THE SECRETARY'S DESK BOOK

A MODERN GUIDE TO CORRECT ENGLISH WITH APPROVED FORMS FOR BUSINESS, OFFICIAL, AND SOCIAL CORRESPONDENCE, AND OTHER USEFUL INFORMATION

Revised Edition

Including

THE WINSTON DICTIONARY

THE JOHN C. WINSTON COMPANY

PHILADELPHIA · TORONTO

FIRST PRINTING OF NEW EDITION, NOVEMBER, 1951
SECOND PRINTING, APRIL, 1952

MADE IN THE UNITED STATES OF AMERICA J-2-52

CONTENTS

PART I

THE RÔLE OF THE SECRETARY

MECHANICS AND CORRECT USAGE

USEFUL INFORMATION

FORMS OF BUSINESS WRITING

PART II

ACKNOWLEDGMENTS

The increasing use of written communication in the business world is making us increasingly conscious of the power and importance of exact and adequate expression. The well-written letter, the expressive sentence, the exact word wield an influence which is felt and acknowledged in business, in social life, in public affairs. A book which helps the individual to say what he wants to say and to say it well—on paper or otherwise—has never been so much needed as it is now. It is to meet this need that the Secretary's Manual has been prepared.

Grateful acknowledgment is made to the following persons and organizations for permission to use their helpful suggestions and material in the preparation of this book: Bureau of Commercial and Industrial Affairs, the Boston Chamber of Commerce; the Mask and Wig Club of the University of Pennsylvania; Bureau of Municipal Research, Philadelphia; the Thomas Skelton Harrison Foundation, and Clarence G. Shenton, Director; The Travelers Aid Society, for the Foreword from the report "When the World Leaves Home"; Chamber of Commerce of the United States of America, for the Foreword from "The City Manager Plan of Municipal Government"; United States Geographic Board; United States Department of the Interior, Office of Education, for letter of transmittal from *Bulletin* No. 17, "Typical Child Care and Parenthood Education in Home Economics Departments"; Family Society of Philadelphia, and Miss Betsy Libbey, General Secretary; The Charity Organization Society of the city of New York, and Lawson Purdy, Secretary; Syracuse Alumnæ Club, Philadelphia; Greenwich House, New York City; Stanford University; Swarthmore College; J. B. Douglas, the United Engineers and Constructors, Inc.; Major General C. H. Bridges, The

Adjutant General, Washington; Miss Dorothy Knudsen, Manager, Finance Department, Philadelphia Chamber of Commerce; Mr. Robert F. Allen, Head of English Department, East Boston High School; Mr. Charles R. Brockmann, The H. W. Wilson Company; Mr. Carl H. Milam, Secretary, American Library Association; Mr. Carl L. Cannon, the New York Public Library; Miss Dorothy E. Hertlein, The Western Union Telegraph Company; Mr. R. B. Shipley, Chief, Passport Division, United States Department of State; Mr. Samuel McCrae Cavert, General Secretary, The Federal Council of the Churches of Christ in America; Miss Eleanor Campion, Union Library Catalogue, Philadelphia; Mr. K. Doyle, United States Department of Commerce, Philadelphia; Elmer P. Thompson, Air Transport Association of America; The University of Chicago Press, for a selection from *A Manual of Style.*

THE RÔLE OF THE SECRETARY

Whether she is a lone assistant, the mainstay of the "one-man" office, or a single cog in the complex wheel of the large corporation, the secretary is always an integral part of the business or social world in which she works. The executive cannot realize his ideas without her; an enterprise cannot function without her services. The rôle of the secretary is a responsible one and the competent secretary should constantly be aware of her obligations.

Punctuality

This is the prime responsibility of any employee, and particularly in the case of the secretary. Her employer is dependent upon her for the execution of his own duties, and it is essential that she be at her desk at the appointed hour each day.

Efficiency

It is presumed that the secretary is adequately trained in stenography. Her regular duties, however, will cover a much wider range of knowledge than that acquired in the business school. In most instances, common sense and sound judgment will be her guides. Remember that doing the job correctly and promptly are not sufficient; checking and rechecking are necessary to insure accuracy.

A certain procedure should be developed and followed for each job. It is wise to record this procedure in a notebook or file for future reference, or for the use of one's successor. This orderliness will facilitate the location of materials and information quickly and will foster a pride of accomplishment.

Neatness is no less important. Tidiness is reflected in

artistically typewritten letters, clean carbon copies, well-kept typewriters and other office machinery, and the attractive appearance of desks, supply cabinets and the office in general. The appearance of the secretary herself is discussed later.

The future wishes of an employer can often be anticipated, and these should be fulfilled before requested whenever possible. When routine tasks are completed without delay, there is time to consider new ideas which contribute to the secretary's mental growth and benefit the employer or business.

Loyalty

A loyal employee will, of course, guard an employer's confidential business matters with the greatest care, avoiding such affairs as the subject of conversation inside or outside the office. Business loyalty also implies a faithfulness to one's fellow employees—a willingness to share helpful information without jealousy, an effort to overlook shortcomings in others, and a ready acceptance of as well as offering of constructive criticism.

Respect for the Public

It is hoped that one's employer and fellow employees warrant respect by their character as well as position. This is not always the case, and the secretary must often employ the utmost tact and discretion in dealing with her associates.

When it comes to contacts with strangers—her employer's or firm's public—this is doubly true. The secretary represents her employer and regardless of a caller's mission, be it in person or by telephone or letter, the secretary is obliged to serve graciously. A courteous and considerate welcome should always be extended in manners, voice and facial expression.

Addressing a caller by name is flattering and has been accepted as a fundamental point of salesmanship. Language which is free from slang and vulgarisms should be used in conversation with a pleasant, well-modulated voice. In telephone conversations, clear enunciation and correct pronunciation are especially important.

Personality and Appearance

Dress

Tailored suits and dresses, simple accessories, and polished shoes which do not sacrifice comfort for beauty are the signs of suitable office attire. Expensive clothes are not necessary; elaborate dress and gaudy jewelry are never appropriate.

Posture and Poise

The first impression made by striking carriage in walking is always favorable, but remains so only if followed by the daily exercise of good posture in sitting and standing. The practice of deep breathing, holding one's head high and pulling in the abdomen is helpful.

Poise comes with self-confidence based on knowledge. The secretary who is assured of adequate preparation, both physical and mental, performs her work with ease. She avoids those mannerisms which might be annoying to others—chewing gum, picking teeth, cleaning or biting fingernails, and combing hair or applying cosmetics in public.

Cleanliness and Health

These are the physical preparations which poise demands. Daily attention to well-groomed hair, carefully-applied cosmetics, clean hands and manicured nails should be a part of the personal routine which also includes the daily change of clothing. It is practical to establish the habit of laundering hosiery and lingerie nightly.

Good physical health depends largely upon the secretary's wise use of leisure time. Daily office work should be balanced with activities that include fresh air, proper exercise, rest, good food and happy surroundings. These will insure against absenteeism and will enable the secretary to withstand the trials of a busy business day without suffering abnormal fatigue.

Regular medical and dental examinations will reveal physical disorders in their early stages, and will detect such minor but offensive disturbances as halitosis (bad breath).

Mental Outlook

A healthy mental attitude is as necessary as physical well-being for the poised secretary. Mental stimulation requires the constant search for new knowledge—on the job and during leisure hours.

The alert and curious secretary entertains new ideas and is ready to offer worth-while suggestions to her employer and fellow employees. A cheerful and coöperative temperament can change drudgery into pleasantry by bringing enthusiasm into the performance of routine tasks.

Be awake to opportunities for learning. Cultivate a hobby; take part in an organized group activity. There are courses given on every conceivable subject, discussion groups, lectures, plays and concerts. Using library facilities keeps one's mind open to new ideas. Mix thought with recreation, and remember that the good secretary is the well-balanced personality.

MECHANICS AND CORRECT USAGE

CHAPTER I

CAPITALIZATION

The rules governing the use of capital letters are set forth below according to common usage among the best known writers and printers, together with examples showing this use according to each rule.

1. Proper nouns. Proper nouns, and adjectives derived from proper nouns, should begin with a capital.

William	Ohio	Platonic
Boston	United States	German

2. First word of sentence. The first word of every sentence or a word standing for a sentence should begin with a capital letter.

Anyone who has anything to say cannot fail to be understood. Begone!

RALEIGH

3. Poetry. The first word of every line of poetry should begin with a capital letter.

It matters not how strait the gate,
How charged with punishments the scroll,
I am the master of my fate:
I am the captain of my soul.

W. E. HENLEY

Exception: In much modern poetry, this rule is applied only to the first line of a stanza.

Winding through the dusk of the temple,
huge, forbidding, gray,
looming above the dark waters of the Nile,
passes the funeral procession of Osiris.

— FRANCIS JAMES, "Pharaoh"

4. Quotation. The first word of every direct quotation should begin with a capital letter.

In a recent address, Sir Stafford Cripps said, "No skill and no ingenuity of mankind, no material inventions or discoveries can save civilization if we depart from those principles which Christ taught us must be the basis of Christian life."

Exception: Do not capitalize the first word of an interrupted quotation within the sentence.

"No," he said, "do not go."

5. Word following a colon. The first word after a colon should be capitalized if it begins a complete independent sentence.

There is much to be said for the old proverb: A stitch in time saves nine.

Do not capitalize the first word after a colon in an enumeration or a list.

Our office manager ordered the following articles for our office: desks, tables, chairs, bookcases, and rugs.

6. *I, O, Oh.* The words *I* and *O* should be capitalized. The word *oh* should be treated as an ordinary word, and should be capitalized only when standing alone or when beginning a sentence.

O rowan tree, O rowan tree! thou'lt aye be dear to me!

CAROLINA NAIRNE

Oh where! and oh where! is your Highland laddie gone?

7. *Whereas*, *Resolved*, *That*. Begin with a capital letter the words *whereas* or *resolved* when used in a formal resolution, and the first word following each such word; also the word *that* following such an expression as, *Know all men by these presents* (see page 280).

WHEREAS, It appears desirable that public recognition should be accorded to the achievements of A. B., therefore be it

Resolved, That this meeting recommend . . .

In typewritten work, the words *whereas* and *resolved* are usually printed entirely in capitals.

8. Roman numerals. Names or abbreviations followed by capitalized Roman numerals should begin with capitals.

Vol. X, Div. II, Figure XV, Act VI.

9. Titles of books, plays, operas, etc. The first word and all important words of titles of books, plays, operas, lectures, pictures, and the like, should begin with a capital. Such words as *a, an, the, of,* are not capitalized unless they begin the title.

The Book of Courage	Three Thirds of a Man
Old English	The Pot of Basil

10. Capitalize the words *father, mother, brother, sister, uncle, aunt,* and like terms when used in direct address or when preceding the name of a relative. They are not capitalized when preceded by a possessive pronoun, or by an article.

May I go with you, Mother?
I know Aunt Mary will be surprised to see us.
I saw my sister standing on the doorstep. She took the place of a mother of the children.

11. Salutation of a letter. The first word and all important words of the salutation and the first word following the salutation, should be capitalized. *Mr., Mrs.* and *Dr.* are permissible abbreviations.

Sir:	Madam:
Dear Sir:	Dear Madam:
Gentlemen:	Ladies:
My dear Sir:	My dear Madam:
My dear Professor Black:	My dear Mrs. Black:
Dear Doctor Bailey:	Dear Mrs. Bailey:
Dear Father:	My dear Mother:

Dear Sir and/or Madam

12. Complimentary close. The first word only of the complimentary close of a letter should begin with a capital.

Cordially yours	Yours very truly	Your sincerely
Faithfully yours	Fraternally yours	Very truly yours
Yours faithfully	Sincerely yours	Yours truly

13. Corporations, companies, works, services, associations, inc., ltd. The first word, and all important words, of the names of corporations, companies, partnerships and the abbreviations *inc.* and *ltd.* if they are part of the incorporated name, should be capitalized. Care should be taken to follow the practice of the organization itself.

The John C. Winston Company
National Fire Protection Association
The Goodyear Tire & Rubber Company, Inc.
Baldwin Locomotive Works
Fox Film Corporation
A. and F. Pears, Ltd.

14. Personified names. All names that are personified should begin with a capital.

Now Nature hangs her mantle green
On every blooming tree
And spreads her sheets o' daisies white
Out o'er the grassy lea.

ROBERT BURNS

He gave to Misery (all he had) a tear,
He gained from Heaven ('twas all he wished) a friend.

THOMAS GRAY

15. Substitutes, epithets. A substitute for a proper name, or an epithet used as part of a proper name, should be capitalized.

Bloody Mary
The Emancipator
Peter the Hermit
The Angel of the Battle Field
The Bard of Avon
The Maid of Orleans

16. Titles. All titles of honor and respect, whether civil, religious, military, or academic, if they precede the name of the person, and all academic degrees that follow the name, whether abbreviated or spelled out, begin with capitals. All titles that refer to certain individuals, used either before the name or instead of the name, and all abbreviations of orders and of names of decorations and their titles, begin with capitals. The particles *d'*, *da*, *de*, *della*, *di*, *du*, *l'*, *la*, *le*, *van*, *von*, usually are not capitalized if they are preceded by a title or a given name. Since American usage varies on the proper form to be used, individual preference should be followed when ascertainable, especially if the form in which it is written is important.

The Duke of Edinburgh	General von Gesler
President Truman	Henry van Dyke
President Roosevelt	Camillo di Cavour
Sir Oliver Lodge, F.R.S., D.Sc.	Lucca della Robbia
Du Maurier	Sir William d'Avenant
Leconte de Lisle	Jean de Reszke

17. Government and official titles. The names of specific legislative bodies, executives, and chief magistrates (national, state, or municipal) should begin with capitals, as: Congress, Parliament, Legislature, General Assembly, Senate, Court, Judge, Assembly, Common Council, Board of Aldermen, Selectmen, Alderman Johnson, the State of New Hampshire, State Government, City Government, National Government, Federal Government, the President of the United States, the Vice President, the Governor of Arizona, the Mayor of Philadelphia, the Cabinet, the Council, the Ministry, the Electoral College; likewise the words *Administration* when referring to the United States Government, and *Nation* when used to designate the United States, or any specific nation.

18. Commissioned officers, Army. Titles of all commissioned officers in the Army and all names of military units are capitalized.

The Chief of Staff	Chief of Chaplains
General	Quartermaster General
Lieutenant General	Chief of Staff U. S. Army Air Force
Major General	Chief of Staff U. S. Army
Brigadier General	Judge Advocate General
Colonel	Provost Marshall General
Lieutenant Colonel	Chief of Ordnance
Major	Chief of Chemical Corps
Captain	Chief of Engineers
Lieutenant (first and second)	Chief Signal Officer
Surgeon General	Chief of Army Transportation
The Adjutant General	First Army
Inspector General	

Exceptions: Do not begin with capitals titles of noncommissioned officers, such as corporal and sergeant, except when they precede a name. The words *corps, company, battalion, division,* when not used as part of a name, do not begin with capitals; nor do the expressions *regular army, general headquarters, general staff, artilleryman,* and the like.

19. Commissioned officers, Navy. All titles of rank are capitalized.

Admiral	Chief, Bureau of Naval Personnel
Vice Admiral	Chief, Bureau of Ordnance
Rear Admiral	Chief, Bureau of Ships
Commodore	Chief, Bureau of Aeronautics
Captain	Chief, Bureau of Supplies and Accounts
Commander	Chief, Bureau of Medicine and Surgery
Lieutenant Commander	Chief, Bureau of Yards and Docks
Lieutenant (senior and junior grades)	Commandant U. S. Coast Guard
Commander in Chief United States Fleet	Commandant U. S. Marine Corps
Chief of Naval Operations	Judge Advocate General

Exceptions: Do not begin with capitals titles of petty and warrant officers, nor the words *cadet* and *midshipman,* except when used with the name of a person. Do not capitalize such expressions as *naval station, naval appropriation,* and *navy yard,* when used in a general sense.

20. Government boards, bureaus, etc. Names of government boards, bureaus, divisions, commissions, surveys, services, and the like, should begin with capitals.

Navy Consulting Board	Interstate Commerce Commission
Bureau of the Census	Geological Survey
Division of Foreign Loans	Reclamation Service

21. County, town, ward, precinct. Words indicating a division of a state, such as a county, a town, a ward, or a precinct, begin with capitals when used with or as proper nouns.

Orange County	Springfield Township
St. Charles Parish	Third Ward
Fifth Precinct	Borough of Manhattan

22. Congress, regiments, dynasties. The names of sessions of Congress, of regiments, of dynasties, and words when used alone to specify definite places, institutions, or bodies, should begin with capitals.

the Eighty-second Congress	the Crown (ruler of a country)
the Fighting Sixty-ninth	the Isthmus (Panama)
the Ming Dynasty	Street (financial center)
Federal (the United States)	Exchange (stock)
Presidency (of any country)	Commonwealth (a state)
Union (the United States)	

23. Streets, parks, avenues, courts. The names of streets, parks, avenues, courts, etc. should begin with capitals.

Chestnut Street	Roosevelt Boulevard
Bevan's Court	Washington Square
Conestoga Road	Fifth Avenue
Columbus Circle	Sheridan Drive
Fairmount Park	Earlham Terrace
Allen Lane	St. James's Place
Lincoln Way	

24. Deity. Names of the Deity and pronouns referring to the Deity, except *who, whose, whom,* are capitalized. Pronouns closely following or preceding a reference to the Deity, however, are usually not capitalized.

"Trust Him who rules all things" (*but:* "When God had worked six days, he rested the seventh").

After Jesus' Resurrection, he appeared to the two disciples on the way to Emmaus.

Before his Ascension, Jesus promised his disciples that he would send them a Comforter.

I know
My God commands, whose power no power resists.
ROBERT GREENE

Holy, Holy, Holy, Lord God Almighty . . .

Exception: In all Bible texts no pronouns (except *I*) referring to God or Jesus Christ are capitalized.

God is a spirit: and they that worship him must worship him in spirit and in truth.

John 4:24

25. The Virgin. The Virgin, Virgin Mary, Blessed Virgin, Our Lady, and similar titles referring to the Mother of Jesus, should begin with a capital. But *goddess*, when referring to a heathen deity, should not begin with a capital.

26. Books of the Bible. The names of the books of the Bible, and the abbreviated forms of these names, should be capitalized.

The Book of Joshua
Ecclesiastes; or, The Preacher
The Acts of the Apostles
The Epistle of Paul to Philemon
The Revelation of Saint John the Divine

Gen. 4:9 Ex. 2:6 Ps.(Pss.) Song of Sol. Jas.

27. The Evil One. The names of the Evil One should begin with capitals.

Satan Satanic Majesty the Devil the Adversary

Exception: When used as an expletive or as a general term for any demon, the word *devil* is not capitalized.

There's the devil to pay!
Oh, the devil!

28. Versions of the Bible. Names of the versions of the Bible, biblical terms such as Gospel, and names of the parables, should begin with capitals.

the King James Version	the Prophets
the Revised Version	the Last Supper
the Douay Bible	the Parable of the Sower
the Vulgate	the Parable of the Draft of Fishes
the Modern Readers' Bible	the Synoptic Gospels

Exception: the words *scriptural* and *biblical* when used as adjectives should not be capitalized.

29. Sacred books. Begin with capital letters the names of sacred books of all faiths.

the Torah	the Koran
the Talmud	the Zend-Avesta
the Vedas	the Dhammapada

30. Religious denominations. The first word and principal words of the names of religious denominations, monastic orders, creeds, and confessions of faith, begin with capitals.

the Presbyterian Church	the Protestant Episcopal Church
the Church of Rome	the Order of St. Benedict
the Society of Jesus	the Westminster Confession of Faith
the Apostles' Creed	

31. Societies, conventions, etc. Begin with capitals the names of societies, institutions, conventions, boards, bureaus, committees, departments, expositions, political alliances, treaties, charters, statutes.

Magna Charta	Department of Exports
Treaty of Utrecht	The American Society of Mechanical Engineers
Triple Alliance	
Coalition	the National Republican Convention
City Welfare Bureau	American National Red Cross
Soldiers' Home	Ways and Means Committee
Board of Health	Bill of Rights

32. School, building, square, etc. Begin with a capital such words as school, building, square, hotel, club, library, museum, university, when used with and as proper nouns.

Horace Mann School	Washington Square
Chrysler Building	Brown Palace Hotel
University Club	Carnegie Library
Metropolitan Museum	

33. Words used with proper nouns. In combinations of common nouns with proper nouns, capitalize as follows:

(*a*) Begin with a capital these words when they follow, or are used as, proper nouns:

peak	harbor	mountain	river
falls	hill	range	spring
island	ferry	ocean	canal

Haines Falls	Benton Harbor	Silver Spring
Arctic Ocean	Bunker Hill	Hudson River
Staten Island	Gores Range	Welland Canal
Peters Mountain	Pikes Peak	Block Island Ferry

(*b*) Begin with a capital letter these words both when they follow and precede the proper noun and when they are used as proper nouns:

bay	desert	isle	mount	sea
camp	fort	lake	pass	point
channel	creek	valley	volcano	strait

Delaware Bay	Mojave Desert	Isle Royale
Camp Sheridan	Fort Smith	City Point
Lake Erie	Chilkoot Pass	Mount Marcy
Davis Strait	Kilauea Volcano	Sea of Marmora
English Channel	Cedar Creek	Mississippi Valley

34. Epochs, periods, ages. Begin with a capital the names of epochs and periods in history, literature, or language, and in geological ages and strata.

the Age of Discovery	Renaissance
Elizabethan Age	the Pleistocene Period of the Cen-
Niagara Epoch	ozoic Era

35. Historical events. The names of important historical events should begin with a capital letter.

the Mayflower Compact	the Mexican Cession
Peace of Paris	the Louisiana Purchase
the Captivity	the Restoration
the French Revolution	the Inquisition

36. Wars. Names of conflicts or wars should begin with capital letters.

the Whiskey Rebellion	Battle of Gettysburg
World War II	the Haymarket Riots
Battle of the Marne	Siege of Yorktown
Wars of the Roses	the Philippine Insurrection

37. Geographical names. Begin with capitals such geographical names as North Pole, the Pole, Tropic of Cancer, South Temperate Zone, Canal Zone, Equator, Old World, New World, the East Indies, the Orient, the

Central States, Far East, Atlantic Slope, the Great Lakes, the Eastern Hemisphere; also, nouns referring to inhabitants of certain parts of the country.

Southerner Westerner

EXCEPTIONS: polar regions, the arctics, temperate zone, the tropics.

38. Points of the compass. Points of the compass, when they designate geographical sections of a country, should begin with capitals.

The North and the South settled the slavery question for all time.

NOTE: Do not capitalize such words when they refer only to direction.

The storm came from the east.

39. Scientific names. In botany, geology, zoölogy, or medicine, the scientific names of divisions, families, and genera, but not of species, begin with capitals.

Pteridium equilinum	Hemoptysis	Crustacea
Cistus canadensis	Herbivora	Cenozoic

40. Days, months, stars, planets. The names of the days of the week and of the months of the year, and the names of the stars, planets, and star groups, should be capitalized.

Tuesday	Capella	M 13
August	Caius Major	47 Tuscanae
Neptune	Milky Way	Coalsack

Exceptions: the words *spring*, *summer*, *fall*, *autumn*, and *winter* are not capitalized.

41. Holidays. Names of all holidays and holy days begin with capitals.

New Year's Day	Christmas
Memorial Day	Good Friday
Labor Day	Passover
Thanksgiving	Atonement

42. Do not use capitals. Proper nouns and the derivatives of proper nouns, which through common use have lost their original significance and acquired special meanings, should not be capitalized.

macadam	artesian well	levant leather
boycott	chinaware	paris green
oriental rug	brussels lace	pasteurization

43. Items in an order. Items cited in an order are often capitalized.

30 doz. Men's Handkerchiefs No. 8
12 doz. Men's White Broadcloth Golf Shirts No. 6, size 15
30 doz. Summer Silk Men's Hose, Nos. 10–11½

44. Checks, notes, drafts. Sums of money when written in words on formal statements, or on checks, promissory notes, drafts, etc., are often capitalized.

Enclosed is a check for Two Hundred Forty Dollars in payment of my account.

Three months after date I promise to pay to Samuel Brown Six Hundred Fifty-three Dollars.

Pay to the order of T. W. Atwood Seven Hundred Seventy Dollars.

NOTE: For the use of *and* between figures and numbers, see page 162, § 2.

45. Hyphenated Compounds. Capitalization affects only the first letter of a hyphenated compound.

When a hyphenated compound containing no proper nouns or adjectives is capitalized, it is written as follows:

Clean-up Week
Twenty-fourth Yearbook
Summary of the Income-tax Law

A proper noun or adjective used in a hyphenated compound retains its capital:

The Berlin-Baghdad railway	Pre-Raphaelite
anti-Semitic	Sir Cecil Spring-Rice

CHAPTER II

PUNCTUATION

The first use of a system of punctuation marks has been attributed to Aldus Manutius, an Italian printer of the fifteenth century. From this rather crude beginning our present system of marks to be used for special purposes has been evolved gradually. The use of these marks today is directed by simple rules based upon the purpose of punctuation, which may be defined as follows:

> **Punctuation,** in writing or printing, the division of a composition into parts, as sentences or parts of sentences, for the sake of clearness, by means of marks devised for the purpose.[1]

The present tendency among most writers, printers, and publishers is opposed to an extravagant use of marks of punctuation. Notwithstanding this tendency, the importance of the accurate use of punctuation is illustrated daily by serious errors that creep into the correspondence of business houses or the printed pages of our daily newspapers. The need for correct punctuation may be shown by one or two illustrations.

In April, 1872, a tariff act was enacted by the Congress of the United States. The official copy of this act contained the following provision in its fifth section: "That on and after the first day of August next, the importation of the articles enumerated and described in this section shall be exempt from duty, that is to say: . . . Fruit, plants tropical and semi-tropical for the purpose of propagation or cultivation; . . ."

The error of placing a comma instead of a hyphen after the word "fruit" was not corrected until May, 1874, with

[1] *The Winston Dictionary.*

the result that many thousands of dollars were lost to the United States through the admission of fruits free of duty.

A member of Parliament was apologizing to a fellow member. "I said that the honorable member was a prevaricator, it is true; and I am sorry for it." The *London Times* printed the apology thus: "I said that the honorable member was a prevaricator. It is true, and I am sorry for it."

Properly handled, punctuation helps the reader to get at the meaning of the printed page, for it serves to separate words that do not belong together and to unite words that do.

The rules which follow, it is hoped, will be found useful to those whose work demands a general knowledge of the laws governing the more common uses of the marks of punctuation.

The Period

1. At end of sentence. A period is placed at the end of a declarative and an imperative sentence, whether complete or incomplete, and after indirect and rhetorical questions.

> There is not a moment without some duty.
>
> Go bid the priests do present sacrifice,
> And bring me their opinions of success.
>
> SHAKESPEARE, *Julius Cæsar*
>
> Will you please answer the telephone.

2. After abbreviation. Place a period after an abbreviation.

Smith *vs.* Jones	Ph.D.	f.o.b.
10 W. Broadway	LL.D.	viz.
	Rev.	

Exceptions:

(a) The French abbreviations for Madame (Mme), for Mademoiselle (Mlle), and for Compagnie (Cie) do not have a period. The period is generally omitted after the abbreviation for manuscript, MS (pl. MSS), and after a letter used to designate a name, as, Mr. X, Mrs. Y.

(b) Write without a period such expressions as IOU, SOS, OK, A1, c/o, %.

(*c*) Do not used a period after the abbreviations of the names of epochs in the development of a language.

OE (Old English) MHG (Middle High German)

(*d*) Do not use a period after Roman numerals that are a part of proper names.

George VI Pope Pius XII
Alfonso XIII John Wesley Jones II

(*e*) Use no periods after chemical symbols.

TNT H_2O Zn Cu Pb

(*f*) Use no periods after box heads, running heads, legends that do not make more than a single line of type, chapter titles, display lines, and items in enumerated lists, (Compare § 9, page 22.)

3. Money and Decimals. Place a period before every decimal fraction, between dollars and cents when numerically expressed, and after the abbreviations *s.* and *d.* for the denominations of English money. Do not use a period after a series of figures representing sums of money in even dollars.

4.5 2.75 $11.04 $.75 £10 15*s.* 6*d.*

I enclose a check for $175 to be applied on my account.

NOTE: The percentage sign (%) is never used when the decimal point appears; for .5% would mean .5 of .01, or .005, whereas 5% really means .05.

4. Divisions of an outline. Use a period after Roman numerals, letters, and figures when they are used to designate the divisions of an outline; also when used in a table of contents to designate chapters.

I. The Nature of Exposition
A. Definitions
B. Illustrations

1. The order of time
2. The order of place
3. The order of logical relationship
4. The order of importance

I. The Nominative Case . . .
II. The Possessive Case . . .
III. The Objective Case . . .

5. Period with quotation marks. The period is always placed inside the quotation marks. This is an invariable rule, and applies to typed material as well as to printed matter.

6. Period with parentheses. If parenthetical matter, even a complete statement, forms part of the sentence, no period is placed inside the closing parenthesis. But if parenthetical matter is independent of, and forms no part of, a preceding sentence, the closing punctuation is placed within the closing parenthesis.

There are five privileged motions; why they are so called has been explained already (Cushing, 136–159).

The officer took off his coat. (The bright sunlight had warmed us all up.)

7. Ellipses. Leaders (periods in a series) are used to indicate that the preceding statement is unfinished. Usually three periods are used.

"We are coming, Father Abraham . . ."

8. Hours and minutes. A period may be used in expressions of time between the figures for hours and for minutes.

1:45 P.M. 2.30 o'clock

See also § 2 at bottom of page 27.

9. Side heads. A period may be used after side heads not set on separate lines. (See also § 6, page 36.)

Balloons and airships. Balloons continue to rise . . .

The Comma

1. In series. A comma should be placed after each member of a series printed without conjunctions as part of a continuous sentence. The best usage requires a comma before *and*, *or*, and *nor* when connecting the last two words of a series without other connectives.

In business, three things are necessary: knowledge, temper, and time.

FELTHAM

Her voice was ever soft, gentle, and low, an excellent thing in woman.

SHAKESPEARE

For three days the battle was fought bitterly, stubbornly, and cruelly.

2. Direct address. Use a comma, or commas, to set off from the rest of the sentence a word or words used in direct address or in a salutation.

You, madam, are one of the selected list.

Lord God of Hosts, be with us yet,
Lest we forget—lest we forget.

KIPLING

3. Appositive. Use commas to set off an appositive.

John Burroughs, the naturalist, knew more about the habits of bees than any other man.

At noon the coach reached Alloway, the birthplace of Robert Burns, the Scottish poet.

NOTE: When the appositive is a closely modifying phrase, no commas are required.

the naturalist Burroughs	Rufus himself
the poet Burns	my brother Frank

4. Break in continuity. Use commas to indicate a break in the continuity of the thought of a sentence when the interruption is slight; otherwise use dashes or parentheses.

The sweetest voices in the world, if any voice may properly be called sweet, come from Italy.

5. Short quotation. Use a comma to separate a short quotation from the rest of the sentence.

"I mean to stand upon the Constitution," replied Webster.

NOTE: Like the period, the comma is always placed inside quotation marks. This is an invariable rule.

6. Omission of a word. Use a comma to show the ellipsis of a word or words from a construction.

Washington was born in 1732; Jefferson, in 1743; and Lincoln, in 1809.

7. Dates, references, etc. A comma may be used to separate parts of dates, references, geographical locations, and addresses. Note that a colon is often used between chapter and verse numbers.

Commencement at Windsor College begins Monday, June 15, 19—.

For the various meanings of Romanticism, see Bliss Perry, *A Study of Prose Fiction,* Ch. X., pp. 258–283.

The Republic Steel Company is located in Pittsburgh, Pennsylvania.

John's address is 114 Raleigh Street, Rochester, New York.

Luke 3:7.

8. Words or phrases in pairs. Use a comma to separate words or phrases that are arranged in pairs.

Sink or swim, live or die, survive or perish, I give my hand and my heart to this vote.

DANIEL WEBSTER

9. Parts of a sentence. A comma should separate the different parts of a sentence whose meaning would not be clear without punctuation.

Ruth, your sister is calling you.
Ruth, your sister, is calling you.
After eating, the dog ceased barking.

10. Nonrestrictive clauses. Use a comma to set off a nonrestrictive clause. Restrictive clauses are not set off by commas.

I plan to go to Boston, whence I shall sail for Gibraltar.

George Washington, who was the first President of the United States, was born in Virginia.

The man who broke his leg was sent to the hospital.

NOTE: The use of the comma with nonrestrictive (nonessential) clauses gives more difficulty, perhaps, than any other comma use. Does the clause merely give information, or does it limit the thought of the main clause? If it merely gives information, it is nonrestrictive and must be separated by commas from the rest of the sentence. But if it limits the thought of the main clause, it is restrictive and should not be set off from the rest of the sentence by commas.

For example, in the second sentence, the clause *who was the first President* is only added information about Washington. It has nothing whatever to do with his being born in Virginia. If it were omitted, the remaining statement would be unchanged in meaning. The clause should therefore be set off by commas.

On the other hand, in the sentence, *The man who broke his leg was sent to the hospital,* the clause *who broke his leg* limits or restricts the application of *sent to the hospital* to one definite person. No commas should separate it from the rest of the sentence.

11. Elements of a sentence. Any element of a sentence that is grammatically independent of the rest of the sentence must be set off by a comma.

Looking to the east, we saw a high cliff.

12. Introductory words. Use a comma to set off such words as *yes, no, indeed, surely, therefore, however, moreover,* and the like, when used as introductory words. They should be set off by commas when they occur within the sentence. When the words *therefore* and *moreover* begin the sentence and are followed immediately by the subject, they should be followed by a comma.

Therefore, my beloved brethren, . . .

Bible

No, the heart that has truly loved never forgets.

MOORE

It did not appear, however, that there was anything remarkably tremendous about Barbara.

DICKENS

13. Phrase or clause out of order. Use a comma to set off a phrase or a clause out of its natural order.

By gnawing through a dyke, even a rat may drown a nation.

BURKE

If you would divine the future, study the past.

CONFUCIUS

14. Coördinate clauses. Use a comma to separate two coordinate clauses joined by *and, for, but, or, nor, neither,* if there is a change of subject and the clauses are not closely connected in thought.

God heals, and the doctor takes the fee.

FRANKLIN

I cannot see, for the mist is in my eyes.

15. Digits. Use a comma in pointing off the digits of a large number into groups of three.

1,157	12,444	156,000	2,076,959

Exception: Use no comma in date or page numbers.

p. 1276	4000 B. C.

16. Measures, weights, etc. Use no comma between the parts of a designation of measurement, weight, dimension, or of a sum of money.

12 ft. 9 in.	£10 9s. 3d.	5 hr. 3 min.	9 lb. 4 oz.

17. Interjection. Use a comma after the interjection "oh" when used in a mild exclamation. Use an exclamation point after "oh" when the sentence expresses wonder or extreme surprise.

Oh, East is East, and West is West . . .
Oh! listen to that roar!

THE SEMICOLON

As a mark of punctuation, the semicolon is intermediate between the period and the comma. Often it is the mark of an unfinished thought. Consequently, to minds beset with doubts, the semicolon is indispensable.

1. Compound sentence. Use a semicolon to separate the independent clauses of a compound sentence, or to mark a more important break in a sentence than can be indicated by a comma.

We demand that big business give people a square deal; in return we must insist that when anyone engaged in big business honestly endeavors to do right, he shall himself be given a square deal. — ROOSEVELT

2. Enumerated items. Use a semicolon to separate parts of a sentence or enumeration which themselves are punctuated by commas.

Among those who attended the banquet were Mr. and Mrs. Jonathan Roberts, of Boston; Mr. Jack McNamee, of Albany; Dr. and Mrs. Sydney Porter, of Philadelphia; and Miss Josephine Preston, a guest of the Porters.

3. Namely, viz., etc. Place a semicolon before the expressions, *namely, viz., for example, e.g., that is, i.e., for instance, however, hence, moreover,* and the like when they introduce a sentence, a principal statement, or an enumeration of examples or explanations (see p. 25, rule 12; p. 160, rule 14).

We are indebted to the Greeks for the three main styles of architecture; namely, the Corinthian, the Doric, and the Ionic.

4. Sections of a book. Use a semicolon to set off references to the various sections of a book.

Matt. 1:18; 12:46; 26:7; 27:56; 28:1.
Hosmer, *The Appeal to Arms*, 99–111; 186–200

5. Quotation marks. The semicolon should be placed outside quotation marks.

THE COLON

1. Salutation. Place a colon after the salutation of a letter, and after a speaker's introductory remark.

My dear Sir: Dear Doctor Mawson: Sir: Gentlemen:
Mr. Toastmaster, Ladies, and Gentlemen:

2. Hours, minutes, etc. A colon is often placed between hours and minutes indicating exact time; between the number of the volume and the page cited in references; between the chapter and the verse when indicating passages from the Bible; and between the parts of a title.

10:50 A.M. II Sam. 3:8–12; Vol. X: 25–80

The Outline of Science, I:243
Art Through the Ages: An Introduction to Its History and Significance

3. References. In literary references, a colon is usually placed between the city of publication and the name of the publisher.

Lassie Come-Home. Philadelphia: Winston

4. Direct quotation. Place a colon before an extended direct quotation.

In the midst of his great speech Burke said: "When we speak of the commerce with our colonies, fiction lags after truth; invention is unfruitful; and imagination, cold and barren."

5. Explanation of a statement. Place a colon before an extended explanation of a preceding statement.

There are four ingredients in conversation: the first is truth; the next, good sense; the third, good humor; and the fourth, wit.

SIR W. TEMPLE

6. Introductory statement. Place a colon after an introductory statement preceding an enumeration or illustration.

The best-known works of Edith Wharton are: *The Valley of Decision, The House of Mirth,* and *The Age of Innocence.*

7. Supplementary phrase or clause. If a phrase or a clause explains or amplifies what precedes it, a colon is used between the clauses.

Commercial flying is not romance: it is service.

THE EXCLAMATION POINT

The exclamation point, like the period, may indicate the end of a complete statement. By its use, a writer may add more feeling, more emotion, to his writing than is indicated by a period.

1. Emotion, supplication, etc. Use the exclamation point to indicate emotion, supplication, passion, command, surprise, or strong feeling.

How sweet the moonlight sleeps upon this bank!
SHAKESPEARE

To arms! they come! the Greek! the Greek!
FITZ-GREENE HALLECK

Ay, tear her tattered ensign down!
HOLMES

They're the spawn of Hell!
SCOLLARD

Honor the Light Brigade,
Noble six hundred!
TENNYSON

Hats off!
The flag is passing by!
BENNETT

Oh, for shame! Fie! Good! Hurrah!

2. Exclamatory sentence. Use an exclamation point at the end of an exclamatory sentence that begins with an interjection.

O welcome, thou that bring'st the summer nigh!
WILLIAM MORRIS

O little town of Bethlehem,
How still we see thee lie!
PHILLIPS BROOKS

3. Word used independently. Use an exclamation point after a word of exclamation used independently.

Alas! Why gnaw you so your nether lip?
SHAKESPEARE

Ah, ha! Come, some music.
Bah! That sounds ridiculous.

4. Interrogative pronoun or adverb. Use an exclamation point after an exclamation that begins with an interrogative pronoun or adverb.

What a piece of work is man! how noble in reason! how infinite in faculty!
SHAKESPEARE

Interrogation Point

1. Direct question. Place an interrogation point after every direct question.

What were some of the things which prehistoric man knew?
Did you go?
Of course you went?

Note: The last sentence is declarative in form, but interrogative in purpose and punctuation.

2. The rhetorical question. A rhetorical question, that is, a statement that is framed in the form of a question for the sake of effect, does not require a question mark. A short rhetorical question, however, may be followed by a question mark or by an exclamation point.

Were ever words more fitly spoken.
Will you please send us your new fall catalog of musical supplies.
Who cares? What's the use!

3. Doubt or query. Use an interrogation point to indicate a doubt or a query.

Xerxes (? – 465 B. C.) was king of Persia.
Doctor Cook discovered (?) the North Pole in 1912.

4. With quotation marks or parentheses. Place an interrogation point inside quotation marks only when the quoted matter constitutes a question. If matter in parentheses, occurring within or at the end of a sentence, constitutes a question, place an interrogation point inside the closing parenthesis; if a sentence containing a parenthesis is interrogative independently of the parenthesis, place an interrogation point outside the parenthesis.

I heard him say, "Who spoke?"
What is meant by "Water seeks its own level"?
Poe's work as a critic (Who can deny that he still remains America's foremost literary critic?) calls for much comment.
Have you done your exercises (that is, the ones assigned on Monday)?

Quotation Marks

1. Quoted matter. Inclose in quotation marks all matter that is quoted in the exact words of a speaker or a writer.

"Charge, Chester, charge! On, Stanley, on!" were the last words of Marmion.

Scott

The park guard shouted to the boys, "Hands off!"

2. Beginning each paragraph. If the quotation comprises two or more paragraphs from the work of an author, quotation marks are placed at the beginning of each paragraph, but the closing quotation marks appear only at the end of the quotation.

"Only yesterday, we laid to rest the mortal remains of our beloved President, Franklin Delano Roosevelt. At a time like this, words are inadequate. The most eloquent tribute would be a reverent silence. . . .

"In His infinite wisdom, Almighty God has seen fit to take from us a great man who loved, and was beloved by, all humanity.

"No man could possibly fill the tremendous void left by the passing of that noble soul. No words can ease the aching hearts of untold millions of every race, creed and color. The world knows it has lost a heroic champion of justice and freedom."

Harry S. Truman
First Message to Congress

3. Unusual or peculiar terms. Inclose in quotation marks unusual or peculiar terms. Be on guard, however, against using quotation marks too freely in this way.

Mrs. Pringle's "high teas" were the chief social events of our Sunday afternoons.

Less good: Mr. Peacock was appointed "master of the hounds."

4. Pictures, ships, airplanes, chapters of books, and poems. Inclose in quotation marks book-chapter titles, and names of poems, etc.; some authorities include under this rule the names of ships, airplanes, pictures, and works of art. Often, however, such words are italicized.

Perugino's *Crucifixion* "The Thunderbolt"
U. S. S. *Saratoga* Longfellow's "Hiawatha"

The name "Florence" is always connected with the Renaissance.

The first chapter was called, innocently enough, "The Summerhouse."

5. Single quotation marks. Use single quotation marks to inclose a quotation occurring within a quotation.

"Speaking with great humility, General Eisenhower said: 'Had I possessed the military skill of a Marlborough, the wisdom of Solomon, I still would have been helpless without the loyalty, vision and generosity of thousands of British and Americans.'"

NOTE: Should a third quotation occur within the second quotation, double quotation marks should be used.

When punctuating quotations, place the period and the comma within the quotation marks; the colon and the semicolon outside the quotation marks; the exclamation and interrogation points, within the quotation marks when they form parts of the quotations, otherwise outside.

"All right," I said, "suppose I do."

It was "Rolling Down to Rio"; the notes were unmistakable.

APOSTROPHE

1. Possessive case. Use an apostrophe in forming the possessive case. This is the most common use of the apostrophe.

(*a*) The possessive of any singular noun may be formed by adding an apostrophe and *s*.

the man's house Horace's Odes
Brown's lectures Keats's "Endymion"

(*b*) The possessive of a plural noun ending in *s* is formed by adding the apostrophe only; the possessive of a plural noun not ending in *s* is formed by adding the apostrophe and *s*.

the boys' coats men's clothing
ladies' watches women's hats

(*c*) Nouns of two or more syllables ending in the sound of *s* may form the possessive by adding the apostrophe only; words of one syllable, ending in *s* sound (except names ending in *-ce*), by adding an apostrophe and *s*, the possessive of plural proper nouns, by adding an apostrophe only.

Dickens' novels	Burns's
Xerxes' army	for conscience' sake
Jesus' sayings	for appearance' sake
Berlioz's compositions	

The Williamses' and Powerses' cars collided.

(See rules 4-8, p. 38).

2. Plural of numerals and proper names. The apostrophe and *s* should be used to form the plural of numerals not spelled out, and of letters of the alphabet. Proper names of more than one syllable, if they end in *s*, sometimes form the plural with the apostrophe and *s*, sometimes with the apostrophe alone, and sometimes according to the method used for common nouns (see p. 42, § 2).

the 1860's (*but:* the sixties)	the Voorhees of New York
at sixes and sevens	the three R's
the W. C. T. U.'s	the 2's and 4's

3. Omission, contraction. An apostrophe is used to indicate the omission of a letter or letters in the contraction of a word, or the omission of figures in a number.

don't	haven't	won't	I'll	o'er
the class of '94		the boys of '61		

4. Name of firm. The sign of possession is added only to the last word of a firm or corporate name consisting of two or more parts. (See also § 7, page 39.)

Strawbridge and Clothier's store

If separate ownership is implied, each name has the possessive form.

Drexel's and Morgan's banks

5. *Anyone else's*. The possessive of such expressions as *anyone else, anybody else* may be made in two ways: by adding the apostrophe and *s* to the first word, as *anyone's else,* or by adding them to the second word, as *anyone else's.* Good usage seems to prefer the latter form: *anyone else's.*

Parentheses

1. Explaining or qualifying. An expression inserted in a sentence solely for the purpose of explaining or qualifying should be inclosed in parentheses.

> "Then you will lose your *frite*" (for so the captain always pronounced the word freight), shouted Bryon.
>
> TRELAWNEY

> Certain consonants (*s, sh, z*) have a hissing sound.
> *Mrs.* has no plural: *Mrs. Smith* (one), the *Mrs. Smiths* (more than one).

2. Division letters or figures. Division letters or figures within a paragraph should be inclosed in parentheses.

> Discuss the junior position in a receiving department under the following headings: (*a*) Duties (*b*) Educational requirements (*c*) Character of work (*d*) Opportunities for promotion.

NOTE: Parentheses are not used with Roman numerals.

3. Bibliographical references. Use parentheses to enclose bibliographical references.

> See *Encyclopedia Britannica* (Fourteenth Edition), Vol. 16.
> Irrigation makes desert land fruitful (see Figure 33).
> Dickens, *Christmas Stories* (London, 1854).

4. Dates. Use parentheses to inclose references to dates.

> Theodore Roosevelt (1858–1919)

5. Punctuation. A mark of punctuation is placed after the closing parenthesis if the sentence into which the parenthetical matter is inserted requires punctuation there regardless of the parenthesis. An interrogation point or an exclamation point is placed before a closing parenthesis if the parenthetical matter requires it; a period is placed before a closing parenthesis only if the parenthetical matter is regarded as a complete sentence, and comes after the end of a sentence of which it is felt to be independent.

The cities of central California, like those of the southern part of the State (Sec. 289), have lacked coal.

Did she wear her *obi* (a kind of sash)?

He quoted figures (Who could contradict them?) to prove his point.

He quoted figures (He was always quoting figures) to prove his point.

He quoted figures to prove his point (as always).

He quoted figures to prove his point. (He was always quoting figures.)

BRACKETS

1. Explanatory notes or omissions. Brackets are used to inclose independent words or phrases inserted as explanatory notes or omissions, or to inclose additions that the author does not deem essential to the sense of the text.

The American [French] General, Lafayette, received his first wound at the Battle of Brandywine.

Printed at London for Tho. Lambert and are to be sold at the sign of the Horse-shoe [in Smithfield].

MACBETH [*looking at his hands*]. This is a sorry sight.
SHAKESPEARE

DASH

1. Change in sense or construction. Use a dash after an unfinished sentence, or to indicate a sudden change in the sense or construction of a sentence, or to show hesitancy in speech.

Your next lesson begins — by the way, there is the bell.

She copied this — you may not believe it — in ten minutes.

"But — but it's true," said Mary. "You saw —"

2. Emphasis. Use a dash to introduce a phrase or clause added to the main clause for emphasis or explanation.

The laborer is worthy of his hire — if his labor is.
Wall Street Journal

The truth about returned laundry — not a cuff in a carload.
Judge

3. End of series of clauses. Use a dash at the end of a series of phrases or clauses that depend on, or are summed up by, a concluding expression.

He lost his wealth, his friends, his home — everything but his honor.

4. References, dates, etc. Use a dash for the word *to* between two numbers representing the first and last of a series of consecutive numbers, as in dates, page references, and the like.

1929–19—   Pages 10–19   Chapters IV–VIII

5. Omission of letters. A dash may be used to indicate the omission of letters in a name.

Mrs. M— of G— Street was also present.

6. Side headings. A dash may be used to separate side headings from the main text. (See also § 9, page 22.)

Balloons and airships — Balloons continue to rise . . .

NOTE: Some printers follow the old custom of punctuating side heads with a period and a dash.

7. Preceding a reference. Use a dash immediately preceding the name of an author or a source of quoted matter.

One trouble with the country is that it wants to raise nothing but cotton and wear nothing but silk.

—*American Lumberman*

An ounce of wit is worth a pound of sorrow.

—RICHARD BAXTER

8. To save repetition. In cataloging books, dashes are used to save the repetition of an author's name; in indexing, dashes are used to save the repetition of a word or words that appear in several successive entries.

Conrad Joseph
—Letters, '28, Doubleday & Co.
—Same, ltd. ed. Random House

CHAPTER III

GRAMMAR

This chapter does not attempt to treat the subject of grammar fully. Only those rules are presented which must be used in ordinary writing and in the correction of common grammatical errors. For a more comprehensive treatment of grammar, consult Ralph B. Allen, *English Grammar*, or Lewis and Lynch, *Grammar to Use*.

CASE

The objective case

1. The object of a verb or of a preposition is in the objective case.

Most violations of this rule occur in the use of pronouns.

> *Whom* did you see? *Not: Who* did you see?
> She gave them to *us* boys. *Not:* She gave them to *we* boys.
> He helped John and *me*. *Not:* He helped John and *I*.
> Between you and *me*. *Not:* Between you and *I*.

One of the most troublesome constructions is that in which a relative pronoun is used as the subject of a clause which is the object of the main verb.

> Right: He saw *whoever* opened the gate.
> Wrong: He saw *whomever* opened the gate.

Here *whoever* is not the object of *saw*, but the subject of the clause *whoever opened the gate*. Hence *whoever* should be nominative. But,

> Right: I know *whom* he saw.

Here the main clause is *I know*, and the object of *know* is the relative clause *whom he saw*. But the objective form *whom* is correct because *whom* is the object of the verb ***saw***.

Guard against putting a pronoun in the objective case merely because it follows the main verb. In order to decide which form is correct to use in a particular instance, determine how the pronoun is used in its own clause.

2. The subject and the object of an infinitive are in the objective case.

> He asked *us* to watch *him*.
> I believe *him* (not *he*) to be the ringleader.
> We knew *her* to be our sister.

The infinitive form *to be,* like other forms of *be,* takes, not an object, but a complement which agrees with the subject in case. (See § 3 following.) Since the subject of the infinitive is in the objective case, the complement agreeing with that subject must also be objective. Therefore objective forms of the pronouns may be correctly used after the infinitive *to be.*

> I thought this man to be *him* (not *he*).
> She knew the guide to be *me* (not *I*).
> He expected the culprits to be *them* (not *they*).

These are awkward constructions, however, and should be avoided.

The nominative case

3. The verb *be* ordinarily requires a following word, called a *complement,* to complete its meaning. The complement agrees with the subject; hence when the subject is in the nominative, the complement must also be in the nominative.

> We knew that it was *she* (not *her*).
> This is *he* (not *him*) whom you seek.

Such expressions as *It is me, Between you and I*, may be accepted by some authorities, but in formal writing the correct forms only should be used: *It is I, Between you and me.*

The possessive case

4. The possessive form of nouns is generally used in names only of persons and animals. It should not be used of inanimate objects.

Wrong: The house's windows, the church's steeple, the mountain's top, the book's pages, the factory's manager.

Right: The windows of the house, the steeple of the church, the top of the mountain, the pages of the book, the manager of the factory.

There are well-recognized exceptions to this rule:

the season's greetings	a nickel's worth
the day's work	a stone's throw

5. A confusion of meaning results when the possessive form of a noun is used to show the object of an action expressed in another noun.

The murder *of Jefford* (not *Jefford's murder*).
The betrayal *of Cæsar* (not *Cæsar's betrayal*).

6. Ordinarily, a noun modifying a gerund is in the possessive case.

John's (not *John*) *finding* the paper will spoil our plans.
A approved of *his* (not *him*) *accepting* the position.

7. Joint possession is shown by the last noun in a series.

Brown & *King's* Department Store (not *Brown's & King's* Department Store).

8. The possessive form of the pronoun *it* is spelled without an apostrophe, *its*. *It's* is the contracted form of *it is*.

Agreement

1. A pronoun must agree with its antecedent in gender and number.

A singular antecedent such as *each, every*, requires a singular pronoun.

Wrong: Everyone had studied *their* lessons.
Right: Everyone had studied *his* lesson.
Wrong: Every man knows that *they* would do the same thing.
Right: Every man knows that *he* would do the same thing.

Avoid the use of *he or she* in referring to an indefinite pronoun. *He* is the correct form to use when the gender of the antecedent is not indicated.

Awkward: I have asked everyone whether *he or she* saw the bird.

Better: I have asked everyone whether *he* saw the bird.

2. The pronominal adjectives *this* and *that* should agree in number with the word modified.

When modifying *kind* and *sort,* which are singular, they should have the singular form. (See page 65.)

I do not like *this kind* of books (not *these kind*).
You always look well in *that sort* of clothes (not *those sort*).

3. A verb agrees with its subject in number and person.

(*a*) Two or more singular subjects connected by *and* take a plural verb.

Copper *and* sulphuric acid *are* what I need.

Guard against the use of *don't* in the third person singular. *Don't* is a shortened form of *do not; he don't* (*he do not*) is obviously incorrect. Use the correct singular form: *he doesn't* (*he does not*).

(*b*) Be careful to make a verb agree with its subject, rather than with a word intervening between it and the subject, or with its complement.

The material *was* (not *were*) oak and white pine.
This series of books *is* (not *are*) excellent for children.
The presentation of the paintings and etchings *was* (not *were*) made at the meeting.
How much *does* (not *do*) a set of those fixtures cost?

(*c*) Words joined to the subject by *with, including, as well as,* and the like, do not affect the number of the subject.

The instructor, as well as the boys, *was* (not *were*) alarmed.
The president, with most of the directors, *was* (not *were*) in favor of the plan.
The house, together with furniture, curtains, and all its contents, *was* (not *were*) sold for $10,000.

(*d*) Singular subjects joined by *or* and *nor* take a singular verb.

Neither McMahon *nor* his cousin *has* come.

(*e*) When two subjects different in person or number are joined by *or* or *nor*, the verb usually agrees with the nearer subject. Such expressions are awkward, however, and should be avoided.

Either Biddle or the auctioneers *are* mistaken.
Either she or I *go* to see him every day.

(*f*) *There* used to introduce a sentence is not really the subject and does not affect the number of the verb.

Wrong: There *is* a piano and a phonograph in the room.
Right: There *are* a piano and a phonograph in the room.

(*g*) Nouns that indicate a group (collective nouns) take a plural verb when the members of the group are considered individually, and a singular verb when the group is considered as a unit.

Right: The committee *has* chosen Jones unanimously.
Right: The committee *disagree* on this point.
Right: The audience *are* taking their seats.
Right: The audience *is* enthusiastic.

(*h*) Words expressing numbers, quantities, or fractions of quantities take singular verbs when the quantity is considered as one unit. When several members of a group are indicated, a plural verb is required.

Three times four *is* (not *are*) twelve.
One third of the cloth *is* mine (one unit indicated).
One third of the class *have* already taken their places (individuals indicated).

(*i*) *Each, every, each one, everyone, anyone, anybody, everybody,* and similar words are singular and are followed by a singular verb.

Each man *carries* a gun.
Everyone *knows* what to do.

(*j*) *None* may take a singular or a plural verb according to its meaning.

None of the band *is* willing to confess.
None *are* better made than mine.

(*k*) Some words always are plural in form and take a plural verb. The most common words of this sort are *trousers, scissors, tidings.*

Wrong: Tidings *was* brought by airplane.
Right: Tidings *were* brought by airplane.

(*l*) Some words, plural in form, take either a plural or a singular verb, according to the meaning expressed.

To this group of words belong *athletics, ethics, æsthetics, mathematics, civics, physics.*

Right: Ethics *is* a difficult course for me.
Right: The ethics of those races *are* different from ours.

Order of Pronouns

When pronouns of more than one person are mentioned together, the order usually followed places the second personal pronoun (*you*) first, and the first personal pronouns (*we, I*) last.

You and I are going to the concert.
The invitation is for *you and us.*

The third personal pronoun (*he, she, it, they*) takes precedence over the first, but follows the second.

You and they will share the season ticket.
He and I do not agree.

Formation of the Plural of Nouns

1. Most plurals are formed by adding *s* to the singular.

books, apples, offices, strangers.

2. Words ending in *x, s, z, sh, ch* form the plural by adding *es.*

box*es*, glass*es*, brooch*es*, index*es*, bush*es*, waltz*es*

3. Words ending in *y* preceded by a consonant form the plural by changing the *y* to *i* and adding *es.*

lily, lil*ies*; lady, lad*ies*; security, securit*ies*

4. Words ending in *y* preceded by a vowel form the plural in the usual manner, by adding *s*.

Key, keys; delay, delays; valley, valleys; money, moneys

5. The following nouns ending in *f* or *fe* form the plural by changing the *f* or *fe* to *v* and adding *es*.

Singular	*Plural*	*Singular*	*Plural*
beef	beeves	self	selves
calf	calves	sheaf	sheaves
elf	elves	shelf	shelves
half	halves	thief	thieves
knife	knives	wharf	wharves
leaf	leaves	wife	wives
loaf	loaves	wolf	wolves
life	lives		

Some nouns have two plural forms.

hoof, hoofs, hoo*ves;* scarf, scarfs, scar*ves*; money, mon*ies* (sums of)

Other nouns ending in *f* or *fe* form the plural in the usual manner, by adding *s*.

roof, roofs; belief, beliefs

6. Nouns ending in *o* preceded by a consonant form the plural by adding *es*.

potato*es*, tomato*es*, mosquito*es*, echo*es*, hero*es*

There are many exceptions to this rule. Among the common ones are:

halos, altos, dynamos, pianos, solos

7. Nouns ending in *o* preceded by a vowel form the plural in the usual way, by adding *s*.

cameos, folios

8. Some nouns form the plural by changing an internal vowel or by adding a syllable ending in *n*.

Mouse, mice; tooth, teeth; man, men; child, children; ox, oxen

9. A few nouns have the same form in the plural as in the singular.

deer, sheep, trout, heathen, salmon, elk, Japanese, grouse

10. Some nouns have two plurals differing in meaning.

brother { brothers (relatives)
brethren (members of a society)

fish { fishes (considered individually, or referring to different species of fish)
fish (considered individually or collectively)

11. Numbers, letters, and names of words form the plural by adding the apostrophe and *s*.

The *a's* and the *6's* are poorly made.
There are too many *and's* in the sentence.

12. Compound nouns usually form the plural on the principal word in the combination.

fathers-in-law, men-of-war, attorneys general, passers-by

13. Nouns ending in *-ful* form the plural by adding *s* to the last syllable.

cupfuls, spoonfuls

When more than one cup or spoon is meant, write two separate words: cups full, spoons full.

She used three *cupfuls* of flour in the pudding.
He brought the two *cups full* of milk.

14. Proper nouns form the plural like common nouns. (See page 33, § 2.) But proper nouns ending in *y* preceded by a consonant do not change the *y* to *i*.

Jones, Joneses; Smith, Smiths; *but:* Mary, Marys

The plural of *Miss* is *Misses.*

Mesdames, the plural of *Madame,* is used as the plural of *Mrs.*

Messrs., the abbreviation of the French *Messieurs,* is used as the plural of *Mr.*

Title and name are never pluralized together. When the title is pluralized, the noun is not changed, and vice versa.

Right: the Miss*es* Smith, or the Miss Smith*s*.
Wrong: the Miss*es* Smith*s*

15. Some words borrowed from foreign languages retain the foreign plural. In some instances a word has both a foreign and an English plural. The most common nouns of this group are given below.

Words ending in *us*, forming the plural by changing *us* to *i:*

alumnus	alumni
terminus	termini

Words ending in *a*, forming the plural by changing the *a* to *ae* (usually printed *æ*):

alumna	alumnæ
vertebra	vertebræ
formula	formulæ, formulas

Words ending in *is*, forming the plural by changing *is* to *es:*

oasis	oases
thesis	theses
parenthesis	parentheses
analysis	analyses
crisis	crises
axis	axes

Words ending in *on*, forming the plural by changing the *on* to *a:*

phenomenon	phenomena

Words ending in *um*, forming the plural by changing *um* to *a:*

datum	data
stratum	strata (rarely, stratums)
curriculum	curricula, curriculums
memorandum	memoranda, memorandums

Words ending in *eau*, forming the plural by adding *x:*

beau	beaux, beaus
trousseau	trousseaux
tableau	tableaux, tableaus

Voice, Mood, and Tense

Voice

1. The passive voice is generally less forceful than the active voice. Careless use of the passive weakens the tone of a sentence.

Poor: Your letter has been received by us.
Better: We received your letter.

Mood. The subjunctive

2. The subjunctive mood is now seldom used except to express condition (usually contrary to fact) or desire, in such sentences as the following:

If you *were* going to see her, what should you say?
If I *were* you, I should answer at once.
I wish I *were* going to hear him.
Oh, if I *were* only far away from here!

Tense

3. The present tense is used to express present time, and to make statements regarded as customarily or universally true. In a quoted statement of this kind following a verb in the past tense, the present tense shows the feeling of the speaker that the quoted statement is true; the past tense implies nothing as to its truth.

Right: He told us that some of the mushrooms in his garden *were* poisonous.

Right: He reminded us that some varieties of mushroom *are* poisonous.

Statements of permanent truth or of criticism about books, as in a book review, are usually expressed in the present tense.

Right: *Dynasts*, by Thomas Hardy, *is* based on the Napoleonic Wars.

Do not use the present tense to describe past events.

Wrong: Yesterday he *walks* up and *says* "Hello."
Right: Yesterday he *walked* up and *said* "Hello."

4. The past tense of the verb is never used with the auxiliary *have, has.* The past form of the verb always stands alone. Hence, such forms as *have saw, have went, have broke* are not permissible. The auxiliary must be omitted, or combined with the participle to form the present perfect tense.

Wrong: I *have saw* my mother.
Right: I *saw* (or, *have seen*) my mother.
Wrong: We *have came* to hear the concert.
Right: We *came* (or, *have come*) to hear the concert.

5. The present perfect tense must be carefully distinguished from the past tense. The past tense expresses action completed in past time. The present perfect tense expresses action which is past in relation to the present moment (the moment of speaking or writing) but which may continue up to and into the present moment.

I *have been* laughing.
We *have* not yet *heard* from John (not: We *did* not yet *hear.*)
My father *has made* many visits to Germany.

6. The future tense is formed with the auxiliaries *shall* and *will.* Although the use of *will* for *shall* is spreading, careful writers still observe the distinction between them.

To express simple future time, use *shall* with the first person, *will* with the second and third persons.

I shall go (I intend to go).	We shall go.
You will go (you intend to go).	You will go.
He will go (he intends to go).	They will go.

To express determination, obligation, or necessity, use *will* with the first person, *shall* with the second and third persons.

I will go (I am determined to go).	We will go.
You shall go (you must go).	You shall go.
He shall go (he must go).	They shall go.

In a question, use the auxiliary expected in the answer.

Shall you go? (Answer expected, I shall go).
Will you go? (Answer expected, I will go).

7. In general, *should* and *would* follow the rules for the use of *shall* and *will.* But *should* is used for all persons to express condition or purpose in a subordinate clause.

She said that she *would* go.
If I *should* return, I should not expect to find you here.
If he *should* fail, we should all be lost.

Infinitives

8. The tense of the infinitive depends on the tense of the main verb.

(*a*) If the action of the infinitive is future to that of the main verb, or is going on at the same time as that of the main verb, the present tense of the infinitive is required, even though the main verb is in the past tense.

Wrong: I intended *to have gone.*
Right: I intended *to go.*
Wrong: She expected *to have seen* me at the rehearsal.
Right: She expected *to see* me at the rehearsal.

(*b*) When the action of the infinitive has been completed before the time of the action expressed in the main verb, the perfect infinitive should be used.

Wrong: He is reported *to be killed.*
Right: He is reported *to have been* killed.
Right: I am glad *to have seen* the Alps.
Right: He was thought (or, is thought) *to have been* wounded.

9. Avoid splitting the infinitive.

Wrong: He hopes *to always be* ready when he is called.
Right: He hopes *always to be* ready when he is called.
Wrong: He is able *to easily shape the clay.*
Right: He is able *to shape the clay easily.*

Principal parts

10. Correct usage of verbs requires a knowledge of their principal parts. The following table includes most of the commonly used troublesome verbs. The dictionary gives the principal parts of every verb it defines and should be consulted whenever a question of verb form arises.

Principal Parts of Verbs

Forms in parentheses are permissible but not preferred in modern usage.

Present	*Past*	*Past Participle*
am or be	was	been
arise	arose	arisen
awake	awoke (waked)	awaked (awoke)
bear	bore	borne, born[1]
beat	beat	beat, beaten
begin	began	begun
bend	bent	bent
bid	bade, bid	bidden, bid
bid (to make an offer)	bid	bid
blow	blew	blown
break	broke	broken
bring	brought	brought
burst	burst	burst
catch	caught	caught
choose	chose	chosen
come	came	come
deal	dealt	dealt
dive	dived	dived
do	did	done
draw	drew	drawn
dream	dreamed (dreamt)	dreamed (dreamt)
drink	drank	drunk
drive	drove	driven
eat	ate	eaten
fall	fell	fallen
fight	fought	fought
flee	fled	fled
fly	flew	flown
forget	forgot	forgotten, forgot
forsake	forsook	forsaken
freeze	froze	frozen
get	got	got (gotten)
give	gave	given
go	went	gone
grow	grew	grown
hang (an object)	hung	hung
hang (a person)	hanged	hanged
hide	hid	hidden (hid)

[1] *Born* is used only in the passive voice, in the sense *to be produced* or *brought forth*, when not followed by *by*.
He was *born* in 1912; she has *borne* three sons.

Present	*Past*	*Past Participle*
know	knew	known
lay	laid	laid
lead	led	led
lend	lent	lent
lie	lay	lain
prove	proved	proved (not proven)
ride	rode	ridden
ring	rang	rung
rise	rose	risen
run	ran	run
say	said	said
see	saw	seen
set	set	set
shake	shook	shaken
shine	shone	shone
show	showed	shown
shrink	shrank	shrunk
sing	sang	sung
sink	sank (sunk)	sunk
sit	sat	sat
slay	slew	slain
sleep	slept	slept
slide	slid	slid (slidden)
sneak	sneaked	sneaked
speak	spoke	spoken
spring	sprang (sprung)	sprung
steal	stole	stolen
stick	stuck	stuck
sting	stung	stung
stride	strode	stridden
strive	strove	striven
swear	swore	sworn
swim	swam	swum
take	took	taken
teach	taught	taught
tear	tore	torn
throw	threw	thrown
wear	wore	worn
weave	wove	woven
wet	wet (wetted)	wet
win	won	won
wring	wrung	wrung
write	wrote	written

ADJECTIVES AND ADVERBS

1. Adjectives modify nouns and pronouns, while adverbs modify verbs, adjectives, or other adverbs. Do not use an adjective where the sentence requires an adverb.

Wrong: The teacher spoke *clear* and *emphatic.*

The adjectives *clear* and *emphatic* are incorrectly used here to modify the verb *spoke.* Adverbs are required.

Right: The teacher spoke *clearly* and *emphatically.*

The adjective *sure* is often wrongly used as an adverb.

Wrong: This *sure* is a hard problem.
Right: This *surely* is a hard problem.

2. Most adverbs are formed by adding *-ly* to the adjective.

rapid, rapid*ly*; steady, steadi*ly*

But some adjectives end in *-ly,* and have no corresponding adverbs: lone*ly,* love*ly.*

The words *thus, much, straight, fast,* and *first* may be used as adverbs, and *-ly* should not be added to them.

3. The adjective and the adverb forms of a word may be alike. *Slow, fast, quick, ill, well, cheap, wrong, much, first,* are both adjectives and adverbs.

Some of these words also have adverb forms ending in *-ly.*

Right: Drive slow; drive slow*ly.*
Right: Turn quick; turn quick*ly.*

4. The verbs *look, sound, taste, smell, feel,* and the like, may be followed by an adjective modifying the subject (The food tastes *good*) or by an adverb modifying the verb (The boy looked *carefully*). Use an adverb only when it is clear that the verb (and not the subject) is modified.

The flower smells *sweet* (not *sweetly*).
I feel *bad* (not *badly,* unless you mean that your sense of touch is poor).

After the verb *feel, well* should be used to express physical health, *good* to express good spirits.

Right: I feel *well* (I am in good health).
Right: I feel *good* (I am happy).

After *look,* do not use *good* referring to personal appearance.

Wrong: You look *good* in those clothes.
Right: You look *well* in those clothes.

5. The adverb is often misplaced in a sentence. Place it as near as possible to the word it modifies. The word *only,* which is both adverb and adjective, is especially troublesome.

Notice the difference of meaning in the following sentences, resulting from the different placings of *only.*

Only I was a farmer. I *only* was a farmer.
I was *only* a farmer.
I was a farmer *only.*

Comparison of adverbs and adjectives

6. The comparative degree of adjectives is formed by adding *-er* to the adjective, or by using *more* or *less* with the adjective. The superlative degree is formed by adding *-est* to the adjective, or by using *most* or *least* with the adjective.

clear	clearer	clearest
beautiful	more beautiful	most beautiful

Adverbs form the comparative and superlative degrees by the use of *more, most,* or *less, least.*

slowly	more slowly	most slowly

7. Use the comparative form of an adjective or an adverb when comparing two things. Use the superlative form only in comparing more than two things.

She is the tall*er* of the two (not tall*est*).
John is the old*est* of them all (not old*er*).

8. Adjectives and adverbs which express an absolute or perfect condition cannot logically be compared. Common usage, however, sanctions their comparison to express a greater, or the greatest, approximation to the quality referred to. With this group belong *unique, perfect, full, equal, straight, round, universal, unanimous.*

Right: This stick is *straighter* than that one.

Right: This apple is *rounder* than that one (meaning: This apple is *more nearly round* than that one).
Right: In order to establish *a more perfect* union . . .

9. Two negatives make an affirmative. "There was not no one there" means "There was someone there."

Wrong: I did*n't* say *nothing*.
Right: I did*n't* say *anything*, or better, I said *nothing*.

Since *hardly*, *only*, *but*, and *scarcely* are negative in meaning, they should not be used with other negatives.

Wrong: She could*n't hardly* see.
Right: She could *hardly* see.

10. Avoid the use of unnecessary or redundant adverbs. *Up* and *after* are frequently used unnecessarily.

Mix (not: Mix *up*) the eggs and the milk.
Follow (not: Follow *after*) the man ahead.
Finish (not: Finish *up*) your work.

The articles

11. The articles, *a*, *an*, and *the*, should be repeated with connected nouns or adjectives only when the connected words are to be taken separately.

He bought a red and green tie (one tie).
He bought a red and a green tie (two ties).
We met the president and manager of the company (one person).
We met the president and the manager of the company (two persons).

The article may be repeated for emphasis.

My father was a soldier and a gentleman.

The participial phrase

A participle is a verbal adjective; it may end in *-ing* (throw*ing*, runn*ing*, se*eing*) or in *-d*, *-ed*, *-t*, *-en*, and some other letters (lai*d*, harden*ed*, ridd*en*, hur*t*). Because a participle is an adjective, it, and the phrase to which it belongs, must modify a noun or pronoun. When this is kept in mind, the common error known as the "dangling participial phrase" or "hanging participle" may be more easily avoided.

In the sentence "Holding the door open, the mouse quickly ran out," the only noun which the participle *holding* can modify is *mouse.* The absurd meaning is obviously not what the writer intended. To be clear, the sentence should be recast: *She held the door open, and the mouse quickly ran out.*

Wrong: Watching for the airplane, it was seen over the woods.
(*Watching* modifies *it:* meaning impossible.)

Better: Watching for the airplane, we saw it over the woods.
(*Watching* modifies *we:* the meaning intended.)

Wrong: Standing in the doorway, the typewriters could be heard busily clicking.
(*Standing* modifies *typewriters:* meaning absurd.)

Improved: Standing in the doorway, he could hear the typewriters busily clicking.
(*Standing* modifies *he:* meaning intended.)

Prepositions

1. Do not confuse prepositions of similar meaning. Distinguish carefully between such prepositions as *at* and *to, between* and *among, in* and *into, by* and *with.*

At and *to*

To expresses motion toward a thing, while *at* usually indicates place or position.

She was *at* home (not, *to* home).
Now you are coming *to* the point.
Now you are getting *at* the meaning of it.

Between and *among*

Between expresses a relationship to two things; *among,* to more than two things.

The fortune was divided *between* my brother and me.
He divided the prize *among* the crew.

In and *into*

Into implies motion from without inward. *In* describes position within, and does not necessarily imply motion.

They went *into* the house.
They stayed *in* the cellar during the tornado.

By **and** ***with***

Use *by* to express agency of a person or thing, *with* to express instrumentality of a thing.

He was helped *by* a friend.
He was blinded *by* the storm.
He was helped *with* a gift of fifty dollars.

When you are in doubt about the meaning or use of a preposition, consult the dictionary. The chapter on "Diction and Idiom" in this book (page 57) includes some of the more troublesome prepositions.

2. Avoid the use of unnecessary prepositions. *Of* is frequently used unnecessariiy, especially after *off*.

I climbed *off* the platform (not *off of* the platform).

Of is not needed after the verbs *accept* and *remember*.

accept (not accept *of*)   remember (not remember *of*)

From is not needed before the words *hence, whence, thence.*

the city *whence* he comes (not *from whence* he comes)

3. Some authorities condemn the use of a preposition to conclude a sentence, on the ground that a most important place in the sentence should not be given to one of the less important elements. Good idiomatic usage sanctions this construction, however, and permits its use whenever ending a sentence with a preposition is natural and effective.

Conjunctions

1. Words used to connect other words or groups of words are called conjunctions. Common conjunctions are *and, for, but, since, that, as, therefore, moreover, nevertheless.* Since they are not interchangeable, effective writing requires a knowledge of the differences in their meanings and uses. Consult the dictionary whenever you are not sure of the meaning or use of a conjunction.

2. Do not use the conjunction *and* when *or, nor,* or *but* should be used.

Wrong: They did not see the palace *and* the park.
Right: They did not see the palace *nor* the park.

Wrong: The storm was severe, *and* it did not harm the ship.
Right: The storm was severe, *but* it did not harm the ship.

3. *Like* is not a conjunction. *It should never be used in place of the conjunction* **as**.

Wrong: She rides *like* I do.
Right: She rides *as* I do.

Wrong: He dresses just *like* he did in Mexico.
Right: He dresses just *as* he did in Mexico.

4. Correlative conjunctions

Some conjunctions, called correlatives, are used in pairs. When they are so used, each word of the pair must be in the same relative position as the other: that is, each must be placed before the same kind of word.

Common correlatives are:

both . . . and	though . . . yet
not only . . . but also	although . . . yet
either . . . or	since . . . therefore
neither . . . nor	if . . . then

Wrong: She must *either* see her father *or* her mother.
Right: She must see *either* her father *or* her mother.

Wrong: I *both* enjoyed the entertainment *and* the refreshments.
Right: I enjoyed *both* the entertainment *and* the refreshments.

Wrong: Tourists *not only* flock there in the winter, *but also* in spring and summer.
Right: Tourists flock there *not only* in the winter, *but also* in spring and summer.

Chapter IV

DICTION AND IDIOM

Nothing is more of an asset to a secretary than the ability to use words correctly and effectively. Correct pronunciation is essential to good speech, and careful diction is the basis of good writing, while a knowledge of the exact meaning and use of words and phrases is as necessary to the successful meeting and interviewing of people as it is to the competent handling of correspondence.

The increasing importance of letters in carrying on business is causing increased emphasis on their style, and is requiring in the secretary the ability to write letters not only correctly, but also with some individuality and distinction. For that reason the information contained in the following lists is particularly valuable, clarifying, as it does, so many troublesome faults and rectifying common errors of speech and writing.

Troublesome Idioms

The expressions characteristic of a language are called its idioms. Often idioms are illogical word combinations for whose origin no explanation can be given. All that we know is that certain words are used together to mean particular things, and that other combinations, even when more logical, go against the natural speech ways of our language; they are, in other words, unidiomatic. In the following list, those words are included whose meanings or idiomatic combinations are most frequently misused or troublesome. Many others may be found in the dictionary and in such books as *Juta's Phrase and Idiom* or Henderson's *Dictionary of English Idioms.*

Idioms

above: often used as an adjective in such expressions as "the *above* statement," though this usage is condemned by some authorities, who would prefer "the *former* statement" or "the statement *made above.*"

acquiesce: followed by *in,* not *with.*

administer: blows are *dealt;* medicine is *administered.*

advise: in commercial language often used pretentiously for *inform;* as, "We wish to *advise* you that our agent will call next week."

ain't I, aren't I: dialectal or colloquial for *am I not;* not in good general usage.

alike: use without *both* in some constructions.

Wrong: They are *both alike* in this particular.
Right: They are *alike* in this particular.
Right: I have two boys, and try to treat them *alike* (preferably not, *both alike*).

allow: do not use for *assert* or *promise.*

Wrong: He *allowed* that he would be there.

all right: correctly written thus. The single-word form with one *l* (*alright*) has no respectable status, although we have *all together* and *altogether, all ready* and *already.*

allude means to refer indirectly; as, "The speaker *alluded* to the presence of a distinguished guest in the audience."

almost: correct as an adverb. See **most.**

alone: it is better modern prose usage not to give the adjective *alone* the sense of *only.*

Less desirable: Charles *alone* will come.
Preferable: *Only* Charles will come.
Distinguish from: Charles will come *alone* (that is, unaccompanied).

among. See **between.**

angry at is commonly used of things, animals, or causes; if *angry at* is used of a person, the anger covers not merely the point at issue but the whole range of personal relations.

angry with is the idiom that should, as a rule, be used with respect to persons.

anticipate, expect: it is best to regard *anticipate* as implying foretaste of some emotion, usually pleasure, and not to use it for *expect.*

Inadvisable: I do not *anticipate* that it will rain Saturday.
Right: I already *anticipate* the good times we shall have on our camping trip.

any: incorrect in adverbial sense of *at all;* correct as a pronoun or adjective.

Wrong: I cannot encourage you *any.*
Right: I should like to give you tickets, but I haven't *any.*

any place: incorrect for *to any place; anywhere* is usually the appropriate expression.

Wrong: Shall we go *any place* today?
Right: Shall we go *anywhere* today?

apt implies fitness, suitability, or inherent tendency; as, an *apt* reply; a sympathetic person is *apt* to have friends.—**liable** implies at least the threat of sinister or unfavorable results; as, *liable* for damages; *liable* to get hurt.—**likely** implies probability, sometimes promise, such as readily appeals to belief; of the three words, it is the least specialized in meaning.

as, for *that* or *whether:* avoid.

Wrong: I do not know *as* I can tell you.
Right: I do not know *whether* I can tell you.

as, **so:** after negatives, most authorities prefer *so* to *as; so* is more explicit than *as.* Accordingly, some authorities distinguish: *not so warm as yesterday* implies that yesterday was actually warm; *not as warm as yesterday* does not indicate whether yesterday was warm or not.

as to: of doubtful use and should be avoided.

Bad: The question *as to* his fitness was given further consideration.
Better: The question *of* his fitness . . .

To avoid the use of *as to,* use *of, about, concerning.*

as though, as if: **as if** is preferable. *If* gives the exact meaning. *As though* is colloquial.

He looked *as if* he were in pain.

awful, awfully: do not use to intensify an adjective. In using *awful* with nouns, recall that it means *inspiring with awe, solemn.*

Right: The *awful* majesty of God.

back: do not use for *ago.*

Inadvisable: Three days *back* I saw him.
Right: Three days *ago* I saw him.

back of: do not say *in back of.* Idiom sanctions *in front of* but not *in back of.* *Back of* has some currency, but *behind* is generally to be preferred.

balance: do not use for *remainder.*

Wrong: The firm will be in new quarters for the *balance* of the year.

between, of two (occasionally of a larger group within which there is a duality of relation).—**among,** of more than two

Right: What is one *among* so many?
Right (common use): *Between* the adjoining properties there is a fence.
Right (special use): We have also to consider the relations *between* the states.

biweekly, properly, once every two weeks; for twice a week prefer *semiweekly.*

blame it on is better avoided.

Inadvisable: Don't *blame it on* me!
Correct: Don't blame me *for it.*

but, meaning *only:* use no other negative in the same clause.

Wrong: I haven't met *but* four.
Right: I have met *but* four.

but only: do not use both words if the meaning is *except.*

Wrong: No one was there *but only* Charles.
Right: No one was there *but* (or *except*) Charles. Cf. only.

but that, but what. See **that.**

calculate: do not use for *suppose.*

can expresses ability; **may** expresses permission or possibility.

> Right: *May* I leave early tonight?
> Right: *Can* he run a hundred yards in ten seconds?

Occasionally *may* stresses bare possibility; as, he *may* call today, but I do not expect him.

can but means *can only;* **cannot but** is an idiom for *cannot help.* There is sometimes a difference between these in meaning and always in emphasis. *He can but go* means that to go is all that he can do: either the most that he can do or the only thing that he can do. *He cannot but go* means that the circumstances or considerations that lead him to go are overpowering.

cannot but, cannot help: note the constructions that follow these phrases: *cannot but go, cannot help going* illustrate the correct usage; *cannot help but go* is a double construction that should be avoided.

claim: do not use loosely for *say,* or for *assert,* unless there is some question of right or title involved.

> Wrong: He *claims* that he was there.

compare to means to liken to, possibly in only one particular.

compare with means to examine in conjunction with, with respect to qualities, properties, or impressions. Roosevelt might be *compared with* any common citizen; he once *compared* himself *to* a bull moose.

complected: do not use this or its compounds; **complexioned** is correct, but a less awkward construction is often possible.

> Correct but awkward: She is dark-*complexioned.*
> Improved: She has a dark *complexion.*

correspond to implies more definiteness and closeness of correspondence than does **correspond with** in the latter's similar sense. Both are correct. *Correspond with* also means to communicate with by letters back and forth.

data (dā′tȧ): historically a plural and still to be so regarded. The singular, *datum,* is not so often used as is the plural.

Wrong: This data is submitted . . .
Right: These data are submitted . . .

date: avoid in the sense of an *engagement.*

died of, but **sick with.**

Right: He was *sick with* rheumatism, but *died of* pneumonia.

different from is correct. British usage sometimes employs *different to; different than* is to be avoided.

differ from: to be different from.

differ with: to have a personal disagreement with.

discover. See **invent.**

due to: this expression is correct only when *due,* an adjective, modifies some substantive. Its use as an adverbial equivalent of *because of, owing to,* is not sanctioned.

Wrong: He became sick, *due to* the unhealthful fog.
Right: He suffered from sickness, *due to* the unhealthful fog.

each other, of two (occasionally of a larger group within which there is a duality of relation).—**one another,** of more than two. Cf. **between.**

Right: The several conferees then departed, well pleased with *one another.*
Right (common use): James and John saw *each other* often.
Right (special use): I hope the pupils and their advisers will see *each other* often.

enthuse: this word lacks sanction. The noun *enthusiasm,* however, is in thoroughly good repute.

equally as, though grammatically defensible, lacks sanction. Use either word, but not both together.

Poor: This plan is *equally as* good.
Right: The return trip was *equally* delightful.
Right: Your trip was pleasant, and ours was *as* delightful.

The use of *as* is perhaps a trifle less emphatic.

Esq.: do not use with *Mr.*

etc.: abbreviation for *et cetera,* usually translated "and so forth." Do not say *and etc.,* as *et* is the Latin word for *and.*

Wrong: Lead, tin, zinc, *and etc.,* for sale.
Right: Lead, tin, zinc, *etc.,* for sale.

&c., a less formal way of writing the same thing, is rarely used in ordinary composition. *"And the like"* is commonly used in place of *etc.*

The use of *etc.,* when a definite term is called for, is not pleasing, and is particularly objectionable in a sentence meant to be impressive.

Wrong: Yours, *etc.*
Wrong: He was honest, faithful, devoted, *etc.,* through all his service.

every which way: inelegant. Prefer *in all directions.*

expect. See **anticipate.**

facts: do not use with *true.* All *facts* are true. The phrases *supposed facts* and *alleged facts,* seemingly exceptions to the foregoing, make use of a participial idiom not wholly logical, but in accordance with modern usage.

fewer: used of numbers.—**less**: used of amount. We speak of *fewer* fishes or *less* fish; but notice that even with numerals, amount rather than number may be uppermost in thought. *Less than ten years* is better than *fewer than ten years.* Cf. **many, much.**

fix: correct in such uses as *fixing* a site, *fixing* the attention. Do not use for *repair,* except in the sense of making something stable or stationary. We do not *fix* an automobile. Do not use for *arrange;* as, to *fix* the hair; or for *prepare;* as, to *fix* lunch.

gent: do not use for *gentleman.* *Gents' Furnishing Store* is inelegant English.

a great deal of, a good deal of: good colloquialisms, the former having a trifle more dignity.

guess: do not use for *suppose.*

had ought to, hadn't ought to: both forms are wrong, whether the time referred to is past or present. The verb *ought* is incomplete and has no past participle. Say *ought not to, ought not to have.*

had rather, had better, had best: these are all well established in English idiom. *Would rather* is a synonym for *had rather*, but is of no better standing. *Would better* and *would best* may be used, but they are less free, occasionally causing ambiguity with respect to the meaning of *would* and *should*, and affording no real advantage. *Would better* is not an exact synonym for *had better*.

hardly: this word itself carries a negative idea and should not be used with *not.*

Wrong: I could*n't hardly* do it.
Right: I could *hardly* do it.

heaps: do not use for *very much.*

Wrong: I like it *heaps.*

hopes: when used of a single prospect, prefer *hope* to *hopes.*

Inadvisable: I have no *hopes* of seeing him before winter.
Right: I have no *hope* of seeing him before winter.

how, as how: do not use loosely for *that.*

Wrong: He answered *as how* he couldn't return for a week.

identified with: improper for *employed by* or *associated with*, in the business sense.

Wrong: Mr. Jones, the retiring clerk, has long been *identified with* the firm.

in back of: wrong: see **back of.**

inside: used as a preposition, this word should not be followed by *of;* as a noun it may be followed by *of.*

Right: He stayed *inside* the yard.
Right: The *inside* of the house seemed less attractive.

in under: incorrect for *under.*

Wrong: It rolled *in under* the desk.
Right: It rolled *under* the desk.

Note, however, that the emphatic *in* may sometimes be correctly used before *under* to express a special meaning.

Right (special use): They put the coal *in under* the stairs.

Put in is really to be regarded here as a verb phrase.

invent, discover: to *invent* is to devise something that has not previously existed, or, sometimes, to devise something independently of a previous invention; to *discover* is to find something that has previously existed.

kind: say *this kind, that kind,* not *these kind, those kind.*

kind of: do not use in the sense of *slightly.*

Inadvisable: He was *kind of* sickly all last winter.

Kind of and *sort of* should not be followed by *a* or *an.*

Right: This is a new *kind of* rose.

laundered: not *laundried.*

learn: to acquire knowledge.—**teach**: to impart knowledge. The use of *learn* in the sense of *teach* was once correct, but is now definitely wrong.

leave: do not use for *let.* Prefer *let me go* to *leave me go.* Use *let me alone* to mean do not interfere with me; use *leave me alone* to mean depart, allow me to be in solitude.

less. See **fewer.**

let on: avoid in the sense *pretend* or (chiefly with a negative) *make known, disclose.*

Wrong: He *let on* that he was sick.
Wrong: He didn't *let on* that I had told him anything.

let's don't: wrong for colloquial *don't let's.*

liable. See **apt.**

like: **do not use** as a conjunction equivalent to *as if* or *as though.* It may be correctly used as an adjective.

Wrong: It looks *like* it would rain.
Right: It looks *as if* it would rain.
Right: It looks *like* rain.

likely. See **apt.**

loan: some authorities object to any use of *loan* as a verb. It is best, at all events, to restrict such use to the formal placing of a loan as a transaction, as by a bank. For the ordinary verb counterpart of the noun *loan,* use *lend.*

lots of, a lot of, meaning *many, much:* questionable colloquialisms; the former particularly is challenged. Use *a great deal of, a good deal of.*

majority: do not confuse with *plurality.*

many refers to number, and is used with the plural.—**much** refers to quantity, and is used with the singular.

Right: *many* irons, *much* iron; *many* fishes, *much* fish. Cf. fewer, less.

may. See **can.**

Messrs.: the plural abbreviation of the French *messieurs* used as the plural of *mister;* hence, it is used only with a proper name in the plural or with the implication of plurality.

Right: *Messrs.* Wells and Shaw will meet the *Messrs.* Chesterton.

most: do not use for *almost.* Frequently these words indicate very different meanings. *Most intelligent* is very different from *almost intelligent.*

most, more than: these expressions, in instances such as those below, involve different constructions.

Wrong: Your sample is *more* satisfactory than *any* that I have seen.

Right: Your sample is *more* satisfactory than *any other* that I have seen.

Right: Your sample is the *most* satisfactory that I have seen.

Avoid: Your sample is the *most satisfactory of any* that I have seen.

Right: Your sample is the *most satisfactory of all* that I have seen.

much. See **many.**

not but what: avoid.

Inadvisable: *Not but what* I could have overtaken him if I had wished.

Allowable (but elliptical): *Not that I could not* have overtaken him if I had wished.

nowheres: wrong for *nowhere.* Likewise **anywheres** is wrong for *anywhere,* and **somewheres** is wrong for *somewhere.*

off for of or from: avoid.

Wrong: I bought this set *off* the local dealer.
Right: I bought this set *from* (or *of*) the local dealer.

But note that some verbs take *off* as a matter of idiom.

Wrong: He got *off of* the horse.
Right: He got *off* the horse.

one: for the pronoun *one,* meaning a single one, the possessive is *his.*

Right: I saw two of them, and *one* waved *his* hand.

For the impersonal *one* the possessive is commonly *his* in American usage and usually *one's* in modern British usage, though variations in each occur. *One's* seems to some more careful, while to others it sounds stilted, particularly when the term is repeated. *He, him,* referring to *one,* are common in American usage.

Allowable: In the river country, *one* makes *his* way by canoe.

Allowable: If *one* is in the river country, *he* may have to depend on *his* canoe.

Allowable: In the river country, *one* makes *one's* way by canoe.

The reflexive is more closely linked with the word to which it refers than are other forms; hence, *oneself* is not uncommon; but *himself* is also in common use. Use *oneself* rather than *one's self,* which, however, is also allowable.

one another. See **each other.**

only: do not use as a preposition; recast the sentence.

Wrong: *No* one was there *only* Charles.

Right: *Only* Charles was there; or, No one was there *except* Charles.

Cf. **but only.**

only that: prefer *except that* when this is the meaning.

Inadvisable: Your umbrella is better than mine, *only that* the handle is not so convenient.

Right: Your umbrella is better than mine, *except that* the handle is not so convenient.

otherwise than: not *otherwise but.*

Right: How could I be *otherwise than* glad at such an opportunity?

ought. See **had ought.**

party: do not use loosely for *person.* A *person* may be a *party* to a contract, to a suit at law, to an agreement, to a dispute, or in certain other clear-cut relations; but ordinarily *party* signifies a number of persons.

posted: do not use for *informed.*

present, in the sense of *make acquainted,* is considerably more formal than *introduce,* which is usually the suitable term. The imperatives "Meet" and "Shake hands with" are both objectionable as forms of introduction.

promise: distinguish from *assure. Promise* looks toward a later fulfilment by the speaker.

Wrong: I was there yesterday, I *promise* you.
Right: I was there yesterday, I *assure* you.
Wrong: I know what the matter is, I *promise* you.
Wrong: I can tell what the matter is, I *promise* you.
Right: I will tell what the matter is, I *promise* you.

quite some time: avoid; prefer *a good while.*

real: do not use *real* to modify an adjective. *Really* is the correct form. Often *very,* or some livelier synonym, better fits the sense.

Wrong: He was *real* kind to me yesterday.

Possible (but probably inaccurate): He was *really* kind to me yesterday.

Right: He was *extremely* kind to me yesterday.

reckon: do not use for *suppose.*

regards: do not use for *regard.*

Wrong: I talked with him *in regards* to the subscription.
Right: I talked with him *in* (or *with*) *regard* to the subscription.
Right: Emma sends her *regards* to you.

same, the same: do not use in place of an ordinary pronoun. This may be approved in legal usage, and is much used in business correspondence, but it is not our ordinary idiom.

Avoid: I have returned the goods, and wish you would examine *the same.*
Right: I have returned the goods, and wish you would examine *them.*

seeing as how: wrong for *inasmuch as* or *since.*

Wrong: *Seeing as how* he was here, he must know.
Right: *Since* he was here, he must know.

semioccasionally: prefer *occasionally,* or (colloquially) *once in a while.*

settle: do not use for *pay,* if there has been neither confusion nor controversy in the matter.

sick with. See **died of.**

so: avoid the vague use of *so* with adjectives when there is no word to which to refer it. Perhaps not wholly wrong, it quickly tires, and may become irritating.

Inadvisable: They were all *so* good to me and I saw them *so* often and *so* many people have said to me *so* many times . . .
Correct: They were *so* good to me that I shall never forget them.

so after negatives is generally to be preferred to *as.* See **as.**

Undesirable: He is not *as* good *as* Charles.
Improved: He is not *so* good *as* Charles.

so, in the sense of *therefore,* should not be overworked. Too frequent employment of it makes sentences seem childish. A comma preceding it is usually a mistake in punctuation or indicates a structure of a type for which *so* is not suited.

Permissible: We had heard that hostile Indians were near; *so* we went back to the fort.

some place: do not use as an adverb for *somewhere*. Cf. **any place.**

Wrong: It must be here *some place*.
Right: It must be here *somewhere*.
Wrong: Let's go *some place* today.
Right: Let's go *somewhere* today.

spoonfuls: not *spoonsful.*

splendid: do not use profusely and vaguely as a term of praise. By derivation the word means shining. Like similar terms, it is capable of being used figuratively, but it should not be overworked. Similarly, guard against vagueness and inappropriateness in the use of such words as *fine, magnificent, nice, lovely, beautiful, wonderful, great, stunning, awful, fearful, terrible.*

suspicion: not a verb. *Suspect* (sŭs-pĕkt′) is the verb; *suspect* (sometimes, sŭs′pĕkt) is also a noun meaning a person suspected.

teach. See **learn.**

that: preferable to *but that* or *but what* after a word such as *doubt.*

Wrong: I do not doubt *but what* he will be there.
Inadvisable: I do not doubt *but that* he will be there.
Right: I do not doubt *that* he will be there.

After *know, but that* may be used for a special meaning. "Who knows *but that* the King may come?" is a softened and more evenly balanced equivalent of "Who knows *that* the King will *not* come?"

the reason is that: not *the reason is because.*

Wrong: *The reason is because* there is no gasoline.
Right: *The reason is that* there is no gasoline.

thusly: avoid this humorous variant of *thus*.

to: do not use carelessly for *on*.

Wrong: There was a rug *to* the floor.
Right: There was a rug *on* the floor.

In a few idiomatic phrases, in which the idea of attachment or close application underlies, this use is still correct.

Right: a tail *to* the kite, a string *to* the bow, not a shirt *to* one's back.

Note, however, that the proverbial *shirt to one's back* does not mean exactly the same as a *shirt on one's back*.

to, and (with verbs): use *to* rather than *and* with *go, try,* and *come* when purpose is to be expressed.

Inadvisable: I will *go and* see him.
Improved: I will *go to* see him.
Inadvisable: I will *try and* attend the meeting.
Improved: I will *try to* attend the meeting.

Where purpose is absent, or should not receive stress, the construction with *and* may be retained. This principle applies chiefly to invitations with *come*.

Preferable: Won't you *come and* have luncheon with me?

up: implies ascent toward or into a higher place or position.

He walked *up* the hill.

upon: implies a position of rest on the top or surface of an object.

He placed the books *upon* the shelf. But: They went *up on* the roof.

very: be careful not to use overmuch. Do not use carelessly with words that do not admit of being intensified

Wrong: The pickles were *very excellent*.
Right: The pickles were *excellent*.
Wrong: The pain was *very excruciating*.
Right: The pain was *excruciating*.

very (with participles): should be accompanied by another adverb when modifying a participle used as part of a verb. *Very* may be used alone to modify a participle used as an adjective.

Right: He *was very much amused* at her.
Right: He had a *very amused* look on his face.

Very is a much overworked word. It may be omitted in nine cases out of ten without the loss of emphasis.

way: not *ways*, in the sense of a short distance.

Wrong: He was a little *ways* ahead.
Right: He was a little *way* ahead.

Do not use for *away* in the sense of *far into*.

Wrong: He went *way* into the desert.
Right: He went *away* into, or *far into*, the desert.

when: do not use for *than*.

Wrong: I had no sooner taken my place *when* my friend entered.

Right: I had no sooner taken my place *than* my friend entered.

when, where (in definitions): do not use *is when* or *is where* in defining.

Poor: Trolling *is when* you draw the line through the water by the motion of the boat.

Improved: Trolling *is drawing* the line through the water by the motion of the boat.

without: do not use for *unless*.

Undesirable: I shall not go *without* he agrees.
Right: I shall not go *unless* he agrees.
Right: I shall not go *without* his agreeing.

would rather, would best, would better. See **had rather.**

you and I: correct for all nominative constructions.

you and me: correct for all objective constructions.

Wrong: between *you* and *I*.
Right: between *you* and *me*.

Common Errors in Speech and Writing Resulting from Confusion of Words Similar in Sound or Spelling

Many of the common errors in the use of our language are caused by a confusion of words whose sound or spelling is similar. The following list includes those groups of similarities which have been found to be most troublesome.

accept, consent to receive.
except, make an exception of.

adept, skilled or expert (a noun or adjective).
adapt, a verb, to make fit or suitable.
adopt, a verb, to make one's own.

advice (ăd-vīs′), the noun.
advise (ăd-vīz′), the verb.

affect, to influence; also, to pretend to have (a given trait of character); to behave artificially.
effect, to bring about. *Effect* as a noun means result; *affect* is not used as a noun, except in a technical psychological sense. Since to influence is to produce some result, it happens that the noun *effect* may occasionally be employed of an action for which the verb *affect* was used; but its direct connection is with the verb of the same form.

Right: The change *affected* him profoundly (or, had a profound *effect* on him).

Right: As soon as he took office, he *effected* sweeping reforms.

allude, to refer indirectly.
delude, to deceive.
elude, to escape; avoid.

allusion, an indirect reference.
delusion, a false belief.
elusion, the act of escaping or avoiding.
illusion, a false appearance.

Similarly, **allusive, delusive, elusive, illusive.**

already, beforehand.

all ready, colloquial for completely ready; sometimes, every individual ready.

> Compare: I have *already* seen it. I am *all ready* to see it. The visitors were *all* (that is, without exception) *ready* to see it.

altogether, completely.

all together, all in unison; all reckoned in one sum.

altar, a shrine.

alter, to change.

analyst, one who analyzes.

annalist, one who writes annals; a historian.

anecdote, a brief story, usually illustrative of a personal trait.

antidote, a remedy.

ascent, an upward slope; a climb.

assent, consent.

aseptic (*a*-sĕp′tĭk), free from germs of decay; surgically clean.

antiseptic, preventing decay.

audience places emphasis on the group and on its size.

auditors places emphasis on the individuals.

averse, disinclined.

adverse, unfavorable; opposed.

awhile, for or during a short time: used only as an adverb.

for a while, an equivalent expression, in which *while* is a noun.

> Right: ". . . which I have loved long since and lost *awhile.*"
>
> Right: He came *a long while* ago (or, *a while* ago).

beside, at or by the side of.

besides, also; in addition to.

Britain, the country.

Briton, a person.

Brittany, a province in northwestern France.

canvas, a cloth.
canvass (verb or noun), solicit.

capital, the city.
capitol, the building.

casual, happening by chance; accidental.
causal, relating to cause and effect.

censure, to blame; condemn.
censor, to judge as to fitness or propriety; expurgate.
censer, a vessel for burning incense.

census board, popular for Bureau of the Census or its subsidiaries, engaged in enumerating the population.
board of censors. See **censor**, above.

childish, having the weaker qualities of a child; foolish.
childlike, having the good qualities of a child; frank; trustful; innocent.

collision, violent encounter.
collusion, secret understanding; complicity.

compliment, an expression of approval or admiration.
complement, that which serves to complete.

comprehensible, understandable; capable of being comprehended or understood.
comprehensive, capable of comprehending, or including; inclusive of much: often contrasted with *compendious*.

condemnation, denunciation; censure.
commendation, praise.
conscious, aware.
conscientious, possessing or characterized by a sensitive conscience.

contemptuous, entertaining or expressing contempt.
contemptible, worthy of contempt.

continual refers to time and may apply to what is periodically interrupted and resumed.

continuous applies to that which is uninterrupted, and may refer to time or space.

a *continual* wailing, but a *continuous* wall

Distinguish also from **perpetual**, everlasting; without end.

correspondent, one who writes letters or articles.
corespondent (kō″rê-spŏn′dĕnt), a joint respondent or defendant in a suit, usually a divorce suit.

council, a deliberative body.
counsel, advice; also, an adviser.
consul, a representative of a foreign government; also, a Roman executive magistrate.

Distinguish likewise *councilor*, *counselor*.

credible, worthy of belief.
creditable, worthy of receiving credit or praise.
credulous, foolishly disposed to believe.

Cf. **incredible, incredulous.**

currant, a fruit.
current, a continuous flow; what is passing.

depositary, preferred for a person.
depository, preferred for a place.

deprecate, to plead against; disapprove; view with regret.
depreciate, to diminish in value; speak slightingly of.

desert (dê-zûrt′), (verb), to abandon; also (noun), due reward; merit.
dessert (dĕ-zûrt′), (noun), a course usually served at the end of a dinner or luncheon.
desert (dĕz′ẽrt), a solitary place: the noun corresponding to the verb *desert*, to abandon (listed above), but differently pronounced.

detract, to draw away; withdraw; also, to defame.
distract, to draw (the attention) in various directions; confuse; disorder.

device (dḗ-vīs′), the noun.
devise (dḗ-vīz′), commonly a verb; also a noun in certain legal senses.

dictaphone, the business phonograph.
dictograph, the detective phonographic device.

diseased (dĭ-zēzd′), afflicted with disease.
deceased (dḗ-sēst′), dead: chiefly a legal term.
disinterested, impartial; without selfish interest.
uninterested, unmoved; unresponsive; without emotional interest.

dispense, to deal out; administer.
dispense with, to do without.

disposition, arrangement; also, inclination; temper; habit of mind.
deposition (dĕp″ṓ-zĭsh′ŭn; dē″pṓ-zĭsh′ŭn), sworn testimony obtained out of court; also, the act of placing in trust; also, removal from an office, especially from a kingship; also, sediment.

distinct, clear.
distinctive, individual; characteristic.
distinguished, celebrated.

divers, various; sundry.
diverse, of different natures.

Contrast: They were actuated by *divers* motives.
They were actuated by *diverse* motives.

duel, a combat between two persons.
dual, expressing, or composed of, two.

economical, thrifty.
economic, pertaining to economics.

elegy, a reflective song or poem dealing with death.
eulogy, formal praise, not necessarily of one dead; an encomium.

elicit, to draw forth; educe.
illicit, illegal.

emigrant, one who moves from a country.
immigrant, one who moves into a country: note the doubling of the *m*.

eminent, distinguished.
imminent, impending.
immanent, indwelling; as, the conception of an *immanent* deity.

epithet, an adjective or a phrase denoting a characteristic.
epitaph, an inscription on a monument.

etymology, the science of the derivation of words.
entomology, the science that treats of insects.

exceed, to go beyond; implying excess.
excel, to surpass: usually implying excellence.

exceedingly, very greatly.
excessively, too greatly.

exceptional, unusual; out of the ordinary.
exceptionable, open to criticism or objection.

excite, to rouse.
incite, to rouse or instigate to a particular action.

expect relates to the future.
suspect relates usually to the present, sometimes to the past or the future, and often implies something unfavorable or unpleasant. Sometimes *suppose* is better than either *suspect* or *expect.*

Right: I *expect* he will be there tomorrow.
Wrong: I *expect* he is now coming up the stairs.
Right: I *suspect* he is now coming up the stairs.
Wrong: I *expect* that you wish to see me.
Right: I *suppose* that you wish to see me.

expiate, to atone for.
expatiate, to talk freely and at length.
expatriate, to exile; banish.

extant, continuing to exist; not destroyed, extinct, or lost.
existent, existing: having actual being. The distinction is not wide; the second form is much the commoner; the difference in spelling should be noted.
extent, measure; compass.

farther, preferred for distance; as, the *farther* limit, the *farther* star: occurring more often as an adverb than as an adjective; as, to travel *farther*.
further, preferred for time or degree; as, a *further* instance, a *further* increase: occurring also as an adverb; as, to investigate *further*.

ferment, to produce fermentation in; hence, to excite or to become excited.
foment, to bathe with medication; to foster; hence, usually, to incite; instigate; as, to *foment* revolt.

formerly, at a former time.
formally, in a formal manner.

forth, forward or out.
fourth, one of four equal parts that make up a whole.

guerrilla (gĕ-rĭl′ȧ), a combatant in irregular warfare.
gorilla (gȯ-rĭl′ȧ), a manlike ape.

hanged, executed by hanging.
hung, past tense and past participle of *hang* in other senses.

healthy, possessing health; revealing health.
healthful, imparting or favorable to health; wholesome.

hoard, supplies or treasures secretly amassed.
horde, a multitude or swarm, as of wandering barbarians.

human, pertaining to mankind; having qualities common to mankind.
humane, benevolent or compassionate.

hypocritical, deceitful.
hypercritical, excessively critical.

imperative, urgent; authoritative; unavoidable.
imperious, dictatorial; overbearing; also, sometimes, overmastering.
imperial, pertaining to empire; also, magnificent in display or manner.

incredible, not worthy of belief: seldom used of persons. Cf. **credible.**
incredulous, not disposed to believe; skeptical.

indict (ĭn-dīt′), to charge with a crime.
indite (ĭn-dīt′), to write; compose.

ingenious, clever; skilfully contrived.
ingenuous, frank; artless.

instance, an illustration or example; also, a request.
instants, particular moments of time; seconds.

interstate, between states.
intrastate, within a state.
intestate (ĭn-tĕs′tāt), not having made a will.

irreverent, lacking in reverence.
irrelevant, lacking in pertinence; off the subject. Notice the difference in the position of the *v* sound and in the final vowel.

its, belonging to *it.*
it's, a contraction meaning *it is, 'tis.*

later, refers to time.
latter refers usually to position, as in a list or in casual mention.

leave, departure; also, permission.
lief, gladly. Do not use *leave* or *leaves* as an adverb.

Right: I gave him *leave* to go.
Right: I'd as *lief* go.
Wrong: I'd as *leave* go.

lie (past tense *lay,* past participle *lain*), to recline; intransitive.

lay (past tense and past participle *laid*), to place; mainly, but not exclusively, transitive.

loose (lo͞os), unfastened; also, to unfasten.
lose (lo͞oz), to fail to keep; be deprived of.

luxuriant, fertile; abundant; profuse.
luxurious, devoted to luxury.

magnet, iron or steel possessing the power of attraction.
magnate, a person of influence, power, or wealth.

majority, in voting, a portion greater than half of the total number of the votes cast.
plurality, the excess or margin of votes which one candidate has over another.

mantle, a cape or wrap.
mantel, a shelf, as above a fireplace.

neglect, preferred as a noun, when the emphasis is on the instance rather than on the character or attitude.
negligence, preferred when the attitude of mind is to be stressed.

new, recent; not previously known or used.
novel, unusual or strange.
novel, a book of fiction.

noted, distinguished or famous; as, a *noted* physician.
notorious, noted in an unfavorable sense; as, a *notorious* criminal.

observance, the act of keeping, or paying attention to, laws or customs; also, a rite, ceremony, or custom.
observation, the act of noting or examining; also, a remark.

ordnance, artillery; military supplies.
ordinance, an established law or statute.

pagoda (pȧ-gō′dȧ), an eastern temple of many stories, taking the form of a tall, pyramidal tower.
pergola (pûr′gō̄-lȧ), an arbor or trellis.

per cent, used to indicate rate in hundredths; as, six *per cent.*
percentage, the noun; as, it proved difficult to compute the exact *percentage.*

persecute, to pursue in order to injure.
prosecute, to bring suit against or bring to trial.

personal, relating to an individual and his private affairs.
personnel, denoting or pertaining to persons employed in an organization.

pertinent, in *a pertinent question,* should not be confused with **impertinent,** although the meanings of the two words in this phrase approach each other. *Impertinent* has a derived meaning of impolite, which has become its commonest sense. *Pertinent* means bearing closely upon the matter in hand. On those occasions when a question bears directly upon a highly personal matter which it is hardly proper to approach otherwise than distantly, the expression *pertinent question* may refer to what is in fact an *impertinent question.*

Note that **pert,** too, has much the same meaning as *impertinent,* though there is a suggestion of not unpleasing vivacity about the former term.

practical, applicable to practice; workable under real, as opposed to ideal, conditions.
practicable, capable of being put into effect under the existing conditions.

precipitous, very steep, like a cliff; descending rapidly.
precipitate, rash; sudden.

prescribe, advise; order.
proscribe, condemn; forbid.

presumptive, affording ground for supposition: used chiefly as in *presumptive evidence* and in *heir presumptive.*
presumable, capable of being believed or taken for granted.
presumptuous, arrogant.

principle (noun), a rule, law, or general truth.

principal (adjective), chief; also (noun), used in a number of senses in which the idea of "chief" is inherent, as: (1) the headmaster of a school; (2) the sum of money on which interest is computed; (3) a major participant in a crime, as opposed to an accessory; (4) an actor in a main part, as opposed to a member of the supporting cast; etc.

pronunciation, the correct selection, combination, and discrimination through stress, of the sounds recognized in a given language.
enunciation, the correct rendering of the sounds in a given language, often with respect to distinctness.

prophecy (prŏf'ē-sĭ), (noun), prediction.
prophesy (prŏf'ē-sī), (verb), to utter prophecy; predict.

proposal, an offer.
proposition, a statement presented for consideration. Avoid the loose use which has developed within commercial slang.

propose, to offer; sometimes, to offer as a declared intention.
purpose (verb), to form or have the intention.

quite, fully; completely.
quiet, free from noise; peaceful; at rest. The confusion here is chiefly one of spelling.

recipe, preferred of cookery.
receipt, noun corresponding to the verb *receive,* with a number of special meanings; allowable also of cookery.

respectable, worthy of respect.
respectful, showing respect.

respectfully, in a manner indicative of respect.
respectively, with due regard to position or order of mention.

Right: Yours *respectfully.*
Wrong: Yours *respectively.*
Right: The three parcels that I have mentioned were to go to Jones, Smith, and Brown *respectively.*

rout (rout), to put to flight; also, to root up; scoop out; bring to light.
route (rōōt), to send by a certain way.

sensuous, appealing to the senses.
sensual, relating to the grosser senses.

sewage, preferred for the waste matter.
sewerage, preferred, when a single word is to be used, for a sewage system.

sit, be seated; mainly but not exclusively intransitive.
set, to put; mainly but not exclusively transitive.

solidity, the state of being solid, or hard and heavy.
solidarity, the state of being united in opinion, effort, or purpose.
sodality, a fraternal organization.

sometime, formerly; a past, indefinite time; once.

I am sure that I have met you *sometime.*

sometimes, now and then; occasionally; at times.

I'm *sometimes* up; I'm *sometimes* down.

specially, for a particular purpose, a particular care.
especially, in a high degree.

Specially chosen as being *especially* durable.

stationary, not moving.
stationery, writing material.

statue, image.
statute, enactment.

stimulus, that which rouses the mind or senses: often used of a sense impression.
stimulant, a remedy or agent regarded as producing increased functional activity; especially, an intoxicant.

therefore (*th*âr′fōr; *th*ûr′-), for this or that reason.
therefor (*th*âr-fôr′), in return for this or that: rather formal and not very common.

typographical, relating to printing or type.
topographical, relating to maps and charts.

umpire, a judge; an arbiter.
empire, a nation, the sovereign of which is an emperor.

valuable, of much value.
valued, appreciated; of recognized value.

venal, mercenary; corrupt.
venial, pardonable; trivial.

veracious, true; truthful.
voracious, ravenous; greedy.

vocation, preferred for one's primary or recognized calling or profession.
avocation, preferred for an interest secondary to the vocation, which may be a recreation, a hobby, or a second occupation.

waver, to flicker; also, to hesitate.
waiver, relinquishment of a right.

Words Frequently Mispronounced

(The quality of sound denoted by the various diacritical marks is shown in the key at the foot of the page.)

acclimate	å-klī′mât	alumnæ	*ȧ*-lŭm′nē
acumen	*ȧ*-kū′mĕn	alumni	*ȧ*-lŭm′nī
address (*noun*)	å-drĕs′	amateur	ăm″*ȧ*-tûr′
address (*verb*)	å-drĕs′	amenable	*ȧ*-mē′n*ȧ*-bl
admirable	ăd′mĭr-*ȧ*-bl	amenity	*ȧ*-mĕn′ĭ-tĭ
adult	*ȧ*-dŭlt′	anchovy	ăn-chō′vĭ
adversary	ăd′vẽr-sâ-rĭ	antarctic	ănt-ärk′tĭk
advertisement	ăd-vûr′tĭz-mĕ̊nt	apotheosis	ăp″ō̇-thē′ō̇-sĭs
alias	ā′lĭ-ås	apparatus	ăp″*ȧ*-rā′tůs
alibi	ăl′ĭ-bī	applicable	ăp′lĭ-k*ȧ*-bl
Alma Mater	ăl′m*ȧ* mā′tẽr	apricot	ā′prĭ-kŏ̊t
almond	ä′mŭ̊nd	apropos	ăp″rō̇-pō′
alternate (*adj.*)	ăl-tûr′nāt	archangel	ärk′ān′jĕ̊l
alternate (*verb*)	ăl′tẽr-nāt	archbishop	ärch′bĭsh′ŭ̊p

āte, senåte, râre, căt, ȧsk, fär, åffect, commȧ; scēne, ėvent, ĕdge, writẽr, novĕ̊l; mīne, begĭn; cōld, ōbey, côrd, dôg, stŏp, cŏ̊mpare; ūnit, circŭlate, bûrn, cŭt, focůs; mo͞on, fo͝ot; mound; coin; gold; jewel; yellow; sing; child; show; thin; *th*en; hw, *wh*en; zh, azure.

archetype	är'kē-tīp
archipelago	är-kĭ-pĕl'*ȧ*-gō
architect	är'kĭ-tĕkt
arctic	ärk'tĭk
atelier	ȧ"tē-lyā'
athlete	ăth'lēt
athletic	ăth-lĕt'ĭk
aviator	ā'vĭ-ā"tēr
bade	băd
banal	băn'ăl
banquet	băng'kwĕt
bicycle	bī'sĭ-kl
biography	bī-ŏg'r*ȧ*-fĭ
blatant	blā'tănt
bouquet	bōō-kā'
brigand	brĭg'ănd
brooch	brōch
brougham	brōō'ŭm; brōōm
brusque	brŏŏsk
buoy	boi
casualty	kăzh'ū-ăl-tĭ
cello	chĕl'ō
chastisement	chăs'tĭz-mĕnt
chauffeur	shō"fûr'
chic	shēk
chiropodist	kī-rŏp'ō-dĭst
cigarette	sĭg"*ȧ*-rĕt'
clique	klēk
combatant	kŏm'băt-ănt
combative	kŏm'b*ȧ*-tĭv
comparable	kŏm'p*ȧ*-r*ȧ*-bl
comptroller	kŏn-trōl'ēr
condolence	kŏn-dō'lĕns
conduit	kŏn'dĭt
connoisseur	kŏn"ĭ-sûr'
contrary	kŏn'tr*ȧ*-rĭ
contumely	kŏn'tū-mē-lĭ
conversant	kŏn'vēr-sănt
corral	kŏ-răl'
coupon	kōō'pŏn
creek	krēk

culinary	kū'lĭ-nā-rĭ
daguerreotype	d*ȧ*-gĕr'ō-tīp
data	dā't*ȧ*
deaf	dĕf
débris	dā"brē'
decade	dĕk'ād
decadence	dē-kā'dĕns
decadent	dē-kā'dĕnt
decorum	dē-kō'rŭm
defalcate	dē-făl'kāt
defect	dē-fĕkt'
deficit	dĕf'ĭ-sĭt
demise	dē-mīz'
desideratum	dē-sĭd"ēr-ā'tŭm
despicable	dĕs'pĭ-k*ȧ*-bl
detail	dē-tāl'
digest (*noun*)	dī'jĕst
digest (*verb*)	dĭ-jĕst'
diphtheria	dĭf-thē'rĭ-*ȧ*
dirigible	dĭr'ĭ-jĭ-bl
discharge	dĭs-chärj'
discourse	dĭs-kōrs'
dishabille	dĭs"*ȧ*-bēl'
dishevel	dĭ-shĕv'ĕl
divan	dĭ-văn'
drought	drout
egoism	ē'gō-ĭzm
egotism	ē'gō-tĭzm
encore	äṅ"kôr'
envelope	ĕn'vē-lōp
environs	ĕn-vī'rŭnz
epitome	ē-pĭt'ō-mē
exquisite	ĕks'kwĭ-zĭt
extol	ĕks-tŏl'
façade	f*ȧ*-säd'
falcon	fô'kn
fetid	fĕt'ĭd
fiat	fī'ăt
film	fĭlm (one syllable)
finance	fĭ-năns'
flaccid	flăk'sĭd

forehead	fŏr'ĕd
formidable	fôr'mĭ-d*a*-bl
foyer	fwä″yā'
fragile	frăj'ĭl
gallant (*adj.*)	găl'ănt, *n.* gȧlănt'
gaol	jāl
gape	gāp
genealogy	jĕn″ē-ăl'ō-jĭ
genuine	jĕn'ū-ĭn
gesture	jĕs'tûr
giblet	jĭb'lĕt
gibbous	gĭb'ŭs
gist	jĭst
gondola	gŏn'dō-l*a*
gratis	grā'tĭs
grievous	grēv'ŭs
grimace	grĭ-mās'
grimy	grīm'ĭ
guardian	gär'dĭ-ăn
hearth	härth
heinous	hā'nŭs
homage	hŏm'āj
horizon	hō-rī'zŭn
hospitable	hŏs'pĭ-t*a*-bl
ignoramus	ĭg-nō-rā'mŭs
illustrate	ĭ-lŭs'trāt
impious	ĭm'pĭ-ŭs
implacable	ĭm-plā'kȧ-bl
incognito	ĭn-kŏg'nĭ-tō
incomparable	ĭn-kŏm'p*a*-r*a*-bl
indecorous	ĭn″dē-kō'rŭs
indict	ĭn-dīt'
indictment	ĭn-dīt'mĕnt
infamous	ĭn'f*a*-mŭs
inquiry	ĭn-kwīr'ĭ
inveigle	ĭn-vē'gl
irrelevant	ĭ-rĕl'ē-vănt
irreparable	ĭ-rĕp'*a*-rȧ-bl
irrevocable	ĭ-rĕv'ō-kȧ-bl

isolate	ī'sō-lāt
Italian	ĭ-tăl'yăn
lamentable	lăm'ĕn-t*a*-bl
larynx	lăr'ĭngks
lègionnaire	lā″zhyô″nâr'
leisure	lē'zhûr
long-lived	lông'-līvd″
maintenance	mān'tē-năns
mayonnaise	mā″ō-nāz'
memoir	mĕm'wŏr
millionaire	mĭl″yŭn-âr'
mischievous	mĭs'chĭ-vŭs
misconstrue	mĭs-kŏn'stro͞o
misled	mĭs-lĕd'
municipal	mū-nĭs'ĭ-păl
mustache	mŭs-tásh'
nape	nāp
necessarily	nĕs'ē-sā-rĭ-lĭ
oasis	ō-ā'sĭs
obligatory	ŏb'lĭ-g*a*-tō-rĭ
often	ôf'n
oleomargarine	ō″lē-ō-mär'g*a*-rēn
orchestral	ŏr-kĕs'trăl
papier-mâché	pȧ″pyā'-mä″shā'
pathos	pā'thŏs
patois	pȧ″twä'
patriotism	pā'trĭ-ŏt-ĭzm
penal	pē'năl
penalize	pē'năl-īz
peremptory	pĕr'ĕmp-tō-rĭ
pianist	pĭ-ăn'ĭst
piquant	pē'kănt
poignant	poin'ănt
portière	pôr″tyâr'
precedence	prē-sēd'ĕns
precedent (*adj.*)	prē-sēd'ĕnt
precedent (*noun*)	prĕs'ē-dĕnt

ūnit, circŭlate, bûrn, cŭt, focŭs; mo͞on, fo͝ot; mound; coin; gold; jewel
yellow; sing; child; show; thin; *th*en; hw, *wh*en; zh, a*z*ure.

premise (*noun*)	prĕm′ĭs	spontaneity	spŏn″tȧ-nē′ĭ-tĭ
premise (*verb*)	prē-mīz′	squalor	skwŏl′ŏr
presage (*noun*)	prĕs′āj	status	stā′tŭs
presage (*verb*)	prē-sāj′	strata	strā′tȧ
prestige	prĕs-tēzh′	suite	swēt
probably	prŏb′ȧ-blĭ	superfluous	sū-pûr′flōō-ŭs
		synchronous	sĭng′krō-nŭs
quinine	kwī′nīn		
		tepid	tĕp′ĭd
radiator	rā′dĭ-ā″tẽr	theater	thē′ȧ-tẽr
recess	rē-sĕs′	tomato	tō-mā′tō
recondite	rĕk′ŏn-dīt	tribunal	trī-bū′nȧl
renaissance	rĕn″ĕ-säṅs′		
rendezvous	räṅ′dȧ-vōō	vagary	vȧ-gā′rĭ
romance	rō-măns′	vaudeville	vōd′vĭl
		vehement	vē′hē-mĕnt
sacrilegious	săk″rĭ-lē′jŭs	verbatim	vẽr-bā′tĭm
salmon	săm′ŭn	via	vī′ȧ
scintillate	sĭn′tĭ-lāt	vicar	vĭk′ẽr
seismic	sīs′mĭk	vice versa	vī-sē vûr′sȧ
simultaneous	sī″mŭl-tā′nē-ŭs	victuals	vĭt′lz
sinecure	sī′nē-kūr		
sleek	slēk	yolk	yōk

Foreign Words and Phrases

The pronunciation key is the same as that given below for English words, except that the following additional symbols are needed:

kh—the guttural *ch* in German a*ch* (äkh) or i*ch* (ĭkh).

ö—German *schön* or French *feu*. This sound is like a combination of the sounds ō and ā. It is most nearly approximated if ā is pronounced with rounded lips. The nearest English equivalent is the ā sound in such words as *skein, feign*.

ü—German *für* or French *lune*. This sound is like a combination of the ōō and ē sounds, and is most nearly approximated if ē is pronounced with rounded lips. The nearest English equivalent is the ē sound in such words as *tier, fear*.

ṅ—French e*n*fa*n*t, no*m*. The nasalized *n* or *m* is not itself pronounced but indicates that its preceding vowel is pronounced with a nasal intonation. A nasalized *ah* sounds much like *ahng*, with the *g* not articulated.

'—used only in French words, following an *r, l, m,* or *y*, to indicate that the sound of these letters follows so closely upon the preceding sound that it does not make another syllable, as in *être* (âtr'), *simple* (sâṅpl'), or *Espange* (ĕs″-pȧny″). The last word is pronounced almost like ĕs″pȧn′yĕ, but is really in two syllables, as can be seen from the fact that there is no break between the y' and the preceding letter.

āte, senāte, râre, căt, ȧsk, fär, ȧffect, commȧ; scēne, ēvent, ĕdge, writẽr, novẽl; mīne, begĭn; cōld, ōbey, côrd, dôg, stŏp, cŏmpare; ūnit, circūlate, bûrn, cŭt, focŭs; mōōn, fŏŏt; mound; coin; gold; jewel; yellow; sing; child; show; thin; *th*en; hw, *wh*en; zh, azure.

à bas *French* (ȧ bä′), down; down with.
ab extra *Latin* (ăb ĕks′trȧ), from without.
ab initio *Latin* (ăb ĭn-ĭsh′ĭ-ō), from the beginning; from the very first.
ab intra *Latin* (ăb ĭn′trȧ), from within.
ab invito *Latin* (ăb ĭn-vī′tō), unwilling.
à bon marché *French* (ȧ bôn″ mȧr″shā′), at a good bargain; cheap.
ab origine *Latin* (ăb ō-rĭj′ĭ-nē), from the beginning; from the origin.
à compte *French* (ȧ kônt′), on account; in part payment.
ad astra per aspera *Latin* (ăd ăs′trȧ pûr ăs′pē-rȧ), to the stars through hardships.
ad captandum vulgus *Latin* (ăd kăp-tăn′dŭm vŭl′gŭs), to catch the crowd; in order to please.
à deux *French* (ä dö′), for two; between two.
ad finem *Latin* (ăd fī′nĕm), at the end; to the end.
ad infinitum *Latin* (ăd ĭn″fĭ-nī′tŭm), to infinity; endlessly.—*abbr.* **ad inf.**
ad initium *Latin* (ăd ĭn-ĭsh′ĭ-ŭm), at the beginning.—*abbr.* **ad init.**
ad interim *Latin* (ăd ĭn′tē-rĭm), meanwhile; temporarily.—*abbr.* **ad int.**
ad libitum *Latin* (ăd lĭb′ĭ-tŭm), at pleasure.—*abbr.* **ad lib.**
ad nauseam *Latin* (ăd nô′zhē-ăm), literally, to nausea; to (the point of causing) disgust.
ad patres *Latin* (ăd pā′trēz), (gone) to his fathers; dead.
à droite *French* (ȧ drwät′), to the right; on the right.
æquo animo *Latin* (ē′kwō ăn′ĭ-mō), literally, with equal mind; calmly; with equanimity.
affaire d'amour *French* (ä″fâr′ dȧ″mo͞or′), an amour; a love affair.
affaire d'honneur *French* (ȧ″fâr′ dô″nûr′), an affair of honor; a duel.
affaire du cœur *French* (ȧ″fâr′ dü kûr′), an affair of the heart; a love affair.
à fond *French* (ȧ fôn′), to the bottom; thoroughly; fully.

a fortiori *Latin* (ā fôr″shĭ-ō′rī), with stronger reason; more conclusively.

à gauche *French* (ȧ gōsh′), to the left; on the left.

à la bonne heure *French* (ȧ lȧ bôn″ ûr′), just in time: as an exclamation, good; fine.

à la carte *French* (ȧ lȧ kȧrt′), literally, by the card, or bill of fare: used to designate a meal in which each dish is paid for at a specified price: opposite of **table d'hôte.**

à la française *French* (ȧ lȧ fräṅ″sâz′), in the French fashion: in cookery, applied to various dishes, some of them not typically French.

à la mode *French* (ȧ lȧ môd′), in the fashion.

à l'anglaise *French* (ȧ läṅ″glâz′), in the English style: specifically, in cookery, roasted or boiled.

alter ego *Latin* (ăl′tẽr ē′gō̇), another, or second, I; an intimate or bosom friend.

amende honorable *French* (ȧ″mäṅd′ ô″nô″rȧbl′′), satisfaction given or reparation made, publicly, to the injured party.

amor patriæ *Latin* (ā′môr păt′rĭ-ē), love of one's country or native land.

amour propre *French* (ȧ″mo͞or′ prôpr′′), self-esteem.

anno Domini *Latin* (ăn′nō̇ dŏm′ĭ-nī), in the year of the Lord.

ante bellum *Latin* (ăn′tė bĕl′ŭm), before the war: usually taken to mean before the American Civil War.

ante meridiem *Latin* (ăn′tė mė-rĭd′ĭ-ĕm), before noon.—*abbr.* **a.m.**

à pied *French* (ȧ pyā′), on foot.

à plomb *French* (ȧ plôṅ′), plumb; in the perpendicular; hence, with assurance or ease of manner.

a posteriori *Latin* (ā pŏs-tē″rĭ-ō′rī), from the latter; hence, reasoning from effects to causes.

après moi (or **après nous**) **le déluge** *French* (ȧ″prâ″ mwȧ′ (no͞o′) lẽ dā″lüzh′), after me (or us) the deluge: a remark said to have been made by Louis XV to Madame de Pompadour.

a priori *Latin* (ā prĭ-ō′rī), from the former; hence, reasoning from cause to effect.

arbiter elegantiæ *Latin* (är′bĭ-tẽr ĕl″ė-găn′shĭ-ē), judge of elegance; authority in matters of taste: said of Caius Petronius, of Nero's court.

a rivederci *Italian* (ä rē″vā-dâr′chē), until our next meeting; good-by; au revoir.

arrière pensée *French* (ȧ″ryâr′ päṅ″sā′), a thought kept back; mental reservation.

ars longa, tempus fugit *Latin* (ärz lông′gȧ, tĕm′pŭs fū′jĭt), art (is) lasting, time (is) fleeting.

a tempo *Italian* (ä tĕm′pō), in time.

au contraire *French* (ō kôṅ″trâr′), on the contrary.

au courant *French* (ō ko͞o″räṅ′), literally, with the current; up to date; advised; informed.

au fait *French* (ō fâ′), well acquainted; skilful; expert.

au fond *French* (ō fôṅ′), at bottom; fundamentally; in the main.

auf Wiedersehen *German* (ouf vē′dẽr-zā″ẽn), till we meet again; good-by; au revoir.

au naturel *French* (ō nä″tü″rĕl′), in the natural state.

au revoir *French* (ō″ rẽ-vwȧr′), till we meet again; good-by: implying that the separation is to be temporary: distinguished from **adieu,** which implies a farewell, or final leavetaking.

autres temps, autres mœurs *French* (ōtr′″ täṅ′, ōtr′″ mûr′), other times, other ways or customs.

aux armes *French* (ō zȧrm′), to arms.

avec permission *French* (ȧ″vĕk″ pâr″mē″syôṅ′), with permission.

avec plaisir *French* (ȧ″vĕk″ plâ″zēr′), with pleasure.

à votre santé *French* (ȧ vôtr′″ säṅ″tā′), to your health: sometimes given as a toast.

beau monde *French* (bō″ môṅd′), the fashionable world.

beaux arts *French* (bōz är′), the fine arts.

belles-lettres *French* (bĕl=lĕtr′′), studies or writings of the purely literary kind.

bête noire *French* (bât″ nwȧr′), literally, black beast; a bugbear; an object of aversion.

bona fide *Latin* (bō′nȧ fī′dḗ), in good faith.

bon ami *French* (bôṅ ȧ-mē′), good friend.

bon jour *French* (bôṅ″ zhōōr′), good day; good morning.

bon mot *French* (bôṅ″ mō′), a witty saying.

bon soir *French* (bôṅ″ swȧr′), good evening; good night.

bon vivant *French* (bôṅ″ vē-väṅ′), an epicure; a boon companion.

bon voyage *French* (bôṅ″ vwȧ″yȧzh′), a good voyage (or journey) to you.

carpe diem *Latin* (kär′pḗ dī′ĕm), make use of the day; enjoy the present.

carte blanche *French* (kȧrt″ bläṅsh′), a blank paper; hence, unlimited authority.

casus belli *Latin* (kā′sŭs bĕl′ī), an occasion for war; that is, an act which justifies, or might cause, war.

caveat emptor *Latin* (kā′vḗ-ăt ĕmp′tôr), let the buyer beware.

cave canem *Latin* (kā′vḗ kā′nĕm), beware the dog.

c'est à dire *French* (sâ″ tȧ″ dēr′), that is to say; namely.

c'est autre chose *French* (sâ tōtr′″ shōz′), that is another matter; that is a different thing.

ceteris paribus *Latin* (sĕt′ē-rĭs păr′ĭ-bŭs), other things being equal.

chacun à son gout *French* (shȧ″kûṅ′ ȧ″ sôṅ″ gōō′), everyone to his taste.

chef de cuisine *French* (shĕf′ dē küē″zēn′), head cook: usually contracted to **chef.**

chef-d'œuvre *French* (shē-dûvr″), a masterpiece.

chemin de fer *French* (shē-mâṅ′ dē fâr′), a railroad.

cher ami (**chère amie**) *French* (shâr″ ȧ″mē′), dear friend.

cherchez la femme *French* (shâr″shā′ lȧ fȧm′), literally, look for the woman; there's a woman in the case.

chevalier d'industrie *French* (shē-vȧ″lyā′ dâṅ″düs″trē′), a swindler.

chez moi *French* (shā mwä'), at my house.
circa *Latin* (sûr'kȧ), around; round about; about.
cogito, ergo sum *Latin* (kŏj'ĭ-tō, ûr'gō sŭm), I think, therefore I am: a basic principle in Descartes' philosophy.
comme il faut *French* (kô" mēl" fō'), as it should be; proper.
compte rendu *French* (kônt' räṅ-dü'), an account given; a report.
con amore *Italian* (kōn ä-mō'rā), with love; earnestly; enthusiastically.
corpus delicti *Latin* (kôr'pŭs dē-lĭk'tī), the body, or substantial and essential facts, of a crime.
coup de main *French* (ko͞o" dē mâṅ'), a sudden military movement.
coup de maître *French* (ko͞o" dē mâtr''), a master stroke; an act showing ability.
coup d'état *French* (ko͞o" dā"tȧ'), a sudden act in politics, as the overthrow of an existing government.
coup de théâtre *French* (ko͞o" dē tā"ätr''), a sudden action in a play; hence, a theatrical effect.
coup d'œil *French* (ko͞o" dûy''), a rapid glance.
cum laude *Latin* (kŭm lô'dē), with praise.

dame d'honneur *French* (dȧm" dō"nûr'), maid of honor.
de bonne grâce *French* (dē bôn" gräs'), with good grace; willingly.
de facto *Latin* (dē făk'tō), in fact: used of a government actually though not necessarily legally in power.
de gustibus non (est) disputandum *Latin* (dē gŭs'tĭ-bŭs nŏn (ĕst) dĭs"pū-tăn'dŭm), there is no disputing about tastes.
Dei gratia *Latin* (dē'ī grā'shĭ-ȧ), by the grace of God.
de jure *Latin* (dē jo͞or'ē), of right; by right of lawful title.
de novo *Latin* (dē nō'vō), anew.
Deo volente *Latin* (dē'ō vō-lĕn'tĭ), if God wills.—*abbr.* **D.V.**
de profundis *Latin* (dē prō-fŭn'dĭs), out of the depths.
de rigueur *French* (dē rē"gûr'), obligatory; indispensable.
dernier resort *French* (dâr"nyā' rē-sôr'), a last resort.

de trop *French* (dẽ trō̇′), too much; hence, unwelcome.

deus ex machina *Latin* (dē′ůs ĕks măk′ĭ-nȧ), literally, a god (let down) from a machine (as in ancient theaters); an unexpected occurrence (which settles some problem); a superhuman agency.

dolce far niente *Italian* (dȯl′chā fär nyĕn′tā), literally, sweet to do nothing; it is charming to be idle.

Dominus vobiscum *Latin* (dŏm′ĭ-nůs vō̇-bĭs′kům), the Lord (be) with you.

dramatis personæ *Latin* (drăm′ȧ-tĭs pẽr-sō′nē), persons of the drama; the actors.

dulce et decorum est pro patria mori *Latin* (dŭl′sė ĕt dė-kō′-rům ĕst prō păt′rĭ-ȧ mō′rī), it is sweet and fitting to die for one's country.

ecce homo *Latin* (ĕk′sė hō′mō̇), behold the man: words of Pilate at Christ's trial.

édition de luxe *French* (ā″dē″syôṅ′ dẽ lüks′), an expensive edition (of a book).

editio princeps *Latin* (ė-dĭsh′ĭ-ō̇ prĭn′sĕps), a first edition.

en avant *French* (ä″ nȧ″väṅ′), forward.

en effet *French* (ä″ nĕ″fȧ′), in effect; in fact; indeed.

en famille *French* (äṅ″ fȧ″mēy′′), with one's family.

enfant gâté *French* (äṅ″fäṅ′ gä″tā′), a spoiled child.

enfants perdus *French* (äṅ″fäṅ′ pâr″dü′), literally, lost children; a forlorn hope: a military expression.

enfant terrible *French* (äṅ″fäṅ′ tâ″rēbl′′), literally, a terrible child; a child who makes embarrassing remarks.

enfin *French* (äṅ-fâṅ′), at last; finally; in short.

en masse *French* (äṅ″ mäs′), in a body; all together.

en plein jour *French* (äṅ″ plâṅ″ zhōōr′), in open day; before the whole world.

en rapport *French* (äṅ″ rȧ″pôr′), in agreement; in sympathy; in harmony.

entente cordiale *French* (äṅ″täṅt′ kôr″dyȧl′), a cordial understanding: used especially of relations existing between governments.

entr'acte *French* (äṅ″träkt′), interval between acts of a play; hence, performance in the interval.

entre nous *French* (äṅtr″ nōō′), between ourselves.

e pluribus unum *Latin* (ē plōō′rĭ-bŭs ū′nŭm), one out of many; meaning, one government made of many states: motto of the United States of America.

esprit de corps *French* (ĕs″ prē′ dē kôr′), group spirit.

esse quam videri *Latin* (ĕs′ė kwăm vĭ-dē′rī), to be rather than to seem.

ex cathedra *Latin* (ĕks kȧ-thē′drȧ), from the chair; with authority.

exempli gratia *Latin* (ĕg-zĕm′plī grā′shĭ-ȧ), for the sake of example; for instance.—*abbr.* **e.g.**

exeunt *Latin* (ĕk′sė-ŭnt), they go out: used as a stage direction.

ex libris *Latin* (ĕks lī′brĭs), from the books (of): a bookplate inscription.

ex necessitate rei *Latin* (ĕks nė-sĕs″ĭ-tā′tė rē′ī), from the necessity of the case.

ex officio *Latin* (ĕks ŏ-fĭsh′ĭ-ō), by right of office.

ex parte *Latin* (ĕks pär′tė), of one part or side; not disinterested.

ex post facto *Latin* (ĕks pōst făk′tō), literally, from after the deed. **Ex post facto law,** any law which applies to an act committed before the passage of the law.

facile princeps *Latin* (făs′ĭ-lė prĭn′sĕps), easily chief; by far the best.

faux pas *French* (fō″ pä′), a false step; especially, an offense against convention.

femme de chambre *French* (fȧm″ dē shäṅbr″), chambermaid; lady's maid.

festa *Italian* (fĕs′tä), a holiday; festival; entertainment; frequently, a religious festival.

fête champêtre *French* (fât″ shäṅ″pâtr″), a rural or open-air festival.

feu de joie *French* (fö″ dē zhwȧ′), a bonfire; also, a firing of rifles in token of joy.

fiat lux *Latin* (fī'ăt lŭks'), let there be light.
fidus Achates *Latin* (fī'dŭs ȧ-kā'tēz), faithful Achates; hence, a loyal friend: in allusion to the companion of Æneas in Virgil's *Æneid*.
fin de siècle *French* (fâṅ" dẽ syâkl''), end of the century, referring especially to manners and morals characteristic of the end of the nineteenth century.
fortiter in re, suaviter in modo *Latin* (fôr'tĭ-tẽr ĭn rē', swăv'ĭ-tẽr ĭn mō'dȯ), mightily in deed, gently in manner.
Frau *German* (frou), Mrs., the German title for a married woman.
Fräulein *German* (froi'līn), Miss, the German title for an unmarried woman.

gardez bien *French* (gȧr"dā' byâṅ'), take good care; watch out!
gauche *French* (gōsh), clumsy; awkward.
gaucherie *French* (gō"shẽ-rē'), a blunder; a clumsy act.
genius loci *Latin* (jē'nĭ-ŭs lō'sī), spirit of the place.
genre *French* (zhäṅr'), **1**, kind or type; **2**, a realistic presentation of common life in painting or sculpture.
Gesundheit *German* (gẽ-zŏŏnt'hīt), health (to you).
Gott mit uns *German* (gôt mĭt ŏŏns), God with us.
grâce à Dieu *French* (gräs' ȧ dyö'), thanks (be) to God.

haut gout *French* (ō" gōō'), high flavor: used of seasoning.
Herr *German* (hâr), Mr., the German title of respect.
Heimweh *German* (hīm'vā), homesickness.
hic jacet *Latin* (hĭk jā'sĕt), here lies: used in epitaphs.
hoc loco *Latin* (hŏk lō'kȯ), in this place.
hoc tempore *Latin* (hŏk tĕm'pȯ-rē), at this time.
hoi polloi *Greek* (hoi" pô-loi'), the many; the populace; the masses.
homme d'affaires *French* (ôm" dȧ"fâr'), a business man; an agent.
homme de lettres *French* (ôm" dẽ lĕtr''), a man of letters; a literary man.

homme d'esprit *French* (ôm″ dĕs″prē′), a man of wit.
honi soit qui mal y pense *French* (ô″nē″ swȧ′ kē mȧl″ ē päṅs′), literally, shamed be he who thinks evil of it: usually translated, evil be (it) to him who evil thinks.
horribile dictu *Latin* (hŏ-rĭb′ĭ-lė dĭk′tū), horrible to relate.
hors d'œuvre *French* (ôr″ dûvr′′), a relish.
humanum est errare *Latin* (hū-mā′nŭm ĕst ĕ-rā′rė), to err is human.

ibidem *Latin* (ĭ-bī′dĕm), in the same place; on the identical spot.—*abbr.* **ib.**; **ibid.**
ici on parle français *French* (ē″sē′ ôṅ pȧrl′ fräṅ″sâ′), French is spoken here.
idée fixe *French* (ē″dā′ fėks′), a fixed idea; an obsession.
in æternum *Latin* (ĭn ė-tûr′nŭm), forever; always.
in articulo mortis *Latin* (ĭn är-tĭk′ū-lō môr′tĭs), at the point of death.
in extremis *Latin* (ĭn ĕks-trē′mĭs), at the point of death; in the last extremity.
infra dignitatem *Latin* (ĭn′frȧ dĭg″nĭ-tā′tĕm), beneath one's dignity; undignified.—*abbr.* **infra dig.**
in hoc signo vinces *Latin* (ĭn hŏk sĭg′nō vĭn′sēz), in (or by) this sign thou wilt conquer.
in loco *Latin* (ĭn lō′kō), in place; in the proper place.
in loco parentis *Latin* (ĭn lō′kō pȧ-rĕn′tĭs), in the place of a parent.
in medias res *Latin* (ĭn mē′dĭ-ăs rēz), into the midst of things; into full activity.
in memoriam *Latin* (ĭn mė-mō′rĭ-ăm), in memory (of): used upon monuments, in obituary notices, etc.
in omnia paratus *Latin* (ĭn ŏm′nĭ-ȧ pȧ-rā′tŭs), ready for all things.
in perpetuum *Latin* (ĭn pûr-pĕt′ū-ŭm), forever; always; in perpetuity.
in propria persona *Latin* (ĭn prō′prĭ-ȧ pûr-sō′nȧ), in one's own person; in one's own character.
in re *Latin* (ĭn rē), in the matter of; in regard to; concerning.

in situ *Latin* (ĭn sī′tů), in place; in its original position.
in statu quo *Latin* (ĭn stā′tů kwō), in the state in which (it is or was).
inter alia *Latin* (ĭn′tẽr ā′lĭ-*ȧ*), among other things.
inter se *Latin* (ĭn′tẽr sē), among (or between) themselves; mutually.
in toto *Latin* (ĭn tō′tȯ), in the whole; in (its) entirety; in general.
in vacuo *Latin* (ĭn văk′ū-ō), in a vacuum.
ipse dixit *Latin* (ĭp′sė dĭk′sĭt), literally, he himself said it; an unsupported statement; a dictum.
ipso facto *Latin* (ĭp′sȯ făk′tȯ), by the act (or fact) itself; (obvious) from the very facts of the case.
ipso jure *Latin* (ĭp′sȯ jōō′rė), by the law itself; legally.

ja wohl *German* (yä vōl′), yes, indeed; to be sure.
je ne sais quoi *French* (zhẽ nẽ sâ″kwȧ′), literally, I know not what; something inexpressible.
jeu de mots *French* (zhö″ dẽ mō′), a play on words; a pun.
jeu d'esprit *French* (zhö″ dĕs″prē′), literally, a play of mind; something witty.
jeunesse dorée *French* (zhû″nĕs′ dȏ″rā′), literally, gilded youth; rich and fashionable young people.
jubilate Deo *Latin* (jōō″bĭ-lā′tė dē′ō), rejoice in the Lord.

laissez faire *French* (lâ″sā″ fâr′), literally, let (people) do (what they choose); hence, as a noun, noninterference, as of a government in matters of trade and industry.
l'allegro *Italian* (läl-lā′grō), the cheerful (person).
lapsus calami *Latin* (lăp′sůs kăl′*ȧ*-mī), a slip of the pen.
lapsus linguæ *Latin* (lăp′sůs lĭng′gwē), a slip of the tongue.
lapsus memoriæ *Latin* (lăp′sůs mė-mō′rĭ-ē), a slip of the memory.
lares et penates *Latin* (lā′rēz ĕt pė-nā′tēz), *Roman Mythology,* gods of specific localities, especially of the household: now used of one's treasured possessions.
laus Deo *Latin* (lôs′ dē′ō), praise (be) to God.

leb' wohl *German* (lāp″ vōl′), farewell; good-by.
l'état, c'est moi *French* (lā″tȧ′, sâ mwȧ′), it is I who am the state: a saying attributed to Louis XIV.
le tout ensemble *French* (lẽ tōō″ täṅ″säṅbl′′), the whole (taken) together.
lettre de cachet *French* (lĕtr′′ dẽ kȧ″shâ′), a sealed letter.
lex loci *Latin* (lĕks lō′sī), the law of the place.
l'homme propose et Dieu dispose *French* (lôm′ prô″pōz′ ā dyö′ dēs″pōz′), man proposes and God disposes.
literati *Latin* (lĭt″ẽr-ā′tī), men of letters; scholars.
literatim *Latin* (lĭt″ẽr-ā′tĭm), literally.
loco citato *Latin* (lō′kō sī-tā′tō), in the place quoted; in the cited passage.—*abbr.* **loc. cit.**
locum tenens *Latin* (lō′kŭm tē′nĕnz), a substitute; especially, an acting pastor of a church.
locus sigilli *Latin* (lō′kŭs sĭ-jĭl′ī), the place of the seal.—*abbr.* **L.S.**
loquitur *Latin* (lŏ′kwĭ-tẽr), he speaks: used as a stage direction.—*abbr.* **loq.**

ma chère *French* (mȧ″ shâr′), my dear (fem.).
madame *French* (mȧ″dȧm′), Mrs., the French title for a married woman.—*abbr.* **Mme** (without period).
mademoiselle *French* (mȧd″mwȧ″zĕl′), Miss, the French title for an unmarried woman.—*abbr.* **Mlle** (without period).
ma foi *French* (mȧ″ fwä′), literally, my faith; good gracious: an interjection.
magnum bonum *Latin* (măg′nŭm bō′nŭm), a great good.
magnum opus *Latin* (măg′nŭm ō′pŭs), a great work.
maladie du pays *French* (mȧl″ȧ″dē′ dü pâ′ē), homesickness.
mal de mer *French* (mȧl″ dẽ mâr′), seasickness.
mañana *Spanish* (mä-nyä′nä), tomorrow.
mare clausum *Latin* (mā′rē klô′sŭm), a closed sea; a sea within the separate rule of one's state.
mariage de convenance *French* (mȧ″ryȧzh′ dẽ kôṅ″vẽ-näṅs′), a marriage of convenience.
mauvais goût *French* (mō″vâ′ gōō′), bad taste.

memento mori *Latin* (mē̇-mĕn′tō̇ mō′rī), literally, remember to die; hence, a reminder of death.

mens sana in corpore sano *Latin* (mĕnz sā′nȧ ĭn kôr′pō̇-rē̇ sā′nō̇), a sound mind in a sound body.

meum et tuum *Latin* (mē′ŭm ĕt tū′ŭm), mine and thine.

mirabile dictu *Latin* (mĭ-rā′bĭ-lē̇ dĭk′tū̇), wonderful to relate.

mise en scène *French* (mē″ zäṅ″ sân′), stage setting.

modus operandi *Latin* (mō′dŭs ŏp″ē̇-răn′dī), method of operation; manner of working.

modus vivendi *Latin* (mō′dŭs vĭ-vĕn′dī), a manner of living.

mon ami *French* (mô″nȧ″mē′), my friend (masc.).

monde *French* (môṅd), world; the world of fashion and leisure; the sphere of life in which one moves.

monsieur *French* (mẽ-syö′), Mister.—*abbr.* **M.**

morituri (te) salutamus *Latin* (môr″ĭ-tū′rī (tē) săl″ū̇-tā′mŭs), we who are about to die salute thee: the salutation Roman gladiators made to the emperor as they entered the arena.

moyen âge *French* (mwȧ″yâ″ näzh′), Middle Ages.

multum in parvo *Latin* (mŭl′tŭm ĭn pär′vō̇), much in little.

mutatis mutandis *Latin* (mū̇-tā′tĭs mū̇-tăn′dĭs), the necessary changes having been made.

natura abhorret a vacuo *Latin* (nȧ-tū′rȧ ăb-hôr′ĕt ā văk′-ū̇-ō̇), nature abhors a vacuum.

nemine contradicente *Latin* (nĕm′ĭ-nē̇ kŏn″trȧ-dĭ-sĕn′tē̇), no one contradicting; unanimously.—*abbr.* **nem. con.**

ne plus ultra *Latin* (nē plŭs ŭl′trȧ), no more beyond; as a noun, the summit of achievement; the highest degree; as a command, no further.

n'est-ce pas? *French* (nĕs″ pä′), literally, is it not? used after any statement to mean, is it not true?

nicht wahr? *German* (nĭkht″ vär′), literally, not true? used after any statement to mean, isn't that so?

nihil *Latin* (nī′hĭl), nothing.

n'importe *French* (nâṅ″pôrt′), no matter; it matters not.

nisi *Latin* (nī′sī), unless.

noblesse oblige *French* (nô″blĕs′ ô″blēzh′), rank entails responsibility.
noli me tangere *Latin* (nō′lī mē tăn′jē-rė), touch me not.
nom de guerre *French* (nôn″ dē gâr′), literally, a war name; pen name; pseudonym.
nom de plume *French* (nôn″ dē plüm′), a pen name; an author's assumed name.
non compos mentis *Latin* (nŏn kŏm′pŏs mĕn′tĭs), not of sound mind.
nota bene *Latin* (nō′tȧ bē′nė), note well; take notice.—*abbr.* **N.B.**
nouveau riche *French* (nōō″vō′ rēsh′), newly rich: generally used as a noun, and applied to the uncultured who have recently acquired wealth.

obiit *Latin* (ŏb′ė-ĭt), he (or she) died.
obiter dictum *Latin* (ŏb′ĭ-tēr dĭk′tŭm), literally, (something) said by the way; a passing remark; in law, an incidental decision not considered binding.
objet d'art *French* (ôb″zhȃ″ dȧr′), a work of artistic merit.
on dit *French* (ôn″ dē′), they say; it is said.
onus probandi *Latin* (ō′nŭs prō-băn′dī), the burden of proof.
opere citato *Latin* (ŏp′ė-rė sī-tā′tō), in the volume quoted.—*abbr.* **op. cit.**
opus *Latin* (ō′pŭs), a work or composition.
ora pro nobis *Latin* (ō′rȧ prō nō′bĭs), pray for us.
O tempora, O mores *Latin* (ō tĕm′pŏ-rȧ, ō mō′rēz), O the times! O the customs!

pardonnez-moi *French* (pȧr″dô″nā′=mwȧ′), pardon me.
par excellence *French* (pȧr ĕk″sĕ″lȧns′), preëminently.
par exemple *French* (pȧr″ ĕg″zänpl′′), for example.
pari passu *Latin* (pā′rī păs′ū), with equal pace.
passim *Latin* (păs′ĭm), everywhere; throughout.
pâté de foie gras *French* (pä″tā′ dē fwä′grä′), goose-liver pie.
pater familias *Latin* (pā″tēr fȧ-mĭl′ĭ-ăs), father of a family; the male head of a household.

paternoster *Latin* (pā'tẽr-nŏs'tẽr), literally, our Father; the Lord's Prayer; also, the eleventh bead of the rosary, or the entire rosary.

pax vobiscum *Latin* (păks vȯ-bĭs'kŭm), peace be with you.

per annum *Latin* (pûr ăn'ŭm), by the year.

per capita *Latin* (pûr kăp'ĭ-tȧ), by heads; for each individual; as individuals.

per contra *Latin* (pûr kŏn'trȧ), on the contrary.

per diem *Latin* (pûr dī'ĕm), by the day; daily.

per mensem *Latin* (pûr mĕn'sĕm), by the month; each month; monthly.

per se *Latin* (pûr sē), by itself; of itself; intrinsically.

persona non grata *Latin* (pûr-sō'nȧ nŏn grā'tȧ), an unacceptable person; one who is obnoxious.

petite *French* (pẽ-tēt'), small; often with the additional connotation of neatness and grace.

pièce de résistance *French* (pyâs' dẽ rā"zēs"tāṅs'), literally, the resisting piece; the main dish of a meal, or the chief article of any series or collection.

pince-nez *French* (pâṅs"=nā'), eyeglasses: distinguished from spectacles which have bows over the ears.

pis aller *French* (pē" zȧ"lā'), a last shift or resource.

place aux dames *French* (plȧs" ō" dȧm'), (make) room for the ladies.

poeta nascitur, non fit *Latin* (pȯ-ē'tȧ năs'ĭ-tŭr, nŏn fĭt), a poet is born, not made.

poste restante *French* (pôst" rĕs"tāṅt'), general delivery.

post meridiem *Latin* (pōst mē-rĭd'ĭ-ĕm), after noon.—*abbr.* p.m.

pourboire *French* (pōōr"bwȧr'), literally, for drinking; a tip.

pour faire rire *French* (pōōr fâr" rēr'), to create laughter.

pour faire visite *French* (pōōr fâr" vē"zēt'), to pay a visit.

pour passer le temps *French* (pōōr pä"sā' lẽ täṅ'), to pass away the time.

pour prendre congé *French* (pōōr prändr'" kôṅ"zhā'), to take leave.—*abbr.* **P.P.C.**

prima facie *Latin* (prī'mȧ fā'shĭ-ē), at first sight.

primus *Latin* (prī′mŭs), first.
prix fixe *French* (prē fēks′), set price.
pro aris et focis *Latin* (prō ā′rĭs ĕt fō′sĭs), for altars and firesides.
pro bono publico *Latin* (prō bō′nȯ pŭb′lĭ-kȯ), for the public good; for the general welfare.
procès-verbal *French* (prȯ″sâ′=vâr″bȧl′), an authenticated statement of an official proceeding, especially in regard to a criminal charge.
pro et con *Latin* (prō′ ĕt kŏn′), for and against.
profanum vulgus *Latin* (prȯ-fā′nŭm vŭl′gŭs), the unhallowed multitude; the rabble.
pro memoria *Latin* (prō mė-mō′rĭ-*ȧ*), as a memorial.
pro patria *Latin* (prō păt′rĭ-*ȧ*), for one's country.
pro rata *Latin* (prō rā′t*ȧ*), in proportion, according to the share of each.
pro tempore *Latin* (prō tĕm′pȯ-rė), for the time being; temporarily.—*abbr.* **pro tem.**
punctatim *Latin* (pŭngk-tā′tĭm), point for point.

qua *Latin* (kwā), as; in the capacity of.
quelque chose *French* (kĕl″kē shōz′), something.
que voulez-vous? *French* (kē vo͞o′lā=vo͞o″), what will you? what do you wish?
quid pro quo *Latin* (kwĭd prō kwō), literally, something for something; an equivalent; a substitute.
quién sabe? *Spanish* (kyĕn′ sä′bā), who knows?
qui s'excuse, s'accuse *French* (kē″ sĕks″küz′, sȧ″küz′), he who excuses himself, accuses himself.
qui va là? *French* (kē″ vȧ″ lȧ′), who goes there?
qui vive? *French* (kē vēv′), who goes there? literally, who lives? used with *on the* to mean keen, alert.
quod erat demonstrandum *Latin* (kwŏd ĕr′ăt dĕm″ŏn-străn′dŭm), which was to be demonstrated; as was to be proved.—*abbr.* **Q.E.D.**
quod vide *Latin* (kwŏd vī′dė), which see.—*abbr.* **q.v.**
quo jure *Latin* (kwō jo͞o′rė), by what right.

raison d'être *French* (râ″zôṅ″ dâtr′′), reason for existence.
rara avis *Latin* (rā′rȧ ā′vĭs), a rare bird; a rarity; an unusual person or thing.
reductio ad absurdum *Latin* (rē̇-dŭk′shĭ-ō̇ ăd ăb-sûr′dŭm), a reducing to the absurd; a method of proving a proposition by showing the absurdity of all its alternatives, or of disproving it by showing the absurdity of its implication.
répondez s'il vous plaît *French* (rā″pôṅ″dā′ sēl″ vōō″ plâ′), reply if you please; please reply.—*abbr.* **R.S.V.P.**: used on formal invitations.
requiescat in pace *Latin* (rĕk″wĭ-ĕs′kăt ĭn pā′sē̇), may he (or she) rest in peace.
robe de chambre *French* (rôb′ dẽ shäṅbr′′), a dressing gown.

salle à manger *French* (sȧl″ ȧ mäṅ″zhā′), dining room.
sang-froid *French* (säṅ″=frwä′), calmness and composure in trying circumstances.
sans peur et sans reproche *French* (säṅ″ pûr′ ā säṅ″ rẽ-prôsh′), without fear and without reproach.
sans rime et sans raison *French* (säṅ″ rēm′ ā säṅ″ râ″zôṅ′), without rime or reason; unwarranted.
sans-souci *French* (säṅ″=sōō″sē′), without care.
sartor resartus *Latin* (sär′tôr rē-sär′tŭs), the tailor retailored.
sauve qui peut *French* (sōv′ kē″ pö′), save (himself) who can: a cry of rout in battle; hence, as a noun written **sauve-qui-peut,** a complete rout.
savoir-faire *French* (sȧ″vwȧr″=fâr′), the knowing how to do or act; tact; address.
savoir-vivre *French* (sȧ″vwȧr″=vēvr′′), the knowing how to live; good breeding; courteous manners.
semper fidelis *Latin* (sĕm′pẽr fĭ-dē′lĭs), ever faithful.
señor *Spanish* (sā-nyôr′), **1,** Mr.; **2,** a lord or gentleman.
señora *Spanish* (sā-nyō̇′rä), **1,** Mrs.; Madam; **2,** a lady.
señorita *Spanish* (sā″nyō̇-rē′tä), **1,** Miss; **2,** a young lady.
sic passim *Latin* (sĭk păs′ĭm), so everywhere.
sic semper tyrannis *Latin* (sĭk sĕm′pẽr tĭ-răn′ĭs), ever thus to tyrants.

sic transit gloria mundi *Latin* (sĭk trăn′sĭt glō′rĭ-ȧ mŭn′dī), so passes away the glory of the world.

signor *Italian* (sē-nyōr′), **1,** Mr.; **2,** a lord or gentleman.

signora *Italian* (sē-nyō′rä), **1,** Mrs.; Madam; **2,** a lady.

signorina *Italian* (sē″nyō-rē′nä), **1,** Miss; **2,** a young woman.

s'il vous plaît *French* (sēl″ vōō″ plâ′), literally, if it please you; if you please.

sine cura *Latin* (sī′nē kū′rȧ), without care.

sine die *Latin* (sī′nē dī′ē), literally, without day; finally; without appointing a day for reassembling: used with reference to an adjournment.

sine qua non *Latin* (sī′nē kwā nŏn), literally, without which not; an indispensable condition; a necessity.

soi-disant *French* (swȧ′-dē″zäṅ′), self-styled; would-be.

soupçon *French* (sōōp″sôṅ′), a small amount; a trace.

Sprachgefühl *German* (spräkh′gĕ-fül), intuitive sense of what is correct and idiomatic in a language.

status quo *Latin* (stā′tŭs, or stăt′ŭs, kwō), the condition in which (it is).

Sturm und Drang *German* (shtōōrm′ ŏŏnt dräng′), storm and stress.

sub rosa *Latin* (sŭb rō′zȧ), literally, under the rose; secretly.

sub voce *Latin* (sŭb vō′sē), under the (specified) word (as in a dictionary).—*abbr.* **s.v.**

sui generis *Latin* (sū′ī jĕn′ẽr-ĭs), of its own kind; unique.

summa cum laude *Latin* (sŭm-mȧ kŭm lô′dē), with highest praise.

summum bonum *Latin* (sŭm′ŭm bō′nŭm), the supreme good; the highest good.

sursum corda *Latin* (sûr′sŭm kôr′dȧ), lift up (your) hearts.

tableau vivant *French* (tȧ″blō′ vē″väṅ′), a living picture.

table d'hôte *French* (tȧbl″ dōt′), literally, host's table: used to designate a complete meal served at a fixed price: opposite of **à la carte**; formerly, a common table for guests, as at a hotel.

tant mieux *French* (täṅ″ myö′), so much the better.

tempus fugit *Latin* (tĕm′pŭs fū′jĭt), time flies.

terra incognita *Latin* (tĕr′ȧ ĭn-kŏg′nĭ-tȧ), an unknown land; an unexplored region.

tertium quid *Latin* (tûr′shĭ-ŭm kwĭd), literally, a third something; something intermediate; generally, a harmonizing medium between two diverse things.

tête-à-tête *French* (tâ″-tȧ-tât′), literally, head to head; hence, a confidential chat.

thé dansant *French* (tā′ däṅ-säṅ′), a tea at which there is dancing.

tour de force *French* (to͞or″ dẽ fôrs′), a feat of strength; also, an exhibition of skill.

tout à fait *French* (to͞o″ tȧ″ fâ′), quite; wholly; entirely.

tout à l'heure *French* (to͞o″ tȧ″ lûr′), a little while ago; also, very soon; shortly.

tout de suite *French* (to͞o″ dẽ süēt′), immediately.

tout ensemble *French* (to͞o″ täṅ säṅbl′′), the general effect.

ubique *Latin* (ū-bī′kwē), everywhere.

ubi supra *Latin* (ū′bī sū′prȧ), where (stated) above.

ultimum vale *Latin* (ŭl′tĭ-mŭm vā′lē), a last farewell.

una voce *Latin* (ū′nȧ vō′sē), literally, with one voice; unanimously.

und so weiter *German* (o͝ont zō vī′tẽr), and so forth.—*abbr.* **u.s.w.**

usus loquendi *Latin* (ū′sŭs lō-kwĕn′dī), usage in speaking.

ut infra *Latin* (ŭt ĭn′frȧ), as below.

ut supra *Latin* (ŭt sū′prȧ), as above.—*abbr.* **ut sup.**

vade in pace *Latin* (vā′dē ĭn pā′sē), go in peace.

vade mecum *Latin* (vā′dē mē′kŭm), literally, go with me; as a noun, a manual or handbook.

vae victis *Latin* (vē vĭk′tĭs), woe to the conquered.

vale *Latin* (vā′lē), farewell.

Vaterland *German* (fä′tẽr-länt), fatherland.

veni, vidi, vici *Latin* (vē′nī, vī′dī, vī′sī), I came, I saw, I conquered: Julius Cæsar's curt report of a victory, sent to the Roman Senate.

verboten *German* (fĕr-bō′tĕn), forbidden.
vers libre *French* (vâr″ lēbr′′), free line (of poetry); free verse.
via media *Latin* (vī′*ȧ* mē′dĭ-*ȧ*), a middle way; the golden mean.
vice versa *Latin* (vī′sē vûr′s*ȧ*), conversely.
vide *Latin* (vī′dē), see.
vide ut supra *Latin* (vī′dē ŭt sū′pr*ȧ*), see what is stated above.
virginibus puerisque *Latin* (vûr-jĭn′ĭ-bŭs pū″ĕ-rĭs′kwē), for girls and boys.
vis-à-vis *French* (vē″=zȧ″=vē′), face to face.
vis vitae *Latin* (vĭs vī′tē), vital force.
viva voce *Latin* (vī′v*ȧ* vō′sē), by the living voice; hence, orally.
vive la république *French* (vēv′ lȧ rā″pü″blēk′), (long) live the republic.
vive le roi *French* (vēv′ lĕ rwä′), (long) live the king.
voilà *French* (vwȧ″lȧ′), see there! behold!
voilà tout *French* (vwȧ″lȧ′ tōō′), that is all.
volte-face *French* (vôlt″=fȧs), a change of front.
vox populi, vox Dei *Latin* (vŏks pŏp′ū-lī, vŏks dē′ī), the voice of the people (is) the voice of God; the voice of the people is authoritative.

Wanderjahr *German* (vän′dĕr-yär″), a year of wandering.
Wanderlust *German* (vän′dĕr-lŏŏst″), a passion for wandering or traveling.
Weltanschauung *German* (vĕlt′än-shou-ŏŏng), outlook on the world; general point of view.
Weltschmerz *German* (vĕlt′shmärtz), pessimism; weariness of life.

Zeitgeist *German* (tsīt′gīst″), the spirit of the age.
zum Beispiel *German* (tsōōm bī′shpēl″), for example.—*abbr.* **z.B.**

CHAPTER V

SPELLING

To spell correctly is to command one important means of achieving clarity and precision in the use of written language, and it is also to avoid that almost invariable effect of poor spelling — the impression of ignorance, or of carelessness and slovenly workmanship. In business as in social correspondence effectiveness depends partly upon correct spelling, and can rarely be secured without it.

The elimination of errors of spelling becomes a simpler matter when we realize that nearly everyone misspells the same words, and that although there are several hundred thousand words in the English language, only a few hundred of them are commonly misspelled. These misspellings arise from several causes: mistakes in pronunciation, failure to see and read the printed words correctly, the confusion of words that sound alike but are spelled differently. Most of the difficulties may be corrected by the application of a few spelling rules which, with illustrations and lists of words most commonly misspelled, are given in the following pages.

SPELLING RULES

Doubling a final consonant

1. When words of one syllable and words accented on the last syllable end in a single consonant preceded by a single vowel, the final consonant is doubled before a suffix beginning with a vowel.

dip	**di*pp*er**	**occur**	**occu*rr*ence**
red	**re*dd*est**	**equip**	**equi*pp*ed**
fun	**fu*nn*y**	**propel**	**prope*ll*er**
begin	**begi*nn*ing**	**repel**	**repe*ll*ing, repe*ll*ent**

But:	gas	gaseous	chagrin	chagri*n*ed
	transfer	transfe*r*able	infer	infe*r*able

2. If, however, the accent shifts to another syllable when the suffix is added, the final consonant is not doubled.

confer	confe*rr*ed,	confe*rr*ing	*but:* confe*r*ence
prefer	prefe*rr*ed,	prefe*rr*ing	*but:* prefe*r*ence, prefe*r*able
refer	refe*rr*ed,	refe*rr*ing	*but:* refe*r*ence

But: excel excel*l*ence

3. Note that when the last syllable is not accented, or when more than one vowel precedes, the final consonant is not doubled.

repeal	repealing	reason	reasoning
breed	breeding	abandon	abandoned
cheap	cheapest	cater	caterer
cook	cooker	frugal	frugality
broil	broiler	benefit	benefiting

But: cancel cancel*l*ation

Retaining a final consonant

4. Do not drop a final *n* before a suffix beginning with *n*.

sudden	sudde*nn*ess	clean	clea*nn*ess

5. Do not drop a final *l* before a suffix beginning with *l*.

wool	woo*ll*y	fatal	fata*ll*y
final	fina*ll*y	real	rea*ll*y

6. But drop the final *l* from such words as *all* and *full*, when they are combined with other words.

a*l*ready	a*l*together	gracefu*l*
a*l*ways		restfu*l*

Dropping a final silent *e*

7. A silent *e* is dropped from the end of a word before a suffix beginning with a vowel.

change	changing	create	creator
make	making	write	writing
breathe	breathing	force	forcible
love	lovable	guide	guidance

8. But after *c* or *g*, silent *e* is retained before the suffixes *ous* and *able*.

courage	courag*e*ous	change	chang*e*able
advantage	advantag*e*ous	trace	trac*e*able
notice	notic*e*able		

9. Note that silent *e* is usually retained before a suffix beginning with a consonant.

Exceptions: truly, judgment, acknowledgment

Words ending in *c*

10. Add *k* to a word ending in *c* before a suffix beginning with *e*, *i*, or *y*.

picnic	picnic*k*er, picnic*k*ing	colic	colic*k*y
panic	panic*k*y	traffic	traffic*k*er

Words ending in *y*

11. Nouns ending in *y* preceded by a consonant form the plural by changing *y* to *i* and adding *es*.

baby	bab*ies*	history	histor*ies*

12. Many adjectives and adverbs change *y* to *i* before a suffix.

happy	happ*i*ly	cheery	cheer*i*ly
busy	bus*i*ness	pretty	prett*i*ness

13. Verbs ending in *y* preceded by a consonant change *y* to *i* and add *e* before *s* or *d*.

rely	rel*ie*s, rel*ie*d	cry	cr*ie*s, cr*ie*d

14. But before *-ing* the *y* is retained, and verbs ending in *ie* change the *ie* to *y* before *-ing*.

repl*y*ing		t*ie*	t*y*ing
cr*y*ing		l*ie*	l*y*ing

15. Words ending in *y* preceded by a vowel make no change before suffixes.

prey	preyed	valley	valleys
money	moneyed	obey	obeys, obeying
alloy	alloys	allay	allayed

ei and *ie*

16. The most easily remembered statement of the rule for the use of *ei* and *ie* is the old rime:

I before *e*	(bel*ie*ve, repr*ie*ve)
Except after *c*	(rec*ei*ve, rec*ei*pt, c*ei*ling)
Or when sounded as *a*	
As in n*ei*ghbor and w*ei*gh.	

Common exceptions to this rule are:

financier	foreign	weird
neither	leisure	height

Words prefixed by *dis-* and *mis-*

17. When the prefix *dis-* or *mis-* is added to a word, no change is made in the original word. A double *s* occurs only when the original word begins with *s*.

dis *s*ent	dissent	dis *a*gree	disagree
dis *a*ppear	disappear	mis *s*tep	misstep
dis *a*ppoint	disappoint	mis *a*ppropriate	misappropriate
dis *s*atisfy	dissatisfy	mis *s*end	missend
dis *s*ociate	dissociate	mis *s*pell	misspell
dis *s*olve	dissolve		

American and British usage

18. American usage and British usage in spelling differ chiefly on the following points: *-or* and *-our*, *-er* and *-re*, *in-* and *en-*, *-ize* and *-ise*, *-l-* and *-ll-*. Except in letters or manuscripts intended for English readers, follow the American usage.

	American	*British*
-or and *-our*	color	colour
	endeavor	endeavour
	honor	honour
	labor	labour
	neighbor	neighbour
	odor	odour
	vapor	vapour
-er and *-re*	center	centre
	fiber	fibre
	theater	theatre

	American	British
in- and *en-*	inquire	enquire
	intrust	entrust
-l- and *-ll-*	counselor	counsellor
	jeweler	jeweller
	jewelry	jewellery
	modeled	modelled
	penciling	pencilling
	traveler	traveller
	traveling	travelling
	woolen	woollen

The following list of words is always spelled with *-ise* both in the United States and Great Britain. In the spelling of most words not in this list, American usage favors *-ize*, while British usage still favors *-ise*.

advertise	demise	enfranchise	merchandise
apprise	despise	enterprise	premise
chastise	devise	excise	supervise
circumcise	disfranchise	exercise	surmise
comprise	disguise	improvise	surprise
compromise		incise	

Simplified or phonetic spelling

19. Some simplified spelling forms, such as *program, catalog, pedagog,* have been accepted and are in common use. Others, such as *tho, thru, thoro, nite,* are not generally accepted, and should therefore not appear in formal or business correspondence. Whether they are to be used in informal correspondence is largely a matter of personal taste.

Notice that in many words of foreign origin, silent letters have been dropped from digraphs (combinations of two letters that form a single sound, as *ea* in read).

ether (æther) med*ie*val (mediæval)

encyclop*e*dia (encyclopædia)

Troublesome suffixes

20. Care must be exercised in spelling words with the suffixes *-cede, -ceed, -sede; -able, -ible; -er, -or; -ance, -ence; -sion, -tion.*

No rules govern the formation of words with these suffixes, and difficulties with them must be referred to the dictionary. The following lists, while not complete, may prove helpful in spelling and defining these troublesome groups of words.

-ceed, -cede, -sede		*-er* and *-or*	
exceed	accede	adapter	actor
proceed	antecede	adviser	conqueror
succeed	concede	buyer	creditor
	intercede	corrupter	governor
	precede	decanter	inventor
	recede	deserter	oppressor
	secede	dispenser	possessor
		eraser	prosecutor
	supersede	promoter	purveyor

-able and *-ible*

adorable	likable	accessible	infallible
advisable	malleable	admissible	inflexible
believable	manageable	audible	intangible
capable	noticeable	collapsible	intelligible
changeable	palatable	compatible	invincible
chargeable	peaceable	comprehensible	irresistible
debatable	receivable	credible	legible
desirable	regrettable	edible	negligible
excusable	salable	eligible	ostensible
forgivable	serviceable	feasible	permissible
immovable	solvable	flexible	plausible
indispensable	unmistakable	forcible	possible
		gullible	reducible
		horrible	responsible
		incorrigible	reversible
		indefensible	tangible
		indelible	terrible
		indigestible	visible

-ance and *-ence*

abundance	entrance	absence	occurrence
acceptance	expectance	abstinence	persistence
assistance	hesitance	consequence	presence
assurance	instance	convenience	prudence
attendance	irrelevance	eminence	recurrence

-ance		*-ence*	
consonance	perseverance	existence	reference
contrivance	precipitance	independence	residence
dominance	relevance	indigence	resilience
elegance	resistance	inference	reverence
encumbrance	resonance		
endurance			

-sion and *-tion*

In general, the noun suffix *-sion* is used when the corresponding verb (or, sometimes, noun) ends in *nd, de, ge, re, se, ss, mit, vert*. The suffix *-tion* is used with other words. There are numerous exceptions to this rule.[1]

Common words ending in *-sion*

abrasion	expansion	pervasion
adhesion	explosion	perversion
allusion	expression	precision
aversion	extension	regression
cession	illusion	remission
commission	incision	repression
confession	infusion	reversion
confusion	intermission	revision
conversion	inversion	scansion
decision	lesion	session
diffusion	mission	submission
discussion	obsession	subversion
dissension	omission	suffusion
dissuasion	percussion	suppression
elision	permission	suspension
excursion	persuasion	

COMMON WORDS FREQUENTLY MISSPELLED

abridgment	adviser	among
absence	aërated	anæmia
accessible	aërodrome	anæsthetic
accidentally	aesthetic	analysis
accommodate	aggravate	analyze
achievement	airplane	annual
acknowledgment	allotted	anonymous
acquainted	aluminum	answer
acquitted	amateur	anxiety

[1] See *A Manual of Style*, University of Chicago Press.

apiece
apparatus
appreciate
archæology
arctic
argument
arrangement
ascendancy
ascendant
assassinate
association
athletic
attendance
auxiliary

baccalaureate
bachelor
balance
barytone
battalion
bazaar
becoming
behavior
belief
believing
benefiting
besiege
biased
bicycle
biscuit
boisterous
boundary
bulletin
bureaus
burglar
business

calendar
cancellation
canceling
carburetor
catalog
cemetery
chagrined
changeable
colander
column
committal
committee
compel
competition
conferring
controller
conscientious
corroborate
counterfeit
crystallized
cylinder

deceive
defendants
deferred
definite
demurrage
descendant
describe
description
desiccate
despair
develop
dietitian
dilemma
dining room
diocese
diphtheria
disappear
disappoint
disastrous
discipline
dispatch
dissipate
distribution

ecstasy
eliminate
embarrass
emphasize
encouraging
exaggerate
exceed
excerpt
exercise
exhilarate
existence

fascinate
February
fierce
finally
financier
foreclosure
foreigner
fortieth
fourteen
fourth
friend

gelatin
genuineness
government
grammar
guarantee
guardian

hairbreadth
harass
height
hoping
hosiery
hundredths
hygiene

immediately
incidentally
independent
indispensable
inference
infinite
intercede

judgment

keenness
knowledge

laboratory
lacquer
leisure

library
license
likable
liquefy
lovable
lying

maintenance
maneuver
manikin
manual
marriage
masquerade
matinée
mayonnaise
millennium
millinery
millionaire
miniature
miscellaneous
mischievous
misspelled
muscle
mustache

naphtha
negroes
nickel
nineteen
ninetieth
ninety
ninth
noticeable
nucleus

obbligato
occasionally
occurring
offered
omelet
omission
omitted
operate
opportunity
optimistic
outrageous

paid
panicky
parallel
paralysis
parliament
pastime
patient
peaceable
peddler
peremptory
perseverance
perspiration
personal
personnel
persuade
picnicking
pneumonia
politician
politics
possession
prairie
precedence
preparation
prescription
privilege
procedure
proffered
prominent
promissory
psychology
pulmonary
pursue

questionnaire

raccoon
really
receipt
receive
receptacle
recognize
recommend
referred
remodeling
repellent
repetition
rhythm
rime

schedule
secretary
seize
separate
sergeant
serviceable
siege
similar
sincerely
siphon
spaghetti
stopped
stretch
subpoena
succeed
superintendent
supersede
sustenance

technical
television
tendency
tongue
traceable
transferable
Tuesday

unnecessary
useful
usually

vacuum
vengeance
volume

warrant
weather
Wednesday
weird
whether
woolly
writing

yacht

Proper Nouns and Geographic Names Frequently Misspelled

Aeolian
Allegany County (N. Y., Md.)
Alleghany County (Va.)
Allegheny Mountains
Allegheny County (Pa.) and River (N. Y., Pa.)
Argentina (used as name of country, without *Republic*)
Argentine (the adjective, as in the *Argentine Republic*)
Athenaeum

Bayreuth (bī″roit′) (Bavaria)
Bedouin (bĕd′o͝o-ĭn)
Bering Sea, Strait, Island, Glacier
Beyrouth (bā″ro͞ot′) (Syria)
Bosporus
Budapest (bo͝o′da-pĕst″)
Buenos Aires (bwā″nōs ī′rās)

Cape Town
Caribbean Sea
Chile
Chosen (chō′sĕn) (Korea)
Cincinnati

Danzig
Dominican Republic (Santo Domingo)

Eskimo

Filipino
Fond-du-lac (Wis.)

Galilean
Graeco-Roman

Habana (Cuba)
Haiti, Haitian
Hawaii, Hawaiian
Hindu
Hoosac Tunnel
Hoosick Falls

Iraq (ē″räk′)
Iran (ē″rän) (Persia)

Judea

Khartoum

Koran
Kyoto

Leipzig
Luxembourg (the country)
Luxembourg (Gardens and Museum in Paris)

Matawan (N. J.)
Matewan (W. Va.)
Mattawan (Mich.)
Matteawan (N. Y.)
Mechanicville (N. Y.)
Mechanicsville (Pa.)
Mohammedan
Moslem
Muscle Shoals (Ala.)

Newburgh (N. Y.)
Newfoundland
Nürnberg

Pekingese
Philippine
Phoenix
Piraeus
Pittsburgh (Pa.)
Plattsburg (N. Y.)
Pompeii, Pompeian
Poughkeepsie

Rio de Janeiro
Riviera

Salonika (sä-lȯ-nē′kȧ)
Sarajevo (sȧ′rä-yȧ-vȯ)

Serbia
Schenectady
Spitsbergen
Spuyten Duyvil (spī'tĕn dī'vl)
Straits Settlements
Strasbourg (France)

Tehran (te-hrän') (Iran)
The Hague

Tibet
Tokyo
Trieste

Vladivostok

Wilkes-Barre
Woods Hole

Yangtze
Yugoslavia

Variations Given by the United States Geographic Board

China
Chungking (chŏŏng'kĭng')

Czechoslovakia
Bratislava (Pressburg)
Brno (bûr'nŏ) (Brunn)
Praha (prä'hȧ) (Prague)

Denmark
København (Copenhagen)

Finland
Helsinki (Helsingfors)
Tampere (Tammerfors)
Viipuri (Viborg)

Norway
Trondheim (Trondhjem)
Oslo (Christiania)

Poland
Kraków (krä'kōōf) (Cracow)
Lwów (Lvōōf) (Lemberg)

Russia (U.S.S.R.)
Stalingrad (stä-lĕn-gräd')
Dnepropetrovsk (dnyĕp"rŏ-pyĕ-trôfsk')

Sweden
Uppsala (ŭp'sȧ-lȧ) (Upsala)

Turkey
Ankara (äng'kä-rä) (Angora)
Bursa (bōōr'sä) (Brusa)
Edirne (ĕ-dĭr'nĕ) (Adrianople)
Gelibolu (Gallipoli)
Istanbul (ē"stäm-bōōl') (Constantinople)
Izmir (Smyrna)
Mersin (Mersina)
Trabzon (Trebizond)

Yugoslavia
Beograd (bĕ-ō'grȧd) (Belgrade)
Bitolj (bĕ'tŏly') (Monastir)
Dubrovnik (Ragusa)
Split (Spalato)
Zagreb (zä'grĕb) (Agram)

NOTE: The United States Geographic Board makes the following statement:

"Where the conventional English form — sometimes a transliteration — differs from the local official form, the trend both in the United States and abroad is toward the adoption of the local official form, and the discontinuance of the conventional English form. The choice of the form of the name should be made with proper regard for the purposes for which the particular publication [or letter] is intended."

CHAPTER VI

COMPOUNDING AND DIVISION OF WORDS

WORD DIVISION

Dictionaries differ in their systems of syllabification, some recommending division according to pronunciation and some according to derivation, and no absolute rule can be given. In general, follow pronunciation and consult a reputable dictionary whenever a question arises.

Since the division of words at the ends of lines makes reading more difficult, avoid division whenever avoidance is possible. When a word must be divided, however, observe the following rules in making the division:

1. Use a hyphen to indicate syllable division.

2. Divide a word only at the end of a syllable.

3. Divide a word only at the end of a line.

4. Never divide the last word on a page.

5. Do not allow word divisions, with the resulting hyphen, to occur at the end of more than two successive lines.

6. If possible, divide a word so that the syllable or syllables before the hyphen are suggestive of the whole word. Thus, *refer-ence* is a better division than *ref-erence,* and *correspond-ence* is better than *cor-respondence.*

7. Never divide a word of one syllable. This rule applies to such words as *spasm, haven't, James's,* as well as the more easily recognized monosyllables, such as *hopped, come, brain, through, strange.*

8. In general, do not divide a word of two syllables unless the word consists of six or more letters.

Right: thor-ough, con-fide, fran-tic
Not advisable: fu-ry, be-gin, ga-la

9. Do not divide a word so as to leave a single letter in either part. Do not divide a word so as to leave two letters, except when such division is unavoidable.

Wrong: read-y, a-cross, a-malgamate, e-luding, fair-y
Not advisable: pa-pering, deposit-ed, se-curities, re-porter

10. Never separate:

(*a*) one part of an abbreviation from the other part

(*b*) a qualifying sign, such as the dollar sign, from the figures to which it belongs

(*c*) digits in a group of three or fewer

(*d*) marks of subdivisions, such as (*a*), (*1*), from the matter following them.

If possible avoid separating:

(*e*) the given name or names, or the corresponding initials, from the family name

(*f*) degrees or titles from a name.

Vowels and consonants

Syllables are formed about vowel sounds. Each syllable is composed of one and only one vowel sound, though there may be several vowel letters sounded as one, as in th*ough*, r*ea*d, *ai*sle, b*oo*k. If two vowels occurring together are pronounced separately, they form different syllables and may be separated in word division: *curi-osity, sci-ence, ortho-epy.* The vowel sounds are usually easy to distinguish, and difficulties of division are caused not by the vowels but by the intervening consonants. Shall they be kept with the preceding vowel or placed with the following vowel? In the placing of consonants the following rules will be useful:

11. When a single consonant occurs between two vowels, as in *solitude, sobering,* the position of the consonant in syllable division depends on the quality of the preceding vowel.

(*a*) If the preceding vowel is short, the consonant usually remains with it: *sol*-itude (not *so*-litude).

(*b*) If the preceding vowel is long, the consonant usually goes with the following vowel: *so*-bering (not *sob*-ering); *fla*-vor (not *flav*-or).

12. When two (or more) consonants occur between two sounded vowels, the consonants are divided.

for-tify	res-tive	shel-ter	diph-thong
num-ber	baf-fling	par-cel	mon-ster

An exception to this rule occurs when the preceding vowel is long and accented or when the following vowel is accented and the consonants are capable of beginning a separate syllable. Under these conditions, both consonants go with the following vowel.

ni-trate	ana-glyphic	fee-ble
emi-gration	sa-cred	tri-fler

The following rules take precedence over Rules 11 and 12:

13. Words containing a prefix or a suffix should, in general, be divided on the prefix or suffix, except when such a division would clearly contradict the pronunciation.

dis-appear	anti-federal	south-ern
mal-adjust	rain-ing	clos-est

But words having the endings *-able, -ance, -ant, -ence, -ent, -ible, -ic, -ical, -ive, -or* are usually divided according to sound rather than on the suffix.

indispen-sable	signifi-cant	logi-cal
abun-dance	promi-nent	defen-sive
dili-gence	diri-gible	refrac-tor
	anæ-mic	

14. In the division of words whose final consonant is doubled before a suffix, as *occur, occurring,* and *shop, shopping,* the added consonant goes with the suffix: *shop-ping, occur-ring.* But when the word itself ends with a double consonant, the consonants are not divided, and division is made according to Rule 13, on the suffix: *bluff, bluff-ing.*

15. Compound words written with a hyphen should be divided only on the compound. In no case should a division be made which introduces an additional hyphen.

well-being   far-reaching   self-denial

16. The endings *-cial, -cion, -cious, -geous, -gion, -gious, -sion, -tial, -tion,* should never be divided.

gor-geous	*not:*	gorg-eous
con-scious	*not:*	consc-ious
irra-tional	*not:*	irrat-ional
reli-gious	*not:*	relig-ious

17. Never divide the groups *gn, ng, ph, sh, tch, th,* except when the letters are pronounced as separate sounds.

assign-ment	bish-ops	anath-ema
song-ster	graph-ophone	wretch-edly

Compounding of Words

A compound word is made up of two or more separate words used together to make a new word with a different meaning from that which the words have separately. Such a word may be written with a hyphen, as *self-control,* or as one solid word, as *longshoreman.* For many words, usage is so various as to cause their appearance in two or three forms, and we see them written with the hyphen, written solid, and written as separate, unhyphenated words. Dictionaries themselves are not always in agreement. The best that one can do, therefore, is to see that one's own usage agrees with some accepted standard and that it is uniform throughout any one piece of writing. The wisest course is that of choosing a good dictionary and following its practice consistently throughout one's writing.

The following rules deal with the more common difficulties:

Accent

1. In general, if a compound is made up of two words, one of which loses its accent in the combination so that the compound is pronounced with only one accented syllable, as *bedroom*, it should be written solid.

broomstick	airway
bookcase	headache
corkscrew	keyboard
daydream	steamship

Compound adjectives

2. When a word group is used as a single adjective and is placed *before* the word it modifies, the group is written as a hyphenated compound. When a group is placed *after* the word it modifies, or is used other than as an adjective, the words are written separately, without hyphens.

a fair-weather policy	*but:*	a forecast of fair weather
worn-out clothing	*but:*	clothing worn out in a month
a built-in cupboard	*but:*	a cupboard built in for convenience
a birch-bark canoe	*but:*	a canoe built of birch bark
a fresh-water fish	*but:*	a fish that lives in fresh water
a high-school course	*but:*	a course in high school
an out-of-the-way place	*but:*	stepping out of the way
an up-to-date style	*but:*	the style was up to date
EXCEPTION: a two-ply yarn		the yarn was two-ply

3. Note that proper nouns made up of two words, such as *New England, South Carolina, West End,* do not take the hyphen when they are used as adjectives.

a New England farm
a South Carolina product
a West End custom

4. Do not confuse a compound adjective with a series of independent adjectives.

a deep, clear, cold stream
a rare, beautiful, expensive edition

Word groups used as single words

5. Expressions consisting of groups of words commonly used as a single word are usually hyphenated.

brother-in-law
man-of-war
will-o'-the-wisp
four-in-hand
mother-of-pearl
hop-o'-my-thumb
well-to-do
happy-go-lucky

Prefixes

6. Ordinarily a prefix is written solid with its stem.

semiannual
nonresident
antedate
demigod
prepay
anticlimax
sublease
hypercritical
biennial
maladjusted

7. But when a prefix is joined to a proper noun or a proper adjective, a hyphen is used.

Pre-Raphaelite	pro-German	Neo-Catholic
un-American	mid-Victorian	re-examine

8. A hyphen is often used between a prefix and its noun to prevent an awkward piling up of consonants, or mispronunciation of vowels.

co-author re-use bell-like

The diæresis is sometimes used for this purpose:

coöperate	better: co-operate
preëmpt	better: pre-empt

9. When two compound words, each made up of the same verb form and prefix, are spelled alike but have different meanings, use a hyphen in the word which keeps the main verb meaning.

reform	recreation	resign
re-form	re-creation	re-sign

Compounds in *-ed*

10. Use a hyphen with compounds made up of two words the first of which is used as an adjective and the last of which is a noun to which *-d* or *-ed* has been added.

red-headed	broken-hearted	bright-eyed
middle-aged	able-bodied	sure-footed

Compounds with participial endings

11. Use a hyphen in most compounds made up of words the last of which is a participle.

(*a*) Present participles (in *-ing*)

nerve-racking	sweet-smelling
deep-lying	far-reaching

(*b*) Past participles (in *-d*, *-ed*, or *-en*)

deep-laid	worm-eaten
high-flown	gold-filled
time-honored	L-shaped
tongue-tied	sun-tanned
long-winded	

(*c*) But when an adverb is used with a participle, the words are usually written separately.

eagerly awaited	*but:* well-bred
highly colored	

Verb-adverb compounds

12. A compound formed of verb plus adverb and used as a noun is usually hyphenated.

blow-out	round-up
lean-to	show-down
rake-off	stop-over

Numbers

13. Use a hyphen with compound cardinal numbers from twenty-one to ninety-nine and ordinal numbers from twenty-first to ninety-ninth.

thirty-eight tickets
one hundred thirty-eight tickets
the thirty-eighth ticket

Fractions

14. Note that no hyphen is required with a fraction unless the fraction is used as an adjective.

two thirds	two-thirds interest
one half	one-half-pound box

Compounds with a common base

15. Use a hyphen after each of two or more words compounded on a common base.

six- and eight-cylinder cars
two-, three-, and six-room apartments
seven- and eight-year-olds

Compounds with possessive nouns

16. Use a hyphen in compounds whose first word is a possessive noun.

cat's-paw	jew's-harp	swan's-down
death's-head	crow's-foot	bird's-eye

Special words

17. Words compounded with *like* (except words ending in *l*) do not use a hyphen.

boylike	businesslike
godlike	childlike

18. When *any, every, some, no* are combined with other words no hyphen is used. The combinations are sometimes written as two separate words, sometimes as one word. *The Winston Dictionary* gives the following as preferred forms:

everybody	nobody	somebody	anybody
everyone	no one	somehow	anyhow
everything	nothing	someone	anyone
everywhere	nowhere	something	anything
		sometime(s)	anyway
		somewhat	anywhere
		somewhere	

19. Use a hyphen in most titles made by compounding words with *elect, ex-, general, governor,* and *vice* when the proper name or surname is used without initials or given name.

President-elect Lincoln	Attorney-General Cummings
Vice Admiral Rowan	Lieutenant-Governor Shanahan
ex-President Grant	Rear Admiral W. L. Capps

But military titles, such as *major general, surgeon general,* are not hyphenated.

20. All compounds of *self* are hyphenated except *selfsame* and *selfless* and the compounds formed with the personal pronouns.

self-confidence	self-preservation	*but:*
self-centered	self-will	selfsame
self-assertive	self-service	selfless
self-contained	self-control	myself
self-indulgent	self-denial	himself
	self-made	ourselves

Compass directions

21. Write compass directions according to the following examples:

southeast	south-southeast
northwest	north-northwest

Compounds made up of reduplicating word elements

22. Compounds made up of reduplicating word elements are usually hyphenated.

fiddle-faddle	hurdy-gurdy
hoity-toity	willy-nilly
hurly-burly	topsy-turvy

But: flimflam

Foreign phrases

Foreign phrases are not governed by the foregoing rules. To determine whether or not they should be written with hyphens, consult a good dictionary.

23. A few foreign phrases are always hyphenated.

gutta-percha	olla-podrida
major-domo	tête-à-tête

24. Most foreign phrases, however, should be used without a hyphen.

an *ex officio* member	a *laissez faire* theory
an *ex post facto* law	a *table d'hôte* dinner

Unclassified compounds

25. There are a great many compounds which are not accounted for by the foregoing rules. To determine correct usage for these, the only recourse is to a good dictionary.

New compounds

26. There is almost no limit to the number of compounds which may be made if they are formed according to the conditions stated in some one of the rules just given. Because of lack of space, even an unabridged dictionary does not contain more than a few of these possible compounds. They are, however, perfectly good words if they are formed correctly, and they may be used freely. The largest group of these compounds which may be coined at will is that formed of words combined with one of the prefixes, *co-*, *re-*, *pro-*, etc. Ordinarily a hyphen should be used with new compounds of this sort.

Compound Words That Use the Hyphen

able-bodied
absent-minded
after-dinner (*adj.*)
aid-de-camp
air-tight
all-round (*adj.*)
alto-cumulus
alto-relievo
anti-Sabbatarian
anti-Semite
anti-trade
armor-bearer
armor-clad
attorney-general
auto-infection
auto-inoculation
auto-intoxication
awe-stricken

bas-relief
basso-relievo
battering-ram
battle-ax
beetle-browed
bird's-eye view
blear-eyed
blood-red
blow-out (*noun*)
blue-sky laws
boot-tree
brand-new
break-up (*noun*)
bric-a-brac
broad-brimmed
broad-gauge
broad-minded
broken-hearted
broken-winded
brother-in-law
bull-neck
bull's-eye
by-law

by-name
by-pass
by-product
by-tone

camp-fire girl
cast-off (*adj.*)
cater-cornered
cat-o'-nine-tails
cat's-eye
cat's-paw
cat-tail
chicken-hearted
chock-full
cirro-cumulus
cirro-stratus
clean-cut
clear-cut
close-hauled
close-mouthed
cloud-burst
cloven-footed
coarse-grained
cold-blooded
cold-hearted
color-blind
court-martial
court-plaster
cousin-german
cow-puncher
crack-brained
Cro-Magnon
cross-country
cross-examine
cross-eyed
cross-fertilization
cross-grained
cross-purpose
cross-question
cross-stitch
crow's-foot
cubby-hole
cul-de-sac
cumulo-stratus
cure-all (*noun*)

cut-off (*noun*)
cut-out (*noun*)

dare-devil
daughter-in-law
deaf-mute
death's-head
deckle-edged
deep-laid
deep-sea (*adj.*)
deep-seated
ditty-bag
double-dealing
double-faced
double-quick
double-surfaced
drawing-room
dry-clean
dumb-bell
dumb-waiter

eagle-eyed
easy-going
even-handed

fag-end
faint-hearted
fair-faced
fair-spoken
fancy-free
far-away (*adj.*)
far-fetched
far-off (*adj.*)
far-reaching
fashion-monger
father-in-law
feeble-minded
first-born
first-class (*adj.*)
first-hand (*adj.*)
first-rate (*adj.*)
flare-up (*noun*)
flat-footed
fleur-de-lis
fly-fishing
foot-and-mouth disease

fore-and-aft (*adj.*)
fore-topgallant
fore-topmast
fore-topsail
forget-me-not
foul-mouthed
four-flusher
four-footed
four-in-hand
four-wheeler
fox-trot (*verb*)
frame-up (*noun*)
free-born
free-for-all
free-hand(ed)
free-hearted
free-living
free-spoken
fresh-water (*adj.*)
full-blooded
full-blown
full-fledged

gaff-topsail
gilt-edged
globe-trotter
go-between
gold-filled
good-by
good-humored
good-natured
good-tempered
great-aunt
great-grandchild
great-granddaughter
great-grandfather
great-grandmother
great-grandson
great-hearted
great-uncle
green-eyed
gutta-percha

half-and-half
half-breed (-bred)
half-caste
half-mast
half-moon
half-witted
hanger-on
happy-go-lucky
hara-kiri
hard-hearted
hawk-eyed
heart-rending
heart-whole
helter-skelter
high-bred
high-colored
high-flown
high-handed
high-minded
high-pressure (*adj.*)
high-speed (*adj.*)
high-spirited
high-strung
high-toned
hit-and-miss (*adj.*)
hitch-hike
hollow-hearted
home-born
home-bred
home-brew
hook-up (*noun*)
horny-handed
horse-chestnut
hot-blooded
hot cross-bun
hurdy-gurdy

ill-bred
ill-favored
ill-natured
ill-starred
ill-tempered
ill-use
Indo-European
iron-bound
iron-gray

jack-in-the-box
jack-in-the-pulpit
Jack-of-all-trades
jack-o'-lantern
jack-tar
jerry-built
jew's-harp
jolly-boat

kick-off (*noun*)
kind-hearted
king-pin
knife-edge
knight-errant(ry)
knock-kneed
knock-out (*noun*)
Know-Nothing
kohl-rabi

labor-saving
lady-killer
lady's-slipper
land-poor
lantern-jawed
law-abiding
left-hand(ed)
leg-of-mutton (*adj.*)
life-giving
light-fingered
light-footed
light-headed
light-hearted
light-minded
line-up (*noun*)
lion-hearted
long-distance (*adj.*)
long-drawn
long-headed
long-lived
long-sighted
long-standing
long-suffering
long-tongued
long-winded

looker-on
lop-eared
lotus-eater
loud-speaker
loving-kindness
low-necked
low-pressure
low-spirited

major-domo
make-believe
make-up (*noun*)
mangel-wurzel
man-of-war
mare's-nest
master-at-arms
matter-of-fact (*adj.*)
mealy-mouthed
merry-go-round
middle-aged
middle-class (*adj.*)
mid-iron
mock-heroic
money-making
moth-eaten
mother-in-law
mother-of-pearl
muzzle-loader

narrow-minded
near-by (*adj.*)
needle-point lace
new-fashioned
Neo-Catholic
north-northeast (-northwest)

off-color
old-fashioned
on-coming
one-horse (*adj.*)
one-sided
one-step
open-eyed
open-handed
open-hearted

open-hearth furnace
open-minded
open-mouthed
orang-utan
out-of-door (*adj.*)
out-of-the-way (*adj.*)
out-patient
outward-bound

Pan-American
Pan-German
panic-stricken
parti-colored
passer-by
pass-key
pea-jacket
pell-mell
penny-wise
pepper-and-salt (*adj.*)
photo-electric
photo-engraving
pigeon-toed
pince-nez
point-blank
poor-spirited
pop-over (*noun*)
porte-cochère
post-mortem
pound-foolish
poverty-stricken
Pre-Raphaelite
prick-eared
prie-dieu
purse-proud

quarter-deck
quick-witted

rain-proof
rake-off (*noun*)
ready-made
red-handed
red-hot
red-letter day
right-hand(ed)
rocking-chair
rocking-horse
round-shouldered
round-up (*noun*)

safe-conduct
safe-deposit box
safe-keeping
scot-free
sea-green
second-class (*adj.*)
second-rate (*adj.*)
second-sight
set-off (*noun*)
set-to (*noun*)
sharp-witted
shepherd's-purse
shock-headed
shoe-tree
short-circuit (*verb*)
short-lived
short-winded
shovel-nosed
show-down (*noun*)
sight-seeing
silver-haired
single-handed
single-hearted
single-minded
sister-in-law
skin-deep
sky-writing (-er)
smooth-faced
snow-blind
snow-bound
snub-nosed
sober-minded(ly)
so-called (*adj.*)
son-in-law
south-southeast (-southwest)
speak-easy
spick-and-span
spindle-legged

square-rigged
square-toed
squint-eyed
stalking-horse
stall-fed
stand-by (*noun*)
Star-Spangled Banner
stem-winding (-winder)
step-down (*noun*)
step-parent
stepping-stone
step-up (*noun*)
stern-wheeler
stiff-hearted
stiff-necked
stock-still
stone-blind
stone-deaf
stop-gap
stop-over
stout-hearted(ly)
strait-jacket
strait-laced
strong-minded
stuck-up (*adj.*)
sugar-loaf (*adj.*)
sure-footed
surgeon-general
swan's-down
sweet-scented
sweet-tempered
swift-footed

table-land
tailor-made
take-off (*noun*)
tender-hearted
thick-skinned
thin-skinned
three-color process
three-decker
three-mile limit
three-piled
three-ply
three-quarter binding
tie-up (*noun*)
time-honored
time-table
title-page
to-do (*noun*)
tom-tom
tongue-tied
top-boot(ed)
top-hamper
top-heavy
top-hole (*adj.*)
topsy-turvy
torpedo-boat destroyer
touch-me-not
trade-mark
trade(s)-union
tragi-comedy (-comic)
treasure-trove
true-blue
trundle-bed
try-square
tutti-frutti
twenty-fourmo
twin-screw (*adj.*)
two-edged
two-faced
two-handed
two-phase
two-ply
two-step

U-boat
ultra-violet
uncalled-for
unheard-of
unlooked-for
up-to-date (*adj.*)

vicar-general

waist-high
wake-robin
walk-over (*noun*)

wall-eye(d)
warm-blooded
warm-hearted(ly)
water-logged
water-tight
web-fingered
well-balanced
well-being
well-born
well-bred
well-doer (-doing)
well-favored
well-found
well-meaning
well-nigh
well-spoken
well-to-do
well-wisher
whipper-in
white-hot
whole-hearted
wide-awake (*adj.*)
wild-goose chase
will-o'-the-wisp
wind-broken
wind-up (*noun*)
witch-hazel
wonder-worker
wood-note
worldly-wise
world-weary
world-wide
worm-eaten
worn-out (*adj.*)
would-be
write-up (*noun*)

X-ray (*adj.*)

yellowhammer
yo-heave-ho

Write the Following as Separate, Unhyphenated Words (*but see* § 2, p. 123)

A battery
air bladder
air brake
air cushion
air cylinder
air gas
air gun
air hole
air lane
air line
air lock
air plant
air pump
air spring
army worm

baking powder
ballad monger
ball bearing
ballot box
bank bill
bank book
bank discount
bank draft
bank note
basket ball
bass drum
bass tuba
bass viol
bay rum
bay tree
bay window
B battery
bear baiting
beauty spot
bee line
bell buoy
bell jar
bell metal
betel nut

birch bark (*noun*)
black bass
black damp
black fly
black list
blood money
blood poisoning
blood pressure
blood relation
blood vessel
blotting paper
blue grass
blue gum
blue laws
blue print
boa constrictor
board foot
board walk
boat hook
boiler plate
boll weevil
bone dry
bowie knife
bow window
boy scout
brain storm
breeches buoy
bridle path
Bristol board
broom corn
bucket shop
bull baiting
burning bush
burning glass
bus boy

camp meeting
candle power
cannon ball
cannon shot
carbon dioxide
carbon monoxide
carrier pigeon
case knife
cash register

cast iron
castor oil
chafing dish
chamber music
cheval glass
chewing gum
chimney piece
chimney pot
chimney sweep
chop suey
civil service
clasp knife
clearing house
cliff dweller
closed shop
coal gas
coal heaver
coal hod
coal oil
coal tar
coaster brake
coast guard
coat of arms
coat of mail
cold sore
color blindness
commander in chief
conning tower
copy book
corner stone
corn meal
cottage cheese
cotton gin
county seat
crank shaft
cross reference
crow's nest
cube root
cut glass

darning needle
day school
dead center
dead march
dead reckoning

dead set
dead weight
death damp
death mask
death rate
death rattle
death warrant
decoy duck
dessert spoon
dining car
dining room
diving bell
dormer window
double bass
double entry
draft horse
dragon fly
dressing gown
dripping pan
dry dock
dry goods
dry rot

ear trumpet
eider down
eye opener

face card
feed bag
feed pipe
feed pump
fellow feeling
finger board
finger bowl
finger post
finger print
fire boat
fire box
fire bug
fire eater
fire engine
fireless cooker
fire plug
fire ship
fire trap

first fruits
flash light
fox trot (*noun*)
free lance
freight car

glass blower
good will
goose step

hair line
half sister
hand screw
high ball
high school
home rule
home run
house boat

ice box

jack rabbit
jay walker
jig saw

knot hole

lady finger
lamb's wool
lap dog
lily of the valley
living room
lock step
lock stitch
looking glass

main topmast
main topsail
main yard
marsh mallow
melting pot
mill pond
minute hand
money changer
money order
music box
music hall

note paper

pepper pot
pier glass
pile driver
pill box
pine cone
pole vault
poll tax
pop corn
post card
post office
pot roast
press agent
press gang
proof reader
pug nose
push button
pussy willow
putting green

quarter section

rear admiral
road house
roller coaster
roller skate
rolling stock
roof garden
rope ladder

safety match
safety valve
sal soda
sal volatile
screw driver
screw propeller
sea anchor
sea anemone
sea bass
sea lion
sealing wax
search warrant
sea wall
shell shock
shooting star
short circuit (*noun*)
shoulder blade
shoulder strap
side line
side show
single file
sky pilot
sleeping car
sling shot
smelling salts
smoke screen
snare drum
soap bubble
steam engine
steam roller
steel wool
steeple jack
stop watch
sugar cane
sweet corn

tea ball
terra cotta
test tube
tiger lily
tight rope
time clock
title deed
title rôle
trolley car
trolley line
tuning fork
turning point

war cry
war dance
war paint
water cress
water glass
water meter
water polo
water tower
water wheel
well off

X Ray (*noun*)

CHAPTER VII

ABBREVIATIONS

As a rule, the use of abbreviations should be avoided in ordinary and formal writing.

There are several reasons why abbreviations are not in good taste. They are shortened forms of words, and their use conveys the impression of haste or carelessness, or of compactness and brevity at the expense of appearance. The use of abbreviations also shows a lack of consideration for the reader, who may find them unfamiliar and difficult to read and understand. In lists and tables, however, in footnotes and parenthetical matter, and indeed wherever the saving of space is very important, abbreviations are allowable. In using them, observe the following rules.

Standard forms

1. Some words are abbreviated in several ways. Use only the accepted or officially recognized form.

Calif. (*not* Cal.) Sept. (*not* Sep.) cm. (*not* centim.)

2. There are a few abbreviations which are widely used and are always permissible.

A.D., B.C., Mr., Mrs., i.e., e.g., viz., etc., f.o.b., c.o.d.

Punctuation

3. Place a period after an abbreviation.

P.M. Jan. No. pp. U. S. A.

Exceptions: Do not place a period after:

(1) Names of language periods or epochs
OE (Old English)
MHG (Middle High German)

(2) The French abbreviations *Mlle*, *Mme*, and *Cie*

(3) The abbreviations for book formats and for manuscript as, *8vo, 12mo, MS*
(4) Such business expressions as *A1, c/o, %, per cent*
(5) The expressions *IOU* and *SOS*
(6) Such mathematical abbreviations as *cos, sec, tan*
(7) Initials standing for technical publications, as *PMLA*.
(8) Names of government agencies, airline companies and other well-known organizations, as FBI (Federal Bureau of Investigation), AL (American Legion).

The names of radio and television stations are not abbreviations and do not take periods: *WJZ, WFIL-TV*.

4. Be careful to distinguish between an abbreviation and a contraction, which is written with an apostrophe instead of a period, and between an abbreviation and a chemical symbol or a formula, which has neither apostrophe nor period.

Contraction	*Symbol or Formula*	*Abbreviation*
won't	Fe	ave.
can't	H_2O	Feb.
don't	$V = lwh$	A.A.U.W.

Capitalization

5. Capitalize an abbreviation if the word for which it stands takes a capital.

Nov. La. yd. ibid.

6. Most abbreviations consisting of one letter are capitalized. The following are among those that are commonly printed in small letters: *s.* (shilling or shillings), *d.* (penny or pence), *r.p.m., i.e., e.g., cwt.*

7. In abbreviations of academic degrees or honorary awards or titles, capitalize a single letter standing for a word, but only the first letter if two or more letters stand for a word. Initial letters doubled to indicate the plural should both be capitalized.

A.B. F.R.S. Ph.D. LL.D.

Plurals

8. The plurals of most abbreviations are formed by adding *s* to the singular, but many are the same for both.

Titles and names of persons

9. When a title is followed by a surname without a Christian name or initials, it always should be spelled out.

Exceptions: *Mr., Mrs., Messrs., MM, Mme, Mlle* are never spelled out.

Correct	*Incorrect*
Professor Westcott	Prof. Westcott
General Holmes	Gen. Holmes
Captain Drury	Capt. Drury
Doctor Jones	Dr. Jones

10. The titles *Esquire, Senior,* and *Junior* following a name may be abbreviated. They are written variously with and without a preceding comma and a following period, with and without a capital letter. The most commonly accepted form uses comma, capital, and period.

James J. Dugan, Jr.
W. Randolph Church, Sr.
Wallace Channing, Esq.

11. *Dr.* and *Esq.* are never used with any other title.

Patrick J. Monahan, Esq. *not: Mr.* Patrick J. Monahan, *Esq.*
Dr. James A. Reed *not: Dr.* James A. Reed, *M.D.*

12. *Reverend* and *Honorable* may be abbreviated when used with a full name. They should never be used with a last name only, or abbreviated when the office of the person is given with his name. Ordinarily the abbreviations are not used with *the* or *Mr.*

Incorrect	*Correct*
Reverend Smith	The Reverend Henry Smith
Rev. Smith	The Rev. Henry Smith
The Hon. Jones	Hon. James J. Jones *or* The Honorable James J. Jones
Rt. Rev. William Williams, Bishop of Tennessee	Right Reverend William Williams, Bishop of Tennessee
Hon. John Smith, Secretary of the Treasury	Honorable John Smith, Secretary of the Treasury
The Rev. Mr. Jones	The Reverend Mr. Jones

13. Do not abbreviate personal names except in copying signatures in which the author prefers to use an abbreviation.

Company names

14. Follow company usage in abbreviating firm or company names. *Co., Ltd., Bros., &, Inc.,* should be used only as the companies themselves use these abbreviations. Companies incorporated under the Companies Act by the Parliament of Canada are required to use *Limited* in full.

Poèt et Cie
Farson & Farson, Contractors
Brown and Brown
Marx Bros.
Haynemann Brothers
Harris, Langenwalter, Smith, and Company
James Tyson & Company
Pennsylvania Oil Company
George Allen & Unwin, Ltd.
Bond Bros. & Co.
McClelland & Stewart, Limited

Letters

15. In the heading and inside address of a letter, do not abbreviate the name of the month, the name of the city, or the words *street* and *avenue.* Abbreviation of the state name is permissible, but should be avoided. Personal and company names should not be abbreviated except in following the personal or company usage. In the salutation, the only permissible abbreviations are *Mr., Mrs., Dr.* On the envelope, abbreviations may be used in the return address but should be avoided in the main address. If the postal zone is known, the number should be used in the address.

1602 Walnut Street
Philadelphia 3, Pennsylvania
May 12, 19—.

James A. Wright, Ph.D.
Dean, Windsor College
Windsor, Maryland

My dear Dr. Wright:

Miscellaneous

16. Never begin a sentence with an abbreviation.

17. Do not abbreviate the names of cities, except the word *Saint,* which is always abbreviated.

St. Paul, St. Louis *but not:* Phila., N. Y., Chi.

18. Do not use the abbreviations *2nd, 3rd, 5th, 21st,* etc. Do not use *firstly, secondly,* and the like as adverbs: use *first, second.* These words are adjectives, adverbs, and nouns.

19. Do not abbreviate units of measure except when they are used with a number; as, 3 ft., 4 oz., 8 in.

But not: The auto traveled fifty ft. before stopping.

20. Do not abbreviate parts of geographic names except in lists, tables, etc., when there is not space enough to write the name in full. Then the first parts of such names as *Fort Worth, Point Jefferson, Mount Rainier,* may be abbreviated: *Ft. Worth, Pt. Jefferson, Mt. Rainier.*

21. Do not use the abbreviations *U. S.* and *U. S. A.* in ordinary writing, except in giving the names of ships, government bureaus, government publications, and the like.

U. S. S. *Idaho*
U. S. Bureau of Standards

OFFICIAL ABBREVIATIONS FOR NAMES OF STATES, TERRITORIES, AND UNITED STATES POSSESSIONS

Alabama	Ala.	Indiana	Ind.
Arizona	Ariz.	Kansas	Kans.
Arkansas	Ark.	Kentucky	Ky.
California	Calif.	Louisiana	La.
Canal Zone	C. Z.	Maryland	Md.
Colorado	Colo.	Massachusetts	Mass.
Connecticut	Conn.	Michigan	Mich.
Delaware	Del.	Minnesota	Minn.
District of Columbia	D. C.	Mississippi	Miss.
Florida	Fla.	Missouri	Mo.
Georgia	Ga.	Montana	Mont.
Hawaii	T. H.	Nebraska	Nebr.
Illinois	Ill.	Nevada	Nev.

New Hampshire	N. H.	Rhode Island	R. I.
New Jersey	N. J.	South Carolina	S. C.
New Mexico	N. Mex.	South Dakota	S. Dak.
New York	N. Y.	Tennessee	Tenn.
North Carolina	N. C.	Texas	Tex.
North Dakota	N. Dak.	Vermont	Vt.
Oklahoma	Okla.	Virginia	Va.
Oregon	Oreg.	Washington	Wash.
Pennsylvania	Pa.	West Virginia	W. Va.
Philippine Islands	P. I.	Wisconsin	Wis.
Puerto Rico	P. R.	Wyoming	Wyo.

Do not abbreviate Alaska, Iowa, Idaho, Maine, Ohio, Utah, Samoa, Guam, Virgin Islands.

Days and Months

Sun.	Jan.	July
Mon.	Feb.	Aug.
Tues.	Mar.	Sept.
Wed.	Apr.	Oct.
Thurs.	May	Nov.
Fri.	June	Dec.
Sat.		

Academic Degrees

A.B. or B.A.	Bachelor of Arts
A.M. or M.A.	Master of Arts
A.R.A.	Associate of the Royal Academy of Arts
A.R.I.B.A.	Associate of the Royal Institute of British Architects
B.Arch.	Bachelor of Architecture
B.C.E.	Bachelor of Civil Engineering
B.C.L.	Bachelor of Civil Law
B.D.	Bachelor of Divinity
B.L.	Bachelor of Law
B.Mus.	Bachelor of Music
B.S. or B.Sc.	Bachelor of Science
B.S.C.	Bachelor of Science in Commerce
B.S.E.	Bachelor of Science in Education
C.E.	Civil Engineer
D.C.L.	Doctor of Civil Law
D.D.	Doctor of Divinity
D.D.S.	Doctor of Dental Surgery
D.O.	Doctor of Osteopathy

D.Pd. or Pd.D.	Doctor of Pedagogy
D.Sc.	Doctor of Science
D.V.M.	Doctor of Veterinary Medicine
E.E.	Electrical Engineer
F.A.C.S.	Fellow of American College of Surgeons
F.A.I.A.	Fellow of American Institute of Architects
F.B.A.	Fellow of the British Academy
F.B.S.	Fellow of the Botanical Society
F.G.S.	Fellow of the Geological Society
F.R.A.S.	Fellow of the Royal Astronomical Society
F.R.C.P.	Fellow of the Royal College of Physicians
F.R.C.S.	Fellow of the Royal College of Surgeons
F.R.Econ.Soc.	Fellow of the Royal Economic Society
F.R.G.S.	Fellow of the Royal Geographic Society
F.R.I.B.A.	Fellow of the Royal Institute of British Architects
F.R.S.	Fellow of the Royal Society
F.S.A.	Fellow of the Society of Antiquaries
G.P. or Ph.G.	Graduate in Pharmacy
J.C.L.	Licentiate in Canon Law
L.H.D.	Doctor of Humanities
Litt.B.	Bachelor of Letters
Litt.D.	Doctor of Letters
LL.B.	Bachelor of Laws
LL.D.	Doctor of Laws
M.B.A.	Master of Business Administration
M.D.	Doctor of Medicine
M.E.	Mechanical *or* Military *or* Mining Engineer
M.S.	Master of Science
Mus.Doc. (D.)	Doctor of Music
P.C.	Pharmaceutical Chemist
Ph.B.	Bachelor of Philosophy
Ph.D.	Doctor of Philosophy
Ph.M.	Master of Philosophy
Phar.D.	Doctor of Pharmacy
R.N.	Registered Nurse
S.J.D.	Doctor of Juridical Science
S.T.B.	Bachelor of Sacred Theology
S.T.D.	Doctor of Sacred Theology
S.T.M.	Master of Sacred Theology

Old Testament (O. T.)

Gen.	Genesis	Num.	Numbers
Ex.	Exodus	Deut.	Deuteronomy
Lev.	Leviticus	Josh.	Joshua

Judges	Judges
Ruth	Ruth
I and II Sam.	I and II Samuel
I and II Kings	I and II Kings
I and II Chron.	I and II Chronicles
Ezra	Ezra
Neh.	Nehemiah
Esther	Esther
Job	Job
Ps. (Pss.)	Psalms
Prov.	Proverbs
Eccles.	Ecclesiastes
Cant.	Canticles; the Song of Solomon
Isa.	Isaiah
Jer.	Jeremiah
Lam.	Lamentations
Ezek.	Ezekiel
Dan.	Daniel
Hos.	Hosea
Joel	Joel
Amos	Amos
Obad.	Obadiah
Jon.	Jonah
Mic.	Micah
Nah.	Nahum
Hab.	Habakkuk
Zeph.	Zephaniah
Hag.	Haggai
Zech.	Zechariah
Mal.	Malachi

NEW TESTAMENT (N. T.)

Matt.	Matthew
Mark	Mark
Luke	Luke
John	John
Acts	The Acts
Rom.	Romans
I and II Cor.	I and II Corinthians
Gal.	Galatians
Eph.	Ephesians
Philip.	Philippians
Col.	Colossians
I and II Thess.	I and II Thessalonians
I and II Tim.	I and II Timothy
Tit.	Titus
Philem.	Philemon
Heb.	Hebrews
James	James
I and II Pet.	I and II Peter
I, II, and III John	I, II, and III John
Jude	Jude
Rev.	Revelation

APOCRYPHA (APOC.)

I and II Esd.	I and II Esdras
Tob.	Tobit
Jud.	Judith
Rest of Esther	Additions to Esther
Wisd. of Sol.	Wisdom of Solomon
Ecclus.	Ecclesiasticus
Bar.	Baruch
Song of Three Children	Song of the Three Holy Children
Sus.	History of Susannah
Bel and Dragon	Bel and the Dragon
Pr. of Man.	Prayer of Manasses
I, II, III, and IV Macc.	I, II, III, and IV Maccabees

DEPARTMENTS OF THE FEDERAL GOVERNMENT

AEC—Atomic Energy Commission
ANC—Army Nurse Corps
ARA—Agricultural Research Administration
ATC—Air Training Command
AUS—Army of the United States
BAE—Bureau of Agricultural Economics
BLS—Bureau of Labor Statistics
CAA—Civil Aeronautics Administration
CAB—Civil Aeronautics Board
CAC—Coast Artillery Corps
CSC—Civil Service Commission
DC—Dental Corps
ECA—Economic Cooperation Administration
FBI—Federal Bureau of Investigation
FCA—Farm Credit Administration
FCC—Federal Communications Commission
FCIC—Federal Crop Insurance Corporation
FDA—Food and Drug Administration
FDIC—Federal Deposit Insurance Corporation
FPC—Federal Power Commission
FRS—Federal Reserve System
FTC—Federal Trade Commission
FWA—Federal Works Agency
GAO—General Accounting Office
GPO—Government Printing Office
HC—Hospital Corps
HHFA—Housing and Home Finance Agency
ICC—Interstate Commerce Commission
MC—Medical Corps
NACA—National Advisory Committee for Aeronautics
NG—National Guard
NLRB—National Labor Relations Board
NRC—National Research Council
OEM—Office of Emergency Management
PBA—Public Buildings Administration
PRA—Public Roads Administration
QMC—Quartermaster Corps
REA—Rural Electrification Administration
RFC—Reconstruction Finance Corporation
RRB—Railroad Retirement Board
SCS—Soil Conservation Service
SEC—Securities and Exchange Commission
TVA—Tennessee Valley Authority
USA—United States Army
USCG—United States Coast Guard
USMA—United States Military Academy
USMC—United States Marine Corps
USNA—United States Naval Academy
VA—Veterans' Administration

ORGANIZATIONS

AAA—American Automobile Association
AAAS—American Academy of Arts and Sciences; American Association for the Advancement of Science
AAU—Amateur Athletic Union
AAUW—American Association of University Women
AF & AM—Ancient Free and Accepted Masons
AF of L—American Federation of Labor
ALA—American Library Association
AMA—American Medical Association
AL—American Legion
BPOE—Benevolent and Protective Order of Elks
CIO—Congress of Industrial Organization
DAR—Daughters of the American Revolution
KC—Knights of Columbus
MLA—Modern Language Association
NCAAAA—National Collegiate Amateur Athletic Association of America

NEA—National Education Association
RC—Red Cross
SA—Salvation Army
SPCA—Society for the Prevention of Cruelty to Animals
SPCC—Society for the Prevention of Cruelty to Children
YMCA—Young Men's Christian Association
YMHA—Young Men's Hebrew Association
YWCA—Young Women's Christian Association
YWHA—Young Women's Hebrew Association

HONORS AND TITLES

American

A.M.—Air Medal
B.S.M.—Bronze Star Medal
D.F.C.—Distinguished Flying Cross (Army and Navy)
D.S.C.—Distinguished Service Cross (Army and Navy)
D.S.M.—Distinguished Service Medal (Army and Navy)
L.M.—Legion of Merit
M.H.—Medal of Honor (Army and Navy)
N.C.—Navy Cross
O.L.C.—Oak-leaf Cluster
P.H.—Order of the Purple Heart
S.M.—Soldier's Medal

British

C.B.E.—Commander of the Order of the British Empire
C.I.E.—Companion of the Order of the Indian Empire
C.M.G.—Companion of St. Michael and St. George
C.S.I.—Companion of the Order of the Star of India
C.V.O.—Commander of the Royal Victorian Order
D.B.E.—Dame Commander Order of British Empire
D.S.C.—Distinguished Service Cross
D.S.O.—Distinguished Service Order
D.F.C.—Distinguished Flying Cross
G.B.E.—Knight or Dame Grand Cross Order of the British Empire
G.C.B.—Knight Grand Cross of the Bath
G.C.I.E.—Knight Grand Commander of the Indian Empire
G.C.M.G.—Knight Grand Cross of St. Michael and St. George
G.C.S.I.—Knight Grand Commander of the Star of India
G.C.V.O.—Knight or Dame Grand Cross of the Royal Victorian Order
K.B.E.—Knight Commander Order of the British Empire
K.C.—King's Counsel
K.C.B.—Knight Commander of the Bath
K.C.I.E.—Knight Commander of the Indian Empire
K.C.M.G.—Knight Commander of St. Michael and St. George
K.C.S.I.—Knight Commander of the Star of India
K.C.V.O.—Knight Commander of the Royal Victorian Order
K.G.—Knight of the Order of the Garter
K.P.—Knight of the Order of St. Patrick
M.B.E.—Member Order of the British Empire
M.C.—Military Cross
M.V.O.—Member Royal Victorian Order
O.M.—Order of Merit
Q.C.—Queen's Counsel
R.F.A.—Royal Field Artillery
R.H.A.—Royal Horse Artillery
R.H.G.—Royal Horse Guards
R.A.F.—Royal Air Force
R.A.M.C.—Royal Army Medical Corps
R.N.—Royal Navy
R.N.V.R.—Royal Naval Volunteer Reserve

H.B.M.—His Britannic Majesty

H.I.H.—His (*or* Her) Imperial Highness
H.I.M.—His (*or* Her) Imperial Majesty
H.M.—His (*or* Her) Majesty
H.M.S.—His Majesty's Ship Service
H.R.H.—His (*or* Her) Royal Highness
H.S.H.—His (*or* Her) Serene Highness
O.H.M.S.—On his Majesty's Service

Common Abbreviations of Railroads

A. C. L.	Atlantic Coast Line
A. B. & C.	Atlanta, Birmingham & Coast
A. T. & S. F.	Atchison, Topeka & Santa Fe
B. & A.	Boston and Albany
B. & L. E.	Bessemer & Lake Erie
B. & M.	Boston & Maine
B. & O.	Baltimore & Ohio
C. N.	Canadian National
C. P.	Canadian Pacific
C. & A.	Chicago & Alton
C. B. & Q.	Chicago, Burlington & Quincy
C. C. C. & St. L.	Cleveland, Cincinnati, Chicago & St. Louis
C. & E. I.	Chicago & Eastern Illinois
C. M. St. P. & P.	Chicago, Milwaukee, St. Paul & Pacific
C. & N.W.	Chicago & Northwestern
C. & O.	Chesapeake & Ohio
C. P. R.	Canadian Pacific Railway
C. R. I. & P.	Chicago, Rock Island & Pacific
C. St. P. M. & O.	Chicago, St. Paul, Minneapolis & Omaha
D. L. & W.	Delaware, Lackawanna & Western
D. & R. G.	Denver & Rio Grande
G. M. & N.	Gulf, Mobile & Northern
G. N.	Great Northern
I. C.	Illinois Central
K. C. S.	Kansas City Southern
L. & N.	Louisville & Nashville
L. V.	Lehigh Valley
M. C.	Michigan Central
M-K-T	Missouri-Kansas-Texas
Mo. P.	Missouri Pacific
N. C. & St. L.	Nashville, Chattanooga & St. Louis
N. P.	Northern Pacific
N. & W.	Norfolk & Western
N. Y. C. R. R.	New York Central Railroad

N. Y. N. H. & H.	New York, New Haven & Hartford
P. M.	Pere Marquette
P. R. R.	Pennsylvania Railroad
P. & R.	Philadelphia & Reading
S. A. L.	Seaboard Air Line
S. P.	Southern Pacific
S. R.	Southern Railway System
T. H. & B.	Toronto, Hamilton & Buffalo
T. & P.	Texas & Pacific
T. P. & W.	Toledo, Peoria & Western
U. P.	Union Pacific
W. M.	Western Maryland
W. & L. E.	Wheeling & Lake Erie
Wab.	Wabash Railroad

Common Abbreviations of Airlines

AAL	American Airlines System
AOA	American Overseas Airlines
ASA	Alaska Airlines
BCPA	British Commonwealth Pacific Airlines
BOAC	British Overseas Airways
CAI	Colonial Airlines
CAL	Continental Air Lines
CAP	Capital Airlines
CPA	Canadian Pacific Air Lines
DAL	Delta Air Lines
EAL	Eastern Air Lines
EML	Empire Air Lines
KIM	Royal Dutch Airlines
NAL	National Airlines
NEA	Northeast Airlines
NWA	Northwest Airlines
PAA	Pan American Airways System
QCA	Queen Charlotte Air Lines, Ltd.
TCA	Trans-Canada Air Lines
TWA	Trans-World Airlines
UAL	United Air Lines
WAL	Western Air Lines
WCA	West Coast Airlines

Common Abbreviations Used in Writing and Printing

a.	acre
abbr., abbrev.	abbreviated; abbreviation
Abp.	Archbishop

abr.	abridged
abs.	abstract
acct.	account (also written a/c); accountant
A.D. (Lat. *anno Domini*)	in the (specified) year of our Lord
ad fin (Lat. *ad finem*)	at the end
ad inf. (Lat. *ad infinitum*)	to infinity
ad init. (Lat. *ad initium*)	the beginning
ad int. (Lat. *ad interim*)	in the meantime
a/v (Lat. *ad valorem*)	according to value
Adv.	Advent; advertisement
æ., æt., ætat. (Lat. *ætatis*)	of age, aged
A. F. of L.	American Federation of Labor
agt.	against; agent
alt.	alternate; altitude; alto
a.m., A.M. (Lat. *ante meridiem*)	before noon
amt.	amount
anat.	anatomy, anatomist
anc.	ancient
Angl. Ch.	Anglican Church
Ang.-Sax., A.S., A-S.	Anglo-Saxon
anon., an.	anonymous
ans.	answer
app.	appendix; appointed
approx.	approximately
Apr., Ap., Apl.	April
aq. (Lat. *aqua*)	water
ar.	arrival or arrive
Ar.	Arabia; Arabian; Arabic
A. R. (Lat. *anno regni*)	in the (specified) year of the reign
Arab., Ar.	Arabian, Arabic
Aram.	Aramaic
arch.	archaic; archipelago; architecture
Arch.	Archibald
archæol.	archæology

Archd.	Archdeacon; Archduke
art.	article; artificial; artillery; artist
asst.	assistant
assoc.	associate; association (also, assn.)
atty.	attorney
aux.	auxiliary
avoir., avdp.	avoirdupois
ave.	avenue
bar.	barometer, barometric
bbl.	barrel
B.C.	Before Christ
b.e.	bill of exchange
b.l.	bill of lading
bldg.	building
Bp.	Bishop
bro.	brother
B.T.U.	British thermal unit
bu.	bushel
bul.	bulletin
Bvt.	Brevet
cf. (Lat. *confer*)	compare (also, comp., cp.)
c.f. & i., c.i. & f., c.i.f.	cost, freight, and insurance
cg.	centigram
C.G.	Coast Guard; Commanding General; Commissary General; Consul General
chap., c.	chaplain; chapter; c., chapter, in law citations only
cl.	centiliter
cm.	centimeter
c.o.	care of (also written c/o); carried over
Co	cobalt
Co.	company; county
C.O.	Commanding Officer; conscientious objector
cod.	codex
C.O.D.	cash, *or* collect, on delivery
cont.	containing; contents; continent; continue(d)
cor.	corner, cornet
c.p.	candle power; chemically pure
C.P.	Common Pleas; Common Prayer; Court of Probate
C.P.A.	Certified Public Accountant

cr.	credit, creditor
ct.	cent (also c.); count
cu.	cubic
cwt. (Lat. *centum* + weight)	hundredweight(s)
d.	date; daughter; day; dead; degree; deputy; died; dime; dollar; pence
def.	defendant (also, dft.); definition
deg.	degree
del.	delegate; (Lat. *delineavit*), he (*or* she) drew it
dept.	department
der., deriv.	derivative, derived
dg.	decigram
diam.	diameter
dict.	dictator; dictionary
disc.	discount; discovered, discoverer
dist.	distant
div.	divide, divided, dividend
dl.	deciliter
dm.	decimeter
do.	ditto
dol.	dollar, dollars
dom.	dominion
doz.	dozen(s)
dr.	dram. debtor
Dr.	Doctor
D.R.	Dutch Reformed
dwt.	pennyweight
E.	East
ea.	each
E. & O.E.	errors and omissions excepted
ed.	edited, edition, editor
e.g. (Lat. *exempli gratia*)	for the sake of the example, for example
eq.	equal; equation; equator; equivalent (also equiv.)
Esq.	Esquire
et al. (Lat. *et alibi*)	and elsewhere; (Lat. *et alii*), and others
etc. (Lat. *et. cetera*)	and other things, and so forth
et seq. (Lat. *et sequens*)	and the following
ex.	example
ex div.	ex (without) dividend

exec.	executive, executor
exp.	export; express
f.	farthing; fathom
fig.	figure
f.o.b.	free on board
fol.	folio
fr.	franc (also, f.); from
Fr.	father; France; (*Ger.*) Frau; French; Friday (also F., Fri.); Friar
frt.	freight
ft.	foot, feet; fort
g.	gauge; gulf
gal.	gallon
gi.	gill(s)
gov.	governor
G. I.	Government Issue
gr.	gram
gtt. (Lat. *guttae*)	drops
hdkf.	handkerchief
hdqrs.	headquarters
hg.	hectogram, heliogram
hhd.	hogshead(s)
hl.	hectoliter
hm.	hectometer
hr.	hour
ht.	height
hyp.	hypothesis
ib., ibid. (Lat. *ibidem*)	in the same place
id. (Lat. *idem*)	the same
i.e. (Lat. *id est*)	that is
I.E.	Indo-European
i.h.p.	indicated horse power
in.	inch
in loc. cit. (Lat. *in loco citato*)	in the place cited
int.	interest
inv.	invoice
isl.	island
ital.	italic(s)

J.	judge
JJ.	justices
Jr.	junior
k.	king; knight
kg.	kilogram
kl.	kiloliter
km.	kilometer
lat.	latitude
lb. (Lat. *libra*)	pound
l.c.	lower case; letter of credit (also written L/C)
L. C.	Lower Canada
ld.	lead: used in proof reading
l.f.	lightface
L.F.C.	Low-Frequency Current
Lieut, Lt.	Lieutenant
loc. cit. (Lat. *loco citato*)	in the place cited
log.	logarithm
long.	longitude
l.t.	long ton
ltd.	limited
mdse.	merchandise
meas.	measure
mem.	memento; memoir; memorandum; memorial
mfd.	manufactured
mfg.	manufacturing
mfr.	manufacturer
mg.	milligram(s)
mgr.	manager
misc.	miscellaneous
mo.	month
ms, MS	manuscript
mt.	mount, mountain
neg.	negative
neut.	neuter
N.	North
nol. pros. (Lat. *nolle prosequi*)	to be unwilling to prosecute
non seq. (Lat. *non sequitur*)	it does not follow

ob. (Lat. *obit*)	he (*or* she) died
obs.	obsolete
op. (Lat. *opus*)	work
oz.	ounce(s)
p. (*pl.* pp.)	page
par.	paragraph; parallel; parenthesis
part.	participle
payt.	payment
p.c.	per cent
pd.	paid
per an. (Lat. *per annum*)	by the year
per ct., p.c. (Lat. *per centum*)	per cent
per pro. (Lat. *per procurationem*)	by proxy
pfd.	preferred
pinx., pnxt., pxt. (Lat. *pinxit*)	he (*or* she) painted it
pk.	peck
pkg.	package
pl.	plural
p.m. P.M.(Lat. *post meridiem*)	afternoon
pol. econ.	political economy
poss.	possession, possessive
pref.	preface; preferred; prefix
Pres.	President
prin.	principal
pron.	pronominal, pronoun; pronounced
Prot.	Protestant
pro tem. (Lat. *pro tempore*)	for the time being; temporarily
Prov.	Proverbs; province; Provost
prox. (Lat. *proximo mense*)	in the next, or coming, month
Ps.	Psalm(s)
pt.	pint
Q.E.D. (Lat. *quod erat demonstrandum*)	which was to be demonstrated
Q.E.F. (Lat. *quod erat faciendum*)	which was to be done

qr.	quarter; quire
qt.	quart
q.v. (Lat. *quod vide*)	which see
qy.	query
r.	river; right; road
R.C.	Red Cross; Roman Catholic
rd.	rod
R.D.	Rural Delivery
ref.	referee; reference
regt.	regent; regiment
retd.	returned
rev.	revenue; reverse; revise(d)
rom.	roman (type)
r.p.m.	revolutions per minute
R.O.T.C.	Reserve Officers' Training Corps
R.P.O.	Railroad Post Office
R.R.	railroad
R.S.F.S.R.	Russian Socialist Federal Soviet Republic
Ry.	Railway
S.A.T.C.	Students' Army Training Corps
sch.	schooner
scil., sc., ss. (Lat. *scilicet*)	namely
scr.	scruple
sculp.	sculptor, sculpture
sec	secant; sec., second
sect., sec.	section
secy.	secretary
ser.	series
sergt.	sergeant
sp. gr.	specific gravity
s., S.	shilling(s), South
sm. caps., s. c.	small capitals
SOS	a signal call of distress consisting of the letters *s o s* (- - - — — — - - -) of the international Morse alphabet
sov.	sovereign
sq.	square
sq. in.	square inch
sq. mi.	square mile
Sr.	Senior
St.	street; Saint

str.	strait
subj.	subject
suff.	suffix
Supt.	Superintendent
surg.	surgeon
syn.	synonym
t.b.	tubercle bacillus *or* tuberculosis
tel.	telegram; telegraph; telephone
tr.	transfer; transitive; transpose
ult.	ultimate(ly); (Lat. *ultimo*), in the month preceding the current month
univ.	universal(ly); university
U.S.A.	United States of America; United States Army
U.S.S.R.	Union of Soviet Socialist Republics
v.	verb; verse; valve
v.a.	verb active
var.	variant
Vat.	Vatican
v.i.	verb intransitive
vid., v. (Lat. *vide*)	see
viz. (Lat. *videlicet*)	namely, to wit
vocab.	vocabulary
vol.	volcano, volcanic; volume; volunteer
v.r.	verb reflexive
V.R. (Lat. *Victoria regina*)	Queen Victoria
vs. (Lat. *versus*)	against
v.s. (Lat. *vide supra*)	see above
v.t., v.tr.	verb transitive
W.	West
wk., w.	week
w.l.	wave length
wt.	weight
yd.	yard
yr., y.	year; younger; your

CHAPTER VIII

ITALICS AND NUMBERS

ITALICS

Italic type is used mainly for two purposes: emphasis, and display or distinction. It is indicated in unprinted matter by one line drawn beneath a word.

Emphasis

The use of italics for emphasis is to be avoided, as the other uses of italics may interfere with the emphatic use or be mistaken for it, and too much italic spoils the appearance of a page. Sometimes, however, italics are needed to bring out the meaning of a sentence by showing emphasis on a particular word which does not receive natural stress.

"What!" he cried, "Jim Bryant *here!*"

Display or Distinction

Italics are generally used to make a word or a phrase stand out from its context. Quotation marks are sometimes employed, but present-day usage tends more and more to use italics for this purpose.

1. Books, periodicals, etc. Italicize titles of books, periodicals, musical compositions, names of ships and aircraft, and works of art.

Meredith's *The Tragic Comedians*	*U. S. S. New York*
Mozart, *Symphony in G Minor*	*Spirit of St. Louis*
the *Perseus* of Cellini	*U—3*
the Beethoven *Missa Solemnis*	*DC–6*
Concert Champêtre	

Note that *the* should be italicized when it is part of the title of books, periodicals, and also in newspaper titles, unless the company that owns the paper uses it otherwise. In magazine titles, also, *the* occurring as the first word is usually not italicized in informal references.

The New York Times	Tennyson's *The Lotos-Eaters*
The Saturday Evening Post	*The Herald-Tribune*
The Cleveland Plain Dealer	the *Field and Stream* magazine

2. Words and letters. Italicize words or letters when referred to by name.

There are too many *and's*.
He erased every *h* on the page.

3. Scientific names. In bacteriological, botanical, geological, and zoölogical matter, scientific names consisting of the genus and species are usually italicized.

Closterium pasteuriana	*Cistus canadensis*
Pteridum equilium	

4. Resolved. Italicize the word *Resolved* in a resolution.

Therefore be it *Resolved,* That this organization. . .

In typewritten work, *Resolved* is generally typed in solid capitals.

5. Plaintiff and defendant. Italicize the names of plaintiff and defendant in legal citations.

Cooker v. *Lanahan* (78 U. S. 415)

6. Subdivisions. Italicize small letters and arabic numerals used in subdivisions.

I. . . . .
(*a*). . . . .
(*b*). . . . .
(*1*). . . . .

7. *To be continued.* The words *Continued* and *To be continued* preceding or concluding a portion of an article should be set in italics.

8. Algebraic symbols. Italicize algebraic symbols and equations. Numbers are not italicized.

$x(y - z) = 10$ the nth power

9. Errata. The words *for* and *read* in lists of errata, and the words *see also* in cross-index references are printed in italics.

See also Murry
for patrol *read* petrol

10. Names of ships. Italicize the names of ships. These are sometimes inclosed in quotation marks, but the tendency is to print them in italics. Some newspapers, however, print them in small capitals, and some do not distinguish them in any way.

The *Berengaria* sailed yesterday.

11. English money. Italicize *s.* and *d.* after sums of English money: 10*s.* 6*d.*

12. Definitions. A word or phrase introduced into a passage for the purpose of definition and discussion is italicized.

Smaller plants that multiply by a process called *fission*, composed of spherical. . . .

13. Letters, speeches, reports. In material that is to be printed, italicize all address lines in letters, speeches, and reports, and the title following a signature.

Mr. Chairman, Ladies and Gentlemen:

Miss Charlotte Guthrie
21 Washington Lane
Richmond, Virginia

Dear Miss Guthrie:

Very truly yours,
Austin P. Dobson, *Secretary*

14. Reference. The following words used in references are printed in italics.

ad loc.	*idem*	*post*	*ex parte*
ante	*infra*	*sc.*	*in the matter of*
circa	*loc. cit.*	*supra*	*via*
et al.	*op. cit.*	*vide*	*sc.*
ibid	*passim*	*in re*	*ad lib.*

Do not italicize the following:

c.f.	etc.	i.e.	viz.
e.g.	f. and ff.	q.v.	v. and vs.

The last of these, or indeed any of them, may be italicized when they might be misunderstood if not so printed, as when between two words not italicized.

15. Foreign words and phrases. Foreign words and phrases which have not become completely Anglicized should be printed in italics. It is often difficult to determine whether a word is sufficiently Anglicized to be written without italics. A good dictionary will usually give the status, and the following brief, suggestive lists may prove helpful.

Words to be italicized:

au courant
autres temps, autres mœurs
beau monde
belles-lettres
bon mot
chez moi
cinquecento
comédienne
comme il faut
congé
danseuse
déjeuner
deus ex machina
élan
en rapport
entente cordiale
femme de chambre
fin de siècle
garçon
gendarme
mise en scène
moyen âge
pâté
pièce de résistance
pourboire
prie-dieu
raison d'être
recherché
salon
soupçon
tant mieux
tour de force
Wanderlust
Zeitgeist

Words not to be italicized:

addenda (-um)
aid-de-camp
alias
beau ideal
café
camouflage
clientele
corrigenda (-um)
data (-um)
demimonde
dilettante
éclat
entrée
façade
gratis
habitué
levee
mandamus
matinée
onus
parvenu
paterfamilias
patois
post obit
protégé
régime
reveille
sauerkraut
versus
via
vice versa
viva voce

The Writing of Numbers

The question of when to write numbers as figures and when to write numbers as words is simplified by the fact that usage is fairly well defined in the matter. In the following rules, the approved practice in the writing of numbers is given.

General

1. **Numbers at beginning of sentence.** Spell out a number which begins a sentence, even though it would be written in figures within the sentence. It is well to avoid beginning a sentence with a large number which, if occurring within the sentence, would be given in figures.

One hundred twenty-three men were trapped in the mine for fourteen hours.
Five dollars and seventy cents was all we had.

2. ***And* with numbers.** While not incorrect, *and* is usually not necessary between the figures in a number except between a whole number and a fraction.

five hundred twenty　　three *and* three eighths

Note that *and* is often used in legal documents and official proclamations after the designation of hundreds.

in the year of our Lord, one thousand nine hundred *and* fifty-one
nineteen hundred *and* fifty-one

3. **Ages.** Spell out the numbers used in giving the age of a person or of an object.

ninety years old　　a two-year-old colt
a three-months-old baby　　a century-old church

4. **Military bodies, sessions of Congress, etc.** Spell out numbers of military bodies, of sessions of Congress, of Egyptian dynasties, of political divisions.

Eighty-second Congress　　British Eighth Army
Tenth Ward　　Twelfth Dynasty

5. Balloting. Write as figures the results of balloting.

There were 17 votes cast in favor of the motion, 23 against it.

6. Page and chapter numbers. Write as figures page, chapter, and section numbers, and numbers used as footnotes.

page 71 chapter 12 section 8

Money and amounts

7. Numbers. Treat all numbers alike in a group. Spell out numbers of one and two digits. But if the accompanying paragraph contains several related numbers of various digits, then all should be expressed in digits. Avoid combinations of figures with the words; such as, 100 million, 1 billion.

We had to pay $14.75 for the silk and $3.30 for the lining. Thread and buttons cost 63 cents, and the dressmaker's bill was $10—altogether, $28.68.

8. Cents. Always spell out a sum in cents unless other amounts are mentioned.

We enclose thirty-seven cents in stamps.

9. Dollar sign. Do not use the dollar sign for amounts less than a dollar.

I paid seventy-five cents (*not:* I paid $.75).

10. Even dollars. Do not write *.00* after a figure designating an even number of dollars.

He owed us $575 (*not* $575.00).

11. Mixed amounts. For mixed amounts use the dollar sign and write the numbers as figures.

The bill amounts to $3.17.

12. Round numbers. Spell out all amounts expressed in one or two words, and all round numbers (approximate figures in units of 100 for numbers of 1,000 or less, and in units of 1,000 for larger numbers). A number such as

1,500 should be written as fifteen hundred rather than as one thousand five hundred.

two thousand pounds	seventy-five dollars
eight hundred people	twelve million dollars

But:

2,576 pounds	$175
857 people	$12,780,000

13. Mixed numbers. Use figures for mixed numbers.

$16\frac{2}{3}$ $87\frac{1}{2}$ $59\frac{3}{4}$

14. Fractions. Spell out fractions standing alone.

three fourths of a mile one eighth of a pound

15. Numbers as adjectives. Spell out a sum used as an adjective.

three-million-dollar fortune
hundred-yard dash
ten-foot pole

16. Decimals and per cents. Always use figures for decimals and per cents.

They recovered .6 of a grain from the scrapings.
He learned that 25 per cent of the class had failed.

17. Parentheses. In ordinary business writing and correspondence, it is not necessary to repeat in parentheses an amount that has been spelled out. When repetition is necessary, as in legal writing, use the parentheses as follows:

We agree to pay fifty dollars ($50) a month. *Not:* fifty dollars (50).

Enclosed is a check for one hundred twenty-five dollars ($125). *Not:* one hundred twenty-five (125) dollars.

Time

18. Time of day. When exact time of day is given in hours and minutes, use figures. Spell out other expressions.

3:15 8:35 half-past two three o'clock a quarter to ten

19. A.M. and P.M. The abbreviations *a.m.* and *p.m.* should be written in small capitals (A.M., P.M.) and used only with figures. They should never be used with words.

3:15 P.M. 8:35 A.M.

20. Punctuation. A colon should be used to separate the figures standing for hours and minutes.

3:15 P.M.

Dates

21. Numbers in dates. The numbers in dates should ordinarily be written as figures.

He was born on September 1, 1863.
in 1918 '98 the winter of 1778

22. Formal writing. In formal and legal writing, dates are usually written out.

nineteen hundred fifty-one
one thousand nine hundred and fifty-one nineteen fifty-one

23. Dates in letters. In letters, dates should be written as follows:

(*a*) *Headings.* The date should be written in figures in a letter heading.

June 13, 19—
13, June, 19— (occasional British practice)

(*b*) *Body of letter.* The following forms are permissible in the body of a letter.

He sailed May 16.
He sailed May sixteenth.
He sailed on the sixteenth.

(*c*) A date written as 3/11/— might be interpreted as November 3, 19—, or March 11, 19—. To avoid a misunderstanding, do not write a date in this manner. Better is 3/xi/— (meaning the third of November, 19—). This usage is perhaps more British than American.

(*d*) Avoid the forms *3rd, 4th, 21st, 22nd,* and the like.

Measures and Distances

24. Dimensions, weights, etc. Write as figures dimensions weights, measures, distances, and degrees, except degrees of inclination. But fractional amounts should be spelled out.

31 miles	8 pounds	4 yards	18 bushels
45° 18′	96° F.	12° C.	6 by 8 feet

an angle of forty-five degrees
three fourths of a bushel
half a mile

Streets

25. Street names. As a general rule, write out a number below 100 used as the name of a street. In mail addresses, however, and wherever lack of space requires the use of a shorter form, figures may he used for numbers above 12. Avoid the use of *st, nd, rd,* and *th,* with the numbers.

Fifty-first Street	Permissible: 51 Street
Second Avenue	To be avoided: 2nd Avenue
134 Street	134th Street

Do not abbreviate the words *South, North, East,* and *West* with a number used as the name of a street.

South 134 Street *not:* S. 134 Street

26. Street numbers. Write as figures the street numbers of buildings. Connect with *and* two consecutive numbers on a street.

512 Fifth Avenue	1016 and 1018 South 17 Street
29 St. James Court	

ROMAN NUMERALS

I	one	V	five
II	two	VI	six
III	three	VII	seven
IV or IIII	four	VIII	eight

IX or VIIII	nine
X	ten
XI	eleven
XII	twelve
XIII	thirteen
XIV or XIIII	fourteen
XV	fifteen
XVI	sixteen
XVII	seventeen
XVIII	eighteen
XIX	nineteen
XX	twenty
XXX	thirty
XL or XXXX	forty
L	fifty
LX	sixty
LXX	seventy
LXXX	eighty
XC or LXXXX	ninety
C	one hundred
CC	two hundred
CCC	three hundred

CCCC	four hundred
D	five hundred
DC	six hundred
DCC	seven hundred
DCCC	eight hundred
DCCCC or CM	nine hundred
M or ⊘, or ○○	one thousand
MCMXXV	one thousand nine hundred twenty-five
*$\overline{II}$ or MM, or ⊘⊘,	two thousand
$\overline{V}$	five thousand
$\overline{VIII}$	eight thousand
$\overline{X}$ or ⊚	ten thousand
$\overline{XXX}$	thirty thousand
$\overline{XL}$	forty thousand
$\overline{L}$	fifty thousand
$\overline{XC}$	ninety thousand
$\overline{C}$ or ◎	one hundred thousand
$\overline{M}$ or ⌈x⌉	one million

* A line placed over a Roman numeral multiplies its value by 1000.

USEFUL INFORMATION

CHAPTER IX

ALPHABETIC FILING

Each business office adapts and modifies a filing system to meet its own needs. Many offices have developed their own special rules for certain points of filing procedure. In general, however, the following rules for alphabetic filing are used.

How to alphabetize

1. To alphabetize a group of words, arrange the words according to the alphabetic order of their first letters. When first letters are alike, the order of words depends on the alphabetic sequence of the second letters, then of the third, etc. Sometimes every letter of a word must be used to determine the alphabetic order of the word.

Not alphabetized	*Alphabetized*
Cowdrey	Bain
Balley	Bainter
Stoney	Balley
Bain	Cowdrey
Stoner	Montrose
Sloane	Randall
Bainter	Sloane
Slosson	Slosson
Smythe	Smyth
Montrose	Smythe
Randall	Stoner
Smyth	Stoney

2. Whenever variations in spelling occur, make cross references under every variation.

Raeburn *see also* Rayburn
Rayburn *see also* Raeburn

Names of persons

3. Names for filing should be written or filed as if written with surname first, given name or initials second.

	Filed as
Robert J. Barclay	Barclay, Robert J.
J. M. Bryce	Bryce, J. M.
Francis Martin Connolly	Connolly, Francis Martin
C. Hamilton Fish	Fish, C. Hamilton

4. Titles such as *Dr., Jr., Rev., Prof.*, are always placed at the end of a name, in parentheses, and disregarded in filing.

	Filed as
Mrs. Gertrude Chase	Chase, Gertrude (Mrs.)
Prof. Henry Hastings	Hastings, Henry (Prof.)
James J. McCallum, Jr.	McCallum, James J. (Jr.)
William Lyon Phelps, LL.D.	Phelps, William Lyon (LL.D.)
Dr. Leon Rosenthal	Rosenthal, Leon (Dr.)

5. But when a foreign title is used as part of the name, file exactly as written, with title first, and make a cross reference under the name.

	Cross reference
Lady Alice	Alice, Lady *see* Lady Alice
Lord Gray	Gray, Lord *see* Lord Gray

6. An initial always precedes a name beginning with the same letter.

	Alphabetized as
Franklin Simon	Simon, F.
F. Matthew Simon	Simon, F. M.
F. Simon	Simon, F. Matthew
F. W. Simon	Simon, F. Warren
F. Warren Simon	Simon, Franklin

7. Abbreviations are treated as if spelled out.

Chas. *as* Charles   Wm. *as* William

8. Surnames compounded with *du, de, d', della, von, van, le, la, l', Mc, M', Mac, O'*, etc., are filed as if written in one word. Apostrophes are disregarded.

	Filed as
della Robbia	Dellarobbia
du Pont	Dupont
La Crosse	Lacrosse
Mac Lean	Maclean
McGregor	Mcgregor
O'Brien	Obrien
Von Tassel	Vontassel

9. A hyphenated personal name is alphabetized exactly as spelled and is treated as one word. Always make a cross reference from the second of the two names.

Henry Forbes-Watson, *filed as if written* Forbeswatson, Henry

Cross reference under Watson, Henry Forbes-

Names of business companies and institutions

10. The name of a company or an institution is filed alphabetically as written, except for the instances noted in the rules that follow. Cross references should be used wherever greater convenience will result.

Filed as written

International Harvester Co.
Cranford Real Estate Corporation
Harper Paving Co.
Dr. Reed Cushion Shoe Co.

11. No exception to this rule is made when words such as *new, saint, north, south,* etc., begin the title; but any word which occurs in company names sometimes as one word and sometimes as two words is treated as one word. Thus *North Eastern* is treated as *Northeastern, South Western* as *Southwestern, Inter State* as *Interstate.*

	Filed as
New American Cigar Co.	New American Cigar Co.
North German Lloyd	North German Lloyd
North Western Radio Corporation	Northwestern Radio Corporation
New York Canning Co.	New York Canning Co.
Inter State Auto Parts Co.	Interstate Auto Parts Co.
South East Laundry Co.	Southeast Laundry Co.

12. *The* occurring anywhere in a firm name is placed in parentheses and disregarded in filing. When *the* occurs at the beginning of the company name, it is placed at the end.

	Filed as
The Fireside Stove Company	Fireside Stove Co. (The)
Jackson the Florist	Jackson (the) Florist

13. *And*, *&*, *of*, etc., are disregarded in alphabetizing company names.

	Alphabetized as
Haynes & Ehrhart	Haynes, Ehrhart
Daughters of the American Revolution	Daughters American Revolution
Committee for Prison Reform	Committee Prison Reform
Cathedral of St. James	Cathedral St. James

14. When the name of a business house or institution includes the full name of a person, reverse the order of the given name and surname, and alphabetize with surname first, given name second, and other parts of the business title following.

	Alphabetized as
Harris F. Baker Company	Baker, Harris F., Company
Martha Cook Home for Aged	Cook, Martha, Home Aged
J. L. Holmes & Sons	Holmes, J. L., Sons

15. Hyphenated business names are treated as separate words. Compare with § 9 page 173.

	Alphabetized as
Smith-Jones Realty Co.	Smith Jones Realty Co.
Ray-O-Light Corporation	Ray O Light Corporation

16. *S* after an apostrophe is disregarded in alphabetizing. Thus *Smith's* and *Smith* are of equal rank, and the order in which they are filed will depend upon the rest of the name.

Alphabetized

Smith's Drug Store
Smith, John W.
Smithson, Henry A.

17. But *s* preceding an apostrophe is considered.

Alphabetized
Friend, Charles E.
Friendly Club (The)
Friends' Benevolent Association
Friendwin Home (The)

18. Numbers in a name are filed as if spelled out.

57th Street Garage	Fifty-seventh Street Garage
8th Avenue Hotel	Eighth Avenue Hotel

19. When several different companies have the same name, alphabetize by towns, and if necessary by States, in which the companies are located.

Greenburg Clothing Company, Cleveland
Greenburg Clothing Company, Dallas
Greenburg Clothing Company, Washington, Conn.
Greenburg Clothing Company, Washington, Tenn.

Government names and titles

20. Titles and names of bureaus of governments are filed under the name of the country, with title or name of bureau second.

German Treasury Dept.	Germany, Treasury (Dept.)
Kingdom of Belgium Bureau of Railways	Belgium, Railways (Bureau of)

21. Titles of United States government officials or departments are filed under *United States Government,* with department or title as a subtitle.

	Filed as
United States Children's Bureau	United States Government, Federal Security Agency, Children's Bureau
Treasury Department of the United States	United States Government, Treasury (Dept. of)
United States Bureau of Indian Affairs	United States Government, Interior (Dept. of), Bureau of Indian Affairs

	Filed as
Collector of Internal Revenue	United States Government, Treasury (Dept. of), Internal Revenue (Bur. of) Collector

22. State and municipal government departments and titles are filed under the name of state or city.

	Filed as
Territory of Alaska	Alaska, Territory of
City of Denver	Denver, City of
Borough of Manhattan	Manhattan, Borough of

23. The words *department*, *commission(er)*, *bureau*, etc., are placed in parentheses at the end of a title except when they are part of a corporate name.

	Filed as
Bureau for Jewish Children	Bureau Jewish Children
Bureau of Part-time Work	Bureau Part Time Work
But:	
Bureau of Street Cleaning of Nashville	Nashville Street Cleaning (Bureau of)
Indiana Department of Justice	Indiana Justice (Dept. of)
Westchester County Board of Health	Westchester (County of) Health (Board of)

CHAPTER X

REFERENCE SOURCES FOR THE SECRETARY

An important part of the secretary's equipment is her ability to find particular and accurate information on any special subject. A few of those reference books which she has occasion to use most frequently may be conveniently kept in her office. Many, however, are too voluminous or expensive, and many others are too seldom used to be kept on the office shelf. These may usually be consulted in any good public library.

The following list gives some of the best or most common books of reference in the various fields of knowledge which may come within the secretary's province. It is by no means exhaustive, either in scope or content. A much more extensive list is contained in a *Guide to Reference Books*, by Isadore Mudge, which furnishes an alphabetic index of all important reference books.

Indexes and guides

The amount of information in print is vast; yet it is often difficult to find the particular information which one desires and needs. Guides and indexes exist for most kinds of printed matter, however, and the knowledge of how to use them is a necessary and important part of every secretary's training.

For general periodical (magazine) literature, the most important index is *The Readers' Guide to Periodical Literature*, published by The H. W. Wilson Company. This is a monthly and annual index by title, subject, and author, of articles in most current periodicals of general interest. In a recent issue, nearly one hundred fifty periodicals are listed.

Indexes to periodicals

Readers' Guide to Periodical Literature. New York: Wilson. A monthly and annual index by title, subject, and author of articles in most current periodicals of general interest.

International Index to Periodicals. New York: Wilson. An index of the same type as the *Readers' Guide,* but indexing scholarly and scientific periodicals and foreign publications.

Poole's Index to Periodical Literature. Boston: Houghton. An index to articles which appeared in periodicals from 1802 to 1907. Contains no author entries, only subjects and titles. Valuable as an index to old material.

Industrial Arts Index. New York: Wilson. A monthly and annual index to a selected list of engineering, trade, and business periodicals.

The Industrial Market Data Book. Chicago: Advertising Publications, Inc. A directory of market, trade, and class publications in addition to a presentation of market conditions in the various industries.

Social Science Abstracts. New York: Soc. Sci. Abstr. An index to world periodical literature in the social sciences, with abstracts of important articles.

Bulletin of the Public Affairs Information Service. New York: Pub. Aff. Inf. Serv. A publication appearing in weekly, bimonthly, and annual issues, containing a subject index to books, documents, periodical articles, multigraphed material, etc., and including summaries of recent events and developments in sociology, political science, and economics.

New York Times Index. New York: N. Y. Times. A quarterly index to articles appearing in the daily and Sunday *Times.*

Other specialized indexes include the *Book Review Digest, Index to Legal Periodicals,* the *Filmstrip* and *Educational Film Strip Guides,* and the *Art, Education, Agricultural, Essay and General Literature, Biography* and *Bibliographic Indexes.*

Indexes to books

Guide to Reference Books, by Isadore Mudge. Chicago: A.L.A. A descriptive index to all important reference books.

Introduction to Reference Books, by Arthur Denis Roberts. London: Library Association.

Cumulative Book Index. New York: Wilson. A world list of books in the English language, listed by author, publisher, subject, and title. A supplement is issued monthly.

The Publishers' Weekly. New York: Bowker. Contains lists of new publications of the week and of books announced for publication.

The Publishers' Trade List Annual. New York: Bowker. Contains the annual catalogs of American Publishers.

United States Catalog. New York: Wilson. A catalog of books published in the United States prior to 1928. Gives author, title, edition, date, publisher, price, and paging.

Reference Catalogue of Current Literature. London: Whitaker. An English catalog containing full titles of books in print and on sale, with the prices at which they may be obtained. Appears annually, and is supplemented by quarterly issues of *Whitaker's Cumulative Book List.*

American Business Directories. Washington: Government Printing Office. A publication of the U. S. Department of Commerce designed to help businessmen locate sources of supply and lists of prospective customers.

Encyclopedias, dictionaries, and atlases

Book of Knowledge. New York: Grolier Society, Inc.

Britannica Junior Encyclopedia. Chicago: Ency. Brit.

Columbia Encyclopedia. New York: Columbia U. Press.

Encyclopedia Americana. Chicago: Americana Corp.

Encyclopædia Britannica, Britannica Book of the Year. Chicago: Ency. Brit.

Modern Wonder Book of Knowledge. Philadelphia: Winston.

New International Encyclopedia. New York: Funk and Wagnalls.

World Book Encyclopedia. Chicago: Quarrie Corp.

The usefulness of a dictionary is not limited to its information about words. Besides the meaning, pronunciation, derivation, spelling, hyphenation, syllabification, and use of words, a dictionary usually contains maps and statistical geographical information; translations of foreign phrases; commonly used abbreviations and their meanings; signs and symbols used in various languages and professions; names of persons and places; characters in fiction, history, and legend. Among the standard general dictionaries are:

American Everyday Dictionary. New York: Random House.

Dictionary of the English Language. New York: Collier.

Webster's New International Dictionary. Springfield: Merriam.

New Practical Standard Dictionary. New York: Funk & Wagnalls.

The Winston Dictionary. Philadelphia: Winston.

The following are typical of the many dictionaries pertaining to special subjects.

Shorthand Dictionary, John R. Gregg. New York: Gregg.

Dictionary of Commercial Correspondence in English, French, German, Spanish, Italian, Portuguese, and Russian. New York: Pitman.

Blakiston's New Gould Medical Dictionary. Philadelphia: Blakiston.

Medical Dictionary, by T. Stedman. Baltimore: Williams and Wilkins.

Bouvier's Law Dictionary. Cleveland: Banks-Baldwin.

Webster's Biographical Dictionary and *Webster's Geographical Dictionary*. Springfield: Merriam.

Good atlases include the following:

The Times Survey of Canada and World Trade. London: Times Publishing Co.

Commercial Atlas and Marketing Guide. New York: Rand McNally.

International Atlas and *Cosmopolitan Atlas*. New York: Rand McNally.

Advanced Reference Atlas and *Universal World Atlas*. New York: Hammond and Co.

Business and financial directories and handbooks

Reference Book. New York: Dun and Bradstreet, Inc. This credit rating book is available to subscribers to the Dun and Bradstreet service for their confidential use. Business firms throughout the United States are listed, alphabetically by states and towns within the states, with estimated capital and credit standing given for each firm.

Poor's Register of Directors and Executives of the United States and Canada. New York: Standard and Poor's Corp. Contains lists of directors of various corporations, with their business standing and connections.

Kelly's Directory of Merchants, Manufacturers, and Shippers of the World. An annual guide to the export, import, shipping, and manufacturing industries. New York: Cambridge Special Agency, Inc.

Thomas' Register of American Manufacturers. New York: Thomas Publishing Company. A catalog for buyers.

Moody's Manual of Investments. New York: Moody's investors' service. An annual including separate volumes on railroads, industrial conditions, banking and finance, public utilities, and foreign and domestic securities. Lists of corporations are included, with names of directors, statements of income, assets, and liabilities.

Foreign Commerce Year Book. Wash.: U. S. Dept. of Commerce. Contains detailed information on business conditions in some 60 foreign countries.

Lloyd's Calendar. London: Lloyd's. A year book of shipping information.

Bankers' Almanac and Year Book. London: Skinner. A British directory including lists of the principal banks of the world, and of principal insurance offices.

Rand McNally Bankers' Directory with List of Attorneys and Investment Houses. New York: Rand McNally.

United States Official Postal Guide. Washington: Post Office Department. Gives domestic and international rates.

National Associations of the United States. Wash.: Govt. Printing Office. Contains detailed information on more than 4,000 trade, professional, civic and other associations.

Business Service Check-List. Wash.: U. S. Dept. of Commerce. A weekly guide to all publications of the department.

Selected U. S. Govt. Publications. Wash.: Govt. Printing Office. Semimonthly list.

Western Union Code Book.

Bentley Code Book.

Acme Code Book.

Official handbooks

United States Laws and Statutes. Wash.: Govt. Printing Office. A code of laws in force up to the year 1936.

United States Statutes at Large. Wash.: Govt. Printing Office. Laws made since 1936.

Official Register of the United States. Washington: Civil Service Commission. A list of all the principal officials in the government employ.

Official Congressional Directory for the Use of the United States Congress. Published several times a year by the Government Printing Office. Contains authentic biographical and statistical information about members of Congress, the Cabinet, Executive Departments, the Supreme Court, the diplomatic representatives of the United States abroad, and the representatives of foreign countries in the United States.

U. S. Government Organization Manual. Wash.: Govt. Printing Office.

Register of the Department of State. Washington: U. S. Department of State. Contains statistical, historical, and biographical information about the foreign service and the State Department.

Foreign Office List and Diplomatic and Consular Year Book. London: Harrison and Sons. A yearbook containing lists of those in the British diplomatic and consular service.

Professional directories

Only a few of the many professional directories are listed here.

American Medical Directory, a register of legally qualified physicians in the United States and its possessions, and in Canada. Chicago: American Medical Association.

American Dental Directory. Chicago: American Dental Association.

American Library Directory. New York: Bowker. A classified list of libraries, librarians and statistical data.

Martindale-Hubbell Law Directory. Summit, N. J.: M-H, Inc. A complete legal service.

Educational directories

Sargent's Handbook of Private Schools. Boston: Sargent. An annual containing information about private schools in the United States, and those in foreign countries accepting American children.

Your Guide. New York: Official Surveys, Inc. A camp and school directory and buyer's guide.

Patterson's American Educational Directory. Chicago: American Education Company. An annual publication containing information about public and private schools and colleges throughout the country, and lists of educational officials and directors of the institutions listed.

American Universities and Colleges. Wash.: American Council on Education. Gives summaries and discussions of present resources and organization of American colleges and universities, and an alphabetical list of accredited colleges and universities, with information about their history, organization, requirements, fees, scholarship funds, etc.

Education Directory. Wash.: Federal Security Agency. Includes data on various types of educational institutions. Published in four parts: *Federal Government and States, Counties and Cities, Higher Education,* and *Education Associations.*

Lovejoy's Guide to American Colleges and Universities. New York: Simon and Shuster.

Universities of the World Outside the United States. Wash.: American Council on Education.

Handbook of Technical Societies and Institutions of the United States and Canada. Published by the Research Information Service of the National Research Council. Washington.

Literary and classical handbooks, and style books

Crowell's Handbook for Readers and Writers. New York: Crowell. A dictionary of famous characters and plots in fiction, legend, drama, and poetry.

An Index to Poetry and Recitations, Granger. Chicago: McClurg. Contains title, author, and first line indexes to more than 50,000 poems.

Bartlett's Familiar Quotations. New York: Little, Brown.

International Encyclopedia of Prose and Poetical Quotations, Walsh. Philadelphia: Winston.

Oxford Dictionary of Quotations. New York: Oxford University Press.

Reader's Digest of Books, Keller. New York: Macmillan. Brief summaries of important books in many fields.

Roget's Thesaurus of English Words and Phrases. London and New York: Longmans. An extensive list of synonyms and antonyms, arranged according to ideas expressed.

New Rhyming Dictionary. Los Angeles: National Poetry Assn.

Business Terms, Phrases and Abbreviations. New York: Pitman.

Style Book for Typists, Julius Nelson. New York: Gregg.

Style Manual of the Government Printing Office.

Stylebook in English—A Secretary's Manual, Raymond Pence. New York: Odyssey.

A Manual of Style. Chicago: University of Chicago Press. Contains information about the making of books, including suggestions for authors, typographical rules, and specimens of type.

English Grammar, Ralph B. Allen. New York: American Book Co.

Grammar to Use, Lewis and Lynch. Philadelphia: Winston.
Styles of Address, Measures. New York: Thos. Y. Crowell. Correct forms for various countries.
Business Letter English, Robertson and Carmichael. New York: Gregg.
Business Letters and How to Write Them, Brown and Doris. New York: Prentice-Hall.
Business Letter—Its Principles and Problems, Carl Naether. New York: Appleton.
Business Phrases in Six Languages, De Levie. New York: Pitman.
Get It Right, Opdyke. New York: Funk & Wagnalls.
The Executive's Desk Book, Philadelphia: Winston.

Religious handbooks and directories

Irwin's Bible Commentary. Philadelphia: Winston. A one-volume commentary with an introduction to each book of the Bible and 25,000 text references.
Cruden's Complete Concordance. Philadelphia: Winston.
World Christian Handbook. New York: Friendship Press. Contains statistics for missionaries.
Yearbook of American Churches. Published biennially for the Federal Council of Churches. Lebanon, Pa.: Sowers. Contains current directory and statistical information.
Official Catholic Directory. New York: Kenedy. A yearbook containing detailed statistical information about the organization, clergy, schools, religious orders, etc., of the Roman Catholic Church in the United States, Great Britain, Ireland, Canada, Cuba, and Mexico.
American Jewish Year Book. Philadelphia: Jewish Publication Society of America. Contains statistical information, and biographical sketches of prominent Jews.
Yearbooks of the various Protestant denominations.

Reference books of general and statistical information

Cushing's Manual of Parliamentary Practice, Luther S. Cushing. Philadelphia: Winston.
American Year Book. New York: Doubleday, Doran. A record of events and progress, having articles by specialists.
New International Year Book. Published as a yearly supplement to the *New International Encyclopedia*. New York: Funk and Wagnalls. A compendium of world information, especially useful for American affairs.

The World Almanac and Book of Facts. New York: The World-Telegram. An almanac and book of facts, containing statistics on industrial, political, financial, and other subjects.
Information Please Almanac. New York: Doubleday.
Bulletin Almanac.
Chicago Daily News Almanac.
Brooklyn Eagle Almanac.

City directories, almanacs, and pamphlets issued by local chambers of commerce give valuable local statistical and commercial information.

Whitaker's Almanack. London: Whitaker. Especially useful for statistics of the British Empire.
Statesman's Year-book. New York: Macmillan. Contains reliable descriptive and statistical information about governments of the world.
South American Handbook. New York: H. H. Wilson. An annual publication containing information about the countries and resources of Central and South America, Mexico, and Cuba.
Heaton's Commercial Handbook of Canada. Toronto: Heaton. A Canadian yearbook giving annual statistics and information about industry and commerce. Contains a postal and shipping guide, customs tariff information, and directories of trade publications and manufacturers.

Census reports and statistical publications of the United States and foreign countries contain useful information.

Statistical Abstract of the United States. Wash.: Govt. Printing Office. Contains statistics on many subjects: population, area, immigration, wealth, education, etc.
Statistical Supplement. Wash.: Govt. Printing Office. Published biennially to supplement the monthly *Survey of Current Business.* Gives data for a wide variety of business fields, such as national income, production figures, and prices for retail, wholesale and manufacturing levels.
N. W. Ayer and Son's Directory of Newspapers and Periodicals. Philadelphia: Ayer. A guide to publications printed in the United States and its Possessions, the Philippine Commonwealth, the Dominions of Canada and Newfoundland, Bermuda, Cuba and the West Indies. Includes classified lists, maps and descriptions of the states, cities and towns in which the population exceeds 2,500.

Biographical reference books

Biographical information about persons who lived in the past is to be found in encyclopedias and historical reference books. The names of contemporary men and women, however, can seldom be found in encyclopedias, and must be looked for in books such as are listed below. These books contain brief biographical sketches.

Who's Who (principally English).
Who's Who in America.
Who's Who in American Art.
Who's Who in American Education.
Who's Who in Canada.
Who's Who in Commerce and Industry.
Who's Who in Engineering.
Who's Who in Furs.
Who's Who in Latin America.
Who's Who in Railroading.
Who's Who in World Medicine.

There are also numerous *Who's Who* directories that cover particular regions of the United States such as the West, Central States, New England, etc.

Information about the nobility of the continent and their titles and estates is contained in the following books:

Burke's Peerage. London: Burke Publishing Company. A genealogical and heraldic history of peerage and baronetage, published annually. Contains lists and brief accounts of bishops, royal families, knights, and barons, and members of the Privy Council, with full lineages and a guide to relative precedence and orders of knighthood.

Kelly's Handbook of the Titled and Landed Classes. New York: Cambridge Special Agency, Inc.

Titles and Forms of Address, Armiger. New York: Macmillan. A guide to the correct use of British titles and honors.

Registers of society and women's clubs

Social Register. Published in New York, Philadelphia, and the larger cities throughout the country. Gives names and addresses of the people who are socially prominent in the particular district for which the book is issued.

Blue Book. Similar to the *Social Register* and published in different cities of the country.
Dau's Blue Books.
Annual Register of Women's Clubs. An annual directory of women's clubs and national organizations, with a directory of professional lecturers, entertainers, and musicians.

Travel guides

Baedeker guide books for different countries.
Blue Guides (Guides Bleues). New York: Rand McNally.
Your Trip Abroad, Richard Joseph. New York: Doubleday. Covers Europe, South and Central America.
The World in Color. New York: McGraw. Series of volumes including maps, travel guides, etc.
American Guide Series. Set of 48 books on each of the United States.
Official Guide of the Railroads and Steam Navigation Lines in the United States, Canada, Puerto Rico, Mexico, and Cuba. New York: National Railway Publishing Company. Monthly issues bring the railroad and steamship information up-to-date. Also includes airline schedules.
Official Airline Guide. Chicago: Wayne W. Parrish. A monthly publication giving world-wide airline schedules, fares, and other information.
Official Hotel Red Book and Directory. New York. American Hotel Association.
American Automobile Association guide books and accommodations directory.
Leahy's Hotel Guide and Travel Atlas. Chicago: American Hotel Register Co. Covers travel in the United States, Canada and Mexico.

CHAPTER XI

THE MANUSCRIPT

PREPARATION, TYPOGRAPHY, PROOF READING

A secretary's duties often include responsibility for the various details connected with the publication of a manuscript. How to prepare the manuscript for the publishers, how to send it, how to read and mark the printers' proofs are matters which often prove perplexing even to the experienced secretary. The material in this chapter is designed to give information on these important points.

The manuscript should be made as perfect as possible, so that it will not be necessary to make changes in proof, as such changes are expensive.

PREPARATION OF THE MANUSCRIPT

Before sending a manuscript to the publisher, read it through carefully. See that it contains no errors in spelling, punctuation, or grammatical usage, and that the sentences express clearly the ideas to be conveyed. After the proofs are returned from the printer, a change of wording is both difficult and expensive. Careful editing of the manuscript will usually make changes in the proofs unnecessary.

Appearance

Use bond paper of good quality. The sheets should be of uniform size, preferably eight and one half by eleven inches. Use only one side of the paper.

Typewrite all manuscript material in double space.

Allow plenty of margin space for corrections. A margin one and one half inches wide is ordinarily suitable for the upper and left margins, while less space is required at the right and at the bottom of the page.

Never send a carbon or mimeographed copy of a manuscript to the publisher. Send the original typewritten copy and keep the carbon copy as a duplicate to guard against loss of the original.

Do not sew or tie together the pages of a manuscript. Fasten the pages of each chapter with clips or pins which may be removed easily without tearing the paper. Many authors prefer not to fasten the pages, as clips mark them and spoil their freshness.

Numbering

Number all pages consecutively with Arabic numerals. Place the number in the middle of each page at the top, or in the upper right-hand corner.

Number all chapters consecutively with Roman numerals.

Begin every chapter on a new sheet of paper. Write the chapter number and title at the top of the first page.

Corrections

Corrections of single words or very short sentences should be written on separate sheets, cut to the proper size, and pasted carefully over the corrected portion of the manuscript. Never attach a part of a sheet to a manuscript page by clips or pins, or by glue at one side only, for the attached sheet is likely to be torn off and lost in handling.

When extra pages must be inserted, indicate plainly on the manuscript and the extra pages where the insertion is to be made. For example, if three pages of additional text are to be inserted within or at the bottom of page 110 of the manuscript, write at the appropriate place in the margin of page 110, "Insert pages 110*a–c*" and number the pages to be inserted 110*a*, 110*b*, 110*c*. At the bottom of page 110, write "110*a* follows." Place the extra pages immediately after the page which they follow in the manuscript.

To indicate that one or more consecutive pages are to be omitted from a set of pages already numbered, mark the page preceding the omission with its own number and that of the last omitted page. For example, if pages 63 and 64 are to be withdrawn, mark page 62 as 62–64.

Reference material

Spell out all references to publications. Use abbreviations only when making repeated references to a publication. Do not use any abbreviations which you do not wish to appear in the published book or article.

Number all footnotes consecutively throughout each chapter, using Arabic numerals. Federal bureaus and some technical magazines require all footnotes to be placed on separate sheets at the end of the manuscript so that all small-type printing may be done at the same time. Ordinarily, however, a footnote should be placed in the text of the manuscript, immediately below the sentence to which it refers, and separated from the text by lines across the page above and below it. The number of the footnote should precede the note, and should be written somewhat above the level of the line; the corresponding number in the text should follow the word to which the note refers.

When an index is required, make it after the page proof of the manuscript has been returned from the printer. Detailed instruction is given in Chapter XIII, pages 207–209.

Copyrights and illustrations

The securing of copyrights is usually left to the publisher.

If the author makes use in his manuscript of any copyrighted material from another publication, he must secure permission to use that material from the author or the publisher or both, and must acknowledge the use of it in the manner prescribed by the publisher. Information concerning copyrightable material and other provisions of the copyright law is contained in Chapter XII, pages 197–199.

Since the nature and arrangement of the illustrations directly affect the make-up of a book or article, the publisher should always be consulted before any decision is made about them. If any drawings or photographs are submitted with the manuscript, they should be numbered consecutively throughout the entire manuscript. Use Roman numerals for numbering tables, maps, charts, photographs, and plates, and use Arabic numerals for text illustrations.

Sending the manuscript

Wrap the manuscript carefully for mailing. Do not roll it, but send it flat in a box or an envelope plainly marked with the publisher's address and with the author's return address. Always register or insure the package.

Proof Reading

Kinds of proof

The first proofs to be returned from the printer are called the *galley proofs*. These proofs are usually revised and corrected by the publisher's proof reader before they are sent to the author for his corrections. The author may request a second galley proof from the corrected material. The galley proofs should be read and corrected with great care so that all errors may be eliminated before further proofs are made, for every correction of text indicated on later proofs is both difficult and expensive.

The *page proofs* are made from the corrected galley proofs, in the form of numbered pages as they are to appear when published. Ordinarily, these are the last proofs sent to the author. The *foundry proofs* are made after the type is locked up for the casting of the book plates. These proofs, and the final or *plate proofs*, are rarely sent to the author, except by special request.

Suggestions for reading proof

It is well to keep in mind the following directions.

Read all proofs carefully, word by word, for errors in text and in typography. It is a good plan to read proofs through several times, each time with a definite purpose in mind: one reading for punctuation, grammar, correspondence with manuscript, etc.; another reading for typographical errors; another for appearance and general effect.

Make all corrections in ink of a different shade from that used by the professional proof reader.

Make every correction in the margin opposite the line in which the error occurs, making the proper mark in the text for each marginal correction. If more than one error appears in the same line, make the corrections in the order of their occurrence and separate each from the one following by a slant line, thus: ¶ / , / l.c.

To indicate that a word is to be printed in large capitals, underline the word three times and write *caps* in the margin. Two underlines, and *s. c.* written in the margin, indicate that a word is to be written in small capitals. One line beneath a word and *ital.* written in the margin indicate that the word is to be printed in italics, while a wavy underline and *bf* in the margin call for boldface type. A line drawn through a capital letter, and the marginal note *l. c.*, show that the letter is to be in lower-case type.

Use a caret (‸) to show where a correction or additional copy is to be inserted in the text.

If you think that text corrected by the professional should remain without the indicated correction, cross out the marks in the margin and write *stet* (let it stand).

Do not erase any marks made in the margin. If necessary, cross them out, or rewrite symbols or corrections.

Be sure to answer all queries of the copy reader or the professional proof reader. If you do not agree with his suggestions, cross them out or answer them in full. If you do agree, cross out his question mark.

Return the proofs promptly to the publisher so that the printing will not be delayed.

Return the original manuscript with the corrected proof.

Proof-Readers' Marks

Most publishing companies furnish a set of proof-readers' marks with the galley proofs. The author should always make use of them. Usually they will conform with the standard proof-readers' marks which are given below.

Marks used to indicate deletion

℘	Dele or delete: take ~~it~~ out.
℘ (closed)	Take out and clo(p)se up space.
⁀	Clo se up space.
âe/fî	Make a ligature (âe, fî, etc.).

Marks used to indicate retention

stet	Let it stand. Retain what has been ~~crossed~~ out.
Out s.c.	Out, see copy, denotes matter omitted ^ which may be found in the manuscript.

Marks used to indicate spacing

#	Put^in space.
even #	Bad^ spacing;^space^more^evenly.
⊥	Push down the space which shows.
ld	Insert lead or space between the lines.

Marks used to indicate forms of type

≡	Set in CAPITALS.
=	Set in SMALL CAPITALS.
lc	Set in lower case.
ital	Set in *italics*.
rom	Set in roman type.
bf	Set in **boldface** type.

Marks used to indicate forms of letters

wf	Wrong f/ont: use same size and style as rest of text.
×	Change the worn or broken type.

Marks used to indicate position of letters

ꝺ	Reverse the letters which are printed u/side down.
tr	Transpsoe these letters words and.

Marks used to indicate alignment of letters

=	Straighten alignment.
ǁ	//Straighten the end of the line.
⌐	Raise the letter.
⌴	Lower the letter.

Marks used to indicate position of words

center	Put in the middle of the line.
run on	Carry over to the next line.
run back	Run back to the line above.

Marks used to indicate position of paragraphs

#	^Make a paragraph.
no #	^Do not start a new paragraph here. Join the following matter to the preceding paragraph.

Marks used to indicate the position of lines

□	^Indent one em-quad space.
]	Bring to the right.
[	Bring to the left.

Marks used to indicate punctuation

⊙	Insert period.
,	Insert comma.
/=/	Insert hyphen.
‘‘	Insert quotation marks.
*	Insert asterisk.
’	Insert apostrophe.
em	Insert em dash.
en	Insert en dash.

Qy **Query to the author**

sp. **A circled number or abbreviation is to be spelled out in full**

Copy of Proof Showing Proof-reader's Marks

"The estate is yours beyond a doubt," replied a lawyer. "It matters nothing what your faather signed, you
are the heir of *entail*. But your uncle is a man to fight
the indefensible; and it would be likely that your identity
he would call in question. A lawsuit is always expensive,
and a fa mily lawsuit always scandalous; besides which,
if any of your doings with your friend Mr. Thomson
were to come out, we might find that we had burned
our fingers. The kidnapping,to be sure, would be a
court card upon our side, if we could only prove it.
But it may be difficult to prove; and my advice (upon
the whole) is to make a very easy bargain with your
Uncle, perhaps even leaving him at Shaws, where he
has taken root for a quarter of a century, and contenting yourself in the meanwhile with a fair provision."
I told him I was very willing to be ieasy, and that to
carry family concerns before the public was a step from
which I was naturally much averse. In the menatime
(thinking to myself) I began to see the out lines of that
scheme on which we afterwards acted.

"The great affair," I asked, is to bring home to him
the kidnapping."

"Sorely," said Mr. Rankeillor, "and if posssible, out
of court. For mark you here, Mr. David: we could no
doubt find some men of the *Covenant* who would swear
to your reclusion, but once they were in the box, we
could no longer check theer testimony, and some word
of your friend Mr. Thomson must certainly crop out.
Which (from what you have let fall I cannot think to
be desirable.

From Kidnapped
Robert Louis Stevenson

Copy of Proof After Corrections Have Been Made

"The estate is yours beyond a doubt," replied the lawyer. "It matters nothing what your father signed, you are the heir of entail. But your uncle is a man to fight the indefensible; and it would be likely your identity that he would call in question. A lawsuit is always expensive, and a family lawsuit always scandalous; besides which, if any of your doings with your friend Mr. Thomson were to come out, we might find that we had burned our fingers. The kidnapping, to be sure, would be a court card upon our side, if we could only prove it. But it may be difficult to prove; and my advice (upon the whole) is to make a very easy bargain with your uncle, perhaps even leaving him at Shaws, where he has taken root for a quarter of a century, and contenting yourself in the meanwhile with a fair provision."

I told him I was very willing to be easy, and that to carry family concerns before the public was a step from which I was naturally much averse. In the meantime (thinking to myself) I began to see the outlines of that scheme on which we afterwards acted.

"The great affair," I asked, "is to bring home to him the kidnapping?"

"Surely," said Mr. Rankeillor, "and if possible, out of court. For mark you here, Mr. David: we could no doubt find some men of the *Covenant* who would swear to your reclusion; but once they were in the box, we could no longer check their testimony, and some word of your friend Mr. Thomson must certainly crop out. Which (from what you have let fall) I cannot think to be desirable."

From *Kidnapped*
Robert Louis Stevenson

CHAPTER XII

COPYRIGHTS, TRADE-MARKS, PATENTS

What is copyrightable or patentable material, and under what conditions a copyright or patent may be granted or a trade-mark registered, may be learned from the following paragraphs. How to apply for copyright or patent, and the full requirements and provisions of the United States law in the matter may be learned on application to the Register of Copyrights, Library of Congress, Washington, D. C., or to the Commissioner of Patents, the Patent Office, Washington, D. C.

COPYRIGHTS

According to the United States Copyright Law, copyrightable material is classified as:

(*a*) Books (including composite and cyclopedic works, directories, gazetteers, and other compilations)

(*b*) Periodicals, including newspapers

(*c*) Lectures, sermons, addresses, (prepared for oral delivery)

(*d*) Dramatic or dramatico-musical compositions

(*e*) Musical compositions

(*f*) Maps

(*g*) Works of art; models or designs for works of art

(*h*) Reproductions of a work of art

(*i*) Drawings or plastic work of a scientific or technical character

(*j*) Photographs

(*k*) Prints and pictorial illustrations

(*l*) Motion-picture photoplays

(*m*) Motion pictures other than photoplays.

Any printed literary, musical, or dramatic work to be copyrightable in the United States must be completely manufactured in the United States, except the original text of a book of foreign origin printed in a language other than English.

No material is copyrightable upon which a renewal of the original copyright has expired, or which is published by the government or by a government official in his official capacity. No material is copyrightable which has not been copyrighted by the original author or owner, or the publisher, at the time of publication. But abridgments, adaptations, arrangements, compilations, etc., of noncopyrightable material, or of copyrighted material with the permission of the copyright holder, and works republished including new material, are considered to be new works and copyrightable as such.

Anything which has been copyrighted must contain a notice to that effect. In books and printed matter, the notice must contain the name of the copyright holder and the year in which the copyright was secured. The notice is usually placed on the back of the title page and is phrased like the following illustration:

Copyright, 1950, by
The John C. Winston Company

Pictures, or other objects on which a full notice like that above cannot be placed, are marked with the letter *C* inclosed in a circle, ©, accompanied by the name of the copyright holder or a symbol (such as initials) for his name. If only the symbol is used with the copyright mark, however, the name must appear at some other place on the object.

The duration of a copyright is twenty-eight years; within one year of which time it may be renewed for another twenty-eight-year period. Fifty-six years is the longest period of duration of a copyright on a particular work.

A person not a citizen of the United States may secure a copyright on his work if he is a resident of the United States at the time of publication of his work, or if he is a citizen of a country which protects American citizens by granting copyrights to them.

The United States has copyright relations with most of the important countries of the world. For specific information on particular countries, consult the Copyright Office, The Library of Congress, Washington, D. C.

The United States is not a member of the International Copyright Union, but American citizens may obtain copyrights in those foreign countries (see preceding paragraph) with which the United States has reciprocal copyright treaties or agreements.

Trade-Marks

A trade-mark may be a word, a symbol, a design, a picture, or any original or distinguishing mark or sign which indicates the origin of an article or distinguishes it from other similar articles. To satisfy the registration requirements of originality and distinguishing power, a trade-mark may not be:

(*a*) a geographical term, as *Philadelphia* shoes, *Eastern* asbestos;

(*b*) a description of quality, as *Superior* silks, *Fine* sugar.

A trade-mark must be in actual use in business before it can be registered. In case there are several applications for the same trade-mark, the decision is made on the basis of priority of actual adoption of the trade-mark among the applicants. The words *Trade-mark registered* must be printed on every trade-marked article.

A trade-mark permit is issued for a period of twenty years and may be renewed for the same length of time.

Patents

A patent may be secured on any article, machine, or device which is considered by the Patent Office to be new and useful. By *new* is meant not merely different in size, shape, or arrangement from a previously patented article, but embodying a new principle, or an original adaptation or improvement or combination which forms a new product. An improvement which would naturally occur to any skilled mechanic is not considered new by the Patent Office.

Application for a patent must be filed before the invention has been on sale or in public use for two years. The application must contain a full and complete description of the invention. Omission of any part of the details, if discovered, automatically causes the forfeiture of the patent.

Every patented article must contain a notice giving either the date of issue of the patent or its serial number as shown on the patent certificate.

A patent for a design will be granted in the United States only to the inventor, irrespective of his age, color, nationality, race, or sex. The patent is valid for a period of seventeen years. It may be renewed only by a special act of Congress, which is rarely passed.

The United States is a member of the International Patent Union (International Union for Protection of Industrial Property), to which most countries of the world belong, and American citizens have the advantages and protection accorded to all citizens of member countries. This organization fixes the conditions under which patents may be secured in foreign countries, and protects foreign holders of patents in those countries.

CHAPTER XIII

BIBLIOGRAPHIES AND INDEXES

PREPARING A BIBLIOGRAPHY

A bibliography is a list of the printed sources of information on a particular subject, prepared for the purpose of assembling and presenting those sources in the most convenient form. The requisites of a good bibliography are therefore two: completeness, and convenience of arrangement.

Sometimes a bibliography contains only the sources used in the preparation of a particular report. In that case, the titles to be included are automatically limited. They are chosen by the compiler of the report and require no selection by the bibliographer. When, however, the bibliography is designed to present the source material on a subject, for the use of those investigating that subject, the task of the bibliographer is much more difficult, for the bibliography must be at once comprehensive and selective. It must be comprehensive, for no usable material may be overlooked or omitted. It must be selective, for all unreliable or unsatisfactory material must be excluded, or, if included, must be labeled with the nature of its contents. The preparation of such a bibliography demands that the compiler acquaint himself in so far as is possible with all the material available on the subject; and it calls for the exercise of intelligence, care, and discrimination in the selection of the material to be included in the list.

Convenience of arrangement in a bibliography may be secured by the use of the customary form for bibliographical lists, illustrated in the following pages. Within this form occur variations in punctuation, capitalization, and spacing, as shown in the illustrations. The selection of the particular variation to be used for a bibliography will depend somewhat upon the nature and purpose of the bibliography and upon customary usage or precedent within the organization for which the bibliography is compiled.

A bibliography is always arranged in alphabetic order. Ordinarily the author's name is listed first. It is followed by the name of the book or article, and by the details of publication. When a book is referred to, these details are: place of publication, name of publisher, and date of publication. When a magazine is referred to, these details are: name of magazine, volume and number, page numbers, and date of issue. Sometimes this order is changed for the sake of clearness or emphasis, particularly in a bibliography of magazine articles, where the order frequently used is as follows: name of periodical, volume and number, page numbers, date of issue, name of article, name of author.

Occasionally a bibliography alphabetized by authors' names will also contain references to publications for which no author is given, as a bulletin or report. In that case the names of such publications and the authors' names are given in one alphabetic list.

In minor details, the practice in bibliography making is so varied that at first glance it seems confusing. Although no common standard or norm of practice exists, modern usage tends always to greater simplification and the abolition of unnecessary mechanical aids, such as quotation marks, italics, and many capitals. Any form may be used which is simple, and which makes the bibliography clear, easy to understand, and easy to use.

Authors' names

Ordinarily the name of the author is written in capital letters.

Write the name of the author with surname first, given name or initial second, and middle name or initial last.

When a book has more than one author, write each name in the manner suggested above, giving the names in the order of their appearance on the title page of the book.

FISHER, MARGUERITE J. and BISHOP, D. G., *Municipal and Other Local Governments*, New York: Prentice-Hall, 1950.

MATHESON, J. K., and BOVILL, E. W., *East African Agriculture*, New York: Oxford University Press, 1950.

When listing other works by the same author immediately after the first reference, use a dash in place of the author's name.

STEVENSON, ROBERT L., *Treasure Island*
————*Virginibus Puerisque*
————*Kidnapped*

Book references, and titles of books

Ordinarily the name of a book is written in italics.

A subtitle or a reference to a particular part of a book should follow the name of the book, and should be separated from it by a colon.

FLEW, ROBERT NEWTON, *Idea of Perfection in Christian Theology: an Historical Study of the Christian Ideal for the Present Life*, New York: Oxford University Press, 1950.

OVERSTREET, H. A., *The Mature Mind:* Criteria of Maturity, p. 42, New York: Norton and Co., Inc., 1949.

When making a reference to a work which has just been named, use the abbreviations *ibid.* (Latin *ibidem*, in the same place) or *op.cit.* (Latin *opere citato*, in the work cited) to stand for everything that would otherwise have to be repeated.

A Manual of Style: Planning a Book, p. 1, Chicago: The University of Chicago Press, 1949.

Ibid., Specimens of Type, p. 279.

Magazine articles

The name of a magazine is usually written in italics, and the name of a magazine article is placed in quotation marks.

The volume of the magazine, the date of issue, and the page numbers of the article should always be given.

EINSTEIN, ALBERT, "On the Generalized Theory of Gravitation," *Scientific American*, vol. 182, pp. 13–17, April, 1950.

Ordinarily the issue number of the magazine is given, as well as the volume number.

THRUELSEN, RICHARD, "Nature's Million-Dollar Mistake," *The Saturday Evening Post*, vol. 222, no. 49, pp. 32–33, June 3, 1950.

Abbreviation and punctuation

The abbreviations ordinarily used are *vol.* for volume, *no.* for number, *chap.* for chapter, *p.* (plural *pp.*) for page. Other abbreviations, such as those for months, names of cities, names of publishers, should be used only in extensive bibliographies, or where limitations of space require shortened forms. An abbreviated form should not be used if it is likely to be misunderstood by a reader.

Usage varies widely in the punctuation of bibliographies. Sometimes a period is used to separate all the items.

LINSLEY, H. E., *Practical Ideas for Machinists.* New York. McGraw. 1950.

Sometimes a comma is used to separate all the items.

SIDNEY, MARGARET, *Our Davie Pepper*, New York, Grosset, 1950.

Sometimes both comma and period are used.

ROSENKAMPFF, ARTHUR HENRY, and WALLACE, W. C., *Bookkeeping and Accounting: Principles and Practice.* New York, Prentice-Hall, 1950.

Usually a colon is used between the place of publication and the name of the publisher. A colon is also used to separate a book title from subtitle or from a particular section of the book to which reference is made (see preceding page).

Philadelphia: John C. Winston Company, 1950.

MOTT, FRANK LUTHER. *American Journalism: A History of Newspapers in the United States Through 260 Years—1690 to 1950.* New York, Macmillan, 1950.

Typography and arrangement

Special typography is available when a bibliography is printed, but cannot be used when a list is merely typewritten. Effective spacing will often take the place of italics in book titles and make quotation marks unnecessary. When the name of author, book, and publisher are written in continuous prose, however, italics and quotation marks are very useful to distinguish the separate items.

The following bibliography illustrates an informal style frequently used. Notice in book titles the absence of capital letters and italics.

BOSANQUET, B. Logic. Oxford.
LOOMIS, C. P., and BEEGLE, J. A. Rural social systems. Prentice-Hall.
KNIGHT, ARTHUR. Ideas on film. Saturday Review of Literature. May 27, 1950.
SIMMONS, EDWIN. Writing for military magazines. The Writer 62: 4. April, 1949.

A simplified form, with abbreviations, is often used in extensive bibliographies. Names of authors and books are written alike, in ordinary type.

Comer, H. D. The payment plan of retailing men's clothing. Ohio State University.
Duncan, R. Equipment obligations. Appleton. N. Y.
Estrich, W. A. Law of installment sales of goods. Lawyers' Co-operative Pub. Co. Rochester, N. Y.
Griffin, B. W. Installment sales and collections. Prentice-Hall, Inc.
Installment buying. Farmers' Loan and Trust Co. N. Y.
Marvin, Donald M. Partial payment plan. American Management Assn. N. Y.
Schweppe, G. A. Installment selling in department stores. Textile Pub. Co. N. Y.

A still more simple form of bibliography lists first the full title of the book in capital letters. The name of the author follows, with the given name preceding the surname. The publisher's name is listed only if there is no author named. Details of publication, such as date and place, are usually omitted.

Constitutional Limitations	Thomas M. Cooley
Construction of Oblique Arches, The	E. A. Grosvenor
Contemporary History of the World	John Hart
Contemporary Socialism	John Rae
Continuous Current Dynamos	J. Fisher-Hinnen
Continuous Railway Brakes	Michael Reynolds
Contributions to the Physical History of the British Isles	Edward Hull
Cook's Otto's German Grammar	William Cook
Cooperative Commonwealth, The	Laurence Gronlund
Coordinate Geometry	S. L. Loney
Cours de Mecanique Analytique	Ernest Posquier
Crabb's English Synonyms	George Crabb
Crystallography	A. J. Lewis
Cyclopedia of American Horticulture	The Macmillan Co.
Cyclopedia of Engineering	American Technical Society

The following list[1] illustrates a style sometimes used for references to parts of books.

DARTNELL REPORT. "A Study of Salaries Paid to Executives in Principal Lines of Business." Dartnell Corporation, Chicago.

FREDERICK, J. GEORGE. *Modern Salesmanagement*, chap. i, "The Salesmanager Himself and His Point of View"; chap. xxxiii, "Imagination and Vision." D. Appleton and Company, New York.

HESS, HERBERT V. *Creative Salesmanship*, chap. xxi, "The Salesmanager and His Technic." J. B. Lippincott Company, Philadelphia.

JONES, JOHN G. *Salesmanship and Sales Management*. Modern Business, vol. 7, Part II, chap. i, "The Sales Manager, His Qualifications and Duties." Alexander Hamilton Institute, New York.

[1] From Tosdal, Harry R., *Problems in Sales Management*, page 124, published by McGraw Hill Book Company.

Preparing an Index

Like a bibliography, an index presents reference material in a convenient and usable form. It is a key to the contents of a book and determines much of its usefulness if the book contains material any part of which is to be used for reference. Since an index makes the contents of a book available for reference use, all scientific or technical books, pamphlets, or reports, except the very brief ones, should be indexed.

The usefulness of an index depends upon its completeness and accuracy. It depends also upon the way in which its subject-items are listed: whether they are listed under the captions or "catch words" for which a reader is likely to look in hunting for material, and whether all the probable captions for one subject are listed, either as direct references or as cross references.

In choosing index captions, the indexer must keep the user of the index constantly in mind. If he asks himself "For what word in the index should I look if I were hunting for material on this subject?" he will find his task easier. If a subject has several phases, it will need as many sub-entries. If it might be worded in any one of several ways, separate entries should be made for all the probable variations. For instance, in a report on Plant Culture, plant enemies might very well be indexed under *Plant enemies; Parasites, harmful; Enemies, plant;* as well as under the individual names of the separate plant enemies.

If an index is to be made for typewritten or mimeographed material, the work can be begun as soon as the page numbers are known. If a printed report or a book is being indexed, however, the work can rarely be begun before the page proofs are returned from the printer. As soon as these proofs are returned, the work of indexing should be started.

Small cards — the 3-by-5-inch size is good — should be used in making the index. Go through the manuscript or proofs carefully to find all items that should be indexed. These are sometimes underlined for the sake of ease in checking. Every item, with its page number, is written on a separate card. When the work of transcribing items is complete, check all the entries for page numbers. Then alphabetize the cards (see Chapter IX, page 171). Group with the main subject card all cards containing items which should be subentries, and arrange them either alphabetically or in the order of their occurrence in the manuscript. The subentries may then be listed on one card (or more if necessary) for ease in handling, and the original cards removed. The page numbers for a subject to which there are a number of references should also be grouped on one card.

Printers will sometimes set type directly from the index cards. Ordinarily, however, the card entries when finally arranged should be typewritten on manuscript paper and sent in that form to the printer or the mimeographer.

Various methods of spacing and kinds of type are used in printing an index. The style chosen depends largely on the nature of the index and whether it contains subentries or scientific matter.

For most indexes, indention is sufficient to show all necessary distinctions, as in the index below:

- Telegraph messengers, 184
- Telephone, 90–98, 186
    - answering the, 186
    - calls, classes of, 92
        - emergency, 94
        - local, 93
        - long-distance, 95
        - person-to-person, 95, 97
        - special, 95
        - station-to-station, 94–97
    - coin box, 94
    - directory, 63
    - equipment, 91
    - facts about the, 90
    - information, 93
    - machine switching, 96
        - dial, 96
        - local calls, 97
        - special calls, 97

Occasionally a dash is used to indicate subentries:

The paragraph form is sometimes used for subentries. This form is less convenient for the reader, but saves space.

Special typography is made use of for a specialized index:

[1] From Gray's *New Manual of Botany*, By the President and Fellows of Harvard College. Used by permission of American Book Company, publishers.

CHAPTER XIV

PLANNING ITINERARIES

The working equipment of a secretary should include a certain amount of information which will help her to plan itineraries for her employer. She should have a knowledge of all available means of transportation to and from the city in which she works, for any one may be necessary to her employer at one time or another. Railroad trunk and connecting lines, airplane services, bus, interurban, and steamship lines — she should know which of these are possible and which are practicable for different kinds of trips. She must be able to read and interpret a railroad time-table, and to discover from it whether a particular train has Pullman services, whether it carries dining and sleeping cars, or parlor, club, and observation cars. She should also have some knowledge of the services offered by various travel agencies, and of how to make use of them. This information furnishes a good working basis for the planning of any itinerary.

In planning a particular itinerary, the secretary must consider both the purposes of the trip and the personal preferences of her employer. If the trip is to be a purely business one, the itinerary must be planned so that no time will be lost in unnecessary traveling or delays. This is more easily accomplished if the trip can be confined to one district or territory and does not attempt to include points too widely separated, as New England and the South or Middle West. A trip of four or five days should be planned so that it is not extended unnecessarily by being made to include the non-business days of the week-end. Appointments should be as carefully planned as possible to avoid long delays and hurried intervals. The fastest and shortest route should be chosen, and if possible all Pullman and hotel reservations should be made several days before the beginning of the trip. The personal tastes of the employer should also be considered in choosing a travel route—whether he prefers day to night travel, an upper to a lower berth, one railroad to another serving the same territory, airplane or automobile to train travel, a particular hotel to others in the same city.

Sometimes a simple itinerary such as the following is desired, listing only travel arrangements.

ITINERARY OF MRS. REESEMAN

Lv North Phila.	4:50 P.M.	Mon., June 16	Pennsylvania R.R. Car 56, Lower 4
Ar Chicago	11:00 A.M.	Tues., June 17	
Lv Chicago	10:15 P.M.	Tues., June 17	Santa Fe Car 237 Lower 10
Ar Grand Canyon	8:15 A.M.	Fri., June 20	
Lv Grand Canyon	8:30 P.M.	Fri., June 20	Sante Fe Car 237 Lower 10
Ar Los Angeles	2:15 P.M.	Sat., June 21	
(June 21 to June 30, *Biltmore Hotel*, Los Angeles, California)			
Lv Los Angeles	6:10 P.M.	Mon., June 30	Southern Pacific Car 14 Lower 7
Ar Merced	5:23 A.M.	Tues., July 1	

A full itinerary should include memoranda on the following points: time and place of arrival and departure of every train and airplane taken; hotels at which reservations have been made; the time and place of all appointments; and where to find any special papers that are being taken on the trip. It should be arranged in a form which makes it easy to grasp at a glance, and typed on paper which will withstand constant handling. When completed it will probably look somewhat like the accompanying itinerary.

Itinerary of Mr. Stevens

July 13–July 17

Pittsburgh, Cincinnati, Cleveland

Standard Time

Tuesday July 13	10:35 P.M.	Leave Philadelphia (North Philadelphia station, Pennsylvania R. R.).
Wednesday July 14	6:55 A.M.	Arrive Pittsburgh.
	9:00 A.M.	Appointment with Mr. Clark Robbins at Bankers' Trust Building. (Telephone, Commercial 3720.) Papers for contract in envelope No. 1, marked *Contract*.
	11:00 A.M.	Conference with agents for Pittsburgh territory, arranged by Mr. Powers, at the *Drake*. Papers in envelope No. 2, marked *Conference*.
	1:50 P.M.	Leave Pittsburgh (*via* TWA, Flight 63).
	4:00 P.M.	Arrive Cincinnati.
	6:30 P.M.	Mr. Loeb and Mr. Granger will meet you for dinner at the *Gibson*.
Thursday July 15	10:00 A.M.	Call on Mr. Eisenbluth at 2104 Robertson Avenue.
	12:30 P.M.	Luncheon with Mr. Harris of Harris & Slocum at the *Crescent*.
	3:30 P.M.	Leave Cincinnati (*via* Big Four).
	9:50 P.M.	Arrive Cleveland. Headquarters at the *Hollenden*.
Friday July 16	9:30 A.M.	Mr. Tyndal will call for you and take you to the plant. Inspection of new machinery. Conference with Mr. Roberts about production reports.
	2:00 P.M.	Conference with architects at the plant. Mr. Sloane will represent Williams, Sloane & Harvey. Our suggestions are in the manila folder marked *Plans*.

		Dinner with Mr. Tyndal.
	8:20 P.M.	Leave Cleveland (*via* P. R. R.).
Saturday July 17	7:47 A.M.	Arrive Philadelphia (Broad Street Station).

Useful books

In the planning of itineraries, several books will be useful to the secretary. *The Official Railway and Steam Navigation Guide* contains the time-tables of all the railroads and steam navigation lines in the United States and Canada. The American Hotel Association *Red Book* and the American Automobile Association guide books are useful in the selection of hotels and the planning of automobile trips.

The individual airlines issue brochures giving complete air travel information.

Passports

The Department of State gives the following as essential requirements for anyone applying for a passport:

1. An application for a passport must be executed before a clerk of a Federal court or a State court authorized by law to naturalize aliens, or before an agent of the Department of State. AN APPLICATION EXECUTED BEFORE ANY OTHER OFFICIAL WILL NOT BE ACCEPTED.

In Washington it is desired that applications be executed in the Passport Division of the State Department.

Necessary Proof to Establish American Citizenship

IMPORTANT.—*All documents, such as birth certificates, baptismal certificates, certified copies of records, affidavits, etc.,* submitted as evidence of the American citizenship of an applicant for a passport must give the *place* and *date* of birth and bear the *seal* of the office and *signature* of the officer before whom such documents were executed or by whom they were issued. Birth and baptismal certificates to be acceptable must show that the birth or baptism was recorded shortly after birth.

2. A native American citizen must submit with his application for a passport a birth certificate, or, if such a certificate is not obtainable, a baptismal certificate or a certified copy of the record of baptism. If either of these certificates is not obtainable,

the applicant should submit in lieu thereof an affidavit executed by a parent, brother, sister, or other relative, preferably an older person, or the physician who attended the birth, setting forth the date and place of birth of the applicant. If an affidavit of a relative or physician cannot be obtained, an affidavit of some other reputable person having knowledge of facts, which enable him to testify as to the place and date of birth, should be submitted. In the affidavit a brief statement should be made showing how and through what source knowledge of the place and date of birth was acquired.

3. A person who claims American citizenship through birth abroad of a native or naturalized American father or mother should prove the parent's birth in the United States or naturalization as a citizen of this country by documentary evidence of the kind indicated in paragraph 2 or 6.

4. (*a*) A woman who was married to an American citizen prior to September 22, 1922, must submit evidence of her husband's American citizenship.

(*b*) An American woman who lost American citizenship by marriage to an alien, but who alleges that after the termination of the marital relation and prior to September 22, 1922, she resumed American citizenship, must submit evidence that she was an American citizen at the time of marriage. If the marital relation is alleged to have been terminated by divorce, a certified copy of the decree of court granting the absolute divorce should be submitted. A legal separation or an interlocutory decree of divorce does not terminate marriage.

(*c*) An American woman who was married to an American citizen or to an alien on or after September 22, 1922, must submit evidence of her own citizenship.

(*d*) An American woman who lost citizenship by marriage to an alien prior to September 22, 1922, and resumed American citizenship after that date must submit documentary evidence of her naturalization.

5. A person who claims American citizenship by naturalization must submit with his application a certificate of naturalization.

6. (*a*) A person who claims citizenship through the naturalization of a parent may submit with his appplication the naturalization certificate of the parent through whom he derived citizenship, or a certificate of derivative citizenship issued by the Commissioner of Immigration and Naturalization under the provisions of the naturalization laws.

(*b*) A woman who claims citizenship through the naturalization of her husband prior to September 22, 1922, may submit the latter's certificate of naturalization or a derivative certificate of citizenship issued by the Commissioner of Immigration and Naturalization under the provisions of the naturalization laws.

7. An applicant who holds an expired or unexpired passport issued since January 2, 1918, should submit the old passport for cancellation. Such document will be accepted as evidence of citizenship if proper documentary evidence of American nationality was submitted with the previous application. If a previous passport, issued since January 2, 1918, which has definitely expired cannot be presented for surrender or cancellation, it is necessary to state briefly in the new application the disposition of the previous passport. However, if the previous passport has not definitely expired, it is necessary to submit under oath a separate statement setting forth in circumstantial detail the disposition of the valid passport.

Photographs

8. Two *recently taken* photographs (duplicates) must be submitted of each person named in application, one affixed to the application, the other, signed by the applicant, must accompany the application unattached. A *group photograph* should be used when a wife, or wife and children, are included in one application. Photographs must be full face, on thin paper, with a light background, and not over 3 by 3 inches nor less than 2½ by 2½ inches in size. Snapshot, newspaper, magazine, or full length photographs will not be accepted. Photographs printed on photographic paper, the back of which is glazed, will not adhere to passports and therefore will not be accepted.

Identifying Witness

9. The identifying witness *must appear in person with the applicant* and fill in and sign the affidavit (on the application form) before a clerk of court or an agent of the Department of State. The identifying witness should be an adult American citizen (man or woman), who is able to state under oath that he has known the applicant for at least two years; that the applicant is the person he represents himself to be; and that the facts stated in the application are true to the best of the witness's knowledge and belief. An expired American passport bearing a signed photograph may be used as identification in lieu of an identifying witness. In cases of persons who have not previously obtained passports, the applicant or the witness must be known

to the clerk of court or the Passport Agent, or the applicant or the witness must be able to establish his identity, beyond reasonable doubt, by documentary evidence which should be *listed* on the application. If the applicant or the witness is not known to the clerk of court or Passport Agent and conclusive documentary evidence of the identity of either cannot be presented, the applicant will be required to obtain as a witness to his application an American citizen established in a recognized profession or business and having his office or place of business within the jurisdiction of the court or passport agency. However, if a clerk of court or a Passport Agent considers that an applicant has not been satisfactorily identified, he may forward the application to the Department of State with a statement of the facts in the case and give the names of two or more persons with whom the Department may communicate in order to satisfy itself of the identity and citizenship of the applicant. A husband or wife is not acceptable as an identifying witness of the spouse unless his or her identity is established to the satisfaction of the clerk of court or Passport Agent.

Letters from Business Concerns and from Missionary Organizations

10. Applications of persons proceeding abroad on business must be accompanied by a letter from the head of the firm, or in his absence from the person in charge, showing the countries to be visited and the necessity for travel therein. When a missionary applies for a passport he should submit to the Department a letter showing the name of the organization which he represents, the station to which he wishes to proceed, whether he has previously served abroad as a missionary, whether he is returning to a station previously occupied, whether he will be replacing a missionary who is returning to the United States and, if so, the name of the missionary, or whether he will be an addition to the existing missionary staff. The letter should also show the date or the approximate date of the proposed departure and the travel arrangements which have been made.

Passport Applications from Persons Subject to the Draft

11. Passport applications may be accepted from persons who are of military draft age. However, such persons should keep their local boards advised of their whereabouts.

Fees for Passport and Application

12. The total of the fees for passport and application is $10. ($9 must accompany the application to Washington and should

be in the form of currency or a postal money order made payable to the Secretary of State, Washington, D. C., and $1 paid to the clerk of court or agent before whom the application is executed). No fee is collected for the issuance or renewal of a passport to a person who is proceeding abroad on official business or to members of his household who desire to accompany or join him but the fee of $1 for the execution of the application for a passport must be collected. Drafts or checks will not be accepted either for the issue of passports or the renewal thereof.

13. Under the act of May 16, 1932, a passport is valid for 2 years from date of issue unless limited to a shorter period. It may be renewed for a period of 2 years upon payment of a fee of $5, but the final date of expiration shall not be more than 4 years from the original date of issue. A passport which was issued within the period of 4 years prior to the time when application for renewal is made may be renewed.

Requests for renewal may be made by personal application or letter addressed to the Department of State, a Passport Agent, a Consular Officer of the United States, or the Chief Executives of Hawaii, Puerto Rico, the Virgin Islands, Guam, or American Samoa, and the fee, in currency or postal money order, should accompany each request.

Persons proceeding abroad are urgently requested to make inquiry of the consuls of the countries to be visited for authentic information concerning visas.

Money

Travelers' checks have proved to be both a safe and a convenient way of carrying money. If issued by a reputable company (as The American Express, Thomas Cook, the American Bankers' Association), they will be accepted by any bank and by most stores and business houses, both in America and in other countries. They are issued in small and large denominations. A letter of credit is also a useful method of carrying money, but since the letter of credit is recognized only by specified banks in certain cities, it lacks the convenience of travelers' checks, which have become a kind of international currency.

Information concerning values of foreign monies may be obtained from local banks or from the Customs Information Exchange, New York, N. Y.

CHAPTER XV

USING THE TELEPHONE

For today's modern office, perhaps the most indispensable service is the telephone. The rapid pace of twentieth-century business is entirely dependent on the alertness and efficiency of the vast network of telephone connections throughout the world, whether they be local or long-distance calls to and from countless business firms and private individuals, or merely intra-office conversations.

Because so many of the private secretary's daily duties for her employer are performed "over the phone," it is important that she be expertly groomed in telephone etiquette and that she be familiar with the functions and services of the telephone company. As "middleman" for the communicant and her employer, the secretary should be at all times the friendly, attentive, well-mannered and intelligent "voice" of her firm.

An understanding of the functions and services of the telephone presupposes a knowledge of the following fundamentals.

Local Service

Incoming calls should be handled with efficiency and promptness, as the manner of replying may create a favorable or unfavorable impression. With a view toward economy of time, always identify yourself and your firm immediately. Learn the name of the person or firm making the call; then obtain the purpose of the message and offer such information as will satisfy the caller.

In the absence of executives from the office, handle all

telephone business with poise, asking and answering questions thoughtfully yet promptly. Refer the caller, if necessary, to a more informed member of the office staff, transfer the call to another department, or merely record the message—completely and clearly—for a return call. A pad and pencil should always be handy near the telephone. If the secretary has access to requested information but cannot locate it without some delay, it is courteous to suggest returning the call when this data is available.

Outgoing calls are transmitted on manual or dial telephones. The most important step in either case is to locate the correct number. When in doubt about a number, consult the telephone directory. It is helpful to keep an index of those numbers which are used frequently near the telephone. If for some reason the desired number cannot be located, call "Information" before initiating the call.

Manual telephone. When using this instrument, you will be dealing directly with the operator. Remember to give the correct number slowly and distinctly to the operator's "Number please" question. A "busy signal" or the operator herself will indicate when the line is already in use. If a wrong number is received or a "cut off" occurs, recall the operator by moving the receiver hook up and down.

Dial telephone. With this telephone, the call is placed without the aid of the operator. When the "dial tone" is audible, proceed to dial the key letters and numbers in their exact order, being careful that each turn is satisfactorily completed. If dialing has been accurate, the call will be realized or a "busy signal" will indicate that the line is not free. If a call is not completed successfully, dial "Information," where operators are available to assist you. It is necessary to break each connection before redialing a different number.

PBX. Many business calls are established through a Private Branch Exchange (PBX). This means that the firm has its own switchboard and employs an operator who receives all incoming and outgoing calls. Through a complex network of extension telephones to various offices and desks, all calls are made through this switchboard. However, individuals who wish to make outgoing calls may secure a direct line from their switchboard operator upon request.

Emergency calls. Fire and police calls may be made without locating the directory number. For manual calls, simply await the operator's signal; then relay the message with your name and address. The dial telephone requires that you dial either the proper number as listed in the Emergency Directory (on first page of the telephone directory), or "Operator" in order to get information of this nature to the proper agencies.

Long-Distance Calls

Long-distance or toll calls are put through to areas outside local service limits. The charge is determined by the distance, type of service, time of day and minutes used for conversing. With a manual telephone, the long-distance operator must be asked for; with a dial telephone, a specific long-distance number must be dialed. The operator will expect to hear your name and telephone number; the name, number or any pertinent information you can offer about the person called; and the type of service desired.

Station-to-station calls are practical when you are willing to talk to anyone answering your ring. These calls are handled more rapidly than person-to-person arrangements. Charges begin at the time the party or the switchboard answers.

Person-to-person calls are sensible when you desire to speak to a particular person, department or switchboard extension. Rates for these calls are higher in view of the extra service required to handle them. However, charges do not begin until the specified party is located. When charges are to be reversed (paid for at the end of the line), that fact should be made known at the time the call is placed.

The designated party must agree to accept these charges before the call is completed.

Messenger service makes possible long-distance calls to persons who do not have telephones. For an extra charge, a messenger will be sent to notify the party of the call and to arrange for the use of a telephone.

Conference calls can be arranged through the conference service offered by the telephone company to establish group conversations over long-distance wires. It is possible for individuals in any part of the country to get into direct communication with one another at the same time.

Teletypewriter service makes possible the transmission of typewritten material over long-distance lines. Communication between an office and the local telegraph system, as well as between offices in different cities, can be established by installing teletypewriter machines.

Overseas and *ship-to-shore service* is available to principal countries and to many larger ships within transmission range. Information concerning this service may be obtained from the "long-distance" operator.

CHAPTER XVI

BUSINESS FORMS

While oral agreements are valid, written agreements are almost always more binding. Even honest men sometimes forget their promises, and much misunderstanding may be avoided if there is a simple, written agreement to which to refer. Most employers realize this, but the good secretary will make it a practice to remind her employer to use the following forms when necessary.

Notes on Demand

(1) $300 *New York, February —, 19—*

On demand, I promise to pay *Samuel Huestis*, or Order, Three Hundred Dollars, value received.

JAMES SMITH

(2) $205.50 *Brooklyn, July —, 19—*

For value received, I promise to pay *Charles Greene*, or Bearer, Two Hundred Five Dollars, Fifty Cents, on demand, with interest.

CHARLES P. HUESTIS

Note on Time

(3) $275 *Jersey City, April —, 19—*

Ninety days after date, I promise to pay *Holland & Glover*, or Order, Two Hundred Seventy-five Dollars, value received.

VINCENT L. DILL

A Joint Note

(4) $350.75 *New York, June —, 19—*

Six months after date, we severally and jointly promise to pay *George Snyder*, or Order, Three Hundred Fifty Dollars, Seventy-five Cents, value received.

JAMES BRUCE
PHILIP COZENS

Bank Note

(5) $800 *Newburgh, July —, 19—*

Sixty days after date, I promise to pay *S. G. & B. Jones*, or Order, at the Chemical Bank, Eight Hundred Dollars, value received.

N. C. GOLDSMITH

Remarks: These are the usual forms of notes. A note on demand, as No. 1, is due at any time when demanded. A note payable to S. H. or *Order* may be sold or negotiated if S. H. writes his name upon the back; and if payable to S. H. or *Bearer*, it may be sold without being endorsed, and will be good to the holder. In the State of Pennsylvania the words *without defalcation* are inserted after *dollars*.

When two or more persons sign a note "severally and jointly," each is responsible for its payment. The words *value received* should be written on a note to make it valid.

A person endorsing a note, or writing his name across the back, becomes responsible for its payment. If, however, the person thus endorsing is not notified when the note becomes due of its nonpayment by the drawer, he can no longer be held responsible for its payment. A partial payment should always be endorsed on the note.

Note not Negotiable

$700 *New York, December —, 19—*

Ten days after date, I promise to pay to *Matthew Smith*, Seven Hundred Dollars, value received.

JAMES OTHELLO BRICKS

Note Negotiable by Endorsement

$310 *Brooklyn, L. I., June —, 19—*

Twenty days after date, I promise to pay to the order of *John Doe*, Three Hundred Ten Dollars, value received. RICHARD THIRD

Note Negotiable without Endorsement

$1000 *New Orleans, September —, 19—*

Two months after date, I promise to pay to *Joseph Suds*, or Bearer, One Thousand Dollars, value received. MARTIN T. SMITH

Joint Negotiable Note Payable at a Bank

$1100 *New York, December —, 19—*

Four months after date, we promise to pay *Henry Jones*, or Order, Eleven Hundred Dollars, at the Colonial Bank, New York.

DOE, ROE & CO.

Negotiable Note Payable in Merchandise

$300 *Boston, October —, 19—*

Thirty days after date, for value received, I promise to pay to *Edward Somers*, or Order, Three Hundred Dollars in merchantable corn, at the current price.

ALEXANDER GLENDENING

Form of a Judgment Note

$900

For value received, I promise to pay to *Henry Richards*, or Order, the sum of Nine Hundred Dollars, ninety days after date; and I hereby nominate, constitute, and appoint the said *Henry Richards*, or any Attorney at Law of this State, my true and lawful Attorney irrevocable, for me, and in my name, to appear in any Court of Record of this State, at any time after the Promissory Note above becomes due, and to waive all process and service thereof, and to confess judgment in favor of the holder hereof for the sum that may be due and owing hereon, with interest and costs, and waiving all errors, etc.

In Witness whereof, I have hereunto set my hand and seal at the City of Cincinnati, State of Ohio, this tenth day of May, one thousand nine hundred and fifty-one.

E. D. ABBOTT [SEAL]

Sealed and delivered in the presence of
E. LYON, JOHN SUTHERLAND

NOTE: The principal difference between a Sealed Note and one without a Seal is that the former must be first paid in the settlement of a decedent's estate, and is not barred by the Statute of Limitations.

In general, never sign a receipt, affidavit, or the like, without making a copy. It is much safer to have a copy than to trust to memory the contents of a signed paper.

Receipt on Account

New York, April —, 19—

Received from *Zachary Taylor*, Seventy-five Dollars on account.

LUKE F. COZANS

Receipt in Full

New York, May —, 19—

Received from *Messrs. Sutherland & Abbott*, One Hundred Four $\frac{73}{100}$ Dollars, in full of account to date.

\$104 $\frac{73}{100}$ WILLIAM J. BUNCE

A receipt, such as the first, acknowledges the partial payment of a debt, and such as the second, of all claims excepting negotiable notes.

Due Bill

\$25 *Hudson, February —, 19—*

Due *John Smith*, Twenty-five Dollars on demand, value received.

JOHN JONES

Order for Money

\$75 *New York, June —, 19—*

Mr. George W. Strong:

Please pay *Daniel Fanshaw*, or Order, Seventy-five Dollars, and charge to the account of ROBERT H. ELTON

Remarks —An Order may be written payable to B. C. or Order, or to B. C. or Bearer. If written in the former manner, B. C. can dispose of it, if he writes his name upon the back. If payable to B. C. or Bearer, it will be good to the holder.

Business Laws in Daily Use.

The following compilation of business law contains the essence of a large amount of legal verbiage:

If a note is lost or stolen, it does not release the maker; he must pay it if the consideration for which it was given and the amount can be proved.

Notes bear interest only when so stated.

Principals are responsible for the acts of their agents.

Each individual in a partnership is responsible for the whole amount of the debts of the firm, except in cases of special partnership.

An agreement without consideration is void.

A note made on Sunday is void.

Contracts made on Sunday cannot be enforced.

A note by a minor is void.

A contract made with a minor is void.

A note obtained by fraud, or from a person in a state of intoxication, cannot be collected.

A receipt for money is not always conclusive.

The acts of one partner bind all the rest.

The maker of an "accommodation" bill or note (one for which he has received no consideration, having lent his name or credit for the accommodation of the holder) is not bound to the person accommodated, but is bound to all other parties precisely as if there was a good consideration.

Checks or drafts must be presented for payment without unreasonable delay.

If the drawee of a check or draft has changed his residence, the holder must use due or reasonable diligence to find him.

If one who holds a check, as payee or otherwise, transfers it to another, he has a right to insist that the check be presented that day, or, at farthest, on the day following.

A note indorsed in blank (the name of the indorser only written), is transferable by delivery, the same as if made payable to bearer.

If the time of payment of a note is not inserted, it is held payable on demand.

An indorsee has a right of action against all whose names were on the bill when he received it.

If the letter containing a protest of non-payment be put into the post office, any miscarriage does not affect the party giving notice.

If two or more persons as partners are jointly liable on a note or bill, due notice to one of them is sufficient.

If a note or bill is transferred as security, or even as payment of a pre-existing debt, the debt revives if the bill or note be dishonored.

All claims which do not rest upon a seal or judgment must be sued within six years from the time when they arise.

Part payment of a debt which has passed the time of statutory limitation revives the whole debt, and the claim holds good for another period of six years from the date of such partial payment.

If, when a debt is due, the debtor is out of the State, the "six years" do not begin to run until he returns. If he afterward leave the State, the time forward counts the same as if he remained in the State.

An oral agreement must be proved by evidence. A written agreement proves itself. The law prefers written to oral evidence, because of its precision.

Ignorance of the law excuses no one.

The law compels no one to do impossibilities.

A contract made with a lunatic is void.

It is a fraud to conceal a fraud.

Signatures made with a lead-pencil are good in law.

"Value received" is usually written in a note, and should be, but is not necessary. If not written, it is presumed by the law or may be supplied by proof.

No consideration is sufficient in law if it be illegal in its nature.

Checks or drafts should be presented during business hours, but in this country, except in the case of banks, the time extends through the day and evening.

The time of payment of a note must not depend upon a contingency. The promise must be absolute.

A bill may be written upon any paper or substitute for it, either with ink or pencil.

The payee should be distinctly named in the note, unless it is payable to bearer.

Notice of protest may be sent either to the place of business or of residence of the party notified.

The loss of a bill or note is not sufficient excuse for not giving notice of protest.

An indorsement may be written on the face or back.

FORMS OF BUSINESS WRITING

CHAPTER XVII

LETTERS: THEIR COMPOSITION AND TONE

It is a far cry from the Amarna letters of Middle Egypt to modern business correspondence or to the more colorful social letter. Aside from the difference in mechanical make-up, the subject matter of the letters of the ancients had little to commend it to consideration today, if we can judge by the fragmentary examples left us, which are stripped of the courteous language of the modern letter.

TONE

Most of the letters written today pertain to business. Probably the business letter has contributed more to the growth of business than any other one thing. This is because the modern business letter is not a stereotyped form of expression employed by everyone who needs to communicate with his fellow men on topics pertaining to his vocation. The business letter today breathes personality — it has *tone.* It inevitably reflects the character of the writer, and it should be carefully adapted to the characteristics of the person to whom it is sent.

One would not think of writing a letter to a farmer about the purchase of harvesting machinery in the same juvenile tone that would be employed in a letter that attempts to sell to a youth a subscription to *Boys' Life.* The appeal to the farmer must be made through his need of modern harvesting machinery, and argument must be substantiated by fact. Generalizations will not do. The farmer must be convinced of his need. The letter should not be couched in high-sounding phrases. Plain talk appeals to him, as does a matter-of-fact, frank tone. He will give consideration to a letter that guarantees value received and satisfaction in the product that is being sold.

On the other hand, a letter to a boy must be adapted to the mind of a boy. Its tone, language, and diction must produce the effect of simplicity. But it must also be dignified, and the appeal must be directed to the motives and instincts of boyhood.

Characteristics of a Good Business Letter

Much business correspondence today is dictated. It requires skill to be able to dictate a well-balanced letter, one that conveys to the reader the exact meaning which the dictator intends to convey, and which at the same time creates good will and friendship.

A good business letter is clear, concise, and courteous. It does not require rereading in order to be understood. A carefully planned letter is seldom vague or incoherent. If a letter is not understandable to the reader, it probably has been carelessly prepared. Unusual terms and technical expressions should be avoided.

The excessively long sentence is often responsible for involved statements that are difficult to read and to understand. On the other hand, the writer should not fill his letter with sentences that are too short. Of course there is no set limit to the length of a sentence, but if the reader is required to read sentences that are invariably long, his attention to the subject may be taxed to the limit; and when his attention begins to grow weak, he is likely to lose interest in the purpose of the letter.

The beginning sentence should give a hint of the purpose of the letter. It should contain something that will attract the reader's attention, something that will interest him. Stilted expressions, such as "Yours of the ninth instant received and contents duly noted," mean nothing and should be avoided. By using meaningless statements at the beginning of a letter, the writer misses the opportunity to arouse the reader's interest.

The sample letters which follow will serve to illustrate what is meant by stilted expressions. The first letter is a "dead-language" letter typical of many poor business letters. The phrases in italics are awkward or overworked expressions that should not find place in any letter.

Dear Reader:

We *beg to call your attention* to the fact that a part of this chapter is devoted to the question of letter lingo, in the hope that everyone who reads it will resolve that from now on and forevermore he will omit these time-worn expressions from his daily dictation.

When dictating an answer to an ordinary, everyday business letter, do you think it adds anything of interest to your message to tell your reader that you *have duly received his favor of the 16th inst.*, and that *same being to hand* you *wish to state in reply that . . . ?*

Do you *attach hereto* the memorandum that you are sending him, or do you *beg to hand it to him herewith?* Do you believe that he will know exactly what you mean when you say that the matter to which he referred in his *letter of recent date* will have your *immediate attention* and that you *will see to it* that shipments are sent forward at the *earliest possible moment?*

In reply to these questions which are *respectfully submitted herewith, would ask* that you *carefully note contents of this letter* and observe how much of interest and sense such expressions add to the message itself. Due to the fact that these unnecessary flourishes are costing American business organizations many thousands of dollars daily, *would suggest* that your customer-reader would *thank you in advance* if you would omit them altogether and write him as though you considered him a normal human being.

Thanking you for your kind attention and *trusting that* you will follow the suggestions made in this communication, we *wish to remain,*

Courtesy the Boston Chamber of Commerce

Following is another example of what a business letter should not be. This is said to be the worst letter that ever was written.

Yours of the 27th inst. at hand and contents duly noted. In reply would say same shall receive our best attention at earliest possible moment. We take pleasure in handing you herewith our latest investment listings, attached hereto, as per your request. Through an oversight on the part of our mailing clerk, the statement sent in compliance with your esteemed favor of the 12th ult. was wrongly addressed and has accordingly been returned to us. Regret the delay thus caused but beg to be permitted to say that we take pleasure in enclosing duplicate herewith. At present writing we are unable to quote on Siberian securities, owing to unforeseen circumstances arising in connection with shipping, but beg to inform you that in so far as we are able to foresee, the old prices will prevail during the coming season. Whatever the case may be, we are pleased to advise you that quotation shall go forward to your address immediately on receipt of same at our office. Hoping this communication may prove satisfactory in every respect, assuring you of our best attention at all times, and awaiting your further commands, beg to remain . . .

In contrast to these two letters, following is a letter which shows that it was more carefully thought out. The writer knew what he wanted to say and he has said it in the simple, clear style that a carefully planned business letter should have.

My dear Mr. Jones:

Increasingly advertisers realize that their biggest mission is to educate. Let the public know all about your business, your factory, your product, and if your business, your factory, your product are what they should be, you are bound to prosper.

This has been the policy of the World Baking Company in the preparation of the year's schedule of trade-paper advertising reproduced in miniature in the attached booklet.

This miniature reproduction does not give the full effect of the originals as they appear in full size and full color in millers' and bakers' trade papers, but it does tell the story. It tells the story of the company, its ideals, its aspirations, its problems, and its methods of solving those problems.

It is the hope and belief of the officers and directors of this company that this recital will interest you as one of our stockholders. We feel that the booklet prepared by our advertising department contains a story of a business and a business institution which you will find well worth while perusing.

Very truly yours,
WORLD BAKING COMPANY

There can be no hard and fast rules set down about the content of the business letter. Its effectiveness depends very much upon the temperament of the writer and of the recipient. In any case, a business letter should be dignified and courteous. An occasion never arises for writing a letter that will offend. The business correspondent, no matter what the provocation may be, should remember that a letter *can* be a good business letter and at the same time be friendly. We all know that a friendly, courteous, painstaking effort to obtain an audience with a correspondent will go a long way toward establishing cordial business relations. Such letters always are taken as representative of the company from which they are received.

In its form, a business letter differs from a social letter only in having a slight additional degree of formality. Each has a specific message to convey and the principle of construction is the same. The business letter is as brief and explicit as possible without being curt. The social letter may be drawn out, through intimacy, to greater length.

THE MECHANICS OF LETTER WRITING

A well-planned, carefully phrased letter requires an attractive form. Like the successful salesman, it must go forth in a garb "neat, not gaudy." It must be orderly in its make-up. It must give the appearance of careful preparation before going forth on its errand. It must make a favorable impression on its reader before he begins to read it. In other words, its "How do you do" to its recipient must be such as to win for it a cordial welcome.

The heading

The heading of the letter, with the exception of the date, is included in the letterhead. Sometimes the date is placed in the center of the sheet of paper, but more often at the right below the letterhead, with the last figure of the date marking the right-hand margin of the body of the letter. The date should give the year, month, and day, with the month written out, and the day of the month indicated in cardinal numerals. *St, nd, rd,* and *th* should not be used after a date: May 3, 19—, *not* May 3rd.

The salutation

The salutation is the complimentary greeting that is used to begin a letter. It should be placed two spaces below the inside address, flush with the margin. In business letters, the salutation is always followed by a colon, but a comma may follow the salutation in personal letters. The form of the salutation will depend upon the relation between the person addressed and the writer. In business letters, *Gentlemen, Ladies, Dear Sir,* and *Dear Madam* are the most common salutations, the first two being used when addressing a company or corporation, the last two when addressing a man or a woman.

If the person addressed is known personally to the writer, the forms *Dear Mr. Webster* or *Dear Miss Roberts* or *Dear Mrs. Stevens* may be used. When writing to a public official of high rank, the more formal salutation, *Sir,* is employed.

Following are the more commonly used forms of salutation.

Official
Sir:
Madam:

Formal
My dear Sir:
My dear Madam:
My dear Mr. Smith:
My dear Mrs. Smith:
My dear Miss Smith:

Semiformal
Dear Sir:
Dear Madam:
Gentlemen:
Ladies:

Informal
Dear Mr. Smith:
Dear Mrs. Smith:
Dear Miss Smith:

The inside address

The name and address of the company or the individual to whom the letter is addressed is written at the left of the letter page, slightly below the heading. There are two forms in common use: the block form, in which every line of the address begins flush with the margin; and the indented form. From the standpoint of utility, the block form is preferable, as it saves the time of the typist. Whichever form is used in the address should also be used in heading, signature, and envelope address. In the indented form, closed or full punctuation may be used, but in the block form, open punctuation is usually adopted.

A title is used with the name of an individual: *Mr.*, *Mrs.*, *Miss*, *Professor*, *Dr.*, *Hon.*, *Rev.*, *Captain*, *Major*, *Dean*, *Ph.D.*, *LL.D.*, or the like. If the letter is addressed to a company, no title is used when the name is followed by the words *Company*, *Incorporated* or their abbreviations. But if these words do not follow the name of the company, the abbreviation *Messrs.* is sometimes used. However, the use of this French abbreviation is more common in England and Canada than in the United States. In addressing a company or an individual, be sure to write the name exactly as the company or individual writes it. Do not take liberties with names. By doing so, you may offend.

Forms of address for distinguished individuals will be found on pages 261–265.

Body of the letter

The body of the letter contains the real communication. The dictator should assist the typist in its arrangement by indicating the beginning of each paragraph. Paragraphing is of great importance, if for nothing else than for the artistic effect. It is equally important, however, in classifying the writer's ideas. Every paragraph should treat of one subject only. When the writer's thought changes, a new paragraph should be made.

Double spacing should be allowed between the salutation and the letter proper. Care should be used in determining the spacing and margins of the body of the letter.

The body of the letter should be so planned that the complimentary close and the signature will not be crowded into the lower margin. If more than one page is needed to complete the letter, the second sheet should be numbered at the top with the initials of the person to whom the letter is addressed, and the date; as, *2 - J.A.R.......Jan. 2, 19—*. If the first page has no letterhead, the second page should be numbered and the name of the writer should be written across the top of the page.

In interoffice correspondence, each paragraph may be labeled with its subject, or may be written on a separate sheet.

Paragraphs are usually begun with an indented line. Some writers prefer the block form or the "hanging indention," but these forms are for the most part looked upon as innovations. Double spaces are often left between the paragraphs if the body of the letter has been typed in single space.

The body of a letter must be carefully punctuated. Care must also be used in the spacing between words and lines, and in the division of words at the end of lines. The dictionary is the secretary's safest guide in dividing words, as in spelling them.

The complimentary close

The complimentary close of a letter is a leave-taking of the person addressed, and is to a letter what "good-by" is to a personal parting. It is written or typed two or three spaces below the last line of the body of the letter, midway between the right and left margins. The form used should be appropriate to the person addressed. A list follows of the most common forms in use today.

Friendly	*Business*	*Official*
Sincerely yours	Yours truly	Respectfully
Yours sincerely	Truly yours	Respectfully yours
Cordially yours	Yours very truly	*Informal*
Yours cordially	Very truly yours	Yours gratefully
Faithfully yours	Yours faithfully	Fraternally yours

Only the first word of the complimentary close is capitalized, and a comma is placed after the last word.

The signature

As the word implies, the signature designates the writer, or the company he represents, or both. In the last case, the company name is typed, and the writer's name is written underneath it, with his official position typed at the right of, or beneath, his name. If the writer of the letter is not an executive, the word *by* is usually placed before his name.

No title should appear before a man's signature. If the writer be a married woman, the common form is

Frances Hill Devon
(Mrs. Philip Snowden Devon)

A widow writes her name exactly as she wrote it before the death of her husband. An unmarried woman usually writes her name with the word *Miss* in parentheses preceding it. A divorced woman may assume her maiden name with or without *Mrs.*; or she may retain her husband's name with *Miss* or *Mrs.*

The signature follows the complimentary close, one or two spaces directly below or to the right. It should follow the form, block or indented, which is used in the address. The name should be written plainly and always with the same use of initials and given name.

Examples of Types of Letters

Sales Letters

Dear Sir:

Popular imagination has ever been stirred by the colorful tales of English voyagers in Elizabethan times—Frobisher, Drake, Raleigh, and their fellows, braving the unknown Atlantic and bringing back precious freight of foreign wealth. No less thrilling are the deeds of those mighty Elizabethan adventurers into the countries of the mind, the men who brought into English speech and English literature the treasure-trove of foreign letters. To us, indeed, the Elizabethan Age would not be Elizabethan without Hoby and North and Florio!

How these men and others brought the Renaissance to England, is the theme of a most attractive book, by Dr. F. O. Matthiessen of Harvard University, which we have just published with the title *Translation: an Elizabethan Art.*

By a detailed analysis of a representative group of Elizabethan translations, Dr. Matthiessen has been able to suggest the purpose and importance as well as the literary qualities of all these works. He has a deep appreciation of his originals and is therefore able to impart to his pages both vividness and interest. After reading him, you will agree that the Elizabethan translations are worthy of a high place in the history of English literature and deserve much credit for their help in developing the English language and in broadening the English mind. We commend the book to all faithful admirers of vigorous English prose.

Dr. Matthiessen's *Translation: An Elizabethan Art* is a volume of 242 pages. The price is $2.50 a copy, postpaid. We shall be glad to send you a copy, with invoice payable in thirty days.

Very truly yours,

Dear Madam:

What will be the prevailing colors in hosiery this season? Wouldn't you be pleased to have the word of an expert on this important question? We know you would, for you have taken the trouble to write to us concerning our advertisement in *Vogue*. You will, moreover, be pleased to learn that it is possible for you to see, in your own home, the first of this season's production of hosiery, and to learn what will be the newest shades.

Our colorists are in touch with the shoe and dress-goods experts all the time. They learn months in advance when a new shade is to appear in cloth or leather. This forethought means that our customers can always depend on *Colonial Dame Hosiery.*

It is not necessary for you to carry shoes or dresses down town when you want to match them in hosiery. Simply send for me, and I will call at your house at your convenience with samples of our full line of thirty-five new colors.

Put the enclosed card in the mail today if you want to see what will be in style this spring.

Yours very truly,

Dear Sir:

Out in Yellowstone National Park the great geyser known as Old Faithful spouts a never-failing column of boiling water 150 feet into the air. It is estimated that 250,000 gallons of hot water are liberated with every play, and each play lasts from four to seven minutes.

Suppose that you could have a pipe line from "Old Faithful" to your house. Wouldn't it be fine to have all the hot water you could use without having to build a fire? You can enjoy just such a hot-water service if you install an *Automatic Gas Water Heater.*

This water heater is placed in the cellar and is connected with the water and gas supply. You never have to go near it or give it any attention whatever. The moment that you open any hot-water faucet in your house, the flow of water turns on and ignites the gas, and the water is heated as it runs.

Thousands of satisfied users know that this water heater operates with perfect satisfaction at all times, and gives piping-hot water at any time and in any quantity desired.

If you will let me know when it will be convenient for you to have me call, I shall be pleased to answer any questions and give you figures for installing this hot-water service in your home.

Very truly yours,

ORDER LETTER

337 Charles Street
Terre Haute, Indiana
October 31, 19—

Ditson and Healy, Inc.
Chicago, Illinois

Gentlemen:

Please send me by parcel post the following items from your Fall Catalog of Musical Supplies:

		List Price	
2 quires 13A music paper	@	$1.10	$2.20
2 quires 2A music paper	@	1.10	2.20
4 doz. No. 75 blank music books	@	3.10	12.40
			$16.80

I am enclosing my personal check for $16.80 in payment of the goods listed.

Yours truly,
JOSEF LEVIN

LETTERS ACKNOWLEDGING AN ORDER

June 30, 19—

Mr. James O. Foster
220 North Fourth Street
Bristol, Connecticut

Dear Sir:

Your order, made through our representative, Mr. Allen, for four boxes of double-thick glass to be shipped by freight, and six panes of leaded glass to be shipped by express, will be sent today.

We thank you for the order, and trust that it will be the beginning of a long and pleasant business relation between us.

Very truly yours,
GEORGE BLAKE
Manager

International Machine Company
Sao Paulo, Brazil

Gentlemen:

We thank you for the order transmitted to us by cable, which we will forward to the mill for final approval and acceptance under conditions as stipulated below.

Quantity: 20 machines set up
Description: 5 machines thirteen gauge
5 machines fourteen gauge
5 machines fifteen gauge
5 machines twelve gauge
Quality: Checkered head countersunk wire nail machines, American Machine Company's make.
Price: $2,000 (two thousand dollars American gold) each C.I.F. Sao Paulo, Brazil.
Terms: Payment to be made in New York on presentation of complete set of ocean documents; confirmed irrevocable letter of credit to be established to our order for full amount of order, available for payment thirty days from date; credit to be established by you by cable.
Shipment: Shipment will be made at once from the mill.
Remarks: This order is accepted with the understanding that we will not be responsible for delays due to conditions beyond our control, and is subject to our receiving Federal export license within the specified time.

Respectfully yours,
AMERICAN EXPORT CORPORATION
By James McClettan

CREDIT LETTER

Dear Sir:

We thank you for the order which you have placed with our representative, Mr. Johnson.

We have not had the pleasure of doing business with you before, but we shall try to serve you so well that we can expect a continuance of your patronage.

As is customary with all business houses, we are obliged to seek information that will enable us to determine the amount of credit to which a new customer is entitled. To facilitate these investigations, we shall appreciate your giving us the names of a few houses with whom you have been dealing.

For your convenience in replying, we enclose an addressed, stamped envelope. May we hear from you by return mail.

Yours very truly,

COLLECTION LETTERS

Dear Mr. Benson:

In looking over the books this morning, I noticed that your bill for goods delivered in April has not been paid. The matter is not worrying me at all, but I thought you might be glad to have it brought to your attention. If convenient, perhaps you will send us a check before the close of the month.

Cordially yours,

ARNOLD WHEELER,

Treasurer

Dear Sir:

We wish to call your attention to the enclosed statement of your account, which was due September 15.

We shall very much appreciate your check for the amount due, $317.63.

Very truly yours,

Dear Sir:

No doubt you have overlooked the statement of your overdue account, which we sent you September 21. We are confident that this reminder will bring the matter to your attention and that you will mail us at once your check for $317.63.

Very truly yours,

Dear Sir:

We dislike to annoy you, but your failure to give any attention to your overdue account, which amounts to $317.63, compels us to bring it to your attention again.

We hope that you will not make it necessary for us to write about this again, and that you will send us a remittance at once.

Very truly yours,

Crawford, Indiana
December 28, 19—

Smith, Brown and Jones
Billings
Montana

Gentlemen:

A feather is not heavy: but have you ever carried a feather bed upstairs?

One small account does not burden anyone. Hundreds of them, however, often make a heavy load.

Furthermore, the profit on a small account may be spent easily for postage before the account is paid.

You do not want to appear to be unfair about the small amount that you owe us: $4.50 since August 27.

Will you not, then, send us a check for the small amount so that we may balance your account. A stamped, return envelope is enclosed.

Very truly yours,

Z : b JOHN ROBERTS & COMPANY

LEGAL LETTER

Dear Sir:

We are returning by registered mail, as requested in your letter of March 31, the certificate for fifty shares of the Spencer Manufacturing Company's First Preferred Stock, which was registered in the name of Harriet L. Smith.

This certificate was returned by our New York correspondent with the statement that the following papers must be submitted to them before payment may be effected:

Certified copy of the will
New York State waiver
Signature of the executor guaranteed
Assignment of the Spencer Manufacturing Company erased and erasure guaranteed

If you will have these papers prepared and mail them to us, we shall be pleased to proceed with the collection.

Yours truly,

FOLLOW-UP LETTER

Dear Sir:

Did you ever have a good customer stop trading with you? If so, what did you do? Very likely you waited until you saw him again and then said to him, "We haven't sold you anything lately, Mr. Smith. What is the matter?"

You made a straight-from-the-shoulder attempt to find the real reason for his leaving you. Then Mr. Smith probably told you frankly his reasons. If they were just and you had made a mistake, you did your level best to straighten out the matter.

That is our attitude of mind in writing you this morning. We have not had an order from you for some time. We should like to know the "real reason why."

If we have failed to serve you properly in any way, we want to know it. Our efforts to serve in the best possible manner are always sincere. We know it is only by following this rule rigidly that we can hope to see our business grow as we should like to have it grow.

Put yourself in our place for a moment. Then turn this sheet over and answer this letter as you would like to have it answered if you had written it. Be frank, for that is the kind of answer we want.

We await your reply with the deepest interest.

Very truly yours,

LETTER OF COMPLAINT

34 Center Street
St. Charles, Missouri
June 30, 19—

Hartley & Wells Company
Columbia, Missouri
Gentlemen:

On June 9 I wrote you ordering one set of assortment #12, Fourth of July Fireworks, priced at $7.50, and I enclosed my check in payment. The canceled check was returned with my bank statement today, but the fireworks have not yet arrived.

Of course I realize the pressure of business upon you at this season in this department, but the goods ordered will naturally be of no use to me after next Saturday.

Will you please look the matter up, and send the goods through, marked *Rush*.

Very truly yours,
ANDREW T. SAMPSON

ADJUSTMENT LETTERS

HARTLEY & WELLS COMPANY
Columbia
Missouri

Claim Department

July 2, 19

Mr. Andrew T. Sampson
34 Center Street
St. Charles, Missouri

Subject: Nonarrival of goods

Dear Mr. Sampson:

Your letter of June 30, regarding the delay in delivering to you one set #12 Assorted Fireworks, has been referred to this department.

On consulting our files I find that your letter was received on June 11, and the order sheet is marked "Filled and forwarded June 17."

I have given personal directions that a duplicate set be sent to you today by express. If through any mischance this should not reach you by July 4, will you please return it at our expense, and let us return the amount of your check. We deeply regret that you have been subjected to this annoyance and disappointment.

Yours very truly,
WILLIAM C. FAIRBANKS

Mrs. B. Oberholdt
2469 Williams Street
Fond du Lac, Wisconsin

Dear Madam:

We are informed by our representative who calls for your weekly orders of an error in your last order delivered September 1. We understand that you received a pint of grape juice instead of the jar of Welch's Grapelade which you had ordered, and that you did not receive the one-half-pound box of Arrowroot Crackers. We regret this error very much.

If you do not wish to keep the grape juice, please have it returned to us for credit. We will also credit your account with the box of Arrowroot Crackers.

We assure you that we shall take every precaution to avoid errors of this nature in the future.

Very truly yours,
EDWARD ATWOOD

Mrs. Alice Penuel
427 Dauphin Street
Lexington, Kentucky

Dear Madam:

Evidently your goods have been lost on the way. We do not want you to be put to any further trouble, so we shall make a new shipment which we feel sure will reach you promptly, and we shall take up the matter with the transportation company ourselves. There will be no charges for you to pay on the new shipment.

After you have had the agent make a notation of the shortage, please send to us in the enclosed envelope the receipt which he gave you when you paid the charges. This will help us to take up the matter with his company.

If after you get one shipment the other should arrive, please leave it at the station and return this letter to us with the notice you received from the agent.

Yours truly,

William Dage

Letter Refusing a Claim

Burk Canning Company
Dover, Delaware

Attention of Mr. C. J. Burk[1]

Gentlemen:

We have taken up your claim with our agent at Pittsburgh. He is unable to furnish us with a record of this shipment, and has not been successful in securing full information from the Reed Can Manufacturing Company. He further states that at no time has the claim been presented to him.

Since you did not take action within the four-month period allowed by this company, I very much regret that we are unable to allow the claim.

Very truly yours,

Frederick James
Claim Agent

[1] "Attention of ———" or "attention: Mr. Burk" or "Mr. C. J. Burk" is usually placed on a separate line between the last line of the inside address and the salutation, and to the right.

LETTERS OF INQUIRY

Gentlemen:

The students of the Media High School will give, in the early part of May, a play based on the story of the "Pied Piper of Hamelin." In advertising this play we should like to have printed posters bearing a picture of the Piper. For this purpose will you lend us the cuts of a picture printed on page 30 of a book published by you entitled *The Pied Piper of Hamelin?*

In case you cannot lend us the cuts, will you object if we have a flat cut made of the Piper?

The courtesy of a prompt reply will be greatly appreciated.

Very truly yours,

Philadelphia, June 16, 19—

The Frazier Preparatory School
Washington City
New York

Gentlemen:

Will you please send me a catalog of your school and let me know whether a boy who has completed the work in the elementary schools of Philadelphia can enter without examination.

Very truly yours,
MIRIAM J. CORDER

Mrs. Benjamin Corder
3840 Trenton Street
Philadelphia, Pa.

ANSWER TO INQUIRY

My dear Sir:

It is a genuine pleasure to learn of your interest in the Hamilton Course and Service.

Your interest will grow, I am sure, as you learn more about our work. Thousands of ambitious business men are using our Course and Service as a definite means of preparing for greater responsibilities and larger incomes.

Our representative, Mr. Smiley, is writing you today at considerable length, explaining just what we have to offer.

This note is merely to express my personal pleasure at receiving your inquiry, and my hope that you will find it possible to take advantage of the specially reduced fee now available.

Very truly yours,

LETTER CONFIRMING A TELEGRAM

Messrs. Morgan & Company
31 Wall Street
New York, N. Y.

Gentlemen:

This confirms our telegram of this morning:

"Sell one hundred Philadelphia and Reading first preferred
Buy fifty Amalgamated Copper"

Yours truly,
GEORGE DEWEY

LETTER OF TESTIMONIAL

Mr. William E. Hodge
248 Cashman Avenue
Buffalo, New York

Dear Sir:

I have examined with some care the relief maps made by Mr. George Thorne-Thompson and regard them as distinctly superior in several respects to any of the older physical maps.

Teachers of history as well as of geography will find them serviceable in many ways, particularly in showing the relation of physiographic features to the movements of population.

Very truly yours,
JAMES ROGERS

LETTER MAKING A RESERVATION

June 8, 19—

Mr. Alfred M. Carino
Hotel Seaview
Asbury Park, New Jersey

Dear Sir:

Please reserve rooms 316 and 318 for eight weeks beginning July first, at the terms stated in your letter of June third. We shall arrive on the train that reaches Asbury Park at 4:30 P.M., Daylight Time. Please send a conveyance for four persons and three large trunks.

Very truly yours,
KATHERINE T. SWEENEY

Mrs. Roger Sweeney
Jenkintown
Pennsylvania

APPOINTMENT LETTERS

August 17, 19—

Dear Mr. Henry:

Mr. Fraser will be in our office at 10: 30 A.M., Monday, August 24, with samples of juveniles and fiction. Please let me know the most convenient time for you to call and examine his samples.

Sincerely yours,
EDNA CARVER

August 17, 19—

Dear Mr. Budd:

Mr. Penhallow was just leaving when your letter was delivered. He asked me to inform you that he will be glad to see you Friday, August 21, at three o'clock.

Very truly yours,
E. P. MORTON
Secretary

LETTER OF APPLICATION

28 Merriam Avenue
Elyria, Colorado
June 23, 19—

Mr. B. R. Jackson
644 Main Street
Denver, Colorado

Dear Mr. Jackson:

In the *Denver Post* this morning, I notice your advertisement for a boy to learn the jewelry business. As I am just graduating from the Elyria High School, I wish to make application for the position.

I am eighteen years old and have the ordinary grammar- and high-school training. In high school I have taken a commercial course and have received good marks throughout the four years. During the summers, holidays, and on Saturdays for the last two years I have worked at Dow's Drug Store, in Elyria.

For further information, I refer you to:

Mr. Arthur C. Barnes
Principal, Elyria High School
Mr. F. J. Dow,
98 Shirley Street, Elyria

I shall be glad to call at your store for an interview at your convenience.

Yours truly,
JAMES F. BROWN

LETTER OF REFERENCE

Mr. John M. Haines
North High School
Rochester, New York

Dear Mr. Haines:

We have an application for a position from Paul H. Thompson, 917 Cottage Street, a graduate of your high school.

We shall appreciate very much any information that you may send us concerning him. We are interested in knowing particularly the kind of record he made in his studies and how he got along with his fellow students. Any other information you may wish to send us about him will be very much appreciated.

We enclose a stamped, addressed envelope for your reply.

Very truly yours,
HERMAN COLLINS

LETTERS OF RECOMMENDATION

Mr. John T. Page
Page Steel Works
Portland, Oregon

Dear Mr. Page:

Mr. John T. Byer has been employed as secretary to the President of this Company for the past two years. He has proved himself accurate, painstaking, and thorough, and has shown remarkable understanding of business methods.

He leaves us of his own accord because he wishes to locate farther west. We most heartily recommend him for any position which he feels he is qualified to fill.

Very truly yours,
POWERS AND WRAITH
E. H. Powers, President

Philadelphia, June 24, 19—

Miss Ellen Ransome, Director
The Secretarial Placement Service
31 East Forty-first Street
New York City

Dear Miss Ransome:

I am glad of the opportunity to recommend Miss Edna Morton, who has been my secretary for two years. During the time she has been with me she has made herself almost indispensable to me in my work, and I greatly regret the circumstances which necessitate her leaving me and going to New York.

Miss Morton is not only an expert stenographer: she is also an unusually intelligent and capable young woman. I recommend her heartily to anyone who is fortunate enough to secure her services.

Sincerely yours,
JAMES PENHALLOW

My dear Mr. Bucannon:

I understand that there is or is about to be a vacancy in the position of Cashier for this company. May I take the liberty of suggesting Mr. M. J. Fernon for promotion to that position.

Of his training and special qualifications for the position it would be presumptuous of me to speak, for you are better able to judge concerning them than I. I should like to call your attention to his long service with the company and to the high esteem in which he is held by all who have been associated with him. I feel sincerely that, all other considerations being equal, it would greatly aid the spirit of good will in the department were Mr. Fernon to receive the appointment.

Respectfully yours,
EDGAR F. SLOAN

Mr. John C. Bucannon
New York City

LETTERS OF INTRODUCTION

451 Park Avenue
New York City
June 4, 19—

My dear Reid:

This will introduce my friend Mr. Robert Cabell, of this city, who will be in Chicago during July and August.

"Bob" Cabell is an A-1 tennis player — in fact,the champion of the Long Island Tennis Club. Knowing your interest in the game, I feel sure that you and he will hit it off. If you can put him up at the Bayside Club, you need not worry about winning that cup this summer.

At any rate, be sure that I shall appreciate any courtesies shown him.

With kind regards,
H. T. GRISWOLD

January 31, 19—

Professor T. C. Harrison, Ph.D.
Allwine University
Washington, D. C.

Dear Professor Harrison:

May I introduce to you my friend Dr. Trescott Fordyce, with whose work in the field of astronomy you are probably familiar. He is very eager to visit your observatory and to discuss a matter which he believes will be of interest to you.

Sincerely yours,
HARRISON CAPE

Portland, Maine
July 16, 19—

Mr. Thomas Winthrop
Metropolitan Building
New York City

Dear Mr. Winthrop:

This letter will introduce to you Mr. James E. Smith, a young mechanical engineer, recently graduated from Cornell University. I know him to be a man of energy and ability, and have found his services in my office invaluable during his vacations.

He is willing to do any kind of work to gain a foothold in New York, and if you or any of your friends can assist him in securing a position, I am sure you will not regret it.

Sincerely yours,
STEPHEN MANN

225 Broadway
New York City
July 6, 19—

Dear Mr. Thomas:

I am glad to introduce to you the bearer of this note, Mr. Fred Cooke, who is personnel manager for the Horton Steel Company of Pittsburgh.

I have known Mr. Cooke for a number of years, and believe he is one of the best men in his line in the country. You have doubtless heard of his "Welfare Bonus Plan."

He has another idea which seems to me just as big as the bonus plan, and I am sure you will be as interested in it as I am.

He will tell you my answer to his proposal. Perhaps you will let me know what you think of the whole thing.

Sincerely yours,
R. A. MILLER

LETTER OF CONGRATULATION

Dear George:

Congratulations! I just learned of your good luck through John McCarthy. I should not say "good luck," for I am sure that you deserve the honor, and evidently the President feels as I do. All good wishes for your success.

Sincerely yours,
BOYD

LETTERS OF CONDOLENCE

Dear Charles:

May I extend to you my sincere sympathy in your sorrow. A friendship such as existed between you and Jack is rare, and I can understand how deeply his passing must have affected you. Please call upon me for anything that I can do at this time.

FRANK

Dear Sarah:

Words cannot express my sympathy for you in the loss of your mother. I am sure that your devotion to her and your efforts to make the last years of her life happy and carefree must be a source of consolation to you.

REBECCA

Dear Henry:

You have my deepest sympathy in the sorrow that has come to you. Your friendship with your father was unusually close, and I know what grief his loss must bring to you. I am sure that you have many pleasant memories of him to sustain you, and that you will find comfort in the memory of his love for you and of your filial devotion to him. Everyone admired him, and to me his sudden passing was a severe shock.

If there is anything that I can do to assist you at this sad time, please let me know.

Sincerely yours,

Formal Invitation

Formal invitations for weddings, dinners and other formal affairs are always engraved.

Mr. and Mrs. John P. Brown
request the pleasure of
Mr. and Mrs. Howard Prichard's*
company at dinner
on Wednesday, April seventh
at eight o'clock,
1632 West Ashley Street

R.s.v.p.

Formal Acceptance

Mr. and Mrs. Howard Prichard accept with pleasure Mr. and Mrs. John P. Brown's kind invitation for dinner on Wednesday, April seventh, at eight o'clock.

16 Bent Road, Arlington
March twenty-fifth

Formal Regret

Mr. and Mrs. Howard Prichard regret that owing to a previous engagement they are unable to accept Mr. and Mrs. John P. Brown's kind invitation for dinner on Wednesday, April seventh, at eight o'clock.

16 Bent Road, Arlington
March twenty-fifth

* Either engraved, or written by hand.

INFORMAL INVITATION

Note. An informal invitation is always written by hand, usually by the hostess or her secretary.

Dear Anne:

Can you and Charles come to dinner with us on Tuesday, March the third? Billie and I want so much to see you both before we leave for our western trip.

We are also asking those delightful young Farrands — you remember falling in love with her at Jane Dorlon's bridge. I know Charles will like her husband, too.

Eight o'clock is the hour. We do hope you can make it.

Always yours,

MARGARET

INFORMAL ACCEPTANCE

Dear Margaret:

Charles and I are delighted to accept for Tuesday, the third, at eight. I'm eager to hear your plans for the trip and also to see pretty Mrs. Farrand again. Thank you for thinking of us.

With love,

ANNE

THE DÉBUTANTE

MR. AND MRS. PRESCOTT PARMELEE

REQUEST THE PLEASURE OF

....

COMPANY AT A DANCE IN HONOUR OF THEIR DAUGHTER

MISS LUCY PARMELEE

ON TUESDAY EVENING, THE THIRD OF MARCH

AT TEN O'CLOCK

FIFTEEN MASCOMA ROAD

R.s.v.p.

At Home, Dancing

MR. AND MRS. GREVILLE STOCKTON
AT HOME
ON THURSDAY, THE FOURTH OF MARCH
AT TEN O'CLOCK
TWENTY EAST SIXTY-NINTH STREET

The favour of an answer is requested — Dancing

Musicale

MRS. KENNETH HOPE PRESTON
REQUESTS THE PLEASURE OF
....
COMPANY AT A MUSICALE
ON MONDAY, THE TWENTY-THIRD OF MARCH
AT FOUR O'CLOCK
52 STUYVESANT PARKWAY

R.s.v.p.

At Home

MRS. JAY DURWARD HOYT
MISS PAULA HOYT
WILL BE AT HOME
SATURDAY, THE NINTH OF FEBRUARY
FROM FOUR UNTIL SEVEN O'CLOCK
145 SOUTH PROSPECT STREET

DANCING

At Home

> Mr. and Mrs. Henry Martin Hardy
> At Home
> Friday afternoon
> October the fifteenth
> from four until six o'clock
> "Fairview"
> Chestnut Hill

Wedding Invitation

> MR. AND MRS. ARTHUR DAVIDSON
> REQUEST THE HONOUR OF YOUR PRESENCE
> AT THE MARRIAGE OF THEIR DAUGHTER
> BEATRICE
> TO
> MR. FRANK LINDLEY DARNELL
> ON SATURDAY THE TWELFTH OF JUNE
> AT TWELVE O'CLOCK NOON
> ST. DOMINICK'S CHURCH
> NEW YORK

Card to Church

> Please present this card
> at St. Dominick's Church
> on Saturday, the twelfth of June
> at twelve o'clock

Words and Expressions to Be Avoided When Writing a Letter

Above:	The use of such expressions as *the above statement* is condemned by some authorities.
According to our records:	Everyone knows that you get information from your records.
Advise:	A greatly overworked word.
All forms of participial endings, such as *trusting*, *hoping*, *thanking*, *wishing*, with *we remain*, *we are*, etc., as, *Thanking you in advance, we remain:*	Remember that the *last* sentence will generally leave its impression — good or bad. Make the closing sentence complete and direct; as, *We shall appreciate an early reply.*
Assuring you of our prompt attention:	Should you use this if you were talking to your correspondent? Be natural. Give a definite date when possible: *we will ship your order tomorrow.* Such an expression as *We assure you that the matter will have our prompt attention* may be used where a definite date cannot be given.
At an early date:	This expression should be avoided.
At hand:	Trite.
Attached find:	If anything is attached to the letter, say *attached is.* Of course it will be found. It could not be attached under separate cover.
Attached hereto:	Omit *hereto.*
Awaiting your further orders:	Why not ask in a direct way?
Beg: in **Beg to state** **Beg to advise**	To beg means to ask something for nothing. If you are in the

Beg to inform
Beg to acknowledge begging mood, these are apt statements, but surely you are not, even if you are wont to use these expressions.

Complaint: A rather rough word to use in a letter. Express your regret over any unpleasant incident that may necessitate correspondence.

Contents duly noted: An unnecessary space filler. These words are meaningless.

Dictated but not read (signed, or corrected): Discourteous. Letter should be returned with notation, "Received but not read."

Even date or recent date: To be clear, mention the exact date.

For your information wish to advise: This expression sounds pretentious. Be natural and you will be more effective.

Hand you: *Send you* is clearer. How can one hand anything to another in a letter?

Has come to hand: If you answer a letter, the sender will know that his has been received.

I have before me your letter: Your correspondent does not care where you have his letter.

Inclosed (enclosed) herewith: *Herewith* is unnecessary.

Inclosed (enclosed) please find:
Inclosed (enclosed) you will find: Use *inclosed is.* Arrange the inclosure so that the reader will find it.

Inclosed (enclosed) under separate cover: Make a definite statement: *We are sending to you by parcel post.*

In due course: Say definitely when you will do it.

In re: Has no place in an English letter.

In reply wish to state: Go ahead and say it.

Inst., prox., ult.: Abbreviations of words borrowed from the Latin. It is more courteous to specialize in English, the language of your correspondent.

Kind: A perfectly good word, but often misused in letter writing. Ordinary business correspondence is neither kind nor unkind.

Kindly: You would not say an unkind thing in a letter. Do not imply it by using *kindly*.

Oblige: Awkward. Resembles the last bow of a high-school declaimer.

Our Mr. Foster: It is better to say, *Mr. Foster, our representative.*

Per, as per: Appropriate in a Latin phrase, as *per annum, per capita.* For *three dollars per day,* say *three dollars a day. As per* should be avoided.

Please be advised that: Usually superfluous.

Proposition: Business slang; you mean *proposal* or *undertaking.*

Permit me to say: You may say anything you please on paper, without permission.

Referring to the matter:
Referring to your favor:
Regarding your communication of: Stilted ways of introducing a subject.

Same (as a pronoun): Much better to mention what you are writing about, or say *it, they,* etc.

State: An overworked verb. Use *say.*

The above subject;
Under the above subject: Why imply that you are backing up to find where you first started?

The writer wishes to say: Do not avoid *I* in this case. Write as you would speak.

This is in reply to: Perfectly obvious from the contents of your letter.
This is to inform you:

This letter is for the purpose of asking: Why not ask without all this preliminary?

Under separate cover: Rather tell how it is being sent — by mail, by parcel post, or by express.

Up to this writing: An awkward expression; avoid.

We or I: When speaking of a company, use *we;* when of an individual, use *I*. Avoid too frequent use of *we* or *I*, especially at the beginning of the letter itself or of sentences within the letter. But do not omit *I* when the sentence requires it.

We see by your letter: Someone has called this "a setting-up exercise," implying that the user of it is getting ready to think. He is sparring for time. Similar expressions are:

We take pleasure in sending you herewith:
We wish to call your attention to the fact that:
We wish to inform you that:
We wish to notify you that:
We wish to advise you:
We would advise:

Wish to say: Do not omit the subject of a sentence.
Would say that:
Would ask that:
Would state:

You can get me on the phone: *You can reach me by telephone* is much more dignified.

FORMS OF ADDRESS
LETTERS TO PERSONS OF RANK

To Whom	Envelope Address	Salutation and Complimentary Close: Formal Letter	Salutation and Complimentary Close: Informal Letter
The President	The President The White House Washington, D. C.	Mr. President: Respectfully,	My dear Mr. President: Very respectfully yours,
The Vice President	The Vice President United States Senate Washington, D. C.	Sir: Very truly yours,	My dear Mr. Vice President: Sincerely yours,
The Chief Justice	The Chief Justice The Supreme Court Washington, D. C.	Sir: Very truly yours,	My dear Mr. Chief Justice: Sincerely yours,
Associate Justice of the Supreme Court	Mr. Justice —— —— The Supreme Court Washington, D. C.	Sir: Very truly yours,	My dear Mr. Justice: Sincerely yours,
Member of the Cabinet	The Honorable * The Secretary of State. (or for a private letter) The Honorable —— —— Secretary of State Washington, D. C.	Sir: Very truly yours,	My dear Mr. Secretary: Sincerely yours,
Senator (U.S. or State)	The Honorable —— —— United States Senate Washington, D. C.	Sir: Very truly yours,	My dear Senator ——: Sincerely yours,
Representative (U.S. or State)	The Honorable —— —— House of Representatives Washington, D. C.	Sir: Very truly yours,	My dear Mr. ——: Sincerely yours,

* With the exception of Cabinet officers and Governors of States. "The Honorable" is used only in addressing an officer by name. For forms of address not given here, see the United States Department of State Style Manual.

LETTERS TO PERSONS OF RANK

To Whom	Envelope Address	Salutation and Complimentary Close: Formal Letter	Salutation and Complimentary Close: Informal Letter
Governor (State, Territory, or Possession)	The Honorable † The Governor of New York Albany, New York	Sir: I have the honor to be, Sir, Your obedient servant,	My dear Governor: Sincerely yours,
Mayor	The Honorable —— —— Mayor of Buffalo New York	Sir: Very truly yours,	My dear Mayor ——: Sincerely yours,
Judge	The Honorable —— —— State Circuit Court Building Chicago, Illinois	Sir: Very truly yours,	My dear Judge ——: Sincerely yours,
American Ambassador or Minister	The Honorable —— —— The American Ambassador or The American Minister London, England	Sir: Very truly yours,	My dear Mr. Ambassador: Sincerely yours,
Foreign Ambassador or Minister	His Excellency The Ambassador of France Washington, D. C.	Excellency: Very truly yours,	My dear Mr. Ambassador: I am, my dear Mr. Ambassador: Sincerely yours,
Prime Minister (Canada)	The Right Honorable —— ——, P.C.,M.P. Prime Minister of Canada Ottawa, Canada	Honourable and dear Sir: I have the honor to be, Sir, Your obedient servant,	My dear Mr. Prime Minister: I am, my dear Mr. Prime Minister, Sincerely yours,
Canadian Senator	The† Honourable —— —— Parliament Buildings Ottawa, Canada	Sir: Yours very truly,	My dear Senator: Believe me, Yours very sincerely,

† See page 261.
* The title, "The Honourable," is given to all Canadian Senators, the Speaker of the House and members of the Canadian Privy Council. Members of the United Kingdom Privy Council bear the title, "The Right Honourable." For other Canadian titles, consult *Styles of Address* by Howard Measures.

LETTERS TO PERSONS OF RANK

To Whom	Envelope Address	Salutation and Complimentary Close: Formal Letter	Salutation and Complimentary Close: Informal Letter
Member of Canadian Dominion Parliament	——,——, Esq., M. P. Parliament Buildings Ottawa, Canada	Sir: Yours very truly,	Dear Mr. ——: Believe me, Yours very sincerely,

LETTERS TO THE CLERGY

To Whom	Envelope Address	Salutation and Complimentary Close: Formal Letter	Salutation and Complimentary Close: Informal Letter
Protestant Bishop	The Right Reverend or —— ——, D.D., LL.D. Bishop of Washington Washington, D. C.	Right Reverend Sir: Respectfully yours,	My dear Bishop: Sincerely yours,
Protestant Clergyman	The Reverend —— —— (or if he has the degree in Divinity) —— ——, D.D. local address	Reverend Sir: Very truly yours,	My dear Mr. ——: (or if he has the degree in Divinity) My dear Dr. ——: Sincerely yours,
Rabbi	Rabbi —— —— (or if he has a higher degree) Dr. —— —— local address	Sir: Very truly yours,	My dear Rabbi ——: or My dear Dr. ——: Sincerely yours,
Pope	His Holiness The Pope or Pope Pius XII Vatican City Rome, Italy	Your Holiness:	Respectfully yours, or (if the writer is a Catholic) Sincerely yours in Christ,
Cardinal	His Eminence —— Cardinal —— local address	Your Eminence:	(same as for The Pope)

LETTERS TO THE CLERGY

To Whom	Envelope Address	Salutation and Complimentary Close: Formal Letter	Salutation and Complimentary Close: Informal Letter
Archbishop	The Most Reverend —— ——, D.D. Archbishop of New York	Your Excellency: (ecclesiastical) or Most Reverend Sir: (general)	(same as for Cardinal)
Bishop	The Most Reverend —— ——, D.D. Bishop of Buffalo	(same as Archbishop)	(same as for Archbishop)
Monsignor	The Right Reverend Msgr. —— —— local address	Right Reverend and dear Monsignor:	Respectfully yours,
Priest (secular)	The Reverend —— —— —— Church local address	My dear Father ——:	Sincerely yours,
* Priest (Religious Order)	The Reverend —— ——, M.M. local address	My dear Father ——:	Sincerely yours,
* Brother	Brother —— ——, C.F.X.	My dear Brother ——:	Sincerely yours,
* Superior of Sisterhood	The Reverend Mother Superior name of order and institution local address	My dear Reverend Mother:	Sincerely yours,
* Sister	Sister —— —— name of order and/or institution	My dear Sister:	Sincerely yours,

* Consult the Official Catholic Directory. Forms of address differ according to order, institution and/or congregation.

Officers of the Army and the Navy

It is the custom in the Army, the Navy, and the Marine Corps formally to introduce officers by title; as, Lieutenant Bowers, Colonel Richards, Ensign Peters, Commander Loucks. No distinction in presentation is made in either the Army or the Navy between first and second lieutenants or lieutenants, junior and senior grades. Each, in both services, is introduced as "lieutenant" Smith, Jones, and the like. But the arm of the service in which an officer is serving usually is designated.

Lieutenants in the Army and the Navy and ensigns in the Navy are designated "junior officers," and each is addressed as "Mr." when spoken to either by another officer or by a civilian. Senior officers are spoken to by title and surname.

Rank in the Army and the Navy

The Army	*The Navy*
General	Admiral
Lieutenant General	Vice Admiral
Major General	Rear Admiral
Brigadier General	Commodore
Colonel	Captain
Lieutenant Colonel	Commander
Major	Lieutenant Commander
Captain	Lieutenant, Senior Grade
First Lieutenant	Lieutenant, Junior Grade
Second Lieutenant	Ensign

The Marine Corps is an arm of the Navy. The Major General Commandant is of rank equal to a Rear Admiral or to a Major General of the Army. The Air Force is a separate department of the National Military Establishment, with the same rank as the Army.

In writing to officers of the Armed Forces, use the title and full name for the envelope address. In formal letters, "Dear Sir:" and "Very truly yours," are used. In informal letters, "My dear —— ——:" and "Sincerely yours."

Chapter XVIII

DOMESTIC AND INTERNATIONAL TELEGRAPH MESSAGES

As high-speed business grows more and more complex with the passing of time, the telegraph and cable industries have grown apace by instituting and improving their service to the public. With these improvements in methods to be followed in the use of the great services of telegraph companies, greater responsibility has been placed upon the public to be up-to-date in knowledge of the proper use of the telegraph service, as an aid to business development.

The Text of Telegrams

Since the cost of messages is figured on the number of words used in each message, skill is required in composing a telegram in order to employ the fewest words possible without injury to its sense and clarity in any way. To accomplish this, conciseness must be the keynote of the well-worded telegram. Every word in it must be essential to the meaning of the message, and no word should be omitted that will add to its clarity.

When writing a telegram, remember that nouns and verbs express thoughts more concisely than any other parts of speech; adjectives and adverbs are next in importance. Such words as *that, the, a, an, and, are, am, to, with, I, we:* in other words, articles, pronouns, copulative verbs, and prepositions often may be omitted without changing the meaning.

Do not use the word "stop" instead of a period at the end of a sentence. It will be charged for if used. Punctuation is permissible and is free when used in any message to be sent to points in the United States, Canada, Mexico and elsewhere on the North American continent.

Paragraphs are likewise permissible and will be transmitted as indicated in the message without charge.

In domestic telegrams, any dictionary word in the Dutch, English, French, German, Italian, Latin, Portuguese and Spanish languages is counted as one word. In international overseas messages, dictionary words in any language are counted at the rate of fifteen characters per word.

Other things to be remembered in writing a message are:

1. Necessary words in the address and signature are sent free in all messages within North America. They are charged for in international overseas messages.

2. Proper names from any language are counted according to the number of words they contain: *El Paso, South Carolina, United States, Oklahoma City* count as two words each; *Van der Goess* counts three words; *D'Angelo* counts one word.

3. Initials are counted as separate words when they are separated by spaces but count as one word for each five characters when written without spaces. For example, *J O Smith* counts as three words, but *JO Smith* counts as two words.

4. Abbreviations in common usage are counted at the rate of five characters to the word. Therefore such abbreviations as *FOB, COD, OK, AM, PM, SS, CWT, LB, FT* count as one word each. Abbreviations of place names count as full words: *Can.* costs as much to send as *Canada.*

5. Do not write figures as words. Every five figures or fraction of five figures are counted as one word, except that in the case of messages to Canada each figure counts as one word.

6. In domestic messages to points in North America except Canada, the signs $, %, &, #, ′ (for feet), ″ (for inches) count as a character. In messages to Canada and to overseas points, such signs count as one word each, except that to overseas points the signs $, & and # are not admissible and the % mark is transmitted as o/o and counts as three characters.

Code and cipher

To reduce the number of words in a message, or to secure secrecy, messages are often sent in secret (code or cipher) language. Code words are words especially selected or coined and given an arbitrary meaning or dictionary words used with an arbitrary meaning. A special private code may be used, or code words found in such code books as the *Bentley, Acme, Western Union, American Express,* and others. Messages in cipher make use of combinations of numbers or letters.

Code language may be used in all domestic telegrams, but only in full-rate international overseas messages. It may not be used in domestic telegram addresses, but may be used in addresses of all classes of international overseas messages.

Time differences

Time differences must be considered in the sending of domestic and overseas messages. In the United States there are four standard time belts, in which the time is successively one hour earlier as one goes west, and one hour later as one goes east. Daylight-saving time, one hour earlier than standard time, is used in many cities and must also be reckoned with in sending a telegram.

Classes of Service

Telegrams—**1.** Full-rate telegrams, the fastest service. The minimum charge is for ten words; in excess of ten words, a low extra-word rate is charged. The cost for a ten-word telegram ranges from 35 cents to $1.45.

2. Day letter service comprises messages of fifty words or less which may be sent less speedily and still serve its purpose. The cost is approximately that of a seventeen-word full-rate telegram.

3. Night letters may be filed up to 2:00 A.M. for delivery the next morning. The rate for twenty-five words varies from thirty to ninety-five cents. The rates decrease progressively as the length of message increases.

4. Serial Service should be used when intermittent correspondence is made with one addressee during the course of a day. A minimum of fifteen text words in each instalment is counted with a minimum aggregate of fifty text words a day charged for. Each instalment must bear the mark "Ser."

International Overseas Messages—In these messages, each word in the address, text, and signature is charged.

In plain language messages, each dictionary word not exceeding fifteen letters is counted as a single word. Non-dictionary code words and figure groups are counted at the rate of five, or fraction of five, characters to the line.

Fraction bars, periods, commas, colons, and dashes grouped with figures are counted as one figure each. Punctuation marks are transmitted only on specific request and are charged for as one word each. A dollar sign (transmitted DOLLARS or DOLS) or a pound sterling mark (transmitted STERLING or STLG) counts as a separate word.

The name of the country of destination is seldom necessary in the address. Unregistered addresses should not be unduly shortened.

Two classes of international message service are in use:

1. Ordinary or full-rate international overseas messages–the standard fast service at full rates.

2. Letter Telegram service is an inexpensive service for plain language messages, with delivery generally being made the day after the filing date. They are designated by LT, charged for at one-half of the ordinary rate, with a minimum charge for 22 words.

Domestic and International Telegraph Money Orders—Money may be sent to any place in the world by telegraph. In addition to the money order, for which a small fee is charged, the sender may add a regular message at the per word rate to the destination point.

Chapter XIX

REPORTS, BRIEFS, AND LEGAL FORMS

Reports

The purpose of a report is to present information about a particular subject to a selected group of people. It may be a statement in the nature of a summary of past transactions or of current conditions. Such a report is frequently periodic and must be prepared at regular intervals, as, for example, a monthly report on market conditions, or on the health of employees. Or it may be an analysis of a special problem or situation, made with a view to determining a projected course of action, as a report on the feasibility and cost of construction of a subway.

Whether or not the report is the result of an extended and thorough research and embodies the findings of an expert, it must present accurate information secured from reliable sources. The report writer must find the facts and draw conclusions only on the basis of the factual evidence presented.

Accuracy is the essential quality of the material presented in a report. Hardly less important, however, is the way in which that material is presented, for the usefulness of the report depends upon the manner of presentation. The report must be so written as to be read easily and understood readily by those to whom it is addressed. It must, therefore, be clear; that is, it must be so arranged and organized that the divisions and subdivisions follow in logical order, and so written, in simple, forceful language, that the material is easily comprehended. It must be complete, giving all necessary information. It must be free from all unnecessary or irrelevant material, and must deal directly with the subject of the report; in other words, it must be concise, and as brief as completeness allows. Also, the important material must be made to stand out clearly, so that for later reference the report may be used quickly and easily.[1]

Many reports are of such nature that they may be made on special report forms standardized within an organization. For the purpose of this chapter, such reports may be disregarded and the discussion confined to the preparation of reports which cannot be made on company forms.

When a report is not more than two or three pages in length, it is often made in the form of a letter. Such a report observes all the requirements of a good business letter. The manner of presentation may be formal, with the points carefully tabulated, or it may be informal, as in the following example:

February 23, 19—

Dr. Clarence A. Dykstra, City Manager
150 City Hall
Cincinnati, Ohio

Dear Dr. Dykstra:

When you were in Philadelphia you asked me to get for you information on the Philadelphia zoölogical garden and on the rates paid for electric power used by the bureau of water for pumping. I have obtained from the Zoölogical Society of Philadelphia and the Bureau of Water the information that you requested, and I am glad to transmit it to you.

The Zoölogical Society of Philadelphia is a private organization chartered by an act of the State Legislature in 1859. By the act of incorporation the society was authorized to occupy, with the consent of city councils, a part of Fairmount Park. Consent to occupy a designed park site was granted by an ordinance of councils approved April 15, 1859. The garden is, therefore, located on park land owned by the city.

The society has eight classes of membership, differentiated according to the amount paid annually or in lump sum to the society. In 1930, the membership was 2,400. Income is obtained from these members, from admission charges, from

[1] See Baker, Ray Palmer, *Preparation of Reports*, p. 43.

rent charged a restuarant, from sales of guidebooks, donkey rides, souvenirs, post cards and the like, from interest on investments, and from an appropriation of city council made to the Commissioners of Fairmount Park for the maintenance of the garden. For adults the admission charge is 35 cents, and for children 5 to 12 years old, 15 cents; children under 5 are admitted free when accompanied by an adult. The city appropriation carries the provision that a designated number of admission tickets shall be given to the Board of Public Education for public and other, except parochial, school children, and to the superintendent of parochial schools. In addition to 200,000 of these free admissions, there were, from March 1, 1929, to March 1, 1930, 281,755 town tickets for parties of 50 or more, 1733 admissions to members, 7,139 loanholders' single tickets, and 9,912 free admissions, from charitable institutions, donors' tickets, etc.

Concerning the cost of electric power for pumping water, about which you also inquired, I am giving the average costs per kilowatt hour for the amount of power used. This would seem to be a better indication of the actual cost than the schedule of rates. As the amount of power used at the several pumping stations varies, the cost also varies. The costs for high-service stations run somewhat higher than the following rates and these stations were included when computing the average costs. I have given the average high-service pumpage in order to show its relative importance.

Station	*Cost of Power per Kilowatt Hour*	*Total Average Daily Pumpage, Gallons*	*Average Daily High-service Pumpage, Gallons*
Torresdale..........	$0.0088	180,000,000	4,000,000
Shawmont..........	.0079	25,000,000	6,000,000
Belmont............	.0083	58,000,000	4,500,000

The estimated total power consumption for 1930 (the actual figures are not yet computed) is 74,580,500 kilowatt hours, and the cost estimated for budget purposes is $730,000. You will note at once that, in the above tabulation, the power cost per kilowatt hour is greatest at the station that pumps the most water. This is because the water is pumped against a low head, and, although a large quantity is raised, not too much power is needed to do it. If there are other details of cost that you would like to have, the officials of the Bureau of Water will be glad to supply them.

I believe that I have given you the information that you desired. Should there be any further data that you would like to have, I shall be glad to get them for you. It was a pleasure to be with you when you were here, and I hope that you found something of interest in your visit.

Yours very truly,

A. C. Howland
Staff Engineer

A longer report is often printed, especially if it is addressed to the public or is of great length. If the report is not printed, it is typed or mimeographed on sheets of paper which may be bound or fastened together in pamphlet form. Care should be taken in the selection of the paper for the report. It should be of a size convenient for reading and filing. It should be tough, for the report may have to withstand much handling. It should preferably not have a glossy finish unless half-tone illustrations must be used. The margin on the side which is fastened should be given extra width to allow for binding. A title-page and full table of contents should be prepared.

The report usually consists of three parts: the introduction, the body or text, and the conclusion. The introduction is often made in the form of a letter of transmittal calling attention to the purpose, scope, and significance of the report, or emphasizing its important points.

LETTER OF TRANSMITTAL

Department of the Interior
Bureau of Education
Washington, D. C.,

SIR:

The growth of child-care and parenthood education from the elementary school through college and university has been so rapid in home-economics departments of recent years that it seems appropriate briefly to set forth the progress made in this comparatively new field of education. Emmeline S. Whitcomb, specialist in home economics, has, at my request, surveyed child-care and parenthood education as it occurs in these fields of educational endeavor and reports her findings in the accompanying manuscript. I recommend that it be published under the title "Typical Child-care and Parenthood Education in Home-economics Departments."

Respectfully submitted,

J. J. Tigert, Commissioner

The Secretary of the Interior

When no special introduction is necessary, the report is often introduced by such statements as the following:

To the Council:
Gentlemen:
The Nominating Committee of 19— herewith submits to the Council its report with the committee's nominations for positions to be filled by election of the membership in 19—.

To the Board of Trustees:
Gentlemen:
I have the honor to present the annual report of the Treasurer for the fiscal year ending August 31, 19—.

To the President:
Sir:
I take pleasure in presenting my report for the year 19—.

When a report is intended for the general public, a short foreword takes the place of the letter of transmittal.

FOREWORD

Requests for information on the City-manager Plan of Municipal Government from Chambers of Commerce and business men have shown a marked increase in the last two years. To find out how business men appraise this plan, secretaries of Chambers of Commerce in City-manager cities were requested to give us the judgment of their business men on the success or failure of this form of municipal government in their communities, including the advantages and disadvantages indicated by their local experience. A summary of this opinion is reproduced in this report, which contains comments from sixty-seven cities. Most of these expressions are favorable to the City-manager Plan. But it is a fact that a number of cities which have operated under this plan have discarded it for some other form of municipal government.

For purpose of reference, there is included here a list of pamphlet material on the City-manager plan, a directory of City-manager cities, and a list of cities that have abandoned the City-manager Plan.

F. Stuart Fitzpatrick, Manager
Civic Development Department
United States Chamber of Commerce

The text of a long report is often preceded by a brief abstract or synopsis, containing a statement of the important conclusions or recommendations reached in the report and of the nature and results of the investigations which led to those conclusions. For the reader who cannot read the whole report, or who wishes an authoritative statement of its gist and import, this preliminary summary is very useful.

INTRODUCTORY SUMMARY

The purpose of this report is to discuss methods of handling force account on unit-price contracts for public works in a large city. Practices are analyzed and compared with practices in other cities. The report ends with a summary of conclusions and recommendations.

Prior to the analysis of particular force-account practices, the report defines "unit-price contract" and discusses the problem presented under such contracts by work which is part of the project contracted for, but which is not foreseen when the contract is let, and which is not covered by the price bid. "Force account" is then defined and shown to be one of the methods of performing and paying for extra work.

Then follows the report proper. For the sake of clearness and emphasis, it is usually organized in sections with headings and subheadings. Underscorings, changes in type and spacing, or other methods which will help to make the meaning clear, are also used.

The conclusion states the results of the investigations described in the report, and makes the applications of those results to the problem under consideration. It contains the recommendations and suggestions made in consequence of the data presented.

SUMMARY OF RECOMMENDATIONS

To remedy the present shortcomings and to enable the bureau to serve the court and the community with maximum efficiency, the following recommendations are submitted:

Function

1. The bureau's index should serve as the sole index to all the records of the six probation divisions, replacing the present divisional indexes. This would be a new function for the bureau.

Completeness and Promptness of Registration

2. Every division should be required to register every new case within 24 hours after the case is initiated; and these regulations should be enforced by the chief probation officer.

Personnel

3. Four workers, including the clerk-in-charge, should be assigned to, and should give continuous service in, the bureau.
4. The clerk-in-charge should receive a higher salary than other workers in the bureau.
5. Job specifications should be utilized in employing new workers.

Equipment

6. The files should be equipped with sliding wooden leaves and should be protected with wooden covers when the office is not in use.
7. The Russell index filing system should be installed in the name index, replacing the group-name system.
8. Card forms used in the indexes should be strictly standardized as to size and thickness. Notification blanks also should be standardized as to size.

Methods of Operation

9. Notifications should be dated, and a rubber stamp should be used for reporting unidentified queries.
10. The statistical system should be revised.
11. An office manual should be compiled and put into use.

A report may have several appendixes containing supplementary material. Graphs, tables, charts, maps, illustrations not placed in the text, notes, special sub-reports, and an index make up these appendixes. Special care should be taken to reproduce exactly and distinctly all supplementary matter, such as graphs and charts, that cannot be used in the original. An index should be made for all reports of any length or complexity.

Briefs

Closely related to the report is the brief, for like the report the brief presents ordered information on a particular subject. As in the report, that information must be arranged in logical order and pared of all irrelevant material.

The distinctive features of the brief grow out of its special purpose, which is to present a summary of essential information in such a way that that information can be read in a moment and grasped at once. The making of a good brief requires, on the part of the secretary, the ability to select essential facts, to state them clearly, and to arrange them logically.

The necessary terseness, compactness, logical arrangement, and emphasis of important points are ordinarily best secured by the use of the outline form. The confinement of material within main heads and subheads makes the relative importance of the different items unmistakably clear, and reveals as well the interrelation between those items. If the outline form is not used, the material in the brief must be arranged in such a way that each separate point stands out clearly.

The kinds of briefs most frequently required are briefs of reports, briefs of correspondence, and special professional briefs, such as legal briefs.

The accompanying report is taken from a Bulletin of the American Library Association. The summary following it is a type of brief which secretaries are frequently required to make. A comparison of the summary with the report will make clear the important feature of the brief—the presentation of the essential substance of the original material in the fewest possible words.

Members of the Council, American Library Association:

The Finance Committee hereby certifies that the estimate of income, for the fiscal year ending August 31, 19—, has been approved by the committee, and that the accounts of the Association for the fiscal year ending August 31, 19— have been audited and found to be correct.

In past years the report of the Finance Committee has ended with the preceding brief statement. This year, however, the committee feels that a word of explanation should be made and a suggestion presented to Council.

As chairman of the Finance Committee for the past four years, I have participated in making the estimates of income upon which the budget has been based. In this time there has been consistent difference of opinion among those participating as to what the estimates should be. Regardless of whose opinion prevailed, the estimates were not, and could not be, correct enough to rely upon. We were consistent in only one thing—we always overestimated.

This year the Finance Committee has adopted a new policy in estimating income. We have estimated income for the fiscal year ending August 31, 19— to be the amount of money *actually* received by the Association as income for the fiscal year ending August 31, 19—, the preceding year. This idea did not originate with the Finance Committee, but was a suggestion referred from the Executive Board. The committee looks upon it with great favor. In fact, we think it is foolproof. It is an improvement on the pay-as-you-go plan; instead, we go only as we have paid.

The committee feels that it has these distinct advantages: (1) It provides a known income base—with no more uncertainty or guesswork. (2) With an increase or decrease in income, the Executive Secretary and Executive Board have the whole year ahead of them in which to make their adjustments.

The only danger in the situation is failure in succeeding years of the Finance Committee to adhere to this policy in making estimates. We, therefore, respectfully suggest to Council that this method of estimating be followed for the next several years and, if it proves successful, Council might then wish to make it a permanent method of estimating income.

The Finance Committee, as set up by the constitution, is an arm of Council with functions primarily that of "watchdog of income." Recently there have come from various sources suggestions that the Finance Committee have its functions broadened to cover ways and means of increasing income. The present committee has no particular feeling as to the propriety of adding such function to the committee, but does present the situation to Council for its reaction and opinion.

A.L.A. Finance Committee
Nancy Elizabeth Hoyle
G. Flint Purdy
Walter Brahm, Chairman

SUMMARY OF THE REPORT OF THE FINANCE COMMITTEE

The income estimate for the forthcoming fiscal year has been approved and the accounts for the fiscal year just ended have been audited and found correct. The adoption of a new policy in estimating income based upon the method used in determining the present estimate, has been proposed. For the first time, income for the forthcoming fiscal year has been estimated to be the amount of money *actually* received during the preceding year. This method has the following advantages over the former "pay-as-you-go" plan: (1) It provides a known income base, eliminating the former guesswork which always resulted in overestimation; (2) in case of income changes requiring adjustments, the Executive Secretary and Board have the full year ahead of them. This new method can be tried for several years and, if successful, be established as a permanent procedure. The possibility of broadening the committee's functions to include ways and means of increasing income was also suggested.

LEGAL FORMS

The business secretary is often called upon to fill out legal forms for her employer, and occasionally she is requested to prepare such forms herself, particularly the *Power of Proxy* and the *Power of Attorney.* Therefore she should be familiar with the ordinary forms of such papers.

POWER OF PROXY

KNOW ALL MEN BY THESE PRESENTS

THAT I, the undersigned, hereby constitute and appoint Albert Stevens, or, if he does not act, Russel Johnston or James Atwood, my true and lawful attorney, for me and in my name and stead, to attend the annual meeting of the stockholders of The Madison Chemical Manufacturing Company on May 30, 19—, as well as any adjournments of the said meeting; and to vote on all matters that may be submitted at the said meeting or at any adjournments thereof, and at all elections then and there held, according to the discretion of my said attorney, the number of shares which I should be entitled to vote if I were then personally present; and to sign any consents: hereby confirming all that my said attorney shall do by virtue hereof.

WITNESS my hand and seal this .... day of ...., A. D. 19—.

[Signed] Samuel Nichols [L. S.]

Signed, sealed, and delivered
in the presence of
[Signed] Loyd Aldridge

Chapter XX

PARLIAMENTARY PROCEDURE AND MINUTES

The secretary of an organization should be familiar with the common principles of parliamentary procedure which are presented in the following pages. For detailed information, one of the several manuals on parliamentary procedure should be consulted.

Holding a meeting

No business can be legally transacted at a meeting of any organization unless a quorum is present. Usually a quorum is a majority of the members. It may, however, be fixed at any number by rule of the society.

When a quorum is present, the usual conduct of the meeting is as follows. The presiding officer (president, chairman, moderator) takes the chair and calls the meeting to order. He then presents, in their order, the items of business to be considered. The regular order of business to be followed in a meeting usually is determined by rule of the organization. If the organization has not adopted an order of business the usual order is:

Roll call
Reading of minutes of previous meeting
Approval of minutes
Reports of officers
Reports of standing committees
Reports of special committees
Unfinished business
New business
Adjournment

Motions

Any member who desires to make a motion should rise and address the chairman by his correct title: "Mr. Chairman" or "Mr. President" or "Madame Chairman." When the chairman has recognized him by announcing his name, the member proceeds with his motion.

The usual form of a motion is "I move that . . . ," or "I wish to make the motion that . . . " A long or very important motion should be in writing so that it can be given to the secretary for exact recording. Such a motion is frequently put into the form of a resolution.

Usually a motion must be seconded by a member of the organization in order to be before the meeting for consideration. The seconder need not wait for recognition from the chairman. In a small group, he need not rise, but merely calls out as he sits, "I second the motion," or "I second it." In a large assembly, the seconder should rise and say, "Mr. Chairman, I second that motion." The chairman then repeats the motion saying, "It has been moved and seconded that . . . " If the motion is debatable, discussion and debate may then follow. If the motion is not debatable, the vote is taken on the motion at once. Nominations, or inquiries of any kind, do not need to be seconded.

Kinds of motion

A motion which introduces a particular subject or brings it before a meeting for consideration is called a *main* motion. Such a motion is debatable and subject to amendment. Any other motions, except other main motions, can be made while it is pending. (A motion is said to be pending after it has been stated by the chairman, but before it has been voted upon.) Motions which arise out of other motions are known as *incidental* and *subsidiary* motions. These motions must be acted upon by a meeting before the main motions to which they apply can be acted upon. In other words, they take precedence over a main motion. A few motions may not be debated or amended. When made, they take precedence over all other motions and must be acted upon at once. These are called *privileged* motions.

Precedence of motions

The precedence of motions often becomes an important factor in the transaction of business in a meeting, and consequently a knowledge of the correct order of precedence is important to anyone who must be familiar with parliamentary practice.

The general principle underlying the order of precedence is that when several motions concerning the same matter are pending, the motion that ranks highest must be considered first. Thus, when an amendment is proposed to a main motion which is before an assembly for consideration, the amendment must be voted upon before the main motion to which it applies can be voted upon. In other words, the motion to amend takes precedence over the main motion. If then, before the motion to amend is put to the vote, a motion to lay the main motion on the table is made, this new motion must be considered before the amendment can be voted upon. If a motion to adjourn the assembly should then be made before the motion to lay on the table is voted upon, the motion to adjourn would take precedence over all the previous motions. It would have to be voted upon first, since if the assembly decided to adjourn, no action on any of the other motions would be required.

The assembly would vote on the four motions in the order of precedence, as follows:

> First, the motion to adjourn; if this is lost, then
> Second, the motion to lay on the table; if this is lost, then
> Third, the motion to amend; and
> Fourth, the main motion.

The general order of precedence of motions is: first, privileged motions; then, subsidiary and incidental motions; and last, main motions. The order of precedence of particular motions is indicated in the table given on the following page.

LIST OF MOTIONS AND RULES THAT APPLY TO THEM

Thirteen of the motions have a definite order of precedence, indicated by numbers from 1 to 13. Applications of rules are indicated by an asterisk (*).

	RULES															
MOTIONS	Order of precedence	Debatable	Non-debatable	Amendable	Non-amendable	Second required	Second not required	Majority vote required	Two-thirds vote required	May interrupt speaker	May not interrupt speaker	Debate limited	Renewable after debate	Not renewable at same session	May be reconsidered	Cannot be reconsidered
Adjourn	2		*		*	*		*			*		*			*
Adjourn, Fix time to	1			*		*		*			*	*	*		*	
Adopt resolution	13	*		*		*		*			*			*		
Amendment	11	*		*		*		*			*	*			*	
Appeal from chair					*	*		*		*		*				
Call for previous question	7		*		*	*			*		*		*		*	
Commit or refer	10			*		*		*		*		*	*		*	
Expunge a resolution		*				*			*		*					
Lay on the table	6		*			*		*			*	*	*			
Limit or extend time for debate	8			*		*			*		*	*	*		*	
Main motion	13	*		*		*					*			*	*	
Objection to consider question			*		*		*		*	*				*	*	
Orders of the day, Call for	5		*				*			*			*			
Orders, To create general		*		*		*		*			*		*			
Orders, To create special		*		*		*			*		*		*			
Parliamentary inquiry, Rise to			*				*			*						
Point of order, Rise to			*				*	*		*						
Postpone indefinitely	12	*			*	*		*			*	*			*	
Postpone to certain time	9			*		*		*			*	*			*	
Previous question, Call for	7		*			*			*		*		*		*	
Privilege, Question of	4		*				*			*			*			
Recess	3			*		*		*			*	*	*			
Reconsider		*				*		*		*		*				
Refer	10			*		*		*			*	*	*		*	
Rescind		*				*			*		*					
Substitute		*		*		*		*			*	*			*	
Suspend rules			*			*			*							
Take from table	6		*			*		*					*			
Withdrawal of motion			*		*		*	*			*		*		*	

Amendments

An amendment to a motion can be proposed only after the motion has been presented for debate and discussion by the chairman of the meeting. As has been indicated, a motion to amend must be voted upon before the main motion can be voted upon. An amendment may be amended, but the amendment to an amendment cannot be amended.

Voting

There are several methods of taking the vote. The usual method is *viva voce* (by the voice). A vote may also be taken by rising, show of hands, ballot, and roll call answered by "yea" and "nay." When the vote is taken *viva voce* or by rising or show of hands, the affirmative vote is usually called for first. Then the negative vote is taken, and the chairman announces the result of the vote. In a small group, the chairman may count the vote himself. In a large group, the chairman may appoint tellers to assist in counting the vote. When the vote is by ballot, tellers are always appointed. In counting ballots, blank ballots are disregarded. Fraudulent or illegal votes are counted in the total number of votes cast, but are not allowed to count for any candidate.

The formality of voting may be dispensed with on questions of small importance if the meeting is in general agreement about the matter to be decided. In this case, voting is said to be by general consent. For example, when the minutes have been read, a vote of approval and adoption may be assumed after opportunity for corrections has been given and necessary corrections made. The chairman need not require a vote of adoption, but instead usually says, "If there are no (further) corrections, the minutes stand approved as read."

At any time before the vote is finally announced, a member may change his vote. After the vote has been announced, the permission of the society is required before a member may change his vote. Ordinarily the chairman does not vote except when his vote would be decisive, as, for instance, when it would make or break a tie.

Voting by proxy

When the rules of an organization allow, a member who cannot be present at a meeting may appoint someone to attend the meeting and act in his stead. The person so appointed is called a *proxy*. A member's proxy has power of attorney to vote and make all decisions which the member himself would be required to make at the meeting. The proxy need not be a member of the organization whose meeting he attends. At stockholders' meetings, where the power of proxy is most often used, the fact that the proxy is not a member of the company makes little difference. But when the society is of a different sort—religious or academic or social—the proceedings may be of such nature that nonmembers should not be present or allowed to participate. For this reason, proxies to meetings of all except strictly business organizations should, if possible, be members of the organizations in whose proceedings they participate.

Constitution and by-laws

The constitution and by-laws consist of the rules of organization and conduct by which a society is governed. The more important of these rules are usually called the constitution, while those of less importance are called the by-laws, the standing rules, or the rules of order. In business organizations a charter frequently takes the place of a constitution.

The constitution should contain statements on the following points: name and purpose of the organization; qualifications required for membership; the name, number, and duties of officers and the method of their election; and the method of making amendments to the constitution. The by-laws should include all necessary additional rules and regulations.

Duties of officers

The duties of the various officers of an organization are defined in the constitution of that organization. Naturally these duties may differ somewhat in different organizations, as the organizations themselves differ in nature and purpose. In general, however, the duties of presiding officer, secretary, and treasurer are as follows.

The presiding officer

1. To open a meeting by taking the chair and calling the members to order.
2. To announce the business before the meeting in the order in which it is to be acted upon.
3. To recognize members who address the chair and are entitled to speak.
4. To receive all motions and propositions put by the members, and to submit these motions and propositions for consideration by the meeting.
5. To state and put to vote all questions which have been moved or which naturally arise in the course of the meeting, and to announce the result of the vote.
6. To enforce the observance of order and decorum among the members.
7. To restrain within the rules of order members who are engaged in debate.
8. To name the members who are to serve on committees, unless these committees are appointed by the meeting.
9. To inform the meeting whenever necessary on points of order or practice pertaining to the business in hand.
10. To authenticate by his signature, whenever necessary, all acts, proceedings, and orders of the organization.

The secretary

1. To take notes and keep record of all things done and passed in the meetings of the society.
2. To read all papers, such as correspondence, which are ordered read by the organization.
3. To call the roll and take note of absent members.
4. To notify delegates of their appointment and furnish them with credentials and all necessary papers.

5. To notify committees of their appointment and of any business referred to them.
6. To call the roll and count the votes when a roll-call vote is taken.
7. To sign with the president, when required, all orders on the treasurer for expenses of the organization.
8. To send out to members notices of all called or special meetings, and of all regular meetings if the society requires it.
9. To take charge of all correspondence of the society.
10. To notify new members of election to membership, and resigning members of the action taken upon their resignations.
11. To take charge of and keep all papers and records of the organization which are not especially assigned to the keeping of the treasurer, the librarian, etc. These include (1) a journal of minutes and proceedings; (2) a journal containing names and addresses of members; (3) a journal containing the constitution and by-laws of the organization; (4) files of correspondence, of committee reports, and the like.

Before each meeting the secretary should make out and give to the chairman an order of business for that meeting, noting in proper order everything that is to be brought before the meeting. In case the president and vice president are both absent, the secretary presides until the election of a temporary chairman.

In some organizations the duties of the secretary are divided between a *corresponding* and a *recording* secretary. The corresponding secretary has charge of all correspondence, the sending out of notices, and any other of the secretary's duties which the society delegates to him. The remaining duties fall upon the recording secretary.

The treasurer

1. To collect and hold all fees and incoming funds.
2. To pay out money from the society's funds for all authorized expenses.
3. To keep a written record of all money received and expended for the organization.

4. To make a regular report to the organization of its financial condition.
5. To keep a file of all receipts and vouchers.

The treasurer is thus really the banker of the society. As his accounts must be audited for all inaccuracies, the report to the organization need not be detailed. A simple report like the following is usually sufficient:

REPORT OF THE TREASURER OF ——— FOR THE YEAR ENDING JUNE 30, 19—

Receipts		
Balance on hand, July 1, 19—		$43.50
Membership fees	$50.00	
Initiation fees	25.00	
Sales at annual exhibit	76.23	
Contributions	10.00	161.23
Total		$204.73
Expenditures		
Stationery, stamps, printing, etc.	$12.00	
Equipment	15.00	
Entertainment expenses	27.08	
Exhibit expenses	19.37	
Scholarship	100.00	173.45
Balance on hand, June 30, 19—		31.28
Total		$204.73

[Signed] JOHN SMITH,
Treasurer.

MINUTES

The minutes of a meeting are an official record of the transactions and important events of that meeting. They must be impersonal and exact in statement and they must be complete. They must also be as brief as possible and must exclude all details not necessary to a narration of the important transactions.

The order of business for a meeting provides the skeleton of the minutes. See order on page 281.

The name of the organization and the date, hour, and place of meeting are always written at the beginning of the minutes, and the hour of adjournment is stated at the end. Minutes of the meetings of boards of directors of corporations, and usually of all small groups, should include the names of those present. All motions should be recorded exactly, in wording and in the order of their occurrence, and as much of the discussions should be reported as seems necessary to give the sense of the meeting. Copies of all documentary material presented in the meeting, such as officers' or committees' reports, notices, and legal papers, should be preserved in the minutes.

The minutes should always be signed by the one recording them. In some organizations it is customary for the president, as well as the secretary, to sign the minutes. Both signatures should be given when the minutes are published.

The style used in the writing of minutes is fixed by custom, and usually is or becomes traditional within an organization. The minutes of the meeting of a board of directors of a large corporation will ordinarily be more formal than those of a committee or academic organization.

The following illustrations show the types of minutes most frequently used.

Minutes of a board of directors:

MINUTES
Of a Special Meeting
Of the Board of Directors of the
Drexel Finance Corporation

A special meeting of the Board of Directors was convened at the office of the Company, 1600 Walnut Street, Philadelphia, Pennsylvania, at 10 A.M., May 20, 19—. The following directors were present: Samuel F. Preston, P. F. McHenry,

Henry F. Williamson, George W. Sternberg, and Michael H. Evans.

A waiver of notice of the time, place, and object of the meeting, signed by all the directors, was presented. The waiver is attached and hereby made a part of these minutes.

The President of the Company, Samuel F. Preston, presented a plan for merging the Drexel Finance Corporation with the Provident Loan Company of Philadelphia, the enlarged organization to be known as the Drexel Finance and Loan Corporation.

After considerable discussion, it was moved by Mr. P. J. McHenry that the plan of reorganization submitted by the President be printed and copies distributed to all the stockholders, and that final action on the plan be deferred until the next regular annual meeting of the Board of Directors. The motion was duly seconded by Mr. George W. Sternberg. Upon being put to a vote the motion was carried, Mr. Evans voting in the negative.

There being no further business, upon motion duly made and seconded the meeting was adjourned.

(Signed) P. J. MCHENRY
Secretary

May 10, 19—.

THE DREXEL FINANCE COMPANY
Philadelphia, Pennsylvania

Gentlemen:

I hereby waive notice of the special meeting of the Board of Directors of the Drexel Finance Company, to be held on the twentieth day of May, 19—, at 10 A.M., at 1600 Walnut Street, Philadelphia, to consider a plan for merging with the Provident Loan Company.

(Signed) ....

CHAPTER XXI

RESOLUTIONS

The tendency toward simplicity has affected the writing of resolutions to produce greater flexibility in their form and style. Although *Whereas* and *Resolved* are still used for most resolutions, the wording has grown much less pompous and formal, especially in resolutions of sympathy and congratulation, and the effect is consequently that of greater sincerity, dignity, purposefulness, and good faith.

A resolution ordinarily consists of two parts: the reasons for the resolution, and the resolution proper. The reasons are usually stated first and introduced by the word *Whereas*, and the resolution itself follows and is prefixed by the word *Resolved*. Occasionally this order is reversed and the resolution stated first; and in some resolutions, particularly in resolutions of sympathy, the words *Whereas* and *Resolved* are omitted in order to avoid an impersonal, formal tone, and to express more simply and adequately a sincere personal feeling on the part of those making the resolution.

If *Whereas* and *Resolved* are used, they are always capitalized and followed by a comma and the first word after them is capitalized. *Whereas* is usually written in capitals, and *Resolved* is ordinarily written in italics.

A resolution to provide funds

Resolved, That the expenses of further conducting the studies and investigations authorized by H. Res. 137, Eighty-first Congress, incurred by the Committee on the Judiciary, acting as a whole or by subcommittee, not to exceed an additional $45,000, including expenditures for the employment of such experts, clerical, stenographic, special counsel, and other assistants, shall be paid out of the contingent fund of the

House on vouchers authorized by said committee, signed by the chairman thereof and approved by the Committee on House Administration.

Resolution opposing a Congressional bill

WHEREAS, Bill H.R. 2945 for postal rate increases calls for radically revised rate schedules with jumps ranging up to 300 per cent; and

WHEREAS, These proposed increases will most certainly cause hundreds of religious, educational, agricultural and general interest periodicals to cease publication; and

WHEREAS, Low postal rates for books, newspapers and magazines have long been considered a boon to the American home and a service well worth preserving—and upon which a vast business structure of publishing and printing has been erected: Therefore be it

Resolved, That the Chamber of Commerce of Philadelphia, while in no way adverse to a moderate advance in postal charges in keeping with increased costs of operating the service, is strongly opposed to a revolutionary revision of rates as contained in H.R. 2945; and be it

Resolved further, That any revision of H.R. 2945 or any new bill on this subject should confine advances in second class rates to not more than 25 per cent spread out over a period of not less than five years.

A resolution included with a report

Before I close my report, I would like to bring the following resolution to the attention of the General Committee:

We hereby resolve that the members of District #3 respectfully request a representative or Commissioner from the Women's Grand Lodge to the National Board. Such a woman would provide the District with the current policy and action of the League. This will enable us to project such policy and action through the 91 chapters in our District who are already engaged in active participation of the present program and who desire to enlarge their activities.

A resolution expressed in legal terms

Be it *Resolved*, That the President and the Secretary be authorized to execute on behalf of the College and affix its corporate seal and the Secretary be appointed its attorney to acknowledge and deliver the deed from Swarthmore College to The Philadelphia, Baltimore, and Washington Railroad

Company for *all that certain* piece or parcel of land *situate* in the County of Delaware and State of Pennsylvania, bounded and described as follows, viz.: *Beginning* at a point in the northerly line of land of The Philadelphia, Baltimore, and Washington Railroad Company and in the easterly line of Chester Avenue, sixty feet wide, at the distance of twenty-one feet and sixty-nine one-hundredths of a foot measured north eight degrees no minutes east, along the said line of avenue, from the tangent of the center line of the southbound track of The Philadelphia, Baltimore, and Washington Railroad Company produced south seventy-seven degrees forty-nine minutes thirty seconds west from the point of tangent of the said center line; extending from the said beginning point north eight degrees no minutes east, along said easterly line of Chester Avenue, four hundred and ninety-two feet and one one-hundredth of a foot to a point; thence by other land of the Swarthmore College as follows, viz.: First, southwardly, on a line curving to the left having a radius of fifty-three feet and a chord whose bearing is south seven degrees no minutes east and whose length is twenty-seven feet, and forty-three one-hundredths of a foot, the distance of twenty-seven feet and seventy-five one-hundredths of a foot to a point; Second, south twenty-two degrees no minutes east eighty-five feet and seventy-two one-hundredths of a foot to a point; Third, southwardly, on a line curving to the right with a radius of sixty feet and a chord whose bearing is south eight degrees nine minutes east and whose length is twenty-eight feet and seventy-three one-hundredths of a foot, the distance of twenty-nine feet and one one-hundredth of a foot to a point; Fourth, south five degrees forty-two minutes west eighty-two feet and fifty-one one-hundredths of a foot to a point; Fifth, southwardly, on a line curving to the left with a radius of ninety feet and a chord whose bearing is south three degrees thirteen minutes east and whose length is twenty-seven feet and nine-tenths of a foot, the distance along said curve of twenty-eight feet and one one-hundredth of a foot to a point; and, Sixth, south twelve degrees eight minutes east two hundred and sixteen feet and one one-hundredth of a foot to a point in the said northerly line of land of the Railroad Company distant nineteen feet and sixty-four one-hundredths of a foot northwardly from and measured at right angles to the said tangent of the center line of the southbound track; and thence south seventy-eight degrees six minutes west, by the said land of The Philadelphia, Baltimore, and

Washington Railroad Company, one hundred and fifty feet to the place of beginning; *containing* thirty-five thousand and twelve square feet, more or less, in consideration whereof the College shall receive from The Philadelphia, Baltimore, and Washington Railroad Company a quit-claim deed for all its interest in 15,868 square feet, more or less, lying north of the Railroad and west of Chester Road now occupied by the Railroad as a driveway and parking space for the existing railroad station, together with receiving from the Railroad Company the sum of __________ dollars in cash.

Be it further *Resolved*, That the President and the Secretary be authorized to execute on behalf of the College and affix its corporate seal and that the Secretary be appointed its attorney to acknowledge and deliver a Release for Damages from Swarthmore College to The Philadelphia, Baltimore, and Washington Railroad Company upon receipt of the sum of __________ dollars and upon completion of the work yet to be done.

Resolutions stating the policy of an organization

WHEREAS, The Chamber of Commerce of Philadelphia recognizes that the construction industry is doing everything in its power to overcome the housing shortage; and

WHEREAS, It is recognized that legislative assistance is now required to provide more and better housing for lowest income groups (particularly in the bracket under $2,500 per annum for a worker family of four); Therefore be it

Resolved, That financial and other legislative assistance be given to the Redevelopment Authority of Philadelphia, and other public bodies similarly dedicated, so that the city may shortly enjoy the benefits from the improvements contemplated; be it further

Resolved, That, after receiving such aid, these public agencies first should make certain that every possible advantage is taken of existing housing through remodeling and redevelopment; be it further

Resolved, That any subsidized housing program should provide the minimum essentials for health and comfort and that, in return for governmental aid, the occupants be held accountable for cleanliness and reasonable maintenance of the property, and that, within a reasonable time, they be removed upon receipt of evidence that family income has risen appreciably above $2,500 per annum; be it further

Resolved, That Philadelphia be granted home rule for the planning, financing and carrying out of housing projects which are supported by state and federal funds.

The following resolution was adopted by the Children's Bureau of Philadelphia:

Recognizing the intimate relation of sanitation and housing to the health, not only of the poor and sick of Philadelphia, but of all citizens, we are keenly interested in the appointment to the position of Chief of the Division of Housing and Sanitation. We believe it essential that the person to be appointed should be qualified by training and experience to administer expertly the important duties of this position. Upon his work of housing and sanitary inspection depends the safety and well-being of every home dweller in Philadelphia. The Chief of the Division is an important factor in epidemic control since to him falls the task of eliminating conditions that predispose to disease. We believe, therefore, that he should have knowledge of preventive medicine and should have had special training and experience in sanitary work.

Resolution interpreting the action of a body

PUBLIC WORKS AND IMPROVEMENTS

WHEREAS, Various acts of Congress enacted during the present Congress have authorized the construction of public buildings and the prosecution of other public works and improvements, and provided appropriations for carrying out such authorizations: Therefore be it

Resolved by the House of Representatives (the Senate concurring), That it is the sense of the Congress that the letting of contracts and the beginning of construction under the several Acts of Congress heretofore enacted authorizing the construction of public buildings and the prosecution of other public works and improvements throughout the United States, and appropriation Acts enacted pursuant thereto, shall be expedited to the fullest extent possible, within the limitations provided by law, to the end that unemployment prevailing throughout the country may be relieved.

Resolution of authorization and confirmation of sale

Be it *Resolved by the Council of American Library Association*, That the Executive Board be authorized from time to time to sell, mortgage or otherwise dispose of any and all real estate now and hereafter owned by American Library Association or any part thereof or any interest therein;

And further *Resolved*, That this resolution and the authority herein granted shall continue and prevail until this resolution is specifically rescinded or annulled by the Council.

Resolved by the Council of American Library Association, That the sale of the parcel located in Chicago, Illinois, described as follows:

> The West 74¾ feet of Lot 6 in the Assessor's Division of Block 47 in Kinzie's Addition to Chicago for $100,000

and the conveyance of such property to the purchaser thereof is hereby in all respects ratified, approved and confirmed.

Resolution of thanks

The following resolution was adopted by the Charity Organization Society of the City of New York, in appreciation of the appeal published by the *Evening Post*.

WHEREAS, the *New York Post* has again this year made its annual appeal for old couples ineligible for the old-age pension, in the same effective manner as in other years, and is thereby making it possible for the Charity Organization Society to care for some of these aged couples in their own homes,

Resolved, that the Charity Organization Society records its appreciation of the help the Society is receiving from the *New York Post* in caring for these needy folk and directs the Secretary to express its thanks to the *New York Post* for this assistance.

Resolution of congratulation

The following resolution was sent by the faculty of Stanford University to the late David Starr Jordan, Chancellor Emeritus, on his seventy-ninth birthday:

Dr. David Starr Jordan
Chancellor Emeritus
Stanford University, California
DEAR SIR:

We, the members of the faculties of the Leland Stanford Junior University, congratulate you and Mrs. Jordan, and give you our warmest best wishes on your seventy-ninth birthday. Those of us who have the longest association with you, and those who have joined us later, know that the University, as it is today, is the outcome of that small beginning made under your leadership nearly forty years ago. With originality, vision, and courage, in thought, speech, and act, you laid the foundations of an establishment for the training of youth in usefulness to themselves and their fellows. Emphasizing that it is more important to be right than to be rich, and that success in life is measured in terms of service, you have won recognition in the world of ideas—in academic life and in the world of science—and also in the world of action which calls itself practical. We, your friends, delight to do you honor and to wish you all the satisfactions of a life of great usefulness because of its independent devotion to realizable ideals.

Faithfully yours,

Resolutions of sympathy and appreciation

It is with much sympathy that we learn of Mr. W———'s recent illness and of his desire for that reason to be relieved of the responsibility of membership on this Board. We believe that it would not be fitting to do otherwise than grant his request, but we hope to welcome him back to our ranks at an early date.

We cannot, however, allow his present withdrawal to pass without some mention of our gratitude for the wise and effective service he has given us for more than ten years. In 19—, when the fortunes of this organization were low, he became a member of the committee that was created to put the organization on a sound financial basis. Consequently he became chairman of our Executive Committee and later, President. During his service in these two offices he brought about a notable improvement in the organization of the Board and its committees, and greatly invigorated the Society's work by bringing into more effective and sympathetic contact its Board and staff. After his retirement as President, he kept up his interest and effectively contributed to the solution of current problems. We owe and shall always owe much to his leadership.

In 19—, Jonathan D——— was elected a Director of this Society. For twenty-eight years he has been a stanch and understanding friend of the Society and a dependable counselor of its officers and staff. Unassuming, and a gentleman in the highest meaning of that word, it may be questioned how many of his fellow directors, even, have a full appreciation of how much dependence those actively in the work have placed on the judgment of Mr. D——— throughout his more than a quarter of a century of service as Director, as Chairman of the Executive Committee, as Vice President, and as President. Even when he had given his service to the country at Washington, and later when his health was impaired, he graciously gave of his busy hours to aid in the solution of troublesome problems.

It is with a deep sense of gratitude to Mr. D——— that the Directors of the Society record upon their minutes their sorrow at the loss of this outstanding member of the Board, and direct that a copy of this statement be forwarded to Mrs. D———.

Resolved, That the Board of Governors learns with very deep regret of the sudden and untimely death on Friday, January 30, 19—, of Paul Radford, who was one of the Club's active workers and whose devotion was an inspiration to all our members; and be it further

Resolved, That copies of this resolution be sent to all Club members as well as to members of the immediate family of the deceased.

Resolution to petition the President

"WHEREAS, many hundreds of thousands of American citizens among the sharecroppers and cotton wage workers throughout the rural South are undernourished (in many cases face starvation), and have disastrously unbalanced diets; and

"WHEREAS, many food crops have large surpluses which could be purchased and distributed to these deprived American workers by the Surplus Commodities Corporation through its food-stamp plan or a modified form of it. Especially important are such surpluses as fruit juices, milk, dried and fresh fruits, canned fruits and vegetables, eggs, cheese, and meats which the Surplus Commodities Corporation is already purchasing;

"Therefore, be it *Resolved,* That we petition President Franklin D. Roosevelt; Claude R. Wickard, Secretary of Agriculture; Milo Perkins, Administrator, Surplus Commodities Corporation; and all Members of Congress to take such necessary steps to get these surplus foods to these hundreds of thousands of sharecroppers and cotton wage workers, under some modified form of the food-stamp plan which can meet the pocketbooks of these shamefully exploited workers and will safeguard that the food gets distributed to these people without interference or discrimination by landlords or their agents."

INDEX

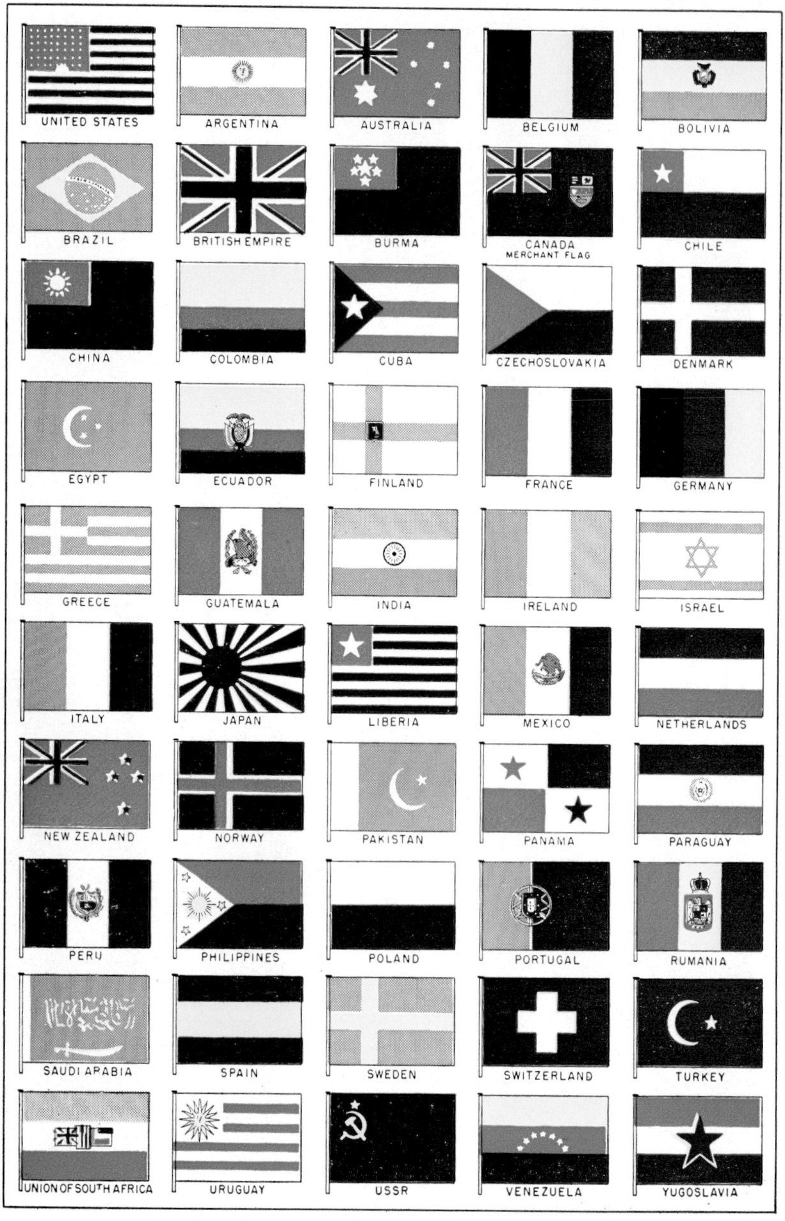

FLAGS OF THE LEADING NATIONS OF THE WORLD

THE WINSTON DICTIONARY

for Home, School and Office

With Every Word Defined
So That Its Use and Meaning
Can Be Easily Understood

ILLUSTRATED

THE JOHN C. WINSTON COMPANY

PHILADELPHIA
TORONTO

PRINTED IN U. S. A.

J-1-54

CONTENTS

ILLUSTRATIONS

Full-page Line Drawings

Part-page Line Drawings

PREFACE

A New Book on a New Plan. The Winston Dictionary has been made to embody two fundamentally new policies—simplicity and clearness of definition, and practical facility of use. One would suppose, indeed, that these two obvious policies would be followed in any dictionary; yet the art and practice of dictionary making have been too deeply incrusted with tradition to keep abreast of the times. Actual use of the dictionaries available reveals many definitions harder to understand than the words defined; and, to increase the difficulty, dictionary makers have usually failed to take advantage of the typographical and editorial devices which make for easy and convenient use. No wonder the dictionary habit languishes when a searcher for information cannot find it in a shape he can readily understand and use; and in young people, particularly, the discouragement is likely to be so great that the habit will never be formed.

Simplicity and Clearness. The Winston Dictionary makes each entry immediately clear. At considerable expense of space it defines every word in simple, everyday language, so that even a child can find and apply the needed information at once, without the burden (which few will assume) of consulting some distant page for further explanations.

The necessity of compressing much information into little space has developed a stilted dictionary style very hard to understand, and has hitherto been deemed a sufficient excuse for self-definition and for the use of technical and abstruse words. For example, a reader may look up *contagious*, and find that it means "communicable or spreading by contagion." This is practically self-definition; so he looks up *contagion*, the key word, which he finds to be "transmission of disease." Under *transmission*, some hundreds of pages away, he finds "the act of transmitting; state of being transmitted." He may look below to the verb *transmit* and find the ultimate key to his problem; or he may satisfy himself with a guess long before he has run the definition down by such repeated references.

Facility of Use. Every possible effort has been made to create a book which will yield its information in the quickest way. The typography is an outstanding feature. Each main entry is printed in large, bold-faced type, so that the desired word is strikingly easy to locate on the page. The type used in the body of the definitions is also of a broader face than usual and has a correspondingly greater legibility. The definitions, as has been pointed out, are so simply worded as never to require the reader to search further for the explanation of an obscure or technical term. Moreover, in the case of variant spellings of the same word, as *calcimine* and *kalsomine*, the definition is given under each entry (with indication of the preferred form), so that the searcher is spared the exasperation of finding under *kalsomine* some such expression as "variant of *calcimine*, which see"; and similarly with alternative terms for the same concept, as *swingletree* and *whippletree*, *ornithorhynchus* and *duckbill.*

Wealth of Verbal Illustration. Thousands of words are much more easily understood from their context in sentences than from formal definitions. For this reason, the Winston Dictionary gives many more illustrative sentences and phrases than any other dictionary of the same scope.

Pictorial Illustrations. In a similar way the meanings of many words can be immediately made clear by pictures. The illustrations in this dictionary are new pictures prepared for their teaching value in clarifying the meanings of words that need pictorial illumination.

Pronunciation. The pronunciation of words is indicated by a phonetic respelling with diacritical markings. The system is a simplified adaptation of those in most common use in school and college textbooks. As a further aid to the quick pronunciation of each word, the Key to Pronunciation is given at the foot of each page.

Vocabulary. The selection of the vocabulary of the Winston Dictionary has been made with particular care. It includes not only all the words in ordinary use, but also the vocabularies of science, history, civics, and current events that are increasingly coming into use in both elementary and secondary schools. Particular attention has been given to the very considerable new vocabulary that has grown out of the World War, radio, aviation, and the advance of general science.

Special Features. The Winston Dictionary includes several unusual features calculated to furnish essential information and to stimulate scholarly interest. Not only does it give in convenient form the tables of *Weights and Measures, Abbreviations*, etc., usually found in such volumes, but it also gives a most valuable chapter entitled *How Our Language Has Grown*, which should be mastered by every English-speaking person. *Word Formation* is treated in a special appendix, in which are listed the common prefixes and suffixes, and the most important Greek and Latin stems appearing in English words, this appendix thus serving as a practical word list for the study of etymology. Another feature of unusual value is a *Dictionary of Mythology*, which is particularly needed in explaining allusions to the religions not only of the Greeks and Romans but also of the Teutonic races and those of ancient Egypt and India. In the *Dictionary of Persons and Places* will be found the outstanding characters whose names stand for achievement in government, art, literature, science, politics, philanthropy, and other branches of human activity, and the more important geographical names, with statistical information. The *Glossary of Business Terms* is also of great value in these days when the practical affairs of life are claiming more and more attention in school and home.

HOW OUR LANGUAGE HAS GROWN

The study of a foreign language may have given you your first realization of the relationship between English and the other languages of the world. When you begin the study of a foreign speech, you are surprised to find how many words in the language you are studying are like English words. If you study Latin, you will meet, for instance, the word *parens,* which by the simple change of the *s* to *t* becomes our English word *parent.* The words *rumor, November, animal* are exactly like the English words; *trānsfero* 'transfer,' *arma* 'arms,' and a great many more are easily recognized by their resemblance to English words.

If you study French, you will have the same experience. In French you will find, for instance, *annoncer* 'announce,' *consoler* 'console,' and a large number of other words much like their English equivalents.

The English language, therefore, bears a certain resemblance to several other languages. A very large proportion of its vocabulary is derived from French and Anglo-Saxon, themselves closely related languages, and from Latin; and its structure and fundamental vocabulary show that it is related to Greek, Russian, Sanskrit, and the other languages comprising what is known as the Indo-European family of languages. And, as is the case with the descendants of human families, English has some traits from all the languages which have helped to make her what she is.

The story of the birth and development of English is most interesting. Twelve or thirteen centuries ago England was not the busy, important island she is now, but was covered with forests and inhabited by the Britons, a people belonging to a race called the Celts. They used one of the forms of the Celtic language, for no *English* language was then in existence.

Over on the low coastal lands of Europe, where your maps show you Denmark and Holland and northern Germany, lived tribes of hardy pirates called the Angles, the Saxons, and the Jutes. These peoples spoke a Teutonic language, somewhat like the present German language, or perhaps more like the Dutch spoken in Holland. The pirates, in their many-oared boats, made their way to the coast of Britain in search of food or of treasure. But once on the shores of the island, they found this land so much pleasanter than their own cold and stormy home on the other side of the North Sea that many of them decided to stay and make new homes for themselves in Britain.

And thus grew up in Britain the English tongue, or Anglo-Saxon, often called *Old English* to distinguish it from modern English, a result of the mixture of the dialects spoken by the two strongest invading tribes. The name of the country, too, was changed, and became Angleland or Engelond, taking the name of one of the pirate tribes. From this it is easy to see how the name became *England* and the language came to be called *English.*

Though at first many Anglo-Saxon words seem entirely unfamiliar, a closer study will show you a number whose resemblance to English is easily recognizable. *Morgen tid* is easily converted into *morning tide.* *Godes* means *of God* or *God's,* for the apostrophe has come to take the place of the *e* in the Old English possessive. *Condel* becomes *candle* by only a slight change, and *beorht* shifts the position of *r* and becomes *bright.*

A rather hasty study shows how nearly related are modern English and Old English. But there is another interesting fact to be observed in this study. The life of these people was so simple that it was occupied chiefly with the simplest needs of existence—eating and drinking and keeping themselves alive in spite of many foes. It naturally followed that the words that have been inherited by modern English from the Anglo-Saxon tongue are for the most part simple words. These simple words are sometimes called *homely* words, because they "come home" to people as the everyday words of everyday life. Such words are *home, light, fire, God.* In this list are also included most of our common prepositions and conjunctions, such as *to, from, over, and.*

A new element was brought into the language, however, by the introduction of Christianity in the sixth and seventh centuries. The English were heathen, worshiping many gods who, they believed, presided over the forces of nature. Thus there were Thor, the thunderer, famous for his strength, and Balder, the sun god, and many others. But in the year 597 there came from Rome a missionary of the Christian religion, named Saint Augustine. Other missionaries followed him, who established the church in Britain and converted many of the people. The church services were read in Latin. And so there came into the language a number of Latin words, some of them having a Greek origin. These words, for the most part, have to do with religion and the church, as *bishop, priest, creed,* and similar words. Such words do not come to us in the exact Latin form. As they were used by the Anglo-Saxons, they came to be slightly changed. The word *bishop* will show how such modifications came about. The Latin form was *episcopus* (compare the English word *episcopal* 'pertaining to a bishop'); under the influence of the Anglo-Saxon it became *biscop,* for the tendency of the simple, unlearned English was to shorten the long, ponderous Latin words, and to change the *p* to a *b;* our modern word is *bishop,* the *sc* being changed to *sh* for the sake of greater smoothness in pronunciation. Similar changes took place in many of the other Latin words which at this time enriched the language.

But the most important new element was yet to come. In 1066 a band of men from the continent of Europe, under the leadership of William of Normandy, known as William the Conqueror, landed in England. These people, known as Normans, or Norman French, came from a district in the northwestern part of France, called Normandy. As their name shows, the Normans were originally Northmen, from the shores of Denmark, Sweden, and Norway. During their piratical raids they had often landed on the coast of France, and being pleased with the fertile soil and the balmy climate, had at last forced the king of France to grant them some territory, and made permanent homes for themselves in the land.

But the Northmen had adopted the civilization and, in large part, the language of the French. This language was a form of the Latin language, for the Gauls, ancestors of the French, had been subjects of the Romans and had used their speech, adapting it to their own speech and needs. Thus the Norman-French spoken by William of Normandy and his followers was a tongue founded on the Latin, or, as it is often called, a Romance language, because it was one of those languages based on the speech of the Romans.

Thus was brought into England an entirely new element. And it had come to stay; for the Normans in a great battle conquered the Saxon king, Harold, and William became king of England. As the Normans were now the ruling race on the island, French became the language used in law courts, the language of literature, of the rich, and of the nobles. French was taught in the schools. It was used at the court of the king. It was the language of writing.

The English, however, who hated the Normans as their conquerors and despised the French language as the language of the conquerors, clung to their native tongue. Thus for a long time the two languages existed side by side—French, the language of the noble, rich, and educated; English, the speech of the simple and the poor.

As time wore on, however, contempt on one hand and bitter hatred on the other gave way to a feeling of interest and friendship. The people ceased to be French and Anglo-Saxon, and became Englishmen, citizens of a common country. It thus became more and more necessary that all the people be able to communicate with each other; the Normans used more English, the English more French. The result was a new language, the slow growth of many years, the vocabulary of which was a mixture of native English and Norman-French, the grammar, largely English.

As we noticed that the words expressing simple, homely ideas are largely from Anglo-Saxon, so the language of learning and formal speech is from the French; for the Norman-French were more highly civilized and educated than the Saxons. As the French had Latin as its foundation, a large Latin element came into English, in changed form, with the French, and it often happened that a French word was adopted with nearly the same meaning as a Saxon word already in use, the French word serving to invest the idea named with an air of learning, elegance, or culture. The following pairs of words, from native English and from Latin-French sources. respectively, will help to make this clear:

home—residence	hide—conceal	break—destroy
show—signify	freeze—congeal	keep—maintain
help—relieve	get—acquire	kind—gracious
dear—precious	king—sovereign	buy—purchase
hard—difficult	horseman—cavalier	feeling—sentiment

It is thus to Anglo-Saxon that we look back as the source of our familiar, everyday speech; to Latin, directly or through French, as that tongue which has enriched and dignified our language with the terms of science, learning, and more formal speech. For as education became more general, the similarity of the French words to the parent Latin made it easy and natural to borrow words directly from the Latin; and in the sixteenth century, especially, a host of words were adopted from the Latin, and also from the Greek. In modern times this tendency has not been altogether lost; the investigators in science and technical fields continually fall back upon the treasures of the Latin and Greek vocabularies to name the new concepts arising in the progress of their work.

As a result of these many additions to the English vocabulary, the language has become wonderfully rich and expressive, but it is not alone dependent upon borrowing for additions to its word stock. Quite as many words are made by uniting stems, or by joining a prefix or a suffix to a stem, thus making compounds of various kinds. The habit of making a new word by combining two other words was a strong one in Anglo-Saxon, as it is still in modern German. The Anglo-Saxon said *book-house* for *library*, and *tree-wright* for *carpenter*, and the English language of today is given to making similar ones, such as *boathouse, bathhouse, storehouse, smokehouse, fire house, greenhouse*, etc., *shipwright, wheelwright, playwright*, and many more such words, which in most cases require no explanation and are consequently called self-explaining compounds. When we say *railroad, trolley car, steamboat, blacksmith, waterworks, department store*, and *life-insurance company*, we are using such self-explaining compounds, whether we write the elements joined or separate.

When, as explained above, we resort to borrowing from other languages, the process of adaptation is equally interesting. Most words of more than one syllable are formed of two or more distinct parts. The most important part, or foundation, of the word—the part that really gives the *thought* of the word—is called the *root* or the *stem*. For instance, in the word *marine*, the stem is *mar-*, from the Latin word *mare* (pronounced mä'rā), meaning sea. Thus *marine* means pertaining to the sea; we have extended its meaning so that we say that marines are soldiers of the sea, and marine trade means trade on the sea. The same stem appears in the words *maritime* and *mariner*. The stem of the word *dictate* is *dict-*, meaning speak or say, a stem which we find also in such words as *predict*, to say before or foretell, *contradict*, to say against or oppose, and in *dictionary*. The stem of the Latin word for foot is *ped-*, which occurs as a stem in *pedal*, *quadruped*, and *pedestrian*.

In many words there are two parts of equal importance, or two stems. Such a word is *phonograph*. *Phon-* is a Greek stem meaning sound, found also in *telephone*, *megaphone*, and other words. *Graph-* is also a Greek stem meaning write; you will recognize it in such words as *telegraph*, *autograph*, and *paragraph*. A phonograph, then, in its literal meaning, is a contrivance that writes sounds.

The word *thermometer* is another two-stem word. *Therm-* is from a Greek word meaning heat, and *meter* is from a common stem meaning measure, so that a thermometer is an instrument that measures heat. A thermostat is a device for keeping the temperature of a room always the same; for *therm-*, as we have seen, means heat, and *stat-* is from a Greek word meaning to stand still. Many more such words of two stems you will find from a study of an unabridged dictionary.

Words of one stem, however, are much more common than those of two or more. Most words have just one important part, whose meaning is more or less changed by a less important syllable. If this syllable is put before a stem, it is called a *prefix;* if it is added after a stem, it is called a *suffix*.

A knowledge of prefixes and suffixes is a great help to a fuller understanding of English words. A prefix usually alters the fundamental meaning of the word; a suffix changes the part of speech. Thus if to the word *take* we prefix *mis-*, the meaning becomes to take wrongly, or to make an error; for *mis-*, means wrongly. If, however, we add to *mistake* the suffix *-en*, the word is changed from a verb to an adjective, though the fundamental meaning of the word is not changed. Again, to prefix *trans-* to the word *plant* adds to the original meaning the idea of removal from place to place, but to add to *transplant* the suffix *-able* merely makes the word an adjective without changing the thought.

A few cases will illustrate the extent to which words may be built up from stems, prefixes, and suffixes. Though the literal meaning of such a word is by no means always the same as the meaning in common use, yet the literal meaning helps decidedly in the understanding of the word. Thus, to take a word with Latin elements, the prefix *trans-* means across, the stem *lat-* means to carry, and the suffix *-ion* means the act or state; but *translation*, literally the act of carrying across, is most commonly used of the special carrying or transference from one language to another; and similarly *bene-fact-or*, literally a well-do-er, one who does well, comes to mean one who confers a benefit. In the case of native English words, the elements sometimes merge so completely into one another as almost to lose their identity: we may not think of a *seer* as a *see-er*; the *s* sound added to *one* and *two* in *once* and *twice*, representing an old adverbial suffix, is not now felt as such; and the suffix *-th* used to form abstract nouns, though easily recognized in *strength*, *width*, *height* (for older *heighth*), etc., is less obvious in *youth* (young-ness), *health* (whole-ness), *filth* (foul-ness), *birth* (a bearing), *sloth* (slow-ness), *aftermath* (after-mowing).

Some of the common prefixes, suffixes, and combining forms from Latin and Greek are included in the list given on the next page. Notice that a prefix frequently becomes changed in form for the sake of greater ease in pronunciation. Thus *ad-*, meaning *to* or *for* or *against*, becomes *ac-* when used with a stem whose first letter is *c*, as in the words *accept* (*ac-*, to; *-cept*, take: take to oneself) and *accede* (*ac-*, to; *-cede*, come, go: agree). When *ad-* is placed before a stem beginning with *f*, the *d* becomes *f*. Such a change has taken place, for instance, in the word *affix* (*af-*, to; *-fix*, fasten: attach). Again, *con-* becomes *col-* when used before a stem whose initial letter is *l*, as in the word *collect* (*col-*, together; *-lect*, gather: gather together). Though there are hybrid words, (that is, words in which the elements are derived from different languages), such as *auto-mobile*, *false-hood*, *book-case*, most compounds (as *wheel-wright*, *bene-factor, tele-phone*) and words made by joining a prefix to a stem (as *over-board, circum-scribe, syl-logism*) are composed of elements from the same language; hence the examples given below with the prefixes and suffixes from Latin and Greek will be found to illustrate Latin and Greek stems in English.

Word	Prefix	Stem	Suffix	Literal Meaning	Common Meaning
transportation	*trans-* across	*port-* carry	*-ation* act or state	act of carrying across	act, means, or system of carrying
portable		*port-* carry	*-able* able to be	capable of being carried	easily carried
pacify		*pax (pac-)* peace	*-fy* to make	to make peaceful	to soothe or quiet
preferment	*pre-* before	*fer-* carry	*-ment* resulting state	result of being carried before	advancement ahead of others
supervisor	*super-* over	*vid- (vis-)* see	*-or* one who, that which	one who sees over	an overseer
antipathy	*anti-* against	*path-* feeling	*-y* state or condition	state of feeling against	aversion or strong dislike

The following prefixes and suffixes from Latin and Greek are common in English. Fuller lists are given in the appendix on Word Formation, page 907.

Prefixes	Used in Words
a-, ab-, away from	*a*-vert, *ab*-duct, *ab*-stract, *ab*-sent, *ab*-normal
ad-, ac-, af-, ag-, al-, etc., to, at	*ad*-here, *ad*-just, *af*-fix, *ac*-cept
ante-, before	*ante*-date, *ante*-cedent
anti-, ant-, against (Greek)	*anti*-slavery, *anti*-septic, *ant*-agonist
auto-, self (Greek)	*auto*-mobile, *auto*-graph, *auto*-biography
bi-, two	*bi*-sect, *bi*-cycle, *bi*-ped
circum-, around	*circum*-ference, *circum*-stance
con-, col-, com-, co-, cor-, with or together	*con*-nect, *col*-lect, *co*-öperate
de-, away from, from, down	*de*-tach, *de*-scend, *de*-pend
equi-, equal	*equi*-distant, *equi*-angular
ex-, ec-, e-, out, from	*ex*-cept, *ec*-centric, *e*-volve
in-, il-, im-, ir-, en-, etc., in, on; also, not	*in*-dorse, *in*-clude, *il*-legal
inter-, between	*inter*-pose, *inter*-cede
mon-, mono-, one, alone (Greek)	*mono*-tone, *mono*-log
per-, through: used also as intensive	*per*-forate, *per*-fervid
post-, after, behind	*post*-pone, *post*-script
pre-, before	*pre*-pare, *pre*-cede
pro-, before, for, forth, forward	*pro*-vide, *pro*-cession, *pro*-pose
re-, red-, back, again	*re*-gain, *re*-read, *red*-olent
sub-, suc-, suf-, sug-, sup-, under	*sub*-ject, *suf*-fer, *sup*-port
trans-, across	*trans*-fer, *trans*-pose, *trans*-port
uni-, one	*uni*-form, *uni*-corn

Suffixes	Used in Words
-able, -ible, capable of being	measur-*able*, percept-*ible*
-age, amount, state	mile-*age*, cour-*age*
-ance, -ence, relation to, condition of	appear-*ance*, independ-*ence*
-ar, -ary, relating to	muscul-*ar*, pulmon-*ary*
-ate, to act, to cause	anim-*ate*
-ation, action, condition	form-*ation*, civiliz-*ation*, degener-*ation*
-cy, quality, state	pira-*cy*, luna-*cy*
-fy, to make	satis-*fy*, horri-*fy*
-ic, -ical, pertaining to, like	geometr-*ic*, class-*ical*,
-ion, action, being, condition	miss-*ion*, rebell-*ion*
-ious, full of	relig-*ious*, suspic-*ious*
-ize, (Br. *-ise*), to make like, affect with	pulver-*ize*, oxid-*ize*
-ive, having the character, given to	talkat-*ive*, posit-*ive*
-ment, resulting state or condition	astonish-*ment*, banish-*ment*, atone-*ment*
-ous, full of, of the nature of	peril-*ous*, wondr-*ous*
-ty, condition or character	digni-*ty*, puri-*ty*

The Latin roots, prefixes, and suffixes, however, form by no means the whole of the English language. They have been spoken of first because they are the easiest to understand, as they are little changed in form and meaning from the original. The real strength of the language, the bulk of the familiar, simpler words, the words of common, everyday speech, as, *house, man, woman, child, give, take, buy, sell, sweet, sour, long, short, in, out, to, from, I, you, he, she,* etc., are Teutonic in origin.

A study of the following list of Anglo-Saxon words and related words of modern English, and of Anglo-Saxon prefixes and suffixes, will give some idea of the influence of the Teutonic element in familiar speech. For a fuller list of prefixes and suffixes, see appendix on Word Formation, page 907.

Word Stems

bacan: bake, baker
bēaten: beat, beater
beran: bear, bearer, bearable
bindan: bind, [1]bond, [3]bound
bītan: bite, bitten, bit
būgan: bow, bough
cat: cat, kitten
cēap: cheap, chapman
clīofan: cleave, cleft, cliff
cnāwan: know, knew, knowledge
cunnan. cunning
dæg: day
dǣlan: deal
dragan: draw, drag, dray
faran: far, fare, farewell
flēon: flee, fled
hlāf: loaf
hām: home, [2]ham
hēafod: head
licgan: lie, lay
mæg: may, might, mighty
rǣdan: read, riddle
stān: stone
tredan: tread, trot
trēow: true, truth
witan: wit, wot, witty

Prefixes

al-, all-, quite: *al*-one, *al*-most, *al*-mighty
an-, a-, on: *a*-bed, *a*-board
for-, thoroughly: *for*-give, *for*-get
fore-, before: *fore*-bode, *fore*-cast
gegn-, gēan-, back or again: *gain*-say
in-, in: *in*-come, *in*-step, *in*-land
mis-, wrong: *mis*-lead, *mis*-trust, *mis*-deed
of-, off-, from: *off*-spring, *off*-shoot
ofer-, above or over: *over*-cast, *over*-throw
twi-, two: *twi*-light
un-, not: *un*-holy, *un*-do, *un*-bind
under-, under: *under*-stand, *under*-bid
ūt-, out: *out*-come, *out*-run
with-, against: *with*-stand

SUFFIXES

-*dōm*, power, office, or state: king-*dom*, prince-*dom*, free-*dom*

-*ede*, characterized by: dogg-*ed*, quick-witt-*ed*

-*en*, pertaining to or of the nature of: gold-*en*, wool-*en*

-*er*, one who or that which: bak-*er*, work-*er*

-*feald*, times or multiplied by: mani-*fold*, two-*fold*

-*hād*, state or rank: boy-*hood*, man-*hood*

-*ing*, (originally son of), part of: farth-*ing* (fourth part)

-*isc*, of the nature of: child-*ish*, fool-*ish*

-*lēas*, loose from or without: hope-*less*, power-*less*

-*līce*, -*līc*, *lic*, like: home-*ly*, love-*ly*, lady-*like*

-*ling*, diminutive: duck-*ling*, gos-*ling*

-*ling*, -*long*, in the direction of: head-*long*

-*ness*, state, quality, or condition: good-*ness*, black-*ness*.

-*scipe*, originally, shape or form: used to make abstract nouns: king-*ship*, wor-*ship*, hard-*ship*

-*sum*, apt or adapted to: tooth-*some*, win-*some*

-*ung*, -*ing*, verbal noun suffix: sing-*ing*

-*weard*, in the direction of: back-*ward*

-*wīse* (not a suffix in Anglo-Saxon), way or manner: no-*wise*, like-*wise*

Year by year, century by century, English has grown and changed. How different from present-day English, for instance, is the language of Shakespeare! New words have come into the language from foreign tongues, and often old words have dropped out of use altogether or come gradually to have new meanings. Thus the old word *clept*, meaning named, and *an*, meaning if, are no longer used. The word *humorous* originally meant, not funny or causing laughter, but full of whims. *Straight* meant at one time immediately, and *presently* had once the same meaning: when a man said, "I will come *straight* (or *presently*)," he meant *immediately*, and not *in a short time*. Other words have acquired new meanings through being misunderstood. Thus the expression *an humble pie* (or, as now used, *humble pie*) is the result of the wrong division of *a numble pie*, the *numbles* being the heart, liver, and lungs of a deer, from which was made a pie to be served to the servants; so that *to eat (h)umble pie* formerly meant to be in the position of a servant, but now means to humble oneself or to apologize.

The English language is a "going concern." Its business is expanding constantly and there is continual need for new words to meet the demands made upon it. In these times of intense living and rapid progress we are daily finding new things, inventing new things, thinking new things, for which we need new words. Anything that affects a great many people or receives extensive consideration adds its quota of words to the vocabulary. Thus, the automobile has been responsible for many words now in common use. Some of these are old words given a special meaning, such as *radiator*, *speedometer*, *gear*, *cylinder*, *muffler*, *magneto*, *storage battery*, *jack;* others are more definitely limited in their use to the automobile, such as *windshield*, *chauffeur*, *brake bands*, *inner tube*, *spare*, *balloon tire*, *piston rings*, *carburetor*, *skid*, *park*. The motion picture is responsible for the common use or readaptation of words such as *photoplay*, *screen*, *animated cartoon*, *reel*, *cinema*, *release*. The war was fruitful in new words: *tank*, *camouflage*, *doughboy*, *barrage*, *dugout*, *no man's land*, *slacker*, *conscientious objector*, *tear gas* are examples. The development of the airplane has given us such words as *seaplane*, *bombing plane*, *airdrome*, *ace*, *zoom*, *nose dive*, *tail spin*. And most recently, the rapid development of radio transmission with its wide appeal has caused many people to talk about *rheostat*, *grid leak*, *variable condenser*, *radio-frequency*, *tube*, *aërial*, *antenna*, *cat whisker*, *vernier*, *ear phones*, *loud-speaker*, *crystal detector*, to say nothing of *static* and *broadcast*. In the colloquial speech, every year witnesses a new crop of slang expressions which come and go, generally without leaving any permanent trace on the language, but occasionally winning on their merit a right to general acceptance. Such words are *mob* (Latin *mobile vulgus*, the volatile common people), to *pit* (one person or team against another, a term originating in cock fighting), *logrolling*, etc. At the present time *sweater*, *skyscraper*, *bleachers*, *auto*, *phone*, *mollycoddle*, *hustle*, *stunt*, *moonshiner*, to mention typical examples, have either thrown off their colloquial character or are sanctioned through being used by persons of discriminating taste.

Though the Anglo-Saxon language forms, as has been shown, the basis of the English language, and the Latin has made a very large contribution, many words in our vocabulary have been transferred bodily from languages other than these two. In fact, the English vocabulary is made up of so many elements from different languages that it has become extremely cosmopolitan. It is favorably disposed towards taking in any new word that promises to be useful, irrespective of its source. In this respect, the English language is like America: it has remarkable powers of assimilation, and once a word is adopted, that word becomes so thoroughly a part of the language that we no longer think of it as a foreign word. Italy, Spain, India, Arabia, the West Indies, all have contributed their share. From Italy we have borrowed many terms pertaining to music and to the refinements of cultured life. Such words are *libretto*, *crescendo*, *balcony*, *cameo*, *intaglio*, *catacomb*. Spain has contributed many words naming commercial products, as *indigo*, *guava*, *vanilla*, *alligator*, as well as some others such as *matador* and *mosquito*. From Holland and Scandinavia come words pertaining to commerce and the sea, among which are *schooner*, *wagon*, *yacht*, *skipper*, *sloop*. India and Arabia with their products sent words naming them, such as *chintz*, *candy*, *orange*, *borax*, *divan*, *alcohol*, *amber*, *coffee*, *cotton*. Biblical literature brings us Hebrew terms, as *cherub*, *jubilee*, *amen*, *alleluia*, *ephod*.

America's contributions to the English language have come from the Mexicans, from the peoples of South America and the West Indies, and from the North American Indians. From Mexico come *chocolate*, *coyote*, *tomato;* from South America, *tapioca*, *guano*, *jaguar*, *quinine*, *alpaca;* from the West Indies, *hurricane*, *maize*, *potato*. The North American Indians have given us such terms as *moccasin*, *moose*, *raccoon*, *tobacco*, *squaw*, *papoose*, *succotash*—words which name things common in an Indian's daily life.

In this way has the whole world contributed and still is contributing to the languages of the English-speaking peoples. What wonder, then, that the English tongue is full and rich and flexible? Its wealth of meaning, its beauty, its power, are the result of centuries of growth and of the gifts bestowed by East and West, by North and South. Such a heritage may well be the pride of every Englishman and every American.

DIRECTIONS FOR THE USE OF THIS BOOK

I. GENERAL DIRECTIONS

Hyphens. In the main listing, in which accent is not indicated, a light hyphen is used to mark division into syllables, and heavy hyphen to separate the parts of a compound word; as, **self-de-ni-al.** In the pronunciation, the light hyphen is omitted under an accent, and a double hyphen, retained even under an accent, is used in compound words; as, sĕlf″=dē-nī′ăl. In variants and derivatives, printed in boldface, usually without pronunciation, the heavy hyphen is used in compound words, even under an accent; the lighter hyphen is used between syllables, except under an accent.

Variant Spellings. If two or more variations of the spelling of a single word exist, as *calcimine* and *kalsomine*, *gauge* and *gage*, each is listed in its proper alphabetical place, with pronunciation, grammatical information, *and definition.* With the listing of the preferred form appears a full definition of all the uses of the word, followed by "Also" and the permissible, but not preferred, variant form. With the listing of the permissible variant form, there is a complete, though concise, definition, followed (1) by "Also" and the preferred variant form, marked *Pfd. S.* (preferred spelling); or (2), in case the definition under the preferred form gives additional information, by "See" and the preferred form, marked *Pfd. S.* A variant, however, which, if entered in alphabetical order, would appear in the immediate neighborhood of the preferred form, is listed at the end of the definition of the preferred form, but is not given main entry. Thus *silvan* and *sylvan* are entered and defined in their respective alphabetical places; but *programme* is listed as a variant, without a special definition, at the end of the entry of *program.*

Proper Names. Included within the main vocabulary are Biblical and mythological names, and the names of characters conspicuous in literature or familiar in allusion, as *King Arthur, Ali Baba, Don Quixote.* For convenience in special study, the mythological names, with many additions, are assembled in a special Appendix; and another Appendix contains the names of a very carefully selected list of outstanding persons (except Biblical characters) and places.

Foreign Words which are so frequently used as to be a part of the educated person's vocabulary, though still felt to be foreign, are included in the main text of the Dictionary, marked with an asterisk [*]. Words that have come to be regarded as English, even though of foreign form, are included in the vocabulary with no special mark, as *abattoir, wigwam, acropolis, kindergarten, stucco, bonanza.* A special Appendix contains a very liberal selection of the foreign words, phrases, and quotations likely to be heard or met with in reading.

Homographs. Words spelled alike but from different sources and, usually, of different meanings, are given separate listings, each preceded by a small numeral, as ^{1}*bark*, the outer covering of a tree, ^{2}*bark*, the cry of a dog, and ^{3}*bark*, a kind of boat.

Prefixes and Suffixes are given in their alphabetical place in the vocabulary, and are treated with unusual fulness. For convenience in special study, they are assembled, with additions, in a special Appendix.

Pronunciation. Every main listing is followed immediately by its pronunciation in parentheses, except in the case of expressions consisting of two or more words each of which is listed elsewhere. The pronunciation of inflectional forms and derivatives is given whenever not completely regular. After a pronunciation has been given in full, an alternative pronunciation or the pronunciation of an inflectional form or derivative is sometimes abbreviated by omitting a part of the word which is pronounced the same way in all the forms; as, **de-ter-mine** (dē-tûr′-mĭn), [*p.t.* and *p.p.* -mined (-mĭnd), *p.pr.* -min-ing].

Grammatical Information. The part of speech of each word is given by the appropriate abbreviation immediately following the pronunciation. The plurals of nouns, comparatives and superlatives of adjectives, and principal parts of verbs are given in light brackets whenever they are in any way irregular; but see the following section for fuller details.

Expressions and Word Groups which have acquired a special meaning not immediately obvious, as *wave length*, *New Testament*, are given in bold-faced type under the word in the expression which appears most likely to be looked up. In many doubtful cases such expressions are given under more than one word, as *heir apparent*. Some expressions, conventionally printed as two words, are in practical use treated as one, and are listed in the vocabulary as independent words, as *army worm*, *spinning wheel*, *steam engine*.

Derivatives. Important derivative words frequently met with are as a rule listed in the main vocabulary with full definitions. The meanings of some derivatives, however, can be easily and directly inferred from the definition of the basic word, as *rapidly* from *rapid*, *whiteness* from *white*. Such words are given in bold-faced type, without definition, following the definition of the basic word, with syllabification, accent, and, in case of need, pronunciation. Derivatives which have developed special meanings of their own, as *contractor*, *adorable*, *suspenders*, are listed and defined separately.

II. SPELLING AND PRONUNCIATION OF INFLECTIONAL FORMS

Plural of Nouns.

1. Add *-s* (pronounced *s*) if the singular ends in the sound of *f*, *k*, *p*, *t*, or *th* as in *bath*—that is, any sound with which the sound of *s* readily combines; as, *puffs*, *rakes*, *tops*, *hopes*, *hats*, *births*.

2. Add *-s* (pronounced *z*) if the singular ends:

(*a*) In a vowel sound; as, *trees*, *laws*.

(*b*) In the sound of *b*, *d*, *g*, *ng*, *l*, *m*, *n*, *r*, *v*, or *th* as in *bathe*—that is, any voiced consonant sound with which the sound of *z* readily combines; as, *cabs*, *odes*, *bags*, *tongs*, *bells*, *plumes*, *tins*, *fires*, *Slavs*, *tithes*.

3. Add *-es* (pronounced *ĕz*, *ĭz*) if the singular ends in a sibilant, or hissing sound, whether voiced or unvoiced—that is, in the sound of *s*, *sh*, *ch*, *z*, *zh*, or *j*—and has no final silent *-e;* as, *dresses*, *marshes*, *matches*, *topazes*.

4. Add *-s* if the singular ends in a sibilant sound and has a final silent *-e*, the final *e* combining with the *s* to form an additional syllable, pronounced *ĕz*, *ĭz;* as, *laces*, *mustaches*, *avalanches*, *breezes*, *garages*, *edges*.

Plurals formed according to the rules stated above are considered regular, and are not given in the Dictionary unless required for some special reason.

The following classes of irregular plurals are noted for reference, but the examples are not exhaustive:

5. Nouns ending in *-o* preceded by a vowel form the plural in *-os* (pronounced *ōz*); as, *cameos*, *folios;* nouns ending in *-o* preceded by a consonant usually form the plural in *-oes;* as, *echoes*, *heroes*, *mosquitoes*, *mottoes*, *negroes*, *potatoes*, *tomatoes*, etc.; but musical terms ending in *-o* add *-s* only, whether a vowel or a consonant precedes the *o;* as, *altos*, *adagios*.

6. Nouns ending in *-y* preceded by a consonant form the plural by changing the *y* to *i* and adding *-es* (the *-ies* being pronounced *ĭz*); as, *lady*, *ladies;* but nouns ending in *-y* preceded by a vowel add *-s* (pronounced *z*); as, *turkey*, *turkeys*.

7. A few nouns ending in the sound of *f* change the *f* to *v* and add *-es* (pronounced *z*); as, *loaf*, *loaves;* *wife*, *wives*.

8. A few plurals are formed without the addition of *-s*. Such are *geese*, *mice*, *children*, *oxen*, *deer*, *sheep;* foreign plurals, as *theses*, *alumni*, *phenomena*, *cherubim;* *dice*, in which the *s* of *dies* has been changed to *c* and transposed; and other scattered cases.

Third Person Singular of Verbs.

The third person singular indicative active of all regular and most irregular verbs is formed according to rules 1–4 for the plural of nouns; as, *gets, hears, wishes, rises.*

Principal Parts of Verbs.

1. Regular verbs add *-ed* to the infinitive to form the past tense and past participle, and *-ing* to form the present participle. The *-ing* is always pronounced as an additional syllable.

2. If the infinitive ends in *-d* or *-t* not silent, the *-ed* is pronounced *ĕd;* as, *ended, heated.*

3. If the infinitive ends in the sound of *b, g, ng, j, l, m, n, r, v, z, zh,* or *th* as in *bathe*—that is, any voiced consonant except *d*—, or in a vowel sound, the *-ed* is pronounced *d;* as, *hurled, hurrahed;* but note rules 5 and 6 below.

4. If the infinitive ends in the sound of *f, k, p, s, sh, ch, th* as in *bath*—that is, any unvoiced consonant except *t*—, the *-ed* is pronounced *t;* as, *amassed, attacked, marched;* but note 5 and 6.

Principal parts derived according to the rules stated above are considered regular, and are not given in the Dictionary unless required for some special reason.

The following classes of irregularly formed parts are noted for reference, but the examples are not exhaustive:

5. (*a*) Final *-e*, whether silent or not, is dropped before *-ed;* as, *agreed, judged.*

(*b*) Final silent *-e* preceded by a consonant is dropped before *-ing;* as, *racing, judging;* but observe a few special cases, as *singeing, dyeing,* in which the omission of the *e* would cause confusion. In words where final silent *-e* is preceded by a consonant and *l* or *r*, those letters unite with *-ing* to form a single syllable; as, *tumbling* from *tumble, centring* from the British spelling *centre.*

(*c*) Final *-y* preceded by a consonant is changed to *i* before *-ed*, but is retained before *-ing;* as, *cried; flying; replied, replying.*

(*d*) Final silent *-e* preceded by *i* is dropped and the *i* is changed to *y* before *-ing;* as, *dying, lying.*

6. Monosyllabic verbs, or polysyllables accented on the last syllable, ending in a single consonant preceded by a single vowel, double the final consonant before *-ed* or *-ing;* as, *plan, planned, planning; prefer, preferred, preferring.*

7. A considerable number of verbs have entirely irregular parts; as, *buy, bought, buying; bear,* past tense *bore,* past participle *borne,* present participle *bearing.* A few are defective, as *can* (no infinitive form), past tense *could.*

8. In British usage, verbs ending in unaccented *-el* double the *l* before *-ed* and *-ing;* as, *travelled, revelling.* These forms are not preferred in American usage, and are not recorded in this book.

Comparison of Adjectives and Adverbs.

1. Adjectives of one syllable are regularly compared by adding *-er* and *-est* to the positive degree to form respectively the comparative and superlative; as, *old, older, oldest.*

2. A final silent *-e* is dropped before these endings; as, *fine, finer, finest.*

3. Adjectives of more than two syllables are regularly compared by using the words *more* and *most* with the positive; as, *beautiful, more beautiful, most beautiful.* (See chart on next page.)

4. Adjectives of two syllabes are compared by adding *-er, -est* (but see rule 2), if the resulting form is easily pronounced; otherwise they are compared by the use of *more* and *most.* Usage varies according to individual taste; but the table given on the next page shows the general tendency.

5. Adverbs are usually compared by the use of *more* and *most,* though a few use *-er* and *-est;* as, *near, nearer, nearest; often, oftener, oftenest.* Some adverbs are not compared; as, *here, there, now, then.*

Comparatives and superlatives formed in accordance with the rules stated above are considered regular, and are not given in the Dictionary unless required for some special reason.

The following cases of irregular comparison are noted for reference, but the examples are not exhaustive:

6. Monosyllabic adjectives or polysyllables accented on the last syllable, ending in a single consonant preceded by a single vowel, double the final consonant before *-er* and *-est;* as, *big, bigger, biggest.*

7. Adjectives ending in *-y* change the *y* to *i* before *-er* and *-est;* as, *happy, happier, happiest.*

8. A number of the commoner adjectives, and a few adverbs, are entirely irregular; as, *good, better, best; ill, worse, worst; far, farther, farthest.*

9. Many adverbs which may function also as prepositions have an adjective function when compared, forming the comparative in *-er* and the superlative by adding *-most* to the positive or comparative; as, *in, inner, inmost* or *innermost.* Some adverbs have only the superlative; as, *fore, foremost.*

Adjectives ending in unaccented	Use in comparison	As in the following examples:
-y, -ly	usually suffixes *-er, -est*	hardy, lovely;
-en, -ful, -some	either method; more often suffixes	rotten, wooden, helpful, handsome;
-al, -ile, -et	usually *more* and *most*	formal, facile, dulcet;
-ous, or other suffix containing a sibilant	usually *more* and *most*	gracious, peevish;
-like, -ine, or other suffix containing a long vowel	usually *more* and *most*	lifelike, bovine;
-ed, -ing, forming participial adjectives	almost always *more* and *most;* sometimes suffixes if the participial sense is lost	refined, stirring, conceited.

III. GUIDE TO PRONUNCIATION

The pronunciation of every main listing, and of all forms or derivatives concerning which any doubt could arise, is given by respelling within parentheses according to a simple phonetic key, accessible throughout the Vocabulary at the foot of the page. The following notes are intended as an amplification of this key. It should be borne in mind that these notes are an explanation of the *symbols used in the key,* rather than of English spelling. Each of the symbols stands for one, and only one, specific sound value; but in many cases the sound value is represented in ordinary English spelling by any of several letters or combinations of letters, as shown by the illustrative words.

The principal stress in a word of two or more syllables is indicated by a primary accent ['] placed after the syllable to be stressed. A secondary accent is indicated by this same mark doubled ["]. A word may have a primary accent and no more, as *sea'man;* a primary and one or more secondary accents, as *ear'mark", huck'le-ber"ry, au"to-in-tox"i-ca'tion;* or, occasionally, two primary accents, as *back'bone'.*

Symbols for English Sounds

ā as in *a*te, p*a*le, f*a*vor, prev*ai*l, w*ei*gh, pl*a*y, st*ea*k, v*ei*l, th*e*y, su*è*de (long *a*): in accented, sometimes in unaccented, syllables.

ȧ as in foli*a*ge, sen*a*te, legisl*a*tive: usually the equivalent of a long *a* sound in an unaccented syllable.

â as in r*a*re, p*a*rent, prep*a*re, th*e*re, *ai*r, h*ei*r, b*ea*r, w*ea*r: usually in an accented syllable before *r.*

ă as in c*a*t, g*a*rret, c*a*nteen (short *a*): in accented and unaccented syllables.

ȧ as in *a*sk, comm*a*nd (intermediate *a*).

ä as in c*a*lm, f*a*ther (broad or Italian *a*).

ȧ as in loc*a*l, *a*ffect, *a*pply: usually equivalent to short *a* in an unaccented syllable ending in a consonant.
ȧ as in ban*a*n*a*, p*a*rade, sof*a*, comm*a*, retali*a*tory (indeterminate *a*): usually equivalent to intermediate *a* in an unaccented syllable not ending in a consonant.
ē as in *e*ven, sc*e*ne, str*ea*m, m*ee*t, s*ei*ze, p*eo*ple, k*ey*, mach*i*ne, y*ie*ld, C*æ*sar, c*œ*liac (long *e*): in accented and sometimes in unaccented syllables.
ė as in *e*vent, cr*e*ate: usually the equivalent of long *e* in an unaccented syllable.
ĕ as in def*e*ct, *e*dge, *e*nd*e*d, *æ*sthetic (short *e*): in accented and unaccented syllables.
ĕ as in nov*e*l, rec*e*nt: usually equivalent to short *e* in an unaccented syllable.
ẽ as in writ*e*r, th*e*, conf*e*rence, elix*i*r, alt*a*r, act*o*r: frequently occurring before *r;* sometimes final; always in an unaccented syllable.
ī as in f*i*ne, del*igh*t, *i*dea, fl*y*, *ai*sle, *aye*, h*eigh*t, *eye*, t*ie* (long *i*): in accented and unaccented syllables.
ĭ as in s*i*t, d*i*ssect, m*y*th: used also for final *y*, as in lovel*y*, seeml*y*, and for *ie* in such forms as lad*ie*s, hurr*ie*s: in accented and unaccented syllables.
ō as in h*o*pe, ech*o*, f*oa*m, d*oe*, bl*ow*, s*ew*, b*eau*, th*ough*, d*oo*r, y*eo*man (long *o*): in accented and unaccented syllables.
ō as in potato, *o*bey, cor*o*net: usually equivalent to long *o* in an unaccented syllable.
ô as in c*o*rd, ad*o*rn, c*a*ll, l*aw*, c*augh*t, f*ough*t (intermediate *o*): in accented, sometimes in unaccented, syllables.
ô as in d*o*g, s*o*ft, obl*o*ng, g*o*ne (open *o*): in accented and unaccented syllables.
ŏ as in c*o*ral, h*o*t, *o*blation, wh*a*t (short *o*): in accented and unaccented syllables.
ŏ as in c*o*mpare, c*o*nnect: usually equivalent to short *o* in an unaccented syllable.
ū as in c*u*re, *u*nit, *yew*, *you*, curf*ew*, f*eu*d (long *u*): in accented and sometimes in unaccented syllables.
ū as in *u*nite, circ*u*late, h*u*mane: usually equivalent to long *u* in an unaccented syllable.
û as in b*u*rn, occ*u*r, f*u*r, m*y*rtle, w*o*rd, ref*e*r, l*ea*rn, m*i*rth, amat*eu*r: usually in an accented syllable, before an *r* in the same syllable.
ŭ as in h*u*rry, *u*pset, c*u*t, h*o*ney, en*ou*gh (short *u*): in accented and unaccented syllables.
ŭ as in foc*u*s, s*u*pport, s*u*cceed: usually equivalent to short *u* in an unaccented syllable.
ōō as in b*oo*t, f*oo*l, d*o*, tr*ue*, r*u*le, thr*ew*, rh*eu*matism, s*ou*p: in accented, sometimes in unaccented, syllables.
ŏŏ as in f*oo*t, p*u*t, tearf*u*l, c*ou*ld: in accented and unaccented syllables.
oi as in b*oi*l, garg*oy*le.
ou as in g*ou*t, h*ow*l, s*au*erkr*au*t, b*ough*.
g as in *g*et, *g*old, *gh*ost (hard *g*).
j as in *j*oy, *g*entleman, a*g*e, e*dg*e, cor*d*ial (soft *g*).
y as in *y*et, *y*ear, *y*ou.
ng as in so*ng*, to*ng*ue, u*n*cle, fi*n*ger.
ch as in *ch*in, ca*tch*, ques*t*ion, righ*te*ous.
sh as in *sh*ow, *s*ure, ac*ti*on, ten*si*on, tena*ci*ous, ceta*ce*an, ma*ch*ine.
zh as in a*z*ure, mea*s*ure, provi*si*on, rou*g*e.
th as in *th*in, ba*th*, e*th*er (voiceless).
th as in *th*en, ba*th*e, ei*th*er (voiced).
hw as in *wh*en, *wh*y, *wh*ere.
b, d, f, h, k, l, m, n, p, r, s, t, v, w, z, are used with their ordinary English values.
c, q, x, are not used in indicating pronunciation. The letter *c* in the conventional spelling is generally equivalent to **k** or **s**; *q*(*u*) = **k**(**w**); and *x* = **ks** or **gz**, or, initially, **z**.

Sounds in Foreign Languages

The trained ear can perceive many small differences between sounds in foreign languages and the nearly equivalent English sounds, which most persons cannot perceive at all, or, if they do, cannot exactly imitate. Some foreign sounds, however, are so strikingly different from any English sounds that an attempt should be made by every educated person to pronounce them with a fair degree of correctness. The symbols used to represent these sounds are given below.

kh the guttural *ch* in German a*ch* (äkh) or Scottish lo*ch* (lôkh): used also for the very similar sound in German i*ch* (ĭkh).

ṅ the French nasal, as in e*nfant* (äṅ″-fäṅ′), bi*en* (byâṅ), n*om* (nôṅ).

ö used for the sound of umlauted *o* in German (written *ö* or, sometimes, *oe*), as in sch*ö*n (shön), G*oe*the (gö′tẽ); also in French words for *eu* final and before *s*, *x*, *z*, *t*, as in f*eu* (fö), dans*eu*se (däṅ″söz′), eût (ö). French *eu* in other cases is pronounced like **û** in the key, as in p*eu*r (pûr), dans*eu*r (däṅ″sûr′).

ü for the sound of umlauted *u* in German, as in f*ü*r (für), L*ü*beck (lü′běk), and for *u* in French, as in l*u*ne (lün), d*u* (dü).

The symbol ẽ is used in English for the neutral unaccented vowel, as in writ*er* (rīt′ẽr) or in the definite article when unstressed (*th*ẽ); for the unstressed final *e* so common in German, as in hab*e* (hä′bẽ); and for certain cases of French mute *e*. In pronouncing French, however, the ẽ should be reduced to almost nothing. Thus *tout de suite* (too͞″ dẽ süēt′) is pronounced almost as too͞d″ süēt′.

The short open *o* so common in German and French, as in German d*o*ch, s*o*llen, French h*o*mme, acc*o*rder, is represented by the key symbol **ô**, usually to be pronounced very short.

The apostrophe ['] following an **r**, **l**, **m**, or **y** in French pronunciations indicates that the letter so marked is to be pronounced almost as ẽr, ẽl, ẽm, yẽ, but so closely with the preceding sound as not to make an additional syllable; as, *être* (âtr′: not as two syllables); *simple* (sâṅpl′); *rheumatisme* (rü″må″tĕsm′′); *Espagne* (ĕs″päny′′).

In the phonetic respelling of French words, one should observe carefully the combinations vowel + y and ü + vowel, as in *canaille* (kå″nȧy′′), *suis* (süē). If the manner of printing shows that the two letters are within the same syllable, the y and ü should be pronounced somewhat like vowels, but should not be given full syllabic value. The English words *yes* and *we*, for example, consist of ē + ĕs, and o͞o + ē, each run into one syllable; and similarly ȧ and y, as in the French pronunciation of *canaille* (kå″nȧy′′), and ü and ē, as in the pronunciation of *suis* (süē), must be run together into one syllable.

In French, all full syllables are pronounced with nearly equal stress; but there is usually a rising inflection or slight stress on the last syllable, which has somewhat the effect of the English accent. In this book, French words are shown with a primary accent on the last syllable, representing the rising inflection or slight stress, and with secondary accents on all other full syllables.

IV. ABBREVIATIONS USED IN THIS BOOK

An asterisk [*] indicates that the word so marked is felt to be foreign.
Small figures, 1, 2, etc., are placed before homographs for convenience of reference.
Figures are used in illustrations and captions to indicate relative size; as, **1/2**, or **×2**, indicates that the cut is one half, or twice, natural size.

abbr.	abbreviation	*fem.*	feminine	*Port.*	Portuguese
A. D.	*anno Domini* = in the year of our Lord	*Fr.*	French	*poss.*	possessive
adj.	adjective	*Ger.*	German	*p.p.*	participle, past
adv.	adverb	*Gk.*	Greek	*p.pr.*	participle, present
Ant.	antonyms	*illus.*	illustration	*prep.*	preposition
B. C.	before Christ	*interj.*	interjection	*pres.*	present
Br.	British	*It.*	Italian	*pron.*	pronoun
C.	centigrade	*Jap.*	Japanese	*p.t.*	past tense
cf.	*confer* = compare; see	*Lat.*	Latin	*ref.*	reference
Colloq.	colloquial (ism)	*lit.*	literally	*Rom.*	Roman
comp.	comparative	*masc.*	masculine	*Russ.*	Russian
conj.	conjunction	*n.*	noun	*Scot.*	Scotch
def.	definition	*neut.*	neuter	*sing.*	singular
Dial.	dialect; dialectal	*nom.*	nominative	*Span.*	Spanish
dim.	diminutive	*obj.*	objective	*specif.*	specifically
Du.	Dutch	*Obs.*	obsolete	*St.*	Saint
Eng.	English	*opp.*	opposite	*Syn.*	synonyms
esp.	especially	*orig.*	originally	*U. S.*	United States
etc.	*et cetera* = and so forth	*p.adj.*	participial adjective	*v.aux.*	verb, auxiliary
F.	Fahrenheit	*Pfd. S.*	preferred spelling	*v.i.*	verb, intransitive
		pl.	plural	*v.t.*	verb, transitive

THE WINSTON DICTIONARY

A

[1]**a** (*ȧ*; when stressed, ā), *indefinite article*, a contracted form of [1]*an*, used before words beginning with a consonant sound or a sounded *h* (as, *a* man, *a* unit, *a* house): **1**, one; any; **2**, (orig. a prep.: see [2]*a*), to, for, or in each; as, once *a* year.

[2]**a** (*ȧ*), *prep*., often felt to be the article, or joined to the following word with or without a hyphen: in; on; into; to; at; as, once *a* year; to go *a*-Maying; *a*fire; *a*float.

a- (*ȧ*-), *prefix*, **1**, (see [2]*a*), in; on; into; to; at; as, *a*fire; *a*shore; **2**, up; as, *a*rise; **3**, of; as, *a*kin; **4**, from; as, *a*vert; **5**, (before vowels, *an-*), without; not; as, *a*pathy; *an*archy.

Aar-on (âr′ŭn), *n*. in the Bible, the brother of Moses; the first high priest of the Hebrews (Exodus 4:13–16).

a-back (*ȧ*-băk′), *adv*. backward: said of sails pressed back against the mast: **taken aback**, surprised; disconcerted.

ab-a-cus (ăb′*ȧ*-kŭs), *n*. [*pl*. abacuses (-ĕz); abaci (-sī)], **1**, a device used for counting, consisting of beads or balls strung on wires or rods set in a frame; **2**, in architecture, a flat plate, as of stone, forming the top section of the capital of a column or pillar (see *architrave*, illus.).

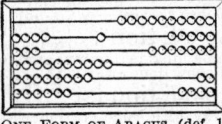

One Form of Abacus (def. 1)

a-baft (*ȧ*-bȧft′), *adv*. at, toward, or in the direction of, the stern, or back part of a ship; astern:—*prep*. toward the stern from; behind; as, *abaft* the funnel.

ab-a-lo-ne (ăb″*ȧ*-lō′nē), *n*. any of various sea mollusks, used for food in the Orient, whose shells are used for making buttons and beads.

[1]**a-ban-don** (*ȧ*-băn′dŭn), *v.t*. **1**, to give up entirely; as, to *abandon* a sinking ship; **2**, to desert; forsake; **3**, to yield (oneself) without restraint, as to an emotion or impulse.—*n*. **a-ban′don-ment**.

Syn. forsake, desert. To *abandon* is to leave entirely; as, the mother *abandoned* her child. To *forsake* is to leave by ceasing to stay with; as, he *forsook* his friends in time of need. To *desert* is to leave by breaking the bonds of faithfulness or honor; as, he *deserted* his wife; the soldier *deserted* his post.

[2]**a-ban-don** (*ȧ*-băn′dŭn; *Fr*. ȧ″bäṅ″dôṅ′), *n*. freedom of manner; dash; complete surrender to natural impulses.

a-ban-doned (*ȧ*-băn′dŭnd), *p.adj*. **1**, unrestrained; as, *abandoned* mirth; **2**, shameless; wicked.

a-base (*ȧ*-bās′), *v.t*. [*p.t*. and *p.p*. a-based′ (-bāst′), *p.pr*. a-bas′ing], **1**, to humble or degrade; deprive of self-respect; **2**, to lower or cast down, as in rank or office; **3**, to dishonor.—*n*. **a-base′ment**.

a-bash (*ȧ*-băsh′), *v.t*. to put to shame; disconcert.—*n*. **a-bash′ment**.

a-bate (*ȧ*-bāt′), *v.t*. [*p.t*. and *p.p*. a-bat′ed, *p.pr*. a-bat′ing], **1**, to lessen; diminish; **2**, to put an end to: obsolete except in law:—*v.i*. to decrease; moderate; subside; as, the storm *abates*.—*n*. **a-bate′ment**.

ab-a-tis (ăb′*ȧ*-tĭs; *Fr*. ȧ″bȧ″tē′), *n*. **1**, a barricade or defense of felled trees with sharpened branches pointed toward the enemy; **2**, in modern warfare, a barbed-wire entanglement. Also, **ab′at-tis**.

A bat-ter-y in radio, a battery, of low voltage and high amperage, connected across the terminals of the filament of a vacuum tube, the purpose of which is to heat the filament and thus cause the emission of negative electrons.

a-bat-toir (ăb″*ȧ*-twär′; *Fr*. ȧ″bȧ″-), *n*. a building in which animals are killed for market; a slaughterhouse.

Ab-ba (ăb′*ȧ*), *n*. **1**, father: a name for God found in the New Testament (Mark 14:36); **2**, a title of a bishop, used in some Eastern churches.

ab-ba-cy (ăb′*ȧ*-sĭ), *n*. [*pl*. abbacies (-sĭz)], the office or term of an abbot.

***ab-bé** (ȧ″bā′), [Fr.], *n*. **1**, an abbot; **2**, in France, a title of a priest or theological scholar in the Roman Catholic Church.

ab-bess (ăb′ĕs), *n*. the head of a nunnery, or community of women devoted to a religious life; a mother superior.

ab-bey (ăb′ĭ), *n*. [*pl*. abbeys (-ĭz)], **1**, an institution where a group of men or women live apart from the world, as in a monastery or a nunnery, and devote themselves to a religious life; **2**, the building in which they live; **3**, their church.

ab-bot (ăb′ŭt), *n*. the head of a monastery, or community of men devoted to a religious life; a father superior.—*n*. **ab′bot-cy** (ăb′ŭt-sĭ).—*n*. **ab′bot-ship**.

ab-bre-vi-ate (ă-brē′vĭ-āt), *v.t*. [*p.t*. and *p.p*. -at″ed, *p.pr*. -at″ing], to shorten; esp., to shorten (a word) by cutting off a part, as in *Dec*. for *December*, or *U.S*. for *United States*.—*n*. **ab-bre′vi-a″tor**.

ab-bre-vi-a-tion (ă-brē″vĭ-ā′shŭn), *n*. a cutting short; esp., the shortened or contracted form of a word or phrase, as *U.S*. for *United States*.—*abbr*. **abbr**.

Ab-di-as (ăb-dī′ăs), *n*. Obadiah: so called in the Douay Bible.

ab-di-cate (ăb′dĭ-kāt), *v.t.* [*p.t.* and *p.p.* -cat″ed, *p.pr.* -cat″ing], to give up or withdraw from; as, the king was forced to *abdicate* his throne:—*v.i.* to give up sovereign power.—*n.* **ab″di-ca′tion.**—*n.* **ab′di-ca″tor.**
Syn. surrender, renounce. (See resign.)

ab-do-men (ăb-dō′mĕn), *n.* the large cavity of the body below the diaphragm, containing the digestive organs.—*adj.* **ab-dom′i-nal.**

ab-duct (ăb-dŭkt′), *v.t.* **1,** to carry off by stealth or force; kidnap; as, to *abduct* a child; **2,** in anatomy, to draw away (a limb) from the mid line of the body.—*n.* **ab-duc′tion.**—*n.* **ab-duc′tor.**

a-beam (ȧ-bēm′), *adv.* opposite the middle part of a ship's side; in a direction at right angles to a ship's keel.

a-bed (ȧ-bĕd′), *adv.* in bed; as, the sluggard lies late *abed;* also, on a bed.

A-bed-ne-go (ȧ-bĕd′nē-gō), *n.* in the Bible, a Jewish captive in Babylon who, with Meshach and Shadrach, survived the fiery furnace (Daniel 3).

A-bel (ā′bĕl), *n.* in the Bible, the second son of Adam and Eve, slain by his brother Cain (Genesis 4).

ab-er-ra-tion (ăb″ĕr-ā′shŭn), *n.* **1,** a wandering from the right way or from a normal type or course; error; **2,** mental disorder.

a-bet (ȧ-bĕt′), *v.t.* [*p.t.* and *p.p.* a-bet′ted, *p.pr.* a-bet′ting], to encourage; aid or assist, esp. in an act of a criminal nature.—*n.* **a-bet′ter; a-bet′tor.**—*n.* **a-bet′ment.**
Syn. aid, assist, countenance, sanction, support, sustain, uphold.

a-bey-ance (ȧ-bā′ăns), *n.* a holding or keeping inactive for a time; a holding over; temporary inactivity.

ab-hor (ăb-hôr′), *v.t.* [*p.t.* and *p.p.* -horred′ (-hôrd′), *p.pr.* -hor′ring], to shrink from with horror, dread, or disgust; loathe.
Syn. despise, detest, hate, dislike.

ab-hor-rence (ăb-hŏr′ĕns), *n.* a feeling of detestation; loathing.

ab-hor-rent (ăb-hŏr′ĕnt), *adj.* hateful; repulsive; repugnant.

a-bide (ȧ-bīd′), *v.i.* [*p.t.* and *p.p.* a-bode′ (-bōd′) or a-bid′ed, *p.pr.* a-bid′ing], to dwell; reside; remain; continue:—*v.t.* **1,** to put up with; tolerate; **2,** to wait for.
Syn. lodge, sojourn, stop, live.

a-bid-ing (ȧ-bīd′ĭng), *p.adj.* staying; steadfast; as, an *abiding* faith; *abiding* purpose.—*adv.* **a-bid′ing-ly.**

a-bil-i-ty (ȧ-bĭl′ĭ-tĭ), *n.* [*pl.* abilities (-tĭz)], power or capacity to do or act; mental gifts; skill; talent.
Syn. capacity, talent. *Ability* is the general term for power, either physical or mental; as, he has *ability* as a speaker. *Capacity* signifies the native strength of the mind, developed or not; as, he has a greater natural *capacity* than his brother. *Talent* means unusual ability, developed by training; as, a musician of *talent.*

ab-ject (ăb′jĕkt), *adj.* cast down; ignoble; mean; hopeless; as, *abject* poverty.—*adv.* **ab′ject-ly.**—*n.* **ab′ject-ness.**
Syn. groveling, slavish, cringing, beggarly, despicable.—*Ant.* dignified, elevated, lofty.

ab-jure (ăb-jo͝or′), *v.t.* [*p.t.* and *p.p.* -jured′ (-jo͝ord′), *p.pr.* -jur′ing], to renounce or give up upon oath; recant; disavow; withdraw formally from; as, to *abjure* allegiance.—*n.* **ab″ju-ra′tion.**—*n.* **ab-jur′er.**
Syn. retract, abandon, forswear.—*Ant.* maintain, uphold, support.

ab-la-tive (ăb′lȧ-tĭv), *adj.* in grammar, designating, or pertaining to, a case, esp. in Latin, denoting primarily place from which:—*n.* the ablative case; also, a word in that case.

a-blaze (ȧ-blāz′), *adj.* and *adv.* on fire; well alight; in a blaze; hence, eager; in a state of excitement; ardent.

a-ble (ā′bl), *adj.* **1,** possessed of sufficient power or means; as, he is not *able* to pay so much; **2,** well qualified mentally; clever; talented; competent; as, an *able* lawyer.—*adv.* **a′bly.**

-a-ble (-ȧ-bl), *adj. suffix,* meaning: **1,** able to; as, dur*able;* delect*able;* **2,** capable of being; as, read*able;* **3,** fit to be; as, laud*able;* detest*able;* **4,** inclined to; characterized by; as, peace*able;* season*able.* Also, in certain combinations, -i-ble or -ble; as, poss*ible;* terr*ible;* vis*ible;* no*ble.*

a-ble-bod-ied (ā′bl-bŏd″ĭd), *adj.* physically strong and sound; capable or efficient for duty.

a-bloom (ȧ-blo͞om′), *adj.* and *adv.* in blossom or in flower; blooming.

ab-lu-tion (ăb-lū′shŭn), *n.* **1,** a washing or cleansing of the body; **2,** a ceremonial washing done as a religious duty; **3,** the liquid used in washing.

ab-ne-gate (ăb′nē-gāt), *v.t.* [*p.t.* and *p.p.* -gat″ed, *p.pr.* -gat″ing], to refuse (a thing) to oneself; reject; give up or surrender.—*n.* **ab″ne-ga′tion.**

ab-nor-mal (ăb-nôr′măl), *adj.* irregular; deformed; unnatural; not conforming to rule or type.—*adv.* **ab-nor′mal-ly.**—*n.* **ab″nor-mal′i-ty.**

a-board (ȧ-bōrd′), *adv.* on or within a ship or railroad train: **close aboard,** close alongside:—*prep.* on board of; on or within (a ship or vehicle).

[1]**a-bode** (ȧ-bōd′), one form of the past tense and past participle of *abide.*

[2]**a-bode** (ȧ-bōd′), *n.* **1,** a place of continued residence; a dwelling; home; **2,** the act of staying in a place.

a-bol-ish (ȧ-bŏl′ĭsh), *v.t.* to do away with; put an end to; as, a war to *abolish* slavery.—*adj.* **a-bol′ish-a-ble.**

ab-o-li-tion (ăb″ō-lĭsh′ŭn), *n.* **1,** the act of destroying or doing away with something; extinction; annulment; **2,** the state of being done away with.

ab-o-li-tion-ist (ăb″ō-lĭsh′ŭn-ĭst), *n.* a person who favors doing away with some law or custom; esp., one of those who, during the Civil War, believed that negro slavery should be ended.

a-bom-i-na-ble (ȧ-bŏm′ĭ-nȧ-bl), *adj.* hateful; odious; offensive; unclean; vile.—*adv.* **a-bom′i-na-bly.**

a-bom-i-nate (ȧ-bŏm′ĭ-nāt), *v. t.* [*p.t.* and *p.p.* -nat″ed, *p.pr.* -nat″ing], to regard with feelings of disgust or hatred; abhor; detest; loathe.

a-bom-i-na-tion (ȧ-bŏm″ĭ-nā′shŭn), *n.* detestation; hatred or disgust; also, anything vile or hateful.
Syn. nuisance, annoyance, offense, shame.

ab-o-rig-i-nal (ăb″ō-rĭj′ĭ-năl), *adj.* original; first, existing from the beginning, or from prehistoric times:—*n.* an animal or plant which has originated in a given place.—*adv.* **ab″o-rig′i-nal-ly.**

ab-o-rig-i-nes (ăb″ō-rĭj′ĭ-nēz), *n.pl.* **1,** the first or earliest known inhabitants of a country; **2,** the native animals or plants of a given region.

a-bor-tion (ȧ-bôr′shŭn), *n.* **1,** a birth which occurs before the normal time; **2,** any fruit which fails to mature; **3,** any failure to complete what has been begun.—*adj.* **a-bor′tion-al.**

a-bor-tive (ȧ-bôr′tĭv), *adj.* **1,** born too soon; **2,** imperfectly developed; **3,** unsuccessful; coming to nothing.

a-bound (ȧ-bound′), *v.i.* **1,** to exist or occur in great numbers or quantity; 2, to be abundantly supplied; teem: followed by *in* or *with;* as, the sea *abounds* with fish.

a-bout (ȧ-bout′), *adv.* 1, around; on every side; 2, near by; 3, in a reversed position; half around; as, to face *about;* 4, in rotation; as, turn *about* is fair play; 5, in a state of action; as, he is up and *about:*—*prep.* 1, concerning; relating to; as, a story *about* a bear; connected with; as, something wrong *about* the plan; 2, around; on all sides of; as, the things *about* us; 3, near or close to; on the person of; as, I haven't a dollar *about* me; 4, near to in number, degree, etc.; as, to stay *about* an hour; 5, here and there in; on or to different parts of; as, to travel *about* the state; 6, on the point of; intending: with a verbal noun or an infinitive; as, *about* to go.

a-bove (ȧ-bŭv′), *adv.* 1, in a higher place; overhead; 2, specif., in heaven; 3, before, esp. in a book or writing; as, from what has been said *above:*—*prep.* 1, over; higher than; 2, superior to; as, to be *above* deceit; 3, beyond; in excess of; surpassing; as, happiness *above* measure.

a-bove-board (ȧ-bŭv′bōrd″), *adv.* openly; without trickery:—*adj.* fair and open: a figure from card playing.

ab-rade (ăb-rād′), *v.t.* [*p.t.* and *p.p.* -rad′ed, *p.pr.* -rad′ing], to wear or rub away; injure or break (a surface) by rubbing or friction; scrape off.

A-bra-ham (ā′brȧ-hăm), *n.* in the Bible, the first great patriarch of the Hebrews, founder of the nation: orig. called *Abram* (Genesis 11).

ab-ra-sion (ăb-rā′zhŭn), *n.* 1, a wearing or rubbing away, as of coins by constant handling; 2, an injury, as to the skin, from rubbing or scraping.

ab-ra-sive (ăb-rā′sĭv), *adj.* tending to rub, wear, or scrape away:—*n.* a substance, as sand or emery, used to wear away or polish.

a-breast (ȧ-brĕst′), *adv.* 1, side by side; 2, in the same line; equally advanced; as, *abreast* of the times.

***a-bri** (ȧ″brē′), [Fr.], *n.* a shelter from enemy shells, as a cellar or dugout.

a-bridge (ȧ-brĭj′), *v.t.* [*p.t.* and *p.p.* a-bridged′ (-brĭjd′), *p.pr.* a-bridg′ing], 1, to shorten or condense, as in making a smaller or more concise dictionary from a larger one; 2, to curtail or cut down, as liberties or authority.—*n.* **a-bridg′ment.**

a-broad (ȧ-brôd′), *adv.* 1, widely; far and wide; 2, beyond the limits of house or country; out of doors; 3, in or to a foreign country; as, to go *abroad.*

ab-ro-gate (ăb′rō-gāt), *v.t.* [*p.t.* and *p.p.* -gat″ed, *p.pr.* -gat″ing], to abolish, annul, or repeal by authority.—*n.* **ab″ro-ga′tion.**—*adj.* **ab′ro-ga-tive.**

ab-rupt (ăb-rŭpt′), *adj.* 1, rising or dropping at a sharp angle from a certain level; ending suddenly; steep; 2, sudden; 3, unceremonious; 4, disconnected.—*adv.* **ab-rupt′ly.**—*n.* **ab-rupt′ness.**

Syn. sharp, precipitous. (See steep.)

Ab-sa-lom (ăb′sȧ-lŏm), *n.* in the Bible, the favorite son of King David, slain while rebelling against his father's authority (2 Samuel 18).

ab-scess (ăb′sĕs), *n.* a collection of pus in the tissues of the body; a boil.

ab-scond (ăb-skŏnd′), *v.i.* to flee or retire in haste, often secretly; hide oneself; disappear, often to avoid the law.—*n.* **ab-scond′ence.**—*n.* **ab-scond′er.**

ab-sence (ăb′sĕns), *n.* 1, the state or period of being away; 2, lack; want; 3, abstraction of thought; inattention; as, *absence* of mind.

ab-sent (ăb′sĕnt), *adj.* 1, not present; away; 2, lacking; 3, buried in thought; preoccupied:—*v.t.* (ăb-sĕnt′), to withdraw (oneself); keep (oneself) away.

ab-sen-tee (ăb″sĕn-tē′), *n.* one who is or stays away from a given place, situation, duty, or the like; esp., a landlord so doing.—*n.* **ab″sen-tee′ism.**

ab-sent-ly (ăb′sĕnt-lĭ), *adv.* in an inattentive manner.

ab-sent–mind-ed (ăb′sĕnt=mīn″dĕd), *adj.* inattentive; abstracted; preoccupied; forgetful.—*adv.* **ab″-sent–mind′ed-ly.**—*n.* **ab″sent–mind′ed-ness.**

ab-sinth (ăb′sĭnth), *n.* a green, aromatic, alcoholic liquor containing wormwood, anise, etc. Also, **ab′sinthe.**

ab-so-lute (ăb′sō-lūt), *adj.* 1, free from any limitation or condition: applied esp. to a government in which the ruler is free to act unrestrained by any law; 2, perfect; complete; as, *absolute* quiet prevailed; 3, positive; real; unquestionable; 4, unmixed; pure; free from everything else. —*adv.* **ab′so-lute-ly.**—*n.* **ab′so-lute-ness.**

Syn. supreme, arbitrary, unconditional.

ab-so-lu-tion (ăb″sō-lū′shŭn), *n.* 1, the act of releasing from an obligation, or freeing from the consequences of sin; 2, the declaring an accused person innocent of a charge; acquittal; 3, forgiveness of sins in the sacrament of penance.

ab-so-lut-ism (ăb′sō-lūt″ĭzm), *n.* 1, the state of being without limitation; 2, the principles underlying despotic government; 3, in theological doctrine, predestination; foreordination by God of one's salvation or damnation.—*n.* **ab′so-lut″ist.**

ab-solve (ăb-sŏlv′), *v.t.* [*p.t.* and *p.p.* -solved′ (-sŏlvd′), *p.pr.* -solv′ing], 1, to release or set free, as from an obligation; 2, to clear of crime or guilt; acquit.—*adj.* **ab-solv′a-ble.**—*adj.* **ab-solv′ent.**

ab-sorb (ăb-sôrb′), *v.t.* 1, to drink in; suck or swallow up; as, a sponge *absorbs* water; 2, to engross or engage (the attention) wholly; 3, to occupy (a person) fully. —*adj.* **ab-sorb′a-ble.**—*n.* **ab-sorb″a-bil′i-ty.**

ab-sorb-ent (ăb-sôr′bĕnt), *adj.* having a tendency to suck or soak up, or drink in, liquids or the like; as, *absorbent* cotton:—*n.* an absorbent substance.

ab-sorb-ing (ăb-sôr′bĭng), *p.adj.* engaging the attention fully; intensely interesting.—*adv.* **ab-sorb′ing-ly.**

ab-sorp-tion (ăb-sôrp′shŭn), *n.* 1, the process or act of taking or sucking in, or swallowing up; 2, the mental state of being entirely occupied or engrossed. —*adj.* **ab-sorp′tive.**

ab-stain (ăb-stān′), *v.i.* to refrain; hold aloof; keep oneself away; as, to *abstain* from the use of tobacco.

Syn. fast, desist.—*Ant.* indulge, gratify.

ab-stain-er (ăb-stān′ẽr), *n.* one who voluntarily goes without something; esp., one who does not use intoxicating liquor; a teetotaler.

ab-ste-mi-ous (ăb-stē′mĭ-ŭs), *adj.* moderate and sparing in the use of food and drink; temperate.—*adv.* **ab-ste′mi-ous-ly.**—*n.* **ab-ste′mi-ous-ness.**

ab-sti-nence (ăb′stĭ-nĕns), *n.* self-denial; specif., the partial or total giving up of food or of alcoholic drink.—*adj.* **ab′sti-nent.**—*adv.* **ab′sti-nent-ly.**

Syn. moderation, sobriety, temperance.

ab-stract (ăb′străkt), *n.* 1, a summing up of the principal parts of a book, article, etc.; brief summary; 2, a quality, idea, or the like, considered as existing alone, having no connection with anything else: **in the abstract,** with reference only to theoretical considerations, and not based upon actual facts:—*adj.* **1**, considered apart from concrete facts or a real situation; as, *abstract* justice; **2**, difficult; complicated; hard to understand; **3**, expressing a quality apart from anything having the quality; as, *strength* and *swiftness* are *abstract* nouns:—*v.t.* (ăb-străkt′), **1**, to take or draw away; steal; **2**, to reduce to a summary; abridge; **3**, to turn away the attention of.—*adv.* **ab′stract-ly.**—*n.* **ab′stract-ness.**

Syn., *v.* detach, remove, withdraw, divert.

ab-stract-ed (ăb-străk′tĕd), *p.adj.* absent-minded; inattentive; preoccupied; lost in thought.—*adv.* **ab-stract′-ed-ly.**—*n.* **ab-stract′ed-ness.**

ab-strac-tion (ăb-străk′shŭn), *n.* **1**, absence of mind; abstractedness; **2**, a taking away; theft; **3**, the process of mentally separating a quality from the object of which it is a part; also, the quality so separated; **4**, hence, something unreal.

ab-struse (ăb-stro͞os′), *adj.* obscure; hidden; hard to understand.—*adv.* **ab-struse′ly.**—*n.* **ab-struse′ness.**

ab-surd (ăb-sûrd′), *adj.* contrary to reason or sense; ridiculous; silly.—*adv.* **ab-surd′ly.**—*n.* **ab-surd′ness.**

Syn. foolish, incorrect, monstrous, senseless, wild, nonsensical.—*Ant.* wise, sensible.

ab-surd-i-ty (ăb-sûr′dĭ-tĭ), *n.* [*pl.* absurdities (-tĭz)], **1**, the state of being ridiculous; **2**, something that is ridiculous, unreasonable, or silly.

a-bun-dance (ȧ-bŭn′dăns), *n.* plenty; profusion; more than enough; as, an *abundance* of riches.

a-bun-dant (ȧ-bŭn′dănt), *adj.* ample; plentiful; more than enough.—*adv.* **a-bun′dant-ly.**

a-buse (ȧ-būz′), *v.t.* [*p.t.* and *p.p.* a-bused′ (-būzd′), *p.pr.* a-bus′ing], **1**, to use improperly; misuse; **2**, to maltreat; treat rudely or wrongfully; **3**, to use violent or insulting language toward; upbraid; **4**, to violate or ravish:—*n.* (ȧ-būs′), **1**, mistreatment; improper or excessive use; **2**, violent or insulting speech; **3**, a corrupt practice or vicious habit.—*n.* **a-bus′er.**

Syn., *v.* reproach, defame, slander.—*Ant.*, *v.* commend, praise.

a-bu-sive (ȧ-bū′sĭv), *adj.* **1**, inclined to indulge in cruel treatment; **2**, inclined to use harsh or insulting language; also, of language, harsh or insulting.—*adv.* **a-bu′sive-ly.**—*n.* **a-bu′sive-ness.**

a-but (ȧ-bŭt′), *v.i.* [*p.t.* and *p.p.* a-but′ted, *p.pr.* a-but′ting], to border (upon); be in contact at one end: with *on*, *upon*, *against;* as, the house *abuts* on the hill.

a-but-ment (ȧ-bŭt′mĕnt), *n.* **1**, that which borders upon something else; **2**, a pier or other structure supporting the end of an arch or bridge (see [1]*arch*, illus.).

a-byss (ȧ-bĭs′), *n.* a deep or bottomless chasm.—*adj.* **a-bys′mal** (ȧ-bĭz′măl).

Ab-ys-sin-i-an (ăb″ĭ-sĭn′ĭ-ăn), *adj.* pertaining to Abyssinia (now officially called *Ethiopia*), a country of Africa east of the upper part of the Nile:—*n.* a native of Abyssinia, or Ethiopia.

ac- (ăk-), *prefix*, a form of *ad-*, (which see), used before *c* and *q;* as, accede; acquire.

-ac (-ăk), *adj. suffix*, influenced or affected by; having; as, ammoni*ac;* pertaining to; as, pericardi*ac:* often forming adjectives used as nouns; as, mani*ac*.

a-ca-cia (ȧ-kā′shȧ), *n.* **1**, any of a genus (*Acacia*) of flowering trees or shrubs growing in warm regions and producing tannin, medicines, perfumes, and an intoxicating liquor; **2**, the dried juice from two of these trees: usually called *gum arabic;* **3**, the false acacia, or common locust tree.

ac-a-dem-ic (ăk″ȧ-dĕm′ĭk), *adj.* **1**, pertaining to a school, college, academy, or the like, or to higher learning; **2**, scholarly; hence, theoretical, but not practical; formal; as, an *academic* discussion.—*adj.* **ac″a-dem′i-cal.**—*adv.* **ac″a-dem′i-cal-ly.**

a-cad-e-mi-cian (ȧ-kăd″ē-mĭsh′ăn), *n.* a member of an academy, or society of learned men.

a-cad-e-my (ȧ-kăd′ē-mĭ), *n.* [*pl.* academies (-mĭz)], **1**, a private school or seminary for the teaching of the higher branches of education; **2**, a school for instruction in a special subject; **3**, an association or society of men famous in literature, science, and art; **4**, a building devoted to educational purposes.

A-ca-di-an (ȧ-kā′dĭ-ăn), *adj.* of or pertaining to Acadia, or Nova Scotia:—*n.* a native of Acadia.

a-can-thus (ȧ-kăn′thŭs), *n.* [*pl.* acanthuses (-ĕz); acanthi (-thī)], a plant of southern Europe, characterized by deeply cleft leaves. In Greek art the leaves are frequently used, in conventionalized form, as a decoration on the tops of Corinthian pillars.

ACANTHUS AS DECORATION

ac-cede (ăk-sēd′), *v.i.* [*p.t.* and *p.p.* -ced′ed, *p.pr.* -ced′ing], **1**, to agree or yield; as, to *accede* to some request; **2**, to succeed, as to a throne.

Syn. assent, consent, acquiesce, comply, coincide, concur, approve.

ac-cel-er-ate (ăk-sĕl′ẽr-āt), *v.t.* [*p.t.* and *p.p.* -at″ed, *p.pr.* -at″ing], **1**, to hasten; cause to move or advance faster; **2**, to cause to occur earlier.—*adj.* **ac-cel′er-a-tive.**—*adj.* **ac-cel′er-a-to-ry.**

Syn. hurry, promote, quicken, further.—*Ant.* delay, hinder, impede, retard.

ac-cel-er-a-tion (ăk-sĕl″ẽr-ā′shŭn), *n.* **1**, increase in speed; also, the state of being increased in speed; **2**, change in velocity, as regards either speed or direction; also, the rate of such change.

ac-cel-er-a-tor (ăk-sĕl′ẽr-ā″tẽr), *n.* **1**, one who or that which increases speed; **2**, any mechanical attachment or device for increasing speed; specif., in an automobile, the throttle, or lever which regulates the amount of gasoline fed to the motor.

ac-cent (ăk′sĕnt), *n.* **1**, the stress laid by the voice upon a particular syllable of a word, so as to render it more prominent than the rest; **2**, any of several characters used in writing and printing to show which syllable is to be stressed [′, ″, ˎ], or to indicate the pronunciation of a vowel [′, ˋ, ^]; **3**, a peculiarity of pronunciation or expression distinguishing the language of a particular part of a country, or the pronunciation of one speaking a foreign language; **4**, in *pl.*, speech; language; **5**, the emphasis placed upon certain notes of a bar of music, or the mark indicating it:—*v.t.* (ăk-sĕnt′; ăk′sĕnt), **1**, to pronounce with special stress; also, to mark with a sign for special stress; **2**, to dwell upon or emphasize, as a passage of music.—*adj.* **ac-cen′tu-al.**

ac-cen-tu-ate (ăk-sĕn′tū-āt), *v.t.* [*p.t.* and *p.p.* -at″ed, *p.pr.* -at″ing], **1**, to emphasize or stress in speaking or writing; **2**, to lay stress upon; make prominent, as opinions.—*n.* **ac-cen″tu-a′tion.**

ac-cept (ăk-sĕpt′), *v.t.* **1**, to take or receive with approval, as a gift or an office; **2**, to agree to, or acquiesce in; as, to *accept* his terms; **3**, to recognize as true; as, to *accept* his excuse; **4**, to agree to pay; as, to *accept* a draft; **5**, to resign oneself to; as, he *accepted* his hard lot.

Syn. assent, accede, admit.

ac-cept-a-bil-i-ty (ăk-sĕp″tȧ-bĭl′ĭ-tĭ), *n.* the quality of being welcome or agreeable.

ac-cept-a-ble (ăk-sĕp′tȧ-bl), *adj.* pleasing; welcome; agreeable; as, an *acceptable* donation.—*adv.* **ac-cept′a-bly.** —*n.* **ac-cept′a-ble-ness.**

ac-cept-ance (ăk-sĕp′tăns), *n.* **1,** the act of taking what is offered, esp. with approval; **2,** the generally understood meaning; as, the usual *acceptance* of the word; **3,** agreement to pay; as, the *acceptance* of a bill of exchange.

ac-cep-ta-tion (ăk″sĕp-tā′shŭn), *n.* **1,** the meaning in which a word or statement is generally understood; **2,** the act of being received or acknowledged.

ac-cep-tor (ăk-sĕp′tẽr; -tôr), *n.* one who accepts; specif., in commerce, the person who receives and agrees to pay a bill of exchange. Also, **ac-cept′er.**

ac-cess (ăk′sĕs; ăk-sĕs′), *n.* **1,** admittance or approach to a person or place; as, to have *access* to the president; **2,** means of approach or admission; as, the *access* to a building; **3,** addition or increase, as of land; **4,** an attack, as of disease.

ac-ces-sa-ry (ăk-sĕs′ȧ-rĭ), *n.* [*pl.* accessaries (-rĭz)], one who or that which aids in an action; an accompaniment:—*adj.* contributing. See **ac-ces′so-ry,** *Pfd. S.*

ac-ces-si-bil-i-ty (ăk-sĕs″ĭ-bĭl′ĭ-tĭ), *n.* the condition of being easily reached or approached.

ac-ces-si-ble (ăk-sĕs′ĭ-bl), *adj.* **1,** easy to reach; as, the garden is *accessible;* **2,** open to influence; as, the man was *accessible;* **3,** attainable; as, his ambitions are *accessible.*—*adv.* **ac-ces′si-bly.**

ac-ces-sion (ăk-sĕsh′ŭn), *n.* **1,** a coming (to), as by succession or by right; as, the *accession* of a prince to the throne; **2,** something added; increase; as, he received a small *accession* to his property.
Syn. increment, addition.

ac-ces-so-ry (ăk-sĕs′ō-rĭ), *adj.* aiding a design or assisting a chief agent; contributory; additional; aiding in a crime:—*n.* (ăk-sĕs′ō-rĭ; ăk′sĕs-ō″rĭ), [*pl.* accessories (-rĭz)], **1,** one who or that which aids the principal agent; **2,** usually in *pl.,* an additional thing; an article connected with a given line of trade; as, toilet *accessories;* **3,** one who, though not present, aids or abets in a crime; an agent or accomplice. Also, **ac-ces′sa-ry.** —*adv.* **ac-ces′so-ri-ly.**—*adj.* **ac″ces-so′ri-al.**
Syn., n. ally, confederate, helper.

ac-ci-dence (ăk′sĭ-dĕns), *n.* **1,** the difference in the form of a word due to changes in case or tense; **2,** the simple or rudimentary part of grammar dealing with such changes; **3,** the elements of any subject.

ac-ci-dent (ăk′sĭ-dĕnt), *n.* **1,** an unexpected or unforeseen event, generally unfortunate; **2,** something not essential or important; an incidental feature; **3,** in grammar, a change of form.
Syn. incident, adventure, chance, mishap.

ac-ci-den-tal (ăk″sĭ-dĕn′tăl), *adj.* **1,** happening by chance or unexpectedly; casual; as, an *accidental* meeting; **2,** not important; nonessential; as, an *accidental* part:—*n.* **1,** that which happens unexpectedly; **2,** a sign [♭, ♭♭, ♯, or ×] used in music to lower or raise the note before which it is placed; also, a note so raised or lowered.—*adv.* **ac″ci-den′tal-ly.**—*n.* **ac″ci-den′tal-ness.**
Syn., adj. unexpected, fortuitous, haphazard.—*Ant.* planned, certain, designed.

ac-claim (ă-klām′), *v.t.* **1,** to applaud; **2,** to hail or proclaim by shouting; as, they *acclaimed* him king:—*v.i.* to shout applause:—*n.* a shout of joy or praise.

ac-cla-ma-tion (ăk″lȧ-mā′shŭn), *n.* **1,** a shout of applause; an outburst of joy or praise; **2,** an oral vote for or against a resolution.—*adj.* **ac-clam′a-to-ry.**
Syn. cheers, approval, plaudit, praise.—*Ant.* derision, contempt, scorn.

ac-cli-mate (ă-klī′măt), *v.t.* [*p.t.* and *p.p.* -mat-ed, *p.pr.* -mat-ing], to accustom to different or foreign conditions of climate; as, to *acclimate* a plant to a new country:—*v.i.* to become used to new conditions. Also, **ac-cli′ma-tize.**

ac-cli-ma-tion (ăk″lĭ-mā′shŭn), *n.* the process of becoming used to new or different conditions of temperature, moisture, etc. Also, **ac-cli″ma-ti-za′tion.**

ac-cliv-i-ty (ă-klĭv′ĭ-tĭ), *n.* [*pl.* acclivities (-tĭz)], an ascent or upward slope of the earth, as the side of a hill.

ac-co-lade (ăk″ō-lād′; ăk″ō-läd′), *n.* the salutation used in conferring knighthood, formerly consisting of a kiss or embrace, now usually a tap on the shoulder with the flat of the sword.

ac-com-mo-date (ă-kŏm′ō-dāt), *v.t.* [*p.t.* and *p.p.* -dat″ed, *p.pr.* -dat″ing], **1,** to adapt or make fit or suitable; as, to *accommodate* the shape of the parcel to the bag; **2,** to adjust; settle, as differences between persons; **3,** to supply or furnish; do a favor to; as, to *accommodate* with a loan; **4,** to provide with lodging.
Syn. serve, oblige, adapt, fit, suit.

ac-com-mo-dat-ing (ă-kŏm′ō-dāt″ĭng), *p.adj.* obliging; adapting oneself to the desires of others. —*adv.* **ac-com′mo-dat″ing-ly.**

ac-com-mo-da-tion (ă-kŏm″ō-dā′shŭn), *n.* **1,** adaptation; as, the *accommodation* of the eye to near objects; **2,** the adjustment of differences; **3,** an obliging spirit; as, he is full of *accommodation;* **4,** the thing that helps; as, this is a great *accommodation;* **5,** a loan of money; credit; **6,** a train stopping at many way stations: also called *accommodation train.*

ac-com-pa-ni-ment (ă-kŭm′pȧ-nĭ-mĕnt), *n.* that which goes with something; a thing added to the principal thing for ornament or harmony; as, the violin and harp were a pleasing *accompaniment* to the voice of the singer.

ac-com-pa-ny (ă-kŭm′pȧ-nĭ), *v.t.* [*p.t.* and *p.p.* -nied (-nĭd), *p.pr.* -ny-ing], **1,** to go with; escort; **2,** to join with; as, she *accompanied* the words with a meaning glance; **3,** in music, to supply the instrumental or vocal background for.—*n.* **ac-com′pa-nist.**
Syn. attend, follow, conduct.

ac-com-plice (ă-kŏm′plĭs), *n.* an associate or companion in crime.
Syn. confederate, accessory, abetter, assistant, partner, colleague, ally.

ac-com-plish (ă-kŏm′plĭsh), *v.t.* **1,** to bring to pass; as, she *accomplished* her purpose; **2,** to complete; finish; as, they *accomplished* the task.
Syn. execute, achieve, perfect. (See effect.)

ac-com-plished (ă-kŏm′plĭsht), *p.adj.* completed; polished; finished; as, an *accomplished* dancer.

ac-com-plish-ment (ă-kŏm′plĭsh-mĕnt), *n.* **1,** the completion of an act or undertaking; fulfillment; **2,** attainment; skill in some art.
Syn. qualification, acquirement.

ac-cord (ă-kôrd′), *v.t.* to give; grant; as, to *accord* due praise:—*v.i.* **1,** to be in harmony; as, his views *accord* with mine; **2,** in music, to agree in pitch and tone:—*n.* **1,** agreement; harmony, esp. of sounds; **2,** impulse: with *own;* as, of his own *accord.*
Syn., v. agree. *Agree* is the general term

expressing exact sameness of mind or feelings; as, he *agrees* with that statement. *Accord* implies resemblance, rather than identity; as, the gloomy day *accorded* with my feelings.

ac-cord-ance (ă-kôr′dăns), *n.* agreement; harmony; as, his acts were in *accordance* with his belief.—*adj.* **ac-cord′ant.**—*adv.* **ac-cord′ant-ly.**

ac-cord-ing (ă-kôrd′ĭng), *p.adj.* agreeing; harmonizing: **according as,** just as: **according to,** in agreement with; as, he acted *according to* his belief.

ac-cord-ing-ly (ă-kôrd′ĭng-lĭ), *adv.* **1,** in agreement; suitably; as, he believed he was right and acted *accordingly;* **2,** consequently; so; as, *accordingly,* I went.

ac-cor-di-on (ă-kôr′dĭ-ŭn), *n.* a small keyed musical instrument which opens and shuts like a bellows, producing sound by the play of the wind upon metallic reeds.

Accordion

ac-cost (ă-kŏst′), *v.t.* to speak to first; salute; greet; address.

ac-count (ă-kount′), *v.t.* to consider; estimate; as, he *accounts* the cost:—*v.i.* **1,** to give a reckoning; **2,** to answer; as, he must *account* to me; **3,** to give or serve as an explanation; as, that *accounts* for it:—*n.* **1,** a reckoning; as, to take into *account;* **2,** often in *pl.*, a record of business dealings; as, he kept *accounts;* **3,** a record; notice; as, he took *account* of the fact; **4,** a reason; consideration; as, on this *account;* **5,** a report; as, to give an *account;* **6,** estimation; importance; as, of no *account.*

Syn., *n.* description, narration, recital.

ac-count-a-bil-i-ty (ă-koun″tȧ-bĭl′ĭ-tĭ), *n.* responsibility for carrying out an obligation or trust.

ac-count-a-ble (ă-koun′tȧ-bl), *adj.* **1,** answerable; responsible; as, man is *accountable* for his actions; **2,** capable of being explained; explicable; as, that is quite *accountable.*—*adv.* **ac-count′a-bly.** —*n.* **ac-count′a-ble-ness.**

ac-count-an-cy (ă-koun′tăn-sĭ), *n.* the art or practice of one skilled in bookkeeping.

ac-count-ant (ă-koun′tănt), *n.* one skilled in the keeping, examining, and adjusting of accounts.

ac-cou-ter (ă-ko͞o′tẽr), *v.t.* to dress; equip; array in military dress or clothing; outfit, as a soldier. Also, **ac-cou′tre** [*p.t.* and *p.p.* -tred (-tẽrd), *p.pr.* -tring].

ac-cou-ter-ments (ă-ko͞o′tẽr-měnts), *n.pl.* **1,** dress; personal equipment or outfit; **2,** the equipment of a soldier except for arms and clothing. Also, **ac-cou′-tre-ments.**

ac-cred-it (ă-krĕd′ĭt), *v.t.* **1,** to create confidence in; as, he *accredits* the man by his friendship; **2,** to send with credentials, as an ambassador; **3,** to accept as true; as, I do not *accredit* the rumor.

ac-cre-tion (ă-krē′shŭn), *n.* **1,** growth by natural enlargement, or by external addition; as, the channel was filled by an *accretion* of shifting sand; **2,** the formation caused by such processes; also, the matter added.

ac-crue (ă-kro͞o′), *v.i.* [*p.t.* and *p.p.* -crued′ (-kro͞od′), *p.pr.* -cru′ing], **1,** to grow; increase; **2,** to come naturally: used esp. of interest on money.—*n.* **ac-cru′al.**

ac-cu-mu-late (ă-kū′mū-lāt), *v.t.* [*p.t.* and *p.p.* -lat″ed, *p.pr.* -lat″ing], to collect or bring together; amass; heap up:—*v.i.* to increase in size, number, or quantity.—*n.* **ac-cu′mu-la″tor.**

Syn. gather, assemble, aggregate, hoard. —*Ant.* disperse, scatter, divide.

ac-cu-mu-la-tion (ă-kū″mū-lā′shŭn), *n.* **1,** an amassing; a collecting together; **2,** a heap; collection.

ac-cu-mu-la-tive (ă-kū′mū-lā-tĭv), *adj.* tending to, or disposed to, collect or heap up; inclined to hoard. —*adv.* **ac-cu′mu-la-tive-ly.**

ac-cu-ra-cy (ăk′ū-rȧ-sĭ), *n.* the quality of being correct; conformity with truth; exactness or precision.

ac-cu-rate (ăk′ū-răt), *adj.* conforming to fact; free from error; precise. —*adv.* **ac′cu-rate-ly.**—*n.* **ac′cu-rate-ness.**

Syn. exact, truthful. (See correct.)

ac-cursed (ă-kûrst′; ă-kûr′sĕd), *adj.* **1,** doomed to destruction; **2,** miserable; detestable. Also, **ac-curst′.**

ac-cu-sa-tion (ăk″ū-zā′shŭn), *n.* **1,** a charge of wrongdoing; **2,** the act of charging with wrongdoing or the state of being so charged.

ac-cu-sa-tive (ă-kū′zȧ-tĭv), *adj.* designating, or pertaining to, that case which indicates the direct object of a verb or, in English, the object of a preposition; objective:—*n.* the accusative case.

ac-cu-sa-to-ry (ă-kū′zȧ-tō-rĭ), *adj.* pertaining to, or containing, a charge of wrongdoing.

ac-cuse (ă-kūz′) *v.t* [*p.t.* and *p.p.* -cused′ (-kūzd′), *p.pr.* -cus′ing], to charge with guilt or blame; find fault with; as, to *accuse* one of theft.—*n.* **ac-cus′er.**

Syn. censure, blame, reproach.

ac-cus-tom (ă-kŭs′tŭm), *v.t.* to make familiar with by use; as, to *accustom* oneself, or another, to new conditions.

ac-cus-tomed (ă-kŭs′tŭmd), *p.adj.* frequent; usual; habitual.

ace (ās), *n.* **1,** a unit; a card or die marked with a single spot; **2,** a very small quantity; **3,** in tennis or similar games, an earned point; **4,** an aviator who has brought down at least five enemy airplanes.

-a-ceous (-ā′shŭs), *adj. suffix,* belonging or pertaining to, or like; as, her*baceous;* in botany, belonging to a (given) family; as, lili*aceous.*

a-cerb-i-ty (ȧ-sûr′bĭ-tĭ), *n.* [*pl.* acerbities (-tĭz)], **1,** sourness, as of unripe fruit; sharpness; **2,** harshness or severity of temper or expression.

ac-er-ose (ăs′ẽr-ōs), *adj.* needle-shaped (see *leaf,* illus.).

ac-e-tab-u-lum (ăs″ē-tăb′ū-lŭm), *n.* [*pl.* acetabula (-lȧ)], the socket in the hip bone that receives the head of the thigh bone (see *pelvis,* illus.).

ac-et-an-i-lide (ăs″ĕt-ăn′ĭ-lĭd; -lĭd), *n.* a white substance used as a medicine to lessen fever. Also, **ac″et-an′i-lid.**

a-ce-tic (ȧ-sē′tĭk; ȧ-sĕt′ĭk), *adj.* pertaining to, or like, vinegar; sour.

a-cet-y-lene (ȧ-sĕt′ĭ-lēn), *n.* a colorless gas, the most brilliant illuminating gas known, used for lighting purposes and in cutting and welding metals.

A-chæ-an (ȧ-kē′ăn), *adj.* pertaining to Achaia, a province of ancient Greece, or to Greece in general:—*n.* a native of Achaia; a Greek. Also, **A-cha′ian** (ȧ-kā′yăn).

A-cha-tes (ȧ-kā′tēz), *n.* in Vergil's "Æneid," the faithful companion of Æneas; hence, any faithful friend.

ache (āk), *n.* pain, more or less constant:—*v.i.* [*p.t.* and *p.p.* ached (ākt), *p.pr.* ach′ing (āk′ĭng)], to suffer, or be in pain, bodily or mental; as, my tooth *aches;* my heart *aches.*

Ach-er-on (ăk′ẽr-ŏn), *n.* in mythology, the River of Woe, one of the rivers in Hades: hence, Hades itself.

a-chieve (*ȧ*-chēv′), *v.t.* [*p.t.* and *p.p.* a-chieved′ (-chēvd′), *p.pr.* a-chiev′ing], **1,** to perform; carry out; accomplish; as, to *achieve* a great work; **2,** to gain or bring to a successful end by an effort; as, to *achieve* one's goal:—*v.i.* to bring about a desired result.

Syn. do, fulfil, execute, win. (See effect.)

a-chieve-ment (*ȧ*-chēv′mĕnt), *n.* **1,** accomplishment; as, the *achievement* of his purpose; **2,** a successful action; something carried out by boldness and ability; as, a brilliant *achievement.*

A-chil-les (*ȧ*-kĭl′ēz), *n.* the greatest Greek of the Trojan War, vulnerable only in the heel: hero of Homer's "Iliad."

ach-ing (āk′ĭng), *p.adj.* enduring or causing pain; painful.—*adv.* **ach′ing-ly.**

ach-ro-mat-ic (ăk″rō-măt′ĭk), *adj.* colorless: used to describe a lens that allows light to pass through without separating it into colors.

ac-id (ăs′ĭd), *adj.* sour; sharp or biting to the taste, as vinegar:—*n.* **1,** a sour substance, often liquid; **2,** in chemistry, that which combines with a base to form a salt.

Syn., adj. tart, acrid. (See bitter.)

a-cid-i-fy (*ȧ*-sĭd′ĭ-fī), *v.t.* and *v.i.* [*p.t.* and *p.p.* -fied (-fīd), *p.pr.* -fy″ing], to make, or become, sour or acid.

a-cid-i-ty (*ȧ*-sĭd′ĭ-tĭ), *n.* sourness; tartness. Also, **ac′id-ness.**

a-cid-u-late (*ȧ*-sĭd′ū-lāt), *v.t.* [*p.t.* and *p.p.* -lat″ed, *p.pr.* -lat″ing], to make sour or slightly acid.

a-cid-u-lous (*ȧ*-sĭd′ū-lŭs), *adj.* somewhat acid; sourish.

-a-cious (-ā′shŭs), *adj. suffix,* abounding in or inclined to; as, mend*acious;* fall*acious;* aud*acious;* pugn*acious.*

ac-knowl-edge (ăk-nŏl′ĕj), *v.t.* [*p.t.* and *p.p.* -edged (-ĕjd), *p.pr.* -edg-ing], **1,** to admit or own to be true, as a fault; **2,** to recognize; as, to *acknowledge* an acquaintance by bowing; **3,** to admit the authority of; as, anarchy *acknowledges* no government; **4,** to admit the receipt of; as, to *acknowledge* a letter; **5,** to admit in a legal sense; as, to *acknowledge* a signature.

Syn. avow, grant, allow, concede.—*Ant.* disavow, deny, repudiate, disclaim.

ac-knowl-edg-ment (ăk-nŏl′ĕj-mĕnt), *n.* **1,** the admission or recognition of a truth; **2,** a thing done or given as a reward; **3,** a confession; avowal; **4,** a declaration made in legal form, or the paper officially certifying to it; **5,** an expression of appreciation; **6,** a receipt.

ac-me (ăk′mē), *n.* the highest point; perfection; as, the *acme* of grace.

ac-o-lyte (ăk′ō-līt), *n.* an attendant; an assistant, as the boy who serves a priest during religious services.

ac-o-nite (ăk′ō-nīt), *n.* **1,** any of several related plants with blue or purple flowers, esp. the monkshood; **2,** a medicine made from this plant, used to slow the pulse and check fever.

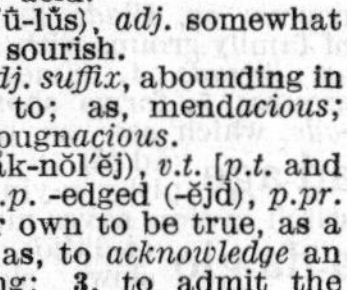

OAK LEAF AND ACORNS

a-corn (ā′kôrn; ā′kẽrn), *n.* the seed of the oak, a small nut with its base held in a natural woody cup.

a-cous-tic (*ȧ*-kōōs′-tĭk; *ȧ*-kous′tĭk), *adj.* **1,** having to do with the sense of hearing; **2,** pertaining to the science of sound; as, the *acoustic* properties of the room. Also, **a-cous′ti-cal.**—*adv.* **a-cous′ti-cal-ly.**

a-cous-tics (*ȧ*-kōōs′tĭks; *ȧ*-kous′tĭks), *n. pl.* **1,** used as *sing.*, the science of sound; **2,** used as *pl.*, the qualities of an auditorium that determine how well sound can be heard in it.

ac-quaint (ă-kwānt′), *v.t.* to notify, make familiar with; as, to *acquaint* oneself with the facts of the case.

ac-quaint-ance (ă-kwān′tăns), *n.* **1,** personal knowledge; as, to have first-hand *acquaintance* with the facts; **2,** a person whom one knows slightly.—*n.* **ac-quaint′ance-ship″.**

ac-quaint-ed (ă-kwān′tĕd), *p.adj.* having personal or mutual knowledge through contact.

ac-qui-esce (ăk″wĭ-ĕs′), *v.i.* [*p.t.* and *p.p.* -esced′ (-ĕst′), *p.pr.* -esc′ing], to agree by not objecting; quietly comply or submit: usually followed by *in;* as, to *acquiesce* in a decision.—*adj.* **ac″qui-es′cent.**—*adv.* **ac″qui-es′cent-ly.**

Syn. agree, accede, comply, consent.

ac-qui-es-cence (ăk″wĭ-ĕs′ĕns), *n.* the act of submitting; silent assent; patient acceptance.

ac-quire (ă-kwīr′), *v.t.* [*p.t.* and *p.p.* -quired′ (-kwīrd′), *p.pr.* -quir′-ing], to gain or obtain possession of, as by physical or mental effort; as, to *acquire* a habit.—*adj.* **ac-quir′a-ble.**—*n.* **ac-quir′er.**

Syn. procure, secure. (See get.)

ac-quire-ment (ă-kwīr′mĕnt), *n.* **1,** the act of gaining, as knowledge, skill, and the like; **2,** attainment; that which is gained through effort.

ac-qui-si-tion (ăk″wĭ-zĭsh′ŭn), *n.* **1,** the act of gaining possession; as, the *acquisition* of property; **2,** that which is gained, esp. a material possession.

ac-quis-i-tive (ă-kwĭz′ĭ-tĭv), *adj.* able or inclined to get or gain for oneself, esp. property or money; acquiring.—*adv.* **ac-quis′i-tive-ly.**—*n.* **ac-quis′i-tive-ness.**

ac-quit (ă-kwĭt′), *v.t.* [*p.t.* and *p.p.* -quit′-ted, *p.pr.* -quit′ting], **1,** to discharge, as a debt; **2,** to pronounce not guilty; as, the prisoner was *acquitted;* **3,** to relieve (oneself) of responsibility for; as, to *acquit* oneself of blame; **4,** to conduct (oneself): behave; as, she *acquitted* herself well.

Syn. pardon, forgive, clear.

ac-quit-tal (ă-kwĭt′ăl), *n.* **1,** the act of discharging a duty, obligation, etc.; also, the state of being released from such duty or obligation; **2,** a judicial declaration of "not guilty."

ac-quit-tance (ă-kwĭt′ăns), *n.* **1,** a discharge or release from debt, accusation, or other liability; **2,** a receipt in full; quittance.

a-cre (ā′kẽr), *n.* **1,** a measure of land area containing 160 square rods, or 43,560 square feet: about equivalent to the area of a field 208 feet square; **2,** a field; **3,** in *pl.*, lands or landed estates: **God's acre,** a churchyard.

a-cre-age (ā′kẽr-āj), *n.* **1,** the number of acres in a tract of land; **2,** land in large areas rather than in small lots.

ac-rid (ăk′rĭd), *adj.* **1,** sharp or bitter to the taste, as vinegar; pungent; irritating; **2,** having a sharp temper.—*adv.* **ac′rid-ly.** *n.* **a-crid′i-ty.**—*n.* **ac′rid-ness.**

ac-ri-mo-ni-ous (ăk″rĭ-mō′nĭ-ŭs), *adj.* bitter; sarcastic; stinging; caustic: said of language or temper.—*adv.* **ac″ri-mo′ni-ous-ly.**

ac-ri-mo-ny (ăk′rĭ-mō-nĭ), *n.* bitterness; severity of temper or speech.

Syn. sharpness, tartness, sourness, harshness.—*Ant.* gentleness, courtesy, blandness.

ac-ro-bat (ăk′rō-băt), *n.* one who performs skilled or daring gymnastic feats, such as tumbling, vaulting, etc. —*adj.* **ac″ro-bat′ic.**—*adv.* **ac″ro-bat′i-cal-ly.**

a-crop-o-lis (*ȧ*-krŏp′ō-lĭs), *n.* [*pl.* acropolises (-ĕz); *Gk.* acropoleis (-lĭs)], the highest part or citadel of a Grecian city, usually the site of the original settlement: **Acropolis**, the citadel of Athens.

a-cross (*ȧ*-krôs′), *adv.* from side to side; crosswise:—*prep.* **1**, from side to side of; from one side to another of; as, to swim *across* a stream; **2**, on the opposite side of; as, she lives *across* the street.

a-cros-tic (*ȧ*-krŏs′tĭk), *n.* a composition, usually in verse, in which a given set of letters taken in order, as the first letter of each line, forms a motto, phrase, name, or word.

act (ăkt), *n.* **1**, a deed or performance; that which is done; **2**, the process of doing; **3**, a decree, edict, or law; also, the judgment of a court; **4**, a formal writing; as, an *act* of sale; **5**, one of the principal divisions of a drama or play: **Acts**, a book of the New Testament: called in full *Acts of the Apostles:*—*v.t.* to perform or play, as on the stage; personate; feign:—*v.i.* **1**, to exert force or energy; as, to *act* as driver; **2**, to behave; as, to *act* queerly; **3**, to perform on the stage.

act-ing (ăk′tĭng), *p.adj.* doing the duties of another, as those of an official; as, the *acting* chairman:—*n.* **1**, the performance of a part on the stage; **2**, false or insincere behavior; as, his joy was only *acting.*

ac-tin-ic (ăk-tĭn′ĭk), *adj.* designating, or pertaining to, the property possessed by radiant energy of producing chemical effects, as in photography; as, *actinic* rays.

ac-tion (ăk′shŭn), *n.* **1**, the state of being in motion, as opposed to that of being at rest; **2**, the doing of something; esp., in *pl.*, conscious acts; conduct; behavior; **3**, the effect of one body or substance upon another; **4**, a suit begun by one party against another in a court of law; **5**, the effective or acting part of a mechanism, as in a piano; **6**, a military or naval engagement.

Syn. act, operation. (See battle.)

ac-tion-a-ble (ăk′shŭn-*ȧ*-bl), *adj.* giving grounds for a lawsuit.

ac-tive (ăk′tĭv), *adj.* **1**, having or using the power or quality of motion or force; **2**, brisk; lively; **3**, in action; operating; working; as, an *active* volcano; **4**, in grammar, designating, or pertaining to, the voice or form of the verb which represents the subject as the doer of the action asserted by the verb: opp. of *passive.*—*adv.* **ac′tive-ly.**

Syn. sprightly, alert, agile, nimble, quick, supple, prompt, vigilant, industrious.

ac-tiv-i-ty (ăk-tĭv′ĭ-tĭ), *n.* [*pl.* activities (-tĭz)], **1**, the quality of doing or acting; **2**, quickness in doing; brisk movement; **3**, in *pl.*, things done, esp. along a certain line; conduct. Also, **ac′tive-ness.**

ac-tor (ăk′tẽr), *n.* **1**, a doer; **2**, one who takes the part of a character in a play; a theatrical or motion-picture player.

ac-tress (ăk′trĕs), *n.* a woman who performs on the stage or before the motion-picture camera.

ac-tu-al (ăk′tū-ăl), *adj.* existing in fact; real as opposed to merely possible; existent; present.

Syn. positive, genuine, certain.

ac-tu-al-i-ty (ăk″tū-ăl′ĭ-tĭ), *n.* [*pl.* actualities (-tĭz)], **1**, reality; fact; **2**, that which is in full existence.

ac-tu-al-ly (ăk′tū-ăl-ĭ), *adv.* really; in truth; as a matter of fact.

ac-tu-a-ry (ăk′tū-ā-rĭ), *n.* [*pl.* actuaries (-rĭz)], **1**, one who is skilled in computing insurance risks, premiums, etc.; **2**, *Rare*, a clerk or notary.—*adj.* **ac″tu-a′ri-al.**

ac-tu-ate (ăk′tū-āt), *v.t.* [*p.t.* and *p.p.* -at″ed, *p.pr.* -at″ing], **1**, to move or incite to effort; as, men are *actuated* by various motives; **2**, to put into motion; as, the connecting rod *actuates* the driving wheels of a locomotive.—*n.* **ac″tu-a′tion.**

a-cu-men (*ȧ*-kū′mĕn), *n.* quickness of perception; penetration; discrimination; keenness of insight.

a-cu-mi-nate (*ȧ*-kū′mĭ-nāt), *adj.* pointed; having a tapering end, as a leaf (see *leaf*, illus.).

a-cute (*ȧ*-kūt′), *adj.* **1**, sharp-pointed; **2**, mentally keen; clever; quick of perception; **3**, severe, as pain or symptoms attending a disease; **4**, of sounds, high in pitch; shrill; **5**, of an angle, less than a right angle (see [1]*angle*, illus.): **acute accent**, a mark [′] used in writing and printing to indicate stress or some special sound quality.—*adv.* **a-cute′ly.**—*n.* **a-cute′ness.**

Syn. shrewd, intelligent, penetrating, piercing, keen.

-a-cy (-*ȧ*-sĭ) *n. suffix*, meaning quality, state, or office; as, accur*acy*; magistr*acy.*

ad- (ăd-), *prefix*, [remaining unchanged before a following vowel and *d, h, j, m*, or *v*, as in *ad*equate, *ad*duce, *ad*here, *ad*jective, *ad*mire, *ad*vent, or changed according to the initial sound of the word to which it is prefixed, as in *ab*breviate, *ac*cede, *af*fect, *ag*gregate, *al*lusion, *an*notate, *ap*ply, *ac*quiesce, *ar*rogate, *as*sociate, *as*cend, *as*pire, *as*tringent *at*tract], meaning to, toward, in addition to, etc.: sometimes merely intensifying the meaning of the word to which it is attached.

-ad (-ăd), *n. suffix*, forming: **1**, collective numerals; as, tri*ad;* **2**, names of epic poems; as, Ili*ad;* **3**, patronymics, or names of family groups with a common designation; as, dry*ad;* **4**, names of some family plant groups; **5**, forms shortened from the suffix *-ade*, which see; as, ball*ad;* sal*ad.*

ad-age (ăd′āj), *n.* an ancient proverb or pithy saying in current use, as "a stitch in time saves nine."

a-da-gio (*ȧ*-dä′jō), *adj.* and *adv.* in music, slow; slowly:—*n.* [*pl.* adagios (-jōz)], a piece of music in which the movement is slow.

Ad-am (ăd′ăm), *n.* in the Bible story of the creation, the first man.

ad-a-mant (ăd′*ȧ*-mănt), *n.* a real or imaginary stone of great hardness; any substance of extreme hardness, such as the diamond; figuratively, something unyielding; as, a will of *adamant.*

ad-a-man-tine (ăd″*ȧ*-măn′tĭn), *adj.* **1**, very hard and strong; impenetrable; **2**, unyielding; inflexible.

Ad-am's ap-ple a cartilage forming the fore part of the human voice box, or larynx, noticeable, esp. in men, as an enlargement in the front of the throat.

a-dapt (*ȧ*-dăpt′), *v.t.* to make suitable; conform; as, to *adapt* oneself to conditions; remodel or fit by alteration; as, to *adapt* a story for the stage.—*adj.* **a-dapt′a-ble.**

a-dapt-a-bil-i-ty (*ȧ*-dăp″t*ȧ*-bĭl′ĭ-tĭ), *n.* the quality of being able to conform to conditions.

ad-ap-ta-tion (ăd″ăp-tā′shŭn), *n.* **1**, the act of adjusting; **2**, the state of being adjusted or fitted; **3**, something which has been changed to fit given conditions.

add (ăd), *v.t.* **1**, to join or unite into a whole; esp., to sum up (a set of numbers); find the total of; **2**, to bring (additional items); as, to *add* stones to a pile; **3**, to go on to say.—*adj.* **add′i-ble.**—*n.* **add″i-bil′i-ty.**—*n.* [1]**add′er.**

Syn. affix, append. (See combine.)

ad-den-dum (ă-dĕn′dŭm), *n.* [*pl.* addenda (-d*ȧ*)], a thing to be joined or added to something, as an appendix to a book.

ad-der (ăd′ẽr), *n.* **1**, any of several harmless American snakes; **2**, the poisonous viper of Europe.

ad-dict (ă-dĭkt′), *v.t.* to devote or give oneself up to: often in a bad sense:—*n.* (ăd′ĭkt), one who is devoted to something, esp. to a drug.—*n.* **ad-dic′tion.**

ad-di-tion (ă-dĭsh′ŭn), *n.* **1**, the act, process, or result of summing up numbers; **2**, the uniting of two or more numbers in one sum; **3**, a thing which is added or joined; as, an *addition* to a house.
Syn. increase, enlargement.

ad-di-tion-al (ă-dĭsh′ŭn-ăl), *adj.* joined; extra; more; supplemental.—*adv.* **ad-di′tion-al-ly.**

ad-di-tive (ăd′ĭ-tĭv), *adj.* **1**, proper to be added; having a tendency to increase; **2**, pertaining to addition.

ad-dle (ăd′l), *adj.* **1**, rotten: applied to eggs; **2**, muddled or confused: **addle-headed**, or **addle-pated**, stupid; weak-brained; muddled:—*v.t.* and *v.i.* [*p.t.* and *p.p.* -dled (-ld), *p.pr.* -dling], to make, or become, corrupt; spoil.

ad-dress (ă-drĕs′), *v.t.* **1**, to speak or write to; **2**, to direct, as a letter; **3**, to apply or direct (one's energy or skill) to a duty, task, etc.; **4**, to woo or to pay court to, as a lover:—*n.* **1**, a speech delivered or written; **2**, manners and bearing; **3**, tact; cleverness; **4**, a person's place of residence; the place to which one's mail is directed.
Syn., v. salute, greet, accost, court.

ad-dress-ee (ă-drĕs″ē′), *n.* one to whom anything, as a letter or a package, is directed, esp. by mail.

ad-dres-so-graph (ă-drĕs′ō-grăf), *n.* a machine used to direct circulars, letters, etc.: a trade name.

ad-duce (ă-dūs′), *v.t.* [*p.t.* and *p.p.* -duced′ (-dūst′), *p.pr.* -duc′ing], to bring forward as a reason; present or offer as proof or evidence in support of some statement; cite.—*adj.* **ad-duc′i-ble.**

-ade (-ād), *n. suffix*, denoting: **1**, something done; as, escap*ade;* **2**, something going on or taking place; as, par*ade;* **3**, something made or created; as, lemon*ade;* masquer*ade;* **4**, a group formed of similar units; as, dec*ade.*

ad-e-noid (ăd′ē-noid), *n.* usually in *pl.*, a growth of spongy or netlike tissue in the passage leading from the nose to the throat, often causing difficulty in breathing:—*adj.* in the form of a gland.

a-dept (ȧ-dĕpt′), *adj.* well skilled:—*n.* one who is fully proficient or skilled in an art; an expert.—*n.* **a-dept′ness.**

ad-e-qua-cy (ăd′ē-kwȧ-sĭ), *n.* suitability for a particular purpose.

ad-e-quate (ăd′ē-kwȧt), *adj.* equal to requirement; enough.—*adv.* **ad′e-quate-ly.**—*n.* **ad′e-quate-ness.**
Syn. competent, suitable.

ad-here (ăd-hēr′), *v.i.* [*p.t.* and *p.p.* -hered′ (-hērd′), *p.pr.* -her′ing], **1**, to stick fast as if glued; **2**, to become attached or devoted, as to a principle or a political party.

ad-her-ence (ăd-hēr′ĕns), *n.* **1**, the act or state of holding fast; **2**, steadfast attachment or devotion.

ad-her-ent (ăd-hēr′ĕnt), *n.* one who holds fast; a follower or supporter, as of a political party:—*adj.* sticking fast; adhering; clinging.
Syn., n. ally, upholder, defender, backer.

ad-he-sion (ăd-hē′zhŭn), *n.* **1**, the state of being stuck together, united, or attached; **2**, firmness in opinion; as, a man's *adhesion* to truth; **3**, a place, as in a wound, where tissues which are ordinarily separate have stuck together.
Syn. adherence, attachment, faithfulness, fidelity, devotion.

ad-he-sive (ăd-hē′sĭv), *adj.* **1**, holding fast; **2**, sticky; gummed for use; as, *adhesive* tape:—*n.* a sticky substance, as glue, or mucilage.—*adv.* **ad-he′sive-ly.**—*n.* **ad-he′sive-ness.**

a-dieu (ȧ-dū′; *Fr.* ȧ-dyö′), *n.* [*pl.* **adieus** (ȧ-dūz′); *Fr.* adieux (ȧ-dyö′)], a farewell; good wishes at parting:—*interj.* good-by; farewell.

ad-i-pose (ăd′ĭ-pōs), *adj.* pertaining to fat; fatty:—*n.* animal fat.—*n.* **ad′i-pose-ness.**—*n.* **ad″i-pos′i-ty.**

ad-ja-cen-cy (ă-jā′sĕn-sĭ), *n.* the state or quality of being close; nearness. Also, **ad-ja′cence.**

ad-ja-cent (ă-jā′sĕnt), *adj.* **1**, near; close, adjoining; **2**, in geometry; designating either of two angles having a common vertex and a common side between them (see [1]*angle*, illus.).
Syn. bordering, neighboring.

ad-jec-tive (ăj′ĕk-tĭv), *n.* a part of speech expressing quality or condition; a word used to qualify, limit, or define a noun or pronoun.—*adv.* **ad′jec-tive-ly.**—*adj.* **ad″jec-ti′val** (-tī′-).—*adv.* **ad″jec-ti′val-ly.**

ad-join (ă-join′), *v.i.* to lie or be situated close together, as two lots of land:—*v.t.* to lie next to; as, his property *adjoins* his brother's.—*p.adj.* **ad-join′ing.**

ad-journ (ă-jûrn′), *v.t.* to put off to another day or time; as, they *adjourned* the meeting; also, to bring (a meeting) to a close:—*v.i.* to cease business for a time; as, the court *adjourned.*
Syn. postpone, close, end, suspend.

ad-journ-ment (ă-jûrn′mĕnt), *n.* the act of putting off or postponing; the postponement of a meeting till another specified time, or indefinitely.

ad-judge (ă-jŭj′), *v.t.* [*p.t.* and *p.p.* -judged′ (-jŭjd′), *p.pr.* -judg′ing], **1**, to decide (a dispute) according to law; **2**, to award or assign; bestow; **3**, to sentence; condemn; **4**, to consider; hold; as, I *adjudge* him unworthy of esteem.

ad-ju-di-cate (ă-jōō′dĭ-kāt), *v.t.* [*p.t.* and *p.p.* -cat″ed, *p.pr.* -cat″ing], to hear, or try, and decide (a case) officially, as in a court of law, or unofficially, on its merits; adjudge.—*n.* **ad-ju″di-ca′tion.**—*n.* **ad-ju′di-ca″tor.**

ad-junct (ăj′ŭngkt), *n.* **1**, something added to another thing, but not a necessary part of it; **2**, in grammar, a qualifying word; modifier.—*adj.* **ad-junc′tive.**
Syn. addition, appendage.

ad-ju-ra-tion (ăj″ōō-rā′shŭn), *n.* **1**, a solemn charging on oath; **2**, a solemn oath.

ad-jure (ă-jōōr′), *v.t.* [*p.t.* and *p.p.* -jured′ (-jōōrd′), *p.pr.* -jur′ing], to command on oath under pain of a penalty; charge solemnly; entreat earnestly.

ad-just (ă-jŭst′), *v.t.* **1**, to fit, or bring into harmony; adapt; **2**, to make accurate; regulate, as mechanism; **3**, to settle or bring to a satisfactory state; as, to *adjust* accounts.—*adj.* **ad-just′a-ble.**

ad-just-er (ă-jŭs′tẽr), *n.* one who regulates, sets right, or fits; esp., one who settles the amount of claims in cases of losses by fire, as an insurance agent.

ad-just-ment (ă-jŭst′mĕnt), *n.* the act of regulating or setting right; settlement or arrangement.

ad-ju-tan-cy (ăj′ōō-tăn-sĭ), *n.* the office of an army officer who assists the commanding officer.

ad-ju-tant (ăj′o͞o-tănt), *n.* **1**, a helper; **2**, a regimental staff officer who assists the commanding officer; **3**, a large stork, common in India: **adjutant general,** [*pl.* adjutants general], the chief staff officer of an army, through whom are sent all orders and messages from the commanding general.

ADJUTANT (def. 3)

ad-min-is-ter (ăd-mĭn′ĭs-tẽr), *v.t.* **1**, to manage or conduct, as affairs; **2**, to supply or give, as justice or relief; **3**, to cause to take, as an oath; **4**, in law, to settle, as an estate:—*v.i.* **1**, to tend or help toward some purpose; as, to *administer* to his peace of mind; **2**, to manage affairs; **3**, in law, to settle an estate.
Syn. conduct, execute, regulate, inflict.

ad-min-is-tra-tion (ăd-mĭn″ĭs-trā′shŭn), *n.* **1**, the official part of a government or the part which enforces or carries out the laws; **2**, the act of managing, dispensing, or giving, as government, justice, medicine, relief, a sacrament, or a deceased person's estate.

ad-min-is-tra-tive (ăd-mĭn′ĭs-trā-tĭv), *adj.* pertaining to the management of affairs or government; executive.—*adv.* **ad-min′is-tra-tive-ly.**

ad-min-is-tra-tor (ăd-mĭn′ĭs-trā″tẽr), *n.* **1**, one who manages, directs, or governs affairs; **2**, one appointed legally to manage or settle an estate; an executor.—*n.* **ad-min′is-tra″tor-ship.**

ad-min-is-tra-trix (ăd-mĭn″ĭs-trā′trĭks), *n.* [*pl.* administratrices (-trā-trī′sēz)], a woman appointed by law to settle a deceased person's estate; an executrix.

ad-mi-ra-ble (ăd′mĭ-rȧ-bl), *adj.* worthy of wonder and approval; excellent.—*adv.* **ad′mi-ra-bly.**

ad-mi-ral (ăd′mĭ-răl), *n.* **1**, a naval officer of the highest rank, as the commander in chief of a fleet; **2**, the chief ship, or flagship, of a fleet.

ad-mi-ral-ty (ăd′mĭ-răl-tĭ), *n.* [*pl.* admiralties (-tĭz)], **1**, the office and authority of an admiral; **2**, a department, or its officers, having entire charge of naval affairs; **3**, the court or law dealing with questions or offenses connected with the sea.

ad-mi-ra-tion (ăd″mĭ-rā′shŭn), *n.* **1**, wonder mingled with approval excited by beauty or excellence; **2**, a thing exciting wonder.

ad-mire (ăd-mīr′), *v.t.* [*p.t.* and *p.p.* -mired′ (-mīrd′), *p.pr.* mir′ing], to regard with delighted approval and surprise.—*n.* **admir′er.**—*adv.* **ad-mir′ing-ly.**
Syn. esteem, honor, respect.—*Ant.* abhor, disapprove, dislike, scorn.

ad-mis-si-ble (ăd-mĭs′ĭ-bl), *adj.* **1**, worthy of being allowed to enter; **2**, allowable; permissible.—*adv.* **ad-mis′si-bly.**—*n.* **ad-mis″si-bil′i-ty.**

ad-mis-sion (ăd-mĭsh′ŭn), *n.* **1**, the power or permission to enter; admittance; acceptance; **2**, acknowledgment that something is true; as, he made full *admission* of his guilt; **3**, the point so granted; **4**, the price of entrance, as to a theater.
Syn. (see admittance).

ad-mit (ăd-mĭt′), *v.t.* [*p.t.* and *p.p.* -mit′ted, *p.pr.* -mit′ting], **1**, to permit to enter; **2**, to allow in argument; concede; as, to *admit* a point; **3**, to permit to have certain privileges; as, to *admit* to bail; **4**, to be capable of; as, it *admits* no other meaning.
Syn. own, acknowledge; suffer, tolerate.

ad-mit-tance (ăd-mĭt′ăns), *n.* **1**, the act of letting in; **2**, the power or permission to enter.
Syn. entrance, admission. *Admittance* refers to the permission or opportunity to enter a place; as, "No *admittance* to vehicles." *Entrance* indicates the passing from the outside to the inside; as, his *entrance* into the room. *Admission* indicates that certain rights or privileges accompany the permission to enter; as, *admission* to the theater.

ad-mix (ăd-mĭks′), *v.t.* to mix, or combine, with something else.

ad-mix-ture (ăd-mĭks′tūr), *n.* **1**, the act of mixing; **2**, that which is added by mixing.

ad-mon-ish (ăd-mŏn′ĭsh), *v.t.* **1**, to reprove gently; as, he *admonished* me for my fault; **2**, to urge; exhort; as, he *admonished* me to do better; **3**, to remind.
Syn. counsel, rebuke. (See advise.)

ad-mo-ni-tion (ăd″mō-nĭsh′ŭn), *n.* gentle reproof or warning.

ad-mon-i-to-ry (ăd-mŏn′ĭ-tō-rĭ), *adj.* giving gentle reproof.

a-do (ȧ-do͞o′), *n.* fuss; haste; trouble; as, much *ado* about nothing.

a-do-be (ȧ-dō′bē), *n.* **1**, brick dried in the sun, used in southwest America and Mexico; **2**, a structure made of such brick.

ad-o-les-cence (ăd″ō-lĕs′ĕns), *n.* the period during which a person passes from childhood to mental and physical maturity; youth.

ad-o-les-cent (ăd″ō-lĕs′ĕnt), *adj.* growing up; passing from childhood to manhood or womanhood; youthful.

A-do-nis (ȧ-dō′nĭs), *n.* in mythology, a beautiful youth beloved by Venus.—*adj.* **A-don′ic.**

a-dopt (ȧ-dŏpt′), *v.t.* to choose or take to be one's own, as a child, an opinion, or a course of action.—*p.adj.* **a-dopt′ed.**—*n.* **a-dopt′er.**—*adj.* **a-dop′tive.**

a-dop-tion (ȧ-dŏp′shŭn), *n.* **1**, the act of taking as one's own, as a child; **2**, the act of accepting and putting into use; as, the *adoption* of reformed spelling.

a-dor-a-ble (ȧ-dōr′ȧ-bl), *adj.* worthy of worship or the utmost love.—*adv.* **a-dor′a-bly.**—*n.* **a-dor′a-ble-ness.**

ad-o-ra-tion (ăd″ō-rā′shŭn), *n.* the act of worship; profound reverence; the utmost love.

a-dore (ȧ-dōr′), *v.t.* [*p.t.* and *p.p.* a-dored′ (-dōrd′), *p.pr.* a-dor′ing], **1**, to pay divine honors to; honor highly; **2**, to love intensely; admire greatly:—*v.i.* to offer worship.—*p.adj.* **a-dor′ing.**—*n.* **a-dor′er.**

a-dorn (ȧ-dôrn′), *v.t.* to beautify; ornament; decorate; bedeck.

a-dorn-ment (ȧ-dôrn′mĕnt), *n.* ornament; decoration.

a-down (ȧ-doun′), *adv.* *Archaic* or *Poetic,* down; downward; below:—*prep.* *Archaic* or *Poetic,* down.

ad-re-nal-ine (ăd-rē′năl-ĭn; -ēn), *n.* a powerful drug used by hypodermic injection to stimulate the heart. Also, **ad-re′nal-in.**

a-drift (ȧ-drĭft′), *adj.* and *adv.* floating at random; at the mercy of the wind; drifting without anchor.

a-droit (ȧ-droit′), *adj.* skilful; expert; clever; cunning; ready in invention.—*adv.* **a-droit′ly.**—*n.* **a-droit′ness.**
Syn. deft, dexterous. (See clever.)

ad-u-la-tion (ăd″ū-lā′shŭn), *n.* excessive or hypocritical praise; flattery.—*adj.* **ad′u-la-to-ry.**

a-dult (ȧ-dŭlt′), *adj.* grown up to full maturity, size, and strength:—*n.* one who or that which is grown up.

a-dul-ter-ant (*ȧ*-dŭl′tẽr-ănt), *n.* something of inferior quality mixed with a substance apparently genuine:—*adj.* making inferior or impure; making false what is supposed to be genuine.

a-dul-ter-ate (*ȧ*-dŭl′tẽr-āt), *v.t.* [*p.t.* and *p.p.* -at″ed, *p.pr.* -at″ing], to corrupt, debase, or make impure by mixing in a foreign or poorer substance; as, to *adulterate* candy.—*n.* **a-dul′ter-a″tor**

a-dul-ter-a-tion (*ȧ*-dŭl″tẽr-ā′shŭn), *n.* the substitution or placing of something of an inferior quality in a mixture with the intention of passing it for the genuine article.

a-dul-ter-y (*ȧ*-dŭl′tẽr-ĭ), *n.* [*pl.* adulteries (-ĭz)], the act of breaking the marriage vow of faithfulness.—*n.* **a-dul′ter-er.** —*n.fem.* **a-dul′ter-ess.**—*adj.* **a-dul′ter-ous.**

ad-um-brate (ăd-ŭm′brāt), *v.t.* [*p.t.* and *p.p.* -brat-ed, *p.pr.* -brat-ing], **1,** to sketch or outline faintly; **2,** to indicate, esp. in advance; foreshadow; **3,** to overshadow.—*n.* **ad″um-bra′tion.**

***ad va-lo-rem** (ăd v*ȧ*-lō′rĕm), [Lat.], by value; according to value: **ad-valorem duty,** an import duty or charge on goods at a certain rate per cent based on their cost at the port of shipment.

ad-vance (ăd-våns′), *v.i.* [*p.t.* and *p.p.* -vanced′ (-vånst′), *p.pr.* -vanc′-ing], to go forward:—*v.t.* **1,** to cause to go forward; **2,** to propose; as, to *advance* an opinion; **3,** to increase; as, to *advance* prices; **4,** to further; as, to *advance* a cause; **5,** to make a payment of beforehand:—*n.* **1,** a moving forward; **2,** improvement; **3,** an addition or rise in value; **4,** usually in *pl.*, an approach, as toward acquaintance; **5,** a loan; **6,** payment beforehand:—*adj.* being or occurring before; as, an *advance* sale of tickets; an *advance* agent.—*p.adj.* **ad-vanced′.**
Syn., v. promote, exalt, improve, elevate.

ad-vance-ment (ăd-våns′mĕnt), *n.* furtherance; progress; progression; promotion.

ad-van-tage (ăd-vån′tāj), *n.* **1,** a state of advance or forwardness; **2,** superior position; **3,** a benefit; any circumstance that aids or assists; as, the *advantage* of a good education; **4,** in lawn tennis, the first point scored after the score is deuce.

ad-van-ta-geous (ăd″văn-tā′jŭs), *adj.* beneficial; profitable; favorable.—*adv.* **ad″van-ta′geous-ly.**

ad-vent (ăd′vĕnt), *n.* a coming or arrival; as, the *advent* of winter: **Advent,** the period of the year including the four Sundays before Christmas, which prepares for the coming of Jesus Christ.

Ad-vent-ism (ăd′vĕn-tĭzm), *n.* the doctrine that Christ is coming a second time to establish a personal kingdom on earth.—*n.* **Ad′vent-ist.**

ad-ven-ti-tious (ăd″vĕn-tĭsh′ŭs), *adj.* happening by chance; casual; accidental; produced out of normal and regular order.—*adv.* **ad″ven-ti′tious-ly.**

ad-ven-ture (ăd-vĕn′tūr), *n.* **1,** a bold undertaking; a daring feat; the encountering of risks; **2,** a remarkable experience; **3,** the taking part in an uncertain enterprise, esp. in business:—*v.t.* and *v.i.* [*p.t.* and *p.p.* -tured (-tūrd), *p.pr.* -tur-ing], to risk; dare.—*adj.* **ad-ven′ture-some.**

ad-ven-tur-er (ăd-vĕn′tūr-ẽr), *n.* **1,** one who engages in new and dangerous enterprises; **2,** a soldier of fortune; **3,** one who seeks distinction by false show or pretense; one who lives by his wits.

ad-ven-tur-ess (ăd-vĕn′tūr-ĕs), *n.* a woman who seeks distinction by false show or pretense.

ad-ven-tur-ous (ăd-vĕn′tūr-ŭs), *adj.* **1,** inclined to incur danger; rash; venturesome; **2,** requiring courage; as, an *adventurous* enterprise.

ad-verb (ăd′vûrb), *n.* a word used to modify a verb, an adjective, or another adverb, by expressing time, place, manner, or the like.

ad-ver-bi-al (ăd-vûr′bĭ-ăl), *adj.* modifying a verb, adjective, or adverb.—*adv.* **ad-ver′bi-al-ly.**

ad-ver-sa-ry (ăd′vẽr-sā-rĭ), *n.* [*pl.* adversaries (-rĭz)], an enemy; foe; opponent; antagonist.

ad-ver-sa-tive (ăd-vûr′s*ȧ*-tĭv), *adj.* expressing opposition or antithesis, as the conjunctions *but, though, yet.*

ad-verse (ăd′vẽrs), *adj.* opposed; opposite; unfavorable; contrary; hostile; unfortunate; as, *adverse* circumstances.—*adv.* **ad′verse-ly.**—*n.* **ad′verse-ness.**

ad-ver-si-ty (ăd-vûr′sĭ-tĭ), *n.* [*pl.* adversities (-tĭz)], the reverse or opposite of prosperity; misery; distress or unhappiness; misfortune.
Syn. hardship, trouble, affliction, suffering. —*Ant.* prosperity, happiness, blessing, joy.

ad-vert (ăd-vûrt′), *v.i.* to turn one's attention; refer incidentally; allude; as, to *advert* to what we were saying a while ago.

ad-vert-ence (ăd-vûr′tĕns), *n.* attention; notice; heed.

ad-vert-ent (ăd-vûr′tĕnt), *adj.* attentive; heedful.—*adv.* **ad-vert′ent-ly.**

ad-ver-tise (ăd′vẽr-tīz″; ăd″vẽr-tīz′), *v.t.* [*p.t.* and *p.p.* -tised″ (-tīzd″), *p.pr.* -tis″ing], to give notice to; turn the attention of others to; announce; inform; publish:—*v.i.* to give notice, as in a newspaper, etc. Also, **ad′ver-tize″; ad″ver-tize′.** —*n.* **ad′ver-tis″er; ad′ver-tiz″er.**

ad-ver-tise-ment (ăd-vûr′tĭz-mĕnt; ăd″vẽr-tīz′mĕnt), *n.* a printed notice, esp. regarding goods offered for sale; an announcement; a bringing into notice. Also, **ad-ver′tize-ment; ad″ver-tize′ment.**

ad-vice (ăd-vīs′), *n.* **1,** an opinion given that is worthy to be followed; counsel; as, I have come to you for *advice* concerning my choice of a college; **2,** usually in *pl.*, information given by letter, telegram, etc.; as, *advices* from Europe come swiftly by cable.
Syn. suggestion, instruction, caution.

ad-vis-a-ble (ăd-vīz′*ȧ*-bl), *adj.* proper to be done; in accordance with good judgment; prudent; expedient or suitable.—*adv.* **ad-vis′a-bly.**—*n.* **ad-vis′a-ble-ness.** —*n.* **ad-vis″a-bil′i-ty.**

ad-vise (ăd-vīz′), *v.t.* [*p.t.* and *p.p.* -vised′ (-vīzd′), *p.pr.* -vis′ing], **1,** to counsel, as a change in a course of action; **2,** to notify; inform; **3,** to recommend as wise, prudent, etc.—*n.* **ad-vis′er.**
Syn. instruct, admonish, counsel. To *advise* is to give wise suggestions as to future action, such suggestions being based on professional knowledge or wide experience; as, a doctor *advises* his patient. To *instruct* is to give clear and positive directions as to a future course of conduct; as, an employer *instructs* an employee as to the nature of his duties. To *admonish* is gently to reprove errors and faults in order to prevent them in the future; as, a mother *admonishes* her daughter as to the dangers of insincerity. To *counsel* is to give an opinion on a serious matter from a fund of superior wisdom and knowledge; as, a clergyman *counsels* his flock.

ad-vis-ed-ly (ăd-vīz′ĕd-lĭ), *adv.* with caution; purposely; not hastily.

ad-vise-ment (ăd-vīz′mĕnt), *n.* consideration; as, I will take the matter under *advisement.*

ad-vi-so-ry (ăd-vī'zō-rĭ), *adj.* having power to suggest or to counsel; as, an *advisory* committee.

ad-vo-ca-cy (ăd'vō-kȧ-sĭ), *n.* the act of pleading for, supporting, or recommending, as a policy.

ad-vo-cate (ăd'vō-kāt), *n.* **1**, one who pleads the cause of another in a court of law; **2**, a pleader in favor of any person or thing; as, an *advocate* of peace:—*v.t.* (ăd'vō-kāt), [*p.t.* and *p.p.* -cat″ed, *p.pr.* -cat″ing], to defend publicly, as a policy or plan; plead for.

adz (ădz), *n.* a cutting tool, somewhat like a short, heavy hoe, having a blade at right angles to the handle, and used in shaping and finishing timber. Also, **adze.**

æ-dile (ē'dīl), *n.* in ancient Rome, an official who had charge of public and private buildings, public games, etc.

æ-gis (ē'jĭs), *n.* **1**, in mythology: **a**, the storm cloud around the thunderbolt, the especial weapon of Zeus; **b**, a breastplate or shield, bordered with serpents, carried by Athena; **2**, any protecting power or influence. Also, **e'gis.**

Æ-ne-as (ē-nē'ăs), *n.* in Homer's "Iliad," the son of Anchises and Aphrodite, a Trojan prince and hero whose wanderings are the subject of Vergil's "Æneid."

Æ-ne-id (ē-nē'ĭd), *n.* the Latin epic poem by Vergil, telling of the wanderings of Æneas and his companions from Troy to Italy after the fall of Troy.

Æ-o-li-an (ē-ō'lĭ-ăn), *adj.* pertaining to Æolus, the god of the winds, or to Æolis, an ancient country of Asia Minor: **æolian**, pertaining to the wind: **æolian harp**, an instrument, the strings of which give out musical sounds when the wind blows through them. Also, **E-o'li-an; e-o'li-an.**

Æ-o-lus (ē'ō-lŭs), *n.* in mythology, king and god of the winds, which he kept imprisoned in a cavern.

æ-on (ē'ŏn), *n.* a period of time too long to measure; an age. Also, **e'on.**

a-ër-ate (ā'ēr-āt), *v.t.* [*p.t.* and *p.p.* -at″ed, *p.pr.* -at″ing], **1**, to charge with gas, as with air or carbon dioxide; **2**, to expose to the action of air; **3**, to treat with oxygen: **aërated bread**, bread raised by charging the dough with gas, instead of using yeast or baking powder.—*n.* **a″ër-a'tion.**—*n.* **a'ër-a″tor.**

a-ë-ri-al (ā-ē'rĭ-ăl), *adj.* **1**, relating to the air; existing or happening in the air; airy; **2**, hence, high; lofty; **3**, not real or substantial; imaginary; as, *aërial* flights of fancy:—*n.* in radio systems, one or more wires suspended in the air to receive or radiate energy; an antenna.—*adv.* **a-ë'ri-al-ly.**

ae-rie (ē'rĭ; ā'ēr-ĭ), *n.* **1**, the nest of an eagle or other bird of prey, as on a lofty crag; **2**, a human dwelling in a similar place; **3**, a brood of eagles, hawks, or similar birds. Also, **ae'ry; ey'rie; ey'ry.**

a-ër-i-form (ā'ēr-ĭ-fôrm), *adj.* having the form of air; gaseous.

a-ër-i-fy (ā'ēr-ĭ-fī), *v.t.* [*p.t.* and *p.p.* -fied (-fīd), *p.pr.* -fy″ing], to combine with air; fill with air.

a-ër-o-drome (ā″ēr-ō-drōm″), *n.* **1**, a building where flying machines are stored and tested; **2**, a ground or field used for airplane instruction and practice. Also, **air'drome″**, *Pfd. S.*

a-ër-o-foil (ā'ēr-ō-foil″), *n.* any thin winglike structure, flat or curved, designed to support bodies by its reaction on the air through which it moves.

a-ër-o-gram (ā'ēr-ō-grăm″), *n.* a message sent by wireless telegraphy.

a-ër-o-gun (ā'ēr-ō-gŭn″), *n.* a gun for use against aircraft.

a-ër-o-lite (ā'ēr-ō-līt), *n.* a meteorite or shooting star; a meteoric stone. Also, **a'ër-o-lith** (-lĭth).

a-ër-ol-o-gy (ā″ēr-ŏl'ō-jĭ), *n.* the science of the air; the study dealing with atmospheric laws and conditions.—*adj.* **a″ër-o-log'i-cal.**—*n.* **a″ër-ol'o-gist.**

a-ër-o-me-chan-ic (ā″ēr-ō-mē-kăn'ĭk), *n.* one who is expertly trained in the adjustment and repair of flying machines.—*adj.* **a″ër-o-me-chan'i-cal.**

a-ër-om-e-ter (ā″ēr-ŏm'ē-tēr), *n.* an instrument for weighing and measuring gases, esp. the air.—*n.* **a″ër-om'e-try.**—*adj.* **a″ër-o-met'ric.**

a-ër-o-naut (ā'ēr-ō-nôt), *n.* an aërial navigator; an aviator or balloonist.—*n.* **a'ër-o-naut″ism.**

a-ër-o-nau-tic (ā″ēr-ō-nô'tĭk), *adj.* relating to the science or art of flying. Also, **a″ër-o-nau'ti-cal.**

a-ër-o-nau-tics (ā″ēr-ō-nô'tĭks), *n. pl.* used as *sing.* aërial navigation, as in an airplane; also, the science or art of traveling in the air.

a-ër-o-plane (ā'ēr-ō-plān″), *n.* an aircraft or flying machine, kept aloft by the reaction of motor-propelled planes upon the air. See **air'plane″**, *Pfd. S.*

a-ër-o-plan-ist (ā'ēr-ō-plān″ĭst), *n.* the operator of an airplane.

a-ër-o-stat (ā'ēr-ō-stăt), *n.* a balloon; a flying machine.

a-ër-o-stat-ics (ā″ēr-ō-stăt'ĭks), *n. pl.* used as *sing.* the branch of science that deals with the mechanical properties of air and of gases not in motion, and with the balance between them: used in connection with the operation of gas balloons or lighter-than-air flying machines.—*adj.* **a″ër-o-stat'ic; a″ër-o-stat'i-cal.**

a-ër-o-sta-tion (ā″ēr-ō-stā'shŭn), *n.* that part of the science of aërial navigation that deals with lighter-than-air flying machines, or aircraft not provided with motive power.

a-ër-o-view (ā'ēr-ō-vū″), *n.* a view from an airplane above the earth.

Æs-cu-la-pi-us (ĕs″kū-lā'pĭ-ŭs), *n.* the Roman god of medicine: identical with the Greek god *Asclepius.*—*adj.* **Æs″cu-la'pi-an.**

Æ-sir (ē'sĭr; â'sĭr), *n.pl.* in Norse mythology, the older or chief gods, including Odin, Thor, Tyr, Balder, Forseti, Heimdall, Loki, etc., who lived with Frigg, Freya, and other goddesses in Asgard: distinguished from the *Vanir*, who lived in Vanaheim.

æs-thete (ĕs'thēt), *n.* **1**, one who has, or aspires to have, a cultivated taste for the beautiful in nature or art; one sensitive to beauty; **2**, a pretender to such taste or sensitiveness. Also, **es'thete.**

æs-thet-ic (ĕs-thĕt'ĭk), *adj.* **1**, pertaining to beauty; **2**, appreciating the beautiful; having a cultivated, artistic taste. Also, **es-thet'ic.**—*adj.* **æs-thet'i-cal.**—*adv.* **æs-thet'i-cal-ly.**

æs-thet-ics (ĕs-thĕt'ĭks), *n. pl.* used as *sing.* the science or theory of the beautiful in nature or art. Also, **es-thet'ics.**

a-far (ȧ-fär'), *adv.* at, to, or from, a distance; as, the sound came from *afar.*

af-fa-bil-i-ty (ăf″ȧ-bĭl'ĭ-tĭ), *n.* friendly, easy courtesy.

af-fa-ble (ăf'ȧ-bl), *adj.* easy to approach; courteous in speech and manner; friendly.—*adv.* **af'fa-bly.**—*n.* **af'fa-ble-ness.**

af-fair (ă-fâr'), *n.* **1**, an event or proceeding referred to indefinitely; as, the *affair* went off smoothly; **2**, that which is done, or is to be done; **3**, often in *pl.*, business of any kind: as, one's private *affairs.*

[1]**af-fect** (ă-fĕkt′), *v.t.* to produce an effect upon; modify; influence; as, heat *affects* the body.

[2]**af-fect** (ă-fĕkt′), *v.t.* **1**, to pretend to do or have; also, to do for effect; as, to *affect* the manner of a bored person; **2**, to show a liking for; be fond of.

af-fec-ta-tion (ăf″ĕk-tā′shŭn), *n.* **1**, the assuming of a manner which is not one's own; **2**, display; **3**, pretense.

af-fect-ed (ă-fĕk′tĕd), *p.adj.* **1**, attacked, as by disease; **2**, not natural; as, *affected* manners.—*adv.* **af-fect′ed-ly.**

af-fect-ing (ă-fĕk′tĭng), *p.adj.* having power to excite the emotions; pathetic.—*adv.* **af-fect′ing-ly.**

af-fec-tion (ă-fĕk′shŭn), *n.* **1**, the state of having the feelings touched or excited; **2**, inclination; attachment; fondness; **3**, disease; as, an *affection* of the eyes.
Syn. love, attraction, liking.

af-fec-tion-ate (ă-fĕk′shŭn-ăt), *adj.* having or expressing love; kind; fond.—*adv.* **af-fec′tion-ate-ly.**

af-fi-ance (ă-fī′ăns), *n.* **1**, trust; faith; **2**, a marriage contract:—*v.t.* [*p.t.* and *p.p.* -anced (-ănst), *p.pr.* -anc-ing], to betroth, or bind by promise of marriage.

af-fi-da-vit (ăf″ĭ-dā′vĭt), *n.* a sworn statement in writing, esp. one made before a properly authorized officer.

af-fil-i-ate (ă-fĭl′ĭ-āt), *v.t.* [*p.t.* and *p.p.* -at″ed, *p.pr.* -at″ing], **1**, to adopt; receive into a family as a son or daughter; **2**, to receive into a society or club; **3**, to join; as, to *affiliate* oneself with a certain set of people:—*v.i.* to be intimately connected or associated: followed by *with;* as, he *affiliated* with a number of learned societies.—*n.* **af-fil″i-a′tion.**

af-fin-i-ty (ă-fĭn′ĭ-tĭ), *n.* [*pl.* affinities (-tĭz)], **1**, nearness of kin; **2**, relationship by marriage, in distinction to relationship by blood; **3**, a natural liking for a person; also, one of two persons naturally drawn to each other; **4**, physical or chemical attraction; **5**, in zoölogy, a relationship between species or groups depending on likeness of structure.
Syn. similarity, resemblance, attraction.—*Ant.* dislike, repulsion, aversion.

af-firm (ă-fûrm′), *v.t.* to assert strongly:—*v.i.* **1**, to confirm a judgment, decree, or order, in court; **2**, to assert something with confidence; **3**, in law, to make a solemn statement, as before a magistrate, but without taking oath.
Syn. maintain, allege. (See assert.)

af-fir-ma-tion (ăf″ẽr-mā′shŭn), *n.* **1**, the act of asserting or declaring anything to be true; **2**, a solemn statement, as in court, made without taking an oath.

af-firm-a-tive (ă-fûr′mȧ-tĭv), *n.* that which declares; a statement which asserts that a fact is so:—*adj.* **1**, positive; confident; **2**, answering, or consisting of, "yes"; as, an *affirmative* answer; **3**, in a debate, supporting a motion or proposition as stated.—*adv.* **af-firm′a-tive-ly.**

af-fix (ă-fĭks′), *v.t.* to attach; fasten to:—*n.* (ăf′ĭks), a letter or syllable put at the beginning or end of a word; a suffix or prefix.

af-flict (ă-flĭkt′), *v.t.* to cause prolonged pain to body or mind; distress; cast down; trouble grievously.

af-flic-tion (ă-flĭk′shŭn), *n.* distress; prolonged pain of body or mind.
Syn. pain, calamity, misfortune, adversity.

af-flu-ence (ăf′lo͞o-ĕns), *n.* an abundant supply, as of thoughts, words, or riches; wealth.

af-flu-ent (ăf′lo͞o-ĕnt), *adj.* **1**, having abundance; wealthy; **2**, flowing freely:—*n.* a stream or river that flows into another.—*adv.* **af′flu-ent-ly.**

af-ford (ă-fōrd′), *v.t.* **1**, to supply; produce; yield; as, singing *affords* him pleasure; **2**, to be able to bear the expense of, as in money or effort.

af-fray (ă-frā′), *n.* **1**, a noisy quarrel; **2**, in law, the fighting of two or more persons in a public place.

af-fright (ă-frīt′), *v.t.* to frighten; terrify; alarm; confuse:—*n.* fear; fright.

af-front (ă-frŭnt′), *v.t.* **1**, to insult intentionally; **2**, to front upon; face.
Syn. annoy, displease, insult, irritate offend, nettle, slight, provoke.—*Ant.* gratify, oblige, conciliate.

Af-ghan (ăf′găn), *n.* a native of Afghanistan, a small country in Asia:—*adj.* relating to Afghanistan: **afghan,** a crocheted or knitted wool blanket.

a-field (ȧ-fēld′), *adv.* **1**, to, in, or on, the field; **2**, astray; out of the way.

a-fire (ȧ-fīr′), *adj.* and *adv.* on fire; as, a house *afire;* to set *afire.*

a-flame (ȧ-flām′), *adj.* and *adv.* on fire; ablaze; as, *aflame* with patriotism.

a-float (ȧ-flōt′), *adj.* and *adv.* **1**, borne on the water; on shipboard; **2**, in circulation, as a rumor; **3**, adrift; moving.

a-foot (ȧ-fo͝ot′), *adv.* **1**, on foot; as, they traveled *afoot;* **2**, astir; stirring; about, as a rumor.

a-fore-said (ȧ-fōr′sĕd″), *adj.* said or spoken of before.

a-fore-thought (ȧ-fōr′thôt″), *adj.* planned, designed, or thought beforehand.

a-fore-time (ȧ-fōr′tīm″), *adv.* formerly; previously.

a-foul (ȧ-foul′), *adj.* and *adv.* in entanglement or collision; as, to fall *afoul* of an obstacle.

a-fraid (ȧ-frād′), *adj.* frightened; filled with fear.
Syn. frightened. *Afraid* expresses a general state of fear; as, he is *afraid* of snakes. *Frightened* names a sudden, intense, and usually temporary, attack of fear; as, the barking of the dog *frightened* her.—*Ant.* bold, brave.

af-reet (ăf′rēt; ȧ-frēt′), *n.* a powerful and evil spirit, demon, or monstrous giant, in Arabian legends. Also, **af′rit; af′rite.**

a-fresh (ȧ-frĕsh′), *adv.* again; anew; newly; over again.

Af-ri-can (ăf′rĭ-kăn), *n.* a native of Africa:—*adj.* relating to Africa: **African lily,** a cultivated plant of the lily family, orig. from South Africa, bearing bright blue flowers (see *inflorescence,* illus.).

aft (ȧft), *adj.* and *adv.* toward the stern or back part of a ship: a nautical term.

aft-er (ȧf′tẽr), *adj.* **1**, next; subsequent; later; as, in *after* days; **2**, behind in place; as, the *after* part of a ship:—*adv.* behind; subsequently in time or place:—*prep.* **1**, in succession to; as, you come *after* me; **2**, later than; as, Monday comes *after* Sunday; **3**, in imitation of; as, do it *after* me; **4**, according to; in the manner of; as, a painting *after* Raphael; **5**, next to in rank or excellence; **6**, in pursuit of; as, to run *after* a rabbit; **7**, by the name of; as, named *after* his father: **after all,** all things considered; on the whole:—*conj.* later than.

aft-er-clap (ȧf′tẽr-klăp″), *n.* something unexpected happening after an affair is supposed to be at an end.

aft-er-damp (ȧf′tẽr-dămp″), *n.* the suffocating gas found in coal mines after an explosion of fire damp: distinguished from *choke damp.*

aft-er-glow (ȧf′tẽr-glō″), *n.* the reflection left in the west after sunset.

aft-er-math (ȧf′tẽr-măth), *n.* **1**, a second mowing in a season; **2**, that which follows any condition or circumstance.

aft-er-most (ȧf′tẽr-mōst), *adj.* superlative of *after:* last; hindmost.

aft-er-noon (ȧf″tẽr-nōōn′), *n.* the time between noon and evening.

aft-er-thought (ȧf′tẽr-thôt″), *n.* reflection begun after an act is finished; esp., an idea that comes too late.

aft-er-wards (ȧf′tẽr-wẽrdz), *adv.* at a later time; subsequently. Also, **aft′er-ward.**

a-gain (ȧ-gĕn′; *Br.* -gān′), *adv.* **1**, a second time; once more; **2**, in return; **3**, further; on the other hand: **again and again**, repeatedly.

a-gainst (ȧ-gĕnst′; *Br.* -gānst′), *prep.* **1**, in contact with; near to; as, the table is *against* the wall; **2**, opposite to; facing toward; in the direction of; as, over *against* Jericho; **3**, in opposition to; as, I am *against* the plan; **4**, in preparation for; as, money laid by *against* a rainy day; **5**, in exchange for; as an offset to; as, payment *against* a loan.

Ag-a-mem-non (ăg″ȧ-mĕm′nŏn), *n.* in mythology, king of Mycenæ, son of Atreus, brother of Menelaus, and commander in chief of the Greeks at the siege of Troy.

a-gape (ȧ-gȧp′; ȧ-gāp′), *adj.* and *adv.* gaping; with the mouth wide open in a state of astonishment or eager attention.

ag-a-ric (ăg′ȧ-rĭk; ȧ-găr′ĭk), *n.* any of a family of mushrooms, esp. the common field and cultivated mushroom.

ag-ate (ăg′ȧt), *n.* **1**, a precious stone, with colors in stripes, clouds, etc.; **2**, a boy's playing marble; **3**, a small size of type, approximately 5½ point, the size used in the text of this book (see *type*).

a-ga-ve (ȧ-gā′vē), *n.* any of a genus (*Agave*) of American plants, including the century plant and some other fiber-producing plants.

age (āj), *n.* **1**, a particular period of time in life or in history; **2**, the length of time already lived; **3**, *Colloq.*, a long or weary time:—*v.i.* and *v.t.* [*p.t.* and *p.p.* aged (ājd), *p.pr.* ag′ing], to grow, or cause to grow, old.

-age (-ĭj), *n. suffix*, denoting: **1**, a collection, sum, etc.; as, foli*age;* mile*age;* **2**, the act or process; as, pass*age;* mass*age;* **3**, fees for or cost of; as, cart*age;* **4**, condition; rank; as, bond*age;* peer*age.*

ag-ed (āj′ĕd; ājd), *p.adj.* **1**, old; far on in years; **2**, (ājd), having (a specified number of) years; as, a child *aged* three.

a-gen-cy (ā′jĕn-sĭ), *n.* [*pl.* agencies (-sĭz)], **1**, operation; action; **2**, the business of one who acts for another; **3**, a place where business is done for another person or firm; **4**, means.

a-gen-da (ȧ-jĕn′dȧ), [Lat.], *n. pl.* [*sing.* agendum (-dŭm)], things to be done; specif., items on a program of business to be brought before a committee or conference.

a-gent (ā′jĕnt), *n.* **1**, one who acts, esp. for another; **2**, an active power or cause; as, to use a chemical *agent.*

Syn. actor, doer, factor, operator, performer.

Ag-ge-us (ă-gē′ŭs), *n.* Haggai: so called in the Douay Bible.

ag-glom-er-ate (ă-glŏm′ẽr-āt), *v.t.* [*p.t.* and *p.p.* -at″ed, *p.pr.* -at″ing], to gather into a cluster or heap; accumulate:—*adj.* (ă-glŏm′ẽr-ȧt), gathered into a heap or cluster:—*n.* a mixed collection or heap of things.—*n.* **ag-glom″er-a′tion.**

ag-glu-ti-nate (ă-glōō′tĭ-nāt), *v.t.* [*p.t.* and *p.p.* -nat″ed, *p.pr.* -nat″ing], to unite, as by glue:—*adj.* glued together; adhering.—*adj.* **ag-glu′ti-na-tive.**

ag-gran-dize (ăg′răn-dīz), *v.t.* [*p.t.* and *p.p.* -dized (-dīzd), *p.pr.* -diz″ing], **1**, to make greater in power, rank, or riches; enlarge; extend; **2**, to glorify; exalt.—*n.* **ag-gran′dize-ment.**

ag-gra-vate (ăg′rȧ-vāt), *v.t.* [*p.t.* and *p.p.* -vat″ed, *p.pr.* -vat″ing], **1**, to add to or increase, as a burden; to make heavier or worse; **2**, *Colloq.*, to trouble or annoy; irritate.—*p.adj.* **ag′gra-vat″ing.**—*adv.* **ag′gra-vat″ing-ly.**

Syn. heighten, intensify, magnify.—*Ant* diminish, lessen, reduce.

ag-gra-va-tion (ăg″rȧ-vā′shŭn), *n.* **1**, the act of increasing or making heavier; **2**, a circumstance that adds to or increases: often used in connection with crimes, offenses, or hardships; **3**, *Colloq.*, exasperation; irritation; provocation.

ag-gre-gate (ăg′rē-gāt), *v.t.* [*p.t.* and *p.p.* -gat″ed, *p.pr.* -gat″ing], **1**, to collect or bring together; **2**, *Colloq.*, to amount to; as, his debts *aggregated* fifty dollars:—*n.* (ăg′rē-gȧt), **1**, the entire number; total; as, the *aggregate* of his debts; **2**, a mass formed by the union of similar particles:—*adj.* formed into a mass or total; as, the *aggregate* amount.

ag-gre-ga-tion (ăg″rē-gā′shŭn), *n.* a collection of units gathered into one whole or mass.

ag-gres-sion (ă-grĕsh′ŭn), *n.* unprovoked attack or assault; an act of unfriendliness or offense, as an unlawful entering upon another's rights or territory.

ag-gres-sive (ă-grĕs′ĭv), *adj.* **1**, moving forward with vigor; **2**, quick to attack, or to press or support a cause.—*adv.* **ag-gres′sive-ly.**—*n.* **ag-gres′sive-ness.**

ag-gres-sor (ă-grĕs′ẽr), *n.* one who attacks or injures another without just cause; one who makes the first move in a quarrel.

ag-grieve (ă-grēv′), *v.t.* [*p.t.* and *p.p.* -grieved′ (-grēvd′), *p.pr.* -griev′ing], to bear heavily upon; oppress; cause sorrow to; afflict, esp. by unjust treatment.

a-ghast (ȧ-gȧst′), *adj.* struck with sudden surprise, horror, or terror.

ag-ile (ăj′ĭl; *Br.* ăj′īl), *adj.* quick-moving; active; nimble: said of the mind or body.—*adv.* **ag′ile-ly.**

a-gil-i-ty (ȧ-jĭl′ĭ-tĭ), *n.* nimbleness; quickness; briskness.

ag-i-o (ăj′ĭ-ō; ā′jĭ-ō), *n.* [*pl.* agios (-ōz)], **1**, the premium paid when one kind of money is exchanged for another; discount; **2**, loosely, money changing.

ag-i-tate (ăj′ĭ-tāt), *v.t.* [*p.t.* and *p.p.* -tat″ed, *p.pr.* -tat″ing], **1**, to stir violently; **2**, to excite; disturb; **3**, to discuss; keep constantly before the public.

ag-i-ta-tion (ăj″ĭ-tā′shŭn), *n.* **1**, the act of exciting or arousing; **2**, the motion, interest, or excitement so produced; **3**, open, active discussion or promotion, as of a civic or political project.

ag-i-ta-tor (ăj′ĭ-tā″tẽr), *n.* **1**, one who makes a political or industrial disturbance; **2**, an implement for stirring.

a-gley (ȧ-glē′; ȧ-glī′), *adv.* askew· wrong. Also, **a-glee′.**

a-glow (ȧ-glō′), *adv.* in a glow:—*adj.* glowing; flushed with pleasure or excitement; as, her cheeks were all *aglow.*

ag-no-men (ăg-nō′mĕn), *n.* [*pl.* agnomina (-nŏm′ĭ-nȧ)], an additional title or name applied to a person, as in Frederick *the Great;* an epithet.

ag-nos-tic (ăg-nŏs′tĭk), *n.* one who denies that man knows the final or essential nature of things; one who neither affirms nor denies the existence of God:—*adj.* **1**, relating to those who deny all knowledge of

God, or of the nature of things.
Syn., *n.* disbeliever, unbeliever, freethinker, infidel, heretic, skeptic.

ag-nos-ti-cism (ăg-nŏs′tĭ-sĭzm), *n.* the belief or doctrine that the existence of God and the essential nature of things are not matters of certain knowledge.

***Ag-nus De-i** (ăg′nŭs dē′ī), [Lat.], **1**, the Lamb of God: a title applied to Jesus by John the Baptist (John 1:29); **2**, an emblem of Christ in the form of a lamb, often bearing a banner marked with a cross.

a-go (ȧ-gō′), *adj.* gone; past: used always after the noun; as, a thousand years *ago:*—*adv.* in past time; as, long *ago.*

a-gog (ȧ-gŏg′), *adv.* and *adj.* in a state of eager desire; highly excited by eagerness or curiosity; astir; alive with interest; as, the village was all *agog.*

a-go-ing (ȧ-gō′ĭng), *adv.* and *adj.* in motion; as, to set *agoing.*

ag-o-nize (ăg′ō-nīz), *v.i.* [*p.t.* and *p.p.* -nized (-nīzd), *p.pr.* -niz″ing], to suffer extreme pain; make great effort of any kind:—*v.t.* to cause to suffer greatly.—*p. adj.* **ag′o-niz″ing.**

ag-o-ny (ăg′ō-nĭ), *n.* [*pl.* agonies (-nĭz)], **1**, intense suffering; extreme mental or physical pain; **2**, death struggle.

a-gra-ri-an (ȧ-grā′rĭ-ăn), *adj.* **1**, relating to land, or to the right or manner of holding real estate; **2**, growing wild in the fields:—*n*, one who is in favor of an equal division of public lands.—*n.* **a-gra′ri-an-ism.**

a-gree (ȧ-grē′), *v.i.* [*p.t.* and *p.p.* a-greed′ (-grēd′), *p.pr.* a-gree′ing], **1**, to harmonize physically, mentally, or morally; **2**, to yield assent; consent; accede; **3**, to accord; come to one opinion; **4**, to be similar; match; **5**, to be suitable as diet; as, strawberries do not *agree* with everybody.
Syn. concur, acquiesce. (See accord.)

a-gree-a-ble (ȧ-grē′ȧ-bl), *adj.* **1**, pleasing to the mind or senses; **2**, conformable; suitable; **3**, *Colloq.*, willing. —*n.* **a-gree″a-bil′i-ty.**—*n.* **a-gree′a-ble-ness.** —*adv.* **a-gree′a-bly.**
Syn. pleasant, amiable, charming.

a-gree-ment (ȧ-grē′mĕnt), *n.* **1**, harmony of opinions or feelings; **2**, in grammar, the correspondence of one word with another in gender, number, case, or person; **3**, a compact; contract; mutual understanding.
Syn. bargain. (See contract.)

ag-ri-cul-ture (ăg′rĭ-kŭl″tŭr), *n.* cultivation of the soil; husbandry; farming.—*n.* **ag″ri-cul′tur-ist.**—*adj.* **ag″ri-cul′tur-al.**—*adv.* **ag″ri-cul′tur-al-ly.**

a-ground (ȧ-ground′), *adj.* and *adv.* on the ground; like a ship whose keel touches the bottom; stranded: opp. of *afloat.*

a-gue (ā′gū), *n.* **1**, a malarial fever recurring at regular intervals and attended by chills and sweating; **2**, a chill.

ah (ä), *interj.* an exclamation expressing sudden, but mild, emotion, as pity.

a-ha (ȧ-hä′), *interj.* expressing triumph, surprise, or contempt.

A-hab (ā′hăb), *n.* a king of Israel led into the worship of idols by his wife, Jezebel (1 Kings 16–22).

A-has-u-e-rus (ȧ-hăz″ū-ē′rŭs; ȧ-hăs′-), *n.* in the Bible, the name of each of two great kings of the Medes and Persians (Esther 1).

a-head (ȧ-hĕd′), *adv.* to or in the front; forward; onward.

a-hem (ȧ-hĕm′), *interj.* a clearing of the throat to attract attention.

a-hoy (ȧ-hoi′), *interj.* a term used in hailing a vessel; as, ship *ahoy!*

a-i (ä′ē), *n.* either of two sloths of South America; so called from the cry.

aid (ād), *v.t.* to assist; help:—*n.* **1**, help; assistance; also, something that is of assistance; **2**, (often, *aide*), a person that helps, as in a church social.
Syn., *v.* sustain, relieve, succor. (See help.)

aid-de-camp (ād′=dē=kămp″; *Fr.* ād′=dē=kăṅ″), *n.* [*pl.* aids-de-camp (ādz′=; ād′=)], an officer who assists a general: also called *aide.* Also, **aide′-de-camp″** [*pl.* aides=de=camp (ādz′=)].

aide (ād), *n.* **1**, an aid-de-camp; **2**, (also, *aid*), a person who aids or assists.

ai-grette (ā-grĕt′; ā′grĕt), *n.* a plume of gems, or esp. of feathers, worn on helmets and as an article of woman's headdress. Also, **ai′gret; e′gret.**

ail (āl), *v.t.* to give or cause pain or discomfort to; as, something *ails* the child:—*v.i.* to feel pain.

ai-le-ron (ā′lĕ-rŏn; *Fr.* â″lĕ-rôṅ′), *n.* a small hinged part of a wing on an airplane, operated by the pilot, for controlling the horizontal balance of the machine (see *airplane*, illus.).

ail-ment (āl′mĕnt), *n.* a slight disorder or disease of the body or mind; sickness; illness; indisposition.

aim (ām), *v.i.* **1**, to endeavor; **2**, to point a weapon at something:—*v.t.* **1**, to point (a weapon) with the purpose of hitting; **2**, to direct against; as, to *aim* a remark at anyone: —*n.* **1**, a purpose; an endeavor; **2**, a target; **3**, the pointing of a weapon.
Syn., *n.* mark, object, design.

aim-less (ām′lĕs), *adj.* without definite intention; purposeless.—*adv.* **aim′-less-ly.**—*n.* **aim′less-ness.**

Ai-nu (ī′nōō), a member of an aboriginal, now dwindling, race of Japan.

air (âr), *v.t.* **1**, to expose to the air; dry thoroughly, as clothes; **2**, to display; bring into public notice; as, to *air* one's views:—*n.* **1**, that combination of gases which supports life in the earth's atmosphere; the atmosphere; **2**, light wind; **3**, external manner; behavior; as, she had a gay *air;* **4**, in *pl.*, affected manners; **5**, in music, a melody: **air base**, a station for the housing, repair, and operation of aircraft: **air bladder**, a sac in a fish, filled with gas, useful for regulating its position in the water: **air brake**, a brake operated by compressed air: **air castle**, a visionary fancy; daydream: **air chamber**, a compartment filled with air, as in a lifeboat: **air gas**, an illuminating gas made from air charged with the vapor of petroleum, naphtha, etc.: **air gun**, a gun from which the projectile is expelled by compressed air: **air hole**, **1**, a local region in the atmosphere in which, as a result of irregular air currents, an aircraft receives little or no support, and drops as if into a hole; **2**, a spot in the ice not frozen over: **air line**, **1**, a straight line between two places; a bee line; **2**, a system of air transportation, or the company which owns and operates such a system: **air liner**, a passenger airplane traveling regularly over a definite route: **air lock**, an air-tight antechamber in a submarine caisson: **air mail**, mail carried by aircraft; also the system of so carrying it: **air pocket**, an air hole: **air pump**, a machine for compressing air, or for drawing it from or forcing it into an air-tight vessel: **air raid**, a military attack during which bombs are dropped on a target from aircraft: **air sleeve**, a cone, usually cloth, supported at the larger end, and above the ground, to show wind direction.

air-con-di-tion (âr′=kŏn-dĭsh″ŭn), *v.t.* to provide wanted temperature, humidity, and purity by circulating treated air within a structure.—*n.* **air-con-di′tion-ing.**

air-craft (âr′kraft″), *n.* [*pl.* aircraft], any form of machine for flying through the air, as an airplane or balloon.

Aire-dale (âr′dāl″), *n.* a terrier of a large, rough-coated breed, tan, with dark gray or grizzled back and sides.

air-field (âr′fēld), *n.* a cleared, flat area for airplane take-off and landing.

air-ing (âr′ĭng), *n.* **1**, a walk, ride, or drive in the open air; **2**, exposure to the air or fire for warming or drying.

air-lift (âr′lĭft), *n.* a military airplane service ferrying supplies and personnel over enemy-held territory. Also **air lift.**

-al (-ăl), *adj. suffix*, of, like, or pertaining to: as, fat*al;* natur*al:*—*n. suffix*, that which is like or pertaining to; as, recit*al;* withdraw*al.*

al-a-bas-ter (ăl′ȧ-bȧs″tẽr), *n.* **1**, a white, marblelike mineral, found chiefly in Italy; **2**, a banded, partly transparent mineral used by the ancients for vases and perfume bottles.

***à la carte** (ȧ lȧ kȧrt′), [Fr.], according to the card, or bill of fare: used of a meal in which each dish is paid for at a specified price, contrasted with *table d'hôte.*

a-lack (ȧ-lăk′), *interj.* an exclamation expressing blame, sorrow, or surprise.

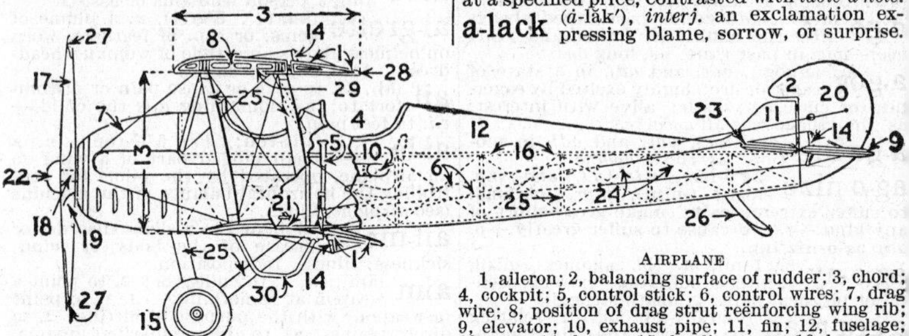

AIRPLANE

1, aileron; 2, balancing surface of rudder; 3, chord; 4, cockpit; 5, control stick; 6, control wires; 7, drag wire; 8, position of drag strut reënforcing wing rib; 9, elevator; 10, exhaust pipe; 11, fin; 12, fuselage; 13, gap; 14, horns; 15, landing gear; 16, longéron; 17, propeller blade; 18, propeller hub; 19, propeller root; 20, rudder; 21, rudder bar; 22, spinner; 23, stabilizer; 24, stays; 25, struts; 26, tail skid; 27, tipping; 28, trailing edge; 29, wing rib; 30, wing skid. (See also *empennage, dihedral, monoplane,* illus.)

air-plane (âr′plān″), *n.* a motor-propelled aircraft or flying machine kept aloft by the reaction of winglike planes upon the air. Also, **a′ër-o-plane″.**

air-port (âr′pōrt″), *n.* a place, either inland or on the seaboard, possessing facilities for the landing, departure, loading, fueling, or repairing of airships.

air-scape (âr′skāp), *n.* a view of a landscape from a lofty position, as from an airship.

air-ship (âr′shĭp″), *n.* **1**, any large machine for navigating the air; **2**, esp., a machine supported by gas-filled bags and propelled through the air by mechanical power, as the dirigible balloon.

air-strip (âr′strĭp), *n.* a runway for the take-off and landing of airplanes.

air–tight (âr′-tīt″), *adj.* so thoroughly closed that no air can enter.

air-way (âr′wā), *n. Aëro.*, a main thoroughfare or highway through the air, from one airport to another.

air-y (âr′ĭ), *adj.* [*comp.* air′i-er, *superl.* air′i-est], **1**, exposed to, or in, the air; breezy; **2**, unsubstantial; **3**, gay.—*adv.* **air′i-ly.**—*n.* **air′i-ness.**

aisle (īl), *n.* **1**, a passageway leading to the seats in a church or other place of assembly; **2**, an alleylike space, as in a store.

¹a-jar (ȧ-jär′), *adj.* and *adv.* slightly turned or opened, as a door.

²a-jar (ȧ-jär′), *adj.* and *adv.* out of harmony; as, his nerves were *ajar.*

A-jax (ā′jăks), *n.* **1**, in Homer's "Iliad," the son of Telamon, and, next to Achilles, the bravest of the Greeks: typical of brute strength without cleverness; **2**, the son of Oïleus, King of Locris, and second only to Achilles in fleetness: also called *Ajax the Less.*

a-kim-bo (ȧ-kĭm′bō), *adj.* and *adv.* with the hands on the hips and the elbows turned outward.

a-kin (ȧ-kĭn′), *adj.* and *adv.* **1**, of kin; related by blood; **2**, allied by nature, or having the same properties; similar.

al- (ăl-), *prefix*, a form of *ad-*, used for euphony before *l-* as, *al*leviate. See **ad-.**

a-lac-ri-ty (ȧ-lăk′rĭ-tĭ), *n.* eager readiness; joyous activity; briskness; as, to move with *alacrity.*—*adj.* **a-lac′ri-tous.**

A-lad-din (ȧ-lăd′ĭn), *n.* the hero of a story in the "Arabian Nights," who possessed a magic lamp.

al-a-mode (ăl′ȧ-mōd″; ȧ″lȧ-mōd′), *adv.* in the fashion:—*adj.* **1**, fashionable; **2**, served in some special manner, as pie with ice cream or beef with vegetables:—*n.* a thin, light, glossy black silk. Also, ***à la mode′*** (ȧ lȧ môd′).

a-larm (ȧ-lärm′), *v.t.* **1**, to arouse to a sense of danger; **2**, to strike with fear of danger:—*n.* **1**, a call to arms; **2**, a warning of danger; **3**, the fear of danger; **4**, a device to warn, as a fire whistle: **alarm clock**, a clock with a bell, adjustable to ring at a set time.

Syn., *v.* frighten, appall, terrify; *n.* (see horror).—*Ant.*, *v.* cheer, encourage, reassure.

a-larm-ing (ȧ-lärm′ĭng), *p.adj.* exciting apprehension or fear.

a-larm-ist (ȧ-lärm′ĭst), *n.* one who excites fear by exaggerating bad news or foretelling calamities.

a-la-ry (ā′lȧ-rĭ; ăl′ȧ-rĭ), *adj.* pertaining to wings; wing-shaped.

a-las (ȧ-lȧs′), *interj.* an exclamation expressing unhappiness.

alb (ălb), *n.* a church vestment of white linen worn over the cassock.

Al-ba-ni-an (ăl-bā′nĭ-ăn), *adj.* of or pertaining to Albania, a country in southeastern Europe:—*n.* **1**, a native of Albania; **2**, the language of Albania.

al-ba-tross (ăl′bȧ-trôs), *n.* **1**, a large sea bird of southern seas and the Pacific Ocean, capable of long-continued flight; **2**, a soft woolen material.

1/30

WANDERING ALBATROSS

al-be-it (ôl″bē′ĭt), *conj.* although; even though; notwithstanding.

al-bi-no (ăl-bī′nō), *n.* [*pl.* albinos (-nōz)], **1**, a person with abnormally white skin and hair, and pinkish eyes; **2**, an animal or plant paler in color than most of its kind.

Al-bi-on (ăl′bĭ-ŭn), *n.* a poetic name for England.

al-bum (ăl′bŭm), *n.* a blank book in which to insert autographs, photographs, stamps, or the like.

al-bu-men (ăl-bū′mĕn), *n.* **1**, the white of an egg; **2**, a thick, sticky substance found in many animals or plants.

al-bu-min (ăl-bū′mĭn), *n.* any of a class of chemical substances belonging to the proteins: found in the blood, milk, and muscles, and in plants, and used in sugar refining and other industries.

al-bu-mi-nous (ăl-bū′mĭ-nŭs), *adj.* containing, or pertaining to, albumen or albumin. Also, **al-bu′mi-nose.**

al-bur-num (ăl-bûr′nŭm), *n.* the outer shell of lighter-colored wood in a tree trunk, between the bark and the heartwood: also called *sapwood.*

al-cal-de (äl-käl′dā), *n.* in Spanish countries, a mayor or judge.

al-che-mist (ăl′kē-mĭst), *n.* one who studied or practiced alchemy, or medieval chemistry.

al-che-my (ăl′kē-mĭ), *n.* the chemistry of the Middle Ages, esp. as devoted to the search for a means of prolonging life and of transmuting or changing the common metals into gold.—*adj.* **al-chem′ic.**

al-co-hol (ăl′kō-hŏl), *n.* **1**, a colorless liquid made by the fermentation of a watery sugar solution, forming the intoxicating substance in all fermented and distilled liquors: a powerful solvent, antiseptic, and medicine; **2**, any of various related chemical substances: **wood alcohol,** a poisonous liquid, much used commercially as a fuel and a solvent.—*adj.* **al″co-hol′ic.**

al-co-hol-ism (ăl′kō-hŏl-ĭzm), *n.* a diseased condition produced by the use of fermented or distilled liquors.

Al-co-ran (ăl″kō-rän′; ăl′kō-răn), *n.* the sacred book of the Mohammedans; the Koran (which see). Also, **Al″ko-ran′.**

al-cove (ăl′kōv; ăl-kōv′), *n.* **1**, a recess in a room, as for a bed or bookcases; **2**, a retired spot, as in a garden.

Al-deb-a-ran (ăl-dĕb′ȧ-răn), *n.* a red star of the first magnitude, the brightest in the constellation Taurus.

al-der (ôl′dẽr), *n.* any of a certain genus of trees and shrubs growing in moist land, the bark of which is used in tanning.

al-der-man (ôl′dẽr-măn), *n.* [*pl.* aldermen (-mĕn)], **1**, in English and Irish municipalities, a magistrate next in rank to the mayor; **2**, in the U. S., one with varied powers and duties, representing a city ward or district.

ale (āl) *n.* a light-colored beer made from malt.

a-lee (ȧ-lē′), *adj.* and *adv.* on the lee or sheltered side of the ship; away from the wind: opp. of *aweather:* a nautical term.

a-lem-bic (ȧ-lĕm′bĭk), *n.* formerly, the cover or lid of an apparatus used in distilling; later, the apparatus itself; hence, anything that refines or purifies.

a-lert (ȧ-lûrt′), *adj.* on the watch; active; brisk; ready; vigilant:—*n.* a warning signal; a guarding against surprise: **on the alert,** ready to act; on the lookout.—*adv.* **a-lert′ly.**—*n.* **a-lert′ness.**

Syn., adj. attentive, observant, prompt.

Al-ex-an-drine (ăl″ĕg-zăn′drĭn), *n.* a verse of six feet of two syllables each, the accent falling on the second syllable of each foot.

al-fal-fa (ăl-făl′fȧ), *n.* a deep-rooted plant of the pea family, which grows from one to four feet in height and produces from two to six crops a year. In the western U. S. it is the staple hay and forage plant.

al-ga (ăl′gȧ), *n.* [*pl.* algæ (-jē)], a marine or fresh-water simple plant of any of various classes, ranging from one-celled organisms to very long plants, as seaweed, pond scums, etc.—*adj.* **al′gal.**

al-ge-bra (ăl′jē-brȧ), *n.* a branch of mathematics which extends the field of arithmetic by using letters and other symbols to represent quantities.—*adj.* **al″ge-bra′ic; al″ge-bra′i-cal.**—*n.* **al′ge-bra″ist.**

Al-ham-bra (ăl-hăm′brȧ), *n.* the Moorish royal palace at Granada, Spain.—*adj.* **Al″ham-bresque′.**

a-li-as (ā′lĭ-ăs), *n.* [*pl.* aliases (-ĕz)], an assumed name:—*adv.* otherwise named; as, Sawyer, *alias* Slippery Sam.

A-li Ba-ba (ăl′ĭ bä′bȧ; ä′lē bä′bä), a youth in one of the stories of the "Arabian Nights," who, by the magic words *open sesame,* enters the cave of the Forty Thieves.

al-i-bi (ăl′ĭ-bī), *n.* the plea of having been elsewhere at the time an offense was committed; also, incorrectly, an excuse.

al-ien (āl′yĕn), *n.* **1**, a foreigner; a person living in a country other than his own without the rights of citizenship; **2**, a stranger:—*adj.* **1**, foreign; strange; **2**, living in a country not one's own; **3**, different; hostile; as, acts *alien* to his principles.

al-ien-a-ble (āl′yĕn-ȧ-bl), *adj.* **1**, capable of being made indifferent or hostile in feeling; **2**, transferable, as property, by sale or gift.—*n.* **al″ien-a-bil′i-ty.**

al-ien-ate (āl′yĕn-āt), *v.t.* [*p.t.* and *p.p.* -at″ed, *p.pr.* -at″ing], to estrange or turn away, as the affections; transfer to another, as property.

al-ien-a-tion (āl″yĕn-ā′shŭn), *n.* **1**, a withdrawing or an estrangement, as of feeling or the affections; **2**, mental derangement; insanity.

al-ien-ist (āl′yĕn-ĭst), *n.* a doctor who specializes in mental diseases.

[1]**a-light** (ȧ-līt′), *adj.* and *adv.* lighted; in a flame.

[2]**a-light** (ȧ-līt′), *v.i.* [*p.t.* and *p.p.* a-light′ed or a-lit′(-lĭt′)], **1**, to dismount; **2**, to descend and settle, as birds.

a-lign (ȧ-līn′), *v.t.* and *v.i.* to place, or become arranged, in a straight line; form in line, as troops. Also, **a-line′.**

a-lign-ment (ȧ-līn′mĕnt), *n.* the act of arranging in line; also, the state of being so adjusted. Also, **a-line′ment.**

a-like (ȧ-līk′), *adj.* resembling one another; similar:—*adv.* in the same manner.

Syn., adj. similar, identical. *Alike* implies an actual sameness in definite respects between persons or things; as, the brothers looked *alike. Similar* is used to indicate merely a general likeness; as, the conditions were *similar. Identical* means the very same; as, the signatures on the will and the letter were *identical.*—*Ant., adj.* dissimilar, different, unlike.

al-i-ment (ăl′ĭ-mĕnt), *n.* food; nutriment; hence, that which sustains or supports.—*adj.* **al″i-men′tal.**

al-i-men-ta-ry (ăl″ĭ-mĕn′tȧ-rĭ), *adj.* pertaining to food; nutritious or nourishing: **alimentary canal,** the great duct or tube through which food is conveyed to the stomach and assimilated, the unused matter being carried off.

al-i-mo-ny (ăl′ĭ-mō-nĭ), *n.* means of living; an allowance made by decree of court to a wife out of her husband's estate, as on separation or divorce,

al-i-quot (ăl′ĭ-kwŏt), *adj.* contained in something else an exact number of times; as, 5 is an *aliquot* part of 15.

a-live (*ȧ*-līv′), *adj.* **1**, having life; **2**, in a state of action; sprightly; attentive; sensitive; as, he is *alive* in every fiber; **3**, full of living things; as, *alive* with flies.

al-ka-li (ăl′k*ȧ*-lī; -lĭ), *n.* [*pl.* alkalies; alkalis (-līz; -lĭz)], one of a class of substances, as soda or potash, having the common properties of combining with acids to form salts, of combining with fats to form soap, and of changing the tint of many coloring matters; a base.—*adj.* **al′ka-line.**

al-ka-loid (ăl′k*ȧ*-loid), *n.* in chemistry, any of a class of basic, organic compounds containing nitrogen, usually very poisonous, to which is due the active medicinal or harmful character of plants in which they occur, as morphine from the opium poppy, or nicotine from tobacco.

Al-ko-ran (ăl″kō-rän′; ăl′kō-răn), *n.* the sacred book of the Mohammedans; the Koran (which see). Also, **Al″co-ran′**, *Pfd. S.*

all (ôl), *adj.* **1**, the whole quantity of, as substance, duration, extent, amount, quality, or degree; as, *all* men; beyond *all* doubt; **2**, as much as possible; as, with *all* speed; **3**, nothing but; as, *all* work and no play:—*pron.* the whole; the whole quantity:—*n.* **1**, a whole; **2**, one's entire possessions:—*adv.* wholly; entirely; completely.

Al-lah (äl′*ȧ*; ȧl-lä′), *n.* the Mohammedan name for God.

Al-lan–a–Dale (ăl″ăn-*ȧ*-dāl′), *n.* one of the leaders of Robin Hood's band, and chief minstrel to the outlaw.

al-lay (*ȧ*-lā′), *v.t.* **1**, to quiet or calm; assuage; pacify; as, to *allay* his anger; **2**, to abate or lessen; as, to *allay* his pain.

Syn. lighten, moderate, reduce, relieve.—*Ant.* agitate, arouse, excite, provoke.

al-le-ga-tion (ăl″ē-gā′shŭn), *n.* **1**, the act of asserting; **2**, that which is asserted or offered as a plea or excuse; as, his *allegation* explains his act; **3**, a statement, as in a suit, of that which one is prepared to prove.

al-lege (ă-lĕj′), *v.t.* [*p.t.* and *p.p.* -leged′ (-lĕjd′), *p.pr.* -leg′ing], **1**, to produce as argument, plea, or excuse; **2**, to affirm; declare; assert; as, he *alleges* that he was there.

Syn. aver, adduce. (See assert.)

al-le-giance (ă-lē′jăns), *n.* **1**, the tie or obligation of a person to his sovereign or state; **2**, fidelity to a cause or person; **3**, the duty of loyalty.

al-le-gor-i-cal (ăl″ē-gŏr′ĭ-kăl), *adj.* figurative; describing by resemblance, as a parable. Also, **al″le-gor′ic.**—*adv.* **al″le-gor′i-cal-ly.**

al-le-go-rize (ăl′ē-gō-rīz), *v.t.* [*p.t.* and *p.p.* -rized (-rīzd), *p.pr.* -riz″ing], **1**, in a story, to represent (a quality or idea) in the likeness of a person or thing; **2**, to interpret symbolically, or give a figurative meaning to; as, he *allegorized* the story:—*v.i.* to represent ideas by concrete things.

al-le-go-ry (ăl′ē-gō-rĭ), *n.* [*pl.* allegories (-rĭz)], **1**, the representing of ideas in a story by actual persons or things; **2**, such a story itself; as, "Pilgrim's Progress" is a great *allegory*.—*n.* **al′le-go-rist.**

*__al-le-gret-to__ (äl″lā-grĕt′tō), [It.], *adj.* and *adv.* in music, somewhat fast or lively, between *andante* (slow) and *allegro* (fast):—*n.* in music, a movement played in a moderately fast and lively tempo.

*__al-le-gro__ (äl-lā′grō), [It.], *adj.* and *adv.* in music, fast; lively:—*n.* in music, a movement played very fast, the only quicker movements being *presto* and *vivace.*

al-le-lu-ia (ăl″ē-lo͞o′y*ȧ*), *interj.* praise ye the Lord:—*n.* a song or cry of praise and joy. See **hal″le-lu′jah,** *Pfd. S.*

al-ler-gy (ăl′ẽr-jĭ). *n.* an extreme sensitivity to certain substances coming to the body from without, as certain kinds of pollen or dust.—*adj.* **al-ler′gic** (ă-lûr′jĭk).

al-le-vi-ate (ă-lē′vĭ-āt), *v.t.* [*p.t.* and *p.p.* -at″ed, *p.pr.* -at″ing], to lighten; lessen; make easier; mitigate; as, to *alleviate* suffering.—*n.* **al-le″vi-a′tion.**

[1]**al-ley** (ăl′ĭ), *n.* [*pl.* alleys (-ĭz)], **1**, a narrow passage in a building; **2**, a narrow way in a city; **3**, a long, narrow inclosure; as, a bowling *alley.*

[2]**al-ley** (ăl′ĭ), *n.* [*pl.* alleys (-ĭz)], a large marble, often colored: so called because originally made of alabaster.

al-ley-way (ăl′ĭ-wā″), *n.* a short or narrow passageway.

All Fools' Day April 1, observed by playing harmless tricks.

all hail all health! a phrase of salutation or greeting.

All-hal-lows (ôl″hăl′ōz), *n.pl.* used as *sing.* All Saints' Day, celebrated on November 1, in honor of all saints.

al-li-ance (ă-lī′ăns), *n.* **1**, relation or connection by birth or marriage; **2**, union between nations or parties; **3**, the nations or parties included in the union.

al-li-ga-tor (ăl′ĭ-gā″tẽr), *n.* **1**, any of a genus (*Alligator*) of reptiles in the crocodile family, with a short, broad snout

ALLIGATOR

and long teeth, living in marshes and along river banks, mainly in the southeastern U. S.; **2**, loosely, any crocodile.

al-lit-er-a-tion (ă-lĭt″ẽr-ā′shŭn), *n.* the repetition of the same initial sound in closely succeeding words, as in *r*ack and *r*uin, to *d*o or *d*ie.

al-lit-er-a-tive (ă-lĭt′ẽr-ā-tĭv), *adj.* having the same initial sound in words closely succeeding or directly following each other; as, *alliterative* verse.

al-lo-cate (ăl′ō-kāt), *v.t.* [*p.t.* and *p.p.* -cat″ed, *p.pr.* -cat″ing], to assign or allot; distribute; apportion; as, to *allocate* shares.—*n.* **al″lo-ca′tion.**

al-lo-di-al (ă-lō′dĭ-ăl), *n.* land owned free of rent or feudal obligation:—*adj.* pertaining to land so held. *Pfd. S.*, **a-lo′di-al.**

al-lo-path (ăl′ō-păth), *n.* one who favors or practices the system of curing disease known as allopathy.

al-lop-a-thy (ă-lŏp′*ȧ*-thĭ), *n.* a method of treating disease by giving remedies which will bring on conditions or symptoms different from those accompanying the disease to be cured: a term devised to name the usual or standard practice, to distinguish it from *homeopathy*, which see.—*n.* **al-lop′a-thist.**—*adj.* **al″lo-path′ic** (ăl″ō-păth′ĭk).

al-lot (ă-lŏt′), *v.t.* [*p.t.* and *p.p.* -lot′ted, *p.pr.* -lot′ting], **1**, to distribute or divide, as by lot; **2**, to apportion, as shares; **3**, to assign or grant for a specific purpose.

al-lot-ment (ă-lŏt′mĕnt), *n.* **1**, the act of dividing or distributing; apportionment; **2**, that which is so divided; an allowance.

al-low (ă-lou′), *v.t.* **1**, to permit, consent to, or approve (an act); **2**, to grant permission to (a person); **3**, to admit, concede, or acknowledge, as a claim; **4**, to assign, grant, or set apart for a special purpose, or as a deduction or addition; as, to *allow* ten days for the trip; to *allow* ten per cent for breakage; **5**, to give; yield; grant; let one have:—*v.i.* to make concession or provision: used with *for*.

al-low-a-ble (ă-lou′*ȧ*-bl), *adj.* permissible; not forbidden or improper; acceptable.—*adv.* **al-low′a-bly.**

al-low-ance (ă-lou′ăns), *n.* **1**, admission; concession; sanction or approval; **2**, a definite sum or quantity granted; as, an *allowance* of spending money or food:—*v.t.* to limit to a fixed expenditure or consumption, as of money or food.

al-loy (ă-loi′), *n.* **1**, any mixture of metals; **2**, a baser metal used in mixture with a finer one; **3**, an admixture of good with evil:—*v.t.* **1**, to melt together or otherwise mix (two or more metals) so as to form a uniform compound; **2**, esp., to debase or reduce in standard or quality by mixture; as, to *alloy* gold or silver with copper.

all right *Colloq.*, Correct(ly); satisfactory. *Slang*, certainly.—**alright**, a popular form, not recognized as good usage.

all–round (ôl′=round″), *adj.* versatile, or many-sided; capable of doing many things; as, a good *all-round* workman.

All Saints' Day November **1**, celebrated in honor of all the saints; the day following Halloween.

All Souls' Day November 2, set apart by certain churches for prayer for the souls in purgatory.

all-spice (ôl′spīs″), *n.* **1**, the fruit or berry of the pimento, a tree of the West Indies; **2**, a spice made from it, supposed to combine the flavors of cinnamon, nutmeg, and cloves.

al-lude (ă-lūd′), *v.i.* [*p.t.* and *p.p.* -lud′ed, *p.pr.* -lud′ing], to refer indirectly: used with *to;* as, to *allude* to his misfortune.

al-lure (ă-lūr′), *v.t.* [*p.t.* and *p.p.* -lured′ (-lūrd′), *p.pr.* -lur′ing], to tempt by the offer of something really or apparently good or pleasurable; entice; attract.

al-lure-ment (ă-lūr′mĕnt), *n.* the act of attracting; temptation.

al-lur-ing (ă-lūr′ĭng), *p.adj.* tempting; enticing; fascinating.

al-lu-sion (ă-lū′zhŭn), *n.* **1**, a slight mention of something; a casual reference, as to a person or event; **2**, a comparison or reference for illustration; as, a literary *allusion*.

al-lu-sive (ă-lū′sĭv), *adj.* having reference to something not definitely or fully expressed; suggestive.—*adv.* **al-lu′sive-ly.**—*n.* **al-lu′sive-ness.**

al-lu-vi-al (ă-lū′vĭ-ăl), *adj.* relating to, or composed of, clay, mud, or other material deposited by running water.

al-lu-vi-um (ă-lū′vĭ-ŭm), *n.* [*pl.* alluviums (-ŭmz); alluvia (-*ȧ*)], **1**, a deposit of earth, sand, clay, etc., left by running water; **2**, land so made.

al-ly (ă-lī′), *v.t.* [*p.t.* and *p.p.* -lied′ (-līd′), *p.pr.* -ly′ing], **1**, to unite by marriage, treaty, league, or confederacy; **2**, to bind, as by friendship; connect, as by resemblance:—*n.* [*pl.* allies (ă-līz′)], one united, related, or associated by these means; a confederate.

Syn., n. partner, colleague, associate. *Ally* is used of an associate in affairs of state, esp. as applied to associates in war; as, Great Britain was an *ally* of France. *Partner* is used of an associate in business, in dancing, or on the same side in a game; as, he was my *partner* in the waltz. *Colleague* is applied to one of a body of professional, religious, or academic persons; as, the doctor was a *colleague* of mine. *Associate* names one who works with others in a business or profession; as, they were *associates* in the printing business.

Al-ma Ma-ter (ăl′m*ȧ* mā′tẽr; äl′m*ȧ* mä′tẽr), the college or other school in which one has been educated.—Also **al′ma ma′ter.**

al-ma-nac (ôl′m*ȧ*-năk), *n.* a yearbook, or calendar, giving the order of the days of the week and month, facts about the heavens, tide tables, church festivals and fasts, and other varied information.

al-might-y (ôl-mīt′ĭ), *adj.* possessing all power; of unlimited might: **the Almighty**, the omnipotent God.

al-mond (ä′mŭnd; ăl′mŭnd), *n.* **1**, the nutlike kernel of the fruit of a small tree somewhat like the peach; **2**, the tree itself; **3**, anything almond-shaped.

al-mon-er (ăl′mŭn-ẽr), *n.* one who dispenses or distributes charity.

al-most (ôl′mōst), *adv.* nearly; very nearly; well-nigh; all but.

alms (ämz), *n.pl.*, often used as *sing.*, **1**, charity; **2**, anything freely given to relieve the poor.

alms-house (ämz′hous″), *n.* a house supported by private or public charity and used as a home for the poor.

a-lo-di-al (ă-lō′dĭ-ăl), *adj.* pertaining to land held in unrestricted ownership, free of rent or feudal obligation: opp. of *feudal:*—*n.* formerly, land thus held: equivalent to land held in fee simple. Also, **al-lo′di-al.**

al-oe (ăl′ō), *n.* any of a number of plants with thick, spiny leaves, native in the warm climates of the Old World: **American aloe**, the century plant.

al-oes (ăl′ōz), *n.pl.*, usually used as *sing.*, **1**, a bitter drug, made from the juice of the leaves of some kinds of aloe; **2**, the fragrant resin or wood of the aloe tree.

a-loft (*ȧ*-lôft′), *adv.* **1**, on high; far above the earth; **2**, at the masthead, or on the higher yards or rigging of a ship.

a-lo-ha (ä-lō′hä), *n.* love: used also in Hawaii as a salutation or farewell.

a-lone (*ȧ*-lōn′), *adj.* and *adv.* without or apart from another; solitary; single.

a-long (*ȧ*-lông′), *prep.* by the length of; lengthwise of:—*adv.* **1**, in a line parallel with the length; **2**, onward; as, let us walk *along:* **along with**, in company with.

a-long-side (*ȧ*-lông′sīd″), *adv.* by the side; side by side: **alongside of**, beside:—*prep.* by the side of; beside.

a-loof (ă-lōōf′), *adj.* and *adv.* **1**, at a distance but within sight; **2**, purposely keeping apart; as, to stand *aloof*.—*n.* **a-loof′ness.**

a-loud (*ȧ*-loud′), *adv.* **1**, with raised voice; **2**, audibly.

alp (ălp), *n.* a lofty mountain: **the Alps**, a mountain chain of Europe.

al-pac-a (ăl-păk′*ȧ*), *n.* **1**, a sheeplike animal native to the Andes of Chile and Peru; **2**, the cloth made from the long, soft, silky wool of this animal.

al-pen-horn (ăl′pĕn-hôrn″), *n.* a long horn, used in the Alps.

al-pen-stock (ăl′pĕn-stŏk″), *n.* a stout staff, tipped with a spike, used by mountain climbers.

al-pha (ăl′f*ȧ*), *n.* the first letter [α, Α] of the Greek alphabet, approximately equivalent to English *a;* hence, the first or beginning of anything.

al-pha-bet (ăl′f*ȧ*-bĕt), *n.* the letters used in writing a language, arranged in their usual order.

al-pha-bet-i-cal (ăl″fȧ-bĕt′ĭ-kăl), *adj.* **1**, pertaining to the alphabet; **2**, designating the order in which the alphabet of a language is ordinarily arranged; also, arranged in an order based upon that of the letters of the alphabet; as, an *alphabetical* list of names. Also, **al″pha-bet′ic.**—*adv.* **al″pha-bet′i-cal-ly.**

al-pha-bet-ize (ăl′fȧ-bĕt-īz), *v.t.* [*p.t.* and *p.p.* -ized (-īzd), *p.pr.* -iz″ing], to arrange in alphabetical order.

Al-pine (ăl′pĭn; -pīn), *adj.* pertaining to the Alps: **alpine,** pertaining to any lofty mountain or mountain range.

al-read-y (ôl-rĕd′ĭ), *adv.* by or before a particular time; beforehand.

Al-sa-tian (ăl-sā′shăn), *adj.* pertaining to Alsace:—*n.* an inhabitant or native of Alsace.

al-so (ôl′sō), *adv.* in like manner; likewise; too; besides.

Al-ta-ir (ăl-tä′ĭr), *n.* the brightest star in the constellation Aquila.

al-tar (ôl′tẽr), *n.* **1**, a raised place of earth or stone, on which to offer sacrifice or burn incense; **2**, in the Christian church, the communion table.

ANCIENT ALTAR

al-ter (ôl′tẽr), *v.t.* to cause to change; modify:—*v.i.* to become different.—*adj.* **al′ter-a-ble.**—*adj.* **al′ter-a-tive.**

al-ter-a-tion (ôl″tẽr-ā′shŭn), *n.* **1**, a change of form or state; **2**, the act of making the change; **3**, the effect caused by changing.

al-ter-cate (ăl′tẽr-kāt; ôl′-), *v.i.* [*p.t.* and *p.p.* -cat″ed, *p.pr.* -cat″ing], to quarrel or dispute in words; wrangle.

al-ter-ca-tion (ăl″tẽr-kā′shŭn; ôl″-), *n.* a dispute; angry debate.

al-ter-nate (ăl′tẽr-nāt; ôl′-), *v.t.* [*p.t.* and *p.p.* -nat″ed, *p.pr.* -nat″ing], to cause to occur by turns; interchange regularly:—*v.i.* to act or take place by turns; as, day *alternates* with night: **alternating current,** an electrical current that reverses its direction periodically:—*adj.* (ăl-tûr′nȧt; ăl′tẽr-nȧt; ôl-), **1**, taking place by turns; first one and then the other; **2**, every other (one); **3**, in botany, branching singly from a stem at different levels:—*n.* a substitute; one appointed to act for another.—*adv.* **al-ter′nate-ly.**—*n.* **al-ter′nate-ness.**

al-ter-na-tion (ăl″tẽr-nā′shŭn; ôl″-), *n.* the taking turns or the following in succession, one after another; as, the *alternation* of day and night.

al-ter-na-tive (ăl-tûr′nȧ-tĭv; ôl-), *adj.* giving the choice of two things, only one of which may be taken, done, etc.:—*n.* a choice between two things or possible courses; as, his only *alternative* to death was flight.—*adv.* **al-ter′na-tive-ly.**

Syn., n. option, election, preference.

al-though (ôl-*th*ō′), *conj.* though; even if; notwithstanding. Also, **al-tho′.**

al-tim-e-ter (ăl-tĭm′ē-tẽr), *n.* an instrument for measuring altitude; esp., a barometer marked to show altitude instead of pressure: used on airplanes.

al-ti-tude (ăl′tĭ-tūd), *n.* **1**, space extended upward; height; as, the *altitude* of a mountain; **2**, highest point or degree; as, the *altitude* reached by a balloon.

al-to (ăl′tō), *adj.* high:—*n.* [*pl.* altos (-tōz)], **1**, the part sung by the lowest female voice; contralto; **2**, a person with such a voice, or the voice itself; **3**, the tenor violin or viola.

al-to-geth-er (ôl″to͞o-gĕ*th*′ẽr), *adv.* wholly; completely; entirely; without exception.

al-tru-ism (ăl′tro͞o-ĭzm), *n.* devoted regard for the interests of others: opp. of *egoism.*

al-tru-ist (ăl′tro͞o-ĭst), *n.* a person devoted to the welfare of others.—*adj.* **al″tru-is′tic.**—*adv.* **al″tru-is′ti-cal-ly.**

al-um (ăl′ŭm), *n.* a white, transparent, salt-like substance largely used in medicine and industry. Common alum is a double sulphate of aluminum and potassium.

a-lu-mi-na (ȧ-lū′mĭ-nȧ), *n.* a compound of aluminum and oxygen: the main part of all clays: largely used in dyeing and calico printing.

a-lu-mi-num (ȧ-lū′mĭ-nŭm), *n.* a bluish white metal noted for its lightness: the most plentiful of all metallic substances, but never found in a pure state. Also, **al″u-min′i-um.**—*adj.* **a-lu′mi-nous.**

a-lum-nus (ȧ-lŭm′nŭs), *n.* [*pl.* alumni (-nī)], a male graduate of a school, college, or university.—*n.fem.* **a-lum′na** [*pl.* alumnæ (-nē)].

al-ways (ôl′wāz; ôl′wȧz), *adv.* at all times; constantly; ever; continually. Also, *Archaic,* **al′way.**

a-lys-sum (ȧ-lĭs′ŭm), *n.* any of several plants bearing small, yellow or white, sweet-scented flowers: commonly called *sweet alyssum.*

am (ăm), the first person singular present indicative of the verb *be.*

a-main (ȧ-mān′), *adv.* with force or violence; suddenly; at full speed.

a-mal-gam (ȧ-măl′găm), *n.* **1**, any metallic mixture of which mercury is the chief ingredient; **2**, a mixture or compound of different things.

a-mal-ga-mate (ȧ-măl′gȧ-māt), *v.t.* [*p.t.* and *p.p.* -mat″ed, *p.pr.* -mat″ing], **1**, to alloy or mix (mercury) with another metal; **2**, to mix to form a compound:—*v.i.* to mix or combine so as to make uniform; as, one race *amalgamates* with another.

Syn. unite, blend, compound.

a-mal-ga-ma-tion (ȧ-măl″gȧ-mā′shŭn), *n.* **1**, the act of mixing mercury with another metal; **2**, the separation of precious metals from the mother rock by means of mercury; **3**, the blending or mixing of different elements or things; **4**, the union or consolidation, as of businesses.

a-man-u-en-sis (ȧ-măn″ū-ĕn′sĭs), *n.* [*pl.* amanuenses (-sēz)], one who writes for, or at the dictation of, another person; a secretary.

am-a-ranth (ăm′ȧ-rănth), *n.* **1**, an imaginary flower said by poets to be unfading; **2**, any of several bright plants, as the cockscomb; **3**, a color mixture in which the chief ingredient is magenta, a dark red dye.

am-a-ran-thine (ăm″ȧ-răn′thĭn), *adj.* **1**, never fading; undying; **2**, of a purplish color.

a-mass (ȧ-măs′), *v.t.* and *v.i.* to collect into a heap; gather together in great quantity; accumulate.

am-a-teur (ăm″ȧ-tûr′; ăm′ȧ-tûr), *n.* **1**, one who practices any art, study, or sport for pleasure but not for money; **2**, one whose work lacks professional finish.—*adj.* **am″a-teur′ish.**—*n.* **am″a-teur′ish-ness.**

am-a-tive (ăm′ȧ-tĭv), *adj.* full of love; loving.—*n.* **am′a-tive-ness.**

am-a-to-ry (ăm′ȧ-tō-rĭ), *adj.* relating to, or expressive of, love.

a-maze (ȧ-māz′), *v.t.* [*p.t.* and *p.p.* a-mazed′ (-māzd′), *p.pr.* a-maz′ing], to bewilder with fear or wonder; astonish; perplex.—*adv.* **a-maz′ed-ly.**—*n.* **a-maz′ed-ness.**

a-maze-ment (ȧ-māz′mĕnt), *n.* astonishment; perplexity or bewilderment arising from sudden surprise.
Syn. awe, wonder, surprise, confusion.

a-maz-ing (ȧ-māz′ĭng), *adj.* very wonderful; astonishing; astounding; bewildering.—*adv.* **a-maz′-ing-ly.**

Am-a-zon (ăm′ȧ-zŏn), *n.* one of a fabulous race of female warriors: **amazon,** a tall, strong, or masculine woman.

Am-a-zo-ni-an (ăm″ȧ-zō′nĭ-ăn), *adj.* **1,** pertaining to an Amazon; warlike; masculine; **2,** pertaining to the Amazon river:—*n.* an Amazon.

am-bas-sa-dor (ăm-băs′ȧ-dẽr), *n.* **1,** a government agent of highest rank representing his country's interests at a foreign capital; **2,** any representative or agent of another charged with a special mission: **ambassador extraordinary,** a minister or agent sent on a special mission by the government of one country to that of another: **ambassador plenipotentiary,** an agent sent by one country to another with full powers to make a treaty or an agreement. Also, **em-bas′sa-dor.**—*n. fem.* **am-bas′sa-dress.**—*adj.* **am-bas″-sa-do′ri-al.**

am-ber (ăm′bẽr), *n.* a yellowish resin, capable of high polish, found on the shores of the Baltic:—*adj.* **1,** made of amber; **2,** yellowish in color; as, an *amber* sky.

am-ber-gris (ăm′bẽr-grēs), *n.* a waxy substance coming from the sperm whale: used in perfumery.

am-bi-dex-trous (ăm″bĭ-dĕks′trŭs), *adj.* **1,** able to use both hands with equal skill; **2,** two-sided.—*adv.* **am″bi-dex′trous-ly.**

am-bi-ent (ăm′bĭ-ĕnt), *adj.* surrounding; inclosing; investing; encompassing; as, *ambient* light.

am-bi-gu-i-ty (ăm″bĭ-gū′ĭ-tĭ), *n.* [*pl.* ambiguities (-tĭz)], **1,** vagueness; uncertainty; **2,** an expression whose meaning can be taken in two or more ways.

am-big-u-ous (ăm-bĭg′ū-ŭs), *adj.* doubtful; having two or more possible meanings.—*adv.* **am-big′u-ous-ly.**—*n.* **am-big′u-ous-ness.**
Syn. uncertain, obscure, vague.—*Ant.* clear, plain, definite, specific.

am-bi-tion (ăm-bĭsh′ŭn), *n.* **1,** an eager desire to obtain some object, as wealth or power; **2,** the thing desired.

am-bi-tious (ăm-bĭsh′ŭs), *adj.* **1,** eager for advancement; strongly desirous; as, *ambitious* of wealth; **2,** determined to succeed; **3,** requiring great skill or effort for success; as, an *ambitious* program.—*adv.* **am-bi′tious-ly.**

am-ble (ăm′bl), *v.i.* [*p.t.* and *p.p.* -bled (-bld), *p.pr.* -bling], **1,** of people, to go at an easy pace; meander; **2,** of horses, to go at a certain gait in which the animal lifts the two feet on the same side together:—*n.* **1,** a peculiar gait of a horse; a pace; **2,** any easy gait.—*n.* **am′bler.**—*adj.* **am′bling.**

am-bro-si-a (ăm-brō′zhĭ-ȧ; -zĭ-ȧ), *n.* **1,** in mythology, the food of the gods; **2,** anything exquisitely pleasing to taste or smell; **3,** ragweed.—*adj.* **am-bro′si-al.**

am-bro-type (ăm′brō-tīp), *n.* a type of photograph taken on glass, in which the light parts are produced in silver, the background, through the clear glass, forming the dark parts.

am-bu-lance (ăm′bū-lăns), *n.* **1,** an inclosed vehicle for carrying the sick and wounded; **2,** a field hospital.

am-bu-la-to-ry (ăm′bū-lȧ-tō-rĭ), *adj.* **1,** pertaining to walking; **2,** having power to walk:—*n.* [*pl.* ambulatories (-rĭz)], a place to walk; a covered way.

am-bus-cade (ăm″bŭs-kād′), *n.* **1,** an ambush; a place where troops lie hidden to attack unexpectedly; also, troops so hidden; **2,** a lying in ambush:—*v.i.* [*p.t.* and *p.p.* -cad′ed, *p.pr.* -cad′ing], to lie in hiding:—*v.t.* to place (troops) in ambush.

am-bush (ăm′bo͝osh), *n.* **1,** a concealed station from which to attack the enemy unexpectedly; **2,** troops so attacking; **3,** the act of lying in wait for such a purpose:—*v.t.* to waylay; attack from ambush.

a-me-ba (ȧ-mē′bȧ), *n.* [*pl.* amebas (-bȧz); amebæ (-bē)], a microscopic animal: one of the simplest forms of animal life. Also, **a-mœ′ba,** *Pfd. S.*

a-meer (ȧ-mēr′), *n.* a prince; governor; esp., the Mohammedan ruler of Afghanistan. Also, **a-mir′.**

a-mel-io-rate (ȧ-mēl′yō-rāt), *v.t.* [*p.t.* and *p.p.* -rat″ed, *p.pr.* -rat″ing], to make better:—*v.i.* to grow better; improve.—*adj.* **a-mel′io-ra-tive.**

a-mel-io-ra-tion (ȧ-mēl″yō-rā′shŭn), *n.* improvement.

a-men (ā″mĕn′; ä″mĕn′), *adv.* and *interj.* verily; so be it: a word used at the end of a prayer or in solemn assent:—*n.* the saying of the word *amen.*

a-me-na-ble (ȧ-mē′nȧ-bl), *adj.* **1,** easy to lead; ready to accept advice; as, *amenable* to criticism; **2,** accountable; liable; as, *amenable* to the law.—*adv.* **a-me′na-bly.**—*n.* **a-me″na-bil′i-ty.**

a-mend (ȧ-mĕnd′), *v.t.* **1,** to change for the better; improve; correct; **2,** to change formally or with authority.

a-mend-a-to-ry (ȧ-mĕn′dȧ-tō-rĭ), *adj.* corrective; as, an *amendatory* clause was added to the law.

a-mend-ment (ȧ-mĕnd′mĕnt), *n.* **1,** a change for the better; **2,** the alteration or change of a government document, or an addition to it.

a-mends (ȧ-mĕndz′), *n.pl.* payment or satisfaction for loss or injury.

a-men-i-ty (ȧ-mĕn′ĭ-tĭ), *n.* [*pl.* amenities (-tĭz)], pleasantness; geniality.

am-ent (ăm′ĕnt; ā′mĕnt), *n.* a hanging, spike-shaped flower cluster, as of the willow or birch; a catkin (see *inflorescence,* illus.).—*adj.* **am″en-ta′ceous.**

a-merce (ȧ-mûrs′), *v.t.* [*p.t.* and *p.p.* a-merced′ (-mûrst′), *p.pr.* a-merc′ing], to punish by a fine or by taking away any right or privilege.—*n.* **a-merce′ment.**

A-mer-i-can (ȧ-mĕr′ĭ-kăn), *adj.* pertaining to, or situated in, America, or, specif., the U. S.: **American plan,** a method whereby board, lodging, and service at a hotel are charged for at a fixed rate per day or week:—*n.* an inhabitant of America; esp., a citizen of the U. S.

A-mer-i-ca-na (ȧ-mĕr″ĭ-kā′nȧ), *n. pl.* writings, records, objects, or the like, relating to America.

A-mer-i-can-ism (ȧ-mĕr′ĭ-kăn-ĭzm), *n.* **1,** a phrase, word, trait, custom, or object, peculiar to, or originating in, the U. S.; **2,** the spirit of loyalty to American ideals and institutions.

A-mer-i-can-ize (ȧ-mĕr′ĭ-kăn-īz), *v.t.* [*p.t.* and *p.p.* -ized (-īzd), *p.pr.* -iz″ing], to bring into agreement or accord with the manners and customs of the U. S.—*n.* **A-mer″i-can-i-za′tion.**

am-e-thyst (ăm′ē-thĭst), *n.* a violet-purple variety of quartz or rock crystal.—*adj.* **am″e-thys′tine.**

a-mi-a-bil-i-ty (ā″mĭ-ȧ-bĭl′ĭ-tĭ), *n.* friendliness; good nature.

a-mi-a-ble (ā′mĭ-ȧ-bl), *adj.* friendly; lovable; kindly.—*adv.* **a′mi-a-bly.**
Syn. attractive, pleasant, agreeable.

am-i-ca-ble (ăm′ĭ-kȧ-bl), *adj.* friendly; peaceable.—*adv.* **am′i-ca-bly.**—*n.* **am″i-ca-bil′i-ty.**

[1]**am-ice** (ăm′ĭs), *n.* an oblong piece of white linen worn around the neck, under the alb, by priests at the celebration of the Eucharist.

[2]**am-ice** (ăm′ĭs), *n.* a hood or cape of gray fur, once worn by religious orders.

a-mid (ȧ-mĭd′), *prep.* in the middle of; among. Also, **a-midst′.**

a-mid-ships (ȧ-mĭd′shĭps), *adv.* in the middle of a ship.

a-mir (ȧ-mēr′), *n.* a prince; governor; esp., the Mohammedan ruler of Afghanistan. Also, **a-meer′**, *Pfd. S.*

A-mos (ā′mŭs), *n.* **1**, in the Bible, a prophet in Israel; **2**, the book of the Old Testament containing his prophecies.

a-mount (ȧ-mount′), *v.i.* **1**, to reach; be equal: with *to;* as, his answer *amounted* to a threat; **2**, to add up or be equal, as to a certain sum:—*n.* the total sum.

a-mour (ȧ″mōōr′), *n.* a love affair; esp., a secret affair.

am-pere (ăm-pâr′; -pēr′), *n.* the unit of measurement of the strength of an electrical current.—*n.* **am-per′age.**

Am-phib-i-a (ăm-fĭb′ĭ-ȧ), *n.pl.* a class of animals including frogs, toads, and the like, which pass their early life in water and their adult life on land.

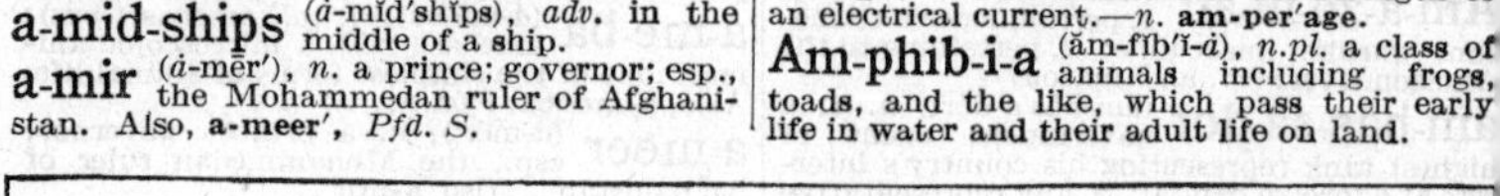

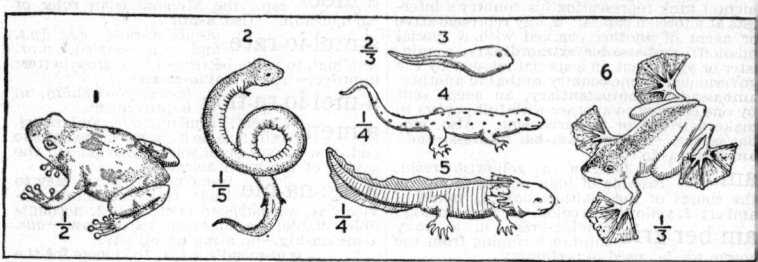

AMPHIBIANS: 1, tree toad; 2, Congo snake; 3, tadpole; 4, spotted salamander; 5, axolotl; 6, flying frog.

a-miss (ȧ-mĭs′), *adj.* wrong; faulty:—*adv.* wrongly; out of the way.

am-i-ty (ăm′ĭ-tĭ), *n.* [*pl.* amities (-tĭz)], friendship; peaceful relations.

am-me-ter (ăm′mē″tẽr), *n.* an instrument that measures the amount of electricity in a current.

am-mo-ni-a (ă-mō′nĭ-ȧ), *n.* **1**, a clear, pungent gas readily soluble in water, used in medicine, for manufacturing ice, etc.; **2**, a solution of this gas in water for the household.—*adj.* **am-mo′ni-ac.**

am-mo-ni-um (ă-mō′nĭ-ŭm), *n.* in chemistry, the base in a salt formed by combining ammonia with an acid: not found except in combination.

am-mu-ni-tion (ăm″ū-nĭsh′ŭn), *n.* formerly, military stores; now, the material used in the discharge of cannon, firearms, and the like.

am-ne-si-a (ăm-nē′sĭ-ȧ; -zĭ-ȧ), *n.* **1**, loss of memory; **2**, esp., inability to recall or understand a familiar word.

am-nes-ty (ăm′nĕs-tĭ), *n.* [*pl.* amnesties (-tĭz)], a general pardon for political offenses against the government.

a-mœ-ba (ȧ-mē′bȧ), *n.* [*pl.* amœbas (-bȧz); amœbæ (-bē)], a one-celled, microscopic animal found in ponds: one of the simplest forms of life. Also, **a-me′ba.**

a-mong (ȧ-mŭng′), *prep.* **1**, in the midst of; surrounded by; in the group with; **2**, by the united action of; as, *among* them all, they succeeded; **3**, in the time of; as, *among* the ancient Greeks, **4**, by distribution to; as, divided *among* them. Also, **a-mongst′.**

Syn. (see between).

am-o-rous (ăm′ō-rŭs), *adj.* fond of the opposite sex; loving.

a-mor-phous (ȧ-môr′fŭs), *adj.* **1**, formless; of no definite shape or character; **2**, not crystallized.

a-mor-tize (ȧ-môr′tīz; -tĭz), *v.t.* [*p.t.* and *p.p.* -tized (-tīzd), *p.pr.* -tizing], to pay off or satisfy (a debt) by means of a sinking fund, or money regularly set aside for the purpose.—*n.* **a-mor″ti-za′tion.**

am-phib-i-an (ăm-fĭb′ĭ-ăn), *n.* an animal living both on land and in water:—*adj.* relating to animals that live both on land and in water; amphibious.

am-phib-i-ous (ăm-fĭb′ĭ-ŭs), *adj.* **1**, having the power of living both on land and in water; amphibian; **2**, hence, having two natures.—*adv.* **am-phib′i-ous-ly.**

am-phi-the-a-ter (ăm″fĭ-thē′ȧ-tẽr), *n.* **1**, an oval or circular

AMPHITHEATER: THE COLOSSEUM.

building with rows of seats rising around a central space; **2**, anything resembling such a structure; **3**, the scene of a contest. Also, **am″phi-the′a-tre.**

am-ple (ăm′pl), *adj.* **1**, full; large; extensive; as, an *ample* waist; **2**, abundant; sufficient for all needs.

am-pli-fi-ca-tion (ăm″plĭ-fĭ-kā′shŭn), *n.* enlargement; extension; as, the *amplification* of a subject.

am-pli-fi-er (ăm′plĭ-fī″ẽr), *n.* **1**, one who or that which makes larger; **2**, in electricity, a vacuum tube used to enlarge feeble electric impulses, as in radio sets.

am-pli-fy (ăm′plĭ-fī), *v.t.* [*p.t.* and *p.p.* -fied (-fīd), *p.pr.* -fy″ing], to make larger or more full; develop:—*v.i.* to add to what has been said or written; expand.

am-pli-tude (ăm′plĭ-tūd), *n.* **1**, extension in space, esp. breadth and width; scope; **2**, largeness of mind; breadth of thought; dignity; **3**, in physics, the maximum value of a periodically varying quantity.

am-ply (ăm′plĭ), *adv.* liberally; abundantly; sufficiently.

am-pu-tate (ăm′pū-tāt), *v.t.* [*p.t.* and *p.p.* -tat″ed, *p.pr.* -tat″ing], in surgery, to cut off, as a human limb or part of a limb.—*n.* **am′pu-ta″tor.**

am-pu-ta-tion (ăm″pū-tā′shŭn), *n.* the act of cutting off a limb or part of a limb.

a-muck (ȧ-mŭk′), *adv.* in a frenzied way: **run amuck,** to run wild; rampage.

am-u-let (ăm′ū-lĕt), *n.* a charm worn to protect against disease or bad luck; a talisman.

a-muse (ȧ-mūz′), *v.t.* [*p.t.* and *p.p.* a-mused′ (-mūzd′), *p.pr.* a-mus′ing], to entertain; as, to *amuse* children with toys.—*p. adj.* **a-mus′ing.**—*adv.* **a-mus′ing-ly.**

a-muse-ment (ȧ-mūz′mĕnt), *n.* **1,** that which diverts or entertains; a pastime; **2,** mental diversion.
Syn. diversion, recreation, entertainment.

[1]**an** (ăn), *indefinite article,* any; each: used before words beginning with a vowel sound or silent *h;* as, *an* egg; *an* hour.

[2]**an** (ăn), *conj. Archaic,* and; if; as, go, *an* it please you.

an- (ăn-), *prefix,* **1,** on; in; as, *an*on; **2,** a form of Lat. *ad;* as, *an*nounce; **3,** against; as, *an*swer; **4,** not; without; as, *an*archy; **5,** used before a vowel for *ana-,* which see.

-an (-ăn), *adj. suffix,* pertaining to or belonging to; as, Americ*an:*—*n. suffix,* one of; an inhabitant of; as, an Americ*an.*

an-a- (ăn′ȧ-), [Gk.], *prefix,* [*an-* before a vowel; as, *an*ode], up; back; anew; again· as, *ana*tomy; *ana*basis.

-a-na (-ā′nȧ; -ăn′ȧ), [Lat.], *n.pl. suffix,* things pertaining to; sayings or anecdotes of; information upon; as, Americ*ana.*

a-nab-a-sis (ȧ-năb′ȧ-sĭs), *n.* [*pl.* anabases (-sēz)], a military advance into a country: **Anabasis,** the account by Xenophon of the march, in 401 B. C., of the 10,000 Greek mercenaries, under Cyrus, to the Euphrates, and their return.

an-ach-ro-nism (ăn-ăk′rō-nĭzm), *n.* an error in the order of time; a mistake in the date of an event; esp., the placing of something in a wrong time, as a clock in ancient Rome.—*adj.* **an-ach″ro-nis′tic.**

an-a-con-da (ăn″ȧ-kŏn′dȧ), *n.* **1,** a very large tropical snake which crushes its victims, usually birds and small animals; **2,** a python or boa constrictor.

a-næ-mi-a (ȧ-nē′mĭ-ȧ), *n.* the condition of not having enough blood, or of having blood of poor quality. Also, **a-ne′-mi-a.**—*adj.* **a-næ′mic.**

an-æs-the-si-a (ăn″ĕs-thē′sĭ-ȧ; ăn″ĕs-thē′zhĭ-ȧ), *n.* a loss of bodily feeling; insensibility, esp. to pain: often induced by drugs, or by the inhaling of gas or ether, as for an operation. Also, **an″es-the′si-a.**—*v.t.* **an-æs′the-tize.**

an-æs-thet-ic (ăn″ĕs-thĕt′ĭk), *adj.* **1,** pertaining to loss of sensation; **2,** taking away bodily feeling, or causing unconsciousness:—*n.* an anæsthetic gas or drug, as ether or cocaine. Also, **an″es-thet′ic.**

an-a-gram (ăn′ȧ-grăm), *n.* **1,** a word or sentence obtained by changing the order of the letters of another word or sentence; **2,** a word formed by the letters of another word read backwards, as *live* from *evil.*

a-nal (ā′năl), *adj.* relating to the anus, or lower opening of the large intestine.

an-al-ges-ic (ăn″ăl-jĕs′ĭk), *adj.* **1,** pain-dulling; **2,** insensible to pain.—*n.* **an″al-ge′si-a.**

a-nal-o-gous (ȧ-năl′ō-gŭs), *adj.* having resemblance; corresponding in certain ways.—*adv.* **a-nal′o-gous-ly.**

an-a-logue (ăn′ȧ-lŏg), *n.* that which has some resemblance to, or corresponds to, something else. Also, **an′a-log.**

a-nal-o-gy (ȧ-năl′ō-jĭ), *n.* [*pl.* analogies (-jĭz)], partial agreement or resemblance between things somewhat different; as, to make an *analogy* between food for the body and fuel for a stove.—*adj.* **an″a-log′i-cal.**—*adv.* **an″a-log′i-cal-ly.**

a-nal-y-sis (ȧ-năl′ĭ-sĭs), *n.* [*pl.* analyses (-sēz)], the division or separation of a thing into the parts that compose it; as, *analysis* of a chemical compound; *analysis* of a sentence or of an argument.

an-a-lyst (ăn′ȧ-lĭst), *n.* one who separates things into the parts that compose them, esp. in chemistry or mathematics.

an-a-lyt-i-cal (ăn″ȧ-lĭt′ĭ-kăl), *adj.* separating, or tending to separate, into parts; as, *analytical* chemistry; an *analytical* habit of mind. Also, **an″a-lyt′ic.**—*adv.* **an″a-lyt′i-cal-ly.**

an-a-lyze (ăn′ȧ-līz), *v.t.* [*p.t.* and *p.p.* -lyzed (-līzd), *p.pr.* -lyz″ing], **1,** to separate into parts; **2,** to examine critically. Also, **an′a-lyse.**—*n.* **an′a-lyz″er.**

An-a-ni-as (ăn″ȧ-nī′ăs), *n.* in the Bible, a follower of the apostles, who, with his wife Sapphira, was struck dead for lying (Acts 5); hence, a liar.

an-a-pest (ăn′ȧ-pĕst), *n.* a poetic foot or measure consisting of three syllables, with the accent on the last; as, I am mon′ | arch of all′ | I survey′. Also, **an′a-pæst.**—*adj.* **an″a-pes′tic.**

a-nar-chic (ȧ-när′kĭk), *adj.* **1,** relating to the political theory called anarchy; **2,** in a state of lawlessness or disorder. Also, **a-nar′chi-cal.**

an-arch-ism (ăn′ȧr-kĭzm), *n.* **1,** the political teaching that all government is unnecessary, and therefore evil; **2,** the support of lawlessness.

an-arch-ist (ăn′ȧr-kĭst), *n.* **1,** one who regards all government as evil and believes, as a political ideal, in living without any government; **2,** any person who stirs up violent revolt against established rule.

an-arch-y (ăn′ȧr-kĭ), *n.* **1,** the absence or lack of government; hence, a lawless condition of society; **2,** terrorism; disorder; confusion in general; **3,** the theory of absolute individual liberty.

a-nath-e-ma (ȧ-năth′ē-mȧ), *n.* **1,** the solemn denunciation or curse of the church, esp. in excommunication; **2,** a prayer that calamity may fall upon a thing or person; **3,** the thing or person so cursed.

a-nath-e-ma-tize (ȧ-năth′ē-mȧ-tīz), *v.t.* [*p.t.* and *p.p.* -tized (-tīzd), *p.pr.* -tiz″ing], to pronounce a curse against; curse:—*v.i.* to utter denunciations; curse.—*n.* **a-nath″e-ma-ti-za′tion.**

an-a-tom-ic (ăn″ȧ-tŏm′ĭk), *adj.* relating to dissection, or to the parts or structure of the body. Also, **an″a-tom′i-cal.**—*adv.* **an″a-tom′i-cal-ly.**

a-nat-o-mist (ȧ-năt′ō-mĭst), *n.* one learned in the structure of plants and animals, or skilled in their dissection.

a-nat-o-mize (ȧ-năt′ō-mīz), *v.t.* [*p.t.* and *p.p.* -mized (-mīzd), *p.pr.* -miz″ing], **1,** to dissect; study the structure of; **2,** to analyze.—*n.* **a-nat″o-mi-za′tion.**

a-nat-o-my (ȧ-năt′ō-mĭ), *n.* [*pl.* anatomies (-mĭz)], **1,** the art or science of dissection or of the structure of plants and animals, esp. of man; **2,** the structure or construction of any living form; **3,** a descriptive account of such structure.

-ance (-ăns), *n. suffix,* denoting action, process, quality, or state; as, assist*ance;* hindr*ance;* brilli*ance.* Also, **-an-cy.**

an-ces-tor (ăn′sĕs-tẽr), *n.* a person from whom one is descended in direct line; a forefather: progenitor.—*n.fem.* **an′ces-tress.**—*adj.* **an-ces′tral.**

an-ces-try (ăn′sĕs-trĭ), *n.* [*pl.* ancestries (-trĭz)], **1,** the line of one's descent traced from a period more or less remote; **2,** the persons of such a line; lineage.

An-chi-ses (ăn-kī′sēz), *n.* in mythology, the father of Æneas, on whose shoulders he was carried from Troy.

an-chor (ăng′kẽr), *n.* **1,** a heavy iron implement for securing a vessel to the ground under water; **2,** any similar thing to hold fast a movable object; **3,** hence, that on which one depends for security: **anchored,** *adj.* in heraldry, suggesting an anchor in shape (see *cross,* illus.):—*v.t.* to hold fast:—*v.i.* to become fixed.

ANCHOR
A, stock
B, shank
C, C, arms
D, crown
E, E, flukes
O, shackle

an-chor-age (ăng′kẽr-ȧj), *n.* **1,** a suitable or customary place for the securing of vessels to the ground under water; place for anchoring; **2,** the hold attained by an anchor; **3,** harbor dues for mooring vessels.

an-cho-ret (ăng′kō-rĕt), *n.* one who willingly leaves the world and lives alone, to devote his time to the study of religion or philosophy; a recluse; a hermit. Also, **an′cho-rite.**—*n.fem.* **an′cho-ress.**

an-cho-vy (ăn-chō′vĭ; ăn′chō-vĭ), *n.* [*pl.* anchovies (-vĭz)], a very small herring common in the Mediterranean, noted for its peculiar flavor, and used for pickling and as a sauce.

an-cient (ān′shĕnt), *adj.* **1,** of or relating to the early history of the world; of past times or remote ages; **2,** hence, of great age or antiquity:—*n.* one who lived in times long ago; also, an aged person.—*adv.* **an′cient-ly.**—*n.* **an′cient-ness.**

-an-cy (-ăn-sĭ), *n. suffix,* denoting action, process, quality, or state. See **-ance.**

and (ănd), *conj.* a word connecting a word, clause, or sentence with one of like kind and equal rank that precedes it.

***an-dan-te** (ăn-dăn′tā; ăn-dăn′tē), [It.], *adj.* in music, moderately slow; moving easily and smoothly:—*n.* in music, a moderately slow, smooth movement.

and-i-ron (ănd′ī″ûrn), *n.* one of two metal supports or rests for holding logs in a fireplace; a firedog.

An-drom-a-che (ăn-drŏm′ȧ-kē), *n.* in Homer's "Iliad," the wife of Hector of Troy.

An-drom-e-da (ăn-drŏm′ē-dȧ), *n.* **1,** in mythology, a Greek maiden rescued from a sea monster by Perseus; **2,** in astronomy, a northern constellation.

-ane (-ān), *adj. suffix,* meaning pertaining to: often used to differentiate from a similar form ending in *-an;* as, urb*an*, urb*ane;* hum*an*, hum*ane*. See **-an.**

an-ec-dote (ăn′ĕk-dōt), *n.* a brief story of an entertaining character; a terse and pithy account of some incident, usually about a well-known person.—*adj.* **an′ec-dot″al.**

Syn. story, tale. An *anecdote* is a short and entertaining account of some detached incident. A *story* is the narration of real or imagined incidents with a well-organized plot. A *tale* is a loosely constructed narrative in which there is practically no plot.

a-ne-mi-a (ȧ-nē′mĭ-ȧ), *n.* the condition of not having enough blood, or of having blood of poor quality. Also, **a-næ′-mi-a,** *Pfd. S.*—*adj.* **a-ne′mic.**

an-e-mom-e-ter (ăn″ē-mŏm′ē-tẽr), *n.* a wind gauge; an instrument which measures the force of the wind.

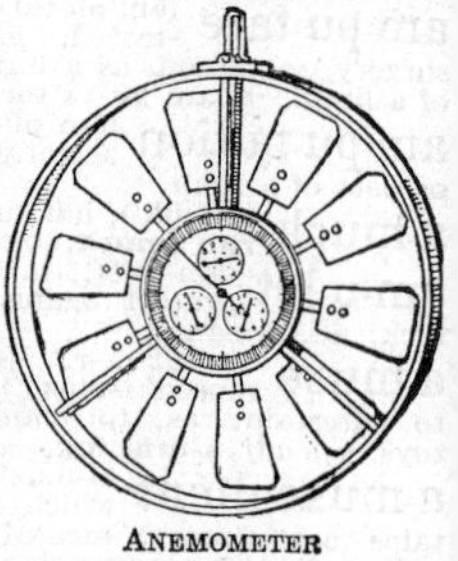

ANEMOMETER

a-nem-o-ne (ȧ-nĕm′ō-nē; ăn″ē-mō′nē), *n.* any of several plants of the crowfoot family; esp., the windflower, or wood anemone: **sea anemone,** any of several sea animals, with soft, tubular bodies crowned with numerous tentacles somewhat resembling a chrysanthemum in appearance.

an-er-oid (ăn′ẽr-oid), *adj.* not containing a liquid, such as quicksilver; as, an *aneroid* battery: **aneroid barometer,** an instrument in which air pressure is shown by a pointer controlled by the movements of the elastic top of a closed box from which the air has been partially exhausted: used in measuring altitudes.

an-es-the-si-a (ăn″ĕs-thē′sĭ-ȧ; -zhĭ-ȧ), *n.* a loss of bodily feeling. See **an″æs-the′si-a,** *Pfd. S.*

an-es-thet-ic (ăn″ĕs-thĕt′ĭk), *adj.* relating to or producing loss of sensation:—*n.* a gas or drug which produces insensibility. See **an″æs-thet′ic,** *Pfd. S.*

a-new (ȧ-nū′), *adv.* afresh; over again; in a new manner or style.

an-gel (ān′jĕl), *n.* **1,** a messenger of God, one of an order of spiritual beings supposed to form a connection between the seen and the unseen worlds; sometimes, a spirit of evil; as, a fallen *angel;* **2,** an old English gold coin bearing an image of the archangel Michael; **3,** a very lovely person.

an-gel-ic (ăn-jĕl′ĭk), *adj.* **1,** relating to the angels; **2,** pure; saintly. Also, **an-gel′i-cal.**—*adv.* **an-gel′i-cal-ly.**

An-ge-lus (ăn′jē-lŭs), *n.* **1,** a prayer or devotion in memory of the annunciation by the angel Gabriel of the incarnation of Christ; also, the church bell rung to announce the time of such devotions; **2,** a famous painting by J. F. Millet.

an-ger (ăng′gẽr), *n.* excessive emotion or passion aroused by a sense of injury or wrong; wrath:—*v.t.* to provoke to resentment; excite to wrath; enrage.

Syn., n. fury, ire, resentment, indignation.

an-gi-na (ăn′jĭ-nȧ; ăn-jī′nȧ), *n.* any disease, esp. of the throat, shown by spasmodic, convulsive attacks: **angina pectoris** (pĕk′tō-rĭs), a painful muscular spasm of the chest, due to heart disease, and often fatal.

[1]**an-gle** (ăng′gl), *n.* **1,** the figure formed by lines or surfaces meeting; **2,** the space be-

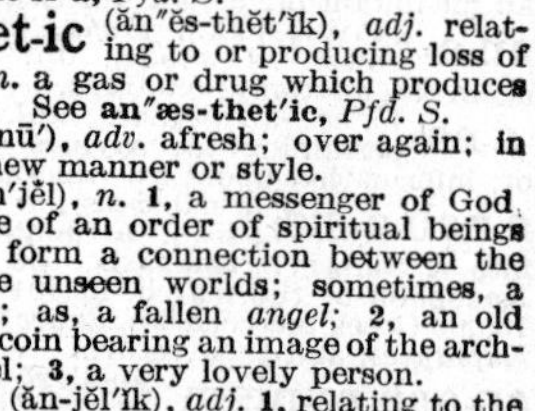

ANGLES
O, vertex; XOP, acute angle; XOY, right angle; XOG, obtuse angle; XOD, straight angle; XOE, reflex angle; XOP and POY, complementary angles; XOP and POD, supplementary angles; POY and YOG, adjacent angles.

tween such lines or surfaces; a corner; nook; **3**, the difference in direction of such lines or surfaces; **4**, a sharp edge; **5**, a point of view: as, to see things from all *angles*.

²an-gle (ăng′gl), *v.i.* [*p.t.* and *p.p.* -gled (-gld), *p.pr.* -gling], **1**, to fish with hook and line; **2**, to use tricks in obtaining something; as, to *angle* for a compliment.

An-gle (ăng′gl), *n.* a member of a Germanic tribe which invaded Britain in the fifth century after Christ and later gave its name (England = *Angle*land) to the island. —*adj.* **An′gli-an.**

an-gler (ăng′glẽr), *n.* **1**, one who fishes with rod and line; **2**, a fish with a large mouth and wormlike growths on the head, that feeds on smaller fish.

an-gle-worm (ăng′gl-wûrm″), *n.* an earthworm used as bait.

An-gli-can (ăng′glĭ-kăn), *adj.* **1**, English; **2**, related to the Established Church of England and to churches in accord with it:—*n.* a member of the Church of England, or of any church in accord with it.—*n.* **An′gli-can-ism.**

An-gli-cize (ăng′glĭ-sīz), *v.t.* [*p.t.* and *p.p.* -cized (-sīzd), *p.pr.* -ciz″ing], to make English; make to agree with English manners and customs.

An-glo-A-mer-i-can (ăng″glō-*ȧ*-mĕr′-ĭ-kăn), *adj.* relating to both England and the U. S., as to commerce, population, and the like:—*n.* an American citizen of English descent.

An-glo-ma-ni-a (ăng″glō-mā′nĭ-*ȧ*), *n.* an excessive respect for, or imitation of, that which is English.

An-glo-Sax-on (ăng″glō-săk′sŭn), *adj.* relating to the settlers in England from the fifth century to the Norman Conquest, or to their language:—*n.* **1**, one of these settlers; also, their language; **2**, any member of a race descended from them.

An-go-ra (ăng-gō′r*ȧ*), *n.* a town in Asia Minor: **Angora cat,** a cat prized for its long, silky hair: **Angora goat,** a goat, native to Asia Minor, noted for its silky hair: **Angora wool,** a fluffy, soft wool: **angora,** a light cloth made from the hair of Angora goats.

an-gry (ăng′grĭ) *adj.* [*comp.* an′gri-er, *superl.* an′gri-est], inflamed with wrath; provoked; enraged.—*adv.* **an′gri-ly.**

an-guish (ăng′gwĭsh), *n.* intense mental or physical suffering; acute pain; torture; torment; agony.

an-gu-lar (ăng′gū-l*ȧ*r), *adj.* **1**, having an outline in which lines or surfaces meet or intersect; **2**, sharp-cornered; pointed, or full of points; **3**, bony; awkward. —*adv.* **an′gu-lar-ly.**—*n.* **an″gu-lar′i-ty.**

an-il (ăn′ĭl), *n.* a West Indian plant from which indigo is made.

an-ile (ăn′īl; -ĭl), *adj.* like an old woman; imbecile.—*n.* **a-nil′i-ty** (*ȧ*-nĭl′ĭ-tĭ).

an-i-line (ăn′ĭ-lĭn; -lēn), *n.* a colorless oily compound which is the base or starting point in the preparation of many rich dyes. Also, **an′i-lin.**

an-i-mad-ver-sion (ăn″ĭ-măd-vûr′-shŭn), *n.* censure; blame; also, a criticizing remark.

an-i-mad-vert (ăn″ĭ-măd-vûrt′), *v.i.* to pass unfavorable comment; criticize: with *on* or *upon.*

an-i-mal (ăn′ĭ-măl), *n.* **1**, a living creature possessing feeling and voluntary motion: distinguished from *plant;* **2**, any one of the lower animals: distinguished from *man;* **3**, a brutish person:—*adj.* **1**, designating, or pertaining to, the broad group of living organisms not classified as plants; as, the *animal* kingdom; **2**, pertaining to the lower animals; **3**, pertaining to the senses; carnal.

Syn., *n.* brute, beast. *Animal* is applied to all living, moving, feeling beings, as distinguished from plants and lifeless objects. *Brute* is applied to animals thought of as savage or not endowed with reason. *Beast* is applied to the larger four-footed animals, esp. in distinguishing them from reptiles and birds. Figuratively, applied to man, these are all terms of reproach. A man called an *animal* is one whom the lower nature controls. A *brute* is one whom cruelty and dulled senses sway; as, her husband was a *brute.* A *beast* is one who gives way to sensuality, or who is content to live in low and filthy surroundings; as, his drunken habits made a *beast* of him.

an-i-mal-cule (ăn″ĭ-măl′kūl), *n.* any very minute, free-swimming animal or animal-like form of life.—*adj.* **an″i-mal′cu-lar.**

an-i-mal-ism (ăn′ĭ-măl-ĭzm), *n.* **1**, the state or activity of animals, esp. those lower than man; **2**, the state in human beings of being influenced merely by the sensual instincts; **3**, the theory which regards mankind as mere animals.

an-i-mate (ăn′ĭ-māt), *v.t.* [*p.t.* and *p.p.* -mat″ed, *p.pr.* -mat″ing], **1**, to impart life to; **2**, to inspire with energy or action; enliven:—*adj.* (ăn′ĭ-măt), **1**, endowed with life; **2**, full of spirit and vigor.—*p.adj.* **an′i-mat″ed.**—*adv.* **an′i-mat″ed-ly.**

an-i-ma-tion (ăn″ĭ-mā′shŭn), *n.* **1**, the act of giving life or spirit; **2**, the state of having life; vivacity; eagerness.

an-i-mism (ăn′ĭ-mĭzm), *n.* **1**, the doctrine of the existence of a soul or spirit as distinguished from matter; **2**, the belief that spirit or soul is the essential principle of life; **3**, the belief that every object possesses a soul; **4**, loosely, spiritualism as distinguished from materialism.—*n.* **an′i-mist.**—*adj.* **an″i-mis′tic.**

an-i-mos-i-ty (ăn″ĭ-mŏs′ĭ-tĭ), *n.* [*pl.* animosities (-tĭz)], hostility; hatred; enmity.

an-i-mus (ăn′ĭ-mŭs), *n.* [*pl.* animi (-mī)], **1**, moving spirit, or purpose: mind; **2**, disposition; inclination; **3**, hostile intention; malicious purpose.

an-i-on (ăn′ī-ŏn), *n.* a negatively charged ion which is set free at the positive electrode, or anode: opp. of *cation.*

an-ise (ăn′ĭs), *n.* **1**, a plant of the parsley family, native in the eastern Mediterranean region and yielding spicy seeds; **2**, the seed of this plant.

an-kle (ăng′kl), *n.* the joint connecting the foot with the leg; also, the region of this joint.

an-klet (ăng′klĕt), *n.* **1**, an ornamental ring for the ankle; **2**, a fetter or shackle; **3**, a support for the ankle.

an-nal-ist (ăn′ăl-ĭst), *n.* a compiler of a narrative of events as they occur year by year.—*adj.* **an″nal-is′tic.**

an-nals (ăn′ălz), *n.pl.* **1**, a description, history, or register issued from time to time, of events as they happen; **2**, records.

Syn. (see history).

an-neal (ă-nēl′), *v.t.* **1**, to heat so as to set colors in, as glass; **2**, to heat, and cool slowly, so as to soften and make less brittle, as glass or metals; hence, to temper; toughen; make lasting.

an-nex (ă-nĕks′), *v.t.* to unite, as a smaller thing to a greater; as, to *annex* a conquered province to a kingdom; hence, to attach as a consequence or condition:—*n.* (ă-nĕks′; ăn′ĕks), something attached to something else; esp., a small building adjoining a larger one.—*adj.* **an-nex′a-ble.**

an-nex-a-tion (ăn″ĕk-sā′shŭn), *n.* **1**, the act of adding or joining;

as, the *annexation* of territory; **2**, that which is joined or added, as territory.

an-nex-a-tion-ist (ăn″ĕk-sā′shŭn-ĭst), *n.* one who believes in, or promotes, the addition of territory to his own country, as by conquest or purchase.

an-ni-hi-late (ă-nī′hĭ-lāt), *v.t.* [*p.t.* and *p.p.* -lat″ed, *p.pr.* -lat″ing], **1**, to blot out; wipe out of existence; **2**, to destroy completely the character or effect of.

an-ni-hi-la-tion (ă-nī″hĭ-lā′shŭn), *n.* the act or state of wiping out of existence; total destruction.

an-ni-ver-sa-ry (ăn″ĭ-vûr′sȧ-rĭ), *n.* [*pl.* anniversaries (-rĭz)], **1**, the return after a year, or any number of years, of the date of an event; **2**, the commemoration of an event, esp. a notable one; **3**, a day for such commemoration.

***an-no Do-mi-ni** (ăn′ō dŏm′ĭ-nī) in the (stated) year of the Christian era: used with dates.—*abbr.* **A. D.**

an-no-tate (ăn′ō-tāt), *v.t.* [*p.t.* and *p.p.* -tat″ed, *p.pr.* -tat″ing], to make notes upon or about by way of explanation or criticism, as on a book:—*v.i.* to make comments or notes.—*n.* **an′no-ta″tor.**

an-no-ta-tion (ăn″ō-tā′shŭn), *n.* a note of explanation, comment, or criticism, made in connection with any text.

an-nounce (ă-nouns′), *v.t.* [*p.t.* and *p.p.* -nounced′ (-nounst′), *p.pr.* -nounc′ing], **1**, to proclaim or make known, formally or in a public manner; publish; **2**, to state formally the presence or approach of.
Syn. reveal, herald. (See declare.)

an-nounce-ment (ă-nouns′mĕnt), *n.* **1**, the act of proclaiming or declaring; **2**, that which is set forth or made known; proclamation.

an-noy (ă-noi′), *v.t.* to vex or trouble by repeated, irritating acts.

an-noy-ance (ă-noi′ăns), *n.* **1**, the act of causing vexation; **2**, a sense of being troubled or vexed; **3**, the thing or act which bothers or vexes.
Syn. irritation, nuisance, trouble.

an-noy-ing (ă-noi′ĭng), *p. adj.* vexing; teasing; irritating; troubling.—*adv.* **an-noy′ing-ly.**

an-nu-al (ăn′ū-ăl), *adj.* **1**, happening, pertaining to, or returning, once in twelve months; yearly; **2**, done, reckoned, or published yearly; as, *annual* income; an *annual* report; **3**, lasting but one year or season, as a plant:—*n.* **1**, a publication appearing once a year; **2**, a plant living only one year or season.—*adv.* **an′nu-al-ly.**

an-nu-i-tant (ă-nū′ĭ-tănt), *n.* one who is in receipt of, or is entitled to receive, a certain sum of money each year.

an-nu-i-ty (ă-nū′ĭ-tĭ), *n.* [*pl.* annuities (-tĭz)], a sum of money payable in yearly instalments.

an-nul (ă-nŭl′), *v.t.* [*p.t.* and *p.p.* -nulled′ (-nŭld′), *p.pr.* -nul′ling], to abolish or do away with, as a law, decree, or compact.—*n.* **an-nul′ment.**

an-nu-lar (ăn′ū-lȧr), *adj.* pertaining to a ring or rings; ring-shaped: **annular eclipse**, an unusual type of solar eclipse, occurring when the moon is at its greatest distance from the earth, in which the sun appears as a circle of light surrounding the dark body of the moon; **annular ligament**, the ligament which encircles the wrist or the ankle.—*adv.* **an′nu-lar-ly.**

an-nun-ci-ate (ă-nŭn′shĭ-āt), *v.t.* [*p.t.* and *p.p.* -at″ed, *p.pr.* -at″ing], to make known officially or publicly; bring tidings of; announce.

an-nun-ci-a-tion (ă-nŭn″sĭ-ā′shŭn; -shĭ-ā′shŭn), *n.* **1**, the act of making known or that which is made known; proclamation; **2**, esp., the announcement by the angel Gabriel to Mary of the coming birth of Jesus (Luke 1 : 28–33): **Annunciation**, in the Roman Catholic and Anglican Churches, the feast day, March 25, celebrating this event: also called *Lady Day.*

an-nun-ci-a-tor (ă-nŭn′shĭ-ā″tẽr), *n.* one who or that which announces; esp., an indicator used in hotels, elevators, etc., as a signal to show where attendance is required.

an-ode (ăn′ōd), *n.* in an electrolyte, vacuum tube, or other electrical apparatus, the place at which the current enters: opp. of *cathode.*—*adj.* **a-nod′ic.**

an-o-dyne (ăn′ō-dīn), *adj.* assuaging or relieving pain:—*n.* a drug which relieves pain; an opiate.

a-noint (ȧ-noint′), *v.t.* to pour oil or other liquid upon, esp. in a religious ceremony, or by way of consecration; consecrate.—*n.* **a-noint′er.**

a-nom-a-lous (ȧ-nŏm′ȧ-lŭs), *adj.* different from the common order; abnormal; irregular; peculiar.—*adv.* **a-nom′a-lous-ly.**

a-nom-a-ly (ȧ-nŏm′ȧ-lĭ), *n.* [*pl.* anomalies (-lĭz)], a turning from the natural order; anything that deviates from the common rule.

a-non (ȧ-nŏn′), *adv.* **1**, soon; in a little while; **2**, at another time; again.

a-non-y-mous (ȧ-nŏn′ĭ-mŭs), *adj.* **1**, having no name; **2**, without the author's name; as, an *anonymous* letter.—*abbr.* **anon.**—*adv.* **a-non′y-mous-ly.**—*n.* **an″o-nym′i-ty** (ăn″ō-nĭm′ĭ-tĭ).

A-noph-e-les (ȧ-nŏf′ĕ-lēz), *n.* the only genus of mosquito whose bite may transmit malaria.

an-oth-er (ă-nŭth′ẽr), *pron.* an additional or different person or thing; as, I have one, but want *another:* also used reciprocally, as correlative of *one;* as, love one *another:*—*adj.* **1**, additional; as, please give me *another* orange; **2**, different; as, he has become *another* man.

an-sate (ăn′sāt), *adj.* having a handle: **ansate cross**, a T-shaped cross with a loop at the top as a handle (see *cross*, illus.).

an-swer (ȧn′sẽr), *n.* **1**, a response or rejoinder; a reply to a charge; **2**, a solution, as of a mathematical problem:—*v.t.* **1**, to speak, write, or act in reply to; as, to *answer* the bell; *answer* a letter; **2**, to correspond to; as, he *answers* the description; **3**, to be sufficient for; as, this *answers* the purpose:—*v.i.* **1**, to speak, write, or act in reply; **2**, to be sufficient; **3**, to be accountable; as, he had to *answer* for his sins.

an-swer-a-ble (ȧn′sẽr-ȧ-bl), *adj.* **1**, admitting of a satisfactory reply; as, that question is not *answerable;* **2**, accountable; responsible; liable.

ant (ȧnt), *n.* a small insect, social like the bees and famed for its industry.

-ant (-ănt), *adj. suffix*, having the same force as the present participle of the root employed; as, regn*ant*, reigning; defi*ant*, defying:—*n. suffix*, denoting the doer of the action indicated by the root; as, claim*ant*.

ant-ac-id (ănt-ăs′ĭd), *adj.* tending to overcome an acid condition; hence, a basic remedy used to overcome acidity, as in the stomach.

An-tæ-us (ăn-tē′ŭs), *n.* in mythology, a giant who was invincible while touching the earth, his mother: conquered by Hercules, who lifted him up into the air and there throttled him.

an-tag-o-nism (ăn-tăg′ō-nĭzm), *n.* the active opposition of two opposing forces; hostility; animosity; also, an opposing force or principle.

an-tag-o-nist (ăn-tăg′ō-nĭst), *n.* **1**, one who contends with another in combat or argument; **2**, a rival.

an-tag-o-nis-tic (ăn-tăg″ō-nĭs′tĭk), *adj.* **1**, contending; **2**, in opposition; as, the muscle bending a joint is *antagonistic* to the muscle straightening it; **3**, unfriendly.—*adv.* **an-tag″o-nis′ti-cal-ly.**

an-tag-o-nize (ăn-tăg′ō-nīz), *v.t.* [*p.t.* and *p.p.* -nized (-nīzd), *p.pr.* -niz″ing], **1**, to oppose actively; compete with; **2**, to neutralize; counteract; as, one substance *antagonizes* another; **3**, to make hostile; as, her manner *antagonizes* people.

ant-arc-tic (ănt-ärk′tĭk), *adj.* opposite to the arctic, or north, pole; relating to the south polar regions: **Antarctic Ocean,** the south polar ocean.

An-ta-res (ăn-tā′rēz), *n.* a red star of the first magnitude, the brightest in the constellation Scorpio.

an-te- (ăn′tē-), [Lat.], *prefix*, before in time, place, or position; as, *ante*date; *ante*room: also found in forms *anti-*, *an-*; as, *anti*cipate; *an*cestor.

ant-eat-er (ănt′ēt″ẽr), *n.* any of several animals which feed upon ants.

SPINY ANTEATER ($\frac{1}{12}$)

***an-te bel-lum** (ăn′tē bĕl′ŭm), [Lat.], literally, before the war; usually, before the American Civil War.

an-te-cede (ăn″tē-sēd′), *v.t.* [*p.t.* and *p.p.* -ced′ed, *p.pr.* -ced′ing], **1**, to precede or go before in time or space; **2**, to excel; outdo; surpass.

an-te-ced-ence (ăn″tē-sēd′ĕns), *n.* the act or state of going before; precedence. Also, **an″te-ced′en-cy.**

an-te-ced-ent (ăn″tē-sēd′ĕnt), *n.* **1**, someone or something which goes before or precedes; **2**, the word to which a pronoun refers; **3**, the first of the two terms of a ratio; **4**, in *pl.*, the previous events or influences in a person's life:—*adj.* going before; preceding.—*adv.* **an″te-ced′ent-ly.**

an-te-cham-ber (ăn′tē-chām″bẽr), *n.* **1**, an apartment leading into the principal room; **2**, an outer room where persons wait for an interview.

an-te-date (ăn′tē-dāt″), *v.t.* [*p.t.* and *p.p.* -dat″ed, *p.pr.* -dat″ing], **1**, to give an earlier date to than the right one; as, to *antedate* a check; **2**, to occur at an earlier time; as, the Civil War *antedated* emancipation:—*n.* a date earlier than a given date.

an-te-di-lu-vi-an (ăn″tē-dĭ-lū′vĭ-ăn), *adj.* **1**, of or relating to the time before the Flood; **2**, pertaining to very ancient times; antiquated:—*n.* **1**, one who or that which lived before the Flood; **2**, an old or old-fashioned person.

an-te-lope (ăn′tē-lōp), *n.* any of a large group of animals including the gazelles, gnus, and others.

an-te-me-rid-i-an (ăn″tē-mē-rĭd′ĭ-ăn), *adj.* **1**, occurring before noon; **2**, relating to the forenoon.

***an-te me-ri-di-em** (ăn″tē mē-rĭd′ĭ-ĕm), [Lat.], before noon.—*abbr.* **A. M.; a. m.**

an-te-na-tal (ăn″tē-nā′tăl), *adj.* occurring or existing before birth.

an-ten-na (ăn-tĕn′ȧ), *n.* [*pl.* antennæ (-ē); antennas (-ȧz)], **1**, one of the feelers upon the heads of insects; **2**, a wire or wires supported in the air, for transmitting the electromagnetic waves of radio systems.

an-te-nup-tial (ăn″tē-nŭp′shăl), *adj.* preceding marriage; as, an *antenuptial* agreement about property.

an-te-pe-nult (ăn″tē-pē′nŭlt; -pē-nŭlt′), *n.* the last syllable but two in a word. Also, **an″te-pe-nul′ti-ma.**

an-te-pe-nul-ti-mate (ăn″tē-pē-nŭl′tĭ-māt), *adj.* relating to the last but two in a series:—*n.* **1**, that which is last but two; **2**, an antepenult.

an-te-ri-or (ăn-tē′rĭ-ẽr), *adj.* **1**, being before, or toward the front, in space; **2**, being before in time; earlier.

an-te-room (ăn′tē-rōōm″), *n.* a room before, or leading to, another; an antechamber.

an-them (ăn′thĕm), *n.* **1**, orig., in church music, a composition with parts sung alternately; **2**, a composition from the Bible or the liturgy set to sacred music; **3**, a song of praise or triumph.

an-ther (ăn′thẽr), *n.* in a flower, the part of the stamen which produces the pollen (see *flower*, [2]*style*, illus.).

an-thol-o-gy (ăn-thŏl′ō-jĭ), *n.* [*pl.* anthologies (-jĭz)], a collection of choice literary extracts from different authors.—*n.* **an-thol′o-gist.**—*adj.* **an″tho-log′i-cal.**

an-thra-cite (ăn′thrȧ-sīt), *n.* a hard coal burning without smoke and giving intense heat.

an-thrax (ăn′thrăks), *n.* [*pl.* anthraces (-sēz)], a contagious disease of animals, esp. of cattle and sheep.

an-thro-poid (ăn′thrō-poid), *adj.* manlike:—*n.* one of the higher apes resembling man, such as the gorilla.

an-thro-pol-o-gist (ăn″thrō-pŏl′ō-jĭst), *n.* one who studies the science and history of the human race.

an-thro-pol-o-gy (ăn″thrō-pŏl′ō-jĭ), *n.* the science of mankind; a systematic study of man as regards his origin, nature, races, and the like.—*adj.* **an″thro-po-log′ic; an″thro-po-log′i-cal.**

an-thro-po-met-ric (ăn″thrō-pō-mĕt′rĭk), *adj.* relating to the measurement or proportions of the different parts of the human body.

an-thro-po-mor-phic (ăn″thrō-pō-môr′fĭk), *adj.* manlike.—*adj.* **an″thro-po-mor′phous.**

an-thro-po-mor-phism (ăn″thrō-pō-môr′fĭzm), *n.* **1**, the process of ascribing to God the feelings and conduct of human beings; **2**, the process of ascribing human qualities to lower animals or to objects.

an-ti (ăn′tī; -tĭ), *n.* [*pl.* antis (-tīz; -tĭz)], *Colloq.*, one opposed to any specified policy or proposal.

an-ti- (ăn′tĭ-), [Gk.], *prefix*, [before a vowel sometimes written *ant-*; as, *ant*acid], against; preventive of; opposite of; as, *anti*slavery; *anti*climax.

an-ti-air-craft (ăn″tĭ-âr′krȧft″), *adj.* directed against airships; as, *antiaircraft* guns.

an-tic (ăn′tĭk), *n.* a funny trick or action:—*adj.* absurd; fantastic; grotesque.

An-ti-christ (ăn′tĭ-krīst), *n.* **1**, an opponent of Christ; **2**, esp., the great personal opponent expected by many to appear before the end of the world, bringing evil (1 John 2 : 22).

an-tic-i-pate (ăn-tĭs′ĭ-pāt), *v.t.* [*p.t.* and *p.p.* -pat″ed, *p.pr.* -pat″ing], **1**, to look forward to; expect; as, to *anticipate* an early answer; **2**, to look forward to with pleasure; as, to *anticipate* a party; **3**, to do or consider before the proper time, esp.

needlessly: **4**, to foresee and prevent; as, to *anticipate* all objections.—*adj.* **an-tic′i-pa-to-ry.**—*adj.* **an-tic′i-pa-tive.**

Syn. apprehend, hope, contemplate, await.

an-tic-i-pa-tion (ăn-tĭs″ĭ-pā′shŭn), *n.* **1**, the act of taking beforehand; **2**, expectation; **3**, hope; **4**, something done or considered before its proper time; **5**, a prevention.

an-ti-cli-max (ăn″tĭ-klī′măks), *n.* **1**, a ludicrous or ridiculous drop in thought and expression; **2**, an abrupt descent from the mention of more important to less important things.

an-ti-cli-nal (ăn″tĭ-klī′năl), *adj.* in geology, sloping in opposite directions from a central axis: used of rock strata: opp. of *synclinal*:—*n.* **1**, an axis from which strata of rock slope in different directions; **2**, a fold of rock strata sloping on opposite sides away from a central axis (see *synclinal*, illus.). Also, *n.* **an′ti-cline.**

an-ti-dote (ăn′tĭ-dōt), *n.* **1**, a substance which counteracts the effects of poison or disease; **2**, that which annuls, counteracts, or tends to prevent evil; **3**, a remedy.—*adj.* **an′ti-dot″al.**

an-ti-fe-brile (ăn″tĭ-fē′brĭl), *adj.* tending to cure or prevent fever.

An-tig-o-ne (ăn-tĭg′ō-nē), *n.* in mythology, the daughter of Œdipus and Jocasta, famed for filial love and faithfulness, who served as guide for her blind father until his death: heroine of tragedies by Sophocles and Euripides.

an-ti-ma-cas-sar (ăn″tĭ-mȧ-kăs′ȧr), *n.* a cover for the back or arms of a chair, sofa, etc.; a tidy.

an-ti-mo-ny (ăn′tĭ-mō-nĭ), *n.* a white, shining, metallic element, used in various important alloys, as pewter, Babbitt metal, type metal, etc., and in certain medicines, as tartar emetic.

an-tin-o-my (ăn-tĭn′ō-mĭ), *n.* [*pl.* antinomies (-mĭz)], **1**, the opposition of one rule, law, or principle to another; **2**, any rule or law, so opposed.

an-tip-a-thy (ăn-tĭp′ȧ-thĭ), *n.* [*pl.* antipathies (-thĭz)], **1**, a strong aversion or dislike: used with *to*, *against*, *between*, or *for*; **2**, that which arouses dislike.

Syn. distaste, hatred, hostility, repulsion.

an-ti-phon (ăn′tĭ-fŏn), *n.* a musical response, as in a chant.

an-tiph-o-nal (ăn-tĭf′ō-năl), *adj.* relating to responsive singing:—*n.* **1**, a book of anthems; **2**, a collection of musical responses, chants, or hymns.

an-tiph-o-ny (ăn-tĭf′ō-nĭ), *n.* [*pl.* antiphonies (-nĭz)], **1**, the alternate or responsive singing by a choir divided into two parts, each part rendering alternately verses of a hymn or anthem; **2**, a musical setting of verses arranged for alternate singing.

an-tip-o-dal (ăn-tĭp′ō-dăl), *adj.* **1**, relating to the opposite sides of the globe; **2**, diametrically opposite.

an-ti-pode (ăn′tĭ-pōd), *n.* [*pl.* antipodes (-pōdz)], **1**, one who resides on the opposite side of the earth; **2**, that which is directly opposite to something else.

an-tip-o-des (ăn-tĭp′ō-dēz), *n.pl.* **1**, those who, residing at opposite sides of the globe, have their feet directly opposed to one another; **2**, two portions of the earth's surface which are exactly opposite to each other; **3**, sometimes used erroneously as collective *sing.*, the direct opposite of a person, place, or condition.

an-ti-py-rine (ăn″tĭ-pī′rĭn), *n.* a drug, obtained from coal tar, used for the relief of neuralgia, nervous headaches, and fevers. Also, **an″ti-py′rin.**

an-ti-qua-ri-an (ăn″tĭ-kwâ′rĭ-ăn), *adj.* relating to ancient times or things:—*n.* a student of ancient things; an antiquary.

an-ti-qua-ry (ăn′tĭ-kwā-rĭ), *n.* [*pl.* antiquaries (-rĭz)], one who collects, studies, or deals in ancient objects, for enjoyment or business.

an-ti-quat-ed (ăn′tĭ-kwāt″ĕd), *adj.* old-fashioned; obsolete; ancient.

an-tique (ăn-tēk′), *adj.* pertaining to a former age; ancient:—*n.* something of great age; a relic of ancient times.

an-tiq-ui-ty (ăn-tĭk′wĭ-tĭ), *n.* [*pl.* antiquities (-tĭz)], **1**, great age; **2**, the early ages; **3**, the people or races of ancient times; **4**, that which belonged to, or survives from, ancient times; a relic.

an-ti-sep-tic (ăn″tĭ-sĕp′tĭk), *adj.* destroying germs, esp. of disease or decay:—*n.* any antiseptic substance.

an-ti-slav-er-y (ăn″tĭ-slāv′ẽr-ĭ), *adj.* opposed to slavery, esp., formerly, Negro slavery in the South:—*n.* opposition to human slavery.

an-tith-e-sis (ăn-tĭth′ē-sĭs), *n.* [*pl.* antitheses (-sēz)], **1**, opposition; contrast; **2**, expression by opposition of words or ideas; **3**, a figure of speech that shows contrast; as, "To err is human; to forgive, divine."—*adj.* **an″ti-thet′ic; an″ti-thet′i-cal.**—*adv.* **an″ti-thet′i-cal-ly.**

an-ti-tox-in (ăn″tĭ-tŏk′sĭn), *n.* a substance formed in the tissues of a plant or animal by the action of a disease germ poison, and having the power to neutralize this poison; esp., a substance introduced into the blood to prevent or cure a disease by neutralizing the poison made by the germ which causes the disease.

an-ti–trade (ăn′tĭ-trād″), *n.* a tropical wind blowing steadily above, and in an opposite direction to, the trade wind, which blows easterly toward the equator.

ant-ler (ănt′lẽr), *n.* a part or the whole of a horn which is shed annually, as in the deer family.

an-to-nym (ăn′tō-nĭm), *n.* a word which is the opposite in meaning of another word in the same language: opp. of *synonym*.—*abbr.* **ant.**

a-nus (ā′nŭs), *n.* the opening at the lower end of the large intestine.

an-vil (ăn′vĭl), *n.* a block, usually of iron faced with steel, on which metals are hammered and shaped.

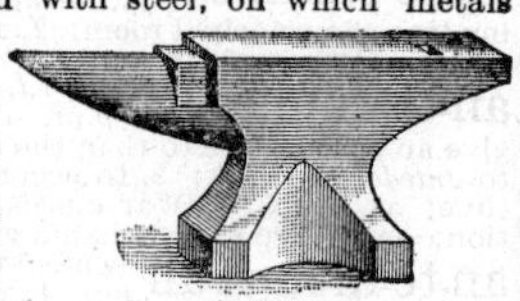

ANVIL

anx-i-e-ty (ăng-zī′ē-tĭ), *n.* [*pl.* anxieties (-tĭz)], **1**, a condition of mental uneasiness, arising from fear or solicitude: **2**, eager desire; great longing.

Syn. concern, dread, trouble. (See care.)

anx-ious (ăngk′shŭs), *adj.* **1**, deeply concerned; greatly troubled; **2**, very solicitous; **3**, desirous; as, *anxious* to please—*adv.* **anx′ious-ly.**—*n.* **anx′ious-ness.**

an-y (ĕn′ĭ), *adj.* one, indeterminately or indefinitely; some; one of an indefinite number, quantity, or degree:—*pron.* **1**, one; anyone; **2**, in *pl.*, some:—*adv.* to any extent; at all; in any degree.

an-y-bod-y (ĕn′ĭ-bŏd″ĭ), *n.* **1**, an ordinary person; any person; **2**, some one of importance; as, is he *anybody?*

an-y-how (ĕn′ĭ-hou), *adv.* **1**, in any way or manner; carelessly; **2**, in any case:—*conj.* at any rate; nevertheless.

an-y-one (ĕn'ĭ-wŭn), *n.* a person taken at random; any person.

an-y-thing (ĕn'ĭ-thĭng), *n.* a thing of any sort; any object, state, act, event, or fact, whatever.

an-y-way (ĕn'ĭ-wā), *adv.* in any manner; anyhow:—*conj.* no matter what happens; nevertheless.

an-y-where (ĕn'ĭ-hwâr), *adv.* in or at any place.

an-y-wise (ĕn'ĭ-wīz), *adv.* **1**, in any way or manner; anyhow; **2**, at all.

An-zac (ăn'zăk), *n.* a name given in 1915 to the troops from the Commonwealth of Australia and the Dominion of New Zealand in the British Empire: composed of the initial letters of *Australia* and *New Zealand Army Corps.*

a-o-rist (ā'ō-rĭst), *n.* in Greek grammar, a tense of the verb which denotes simply past action or occurrence, with no indication of continuance, repetition, completion, or the like, suggested by some other tenses.

a-or-ta (ā-ôr'tȧ), *n.* [*pl.* aortas (-tȧz)], the chief artery which carries the blood from the heart to all parts of the body except the lungs.—*adj.* **a-or'tic.**

a-pace (ȧ-pās'), *adv.* quickly; at a quick pace; speedily; rapidly.

A-pa-che (ȧ-pä'chā; ȧ-păch'ē), *n.* one of a tribe of American Indians orig. inhabiting what is now part of New Mexico, Arizona, and Mexico: **apache** (ȧ"pȧsh'), [*pl.* apaches (ȧ"pȧsh')], a member of a gang of desperate criminals infesting Paris; gangster.

a-pa-ra-dor (ä-pä-rä-dōr'), [Sp.], a sideboard, cupboard, or chest.

a-part (ȧ-pärt'), *adv.* **1**, separately in place, time, or purpose; aside; **2**, asunder.

a-part-ment (ȧ-pärt'mĕnt), *n.* **1**, a separate room or several connected rooms of a building; two or more rooms of a house set apart as a home; **2**, in *pl.*, any suite of rooms; also, a building containing such suites: also called *apartment house.*

ap-a-thet-ic (ăp"ȧ-thĕt'ĭk), *adj.* without feeling or emotion; passionless; languid. Also, **ap"a-thet'i-cal.**—*adv.* **ap"a-thet'i-cal-ly.**

ap-a-thy (ăp'ȧ-thĭ), *n.* [*pl.* apathies (-thĭz)], lack of feeling; want of passion or emotion; indifference.

ape (āp), *n.* **1**, a tailless monkey resembling man in structure and organs, half erect, with very long arms; esp., the gorilla, chimpanzee, orang-utan, etc.; **2**, a silly mimic; a fool:—*v.t.* [*p.t.* and *p.p.* aped (āpt), *p.pr.* ap'ing], to mimic; imitate.—*n.* **ap'er-y.**

Syn., v. mock. (See imitate.)

a-peak (ȧ-pēk'), *adv.* in, or nearly in, an upright position: a nautical term.

a-pe-ri-ent (ȧ-pē'rĭ-ĕnt), *n.* a mild laxative medicine or food, such as figs or prunes:—*adj.* gently laxative.

ap-er-ture (ăp'ĕr-tūr), *n.* an opening; a gap, hole, chasm, or passage; specif., in a camera, the hole, or its size, through which light passes to the plate.

a-pex (ā'pĕks), *n.* [*pl.* apexes (ā'pĕk-sĕz); in technical writing, sometimes apices (ăp'ĭ-sēz)], a point, tip, or summit.

a-pha-si-a (ȧ-fā'zhĭ-ȧ), *n.* loss of the power of speech, or the proper use of words, due to disease or injury of the brain.—*adj.* and *n.* **a-pha'sic.**

a-phel-i-on (ȧ-fēl'yŭn; ȧ-fē'lĭ-ŏn), *n.* [*pl.* aphelia (-yȧ; -lĭ-ȧ); aphelions (-yŭnz; -lĭ-ŏnz)], that point in the orbit or path of a planet or a comet which is farthest from the sun: opp. of *perihelion.*

a-phid (ā'fĭd; ăf'ĭd), *n.* a plant louse, a small insect, wingless in its early life, parasitic on garden and house plants.

a-phis (ā'fĭs), *n.* [*pl.* aphides (ăf'ĭ-dēz)], an aphid, or plant louse.

aph-o-rism (ăf'ō-rĭzm), *n.* a concise or brief statement of a precept; a maxim.—*n.* **aph'o-rist.**—*adj.* **aph"o-ris'tic.**

Aph-ro-di-te (ăf"rō-dī'tē), *n.* in mythology, the Greek goddess of love and beauty: identified with *Venus:* **aphrodite,** a kind of richly colored butterfly.

a-pi-a-ry (ā'pĭ-ā-rĭ), *n.* [*pl.* apiaries (-rĭz)], a place where bees are kept; also, a collection of hives.

ap-i-ces (ăp'ĭ-sēz), *n.pl.* points: Latin plural of *apex*, used esp. in technical or scientific writings.

a-pi-cul-ture (ā'pĭ-kŭl"tūr), *n.* the raising and care of bees.

a-piece (ȧ-pēs'), *adv.* to or for each person or thing; each; severally.

ap-ish (āp'ĭsh), *adj.* like an ape in manners; silly; affected; foppish; foolish; prone to servile imitation.

***a-plomb** (ȧ"plôṅ'), [*Fr.*], *n.* self-possession; assurance; self-confidence.

ap-o- (ăp-ō-), [Gk.], *prefix*, [before a vowel, *ap-;* before the aspirate, *aph-*], **1**, from; off; as, *apo*stle; **2**, used intensively; as, *apo*plexy; **3**, used as a negative; as, *apo*calypse.

a-poc-a-lypse (ȧ-pŏk'ȧ-lĭps), *n.* revelation; discovery; disclosure: **Apocalypse,** the last book of the New Testament, called the Revelation of St. John the Divine.—*adj.* **a-poc"a-lyp'tic.**

a-poc-ry-pha (ȧ-pŏk'rĭ-fȧ), *n.pl.*, erroneously used as *sing.* [whence *pl.* apocryphas (-fȧz)], a writing or statement of doubtful authorship **Apocrypha,** certain writings printed in some editions of the Bible between the Old and New Testaments, which are accepted as authentic by some Christians and rejected by others.

a-poc-ry-phal (ȧ-pŏk'rĭ-făl), *adj.* **1**, of doubtful authority; fictitious; false; **2**, pertaining to the Apocrypha.

ap-o-gee (ăp'ō-jē), *n.* **1**, that point in the orbit or path of a planet, esp. of the moon, which is most distant from the earth: opp. of *perigee;* **2**, the highest or most distant point; **3**, the climax; culmination.

A-pol-lo (ȧ-pŏl'ō), *n.* in mythology, the god of the sun, music, poetry, eloquence, medicine, and the fine arts: son of Jupiter and Leto, and twin brother of Diana: identified with *Helios*, the sun god.

a-pol-o-get-ic (ȧ-pŏl"ō-jĕt'ĭk), *adj.* defending by words or argument; making defense or excuse. Also, **a-pol"o-get'i-cal.**—*adv.* **a-pol"o-get'i-cal-ly.**

a-pol-o-gist (ȧ-pŏl'ō-jĭst), *n.* one who defends a person or cause by argument, spoken or written.

a-pol-o-gize (ȧ-pŏl'ō-jīz), *v.i.* [*p.t.* and *p.p.* -gized (-jīzd), *p.pr.* -giz"ing], **1**, to make an excuse; **2**, to express regret or make amends for anything said or done, on one's own behalf or that of another.

ap-o-logue (ăp'ō-lŏg), *n.* a fable or tale which teaches a useful lesson or moral truth, such as Æsop's fables.

a-pol-o-gy (ȧ-pŏl'ō-jĭ), *n.* [*pl.* apologies (-jĭz)], **1**, a vindication or excuse; an explanation by way of amends; **2**, something spoken, written, or offered in defense; **3**, a poor substitute; a makeshift.

Syn. justification. (See excuse.)

ap-o-plec-tic (ăp"ō-plĕk'tĭk), *adj.* **1**, relating to, or of the nature of, the physical state caused by too high blood pressure; **2**, afflicted, or threatened, with apoplexy. Also, **ap"o-plec'ti-cal.**

ap-o-plex-y (ăp'ō-plĕk"sĭ), *n.* the sudden loss of consciousness, resulting from a broken blood vessel in the brain.

a-port (ȧ-pōrt′), *adv.* on or toward the left side; as, rocks *aport.*

a-pos-ta-sy (ȧ-pŏs′tȧ-sĭ), *n.* [*pl.* apostasies (-sĭz)], the giving up of what one has professed or believed, as faith, principles, or party.

a-pos-tate (ȧ-pŏs′tāt), *n.* **1**, one who has forsaken his faith or party; **2**, one who abandons his profession after having been in holy orders; a renegade:—*adj.* false; traitorous.

a-pos-tle (ȧ-pŏs′l), *n.* **1**, one charged with a high mission; **2**, one of the twelve persons specially selected by Christ to teach his gospel (Luke 6:13); **3**, the first missionary who plants the Christian faith in any region; hence, one who labors with special success as a moral or social reformer: **Apostles' Creed**, an early, widely accepted statement of Christian belief, in its present wording dating from about A. D. 500.

ap-os-tol-ic (ăp″ŏs-tŏl′ĭk), *adj.* **1**, of or relating to the twelve followers of Christ, or to their times, doctrine, or practice; **2**, handed down from the apostles; **3**, papal. Also, **ap″os-tol′i-cal.**

a-pos-tro-phe (ȧ-pŏs′trō-fē), *n.* **1**, a breaking off in a speech to address directly a person or persons who may or may not be present; **2**, the sign ['] used to denote the omission from a word of one or more letters, as *I'll* for *I will*, or to mark the possessive case of nouns.

a-pos-tro-phize (ȧ-pŏs′trō-fīz), *v.i.* [*p.t.* and *p.p.* -phized (-fīzd), *p.pr.* -phiz″ing], to break off in a speech to address a person or persons, present or absent, for rhetorical effect:—*v.t.* to address in this manner for rhetorical effect.

a-poth-e-ca-ry (ȧ-pŏth′ē-kā-rĭ), *n.* [*pl.* apothecaries (-rĭz)], one who prepares and sells medicines and drugs; a pharmacist; druggist: **apothecaries' weight**, the weight used for dispensing drugs: distinguished from *troy weight* (see page 939).

ap-o-thegm (ăp′ō-thĕm), *n.* a short, pithy, instructive saying; a maxim. Also, **ap′oph-thegm** (ăp′ō-thĕm).

ap-o-the-o-sis (ăp″ō-thē′ō-sĭs; ȧ-pŏth″ē-ō′sĭs), *n.* [*pl.* apotheoses (-sēz)], **1**, deification, or the bestowing of divine honors upon a person, as in Rome upon a deceased emperor; **2**, glorification.

ap-o-the-o-size (ăp″ō-thē′ō-sīz), *v.t.* [*p.t.* and *p.p.* -sized (-sīzd), *p.pr.* -siz″ing], to exalt or elevate to the rank of a god; deify; glorify.

ap-pall (ă-pôl′), *v.t.* to frighten, depress, or discourage by fear; shock; dismay; terrify. Also, **ap-pal′.**

ap-pall-ing (ă-pôl′ĭng), *p.adj.* inspiring horror or dismay; frightful. —*adv.* **ap-pall′ing-ly.**

ap-pa-ra-tus (ăp″ȧ-rā′tŭs), *n.* [*pl.* apparatus; apparatuses (-ĕz)], **1**, an outfit of tools, utensils, or instruments adapted to, or necessary for, the accomplishment of any branch of work, or for the performance of an experiment or operation; **2**, the organs which are necessary to the performance of some natural process; as, the digestive *apparatus.*

ap-par-el (ă-păr′ĕl), *n.* clothing or dress: —*v.t.* to clothe; fit out.

ap-par-ent (ă-pâr′ĕnt; -păr′-), *adj.* **1**, open to view; **2**, capable of being easily understood; evident; **3**, seeming, rather than true or real: **heir apparent**, an heir whose rights cannot be nullified if he survive the ancestor: opp. of *heir presumptive*, whose right may be superseded by the birth of a nearer relative.—*adv.* **ap-par′ent-ly.**

Syn. likely, probable, obvious.

ap-pa-ri-tion (ăp″ȧ-rĭsh′ŭn), *n.* **1**, the act of becoming visible; **2**, an appearance of something not real or tangible; **3**, a ghost or specter.—*adj.* **ap″pa-ri′tion-al.**

ap-peal (ă-pēl′), *v.t.* to transfer or refer to a superior court or judge; as, to *appeal* a case:—*v.i.* **1**, to refer to another person, as for aid, mercy, authority; **2**, hence, to excite the interest; make a favorable impression; as, the building *appeals* to one's sense of beauty:—*n.* **1**, a call for aid, sympathy, or authority; **2**, hence, sympathetic interest or the means of exciting it; **3**, the transfer of a case from a lower to a higher court.—*p.adj.* **ap-peal′ing.**—*adv.* **ap-peal′ing-ly.**

ap-pear (ă-pēr′), *v.i.* **1**, to come or be in sight; **2**, to seem; as, he *appears* to be very ill; **3**, to come before the public.

ap-pear-ance (ă-pēr′ăns), *n.* **1**, the act of becoming visible; **2**, the object seen; an apparition; **3**, outward show; **4**, the act of coming before the public; the coming into, or the being present in, court; **5**, look, bearing, or aspect.

ap-pease (ă-pēz′), *v.t.* [*p.t.* and *p.p.* -peased′ (-pēzd′), *p.pr.* -peas′-ing], to quiet; pacify; as, to *appease* anger.

ap-pel-lant (ă-pĕl′ănt), *n.* **1**, one who appeals to a higher court; **2**, one who appeals in any way.

ap-pel-late (ă-pĕl′āt), *adj.* relating to, or dealing with, appeals; as, an *appellate* court; an *appellate* judge.

ap-pel-la-tion (ăp″ĕ-lā′shŭn), *n.* **1**, the name, title, or designation by which a person or thing is called or known; **2**, the act of naming or calling; **3**, the act of appealing from a lower to a higher court.

ap-pel-la-tive (ă-pĕl′ȧ-tĭv), *adj.* designating by name:—*n.* a title or name; an appellation.

ap-pel-lee (ăp″ĕ-lē′), *n.* one against whom an appeal is made to a higher court or jurisdiction.

ap-pend (ă-pĕnd′), *v.t.* **1**, to attach or hang, as a seal; **2**, to add; annex, as supplementary matter to a book.

ap-pend-age (ă-pĕn′dāj), *n.* **1**, something added or attached which is a proper part of a greater thing, such as an arm; **2**, something added that is not a necessary part, as a porch to a house.

Syn. attachment, adjunct, addition.

ap-pen-di-ci-tis (ă-pĕn″dĭ-sī′tĭs), *n.* inflammation of the vermiform appendix.

ap-pen-dix (ă-pĕn′dĭks), *n.* [*pl.* appendixes (-dĭk-sĕz); appendices (-dĭ-sēz)], **1**, that which is added as supplemental; as, the *appendix* to a book; **2**, the vermiform appendix, a wormlike sac, ordinarily three or four inches long, situated, in man, at the beginning of the large intestine.

ap-per-cep-tion (ăp″ĕr-sĕp′shŭn), *n.* **1**, the act of the mind by which it becomes conscious of its ideas as its own; **2**, in psychology, the process by which past experiences affect the sensations of the moment, resulting in perception.

ap-per-tain (ăp″ĕr-tān′), *v.i.* to belong to by right, nature, and custom; be associated; pertain.

ap-pe-tite (ăp′ē-tīt), *n.* **1**, a physical craving for food; **2**, the desire to satisfy a want; **3**, a mental longing.

ap-pe-tiz-er (ăp′ē-tīz″ĕr), *n.* **1**, something that excites the desire for anything; **2**, anything that gives a relish for food.—*adj.* **ap′pe-tiz″ing.**

ap-plaud (ă-plôd′), *v.t.* to express approval or approbation of, esp. by a clapping of the hands; commend:—*v.i.* to clap the hands or otherwise show approval.

ap-plause (ă-plôz′), *n.* the public expression of approval, as by clapping.

ap-ple (ăp′l), *n.* **1**, the round, fleshy fruit of a well-known tree almost universally cultivated in temperate regions, of which there are many varieties; **2**, the tree itself; **3**, any of various fruits or plants; as, the May *apple.*

ap-pli-ance (ă-plī′ăns), *n.* **1**, the act of putting into use; **2**, something used as a means to an end; as, the *appliances* of a trade; the *appliances* of war.

ap-pli-ca-ble (ăp′lĭ-kȧ-bl), *adj.* fit; suitable; appropriate; as, that remark was not *applicable* to me.—*adv.* **ap′pli-ca-bly.**—*n.* **ap″pli-ca-bil′i-ty.**

ap-pli-cant (ăp′lĭ-kănt), *n.* one who asks, requests, or applies for something; a candidate, as for a position.

ap-pli-ca-tion (ăp″lĭ-kā′shŭn), *n.* **1**, the act of putting on; as, an *application* of heat; **2**, the thing put on; **3**, the practical demonstration of a principle; **4**, the act of requesting; **5**, a request; **6**, close attention; **7**, connection; appropriateness.

ap-plied (ă-plīd′), *p.adj.* used, esp. for a practical purpose; as, *applied* mechanics: often opp. of *theoretical.*

***ap-pli-qué** (ȧ″plē″kā′), [Fr.], *n.* an ornamentation for dress or upholstery, cut from one material and laid upon a foundation of another:—*adj.* laid on.

ap-ply (ă-plī′), *v.t.* [*p.t.* and *p.p.* -plied′ (-plīd′), *p.pr.* -ply′ing], **1**, to bring into contact with something; lay on; **2**, to put into practice; as, *apply* your principles to your actions; **3**, to devote to a particular purpose; fix upon; as, *apply* yourself to study:—*v.i.* **1**, to ask; petition; **2**, to have some connection; as, this does not *apply* to you.

ap-point (ă-point′), *v.t.* **1**, to establish by decree; assign; **2**, to name for an office; **3**, to equip.—*n.* **ap-point′er.**

ap-point-ee (ă-poin″tē′), *n.* one chosen to fill an office.

ap-point-ment (ă-point′mĕnt), *n.* **1**, the act of assigning to an office; **2**, the position or office assigned; **3**, an engagement; arrangement to meet by mutual agreement; **4**, in *pl.*, furniture or equipment.

ap-por-tion (ă-pōr′shŭn), *v.t.* to distribute by some rule; allot.—*n.* **ap-por′tion-ment.**

Syn. assign, appoint, divide, allocate.

ap-po-site (ăp′ō-zĭt), *adj.* appropriate; suitable; well adapted; fit.—*adv.* **ap′po-site-ly.**—*n.* **ap′po-site-ness.**

ap-po-si-tion (ăp″ō-zĭsh′ŭn), *n.* **1**, the act of placing side by side; **2**, the state of being so placed; **3**, esp., the relation between a word or phrase and another placed beside it, without a connective, as in the phrase *St. Mark, the Evangelist.*

ap-pos-i-tive (ă-pŏz′ĭ-tĭv), *adj.* explanatory:—*n.* a word or phrase in apposition.—*adv.* **ap-pos′i-tive-ly.**

ap-prais-al (ă-prāz′ăl), *n.* **1**, the act of valuing or putting a price upon; **2**, the valuation so placed.

ap-praise (ă-prāz′), *v.t.* [*p.t.* and *p.p.* -praised′ (-prāzd′), *p.pr.* -prais′ing], to set a price upon; value, esp. officially.

ap-praise-ment (ă-prāz′mĕnt), *n.* **1**, the act of determining a value; **2**, an authorized estimate or valuation.

ap-prais-er (ă-prāz′ẽr), *n.* one who estimates; esp., a person licensed to estimate the value of goods or estates.

ap-pre-ci-a-ble (ă-prē′shĭ-ȧ-bl), *adj.* capable of being estimated; perceptible; as, there is no *appreciable* difference between them.—*adv.* **ap-pre′ci-a-bly.**

ap-pre-ci-ate (ă-prē′shĭ-āt), *v.t.* [*p.t.* and *p.p.* -at″ed, *p.pr.* -at″ing], **1**, to value; estimate the worth of; esteem highly; prize; **2**, to be sensitive to; distinguish; as, to *appreciate* fine distinctions; **3**, to raise in value; as, to *appreciate* a country's paper money: opp. of *depreciate:*—*v.i.* to rise in price or value, as paper money.

ap-pre-ci-a-tion (ă-prē″shĭ-ā′shŭn), *n.* **1**, the just valuation or recognition of worth; **2**, sympathetic understanding; **3**, a rise in value.

ap-pre-ci-a-tive (ă-prē′shĭ-ā-tĭv), *adj.* **1**, showing esteem or interest; as, an *appreciative* audience; **2**, showing gratitude; as, *appreciative* of help.—*adv.* **ap-pre′ci-a-tive-ly.**—*n.* **ap-pre′ci-a-tive-ness.**

ap-pre-hend (ăp″rē-hĕnd′), *v.t.* **1**, to take or lay hold of; seize; arrest; **2**, to take mental hold of; as, to *apprehend* his meaning; **3**, to anticipate with fear:—*v.i.* **1**, to incline to believe; **2**, to catch the meaning; **3**, to look forward with fear.

ap-pre-hen-si-ble (ăp″rē-hĕn′sĭ-bl), *adj.* capable of being conceived; understandable.

ap-pre-hen-sion (ăp″rē-hĕn′shŭn), *n.* **1**, the act of seizure or of laying hold of; arrest; **2**, mental grasp; perception; **3**, anticipation of evil; anxiety; misgiving; **4**, sentiment; opinion.

ap-pre-hen-sive (ăp″rē-hĕn′sĭv), *adj.* **1**, quick to learn or grasp; **2**, fearful of evil; worried.—*adv.* **ap″pre-hen′sive-ly.**—*n.* **ap″pre-hen′sive-ness.**

ap-pren-tice (ă-prĕn′tĭs), *n.* **1**, one bound by agreement to serve another a certain number of years in order to learn a trade or craft; **2**, a novice, or one slightly versed in anything:—*v.t.* [*p.t.* and *p.p.* -ticed (-tĭst), *p.pr.* -tic-ing], to put under a master for instruction in a trade or craft.

ap-pren-tice-ship (ă-prĕn′tĭs-shĭp), *n.* **1**, the term of service, or time served, while learning a trade; **2**, the state of being bound to such service.

ap-prise (ă-prīz′), *v.t.* [*p.t.* and *p.p.* -prised′ (-prīzd′), *p.pr.* -pris′ing], to give notice to; warn; inform. Also, **ap-prize′.**

ap-prize (ă-prīz′), *v.t.* [*p.t.* and *p.p.* -prized′ (-prīzd′), *p.pr.* -priz′ing], **1**, to put a value upon; appraise; **2**, (also, *apprise*), to warn or advise.

ap-proach (ă-prōch′), *v.i.* to draw or be near:—*v.t.* **1**, to come near to in quality, character, or condition; as, this *approaches* my ideal; **2**, to make overtures to; sound; as, they *approached* him on the subject:—*n.* **1**, the act of drawing near; **2**, way of drawing near; as, the *approaches* to the city; **3**, in golf, a shot made in order to place the ball on the green.—*adj.* **ap-proach′-a-ble.**

ap-pro-ba-tion (ăp″rō-bā′shŭn), *n.* the act of pronouncing good; commendation; sanction.

ap-pro-pri-ate (ă-prō′prĭ-āt), *v.t.* [*p.t.* and *p.p.* -at″ed, *p.pr.* -at″ing], **1**, to take to oneself; claim or use, as by an exclusive or sole right; as, he *appropriates* all the praise; **2**, to set apart or assign to a particular use, often by legislative act, as money for good roads:—*adj.* (ă-prō′prĭ-ăt), fit; suitable; proper.—*adv.* **ap-pro′pri-ate-ly.**—*n.* **ap-pro′pri-ate-ness.**

ap-pro-pri-a-tion (ă-prō″prĭ-ā′shŭn), *n.* **1**, the act of setting apart for a particular use or person; **2**, the act of taking to oneself; **3**, anything set apart, esp. a grant of money by the government for a special purpose.

ap-prov-al (ă-prōōv′ăl), *n.* approbation; sanction; ratification; consent.

ap-prove (ă-prōōv′), *v.t.* [*p.t.* and *p.p.* -proved′ (-prōōvd′), *p.pr.* -prov′ing], **1**, to test or demonstrate; **2**, to ratify;

pronounce efficient or sufficient; **3,** to be pleased or satisfied with; commend:—*v.i.* to express satisfaction: usually with *of*.—*p. adj.* **ap-prov′ing.**—*adv.* **ap-prov′ing-ly.**

ap-prox-i-mate (ă-prŏk′sĭ-māt), *v.t.* [*p.t.* and *p.p.* -mat″ed, *p.pr.* -mat″ing], **1,** to come close to; as, to *approximate* the answer; **2,** to cause to approach; as, to *approximate* the tips of two fingers:—*v.i.* to approach closely; be nearly equal:—*adj.* (ă-prŏk′sĭ-māt), **1,** near in resemblance; **2,** almost equal; **3,** nearly correct; fairly accurate, as an answer.—*adv.* **ap-prox′i-mate-ly.**

ap-prox-i-ma-tion (ă-prŏk″sĭ-mā′-shŭn), *n.* **1,** the act of approaching closely; **2,** the result of such approach, as a nearly correct estimate.—*adj.* **ap-prox′i-ma-tive.**

ap-pur-te-nance (ă-pûr′tē-năns), *n.* **1,** that which belongs or relates to something else; an adjunct or appendage; **2,** that which belongs to an estate or property, as trees and shrubbery.

ap-pur-te-nant (ă-pûr′tē-nănt), *adj.* accessory; incident:—*n.* an adjunct or appendage.

a-pri-cot (ā′prĭ-kŏt; ăp′rĭ-), *n.* **1,** the round, orange-colored fruit of a tree allied to both the plum and the peach; **2,** the tree itself.

A-pril (ā′prĭl), *n.* the fourth month of the year, containing 30 days: **April fool,** one who is imposed upon or deceived on April 1, or All Fools' Day.—*abbr.* **Apr.**

***a pri-o-ri** (ā prī-ō′rī; ä prĭ-ō′rē), [Lat.], from the former; characterizing an argument proceeding from cause to effect.

a-pron (ā′prŭn; ā′pûrn), *n.* **1,** an article made of cloth, leather, or other material, worn on the front of a person's clothes for protection or ornament; **2,** a leathern covering for use in an open carriage; **3,** anything like an apron in form or use.

ap-ro-pos (ăp″rō-pō′), *adv.* **1,** approximately; to the point; **2,** seasonably; **3,** with reference (to); as, *apropos* of that remark; by the way:—*adj.* **1,** seasonable; **2,** appropriate. Also, ***à″ pro″pos′** (ȧ″ prô″pō′).

apse (ăps), *n.* a semicircular recess covered with a half dome, at the end of a building, esp. at the eastern end of a church.

apt (ăpt), *adj.* **1,** suitable; pertinent; appropriate; **2,** liable; inclined; prone; **3,** ready; expert; quick of comprehension.—*adv.* **apt′ly.**—*n.* **apt′ness.**

Syn. likely, liable. *Apt* expresses an inherent tendency; as, a beautiful girl is *apt* to be vain. *Likely* implies probability and generally suggests something favorable; as, she is *likely* to succeed. *Liable* indicates exposure to disadvantages or unpleasant situations; as, a careless driver is *liable* to accident.

ap-ter-yx (ăp′tēr-ĭks), *n.* any of a genus (*Apteryx*) of birds of New Zealand, about the size of a hen, nearly extinct, with undeveloped wings concealed by the hairlike feathers: also called *kiwi.*

APTERYX (1/10)

apt-i-tude (ăp′tĭ-tūd), *n.* **1,** capacity for anything; **2,** fitness; **3,** readiness in learning; as, an *aptitude* for languages.

***a-qua** (ā′kwȧ), [Lat.], *n.* water: a term used in pharmacy to indicate the addition of water.—*abbr.* **aq.; Aq.**

a-qua-ma-rine (ā″kwȧ-mȧ-rēn′), *n.* a transparent beryl, bluish green in color, used as a gem.

aq-ua-plane (ăk′wȧ-plān″), *n.* a plank pulled swiftly over the surface of water, so that a person can stand on it.

aq-ua-relle (ăk″wȧ-rĕl′), *n.* a painting in water colors.

a-qua-ri-um (ȧ-kwā′rĭ-ŭm), *n.* [*pl.* aquariums (-ŭmz); aquaria (-ȧ)], **1,** a tank or globe in which water plants and animals, such as goldfish, are kept; **2,** a building for collections of water plants and animals.

A-qua-ri-us (ȧ-kwā′rĭ-ŭs), *n.* a constellation, the Water Bearer; also, the 11th sign of the zodiac (see *zodiac,* illus.).

a-quat-ic (ȧ-kwăt′ĭk), *adj.* **1,** relating to water; **2,** growing or living in or upon water; **3,** performed in or upon water; as, *aquatic* sports:—*n.* **1,** an animal or plant that lives in water; **2,** in *pl.,* water sports.

***a-qua vi-tæ** (ā′kwȧ vī′tē), [Lat.], literally, water of life; hence, brandy; formerly, alcohol or other spirits.

aq-ue-duct (ăk′wē-dŭkt), *n.* a conduit or artificial channel for conducting water from a distant source, such as the Catskill *aqueduct* in New York.

a-que-ous (ā′kwē-ŭs), *adj.* **1,** of the nature of, or abounding in, water; watery; **2,** formed in, or by means of, water.

Aq-ui-la (ăk′wĭ-lȧ), *n.* in astronomy, the Eagle, a northern constellation.

aq-ui-line (ăk′wĭ-lĭn; -līn), *adj.* **1,** relating to, or resembling, an eagle; **2,** curved, as the beak of an eagle; hooked; prominent; as, an *aquiline* nose.

ar (är), *n.* in the metric system, a certain measure of surface. See ²**are,** *Pfd. S.*

-ar (-ȧr), *adj. suffix,* like or pertaining to; as, famili*ar;* lun*ar;* popul*ar:*—*n. suffix,* **1,** a thing like or pertaining to; as, alt*ar;* exempl*ar;* **2,** a doer or agent; as begg*ar;* li*ar.*

Ar-ab (ăr′ăb), *n.* **1,** a native of Arabia; **2,** a desert dweller; a member of one of the Arabic races spread over the African and Syrian deserts; **3,** a homeless street urchin:—*adj.* pertaining to Arabia or its people.

ar-a-besque (ăr″ȧ-bĕsk′), *n.* a kind of ornamentation in low relief consisting of the representation of plants, fruits, flowers, foliage, etc., fancifully combined or oddly grouped.

A-ra-bi-an (ȧ-rā′bĭ-ăn), *adj.* of or pertaining to Arabia or the Arabs: **Arabian Nights,** an ancient collection of tales of Persia, Arabia, etc.: also called *Arabian Nights' Entertainments,* and *Thousand and One Nights:*—*n.* an Arab; a native of Arabia.

Ar-a-bic (ăr′ȧ-bĭk), *adj.* Arabian; pertaining to Arabia or the Arabs: **Arabic numerals,** the figures 0, 1, 2, 3, etc., of Hindu origin, used by the Arabs and introduced into Europe in the 12th century: distinguished from *Roman numerals:*—*n.* the Semitic language used by the Arabs.—*n.* **Ar′a-bist.**

ar-a-ble (ăr′ȧ-bl), *adj.* suited to the purposes of cultivation; as, *arable* land.

a-rach-nid (ȧ-răk′nĭd), *n.* any of a class (*Arachnida*) of invertebrate animals including spiders, scorpions, mites, certain ticks, etc. (see *crustacean,* illus.).—*adj.* and *n.* **a-rach′ni-dan.**

ar-bi-ter (är′bĭ-tēr), *n.* **1,** a person having the power to decide a dispute; an umpire or judge; **2,** one who controls a result or decision.—*n.fem.* **ar′bi-tress.**

ar-bit-ra-ment (är-bĭt′rȧ-mĕnt), *n.* **1,** the right or power of deciding; **2,** the act of deciding; also, the decision of chosen judges or umpires; an award.

ar-bi-tra-ry (är′bĭ-trā-rĭ), *adj.* **1,** not fixed by rule or law; **2,** ca-

pricious; unreasonable; **3**, imperious; despotic.—*adv.* **ar′bi-tra-ri-ly.**

ar-bi-trate (är′bĭ-trāt), *v.t.* [*p.t.* and *p.p.* -trat″ed, *p.pr.* -trat″ing], **1**, to act or decide as judge in (a dispute); settle (a dispute) by discussion; **2**, to refer (a dispute) to arbitrators:—*v.i.* to settle a dispute through arbitrators, by means of discussion and agreement.—*adj.* **ar′bi-tra-ble.**

ar-bi-tra-tion (är″bĭ-trā′shŭn), *n.* **1**, the settlement of a dispute by a group of persons chosen by those on each side; **2**, settlement of a question by mutual agreement; as, disputes between modern nations should be settled by *arbitration*.

ar-bi-tra-tor (är′bĭ-trā″tẽr), *n.* one chosen by the parties in a dispute to settle the difference between them; one who has power to decide.

ar-bor (är′bẽr), *n.* a bower formed by trees or vines trained over a latticework so as to make a roof; a shaded nook or walk.

Ar-bor Day a day legally set apart in certain states for the planting of trees and shrubs.

ar-bo-re-al (är-bō′rē-ăl), *adj.* like, or pertaining to, a tree or trees; attached to, or living among, trees.

ar-bo-res-cent (är″bō-rĕs′ĕnt), *adj.* **1**, treelike; **2**, branching like a tree; as, an *arborescent* mineral.

ar-bo-re-tum (är″bō-rē′tŭm), *n.* [*pl.* arboretums (-tŭmz)], a place in which rare trees are cultivated and exhibited for scientific and educational purposes.

ar-bo-ri-cul-ture (är′bō-rĭ-kŭl″tŭr), *n.* the art of cultivation of trees or shrubs.

ar-bor vi-tæ (vī′tē), an evergreen tree extensively cultivated in gardens. Also, *n.* **ar″bor-vi′tæ.**

ar-bu-tus (är′bū-tŭs; är-bū′tŭs), *n.* **1**, any of a genus (*Arbutus*) of evergreen trees, with many-seeded berries; **2**, a creeping plant of the heath family, with small, fragrant flowers; the Mayflower: often called *trailing arbutus*.

arc (ärk), *n.* **1**, a curved line; any section of a curve forming part of a circle; **2**, in astronomy, the portion of a circle described by the sun or any heavenly body in its apparent passage through the heavens; **3**, the curved band of light formed between two electrodes, caused by the passage of an electric current: also called *voltaic arc:* **arc light,** a lamp, as for a street, lighted by a voltaic arc.

ar-cade (är-kād′), *n.* **1**, a row of arches supported by pillars; **2**, an arched gallery, or promenade, often lined with shops.

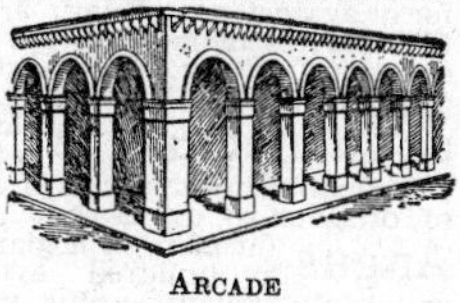

ARCADE

Ar-ca-di-a (är-kā′dĭ-ȧ), *n.* **1**, a mountain district in ancient Greece, inhabited by simple, contented shepherds and huntsmen; **2**, hence, any region or scene of simple pleasure or quiet happiness. Also, **Ar′ca-dy** (är′kȧ-dĭ).

Ar-ca-di-an (är-kā′dĭ-ăn), *adj.* ideally rural and peaceful:—*n.* **1**, a dweller in Arcadia; **2**, one having simple pastoral tastes.

ar-ca-num (är-kā′nŭm), *n.* [*pl.* arcana (-nȧ); arcanums (-nŭmz)], **1**, usually in *pl.*, a mystery; **2**, in medieval alchemy, the vital secret of something in nature; a secret remedy.

[1]**arch** (ärch), *n.* **1**, a structure of brick or masonry, the wedge-shaped parts of which follow a curved line: usually forming the top of a door, window, or gateway; **2**, an

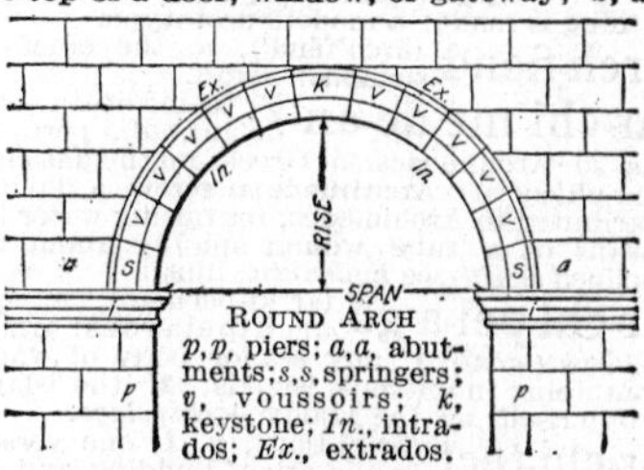

ROUND ARCH
p,p, piers; *a,a*, abutments; *s,s*, springers; *v*, voussoirs; *k*, keystone; *In.*, intrados; *Ex.*, extrados.

opening or passage covered by such a structure; **3**, an arch-shaped curve, as an eyebrow:—*v.t.* **1**, to cover with a curved structure; **2**, to bend or curve:—*v.i.* to form a bent or curved top or covering; curve.

[2]**arch** (ärch), *adj.* **1**, chief; of the first rank; as, an *arch* villain; **2**, shrewd; mischievous; roguish.

arch- (ärch-; ärk-), *prefix*, meaning chief or principal; as, *arch*deacon; *arch*bishop.

Ar-chæ-an (är-kē′ăn), *adj.* designating, or pertaining to, the geologic age next after the Azoic, or oldest period of geologic time. Also, **Ar-che′an.**

ar-chæ-ol-o-gist (är″kē-ŏl′ō-jĭst), *n.* one versed in the study of ancient things, esp. prehistoric remains; an antiquary. Also, **ar″che-ol′o-gist.**

ar-chæ-ol-o-gy (är″kē-ŏl′ō-jĭ), *n.* the science of antiquities; esp., the study of prehistoric remains, or the relics of the early races of mankind. Also, **ar″che-ol′o-gy.**—*adj.* **ar″chæ-o-log′ic; ar″chæ-o-log′i-cal.**

ar-cha-ic (är-kā′ĭk), *adj.* relating to a remote period; old-fashioned; of words, no longer in common use.

ar-cha-ism (är′kā-ĭzm), *n.* an antiquated or old-fashioned word, expression, or idiom; also, the use of such words, expressions, or idioms.

arch-an-gel (ärk′ān′jĕl), *n.* an angel of the highest order.

arch-bish-op (ärch′bĭsh′ŭp), *n.* the chief of the bishops of a church district or ecclesiastical province in the Greek, Roman, and English churches.

arch-bish-op-ric (ärch″bĭsh′ŭp-rĭk), *n.* the office, district, or province of an archbishop; the province over which the archbishop has authority.

arch-dea-con (ärch′dē′kn), *n.* a church officer ranking next below a bishop; a chief deacon.

arch-duch-ess (ärch′dŭch′ĕs), *n.* **1**, the wife of an archduke; **2**, a daughter of the imperial family formerly reigning in Austria.

arch-duch-y (ärch′dŭch′ĭ), *n.* [*pl.* archduchies (-ĭz)], the territory or rank of an archduke or archduchess.

arch-duke (ärch′dūk′), *n.* a prince of the former imperial house of Austria.—*adj.* **arch″du′cal.**

arch-en-e-my (ärch′ĕn′ē-mĭ), *n.* [*pl.* archenemies (-mĭz)], a principal enemy; esp., Satan.

arch-er (är′chẽr), *n.* one skilled in using the bow and arrow: **Archer, 1**, a southern constellation; Sagittarius; **2**, the ninth sign of the zodiac (see *zodiac*, illus.).

arch-er-y (är′chẽr-ĭ), *n.* **1**, the art, practice, or skill of one who uses the bow and arrow; **2**, archers collectively.

ar-che-type (är'kē-tīp), *n.* the original pattern upon or after which a thing is made; a model; prototype.

arch-fiend (ärch'fēnd'), *n.* the chief of demons; Satan.

Ar-chi-me-de-an (är″kĭ-mē'dē-ăn;-mē-dē'ăn), *adj.* pertaining to Archimedes, a Greek mathematician and physicist: **Archimedean screw,** a device, attributed to Archimedes, for raising water by means of a tube wound spirally about an inclined shaft (see *hydraulic*, illus.).

ar-chi-pel-a-go (är″kĭ-pĕl'ȧ-gō), *n.* [*pl.* archipelagoes; archipelagos (-gōz)], **1,** any sea or body of water containing numerous islands; **2,** the island group itself; as, the Malay *Archipelago.*

ar-chi-tect (är'kĭ-tĕkt), *n.* **1,** one versed in the art of building and its various styles; **2,** one who plans or designs buildings and superintends their construction; **3,** hence, one who plans or devises any complicated structure; a designer; maker.

ar-chi-tec-tur-al (är″kĭ-tĕk'tûr-ăl), *adj.* of or pertaining to the art of building, or in harmony with its rules.—*adv.* **ar″chi-tec'tur-al-ly.**

ar-chi-tec-ture (är'kĭ-tĕk″tûr), *n.* **1,** the science or art of building, esp. of fine or beautiful building; **2,** the method or style of building; as, Gothic *architecture;* **3,** construction; workmanship.

ar-chi-trave (är'kĭ-trāv), *n.* the lowest division of an entablature, or horizontal structure supported by columns; that part which rests immediately on the columns of a building or other structure.

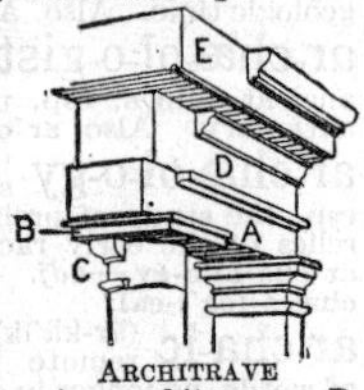

ARCHITRAVE
A, architrave; B, abacus; C, capital; D, frieze; E, cornice; A+D+E, entablature.

ar-chive (är'kīv), *n.* **1,** a record preserved as evidence; **2,** in *pl.:* **a,** the place where public or state records are kept; **b,** state or public documents, or records of historical value.—*n.* **ar'chi-vist.**

arch-ly (ärch'lĭ), *adv.* in a coy manner; roguishly; playfully.

arch-ness (ärch'nĕs), *n.* coyness; roguishness; playfulness.

ar-chon (är'kŏn), *n.* **1,** a chief magistrate of ancient Athens; **2,** in modern Greece, an official.

arch-way (ärch'wā″), *n.* an opening or passage beneath a curved or vaulted roof, or under an arch.

arc-tic (ärk'tĭk), *adj.* relating to the region of the north pole; polar; northern; frigid: **arctic circle,** an imaginary circle parallel to the equator and distant 23° 28′ from the north pole: **Arctic Ocean,** the north polar ocean:—*n.* in the U. S., a high, warmly lined, waterproof overshoe.

Arc-tu-rus (ärk-tū'rŭs), *n.* in astronomy, the brightest star in the constellation Boötes.

-ard (-ȧrd), *suffix,* [sometimes in form *-art;* as, bragg*art*], used to form nouns denoting one with an excess of a quality: often of an adverse meaning; as, drunk*ard;* lagg*ard.*

ar-dent (är'dĕnt), *adj.* **1,** hot; burning; fiery; warm; glowing; **2,** passionate; eager; zealous; vehement: **ardent spirits,** alcoholic liquids, such as brandy, whisky, etc.—*n.* **ar'den-cy.**—*adv.* **ar'dent-ly.**

ar-dor (är'dẽr), *n.* **1,** intense heat; **2,** warmth of affection or passion; eager desire; zeal. Also, **ar'dour.**

ar-du-ous (är'dū-ŭs), *adj.* **1,** steep; hard to climb; **2,** attended with great labor or exertion; difficult.—*adv.* **ar'du-ous-ly.**—*n.* **ar'du-ous-ness.**

¹are (är), present indicative plural, in all three persons, of the verb *be.*

²are (är), *n.* in the metric system, a measure of surface; 100 square meters, equal to 119.6 square yards. Also, **ar** (är).

a-re-a (ā'rē-ȧ), *n.* [*pl.* areas (-ȧz)], **1,** any flat surface having bounds, whether natural or artificial; **2,** any defined extent of land surface; **3,** the space occupied by a building; esp., the sunken space at its base, separating it from the street and affording light to the basement; **4,** extent; range; scope; region; tract; **5,** in geometry, the amount of surface of a plane or solid figure.

a-re-na (ȧ-rē'nȧ), *n.* [*pl.* arenas (-nȧz); arenæ (-nē)], **1,** the central inclosed space of a Roman amphitheater, in which the gladiatorial contests took place; **2,** hence, a scene or field for combat or exertion of any kind; as, the western *arena* of the World War.

Ar-e-op-a-gus (ăr″ē-ŏp'ȧ-gŭs), *n.* **1,** the highest court of ancient Athens, so named from its situation on the Hill of Ares (Mars); **2,** hence, any high court or tribunal; **3,** the Hill of Ares itself.

A-res (ā'rēz), *n.* in Greek mythology, the god of war, son of Zeus and Hera: identified with the Roman *Mars.*

Ar-e-thu-sa (ăr″ē-thū'sȧ), *n.* in mythology, a wood nymph whom Artemis changed into a stream.

ar-gent (är'jĕnt), *adj.* made of, or resembling, silver; silvery white.

Ar-go (är'gō), *n.* in mythology, the ship which carried Jason and the Argonauts on their quest for the Golden Fleece.

ar-gon (är'gŏn), *n.* a colorless, odorless, gaseous element found in the air.

Ar-go-naut (är'gō-nôt), *n.* **1,** one of the band of Greek heroes who sailed with Jason in quest of the Golden Fleece; **2,** hence, one of the gold seekers who went to California in 1849.—*adj.* **Ar″go-nau'tic.**

ar-go-sy (är'gō-sĭ), *n.* [*pl.* argosies (-sĭz)], a large merchant vessel filled with costly goods.

ar-gue (är'gū), *v.i.* [*p.t.* and *p.p.* -gued (-gūd), *p.pr.* -gu-ing], **1,** to offer reasons in support of, or in opposition to, a proposition, opinion, or measure; **2,** to reason; contend in debate:—*v.t.* to debate; prove; discuss by reasoning.

ar-gu-ment (är'gū-mĕnt), *n.* **1,** a presentation of proofs of, or reasons for or against, something; **2,** a discussion, controversy, or debate; **3,** the subject of a discourse or writing; **4,** an abstract or summary of a book.—*n.* **ar″gu-men-ta'tion.**

ar-gu-men-ta-tive (är″gū-mĕn'tȧ-tĭv), *adj.* **1,** consisting of, or exhibiting a process of, reasoning; **2,** fond of, or given to, discussion.

Ar-gus (är'gŭs), *n.* a giant fabled to have a hundred eyes: **Argus-eyed,** watchful; vigilant: **argus,** a watchful person.

a-ri-a (ä'rĭ-ȧ; ā'rĭ-ȧ), *n.* **1,** an air; a melody or tune for a single voice with accompaniment; **2,** an elaborate solo part in a cantata, oratorio, or the like.

Ar-i-ad-ne (ăr″ĭ-ăd'nē), *n.* in mythology, the daughter of King Minos of Crete, who assisted Theseus to kill the Minotaur and escape from the Labyrinth.

A-ri-an (ā'rĭ-ăn), *adj.* relating to the doctrines of Arius, a theologian of the fourth century, who taught that Christ was the noblest of men, but that he was not divine.

-a-ri-an (-ā'rĭ-ăn), *adj.* and *n. suffix,* expressing: **1,** occupation; as, veteri-

narian; **2,** religious affiliation; habit of thought; as, Unit*arian;* **3,** age; as, nonagen*arian.*

ar-id (ăr′ĭd), *adj.* having little or no rainfall; very dry; parched; barren.—*n.* **a-rid′i-ty.**—*n.* **ar′id-ness.**

A-ri-es (ā′rĭ-ēz), *n.* **1,** a constellation, the Ram; **2,** the first of the twelve signs of the zodiac, entered by the sun about March 21 (see *zodiac*, illus.).

a-right (*ȧ*-rīt′), *adv.* correctly; in a proper way or form.

a-rise (*ȧ*-rīz′), *v.t.* [*p.t.* a-rose′ (-rōz′), *p.p.* a-ris′en (-rĭz′n), *p.pr.* a-ris′ing], **1,** to change to a standing position from one of sitting, kneeling, or lying; **2,** to ascend; come into view, as the sun; **3,** to spring up; originate.
Syn. flow, spring, proceed, rise, issue.

a-ris-tate (*ȧ*-rĭs′tāt), *adj.* in botany, **1,** bearded, as grain; **2,** having a sharp, spinelike tip (see *leaf*, illus.).

ar-is-toc-ra-cy (ăr″ĭs-tŏk′r*ȧ*-sĭ), *n.* [*pl.* aristocracies (-sĭz)], **1,** government by persons of the highest rank in a state; **2,** a state so governed; **3,** the nobility or chief persons in a state; **4,** those regarded as superior to the rest of their community in rank, wealth, or intellect.

a-ris-to-crat (*ȧ*-rĭs′tō-krăt; ăr′ĭs-tō-), *n.* **1,** a personage of high rank or noble birth, or one who has traits suited to such rank; **2,** one who upholds aristocracy or favors government by the few.—*adj.* **ar″is-to-crat′ic** (ăr″ĭs-tō-krăt′ĭk; *ȧ*-rĭs″-).

a-rith-me-tic (*ȧ*-rĭth′mē-tĭk), *n.* the science of numbers; the art of reckoning by figures.—*abbr.* **arith.**

a-rith-met-i-cal (ăr″ĭth-mĕt′ĭ-kăl), *adj.* of or relating to the science of numbers.—*adv.* **ar″ith-met′i-cal-ly.**

a-rith-me-ti-cian (*ȧ*-rĭth″mē-tĭsh′ăn; ăr″ĭth-), *n.* one skilled in the science of numbers.

-a-ri-um (-ā′rĭ-ŭm), [Lat.], *n. suffix*, denoting place where; as, herb*arium.*

ark (ärk), *n.* **1,** a chest; **2,** the oblong box containing the Covenant, or tables of the Law, in the Jewish Tabernacle (Exodus **25;** **1** Kings 8); **3,** the ship in which Noah and his family remained during the Deluge (Genesis **6**); **4,** hence, a place of safety or refuge.

¹arm (ärm), *n.* **1,** the limb of the human body which extends from the shoulder to the hand; **2,** the anterior or fore limb of any animal having a backbone; **3,** any projecting organ or part of a main body or trunk, as the branch of a tree; **4,** strength or power.

²arm (ärm), *n.* **1,** usually in *pl.*, a weapon; **2,** a branch of the military service, as the infantry:—*v.t.* **1,** to furnish with weapons or armor; **2,** to fortify; as, to *arm* against disease:—*v.i.* to fit oneself with arms.

ar-ma-da (är-mā′d*ȧ*), *n.* an armed fleet: **Invincible Armada,** the Spanish fleet sent against England in 1588.

ar-ma-dil-lo (är″m*ȧ*-dĭl′ō), *n.* [*pl.* armadillos (-ōz)], any of several South American burrowing animals having the body and head covered with bony plates.

ar-ma-ment (är′m*ȧ*-mĕnt), *n.* **1,** a body of forces prepared for war, either military, naval, or aërial; **2,** the cannon and small arms of a fort or warship; **3,** the equipment of guns of a warship; **4,** the equipment or act of equipping, as for defense.

ar-ma-ture (är′m*ȧ*-tūr), *n.* **1,** armor; that which serves as a means of defense; **2,** any covering used for a purpose similar to armor; **3,** in dynamo-electric machines, that part which by its movement causes a current, as in a dynamo, or which is caused to move when a current is passed through it, as in a motor; **4,** a piece of soft iron used to connect the poles of a magnet.

arm-chair (ärm′châr″), *n.* a chair with supports for the forearms.

Ar-me-ni-an (är-mē′nĭ-ăn), *adj.* pertaining to the mountainous country in the northeastern part of Asia Minor, or to its people:—*n.* **1,** a native of this country; **2,** the language of this country.

arm-ful (ärm′fo͝ol), *n.* [*pl.* armfuls (-fo͝olz)], as much as the arms can hold.

arm-hole (ärm′hōl″), *n.* an opening for the arm in a garment.

ar-mi-stice (är′mĭ-stĭs), *n.* a brief pause in war by agreement of the opposing forces; a truce.

ar-m-let (ärm′lĕt), *n.* **1,** a small creek or inlet of the sea; **2,** a band, as of gold, worn on the arm.

ARMLETS

ar-mor (är′mẽr), *n.* **1,** defensive weapons; protective covering for the body in battle; **2,** the steel plating of a warship; **3,** any protective covering, as the scales of a fish:—*v.t.* to furnish or invest with a protective covering. Also, **ar′mour.**—*p.adj.* **ar′mored.**

ar-mor-bear-er (är′mẽr-bâr″ẽr), *n.* in olden times, an attendant who carried the arms and armor of a warrior or knight. Also, **ar′mour-bear″er.**

ar-mor-clad (är′mẽr-klăd″), *adj.* protected by iron or steel armor:—*n.* a war vessel protected by steel plating. Also, **ar′mour-clad″.**

ar-mor-er (är′mẽr-ẽr), *n.* **1,** formerly, a maker of weapons, shields, etc.; also, one who had charge of the military outfit of another, as of a knight; **2,** the keeper of the weapons of a troop or battleship. Also, **ar′mour-er.**

ar-mo-ri-al (är-mō′rĭ-ăl), *adj.* relating to armor or to coats of arms:—*n.* a book or dictionary of heraldic devices or coats of arms, with the names of persons entitled to use them.

ARMOR

1, basinet; 2, jeweled rim of basinet; 3, gorget; 4, 5, pauldrons; 6, rerebrace; 7, gauntlet; 8, dagger; 9, skirt, composed of tassets; 10, large, bottom tasset, forming tuille; 11, cuisse; 12, knee piece; 13, greave; 14, spur strap; 15, solleret; 16 sword.

ar-mor plate the iron or steel plate with which a fort or ship is covered for greater protection against shell fire. Also, **ar′mour plate.**

ar-mor-y (är′mẽr-ĭ), *n.* [*pl.* armories (-ĭz)], **1,** a place for the storing of weapons; also, weapons collectively; **2,** a place for the assembling of soldiers, usually containing a drill hall, offices, etc.; **3,** a manufactory of weapons. Also, **ar′mour-y.**

arm-pit (ärm′pĭt″), *n.* the hollow beneath the arm near the shoulder.

arms (ärmz), *n.pl.* **1,** weapons of offense or defense; **2,** the military service; as, a call to *arms;* war as a profession; **3,** heraldic bearings or devices; as, the coat of *arms* of the United States: **small arms,** pistols, rifles, etc.

ar-my (är′mĭ), *n.* [*pl.* armies (-mĭz)], **1,** a body of men trained and equipped for war on land, and organized in regiments, brigades, or similar divisions under proper officers; forces; troops; **2,** a great number or multitude; a host; an array; **3,** an organized body of persons engaged in moral warfare: **standing army,** a body of professional soldiers kept permanently in service.

ar-my worm the very destructive larva of a moth, so called because of the great numbers in which it marches across a country, stripping the land of all young grain and grasses.

ar-ni-ca (är′nĭ-kȧ), *n.* **1,** any of a genus (*Arnica*) of perennial, medicinal herbs; **2,** a valuable remedy for bruises made from the roots or flowers of one of these herbs.

a-ro-ma (ȧ-rō′mȧ), *n.* the odor of plants or other substances, generally of an agreeable or spicy nature; perfume; fragrance.

ar-o-mat-ic (ăr″ō-măt′ĭk), *adj.* fragrant; spicy:—*n.* a plant, herb, or drug yielding a fragrant smell, as ginger, cinnamon, etc. Also, *adj.* **ar″o-mat′i-cal.**
Syn., adj. (see odorous).

a-rose (ȧ-rōz′), past tense of the intransitive verb *arise.*

a-round (ȧ-round′), *adv.* **1,** in a circle; **2,** on every side; roundabout:—*prep.* **1,** about; on all sides; **2,** throughout; as, to go *around* the city.

a-rous-al (ȧ-rouz′ăl), *n.* **1,** the act of awakening; **2,** the state of being awakened or stirred to action.

a-rouse (ȧ-rouz′), *v.t.* [*p.t.* and *p.p.* aroused′ (-rouzd′), *p.pr.* a-rous′ing], **1,** to excite or stir to action; put in motion that which is at rest; **2,** to awaken from sleep or a state of rest:—*v.i.* to waken; become active.

a-row (ȧ-rō′), *adv.* in a line; in order; successively.

***ar-peg-gio** (är-pĕd′jō), [It.], *n.* [*pl.* arpeggios (-jōz)], in music, the tones of a chord produced in rapid succession, as in playing a harp.

ar-que-bus (är′kwē-bŭs), *n.* a kind of gun in use before the musket. Also, **har′que-bus,** *Pfd. S.*

ar-raign (ă-rān′), *v.t.* **1,** to call to account; **2,** to summon (a prisoner) into court to answer a charge.—*n.* **ar-raign′ment.**
Syn. accuse, charge, cite, impeach, indict.
—*Ant.* acquit, discharge, excuse, exonerate.

ar-range (ă-rānj′), *v.t.* [*p.t.* and *p.p.* -ranged′ (-rānjd′), *p.pr.* -rang′ing], **1,** to put in proper order or sequence; classify; **2,** to adjust or settle; **3,** in music, to adapt, as a song or piano accompaniment.

ar-range-ment (ă-rānj′mĕnt), *n.* **1,** the act of putting in proper form or order; **2,** that which is ordered or disposed; **3,** the method or style of disposition; **4,** preparation; **5,** classification, as of specimens; **6,** settlement; adjustment, as of an argument; **7,** adaptation, as of a musical composition.

ar-rant (ăr′ănt), *adj.* **1,** notorious: usually in a bad sense; **2,** thorough; downright; as, an *arrant* coward.

ar-ras (ăr′ăs), *n.* tapestry; hangings covering the walls of a room, usually made of rich figured material.

ar-ray (ă-rā′), *n.* **1,** order; **2,** the grouping or arrangement of a body of men when drawn up for battle; **3,** an orderly collection or series of things imposingly displayed; **4,** clothing; esp., gay clothing; apparel:—*v.t.* **1,** to place or dispose in order; **2,** to marshal; **3,** to deck or dress.

ar-rear (ă-rēr′), *n.,* usually in *pl.,* that which is undone, outstanding, or unpaid; as, *arrears* in rent: **in arrears or in arrear,** behindhand.

ar-rear-age (ă-rēr′āj), *n.* **1,** the state or condition of being behindhand; **2,** that which remains unpaid or overdue; arrears.

ar-rest (ă-rĕst′), *v.t.* **1,** to stop or stay; check or hinder the action or motion of; **2,** to seize, take, or apprehend by legal authority; **3,** to seize and fix, as the eye or attention:—*n.* **1,** the act of seizing; **2,** stoppage; a holding back by force or restraint; **3,** the state of being seized or detained by legal authority.
Syn., v. capture, hold, detain, secure.

ar-riv-al (ă-rīv′ăl), *n.* **1,** the act of coming to a place, or reaching a destination from a distance; **2,** attainment of any object; **3,** the person or thing coming, or that has come, to a place.

ar-rive (ă-rīv′), *v.i.* [*p.t.* and *p.p.* -rived′ (-rīvd′), *p.pr.* -riv′ing], **1,** to come to, or reach, a destination; **2,** to reach a point or stage; **3,** to gain or accomplish an object; attain to a state or result: with *at;* **4,** *Colloq.,* to succeed, as in business.

ar-ro-gance (ăr′ō-găns), *n.* a feeling of personal superiority; an exorbitant or undue claim to dignity, rank, or estimation; a lordly contempt of others.

ar-ro-gant (ăr′ō-gănt), *adj.* estimating one's importance too highly; overbearingly haughty.—*adv.* **ar′ro-gant-ly.**
Syn. proud, disdainful, insolent, assuming.

ar-ro-gate (ăr′ō-gāt), *v.t.* [*p.t.* and *p.p.* -gat″ed, *p.pr.* -gat″ing], to take, assume, or demand unduly; claim with presumptuous pride; appropriate wrongfully; usurp; as, to *arrogate* a power.

ar-ro-ga-tion (ăr″ō-gā′shŭn), *n.* the act of making unjust claims; the act of taking more than one is entitled to.

ar-row (ăr′ō), *n.* **1,** a slender, pointed shaft, usually feathered and barbed, made to be shot from a bow; **2,** a figure on maps and the like, to indicate direction.—*adj.* **ar′row-y.**

ar-row-head (ăr′ō-hĕd″), *n.* **1,** the head of an arrow; **2,** any of several aquatic or water plants, so named from the shape of their leaves.

ar-row-root (ăr′ō-rōōt″), *n.* a tropical American plant, or a food starch obtained from its fleshy roots.

ar-roy-o (ă-roi′ō), *n.* [*pl.* arroyos (-ōz)], a small stream or its dry bed.

ar-se-nal (är′sē-năl), *n.* a building for storing or making arms and military equipment for land or naval service.

ar-se-nic (är′sē-nĭk), *n.* **1,** a brittle, metallic element; **2,** a poisonous compound of this element with oxygen: also called *white arsenic.*

ar-son (är′sŭn), *n.* the malicious or intentional setting fire to, and burning of, any building.

¹art (ärt), *Archaic* or *Poetic,* the second person singular indicative present of *be.*

²art (ärt), *n.* **1,** the use of means to the accomplishment of some end; **2,** the application of skill to bring about some result; also, an occupation requiring such skill; as, the *art* of engineering; **3,** hence, practical skill or its application; as, the *art* of making good candy; **4,** cleverness in contrivance; **5,** æsthetic quality; the application of skill and taste to the production of beautiful things, esp. in painting, engraving, sculpture, music, literature, and dancing, known in a group as the *fine arts;* **6,** a branch of learning, esp. one of the group of studies in the ordinary college course, known collectively as the *liberal arts.*

Ar-te-mis (är′tē-mĭs), in Greek mythology, sister of Phœbus Apollo and goddess of the moon and of the hunt: also called *Phœbe* and, by the Romans, *Diana.*

ar-te-ri-al (är-tē′rĭ-ăl), *adj.* relating to the large blood vessels that carry blood from the heart.

ar-ter-y (är′tẽr-ĭ), *n.* [*pl.* arteries (-ĭz)], **1**, one of a system of tubes which carry blood from the heart; **2**, any great channel; as, an *artery* of trade.

ar-te-sian well (är-tē′zhăn), **1**, a well made by boring deep enough to reach water which will rise naturally to the surface under internal pressure; **2**, loosely, any deeply bored well.

art-ful (ärt′fo͝ol), *adj.* **1**, cunning; crafty; **2**, skilful; **3**, artificial; unreal.—*adv.* **art′ful-ly.**—*n.* **art′ful-ness.**
Syn. sly, tricky, insincere. (See wily.)

ar-thro-pod (är′thrō-pŏd), *n.* any of a phylum (*Arthropoda*) of invertebrates with jointed appendages, including the centipedes, insects, spiders, and crustaceans (crabs, lobsters, etc.).

Ar-thur (är′thŭr), *n.* a Celtic chieftain of Britain in the sixth century, who, with his Knights of the Round Table, is the subject of many romances.—*adj.* **Ar-thu′ri-an.**

ar-ti-choke (är′tĭ-chōk), *n.* **1**, a tall plant of the aster family, having a flower head that is used for food; **2**, a kind of American sunflower, having a tuberous root, eaten as a vegetable.

ar-ti-cle (är′tĭ-kl), *n.* **1**, a separate member or part of anything, as a single part in a treatise, creed, or the like; **2**, a complete prose composition in a newspaper, magazine, or the like; **3**, a material thing, as one of a class; as, an *article* of clothing; **4**, in grammar, the word *a*, *an*, or *the*, used before a noun to limit it:—*v.t.* [*p.t.* and *p.p.* -cled (-kld), *p.pr.* -cling], **1**, to bind by written agreement, as an apprentice; **2**, to state in the form of articles; set forth in detail.

ar-tic-u-lar (är-tĭk′ū-lȧr), *adj.* relating to the joints.

ar-tic-u-late (är-tĭk′ū-lāt), *v.t.* [*p.t.* and *p.p.* -lat″ed, *p.pr.* -lat″ing], **1**, to unite by a joint; as, to *articulate* bones to make a skeleton; **2**, to utter in distinct syllables; speak as a human being:—*v.i.* **1**, to utter distinct sounds; **2**, to connect: followed by *with*:—*adj.* (är-tĭk′ū-lĭt), **1**, jointed; formed with joints; **2**, uttered with distinctness; **3**, arranged systematically; as, an *articulate* account.—*adv.* **ar-tic′u-late-ly.**

ar-tic-u-la-tion (är-tĭk″ū-lā′shŭn), *n.* **1**, the act of forming spoken sounds; **2**, speech in regard to its distinctness; also, a distinct sound, esp. a consonant; **3**, the act of joining; **4**, a joint between bones; **5**, the point of union between parts of a plant.

ar-ti-fice (är′tĭ-fĭs), *n.* **1**, skill in contrivance; **2**, a ruse, wile, or trick.
Syn. deceit, cunning, craft.

ar-tif-i-cer (är-tĭf′ĭ-sẽr), *n.* **1**, a skilled or artistic worker; craftsman; **2**, a clever contriver; **3**, an inventor.

ar-ti-fi-cial (är-tĭ-fĭsh′ăl), *adj.* **1**, made by art; **2**, produced by human skill; as, *artificial* heat; **3**, assumed; affected; not genuine or natural.—*adv.* **ar″ti-fi′cial-ly.**
Syn. fictitious, spurious, counterfeit.

ar-ti-fi-ci-al-i-ty (är″tĭ-fĭsh″ĭ-ăl′ĭ-tĭ), *n.* [*pl.* artificialities (-tĭz)], **1**, the state or quality of being unreal or unnatural; **2**, that which is affected.

ar-til-ler-y (är-tĭl′ẽr-ĭ), *n.* **1**, mounted cannon; great guns; **2**, the officers and men handling an army's cannon.—*n.* **ar-til′ler-ist.**

ar-ti-san (är′tĭ-zăn), *n.* a trained workman; mechanic; handicraftsman. Also, **ar′ti-zan.**
Syn. artist, artificer, craftsman, laborer.

art-ist (är′tĭst), *n.* **1**, a person of especial talent in painting, sculpture, music, literature, or the like; **2**, a worker who shows marked creative power in his craft.

ar-tis-tic (är-tĭs′tĭk), *adj.* **1**, pertaining to art or artists; **2**, conceived and executed with skill; as, an *artistic* ending to a play or book; **3**, displaying perfection of design, coloring, and the like; **4**, easily moved by beauty; appreciating beauty; as, an *artistic* temperament.—*adv.* **ar-tis′ti-cal-ly.**

art-less (ärt′lĕs), *adj.* **1**, lacking skill; clumsy; also, without knowledge of the arts; **2**, free from guile; honest; simple; natural; unaffected; sincere.—*adv.* **art′less-ly.**—*n.* **art′less-ness.**
Syn. candid, guileless. (See open.)

a-rum (ā′rŭm), *n.* any of numerous plants, as the skunk cabbage and jack-in-the-pulpit, with small flowers crowded on a spadix, or fleshy spike, often covered with a spathe, or leaflike sheath.

-a-ry (-ȧ-rĭ), *n. suffix,* forming the names of persons, places, or things; as, not*ary;* libr*ary;* diction*ary:*—*adj. suffix,* pertaining to or characterized by; as, liter*ary;* honor*ary.*

Ar-yan (är′yăn; ăr′ĭ-ăn), *adj.* **1**, designating, or pertaining to, a group of languages having a common origin, also called *Indo-European*, including Sanskrit, Persian, Greek, Latin, Teutonic, etc., or their modern derivatives, as Italian, English, German, etc.; **2**, designating, or pertaining to, a race speaking any of these languages:—*n.* **1**, a language of Aryan origin; **2**, a member of an Aryan race.

as (ăz), *adv.* equally; in like manner; similarly; as, just *as* good: often used in correlation with *so* or *as;* as, he cannot run so fast *as* I can:—*conj.* **1**, because; as, he sat down, *as* he was tired; **2**, for example; **3**, in the form or character of; as, he enters the contest *as* a professional; **4**, while; when; **5**, in the way in which; as, he speaks *as* a master; **6**, *Colloq.*, that; as, I do not know *as* I can: **as is**, without guarantee as to condition; as, an automobile sold *as is:*—*relative pron.* that; which: used after *such*, *same*, etc.

as-a-fet-i-da (ăs″ȧ-fĕt′ĭ-dȧ), *n.* a drug with offensive odor and bitter taste, made from the roots of certain Oriental plants of the parsley family. Also, **as″a-fœt′i-da; as″sa-fet′i-da.**

as-bes-tos (ăs-bĕs′tŏs; ăz-bĕs′tŏs), *n.* a fibrous, incombustible material used in fireproof curtains, roofing, and the like. Also, **as-bes′tus.**

as-cend (ă-sĕnd′), *v.i.* **1**, to take an upward direction; rise; **2**, to rise from an inferior to a superior position; **3**, to slope upward; **4**, to rise from a lower to a higher pitch:—*v.t.* **1**, to mount; climb; **2**, to go toward the source of, as a river.—*n.* **as-cend′ance; as-cend′ence.**

as-cend-ant (ă-sĕn′dănt), *adj.* **1**, rising; **2**, superior; predominant; **3**, above the horizon:—*n.* **1**, superiority; **2**, a commanding influence; predominance; **3**, an ancestor: opp. of *descendant.* Also, **as-cend′ent.**—*n.* **as-cend′an-cy; as-cend′en-cy.**

as-cen-sion (ă-sĕn′shŭn), *n.* the act of moving upward; a rising: **Ascension**, the ascent of Christ into heaven: **Ascension Day**, the Thursday, 40 days after Easter, on which is celebrated Christ's ascension into heaven (Acts 1:9): also called *Holy Thursday.*—*adj.* **as-cen′sion-al.**

as-cent (ă-sĕnt′), *n.* **1**, the act of rising, or of reaching a height, as by climbing; **2**, an upward slope; **3**, a hill or high place.

as-cer-tain (ăs″ẽr-tān′), *v.t.* to make certain; find out; determine definitely by test or examination.—*adj.* **as″cer-tain′a-ble.**—*n.* **as″cer-tain′ment.**

artifact or artefact (both correct)

as-cet-ic (ă-sĕt′ĭk), *adj.* **1**, severely self-denying; **2**, pertaining to those who renounce worldly things for self-discipline; hence, exceedingly rigid in the exercise of religious duties:—*n.* **1**, one who gives up the things of the world and devotes himself to religious exercises; **2**, one who subjects himself to severe methods of living; a hermit; recluse.—*adv.* **as-cet′i-cal-ly.**

as-cet-i-cism (ă-sĕt′ĭ-sĭzm), *n.* **1**, the condition or mode of life adopted by one who renounces worldly affairs; **2**, the belief that such a life is a means of salvation; **3**, severe self-denial.

as-cribe (ăs-krīb′), *v.t.* [*p.t.* and *p.p.* -cribed′ (-krībd′), *p.pr.* -crib′ing], **1**, to attribute, impute, or refer, as to a cause; **2**, to consider to belong to; **3**, to assign; set down; as, losses may often be *ascribed* to imprudence.—*adj.* **as-crib′a-ble.**—*n.* **as-crip′tion.**

a-sep-tic (ȧ-sĕp′tĭk), *adj.* free from the germs of disease; surgically clean.—*n.* **a-sep′ti-cism.**—*v.t.* **a-sep′ti-cize.**

As-gard (ăs′gärd), *n.* in Norse mythology, the residence of the gods called Æsir, situated at the zenith and reached by the rainbow bridge Bifrost.

[1]ash (ăsh), *n.* **1**, a common timber and shade tree belonging to the olive family; **2**, the wood of the ash tree; hence, something made of the wood, as a staff or the shaft of a spear or lance.—*adj.* **[1]ash′en.**

[2]ash (ăsh), *n.* **1**, what remains of a body or substance that is burned; **2**, in *pl.*: **a**, the waste of burned substances, as wood; **b**, the remains of a human body.—*adj.* **[2]ash′en.**

a-shamed (ȧ-shāmd′), *adj.* **1**, affected or touched by contempt or disgrace; **2**, cast down or dejected by conscious guilt; abashed by a sense of indecorum or misbehavior; **3**, reluctant or hesitating through fear of reproach.—*adv.* **a-sham′ed-ly.**

a-shore (ȧ-shōr′), *adv.* on shore; to the shore; as, a ship driven *ashore.*

Ash Wednes-day the first day of Lent: so called because of the former custom of sprinkling ashes on the heads of penitents.

ash-y (ăsh′ĭ), *adj.* [*comp.* ash′i-er, *superl.* ash′i-est], **1**, pertaining to ashes; covered with ashes; **2**, pale gray.

A-sian (ā′shăn; ā′zhăn), *adj.* belonging to the continent of Asia.

A-si-at-ic (ā″shĭ-ăt′ĭk; ā″zhĭ-), *adj.* pertaining to, or characteristic of, Asia or its natives:—*n.* a native of Asia.

a-side (ȧ-sīd′), *adv.* **1**, on or to one side; out of a given direction; **2**, apart; away from:—*n.* **1**, a speech or remark made in a lower tone than the rest of the conversation, and assumed to be heard only by the person for whom it is intended; **2**, something apart from the main issue.

as-i-nine (ăs′ĭ-nīn), *adj.* relating to the ass; having the nature or qualities of an ass; hence, obstinate; stupid; silly; as, an *asinine* remark.—*n.* **as″i-nin′i-ty.**

ask (ȧsk), *v.t.* **1**, to request; seek to obtain by words; petition or beg for; **2**, to claim or demand; expect or require; as, what price do you *ask?* **3**, to question; inquire respecting; as, to *ask* the way; **4**, to invite:—*v.i.* **1**, to make request; **2**, to inquire.

Syn. crave, beseech, solicit.

a-skance (ȧ-skăns′), *adv.* sideways; awry; from the corner of the eye; disdainfully; distrustfully. Also, **a-skant′.**

a-skew (ȧ-skū′), *adv.* awry; out of order or position:—*adj.* crooked.

a-slant (ȧ-slȧnt′), *adv.* not at right angles; obliquely:—*adj.* sloping; oblique:—*prep.* across in a slanting position.

a-sleep (ȧ-slēp′), *adj.* and *adv.* in a state of slumber; dormant; unconscious; numbed.

a-slope (ȧ-slōp′), *adv.* and *adj.* in a sloping position or direction.

asp (ăsp), *n.* **1**, (also, *aspic*), a small poisonous snake of Egypt; **2**, the common viper, or adder, of Europe.

Asp (def. 1) 1/6

as-par-a-gus (ăs-păr′ȧ-gŭs), *n.* any of a large genus (*Asparagus*) of plants of the lily family; esp., the common garden variety, having, when young, tender edible shoots, much used as a vegetable.

as-pect (ăs′pĕkt), *n.* **1**, appearance, esp. to the mental vision; look; view; **2**, a way of looking; expression; mien; air; as, her *aspect* was stern; **3**, a side or part facing in any given direction; prospect; **4**, a phase; view.

asp-en (ăs′pĕn; ȧs′pĕn), *n.* a kind of poplar tree whose leaves tremble in the slightest breeze:—*adj.* **1**, relating to such a tree; **2**, quivering like a leaf of such a tree; tremulous; shaking.

as-per-i-ty (ăs-pĕr′ĭ-tĭ), *n.* [*pl.* asperities (-tĭz)], **1**, roughness of surface; unevenness; **2**, roughness or harshness of sound; **3**, sourness; bitterness of taste or temper; crabbedness; moroseness.

as-perse (ăs-pûrs′), *v.t.* [*p.t.* and *p.p.* -persed′ (-pûrst′), *p.pr.* -pers′ing], **1**, to spread false reports against (a person or his character); slander; **2**, to sprinkle.—*n.* **as-per′sion.**

Syn. defame, malign, revile, decry, libel.—*Ant.* defend, eulogize.

as-phalt (ăs′fălt), *n.* a black mineral pitch used for paving, roofing, and cementing:—*v.t.* to pave or cover with such substance. Also, *n.* **as-phal′tum.**—*adj.* **as-phal′tic.**

as-pho-del (ăs′fō-dĕl), *n.* **1**, any one of several plants of the lily family; **2**, the daffodil: so called by the older English poets; **3**, in mythology, the flower of the dead, probably the narcissus, its pale blossoms covering the meadows of Hades.

as-phyx-i-a (ăs-fĭk′sĭ-ȧ), *n.* a stopping of the pulse; the lifeless condition caused by the stopping of the breath, as in choking, drowning, etc.; suffocation.

as-phyx-i-ate (ăs-fĭk′sĭ-āt), *v.t.* [*p.t.* and *p.p.* -at″ed, *p.pr.* -at″ing], to suffocate; cause death or its symptoms to, by depriving of oxygen.—*n.* **as-phyx″i-a′tion.**

[1]as-pic (ăs′pĭk), *n.* a poisonous asp, or Egyptian viper. See **asp**, *Pfd. S.*

[2]as-pic (ăs′pĭk), *n.* a clear meat jelly containing fowl, game, or fish.

[3]as-pic (ăs′pĭk), *n.* the spike lavender, yielding a volatile oil.

as-pir-ant (ăs-pīr′ănt), *adj.* ambitious:—*n.* one who seeks to attain, or is ambitious for, some high object, position, or honor; a candidate.

as-pi-rate (ăs′pĭ-rāt), *v.t.* [*p.t.* and *p.p.* -rat″ed, *p.pr.* -rat″ing], to pronounce with a full breathing; prefix, or add the sound of, the letter *h:*—*n.* (-rȧt), the sound of the letter *h*, as in *horse:*—*adj.* (-rȧt), pronounced with the audible breath.

as-pi-ra-tion (ăs″pĭ-rā′shŭn), *n.* **1**, the act of breathing; a breath;

2, the desire for something higher or better than that already possessed; ambition.

as-pir-a-to-ry (ăs-pīr′ȧ-tō-rĭ), *adj.* relating to breathing; suited to the inhaling of air.

as-pire (ăs-pīr′), *v.i.* [*p.t.* and *p.p.* -pired′ (-pīrd′), *p.pr.* -pir′ing], **1**, to seek after or desire with longing; yearn for that which is better or nobler; **2**, to ascend; soar.

as-pi-rin (ăs′pĭ-rĭn), *n.* a drug, usually a white powder or pellet, used as a remedy for rheumatism, headache, colds, etc.

a-squint (ȧ-skwĭnt′), *adv.* out of the corner of the eye; askance; furtively:—*adj.* furtive.

ass (ăs), *n.* **1**, an animal of the horse family having longer ears and a shorter mane than the horse; **2**, a dull, stupid fellow.

as-sa-fet-i-da (ăs″ȧ-fĕt′ĭ-dȧ), *n.* a drug with a persistent odor and bitter taste. Also, **as″sa-fœt′i-da.** See **as″a-fet′i-da,** *Pfd. S.*

as-sa-gai (ăs′ȧ-gī), *n.* **1**, a slender spear, usually tipped with iron, used by the natives of South Africa; **2**, a South African tree of the dogwood family, from which such spears are made. Also, **as′se-gai.**

as-sail (ă-sāl′), *v.t.* **1**, to fall upon or attack violently; **2**, to attack with argument or abuse.—*adj.* **as-sail′a-ble.**

as-sail-ant (ă-sāl′ănt), *adj.* assaulting; attacking:—*n.* one who or that which attacks.

as-sas-sin (ă-săs′ĭn), *n.* one who kills, or attempts to kill, secretly, as the appointed agent for another or others, or for reward; hence, a murderer.

as-sas-si-nate (ă-săs′ĭ-nāt), *v.t.* [*p.t.* and *p.p.* -nat″ed, *p.pr.* -nat″ing], to kill by secret or treacherous means; slay suddenly or unawares; murder by sudden or treacherous violence.—*n.* **as-sas′si-na″tor.**
Syn. dispatch, slaughter. (See kill.)

as-sas-si-na-tion (ă-săs″ĭ-nā′shŭn), *n.* the act of slaying in secret, sometimes at the bidding of others or for reward; murder.

as-sault (ă-sôlt′), *n.* **1**, an attack with violence by physical means; an onslaught; **2**, an attack by military force; **3**, a violent attack by moral force, as by use of argument or hostile words; **4**, an unlawful attempt or threat to do bodily violence or injury to another: called *assault and battery* if the other person is actually struck; **5**, the charge of an attacking party on a fortified position:—*v.t.* **1**, to attack violently; **2**, to storm, as by armed force; **3**, to attack by moral force; **4**, to threaten or attempt bodily violence or injury to (another).—*n.* **as-sault′er.**

as-say (ă-sā′), *n.* **1**, the act or process of finding the quantity or proportion of any one or more metals in a metallic compound, ore, or alloy; esp., the testing of gold or silver coin or bullion to see if it is of standard purity; **2**, the substance or metal to be tested; **3**, the result of the test; **4**, in the days of chivalry, a trial by danger; also, risk; adventure:—*v.t.* **1**, to subject to analysis; find the quantity or proportion of one or more of the elements of, as in an alloy; **2**, hence, to test the value of.—*adj.* **as-say′a-ble.**

as-say-er (ă-sā′ẽr), *n.* one who analyzes or assays ores or metals; esp., an officer of the mint appointed to test the purity of bullion and coin.

as-sem-blage (ă-sĕm′blāj), *n.* **1**, the act of gathering together; also, the state of being collected in one place; **2**, a group or collection of persons or particular things; hence, a congregation or audience; as, a political *assemblage;* **3**, the fitting together of parts and of pieces, as of machinery.

as-sem-ble (ă-sĕm′bl), *v.t.* [*p.t.* and *p.p.* -bled (-bld), *p.pr.* -bling], **1**, to collect or gather together into one place or body; congregate; **2**, to fit together, as parts of machinery:—*v.i.* to meet or come together; convene.—*n.* **as-sem′bler.**

as-sem-bly (ă-sĕm′blĭ), *n.* [*pl.* assemblies (-blĭz)], **1**, a collection or company of persons brought together in one place and for a common object, whether religious, educational, political, or social; a meeting; congregation; **2**, a legislative body; **3**, a bugle call to bring troops together; the second beating of a drum before a march, upon which the soldiers strike their tents.

as-sem-bly-man (ă-sĕm′blĭ-măn), *n.* [*pl.* assemblymen (-mĕn)], a member of a legislative, or lawmaking, body: **Assemblyman,** in certain states, a member of the lower division of the legislature.

as-sent (ă-sĕnt′), *v.i.* to admit as true; concede; agree; consent:—*n.* the act of agreeing; consent; acquiescence; approval; concurrence.
Syn., v. consent. To *assent* is to agree by act of the understanding; as, we *assent* to a religious doctrine. To *consent* is to agree by act of will or through the influence of the feelings; as, we *consent* to do a favor.

as-sert (ă-sûrt′), *v.t.* **1**, to maintain; declare positively or with assurance; affirm; **2**, to defend by words; as, to *assert* our rights.—*n.* **as-sert′er; as-ser′tor.**
Syn. claim, affirm, allege, maintain. To *assert* is to declare boldly; as, he *asserted* his rights. To *claim* is to assert one's title or right to a thing; as, he *claimed* the property. To *affirm* is to declare the truth of an assertion; as, he *affirmed* the statement. To *allege* is to state without proving; as, he *alleged* it was wrong. To *maintain* is to support an assertion; as, he *maintained* his innocence.

as-ser-tion (ă-sûr′shŭn), *n.* **1**, the act of declaring positively; **2**, that which is affirmed; **3**, a positive declaration without attempt at proof; an unconfirmed statement or affirmation.

as-ser-tive (ă-sûr′tĭv), *adj.* positive; confident in statement; dogmatic.—*n.* **as-ser′tive-ness.**

as-sess (ă-sĕs′), *v.t.* **1**, to fix or determine, as damages; **2**, to fix, rate, or set a certain charge upon, as a tax; value officially for the purpose of taxation; as, the property was *assessed* too high.—*adj.* **as-sess′a-ble.**

as-sess-ment (ă-sĕs′mĕnt), *n.* **1**, the act of determining an amount to be paid; **2**, an official valuation of property, or income, for the purpose of taxation; **3**, the tax paid on property; **4**, any fixed tax; a share of joint expenses.

as-ses-sor (ă-sĕs′ẽr), *n.* one appointed to estimate the value of property for the purpose of taxation.

as-set (ăs′ĕt), *n.* **1**, any item of one's property; hence, anything that is a help rather than a hindrance; **2**, in *pl.*, all the property of a person, firm, or estate which may be used to pay his or its debts: opp. of *liabilities;* hence, property in general.

as-sev-er-ate (ă-sĕv′ẽr-āt), *v.t.* [*p.t.* and *p.p.* -at″ed, *p.pr.* -at″ing], to affirm or aver positively or with solemnity.
Syn. maintain, assert, declare.

as-sev-er-a-tion (ă-sĕv″ẽr-ā′shŭn), *n.* a solemn affirmation, as upon oath; an emphatic assertion.

as-si-du-i-ty (ăs″ĭ-dū′ĭ-tĭ), *n.* [*pl.* assiduities (-tĭz)], close application or unremitting attention; diligence; perseverance; constancy.

as-sid-u-ous (ă-sĭd′ū-ŭs), *adj.* constant in application; devoted;

attentive; perseveringly diligent; unremitting.—*adv.* **as-sid′u-ous-ly.**

as-sign (ă-sīn′), *v.t.* and *v.i.* **1,** to allot; apportion; set apart for a particular purpose; point out exactly; **2,** to transfer or make over to another, as for the benefit of creditors:—*n.* one to whom property or interest is left or made over by will or deed; as, a deed to a man, his heirs, and *assigns.*—*adj.* **as-sign′a-ble.**—*n.* **as-sign′er.**

as-sig-na-tion (ăs″ĭg-nā′shŭn), *n.* **1,** the act of apportioning; **2,** that which is apportioned; **3,** an appointment for meeting: used chiefly of love affairs and now usually in a bad sense.

as-sign-ee (ăs″ĭ-nē′), *n.* one to whom anything is made over, either in trust or for his own use and enjoyment.

as-sign-ment (ă-sīn′mĕnt), *n.* **1,** a setting apart for some particular person or use; an allotment; **2,** a thing marked out or designated; **3,** in law: **a,** transfer of title or interest; **b,** the document effecting such transfer; **c,** the thing transferred.

as-sign-or (ăs″ĭ-nôr′), *n.* one who transfers an interest.

as-sim-i-late (ă-sĭm′ĭ-lāt), *v.t.* [*p.t.* and *p.p.* -lat″ed, *p.pr.* -lat″ing], **1,** to bring to likeness or agreement with something else; **2,** to absorb or take into itself, as nourishment:—*v.i.* **1,** to become similar; harmonize; **2,** to be absorbed into the substance of a body, as food.—*adj.* **as-sim′i-la-tive.**

as-sim-i-la-tion (ă-sĭm″ĭ-lā′shŭn), *n.* **1,** the act or process of bringing into agreement or harmony; **2,** the state of being absorbed, or of becoming a part of; as, the *assimilation* of food by the body in the process of digestion.

as-sist (ă-sĭst′), *v.t.* **1,** to act as a helper to; **2,** to aid; give support to; attend; relieve:—*v.i.* to lend help or aid.

Syn. succor, sustain. (See help.)

as-sist-ance (ă-sĭs′tăns), *n.* help; aid; succor; support.

as-sist-ant (ă-sĭs′tănt), *adj.* helping; lending aid; auxiliary:—*n.* one who or that which helps; an auxiliary.

as-size (ă-sīz′), *n.* **1,** a court or session of justice for the trial by jury of civil or criminal cases; **2,** in English history, an ordinance fixing the weight, measure, and price of articles of general use sold in market; as, the *assize* of bread and ale; **3,** usually in *pl.*, the sessions held regularly in each county of England by judges of the superior courts; also, the time and place of such sessions, or the court itself: **great assize,** last judgment.

as-so-ci-ate (ă-sō′shĭ-āt), *n.* **1,** a companion; **2,** a confederate; an ally; **3,** one belonging to a society or institution:—*adj.* **1,** joined in interest, object, or purpose; **2,** sharing office or employment, as a colleague or partner; **3,** connected by habit, function, or sympathy:—*v.t.* (ăs-sō′shĭ-āt), [*p.t.* and *p.p.* -at″ed, *p.pr.* -at″ing], **1,** to unite; combine; **2,** to connect in thought, as ideas; **3,** to join or unite as an ally, friend, accomplice, or the like: with *with:*—*v.i.* **1,** to unite in company; have fellowship; **2,** to be connected, as ideas.—*adj.* **as-so′ci-a-tive.**

Syn., n. partner, colleague. (See ally.)

as-so-ci-a-tion (ă-sō″sĭ-ā′shŭn; ă-sō″shĭ-ā′shŭn), *n.* **1,** the act of joining together; also, the state of fellowship; the union of persons, as in a society; **2,** a body of persons organized for a common object; a corporation; **3,** a connection of ideas; that which is mentally connected with a thing.—*adj.* **as-so″ci-a′tion-al.**

Syn. combination, company, partnership.

as-so-nance (ăs′ō-năns), *n.* **1,** resemblance of sound; **2,** partial similarity; **3,** hence, rime in which vowels correspond but consonants do not, as in *baby* and *lady; foolish* and *crooning.*

as-so-nant (ăs′ō-nănt), *adj.* having resemblance of sound.

as-sort (ă-sôrt′), *v.t.* to divide or separate into lots, classes, or kinds; classify; arrange: **assorted,** picked out so as to be different; various:—*v.i.* **1,** to agree; be in accordance; **2,** to associate (with).

as-sort-ment (ă-sôrt′mĕnt), *n.* **1,** the act of separating and arranging; **2,** a classified collection of articles or goods of a varied character; as, the box contains a choice *assortment* of candy.

as-suage (ă-swāj′), *v.t.* [*p.t.* and *p.p.* -suaged′ (-swājd′), *p.pr.* -suag′ing], **1,** to soften or soothe; allay or lessen, as pain or grief; **2,** to appease or pacify, as passion:—*v.i.* to grow less; subside.

as-sume (ă-sūm′), *v.t.* [*p.t.* and *p.p.* -sumed′ (-sūmd′), *p.pr.* -sum′ing], **1,** to take to; take upon oneself, esp. without authority; **2,** to take for granted; **3,** to take up, or into, as in partnership; **4,** to undertake; **5,** to pretend to possess:—*v.i.* to be arrogant; presume.—*p.adj.* **as-sum′ing.**—*adj.* **as-sum′a-ble.**—*adv.* **as-sum′a-bly.**

as-sump-tion (ă-sŭmp′shŭn), *n.* **1,** the act of taking to or upon oneself; **2,** the act of taking for granted; also, the thing supposed; **3,** the bodily taking of a person to heaven; as, the *assumption* of the Virgin Mary; **4,** the agreement of one to whom property is transferred to pay charges previously incurred upon it by the transferor.—*adj.* **as-sump′tive.**

as-sur-ance (ă-shŏŏr′ăns), *n.* **1,** the act or state of being sure; **2,** the act of inspiring, or expressing, certain expectation; confidence; **3,** that which produces a pledge; certain proof; clear evidence; **4,** self-possession; self-reliance; courage; **5,** impudence; **6,** a contract for payment in case of fire or loss; insurance.

as-sure (ă-shŏŏr′), *v.t.* [*p.t.* and *p.p.* -sured′ (-shŏŏrd′), *p.pr.* -sur′ing], **1,** to make sure or certain; **2,** to inspire confidence in by declaration or promise; free from uncertainty; **3,** to insure, as against loss by fire or death.—*n.* **as-sur′er.**

as-sured (ă-shŏŏrd′), *p.adj.* **1,** made certain; guaranteed; **2,** self-possessed; confident; **3,** insured:—*n.* a person in whose favor an insurance policy stands.—*n.* **as-sur′ed-ness.**

as-sur-ed-ly (ă-shŏŏr′ĕd-lĭ), *adv.* certainly; without doubt.

As-syr-i-an (ă-sĭr′ĭ-ăn), *adj.* relating to Assyria, its people, or their language:—*n.* **1,** a native of Assyria; **2,** the language of Assyria.

as-ter (ăs′tẽr), *n.* any plant of a large, widely distributed genus (*Aster*) of the composite family, having flowers with variously colored rays about a yellow center.

as-ter-isk (ăs′tẽr-ĭsk), *n.* the figure of a star [*] used in printing or writing as a reference mark, or to indicate letters or words omitted [* * *]:—*v.t.* to mark with such a star.

a-stern (ȧ-stûrn′), *adv.* **1,** at or toward the rear end of a ship; backward; **2,** behind a ship.

as-ter-oid (ăs′tẽr-oid), *n.* one of the many small planets between Jupiter and Mars:—*adj.* starlike; star-shaped.

asth-ma (ăz′mȧ; ăs′mȧ), *n.* a disease attended by difficulty of breathing.

asth-mat-ic (ăz-măt′ĭk; ăs-măt′ĭk), *adj.* affected with difficulty in breathing:—*n.* a person suffering from a disease attended by difficulty in breathing.

a-stig-ma-tism (ȧ-stĭg′mȧ-tĭzm), *n.* **1**, a defect in the eye because of which the rays of light from an outside point do not meet in a point on the retina, so that the vision is blurred; **2**, the same defect in a lens.—*adj.* **as″tig-mat′ic.**

a-stir (ȧ-stûr′), *adj.* and *adv.* on the move; in activity.

as-ton-ish (ăs-tŏn′ĭsh), *v.t.* to strike with sudden wonder; surprise; bewilder; amaze.—*n.* **as-ton′ish-er.**

as-ton-ish-ing (ăs-tŏn′ĭsh-ĭng), *p.adj.* wonderful; surprising.

as-ton-ish-ment (ăs-tŏn′ĭsh-mĕnt), *n.* **1**, extreme surprise; **2**, that which causes amazement or wonder.
Syn. bewilderment, confusion, perplexity.

as-tound (ăs-tound′), *v.t.* to strike with amazement; shock; alarm.—*p.adj.* **as-tound′ing.**—*adv.* **as-tound′ing-ly.**

a-strad-dle (ȧ-străd′l), *adv.* with one leg on each side of something.

as-tra-khan (ăs′trȧ-kăn; ăs″trȧ-kăn′), *n.* **1**, the skin of young lambs, the curly wool of which looks like fur, obtained from Astrakhan, in Russia; **2**, an imitation of this wool or fur. Also, **as′tra-chan.**

as-tral (ăs′trăl), *adj.* relating to, or proceeding from, the stars; starry.—*adv.* **as′tral-ly.**

a-stray (ȧ-strā′), *adv.* out of the right way or proper place; wandering.

a-stride (ȧ-strīd′), *adv.* with the legs wide apart; astraddle.

as-trin-gen-cy (ăs-trĭn′jĕn-sĭ),*n.* **1**, power or tendency to bind or contract; **2**, harshness; severity.

as-trin-gent (ăs-trĭn′jĕnt), *adj.* **1**, binding; contracting: opp. of *laxative:* **2**, harsh or severe:—*n.* a substance or medicine that contracts the tissues and checks discharges.—*adv.* **as-trin′gent-ly.**

as-tro-labe (ăs′trō-lāb), *n.* an instrument formerly used, esp. in navigation, to measure the altitude of heavenly bodies: now replaced by the sextant.

as-trol-o-ger (ăs-trŏl′ō-jẽr), *n.* one who claims to foretell events by means of the heavenly bodies.

as-trol-o-gy (ăs-trŏl′ō-jĭ), *n.* the practice and system of predicting events by the position and mysterious influence on human affairs of the sun, moon, and planets.—*adj.* **as″tro-log′ic; as″tro-log′i-cal.**—*adv.* **as″tro-log′i-cal-ly.**

as-tron-o-mer (ăs-trŏn′ō-mẽr), *n.* one who studies the stars, planets, and other heavenly bodies.

as-tro-nom-i-cal (ăs″trō-nŏm′ĭ-kăl), *adj.* relating to, or according to, the laws of the heavenly bodies: **astronomical signs,** the signs of the zodiac: **astronomical year,** the length of time between two spring equinoxes or two fall equinoxes: also called *equinoctial, natural,* or *solar, year.*—*adv.* **as″tro-nom′i-cal-ly.**

as-tron-o-my (ăs-trŏn′ō-mĭ), *n.* the science which treats of the heavenly bodies, their composition, their distances, their motions, and the laws which control them.—*adj.* **as″tro-nom′ic.**

as-tute (ăs-tūt′), *adj.* shrewd; keen; cunning; crafty; subtle.—*adv.* **as-tute′ly.**—*n.* **as-tute′ness.**
Syn. acute, sharp, sagacious, skilled, wily.

a-sun-der (ȧ-sŭn′dẽr), *adv.* apart; separately; into parts.

a-sy-lum (ȧ-sī′lŭm), *n.* [*pl.* asylums (-lŭmz); asyla (-lȧ)], **1**, a place of refuge or security; **2**, an institution for the care or relief of the aged, poor, or afflicted.

at (ăt), *prep.* expressing: **1**, simple presence or position in, on, near by, or the like; as, *at* the center; **2**, position, state, condition, or the like; as, *at* dinner; **3**, relative position, price, or the like; as, *at* the beginning; *at* ten cents each; **4**, direction through, toward, or the like; as, to start *at* a task; **5**, cause; as, impatient *at* interruptions.

At-a-lan-ta (ăt″ȧ-lăn′tȧ), *n.* in mythology, a beautiful, fleet-footed, valiant Greek heroine, who took part in the Calydonian boar hunt and in the Argonautic Expedition, and who was defeated through trickery in a foot race.

at-a-vism (ăt′ȧ-vĭzm), *n.* **1**, inheritance from a distant ancestor of a trait not possessed by nearer ancestors; also, reversion to an earlier type; **2**, the return of any disease from which an ancestor in remote generations has suffered.—*adj.* **at″a-vis′tic.**

ate (āt), past tense of the transitive and intransitive verb *eat.*

-ate (-āt), *adj. suffix,* in adjectives derived from the Latin past participle; as, orn*ate:*—*v. suffix,* forming verbs derived from Latin verbs, most often of the first conjugation; as, nomin*ate:*—*n. suffix,* denoting: **1**, function; as, potent*ate;* **2**, persons or things; as, deleg*ate.*

***a-te-lier** (ȧ″tē-lyā′), [Fr.], *n.* **1**, a workshop; **2**, a studio, esp. that of a painter or sculptor.

***a tem-po** (ä tĕm′pō), [It.], in music, in time: used to direct a return to the regular tempo.

a-the-ism (ā′thē-ĭzm), *n.* disbelief in, or denial of, the existence of a God or Supreme Being.

a-the-ist (ā′thē-ĭst), *n.* one who disbelieves in, or denies, the existence of a God.—*adj.* **a″the-is′tic; a″the-is′ti-cal.**—*adv.* **a″the-is′ti-cal-ly.**

A-the-na (ȧ-thē′nȧ), *n.* in Greek mythology, the goddess of wisdom, the industrial arts, and war: the Roman *Minerva.*

ath-e-næ-um (ăth″ē-nē′ŭm), *n.* [*pl.* athenæums (-ŭmz); athenæa (-ȧ)], **1**, orig., a temple sacred to Athena; **2**, an institution or club devoted to the study of literature and art; **3**, a building used as a library or reading room. Also, **ath″e-ne′um.**

A-the-ni-an (ȧ-thē′nĭ-ăn), *adj.* pertaining to Athens, Greece, or to its culture:—*n.* a native or a citizen of Athens.

a-thirst (ȧ-thûrst′), *adj.* **1**, thirsty; **2**, having a keen desire; eager.

ath-lete (ăth′lēt), *n.* one trained to contend in feats of physical strength; one of great physical power and endurance.

ath-let-ic (ăth-lĕt′ĭk), *adj.* **1**, of or relating to those trained for physical contests, or to their performances; **2**, strong; robust; vigorous; muscular.—*adv.* **ath-let′i-cal-ly.**—*n.* **ath-let′i-cism.**

ath-let-ics (ăth-lĕt′ĭks), *n. pl.*, sometimes used as *sing.*, **1**, any system of training by gymnastic exercises or athletic sports; **2**, athletic sports collectively.

a-thwart (ȧ-thwôrt′), *adv.* across; from side to side; crosswise:—*prep.* **1**, across the course or direction of, as of a ship; **2**, from side to side of.

-at-ic (-ăt′ĭk), *adj. suffix,* pertaining to; characterized by; as, err*atic:* lymph*atic:* the adjectives often becoming nouns; as, lun*atic.*

a-tilt (ȧ-tĭlt′), *adj.* and *adv.* **1**, in the position or with the action of a person making a thrust; **2**, in a tilted position.

-a-tion (-ā′shŭn), *n. suffix,* indicating: **1**, act or process; as, cre*ation;* **2**, condition or state; as, starv*ation;* emaci*ation;* **3**, a thing that is formed or made; as, plant*ation.* Also, **-sion; -tion; -ion.**

-a-tive (-ȧ-tĭv; -ā-tĭv), *adj. suffix,* pertaining to; characterized by; as, form*ative;*

decor*ative*: the adjectives often becoming nouns; as, nomin*ative*; rel*ative*.

At-lan-tic (ăt-lăn′tĭk), the ocean which separates Europe and Africa from America:—*adj.* pertaining to this ocean.

At-lan-tis (ăt-lăn′tĭs), *n.* a fabled island which, according to ancient writers, existed in the Atlantic Ocean west of the Pillars of Hercules, or Gibraltar, and was later submerged by an earthquake.

at-las (ăt′lăs), *n.* **1**, a bound volume of maps or charts; **2**, the highest vertebra of the neck, supporting the skull: **Atlas**, in mythology, that one of the Titans condemned to bear up the heavens.

ATLAS

At-li (ät′lē), *n.* in the story of the Volsungs, the king of the Huns, who treacherously slew the brothers of his wife, Gudrun, to get their treasure, and was slain in revenge by Gudrun: called *Etzel* in the Nibelungenlied.

at-mos-phere (ăt′mŏs-fēr), *n.* **1**, the air which surrounds the earth; **2**, the envelope of gas around any heavenly body; **3**, a surrounding influence.

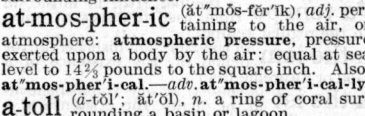

at-mos-pher-ic (ăt″mŏs-fĕr′ĭk), *adj.* pertaining to the air, or atmosphere: **atmospheric pressure**, pressure exerted upon a body by the air: equal at sea level to 14⅔ pounds to the square inch. Also, **at″mos-pher′i-cal.**—*adv.* **at″mos-pher′i-cal-ly.**

a-toll (ȧ-tŏl′; ăt′ŏl), *n.* a ring of coral surrounding a basin or lagoon.

at-om (ăt′ŭm), *n.* **1**, the smallest distinct chemical unit of a substance, itself composed of electrical particles; **2**, a tiny bit.

a-tom-ic (ȧ-tŏm′ĭk), *adj.* **1**, relating to atoms; **2**, very minute: **atomic bomb**, a highly destructive bomb, in which the energy released by nuclear fission is used to produce explosion: **atomic energy**, the force released in the fission of the atom: **atomic theory**, the theory that elements consist of atoms which, when combined with one another, form chemical compounds, and which are composed of smaller electrical particles: **atomic weight**, the relative weight of an atom of a chemical element on a scale which by arbitrarily assigning 16 to oxygen gave approximately whole numbers to all the elements and set that of hydrogen at 1. The atomic weight is equal numerically to the total number of protons and neutrons in the nucleus of the atom.

at-om-ize (ăt′ŭm-īz), *v.t.* [*p.t.* and *p.p.* -ized (-īzd), *p.pr.* -iz″ing], **1**, to reduce to very fine particles; **2**, to spray. Also, **at′om-ise.**

at-om-iz-er (ăt′ŭm-īz″ẽr), *n.* an instrument for changing a liquid to a very fine spray.

at-o-my (ăt′ō-mĭ), *n.* [*pl.* atomies (-mĭz)], **1**, an atom; a mite; **2** a pygmy.

a-tone (ȧ-tōn′), *v.i.* and *v.t.* [*p.t.* and *p.p.* a-toned′ (-tōnd′), *p.pr.* a-ton′ing], to make amends (for).—*n.* **a-tone′ment.**

A-treus (ā′trōōs; ā′trē-ŭs), *n.* in mythology, the father of Menelaus and Agamemnon, famous heroes in the Trojan War.

a-tri-um (ā′trĭ-ŭm), *n.* [*pl.* atria (-ȧ); atriums (-ŭmz)], **1**, the hall or principal room in an ancient Roman house; **2**, any of certain cavities, especially in the heart.

a-tro-cious (ȧ-trō′shŭs), *adj.* extremely wicked; outrageous.—*adv.* **a-tro′cious-ly.**—*n.* **a-tro′cious-ness.**

a-troc-i-ty (ȧ-trŏs′ĭ-tĭ), *n.* [*pl.* atrocities (-tĭz)], **1**, a cruel or outrageous deed; **2**, *Colloq.*, something ugly or very faulty.

at-ro-phy (ăt′rō-fĭ), *n.* a wasting of the body, or any part of it, due to the lack of food or imperfect nourishment:—*v.i.* [*p.t.* and *p.p.* -phied (-fĭd), *p.pr.* -phy-ing] to waste or wither away:—*v.t.* to cause to waste.—*adj.* **a-troph′ic.**

at-ro-pine (ăt′rō-pĭn), *n.* a poisonous substance obtained from plants of the nightshade family. Also, **at′ro-pin.**

At-ro-pos (ăt′rō-pŏs), *n.* in mythology, that one of the three Fates who cut off the thread of life after Clotho had spun it and Lachesis had measured it.

at-tach (ă-tăch′), *v.t.* **1**, to fasten, or fix, to or on; connect; **2**, to assign, as to a military company; appoint; **3**, to affix, as a signature; **4**, to attribute; as, to *attach* importance; **5**, to attract by affection; **6**, to take by law:—*v.i.* to be fixed; adhere.—*adj.* **at-tach′a-ble.**

at-ta-ché (ă-tă-shā′; *Fr.* å″tå″shā′), *n.* [*pl.* attachés (-shāz′)], one who is attached to an embassy, legation, or staff, as an aide or assistant.

at-tach-ment (ă-tăch′mĕnt), *n.* **1**, the act of binding; also, the state of being bound; **2**, affection; fidelity; **3**, that by which connection is made: also, the thing connected or the point of connection; bond; **4**, something added, as an additional part of a machine; **5**, legal seizure of goods; also, the writ of seizure.

at-tack (ă-tăk′), *v.t.* **1**, to set upon; assault; **2**, to assail violently in speech or writing; **3**, to start to have an effect upon, esp. harmfully, as a disease; **4**, to begin vigorously, as a fresh piece of work:—*v.i.* to make an assault:—*n.* **1**, the act of assaulting; onset; bitter criticism; **2**, the first step of an undertaking; **3**, offensive movement; **4**, a seizure, as of indigestion.

Syn., *v.* beset, besiege, combat, encounter.
Ant., *v.* defend, protect, befriend, shelter.

at-tain (ă-tān′), *v.t.* **1**, to reach, as in time, experience, or the like; **2**, to achieve; gain; accomplish:—*v.i.* to arrive.—*adj.* **at-tain′a-ble.**—*n.* **at-tain″a-bil′i-ty.**

Syn. acquire, procure. (See get.)

at-tain-der (ă-tān′dẽr), *n.* the taking away from persons under sentence of death or outlawry of all civil or legal rights until death or pardon.

at-tain-ment (ă-tān′mĕnt), *n.* **1**, the act of arriving at, as the result of effort; **2**, that which is reached; an acquirement; **3**, a personal accomplishment; as, he has many delightful *attainments*.

Syn. acquisition, achievement.

at-taint (ă-tānt′), *v.t.* **1**, to affect; taint; **2**, to sully or stain by disgrace.

at-tar (ăt′ȧr), a fragrant oil extracted from the petals of flowers, esp. roses. Also, **ot′tar; ot′to.**

at-tempt (ă-tĕmpt′), *v.t.* to make an effort to do; try; endeavor to perform; attack:—*n.* trial; endeavor; effort.

at-tend (ă-tĕnd′), *v.t.* **1**, to wait upon; care for, as a patient; **2**, to escort; accompany; **3**, to be present at, as church:—*v.i.* **1**, to give heed; as, *attend* to prayer; **2**, to be present; **3**, to be in waiting; **4**, to look after something.—*n.* **at-tend′er.**

at-tend-ance (ă-tĕn′dȧns), *n.* **1**, the act, or record, of being present; **2**, the act of caring for; **3**, the number of persons present; **4**, a retinue.

at-tend-ant (ă-tĕn′dȧnt), *n.* **1**, one who waits or serves; a retainer; **2**, one who is habitually present, as at church; **3**, that which accompanies:—*adj.* **1**, present; **2**, accompanying or immediately following; as, intemperance, with all its *attendant* evils.

at-ten-tion (ă-tĕn′shŭn), *n.* **1**, the act or faculty of applying the mind;

concentration; thought; 2, a mark of courtesy; consideration; 3, an attitude of motionless erectness; as, come to *attention.*

at-ten-tive (ă-tĕn′tĭv), *adj.* 1, heedful; intent; 2, polite; courteous.—*adv.* **at-ten′tive-ly.**—*n.* **at-ten′tive-ness.**

Syn. thoughtful, considerate, alert.—*Ant.* abstracted, careless, negligent.

at-ten-u-ate (ă-tĕn′ū-āt), *v.t.* [*p.t.* and *p.p.* -at″ed, *p.pr.* -at″ing], 1, to make thin or slender; 2, to thin out by dilution; 3, to weaken; reduce; 4, to lessen in intensity, as a current of electricity:—*v.i.* to become thin, slender, or fine; lessen:—*adj.* (ă-tĕn′ū-āt), thin; slender.

at-ten-u-a-tion (ă-tĕn″ū-ā′shŭn), *n.* 1, the act or process of making slender, or of thinning out by dilution; 2, slenderness; extreme thinness; 3, the act of lessening in intensity, as an electric current.

at-test (ă-tĕst′), *v.t.* 1, to bear witness to; certify as genuine; esp., to confirm by signing or by oath; 2, to give proof of; as, his acts *attest* his good will:—*n.* 1, testimony; witness; 2, a sign or proof of genuineness; esp., a sign in legal form on a document.

at-tes-ta-tion (ăt″ĕs-tā′shŭn), *n.* 1, the act of certifying; 2, testimony or evidence given on oath, or by official declaration; 3, a swearing in, as of witnesses.

at-tic (ăt′ĭk), *n.* the space immediately beneath the roof of a house, above the ceiling of the room below; a loft.

At-tic (ăt′ĭk), *adj.* 1, relating to Attica, in Greece; 2, pure; refined; classical: used esp. of literary style.

at-tire (ă-tīr′), *n.* dress; clothes:—*v.t.* [*p.t.* and *p.p.* -tired′ (-tīrd′), *p.pr.* -tir′-ing], to dress; clothe; array; adorn.

at-ti-tude (ăt′ĭ-tūd), *n.* 1, bodily position or posture; 2, habitual mental reaction or point of view.

at-tor-ney (ă-tûr′nĭ, *n.* [*pl.* attorneys (-nĭz)], a lawyer or legal representative; one legally qualified to act for another in business or in actions at law: also called *attorney at law:* **power of attorney,** a legal authorization allowing a person to do business for another.—*n.* **at-tor′ney-ship.**

at-tor-ney-gen-er-al (ă-tûr″nĭ-jĕn′-ẽr-ăl), *n.* [*pl.* attorney-generals; attorneys-general], the chief law officer appointed to act for a government; the chief law officer of a state.

at-tract (ă-trăkt′), *v.t.* 1, to draw to or toward a place; cause to approach: used esp. of physical forces: opp. of *repel;* 2, to draw by moral influence; invite; allure.

Syn. entice, interest, charm, fascinate.

at-trac-tion (ă-trăk′shŭn), *n.* 1, the power or act of drawing to or toward; 2, esp., a force operating between bodies or particles of matter which draws them together, as in gravitation: opp. of *repulsion;* 3, that which charms; fascination.

at-trac-tive (ă-trăk′tĭv), *adj.* charming; alluring; inviting.—*adv.* **at-trac′tive-ly.**—*n.* **at-trac′tive-ness.**

[1]**at-trib-ute** (ă-trĭb′ūt), *v.t.* [*p.t.* and *p.p.* -ut-ed, *p.pr.* -ut-ing], to impute; ascribe; assign.—*adj.* **at-trib′ut-a-ble.**

[2]**at-tri-bute** (ăt′rĭ-būt), *n.* a trait; characteristic; quality.

at-tri-bu-tion (ăt″rĭ-bū′shŭn), *n.* 1, the act of imputing a quality or characteristic to a person or thing; 2, an ascribed quality or character; designation.

at-trib-u-tive (ă-trĭb′ū-tĭv), *n.* 1, a word denoting a quality or characteristic; 2, a word joined to and describing a noun; an adjective or adjective phrase:—*adj.* in grammar, designating an adjective which stands immediately with its qualified noun, as in *red bricks:* distinguished from *predicative,* as in *bricks are red.*—*adv.* **at-trib′u-tive-ly.**

at-tri-tion (ă-trĭsh′ŭn), *n.* 1, the act of wearing by rubbing; abrasion; 2, the state of being worn; 3, grief for sin arising chiefly from fear of punishment.

at-tune (ă-tūn′), *v.t.* [*p.t.* and *p.p.* -tuned′ (-tūnd′), *p.pr.* -tun′ing], 1, to put in tune; 2, to bring into accordance or harmony; adjust.—*n.* **at-tune′ment.**

a-typ-i-cal (ȧ-tĭp′ĭ-kăl), *adj.* not showing the characteristics of its group; irregular. Also, **a-typ′ic.**—*adv.* **a-typ′i-cal-ly.**

au-burn (ô′bŭrn), *adj.* reddish brown: said usually of the hair.

auc-tion (ôk′shŭn), *n.* a public sale of property or goods where offers, or bids, are made by prospective purchasers and the goods sold to the highest bidder: **auction bridge,** a variety of the game of bridge whist in which the players bid for the privilege of naming the trump suit and playing the hand:—*v.t.* to sell to the highest bidder.

auc-tion-eer (ôk″shŭn-ēr′), *n.* one licensed to sell property or goods by public sale:—*v.t.* to sell at auction.

au-da-cious (ô-dā′shŭs), *adj.* 1, bold; daring; spirited; 2, insolent; impudent.—*adv.* **au-da′cious-ly.**

au-dac-i-ty (ô-dăs′ĭ-tĭ), *n.* [*pl.* audacities (-tĭz)], 1, boldness; daring; spirit; 2, presumptuousness; impudence.

au-di-ble (ô′dĭ-bl), *adj.* loud enough to be heard.—*adv.* **au′di-bly.**

au-di-ence (ô′dĭ-ĕns), *n.* 1, an assembly of hearers; 2, admittance to a formal interview with one of high position; 3, the act of listening or giving attention.

au-dit (ô′dĭt), *n.* 1, an official examination of claims or accounts; 2, a regular settlement of accounts; 3, a statement of account; a balance sheet:—*v.t.* to examine and adjust, as accounts or claims:—*v.i.* to act as examiner of accounts.

au-di-tion (ô-dĭsh′ŭn), *n.* 1, the sense or act of hearing; 2, a hearing, esp. for judging the skill of a performer.

au-di-tor (ô′dĭ-tẽr), *n.* 1, a hearer or listener; 2, a person appointed to examine and verify accounts and claims.

au-di-to-ri-um (ô″dĭ-tō′rĭ-ŭm), *n.* [*pl.* auditoriums (-ŭmz); auditoria (-ȧ)], the space in a theater or other public building assigned to the audience.

au-di-to-ry (ô′dĭ-tō-rĭ), *adj.* relating to hearing, or to the sense or organs of hearing:—*n.* [*pl.* auditories (-rĭz)], 1, an audience; 2, an auditorium.

au-ger (ô′gẽr), *n.* a tool for boring holes larger than those bored by a gimlet (see *tool,* illus.).

aught (ôt), *n.* 1, anything; any part; 2, in arithmetic, a cipher; hence, nothing:—*adv.* in any way; at all. Also, **ought.**

aug-ment (ôg-mĕnt′), *v. t.* to increase in size or extent:—*v.i.* to grow larger; increase.—*adj.* **aug-men′ta-tive.**

***au gra-tin** (ō″ grȧ″tăṅ′), [Fr.], cooked with a top crust of bread crumbs and cheese and browned in an oven.

au-gur (ô′gŭr), *n.* 1, in ancient times, one who officially foretold events by natural signs or omens, such as the flight of birds, thunder and lightning, etc.; 2, one who professes to foretell events by omens; a soothsayer; prophet:—*v.i.* to infer from signs or omens:—*v.t.* 1, to predict; infer; 2, to betoken.

Syn., v. forebode, portend, prophesy, foretell.

au-gu-ry (ô′gū-rĭ), *n.* [*pl.* auguries (-rĭz)], 1, the art or practice of foretelling events by reference to natural signs or omens; 2, an omen; a prediction.

au-gust (ô-gŭst′), *adj.* **1**, imposing; having grandeur and dignity; majestic; of a nature to inspire awe and reverence; solemn; awful; **2**, of high rank; eminent; noble.—*adv.* **au-gust′ly.**—*n.* **au-gust′ness.**
Syn. grand, great, kingly, venerable.

Au-gust (ô′gŭst), *n.* the eighth month of the year, having 31 days: named for the Roman emperor Augustus.—*abbr.* **Aug.**

Au-gus-tan (ô-gŭs′tăn), *adj.* **1**, relating to the age of Augustus Cæsar, or to any age, esp. in literature, that resembles his in brilliance and classical standards; **2**, classical:—*n.* a writer of the classical period of any literature.

auk (ôk), *n.* any of several diving birds, including the extinct great auk of the North Atlantic, with small wings used as paddles, and a heavy body.

AUKS (1/14)

auld (ôld; äld), *adj.* old: **auld lang syne**, long since; days gone by, esp. those that seem happy and full of sweet memories.

aunt (ȧnt), *n.* the sister of one's father or mother; also, an uncle's wife.

au-ra (ô′rȧ), *n.* a supposed influence, force, or matter issuing from the human body and surrounding it like an atmosphere.

au-ral (ô′răl), *adj.* **1**, pertaining to the ear or to the sense of hearing; **2**, perceived or received by the ear.

au-re-ate (ô′rē-āt), *adj.* golden; gilded; splendid.

au-re-ole (ô′rē-ōl), *n.* **1**, a halo or bright cloud surrounding the figures of Christ, the Virgin, and the saints, as represented by the painters: also, *aureola* (ô-rē′ō-lȧ); **2**, the fringe of radiance about the sun or other heavenly body as seen through the telescope.

au-re-o-my-cin (ô″rē-ō-mī′sĭn), *n.* a golden-colored antibiotic produced by a fungus.

au-ri-cle (ô′rĭ-kl), *n.* **1**, that part of the ear which projects from the head; the outer ear; **2**, one of the two chambers of the heart which receive the blood from the veins and transmit it to the ventricles.

au-ric-u-lar (ô-rĭk′ū-lȧr), *adj.* **1**, relating to the ear or to the sense of hearing; **2**, privately addressed, as to the priest in the confessional; **3**, perceived by the ear; known by report; **4**, ear-shaped; **5**, pertaining to the chambers of the heart.

au-ric-u-late (ô-rĭk′ū-lāt), *adj.* having ears or ear-shaped appendages or parts (see *leaf*, illus.).

au-rif-er-ous (ô-rĭf′ẽr-ŭs), *adj.* gold-bearing; yielding or containing gold; as, *auriferous* quartz or strata.

au-ri-form (ô′rĭ-fôrm), *adj.* having the form of the human ear; ear-shaped; as, an *auriform* shell.

Au-ri-ga (ô-rī′gȧ), *n.* in astronomy, a northern constellation, the Wagoner, containing the star Capella.

au-rist (ô′rĭst), *n.* a specialist in diseases of the ear.

au-rochs (ô′rŏks; ou′rŏks), *n.* **1**, the European wild ox, extinct since the 17th century; **2**, (inaccurately) the European bison, a nearly extinct species, similar to the American bison: now found only in Lithuania and the Caucasus, where it is strictly protected.

au-ro-ra (ô-rō′rȧ), *n.* **1**, the rising light of the morning; the dawn; break of day; **2**, the aurora australis or aurora borealis: **Aurora**, the Roman goddess of dawn: identified with the Greek *Eos*.—*adj.* **au-ro′ral.**

au-ro-ra aus-tra-lis (ô-strā′lĭs), the night lights of the southern polar sky, probably due to electrical disturbances in the upper atmosphere.

au-ro-ra bo-re-a-lis (bō″rē-ā′lĭs), the brilliant radiance of the sky in far northern latitudes at night, probably due to electrical disturbances in the upper atmosphere: also called *northern lights.*

aus-pice (ôs′pĭs), *n.* [*pl.* auspices (-pĭ-sĕz)], **1**, an omen or sign drawn from birds; **2**, an omen or sign in general; as, an *auspice* of good fortune; **3**, usually in *pl.*: **a**, protection; patronage; as, under the *auspices* of the club; **b**, favoring circumstances.

aus-pi-cious (ôs-pĭsh′ŭs), *adj.* **1**, having promise of success or happiness; favorable; **2**, fortunate; prosperous. —*adv.* **aus-pi′cious-ly.**—*n.* **aus-pi′cious-ness.**
Syn. (see propitious).

aus-tere (ôs-tēr′), *adj.* **1**, severely simple; not adorned; **2**, severe or strict; rigid in character or mode of living; **3**, sour; harsh; rough to the taste.—*adv.* **aus-tere′ly.** —*n.* **aus-tere′ness.**
Syn. rigid, rigorous, stern, harsh.—*Ant.* affable, mild, gentle, soft.

aus-ter-i-ty (ôs-tĕr′ĭ-tĭ), *n.* **1**, a harshness of attitude or judgment toward others, or toward indulgent modes of living; rigid morality or discipline; **2**, bare simplicity or severity, as of literary style, or of manner of living.

aus-tral (ôs′trăl), *adj.* southern; characteristic of the south.

Aus-tral-a-sian (ôs″trăl-ā′shăn), *adj.* pertaining to the region of Australia and the adjacent islands:—*n.* a native or inhabitant of this region.

Aus-tra-li-an (ôs-trā′lĭ-ăn; ôs-trāl′yăn), *adj.* pertaining to the island continent Australia:—*n.* a native or inhabitant of this region.

Aus-tri-an (ôs′trĭ-ăn), *adj.* pertaining to Austria:—*n.* a native or inhabitant of Austria.

au-tarch-y (ô′tär-kĭ), *n.* in economics, the state of a country in which it does not depend upon any other country in any way, and hence can satisfy its wants without importing goods from abroad.

au-then-tic (ô-thĕn′tĭk), *adj.* **1**, genuine; original; **2**, duly authorized; true; trustworthy. Also, **au-then′ti-cal.**—*adv.* **au-then′ti-cal-ly.**—*n.* **au″then-tic′i-ty.**

au-then-ti-cate (ô-thĕn′tĭ-kāt), *v.t.* [*p.t.* and *p.p.* -cat″ed, *p.pr.* -cat″ing], to establish as true or genuine, as the authorship of a book, or, by legal proceedings, a claim to property.—*n.* **au-then″ti-ca′tion.**

au-thor (ô′thẽr), *n.* **1**, the beginner or originator of anything, as of a movement or reform; **2**, one who composes or writes a book, articles, etc.; esp., one who makes a profession of writing; also, the collective writings of an author.—*n. fem.* **au′thor-ess.**—*n.* **au′thor-ship.**

au-thor-i-ta-tive (ô-thŏr′ĭ-tā-tĭv), *adj.* **1**, having the right to demand obedience, respect, and confidence; **2**, with the air of being duly empowered;

dictatorial; positive; commanding.—*adv.* **au-thor'i-ta-tive-ly.**—*n.* **au-thor'i-ta-tive-ness.**

au-thor-i-ty (ô-thŏr'ĭ-tĭ), *n.* [*pl.* authorities (-tĭz)], **1**, the power or right to act or command; dominion; **2**, personal power derived from respect or reputation; influence; **3**, justification or support for a statement or action, as a quotation or law; also, one to whom appeal or reference can be made, as an expert or specialist; **4**, a person with power to act for another; **5**, in *pl.*, those in power; legal or government officials.

au-thor-i-za-tion (ô"thŏr-ĭ-zā'shŭn), *n.* the act of having legal power; sanction; warrant.

au-thor-ize (ô'thŏr-īz), *v.t.* [*p.t.* and *p.p.* -ized(-īzd), *p.pr.* -iz"ing], **1**, to clothe with power; give (a person) the right to act or command; **2**, to approve; allow; sanction, as acts or expenditures: **Authorized Version**, a version of the Bible, commonly used by English-speaking Protestants, translated in 1611 with the sanction of King James I.

au-to (ô'tō), *n.* [*pl.* autos (-tōz)], *Colloq.*, an automobile:—*v.i.* to ride or travel in an automobile.

au-to- (ô'tō-), a prefix or combining form from the Greek, meaning self, oneself; as, *auto*biography; *auto*mobile.

au-to-bi-o-graph-ic (ô"tō-bī"ō-grăf'ĭk), *adj.* relating to a life history of oneself. Also, **au"to-bi"o-graph'i-cal.**—*adv.* **au"to-bi"o-graph'i-cal-ly.**

au-to-bi-og-ra-phy (ô"tō-bī-ŏg'rȧ-fĭ), *n.* [*pl.* autobiographies (-fĭz)], a biography, account, or character sketch of a person written by himself.—*n.* **au"to-bi-og'ra-pher.**

au-to-boat (ô'tō-bōt"), *n.* a boat driven by motor power.

au-to-bus (ô'tō-bŭs"), *n.* [*pl.* autobusses; autobuses (-ĕz)], an omnibus propelled by motor power within itself.

au-to-car (ô'tō-kär"), *n.* a carriage or wagon moved by motor power within itself; an automobile.

au-toc-ra-cy (ô-tŏk'rȧ-sĭ), *n.* [*pl.* autocracies (-sĭz)], **1**, absolute supremacy; independent power; **2**, government by one invested with absolute authority.

au-to-crat (ô'tō-krăt), *n.* **1**, an absolute prince or sovereign; one who rules without restriction; **2**, hence, one whose authority is not disputed in any group; a dictatorial or despotic person.—*adj.* **au"to-crat'ic; au"to-crat'i-cal.**—*adv.* **au"to-crat'i-cal-ly.**

au-to-cy-cle (ô'tō-sī"kl), *n.* a motor cycle; a bicycle with motor power.

au-to-gi-ro (ô"tō-jī'rō), *n.* [*pl.* autogiros (-rōz)], a type of airplane having above the fuselage four horizontal, windmill-like blades.

au-to-graph (ô'tō-grȧf), *adj.* written in one's own handwriting:—*n.* **1**, a person's own handwriting or signature; **2**, a manuscript written by the author himself:—*v.t.* to sign one's signature in, as a book.—*adj.* **au"to-graph'ic.**—*n.* **au-tog'ra-phy.**

au-to–in-tox-i-ca-tion (ô"tō=ĭn-tŏk"sĭ-kā'shŭn), *n.* poisoning, or the state of being poisoned, by substances produced in one's own body.

au-to-mat (ô'tō-măt), *n.* a self-operating device; esp., a restaurant in which food is secured by inserting coins in slots.

au-to-mat-ic (ô"tō-măt'ĭk), *adj.* **1**, having the power of self-motion or self-action; **2**, done unconsciously or from force of habit:—*n.* **1**, a magazine pistol which fires, ejects the shell, reloads, and cocks with each pull of the trigger; **2**, a rifle which discharges rapidly as long as the trigger is held down.—*adv.* **au"to-mat'i-cal-ly.**

au-tom-a-ton (ô-tŏm'ȧ-tŏn), *n.* [*pl.* automata (-tȧ); automatons (-tŏnz)], **1**, a thing that moves, or seems to move, spontaneously; **2**, a self-acting machine, esp. one made to imitate living beings, as a mechanical doll; hence, one whose actions are unthinking or mechanical.

au-to-mo-bile (ô"tō-mō'bĭl; -mō-bēl'), *n.* a vehicle moved by a source of power within itself; esp., a motor car; an autocar:—*v.i.* [*p.t.* and *p.p.* -biled (-bĭld; -bēld'), *p.pr.* -bil-ing], to ride in, or drive, an automobile:—*adj.* self-moving.

au-to-mo-bil-ist (ô"tō-mō'bĭl-ĭst), *n.* one who uses or controls a motor car, esp. for pleasure.

au-to-mo-tive (ô"tō-mō'tĭv), *adj.* **1**, self-propelling; **2**, pertaining to mechanisms which move under their own power, as automobiles, airplanes, etc.

au-ton-o-mist (ô-tŏn'ō-mĭst), *n.* a believer in self-government.

au-ton-o-mous (ô-tŏn'ō-mŭs), *adj.* self-governing; independent in government.—*adj.* **au"to-nom'ic.**

au-ton-o-my (ô-tŏn'ō-mĭ), *n.* [*pl.* autonomies (-mĭz)], **1**, the power or right of self-government; the state of political independence; **2**, a self-governing state; **3**, personal freedom.

au-top-sy (ô'tŏp-sĭ), *n.* [*pl.* autopsies (-sĭz)], a post-mortem examination, or the inspection of a dead body, to find out the cause of death.

au-to-sug-ges-tion (ô"tō-sŭg-jĕs'chŭn), *n.* the act of impressing a belief upon one's own mind, or of affecting one's physical condition, sensations, or behavior by a mental attitude, as in the treatment of certain diseases.

au-to-truck (ô'tō-trŭk"), *n.* a self-moving truck; a motor truck.

au-tumn (ô'tŭm), *n.* **1**, the season between summer and winter, beginning about September 22, and ending about December 21: often called *fall*, because of the falling of the leaves; **2**, a period of decline or decay; as, the *autumn* of life.

au-tum-nal (ô-tŭm'năl), *adj.* **1**, pertaining or peculiar to the fall; produced or gathered in the fall; **2**, relating to the period of life when middle age is passing: **autumnal equinox**, the time of the sun's southward passage across the equator, about September 22.—*adv.* **au-tum'nal-ly.**

aux-il-ia-ry (ôg-zĭl'yȧ-rĭ), *adj.* helping; aiding; assisting:—*n.* [*pl.* auxiliaries (-rĭz)], **1**, a helper; an assistant; a confederate or ally; aid of any kind; **2**, a verb, such as *be, have, can, might*, which helps to form the moods and tenses of other verbs; **3**, in *pl.*, foreign troops in the service of a nation at war.

a-vail (ȧ-vāl'), *v.i.* **1**, to be of use, value, or service; **2**, to serve for a purpose; as, money does not *avail* on a desert island:—*v.t.* to benefit or help: **avail oneself of**, to take advantage of, or profit by; as, I *availed* myself of his offer:—*n.* use; means toward an end.

Syn., *n.* utility, service, benefit, advantage.

a-vail-a-ble (ȧ-vāl'ȧ-bl), *adj.* **1**, usable; suitable for one's purpose; as, an *available* candidate; **2**, at hand; as, ten cars are *available*.—*n.* **a-vail"a-bil'i-ty.**

av-a-lanche (ăv'ȧ-lȧnch), *n.* **1**, the sudden sliding of a mass of snow and rock, or the like, down a mountain slope; **2**, anything that overwhelms by sudden and resistless force; as, an *avalanche* of woe.

av-a-rice (ăv'ȧ-rĭs), *n.* a greedy desire for wealth; covetousness; cupidity.

av-a-ri-cious (ăv"ȧ-rĭsh'ŭs), *adj.* eager to possess and to keep

riches; greedy for gain; grasping; miserly.—*adv.* **av″a-ri′cious-ly.**—*n.* **av″a-ri′cious-ness.**
Syn. covetous, close, stingy.—*Ant.* generous, prodigal.

a-vast (ȧ-vȧst′), *interj.* stop! cease! hold! a nautical term.

a-vaunt (ȧ-vônt′; ȧ-vȧnt′), *interj.* away! depart! begone! expressing contempt or abhorrence.

a-ve (ā′vē; *Lat.* ä′vā), *interj.* hail! farewell! —*n.* a salutation: **Ave Maria** (also, *Ave; Ave Mary*), a prayer to the Virgin.

a-venge (ȧ-vĕnj′), *v.t.* [*p.t.* and *p.p.* a-venged′ (-vĕnjd′), *p.pr.* a-veng′-ing], to inflict injury in return for:—*v.i.* to execute vengeance; require satisfaction for injury; as, time *avenges*.—*n.* **a-veng′er.**
Syn. revenge. To *avenge* is to exact just punishment from motives free from malice, often from a sense of duty; as, to *avenge* an insult. To *revenge* is to exact punishment from personal malice or to retaliate for some real or imaginary injury; as, he swiftly *revenged* his father's ruin.

av-e-nue (ăv′ĕ-nū), *n.* **1,** a way of approach to, or departure from, a place; **2,** a wide roadway or drive, usually bordered by trees; a broad street; **3,** means of access or attainment; as, hard work is the surest *avenue* to success.
Syn. road, highway, thoroughfare. (See way.)

a-ver (ȧ-vûr′), *v.t.* [*p.t.* and *p.p.* a-verred′ (-vûrd′), *p.pr.* a-ver′ring], **1,** to affirm positively; assert; **2,** in law, to prove to be true; verify.—*n.* **a-ver′ment.**

av-er-age (ăv′ẽr-ȧj), *n.* **1,** something thought of as being of a usual or ordinary character, midway between extremes; **2,** a mean; the result obtained by dividing the sum of several different quantities by the number of quantities; as, the *average* of 5, 8, and 14 is 9:—*adj.* **1,** pertaining to an average or mean; **2,** arrived at by dividing the sum of several quantities by their number; **3,** ordinary:—*v.t.* [*p.t.* and *p.p.* -aged (-ȧjd), *p.pr.* -ag-ing], **1,** to find the mean of, as a series of numbers; **2,** to divide or distribute proportionally; **3,** to do or get according to a prevailing rate; as, the automobile *averaged* 20 miles an hour.—*adv.* **av′er-age-ly.**
Syn., adj. (see mean).

A-ver-nus (ȧ-vûr′nŭs), *n.* **1,** a lake in Italy, supposed by the ancient Romans to lead to the infernal regions; **2,** the infernal regions.—*adj.* **A-ver′ni-an.**

a-verse (ȧ-vûrs′), *adj.* **1,** unwilling; reluctant; disinclined; as, he was *averse* to entering the contest; **2,** having a repugnance to; as, *averse* to war.—*adv.* **a-verse′ly.**—*n.* **a-verse′ness.**

a-ver-sion (ȧ-vûr′shŭn), *n.* **1,** opposition of mind; fixed dislike; **2,** the object or cause of dislike.
Syn. hatred, disgust, antipathy.

a-vert (ȧ-vûrt′), *v.t.* **1,** to turn aside or away; turn or ward off; **2,** to prevent; as, to *avert* a strike.—*adj.* **a-vert′i-ble.**
Syn. hinder, obstruct, preclude.

A-ves-ta (ȧ-vĕs′tȧ), *n.* the bible or sacred scriptures of Persia, part of which is attributed to Zoroaster.

a-vi-a-ry (ā′vĭ-ā-rĭ), *n.* [*pl.* aviaries (-rĭz)], a house or inclosure for the keeping and rearing of birds.—*n.* **a′vi-a-rist.**

a-vi-ate (ā′vĭ-āt), *v.i.* [*p.t.* and *p.p.* -at″ed, *p.pr.* -at″ing], to operate a flying machine; navigate the air.

a-vi-a-tion (ā″vĭ-ā′shŭn), *n.* the art or science of flying, esp. in airplanes; management of airplanes. (See illus. next page; see also *airplane, monoplane, empennage, dihedral,* illus.).

a-vi-a-tor (ā′vĭ-ā″tẽr), *n.* the operator or driver of an airplane; an expert in aviation.—*n.fem.* **a′vi-a″tress; a″vi-a′trix.**

a-vi-cul-ture (ā′vĭ-kŭl″tūr), *n.* the breeding and rearing of birds.

av-id (ăv′ĭd), *adj.* eager; greedy.—*adv.* **av′id-ly.**

a-vid-i-ty (ȧ-vĭd′ĭ-tĭ), *n.* greediness; strong appetite; eagerness; intenseness of desire; covetousness.

av-o-ca-tion (ăv″ō-kā′shŭn), *n.* **1,** a secondary or occasional occupation; **2,** a diversion or distraction; **3,** loosely, one's regular business.

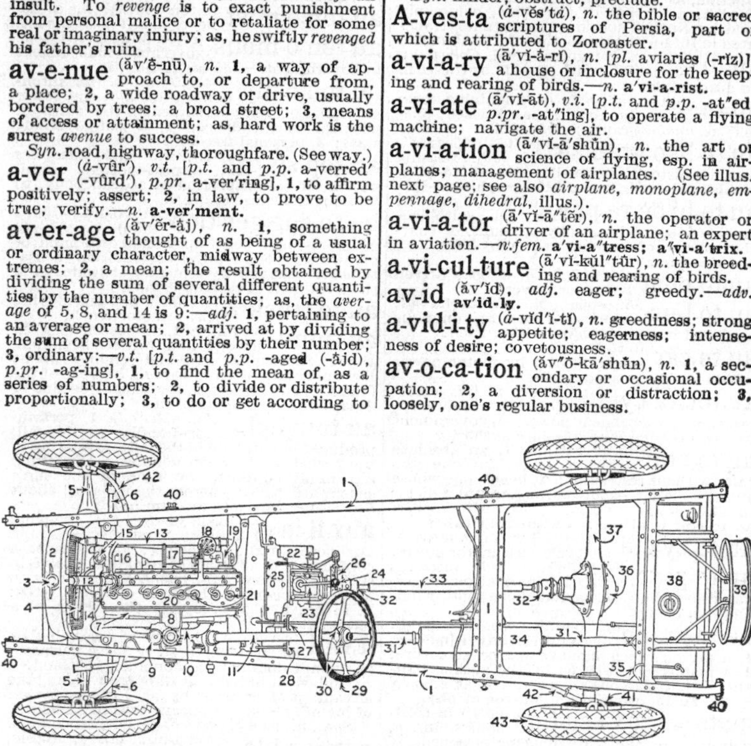

Chassis and Working Parts of Modern Eight-Cylinder Automobile

1, chassis frame of steel; 2, radiator; 3, radiator cap; 4, fan; 5, front axle; 6, cross tube of steering gear; 7, exhaust manifold; 8, mixture heater; 9, carburetor; 10, intake manifold; 11, steering column; 12, water connection from engine to radiator; 13, water return from radiator; 14, thermostat controlling water circulation; 15, engine oil filling cap; 16, electric generator; 17, horn; 18, ignition distributor; 19, water pump; 20, engine; 21, spark plugs; 22, starting motor; 23, transmission housing; 24, gear-shift lever; 25, emergency-brake lever; 26, emergency brake on driving shaft; 27, service foot-brake pedal, for hydraulic brakes; 28, clutch pedal; 29, steering wheel; 30, throttle and spark controls; 31, exhaust pipe; 32, universal joint; 33, propeller shaft; 34, muffler; 35, gasoline line; 36, differential housing; 37, rear axle housing, inclosing the driving shafts; 38, gasoline tank; 39, spare tire rim and rack; 40, spring shackle grease cup; 41, brake drum and brake bands of service brake; 42, hydraulic brake line; 43, low-pressure balloon tire.

TYPES IN THE EVOLUTION OF THE AMERICAN AUTOMOBILE

1, 1786: Murdock steam wagon; 2, 1894: one-cylinder gasoline motor car; high wheels, engine under seat, speed 7 or 8 miles per hour: at that time called *motor cycle;* 3, 1900: more distinctive type; one-cylinder engine, smaller wheels; 4, 1902: four-cylinder, air-cooled engine, in front; steering wheel, hood, mud guards, pneumatic tires; 5, 1904: touring car, two-cylinder engine; beginning of heavier type with greater power; 6, 1905: touring car with side doors; 7, 1906: touring car with permanent top and glass windshield; 8, 1907: touring car with folding top; approximation to streamline body; 9, 1908 limousine; an early glass-inclosed body; 10, 1910: touring car, typical of the general adoption of sliding-gear transmission; 11, 1913: four-door touring car.—From this time on, development was along the line of body design, operating efficiency, and special features making for comfort and convenience.—12, 1925: sedan; 13, streamlined two-door sedan of 1950.

EVOLUTION OF THE AMERICAN AUTOMOBILE

a-void (ȧ-void′), *v.t.* **1**, to keep away from; shun; abstain from; **2**, to make void, as a contract.—*adj.* **a-void′a-ble.**—*adv.* **a-void′a-bly.**
Syn. elude, escape, evade; annul, cancel.

a-void-ance (ȧ-void′ăns), *n.* **1**, the act of shunning anything; **2**, the act of voiding; annulment.

av-oir-du-pois (ăv″ẽr-dŭ-poiz′), *n.* a system of weight in which the unit is a pound consisting of sixteen ounces: used for weighing all commodities except precious metals, gems, and drugs.

a-vouch (ȧ-vouch′), *v.t.* **1**, to affirm or acknowledge openly; **2**, to maintain; declare positively; guarantee; admit.

a-vow (ȧ-vou′), *v.t.* to declare openly; acknowledge frankly; admit.—*p.adj.* **a-vowed′.**—*adv.* **a-vow′ed-ly.**
Syn. aver, confess, affirm, state.

a-vow-al (ȧ-vou′ăl), *n.* an open declaration; a frank acknowledgment.

a-vun-cu-lar (ȧ-vŭng′kū-lẽr), *adj.* pertaining to, or like, an uncle.

a-way (ȧ-wā′), *adv.* **1**, at or to a distance; off; hence, aside; as, to look *away;* **2**, out of one's possession; as, to give *away;* **3**, continuously; as, to work *away;* **4**, out of existence; as, to die *away;* **5**, absent; as, to stay *away:* **right away**, immediately.

awe (ô), *n.* solemn fear; the feeling inspired by viewing something sublime; deep admiration and respect; reverence:—*v.t.* [*p.t.* and *p.p.* awed (ôd), *p.pr.* aw′ing], **1**, to cause feelings of solemn respect or fear in; as, *awed* by the scene; **2**, to restrain by fear or respect.
Syn., *n.* dread, terror, veneration.

a-wea-ry (ȧ-wē′rĭ), *adj. Poetic*, tired; weary; exhausted.

a-weath-er (ȧ-wĕth′ẽr), *adv.* toward the wind: opp. of *alee.*

awe-some (ô′sŭm), *adj.* **1**, appalling; causing terror; weird; **2**, expressing awe.—*adv.* **awe′some-ly.**—*n.* **awe′some-ness.**

aw-ful (ô′fo͞ol), *adj.* **1**, inspiring or impressing with great fear or reverence; as, the *awful* majesty of God; **2**, of a dreadful or appalling nature; solemn.—*n.* **aw′ful-ness.**—*adv.* **aw′ful-ly.**

Types of Airplane Used in Aviation: 1, transport plane; 2, Navy pursuit plane; 3, amphibian; 4, scout or racing plane; 5, bomber; 6, Autogiro; 7. clipper: a hydro-airplane.

a-wait (ȧ-wāt′), *v.t.* **1**, to wait or look for; expect; **2**, to be ready for; **3**, to be in store for; as, misfortune *awaits* him.

a-wake (ȧ-wāk′), *v.t.* [*p.t.* and *p.p.* a-woke′ (-wōk′) or a-waked′ (-wākt′), *p.pr.* a-wak′ing], **1**, to arouse from sleep, or from a state like it; **2**, to put into action; **3**, to infuse new life into:—*v.i.* **1**, to cease to sleep; **2**, to rouse oneself; become alert:—*adj.* not sleeping; roused from sleep or inactivity; in a state of vigilance or action.

a-wak-en (ȧ-wāk′n), *v.t.* and *v.i.* to rouse from sleep; awake.
Syn. stir, arouse, excite, stimulate.

a-wak-en-ing (ȧ-wāk′n-ĭng), *n.* **1**, the act of rousing from sleep; **2**, an arousing, as of attention; a revival:—*adj.* rousing; exciting; stirring.

a-ward (ȧ-wôrd′), *v.t.* to assign, as by judicial sentence; bestow; grant after due consideration, as between contestants:—*n.* **1**, a judgment or sentence arrived at with care; decision; **2**, that which is given as the result of careful judging.

a-ware (ȧ-wâr′), *adj.* **1**, conscious; possessing knowledge; as, *aware* of the facts; **2**, on guard; vigilant.—*n.* **a-ware′ness.**

a-wash (ȧ-wŏsh′), *adj.* and *adv.* **1**, level with, or just above the surface of, the water; **2**, tossed about by the waves.

a-while (ȧ-hwīl′), *adv.* during or for a short time; as, stay *awhile.*

awk-ward (ôk′wẽrd), *adj.* **1**, unskilful; ungraceful; ungainly; clumsy; **2**, difficult to deal with; embarrassing; as, an *awkward* situation.—*adv.* **awk′ward-ly.**—*n.* **awk′ward-ness.**
Syn. clumsy. *Awkward* implies a lack of grace in motion; as, he has an *awkward* gait. *Clumsy* implies something that is ungainly and heavy in movement; as, a duck is *clumsy* on land.—*Ant.* adroit, dexterous, skilful.

awl (ôl), *n.* a pointed tool for making small holes, as in leather or wood.

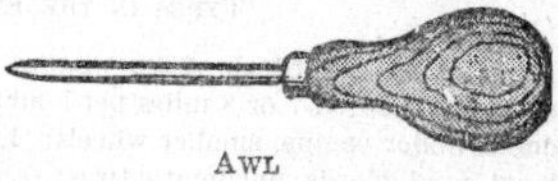

Awl

awn (ôn), *n.* one of the bristlelike extensions which form the beard of a head of barley, oats, and the like.

awn-ing (ôn′ĭng), *n.* a rooflike covering, as canvas, stretched upon a frame and used above or before any place as a shelter from rain or sun.

a-woke (ȧ-wōk′), past tense of the transitive and intransitive verb *awake.*

a-wry (ȧ-rī′), *adj.* **1**, turned or twisted toward one side; as, his face was *awry* with pain; **2**, not straight; crooked; as, her cap was *awry;* **3**, perverse:—*adv.* **1**, out of a straight line; crookedly; **2**, in a twisted fashion; **3**, perversely.

ax (ăks), *n.* **1**, a tool, consisting of an iron head with a cutting edge of steel, attached to a handle, used for hewing timber and chopping wood; **2**, a similar implement, used as a weapon of defense. Also, **axe.**

ax-i-al (ăk′sĭ-ăl), *adj.* pertaining to an axis, or central line.

ax-il (ăk′sĭl), *n.* the angle formed by the upper side of a leaf or branch with the stem or trunk to which it is attached.

ax-il-la-ry (ăk′sĭ-lă-rĭ), *adj.* **1**, pertaining to the armpit; **2**, in botany, rising from, or pertaining to, an axil.

ax-i-om (ăk′sĭ-ŭm), *n.* **1**, a self-evident truth; a statement generally accepted as true; **2**, one of the self-evident principles of an art or science.

Syn. adage, byword, maxim, proverb.

ax-i-o-mat-ic (ăk″sĭ-ō-măt′ĭk), *adj.* **1**, self-evident; proverbial; **2**, of the nature of an accepted principle. Also, **ax″i-o-mat′i-cal.**—*adv.* **ax″i-o-mat′i-cal-ly.**

ax-is (ăk′sĭs), *n.* [*pl.* axes (-sēz)], **1**, a straight line about which a body may rotate or turn; as, the earth's *axis;* **2**, a central column or stem in a spikelike cluster of flowers or leaves: **Axis,** Germany, Italy, and their allies as a political bloc.

ax-le (ăk′sl), *n.* the bar or spindle on which a wheel turns.

ax-le-tree (ăk′sl-trē″), *n.* a bar between opposite wheels of a vehicle, as a wagon, on the ends of which the wheels turn.

ax-o-lotl (ăk′sō-lŏtl), *n.* a salamander found from the northern U. S. to central Mexico: so called within its southern range, where it does not develop into the adult form, but lives and reproduces in its larval stage (see *amphibian,* illus.).

a-yah (ä′yȧ), *n.* in the Far East, a native woman employed as a child's nurse or lady's maid.

[1]**aye** (ā), *adv.* always; forever; continually. Also, **ay.**

[2]**aye** (ī), *adv.* yes; yea; even so; indeed:—*n.* [*pl.* ayes (īz)], a vote in the affirmative; an expression of assent. Also, **ay.**

Ayr-shire (âr′shẽr; -shĭr), *n.* one of a fine breed of dairy cattle raised in Ayrshire, Scotland.

a-za-le-a (ȧ-zā′lē-ȧ), *n.* any of several species of shrub of the heath family, cultivated for its flowers.

A-zo-ic (ȧ-zō′ĭk), *adj.* designating, or pertaining to, the oldest era of the earth's geological history, containing no definite evidences of life.

Az-tec (ăz′tĕk), *n.* **1**, a member of the race which founded the Mexican empire, conquered by Cortez in 1519: **2**, the language of this race:—*adj.* relating to the race of Aztecs.

az-ure (ăzh′ŭr; ā′zhŭr), *adj.* like the clear blue of the sky; sky blue:—*n.* **1**, the clear blue sky; **2**, a sky-blue color; light blue.

B

baa (bä; bȧ), *v.i.* [*p.t.* and *p.p.* baaed (bäd; bȧd), *p.pr.* baa′ing], to bleat or cry, as a sheep:—*n.* the bleating of a sheep or lamb.

Ba-al (bā′ăl), *n.* [*pl.* Baals (-ălz); Baalim (-ȧ-lĭm)], **1**, the sun god, or supreme being, esp. of the Phœnicians before the time of Christ; **2**, an idol.—*adj.* **Ba′al-ish.**

Bab-bitt met-al (băb′ĭt), an alloy of tin, copper, and antimony: used in bearings to lessen friction.—*n.* and *v.t.* **bab′bitt.**—*n.* **bab′bitt-ing.**

bab-ble (băb′l), *v.i.* [*p.t.* and *p.p.* -bled (-ld), *p.pr.* -bling], **1**, to utter indistinct or imperfect sounds; **2**, to prattle; talk childishly; **3**, to chatter; **4**. to murmur constantly, as a brook:—*v.t.* **1**, to utter indistinctly or imperfectly; **2**, to tell, as secrets:—*n.* **1**, foolish talk; **2**, a confused prattle; **3**, a continuous murmuring sound.—*n.* **bab′bler.**

babe (bāb), *n.* an infant or young child; as, a *babe* in arms.

Ba-bel (bā′bĕl), *n.* in the Bible, the city and tower where the confusion of languages took place (Genesis 11): **babel,** tumult; confusion; a place of confusion.

bab-i-rous-sa (băb″ĭ-rōō′sȧ), *n.* the wild hog of Eastern Asia, having four upturned, hornlike tusks.

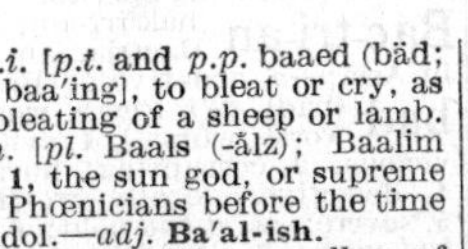

BABIROUSSA ($\frac{1}{48}$)

ba-boon (bă-bōōn′), *n.* any of several large, Old World monkeys, usually short-tailed, with doglike face.

ba-by (bā′bĭ), *n.* [*pl.* babies (-bĭz)], a child in arms; an infant; a small child: **baby bond,** *Colloq.*, a bond having a face value of $100.—*adj.* **ba′by-ish.**—*n.* **ba′by-hood.**

Bab-y-lon (băb′ĭ-lŏn), *n.* any rich but vicious city: in allusion to the luxury and wickedness of ancient Babylon.—*adj.* **Bab″y-lo′ni-an.**—*adj.* **Bab″y-lo′nish.**

bac-ca-lau-re-ate (băk″ȧ-lô′rē-āt), *n.* the degree of bachelor, or first degree, given by universities and colleges:—*adj.* relating to the degree of bachelor: **baccalaureate sermon,** a farewell sermon delivered to a graduating class.

bac-cha-nal (băk′ȧ-năl), *adj.* pertaining to Bacchus or to a feast in his honor; riotous:—*n.* **1**, a follower, priest, or priestess of Bacchus; **2**, a drunken reveler; **3**, a dance or song to honor Bacchus; **4**, in *pl.:* **a**, the Bacchanalia; **b**, a riotous feast.

Bac-cha-na-li-a (băk″ȧ-nā′lĭ-ȧ), *n.pl.* a feast to Bacchus, the god of wine: **bacchanalia,** drunken revels.—*adj.* **bac″cha-na′li-an.**

bac-chant (băk′ănt), *n.* a worshiper of Bacchus, god of wine; hence, a drunken reveler.—*n.fem.* **bac-chante′** (bȧ-kănt′; băk′ănt; bȧ-kăn′tē).

Bac-chus (băk′ŭs), *n.* the Roman god of wine: the Greek *Dionysus.*

bach-e-lor (băch′ē-lẽr), *n.* **1**, an unmarried man; **2**, one who has taken the first degree in any field of learning at a college or university; **3**, orig., a young knight in the service of one more experienced.—*n.* **bach′e-lor-hood.**—*n.* **bach′e-lor-ship.**

bach-e-lor's–but-ton (băch′ē-lẽrz-bŭt′n), *n.* any of several flowering garden plants, esp. the cornflower, or bluebottle.

ba-cil-lus (bȧ-sĭl′ŭs), *n.* [*pl.* bacilli (-ī)], any of a large genus (*Bacillus*) of one-celled vegetable organisms, of characteristic rodlike shape, visible only under the microscope: in some varieties the cause of disease, though usually harmless

1**back** (băk), *n.* **1**, the hinder part of the body of man; in other animals, the surface from the neck to the end of the backbone: **2**, the opposite of the front; the hinder part of anything; **3**, the side of anything away from, or out of sight of, the beholder; **4**, the part of a book where the leaves are sewed in; **5**, the part of a knife, sword, etc., opposite to the cutting edge; **6**, the vertical part of a chair, sofa, etc., used to support the spine; **7**, in athletic games, a position behind the front line; also, a player in such a position:—*v.t.* **1**, to furnish with a back; **2**, to get upon the back of, or mount; **3**, to second or support: often with *up;* **4**, to bet on the successful outcome of; **5**, to sign or indorse; **6**, to cause to move to the rear:—*v.i.* to move backward; specif., to shift counterclockwise, as from east through northeast to north: said of the wind: opp. of *veer:*—*adj.* **1**, lying or being behind as to time, situation, or direction; **2**, moving backward; **3**, overdue; **4**, no longer current; as, *back* numbers of a magazine.

2**back** (băk), *adv.* **1**, to or toward the rear; **2**, to or toward a former place, state, or condition; **3**, to or toward time past; **4**, in withdrawal; as, to take *back* hasty words; **5**, in concealment or reserve; as, to keep *back* part of the truth; **6**, in return; as, to pay *back*.

back-bite (băk′bīt″), *v.t.* [*p.t.* -bit″ (-bĭt″), *p.p.* -bit″ten (-bĭt″n) or -bit, *p.pr.* -bit″ing], to slander or speak evil of (one who is not present).—*n.* **back′bit″er.**

back-bone (băk′bōn′), *n.* **1**, the spine; **2**, firmness; moral courage.

back-er (băk′ẽr), *n.* one who aids or bets on another, esp. in a contest.

back-gam-mon (băk′găm-ŭn), *n.* a game played with dice by two persons, each with fifteen pieces, or men, on spaces marked upon a board.

back-ground (băk′ground″), *n.* **1**, the distant portions of the landscape; **2**, the portion of a picture farthest away from the spectator, or lying between or above the chief figures; also, the whole of a surface upon which patterns or designs are executed, or against which anything can be viewed; **3**, a place obscure or out of sight; retirement; obscurity; **4**, a person's general education or culture.

back-hand (băk′hănd″), *n.* handwriting which slopes upward to the left:—*adj.* **1**, made with the back of the hand, or with the hand turned backward; as, a *backhand* stroke; **2**, insincere.—*adj.* **back′hand″ed.**

back-ing (băk′ĭng), *n.* **1**, something placed behind to support or strengthen; **2**, aid or support given to a person or cause.

back-log (băk′lôg″), *n.* a log of wood placed near the back of a fireplace as a rear support for a fire.

back-sheesh (băk′shēsh), *n.* in the Orient, a tip. Also, **back′shish; bak′shish;** *Pfd. S.*, **bak′sheesh.**

back-side (băk′sīd′), *n.* **1**, (usually, *back side*), the hind part of anything, or that which its opposed to the front; **2**, the hind part of an animal.

back-slide (băk″slīd′; băk′slīd″), *v.i.* [*p.t.* -slid′ (-slĭd′), *p.p.* -slid′den (-slĭd′n) or -slid′, *p.pr.* -slid′ing], to slip back; gradually turn away or fall away from a religion once believed in.—*n.* **back″slid′er.**

back-stay (băk′stā″), *n.* **1**, any rear support; **2**, a long rope stretched from the masthead to the side of the ship, to assist in supporting the mast: a nautical term (see *rigging*, illus.).

back-ward (băk′wẽrd), *adj.* **1**, directed to the rear; **2**, moving or done opposite to the normal way; reversed; **3**, reluctant; hesitating; retiring; bashful; **4**, behind in learning or progress; dull; as, a *backward* pupil; **5**, behindhand; late:—*adv.* **1**, toward the rear; **2**, with the back coming first or foremost; **3**, from better to worse; **4**, in a reverse direction. Also, *adv.* **back′wards.** —*adv.* **back′ward-ly.**—*n.* **back′ward-ness.**

back-water (băk′wô″tẽr), *n.* **1** water held back by a dam or weir; water thrown back, as by the paddles of a steamer; **2**, an inlet from the sea, parallel with the coast and without current.

back-woods (băk′wo͝odz′), *n.pl.* forests or partly cleared land on the outskirts of a newly settled country; hence, any thinly settled district far from any town or city.—*n.* **back″woods′man.**

ba-con (bā′kn), *n.* the salted and dried or smoked flesh of the hog, esp. that from the back and sides.

bac-te-ri-a (băk-tē′rĭ-ȧ), *n. pl.* [*sing.* **bacterium** (-rĭ-ŭm)], a widely distributed group of microscopic, one-celled vegetable organisms, living on organic matter, dead or alive, and causing in their many forms a great variety of processes and conditions affecting animal and vegetable life, as decay, fermentation, soil enrichment, and, in some cases, disease.—*adj.* **bac-te′ri-al.**

bac-te-ri-ol-o-gy (băk-tē″rĭ-ŏl′ō-jĭ), *n.* the scientific study of bacteria, microbes, or disease germs.—*adj.* **bac-te″ri-o-log′i-cal.**—*n.* **bac-te″ri-ol′o-gist.**

bac-te-ri-um (băk-tē′rĭ-ŭm), *n.* **1**, singular of *bacteria*, which see; **2**, any of a large genus (*Bacterium*) of rod-shaped bacteria, including both harmless and disease-producing species.

Bac-tri-an (băk′trĭ-ăn), *adj.* pertaining to Bactria, an ancient province in Asia:—*n.* a native of Bactria.

bad (băd), *adj.* [*comp.* worse (wûrs), *superl.* worst (wûrst)], **1**, evil; morally wicked; vicious; **2**, corrupting; hurtful; **3**, offensive; **4**, defective; legally worthless, as a coin; **5**, severe; as, a *bad* cold; **6**, unfortunate; as, *bad* news; **7**, ill; sick: **in bad form**, not in good taste:—*n.* that which is wrong, corrupting, or the like.—*adv.* **bad′ly.**—*n.* **bad′ness.**

Syn., adj. evil, wicked, naughty. *Bad* is the opposite of *good*, and often implies merely the unsatisfactory nature, poor quality, or defective condition of the thing described; as, a *bad* orange; *bad* manners. When not so used, *bad* means harmful or injurious; as, a *bad* accident. *Evil* usually describes that which is morally bad; as, *evil* thoughts. *Wicked* implies not only evil principles but evil practices: as, *wicked* actions. *Naughty* means disobedient; as, a *naughty* child.—*Ant., adj.* good, beneficent, moral, right.

bade (băd), past tense of the irregular verb *bid* in senses other than offer (a price).

badge (băj), *n.* **1**, a distinctive mark, sign or token to denote the occupation, association, or achievements of the person by whom it is worn; **2**, the mark or token of anything:—*v.t.* [*p.t.* and *p.p.* badged (băjd), *p.pr.* badg′ing], to decorate with a badge.

1**badg-er** (băj′ẽr), *n.* a hairy, flesh-eating, burrowing mammal:—*v.t.* to tease, as the badger in the sport of badger baiting; hence, to annoy; pester; worry.

2**badg-er** (băj′ẽr), *n. Dial.*, a peddler:—*v.t.* to beat down; cheat.

***ba-di-nage** (bȧ″dē″nȧzh′; băd′ĭ-nāj), [Fr.], *n.* light or playful jesting or banter; good-humored pleasantry:—*v.t.* [*p.t.* and *p.p.* -naged′ (-näzhd′; -nājd), *p.pr.* -nag′ing], to tease playfully; banter.

baf-fle (băf'l), *v.t.* [*p.t.* and *p.p.* -fled (-ld), *p.pr.* -fling], **1**, to bring to nothing the efforts of, by placing difficulties in the way; hence, to hinder, foil, or check; **2**, to turn from a straight course, as ships by variable winds:—*n.* any of various devices for deflecting or checking heated gases or liquids: also called *baffle plate* (see *gas engine*, illus.).—*n.* **baf'fle-ment.**—*n.* **baf'fler.**

Syn. balk, frustrate, counteract, checkmate.

baff-y (băf'ĭ), *n.* [*pl.* baffies (-ĭz)], in golf, a wooden club used to play upward, or lofting, shots.

bag (băg), *n.* **1**, a sack; pouch; wallet; **2**, the amount contained in a bag, as of grain; **3**, a sac or receptacle in animal bodies, containing a fluid or other substance, as the bee's honey bag or the cow's udder; **4**, all the game secured by a sportsman in a day:—*v.t.* [*p.t.* and *p.p.* bagged (băgd), *p.pr.* bag'ging], **1**, to inclose in a bag; **2**, to secure or capture, as game:—*v.i.* to bulge; hang down like a full or loose bag.

bag-a-telle (băg″ȧ-tĕl'), *n.* **1**, a trifle; **2**, a game played with a billiard cue and nine balls on an oblong board containing nine holes; **3**, a short, light piece of music for the piano.

bag-gage (băg'āj), *n.* **1**, the tents, clothing, utensils, etc., of an army; **2**, the trunks, packages, etc., which a traveler takes with him; luggage; **3**, a worthless woman; **4**, *Colloq.*, a playful, saucy young woman; a flirt.

bag-ging (băg'ĭng), *n.* coarse cloth or other material used for bags.

bag-gy (băg'ĭ), *adj.* [*comp.* bag'gi-er, *superl.* bag'gi-est], loose or flabby in appearance; swelled, loose, or puffed out like a bag.

bag-pipe (băg'pīp″), *n.*, usually in *pl.*, a shrill-toned Scottish musical instrument consisting of a leathern windbag from which air is forced by the performer's arm into pipes, one pipe, called the *chanter*, giving the melody.—*n.* **bag'pip″er.**

baht (bät), *n.* the monetary unit of Siam, equivalent to about 44 cents.

¹bail (bāl), *v.t.* in law: **1**, to deliver, as personal property, to be returned at a specific time or after a specific purpose has been accomplished; **2**, to deliver, as a defendant or prisoner, to persons who become security for his appearance when summoned; **3**, to procure security for the appearance of, as a prisoner or defendant when summoned:—*n.* in law: **1**, temporary freedom given a defendant or prisoner when security is entered for his appearance when summoned; **2**, security so given; **3**, the person giving such security.—*adj.* **¹bail'a-ble.**

²bail (bāl), *v.t.* **1**, to empty of water by dipping, as a boat; **2**, to dip out, as water, with a pail or other vessel:—*n.* the pail or scoop used in dipping water out of a boat. Also, **²bale.**—*adj.* **²bail'a-ble.**—*n.* **bail'er.**

³bail (bāl), *n.* **1**, a bar, hung in a stable without stalls, to keep the animals apart; **2**, in cricket, either of two wooden crosspieces placed end to end on the wickets.

⁴bail (bāl), *n.* **1**, a semicircular support, as for a wagon cover; **2**, the handle of a pail, kettle, or the like.

bail-ie (bāl'ĭ), *n.* in Scotland, a city officer somewhat resembling an alderman.

bail-iff (bāl'ĭf), *n.* **1**, a sheriff's officer or constable; **2**, in England, an overseer or under steward on an estate.

bail-i-wick (bāl'ĭ-wĭk), *n.* the district within which a sheriff or bailiff has legal power.

bail-ment (bāl'mĕnt), *n.* a delivery of goods or money in trust to another, esp. as surety for a prisoner or for an accused person.

bairn (bârn), *n.* a child; also, a son or daughter of any age.

¹bait (bāt), *v.t.* **1**, to harass or provoke, as an animal, by the setting on of dogs, etc., for sport; set upon; hence, to torment; annoy persistently; **2**, to prepare, as a hook, trap, or snare, by covering with food; **3**, *Obs.*, to give food or drink to upon a journey; feed (an animal); as, to *bait* horses:—*v.i.* *Obs.*, to take food or drink upon a journey; hence, to stop for rest.—*n.* **bait'er.**

²bait (bāt), *n.* **1**, any substance used to entice or allure fish or other animals with a view to catching them; **2**, temptation; **3**, refreshment taken on a journey.

baize (bāz), *n.* a coarse woolen stuff, with a long nap, used for table covers.

bake (bāk), *v.t.* [*p.t.* and *p.p* baked (bākt), *p.pr.* bak'ing], **1**, to cook or prepare, as food, in an oven; **2**, to dry and harden by dry heat, as bricks:—*v.i.* **1**, to prepare and cook food in an oven; also, to be cooked in an oven, as food; **2**, to become hard by heat.

bak-er (bāk'ẽr), *n.* one whose business it is to make bread, biscuits, cakes, etc.: **baker's dozen**, thirteen.

bak-er-y (bāk'ẽr-ĭ), *n.* [*pl.* bakeries (-ĭz)], a place where bread, cakes, pies, etc., are made or sold.

bak-ing (bāk'ĭng), *n.* the quantity of bread, pies, and the like, made at one time; a batch: **baking powder**, a white powder containing bicarbonate of soda and an acid or acid salt: used to raise biscuits, cakes, and the like.

bak-sheesh (băk'shēsh), *n.* in the Orient, a gratuity; a tip. Also, **back'sheesh; back'shish; bak'shish.**

Ba-laam (bā'lȧm), *n.* in the Bible, a prophet who was chided by his ass (Numbers 22 : 28).

bal-ance (băl'āns), *n.* **1**, an apparatus for weighing, consisting in its simplest form of a beam pivoted near its middle, with hooks, platforms, or pans at the ends; **2**, equal poise of the two sides of a scale; hence, equal poise of any opposing forces; equilibrium or steadiness; **3**, mental poise; steadiness of mind; sanity; **4**, an equality between the totals of two sides of an account; also, the excess shown on either side; the sum or weight necessary to make two unequal sums or weights equal; **5**, in a watch, the wheel which regulates the rate of running; the balance wheel: **Balance, 1**, the constellation Libra; **2**, the seventh sign of the zodiac (see *zodiac*, illus.):—*v.t.* [*p.t.* and *p.p.* -anced (-ănst), *p.pr.* -anc-ing], **1**, to weigh by means of a balance; **2**, to weigh by means of the mind; hence, to compare or estimate; **3**, to set off, as one thing against another; **4**, to find out the difference between the debits and credits of, or to bring about an equality between; as, to *balance* an account; **5**, to cause to be steady or in equilibrium: **balanced surface**, a steering or control surface, as a rudder or elevator on an airplane, part of which extends ahead of the pivot or hinge (see *airplane, empennage*, illus.):—*v.i.* **1**, to be of equal weight, force, or amount; **2**, to keep one's poise or equilibrium.—*n.* **bal'anc-er.**

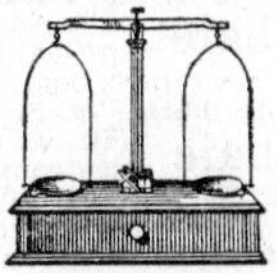

BALANCE (def. 1)

Syn., *n.* counterpoise. (See remainder.)

bal-ance of pow-er **1**, such a division of power among certain nations as guarantees the independence of each; **2**, the power of a small party which can join with either of two larger ones and so determine which shall win.

bal-ance of trade the difference between the actual value in money of the imports and exports of a country during a given period.

bal-ance sheet a statement made to show the condition of a business, by listing its capital or assets, its liabilities or debts, and its profit or loss.

bal-ance wheel a wheel, as in a watch, to regulate motion.

bal-bo-a (bäl-bō'ä), [Span.], *n.* the monetary unit of Panama, equal to $1.00.

bal-brig-gan (băl-brĭg'ăn), *n.* a knitted cotton fabric for underwear.

bal-co-ny (băl'kō-nĭ), *n.* [*pl.* balconies (-nĭz)], **1**, a platform or gallery built out from the wall of a building, and inclosed by a railing; **2**, in a theater, a gallery of seats above the main floor.

bald (bôld), *adj.* **1**, destitute of hair; **2**, without the usual covering of feathers, fur, hair, foliage, etc., on the head, summit, or top; **3**, unadorned; bare; **4**, without disguise; as, a *bald* statement; **5**, as applied to birds, having a white spot or patch on the head; as, the *bald* eagle.—*adv.* **bald'ly.**—*n.* **bald'ness.**

Bal-der (bôl'dẽr), *n.* in Norse mythology, the sun god, son of Odin and Frigg, worshiped as the god of peace, brightness, goodness, and wisdom, and killed through Loki's malice. Also, **Bal'dr.**

bal-der-dash (bôl'dẽr-dăsh), *n.* nonsense; a foolish jumble of words; silly talk or writing; bombast; jargon.

bal-dric (bôl'drĭk), *n.* a broad belt, often richly decorated, worn around the waist, or over one shoulder and across the breast, usually to support a bugle or sword.

1**bale** (bāl), *n.* a large, closely pressed, bound package of merchandise, prepared for storage or transportation:—*v.t.* [*p.t.* and *p.p.* baled (bāld), *p.pr.* bal'ing], to make or pack into bales.

2**bale** (bāl), *v.t.* [*p.t.* and *p.p.* baled (bāld), *p.pr.* bal'ing], **1**, to empty of water, as a container, boat, etc.; **2**, to dip out, as water. See 2**bail**, *Pfd. S.*—*n.* **bal'er.**

3**bale** (bāl), *n.* in poetry, evil or ruin; a disastrous influence; woe.

bale-ful (bāl'fōōl), *adj.* **1**, full of deadly intent; direful; woeful; destructive; **2**, wretched; miserable.—*adv.* **bale'ful-ly.**—*n.* **bale'ful-ness.**

balk (bôk), *n.* **1**, a strip or ridge of land left unplowed; **2**, a thick, heavy piece of timber; **3**, a barrier or check; disappointment:—*v.t.* to hinder; thwart; check or disappoint:—*v.i.* **1**, to stop short; **2**, to swerve.—*adj.* **balk'y.**—*n.* **balk'i-ness.**

1**ball** (bôl), *n.* **1**, a round or roundish body or mass; a sphere; esp., such a body, solid or inflated, used in playing a game; **2**, a bullet or other missile shot from firearms; **3**, the globe or earth; also, any celestial body; **4**, a game played with a ball, which is kicked, pitched, or knocked; esp., in America, baseball; **5**, in baseball, a pitched ball, not struck at, which does not pass over the home plate between the levels of the batsman's shoulders and knees:—*v.t.* to make into a round mass:—*v.i.* to form or gather into a round mass.

2**ball** (bôl), *n.* a large, formal social gathering for dancing.

bal-lad (băl'ăd), *n.* **1**, a short, popular, narrative poem, adapted or suitable for reciting or singing; **2**, a simple song, often sentimental.—*n.* **bal'lad-ry.**

bal-last (băl'ȧst), *n.* **1**, heavy material carried by a ship to balance or steady it; **2**, sand carried in the car of a balloon to steady it; **3**, gravel filling the space between the sleepers or ties of a railway; **4**, that which gives strength to the character:—*v.t.* **1**, to place heavy material in or on in order to steady or balance; **2**, to strengthen or give steadiness to; **3**, to fill in, as the bed of a railroad, with gravel and stone.

ball bear-ing a method of reducing friction by causing a shaft to rest upon or be surrounded by loose balls of metal partly contained in sockets and turning with the shaft.—*adj.* **ball'-bear'ing.**

bal-let (băl'ā"; *Rare,* băl'ĕt), *n.* **1**, an artistic dance; **2**, a complete pantomime or play in which a story is told, and actions, characters, and passions are shown by gestures, accompanied by music and dancing; **3**, the company of persons who perform the dance or the play.

bal-lis-tics (bă-lĭs'tĭks), *n. pl.* used as *sing.* that branch of gunnery which deals with the science of the motion and impact of projectiles.

bal-lo-net (băl"ō-nĕt'), *n.* a small compartment inside a balloon, for controlling the ascent or descent and for preventing the outer envelope from collapsing.

bal-loon (bă-lōōn'), *n.* **1**, a large bag of prepared silk or other material, which, when filled with a lighter-than-air gas, such as hydrogen, ascends and floats in the air; **2**, a large, inflated ball: **fire balloon,** a balloon made buoyant by inflation with hot air, heated by a fire beneath: **balloon tire,** a low-pressure automobile tire of large diameter:—*v.i.* **1**, to go up in a balloon; **2**, to expand or swell out.—*n.* **bal-loon'ist.**

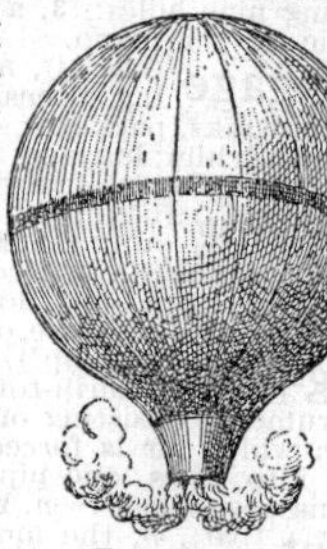

FIRE BALLOON

bal-lot (băl'ŭt), *n.* **1**, orig., a little ball used for secret voting; **2**, a ball, ticket, or paper by which a secret vote is registered or taken; **3**, the system of secret voting by the use of a printed form; **4**, election by secret vote; also, the total number of votes cast or recorded:—*v.t.* and *v.i.* to vote or choose by using a printed form or ticket.

ball-room (bôl'rōōm"), *n.* a large room or hall intended for dancing.

bal-ly-hoo (băl'ĭ-hōō), *n.* **1**, noisy talk before a cheap show, to attract patrons; **2**, extravagant commendation.

balm (bäm), *n.* **1**, an oily, gummy substance coming from certain trees or shrubs, used for healing or soothing; balsam; **2**, anything that heals or soothes pain; **3**, a healing ointment; **4**, any of several aromatic plants of the mint family: **balm of Gilead,** (gĭl'ē-ăd), **1**, any of various kinds of fragrant resin, as that of the evergreen tree of Arabia; also, the tree itself; **2**, the balsam fir.

Bal-mor-al (băl-mŏr'ăl), *n.* **1**, a durable, striped woolen stuff; **2**, a laced walking shoe; **3**, a flat Scotch cap.

balm-y (bäm'ĭ), *adj.* [*comp.* balm'i-er, *superl.* balm'i-est], soft, mild, or soothing, as air.—*adv.* **balm'i-ly.**—*n.* **balm'i-ness.**

bal-sa (băl'sȧ; bôl'-), *n.* a raft made of two hollow cylinders: **balsa wood,** a kind of very light wood from South America.

bal-sam (bôl'săm), *n.* **1**, an oily, fragrant substance obtained from certain trees or shrubs, and used for medicine or in perfumery; balm; **2**, any of several trees, shrubs, or plants, as the balsam fir, yielding an oily, resinous substance; **3**, anything soothing or healing.—*adj.* **bal-sam'ic.**

bal-us-ter (băl′ŭs-tẽr), *n.* one of a set of small pillars that support the handrail, as of a parapet or balustrade.

bal-us-trade (băl″ŭs-trād′), *n.* a row of small pillars, or balusters, topped by a protective rail.

BALUSTRADE

***bam-bi-no** (băm-bē′nō) [It.], *n.* [*pl.* bambini (-nē)], **1,** a child or baby; **2,** a figure of the infant Christ wrapped in swaddling clothes.

bam-boo (băm-bōō′), *n.* any of certain tropical grasses having hard, thick-jointed stems, used for furniture, poles, canes, etc.

1**ban** (băn), *n.* **1,** a public announcement or edict; **2,** in feudal times, a military summons to the king's vassals; **3,** a decree of excommunication by the church; **4,** an authoritative prohibition; **5,** condemnation, as by public opinion; **6,** in *pl.* (usually, *banns*), publication of an intended marriage.

2**ban** (băn), *v.t.* [*p.t.* and *p.p.* banned (bănd), *p.pr.* ban′ning], **1,** to curse; call evil down upon; **2,** to forbid; prohibit.

ban-al (băn′ăl; bā′năl), *adj.* commonplace; trivial; hackneyed; trite.

ba-nal-i-ty (bȧ-năl′ĭ-tĭ), *n.* [*pl.* banalities (-tĭz)], a commonplace and trivial remark, idea, etc.

ba-na-na (bȧ-nä′nȧ; bȧ-năn′ȧ), *n.* **1,** a tropical, treelike plant, growing about 20 feet high, which bears a fruit used as food; **2,** the fruit of the plant.

1**band** (bănd), *n.* **1,** that which ties together; that which holds in place; a bond; **2,** a restraining or uniting influence; **3,** a thin, flat, flexible strip used for binding or supporting; a strip of trimming or lining, as of a hat: **band saw,** a saw in the form of an endless belt running on pulleys:—*v.t.* to tie or mark with a band.

2**band** (bănd), *n.* **1,** a company, as of soldiers, united by a common purpose; **2,** a company of musicians, esp. one playing on instruments that are particularly suited to music out of doors:—*v.t.* to unite into a troop, confederacy, etc.:—*v.i.* to unite; confederate: often with *together*.

band-age (băn′dāj), *n.* **1,** a strip of cotton or other material used in dressing and binding up wounds, sprains, etc.; **2,** a band:—*v.t.* [*p.t.* and *p.p.* -aged (-dājd), *p.pr.* -ag-ing], to dress, cover, or bind, as wounds, with a strip of any soft material.

ban-dan-na (băn-dăn′ȧ), *n.* a large, bright-colored, silk or cotton handkerchief, having a red or blue background with yellow or white dots or figures upon it. Also, **ban-dan′a.**

band-box (bănd′bŏks″), *n.* a light pasteboard box for holding hats.

ban-deau (băn-dō′; băn′dō), *n.* [*pl.* bandeaux (-dōz′)], a narrow band or fillet, as of ribbon, worn above the forehead or around the hair.

ban-de-role (băn′dē-rōl), *n.* a little flag or streamer; a small flag carried as a pennant at the head of a lance or mast. Also, **ban′de-rol.**

ban-dit (băn′dĭt), *n.* [*pl.* bandits (-dĭts); banditti (-dĭt′ĭ)], an outlaw; brigand; robber; highwayman.

ban-do-leer (băn″dō-lēr′), *n.* a broad leather belt, worn over the shoulder, with loops for holding cartridges. Also, **ban″do-lier′.**

1**ban-dy** (băn′dĭ), *v.t.* [*p.t.* and *p.p.* -died (-dĭd), *p.pr.* -dy-ing], **1,** to knock or toss to and fro, as a ball; **2,** to give and take; exchange; as, to *bandy* words:—*v.i.* to give and take; contend.

2**ban-dy** (băn′dĭ), *n.* [*pl.* bandies (-dĭz)], **1,** hockey; **2,** a hockey stick.

3**ban-dy** (băn′dĭ), *adj.* bent or bowed outward, as at the knees.

bane (bān), *n.* a cause of ruin or destruction; woe; as, war is the *bane* of society.—*adj.* **bane′ful.**—*adv.* **bane′ful-ly.**

Syn. ruin, injury, destruction, pest.

1**bang** (băng), *v.t.* **1,** to beat, as with a club or cudgel; thump; **2,** to produce a loud sound by or from; as, to *bang* the door:—*v.i.* **1,** to make a loud noise; **2,** to thump violently:—*n.* **1,** a heavy blow; whack; **2,** a loud, sudden noise; explosive sound:—*adv.* **1,** all at once; abruptly; explosively; **2,** with a violent blow.

2**bang** (băng), *v.t.* to cut straight across, as the hair over the forehead:—*n.*, usually in *pl.*, a short fringe of hair cut straight across over the forehead.

ban-gle (băng′gl), *n.* **1,** an ornamental ring worn upon the wrists and ankles in India and Africa; **2,** one of several slender bracelets worn together.

ban-ian (băn′yăn), an East Indian tree, the branches of which form roots that become trunks. See **ban′yan,** *Pfd. S.*

ban-ish (băn′ĭsh), *v.t.* **1,** to condemn to exile; expel from the country as a punishment; drive away; **2,** to dispel from the mind.—*n.* **ban′ish-er.**

Syn. exile, expel. These words agree in the idea of putting out, either by civil authority or by other compulsion. To be *banished* is to be put out of a country, not necessarily one's own. To be *exiled* is to be driven out of one's own country, either for a definite time or forever. To be *expelled* is to be cast out by force or dismissed by compulsion; as, an undesirable alien may be *expelled* from a country, or a rowdy from a club.

ban-ish-ment (băn′ĭsh-mĕnt), *n.* **1,** the act of expelling; **2,** the state of being expelled; expulsion; **3,** exile.

ban-is-ter (băn′ĭs-tẽr), *n.* **1,** a baluster; **2,** in *pl.*, a balustrade.

ban-jo (băn′jō), *n.* [*pl.* banjos (-jōz)], a stringed musical instrument somewhat like a guitar, having a long neck, and a body like a tambourine.—*n.* **ban′jo-ist.**

1**bank** (băngk), *n.* **1,** a heap, mound, or ridge of earth; **2,** a steep slope; **3,** the land at the edge or margin of a river or watercourse; **4,** an elevation or rising ground beneath the sea or at the mouth of a river; a shoal; as, the *Banks* of Newfoundland; **5,** a moundlike formation, as of snow, massed clouds, etc.:—*v.t.* **1,** to defend or fortify with a bank; **2,** to pile or heap up; **3,** to cover (a fire) with ashes or packed coal, to prevent rapid burning; **4,** to incline (an airplane) laterally, as in turning to left or right: **right bank,** to turn (an airplane) to the right, with the right wing down.

2**bank** (băngk), *n.* **1,** a rowers' bench or a row of oars, as in a medieval galley; **2,** a row or rank, esp. of organ keys.

3**bank** (băngk), *n.* **1,** an institution which deals in money and credit, where money may be deposited for safe-keeping; **2,** the office of a banking company; **3,** in gambling, the fund of the dealer; **4,** a reserve, as in dominoes, from which players may draw; a pool:—*v.t.* to place (money) in a bank:—*v.i.* **1,** to have an account with a bank; **2,** to conduct a banking business; **3,** in gambling, to hold the funds; **4,** *Colloq.*, to rely; with *on.*

bank bill **1,** a note issued by a bank, payable on demand, and current as money; **2,** a draft or bill of exchange of a bank, payable on demand.

bank book a depositor's pass book in which charges and deposits on his account are recorded.

bank cred-it the amount a person, on giving proper security, is allowed to draw upon a bank.

bank dis-count simple interest, at a given rate, on the principal of a note or bill of exchange, deducted on the day of discount.

bank-er (băngk'ẽr), *n.* **1**, a person or corporation engaged in lending, exchanging, issuing, or caring for money; **2**, in gambling, the keeper of the funds.

bank-ing (băngk'ĭng), *n.* the business of lending, exchanging, issuing, or caring for money.

bank note a promissory note issued by a legally authorized bank, payable on demand, and current as money.

bank-rupt (băngk'rŭpt), *n.* a person legally declared to be unable to pay his debts:—*adj.* unable to meet one's obligations; insolvent:—*v.t.* **1**, to exhaust the financial credit of; **2**, to impoverish; as, to *bankrupt* a corporation.

bank-rupt-cy (băngk'rŭpt-sĭ), *n.* [*pl.* bankruptcies (-sĭz)], **1**, the state of being legally insolvent, or unable to pay all debts; **2**, failure in business; **3**, hence, utter lack, as of pride or hope.

ban-ner (băn'ẽr), *n.* a piece of cloth or silk attached to a pole or staff, and usually worked with some device or motto; an ensign, standard, or flag, as of a state or order:—*adj.* leading; foremost; also, unusually good; as, a *banner* year.

ban-nock (băn'ŭk), *n.* a thick cake made of meal, baked on a hot stone or griddle.

banns (bănz), *n.pl.* notice, in church, of a proposed marriage. Also, **bans.**

ban-quet (băng'kwĕt), *n.* an elaborate or costly feast or sumptuous entertainment:—*v.t.* and *v.i.* to feast.

ban-quette (băng-kĕt'), *n.* a level bank or platform behind a parapet or earthwork, for soldiers to fire from (see *rampart, terreplein*, illus.).

ban-shee (băn'shē), *n.* in Ireland and some parts of Scotland, a spirit whose wailing was believed to foretell death. Also, **ban'shie.**

ban-tam (băn'tăm), *n.* a domestic fowl of any of numerous small breeds.

ban-ter (băn'tẽr), *n.* good-natured pleasantry or teasing:—*v.t.* to attack in jest; make fun of with good humor.—*adv.* **ban'ter-ing-ly.**

Syn., *n.* chaff, mockery, ridicule, jeering, derision, raillery.

bant-ling (bănt'lĭng), *n.* a young child; a brat.

ban-yan (băn'yăn), *n.* an East Indian tree, the branches of which send out aërial roots that grow down to the ground and form new trunks. Also, **ban'ian.**

ban-za-i (bän'zä'ē), *interj.* in Japan, hurrah! live forever! a battle cry and salutation to the emperor.

ba-o-bab (bā'ō-băb; bä'ō-), *n.* an African tree with a very thick trunk and an edible fruit called *monkey bread.*

bap-tism (băp'tĭzm), *n.* **1**, the sacrament of immersion or sprinkling with water, symbolizing the washing away of sin, and admitting to membership in some Christian churches; **2**, an experience or trial that purifies or tests; as, a *baptism* of fire.—*adj.* **bap-tis'mal.**—*adv.* **bap-tis'mal-ly.**

Bap-tist (băp'tĭst), *n.* **1**, orig., one who administered baptism; as, John the *Baptist;* **2**, one of that church which believes that Christians should receive baptism only as adults, after publicly declaring their faith, and by complete immersion rather than by sprinkling.—*abbr.* **Bapt.**

Baobab

bap-tis-ter-y (băp'tĭs-tẽr-ĭ), *n.* [*pl.* baptisteries (-ĭz)], a building or part of a church in which baptism is performed. Also, **bap'tis-try.**

bap-tize (băp-tīz'), *v.t.* [*p.t.* and *p.p.* -tized' (-tīzd'), *p.pr.* -tiz'ing], **1**, to sprinkle or pour water on, or immerse in water, as a religious ceremony, esp. in admitting to a Christian church; **2**, to purify; **3**, to christen; name.—*n.* **bap-tiz'er.**

[1]**bar** (bär), *n.* **1**, a rigid piece of wood, metal, or other solid matter, long in proportion to its thickness; **2**, a quantity contained in such a shape; as, a *bar* of chocolate; **3**, a rail; a barrier; anything which impedes or obstructs; **4**, a bank of sand, gravel, or the like, obstructing navigation; **5**, the place in court where prisoners are stationed for trial or sentence; **6**, the body of persons authorized to appear in court to try cases; lawyers as a class; **7**, any tribunal, as that of public opinion; **8**, a counter where liquor is sold as a beverage, or a room containing such a counter; **9**, a band or stripe; **10**, in music, one of the upright lines drawn through the staff of a piece of music, dividing it into equal measures of time:—*prep.* but; except: mainly in the expression *bar none:*—*v.t.* [*p.t.* and *p.p.* barred (bärd), *p.pr.* bar'ring], **1**, to fasten with a bar; **2**, to hinder; obstruct; prevent; as, the police *barred* the way.

[2]**bar** (bär), *n.* in physics, a unit of pressure, equivalent to one dyne per square centimeter.

[1]**barb** (bärb), *n.* the sharp point extending backward in an arrow, fishhook, etc.; hence, any similar sharp projection:—*v.t.* to furnish with barbs.

[2]**barb** (bärb), *n.* a horse of a swift and hardy breed, originally brought by the Moors from Africa to Spain.

bar-ba-ri-an (bär-bā'rĭ-ăn), *n.* **1**, in history, a foreigner, usually in a belittling sense; **2**, a man in a rude state, but above that of the savage; **3**, an uncultivated person:—*adj.* rude; uncivilized; savage.—*n.* **bar-ba'-ri-an-ism.**

bar-bar-ic (bär-băr'ĭk), *adj.* **1**, relating to, or like, uncivilized people; **2**, roughly gorgeous; as, *barbaric* splendor.

bar-ba-rism (bär'bȧ-rĭzm), *n.* **1**, a word or expression not in good usage; **2**, an uncivilized state; rudeness; ignorance of art and literature.

bar-bar-i-ty (bär-băr'ĭ-tĭ), *n.* [*pl.* barbarities (-tĭz)], **1**, brutal or inhuman conduct, as, the *barbarities* of war; **2,** in art, a violation of good taste.

bar-ba-rize (bär′bȧ-rīz), *v.t.* and *v.i.* [*p.t.* and *p.p* -rized (-rīzd), *p.pr.* -riz″ing], to make or become rude or uncivilized.—*n.* **bar″ba-ri-za′tion.**

bar-ba-rous (bär′bȧ-rŭs), *adj.* **1,** pertaining to, or like, an uncivilized person; outlandish; rude; **2,** cruel; inhuman; **3,** of language, illiterate; harsh in sound; **4,** foreign in nationality, speech, or customs.—*adv.* **bar′ba-rous-ly.**

Syn. brutal, savage, merciless.

bar-be-cue (bär′bē-kū), *n.* **1,** the carcass of an ox, pig, etc., roasted whole; **2,** an out-of-door feast at which animals are roasted whole:—*v.t.* [*p.t.* and *p.p.* -cued (-kūd), *p.pr.* -cu″ing], to dress and roast whole, as an ox.

barbed (bärbd), *p.adj.* having a sharp point turned back: **barbed wire,** twisted wire with sharp, thornlike projections.

bar-bel (bär′bĕl), *n.* **1,** one of the threadlike, soft processes hanging from the jaws or nostrils of certain fishes; **2,** a large fresh-water fish having such appendages.

bar-ber (bär′bẽr), *n.* one whose business is shaving, or cutting and dressing the hair:—*v.t.* to shave, or trim the hair of.

bar-ber-ry (bär′bĕr-ĭ), *n.* [*pl.* barberries (-ĭz)], **1,** any of several prickly shrubs bearing berries which turn red in the fall; **2,** the fruit of such shrubs.

bar-bette (bär-bĕt′), *n.* **1,** a platform from which to fire cannon over a parapet; **2,** on a battleship, an armored structure protecting the bases of guns or turrets.

bar-bi-can (bär′bĭ-kăn), *n.* a tower or other outpost which defends the entrance to a castle or city.

bar-ca-role (bär′kȧ-rōl), *n.* a simple, popular song sung by Venetian gondoliers. Also, **bar′ca-rolle.**

bard (bärd), *n.* **1,** in ancient times, a poet and singer; **2,** any poet.

[1]**bare** (bâr), *adj.* **1,** uncovered; naked; **2,** hav.ng the head uncovered; **3,** unconcealed; **4,** unadorned; **5,** unfurnished; **6,** threadbare; **7,** simple; scanty; mere; as, the criminal received *bare* justice:—*v.t.* [*p.t.* and *p.p.* bared (bârd), *p.pr.* bar′ing], to uncover; expose; reveal.—*n.* **bare′ness.**

[2]**bare** (bâr), archaic past tense of the irregular verb [2]*bear.*

bare-back (bâr′băk″), *adj.* and *adv.* seated on a horse which wears no saddle or other back-covering; as, a *bareback* rider; to ride *bareback.*—*adj.* **bare′backed″.**

bare-faced (bâr′fāst″), *adj.* **1,** without concealment; not disguised; **2,** shameless; impudent.—*adv.* **bare′faced″ly.**

bare-ly (bâr′lĭ), *adv.* **1,** scarcely; hardly; **2,** nakedly; **3,** openly; **4,** merely.

bar-gain (bär′gĕn; -gĭn), *n.* **1,** an agreement on the terms of a transaction; **2,** the terms agreed upon; **3,** that which is offered at a low price; also, the result of buying under these terms:—*v.i.* to make an agreement; haggle:—*v.t.* to hand over for a consideration; trade.—*n.* **bar′gain-er.**

Syn., n. (see contract).

barge (bärj), *n.* **1,** a large, flat-bottomed vessel, used in loading and unloading ships, and for carrying freight on rivers and canals; **2,** a pleasure boat; **3,** a large double-banked boat of a warship, used by a flag officer:—*v.i.* [*p.t.* and *p.p.* barged (bärjd), *p.pr.* barg′ing], *Colloq.*, to move ponderously.—*n.* **barge′man.**

barge-board (bärj′bōrd″), *n.* a board close under an overhanging roof of a gable end, placed so as to conceal the rafters (see *frame house*, illus.).

bar-i-tone (băr′ĭ-tōn), *n.* **1,** a male voice between tenor and bass; **2,** a person having such a voice:—*adj.* having a range of voice between tenor and bass. Also, **bar′y-tone,** *Pfd. S.*

ba-ri-um (bā′rĭ-ŭm; bâr′ĭ-), *n.* a soft, silver-gray, alkaline metallic element, obtained by decomposing its chloride by an electric current: **barium sulphate,** a heavy, white mineral, used in paints.

[1]**bark** (bärk), *n.* the outer covering of the trunk, branches, etc., of trees and other woody plants:—*v.t.* **1,** to remove by stripping; peel; **2,** to scrape the skin from; as, to *bark* the knee.

[2]**bark** (bärk), *n.* the sound made by a dog, or any such sound:—*v.i.* to utter a bark, as a dog.

[3]**bark** (bärk), *n.* **1,** a small three-masted vessel with foremast and mainmast square-rigged and mizzenmast fore-and-aft-rigged (see *ship*, illus.); **2,** *Poetic,* any small ship. Also, **barque.**

bark-en-tine (bär′kĕn-tēn), *n.* a three-masted vessel with foremast square-rigged and mainmast and mizzenmast fore-and-aft-rigged (see *ship*, illus.).

bar-ley (bär′lĭ), *n.* **1,** a grain used as a food and in the manufacture of malt liquors; **2,** the plant which yields the grain.

bar-ley-corn (bär′lĭ-kôrn″), *n.* a grain of barley: **John Barleycorn,** the personification of strong drink.

barm (bärm), *n.* the foam rising upon malt liquors when fermenting, used as leaven; yeast.—*adj.* **barm′y.**

bar-maid (bär′mād″), *n.* in England, a girl or woman who serves food and drink in the liquor roon of an inn.

Bar-me-cide (bär′mē-sīd), *adj.* unreal; sham:—*n.* **1,** a wealthy Persian in the "Arabian Nights," who invited a beggar to a meal, but served him only imaginary food; **2,** hence, a giver of unreal or disappointing benefits.

barn (bärn), *n.* a farm building for keeping produce, implements, or live stock.

Bar-na-bas (bär′nȧ-bȧs), *n.* in the Bible, Paul's companion on his first missionary journey.

bar-na-cle (bär′nȧ-kl), *n.* any of several small sea animals living in white shells and fastening themselves to rocks or the bottom of ships.

barn-storm-er (bärn′stôr″mẽr), *n.* an aviator who flies without fixed schedule, exhibiting, or taking up passengers for a fee.—*v.i.* **barn′storm″.**

barn-yard (bärn′yärd″), *n.* an inclosure about or before a barn.

bar-o-gram (băr′ō-grăm), *n.* the record of variations in air pressure made by a barograph.

bar-o-graph (băr′ō-grȧf), *n.* a self-registering instrument for recording air pressure.

ba-rom-e-ter (bȧ-rŏm′ē-tẽr), *n.* an instrument for measuring air pressure: used to foretell changes of weather, or to measure altitudes.—*adj.* **bar″o-met′ric** (băr″ō-mĕt′rĭk); **bar″o-met′ri-cal.**—*adv.* **bar″o-met′ri-cal-ly.**

bar-on (băr′ŭn), *n.* **1,** in English history, one who held an estate directly from the king; **2,** in Great Britain and other countries, a noble of the lowest rank within the nobility, or the rank itself.—*n.fem.* **bar′on-ess.**

bar-on-age (băr′ŭn-āj), *n.* **1,** formerly, the whole body of British peers; **2,** now, the body of peers of the lowest rank, or the rank itself.

bar-on-et (băr′ŭn-ĕt), *n.* **1,** a degree of honor next below baron and above knight; **2,** a person holding this degree. —*abbr.* **Bart.**—*n.* **bar'on-et-cy.**

bar-on-y (băr'ō-nĭ), *n.* [*pl.* baronies (-nĭz)], the rank or domain of a baron. —*adj.* **ba-ro'ni-al.**

ba-roque (bȧ-rōk'), *adj.* **1,** odd or irregular in shape: used esp. of a kind of pearl; **2,** ornate; rococo: used of architecture.

ba-rouche (bȧ-rōōsh'), *n.* a carriage with a driver's seat, two seats facing each other, and a folding top.

barque (bärk), *n.* a small three-masted vessel. See [3]**bark,** *Pfd. S.*

bar-rack (băr'ȧk), *n.*, usually in *pl.*, a large structure or a row of buildings for lodging soldiers or, temporarily, any company of men, as workmen.

bar-rage (bȧ"räzh'; bär'ĭj), [Fr.], *n.* a volley of missiles of any sort, as a curtain of bursting shells, fired so as to fall in a line in front of advancing troops, in order to protect them from attack.

bar-rel (băr'ĕl), *n.* **1,** a round, bulging cask or vessel, of greater length than breadth, and having flat ends or heads; **2,** the quantity which a barrel should contain; **3,** anything like a barrel in shape; **4,** the heavy, main tube of a gun; **5,** the body of a windlass, about which the cable winds (see *capstan,* illus.). **barrel organ,** a portable musical instrument, usually turned by a crank:—*v.t.* to put or pack in a barrel.

bar-ren (băr'ĕn), *adj.* **1,** unable to bear young; sterile; **2,** not bearing fruit, as a plant; **3,** not producing vegetation; not fertile, as land; **4,** without profit; empty; as, *barren* labor; **5,** dull in mind; stupid:—*n.*, usually in *pl.*, a sandy, wooded tract.—*adv.* **bar'ren-ly.**—*n.* **bar'ren-ness.**

bar-rette (bä-rĕt'; bȧ-rĕt'), *n.* a bar with a clasp for holding a woman's hair in place.

bar-ri-cade (băr"ĭ-kād'), *n.* **1,** a fort made in haste of such materials as are nearest to hand, and serving to obstruct an enemy or shield a besieged party; **2,** any bar or obstruction:—*v.t.* [*p.t.* and *p.p.* -cad'ed, *p.pr.* -cad'ing], to obstruct or stop up; fortify or inclose by a barrier.

bar-ri-er (băr'ĭ-ẽr), *n.* **1,** anything that obstructs progress, approach, or attack; **2,** a fence or wall to shut out trespassers; **3,** a limit or boundary: **barrier reef,** a coral reef skirting a coast.
Syn. bar, hindrance, obstacle, obstruction.

bar-ring (bär'ĭng), *prep.* excepting; leaving out of account; as, *barring* accident, we shall go.

bar-ris-ter (băr'ĭs-tẽr), *n.* in England, a lawyer who practices in the superior courts; an attorney.

bar-room (bär'rōōm"), *n.* a room in which liquor is sold over a counter.

[1]**bar-row** (băr'ō), *n.* a shallow, boxlike container carried by means of bars or with a wheel at one end and shafts at the other, for wheeling or carrying goods.

[2]**bar-row** (băr'ō), *n.* **1,** a mound over a grave; **2,** an animal's burrow.

bar-ter (bär'tẽr), *n.* the trade or exchange of one thing for another, instead of for money:—*v.t.* to give in exchange for something:—*v.i.* to trade by barter.—*n.* **bar'ter-er.**

Bart-lett (bärt'lĕt), *n.* a variety of large, juicy pear: also called *Bartlett pear* (see *fruit,* illus.).

bar-y-tone (băr'ĭ-tōn), *adj.* **1,** a male voice between tenor and bass; **2,** a person with such a voice:—*adj.* having a range between tenor and bass. Also, **bar'i-tone.**

ba-salt (bȧ-sôlt'; băs'ôlt), *n.* any of a group of hard greenish black rocks of volcanic origin. —*adj.* **ba-salt'ic.**

bas-cule (băs'kūl), *n.* an apparatus in which one end balances the other; a counterpoised lever: **bascule bridge,** a counterpoised drawbridge.

[1]**base** (bās), *n.* **1,** the part of a thing on which it rests; **2,** a principal or fundamental ingredient of anything; hence, an essential part; as, this is the *base* of my argument; **3,** the line or point from which an operation starts, as in surveying; **4,** in some games, a station or goal; **5,** in chemistry, that which combines with an acid to form a salt; also, the hydroxide of a positive or metallic element, such as sodium hydroxide; **6,** a secure or fortified location used as a starting point for operations, for storage of supplies, etc.: **base hit,** in baseball, a hit by which the batsman reaches first base without error by an opponent, and without forcing a base runner:—*v.t.* [*p.t.* and *p.p.* based (bāst), *p.pr.* bas'ing], to lay a foundation for; hence, to justify; as, I *base* my plea on their innocence. —*adj.* **base'less.**—*adj.* **bas'al.**
Syn., n. support, basis, foundation, ground.

[2]**base** (bās), *adj.* **1,** worthless; inferior; **2,** alloyed with inferior metal; as, a *base* coin; **3,** ignoble; morally low; **4,** (commonly, *bass*), deep or grave in sound; low-pitched; **5,** *Archaic:* **a,** baseborn; **b,** not high; short.—*adv.* **base'ly.**—*n.* **base'ness.**
Syn. vile, mean, servile, dishonorable, despicable, degraded, contemptible.

base-ball (bās'bôl'), *n.* **1,** a game, popular in the United States, played with bat and ball by nine players on a side; the field has four *bases,* in the shape of a diamond; **2,** the ball used in this game.

base-board (bās'bōrd"), *n.* a wide molding on the lower part of the wall of a room, touching the floor.

base-born (bās'bôrn"), *adj.* **1,** of humble parentage; plebeian; **2,** illegitimate; born out of wedlock.

base line **1,** a measured line used in surveying and triangulation; **2,** in baseball, a line between bases.

base-man (bās'măn), *n.* [*pl.* basemen (-mĕn)], *n.* in baseball, a player stationed at the first, second, or third base. Also, **base man.**

base-ment (bās'mĕnt), *n.* the lowest story of a building, beneath the main floor; sometimes, the ground floor.

bash-ful (băsh'fōōl), *adj.* shy; easily embarrassed.—*adv.* **bash'ful-ly.**—*n.* **bash'ful-ness.**
Syn. timid, retiring, coy. (See shy.)

bas-ic (bās'ĭk), *adj.* **1,** fundamental; as, a *basic* principle; **2,** in chemistry, having the properties of a base; alkaline.—**Basic English,** 850 common English words, which, with inflections and derivations, may serve as the foundation for an international language.—*adv.* **ba'sic-al-ly.**

ba-sil-i-ca (bȧ-sĭl'ĭ-kȧ), *n.* [*pl.* basilicas (-kȧz)], **1,** in ancient Rome, a hall of simple oblong design used as a court or for an assembly; **2,** a church built on such a plan.—*adj.* **ba-sil'i-can.**

bas-i-lisk (băz'ĭ-lĭsk; băs'-), *n.* **1,** in legend, a kind of serpent, lizard, or dragon, whose breath and look were supposed to be fatal; **2,** any of several tropical lizards.

ba-sin (bā'sn), *n.* **1,** a round, wide vessel for holding water or other liquid; **2,** the quantity such a vessel will hold; **3,** a pond, dock, or other reservoir for water; **4,** all the land drained by a river and its tributaries.

ba-sis (bā'sĭs), *n.* [*pl.* bases (-sēz)], **1,** a base or foundation; **2,** the groundwork or first principle, as of an argument or belief; **3,** the chief ingredient, as of a food.

bask (bȧsk), *v.i.* **1**, to lie in warmth; as, to *bask* in the sun; **2**, to be at ease and thriving under kindly influences:—*v.t.* to expose to cheerful heat.

bas-ket (bȧs′kĕt), *n.* **1**, a vessel made of rushes, twigs, reeds, or other flexible material, interwoven; **2**, the amount which such a vessel will hold.—*n.* **bas′ket-work″.**

bas-ket ball 1, a popular game, usually played in a gymnasium, by teams of five on a side, in which the ball must be thrown into elevated goals, or *baskets*, at each end; **2**, a spherical air-filled ball used in the game. Also, *n.* **bas′ket-ball″.**

bas-ket-ry (bȧs′kĕt-rĭ), *n.* the art of making baskets.

Basque (bȧsk), *n.* **1**, one of a people living in the western Pyrenees; **2**, their language:—*adj.* pertaining to the Basques or their language.

basque (bȧsk), *n.* a woman's bodice with a short tunic; also, such a tunic.

bas-re-lief (bä″=rē-lēf′; bȧs″=), *n.* low relief; in sculpture, a form of cutting in which the figures stand out very slightly from the background. Also, **bas″so-re-lie′vo** (bȧs″ō=rē-lē′vō), [*pl.* basso-relievos (=rē-lē′vōz)].

[1]**bass** (bȧs), *n.* any of various edible and game fishes, found in both fresh and salt waters.

[2]**bass** (bȧs), *n.* the American linden or its wood: also called *basswood*.

[3]**bass** (bās), *adj.* deep; low-toned; low in pitch:—*n.* **1**, a deep, solemn tone; **2**, in music: **a**, the lowest part in a musical composition; **b**, the lowest tones of a male voice or of an instrument; **c**, a large, violinlike orchestral instrument; also called *bass viol*, which see: **bass clarinet**, a large deep-toned orchestral instrument of the wood-wind group (see *musical instrument*, illus.): **bass clef**, in music, a sign fixed on the fourth line from the bottom of the bass staff: **bass drum**, the largest of the drums (see *drum, musical instrument*, illus.): **bass staff**, in music, the five parallel lines, with the spaces between, on which the notes of the bass and frequently the tenor parts of a piece of music are written (see *degree*, illus.): **bass tuba**, an orchestral instrument of the trumpet family, the lowest in tone of the brass-wind group (cf. *musical instrument*, illus.): **bass viol**, a large orchestral instrument, similar in shape to the violin, the largest and lowest-toned of the stringed instruments: also called *bass; double bass; contrabass* (see *musical instrument*, illus.).

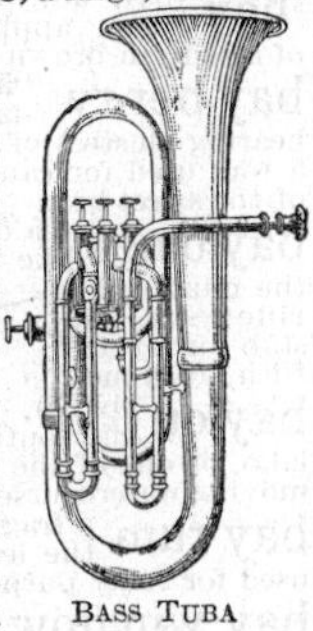
BASS TUBA

bas-si-net (bȧs′ĭ-nĕt), *n.* a wicker basket with a hood at one end, used as a cradle for young children.

bas-soon (bă-sōōn′), *n.* **1**, a wind instrument of deep tones, having a long curved mouthpiece, and a doubled wooden tube (see *musical instrument*, illus.); **2**, an organ stop producing a similar sound.

bass-wood (bȧs′wŏŏd″), *n.* the American linden: also called *bass*.

bast (bȧst), *n.* **1**, the tough, inner fibrous bark of various trees, esp. of the linden; **2**, rope or matting made from this bark.

Bast (bȧst), *n.* an Egyptian goddess representing the life-giving power of the sun (see *idol*, illus.).

bas-tard (băs′tȧrd), *n.* **1**, a child whose parents were not married; **2**, an animal of inferior quality or breed:—*adj.* **1**, begotten and born out of lawful wedlock; **2**, not genuine; false.—*n.* **bas′tar-dy.**

[1]**baste** (bāst), *v.t.* [*p.t.* and *p.p.* bast′ed, *p.pr.* bast′ing], to sew slightly, or fasten in position temporarily with long stitches, as in dressmaking.

[2]**baste** (bāst), *v.t.* [*p.t.* and *p.p.* bast′ed, *p.pr.* bast′ing], to moisten (roasting meat) to prevent burning.

[3]**baste** (bāst), *v.t.* [*p.t.* and *p.p.* bast′ed, *p.pr.* bast′ing], to beat; thrash.

bas-tile (bȧs-tēl′; bȧs′tĭl), *n.* (also, *bastille*), a tower or fortification used for the defense of a fortified place: **Bastille**, an old castle in Paris used as a state prison, destroyed by the people in 1789.

bas-ti-na-do (băs″tĭ-nā′dō), *n.* [*pl.* bastinadoes (-dōz)], an Oriental form of punishment, consisting of beating an offender upon the soles of his feet with a stick or rod:—*v.t.* to beat on the soles of the feet with a stick or cudgel; flog. Also, **bas″ti-nade′.**

bas-tion (băs′chŭn), *n.* an earthwork faced with brick or stone, projecting from the main body of a fort, commanding the outworks and grounds before it.

[1]**bat** (băt), *n.* **1**, a heavy stick or club, esp. one used in cricket, baseball, etc.; also, a racket; **2**, in baseball, cricket, etc., a batsman; batter; **3**, a piece of a brick; **4**, a sheet of cotton or wool; **5**, *Colloq.*, a hard blow; **6**, *Slang*, a care-free good time; a spree:—*v.t.* [*p.t.* and *p.p.* bat′ted, *p.pr.* bat′ting], to hit or strike with, or as with, a bat or club:—*v.i.* **1**, to use a bat in games; **2**, to enjoy an irresponsible good time.

[2]**bat** (băt), *n.* any of an order of insect-eating animals, with soft, furry body, and wings formed by skin stretched between the fingers, legs, and tail, which fly by night.

batch (băch), *n.* **1**, the quantity of bread baked at one time; **2**, a quantity of anything produced at one time; also, a group or collection of similar things.

bate (bāt), *v.t.* and *v.i.* [*p.t.* and *p.p.* bat′ed, *p.pr.* bat′ing], to abate; moderate; as, with *bated* breath.

ba-teau (bȧ-tō′), *n.* [*pl.* bateaux (-tōz′)], a light, flat river boat, used esp. in Canada and Louisiana.

bath (bȧth), *n.* [*pl.* baths (bȧ*th*z)], **1**, the act of washing or covering the body with water, or of exposing it to any other fluid or vapor; **2**, the state of being covered with a fluid, as sweat; **3**, a vessel holding water for bathing; **4**, a building or room fitted up for bathing purposes; **5**, a vessel containing a liquid for treating an object put in it; also, the process of treatment, or the liquid used.

bathe (bā*th*), *v.t.* [*p.t.* and *p.p.* bathed (bā*th*d), *p.pr.* bath′ing], **1**, to put into water or other liquid; **2**, to wash; lave; wet; **3**, to spread over; put into or surround with anything, as vapor or light:—*v.i.* to take a bath.—*n.* **bath′er.**

bath-house (bȧth′hous″), *n.* a house with dressing rooms for bathers.

ba-thos (bā′thŏs), *n.* a ridiculous descent from the lofty to the commonplace in writing or speech; an anticlimax.—*adj.* **ba-thet′ic** (bȧ-thĕt′ĭk).

bath-room (bȧth′rōōm″), *n.* a room containing a tub for bathing and, usually, other toilet facilities.

ba-tiste (bȧ-tēst′), *n.* a fine cotton lawn or muslin.

ba-ton (bă″tôṅ′; băt′ŭn), [Fr.], *n.* **1**, a staff used as a weapon, or as a badge of office; **2**, the stick used by the leader of a chorus or an orchestra for beating time.

bats-man (băts′măn), *n.* [*pl.* batsmen (-mĕn)], in baseball, cricket, etc., the one who wields the bat.

bat-tal-ion (bă-tăl′yŭn), *n.* a body of foot soldiers, usually forming about one third of a regiment.

[1]**bat-ten** (băt′n), *n.* a narrow strip of wood used to nail across two boards, to fasten a piece of canvas to the deck of a ship, or the like; a cleat:—*v.t.* to fasten with such strips; as, *batten* down the hatches.

[2]**bat-ten** (băt′n), *v.t.* and *v.i.* to make or become fat by plenteous living.

[1]**bat-ter** (băt′ẽr), *v.t.* and *v.i.* to strike with heavy, repeated blows, so as to bruise, shatter, or destroy; injure:—*n.* a thick, liquid mixture of several materials, as flour, eggs, etc., beaten together and used in cookery.—*n.* **bat′ter-er.**

Syn., *v.* beat, pound, bruise, demolish.

[2]**bat-ter** (băt′ẽr), *n.* one that hits with a bat or club; specif., a batsman.

bat-ter-ing–ram (băt′ẽr-ĭng=răm″), *n.* a large, iron-headed beam, used in ancient days to beat down the walls of besieged places.

bat-ter-y (băt′ẽr-ĭ), *n.* [*pl.* batteries (-ĭz)], **1**, the act of beating another; as, in law, assault and *battery;* **2**, a number of large guns with their accompaniment of officers, men, and equipment, for field operations; also, the guns of a battleship; **3**, any raised work where guns are mounted and gunners protected; **4**, an apparatus for producing electricity.

bat-ting (băt′ĭng), *n.* **1**, wool or cotton prepared in sheets; **2**, the act of hitting or striking, as in a ball game.

bat-tle (băt′l), *n.* a fight or encounter between opposing forces; a combat; a contest or struggle for mastery:—*v.i.* [*p.t.* and *p.p.* -tled (-ld), *p.pr.* -tling], to contend in a fight; struggle.—*n.* **bat′tle-field″.**

Syn., *n.* conflict, engagement, skirmish, action, fight. A *battle* is a combat between large bodies of organized forces, whether on land or sea. *Conflict* names a long, bitter struggle which includes many battles, or a single sharp encounter between individuals. *Engagement*, another word for *battle*, has less force, though it may indicate an extensive operation. *Skirmish* names a minor act of war, incident to scattered troops; as, the scouting parties met in a *skirmish. Action* may name a minor act of war or a single operation of fighting. *Fight* is a more general word, applying to a serious struggle, a short, fierce combat, or a brawl.

bat-tle–ax (băt′l=ăks″), *n.* a broad-faced ax formerly used as a weapon. Also, **bat′tle–axe″.**

bat-tle-dore (băt′l-dōr), *n.* a kind of light racket used for playing battledore and shuttlecock, a game in which a light ball is tossed back and forth between two players with rackets.

bat-tle-ment (băt′l-mĕnt), *n.*, usually in *pl.*, a wall or parapet with open spaces along the top line, used in ancient times for defense and later for decoration.—*adj.* **bat′tle-ment-ed.**

bat-tle-plane (băt′l-plān″), *n.* an airplane equipped with machine guns, bombs, and the like.

bat-tle-ship (băt′l-shĭp″), *n.* a large, strongly armored ship carrying heavy guns.

bau-ble (bô′bl), *n.* **1**, a trifling piece of finery; anything showy or gay but without real value; as, Christmas trees are trimmed with many pretty *baubles;* **2**, a child's plaything; **3**, formerly, the wand or staff carried by a court jester or king's fool.

Ba-va-ri-an (bȧ-vā′rĭ-ăn), *adj.* of or pertaining to Bavaria, a state in Germany, or the dialect of High German spoken there:—*n.* **1**, a native or citizen of Bavaria; **2**, the Bavarian dialect.

baw-bee (bô-bē′), *n.* **1**, a small Scottish coin about equal in value to a cent; **2**, any small coin.

bawd-y (bôd′ĭ), *adj.* obscene; immoral; indecent; lewd.—*adv.* **bawd′i-ly.** —*n.* **bawd′i-ness.**

bawl (bôl), *v.i.* to cry out with a loud, full, and sustained sound:—*v.t.* to proclaim loudly; shout:—*n.* a loud, prolonged cry.—*n.* **bawl′er.**

[1]**bay** (bā), *n.* **1**, a curve or recess in the shore of a sea or lake; an arm of the sea; **2**, a remote hollow among hills.

[2]**bay** (bā), *n.* **1**, a principal division in the arrangement of a structure; an alcove or recess; **2**, the part of a window between two of the vertical bars of the frame; **3**, a bay window; **4**, a place for storage, as in a barn, for fodder.

[3]**bay** (bā), *n.* **1**, any of several trees and shrubs, including the sweet bay in America, and the laurel in England; **2**, an honorary garland or crown, formerly composed of woven laurel leaves, given to conquerors and successful poets.

[4]**bay** (bā), *n.* **1**, the deep-toned, prolonged cry of a dog; **2**, the state or position of a person or animal compelled by close pursuit to turn and face an enemy or a danger when no escape is possible; as, a stag at *bay:*—*v.i.* to bark with a deep sound, as hounds in the chase:—*v.t.* to pursue with barking.

[5]**bay** (bā), *adj.* red or reddish brown in color: applied to horses:—*n.* a horse of a reddish brown color.

bay-ber-ry (bā′bĕr-ĭ), *n.* [*pl.* bayberries (-ĭz)], **1**, a low-growing shrub bearing clusters of round berries, which yield a wax used for candles; **2**, the waxy berries of the sweet bay.

bay-o-net (bā′ō-nĕt), *n.* a short dagger-like instrument attached to the muzzle of a rifle:—*v.t.* to stab or attack with a bayonet.

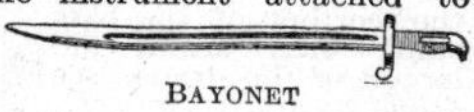

BAYONET

bay-ou (bī′o͞o), *n.* [*pl.* bayous (-o͞oz)], in the southern U. S., the outlet of a lake, or one of the mouths of a river; a slow-moving watercourse.

bay rum a fragrant liquid, prepared from the leaves of the bayberry and used for toilet purposes.

bay win-dow the window or windows forming a recess in a room, and extending outward from the wall.

ba-zaar (bȧ-zär′), *n.* **1**, in the East, a market place or exchange; **2**, a hall or series of rooms with stalls for the sale of goods; **3**, a sale of fancy articles, usually in aid of some charity. Also, **ba-zar′.**

B bat-ter-y in electricity, the battery used to produce the current from the plate to the filament in a vacuum tube, supplying the plate potential.

be (bē), *v.i.* [*pres. indicative sing.* am, art, is, *pl.* are; *p.t. sing.* was, *pl.* were; *p.p.* been (bĭn); *p.pr.* be′ing], **1**, to exist; live; have actual place as a fact; as, whatever *is*, is right; **2**, to come into existence; happen; as, such things should not *be;* **3**, to stay; remain; last; as, let it *be;* **4**, to befall: with *to* or *unto;* as, peace *be* unto you; **5**, to mean; as, it *is* nothing to me; **6**, to have place in, or experience of (a given situation or condition); as, to *be* at the play, in pain, on time; to fit (a given description); as, to *be* brave; to coincide in identity with; as, she *is* my sister:—*v. aux.* **1**, used with present participle to make progressive form; as, he *is* walking; **2**, used with past participle to form passive voice.

be- (bē-) *prefix*, **1**, to cause to be; make: used to form transitive verbs from adjectives, nouns, and intransitive verbs; as, *be*foul; **2**, all around; all over; completely; thoroughly; as *be*dabble; *be*deck; **3**, to call: used to form transitive verbs from nouns; as *be*devil; *be*friend; **4**, to surround with; behave toward as; affect with: used to form transitive verbs from nouns; as, *be*cloud; *be*dew; *be*witch; **5**, off; away: used with privative force; as, *be*head; *be*reave; **6**, adding a tone of contempt or jocularity to a participial adjective; as, *be*wigged.

beach (bēch), *n.* the portion of the shore of the sea or of a lake which is washed by the waves, esp. the sandy or pebbly part: **beach comber, 1**, a long, curling wave rolling in from the ocean; **2**, one who waits about wharves or along the shore on the lookout for wreckage or plunder:—*v.t.* to run or haul up, as a vessel or boat, upon the beach: —*v.i.* to land on a beach; strand.

bea-con (bē'kn), *n.* **1**, a signal of warning or guidance, on sea or land; formerly, a fire lighted on a hill or in a high tower to signal danger, assemble troops, etc.; **2**, hence, any guiding light:—*v.t.* to light up, as a signal; furnish with beacons:—*v.i.* to shine, as a warning light.

bead (bēd), *n.* **1**, a little ball of any material, such as wood, glass, pearl, etc., pierced through and intended to be strung with others to form an ornament, a necklace, a rosary, etc.; **2**, any small body shaped like a little globe; **3**, a drop or bubble; as, a *bead* of perspiration; **4**, a narrow, rounded molding or projecting band; **5**, a small knob of metal at the end of a gun barrel, used in taking aim: **to draw a bead**, to take aim:— *v.t.* to ornament with beads.—*adj.* **bead'y**.

bead-ing (bēd'ĭng), *n.* **1**, bead ornaments; beads collectively; **2**, froth on liquors; **3**, a kind of openwork trimming through which ribbon or tape is run.

bea-dle (bē'dl), *n.* **1**, a messenger or crier of a court; **2**, a parish officer with various small duties connected with a church.

bea-gle (bē'gl), *n.* **1**, a small hound used for hunting hares; **2**, a bailiff.

beak (bēk), *n.* **1**, the bill of a bird, esp. of a bird of prey; the long, sharp mouth of some insects and other animals; **2**, anything which is pointed or shaped like the bill of a bird; **3**, the powerful projection of steel forming part of the bow of modern war vessels.—*adj.* **beaked**.

beak-er (bēk'ẽr), *n.* **1**, a large drinking cup or vessel with a wide mouth; **2**, an open-mouthed vessel with a projecting lip, used as a container in laboratories.

beam (bēm), *n.* **1**, a long piece of timber, iron, or steel, used to support the rafters of a building or as part of an engine, loom, or the like; **2**, one of the principal crosswise horizontal timbers of a building or ship; **3**, the extreme breadth of a ship; **4**, the bar of a balance on which the scale pans are hung; **5**, the principal stem of a deer's horns which bears the antlers; **6**, a ray or the parallel rays of light given out from the sun or any other body which gives forth light: **beam compass**, an instrument used for drawing large circles: —*v.t.* to send forth, as light:—*v.i.* to shine.

beam-ing (bēm'ĭng), *p.adj.* **1**, radiant; bright; cheerful; **2**, giving forth rays.—*adv.* **beam'ing-ly**.

bean (bēn), *n.* **1**, the smooth, kidney-shaped seed of many plants; **2**, the plant itself; **3**, popularly, any of certain other seeds or fruits resembling true beans.

[1]**bear** (bâr), *n.* **1**, a large four-footed animal, widely distributed in various species, having long, shaggy fur and a five-toed foot; **2**, an animal suggestive of a bear; as, the ant *bear;* **3**, a person with rough, uncouth, or surly manners; **4**, on the stock exchange, one who attempts to lower the prices of stocks in order to take advantage of the resulting slump: opp. of *bull:* **bear market**, on the stock exchange, a market in which prices are falling: **bear baiting**, the sport of setting dogs to fight with captive bears: **Bear**, either of two groups of stars in the Northern Hemisphere, called *Great Bear*, *Ursa Major*, or *Great Dipper*, and *Little Bear*, *Ursa Minor*, or *Little Dipper:*— *v.t.* to attempt to lower the price of, as stocks, or the prices in, as a market.

[2]**bear** (bâr), *v.t.* [*p.t.* bore (bōr) or, *Archaic*, bare (bâr), *p.p.* borne (bōrn) or born (bôrn), (*born* is properly used only in the passive voice of sense 10 when *by* does not follow; as, a son was *born* to him; was *born* in 1800; a son *borne* by his first wife), *p.pr.* bear'ing], **1**, to sustain, support, or hold up; **2**, to carry or convey; **3**, to suffer or endure; **4**, to be accountable for, as blame; **5**, to possess, wear, or use, as a weapon; **6**, to have in or on; **7**, to keep, esp. in the mind; **8**, to admit or be capable of; as, his conduct will not *bear* examination; **9**, to show, as testimony; **10**, to bring forth or produce; **11**, to behave:—*v.i.* **1**, to be capable of supporting; **2**, to be fruitful; **3**, to press or weigh: with *upon* or *against;* **4**, to tend; be in, or have, a certain direction, as of the compass; **5**, to refer; as, this *bears* on our discussion.—*adj.* **bear'a-ble.**—*n.* **bear'a-ble-ness.**—*adv.* **bear'a-bly.**

Syn. endure, suffer, stand. To *bear* is to hold up a load or burden that taxes the strength. *Bear* may be used in connection with small or with serious things; as, she could not *bear* the noise; she *bore* her misfortunes bravely. To *endure* is to bear by bracing oneself against pain and suffering, and may imply long hardship. To *suffer* is to put up with by refraining from objection. To *stand* is to bear gamely; as, he *stood* his punishment well.

beard (bērd), *n.* **1**, the hair that grows on the human face, chiefly of men; **2**, anything which resembles this hairy growth; **3**, the growth of bristlelike hairs on the heads of barley and other grains; **4**, any of various points or projections, as the point projecting backward on an arrowhead:—*v.t.* **1**, to take by the beard; **2**, to oppose face to face; defy; as, to *beard* the lion in his den.—*p.adj.* **beard'-ed.**—*adj.* **beard'less.**

bear-er (bâr'ẽr), *n.* **1**, one who or that which carries or sustains; **2**, a tree or plant that yields a good crop of fruit; **3**, a pallbearer; **4**, one who holds a check or other order for the payment of money.

bear-ing (bâr'ĭng), *n.* **1**, the act of enduring with patience; **2**, the manner of carrying the head and body; as, I knew him by his *bearing;* **3**, behavior; **4**, meaning or significance; **5**, the act or power of producing; **6**, a part of a machine that supports friction; **7**, the direction or point of the compass in which an object is seen; also, the position of one object with respect to another; **8**, an emblem or charge in a coat of arms.

bear-ish (bâr'ĭsh), *adj.* **1**, rude; surly; as, *bearish* behavior; **2**, characterized by falling prices, as the stock market.

beast (bēst), *n.* **1**, a four-footed animal, as distinguished from a bird, insect, fish, or man; **2**, a rude or coarse person.

Syn. (see animal).

beast-ly (bēst'lĭ), *adj.* brutal; low; vile; beastlike; as, *beastly* habits; a *beastly* man.—*n.* **beast'li-ness.**

beat (bēt), *v.t.* [*p.t.* beat, *p.p.* beat or beat′en (bēt′n), *p.pr.* beat′ing], **1**, to strike with repeated blows; **2**, to thrash or punish with blows; **3**, in hunting, to range over, as a thicket, in order to drive out game; **4**, to flutter, as wings; **5**, to excel; defeat; vanquish; **6**, in cooking, to mix by stirring or striking with a spoon or fork; **7**, in music, to measure (time) by strokes; **8**, to sound (a signal), as by sounding a drum:—*v.i.* **1**, to strike repeatedly; **2**, to throb; **3**, to fall with violence; **4**, to give forth sound when struck; **5**, to sail against the wind by tacking; **6**, *Colloq.*, to win in a contest:—*n.* **1**, a stroke which is made again and again; **2**, a round or course which is frequently gone over; as, the policeman's *beat;* **3**, in music, the rise and fall of the stroke marking the divisions of time.—*n.* **beat′er.**

Syn., *v.* strike, pommel, smite, bang, pound, batter, bruise, maul; overcome, conquer.

beat-en (bēt′n), *p.adj.* **1**, shaped by beating; **2**, worn by use, as by the tread of feet; **3**, conquered; **4**, exhausted; **5**, baffled; outwitted.

be-a-tif-ic (bē″ȧ-tĭf′ĭk), *adj.* having power to make perfectly happy; blissful: **beatific vision,** the direct vision of God, regarded as enjoyed by the angels and saints.

be-at-i-fy (bē̆-ăt′ĭ-fī), *v.t.* [*p.t.* and *p.p.* -fied (-fīd), *p.pr.* -fy″ing], **1**, to make happy; bless with complete heavenly enjoyment; **2**, in the Roman Catholic Church, to declare (a dead person) publicly to have attained the rank of the blessed, and the right to religious honor.—*n.* **be-at″i-fi-ca′tion.**

beat-ing (bēt′ĭng), *n.* **1**, a striking or flogging, as in punishment; **2**, a pulsing or throbbing; **3**, a defeat.

be-at-i-tude (bē̆-ăt′ĭ-tūd), *n.* bliss of the highest kind; blessedness: **the Beatitudes,** nine declarations made in the Sermon on the Mount (Matthew 5: 3–12) with regard to the blessedness of those who have certain virtues.

beau (bō), *n.* [*pl.* beaus; beaux (bōz)], **1**, a man who strictly follows the fashion; a fop. **2**. an escort, a lover.

beau i-de-al the highest ideal of perfection.

beau-te-ous (bū′tē-ŭs), *adj.* beautiful; lovely.—*adv.* **beau′te-ous-ly.**

beau-ti-ful (bū′tĭ-fo͝ol), *adj.* possessing qualities which delight the mind and senses; lovely.—*adv.* **beau′ti-ful-ly.**

Syn. handsome, pretty, comely. *Beautiful* implies the possession of such qualities as delight the eye, ear, and mind. A *beautiful* object has delicacy of outline, exquisite color, or harmony of proportion; a *beautiful* person adds to these outer graces the charm of loveliness. *Handsome* describes that which is well-proportioned, but does not necessarily include any idea of beautiful; a *handsome* man may be a scoundrel, a *handsome* house merely impressive. *Pretty* implies that which is attractive in a dainty and diminutive way. *Pretty* is often used of things not small to express the idea that they are pleasing to the senses; as, a *pretty* room. *Comely* describes a person, who, though not beautiful, is attractive in looks.

beau-ti-fy (bū′tĭ-fī), *v.t.* [*p.t.* and *p.p.* -fied (-fīd), *p.pr.* -fy″ing], to make charming; adorn:—*v.i.* to become lovely.—*n.* **beau′ti-fi″er.**

beau-ty (bū′tĭ), *n.* [*pl.* beauties (-tĭz)], **1**, that combination of qualities which is pleasing to the eye or ear, or is satisfying in a moral sense; **2**, a particular grace or charm; **3**, a beautiful thing or person, esp. a woman: **beauty spot,** a small black patch placed on the face to increase its charm.

beaux (bōz), *n.* one of the plural forms of the noun *beau.*

[1]**bea-ver** (bē′vẽr), *n.* **1**, a small fur-bearing animal living in water and on land, having a broad, flat, powerful tail, strong teeth formed for gnawing, and webbed hind feet: remarkable for its building of dams and huts; **2**, its fur; **3**, a gentleman's high hat, formerly made of fur of the beaver; **4**, a heavy woolen cloth: **beaver tree,** the sweet bay, common in the southeastern U. S.: so called because beavers eat its bark.

[2]**bea-ver** (bē′vẽr), *n.* **1**, a movable piece of armor for protecting the lower part of the face when the upper part was protected by the visor; **2**, later, a visor.

be-calm (bē̆-käm′), *v.t.* to make still: **becalmed,** motionless, as a ship, because of a lack of wind.

be-came (bē̆-kām′), past tense of the irregular verb *become.*

be-cause (bē̆-kôz′), *adv.* by reason: with *of;* as, you are ill *because* of your imprudence:—*conj.* for the reason that; since; inasmuch as; as, we came in *because* it rained.

be-chance (bē̆-chȧns′), *v.t.* and *v.i.* [*p.t.* and *p.p.* -chanced′ (-chȧnst′) *p.pr.* -chanc′ing], to befall; happen (to).

[1]**beck** (bĕk), *n.* a little brook or the valley through which it runs.

[2]**beck** (bĕk), *n.* a nod or other gesture full of meaning, as of command.

beck-et (bĕk′ĕt), *n.* in ships, a contrivance, as a hook or bracket, to hold in place small spars or loose ropes.

beck-on (bĕk′n), *v.i.* and *v.t.* to signal by a motion of the head or hand; call by signs; as, she *beckoned* him to stay.

be-cloud (bē̆-kloud′), *v.t.* to darken; obscure; dim.

be-come (bē̆-kŭm′), *v.i.* [*p.t.* -came′ (-kām′), *p.p.* -come′, *p.pr.* -com′-ing], **1**, to pass from one state to another; **2**, to come or grow to be:—*v.t.* **1**, to suit; be fitting for; **2**, to agree with; grace or adorn.

be-com-ing (bē̆-kŭm′ĭng), *p.adj.* **1**, proper; befitting; suitable; **2**, suitable or harmonious, and hence serving to adorn; as, a *becoming* hat.—*adv.* **be-com′-ing-ly.**—*n.* **be-com′ing-ness.**

Syn. decent, seemly, suitable.—*Ant.* indecent, unbecoming, awkward.

bed (bĕd), *n.* **1**, an article of furniture upon which one rests or sleeps; **2**, anything which serves as a resting place, or in which something lies or is embedded; as, the *bed* of a railroad; **3**, a portion of a garden prepared and set apart for plants; **4**, the bottom of a river or any body of water; **5**, a layer of rock; **6**, a foundation or any firm support, as for a machine (see *lathe*, illus.):—*v.t.* [*p.t.* and *p.p.* bed′ded, *p.pr.* bed′ding], **1**, to furnish with a bed; **2**, to plant, as flowers; **3**, to embed; set permanently in place, as a stone:—*v.i.* **1**, to go to bed; **2**, to form a compact layer.

be-dab-ble (bē̆-dăb′l), *v.t.* [*p.t.* and *p.p.* -bled (-ld), *p.pr.* -bling], to sprinkle; splash; wet.

be-daub (bē̆-dôb′), *v.t.* to smear over with something oily or dirty.

be-daz-zle (bē̆-dăz′l), *v.t.* [*p.t.* and *p.p.* -zled (-ld), *p.pr.* -zling], to dazzle; bewilder; confuse.

bed-bug (bĕd′bŭg″), *n.* a blood-sucking, flat-bodied insect, of vile odor, sometimes infesting furniture, esp. beds.

bed-ding (bĕd′ĭng), *n.* **1**, the materials of a bed, whether for man or beast; **2**, a foundation of any kind.

be-deck (bē̆-dĕk′), *v.t.* to adorn; decorate; ornament; garnish.

be-dew (bē̆-dū′), *v.t.* to moisten with, or as with, dew.

bed-fel-low (bĕd′fĕl″ō), *n.* one who shares another's bed.

be-dim (bē-dĭm′), *v.t.* [*pt.* and *p.p.* -dimmed′ (-dĭmd′), *p.pr.* -dim′ming], to darken; cloud; dim; as, tears *bedim* the eyes.

be-diz-en (bē-dĭz′n; -dī′zn), *v.t.* to deck or adorn with vulgar finery.—*n.* **be-diz′en-ment.**

bed-lam (bĕd′lăm), *n.* a madhouse; an asylum or hospital for lunatics; hence, any scene of uproar and confusion.

Bed-ou-in (bĕd′ōō-ĭn; -ēn), *n.* [*pl.* Bedouins (-ĭnz); Bedouin], a wandering Arab or tent dweller of Arabia, Syria, and northern Africa:—*adj.* pertaining to such nomads. Also, **Bed′u-in.**

be-drag-gle (bē-drăg′l), *v.t.* [*p.t.* and *p.p.* -gled (-ld), *p.pr.* -gling], to make wet and dirty by dragging, as garments, in mud, rain, or dust.

bed-rid-den (bĕd′rĭd″n), *adj.* confined to bed by age or sickness; as, a *bedridden* invalid. Also, **bed′rid″.**

bed rock in mining, the solid rock underlying the superficial upper crust; solid bottom.

bed-room (bĕd′rōōm″), *n.* a sleeping room; a room holding a bed.

bed-stead (bĕd′stĕd), *n.* the framework supporting a bed.

bed-tick (bĕd′tĭk″), *n.* a bag or case of strong linen or cotton for containing the padding material of a mattress.

bee (bē), *n.* **1,** any of certain insects, some of which store up the pollen of flowers for food, or make honey and wax; esp., the honeybee, kept in hives for the sake of its honey and wax; **2,** an industrious person; **3,** a social meeting for work on behalf of a neighbor or charity, or for some other purpose; as, a spelling *bee;* a quilting *bee.*

bee-bread (bē′brĕd″), *n.* a brown, bitter substance, consisting of the pollen of flowers, and stored by bees as food.

beech (bēch), *n.* any of various trees yielding a hard timber and edible triangular nuts.—*adj.* **beech′en.**—*adj.* **beech′y.**

bee eat-er a brightly colored bird of the Old World, that feeds on bees.

beef (bēf), *n.* [*pl.* beeves (bēvz)], **1,** the flesh of an ox, bull, or cow, prepared for food; **2,** an ox, cow, or bull full grown.

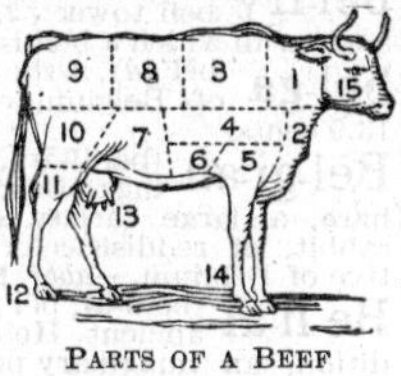

PARTS OF A BEEF

1, neck; 2, shaking piece and brisket; 3, chuck ribs; 4, ribs; 5, clod; 6, plate; 7, flank; 8, loin; 9, rump; 10, round; 11, leg; 12, foot; 13, udder; 14, shin; 15, cheek.

beef-eat-er (bēf′ēt″ẽr), *n.* **1,** one who eats beef; hence, a large, fleshy person; **2,** popularly, in England, one of the yeomen of the guard who attend the king on state occasions; also, one of the guards of the Tower of London.

beef-steak (bēf′stāk″), *n.* a slice of beef suitable for broiling or frying.

beef-y (bēf′ĭ), *adj.* [*comp.* beef′i-er, *superl.* beef′i-est], brawny; fat; hence, dull.

bee-hive (bē′hīv″), *n.* a box made to house a swarm of bees, and serving for the storage of honey.

bee line **1,** the straight course pursued by a bee returning laden to the hive; **2,** hence, the most direct way from one point to another.

Be-el-ze-bub (bē-ĕl′zē-bŭb), *n.* in the Bible, the prince of demons or devils; hence, the Devil himself.

been (bĭn; *Br.* bēn), past participle of the irregular verb *be.*

beer (bēr), *n.* **1,** any of several fermented liquors, generally made from malted barley, with something added to give a bitter flavor; **2,** a fermented extract of the roots and other parts of various plants; as, ginger *beer;* spruce *beer.*—*adj.* **beer′y.**

beest-ings (bēs′tĭngz), *n.pl.* the first milk from a mammal, esp. a cow, after bringing forth young. Also, **biest′ings.**

bees-wax (bēz′wăks″), *n.* a tough, yellowish brown substance made by bees, and used in building the comb:—*v.t.* to rub wax on.

beet (bēt), *n.* a plant cultivated for its sweet, edible root, and as a source of sugar; also, the root.

¹bee-tle (bē′tl), *n.* a member of a group of insects having four wings, the outer pair being hardened and serving as a horny covering.

²bee-tle (bē′tl), *n.* **1,** a heavy wooden mallet; **2,** a kind of pestle:—*v.t.* [*p.t.* and *p.p.* -tled (-tld), *p.pr.* -tling], **1,** to use a heavy wooden mallet on; **2,** to stamp, mangle, or finish, as cotton cloth, with, or as with, a heavy wooden mallet.

³bee-tle (bē′tl), *v.i.* [*p.t.* and *p.p.* -tled (-tld), *p.pr.* -tling], to jut out; overhang, as a cliff:—*adj.* prominent: **beetle-browed,** having overhanging brows; hence, gloomy; sullen.

beeves (bēvz), *n.* plural of the noun *beef;* beef cattle collectively.

be-fall (bē-fôl′), *v.t.* [*p.t.* -fell′ (-fĕl′), *p.p.* -fall′en (-fôl′n), *p.pr.* -fall′ing], to happen or occur to:—*v.i.* to come to pass.

be-fit (bē-fĭt′), *v.t.* [*p.t.* and *p.p.* -fit′ted, *p.pr.* -fit′ting], to be worthy of; be suitable or appropriate for.—*p.adj.* **be-fit′ting.**—*adv.* **be-fit′-ting-ly.**

be-fog (bē-fŏg′), *v.t.* [*p.t.* and *p.p.* -fogged′ (-fŏgd′), *p.pr.* -fog′ging], to envelop in a fog or mist; hence, to confuse.

be-fool (bē-fōōl′), *v.t.* to deceive; lead astray; delude.

be-fore (bē-fōr′), *prep.* **1,** in front of; **2,** preceding in space, time, or rank; **3,** in presence or sight of:—*adv.* in front; in advance, previously; formerly:—*conj.* **1,** earlier than; **2,** rather than.

be-fore-hand (bē-fōr′hănd″), *adv.* in advance; before the time:—*adj.* forehanded; early.

be-foul (bē-foul′), *v.t.* to soil; dirty; pollute; foul.

be-friend (bē-frĕnd′), *v.t.* to act as a friend to; aid or shield.

be-fud-dle (bē-fŭd′l), *v.t.* [*p.t.* and *p.p.* -dled (-ld), *p.pr.* -dling], to confuse; becloud, as with liquor.

beg (bĕg), *v.t.* and *v.i.* [*p.t.* and *p.p.* begged (bĕgd), *p.pr.* beg′ging], **1,** to ask in charity; **2,** to ask (a person) earnestly; beseech; **3,** to ask as a favor: **beg the question,** to take for granted, or assume by implication, the truth of a matter in dispute.

Syn. implore, solicit, supplicate.

be-gan (bē-găn′), past tense of the irregular verb *begin.*

be-gat (bē-găt′), archaic past tense of the verb *beget.*

be-get (bē-gĕt′), *v.t.* [*p.t.* -got′ (-gŏt′) or, *Archaic,* -gat′ (-găt′), *p.p.* -got′ or -got′ten (-gŏt′n), *p.pr.* -get′ting], **1,** to become the father of; **2,** to produce; cause to exist; as, idleness *begets* discontent.—*n.* **be-get′ter.**

beg-gar (bĕg′ẽr), *n.* **1,** one who asks with humility; **2,** one who gets a living by asking for alms; **3,** one who is reduced to extreme poverty; **4,** a rogue; scamp: often humorously:—*v.t.* **1,** to take everything away from; **2,** to use up all the possibilities of; as, the horrors of a battlefield *beggar* description.

beg-gar-ly (bĕg′ẽr-lĭ), *adj.* like one in great poverty; poor; contemptible.—*n.* **beg′gar-li-ness.**

Syn. abject, sordid, wretched, squalid, mean.

beg-gar–ticks (bĕg′ẽr=tĭks″), *n.pl.* used as *sing.* any of several weeds with seeds that stick to clothing, the fur of animals, etc.; also, used as *pl.*, the prickly seeds of such plants.

beg-gar-y (bĕg′ẽr-ĭ), *n.* the act or state of one who asks alms.

be-gin (bē-gĭn′), *v.i.* [*p.t.* -gan′ (-găn′), *p.p.* -gun′ (-gŭn′), *p.pr.* -gin′ning], **1,** to come into existence; arise; **2,** to take the first step or do the first act; start:—*v.t.* **1,** to cause to be; **2,** to commence.—*n.* **be-gin′ner.**

Syn. commence. *Begin* and *commence* are identical in meaning, but *commence* is more formal than *begin*. *Commence* is often used to indicate the starting of some definite course of action; as, to *commence* a lawsuit. *Begin* is used to indicate the starting point or first step of anything; as, to *begin* to make a dress.—*Ant.* delay, postpone.

be-gin-ning (bē-gĭn′ĭng), *n.* **1,** the first cause; **2,** the act of entering upon a course of action; the first stage of anything; **3,** the starting point.

be-gone (bē-gôn′), *interj.* go away! depart! as, *begone* from my sight!

be-go-ni-a (bē-gō′nĭ-*ȧ*), *n.* any of a number of plants cultivated for their ornamental leaves and flowers.

be-got (bē-gŏt′), past tense and past participle of the irregular verb *beget*: **begotten,** past participle of the verb *beget*.

be-grime (bē-grīm′), *v.t.* [*p.t.* and *p.p.* -grimed′ (-grīmd′), *p.pr.* -grim′ing], to soil with dirt deeply rubbed in.

be-grudge (bē-grŭj′), *v.t.* [*p.t.* and *p.p.* -grudged′ (-grŭjd′), *p.pr.* -grudg′ing], **1,** to grumble at; **2,** to envy the possession of; **3,** to give reluctantly.—*adv.* **be-grudg′ing-ly.**

be-guile (bē-gīl′), *v.t.* [*p.t.* and *p.p.* -guiled′ (-gīld′), *p.pr.* -guil′ing], **1,** to impose upon or deceive by a trick; mislead; **2,** to cause to pass pleasantly, as the time; **3,** to divert; entertain.—*n.* **be-guile′ment.**

be-gun (bē-gŭn′), past participle of the irregular verb *begin*.

be-half (bē-häf′), *n.* advantage; support; stead; interest; as, on my *behalf*.

be-have (bē-hāv′), *v.t.* [*p.t.* and *p.p.* -haved′ (-hāvd′), *p.pr.* -hav′ing], to conduct, carry, or manage: used reflexively; as, he *behaves* himself well:—*v.i.* **1,** to act; **2,** to conduct oneself in a proper manner.

be-hav-ior (bē-hāv′yẽr), *n.* conduct and manners; bearing; deportment. Also, **be-hav′iour.**

be-hav-ior-ist (bē-hāv′yẽr-ĭst), *n.* in psychology, one who studies actual conduct, speech, and other responses, or behavior, rather than supposed or theoretical states of consciousness.—*n.* **be-hav′ior-ism.** —*adj.* **be-hav″ior-is′tic.**

be-head (bē-hĕd′), *v.t.* to execute by cutting off or severing the head.

be-held (bē-hĕld′), past tense and past participle of the verb *behold*.

be-he-moth (bē′hē-mŏth; bē-hē′mŏth), *n.* in the Bible, an enormous animal, probably the hippopotamus (Job 40: 15–24); hence, any very large animal.

be-hest (bē-hĕst′), *n.* a command; order; as, to do his master's *behest*.

be-hind (bē-hīnd′), *prep.* **1,** at the back of; on the other side of; **2,** remaining after; **3,** inferior to; **4,** in a position to support:—*adv.* **1,** at the back; in the rear; **2,** toward the back; **3,** out of sight; **4,** past in point of time; **5,** in arrears.

be-hind-hand (bē-hīnd′hănd″), *adj.* and *adv.* **1,** back in time or in progress; **2,** in arrears in payment.

be-hold (bē-hōld′), *v.t.* [*p.t.* -held′ (-hĕld′), *p.p.* -held′ or, *Archaic,* -hold′en (-hōl′dn), *p.pr.* -hold′ing], to fix the eyes upon; look at; observe with care:—*v.i.* **1,** to look; **2,** to direct or fix the mind.—*n.* **be-hold′er.**

be-hold-en (bē-hōl′dn), *adj.* indebted; bound in gratitude; as, the world is much *beholden* to its great inventors.

be-hoof (bē-hōōf′), *n.* a thing which benefits; advantage.

be-hoove (bē-hōōv′), *v.t.* [*p.t.* and *p.p.* -hooved′ (-hōōvd′), *p.pr.* -hoov′ing], to be necessary, or fit, for; as, it will *behoove* you to stay. Also, **be-hove′** (bē-hōv′).

be-ing (bē′ĭng), *n.* **1,** mortal life; the state of existing; **2,** that which exists; **3,** a person; as, man is a rational *being*: **the Supreme Being,** God.

be-jew-el (bē-jū′ĕl; bē-jōō′ĕl), *v.t.* to ornament with many gems.

bel (bĕl), *n. Phys.*, a unit for measuring differences in sound intensity.

be-la-bor (bē-lā′bẽr), *v.t.* to beat with hard blows, as a horse; thrash; assail. Also, **be-la′bour.**

be-lat-ed (bē-lāt′ĕd), *p.adj.* **1,** delayed; **2,** overtaken by darkness.

be-lay (bē-lā′), *v.t.* [*p.t.* and *p.p.* -layed′ (-lād′), *p.pr.* -lay′ing], to make fast, as a running rope, by winding around a pin, cleat, or the like: **belay!** hold! enough!

belch (bĕlch), *v.t.* **1,** to discharge (gas) from the stomach through the mouth; **2,** to throw out with force or violence; as, factory chimneys *belch* forth black smoke:—*v.i.* **1,** to force wind from the stomach; **2,** to throw out with force:—*n.* the act of forcing out wind from the stomach.

bel-dam (bĕl′dăm), *n.* **1,** orig., a grandmother; **2,** an ugly old woman; a hag. Also, **bel′dame.**

be-lea-guer (bē-lē′gẽr), *v.t.* to besiege; surround with an army so as to make escape impossible.

Syn. attack, encompass, blockade, beset.

bel-fry (bĕl′frĭ), *n.* [*pl.* belfries (-frĭz)], **1,** a bell tower; **2,** that part of a tower in which a bell is hung.

BELFRY

bel-ga (bĕl′g*ȧ*), *n.* the monetary unit of Belgium, equivalent to 13.9 cents.

Bel-gi-an (bĕl′jĭ-ăn), *adj.* pertaining to Belgium: **Belgian hare,** a large variety of domestic rabbit, of reddish color:—*n.* a native of Belgium.—*abbr.* **Belg.; Bel.**

Be-li-al (bē′lĭ-ăl; bēl′yăl), *n.* in ancient Hebrew tradition, an imaginary person representing evil; Satan.

be-lie (bē-lī′), *v.t.* [*p.t.* and *p.p.* -lied′ (-līd′), *p.pr.* -ly′ing], **1,** to speak falsely about; slander; **2,** to show to be false; **3,** to misrepresent; **4,** to give the lie to; fail to accord with; as, his acts *belie* his words.—*n.* **be-li′er.**

be-lief (bē-lēf′), *n.* **1,** the acceptance of something as true; trust in the truthfulness of another; **2,** the body of teachings considered true by any group of people; creed; **3,** opinion.

Syn. credit, faith, confidence, conviction.—*Ant.* disbelief, distrust, doubt, unbelief.

be-liev-a-ble (bē-lēv′*ȧ*-bl), *adj.* capable or worthy of being accepted as truth; trustworthy.

be-lieve (bē-lēv′), *v.t.* [*p.t.* and *p.p.* -lieved′ (-lēvd′), *p.pr.* -liev′ing], **1,** to accept as true, esp. without personal knowledge; **2**, to trust the word of; place confidence in; **3**, to think; hold (an opinion):—*v.i.* **1**, to have faith; **2**, to be sure of the truth of anything; **3**, to judge; suppose.—*p.adj.* **be-liev'ing.**—*adv.* **be-liev'ing-ly.**

be-liev-er (bē-lēv'ēr), *n.* **1**, one who accepts as truth something not seen, as a religious faith; **2**, a Christian.

be-lit-tle (bē-lĭt'l), *v.t.* [*p.t.* and *p.p.* -tled (-ld), *p.pr.* -tling], **1**, to cause to appear small; **2**, to speak slightingly of.

[1]**bell** (bĕl), *n.* **1**, a hollow metal vessel, usually cup-shaped, which gives a clear, ringing sound when struck; **2**, anything shaped like a bell, as the corolla of a flower, or the flare at the mouth of a horn, trumpet, or the like (see *saxophone*, illus.); **3**, in *pl.*, on shipboard, strokes on a bell to mark the time in half-hour intervals:—*v.t.* to put a bell on:—*v.i.* to blossom into bell-shaped flowers.

[2]**bell** (bĕl), *v.i.* to bellow, as a deer:—*n.* a roar; a bellowing sound.

bel-la-don-na (bĕl″*ȧ*-dŏn'*ȧ*), *n.* a European herb yielding atropine, used in medicine, as to relieve pain and to expand the pupils of the eyes.

bell buoy a warning buoy with a bell which is made to ring by the motion of the waves.

belle (bĕl), *n.* a beautiful woman; a very popular young lady.

Bel-ler-o-phon (bĕ-lĕr'ō-fŏn), *n.* in mythology, a Grecian hero who, mounted on the winged horse Pegasus, killed the Chimera, a fire-breathing monster.

***belles-let-tres** (bĕl″=lĕtr'), [Fr.], *n.pl.* **1**, literature regarded as an art; finished, elegant writing; **2**, the study and criticism of such literature. —*adj.* **bel″le-tris'tic.**

bel-li-cose (bĕl'ĭ-kōs), *adj.* inclined to fight; quarrelsome.—*adv.* **bel'li-cose″ly.**—*n.* **bel″li-cos'i-ty.**

bel-lig-er-ence (bĕ-lĭj'ẽr-ĕns), *n.* **1**, the act or state of waging war; warfare; **2**, the quality of being warlike. Also, **bel-lig'er-en-cy.**

bel-lig-er-ent (bĕ-lĭj'ẽr-ĕnt), *adj.* **1**, waging war; **2**, relating to war; **3**, quarrelsome:—*n.* a power or person carrying on war.—*adv.* **bel-lig'er-ent-ly.**

bell jar a bell-shaped glass vessel used in laboratories.

bell-man (bĕl'măn), *n.* [*pl.* bellmen (-mĕn)], one who uses a bell to attract attention to a public announcement of news of any sort; a town crier.

bell met-al a variety of bronze; a mixture of copper and tin, of which bells are made.

Bel-lo-na (bĕ-lō'n*ȧ*), *n.* in mythology, the goddess of war.

bel-low (bĕl'ō), *v.i.* **1**, to utter a full, roaring sound, as a bull; **2**, to roar, as the sea, cannon, etc.; **3**, to cry out noisily; bawl:—*v.t.* to utter with a loud, full voice; as, he *bellowed* out his orders:—*n.* **1**, the roar of a bull or similar animal; **2**, a loud, resounding cry.—*n.* **bel'low-er.**

bel-lows (bĕl'ōz; -ŭs), *n.* [*pl.* bellows], an instrument for producing a current of air, used for various purposes, such as blowing fires or filling the pipes of an organ.

bell-weth-er (bĕl'wĕ*th*″ẽr), *n.* a male sheep, or wether, wearing a bell, and acting as leader of the flock.

bel-ly (bĕl'ĭ), *n.* [*pl.* bellies (-ĭz)], **1**, that part of the human body between the breast and the thighs, containing the bowels; the abdomen; **2**, the corresponding part in the lower animals; **3**, the part of anything that swells out into a larger size; as, the *belly* of a flask:—*v.i.* [*p.t.* and *p.p.* -lied (-ĭd), *p.pr.* -ly-ing], to swell and extend; bulge out, as sails in the wind:—*v.t.* to cause to swell out; as, the wind *bellies* the sails.

bel-ly-band (bĕl'ĭ-bănd″), *n.* a band fastened around the belly, as of a horse; a girth (see *harness*, illus.).

be-long (bē-lŏng'), *v.i.* **1**, to be the property, concern, or business: with *to;* as, this *belongs* to your department; **2**, to be a part or member, as of a society: with *to;* **3**, to be suitable or proper, as a right or duty; **4**, to be a native or inhabitant of a place; as, he *belongs* in the East; to have a fixed or usual location; as, the book *belongs* on the shelf.

be-long-ing (bē-lŏng'ĭng), *n.* **1**, that which is one's own; **2**, usually in *pl.*, property; possessions; goods.

be-lov-ed (bē-lŭv'ĕd; bē-lŭvd'), *adj.* regarded with grea' affection:—*n.* one who is greatly loved.

be-low (bē-lō'), *prep.* **1**, farther down or lower than in rank, place, or excellence; lower in value, price, etc.; **2**, unworthy of; as, the act was *below* him:—*adv.* **1**, lower in place, with regard to something else; beneath; hence, on the earth; also, in hell; **2**, in a lower rank or grade; under.

Bel-shaz-zar (bĕl-shăz'*ȧ*r), *n.* in the Bible, the last king of Babylon, who was warned by handwriting on the wall, and killed the same night (Daniel 5).

belt (bĕlt), *n.* **1**, a girdle or band used around the waist, esp. one worn as a mark of rank; **2**, anything like a band, which encircles, restrains, or supports; a strip; **3**, a region which produces certain vegetation; as, the timber *belt;* **4**, an endless band connecting two wheels, pulleys, or cylinders, and passing motion from one to the other; as, the *belt* connecting the two wheels of a sewing machine:—*v.t.* **1**, to encircle, as with a band or girdle; surround; **2**, to gird on, as a sword.

belt-ed (bĕl'tĕd), *p.adj.* **1**, wearing a distinctive belt; as, a *belted* knight; **2**, marked or adorned with a band or circle; as, the *belted* kingfisher.

belt-ing (bĕl'tĭng), *n.* **1**, material from which belts are made; **2**, belts collectively or in general.

bel-ve-dere (bĕl″vē-dēr'; *It.* bĕl″vȧ-dā'rȧ), *n.* an open structure at the top of a house, affording a wide view; also, a summerhouse built on a little hill.

be-mire (bē-mīr'), *v.t.* [*p.t* and *p.p.* -mired' (-mīrd'), *p.pr.* -mir'ing], **1**, to soil by passing through mud; **2**, to fix in the mud.

be-moan (bē-mōn'), *v.i.* to lament; bewail:—*v.t.* to grieve for or over.

be-muse (bē-mūz'), *v.t.* [*p.t.* and *p.p.* -mused' (-mūzd'), *p.pr.* -mus'ing], to confuse; daze; stupefy, as with liquor.

bench (bĕnch), *n.* **1**, a long seat; **2**, a strong table on which mechanics do their work; **3**, the seat where judges sit in court; hence, the persons who sit as judges; the court; **4**, a natural ledge or terrace in rock: **bench mark**, a mark, as a low metal peg, fixed in the ground and used as a reference point in leveling and surveying: **bench warrant**, a legal paper, providing for the arrest of an offender, given out by a court or judge, as distinguished from a justice's warrant given out by a magistrate.

[1]**bend** (bĕnd), *v.t.* [*p.t.* and *p.p.* bent (bĕnt), *p.pr.* bend'ing], **1**, to strain, or make taut, as the string of a bow; **2**, to curve or make crooked; also, to cause to yield; **3**, to turn; incline; deflect; **4**, to direct to a certain point, as one's energies; **5**, to fasten, as a sail to a spar:—*v.i.* **1**, to be, or to become, curved or crooked; **2**, to be turned toward, or away from, something; **3**, to bow or stoop; hence, to submit; **4**, to devote one's attention to

something:—*n.* **1**, a curve; crook; **2**, the act of bending or bowing.—*n.* **bend'er.**

[2]**bend** (bĕnd), *n.* **1**, a knot, as in a rope on shipboard (see *knot*, illus.); **2**, half a trimmed hide (see *leather*, illus.); **3**, in heraldry, a diagonal band on the shield from an upper corner, esp. that on the (wearer's) right: **bend sinister**, a bend from the upper left corner.

be-neath (bē-nēth'; bē-nēth'), *prep.* **1**, lower in place, with reference to something above; **2**, under the pressure of; **3**, lower than, in rank, dignity, or excellence; **4**, unworthy of:—*adv.* in a lower place; below.

ben-e-dict (bĕn'ē-dĭkt), *n.* a newly married man, esp. one who has been long a bachelor: from *Benedick* in Shakespeare's 'Much Ado About Nothing.''

ben-e-dic-tion (bĕn"ē-dĭk'shŭn), *n.* **1**, the act of blessing; **2**, a solemn blessing or expression of kind wishes; **3**, the short blessing pronounced at the close of public worship.—*adj.* **ben"e-dic'to-ry.**

ben-e-fac-tion (bĕn"ē-făk'shŭn), *n.* **1**, the act of conferring a benefit, or a benefit conferred; **2**, a charitable gift.
Syn. alms, charity, donation, bequest, gift.

ben-e-fac-tor (bĕn"ē-făk'tẽr), *n.* one who does a favor or performs an act of kindness; a friendly helper or patron.—*n.fem.* **ben"e-fac'tress.**

ben-e-fice (bĕn'ē-fĭs), *n.* **1**, orig., an estate in lands granted for life only, and held at the pleasure of the donor; **2**, a church in possession of a regular income, as from funds or property; **3**, the income itself.

be-nef-i-cent (bē-nĕf'ĭ-sĕnt), *adj.* doing or producing good; kindly.—*adv.* **be-nef'i-cent-ly.**—*n.* **be-nef'i-cence.**
Syn. bountiful, generous, liberal, benevolent.

ben-e-fi-cial (bĕn"ē-fĭsh'ăl), *adj.* useful; helpful; advantageous; profitable.—*adv.* **ben"e-fi'cial-ly.**

ben-e-fi-ci-a-ry (bĕn"ē-fĭsh'ĭ-ā-rĭ), *n.* [*pl.* beneficiaries (-rĭz)], **1**, one who receives anything as a gift, benefit, or advantage; hence, the person who receives the proceeds of a will or insurance policy; **2**, a priest who has been given a church living:—*adj.* of the nature of a charity or donation.

ben-e-fit (bĕn'ē-fĭt), *n.* **1**, an act of kindness; a favor conferred; **2**, whatever promotes the happiness and well-being of a person or thing, or adds to the value of property; **3**, a theatrical performance, the proceeds of which go to one of the actors, a cause, or the like:—*v.t.* to do good to; be of service to:—*v.i.* to gain advantage; improve.
Syn., n. profit, advantage, service, use.

be-nev-o-lence (bē-nĕv'ō-lĕns), *n.* **1**, the desire to do good; charitableness; good will; **2**, an act of kindness; **3**, a royal tax formerly imposed upon the people under the name of a gift to the ruler.
Syn. beneficence, humanity, tenderness.

be-nev-o-lent (bē-nĕv'ō-lĕnt), *adj.* kindly; charitable; ready to give to good objects.—*adv.* **be-nev'o-lent-ly.**

Ben-gal light (bĕn-gôl'), a firework: also used for signaling at sea because of its steady, bright blue light.

be-night-ed (bē-nīt'ĕd), *adj.* **1**, enshrouded in darkness; overtaken by night; **2**, ignorant; depraved.

be-nign (bē-nīn'), *adj.* **1**, of a kind or gentle disposition; **2**, favorable; **3**, healthful; as, a *benign* influence.—*adv.* **be-nign'ly.**

be-nig-nant (bē-nĭg'nănt), *adj.* **1**, kind; condescendingly gracious; **2**, genial; helpful; gentle.—*n.* **be-nig'nan-cy.**

be-nig-ni-ty (bē-nĭg'nĭ-tĭ), *n.* [*pl.* benignities (-tĭz)], **1**, kindliness of nature; graciousness; gentleness; as, *benignity* of manner; **2**, a kindly act.

ben-i-son (bĕn'ĭ-zn; -sn), *n.* a blessing; a benediction.

Ben-ja-min (bĕn'jȧ-mĭn), *n.* in the Bible, the youngest son of Jacob and Rachel; also, the tribe descended from him (Genesis 35:18).

[1]**bent** (bĕnt), past tense and past participle of the verb [1]*bend*:—*p.adj.* **1**, curved; crooked; **2**, strongly inclined; determined:—*n.* **1**, a mental bias; tendency; as, a *bent* for music; **2**, limit of endurance: now only in the expression *to the top of one's bent.*

[2]**bent** (bĕnt), *n.* a reedlike grass; hence, any of various stiff, wiry grasses.

be-numb (bē-nŭm'), *v.t.* to stupefy; deprive of feeling; deaden; as, a foot *benumbed* by cold.

ben-zene (bĕn'zēn; bĕn-zēn'), *n.* a clear, colorless liquid, containing carbon and hydrogen, very easily set on fire: used for dissolving fats, as a motor fuel, and in the manufacture of dyes.

ben-zine (bĕn'zĭn; bĕn'zēn), *n.* a light oil obtained from petroleum, similar to benzene but less volatile: used as a motor fuel, solvent, etc.

ben-zo-in (bĕn'zō-ĭn; -zoin), *n.* the fragrant juice of a tree of Sumatra and near-by regions: used chiefly in toilet preparations, perfumes, and incense. Also, **ben'zo-ine.**—*adj.* **ben-zo'ic.**

ben-zol (bĕn'zōl; -zŏl), *n.* a nearly colorless liquid, commercial benzene, obtained from coal tar: used as a motor fuel and as a solvent. Also, **ben'zole.**

Be-o-wulf (bā'ō-wo͝olf), *n.* the warlike hero of an Anglo-Saxon epic poem of the seventh or eighth century; also, the poem, containing about 3,000 lines.

be-queath (bē-kwēth'), *v.t.* **1**, to give or leave by will; **2**, to hand down; transmit by inheritance.—*n.* **bequeath'al.**—*n.* **be-queath'ment.**

be-quest (bē-kwĕst'), *n.* **1**, the act of leaving by will; **2**, something left by will; a legacy.

be-rate (bē-rāt'), *v.t.* [*p.t.* and *p.p.* -rat'ed, *p.pr.* -rat'ing], to scold; chide harshly; rebuke severely.

Ber-ber (bûr'bẽr), *n.* **1**, a member of a native North African race; **2**, any Moor or native of Barbary.

be-reave (bē-rēv'), *v.t.* [*p.t.* and *p.p.* -reaved' (-rēvd') or -reft' (-rĕft'), *p.pr.* -reav'ing], to deprive; make destitute; leave desolate; as, to *bereave* her of children.

be-reave-ment (bē-rēv'mĕnt), *n.* **1**, the state of being deprived of something prized; **2**, the loss of a relative or friend by death.

be-reft (bē-rĕft'), past tense and past participle of the verb *bereave.*

bé-ret (bā"rĕ'), *n.* a round, soft peasant's cap: **beret** (bĕ-rā'), a soft, brimless cap, worn informally by men or women.

berg (bûrg), *n.* a large floating mass of ice; an iceberg.

[1]**ber-ga-mot** (bûr'gȧ-mŏt), *n.* **1**, a fruit cultivated in southern Europe, the rind of which yields an oil much used in perfumery; **2**, the tree yielding this fruit; **3**, any of several plants of the mint family, esp. a wild North American plant bearing a showy head of lilac or pink flowers.

[2]**ber-ga-mot** (bûr'gȧ-mŏt), *n.* a certain fine variety of pear.

berm (bûrm), *n.* **1**, a horizontal ledge on a slope; **2**, in fortification, a ledge at the base of a parapet, to prevent dislodged fragments of the parapet from filling the ditch (see *rampart*, illus.); in the World War, a narrow ledge cut along the trench walls, to prevent earth from falling into the trench.

ber-ry (bĕr′ĭ), *n.* [*pl.* berries (-ĭz)], **1**, any small pulpy fruit, as the strawberry; **2**, in botany, any simple fruit with many seeds contained in a pulp, as the tomato or grape; **3**, the dry seed or kernel of certain plants, as of the coffee:—*v.i.* [*p.t.* and *p.p.* -ried (-ĭd), *p.pr.* -ry-ing], to bear, produce, or gather berries.

ber-serk (bûr′sûrk), *n.* **1**, in myth and folklore, a strong, fierce warrior, able to assume the form of the bear or the wolf, and almost invincible in battle; **2**, a bold, furious fighter; one given to fits of violence. Also, **ber′serk-er.**

berth (bûrth), *n.* **1**, enough room at sea for a ship to throw an anchor in; **2**, a station which a ship occupies at port; **3**, a bunk or bed for a passenger on a ship or railroad car; **4**, a situation or appointment:—*v.t.* **1**, to give anchorage to; **2**, to give a bed to.

ber-tha (bûr′thȧ), *n.* a kind of cape or collar, often of lace, used as a trimming for a woman's dress: **Big Bertha,** *Slang,* in the World War, a large, long-range, German cannon.

ber-yl (bĕr′ĭl), *n.* a precious stone of varying colors, commonly green or greenish blue; as, the aquamarine and the emerald are *beryls.*—*adj.* **ber′yl-line.**

be-seech (bē-sēch′), *v.t.* [*p.t.* and *p.p.* -sought′ (-sôt′), *p.pr.* -seech′-ing], **1**, to entreat; implore; as, I *beseech* you to hear me; **2**, to beg eagerly for; as, I *beseech* your favor.—*p.adj.* **be-seech′ing.**—*adv.* **be-seech′ing-ly.**—*n.* **be-seech′ing-ness.**

be-seem (bē-sēm′), *v.t.* and *v.i.* to be suitable or becoming to; befit.

be-set (bē-sĕt′), *v.t.* [*p.t.* and *p.p.* -set′, *p.pr.* -set′ting], **1**, to set or stud, as with ornaments; **2**, to assail; harass; **3**, to hem in; surround; as, a spy is constantly *beset* with dangers.—*p.adj.* **be-set′ting.**
Syn. encompass, besiege, attack, beleaguer.

be-shrew (bē-shrōō′), *v.t.* to call down evil upon: used as a mild curse.

be-side (bē-sīd′), *prep.* **1**, at or by the side of; near by; as, sit *beside* me; **2**, in comparison with; as, my work is poor *beside* yours; **3**, away from; as, *beside* the point: **beside oneself,** greatly disturbed; almost out of one's senses.

be-sides (bē-sīdz′), *adv.* more than that; in addition; also; as well:—*prep.* over and above; other than.

be-siege (bē-sēj′), *v.t.* [*p.t.* and *p.p.* -sieged′ (-sējd′), *p.pr.* -sieg′ing], to surround with armed forces; lay siege to; harass in any way.—*n.* **be-sieg′er.**

be-smirch (bē-smûrch′), *v.t.* to soil; dishonor; as, to *besmirch* a man's reputation.

be-som (bē′zŭm), *n.* a brush or bundle of twigs for sweeping; a broom.

be-sot (bē-sŏt′), *v.t.* [*p.t.* and *p.p.* -sot′ted, *p.pr.* -sot′ting], to make brutish, as with drink; stupefy.—*p.adj.* **be-sot′ted.**

be-sought (bē-sôt′), past tense and past participle of the verb *beseech.*

be-spat-ter (bē-spăt′ẽr), *v.t.* **1**, to scatter about; **2**, to soil by splashing with wet mud or the like; **3**, to slander; injure by speaking evil of.

be-speak (bē-spēk′), *v.t.* [*p.t.* -spoke′ (-spōk′), *p.pr.* -speak′ing], **1**, to ask for beforehand; **2**, to order or arrange in advance; **3**, to show or give evidence of, as by signs or marks; as, the relics left by the Aztecs *bespeak* a high degree of civilization.

Bes-se-mer proc-ess (bĕs′ē-mẽr), a process for making steel, in which air is blown through molten cast iron to remove impurities: now used also for other metals, as copper.

best (bĕst), *adj.* superlative of *good:* **1**, having the highest degree of goodness or excellence; **2**, most desirable, suitable, advantageous, etc.; **3**, largest:—*n.* **1**, the highest state of excellence; **2**, the greatest endeavor; all one can do or show; **3**, the people of highest standing; **4**, finest or dress clothes:—*adv.* superlative of *well:* **1**, in the highest degree; **2**, with most advantage or success:—*v.t.* to get the better of; surpass.

be-stead (bē-stĕd′), *v.t.* [*p.t.* and *p.p.* -stead′ or -sted′ (-stĕd′), *p.pr.* -stead′ing], **1**, to help; be of profit to; **2**, (only in *p.p.*), to put in a (specified) situation or condition; as, many are worse *bestead* than he.

bes-tial (bĕs′chăl), *adj.* **1**, pertaining to the lower animals; **2**, having the qualities of a beast; savage; brutal; as, the Roman gladiatorial contests were *bestial* amusements.—*adv.* **bes′tial-ly.**

bes-tial-i-ty (bĕs-chăl′ĭ-tĭ; bĕs″chĭ-ăl′ĭ-tĭ), *n.* [*pl.* bestialities (-tĭz)], the qualities or nature of a beast; conduct unworthy of human nature; brutality.

be-stir (bē-stûr′), *v.t.* [*p.t.* and *p.p.* -stirred′ (-stûrd′), *p.pr.* -stir′ring], to put into brisk or vigorous action; move with life and vigor; as, to *bestir* oneself.

be-stow (bē-stō′), *v.t.* **1**, to lay up in store; deposit in safe-keeping; **2**, to use or apply; **3**, to give or confer; as, to *bestow* a person in marriage; *bestow* gifts and honors.
Syn. grant, present. (See give.)

be-stow-al (bē-stō′ăl), *n.* **1**, the act of giving or conferring; **2**, that which is given.—*n.* **be-stow′ment.**

be-strew (bē-strōō′), *v.t.* [*p.t.* -strewed′ (-strōōd′), *p.p.* -strewed′ or -strewn′ (-strōōn′), *p.pr.* -strew′ing], **1**, to strew or scatter over; as, to *bestrew* flowers; **2**, to cover with things scattered; as, to *bestrew* a place with flowers. Also, **be-strow′.**

be-stride (bē-strīd′), *v.t.* [*p.t.* -strode′ (-strōd′) or, *Obs.*, -strid′ (-strĭd′), *p.p.* -strid′den (-strĭd′n) or, *Obs.*, -strid′, *p.pr.* -strid′ing], **1**, to stand or sit on with one leg on each side; straddle, as a horse; **2**, to pass or step over, as with long strides.

bet (bĕt), *n.* **1**, the act of wagering; **2**, that which is laid, staked, or pledged on any event or contest, the outcome of which is uncertain; **3**, that on which a wager is made; as, he is a safe *bet:*—*v.t.* [*p.t.* and *p.p.* bet or bet′ted, *p.pr.* bet′ting], to stake or wager, as on the possibility of some future happening:—*v.i.* to lay a wager.

be-ta (bē′tȧ: bā′tȧ), *n.* the second letter [β, B] in the Greek alphabet, corresponding in general to the English *b:* **beta rays,** the most important of the three kinds of rays sent forth by radioactive substances such as radium, having power to penetrate many objects usually opaque, and used in treating certain diseases.

be-take (bē-tāk′), *v.t.* [*p.t.* -took′ (-tŏŏk′), *p.p.* -tak′en (-tāk′n), *p.pr.* -tak′ing], to take (oneself): with *to;* as, to *betake* oneself to a place of safety.

be-tel (bē′tl), *n.* a climbing pepper which grows in the East Indies, the leaves of which, with the nutlike seed of a certain palm, are chewed by the natives.

Bet-el-geuse (bĕt″ĕl-gûz′; *Br.* bĕt″ĕl-jô′zȧ), *n.* a bright, reddish variable star of the first magnitude in the constellation Orion. Also, **Bet″el-geux′.**

***bete noire** (bât nwär), [Fr.], literally, a black beast; something especially disliked; an aversion; a bugbear.

be-think (bē-thĭngk′), *v.t.* and *v.i.* [*p.t.* and *p.p.* -thought′ (-thôt′), *p.pr.* -think′ing], to call to mind; consider: used reflexively; as, to *bethink* oneself of the past.

be-thought (bē-thôt′), past tense and past participle of the irregular verb *bethink*.

be-tide (bē-tīd′), *v.t.* [*p.t.* and *p.p.* -tid′ed, *p.pr.* -tid′ing], to happen to; befall; as, woe *betide* the wanderer.—*v.i.* to happen; come to pass.

be-times (bē-tīmz′), *adv.* **1**, in good season or time; before it is too late; as, come *betimes* in the morning; **2**, soon.

be-to-ken (bē-tō′kn), *v.t.* to give promise of; signify; as, a large nut crop is said to *betoken* a cold winter.
Syn. indicate, foreshow, signify.

be-took (bē-to͝ok′), past tense of the irregular verb *betake*.

be-tray (bē-trā′), *v.t.* **1**, to give over into the hands of an enemy by treachery; as, Judas *betrayed* his Master for thirty pieces of silver; **2**, to fail to be true to, through fraud or unfaithfulness; as, to *betray* a trust; **3**, to disclose, as a secret or that which one is bound in honor not to make known; **4**, to deceive; **5**, to indicate or show; as, his manner *betrays* uneasiness.—*n.* **be-tray′er**.—*n.* **be-tray′al**.

be-troth (bē-trōth′; -trŏth′), *v.t.* **1**, to promise to give in marriage, as a daughter; **2**, to promise to marry.

be-troth-al (bē-trôth′ăl; bē-trōth′ăl), *n.* **1**, an engagement to marry; the state of being engaged; **2**, a promise to marry made between a man and a woman.

1**bet-ter** (bĕt′ẽr), *adj.* comparative of *good*: **1**, having good qualities in a greater degree than another; **2**, preferable; as, it is *better* to walk than to wait for a car; **3**, improved in health; **4**, more; larger; greater:—*adv.* comparative of *well*: **1**, in a more excellent manner; **2**, in a higher degree; **3**, more, as to value, time, extent, etc.:—*v.t.* **1**, to improve the condition of, morally, physically, financially, etc.; **2**, to surpass:—*v.i.* to grow or become better:—*n.* **1**, that which excels something else; **2**, advantage: with *the*; as, he got the *better* of his opponent; **3**, usually in *pl.*, a superior; as, respect for one's *betters*.
Syn., *v.* correct, reform, amend, surpass.

2**bet-ter** (bĕt′ẽr), *n.* one who wagers or lays bets. Also, **bet′tor**.

bet-ter-ment (bĕt′ẽr-mĕnt), *n.* a making more suitable or excellent; an improvement; in law, the improvement of lands or houses which increases their value.

be-tween (bē-twēn′), *prep.* **1**, in the space or time which separates; as, *between* dark and daylight; **2**, from one to another of; as, a look passed *between* them; **3**, by the joint action of; as, *between* us we shall succeed; **4**, in common; as, we had only one horse *between* us; **5**, involving the mutual relation of; as, the contest *between* old and new; **6**, by comparison of; as, a choice *between* evils:—*adv.* in, into, or across intervening space, position, line, relation, etc.; in the meantime; in the interval.
Syn., *prep.* among. *Between* is used generally with only two objects; as, he sat *between* his wife and child. It may be used with more than two objects in cases where *among* does not convey the relation intended; as, an agreement *between* the three brothers. *Among* is used with more than two objects; as, he struck the ball *among* the spectators.

be-twixt (bē-twĭkst′), *prep.* and *adv.* between; as, he stood *betwixt* two perils.

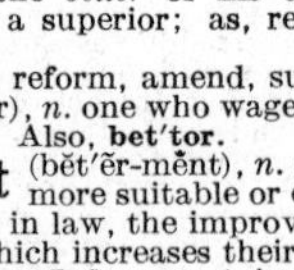

ONE TYPE OF BEVEL

bev-el (bĕv′ĕl), *v.t.* **1**, to cut to an angle other than a right angle; **2**, to give a sloping edge to; as, to *bevel* the edge of a table:—*v.i.* to slant or incline off to an oblique angle:—*n.* **1**, the angle that one line or surface makes with another when they are not perpendicular to each other; **2**, an instrument consisting of two rules, opening at any angle, used for drawing angles:—*adj.* aslant; oblique.

bev-er-age (bĕv′ẽr-āj), *n.* **1**, a drink of any description, as water or lemonade; **2**, liquor for drinking.

bev-y (bĕv′ĭ), *n.* [*pl.* bevies (-ĭz)], **1**, a company or assembly of persons, esp. of girls or women; **2**, a flock of birds, esp. of quail or larks.
Syn. covey, drove. (See herd.)

be-wail (bē-wāl′), *v.t.* to mourn or weep aloud for; lament:—*v.i.* to express grief or sorrow.—*n.* **be-wail′er**.

be-ware (bē-wâr′), *v.i.* [usually used as an imperative, but sometimes inflected: *p.t.* and *p.p.* -wared′ (-wârd′), *p.pr.* -war′ing], to be on one's guard; be cautious:—*v.t.* to look out for; as, *beware* the dog.

be-wigged (bē-wĭgd′), *adj.* wearing a wig, as a judge.

be-wil-der (bē-wĭl′dẽr), *v.t.* **1**, to perplex or confuse; puzzle; **2**, to cause to lose one's way.—*p.adj.* **be-wil′dered**.—*adv.* **be-wil′dered-ly**.
Syn. confound, mystify. (See perplex.)

be-wil-der-ment (bē-wĭl′dẽr-mĕnt), *n.* **1**, the state of being greatly puzzled; **2**, a tangled or confused network; as, a *bewilderment* of passages.

be-witch (bē-wĭch′), *v.t.* **1**, to cast a spell over; **2**, to fascinate; charm.

be-witch-ing (bē-wĭch′ĭng), *p.adj.* having power to fascinate; charming.—*adv.* **be-witch′ing-ly**.—*n.* **be-witch′ment**.

be-wray (bē-rā′), *v.t.* to betray; as, his words *bewray* him.

bey (bā), *n.* **1**, a governor of a province or district in Turkey; **2**, a title of respect used after a name.

be-yond (bē-yŏnd′), *prep.* **1**, at or on the farther side of; as, *beyond* the hills; **2**, farther than; past; as, she looked *beyond* him; **3**, out of the reach of; as, *beyond* medical aid; **4**, above; as, *beyond* his hopes; **5**, outside the experience or knowledge of; too much for; as, algebra was *beyond* him:—*adv.* at a distance; yonder:—*n.* that which lies on the farther side; esp., existence after death: usually with *the*.

bez-ant (bĕz′ănt; bē-zănt′), *n.* a gold coin of Byzantium or Constantinople, in use in Europe from the 6th to the 16th century; also, a silver coin.

bez-el (bĕz′ĕl), *n.* **1**, the slope at the edge of a cutting tool; **2**, the oblique face of a cut gem; **3**, the rim which surrounds and fastens a gem in its setting; a grooved rim into which a watch crystal is fitted.

be-zique (bē-zēk′), *n.* a game played with packs of cards from which the cards of two to six spots have been removed.

bi- (bī-), [Lat.], *prefix*, two; twice; doubly; as, *bi*lateral; specif., lasting two or occurring every two (intervals); as, *bi*ennial; coming or occurring twice; as, *bi*weekly: in this sense preferably *semi-*, to avoid ambiguity.

bi-an-nu-al (bī-ăn′ū-ăl), *adj.* occurring twice a year; semiannual.—*adv.* **bi-an′nu-al-ly**.

bi-as (bī′ăs), *n.* **1**, an oblique line made diagonally across the threads of a dress material; **2**, a leaning of the mind toward a particular thing, desire, or opinion; prejudice:—*v.t.* **1**, to give a particular direction to; influence; as, the newspapers we read *bias* our opinions; **2**, in radio, to modify (the grid potential in a vacuum tube):—*adv.* in a slanting manner.

bib (bĭb), *n.* a cloth placed under a child's chin to protect the clothes.

bib-ber (bĭb'ẽr), *n.* a man who drinks frequently; a tippler.

bib-cock (bĭb'kŏk''), *n.* a faucet having a turned-down nozzle.

Bi-ble (bī'bl), *n.* **1,** the sacred writings of the Old and New Testaments, whether in the original tongue or translated; the Scriptures; **2,** a book of the sacred writings of any people: **Douay Bible,** an English version of the Bible, translated from the Vulgate, commonly used by English-speaking Roman Catholics.

Bib-li-cal (bĭb'lĭ-kăl), *adj.* pertaining to the Bible; scriptural.—*adv.* **Bib'li-cal-ly.**

bib-li-o- (bĭb'lĭ-ō-), a combining form from the Greek word meaning book; as, *biblio*phile; *biblio*grapher.

bib-li-og-ra-pher (bĭb''lĭ-ŏg'rȧ-fẽr), *n.* one who writes about books, esp. in regard to their authorship, date of printing, editions, etc.

bib-li-og-ra-phy (bĭb''lĭ-ŏg'rȧ-fĭ), *n.* [*pl.* bibliographies (-fĭz)], **1,** a history or description of books, their authors, material, style of printing, dates, editions, etc.; **2,** a list of books relating to any given subject or author.

bib-li-o-ma-ni-a (bĭb''lĭ-ō-mā'nĭ-ȧ), *n.* a craze for collecting and possessing books, esp. rare and curious ones.

bib-li-o-phile (bĭb'lĭ-ō-fĭl; -fīl), *n.* a lover of books. Also, **bib'li-o-phil.**—*n.* **bib''li-oph'i-lism.**

bib-u-lous (bĭb'ū-lŭs), *adj.* **1,** readily soaking up fluids; spongy; **2,** fond of drinking.—*adv.* **bib'u-lous-ly.**

bi-cam-er-al (bī-kăm'ẽr-ăl), *adj.* two-chambered; esp., consisting of two legislative chambers.

bi-car-bon-ate (bī-kär'bŏn-āt), *n.* a salt of carbonic acid which still has in it some of the hydrogen of the acid.

bi-cen-te-na-ry (bī-sĕn'tē-nă-rĭ), *n.* [*pl.* bicentenaries (-rĭz)], the 200th anniversary of any event, or its celebration:—*adj.* **1,** occurring once in 200 years; **2,** pertaining to a 200th anniversary.

bi-cen-ten-ni-al (bī''sĕn-tĕn'ĭ-ăl), *n.* the 200th anniversary of an event, or its celebration:—*adj.* **1,** consisting of 200 years; **2,** occurring once in 200 years.

bi-ceps (bī'sĕps), *n.* a muscle, one end of which has two heads, or places of attachment; esp., the large muscle on the front of the upper arm.

bi-chlo-ride (bī-klō'rīd; -rĭd), *n.* **1,** a compound containing twice as much chlorine as is found in another chloride of the same element; **2,** specif., bichloride of mercury, a deadly poison, used as an antiseptic. Also **bi-chlo'rid.**

bick-er (bĭk'ẽr), *v.i.* **1,** to engage in petty quarreling; wrangle; **2,** to move rapidly with a noise; babble, as a stream; patter, as rain; flicker, as flame:—*n.* an angry or petty dispute.—*n.* **bick'er-er.**

bi-cus-pid (bī-kŭs'pĭd), *adj.* having two points:—*n.* in man, one of eight teeth, placed in pairs, two on each side of each jaw, between the canines and the molars.—*adj.* **bi-cus'pid-ate.**

bi-cy-cle (bī'sĭ-kl), *n.* a light vehicle having a metal frame, two wheels, one behind the other, and a saddle for the rider, worked by means of treadles:—*v.i.* [*p.t.* and *p.p.* -cled (-kld), *p.pr.* -cling], to ride on such a vehicle.—*n.* **bi'cy-cler.**—*n.* **bi'cy-clist.**

bid (bĭd), *v.t.* [*p.t.* bade (băd) or bid, *p.p.* bid'den (bĭd'n) or bid, *p.pr.* bid'ding; in sense 3, *p.t.* and *p.p.* bid, *p.pr.* bid'ding], **1,** to make an offer of, as at auctions, in certain card games, and the like; **2,** to invite; **3,** to propose as a price; offer or express by words: as, to *bid* a dollar, or to *bid* a welcome; **4,** to command; order or direct:—*v.i.* to make an offer; offer a price:—*n.* an offer.—*n.* **bid'der.**

bid-da-ble (bĭd'ȧ-bl), *adj.* obedient; docile; as, a *biddable* child.

bid-ding (bĭd'ĭng), *n.* **1,** an order; command; **2,** an invitation; **3,** the act of offering a price, as at auction.

bide (bīd), *v.i.* [*p.t.* and *p.p.* bode (bōd) or bid'ed, *p.pr.* bid'ing], **1,** to remain; continue; wait; **2,** to live; dwell:—*v.t.* **1,** to endure; **2,** to wait for; as, I *bide* my time.

bi-den-tal (bī-dĕn'tăl), *adj.* having two teeth, or two toothlike projections.—*adj.* **bi-den'tate.**

bi-en-ni-al (bī-ĕn'ĭ-ăl), *adj.* **1,** happening once in two years; as, a *biennial* convention; **2,** continuing or existing for two years, as plants:—*n.* **1,** a plant which produces roots and leaves in the first year, and flowers, fruit, and seed in the second, and then dies; **2,** an event which is held once in two years.—*adv.* **bi-en'ni-al-ly.**

bier (bēr), *n.* **1,** a frame on which a corpse or coffin is placed or carried to the grave; **2,** loosely, a coffin; tomb.

biest-ings (bēs'tĭngz), *n.pl.* the first milk from a cow after calving. See **beest'ings,** *Pfd. S.*

bi-fo-cal (bī-fō'kăl), *adj.* having two focal lengths, as a lens:—*n.* a lens ground to form a combination of two lenses, as for near- and long-distance eyeglasses.

bi-fo-li-ate (bī-fō'lĭ-āt), *adj.* in botany, having two leaves.

Bif-rost (bēf'rŏst), *n.* in Norse mythology, the rainbow bridge connecting Asgard, the abode of the chief gods, with Midgard, the earth.

bi-fur-cate (bī-fûr'kāt; bī'fûr-kāt), *v.i.* [*p.t.* and *p.p.* -cat-ed, *p.pr.* -cat-ing], to divide in two directions:—*adj.* (bī-fûr'kāt), divided into two branches; forked, as a root.—*n.* **bi''fur-ca'tion.**

big (bĭg), *adj.* [*comp.* big'ger, *superl.* big'gest], **1,** large; bulky; grown up; **2,** full of importance; pompous; **3,** full to overflowing; as, *big* with grief; teeming; as, *big* with promise; **4,** pregnant.—*n.* **big'ness.**

big-a-mist (bĭg'ȧ-mĭst), *n.* one who has more than one husband or wife at one time.

big-a-my (bĭg'ȧ-mĭ), *n.* the crime of having two wives or husbands at one time.—*adj.* **big'a-mous.**

big-horn (bĭg'hôrn''), *n.* the wild sheep of the Rocky Mountains.

bight (bīt), *n.* **1,** a bend in a coast line, forming a bay; **2,** a small bay between two headlands; **3,** a loop in a rope.

big-ot (bĭg'ŭt), *n.* **1,** one who is unreasonably and blindly attached to a particular creed, church, or party; **2,** one who will not allow to others the enjoyment of opinions which differ from his own.

big-ot-ed (bĭg'ŭt-ĕd), *adj.* **1,** obstinately attached to a creed or an idea; **2,** unwilling to allow to others opinions differing from one's own; illiberal.

Syn. intolerant, prejudiced, biased.—*Ant.* liberal, tolerant, unbiased.

big-ot-ry (bĭg'ŭt-rĭ), *n.* [*pl.* bigotries (-rĭz)], **1,** the state of mind of a prejudiced, illiberal person; **2,** obstinate devotion to a creed or belief; intolerance.

big tree a giant tree of California, akin to the redwood.

big-wig (bĭg'wĭg''), *n.* *Slang,* an important person of authority or rank, such as formerly wore a wig.

*__bi-jou__ (bē″zhōō′; bē′zhōō), [Fr.], *n.* [*pl.* bijoux (bē″zhōō′; -zhōōz′; bē′zhōō; -zhōōz)], a jewel; trinket.

bi-la-bi-al (bī-lā′bĭ-ăl), *n.* a sound formed by both lips, as *p, b, m*:—*adj.* **1**, in botany, having two lips, as the corolla of the mint flower: preferably, *bilabiate* (-āt); **2**, in phonetics, formed by both lips, as *p*.

bi-lat-er-al (bī-lăt′ẽr-ăl), *adj.* relating to, or having, two sides; two-sided.—*adv.* **bi-lat′er-al-ly.**

bil-ber-ry (bĭl′bĕr-ĭ), *n.* [*pl.* bilberries (-ĭz)], **1**, any of several shrubs of the heath family, bearing berries resembling blueberries, some being sweet; **2**, the fruit; **3**, in Europe, the whortleberry.

bil-bo (bĭl′bō), *n.* [*pl.* bilboes (-bōz)], **1**, a rapier or sword; **2**, in *pl.*, a bar of iron with sliding shackles, once used to fetter prisoners.

bile (bīl), *n.* **1**, a bitter, yellow or greenish fluid secreted from the blood by the liver; **2**, a fit of anger; ill humor.

bilge (bĭlj), *n.* **1**, the bulging part of a cask; **2**, the broadest part of a ship's bottom, on which the vessel rests when aground; **3**, *Slang*, nonsense; twaddle: **bilge water,** water which gathers in the bottom of a ship, usually very disagreeable in odor:—*v.i.* [*p.t.* and *p.p.* bilged (bĭljd), *p.pr.* bilg′ing], to spring a leak by a break in the bottom, or bilge, as a ship:—*v.t.* **1**, to stave in the bottom of; **2**, to cause to swell out.

bil-i-a-ry (bĭl′ĭ-ȧ-rĭ), *adj.* pertaining to, or carrying, bile; as, a *biliary* duct: **biliary calculus,** gallstone.

bi-lin-gual (bī-lĭng′gwăl), *adj.* pertaining to two languages; speaking two languages.—*adv.* **bi-lin′gual-ly.**

bil-ious (bĭl′yŭs), *adj.* **1**, having the liver out of order; **2**, of or pertaining to the bile; **3**, ill-tempered; peevish.—*adv.* **bil′ious-ly.**—*n.* **bil′ious-ness.**

bi-lit-er-al (bī-lĭt′ẽr-ăl), *adj.* consisting of two letters:—*n.* a word, root, or syllable of two letters.

bilk (bĭlk), *v.t.* to deceive or defraud; cheat:—*n.* **1**, a dishonest person; swindler; **2**, a dishonest act; trick.

[1]**bill** (bĭl), *n.* **1**, a draft of a proposed law presented to a legislature; **2**, an account of money owed for goods sold, services given, or work done; **3**, a petition; **4**, a U. S. bank or government note, used as money; also, a bill of exchange; **5**, a printed advertisement; a poster; **6**, a paper giving a list of particulars; as, the *bill* of the races; **7**, in law, a written statement setting forth certain particulars, as the items composing a plaintiff's claim; **8**, in a criminal case, a written accusation to be presented to a grand jury: **bill of entry,** a written account of goods entered at a custom-house: **bill of exchange,** a written order from one person, the drawer, to another, the acceptor, to pay a certain sum at a fixed time; a draft: **bill of health,** an official certificate given to the master of a vessel at time of sailing, recording the state of health of passengers and crew: **bill of lading,** a receipt issued by a railroad, shipping company, or other carrier, to the shipper, acknowledging responsibility for the shipment of goods and promising to make delivery to the person or place designated: **bill of sale,** a formal paper transferring to a buyer the title to personal property:—*v.t.* **1**, to advertise by posters; enter on a program; announce; **2**, to make a list of, as goods; **3**, to charge (a person); send a statement of indebtedness to; **4**, to ship by freight; as, *billed* to Chicago.

[2]**bill** (bĭl), *n.* **1**, the beak of a bird; **2**, the jaw of a turtle:—*v.i.* to join bills; as, doves *bill* and coo; hence, to caress.

[3]**bill** (bĭl), *n.* **1**, in ancient times, a pike or halberd with a narrow, hook-shaped blade, usually with spikes on the back and outer end; **2**, a farmer's tool consisting of a blade with a hook at the end, for cutting brush or pruning; a billhook.

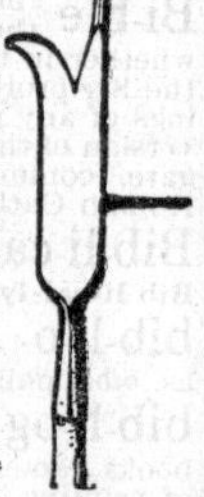
[3]BILL

[1]**bil-let** (bĭl′ĕt), *n.* **1**, a small stick or log of wood used for fuel; **2**, a short bar of iron or steel.

[2]**bil-let** (bĭl′ĕt), *n.* **1**, a note or short letter; **2**, a ticket directing a soldier to board and lodge at a certain house; **3**, a place where a soldier is lodged; in the World War, a rest camp; **4**, a situation; appointment:—*v.t.* to quarter or lodge:—*v.i.* to be quartered or lodged, as soldiers.

*__bil-let-doux__ (bĭl′ē-dōō′; bē″yâ″-dōō′), [Fr.], *n.* [*pl.* billets-doux (bĭl′ē-dōōz′; bē″yâ″-dōō′)], a love letter.

bill-head (bĭl′hĕd″), *n.* a printed form, with a business address at the top, for the issuing of a bill or statement of an account.

bill-hook (bĭl′ho͝ok″), *n.* a tool with a hooked point used for pruning.

bil-liards (bĭl′yȧrdz), *n.* a game played on an oblong, cloth-covered table, with ivory balls and a cue.

bil-lings-gate (bĭl′ĭngz-gāt″), *n.* coarse and abusive language.

bil-lion (bĭl′yŭn), *n.* in the U. S. and France, one thousand millions: written 1,000,000,000; in England and Germany, a million millions: written 1,000,000,000,000.—*adj.* and *n.* **bil′lionth.**

bil-low (bĭl′ō), *n.* **1**, a great wave of the sea swelled by the wind; **2**, hence, anything that sweeps on with increasing force or volume:—*v.i.* to rise and roll in large waves.—*adj.* **bil′low-y.**

bil-ly (bĭl′ĭ), *n.* [*pl.* billies (-ĭz)], **1**, a bludgeon or club; **2**, a camper's tin kettle.

bi-met-al-lism (bī-mĕt′ăl-ĭzm), *n.* the policy of using two metals, as gold and silver, in the money of a country as a standard at a fixed relative value.—*n.* **bi-met′al-list.**—*adj.* **bi″me-tal′lic.**

bi-month-ly (bī-mŭnth′lĭ), *adj.* occurring once every two months; as, a *bimonthly* meeting; also, lasting two months.

bin (bĭn), *n.* a box or compartment used as a storage place; as, a coal *bin*.

bi-na-ry (bī′nȧ-rĭ), *adj.* consisting of two things or parts; as, water is a *binary* compound because it is composed of two substances, hydrogen and oxygen.

bind (bīnd), *v.t.* [*p.t.* and *p.p.* bound (bound), *p.pr.* bind′ing], **1**, to make fast with a cord or band; **2**, to confine or hold by physical force; **3**, to unite by bonds of affection, loyalty, or duty; hold by any moral tie; **4**, to protect, strengthen, or adorn, by a band, border, or cover; **5**, to oblige by a promise, law, duty, etc.; **6**, to fasten together in a cover, as a book:—*v.i.* **1**, to tie up something; as, to reap and *bind;* **2**, to have the force of a duty or necessity; **3**, to be too tight:—*n.* anything which holds or ties.—*n.* **bind′er.**

bind-er-y (bīn′dẽr-ĭ), *n.* [*pl.* binderies (-ĭz)], a place where books are fastened into covers.

bind-ing (bīn′dĭng), *n.* **1**, the act of making fast; **2**, a bandage; **3**, the cover of a book; **4**, something that secures the edges of cloth from fraying:—*adj.* holding; compelling, as an agreement: **binding posts,** metallic fixtures to which wires are fastened on electrical apparatus.

bind-weed (bīnd'wēd″), *n.* **1**, any plant of a large group containing the morning-glory; **2**, a weak, trailing vine of the buckwheat family.

bine (bīn), *n.* the twining stem of a hop vine or other climbing plant.

bin-na-cle (bĭn'ȧ-kl), *n.* a case or box near the steering wheel of a ship, containing the ship's compass.

bin-o-cle (bĭn'ō-kl), *n.* a field or opera glass with two tubes for the use of both eyes at once; a binocular.

bin-oc-u-lar (bĭn-ŏk'ū-lȧr; bī-nŏk'ū-lȧr), *adj.* adapted to the use of both eyes at the same time; as, *binocular* glasses:—*n.* any glass fitted for use of both eyes at one time, as a field glass or opera glass.

bi-no-mi-al (bī-nō'mĭ-ăl), *adj.* **1**, in algebra, consisting of two terms; **2**, having two names: **binomial theorem**, a rule or method invented by Sir Isaac Newton for writing out any power of a binomial:—*n.* **1**, in algebra, an expression consisting of two terms connected by the sign plus [+] or minus [−], as $a+b$; **2**, in biology, a name consisting of two parts.

bi-o-graph (bī'ō-gráf), *n.* a device for throwing moving pictures upon a screen; a cinematograph.

bi-og-ra-pher (bī-ŏg'rȧ-fēr), *n.* one who writes the life of a person; as, Boswell was Johnson's *biographer*.

bi-og-ra-phy (bī-ŏg'rȧ-fĭ), *n.* [*pl.* biographies (-fĭz)], **1**, the written history of a person's life; **2**, such writings in general.—*adj.* **bi″o-graph'ic; bi″o-graph'i-cal.**—*adv.* **bi″o-graph'i-cal-ly.**

bi-ol-o-gy (bī-ŏl'ō-jĭ), *n.* the science which deals with the origin and life history of plants and animals, including *botany* and *zoölogy*.—*abbr.* **biol.**—*n.* **bi-ol'o-gist.**—*adj.* **bi″o-log'i-cal; bi″o-log'ic.**—*adv.* **bi″o-log'i-cal-ly.**

bi-ped (bī'pĕd), *n.* an animal having two feet, as man:—*adj.* having two feet.—*adj.* **bi'pe-dal** (bī'pē-dăl; bĭp'ē-dăl).

bi-plane (bī'plān″), *n.* an airplane with two supporting surfaces or guiding boards, one above the other, as in the Wright machine (see *airplane, aviation*, illus.).

birch (bûrch), *n.* **1**, any of several trees or shrubs which have a close-grained wood and smooth outer bark which in some varieties may be removed in thin, papery sheets; **2**, a rod formed of birch twigs, used for punishment; **3**, a birch-bark canoe:—*adj.* made of birch:—*v.t.* to punish with a birch rod; flog; whip.

birch bark the smooth outer bark of any of several varieties of birch, esp. the white paper birch: **birch–bark,** *adj.* made of birch bark.

birch-en (bûr'chn), *adj.* relating to, or consisting of, birch.

bird (bûrd), *n.* **1**, a warm-blooded, feathered, egg-laying vertebrate animal, generally having wings; **2**, any small bird shot by a gunner, as distinguished from a waterfowl; **3**, *Slang*, a queer or inefficient person: **bird of paradise,** any of several birds found in New Guinea and neighboring islands, noted for their beautiful plumage: **bird of passage, 1**, a bird which goes from one region to another with a change of seasons; **2**, hence, a person who does not remain long in one place: **bird of prey,** any flesh-eating bird, as a hawk:—*v.i.* to shoot or catch birds.

bird-lime (bûrd'līm″), *n.* a sticky substance prepared from holly bark, and used for catching small birds.

bird-man (bûrd'măn″), *n.* [*pl.* birdmen (-mĕn″)], an aviator; the pilot or operator of an airplane.

bird's–eye (bûrdz'-ī″), *adj.* **1**, seen from above, as by a flying bird; hence, general, not detailed; as, a *bird's-eye* view of New York; **2**, marked with spots resembling a bird's eye; as, *bird's-eye* maple.

bi-reme (bī'rēm), *n.* an ancient boat or galley, having two banks of oars.

birth (bûrth), *n.* **1**, the act of coming into life; **2**, the fact of being born; **3**, the act of bringing forth; **4**, that which is born; **5**, descent; as, Abraham Lincoln was a man of humble *birth;* **6**, inherited disposition or bent; **7**, an origin; a beginning.

birth-day (bûrth'dā″), *n.* the day on which one is born; also, the anniversary of such a day.

birth-mark (bûrth'märk″), *n.* **1**, a mark on the skin at birth; **2**, hence, any striking abnormality or defect, whether physical or mental, dating from birth.

birth-place (bûrth'plās″), *n.* the place of one's birth; place of origin.

birth rate the rate at which births occur: usually given as so many births each year per thousand of inhabitants.

birth-right (bûrth'rīt″), *n.* **1**, any right, privilege, or possession to which a person is entitled by birth; **2**, the right of the first born.

bis-cuit (bĭs'kĭt), *n.* **1**, a flat cake of unraised bread, baked hard and dry; a cracker; **2**, in the U. S., a small, baked cake of raised bread dough; **3**, unglazed pottery after one baking.

bi-sect (bī-sĕkt'), *v.t.* **1**, to divide into two parts; **2**, in geometry, to divide into two equal parts.—*n.* **bi-sec'tion.**

bi-sec-tor (bī-sĕk'tēr), *n.* that which divides an object into two equal parts.

bish-op (bĭsh'ŭp), *n.* **1**, a spiritual overseer; **2**, the spiritual head or ruler of a diocese or church district; **3**, one of the pieces used in playing chess.

bish-op-ric (bĭsh'ŭp-rĭk), *n.* **1**, the office of a bishop; **2**, a diocese, or church district presided over by a bishop.

bis-muth (bĭz'mŭth; bĭs'mŭth), *n.* a heavy, pinkish, brittle metal used in alloys.

bi-son (bī'sŭn), *n.* **1**, a wild, oxlike animal of America, popularly called *buffalo*, which has now almost disappeared; **2**, an animal like the ox, nearly extinct, but still found in Lithuania.

[1]**bisque** (bĭsk), *n.* an unglazed white porcelain, used for statuettes.

[2]**bisque** (bĭsk), *n.* **1**, a thick, rich soup made from meat, fish, or tomatoes; **2**, a kind of ice cream containing crushed macaroons. Also, **bisk.**

[1]**bit** (bĭt), past tense and past participle of the verb *bite:*—*n.* **1**, a tool for boring holes, as an auger (see *tool*, illus.); **2**, the cutting part of a tool, as the blade in a plane; **3**, the metal mouthpiece of a bridle; **4**, any force which checks or restrains; **5**, the part of a key that enters the lock and acts on the bolts and tumblers (see [1]*key*, illus.):—*v.t.* [*p.t.* and *p.p.* bit'ted, *p.pr.* bit'ting], **1**, to put a bridle upon; **2**, to put a bit in the mouth of; **3**, to check; restrain.

[2]**bit** (bĭt), *n.* **1**, a small piece of anything; **2**, somewhat; a little; **3**, a little while; as, wait a *bit;* **4**, any small coin: **two bits,** 25 cents: **not a bit,** not at all; none at all.

bitch (bĭch), *n.* the female of the dog, wolf, fox, etc.

bite (bīt), *v.t.* [*p.t.* bit (bĭt), *p.p.* bit'ten (bĭt'n) or bit, *p.pr.* bit'ing], **1**, to seize, grip, or cut, as with the teeth or part of a machine; sting, as an insect; **2**, to cut into, as with a sword; **3**, to cause smarting pain to, as cold;

4, to eat into; corrode, as acid:—*v.i.* 1, to seize, as with teeth or part of a machine; 2, to be pungent; sting, as ammonia; 3, to take a bait, as a fish; seize a chance; 4, to corrode, as an acid:—*n.* 1, the act of seizing, as with teeth; 2, a wound made by the teeth, or by a sting; 3, a mouthful. 4, a hold or grip. 5, a smarting sensation.—*n.* **bit'er.**

bit-ing (bīt'ĭng), *p.adj.* sharp; cutting; sarcastic.—*adv.* **bit'ing-ly.**

bitt (bĭt), *n.* a post or, usually, one of a pair of posts of wood or iron on a ship to which cables, ropes, etc., are made fast:—*v.t.* to put round the cable posts.

bit-ten (bĭt'n), a form of the past participle of the verb *bite.*

bit-ter (bĭt'ẽr), *adj.* 1, having a sharp or harsh taste; 2, sharp to the feeling; as, *bitter* cold; 3, painful; grievous; as, *bitter* woe; 4, severe; sarcastic; as, *bitter* words; cruel; as, a *bitter* enemy; 5, expressing grief; as, a *bitter* cry:—*n.* 1, any substance that is sharp or harsh to the taste; 2, in *pl.*, liquor in which herbs or roots are soaked.—*adv.* **bit'ter-ly.**—*n.* **bit'ter-ness.**—*adj.* **bit'ter-ish.**

Syn., *adj.* sour, acid, tart, biting, acrid, stinging, sharp, keen. *Bitter* describes a biting, sharp taste. *Sour* and *acid* describe a taste similar to that of vinegar. *Tart* describes a slightly stinging taste. Figuratively, *bitter* describes that which afflicts both mind and body painfully; as, *bitter* grief. Used of words, *bitter* means stinging and severe. *Sour* is applied to one who is crabbed, or habitually ill-humored. *Acid* speech is cutting and severely critical. *Tart* speech is biting but not always unpleasant in its effect.

¹bit-tern (bĭt'ẽrn), *n.* any of several wading birds related to the heron.

²bit-tern (bĭt'ẽrn), *n.* in salt manufacture, the brine remaining after the salt is extracted.

bit-ter-sweet (bĭt'ẽr-swēt''), *n.* 1, a vine of the nightshade family; 2, an American twining shrub showing in the fall scarlet seeds in open pods:—*adj.* mingling bitter and sweet, or pain and pleasure.

bi-tu-men (bĭ-tū'mĕn; bĭt'ū-mĕn), *n.* a mixture of sticky or solid hydrocarbons found in the earth, as mineral pitch or asphalt.

bi-tu-mi-nous (bĭ-tū'mĭ-nŭs), *adj.* like or containing bitumen: **bituminous coal,** coal containing a large amount of bitumen: commonly called *soft coal,* and distinguished from anthracite, or *hard coal.*

bi-valve (bī'vălv), *n.* a shellfish whose shell is composed of two plates, or valves, connected by a ligament, as the oyster:—*adj.* having two valves.—*adj.* **bi'-valved.**—*adj.* **bi-val'vu-lar.**

biv-ouac (bĭv'wăk; bĭv'o͝o-ăk), *n.* a camp of soldiers in the open air, without tents; hence, any temporary camp:—*v.i.* [*p.t.* and *p.p.* -ouacked (-wăkt; -o͝o-ăkt), *p.pr.* -ouack-ing], to encamp at night in the open without shelter.

bi-week-ly (bī''wēk'lĭ), *adj.* occurring or appearing every two weeks; as, a *biweekly* magazine:—*n.* [*pl.* biweeklies (-lĭz)], a periodical issued once in two weeks:—*adv.* once every two weeks.

bi-zarre (bĭ-zär'), *adj.* odd in manner or appearance; fanciful; grotesque.

blab (blăb), *v.t.* [*p.t.* and *p.p.* blabbed (blăbd), *p.pr.* blab'bing], to tell thoughtlessly:—*v.i.* to tell tales; talk unwisely:—*n.* one who lets out secrets, or tells tales.—*n.* **blab'ber.**

black (blăk), *adj.* 1, entirely without light: opp. of *white;* 2, wrapped in darkness; 3, dismal; forbidding; threatening; sullen; 4, without moral light or goodness; evil; 5, dark-skinned, as a negro: **black art,** the art practiced by witches and magicians; magic; necromancy: **black market,** a market for goods unlawfully sold:—*n.* 1, the darkest color: opp. of *white;* 2, a black color or dye; 3, a negro; 4, mourning:—*v.t.* to blacken; as, to *black* boots.—*adj.* **black'ish.**—*adv.* **black'-ly.**—*n.* **black'ness.**

black-a-moor (blăk'ȧ-mo͝or), *n.* a negro: esp., an African Negro.

black-ball (blăk'bôl''), *v.t.* to reject or exclude, as a candidate, by, or as by, placing black balls in the ballot box.

black-ber-ry (blăk'bĕr-ĭ), *n.* [*pl.* blackberries (-ĭz)], 1, any of several brambles bearing a small, dark, juicy fruit; 2, the fruit itself.

black-bird (blăk'bûrd), *n.* 1, an English song bird of the thrush family; 2, any of several birds of North America, related to the bobolinks and meadow larks, esp. the purple grackle.

black-board (blăk'bōrd''), *n.* a large slate, or a board painted black, to be written or drawn upon with chalk.

black-cap (blăk'kăp''), *n.* 1, any of several black-crowned birds, as the chickadee; 2, the black raspberry.

black death the deadly plague which swept Asia and Europe in the 14th century.

black-en (blăk'n), *v.i.* to grow black or dark:—*v.t.* 1, to make black; soil; 2, to speak evil of.—*n.* **black'en-er.**

black flag the flag of a pirate, decorated with a skull and crossbones.

black fly 1, a small, troublesome fly, with a black body, abundant in the forests of the northern U. S. and of Canada; 2, a kind of plant louse which attacks the bean plant.

Black Fri-ar a monk of the Dominican order: so called from the black gown worn by these monks.

black-guard (blăg'ärd), *n.* a foul-mouthed and abusive scoundrel:—*adj.* 1, vicious; low; vile; 2, abusive:—*v.t.* to revile.—*adv.* **black'guard-ly.**

Black Hand a secret society organized to force money from people by threats of injury; esp., such a society among the Italians.

black-ing (blăk'ĭng), *n.* a mixture for giving a black polish to boots and shoes, stoves, etc.

black-jack (blăk'jăk''), *n.* 1, a small club with a flexible handle, used as a weapon; 2, the pirate flag.

black lead a substance made of graphite and clay, but no lead: used in pencils.

black-leg (blăk'lĕg''), *n.* 1, a dishonest, cheating gambler; swindler. 2, a strike breaker; scab.

black let-ter a style of type used in early manuscripts and in the first printed books.—*adj.* **black'-let''ter.**

black list a list of persons who are considered deserving of punishment, or exclusion from employment: **black-list** (blăk'lĭst''), *v.t.* to put on a black list.

black-mail (blăk'māl''), *n.* 1, a tax formerly paid to freebooters on the Scottish border to secure protection from theft; 2, hence, the securing of money by threats, esp. of public exposure:—*v.t.* to secure money from by threats.—*n.* **black'mail''er.**

black-out (blăk'out''), *n.* the extinction of lights visible out of doors.

black-smith (blăk'smĭth''), *n.* a person who works in iron.

black-snake (blăk'snāk''), *n.* 1, any of several very dark, swift, nonpoisonous snakes; 2, a heavy whip of braided cowhide. Also, **black snake.**

black-thorn (blăk′thôrn″), *n.* 1, a thorny shrub of the rose family; the sloe; 2, a stick cut from its stem.

blad-der (blăd′ẽr), *n.* 1, a sac of muscle or membrane in animals, in which a fluid is collected; esp., the urinary bladder; 2, any sac or blister, containing fluid or air; 3, anything puffed up or inflated.

blade (blād), *n.* 1, the leaf of a grass; the broad part of any leaf; 2, the cutting part of a knife or other instrument; 3, anything like the broad part of a knife; as, the *blade* of an oar; 4, a swordsman; 5, a dashing fellow:—*v.i.* [*p.t.* and *p.p.* blad′ed, *p.pr.* blad′ing], to put forth blades, as grass. —*p.adj.* **blad′ed.**

blain (blān), *n.* a blister; an inflamed sore or swelling.

blam-a-ble (blām′ȧ-bl), *adj.* deserving of blame or censure; faulty.—*adv.* **blam′a-bly.**—*n.* **blam′a-ble-ness.**

blame (blām), *n.* 1, an expression of disapproval; censure; 2, a fault; responsibility for anything wrong:—*v.t.* [*p.t.* and *p.p.* blamed (blāmd), *p.pr.* blam′ing], to find fault with; reproach.

Syn., v. condemn, reprove, upbraid, censure.

blame-less (blām′lĕs), *adj.* free from fault or wrongdoing.—*adv.* **blame′less-ly.**—*n.* **blame′less-ness.**

blame-wor-thy (blām′wûr″thĭ), *adj.* deserving reproof.

blanch (blȧnch), *v.t.* 1, to take the color out of; make white; as, to *blanch* celery; 2, to scald quickly so as to remove the skin, as almonds:—*v.i.* to become white; of persons, to turn pale, as from fear or cold.

blanc-mange (blȧ-mänzh′; -mäṅzh′), *n.* a white dessert composed of some jellylike or starchy substance combined with milk.

bland (blănd), *adj.* 1, soft-spoken; affable; 2, mild; soothing; gentle; as, a *bland* smile.—*adv.* **bland′ly.**—*n.* **bland′ness.**

blan-dish (blăn′dĭsh), *v.t.* to flatter; fondle; coax; wheedle.

blan-dish-ment (blăn′dĭsh-mĕnt), *n.* a flattering or soothing expression; cajolery; wheedling.

blank (blăngk), *n.* 1, any empty space; 2, a printed paper with spaces to be filled in; 3, a piece of metal, as for a coin, ready for stamping:—*adj.* 1, free from writing or print; 2, without variety or interest; 3, fruitless; vacant; empty; 4, utter; absolute; as, *blank* silence; 5, unbroken in surface; as, a *blank* wall; 6, not stamped.—*adv.* **blank′-ly.**—*n.* **blank′ness.**

Syn., adj. (see empty).

blan-ket (blăng′kĕt), *n.* 1, a soft, heavy, woolen cloth, used as a bed covering, a cover for a horse, etc.; 2, a covering of any material; as, a waterproof *blanket:* —*v.t.* to cover, as with a blanket.

blank verse unrimed verse; esp., in English literature, verse written in unrimed iambic pentameter.

blare (blâr), *n.* a harsh noise like the blast of a trumpet:—*v.i.* [*p.t.* and *p.p.* blared (blârd), *p.pr.* blar′ing], to give forth a loud, brazen sound like that of a trumpet: —*v.t.* to sound loudly, trumpet forth.

blar-ney (blär′nĭ), *n.* soft, coaxing speech; flattery: **Blarney stone,** a stone in the wall of Blarney Castle, Ireland which is said to confer the gift of flattery upon those who kiss it:—*v.t.* to influence or deceive by soft, coaxing speeches; humbug with flattery.

***bla-sé** (blä″zā′), [Fr.], *adj.* wearied by too much pleasure, so as to have lost the power of enjoyment.

blas-pheme (blas-fēm′), *v.t.* [*p.t.* and *p.p.* -phemed′ (-fēmd′), *p.pr.* -phem′ing], to speak irreverently of, or profanely or falsely about (God):—*v.i.* to talk irreverently or profanely; deny the being of God.—*n.* **blas-phem′er.**—*adj.* **blas′phe-mous.** —*adv.* **blas′phe-mous-ly.**

blas-phe-my (blȧs′fē-mĭ), *n.* [*pl.* blasphemies (-mĭz)], impious, profane, or mocking speech concerning God or sacred things.

blast (blȧst), *n.* 1, a strong gust of wind, 2, a forcible stream of air or gas from an opening; as, a *blast* of heat from a furnace; 3, the sound produced by blowing a wind instrument; 4, a sudden harmful influence upon plants or animals; a blight; 5, the explosion of gunpowder, dynamite, etc., in rending or removing rocks, or the charge so used:—*v.t.* 1, to injure; cause to fade or wither by some evil influence; ruin; destroy; 2, to break open or shatter by any explosive agent.—*n.* **blast′er.**

blast-ed (blȧs′tĕd), *p.adj.* 1, blighted; withered; shriveled; 2, *Colloq.*, accursed; detestable.

bla-tant (blā′tănt), *adj.* 1, bawling; noisy; 2, conspicuous; coarse.—*adv.* **bla′tant-ly.**—*n.* **bla′tan-cy.**

blath-er (blăth′ẽr; blȧth′ẽr), *n.* foolish talk:—*v.i.* and *v.t.* to talk or say foolishly. Also, **bleth′er.**

[1]**blaze** (blāz), 1, a fire; a body of bright flame; 2, intense direct light, as brilliant sunlight; 3, a sudden bursting out of some quality or emotion; ardor; 4, brilliant display; splendor; brightness:—*v.i.* [*p.t.* and *p.p.* blazed (blāzd), *p.pr.* blaz′ing], 1, to burst into flame; burn; 2, to glow or shine brightly; 3, to be lighted up; 4, to show sudden emotion:—*v.t.* to cause to burn or flame.

Syn., v. (see burn).

[2]**blaze** (blāz), *v.t.* [*p.t.* and *p.p.* blazed (blāzd), *p.pr.* blaz′ing], to spread abroad; proclaim news of.

[3]**blaze** (blāz), *n.* 1, a white spot on the face of a horse or other animal; 2, a mark made on a tree by removing a portion of the bark:—*v.t.* [*p.t.* and *p.p.* blazed (blāzd), *p.pr.* blaz′ing], 1, to mark, as a tree, by chipping off a portion of the bark, 2, to indicate, as a path or boundary, by such marks.

blaz-er (blāz′ẽr), *n.* a brightly colored or striped jacket, orig. worn at tennis, cricket, etc.

bla-zon (blā′zn), *n.* 1, a coat of arms; 2, a description of the figures on a coat of arms, banner, or the like, in the technical language of heraldry; 3, showy display:—*v.t.* 1, to explain or outline (the figures on a coat of arms, banner, etc.); 2, to decorate in color, as a shield; inscribe; 3, to proclaim; as, his face *blazons* his evil deeds.—*n.* **bla′zon-ment.**

bla-zon-ry (blā′zn-rĭ), *n.* 1, figures on coats of arms; 2, the art of describing and explaining coats of arms and armorial bearings; 3, bright display.

-ble (-bl), *adj. suffix,* in words from Latin; as, no*ble;* hum*ble.* See **-a-ble; -ile.**

bleach (blēch), *v.t.* to make white or whiter by a chemical process or by exposing to the sun's rays:—*v.i.* to grow or become white.—*n.* **bleach′er.**

bleach-ers (blēch′ẽrz), *n.pl.* the roofless space or seats for spectators at baseball and other games.

bleak (blēk), *adj.* 1, exposed to wind and cold; unsheltered; 2, piercing; cold; cutting; as, a *bleak* wind; 3, gray and cheerless.—*adv.* **bleak′ly.**—*n.* **bleak′ness.**

blear (blēr), *adj.* sore or dim from a watery discharge: said of the eyes: —*v.t.* 1, to make sore or watery, as the eyes;

2, to dim or obscure; hence, to deceive or hoodwink.—*adj.* **blear'-eyed"**.

blear-y (blēr'ĭ), *adj.* dull; blurry; sore.—*n.* **blear'i-ness.**

bleat (blēt), *n.* the cry of a sheep, goat, or calf:—*v.i.* to cry as, or like, a sheep.

bleb (blĕb), *n.* a blister; bubble; specif., a bubble in a solid substance that has been fluid; as, a *bleb* in glass.—*adj.* **bleb'by.**

bled (blĕd), past tense and past participle of the verb *bleed.*

bleed (blēd), *v.i.* [*p.t.* and *p.p.* bled (blĕd), *p.pr.* bleed'ing], **1**, to give forth or lose blood; shed one's blood; **2**, to lose sap or juice; as, trees *bleed* if trimmed after the sap is up in the spring; **3**, to be filled with sympathy or pity; as, all hearts *bleed* for the sufferers:—*v.t.* **1**, to take blood or sap from; **2**, *Colloq.*, to extort money from.

blem-ish (blĕm'ĭsh), *n.* any defect or deformity, physical or moral:—*v.t.* to injure; mar; disfigure.

Syn., n. defect, flaw. A *blemish* is a disfiguring mark which mars the appearance of an object: as, a scratch on a table is a *blemish.* A *defect* is a lack of something which is essential and spoils completeness; as, a *defect* in a motor. *Flaw* names an injury or fault in the structure of an object; as, a *flaw* in a mirror.

[1]**blench** (blĕnch), *v.i.* to start or shrink back; quail; flinch.

[2]**blench** (blĕnch), *v.t.* to make white or pale:—*v.i.* to grow pale.

blend (blĕnd), *v.t.* [*p.t.* and *p.p.* blend'ed or blent (blĕnt), *p.pr.* blend'ing], to mix together, so that the things mixed cannot be separated or distinguished from each other: —*v.i.* to mingle; shade into each other: said of colors:—*n.* **1**, a thorough mixture of colors, liquids, tobaccos, teas, etc.; **2**, a shading or merging, as of one color or flavor into another.

Syn., v. merge, fuse, combine. (See mix.)

bless (blĕs), *v.t.* [*p.t.* and *p.p.* blessed or blest (blĕst), *p.pr.* bless'ing], **1**, to set apart for a holy purpose; **2**, to call down a blessing upon; **3**, to give happiness to; as, O Lord, *bless* thy people; **4**, to praise or extol; **5**, to keep; guard: now only in exclamations; as, *bless* my soul!

bless-ed (blĕs'ĕd; *Poetic,* blĕst), *p.adj.* **1**, holy; worthy of reverence; **2**, supremely happy; **3**, enjoying or relating to heavenly bliss: **the blessed,** in the Roman Catholic Church, those in heaven who are entitled to public religious honor.—*adv.* **bless'ed-ly.**—*n.* **bless'ed-ness.**

bless-ing (blĕs'ĭng), *n.* **1**, an appeal for happiness or holiness for another; a benediction; **2**, that which causes prosperity; a divine benefit or gift; a mercy or boon; **3**, a brief prayer of thanksgiving said before or after a meal.

blest (blĕst), past tense and past participle of the verb *bless:*—*p.adj.* blessed.

bleth-er (blĕth'ẽr), *v.i.* to talk nonsense:—*n.* silly, talk. Also, **blath'er,** *Pfd.S.*

blew (bloo͞), past tense of the transitive and intransitive verb *blow.*

blight (blīt), *n.* **1**, a disease that causes plants to wither partly or wholly; smut; mildew; **2**, anything which causes such a disease, as certain fungi, insects, etc.; **3**, anything which serves to check, nip, or destroy; as, the *blight* of sin:—*v.t.* **1**, to affect with a withering disease or baleful influence; blast; **2**, hence, to destroy; frustrate.

blight-y (blīt'ĭ), *n.* a corruption of an East Indian word meaning "foreign country," esp. England; in the World War, used by the British soldiers to signify home, or Britain; as, back to *blighty* on a furlough.

blimp (blĭmp), *n.* a small, dirigible balloon used to locate submarines.

blind (blīnd), *adj.* **1**, without the sense of sight; sightless; also, pertaining to those without sight; **2**, unable or unwilling to understand, judge, or realize; **3**, heedless; unthinking; as, *blind* haste; **4**, without rule or reason; as, *blind* instinct; **5**, hidden; **6**, closed at one end; as, a *blind* alley; **7**, hard to understand; as, a *blind* statement: **blind tiger,** *U. S. Slang,* a place where intoxicants are illegally sold on the sly: also called *blind pig:*—*n.* **1**, anything which serves to hinder or obstruct vision, or hinders the passage of light, as a window shade, a hinged shutter for windows, a blinker on a horse's bridle, and the like; **2**, something to mislead the eye or the understanding; as, a *blind* of boughs and leaves is used to hide camera and men in photographing wild animals; **3**, a trick; ruse. —*v.t.* **1**, to deprive of sight or judgment; dazzle; **2**, to eclipse or hide.—*adv.* **blind'ly.**

blind-er (blīn'dẽr), *n.* **1**, one who or that which prevents from seeing; **2**, a blinker on a horse's bridle (see *harness,* illus.).

blind-fold (blīnd'fōld"), *adj.* **1**, having the eyes covered so as to be unable to see; **2**, hence, reckless:—*v.t.* **1**, to cover the eyes of, as with a bandage; **2**, to mislead.

blind-man's buff (blīnd'mănz"), a game in which someone who is blindfolded must catch and name one of the other players.

blind-ness (blīnd'nĕs), *n.* want of sight, wisdom, or understanding.

blind spot a small area on the retina of the eye which is not affected by or sensitive to light.

blind-worm (blīnd'wûrm"), *n.* a small, slender, limbless lizard with tiny eyes, so named from the popular belief that it cannot see; the slowworm.

blink (blĭngk), *v.i.* **1**, to wink quickly; see through half-shut eyes; **2**, hence, to get a quick glimpse; **3**, to twinkle; glimmer: —*v.t.* **1**, to wink rapidly, as the eyes; **2**, to shut one's eyes to; ignore (what one is looking at); as, he *blinks* a question:—*n.* **1**, a glimpse; **2**, the time of a wink; a twinkling; **3**, a glimmer; also, at sea, light on the horizon reflected from distant ice.

blink-er (blĭngk'ẽr), *n.* **1**, one who winks or evades; **2**, a leather flap placed one on each side of a horse's bridle to prevent him from seeing objects beside or behind him.

bliss (blĭs), *n.* **1**, the highest degree of happiness; the perfect joy of heaven; **2**, gladness; **3**, a cause of joy.

bliss-ful (blĭs'fo͝ol), *adj.* filled with gladness or joy; extremely happy.—*adv.* **bliss'ful-ly.**—*n.* **bliss'ful-ness.**

blis-ter (blĭs'tẽr), *n.* **1**, a small, bladderlike swelling on the skin, containing watery matter, as from a burn, friction, etc.; **2**, a similar swelling on the surface of a leaf, on painted boards, in glass, etc.; **3**, any substance used to produce such swellings:—*v.t.* to cause blisters to come upon:—*v.i.* to rise in, or become covered with, blisters.

blithe (blīth), *adj.* gay; joyous; glad; cheery; happy.—*adv.* **blithe'ly.**—*adj.* **blithe'some.**

blitz (blĭts), a sudden, violent, overwhelming attack.

bliz-zard (blĭz'ȧrd), *n.* a furious hurricane of wind accompanied by fine driving snow and intense cold.

[1]**bloat** (blōt), *v.t.* to cure (herring) by smoking.

[2]**bloat** (blōt), *v.t.* **1**, to cause to swell or distend, as with water or air; inflate; **2**, hence, to make vain:—*v.i.* to become puffed out or distended:—*adj.* puffy:—*n.* in animals, a large accumulation of gas in the abdomen.

bloat-er (blōt′ẽr), *n.* a large herring, salted, smoked, and half dried.

***bloc** (blôk), [Fr.], *n.* a political group which votes and acts for one purpose.

1block (blŏk), *n.* **1**, a solid piece of wood, stone, metal, etc.; esp., one prepared for building, or for use in chopping, pounding for attention, mounting a horse, etc.; also, a form used to mold hats, display wigs, or the like; **2**, the thick piece of wood supporting the neck of a person about to be beheaded; **3**, a pulley: often called *pulley block;* also, a system of pulleys in a frame or shell called, with the rope which operates it, *block and tackle;* **4**, a connected row of houses or shops; a large store or office building; **5**, a portion of a city bounded by two successive parallel streets in each direction, intersecting at right angles: also called *square;* also, the length of one side of such a square; **6**, a mass or division of something taken as a unit; as, a *block* of stock; a *block* of theater seats:—*v.t.* **1**, to secure or hold up, as by squared wooden supports; **2**, to mold or place on a form, as hats; **3**, to outline roughly; plan without details: usually with *out.*

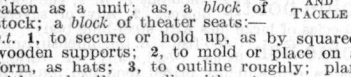

BLOCK AND TACKLE

2block (blŏk), *n.* **1**, an obstruction or impediment; **2**, the state of being obstructed:—*v.t.* to obstruct: often with *up.*

block-ade (blŏk-ād′), *n.* the shutting up of a place, as a port, by ships or troops of an enemy in order to prevent anything from coming in or going out, and thus force surrender:—*v.t.* [*p.t.* and *p.p.* -ad′ed, *p.pr.* -ad′ing], to surround (a place) with a blockade.—*n.* **block-ad′er.**

block-head (blŏk′hĕd″), *n.* a stupid fellow; a dolt.

block-house (blŏk′hous″), *n.* a fortress of heavy timber, with projecting upper story, having loopholes in the walls for the firing of guns.

block sys-tem an automatic system providing for the safe passage of railway trains, by which the line is divided into short sections called blocks, no train being allowed to leave a section until the next section is signaled clear.

blond (blŏnd), *adj.* **1**, having a fair complexion, light hair, and blue or gray eyes; **2**, of a fair color:—*n.* a person of very fair complexion, blue or gray eyes, and light hair. Also, *fem.* **blonde.**

blood (blŭd), *n.* **1**, the red fluid which circulates in the heart, arteries, and veins of animals supplying the body with food and oxygen; **2**, any vital fluid, such as sap; **3**, kinship; as, near in *blood;* **4**, descent; esp. noble lineage; as, a prince of royal *blood;* **5**, a man of spirit; as, a young *blood;* **6**, temper; mettle; as, his *blood* was up; **7**, slaughter or murder.

blood bank a reserve supply of blood or plasma for transfusion.

blood-ed (blŭd′ĕd), *adj.* of the best stock or breed.

blood heat the normal temperature of the human blood in health which is 98.6° Fahrenheit.

blood-hound (blŭd′hound″), *n.* **1**, one of a breed of large dogs remarkable for their acute sense of smell, employed to track wounded game and escaped prisoners or criminals; **2** hence, a detective.

blood-less (blŭd′lĕs), *adj.* **1**, run down physically; pale; **2**, lifeless; spiritless; **3**, cold-hearted; unfeeling; **4**, without bloodshed; as, a *bloodless* victory.—*adv.* **blood′less-ly.**—*n.* **blood′less-ness.**

blood mon-ey **1**, money obtained at the cost of another's life; as, Judas, when he betrayed Jesus, received thirty pieces of silver as *blood money;* **2**, the reward paid for the capture of a murderer; **3**, money formerly paid by the slayer to the next of kin of a slain person, as to avoid a feud.

blood plas-ma **1**, the fluid portion of unclotted blood; **2**, blood from which the red cells have been removed, treated, and usually dried, for use in transfusion.

blood-red (blŭd′=rĕd″), *adj.* of the color of blood; very red.

blood-root (blŭd′ro͞ot″), *n.* a plant of the poppy family, having thick red roots and orange-red sap, and bearing a white flower which blooms in early spring.

blood-shed (blŭd′shĕd″), *n.* slaughter; esp., destruction of human life, as in war or murder.

blood-shot (blŭd′shŏt″), *adj.* red and inflamed: said of the eyes.

blood-stone (blŭd′stōn″), *n.* a dark green variety of quartz spotted with red jasper.

blood-suck-er (blŭd′sŭk″ẽr), *n.* **1**, an animal that sucks blood; esp., a leech; **2**, one who forces money from another; an extortioner.

blood-thirst-y (blŭd′thûrs″tĭ), *adj.* murderous; eager to kill; cruel.—*adv.* **blood′thirst″i-ly.**—*n.* **blood′-thirst″i-ness.**

blood type any one of four classes into which human blood is divided according to red cell clumping tendencies.

blood-y (blŭd′ĭ), *adj.* [*comp.* blood′i-er, *superl.* blood′i-est], **1**, relating to, containing, or resembling blood; **2**, blood-stained; **3**, cruel; murderous; attended with slaughter.—*adv.* **blood′i-ly.**—*n.* **blood′i-ness.**

1bloom (blo͞om), *n.* **1**, the blossom or flower borne by a plant; **2**, the state of being in flower or having flowers; **3**, a state or period of health or growth; prime; **4**, the delicate, waxy or powdery coating on certain fruits and leaves; also, any surface coating suggesting this, as on a new coin:—*v.i.* **1**, to produce blossoms; flower; **2**, to glow with youth and freshness; flourish.

2bloom (blo͞om), *n.* **1**, a mass of wrought iron from a forge or furnace, shaped into a rough bar, and ready for forging or rolling; **2**, a lump of molten glass.

bloom-ers (blo͞o′mẽrz), *n.pl.* loose wide pants gathered at the bottom with elastic, worn as underwear by little girls, and once common as part of women's gym suits.

bloom-ing (blo͞o′mĭng), *p.adj.* **1**, blossoming; in flower; **2**, thriving in health, vigor, and beauty.—*adv.* **bloom′ing-ly.**

blos-som (blŏs′ŭm), *n.* **1**, the flower of a plant; **2**, the state of flowering:—*v.i.* **1**, to put forth flowers; **2**, to flourish.

blot (blŏt), *n.* **1**, a spot or stain; **2**, a wiping out or erasure; **3**, a spot on the reputation; disgrace:—*v.t.* [*p.t.* and *p.p.* blot′ted, *p.pr.* blot′ting], **1**, to spot or stain, as with ink; **2**, to dishonor; **3**, to impair; damage; **4**, to dry (ink) with absorbent paper; **5**, to cancel: usually with *out;* **6**, to destroy utterly; as, Sodom was *blotted* out; **7**, to darken or hide; as, a cloud *blots* out the moon:—*v.i.* **1**, to make a blot or blots; **2**, to become covered with blots.

blotch (blŏch), *n.* **1**, a large irregular spot, as of ink; **2**, a coarse eruption; as, a *blotch* of pimples on the face:—*v.t.* to mark or disfigure with irregular blots or spots.—*adj.* **blotch′y.**

blot-ter (blŏt′ẽr), *n.* **1**, something intended to dry or absorb wet ink; a piece of blotting paper; **2**, a book in which entries are made of events as they occur.

blot-ting pa-per paper specially made to absorb wet ink.

blouse (blouz; blous), *n.* **1**, a loose outer garment originally worn by workmen; **2**, any similar garment.

[1]**blow** (blō), *v.i.* [*p.t.* blew (blōō), *p.p.* blown (blōn), *p.pr.* blow'ing], to burst into bloom; be in flower:—*n.* a flower; blossom.

[2]**blow** (blō), *v.t.* [*p.t.* blew (blōō), *p.p.* blown (blōn), *p.pr.* blow'ing], **1**, to cause to move or send forward by a current of air; **2**, to inflate, as glass; **3**, to puff up, as by vanity; **4**, to cause to sound by forcing air through, as a whistle; **5**, to clear by forcing air through, as a tube or nostril; **6**, to cause or permit to pant for breath; **7**, to lay eggs in, as flies in raw meat; **8**, to scatter or shatter by explosives: usually with *up*, *open*, etc.; **9**, hence, *Colloq.*, to scold; chide: with *up*:—*v.i.* **1**, to move, as does a current of air; **2**, to send forth air, as a bellows; eject steam, a spout of water, etc.; **3**, to give forth sound when air is forced through, as a wind instrument; **4**, to pant; breathe quickly and with gasps; **5**, *Colloq.*, to brag; talk loudly:—*n.* **1**, the act of causing a current of air to move; **2**, a gale; puff of fresh air.

[3]**blow** (blō), *n.* **1**, a sudden, hard stroke with the hand or a weapon; **2**, a calamity or misfortune.

Syn. stroke, shock, knock, cuff, lash. A *blow* is a sudden violent striking, as by the clenched fist or a heavy object. A *stroke* is a long-drawn blow; as, the *stroke* of a whip; or it is a sweeping motion given with force and exactness; as, the *stroke* of a swimmer. Figuratively, *blow* names a sudden calamity or unpleasant surprise; as, his death was a great *blow*. *Stroke* is applied to a sudden, prostrating attack; also to any strikingly successful effort; as, a *stroke* of luck.

blow-er (blō'ẽr), *n.* **1**, one who blows; **2**, a device for causing a current of air.

blow-fly (blō'flī″), *n.* [*pl.* blowflies(-flīz″)], any of several flies which lay eggs on meat or in wounds.

blow-gun (blō'gŭn″), *n.* a tube from which missiles, such as arrows, are driven by the breath.

blown (blōn), past participle of the verb *blow*:—*p.adj.* **1**, winded, as from running or fatigue; **2**, tainted, as meat; **3**, infested with fly eggs.

blow-pipe (blō'pīp″), *n.* a tube by means of which a current of air or gas is driven through a flame to increase the heat and to direct it upon a substance to be heated.

blowz-y (blouz'ĭ), *adj.* [*comp.* blowz'i-er, *superl.* blowz'i-est], **1**, ruddy-faced; high-colored; coarse-complexioned, as by exposure to the weather; **2**, frowzy; disordered by wind, as the hair. Also, **blowzed.**

blub-ber (blŭb'ẽr), *v.i.* to weep noisily and so as to disfigure the face:—*v.t.* **1**, to disfigure (the face) with weeping; **2**, to utter sobbingly:—*n.* **1**, the act of weeping noisily; **2**, the fat of whales and some other large, marine animals: a source of oil; **3**, a kind of jellyfish.

blu-cher (blōō'chẽr; blōō'kẽr), *n.* **1**, a strong half-boot; **2**, a shoe in which the tongue and toe are made of one piece of leather.

bludg-eon (blŭj'ŭn), *n.* a short, heavy-headed stick used as a weapon:—*v.t.* to strike with, or as if with, a club:—*v.i.* to strike; batter.—*n.* **bludg'eon-ing.**

blue (blōō), *adj.* **1**, of the color of the clear sky; azure; **2**, low-spirited; dismal; as, the news made her *blue;* **3**, severely moral; as, the *blue* laws; **4**, purplish; discolored, as from a bruise; **5**, of blood, venous: opp. of *red*, or arterial; **6**, without promise; gloomy; as, a *blue* prospect: **blue blood,** **1**, in stock breeding, blood of a pure breed; **2**, blood of a noble or aristocratic family:—*n.* **1**, the color of the clear sky; azure; a certain one of the primary colors of the solar spectrum; **2**, a dye or powder that produces this color; **3**, in *pl.*, *Colloq.*, melancholy; low spirits:—*v.t.* [*p.t.* and *p.p.* blued (blōōd), *p.pr.* blu'ing or blue'ing], **1**, to make or dye the color of the clear sky or any hue like it; **2**, to treat with bluing.—*adv.* **blue'ly.**—*n.* **blue'ness.**

Blue-beard (blōō'bērd″), *n.* in folklore, a tyrannous husband who murdered many wives.

blue-bell (blōō'bĕl″), *n.* any of several plants bearing bell-shaped, blue flowers, as the harebell of Scotland.

blue-ber-ry (blōō'bĕr-ĭ), *n.* [*pl.* blueberries (-ĭz)], **1**, any of several plants of the heath family, bearing round, blue berries; **2**, the fruit itself.

blue-bird (blōō'bûrd″), *n.* any of several song birds of the thrush family, the males being blue above and cinnamon and white or blue and white below.

blue-bot-tle (blōō'bŏt″l), *n.* **1**, the cornflower; **2**, any of several species of large flies with steel-blue body.

blue-fish (blōō'fĭsh″), *n.* [*pl.* bluefish; bluefishes (-ĕz)], any of various fishes, esp. a highly prized food fish found in western Atlantic waters.

blue-jack-et (blōō'jăk″ĕt), *n.* a sailor; an enlisted man in the navy.

blue laws **1**, certain very strict laws said to have been made by the Puritans of New Haven, Connecticut; **2**, hence, any severe religious laws, esp. in regard to Sunday amusements.

blue pe-ter a blue flag with a white square in the center, used when a ship is about to sail.

blue rib-bon usually, the highest award in a competition, as at a dog show; a prized honor.

blue-sky laws laws aimed to prevent the sale of fraudulent stocks, bonds, or other securities.

blue-stock-ing (blōō'stŏk″ĭng), *n.* a scholarly woman, so interested in books that she cares for little else.

blu-et (blōō'ĕt), *n.* a low-growing meadow plant of the U.S., with small, bluish flowers: also called *innocence.*

[1]**bluff** (blŭf), *adj.* **1**, having a broad, flattened front; **2**, rising steeply or boldly, as a cliff; **3**, rough and hearty; abrupt; as, a *bluff* man:—*n.* a high, steep bank, cliff, or headland.—*adv.* **bluff'ly.**—*n.* **bluff'ness.**

Syn., *adj.* curt, brusque, rough; rude, gruff.—*Ant.*, *adj.* gentle, considerate, civil, polite, gracious.

[2]**bluff** (blŭf), *v.t.* to deceive, esp. by manner or speech, in order to accomplish one's own ends:—*v.i.* to deceive, or attempt to deceive, by assuming an air of confidence or strength:—*n.* **1**, the act of assuming a misleading manner; **2**, a bold manner intended to mislead.—*n.* **bluff'er.**

blu-ing (blōō'ĭng), *n.* a bluish preparation, as of indigo, used in laundering. Also, **blue'ing.**

blu-ish (blōō'ĭsh), *adj.* somewhat blue; shading into blue.—*n.* **blu'ish-ness.**

blun-der (blŭn'dẽr), *n.* a stupid mistake; a serious error:—*v.i.* **1**, to make a bad mistake from stupidity, ignorance, etc.; err stupidly; **2**, to move or act clumsily:—*v.t.* to do or utter stupidly.—*p.adj.* **blun'der-ing.**—*adv.* **blun'der-ing-ly.**—*n.* **blun'der-er.**

Syn., *n.* error, mistake, oversight. *Error*, the general term, names any departure from right or truth; as, an *error* in judgment; an error in writing. *Mistake* and *blunder* name kinds of error. A *mistake* is an error due to carelessness, inattention, or misunderstanding; as, he made a *mistake* in addition. A *blunder* is more serious than a *mistake* or an *error;* it is usually caused by stupidity or ignorance; as, his failure to apologize was a *blunder.*

blun-der-buss (blŭn′dẽr-bŭs), *n.* **1,** an old-fashioned, short gun with a flaring muzzle; **2,** a stupid fellow.

blunt (blŭnt), *adj.* **1,** having a thick or rounded edge or point; not sharp; **2,** dull in understanding; stupid; **3,** abrupt in speech or manner; plain-spoken:—*v.t.* **1,** to dull the edge or point of; **2,** to make weaker or less keen:—*v.i.* to become dull; lose keenness.—*adv.* **blunt′ly.**—*n.* **blunt′ness.**

blur (blûr), *v.t.* [*p.t.* and *p.p.* blurred (blûrd), *p.pr.* blur′ring], **1,** to make indistinct in outline; dim; **2,** to stain; blemish:—*v.i.* to become indistinct in outline:—*n.* **1,** a smudge; smear, as of ink; **2,** an indistinct or confused appearance.—*adj.* **blur′ry.**

blurb (blûrb), *n. Slang,* a short write-up concerning an author or his work, often issued as an announcement of a book or printed at the beginning of a story in a magazine.

blurt (blûrt), *v.t.* to speak out suddenly and without thought; utter unwisely: usually with *out;* as, to *blurt* out a secret.

blush (blŭsh), *v.i.* **1,** to redden or become rosy in the cheeks, as from shame or confusion; **2,** to feel shame: with *for* or *to:* —*n.* **1,** the red color that rises in the cheeks or face through shame, confusion, modesty, etc.; **2,** a red or reddish color; rosy tint.—*adv.* **blush′ing-ly.**

blus-ter (blŭs′tẽr), *v.i.* **1,** to be windy and boisterous, as the weather; **2,** to talk in a noisy, threatening style; bully:—*v.t.* to utter with noisy violence: with *forth* or *out:*—*n.* **1,** the noise and violence of a storm, or of the wind in gusts; **2,** noisy talk; empty threats.—*n.* **blus′ter-er.**—*adj.* **blus′ter-y.**

blus-ter-ing (blŭs′tẽr-ĭng), *p.adj.* **1,** gusty; stormy; **2,** overbearing; swaggering; noisy.—*adv.* **blus′ter-ing-ly.**—*adj.* **blus′ter-ous; blus′trous.**

bo-a (bō′ȧ), *n.* [*pl.* boas (-ȧz)], **1,** any one of various large nonpoisonous snakes, some of which are able to crush prey as large as a deer in their coils: popularly used to include certain Old World pythons; **2,** a long, round fur or feather neck piece for women.

bo-a con-stric-tor a boa, reaching eleven feet in length, found in tropical America, remarkable for its power of crushing its prey to death in its coils.

Boa Constrictor ($\frac{1}{30}$)

boar (bōr), *n.* **1,** the male of swine: **2,** the wild hog.—*adj.* **boar′ish.**

board (bōrd), *n.* **1,** a thin, flat piece of wood, longer than it is broad; **2,** a table for, or spread with, food: so called because a table at first was a wooden board; **3,** hence, the food served, esp. when at a fixed price; **4,** a group of directors, officers, etc., organized to act together for a special purpose; **5,** pasteboard, as for a book cover; **6,** a thin piece of wood or pasteboard prepared for a definite use; as, a checker*board;* a bulletin *board;* **7,** the side of a ship; as, over*board;* **8,** in *pl.,* the stage of a theater: **by the board, 1,** of a ship's mast, gone or broken off; **2,** hence, wrecked; lost: **on board,** on a ship or in a train:—*v.t.* **1,** to cover with flat timbers; **2,** to furnish with food, or food and lodging, in return for money; **3,** to cause to be lodged and fed, as a horse at a stable; **4,** to go on (a ship) or enter (a train):—*v.i.* to be regularly supplied with meals, or with meals and lodging, at a fixed charge.

board-er (bōr′dẽr), *n.* **1,** one who is regularly supplied with food, or with food and lodging, at a fixed price by the day or week; **2,** one who gets upon a ship, esp. an enemy ship.

board foot a volume equal to that of a timber one foot square and one inch thick: used in measuring lumber.

board-ing (bōrd′ĭng), *n.* **1,** light timber; also, a covering of light timber; **2,** the act of going on a ship; **3,** the act of supplying, or state of being supplied with, food and lodging, for a stated sum. **boarding house,** a house where people are regularly supplied with meals, and sometimes lodging, at a fixed price: **boarding school,** a school where the pupils are lodged and fed.

board meas-ure the measurement of lumber in board feet.

boast (bōst), *v.i.* **1,** to brag; speak of oneself or one's belongings in loud and vain terms; **2,** to exult:—*v.t.* **1,** to brag of; **2,** to possess as a thing to be proud of; as, he *boasted* a fine ranch:—*n.* **1,** a proud, vainglorious speech; **2,** a cause of pride, vanity, or praiseworthy triumph.—*n.* **boast′er.**

boast-ful (bōst′fo͝ol), *adj.* given to bragging, or full of vanity.—*adv.* **boast′ful-ly.**—*n.* **boast′ful-ness.**

boat (bōt), *n.* **1,** a small, open vessel, usually moved by oars or power but often by means of a sail; a ship; hence, any vessel for navigating the water; **2,** an open dish resembling a ship in form:—*v.i.* to go in a small open vessel; row; sail:—*v.t.* to transport or put in a boat.—*n.* **boat′man.**

boat hook a pole, usually having a sharp point and a hook, used in holding a small boat to a ship's side or to a wharf, or for pushing off.

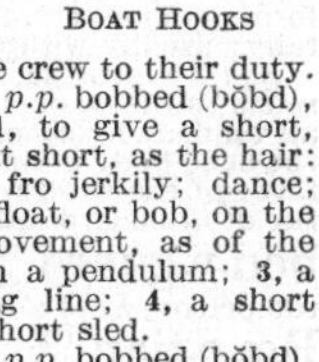

Boat Hooks

boat-ing (bōt′ĭng), *n.* the act of sailing or rowing, particularly when done as a pastime.

boat-swain (bōt′swān; bō′sn), *n.* an under officer of a ship, who has charge of the rigging, anchors, and cordage, and who calls the crew to their duty.

[1]**bob** (bŏb), *v.t.* [*p.t.* and *p.p.* bobbed (bŏbd), *p.pr.* bob′bing], **1,** to give a short, jerky motion to; **2,** to cut short, as the hair: —*v.i.* **1,** to move to and fro jerkily; dance; curtsy; **2,** to fish with a float, or bob, on the line:—*n.* **1,** a jerking movement, as of the head; **2,** a weight, as on a pendulum; **3,** a cork or float on a fishing line; **4,** a short haircut for women; **5,** a short sled.

[2]**bob** (bŏb), *v.t.* [*p.t.* and *p.p.* bobbed (bŏbd), *p.pr.* bob′bing], to strike; give a blow to; jog; rap:—*n.* a light blow; rap.

[3]**bob** (bŏb), *n.* [*pl.* bob], *Slang,* in England, a shilling.

bob-bin (bŏb′ĭn), *n.* **1,** one of the pins or small cylinders of wood used to carry and steady the threads in making pillow lace; **2,** a spool or reel with a head at one or both ends, used on machines to hold yarn or thread for spinning, weaving, or sewing.

bob-bi-net (bŏb″ĭ-nĕt′; bŏb′ĭ-nĕt), *n.* a machine-made cotton netting.

bob-by (bŏb′ĭ), *n.* [*pl.* bobbies (-ĭz)], *Slang*, in England, a policeman.

bob-o-link (bŏb′ō-lĭngk), *n.* an American song bird: also called, in certain localities, *ricebird; reedbird.*

bob-sled (bŏb′slĕd″), *n.* a sled made of two short sleds, called *bobs*, placed one behind the other and joined by a plank: used for hauling lumber and, when smaller, for coasting.

bob-stay (bŏb′stā″), *n.* in a sailing vessel, a rope or chain from the end of the bowsprit to the stem, to hold the bowsprit down (see *rigging*, illus.).

bob-tail (bŏb′tāl″), *n.* **1,** a short tail or a tail cut short; **2,** hence, an animal with such a tail.—*adj.* **bob′tailed″.**

bob-white (bŏb′hwīt″), *n.* **1,** the common American quail or partridge, **2,** the cry of this bird.

Boche (bôsh), *n.* [*pl.* Boches (bôsh)], **1,** a savage revolutionist; **2,** in the World War, a German soldier.

bode (bōd), *v.t.* [*p.t.* and *p.p.* bod′ed, *p.pr.* bod′ing], to portend; be a sign of future events, esp. of evil.

bod-ice (bŏd′ĭs), *n.* **1,** the close-fitting waist or body of a woman's dress; **2,** a wide belt or girdle, laced and tight-fitting.

bod-ied (bŏd′ĭd), *p.adj.* having a material form or body: usually in compounds; as, able-*bodied* seamen.

bod-i-less (bŏd′ĭ-lĕs), *adj.* having no concrete form; not made up of matter; immaterial.

bod-i-ly (bŏd′ĭ-lĭ), *adj.* **1,** having material form; **2,** pertaining to, or belonging to, the body; as, *bodily* sickness or harm:—*adv.* **1,** in person; **2,** entirely; completely.

bod-kin (bŏd′kĭn), *n.* **1,** a pointed instrument for piercing holes in embroidery; **2,** a blunt needle with a large eye for drawing tape or ribbon through a hem, eyelets, or the like; **3,** a long pin to fasten up the hair; **4,** an instrument for picking type from a form.

bod-y (bŏd′ĭ), *n.* [*pl.* bodies (-ĭz)], **1,** the form and substance of an animal, living or dead; **2,** the trunk or main portion of an animal or thing; **3,** a person; **4,** an aggregate of persons or things; as, a legislative *body;* a *body* of facts; **5,** a mass of matter; as, a heavenly *body;* **6,** consistency; substance; as, this silk has very little *body:* **body politic, 1,** the people of a nation, state, or community regarded as a political unit; **2,** the people collectively:—*v.t.* [*p.t.* and *p.p.* bod′ied (-ĭd), *p.pr.* bod′y-ing], **1,** to furnish with a material form; embody; **2,** to represent; picture mentally: usually with *forth.*

Syn., n. corpse, remains, carcass. *Body* refers to the whole physical being of a man or an animal, living or dead. *Corpse* refers to the dead body of man, and is often avoided in favor of the word *remains. Carcass* refers to the dead body of an animal.

bod-y-guard (bŏd′ĭ-gärd″), *n.* **1,** a guard, of one or more, to protect the person, as of a ruler; **2,** a retinue; escort.

Bœ-o-tian (bē-ō′shăn), *adj.* pertaining to Bœotia, in ancient Greece, derided for its dull, slow-witted people; hence, dull; stupid:—*n.* **1,** a native of Bœotia; **2,** a stupid person.

Boer (bo͝or), *n.* a South African colonist or farmer of Dutch descent.

bog (bŏg), *n.* a tract of wet, spongy ground, composed of partially decayed vegetable matter; a quagmire; marsh:—*v.i.* [*p.t.* and *p.p.* bogged (bŏgd), *p.pr.* bog′ging], to sink in a marsh:—*v.t.* to cause to sink, as in a marsh or quagmire.

bog-gle (bŏg′l), *v.i.* [*p.t.* and *p.p.* -gled (-ld), *p.pr.* -gling], **1,** to hesitate; waver; esp., to shy, as a horse; **2,** to demur; dissemble; **3,** to act clumsily; bungle:—*v.t.* to make a botch of:—*n.* **1,** a scruple; **2,** a blunder.

bog-gy (bŏg′ĭ), *adj.* [*comp.* bog′gi-er, *superl.* bog′gi-est], full of wet, muddy places; marshy; swampy.

bo-gus (bō′gŭs), *adj.* counterfeit; not genuine; fictitious; sham.

bo-gy (bō′gĭ), *n.* [*pl.* bogies (-gĭz)], a hobgoblin; specter; bugbear; ghost. Also, **bo′gie; bo′gey.**

Bo-he-mi-an (bō-hē′mĭ-ăn), *n.* **1,** a native of Bohemia; **2,** the language of Bohemia; **3,** one interested in art, literature, etc., who is indifferent to the conventions of social life; **4,** a gypsy:—*adj.* **1,** pertaining to Bohemia; **2,** disregarding conventions; free and easy.—*n.* **Bo-he′mi-an-ism.**

¹boil (boil), *v.i.* **1,** to bubble through the action of heat; become so hot as to bubble and change into vapor: said of a liquid; **2,** to be cooked in boiling water; **3,** to seethe with an agitation like that of boiling; **4,** to be excited by passion and anger:—*v.t.* **1,** to heat (a liquid) to the temperature at which the vapor rises to the top in bubbles; **2,** to cook in, or subject to, a boiling liquid:—*n.* **1,** the act or state of bubbling from the effect of heat; **2,** a submerging in boiling water.

²boil (boil), *n.* an inflamed, festering sore in the skin.

boil-er (boil′ẽr), *n.* **1,** a strong metallic vessel in which steam is produced for driving engines; **2,** a tank for storing hot water; **3,** a vessel in which a liquid is heated.

boil-ing (boil′ĭng), *p.adj.* heated to the point of bubbling; also, seething, as with passion:—*n.* **1,** the act of bubbling as a result of heat; **2,** the effect of subjecting to the action of hot liquid: **boiling point,** the temperature at which the vapor from a liquid overcomes the air pressure and rises in bubbles.

bois-ter-ous (bois′tẽr-ŭs), *adj.* **1,** violent; rough; stormy; **2,** noisy; rude; turbulent.—*adv.* **bois′ter-ous-ly.**—*n.* **bois′ter-ous-ness.**

bold (bōld), *adj.* **1,** courageous; fearless; venturesome; **2,** planned or carried out with daring and spirit; **3,** steep; abrupt, as a cliff; **4,** prominent; in high relief; **5,** venturing beyond the commonplace; mentally vigorous; as, a *bold* mind; **6,** impudent; presuming, as a speech.—*adv.* **bold′ly.**—*n.* **bold′ness.**

Syn. brave, daring, undaunted, brazen.

bold-face (bōld′fās″), *n.* a type with black, heavy face.—*adj.* **bold′-faced″.**

¹bole (bōl), *n.* the trunk or stem of a tree, or anything resembling it.

²bole (bōl), *n.* any of several kinds of easily crumbled clay.

bo-le-ro (bō-lā′rō), *n.* [*pl.* boleros (-rōz)], **1,** a lively Spanish dance; **2,** the music for such a dance; **3,** a short jacket.

bol-i-var (bŏl′ĭ-vȧr), *n.* the monetary unit of Venezuela, equal to 19.3 cents.

bo-li-via-no (bō-lē-vyä′nō), *n.* [*pl.* bolivianos (-nōz; -nōs)], the monetary unit of Bolivia, equal to 38.93 cents.

boll (bōl), *v.i.* to go to seed:—*n.* the pod or seed vessel of a plant, as of flax: **boll weevil,** a grayish beetle about $\frac{1}{4}$ of an inch long, the larvæ of which infest the cotton plant.

boll-worm (bōl′wûrm″), *n.* a larva which feeds on cotton, corn, etc.

bo-lo (bō′lō), *n.* [*pl.* bolos (-lōz)], a large, heavy knife used in the Philippines.

Bol-she-vi-ki (bŏl″shĕ-vē′kē), *n.pl.* [*sing.* Bolshevik], the followers

BIRDS OF NORTH AMERICA

1. Mocking bird. 2. Humming bird. 3. Catbird. 4. House wren. 5. Carolina cuckoo. 6. Cedar bird. 7. Baltimore oriole. 8. Chicken hawk (male). 9. Blue yellow-backed warbler. 10. Great horned owl. 11. Brown thrasher. 12. Australian weaver bird (recently introduced in America). 13. Cardinal (male). 14. Wild turkey. 15. Kingfisher. 16. Pearl's egret heron. 17. Woodpecker.

of the political party of revolutionary socialism which established the soviet form of government in Russia in 1917.—*adj.* **Bol'she-vik.**

Bol-she-vism (bŏl'shĕ-vĭsm), *n.* the theory of government of the Bolsheviki; revolutionary socialism.—*adj.* and *n.* **Bol'she-vist.**

bol-ster (bōl'stẽr), *n.* **1**, a long pillow or cushion used to support the head, as on a bed; **2**, a cushioned pad to ease pressure, deaden noise, etc.; **3**, a structure placed over the axles of a wagon or truck to support the body:—*v.t.* **1**, to support with a pillow or cushion; prop: usually with *up;* **2**, to abet; countenance: with *up;* **3**, to pad.

[1]**bolt** (bōlt), *n.* **1**, a short, thick, heavy-headed arrow; dart; **2**, hence, anything coming dartingly or suddenly, as a flash of lightning; a thunderbolt; **3**, a metal pin or rod for fastening together or holding in place parts of machinery, furniture, etc., threaded at one end, and sometimes at both, to hold a nut; **4**, a sliding catch for a door or gate; that part of a lock which is shot or drawn back by the key; **5**, a roll of cloth, usually containing about 40 yards; **6**, a sudden dashing or darting away, as of a horse; **7**, in politics, a refusal to support a party policy or nominee:—*v.t.* **1**, to shoot; expel with force; **2**, to blurt out unexpectedly; **3**, to fasten with a sliding catch, as a door; **4**, to fasten together with metal pins, as metal plates; **5**, to swallow (food) very rapidly, or without chewing; **6**, in U. S. politics, to refuse to support (the candidate or policy of one's own party); break away from (one's party):—*v.i.* **1**, to dash or dart away suddenly; run away, as a horse; **2**, to fall swiftly and with force; shoot down; **3**, in U. S. politics, to refuse to support a party, candidate, or policy.

[2]**bolt** (bōlt), *adv.* directly and suddenly, like a dart: **bolt upright**, erect.

[3]**bolt** (bōlt), *v.t.* **1**, to sift, as flour from bran; **2**, to examine minutely.

[1]**bolt-er** (bōl'tẽr), *n.* **1**, a horse given to running away suddenly; **2**, in politics, one who refuses to support his party.

[2]**bolt-er** (bōl'tẽr), *n.* a machine for separating flour from bran.

bomb (bŏm; bŭm), *n.* **1**, a hollow iron ball or shell filled with an explosive material, fired from a gun or exploded by concussion or by a fuse; **2**, any shell similarly constructed and thrown by the hand or dropped from an airship: **incendiary bomb**, a shell that, when exploded, throws out a flaming liquid which sets fire to anything combustible within a large area.

bom-bard (bŏm-bärd'; bŭm-bärd'), *v.t.* **1**, to attack with cannon; fire shot or shell at or into; **2**, to assail persistently with missiles: often used figuratively; as, *bombarded* with questions.

bom-bard-ment (bŏm-bärd'mĕnt; bŭm-), *n.* **1**, a continuous attack with shot and shell, rockets, missiles, etc.; the act or process of shelling a town or fort; **2**, a persistent attack.

bom-bast (bŏm'băst; bŭm'-), *n.* high-sounding words; inflated language or style with little meaning.

bom-bas-tic (bŏm-băs'tĭk; bŭm-), *adj.* **1**, pompous; inflated; ranting; **2**, given to high-sounding language.—*adv.* **bom-bas'ti-cal-ly.**

bom-ber (bŏm'ẽr; bŭm'ẽr), *n.* an airplane or other aircraft used in bombing (see *aviation*, illus.).

bomb-proof (bŏm'prōōf"; bŭm'-), *adj.* secure against damage, or resisting injury, from the explosive force of shells:—*n.* a structure or chamber secure against explosive shells.

bomb-shell (bŏm'shĕl"; bŭm'-), *n.* **1**, an explosive missile, or bomb; **2**, anything very sudden and surprising.

***bo-na fi-de** (bō'nȧ fī'dē), [Lat.], literally, in good faith; genuine.

bo-nan-za (bō-năn'zȧ), *n. U. S. Slang,* a rich vein of ore in a mine; hence, any unexpected good fortune.

bon-bon (bŏn'bŏn"; *Fr.* bôṅ"bôṅ'), *n.* a confection; candy; sweetmeat.

[1]**bond** (bŏnd), *n.* **1**, that which fastens, ties, or confines; **2**, in *pl.*, fetters; imprisonment; **3**, a binding agreement; **4**, a force or an influence which unites; as, the *bond* of kinship; **5**, in law: **a**, security given for another; bail; **b**, an obligation in writing and under seal; **6**, a promise by a corporation or government to pay an investor, in return for the use of his credit, a principal sum on a certain date, with interest; **7**, a guarantee that owners of imported goods, liable to duty and held in a warehouse pending disposal, will pay the duty when the goods are removed for sale:—*v.t.* **1**, in law: **a**, to place under the conditions of a bond; **b**, to secure or assure, as payment or the faithful performance of duty; **2**, to put or hold (dutiable goods) in a warehouse, on security that the duties will be paid when the goods are released for sale; **3**, to require a pledge of property or security from; **4**, to mortgage; **5**, in building, to connect or bind together by a special arrangement, as timbers or stones; **6**, in electricity, to connect so as to lessen resistance to the passage of current at a particular point.

[2]**bond** (bŏnd), *adj.* in servitude or slavery; captive.

bond-age (bŏn'dĭj), *n.* serfdom; physical or moral slavery or subjection; imprisonment; servitude.

bond-ed (bŏn'dĕd), *p.adj.* **1**, held in bond, or under pledge, for payment of import duties; **2**, secured by written agreement, as a debt: **bonded warehouse**, a place in which goods are kept under bond.

bond-hold-er (bŏnd'hōl"dẽr), *n.* the holder or owner of a bond.

[1]**bonds-man** (bŏndz'măn), *n.* [*pl.* bondsmen (-mĕn)], one who becomes surety for another's debt, appearance for trial, or the like.

[2]**bonds-man** (bŏndz'măn), *n.* [*pl.* bondsmen (-mĕn)], a slave or serf. Also, **bond'man.**—*n. fem.* **bonds'wom"an.**

bone (bōn), *n.* **1**, the hardened tissue forming the skeleton of the higher orders of animals; **2**, one of the parts or pieces of an animal skeleton; **3**, a stay of whalebone, steel, etc., for a corset; **4**, any of certain substances resembling bone, as ivory; **5**, a joint of meat; **6**, in *pl.:* **a**, the whole skeleton; remains; **b**, dice; **c**, pieces of bone or ivory held between the fingers and rattled together as an accompaniment to music: **bone dry**, **1**, very dry, as a sun-dried bone; **2**, *Slang*, free from the legal sale of intoxicants: said of states and countries which prohibit by law all traffic in alcoholic liquors:—*v.t.* [*p.t.* and *p.p.* boned (bōnd), *p.pr.* bon'ing], **1**, to remove the bones from; **2**, to stiffen with whalebone, as a dress; **3** *Slang*, to study; cram.—*adj.* **bone'less.**

bone dust bone ground fine to use as fertilizer: also called *bone meal.*

[1]**bon-er** (bōn'ẽr), *n.* a worker who cuts bones from meat.

[2]**bon-er** (bōn'ẽr), *n. Slang*, a silly, stupid error, either of speech or action.

bone-set (bŏn'sĕt"), *n.* thoroughwort, a wild plant with medicinal properties, widely distributed in the U. S.

bon-fire (bŏn'fīr"), *n.* any large fire made in the open air, as to celebrate an event or to destroy rubbish or trash.

7

bon-ho-mie (bŏn″ō-mē′; *Fr.* bô″nô″mē′), *n.* good nature; a frank, pleasant, easy manner. Also, **bon″hom-mie′.**

***bon mot** (bôṅ″ mō′), [Fr.], [*pl.* bons mots (bôṅ″ mō′)], a witty saying.

***bonne** (bôn), [Fr.], *n.* a French maid, esp. a nursemaid.

bon-net (bŏn′ĕt), *n.* **1,** a soft woolen cap worn by men in Scotland; **2,** a woman's or child's outdoor head covering, usually having strings, but no brim; **3,** anything resembling such a head covering in shape or use:—*v.t.* to provide with a bonnet.

bon-ny (bŏn′ĭ), *adj.* [*comp.* bon′ni-er, *superl.* bon′ni-est], **1,** comely; pretty; **2,** cheerful; gay. Also, **bon′nie.**

bon-ny-clab-ber (bŏn′ĭ-klăb″ẽr), *n.* milk that has thickened in souring.

***bon ton** (bôṅ″ tôṅ′), [Fr.], **1,** the style of persons in high society; **2,** fashionable society; **3,** the height of fashion.

bo-nus (bō′nŭs), *n.* [*pl.* bonuses (-ĕz)], **1,** a sum given, or paid, over and above what is strictly due, as in dividends, profits, or wages; **2,** an additional payment made to the shareholders in a company out of the profits.

bon-y (bōn′ĭ), *adj.* [*comp.* bon′i-er, *superl.* bon′i-est], **1,** like, or full of, bones; **2,** having prominent or conspicuous bones.

boo (bo͞o), *interj.* **1,** an expression of dislike, aversion, or contempt; **2,** an exclamation made to frighten:—*v.i.* to utter the sound *boo,* as to frighten someone.

boo-by (bo͞o′bĭ), *n.* [*pl.* boobies (-bĭz)], **1,** a dunce; a stupid fellow; **2,** in a game, the player with the poorest score.

boo-dle (bo͞o′dl), *n. Slang,* money paid for votes or political influence; bribe money; graft.

boo-hoo (bo͞o′ho͞o″; bo͞o″ho͞o′), *n.* loud crying, weeping, or laughter:—*interj.* expressing the sound of loud weeping:—*v.i.* (bo͞o″ho͞o′), to cry loudly: usually used humorously or in derision.

book (bo͝ok), *n.* **1,** a collection of sheets of paper and other material, blank, written, or printed, bound together in a volume; **2,** a composition of some length on a particular subject, printed and bound; **3,** a main division, section, or part of a literary composition; **4,** a volume of blank pages prepared for recording commercial transactions or official records; **5,** in card playing, a certain number of tricks held by one side; **6,** in horse racing, a list of horses entered and the bets laid on them: **the Book,** the Bible: **Book of Common Prayer,** the official service book of the Church of England and the Protestant Episcopal Church:—*v.t.* **1,** to enter or register; as, to *book* an order; **2,** to engage beforehand, as rooms; to reserve transportation for.

book-bind-er (bo͝ok′bīn″dẽr), *n.* one whose business or occupation it is to bind books.—*n.* **book′bind″ing.**—*n.* **book′bind″er-y.**

book-case (bo͝ok′kās″), *n.* a set of shelves for books.

book-ish (bo͝ok′ĭsh), *adj.* **1,** fond of study; given to reading; **2,** better acquainted with books than with men; learned; **3,** making a display of learning; as, *bookish* talk.—*adv.* **book′ish-ly.**—*n.* **book′ish-ness.**

book-keep-ing (bo͝ok′kēp″ĭng), *n.* the art of recording accounts or business transactions in a regular and systematic manner.—*n.* **book′keep″er.**

book-let (bo͝ok′lĕt), *n.* a small volume, usually intended either for ornament or for advertising purposes.

book-mak-er (bo͝ok′māk″ẽr), *n.* **1,** one who writes or publishes books; **2,** a professional betting man.

book-plate (bo͝ok′plāt″), *n.* a label in a book giving its classification in a library, or the name of the owner: sometimes called *ex libris.*

book-worm (bo͝ok′wûrm″), *n.* **1,** any of various kinds of insects that live in and injure books; **2,** a person who is unusually devoted to reading and study.

[1]**boom** (bo͞om), *n.* **1,** a chain or line of floating timbers used, as on a river, to stop traffic, or to confine saw logs; also, the area so inclosed; **2,** a long pole or spar attached either to a ship's mast to extend the sail, or to a derrick's mast to steady or guide in hoisting.

[2]**boom** (bo͞om), *n.* a deep, hollow sound, as of breakers or cannon; also, the hollow cry of the bittern:—*v.i.* and *v.t.* to make, or give forth with, a deep, hollow sound.

[3]**boom** (bo͞om), *n.* **1,** a sudden increase of business activity; a rapid rise in prices; also, rapid growth in development and population; **2,** a vigorous campaign for a political candidate or cause:—*v.i.* to grow with a rush; be prosperous:—*v.t.* to cause to grow rapidly, as a town; push with vigor or spirit, as a candidate for office.—*n.* **boom′er.**

boom-er-ang (bo͞om′ẽr-ăng), *n.* **1,** a weapon used by the Australian natives, consisting of a piece of flat curved hard wood, which, when thrown by the hand in a certain manner, makes a number of curves, and finally returns to the thrower; **2,** hence, any plot or action the result of which recoils upon the maker to his disadvantage.

[1]**boon** (bo͞on), *n.* **1,** a benefit; blessing; gift; privilege; **2,** *Obs.,* a petition.
Syn. bequest, present, grant, donation.

[2]**boon** (bo͞on), *adj.* **1,** jovial; merry; convivial: as, a *boon* companion; **2,** *Archaic* or *Poetic,* kind; bounteous.

boor (bo͞or), *n.* **1,** a peasant; **2,** a rustic; **3,** a rude, ill-mannered person.

boor-ish (bo͞or′ĭsh), *adj.* **1,** clownish; awkward in manner; ungainly; **2,** ignorant; without culture.—*adv.* **boor′ish-ly.**—*n.* **boor′ish-ness.**

boost (bo͞ost), *v.t. U. S. Colloq.,* to lift by pushing from behind; hence, to promote:—*n. U. S. Colloq.,* a push or shove that aids one to rise or advance.—*n.* **boost′er.**

[1]**boot** (bo͞ot), *n.* **1,** a leather covering for the foot and the lower part of the leg. **2,** an old instrument of torture, made to squeeze or crush the lower part of the leg; **3,** a place for baggage, as at the back of a coach or automobile; **4,** anything resembling a boot:—*v.t.* **1,** to put boots on; **2,** to kick with the boot; **3,** to torture with the boot.

[2]**boot** (bo͞ot), *n. Obs.:* **1,** remedy; help; **2,** profit: **to boot,** in addition, as to the terms of a bargain:—*v.t.* **1,** to profit; benefit; as, it *boots* me nothing: usually used impersonally; **2,** *Obs.:* **a,** to remedy; **b,** to give (something) to equalize the exchange.

boot-black (bo͞ot′blăk″), *n.* one whose occupation is to polish shoes.

boot-ee (bo͞o-tē′), *n.* a little boot; a lady's, or child's, light boot or half-boot.

Bo-ö-tes (bō-ō′tēz), *n.* in astronomy, a constellation, the Herdsman, whose brightest star is Arcturus.

booth (bo͞o*th*; bo͞oth), *n.* **1,** a covered stall or other temporary structure made of boards, canvas, etc.; **2,** a stand, as at a fair or market, where goods are exhibited.

boot-jack (bo͞ot′jăk″), *n.* an instrument for pulling off boots or shoes.

boot-leg-ger (bo͞ot′lĕg″ẽr), *n. U. S. Colloq.,* one who engages in the business of making or marketing alcoholic liquors in violation of law.—*v.i.* **boot′-leg″.**—*n.* **boot′leg″ging.**

boot-less (bōōt′lĕs), *adj.* without avail; without advantage; useless; as, a *bootless* errand.

boots (bōōts), *n.pl.* used as *sing.* the servant in a hotel who cleans and polishes the shoes of the guests; a bootblack.

boot-tree (bōōt′-trē″), *n.* a device on which to stretch boots or keep them from losing their shape.

boo-ty (bōō′tĭ), *n.* [*pl.* booties (-tĭz)], **1,** food, guns, etc., taken from the enemy in war; plunder; **2,** that which is seized by violence and robbery; **3,** any rich spoil.

booze (bōōz), *v.i.* [*p.t.* and *p.p.* boozed (bōōzd), *p.pr.* booz′ing], to drink to excess; tipple:—*n. Colloq.*, **1,** liquor; drink; **2,** a spree.—*n. Colloq.*, **booz′er.**

bo-peep (bō-pēp′), *n.* a quick peeping out and withdrawing, in a child's game of this name.

bo-rac-ic (bō-răs′ĭk), *adj.* pertaining to, or produced from, boron; boric: **boracic acid,** a colorless crystalline compound, largely used in solution as a wash for the eyes and for antiseptic purposes; boric acid.

bo-rat-ed (bō′rāt-ĕd), *adj.* mixed or filled with borax or boric acid; as, *borated* talcum powder.

bo-rax (bō′răks), *n.* a white, crystalline salt composed of sodium, boron, and oxygen: used as a flux, and as a cleaning agent and antiseptic.

bor-der (bôr′dẽr), *n.* **1,** the outer part or edge of anything; a margin; **2,** a rim; boundary; frontier; verge; **3,** an edging outlining anything, as a narrow flower bed along a path:—*v.t.* **1,** to make a decorative margin about; **2,** to be next to:—*v.i.* **1,** to touch at the edge or boundary: with *on* or *upon;* **2,** to approach: with *on* or *upon;* as, his ability *borders* upon genius.

Syn., *n.* margin, edge, rim, brim, brink, coast, shore. A *border* is that portion of a surface just within the boundary line, or the boundary or limiting line itself; as, the *border* between the United States and Canada. A *margin* is a definite border, as the blank space surrounding the printed part of a page. *Edge* names the extreme line or limit of a border; as, the *edge* of the horizon; the *edge* of a knife. *Rim, brim,* and *brink* name different kinds of edge. A *rim* is the edge of any vessel or opening, but usually of a curved one; as, the *rim* of a barrel. A *brim* is the outer, upper edge of a hollow vessel; as, the *brim* of a cup. A *brink* is the edge of a steep or deep place; as, the *brink* of a pool. A *coast* is the bordering sea line of a country or continent; as, the *coast* of France. A *shore* is the land bordering any body of water; as, the *shore* of a lake.

bor-der-er (bôr′dẽr-ẽr), *n.* one who dwells on the edge of a district.

bor-der-land (bôr′dẽr-lănd″), *n.* **1,** land forming a frontier; **2,** an uncertain or doubtful district; as, the *borderland* between right and wrong.

[1]**bore** (bōr), *v.t.* [*p.t.* and *p.p.* bored (bōrd), *p.pr.* bor′ing], **1,** to pierce or drill a hole in, as with an auger; **2,** to form (a hole) by piercing or drilling, as with an auger; **3,** to force (a passage) with effort:—*v.i.* **1,** to make a hole; pierce; **2,** to be drilled by an instrument; **3,** to push forward toward a certain point:—*n.* **1,** a hole made by, or as if by, piercing or drilling; **2,** hence, the cavity or hollow of a gun, pipe, or tube; **3,** the inside diameter of a drilled hole; caliber; **4,** a hole, as one drilled into the earth.

[2]**bore** (bōr), *v.t.* [*p.t.* and *p.p.* bored (bōrd), *p.pr.* bor′ing], **1,** to weary by tiresome repetition or by dulness; **2,** to annoy:—*n.* **1,** any person or thing that causes dull weariness; **2,** an annoyance.

[3]**bore** (bōr), *n.* a sudden and violent inrush of the flood tide occurring in certain rivers and estuaries: also called *eagre.*

[4]**bore** (bōr), one of the forms of the past tense of the irregular verb *bear.*

bo-re-al (bō′rē-ăl), *adj.* pertaining to the north or the north wind.

Bo-re-as (bō′rē-ăs), *n.* the north wind: one of the names by which the Greeks personified the four winds.

bore-dom (bōr′dŭm), *n.* mental weariness produced by monotony or by lack of interest in life.

bor-er (bōr′ẽr), *n.* **1,** one who or that which pierces or drills a hole, as an auger; **2,** an insect or other animal that drills holes.

bo-ric (bō′rĭk), *adj.* pertaining to, or containing, boron; boracic: **boric acid,** a crystalline compound used in solution as an antiseptic; boracic acid.

bo-ride (bō′rīd; bō′rĭd), *n.* a compound of boron with some metallic substance. Also, **bo′rid.**

born (bôrn), past participle of the verb *bear* when used passively in reference to birth:—*p.adj.* **1,** brought forth or into being, as offspring; **2,** natural; made of a certain character by birth; ingrained.

borne (bōrn), past participle of the verb *bear:* used when not referring to birth, or when referring to birth and associated with mention of the mother; as, two children *borne* by one mother; she has *borne* a child.

bo-ron (bō′rŏn), *n.* a nonmetallic element somewhat like carbon and silicon in chemical behavior.

bor-ough (bŭr′ō), *n.* a town which is organized into a self-governing body under a mayor and other officers.

bor-row (bŏr′ō), *v.t.* **1,** to obtain the use of, with the understanding that the article obtained is to be returned; **2,** to take; copy; adopt; as, many republics *borrow* their constitutions from the U. S.; **3,** in arithmetical subtraction, to take a unit from any given denomination in order to add ten to the next lower denomination:—*v.i.* **1,** to obtain something with the intention of returning it; **2,** to copy or adopt another's thought or words.—*n.* **bor′row-er.**

bosh (bŏsh), *n. Colloq.*, absurd or empty talk; utter nonsense.

bosk (bŏsk), *n.* a grove; thicket; a small wood.—*adj.* **bosk′y.**—*n.* **bos′ki-ness.**

bos-om (bŏŏz′ŭm), *n.* **1,** the breast of a human being; **2,** the part of a garment which covers the breast; **3,** the breast as the seat of the affections or passions, or as the center of emotions or desires; the heart; **4,** hence, any deep, central place; as, the *bosom* of the lake:—*adj.* **1,** intimate; beloved; as, a *bosom* friend; **2,** worn on the breast:—*v.t.* **1,** to place or carry close to the heart; keep tenderly; **2,** to conceal.

[1]**boss** (bôs), *n.* **1,** a knob; stud; a circular ornament, as of metal, which stands out from a flat surface, as of a shield; **2,** in geology, a hill or mountain of igneous rock:—*v.t.* to ornament with knobs.—*adj.* [1]**boss′y.**

[2]**boss** (bôs), *n.* **1,** a superintendent of workmen; foreman; **2,** the dictator of a political organization:—*v.t. Colloq.*, to hold mastery over; manage; direct:—*v.i. Colloq.*, to be master.—*adj. Colloq.*, [2]**boss′y.**

bo-tan-ic (bō-tăn′ĭk), *adj.* pertaining to botany, the science which treats of the study of plant life. Also, **bo-tan′i-cal.**—*adv.* **bo-tan′i-cal-ly.**

bot-a-nize (bŏt′ȧ-nīz), *v.i.* [*p.t.* and *p.p.* -nized (-nīzd), *p.pr.* -niz″ing], to seek after plants for the purpose of studying them; go into the fields to study plants as they grow.—*n.* **bot′a-niz″er.**

bot-a-ny (bŏt′ȧ-nĭ), *n.* [*pl.* botanies (-nĭz)], the science which treats of plants, their forms, classes, etc.; also, a textbook on this science.—*n.* **bot′a-nist.**

botch (bŏch), *n.* **1,** a patch badly or clumsily put on; **2,** bungling work:—*v.t.* **1,** to spoil; disfigure; **2,** to mend clumsily:—*v.i.* to do a poor piece of work.—*n.* **botch′er.**

botch-y (bŏch′ĭ), *adj.* [*comp.* botch′i-er, *superl.* botch′i-est], poorly or clumsily done; poorly repaired.

bot-fly (bŏt′flī″), *n.* [*pl.* botflies (-flīz″)], any of several flies which in one stage live on horses and other animals.

both (bōth), *adj.* two at once or together; as, *both* soldiers were killed:—*pron.* the two together; as, he saw *both:*—*conj.* as well; not only; as, *both* the living and the dead:—*adv.* equally; also; too; as, cruelty spoils goodness and beauty *both.*

both-er (bŏ*th*′ẽr), *v.t.* to annoy; tease; worry; give trouble to:—*v.i.* **1,** to feel trouble or care; **2,** to be troublesome:—*n.* **1,** a source of worry; annoyance; perplexity; **2,** one who gives trouble.

both-er-a-tion (bŏ*th*″ẽr-ā′shŭn), *n.* **1,** the act of annoying or bothering; **2,** the state of being vexed, annoyed, or perplexed:—*interj.* confound it!

both-er-some (bŏ*th*′ẽr-sŭm), *adj.* troublesome; annoying; causing worry or perplexity.

bots (bŏts), *n.pl.* [*sing.* bot (bŏt)], the larvæ, or first stage, of the botfly, which live on horses, oxen, sheep, etc. Also, **botts.**

bot-tle (bŏt′l), *n.* **1,** a hollow, narrow-necked vessel without handles, made of glass or earthenware, for holding liquids; **2,** the contents of such a vessel:—*v.t.* [*p.t.* and *p.p.* -tled (-ld), *p.pr.* -tling], **1,** to put into such vessels; **2,** to shut in or to hold back; as, to *bottle* up one's feelings.—*n.* **bot′tler.**

bot-tom (bŏt′ŭm), *n.* **1,** the lowest part of anything; the base; foundation; root; **2,** the ground under any body of water; **3,** low land; **4,** the power to endure; **5,** the part of a vessel below the water line; hence, a ship:—*adj.* lowest; undermost:—*v.t.* **1,** to found or build upon; **2,** to furnish with a foundation.—*adj.* **bot′tom-less.**

bou-doir (bo͞o′dwär″), *n.* a small room, esp. a lady's private sitting room.

bough (bou), *n.* a limb or branch of a tree, esp. a main branch.

bought (bôt), past tense and past participle of the verb *buy.*

***bou-illon** (bo͞o″yôṅ′; bo͝ol″yôṅ′; bo͝ol′-yŏn), [Fr.], *n.* clear soup or broth made from beef or other meat.

boul-der (bōl′dẽr), *n.* **1,** a large stone worn or rounded by running water; **2,** a large weatherworn rock detached from its original bed. Also, **bowl′der.**

bou-le-vard (bo͞o′lē-värd), *n.* **1,** a broad street or avenue, usually bordered with trees; **2,** in a fortification, a paved way along a rampart, on the original ground level (see *rampart, terreplein,* illus.).

bounce (bouns), *v.t.* [*p.t.* and *p.p.* bounced (bounst), *p.pr.* bounc′ing], **1,** to cause to rebound; **2,** to toss:—*v.i.* **1,** to rebound; **2,** to spring suddenly; **3,** to come in or go out noisily:—*n.* **1,** an elastic motion; **2,** a sudden bound or spring; a heavy thump; **3,** brag; boasting.

bounc-er (boun′sẽr), *n.* **1,** one who or that which bounds or springs; **2,** someone or something unusually big.

bounc-ing (boun′sĭng), *p.adj.* **1,** large; strapping; **2,** active; strong; lively; **3,** boastful.

1**bound** (bound), *v.i.* **1,** to leap or spring lightly; **2,** to rebound; recoil:—*v.t.* to cause to spring back or recoil:—*n.* **1,** a light, elastic step or leap; a rebound; **2,** the space covered by such a leap.

2**bound** (bound), *v.t.* **1,** to set a limit to; restrict; **2,** to form the limiting line to; lie adjacent to; **3,** to name the countries or waters surrounding; as, to *bound* Canada:—*n.* **1,** that which defines or confines; a limit; **2,** in *pl.,* extent of territory within certain limits; hence, range of action, thought, etc., within certain limits.

Syn., v. limit, inclose, terminate.

3**bound** (bound), past tense and past participle of the verb *bind:*—*p.adj.* **1,** tied; confined; **2,** obliged; compelled; **3,** apprenticed; **4,** made fast between covers, as a book; **5,** *U. S. Colloq.,* purposed; determined; certain.

4**bound** (bound), *adj.* all ready to go; having started: with *for* or *to.*

bound-a-ry (boun′dȧ-rĭ), *n.* [*pl.* boundaries (-rĭz)], **1,** a limiting line; **2,** that which marks the extent or limit of anything, as a frontier.

bound-en (boun′dn), *adj.* **1,** under obligation; **2,** binding.

bound-less (bound′lĕs), *adj.* without limits; unlimited; vast.

boun-te-ous (boun′tē-ŭs), *adj.* **1,** giving freely; **2,** freely given.—*adv.* **boun′te-ous-ly.**—*n.* **boun′te-ous-ness.**

boun-ti-ful (boun′tĭ-fo͝ol), *adj.* **1,** liberal in bestowing gifts or favors; generous; **2,** plentiful.—*adv.* **boun′ti-ful-ly.**—*n.* **boun′ti-ful-ness.**

Syn. bounteous, abundant, ample.—*Ant.* stingy, close, miserly.

boun-ty (boun′tĭ), *n.* [*pl.* bounties (-tĭz)], **1,** generosity in giving gifts or favors; **2,** that which is freely given; **3,** a premium or allowance offered by a government to encourage enlistment or industry.

bou-quet (bo͞o-kā′), *n.* **1,** a bunch of flowers; nosegay; **2,** an aroma, as of wine; perfume.

1**bour-geois** (bûr-jois′), *n.* in printing, a size of type, nearly equivalent to 9 point (see *type*).

2***bour-geois** (bo͞or″zhwȧ′), [Fr.], *n.* **1,** a French citizen between the gentleman and the peasant in social position; a shopkeeper; **2,** in Russia, one who owns property and hence is suspected of being hostile to the proletariat, or wage earners; **3,** in other countries, one of the middle class:—*adj.* belonging to the middle class; hence, commonplace and lacking distinction.

***bour-geoi-sie** (bo͞or″zhwȧ″zē′), [Fr.], *n.* the middle classes of a country, esp. of France.

bour-geon (bûr′jŭn), *v.i.* to bud:—*n.* a bud. Also, **bur′geon,** *Pfd. S.*

1**bourn** (bōrn), *n.* in Great Britain, a brook; rivulet. Also, **bourne; burn.**

2**bourn** (bōrn; bo͞orn), *n.* **1,** a boundary; limit; **2,** a place aimed at; a goal.

bourse (bo͞ors), *n.* an exchange for the transaction of business; esp., the stock exchange of Paris.

bout (bout), *n.* **1,** a going and returning, as in mowing; **2,** as much work as is performed in a single turn; **3,** a set-to, as at boxing; contest; **4,** a spell of drunkenness or illness; **5,** a turn or loop.

***bou-ton-nière** (bo͞o″tô″nyâr′), [Fr.], *n.* a very small bouquet worn in a man's buttonhole.

bo-vine (bō′vīn; -vĭn), *adj.* **1,** pertaining to the family of mammals that includes sheep, horned cattle, etc.; **2,** oxlike; patient; stolid.

1**bow** (bou), *v.t.* **1,** to cause to bend or become curved; **2,** to bend, as the head or body, in respect; **3**, to humiliate; oppress; crush; **4**, to usher in or out; **5**, to express, as thanks or respect, by bending the head or body:—*v.i.* **1**, make a bow, as in repsect or submission; **2**, to bow or nod the head in greeting or salutation: often with *to:*—*n.* a bending of the head or body in greeting or respect.

²**bow** (bō). *n.* **1**, anything curved, as a rainbow, the rim or curved end of spectacles, the curved handle on the stem of a key, etc.; **2**, a weapon of elastic wood, bent by a string attached to both ends, which drives an arrow by its rebound when released; **3**, a staff of pliant wood strung with tightly stretched horsehair, for playing instruments of the violin class; **4**, a knot with a loop or loops, as of ribbon:—*v.t.* to bend or curve like a bow:—*v.i.* **1**, to become bent or curved; **2**, to play with a bow, as the violin.

³**bow** (bou), *n.* **1**, the fore part or prow of a vessel or an airship; **2**, the foremost oarsman in a boat.

bow-el (bou′ĕl), *n.* **1**, an intestine; **2**, in *pl.:* **a**, the intestines of an animal, esp. man; **b**, the interior parts of the earth; **c**, the seat of tenderness; hence, compassion.

¹**bow-er** (bou′ẽr), *n.* a shelter made of boughs or twining plants; an arbor:—*v.t.* to surround, as with foliage or boughs; embower.—*adj.* ¹**bow′er-y.**

²**bow-er** (bou′ẽr), *n.* an anchor carried at the bow of a ship.

²**bow-er-y** (bou′ẽr-ĭ), *n.* [*pl.* boweries (-ĭz)], a farm with its buildings: so called by the early Dutch settlers in New York: **Bowery,** a street in New York City, once famous because of the vulgarity and flashiness of its cheap amusement resorts.

bow-ie knife (bō′ĭ; bōō′ĭ), a strong hunting knife; loosely, any sheath knife.

bow-knot (bō′nŏt″), *n.* a slipknot, as of ribbon, with a single or double loop, easily untied.

¹**bowl** (bōl), *n.* **1**, a low, concave vessel for holding liquids; **2**, a large drinking cup; **3**, the hollow part of anything, or anything shaped like a bowl; as, the *bowl* of a spoon; esp., a large, curved amphitheater; **4**, the contents of a bowl.

²**bowl** (bōl), *n.* **1**, a ball of wood used in the games of bowls and skittles, weighted so as to make it run a curved course; **2**, in *pl.*, in England, a game played with such balls; ninepins; tenpins:—*v.i.* **1**, to play with bowls; **2**, in cricket, to serve the ball with a stiff or straight arm; **3**, to roll a bowl or ball; **4**, to move rapidly and smoothly along:—*v.t.* **1**, to roll, as a bowl or ball; **2**, in cricket, to put out (a batsman) by bowling; **3**, to knock down; disconcert; stun momentarily; as, to *bowl* anyone over.—*n.* **bowl′er.**

bowl-der (bōl′dẽr), *n.* any detached and rounded or worn piece of rock. See **boul′der,** *Pfd. S.*

bow-leg (bō′lĕg″), *n.* a crooked leg; a leg bowed or curved outward.—*adj.* **bow′-leg″ged** (bō′-lĕg″ĕd; -lĕgd″).

bow-line (bō′lĭn; -līn), *n.* **1**, a rope fastened near to the weather edge of a square sail, to keep the ship nearer the wind; **2**, a special kind of loop knot which will not slip, and which can be easily untied (see *knot*, illus.).

bowl-ing (bōl′ĭng), *n.* **1**, the sport of playing at bowls; **2**, the game itself; **3**, in cricket, the act of delivering the ball: **bowling alley,** a place for playing bowls: **bowling green,** a level, smooth lawn on which the game of bowls is played.

¹**bow-man** (bō′măn), *n.* [*pl.* bowmen (-mĕn)], an archer; one who uses a bow and arrows.

²**bow-man** (bou′măn), *n.* [*pl.* bowmen (-mĕn)], the oarsman nearest the bow of the boat.

bow-sprit (bō′sprĭt; bou′sprĭt), *n.* a large spar running out from the forward end of a ship.

bow-string (bō′strĭng″), *n.* **1**, the string of a bow; **2**, the string used by the Turks for strangling criminals; **3**, hence, execution by strangling:—*v.t.* [*p.t.* and *p.p.* -stringed″ (-strĭngd″) or -strung″ (-strŭng″), *p.pr.* -string″ing], to strangle with a bowstring.

¹**box** (bŏks), *n.* a slap on the face, or a cuff on the ear:—*v.t.* to buffet or strike with the fist or hand:—*v.i.* to fight with the fists; spar with boxing gloves.

²**box** (bŏks), *n.* any of a genus of evergreen trees or shrubs, one species being much used for hedges: also called *box tree.*

³**box** (bŏks), *n.* **1**, a case or container for solids, usually with a lid; **2**, the quantity that such a container does, or can, hold; **3**, the driver's seat on a coach or carriage; **4**, a separate compartment in a theater, restaurant, etc.; **5**, a shed or structure resembling a box, as the shelter for a sentry or signalman; **6**, in baseball, the place where the pitcher stands, or where the batsman stands; **7**, a case for inclosing or protecting a part, as a bearing: **box office,** a ticket office, esp. of a theater:—*v.t.* **1**, to provide or furnish with a solid case or covering; **2**, to shut up in, or inclose in, a solid case; pack; stow: sometimes with *up.*—*n.* ¹**box′er.**

²**box-er** (bŏk′sẽr), *n.* a pugilist; one who fights with gloved fists: **Boxer,** a member of the Chinese secret society which in 1900 attempted to rid China of all foreigners by massacre.

¹**box-ing** (bŏk′sĭng), *n.* **1**, the act of putting into a box; **2**, the material used for making boxes; **3**, an inclosure resembling a box; casing.

²**box-ing** (bŏk′sĭng), *n.* the art of fighting with the fists or sparring with gloves; pugilism: **boxing gloves,** gloves padded for sparring.

box-wood (bŏks′wŏŏd″), *n.* the hard, tough, close-grained wood of the box tree (see ²*box*).

boy (boi), *n.* **1**, a male child from birth to about sixteen years of age; a young lad; **2**, a male servant, used esp. of Orientals and negroes.

boy-cott (boi′kŏt), *v.t.* **1**, to refuse as a group to trade or associate with (a person or company); **2**, to refuse to trade in (a thing):—*n.* a combination to withhold or prevent trade, as for forcing down prices.

boy-hood (boi′hŏŏd), *n.* **1**, the state or time of being a boy; **2**, boys collectively; as, the *boyhood* of America.

boy-ish (boi′ĭsh), *adj.* **1**, pertaining to a boy or boyhood; **2**, childish; youthful.—*adv.* **boy′ish-ly.**—*n.* **boy′ish-ness.**

boy scout a member of an organization for training boys in character and self-reliance by means of camp life and civic service.

brace (brās), *n.* **1**, that which steadies a thing, or holds it tightly or supports it firmly, as a prop or bandage; **2**, a pair; as, a *brace* of pistols; **3**, a curved line, as { or }, connecting two or more lines of print, staffs of music, or the like; **4**, a curved implement for holding and turning boring tools (see *tool*, illus.); **5**, a timber to strengthen the framework of a building:—*v.t.* [*p.t.* and *p.p.* braced (brāst), *p.pr.* brac′ing], **1**, to bind; strengthen; furnish with supports; **2**, to stimulate: often with *up:*—*v.i.* to rouse oneself to greater effort: with *up.*

brace-let (brās′lĕt), *n.* an ornamental band or ring for the wrist.

brac-er (brās'ẽr), *n.* **1**, that which supports; **2**, a tonic; stimulant; **3**, a guard for the wrist.

bra-chi-um (brā'kĭ-ŭm), *n.* [*pl.* brachia (-*ȧ*)], **1**, the part of the arm from the shoulder to the elbow; **2**, that which in animals represents an arm; a fore limb; **3**, a process like an arm.—*adj.* **bra'chi-al.**

brac-ing (brās'ĭng), *p.adj.* giving strength or vigor; as, *bracing* air.

brack-en (brăk'n), *n.* any of various large ferns.

brack-et (brăk'ĕt), *n.* **1**, a supporting piece projecting from a wall; **2**, a single or jointed gas pipe projecting from a wall or pillar; **3**, one of two marks [ ], used to inclose a word, or to separate a certain part from the rest of the text:—*v.t.* **1**, to furnish with brackets; **2**, to couple together.

brack-ish (brăk'ĭsh), *adj.* **1**, saltish; **2**, hence, distasteful.

bract (brăkt), *n.* a leaflike appendage on the side of a flower stalk or beneath the flower.—*adj.* **brac'te-al.**—*adj.* **brac'te-ate.** —*adj.* **brac'te-o-late.**

brad (brăd), *n.* **1**, a small, slender nail, sometimes flat, having a projection on one side, but no head; **2**, a small, wire nail.

brad-awl (brăd'ôl″), *n.* a straight awl having a chisel edge.

brae (brā; brē), *n.* a hillside or slope; sloping ground.

brag (brăg), *v.t.* [*p.t.* and *p.p.* bragged (brăgd), *p.pr.* brag'ging], to boast of; vaunt:—*v.i.* to boast; speak swaggeringly:—*n.* **1**, boasting; **2**, a thing boasted of; **3**, one who boasts.—*n.* **brag'ger.**

brag-ga-do-ci-o (brăg″*ȧ*-dō'shĭ-ō), *n.* **1**, a boaster; a swaggerer; **2**, empty boasting; brag.

brag-gart (brăg'*ȧ*rt), *n.* a boaster; vain fellow:—*adj.* boastful.

[1]**Brah-ma** (brä'm*ȧ*), *n.* a useful variety of large domestic fowl.

[2]**Brah-ma** (brä'm*ȧ*), *n.* the first member of the trinity in Hindu religion; the Creator. Also, **Brahm.**

Brah-man (brä'măn), *n.* [*pl.* Brahmans (-mănz)], a Hindu of the sacred, or priestly, caste. Also, **Brah'min.**—*adj.* **Brah-man'ic; Brah-man'i-cal.**

Brah-man-ism (brä'măn-ĭzm), *n.* the religious and social system of the Hindus, among whom the Brahmans form the highest caste. Also, **Brah'-min-ism.**

braid (brād), *v.t.* **1**, to weave; intertwine; plait; **2**, to trim or outline with a narrow band:—*n.* **1**, a plaited band; **2**, a narrow, flat band, as of tape or ribbon, used for trimming and binding.

Braille (brāl), *n.* **1**, a system of printing for the blind in which points raised above the surface are used to represent letters; **2**, the symbols themselves.

brain (brān), *n.* **1**, in higher animals, the mass of nervous tissue filling the skull; the seat of the higher activities of the mind; **2**, in many lower animals, a nerve center in the head; the chief nerve center of the animal:—*v.t.* to dash out the brains of.

brain-less (brān'lĕs), *adj.* without understanding; without wit.—*adv.* **brain'less-ly.**—*n.* **brain'less-ness.**

brain-pan (brān'păn″), the cranium; the part of the skull inclosing the brain (see *skull,* illus.).

brain-y (brān'ĭ), *adj.* [*comp.* brain'i-er, *superl.* brain'i-est], *U. S. Colloq.*, mentally acute; sharp-witted.

braise (brāz), *v.t.* [*p.t.* and *p.p.* braised (brāzd), *p.pr.* brais'ing], to stew or broil (as meat) in a covered vessel.

[1]**brake** (brāk), *n.* **1**, a device for checking the motion of a wheel, vehicle, etc.; **2**, an instrument for separating the fiber from flax, hemp, etc.; **3**, a heavy harrow; **4**, any long lever, as a pump handle; **5**, a baker's kneading trough; **6**, a frame for holding the foot of an unruly horse while it is being shod; **7**, (usually, *break*), a kind of wagonette: **brake shoe**, that part of a brake which presses against the wheel:—*v.t.* [*p.t.* and *p.p.* braked (brākt), *p.pr.* brak'ing], **1**, to stop or retard, as a wheel or vehicle, by applying a check; **2**, to crush or bruise, as flax; **3**, to break up, powder, or grind with a harrow; **4**, to knead:—*v.i.* to operate a brake, as on a railroad car; also, to be employed for this purpose, or as assistant to the conductor.

[2]**brake** (brāk), *n.* a large fern common in temperate latitudes on waste lands.

[3]**brake** (brāk), *n.* a place overgrown with shrubs and brambles; a thicket.

brake-man (brāk'măn), *n.* [*pl.* brakemen (-mĕn)], one who operates the brakes, as on a railroad car; also, one who acts as an assistant to the conductor.

bram-ble (brăm'bl), *n.* **1**, the English blackberry; **2**, any prickly bush or shrub.—*adj.* **bram'bly.**

bran (brăn), *n.* the husks of wheat, rye, etc., separated from the flour by sifting or bolting.—*adj.* **bran'ny.**

branch (brȧnch), *n.* **1**, a shoot or limb from a main bough; **2**, hence, anything resembling this; as, a *branch* of a river; **3**, any member or part of a body or system; a department; **4**, a section or subdivision; esp., a division of a family descended from some particular ancestor:—*adj.* turning aside from the trunk or main body; as, the *branch* roads of a railway system:—*v.i.* to divide from the main body; diverge: with *out.*

brand (brănd), *n.* **1**, a burning piece of wood; **2**, a mark burned with a hot iron, as upon cattle; also, the iron used; **3**, a trade-mark; hence, any particular kind or make of goods; **4**, a mark of disgrace; **5**, *Poetic*, a sword:—*v.t.* **1**, to mark with a hot iron, or by other means; **2**, hence, to impress deeply upon the mind; **3**, to disgrace.—*n.* **brand'er.**

bran-dish (brăn'dĭsh), *v.t.* to move, wave, or shake, as a raised weapon; flourish, as with a challenge.—*n.* **bran'dish-er.**

brand-new (brănd'=nū'), *adj.* quite new. Also, **bran'-new'.**

bran-dy (brăn'dĭ), *n.* [*pl.* brandies (-dĭz)], an alcoholic liquor distilled from wine or the juice of grapes or other fruits.—*adj.* **bran'died.**

brant (brănt), *n.* a small, dark-colored wild goose of northern waters.

[1]**brash** (brăsh), *adj. Colloq.*, saucy; pert; also, quick-tempered.

[2]**brash** (brăsh), *adj.* easily broken; brittle, as some kinds of timber.

[1]**bra-sier** (brā'zhẽr), *n.* a pan for burning charcoal. Also, **bra'zier**, *Pfd. S.*

[2]**bra-sier** (brā'zhẽr), *n.* one who works in brass. Also, **bra'zier** *Pfd. S.*

brass (brȧs), *n.* **1**, an alloy made by mixing copper with zinc, or, sometimes, tin; **2**, *Slang:* **a**, money; **b**, impudence; **3**, in *pl.*, instruments, vessels, ornaments, etc., made of a copper and zinc alloy, esp. the brass winds: **brass winds**, in an orchestra, those wind instruments (also called *brass-wind instruments*) which are made of brass, as the trumpet, trombone, etc. (see *musical instrument*, illus.).

bras-sard (brăs'*ȧ*rd, br*ȧ*-särd'), *n.* **1**, (usually, *brassart*), orig., a piece of armor for the upper arm, or, later, for the whole arm (see *reredos*, illus.); **2**, a badge worn on the arm as an emblem of rank, a symbol of mourning, etc.

***bras-sière** (brä″syâr′), [Fr.], *n.* an underwaist worn by women.

brass-y (bràs′ĭ), *adj.* [*comp.* brass′i-er, *superl.* brass′i-est], **1**, made of, or like, brass; **2**, *Slang*, impudent; brazen:—*n.* [*pl.* brassies (-ĭz)], a club of a special kind, used in the game of golf. Also, *n.* **brass′ie; brass′ey.**—*adv.* **brass′i-ly.**—*n.* **brass′i-ness.**

brat (brăt), *n.* a child: used contemptuously.

bra-va-do (brȧ-vä′dō; -vā′dō), *n.* [*pl.* bravadoes; bravados (-dōz)], bragging pretense of courage or indifference; boastful defiance.

brave (brāv), *adj.* **1**, bold; courageous; fearless; as, a *brave* general; *brave* deed; **2**, making a fine show; as, *brave* attire:—*n.* **1**, an Indian warrior; **2**, a courageous man:—*v.t.* [*p.t.* and *p.p.* braved (brāvd), *p.pr.* brav′ing], to meet with courage; defy; as, a soldier must *brave* danger and hardships:—*adv.* **brave′ly.**—*n.* **brave′ness.**

brav-er-y (brāv′ẽr-ĭ), *n.* [*pl.* braveries (-ĭz)], **1**, the quality of being fearless; gallantry; heroism; **2**, *Archaic*, bright show.

Syn. courage, valor, pluck. These words agree in that they express resistance to some opposing power. *Courage*, the noblest term, is that quality of character which meets dangers without fear under all circumstances; as, the *courage* of a hero. *Bravery* is a more common trait than *courage* and is often present only at the moment of need or danger; as, the *bravery* of a fireman. *Valor* combines the daring of *bravery* with the ability of *courage* to lead and endure; as, the *valor* of a soldier. *Pluck* implies courage and a determination to overcome difficulties; as, a man of *pluck*.

[1]**bra-vo** (brä′vō), *interj.* well done! good!—*n.* [*pl.* bravos (-vōz)], a shout of applause; as, the hall rang with *bravos*.

[2]**bra-vo** (brä′vō; brā′-), *n.* [*pl.* bravoes; bravos (-vōz)], a hired assassin; a bandit.

braw (brô), *adj. Scot. Dial.*, strong; fine; brave; handsome; as, a *braw* laddie.—*adv.* **braw′ly.**

brawl (brôl), *n.* **1**, a noisy quarrel; **2**, the noise of a rushing brook:—*v.i.* **1**, to quarrel or wrangle noisily; **2**, to make a loud noise, as of water rushing over a rocky bed.—*n.* **brawl′er.**—*adv.* **brawl′ing-ly.**

brawn (brôn), *n.* **1**, firm, strong muscles, esp. of the arm or leg; **2**, muscular strength; **3**, boar's flesh, esp. when prepared by boiling, pickling, and pressing.

brawn-y (brôn′ĭ), *adj.* [*comp.* brawn′i-er, *superl.* brawn′i-est], muscular; strong; as, the blacksmith has a *brawny* arm.—*n.* **brawn′i-ness.**

[1]**bray** (brā), *n.* a loud, harsh sound, as the cry of the ass, or the blast of a trumpet:—*v.t.* to utter in a loud, harsh way:—*v.i.* to utter a loud, harsh sound or cry.

[2]**bray** (brā), *v.t.* to pound or beat fine or small, esp. in a mortar.

[1]**braze** (brāz), *v.t.* [*p.t.* and *p.p.* brazed (brāzd), *p.pr.* braz′ing], **1**, to join with hard solder of brass and zinc; **2**, to harden.

[2]**braze** (brāz), *v.t.* [*p.t.* and *p.p.* brazed (brāzd), *p.pr.* braz′ing], to make of, or like, brass; ornament with brass.

bra-zen (brā′zn), *adj.* **1**, made of brass; resembling, or sounding like, brass; **2**, impudent; shameless:—*v.t.* to face with impudence: with *out*.—*adv.* **bra′zen-ly.**—*n.* **bra′zen-ness.**

[1]**bra-zier** (brā′zhẽr), *n.* an open pan for holding burning charcoal or coals. Also, **bra′sier.**

[2]**bra-zier** (brā′zhẽr), *n.* one who works in brass. Also, **bra′sier.**

Bra-zil-ian (brȧ-zĭl′yȧn), *adj.* pertaining to Brazil:—*n.* a resident in, or native of, Brazil.

Bra-zil nut (brȧ-zĭl′), an edible nut, the seed of a South American tree.

breach (brēch), *n.* **1**, the act of making an opening or separation; **2**, the breaking of a law, a contract, or any other obligation; **3**, a gap; **4**, a rupture of friendly relations; a quarrel: **breach of promise**, failure to keep one's promise, esp. a promise to marry:—*v.t.* to make an opening in.

bread (brĕd), *n.* **1**, dough made from the flour or meal of some kind of grain, and baked; **2**, food in general; **3**, hence, livelihood; as, he works hard for his daily *bread*:—*v.t.* to cover with bread crumbs before cooking; as, to *bread* cutlets.—*p.adj.* **bread′ed.**

bread-fruit (brĕd′frōōt″), *n.* **1**, the fruit of a tree native to the Pacific islands: when roasted, somewhat like bread; **2**, the tree which bears this fruit.

bread-stuff (brĕd′stŭf″), *n.* any material, such as corn, flour, or meal, from which bread is made.

breadth (brĕdth), *n.* **1**, the measure of any surface from side to side; hence, spaciousness; extent; **2**, freedom from narrowness; liberality; **3**, a piece of fabric of uniform width; as, two *breadths* of cloth are needed for the skirt.

break (brāk), *v.t.* [*p.t.* broke (brōk) or, *Archaic*, brake (brāk), *p.p.* bro′ken (brō′kn) or, *Obs.* or *Archaic*, broke, *p.pr.* break′ing], **1**, to separate into pieces by a blow or strain; fracture, as a bone; **2**, to force (a way, path, crack, hole, or the like) into or through something; **3**, to destroy the arrangement or completeness of; as, to *break* ranks; to *break* a dollar bill; **4**, to weaken the force of, as a fall, a blow, the wind; **5**, to set aside, violate, or fail to obey, as a promise or a law; **6**, to degrade, as an officer to the ranks; **7**, to tell cautiously; disclose, as bad news; **8**, to tame, as a horse; **9**, to plow or dig up, as ground; **10**, to make bankrupt; **11**, to discontinue: with *off*; **12**, to excel (a record); **13**, to destroy the health or vitality of; **14**, to interrupt, as silence, or an electric circuit:—*v.i.* **1**, to separate into pieces suddenly; burst; **2**, to change abruptly, as a gait, tone, etc.; **3**, to fail in health; weaken; **4**, to become bankrupt; **5**, to burst forth violently, as a storm or cry; **6**, to be scattered, as clouds; **7**, to come, as the dawn; **8**, to occur or turn out in a specified way; as, luck *broke* against him; **9**, to quarrel; rupture friendship; **10**, to lose musical quality suddenly, as a voice; also, to change in tone, as a boy's voice at puberty:—*n.* **1**, an opening; interruption; breach; a gap or rent; pause; **2**, that which causes a gap, interruption, rent, etc.; **3**, a first appearance or marked change; as, the *break* of day; **4**, a sudden fall in prices; as, a *break* in the stock market; **5**, the point where one register, or quality, changes to another, as of a voice or the tones of an instrument; **6**, (also, *brake*), a large wagonette; **7**, *U. S. Colloq.*, a blunder of speech or action.—*adj.* **break′a-ble.**

Syn., *v.* crush, rend, tear, destroy, smash, crack, split, shiver, shatter.

break-age (brāk′ĭj), *n.* **1**, the act of breaking; **2**, the state of being broken; **3**, an allowance for things broken by accident, as in moving.

break-bone fe-ver (brāk′bōn″), an infectious, eruptive disease of the tropics: also called *dengue*.

break-down (brāk′doun″), *n.* **1**, a physical collapse; **2**, a failure; stoppage; downfall; as, the *breakdown* of the empire; **3**, a noisy, shuffling negro dance.

break-er (brāk'ẽr), *n.* **1**, one who or that which separates by force; esp., a machine to crush coal, rocks, etc.; **2**, a wave which dashes itself into foam, as against the shore or a rock or reef.

break-fast (brĕk'fȧst), *n.* the first meal of the day:—*v.t.* to provide with, or entertain at, the morning meal:—*v.i.* to eat the morning meal.

break-neck (brāk'nĕk"), *adj.* dangerously fast; involving risk of life; as, a *breakneck* pace.

break-wa-ter (brāk'wô"tẽr), *n.* any structure built to withstand the force of the waves; a sea wall.

1**bream** (brēm), *n.* **1**, a deep-bodied, fresh-water European fish of the carp family; **2**, in the U. S., any of various fresh-water sunfishes.

2**bream** (brēm), *v.t.* to clear (a ship's bottom) of shells, seaweed, ooze, and the like, by heating with torches and scraping.

breast (brĕst), *n.* **1**, the fore part of the body between the neck and the abdomen; **2**, either one of the glands found on the chest of man, and some other mammals, for the secretion of milk; **3**, anything resembling the breast; **4**, the seat of the affections:—*v.t.* **1**, to present the front to; **2**, to oppose manfully or openly; as, to *breast* a storm of opposition.

breast-bone (brĕst'bōn"), *n.* a thin, flat bone in the front part of the chest to which most of the ribs are joined.

breast-pin (brĕst'pĭn"), *n.* an ornamental pin worn at the throat.

breast-plate (brĕst'plāt"), *n.* **1**, a portion of armor covering the front of the body; **2**, in the Bible, a square ornament worn by the Jewish high priest, bearing twelve precious stones engraved with the names of the twelve tribes of Israel.

breast wheel a type of water wheel to which the water is admitted at about the level of the axle of the wheel (see *hydraulic*, illus.).

breast-work (brĕst'wûrk"), *n.* a hastily constructed defensive wall or parapet of moderate height.

breath (brĕth), *n.* **1**, the air drawn into and forced out of the lungs; **2**, a single act of drawing in or forcing out air from the lungs; hence, an instant; pause; **3**, the power to use the lungs freely; as, to lose one's *breath;* hence, life; strength; **4**, a whiff of something sweet-scented; **5**, a light breeze; hence, a rumor; gossip; **6**, a film produced by the breath, as on a mirror: **under one's breath**, in a low or whispered tone.

breathe (brē*th*), *v.i.* [*p.t.* and *p.p.* breathed (brē*th*d), *p.pr.* breath'ing], **1**, to draw air into the lungs and force it out again; be alive; **2**, to rest from action; **3**, to exhale; **4**, to blow softly:—*v.t.* **1**, to draw into and force out of the lungs, as air; **2**, to give forth; as, the flower *breathes* perfume; **3**, to express; **4**, to whisper softly; as, to *breathe* a secret; **5**, to infuse; as, to *breathe* courage into the expedition.—*adj.* **breath'a-ble.**

breath-ing (brē*th*'ĭng), *n.* **1**, the act of drawing in air to the lungs and forcing it out again; **2**, air in gentle motion; **3**, a pause; **4**, in Greek grammar, a mark ['], called *rough breathing*, or ['], called *smooth breathing*, over an initial vowel, to show that the *h*-sound is or is not to be given:—*p.adj.* **1**, able to breathe; living; **2**, lifelike.

breath-less (brĕth'lĕs), *adj.* **1**, spent with action, or out of breath; **2**, without breath, or dead; **3**, holding the breath; as, *breathless* with fear; **4**, eager; excited; as, *breathless* attention; **5**, motionless, as air.—*adv.* **breath'less-ly.**

bred (brĕd), the past tense and past participle of the verb *breed.*

breech (brēch), *n.* **1**, the buttocks; **2**, the hinder part of anything; **3**, the part of a firearm behind the part which contains the powder:—*v.t.* **1**, to put into breeches; **2**, to whip on the breech, or buttocks; **3**, to fasten (a cannon on shipboard) by a rope.

breech-es (brĭch'ĕz), *n.pl.* **1**, short trousers, made to cover the legs from the knees to the waist; **2**, *Colloq.*, trousers: **breeches buoy**, a life-saving device consisting of short-legged canvas breeches attached below a cork ring, by which persons can be hauled along a rope to the shore.

breech-ing (brĭch'ĭng; brēch'-), *n.* **1**, in a horse's harness, a heavy strap which passes behind the horse's body (see *harness*, illus.); **2**, the parts that make up the breech of a gun; **3**, a flogging; **4**, on a ship, a rope for securing a gun to the ship's side.

breech-load-er (brēch'lōd"ẽr), *n.* a firearm loaded at the breech, or back, instead of at the muzzle.—*adj.* **breech'-load"ing.**

breed (brēd), *v.t.* [*p.t.* and *p.p.* bred (brĕd), *p.pr.* breed'ing], **1**, to produce, as offspring; hatch; **2**, to cause; as, to *breed* trouble; **3**, to train; rear; **4**, to propagate, as cattle; **5**, to be the native place of; as, a swamp *breeds* mosquitoes:—*v.i.* **1**, to bear young; **2**, to be born; come into being:—*n.* **1**, the offspring of one stock; a race; strain; as, horses or cattle of good *breed;* **2**, a class or kind.—*n.* **breed'er.**

breed-ing (brēd'ĭng), *n.* **1**, the process of producing young; **2**, the training of the young; **3**, hence, the result of training; good manners; behavior; as, a person of good *breeding.*

Syn. nurture. (See education.)

1**breeze** (brēz), *n.* **1**, refuse ashes and coke dust, used in burning bricks in a kiln; **2**, house sweepings; refuse.

2**breeze** (brēz), *n.* a gadfly; a botfly: also called *breeze fly.* Also, **breese.**

3**breeze** (brēz), *n.* a fresh but gentle wind; a moderate wind.

breez-y (brēz'ĭ), *adj.* [*comp.* breez'i-er, *superl.* breez'i-est], **1**, airy; fresh; **2**, brisk; vivacious; as, a *breezy* manner.

breth-ren (brĕ*th*'rĕn), *n. pl.* brothers: used in solemn address, and of the members of a profession or brotherhood, esp. a religious order.

Bret-on (brĕt'ŭn), *n.* **1**, a native of Brittany, a district in northwestern France; **2**, the native language of Brittany:—*adj.* relating to Brittany.

breve (brēv), *n.* **1**, a command from a sovereign or pope; **2**, a mark [˘] used to indicate a short vowel.

bre-vet (brē-vĕt'; brĕv'ĕt), *n.* **1**, an official note to an officer in the army giving him a higher nominal rank, but without change of duty or increase of pay; thus, a *brevet* major serves and is paid as captain; **2**, the promotion itself:—*v.t.* [*p.t.* and *p.p.* bre-vet'ted or brev'et-ed, *p.pr.* bre-vet'ting or brev'et-ing], to promote in such a manner:—*adj.* conferring or taking rank by brevet.

bre-vi-a-ry (brē'vĭ-ā-rĭ), *n.* [*pl.* breviaries (-rĭz)], a book containing the daily service and prayers of the Roman Catholic and the Greek churches.

bre-vier (brē-vēr'), *n.* a size of type, equivalent to 8 point (see *type.*).

brev-i-ty (brĕv'ĭ-tĭ), *n.* [*pl.* brevities (-tĭz)], **1**, shortness; **2**, the quality of being brief; conciseness.

brew (brōō), *v.t.* **1**, to prepare a mixture by boiling and fermenting; **2**, to make by fermentation, as beer; **3**, to make by infu-

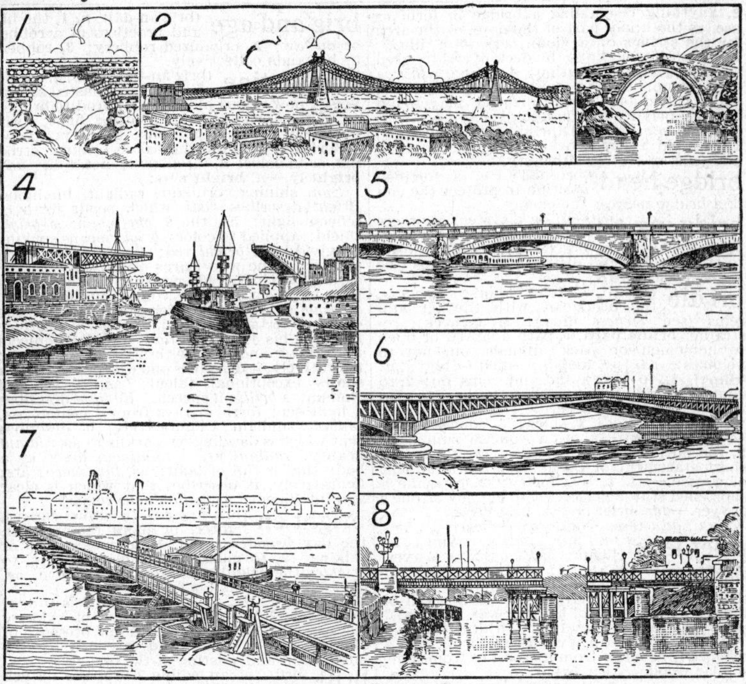

PRINCIPAL TYPES OF BRIDGE CONSTRUCTION

1, old wooden bridge; 2, steel suspension bridge; 3, single-arch stone bridge; 4, swing drawbridge; 5, concrete bridge; 6, steel bridge; 7, military pontoon bridge; 8, rolling drawbridge.

sion, as tea, or by mixing, as punch; **4,** to bring about; plot; as, to *brew* mischief:—*v.i.* **1,** to make a liquor, as by fermentation or infusion; **2,** to gather; grow in force; as, a storm *brews*:—*n.* **1,** the process of making by fermentation or infusion; **2,** the liquor so made; **3,** the quality, brand, or kind of such liquor.—*n.* **brew'er.**

brew-er-y (broo͞'ẽr-ĭ), *n.* [*pl.* breweries (-ĭz)], a building where beer or other liquors are made; also, the apparatus for making such liquors: also called *brewhouse.*

brew-ing (broo͞'ĭng), *n.* **1,** the making of beer and other malt liquors; **2,** all the liquor made at one time.

[1]**bri-ar** (brī'ẽr), *n.* **1,** any thorny plant: **2,** a thorn; **3,** a patch of thorny bushes. See [1]**bri'er,** *Pfd. S.*—*adj.* **bri'ar-y.**

[2]**bri-ar** (brī'ẽr), *n.* the white heath; also, a tobacco pipe made from its root or from some similar wood. Also, **bri'er,** *Pfd. S.*

bri-ar root **1,** the root of the white heath, used in making tobacco pipes; **2,** a pipe made of this wood. See **bri'er root,** *Pfd. S.*

bribe (brīb), *n.* **1,** a gift made or promised with the object of causing one to do some act against what he believes to be truth, justice, or uprightness; **2,** a thing that leads astray or allures:—*v.t.* [*p.t.* and *p.p.* bribed (brībd), *p.pr.* brib'ing], to influence wrongly by a gift:—*v.i.* to influence a person by offering a gift.—*n.* **brib'er.**—*adj.* **brib'a-ble.**

brib-er-y (brīb'ẽr-ĭ), *n.* [*pl.* briberies (-ĭz)], the act of paying a person to do some specified, usually dishonorable, thing.

bric-a-brac (brĭk'=ȧ=brăk"), *n.* rare or antique objects of art; knickknacks.

brick (brĭk), *n.* **1,** a block of clay dried in the sun or burned in a kiln; **2,** *Slang,* a fine fellow:—*adj.* made of, or like, brick:—*v.t.* **1,** to lay or build with bricks; **2,** to surround or wall in with bricks.—*n.* **brick'work".**

brick-bat (brĭk'băt"), *n.* a piece of brick, esp. one used as a missile.

brick-kiln (brĭk'kĭl"; -kĭln"), *n.* a furnace in which bricks are baked.

brick-lay-er (brĭk'lā"ẽr), *n.* one whose occupation is to lay bricks in buildings, walls, etc.—*n.* **brick'lay"ing.**

brid-al (brīd'ăl), *n.* a wedding:—*adj.* pertaining to a bride or wedding.

bride (brīd), *n.* a woman newly married, or about to be married.

bride-groom (brīd'groo͞m"), *n.* a man newly married, or on the point of being married.

brides-maid (brīdz'mād"), *n.* a woman who acts as an attendant on a bride at her wedding.

bride-well (brīd'wĕl), *n.* a house of correction for disorderly persons.

bridge (brĭj), *n.* **1,** a structure, as of iron, stone, or wood, built to carry a road or path across a river, road, valley, etc.;

2, anything resembling a bridge in form or use, as the upper part of the nose, or the arch for the strings on a violin (see *violin*, illus.); 3, the platform above the deck of a ship, used as an observation station; 4, bridge whist, a card game; also, a development of bridge whist, called *auction*, in which the players bid for the privilege of naming the trump:—*v.t.* [*p.t.* and *p.p.* bridged (brĭjd), *p.pr.* bridg'ing], 1, to build a bridge over; span; 2, hence, to pass; get over, as a difficulty.

bridge-head (brĭj'hĕd″), *n.* a fortified position to protect the end of a bridge nearest the enemy.

bridg-ing (brĭj'ĭng), *n.* a system of braces between two beams; usually, X-shaped wooden braces between floor joists to stiffen them and distribute the strains (see *frame house*, illus.).

bri-dle (brī'dl), *n.* 1, in a horse's harness, the headgear, with the bit and reins (see *harness*, illus.); 2, a check; restraint: **bridle path**, a path adapted or open to horsemen or pack animals, but not to vehicles:—*v.t.* [*p.t.* and *p.p.* -dled (-dld), *p.pr.* -dling], 1, to put a bit and reins on; 2, to control; guide:—*v.i.* to hold the head up, or toss it, as a sign of pride, scorn, or anger.

brief (brēf), *adj.* 1, short; 2, concise; condensed:—*n.* 1, a concise summary; 2, the outline of an argument; 3, a lawyer's short statement or outline for the argument of a case:—*v.t.* 1, to shorten; 2, to make a shortened statement of; 3, to employ as one's lawyer.—*adv.* **brief'ly.**—*n.* **brief'ness.**
Syn., adj. terse, curt. (See short.)

brief-less (brēf'lĕs), *adj.* having no clients; as, a *briefless* lawyer.

1**bri-er** (brī'ẽr), *n.* 1, a thorny plant or shrub; as, the *brier* rose; 2, a thorn; as, a blackberry *brier;* 3, a patch of thorny bushes. Also, **bri'ar.**—*adj.* **bri'er-y.**

2**bri-er** (brī'ẽr), *n.* 1, the white heath, a European evergreen shrub; 2, a tobacco pipe made from its root, or from some similar wood. Also, **bri'ar.**

bri-er root 1, the root of any of several plants, as the white heath or the mountain laurel, used in making tobacco pipes; 2, a tobacco pipe made from such a root. Also, **bri'ar root.**

1**brig** (brĭg), *n.* a two-masted, square-rigged vessel: **hermaphrodite brig**, a two-masted vessel on which the foremast is square-rigged and the mainmast fore-and-aft-rigged (see *ship*, illus.).

BRIG

2**brig** (brĭg), *n.* a place on a ship for imprisoning offenders; a ship's prison.

bri-gade (brĭ-gād'), *n.* 1, a subdivision of an army, usually consisting of two or more regiments, under the command of a brigadier general; 2, an organized body acting under authority; as, a fire *brigade:*—*v.t.* [*p.t.* and *p.p.* -gad'ed, *p.pr.* -gad'ing], to form into such a brigade, as troops.

brig-a-dier (brĭg″ȧ-dēr'), *n.* an officer commanding a brigade, and ranking next below a major general: often called *brigadier general.*

brig-and (brĭg'ănd), *n.* a robber; a member of a gang of robbers, often living in mountainous districts.

brig-and-age (brĭg'ăn-dāj), *n.* 1, the life and practices of a robber or outlaw; 2, organized robbery; 3, robbers or brigands collectively.

brig-an-tine (brĭg'ăn-tēn; -tīn), *n.* a kind of small, two-masted sailing vessel, now rigged like a hemaphrodite brig.

bright (brīt), *adj.* 1, showing light; brilliant; 2, glorious; 3, witty; lively; 4, fortunate; 5, glowing, as in beauty; striking, as in color; 6, intelligent; not dull.—*adv.* **bright'ly.**—*n.* **bright'ness.**
Syn. shining, brilliant, radiant, luminous. *Bright* describes that which sends forth or reflects light; as, the *bright* moon; a *bright* shield; applied to colors, *bright* means striking or vivid; as, *bright* red; figuratively, *bright* applies to one who learns quickly and easily; as, a *bright* child. *Shining* is applied to objects that have a steady or continuous light; as, *shining* gold; figuratively, it describes the effect of certain feelings; as, his *shining* face revealed his joy. *Brilliant* describes objects that glitter and flash with light, as diamonds; figuratively, it describes one who or that which shows exceptional talent; as, a *brilliant* woman; a *brilliant* speech. *Radiant* describes a light sent forth in rays from a center; as, *radiant* sunlight; figuratively, it describes that which is dazzling or sparkling; as, *radiant* beauty; *radiant* joy. *Luminous* describes a body that is full of light; as, *luminous* stars; figuratively, it describes that which is clear and intelligent; as, a *luminous* remark.

bright-en (brīt'n), *v.i.* to grow clearer, lighter, or more radiant; as, the day *brightens:*—*v.t.* 1, to make light or shining; 2, to make gay or cheerful; as, to *brighten* the neighborhood; 3, to improve; as, his going *brightens* his future.

Bright's dis-ease any of several forms of kidney disease, marked by the persistent presence of albumin in the urine, and attended by disintegration and wasting of the organs.

brill (brĭl), *n.* an edible European flatfish resembling the turbot.

bril-liance (brĭl'yăns), *n.* 1, glitter; great brightness; splendor; 2, excellence; distinction; 3, outstanding intellectual ability. Also, **bril'lian-cy.**

bril-liant (brĭl'yănt), *adj.* 1, sparkling; glittering; 2, having exceptional talent or culture; 3, distinguished by splendid mental ability; as, a *brilliant* career:—*n.* 1, a diamond or other precious stone, cut to show its sparkling quality; 2, the smallest size of type; 3, a kind of cotton fabric with a raised pattern.—*adv.* **bril'liant-ly.**
Syn., adj. (see bright).

bril-lian-tine (brĭl'yăn-tēn), *n.* 1, a mixture for giving a gloss to the hair; 2, a glossy fabric of fine quality, somewhat like alpaca.

brim (brĭm), *n.* 1, the edge or margin, as of a fountain; 2, the projecting edge, as of a hat; 3, the rim, as of a cup:—*v.t.* [*p.t.* and *p.p.* brimmed (brĭmd), *p.pr.* brim'ming], to fill to the upper edge of:—*v.i.* to be full to the very top or edge.—*adj.* **brim'less.**
Syn., n. (see border).

brim-ful (brĭm'fo͝ol'), *adj.* full to the edge; completely filled.

brim-stone (brĭm'stōn), *n.* sulphur:—*adj.* 1, made of sulphur; 2, of the yellow color of sulphur.

brin-dled (brĭn'dld), *adj.* of a gray or dark yellow color, with dark spots or streaks; as, a *brindled* cat.

brine (brīn), *n.* 1, salt water; 2, the ocean; 3, tears:—*v.t.* [*p.t.* and *p.p.* brined (brīnd), *p.pr.* brin'ing], 1, to soak in salt water, as meat; 2, to salt, as hay.

bring (brĭng), *v.t.* [*p.t.* and *p.p.* brought (brôt), *p.pr.* bring'ing], **1**, to convey or lead to a point where the speaker is or is supposed to be; fetch; **2**, to yield; cause the possession of; as, sleep *brings* relief from care; **3**, to persuade; influence; as, I cannot *bring* him to forgive you; **4**, to procure in exchange, as a price; **5**, to conduct; carry; as, the boat *brought* me to the shore; **6**, in law, to institute; as, to *bring* suit for libel: **bring about**, to cause to happen: **bring down the house**, to call forth great applause: **bring forward**, **1**, to introduce, as a proposal; **2**, to carry forward, as a sum: **bring home**, to make vividly clear; as, he *brought home* my error to me: **bring round or over**, to cause to change opinions, sides, etc.: **bring to**, **1**, to resuscitate, as from a faint; **2**, to cause (a ship) to come to a standstill: **bring to bear**, to cause to have influence: **bring to book**, to call to account: **bring up**, **1**, to rear from childhood; educate; **2**, to stop suddenly.—*n.* **bring'er.**

Syn. fetch, carry, bear, convey, transport. To *bring* a thing is to come with it; as, to *bring* a book. To *fetch* is to go for something and bring it; as, to *fetch* some water. To *carry* is to take from one place to another; as, to *carry* a message.

brink (brĭngk), *n.* the edge, margin or border, esp. of a steep place.

Syn. (see border).

brin-y (brīn'ĭ), *adj.* [*comp.* brin'i-er, *superl.* brin'i-est], very salty; as, the *briny* ocean; *briny* tears.

***bri-quet** (brē"kā'), [Fr.], *n.* a steel for striking a light; a tinder box.

bri-quette (brĭ-kĕt'), *n.* a brick-shaped mass of coal dust, held together by a cementing material and used for fuel. Also, [2]**bri-quet'.**

Bri-se-is (brī-sē'ĭs), *n.* in Homer's "Iliad," a beautiful captive girl, allotted to Achilles, but seized by Agamemnon to replace his lost Chryseis, thus arousing the wrath of Achilles.

brisk (brĭsk), *adj.* **1**, lively; animated; active; swift; nimble; **2**, burning freely; as, a *brisk* fire; **3**, keen, as air; sparkling, as certain liquors:—*v.t.* and *v.i.* to make or become lively or swift: generally with *up.* —*adv.* **brisk'ly.**—*n.* **brisk'ness.**

bris-ket (brĭs'kĕt), *n.* the front part of the breast of an animal whose flesh is used for food (see *beef*, illus.).

bris-tle (brĭs'l), *n.* **1**, a short, stiff, coarse hair, esp. upon the back and sides of the hog; **2**, any stiff, sharp hair:—*v.t.* [*p.t.* and *p.p.* -tled (-ld), *p.pr.* -tling], **1**, to cause to stand up in a stiff, prickly way; **2**, to furnish with bristles, as a brush:—*v.i.* **1**, to stand up in a stiff, prickly way; **2**, to be covered with, or full of, sharp points; as, the battle front *bristles* with bayonets; **3**, to become angry; as, to *bristle* up at an insulting remark.

bris-tly (brĭs'lĭ), *adj.* covered with stiff, sharp hair; rough.

Bris-tol board (brĭs'tŭl), a thick, smooth, and sometimes glazed, white cardboard.

brit (brĭt), *n.* **1**, the young of the herring and sprat; **2**, small fry upon which whales feed, esp. certain herring. Also, **britt.**

Bri-tan-ni-a (brĭ-tăn'ĭ-ȧ), *n.* Great Britain; also, the female figure symbolizing it.—*adj.* **Bri-tan'nic.**

bri-tan-ni-a met-al a white metal mixture of tin, copper, antimony, and zinc: used in making tableware: also called *britannia.*

Brit-ish (brĭt'ĭsh), *adj.* **1**, of or relating to Great Britain or its inhabitants; **2**, relating to the ancient Britons:—*n.* the language spoken by the ancient Britons.

Brit-on (brĭt'ŭn), *n.* **1**, a member of one of the Celtic tribes of ancient Britain; **2**, a native of Great Britain.

brit-tle (brĭt'l), *adj.* easily broken; fragile; breakable; not tough or tenacious. —*n.* **brit'tle-ness.**

Syn. fragile, delicate, frail. *Brittle* describes substances that break easily, esp. as the result of a blow or jar; as, *brittle* china; *brittle* candy. *Fragile* is applied to objects which, because of delicate structure, may be easily broken; as, *fragile* beads. *Delicate* describes something sensitive or easily injured; as, a *delicate* instrument. *Frail* suggests an inherent weakness; as, a *frail* child.

broach (brōch), *n.* a sharp-pointed tool, as a spike or skewer; any boring tool:—*v.t.* **1**, to tap or pierce, as a keg of wine; **2**, to begin a discussion about; as, it is difficult to *broach* an unpleasant subject.

broad (brôd), *adj.* **1**, wide; as, a *broad* road; **2**, ample; vast; **3**, liberal; as, *broad* opinions; **4**, comprehensive, as a discussion; **5**, open; clear; as, *broad* daylight; **6**, evident; bold; as, a *broad* hint; **7**, indelicate, as a joke; **8**, pronounced with the mouth relatively open, as the *a* in *father.*—*adv.* **broad'ly.**—*n.* **broad'ness.**

Syn. extensive, large; tolerant, catholic.—*Ant.* narrow, intolerant, prejudiced.

broad ar-row a mark by which the British government distinguishes its property.

broad-ax (brôd'ăks"), *n.* **1**, a broad-edged ax for cutting timber; **2**, an ancient military weapon with a wide blade. Also, **broad'axe".**

broad-brim (brôd'brĭm"), *n.* a hat like those worn by Friends, or Quakers: **Broadbrim**, *Colloq.*, a Quaker.

broad-cast (brôd'kȧst"), *v.t.* [*p.t.* and *p.p.* -cast" or -cast"ed, *p.pr.* -cast"ing], **1**, to scatter or throw by hand in all directions, as seed; **2**, to spread abroad, as news; **3**, to send out messages or sound by radio from a central station; radiocast; as, to *broadcast* a program of music or a speech:—*adj.* scattered far and wide; widely disseminated:—*adv.* so as to scatter widely:—*n.* **1**, a casting or scattering of seed far and wide; **2**, anything broadcast, as a program, speech, or baseball game, by radio.

broad-cloth (brôd'klŏth), *n.* **1**, a fine woolen cloth with a smooth surface, usually of double width; **2**, a fine, silky wash fabric.

broad-en (brôd'n), *v.i.* to grow wide or wider:—*v.t.* to make wider.

broad-gauge (brôd'=gāj"), *adj.* **1**, of a railway, having rails more than the standard 56½ inches apart; **2**, broad-minded; liberal.

broad-mind-ed (brôd'=mīn"dĕd; =mīn"dĭd), *adj.* liberal in opinions; tolerant.

broad seal the public seal of a country, esp. the official or great seal used by England.

broad-side (brôd'sīd"), *n.* **1**, the entire side of a ship above the water line; **2**, all the cannon on one side of a warship; also, a discharge from all of these at one time; **3**, a sheet printed on one side only, and containing information of a popular character; **4**, *Colloq.*, a printed or verbal attack on some public person:—*adv.* with the side turned or exposed.

broad-sword (brôd'sōrd"), *n.* a sword with a wide cutting blade.

Brob-ding-nag-i-an (brŏb"dĭng-năg'ĭ-ăn), *adj.* **1**, resembling an inhabitant of the fabled country of Brobdingnag in Swift's "Gulliver's Travels"; **2**, hence, colossal; gigantic:—*n.* a giant.

bro-cade (brō-kād′), *n.* a rich silken material woven with gold and silver threads, or ornamented with raised figures in silk or velvet, in designs of flowers, fruits, etc.:—*v.t.* [*p.t.* and *p.p.* -cad′ed, *p.pr.* -cad′ing], to decorate or weave with a raised pattern.—*p.adj.* **bro-cad′ed.**

bro-ca-tel (brō′kȧ-tĕl; brŏk′ȧ-tĕl), *n.* **1,** a fabric with woven figures, coarser than brocade, made of silk and wool, silk and cotton, or pure wool; **2,** a marble of various colors, obtained from Italy and Spain. Also, **broc″a-telle′.**

broc-co-li (brŏk′ō-lĭ), *n.* the cauliflower; a plant of the mustard family, akin to the common cabbage.

bro-chure (brō-shür′), *n.* **1,** a booklet dealing with a subject of passing interest; **2,** any pamphlet or booklet.

bro-gan (brō′găn), *n.* a coarse, heavy shoe laced or buckled over the instep.

1**brogue** (brōg), *n.* a coarse, rough shoe of untanned hide.

2**brogue** (brōg), *n.* a dialectal pronunciation of English, esp. that common in Ireland.

1**broil** (broil), *v.t.* to cook directly over a hot fire, as on a gridiron or a fork:—*v.i.* **1,** to be exposed to great heat; **2,** to be heated by excitement:—*n.* something cooked directly over a hot fire.

2**broil** (broil), *n.* a noisy quarrel; brawl:—*v.i.* to engage in a noisy quarrel.

broil-er (broil′ẽr), *n.* **1,** a utensil for cooking food directly over the fire; **2,** a bird suitable to be so cooked.

broke (brōk), past tense and obsolete past participle of the verb *break.*

bro-ken (brō′kn), *p.adj.* **1,** not entire; in pieces; **2,** rough; hilly; as, *broken* country; **3,** transgressed; as, a *broken* law; **4,** bankrupt; **5,** subdued; crushed; as, a *broken* spirit; **6,** infirm; **7,** imperfect; as, *broken* English; **8,** interrupted; as, *broken* sleep; **9,** trained to obedience: used esp. of a horse; **10,** disorganized, as an army.—*adv.* **bro′ken-ly.**—*n.* **bro′ken-ness.**

bro-ken–heart-ed (brō′kn=härt″ĕd), *adj.* overcome by grief and misery; not to be comforted.

bro-ker (brō′kẽr), *n.* a dealer in drafts, notes, money, stocks, etc.; one who transacts business for another.

bro-ker-age (brō′kẽr-āj), *n.* **1,** the business of a broker; **2,** the fee or commission charged by brokers.

bro-mide (brō′mīd; brō′mĭd), *n.* **1,** a compound of bromine and some metal; as, potassium *bromide:* a drug with a soothing effect; **2,** *Colloq.:* **a,** a person who thinks and talks in a commonplace way; **b,** a commonplace person or remark. Also, **bro′-mid.**—*adj. Colloq.,* **bro-mid′ic.**

bro-mine (brō′mĭn; brō′mēn), *n.* a reddish brown liquid element with a disagreeable odor: used in making dyes. Also, **bro′min.**—*adj.* **bro′mic.**

bron-chi (brŏng′kī), *n.pl.* [*sing.* bronchus (-kŭs)], the two principal branches of the windpipe, or trachea.

bron-chi-a (brŏng′kĭ-ȧ), *n.pl.* the group of tubes into which each of the bronchi divides, forming the larger air passages of the lungs.

bron-chi-al (brŏng′kĭ-ăl), *adj.* pertaining to the bronchi or the bronchia.

bron-chi-tis (brŏng-kī′tĭs), *n.* an inflammation of the mucous lining of the bronchi or bronchial tubes.—*adj.* **bron-chit′ic** (brŏng-kĭt′ĭk).

bron-cho (brŏng′kō), *n.* [*pl.* bronchos (-kōz)], in the western U. S., any native small horse; a mustang. Also, **bron′co.**

bron-chus (brŏng′kŭs), *n.* [*pl.* bronchi (-kī)], either of the two principal branches of the windpipe, or trachea, which subdivide into tubes called *bronchia.*

bron-to-sau-rus (brŏn″tō-sô′rŭs), *n.* any of a group of enormous, four-legged, prehistoric reptiles, fossil remains of which have been found in western North America.

bronze (brŏnz), *n.* **1,** an alloy of eight or nine parts copper to one of tin; **2,** a work of art cast or wrought in this alloy; **3,** a yellowish or reddish brown, the color of bronze; also, a pigment or wash of this color:—*adj.* made of, or resembling, bronze: **bronze age,** the age supposed to follow the iron age: so called because the weapons of man in that period were made of bronze:—*v.t.* [*p.t.* and *p.p.* bronzed (brŏnzd), *p.pr.* bronz′ing], to make of the color of bronze; tan.

brooch (brōch; bro͞och), *n.* an ornamental pin with a clasp; a breastpin.

brood (bro͞od), *n.* **1,** all the young birds, as chicks, hatched at one time; **2,** all the young of one mother; **3,** kind; breed; species:—*v.i.* **1,** to sit on eggs, as a hen; **2,** to linger over sorrowfully: with *on* or *over:*—*v.t.* **1,** to sit over, cover, and cherish, as eggs; **2,** to cherish in the mind; ponder.—*adj.* **brood′y.**

1**brook** (bro͝ok), *n.* a small, natural stream of water: **brook trout,** a medium-sized North American fresh-water game fish.—*n. dim.* **brook′let.**

2**brook** (bro͝ok), *v.t.* to bear; put up with; as, I will *brook* no delay.

broom (bro͞om), *n.* **1,** a stiff brush used for sweeping; **2,** any of a group of shrubs of the pea family with stiff, slender branches; esp., the Scotch broom.

broom corn *n.* a cornlike grass growing eight to ten feet high: used in making brooms.

broom-stick (bro͞om′stĭk″), *n.* the handle of a broom.

broth (brôth), *n.* thin soup made by cooking meat slowly in water.

broth-er (brŭth′ẽr), *n.* [*pl.* brothers (-ẽrz); brethren (brĕth′rĕn)], **1,** a male who has the same father and mother as another; **2,** a member of a family or race; **3,** one closely united to another or others by a common interest; also, a member of a religious order; **4,** in *pl.,* human beings in general; fellow creatures.

broth-er-hood (brŭth′ẽr-ho͝od), *n.* **1,** the state or quality of being a brother; **2,** an association of men for any purpose; a fraternity; also, the members of such an order taken together; **3,** fellowship; as, the *brotherhood* of man.

broth-er–in–law (brŭth′ẽr=ĭn=lô″), *n.* [pl. brothers-in-law (-ẽrz=)], **1,** a brother of one's husband or wife; **2,** the husband of one's sister.

Broth-er Jon-a-than (jŏn′ȧ-thăn) a humorous imaginary character representing New England, or, more broadly, the United States.

broth-er-ly (brŭth′ẽr-lĭ), *adj.* **1,** pertaining to, or like, a brother; as, *brotherly* love; **2,** affectionate; kind:—*adv.* in a way characteristic of, or suitable to, a brother.—*n.* **broth′er-li-ness.**

brough-am (bro͞o′ŭm; bro͞om; *Br.* brō′ŭm), *n.* a light, closed carriage with a straight front; also, an automobile with a body resembling that of a brougham.

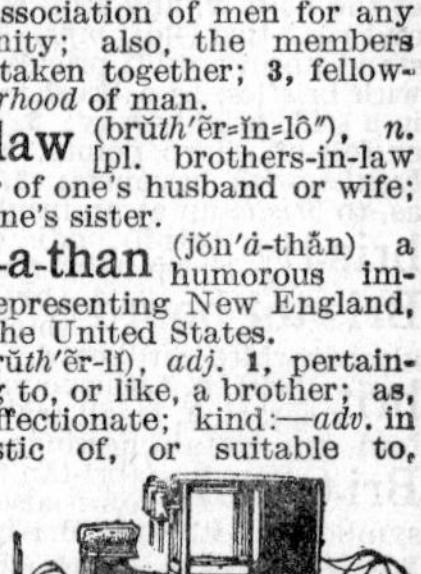
BROUGHAM

brought (brôt), past tense and past participle of the verb *bring*.

brow (brou), *n.* **1**, the forehead; **2**, the arch of hair over the eye; **3**, the countenance as a whole; **4**, the edge of a steep place; the upper portion of a hill.

brow band in a horse's harness, a strap of the bridle which passes in front of the horse's head (see *harness*, illus.).

brow-beat (brou'bēt″), *v.t.* [*p.t.* -beat″ (-bēt″), *p.p.* -beat″ or -beat″en (-bēt″n), *p.pr.* -beat″ing], to frighten by stern looks or words.

brown (broun), *adj.* of a dusky color between black and orange: **brown study**, a condition of being in deep thought; absent-mindedness: **brown sugar**, sugar not refined, or only partly refined, as distinguished from crystallized sugar:—*n.* a dark color between black and orange; also, any coloring matter producing this color:—*v.i.* and *v.t.* to become or to make brown.—*adj.* **brown'ish.**

brown-ie (broun'ĭ), *n.* a good-natured elf supposed to perform certain useful household tasks by night, as sweeping, churning, etc. Also, **brown'y.**

brown-stone (broun'stōn″), *n.* a kind of brown sandstone, used for building purposes.

browse (brouz), *n.* the tender shoots or twigs of shrubs and trees fit for the food of cattle and other animals:—*v.t.* [*p.t.* and *p.p.* browsed (brouzd), *p.pr.* brows'ing], **1**, to eat; nibble off; crop; **2**, to pasture on; graze on; as, the cattle *browse* the meadow:—*v.i.* **1**, to eat or nibble off twigs or buds; **2**, to graze; feed; **3**, to read scattered passages at leisure, as in a book or in various books.

bru-in (brōō'ĭn), *n.* the brown bear: so called in popular tales. Also, **Bru'in.**

bruise (brōōz), *n.* an injury to the flesh, as of an animal or a plant, caused by a blow:—*v.t.* [*p.t.* and *p.p.* bruised (brōōzd), *p.pr.* bruis'ing], **1**, to injure, crush, or indent by a blow or pressure without cutting; **2**, to crush by beating or pounding:—*v.i.* to fight with the fists; box.

bruis-er (brōōz'ẽr), *n.* **1**, a boxer; pugilist; hence, a strong, brutal person; **2**, a machine for crushing grain, etc.

bruit (brōōt), *n.* report, rumor:—*v.t.* to report; spread abroad.

bru-nette (brōō-nĕt'), *n.* a girl or woman with dark skin, hair, and eyes:—*adj.* having such coloring. Also, **bru-net'.**

Brun-hild (brōōn'hĭlt), *n.* in mythology, a queen in Iceland whom King Gunther, by the magic aid of Siegfried, won as bride: also called, as the chief figure in Wagner's "Die Walküre," *Brünnehilde.*

brunt (brŭnt), *n.* the heaviest part of a shock, strain, attack, or burden; as, to bear the *brunt* of an attack.

brush (brŭsh), *n.* **1**, an implement made of bristles, feathers, hair, or other material fixed in a back or handle: used for cleaning, smoothing, applying paint, etc.; **2**, the bushy tail of a fox; **3**, a thicket of small trees or a section of country covered with such growth; **4**, a slight battle; skirmish; **5**, the act of cleaning or smoothing with a brush; also, a light touch; **6**, thin metallic plates or wires bound together, to conduct a current to or from an electric motor or dynamo:—*v.t.* **1**, to sweep, cleanse, or rub with a brush; **2**, to remove by a brush; **3**, to touch lightly in passing:—*v.i.* **1**, to move with haste; **2**, to skim over with a light touch.—*adj.* **brush'y.**

brush hook a hooklike hacking tool for cutting small trees.

brush-wood (brŭsh'wŏŏd), *n.* **1**, a dense growth of bushes; thicket; **2**, small wood, suitable for a fire.

brusque (brŏŏsk; brŭsk), *adj.* blunt; abrupt in manner. Also, **brusk.**

Brus-sels (brŭs'ĕlz), *n.* the capital city of Belgium: **brussels carpet**, a strong kind of woolen carpet: **brussels lace**, various kinds of costly lace, orig. made at Brussels: **brussels sprouts**, a vegetable consisting of small green heads, each like a tiny cabbage, one or two inches in diameter.

bru-tal (brōō'tăl), *adj.* **1**, savage; cruel; inhuman; unfeeling; **2**, rude; coarse.—*adv.* **bru'tal-ly.**

bru-tal-i-ty (brōō-tăl'ĭ-tĭ), *n.* [*pl.* brutalities (-tĭz)], **1**, pitiless cruelty; savageness; inhumanity; **2**, a savage act.

bru-tal-ize (brōō'tăl-īz), *v.t.* [*p.t.* and *p.p.* -ized (-īzd), *p.pr.* -iz″ing], to make cruel or inhuman; as, war tends to *brutalize* men.

brute (brōōt), *adj.* **1**, inhuman; without reason or intelligence; **2**, merely material; as, *brute* earth; **3**, lacking in the finer feelings; unthinking; **4**, like a beast; hence, cruel; **5**, rough; uncivilized:—*n.* **1**, a beast; **2**, an inhuman person; as, a lazy *brute*.
Syn., *n.* (see animal).

brut-ish (brōōt'ĭsh), *adj.* savage; stupid; coarse.—*n.* **brut'ish-ness.**

Bryn-hild (brün'hĭlt), *n.* in the Volsunga saga, a Valkyrie, disobedient to Odin, who was wakened by Sigurd (Siegfried) from a magic sleep. Also, **Brün″ne-hil'de.** See **Brun'hild.**

bub-ble (bŭb'l), *n.* **1**, a small globe of water or other fluid filled with air or gas; **2**, a small body of air or gas rising to the surface of a liquid or held within a solidified fluid, as glass; **3**, anything unreal or fanciful, as an empty scheme to deceive people into investing their money without offering anything of value in exchange:—*v.i.* [*p.t.* and *p.p.* -bled (-ld), *p.pr.* -bling], to rise in bubbles; run with a gurgling sound.

bu-bon-ic (bū-bŏn'ĭk), *adj.* pertaining to a kind of infectious inflammation, esp. of the groin: **bubonic plague**, a fatal, contagious, epidemic disease, accompanied by swelling of the lymphatic glands in neck, armpit, and groin: generally transmitted through the bites of fleas which have become infected by feeding on infected rats: also called *The Plague*, as in London in 1667.

buc-ca-neer (bŭk″ȧ-nēr'), *n.* **1**, a pirate; a sea robber; **2**, esp., one of the pirates who, during the 17th century, made raids on the Spaniards in America.

bu-cen-taur (bū-sĕn'tôr), *n.* **1**, an imaginary monster, half man and half bull; **2**, the state barge of Venice, used by the doges, or former rulers, in the annual ceremony of wedding the city to the Adriatic.

Bu-ceph-a-lus (bū-sĕf'ȧ-lŭs), *n.* **1**, the charger of Alexander the Great; **2**, humorously, any saddle horse.

[1]**buck** (bŭk), *n.* **1**, the male of the deer, rabbit, hare, etc., of which the female is called *doe;* **2**, a gay fellow; **3**, a male Indian or negro; **4**, the sudden, vertical leap of a horse or mule, intended to throw off a load; **5**, *Slang*, a dollar; **6**, in card games, a marker passed from player to player, to keep track of the deal: **to pass the buck**, to shift responsibility, or any unpleasant task, to another:—*v.i.* to make a sudden, vertical leap in the air, so as to throw off a rider or load: said of a horse or mule:—*v.t.* **1**, to throw off by a sudden, vertical leap; **2**, in the army, to punish by fastening the arms in front of the bent knees and thrusting a stick over the arms and through the opening left below the knees.—*adj.* **buck'ish.**—*adv.* **buck'ish-ly.**

[2]**buck** (bŭk), *n.* a mixture of suds and lye:—*v.t.* to wash or soak in suds or lye.

buck-board (bŭk'bōrd''), *n.* a light wagon in which the body and springs are replaced by a long, elastic board, supported directly by the axles.

buck-et (bŭk'ĕt), *n.* **1**, a deep, cylindrical vessel for drawing or holding water, etc., or anything resembling it in appearance or use; **2**, the scoop of a dredging machine or of a grain elevator: **bucket shop,** an office for gambling in stocks, grain, etc., by going through the forms of buying and selling with no actual purchases or sales.

buck-eye (bŭk'ī''), *n.* **1**, the American horse-chestnut tree; **2**, (usually, *bugeye*), a certain type of sailboat, used esp. on Chesapeake Bay (see *ship*, illus.): **Buckeye,** a native of Ohio, the Buckeye State.

[1]**buck-le** (bŭk'l), *n.* **1**, a metal clasp with a device for fastening the ends of two straps or of the same strap; **2**, a similar ornament for a dress, a hat, etc.:—*v.t.* [*p.t.* and *p.p.* -led (-ld), *p.pr.* -ling], **1**, to fasten with a buckle; join together; **2**, to apply (oneself) with energy:—*v.i.* **1**, to be held together by means of a buckle; **2**, to set to work energetically; **3**, to struggle; grapple.

[2]**buck-le** (bŭk'l), *n.* a bend or kink in a piece of metal, as in a saw blade:—*v.i.* [*p.t.* and *p.p.* -led (-ld), *p.pr.* -ling], **1**, to bend or warp, as metal, under pressure or from heat; **2**, *Colloq.*, to yield:—*v.t.* to cause to bend, crumple, or curl, by the application of heat or pressure.

buck-ler (bŭk'lẽr), *n.* a kind of ancient shield, composed of wood or wicker, covered with skin or leather, and worn on the left arm; hence, any protection resembling a shield.

buck-ram (bŭk'răm), *n.* **1**, coarse cloth of linen, cotton, or hemp stiffened with glue; **2**, hence, stiffness:—*adj.* **1**, made of, or resembling, such cloth; **2**, hence, stiff; formal; precise.

buck-saw (bŭk'sô''), *n.* a saw set in a light frame and worked with both hands· used for sawing firewood.

buck-shot (bŭk'shŏt''), *n.* shot of large size: so called from its use formerly in shooting deer.

buck-skin (bŭk'skĭn''), *n.* **1**, the skin of a buck; **2**, a soft, grayish yellow leather made from the skin of a deer or of a sheep; **3**, in *pl.*, clothes made of such skin: **Buckskin,** an American soldier in the Revolutionary Army:—*adj.* made of such skin; as, a *buckskin* coat.

buck-wheat (bŭk'hwēt''), *n.* a plant cultivated for its triangular seeds, which are ground into meal and used for food; also, the flour made from the seeds.

bu-col-ic (bū-kŏl'ĭk), *adj.* relating to country affairs and to a shepherd's life and occupation; pastoral; rustic:—*n.* a poem which deals with such matters.

bud (bŭd), *n.* **1**, the tip of a root, stem, or branch which may develop into a branch, leaf, or flower; **2**, a young girl in her first season in society:—*v.t.* [*p.t.* and *p.p.* bud'ded, *p.pr.* bud'ding], to graft:—*v.i.* **1**, to put forth or produce new shoots; begin to grow; sprout; **2**, to be like a young flower in youth and freshness.

Bud-dha (bo͝od'ȧ), *n.* **1**, a person embodying divine wisdom; **2**, specif., Gautama Siddhartha, the founder of Buddhism, a religion of eastern Asia.

Bud-dhism (bo͝od'ĭzm), *n.* a religion of eastern Asia, named for its founder, which teaches self-denial, virtue, and wisdom.—*n.* and *adj.* **Bud'dhist.**

bud-dy (bŭd'ĭ), *n.* [*pl.* buddies (-ĭz)], *Colloq.*, **1**, brother; little boy; **2**, a close friend; esp., in the army, a fellow soldier.

[1]**budge** (bŭj), *v.i.* [*p.t.* and *p.p.* budged (bŭjd), *p.pr.* budg'ing], to move from one's place; stir:—*v.t.* to cause to move; stir; as, I can't *budge* the box.

[2]**budge** (bŭj), *n.* lambskin dressed like fur and used for linings and edgings:—*adj.* trimmed with lambskin, as a scholar's gown; hence, scholarly; pompous.

budg-et (bŭj'ĕt), *n.* **1**, a bag with its contents; hence, a quantity or store; as, a *budget* of news; **2**, the annual estimate of the financial needs for the year to come of an individual, a nation, or an organization.

buff (bŭf), *n.* **1**, a thick, flexible, dull yellow leather prepared from the skin of the buffalo, ox, etc., and dressed with oil; **2**, a coat made from this skin; **3**, a pale or faded yellowish orange color; **4**, a polishing wheel; **5**, *Colloq.*, the bare skin:—*adj.* **1**, made of thick, oiled leather; **2**, of a dull, light yellow color:—*v.t.* to polish with an implement covered with buff leather.

buf-fa-lo (bŭf'ȧ-lō), *n.* [*pl.* buffaloes (-lōz)], **1**, a large animal of the ox family; also, any one of various wild oxen, such as the East Indian water buffalo and the South African Cape buffalo; **2**, popularly, the North American bison.

[1]**buff-er** (bŭf'ẽr), *n.* any device which serves to deaden the shock caused by the striking together of two bodies, esp. such a device on the end of a railway car.

[2]**buff-er** (bŭf'ẽr), *n.* an elderly or old-fashioned, inefficient fellow.

[1]**buf-fet** (bŭf'ĕt), *n.* **1**, a blow with the hand; **2**, any blow:—*v.t.* **1**, to strike with the hand or fist; box; beat; **2**, to struggle against; as, to *buffet* the waves:—*v.i.* to fight with blows; force a way; as, to *buffet* with the waves.

[2]**buf-fet** (bo͞o-fā'; bŭf'ĕt; *Fr.* bü''fā'), *n.* **1**, a sideboard; **2**, a counter for refreshments; also, a restaurant equipped with such a counter: **buffet luncheon**, a light meal served to guests seated or standing about a room.

buf-foon (bŭ-fo͞on'), *n.* one who amuses others by low jests, antics, odd gestures, etc., as a clown.

buf-foon-er-y (bŭ-fo͞on'ẽr-ĭ), *n.* [*pl.* buffooneries (-ĭz)], the pranks of a clown or low comedian; vulgar tricks.

bug (bŭg), *n.* **1**, an insect, esp. a crawling insect, as a bedbug; **2**, *Colloq.*, a disease germ.—*adj.* [1]**bug'gy.**

bug-a-boo (bŭg'ȧ-bo͞o''), *n.* [*pl.* bugaboos (-bo͞oz'')], a fancied cause of fear; esp., an unreal terror used to frighten children into obedience.

bug-bear (bŭg'bâr''), *n.* **1**, an imaginary cause of fear; bugaboo; **2**, an object of dislike or terror.

bug-eye (bŭg'ī''), *n.* a certain kind of sailboat, used esp. on Chesapeake Bay (see *ship*, illus.). Also, **buck'eye''.**

[2]**bug-gy** (bŭg'ĭ), *n.* [*pl.* buggies (-ĭz)], a light four-wheeled carriage.

[1]**bu-gle** (bū'gl), *n.* a cylindrical glass bead, usually black, used for trimming, as on a dress.

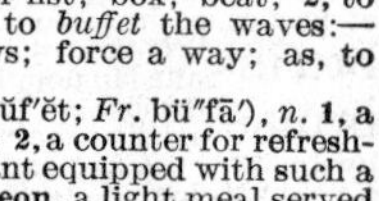

[3]BUGLE (def. 2)

[2]**bu-gle** (bū'gl), *n.* any of various common plants of the mint family.

[3]**bu-gle** (bū'gl), *n.* **1**, a hunting horn; **2**, a military wind instrument similar to the horn, with or without valves and keys:—*v.t.* [*p.t.* and *p.p.* -gled (-gld), *p.pr.* -gling], to sound (a call) on the bugle:—*v.i.* to sound the bugle; give a bugle call.

bu-gler (bū'glẽr), *n.* one who plays or sounds signals on the bugle.

buhl (bo͞ol), *n.* cabinetwork or furniture inlaid with tortoise shell, yellow and white metal, etc.; also, this style of decoration.

buhr-stone (bûr′stōn″), *n.* a rock used to make a grindstone. Also, **burr′stone″; bur′stone″.**

build (bĭld), *v.t.* [*p.t.* and *p.p.* built (bĭlt) or, *Archaic,* build′ed, *p.pr.* build′ing], **1,** to construct; erect, as a house; **2,** to form by art; **3,** to rest on or found, as hopes or plans; **4,** to establish, as a business:—*v.i.* **1,** to construct a building; **2,** to depend or rely: with *on* or *upon:*—*n.* manner of construction; figure; form.—*n.* **build′er.**

build-ing (bĭl′dĭng), *n.* **1,** the art or business of erecting houses, churches, etc.; **2,** the act of constructing, raising, or establishing; **3,** a structure, as a house, church, or the like.

Syn. edifice, structure. *Building,* the common term, applies to anything with walls and a roof. *Edifice* suggests a large, important, or magnificent building. *Structure* applies more to the form and arrangement of a building, although, like *edifice,* it may be applied to buildings of some size and importance.

bulb (bŭlb), *n.* **1,** an onion-shaped root formed of thick, overlapping layers; **2,** a kind of leaf bud; **3,** any swelling or rounded portion, as of a stem or tube; **4,** a small glass globe containing an electric light.

bulb-ous (bŭl′bŭs), *adj.* **1,** bulb-shaped; **2,** growing from a bulb.

bul-bul (bo͝ol′bo͝ol), *n.* the Persian nightingale.

Bul-ga-ri-an (bo͝ol-gā′rĭ-ăn; bŭl-gā′rĭ-ăn), *adj.* of or pertaining to Bulgaria, its people, or its language:—*n.* **1,** one of an ancient Finnish race who conquered the Slavs of the Balkan peninsula; **2,** an inhabitant of Bulgaria; **3,** its language.—*n.* **Bul′gar.**

bulge (bŭlj), *n.* **1,** a swelling outward; **2,** the part of a wall, ship, or the like, which swells out; **3,** a sudden rise in price: as, a *bulge* in stocks:—*v.i.* [*p.t.* and *p.p.* bulged (bŭljd), *p.pr.* bulg′ing], to swell out:—*v.t.* to bend outward.—*adj.* **bulg′y.**

bulk (bŭlk), *n.* **1,** the extent of an object; size; volume; **2,** the main mass or body; the greater part or number; **3,** the cargo of a ship when stowed:—*v.i.* **1,** to increase in volume; grow larger; **2,** to loom up, as in size or importance; **3,** to form into a tight or compact mass.

bulk-head (bŭlk′hĕd″), *n.* **1,** an upright partition in a vessel, which separates one part of it from another; **2,** a structure built to stand the pressure of water, air, or earth.

bulk-y (bŭl′kĭ), *adj.* [*comp.* bulk′i-er, *superl.* bulk′i-est], massive; ponderous; of great size.—*adv.* **bulk′i-ly.**—*n.* **bulk′i-ness.**

[1]**bull** (bo͝ol), *n.* **1,** the male of any animal of the ox family or of various other large animals, such as the whale, elephant, etc.; **2,** a dealer in stocks who endeavors to raise the price of stock: opp. of *bear:* **bull market,** a market in which the prices of stocks are rising: **Bull, 1,** the constellation Taurus; **2,** the second sign of the zodiac (see *zodiac,* illus.).

[2]**bull** (bo͝ol), *n.* **1,** orig., a seal affixed to an official paper; **2,** an official document; an edict; **3,** a document containing a decree or declaration of the Pope.

[3]**bull** (bo͝ol), *n.* an absurd blunder in speaking, usually a contradiction of terms: often called *Irish bull.*

bull bait-ing the sport of attacking bulls with dogs.

bull-dog (bo͝ol′dôg″), *n.* a variety of powerful, medium-sized dog, remarkable for its courage and fierceness, and for its strong grip: formerly used for baiting bulls:—*adj.* having courage and the quality of holding to a thing; as, a *bulldog* firmness of mind.

bull-doze (bo͝ol′dōz″), *v.t.* [*p.t.* and *p.p.* -dozed″ (-dōzd″), *p.pr.* -doz″-ing], to bully; frighten.

bull-doz-er (bo͝ol′dōz″ẽr), *n.* **1,** a machine used in grading and road-building: a powerful tractor, pushing a broad horizontal scraper; **2,** a person who forces another by bluster or violence; also, anything used to threaten, as a weapon; **3,** a heavy machine for bending and shaping metal into shorter and thicker form, as a press.

bul-let (bo͝ol′ĕt), *n.* a small lead ball for shooting from a gun.

bul-le-tin (bo͝ol′ĕ-tĭn), *n.* **1,** a brief announcement or official report on some matter or event of public interest; **2,** a periodical publication:—*v.t.* to publish or announce in a brief authorized statement.

bull-fight (bo͝ol′fīt″), *n.* a combat held for public amusement, between armed men and a bull.—*n.* **bull′fight″er.**

bull-finch (bo͝ol′fĭnch″), *n.* any of several finches, esp. a common, handsome British song bird.

bull-frog (bo͝ol′frŏg″), *n.* the largest of the North American frogs, remarkable for its loud, bellowing croak.

bull-head (bo͝ol′hĕd″), *n.* any of various big-headed fishes, as a catfish.

bul-lion (bo͝ol′yŭn), *n.* **1,** gold or silver uncoined or valued only as metal; **2,** heavy twisted fringe of fine gold or silver wire: used for epaulets, on flags, etc.

bull moose a large male animal of the deer family, of great strength and endurance (see *moose,* illus.): **Bull Moose,** a member of the Progressive political party formed in **1912** by Theodore Roosevelt.

bull-ock (bo͝ol′ŭk), *n.* a castrated male of the ox family; steer.

bull's–eye (bo͝olz′-ī″), *n.* **1,** a bulging lens used to center light rays from a lamp upon a small spot; also, a lantern having such a lens; **2,** a round piece of thick glass in a floor, to admit light; **3,** the center of a target, or a shot that hits it.

bul-ly (bo͝ol′ĭ), *n.* [*pl.* bullies (-ĭz)], **1,** one who rules over others by threats; **2,** an overbearing fellow:—*v.t.* [*p.t.* and *p.p.* bul′lied (-ĭd), *p.pr.* bul′ly-ing], to rule with bluster and threats:—*v.i.* to be noisy and quarrelsome:—*adj. Slang,* excellent; very good.

bul-rush (bo͝ol′rŭsh″), *n.* any of various rushes growing in water or marshes, with long, slender stalks.

bul-wark (bo͝ol′wẽrk), *n.* **1,** a barrier or wall built for defense; **2,** esp., a mound of earth raised around a place as a defense against cannon shot; an earthwork; a rampart; **3,** the boarding round the sides of a ship, above the level of the deck; **4,** any means of protection or defense.

bum (bŭm), *v.i.* [*p.t.* and *p.p.* bummed (bŭmd), *p.pr.* bum′ming], **1,** *Rare,* to make a humming sound; **2,** *Colloq.,* to spend time idly; loaf:—*v.t. Colloq.,* to sponge:—*n. Colloq.,* a loafer; an idle or dissolute fellow:—*adj.* [*comp.* bum′mer, *superl.* bum′mest], *Colloq.,* poor; bad.—*n.* **bum′mer.**

bum-ble-bee (bŭm′bl-bē″), *n.* any of various kinds of large, hairy, social bees.

bump (bŭmp), *n.* **1,** a shock from a blow, **2,** a swelling due to a knock or blow —*v.t.* **1,** to bring violently together; **2,** to strike against:—*v.i.* to strike together heavily.

[1]**bump-er** (bŭm′pẽr), *n.* **1,** an overflowing cup, esp. as used in drinking a toast; **2,** *Colloq.,* anything unusually large, as a harvest:—*adj.* very large; as, a *bumper* crop.

[2]**bump-er** (bŭm′pẽr), *n.* **1,** anything that hits against something else; **2,** a device to deaden the shock of a collision; a fender, as on an automobile; buffer.

bump-kin (bŭmp′kĭn), *n.* an awkward, clumsy countryman.

bump-tious (bŭmp′shŭs), *adj.* conceited; forward; self-assertive.—*adv.* **bump′tious-ly.**—*n.* **bump′tious-ness.**

bun (bŭn), *n.* a small light cake or slightly sweetened biscuit. Also, **bunn.**

bunch (bŭnch), *n.* **1,** a lump; **2,** a cluster; **3,** a collection of things of the same kind grouped or fastened together:—*v.i.* **1,** to stick out clumsily; **2,** to form a cluster:—*v.t.* **1,** to form into a cluster; **2,** to gather into folds; **3,** to group together.—*adj.* **bunch′y.**
Syn., *n.* (see bundle).

bun-co (bŭng′kō), *n.* a swindling game or scheme:—*v.t.* [*p.t.* and *p.p.* -coed (-kōd), *p.pr.* -co-ing], to swindle or cheat by trickery. Also, **bun′ko.**

bun-combe (bŭng′kŭm), *n.* **1,** the making of speeches to gain public applause; **2,** anything said or done for mere show. Also, **bun′kum.**

bun-dle (bŭn′dl), *n.* **1,** a number of things bound together; **2,** a quantity of something in one mass; as, a *bundle* of carpet; **3,** a definite quantity of certain goods, as two reams of paper; **4,** a group; collection:—*v.t.* [*p.t.* and *p.p.* -dled (-dld), *p.pr.* -dling], **1,** to tie in a mass or roll; **2,** to send off in a hurry: with *off* or *out*:—*v.i.* to pack up and start in haste: with *out*, *off*, or *away*.
Syn., *n.* bunch, package, parcel. A *bundle* is a group of things tied or rolled together; as, a *bundle* of clothes. A *bunch* is a collection of like things growing together or fastened together; as, a *bunch* of radishes; a *bunch* of flowers. A *package* is something wrapped for carrying, sending, or storing; as, a parcel-post *package*. A *parcel* is a small package.

bung (bŭng), *n.* **1,** a large cork for stopping the hole in a cask or barrel; **2,** the hole itself: **bunghole,** the hole in a cask or barrel stopped with a bung:—*v.t.* **1,** to stop with such a cork; **2,** to close or shut up.

bun-ga-low (bŭng′gȧ-lō), *n.* a one-story house, generally surrounded by a porch or veranda.

bun-gle (bŭng′gl), *v.i.* and *v.t.* [*p.t.* and *p.p.* -gled (-gld), *p.pr.* -gling], to perform in a clumsy manner:—*n.* a clumsy performance; botch.—*n.* **bun′gler.**—*adj.* **bun′gle-some.**—*p.adj.* **bun′gling.**

bun-ion (bŭn′yŭn), *n.* a swelling on a joint, usually on the first joint of the great toe. Also, **bun′yon.**

[1]**bunk** (bŭngk), *n.* a shelf or recess used for a bed in a ship, sleeping car, etc.:—*v.i.* **1,** to sleep in a bunk; **2,** to go to bed.

[2]**bunk** (bŭngk), *n.* *Slang*, speech without meaning or truth; humbug.

bunk-er (bŭngk′ẽr), *n.* **1,** a large bin, esp. for coal on shipboard; **2,** any rough, hazardous ground on a golf links.

bun-ny (bŭn′ĭ), *n.* [*pl.* bunnies (-ĭz)], a squirrel or rabbit: a pet name.

Bun-sen burn-er (bo͝on′sĕn; bŭn′-), a gas burner for laboratory use, consisting of a tube a few inches in length, with small holes at the bottom, forming a mixture of air and gas which burns with a blue, intensely hot flame.

[1]**bunt** (bŭnt), *v.t.* **1,** to butt or push, as with head or horns; **2,** in baseball, to bat (the ball) a short distance infield:—*v.i.* **1,** to butt; push; **2,** in baseball, to bat the ball a short distance infield:—*n.* **1,** a push, as with horns; **2,** in baseball, a short hit to the infield.

[2]**bunt** (bŭnt), *n.* the baggy middle part of a square sail, of a fishing net, etc.

[1]**bun-ting** (bŭn′tĭng), *n.* any of various birds akin to the finches.

[2]**bun-ting** (bŭn′tĭng), *n.* a light, loosely woven fabric, used for flags. Also, **bun′tine** (bŭn′tĭn).

bunt-line (bŭnt′lĭn; bŭnt′līn), *n.* one of the ropes attached to a square sail to draw the sail up to the yards.

buoy (boi; bo͞o′ĭ; bwoi), *n.* **1,** a floating body moored to the bottom to show the position of rocks or shoals beneath the water, or to mark a channel; **2,** a device to support a person in the water to prevent drowning: usually called *life buoy*:—*v.t.* **1,** to keep afloat in a fluid: usually with *up*; **2,** to mark with floats to indicate a channel; **3,** to support; sustain; as, to *buoy* up one's hope.

buoy-an-cy (boi′ăn-sĭ; bo͞o′ĭ-ăn-sĭ), *n.* **1,** the property of floating on or in a liquid; **2,** the power of a fluid to hold up or partially hold up a body in it; **3,** gaiety of spirits; cheerfulness.

buoy-ant (boi′ănt; bo͞o′ĭ-ănt), *adj.* **1,** able to float in a fluid; **2,** sustaining, as a fluid; **3,** gay; light-hearted; vivacious.—*adv.* **buoy′ant-ly.**
Syn. sprightly, hopeful, cheerful.

[1]**bur** (bûr), *n.* **1,** the rough, prickly seed case of certain plants, as the burdock; **2,** the burdock; **3,** hence, something that clings persistently. Also, **burr.**

[2]**bur** (bûr), *n.* **1,** a guttural or throaty pronunciation of the *r*-sound; **2,** a humming sound:—*v.i.* [*p.t.* and *p.p.* burred (bûrd), *p.pr.* bur′ring], **1,** to speak with a rough or guttural tone; **2,** to make a humming noise:—*v.t.* to utter in a roughened, guttural tone. See [2]**burr,** *Pfd. S.*

bur-bot (bûr′bŏt), *n.* either of two kinds of codfish having hairlike filaments on the nose and chin.

[1]**bur-den** (bûr′dn), *n.* **1,** something borne or carried; a load; **2,** a load upon mind or spirit, as of grief; **3,** something the carrying of which hinders progress; **4,** the bearing of loads or packs; as, a beast of *burden*; **5,** the capacity of a vessel for carrying cargo; tonnage:—*v.t.* **1,** to load; **2,** to put too much upon; oppress. Also, [1]**bur′then.**

[2]**bur-den** (bûr′dn), *n.* **1,** a refrain in a song or ballad, repeated frequently; **2,** something often repeated and much dwelt upon; **3,** topic; gist. Also, [2]**bur′then.**

bur-den-some (bûr′dn-sŭm), *adj.* hard to bear; very oppressive. Also, **bur′then-some.**

bur-dock (bûr′dŏk), *n.* any of several large wayside weeds with burlike fruit and rough, broad leaves, whose seed pods cling to clothing or fur.

bu-reau (bū′rō; *Br.* bū-rō′), *n.* [*pl.* bureaus; bureaux (-rōz)], **1,** a chest of drawers for clothing; **2,** a desk or writing table furnished with drawers; **3,** an office; as, a *bureau* of information; **4,** a government department for the transaction of public business; as, the Secret Service *Bureau*.

bu-reau-cra-cy (bū-rō′krȧ-sĭ; bū-rŏk′rȧ-sĭ), *n.* [*pl.* bureaucracies (-sĭz)], **1,** government by bureaus, or departments, each under a head or chief, and forming a well-organized system; **2,** officials of the government spoken of collectively.

bu-rette (bū-rĕt′), *n.* a finely graduated glass tube, from which a small, measured quantity of a liquid or gas can be drawn off at a time: used in chemical analysis. (See illus. next page.)

burg (bûrg), *n.* *Obs.*, a fortified town; *U. S. Slang*, a town or city.

bur-geon (bûr′jŭn), *v.i.* to send forth buds; sprout:—*n.* a young shoot; bud. Also, **bour′geon.**

bur-gess (bûr′jĕs), *n.* **1**, a citizen or freeman of a borough; **2**, in Pennsylvania, the chief administrative officer of a borough; **3**, in Connecticut, a member of the town council; **4**, formerly, in Maryland and Virginia, a member of the lower house of the legislature.

burgh (bûrg; *Scot.* bŭr′ō), *n.* in Scotland, a corporate town; borough.

burgh-er (bûr′gẽr), *n.* a citizen, usually of an earlier time, of a borough or town; as, the *burghers* of Ghent.

bur-glar (bûr′glẽr), *n.* one who breaks into a building at night to steal.

bur-gla-ry (bûr′glȧ-rĭ), *n.* [*pl.* burglaries (-rĭz)], the act or crime of breaking into a building, esp. at night, to steal.—*adj.* **bur-gla′ri-ous.**

bur-go-mas-ter (bûr′gō-mȧs″tẽr), *n.* **1**, the chief magistrate of a town in Holland, Flanders, or Germany, corresponding to *mayor;* **2**, a large arctic gull.

Bur-gun-di-an (bûr-gŭn′dĭ-ăn), *n.* a member of a Germanic tribe that established the kingdom of Burgundy on the Rhone River, in ancient Gaul, in the fifth century:—*adj.* pertaining to the Burgundians, or to the kingdom of Burgundy on the Rhone.

Bur-gun-dy (bûr′gŭn-dĭ), *n.* a wine, red or white, made in Burgundy, France.

bur-i-al (bĕr′ĭ-ăl), *n.* the act of placing a body in the grave; interment.

bu-rin (bū′rĭn), *n.* a pointed engraving tool of steel.

burl (bûrl), *n.* **1**, a small knot or lump in thread or cloth; **2**, a knot on a tree:—*v.t.* to pick knots and loose threads from, as in finishing cloth.—*adj.* ¹**burl′y.**

bur-lap (bûr′lăp), *n.* a coarse fabric made of jute or hemp: used for bagging, curtains, etc. Also, *n.pl.* used as *sing.*, **bur′laps.**

bur-lesque (bûr-lĕsk′), *n.* **1**, a ridiculous, overdrawn representation; a parody; **2**, a composition in which a trifling subject is treated as a subject of dignity or importance:—*v.t.* and *v.i.* [*p.t.* and *p.p.* -lesqued′ (-lĕskt′), *p.pr.* -les′quing], to ridicule by caricatured representation:—*adj.* tending to excite mirth by exaggerating peculiarities.

Syn., *n.* (see parody).

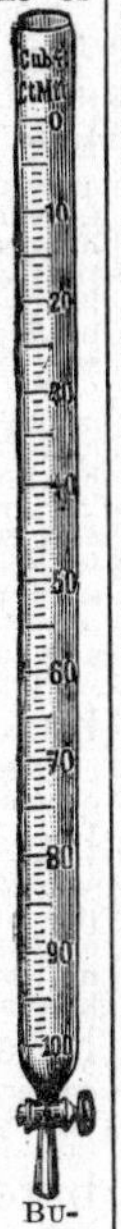

BURETTE

²**bur-ly** (bûr′lĭ), *adj.* [*comp.* bur′li-er, *superl.* bur′li-est], **1**, bulky; large; muscular; **2**, rough; noisy.—*n.* **bur′li-ness.**

bur mar-i-gold any of several coarse herbs of the aster family, with small, dry seed pods.

Bur-mese (bûr″mēz′; bûr″mēs′), *n.* [*pl.* Burmese], **1**, a native of Burma; **2**, the language of the Burmese:—*adj.* pertaining to Burma, its people, or its language.—*n.* and *adj.* **Bur′man.**

¹**burn** (bûrn), *n.* in Great Britain, a brook. Also, **bourn; bourne.**

²**burn** (bûrn), *v.t.* [*p.t.* and *p.p.* burned (bûrnd). or burnt (bûrnt), *p.pr.* burn′ing], **1**, to destroy or injure by fire; **2**, to reduce to ashes; **3**, to scald or sear; **4**, to inflame or tan (the skin); **5**, to affect with a burning feeling; **6**, to expose intentionally to the action of fire, as wood to make charcoal; **7**, in surgery, to apply heat or acid to for curative purposes; cauterize:—*v.i.* **1**, to be on fire; **2**, to suffer from, or be injured by, too much heat; **3**, to be inflamed with passion or desire; as, he *burns* to win fame; **4**, to feel a sensation of heat:—*n.* an injury caused by fire; any damage caused by too much heat.

Syn., *v.* blaze, scorch, singe. *Burn* is the general term; the others are methods of burning. To *burn* is to change, injure, or destroy completely by fire; as, to *burn* one's finger; to *burn* coal. To *blaze* is to burn with a bright flame, as oil. To *scorch* and to *singe* indicate surface burning. To *scorch* is more serious and implies injury in color or texture; as, to *scorch* with an iron. To *singe* is to burn slightly; as, to *singe* the hair.

burn-er (bûr′nẽr), *n.* **1**, one who burns or sets fire to anything; **2**, the part of a lamp, gas fixture, or the like, from which the flame comes; as, a Bunsen *burner.*

burn-ing glass a lens of glass, used to set fire to or melt something by bringing the direct rays of the sun to a point, or focus, on it.

burn-ing point the temperature at which the vapor from a volatile oil will take fire and continue to burn: distinguished from *flashing point.*

bur-nish (bûr′nĭsh), *v.t.* to polish by rubbing or friction, as metal; make smooth and shining:—*n.* polish; brightness. —*n.* **bur′nish-er.**—*n.* **bur′nish-ment.**

Syn., *n.* luster, shine, glossiness.

bur-noose (bûr-no͞os′; bûr′no͞os), *n.* **1**, a cloak and hood combined, worn by Moors and Arabs; **2**, a similar cloak worn by women. Also, **bur-nous′.**

burnt (bûrnt), a form of the past tense and past participle of the verb *burn:*—*p.adj.* charred, destroyed, or affected by fire.

¹**burr** (bûr), *n.* **1**, a prickly seed case; **2**, the burdock. See ¹**bur**, *Pfd. S.*

²**burr** (bûr), *n.* **1**, a thin ridge or roughness left by a tool in cutting or shaping metal; **2**, a rough, humming sound; **3**, a rough, guttural pronunciation of *r:*—*v.i.* **1**, to pronounce *r* with a rough or guttural sound; speak in a rough, harsh tone; **2**, to make a humming noise:—*v.t.* **1**, to make a rough, projecting edge upon; **2**, to utter with a roughened, guttural tone. Also, **bur.**

bur-ro (bo͝or′ō; bŭr′ō), *n.* [*pl.* burros (-ōz)], in the southwestern U. S., a donkey.

bur-row (bûr′ō), *n.* **1**, a hole in the ground dug by a rabbit or other animal as a refuge or home; **2**, a similar shelter:—*v.i.* **1**, to dig a hole in the earth, as for shelter; **2**, to work a way in or down:—*v.t.* to make burrows in, or build by burrowing; as, to *burrow* a cave.—*n.* **bur′row-er.**

burr-stone (bûr′stōn″), *n.* a rock used for millstones. Also, **buhr′-stone″**, *Pfd. S.*

bur-sa (bûr′sȧ), *n.* [*pl.* bursas (-sȧz); bursæ (-sē)], a small sac or cavity in the body, esp. between joints (see *knee*, illus.).

bur-sar (bûr′sẽr), *n.* **1**, the treasurer of a college; **2**, in Scotland, a university student who receives an allowance for his support while studying.

burst (bûrst), *v.i.* [*p.t.* and *p.p.* burst, *p.pr.* burst′ing], **1**, to break open by flying to pieces; **2**, to explode; **3**, to break suddenly into action, speech, or feeling: usually with *out, upon, into,* etc.; as, to *burst* into tears; **4**, to appear or disappear suddenly; as, a scene *bursts* upon the view:—*v.t.* to break by violence; open suddenly:—*n.* **1**, a violent or sudden breaking forth; as, a *burst* of applause; **2**, a sudden explosion; **3**, a rush; spurt.

¹**bur-then** (bûr′*th*n), *n.* **1**, a load; **2**, a weight of grief or care; **3**, an encumbrance; **4**, the bearing of packs; **5**, the carrying capacity of a vessel:—*v.t.* **1**, to load; **2**, to oppress. See ¹**bur′den**, *Pfd. S.*—*adj.* **bur′then-some.**

[2]**bur-then** (bûr′*th*n), *n.* **1**, a refrain; **2**, a subject much dwelt upon; **3**, topic; gist. See [2]**bur′den,** *Pfd. S.*

bur-y (bĕr′ĭ), *v.t.* [*p.t.* and *p.p.* bur′ied (bĕr′ĭd), *p.pr.* bur′y-ing], **1**, to place in a grave, tomb, etc., usually with ceremony; **2**, to cover from sight; conceal, as treasure; **3**, to hide; keep secret; **4**, to forget; **5**, to engross; as, to *bury* oneself in a book.

bus (bŭs), *n.* [*pl.* busses; buses (bŭs′ĕz)], an omnibus; a large public vehicle.

[1]**bush** (bo͝osh), *n.* **1**, a shrub or low-growing plant which develops some wood in its stem; **2**, a wide-spreading growth of low, shrubby plants, or a region covered with such a growth; hence, an uncleared forest region: used esp. of uncultivated or forest land in Australia:—*v.i.* to put out small branches thickly; grow thickly, like a bush.

[2]**bush** (bo͝osh), *n.* in machinery, a lining used to reduce friction; a bushing.

[1]**bush-el** (bo͝osh′ĕl), *n.* **1**, a unit of dry measure, containing four pecks; **2**, a container holding that amount.

[2]**bush-el** (bo͝osh′ĕl), *v.t.* to mend or alter, as men's clothes.—*n.* **bush′el-er.** —*n.* **bush′el-man.**

bush-ing (bo͝osh′ĭng), *n.* a metallic, detachable lining for a hole.

bush-man (bo͝osh′măn), *n.* [*pl.* bushmen (-mĕn)], in Australia, an inhabitant of the bush.

Bush-man (bo͝osh′măn), *n.* [*pl.* Bushmen (-mĕn)], one of an aboriginal tribe in southwest Africa, similar to, but lower than, the Hottentots.

bush-rang-er (bo͝osh′rān″jẽr), *n.* **1**, one who leads a wandering life in an uncleared forest region; **2**, an escaped criminal living a lawless life in the bush or forest lands of Australia.

bush-whack-er (bo͝osh′hwăk″ẽr), *n.* **1**, a backwoodsman; **2**, in the Civil War, a Confederate guerrilla fighter; **3**, a tool for cutting brushwood.—*n.* **bush′whack″ing.**

bush-y (bo͝osh′ĭ), *adj.* [*comp.* bush′i-er, *superl.* bush′i-est], **1**, thick and spreading like a bush; **2**, overgrown with shrubs.—*adv.* **bush′i-ly.**—*n.* **bush′i-ness.**

busi-ness (bĭz′nĕs), *n.* **1**, employment; trade; profession; **2**, something necessary to be done; duty; mission; **3**, concern; as, it is no *business* of mine; **4**, affair; matter; **5**, a commercial enterprise; **6**, commercial or financial activities:—*adj.* pertaining to commercial pursuits.—*adj.* **busi′ness-like″.**

Syn., *n.* commerce, trade, profession, occupation, craft, calling. A *business* is an interest that is followed for gain or as a means of securing a living. Collectively, *business* names those occupations that have to do with mercantile or financial interests; as, the banking *business:* the grocery *business. Commerce* is business on a large scale, involving the buying, selling, and transportation of goods; as, interstate *commerce. Commerce* and *trade* are like terms, but *trade* may also be applied to a much smaller unit; as, the *trade* of a village, or world *trade. Trade* in its special sense names any of the occupations carried on by manual labor, except those connected with agriculture; as, he is a carpenter by *trade.* A *profession* is a business that requires specialized training and implies mental rather than physical labor; as, the *profession* of medicine.

busk (bŭsk), *n.* **1**, a stiffened garment for the upper part of the body, as a corset or doublet; **2**, a corset stay.

bus-kin (bŭs′kĭn), *n.* **1**, a kind of high, laced shoe; **2**, a high shoe with thick sole worn by ancient tragic actors; **3**, hence, tragedy.—*adj.* **bus′kined** (bŭs′kĭnd).

buss (bŭs), *n.* a kiss; a smack:—*v.t.* and *v.i.* to kiss: now archaic.

bust (bŭst), *n.* **1**, the human chest or thorax; the breast or bosom; **2**, a piece of sculpture representing the head, shoulders, and breast of a person.

bus-tard (bŭs′tȧrd), *n.* any of the Old World, cranelike game birds, resembling the ostrich, but smaller.

[1]**bus-tle** (bŭs′l), *n.* tumult; noisy activity: —*v.i.* [*p.t.* and *p.p.* -tled (-ld), *p.pr.* -tling], to be noisily busy; move about quickly; as, to *bustle* about a room.—*p.adj.* **bus′tling.**—*adv.* **bus′tling-ly.**

Syn., *n.* stir, agitation, fuss, commotion.

[2]**bus-tle** (bŭs′l), *n.* a pad or framework formerly worn by women beneath the skirt at the back.

bus-y (bĭz′ĭ), *adj.* [*comp.* bus′i-er, *superl.* bus′i-est], **1**, earnestly, actively, or closely at work; **2**, characteristic of, or pertaining to, industry or diligence; as, the *busy* hum of the factory; **3**, bustling; full of activities; as, a *busy* day; **4**, in use, as a telephone line; **5**, meddlesome:—*v.t.* [*p.t.* and *p.p.* bus′ied (-ĭd), *p.pr.* bus′y-ing], to keep constantly engaged; occupy.—*adv.* **bus′i-ly.**

Syn., *adj.* diligent, industrious, engaged, occupied. *Busy* means keeping earnestly and actively at work. It also describes one who has much to do; as, a *busy* man. Sometimes it carries the sense of occupied; as, he is too *busy* to see you. *Diligent* describes one who is carefully and busily engaged in following some pursuit; as, a *diligent* student. *Industrious* describes one who is habitually busy and applies himself closely; as, an *industrious* workman.—*Ant.*, *adj.* idle, indolent, lazy.

bus-y-bod-y (bĭz′ĭ-bŏd″ĭ), *n.* [*pl.* busybodies (-ĭz)], one who officiously concerns himself with the affairs of others; a meddler.

but (bŭt), *adv.* only; as, speak *but* a word:—*prep.* except; as, I can bear all *but* that: —*conj.* **1**, still; yet; as, poor *but* honest; **2**, on the contrary; as, you go, *but* I stay; **3**, except; as, *but* for that, I could go; **4**, that; as, I do not doubt *but* it is true; that not; as, who knows *but* he will succeed?

butch-er (bo͝och′ẽr), *n.* **1**, one who kills animals for food; **2**, a meat dealer; **3**, a cruel and bloody murderer:—*v.t.* **1**, to kill animals for food; **2**, to murder brutally and cruelly; **3**, to botch or mangle; ruin.

butch-er bird any of several shrikes, birds that hang or impale their prey upon thorns.

butch-er-y (bo͝och′ẽr-ĭ), *n.* [*pl.* butcheries (-ĭz)], **1**, a place where animals are killed for food; **2**, the business of killing cattle; **3**, horrible, cruel, and unnecessary slaughter, as of noncombatants.

but-ler (bŭt′lẽr), *n.* a manservant in a household, who has charge of the dining room, silver, etc.; the chief manservant in a large household.

[1]**butt** (bŭt), *n.* **1**, the blunt end of anything, as a whip; **2**, in shipbuilding, the square end of a timber which meets another endways; **3**, any of several kinds of hinge or joint; **4**, a square-trimmed leather hide (see *leather*, illus.):—*v.t.* to strike as with the end of a heavy timber:—*v.i.* to join together end to end, as timbers.

[2]**butt** (bŭt), *n.* a push delivered by the head of an animal, as a goat:—*v.t.* **1**, to strike by thrusting; **2**, to strike with the lowered head; **3**, to place the end of against a flat surface:—*v.i.* **1**, to strike anything with the head; **2**, to collide: with *into;* **3**, to abut: with *on* or *upon:* **butt in,** to intrude.

[3]**butt** (bŭt), *n.* **1**, a target; also, the embankment back of it; **2**, that at which anything is aimed; **3**, hence, one at whom jest or ridicule is directed; **4**, in *pl.*, a shooting range.

[4]**butt** (bŭt), *n.* a large cask or vessel, as for wine or beer.

butte (būt), *n.* a steep hill or ridge standing alone.

but-ter (bŭt′ẽr), *n.* **1**, the fatty or oily substance obtained from cream or milk by churning; **2**, any of several butterlike substances:—*v.t.* to spread or season with this fat.—*adj.* [1]**but′ter-y.**

but-ter-cup (bŭt′ẽr-kŭp″), *n.* any of several yellow, cup-shaped wild flowers, growing esp. in meadows.

but-ter-fly (bŭt′ẽr-flī″), *n.* [*pl.* butterflies (-flīz″)], **1**, any of an order of insects with four down-covered, brightly colored wings, which fly by day; **2**, a gay idler: **butterfly valve,** a valve or damper in a pipe, consisting of a disk, or flat plate, turning on an axis within the pipe.

but-ter-ine (bŭt′ẽr-ēn; bŭt′ẽr-ĭn), *n.* artificial butter; oleomargarine.

but-ter-milk (bŭt′ẽr-mĭlk″), *n.* the liquid remaining when cream or milk has been churned and the fat removed.

but-ter-nut (bŭt′ẽr-nŭt″), *n.* the North American white walnut or its edible fruit.

[2]**but-ter-y** (bŭt′ẽr-ĭ), *n.* [*pl.* butteries (-ĭz)], a room or closet in which provisions are kept; the butler's pantry.

but-tock (bŭt′ŭk), *n.* **1**, usually in *pl.*, either side of the rump or hinder part of a man or animal; **2**, the part of a ship under the stern.

but-ton (bŭt′n), *n.* **1**, any small, rounded object used for fastening or ornamenting a garment: **2**, a pivoted fastening for a door, window, etc.; **3**, the knob at the end of a fencing foil; **4**, a small knob operating a switch in an electric circuit; **5**, any small, rounded object, as the bud of a plant; **6**, in *pl.*, young mushrooms; **7**, in *pl.* used as *sing.*, a page boy:—*v.t.* to fasten or furnish with buttons:—*v.i.* to be capable of being fastened by buttons.—*n.* **but′ton-er.**

but-ton-hole (bŭt′n-hōl″), *n.* a stitched hole for a button to pass through:—*v.t.* [*p.t.* and *p.p.* -holed″ (-hōld″), *p.pr.* -hol″ing], **1**, to hold in conversation against the will; **2**, to furnish with buttonholes; **3**, to edge with the stitching used in finishing buttonholes, as cloth.

but-ton-wood (bŭt′n-wo͝od″), *n.* a large North American plane tree: so called because of its small, round, rough, buttonlike fruit; a sycamore.

but-tress (bŭt′rĕs), *n.* **1**, masonry or brickwork built against a wall to afford support; **2**, any prop or support:—*v.t.* to support, as by a buttress.

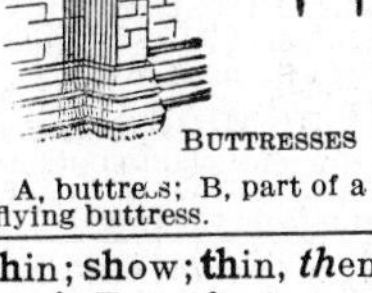

BUTTRESSES

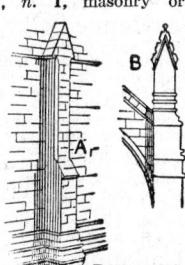

A, buttress; B, part of a flying buttress.

bux-om (bŭk′sŭm), *adj.* **1**, robust; handsome; **2**, lively; vigorous; energetic.

buy (bī), *v.t.* [*p.t.* and *p.p.* bought (bôt), *p.pr.* buy′ing], **1**, to obtain by paying an agreed price; **2**, to gain at a sacrifice; as, to *buy* peace by giving up one's own way; **3**, to serve to get; as, money cannot *buy* happiness; **4**, to bribe; win over by the payment of money:—*v.i.* to make a purchase.—*n.* **buy′er.**

buzz (bŭz), *n.* **1**, a constant humming noise, as of bees; **2**, a confused or blended murmur, as of many voices; **3**, a whispered report or rumor:—*v.i.* **1**, to make a low humming sound; **2**, to speak with a low humming voice:—*v.t.* **1**, to spread secretly, as gossip; **2**, to cause to give a buzzing sound.

buz-zard (bŭz′ȧrd), *n.* **1**, any of several hawklike birds of prey of America and Europe; **2**, esp., in America, the turkey buzzard, properly a vulture.

buzz-er (bŭz′ẽr), *n.* an electric instrument for signaling.

by (bī), *prep.* **1**, next or near to; as, a chair *by* the window; **2**, along; over; as, a road *by* the river; **3**, in, on, or at; as, *by* night; *by* land; **4**, past and beyond; as, to go *by* the spot; **5**, after; according to; as, known *by* his gait; **6**, not any later than; as, to finish *by* two o'clock; **7**, through the agency of; as, to send word *by* messenger; **8**, through the action of; as, a poem *by* Shelley; **9**, because of; as, to succeed *by* industry; **10**, to the amount of: used after comparatives; as, taller *by* several inches; **11**, with regard to; as, to deal unfairly *by* a friend; **12**, with the witness of: used in oaths; as, to swear *by* the Book; **13**, according to; as, to judge *by* appearances; **14**, in the measure of; as, sell *by* the pound; wages *by* the week; **15**, at sea, one point in the direction of; as, north *by* east: **by the way, 1**, on the road; **2**, incidentally:—*adv.* **1**, near; beside; as, to stand *by;* **2**, aside; as, lay your armor *by;* **3**, past; as, he drove *by:* **by and by,** after a little while; hereafter: **by and large,** speaking generally; regarding all sides of the question

by- (bī-), *prefix*, secondary; out of the direct road; as, *by*path.

bye (bī), *n.* **1**, in cricket, a run scored on a ball which the batsman has not touched and which the wicket keeper has failed to stop; **2**, (also, *by*), something secondary: obsolete except in *by the bye, by the by*, by the way.

by-gone (bī′gŏn″), *adv.* past; gone by:—*n.* something in the past.

by–law (bī′-lô″), *n.* a rule adopted by an association to add to the provisions of a constitution or charter.

by–pass (bī′-pȧs″), *n.* a side passage for the flow of a fluid or something likened to it in a path parallel to the main path; esp., an outlet in a gas fixture by which a small flame, or pilot light, is kept burning when the main flame is extinguished: **by-pass condenser,** in radio, a condenser connected across the terminals of a telephone or other instrument to facilitate the passage of certain currents in the plate circuit (see *radio*, illus.).

by-path (bī′pȧth″), *n.* a private or retired path; a side path.

by-play (bī′plā″), *n.* on the stage, action of the players not directly connected with the main situation.

by–prod-uct (bī′-prŏd″ŭkt), *n.* something produced during a manufacturing process, in addition to the principal thing manufactured, as sawdust in a sawmill; a secondary product.

by-stand-er (bī′stăn″dẽr), *n.* one standing by or looking on, but not taking part; a spectator.

by-way (bī′wā″), *n.* a private or secluded road or path.

by-word (bī′wûrd″), *n.* **1**, a proverb or saying; **2**, a nickname; **3**, an object of scorn or ridicule.

By-zan-tine (bĭ-zăn′tĭn; bĭz′ăn-tĭn; -tīn), *adj.* pertaining to Byzantium, now called Constantinople:—*n.* a native of Byzantium, or of Constantinople.

C

Ca-a-ba (kä'ȧ-bȧ; kä'bȧ), *n.* the shrine at Mecca, the chief object of pilgrimage of Mohammedans, toward which they face when praying. It contains a black stone said to be a ruby brought from heaven, and made black by the sins of those who have touched it. Also, **Ka'a-ba.**

cab (kăb), *n.* **1,** a public carriage with two or four wheels, drawn by one horse; **2,** the shelter for the driver of a locomotive.

ca-bal (kȧ-băl'), *n.* **1,** a secret scheme; an intrigue; **2,** a secret combination of a few persons for carrying out some special plan, usually evil:—*v.i.* [*p.t.* and *p.p.* -balled' (-băld'), *p.pr.* -bal'ling], to unite in secret with others to effect some design.

cab-a-la (kăb'ȧ-lȧ), *n.* **1,** a secret system of the Jewish rabbis for finding the hidden meaning of the first five books of the Bible; **2,** hence, any occult or mystic philosophy. Also, **cab'ba-la.**

cab-a-lism (kăb'ȧ-lĭzm), *n.* secret, mysterious doctrine. Also, **cab'ba-lism.**—*n.* **cab'a-list.**

cab-a-lis-tic (kăb"ȧ-lĭs'tĭk), *adj.* mysterious; suggesting the secret; occult; mystical. Also, **cab"ba-lis'tic.**—*adv.* **cab"a-lis'ti-cal-ly.**

ca-bane (kȧ"bȧn') [Fr.], *n.* a framework to stiffen the wings of an airplane over the fuselage (see *monoplane*, illus.) or at the outer ends of the upper wings.

cab-a-ret (kăb"ȧ-rā'; *Fr.* kȧ"bȧ"rĕ'), *n.* a restaurant in which guests are entertained while at meals by dancing and vaudeville acts.

cab-bage (kăb'āj), *n.* **1,** a European plant of the mustard family, cultivated as a vegetable for its compact head of leaves; **2,** the terminal bud of a palm: **cabbage palm,** any of several species of palm with an edible terminal bud.

cab-in (kăb'ĭn), *n.* **1,** a small hut, cottage, or room; **2,** a room in a ship for officers or passengers:—*v.t.* to confine in a small space; hem in.

cab-i-net (kăb'ĭ-nĕt), *n.* **1,** a small apartment; private room; **2,** a piece of furniture to hold objects of art, curiosity, etc.; **3,** a committee of the heads of governmental departments; as, the President appoints his own *cabinet*:—*adj.* **1,** secret; **2,** small; as, a *cabinet* organ; **3,** of or pertaining to the advisory council of the chief executive of a nation; as, a *cabinet* meeting.

cab-i-net-mak-er (kăb'ĭ-nĕt-māk"ẽr), *n.* a worker in fine woods; usually, a maker of fine household furniture.—*n.* **cab'i-net-work".**

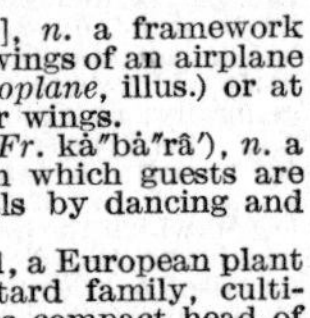

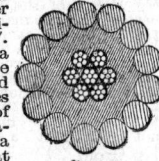

CABLE
Section of submarine cable, with seven cores of twisted copper wires, surrounded by hemp packing, protected by outer ring of iron wires.

ca-ble (kā'bl), *n.* **1,** a large strong rope or chain; **2,** an insulated bundle of electric wires covered with a waterproof substance, as for a submarine telegraph line; **3,** a measure of distance used at sea, equal to about 100 fathoms:—*v.t.* [*p.t.* and *p.p.* -bled (-bld), *p.pr.* -bling], **1,** to fasten with a cable; **2,** to send (a message) or communicate with (a person) by submarine telegraph.

ca-ble-gram (kā'bl-grăm"), *n.* a message sent by submarine cable.

ca-boose (kȧ-bōōs'), *n.* **1,** the kitchen of a ship; **2,** the trainmen's car attached to the end of a freight train.

cab-ri-o-let (kăb"rĭ-ō-lā'), *n.* **1,** a covered carriage with two or four wheels, drawn by one horse; **2,** an inclosed automobile with a top which folds back.

ca-ca-o (kȧ-kā'ō; kȧ-kä'ō), *n.* **1,** a small evergreen tree of tropical America and the West Indies; **2,** the seeds of this tree, from which cocoa and chocolate are made.

cache (kȧsh), *n.* a hiding place for food or supplies:—*v.t.* [*p.t.* and *p.p.* cached (kȧsht), *p.pr.* cach'ing], to hide away, as provisions or supplies.

cach-in-nate (kăk'ĭ-nāt), *v.i.* [*p.t.* and *p.p.* -nat"ed, *p.pr.* -nat"ing], to laugh boisterously.—*n.* **cach"in-na'tion.**—*n.* **cach'in-na"tor.**

ca-cique (kȧ-sēk'), *n.* **1,** a native prince or chieftain in Mexico, Peru, and the West Indies; **2,** in the Philippines, a landholder, esp. one whose property is extensive.

cack-le (kăk'l), *n.* **1,** the cry of a hen or goose; **2,** chatter; idle talk:—*v.i.* [*p.t.* and *p.p.* -led (-ld), *p.pr.* -ling], **1,** to cry like a goose, or like a hen which has laid an egg; **2,** to giggle; prattle.

cac-tus (kăk'tŭs), *n.* [*pl.* cactuses (-ĕz); cacti (-tī)], any of a family of prickly or spiny desert plants, some of which bear showy flowers.

cad (kăd), *n.* **1,** a vulgar, ill-bred fellow of mean principles; **2,** in England, a loafer.

ca-da-ver (kȧ-dā'vẽr; kȧ-dăv'ẽr), *n.* a dead body, esp. of a person.

ca-dav-er-ous (kȧ-dăv'ẽr-ŭs), *adj.* like a corpse; pale; ghastly.

cad-die (kăd'ĭ), *n.* a lad who carries the clubs for golf players. Also, [1]**cad'dy; cad'ie; cad'y.**

cad-dis (kăd'ĭs), *n.* **1,** a kind of lint; **2,** *Obs.*: **a,** fibrous wadding; **b,** a coarse, woolen yarn. Also, **cad'dice.**

cad-dis fly an insect whose larva, growing in water, and called *caddis worm,* lives in and drags about a silk-lined case covered with bits of wood and sand.

cad-dish (kăd'ĭsh), *adj.* mean; unmanly; ill-bred.—*adv.* **cad'dish-ly.**—*n.* **cad'dish-ness.**

[2]**cad-dy** (kăd'ĭ), *n.* [*pl.* caddies (-ĭz)], a small box for storing tea.

ca-dence (kā'dĕns), *n.* **1,** the rise and fall of the voice in reading or speaking; **2,** rhythm, as in music; also, a musical run or trill; **3,** a uniform time and pace in marching; **4,** in music, a group of chords at the end of a division of a composition.

ca-det (kȧ-dĕt'), *n.* **1,** a student in a naval or military academy; **2,** a younger son.—*n.* **ca-det'ship.**

ca-di (kä'dĭ; kā'dĭ), *n.* [*pl.* cadis (-dĭz)], a Mohammedan judge, usually over a village. Also, **ka'di.**

cad-mi-um (kăd'mĭ-ŭm), *n.* a rare metallic element, bluish white in color, easily fusible, malleable, and ductile: chiefly used in alloys.

Cad-mus (kăd'mŭs), *n.* in mythology, a Phœnician prince who killed a dragon, planted its teeth and built Thebes with the help of five of the soldiers who sprang up from the teeth.

ca-du-ce-us (kȧ-dū′sē-ŭs), *n.* [*pl.* caducei (-ī)], the winged, serpent-twined staff carried by Mercury, the messenger of the gods.—*adj.* **ca-du′ce-an.**

CADUCEUS

cæ-cum (sē′kŭm), *n.* [*pl.* cæca (-kȧ)], the upper end of the large intestine.

Cæ-no-zo-ic (sē″nō-zō′ĭk), *adj.* in geology, designating the era immediately following the Mesozoic, and preceding the Recent. See **Ce″no-zo′ic,** *Pfd. S.*

Cæ-sar (sē′zȧr), *n.* **1,** a Roman emperor: taken as a title by the first Roman emperor who was an adopted son of Julius Cæsar; **2,** hence, any dictator.

cæ-su-ra (sē-zū′rȧ; sē-sū′rȧ), *n.* a pause or division in scanning verse. Also, **ce-su′ra.**—*adj.* **cæ-su′ral.**

ca-fé (kȧ″fā′; kȧ′fā″), *n.* a coffeehouse; a restaurant.

caf-e-te-ri-a (kăf″ē-tē′rĭ-ȧ), *n.* a lunch room or restaurant where the patrons serve themselves.

caf-fe-ine (kăf′ē-ĭn; -ēn), *n.* a bitter, stimulating substance found in coffee, kola, and tea. Also, **caf′fe-in.**

caf-tan (kăf′tăn; kȧf-tän′), *n.* a girdled, long-sleeved gown worn in Eastern countries. Also, **kaf′tan.**—*adj.* **caf′taned.**

cage (kāj), *n.* **1,** a box or inclosure furnished with bars for confining birds or other animals; **2,** a basket for raising and lowering men in a mine shaft; **3,** anything resembling a cage in form or effect; **4,** the boxlike compartment or car of an elevator, in which passengers are carried:—*v.t.* [*p.t.* and *p.p.* caged (kājd), *p.pr.* cag′ing], to confine, as in a cage; shut up.

Ca-ia-phas (kā′yȧ-făs; kī′ȧ-), *n.* in the Bible, a Jewish high priest presiding at the trial of Jesus (Matthew 26:57).

cai-man (kā′măn), *n.* an alligator of tropical America. See **cay′man,** *Pfd.S.*

Cain (kān), *n.* **1,** in the Bible, the son of Adam and brother of Abel, whom he killed (Genesis 4:1–10); **2,** hence, a murderer.

cairn (kârn), *n.* a cone-shaped heap of stones erected as a monument, esp. those in the British Isles, apparently the work of the early Britons.—*adj.* **cairned.**

cairn-gorm (kârn′gôrm″), *n.* a yellow or brown quartz or rock crystal, used as a gem.

cais-son (kā′sŏn), *n.* **1,** an ammunition wagon; **2,** a box filled with explo-

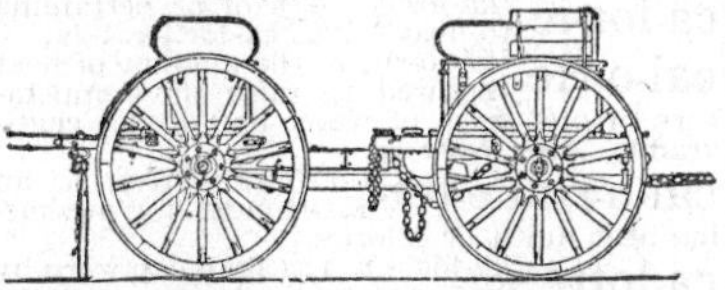

ARTILLERY CAISSON (def. 1)

sives for firing a mine; **3,** a water-tight box or casing used for building structures in water; **4,** a structure for raising sunken vessels.

cai-tiff (kā′tĭf), *n.* a mean, cowardly wretch:—*adj.* vile; cowardly.

ca-jole (kȧ-jōl′), *v.t.* and *v.i.* [*p.t.* and *p.p.* -joled′ (-jōld′), *p.pr.* -jol′ing], to coax or deceive by flattery; wheedle; cheat.

ca-jol-er-y (kȧ-jōl′ẽr-ĭ), *n.* [*pl.* cajoleries (-ĭz)], the act of deceiving with flattery; wheedling.

cake (kāk), *n.* **1,** a small mass of dough, sweetened and baked; **2,** a pancake; **3,** any compressed or solidified mass, esp. if thin or flat:—*v.i.* and *v.t.* [*p.t.* and *p.p.* caked (kākt), *p.pr.* cak′ing], to form into a hard mass; as, dry weather causes mud to *cake.*

cal-a-bash (kăl′ȧ-băsh), *n.* **1,** the hard-shelled fruit of a tree of tropical America; **2,** a vessel or implement made from the dried shell of this fruit.

CALABASH

cal-a-boose (kăl″ȧ-bōōs′), *n.* a jail; lockup.

ca-lam-i-tous (kȧ-lăm′ĭ-tŭs), *adj.* producing, or resulting from, disaster; as, *calamitous* floods.—*adv.* **ca-lam′i-tous-ly.**—*n.* **ca-lam′i-tous-ness.**

ca-lam-i-ty (kȧ-lăm′ĭ-tĭ), *n.* [*pl.* calamities (-tĭz)], **1,** any cause that produces evil, disaster, or extreme misfortune; **2,** distress; affliction.

Syn. accident, mishap, catastrophe.

cal-a-mus (kăl′ȧ-mŭs), *n.* [*pl.* calami (-mī)], **1,** a slender, climbing palm, producing rattan canes; **2,** a flute or pipe made of this palm; **3,** the sweet flag.

ca-lash (kȧ-lăsh′), *n.* **1,** a light carriage with low wheels and a folding top; **2,** a large hood supported on hoops, formerly worn by English women.

cal-ca-re-ous (kăl-kā′rē-ŭs), *adj.* of the nature of, or containing, carbonate of lime; as, *calcareous* earth.

cal-cif-er-ous (kăl-sĭf′ẽr-ŭs), *adj.* containing or producing carbonate of lime, as certain rocks.

cal-ci-fy (kăl′sĭ-fī), *v.t.* and *v.i.* [*p.t.* and *p.p.* -fied (-fīd), *p.pr.* -fy″ing], to make or become hard by the addition of lime.

cal-ci-mine (kăl′sĭ-mīn; kăl′sĭ-mĭn), *n.* a white or tinted wash for walls or ceilings:—*v.t.* [*p.t.* and *p.p.* -mined (-mīnd; -mĭnd), *p.pr.* -min″ing], to cover with such a wash. Also, incorrectly, **kal′so-mine.**

cal-cine (kăl-sīn′; kăl′sĭn), *v.t.* [*p.t.* and *p.p.* -cined′ (-sīnd′; -sĭnd), *p.pr.* -cin′ing], to reduce (a substance) to powder by heat:—*v.i.* to become powder under the influence of heat.—*n.* **cal″ci-na′tion.**

cal-cite (kăl′sīt), *n.* calcium carbonate; natural lime, chalk, marble, etc.

cal-ci-um (kăl′sĭ-ŭm), *n.* a soft, white, metallic element occurring in nature only in combination, as in lime, marble, chalk, etc., because of its strong chemical activity: **calcium carbide,** a compound of calcium and carbon which, when combined with water, gives off acetylene gas: **calcium chloride,** a compound of calcium and chlorine, used as a disinfectant and as a drying agent: **calcium light,** an intense white light: also called *limelight.*

cal-cu-la-ble (kăl′kū-lȧ-bl), *adj.* capable of being determined or reckoned.—*adv.* **cal′cu-la-bly.**

cal-cu-late (kăl′kū-lāt), *v.t.* [*p.t.* and *p.p.* -lat″ed, *p.pr.* -lat″ing], **1,** to add, subtract, multiply, or divide any sum to find the result; **2,** to determine by any process of reasoning; estimate; as, no one can *calculate* the benefits of electricity to the world:—*v.i.* **1,** to make a computation; **2,** to conclude by reasoning; **3,** to rely: with *on* or *upon.*

Syn. compute, number, rate.

cal-cu-la-tion (kăl″kū-lā′shŭn), *n.* **1,** the use of numbers in reckoning a problem; also, the result obtained; **2,** a result of reasoning or inference; estimate.

cal-cu-la-tive (kăl′kū-lā-tĭv), *adj.* **1,** of or pertaining to computation; **2,** inclined to compute or reckon.

cal-cu-la-tor (kăl′kū-lā″tẽr), *n.* one who, or a machine that, computes or reckons, as an adding machine.

cal-cu-lous (kăl′kū-lŭs), *adj.* stony; gritty; as, a *calculous* mass.

cal-cu-lus (kăl′kū-lŭs), *n.* [*pl.* calculi (-lī)], **1,** any branch of mathematics involving calculation, esp. differential calculus and integral calculus; **2,** a hard substance sometimes formed in the kidneys, bladder, or gall bladder, as a gallstone.

cal-dron (kôl′drŭn), *n.* a large kettle or boiler. Also, **caul′dron.**

cal-en-dar (kăl′ĕn-dȧr), *n.* **1,** a method of reckoning time, esp. as to the length and divisions of a year; **2,** an arrangement, as on a card or sheets of paper, setting forth the days, weeks, and months of a year; **3,** an almanac; **4,** a register or list; **5,** a list of cases arranged for trial:—*v.t.* to register or place on a list. Also, **kal′en-dar.**

cal-en-der (kăl′ĕn-dẽr), *n.* a machine containing heated rollers for smoothing and glazing paper or cloth:—*v.i.* to press in a smoothing machine, as paper.

cal-ends (kăl′ĕndz), *n.pl.* in ancient Rome, the first day of the month.

[1]**calf** (kȧf), *n.* [*pl.* calves (kȧvz)], **1,** the young of the cow; **2,** the young of other large mammals, as the whale, elephant, etc.; **3,** leather made from the skin of a calf; **4,** a mass of ice breaking from an iceberg.

[2]**calf** (kȧf), *n.* [*pl.* calves (kȧvz)], the fleshy hinder part of the human leg between the knee and ankle.

calf-skin (kȧf′skĭn″), *n.* **1,** the skin of a calf; **2,** leather made of the skin of a calf, widely used for shoes, belting, etc.

cal-i-ber (kăl′ĭ-bẽr), *n.* **1,** the diameter of a round body; **2,** esp., the inside diameter of the barrel of a gun, cannon, or the like; **3,** mental capacity or intellectual power. Also, **cal′i-bre.**

cal-i-brate (kăl′ĭ-brāt), *v.t.* [*p.t.* and *p.p.* -brat″ed, *p.pr.* -brat″ing], **1,** to compare (an instrument or device) with a standard to determine accuracy or to produce a scale; as, to *calibrate* a thermometer; **2,** to find the diameter of, as a tube or gun barrel.

cal-i-co (kăl′ĭ-kō), *n.* [*pl.* calicoes; calicos (-kōz)], white or printed cotton cloth:—*adj.* made of, or similar to, calico.

cal-i-per (kăl′ĭ-pẽr), *n.*, often in *pl.*, a device, often resembling a compass with bent legs, used in determining inside or outside diameters, thicknesses, or the like (see *tool*, illus.):—*v.t.* and *v.i.* to measure with a caliper. Also, **cal′li-per.**

ca-liph (kā′lĭf; kăl′ĭf), *n.* among the Mohammedans, one having supreme power in religion and government. Also, **ca′lif; ka′lif; kha′lif; kha′liff.**

cal-is-then-ics (kăl″ĭs-thĕn′ĭks), *n.pl.* **1,** used as *sing.*, the art of promoting health by physical exercise; **2,** simple athletic gymnastics. Also, **cal″lis-then′ics.**—*adj.* **cal″is-then′ic.**

[1]**calk** (kôk), *v.t.* to drive oakum, or hemp rope fiber, into the seams of (a ship) to keep out water. Also, **caulk.**—*n.* **calk′er.** —*n.* **calk′ing.**

[2]**calk** (kôk), *n.* a pointed piece of metal projecting downward from the shoe of a horse, or from a man's boot, to prevent slipping:—*v.t.* to furnish with calks.

call (kôl), *v.t.* **1,** to utter in a loud voice; announce; **2,** to send for; **3,** to attract the attention of, by loud speech; **4,** to rouse from sleep; **5,** to choose for an office; as, to *call* a minister; **6,** to give a name to; **7,** to assemble; as, to *call* a meeting; **8,** to put in a certain class; as, I *call* him my friend; **9,** in business, to make a formal demand for payment of; as, to *call* a loan:—*v.i.* **1,** to cry out loudly; **2,** to make a brief visit: with *on* or *upon;* **3,** to request something from someone: with *on* or *upon;* as, the chairman *called* on him for his opinion:—*n.* **1,** a cry to gain attention; **2,** a summons; **3,** an official invitation or request; **4,** an impulse to some special work; as, a *call* to preach; **5,** a claim or right; a demand; as, the *call* of humanity; **6,** a short visit; **7,** the cry or note of an animal or bird: —*adj.* in business, subject to payment on demand; as, a *call* loan.—*n.* **call′er.**

cal-la (kăl′ȧ), *n.* a well-known cultivated plant bearing a spike of small flowers surrounded by a large, white sheath, or spathe, resembling a lily: also called *calla lily.*

cal-lig-ra-phy (kă-lĭg′rȧ-fĭ), *n.* **1,** elegant or beautiful writing or penmanship; **2,** any handwriting. Also, **ca-lig′ra-phy.**—*adj.* **cal″li-graph′ic.**

call-ing (kôl′ĭng), *n.* **1,** the act of summoning; **2,** a summons or invitation; **3,** a vocation; trade; **4,** a crying aloud.

Cal-li-o-pe (kă-lī′ō-pē), *n.* in mythology, the Muse of epic poetry and eloquence: **calliope,** a mechanical organ in which the notes are produced from a series of steam whistles sounded from a keyboard.

cal-los-i-ty (kă-lŏs′ĭ-tĭ), *n.* [*pl.* callosities (-tĭz)], **1,** hardness; lack of sensitiveness; **2,** a thick or hardened place on skin or on bark.

cal-lous (kăl′ŭs), *adj.* **1,** hardened, as the skin at a callus; **2,** unfeeling.—*adv.* **cal′lous-ly.**—*n.* **cal′lous-ness.**

cal-low (kăl′ō), *adj.* **1,** unfledged; **2,** very young and inexperienced; as, a *callow* youth.—*n.* **cal′low-ness.**

cal-lus (kăl′ŭs), *n.* [*pl.* calluses (-ĕz); calli (-ī)], **1,** the bony matter which unites the ends of fractured bones; **2,** a thick, hard place on the skin; **3,** the protective covering formed over the cut or wounded surface of a plant.

calm (käm), *n.* stillness; serenity:—*v.t.* **1,** to quiet; **2,** to pacify:—*v.i.* to become quiet: with *down:*—*adj.* **1,** still; **2,** undisturbed.—*adv.* **calm′ly.**—*n.* **calm′ness.**

Syn., adj. tranquil, placid, peaceful, serene. *Calm* describes a state free from noise, disturbance, or violent emotion; as, a *calm* night. *Tranquil* suggests a quiet that lies more in the nature of the object or person than *calm;* as, a *tranquil* scene. *Placid* suggests peace and contentment; as, a *placid* sheet of water; a *placid* temper. *Peaceful* implies something which is undisturbed and at peace; as, a *peaceful* mind; a *peaceful* country.

cal-o-mel (kăl′ō-mĕl), *n.* mercurous chloride: used as a medicine to move the bowels.

ca-lor-ic (kȧ-lŏr′ĭk), *adj.* of or pertaining to heat.—*adv.* **ca-lor′i-cal-ly.**

cal-o-rie (kăl′ō-rĭ), *n.* the amount of heat required to raise the temperature of one gram of water one degree centigrade. Also, **cal′o-ry.**

cal-o-rim-e-ter (kăl″ō-rĭm′ē-tẽr), *n.* an instrument for measuring heat units, or calories.

ca-lotte (kȧ-lŏt′), *n.* **1,** a skull cap worn by Roman Catholic clergymen; **2,** the close-fitting crown of any headdress; as, the *calotte* of a helmet; **3,** a dome, or caplike ceiling; a caplike covering for a spire.

cal-trop (kăl′trŏp), *n.* **1,** in ancient warfare, a small four-pronged instrument used to obstruct the advance of cavalry by piercing the feet of the horses; **2,** any of several plants with spiny heads, as the star thistle. Also, **cal′trap.**

cal-u-met (kăl′ū-mĕt), *n.* the tobacco pipe of the

CALUMET

North American Indians, smoked as a symbol of peace or to confirm treaties or alliances.

ca-lum-ni-ate (kȧ-lŭm′nĭ-āt), *v.t.* [*p.t.* and *p.p.* -at″ed, *p.pr.* -at″ing], to accuse falsely and with ill will:—*v.i.* to start evil reports for the purpose of injuring another's character.—*n.* **ca-lum″ni-a′tion.**—*n.* **ca-lum′ni-a″tor.**

ca-lum-ni-ous (kȧ-lŭm′nĭ-ŭs), *adj.* slanderous; defamatory; injurious.—*adv.* **ca-lum′ni-ous-ly.**

cal-um-ny (kăl′ŭm-nĭ), *n.* [*pl.* calumnies (-nĭz)], a false accusation made purposely to injure; slander.

Cal-va-ry (kăl′vȧ-rĭ), *n.* the place where Jesus was crucified: **calvary,** [*pl.* calvaries (-rĭz)], in Roman Catholic countries, a representation of the crucifixion.

calve (kȧv), *v.i.* [*p.t.* and *p.p.* calved (kȧvd), *p.pr.* calv′ing], to bring forth young: said of the cow, doe, whale, etc.

Cal-vin-ism (kăl′vĭn-ĭzm), *n.* **1,** the doctrines of John Calvin (1509–64), the Swiss reformer, who taught that God predestines man, and elects those who are to be saved; **2,** a modified form of this doctrine.—*n.* **Cal′vin-ist.**—*adj.* **Cal″vin-is′tic.**

Ca-lyp-so (kȧ-lĭp′sō), *n.* in mythology, a sea nymph, who detained Odysseus seven years on her island.

ca-lyx (kā′lĭks; kăl′ĭks), *n.* [*pl.* calyxes (kā′lĭks-ĕz); calyces (kăl′ĭ-sēz)], the circle of small leaves beneath the petals of a flower, sometimes forming one cup.

cam (kăm), *n.* a device used in certain machines for changing circular motion into straight-line or back-and-forth motion.

cam-bi-um (kăm′bĭ-ŭm), *n.* the layer of growing tissue which lies between the sapwood and the bark of trees, and produces the new wood and the new bark.

Cam-bri-an (kăm′brĭ-ăn), *adj.* **1,** pertaining to, or having reference to, one of the earliest geologic eras; **2,** pertaining to Wales or the Welsh.

cam-bric (kām′brĭk), *n.* **1,** a fine, thin, white linen fabric; **2,** a fine cotton imitation of this: also called *cambric muslin:*—*adj.* pertaining to, or made of, either one of these fabrics.

came (kām), past tense of the intransitive verb *come.*

cam-el (kăm′ĕl), *n.* a large four-footed cud-chewing animal, of which there are two kinds: the Arabian camel or dromedary, with a single hump, and the Bactrian camel, with two humps.

BACTRIAN CAMEL ($\frac{1}{80}$)

ca-mel-li-a (kȧ-mĕl′ĭ-ȧ; kȧ-mēl′yȧ), *n.* a hothouse shrub of Asia, with shining evergreen leaves, cultivated for its double red or white flowers; the Japan rose.

ca-mel-o-pard (kȧ-mĕl′ō-pärd), *n.* the giraffe.

Cam-e-lot (kăm′ē-lŏt), *n.* the place in England where King Arthur, of ancient legend, had his palace and court.

cam-e-o (kăm′ē-ō), *n.* [*pl.* cameos (-ōz)], **1,** a precious stone or shell on which raised figures are engraved: opp. of *intaglio;* **2,** carving in relief.

cam-er-a (kăm′ẽr-ȧ), *n.* [*pl.* cameras (-ȧz)], **1,** a chamber; **2,** in photography, the apparatus, usually consisting of a box fitted with a lens for admitting light through an aperture, by which images can be thrown on a plate sensitive to light.

cam-let (kăm′lĕt), *n.* **1,** an Eastern or Oriental fabric of great beauty; **2,** any imitation of it.

cam-o-mile (kăm′ō-mīl), *n.* a strongly scented plant of the composite family, formerly used in medicine. Also, **cham′o-mile.**

ca-mou-flage (kăm′o͞o-fläzh″; *Fr.* kȧ″mo͞o″flȧzh′), *n.* **1,** in war, the art of disguising military roads, guns, battleships, etc., by the use of shrubbery, painted scenery, and the like; **2,** disguise of this kind; hence, pretense:—*v.t.* and *v.i.* [*p.t.* and *p.p.* -flaged″ (-fläzhd″), *p.pr.* -flag″ing], to disguise; conceal.—*n.* **ca″mou″fleur′** (kȧ″mo͞o″flûr′).

camp (kămp), *n.* **1,** the ground occupied by an army, with tents, huts, etc.; **2,** a place where tents are put up for shelter; as, a fishing *camp;* **3,** the persons in an encampment: **camp meeting,** an outdoor religious gathering, generally lasting several days: **camp stool,** a folding stool:—*v.i.* to live temporarily, esp. in tents: often with *out.*

cam-paign (kăm-pān′), *n.* **1,** a series of military operations; **2,** the period during which an army carries on active operations in the field; **3,** a series of operations designed to produce a certain result; as, a political *campaign:*—*v.i.* to serve in such a series of operations.—*n.* **cam-paign′er.**

cam-pa-ni-le (kăm″pȧ-nē′lĭ; *It.* käm″pä-nē′lā), *n.* [*pl.* campaniles (-lĭz); campanili (-lē)], a bell tower, esp. one detached from the body of a church.

CAMPANILE

camp–fire girl a member of The Camp Fire Girls of America, an organization aiming to promote useful, healthy womanhood through supervised outdoor life.

cam-phor (kăm′fẽr), *n.* a whitish substance which wastes away on exposure to the air, obtained from various trees and plants of eastern Asia: **camphor tree,** an Asiatic tree of the laurel family, from the wood of which camphor is obtained.—*adj.* **cam-phor′ic.**

cam-phor-ate (kăm′fẽr-āt), *v.t.* [*p.t.* and *p.p.* -at″ed, *p.pr.* -at″ing], to saturate or treat with camphor; as, *camphorated* oil; *camphorated* vaseline.

cam-pus (kăm′pŭs), *n.* in America, the grounds of a school or college.

¹can (kăn), *v. aux.* followed by infinitive without *to,* [*p.t.* could (ko͝od)], **1,** to be able; **2,** to possess power physically, morally, or mentally; **3,** *Colloq.,* to be permitted.
Syn. (see may).

²can (kăn), *n.* a small metal vessel, usually cylindrical, for holding liquids or preserving solids: in Great Britain, called *tin:*—*v.t.* [*p.t.* and *p.p.* canned (kănd), *p.pr.* can′ning], **1,** to put up in metal or glass containers, as fruit, for preservation; **2,** *Slang,* to get rid of; stop.

Ca-naan (kā′năn), *n.* in the Bible: **1,** a son of Ham and grandson of Noah (Genesis 10:6); **2,** the "Promised Land" of the Israelites; Palestine.—*adj.* **Ca′naan-it″ish.**—*n.* **Ca′naan-ite.**

Ca-na-di-an (kȧ-nā′dĭ-ăn), *n.* a native or citizen of Canada:—*adj.* pertaining to Canada.

ca-nal (kȧ-năl′), *n.* **1,** a man-made navigable waterway; also, a similar channel for irrigation; **2,** a tube for the passage of fluids; as, the alimentary *canal;* **3,** in architecture, a channel or groove: **Canal Zone,** a strip of land extending five miles on either side of the Panama Canal, held under perpetual lease by the U. S.

ca-nal-ize (kȧ-năl′īz; kăn′ȧ-līz), *v.t.* [*p.t.* and *p.p.* -ized (-īzd), *p.pr.* -iz-ing], **1,** to furnish with canals; **2,** to cause to resemble a canal.

ca-nard (kȧ-närd′; *Fr.* kȧ″nȧr′), *n.* a ridiculous rumor sent abroad to deceive the people.

ca-na-ry (kȧ-nā′rĭ), *n.* [*pl.* canaries (-rĭz)], **1,** a light wine, made in the Canary Islands; **2,** a light yellow color; **3,** a small singing bird with yellow, or greenish and yellow, plumage, native to the Canary Islands: often called *canary bird:*—*adj.* light yellow in color.

can-cel (kăn′sĕl), *v.t.* **1,** to deface writing by drawing lines across it; **2,** to mark so as to render valueless, as a stamp; **3,** to annul, as a contract; **4,** to withdraw, as an order; **5,** in mathematics, to strike out, as in taking out a common factor from the numerator and denominator of a fraction.
Syn. abolish, efface, repeal. (See erase.)

can-cel-la-tion (kăn″sĕ-lā′shŭn), *n.* **1,** the act of annulling or revoking; **2,** the act of destroying the force, value, or legal authority of; **3,** in mathematics, the process of striking out figures.

Can-cer (kăn′sẽr), *n.* **1,** a constellation, the Crab; **2,** the fourth sign of the zodiac, entered by the sun at the summer solstice, when it is farthest north of the equator, about June 21 (see *zodiac,* illus.): **tropic of Cancer,** the parallel of latitude 23° 27′ north of the equator, which marks the northern boundary of the torrid zone (see *zone,* illus.).

can-cer (kăn′sẽr), *n.* **1,** a disease characterized by a dangerous tumor or growth which often causes death; **2,** any consuming evil.—*adj.* **can′cer-ous.**

can-de-la-brum (kăn″dē-lā′brŭm), *n.* [*pl.* candelabra (-brȧ); candelabrums (-brŭmz)], **1,** (also, *candelabra* [*pl.* -bras (-brȧz)]), an ornamented branched candlestick; **2,** formerly, a lamp stand.

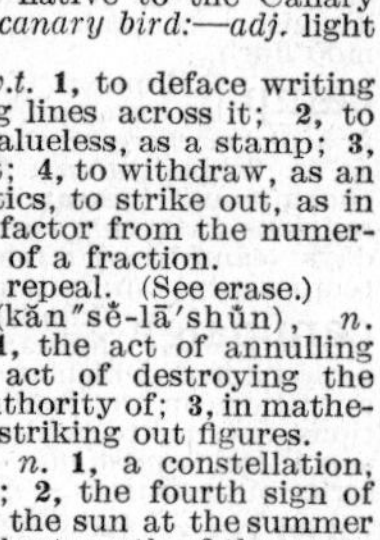
CANDELABRUM

can-did (kăn′dĭd), *adj.* **1,** honest; outspoken; sincere: applied to persons; **2,** unprejudiced; fair; as, give me your *candid* opinion.—*adv.* **can′did-ly.**—*n.* **can′did-ness.**
Syn. artless, truthful, blunt. (See open.)

can-di-da-cy (kăn′dĭ-dȧ-sĭ), *n.* [*pl.* candidacies (-sĭz)], the position or state of one who presents himself, or is presented by others, as a contestant for an office, position, or honor. Also, **can′di-da-ture.**

can-di-date (kăn′dĭ-dāt), *n.* one who offers himself, or is proposed by others, to fill some office; as, Henry Clay was twice a *candidate* for the presidency.

can-died (kăn′dĭd), *p.adj.* **1,** preserved with, or covered with, a hard coat of sugar; **2,** changed to sugar; **3,** sweet; flattering; honeyed.

can-dle (kăn′dl), *n.* **1,** a slender, rounded body of tallow, wax, or other fatty material, inclosing a wick of cotton, and used to furnish light; **2,** anything resembling a candle in form or purpose; **3,** in electricity, a unit of intensity of light:—*v.t.* [*p.t.* and *p.p.* -dled (-dld), *p.pr.* -dling], to test or examine (eggs) by holding between the eye and a small light, as of a candle.

can-dle-light (kăn′dl-līt″), *n.* **1,** the light of a candle or candles; light produced by artificial means; **2,** twilight.

Can-dle-mas (kăn′dl-mȧs), *n.* February 2, the day of the feast of the Purification of the Virgin Mary.

can-dle pow-er the lighting power of a standard candle taken as a measure to determine the illuminating power of any kind of light.

can-dle-stick (kăn′dl-stĭk″), *n.* a device for holding, or a support for, a candle or candles.

can-dor (kăn′dẽr), *n.* **1,** openness; frankness; as, *candor* of speech; **2,** fairness; as, to judge with *candor.* Also, **can′dour.**

can-dy (kăn′dĭ), *n.* [*pl.* candies (-dĭz)], **1,** a confection of sugar, combined with flavoring or coloring substances; **2,** any sweetmeat made of, or covered with, sugar or molasses:—*v.t.* [*p.t.* and *p.p.* -died (-dĭd), *p.pr.* -dy-ing], **1,** to make into, or cause to become, sugar; **2,** to preserve in sugar:—*v.i.* **1,** to become coated with sugar; **2,** to sugar.

can-dy-tuft (kăn′dĭ-tŭft″), *n.* a low-growing plant bearing clustered or tufted flowers, sometimes grown in gardens.

cane (kān), *n.* **1,** the woody stem of certain palms, grasses, and other plants, as the bamboo, sugar cane, rattan, etc.; **2,** a walking stick:—*v.t.* [*p.t.* and *p.p.* caned (kānd), *p.pr.* can′ing], **1,** to beat with a walking stick; **2,** to furnish with parts made of grasses, rattan, etc.; as, to *cane* chairs.—*adj.* **can′y.**

cane-brake (kān′brāk″), *n.* a dense growth of palms or canes.

ca-nine (kȧ-nīn′; kā′nīn), *adj.* **1,** pertaining to dogs; **2,** having the nature or qualities of a dog; doglike; **3,** designating, or pertaining to, the sharp-pointed teeth next to the incisors: **canine tooth,** one of four sharp-pointed teeth, one on each side of the upper and lower jaws of most animals:—*n.* **1,** in the human mouth, one of the canine teeth; **2,** humorously, a dog.

Ca-nis (kā′nĭs), *n.* the principal genus of the dog family, which includes dogs, wolves, and jackals: **Canis Major,** a constellation, the Great Dog, following Orion and containing Sirius, the Dog Star, brightest of all the fixed stars: **Canis Minor,** a constellation, the Lesser Dog, east of Orion and containing the star Procyon.

can-is-ter (kăn′ĭs-tẽr), *n.* **1,** a metal box or case for tea, coffee, etc.; **2,** a shell containing shot, or scraps of iron, which explodes when fired from a cannon.

can-ker (kăng′kẽr), *n.* **1,** anything which causes rot or decay, or destroys by gradual eating or wearing away; **2,** a gangrenous ulcer, particularly in the mouth; **3,** a popular name for certain small white sores in the mouth:—*v.t.* to infect with poisonous influence:—*v.i.* to become diseased; be infected with disease.—*adj.* **can′ker-ous.**

can-ker-worm (kăng′kẽr-wûrm″), *n.* **1,** a caterpillar destructive to trees or plants; **2,** something, as sorrow or evil, that destroys one's happiness.

can-na (kăn′ȧ), *n.* **1,** any of certain tropical American plants with large leaves and flowers; **2,** the flower of any of these plants.

canned (kănd), *p. adj.* preserved in a tin or glass receptacle; as, *canned* meat.

can-nel (kăn′ĕl), *n.* a soft coal that burns with a clear, bright flame: also called *cannel coal.*

can-ner-y (kăn′ẽr-ĭ), *n.* [*pl.* canneries (-ĭz)], an establishment for preserving meat, fish, etc., in cans.

can-ni-bal (kăn′ĭ-băl), *n.* **1**, a human being who eats human flesh; **2**, any animal that eats the flesh of its own kind:—*adj.* pertaining to, or like, a cannibal.—*n.* **can′ni-bal-ism.**—*adj.* **can″ni-bal-is′tic.**

can-non (kăn′ŭn), *n.* [*pl.* cannons (-ŭnz); collectively, cannon], a large gun which hurls shells, etc., by means of explosives; a piece of artillery.—*n.* **can″non-eer′.**

can-non-ade (kăn″ŭn-ād′), *n.* a continuous discharge of artillery against a town, fort, etc.:—*v.t.* [*p.t.* and *p.p.* -ad′ed, *p.pr.* -ad′ing], to attack with artillery.

can-non ball orig., the round projectile discharged by a cannon; later, any missile for cannon.

can-non bone the bone from the hock joint to the fetlock, found on hoofed animals.

can-not (kăn′nŏt), a negative form of the verb *can.*

can-ny (kăn′ĭ), *adj.* [*comp.* can′ni-er, *superl.* can′ni-est], **1**, shrewd; cautious; as, the Scotch are a *canny* race; **2**, thrifty; **3**, *Scot.:* **a**, quiet; gentle; **b**, trustworthy. Also, **can′nie.**—*adv.* **can′ni-ly.**

ca-noe (kȧ-nōō′), *n.* any light boat, as of birch bark, canvas, or thin wood, driven forward by paddles:—*v.i.* [*p.t.* and *p.p.* -noed′ (-nōōd′), *p.pr.* -noe′ing], to paddle or sail in a light boat.—*n.* **ca-noe′ist.**

¹can-on (kăn′ŭn), *n.* **1**, a generally accepted law or rule governing any phase of art, science, or conduct; a standard of criticism; **2**, in church government, an authoritative rule of discipline or doctrine; **3**, the books of the Bible received as authoritative by the Christian Church; **4**, a catalog of saints in the Roman Catholic Church; **5**, the works of an author recognized as genuine; as, the Chaucer *canon;* **6**, a very large size of type, equivalent to 48 point.

²can-on (kăn′ŭn), *n.* a clergyman, with various duties, attached to a cathedral; a member of a cathedral chapter.

ca-ñon (kăn′yŭn), *n.* in the U. S., a narrow, deep gorge or ravine with very steep sides. Also, **can′yon.**

ca-non-i-cal (kȧ-nŏn′ĭ-kăl), *adj.* **1**, pertaining to, or conforming to, laws or rules of the church; **2**, pertaining to, or included among, the books of the Bible which are accepted as authoritative; **3**, accepted as a rule: **canonicals,** *n.pl.* the dress or vestments prescribed to be worn by a clergyman when officiating at religious services.—*adv.* **ca-non′i-cal-ly.**

can-on-ize (kăn′ŭn-īz), *v.t.* [*p.t.* and *p.p.* -ized (-īzd), *p.pr.* -iz″ing], to declare a deceased person a saint and enter his name in the catalog of the saints.—*n.* **can″on-i-za′tion.**

can-o-py (kăn′ō-pĭ), *n.* [*pl.* canopies (-pĭz)], **1**, a covering fixed above a bed, or hung over a throne; **2**, any overhanging covering, as the arch of the sky:—*v.t.* [*p.t.* and *p.p.* -pied (-pĭd), *p.pr.* -py-ing], to cover with, or as with, an overhanging shelter; as, the elm that *canopies* your home.

¹cant (kănt), *n.* **1**, a whining manner of speech; esp., the whining speech used by beggars; **2**, the slang spoken by thieves, gypsies, etc.; **3**, the words and phrases peculiar to a certain trade, profession, party, sect, etc.; **4**, the insincere use of certain phrases and forms of speech, esp. in religion:—*v.i.* **1**, to use language peculiar to some class or occupation; **2**, to speak in an affected or hypocritical way; **3**, to make whining pretensions to goodness.—*n.* **¹cant′er.**

²cant (kănt), *n.* **1**, a sloping position; an inclination; **2**, a sudden, forceful thrust or toss resulting in a change of course or position:—*v.t.* **1**, to give a tilt or slant to; **2**, to throw with sudden force:—*v.i.* to lean.

can't (kȧnt; känt), *Colloq.*, the contraction of the negative form *cannot.*

can-ta-loupe (kăn′tȧ-lōōp; kăn′tȧ-lōp), *n.* a muskmelon of delicate flavor. Also, **can′ta-loup.**

can-tan-ker-ous (kăn-tăng′kẽr-ŭs), *adj. Colloq.*, ill-tempered; unreasonable.—*adv.* **can-tan′ker-ous-ly.**—*n.* **can-tan′ker-ous-ness.**

can-ta-ta (kȧn-tä′tȧ), *n.* a poem or story set to music.

can-teen (kăn-tēn′), *n.* **1**, a kind of shop in barracks or camp where provisions and supplies are sold; **2**, a vessel used by soldiers for carrying water or other liquid when on the march; **3**, a box containing mess utensils, etc., for officers on active service.

²can-ter (kăn′tẽr), *n.* an easy gallop:—*v.i.* and *v.t.* to move, or cause to move, in an easy gallop.—*n.* **can′ter-er.**

can-thar-i-des (kăn-thăr′ĭ-dēz), *n.pl.* in medicine, a preparation made from Spanish flies, dried and powdered: used for blistering.

cant hook **1**, a movable iron hook at or near the end of a wooden handle or lever: used to handle or turn over logs, etc.; **2**, the implement itself.

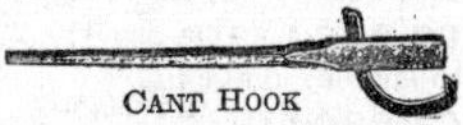

CANT HOOK

can-ti-cle (kăn′tĭ-kl), *n.* **1**, a song; **2**, a passage of the Bible arranged for chanting in church service: **Canticles, in** the Bible, the Song of Solomon.

can-ti-le-ver (kăn′tĭ-lē″vẽr; kăn′tĭ-lĕv″-ẽr), *n.* **1**, a bracket or block projecting from the wall of a house, to support a balcony, cornice, etc.; **2**, a form of bridge truss, usually supported on a pier, balanced or counterpoised and projecting toward a similar truss on the opposite side of the space bridged, with which it is connected directly or by a girder. Also, **can′ta-le″ver.**

can-to (kăn′tō), *n.* [*pl.* cantos (-tōz)], a division of a long poem, corresponding to a chapter of prose.

can-ton (kăn′tŏn; kăn-tŏn′), *n.* **1**, a district or division of a territory; **2**, one of the states of Switzerland; **3**, a rectangular division in one of the upper corners of an escutcheon or flag:—*v.t.* **1**, to assign separate quarters to; as, to *canton* troops; **2**, to divide into districts.

Can-ton flan-nel a strong cotton cloth with long, fleecy nap.

can-ton-ment (kăn′tŏn-mĕnt; kăn-tŏn′-; kăn-tōōn′-), *n.* the place assigned to troops for quarters.

can-vas (kăn′vȧs), *n.* **1**, a coarse, heavy cloth of hemp, cotton, or flax, used for tents, sails, etc., and as a surface for oil painting; **2**, an article made of this cloth, as a sail; **3**, an oil painting:—*adj.* made of this coarse cloth, as a sail.

can-vas-back (kăn′vȧs-băk″), *n.* a North American wild duck.

can-vass (kăn′vȧs), *n.* **1**, a close inspection or examination; discussion; **2**, a solicitation of votes, interest, orders, etc.:—*v.t.* **1**, to examine; discuss thoroughly; as, to *canvass* a subject; **2**, to ask for votes or opinions; **3**, to traverse (a district) for the purpose of securing votes, interest, orders, etc.; as, a book agent may *canvass* a town:—*v.i.* to seek for orders, or solicit; as, he *canvassed* for subscriptions.—*n.* **can′vass-er.**

can-yon (kăn′yŭn), *n.* a deep, narrow gorge. See **ca′ñon,** *Pfd. S.*

caout-chouc (kōō′chŏŏk; kou′chŏŏk), *n.* the gum obtained from the juice of many tropical plants: commonly called *India rubber*.

cap (kăp), *n.* **1**, a covering for the head, usually without a brim; **2**, anything resembling such a head covering, as a mushroom top, kneecap, etc.; **3**, a small copper or brass shell used in exploding gunpowder (see *shell*, illus.); **4**, the top or summit; **5**, writing paper of various large sizes:—*v.t.* [*p.t.* and *p.p.* capped (kăpt), *p.pr.* cap'ping], **1**, to cover with, or as with, a cap; **2**, to cover the top or end of; **3**, to complete; match; reach the very limit of; as, to *cap* the climax; *cap* the day.

ca-pa-bil-i-ty (kā"pȧ-bĭl'ĭ-tĭ), *n.* [*pl.* capabilities (-tĭz)], **1**, the quality of being able to do; **2**, in *pl.*, mental attainments; as, he has unusual *capabilities*.

ca-pa-ble (kā'pȧ-bl), *adj.* **1**, having power, skill, or ability; as, a *capable* servant; **2**, receptive; open to influence; as, a *capable* student.—*adv.* **ca'pa-bly.**—*n.* **ca'pa-ble-ness.**

Syn. able, competent, efficient, skilful.

ca-pa-cious (kȧ-pā'shŭs), *adj.* roomy; able to hold much; as, a *capacious* trunk; a *capacious* car.—*adv.* **ca-pa'cious-ly.**—*n.* **ca-pa'cious-ness.**

ca-pac-i-tate (kȧ-păs'ĭ-tāt), *v.t.* [*p.t.* and *p.p.* -tat"ed, *p.pr.* -tat"ing], to enable; make fit.

ca-pac-i-ty (kȧ-păs'ĭ-tĭ), *n.* [*pl.* capacities (-tĭz)], **1**, the power of receiving or containing; **2**, the power of containing a certain quantity exactly; **3**, the amount that can be contained; as, the *capacity* of the cask is four gallons; **4**, ability; esp., mental ability; as, suit the instruction to the *capacity* of the child; **5**, profession; position; as, Goldsmith once served in the *capacity* of a teacher.

Syn. (see ability).

cap-a-pie (kăp"=ȧ=pē'), *adv.* from head to foot; as, a knight fought armed *cap-a-pie*. Also, **cap"-à-pie'.**

ca-par-i-son (kȧ-păr'ĭ-sŭn), *n.* **1**, an ornamental covering for a horse; **2**, gay or rich clothing:—*v.t.* **1**, to cover with rich clothing, as a horse; **2**, to adorn with rich dress; as, to *caparison* in velvet.

[1]**cape** (kāp), *n.* a circular cloak, short or long, without sleeves.

[2]**cape** (kāp), *n.* a point of land projecting into a body of water.

Ca-pel-la (kȧ-pĕl'ȧ), *n.* the brightest star in the constellation Auriga.

[1]**ca-per** (kā'pẽr), *n.* **1**, a playful leap or spring; skip; **2**, a prank:—*v.i.* to skip or jump playfully; frolic.

[2]**ca-per** (kā'pẽr), *n.* **1**, a Mediterranean plant, the flower buds of which are pickled and used as a seasoning; **2**, in *pl.*, the buds of this plant.

cap-il-lar-i-ty (kăp"ĭ-lăr'ĭ-tĭ), *n.* **1**, the condition or state of being capillary; **2**, in physics, the action by which the surface of a liquid is raised or lowered where in contact with a solid: seen best in very small tubes when dipped in a liquid.

cap-il-la-ry (kăp'ĭ-lā-rĭ; kȧ-pĭl'ȧ-rĭ), *n.* [*pl.* capillaries (-rĭz)], **1**, a tube with a small bore; **2**, in anatomy, one of the minute blood vessels connecting the arteries with the veins:—*adj.* **1**, resembling a hair; slender; **2**, pertaining to the minute tubes or vessels of the body; **3**, pertaining to capillarity: **capillary attraction**, the power possessed by porous bodies, or by tubes of small bore, of drawing up a fluid; as, a blotter absorbs ink by *capillary attraction*: **capillary tube**, a tube of very small bore.

[1]**cap-i-tal** (kăp'ĭ-tăl), *adj.* **1**, punishable by death; as, a *capital* crime; **2**, in writing and printing, designating a letter of the kind called *upper-case*, as A, B, C, etc., larger than the common, or *lower-case*, letters, as a, b, c, etc., and often of different shape; **3**, first in importance; chief; principal; as, the *capital* points in a discussion; **4**, good; first-rate; as, a *capital* plan:—*n.* **1**, the city or town chosen as the seat of government in a country or state; **2**, a letter of the kind called *upper-case*, as A, B, C, etc.; a capital letter; **3**, the total face value of the shares of stock of a corporation, or the amount of money invested in any particular business; **4**, stock or resources of any kind, moral or physical; **5**, the actual goods purchased by invested money, esp. such goods as are used for the production of further wealth, as machinery, buildings, or railroad equipment; **6**, accumulated wealth; the amount of property belonging to an individual at any time.—*adv.* **cap'i-tal-ly.**

Syn., *adj.* leading, cardinal, important, vital.

[2]**cap-i-tal** (kăp'ĭ-tăl), *n.* in architecture, the ornamental head or top of a column, pillar, or pilaster.

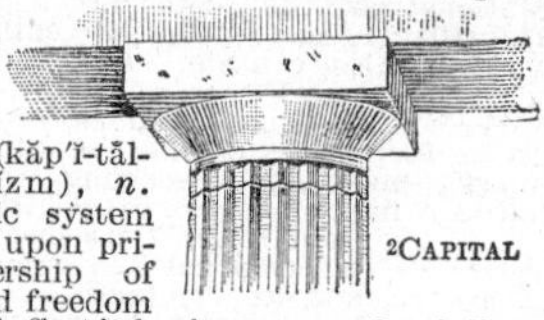

[2]CAPITAL

cap-i-tal-ism (kăp'ĭ-tăl-ĭzm), *n.* an economic system which rests upon private ownership of property and freedom of individual effort in business: opp. of *socialism*.

cap-i-tal-ist (kăp'ĭ-tăl-ĭst), *n.* **1**, a person who owns wealth in the form of factories, railroads, etc.; **2**, a person of large wealth which may be used in promoting business enterprises.—*adj.* **cap"i-tal-is'tic.**

cap-i-tal-i-za-tion (kăp"ĭ-tăl-ĭ-zā'shŭn), *n.* **1**, the act of changing or converting into money for use in business; **2**, the face value of the stocks and bonds of a business; **3**, the act of writing or printing with capital letters.

cap-i-tal-ize (kăp'ĭ-tăl-īz), *v.t.* [*p.t.* and *p.p.* -ized (-īzd), *p.pr.* -iz"-ing], **1**, to estimate the principal sum needed to bring in (a given income); **2**, to convert into available money for use in business; **3**, to make use of; turn to account; **4**, to write or print with capital letters.

cap-i-ta-tion (kăp"ĭ-tā'shŭn), *n.* **1**, the counting of heads, that is, of individuals; **2**, the levying of a tax on each individual; **3**, a poll tax; **4**, any uniform fee paid by each individual of a group.

Cap-i-tol (kăp'ĭ-tŏl), *n.* **1**, the temple of Jupiter at Rome; **2**, the building occupied by Congress at Washington; **3**, (often, *capitol*), the building occupied by a state legislature; a statehouse.

Cap-i-to-line (kăp'ĭ-tō-līn; kȧ-pĭt'ō-līn), *adj.* designating, or pertaining to, one of the seven hills of Rome, where stood the Temple of Jupiter:—*n.* the Capitoline hill, one of the seven hills of Rome.

ca-pit-u-late (kȧ-pĭt'ū-lāt), *v.i.* [*p.t.* and *p.p.* -lat"ed, *p.pr.* -lat"ing], to surrender, as to an enemy, on conditions agreed upon.—*n.* **ca-pit'u-la"tor.**

ca-pit-u-la-tion (kȧ-pĭt"ū-lā'shŭn), *n.* **1**, the act of surrendering; **2**, a summary of the heads of a subject.

ca-pon (kā'pŏn), *n.* a castrated cock which has been fattened for the table.—*v.t.* **ca'pon-ize.**

ca-price (kȧ-prēs'), *n.* **1**, the tendency to sudden, unreasoning change of purpose; **2**, a whim.

ca-pri-cious (kȧ-prĭsh'ŭs), *adj.* unsteady; fickle; as, a *capricious* temper. — *adv.* **ca-pri′cious-ly.** — *n.* **ca-pri′-cious-ness.**

Syn. changeable, moody, shifting.

Cap-ri-corn (kăp′rĭ-kôrn), *n.* **1,** a constellation, the Goat; **2,** the tenth sign of the zodiac, entered by the sun at the winter solstice, when it is farthest south of the equator, about December 21 (see *zodiac,* illus.): **tropic of Capricorn,** the parallel of latitude 23° 27′ south of the equator, which marks the southern boundary of the torrid zone (see *zone,* illus.). Also, **Cap″ri-cor′nus.**

cap-ri-fi-ca-tion (kăp″rĭ-fĭ-kā′shŭn), *n.* an artificial method of fertilizing with pollen the fruit of the cultivated fig in order to hasten its ripening and improve the fruit.

cap-ri-fig (kăp′rĭ-fĭg″), *n.* **1,** the wild fig of Asia Minor and southern Europe; **2,** the fruit of the wild fig.

cap-ri-ole (kăp′rĭ-ōl), *n.* a leap of a horse made without advancing:—*v.i.* [*p.t.* and *p.p.* -oled (-ōld), *p.pr.* -ol″ing], to execute such a leap.

cap-si-cum (kăp′sĭ-kŭm), *n.* **1,** any of several varieties of plants of the nightshade family, bearing pungent berries; **2,** the dried and powdered fruit of these plants, including cayenne and other peppers.

cap-size (kăp-sīz′), *v.i.* [*p.t.* and *p.p.* -sized′ (-sīzd′), *p.pr.* -siz′ing], to be overturned; upset: said of a boat:—*v.t.* to upset, as a boat.

cap-stan (kăp′stăn), *n.* an upright drum or cylinder revolving upon an iron pivot and worked by bars or levers: used for raising weights, as the anchor of a ship, by means of a rope.

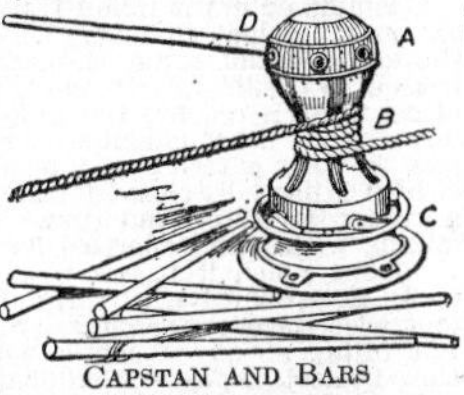

CAPSTAN AND BARS

A, capstan head; B, barrel; C, pawl rim and pawls; D, capstan bar.

cap-stone (kăp′stōn″), *n.* **1,** the top stone of a structure; **2,** one of a row of flat stones laid along the top of a wall.

cap-sule (kăp′sūl), *n.* **1,** a metallic seal or cover for a bottle; **2,** a small envelope of gelatin inclosing medicine; **3,** a seed vessel which bursts when ripe; **4,** a skinlike sac inclosing some part or organ of the body.—*adj.* **cap′su-lar.**

cap-tain (kăp′tĭn), *n.* **1,** one in authority over others acting in a group; **2,** in the army, the commander of a company; **3,** in the navy, an officer commanding a ship of war; **4,** the master of a merchant vessel; **5,** the head of a team or side in an athletic game:—*v.t.* to act as leader or captain of; lead.—*abbr.* **Capt.; Cap.**—*n.* **cap′tain-cy.**

cap-tion (kăp′shŭn), *n.* **1,** the heading of a written or printed chapter, section, page, or article; **2,** the title of an illustration; a legend.

cap-tious (kăp′shŭs), *adj.* ready to find fault or take offense; as, a *captious* customer.—*adv.* **cap′tious-ly.**—*n.* **cap′tious-ness.**

Syn. fretful, cross, peevish, petulant.

cap-ti-vate (kăp′tĭ-vāt), *v.t.* [*p.t.* and *p.p.* -vat″ed, *p.pr.* -vat″ing], to enslave or hold captive by beauty or excellence; charm; fascinate.—*n.* **cap″ti-va′tion.**

cap-tive (kăp′tĭv), *adj.* **1,** made prisoner; held in bondage; **2,** held by ties of affection, loyalty, etc.; also, fascinated; **3,** pertaining to a prisoner:—*n.* **1,** one who is taken prisoner, esp. in war; **2,** one fascinated.

cap-tiv-i-ty (kăp-tĭv′ĭ-tĭ), *n.* [*pl.* captivities (-tĭz)], **1,** the state of being taken or held prisoner, esp. in war; **2,** a condition of bondage.

cap-tor (kăp′tẽr), *n.* one who takes a person or thing prisoner.

cap-ture (kăp′tūr), *n.* **1,** the act of seizing or taking, as a prisoner or a prize; arrest; **2,** the person or the thing taken:—*v.t.* [*p.t.* and *p.p.* -tured (-tūrd), *p.pr.* -tur-ing], **1,** to take or seize by force, skill, surprise, or trick; **2,** to make a prisoner or prize of.—*n.* **cap′tur-er.**

Cap-u-chin (kăp′ū-chĭn; kăp″ū-shēn′), *n.* a monk of one of the Franciscan orders, wearing a long, pointed hood.

car (kär), *n.* **1,** a wheeled vehicle running on tracks to carry passengers, baggage, or freight; **2,** the basket suspended beneath a balloon to contain the balloonist; **3,** an automobile; **4,** the cage of an elevator; **5,** in poetry, a chariot of war or state.

***ca-ra-ba-o** (kä″rä-bä′ō), *n.* [*pl.* carabaos (-ōz)], a water buffalo, used as a draft animal in the Philippine Islands.

car-a-cole (kăr′ȧ-kōl), *n.* a half turn which a horseman makes, either to the right or left:—*v.i.* [*p.t.* and *p.p.* -coled (-kōld), *p.pr.* -col-ing], to move in such a way; wheel. Also, **car′a-col** (kăr′ȧ-kŏl).

ca-ra-cul (kä″rȧ-ko͞ol′; popularly, kăr′ȧ-kŭl), *n.* a valuable fur from the young astrakhan, or curly-haired sheep of Asia. Also, **ka″ra-kul′**, *Pfd. S.*

ca-rafe (kȧ-råf′), *n.* a glass water bottle for the table; a decanter.

car-a-mel (kăr′ȧ-mĕl), *n.* **1,** burnt sugar, used for coloring foods, or as a flavoring; **2,** a kind of sweetmeat.

car-at (kăr′ăt), *n.* **1,** a unit of weight for precious stones, and, sometimes, precious metals; one fifth of a gram; **2,** a 24th part: used to express the fineness of gold; as, gold 22 *carats* fine contains 22 parts of gold and 2 of an alloy. Also, **kar′at.**

car-a-van (kăr′ȧ-văn; kăr″ȧ-văn′), *n.* **1,** in the Orient, a company traveling together for safety, esp. across a desert; **2,** any large number of persons journeying together; **3,** a large covered wagon; a van.

car-a-van-sa-ry (kăr″ȧ-văn′sȧ-rĭ), *n.* [*pl.* caravansaries (-rĭz)], **1,** in the Orient, a kind of inn with a spacious court, where caravans rest at night; **2,** a large hotel. Also, **car″a-van′se-rai** (-sē-rī).

car-a-vel (kăr′ȧ-vĕl), *n.* a small vessel used from the 15th to the 17th century by Spanish and Portuguese sailors, with narrow, high poop and three-cornered sails. Also, **car′vel.**

COLUMBUS'S CARAVEL

car-a-way (kăr′ȧ-wā), *n.* a plant of the parsley family, whose seed is used to flavor small cakes, etc.

car-bide (kär′bīd; kär′bĭd), *n.* a compound of carbon with a metal.

car-bine (kär′bīn), *n.* a short, light rifle used chiefly by cavalry.

car-bo-hy-drate (kär″bō-hī′drāt), *n.* a compound of carbon, hydrogen, and oxygen, as sugar or starch.

car-bo-lat-ed (kär′bō-lāt″ĕd), *adj.* treated with carbolic acid; as, *carbolated* vaseline.

car-bol-ic (kär-bŏl′ĭk), *adj.* pertaining to a weak acid obtained from coal tar: **carbolic acid,** a strong poison obtained from coal tar: largely used as a germicide and disinfectant; phenol.

car-bo-lize (kär′bō-līz), *v.t.* [*p.t.* and *p.p.* -lized (-līzd), *p.pr.* -liz″ing], to treat or mix with carbolic acid.

car-bon (kär′bŏn), *n.* **1,** a nonmetallic element occurring in nature as the diamond and as graphite, and in coal, and found in combination in all animal and vegetable substances; **2,** one of two rods of hard carbon used in the terminals between which the current passes in an arc light: **carbon copy,** a copy of a written sheet made by the use of carbon paper: **carbon dioxide,** a heavy, colorless gas produced by burning carbonaceous material, by respiration, etc.: also called *carbonic-acid gas:* **carbon monoxide,** a colorless, odorless, poisonous gas present in coal gas, and produced by an incomplete burning of carbonaceous matter: **carbon paper,** tissue paper so treated with carbon that, when placed between sheets of paper, it will transfer to the lower what is written or typed on the upper.—*adj.* **car″bo-na′ceous.**

car-bon-ate (kär′bŏn-āt), *n.* a salt formed by the union of carbonic acid with a base:—*v.t.* [*p.t.* and *p.p.* -at″ed, *p.pr.* -at″ing], to charge with carbonic-acid gas, or carbon dioxide.

car-bon-ic (kär-bŏn′ĭk), *adj.* pertaining to carbon: **carbonic acid,** an acid formed by dissolving carbon dioxide gas in water: very easily broken up again into water and carbon dioxide.

car-bon-if-er-ous (kär″bŏn-ĭf′ẽr-ŭs), *adj.* containing or yielding carbon or coal.

car-bon-ize (kär′bŏn-īz), *v.t.* [*p.t.* and *p.p.* -ized (-īzd), *p.pr.* -iz″ing], **1,** to convert into carbon by fire, or an acid; **2,** to coat with carbon.—*n.* **car″bon-i-za′tion.**

car-bo-run-dum (kär″bō-rŭn′dŭm), *n.* an artificial compound of carbon and silicon; a very hard substance, used in grinding and polishing.

car-boy (kär′boi), *n.* a large glass bottle, protected by basketwork, used to contain or carry certain acids.

car-bun-cle (kär′bŭng-kl), *n.* **1,** a deep red garnet cut without facets; **2,** a local inflammation of the skin and deeper tissues.

car-bu-ret (kär′bū-rĕt), *v.t.* to combine with carbon or a hydrocarbon.

car-bu-ret-or (kär′bū-rĕt″ẽr), *n.* an apparatus used to charge air with gas from gasoline for producing light or power; as, the *carburetor* supplies the fumes of gasoline, mixed with air, to the motor of an automobile. Also, **car′bu-ret″er; car′bu-ret″tor.** (See illus. next column.)

car-cass (kär′kȧs), *n.* [*pl.* carcasses (-ĕz)], **1,** the dead body of an animal; **2,** in contempt, the corpse, or the living body, of a human being; **3,** the decaying remains of a bulky thing; **4,** the framework or skeleton of a building, ship, etc. Also, **car′case.**
Syn. (see body).

1**card** (kärd), *n.* **1,** a piece of pasteboard, printed or plain, used for various social or business purposes; as, a post *card;* a calling *card;* **2,** a small piece of pasteboard printed with certain devices or figures, used for playing games; **3,** in *pl.,* any game or games played with cards; card playing; **4,** a short business advertisement, as in a newspaper or magazine; **5,** the dial of a mariner's compass.

2**card** (kärd), *n.* an instrument for raising the nap on cloth or for combing the fibers of wool, flax, or cotton, to prepare the material for weaving or spinning:—*v.t.* to comb, as wool, flax, etc., with, or as with, such an instrument.—*n.* **card′er.**

car-da-mom (kär′dȧ-mŭm), *n.* **1,** the aromatic seed capsule of any of several Oriental plants of the ginger family; **2,** any of the plants. Also, **car′da-mon; car′da-mum.**

card-board (kärd′bōrd″), *n.* pasteboard of different qualities: used in making cards, posters, and the like.

car-di-ac (kär′dĭ-ăk), *adj.* **1,** pertaining to, or situated near, the heart; **2,** quickening the heart's action; **3,** pertaining to a certain part of the stomach:—*n.* a medicine which increases the heart's action.

car-di-gan (kär′dĭ-găn), *n.* a knitted woolen jacket or waistcoat: also called *cardigan jacket.*

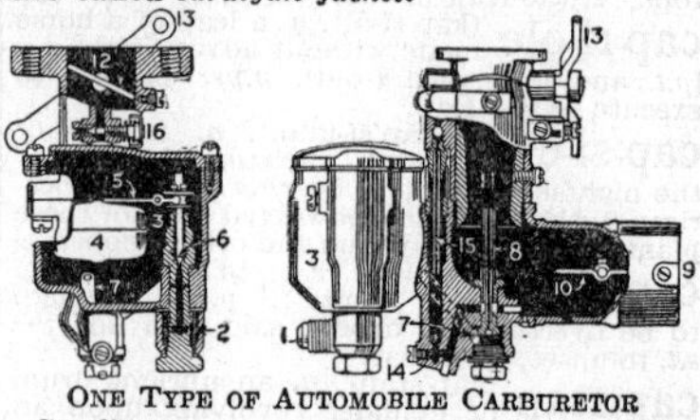

One Type of Automobile Carburetor

Gasoline enters at union 1, passing through filter screen 2 to float chamber 3. Float 4 rises with the gasoline and acting through float lever 5, connected to needle valve 6, shuts off the flow of gasoline when it reaches the proper level. Gasoline flows from float chamber through passage 7 to jets 8. Air entering at 9 passes choke valve 10 (which is partially closed for starting, to give motor a richer mixture) and draws gasoline from jets, mixing with it in vaporized form in Venturi tube 11, from which it passes to motor through butterfly throttle valve 12. Hand throttle lever and foot accelerator are connected to butterfly lever 13. For idling speed of motor with throttle nearly closed, gasoline passes from float chamber to idling well 14, thence to idling jet 15, where it is mixed with air admitted by idling adjusting screw 16 and enters main gas passage immediately above butterfly valve 12.

car-di-nal (kär′dĭ-năl), *adj.* **1,** chief; important; as, justice is one of the *cardinal* virtues; **2,** pertaining to the cardinals of the Roman Catholic Church; **3,** of the rich red color worn by these dignitaries: **cardinal bird,** an American finch having brilliant red plumage, a conspicuous crest, and a large red bill: **cardinal numbers,** the numbers *one, two, three,* etc., in distinction from the ordinal numbers, *first, second, third,* etc.: **cardinal points,** north, east, south, west: **cardinal winds,** winds which blow directly from the north, east, south, and west:—*n.* **1,** a high official in the Roman Catholic Church, appointed by the Pope, and a member of his council; **2,** a rich red color; **3,** the cardinal bird.

car-di-nal-ate (kär′dĭ-năl-āt), *n.* the rank, dignity, or office of a cardinal.—*n.* **car′di-nal-ship″.**

care (kâr), *n.* **1,** uneasiness of mind; anxiety; **2,** the cause of such uneasiness, as a duty or burden; **3,** charge or oversight; as, under a nurse's *care;* **4,** attention; watchfulness; **5,** an object of watchful attention and regard:—*v.i.* [*p.t.* and *p.p.* cared (kârd), *p.pr.* car′ing], **1,** to be anxious, concerned, or interested; **2,** to desire or wish; as, she did not *care* to go; **3,** to have a fondness: with *for.*

Syn., n. anxiety, solicitude, concern, worry. *Care* is a troubled uneasiness of mind resulting from responsibility, duty, overwork, etc.; as, worn by *care*. *Anxiety* is a state of mental distress or pain, felt toward some uncertain event; as, an illness may cause *anxiety*. *Solicitude* is a milder form of *anxiety:* the word implies a tender hope or an active effort in behalf of loved ones; as, the *solicitude* of a mother for her child. *Concern* suggests an earnest desire for the good of some person, or an active and sympathetic interest in some object or thing; as, *concern* for her safety. *Worry* names a nervous mental state that is filled with care and anxiety; as, too much work may dispose one to *worry*.—*Ant., n.* heedlessness, inattention, negligence.

ca-reen (kȧ-rēn′), *v.t.* to turn (a ship) over on one side for the purpose of closing leaks, cleansing, or repairing:—*v.i.* to incline on one side, as a ship under sail.

ca-reer (kȧ-rēr′), *n.* **1**, a swift charge; hence, speed; **2**, a general course of action; progress, esp. when remarkable; as, it is interesting to read of the *careers* of great men; **3**, an occupation or calling:—*v.i.* to move or run rapidly.

care-ful (kâr′fo͝ol), *adj.* **1**, done or made with care; **2**, attentive; concerned: usually with *of;* as, *careful* of her dress; **3**, watchful; cautious; thoughtful; **4**, *Obs.:* **a**, sorrowful; **b**, anxious:—*adv.* **care′ful-ly**.—*n.* **care′ful-ness**.

Syn. cautious, prudent, discreet, wary. *Careful* describes one who is watchful and tries in every way to act wisely; as, a *careful* driver. *Cautious* describes one who guards against possible danger or loss because of fear or timidity; as, a *cautious* swimmer. *Prudent* describes one who is wise and practical, but who also takes care of the future by careful saving and investment; as, a *prudent* business man. *Discreet* describes one who or that which is characterized by caution and judgment; as, *discreet* conduct. —*Ant.* heedless, careless, negligent.

care-less (kâr′lĕs), *adj.* **1**, neglectful; heedless; **2**, free from trouble or responsibility.—*adv.* **care′less-ly**.—*n.* **care′less-ness**.

Syn. indifferent, thoughtless, reckless.—*Ant.* attentive, accurate, thoughtful.

ca-ress (kȧ-rĕs′), *n.* any act expressing affection; an embrace:—*v.t.* to touch with affection; fondle; embrace.—*adv.* **ca-ress′ing-ly**.

car-et (kăr′ĕt; kā′rĕt), *n.* a mark [∧] used in writing, or in correcting proofs, to indicate the place where something is omitted or is to be added.

care-worn (kâr′wōrn″), *adj.* showing the marks of anxiety; harassed.

car-go (kär′gō), *n.* [*pl.* cargoes (-gōz)], the lading or freight of a ship; load.

Syn. freight. *Cargo* refers to merchandise taken on board a vessel for shipment; a ship's *cargo* is sometimes referred to as *freight*, but *freight* is also applied, esp. in the U. S., to loads shipped on land.

car-i-bou (kăr′ĭ-bo͞o; kăr″ĭ-bo͞o′), *n.* the North American reindeer.

car-i-ca-ture (kăr′ĭ-kȧ-tūr), *n.* a picture or description of a person or thing, in which the defects or peculiarities are exaggerated so as to produce a laughable effect:—*v.t.* [*p.t.* and *p.p.* -tured (-tūrd), *p.pr.* -tur″ing], to represent in a ridiculous or exaggerated style.—*n.* **car′i-ca-tur″ist**.

Syn., n. mimicry, burlesque. (See parody.)

ca-ri-es (kā′rĭ-ēz), *n.* the ulceration and decay of a bone or tooth, causing its gradual destruction.—*adj.* **ca′ri-ous**.

cark-ing (kärk′ĭng), *adj. Archaic*, causing vexation or distress; distressing; as, *carking* care.

carl (kärl), *n.* **1**, *Archaic* or *Historical*, a peasant; **2**, *Scot.*, a boor; churl.

Car-mel-ite (kär′mĕl-īt), *n.* a member of an order of begging friars founded on Mount Carmel, Syria, in 1156; a White Friar:—*adj.* pertaining to this order.

car-min-a-tive (kär-mĭn′ȧ-tĭv; kär′-mĭ-nā-tĭv), *adj.* tending to relieve the stomach and bowels of gas; relieving colic:—*n.* a remedy for colic, griping, or flatulence.

car-mine (kär′mĭn; kär′mīn), *n.* **1**, the rich crimson coloring matter obtained from the cochineal insect; **2**, this color.

car-nage (kär′nāj), *n.* great slaughter, as in battle; bloodshed.

Syn. butchery, massacre.

car-nal (kär′năl), *adj.* pertaining to the body, its passions and its appetites; sensual; as, a *carnal* appetite: opp. of *spiritual*.—*adv.* **car′nal-ly**.

[1]**car-na-tion** (kär-nā′shŭn), *n.* **1**, a light rose pink; flesh color; **2**, in *pl.*, the parts of a painting representing flesh.

[2]**car-na-tion** (kär-nā′shŭn), *n.* any of several cultivated pinks.

car-nel-ian (kär-nēl′yăn), *n.* a bright red variety of chalcedony: used for jewelry and seals. Also, **cor-nel′ian**.

car-ni-val (kär′nĭ-văl), *n.* **1**, the season of rejoicing before Lent, observed in Roman Catholic countries; **2**, any feasting or revelry.

car-ni-vore (kär′nĭ-vōr), *n.* **1**, any of an order (*Carnivora*) of animals that feed chiefly on flesh, including the cat, dog, bear, etc.; **2**, an insect-devouring plant.

car-niv-o-rous (kär-nĭv′ō-rŭs), *adj.* **1**, feeding on flesh; flesh-eating; **2**, of or pertaining to the carnivores, or flesh-eating animals.

car-ol (kăr′ŭl), *n.* a song of joy or praise; as, a Christmas *carol:*—*v.t.* and *v.i.* to sing in joy; warble; sing joyously.—*n.* **car′ol-er**; **car′ol-ler**.

Car-o-le-an (kăr-ō-lē′ăn), *adj.* pertaining to Charles I or Charles II of England: used esp. of period furniture typical of their reigns. Also, **Car′o-line** (kăr′ō-līn; kăr′ō-lĭn).

car-om (kăr′ŭm), *v.i.* to move swiftly in a slanting line, as a billiard ball:—*n.* **1**, in billiards, the striking of a ball against two others in succession; **2**, any such shot in other games; **3**, in *pl.*, a game somewhat resembling billiards, played on a square board.

ca-rot-id (kȧ-rŏt′ĭd), *n.* one of the two principal arteries, one on either side of the neck, which convey the blood to the head:—*adj.* pertaining to either or both of the two great arteries of the neck.

ca-rous-al (kȧ-rouz′ăl), *n.* a carouse; revelry; drinking match or bout.

ca-rouse (kȧ-rouz′), *n.* **1**, a feast or festival; **2**, a noisy drinking bout or revel:—*v.i.* [*p.t.* and *p.p.* -roused′ (-rouzd′), *p.pr.* -rous′ing], to drink heartily and with noisy jollity; revel.—*n.* **ca-rous′er**.

ca-rou-sel (kăr″o͞o-zĕl′), *n.* **1**, a merry-go-round; **2**, *Obs.*, a kind of military pageant. Also, **car″rou-sel′**, *Pfd. S.*

[1]**carp** (kärp), *v.i.* to find unreasonable fault; cavil: with *at*.—*n.* **carp′er**.—*p.adj.* **carp′ing**.

[2]**carp** (kärp), *n.* any of a family of long-lived fresh-water fishes, esp. the goldfish, cultivated in ponds for their vivid color or hardy growth.

car-pal (kär′păl), *adj.* pertaining to the carpus, or wrist:—*n.* a wrist bone.

car-pel (kär′pĕl), *n.* a simple one-celled seed vessel, or one of the parts of a compound pistil.

car-pen-ter (kär′pĕn-tẽr), *n.* one who works in timber, and builds or repairs the woodwork of houses, ships, etc.

car-pen-try (kär′pĕn-trĭ), *n.* the art of cutting and joining timber.

car-pet (kär′pĕt), *n.* **1**, a thick woven or felted fabric; esp., a number of breadths of this fabric used as a floor covering; **2**, a soft covering upon which one may walk; as, a *carpet* of grass: **carpet beetle**, a small beetle whose larvæ destroy carpets and other woolen fabrics:—*v.t.* to cover with, or as with, a carpet.

car-pet-bag (kär′pĕt-băg″), *n.* a traveling bag, orig. made of carpet-like material stretched over a frame.

car-pet-bag-ger (kär′pĕt-băg″ẽr), *n.* one traveling with only a carpetbag; esp., a political adventurer from the North in the Southern States after the Civil War: a term of contempt.

car-pet-ing (kär′pĕt-ĭng), *n.* **1**, cloth for carpets; **2**, carpets in general.

car-pet knight **1**, one upon whom the honor of knighthood or other distinction has been conferred for other than active service; **2**, a stay-at-home soldier; a ladies' man.

car-pus (kär′pŭs), *n.* [*pl.* carpi (-pī)], the wrist, or the wrist bones.

car-riage (kăr′ĭj), *n.* **1**, the act of conveying or transporting; **2**, cost of transporting; **3**, the business of conveying goods or passengers; **4**, a wheeled vehicle; **5**, a wheeled stand or support, as of a cannon; **6**, any part of a machine which carries another part, as in a typewriter; **7**, behavior; manner of bearing oneself; as, an erect *carriage* is necessary to correct breathing.

car-rick bend (kăr′ĭk), a certain kind of knot (see *knot*, illus.).

car-ried (kăr′ĭd), past tense and past participle of the verb *carry*.

car-ri-er (kăr′ĭ-ẽr), *n.* **1**, one who or that which transports or conveys; **2**, one whose business is to transport goods for others; **3**, a device, as in a machine, for guiding something, as slides in a magic lantern; **4**, a messenger; **5**, a basket, as of fruit; **6**, one who, while apparently well, carries disease germs: **carrier pigeon**, a variety of pigeon trained to carry letters, messages, etc.

car-ri-on (kăr′ĭ-ŭn), *n.* dead or decaying flesh:—*adj.* pertaining to, or feeding on, such flesh.

car-rot (kăr′ŭt), *n.* **1**, a plant with an orange-yellow tapering root used for food; **2**, the root itself.—*adj.* **car′rot-y.**

car-rou-sel (kăr″ōō-zĕl′), *n.* **1**, a merry-go-round; **2**, *Obs.*, a kind of military pageant. Also, **ca″rou-sel′.**

car-ry (kăr′ĭ), *v.t.* [*p.t.* and *p.p.* -ried (-ĭd), *p.pr.* -ry-ing], **1**, to support completely from one point to another; bear; **2**, to serve as the means of conveying; as, the atmosphere *carries* sound waves; **3**, to lead; conduct; direct; as, to *carry* an undertaking to success; **4**, to put forward; as, to *carry* a case into court; transfer; as, to *carry* an amount from one page of a ledger to the next; **5**, to bring to a desired end; win a victory in; as, to *carry* an election; **6**, to secure the passage of, as a bill in Congress; **7**, to direct or influence mentally; as, to *carry* an audience; **8**, to hold (oneself); behave; **9**, to support or hold up, as columns upholding a roof; **10**, to keep for sale or use, as a stock of goods; **11**, to bear the cost of for another; as, to *carry* an account: **carry arms**, to hold the rifle vertical in the right hand with the right arm hanging at full length: **carry away**, to transport with joy, admiration, passion, etc.: **carry on**, to conduct or manage, as a business: **carry out**, to obey or execute, as the orders or wishes of another:—*v.i.* **1**, to perform the act of bearing or conveying; **2**, to possess or exert propelling force, as a gun; **3**, to have power to reach a distance, as a voice: **carry on**, **1**, to frolic gaily and thoughtlessly; **2**, in the British army during the World War, to proceed with whatever had been ordered; hence, popularly, to endure; keep on in spite of hardships:—*n.* [*pl.* carries (-ĭz)], **1**, the distance over which a gun will hurl a projectile; **2**, in the northern U. S. and Canada, land between two navigable streams or lakes over which a boat must be carried: also called *portage*.

Syn., *v.* convey, transport. (See bring.)

car-ry-all (kăr′ĭ-ôl″), *n.* a light, covered carriage for family use.

cart (kärt), *n.* **1**, a two-wheeled vehicle for carrying heavy goods; **2**, a light delivery wagon used by tradesmen, etc.:—*v.t.* to carry or convey in a cart.—*n.* **cart′er.**

cart-age (kär′tāj), *n.* the act of, or charge made for, transporting something by a cart or truck.

***carte blanche** (kårt blănsh), [Fr.], **1**, a blank paper; **2**, a signed sheet of paper given to another to be filled up as he pleases; **3**, hence, absolute freedom of action; unlimited authority.

car-tel (kär′tĕl; kär-tĕl′), *n.* **1**, a written agreement between hostile states regarding the exchange of prisoners; **2**, a written challenge to single combat; **3**, *Com.*, in Europe, a number of industrial establishments which combine by agreement to regulate the output of each, fix prices, etc.

Car-tha-gin-i-an (kär″thȧ-jĭn′ĭ-ăn), *adj.* of or pertaining to the city of Carthage:—*n.* a native of ancient Carthage.

car-ti-lage (kär′tĭ-lāj), *n.* **1**, a tough solid, elastic, animal tissue or gristle; **2**, a part consisting of this material.

car-ti-lag-i-nous (kär″tĭ-lăj′ĭ-nŭs), *adj.* **1**, pertaining to, or in the form of, gristle, or cartilage; **2**, having a skeleton of gristle, as sharks.

car-tog-ra-phy (kär-tŏg′rȧ-fĭ), *n.* the art of drawing maps or charts.—*n.* **car-tog′ra-pher.**

car-ton (kär′tŏn), *n.* **1**, a pasteboard box; **2**, pasteboard for making boxes.

car-toon (kär-tōōn′), *n.* **1**, a picture, often amusing, dealing with a subject by caricature or symbols; **2**, a full-sized sketch of a design for a decoration or painting:—*v.t.* to caricature.—*n.* **car-toon′ist.**

car-tridge (kär′trĭj), *n.* **1**, a case of cardboard, metal, or other material, containing the powder, or powder and ball, for a firearm; **2**, a roll of protected films, suggesting a cartridge, for a camera.

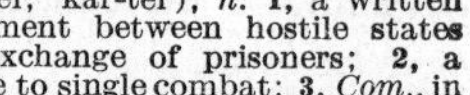

CARTRIDGE, 30 CALIBER

carve (kärv), *v.t.* [*p.t.* and *p.p.* carved (kärvd), *p.pr.* carv′ing], **1**, to form, as a design, by cutting; **2**, to cut or grave, as stone, wood, or metal; **3**, to decorate by cutting; **4**, to cut into slices; as, to *carve* meat; **5**, to mark with lines or furrows; as, her face was *carved* with wrinkles:—*v.i.* **1**, to make graven work or figures; **2**, to cut up meat.—*n.* **carv′er.**

car-vel (kär′vĕl), *n.* formerly, a small Spanish vessel. See **car′a-vel**, *Pfd. S.*

carv-ing (kärv′ĭng), *n.* **1**, the act or art of one who sculptures or designs by cutting; **2**, the work so accomplished;

3, ornamental sculpture, as of wood, stone, ivory, or the like.

car-y-at-id (kăr″ĭ-ăt′ĭd), *n.* [*pl.* caryatids (-ĭdz); caryatides (-ĭ-dēz)], a supporting column in the form of a woman.

CARYATID

cas-cade (kăs-kād′), *n.* **1,** a small waterfall; **2,** anything like a waterfall, as a fall of lace.

¹case (kās), *n.* **1,** literally, that which befalls or happens; **2,** a peculiar state, condition, or set of circumstances; **3,** a special instance or example of a general condition; as, it was a *case* of insubordination; **4,** a person exhibiting any given disease; a patient; **5,** an action or suit at law or in equity; **6,** a form in the declension of a noun, pronoun, or adjective, showing its relation to other words; also, the relation.

Syn. event, situation, plight, contingency.

²case (kās), *n.* **1,** a covering or container; **2,** the contents of a covering or container, or the amount of this content; **3,** a glass box used for purposes of exhibition; as, a jeweler's show *case;* **4,** a frame or casing, as of a window; **5,** in printing, a shallow tray for type, divided into the *upper case,* which contains the capitals, and the *lower case,* which contains small letters, figures, etc.:—*v.t.* [*p.t.* and *p.p.* cased (kāst), *p.pr.* cas′ing], to protect with, or inclose in, a cover or container.

case-hard-en (kās′här″dn), *v.t.* **1,** to harden the surface of (metal); **2,** to make insensible or callous.

ca-se-in (kā′sē-ĭn), *n.* a proteid found in milk, forming the main part of cheese and of curd.

case knife **1,** a knife provided with a sheath; **2,** a table knife.

case-mate (kās′māt), *n.* **1,** a shell-proof vault in a thick wall, having openings through which cannon may be

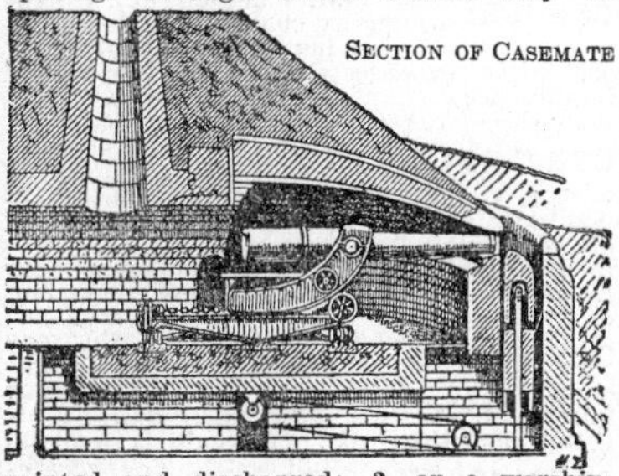

SECTION OF CASEMATE

pointed and discharged; **2,** on a warship, an armored inclosure with openings for guns.

case-ment (kās′mĕnt), *n.* a window sash made to open on hinges; loosely, any window.

ca-se-ous (kā′sē-ŭs), *adj.* pertaining to, or resembling, cheese.

¹cash (kăsh), *n.* **1,** money; esp., ready money; **2,** money paid for an article at the time of purchase; **3,** in banking, strictly, coin, but also paper money, bank notes, and commercial paper easily exchanged for coin:—*v.t.* to exchange for money in coin or bills; as, to *cash* a check.

²cash (kăsh), *n.* [*pl.* cash], any of several Chinese and Indian coins of slight value; esp., a Chinese coin with a hole.

cash-book (kăsh′bŏŏk″), *n.* a book in which an account is kept of money received or paid out.

ca-shew (kȧ-shōō′), *n.* **1,** a tropical American tree; **2,** its edible nut.

¹cash-ier (kăsh-ēr′), *n.* an official whose duty it is to pay bills and debts and to receive remittances: **cashier's check,** a check drawn by a bank upon its own funds, signed by the cashier.

²cash-ier (kăsh-ēr′), *v.t.* **1,** to dismiss in disgrace from a position of trust or from military service; **2,** to reject; cast away; discard.

cash-mere (kăsh′mēr; kăsh″mēr′), *n.* **1,** a soft woolen fabric for shawls, etc.; **2,** a shawl made of this fabric; **3,** a soft woolen imitation of the real fabric.

cas-ing (kās′ĭng), *n.* **1,** the act of covering with, or placing in, a case; **2,** a covering; **3,** a framework, as of a window.

ca-si-no (kȧ-sē′nō), *n.* [*pl.* casinos (-nōz); casini (-nē)], **1,** in Italy, a small country house; **2,** a public room or building for dancing, gaming, etc.; **3,** (usually, *cassino*), a game of cards.

cask (kȧsk), *n.* **1,** a barrel-shaped vessel for holding liquids; **2,** the quantity contained in such a vessel.

cas-ket (kȧs′kĕt), *n.* **1,** a small chest or box, as for jewels; **2,** a coffin, esp. a costly one.

casque (kȧsk), *n.* a helmet: a poetic term.—*adj.* **casqued** (kȧskt).

Cas-san-dra (kă-săn′drȧ), *n.* **1,** in mythology, a daughter of Priam and Hecuba of Troy, a prophetess condemned never to be believed; **2,** hence, one who constantly predicts misfortune.

cas-sa-va (kă-sä′vȧ), *n.* a plant of tropical America and Africa, cultivated for its roots, which yield a starch; also, the starch, from which tapioca is made.

cas-se-role (kăs′ē-rōl; kăs″ē-rōl′), *n.* **1,** a covered baking dish, often with a metal stand or container; **2,** a saucepan; **3,** a stew made in such a pan.

cas-sia (kăsh′ȧ; kăsh′ĭ-ȧ), *n.* **1,** any of several kinds of tropical plants from which the drug senna is obtained; **2,** the bark of certain tropical plants, used as cinnamon; also, any plant producing it.

cas-si-mere (kăs′ĭ-mēr), *n.* a thin woolen cloth used for garments. Also, **cas′i-mere; ker′sey-mere.**

cas-si-no (kă-sē′nō), *n.* a certain game at cards, played by two or four players. Also, **ca-si′no.**

Cas-si-o-pe-ia (kăs″ĭ-ō-pē′yȧ), *n.* **1,** a constellation near the north polar star, the Lady in the Chair; **2,** in mythology, the wife of King Cepheus of Ethiopia, and mother of Andromeda.

cas-sock (kăs′ŭk), *n.* a long, close-fitting garment worn by clergymen, choristers, etc., under the surplice.

cas-so-wa-ry (kăs′ō-wâ-rĭ), *n.* [*pl.* cassowaries (-rĭz)], a large bird resembling the ostrich, inhabiting Australia and the Papuan Islands.

(1/80)

CASSOWARY

cast (kȧst), *v.t.* [*p.t.* and *p.p.* cast, *p.pr.* cast′ing], **1,** to throw; hurl, often violently; **2,** to send in a certain direction, as a glance or shadow; **3,** to throw down, as in wrestling; **4,** to shed; as, a snake *casts* its skin; **5,** to deposit, often forcibly; as, *cast* him into prison; **6,** to form into a certain shape; as, to *cast* clay into a statue, or metal in a mold; **7,** to calculate, as a bill; **8,** to deposit (a ballot); **9,** to turn or twist; of a ship, to veer; **10**, in the theater: **a**, to assign, as parts in a play to certain actors; **b**, to assign certain parts to:—*v.i.* **1**, to throw the line in angling; **2**, to receive shape in a mold; **3**, to consider; forecast; surmise; **4**, to calculate; **5**, to throw dice; **6**, to turn or twist:—*n.* **1**, the act or manner of throwing; **2**, a thing or quantity thrown; also, the distance so covered; **3**, a throw of dice; hence, fortune; **4**, a turn or twist; esp., a turn of the eye; hence, a slight squint or error in focus; **5**, manner; tendency; as, a humorous *cast* of mind; **6**, shape; expression; as, a gloomy *cast* of countenance; **7**, a faint shade of color; a tinge. **8**, something formed by molding; as, a plaster *cast;* **9**, a throw of a line, as in angling; **10**, a calculation; **11**, the members of a company of actors as assigned to certain parts:—*adj.* **1**, cast-off; **2**, shaped in a mold while fluid.

cas-ta-nets (kȧs′tȧ-nĕts; kȧs″tȧ-nĕts′), *n.pl.* small spoon-shaped shells of hard wood or ivory fastened loosely at the top, shaken with the fingers to beat time to dances and music, esp. Spanish dances.

CASTANETS

cast-a-way (kȧst′ȧ-wā″), *n.* **1**, a person or vessel wrecked on a barren coast; as, Robinson Crusoe was a *castaway;* **2**, a social or moral outcast:—*adj.* **1**, shipwrecked; **2**, thrown aside; rejected; set adrift.

caste (kȧst), *n.* **1**, one of the restricted hereditary divisions of society into which Hindus are separated by Brahman religious law; also, the custom of this division; **2**, any similar division of society, as by wealth, occupation, etc.; **3**, social position.

Syn. class, clan, club, clique. Each of these words names a group of related persons or objects. *Class* is the general term for any group whose members possess common interests and characteristics; as, the working *class:* a social *class;* a *class* in school. *Caste* suggests being born into a particular group; it involves hereditary and sacred distinctions, and its membership is exclusive; as, the Brahman *caste* in India. *Clan* names a group in which the members are bound together by direct descent from an ancestor; as, a Scottish *clan. Club* names a group in which the members have a definite organization and purpose; as, a baseball *club;* a study *club. Clique* names a small, exclusive group, usually within a larger one, and generally has an unfavorable meaning; as, a *clique* in a college; a snobbish *clique.*

cas-tel-lat-ed (kăs′tĕ-lāt″ĕd), *adj.* furnished with turrets and battlements; like a castle.

cast-er (kȧs′tẽr), *n.* **1**, one who or that which throws, molds, calculates, etc.; **2**, (also, *castor*), a cruet or small vessel for holding salt, pepper, vinegar, etc., at table; **3**, (also, *castor*), a small roller on a swivel, fastened under a piece of furniture to help in moving it.—*adj.* **cast′er-less.**

cas-ti-gate (kăs′tĭ-gāt), *v.t.* [*p.t.* and *p.p.* -gat″ed, *p.pr.* -gat″ing], **1**, to correct; chastise; punish; **2**, to subject to severe criticism, as a book.—*n.* **cas″ti-ga′tion.** —*n.* **cas′ti-ga″tor.**

Cas-tile soap (kăs′tēl: kăs-tēl′), a superior kind of soap, orig. made from pure olive oil at Castile, Spain.

Cas-til-ian (kăs-tĭl′yăn), *adj.* of or pertaining to Castile:—*n.* **1**, a native of Castile; **2**, the standard literary form of the Spanish language.

cast-ing (kȧst′ĭng), *n.* **1**, the act or process of forming from melted metal any article according to a given design; **2**, a metal object which has been so shaped; **3**, the process of taking impressions of statues, medals, etc., in some plastic material.

cast-ing vote the deciding vote of a chairman when the votes on opposing sides a e equal.

cast i-ron iron melted and run into molds: **cast-iron**, *adj.* **1**, made of melted or cast iron; **2**, very hard.

cas-tle (kȧs′l), *n.* **1**, a building or group of buildings fortified for defense against an enemy; a fortress; **2**, a strong and imposing mansion of a noble and wealthy person; **3**, one of the pieces at chess: also called *rook:*—*v.t.* [*p.t.* and *p.p.* -tled (-ld), *p.pr.* -tling], to inclose in, or as in, a fortified place or stronghold.

[1]**cas-tor** (kȧs′tẽr), *n.* **1**, a cruet for vinegar, oil, etc.; **2**, a small roller on a swivel, fastened under a piece of furniture to help in moving it. See **cast′er**, *Pfd. S.*

[2]**cas-tor** (kȧs′tẽr), *n.* **1**, a hat, esp. of beaver fur; **2**, an odorous, oily substance obtained from the beaver: used in perfumery; **3**, a heavy, all-wool fabric for overcoats; **4**, *Obs.*, the beaver.

Cas-tor (kȧs′tẽr), *n.* **1**, in mythology, one of the heroes of the Argonautic Expedition, at whose death his twin brother Pollux also asked for death, the two being placed in the sky as the constellation Gemini; **2**, one of the two brightest stars in the zodiacal constellation Gemini, the Twins.

cas-tor bean a plant, orig. from Asia, but now growing in all tropical regions, from which castor oil is made; also, its beanlike seed.

cas-tor oil an oil from the castor bean, used as a medicine.

cas-trate (kăs′trāt), *v.t.* [*p.t.* and *p.p.* -trat-ed, *p.pr.* -trat-ing], to remove the semen-producing glands from (the male).—*n.* **cas-tra′tion.**

cas-u-al (kăzh′ū-ăl; kăz′ū-ăl), *adj.* **1**, happening by chance; accidental, as a meeting; **2**, coming without regularity; as, *casual* expenses; **3**, having an air of indifference; as, a *casual* answer; a *casual* manner.—*adv.* **cas′u-al-ly.**

cas-u-al-ty (kăzh′ū-ăl-tĭ), *n.* [*pl.* casualties (-tĭz)], **1**, an unforeseen event; **2**, an accident, esp. if resulting in bodily injury or death; as, the railroads are responsible for many *casualties;* **3**, in *pl.*, in the army and navy, losses in general, caused by death, wounds, illness, desertion, or discharge.

cas-u-ist (kăzh′ū-ĭst; kăz′ū-ĭst), *n.* one who studies questions of right or wrong in conduct; esp., one who reasons falsely about such questions.—*adj.* **cas″u-is′tic; cas″u-is′ti-cal.**—*adv.* **cas″u-is′ti-cal-ly.**

cas-u-ist-ry (kăzh′ū-ĭs-trĭ; kăz′ū-ĭs-trĭ), *n.* [*pl.* casuistries (-trĭz)], **1**, the science dealing with questions of right or wrong in conduct; **2**, false reasoning as to morals; **3**, hairsplitting distinctions in matters of conduct.

cat (kăt), *n.* **1**, any of a family of flesh-eating animals, including the lion, tiger, etc.; esp., the familiar household pet; **2**, loosely, any catlike animal.

cat-a- (kăt′ȧ-), *prefix*, **1**, down; as, *cata*ract; **2**, under; as, *cata*comb; **3**, against; as, *cata*pult. Also, **kat′a-.**

cat-a-clysm (kăt′ȧ-klĭzm), *n.* **1**, a deluge; flood; **2**, a violent or sudden change of the earth's surface, as from an earthquake; **3**, hence, an upheaval, social or political, such as a great war.

cat-a-comb (kăt′ȧ-kōm), *n.*, usually in *pl.*, an underground burial place with niches hollowed out for the dead; as, the *catacombs* of Rome.

cat-a-falque (kăt′ȧ-fălk), *n.* a temporary, usually draped, structure sometimes used to support the coffin during an imposing funeral.

cat-a-lep-sy (kăt′ȧ-lĕp″sĭ), *n.* a sudden suspension of motion and feeling, with stiffening of the muscles. Also, **cat″a-lep′sis.**—*adj.* **cat″a-lep′tic.**

cat-a-log (kăt′ȧ-lŏg), *n.* an arranged list:—*v.t.* to enter in, or make, a list of. Also, **cat′a-logue.**—*n.* **cat′a-log″er.**

ca-tal-pa (kȧ-tăl′pȧ), *n.* a rapidly growing tree having large leaves, showy flower clusters, and winged seeds in long pods.

cat-a-lyst (kăt′ȧ-lĭst), *n.* in chemistry, a substance that starts or assists chemical action between two or more other substances without itself combining with either of them or undergoing any permanent change: also called *catalyzer* or *catalytic agent.*

cat-a-ma-ran (kăt″ȧ-mȧ-răn′), *n.* **1,** a kind of float or raft made of logs or pieces of wood lashed together and propelled by paddles or sails; **2,** any vessel or craft with twin hulls.

cat-a-mount (kăt′ȧ-mount), *n.* **1,** the European wild cat; **2,** a large, tawny, wild cat of North America: also called *puma* (which see for illus.); *cougar; mountain lion;* **3,** in America, the lynx.

cat-a-pult (kăt′ȧ-pŭlt), *n.* **1,** an ancient military engine for hurling darts and stones; **2,** a forked stick with an elastic band by which stones, dried peas, etc., are thrown:—*v.t.* and *v.i.* to throw or be thrown from, or as from, such an engine.

CATAPULT

cat-a-ract (kăt′ȧ-răkt), *n.* **1,** a large waterfall; **2,** a furious rush or downpour of water; **3,** a disease of the eye in which the vision becomes impaired or is lost.

ca-tarrh (kȧ-tär′), *n.* an inflammation of any mucous membrane, esp. of the air passages in the head and throat; cold in the head.—*adj.* **ca-tarrh′al.**

ca-tas-tro-phe (kȧ-tăs′trō-fē), *n.* **1,** a great calamity or disaster; **2,** the outcome of a dramatic plot.—*adj.* **cat″a-stroph′ic.**

Syn. misfortune, mischance, mishap.

Ca-taw-ba (kȧ-tô′bȧ), *n.* **1,** a light red variety of American grape; **2,** a light wine made from this grape.

cat-bird (kăt′bûrd″), *n.* a common American song bird: so named from one of its notes.

cat-boat (kăt′bōt″), *n.* a small boat with one sail on a mast near the bow (see *ship,* illus.).

cat-call (kăt′kôl″), *n.* **1,** a squeaking sound made in public halls to express disapproval; **2,** an instrument used to make such a sound:—*v.t.* and *v.i.* to deride or to express disapproval by such calls.

catch (kăch), *v.t.* [*p.t.* and *p.p.* caught (kôt), *p.pr.* catch′ing], **1,** to overtake; come in time to reach, as a train; **2,** to seize; lay hold of; **3,** to make captive; **4,** to gain the attention of; charm; as, beauty *catches* the eye; **5,** to perceive by the senses, as a sound or odor; **6,** to grasp mentally, as a meaning; **7,** to be affected by, as a result of contagion or exposure; as, to *catch* measles; **8,** to come upon, or detect; **9,** to secure with a fastening:—*v.i.* **1,** to grasp; take hold; **2,** to snatch: with *at;* **3,** to become entangled; as, a dress may *catch* on a brier; **4,** to spread by contagion, as disease; **5,** to take fire; as, dry tinder *catches* easily; **6,** in baseball, to act as catcher: **catch on,** *Colloq.*, to understand; get a meaning:—*n.* **1,** the act of seizing or grasping; **2,** anything that takes hold and serves to fasten something, as a hook, door latch, etc.; **3,** a choking sensation in the throat; **4,** that which is taken or held; as, a *catch* of fish; **5,** in baseball and similar games, the seizing of the ball while it is in the air; **6,** in music, a round, set to humorous words.—*n.* **catch′er.**

catch-all (kăch′ôl″), *n.* a receptacle for holding many things.

catch-ing (kăch′ĭng), *p.adj.* **1,** contagious; infectious; **2,** captivating; fascinating; as, *catching* ways.

catch-pen-ny (kăch′pĕn-ĭ), *n.* [*pl.* catchpennies (-ĭz)], an article of little value made attractive in order to sell quickly:—*adj.* cheap; made to sell to the unwary or ignorant.

catch-up (kăch′ŭp), *n.* a sauce made by boiling and spicing fruit, mushrooms, tomatoes, or walnuts: used for meat. Also, **cat′sup; ketch′up.**

catch-word (kăch′wûrd″), *n.* **1,** a word or phrase that takes the popular fancy; **2,** in the theater, a cue.

catch-y (kăch′ĭ), *adj.* [*comp.* catch′i-er, *superl.* catch′i-est], **1,** attractive; **2,** quick to win popular approval; as, a *catchy* tune; **3,** captivating; **4,** fitful; uncertain; as, *catchy* weather.

cat-e-chet-i-cal (kăt″ē-kĕt′ĭ-kăl), *adj.* **1,** consisting of questions and answers; as, the *catechetical* method of teaching; **2,** pertaining to instruction in the principles and doctrines of Christianity. Also, **cat″e-chet′ic.**

cat-e-chism (kăt′ē-kĭzm), *n.* **1,** a small book of instruction in the form of questions and answers, esp. in the principles of the Christian religion; **2,** a method of teaching by questions and answers; **3,** a set of questions to be answered by a candidate for a position.

cat-e-chize (kăt′ē-kīz), *v.t.* [*p.t.* and *p.p.* -chized (-kīzd), *p.pr.* -chiz″-ing], **1,** to instruct by means of questions and answers, esp. in the Christian religion; **2,** to ask questions of; question, esp. inquisitively. Also, **cat′e-chise.**

cat-e-chu (kăt′ē-chōō), *n.* any of various substances containing tannin, used in tanning, dyeing, etc.

cat-e-gor-i-cal (kăt″ē-gŏr′ĭ-kăl), *adj.* **1,** pertaining to, or in the form of, a general classification of things; **2,** absolute; unconditional; **3,** precise; clear; positive; explicit; as, a *categorical* answer.—*adv.* **cat″e-gor′i-cal-ly.**

cat-e-go-ry (kăt′ē-gō-rĭ), *n.* [*pl.* categories (-rĭz)], **1,** in logic, one of the classes into which all objects of thought can be divided, such as time, place, quantity, quality, etc.; **2,** any similar wide division or class of persons or objects.

cat-e-na-ry (kăt′ē-nā-rĭ; kȧ-tē′nȧ-rĭ), *n.* [*pl.* catenaries (-rĭz)], **1,** in mathematics, a certain curve formed by a cord suspended by its ends; **2,** in an airship, such a cord used to distribute stress evenly through a fabric:—*adj.* indicating the curve of such a cord.

[1]**ca-ter** (kā′tẽr), *v.i.* **1,** to supply food or amusement; **2,** to supply what is desired or needed: with *to* or *for.*—*n.* **ca′ter-er.**

[2]**ca-ter** (kā′tẽr; kăt′ẽr), *n. Archaic,* **1,** (also, *quatre*), a die, domino, or card bearing a marking of four spots; **2,** in *pl.*, (also,

quaters; quatres), in change ringing, the changes rung on a set, or ring, of nine bells: —*adv. Dial.*, diagonally; obliquely.

cat-er-pil-lar (kăt'ẽr-pĭl″ẽr), *n.* **1**, the wormlike stage in the life of a butterfly or moth, or the similar larva of other insects; **2**, a powerful traction engine operating on an endless belt which turns like a moving track: used for slow, heavy hauling.

cat-er-waul (kăt'ẽr-wôl), *v.i.* **1**, to cry, as cats at night; **2**, hence, to utter harsh sounds.

cat-fish (kăt'fĭsh″), *n.* any of several fishes of a large family, including the common bullhead.

cat-gut (kăt'gŭt″), *n.* a dried and twisted cord made from the intestines of animals, usually sheep, and used as strings for musical instruments, tennis rackets, etc.

ca-thar-tic (kȧ-thär'tĭk), *adj.* cleansing the bowels; purgative:—*n.* a medicine to cause movement of the bowels.

Ca-thay (kă-thā'), *n.* China: now only poetically.

ca-the-dra (kȧ-thē'drȧ; kăth'ē-drȧ), *n.* **1**, the throne of a bishop; **2**, the seat of anyone in authority, as a professor: **ex cathedra** (kăth'ē-drȧ), from the seat or throne; hence, with authority.

ca-the-dral (kȧ-thē'drăl), *n.* the chief church of a diocese or church district under the special charge of the bishop: —*adj.* pertaining to such a church or the diocese of which it is the center.

cath-ode (kăth'ōd), *n.* the terminal by which an electric current leaves the substance through which it passes, known as the negative pole: opp. of *anode:* **cathode rays**, a stream of electrons produced when an electrical discharge is passed through a gas at low pressure.—*adj.* **ca-thod'ic.**

cath-o-lic (kăth'ō-lĭk), *adj.* **1**, universal; general; including all; as, he has a *catholic* taste for literature; **2**, liberal; large-hearted; **3**, fitted to include all mankind: **Catholic**, *adj.* **1**, designating the universal Christian church: so used in the Apostles' Creed; **2**, designating the Church of Rome:—*n.* a member of the Catholic Church, esp. of the Roman Catholic Church.

ca-thol-i-cism (kȧ-thŏl'ĭ-sĭzm), *n.* broadmindedness; tolerance: **Catholicism**, **1**, the teaching or practice of the universal Christian church; **2**, adherence to, or belief in, such a church; **3**, esp., adherence to the doctrine, teaching, and practice of the Roman Catholic Church.

cath-o-lic-i-ty (kăth″ō-lĭs'ĭ-tĭ), *n.* **1**, the quality of being universal; **2**, liberality; tolerance; **3**, the quality of being in harmony with the teachings and practices of a Catholic church: **Catholicity**, the teaching and practice of the Roman Catholic Church.

cat-i-on (kăt'ĭ-ŏn), *n.* the product of electrolytic decomposition formed at the negative electrode, during the passage of a current; a positive ion: opp. of *anion.*

cat-kin (kăt'kĭn), *n.* one of the hanging blossoms of the willow, birch, etc. (see *inflorescence*, illus.).

cat-nip (kăt'nĭp″), *n.* a common plant of the mint family.

cat-o'-nine-tails (kăt″-ō-nīn'-tālz″), *n.* **1**, a whip with nine lashes of knotted cord, formerly used for flogging offenders; **2**, the cat-tail.

cat's-paw (kăts'-pô″), *n.* **1**, a dupe; a person who is deceived into doing something to advance the interests of another; **2**, a kind of knot (see *knot*, illus.).

cat-sup (kăt'sŭp), *n.* a spicy sauce, as for meat. See **catch'up**, *Pfd. S.*

cat-tail (kăt'-tāl″), *n.* a tall marsh plant with long, narrow leaves and brownish, furry spikes of flowers.

cat-tle (kăt'l), *n.* **1**, live stock; esp., oxen, bulls, and cows, kept for profit; **2**, people: used contemptuously: **cattle tick**, a tick infesting cattle, esp. in the warmer parts of America (see illus. page 171).

cat whisk-er in radio, in certain forms of crystal detector, a piece of fine wire used to make light contact with the crystal (see *detector*, illus.).

Cau-ca-sian (kô-kā'shăn; kô-kăsh'ăn), *adj.* **1**, pertaining to the Caucasus, or its inhabitants; **2**, designating, or pertaining to, a division of mankind including the chief races of Europe, northern Africa, and southwestern Asia:—*n.* **1**, a member of the Caucasian race; **2**, a native of the Caucasus. —*adj.* **Cau-cas'ic** (kô-kăs'ĭk).

cau-cus (kô'kŭs), *n.* a meeting of the leaders or members, as of a political party, to decide upon a policy to be submitted to a convention or larger meeting.

cau-dal (kô'dăl), *adj.* **1**, pertaining to a tail; as, the *caudal* fin of a fish; **2**, having a tail-like attachment.

cau-dle (kô'dl), *n.* a gruel-like drink for invalids, of wine or ale, eggs, sugar, spices, and bread crumbs.

caught (kôt), past tense and past participle of the verb *catch.*

caul (kôl), *n.* **1**, a membrane, such as the great omentum; **2**, the enveloping membrane sometimes covering the head of a child at birth; **3**, a net, esp. one for the hair.

caul-dron (kôl'drŭn), *n.* a large kettle or boiler. Also, **cal'dron**, *Pfd. S.*

cau-li-flow-er (kô'lĭ-flou″ẽr), *n.* **1**, a garden variety of cabbage with a compact flowering head; **2**, the flowering head, used as a vegetable.

caulk (kôk), *v.t.* to make tight by filling (the crevices of) with soft material; as, to *caulk* the seams of a ship. Also, **calk**, *Pfd. S.*—*n.* **caulk'er.**

caus-al (kôz'ăl), *adj.* relating to, or expressing, a reason or cause; as, a *causal* event:—*n.* in grammar, a causal word, as *therefore* or *because.*—*adv.* **caus'al-ly.**

cau-sal-i-ty (kô-zăl'ĭ-tĭ), *n.* [*pl.* causalities (-tĭz)], **1**, the relation of cause and effect; the principle that nothing happens without a cause; **2**, the action or agency that brings a thing about.

cau-sa-tion (kô-zā'shŭn), *n.* **1**, the act of bringing about or producing, as a result; **2**, the act or agency producing an effect; **3**, causality.

caus-a-tive (kôz'ȧ-tĭv), *adj.* **1**, effective as an agency or cause; **2**, expressing action which brings about a result: said of a verb.—*adv.* **caus'a-tive-ly.**

cause (kôz), *n.* **1**, one who or that which produces or contributes to a result; **2**, a force or condition from which an effect inevitably follows; **3**, a motive; **4**, a reason; **5**, a subject which arouses discussion; as, the *cause* of international peace; **6**, a side or party; as, the *cause* of prohibition; **7**, in law: **a**, a lawsuit; **b**, ground for action:—*v.t.* [*p.t.* and *p.p.* caused (kôzd), *p.pr.* caus'ing], to produce; bring about.—*adj.* **cause'less.**

Syn., *n.* reason, motive, occasion. *Cause*, the general term, names that which produces effect; whatever happens is from a *cause* that made or produced it. A *reason* is the explanation or argument given for an act or conclusion; thus, *reason* is said to be the cause of the act or conclusion; as, the *reason* for a statement. A *motive* is an impulse which, if allowed to run its course, results in action; it may be a cause for action;

as, desire for fame was her *motive.* An *occasion* is that which gives rise to, and hence causes, action; as, he had *occasion* to go.

cause-way (kôz'wā), *n.* 1, a paved road or pathway, raised, as over wet ground, through shallow water, etc.; 2, a raised sidewalk beside a roadway.

caus-tic (kôs'tĭk), *adj.* 1, having the power of gradually eating away animal tissues by chemical action; 2, sarcastic; as, a *caustic* remark:—*n.* a substance which eats away animal tissues.—*adv.* **caus'ti-cal-ly.**—*n.* **caus-tic'i-ty** (kôs-tĭs'ĭ-tĭ).

cau-ter-ize (kô'tẽr-īz), *v.t.* [*p.t.* and *p.p.* -ized (-īzd), *p.pr.* -iz"ing], to burn or sear with a hot iron, or with some caustic agent, as a wound. Also, **cau'ter-ise.** —*n.* **cau"ter-i-za'tion.**

cau-ter-y (kô'tẽr-ĭ), *n.* [*pl.* cauteries (-ĭz)], 1, a burning or searing, as with a hot iron or a caustic agent; 2, the instrument or substance used to cauterize.

cau-tion (kô'shŭn), *n.* 1, an act or word that conveys a warning; 2, heedfulness; prudence in regard to danger; watchfulness:—*v.t.* to warn or notify of danger.

cau-tion-a-ry (kô'shŭn-ā-rĭ), *adj.* pertaining to, or conveying, a warning; cautioning.

cau-tious (kô'shŭs), *adj.* exercising discretion; careful; heedful; prudent.—*adv.* **cau'tious-ly.**—*n.* **cau'tious-ness.**
Syn. (see careful).

cav-al-cade (kăv"ăl-kād'), *n.* a train or procession of persons, usually on horseback.

cav-a-lier (kăv"ȧ-lẽr'), *n.* 1, a horseman; often, an armed horseman; a knight; 2, a gay adventurer; 3, a lady's escort; a gallant:—*adj.* 1, gay; frank and careless; 2, haughty; as, a *cavalier* refusal: **Cavalier,** *n.* a partisan of Charles I in his struggle with the Parliament in the 17th century:—*adj.* pertaining to the adherents of Charles I.—*adv.* **cav"a-lier'ly.**

cav-al-ry (kăv'ăl-rĭ), *n.* [*pl.* cavalries (-rĭz)], 1, mounted troops; horse soldiers; 2, horsemen collectively.—*n.* **cav'al-ry-man.**

cave (kāv), *n.* a hollow place in the earth; a large natural hole or den:—*v.t.* [*p.t.* and *p.p.* caved (kāvd), *p.pr.* cav'ing], to hollow out:—*v.i.* to fall in or down; give way: usually with *in;* as, the road *caved* in.

cave man a man of the prehistoric, or stone, age, who lived in a cave; hence, a rough, brutal man.

cav-ern (kăv'ẽrn), *n.* a large natural hollow or cavity under ground; den; cave.—*adj.* **cav'erned.**

cav-ern-ous (kăv'ẽr-nŭs), *adj.* 1, hollow like a cavern; 2, containing caverns; 3, filled with small holes.—*adv.* **cav'ern-ous-ly.**

cav-i-ar (kăv"ĭ-är'), *n.* the roe, or eggs, of certain large fishes, esp. the sturgeon, salted and dried. Also, **cav"i-are'.**

cav-il (kăv'ĭl), *v.i.* 1, to find fault without good reason; 2, to raise foolish or frivolous objections: followed by *at;* as, a generous man will not *cavil* at the little faults of his neighbors:—*v.t.* to find unreasonable fault with:— a petty or frivolous objection. —*n.* **cav'il-er.**

cav-i-ty (kăv'ĭ-tĭ), *n.* [*pl.* cavities (-tĭz)], a hollow place within a solid body.
Syn. hole, opening, dent, hollow.

ca-vort (kȧ-vôrt'), *v.i.* *Colloq.*, to prance about, as a horse.

caw (kô), *v.i.* to cry like a crow, rook, or raven:—*n.* the cry of the crow.

cay-enne (kā-ĕn'; kī-ĕn'), *n.* a kind of pepper made from the seeds or fruit of different species of capsicum: also called *red pepper.*

cay-man (kā'măn), *n.* [*pl.* caymans (-mănz)], any of a genus (*Caiman*) of alligators found in tropical America. Also, **cai'man.**

Ca-yu-ga (kā-yōō'gȧ), *n.* one of a tribe of Iroquoian Indians formerly dwelling on Cayuga Lake, New York, but now chiefly residents of Ontario.

Ca-yuse (kī-ūs'), *n.* one of a tribe of western American Indians: **cayuse,** an Indian pony; a mustang.

C clef in music, a sign sometimes used to mark the middle line or the fourth line of a staff as middle C.

cease (sēs), *v.i.* [*p.t.* and *p.p.* ceased (sēst), *p.pr.* ceas'ing], to come to an end; stop: followed by *from* before a noun:—*v.t.* to discontinue.
Syn. pause, desist, terminate, refrain.

cease-less (sēs'lĕs), *adj.* without end; without stop; incessant.—*adv.* **cease'less-ly.**—*n.* **cease'less-ness.**

Ce-cro-pi-a moth (sē-krō'pĭ-ȧ), a large, beautiful North American moth, whose larva spins a cocoon of silk.

ce-dar (sē'dẽr), *n.* 1, any of several evergreen trees of the pine family, having wood of great durability and fragrance; 2, any of several cone-bearing North American trees similar to the true cedar, as the white cedar, red cedar, and arbor vitæ:—*adj.* pertaining to, or made of, cedar.

ce-dar bird a crested American bird about seven inches long, with a row of red, waxlike color patches on the tips of the secondary wing feathers: also called *waxwing; cedar waxwing.*

cede (sēd), *v.t.* [*p.t.* and *p.p.* ced'ed, *p.pr.* ced'ing], 1, to give up or surrender; 2, to grant, as in an argument.

ce-dil-la (sē-dĭl'ȧ), *n.* a mark placed under *c* [ç] to indicate that it has the sound of *s*, as in the French word *leçon.*

ceil (sēl), *v.t.* to furnish or cover with a ceiling.

ceil-ing (sēl'ĭng), *n.* 1, the inner overhead covering of a room, usually made of laths and plaster; 2, the altitude to which an airplane can ascend; 3, the highest price at which a commodity may be sold.

cel-an-dine (sĕl'ăn-dīn), *n.* a biennial herb, used as a purgative.

cel-e-brant (sĕl'ē-brănt), *n.* one who performs a public religious ceremony, esp. the priest officiating at Mass.

cel-e-brate (sĕl'ē-brāt), *v.t.* [*p.t.* and *p.p.* -brat"ed, *p.pr.* -brat"ing], 1, to perform publicly with suitable ceremonies, as a Mass; 2, to make known with praise; honor; 3, to commemorate with suitable observances.—*n.* **cel'e-bra"tor.**
Syn. commemorate, observe, keep. To *celebrate* is to mark an event, anniversary, or public occasion by fitting ceremonies or demonstrations; as, to *celebrate* the Fourth of July. To *commemorate* is to observe the memory of some honored person, or to keep a past event in remembrance by suitable services; as, to *commemorate* Washington's Birthday. To *observe* is to mark religious days or ceremonies with appropriate conduct; as, to *observe* Lent. *Keep* is less formal than *observe,* and is applied chiefly to religious occasions, though it may be used of others; as, to *keep* the Sabbath.

cel-e-brat-ed (sĕl'ē-brāt"ĕd), *p.adj.* famous; illustrious.

cel-e-bra-tion (sĕl"ē-brā'shŭn), *n.* 1, the act of officiating at a ceremony; 2, the act of honoring; 3, an observance in honor of anything.

ce-leb-ri-ty (sē-lĕb′rĭ-tĭ), *n.* [*pl.* celebrities (-tĭz)], **1**, fame; distinction; **2**, a renowned or famous person.

ce-ler-i-ty (sē-lĕr′ĭ-tĭ), *n.* rapidity; swiftness; speed.

cel-er-y (sĕl′ēr-ĭ), *n.* a garden plant the stalks of which, blanched, are used as a salad or vegetable.

ce-les-tial (sē-lĕs′chăl), *adj.* **1**, pertaining to the heavens; as, the sun, the moon, and the stars are *celestial* bodies; **2**, heavenly; divine; **3**, pertaining to the former Chinese empire:—*n.* an inhabitant of heaven: **Celestial**, a native of China.—*adv.* **ce-les′tial-ly.**

Syn., adj. heavenly. *Celestial* and *heavenly*, when used to designate the visible sky, are interchangeable; as, *heavenly* bodies; the *celestial* blue. When not used in the physical sense, *celestial* describes that which comes supposedly from heaven itself; as, a *celestial* messenger; *heavenly* is used more commonly in a spiritual sense, suggesting the qualities of the divine; as, our *heavenly* Father.

cel-i-ba-cy (sĕl′ĭ-bȧ-sĭ; sē-lĭb′ȧ-sĭ), *n.* **1**, the state of being unmarried; **2**, single life, esp. that of a bachelor or of one bound by religious vows of chastity.

cel-i-bate (sĕl′ĭ-bāt), *n.* an unmarried person:—*adj.* single; unmarried.

cell (sĕl), *n.* **1**, a small, close room, as in a monastery or prison; **2**, a tiny, usually microscopic, mass of protoplasm, one of the units of structure of living matter in both plants and animals; **3**, a small, inclosed space, as in a honeycomb, lung, etc.; **4**, a source of electric current, consisting of two electrodes in one or more electrolytes: sometimes called *voltaic cell;* **5**, an apparatus for producing chemical changes by the electric current, consisting of a vessel containing an electrolyte and two electrodes by which the current enters and leaves: usually called *electrolytic cell.*

cel-lar (sĕl′ēr), a vault or room under a building, used for storing provisions, wine, fuel, etc.

cel-lar-age (sĕl′ēr-ȧj), *n.* **1**, cellars; **2**, the space in, or occupied by, cellars; **3**, a charge for storage in a cellar.

cel-lo (chĕl′ō), *n.* [*pl.* cellos (-ōz); celli (-ē)], the violoncello, a large four-stringed musical instrument of the violin class, tuned an octave lower than the viola. Also, **'cel'lo** (chĕl′ō).—*n.* **cel′list.**

cel-lo-phane (sĕl′ō-fān), *n.* a thin, transparent, air- and grease-proof fabric, used for wrapping: a trade name.

cel-lu-lar (sĕl′ū-lȧr), *adj.* pertaining to, consisting of, or like, cells.

cel-lu-loid (sĕl′ū-loid), *n.* a compound of camphor and guncotton, made in imitation of ivory, tortoise shell, etc.

cel-lu-lose (sĕl′ū-lōs), *n.* a substance related to starch, which forms the main part of plant tissue, linen, paper, etc.

Celt (sĕlt), *n.* a member of the Celtic branch of the Aryan race which includes the ancient Gauls and Britons, the Gaelic Scotch, the Irish, the Bretons, and the Welsh. Also, **Kelt** (kĕlt).

Celt-ic (sĕl′tĭk), *adj.* of or pertaining to the Celts or their languages. Also, **Kelt′ic** (kĕl′tĭk).—*abbr.* **Celt.**—*n.* **Celt′i-cism.**

ce-ment (sē-mĕnt′; sĕm′ĕnt), *n* **1**, any substance, such as glue, which will cause objects to stick together as it hardens; **2**, hence, anything creating a firm bond of union; **3**, a kind of mortar which, when wet, hardens slowly into a stonelike mass; **4**, the bony material which covers the root of a tooth (see *tooth*, illus.); **5**, a substance used to fill cavities in teeth:—*v.t.* (sē-mĕnt′), **1**, to cause to stick together; **2**, to unite firmly; **3**, to cover or pave with a mortar called cement:—*v.i.* to join together firmly.—*n.* **cem″-en-ta′tion** (sĕm″ĕn-tā′shŭn; sē″mĕn-tā′shŭn).

cem-e-ter-y (sĕm′ē-tĕr-ĭ), *n.* [*pl.* cemeteries (-ĭz)], a burial ground; graveyard; necropolis.

cen-o-bite (sĕn′ō-bīt; sē′nō-bīt), *n.* a member of a religious community; a monk. Also, **cœ′no-bite** (sē′nō-bīt).

cen-o-taph (sĕn′ō-tȧf), *n.* an empty tomb, or a monument erected in memory of a person buried elsewhere.

Ce-no-zo-ic (sē″nō-zō′ĭk; sĕn″ō-zō′ĭk), *adj.* designating, or pertaining to, the geological era preceding the Recent era, and ending with the ice age:—*n.* the era of the rise of mammals, including man.

cen-ser (sĕn′sēr), *n.* a vessel with holes in the lid, in which incense is burned.

cen-sor (sĕn′sŏr; sĕn′sēr), *n.* **1**, in ancient Rome, one of two magistrates who imposed taxes and regulated the manners and morals of a community; **2**, an official appointed to examine books, manuscripts, plays, motion pictures, etc., before publication, performance, or use, to find out if there is anything immoral or offensive in them; **3**, in time of war, an official who examines all printed matter, mail, newspaper cablegrams or telegrams, etc., in which information of value to the enemy might be written; **4**, one who criticizes manners or morals.—*adj.* **cen-so′ri-al** (sĕn-sō′rĭ-ăl).—*n.* **cen′sor-ship.**

cen-so-ri-ous (sĕn-sō′rĭ-ŭs), *adj.* inclined to find fault; containing criticism or censure.—*adv.* **cen-so′ri-ous-ly.**—*n.* **cen-so′ri-ous-ness.**

cen-sure (sĕn′shŭr), *n.* **1**, blame; reproof; **2**, the act of finding fault:—*v.t.* [*p.t.* and *p.p.* -sured (-shŭrd), *p.pr.* -sur-ing], to find fault with or condemn; as, do not *censure* what you do not understand:—*v.i.* to find fault.—*adj.* **cen′sur-a-ble.**

Syn., v. criticize, blame, upbraid.—*Ant., v.* praise, approve, commend, laud.

cen-sus (sĕn′sŭs), *n.* **1**, in ancient Rome, an enrolling of the people, and a valuation of their property; **2**, an official count of persons, property, or things, with details of sex, age, employment, value, etc.

cent (sĕnt), *n.* **1**, the hundredth part of the monetary unit of value, as, in the U. S., the hundredth part of a dollar; **2**, a hundred: used only in the phrase *per cent.*

cen-taur (sĕn′tôr), *n.* **1**, in mythology, one of a race of beings, half man and half horse, thought of as living in Thessaly; **2**, hence, a skilful horseman.

cen-te-na-ri-an (sĕn″tē-nā′rĭ-ăn), *n.* a person 100 years old or over:—*adj.* pertaining to 100 years.

cen-te-na-ry (sĕn′tē-nȧ-rĭ), *n.* [*pl.* centenaries (-rĭz)], **1**, a period of 100 years; **2**, the 100th anniversary of an event:—*adj.* of or pertaining to 100 years.

cen-ten-ni-al (sĕn-tĕn′ĭ-ăl), *adj.* **1**, consisting of, or enduring, 100 years; **2**. taking place once in 100 years:—*n.* a 100th anniversary.—*adv.* **cen-ten′ni-al-ly.**

cen-ter (sĕn′tēr), *n.* **1**, a point on a straight line equally distant from its extremities; **2**, that point of a circle or sphere which is equally distant from every point of the circumference; **3**, the middle point of anything; that point about which something rotates or revolves; **4**, a point about which things are collected; as, the *center* of a rebellion; the *center* of trouble; the *center* of a town; **5**, certain members of a lawmaking body who hold moderate views between two extremes of opinion:—*v.t.* **1**, to place on or at the middle point; **2**, to gather to a point; concentrate, as the attention:—*v.i.* **1**, to be in the middle; **2**, to gather in one point; as, his interests *center* in his children; **3**, to converge toward the middle, or toward a focus or central point. Also, *n.*, *v.i.*, and *v.t.* **cen'tre** [*p.t.* and *p.p.* cen'tred (-trd), *p.pr.* cen'tring].

cen-ter-board (sĕn'tẽr-bōrd''), *n.* **1**, in a sailboat, a vertical board, like a keel, that may be thrust down through the bottom of the boat into the water, to prevent the boat from being blown sideways; **2**, a boat having such a keel. Also, **cen'tre-board''**.

cen-ter of grav-i-ty the point in a body about which all parts of the body balance each other.

cen-ti-grade (sĕn'tĭ-grād), *adj.* graduated or divided into a hundred equal parts called degrees: **centigrade thermometer**, a thermometer on which the distance between the freezing point of water, called 0°, and the boiling point, called 100°, is divided into 100 equal degrees.—*abbr.* **C.**

cen-ti-gram (sĕn'tĭ-grăm), *n.* a weight equal to the 100th part of a gram, or 0.15432 grain, troy. Also, **cen'ti-gramme.**—*abbr.* **cg.**

cen-ti-li-ter (sĕn'tĭ-lē''tẽr), *n.* a measure of volume equal to the 100th part of a liter, or 0.6102 cubic inch. Also, **cen'ti-li''tre.**—*abbr.* **cl.**

cen-time (säṅ''tēm'; sän'tēm), [Fr.], *n.* a small French coin equal to the 100th part of a franc.—*abbr.* **c.**

cen-ti-me-ter (sĕn'tĭ-mē''tẽr), *n.* a measure of length equal to the 100th part of a meter, or about 0.3937 inch. Also, **cen'ti-me''tre.**—*abbr.* **cm.**

cen-ti-pede (sĕn'tĭ-pēd), *n.* any of an order of small, wormlike animals having many feet attached to a many-jointed, flat body.

cen-tral (sĕn'trăl), *adj.* **1**, relating to, or situated in, the middle; **2**, chief; leading; as, the *central* theme of the discussion.—*adv.* **cen'tral-ly.**—*n.* **cen'tral-ness.**

cen-tral-ize (sĕn'trăl-īz), *v.t.* [*p.t.* and *p.p.* -ized (-īzd), *p.pr.* -iz''ing], **1**, to draw or bring to one chief or middle point; **2**, to bring under one control or system, as local government.—*n.* **cen''tral-i-za'tion.**

cen-tric (sĕn'trĭk), *adj.* starting at, or connected with, a middle point; central. Also, **cen'tri-cal.**

cen-trif-u-gal (sĕn-trĭf'ū-găl), *adj.* **1**, tending, or directed, away from a center: opp. of *centripetal;* **2**, pertaining to, or operated by, centrifugal force; as, a *centrifugal* pump (see *pump*, illus.): **centrifugal force**, the force which causes a body moving in a curved path to tend to go off at a tangent.—*adv.* **cen-trif'u-gal-ly.**

cen-trip-e-tal (sĕn-trĭp'ē-tăl), *adj.* **1**, tending toward a center: opp. of *centrifugal;* **2**, pertaining to, or operated by, centripetal force; **3**, progressing from the outside of an object toward its center: **centripetal force**, the force which prevents a body moving in a curved path from going off at a tangent.—*adv.* **cen-trip'e-tal-ly.**

cen-tu-ple (sĕn'tū-pl), *adj.* increased 100 times:—*v.t.* [*p.t.* and *p.p.* -pled (-pld), *p.pr.* -pling], to increase 100 times; multiply by 100.

cen-tu-ri-on (sĕn-tū'rĭ-ŭn), *n.* in ancient Rome, the captain of a hundred Roman soldiers.

cen-tu-ry (sĕn'tū-rĭ; sĕn'chōō-rĭ), *n.* [*pl.* centuries (-rĭz)], **1**, a hundred; **2**, a hundred years; **3**, in ancient Rome, a subdivision of the people for voting; also, a company of a hundred foot soldiers: **century plant**, the American aloe, or maguey: from the mistaken belief that it blooms only once in a hundred years.—*adj.* **cen-tu'ri-al.**

ce-phal-ic (sē-făl'ĭk), *adj.* of, pertaining to, or located near, the head.

ceph-a-lo-pod (sĕf'ȧ-lō-pŏd''), *n.* any of the highest class of mollusks, including the cuttlefish, octopus, etc.

ce-ram-ic (sē-răm'ĭk), *adj.* of or pertaining to pottery; as, the Greeks excelled in the *ceramic* arts: **ceramics**, *n.pl.* **1**, used as *sing.*, the art of making vases, tiles, etc., of baked clay: contrasted with *vitrics;* **2**, used as *pl.*, pottery executed wholly or partly in clay and baked. Also, **ke-ram'ic** (kē-).

ce-rate (sē'rāt), *n.* a mixture of oil, lard, wax, and other ingredients, used as a plaster upon the skin.

Cer-ber-us (sûr'bẽr-ŭs), *n.* in mythology, the three-headed dog of Hades, which guarded the gates to the lower world; hence, an alert or surly guard or protector.—*adj.* **Cer-be're-an** (sûr-bē'rē-ăn).

cere (sēr), *v.t.* [*p.t.* and *p.p.* cered (sērd), *p.pr.* cer'ing], **1**, to cover or close with wax or cerecloth; **2**, to embalm.

ce-re-al (sē'rē-ăl), *adj.* pertaining to, or producing, wheat or other edible grain:—*n.* **1**, any grass that yields a grain or seed used for human food; **2**, any of these grains, as rice, wheat, oats, etc.; **3**, a grain prepared for human food, esp. breakfast food.

cer-e-bel-lum (sĕr''ē-bĕl'ŭm), *n.* [*pl.* cerebellums (-ŭmz); cerebella (-ȧ)], a lobe at the back of the brain of a higher animal, regarded as a center for habitual movements.—*adj.* **cer''e-bel'lar.**

cer-e-bral (sĕr'ē-brăl), *adj.* pertaining to the brain, esp. to the cerebrum or larger part of the brain.

cer-e-brate (sĕr'ē-brāt), *v.t.* [*p.t.* and *p.p.* -brat''ed, *p.pr.* -brat''ing], to accomplish by the action of the brain:—*v.i.* to exercise the functions of the brain, consciously or unconsciously.—*n.* **cer''e-bra'tion.**

cer-e-brum (sĕr'ē-brŭm), *n.* [*pl.* cerebrums (-brŭmz); cerebra (-brȧ)], the larger part of the brain, lying in front of and above the cerebellum: the seat of consciousness.

cere-cloth (sēr'klôth''), *n.* a cloth soaked or coated with wax or some gummy substance, in which embalmed bodies are wrapped to preserve them.

cere-ment (sēr'mĕnt), *n.*, usually in *pl.*, a shroud for the dead.

cer-e-mo-ni-al (sĕr''ē-mō'nĭ-ăl), *adj.* relating to, or performed with, rites or formalities:—*n.* **1**, ritual; **2**, proper behavior required by custom on a given social occasion.—*adv.* **cer''e-mo'ni-al-ly.**

cer-e-mo-ni-ous (sĕr''ē-mō'nĭ-ŭs), *adj.* **1**, according to established usage; **2**, characterized by formality; **3**, observant of prescribed forms; precise; punctilious.—*adv.* **cer''e-mo'ni-ous-ly.**—*n.* **cer''e-mo'ni-ous-ness.**

cer-e-mo-ny (sĕr'ē-mō-nĭ), *n.* [*pl.* ceremonies (-nĭz)], **1**, a sacred rite or observance; as, the marriage *ceremony;* **2**, a prescribed rite or formality; as, the inaugural *ceremony:* **3**, behavior regulated by the laws of strict etiquette; **4**, sometimes, empty form.

Syn. form, rite, formality. *Ceremony* denotes a display, usually elaborate and impressive, connected with some religious or public occasion; as, the *ceremony* dedicating the chapel. *Form* names a customary or accepted method of action; as, to be initiated in due *form.* A *rite* is a solemn observance sanctioned by custom, and is applied to the ceremonies of any church or order; as, the *rites* of the Roman Catholic Church. *Formality* implies strict adherence to custom or forms, and frequently suggests no more than the habitual performance of social or other duties; as, the *formality* of a social call.

Ce-res (sē'rēz), *n.* in Roman mythology, the goddess of growing vegetation: identified with the Greek goddess *Demeter*.

ce-rise (sē-rēz'), *adj.* bright red; cherry-colored:—*n.* a bright red color.

cer-tain (sûr'tĭn), *adj.* **1**, sure; beyond a doubt; **2**, destined; as, *certain* to happen; **3**, fixed or stated; settled; as, a *certain* time; **4**, dependable; as, a *certain* cure; **5**, indefinite, but presumably known to exist; as, a *certain* city; **6**, confident; as, *certain* of their loyalty.

Syn. secure, positive, undeniable, decided. —*Ant.* doubtful, obscure.

cer-tain-ly (sûr'tĭn-lĭ), *adv.* without fail; surely; undoubtedly.

cer-tain-ty (sûr'tĭn-tĭ), *n.* [*pl.* certainties (-tĭz)], **1**, a thoroughly established fact; **2**, the state or quality of being sure, fixed, or definite; **3**, something that is sure to happen.

cer-tes (sûr'tēz; sûr'tĭz), *n. Archaic*, certainly; in truth.

cer-tif-i-cate (sûr-tĭf'ĭ-kāt), *n.* **1**, a formal statement in writing by an official in public or private service; as, a *certificate* of marriage; **2**, a testimonial as to character or ability: **certificate of deposit**, a certificate issued by a bank stating that a certain amount is set aside and is not to be withdrawn by check:—*v.t.* (sûr-tĭf'ĭ-kāt), [*p.t.* and *p.p.* -cat″ed, *p.pr.* -cat″ing], to give testimony of by means of a written statement; as, to *certificate* a student for college.—*abbr.* **cert.**; **certif.**—*adj.* **cer-tif'i-ca-to-ry.**

cer-ti-fi-ca-tion (sûr″tĭ-fĭ-kā'shŭn), *n.* **1**, the act of confirming the truth of something by a written statement; **2**, a formal notice; **3**, a formal paper testifying to the truth of some matter.

cer-ti-fy (sûr'tĭ-fī), *v.t.* [*p.t.* and *p.p.* -fied (-fīd), *p.pr.* -fy″ing], **1**, to confirm the truth of something by a written statement signed by an official; **2**, to guarantee; as, to *certify* a check.—*adj.* **cer'ti-fi″a-ble.**

cer-ti-tude (sûr'tĭ-tūd), *adj.* assurance; freedom from doubt.

ce-ru-le-an (sē-rōō'lē-ăn), *adj.* azure; sky-colored.

cer-vi-cal (sûr'vĭ-kăl), *adj.* of or pertaining to the neck.

ces-sa-tion (sĕ-sā'shŭn), *n.* the act of ceasing; also, a pause.

Syn. intermission, rest, stop, end, close.

ces-sion (sĕsh'ŭn), *n.* **1**, a formal giving up to another, as of territory, property, or rights; **2**, a legal giving over of one's property to creditors.

cess-pool (sĕs'pōōl″), *n.* **1**, a deep hole in the ground, or the well of a drain, to receive sewage; **2**, hence, any place where filth accumulates.

[1]**ces-tus** (sĕs'tŭs), *n.* [*pl.* cesti (-tī)], in ancient Greece and Rome, a girdle worn by both men and women to hold the tunic in place.

[2]**ces-tus** (sĕs'tŭs), *n.* [*pl.* cestus (-tŭs)], in ancient Greece and Rome, a kind of glove used by boxers, often weighted.

ce-su-ra (sē-zū'rȧ; sē-sū'rȧ), *n.* a slight break or pause in a line of verse. Also, **cæ-su'ra,** *Pfd. S.*

ce-ta-cean (sē-tā'shăn), *n.* any of an order (*Cetacea*) of sea mammals, including the whale, dolphin, porpoise, etc.:—*adj.* of or pertaining to this order.—*adj.* **ce-ta'ceous.**

chafe (chāf), *v.t.* [*p.t.* and *p.p.* chafed (chāft), *p.pr.* chaf'ing], **1**, to make warm by friction; **2**, to wear away or make sore by rubbing; **3**, to anger; annoy; fret; irritate:—*v.i.* **1**, to rub; **2**, to move one body on or against another, causing friction; **3**, to be worn or made sore by rubbing; **4**, to be vexed; fret.

chaf-er (chāf'ẽr), *n.* any of several beetles; esp., the cockchafer.

chaff (chȧf), *n.* **1**, the husks of grain, separated by threshing and winnowing; **2**, straw or hay cut fine for cattle; **3**, anything worthless; **4**, good-natured raillery:—*v.i.* and *v.t.* to tease; make fun (of).

chaf-fer (chăf'ẽr), *n.* the act of bargaining:—*v.i.* to haggle or dispute about a purchase.—*n.* **chaf'fer-er.**

chaf-finch (chăf'ĭnch; chȧf'ĭnch), *n.* a common European song bird: so named from its habits of feeding.

chaff-weed (chȧf'wēd″), *n.* a plant with short, dry, chaffy leaves: also called *false pimpernel.*

chaff-y (chȧf'ĭ), *adj.* [*comp.* chaff'i-er, *superl.* chaff'i-est], **1**, resembling, or full of, chaff; **2**, light or worthless.

chaf-ing dish a small, covered pan, heated by alcohol or electricity, used for cooking at the table.

cha-grin (shȧ-grĭn'; shȧ-grēn'), *n.* vexation due to disappointment or mortification:—*v.t.* to excite vexation in; mortify.

Syn., *n.* confusion, dismay, humiliation, shame, disgust.

chain (chān), *n.* **1**, a series of links or rings joined together; **2**, a measure of 100 links or 66 feet, used in surveying land; **3**, a connected series or succession; as, a *chain* of events; **4**, anything which binds or restrains; **5**, in *pl.*, fetters; bondage:—*v.t.* **1**, to fasten with a chain; **2**, to fetter; restrain.

chain gang a gang of convicts chained together while at work.

chain mail armor made of small metal links woven together.

chain stitch **1**, a fancy stitch resembling a chain, used in crocheting and embroidery; **2**, a loop stitch with a single thread, made by a sewing machine.

chain store one of a number of stores, each under a local manager, controlled and supplied from a central office.

chair (châr), *n.* **1**, a movable seat with a back; **2**, a position of honor, dignity, or authority; a professorship; **3**, the position of presiding officer of an assembly; also, the presiding officer himself.

chair-man (châr'măn), *n.* [*pl.* chairmen (-mĕn)], the presiding officer of an assembly, meeting, public company, etc. —*n.* **chair'man-ship.**—*n. fem.* **chair'wom″an.**

chaise (shāz; *Dial.* shā), *n.* a light carriage with folding top, usually for two persons. Also, **shay.**

chal-ced-o-ny (kăl-sĕd'ō-nĭ; kăl'sē-dō-nĭ), *n.* [*pl.* chalcedonies (-nĭz)], a variety of quartz with a waxy luster, including onyx, agate, etc.

chal-cid (kăl'sĭd), *n.* any of a large group of very small insects, mostly parasitic on the eggs of other species: also called *chalcid fly.*—*n.* and *adj.* **chal-cid'i-an.**

chal-co-py-rite (kăl″kō-pī'rīt), *n.* a yellow sulphide of copper and iron: also called *copper pyrites.*

Chal-de-an (kăl-dē'ăn), *adj.* pertaining to Chaldea, or ancient Babylonia, esp. to its science of astrology:—*n.* **1**, an inhabitant of ancient Babylonia; **2**, one of a Semitic race dominant in Babylonia throughout most of its history; **3**, an astrologer or soothsayer; a seer; **4**, the Semitic language of the Chaldeans. Also, **Chal'dee″.**

chal-dron (chôl'drŭn), *n.* an old English measure for coal, coke, etc.

cha-let (shȧ-lā′; shȧ″lĕ′), *n.* **1**, a Swiss herdsman's hut on a mountain pasture; **2**, a Swiss peasant's cottage; **3**, a house built in the Swiss style.

SWISS CHALET

chal-ice (chăl′ĭs), *n.* **1**, a goblet; **2**, the head of a flower, as the tulip, more or less cup-shaped; **3**, the cup used in celebrating the Lord's Supper.

chalk (chôk), *n.* **1**, a soft, white, limestone rock; **2**, this rock, or something like it, prepared for use in marking, as on a blackboard; **3**, a score in a game:—*v.t.* to mark, rub, or whiten, as with chalk.—*adj.* **chalk′y.**—*n.* **chalk′i-ness.**

CHALICE

chal-lenge (chăl′ĕnj), *n.* **1**, a call to combat, as to a duel; an invitation to a contest, as a debate; **2**, a letter containing such a summons; **3**, a demand for the countersign by a soldier on sentry duty; **4**, an objection made to a person's serving on a jury:—*v.t.* [*p.t.* and *p.p.* -lenged (-ĕnjd), *p.pr.* -leng-ing], **1**, to summon, as to a contest or duel; **2**, to invite, as inspection; **3**, to take exception to, as a statement; **4**, to claim as due; as, he *challenges* one's respect by his honesty; **5**, to demand the countersign from; **6**, to object to, as a juror.—*n.* **chal′leng-er.**

chal-lis (shăl′ĭ; chăl′ĭs), *n.* a light-weight, all-wool dress material; sometimes, a similar material in cotton. Also, **chal′lie.**

cha-lyb-e-ate (kȧ-lĭb′ē-ăt), *adj.* **1**, containing iron, as some mineral waters or springs; **2**, tasting of iron:—*n.* a mineral water or medicine containing iron in solution.

cham-ber (chām′bẽr), *n.* **1**, a room, esp. a sleeping room; **2**, a place where an assembly meets; as, the senate *chamber;* **3**, a hollow space in some object, as a gun; **4**, a bedroom utensil: short for *chamber pot:* **Chamber of Commerce, 1**, an association of business men for furthering the trade interests of its members; **2**, an association of persons organized to further their commercial, economic, social, and civic interests.

cham-bered (chām′bẽrd), *adj.* **1**, having compartments; **2**, having chambers, as a shell.

cham-ber-lain (chām′bẽr-lĭn), *n.* **1**, an officer, usually of high rank, who has charge of the private apartments of a ruler or nobleman; **2**, a male servant who has charge of a suite of rooms; **3**, a treasurer; steward.—*n.* **cham′ber-lain-ship″.**

cham-ber-maid (chām′bẽr-mād″), *n.* a woman having charge of bed chambers, making the beds, etc.

cham-bray (shăm′brā), *n.* a gingham dress fabric with a linen finish, made in plain colors.

cha-me-le-on (kȧ-mē′lē-ŭn), *n.* **1**, any of various lizards which have the power of changing color; **2**, a person of changeable disposition.

cham-fer (chăm′fẽr), *n.* **1**, the surface made by cutting away the square edge or corner of a timber, stone, etc.; a bevel; **2**, a groove; **3**, a tool for cutting a bevel or groove:—*v.t.* **1**, to cut a groove in; **2**, to give a sloping edge to; bevel.

cham-ois (shăm′ĭ; shȧ″mwä′), *n.* **1**, an antelope found on high peaks in Europe and Asia; **2**, (also, *chammy; shammy* (shăm′ĭ), [*pl.* chammies, shammies (-ĭz)]), a soft, thin leather, orig. made from the hide of the chamois, but now prepared from other skins.

cham-o-mile (kăm′ō-mīl), *n.* a creeping plant, from the leaves of which a tonic is made. See **cam′o-mile**, *Pfd.S.*

champ (chămp), *v.t.* and *v.i.* to bite with the teeth repeatedly and impatiently: usually with *on* or *at;* as, a horse *champs* at the bit.

CHAMOIS ($\frac{1}{30}$)

cham-pagne (shăm-pān′), *n.* a light, sparkling, amber-colored wine, made in any of several varieties.

cham-paign (shăm-pān′), *n.* **1**, flat, open country; **2**, a clear level landscape; expanse.

cham-pi-on (chăm′pĭ-ŭn), *n.* **1**, one who defends the cause of another by combat or other means; **2**, a hero; valiant warrior; **3**, a successful competitor against all rivals; **4**, something that has been given first prize, as an animal, plant, etc.:—*adj.* superior to all rivals:—*v.t.* to defend or support.—*n.* **cham′pi-on-ship″.**

chance (chȧns), *n.* **1**, the unforeseen happening of events; fortune; **2**, an unexpected event; **3**, a possibility; a probability; as, a *chance* of success; **4**, opportunity; as, a *chance* of a position; **5**, risk; **6**, an imaginary cause of unexplained events; fate:—*adj.* accidental; unforeseen:—*v.i.* [*p.t.* and *p.p.* chanced (chȧnst), *p.pr.* chanc′ing], to happen:—*v.t.* *Colloq.*, to risk: usually with *it.*

chan-cel (chȧn′sĕl), *n.* in certain churches, the area surrounding the altar.

chan-cel-lor (chȧn′sĕl-ẽr), *n.* **1**, an official secretary to a king or noble; **2**, in some European countries, the chief minister of state; **3**, in many universities, the president: **Chancellor**, in Great Britain, **1**, the highest judge of the realm: called *Lord Chancellor;* **2**, the minister of finance: called *Chancellor of the Exchequer.*—*n.* **chan′cel-lor-ship″.**

chan-cer-y (chȧn′sẽr-ĭ), *n.* **1**, a court of equity, or law based on natural principles; **2**, the principles or practice of such law: **in chancery**, in a helpless position: from the long delays of the old Court of Chancery.

chan-de-lier (shăn″dĕ-lēr′), *n.* a hanging, branching frame for lights.

chan-dler (chăn′dlẽr), *n.* **1**, a maker or seller of candles; **2**, a merchant; as, a tallow *chandler.*—*n.* **chan′dler-y.**

change (chānj), *v.t.* [*p.t.* and *p.p.* changed (chānjd), *p.pr.* chang′ing], **1**, to alter; as, to *change* one's habits; **2**, to exchange; as, to *change* rings with someone; **3**, to give an equivalent for; as, to *change* a dollar bill:—*v.i.* **1**, to vary; **2**, to undergo alteration; **3**, to pass from one place to another:—*n.* **1**, an alteration; a variation; **2**, the quality of variableness in general; as, chance and *change* cannot be avoided; **3**, variety; **4**, small coins taken together; **5**, the difference, returned to a purchaser, between the price of a purchase and the amount paid: **change ringing**, a varied arrangement in the ringing of a peal of bells.—*n.* **chang′er.**

change-a-ble (chān′jȧ-bl), *adj.* **1**, capable of going from one thing to another or from one mood to another;

fickle; **2,** taking now one form or color and now another.—*adv.* **change'a-bly.**—*n.* **change"-a-bil'i-ty.**—*n.* **change'a-ble-ness.**

change-less (chānj'lĕs), *adj.* free from alteration or substitution.—*adv.* **change'less-ly.**—*n.* **change'less-ness.**

change-ling (chānj'lĭng), *n.* **1,** in folklore, an elf child left by fairies in exchange for a human infant; **2,** any child substituted for another.

chan-nel (chăn'ĕl), *n.* **1,** the bed of a stream; **2,** the deepest part of a strait, bay, harbor, etc.; **3,** a piece of water, wider than a strait, separating two large bodies of land; **4,** a long groove or furrow; **5,** a way by which anything may be carried: —*v.t.* to cut or wear grooves or furrows in.

chan-son (shăn'sŏn; shäṅ"sôṅ'), [Fr.], *n.* **1,** a simple lyric, or the music to which it is sung; **2,** an Old French epic.

chant (chȧnt), *v.t.* **1,** to sing; **2,** to praise in song; **3,** to intone:—*v.i.* **1,** to make melody with the voice; **2,** to intone; sing slowly and solemnly:—*n.* **1,** a song; esp., a solemn song; **2,** a special musical composition used in church services, in which a number of words are half sung, half recited in one tone.

chant-er (chȧn'tẽr), *n.* **1,** one who sings or intones; **2,** the pipe in a bagpipe which gives the melody.

chant-ey (shȧn'tĭ; chȧn'tĭ), *n.* [*pl.* chant-eys (-tĭz)], a song sailors and other laborers sing while at work.

chan-ti-cleer (chăn'tĭ-klēr), *n.* a cock: used as if a proper name.

cha-os (kā'ŏs), *n.* **1,** the complete confusion formerly supposed to have prevailed before natural law came into being; **2,** utter confusion or disorder.

cha-ot-ic (kā-ŏt'ĭk), *adj.* very confused; disordered.—*adv.* **cha-ot'i-cal-ly.**

[1]**chap** (chăp), *v.t.* [*p.t.* and *p.p.* chapped (chăpt), *p.pr.* chap'ping], to cause to crack or become rough, as the skin:—*v.i.* to crack or become rough:—*n.* a crack, as in skin.

[2]**chap** (chŏp; chăp), *n.* **1,** a jaw, as of an animal; **2,** in *pl.*, the mouth or the fleshy parts about it. Also, **chop.**

[3]**chap** (chăp), *n.* *Colloq.*, a fellow; youth; a man or boy.

chap-ar-ral (chăp"ȧ-răl'), *n.* a dense thicket of dwarf evergreen oaks, shrubs, or cacti: **chaparral cock,** a large running bird of the cuckoo family, found in the southwestern U. S.

cha-peau (shȧ"pō'), *n.* [*pl.* chapeaux (-pōz'; -pō')], a hat; esp., a hat belonging to an official costume.

chap-el (chăp'ĕl), *n.* **1,** a place of public worship, not so large or important as a church; **2,** a place of worship in a palace, institution, etc.; **3,** in Great Britain, a church affiliated with neither the Established nor the Roman Catholic Church.

chap-er-on (shăp'ẽr-ōn), *n.* a married or older woman who escorts or accompanies young unmarried women in public:—*v.t.* to escort.—*n.* **chap'er-on"age.**

chap-fall-en (chŏp'fôl"n; chăp'fôl"n), *adj.* dejected; crestfallen. Also, **chop'fall"en.**

chap-lain (chăp'lĭn), *n.* a clergyman who performs service in the army, navy, a public institution, etc.—*n.* **chap'-lain-cy.**—*n.* **chap'lain-ship.**

chap-let (chăp'lĕt), *n.* **1,** a wreath or garland for the head; **2,** a rosary or a third part of it; **3,** any string of beads.

chap-man (chăp'măn), *n.* [*pl.* chapmen (-mĕn)], a peddler.

chap-ter (chăp'tẽr), *n.* **1,** a division of a book; **2,** an organized local group of some religious or fraternal order; also, the body of clergy attached to a cathedral; **3,** a meeting of such a body or group.

char (chär), *v.t.* [*p.t.* and *p.p.* charred (chärd), *p.pr.* char'ring], **1,** to burn partially; **2,** to change into charcoal, as wood.

char-ac-ter (kăr'ăk-tẽr), *n.* **1,** a distinctive sign or mark, as a trademark; **2,** a letter or figure representing a sound or number; **3,** a system of these peculiar to a people; as, our common numerals are in the Arabic *character;* **4,** distinctive quality or traits; **5,** a person possessing distinctive qualities; as, a great historical *character;* **6,** individuality; **7,** reputation; **8,** a testimonial; **9,** a personage in a play or novel.

char-ac-ter-is-tic (kăr"ăk-tẽr-ĭs'tĭk), *adj.* pertaining to, or displaying, the mental or moral nature of; typical; as, her *characteristic* kindness:—*n.* a distinguishing mark or quality; essential nature.—*adv.* **char"ac-ter-is'ti-cal-ly.**

Syn., *n.* feature, trait. A *characteristic* is a part of the nature of the person, animal, thing, or group concerned; it is a distinctive, typical mark; as, round heads are a *characteristic* of some races of people. A *feature* is a prominent part of a person or thing; it stands out and arrests the attention; as, her principal *feature* was her eyes; a *feature* of some newspapers is bold headlines. A *trait* is a definite *characteristic*, usually a mental or moral characteristic; as, cheerfulness is an excellent *trait.*

char-ac-ter-ize (kăr'ăk-tẽr-īz), *v.t.* [*p.t.* and *p.p.* -ized (-īzd), *p.pr.* -iz"ing], **1,** to describe as having peculiar or essential qualities; **2,** to mark or distinguish; as, the Angora cat is *characterized* by long, silky hair.—*n.* **char"ac-ter-i-za'tion.**

cha-rade (shȧ-rād'; *Br.* shȧ-räd'), *n.* an acted riddle based on a word with several significant parts or syllables, each of which, as well as the word, is to be guessed from the acting.

char-coal (chär'kōl"), *n.* wood partially burned in such a way as to be good for fuel.

charge (chärj), *v.t.* [*p.t.* and *p.p.* charged (chärjd), *p.pr.* charg'ing], **1,** to load, as a gun; **2,** to command; instruct; **3,** to impute, as a fault; **4,** to accuse; blame; censure; **5,** to demand as a price; **6,** to place (something) on record as due from, or as a debt of; **7,** to rush on or attack; **8,** to impose a duty, trust, or obligation upon; **9,** to electrify; **10,** to renew (a battery); **11,** to instruct, as a jury, by an address at the end of a trial: —*v.i.* **1,** to demand or set a price or sum due; place the price of a thing against one's account; **2,** to make an attack; **3,** to crouch; lie flat: said of a dog:—*n.* **1,** a quantity of material with which a firearm or other apparatus is loaded; **2,** an office or trust; responsibility; **3,** a parish or congregation intrusted to the care of a minister; **4,** an order or command; **5,** the price of an object; **6,** an entry or account of one's indebtedness; **7,** an expense or liability; **8,** an accusation; imputation; **9,** a violent onset or attack; **10,** the quantity of electricity at rest on a conductor; **11,** the quantity of ore, fuel, and flux introduced into a furnace at one time; **12,** an address of instruction to the jury by the presiding judge at the end of a trial; **13,** a heraldic bearing or emblem.

charge-a-ble (chär'jȧ-bl), *adj.* **1,** subject or liable to tax; **2,** liable to an accusation, expense, responsibility, etc.; **3,** capable of being loaded.

***char-gé d'af-faires** (shȧr"zhā' dȧ"fâr'), [Fr.], [*pl.* chargés (shȧr"zhā')], a government official who acts for an ambassador in his absence, or at a court at which no ambassador is received.

charg-er (chär′jẽr), *n.* **1**, a spirited horse; **2**, a large platter; **3**, one who or that which charges.

char-i-ot (chăr′ĭ-ŏt), *n.* **1**, an ancient two-wheeled car for war, state processions, racing, etc.; **2**, a four-wheeled vehicle of the 18th century.—*n.* **char″i-ot-eer′**.

ROMAN CHARIOT: QUADRIGA

char-i-ta-ble (chăr′ĭ-tȧ-bl), *adj.* **1**, merciful; kind and liberal; **2**, forgiving; forbearing; **3**, benevolent; open-handed; **4**, providing for the poor; as, a *charitable* institution.—*adv.* **char′i-ta-bly**.—*n.* **char′i-ta-ble-ness**.

char-i-ty (chăr′ĭ-tĭ), *n.* [*pl.* charities (-tĭz)], **1**, the disposition to think well of others; **2**, generosity to the poor; alms; **3**, universal love and good will; **4**, an institution for the poor, founded by a gift.

cha-ri-va-ri (shä″rē-vä′rē; shȧ-rē″vȧ-rē′; shĭv′ȧ-rē), *n.* a mock serenade; a jumble of discordant sounds.

char-la-tan (shär′lȧ-tăn), *n.* **1**, an impostor; **2**, a pretentious boaster.

Charles's Wain the seven principal stars in the constellation of the Great Bear; the Dipper.

char-lotte russe (shär′lŏt rōōs′), whipped cream or custard inclosed in sponge cake.

charm (chärm), *n.* **1**, orig., a chanted verse supposed to have magic power; **2**, hence, anything which has magic power; **3**, attractiveness; esp., a mysterious allurement; **4**, a trinket worn on a watch fob, etc.:—*v.t.* **1**, to put a spell on; **2**, to overcome by magic; **3**, hence, to lessen, as pain; protect, as by magic; as, he bore a *charmed* life; **4**, to fascinate:—*v.i.* **1**, to work by magic; **2**, to act as a charm; be delightful.—*n.* **charm′er**.

charm-ing (chärm′ĭng), *p.adj.* attractive; with power to cause admiration or give delight; fascinating; pleasing.—*adv.* **charm′ing-ly**.—*n.* **charm′ing-ness**.

char-nel (chär′nĕl), *adj.* **1**, containing dead bodies; **2**, gloomy; dismal: **charnel house**, a common burial tomb for the bodies or bones of the dead; a sepulcher.

Cha-ron (kā′rŏn), in mythology, the boatman who ferried souls across the river Styx in Hades.

chart (chärt), *n.* **1**, a map of any part of a sea, river, etc., for the use of mariners; **2**, the map of a ship's course; **3**, a sheet giving information in tabular form; as, a nurse's *chart*:—*v.t.* to map out.

Syn., *n.* map. A *map* is a representation of all or part of the earth's surface; it may show physical features, political divisions, distribution of population, etc. A *chart* is a particular *map* designed for the use of navigators, showing the position of channels, shallows, rocks, lighthouses, etc.

char-ter (chär′tẽr), *n.* **1**, an official paper bestowing certain rights and privileges; as, King James gave William Penn a *charter* to the province of Pennsylvania; **2**, a written order from the authorities of a society to establish a chapter, lodge, or branch:—*v.t.* **1**, to grant a charter to; **2**, to hire, esp. for one's own use.

char-wom-an (chär′wo͝om″ăn; châr′-wo͝om″ăn), *n.* [*pl.* charwomen (-wĭm″ĕn)], a woman hired by the day to do cleaning and scrubbing in offices and office buildings.

char-y (châr′ĭ; chā′rĭ), *adj.* [*comp.* char′i-er, *superl.* char′i-est], **1**, careful; cautious; **2**, reserved; shy; **3**, frugal or sparing; as, a poor man must be *chary* in the use of his money.—*adv.* **char′i-ly**.—*n.* **char′i-ness**.

Cha-ryb-dis (kȧ-rĭb′dĭs), *n.* in mythology, a greedy woman whom Jupiter transformed into a dangerous whirlpool, between Sicily and Italy: **between Scylla and Charybdis**, having to choose between two evils.

[1]**chase** (chās), *v.t.* [*p.t.* and *p.p.* chased (chāst), *p.pr.* chas′ing], **1**, to pursue with intent to capture or kill, as a fox; hunt; **2**, to drive away; dispel; **3**, to follow persistently:—*v.i.* to follow in pursuit; pursue:—*n.* **1**, eager pursuit with the idea of capturing or killing, esp. of wild animals; **2**, pursuit with the idea of satisfying desire; **3**, that which is pursued; **4**, those taking part in a hunt; **5**, in England, an unfenced game preserve.

Syn., *v.* (see follow).

[2]**chase** (chās), *v.t.* [*p.t.* and *p.p.* chased (chāst), *p.pr.* chas′ing], to decorate, as a metal surface, by embossing, engraving, or the like.

[3]**chase** (chās), *n.* **1**, a groove; a narrow rut or channel; as, the *chase* for a water wheel; **2**, an iron frame into which the pages or columns of type are fastened.

[1]**chas-er** (chās′ẽr), *n.* one who pursues; a hunter.

[2]**chas-er** (chās′ẽr), *n.* **1**, an engraver; **2**, a tool used for decorating metal by engraving, embossing, etc.

chasm (kăzm), *n.* **1**, a deep opening in the earth; a cleft; gap; **2**, a void.

chas-seur (shă″sûr′), *n.* **1**, a huntsman; **2**, a kind of attendant in a European noble household; **3**, a soldier, either of the cavalry or the infantry, trained for rapid pursuit.

chas-sis (shăs′ĭ; chăs′ĭ; chăs′ĭs; *Fr.* shȧ′-sē), *n.* [*pl.* chassis (-ĭz; -ĭ)], **1**, the frame, machinery, and wheels of an automobile (see *automobile*, illus.); **2**, the main framework of an airplane.

chaste (chāst), *adj.* **1**, virtuous; modest; morally pure; esp., sexually pure; **2**, pure in style and execution, as art.—*adv.* **chaste′ly**.—*n.* **chaste′ness**.

chas-ten (chās′n), *v.t.* **1**, to punish for the purpose of making better; **2**, to subdue; as, God *chastens* his people; **3**, to make pure.—*n.* **chas′ten-er**.—*n.* **chas′ten-ing**.

Syn. chastise, punish. To *chasten* is to discipline one in obedience, meekness, purity, etc.; as, we may be *chastened* by hardship. To *chastise* is to try to correct or reform by inflicting physical suffering; as, children may be *chastised* to teach them not to repeat their faults. To *punish* is to inflict penalty for crimes, offenses, or disobedience; as, he was *punished* for stealing.

chas-tise (chăs-tīz′), *v.t.* [*p.t.* and *p.p.* -tised′ (-tīzd′), *p.pr.* -tis′ing], to correct by punishment; as, the parent *chastises* the child.—*n.* **chas-tis′er**.

Syn. (see chasten).

chas-tise-ment (chăs′tĭz-mĕnt), *n.* punishment; discipline.

chas-ti-ty (chăs′tĭ-tĭ), *n.* **1**, moral purity; esp., sexual purity; as, *chastity* is a Christian virtue; **2**, simplicity, as of design or style.

chat (chăt), *v.i.* [*p.t.* and *p.p.* chat′ted, *p.pr.* chat′ting], to talk in an easy, familiar manner:—*n.* **1**, familiar or informal speech; gossip; **2**, any of various song birds.

châ-teau (shă′tō′; *Fr.* shä″tō′), *n.* [*pl.* châteaux (-tōz′; -tō′)], **1**, a French feudal castle; **2**, a large and stately manor house or country seat.

chat-e-laine (shăt′ē-lān; *Fr.* shä″tē-lân′), *n.* **1**, the lady of a château; **2**, a chain worn at the waist, as for keys, trinkets, etc.

chat-tel (chăt′l), *n.*, usually in *pl.*, personal property not including houses or land; movable possessions.

chat-ter (chăt′ẽr), *v.i.* **1**, to utter sounds rapidly and indistinctly; **2**, to utter notes rapidly: said of birds; **3**, to rattle the teeth, as in shivering; **4**, to talk much and say little; **5**, to rattle, as parts of a machine:—*v.t.* to utter rapidly or idly:—*n.* **1**, sounds like those of the magpie, monkey, etc.; **2**, idle, rapid talk; **3**, a rattling of the teeth, as from cold or fear.—*n.* **chat′ter-er.**

chat-ter-box (chăt′ẽr-bŏks″), *n. Colloq.*, an incessant and idle talker, esp. a child.

chat-ty (chăt′ĭ), *adj.* [*comp.* chat′ti-er, *superl.* chat′ti-est], talkative in an easy, familiar way.—*n.* **chat′ti-ness.**

chauf-feur (shō″fûr′; shō′fẽr), *n.* a driver of an automobile, esp. for hire.—*n.fem.* ***chauf″feuse′** (shō″föz′).

Chau-tau-qua (shȧ-tô′kwȧ), *n.* **1**, a system of education by summer schools, programs of lectures, etc.: orig. at Chautauqua, N. Y.; later, a similar program conducted by itinerant lecturers, musicians, etc.; **2**, a system of home instruction by correspondence, under the supervision of a central organization.

chau-vin-ism (shō′vĭn-ĭzm), *n.* blind devotion, as to a country or a cause; esp., braggart patriotism.—*n.* **chau′-vin-ist.**—*adj.* **chau″vin-is′tic.**

cheap (chēp), *adj.* **1**, low in price; **2**, common; mean; of little real value.—*adv.* **cheap′ly.**—*n.* **cheap′ness.**

cheap-en (chēp′n), *v.t.* **1**, to beat down the price of; **2**, to lessen or bring down in price; **3**, to lower, as one's own value:—*v.i.* to become low in price or esteem.

cheat (chēt), *n.* **1**, a fraud or deception; **2**, one who defrauds another, as of money:—*v.t.* **1**, to deceive or defraud; **2**, to escape; elude; as, to *cheat* the gallows; **3**, to wile away; beguile:—*v.i.* to act dishonestly.—*n.* **cheat′er.**

¹check (chĕk), *n.* **1**, a restraint; **2**, a reproof; **3**, a ticket for identifying the holder; **4**, an order or draft on a bank for money; **5**, in chess, a word used as warning that the king is in danger of being captured by the next move; also, the position of the king when in such danger; **6**, a mark showing that something has been examined or verified; **7**, a means of securing accuracy by verifying one thing with another:—*v.t.* **1**, to restrain; stop; **2**, to reprove; **3**, to examine by comparison, or mark as having been examined or verified; **4**, to hold up by a checkrein, as a horse's head; **5**, to deposit for safe-keeping:—*v.i.* **1**, to pause; halt; **2**, to open in cracks, as wood.

²check (chĕk), *n.* **1**, a pattern of squares of alternating colors, as on a checkerboard; **2**, cloth woven with this pattern:—*v.t.* to mark in small squares.

¹check-er (chĕk′ẽr), *n.* **1**, one who or that which checks; **2**, an employee whose duty it is to see that all items in each order are properly assembled for shipment.

²check-er (chĕk′ẽr), *n.* **1**, one of the squares of a pattern marked in alternate squares; also, the pattern itself, or any spot like a square in this pattern; **2**, one of the 24 round pieces used in playing the game of checkers; **3**, in *pl.*, a game played on a checkerboard by two persons:—*v.t.* **1**, to mark with small squares; **2**, to give variety to; mark with irregular changes, as those of prosperity or adversity. Also, **cheq′uer.**

check-er-ber-ry (chĕk′ẽr-bĕr″ĭ), *n.* [*pl.* checkerberries (-ĭz)], **1**, the spicy red fruit of the American wintergreen plant; **2**, the plant itself.

check-er-board (chĕk′ẽr-bōrd″), *n.* a board of 64 squares on which the game of checkers is played.

check-mate (chĕk′māt), *n.* **1**, the winning move at chess; **2**, hence, a complete defeat:—*v.t.* [*p.t.* and *p.p.* -mat-ed, *p.pr.* -mat-ing], **1**, in chess, to make impossible the escape of (the opponent's king), **2**, to defeat utterly; as, to *checkmate* a plan.

check-off (chĕk′ôf″), *n.* a plan whereby dues of union members are deducted from their wages by the employer and paid directly to the union.

check-rein (chĕk′rān″), *n.* a short rein attached to the saddle of a harness to keep a horse from lowering its head (see *harness*, illus.).

cheek (chēk), *n.* **1**, the side of the face below either eye; **2**, a part or surface resembling the human cheek; **3**, among mechanics, one of two corresponding sides; as, the *cheeks* of a lathe; **4**, *Slang*, brazen impudence; bold assurance.—*adj.* **cheek′y.**

cheep (chēp), *n.* **1**, a peep or chirp; **2**, a shrill, feeble noise, as that of a young chicken or a mouse:—*v.i.* to make such a noise.—*n.* **cheep′er.**

cheer (chēr), *n.* **1**, temper or state of heart or mind; esp., a state of gladness or joy; **2**, something which gladdens; esp., that which is furnished for food or entertainment; **3**, a shout of applause; **4**, luck:—*v.t.* **1**, to gladden; **2**, to encourage; applaud; **3**, to greet, esp. with shouts of welcome:—*v.i.* **1**, to become hopeful: with *up;* **2**, to applaud.—*n.* **cheer′er.**

cheer-ful (chēr′fŏŏl), *adj.* happy; full of, or showing, good spirits.—*adv* **cheer′ful-ly.**—*n.* **cheer′ful-ness.**

Syn. cheery, gay, hilarious, mirthful. *Cheerful* describes one who is happy, contented, and habitually free from gloom. *Cheery* describes one who or that which communicates good spirits to others; as, a *cheery* companion; *cheery* words. *Gay* describes one who or that which is sportive, merry, and bright, as a friend, mood, or color.

cheer-less (chēr′lĕs), *adj.* gloomy; forlorn; dismal.—*adv.* **cheer′-less-ly.**—*n.* **cheer′less-ness.**

cheer-y (chēr′ĭ), *adj.* [*comp.* cheer′i-er, *superl.* cheer′i-est], **1**, cheerful; gay; as, a *cheery* voice; **2**, attractive; as, a *cheery* room.—*adv.* **cheer′i-ly.**—*n.* **cheer′i-ness.**

cheese (chēz), *n.* a food consisting of the curd of milk.

cheese-cloth (chēz′klôth″), *n.* a thin, loosely woven cloth resembling that in which cheese is wrapped.

chees-y (chēz′ĭ), *adj.* [*comp.* chees′i-er, *superl.* chees′i-est], containing, like, or appearing like, cheese.

chee-tah (chē′tȧ), *n.* a leopardlike animal found in Persia, India, etc.

chef (shĕf), *n.* a chief or head cook, esp. a French cook.

***chef–d'œu-vre** (shâ″-dûvr′), [Fr.], *n.* [*pl.* chefs-d'œuvre (shâ″-dûvr′)], a masterpiece.

chem-i-cal (kĕm′ĭ-kăl), *adj.* **1**, pertaining to chemistry; **2**, produced by, or used in, operations of chemistry:—*n.* a substance produced by, or used in, a chemical process.—*adv.* **chem′i-cal-ly.**

che-mise (shē-mēz′), *n.* a woman's sleeveless undergarment.

chem-ist (kĕm′ĭst), *n.* **1**, one skilled in chemicals or chemistry; **2**, a dealer in drugs and medicines.

chem-is-try (kĕm′ĭs-trĭ), *n.* **1,** the science which treats of the nature and composition of substances, and the laws which govern their relations; **2,** application of this knowledge to a particular subject; as, the *chemistry* of steel.

che-nille (shē-nēl′), *n.* a tufted cord of soft, fluffy cotton, silk, or worsted: used in trimmings, rugs, etc.

cheque (chĕk), *n.* an order or draft on a bank, esp. in Great Britain. Also, **check.**

cher-ish (chĕr′ĭsh), *v.t.* **1,** to protect; hold dear, as a memory; **2,** to cling to, as a hope.—*n.* **cher′ish-er.**

Cher-o-kee (chĕr″ō-kē′), *n.* one of a tribe of American Indians, orig. inhabiting what is now northern Georgia, North Carolina, etc.: now in Oklahoma.

che-root (shē-rōōt′; chē-), *n.* a cigar, orig. made in India and the Philippine Islands, having square ends.

cher-ry (chĕr′ĭ), *n.* [*pl.* cherries (-ĭz)], **1,** any of several trees or shrubs related to the plum, extensively cultivated, bearing small, smooth, fleshy fruit; also, the fruit or the wood; **2,** a bright red like that of certain cherries:—*adj.* **1,** of the color of the ripe fruit of this tree; **2,** made of wood of the cherry.

cher-ub (chĕr′ŭb), *n.* [*pl.* cherubs (-ŭbz); cherubim (chĕr′ū-bĭm; -ōō-bĭm)], **1,** a representation of a winged child or child's head; hence, a beautiful, innocent child; **2,** in the Bible, a heavenly being (Ezekiel 1:5–11); **3,** a representation of such a being, esp. in connection with the Jewish Ark or Temple.

che-ru-bic (chē-rōō′bĭk), *adj.* of or pertaining to cherubs; angelic.

cher-vo-netz (châr-vô′nĕts), *n.* [*pl.* chervontsi (-vônt′sĭ)], the monetary unit of Soviet Russia, normally worth ten gold rubles, or $5.14½; also, a gold coin worth one chervonetz. Also, **tcher-vo′netz.**

¹chess (chĕs), *n.* any of several pernicious weeds resembling oats and infesting wheat fields.

²chess (chĕs), *n.* a certain game played by two persons or sides, with sixteen variously shaped pieces, or men, to each side, on a checkered board divided into 64 squares. —*n.* **chess′board″.**—*n.* **chess′man.**

CHESSBOARD

The chessmen arranged as at beginning of game: left to right, top and bottom rows—queen's rook (or castle), queen's knight, queen's bishop, queen, king, king's bishop, king's knight, king's rook (or castle); other two rows, pawns.

chest (chĕst), *n.* **1,** a strong case; a box; **2,** the quantity such a box contains; **3,** a treasury or place for keeping a fund; also, the fund itself; **4,** the breast or thorax; **5,** a tight container for gas, steam, etc.

chest-nut (chĕs′nŭt), *n.* **1,** any of a genus of trees of the beech family, bearing nuts within a prickly bur; **2,** the nut; **3,** its light, coarse-grained timber; **4,** a reddish brown color; **5,** a horse of such color; **6,** *Slang,* an old or stale joke:—*adj.* **1,** reddish brown; **2,** made of wood of the chestnut: **horse-chestnut,** a shade tree bearing a nut somewhat similar to a chestnut but larger, formerly used as feed for horses.

che-val glass (shē-văl′), a framed mirror long enough to reflect the full-length figure.

chev-a-lier (shĕv″ȧ-lēr′), *n.* **1,** a knight; **2,** in France, a member of an order of merit; **3,** a gallant young man.

Chev-i-ot (chĕv′ĭ-ŭt; chē′vĭ-ŭt), *n.* a sheep bred on the Cheviot Hills between England and Scotland: **cheviot, 1,** a rough cloth made from the wool of this sheep; **2,** a similar fabric made of cotton.

chev-ron (shĕv′rŭn), *n.* **1,** a design on a coat of arms representing two rafters of a house meeting at the top; **2,** the badge on the coat sleeve of a military officer to show rank.

CHEVRON (def. 1)

chew (chōō; chū), *v.t.* to crush and grind with the teeth; hence, to meditate upon:—*v.i.* to bite repeatedly; hence, to reflect: with *on* or *upon:* **chewing gum,** a gumlike preparation sweetened and flavored for chewing:—*n.* **1,** the act of masticating, or chewing; **2,** that which can be chewed, as a cud or quid.

che-wink (chē-wĭngk′), *n.* a North American bird of the sparrow family: so called from its note.

Chey-enne (shī-ĕn′), *n.* one of a tribe of American Indians, orig. inhabiting the region of the Upper Arkansas River, now living in Oklahoma.

chi (kī), *n.* the 22d letter of the Greek alphabet [χ, Χ], nearly equivalent to English *kh,* but usually transliterated by *ch* and pronounced like *k,* as in *chaos.*

***chia-ro-scu-ro** (kyä″rō-skōō′rō), *n.* **1,** in art, the treatment of light and shade, as in a picture; also, a drawing in black and white; **2,** hence, variation; the use of contrast, as in literature. Also, ***chia′ro-o-scu′ro.**—*n.* **chia″ro-scu′rist.**

***chic** (shēk), [Fr.], *n. Colloq.,* **1,** Parisian elegance in dress; hence, smartness; style; **2,** cleverness; **3,** pertness:—*adj.* stylish.

chi-can-er-y (shĭ-kān′ẽr-ĭ), *n.* [*pl.* chicaneries (-ĭz)], **1.** trickery; **2,** shrewd or sharp dealing or practice.

chick (chĭk), *n.* **1,** the young of a bird, esp. of the hen; **2,** hence, a child.

chick-a-dee (chĭk′ȧ-dē″), *n.* any of various American titmice.

chick-en (chĭk′ĕn), *n.* **1,** the young of a fowl, esp. of the domestic fowl; **2,** *Colloq.,* a child or an inexperienced person.

chick-en–heart-ed (chĭk′ĕn-här″tĕd), *adj.* **1,** timid; **2,** cowardly; lacking courage.

chick-en pox a mild, infectious disease of children.

chick-weed (chĭk′wēd″), *n.* a common wild plant with white blossoms, the seeds of which are used as food for cage birds.

chic-o-ry (chĭk′ō-rĭ), *n.* a plant with bright blue flowers and a tapering root, which, when roasted and ground, is used in adulterating coffee.

chide (chīd), *v.t.* and *v.i.* [*p.t.* chid (chĭd), chid′ed, *p.p.* chid, chid′ed, chid′den (chĭd′n), *p.pr.* chid′ing], to find fault (with); scold.—*n.* **chid′er.**

Syn. blame, rebuke, censure, reprimand.

chief (chēf), *n.* **1**, a commander, leader, or principal person, as in an organization or group; **2**, the principal or most important part:—*adj.* principal; leading; main.

Syn., adj. principal, main. *Chief* indicates foremost or supreme; as, his *chief* interest in life; when used in connection with a title or position it indicates rank; as, *chief* justice; *chief* clerk. *Principal* indicates importance; as, the *principal* citizens; our *principal* motive. *Main* refers to superiority in size, quantity, or extent; as, the *main* building.

chief-ly (chēf′lĭ), *adv.* principally; for the most part; generally.

chief-tain (chēf′tĭn), *n.* a captain, leader, or commander; esp., the military or civil head of a clan or tribe.—*n.* **chief′tain-cy.**—*n.* **chief′tain-ship.**

chif-fon (shĭf′ŏn; *Fr.* shē″fôn′), *n.* a soft, thin, gauze fabric.

chif-fo-nier (shĭf″ō-nēr′), *n.* **1**, a high chest of drawers, usually with a mirror; **2**, an ornamental cabinet. Also, **chif″fon-nier′.**

chi-gnon (shē″nyôn′; shĭn′yŏn), *n.* a roll of hair worn by a woman at the back of the head.

chig-oe (chĭg′ō), *n.* **1**, (also, *chigre, chigger,* or *jigger*), a species of flea of the West Indies and South America, the female of which burrows beneath the human skin, causing a sore; **2**, a similar mite found in the southern U. S.; the jigger.

chil-blain (chĭl′blān″), *n.* soreness or inflammation caused by frost or cold, usually affecting the feet or hands.—*adj.* **chil′blained.**

child (chīld), *n.* [*pl.* children (chĭl′drĕn)], **1**, a son or daughter; offspring; **2**, a baby; **3**, a very young person; **4**, a descendant; as, a *child* of Abraham; **5**, anything regarded as offspring; as, a *child* of the desert; this book is the *child* of her brain.

child-birth (chīld′bûrth″), *n.* the act of bringing forth a child.

childe (chīld), *n. Archaic* or *Poetic*, a youth of noble parentage; also, a knight; as, "*Childe* Roland."

child-hood (chīld′ho͝od), *n.* **1**, the period from infancy to boyhood or girlhood; **2**, the state of being a child.

child-ish (chīld′ĭsh), *adj.* **1**, like a child; **2**, weak; foolish; as, a *childish* impulse in an adult.—*adv.* **child′ish-ly.**—*n.* **child′ish-ness.**

child-less (chīld′lĕs), *adj.* having no child; without a family.—*n.* **child′less-ness.**

child-like (chīld′līk″), *adj.* **1**, like, or belonging to, a child; **2**, becoming to a child; **3**, having the good qualities of a child; lovable; trustful.

Chil-e-an (chĭl′ē-ăn), *adj.* of or pertaining to Chile:—*n.* a native of Chile.

Chil-e salt-pe-ter (chĭl′ĭ; chē′lā), sodium nitrate, found native in Chile and largely used as a fertilizer and in manufacturing.

chil-i (chĭl′ĭ), *n.* [*pl.* chilies (-ĭz)], **1**, the red pod of certain peppers; **2**, any plant bearing such pods. Also, **chil′li.**

chill (chĭl), *n.* **1**, coldness; **2**, a sudden coldness of body with shivering; **3**, a restraint upon enthusiasm; discouragement:—*adj.* **1**, having a moderate degree of coldness; **2**, depressing; **3**, unfriendly; not cordial:—*v.t.* **1**, to make cold; **2**, to discourage; restrain; **3**, to cool suddenly, as molten iron:—*v.i.* **1**, to become cold; **2**, to take cold; **3**, to suffer with ague; **4**, to become hardened on the surface, as iron, by sudden cooling.

chill-y (chĭl′ĭ), *adj.* [*comp.* chill′i-er, *superl.* chill′i-est], **1**, unpleasantly cool; **2**, cool in manner; distant; formal.—*adv.* **chill′i-ly.**—*n.* **chill′i-ness.**

chime (chīm), *n.* **1**, the musical sound made by ringing a set of bells; **2**, a set of tuned bells struck with hammers to produce music; **3**, usually in *pl.*, the mechanism which causes the hammers to strike; **4**, harmony of sounds in general:—*v.i.* [*p.t.* and *p.p.* chimed (chīmd), *p.pr.* chim′ing], **1**, to sound in harmony; **2**, to agree; **3**, to recite in a singsong way:—*v.t.* **1**, to cause to sound in harmony; **2**, to play tunefully upon, as bells; **3**, to announce (the hour) by the ringing of bells; **4**, to recite together.

chi-me-ra (kĭ-mē′rȧ; kī-), *n.* **1**, (also, *Chimæra*), in mythology, a fearful monster which breathed out fire; **2**, a foolish creature of the imagination. Also, **chi-mæ′ra.**

chi-mer-i-cal (kĭ-mĕr′ĭ-kăl; kī-), *adj.* **1**, solely imaginary; fantastic; **2**, preposterous; incapable of becoming real; **3**, given to impossible or impracticable schemes. Also, **chi-mer′ic.**

chim-ney (chĭm′nĭ), *n.* [*pl.* chimneys (-nĭz)], **1**, the passage through which smoke, heated air, etc., escapes; **2**, a glass tube around the flame of a lamp; **3**, the part of a flue above a roof; **4**, a narrow crevice in a cliff, by which one may climb.

chim-ney sweep **1**, one who climbs up a chimney, to clean out the soot; **2**, an apparatus for cleaning a chimney.

chim-pan-zee (chĭm-păn′zē; chĭm″păn-zē′), *n.* a blackish brown ape of central Africa somewhat smaller than the gorilla.

Chimpanzee ($\frac{1}{30}$)

chin (chĭn), *n.* the part of the face below the under lip:—*v.t.* [*p.t.* and *p.p.* chinned (chĭnd), *p.pr.* chin′ning], to pull (oneself) up, while hanging by the hands from a horizontal bar, until one's chin is on a level with the bar.

chi-na (chī′nȧ), *n.* **1**, a fine kind of porcelain; **2**, any crockery; crockery dishes:—*adj.* pertaining to, or made of, porcelain.

chi-na-ware (chī′nȧ-wâr″), *n.* **1**, fine porcelain ware; **2**, dishes in general.

chinch (chĭnch), *n.* **1**, an insect that destroys grass, wheat, and other grains; **2**, a bedbug.

chin-chil-la (chĭn-chĭl′ȧ), *n.* **1**, a small, gnawing, South American animal with a soft, fine, gray fur; **2**, the fur of this animal; **3**, a heavy woolen cloth with curly nap.

Chinchilla ($\frac{1}{5}$)

chine (chīn), *n.* **1**, the backbone of an animal; **2**, a piece of the backbone of an animal with adjoining parts, cut for cooking; **3**, a sharp ridge:—*v.t.* [*p.t.* and *p.p.* chined (chīnd), *p.pr.* chin'ing], to break through the backbone of.

Chi-nese (chī-nēz'; chī-nēs'), *adj.* of or pertaining to China: **Chinese lantern**, an ornamental, collapsible paper lantern in bright colors:—*n.* **1**, [*pl.* Chinese], a native of China; a naturalized inhabitant; **2**, the language of the Chinese.

[1]**chink** (chĭngk), *n.* a narrow crack or opening; a gap:—*v.t.* **1**, to make fissures or cracks in; **2**, to fill the cracks of:—*v.i.* to open in cracks.—*adj.* **chink'y.**

[2]**chink** (chĭngk), *n.* a sharp, metallic, or jingling sound:—*v.t.* to cause to make a metallic sound:—*v.i.* to jingle; clink.

Chi-nook (chĭ-nōōk'), *n.* **1**, an American Indian of any of various northwestern tribes; **2**, a language combining French, English, and Indian.

chin-qua-pin (chĭng'kȧ-pĭn), *n.* **1**, a species of chestnut of the U. S., having a small, sweet, edible nut: also called *dwarf chestnut;* **2**, the nut of this tree; **3**, a related tree of California and Oregon, and its fruit. Also, **chin'ka-pin.**

chintz (chĭnts), *n.* a glazed cotton cloth, printed in various colors. Also, *Obs.*, **chints.**

chip (chĭp), *v.t.* [*p.t.* and *p.p.* chipped (chĭpt), *p.pr.* chip'ping], **1**, to form by cutting with an ax, chisel, etc.; **2**, to cut or break small pieces from:—*v.i.* to break off in small bits:—*n.* **1**, a small piece of stone, wood, etc., cut or broken off; **2**, wood, coarse straw, etc., split into thin strips and woven into hats, mats, etc.; **3**, anything worthless or trivial.

chip-munk (chĭp'mŭngk), *n.* any of several small, striped, squirrel-like animals. Also, **chip'muck.**

Chip-pen-dale (chĭp'ĕn-dāl), *adj.* designating, or pertaining to, a style of furniture made by Thomas Chippendale, an English cabinetmaker who died in 1779:—*n.* a piece of furniture in this style (see *furniture*, illus.).

chip-per (chĭp'ẽr), *adj. Colloq.*, lively; happy.

Chip-pe-wa (chĭp'ē-wä), *n.* one of a tribe of American Indians, orig. living near Lake Sŭperior: also called *Ojibwa.*

chi-rog-ra-phy (kī-rŏg'rȧ-fĭ), *n.* **1**, the art of writing; **2**, the style or character of handwriting.

chi-rop-o-dist (kī-rŏp'ō-dĭst), *n.* one who treats diseases of the feet or hands, esp. corns.—*n.* **chi-rop'o-dy.**

chi-ro-prac-tic (kī″rō-prăk'tĭk), *n.* a system of treatment of bodily disorders by means of manipulating the spine, without the use of drugs or surgery:—*adj.* pertaining to this method.—*n.* **chi″ro-prac'tor.**

chirp (chûrp), *n.* a short, cheerful note, as that of a bird:—*v.i.* **1**, to utter such a note; **2**, to talk merrily:—*v.t.* to utter with, or cheer up by, such a note.

chir-rup (chĭr'ŭp), *v.i.* **1**, to chirp repeatedly, as a cricket; **2**, to make a sound like a chirp:—*v.t.* **1**, to utter with a chirp; **2**, to encourage by such a sound:—*n.* the act or sound of chirping repeatedly.

chis-el (chĭz'ĕl), *n.* an iron or steel tool with a sharp, square end, for cutting wood, stone, or metal (see *tool*, illus.):—*v.t.* and *v.i.* to cut or engrave with such a tool.

chit (chĭt), *n.* **1**, a child; **2**, a pert, forward girl or young woman.

chit-chat (chĭt'chăt), *n.* chatter; prattle; gossip.

chi-tin (kī'tĭn), *n.* the horny substance that forms finger nails and toenails, and the principal part of the hard outer coat of insects, crustaceans, etc.—*adj.* **chi'tin-ous.**

chiv-al-ric (shĭv'ăl-rĭk), *adj.* knightly; of courteous spirit.

chiv-al-rous (shĭv'ăl-rŭs), *adj.* **1**, pertaining to chivalry; **2**, brave; gallant; courteous; as, a gentleman is expected to be *chivalrous* to a lady.—*adv.* **chiv'al-rous-ly.**

chiv-al-ry (shĭv'ăl-rĭ), *n.* **1**, the system of knighthood in the Middle Ages; **2**, the characteristics of a knight, as bravery, nobleness, courtesy, respect for women, etc.; **3**, a body of knights; **4**, the customs and practices of knighthood.

chive (chīv), *n.*, usually in *pl.*, a perennial herb allied to the onion.

chlo-ral (klō'răl), *n.* a colorless and oily liquid formed by the action of chlorine upon alcohol.

chlo-rate (klō'rāt), *n.* a salt of chloric acid.

chlo-ric (klō'rĭk), *adj.* pertaining to, or obtained from, chlorine.

chlo-ride (klō'rīd; klō'rĭd), *n.* a salt of hydrochloric acid: **chloride of lime**, a grayish white powder, used in bleaching and as a disinfectant. Also, **chlo'rid.**

chlo-rine (klō'rĭn; klō'rēn), *n.* a greenish yellow, heavy, highly poisonous gas, used commercially for bleaching and for disinfecting water supplies. Also, **chlo'rin.**

chlo-ro-form (klō'rō-fôrm), *n.* a colorless liquid with sweetish odor, used to make one unconscious of pain:—*v.t.* to give chloroform to.

chlo-ro-phyll (klō'rō-fĭl), *n.* the green coloring matter of plants. Also, **chlo'ro-phyl.**

chock (chŏk), *n.* **1**, a block or wedge to fill in a space so as to prevent motion; **2**, on a ship, a type of casting or wooden part for ropes or cables to run through:—*v.t.* to furnish, wedge, or make fast, with a chock:—*adv.* as tightly or closely as possible.

CHOCK

chock-a-block (chŏk'ȧ-blŏk″), *adj.* **1**, pulled up as high or as close as the blocks will allow: said of ropes or tackle; **2**, hence, as tight or as full as possible; crowded.

chock-full (chŏk'-fōōl″), *adj.* full to capacity; as full as possible. Also, **chuck'-full″.**

choc-o-late (chŏk'ō-lāt), *n.* **1**, a paste of the roasted kernels of the cacao nut; **2**, a beverage prepared from this:—*adj.* having the color of, made of, or flavored with, chocolate.

Choc-taw (chŏk'tô), *n.* **1**, one of a tribe of American Indians, orig. inhabiting the region between the Mobile and Mississippi Rivers in Alabama and Mississippi: now in Oklahoma; **2**, the language of these Indians.

choice (chois), *n.* **1**, the act of choosing; **2**, the thing or person chosen; **3**, the best or preferable part; **4**, a number large enough to choose from:—*adj.* **1**, select; carefully chosen; **2**, careful: with *of;* **3**, uncommon.—*adv.* **choice'ly.**—*n.* **choice'ness.**

choir (kwīr), *n.* **1**, a band of singers, esp. in a church; **2**, the place where they sing. Also, **quire.**

choke (chōk), *v.t.* [*p.t.* and *p.p.* choked (chōkt), *p.pr.* chok'ing], **1**, to stop the breath of by closing the windpipe; **2**, to stifle, strangle, or suffocate; **3**, to block up; clog; **4**, to suppress, as emotion: with *back:*—*v.i.* **1**, to become suffocated; **2**, to become clogged:—*n.* the act or sound of strangling, or of blocking up a passage: **choke**

valve, a valve in the carburetor of a gasoline engine, as in an automobile, which partly closes the air intake (see *carburetor*, illus.).

choke-ber-ry (chōk′bĕr-ĭ), *n.* [*pl.* chokeberries (-ĭz)], **1**, any of several species of North American shrubs of the rose family, cultivated for their showy flowers; **2**, the reddish or black berrylike fruit of any of these shrubs.

choke-cher-ry (chōk′chĕr″ĭ), *n.* [*pl.* chokecherries (-ĭz)], a North American wild cherry, or its fruit.

choke damp a heavy, highly poisonous gas, sometimes produced in wells, mines, and other pits: distinguished from *afterdamp*.

chok-y (chōk′ĭ), *adj.* [*comp.* chok′i-er, *superl.* chok′i-est], **1**, stifling; **2**, tending to strangle or choke, as through strong feeling. Also, **chok′ey**.

chol-er (kŏl′ẽr), *n.* anger; as, he was a man whose *choler* was quickly aroused.

chol-er-a (kŏl′ẽr-ȧ), *n.* a disease, usually fatal, accompanied by violent vomiting: **cholera infantum** (ĭn-făn′tŭm), a disease of infants, accompanied by vomiting and diarrhea: **cholera morbus** (môr′bŭs), an acute disease characterized by violent vomiting, cramps, purging, and prostration.

chol-er-ic (kŏl′ẽr-ĭk), *adj.* high-tempered; excitable.

choose (chōōz), *v.t.* [*p.t.* chose (chōz), *p.p.* chosen (chō′zn), *p.pr.* choos′ing], **1**, to select; **2**, to prefer; **3**, *Colloq.*, to wish; desire: with an infinitive; as, I *choose* to do it:—*v.i.* to make a choice.
Syn. (see elect).

[1]**chop** (chŏp), *v.t.* [*p.t.* and *p.p.* chopped (chŏpt), *p.pr.* chop′ping], **1**, to cut with repeated blows; **2**, to cut into very small pieces; **3**, to cut short, as words:—*v.i.* **1**, to make a quick stroke, as with an ax; **2**, to interrupt:—*n.* **1**, a piece chopped off; **2**, specif., a small piece of mutton, pork, etc., containing a rib or section of bone; **3**, a short, rough movement of the waves; **4**, grain coarsely ground.—*n.* **chop-per.**

[2]**chop** (chŏp), *v.i.* [*p.t.* and *p.p.* chopped (chŏpt), *p.pr.* chop′ping], to shift suddenly, as the wind.

[3]**chop** (chŏp), *n.* **1**, a jaw, as of an animal; **2**, in *pl.*, the mouth or the fleshy parts about it. Also, **chap**, *Pfd. S.*

chop-fall-en (chŏp′fôl″n), *adj.* dejected. Also, **chap′fall″en**, *Pfd. S.*

[1]**chop-py** (chŏp′ĭ), *adj.* [*comp.* chop′pi-er, *superl.* chop′pi-est], full of short, rough waves; as, a *choppy* sea.

[2]**chop-py** (chŏp′ĭ), *adj.* [*comp.* chop′pi-er, *superl.* chop′pi-est], changeable: said of the wind.

chop-sticks (chŏp′stĭks″), *n.pl.* two small sticks used in the East, esp. by the Chinese, instead of a fork.

chop su-ey (sōō′ĭ), a Chinese dish of stewed chicken or pork, vegetables, and seeds.

cho-ral (kō′răl), *adj.* **1**, of or pertaining to a choir; **2**, chanted or sung by a choir; as, a *choral* service.—*n.* **cho′ral-ist.**

[1]**chord** (kôrd), *n.* **1**, the string of a musical instrument; **2**, in mathematics, a straight line joining two points of a curve, esp. two points on the circumference of a circle; **3**, a principal horizontal member in the supporting framework of a bridge; **4**, a tendon, as in the body; **5**, the straight, front-to-back line from edge to edge of an airplane wing (see *airplane*, illus.).

[2]**chord** (kôrd), *n.* in music, a combination of tones sounded simultaneously and in harmony:—*v.t.* to tune; bring into harmony:—*v.i.* to be in harmony.

chore (chōr), *n.* **1**, a small job; **2**, in *pl.*, in the U. S. and provincial England, small or odd jobs; the daily light work of a farm or household.

cho-re-a (kō-rē′ȧ), *n.* a nervous disease; St. Vitus's dance.

cho-ric (kō′rĭk; kŏr′ĭk), *adj.* pertaining to, or like, a chorus.

chor-is-ter (kŏr′ĭs-tẽr), *n.* **1**, a member of a choir, esp. a male singer; **2**, in the U. S., a leader of a choir.

chor-tle (chôr′tl), *v.i.* and *v.t.* [*p.t.* and *p.p.* -tled (-tld), *p.pr.* -tling], to laugh in a chuckling, snorting fashion: a humorous word coined by Lewis Carroll, the author of "Alice in Wonderland."

cho-rus (kôr′ŭs), *n.* **1**, a number of persons singing together; **2**, that part of a musical composition in which the company all sing together; **3**, a piece of music arranged in parts; **4**, a refrain recurring at the end of each verse of a song; **5**, a band of singers and dancers in a Greek play:—*v.t.* and *v.i.* to sing or speak all together.—*n.* **cho′rist.**

chose (chōz), past tense of the verb *choose.*

cho-sen (chō′zn), *p.adj.* selected; picked out; as, a *chosen* few.

chough (chŭf), *n.* a crowlike, Old World bird having all black feathers and red bill and legs.

chow (chou), *n.* **1**, a breed of dogs in northern China, similar to a small Eskimo dog; **2**, *Slang*, food.

chow-chow (chou′chou″), *n.* a mixture; esp., chopped, mixed pickles and mustard, used as a relish.

chow-der (chou′dẽr), *n.* a dish made by stewing fish, shellfish, or certain vegetables, usually with milk; as, clam *chowder;* corn *chowder.*

chrism (krĭzm), *n.* oil blessed by the priest and used in baptism, confirmation, etc.—*adj.* **chris′mal.**

chris-om (krĭz′ŭm), *n.* **1**, consecrated oil; **2**, a white robe placed around a child during baptism.

Christ (krīst), *n.* **1**, the Messiah, whose coming was foretold by the Jewish prophets; **2**, a title of Jesus, as the fulfiller of this prophecy, but later considered as a part of his name, which is in full *Jesus Christ.*

chris-ten (krĭs′n), *v.t.* **1**, to baptize: used esp. of a child; **2**, to name at, or as at, the ceremony of baptism; as, to *christen* a ship "Providence."

Chris-ten-dom (krĭs′n-dŭm), *n.* **1**, that part of the world whose people are Christians; **2**, Christians collectively; the church.

Chris-tian (krĭs′chăn), *n.* **1**, a believer in the religion of Christ; a member of the Christian church; **2**, one considered as a believer in Christ, because of race or habits of life; hence, in America or western Europe, a civilized person:—*adj.* **1**, believing in, or practicing, the religion of Christ; **2**, pertaining to Christ or his teachings; **3**, showing Christlike qualities, as gentleness, humility, service, etc.; **4**, belonging to a race which is considered Christian.

Chris-ti-an-i-ty (krĭs″chĭ-ăn′ĭ-tĭ; krĭs-chăn′ĭ-tĭ), *n.* the religion or doctrines taught by Christ.

Chris-tian-ize (krĭs′chăn-īz), *v.t.* [*p.t.* and *p.p.* -ized (-īzd), *p.pr.* -iz″ing], to convert to Christianity; make Christian.—*n.* **Chris″tian-i-za′tion.**

Chris-tian Sci-ence a system of religious teaching and practice based on the Scriptures, which is applicable to the preservation and recovery of health, without resort to medical treatment: founded in 1866 by Mary Baker Eddy of New Hampshire.

Christ-mas (krĭs′mȧs), *n.* the festival (December 25) which celebrates the birth of Christ.

chro-mat-ic (krō-măt′ĭk), *adj.* pertaining to color: **chromatic scale**

Chromatic Scale, ascending and descending

in music, a scale in which the intervals are half steps: played by striking all the keys, white and black, in order, from any key on a piano to the key an octave above: **chromatics**, *n.pl.* used as *sing.* that branch of optics treating of colors.—*adv.* **chro-mat′i-cal-ly.**

chro-mi-um (krō′mĭ-ŭm), *n.* a metallic element of a grayish white color. Also, **chrome.**

chro-mo (krō′mō), *n.* [*pl.* chromos (-mōz)], a picture printed in colors.

chro-mo-sphere (krō′mō-sfēr), *n.* the luminous envelope of incandescent gases surrounding the sun: seen at times of a total eclipse.—*adj.* **chro″mo-spher′ic** (krō″mō-sfĕr′ĭk).

chron-ic (krŏn′ĭk), *adj.* **1,** continuing for a long time; **2,** of a disease, deep-rooted; lingering; **3,** habitual.

chron-i-cle (krŏn′ĭ-kl), *n.* a record of events in the order of their happening: **Chronicles,** either of two books of the Old Testament, following Kings:—*v.t.* [*p.t.* and *p.p.* -cled (-kld), *p.pr.* -cling], to enter, as in a record; as, history *chronicles* great events.—*n.* **chron′i-cler.**

Syn., n. annals, archives. (See history.)

chron-o-graph (krŏn′ō-grȧf), *n.* **1,** an instrument for marking very short intervals of time, as a stop watch; **2,** an instrument for recording graphically the time or duration of an act or occurrence.

Chronograph

chron-o-log-i-cal (krŏn″ō-lŏj′ĭ-kăl), *adj.* pertaining to, or containing an account of, past events in the order of time; as, in a history textbook, the events are arranged in *chronological* order.—*adv.* **chron″o-log′i-cal-ly.**

chro-nol-o-gy (krō-nŏl′ō-jĭ), *n.* [*pl.* chronologies (-jĭz)], **1,** the science that treats of events and arranges their dates in proper order; **2,** any system of arrangement according to time; **3,** a table or list of events given in proper order of time.—*n.* **chro-nol′o-gist.**

chro-nom-e-ter (krō-nŏm′ē-tēr), *n.* **1,** an instrument for measuring time; **2,** esp., a nautical timepiece so adjusted as not to be disturbed by temperature: used to determine longitude.

chrys-a-lis (krĭs′ȧ-lĭs), *n.* [*pl.* chrysalises (-lĭs-ĕz); chrysalides (krĭ-săl′ĭ-dēz)], **1,** the last stage through which an insect passes before it leaves its case in its perfect form; **2,** the case inclosing it during that stage; a cocoon. Also, **chrys′a-lid.**

chrys-an-the-mum (krĭs-ăn′thē-mŭm), *n.* **1,** a plant allied to the aster family, having large, showy flowers; **2,** a flower of this plant.

Chry-se-is (krī-sē′ĭs), *n.* in Homer's "Iliad," a beautiful captive in the Trojan War, whom Agamemnon was forced to restore to her father.

chrys-o-lite (krĭs′ō-līt), *n.* a green-colored mineral, which, when transparent, is often used as a gem.

chub (chŭb), *n.* any of various carplike, fresh-water fishes.

chub-by (chŭb′ĭ), *adj.* [*comp.* chub′bi-er, *superl.* chub′bi-est], short and plump; as, a *chubby* child.—*n.* **chub′bi-ness.**

¹chuck (chŭk), *v.i.* **1,** to cluck, as a hen; **2,** to make a sound like that of a hen, as in calling fowls or urging a horse:—*n.* the cluck of a hen.

²chuck (chŭk), *v.t.* **1,** to tap or pat in a playful manner; **2,** to fling away; throw; toss:—*n.* **1,** a light tap or pat; a light blow under the chin; **2,** a toss, or short, jerky throw.

³chuck (chŭk), *n.* **1,** a small pebble; **2,** in *pl., Scot.,* a game played with pebbles.

⁴chuck (chŭk), *n.* **1,** a contrivance for securely holding a tool or piece of work in a lathe or drill press; **2,** the part of a side of beef including some of the neck, the shoulder blade, and about three ribs: **chuck ribs,** the ribs of a beef included within the chuck (see *beef,* illus.).

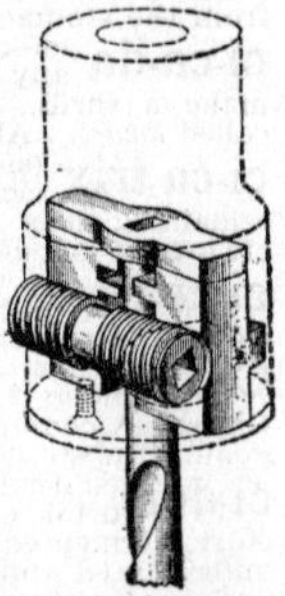

Drill Chuck

chuck-full (chŭk′=fōōl″), *adj.* as full as possible; full to capacity. Also, **chock′-full″**, *Pfd. S.*

chuck-le (chŭk′l), *n.* a quiet, suppressed laugh:—*v.i.* [*p.t.* and *p.p.* -led (-ld), *p.pr.* -ling], to laugh in a quiet, suppressed manner.

chum (chŭm), *n.* **1,** one who lodges in the same apartment; **2,** an old or intimate friend:—*v.i.* [*p.t.* and *p.p.* chummed (chŭmd), *p.pr.* chum′ming], **1,** to occupy the same room; **2,** to be intimately friendly.—*adj.* **chum′my.**

chump (chŭmp), *n.* **1,** a short, thick, heavy piece of wood; **2,** a thick end of meat; **3,** *Slang,* a fool; stupid person.

chunk (chŭngk), *n. Colloq.,* a short, thick person or thing.—*adj.* **chunk′y.**

church (chûrch), *n.* **1,** a building for public Christian worship; **2,** the entire body of Christians; **3,** (usually, *Church*), a particular body or division of Christians; a denomination; as, the Presbyterian *Church;* **4,** an organized body of Christians in a particular place; as, the *church* in Scotland; **5,** a single congregation; parish; **6,** the organized power of a religious body; as, *church* and state opposed each other; **7,** a regular service for Christian worship; as, to go to *church:* **Established Church,** a church authorized, and in part supported, by a state, as the Presbyterian Church in Scotland:—*adj.* pertaining to organized Christianity.—*adj.* **church′ly.**

church-man (chûrch′măn), *n.* [*pl.* churchmen (-mĕn)], **1,** a clergyman; **2,** a member of the church, esp. of an established church, as the Church of England.

church-ward-en (chûrch′wôr″dn), *n.* in the Protestant Episcopal Church, one of two laymen in a parish who look after church property and the poor.

church-yard (chûrch′yärd″), *n.* the ground around a church, esp. when used for burial.

churl (chûrl), *n.* **1**, formerly, a rustic or countryman; **2**, a surly, ill-bred person; **3**, a miser.

churl-ish (chûr′lĭsh), *adj.* **1**, ill-bred; **2**, miserly; **3**, hard to manage; stubborn.—*adv.* **churl′ish-ly.**—*n.* **churl′ish-ness.**

churn (chûrn), *n.* a vessel in which milk or cream is made into butter:—*v.t.* **1**, to make (butter) by violently stirring cream; **2**, to stir by violent motion:—*v.i.* **1**, to stir cream in making butter; **2**, to become a seething mass, as the sea.

chute (shōōt), *n.* **1**, a slanting trough for sending articles down; as, a coal *chute;* **2**, a river fall over which timber is floated; **3**, a toboggan slide:—*v.t.* [*p.t.* and *p.p.* chut′ed, *p.pr.* chut′ing], to send, as logs, down an inclined trough:—*v.i.* to descend.

chut-ney (chŭt′nĭ), *n.* an East Indian pickle composed of fruit, spices, etc. Also, **chut′nee.**

chyle (kīl), *n.* a milklike fluid composed of digested fat, absorbed by the lacteal vessels.—*adj.* **chy′lous.**

chyme (kīm), *n.* the pulpy mass of partly digested food before its passing from the stomach into the small intestine.

ci-ca-da (sĭ-kā′dȧ), *n.* [*pl.* cicadas (-dȧz)], any of a class of insects which make a shrill, chirping sound: commonly called *locust.* Also, **ci-ca′la** (sĭ-kä′lȧ).

ci-ca-trix (sĭ-kā′trĭks; sĭk′ȧ-trĭks), *n.* [*pl.* cicatrices (sĭk″ȧ-trī′sēz)], the scar remaining after a wound has healed. Also, **cic′a-trice** (sĭk′ȧ-trĭs).

ci-ce-ro-ne (chē″chā-rō′nā; sĭs″ē-rō′nē), [It.], *n.* [*pl.* ciceroni (-nē); cicerones (-nēz)], a guide; esp., an Italian guide.

Cid (sĭd; *Span.* thēth), *n.* **1**, a chief or commander; **2**, esp., the hero Ruy Diaz, the Christian champion against the Moors in Spain: the subject of Spanish chronicles, etc.

ci-der (sī′dẽr), *n.* apple juice: used as a drink or for making vinegar: **hard cider,** fermented apple juice: **sweet cider,** unfermented apple juice.

ci-gar (sĭ-gär′), *n.* a small roll of tobacco leaf, used for smoking.

cig-a-rette (sĭg″ȧ-rĕt′), *n.* a small roll made of finely cut tobacco for smoking, usually rolled in thin paper.

cil-i-a (sĭl′ĭ-ȧ), *n.pl.* **1**, the fringe of fine hairs on the eyelids; eyelashes; **2**, similar hairlike processes, as of a cell, or of certain plants.—*adj.* **cil′i-a-ry.**

cil-i-at-ed (sĭl′ĭ-āt″ĕd), *adj.* **1**, covered with cilia, or fine hairs; **2**, having hairlike organs, as certain cells. Also, **cil′i-ate.**

Cim-me-ri-an (sĭ-mē′rĭ-ăn), *adj.* **1**, belonging to the Cimmerii, a people mentioned by Homer as living in constant darkness; **2**, hence, very dark; gloomy.

cinch (sĭnch), *n.* *U. S. Colloq.*, **1**, a saddle girth firmly fastened in place by loops and knots; **2**, hence, a sure grip or hold; **3**, *Slang*, a sure or easy thing.

cin-cho-na (sĭn-kō′nȧ), *n.* **1**, any of a genus of evergreen trees of South America; **2**, the bark, a source of quinine.

cinc-ture (sĭngk′tŭr), *n.* **1**, the act of belting or surrounding; **2**, a belt or girdle worn round the waist; **3**, a raised or carved ring at the bottom and top of a pillar:—*v.t.* [*p.t.* and *p.p.* -tured (-tŭrd), *p.pr.* -turing], to surround with, or as with, a girdle.

cin-der (sĭn′dẽr), *n.* **1**, a live, smoldering coal; **2**, slag from a metal furnace; **3**, in *pl.*, *Colloq.*, ashes.—*adj.* **cin′der-y.**

Cin-der-el-la (sĭn″dẽr-ĕl′ȧ), *n.* **1**, in an old fairy tale, a maiden compelled to serve her stepsisters as a drudge until, aided by her fairy godmother, she marries a prince; **2**, hence, an unappreciated person; a household drudge.

cin-e (sĭn′ĭ), *n.* in the Philippines, a motion picture; movie; photoplay.

cin-e-ma (sĭn′ē-mȧ), *n.* chiefly *Br.*, **1**, a motion-picture theater; also, a photoplay; **2**, a motion-picture camera.

cin-e-mat-o-graph (sĭn″ē-măt′ō-gráf), *n.* **1**, an apparatus for showing a series of pictures so as to give the effect of motion; **2**, the camera which takes such pictures.

cin-e-ra-ri-um (sĭn″ē-rā′rĭ-ŭm), *n.* [*pl.* cineraria (-ȧ)], a place intended to receive the ashes of cremated bodies.—*adj.* **cin′er-a-ry.**

cin-na-bar (sĭn′ȧ-bär), *n.* a compound of sulphur with mercury, used as a pigment: usually called *vermilion.*

cin-na-mon (sĭn′ȧ-mŭn), *n.* **1**, the inner bark of any of several East Indian trees, from which a spice is made; **2**, any tree yielding this bark, as the cassia.

cinque-foil (sĭngk′foil″), *n.* **1**, a plant of the rose family, so called from its five-parted leaves; **2**, an ornament resembling five leaves.

ci-on (sī′ŏn), *n.* **1**, a shoot or bud of a plant, suitable for grafting; **2**, a descendant; child. See **sci′on,** *Pfd. S.*

ci-pher (sī′fẽr), *n.* **1**, in mathematics, zero; naught [symbol **0**]; **2**, hence, a person or thing without value or power; **3**, a secret manner of writing, or the key to it; a code; as, a cablegram sent in *cipher:*—*v.t.* and *v.i.* **1**, to work (arithmetical examples) with figures; **2**, to write with a private alphabet or other secret characters. Also, **cy′pher.**—*adj.* **ci′pher-a-ble.**

Cir-ce (sûr′sē), *n.* **1**, in Homer's "Odyssey," an enchantress who changed the companions of Odysseus into animals; **2**, hence, any enchantress.—*adj.* **Cir-ce′an.**

cir-cle (sûr′kl), *n.* **1**, a plane surface bounded by a single curved line called its circumference, every part of which is equally distant from a point within it, called the center; also, the closed plane curve bounding such a surface; **2**, any flat, round body; **3**, a number of persons or things united by a common bond; as, Goldsmith had a large *circle* of friends; **4**, something circular, as a group of seats in a theater:—*v.i.* [*p.t.* and *p.p.* -cled (-kld), *p.pr.* -cling], **1**, to move around; **2**, to revolve:—*v.t.* to surround.—*n.* **cir′cler.**

cir-clet (sûr′klĕt), *n.* **1**, a small circle; esp., a ring or bracelet; **2**, a circular band; esp., an ornament for the head.

cir-cuit (sûr′kĭt), *n.* **1**, the act of going around anything; **2**, the distance around anything; **3**, a space or district within certain boundaries, as that assigned to a judge; **4**, the route in such a district covered by a judge; **5**, a circular route passed over at regular intervals; **6**, the path of an electric current; **7**, a group of theaters under the same management; **8**, the district and route assigned to a Methodist preacher.

cir-cu-i-tous (sẽr-kū′ĭ-tŭs), *adj.* roundabout; indirect; as, to go by a *circuitous* route.—*adv.* **cir-cu′i-tous-ly.**

cir-cu-lar (sûr′kū-lȧr), *adj.* **1**, of, pertaining to, or like, a circle; **2**, moving in a circle; **3**, roundabout; **4**, published for distribution to a number of persons; as, a *circular* letter:—*n.* a letter or notice for general distribution.—*adv.* **cir′cu-lar-ly.**

cir-cu-lar-ize (sûr′kū-lȧr-īz), *v.t.* [*p.t.* and *p.p.* -ized (-īzd), *p.pr.* -iz″ing], **1**, to make round like a circle; **2**, to send printed circulars to.

cir-cu-late (sûr′kū-lāt), *v.t.* [*p.t.* and *p.p.* -lat″ed, *p.pr.* -lat″ing], to cause to pass from point to point or from one person to another:—*v.i.* **1**, to move around and return to the starting point; **2**, to pass from hand to hand; **3**, to be distributed, as a newspaper; **4**, to be diffused, as air in a room: **circulating decimal**, a repeating decimal, as 1.232323+.—*n.* **cir′cu-la″tor.**

cir-cu-la-tion (sûr″kū-lā′shŭn), *n.* **1**, the act of moving around, or of passing or sending from place to place; **2**, the extent to which a thing is distributed or sent; as, the magazine has a large *circulation;* **3**, movement in a circle around to the starting point; esp., the movement of the blood through the vessels of the body; **4**, the amount of currency, as coin, bills, etc., in actual use.

cir-cu-la-to-ry (sûr′kū-lȧ-tō-rĭ), *adj.* **1**, pertaining to circulation; **2**, circulating; going over a circuit.

cir-cum- (sûr′kŭm-), *prefix*, around; roundabout; as, *circum*navigate.

cir-cum-am-bi-ent (sûr″kŭm-ăm′bĭ-ĕnt), *adj.* inclosing; encompassing; surrounding.

cir-cum-am-bu-late (sûr″kŭm-ăm′bū-lāt), *v.t.* and *v.i.* [*p.t.* and *p.p.* -lat″ed, *p.pr.* -lat″ing], to walk about or around.

cir-cum-cise (sûr′kŭm-sīz), *v.t.* [*p.t.* and *p.p.* -cised (-sīzd), *p.pr.* -cis″ing], **1**, to cut off part or all of the foreskin of; **2**, in the Bible, to cleanse from sin.

cir-cum-ci-sion (sûr″kŭm-sĭzh′ŭn), *n.* **1**, the act of cutting off part or all of the prepuce, the initiatory rite practiced by the Jews, Mohammedans, and others; **2**, in the Bible, spiritual purification: **The Circumcision**, the Jews as a people.

cir-cum-fer-ence (sẽr-kŭm′fẽr-ĕns), *n.* **1**, the line that bounds a circle or any curved plane figure; **2**, the distance around a circular body; circuit.

cir-cum-flex (sûr′kŭm-flĕks), *n.* a mark [˜, ⌒, ˆ] over a vowel or syllable to denote accent, contraction, etc.:—*adj.* **1**, marked with such an accent; **2**, curved or bending round; as, a *circumflex* artery.

cir-cum-lo-cu-tion (sûr″kŭm-lō-kū′shŭn), *n.* **1**, the use of many words where but few are necessary; **2**, indirect or evasive expression.

cir-cum-nav-i-gate (sûr″kŭm-năv′ĭ-gāt), *v.t.* [*p.t.* and *p.p.* -gat″ed, *p.pr.* -gat″ing], to sail completely around, as the earth.—*n.* **cir″cum-nav′i-ga″tor.**—*n.* **cir″cum-nav″i-ga′tion.**

cir-cum-po-lar (sûr″kŭm-pō′lȧr), *adj.* near or about the north or the south pole; as, the *circumpolar* stars.

cir-cum-scribe (sûr″kŭm-skrīb′), *v.t.* [*p.t.* and *p.p.* -scribed′ (-skrībd′), *p.pr.* -scrib′ing], **1**, to inclose within certain lines or boundaries; **2**, hence, to restrict; as, to *circumscribe* the powers of a king; **3**, in geometry, to surround with a figure which touches at every possible point; as, to *circumscribe* a triangle with a circle.—*n.* **cir″cum-scrip′tion.**—*n.* **cir″cum-scrib′er.**

cir-cum-spect (sûr′kŭm-spĕkt), *adj.* cautious; prudent.—*adv.* **cir′cum-spect″ly.**—*n.* **cir′cum-spect″ness.**

cir-cum-spec-tion (sûr″kŭm-spĕk′shŭn), *n.* caution; watchfulness on every side; prudence.

cir-cum-stance (sûr′kŭm-stăns), *n.* **1**, something relative to a fact; an event, detail, or incident; as, an interesting *circumstance* in his life; **2**, a detail tending to prove something; **3**, a minor or unessential detail; **4**, full and particular detail; as, he wrote with *circumstance;* **5**, pomp; display; **6**, usually in *pl.*, state of affairs; material welfare: usually of a person:—*v.t.* [*p.t.* and *p.p.* -stanced (-stănst), *p.pr.* -stanc″ing], to place under limiting conditions.

cir-cum-stan-tial (sûr″kŭm-stăn′shăl), *adj.* **1**, pertaining to circumstances; **2**, presumptive; based on apparent facts; as, *circumstantial* evidence; **3**, detailed; **4**, pertaining to one's material welfare.—*adv.* **cir″cum-stan′tial-ly.**

cir-cum-stan-ti-ate (sûr″kŭm-stăn′shĭ-āt), *v.t.* [*p.t.* and *p.p.* -at″ed, *p.pr.* -at″ing], to prove; verify.

cir-cum-vent (sûr″kŭm-vĕnt′), *v.t.* **1**, to gain an advantage over by stratagem; **2**, to outwit; **3**, to go round.—*n.* **cir″cum-vent′er; cir″cum-ven′tor.**

cir-cum-ven-tion (sûr″kŭm-vĕn′shŭn), *n.* **1**, the act of gaining an advantage by deception or stratagem; **2**, a trick so used.

cir-cus (sûr′kŭs), *n.* [*pl.* circuses (-ĕz)], a large level space, usually within a tent, for feats of horsemanship and displays of skill, with seats for spectators arranged in rows, one above the other; also, the performance in such a space, and the company of performers of the feats.

cir-rho-sis (sĭ-rō′sĭs), *n.* a disease, as of the liver, resulting in an abnormal growth of hardened connective tissue.—*adj.* **cir-rhot′ic** (sĭ-rŏt′ĭk).

cir-ro–cu-mu-lus (sĭr″ō=kū′mū-lŭs), *n.* a cloud formation consisting of small, white, fleecy clouds at a high altitude, sometimes covering nearly the entire sky; mackerel sky.

cir-ro–stra-tus (sĭr″ō=strā′tŭs), *n.* a high, fairly uniform, horizontal sheet of cloud, having the delicacy of the cirrus cloud.

cir-rus (sĭr′ŭs), *n.* [*pl.* cirri (-ī)], a form of cloud spreading in filmy white wisps at a great height.

cis- (sĭs-), *prefix*, on this side; as, *cis*alpine: opp. of *trans-* or *ultra-*.

cis-al-pine (sĭs-ăl′pĭn; -pīn), *adj.* on this side of the Alps, from the point of view of Rome: opp. of *transalpine.*

Cis-ter-cian (sĭs-tûr′shăn), *n.* a monk belonging to a strict clerical order, founded at Cîteaux, in France, in 1098:—*adj.* pertaining to this order of monks.

cis-tern (sĭs′tẽrn), *n.* a pit or reservoir for storing water or other liquids.

cit-a-del (sĭt′ȧ-dĕl), *n.* **1**, a fortress, esp. one defending a city; **2**, any strongly fortified place; any refuge.

ci-ta-tion (sī-tā′shŭn), *n.* **1**, a summons to appear at a court of justice; **2**, the act of quoting, or a passage quoted, as from a book; **3**, mention; esp., in war, honorable mention in the dispatches for bravery.

cite (sīt), *v.t.* [*p.t.* and *p.p.* cit′ed, *p.pr.* cit′ing], **1**, to summon to appear in court; **2**, to quote; as, a minister *cites* as his text a passage from the Bible; **3**, to call to action; incite; **4**, to give honorable mention to, as for bravery in war.

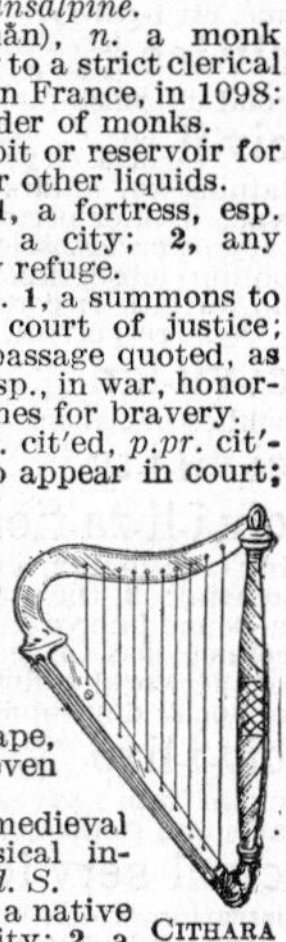
CITHARA

cith-a-ra (sĭth′ȧ-rȧ), *n.* the ancient Greek lyre, triangular in shape, with from seven to eleven strings. Also, **cith′er.**

cith-ern (sĭth′ẽrn), *n.* a medieval guitarlike musical instrument. See **cit′tern**, *Pfd. S.*

cit-i-zen (sĭt′ĭ-zĕn), *n.* **1**, a native of a town or city; **2**, a member of a state or nation who enjoys political rights and privileges, and gives in return his allegiance to the government; **3**, in a general sense, a permanent resident of a city or country; as, the *citizens* of New York; **4**, a civilian; one without military or public office; **5**, loosely, any inhabitant.—*n.* **cit'i-zen-ry.**

cit-i-zen-ship (sĭt'ĭ-zĕn-shĭp″), *n.* the status of a person who owes allegiance to the government in return for his political rights and privileges.

cit-rate (sĭt'rāt), *n.* a salt derived from citric acid; as, sodium *citrate.*

cit-ric (sĭt'rĭk), *adj.* pertaining to, or derived from, citrous fruits: **citric acid**, a sharply sour acid obtained from lemons and oranges.

cit-ron (sĭt'rŭn), *n.* **1**, a small Asiatic tree; **2**, its fruit, like the lemon, but larger and not so acid; **3**, the thick rind of this fruit, used in preserves, confections, etc.

cit-rous (sĭt'rŭs), *adj.* of or pertaining to a genus of trees (*Citrus*) which includes the orange, lemon, lime, citron, grapefruit, etc.: technically called *citrus.*

cit-tern (sĭt'ẽrn), *n.* a medieval guitar-like musical instrument with wire strings which were picked with a quill. Also, **cith'ern; zit'tern.**

cit-y (sĭt'ĭ), *n.* [*pl.* cities (-ĭz)], **1**, a large and important town; **2**, in the U. S. and Canada, a municipality having local self-government; **3**, the inhabitants of such a town collectively.

civ-et (sĭv'ĕt), *n.* **1**, any of various catlike animals; **2**, the fur of these animals; **3**, a thick substance, of a yellowish color and a musklike odor, secreted by these animals: used in perfumes.

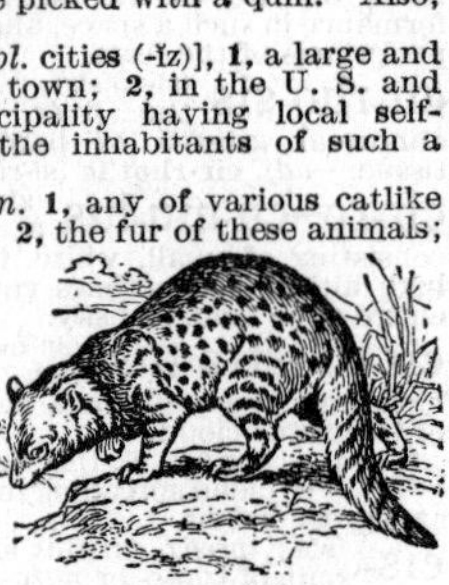

CIVET (1/15)

civ-ic (sĭv'ĭk), *adj.* of or pertaining to a city or citizenship; as, the founding of the city was celebrated by a great *civic* parade.—*adv.* **civ'i-cal-ly.**

civ-ics (sĭv'ĭks), *n.pl.* used as *sing.* the science of city government or of good citizenship.

civ-il (sĭv'ĭl), *adj.* **1**, pertaining to the affairs of a city; **2**, taking place in, or pertaining to, affairs within a nation; as, *civil* war; **3**, of or pertaining to civilians; not military or ecclesiastical; **4**, polite; often, barely polite; observing social etiquette, but with no warmth or cordiality.—*adv.* **civ'il-ly.**
Syn. respectful. (See polite.)

ci-vil-ian (sĭ-vĭl'yăn), *n.* one engaged in civil affairs or pursuits; not a soldier or sailor.

ci-vil-i-ty (sĭ-vĭl'ĭ-tĭ), *n.* [*pl.* civilities (-tĭz)], good breeding; courtesy.

civ-i-li-za-tion (sĭv″ĭ-lĭ-zā'shŭn), *n.* **1**, the act of making or becoming civilized; **2**, a state marked by progress in general; **3**, the state of being refined in manners and improved in arts and letters; culture; refinement; **4**, collectively, those countries of the world which have reached a high stage of social development.

civ-i-lize (sĭv'ĭ-līz), *v.t.* [*p.t.* and *p.p.* -lized (-līzd), *p.pr.* -liz″ing], **1**, to reclaim from a savage state; **2**, to instruct in the arts and refinements of civilized life.

civ-il serv-ice **1**, the departments of the government administration which are not naval, military, judiciary, or legislative; **2**, any government service in which office is secured through competitive public examination.

clab-ber (klăb'ẽr), *v.t.* and *v.i.* to curdle, as milk:—*n.* milk which has become thick by souring.

clack (klăk), *v.i.* **1**, to make a sudden, sharp sound; **2**, to chatter rapidly and continuously; **3**, to cackle, as a fowl:—*n.* **1**, a sudden, sharp sound; **2**, continual prattle.—*n.* **clack'er.**

clad (klăd), past tense and past participle of the verb *clothe:*—*p.adj.* dressed.

claim (klām), *v.t.* to demand as a right, or by authority:—*v.i.* **1**, to be entitled to anything; **2**, to make a claim or assertion:—*n.* **1**, a demand of a right; **2**, the asserting of a fact; **3**, the assertion of a right or title to anything; **4**, the thing demanded; esp., a piece of land which a miner marks out in accordance with mining law.—*adj.* **claim'a-ble.**—*n.* **claim'er.**
Syn., *v.* affirm, maintain, state. (See **assert.**)

claim-ant (klām'ănt), *n.* one who demands anything as his right.

clair-voy-ance (klâr-voi'ăns), *n.* **1**, the power claimed by some persons of seeing objects others cannot see, or of reading minds; **2**, unusual insight.

clair-voy-ant (klâr-voi'ănt), *n.* one who professes to have the power of clairvoyance; a medium:—*adj.* pertaining to clairvoyance.

clam (klăm), *n.* any of several varieties of edible shellfish:—*v.i.* [*p.t.* and *p.p.* clammed (klămd), *p.pr.* clam'ming], to dig for or gather this shellfish.

clam-ber (klăm'bẽr), *v.t.* and *v.i.* to ascend or climb with difficulty.

clam-my (klăm'ĭ), *adj.* [*comp.* clam'mi-er, *superl.* clam'mi-est], soft and sticky; cold and moist.—*adv.* **clam'mi-ly.**—*n.* **clam'mi-ness.**

clam-or (klăm'ẽr), *n.* **1**, a loud and continued outcry; **2**, a loud and persistent demand:—*v.t.* to shout with a loud voice:—*v.i.* to make noisy demands. Also, **clam'our.**—*n.* **clam'or-er.**
Syn., *n.* uproar, racket. (See noise.)

clam-or-ous (klăm'ẽr-ŭs), *adj.* noisy; as. a *clamorous* mob.—*adv.* **clam'or-ous-ly.**—*n.* **clam'or-ous-ness.**
Syn. uproarious, vociferous, obstreperous.

clamp (klămp), *n.* anything that fastens; specif., a piece of wood, metal, etc., used to bring two things together (see *tool*, illus.):—*v.t.* to fasten or bind with such a device.

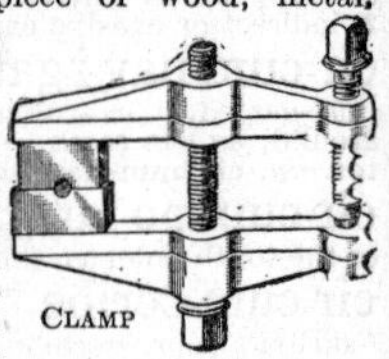

CLAMP

clan (klăn), *n.* **1**, a tribe or association of families united under one chieftain, claiming common ancestry and having the same surname; **2**, a group of persons descended from one ancestor; **3**, a set or clique.
Syn. party. (See caste.)

clan-des-tine (klăn-dĕs'tĭn), *adj.* secret; private; as, the early Christians held *clandestine* meetings in caves.—*adv.* **clan-des'tine-ly.**

clang (klăng), *n.* a loud, sharp, ringing, metallic sound:—*v.i.* and *v.t.* to give out, or cause to give out, such a sound.

clan-gor (klăng'gẽr; klăng'ẽr), *n.* a loud, metallic sound; clamorous noise:—*v.i.* to ring repeatedly and noisily.—*adj.* **clan'gor-ous.**—*adv.* **clan'gor-ous-ly.**

clank (klăngk), *n.* a sharp, harsh, brief, metallic sound:—*v.t.* and *v.i.* to rattle and sound, as chains.

clan-nish (klăn'ĭsh), *adj.* **1**, pertaining to a clan or family; **2**, exclusive;

3, prejudiced; narrow.—*adv.* **clan′nish-ly.**—*n.* **clan′nish-ness.**

clans-man (klănz′măn), *n.* [*pl.* clansmen (-mĕn)], **1**, a member of a clan; **2**, a member of the same clan.

clap (klăp), *v.t.* [*p.t.* and *p.p.* clapped (klăpt), *p.pr.* clap′ping], **1**, to strike together with a quick, sharp noise; **2**, to applaud by striking the hands together noisily; **3**, to put, place, etc., quickly and suddenly; **4**, to strike or slap suddenly:—*v.i.* **1**, to show approval by striking the hands together; **2**, to come together with a quick, sharp noise:—*n.* **1**, a loud noise made by a sudden collision; **2**, applause expressed by striking the hands together; **3**, a blow delivered with suddenness.

clap-board (klăp′bōrd; *Colloq.* klăb′ōrd; klăb′ẽrd), *n.* a long, thin, narrow board for the outside covering of wooden houses:—*v.t.* to cover with such boards.

clap-per (klăp′ẽr), *n.* one who or that which claps or makes a noise; esp., the tongue of a bell.

clap-trap (klăp′trăp″), *n.* any device, expression, trick, language, or show, intended to gain applause or attention.

claque (klȧk), *n.* **1**, an organized body of men paid to applaud at theaters; **2**, hence, a body of servile admirers.—*n.* **claq′uer** (klăk′ẽr).

clar-et (klăr′ĕt), *n.* **1**, the English name for a red table wine of France; **2**, hence, any similar wine; **3**, a deep, purplish red color:—*adj.* purplish red.

clar-i-fy (klăr′ĭ-fī), *v.t.* [*p.t.* and *p.p.* -fied (-fīd), *p.pr.* -fy″ing], **1**, to make clear or bright; **2**, to make intelligible:—*v.i.* to become clear, pure, or transparent.—*n.* **clar″i-fi-ca′tion.**—*n.* **clar′i-fi″er.**

clar-i-net (klăr′ĭ-nĕt″, klăr″ĭ-nĕt′), *n.* a mellow-toned, musical wind instrument (see *musical instrument*, illus.). Also, **clar′i-o-net″.**

CLARINET

clar-i-on (klăr′ĭ-ŭn), *n.* a small, high-pitched trumpet:—*adj.* trumpetlike; rousing.

clar-i-ty (klăr′ĭ-tĭ), *n.* clearness; as, the *clarity* of the air; the *clarity* of an explanation.

clash (klăsh), *v.i.* **1**, to make a loud, harsh noise by striking together; **2**, to be in opposition; disagree; as, their opinions *clash*:—*v.t.* to strike violently together:—*n.* **1**, the noise so produced; **2**, opposition; contradiction.

clasp (klȧsp), *v.t.* **1**, to shut or fasten together with, or as with, a hook or fastener; **2**, to embrace; **3**, to hold firmly:—*n.* **1**, a hook to hold anything close; **2**, a close embrace: **clasp knife**, a knife the blades of which fold into the handle.—*n.* **clasp′er.**

class (klȧs), *n.* **1**, a rank or order of persons having like interests, or of things which are similar; **2**, a number of students of the same rank or status; **3**, a division or grading on the basis of quality; as, the *classes* of passage on a steamer; **4**, a group of animals or plants between a phylum and an order; **5**, a number of objects, events, etc., having characteristics in common:—*v.t.* to arrange according to a system; classify.

Syn., *n.* (see caste).

clas-sic (klăs′ĭk), *n.* **1**, any book or work of art that is, or may properly be regarded as, a standard; **2**, esp., any Greek or Roman piece of literature or work of art; **3**, any author whose productions are of such excellence that they are regarded as standards: **the classics**, Greek and Latin:—*adj.* **1**, of or pertaining to the highest class or rank in literature or art; conforming to the highest standard; **2**, pertaining to, or like, the Greek or Roman authors; pure; refined; clear-cut; modeled after, or like, the highest forms of ancient art or literature. Also, *adj.* **clas′si-cal.**—*adv.* **clas′si-cal-ly.**

clas-si-cism (klăs′ĭ-sĭzm), *n.* **1**, agreement or adherence to classical style; **2**, the principles of the classic style, as representing dignity, elegance, proportion, and simplicity: opp. of *romanticism;* **3**, classical scholarship.—*n.* **clas′si-cist.**

clas-si-fi-ca-tion (klăs″ĭ-fĭ-kā′shŭn), *n.* the act or result of grouping according to some system.

clas-si-fy (klăs′ĭ-fī), *v.t.* [*p.t.* and *p.p.* -fied (-fīd), *p.pr.* -fy″ing], to arrange in groups according to a system; put in order; systematize.—*adj.* **clas′si-fi″a-ble.**

class-mate (klȧs′māt″), *n.* one belonging to the same class as another, as at college.

clat-ter (klăt′ẽr), *v.i.* **1**, to make a rattling sound; **2**, to talk idly and noisily:—*v.t.* to cause to make a rattling sound:—*n.* **1**, a confused noise; **2**, a rattling noise; **3**, idle gossip.—*n.* **clat′ter-er.**

clause (klôz), *n.* **1**, a separate part of a written composition or document; **2**, a division of a sentence containing a subject and predicate of its own.

claus-tral (klôs′trăl), *adj.* pertaining to, or confined in, a cloister.

clav-i-chord (klăv′ĭ-kôrd), *n.* a stringed instrument, forerunner of the piano and having a similar keyboard.

clav-i-cle (klăv′ĭ-kl), *n.* a bone which connects the sternum, or breastbone, and the shoulder blade; the collar bone.—*adj.* **cla-vic′u-lar.**

cla-vi-er (klā′vĭ-ẽr; klȧ-vēr′), *n.* **1**, the keyboard of an organ, piano, or similar instrument; **2**, any stringed instrument having a keyboard; **3**, an instrument for practice, producing no musical tone.

claw (klô), *n.* **1**, a sharp, hooked, horny nail in the foot of an animal or bird; **2**, the whole foot, as of a bird; **3**, anything sharp and hooked like a claw, as the curved end of some hammer heads (see *tool*, illus.); **4**, a pulling or scratching:—*v.t.* and *v.i.* to tear or scratch with, or as if with, claws.

clay (klā), *n.* **1**, soft, plastic earth, used in making pottery, bricks, etc.; **2**, the bodily or earthly nature of man.—*adj.* **clay′ey.**

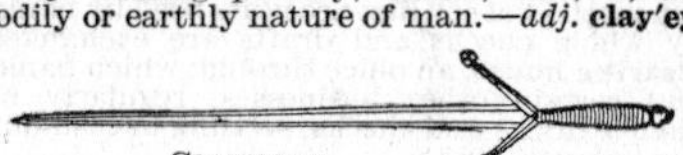

CLAYMORE

clay-more (klā′mōr″), *n.* a two-edged broadsword used by the Scottish Highlanders.

clay stone **1**, an irregular mass of limestone formed in a bed of clay; **2**, a variety of rock containing clay.

-cle (-kl), *n. suffix*, used to form diminutives; as, corpus*cle;* parti*cle*, etc.

clean (klēn), *adj.* **1**, free from dirt; **2**, unadulterated; **3**, free from imperfections; shapely; **4**, free from awkward bungling; **5**, free from defect or error; **6**, cleanly by habit; **7**, morally pure; honorable:—*adv.* wholly; without qualification or limitation:—*v.t.* **1**, to remove dirt from; **2**, to remove, as dirt, by cleaning.—*adv.* **¹clean′ly.**—*n.* **clean′ness.**

Syn., *adj.* cleanly. *Clean* describes a condition free from dirt, soil, or corruption. It is used in the moral as well as the physical sense; as, a *clean* heart. *Cleanly* describes a person who is habitually *clean* and neat.

clean-cut (klēn′=kŭt″), *adj.* well-shaped; definite; precise.

clean-er (klēn'ẽr), *n.* a person or thing that removes dirt, stains, etc.

²clean-ly (klĕn'lĭ), *adj.* [*comp.* clean'li-er, *superl.* clean'li-est], **1,** clean by habit; **2,** cleansing; freeing from dirt and stain.—*adv.* **clean'li-ly.**—*n.* **clean'li-ness.**

Syn. (see clean).

cleanse (klĕnz), *v.t.* [*p.t.* and *p.p.* cleansed (klĕnzd), *p.pr.* cleans'ing], **1,** to free from dirt; **2,** to free from guilt.—*n.* **cleans'er.**

clear (klēr), *adj.* **1,** easily visible; unclouded; undimmed; **2,** pure; unadulterated; **3,** unblemished, as a skin; **4,** untroubled; serene; as, a *clear* conscience; **5,** easily understood; plain; **6,** audible; distinct; as, a *clear* enunciation; **7,** having the power of keen perception; discerning; as, a *clear* mind; **8,** free or rid of responsibility; not hampered by debt; acquitted of blame, etc.; **9,** without further cost to be deducted; net; as, *clear* profit; **10,** certain; sure; **11,** unobstructed, as a view; freed from any obstruction, as land of stumps, etc.:—*v.t.* **1,** to make bright; make free from impurity or disorder; **2,** to free from obstruction; **3,** to remove, as an obstruction, a blemish, refuse, etc.; **4,** to make plain: usually followed by *up, of,* or *from;* as, to *clear* up a puzzling situation; **5,** to prove or declare innocent, as an accused person; **6,** to free from debt or other burden; **7,** to jump over or pass by without touching; as, the horse *cleared* the fence; **8,** to make beyond expenses; **9,** to put through the clearing house, as a check; **10,** to get or give clearance for (a vessel):—*v.i.* **1,** to become bright; become free from mist, etc.; as, the weather *clears;* **2,** to disappear, as mist; **3,** to take out clearance papers; also, to sail; **4,** to settle accounts, as through a clearing house.—*adv.* **clear'ly.**—*n.* **clear'ness.**

Syn., adj. bright, lucid, vivid.—*Ant., adj.* dull, opaque, obscure, vague.

clear-ance (klēr'ăns), *n.* **1,** the act of clearing; removal of obstruction; **2,** a legal certificate issued by a customhouse permitting a vessel to leave port.

clear–cut (klēr'-kŭt"), *adj.* **1,** having a sharp, clearly defined outline; clean-cut; **2,** concise.

clear-ing (klēr'ĭng), *n.* **1,** the act of removing obstructions from; **2,** a tract of land cleared of trees and underbrush; **3,** a method of settling accounts used by banks, by which checks and drafts are exchanged: **clearing house,** an office through which banks, and certain other businesses, regularly exchange drafts and checks, settling in cash only the balances due.

cleat (klēt), *n.* **1,** a piece of wood or iron on ships to keep the ropes from slipping; **2,** a strip of wood nailed across a board to give strength, hold in position, etc.:—*v.t.* to secure or strengthen by a cleat.

CLEAT

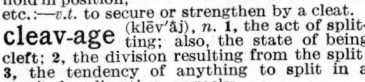

cleav-age (klēv'ăj), *n.* **1,** the act of splitting; also, the state of being cleft; **2,** the division resulting from the split; **3,** the tendency of anything to split in a particular direction, as rocks.

¹cleave (klēv), *v.i.* [*p.t.* cleaved (klēvd) or, *Archaic,* clave (klāv), *p.p.* cleaved, *p.pr.* cleav'ing], to adhere; stick; cling.

²cleave (klēv), *v.t.* [*p.t.* cleft (klĕft), cleaved (klēvd), *Rare,* clove (klōv), or, *Archaic,* clave (klāv), *p.p.* cleft, cleaved, clo'ven (klō'vn), or, *Archaic,* clove, *p.pr.* cleav'ing], **1,** to cut open; cut a way through; split; **2,** to sever; chop off:—*v.i.* to split, esp. along the grain.—*adj.* **cleav'a-ble.**

Syn. tear, rend, rip.

cleav-er (klēv'ẽr), *n.* **1,** a butcher's heavy hatchet; **2,** one who or that which splits.

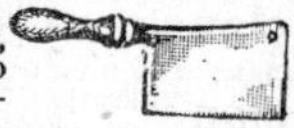

CLEAVER (def. 1)

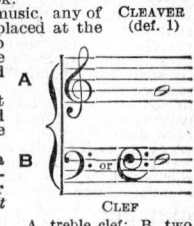

cleek (klēk), *n.* **1,** in golf, an iron-headed club of considerable driving power; **2,** a large iron hook.

clef (klĕf), *n.* in music, any of various signs placed at the beginning of a staff to show the pitch of the notes on each line and space of the staff.

A

B

CLEF

A, treble clef; B, two forms of bass clef.

¹cleft (klĕft), a past tense and past participle of the verb ²*cleave.*

²cleft (klĕft), *n.* a crack; crevice; as, the water trickled from a *cleft* in the rock above us.

clem-a-tis (klĕm'ȧ-tĭs), *n.* any of several plants of the crowfoot family, perennials with yellow, purple, or white flowers.

clem-en-cy (klĕm'ĕn-sĭ), *n.* [*pl.* clemencies (-sĭz)], **1,** compassion; mercy; **2,** applied to the weather, mildness.

clem-ent (klĕm'ĕnt), *adj.* **1,** forgiving; gentle; kind; **2,** of the weather, mild.—*adv.* **clem'ent-ly.**

clench (klĕnch), *v.i.* **1,** to set closely together, as the teeth; **2,** to clinch or settle, as an argument; **3,** (usually, *clinch*), to fasten, as a nail, by hammering down the point; **4,** to grasp firmly:—*n.* a thing that grips or catches.—*n.* **clench'er.**

clep-to-ma-ni-a (klĕp"tō-mā'nĭ-ȧ), *n.* an insane or uncontrollable desire to steal. Also, **klep"to-ma'ni-a,** *Pfd. S.*—*n.* **clep"to-ma'ni-ac.**

clere-sto-ry (klēr'stō"rĭ), *n.* [*pl.* clerestories (-rĭz)], **1,** the highest story of a church, above the aisle roof, having windows; **2,** a similar part, as in a railroad car. Also, **clear'sto"ry.**

cler-gy (klûr'jĭ), *n.* the whole body of men properly ordained as ministers in the Christian church.

cler-gy-man (klûr'jĭ-măn), *n.* [*pl.* clergymen (-mĕn)], a properly ordained minister or preacher.

cler-ic (klĕr'ĭk), *n.* a clergyman:—*adj.* clerical.

cler-i-cal (klĕr'ĭ-kăl), *adj.* **1,** pertaining to the clergy; **2,** pertaining to a clerk, writer, or copyist.—*adv.* **cler'i-cal-ly.**

clerk (klûrk; *Br.* klärk), *n.* **1,** an officer of a church parish with minor duties; **2,** an official who keeps records and does routine business; **3,** an employee in an office who assists generally; a typist; a secretary; **4,** a salesman or saleswoman.—*n.* **clerk'ship.**

clev-er (klĕv'ẽr), *adj.* **1,** skilful; **2,** mentally quick; **3,** ingenious.—*adv.* **clev'er-ly.**—*n.* **clev'er-ness.**

Syn. adroit, skilful, deft, expert. *Clever* describes one who or that which is quick, ready, and adaptable; it may imply physical or mental ability; as, a *clever* boxer; a *clever* remark. *Adroit* implies ability to handle a difficult or dangerous situation with cleverness or tact; as, an *adroit* speaker. *Skilful* implies knowledge or expertness, and is usually the result of practice and habit; as, a *skilful* designer. *Deft* describes persons or movements that are *skilful, clever,* and practiced; as, *deft* fingers. *Expert* suggests practice, skill, experience, and often, specialization; as, an *expert* radio operator.—*Ant.* awkward, clumsy, bungling, slow, stupid, dull.

clev-is (klĕv'ĭs), *n.* a U-shaped iron piece with a pin through the ends, at the end of the tongue of a plow, wagon, etc.

clew (klōō), *n.* **1,** a ball of thread, yarn, etc.; **2,** (usually, *clue*), a guide or key to the solution of a problem, plot, or mystery; **3,** a lower corner of a square sail, or the after corner of a fore-and-aft sail; also, a loop at the corner of a sail:—*v.t.* to haul (a sail) up, as for furling. Also, **clue.**

click (klĭk), *n.* **1,** a slight, sharp sound; **2,** a small bar or tooth acting as a catch by dropping into notches, as on a toothed wheel to prevent it from turning backward; a pawl, or ratchet:—*v.i.* and *v.t.* to make, or cause to make, a short, sharp noise.

cli-ent (klī'ĕnt), *n.* one who consults or employs a lawyer; hence, loosely, a customer or patron.

cli-en-tele (klī"ĕn-tĕl'; *Fr.* klē"äṅ-tâl'), *n.* the body of those who habitually seek a person for professional advice, or who patronize a certain theater, shop, etc.; clients collectively.

cliff (klĭf), *n.* a high, steep face of rock; a precipice: **cliff dweller,** a member of an aboriginal tribe who lived in the southwestern U. S. in dwellings built on the sides of cliffs.

cli-mac-ter-ic (klī-măk'tẽr-ĭk; klī"măk-tẽr'ĭk), *adj.* **1,** of or pertaining to a climax; climactic; **2,** marking, or marked by, a critical period of change:—*n.* any great change, as in physical development.

cli-mate (klī'mĭt), *n.* **1,** the atmospheric and weather conditions of a place, esp. as regards temperature, moisture, etc.; **2,** a place or region characterized by certain weather; clime.—*adj.* **cli-mat'ic.**

cli-max (klī'măks), *n.* **1,** a series of ideas or expressions increasing in force; also, the last of the series; **2,** hence, the highest point, as of excitement.—*adj.* **cli-mac'tic.**

climb (klīm), *v.t.* and *v.i.* **1,** to mount or ascend, as by the hands and feet; ascend with difficulty; **2,** to ascend by twining, as the tendrils of a vine:—*n.* the act of mounting; also, the ascent mounted.—*n.* **climb'er.**—*adj.* **climb'a-ble.**

clime (klīm), *n. Poetic,* a country; region; climate; as, in every *clime.*

clinch (klĭnch), *v.t.* **1,** to rivet; secure; **2,** (also, *clench*), to drive the point of (a nail) sidewise; **3,** to confirm or settle, as a bargain or an argument; **4,** to grasp tightly; **5,** to clench, as the teeth or fingers:—*v.i.* **1,** to fasten something by driving the point, as of a nail, sidewise; **2,** to grapple; hold on firmly:—*n.* **1,** the act of making a fastening on both sides of something; **2,** the fastening by which a tight hold is obtained; **3,** an unanswerable argument: **inside clinch,** a kind of knot (see *knot,* illus.).

cling (klĭng), *v.i.* [*p.t.* and *p.p.* clung (klŭng), *p.pr.* cling'ing], to adhere closely; stick; hold fast by embracing or entwining.

clin-ic (klĭn'ĭk), *n.* **1,** the treatment of patients before a class of students for the instruction of the class; **2,** the body of students itself; **3,** an institution devoted to the study, and often the free treatment, of patients.—*adj.* **clin'i-cal.**—*adv.* **clin'i-cal-ly.**

clink (klĭngk), *v.t.* to strike so as to make a slight, sharp sound:—*v.i.* to make a short, sharp noise:—*n.* **1,** a slight, sharp, tinkling noise; a jingle; **2,** the piercing note of certain birds.

clink-er (klĭngk'ẽr), *n.* a mass of partly burned coal formed into a hard, stony cake, as in a furnace; slag.

clink-er–built (klĭngk'ẽr=bĭlt"), *adj.* built with the outside planking overlapping from above downward, and clinched with nails, as some boats.

cli-nom-e-ter (klī-nŏm'ē-tẽr), *n.* an instrument for determining the dip, or angular inclination, as of a gun, the deck of a ship, etc.—*adj.* **cli"no-met'ric.**

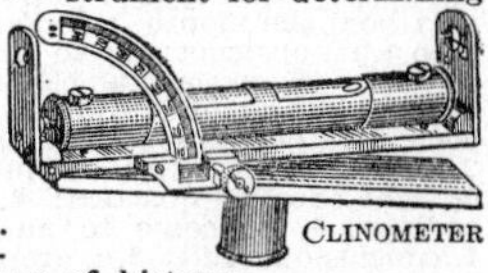
CLINOMETER

Cli-o (klī'ō), *n.* in mythology, the Muse of history.

¹**clip** (klĭp), *v.t.* [*p.t.* and *p.p.* clipped or clipt (klĭpt), *p.pr.* clip'ping], to clasp or hold tightly:—*n.* a clasp, as for holding papers; any device for gripping.—*n.* ¹**clip'per.**

²**clip** (klĭp), *v.t.* [*p.t.* and *p.p.* clipped or clipt (klĭpt), *p.pr.* clip'ping], **1,** to cut or trim with shears or scissors, as the hair, or wool from sheep; **2,** to pare the edge from, as a coin; **3,** to cut short; omit, as final letters, syllables, etc., from words:—*n.* **1,** the act of cutting off with, or as with, shears; **2,** the amount of wool obtained from a single shearing season.—*n.* ²**clip'per.**

³**clip** (klĭp), *v.i.* [*p.t.* and *p.p.* clipped (klĭpt), *p.pr.* clip'ping], *Colloq.,* to move swiftly:—*n.Colloq.,* a fast gait; as, at a good *clip.*

³**clip-per** (klĭp'ẽr), *n.* a vessel built with graceful lines, and rigged for fast sailing.

CLIPPER

clip-ping (klĭp'ĭng), *n.* **1,** the act of cutting; **2,** a piece cut off, as from a newspaper.

clique (klēk), *n.* a social set; an exclusive group.—*adj.* **cli'quish.**
Syn. (see caste).

cloak (klōk), *n.* **1,** a loose outer garment; **2,** hence, that which covers or conceals:—*v.t.* to conceal.

¹**clock** (klŏk), *n.* a mechanical device for keeping time, showing a moving pair of pointers, or hands, on a dial marked with the hours and minutes.

²**clock** (klŏk), *n.* a woven or embroidered ornament on the ankle of a sock or stocking.—*adj.* **clocked.**

clock-wise (klŏk'wīz"), *adj.* and *adv.* in the same direction as the motion of the hands of a clock.

clock-work (klŏk'wûrk"), *n.* **1,** the machinery of a clock; **2,** any mechanism resembling it.

clod (klŏd), *n.* **1,** a lump of earth, turf, or clay; **2,** the earth; **3,** anything material as opposed to soul; **4,** a part of the shoulder, as of a beef, used as meat (see *beef,* illus.); **5,** a stupid fellow.—*adj.* **clod'dy.**

clod-hop-per (klŏd'hŏp"ẽr), *n.* **1,** a rustic; a clown; **2,** in *pl.,* heavy shoes, such as are worn by a plowman.

clog (klŏg), *v.t.* [*p.t.* and *p.p.* clogged (klŏgd), *p.pr.* clog'ging], **1,** to hinder; **2,** to obstruct; **3,** to burden:—*v.i.* **1,** to be hindered; **2,** to stick together:—*n.* **1,** a load or weight; **2,** a kind of wooden shoe; **3,** a dance by one wearing such shoes.—*adj.* **clog'gy.**

clois-ter (klois'tẽr), *n.* **1,** a place of religious retirement; a monastery or nunnery; **2,** an arched way or covered walk inside the walls of a church building or college:—*v.t.* to confine in, or as in, a convent or place of retirement; seclude from the world.

clois-tral (klois'trăl), *adj.* pertaining to, or confined in, a cloister; retired; secluded.

[1]close (klōz), *v.t.* [*p.t.* and *p.p.* closed (klōzd), *p.pr.* clos′ing], **1,** to shut, as a box, the mouth, a knife, etc.; **2,** to fill; stop up; obstruct; **3,** to make contact between, as the parts of an electric circuit; join; **4,** to make an ending to; conclude:—*v.i.* **1,** to come together, as separated parts, as of a cut; **2,** to inclose; shut in; confine; **3,** to grapple or fight at close quarters; **4,** to come to an ending; **5,** to come to an agreement:—*n.* **1,** conclusion; end; **2,** a grapple.—*n.* **clos′er.**

Syn., v. end, conclude, finish, complete, terminate. To *end* is to bring or come to a final point; as, the story *ends* well. To *close* is to bring or come to an end by not continuing; as, he *closed* the letter; school *closed* for the summer. To *conclude* is to bring to a suitable or desirable point; as, we *concluded* our business. To *finish* is to arrive at the end of a thing; it implies the completion of a process; as, we *finished* our plans. To *complete* is to make a thing exactly what it should be; as, he *completed* his task. To *terminate* is to *end* because of the limitations of time or space; as, the dance *terminated* at twelve.

[2]close (klōs), *adj.* **1,** shut; closed; **2,** contracted; narrow; shut in; **3,** stifling; without ventilation; **4,** concealed; hidden; **5,** kept confined; guarded; **6,** inclined to secrecy; **7,** stingy; **8,** near in space, time, etc.; near in thought; coherent; as, *close* thinking; near in the sense of tight; as, *close* weaving; **9,** dear; familiar; **10,** almost equal; as, a *close* race or contest; **11,** fitting tightly or snugly, as a turban to the head; **12,** accurate; precise; as, a *close* copy; almost exactly like; as, a *close* resemblance; **13,** keen; sharply observant; as, *close* scrutiny; **14,** short, as hair cut near to the head; **15,** not open; not accessible; legally shut or restricted, as a season for hunting; admitting only a few, or certain qualified ones; as, a *close* corporation; **16,** of sounds, uttered with a relatively closed position of the speaking parts specially concerned, as the sounds *oo* and *ō*: opp. of *open*:—*adv.* **1,** near in space or time; as, follow *close* after me; **2,** tightly; closely together; **3,** watchfully; **4,** precisely.—*adv.* **close′ly.**—*n.* **close′ness.**

[3]close (klōs), *n.* any inclosed place, as a court; esp., the precinct of a cathedral or abbey.

closed shop a shop which excludes labor of any given kind, usually nonunion labor: opp. of *open shop.*

close-fist-ed (klōs′fĭs″tĕd), *adj.* stingy.—*n.* **close″fist′ed-ness.**

close–hauled (klōs′=hôld″), *adj.* sailing nearly into the wind.

close–mouthed (klōs′=mouthd″; klōs′=moutht″), *adj.* not given to talking; uncommunicative.

clos-et (klŏz′ĕt), *n.* **1,** a small room for privacy or retirement; **2,** a place for storing valuable things; **3,** a water-closet; **4,** the private council chamber of a ruler:—*adj.* **1,** private; secluded; **2,** adapted to seclusion; to be read rather than acted; as, a *closet* play:—*v.t.* to shut up, as in a private room.

clo-sure (klō′zhŭr), *n.* **1,** the act of shutting up; **2,** that which incloses; **3,** (also, *cloture; clôture*), a parliamentary proceeding by which a debate may be stopped, usually by the vote of more than the majority.

clot (klŏt), *v.i.* [*p.t.* and *p.p.* clot′ted, *p.pr.* clot′ting], to thicken, as blood:—*v.t.* to make, form into, or cover with, lumps of thickened fluid:—*n.* a thick, semisolid mass of coagulated fluid.—*adj.* **clot′ty; clot′ted.**

cloth (klôth), *n.* [*pl.* cloths (klôthz; klôths)], **1,** a woven fabric of wool, hair, etc.; **2,** a piece of such fabric; **3,** a woven covering; **4,** the usual dress of any profession, esp. the clerical: **the cloth,** the clerical profession.

clothe (klōth), *v.t.* [*p.t.* and *p.p.* clothed (klōthd) or clad (klăd), *p.pr.* cloth′ing], **1,** to dress; **2,** to cover with, or as with, a garment; **3,** to provide with garments.

clothes (klōthz), *n.pl.* **1,** covering for the body; **2,** coverings for beds.

clothes-press (klōthz′prĕs″), *n.* a wardrobe for wearing apparel.

cloth-ier (klōth′yẽr), *n.* one who makes, or deals in, cloth or clothing.

cloth-ing (klōth′ĭng), *n.* clothes; dress; garments in general.

Clo-tho (klō′thō), *n.* in mythology, the youngest of the three Fates, who spins the thread of life.

clo-ture (klō′tūr), *n.* stoppage of debate (see *closure*). Also, **clô″ture′** (klō″tür′).

cloud (kloud), *n.* **1,** a mass of condensed water floating in the air; **2,** a volume of smoke or dust; **3,** a dimmed appearance or spot, as in marble; **4,** anything threatening in aspect, or casting suspicion on one; **5,** anything that moves in a mass, as arrows, horsemen, etc.; **6,** a light woolen shawl:—*v.t.* **1,** to cover with a mist or cloud; **2,** to make gloomy; **3,** to blacken; sully;—*v.i.* **1,** to grow cloudy; **2,** to become downcast or discouraged.

cloud–burst (kloud′=bûrst″), *n.* an unusually violent downpour of rain, as if from a whole cloud at once.

cloud-less (kloud′lĕs), *adj.* clear; bright; unshadowed; not overcast.—*adv.* **cloud′less-ly.**—*n.* **cloud′less-ness.**

cloud-y (kloud′ĭ), *adj.* [*comp.* cloud′i-er, *superl.* cloud′i-est], **1,** pertaining to a cloud or clouds; **2,** overcast; threatening (rain); **3,** vague; obscure; **4,** not transparent; as, a *cloudy* liquid; **5,** gloomy.—*adv.* **cloud′i-ly.**—*n.* **cloud′i-ness.**

clout (klout), *n.* **1,** a piece of cloth; formerly, a rag; **2,** *Colloq.*, a blow on the head with the hand:—*v.i.* **1,** to patch or mend coarsely; **2,** *Colloq.*, to strike with the hand.

[1]clove (klōv), past tense and archaic past participle of [2]*cleave*: **clove hitch,** a kind of knot (see *knot*, illus.).

[2]clove (klōv), *n.* **1,** the dried flower bud of a tropical evergreen tree of the myrtle family: used as spice; **2,** the tree which produces these buds: **oil of cloves,** the oil extracted from cloves: used in medicine, perfumery, etc.: **clove pink,** a clove-scented variety of pink.

[3]clove (klōv), *n.* one of the bulbs of a compound bulb.

clo-ven (klō′vn), *p.adj.* divided into two parts; split; as, a *cloven* foot: **cloven–footed, 1,** having the foot deeply cleft, as the ox; **2,** devilish.

clo-ver (klō′vẽr), *n.* any of several low-growing plants, usually three-leaved, as the sweet clover, hop clover, white clover, etc. (see *shamrock*, illus.).

clown (kloun), *n.* **1,** a rustic; **2,** a man of coarse manners; boor; **3,** a professional jester; buffoon.

clown-ish (kloun′ĭsh), *adj.* like a clown; rude; coarse; awkward.—*adv.* **clown′ish-ly.**—*n.* **clown′ish-ness.**

cloy (kloi), *v.t.* to fill too full; surfeit, as the appetite.—*n.* **cloy′ment.**

Syn. (see satisfy).

club (klŭb), *n.* **1,** a heavy stick; **2,** one of the suits of playing cards; **3,** a number of persons associated for a common purpose or mutual benefit; **4,** a building or room occupied by such persons:—*v.t.* [*p.t.* and *p.p.* clubbed (klŭbd), *p.pr.* club′bing], **1,** to beat with a cudgel; **2,** to give to a common expense:—*v.i.* **1,** to combine for a common purpose; as, to *club* together to buy a football; **2,** to form a group united by a common interest.

Syn., n. (see caste).

club-foot (klŭb′fo͝ot″), *n.* [*pl.* clubfeet (-fēt″)], a foot deformed from birth.—*adj.* **club′foot″ed.**

cluck (klŭk), *n.* the call of a brooding hen to her chickens:—*v.t.* to call with a cluck:—*v.i.* to make such a call.

clue (klo͞o), *n.* **1,** (usually, *clew*), a ball of thread or yarn; **2,** (also, *clew*), anything that helps to solve a difficulty; a hint; a suggestion; **3,** (usually, *clew*), the lower corner of a sail.

clump (klŭmp), *n.* **1,** a cluster or group, as of trees; **2,** an extra thickness of sole:—*v.t.* **1,** to arrange in a cluster or group; **2,** to furnish (a shoe) with an extra sole:—*v.i.* to tread heavily.

clum-sy (klŭm′zĭ), *adj.* [*comp.* clum′si-er, *superl.* clum′si-est], **1,** awkward; heavy; unskilful; **2,** ill-made; **3,** lacking ease or grace; as, a *clumsy* boy; a *clumsy* action.—*adv.* **clum′si-ly.**—*n.* **clum′si-ness.**
Syn. (see awkward).

clung (klŭng), past tense and past participle of the verb *cling.*

clus-ter (klŭs′tẽr), *n.* **1,** a number of things, such as fruits, of the same kind growing or collected together; a bunch; **2,** a crowd:—*v.i.* to grow or gather in bunches:—*v.t.* to gather or collect into bunches.

[1]**clutch** (klŭch), *n.* a brood or set of eggs for hatching.

[2]**clutch** (klŭch), *v.t.* to grasp, seize, or grip strongly; as, to *clutch* a dagger:—*v.i.* to snatch or seize: with *at:*—*n.* **1,** a tight grasp; **2,** a talon or claw in the act of seizure; hence, often in *pl.*, a cruel grasp; as, keep out of his *clutches;* **3,** a device for gripping or holding, or, in an automobile, for coupling.

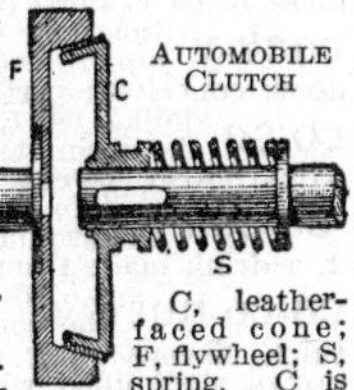

AUTOMOBILE CLUTCH
C, leather-faced cone; F, flywheel; S, spring. C is pressed by S into F, gearing with it by friction.

clut-ter (klŭt′ẽr), *n.* disorder; litter; confusion:—*v.t.* to heap up in disorder and confusion; disarrange.

Cly-tem-nes-tra (klī″tĕm-nĕs′trȧ), *n.* in mythology, the faithless wife of Agamemnon, slain by Orestes.

co- (kō-), *prefix*, a shortened form of *com-*, meaning joint, jointly; as, *co*heir; *co*öperate. See **com-.**

coach (kōch), *n.* **1,** a large, closed, four-wheeled carriage; also, a type of closed passenger automobile; **2,** a tutor, esp. one who prepares another for an examination or an athletic contest; **3,** a railroad passenger car:—*v.t.* to instruct:—*v.i.* to study or train with a tutor.—*n.* **coach′er.**

coach-man (kōch′măn), *n.* [*pl.* coachmen (-mĕn)], one who drives a coach or any carriage.

co-ad-ju-tor (kō″ă-jo͞o′tẽr), *n.* an official helper or assistant.

co-ag-u-late (kō-ăg′ū-lāt), *v.t.* and *v.i.* [*p.t.* and *p.p.* -lat″ed, *p.pr.* -lat″ing], to clot or curdle; thicken; congeal; solidify.—*n.* **co-ag′u-la″tor.**

co-ag-u-la-tion (kō-ăg″ū-lā′shŭn), *n.* **1,** the act of curdling or clotting; **2,** the change from a liquid to a thickened curdlike state, as in soured milk.

co-ag-u-la-tive (kō-ăg′ū-lā-tĭv), *adj.* tending to produce curdling or clotting.

coal (kōl), *n.* **1,** a black, or brownish black, hard, combustible mineral, formed from the vegetation of prehistoric times, taken from the earth and used as fuel; **2,** charcoal; **3,** a glowing bit; an ember: **coal gas,** gas produced by heating coal without air: used for heating and lighting: **coal oil, 1,** petroleum; **2,** any oil obtained from petroleum; esp., kerosene: **coal tar,** a thick, dark liquid obtained from soft coal, used in coating roads, making dyes, etc.:—*v.t.* to furnish with coal:—*v.i.* to take in coal.—*adj.* **coal′y.**—*n.* **coal′er.**

co-a-lesce (kō″ȧ-lĕs′), *v.i.* [*p.t.* and *p.p.* -lesced′ (-lĕst′), *p.pr.* -lesc′ing], to grow together; combine; blend; fuse.

co-a-les-cence (kō″ȧ-lĕs′ĕns), *n.* the act or process of uniting; blending.—*adj.* **co″a-les′cent.**

co-a-li-tion (kō″ȧ-lĭsh′ŭn), *n.* **1,** union in a body or mass; **2,** a temporary combination of persons or parties of opposing aims.

coal-pit (kōl′pĭt″), *n.* **1,** an excavation in the earth from which coal is dug; **2,** a pit in which charcoal is made.

coarse (kōrs), *adj.* **1,** of poor or inferior quality or appearance; **2,** large in texture or size; **3,** not refined; indelicate; gross.—*adv.* **coarse′ly.**—*n.* **coarse′ness.**
Syn. rude, rough, unpolished.—*Ant.* fine, polished, polite.

coars-en (kōr′sn), *v.t.* to make large, rough, or common:—*v.i.* to turn or become harsh, rude, rough, or unrefined.

coast (kōst), *n.* **1,** the land forming the margin or boundary of the sea; **2,** a slide downhill on a sled; **3,** a traveling by the force of gravity:—*v.i.* **1,** to sail along the shore; **2,** to descend by force of gravity, as a sled, bicycle, or airplane:—*v.t.* to sail close to or near to.—*adj.* **coast′al.**
Syn., n. edge, bank, shore. (See border.)

coast-er (kōs′tẽr), *n.* **1,** a vessel engaged in the coasting trade; **2,** one who descends by gravity on a sled, bicycle, etc.

coast guard a member of a crew organized to save life along a coast, or to protect the coast.

coast-ing trade the trade between ports of the same country; coastwise trade.

coast-wise (kōst′wīz″), *adv.* and *adj.* by way of, or along, the coast. Also, *adv.* **coast′ways″.**

coat (kōt), *n.* **1,** an outer, sleeved garment covering the upper part of the body; **2,** any outside covering, as fur, skin, rind, etc.:—*v.t.* to cover or spread over.—*n.* **coat′ing.**

coat of arms 1, orig., a light garment worn by English knights, often bearing the heraldic signs of the wearer's rank or family; **2,** a shield bearing such device or imprint; **3,** a similar shield bearing the insignia of a city, state, or nation; as, the *coat of arms* of the United States.

coat of mail a garment of chain mail or metal scales, formerly worn for protection.

coax (kōks), *v.t.* to wheedle; persuade by flattery:—*v.i.* to use gentle persuasion or flattery.—*n.* **coax′er.**—*adv.* **coax′ing-ly.**

cob (kŏb), *n.* **1,** a lump; a rounded mass; **2,** a corncob; **3.** a strong, thickset pony.

co-balt (kō′bôlt; -bŏlt), *n.* **1,** a steel-gray metallic element, similar to nickel; **2,** a deep blue pigment.—*adj.* **co-bal′tic.**

[1]**cob-ble** (kŏb′l), *n.* a round stone, worn smooth by water, esp. one of a size used for street paving; a cobblestone:—*v.t.* [*p.t.* and *p.p.* -bled (-ld), *p.pr.* -bling], to pave with cobblestones.

[2]**cob-ble** (kŏb′l), *v.t.* [*p.t.* and *p.p.* -bled (-ld), *p.pr.* -bling], to mend or patch up coarsely; repair, esp. shoes:—*v.i.* to work at the business of mending shoes.

cob-bler (kŏb′lẽr), *n.* **1,** one who mends boots and shoes; **2,** a clumsy workman; **3,** a cooling summer drink of iced wine, etc.; as, sherry *cobbler.*

cob-ble-stone (kŏb'l-stōn″), *n.* a rounded stone used for paving.

co-bra (kō'brȧ), *n.* a large, venomous snake of Asia, esp. India, which, when irritated, dilates its neck like a hood.

cob-web (kŏb'wĕb″), *n.* **1,** a spider's web; **2,** hence, a net or snare:—*adj.* made of, or like, a spider's web; flimsy; entangling.—*adj.* **cob'web″by.**

co-ca (kō'kȧ), *n.* a small South American shrub, the dried leaves of which yield a powerful narcotic drug.

co-ca-ine (kō'kȧ-ĭn; -ēn; commonly, kō-kān'), *n.* a powerful drug extracted from coca leaves: used as a local anæsthetic. Also, **co'ca-in.**

coc-cyx (kŏk'sĭks), *n.* [*pl.* coccyges (kŏk-sī'-jēz)], the last bone of the spinal column (see *pelvis,* illus.).

coch-i-neal (kŏch'ĭ-nēl), *n.* **1,** a scarlet dye obtained from the dried body of an insect; **2,** the insect itself.

coch-le-a (kŏk'lē-ȧ), *n.* [*pl.* cochleæ (-ē)], the spiral-shaped part of the inner ear, which contains the endings of the nerve of hearing.—*adj.* **coch'le-ar.**

¹cock (kŏk), *n.* **1,** the male of the common domestic fowl; a rooster; also, his crowing; **2,** any male bird; **3,** a weather vane in the shape of a rooster; **4,** a leader or chief; **5,** a turn valve, tap, faucet, etc.; **6,** the hammer of a firearm, or its position when raised: **cock-and-bull,** *adj. Colloq.,* ridiculous; extravagant: used of a story or an explanation.

²cock (kŏk), *n.* **1,** the act of tilting or turning up jauntily, as a hat or an eye; **2,** the upward turn or tilt so given:—*v.t.* **1,** to turn up or set jauntily on one side; tilt defiantly; **2,** to raise the hammer of (a gun), in readiness for firing.

³cock (kŏk), *n.* a small, cone-shaped pile, esp. of hay:—*v.t.* to stack in piles.

cock-ade (kŏk-ād'), *n.* **1,** a badge or rosette on the hat; **2,** an ornament, like a large button, on a bridle (see *harness,* illus.).

cock-a-too (kŏk″ȧ-tōō'), *n.* any of various white or brilliantly colored parrots, often with conspicuous crests.

cock-a-trice (kŏk'ȧ-trĭs; kŏk'ȧ-trīs), *n.* a fabulous monster said to have been hatched from a cock's egg, and able to kill by a glance of its eye.

cock-boat (kŏk'bōt″), *n.* a small rowboat; tender.

cock-chaf-er (kŏk'chăf″ĕr), *n.* a kind of beetle of America and Europe, destructive to vegetation.

cock-crow (kŏk'krō″), *n.* early morning, when the cock first crows. Also, **cock'crow″ing.**

cock-er (kŏk'ĕr), *n.* a spaniel used in hunting: also called *cocker spaniel.*

cock-er-el (kŏk'ĕr-ĕl), *n.* a young domestic cock less than a year old.

cock-eyed (kŏk'īd″), *adj.* having squinting eyes; hence, crooked.

cock-fight (kŏk'fīt″), *n.* a contest between cocks, esp. between cocks armed with spurs.—*n.* **cock'fight″ing.**

cock-horse (kŏk'hôrs'), *n.* a rocking-horse; hobbyhorse.

¹cock-le (kŏk'l), *n.* **1,** any of various mollusks, esp. an edible European species with two heart-shaped, fluted shells; **2,** one of its shells; **3,** a frail or shallow boat; **4,** in *pl.,* the innermost part of the heart; hence, feelings.

²cock-le (kŏk'l), *n.* any of several plants; esp., the corn cockle that grows as a weed among grain.

cock-loft (kŏk'lôft″), *n.* a loft or attic under a roof.

cock-ney (kŏk'nĭ), *n.* [*pl.* cockneys (-nĭz)], a Londoner: the name given to one born within sound of the bells of Bow Church, Cheapside; esp., an uneducated Londoner.—*adj.* **cock'ney-ish.**

cock-pit (kŏk'pĭt″), *n.* **1,** an inclosed space for cockfighting; **2,** in small vessels, a space aft lower than the deck; **3,** in men-of-war, the quarters of junior officers, used as a hospital during an action; **4,** in an airplane, the well in the body where the pilot's seat is placed (see *airplane,* illus.).

cock-roach (kŏk'rōch″), *n.* a black or brown beetlelike insect found in kitchens, pantries, etc.

cocks-comb (kŏks'kōm″), *n.* **1,** the comb or crest of a cock; **2,** (also, *coxcomb*), a garden plant of the amaranth family, with a crest-shaped, red or yellow flower; **3,** (usually, *coxcomb*), the red edge on a jester's cap; also, the cap; **4,** (usually, *coxcomb*), a conceited fellow; fop.

cock-sure (kŏk'shōōr″; kŏk″shōōr'), *adj.* **1,** absolutely certain or sure; **2,** *Colloq.,* too positive.—*n.* **cock″sure'ness.**

cock-swain (kŏk'swān; kŏk'sn), *n.* the steersman of a ship's boat, a racing shell, etc. See **cox'swain,** *Pfd. S.*

cock-tail (kŏk'tāl″), *n.* **1,** a mixed drink made of spirits, bitters, sugar, and flavoring; **2,** a tasty food served in a glass, often as a first course; as, oyster *cocktail.*

cock-y (kŏk'ĭ), *adj.* [*comp.* cock'i-er, *superl.* cock'i-est], *Colloq.,* impudent; conceited; pert.—*n.* **cock'i-ness.**

co-co (kō'kō), *n.* **1,** a palm which produces the coconut; **2,** the fruit of the coco palm. Also, **¹co'coa.**

²co-coa (kō'kō), *n.* **1,** a powder made from the ground seeds of the cacao tree; **2,** a drink made from the powder.

co-co-nut (kō'kō-nŭt″), *n.* **1,** the fruit of the coco palm, consisting of a thick, fibrous outer coat, and a hard, thin, brown shell lined with a white, meaty substance, and containing a milky liquid; **2,** loosely, the white meaty substance prepared for use as food. Also, **co'coa-nut″.**

co-coon (kō-kōōn'), *n.* **1,** the silky case spun by the larva of many insects, as the silkworm, as a protection while developing into the adult stage; **2,** any similar protective structure.

¹cod (kŏd), *n.* a husk or pod holding the seeds of a plant.

²cod (kŏd), *n.* a large, important food fish found in northern and temperate seas: **cod-liver oil,** an oil obtained from the liver of the cod, useful as a nutritive medicine.

cod-dle (kŏd'l), *v.t.* [*p.t.* and *p.p.* -dled (-ld), *p.pr.* -dling], **1,** to humor or pamper; treat tenderly; **2,** to stew gently; cook by allowing to stand in hot water, as eggs.

code (kōd), *n.* **1,** a body of laws or regulations arranged in a certain order; **2,** a system of military or naval signals; **3,** a system of symbols used for brevity or secrecy; as, the Morse *code;* **4,** a body of principles or standards pertaining to a special field; as, the social *code;* the *code* of honor.

co-dex (kō'dĕks), *n.* [*pl.* codices (kŏd'ĭ-sēz; kō'dĭ-sēz)], an ancient manuscript of a book, esp. of the Bible or the classics.

cod-fish (kŏd'fĭsh″), *n.* the cod, or its flesh served as food.

codg-er (kŏj'ĕr), *n.* **1,** a miser; **2,** an odd or testy old man.

cod-i-cil (kŏd'ĭ-sĭl), *n.* an addition; a supplement to a will.

co-di-fy (kō'dĭ-fī; kŏd'ĭ-fī), *v.t.* [*p.t.* and *p.p.* -fied (-fīd), *p.pr.* -fy″ing], to reduce to a system or code, as laws or regulations.—*n.* **co″di-fi-ca′tion.**

[1]**cod-ling** (kŏd′lĭng), *n.* the young of the cod, an important food fish.

[2]**cod-ling** (kŏd′lĭng), *n.* **1**, an inferior or unripe apple, fit only for stewing; **2**, a kind of apple, long and tapering: **codling moth,** a small moth whose larvæ damage apples, pears, etc. Also, **cod′lin.**

co-ed (kō′ĕd′), *n. U. S. Slang,* a young woman student of a school or college attended by both sexes. Also, **co′-ed′.**

co-ed-u-ca-tion (kō-ĕd″ū-kā′shŭn), *n.* the joint education of both sexes in the same school or college.—*adj.* **co-ed″u-ca′tion-al.**

co-ef-fi-cient (kō″ĕ-fĭsh′ĕnt), *adj.* coöperating:—*n.* **1**, any agent that coöperates or works with another agent; **2**, in mathematics, any symbol or group of symbols placed before another or others as a multiplier; as, in $3y$ the *coefficient* of y is 3.

cœ-no-bite (sē′nō-bīt; sĕn′ō-), *n.* a monk. See **cen′o-bite,** *Pfd. S.*

co-e-qual (kō-ē′kwăl), *adj.* of the same value or importance:—*n.* one of the same value or importance as another.

co-erce (kō-ûrs′), *v.t.* [*p.t.* and *p.p.* -erced′ (-ûrst′), *p.pr.* -erc′ing], to restrain or constrain by force, esp. legally or morally.

co-er-cion (kō-ûr′shŭn), *n.* the act of constraining forcibly; compulsion.—*adj.* **co-er′cive.**
Syn. force, constraint, violence.

co-e-val (kō-ē′văl), *adj.* of the same age or period; of the same duration.

co-ex-ist (kō″ĕg-zĭst′), *v.i.* to exist together in time or place.—*adj.* **co″ex-ist′ent.**—*n.* **co″ex-ist′ence.**

co-ex-tend (kō″ĕks-tĕnd′), *v.t.* and *v.i.* to reach, or cause to reach, the same limits through the same space, time, etc., as another.—*n.* **co″ex-ten′sion.**

co-ex-ten-sive (kō″ĕks-tĕn′sĭv), *adj.* having the same limits or extent of space, time, etc.

cof-fee (kôf′ĭ), *n.* **1**, the seeds of a tropical shrub, used, when roasted and ground, to make a well-known drink; **2**, the drink; **3**, the plant: **coffeehouse,** a house where coffee and other refreshments are sold: **coffeepot,** a covered utensil for making and serving coffee.

cof-fer (kôf′ĕr), *n.* **1**, a casket, chest, or trunk for the storage of valuables; **2**, usually in *pl.*, a treasury; funds; **3**, a caisson or floating dock.

cof-fer-dam (kôf′ĕr-dăm″), *n.* a watertight inclosure built under water and pumped dry, to protect workmen.

cof-fin (kôf′ĭn), *n.* a case or chest in which a corpse is placed for burial:—*v.t.* to inclose in a chest or coffin: **coffin bone,** the foot bone of a horse's foot, inclosed within the hoof.

cog (kŏg), *n.* **1**, the tooth of a gear wheel; **2**, a projection on a beam to be received in a notch on another to join the two together:—*v.t.* [*p.t.* and *p.p.* cogged (kŏgd), *p.pr.* cog′ging], **1**, to furnish with gear teeth; **2**, to join, as timbers, by a cog.

co-gent (kō′jĕnt), *adj.* having great force; convincing; as, a *cogent* reason.—*adv.* **co′gent-ly.**—*n.* **co′gen-cy.**

cog-i-tate (kŏj′ĭ-tāt), *v.i.* [*p.t.* and *p.p.* -tat″ed, *p.pr.* -tat″ing], to reflect:—*v.t.* to meditate upon; plan.—*adj.* **cog′i-ta-tive.**—*n.* **cog″i-ta′tion.**

co-gnac (kō′nyăk), *n.* a very fine French brandy.

cog-nate (kŏg′nāt), *adj.* **1**, related by blood; **2**, of the same, or allied, quality, as sciences; **3**, related in origin; as, *cognate* words or languages:—*n.* a person or thing that is akin to another by blood, derivation, etc.—*n.* **cog-na′tion.**

cog-ni-tion (kŏg-nĭsh′ŭn), *n.* **1**, the act, power, or faculty of knowing and perceiving; **2**, that which is known or perceived.—*adj.* **cog′ni-tive.**

cog-ni-za-ble (kŏg′nĭ-zȧ-bl; kŏn′ĭ-zȧ-bl), *adj.* capable of being known, perceived, or apprehended.

cog-ni-zance (kŏg′nĭ-zăns; kŏn′ĭ-), *n.* **1**, knowledge; apprehension; notice; **2**, range of observation; **3**, the right to exercise the legal power of a court; **4**, a hearing by a court; **5**, a badge, crest, or distinctive mark.

cog-ni-zant (kŏg′nĭ-zănt; kŏn′ĭ-zănt), *adj.* having knowledge (of anything); aware; as, *cognizant* of a situation.

cog-no-men (kŏg-nō′mĕn), *n.* [*pl.* cognomens (-mĕnz); cognomina (-nŏm′ĭ-nȧ)], a surname or family name.

cog-wheel (kŏg′hwēl″), *n.* a wheel with teeth notched in its rim.

co-hab-it (kō-hăb′ĭt), *v.i.* to live together as husband and wife.—*n.* **co-hab″i-ta′tion.**

co-heir (kō-âr′), *n.* a person who inherits jointly with another or others.—*n. fem.* **co-heir′ess.**

co-here (kō-hēr′), *v.i.* [*p.t.* and *p.p.* -hered′ (-hērd′), *p.pr.* -her′ing], **1**, to stick together; **2**, to be consistent, as an argument.

co-her-ence (kō-hēr′ĕns), *n.* **1**, the state or quality of being united; **2**, logical connection. Also, **co-her′en-cy.**

co-her-ent (kō-hēr′ĕnt), *adj.* **1**, sticking together; **2**, logically connected and developed; consistent; as, a *coherent* argument.—*adv.* **co-her′ent-ly.**

co-her-er (kō-hēr′ĕr), *n.* a device for detecting the signals used in wireless telegraphy.

co-he-sion (kō-hē′zhŭn), *n.* **1**, the force that unites particles of the same material; **2**, the act of uniting or sticking together; **3**, the state of being united.

co-he-sive (kō-hē′sĭv), *adj.* **1**, causing to unite or stick together; as, the *cohesive* force which holds a political party together; **2**, capable of sticking together.—*adv.* **co-he′sive-ly.**—*n.* **co-he′sive-ness.**

co-hort (kō′hôrt), *n.* **1**, in ancient Rome, a body of soldiers, the tenth part of a legion; **2**, any body of soldiers; **3**, a band of persons.

coif (koif), *n.* a small, tight-fitting cap:—*v.t.* to cover with, or as with, a coif.

coif-fure (kwȧ″für′; koif′ūr), [Fr.], *n.* **1**, a headdress; **2**, the manner of arranging the hair.

coign (koin), *n.* a projecting stone or angle; a corner: **coign of vantage,** an advantageous position. Also, **coigne; coin.**

coil (koil), *n.* **1**, a rope gathered into a ring; anything like it; a spiral; **2**, a series of connected pipes in windings, layers, etc.; **3**, a continuous spiral of conducting material, as wire:—*v.t.* to gather or wind into circles or spirals:—*v.i.* to wind in rings.

coin (koin), *n.* **1**, a piece of metal legally stamped to be used as money; **2**, coined money collectively; **3**, a corner or angle: also, *coign;* **4**, a wedge-shaped piece of wood or metal:—*v.t.* **1**, to make (coins) by stamping pieces of metal; **2**, to invent, as a new word:—*v.i.* to mint; make coins.

coin-age (koin′āj), *n.* **1**, the process of making pieces of money; **2**, the money made; **3**, the system of metal money used in a country; **4**, the cost of making metal money or the charge for making it; **5**, an invention.

co-in-cide (kō″ĭn-sīd′), *v.i.* [*p.t.* and *p.p.* -cid′ed, *p.pr.* -cid′ing], **1**, to correspond exactly; **2**, to occur at the same time, or be in the same space.

co-in-ci-dence (kō-ĭn′sĭ-dĕns), *n.* **1**, the condition of happening at the same time or occupying the same space; **2**, agreement; **3**, a striking, but apparently accidental, falling together of events.

co-in-ci-dent (kō-ĭn′sĭ-dĕnt), *adj.* exactly corresponding; agreeing, as in time, space, etc.—*adj.* **co-in″ci-den′tal.**

coin-er (koin′ẽr), *n.* one who stamps coins; esp., one who counterfeits money.

coir (koir), *n.* the fiber of coconut husk, used in making cordage, matting, etc.

co-i-tion (kō-ĭsh′ŭn), *n.* a coming together; specif., sexual intercourse.

coke (kōk), *n.* what remains of coal after the gases have been driven off by heating:—*v.t.* and *v.i.* [*p.t.* and *p.p.* coked (kōkt), *p.pr.* cok′ing], to change into coke.

col- (kŏl-) *prefix*, with: a form of *com-* used before *l-* as, *col*laborate. See **com-.**

col-an-der (kŭl′ăn-dẽr), *n.* a strainer; a vessel perforated so as to allow liquids to run through, as in washing vegetables.

col-chi-cum (kŏl′kĭ-kŭm; kŏl′chĭ-kŭm), *n.* **1**, the meadow saffron; **2**, a drug extracted from it.

cold (kōld), *adj.* **1**, producing or feeling chilliness; **2**, of low temperature; chilled; **3**, indifferent; **4**, unresponsive; **5**, not moved; as, the news left him *cold;* **6**, depressing; as, *cold* comfort; **7**, spiritless; dull; **8**, not fresh, as a scent in hunting:—*n.* **1**, a low temperature in one body as compared with another; **2**, the sensation produced by lack of heat; **3**, an inflammation of a mucous membrane, generally affecting the nose or throat. —*adv.* **cold′ly.**—*n.* **cold′ness.**

cold–blood-ed (kōld′-blŭd″ĕd), *adj.* **1**, having blood that takes its temperature from the surroundings: said of certain fishes, reptiles, etc.; **2**, feeling low temperature keenly because of poor circulation; **3**, unfeeling; heartless.

cold sore a fever blister; an eruption about the mouth, usually appearing during a cold or fever.

cold war an international situation in which, without recourse to armed conflict, and without severance of diplomatic relations, openly hostile nations contend for political advantage.

cole (kōl), *n.* any of various plants of the mustard family, as the cabbage.

col-e-op-ter (kŏl″ē-ŏp′tẽr), *n*, any of an order (*Coleoptera*) of insects, comprising the beetles, having a pair of inner, membranous wings, sheathed by a pair of outside, hardened wings.

cole-slaw (kōl′slô″), *n.* a salad of finely cut raw cabbage and dressing.

cole-wort (kōl′wûrt″), *n.* **1**, cole; **2**, a young cabbage; **3**, any cabbage not completely headed.

col-ic (kŏl′ĭk), *n.* a sharp, frequent pain in the abdomen or bowels:—*adj. Med.*, pertaining to the colon.—*adj.* **col′ick-y.**

Col-i-se-um (kŏl″ĭ-sē′ŭm), *n.* a great amphitheater in ancient Rome. See **Col″os-se′um.** *Pfd. S.*

col-lab-o-rate (kŏ-lăb′ō-rāt), *v.i.* [*p.t.* and *p.p.* -rat″ed, *p.pr.* -rat″ing], **1**, to work with another, or others, esp. in literary or scientific production; **2**, to co-operate with the enemy, esp. during enemy occupation.—*n.* **col-lab″o-ra′tion.**—*n.* **col-lab″o-ra′tion-ist.**—*n.* **col-lab′o-ra″tor.**

col-lapse (kŏ-lăps′), *n.* **1**, a falling in or together; **2**, sudden and complete failure; **3**, general prostration; as, the man's *collapse* was caused by overwork:—*v.i.* [*p.t.* and *p.p.* -lapsed′ (-lăpst′), *p.pr.* -laps′ing], **1**, to fall in or together; **2**, to fall completely and suddenly; **3**, to break down physically; **4**, to be brought down to a more compact form.—*adj.* **col-laps′i-ble.**

col-lar (kŏl′ȧr), *n.* **1**, something worn about the neck for use, restraint, or ornament; **2**, a ring around anything: **collar beam**, in a roof truss, a tiebeam connecting opposite rafters on a level above that of the wall plate (see *mansard*, illus.): **collar bone**, the clavicle:—*v.t.* **1**, to seize by the collar; **2**, to put a collar on.

col-late (kŏ-lāt′), *v.t.* [*p.t.* and *p.p.* -lat′ed, *p.pr.* -lat′ing], **1**, to compare critically, as texts; **2**, to examine, as the gathered sheets of a book, before binding.—*n.* **col-la′tor.**

col-lat-er-al (kŏ-lăt′ẽr-ăl), *adj.* **1**, side by side; parallel; **2**, confirming or supporting, as testimony; **3**, incidental; **4**, pertaining to something offered as security, in addition to one's personal obligation; **5**, descended from the same stock, but in a different line:—*n.* security additional to one's obligation.—*adv.* **col-lat′er-al-ly.**

col-la-tion (kŏ-lā′shŭn), *n.* **1**, the act of bringing together for comparison, as books, pages, etc.; **2**, a light meal.

col-league (kŏl′ēg), *n.* an associate in office, or in a profession.
Syn. (see ally).

[1]**col-lect** (kŏl′ĕkt), *n.* a short prayer regularly used as part of a service.

[2]**col-lect** (kŏ-lĕkt′), *v.t.* **1**, to gather together; **2**, to demand and obtain payment of; **3**, to make a hobby of collecting, as stamps; **4**, to regain control of (oneself):—*v.i.* **1**, to accumulate; **2**, to meet or assemble. —*adj.* **col-lect′i-ble; col-lect′a-ble.**

col-lect-ed (kŏ-lĕk′tĕd), *p.adj.* **1**, self-possessed; **2**, brought together. —*adv.* **col-lect′ed-ly.**—*n.* **col-lect′ed-ness.**

col-lec-tion (kŏ-lĕk′shŭn), *n.* **1**, the act of gathering together; **2**, a mass, as of dirt; **3**, an assemblage of works of art, or natural objects; as, there are many art *collections* in America; **4**, a contribution asked for; **5**, the act of receiving or enforcing payment; also, the amount thus secured.

col-lec-tive (kŏ-lĕk′tĭv), *adj.* **1**, making a group taken as a whole; **2**, having the power to bring together; **3**, belonging to a group of individuals; as, *collective* bargaining: **collective noun**, a noun used to name a group or collection, as *army, audience;*—*n.* **1**, a gathering; **2**, a collective noun. —*adv.* **col-lec′tive-ly.**

col-lec-tiv-ize (kŏ-lĕk′tĭv-īz), *v.t.* [*p.t.* and *p.p.* -ized (-īzd), *p.pr.* -iz″ing], to bring (an industry) or to bring the principal industries of (a country) under state control.—*n.* **col-lec′tiv-ism.**

col-lec-tor (kŏ-lĕk′tẽr), *n.* **1**, one who gathers things together, esp. objects of art or of general interest; **2**, an official who collects taxes, debts, or the like.

col-lege (kŏl′ĕj), *n.* **1**, a society of men possessing certain powers and rights, and engaged in some common pursuit; as, the *College* of Physicians; **2**, an educational institution which gives advanced courses; also, one of the separate schools in a university; **3**, a school for special instruction; as, a business *college;* **4**, the building or buildings of such an institution.—*adj.* **col-le′gi-ate.**

col-lide (kŏ-līd′), *v.i.* [*p.t.* and *p.p.* -lid′ed, *p.pr.* -lid′ing], to strike together with force; come into conflict; clash.

col-lie (kŏl′ĭ), *n.* a Scottish sheep dog, with a shaggy coat.

col-lier (kŏl′yẽr), *n.* **1**, a coal digger; **2**, a vessel in the coal trade.

col-lier-y (kŏl'yẽr-ĭ), *n.* [*pl.* collieries (-ĭz)], a coal mine and its surrounding buildings.

col-li-sion (kŏ-lĭzh'ŭn), *n.* the striking together violently of two bodies; concussion; clash; opposition.
Syn. contact, conflict, impact, encounter.

col-lo-cate (kŏl'ō-kāt), *v.t.* [*p.t.* and *p.p.* -cat″ed, *p.pr.* -cat″ing], to set or place side by side, or in relation; arrange.—*n.* **col″lo-ca'tion.**

col-lo-di-on (kŏ-lō'dĭ-ŭn), *n.* a substance made by dissolving guncotton in ether: used in photography, and in surgery as a coating for wounds.

col-loid (kŏl'oid), *adj.* like jelly:—*n.* in chemistry, a substance ordinarily regarded as insoluble, in the form of extremely minute particles which remain suspended indefinitely in a suitable medium; also, the jellylike substance separating from such a suspension upon cooling, evaporation, or the addition of salts.—*adj.* **col-loi'dal.**

col-lo-qui-al (kŏ-lō'kwĭ-ăl), *adj.* used in ordinary conversation; belonging to everyday speech; informal.—*adv.* **col-lo'qui-al-ly.**—*abbr.* **colloq.; coll.**

col-lo-qui-al-ism (kŏ-lō'kwĭ-ăl-ĭzm), *n.* a form of speech, familiar and informal rather than literary.

col-lo-quy (kŏl'ō-kwĭ), *n.* [*pl.* colloquies (-kwĭz)], conversation in the nature of a conference.

col-lude (kŏ-lūd'), *v.i.* [*p.t.* and *p.p.* -lud'ed, *p.pr.* -lud'ing], to conspire; work with others secretly, with evil intent.—*n.* **col-lud'er.**

col-lu-sion (kŏ-lū'zhŭn), *n.* secret agreement for an unlawful or evil purpose.—*adj.* **col-lu'sive.**—*adv.* **col-lu'sive-ly.**

co-logne (kŏ-lōn'), *n.* a perfume made of alcohol and fragrant oils.

¹co-lon (kō'lŏn), *n.* a mark of punctuation [:] indicating a nearly full stop.

²co-lon (kō'lŏn), *n.* the large intestine: in man about six feet long.

³co-lon (kō-lōn'), *n.* [*pl.* colons (-lōnz'); -lones (-lō'nās)], the monetary unit of Costa Rica or of Salvador, equivalent respectively to 46.53 cents or 50 cents.

colo-nel (kûr'nĕl), *n.* the chief officer of a regiment, between lieutenant colonel and brigadier general.—*n.* **colo'nel-cy.**

co-lo-ni-al (kō-lō'nĭ-ăl), *adj.* **1,** pertaining to a colony; specif., pertaining to the thirteen British colonies which later joined to form the United States of America; as, *colonial* rights or customs; **2,** in zoölogy, living together in a community or colony, as certain ants.—*n.* **co-lo'ni-al-ism.**

col-o-nist (kŏl'ō-nĭst), *n.* a member or inhabitant of a colony; a settler.

col-o-nize (kŏl'ō-nīz), *v.t.* [*p.t.* and *p.p.* -nized (-nīzd), *p.pr.* -niz″ing], **1,** to migrate to and settle in; **2,** to bring together in a colony:—*v.i.* to establish a colony.—*n.* **col″o-ni-za'tion.**

col-on-nade (kŏl″ō-nād'), *n.* a row or series of columns.

col-o-ny (kŏl'ō-nĭ), *n.* [*pl.* colonies (-nĭz)], **1,** a body of people who leave their native country and settle in another land, but remain subject to the mother country; **2,** the country thus settled; **3,** a group of people allied by race, interests, etc., living close together as in a colony, as artists; **4,** a number of animals of the same kind living as a community, as ants.

col-or (kŭl'ẽr), *n.* **1,** a property of light depending on its wave length, and causing the hues of the spectrum or rainbow; **2,** a paint; **3,** complexion, esp. a flush on the skin; **4,** a pretext; false show; **5,** character; tone; **6,** in *pl.:* **a,** a badge or ribbon; **b,** the flag of a nation, ship, etc.: **local color,** in literature, such use of detail as makes a story seem likely:—*v.t.* **1,** to give a color to; dye; **2,** to misrepresent; **3,** to lend a certain tone to, as a literary work:—*v.i.* to blush. Also, **col'our.**
Syn., n. shade, tint, hue. *Color* is the general term for that quality that makes the bands of the rainbow appear to the eye as violet, red, yellow, etc.; loosely, *color* also includes black and white. *Shade* refers to degree or intensity of a given *color;* as, pink is a pale *shade* of red. A faint *shade,* a delicate variety of *color,* is a *tint;* as, the shells were beautiful with rose and gray *tints. Hue* refers to that variation of *shade* resulting from slight alterations of a predominant *color;* as, green of a bluish *hue.*

col-or-a-ble (kŭl'ẽr-ȧ-bl), *adj.* **1,** capable of being colored; **2,** deceptive; plausible. Also, **col'our-a-ble.**

col-o-ra-do (kŏl″ō-rä'dō), *adj.* of medium strength: said of cigars.

Col-o-ra-do bee-tle a black-and-yellow striped beetle with red wings; the potato bug.

col-or blind-ness inability to perceive color or, usually, to distinguish between certain specified colors.—*adj.* **col'or–blind″.**

col-ored (kŭl'ẽrd), *p.adj.* **1,** having color; **2,** belonging to a dark-skinned race: applied to negroes or those of negro blood; **3,** exaggerated; heightened in interest by the addition of details; **4,** plausible. Also, **col'oured.**

col-or-ing (kŭl'ẽr-ĭng), *n.* **1,** the act, art, or style of applying or producing color; **2,** material producing color; **3,** appearance; esp., specious or false appearance. Also, **col'our-ing.**

col-or-ist (kŭl'ẽr-ĭst), *n.* one who paints in colors; esp., an artist whose work is notable for its color. Also, **col'our-ist.**

col-or-less (kŭl'ẽr-lĕs), *adj.* **1,** having no color; **2,** uninteresting; **3,** impartial; not biased. Also, **col'our-less.**—*adv.* **col'or-less-ly.**—*n.* **col'or-less-ness.**

co-los-sal (kō-lŏs'ăl), *adj.* huge; like a colossus.—*adv.* **co-los'sal-ly.**
Syn. immense, vast. (See enormous.)

Col-os-se-um (kŏl″ō-sē'ŭm), *n.* an amphitheater in ancient Rome built about A. D. 80 for gladiatorial and other spectacles (see *amphitheater,* illus.). Also, **Col″i-se'um.**

Co-los-si-an (kō-lŏsh'ĭ-ăn; kō-lŏsh'ăn), *n.* **1,** a native or inhabitant of Colossæ; **2,** in *pl.,* a book of the New Testament, containing the Epistle of the apostle Paul to the Christians at Colossæ.—*abbr.* **Col.**

co-los-sus (kō-lŏs'ŭs), *n.* [*pl.* colossuses (-ĕz); colossi (-ī)], **1,** a statue of great size; as, the *Colossus* of Rhodes; **2,** any very great person or object.

col-por-teur (kŏl'pōr″tẽr; *Fr.* kōl″pôr″tûr'), *n.* one who distributes Bibles, religious books, etc.—*n.* **col'por″tage.**

colt (kōlt), *n.* **1,** a young horse; **2,** an inexperienced youth; **3,** a frisky person.

col-ter (kōl'tẽr), *n.* a rolling disk or blade on a plow to cut ahead of the share. Also, **coul'ter.**

colt-ish (kōl'tĭsh), *adj.* like a colt; frisky; playful; gay.—*adv.* **colt'ish-ly.**—*n.* **colt'ish-ness.**

colts-foot (kōlts'fŏŏt″), *n.* a perennial herb with large leaves clustered at the ground, and with yellow flowers at the top of the flower stalk.

Co-lum-bi-an (kō-lŭm'bĭ-ăn), *adj.* of or pertaining to the United

States or to Christopher Columbus, the discoverer of America.

col-um-bine (kŏl′ŭm-bīn), *adj.* pertaining to, or like, a dove or pigeon:—*n.* a spring plant of the crowfoot family, with flowers having five deeply spurred petals, as the mountain columbine.

col-umn (kŏl′ŭm), *n.* **1**, a round pillar to support or adorn a building; **2**, a vertical division of the type on a printed page; **3**, in the army and navy, a formation of a body

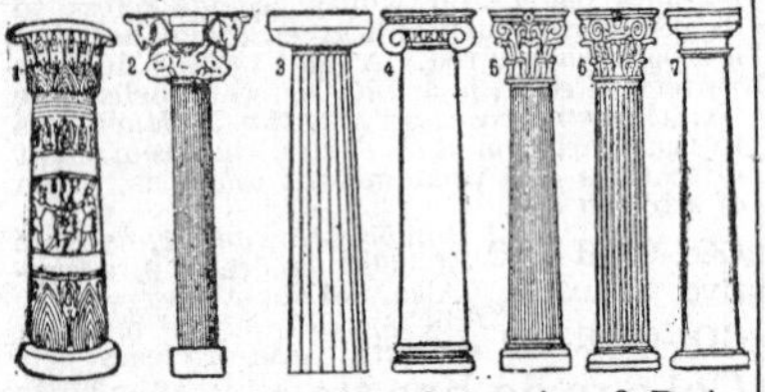

COLUMNS: 1, Egyptian; 2, Assyrian; 3, Doric; 4, Ionic; 5, Corinthian; 6, Composite; 7, Tuscan.

of troops or ships; **4**, anything suggestive of a pillar or shaft; as, a *column* of figures; the spinal *column.*—*adj.* **co-lum′nar** (kō-lŭm′nȧr). —*n.* **co-lum″ni-a′tion.**

col-um-nist (kŏl′ŭm-nĭst), *n.* one who writes a regular article, as in a newspaper, about a column long, composed of comments, contributions, poems, etc.

com- (kŏm-), *prefix,* [*com-* before *b, m, p,* and sometimes *f; col-* before *l; cor-* before *r; co-* before *h, w, gn,* or a vowel; *con-* before any consonant except *b, m, p, l, r, h, w*], **1**, to gether; as, *compose*; **2**, with; as, *compete*; **3**, completely; fully: an intensive; as, *compel.*

¹co-ma (kō′mȧ), *n.* [*pl.* comæ (-mē)], **1**, in a comet, the luminous, cloudy mass at the head; **2**, a silky tuft on some seeds.

²co-ma (kō′mȧ), *n.* profound and prolonged insensibility, due to disease, injury, or poison; stupor; lethargy.

Co-man-che (kō-măn′chē), *n.* one of a fierce predatory tribe of American Indians, orig. living in what is now northern Texas.

com-a-tose (kŏm′ȧ-tōs; kō′mȧ-tōs), *adj.* **1**, affected by, relating to, or in a state of, profound insensibility; **2**, lethargic; drowsy. Also, **com′a-tous** (-tŭs).—*adv.* **com′a-tose″ly.**—**com′a-tose″ness.**

comb (kōm), *n.* **1**, a toothed instrument to separate, adjust, or confine, the hair; also, a toothed ornament for the hair; **2**, the crest of a cock; **3**, the crest of a wave or hill; **4**, a honeycomb; **5**, a currycomb, used in grooming horses; **6**, an instrument for carding wool:—*v.t.* **1**, to dress (the hair) with a toothed instrument; **2**, to cleanse, as wool with a comb; **3**, to search through; investigate thoroughly:—*v.i.* to roll over and break into foam: said of the crest of a wave.

com-bat (kŏm′băt; kŭm′băt), *v.i.* to fight; contend; struggle:—*v.t.* to oppose; resist:—*n.* a struggle; fight.

Syn., n. strife, contest, conflict, battle.

com-bat-ant (kŏm′băt-ănt; kŭm′-), *n.* one who fights:—*adj.* **1**, disposed to fight; **2**, bearing arms; **3**, fighting.

com-ba-tive (kŏm′bȧ-tĭv; kŭm′-; kŏm-băt′ĭv), *adj.* pugnacious; showing a disposition to fight or oppose; as, the fox terrier has a *combative* disposition.—*adv.* **com′ba-tive-ly.**—*n.* **com′ba-tive-ness.**

comb–back (kōm′=băk″), *adj.* designating a kind of chair with vertical rods in the back (see *furniture,* illus.).

comb-er (kōm′ẽr), *n.* **1**, one that combs; **2**, a steep, curling wave.

com-bi-na-tion (kŏm″bĭ-nā′shŭn), *n.* **1**, the act of joining: the state of being united; as, a *combination* of ideas; **2**, the union of bodies or qualities; **3**, an association of persons for a common object; **4**, a suit of underwear; **5**, the series of motions which will unlock a keyless lock.

com-bine (kŏm-bīn′), *v.t.* [*p.t.* and *p.p.* -bined′ (-bīnd′), *p.pr.* -bin′ing], **1**, to unite or join; **2**, to link closely together:—*v.i.* to unite; agree; as, two political parties will *combine* to defeat a third party:—*n.* (often, kŏm′bīn), *Colloq.*, a joining together of persons or groups, sometimes for unlawful purposes.—*adj.* **com-bin′a-ble.**—*n.* **com-bin′er.**

Syn., v. join, unite, add, connect. *Join,* the general term, means to bring together into any degree of closeness. *Combine* may be used of dissimilar objects; as, the *combined* instruments produced harmony; or it may be used of things or people with similarity of purpose; as, to *combine* forces. To *unite* is to *join* things hitherto separate and distinct; as, the thirteen colonies were *united;* they *united* their efforts. To *add* is to put another part to what is already there, forming a unified whole; as, to *add* an ingredient. To *connect* is to tie together by some linking object or relationship; as, the rooms were *connected;* the families were *connected* by marriage.

com-bus-ti-ble (kŏm-bŭs′tĭ-bl), *adj.* capable of taking fire and burning; as, wood and coal are *combustible:*—*n.* any substance which may be burned.—*n.* **com-bus′ti-ble-ness.**—*n.* **com-bus″ti-bil′i-ty.**

com-bus-tion (kŏm-bŭs′chŭn), *n.* **1**, the act of burning; the state of being burned; **2**, in chemistry, the union of an inflammable substance with oxygen, producing light and heat.

come (kŭm), *v.i.* [*p.t.* came (kām), *p.p.* come, *p.pr.* com′ing], **1**, to move toward; draw near: opp. of *go;* **2**, to extend (to a given point); hence, to be equivalent; **3**, to become visible, audible, etc.; as, sounds *come* to the ear; **4**, to arrive; be present; **5**, to issue from or forth from, as from a source; **6**, to occur as a result; **7**, to approach in kind or quality; **8**, to happen.—*n.* **com′er.**

co-me-di-an (kō-mē′dĭ-ăn), *n.* **1**, a comic actor; **2**, a writer of comedy. —*n. fem.* ***co″mé″di-enne′** (kô″mā″dyĕn′).

com-e-dy (kŏm′ē-dĭ), *n.* [*pl.* comedies (-dĭz)], **1**, a humorous play or drama full of lively entertainment, and usually ending happily; **2**, any humorous incident; **3**, the art of writing, or acting in, comedy.

come-ly (kŭm′lĭ), *adj.* [*comp.* come′li-er, *superl.* come′li-est], **1**, graceful; handsome; as, a *comely* person; **2**, suitable; proper, as behavior.—*n.* **come′li-ness.**

Syn. (see beautiful).

co-mes-ti-ble (kō-mĕs′tĭ-bl), *n.* a thing to eat:—*adj.* edible.

com-et (kŏm′ĕt), *n.* a heavenly body moving about the sun and often having a long blazing train or tail.—*adj.* **com′et-a-ry.**

com-fit (kŭm′fĭt), *n.* a dried fruit preserved in sugar; sweetmeat.

com-fort (kŭm′fẽrt), *v.t.* to console; cheer; strengthen:—*n.* **1**, a state of well-being and quiet enjoyment; **2**, consolation; encouragement; **3**, a person or thing that brings ease, assistance, or consolation; **4**, a quilted cover for a bed.

com-fort-a-ble (kŭm′fẽr-tȧ-bl), *adj.* **1**, being at ease; **2**, enjoying contentment or freedom from care:—*n.* a padded quilt for beds.—*adv.* **com′fort-a-bly**

Syn., adj. snug, contented, satisfied.—*Ant., adj.* cheerless, discontented, wretched.

com-fort-er (kŭm′fĕr-tĕr), *n.* **1**, one who consoles or aids; **2**, a long and narrow woolen scarf; **3**, in the U. S., a quilted cover for the bed; a comfortable.

com-fort-less (kŭm′fĕrt-lĕs), *adj.* cheerless; unhappy; miserable.

com-ic (kŏm′ĭk), *adj.* **1**, pertaining to, or like, comedy; **2**, exciting mirth; droll; funny; comical:—*n.* in *pl.*, in a newspaper, cartoonlike pictures intended to amuse.

com-i-cal (kŏm′ĭ-kăl), *adj.* **1**, relating to comedy; **2**, comic; witty; droll; **3**, *Colloq.*, odd; queer.—*adv.* **com′i-cal-ly.**

com-ing (kŭm′ĭng), *n.* an arrival:—*p.adj.* expected; approaching; future.

com-i-ty (kŏm′ĭ-tĭ), *n.* [*pl.* comities (-tĭz)], civility; politeness; esp., acts of courtesy between nations.

com-ma (kŏm′ȧ), *n.* a punctuation mark [,] indicating a slight separation in ideas or construction.

com-mand (kŏ-månd′), *v.t.* **1**, to order or charge with authority; **2**, to control; exercise supreme authority over; lead; **3**, to overlook, as from a height; **4**, to exact; demand with authority; **5**, to be able to obtain:—*v.i.* **1**, to act as a leader; rule; **2**, to overlook:—*n.* **1**, authority; **2**, the act of commanding; **3**, an order or mandate; **4**, a dominating situation; **5**, a naval or military force under the command of a certain officer.

com-man-dant (kŏm″ȧn-dănt′; -dänt′), *n.* an officer in command of a fortified place or a body of troops.

com-man-deer (kŏm″ȧn-dēr′), *v.t.* **1**, to compel to military service; **2**, to take forcibly for military purposes; **3**, *Colloq.*, to seize for personal use.

com-mand-er (kŏ-mån′dĕr), *n.* **1**, one who is a leader; **2**, a military chief or leader; also, the chief officer in various orders; **3**, a naval officer ranking next below a captain.

com-mand-ing (kŏ-månd′ĭng), *p.adj.* impressive; qualified to take charge.—*adv.* **com-mand′ing-ly.**

com-mand-ment (kŏ-månd′mĕnt), *n.* a mandate or order; a precept; law; esp., any one of the Ten Commandments, or Decalog.

com-mem-o-rate (kŏ-mĕm′ō-rāt), *v.t.* [*p.t.* and *p.p.* -rat″ed, *p.pr.* -rat″ing], **1**, to call to remembrance by a solemn act; **2**, to keep alive the remembrance of.—*n.* **com-mem″o-ra′tion.**

Syn. observe, signalize. (See celebrate.)

com-mem-o-ra-tive (kŏ-mĕm′ō-rā-tĭv), *adj.* preserving, or intended to preserve, in memory.

com-mence (kŏ-mĕns′), *v.i.* [*p.t.* and *p.p.* -menced′ (-mĕnst′), *p.pr.* -menc′ing], to come into existence; begin:—*v.t.* to enter upon; perform the first act of.

Syn. start, originate. (See begin.)

com-mence-ment (kŏ-mĕns′mĕnt), *n.* **1**, beginning; origin; **2**, the exercises at which degrees or diplomas are conferred at schools and colleges.

com-mend (kŏ-mĕnd′), *v.t.* **1**, to recommend as worthy of notice; **2**, to praise; **3**, to intrust; **4**, to give the regards of; convey the greetings of.—*adj.* **com-mend′a-ble.**—*adv.* **com-mend′a-bly.**

com-men-da-tion (kŏm″ĕn-dā′shŭn), *n.* **1**, the act of praising; **2**, a reason for approval.

com-mend-a-to-ry (kŏ-mĕn′dȧ-tō-rĭ), *adj.* **1**, serving to present for favorable consideration; **2**, containing praise or approval.

com-men-su-ra-ble (kŏ-mĕn′shōō-rȧ-bl), *adj.* **1**, having, or reducible to, a common measure; as, a yard and a foot are *commensurable;* **2**, comparable by a common standard.—*adv.* **com-men′su-ra-bly.**—*n.* **com-men″su-ra-bil′i-ty.**

com-men-su-rate (kŏ-mĕn′shōō-rāt), *adj.* **1**, reducible to a common measure; **2**, equal; adequate; corresponding in amount; as, our fortunes are often not *commensurate* with our desires:—*v.t.* (kŏ-mĕn′shōō-rāt), [*p.t.* and *p.p.* -rat″ed, *p.pr.* -rat″ing], to reduce to a common measure.—*adv.* **com-men′su-rate-ly.**

com-ment (kŏm′ĕnt), *n.* **1**, a spoken or written remark; esp., a written note by way of explanation, illustration, or criticism; **2**, talk; gossip:—*v.i.* (kŏm′ĕnt; kŏ-mĕnt′), **1**, to write notes of explanation, illustration, or criticism upon the text of an author; **2**, to make observations: with *upon.*—*n.* **com′ment-er.**

com-men-ta-ry (kŏm′ĕn-tā-rĭ), *n.* [*pl.* commentaries (-rĭz)], **1**, an explanation; **2**, a series of explanatory notes, as on passages in the Bible; **3**, an explanatory narrative; as, Cæsar's *Commentaries.*

com-men-ta-tor (kŏm′ĕn-tā″tĕr), *n.* one who writes notes to explain a writing, book, etc.

com-merce (kŏm′ĕrs), *n.* **1**, business intercourse; esp., interchange of merchandise on a large scale; trade; **2**, social intercourse; fellowship.

Syn. (see business).

com-mer-cial (kŏ-mûr′shăl), *adj.* **1**, engaged in, or pertaining to, trade or business; mercantile; **2**, prepared for sale in the market; as, *commercial* soda: **commercial paper**, notes, bills of exchange, trade acceptances, or other evidences of debt, which may be used as security for a loan from a bank.—*adv.* **com-mer′cial-ly.**

com-mer-cial-ism (kŏ-mûr′shăl-ĭzm), *n.* **1**, business principles, habits, methods, or spirit; **2**, the predominance of this spirit in a community; **3**, a business practice or expression.

com-mer-cial-ize (kŏ-mûr′shăl-īz), *v.t.* [*p.t.* and *p.p.* -ized (-īzd), *p.pr.* -iz″ing], **1**, to reduce to a basis of business or trade; **2**, to emphasize, or make dominant, the commercial aspect of.

com-min-gle (kŏ-mĭng′gl), *v.t.* and *v.i.* [*p.t.* and *p.p.* -gled (-gld), *p.pr.* -gling], to mix; blend.

com-mi-nute (kŏm′ĭ-nūt), *v.t.* [*p.t.* and *p.p.* -nut″ed, *p.pr.* -nut″ing], to break into minute fragments; pulverize.—*n.* **com″mi-nu′tion.**

com-mis-er-ate (kŏ-mĭz′ĕr-āt), *v.t.* [*p.t.* and *p.p.* -at″ed, *p.pr.* -at″ing], to feel or express pity for; sympathize or condole with.—*adj.* **com-mis′er-a-tive.**—*n.* **com-mis″er-a′tion.**

com-mis-sar (kŏm′ĭ-sär), *n.* **1**, a commissary (which see); **2**, in Soviet Russia, a member of an administrative body resembling a cabinet, composed mainly of heads of governmental departments.

com-mis-sa-ri-at (kŏm″ĭ-sā′rĭ-ăt), *n.* **1**, the department of an army that furnishes provisions and other supplies; **2**, the officers in this department; **3**, the supplies furnished.

com-mis-sa-ry (kŏm′ĭ-sā-rĭ), *n.* [*pl.* commissaries (-rĭz)], **1**, one to whom some charge or duty is committed by a superior; **2**, an official in charge of the food department of an army.

com-mis-sion (kŏ-mĭsh′ŭn), *n.* **1**, the act of doing or performing: often implying wrongdoing; **2**, the intrusting of business to anyone; **3**, a trust; charge; **4**, the warrant by which anything is done; **5**, one or more persons appointed or elected to perform certain specified duties in business or government; **6**, in commerce, brokerage or allowance; **7**, a document conferring military or naval rank or authority: **commission merchant**, one who acts as agent in selling goods for a commission; also, a middleman:—*v.t.* **1**, to empower; delegate; **2**, in the army and navy, to confer rank or authority upon; **3**, to put into service, as a warship.

com-mis-sion-aire (kŏ-mĭsh″ŭn-âr′; *Fr.* kō-mē″syō-nâr′), *n.* **1**, one intrusted with an errand, as a professional shopper; **2**, in Europe, a hotel attendant who meets trains, boats, etc.

com-mis-sion-er (kŏ-mĭsh′ŭn-ẽr), *n.* **1**, a person holding authority under a commission, or warrant; **2**, an officer in charge of some department of the public service; as, the water *commissioner;* **3**, one of a body governing a political unit, as a city, under public authority.—*n.* **com-mis′sion-er-ship.**

com-mit (kŏ-mĭt′), *v.t.* [*p.t.* and *p.p.* -mit′ted, *p.pr.* -mit′ting], **1**, to give in charge or trust; **2**, to consign to custody, esp. for a short time; as, to *commit* a man for trial; **3**, to refer (a bill) to a committee; **4**, to perform or perpetrate, as a crime; **5**, to bring into risk or danger; also, to pledge: often used reflexively; **6**, to consign for safe-keeping, as by writing down, memorizing, etc.—*adj.* **com-mit′ta-ble.**

com-mit-ment (kŏ-mĭt′mĕnt), *n.* **1**, the act of intrusting or giving in charge; **2**, the state of being consigned, as to prison; **3**, the referring of a bill to a committee; **4**, an evil act; **5**, the act of pledging.—*n.* **com-mit′tal.**

com-mit-tee (kŏ-mĭt′ē), *n.* one or more persons appointed to consider, act on, or report on, any matter.

com-mode (kŏ-mōd′), *n.* **1**, a bureau or chest of drawers; **2**, a covered washstand containing basin, waste pipe, pitcher, etc.; **3**, a boxlike seat with a vessel beneath, serving as a portable water-closet.

com-mo-di-ous (kŏ-mō′dĭ-ŭs), *adj.* **1**, suitable; useful; **2**, affording ample accommodation; roomy.—*adv.* **com-mo′di-ous-ly.**—*n.* **com-mo′di-ous-ness.**

com-mod-i-ty (kŏ-mŏd′ĭ-tĭ), *n.* [*pl.* commodities (-tĭz)], **1**, that which is useful; **2**, an article of commerce; **3**, in *pl.*, in commerce, anything movable that is bought and sold, except animals; goods.

com-mo-dore (kŏm′ō-dōr″), *n.* **1**, in the U. S., a retired naval officer ranking between a captain and a rear admiral; **2**, in Great Britain, the commander of a squadron; **3**, a title of courtesy.

com-mon (kŏm′ŭn), *adj.* **1**, belonging to, or shared by, more than one; as, *common* to the human race; **2**, belonging, or pertaining, to a group or community; public; **3**, usual; frequent; trite; **4**, not worthy of note; inferior; vulgar; commonplace; **5**, in grammar, naming any individual of a class, rather than a specific one; as, "boy" is a *common* noun; also, either masculine or feminine; as, a noun of *common* gender: **common sense**, good judgment in ordinary affairs:—*n.* a tract of open public land.—*n.* **com′mon-ness.**—*adv.* **com′mon-ly.**

Syn., adj. mean, ordinary. (See general, mutual.)—*Ant., adj.* unusual, uncommon, exceptional, extraordinary.

com-mon-al-ty (kŏm′ŭn-ăl-tĭ), *n.* [*pl.* commonalties (-tĭz)], the common people; the commons.

com-mon-er (kŏm′ŭn-ẽr), *n.* **1**, one of the common people; **2**, in Great Britain, a person of low rank; **3**, a member of the British House of Commons.

com-mon law the law of immemorial custom or usage, not in the written statutes of a country.

com-mon-place (kŏm′ŭn-plās″), *n.* **1**, an ordinary topic or remark; **2**, anything ordinary:—*adj.* uninteresting; common; neither new nor striking; dull.—*n.* **com″mon-place′ness.**

com-mons (kŏm′ŭnz), *n.pl.* **1**, the mass of the people; **2**, in a college or university, rations or fare in common; hence, the dining hall where such fare is served: **Commons**, the House of Commons, or lower house of Parliament in Great Britain and Canada.

com-mon-weal (kŏm′ŭn-wēl′), *n. Archaic*, a commonwealth. Also, **com′mon weal.**

com-mon-wealth (kŏm′ŭn-wĕlth″), *n.* the public; the whole body of people in a state; also, a state in which the people rule.

com-mo-tion (kŏ-mō′shŭn), *n.* **1**, violent agitation; tumult; as, a *commotion* of the waves; **2**, insurrection.

com-mu-nal (kŏm′ū-năl; kŏ-mū′năl), *adj.* **1**, pertaining to ownership in common; **2**, pertaining to a commune.

com-mu-nal-ism (kŏm′ū-năl-ĭzm), *n.* the theory that each community or township should be self-governed and the state should be a combination of such communities; self-government on the widest possible scale.—*n.* **com′mu-nal-ist.**

[1]**com-mune** (kŏm′ūn), *n.* the smallest political division in France; hence, a local, self-governing community: **Commune**, the usurping government set up in Paris in 1792, or in 1871.—*n.* **Com′mu-nist.**

[2]**com-mune** (kŏ-mūn′), *v.i.* [*p.t.* and *p.p.* -muned′ (-mūnd′), *p.pr* -mun′ing], **1**, to converse together; take intimate counsel; **2**, to partake of the Eucharist, or Holy Communion.

com-mu-ni-ca-ble (kŏ-mū′nĭ-kȧ-bl), *adj.* capable of being imparted, made known, or conveyed to another; as, a *communicable* disease.

com-mu-ni-cant (kŏ-mū′nĭ-kănt), *n.* **1**, a partaker, esp. of the Eucharist, or Lord's Supper; **2**, one who imparts or makes known.

com-mu-ni-cate (kŏ-mū′nĭ-kāt), *v.t.* [*p.t.* and *p.p.* -cat″ed, *p.pr.* -cat″ing], **1**, to impart; **2**, to make known; tell:—*v.i.* **1**, to partake of the Eucharist, or Lord's Supper; **2**, to be connected; **3**, to hold intercourse.—*n.* **com-mu′ni-ca″tor.**

com-mu-ni-ca-tion (kŏ-mū″nĭ-kā′shŭn), *n.* **1**, an imparting; **2**, the act of making oneself understood; an expression of thoughts or opinions; **3**, means of passing from one place to another; **4**, news; intercourse.

com-mu-ni-ca-tive (kŏ-mū′nĭ-kā-tĭv), *adj.* unreserved; talkative.—*n.* **com-mu′ni-ca-tive-ness.**

com-mun-ion (kŏ-mūn′yŭn), *n.* **1**, intercourse; fellowship; esp., religious fellowship; **2**, common possession; **3**, a religious body with a common faith and administration: **Communion**, the sacrament of the Lord's Supper, or the partaking of it.

*__com-mu-ni-qué__ (kô″mü″nē″kā′), [Fr.], *n.* [*pl.* communiqués (-kā′)], an official report of news or intelligence.

com-mu-nism (kŏm′ū-nĭzm), *n.* **1**, a social organization in which property is held in common; **2**, communalism (which see); **3**, any organization of society in which property is held in common, and the state controls production and the distribution of the products of labor.—*n.* **com-mu-nist.**—*adj.* **com″mu-nis′tic.**

com-mu-ni-ty (kŏ-mū′nĭ-tĭ), *n.* [*pl.* communities (-tĭz)], **1**, a body of persons having common rights, interests, and privileges, living in the same locality; **2**, joint participation, sharing, or ownership; **3**, the people in general: usually with *the*; **4**, likeness; a character in common: **community chest**, a fund, collected annually by popular subscription, for the support of charitable and civic organizations in a given community.

com-mu-ta-tion (kŏm″ū-tā′shŭn), *n.* **1**, the act of substituting, as one kind of payment or service for another; **2**, the putting of something less severe in place of something severe; as, the *commutation* of sentence of death to life imprisonment; **3**, changing the flow of an electrical current, usually so as to cause it to run always in one direction: **commutation ticket**, a ticket, at a reduced rate, for a stated number of passages between fixed points, or for a certain number of meals, or the like.

com-mu-ta-tor (kŏm′ū-tā″tẽr), *n.* a device for regulating the direction of an electrical current, usually resulting in making one continuous flow.

com-mute (kŏ-mūt′), *v.t.* [*p.t.* and *p.p.* -mut′ed, *p.pr.* -mut′ing], **1**, to exchange; substitute; **2**, to reduce the severity of; as, to *commute* a sentence:—*v.i.* to use a commutation ticket; esp., to ride back and forth daily between a suburb and work in the city.—*n.* **com-mut′er**.—*n.* **com-mut′a-ble**.

1**com-pact** (kŏm′păkt), *n.* a contract; covenant; agreement.

2**com-pact** (kŏm-păkt′), *adj.* **1**, closely or firmly united; knit or pressed together; **2**, terse; condensed:—*v.t.* to press or pack closely; make solid:—*n.* (kŏm′păkt), a small cake of some cosmetic preparation, as powder or rouge, inclosed in a metal case.—*adv.* **com-pact′ly**.—*n.* **com-pact′ness**.

1**com-pan-ion** (kŏm-păn′yŭn), *n.* **1**, a comrade or associate; also, one paid to live with another; **2**, one of a pair or set of objects designed to go together:—*v.t.* to accompany:—*v.i.* to associate: usually with *with*.—*adj.* **com-pan′-ion-a-ble**.—*n.* **com-pan′ion-a-ble-ness**.—*n.* **com-pan′ion-ship**.

Syn., *n.* fellow, friend, compeer, ally, chum.

2**com-pan-ion** (kŏm-păn′yŭn), *n.* **1**, a hoodlike covering over a stairway on a ship, leading to a cabin or saloon below; **2**, the stairway itself.

com-pan-ion-ate (kŏm-păn′yŭn-ât), *adj.* pertaining to companionship: **companionate marriage**, the period before the responsibilities of parenthood have been incurred, in a marriage contracted in the usual way, but under conditions such that the parties can legally obtain scientific knowledge of birth control, and, if childless, can secure divorce by mutual consent, without alimony except in special cases.

com-pa-ny (kŭm′pȧ-nĭ), *n.* [*pl.* companies (-nĭz)], **1**, a group of people; **2**, a body of persons associated together; a society; **3**, one's usual associates; **4**, a body of actors; **5**, a guest, or guests; **6**, fellowship; **7**, a firm; **8**, a ship's crew; **9**, a section of a regiment, commanded by a captain: **company union**, in industry, an organization of workers open to all employees in a single plant or company, regardless of the type of work they do.

Syn. assemblage, crowd, host, throng.

com-pa-ra-ble (kŏm′pȧ-rȧ-bl), *adj.* capable of being likened to someone or something.—*adv.* **com′pa-ra-bly**.

com-par-a-tive (kŏm-păr′ȧ-tĭv) *adj.* **1**, pertaining to the act of comparing; **2**, not absolute; estimated by, or resulting from, comparison; relative; **3**, designating, or pertaining to, the second degree in the comparison of adjectives and adverbs, as *greater*, *higher*:—*n.* the comparative degree, or a word in it.—*adv.* **com-par′a-tive-ly**.

com-pare (kŏm-pâr′), *v.t.* [*p.t.* and *p.p.* -pared′ (-pârd′), *p.pr.* -par′ing], **1**, to liken; refer to as similar; **2**, to examine in order to discover likeness and unlikeness; **3**, to name over in order the degrees in the comparison of (adjectives and adverbs):—*v.i.* **1**, to be like or equal; **2**, to be worthy of, or suitable for, comparison.—*n.* **com-par′er**.

com-par-i-son (kŏm-păr′ĭ-sŭn), *n.* **1**, the act or effort of perceiving likenesses or differences; **2**, an illustration or simile; **3**, relative resemblance; **4**, in grammar, the change in form of adjectives and adverbs which shows a difference in degree.

com-part-ment (kŏm-pärt′mĕnt), *n.* **1**, one of the parts into which an inclosed space is divided; a division made by a partition; **2**, a separate section, as of a railway carriage.

1**com-pass** (kŭm′pȧs), *v.t.* **1**, to encircle; walk or go around; **2**, to besiege; **3**, to attain.—*adj.* **com′pass-a-ble**.

2**com-pass** (kŭm′pȧs), *n.* **1**, the boundary of an area; **2**, inclosed space; extent; limits; **3**, any of various instruments designed to indicate the magnetic north or the true north; **4**, the range of tones possible to a given voice or instrument; **5**, in *pl.*, an instrument for drawing circles, transferring measurements, etc., consisting of two small rods joined together at the top by a hinge; dividers.

com-pass card on a mariner's compass, a movable circular dial, divided into 32 equal divisions, or points of the compass, each of 11¼ degrees.

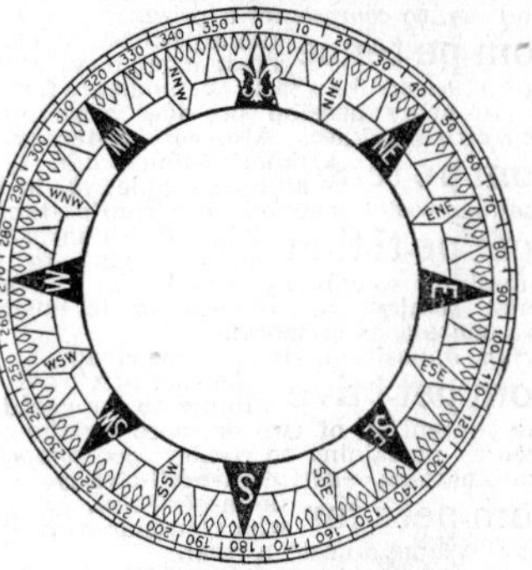

COMPASS CARD

Formerly, a course was given in terms of one of the 32 named points of the compass, as north, north by east, north-northeast, northeast by north, northeast, etc. It is usual now to give the number of degrees from north, up to 360.

com-pas-sion (kŏm-păsh′ŭn), *n.* sorrow for the distress of others.

Syn. sympathy, pity, mercy, tenderness.

com-pas-sion-ate (kŏm-păsh′ŭn-ât), *adj.* sympathetic; merciful.—*adv.* **com-pas′sion-ate-ly**.

com-pat-i-ble (kŏm-păt′ĭ-bl), *adj.* **1**, harmonious; agreeable; **2**, agreeing; consistent.—*adv.* **com-pat′i-bly**.—*n.* **com-pat″i-bil′i-ty**.—*n.* **com-pat′i-ble-ness**.

com-pa-tri-ot (kŏm-pā′trĭ-ŭt), *n.* a fellow citizen or fellow countryman; one of the same country.

com-peer (kŏm-pēr′), *n.* **1**, an equal in rank; **2**, a companion.

com-pel (kŏm-pĕl′), *v.t.* [*p.t.* and *p.p.* -pelled′ (-pĕld′), *p.pr.* -pel′ling], **1**, to urge irresistibly; **2**, to oblige; force; as, circumstances *compel* us to reduce expenses.
Syn. coerce, make, drive, necessitate.

com-pend (kŏm′pĕnd), *n.* an abridgment; summary; compendium.

com-pen-di-ous (kŏm-pĕn′dĭ-ŭs), *adj.* containing the substance of a subject in condensed form; summarized; abridged; compact.—*adv.* **com-pen′di-ous-ly.**—*n.* **com-pen′di-ous-ness.**

com-pen-di-um (kŏm-pĕn′dĭ-ŭm), *n.* [*pl.* compendiums (-ŭmz); compendia (-*a*)], an abridgment; a summary; condensed account of a book or subject; as, a *compendium* of science.
Syn. epitome, abstract, brief, synopsis.

com-pen-sate (kŏm′pĕn-sāt; kŏm-pĕn′sāt), *v.t.* [*p.t.* and *p.p.* -sat″ed, *p.pr.* -sat″ing], **1**, to make a fit return to; recompense; **2**, to make amends for; be equivalent to:—*v.i.* to make amends.

com-pen-sa-tion (kŏm″pĕn-sā′shŭn), *n.* **1**, recompense or payment; whatever makes good any lack or loss; a set-off; payment; amends; as, the man received *compensation* for his injuries; **2**, something given in return for a service or for something of value.

com-pen-sa-tor (kŏm′pĕn-sā″tẽr), *n.* one who or that which compensates or makes amends.

com-pete (kŏm-pēt′), *v.i.* [*p.t.* and *p.p.* -pet′ed, *p.pr.* -pet′ing], to enter into a contest or rivalry with another; contend; as, to *compete* for a prize.

com-pe-tence (kŏm′pē-tĕns), *n.* **1**, fitness; capability; ability; as, *competence* for a task; **2**, moderate fortune; as, an army pension provides a *competence* for a retired soldier. Also, **com′pe-ten-cy.**

com-pe-tent (kŏm′pē-tĕnt), *adj.* **1**, fit; able; suitable; **2**, in law, qualified to act or serve.—*adv.* **com′pe-tent-ly.**

com-pe-ti-tion (kŏm″pē-tĭsh′ŭn), *n.* **1**, the act of trying to gain something sought by another at the same time; rivalry; as, *competition* in business; **2**, a contest, as in sports.
Syn. opposition, strife. (See rivalry.)

com-pet-i-tive (kŏm-pĕt′ĭ-tĭv), *adj.* pertaining to, or based on, the contention of two or more for the same object; pertaining to rivalry; as, *competitive* examinations.—*adv.* **com-pet′i-tive-ly.**

com-pet-i-tor (kŏm-pĕt′ĭ-tẽr), *n.* one who contends with others for the same object; a rival.

com-pi-la-tion (kŏm″pĭ-lā′shŭn), **1**, the act of bringing together; esp., the collecting of material for a book; **2**, a book or the like made from such collecting.

com-pile (kŏm-pīl′), *v.t.* [*p.t.* and *p.p.* -piled′ (-pīld′), *p.pr.* -pil′ing], **1**, to put together in fresh form; as, to *compile* a book; **2**, to arrange in order, as a tabular report.—*n.* **com-pil′er.**

com-pla-cence (kŏm-plā′sĕns), *n.* tranquil self-satisfaction. Also, **com-pla′cen-cy.**

com-pla-cent (kŏm-plā′sĕnt), *adj.* showing satisfaction; pleased with oneself.—*adv.* **com-pla′cent-ly.**

com-plain (kŏm-plān′), *v.i.* **1**, to express grief, pain, resentment, or discontent; **2**, to lament mournfully; **3**, to express suffering; **4**, to make an accusation.—*n.* **com-plain′er.**—*adv.* **com-plain′ing-ly.**
Syn. deplore, murmur, repine, bewail.—*Ant.* rejoice, approve, commend.

com-plain-ant (kŏm-plān′ănt), *n.* **1**, one who grumbles; **2**, a plaintiff, or petitioner.

com-plaint (kŏm-plānt′), *n.* **1**, in law, a formal charge against a party; **2**, an expression of discontent, grief, or pain; **3**, an ailment; disease.

com-plai-sant (kŏm′plā-zănt″; kŏm-plā′zănt), *adj.* courteous; compliant.—*adv.* **com′plai-sant″ly.**—*n.* **com′plai-sance″** (kŏm′plā-zăns″; kŏm-plā′zăns).

com-ple-ment (kŏm′plē-mĕnt), *n.* **1**, full number or quantity; as, the regiment had its *complement* of men; a complete set; **2**, something that completes that which was not complete; **3**, one of two parts which together make up a whole; **4**, a word added to complete the meaning of a predicate; **5**, the color which, when combined with a given color, produces white; **6**, the angle or arc by which a given angle or arc falls short of 90 degrees:—*v.t.* (kŏm′plē-mĕnt″; kŏm″plē-mĕnt′), to complete.

com-ple-men-ta-ry (kŏm″plē-mĕn′t*a*-rĭ), *adj.* forming, or of the nature of, a complement, or completing part: **complementary angles**, two angles which together make a right angle, or 90 degrees (see [1]*angle*, illus.): **complementary colors**, two colors which, when in combination, produce white.

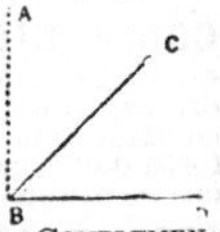

COMPLEMENTARY ANGLES, *ABC* AND *CBD*.

com-plete (kŏm-plēt′), *adj.* **1**, lacking nothing; entire; perfect; full; as, in *complete* armor; **2**, absolute; **3**, finished:—*v.t.* [*p.t.* and *p.p.* -plet′ed, *p.pr.* -plet′ing], to make whole or perfect; finish.—*adv.* **com-plete′ly.**—*n.* **com-plete′ness.**
Syn., *v.* (see close).

com-ple-tion (kŏm-plē′shŭn), *n.* the act of making, or state of being, whole or perfect; accomplishment.

com-plex (kŏm-plĕks′), *adj.* **1**, composed of various parts; not simple; **2**, involved; intricate: **complex sentence**, a sentence consisting of a principal clause and one or more subordinate clauses:—*n.* (kŏm′plĕks), **1**, an intricate or involved thing or situation; **2**, in psychology, a group of ideas on a subject which, when brought to the attention, calls forth a reaction influenced by an emotion, often unsuspected, rather than by reasoning; a habitual emotional attitude of sensitiveness and unreasonableness regarding a given subject.—*adv.* **com-plex′ly.**—*n.* **com-plex′ness.**
Syn., *adj.* complicated, entangled.

com-plex-ion (kŏm-plĕk′shŭn), *n.* **1**, the color of the skin, esp. of the face; **2**, aspect.—*adj.* **com-plex′ioned.**

com-plex-i-ty (kŏm-plĕk′sĭ-tĭ), *n.* [*pl.* complexities (-tĭz)], **1**, the state of being intricate or involved: opp. of *simplicity*; **2**, something involved.

com-pli-a-ble (kŏm-plī′*a*-bl), *adj.* capable of yielding; compliant.—*n.* **com-pli′a-ble-ness.**—*adv.* **com-pli′a-bly.**

com-pli-ance (kŏm-plī′ăns), *n.* **1**, the act or state of yielding or consenting; submission; as, in *compliance* with your desires; **2**, accordance; agreement; complaisance.—*n.* **com-pli′an-cy.**

com-pli-ant (kŏm-plī′ănt), *adj.* disposed to consent; yielding; obliging.—*adv.* **com-pli′ant-ly.**

com-pli-cate (kŏm′plĭ-kāt), *v.t.* [*p.t.* and *p.p.* -cat″ed, *p.pr.* -cat″ing], to make confused or hard to understand; involve:—*adj.* (kŏm′plĭ-kăt), difficult; complex.—*p.adj.* **com′pli-cat″ed.**

com-pli-ca-tion (kŏm″plĭ-kā′shŭn), *n.* **1**, a confusing combination of circumstances; **2**, the state of being hard to understand; difficulty; **3**, an event causing perplexity; **4**, a physical disorder not connected with the main disease, but affecting or bearing relation to it.

com-plic-i-ty (kŏm-plĭs′ĭ-tĭ), *n.* [*pl.* complicities (-tĭz)], partnership in wrongdoing or crime.

com-pli-ment (kŏm′plĭ-mĕnt), *n.* **1**, a formal act or expression of courtesy; **2**, an expression of approval or admiration; delicate flattery:—*v.t.* (kŏm′plĭ-mĕnt″; kŏm″plĭ-mĕnt′), **1**, to flatter; congratulate; praise, **2**, to show respect and affection for, as by a gift.

Syn., *n.* flattery. A *compliment* is a gracious expression of admiration or approval; it may be sincere, or it may be merely a formal expression used to be polite. *Flattery* means exaggerated or insincere praise bestowed directly upon its subject by one who either sees no faults or has secret ends to gain.

com-pli-men-ta-ry (kŏm″plĭ-mĕn′tȧ-rĭ), *adj.* **1**, conveying approval, admiration, or commendation; **2**, expressive of regard or preference; as, *complimentary* language; **3**, given free, as tickets.

com-ply (kŏm-plī′), *v.i.* [*p.t.* and *p.p.* -plied′ (-plīd′), *p.pr.* -ply′ing], to assent; agree; consent.—*n.* **com-pli′er.**

Syn. accede, conform, submit.

com-po-nent (kŏm-pō′nĕnt), *adj.* forming a part; composing; constituent; as, the *component* parts of a machine:—*n.* a necessary part; an ingredient.

com-port (kŏm-pōrt′), *v.t.* to conduct or behave: used reflexively; as, to *comport* oneself in a dignified manner:—*v.i.* to agree; accord· harmonize.

com-port-ment (kŏm-pōrt′mĕnt), *n.* manner of behaving.

com-pose (kŏm-pōz′), *v.t.* [*p.t.* and *p.p.* -posed′ (-pōzd′), *p.pr.* -pos′ing], **1**, to form by combination; **2**, to make up: often in passive; as, bronze is *composed* of copper and tin; **3**, to calm; make tranquil; **4**, to adjust; arrange in proper order; **5**, to set (type):—*v.i.* to engage in composition, as of musical or literary work.

com-posed (kŏm-pōzd′), *p.adj.* tranquil; calm; serene; quiet.—*adv.* **com-pos′ed-ly.**—*n.* **com-pos′ed-ness.**

com-pos-er (kŏm-pōz′ẽr), *n.* one who composes an original work; esp., one who composes music.

com-pos-ite (kŏm-pŏz′ĭt; kŏm′pō-zĭt), *adj.* **1**, made up of distinct

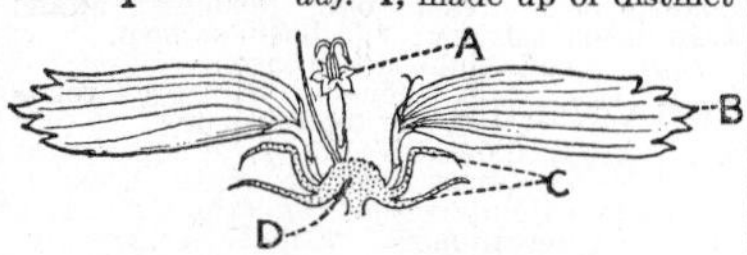

PORTION OF COMPOSITE FLOWER HEAD

A, one of the many fertile disk flowers; B, an infertile ray flower; C, D, section through the involucre (C) and receptacle (D).

parts; as, a *composite* photograph; **2**, in botany, having small flowers arranged compactly in heads, the outer flowers often appearing to be a ring of petals, as in the daisy: **composite,** displaying characteristics of both the Ionic and Corinthian styles of architecture (see *column*, illus.):—*n.* a composition.—*adv.* **compos′ite-ly.**

com-po-si-tion (kŏm″pō-zĭsh′ŭn), *n.* **1**, the union of different things or principles to make a whole; **2**, the act or art of creating an artistic work; **3**, the product of such action; **4**, a schoolroom exercise written for practice in the use of language; **5**, make-up, as of a picture; **6**, the setting up of type; **7**, a substance formed by mingling various materials; **8**, an agreement, as to settle a dispute; compromise.

com-pos-i-tor (kŏm-pŏz′ĭ-tẽr), *n.* one who sets type.

com-post (kŏm′pōst), *n.* a mixture of various substances, such as leaf mold, manure, etc., for fertilizing land.

com-po-sure (kŏm-pō′zhŭr), *n.* tranquillity; serenity.

com-pote (kŏm′pōt), *n.* **1**, fruit stewed in sirup; **2**, a small dish in which stewed fruit is served.

[1]**com-pound** (kŏm-pound′), *v.t.* **1**, to mix or combine together; as, to *compound* drugs; **2**, to join or unite; **3**, to form by mixing or joining; as, to *compound* a medicine; **4**, to settle, as a debt, for less than the amount claimed:—*v.i.* to compromise; bargain:—*adj.* (kŏm′pound), **1**, composed of two or more elements; **2**, in grammar, containing two or more independent clauses; as, a *compound* sentence: **compound interest,** interest which continually becomes greater by adding each interest amount, as it becomes due, to the last principal to make the new principal: **compound number,** a number having several denominations, as 6 feet 10 inches:—*n.* (kŏm′-pound), **1**, a combination of two or more elements or parts; **2**, in chemistry, a substance formed of two or more elements united in definite proportions, and differing in properties from any of them: distinguished from *mixture;* **3**, in grammar, a word composed of two or more elements, themselves usually words, as *housewife*.—*n.* **com-pound′er.**

Syn., *adj.* complex, combined; *v.* (see mix).

[2]**com-pound** (kŏm′pound), *n.* in the East Indies, China, etc., an inclosure containing a factory, residence, or the like, esp. one used by foreigners.

com-pre-hend (kŏm″prē-hĕnd′), *v.t.* **1**, to include or comprise; **2**, to grasp with the mind; understand; as, to *comprehend* an idea; **3**, to imply.

Syn. embrace, contain, embody.

com-pre-hen-si-ble (kŏm″prē-hĕn′sĭ-bl), *adj.* intelligible.—*n.* **com″pre-hen″si-bil′i-ty.**

com-pre-hen-sion (kŏm″prē-hĕn′-shŭn), *n.* the act of understanding or including; understanding; the power to grasp with the mind.

com-pre-hen-sive (kŏm″prē-hĕn′sĭv), *adj.* **1**, including much; full; complete; **2**, able to understand readily and clearly.—*adv.* **com″pre-hen′-sive-ly.**—*n.* **com″pre-hen′sive-ness.**

com-press (kŏm-prĕs′), *v.t.* to press together; condense:—*n.* (kŏm′-prĕs), **1**, a soft pad used in surgery as a dressing or to maintain pressure; **2**, a machine for pressing cotton, etc., into bales.

com-press-i-ble (kŏm-prĕs′ĭ-bl), *adj.* condensable; capable of being forced into a small space; yielding to pressure.—*n.* **com-press″i-bil′i-ty.**

com-pres-sion (kŏm-prĕsh′ŭn), *n.* **1**, the act of making compact or of pressing together; **2**, condensation.

com-pres-sive (kŏm-prĕs′ĭv), *adj.* tending to, or having the power to, press together or make more compact.

com-prise (kŏm-prīz′), *v.t.* [*p.t.* and *p.p.* -prised′ (-prīzd′), *p.pr.* -pris′-ing], to comprehend; contain; include; embrace; as, the British Empire *comprises* many colonies. Also, **com-prize′.**

com-pro-mise (kŏm′prō-mīz), *n.* **1**, a settlement by which each party concedes or gives up something;

2, a combination of two opposite systems, made by sacrifice on the part of each; 3, a line of action which follows a middle course:—*v.t.* [*p.t.* and *p.p.* -mised (-mīzd), *p.pr.* -mis″ing], 1, to settle by mutual concession; 2, to endanger the interests of, as by indirect speech or action:—*v.i.* to settle by adjustment or concession.—*n.* **com′pro-mis″er.**

comp-trol-ler (kŏn-trōl′ẽr), *n.* a public officer who oversees, examines, and certifies accounts. Also, **con-trol′ler,** *Pfd. S.*—*n.* **comp-trol′ler-ship.**

com-pul-sion (kŏm-pŭl′shŭn), *n.* 1, the act of coercing, or the state of being coerced; 2, force; constraint; 3, in psychology, a nervous condition in which a person feels compelled to do certain strange acts.

com-pul-so-ry (kŏm-pŭl′sō-rĭ), *adj.* 1, exercising force; 2, obligatory; enforced.—*adv.* **com-pul′so-ri-ly.**

com-punc-tion (kŏm-pŭngk′shŭn), *n.* mild remorse; uneasiness of conscience; contrition.

com-pu-ta-tion (kŏm″pū-tā′shŭn), *n.* 1, the act of reckoning; calculation; 2, the estimate arrived at; 3, a system of reckoning.

com-pute (kŏm-pūt′), *v.t.* [*p.t.* and *p.p.* -put′ed, *p.pr.* -put′ing], to figure; number; reckon; calculate; as, to *compute* the distance of the moon from the earth.—*adj.* **com-put′a-ble.**—*n.* **com-put′er.**

com-rade (kŏm′răd; kŏm′răd), *n.* an intimate friend; a companion.—*n.* **com′rade-ship.**

[1]**con** (kŏn), *v.t.* [*p.t.* and *p.p.* conned (kŏnd), *p.pr.* con′ning], to study or examine carefully; hence, to commit to memory.

[2]**con** (kŏn), *v.t.* [*p.t.* and *p.p.* conned (kŏnd), *p.pr.* con′ning], to oversee or direct the steering of (a ship):—*v.i.* to direct the steering of a vessel.

[3]**con** (kŏn), *adv.* on the negative side; as, they argued the matter pro and *con.*

con- (kŏn-), *prefix,* [used before any consonant except *b, m, p, l, r, h, w*], 1, together; as, *con*fluence; 2, with; as, *con*text; 3, fully; completely: used intensively; as, *con*gratulate. See **com-.**

con-cat-e-nate (kŏn-kăt′ē-nāt), *v.t.* [*p.t.* and *p.p.* -nat″ed, *p.pr.* -nat″ing], to link together; connect, as in a series.—*n.* **con-cat″e-na′tion.**

con-cave (kŏn′kāv), *adj.* hollow and curved, as the inner surface of a sphere: opp. of *convex:* **concave lens,** a lens one or both sides of which are slightly hollow and curved: **double concave lens,** a lens both sides of which are concave (see *lens,* illus.):—*v.t.* [*p.t.* and *p.p.* -caved (-kāvd), *p.pr.* -cav-ing], to make hollow and curved, as a lens.

con-cav-i-ty (kŏn-kăv′ĭ-tĭ), *n.* [*pl.* concavities (-tĭz)], 1, hollowness; the state of being concave; 2, the inner surface of a rounded, hollow body.

con-ca-vo–con-vex (kŏn-kā″vō-kŏn′vĕks), *adj.* concave on one side, convex on the other, as a lens (see *lens,* illus.).

con-ceal (kŏn-sēl′), *v.t.* to hide; keep secret.—*adj.* **con-ceal′a-ble.**

Syn. hide, secrete, disguise. *Hide,* the general term, means to put under cover, or to put intentionally out of sight. The act of hiding may result from a set purpose, an accident, or a limitation of nature; as, the children *hid* their toys; trees *hide* the garage. To *conceal* is to prevent facts, persons, objects, or purposes, from coming to the observation of others; it is always the act of intention; as, he *concealed* the gun; she *concealed* her feelings. To *secrete* is to place objects beyond the knowledge or observation of all but the person involved; as, stolen goods are *secreted.* To *disguise* is to make a thing seem what it is not; as, the detective was *disguised* as a waiter.

con-ceal-ment (kŏn-sēl′mĕnt), *n.* 1, the act of hiding, or state of being hidden; 2, a place of hiding; shelter.

con-cede (kŏn-sēd′), *v.t.* [*p.t.* and *p.p.* -ced′ed, *p.pr.* -ced′ing], 1, to yield; admit, as a point in a debate; 2, to grant as a right; as, the government *conceded* the franchise to the negro.—*n.* **con-ced′er.**

con-ceit (kŏn-sēt′), *n.* 1, an idea or opinion without sufficient ground; a fanciful notion; 2, an undue belief in one's own powers; vanity; 3, opinion; estimation; as, wise in one's own *conceit.*

con-ceit-ed (kŏn-sēt′ĕd), *adj.* having too good an opinion of oneself; excessively vain.—*adv.* **con-ceit′ed-ly.**

con-ceiv-a-ble (kŏn-sēv′ȧ-bl), *adj.* capable of being imagined; as, a *conceivable* story.—*adv.* **con-ceiv′a-bly.**

con-ceive (kŏn-sēv′), *v.t.* [*p.t.* and *p.p.* -ceived′ (-sēvd′), *p.pr.* -ceiv′ing], 1, to become pregnant with (young); 2, to imagine; 3, to understand; take into the mind:—*v.i.* 1, to think; 2, to become pregnant.

Syn. comprehend, grasp, realize.

con-cen-trate (kŏn′sĕn-trāt; kŏn-sĕn′trāt), *v.t.* [*p.t.* and *p.p.* -trat″ed, *p.pr.* -trat″ing], 1, to bring to one point or common center; 2, to increase in strength; 3, to fix, as the attention:—*v.i.* to approach to, or meet at, a given point.

con-cen-tra-tion (kŏn″sĕn-trā′shŭn), *n.* 1, the act of placing together or the state of being placed together; 2, close attention; 3, condensation: **concentration camp,** a place where troops from various localities are assembled.

con-cen-tric (kŏn-sĕn′trĭk), *adj.* having a common center; as, *concentric* circles were made in the water. Also, **con-cen′tri-cal.**—*adv.* **con-cen′tri-cal-ly.**

con-cept (kŏn′sĕpt), *n.* mental impression of an object; a general idea or notion of a class of objects.

con-cep-tion (kŏn-sĕp′shŭn), *n.* 1, origin; beginning; 2, the act or power of forming a mental image or impression; 3, an idea or notion; 4, the act of becoming pregnant.

con-cern (kŏn-sûrn′), *v.t.* 1, to affect the welfare of; relate or belong to; 2, to interest or engage; as, I am not *concerned* in that; 3, to make uneasy:—*n.* 1, that which belongs or relates to one; business; affair; 2, interest; anxiety; 3, a business firm.

Syn., n. solicitude. (See care.)

con-cern-ing (kŏn-sûrn′ĭng), *prep.* relating to; regarding.

con-cert (kŏn-sûrt′), *v.t.* 1, to contrive or devise together; 2, to adjust or arrange by joint action:—*n.* (kŏn′sẽrt), 1, a musical entertainment; 2, musical harmony; 3, mutual agreement; as, a *concert* of nations; 4, unison of voices; as, to recite in *concert.*

con-cert-ed (kŏn-sûr′tĕd), *p.adj.* mutually planned or agreed upon; simultaneous; as, *concerted* action is most effective.

con-cer-ti-na (kŏn″sẽr-tē′nȧ), *n.* a small musical reed instrument with extensible bellows.

CONCERTINA

con-ces-sion (kŏn-sĕsh′ŭn), *n.* 1, the act of granting or yielding, as a point in dispute; 2, the thing conceded; 3, an acknowledgment or admission.

con-ces-sion-aire (kŏn-sĕsh″ŭn-âr′), *n.* a person holding a concession or grant. Also, in the *U. S.*, **con-ces′sion-er.**

conch (kŏngk; kŏnch; kŏnsh), *n.* a large, spiral sea shell, as that of certain kinds of mollusks.

Conch

con-chol-o-gy (kŏng-kŏl′ō-jĭ), *n.* that part of zoölogy which treats of mollusks and their shells.—*n.* **con-chol′o-gist.** —*adj.* **con″cho-log′i-cal.**

***con-cierge** (kôn″syârzh′), [Fr.], *n.* in France, the doorkeeper or janitor of a hotel or of a private house.

con-cil-i-ate (kŏn-sĭl′ĭ-āt), *v.t.* [*p.t.* and *p.p.* -at″ed, *p.pr.* -at″ing], to win or gain the affections or good will of; as, William Penn wisely tried to *conciliate* the Indians.—*n.* **con-cil′i-a″tor.**

con-cil-i-a-tion (kŏn-sĭl″ĭ-ā′shŭn), *n.* 1, the act of restoring good will, or of banishing hostility; 2, the change of attitude thus brought about.

con-cil-i-a-to-ry (kŏn-sĭl′ĭ-ȧ-tō-rĭ), *adj.* tending to pacify; showing a spirit willing to come half way.

con-cise (kŏn-sīs′), *adj.* condensed; terse; brief; putting much in few words.—*adv.* **con-cise′ly.**—*n.* **con-cise′ness.**

Syn. pithy, succinct. (See short.)

con-clave (kŏn′klāv), *n.* 1, a private meeting of cardinals for the election of a pope; 2, the rooms in which such meetings are held; 3, any private meeting.

con-clude (kŏn-klōōd′), *v.t.* [*p.t.* and *p.p.* -clud′ed, *p.pr.* -clud′ing], 1, to come to a decision about; 2, to determine; settle; 3, to end; as, to *conclude* an argument; 4, to infer; as, to *conclude* that a man is guilty: —*v.i.* 1, to draw an inference; 2, to end.

Syn. terminate. (See close.)

con-clu-sion (kŏn-klōō′zhŭn), *n.* 1, a final determination; 2, a summing up; 3, an inference; judgment; 4, the closing part, as of a discussion; end.

con-clu-sive (kŏn-klōō′sĭv), *adj.* decisive; final; ending argument; as, a *conclusive* answer.—*adv.* **con-clu′sive-ly.**—*n.* **con-clu′sive-ness.**

con-coct (kŏn-kŏkt′), *v.t.* 1, to prepare, as food, by mixing various things together; 2, to form; make up; as, to *concoct* a plot to destroy the government.

con-coc-tion (kŏn-kŏk′shŭn), *n.* 1, the act of preparing or mixing different ingredients; 2, a plan or plot; 3, a mixture of various articles of food.

con-com-i-tant (kŏn-kŏm′ĭ-tănt), *n.* that which accompanies or is combined with something else; an attendant quality or circumstance; as, culture and refinement are not always *concomitants* of wealth:—*adj.* accompanying; combined with; attending; as, *concomitant* circumstances.—*adv.* **con-com′i-tant-ly.**

con-cord (kŏng′kôrd; kŏn′kôrd), *n.* 1, harmony; union; 2, the agreement of words, as in gender, number, and case.

con-cord-ance (kŏn-kôr′dȧns), *n.* 1, agreement; accordance; 2, a dictionary of words or passages, with references to the places where they occur; esp., an index of Bible words.

con-cord-ant (kŏn-kôr′dănt), *adj.* harmonious; agreeing; agreeable.—*adv.* **con-cord′ant-ly.**

con-course (kŏng′kōrs; kŏn′kōrs), *n.* 1, a meeting together; as, a *concourse* of waters; 2, an assembly or crowd; 3, a place, usually not inclosed, where crowds assemble or roads meet.

con-crete (kŏn′krēt; kŏn-krēt′), *adj.* 1, formed into a mass by mixing; 2, pertaining to actual events or things; not abstract or general; 3, specific, not general, in application; 4, consisting of the substance called *concrete*:—*n.* an artificial stone made of cement, sand, and broken stone:—*v.t.* (kŏn-krēt′), [*p.t.* and *p.p.* -cret′ed, *p.pr.* -cret′ing], 1, to form or unite in a mass; 2, to form of, or cover with, concrete.—*adv.* **con′crete-ly.**—*n.* **con′crete-ness.**

con-cre-tion (kŏn-krē′shŭn), *n.* 1, the act or process of forming into a solid mass; 2, the act of covering something with concrete; 3, a hardened mass.

con-cu-bine (kŏng′kū-bīn), *n.* a woman who lives with a man without being his wife; a secondary wife.—*n.* **con-cu′bi-nage.**

con-cur (kŏn-kûr′), *v.i.* [*p.t.* and *p.p.* -curred′ (-kûrd′), *p.pr.* -cur′ring], 1, to agree or unite in action or opinion; 2, to happen at the same time; coincide.

con-cur-rence (kŏn-kŭr′ĕns), *n.* the act of agreeing; agreement; consent; coincidence. Also, **con-cur′ren-cy.**

con-cur-rent (kŏn-kŭr′ĕnt), *adj.* 1, acting in union or conjunction; agreeing; 2, joint and equal in authority; 3, happening or existing at the same time; 4, meeting in, or passing through, a common point, as lines.—*adv.* **con-cur′rent-ly.**

con-cus-sion (kŏn-kŭsh′ŭn), *n.* 1, a shaking; the shock caused by two bodies coming violently together; 2, injury by a fall; as, *concussion* of the brain.

con-demn (kŏn-dĕm′), *v.t.* [*p.t.* and *p.p.* -demned′ (-dĕmd′), *p.pr.* -demn′ing (-dĕm′ĭng; -dĕm′nĭng)], 1, to pronounce or judge guilty; 2, to blame; censure; 3, to declare to be forfeited or taken for public use; as, to *condemn* land; 4, to pronounce to be unfit for use; as, to *condemn* a prison.—*adj.* **con-dem′na-to-ry.**—*n.* **con-demn′er** (kŏn-dĕm′ēr; kŏn-dĕm′nēr).

Syn. disapprove, denounce, upbraid.—*Ant.* approve, justify, exonerate.

con-dem-na-tion (kŏn″dĕm-nā′shŭn), *n.* 1, the act of pronouncing guilty, unfit, forfeited, etc.; 2, the state of being so pronounced.

con-den-sa-ble (kŏn-dĕn′sȧ-bl), *adj.* 1, capable of compression or reduction in size; 2, capable of being made more dense, or of being changed from a gas or vapor to a liquid, as steam.

con-den-sa-tion (kŏn″dĕn-sā′shŭn), *n.* 1, reduction in size; compression; 2, the act of making dense or denser: opp. of *rarefaction;* 3, the change from a gaseous to a liquid form: opp. of *vaporization.*

con-dense (kŏn-dĕns′), *v.t.* [*p.t.* and *p.p.* -densed′ (-dĕnst′), *p.pr.* -dens′ing], 1, to compress; make close or dense; 2, to reduce to a few words without losing the meaning; 3, to bring together at one point; concentrate, as rays of light by a lens; 4, to change from a gas or vapor to a liquid, as steam to water; 5, to increase in intensity, as an electric charge:—*v.i.* 1, to become dense; 2, to pass from gaseous or vaporous to liquid form: opp. of *rarefy.*

con-dens-er (kŏn-dĕn′sēr), *n.* 1, one who or that which makes dense, concentrates, or compresses; 2, a machine for changing gases to liquid or solid form; 3, a lens for concentrating or bringing together rays of light; 4, a device for accumulating or storing up an electric charge.

con-de-scend (kŏn″dē-sĕnd′), *v.i.* to stoop; descend; deign; come down voluntarily to the plane of inferiors.—*adv.* **con″de-scend′ing-ly.**

con-de-scen-sion (kŏn″dē-sĕn′shŭn), *n.* the act of stooping to the level of inferiors; display of courtesy to an inferior.

con-dign (kŏn-dīn′), *adj.* deserved; adequate: usually applied to punishment.—*adv.* **con-dign′ly.**

con-di-ment (kŏn′dĭ-mĕnt), *n.* a seasoning for food; a spicy relish.

con-di-tion (kŏn-dĭsh′ŭn), *n.* **1,** something necessary, demanded or agreed upon: **2,** rank in the social scale; **3,** state of being or of circumstances; **4,** fitness; satisfactory state of being; as, the team is in *condition*:—*v.t.* **1,** to arrange; **2,** to be a necessity of; limit; as, he *conditioned* his gift on their good behavior.

con-di-tion-al (kŏn-dĭsh′ŭn-ăl), *adj.* **1,** of, pertaining to, or dependent upon, certain stipulations or provisions; not absolute; **2,** in grammar, containing a provisional clause.—*adv.* **con-di′tion-al-ly.**

con-di-tioned (kŏn-dĭsh′ŭnd), *p.adj.* **1,** subject to certain stipulations and provisions; as, an order *conditioned* on a low price; **2,** placed in, or having the marks of, certain circumstances; as, a well-*conditioned* horse; **3,** deficient; charged with a record or grade below the passing mark: used of a student.

con-dole (kŏn-dōl′), *v.i.* [*p.t.* and *p.p.* -doled′ (-dōld′), *p.pr.* -dol′ing], to express sympathy for another: with *with.*

con-do-lence (kŏn-dō′lĕns), *n.* sympathy for another's grief; as, a message of *condolence.*

Syn. compassion. (See sympathy.)

con-done (kŏn-dōn′), *v.t.* [*p.t.* and *p.p.* -doned′ (-dōnd′), *p.pr.* -don′ing], to forgive, esp. by seeming to overlook, as a fault.—*n.* **con″do-na′tion.**

con-dor (kŏn′dŏr), *n.* a very large, South American vulture found in the highest parts of the Andes.

con-duce (kŏn-dūs′), *v.i.* [*p.t.* and *p.p.* -duced′(-dūst′), *p.pr.* -duc′ing], to lead or tend toward a result; contribute.

con-du-cive (kŏn-dū′sĭv), *adj.* leading or tending to a result; contributing; as, temperance **is** *conducive* to happiness.—*n.* **con-du′cive-ness.**

con-duct (kŏn-dŭkt′), *v.t.* **1,** to guide; **2,** to direct; manage; **3,** to behave; **4,** to serve as a medium or channel for; transmit, as heat:—*v.i.* **1,** to direct; lead; **2,** to transmit electricity, heat, etc.:—*n.* (kŏn′dŭkt), **1,** personal behavior or practice; **2,** management; **3,** guidance.

Syn., v. direct, manage. *Conduct, direct,* and *manage* express different ways of regulating affairs or guiding men. To *conduct* is to supervise by careful planning and arranging, or by personal leadership; as, to *conduct* a campaign; to *conduct* an orchestra. *Direct* means to point out a way or course for others to follow; it implies the idea of authority; as, to *direct* traffic; an engineer *directs* the construction of a bridge. To *manage* is to take hold of the thing involved and handle it to the last detail; as, to *manage* an office.

con-duct-i-ble (kŏn-dŭk′tĭ-bl), *adj.* capable of being transmitted.—*n.* **con-duct″i-bil′i-ty.**

con-duc-tion (kŏn-dŭk′shŭn), *n.* **1,** the act or process of conveying or transmitting, as water through a pipe; **2,** transmission by a conductor, esp. of heat or electricity; **3,** conductivity.

con-duc-tive (kŏn-dŭk′tĭv), *adj.* having the property of transmitting heat, electricity, etc.—*n.* **con″duc-tiv′i-ty.**

con-duc-tor (kŏn-dŭk′tẽr), *n.* **1,** a leader or guide; a director, as of an orchestra; **2,** one who has charge of a car or train; **3,** a substance which transmits water, heat, or the like.—*n.fem.* **con-duc′tress.**

con-duit (kŏn′dĭt), *n.* **1,** a canal or pipe for carrying water, etc.; **2,** a trough, tube, or subway for electric wires.

cone (kōn), *n.* **1,** a solid body which tapers uniformly to a point from a circular base; **2,** anything of similar shape; **3,** specif., the fruit of the fir, pine, etc. (see *inflorescence,* illus.); **4,** in geometry, a solid generated by the revolution of a right angle around one of its legs; also, more generally, a surface generated by the movement of a straight line, one point of which is fixed.

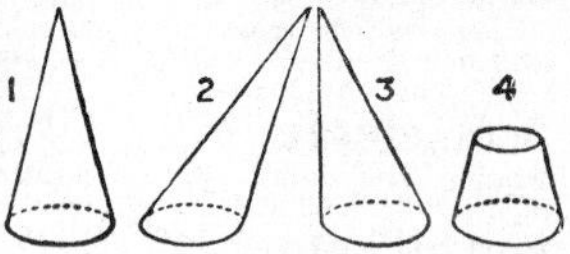

CONES

1, right circular cone; 2, 3, oblique, or scalene, cones; 4, frustum of a cone.

co-ney (kō′nĭ; kŭn′ĭ), *n.* [*pl.* coneys (-nĭz)], a rabbit. See **co′ny,** *Pfd. S.*

con-fab-u-late (kŏn-făb′ū-lāt), *v.i.* [*p.t.* and *p.p.* -lat″ed, *p.pr.* -lat″ing], *Colloq.,* to gossip or chat familiarly.—*n.* **con-fab″u-la′tion.**

con-fec-tion (kŏn-fĕk′shŭn), *n.* **1,** a mixing of ingredients; **2,** anything preserved with sugar; a sweetmeat.

con-fec-tion-a-ry (kŏn-fĕk′shŭn-ā-rĭ), *n.* [*pl.* confectionaries (-rĭz)], **1,** a sweetmeat; **2,** an establishment in which sweetmeats are made or sold; **3,** *Obs.,* one who makes sweetmeats:—*adj.* pertaining to, or like, sweetmeats.

con-fec-tion-er (kŏn-fĕk′shŭn-ẽr), *n.* one who prepares and sells candy, sweetmeats, etc.: **confectioners' sugar,** sugar in the form of a very fine white powder.

con-fec-tion-er-y (kŏn-fĕk′shŭn-ẽr-ĭ; -ẽr-ĭ), *n.* [*pl.* confectioneries (-ĭz)], **1,** candies, ice cream, cakes, preserves, etc.; **2,** the business, or place of business, of a dealer in candies.

con-fed-er-a-cy (kŏn-fĕd′ẽr-ȧ-sĭ), *n.* [*pl.* confederacies (-sĭz)], **1,** persons, states, or nations united for mutual support of any kind; alliance; **2,** conspiracy; unlawful combination: **the Confederacy,** the Confederate States of America, a league of 11 southern states that seceded from the United States **in** 1860 and 1861.

con-fed-er-ate (kŏn-fĕd′ẽr-āt), *v.t.* and *v.i.* [*p.t.* and *p.p.* -at″ed, *p.pr.* -at″ing], to unite in a league:—*adj.* (kŏn-fĕd′ẽr-āt), united by a league or agreement: **Confederate,** pertaining to the Confederate States of America (see *Confederacy*):—*n.* **1,** a member of a league or union; **2,** an ally; esp., an accomplice: **Confederate,** an adherent or defender of the Confederate States of America.

con-fed-er-a-tion (kŏn-fĕd″ẽr-ā′shŭn), *n.* **1,** the act of joining together or forming a league; an alliance; **2,** a union of states.

con-fer (kŏn-fûr′), *v.t.* [*p.t.* and *p.p.* -ferred′ (-fûrd′), *p.pr.* -fer′ring], to give or bestow; as, to *confer* an honor or a medal on a person:—*v.i.* to consult together; converse: with *with;* as, the President *confers* with his cabinet today.—*n.* **con-fer′rer.**

Syn. grant. (See give.)

con-fer-ee (kŏn″fẽr-ē′), *n.* **1,** one who takes part in a conference; **2,** one upon whom something is conferred.

con-fer-ence (kŏn′fẽr-ĕns), *n.* **1,** the act of consulting together formally; **2,** an appointed meeting for discussing some topic or business, as of committees or for arbitration; **3**, a religious convention; as, the annual *conference* of ministers; **4**, a conferring or bestowing.—*adj.* **con″fer-en′tial.**

con-fer-va (kŏn-fûr′vȧ), *n.* [*pl.* confervæ (-vē)], a kind of green, fresh-water alga, or any other similar threadlike plant.—*adj.* **con-fer′val.**

con-fess (kŏn-fĕs′), *v.t.* **1**, to admit or acknowledge, as a fault; **2**, to admit as true; **3**, to profess, as a religious belief; **4**, to reveal; **5**, to hear a confession from: said of a priest; **6**, to tell (one's sins) to a priest:—*v.i.* **1**, to disclose the state of one's conscience to a priest and receive absolution; **2**, of a priest, to hear a confession; **3**, to make an acknowledgment: with *to.*

con-fess-ed-ly (kŏn-fĕs′ĕd-lĭ), *adv.* admittedly; avowedly.

con-fes-sion (kŏn-fĕsh′ŭn), *n.* **1**, the act of acknowledging or admitting; **2**, the act of making known one's sins to a priest; **3**, a profession of belief, as in public worship; a creed; **4**, anything disclosed or acknowledged; an admission.

con-fes-sion-al (kŏn-fĕsh′ŭn-ăl), *n.* the closed place where a priest hears confessions.

con-fes-sor (kŏn-fĕs′ẽr), *n.* **1**, one who admits or acknowledges a wrong; **2**, a priest who hears confessions.

con-fet-ti (kŏn-fĕt′tē), *n.pl.* [*sing.* confetto (-tō)], **1**, orig., bonbons or sweetmeats, or paper imitations, thrown at carnivals, weddings, etc.; **2**, now, usually as *sing.*, small pieces of paper similarly used.

con-fi-dant (kŏn″fĭ-dănt′; kŏn′fĭ-dănt″), *n.* an intimate friend.—*n.fem.* **con″fi-dante′.**

con-fide (kŏn-fīd′), *v.i.* [*p.t.* and *p.p.* -fid′ed, *p.pr.* -fid′ing], to have trust or faith (in); as, the king *confides* in his ministers:—*v.t.* **1**, to put into another's trust or keeping; intrust: with *to;* **2**, to tell, as a secret.—*n.* **con-fid′er.**

con-fi-dence (kŏn′fĭ-dĕns), *n.* **1**, belief; reliance; trust; **2**, faith based on intimate acquaintance; **3**, self-reliance; boldness; assurance; **4**, the telling of something privately and trustfully; also, the thing thus told; a secret.

con-fi-dent (kŏn′fĭ-dĕnt), *adj.* **1**, full of trust; self-reliant; bold; **2**, convinced; sure.—*adv.* **con′fi-dent-ly.**

con-fi-den-tial (kŏn″fĭ-dĕn′shăl), *adj.* **1**, spoken or written as a secret; as, *confidential* correspondence; **2**, intimate; trustworthy; as, a *confidential* secretary; **3**, indicating trust; as, his manner became *confidential.*—*adv.* **con″fi-den′tial-ly.**

con-fid-ing (kŏn-fīd′ĭng), *p.adj.* trustful; full of simple faith; trusting; credulous.—*adv.* **con-fid′ing-ly.**

con-fig-u-ra-tion (kŏn-fĭg″ū-rā′shŭn), *n.* figure or contour; conformation, as of the land.

con-fine (kŏn′fīn), *n.*, usually in *pl.*, a boundary border, or limit; a frontier; as, to keep within the *confines* of the country:—*v.t.* (kŏn-fīn′), [*p.t.* and *p.p.* -fined′ (-fīnd′), *p.pr.* -fin′ing], to restrict within limits; keep within doors; imprison.

con-fine-ment (kŏn-fīn′mĕnt), *n.* **1**, the act of restricting or imprisoning; **2**, restraint, as by illness; esp., illness in childbirth.

con-firm (kŏn-fûrm′), *v.t.* **1**, to strengthen; make firmer; **2**, to make sure; ratify; as, our fears were *confirmed* by the report; **3**, to administer the rite of confirmation, or to receive into church membership.—*adj.* **con-firm′a-ble.**—*n.* **con-firm′er.**

Syn. establish, verify, sustain.

con-fir-ma-tion (kŏn″fẽr-mā′shŭn), *n.* **1**, the act of verifying, ratifying, making sure, etc.; **2**, that which proves; **3**, admission to full communion in certain Christian churches, after baptism.

con-firm-a-to-ry (kŏn-fûr′mȧ-tō-rĭ), *adj.* serving to verify or prove true; helping to establish; corroborative.—*adj.* **con-firm′a-tive.**

con-firmed (kŏn-fûrmd′), *p.adj.* **1**, admitted to full church privileges; **2**, habitual; settled, as a habit or mannerism; **3**, ratified; definitely proved.

con-fis-cate (kŏn′fĭs-kāt; kŏn-fĭs′kāt), *v.t.* [*p.t.* and *p.p.* -cat″ed, *p.pr.* -cat″ing], **1**, to seize as forfeited or as belonging to the state or public treasury; as, the traitor's land was *confiscated;* **2**, to take, as by authority:—*adj.* forfeited; seized.—*adj.* **con-fis′ca-to-ry.**—*n.* **con′fis-ca″tor.**

con-fis-ca-tion (kŏn″fĭs-kā′shŭn), *n.* the act of taking private property for public use; appropriation.

con-fla-gra-tion (kŏn″flȧ-grā′shŭn), *n.* **1**, a great fire; as, there was a terrible *conflagration* in Chicago in 1871; **2**, a great outburst, as of war.

con-flict (kŏn-flĭkt′), *v.i.* **1**, to strike together in collision, or clash; contend; fight; **2**, to disagree; as, opinions that *conflict:*—*n.* (kŏn′flĭkt), **1**, a fight or struggle for the mastery; battle; as, the *conflict* lasted three years; a violent collision; **2**, antagonism, as of ideas.—*n.* **con-flic′tion.**

Syn., *n.* combat, contest, contention. (See battle.)—*Ant.*, *n.* accord, peace.

con-flict-ing (kŏn-flĭkt′ĭng), *p.adj.* opposing; contradictory.

con-flu-ence (kŏn′flōō-ĕns), *n.* **1**, a flowing or coming together of streams, roads, etc.; also, the place where they meet; **2**, a flocking together, as of people.—*adj.* **con′flu-ent.**

con-form (kŏn-fôrm′), *v.t.* to make like; bring into harmony with; as, a foreigner must *conform* his behavior to our customs: usually with *to:*—*v.i.* **1**, to be in harmony with a pattern, standard, method, etc.: with *to;* **2**, to comply; be tractable.—*n.* **con-form′er.**—*n.* **con-form′ance.**

con-form-a-ble (kŏn-fôr′mȧ-bl), *adj.* **1**, like; corresponding; consistent; as, our actions should always be *conformable* with our ideals; **2**, compliant; submissive.—*adv.* **con-form′a-bly.**

con-for-ma-tion (kŏn″fôr-mā′shŭn), *n.* **1**, conformity; adaptation; **2**, the shaping of a thing by orderly arrangement of its parts; **3**, form; structure: as, the *conformation* of the earth's surface.

con-form-ist (kŏn-fôr′mĭst), *n.* one who is in agreement; esp., a member of the Established Church of England.

con-form-i-ty (kŏn-fôr′mĭ-tĭ), *n.* [*pl.* conformities (-tĭz)], **1**, likeness; harmony; **2**, compliance with established forms, esp. religious forms.

con-found (kŏn-found′), *v.t.* **1**, to perplex; bewilder; **2**, to throw into disorder or confusion; **3**, to mingle; mix; confuse; **4**, to rout; bring to nothing; as, science *confounds* superstition; **5**, *Colloq.*, to damn: used as a mild curse.

***con-frère** (kôn″frâr′), [Fr.], *n.* an associate; colleague; as, the professors in a college are *confrères.*

con-front (kŏn-frŭnt′), *v.t.* **1**, to put face to face: with *with;* as, to *confront* a prisoner with evidence; **2**, to face defiantly or with hostility; oppose.

Con-fu-cian-ism (kŏn-fū′shăn-ĭzm), *n.* the system of morals and ethics taught by Confucius, the Chinese sage, and his followers: based on ancestor worship, filial devotion, virtue, and piety.—*n.* **Con-fu'cian-ist.**

con-fuse (kŏn-fūz'), *v.t.* [*p.t.* and *p.p.* -fused' (-fūzd'), *p.pr.* -fus'ing], **1,** to bewilder; perplex; **2,** to mingle; mix; mistake for another.—*adv.* **con-fus'ed-ly.**
Syn. distract, disturb. (See perplex.)

con-fu-sion (kŏn-fū'zhŭn), *n.* **1,** the act of perplexing, embarrassing, etc.; **2,** the state of being abashed or embarrassed; perplexity; loss of self-possession; **3,** disorder; tumult.

con-fute (kŏn-fūt'), *v.t.* [*p.t.* and *p.p.* -fut'ed, *p.pr.* -fut'ing], **1,** to prove to be false or untrue; **2,** to convict of error; as, he was unable to *confute* the debater.—*n.* **con"fu-ta'tion.**—*n.* **con-fut'er.**
Syn. disprove, refute.

***con-gé** (kôn'zhā'; *Br.* kŏn'jē), [Fr.], *n.* **1,** a formal leave taking; **2,** an abrupt dismissal; as, the ambassador received his *congé.* Also, **con'gee** (kŏn'jē).

con-geal (kŏn-jēl'), *v.t.* to thicken; coagulate; freeze; as, when cold *congeals* water, ice is formed:—*v.i.* to harden by cold; grow stiff or solid, as by coagulation.—*adj.* **con-geal'a-ble.**

con-gen-ial (kŏn-jēn'yăl), *adj.* **1,** of kindred spirit; sympathetic; having the same tastes; **2,** agreeable; naturally suited to one's disposition.—*adv.* **con-gen'ial-ly.**—*n.* **con-ge"ni-al'i-ty.**

con-gen-i-tal (kŏn-jĕn'ĭ-tăl), *adj.* existing at birth, not caused by later influences.—*adv.* **con-gen'i-tal-ly.**

con-ger (kŏng'gẽr), *n.* a large marine, or sea, eel: also called *conger eel.*

con-gest (kŏn-jĕst'), *v.t.* **1,** to cause the blood vessels of (an organ or part of the body) to become too full; **2,** to make too full or overcrowded; as, to *congest* traffic:—*v.i.* **1,** to become too full of blood: said of an organ or part of the body; **2,** to gather into a mass; become too full.

con-ges-tion (kŏn-jĕs'chŭn), *n.* **1,** an overcrowded condition, as of traffic; **2,** excessive fulness of the blood vessels; as, *congestion* of the lungs.

con-glom-er-ate (kŏn-glŏm'ẽr-āt), *v.t.* [*p.t.* and *p.p.* -at"ed, *p.pr.* -at"ing], to gather into a round mass:—*adj.* (kŏn-glŏm'ẽr-ăt), collected, clustered, or massed together:—*n.* **1,** a mass of varied materials or elements; **2,** a rock composed of pebbles, gravel, etc., cemented together.

con-glom-er-a-tion (kŏn-glŏm"ẽr-ā'shŭn), *n.* **1,** the act of gathering into a mass; **2,** a mixed collection or accumulation; mixture.

Con-go snake (kŏng'gō), an eel-like animal, about a foot long, found in the southeastern part of the U. S. (see *amphibian,* illus.).

con-grat-u-late (kŏn-grăt'ū-lāt), *v.t.* [*p.t.* and *p.p.* -lat"ed, *p.pr.* -lat"ing], to rejoice with, or express sympathetic pleasure to, on account of some happy event.—*n.* **con-grat'u-la"tor.**

con-grat-u-la-tion (kŏn-grăt"ū-lā'shŭn), *n.* the act of expressing sympathetic pleasure.

con-grat-u-la-to-ry (kŏn-grăt'ū-lȧ-tō-rĭ), *adj.* expressing happiness or sympathetic pleasure over another's good fortune.

con-gre-gate (kŏng'grē-gāt), *v.t.* [*p.t.* and *p.p.* -gat"ed, *p.pr.* -gat"ing], to collect into a crowd, mass, etc.:—*v.i.* to assemble; gather together.

con-gre-ga-tion (kŏng"grē-gā'shŭn), *n.* **1,** the act of assembling, or the state of being assembled; **2,** an assembly of persons, esp. for worship; **3,** those organized into a body for religious activity.

con-gre-ga-tion-al (kŏng"grē-gā'shŭn-ăl), *adj.* pertaining to a congregation, esp. one organized for religious activity: **Congregational,** pertaining to Congregationalism or Congregationalists.

con-gre-ga-tion-al-ism (kŏng"grē-gā'shŭn-ăl-ĭzm), *n.* a form of church government in which each congregation governs itself: **Congregationalism,** the faith of a denomination of Protestant evangelical churches united for joint action, but recognizing each congregation as supreme within its own limits.—*n.* **Con"gre-ga'tion-al-ist.**

con-gress (kŏng'grĕs), *n.* **1,** a coming together; meeting; **2,** a conference; an assembly of delegates for the discussion or settlement of affairs of common interest; **3,** the chief lawmaking body of a republic: **Congress,** the national legislature of the United States of America; as, *Congress* holds its sessions at Washington.

Con-gres-sion-al (kŏn-grĕsh'ŭn-ăl), *adj.* pertaining to Congress: **congressional,** of or pertaining to any assembly.—*n.* **con-gres'sion-al-ist.**

Con-gress-man (kŏng'grĕs-măn), *n.* [*pl.* Congressmen (-mĕn)], a member of the U. S. Congress; esp., a member of the House of Representatives.—*n.fem.* **Con'gress-wom"an.**

con-gru-ent (kŏng'grōō-ĕnt), *adj.* **1,** agreeing; suitable; **2,** in geometry, capable of being placed one upon another so as to coincide.—*n.* **con'gru-ence.**

con-gru-i-ty (kŏn-grōō'ĭ-tĭ), *n.* [*pl.* congruities (-tĭz)], agreement; consistency; fitness; also, an instance of agreement or appropriateness.

con-gru-ous (kŏng'grōō-ŭs), *adj.* **1,** in accord with what is fitting; appropriate; **2,** in geometry, capable of being superposed; congruent.—*adv.* **con'gru-ous-ly.**—*n.* **con'gru-ous-ness.**

con-ic (kŏn'ĭk), *adj.* shaped like a cone, or solid body which tapers regularly to a point from a circular base. Also, **con'i-cal.**—*adv.* **con'i-cal-ly.**

co-ni-fer (kō'nĭ-fẽr), *n.* any of an order of evergreen trees having a cone for fruit, as the spruce.

co-nif-er-ous (kō-nĭf'ẽr-ŭs), *adj.* **1,** bearing cones; as, the pine and fir are *coniferous* trees; **2,** pertaining to a tree of the pine or yew family.

con-jec-tur-al (kŏn-jĕk'tūr-ăl), *adj.* doubtful; implying a guess or opinion; as, a *conjectural* statement.—*adv.* **con-jec'tur-al-ly.**

con-jec-ture (kŏn-jĕk'tūr), *n.* a probable inference; surmise; guess:—*v.t.* [*p.t.* and *p.p.* -tured (-tūrd), *p.pr.* -tur-ing], to imagine; guess; as, we can only *conjecture* what the future holds:—*v.i.* to form opinions by surmise; guess.—*adj.* **con-jec'tur-a-ble.**—*n.* **con-jec'tur-er.**

con-join (kŏn-join'), *v.t.* to join together; associate:—*v.i.* to unite.

con-joint (kŏn-joint'), *adj.* **1,** coöperating; united; **2,** joint; as, *conjoint* action in an enterprise.—*adv.* **con-joint'ly.**

con-ju-gal (kŏn'jōō-găl), *adj.* of or pertaining to marriage.—*adv.* **con'ju-gal-ly.**—*n.* **con"ju-gal'i-ty.**

con-ju-gate (kŏn'jōō-gāt), *v.t.* [*p.t.* and *p.p.* -gat"ed, *p.pr.* -gat"ing], to give the forms of (a verb), covering the various changes according to voice, mood, tense, number, and person:—*v.i.* to unite sexually:—*adj.* (kŏn'jōō-găt), **1,** combined in pairs; **2,** of words, similar in origin.

con-ju-ga-tion (kŏn″jo͞o-gā′shŭn), *n.* 1, the act of joining together; union; 2, in grammar, the process of giving the forms of a verb, indicating voice, mood, tense, number, and person; 3, the inflection so given; 4, a division of verbs inflected in a similar way; 5, a temporary union of two minute animal forms, which in this way exchange material.—*adj.* **con″ju-ga′tion-al.**

con-junct (kŏn-jŭngkt′), *adj.* joined together; conjoined; as, *conjunct* degrees in music.—*adv.* **con-junct′ly.**

con-junc-tion (kŏn-jŭngk′shŭn), *n.* 1, the act of joining; 2, union; connection; 3, the apparent meeting of two or more stars or planets; 4, in grammar, an uninflected word used to connect: **coördinating conjunction,** a conjunction, such as *and,* connecting equal and similar parts: **subordinating conjunction,** a conjunction, such as *if,* introducing a dependent clause.

con-junc-ti-va (kŏn″jŭngk-tī′vȧ), *n.* the mucous membrane lining the inner surface of the eyelids and covering the front part of the eyeball.

con-junc-tive (kŏn-jŭngk′tĭv), *adj.* 1, connective; uniting; 2, in grammar: a, possessing the qualities of a conjunction; as, a *conjunctive* adverb; b, *Rare,* subjunctive:—*n.* in grammar, 1, a word connecting both meaning and construction: opp. of *disjunctive;* 2, the subjunctive mood.—*adv.* **con-junc′tive-ly.**

con-junc-ti-vi-tis (kŏn-jŭngk″tĭ-vī′tĭs), *n.* inflammation of the mucous membrane covering the front part of the eyeball and lining the eyelids.

con-junc-ture (kŏn-jŭngk′tûr), *n.* 1, a holding together; union; 2, a combination of circumstances or causes; a critical time; as, at this *conjuncture* the citizens were asked to be strictly neutral.

con-ju-ra-tion (kŏn″jo͞o-rā′shŭn), *n.* 1, a magic spell; 2, the practice of magic; sorcery.

con-jure (kŭn′jẽr), *v.t.* [*p.t.* and *p.p.* **-jured** (-jẽrd), *p.pr.* -jur-ing], 1, to command or summon by a spell, as an evil spirit; 2, to influence, as if by magic; as, he *conjured* her grief away; 3, (kŏn-jo͝or′), to appeal to solemnly; implore:—*v.i.* to use a magic spell; practice magic.

con-jur-er (kŭn′jẽr-ẽr), *n.* one who produces illusions by magic or sleight of hand; a juggler; as, the *conjurers* of India perform wonders. Also, **con′jur-or.**

con-nate (kŏn′āt; kŏ-nāt′), *adj.* 1, innate; inborn; as, *connate* markings; 2, existing together from birth; 3, of the same origin; cognate, as languages or words.

con-nect (kŏ-nĕkt′), *v.t.* 1, to bind or fasten together; unite; 2, to associate:—*v.i.* to join; be associated.
Syn. (see combine).

con-nect-ed (kŏ-nĕk′tĕd), *p.adj.* 1, marked by coherence; continuous; 2, related; linked together.—*adv.* **con-nect′ed-ly.**—*n.* **con-nect′ed-ness.**

con-nec-tion (kŏ-nĕk′shŭn), *n.* 1, the state of being joined; union; 2, relation or closeness, as of thought; as, in this *connection,* let me say, etc.; 3, the act or means of joining; 4, a bond or tie; 5, relation by marriage or blood; also, a distant relative; 6, one's customers, acquaintances, etc., considered as a group. Also, esp. in Great Britain, **con-nex′ion.**

con-nec-tive (kŏ-nĕk′tĭv), *adj.* fitted for the work of joining: **connective tissue,** a tissue that binds together and supports other tissues; as, tendons are made of *connective tissue:*—*n.* that which joins, as, in grammar, a conjunction.

con-ning tow-er 1, the low, shot-proof pilot house of an armored vessel; 2, on submarines, a low tower on the deck used as a post of observation and as an entrance to the boat.

con-niv-ance (kŏ-nīv′ăns), *n.* the act of secretly encouraging wrong; silent assent, as to wrongdoing.

con-nive (kŏ-nīv′), *v.i.* [*p.t.* and *p.p.* -nived′ (-nīvd′), *p.pr.* -niv′ing], 1, to close the eyes to a wrong or fault; permit secretly that which one should openly oppose; 2, to aid secretly; as, to *connive* at the breaking of a law.—*n.* **con-niv′er.**

con-nois-seur (kŏn″ĭ-sûr′; kŏn″ĭ-sūr′), *n.* a critical and competent judge; as, a *connoisseur* of art.

con-no-ta-tion (kŏn″ō-tā′shŭn), *n.* 1, that which is suggested in addition to the primary meaning; as, the *connotation* of the word "rainbow" includes the seven primary colors; 2, the suggestion of something additional; also, the thing implied; 3, import; meaning.

con-note (kŏ-nōt′), *v.t.* [*p.t.* and *p.p.* -not′ed, *p.pr.* -not′ing], to imply in addition to the primary meaning; as, the word "man" *connotes* life, action, form, etc.
Syn. denote. *Denote,* as contrasted with *connote,* means to have as literal or precise signification; an exact definition of a word expresses what the word *denotes. Connote* means to suggest, or to have as secondary meaning, in addition to or along with the denotation. The word "tiger" *denotes* a large beast of the cat family; it *connotes* the cruelty and swiftness of the cat.

con-nu-bi-al (kŏ-nū′bĭ-ăl), *adj.* of or pertaining to marriage.—*adv.* **con-nu′bi-al-ly.**—*n.* **con-nu″bi-al′i-ty.**

con-quer (kŏng′kẽr), *v.t.* 1, to gain by conquest; overcome; subdue; as, Cæsar *conquered* Gaul; 2, to overcome by moral force, as a habit:—*v.i.* to be victorious.—*adj.* **con′quer-a-ble.**
Syn. surmount, vanquish, defeat, subjugate.

con-quer-or (kŏng′kẽr-ẽr), *n.* a victor; as, the *conqueror* Napoleon.

con-quest (kŏng′kwĕst), *n.* 1, the act of subduing; subjugation; victory; 2, that which is won or overpowered.
Syn. triumph, mastery. (See victory.)

con-san-guin-e-ous (kŏn″săng-gwĭn′ē-ŭs), *adj.* 1, pertaining to blood relationship; 2, descended from the same stock; akin; related by blood.—*adv.* **con″san-guin′e-ous-ly.**

con-san-guin-i-ty (kŏn″săng-gwĭn′ĭ-tĭ), *n.* blood relationship.

con-science (kŏn′shĕns), *n.* 1, the moral sense or consciousness within oneself which determines right and wrong; 2, conduct in accordance with one's sense of right.—*adj.* **con′science-less.**

con-sci-en-tious (kŏn″shĭ-ĕn′shŭs), *adj.* 1, pertaining to the conscience; as, *conscientious* objections; 2, influenced or regulated by conscience; as, a good and *conscientious* man.—*adv.* **con″sci-en′tious-ly.**—*n.* **con″sci-en′-tious-ness.**

con-scious (kŏn′shŭs), *adj.* 1, aware of one's own thoughts and actions or of things outside oneself; 2, known within, or as belonging to, oneself; as, *conscious* superiority; 3, mentally awake; 4, embarrassed; self-conscious.—*adv.* **con′scious-ly.**
Syn. advised, sensible, assured.

con-scious-ness (kŏn′shŭs-nĕs), *n.* 1, the knowledge of that which passes in one's own mind; 2, the state of being aware; sensation; 3, knowledge gained directly of the presence of some object, state, or influence; 4, the entire mental life.

con-script (kŏn-skrĭpt′), *v.t.* to compel to enter the army or navy; as, men were *conscripted* for army service during the Civil War:—*adj.* (kŏn′skrĭpt), registered; enrolled by compulsion in the army:—*n.* one thus enrolled.

con-scrip-tion (kŏn-skrĭp′shŭn), *n.* **1**, the drafting, or compulsory enrollment, of a person for military or naval service; **2**, the draft system.

con-se-crate (kŏn′sē-krāt), *v.t.* [*p.t.* and *p.p.* -crat″ed, *p.pr.* -crat″-ing], **1**, to set apart as sacred; dedicate to the service of God: opp. of *desecrate;* **2**, to hallow:—*adj.* made sacred.—*n.* **con′se-cra″tor.**

con-se-cra-tion (kŏn″sē-krā′shŭn), *n.* **1**, the act of hallowing or sanctifying; **2**, the state of being hallowed or sanctified; **3**, a setting apart for a sacred use or office; **4**, devotion to a cause; **5**, ordination, as of a bishop.

con-sec-u-tive (kŏn-sĕk′ū-tĭv), *adj.* **1**, without interruption in succession; as, *consecutive* days; **2**, composed of parts arranged in due order; as, a *consecutive* story; **3**, designating, or pertaining to, a clause expressing result.—*adv.* **con-sec′u-tive-ly.**—*n.* **con-sec′u-tive-ness.**

con-sen-sus (kŏn-sĕn′sŭs), *n.* general agreement, as, esp., in opinion.—*adj.* **con-sen′su-al.**

con-sent (kŏn-sĕnt′), *n.* **1**, a yielding of the mind or will; **2**, concord; agreement; as, by common *consent:*—*v.i.* **1**, to comply; yield; **2**, to concur; agree.

Syn., v. accede, acquiesce. (See assent.)

con-se-quence (kŏn′sē-kwĕns), *n.* **1**, that which naturally follows a cause; result; **2**, importance; hence, rank or position.

Syn. effect, end, issue. (See result.)

con-se-quent (kŏn′sē-kwĕnt), *adj.* following as a result or natural effect; as, war and the *consequent* poverty:—*n.* **1**, a natural result or effect; that which follows; **2**, in mathematics, the second term of a ratio.—*adv.* **con′se-quent-ly.**

con-se-quen-tial (kŏn″sē-kwĕn′shăl), *adj.* **1**, following as an effect; **2**, self-important; **3**, weighty; important.—*adv.* **con″se-quen′tial-ly.**

con-ser-va-tion (kŏn″sẽr-vā′shŭn), *n.* **1**, the act of keeping from decay, loss, or injury; **2**, official care and preservation, as of such natural resources as coal, oil, forests, etc.

con-serv-a-tism (kŏn-sûr′vȧ-tĭzm), *n.* the tendency to adhere to existing conditions, institutions, laws, etc., and to oppose change or progress.

con-serv-a-tive (kŏn-sûr′vȧ-tĭv), *adj.* **1**, having the tendency or power to preserve or keep, as salt; **2**, naturally opposed to change:—*n.* **1**, that which preserves; **2**, one opposed to hasty changes in political, religious, or civil institutions; as, the *conservative* is seldom progressive: **Conservative**, a member of a political party in Great Britain, opposed to radical reform: distinguished from *Liberal* and *Laborite.*—*adv.* **con-serv′a-tive-ly.**—*n.* **con-serv′a-tive-ness.**

con-serv-a-to-ry (kŏn-sûr′vȧ-tō-rĭ), *adj.* tending to preserve:—*n.* [*pl.* conservatories (-rĭz)], **1**, a greenhouse, esp. a private one; **2**, a public place of instruction, as in music.

con-serve (kŏn-sûrv′), *v.t.* [*p.t.* and *p.p.* -served′ (-sûrvd′), *p.pr.* -serv′-ing], **1**, to preserve from injury or destruction; as, to *conserve* the peace of society; **2**, to preserve with sugar:—*n.* (kŏn-sûrv′; kŏn′sûrv), **1**, preserved or candied fruit; a sweetmeat; **2**, in *pl.*, preserves.

con-sid-er (kŏn-sĭd′ẽr), *v.t.* **1**, to fix the mind upon; **2**, to treat with thoughtfulness; esteem; **3**, to believe; regard as; as, I *consider* him rude; **4**, to make allowance for; as, to *consider* his poverty in imposing a fine:—*v.i.* to deliberate; reflect.

Syn. ponder, weigh, meditate.

con-sid-er-a-ble (kŏn-sĭd′ẽr-ȧ-bl), *adj.* worthy of notice; important; valuable.—*adv.* **con-sid′er-a-bly.**

con-sid-er-ate (kŏn-sĭd′ẽr-āt), *adj.* having regard for others; thoughtful.—*adv.* **con-sid′er-ate-ly.**

con-sid-er-a-tion (kŏn-sĭd″ẽr-ā′shŭn), *n.* **1**, the act of taking thought or reflecting; **2**, claim to notice; importance; **3**, mature thought; as, to take into *consideration* the result of an act; **4**, regard for others; thoughtfulness; **5**, a fee; payment for service rendered; **6**, something to be taken into calculation; reason.

con-sid-er-ing (kŏn-sĭd′ẽr-ĭng), *prep.* taking into account; allowing for; in view of.

con-sign (kŏn-sīn′), *v.t.* **1**, to deliver in a formal manner to another; yield in trust; **2**, to send to another to be sold, cared for, etc., as merchandise; **3**, to set apart; devote; as, the host *consigned* the room to our use.—*adj.* **con-sign′a-ble.**

con-sign-ee (kŏn″sī-nē′; kŏn″sĭ-nē′), *n.* the person to whom goods are shipped; an agent.

con-sign-ment (kŏn-sīn′mĕnt), *n.* **1**, the act of sending goods; **2**, the thing consigned; as, he received a large *consignment* of goods; **3**, the writing by which anything is delivered formally or shipped.

con-sign-or (kŏn-sīn′ẽr; kŏn″sī-nôr′), *n.* the person who sends goods to another. Also, **con-sign′er.**

con-sist (kŏn-sĭst′), *v.i.* **1**, to be made; be composed: followed by *of;* **2**, to have as foundation or nature: followed by *in;* **3**, to have the power of harmonizing; be consistent: followed by *with.*

con-sist-en-cy (kŏn-sĭs′tĕn-sĭ), *n.* [*pl.* consistencies (-sĭz)], **1**, degree of density or firmness; as, the *consistency* of a liquid; **2**, harmony; agreement, esp. between deeds and statements or between conduct and principles; **3**, the state of being consistent. Also, **con-sist′ence.**

con-sist-ent (kŏn-sĭs′tĕnt), *adj.* **1**, solid; not fluid; **2**, not self-contradictory; standing together or in agreement; as, his deeds were *consistent* with his belief.—*adv.* **con-sist′ent-ly.**

Syn. accordant, compatible, harmonious.

con-sis-to-ry (kŏn-sĭs′tō-rĭ; kŏn′sĭs-tō-rĭ), *n.* [*pl.* consistories (-rĭz)], the governing body of a church; also, the place where such a body meets.

con-sol-a-ble (kŏn-sōl′ȧ-bl), *adj.* capable of being comforted or cheered in misfortune or grief.

con-so-la-tion (kŏn″sō-lā′shŭn), *n.* **1**, the act of giving, or state of receiving, sympathy; **2**, a means of relieving mental or physical distress; solace.

con-sol-a-to-ry (kŏn-sŏl′ȧ-tō-rĭ), *adj.* soothing; tending to relieve or comfort; giving solace.

¹con-sole (kŏn-sōl′), *v.t.* [*p.t.* and *p.p.* -soled′ (-sōld′), *p.pr.* -sol′ing], to give comfort to; cheer in sorrow; solace.

²con-sole (kŏn′sōl), *n.* **1**, in architecture, a corbel; a bracketlike support or ornament; **2**, the frame or stand which contains the keys, stops, etc., of a modern pipe organ, at which the performer sits.

con-sol-i-date (kŏn-sŏl′ĭ-dāt), *v.t.* [*p.t.* and *p.p.* -dat″ed, *p.pr.*

-dat″ing], **1**, to make solid; condense; **2**, to strengthen; unite:—*v.i.* **1**, to become solid; **2**, to become united.—*n.* **con-sol′i-da″tor.**—*n.* **con-sol″i-da′tion.**

con-sols (kŏn-sŏlz′; kŏn′sŏlz), *n.pl.* the principal government securities of Great Britain, consolidated in 1751.

***con-som-mé** (kôn″sô″mā′; kŏn″sō-mā′), [Fr.], *n.* a strong, clear soup made from meat and vegetables.

con-so-nance (kŏn′sō-năns), *n.* agreement of sounds; harmony; concord. Also, **con′so-nan-cy.**

con-so-nant (kŏn′sō-nănt), *n.* **1**, a speech sound made by closing or narrowing the mouth or throat; **2**, a letter used as the symbol of such a sound, as *b*, *c*, *d*, etc.:—*adj.* **1**, of musical sounds, harmonious; **2**, consistent; **3**, pertaining to a consonant.—*adj.* **con″so-nan′tal.**—*adv.* **con′so-nant-ly.**

con-sort (kŏn′sôrt), *n.* **1**, a companion; a partner; **2**, a husband or wife; **3**, a ship accompanying another; **4**, agreement:—*v.t.* and *v.i.* (kŏn-sôrt′), to associate; keep company: with *with*.

con-spic-u-ous (kŏn-spĭk′ū-ŭs), *adj.* **1**. plainly visible; striking; obvious; **2**, outstanding; noticeable; **3**, distinguished; notable.—*adv.* **con-spic′u-ous-ly.**—*n.* **con-spic′u-ous-ness.**

con-spir-a-cy (kŏn-spĭr′*ȧ*-sĭ), *n.* [*pl.* conspiracies (-sĭz)], **1**, a plot; a secret combination of persons, as for an unlawful purpose; **2**, any seeming combination of circumstances leading to an event.

con-spir-a-tor (kŏn-spĭr′*ȧ*-tẽr), *n.* one who plots.

con-spire (kŏn-spīr′), *v.i.* [*p.t.* and *p.p.* -spired′ (-spīrd′), *p.pr.* -spir′-ing], **1**, to plan secretly together to commit a crime; combine for an unlawful purpose; **2**, to agree to work to one end; **3**, to work in harmony with other circumstances so as to tend to produce a given result; as, events *conspired* to injure him.—*n.* **con-spir′er.**

con-sta-ble (kŭn′st*ȧ*-bl; kŏn′-), *n.* **1**, in the Middle Ages, a high court official; **2**, an officer of the law, with duties similar, but inferior, to those of a sheriff.—*n.* **con′sta-ble-ship″.**

con-stab-u-la-ry (kŏn-stăb′ū-lā-rĭ), *adj.* pertaining to constables, or police:—*n.* [*pl.* constabularies (-rĭz)], **1**, constables collectively; **2**, an armed force organized for police duty.

con-stan-cy (kŏn′stăn-sĭ), *n.* **1**, firmness of mind; endurance; fidelity; **2**, stability; fixedness.
Syn. faithfulness, devotion, loyalty.

con-stant (kŏn′stănt), *adj.* **1**, faithful; firm; steadfast; true; **2**, unchanging; invariable; regular; **3**, in mathematics, not changing in value:—*n.* **1**, that which does not vary; **2**, in mathematics, a value which remains unchanged.

con-stant-ly (kŏn′stănt-lĭ), *adv.* **1**, in a faithful or regular manner; **2**, continually; invariably.

con-stel-la-tion (kŏn″stĕ-lā′shŭn), *n.* **1**, a group of fixed stars, having a special name; **2**, an assemblage of brilliant and distinguished persons.

con-ster-na-tion (kŏn″stẽr-nā′shŭn), *n.* dismay; terror; horror.

con-sti-pate (kŏn′stĭ-pāt), *v.t.* [*p.t.* and *p.p.* -pat″ed, *p.pr.* -pat″ing], to render (the bowels) inactive: **constipated,** *p.adj.* having bowels which move infrequently or with difficulty.—*n.* **con″sti-pa′tion.**

con-stit-u-en-cy (kŏn-stĭt′ū-ĕn-sĭ), *n.* [*pl.* constituencies (-sĭz)], **1**, the body of electors voting for a representative member, as of Congress; **2**, a body of clients, subscribers, etc.; **3**, the district in which such a body of supporters lives.

con-stit-u-ent (kŏn-stĭt′ū-ĕnt), *adj.* **1**, forming a necessary part; component; as, oxygen and hydrogen are the *constituent* parts of water; **2**, having the power to vote for a representative:—*n.* **1**, an essential or necessary part; **2**, a voter; **3**, one who is represented by another.

con-sti-tute (kŏn′stĭ-tūt), *v.t.* [*p.t.* and *p.p.* -tut″ed, *p.pr.* -tut″ing], **1**, to compose or make up; as, he is delicately *constituted;* **2**, to appoint; **3**, to elect; enact; establish.—*n.* **con′sti-tut″er.**

con-sti-tu-tion (kŏn″stĭ-tū′shŭn), *n.* **1**, the act of establishing; **2**, bodily strength; vitality; **3**, mental temperament; **4**, the principles of organization of a social group; esp., the system of fundamental laws of a nation or state; as, the *Constitution* of the United States.

con-sti-tu-tion-al (kŏn″stĭ-tū′shŭn-ăl), *adj.* **1**, inherent in the fundamental make-up of a person, mental or physical; as, a *constitutional* dislike of hard work; **2**, pertaining to the make-up of a thing; **3**, in accordance with the fundamental law of a state, nation, society, or other group; as, *constitutional* rights:—*n. Colloq.*, a walk for health.—*adv.* **con″sti-tu′tion-al-ly.**

con-sti-tu-tion-al-i-ty (kŏn″stĭ-tū″-shŭn-ăl′ĭ-tĭ), *n.* the quality or state of being in accordance with the fundamental law of some state or society; lawfulness.

con-strain (kŏn-strān′), *v.t.* **1**, to hold down or keep back; as, the handcuffs *constrained* his action; **2**, to urge, drive, or compel; as, his conscience *constrains* him to do right; **3**, to confine; imprison; **4**, to secure or hold tightly.—*n.* **con-strain′er.**

con-strained (kŏn-strānd′), *p.adj.* characterized by unnaturalness or repression.—*adv.* **con-strain′ed-ly.**

con-straint (kŏn-strānt′), *n.* **1**, compulsion; force; necessity; **2**, repression; lack of naturalness; **3**, confinement.
Syn. coercion. (See restraint.)

con-strict (kŏn-strĭkt′), *v.t.* to bind; cramp.—*adj.* **con-stric′tive.**

con-stric-tion (kŏn-strĭk′shŭn), *n.* **1**, compression; **2**, that which compresses; **3**, that which is compressed; a narrowed part.

con-stric-tor (kŏn-strĭk′tẽr), *n.* **1**, that which binds or squeezes; **2**, a serpent that crushes its prey in its coils; **3**, a muscle that contracts part of the body.

con-struct (kŏn-strŭkt′), *v.t.* **1**, to build; form; put together; compose; **2**, to contrive; invent; **3**, in geometry, to represent by means of points, lines, or planes; as, to *construct* an angle equal to a given angle.—*n.* **con-struc′tor; con-struct′er.**

con-struc-tion (kŏn-strŭk′shŭn), *n.* **1**, the act of building; **2**, that which is built; an edifice; **3**, interpretation; **4**, arrangement and grammatical relationship of words in a clause or sentence.—*adj.* **con-struc′tion-al.**

con-struc-tive (kŏn-strŭk′tĭv), *adj.* **1**, capable of, or pertaining to, building; **2**, positive; tending to help or build up rather than to hinder, depress, or destroy: opp. of *destructive;* as, *constructive* criticism suggests improvements; **3**, based on interpretation rather than on express statement; implied; as, *constructive* fraud.—*adv.* **con-struc′tive-ly.**—*n.* **con-struc′tive-ness.**

con-strue (kŏn′stro͞o; kŏn-stro͞o′), *v.t.* [*p.t.* and *p.p.* -strued (-stro͞od), *p.pr.* -stru-ing], **1**, to interpret; explain; as, his act was *construed* as a favor; **2**, in grammar: **a**, to analyze or take apart (a sentence) so as to show the word relationship and make plain the meaning; hence, to translate (a foreign language); **b**, to combine in proper grammatical relation; as, in Latin, to *construe* a verb with the dative.—*n.* **con′stru-er.**—*adj.* **con-stru′a-ble.**

con-sul (kŏn′sŭl), *n.* **1**, an officer commissioned by a government to reside in a foreign port or city, to promote the interests of his country's trade and protect its citizens or subjects; **2**, one of the two joint chief officials of the Roman Republic; **3**, in French history, one of the three joint chief officials of the French Republic (1799–1804).—*n.* **con′sul-ship.**—*adj.* **con′su-lar.**

con-su-late (kŏn′sū-lāt), *n.* **1**, the office and residence of a consul; **2**, the term of office of a consul.

con-sult (kŏn-sŭlt′), *v.t.* **1**, to ask advice of; **2**, to have regard to:—*v.i.* to take counsel together.—*n.* **con-sult′er.**

con-sul-ta-tion (kŏn″sŭl-tā′shŭn), *n.* **1**, the act of conferring; **2**, a conference for mutual counsel; as, a *consultation* of physicians.

con-sume (kŏn-sūm′), *v.t.* [*p.t.* and *p.p.* -sumed′ (-sūmd′), *p.pr.* -sum′ing], **1**, to destroy, as by fire; waste wholly; **2**, to eat or drink up; use up:—*v.i.* to waste away.—*adj.* **con-sum′a-ble.**—*n.* **con-sum′er.**

con-sum-mate (kŏn′sŭ-māt; kŏn-sŭm′ āt), *v.t.* [*p.t.* and *p.p.* -mat″ed, *p.pr.* -mat″ing], to complete; finish; perfect:—*adj.* (kŏn-sŭm′āt; kŏn′sŭ-māt), perfect.—*adv.* **con-sum′mate-ly.**

con-sum-ma-tion (kŏn″sŭ-mā′shŭn), *n.* **1**, conclusion; accomplishment; as, the *consummation* of a wish; **2**, a desired end; goal.

con-sump-tion (kŏn-sŭmp′shŭn), *n.* **1**, the act of using up, or the state of being used up; destruction; **2**, the amount used up; as, the annual *consumption* of sugar; **3**, a gradual wasting away of the body; hence, a wasting disease, esp. pulmonary tuberculosis.

con-sump-tive (kŏn-sŭmp′tĭv), *adj.* **1**, intended to be used up; tending to use up; **2**, pertaining to, inclined to, or afflicted with, pulmonary tuberculosis:—*n.* one afflicted with pulmonary tuberculosis.—*adv.* **con-sump′tive-ly.**

con-tact (kŏn′tăkt), *n.* **1**, a coming together of two things; a touching; close union; **2**, the joining point of two conductors through which an electric current passes; **3**, a means of securing a personal interview; also, the interview, esp. with a prospective customer:—*v.t.* to come into contact with; esp., to interview.

con-ta-gion (kŏn-tā′jŭn), *n.* **1**, the giving of disease to another by direct or indirect contact; **2**, a disease that can be so communicated; **3**, an agency, as a virus, by which disease may be transmitted; **4**, pestilence; corruption; **5**, the communication of an emotion, manner, etc., to another.

con-ta-gious (kŏn-tā′jŭs), *adj.* **1**, transmitted by contact; as, scarlet fever is *contagious;* **2**, carrying infection; hence, unwholesome.—*adv.* **con-ta′gious-ly.**—*n.* **con-ta′gious-ness.**

Syn. infectious. A *contagious* disease is one that can be carried through contact of some kind; as, measles is *contagious.* An *infectious* disease is one that can be spread through germs in the air, water, etc.; as, influenza is *infectious.*

con-tain (kŏn-tān′), *v.t.* **1**, to hold, as a vessel; **2**, to comprehend; include; **3**, to hold or be equivalent to; as, a quart *contains* two pints; **4**, to restrain or hold back; repress: used reflexively; as, she could scarcely *contain* herself; **5**, to be exactly divisible by.—*n.* **con-tain′er.**

con-tam-i-nate (kŏn-tăm′ĭ-nāt), *v.t.* [*p.t.* and *p.p.* -nat″ed, *p.pr.* -nat″ing], to pollute or make impure.—*adj.* **con-tam′i-na-tive.**

Syn. corrupt, defile, taint, sully.

con-tam-i-na-tion (kŏn-tăm″ĭ-nā′shŭn), *n.* **1**, the act of making impure; **2**, that which pollutes; **3**, a taint; as, it is very necessary to keep drinking water from *contamination.*

con-temn (kŏn-tĕm′), *v.t.* [*p.t.* and *p.p.* -temned′ (-tĕmd′), *p.pr.* -temn′ing (-tĕm′ĭng; -tĕm′nĭng)], to scorn; look upon or treat with contempt.

con-tem-plate (kŏn′tĕm-plāt; kŏn-tĕm′plāt), *v.t.* [*p.t.* and *p.p.* -plat″ed, *p.pr.* -plat″ing], **1**, to consider with attention; meditate on; **2**, to look upon as possible or probable; intend; as, to *contemplate* going south:—*v.i.* to meditate.—*n.* **con′tem-pla″tor.**—*n.* **con″tem-pla′tion.**

con-tem-pla-tive (kŏn-tĕm′plȧ-tĭv), *adj.* thoughtful; as, a *contemplative* state of mind.—*adv.* **con-tem′pla-tive-ly.**—*n.* **con-tem′pla-tive-ness.**

con-tem-po-ra-ne-ous (kŏn-tĕm″pō-rā′nē-ŭs), *adj.* living, occurring, or existing at the same time. Also, **co-tem″po-ra′ne-ous.**—*adv.* **con-tem″po-ra′ne-ous-ly.**—*n.* **con-tem″po-ra′ne-ous-ness.**

con-tem-po-ra-ry (kŏn-tĕm′pō-rā-rĭ), *adj.* **1**, existing or occurring at the same time; **2**, belonging to the same time; coeval:—*n.* [*pl.* contemporaries (-rĭz)], a person or thing existing at the same time as another.

con-tempt (kŏn-tĕmpt′), *n.* **1**, the act of scorning; **2**, the state of being scorned; **3**, disdain; scorn; **4**, disobedience to the orders, rules, etc., of a court; also, disorderly conduct in court; **5**, disgrace; shame.

con-tempt-i-ble (kŏn-tĕmp′tĭ-bl), *adj.* meriting scorn.—*adv.* **con-tempt′i-bly.**—*n.* **con-tempt′i-ble-ness.**

Syn. contemptuous. *Contemptible* describes that which deserves disdain or scorn; as, his meanness was *contemptible; contemptible* cowardice. *Contemptuous* describes that which expresses disdain and scorn, and also one who feels disdain and scorn; as, *contemptuous* disapproval; a *contemptuous* critic.

con-temp-tu-ous (kŏn-tĕmp′tū-ŭs), *adj.* disdainful; scornful; as, a *contemptuous* smile.—*adv.* **con-temp′tu-ous-ly.**—*n.* **con-temp′tu-ous-ness.**

Syn. (see contemptible).

con-tend (kŏn-tĕnd′), *v.i.* **1**, to strive in opposition; vie; as, to *contend* for the prize; **2**, to dispute or debate:—*v.t.* to maintain or assert.—*n.* **con-tend′er.**

Syn. contest, struggle, combat.

[1]**con-tent** (kŏn′tĕnt; kŏn-tĕnt′), *n.* **1**, usually in *pl.*, all that which is contained, as in a vessel, bundle, book, etc.; **2**, the subject matter or meaning, as of a sermon or thesis; **3**, usually in *pl.*, extent; capacity, as for holding; size; **4**, the quantity or amount contained.

[2]**con-tent** (kŏn-tĕnt′), *adj.* **1**, satisfied with one's lot, whatever it is; easy of mind and heart; **2**, willing; assenting:—*v.t.* to satisfy; gratify; appease:—*n.* **1**, ease of mind and heart; satisfaction; **2**, the cause of such satisfaction.

con-tent-ed (kŏn-tĕn′tĕd), *p.adj.* gratified; satisfied; serene.—*adv.* **con-tent′ed-ly.**—*n.* **con-tent′ed-ness.**

con-ten-tion (kŏn-tĕn′shŭn), *n.* **1**, contest; debate; quarrel; strife; **2**, a point or statement brought forward to support an argument.

con-ten-tious (kŏn-tĕn′shŭs), *adj.* causing disputes or strife; quarrelsome; as, a *contentious* spirit.—*adv.* **con-ten′tious-ly.**—*n.* **con-ten′tious-ness.**

con-tent-ment (kŏn-tĕnt′mĕnt), *n.* **1,** the state of being satisfied; **2,** satisfaction; content.

con-ter-mi-nous (kŏn-tûr′mĭ-nŭs), *adj.* **1,** contained within the same limits; **2,** having the same boundary; bordering, as states. Also, **co-ter′mi-nous.** —*adj.* **con-ter′mi-nal.**

con-test (kŏn-tĕst′), *v.t.* **1,** to dispute; as, to *contest* an election; **2,** to struggle to gain, as a victory; **3,** to litigate:—*v.i.* to strive; contend; vie:—*n.* (kŏn′tĕst), **1,** a struggle for superiority, as in sports; **2,** a fight; **3,** a litigation.—*adj.* **con-test′a-ble.**
Syn., n. conflict, combat, quarrel.

con-test-ant (kŏn-tĕs′tănt), *n.* one who disputes, opposes, questions, or contends. Also, **con-test′er.**

con-text (kŏn′tĕkst), *n.* the words which are closely connected with any special sentence or word, and which may determine its meaning.—*adj.* **con-tex′tu-al.**

con-ti-gu-i-ty (kŏn″tĭ-gū′ĭ-tĭ), *n.* [*pl.* contiguities (-tĭz)], **1,** nearness; contact; **2,** a continuous mass or series.

con-tig-u-ous (kŏn-tĭg′ū-ŭs), *adj.* touching; adjoining; near.—*adv.* **con-tig′u-ous-ly.**—*n.* **con-tig′u-ous-ness.**

con-ti-nence (kŏn′tĭ-nĕns), *n.* self-control, esp. in regard to passions and desires. Also, **con′ti-nen-cy.**

[1]**con-ti-nent** (kŏn′tĭ-nĕnt), *adj.* temperate; exercising self-control, esp. over passions and desires; virtuous; abstinent.—*adv.* **con′ti-nent-ly.**

[2]**con-ti-nent** (kŏn′tĭ-nĕnt), *n.* one of the large divisions of land on the earth; as, the *continent* of North America: **the Continent,** the mainland of Europe.

con-ti-nen-tal (kŏn″tĭ-nĕn′tăl), *adj.* pertaining to, or characteristic of, a continent: **Continental, 1,** of or pertaining to the mainland of Europe; **2,** in American history, of or pertaining to the colonies at the time of the Revolution:—*n.* **1,** in American history, a colonial soldier during the Revolution; **2,** an inhabitant of Europe.

con-tin-gen-cy (kŏn-tĭn′jĕn-sĭ), *n.* [*pl.* contingencies (-sĭz)], **1,** possibility, but not certainty; **2,** a chance or possible occurrence; also, one occurrence incidental to another. Also, **con-tin′gence.**

con-tin-gent (kŏn-tĭn′jĕnt), *adj.* **1,** possible; **2,** accidental; **3,** conditional; as, a *contingent* liability:—*n.* **1,** a possibility; **2,** a proportionate share; esp., a quota of troops.—*adv.* **con-tin′gent-ly.**

con-tin-u-al (kŏn-tĭn′ū-ăl), *adj.* **1,** occurring again and again; **2,** proceeding without interruption; incessant; constant.—*adv.* **con-tin′u-al-ly.**
Syn. continuous. *Continual* sometimes means unceasing or constant, but often has the idea of occurring or repeating steadily and rapidly; as, *continual* storms. *Continuous* means unbroken or uninterrupted and applies to both time and space; as, a *continuous* performance may be marred by *continual* interruptions.

con-tin-u-ance (kŏn-tĭn′ū-ăns), *n.* **1,** uninterrupted succession; **2,** duration, as of a habit.

con-tin-u-a-tion (kŏn-tĭn″ū-ā′shŭn), *n.* **1,** the act or state of being carried on without interruption; **2,** that which resumes, as part of a story; **3,** a supplementary or additional part: **continuation school,** a school in which pupils old enough to be employed can continue with general or vocational courses without interruption to their employment.

con-tin-ue (kŏn-tĭn′ū), *v.t.* [*p.t.* and *p.p.* -ued (-ūd), *p.pr.* -u-ing], **1,** to carry on without interruption; **2,** to take up again after interruption; resume, as a story; **3,** to retain, as an official in office; **4,** to postpone; prolong, as a law case:—*v.i.* **1,** to remain; abide; **2,** to last; **3,** to persevere.

con-ti-nu-i-ty (kŏn″tĭ-nū′ĭ-tĭ), [*pl.* continuities (-tĭz)], **1,** uninterrupted succession or connection; **2,** close union; **3,** in a motion-picture scenario, the arrangement of events in dramatic order.

con-tin-u-ous (kŏn-tĭn′ū-ŭs), *adj.* connected; uninterrupted; unbroken.—*adv.* **con-tin′u-ous-ly.**
Syn. (see continual).

con-tort (kŏn-tôrt′), *v.t.* to bend or twist violently out of shape; distort.

con-tor-tion (kŏn-tôr′shŭn), *n.* **1,** a twisting or writhing, esp. of the face or body.—*n.* **con-tor′tion-ist.**

con-tour (kŏn′to͞or″; kŏn″to͞or′), *n.* an outline, esp. if curved or sweeping; profile; as, the *contour* of the face or of the land: **contour line,** a line connecting points on a land surface which have the same elevation; also, the indication on a map of such a line.

con-tra- (kŏn′trȧ-), [Lat.], *prefix,* against; opposite; opposite to; contrary; contrary to; as, *contra*dict; *contra*distinction.

con-tra-band (kŏn′trȧ-bănd), *adj.* prohibited; forbidden to be brought in, or shipped out, as in time of war:—*n.* **1,** traffic in forbidden goods; smuggling; **2,** smuggled or forbidden goods: **contraband of war,** certain materials essential to warfare, as munitions, food, etc., which a neutral nation may not supply to the nations at war, except at the risk of seizure and condemnation.

con-tra-bass (kŏn′trȧ-bās″), *adj.* in music, being an octave lower in pitch than another instrument of the same kind:—*n.* a large, deep-toned, orchestral instrument shaped like a violin: also called *bass*, or, usually, *double bass* or *bass viol* (see *musical instrument,* illus.).

con-tra-cep-tion (kŏn″trȧ-sĕp′shŭn), *n.* the act or practice by which conception or pregnancy is artificially prevented.—*adj.* and *n.* **con″tra-cep′tive.**

con-tra-clock-wise (kŏn″trȧ-klŏk′wīz″), *adj.* and *adv.* in a direction opposite to that taken by the hands of a clock. Also, **coun″ter-clock′wise″**, *Pfd. S.*

con-tract (kŏn-trăkt′), *v.t.* **1,** to draw closer together; condense; **2,** to wrinkle, as the brows; **3,** to become affected with, as a disease; acquire; incur, as a debt; **4,** to establish by formal agreement; betroth; **5,** in grammar, to shorten, as in *o'er* for *over:*—*v.i.* **1,** to shrink; **2,** to agree to do something; **3,** to make a promise of marriage:—*n.* (kŏn′trăkt), **1,** a written agreement; as, a *contract* for goods; **2,** a legal agreement, or the document containing it: **contract bridge,** auction bridge in which only so many odd tricks may be counted in the trick score as the declarer contracts to take.—*adj.* **con-trac′tive.**
Syn., n. agreement, bargain. *Agreement,* the most general term, names an arrangement made by general consent of the parties to it; as, an *agreement* to meet for lunch. A *contract* is a formal, binding, and enforceable *agreement;* as, a teacher's *contract. Bargain* is used mainly of buying and selling; as, to make a *bargain* with a dealer.

con-tract-ed (kŏn-trăk′tĕd), *p.adj.* **1,** drawn together; shortened; **2,** narrow; mean; **3,** betrothed.—*adv.* **con-tract′ed-ly.**—*n.* **con-tract′ed-ness.**

con-tract-i-ble (kŏn-trăk′tĭ-bl), *adj.* capable of being shortened or drawn together.—*n.* **con-tract′i-ble-ness.**

con-trac-tile (kŏn-trăk′tĭl), *adj.* tending to, or capable of, shortening or drawing together.—*n.* **con″trac-til′i-ty.**

con-trac-tion (kŏn-trăk′shŭn), *n.* **1,** the act of drawing together; **2,** the state of being drawn together; **3,** shrinkage; decrease; **4,** acquirement, as of a disease; **5,** the shortening of a word by the omission of letters, as *can't* for *cannot.*

con-trac-tor (kŏn-trăk′tẽr), *n.* **1,** one of the parties to a written agreement; **2,** one who undertakes to supply or construct on a large scale for a stated sum; **3,** something that shortens or draws together.

con-tra-dict (kŏn″trȧ-dĭkt′), *v.t.* **1,** to assert the opposite of (a statement); **2,** to deny the words of (another):—*v.i.* to oppose in words; gainsay.—*n.* **con″tra-dict′er; con″tra-dic′tor.**

con-tra-dic-tion (kŏn″trȧ-dĭk′shŭn), *n.* **1,** the act of saying the opposite; denial; **2,** absolute opposition; inconsistency; as, a *contradiction* of terms.

con-tra-dic-to-ry (kŏn″trȧ-dĭk′tō-rĭ), *adj.* **1,** characterized by inconsistency or opposition, as statements; **2,** contrary; denying; as, a *contradictory* person.—*adv.* **con″tra-dic′to-ri-ly.**—*n.* **con″tra-dic′to-ri-ness.**

Syn. inconsistent, opposed. (See opposite.)

con-tra-dis-tinc-tion (kŏn″trȧ-dĭs-tĭngk′shŭn), *n.* distinction by contrast: esp. in *in contradistinction to.*—*adj.* **con″tra-dis-tinc′tive.**

con-tral-to (kŏn-trăl′tō; kŏn-trȧl′tō), *n.* [*pl.* contraltos (-tōz); contralti (-tē)], **1,** the lowest female voice; alto; **2,** a person with such a voice; **3,** the part sung by such a person, as in a quartet.

con-trap-tion (kŏn-trăp′shŭn), *n. Colloq.*, a device or contrivance.

con-tra-ri-e-ty (kŏn″trȧ-rī′ĕ-tĭ), *n.* [*pl.* contrarieties (-tĭz)], **1,** the state or quality of being contradictory, opposed, or perverse; **2,** opposition; inconsistency.

con-tra-ri-wise (kŏn′trȧ-rĭ-wīz″; kŏn-trâ′rĭ-wīz″), *adv.* **1,** conversely; in the opposite way; **2,** on the contrary; **3,** in a contrary manner.

con-tra-ry (kŏn′trȧ-rĭ; kŏn-trâ′rĭ), *adj.* **1,** opposed; contradictory; conflicting; **2,** opposite in direction; **3,** adverse, as a wind; **4,** (often kŏn-trâ′rĭ), perverse; wayward:—*n.* [*pl.* contraries (-rĭz)], **1,** a thing with qualities opposite or contradictory to those of some other thing; **2,** the opposite of some assertion or declaration.—*adv.* **con′tra-ri-ly.**—*n.* **con′tra-ri-ness.**

Syn., adj. discordant. (See opposite.)

con-trast (kŏn-trȧst′), *v.t.* **1,** to place in such a way as to show differences; compare in order to show unlikeness; **2,** to state the difference between:—*v.i.* to be very different, as shown by comparison:—*n.* (kŏn′trȧst), **1,** opposition or striking difference of qualities shown by comparison; **2,** the thing or quality showing such difference.

con-tra-vene (kŏn″trȧ-vēn′), *v.t.* [*p.t.* and *p.p.* -vened′ (-vēnd′), *p.pr.* -ven′ing], **1,** to obstruct; act contrary to; violate, as a treaty; **2,** to dispute, as a statement; defeat.—*n.* **con″tra-ven′tion.**

***con-tre-temps** (kôṅtr′″tāṅ′), [Fr.], *n.* [*pl.* contretemps (-tāṅ′)], an awkward occurrence; a hitch.

con-trib-ute (kŏn-trĭb′ūt), *v.t.* [*p.t.* and *p.p.* -ut-ed, *p.pr.* -ut-ing], to give to some common fund or purpose along with others, as to the Red Cross; furnish, as a share:—*v.i.* **1,** to aid the accomplishment of a common purpose; give to a cause; **2,** to be of use; help to bring about; as, play *contributes* to health.—*n.* **con-trib′u-tor.**

con-tri-bu-tion (kŏn″trĭ-bū′shŭn), *n.* **1,** the act of giving or sharing for a common purpose; **2,** the thing or help given; **3,** a writing furnished to a newspaper or magazine.

con-trib-u-tive (kŏn-trĭb′ū-tĭv), *adj.* **1,** tending, in common with other factors, to produce a result; **2,** giving; lending aid.—*adv.* **con-trib′u-tive-ly.**

con-trib-u-to-ry (kŏn-trĭb′ū-tō-rĭ), *adj.* **1,** giving or lending aid; **2,** of the nature of a contribution; **3,** tending, in common with other factors, to produce a result; as, a *contributory* cause of war.

con-trite (kŏn′trīt), *adj.* **1,** humble; penitent; as, a *contrite* sinner; **2,** resulting from penitence.—*adv.* **con′trite-ly.**—*n.* **con′trite-ness.**

con-tri-tion (kŏn-trĭsh′ŭn), *n.* sincere sorrow for sin or error.

con-triv-ance (kŏn-trīv′ăns), *n.* **1,** the inventive faculty; ingenuity; **2,** the act of working out devices for special uses; **3,** the device or apparatus thus worked out; a scheme.

con-trive (kŏn-trīv′), *v.t.* [*p.t.* and *p.p.* -trived′ (-trīvd′), *p.pr.* -triv′ing], **1,** to devise cleverly; invent; plan; **2,** to manage:—*v.i.* to scheme; as, he *contrived* to escape.—*n.* **con-triv′er.**—*adj.* **con-triv′a-ble.**

Syn. plot, design. (See discover.)

con-trol (kŏn-trōl′), *n.* **1,** a check; restraint; **2,** superintendence; authority; **3,** the apparatus regulating the movement of an airplane:—*v.t.* [*p.t.* and *p.p.* -trolled′ (-trōld′), *p.pr.* -trol′ling], **1,** to restrain; govern; **2,** to regulate.—*adj.* **con-trol′la-ble.**—*adv.* **con-trol′la-bly.**

Syn., v. guide, direct. (See govern.)

con-trol-ler (kŏn-trōl′ẽr), *n.* **1,** one who or that which governs or regulates; **2,** (also, *comptroller*), a public officer who oversees, examines, and certifies accounts.—*n.* **con-trol′ler-ship.**

con-tro-ver-sial (kŏn″trō-vûr′shăl), *adj.* pertaining to, or like, a dispute; contentious.—*adv.* **con″tro-ver′sial-ly.**—*n.* **con″tro-ver′sial-ist.**

con-tro-ver-sy (kŏn′trō-vûr″sĭ), *n.* [*pl.* controversies (-sĭz)], a dispute; argument.

Syn. contention, strife. (See quarrel.)

con-tro-vert (kŏn′trō-vûrt; kŏn″trō-vûrt′), *v.t.* to dispute about; discuss; deny.—*n.* **con′tro-vert″er.**

con-tro-vert-i-ble (kŏn″trō-vûr′tĭ-bl), *adj.* capable of being disputed.—*adv.* **con″tro-vert′i-bly.**

con-tu-ma-cious (kŏn″tū-mā′shŭs), *adj.* stubborn; scornful, esp. of legal authority.—*adv.* **con″tu-ma′cious-ly.**—*n.* **con″tu-ma′cious-ness.**

con-tu-ma-cy (kŏn′tū-mȧ-sĭ), *n.* [*pl.* contumacies (-sĭz)], obstinate or stubborn opposition to lawful authority.

con-tu-me-li-ous (kŏn″tū-mē′lĭ-ŭs), *adj.* showing haughty contempt or scorn; exhibiting insolence or rudeness.—*adv.* **con″tu-me′li-ous-ly.**

con-tu-me-ly (kŏn′tū-mē-lĭ), *n.* [*pl.* contumelies (-lĭz)], **1,** haughty, scornful rudeness; insolent, insulting language or abuse; **2,** an instance of, or the humiliation after, such behavior.

con-tuse (kŏn-tūz′), *v.t.* [*p.t.* and *p.p.* -tused′ (-tūzd′), *p.pr.* -tus′ing], to bruise or injure by a blow.

con-tu-sion (kŏn-tū′zhŭn), *n.* **1,** the act of bruising by a blow; **2,** the condition of being so bruised; **3,** a bruise.

co-nun-drum (kō-nŭn′drŭm), *n.* a riddle or puzzle.

con-va-lesce (kŏn″vȧ-lĕs′), *v.i.* [*p.t.* and *p.p.* -lesced′ (-lĕst′), *p.pr.* -lesc′ing], to recover strength and health after illness; get better; improve.

con-va-les-cence (kŏn″vȧ-lĕs′ĕns), *n.* **1**, the gradual recovery of good health after illness; **2**, the period of such recovery.

con-va-les-cent (kŏn″vȧ-lĕs′ĕnt), *adj.* **1**, recovering health; **2**, of or pertaining to the recovery from illness or the period of recovery:—*n.* one recovering health after illness.

con-vec-tion (kŏn-vĕk′shŭn), *n.* a carrying or transmitting; esp., the transmitting of heat or electricity through a liquid or gas by means of currents.

con-vene (kŏn-vēn′), *v.i.* [*p.t.* and *p.p.* -vened′ (-vēnd′), *p.pr.* -ven′ing], to meet together: used of persons or of an assembly:—*v.t.* to cause to assemble.

con-ven-ience (kŏn-vēn′yĕns), *n.* **1**, suitability; fitness; **2**, freedom from discomfort; ease; accommodation; **3**, that which adds to comfort or makes work easier. Also, **con-ven′ien-cy.**

con-ven-ient (kŏn-vēn′yĕnt), *adj.* **1**, suitable; timely; **2**, affording accommodation; handy; saving work or trouble.—*adv.* **con-ven′ient-ly.**

con-vent (kŏn′vĕnt), *n.* **1**, an association of persons devoted to a religious life: called a nunnery, if made up of women, a monastery, if made up of men; **2**, a building occupied by such an association.

con-ven-ti-cle (kŏn-vĕn′tĭ-kl), *n.* a meeting or an assembly for worship, esp. a private or illegal one.

con-ven-tion (kŏn-vĕn′shŭn), *n.* **1**, the act of meeting; **2**, a formal meeting; esp., a social, commercial, or political assembly, met for some definite object; as, the annual *conventions* of bankers or railroad men; **3**, a diplomatic agreement; **4**, general consent or opinion; **5**, hence, something established thereby; a fixed custom or usage.

con-ven-tion-al (kŏn-vĕn′shŭn-ăl), *adj.* **1**, of or pertaining to an assembly; **2**, pertaining to established customs; **3**, formal; sanctioned by, or growing out of, custom or tradition; **4**, based on accepted models; showing lack of originality; **5**, in art, following fixed rules in design, technique, etc.—*adv.* **con-ven′tion-al-ly.**

con-ven-tion-al-ism (kŏn-vĕn′shŭn-ăl-ĭzm), *n.* **1**, regard for that which is formal or artificial in conduct, art, etc.; **2**, a formality; customary practice or usage.—*n.* **con-ven′tion-al-ist.**

con-ven-tion-al-i-ty (kŏn-vĕn″shŭn-ăl′ĭ-tĭ), *n.* [*pl.* conventionalities (-tĭz)], **1**, adherence to formal or set rules or precedents; **2**, a formality.

con-ven-tion-al-ize (kŏn-vĕn′shŭn-ăl-īz), *v.t.* [*p.t.* and *p.p.* -ized (-īzd), *p.pr.* -iz″ing], to make to conform to custom, as conduct, art, etc.

con-ven-tu-al (kŏn-vĕn′tū-ăl), *adj.* pertaining to, or characteristic of, a convent:—*n.* a member of a convent.

con-verge (kŏn-vûrj′), *v.i.* [*p.t.* and *p.p.* -verged′ (-vûrjd′), *p.pr.* -verg′ing], to tend to meet at one point:—*v.t.* to cause to meet at one point.

con-ver-gence (kŏn-vûr′jĕns), *n.* the act or quality of tending toward one point; a coming together at one point. Also, **con-ver′gen-cy.**

con-ver-gent (kŏn-vûr′jĕnt), *adj.* tending to one point; gradually approaching each other, as lines.

con-ver-sant (kŏn′vẽr-sănt), *adj.* **1**, familiar; fully informed: with *with;* as, *conversant* with the rules; **2**, well acquainted, as with persons.

con-ver-sa-tion (kŏn″vẽr-sā′shŭn), *n.* **1**, informal or familiar talk; **2**, social intercourse; association.—*n.* **con″ver-sa′tion-ist.**

Syn. chat, parley, discourse, colloquy.

con-ver-sa-tion-al (kŏn″vẽr-sā′shŭn-ăl), *adj.* **1**, given to chatty talk; ready to talk; **2**, pertaining to familiar talk.—*adv.* **con″ver-sa′tion-al-ly.**—*n.* **con″ver-sa′tion-al-ist.**

¹con-verse (kŏn-vûrs′), *v.i.* [*p.t.* and *p.p.* -versed′ (-vûrst′), *p.pr.* -vers′ing], **1**, to exchange ideas; talk familiarly; **2**, to engage in intimate intercourse, socially or commercially:—*n.* (kŏn′vûrs), **1**, familiar talk; **2**, intercourse.—*n.* **con-vers′er.**

²con-verse (kŏn′vûrs), *adj.* reversed in order or relationship; opposite:—*n.* **1**, that which is contrary to, or the opposite of, something; **2**, a proposition made by interchanging the terms, as in logic.—*adv.* **con′verse-ly** (kŏn′vẽrs-lĭ; kŏn-vûrs′lĭ).

con-ver-sion (kŏn-vûr′shŭn), *n.* **1**, the act or state of changing from one substance, kind, state, form, etc., to another; **2**, a change in religious belief, as from indifference to faith in a religion, or from one religion to another; as, after his *conversion* he was a better man; **3**, the state of being so changed.

con-vert (kŏn-vûrt′), *v.t.* **1**, to transform, as in form, substance, etc.; **2**, to change from one religion or course to another; cause to undergo a moral change; as, the Christian missionaries try to *convert* the heathen; **3**, to exchange or give for an equivalent:—*n.* (kŏn′vûrt), **1**, one who changes from one belief to another; **2**, one who changes an opinion or a practice.

con-vert-er (kŏn-vûr′tẽr), *n.* **1**, one who or that which changes; **2**, a vessel in which materials undergo change of condition; as, in certain processes, pig iron is changed to steel in a *con erter;* **3**, in electrical usage, a device for changing electrical energy from one form to another, as from an alternating current to a direct current.

con-vert-i-ble (kŏn-vûr′tĭ-bl), *adj.* **1**, capable of being changed, as in substance, form, kind, etc.; **2**, interchangeable; as, *convertible* bonds.—*adv.* **con-vert′i-bly.**—*n.* **con-vert″i-bil′i-ty.**

con-vex (kŏn′vĕks), *adj.* curved on the surface; bulging; as, a *convex* mirror: opp. of *concave:* **convex lens,** a magnifying glass, curved out on one or both sides: **double convex lens,** a lens convex on both sides (see *lens,* illus.):—*n.* a convex body, line, or surface.—*adv.* **con′vex-ly.**

CON-VEX LENS

con-vex-i-ty (kŏn-vĕk′sĭ-tĭ), *n.* [*pl.* convexities (-tĭz)], **1**, the state of curving outward; **2**, a bulging surface, as of a dome.

con-vey (kŏn-vā′), *v.t.* **1**, to carry or transport; as, to *convey* the wheat to market; **2**, to transmit; **3**, to impart, as ideas; communicate; **4**, to transfer to another, as the title to property.—*n.* **con-vey′er; con-vey′or.**—*adj.* **con-vey′a-ble.**

con-vey-ance (kŏn-vā′ăns), *n.* **1**, the act or means of transmitting, communicating, etc.; transport; hence, a vehicle, as an automobile; **2**, the transfer of property from one owner to another; also, the document by which such transfer is made.

con-vey-anc-er (kŏn-vā′ăn-sẽr), *n.* one whose business it is to draw up deeds, etc., transferring property.

con-vey-anc-ing (kŏn-vā′ăn-sĭng), *n.* the business of drawing deeds, leases, etc., and of investigating titles to property.

con-vict (kŏn-vĭkt′), *v.t.* to prove or pronounce guilty of a crime charged:—*n.* (kŏn′vĭkt), a criminal sentenced to prison; one serving his time in prison.

con-vic-tion (kŏn-vĭk′shŭn), *n.* **1,** the act of finding guilty; **2,** the state of being found guilty; **3,** strong belief; as, a *conviction* of what is right; **4,** that which is strongly believed.

con-vince (kŏn-vĭns′), *v.t.* [*p.t.* and *p.p.* -vinced′ (-vĭnst′), *p.pr.* -vinc′-ing], to satisfy by evidence or argument; persuade; cause to believe.—*adv.* **con-vinc′ing-ly.**

Syn. persuade. To *convince* is to satisfy the mind by evidence, proof, or argument. *Persuade* sometimes means the same; as, I am *persuaded* (or *convinced*) that he is right. Usually, however, *persuade* means to win over by personal influence to some act, or to a belief held by another; as, I have *persuaded* her to come to my party.

con-viv-i-al (kŏn-vĭv′ĭ-ăl), *adj.* festive; jovial; gay.—*adv.* **con-viv′i-al-ly.**—*n.* **con-viv″i-al′i-ty.**

con-vo-ca-tion (kŏn″vō-kā′shŭn), *n.* **1,** the act of calling together an assembly, esp. of bishops and clergy, or heads of universities; **2,** a meeting or convention of ministers.—*n.* **con′vo-ca″tor.** —*adj.* **con″vo-ca′tion-al.**

con-voke (kŏn-vōk′), *v.t.* [*p.t.* and *p.p.* -voked′ (-vōkt′), *p.pr.* -vok′ing], to call or summon together; convene; as, Parliament was *convoked* in June.

con-vo-lute (kŏn′vō-lūt), *adj.* rolled inward from one side; rolled together, one part on another.—*adj.* **con′vo-lut″ed.**—*adv.* **con′vo-lute-ly.**

con-vo-lu-tion (kŏn″vō-lū′shŭn), *n.* **1,** a coiling or winding together; **2,** a coil; **3,** one of the irregular folds in the surface of the brain.

con-vol-vu-lus (kŏn-vŏl′vū-lŭs), *n.* [*pl.* convolvuluses (-ĕz); convolvuli (-lī)], any of a genus (*Convolvulus*) of erect, trailing, or twining plants with trumpet-shaped flowers, akin to the morning-glory.

con-voy (kŏn-voi′), *v.t.* to accompany on the way, for protection, by sea or land; as, the ship was *convoyed* into the harbor:—*n.* (kŏn′voi), **1,** a protecting force accompanying ships, goods, persons, etc.; an escort; **2,** the act of escorting or the state of being escorted; as, the ambassador had safe *convoy* home; **3,** one who or that which is so escorted.

con-vulse (kŏn-vŭls′), *v.t.* [*p.t.* and *p.p.* -vulsed′ (-vŭlst′), *p.pr.* -vuls′-ing], to agitate violently; shake; affect with spasms, as of laughter; also, to disturb greatly; throw into a tumult, as with a revolution.

con-vul-sion (kŏn-vŭl′shŭn), *n.* **1,** usually in *pl.*, a violent and unnatural shortening of the muscles; a spasm; fit; **2,** a violent disturbance of the earth, such as an earthquake; **3,** any unusual and extreme agitation or tumult.

con-vul-sive (kŏn-vŭl′sĭv), *adj.* **1,** producing, resulting from, or affected by, abnormal muscular contractions; spasmodic; **2,** pertaining to agitation or physical disturbance.—*adv.* **con-vul′sive-ly.**—*n.* **con-vul′sive-ness.**

co-ny (kō′nĭ; kŭn′ĭ), *n.* [*pl.* conies (-nĭz)], **1,** a small Old World mammal; **2,** *Archaic*, a rabbit; **3,** in the western U. S., a small rodent. Also, **co′ney** [*pl.* coneys (-nĭz)].

coo (kōō), *v.i.* **1,** to cry like a dove or pigeon; **2,** to act or converse in a loving manner:—*v.t.* to utter in a loving, murmuring way:—*n.* the sound uttered by doves and pigeons.—*n.* **coo′er.**

cook (kŏŏk), *v.t.* **1,** to prepare for eating by subjecting to the action of heat, as by boiling, baking, frying, etc.; **2,** *Colloq.*, to alter; tamper with, as accounts; falsify, as a story:—*v.i.* **1,** to act as a cook; **2,** to undergo cooking:—*n.* one who prepares food.

cook-er (kŏŏk′ẽr), *n.* a special apparatus or vessel for preparing food for the table: **fireless cooker,** a device by means of which foods which have been thoroughly heated or partially cooked on the stove are kept hot long enough to complete the process.

cook-er-y (kŏŏk′ẽr-ĭ), *n.* [*pl.* cookeries (-ĭz)], the art or practice of preparing food for the table.

cook-y (kŏŏk′ĭ), *n.* [*pl.* cookies (-ĭz)], a small, flat, sweet cake. Also, **cook′ie.**

cool (kōōl), *adj.* **1,** slightly or moderately cold; **2,** not admitting or retaining heat; as, *cool* clothes; **3,** calm; deliberate; **4,** lukewarm; lacking in cordiality; as, a *cool* reception; **5,** impudent; **6,** *Colloq.*, not exaggerated or overstated; as, he made a *cool* thousand:—*v.t.* **1,** to make slightly cold; chill; **2,** to calm:—*v.i.* to become slightly cold:—*n.* **1,** something slightly cold; **2,** a moderate state of cold: often considered refreshing; as, the *cool* of the evening.—*adj.* **cool′ish.**—*adv.* **cool′ly.**—*n.* **cool′ness.**

cool-er (kōōl′ẽr), *n.* a device that keeps things slightly cold, as an ice box.

coo-lie (kōō′lĭ), *n.* a Chinese or East Indian unskilled laborer. Also, **coo′ly.**

coon (kōōn), *n. Colloq.*, raccoon, a common North American animal.

coop (kōōp), *n.* a cage for fowls, rabbits, etc.; a pen:—*v.t.* to confine in, or as in, a cage; inclose.

coop-er (kōōp′ẽr; kŏŏp′ẽr), *n.* a maker of barrels, casks, etc.

coop-er-age (kōōp′ẽr-āj), *n.* **1,** the business or workshop of a maker of barrels, etc.; **2,** the price for such work.

co-öp-er-ate (kō-ŏp′ẽr-āt), *v.i.* [*p.t.* and *p.p.* -at″ed, *p.pr.* -at″ing], to act or work jointly for a common end; work together to produce the same effect or benefit.—*n.* **co-öp′er-a″tor.**

co-öp-er-a-tion (kō-ŏp″ẽr-ā′shŭn), *n.* **1,** the act of working jointly together for the same end; concurrence; **2,** the association of individuals, as in business, industry, etc., for mutual benefit.

co-öp-er-a-tive (kō-ŏp′ẽr-ā-tĭv), *adj.* **1,** working together for common ends; **2,** belonging, or pertaining, to an organized group so working; as, *coöperative* stores.—*adv.* **co-öp′er-a-tive-ly.**

co-ör-di-nate (kō-ôr′dĭ-nāt), *v.t.* [*p.t.* and *p.p.* -nat″ed, *p.pr.* -nat″-ing], **1,** to place in the same order or class; **2,** to put in harmony; adjust:—*v.i.* **1,** to be of the same order, etc.; **2,** to harmonize:—*adj.* (kō-ôr′dĭ-nāt), **1,** of the same rank or order; as, *coördinate* clauses; **2,** pertaining to things of the same rank:—*n.* one who or that which is of the same rank, order, etc.—*adv.* **co-ör′di-nate-ly.**—*n.* **co-ör″di-na′tion.**

co-ör-di-na-tive (kō-ôr′dĭ-nā-tĭv), *adj.* **1,** adjusted; equal in rank or importance; **2,** making equal in rank; as, a *coördinative* conjunction.

coot (kōōt), *n.* **1,** any of certain birds of the rail family, resembling ducks; **2,** in the U. S., a scoter.

coot-ie (kōōt′ĭ), *n. Slang*, the body louse: a term used by soldiers.

cop (kŏp), *n. Slang*, a policeman: also called *copper*:—*v.t.* [*p.t.* and *p.p.* copped (kŏpt), *p.pr.* cop′ping], *Slang*, to catch; arrest.

co-part-ner (kō-pärt'nẽr), *n.* an associate with others in any undertaking; sharer; sometimes, a business partner.—*n.* **co-part'ner-ship.**

[1]**cope** (kōp), *v.i.* [*p.t.* and *p.p.* coped (kōpt), *p.pr.* cop'ing], to strive or contend evenly; succeed in resisting: often with *with.*

[2]**cope** (kōp), *n.* **1,** a vestment consisting of a long, semicircular cloak or mantle; **2,** something resembling this cloak in shape, as an arched roof; esp., figuratively, the arch of the sky; **3,** a coping, or top layer of a wall:—*v.t.* [*p.t.* and *p.p.* coped (kōpt), *p.pr.* cop'ing], to furnish with a coping; cover, as with a vault.

co-peck (kō'pĕk), *n.* a small, Russian, copper coin, formerly worth about half a cent. Also, **ko'peck,** *Pfd. S.*

Co-per-ni-can (kō-pûr'nĭ-kăn), *adj.* **1,** pertaining to Copernicus, who conceived the sun to be the center of the solar system; **2,** pertaining to his theory.

cope-stone (kōp'stōn″), *n.* **1,** the top stone of a wall; one of the stones of a coping; **2,** the final touch.

Co-phet-u-a (kō-fĕt'ū-ȧ), *n.* an African king who married a beggar maid: used as a subject by Tennyson.

cop-i-er (kŏp'ĭ-ẽr), *n.* **1,** one who makes a reproduction from an original; **2,** an imitator.

cop-ing (kōp'ĭng), *n.* the top masonry of a wall, often sloping so steeply as to shed water.

co-pi-ous (kō'pĭ-ŭs), *adj.* **1,** plenteous; ample; abundant; **2,** profuse in words; voluble.—*adv.* **co'pi-ous-ly.**—*n.* **co'pi-ous-ness.**

cop-per (kŏp'ẽr), **1,** a common, reddish, metallic element, easily worked, and an excellent conductor of heat and electricity; **2,** something made of this metal, as the cent.—*adj.* **cop'per-y.**

cop-per-as (kŏp'ẽr-ȧs), *n.* a green chemical used in dyeing.

cop-per-head (kŏp'ẽr-hĕd″), *n.* a poisonous American snake, akin to the rattlesnake: **Copperhead,** a Northerner whose sympathies lay with the South during the American Civil War.

cop-per-plate (kŏp'ẽr-plāt″), *n.* **1,** a polished copper plate on which something is engraved for printing; **2,** an engraving or a print made from such a plate:—*adj.* **1,** pertaining to the art of engraving on such a plate; **2,** finished; neat.

cop-pice (kŏp'ĭs), *n.* a thicket of small trees or bushes; a copse.

cop-ra (kŏp'rȧ), *n.* the dried meat of the coconut.

copse (kŏps), *n.* a grove or thicket of small trees or bushes; a coppice.

Copt (kŏpt), *n.* a native Egyptian belonging to the race that is descended from the ancient Egyptians.

Cop-tic (kŏp'tĭk), *adj.* of or pertaining to the Copts or their language:—*n.* the language of the Copts.

cop-u-la (kŏp'ū-lȧ), *n.* [*pl.* copulas (-lȧz)], a verb which simply asserts a relationship between the subject and predicate, as, seeing *is* believing, snow *is* white, or the second *is* in the sentence, whatever is, *is* right.

cop-u-late (kŏp'ū-lāt), *v.i.* [*p.t.* and *p.p.* -lat″ed, *p.pr.* -lat″ing], to join or unite, as a pair: used esp. of sexual intercourse.—*n.* **cop″u-la'tion.**

cop-u-la-tive (kŏp'ū-lā-tĭv), *adj.* **1,** uniting; **2,** connecting words or clauses; as, a *copulative* conjunction.

cop-y (kŏp'ĭ), *n.* [*pl.* copies (-ĭz)], **1,** an imitation; duplicate; **2,** a writing exercise from a model; also, the model; **3,** manuscript to be set up in type; **4,** a single one of an edition, as of a book:—*v.t.* [*p.t.* and *p.p.* cop'ied (-ĭd), *p.pr.* cop'y-ing], **1,** to transcribe; reproduce; as, many artists *copy* the works of the masters; **2,** to imitate.
Syn., n. (see duplicate).

cop-y book a book in which are model specimens of handwriting for students to imitate.

cop-y-hold (kŏp'ĭ-hōld″), *n.* **1,** in English law, a tenure of land in which the record of the title is shown only on the rolls of the manorial court; **2,** land held under a tenure recorded in this way.

cop-y-hold-er (kŏp'ĭ-hōl″dẽr), *n.* **1,** in English law, one who holds land by right of a copyhold; **2,** in printing, one who reads to the proof reader the manuscript of matter set up in type.

cop-y-ist (kŏp'ĭ-ĭst), *n.* one who makes reproductions from originals.

cop-y-right (kŏp'ĭ-rīt″), *n.* the exclusive legal right of an artist or author, or his agent, to reproduce, publish, sell, etc., a literary or artistic work for a certain number of years:—*v.t.* to secure a copyright for.

co-quet (kō-kĕt'), *v.i.* [*p.t.* and *p.p.* -quet'ted, *p.pr.* -quet'ting], to flirt; trifle or dally with love, with danger, or the like: with *with.*

co-quet-ry (kō'kĕt-rĭ), *n.* [*pl.* coquetries (-rĭz)], the act of exciting the affection of one of the opposite sex through vanity; flirtation.

co-quette (kō-kĕt'), *n.* a vain woman who trifles with love; a flirt.—*adj.* **co-quet'tish.**—*adv.* **co-quet'tish-ly.**—*n.* **co-quet'tish-ness.**

co-qui-na (kō-kē'nȧ), *n.* a light, fragile rock, found on the coast of Florida, composed of the broken pieces of sea shells: used for buildings, roadbeds, etc.

cor- (kŏr-), a form of *com-* used before *r,* meaning with, together; as, *cor*respond: also used intensively; as, *cor*rode.

cor-a-cle (kŏr'ȧ-kl), *n.* a boat made of basketwork covered with leather, oilcloth, or other waterproof material.

cor-al (kŏr'ăl), *n.* **1,** a hard substance made up of tiny skeletons of certain sea animals; **2,** one of these animals:—*adj.* **1,** made of coral; **2,** red in color, like coral.

cor-al-line (kŏr'ă-lĭn; kŏr'ă-līn), *adj.* **1,** pinkish red, like coral; **2,** pertaining to, or composed of, coral.

cor-bel (kôr'bĕl), *n.* a piece of stone, wood, iron, or the like, projecting from the side of a wall, and used for support.

cord (kôrd), *n.* **1,** a twisted string; a small rope; **2,** often in *pl.,* anything which connects; as, *cords* of love; **3,** a measure of wood, usually equal to 128 cubic feet; **4,** a tendon or nerve:—*v.t.* **1,** to bind or connect with string or rope; **2,** to pile up, as wood, in piles 8 feet by 4 feet.—*p.adj.* **cord'ed.**

cord-age (kôr'dăj), *n.* **1,** cords and ropes collectively, esp. those forming the rigging of a ship; **2,** the number of cords, as of wood, on any given piece of land.

cor-date (kôr'dāt), *adj.* shaped like a heart (see *leaf,* illus.).

cor-dial (kôr'jăl; kôrd'yăl), *adj.* **1,** tending to revive, as a medicine; **2,** hearty; sincere; as, a *cordial* manner:—*n.* **1,** a medicine, food, or drink that revives or cheers; **2,** a sweet, aromatic, alcoholic beverage.—*adv.* **cor'dial-ly.**—*n.* **cor'dial-ness.**

cor-dial-i-ty (kôr-jăl'ĭ-tĭ; kôr″dĭ-ăl'ĭ-tĭ), *n.* sincere geniality; heartiness; as, he greeted us with *cordiality.*

cor-dil-le-ra (kôr″dĭl-yā'rȧ; kŏr-dĭl'ẽr-ȧ), *n.* the main system of parallel mountain ranges of a continent: **the Cordilleras**, the parallel mountain ranges of western North America.

cord-ing (kôr'dĭng), *n.* the ribbed surface of a corded fabric, like corduroy.

cord-ite (kôr'dīt), *n.* a kind of smokeless gunpowder.

cor-do-ba (kôr'dō-vä), *n.* the monetary unit of Nicaragua, equivalent to one gold dollar in U. S. money.

cor-don (kôr'dŏn), *n.* **1**, a ribbon worn as the badge of an order; **2**, a line of men, ships, etc., stationed as sentinels.

cor-do-van (kôr'dō-văn), *n.* a fine Spanish leather, made of goatskin or split horsehide: also called *cordovan leather*.

cor-du-roy (kôr'dŭ-roi"; kôr"dŭ-roi'), *n.* **1**, a stout ribbed or corded cotton cloth with a velvety surface; **2**, in *pl.*, *Colloq.*, trousers, or a suit, made of this material; **3**, in the U. S., a road made of logs laid transversely:—*adj.* **1**, made of a ribbed, durable material called corduroy; **2**, in the U. S., made of logs laid transversely; as, it is rough traveling over a *corduroy* road.

core (kōr), *n.* **1**, the heart or innermost part of anything, esp. of fruit; **2**, the substance or essential point, as of a subject; pith; **3**, a solid form, placed in a mold, which, when metal is poured about it, shapes the interior of a hollow casting; **4**, a bar of soft iron forming the center of an electromagnet or an induction coil:—*v.t.* [*p.t.* and *p.p.* cored (kōrd), *p.pr.* cor'ing], to remove the center, or core, from, as an apple.—*n.* **cor'er.**

co-re-op-sis (kō"rē-ŏp'sĭs; kŏr"ē-ŏp'sĭs), *n.* any of several varieties of plants of the aster family.

co-re-spond-ent (kō"rē-spŏn'dĕnt), *n.* a joint respondent; the person named, jointly with the husband or wife, as the guilty party in a divorce suit. —*n.* **co"re-spond'en-cy.**

co-ri-an-der (kō"rĭ-ăn'dẽr; kŏr"ĭ-), *n.* **1**, a plant of the parsley family, bearing aromatic seeds; **2**, the seed itself, used in flavoring pastries, sweets, etc.

Co-rin-thi-an (kō-rĭn'thĭ-ăn), *adj.* **1**, of or pertaining to Corinth, a luxurious city of ancient Greece; hence, licentious; **2**, designating, or pertaining to, the most highly decorated of the classic orders of architecture, having an ornamented, bell-shaped capital topping a slender column (see *column*, illus.):—*n.* **1**, a native of Corinth; **2** in *pl*, either of two books of the New Testament.—*abbr.* **Cor.**

cork (kôrk), *n.* **1**, the light, elastic, outer layer of bark of a kind of oak; **2**, anything made of cork, as a stopper:—*v.t.* **1**, to stop with a cork, as a bottle; **2**, to hold back or restrain: with *up*:—*adj.* made of cork.—*adj.* **cork'y.**—*adj.* **corked.**

cork-screw (kôrk'skrōō"), *n.* a spirally twisted steel instrument for drawing the corks from bottles:—*adj.* shaped like a corkscrew:—*v.i.* and *v.t.* *Colloq.*, to follow, or cause to follow, a winding course.

corm (kôrm), *n.* a bulblike plant stem, short, and of solid texture, as in the crocus.

cor-mo-rant (kôr'mō-rănt), *n.* **1**, a diving bird that feeds on fish; **2**, a gluttonous person; **3**, an avaricious person.

[1]**corn** (kôrn), *n.* **1**, a grain or seed, esp. of a cereal; **2**, edible cereal grain, as wheat, barley, etc., collectively: the usual sense in Great Britain; **3**, in the U. S., maize or Indian corn; **4**, the plant that produces corn: **corn borer**, a very destructive moth, introduced from Europe in 1917, the larva of which feeds upon many plants, and eats all parts of the corn ear and stalk:—*v.t.* to preserve in salt; season in brine, as beef or tongue.

[2]**corn** (kôrn), *n.* a horny thickening of the skin, esp. on the toe or foot, caused by friction or pressure.

corn-cob (kôrn'kŏb"), *n.* **1**, the woody center of an ear of Indian corn, on which the kernels are set; **2**, a tobacco pipe made of corncob.

corn cock-le a tall weed of the pink family, bearing bright flowers: also called *cornflower*.

corn-crib (kôrn'krĭb"), *n.* in the U. S., a small building for storing corn.

cor-ne-a (kôr'nē-ȧ), *n.* the front, transparent part of the outer coat of the eyeball, which covers the iris and pupil and admits light to the interior.

corned (kôrnd), *p.adj.* preserved or pickled in brine or salt, as, *corned* beef.

cor-nel (kôr'nĕl), *n.* any of various shrubs or low trees, including the dogwoods of Europe and of the U. S.

cor-nel-ian (kôr-nēl'yăn), *n.* a variety of chalcedony: used for jewelry and seals. See **car-nel'ian**, *Pfd. S.*

cor-ner (kôr'nẽr), *n.* **1**, an angle; the point where two lines, sides, or edges meet; **2**, a nook; a secluded place; **3**, a remote point; as, the *corners* of the earth; **4**, an awkward position; a difficult situation; **5**, a condition of monopoly, which causes prices to rise; as, a *corner* in wheat:—*v.t.* **1**, to place in, or drive into, a corner; **2**, to drive or force into some position of difficulty from which there is no escape: **corner the market**, to buy up stock or property, so as to obtain exclusive control of it and dictate the price: a term used in the stock exchange.

cor-ner stone **1**, a stone at the corner of a building, uniting two walls; **2**, a thing of basic importance.

cor-ner-wise (kôr'nẽr-wīz"), *adv.* **1**, diagonally; with the corner toward the front; **2**, so as to form a corner.

[1]**cor-net** (kôr'nĕt; kôr-nĕt'), *n.* **1**, a brass valve instrument, used to give a martial, bold effect (cf. *musical instrument*, illus.); **2**, a cone-shaped paper receptacle for candy; cornucopia.—*n.* **cor'net-ist; cor-net'tist.**

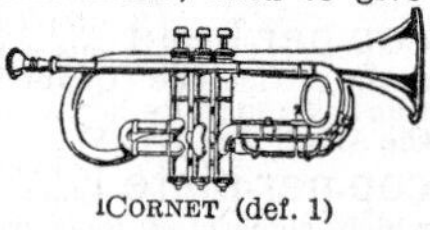

[1]CORNET (def. 1)

[2]**cor-net** (kôr'nĕt; kôr-nĕt'), *n.* **1**, a flag; in the U. S. navy, a flag used for signaling; **2**, a kind of a woman's headdress; the large, white head covering worn by Sisters of Charity.

corn-flow-er (kôrn'flou"ẽr), *n.* **1**, the corn cockle; **2**, the bachelor's-button, a plant having flowery heads of different colors, blue, pink, or white.

cor-nice (kôr'nĭs), *n.* **1**, an ornamental molding placed on a wall near the ceiling; **2**, a horizontal projection forming the top of a wall, column, etc. (see also *architrave*, *entablature*, illus.).—*adj.* **cor'niced.**

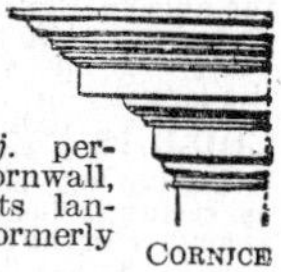

CORNICE

Cor-nish (kôr'nĭsh), *adj.* pertaining to Cornwall, England, its people, or its language:—*n.* the language formerly spoken in Cornwall.

corn meal **1**, coarsely ground corn, usually maize, or Indian corn; **2**, in Scotland, coarse oatmeal.

corn pone in the southern U. S., bread made of corn meal; pone.

corn-stalk (kôrn'stôk"), *n.* a stalk of maize, or Indian corn.

corn-starch (kôrn'stärch"), *n.* starch in the form of a fine powder, made from Indian corn: used for cookery, in making cosmetics, etc.

cor-nu-co-pi-a (kôr″nū-kō′pĭ-*ȧ*), *n.* [*pl.* cornucopias (-*ȧ*z)], **1,** a horn full of fruit and flowers, symbolizing prosperity; **2,** a horn-shaped paper holder for nuts and candy; **3,** plenty; abundance.

co-rol-la (kō-rŏl′*ȧ*), *n.* the petals of a flower collectively, whether separate or united at the edges (cf. *flower*, illus.).

cor-ol-la-ry (kŏr′ō-lā-rĭ; *Br.* kō-rŏl′*ȧ*-rĭ), *n.* [*pl.* corollaries (-rĭz)], **1,** in mathematics, a fact discovered in proving some other fact; an obvious deduction; **2,** a result; an inference.

co-ro-na (kō-rō′n*ȧ*), *n.* [*pl.* coronas (-n*ȧ*z); coronæ (-nē)], **1,** a crown; a garland; **2,** anything at the top resembling a crown; **3,** a halo surrounding a heavenly body, esp. the sun; **4,** a bright discharge produced around electric terminals and wires which carry an alternating current of high potential.

cor-o-nach (kŏr′ō-năkh), *n.* in Scotland and Ireland, a funeral dirge.

cor-o-nal (kŏr′ō-năl; kō-rō′năl), *adj.* of or pertaining to a corona, a crown, or a halo:—*n.* (kŏr′ō-năl), a circlet, wreath, or garland for the head.

cor-o-na-tion (kŏr″ō-nā′shŭn), *n.* the act or ceremony of crowning a king or queen.

cor-o-ner (kŏr′ō-nẽr), *n.* an officer whose chief duty is to investigate, in an inquest, the circumstances of any death supposedly not due to natural causes.

cor-o-net (kŏr′ō-nĕt; kôr′-), *n.* **1,** a small crown for the head, denoting various degrees of rank below that of the sovereign; **2,** an ornamental band or wreath intended to be worn on the head; **3,** the soft part of a horse's foot just above the hoof.

[1]**cor-po-ral** (kôr′pō-răl), *n.* a square of fine white linen placed on the altar beneath the sacred elements during the celebration of the Eucharist.

[2]**cor-po-ral** (kôr′pō-răl), *n.* the lowest noncommissioned officer in the army: **corporal's guard,** a small detachment of men under the command of a corporal; hence, any small group of people.

[3]**cor-po-ral** (kôr′pō-răl), *adj.* pertaining to the human body, as distinguished from, or opposed to, the mind; as, *corporal* punishment.—*n.* **cor″po-ral′i-ty.**

cor-po-rate (kôr′pō-rāt), *adj.* **1,** pertaining to a body of persons united legally, as for doing business; as, *corporate* property; **2,** bodily; in the body; **3,** common; joint; combined; as, *corporate* efforts; **4,** legally established as a body; as, a *corporate* town.—*adv.* **cor′po-rate-ly.**

cor-po-ra-tion (kôr″pō-rā′shŭn), *n.* a number of persons legally acting as one body within the scope of a charter, as a stock company, a municipal group, or the like.

cor-po-re-al (kŏr-pō′rē-ăl), *adj.* having a material body; physical; tangible; as, the body is the *corporeal* habitation of the soul: opp. of *spiritual.*—*adv.* **cor-po′re-al-ly.**—*n.* **cor-po″re-al′i-ty.**

corps (kōr), *n.* [*pl.* corps (kōrz)], **1,** a body of troops for special service; **2,** a body of persons associated in a common work.

corpse (kôrps), *n.* a dead body, usually a human body.

Syn. remains, carcass. (See body.)

cor-pu-lence (kôr′pū-lĕns), *n.* bulkiness or largeness of body; great fatness. Also, **cor′pu-len-cy.**

cor-pu-lent (kôr′pū-lĕnt), *adj.* bulky; fat; having a large, fleshy body; as, a *corpulent* man.

Cor-pus Chris-ti (kôr′pŭs krĭs′tī; krĭs′tĭ), a Roman Catholic festival, celebrated the first Thursday after Trinity Sunday, in honor of the Eucharist, or sacrament of the Lord's Supper.

cor-pus-cle (kôr′pŭs-l), *n.* **1,** a minute particle of matter; **2,** an electron; **3,** in anatomy, a small mass or body; as, a red or white *corpuscle* in the blood.—*adj.* **cor-pus′cu-lar** (kôr-pŭs′kū-l*ȧ*r).

cor-ral (kŏ-răl′; *Span.* kō-räl′), *n.* **1,** a pen for horses or cattle; **2,** an inclosure or wide circle of wagons formed for protection in an encampment:—*v.t.* (kŏ-răl′), [*p.t.* and *p.p.* -ralled′ (-răld′), *p.pr.* -ral′ling], **1,** to drive into, or secure in, a pen or inclosure; **2,** *Colloq.,* to take possession of; appropriate.

cor-rect (kŏ-rĕkt′), *v.t.* **1,** to set straight; make right; **2,** to cure, as a person, of a fault; **3,** to punish for faults; **4,** to counteract; neutralize:—*adj.* **1,** exact; accurate; free from error; **2,** measuring up to or meeting a standard of morals, taste, manners, etc.—*adv.* **cor-rect′ly.**—*n.* **cor-rect′ness.**

Syn., adj. accurate, exact, precise. These words are alike in expressing an agreement with the demands of truth or of some standard. *Correct* means keeping these demands without fault or mistake; as, a *correct* statement. *Accurate* emphasizes the idea of great care in all details; as, *accurate* measurements. *Exact* puts emphasis on absolute agreement with a fact or standard, whether or not this is accomplished by care; as, the *exact* words; the *exact* time. *Precise* sometimes adds to the meaning of *exact* the idea of too great care in details, or fussiness. (See rectify.)

cor-rec-tion (kŏ-rĕk′shŭn), *n.* **1,** the act of pointing out mistakes or of changing something wrong to make it right; **2,** that which is put in the place of something wrong; **3,** reproof; punishment. —*adj.* **cor-rec′tion-al.**

cor-rec-tive (kŏ-rĕk′tĭv), *adj.* tending, or having the power, to make right:—*n.* that which makes right; that which counteracts or neutralizes; an antidote.

cor-rec-tor (kŏ-rĕk′tẽr), *n.* one who or that which sets things right.

cor-re-late (kŏr″ē-lāt′; kŏr′ē-lāt), *v.i.* [*p.t.* and *p.p.* -lat′ed (-lāt′ĕd; -lāt″ĕd), *p.pr.* -lat′ing or lat′ing], to be related by connection, parallelism, etc.:—*v.t.* to put or bring into relation, connection, etc.; connect by exhibiting or discovering a mutual relation.

cor-re-la-tion (kŏr″ē-lā′shŭn), *n.* **1,** a mutual relation; similarity; **2,** the act of bringing into some mutual relationship; **3,** an interdependence of natural happenings; as, the *correlation* of energy.

cor-rel-a-tive (kŏ-rĕl′*ȧ*-tĭv), *adj.* having mutual relation; as, in the sentence, either John or James did it, *either* and *or* are *correlative* conjuctions:—*n.* one of two terms or words that are mutually related.—*adv.* **cor-rel′a-tive-ly.**

cor-re-spond (kŏr″ē-spŏnd′), *v.i.* **1,** to match; as, the hat should *correspond* with the dress; agree; as, his words and acts do not *correspond;* **2,** to write letters.

cor-re-spond-ence (kŏr″ē-spŏn′dĕns), *n.* **1,** communication by letters; also, the letters themselves; **2,** harmony; agreement; similarity.

cor-re-spond-ent (kŏr″ē-spŏn′dĕnt), *adj.* agreeing with; similar:—*n.* **1,** one with whom letters are exchanged; **2,** one who writes for, or is paid to contribute to, a newspaper or magazine.

cor-re-spond-ing (kŏr″ē-spŏn′dĭng), *p.adj.* **1,** agreeing; matching; **2,** holding communication by means of letters.—*adv.* **cor″re-spond′ing-ly.**

cor-ri-dor (kŏr'ĭ-dôr; -dōr), *n.* **1,** a passage, esp. in a large building; **2,** a narrow strip of land, esp. one that connects inland territory with a seaport.

cor-ri-gen-dum (kŏr"ĭ-jĕn'dŭm), [Lat.], *n.* [*pl.* corrigenda (-dȧ)], a fault or error that is to be corrected, esp. an error in a printed book.

cor-ri-gi-ble (kŏr'ĭ-jĭ-bl), *adj.* **1,** capable of being corrected or reformed; **2,** submissive under correction; amenable.—*adv.* **cor'ri-gi-bly.**—*n.* **cor"ri-gi-bil'i-ty.**—*n.* **cor'ri-gi-ble-ness.**

cor-rob-o-rate (kŏ-rŏb'ō-rāt), *v.t.* [*p.t.* and *p.p.* -rat"ed, *p.pr.* -rat"ing], to confirm; make certain; as, to *corroborate* news.—*n.* **cor-rob"o-ra'tion.**

cor-rob-o-ra-tive (kŏ-rŏb'ō-rȧ-tĭv; -rā-tĭv), *adj.* tending to prove, strengthen, verify, or make sure; as, *corroborative* testimony.—*adv.* **cor-rob'o-ra-tive-ly.**—*adj.* **cor-rob'o-ra-to-ry.**

cor-rode (kŏ-rōd'), *v.t.* [*p.t.* and *p.p.* -rod'-ed, *p.pr.* -rod'ing], to eat away gradually, as by chemical action; disintegrate; rust:—*v.i.* to decay; disintegrate.

cor-ro-sion (kŏ-rō'zhŭn), *n.* **1,** the act of eating or wearing away, esp. by chemical action; **2,** a condition produced by the gradual eating or wearing away of some substance, as of metal by rust.

cor-ro-sive (kŏ-rō'sĭv), *adj.* having the power of gradually eating away, as by chemical action: **corrosive sublimate,** mercuric chloride, a white, crystalline, poisonous compound:—*n.* that which eats away or destroys, as an acid.—*adv.* **cor-ro'sive-ly.**

cor-ru-gate (kŏr'ōō-gāt), *v.t.* [*p.t.* and *p.p.* -gat"ed, *p.pr.* -gat"ing], to shape in wrinkles or alternate ridges and grooves; as, time will *corrugate*, or wrinkle, the face: **corrugated iron,** sheet iron pressed into parallel ridges and grooves:—*v.i.* to contract into wrinkles or folds.—*n.* **cor"ru-ga'tion.**

cor-rupt (kŏ-rŭpt'), *v.t.* **1,** to injure; spoil; **2,** to make impure; **3,** to bribe:—*v.i.* to rot; become tainted:—*adj.* **1,** depraved; **2,** putrid; spoiled; **3,** abounding in errors, as a text; **4,** open to bribery; corruptible; as, a *corrupt* lawyer.—*adv.* **cor-rupt'ly.**—*n.* **cor-rupt'ness.**—*n.* **cor-rupt'er.**

cor-rupt-i-ble (kŏ-rŭp'tĭ-bl), *adj.* **1,** capable of being changed for the worse; subject to decay; **2,** capable of being bribed.—*n.* **cor-rupt"i-bil'i-ty.**—*n.* **cor-rupt'i-ble-ness.**—*adv.* **cor-rupt'i-bly.**

cor-rup-tion (kŏ-rŭp'shŭn), *n.* **1,** the act of changing for the worse: applied to loss of purity or honor, or to physical decay; **2,** the state of being changed for the worse; decay; deterioration; impurity; depravity; also, perversion, as of a text.

cor-rup-tive (kŏ-rŭp'tĭv), *adj.* tending to pervert; contaminating.

cor-sage (kôr'sĭj; *Fr.* kôr"sȧzh'), *n.* **1,** the bodice or waist of a woman's dress; **2,** a bouquet of flowers for a woman to wear attached to her dress.

cor-sair (kôr'sâr), *n.* **1,** one who sails on the seas in search of booty; a pirate; **2,** a pirate's armed vessel.

corse (kôrs), *n.* a dead body: used in poetry for *corpse*.

corse-let (kôrs'lĕt), *n.* in former times, armor for the body of a soldier; also, specif., the breastplate. Also, **cors'let.**

cor-set (kôr'sĕt), *n.* a woman's stiffened undergarment, worn to support the figure; stays:—*v.t.* to inclose in stays.

Cor-si-can (kôr'sĭ-kăn), *adj.* pertaining to the island of Corsica or its people:—*n.* **1,** a native of Corsica; **2,** the language of the Corsicans.

***cor-tège** (kôr"tâzh'), [Fr.], *n.* a procession, as of attendants.

Cor-tes (kôr'tĕs), *n.pl.* in Spain or Portugal, the two chambers forming the governing body, or parliament.

cor-tex (kôr'tĕks), *n.* [*pl.* cortices (-tĭ-sēz)], **1,** the rind; **2,** the outer layers of an organ, as of the kidneys or the brain.

co-run-dum (kō-rŭn'dŭm), *n.* an extremely hard mineral used for polishing, occurring in impure form as emery, and in gem varieties as the sapphire.

cor-us-cate (kŏr'ŭs-kāt; kō-rŭs'kāt), *v.i.* [*p.t.* and *p.p.* -cat"ed, *p.pr.* -cat"ing], **1,** to sparkle; gleam, as lightning; **2,** to shine intellectually.—*n.* **cor"us-ca'tion.**

cor-vette (kŏr-vĕt'), *n.* a ship of war, next below a frigate in rank. Also, **cor'vet** (kôr'vĕt).

cor-vine (kôr'vīn; -vĭn), *adj.* of or pertaining to crows; like a crow.

cor-ymb (kŏr'ĭmb; kŏr'ĭm), *n.* in certain plants, a form of flowering in which several flowers are clustered on a central stem, the outer flowers opening first and having longer stalks, so that the cluster is nearly flat on top, as in the hawthorn (see *inflorescence*, illus.).—*adj.* **co-rym'bose** (kō-rĭm'bōs; kŏr"ĭm-bōs'); **co-rym'bous.**

co-se-cant (kō-sē'kănt), *n.* in a right-angled triangle, the ratio of the hypotenuse to the side opposite an acute angle: one of the trigonometric functions.

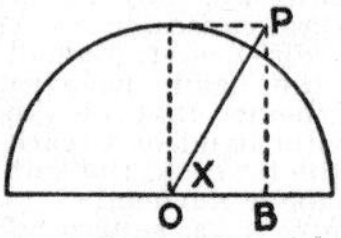

COSECANT

$\frac{OP}{BP}$ = cosecant of angle X.
If BP = 1, the cosecant is equal to OP.

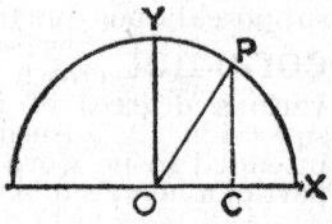

COSINE

$\frac{OC}{OP}$ = cosine of angle XOP.
If OP = 1, the cosine is equal to OC.

co-sine (kō'sīn), *n.* in a right-angled triangle, the ratio of the side adjacent to an acute angle to the hypotenuse: one of the trigonometric functions.

cos-met-ic (kŏz-mĕt'ĭk), *n.* a preparation used to make the skin or hair beautiful:—*adj.* beautifying; esp., designed to beautify the complexion.

cos-mic (kŏz'mĭk), *adj.* **1,** pertaining to the universe and the laws which govern it; hence, orderly, as opposed to chaotic; **2,** vast: **cosmic rays,** radiations similar to X rays, but of greater penetrating power, probably coming from outer space: also called *Millikan rays*. Also, **cos'mi-cal.**—*adv.* **cos'mi-cal-ly.**

cos-mism (kŏz'mĭzm), *n.* a theory of the universe; the philosophy of cosmic evolution.—*n.* **cos'mist.**

cos-mog-o-ny (kŏz-mŏg'ō-nĭ), *n.* [*pl.* cosmogonies (-nĭz)], a theory of the world's origin and growth.

cos-mog-ra-phy (kŏz-mŏg'rȧ-fĭ), *n.* [*pl.* cosmographies (-fĭz)], the science that deals with the description of the general features of the world or the universe.—*n.* **cos-mog'ra-pher.**

cos-mo-pol-i-tan (kŏz"mō-pŏl'ĭ-tăn), *n.* a citizen of the world; one free from local prejudices:—*adj.* at home in any part of the world; free from local prejudices; not provincial.

cos-mop-o-lite (kŏz-mŏp'ō-līt), *n.* one at home in all parts of the world; a cosmopolitan.

cos-mos (kŏz'mŏs), *n.* **1**, order; harmony; **2**, the system of law and order in the universe: opp. of *chaos;* **3**, any harmonious whole developed from complex parts; **4**, any of a genus (*Cosmos*) of plants of the composite family, cultivated for their flowers.

Cos-sack (kŏs'ăk), *n.* one of a warlike tribe of southern Russia, skilled as horsemen.

cos-set (kŏs'ĕt), *n.* a pet lamb; a pet of any kind:—*v.t.* to fondle; pet.

cost (kôst), *v.t.* [*p.t.* and *p.p.* cost, *p.pr.* cost'ing: historically *v.i.*, now a partial *v.t.*, but without passive], **1**, to have (a certain amount) as price; be obtainable for (a certain price); as, the hat *costs* seven dollars; **2**, to require to expend or to be expended, as loss, penalty, consequence, etc.; as, the effort *cost* him much pain; war *costs* many lives:—*v.i.* to involve or cause expenditure, loss, etc.; as, the accident *cost* him dear:—*n.* **1**, charge; expense; the amount paid for anything; **2**, the thing sacrificed to obtain or gain something; outlay, as of labor; **3**, loss; suffering; injury; penalty; **4**, in *pl.*, the expenses of a lawsuit.—*n.* **cost'li-ness.**

cos-tal (kŏs'tăl), *adj.* pertaining to, or situated near, a rib or ribs.

cos-ter-mon-ger (kŏs'tĕr-mŭng"gĕr), *n.* one who peddles fruit, vegetables, fish, etc.

cos-tive (kŏs'tĭv), *adj.* **1**, constipated; **2**, likely to cause constipation.

cost-ly (kôst'lĭ), *adj.* [*comp.* cost'li-er, *superl.* cost'li-est], expensive.
Syn. (see dear).

cos-tume (kŏs'tūm; kŏs-tūm'), *n.* **1**, dress in general; style of dress; **2**, all the outer garments worn at one time, esp. by a woman; **3**, the dress of a given time, period, class, etc.; **4**, historical dress; fancy dress:—*v.t.* (kŏs-tūm'), [*p.t.* and *p.p.* -tumed' (-tūmd'), *p.pr.* -tum'ing], to provide with appropriate garments.—*n.* **cos-tum'er.**

co-sy (kō'zĭ), *adj.* [*comp.* co'si-er, *superl.* co'si-est], comfortable; snug:—*n.* [*pl.* cosies (-zĭz)], **1**, a padded covering for a teapot; **2**, a snug seat. Also, **co'sey;** *Pfd. S.*, **co'zy.**—*adv.* **co'si-ly.**—*n.* **co'si-ness.**

[1]**cot** (kŏt), *n.* **1**, a cottage; hut; **2**, a cover, as for a hurt finger.

[2]**cot** (kŏt), *n.* a small portable bed, esp. one made of canvas.

co-tan-gent (kō-tăn'-jĕnt), *n.* in a right-angled triangle, the ratio between the side adjacent and the side opposite to an acute angle: one of the trigonometric functions.

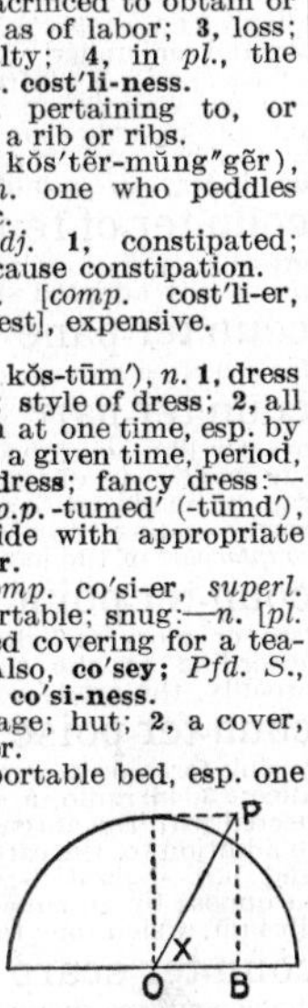

COTANGENT
$\frac{OB}{BP}$ = cotangent of angle X.
If BP = 1, the cotangent is equal to OB.

cote (kōt), *n.* a sheepfold; shelter, esp. for animals at night; also, *Obs.*, a hut.

co-tem-po-ra-ne-ous (kō-tĕm"pō-rā'nē-ŭs), *adj.* living, existing, or occurring at the same time. Also, **con-tem"po-ra'ne-ous**, *Pfd. S.*

co-tem-po-ra-ry (kō-tĕm'pō-rā-rĭ), *n.* [*pl.* cotemporaries (-rĭz)], one living at the same time as another:—*adj.* happening or living at the same time. See **con-tem'po-ra-ry**, *Pfd. S.*

co-te-rie (kō'tē-rĭ; -rē), *n.* a set of persons who meet familiarly; a clique.

co-ter-mi-nous (kō-tûr'mĭ-nŭs), *adj.* having a common boundary. See **con-ter'mi-nous**, *Pfd. S.*

co-til-lion (kō-tĭl'yŭn), *n.* **1**, any of various lively French dances; a quadrille; **2**, a lively dance for eight or more persons; the german; **3**, music for such a dance. Also, ***co"til"lon'** (kô"tē"yôṅ').

cot-tage (kŏt'āj), *n.* a small dwelling; also, a dwelling, big or little, at a summer resort.—*n.* **cot'tag-er.**

[1]**cot-ter** (kŏt'ẽr), *n.* **1**, a cottager; **2**, in Great Britain and Ireland, a tenant farmer. Also, **cot'tar; cot'ti-er.**

[2]**cot-ter** (kŏt'ẽr), *n.* a pin or bolt to fasten together parts of machinery: in some forms called *cotter pin.*

cot-ton (kŏt'n), *n.* **1**, a white, soft, downy substance, resembling wool and inclosing the seeds of certain plants of the mallow family; **2**, the plant producing this substance; **3**, thread or cloth made of cotton: —*adj.* pertaining to, or made of, cotton: **cotton batting,** cotton prepared in rolls for quilting, padding, etc.:—*v.i. Colloq.*, to take a liking: with *to.*—*adj.* **cot'ton-y.**

cot-ton gin a machine for separating the seeds from cotton.

cot-ton-tail (kŏt'n-tāl"), *n.* a wild American rabbit.

cot-ton-wood (kŏt'n-wŏŏd"), *n.* any of several American poplars, having a fluffy, cottony tuft about the seeds.

cot-y-le-don (kŏt"ĭ-lē'dŭn), *n.* a part of a seed containing food to be used to develop the young root, stem, and first true leaves: in many plants appearing above the ground as the seed leaf (see *germination*, illus.). Also, **cot'yl.**—*adj.* **cot"y-le'-don-al.**—*adj.* **cot"y-le'don-ous.**

couch (kouch), *v.t.* **1**, to lay upon a bed or other resting place; **2**, to put into words; as, to *couch* a letter in strong terms; **3**, to lower, as a lance or spear for attack: —*v.i.* **1**, to lie down, as an animal; **2**, to cower: **couch grass,** any of several creeping, spreading grasses (see *inflorescence*, illus.):—*n.* **1**, a bed; sofa; **2**, any place for resting.

couch-ant (kouch'ănt), *adj.* in heraldry, crouching, but with the head up; as, a lion *couchant* (see *lion*, illus.).

cou-gar (kōō'gär), *n.* a large, tawny American animal of the cat family; a puma (which see for illus.): also called *panther; catamount; mountain lion.*

cough (kôf), *v.i.* to expel air from the lungs by a violent effort:—*v.t.* to expel from the lungs or air passages: followed by *up:*—*n.* **1**, the act of coughing; **2**, a disease which makes one cough.

could (kŏŏd), past tense of the auxiliary verb *can.*

cou-lee (kōō'lĭ), *n.* **1**, in western North America, a deep, dry gulch with sides sloping less steeply than those of a cañon; **2**, a sheet of cooled or solid lava.

cou-lomb (kōō-lŏm'), *n.* the practical unit for measuring electricity; the amount of electricity conveyed by one ampere in one second.

coun-cil (koun'sĭl), *n.* **1**, an assembly for consultation; **2**, a municipal governing body; **3**, the deliberation of such a body.

coun-cil-man (koun'sĭl-măn), *n.* [*pl.* councilmen (-mĕn)], a member of an assembly; esp., of the lawmaking body of a city or town.

coun-ci-lor (koun'sĭ-lẽr), *n.* a member of an advisory, deliberative, or governing body. Also, **coun'cil-lor.**

coun-sel (koun'sĕl), *n.* **1**, interchange of opinion; consultation; as, to take *counsel* regarding the course to pursue; **2**, opinion, instruction, advice, etc., as the result of consultation; **3**, a deliberate purpose; plan; **4**, prudence; foresight; **5**, an advocate or lawyer:—*v.t.* **1**, to give advice to; **2**, to recommend; as, I *counsel* patience.
Syn., *v.* (see advise).

coun-se-lor (koun'sĕ-lẽr), *n.* **1**, one who gives advice or counsel; **2**, an advising lawyer: **counselor at law**, a lawyer. Also, **coun'sel-lor.**

1**count** (kount), *v.t.* **1**, to tell off (units) in order to find their number; sum up; enumerate; **2**, to esteem; consider; as, she *counts* herself generous; **3**, to include in an enumeration; as, he *counted* only the best:—*v.i.* **1**, to tell off articles or numbers in order; **2**, to rely: with *on* or *upon;* **3**, to be of worth or value; **4**, to have effect; tell: usually with *heavily, lightly,* or the like:—*n.* **1**, the act of numbering; **2**, the total ascertained.—*adj.* **count'a-ble.**

2**count** (kount), *n.* in France, Spain, Italy, etc., a nobleman, or a title of nobility, equivalent in general to British *earl* and German *graf.*—*n.fem.* **count'ess.**

coun-te-nance (koun'tē-năns), *n.* **1**, the face; **2**, the expression; appearance; **3**, support; **4**, composure; as, he kept *countenance* despite the insult:—*v.t.* [*p.t.* and *p.p.* -nanced (-nănst), *p.pr.* -nanc"-ing], to support; encourage; favor; as, her father would not *countenance* the match.

1**count-er** (koun'tẽr), *n.* **1**, one who or that which keeps count; esp., a piece used to keep the score in a game; **2**, a table in a store at which goods are shown, sold, etc.; **3**, an imitation coin; token.

2**coun-ter** (koun'tẽr), *adj.* contrary; opposite:—*n.* **1**, the opposite or contrary; **2**, a hollow space between parts of a type face (see *type*, illus.); **3**, in boxing, a blow to ward off a blow:—*v.i.* to make an opposite or contrary attack:—*v.t.* **1**, to return (a blow) by another blow; **2**, to combat; oppose:—*adv.* in a contrary direction; in an opposing way or manner.

coun-ter- (koun'tẽr-), *prefix*, in combination with nouns, verbs, adverbs, and participial adjectives, with the following senses: **1**, reciprocation; as, *counter*act; **2**, retaliation; opposition; as, *counter*claim; **3**, oppositeness of direction, tendency, intent, or the like; as, *counter*march; *counter*clockwise; *counter*mand; **4**, correspondence, or a complementary thing, state, etc.; as, *counter*part; *counter*point; *counter*sign; **5**, a duplicate or substitute; as, *counter*feit; *counter*foil.

coun-ter-act (koun"tẽr-ăkt'), *v.t.* to act in opposition to, so as to defeat or hinder; neutralize; bring to nothing.—*adj.* **coun"ter-ac'tive.**—*n.* **coun"ter-ac'tion.**

coun-ter-bal-ance (koun'tẽr-băl"ăns), *n.* an opposed equal force; a counterpoise:—*v.t.* (koun"tẽr-băl'-ăns), [*p.t.* and *p.p.* -anced (-ănst), *p.pr.* -ancing], to oppose by an equal force; offset.

coun-ter-claim (koun'tẽr-klām"), *n.* an opposing claim or demand:—*v.t.* (koun"tẽr-klām'), to make or present, as an opposing claim or demand.

coun-ter-clock-wise (koun"tẽr-klŏk'-wīz"), *adj.* and *adv.* in the direction opposite to that of the motion of clock hands. Also, **con"tra-clock'wise".**

coun-ter-feit (koun'tẽr-fĭt), *v.t.* to copy for a dishonest purpose; forge; imitate with intent to deceive or defraud; as, to *counterfeit* money:—*v.i.* **1**, to carry on deception; **2**, to make imitations, esp. of money:—*adj.* feigned; spurious; forged:—*n.* **1**, an imitation made with intent to deceive; a forgery; **2**, an impostor.—*n* **coun'ter-feit"er.** —*n.* **coun'ter-feit"ing.**

Syn., v. forge. To *counterfeit* is to make imitations of coins, medals, bank bills, or the like, with intent to defraud. To *forge* is to change falsely a written or printed document, or to attach a false signature to such a document, or to a check, note, etc.

coun-ter-foil (koun'tẽr-foil"), *n.* a part attached to a document, as a check, on which a memorandum of its contents may be retained; a stub.

coun-ter-ir-ri-tant (koun"tẽr-ĭr'ĭ-tănt), *n.* in medicine, an agent used to inflame the surface in order to relieve a deep-seated inflammation.

coun-ter-mand (koun"tẽr-månd'; koun'tẽr-månd), *v.t.* **1**, to change (an order or command); revoke (an order); recall; cancel; **2**, to reverse the orders of:—*n.* (koun'tẽr-månd; koun"tẽr-månd'), a contrary order or command.

coun-ter-march (koun'tẽr-märch"), *n.* **1**, a reversal; a returning; **2**, in marching, a sharp turn, as if around a post, and a march back parallel and close to the line of advance:—*v.i.* (koun"tẽr-märch'; koun'tẽr-märch"), **1**, to perform this movement; **2**, to march back.

coun-ter-mine (koun'tẽr-mīn"), *n.* **1**, a mine made to intercept that of an enemy; **2**, a mine placed underground or under water, to destroy similar mines:—*v.i.* (koun"tẽr-mīn'), [*p.t.* and *p.p.* -mined' (-mīnd'), *p.pr.* -min'ing], to place a mine to destroy that of the enemy:—*v.t.* **1**, to oppose by means of countermines; **2**, to defeat or hinder, esp. by hidden means.

coun-ter-of-fen-sive (koun"tẽr-ŏ-fĕn'sĭv), *n.* aggressive operations against an enemy who has previously adopted similar tactics.

coun-ter-pane (koun'tẽr-pān"), *n.* an outer coverlet or quilt for a bed; a spread, often white.

coun-ter-part (koun'tẽr-pärt"), *n.* **1**, a duplicate; **2**, a person exactly like someone else; as, each twin was the *counterpart* of the other; **3**, a thing which can be made to fit exactly; the exact but corresponding reverse; as, the right foot **is a** *counterpart* of the left.

coun-ter-point (koun'tẽr-point"), *n.* the art of combining two or more melodies with a main theme, according to the rules of harmony; more broadly, the art of writing part music.

coun-ter-poise (koun'tẽr-poiz"), *n.* **1**, a counterbalance; an opposing force or power; **2**, a condition of balance; **3**, in radio, a conductor which is connected with the antenna circuit in place of, or in addition to, the earth connection:—*v.t.* [*p.t.* and *p.p.* -poised" (-poizd"), *p.pr.* -pois"ing], to oppose by an equal force; bring into equilibrium; weigh (one thing) against another.

coun-ter-scarp (koun'tẽr-skärp"), *n.* the inner ditch wall, facing the enemy (see *rampart*, illus.).

coun-ter-sign (koun'tẽr-sīn"; koun"tẽr-sīn'), *v.t.* to confirm by signing a document already signed by another; ratify:—*n.* **1**, an additional signature to a document to make it of value; **2**, a word or phrase known to a special group, as a secret password or military watchword.

coun-ter-sink (koun'tẽr-sĭngk"), *v.t.* [*p.t.* and *p.p.* -sunk" (-sŭngk"), *p.pr.* -sink"ing], **1**, to drill (a conelike depression) to receive a screw or bolt; **2**, to drive or sink (a screw or bolt) into such a depression:—*n.* **1**, a tool for drilling such a depression, as for a screw head; **2**, a depression so made.

count-ing-house (koun'tĭng-hous"), *n.* a room or building where business is done and accounts are kept.

count-less (kount'lĕs), *adj.* incapable of being counted; innumerable.

coun-tri-fied (kŭn'trĭ-fīd), *adj.* rural; rustic in manners or appearance. Also, **coun'try-fied.**

coun-try (kŭn′trĭ), *n.* [*pl.* **countries** (-trĭz)], **1**, a tract of land; region; **2**, rural parts; as, "God made the *country* and man made the town"; **3**, one's native land; the land of one's citizenship; **4**, a territory that has a distinct existence as to name, language, government, and the like; also, the people of such a nation; **5**, the people of a nation as a whole; the public:—*adj.* **1**, pertaining to the rural regions; **2**, unpolished; rustic; **3**, pertaining to one's own land.

coun-try–dance (kŭn′trĭ=dȧns″), *n.* a rural dance in which each couple passes between parallel lines made by the other couples.

coun-try-man (kŭn′trĭ-măn), *n.* [*pl.* countrymen (-mĕn)], **1**, one who lives in the rural regions; **2**, one who lives in the same country as another.—*n.fem.* **coun′try-wom″an.**

coun-try-side (kŭn′trĭ-sīd″), *n.* a section or district of the country; also, the people living there.

coun-ty (koun′tĭ), *n.* [*pl.* counties (-tĭz)], **1**, a definite, political district of a country; in the U. S., the division intermediate between state and township; **2**, its inhabitants:—*adj.* pertaining to a county.

coun-ty seat in the U. S., the town or city where a county's government is centered.

***coup** (ko͞o), *n.* **1**, a stroke or blow; **2**, a master stroke of strategy, coming with sudden force: ***coup d'état** (dā″tȧ′), [Fr.], a stroke of state; a sudden act of government changing the political situation.

cou-pé (ko͞o″pā′), *n.* **1**, the front compartment of a French stagecoach; **2**, a half compartment at the end of a European railway carriage; **3**, (ko͞o″pā′; *Colloq.*, ko͞op), a closed four-wheeled carriage or automobile with places for two, three, or four.

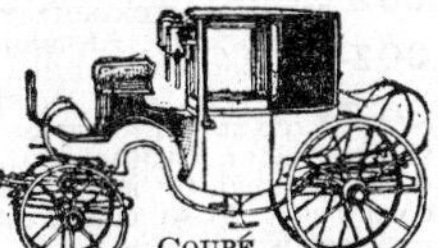

COUPÉ

cou-ple (kŭp′l), *n.* **1**, that which holds together; a leash; bond; **2**, two of the same kind; a pair; brace; **3**, man and wife; **4**, partners at a dance, game, etc.:—*v.t.* [*p.t.* and *p.p.* -pled (-ld), *p.pr.* -pling], **1**, to link or join together, as the cars of a train; **2**, to unite in wedlock:—*v.i.* to form in pairs.

cou-pler (kŭp′lẽr), *n.* one who or that which connects; esp., a device for joining, as railway cars.

cou-plet (kŭp′lĕt), *n.* **1**, two successive lines of verse which rime; a pair of rimes; **2**, a pair; couple.

cou-pling (kŭp′lĭng), *n.* **1**, the act of joining; **2**, that which joins; specif., an iron link uniting two railway cars.

cou-pon (ko͞o′pŏn), *n.* **1**, part of a printed ticket which can be detached or pulled off, such as a ticket for the theater, proving the holder's right to his seat; **2**, a dated certificate attached to a bond, which entitles the holder to the interest.

cour-age (kŭr′āj), *n.* bravery; boldness; fearlessness; valor; fortitude.
Syn. (see bravery).

cou-ra-geous (kŭ-rā′jŭs), *adj.* brave; bold; fearless.—*adv.* **cou-ra′geous-ly.**—*n.* **cou-ra′geous-ness.**

cou-ri-er (ko͞o′rĭ-ẽr; ko͝or′ĭ-ẽr), *n.* **1**, an express messenger; **2**, a traveling attendant who arranges all the details of the journey, as hotel reservations, tickets, etc.

course (kōrs), *n.* **1**, the act of moving onward; progress; career; race; **2**, the ground passed over; a path; a channel through which water flows; **3**, a succession; series, as of lectures; **4**, line of conduct; behavior; **5**, the portion of a meal served at one time; **6**, orderly sequence; as, in due *course;* **7**, a direction, esp. that in which a ship sails; **8**, in golf, the ground over which the game is played; the links: **of course**, as was to be expected; naturally:—*v.t.* [*p.t.* and *p.p.* coursed (kōrst), *p.pr.* cours′ing], **1**, to run through; **2**, to cause to run; pursue.

cours-er (kōr′sẽr), *n.* **1**, one who pursues game with dogs; **2**, *Poetic*, a swift and spirited horse; a racer; war horse.

court (kōrt), *n.* **1**, an inclosed space; esp., a small paved place surrounded by houses; a short street; a blind alley; **2**, a royal palace; **3**, a prince or sovereign and his ministers considered as a ruling power; **4**, an official meeting of a sovereign and his councilors; also, an assembly or reception held by a sovereign; **5**, a level space marked for playing games, as lawn tennis; **6**, a hall of justice; **7**, the place where prisoners are tried; **8**, the judges engaged there; the judge hearing a case; as, the *court* sustained the objection; **9**, the session of a judicial assembly; **10**, flattery paid to one in power; **11**, attention paid by a man to a woman to win her in marriage:—*v.t.* **1**, to pay attention to, as a lover; woo; **2**, to flatter; **3**, to ask, as favors; solicit; invite, as investigation:—*v.i.* **1**, to make love; **2**, to seek favors.

cour-te-ous (kûr′tē-ŭs; kōrt′yŭs), *adj.* courtly; affable; polite.—*adv.* **cour′te-ous-ly.**—*n.* **cour′te-ous-ness.**
Syn. (see polite).

cour-te-san (kōr′tē-zăn; kûr′tē-zăn), *n.* a harlot. Also, **cour′te-zan.**

cour-te-sy (kûr′tē-sĭ; kōr′tē-sĭ), *n.* [*pl.* courtesies (-sĭz)], **1**, politeness combined with kindness; **2**, an act of kindliness, civility, or respect; **3**, favor or consent, as distinguished from right or validity; **4**, (usually, *curtsy*), a slight, respectful bending of the knees by women or girls:—*v.i.* (usually, *curtsy*), [*p.t.* and *p.p.* -sied (-sĭd), *p.pr.* -sy-ing], to make a curtsy.

court-house (kōrt′hous″), *n.* a public building where justice is administered by those legally qualified.

court-ier (kōrt′yẽr), *n.* **1**, one who is attached to a royal court; **2**, one who solicits favor; a flatterer.

court-ly (kōrt′lĭ), *adj.* [*comp.* court′li-er, *superl.* court′li-est], polished; elegant: said of manners.—*n.* **court′li-ness.**

court–mar-tial (kōrt″=mär′shăl), *n.* [*pl.* courts-martial (kōrts″=)], a military or naval court of justice:—*v.t.* to try by such a court.

court–plas-ter (kōrt′=plȧs″tẽr), *n.* a fine fabric covered on one side by an adhesive coating, to be applied to cuts, abrasions, etc.

court-ship (kōrt′shĭp), *n.* the act of wooing or the time so spent.

court-yard (kōrt′yärd″), *n.* an inclosed space adjoining a house.

cous-in (kŭz′n), *n.* **1**, the son or daughter of one's uncle or aunt; **2**, a distant relative.—*adj.* and *adv.* **cous′in-ly.**

cous-in–ger-man (kŭz′n=jûr′măn), *n.* [*pl.* cousins-german (kŭz′nz=)], a first cousin.

cove (kōv), *n.* **1**, a sheltered inlet or creek; **2**, a retired nook.

cov-e-nant (kŭv′ē-nănt), *n.* **1**, a compact; **2**, the promises of God as conditioned and set forth in the Bible; **3**, a solemn agreement of fellowship and faith between members of a church:—*v.t.* and *v.i.* to promise by solemn agreement.

cov-e-nant-er (kŭv′ē-năn-tẽr), *n.* one who enters into an agreement, or makes a covenant.

cov-er (kŭv′ẽr), *v.t.* **1**, to put something over, as a lid; **2**, to conceal; **3**, to overspread, as an area; **4**, to sit upon or incubate, as a hen her eggs; **5**, to include or be sufficient for; as, the book *covers* the topic; **6**, to pass over, as a space or distance; **7**, to shelter; **8**, to hold within aim or range:—*v.i.* **1**, to put on a hat or headdress; **2**, to spread over a surface:—*n.* **1**, that which is laid on something else; **2**, a shelter; protection; as, he went under the *cover* of an escort of soldiers; **3**, a covert, thicket, etc., concealing game; **4**, the table equipment at a meal, esp. that for one person; **5**, a disguise; pretense: **cover charge**, in a restaurant, a fixed fee for table service independent of the charge for food.

cov-ered way in a rampart, a path along the counterscarp, or side of the moat toward the enemy, protected from the enemy's fire by an embankment called the *glacis* (see *rampart*, illus.).

cov-er-ing (kŭv′ẽr-ĭng), *n.* **1**, the act of putting on a cover; **2**, that which covers; wrapper; envelope.

cov-er-let (kŭv′ẽr-lĕt), *n.* a bed quilt; counterpane.

cov-ert (kŭv′ẽrt), *adj.* concealed; covered; disguised; secret:—*n.* **1**, a place that protects or shelters; **2**, a thicket; shelter for game.—*adv.* **cov′ert-ly.**

cov-er-ture (kŭv′ẽr-tūr), *n.* a cover; means of concealment.

cov-et (kŭv′ĕt), *v.t.* to desire eagerly and often guiltily:—*v.i.* to have an extreme or unlawful desire.

cov-et-ous (kŭv′ĕ-tŭs), *adj.* very desirous, esp. of another's property; grasping; avaricious.—*adv.* **cov′et-ous-ly.**—*n.* **cov′et-ous-ness.**

cov-ey (kŭv′ĭ), *n.* [*pl.* coveys (-ĭz)], **1**, a hatch or brood of birds, esp. partridges, quail, etc.; **2**, a company or bevy. *Syn.* (see herd).

[1]**cow** (kou), *n.* [*pl.* cows (kouz); *Poetic* or *Archaic*, kine (kīn)], **1**, a large domestic animal, the mature female of the ox family, kept for its milk; **2**, the female of various other mammals, as the moose, elk, whale, elephant, seal, etc.

[2]**cow** (kou), *v.t.* to depress with fear; intimidate; as, the storm's fury *cowed* him.

cow-ard (kou′ẽrd), *n.* one without courage; a craven; dastard; timid person:—*adj.* **1**, lacking courage; timid; **2**, resulting from timidity; as, a *coward* silence.

cow-ard-ice (kou′ẽr-dĭs), *n.* want of courage; dishonorable fear.

cow-ard-ly (kou′ẽrd-lĭ), *adj.* timid; dastardly; base; befitting a coward; mean.—*n.* **cow′ard-li-ness.**

cow-bird (kou′bûrd″), *n.* an American blackbird: so called because often found with cattle.

cow-boy (kou′boi″), *n.* **1**, a boy who looks after cows; **2**, a mounted employee of a stockman or ranchman, who looks after the cattle while they graze.

cow-catch-er (kou′kăch″ẽr), *n.* a wedge-shaped frame on the front of a locomotive, for removing cows or other obstructions from the track.

cow-er (kou′ẽr), *v.i.* to crouch down, esp. from fear or shame.

cow-herd (kou′hûrd″), *n.* one who tends cattle at pasture.

cow-hide (kou′hīd″), *n.* **1**, the tanned and dressed skin of a cow (see *leather*, illus.); **2**, a whip of braided leather:—*adj.* made of cowhide:—*v.t.* [*p.t.* and *p.p.* -hid″ed, *p.pr.* -hid″ing], to flog with a cowhide.

cowl (koul), *n.* **1**, a monk's hood; **2**, a revolving cover for a chimney; **3**, that part of an automobile body just in front of the windshield.—*adj.* **cowled** (kould).

cow-lick (kou′lĭk″), *n.* a small patch of hair, often above the forehead, which grows peculiarly, as if licked by a cow.

co-work-er (kō″wûr′kẽr), *n.* one who works or coöperates with another; a fellow worker.

cow-pea (kou′pē″), *n.* a twining plant of the bean family, cultivated in the southern U. S. for forage.

cow-pox (kou′pŏks″), *n.* an acute contagious disease of cows, which, when communicated to man, as by vaccination, prevents smallpox for a term of years.

cow-rie (kou′rĭ), *n.* a kind of shell used as money in Africa and parts of Asia. Also, **cow′ry.**

cow-slip (kou′slĭp″), *n.* **1**, a wild English primrose; **2**, in the U. S., the marsh marigold.

cox-comb (kŏks′kōm″), *n.* **1**, (also, *cockscomb*), something resembling a cock's comb, formerly worn by licensed jesters; **2**, (also, *cockscomb*), a vain, conceited fellow; fop; **3**, (usually, *cockscomb*), a garden plant bearing a red or yellow flower.

cox-swain (kŏk′swān; kŏk′sn), *n.* one who steers or has charge of a ship's boat, a racing shell, or the like; a helmsman. Also, **cock′swain.**

coy (koi), *adj.* **1**, bashful; demure; shy; **2**, coquettish.—*adv.* **coy′ly.**—*n.* **coy′ness.**

coy-o-te (kī-ō′tē; kī′ōt), *n.* the prairie wolf of North America.

coz (kŭz), *n.* cousin: used formerly to any relative or close friend.

coz-en (kŭz′n), *v.t.* and *v.i.* to cheat in a petty way; deceive; swindle.

co-zy (kō′zĭ), *adj.* [*comp.* co′zi-er, *superl.* co′zi-est], warm and comfortable; snug:—*n.* [*pl.* cozies (-zĭz)], **1**, a woolen cover, often padded, to keep a teapot warm; **2**, a corner seat. Also, **co′sy; co′sey.**—*adv.* **co′zi-ly.** —*n.* **co′zi-ness.**

[1]**crab** (krăb), *n.* **1**, any of several crustaceans with a broad, flattened body, ten walking legs, and the abdomen, or so-called tail, curled under the body (see *crustacean*, illus.); **2**, any of various mechanical devices, esp. a kind of portable windlass for hoisting: **Crab, 1**, a northern constellation, Cancer; **2**, the fourth sign of the zodiac, which the sun enters about June 21 (see *zodiac*, illus.):—*v.i.* [*p.t.* and *p.p.* crabbed (krăbd), *p.pr.* crab′bing], to fish for crabs.

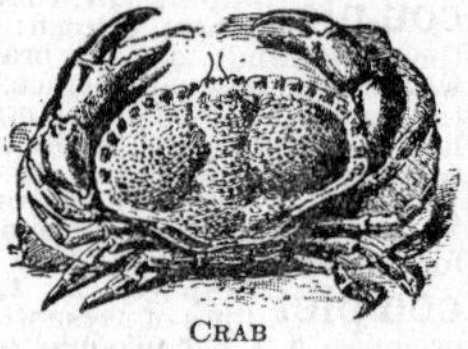

CRAB

[2]**crab** (krăb), *n.* **1**, any of various trees producing small, sour apples, often used in making jelly: usually called *crab apple* or *crab tree;* also, the fruit; **2**, a surly, cranky, sour person:—*adj.* **1**, pertaining to the crab apple; **2**, sour; harsh.

crab ap-ple the fruit of the crab tree (see [2]*crab*); also, the tree.

crab-bed (krăb′ĕd), *adj.* **1**, cross; morose; peevish; **2**, difficult to read; cramped, as writing; **3**, sour.—*adv.* **crab′bed-ly.**—*n.* **crab′bed-ness.**

crack (krăk), *v.i.* **1**, to make a rasping, or sharp, snapping noise; **2**, to break without dividing completely: **crack up**, *Aëro. Slang*, to be wrecked; crash:—*v.t.* **1**, to cause to make a short, rasping sound; cause to snap;

2, to break without separating; 3, to burst, as a nut; 4, to utter, as a joke; 5, to decompose (a substance, as petroleum) by heat or pressure into simpler forms: **crack up**, *Aëro. Slang*, to wreck:—*n.* 1, a sudden, sharp noise; 2, a break, esp. when incomplete; 3, a sharp blow; 4, a dissonant note, as in a boy's voice when changing:—*adj. Colloq.*, first-rate; excellent; as, a *crack* football team.

crack–brained (krăk′=brānd″), *adj.* crazy; senseless; queer.

crack-er (krăk′ẽr), *n.* 1, one who or that which breaks, etc., or causes to break; 2, a boaster; 3, a small explosion; 4, a bonbon that pops with an explosive sound; 5, a thin, brittle biscuit; 6, in the southeastern U. S., a country fellow or poor white.

crack-le (krăk′l), *v.i.* [*p.t.* and *p.p.* -led (-ld), *p.pr.* -ling], to make slight rustling or snapping noises, frequently repeated; as, the leaves *crackle* underfoot:—*v.t.* to cover, as china, with a delicate network of minute cracks; break or crush by repeated blows:—*n.* 1, a noise made by frequent and slight cracks and reports; 2, the making of such a noise; 3, the appearance of the surface glaze on glass or porcelain that has cracked in all directions.

crack-ling (krăk′lĭng), *n.* 1, the giving out of small abrupt reports in quick succession; as, the *crackling* of a fire; 2, the crisp, browned skin of roasted pork.

crack-nel (krăk′nĕl), *n.* a hard, brittle biscuit; a thin, crisp cake.

cracks-man (krăks′măn), *n.* [*pl.* cracksmen (-mĕn)], *Slang.*, a burglar; one who breaks into a house.

cra-dle (krā′dl), *n.* 1, a baby's crib or little bed, often on rockers; 2, infancy; 3, birthplace or origin; as, the *cradle* of liberty; 4, a case for a broken limb; 5, a frame of timbers placed under a ship during building; 6, a steel tool used in engraving; 7, a trough on rockers in which gold-bearing earth is washed; 8, a frame of wood, with long teeth, fastened to a scythe, used in harvesting grain:—*v.t.* [*p.t.* and *p.p.* -dled (-dld), *p.pr.* -dling], 1, to rock or place in a cradle; shelter; 2, to put into any device resembling a cradle; 3, to reap with a scythe having a cradle:—*v.i.* to reap grain with a cradle.

craft (kråft), *n.* 1, ability; skill; esp., artistic, manual skill; 2, artfulness; deceit; cunning; 3, a trade requiring artistic manual ability; also, those employed in such a trade; 4, a vessel; also, vessels collectively.
Syn. art, dexterity, ingenuity, trade.

crafts-man (kråfts′măn), *n.* [*pl.* craftsmen (-mĕn)], a skilled and artistically inclined workman; an artificer.—*n.* **crafts′man-ship.**

craft-y (kråf′tĭ), *adj.* [*comp.* craft′i-er, *superl.* craft′i-est], cunning; artful; deceitful.—*adv.* **craft′i-ly.**—*n.* **craft′i-ness.**
Syn. (see wily).

crag (krăg), *n.* a steep, rugged rock that stands out prominently.

crag-gy (krăg′ĭ), *adj.* [*comp.* crag′gi-er, *superl.* crag′gi-est], rough; rugged; full of broken rocks.—*n.* **crag′gi-ness.**

crake (krāk), *n.* any of several rails, esp. the corn crake, a bird of Europe.

cram (krăm), *v.t.* [*p.t.* and *p.p.* crammed (krămd), *p.pr.* cram′ming], 1, to stuff; fill to overflowing, as with food; 2, to pack or crowd in; 3, to cover (a subject) hastily, as for an examination:—*v.i.* 1, to study hard for an examination; 2, to eat greedily:—*n.* 1, the act of stuffing; 2, one who gathers knowledge hurriedly; also, knowledge so gained.

¹cramp (krămp), *n.* 1, an iron bar to hold blocks of stone, etc., together; 2, a piece of iron or steel, resembling a C, with a tightening screw, used for holding two things together: also called *clamp;* 3, a piece of wood used in shoemaking, to give shape to the upper leather; 4, a hindrance to motion or growth:—*v.t.* 1, to fasten or hold by a mechanical device; 2, to hinder in action or growth; hamper:—*adj.* 1, narrowly hemmed in; restricted; 2, twisted, small, and illegible, as handwriting.

²cramp (krămp), *n.* 1, a spasmodic contraction of the muscles, painful and involuntary; 2, a kind of local paralysis:—*v.t.* to cause to suffer from cramp.

cran-ber-ry (krăn′bĕr-ĭ), *n.* [*pl.* cranberries (-ĭz)], 1, the small, red, acid berry of certain shrubs of the heath family; 2, the shrub itself.

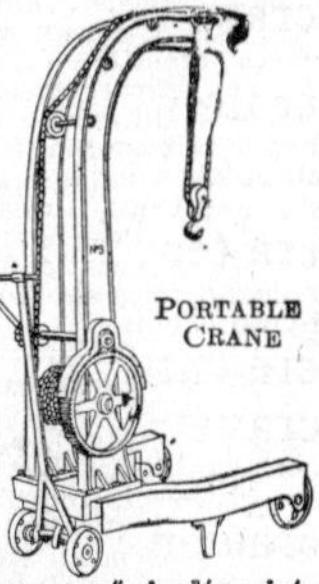

PORTABLE CRANE

crane (krān), *n.* 1, a large wading bird with very long legs and neck, and a long straight bill; 2, a machine for raising heavy weights; as, a traveling *crane:*—*v.t.* and *v.i.* [*p.t.* and *p.p.* craned (krānd), *p.pr.* cran′ing], to stretch or bend (the neck) like a crane, esp. in order to see better, as when in a crowd.

cra-ni-ol-o-gy (krā″nĭ-ŏl′ō-jĭ), *n.* the scientific study of skulls and of their characteristics.—*n.* **cra″ni-ol′o-gist.**

cra-ni-um (krā′nĭ-ŭm), *n.* [*pl.* craniums (-ŭmz); crania (-*ȧ*)], the skull, esp. the part inclosing the brain (see *skull*, illus.).—*adj.* **cra′ni-al.**

¹crank (krăngk), *n.* 1, a device for changing to-and-fro motion to rotary motion, or the opposite, usually consisting of an arm attached at right angles to a shaft which transfers the motion; 2, an elbow-shaped handle, which can be used to give rotary motion to a shaft, wheel, or the like; as, the *crank* of an automobile engine; 3, an elbow-shaped connecting part or support, esp. as used in hanging bells: **crank case**, a case inclosing a crank shaft, as in an automobile engine (see *gas engine*, illus.):—*v.t.* 1, to bend at right angles to an axis; 2, to wind up; turn, esp. by using a crank or the like.

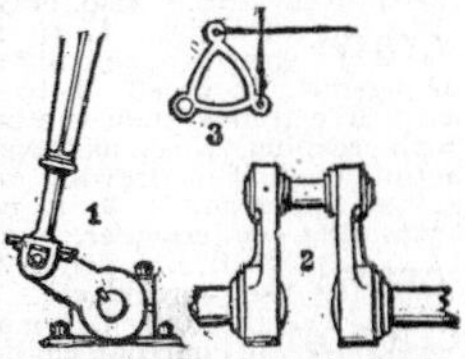

CRANKS: 1, end crank; 2, center crank; 3, bell crank.

²crank (krăngk), *n.* 1, an odd turn of speech or mind; a caprice; 2, *Colloq.*, an eccentric person; a person who pursues one idea exclusively.

³crank (krăngk), *adj.* of a boat, easily upset; cranky: opp. of *stiff.*

crank shaft a shaft driven by a crank. Also, *n.* **crank′shaft″.**

crank-y (krăngk′ĭ), *adj.* [*comp.* crank′i-er, *superl.* crank′i-est], 1, full of whims or irritability; 2, of a boat, liable to be upset; 3, in a shaky or loose condition.—*adv.* **crank′i-ly.**—*n.* **crank′i-ness.**

cran-nied (krăn′ĭd), *adj.* full of chinks or cracks; as, the flower grew in the *crannied* wall.

cran-ny (krăn′ĭ), *n.* [*pl.* crannies (-ĭz)], a crack or chink.

crape (krāp), *n.* **1**,(also, *crêpe*), a thin, black, crinkled silk fabric, used as a sign of mourning; **2**, (usually, *crêpe*), a similar crinkled fabric, as of silk, wool, cotton, etc., often colored.—*adj.* **crap'y.**

[1]**crash** (krăsh), *v.t.* to shatter noisily; dash into pieces:—*v.i.* **1**, to make a loud noise, as of thunder or violent breakage; **2**, of an airplane, to come to earth violently:—*n.* **1**, a shattering; **2**, the sound occasioned by violent breakage, thunder, a burst of loud music, or the like; **3**, the failure of a business; bankruptcy.

[2]**crash** (krăsh), *n.* a kind of coarse linen used for toweling, or as a cover for surfaces that receive hard wear.

crass (krăs), *adj.* **1**, coarse in texture; **2**, dense; stupid; as, *crass* ignorance —*adv.* **crass'ly.**—*n.* **crass'ness.**

crate (krāt), *n.* a wickerwork basket for shipping china, glassware, etc.; hence, a case made of wooden slats, used for shipping goods:—*v.t.* [*p.t.* and *p.p.* crat'ed, *p.pr.* crat'ing], to pack in a case or basket.

cra-ter (krā'tẽr), *n.* **1**, the cup-shaped cavity forming the mouth of a volcano; **2**, a similar cavity, as the pit formed by an explosion.

cra-vat (krȧ-văt'), *n.* a necktie or neckcloth, usually worn by men.

crave (krāv), *v.t.* [*p.t.* and *p.p.* craved (krāvd), *p.pr.* crav'ing], **1**, to ask for with humility; beg earnestly; **2**, to long for eagerly:—*v.i.* to desire greatly; yearn.

cra-ven (krā'vn), *adj.* cowardly; base:—*n.* an abject coward.

crav-ing (krāv'ĭng), *n.* **1**, a strong desire or appetite; yearning; **2**, a begging; petition.—*adv.* **crav'ing-ly.**

craw (krô), *n.* **1**, a bird's first stomach or crop; **2**, an insect's crop.

craw-fish (krô'fĭsh''), *n.* any of several small, fresh-water, lobsterlike animals (see *crustacean*, illus.): **sea crawfish**, the spiny lobster. Also, **cray'fish''** (krā'-).

[1]**crawl** (krôl), *v.i.* **1**, to move slowly by drawing the body along the ground; of persons, to creep; **2**, to have the feeling as of live things upon the body; be infested with creeping things, as the ground:—*n.* **1**, the act of creeping or drawing one's body slowly along the ground; **2**, a certain stroke in swimming.—*n.* **crawl'er.**—*adj.* **crawl'y.**

[2]**crawl** (krôl), *n.* a pen in shallow water for fish, turtles, etc.

cray-on (krā'ŏn), *n.* **1**, a stick or pencil, as of charcoal, chalk, etc.; **2**, a drawing done with such material:—*adj.* drawn with crayon:—*v.t.* to draw with a crayon.

craze (krāz), *v.i.* [*p.t.* and *p.p.* crazed (krāzd), *p.pr.* craz'ing], **1**, to become demented or insane; **2**, to open in slight cracks: said of pottery:—*v.t.* **1**, to produce cracks in (pottery); **2**, to render insane:—*n.* **1**, a passing fashion or infatuation; caprice; **2**, a mania; **3**, a crack in pottery glaze.—*p.adj.* **crazed.**

cra-zy (krā'zĭ), *adj.* [*comp.* cra'zi-er, *superl.* cra'zi-est], **1**, insane; mad; **2**, shaky; unsound, as a ship or building; **3**, *Colloq.*, foolishly eager: **crazy bone**, a place at the back of the elbow which, when struck, gives one a distracting, nervous, tingling sensation. —*adv.* **cra'zi-ly.**—*n.* **cra'zi-ness.**

creak (krēk), *v.i.* to make a sharp, harsh, squeaking sound:—*v.t.* to cause to make such a sound:—*n.* a harsh, grating sound, as from the friction of parts needing oil.

creak-y (krēk'ĭ), *adj.* [*comp.* creak'i-er, *superl.* creak'i-est], apt to make harsh, squeaky noises; as, *creaky* floors.

cream (krēm), *n.* **1**, the rich, oily part of milk, which rises to the top; hence, the choicest part of anything; **2**, a dessert or sweet made of, or like, this substance; **3**, a light yellow color; **4**, a soft cosmetic:—*v.t.* **1**, to skim or take off by skimming; **2**, in cooking: **a**, to beat together into a smooth, creamy mixture, as shortening, sugar, and eggs; **b**, to cook with a dressing of, or like, cream:—*v.i.* to become covered with, or thick like, cream; form a froth.

cream-er-y (krēm'ẽr-ĭ), *n.* [*pl.* creameries (-ĭz)], **1**, a shop where butter and cheese are made or prepared for sale; **2**, a place where cream and milk are sold.

cream of tar-tar a purified, crystallized form of tartar, used in medicine and in cooking.

cream-y (krēm'ĭ), *adj.* [*comp.* cream'i-er, *superl.* cream'i-est], containing, or like, cream; smooth; luscious.

[1]**crease** (krēs), *n.* **1**, a mark, line, or wrinkle left by a fold; **2**, in cricket, one of a set of lines defining the positions of bowler and batsman:—*v.t.* [*p.t.* and *p.p.* creased (krēst), *p.pr.* creas'ing], to make a fold, wrinkle, or similar mark in:—*v.i.* to fall in folds or wrinkles.

[2]**crease** (krēs), *n.* a Malayan dagger. Also, **kris; cris.** See **creese**, *Pfd. S.*

cre-a-sote (krē'ȧ-sōt), *n.* a heavy, oily liquid with a smoky smell, obtained from wood tar: used as an antiseptic. Also, **cre'o-sote**, *Pfd. S.*

cre-ate (krē-āt'), *v.t.* [*p.t.* and *p.p.* -at'ed, *p.pr.* -at'ing], **1**, to cause to come into existence; form out of nothing; **2**, to make, as a product out of raw material; **3**, to invest with a new rank, office, or function; **4**, to originate, as a character.

cre-a-tion (krē-ā'shŭn), *n.* **1**, the act of making, forming, or originating; **2**, the thing made, formed, or originated; original work; esp., the universe or the act by which it was created.

cre-a-tive (krē-ā'tĭv), *adj.* **1**, constructive; capable of originating; as, a *creative* mind; **2**, productive.

cre-a-tor (krē-ā'tẽr), *n.* one who makes, brings into existence, or originates: **Creator**, the Supreme Being; God.

crea-ture (krē'tūr), *n.* **1**, that which has been made or brought into existence; a created living being; **2**, one dependent on, or the tool of, another.

***crèche** (krâsh), [Fr.], *n.* **1**, a day nursery; **2**, an asylum for foundlings.

cre-dence (krē'dĕns), *n.* belief; credit; trust; as, it was difficult to give *credence* to the report.

cre-den-tial (krē-dĕn'shăl), *n.* **1**, that which bears testimony to one's claims or authority; **2**, usually in *pl.*, a letter or certificate given to a person to show that he has a right to confidence or to the exercise of certain authority.

cred-i-ble (krĕd'ĭ-bl), *adj.* believable; not impossible or absurd; trustworthy; as, a *credible* story.—*adv.* **cred'i-bly.** —*n.* **cred''i-bil'i-ty.**

cred-it (krĕd'ĭt), *v.t.* **1**, to believe; trust; have confidence in; **2**, to enter on the credit side of an account; **3**, to ascribe:—*n.* **1**, belief; honor; trust placed in one; **2**, trustworthiness; **3**, character; a good reputation; **4**, that which adds to one's reputation; **5**, sale on trust; **6**, the time allowed for payment of goods sold; **7**, financial standing; **8**, value received: opp. of *debit.*

cred-it-a-ble (krĕd'ĭt-ȧ-bl), *adj.* praiseworthy; deserving esteem. —*adv.* **cred'it-a-bly.**

cred-i-tor (krĕd'ĭ-tẽr), *n.* one to whom another is indebted for money or goods: opp. of *debtor.*

cre-do (krē′dō), *n.* [*pl.* credos (-dōz)], **1,** a creed; in particular, the Apostles' or the Nicene Creed; **2,** the musical setting for the latter, used in the Mass. Also, **Cre′do.**

cre-du-li-ty (krē-dū′lĭ-tĭ), *n.* [*pl.* credulities (-tĭz)], ready belief; esp., an inclination or readiness to believe on insufficient evidence.

cred-u-lous (krĕd′ū-lŭs), *adj.* apt to believe on slight evidence; hence, easily imposed upon.—*adv.* **cred′u-lous-ly.**—*n.* **cred′u-lous-ness.**

creed (krēd), *n.* **1,** a brief, authoritative statement of religious belief; **2,** a summing up or formula of belief in any matter.

creek (krēk), *n.* **1,** a small bay or cove; **2,** a small stream, between a brook and a river in size.

Creek (krēk), *n.* one of a tribe of American Indians, orig. inhabiting the region between the Mobile and Savannah rivers, in Alabama and Georgia: now in Oklahoma.

creel (krēl), *n.* **1,** a wicker fishing basket; **2,** a wickerwork cage, as for catching lobsters:—*v.t.* to put in a wicker basket; catch.

creep (krēp), *v.i.* [*p.t.* and *p.p.* crept (krĕpt), *p.pr.* creep′ing], **1,** to move slowly along the ground, as a worm or reptile; crawl; **2,** to have the feeling as of touching crawling things; **3,** to grow along the ground, as a plant; **4,** to move secretly or stealthily; **5,** to cringe; fawn; **6,** to slip slightly, as cloth or wood:—*n.* **1,** the act of crawling along the ground; **2,** usually in *pl.*, the sensation of being covered with crawling things.

creep-er (krēp′ẽr), *n.* **1,** one who or that which moves slowly, close to or touching the ground; **2,** a plant which clings by rootlets or tendrils to some support; as, the English ivy is an evergreen *creeper;* **3,** any of certain birds which creep; **4,** a grapnel.

creep-y (krēp′ĭ), *adj.* [*comp.* creep′i-er, *superl.* creep′i-est], **1,** shivering; chilled with fear; as, a *creepy* feeling; **2,** marked by creeping; moving with difficulty.—*n.* **creep′i-ness.**—*adv.* **creep′i-ly.**

creese (krēs), *n.* a short dagger with a waved blade, used by Malayans. Also, **cris; kris; crease.**

cre-mate (krē-māt′; krē′māt), *v.t.* [*p.t.* and *p.p.* -mat′ed, *p.pr.* -mat′ing], to reduce to ashes by heat; consume by fire, as a corpse.—*n.* **cre-ma′tor** (krē-mā′tẽr).

cre-ma-tion (krē-mā′shŭn), *n.* a burning; esp., the act or practice of burning, instead of burying, the dead.

crem-a-to-ry (krĕm′ȧ-tō-rĭ, krē′mȧ-tō-rĭ), *adj.* pertaining to cremation:—*n.* [*pl.* crematories (-rĭz)], a furnace or an establishment for burning dead bodies.—*n.* **crem″a-to′ri-um** (-tō′rĭ-ŭm).

***crème** (krâm), [Fr.], *n.* **1,** cream; **2,** in cooking, a white sauce.

Cre-mo-na (krē-mō′nȧ), *n.* a kind of violin, of unequaled excellence, formerly made at Cremona, Italy.

cre-nate (krē′nāt), *adj.* in botany, having a scalloped edge (see *leaf*, illus.).

cren-el-at-ed (krĕn′ĕl-āt″ĕd), *adj.* decorated with indented moldings or scalloped with notches.

Cre-ole (krē′ōl), *n.* a native of the West Indies, or of Louisiana or the Gulf States, of French or Spanish descent:—*adj.* pertaining to a Creole. Also, **cre′ole.**

Cre-on (krē′ŏn), *n.* in mythology, a Theban king, brother-in-law of Œdipus, who caused Antigone to be buried alive.

cre-o-sol (krē′ō-sōl; -sŏl), *n.* a colorless, aromatic, oily liquid resembling phenol or carbolic acid.

cre-o-sote (krē′ō-sōt), *n.* a heavy, oily liquid with a smoky smell, obtained from coal or wood tar: used as an antiseptic. Also, **cre′a-sote.**

crêpe (krâp; krāp), *n.* **1,** (also, *crape*), a soft fabric, as of silk, wool, or cotton, closely woven and wavy in appearance; **2,** (usually, *crape*), a similar black silk fabric, used as a sign of mourning: **crêpe de Chine** (shēn), a fine, thin crêpe made of raw silk, with an almost smooth surface.

crep-i-tate (krĕp′ĭ-tāt), *v.i.* [*p.t.* and *p.p.* -tat″ed, *p.pr.* -tat″ing], to crackle; make a succession of snapping sounds.—*n.* **crep″i-ta′tion.**

crept (krĕpt), past tense and past participle of the intransitive verb *creep.*

cre-scen-do (krĕ-shĕn′dō; krĕ-sĕn′dō), *n.* a gradual increase in force of musical sound; as, the music ended with a loud *crescendo:*—*adv.* and *adj.* slowly growing in force or loudness.—*abbr.* **cres.; cresc.**

cres-cent (krĕs′ĕnt), *adj.* **1,** growing; **2,** shaped like the new moon:—*n.* **1,** an increasing or new moon; **2,** a figure like a new moon; esp., the national emblem of Turkey; **3,** the power or religion of Turkey; Mohammedanism.

CRESCENT

cress (krĕs), *n.* any of numerous small green plants of the mustard family, having crisp, peppery leaves which are used in salads.

cres-set (krĕs′ĕt), *n.* a vessel for holding oil, wood, etc., to be burned and used as a torch or beacon.

Cres-si-da (krĕs′ĭ-dȧ), *n.* in medieval romances based on Homer's "Iliad," the fair but unfaithful love of Troilus.

crest (krĕst), *n.* **1,** a comb or tuft on the head of a fowl or bird; **2,** a tuft of feathers on a helmet, or the helmet itself, **3,** the top of anything, as the ridge of a wave, the summit of a hill or ridge, etc.; **4,** a heraldic device, usually worn above the shield:—*v.t.* **1,** to furnish with, or serve as, a crest; **2,** to surmount, as a hill:—*v.i.* to take the form of a crest or ridge.—*p.adj.* **crest′ed.**

crest-fall-en (krĕst′fôl″n), *adj.* dejected; disappointed; dispirited.

cre-ta-ceous (krē-tā′shŭs), *adj.* containing, or like, chalk; chalky.

Cre-tan (krē′tăn), *adj.* of or pertaining to Crete, an island in the eastern Mediterranean:—*n.* an inhabitant of Crete.

cre-tonne (krē-tŏn′; krē′tŏn), *n.* an unglazed cotton fabric, printed on one side and used for covering chairs, etc.

cre-vasse (krĕ-văs′), *n.* **1,** a deep crack or fissure, as in glacier ice; **2,** in the U. S., a breach in a levee or embankment.

crev-ice (krĕv′ĭs), *n.* a crack; fissure; as, a *crevice* in a wall or rock.

crew (krōō), *n.* **1,** a ship's or boat's company; as, the captain and the sailors form the *crew* of a ship; **2,** a gang of men working together; as, a train *crew;* **3,** a throng; mob.

crew-el (krōō′ĕl), *n.* loosely twisted worsted yarn used in embroidery.

crib (krĭb), *n.* **1,** a rack or manger; **2,** a stall for horses or cattle; **3,** a child's bed; **4,** a small cottage; **5,** a petty theft; **6,** *School Slang*, an illegitimate aid, as a key or a translation, used by a student; **7,** a supporting framework, as of wood, used in building:—*v.t.* [*p.t.* and *p.p.* cribbed (krĭbd), *p.pr.* crib′bing], **1,** to confine; **2,** to furnish with a crib; **3,** *Colloq.*, to steal:—*v.i.* *Colloq.*, **1,** to use a translation or notes improperly; **2,** to steal.

crib-bage (krĭb′āj), *n.* a card game played by two or more persons: **cribbage board,** a board with holes and pegs, used in the game of cribbage for scoring.

crick (krĭk), *n.* a painful stiffness of the muscles of the neck or back.

1crick-et (krĭk'ĕt), *n.* a famous English outdoor game played with wickets, bats, and a ball, by eleven players on each side.—*n.* **crick'et-er.**

2crick-et (krĭk'ĕt), *n.* any of several black, chirping insects.

3crick-et (krĭk'ĕt), *n.* a small, low, wooden stool; footstool.

cried (krīd), past tense and past participle of the verb *cry.*

cri-er (krī'ẽr), *n.* one who cries or proclaims an announcement.

crime (krīm), *n.* **1,** an act which breaks the law and makes the offender liable to punishment; **2,** an offense against morality or the public welfare; as, stealing is a *crime.*

Syn. sin, vice, misdemeanor, wickedness.—*Ant.* virtue, sinlessness.

Cri-me-an (krī-mē'ăn; krĭ-mē'ăn), *adj.* of or pertaining to the Crimea, a Russian peninsula on the Black Sea: **Crimean War,** a war in which France, Great Britain, and Sardinia allied themselves with Turkey against Russia (1854-56):—*n.* a native or an inhabitant of the Crimea.

crim-i-nal (krĭm'ĭ-năl), *n.* one guilty of a grave offense against the law:—*adj.* pertaining to, or guilty of, a grave offense against the law.—*adv.* **crim'i-nal-ly.**

Syn., n. convict, culprit, felon, malefactor.

crim-i-nal-i-ty (krĭm"ĭ-năl'ĭ-tĭ), *n.* the state, quality, or fact of being guilty of a serious offense against the law; guilt; guiltiness.

crim-i-nate (krĭm'ĭ-nāt), *v.t.* [*p.t.* and *p.p.* -nat"ed, *p.pr.* -nat"ing], to accuse or declare guilty of crime; involve in a crime.—*n.* **crim"i-na'tion.**—*adj.* **crim'i-na-tive** (-nā-tĭv).—*adj.* **crim'i-na-to-ry.**

crim-i-nol-o-gy (krĭm"ĭ-nŏl'ō-jĭ), *n.* the science of investigating and studying crime and the methods and characteristics of criminals.—*n.* **crim"i-nol'o-gist.**

1crimp (krĭmp), *v.t.* **1,** to fold or press into plaits; impart a wavy appearance to; **2,** to gash with a knife, as the flesh of a fish before cooking, to make it crisp:—*n.* **1,** the act of pressing, fluting, or frilling; **2,** that which is fluted or pressed into folds; esp., in *pl.*, curled hair.—*n.* **crimp'er.**

2crimp (krĭmp), *n.* in England, one who decoys or entraps men into enlisting as soldiers or sailors:—*v.t.* to entrap for enlistment, as seamen; impress; press.

crim-ple (krĭm'pl), *n.* a wrinkle; rumple: —*v.t.* [*p.t.* and *p.p.* -pled (-pld), *p.pr.* -pling], to cause to wrinkle.

crimp-y (krĭm'pĭ), *adj.* [*comp.* crimp'i-er, *superl.* crimp'i-est], having a wrinkled or plaited appearance; frizzly.

crim-son (krĭm'zn), *n.* a deep red color somewhat like purple:—*adj.* **1,** deep red; **2,** bloody:—*v.t.* to dye with this color:—*v.i.* to blush.

cringe (krĭnj), *v.i.* [*p.t.* and *p.p.* cringed (krĭnjd), *p.pr.* cring'ing], to bend or crouch from fear or pain, or with servility:—*n.* a servile bow.—*n.* **cring'er**

Syn., v. stoop, cower, shrink, wince.

crin-gle (krĭng'gl), *n.* an eye or ring made by a rope on the edge of a sail.

crin-kle (krĭng'kl), *n.* a wrinkle; bend:—*v.t.* [*p.t.* and *p.p.* -kled (-kld), *p.pr.* -kling], to wrinkle; curl:—*v.i.* **1,** to become corrugated or crimped; **2,** to rustle, as silk.—*adj.* **crin'kly.**

crin-o-line (krĭn'ō-lĭn; -lēn), *n.* **1,** a stiff fabric for stiffening a garment; **2,** a skirt so stiffened; also, a hoop skirt.

crip-ple (krĭp'l), *n.* one who is lame or maimed:—*v.t.* [*p.t.* and *p.p.* -pled (-ld), *p.pr.* -pling], to deprive of the use of a limb; disable; impair.

cris (krēs), *n.* a short Malay dagger with a waved blade. Also, **creese,** *Pfd. S.*

cri-sis (krī'sĭs), *n.* [*pl.* crises (-sēz)], **1,** a turning point; time of danger or difficulty; as, a *crisis* in history; **2,** a critical turn in the course of a disease.

crisp (krĭsp), *adj.* **1,** wavy; curled; **2,** brittle; short, as pastry; **3,** cheerful; terse: said of style, manner, etc.; **4,** fresh, as lettuce; bracing, as air:—*v.t.* **1,** to curl; ripple; **2,** to make brittle, as lettuce:—*v.i.* **1,** to form into little curls along an edge; **2,** to become brittle. —*adv.* **crisp'ly.**—*n.* **crisp'ness.**

Cris-pin (krĭs'pĭn), *n.* a shoemaker: in allusion to St. Crispin, the patron saint of shoemakers, whose day is October 25.

criss-cross (krĭs'krôs"), *adj.* crossing in different directions, as lines: —*adv.* in such a way as to cross something else:—*n.* a child's game played on crossed lines: also called *ticktacktoo.*

cri-te-ri-on (krī-tē'rĭ-ŭn), *n.* [*pl.* criteria (-*ȧ*)], a standard, law, or rule by which a correct judgment can be formed; measure; test.

crit-ic (krĭt'ĭk), *n.* **1,** one capable of, or skilled in, judging things; as, a musical *critic;* **2,** one who judges harshly.

crit-i-cal (krĭt'ĭ-kăl), *adj.* **1,** inclined to find fault; as, a *critical* person; **2,** nicely exact; skilled in careful judgment, particularly of literary or artistic works; **3,** pertaining to the turning point of a disease; **4,** involving risk; **5,** decisive; momentous; crucial.—*adv.* **crit'i-cal-ly.**

crit-i-cism (krĭt'ĭ-sĭzm), *n.* **1,** the act or art of judging and defining the merits of a literary or artistic work; as, the author finds honest *criticism* very helpful; **2,** censure; **3,** the principles or method of judging works of art, reasoning, etc.

Syn. comment, disapproval, reflection.

crit-i-cize (krĭt'ĭ-sīz), *v.t.* [*p.t.* and *p.p.* -cized (-sīzd), *p.pr.* -ciz"ing], **1,** to examine or judge as a critic; **2,** to censure:—*v.i.* to review; act as a judge. Also, **crit'i-cise.**—*adj.* **crit'i-ciz"a-ble.**

cri-tique (krĭ-tēk'), *n.* **1,** a careful analysis of a literary or artistic production; review; **2,** the art of criticism.

croak (krōk), *v.i.* **1,** to make a sound like that of a raven; **2,** to grumble:—*v.t.* to utter dismally:—*n.* the low, hoarse sound of the raven or frog.—*n.* **croak'er.**

Cro-a-tian (krō-ā'shăn), *adj.* of or pertaining to Croatia, a district in Yugoslavia:—*n.* **1,** a native of Croatia; **2,** the Croatian language. Also, *n.* **Cro'at.**

cro-chet (krō-shā'), *n.* a kind of knitting made with one hooked needle, in cotton, wool, etc.:—*v.t.* and *v.i.* [*p.t.* and *p.p.* -cheted' (-shād'), *p.pr.* -chet'ing (-shā'ĭng)], to knit with a hooked needle.

1crock (krŏk), *n.* **1,** soot, as on a kettle; **2,** coloring matter which rubs off from cloth:—*v.t.* and *v.i.* to smudge.

2crock (krŏk), *n.* an earthenware vessel:—*v.t.* to put in a crock.

crock-er-y (krŏk'ẽr-ĭ), *n.* earthenware, esp. kitchen dishes, bowls, etc.

crock-et (krŏk'ĕt), *n.* in ancient architecture, a carved ornament, often resembling foliage, on the angles of spires, gables, and canopies.

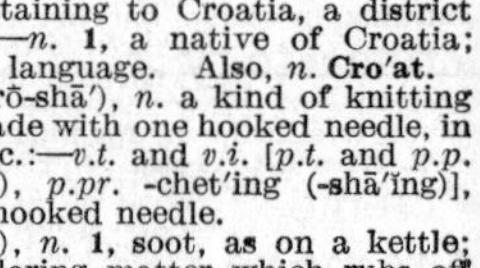

CROCODILE (1/80)

croc-o-dile (krŏk'ō-dīl), *n.* any of several large, lizardlike reptiles, with hard square scales on its back and long tail.—*adj.* **croc″o-dil′i-an** (krŏk″ō-dĭl′ĭ-ăn).

cro-cus (krō′kŭs), *n.* **1**, the earliest spring flower, yellow and white in color, from one class of which saffron is obtained; **2**, a kind of polishing powder.

Crœ-sus (krē′sŭs), *n.* a very wealthy king of the sixth century B. C.; hence, a very wealthy person.

croft (krôft), *n.* **1**, a small field near a house, used for pasture and tillage; **2**, in Scotland, a very small farm.—*n.* **croft′er.**

***croix de guerre** (krwä″ dē gâr′), [Fr.], the French war cross, given only for acts of exceptional bravery under fire.

crom-lech (krŏm′lĕk), *n.* an ancient monument of rough stones, with one huge flat stone resting across the others, forming a rough chamber.

crone (krōn), *n.* a withered old woman; as, a toothless, wrinkled *crone.*

Cro-nus (krō′nŭs), *n.* in Greek mythology, a Titan, deprived of the government of the world by his son Zeus: god of the harvests: identified with the Roman *Saturn.*

cro-ny (krō′nĭ), *n.* [*pl.* cronies (-nĭz)], a familiar friend; chum.

crook (kro͝ok), *n.* **1**, a bend; as, a *crook* in the river; **2**, that which is bent, as a shepherd's or bishop's staff; **3**, the act of bending; **4**, *Colloq.*, a dishonest person; swindler:—*v.t.* to bend; as, to *crook* the finger:—*v.i.* to curve; grow crooked.

crook-ed (kro͝ok′ĕd), *p.adj.* **1**, bent; curved; **2**, not upright in conduct; dishonest.—*adv.* **crook′ed-ly.**—*n.* **crook′ed-ness.**
Syn. twisted, awry, askew.

crook-neck (kro͝ok′nĕk″), *n.* a squash with a recurved neck.

croon (kro͞on), *v.i.* to sing in a soft, plaintive tone:—*v.t.* to sing or hum softly:—*n.* the sound made by singing softly and plaintively.

crop (krŏp), *n.* **1**, the produce of the ground, as corn; harvest, or anything likened to the harvest; as, a *crop* of ice; **2**, a bird's craw; **3**, a stout hunting whip; **4**, hair cut close or short:—*v.t.* [*p.t.* and *p.p.* cropped or cropt (krŏpt), *p.pr.* crop′ping], **1**, to cut off the top or ends of; reap; mow; **2**, to bite off: said of animals; **3**, to cut short, as hair, tail, ears, etc.:—*v.i.* **1**, to appear unexpectedly; **2**, to sprout; as, in all gardens the weeds *crop* out.

crop-per (krŏp′ẽr), *n.* **1**, one who or that which cuts or bites off; **2**, one who raises farm crops on shares; **3**, a pigeon with a large crop; pouter; **4**, *Slang*, a fall headlong, as from a horse; as, the hunter came a *cropper;* hence, a disastrous failure.

cro-quet (krō-kā′), *n.* a lawn game played with mallets, balls, and arches.

cro-quette (krō-kĕt′), *n.* a ball of minced meat, fish, or fowl, seasoned and fried brown.

cro-sier (krō′zhẽr), *n.* the staff of a bishop or abbot, the symbol of his office as a shepherd of God's flock. Also, **cro′zier.**

cross (krôs), *n.* **1**, an ancient instrument of punishment, upon which malefactors were fastened and left to die; **2**, an emblem of the Christian faith and of Christendom; **3**, a model of this instrument; **4**, a variously shaped device in the form of a cross, as in coats of arms, badges of military or knightly orders, etc.; **5**, a mark consisting of two intersecting lines, used as a signature by an illiterate; **6**, suffering or affliction to be borne for Christ's sake; **7**, anything that thwarts, hinders, or tries the patience; **8**, an intermixture of breeds or varieties; the offspring of a male and a female of different varieties of the same species, or of different species: also called *crossbreed:*—*v.t.* **1**, to put or lay across; draw or mark across; move or carry to the

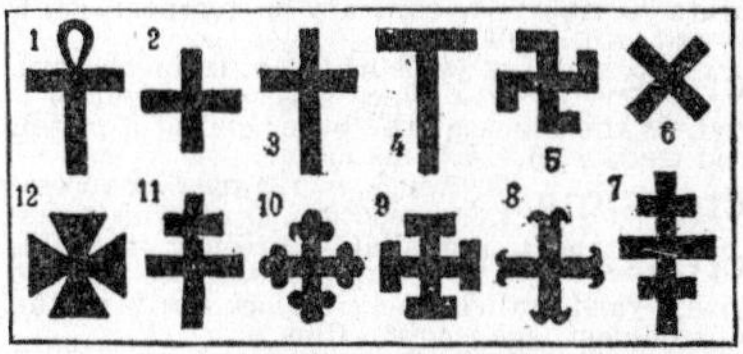

CROSSES: 1, ansate; 2, Greek; 3, Latin; 4, tau; 5, swastika, fylfot, or gammadion; 6, St. Andrew's; 7, papal; 8, anchored; 9, potent; 10, crosslet; 11, patriarchal; 12, pattée.

opposite side; go or travel to the opposite side of; meet and pass; intersect; **2**, to make the sign of the cross upon; **3**, to cancel, as by marking off with intersecting lines: usually with *off* or *out;* **4**, to thwart; oppose; hinder; **5**, to cause to interbreed, as plants or animals of different varieties or species:—*v.i.* **1**, to go, move, or lie from one side to the other; **2**, to meet and pass, going in opposite directions; **3**, to interbreed:—*adj.* **1**, not parallel; transverse; **2**, opposed; counter; contrary; **3**, ill-tempered; out of sorts; peevish; **4**, produced by interbreeding of varieties: **the Cross,** a southern constellation with four bright stars in the form of a cross; the Southern Cross.—*n.* **cross′ness.**—*adv.* **cross′ly.**

cross-bar (krôs′bär″), *n.* a bar or line going crosswise or transversely.—*adj.* **cross′barred″** (krôs′bärd″).

cross-bill (krôs′bĭl″), *n.* any of several kinds of finches having mandibles whose points cross each other.

cross-bones (krôs′bōnz″), *n.pl.* a representation of two bones crossing each other, and usually topped by a skull: a symbol of death.

cross-bow (krôs′bō″), *n.* a shooting weapon, having a bow across the stock, used in the Middle Ages.

cross-breed (krôs′brēd″), *n.* the offspring of two animals or plants of different species or races; a hybrid.—*adj.* **cross′bred″** (krôs′brĕd″).

cross–bun (krôs′=bŭn″), *n.* a bun or small cake marked with a cross, usually eaten on Good Friday.

cross-cut (krôs′kŭt″), *n.* **1**, a transverse way, more direct than the usual road; a short cut; **2**, a crosscut saw: **crosscut saw,** a handsaw with teeth set for cutting across the grain; also, a two-handed lumberman's saw (see *tool,* illus.):—*v.t.* [*p.t.* and *p.p.* -cut″, *p.pr.* -cut″ting], to cut across or through.

crosse (krôs), *n.* the bat used in the game of lacrosse (see *lacrosse,* illus.).

cross–ex-am-i-na-tion (krôs″=ĕg-zăm″ĭ-nā′shŭn), *n.* the questioning or examination of a witness by the opposing counsel.

cross–ex-am-ine (krôs″=ĕg-zăm′ĭn), *v.t.* [*p.t.* and *p.p.* -ined (-ĭnd), *p.pr.* -in-ing], to question or examine (a witness) to test the truth of previous evidence.—*n.* **cross″–ex-am′in-er.**

cross–eyed (krôs′=īd″), *adj.* having the eyes turned inward toward the bridge of the nose; squint-eyed: opp. of *wall-eyed.*—*n.* **cross′–eye″.**

cross–fer-ti-li-za-tion (krôs′=fûr″tĭ-lĭ-zā′shŭn), *n.* the act or process whereby a flower is rendered fruitful by pollen received from another flower.—*v.t.* **cross′–fer′ti-lize.**

cross–grained (krôs′=grānd″), *adj.* **1**, with an irregular grain or fiber; **2**, contrary in temper; as, a *cross-grained* old man.

cross-head (krôs′hĕd″), *n.* in mechanics, a piece across the end of a rod, as the block at the outer end of a piston rod (see *locomotive*, illus.).

cross-ing (krôs′ĭng), *n.* **1**, a passing across; **2**, intersection, as of two streets.

cross-jack (krôs′jăk″; krō′jĕk; krō′jĭk), *n.* a square sail set on the lower yard, called the *crossjack yard*, of the mizzenmast (see *rigging*, illus.).

cross-let (krôs′lĕt), *n.* in heraldry, a small cross: **cross crosslet**, a cross having a small cross at each of the four ends (see *cross*, illus.).

cross-piece (krôs′pēs″), *n.* one part that lies across another.

cross–pol-li-na-tion (krôs″=pŏl″ĭ-nā′-shŭn), *n.* the depositing of pollen, the fertilizing substance, from one flower on the stigma of another, as by insects or wind.—*v.t.* **cross″–pol′li-nate.**

cross–pur-pose (krôs′=pûr″pŭs), *n.* **1**, usually in *pl.*, contrary or conflicting purpose; as, they worked at *cross-purposes* and accomplished nothing; **2**, in *pl.*, a game of questions and answers.

cross–ques-tion (krôs′=kwĕs′chŭn), *v.t.* to cross-examine; question again and again; as, the police were asked to *cross-question* the prisoner.

cross ref-er-ence a reference or specific direction from one part of a book or passage to another.

cross-road (krôs′rōd″), *n.* **1**, a road that crosses a main road, or from one main road to another: **crossroads**, the place where two or more roads cross each other.

cross–stitch (krôs′=stĭch″), *n.* a form of stitch in which one stitch crosses another, forming an H.

cross-tie (krôs′tī″), *n.* a log of wood under rails on a railroad; a sleeper.

cross-trees (krôs′trēz″), *n.pl.* short pieces of timber at the upper ends of masts, to support the rigging.

cross-wise (krôs′wīz″), *adv.* **1**, across; **2**, in the shape of a cross; as, the church was built *crosswise;* **3**, perversely.

cross-word puz-zle (krôs′wûrd″), a problem of placing letters in a diagram of small squares so as to form intersecting words, some reading across and some down, that fit prescribed definitions.

crotch (krŏch), *n.* **1**, a hook or fork; esp., a forked prop or support; **2**, a separation into two parts or branches; as, a *crotch* of a tree.—*adj.* **crotched** (krŏcht).

crotch-et (krŏch′ĕt), *n.* **1**, in music, a quarter note; **2**, any of various small hooks or hooklike instruments; as, a reaping *crotchet;* **3**, a whim or fancy.

crotch-et-y (krŏch′ĕt-ĭ), *adj.* full of whims or fancies; eccentric.

cro-ton (krō′tŭn), *n.* a strong-scented tropical shrub or herb: **croton oil**, a vegetable oil taken from the seeds of the croton plant, used as a purgative.

Cro-ton bug a small, active, winged cockroach.

crouch (krouch), *v.i.* **1**, to stoop low; as, to *crouch* behind a wall; **2**, to cringe:—*n.* a servile cringing; a stooping.

[1]**croup** (kroop), *n.* a child's disease, not infectious, characterized by a sudden attack of difficult breathing, choking, loss of voice, and a peculiarly harsh, gasping cough.—*adj.* **croup′y.**

[2]**croup** (kroop), *n.* the rump, or hind quarters, of a horse.

crou-pi-er (kroo′pĭ-ẽr; kroo-pēr′), *n.* one who collects or pays out the money lost or won at a gaming table.

[1]**crow** (krō), *v.i.* [*p.t.* in sense **1**, crew (kroo); otherwise regular], **1**, to make a shrill sound like that of a barnyard cock; **2**, to boast in triumph: with *over;* **3**, to utter a joyous cry, as an infant:—*n.* **1**, the cry of a barnyard cock; **2**, a similar cry.

[2]**crow** (krō), *n.* **1**, a large, black bird, harsh-voiced, highly intelligent, and often destructive; **2**, any closely related bird, as a rook or raven; **3**, a crowbar: **carrion crow**, **1**, the common European crow; **2**, the black vulture of America: **Crow**, **1**, one of a tribe of American Indians, orig. inhabiting the region of the Yellowstone River, now dwelling at their Montana agency; **2**, a small southern constellation containing four bright stars; Corvus.

crow-bar (krō′bär″), *n.* a long, straight iron lever, flattened at one end.

crowd (kroud), *n.* **1**, a number of persons or things, collected closely together; as, a large *crowd* at the ball game; **2**, the populace, or common people:—*v.t.* **1**, to press closely together, as people or things; **2**, to fill too full; as, to *crowd* a boat; **3**, to force (oneself or one's way) through a throng; hence, to shove; push:—*v.i.* **1**, to assemble; **2**, to push; force oneself.—*n.* **crowd′er.**

Syn., *n.* multitude, rabble. (See throng.)

crow-foot (krō′foot″), *n.* [*pl.* crowfoots (-foots″)], any of a large family of plants, including larkspurs, buttercups, etc.

crown (kroun), *n.* **1**, a wreath, as of flowers, worn by returning conquerors, etc.; hence, an emblem of victory; a reward; a prize; **2**, a royal head covering, as a circlet of gold, jewels, etc.; hence, the sovereign himself, or regal power; **3**, a garland for the head; **4**, anything shaped like, or likened to, a crown, as the top of a hill, the part of a tooth projecting from the gum, an artificial top or body of a tooth, the top of a hat, of the head, or the like; in an anchor, the end of the shank adjacent to the arms; **5**, the perfect state of anything; a finishing touch; **6**, in England, a coin worth five shillings; **7**, the highest part of an arch; a knoblike ornament, as at the converging point of flying buttresses; **8**, the corona of a flower, as of a daffodil; also, in a seed plant, the point of junction between stem and root:—*v.t.* **1**, to put a decorative garland, gold circlet, etc., upon the head of, hence, to mark as having, or invest with, regal power; reward; honor; **2**, to form or occupy the topmost part of; hence, to cap; complete; bring (efforts or exertion) to a fortunate outcome; as, the results *crowned* his efforts with success; **3**, in dentistry, to place an artificial top or grinding surface upon (a tooth).

CROWN
Used at coronation of Queen Victoria.

crown glass **1**, the finest window glass; **2**, a very white, transparent, optical glass.

crown-land (kroun′lănd″), *n.* the land inherited by a sovereign.

crown prince the heir apparent to a throne.

crown prin-cess the wife of a crown prince.

crow's–foot (krōz′=foot″), *n.* [*pl.* crow's-feet (=fēt″)], **1**, one of the wrinkles due to age, at the outer corners of the eyes; **2**, a three-pointed stitch.

crow's nest a lookout or watchtower near a masthead on a ship.

cro-zier (krō'zhẽr), *n.* the staff of a bishop or abbot. Also, **cro'sier,** *Pfd. S.*

cru-cial (kro͞o'shăl), *adj.* **1,** having the form of a cross; **2,** severe; agonizing; **3,** decisive; searching; as, the opportunity to steal was a *crucial* test of his honesty: **crucial ligaments,** two ligaments within the knee joint, which cross each other so as somewhat to resemble an X, and connect the femur and the tibia (see *knee*, illus.).—*adv.* **cru'cial-ly.**

cru-ci-ble (kro͞o'sĭ-bl), *n.* **1,** a pot in a furnace to receive melted metals; **2,** a vessel used by chemists; **3,** a test; chastening.

CRUCIBLE

cru-ci-fix (kro͞o'sĭ-fĭks), *n.* a cross bearing the sculptured figure of Christ upon it.

cru-ci-fix-ion (kro͞o"sĭ-fĭk'shŭn), *n.* the act of crucifying, esp. the nailing of Christ upon the cross; as, *crucifixion* was an ancient form of punishment.

cru-ci-form (kro͞o'sĭ-fôrm), *adj.* cross-shaped, as a church.

cru-ci-fy (kro͞o'sĭ-fī), *v.t.* [*p.t.* and *p.p.* -fied (-fīd), *p.pr.* -fy"ing], **1,** to put to death by nailing the hands and feet to a cross; torture; **2,** to subdue, as the passions.

crude (kro͞od), *adj.* **1,** being in a raw, unprepared state; unrefined; as, all metals are *crude* when taken out of the earth; hence, unripe; raw; immature; imperfect; **2,** uncultured; as, *crude* manners; **3,** wanting in grace or taste; harsh in color.—*adv.* **crude'-ly.**—*n.* **crude'ness.**

cru-di-ty (kro͞o'dĭ-tĭ), *n.* [*pl.* crudities (-tĭz)], **1,** the state or condition of being without maturity, culture, or taste; **2,** an instance of this lack.

cru-el (kro͞o'ĕl), *adj.* **1,** disposed to give pain to others; merciless; hard-hearted; fierce; **2,** painful; unrelenting, as a disease or handicap.—*adv.* **cru'el-ly.**

Syn. barbarous, brutal, inhuman, savage.

cru-el-ty (kro͞o'ĕl-tĭ), *n.* [*pl.* cruelties (-tĭz)], **1,** inhumanity; savageness; **2,** a savage or inhuman deed.

cru-et (kro͞o'ĕt), *n.* a small glass vial, esp. for vinegar, oil, etc., for the dining table; a caster.

cruise (kro͞oz), *v.i.* and *v.t.* [*p.t.* and *p.p.* cruised (kro͞ozd), *p.pr.* cruis'ing], to sail to and fro (over or along the shores of):—*n.* a voyage from place to place.

cruis-er (kro͞oz'ẽr), *n.* **1,** one that sails to and fro; **2,** a man-of-war inferior in armor and armament to a battleship.

crul-ler (krŭl'ẽr), *n.* a ring-shaped or twisted cake, fried brown in deep fat: often called *doughnut*.

crumb (krŭm), *n.* **1,** the soft, inner part of bread; **2,** a fragment of bread; a little piece:—*v.t.* to break into little pieces.

crum-ble (krŭm'bl), *v.t.* [*p.t.* and *p.p.* -bled (-bld), *p.pr.* -bling], to break into crumbs or pieces:—*v.i.* **1,** to disappear gradually; **2,** to fall into small pieces.—*adj.* **crum'bly.**

crum-my (krŭm'ĭ), *adj.* [*comp.* crum'mi-er, *superl.* crum'mi-est], **1,** full of crumbs; **2,** soft, like the soft part of bread. Also, **crumb'y** (krŭm'ĭ).

crump-et (krŭm'pĕt), *n.* a tea cake or muffin, usually toasted.

crum-ple (krŭm'pl), *v.t.* [*p.t.* and *p.p.* -pled (-pld), *p.pr.* -pling], to press into wrinkles; rumple:—*v.i.* to become rumpled or wrinkled; as, her dress *crumpled*.

crunch (krŭnch), *v.t.* to crush or grind noisily; as, a dog likes to *crunch* a bone; grind under foot, as gravel:—*v.i.* to chew audibly; grind noisily; as, the wheels *crunched* in the snow:—*n.* the act or noise of grinding noisily or chewing audibly.

crup-per (krŭp'ẽr), *n.* the looped leather band in a harness, passing close up under a horse's tail (see *harness*, illus.).

cru-sade (kro͞o-sād'), *n.* **1,** historically, a military expedition under the banner of the cross, engaged in by one of the Christian powers to recover the Holy Land; as, in the first real *crusade* Jerusalem was captured; **2,** vigorous concerted action for the defense of some cause, or the advancement of some idea:—*v.i.* [*p.t.* and *p.p.* -sad'ed, *p.pr.* -sad'ing], to engage in a crusade.—*n.* **cru-sad'er.**

cruse (kro͞os; kro͞oz), *n. Archaic,* a small vessel for holding oil, water, etc.

crush (krŭsh), *v.t.* **1,** to press between two opposite bodies; squeeze; break by pressure; as, to *crush* a hat by sitting on it; to *crush* a mineral; **2,** to bruise; as, to *crush* a limb; **3,** to break down; ruin; quell; conquer; as, despair *crushed* his dreams:—*v.i.* to be pressed out of shape or into smaller compass; as, the dresses have *crushed*:—*n.* **1,** a violent compression or collision; **2,** a crowd; **3,** *Colloq.*, a crowded social gathering.—*n.* **crush'er.**

crust (krŭst), *n.* **1,** a hard outside coating or rind; **2,** the exterior solid part of the earth's surface; **3,** a shell or hard covering, as on a loaf of bread; **4,** the pastry casing of a pie:—*v.t.* to cover over with a hard covering:—*v.i.* to become so covered.

crus-ta-cean (krŭs-tā'shăn), *n.* any of a class (*Crustacea*) of animals, most of which live in the water, having a crustlike shell, including crabs, lobsters, shrimps, etc. (See illus. next page.)

crust-y (krŭs'tĭ), *adj.* [*comp.* crust'i-er, *superl.* crust'i-est], **1,** like a crust; **2,** cross; surly; snappish.—*adv.* **crust'i-ly.**—*n.* **crust'i-ness.**

crutch (krŭch), *n.* **1,** a staff with a cross-piece to fit under the arm, used as a support for cripples; **2,** any mechanical device like such a support, as the forked rest on a sidesaddle.

crux (krŭks), *n.* [*pl.* cruxes (-ĕz); cruces (kro͞o'sēz)], **1,** a hard point to settle; **2,** the essential question upon which a decision depends; as, the *crux* of the matter.

cru-zei-ro (kro͞o-thā'rō), *n.* [*pl.* -ros (-rōs)], a monetary unit of Brazil, replacing the *milreis;* equivalent to about five cents.

cry (krī), *v.i.* [*p.t.* and *p.p.* cried (krīd), *p.pr.* cry'ing], **1,** to call aloud; complain loudly; **2,** to shed tears; **3,** of animals, to utter a characteristic sound; howl, bark, low, neigh, etc.:—*v.t.* to utter publicly in giving notice; announce; as, to *cry* the hour of the night:—*n.* **1,** loud or passionate utterance, esp. of weeping or lamentation; as, a *cry* of joy, fear, anger, pain, etc.; an exclamation of wonder or triumph; **2,** outcry; clamor; demand; as, the *cry* for liberty; **3,** the proclamation of goods; as, the peddler's *cry;* **4,** common report; rumor; **5,** the characteristic call of an animal; as, the *cry* of the wolf; **6,** a fit of weeping; **7,** a battle cry; a party catchword.

cry-ing (krī'ĭng), *p.adj.* notorious; demanding notice; as, a *crying* shame.

crypt (krĭpt), *n.* **1,** an underground cell or vault, esp. one used for burial; **2,** a chamber below the main floor, often used as a chapel, as in a cathedral.

cryp-tic (krĭp'tĭk), *adj.* hidden; secret; mystical; occult.

cryp-to-gam (krĭp'tō-găm), *n.* a plant having no true flower or seed.—*adj.* **cryp"to-gam'ic.**—*adj.* **cryp-tog'a-mous** (krĭp-tŏg'ȧ-mŭs).

cryp-to-gram (krĭp′tō-grăm), *n.* a writing in cipher: as, a government uses a *cryptogram* or secret code.—*adj.* **cryp″to-gram′mic.**

crys-tal (krĭs′tăl), *n.* **1**, transparent quartz; **2**, a body formed by a solidifying element or compound, having a regular internal structure, usually inclosed by regularly arranged plane surfaces; **3**, a glass of superior clearness; **4**, the glass over a watch dial:—*adj.* consisting of transparent glass; clear; transparent: **crystal detector,** in radio, an instrument used to rectify the received signal in the receiving set (see *detector*, illus.).

crys-tal-line (krĭs′tăl-ĭn; krĭs′tăl-īn), *adj.* **1**, pertaining to, or having the form of, a crystal; **2**, composed of crystals: opp. of *amorphous;* **3**, clear; transparent; **4**, composed of grains or particles: **crystalline lens,** a transparent body in the eye behind the pupil, which brings together or focuses rays of light on the retina.

crys-tal-li-za-tion (krĭs″tăl-ĭ-zā′shŭn; krĭs″tăl-ī-zā′shŭn), *n.* **1**, the process of taking on a regular or crystalline form; **2**, the act of forming or being made into a definite shape, as ideas, plans, or the like; **3**, the form thus produced.

crys-tal-lize (krĭs′tăl-īz), *v.t.* [*p.t.* and *p.p.* -lized (-īzd), *p.pr.* -liz″-ing], **1**, to cause to form grains or become crystalline; **2**, to give fixed shape to:—*v.i.* **1**, to be converted into grains or become crystalline; **2**, to assume a definite shape.

crys-tal-log-ra-phy (krĭs″tăl-ŏg′rȧ-fĭ), *n.* the science which treats of the properties of crystals.

cub (kŭb), *n.* **1**, the young of certain animals, as the fox, bear, etc.; **2**, a rough, ill-mannered boy.

Cu-ban (kū′băn), *adj.* of or pertaining to Cuba, its inhabitants, or customs:—*n.* a native or an inhabitant of Cuba.

cub-by-hole (kŭb′ĭ-hōl″), *n.* a pigeonhole; a small, inclosed space, often used for storage.

cube (kūb), *n.* **1**, a regular solid body with six equal square sides or faces; **2**, the product obtained by multiplying the square of a quantity by the quantity itself, as 5 × 5 × 5 = 125, the cube of 5:—*v.t.* [*p.t.* and *p.p.* cubed (kūbd), *p.pr.* cub′ing], to raise to the third power.

CUBE

cu-beb (kū′bĕb), *n.* the small spicy berry of a kind of pepper.

cube root that factor of a number which, raised to the third power, produces the given number.

cu-bic (kū′bĭk), *adj.* **1**, having the form or properties of a cube; **2**, having three dimensions; as, a *cubic* yard; **3**, in algebra, of the third degree or power. Also, **cu′bi-cal.**—*adv.* **cu′bi-cal-ly.**

cub-ism (kūb′ĭzm), *n.* a modern school of painting and sculpture characterized by the use of geometrical figures.—*n.* **cub′ist.**

cu-bit (kū′bĭt), *n.* an ancient measure of about eighteen inches.

cuck-old (kŭk′ŭld), *n.* a man whose wife has proved unfaithful.

cuck-oo (kŏŏk′ōō), *n.* **1**, a bird with dark feathers and curved bill that lays its eggs in the nests of other birds; **2**, the characteristic call of this bird.

cu-cum-ber (kū′kŭm-bẽr), *n.* **1**, a creeping plant, the fruit of which is used as a salad or pickle; **2**, the fruit itself.

cud (kŭd), *n.* food brought from the first stomach of certain animals, called *ruminants*, back into the mouth to be chewed; as, the cow chews her *cud.*

cud-dle (kŭd′l), *v.t.* [*p.t.* and *p.p.* -dled (-ld), *p.pr.* -dling], to embrace closely:—*v.i.* to lie close or snug:—*n.* a close and nestling embrace.

cud-dy (kŭd′ĭ), *n.* [*pl.* cuddies (-ĭz)], **1**, a small closet; **2**, a small cabin in which officers of a ship take their meals; also the cook's galley of a small vessel.

cudg-el (kŭj′ĕl), *n.* a short thick stick:—*v.t.* to beat, as with a thick club.

¹cue (kū), *n.* **1**, (usually, *queue*), the tail or end of a thing; esp., a hanging braid of hair; **2**, (usually, *queue*), a line of persons waiting; **3**, the tapering rod used to strike the ball in playing billiards, caroms, etc.

²cue (kū), *n.* **1**, a hint; a suggestion as to what to do, or when to do something already agreed upon; **2**, the last words of an actor's speech, as indicating the time for another actor to enter or speak.

¹cuff (kŭf), *n.* a blow, esp. with the open hand; slap:—*v.t.* to stroke; slap.

²cuff (kŭf), *n.* **1**, a band to wear about the wrist; the fold on the lower part of a sleeve; also, a similar fold about the bottom of men's long trousers; **2**, the wrist-covering part of a long glove.

cui-rass (kwē-rȧs′), *n.* **1**, a piece of armor covering the body from neck to waist; **2**, a breastplate.

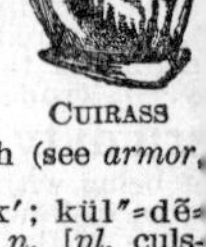
CUIRASS

cui-ras-sier (kwē″rȧ-sēr′), *n.* a mounted soldier wearing a breastplate.

***cui-sine** (kwē-zēn′), [Fr.], *n.* the kitchen, as of a hotel; also, style of preparing and cooking food.

cuisse (kwĭs), [*pl.* cuisses (-ĕz)], a piece of armor to protect the front of the thigh (see *armor*, illus.). Also, **cuish** (kwĭsh).

***cul-de-sac** (kü″-dē-sȧk′; kŭl″-dē-săk′), [Fr.], *n.* [*pl.* culs-de-sac (kü″-dē-sȧk′; kŭlz″-dē-săk′)], a blind alley; a passage open only at one end.

cu-li-na-ry (kū′lĭ-nā-rĭ), *adj.* pertaining to the kitchen, or to the art or process of cooking; as, *culinary* secrets are taught in domestic science.

cull (kŭl), *v.t.* **1**, to pick out; select; gather; as, to *cull* the flowers from a garden; **2**, to subject to the process of selecting:—*n.* something sorted out from the rest: usually inferior; hence, something worthless.

¹culm (kŭlm), *n.* **1**, coal dust; coal refuse, esp. of anthracite coal; **2**, an inferior anthracite coal.—*adj.* **cul-mif′er-ous.**

²culm (kŭlm), *n.* the jointed stem of a grass or sedge.

cul-mi-nate (kŭl′mĭ-nāt), *v.i.* [*p.t.* and *p.p.* -nat″ed, *p.pr.* -nat″ing], to reach the highest point, altitude, or degree; come to a climax; as, Napoleon's career *culminated* in utter defeat.

cul-mi-na-tion (kŭl″mĭ-nā′shŭn), *n.* **1**, the highest point, altitude, degree, etc.; **2**, the attainment of the highest point.

Syn. summit, crown, acme, climax, zenith.

cul-pa-ble (kŭl′pȧ-bl), *adj.* deserving censure; criminal; blameworthy—*adv.* **cul′pa-bly.**—*n.* **cul″pa-bil′i-ty.**

Syn. guilty, wicked, wrong.

cul-prit (kŭl′prĭt), *n.* **1**, one tried before a judge; **2**, one guilty of a crime or fault; an offender.

cult (kŭlt), *n.* **1**, a particular system of worship; **2**, devotion to a person, idea theory, or the like.

cul-ti-vate (kŭl′tĭ-vāt), *v.t.* [*p.t.* and *p.p.* -vat″ed, *p.pr.* -vat″ing], **1**, to till, as the soil; raise by tillage, as crops **2**, to improve by care, labor, or study; **3**, to cherish, as a friendship; foster or promote the growth of, as plants or bacteria; **4**, to devote oneself to, as literature; **5**, to seek the society of; **6**, in the U. S., to loosen the ground about (growing crops).

cul-ti-va-tion (kŭl″tĭ-vā′shŭn), *n.* **1**, the act of tilling; **2**, the state of being tilled; tillage; **3**, culture; **4**, development; **5**, devotion, as to literature.

cul-ti-va-tor (kŭl′tĭ-vā″tẽr), *n.* **1**, one who tills the ground; **2**, an agricultural or farm tool for loosening the ground about crops, as a harrow.

cul-ture (kŭl′tŭr), *n.* **1**, care given to the growth and development of animals and plants; **2**, the breeding of bacteria

cum-ber (kŭm′bẽr), *v.t.* to burden, as with sorrow; hinder; obstruct; as, the road was *cumbered* with rocks.

cum-ber-some (kŭm′bẽr-sŭm), *adj.* burdensome; clumsy.—*adv.* **cum′ber-some-ly.**

cum-brous (kŭm′brŭs), *adj.* troublesome; heavy; weighty; obstructing.—*adv.* **cum′brous-ly.**—*n.* **cum′brous-ness.**

cum-in (kŭm′ĭn), *n.* a dwarf plant of the carrot family; also, its aromatic seeds. Also, **cum′min.**

cum-quat (kŭm′kwŏt), *n.* **1**, a small citrous fruit, chiefly used in preserves; **2**, the tree bearing this fruit. Also, **kum′quat,** *Pfd. S.*

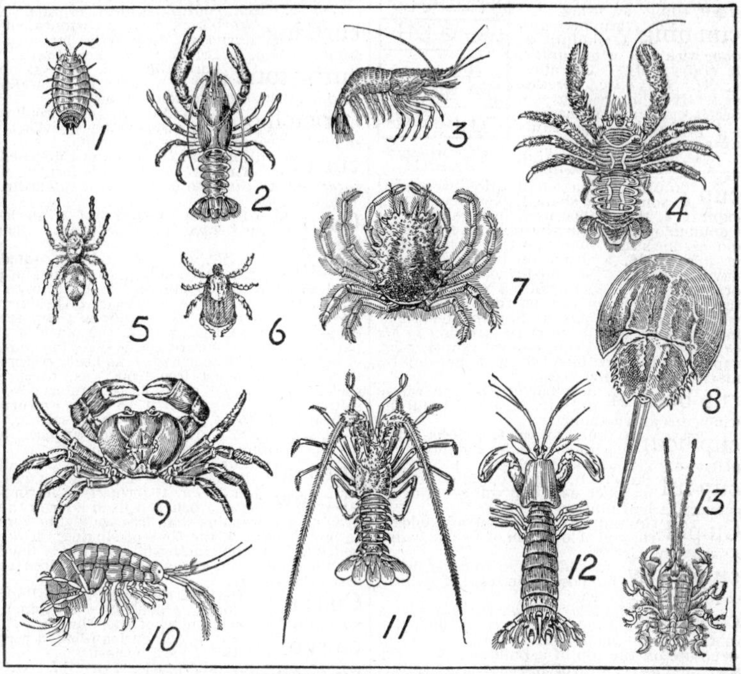

CRUSTACEANS AND ARACHNIDS

1, wood louse, or sow bug; 2, crawfish; 3, prawn; 4, plated lobster; 5, jumping spider; 6, cattle tick; 7, spider crab; 8, king crab; 9, land crab; 10, fresh-water shrimp; 11, spiny lobster; 12, squilla; 13, porcelain crab.

for scientific use; also, the product of such breeding; **3**, improvement secured by practice or training; as, physical *culture;* voice *culture;* **4**, the training of the mental or moral powers; refinement.—*adj.* **cul′tur-al.**

Syn. (see education).

cul-tured (kŭl′tŭrd), *adj.* **1**, tilled; cultivated; **2**, showing the effects of training in taste and manners; educated.

cul-ver-in (kŭl′vẽr-ĭn), *n.* orig., a small firearm; in the 16th century, a long cannon.

cul-vert (kŭl′vẽrt), *n.* a drain or artificial passage for water built under a road, canal, railroad, etc.

cu-mu-late (kū′mū-lāt), *v.t.* [*p.t.* and *p.p.* -lat″ed, *p.pr.* -lat″ing], to add to by heaping together; save.

cu-mu-la-tion (kū″mū-lā′shŭn), *n.* **1**, the act of heaping up; **2**, a gathered mass or heap.

cu-mu-la-tive (kū′mū-lā-tĭv), *adj.* **1**, adding to, or gradually increasing, the number, volume, or strength; formed or made up of portions gathered one after another; as, *cumulative* evidence; **2**, accruing, as dividends or interest, so as to be added to future payments if not paid when due.

cu-mu-lo-stra-tus (kū″mū-lō-strā′tŭs), *n.* a cloud

form or shape combining the characteristics of cumulus and stratus, as in a rounded, piled-up cloud whose base spreads out in a low, horizontal formation.

cu-mu-lus (kū'mū-lŭs), *n.* [*pl.* cumuli (-lī)], **1,** a heap; summit; **2,** a cloud having the appearance of heaped-up masses.—*adj.* **cu'mu-lous.**

cu-ne-i-form (kū-nē'ĭ-fôrm; kū'nē-ĭ-fôrm″), *adj.* having the form of a wedge: said of the arrow-shaped characters of the ancient inscriptions of Assyria and Persia:—*n.* cuneiform writing.

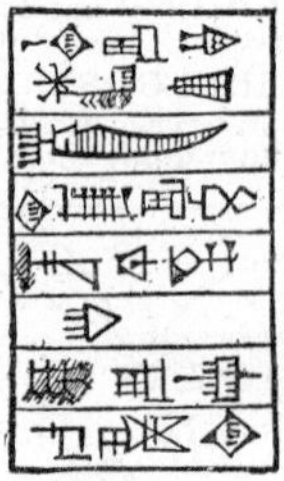

Cuneiform Writing

cun-ner (kŭn'ẽr), *n.* either of two small, edible sea fishes.

cun-ning (kŭn'ĭng), *adj.* **1,** skilful; **2,** done with skill or ingenuity; **3,** crafty; sly; designing; **4,** *U. S. Colloq.*, pretty; attractive; interesting:—*n.* deceit; guile; craftiness.—*adv.* **cun'ning-ly.**—*n.* **cun'-ning-ness.**

Syn., adj. adroit, artful, deceitful, sly. (See wily.)

cup (kŭp), *n.* **1,** a small drinking vessel; **2,** something shaped like a cup; **3,** a cupful; **4,** the chalice used in administering Communion; also, the wine taken at Communion; **5,** one's fate; one's portion of happiness or misery; **6,** a drink or beverage, as of flavored wine; **7,** in medicine, a vessel for drawing blood; **8,** in golf, a small hole in the course, esp. in the putting green, into which the ball is played; **9,** in *pl.*, a state of intoxication: usually in the expression *in his cups*:—*v.t.* [*p.t.* and *p.p.* cupped (kŭpt), *p.pr.* cup'ping], to draw blood from (a person) by means of a cupping glass.

cup-bear-er (kŭp'bâr″ẽr), *n.* one whose duty in office it is to fill the wine cups at a banquet.

cup-board (kŭb'ẽrd), *n.* **1,** a closet fitted with shelves for holding cups, plates, etc.; **2,** any small closet.

cup-ful (kŭp'fo͝ol), *n.* [*pl.* cupfuls (-fo͝olz)], as much as a cup will contain; in cookery, a half pint.

Cu-pid (kū'pĭd), *n.* in Roman mythology, the god of love, son of Venus: called *Eros* by the Greeks.

cu-pid-i-ty (kū-pĭd'ĭ-tĭ), *n.* an eager desire for possession, esp. of wealth; covetousness; greed.

cu-po-la (kū'pō-lȧ), *n.* [*pl.* cupolas (-lȧz)], **1,** a hemispherical or domelike roof; a small dome; **2,** loosely, any small structure on the top of a building; **3,** in the army and navy, a revolving shot-proof turret; **4,** a furnace for melting pig iron in a foundry.

cup-ping (kŭp'ĭng), *n.* the process of drawing blood with a cupping glass: **cupping glass,** a glass cup, from which the air has been partly exhausted, applied to the surface of the body to draw blood to it or out of it.

cur (kûr), *n.* **1,** a mongrel; a dog of inferior breed; **2,** a surly, ill-bred person.

cur-a-ble (kūr'ȧ-bl), *adj.* capable of being healed or cured; as, the patient has a *curable* disease.—*n.* **cur″a-bil'i-ty.**

cu-ra-çao (kū″rȧ-sō'; ko͞o″rȧ-sō'), *n.* a cordial flavored with the dried peel of bitter oranges.

cu-ra-cy (kū'rȧ-sĭ), *n.* [*pl.* curacies (-sĭz)], the employment, office, or district of a curate.

cu-rate (kū'rāt), *n.* a rector's or a vicar's assistant.

cur-a-tive (kūr'ȧ-tĭv), *adj.* pertaining or referring to the healing of diseases; promoting cure; as, sick people go to hot springs for the *curative* waters:—*n.* that which heals or serves to heal.

cu-ra-tor (kū-rā'tẽr), *n.* one having charge of a museum, art gallery, etc.

curb (kûrb), *v.t.* **1,** to restrain; keep within bounds; as, it is hard to *curb* an unruly tongue; **2,** (also, in British usage, *kerb*), to furnish with a protecting rim, as of stone:—*n.* **1,** that which checks, restrains, or subdues; **2,** a part of a horse's bridle (see *harness*, illus.); **3,** (also, in British usage, *kerb*), a protective rim, frame, or edge; curbstone; **4,** (also, *kerb*), the street as a market for buying and selling stocks, bonds, etc.

Syn., v. check, control, subject, repress.

curb-ing (kûrb'ĭng), *n.* **1,** curbstones collectively; **2,** material for curbstones. Also, in British usage, **kerb'ing.**

curb-stone (kûrb'stōn″), *n.* the stone edge of a street or sidewalk. Also, in British usage, **kerb'stone″.**

cur-cu-li-o (kûr-kū'lĭ-ō), *n.* [*pl.* curculios (-ōz)], any of the weevils or snout beetles; as, the apple *curculio.*

curd (kûrd), *n.* the coagulated or thickened part of milk; as, cheese is formed of *curd*:—*v.t.* to cause to curdle:—*v.i.* to curdle.—*adj.* **cur'dy.**

Curd (ko͞ord), *n.* a member of a dark-skinned race of Kurdistan. See **Kurd,** *Pfd. S.*

cur-dle (kûr'dl), *v.t.* [*p.t.* and *p.p.* -dled (-dld), *p.pr.* -dling], to thicken into curd:—*v.i.* **1,** to coagulate; **2,** to thicken.

cure (kūr), *n.* **1,** the act or art of healing; **2,** a remedy; as, quinine is a *cure* for colds; **3,** spiritual charge; **4,** the office of a parish priest or curate:—*v.t.* [*p.t.* and *p.p* cured (kūrd), *p.pr.* cur'ing], **1,** to heal; restore to health; **2,** to set free from; as, to *cure* society of a social evil; **3,** to preserve by salting, drying, etc.:—*v.i.* **1,** to cause a return to health; **2,** to be preserved, as by salting.

***cu-ré** (kü″rā'), [Fr.], *n.* in France, a Roman Catholic parish priest.

cure–all (kūr'-ôl″), *n.* a remedy for all diseases, evils, or ills; a panacea.

cur-few (kûr'fū), *n.* **1,** formerly, the ringing of a bell at a fixed hour in the evening as a warning that fires and lights were to be put out; **2,** the time of ringing; **3,** the bell itself; **4,** the ringing of a bell at a fixed evening hour, esp. as a signal for children to leave the streets.

Cu-ri-a (kū'rĭ-ȧ), *n.* the court of the Pope at Rome, which, like a cabinet, assists in the government of the Church.

cu-ri-o (kū'rĭ-ō), *n.* [*pl.* curios (-ōz)], a rare object of art; a curiosity.

cu-ri-os-i-ty (kū″rĭ-ŏs'ĭ-tĭ), *n.* [*pl.* curiosities (-tĭz)], **1,** eager desire to get knowledge; **2,** inquisitiveness; **3,** something strange or rare.

cu-ri-ous (kū'rĭ-ŭs), *adj.* **1,** anxious to know; inquisitive; prying; **2,** strange; full of mystery; **3,** requiring skill; as, a *curious* carving.—*adv.* **cu'ri-ous-ly.**—*n.* **cu'ri-ous-ness.**

Syn. novel, interesting; meddling, prying.

curl (kûrl), *n.* **1,** a small ring of hair, smoke, etc.; **2,** the act of forming, or state of being formed, into spirals, coils, etc.; **3,** a growth which affects plants, esp. peach trees:—*v.t.* to twist into ringlets; decorate with curls:—*v.i.* to move in spirals, as smoke.

cur-lew (kûr'lū), *n.* any of several wading birds with long, curving bill.

curl-ing (kûr'lĭng), *n.* **1,** the act of making ringlets; **2,** a game played by sliding smooth, lens-shaped stones on the ice.

curl-y (kûr'lĭ), *adj.* [*comp.* curl'i-er, *superl.* curl'i-est], having ringlets or waves; as, *curly* hair.—*n.* **curl'i-ness.**

cur-mudg-eon (kŭr-mŭj'ŭn), *n.* a grasping, churlish fellow.—*adj.* **cur-mudg'eon-ly.**

cur-rant (kŭr'ănt), *n.* **1,** a small seedless raisin; **2,** a common garden shrub; also, its berry.

cur-ren-cy (kŭr'ĕn-sĭ), *n.* [*pl.* currencies (-sĭz)], **1,** a continual passing from hand to hand; circulation, as of bank notes; **2,** the state of being accepted; as, the phrase is in common *currency;* also, the time during which acceptance exists; **3,** that which is generally used for money, as notes and coin; as, the *currency* of the United States includes paper money and gold, silver, nickel, and copper coins.

cur-rent (kŭr'ĕnt), *adj.* **1,** widely circulated; passing from hand to hand; **2,** now passing, as time; as, the *current* year; **3,** generally accepted; common; as, the *current* opinion:—*n.* **1,** a flow or passing: said of fluids; **2,** a body of air or water flowing in a certain direction; as, the boat moved down the river with the *current;* **3,** general course or tendency, as of a stream, rumor, etc.; **4,** a movement of electricity, or the rate of such movement: **alternating current,** a current of electricity that reverses its direction at regular intervals: **direct current,** a current of electricity that flows in one direction only.—*adv.* **cur'rent-ly.**

cur-ric-u-lum (kŭ-rĭk'ū-lŭm), *n.* [*pl.* curriculums (-lŭmz); curricula (-lȧ)], a prescribed regular course of study in a university, school, etc.; as, the school *curriculum* includes cooking and sewing.

cur-ri-er (kŭr'ĭ-ẽr), *n.* one who dresses and colors tanned leather.

cur-rish (kûr'ĭsh), *adj.* pertaining to, or like, a mongrel dog; hence, mean; ignoble.—*adv.* **cur'rish-ly.**—*n.* **cur'rish-ness.**

[1]**cur-ry** (kŭr'ĭ), *v.t.* [*p.t.* and *p.p.* -ried (-ĭd), *p.pr.* -ry-ing], **1,** to rub down and clean, as a horse; **2,** to dress after tanning, as leather: **curry favor,** to seek favor by flattery, servile admiration, etc.

[2]**cur-ry** (kŭr'ĭ), *n.* [*pl.* curries (-ĭz)], **1,** a highly spiced East Indian sauce; **2,** a stew of rice, fowl, etc., seasoned with this condiment.—*adj.* **cur'ried.**

cur-ry-comb (kŭr'ĭ-kōm''), *n.* a metal comb, used to clean horses.

curse (kûrs), *n.* **1,** an oath; **2,** a prayer for injury to come to someone; **3,** that which brings or causes evil or trouble; also, the evil itself:—*v.t.* [*p.t.* and *p.p.* cursed or curst (kûrst), *p.pr.* curs'ing], **1,** to wish, or bring, evil upon; **2,** to torment:—*v.i.* to swear.

curs-ed (kûr'sĕd), *p.adj.* **1,** under a curse; **2,** hateful; detestable; abominable.—*adv.* **curs'ed-ly.**

cur-sive (kûr'sĭv), *adj.* flowing: said of writing in which the letters are joined and the angles often rounded:—*n.* a letter used in such writing, or manuscript written in such characters.—*adv.* **cur'sive-ly.**

cur-so-ry (kûr'sō-rĭ), *adj.* hasty; careless; as, he gave the book a *cursory* reading.—*adv.* **cur'so-ri-ly.**—*n.* **cur'so-ri-ness.**

Syn. desultory, fitful, rapid, discursive.—*Ant.* thorough, critical, painstaking.

curst (kûrst), a form of the past tense and past participle of *curse.*

curt (kûrt), *adj.* **1,** short; **2,** abrupt; rude; as, the child gave a *curt* answer.—*adv.* **curt'ly.**—*n.* **curt'ness.**

Syn. concise, brusque, uncivil. (See short.)

cur-tail (kŭr-tāl'), *v.t.* to cut short; reduce; as, to *curtail* expenses.

Syn. abbreviate, shorten, lessen.

cur-tail-ment (kŭr-tāl'mĕnt), *n.* the act of reducing or shortening.

cur-tain (kûr'tĭn; kûr'tn), *n.* **1,** a hanging screen which can be drawn up or aside; as, a window *curtain;* a stage *curtain;* **2,** anything that serves to conceal: **curtain call,** a summons to an actor to appear and acknowledge applause: **curtain raiser,** a short piece given before the principal play:—*v.t.* to inclose with a screen or the like.

curt-sy (kûrt'sĭ), *n.* [*pl.* curtsies (-sĭz)], a bow; a salutation made by bending the knees and gracefully drooping the body:—*v.i.* [*p.t.* and *p.p.* -sied (-sĭd), *p.pr.* -sy-ing], to salute by making such a gesture. Also, **curt'sey; cour'te-sy** (kûr'tĕ-sĭ).

cur-va-ture (kûr'vȧ-tūr), *n.* **1,** a bending; a curving; as, *curvature* of the spine; **2,** the measure of the bending of a line or surface.

curve (kûrv), *n.* **1,** a bending without angles; **2,** a draftsman's instrument for forming such bendings; **3,** in baseball, a ball so pitched as to turn from its expected course; **4,** in mathematics, a line representing the graph of an equation:—*v.t.* [*p.t.* and *p.p.* curved (kûrvd), *p.pr.* curv'ing], to cause to bend:—*v.i.* to bend:—*adj.* bent without angles.—*n.* **curv'ed-ness.**

cur-vet (kûr'vĕt; kŭr-vĕt'), *n.* a particular leap of a horse; a frisk or bound:—*v.i.* (kŭr-vĕt'; kûr'vĕt), [*p.t.* and *p.p.* -vet'ted or -vet'ed, *p.pr.* -vet'ting or -vet'ing], to leap, as a horse; frisk or bound:—*v.t.* to cause to leap or bound.

cur-vi-lin-e-ar (kûr''vĭ-lĭn'ē-ȧr), *adj.* made up of curved lines; bounded by curved lines. Also, **cur''vi-lin'e-al.**

curv-om-e-ter (kûrv-ŏm'ē-tẽr), *n.* an instrument for measuring the length of curved lines, as on a map.

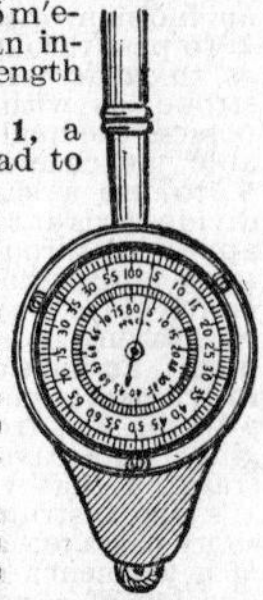

CURVOMETER

cush-ion (ko͝osh'ŭn), *n.* **1,** a pillow or soft pad to sit, lie, or rest upon; **2,** a pillow used in making lace; **3,** the elastic rim of a billiard table:—*v.t.* **1,** to seat upon a soft pad; **2,** to furnish with a soft pad; **3,** to cover up; hence, to suppress; as, to *cushion* complaints:—*v.i.* to make the cue ball strike against the elastic rim of a billiard table.

cusp (kŭsp), *n.* a pointed end, as of a tooth; the horn of a crescent, as of the new moon; a sharp point.—*adj.* **cusped** (kŭspt).

cus-pid (kŭs'pĭd), *n.* a tooth having but one point, as for tearing food; a canine tooth.—*adj.* **cus'pi-dal.**

cus-pi-date (kŭs'pĭ-dāt), *adj.* furnished with, or resembling, a sharp, spearlike point. Also, **cus'pi-dat''ed.**

cus-pi-dor (kŭs'pĭ-dōr; kŭs'pĭ-dôr), *n.* in the U. S., a spittoon.

cus-tard (kŭs'tȧrd), *n.* a mixture of eggs, milk, etc., baked or boiled.

cus-to-di-an (kŭs-tō'dĭ-ăn), *n.* a keeper; one who has the care of anything; as, the *custodian* of a museum.

cus-to-dy (kŭs'tō-dĭ), *n.* **1,** guardianship; care; as, the welfare of a city should be in the *custody* of upright men; **2,** restraint of liberty; imprisonment; as, the *custody* of a prisoner.—*adj.* **cus-to'di-al.**

cus-tom (kŭs'tŭm), *n.* **1,** a usual course of action; a frequent repetition of the same act; **2,** established or recognized usage; as, it is the *custom* to exchange gifts at Christmas; **3,** regular patronage; business support; 4, established usage with the force of law; unwritten law; 5, in *pl.*, duties on imported or, less frequently, exported goods:—*adj.* 1, made to order; as, *custom* shoes; *custom* clothes; 2, accepting only work to be done to order; as, a *custom* tailor.

Syn., *n.* fashion, practice. (See habit.)

cus-tom-a-ry (kŭs′tŭm-ā-rĭ), *adj.* habitual; conventional; common; usual.—*adv.* **cus′tom-a-ri-ly**.

cus-tom-er (kŭs′tŭm-ẽr), *n.* 1, a regular buyer; purchaser; 2, *Colloq.*, a fellow; as, an ugly *customer*.

cus-tom-house (kŭs′tŭm-hous″), *n.* a building where duties or taxes are paid on exported or imported goods, and vessels are entered and cleared.

cut (kŭt), *v.t.* [*p.t.* and *p.p* cut, *p.pr.* cut′ting], 1, to penetrate with an edged instrument; wound thus; 2, to cleave or separate with, or as with, a sharp-edged instrument; as, to *cut* bread; detach or remove thus; as, to *cut* the grass; hew; as, to *cut* down a tree; sever; divide, as a pack of cards at random to prevent cheating; carve, as meat; 3, to cause (teeth) to break through the gums; 4, to shape with a sharp instrument, as a garment: often with *out;* 5, to shorten or reduce by removing a part of, as the hair, expenses, etc.; 6, to do; perform; as, to *cut* a caper; 7, figuratively, to grieve or hurt, as a friend; 8, to pretend not to recognize; 9, to cross, as lines of a geometrical figure; 10, in cricket and tennis, to hit (a ball) with a slicing motion; 11, to dissolve or make less viscous or stiff; as, a strong soap will *cut* the grease in washing dishes; 12, *Colloq.*, to absent oneself from, as a lecture, class, etc.:—*v.i.* 1, to make an incision or gash; as, the knife *cuts* well; 2, to pass through or across by a direct route; as, to *cut* across is shorter; 3, to make a quick stroke, as with a sword, whip, etc.; 4, to possess the quality of being divisible or severable; as, cheese *cuts* more easily than rubber; 5, to use a sharp-edged instrument; 6, to divide cards at random; 7, to have (a tooth) just appearing through the gums: 8, *Slang*, to run away abruptly: **cut up**, to behave in a lively or frivolous way; misbehave:—*n.* 1, the act of cleaving or separating by a sharp instrument; an incision or wound made by a sharp instrument; gash; 2, a sharp stroke, as with a whip; 3, a trench or channel made by digging; an excavated passage, as for a railway track; 4, that which is severed or detached by a sharp instrument; a slice; 5, a straight, short passage; as, a short *cut;* 6, the fashion of a garment; style; shape; 7, the random division of a pack of cards; 8, a particular stroke in cricket or in tennis, which imparts a spin to the ball; 9, a reduction in price; a curtailing, as in expenses; 10, the act of shortening, as a story; also, the part removed; 11, absence, as from a lecture, class, etc.; 12, an act or speech which wounds the feelings; 13, the deliberate ignoring of an acquaintance; 14, the engraved surface from which a picture or the like is printed; also, the picture made from it:—*adj.* 1, divided or separated; 2, gashed; wounded; 3, having the surface ornamented or fashioned, as a gem; 4, not wrought or handmade, as nails; 5, reduced, as in price.

cu-ta-ne-ous (kū-tā′nē-ŭs), *adj.* pertaining to, or affecting, the skin; as, a *cutaneous* disease.

cut-a-way (kŭt′ȧ-wā″), *adj.* cut back from the waist:—*n.* a coat, the skirts of which are cut back from the waist.

cute (kūt), *adj.* *Colloq.*, 1, clever at looking out for oneself; hence, shrewd; sly; as, a *cute* trick; 2, attractive because of beauty or daintiness; as, a *cute* child.—*adv.* **cute′ly**.—*n.* **cute′ness**.

cut glass flint glass cut with facets or figures.

cu-ti-cle (kū′tĭ-kl), *n.* 1, the outer layer of skin: also called *epidermis;* 2, any thin outer covering, as on certain plants.

cu-tis (kū′tĭs), *n.* in anatomy, the true skin which lies under the epidermis.

cut-lass (kŭt′lȧs), *n.* a short, curved sword, used esp. by sailors.

cut-ler (kŭt′lẽr), *n.* one who makes or sells knives or other cutting tools.

cut-ler-y (kŭt′lẽr-ĭ), *n.* edged or cutting tools collectively.

cut-let (kŭt′lĕt), *n.* a slice of meat, cut from the ribs or leg, for broiling or frying; also, a cake made of finely cut meat.

cut–off (kŭt′=ôf″), *n.* 1, that which shortens, as a short or straight road; 2, a new, shorter channel cut by a river across a bend; 3, in engineering, a device for stopping the flow of a fluid, as steam, water, etc.; also, the act of thus shutting off steam, or the point at which it is effected.

cut–out (kŭt′=out″), *n.* 1, a switchlike contrivance to cut off an electric light from the circuit; a circuit breaker; 2, a device by which an internal-combustion engine exhausts directly into the air, instead of, as regularly, through a muffler.

cut-purse (kŭt′pûrs″), *n.* one who cuts purses to steal their contents; hence, a pickpocket.

cut-ter (kŭt′ẽr), *n.* 1, one who cuts out and shapes garments; 2, that which cuts; 3, a light sleigh for two persons; 4, any of various types of boat, as a small, fast-sailing vessel; a man-of-war's boat.

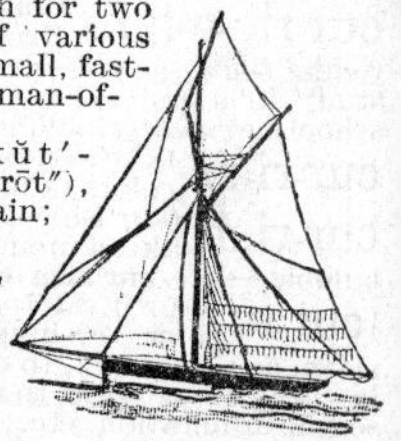

CUTTER

cut-throat (kŭt′-thrōt″), *n.* a murderous villain; a ruffian; thug.

cut-ting (kŭt′ĭng), *p.adj.* 1, dividing, as with an edged instrument; 2, deeply wounding the feelings; sarcastic; as, a *cutting* reply; 3, piercing; chilling; sharp; as, a *cutting* wind:—*n.* 1, a piece cut off or from; a slip; as, to make a *cutting* from a geranium; 2, an incision; 3, an excavation, as for a railway track.

cut-tle (kŭt′l), *n.* the cuttlefish, a fish with ten arms, suckers, two large eyes, and an ink bag containing a dark fluid.

cut-tle-fish (kŭt′l-fĭsh″), *n.* any of several sea animals, belonging to the mollusks, having eight short and two long tentacles, two large eyes, and a hard internal plate, the *cuttle bone* of commerce.

cut-worm (kŭt′wûrm″), *n.* a destructive caterpillar which destroys the young shoots of cabbage, corn, etc.

cy-a-nide (sī′ȧ-nīd; sī′ȧ-nĭd), *n.* a compound of cyanogen with an element or radical; esp., potassium cyanide.

cy-an-o-gen (sī-ăn′ō-jĕn), *n.* a colorless poisonous gas burning with a purple flame, with the odor of peach blossoms, and combining to form cyanides.

cy-an-o-type (sī-ăn′ō-tīp), *n.* a photographic print, as a blue print, made by using a cyanide.

Cyb-e-le (sĭb′ē-lē), *n.* in mythology, the nature goddess of Asia Minor.

cyc-la-men (sĭk′lȧ-mĕn), *n.* any of various plants of the primrose family, with showy flowers.

cy-cle (sī′kl), *n.* 1, a period of time, or order of events, which repeats itself regularly; **2,** a course, as of operations, that is completed and about to start over again; also, the period of such a course; a round; **3,** a complete series; esp., the stories and traditions surrounding some famous event or hero; as, the stories of the Knights of the Round Table make up the Arthurian *cycle;* **4,** an age or long period; **5,** a bicycle or tricycle: **cycle car,** a very light, small vehicle driven by a motor:—*v.i.* [*p.t.* and *p.p.* -cled (-kld), *p.pr.* -cling], **1,** to occur or recur, at regular intervals; **2,** to ride a cycle.—*n.* **cy'cler.**—*n.* **cy'clist.**

cyc-lic (sĭk'lĭk; sī'klĭk), *adj.* pertaining to, belonging to, or moving in, a cycle.

cy-cloid (sī'kloid), *n.* a geometrical curve traced out by any point of a circle rolling along a straight line until it has completed a revolution.—*adj.* **cy-cloi'dal.**

cy-clom-e-ter (sī-klŏm'ē-tẽr), *n.* an instrument for measuring the distance covered by a wheel.

cy-clone (sī'klōn), *n.* **1,** a violent storm in which the wind whirls inward toward a center; **2,** loosely, a tornado or any destructive storm.—*adj.* **cy-clon'ic** (sī-klŏn'-ĭk).—*adv.* **cy-clon'i-cal-ly.**

cy-clo-pe-di-a (sī"klō-pē'dĭ-*ȧ*), *n.* an encyclopedia; a book containing brief information upon all subjects, alphabetically arranged. Also, **cy"clo-pæ'-di-a.**—*adj.* **cy"clo-pe'dic.**

Cy-clops (sī'klŏps), *n.* [*pl.* Cyclopes (sī-klō'pēz)], **1,** in mythology, one of a race of one-eyed giants; **2,** in Homer's "Odyssey," one of a race of one-eyed, gigantic shepherds.—*adj.* **Cy"clo-pe'an.**

cyg-net (sĭg'nĕt), *n.* a young swan.—*adj.* **cyg'ne-ous.**

Cyg-nus (sĭg'nŭs), *n.* a northern constellation, the Swan, in the Milky Way.

cyl-in-der (sĭl'ĭn-dẽr), *n.* **1,** a solid generated by a rectangle which revolves about one of its sides as an axis; also, the surface so formed (see *solid,* illus.); **2,** any body having the form of a cylinder, as the chamber in which force is exerted on the piston of a steam engine, the barrel of a pump, a roller for printing, etc.

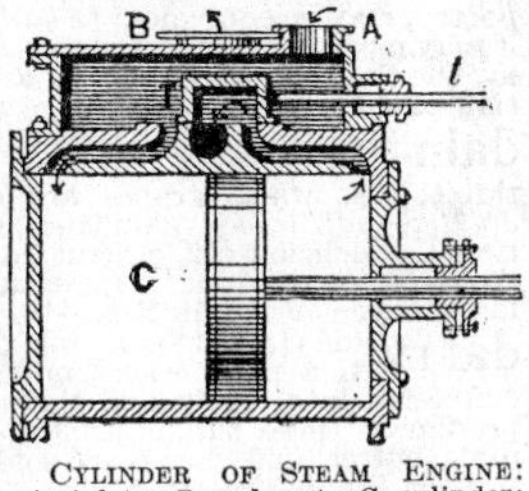

CYLINDER OF STEAM ENGINE: *A,* inlet; *B,* exhaust; *C,* cylinder; *t,* valve stem; *T,* slide valve.

cy-lin-dric (sĭ-lĭn'drĭk), *adj.* having the form, or characteristic qualities, of a cylinder. Also, **cy-lin'dri-cal.**—*adv.* **cy-lin'dri-cal-ly.**

cy-mar (sĭ-mär'), *n.* a loose garment or chemise worn by women.

cym-bal (sĭm'bǎl), *n.,* usually in *pl.,* either of two circular, concave, metal plates which form a musical instrument, played by striking their edges together.

CYMBALS

cyme (sīm), *n.* a certain way of flowering, in which the primary, as well as the secondary, axis terminates in a flower (see *inflorescence,* illus.); hence, any flat or convex flower formation, as the forget-me-not.—*adj.* **cy'mose.**

Cym-ric (kĭm'rĭk; sĭm'rĭk), *adj.* pertaining to the Welsh race or their speech:—*n.* the Welsh language; also, any of certain allied languages. Also, **Kym'ric.**

Cym-ry (kĭm'rĭ), *n.pl.* the Welsh people collectively. Also, **Kym'ry.**

Cyn-ic (sĭn'ĭk), *n.* one of a school of ancient Greek philosophers who taught that virtue, based on self-control and independence, was the only good:—*adj.* pertaining to the doctrine of the Cynics: **cynic,** one who believes that self-interest is the sole motive behind the actions of human beings; hence, a sarcastic, surly person:—*adj.* sarcastic; doubting; sneering.—*adj.* **Cyn'i-cal.**

cyn-i-cal (sĭn'ĭ-kǎl), *adj.* **1,** surly; sarcastic; as, a sneering, *cynical* remark; **2,** given to sneering at purity of thought or high motives.—*adv.* **cyn'i-cal-ly.**—*n.* **cyn'i-cal-ness.**

Cyn-i-cism (sĭn'ĭ-sĭzm), *n.* the philosophy of the Greek Cynics: **cynicism,** the quality of mind that expresses itself in surliness, sarcasm, and lack of faith in disinterested motives.

cy-no-sure (sī'nō-shōōr; sĭn'ō-shōōr), *n.* **1,** an object of general attraction; **2,** anything that attracts attention; as, the *cynosure* of all eyes.

cy-pher (sī'fẽr), *n.* **1,** the character [0] meaning zero; **2,** a secret method of writing and the key to it; **3,** that which is so written; **4,** something of no value:—*v.t.* and *v.i.* **1,** to work out by means of arithmetic; **2,** to write with a private alphabet or other secret characters. See **ci'pher,** *Pfd. S.*

cy-press (sī'prĕs), *n.* **1,** any of a genus (*Cupressus*) of cone-bearing evergreen trees, a branch of which is used as an emblem of mourning; also, any of certain related trees, as the bald cypress of the southern U. S.; **2,** the wood of this tree:—*adj.* pertaining to, or made of, wood of the cypress.

cyst (sĭst), *n.* a sac, or pouch, in animal bodies, sometimes containing diseased matter.—*adj.* **cyst'oid.**

cyst-ic (sĭs'tĭk), *adj.* pertaining to a cyst or to a bladder.

cy-to-plasm (sī'tō-plǎzm), *n.* the protoplasmic substance of a cell exclusive of, and surrounding, the nucleus.

czar (zär; tsär), *n.* an emperor or absolute monarch; a supreme lord or ruler: **Czar,** formerly, the title of a Russian emperor: a form of Cæsar. Also, **tsar; tzar.**

czar-e-vitch (zär'ĕ-vĭch; tsär'-), *n.* formerly, the eldest son of a czar. Also, **tsar'e-vitch; tzar'e-vitch.**

cza-rev-na (zä-rĕv'n*ȧ*; tsä-), *n.* formerly, a daughter of a czar of Russia. Also, **tsa-rev'na; tza-rev'na.**

cza-ri-na (zä-rē'n*ȧ*; tsä-), *n.* formerly, an empress of Russia; the wife of a czar. Also, **tsa-ri'na; tza-ri'na.**

Czech (chĕk), *n.* **1,** a member of the most westerly branch of the Slavonic family, including Bohemians, Moravians, and Slovaks; **2,** the language of these peoples; **3,** a citizen or inhabitant of Czechoslovakia.—*adj.* and *n.* **Czech'ish.**

Czech-o-slav (chĕk'ō-släv"; -slǎv"), *n.* **1,** a member of the Czechish branch of the Slavonic race, including Bohemians, Moravians, and Slovaks; a Czech; **2,** the language of the Czechs.

Czech-o-slo-vak (chĕk'ō-slō-vǎk'; -slō'vǎk), *adj.* pertaining to the Czechs and Slovaks, or to their language; pertaining to the people of Bohemia, Moravia, and northwestern Hungary, or to their language: **Czechoslovak Republic,** a nation formed in central Europe in 1918, including Bohemia, Moravia, and parts of Silesia and Hungary; Czechoslovakia:—*n.* a member of the Czechoslovak race or nation.

D

[1]**dab** (dăb), *n.* a flat, salt-water fish; any of several flounders.

[2]**dab** (dăb), *n. Colloq.*, an expert; a skilful person; a dabster.

[3]**dab** (dăb), *v.t.* [*p.t.* and *p.p.* dabbed (dăbd), *p.pr.* dab′bing], to strike or touch lightly; smear in spots, as paint:—*n.* **1**, a soft blow; **2**, a quick, sharp stroke; **3**, a small, soft lump; **4**, a small portion, as of butter.

dab-bing (dăb′ĭng), *n.* the process of indenting the surface of a stone by a pick-shaped tool.

dab-ble (dăb′l), *v.t.* [*p.t.* and *p.p.* -bled (-ld), *p.pr.* -bling], to wet by dipping slightly and often; spatter:—*v.i.* **1**, to paddle in water, as with the hands; **2**, to do anything in a careless manner; as, to *dabble* in art.—*n.* **dab′bler.**

dab-ster (dăb′stẽr), *n. Colloq.*, **1**, one who is skilled; an expert; as, he is a *dabster* at tennis; **2**, *Obs.*, a trifler.

dace (dās), *n.* **1**, any of several small, European fresh-water fishes, resembling the roach or the chub; **2**, in North America, any of various related fishes, such as the horned dace.

dachs-hund (däks′ho͝ont″; dȧks′ho͞ond), [Ger.], *n.* the German badger dog, a hound with a long body and very short, crooked legs.

dac-tyl (dăk′tĭl), *n.* a metrical foot, consisting of one long or accented, and two short or unaccented, syllables.—*adj.* **dac-tyl′ic.**

dac-tyl-o-gram (dăk′tĭ-lō-grăm″), *n.* a finger-print; the impression made for purposes of identification, as in tracing a criminal.—*n.* **dac″ty-log′ra-phy.**

dad (dăd), *n.* a father: used in intimate or informal speech. Also, **dad′dy** (dăd′ĭ).

dad-dy long-legs (lông′lĕgz″), **1**, a two-winged insect, resembling a large mosquito with long legs; **2**, in America, a small-bodied spiderlike animal with eight very slender, long legs.

da-do (dā′dō; dä′dō), *n.* [*pl.* dadoes (-dōz)], **1**, the lower part of the wall of a room when differently decorated from the upper part; **2**, a covering for the lower part of the wall of a room between the baseboard and the chair rail; **3**, a face of a pedestal, between the base and cornice (see *pedestal*, illus.).

Dæd-a-lus (dĕd′ȧ-lŭs), *n.* in mythology, an Athenian artist, artificer, and architect, who was exiled to Crete, where he built the Labyrinth, and whence he escaped with his son Icarus by flight on wings attached with wax.—*adj.* **Dæ-dal′ian** (dē-dāl′yăn).

dæ-mon (dē′mŏn), *n.* a spirit; devil. See **de′mon**, *Pfd.S.*—*adj.* **dæ-mon-ic.**

daf-fo-dil (dăf′ō-dĭl), *n.* a narrow-leaved, bulbous plant bearing large yellow single or double flowers: a species of narcissus. Also, *Dial.* and *Poetic*, **daf′fo-dil″ly; daf′fy-down-dil″ly.**

daft (dȧft), *adj.* **1**, weak-minded; simple; silly; foolishly enthusiastic; as, he is *daft* on that subject; **2**, in Scotland, gay or light-hearted.

dag-ger (dăg′ẽr), *n.* **1**, a short weapon for stabbing; **2**, a reference mark in printing [†]: **double dagger**, a reference mark [‡] like a dagger with a grip at each end.

da-guerre-o-type (dȧ-gĕr′ō-tīp), *n.* an early method of photography by which the pictures were taken on silver-coated plates; also, a picture taken by this process.

da-ha-be-ah (dä″hȧ-bē′ȧ), *n.* a passenger boat used on the Nile, having a sharp bow and broad stern, and one or two masts with lateen sails. Also, **da″ha-bee′yah** (dä″hȧ-bē′yȧ); **da″ha-bi′ah** (dä″hȧ-bē′ȧ).

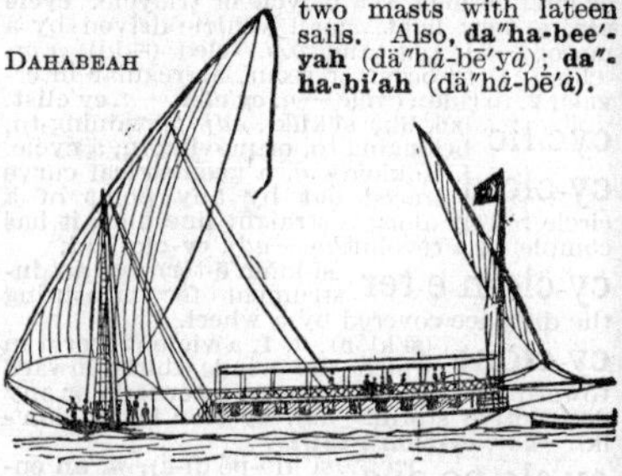

DAHABEAH

dahl-ia (däl′yȧ; often, dāl′yȧ; dăl′yȧ), *n.* [*pl.* dahlias (-yȧz)], a tuberous-rooted plant of the aster family, cultivated for its beautiful blossoms; also, the blossom.

Dail Eir-eann (dāl âr′ĭn; dôl), the Chamber of Deputies of the Irish Free State.

dai-ly (dā′lĭ), *n.* [*pl.* dailies (-lĭz)], a newspaper published each day:—*adj.* occurring or recurring each successive day; diurnal; as, *daily* need of food:—*adv.* on every day; day by day; as, they bring supplies *daily.*

Syn., adj. diurnal. *Daily* describes ordinary events that happen every twenty-four hours; as, *daily* meals; *daily* exercise. *Diurnal*, in poetry, may be equivalent to *daily;* in science, it may mean occupying one day, or active during the daytime only; as, the *diurnal* revolution of the earth; *diurnal* flowers.

dain-ty (dān′tĭ), *n.* [*pl.* dainties (-tĭz)], something choice or delicious; a tidbit; as, white grapes are considered a *dainty:*—*adj.* [*comp.* dain′ti-er, *superl.* dain′ti-est], **1**, delicious; **2**, elegant; delicate; as, a *dainty* piece of china; **3**, sensitive; choice; fastidious.—*adv.* **dain′ti-ly.**—*n.* **dain′ti-ness.**

dai-ry (dā′rĭ; dâr′ĭ), *n.* [*pl.* dairies (-rĭz)], **1**, a place where milk is kept and converted into butter and cheese; **2**, a farm producing these supplies; **3**, a shop where milk, butter, and cheese are sold.—*n.* **dai′ry-ing.**—*n.fem.* **dai′ry-maid″.**

dai-ry-man (dā′rĭ-măn; dâr′ĭ-), *n.* [*pl.* dairymen (-mĕn)], **1**, a man employed in a dairy; **2**, the owner of a dairy.—*n.fem.* **dai′ry-wom″an.**

da-is (dā′ĭs; dās), *n.* a raised platform for a throne or seats of honor.

dai-sy (dā′zĭ), *n.* [*pl.* daisies (-zĭz)], in the U. S., any of various wild field flowers of the aster family, with a yellow or brown center, composed of very small flowers, surrounded by white or yellow ray flowers resembling petals (see *inflorescence*, illus.): also called *oxeye; oxeye daisy.*—*adj.* **dai′sied.**

Da-ko-ta (dȧ-kō′tȧ), *n.* one of a Sioux tribe of American Indians, orig. inhabiting the region of the upper Mississippi.

dale (dāl), *n.* a valley; glen; as, they went up hill and down *dale.*

dalles (dălz), *n.pl.* in the northwestern U. S. and Canada, rapids, esp. those flowing through a gorge.

dal-li-ance (dăl′ĭ-ăns), *n.* the act of trifling, loitering, or playing.

dal-ly (dăl′ĭ), *v.i.* [*p.t.* and *p.p.* -lied (-ĭd), *p.pr.* -ly-ing], **1**, to make sport, esp. amorously; also, to trifle with a person's affections; **2**, to waste time; delay; loiter; as, to *dally* on the road.—*n.* **dal′li-er.**

Dal-ton-ism (dôl′tŭn-ĭzm), *n.* color blindness: so called from John Dalton, who first described it.

¹dam (dăm), *n.* **1**, a bank or wall built so as to hold water; **2**, water so held back; **3**, a sheet of rubber used in dentistry to keep saliva from a tooth:—*v.t.* [*p.t.* and *p.p.* dammed (dămd), *p.pr.* dam′ming], **1**, to confine or raise the level of, as water, by a dam; restrain; **2**, to provide with a dam; confine the waters of, as a stream, by a dam.

²dam (dăm), *n.* a mother: generally used of quadrupeds.

dam-age (dăm′āj), *n.* **1**, injury or harm; as, the flood caused great *damage;* **2**, harm wilfully done to one's reputation, person, or estate; as, the story did great *damage* to the man's reputation; **3**, in *pl.*, compensation awarded to one for injury or loss through the fault of another:—*v.t.* [*p.t.* and *p.p.* -aged (-ājd), *p.pr.* -ag-ing], to injure; harm; hurt; impair.
Syn. (see injury).

dam-a-scene (dăm″ȧ-sēn′; dăm′ȧ-sēn), *v.t.* (also, *damaskeen*), [*p.t.* and *p.p.* -scened′ (-sēnd′), *p.pr.* -scen′ing], to decorate (metal) with etching or inlaid designs, as was done at Damascus:—*adj.* (dăm′ȧ-sēn; dăm″ȧ-sēn′), pertaining to damask or damascening: **Damascene,** pertaining to Damascus.

Da-mas-cus steel (dȧ-măs′kŭs), a flexible steel first made at Damascus: used for sword blades.

dam-ask (dăm′ȧsk), *n.* **1**, silk or linen material woven with elaborate patterns; **2**, a fine twilled linen with patterns made by threads woven so as to reflect the light; **3**, Damascus steel or work; **4**, a deep pink color:—*adj.* **1**, pertaining to, or made of, damask; **2**, made of, or similar to, Damascus steel; **3**, of a deep pink color.

dame (dām), *n.* **1**, a lady of high social rank; **2**, a title formerly used instead of Mistress or Madam; **3**, a school mistress; **4**, a matron; an elderly woman.

damn (dăm), *v.t.* [*p.t.* and *p.p.* damned (dămd), *p.pr.* damn′ing (dăm′ĭng; often dăm′nĭng, in adjective sense)], **1**, to sentence to punishment or death; **2**, to doom to eternal punishment; **3**, to invoke a curse upon; **4**, to condemn as bad, faulty, or as a failure; as, to *damn* with faint praise:—*v.i.* to swear; curse:—*n.* **1**, a curse; **2**, anything as valueless as an oath.

dam-na-ble (dăm′nȧ-bl), *adj.* **1**, deserving to be eternally condemned; **2**, annoying.—*adv.* **dam′na-bly.**

dam-na-tion (dăm-nā′shŭn), *n.* **1**, eternal punishment; **2**, condemnation; severe criticism, as of books.

damned (dămd; *Poetic,* dăm′nĕd), *p.adj.* **1**, condemned to eternal punishment; **2**, condemned as bad or as a failure; **3**, cursed: used as an expletive.

Dam-o-cles (dăm′ō-klēz), *n.* a courtier of the tyrant Dionysius of Syracuse, who, because he envied his master for his wealth and power, was seated beneath a sword held by a single hair, to make him realize the dangers of a tyrant's life.

dam-oi-selle (dăm″ĭ-zĕl′), *n.* a young unmarried woman; a maiden. Also, **dam′o-sel″**; *Pfd. S.*, **dam′sel.**

Da-mon (dā′mŏn), *n.* in mythology, the friend of Pythias (or, more properly, *Phintias*). When the latter, condemned to death by the tyrant Dionysius of Syracuse, asked permission to go home and arrange his affairs, Damon offered his own life as pledge for the return of his friend.

damp (dămp), *n.* **1**, moisture; fog; **2**, depression; discouragement; **3**, fire damp, a poisonous gas sometimes found in coal mines:—*adj.* moist; foggy; humid:—*v.t.* **1**, to moisten; **2**, to discourage; depress; **3**, to check; stifle.—*adv.* **damp′ly.**—*n.* **damp′ness.**
Syn., adj. (see moist).

damp-en (dămp′n), *v.t.* **1**, to make moist or wet; **2**, to depress or discourage.—*n.* **damp′en-er.**

damp-er (dămp′ẽr), *n.* **1**, something which depresses or discourages; **2**, a movable plate to regulate the draft, as in a stove; **3**, a device to check the vibrations of a musical instrument; as, the *damper* in a piano is made of wood covered with felt.

dam-sel (dăm′zĕl), *n.* a maiden; a girl; a young unmarried woman. Also, **dam″oi-selle′** (dăm″ĭ-zĕl′); **dam′o-sel″**; **dam′-o-zel″** (dăm′ō-zĕl″).

dam-son (dăm′zn), *n.* **1**, a small, oval, purple plum, orig. from Damascus; **2**, the tree that bears this fruit.

Dan-a-ë (dăn′ā-ē), *n.* in mythology, a princess of Argos, imprisoned by her father in a brazen tower, and there wooed by Zeus in the form of a golden shower.

dance (dȧns), *v.i.* [*p.t.* and *p.p.* danced (dȧnst), *p.pr.* danc′ing], **1**, to move the body and feet rhythmically to music; perform the figures of a dance; **2**, to skip about; move lightly: used of shadows, objects, etc.:—*v.t.* **1**, to give a dancing motion to; as, to *dance* the baby up and down; **2**, to perform by dancing; as, to *dance* a jig:—*n.* **1**, a regulated movement of the body and feet to a rhythmical musical accompaniment; as, the minuet is an old-time *dance;* **2**, a dancing party, less formal than a ball; **3**, one round of dancing at such a party.—*n.* **danc′er.**

dan-de-li-on (dăn′dē-lī″ŭn), *n.* a common plant having yellow flowers coarsely toothed leaves, and a milky root.

dan-der (dăn′dẽr), *n. Colloq.*, temper anger; indignation; as, to have one's *dander* up.

dan-dle (dăn′dl), *v.t.* [*p.t.* and *p.p.* -dled (-dld), *p.pr.* -dling], **1**, to dance (an infant) up and down, as on the knee or in the arms; **2**, to fondle.—*n.* **dan′dler.**

dan-druff (dăn′drŭf), *n.* the dead, scale-like skin that forms on the scalp. Also, **dan′driff.**

dan-dy (dăn′dĭ), *n.* [*pl.* dandies (-dĭz)], **1**, a fop; a man who gives much attention to dress; as, Beau Brummel was the *dandy* of his time; **2**, *Slang,* something unusually fine:—*adj. Slang,* excellent or very fine. —*adj.* **dan′dy-ish.**

dan-dy-ism (dăn′dĭ-ĭzm), *n.* foppishness; as, Beau Brummel was a noted representative of *dandyism.*

Dane (dān), *n.* a native or inhabitant of Denmark: **great Dane,** a very large and powerful breed of dog.

Dane-law (dān′lô″), *n.* **1**, the code of laws enforced by the Danes in England in the ninth century; **2**, the territory governed by these laws. Also, **Dane′lagh″** (dān′lăkh″; -lä″).

dan-ger (dān′jẽr), *n.* peril; exposure to loss, injury, or death; also, the cause of such exposure.
Syn. peril, risk. These terms are alike in giving the idea of chance or uncertainty. *Danger* is exposure to possible harm or injury in the future; as, the *danger* of shipwreck. *Peril* is danger that is close upon one; as, the *perils* of traffic. *Risk* implies the voluntary taking of chances under probably adverse conditions; as, the *risks* of gambling.

dan-ger-ous (dăn′jẽr-ŭs), *adj.* 1, unsafe; involving, or beset with, danger; perilous; as, it is *dangerous* to play with fire; 2, ready to do harm or injury.—*adv.* **dan′ger-ous-ly.**—*n.* **dan′ger-ous-ness.**

dan-gle (dăng′gl), *v.i.* [*p.t.* and *p.p.* -gled (-gld), *p.pr.* -gling], 1, to hang or swing loosely; 2, to hang about or depend on anyone; follow:—*v.t.* to cause to swing loosely.—*n.* **dan′gler.**

Dan-iel (dăn′yĕl), *n.* 1, in the Bible, a Hebrew prophet captive at Babylon; 2, the book of the Old Testament which contains his history and prophecies.

Dan-ish (dān′ĭsh), *adj.* pertaining to Denmark, its language, or its people:—*n.* the language of Denmark.

dank (dăngk), *adj.* unpleasantly humid or damp; moist; wet; as, *dank* hair; *dank* weeds; a cold, *dank* cave.—*adv.* **dank′ly.**
Syn. (see moist).

***dan-seuse** (dän″söz′), [Fr.], *n.* [*pl.* danseuses (-söz′)], a professional woman dancer; a ballet dancer: ***première danseuse** (prē-myâr′), the leading woman dancer in a ballet.

Daph-ne (dăf′nē), *n.* in mythology, the lovely daughter of the river god Peneus, who, while trying to escape from her wooer, Apollo, was changed into a laurel.

dap-per (dăp′ẽr), *adj.* 1, small and active; 2, trim and neat in appearance.

dap-ple (dăp′l), *adj.* spotted; as, a *dapple* gray horse:—*n.* 1, a spotted animal, esp. a horse; 2, a patch of color on an animal:—*v.t.* [*p.t.* and *p.p.* -pled (-ld), *p.pr.* -pling], to decorate with little spots.

dare (dâr), *v.i.* [*p.t.* dared (dârd) or durst (dûrst), *p.p.* dared, *p.pr.* dar′ing], to have courage; be bold enough; venture: often with a dependent infinitive:—*v.t.* 1, to venture upon; have the courage for; brave; as, to *dare* the perils of arctic travel; 2, to challenge:—*n.* a taunting defiance.

dare–dev-il (dâr′=dĕv″l), *adj.* characteristic of a reckless man:—*n.* a reckless fellow.

dar-ing (dâr′ĭng), *n.* bravery; boldness:—*p.adj.* fearless; bold; venturous.

dark (därk), *adj.* 1, without light; not reflecting light; 2, of colors, approaching black; 3, of a brunette complexion; as, the Indian has a *dark* skin; 4, gloomy; as, a *dark* mood; 5, secret; as, keep it *dark;* 6, mysterious; as, a *dark* saying; 7, ignorant; as, the mind of the savage is *dark;* 8, dastardly; as, a *dark* deed:—*n.* 1, absence of light; a place where there is little or no light; nightfall; 2, secrecy; as, to work in the *dark;* 3, ignorance; as, I am in the *dark* on the subject; 4, a color or shade nearly black.—*adv.* **dark′ly.**—*n.* **dark′ness.**
Syn., adj. dismal, opaque, dim, shadowy.—*Ant., adj.* bright, brilliant, light.

dark-en (där′kn), *v.t.* 1, to make dark; shut out the light from; obscure; 2, to make gloomy; as, the misfortunes of war *darken* many homes; 3, to perplex; puzzle; 4, to pollute:—*v.i.* to become dark.

dark-ling (därk′lĭng), *adj.* dimly seen:—*adv.* in the dark.

dark-room (därk′rōōm″), *n.* a room freed of natural light, for photographic operations.

dark-some (därk′sŭm), *adj.* gloomy; without light; mysterious.

dar-ling (där′lĭng), *n.* one dearly loved; a favorite; pet:—*adj.* greatly cherished; tenderly loved; very dear.

[1]**darn** (därn), *v.t.* to mend, as a hole in a fabric, by interweaving thread or yarn:—*v.i.* to perform the operation of darning:—*n.* the place so mended.

[2]**darn** (därn), *v.t. Colloq.*, to damn:—*n.* a word used to express mild profanity. Also, **durn; dern.**

dar-nel (där′nĕl), *n.* a common weed of the grass family: identified with the tares of the Bible (Matthew 13:24–30).

darn-ing nee-dle 1, a large needle usually with an elongated eye, used in darning; 2, any dragon fly with a long, thin body: often called *devil's darning needle.*

dart (därt), *n.* 1, a small lance or spear; the arrow of a blowgun; 2, anything that wounds sharply, as an insect's sting; 3, a swift, sudden movement:—*v.t.* to throw; as, the invaders *dart* their spears:—*v.i.* to move swiftly; start suddenly and go quickly; as, the fish *dart* through the water.

Dar-win-i-an (där-wĭn′ĭ-ăn), *adj.* relating to Charles Darwin, the naturalist, or to his theory of evolution:—*n.* a believer in Darwinism.

Dar-win-ism (där′wĭn-ĭzm), *n.* the theory of evolution to the effect that the present forms of plants and animals have been produced from simple forms by repeated slight changes transmitted from parent to offspring, those forms surviving which are best fitted to their surroundings.—*n.* **Dar′win-ist.**

dash (dăsh), *v.t.* 1, to throw violently or hastily; hurl; 2, to break by collision; shatter; 3, to splash: with *with;* 4, to ruin; frustrate; as, to *dash* one's hopes; 5, to perform hastily, as writing or sketching: with *off;* 6, to depress; confuse:—*v.i.* to rush with violence; strike on a surface with a violent, noisy motion:—*n.* 1, a collision; 2, a slight addition; as, a *dash* of pepper; 3, decisiveness of manner; as, with vim and *dash;* 4, *Colloq.*, a vulgar display; as, to cut a *dash* with fine clothes; 5, a mark [—] in writing or printing; 6, something that causes discouragement; 7, the striking of water in noisy motion; as, the *dash* of the waves; 8, a sudden rush; 9, a short, very quick race.

dash-board (dăsh′bōrd″), *n.* 1, a mud screen on the front of a carriage or wagon; 2, a baseboard.

dash-een (dăsh″ēn′), *n.* an edible tropical root, similar to the potato in its food characteristics, adapted for cultivation in rich, moist soils: recently introduced into the southern U. S.

dash-er (dăsh′ẽr), *n.* 1, one who or that which dashes; 2, specif., the inner mechanism of an ice-cream freezer, or the part of a churn which is moved up and down to make milk into butter.

dash-ing (dăsh′ĭng), *p.adj.* 1, spirited; bold; as, a *dashing* soldier; 2, showy; gay.—*adv.* **dash′ing-ly.**

das-tard (dăs′tȧrd), *n.* a coward; esp., a base coward:—*adj.* meanly shrinking from danger; cowardly.

das-tard-ly (dăs′tȧrd-lĭ), *adv.* cowardly; slyly base or wicked.—*n.* **das′tard-li-ness.**

da-ta (dā′tȧ), *n.pl.* [*sing.* datum (-tŭm)], a collection of facts; as, the necessary *data* for his report.

[1]**date** (dāt), *n.* 1, the time specified by year, month, and day, as of an occurrence, object, etc.; 2, a period of time; age; 3, the present time: used in *out of date* and *up to date;* 4, *Colloq.*, an engagement for a fixed time:—*v.t.* [*p.t.* and *p.p.* dat′ed, *p.pr.* dat′ing], 1, to mark with a definite time; 2, to find the definite time of:—*v.i.* 1, to bear the statement of a time and place: usually with *from;* 2, to reckon time from a given time, era, event, or the like; belong to the time of something; as, this house *dates* from Revolutionary days.

²date (dāt), *n.* the edible fruit of the date palm, consisting of a drupe with a single seed; also, the tree: **date palm,** a tree with a crown of feathery leaves, and a long trunk, native to Africa and Asia, and yielding edible fruit: now grown in Arizona.

da-tive (dā'tĭv), *adj.* in inflected languages, designating, or pertaining to, the case of a noun or pronoun which expresses the indirect object:—*n.* **1,** the dative case, its equivalent in English being *to* or *for* with the objective case; **2,** a substantive in that case.

da-tum (dā'tŭm), *n.* [*pl.* data (-tȧ)], **1,** usually in *pl.,* something assumed, known, or granted for the basis of an argument or inference; as, statistics used as *data;* **2,** a certain level assumed, from which heights and depths are measured.

daub (dôb), *v.t.* **1,** to cover or smear with mud, plaster, etc.; **2,** to paint coarsely or unskilfully:—*n.* **1,** a cheap kind of plaster; **2,** a coarse or rude painting; **3,** a smear; smudge.—*n.* **daub'er.**

daugh-ter (dô'tẽr), *n.* **1,** the female offspring of human parents; a female descendant; **2,** a woman of a certain country; as, a *daughter* of France; **3,** anything considered as feminine looked at in relation to its source or origin; as, charity is the *daughter* of civilization.—*adj.* **daugh'ter-ly.**

daugh-ter–in–law (dô'tẽr-ĭn-lô''), *n.* [*pl.* daughters-in-law (-tẽrz-)], a son's wife.

daunt (dônt; dônt), *v.t.* to frighten; discourage; dishearten.

daunt-less (dônt'lĕs; dônt'-), *adj.* fearless; persevering; intrepid; as, the *dauntless* captain brought his ship safely through the storm.—*adv.* **daunt'less-ly.** —*n.* **daunt'less-ness.**

dau-phin (dô'fĭn), *n.* the title of the eldest son of each of the kings of France from 1349 to 1830.

dav-en-port (dăv'ĕn-pōrt), *n.* **1,** a kind of small writing desk or table; **2,** a long, low sofa.

Da-vid (dā'vĭd), *n.* in the Bible, the youngest son of Jesse of Bethlehem: second king of Israel, and probable writer of many songs contained in the Psalms.

dav-it (dăv'ĭt; dā'vĭt), *n.* one of a pair of ˥-shaped pieces of iron on the side of a vessel, for suspending or lowering a boat; also, a small crane for hoisting the flukes of the anchor.

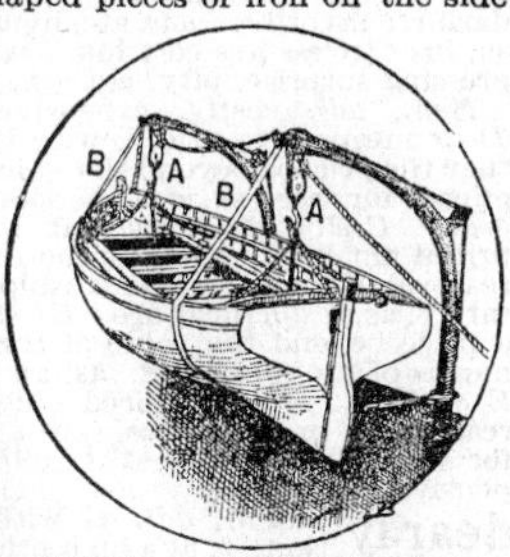

DAVITS: *A,* block and hook supporting boat; *B,* lashing to prevent sway.

da-vy (dā'vĭ), *n.* [*pl.* davies (-vĭz)], a miner's safety lamp surrounded by fine gauze wire, invented by Sir Humphry Davy as a protection against explosions of fire damp: abbreviated from its full name, *Davy lamp.*

Da-vy Jones (jōnz), according to a superstition of sailors, the spirit of the sea: **Davy Jones's locker,** the bottom of the sea, regarded as the grave of drowned sailors and voyagers.

daw (dô), *n.* **1,** a bird of the crow family; a jackdaw; **2,** a simpleton.

daw-dle (dô'dl), *v.i.* [*p.t.* and *p.p.* -dled (-dld), *p.pr.* -dling], to waste time in a trifling manner; loiter.—*n.* **daw'dler.**

dawn (dôn), *v.i.* **1,** to begin to grow light; glimmer; break, as the day; **2,** to begin to develop or show promise; as, *dawning* beauty; **3,** to begin to be evident or plain; as, the solution *dawned* upon him:—*n.* **1,** the first appearance of daylight; as, the cock crows at *dawn;* **2,** beginning or unfolding; as, the *dawn* of history.

day (dā), *n.* **1,** the period of light between sunrise and sunset; daylight; sunshine; **2,** the period of 24 consecutive hours, reckoning from midnight, or from any specified time; **3,** in the East, a distance that can be traveled in 24 hours; **4,** a specified time or period; as, the *day* of chivalry; **5,** the number of hours allowed by law or custom for work; as, an eight-hour *day;* **6,** a conflict, or its result; as, to gain the *day.*

day-bed (dā'bĕd''), *n.* a bed or couch used for resting through the day, or serving as a couch in a room which during the day is used otherwise than as a bedroom.

day-book (dā'bo͝ok''), *n.* a book in which the business accounts of the day's transactions are kept.

day-break (dā'brāk''), *n.* the dawn; as, the birds sang at *daybreak.*

day-dream (dā'drēm''), *n.* an idle fancy; undirected thought:—*v. i.* to dream idly while awake; as, he *daydreams* and builds castles in the air.

day let-ter a telegram with a minimum charge for 50 words, accepted for sending during the day on the understanding that regular telegrams take precedence, and hence sent at a lower rate: distinguished from *night letter.*

day-light (dā'līt''), *n.* **1,** the light of day; **2,** time between dawn and dusk.

day-spring (dā'sprĭng''), *n.* the dawn; beginning.

day–star (dā'-stär''), *n.* **1,** a morning star; **2,** an emblem of hope.

day-time (dā'tīm''), *n.* the hours during which the sun gives light.

daze (dāz), *v.t.* [*p.t.* and *p.p.* dazed (dāzd), *p.pr.* daz'ing], **1,** to confuse; stupefy; **2,** to dazzle:—*n.* the state of being confused or stupefied; as, he was in a *daze* after the blow.—*adv.* **daz'ed-ly.**

daz-zle (dăz'l), *v.t.* [*p.t.* and *p.p.* -zled (-ld), *p.pr.* -zling], **1,** to confuse by a glare of light; **2,** to bewilder by splendor; as, the jewels of the rich *dazzle* the eyes of the poor:—*v.i.* to be confused by excess of light; as, my eyes *dazzle* in the strong light:—*n.* excess of light.—*adv.* **daz'zling-ly.**

de- (dē-; dē-), *prefix,* **1,** down; as, *de*pend; *de*press; **2,** off; away; as, *de*tract; *de*port; **3,** entirely: used with intensive effect; as, *de*note; *de*clare; *de*claim; **4,** reversal or negation; as, *de*capitate; *de*mobilize; **5,** for Latin *dis-:* see *dis-.*

dea-con (dē'kn), *n.* an inferior or subordinate church officer; also, in some churches, a man appointed to assist the minister.—*n.fem.* **dea'con-ess.**

dead (dĕd), *adj.* **1,** having ceased to live; deprived of life; **2,** without life; inanimate; as, *dead* and inert matter; **3,** resembling death; inactive; showing no force, motion, liveliness, etc.: in many figurative uses; as, a *dead* electric wire; a *dead* end to a street; a *dead* market; **4,** disused; obsolete; as, a *dead* language; **5,** complete; utter; as, a *dead* loss; **6,** unerring; sure; as, a *dead* shot; **7,** out of the game or play; as, a *dead* ball; **8,** lacking fire, brilliancy, vivacity, etc.; as, a *dead* social season; **9,** flat; not varied; as, a *dead* level; **10,** in printing, not to be used; as, *dead* copy:—*n.* **1**, one or many dead persons: used with *the;* **2**, the point or time of greatest lifelessness; as, the *dead* of night: —*adv.* **1**, absolutely; completely; utterly; as, you are *dead* right; **2**, exactly; as, *dead* east.

Syn., adj. inanimate, lifeless. *Dead* generally describes that which has had life, but from which life has departed, and emphasizes the fact of death; as, a *dead* body. *Inanimate* describes that which never had life; as, an *inanimate* block of wood. *Lifeless* may describe either, but emphasizes the absence of life; as, a *lifeless* body; a *lifeless* region. Figuratively, *dead* and *lifeless* imply dulness, inaction, and a lack of mental strength; as, a *dead* issue; a *lifeless* party; a *lifeless* speaker. —*Ant., adj.* animate, alive, virile.

dead-beat (dĕd′bēt″), *n.* in physics, a movement with no recoil.

dead cen-ter that position of a crank in which the crank axle, crank pin, and the connecting rod are all in a straight line, so that a push or pull on the connecting rod produces no rotation.

dead-en (dĕd′n), *v.t.* **1**, to lessen the intensity or vigor of; retard; blunt; as, the medicine was given to *deaden* the pain; **2**, to make soundproof, as a wall; **3**, to make tasteless or stale; **4**, to deprive of gloss or brilliancy; **5**, to kill (trees) by girdling.—*n.* **dead′en-er.**—*n.* **dead′en-ing.**

dead-eye (dĕd′ī″), *n.* a round, flat block of wood pierced with three holes to receive lanyards or ropes.

dead-head (dĕd′hĕd″), *n.* **1**, *Colloq.*, a person who has a free pass on railways or for admission to places of amusement, etc.; **2**, a wooden buoy.

dead let-ter **1**, an unclaimed letter, the owner of which cannot be found; **2**, that which has lost force or influence; as, the whipping post is now a *dead letter.*

dead-lock (dĕd′lŏk″), *n.* **1**, a lock worked on one side by a handle and on the other by a key; **2**, a complete standstill; the point when two opposing forces equal each other in strength, so that neither can go ahead.—*adj.* **dead′locked″.**

dead-ly (dĕd′lĭ), *adj.* [*comp.* dead′li-er, *superl.* dead′li-est], **1**, causing death; destructive; fatal; as, Asiatic cholera is a *deadly* disease; **2**, relentless; as, a *deadly* enemy; **3**, resembling death; deathly; as, a *deadly* paleness:—*adv.* **1**, relentlessly; **2**, like death; as, *deadly* pale.—*n.* **dead′li-ness.**

Syn., adj. mortal, fatal. *Deadly* describes that which causes, or can cause, death; as, a *deadly* germ; a *deadly* weapon. *Mortal* also describes that which causes death; as, a *mortal* wound; but, unlike deadly, it may not be applied to a weapon. *Mortal* and *deadly* both describe that which can end only with death, or is merciless; as, *mortal* enmity; a *deadly* feud. *Mortal* also describes those subject to death; as, all men are *mortal.* *Fatal* describes that which causes death or disaster; as, a *fatal* illness; a *fatal* decision.

dead march a piece of solemn music to be played at a funeral.

dead reck-on-ing the method of finding a ship's place at sea by the log and compass.

dead weight **1**, heaviness of, or like that of, a lifeless body; **2**, the weight of a vehicle, as distinguished from that of its load; **3**, freight charged for by weight instead of by bulk.

deaf (dĕf), *adj.* **1**, unable to hear; **2**, unwilling to hear or pay regard to.—*adv.* **deaf′ly.**—*n.* **deaf′ness.**

deaf-en (dĕf′n), *v.t.* **1**, to make unable to hear; **2**, to drown out, as a sound; **3**, to make soundproof.

deaf-en-ing (dĕf′n-ĭng), *p.adj.* **1**, making soundproof; **2**, making unable to hear; **3**, so loud as to drown out other sounds:—*n.* material used in a floor or wall to deaden sound.—*adv.* **deaf′en-ing-ly.**

deaf-mute (dĕf′=mūt′), *n.* one deaf and dumb; one who is dumb from lack of hearing.

[1]deal (dēl), *n.* **1**, a division; part; a portion; **2**, an indefinite, but by implication large, quantity, degree, etc.: often with *great* or *good;* as, it cost me a great *deal* of trouble; **3**, in games, a division of cards to the players; **4**, *Colloq.*, a bargain or secret agreement:—*v.t.* [*p.t.* and *p.p.* dealt (dĕlt), *p.pr.* deal′ing], **1**, to distribute, apportion, or divide, as cards; **2**, to deliver; inflict; as, to *deal* a blow:—*v.i.* **1**, to conduct business; as, they *deal* directly with the farmers; **2**, to carry on a business: with *in;* as, to *deal* in oats; **3**, to be concerned, as to settle something: with *with;* **4**, to behave; comport oneself; as, he *dealt* honorably by his ward.

[2]deal (dēl), *n.* fir or pine cut into planks of various sizes: **standard deal,** a deal cut 9 by 3 inches by 12 feet.

deal-er (dēl′ẽr), *n.* **1**, one who does business with others; a trader; one who buys and sells goods; **2**, one who distributes the cards in a game.

deal-ing (dēl′ĭng), *n.* **1**, conduct toward others; method of doing business; as, fair *dealing;* **2**, in *pl.*, business relations.

dealt (dĕlt), past tense and past participle of the verb *deal.*

dean (dēn), *n.* **1**, the head of a group of clergy in cathedral and collegiate churches; **2**, an administrative officer in a college faculty, often supervising the conduct and studies of the students; **3**, the administrative officer of a college or university next below the president; **4**, the oldest member, in years of service, in a body of men of a certain profession: a term of courtesy.—*n.* **dean′ship.**

dean-er-y (dēn′ẽr-ĭ), *n.* [*pl.* deaneries (-ĭz)], the position, extent of authority, or residence of a dean.

dear (dēr), *adj.* **1**, beloved; highly esteemed: often, as in letters, merely a polite form of address; **2**, expensive; costly; also, charging high prices, as tradesmen; **3**, heartfelt; earnest; as, his *dearest* ambition:—*n.* a darling; favorite:—*adv.* at a high price or rate; as, his carelessness cost him *dear:*—*interj.* expressing surprise, pity, etc.—*n.* **dear′ness.**

Syn., adj. costly, expensive, exorbitant. *Dear* means high-priced, with the suggestion that the price is beyond the value of the thing offered for sale; as, strawberries in winter are *dear.* *Costly* describes that which is high-priced but not necessarily too much so for its real value in fine workmanship, richness, or rarity; as, *costly* furniture. *Expensive* suggests a price beyond the value of the thing or the means of the purchaser; as, an *expensive* car. *Exorbitant* means priced higher than is reasonable or right; as, an *exorbitant* rent for so small a house.—*Ant., adj.* cheap, inexpensive, reasonable.

dear-ly (dēr′lĭ), *adv.* **1**, with great affection; **2**, at a high price or rate; as, he paid *dearly* for his pleasures; **3**, sincerely.

dearth (dûrth), *n.* want; scarcity; as, a *dearth* of coal during a strike.

death (dĕth), *n.* **1**, cessation of life or feeling; the state of having ceased to live; **2**, total loss; as, the *death* of his hopes; **3**, something as terrible as death; as, the disgrace was *death* to him; **4**, slaughter; bloodshed; **5**, a personification of death, as a skeleton with a scythe; **6**, that which causes death, as a plague.

Syn. departure, decease, demise, extinction.

death-bed (dĕth′bĕd″), *n.* **1**, the bed of a person's last sickness and death; **2**, the last hours of life.

death-blow (dĕth′blō″), *n.* **1**, something which causes death; **2**, a shock from which one cannot recover.

death-less (dĕth′lĕs), *adj.* immortal; never dying; as, *deathless* fame.—*adv.* **death′less-ly.**—*n.* **death′less-ness.**

death-ly (dĕth′lĭ), *adj.* **1**, mortal; fatal; deadly; **2**, resembling death; as, a *deathly* stillness:—*adv.* so as to resemble death; as, *deathly* pale.—*n.* **death′li-ness.**

death mask a cast, as of plaster of Paris, taken of the features of one who is dead.

death rate the relation of the number of deaths, during a specified period and in a specified place, to the population: usually reckoned at a proportion of so many per thousand.

death's-head (dĕths′-hĕd″), *n.* a human skull as a conventional symbol, or emblem, of death.

death war-rant **1**, an official order giving power to carry out a sentence of death; **2**, something which ends happiness, hope, or the like.

death-watch (dĕth′wŏch″), *n.* **1**, a watch or guard beside a dying person; **2**, a guard set over a condemned criminal prior to his execution.

de-ba-cle (dē-bä′kl; dē-băk′l), *n.* **1**, a stampede; a disorderly flight in battle; **2**, the breaking up of ice on a river; **3**, a violent flood, carrying with it débris or rubbish in great masses; as, the Mississippi River *debacle* caused great suffering. Also, ***dé′bâ′cle** (dā′bäkl′).

de-bar (dē-bär′), *v.t.* [*p.t.* and *p.p.* -barred′ (-bärd′), *p.pr.* -bar′ring], to shut out; exclude; hinder (from approach, enjoyment, or action): with *from;* as, the railroad gates *debar* people from crossing the tracks.—*n.* **de-bar′ment.**

de-bark (dē-bärk′), *v.i.* to disembark; go ashore from a vessel:—*v.t.* to put ashore from a vessel; unload.

de-bar-ka-tion (dē″bär-kā′shŭn), *n.* the act of going, or putting, ashore from a vessel; as, the *debarkation* of troops.—*n.* **de-bark′ment.**

de-base (dē-bās′), *v.t.* [*p.t.* and *p.p.* -based′ (-bāst′), *p.pr.* -bas′ing], to reduce from a higher to a lower state; lower in character, virtue, purity, value, or the like; as, to *debase* the coinage.—*n.* **de-bas′er.**

de-base-ment (dē-bās′mĕnt), *n.* **1**, the act of lowering in value, character, quality, etc.; **2**, the condition of being so lowered or reduced.

de-bat-a-ble (dē-băt′ȧ-bl), *adj.* disputable; admitting of question or debate; as, the cause of the fire was a *debatable* matter.

de-bate (dē-bāt′), *n.* **1**, contention in words; argument; discussion, as in a legislative assembly; **2**, a formal presentation of arguments on both sides of a question, by several speakers, before an audience:—*v.t.* [*p.t.* and *p.p.* -bat′ed, *p.pr.* -bat′ing], **1**, to discuss by presenting arguments for and against; dispute about; **2**, to meditate upon:—*v.i.* **1**, to discuss a point; **2**, to reflect.

de-bat-er (dē-bāt′ẽr), *n.* a person who takes part in an argument, usually of a formal nature.

de-bauch (dē-bôch′), *v.t.* **1**, to corrupt in morals or principles, as a person; **2**, to pollute; vitiate; misuse, as one's abilities:—*n.* **1**, excess in sensual pleasure, esp. in eating and drinking; **2**, corruption of fidelity.—*p.adj.* **de-bauched′.**—*n.* **de-bauch′er.**

deb-au-chee (dĕb″ō-shē′), a dissipated person; drunkard.

de-bauch-er-y (dē-bôch′ẽr-ĭ), *n.* [*pl.* debaucheries (-ĭz)], intemperance: drunkenness; gluttony; sensuality; corruption of fidelity.

de-ben-ture (dē-bĕn′tūr), *n.* **1**, a written acknowledgment of a debt; **2**, a government voucher for money.

de-bil-i-tate (dē-bĭl′ĭ-tāt), *v.t.* [*p.t.* and *p.p.* -tat″ed, *p.pr.* -tat″ing], to weaken; enfeeble.—*p.adj.* **de-bil′i-tat″ed.**

de-bil-i-ta-tion (dē-bĭl″ĭ-tā′shŭn), *n.* **1**, the act of weakening; **2**, the state of weakness or feebleness.

de-bil-i-ty (dē-bĭl′ĭ-tĭ), *n.* [*pl.* debilities (-tĭz)], weakness; lack of energy or strength; languor.

deb-it (dĕb′ĭt), *n.* an entry in an account showing something owed or due; also, the debtor side of an account: opp. of *credit:*—*adj.* relating to debts:—*v.t.* to charge (a sum due); enter a charge against.

deb-o-nair (dĕb″ō-nâr′), *adj.* **1**, gay and light-hearted; **2**, of gentle manners or breeding; elegant; as, the Frenchman had *debonair* manners. Also, **deb″o-naire′; deb″on-naire′.**—*adv.* **deb″o-nair′ly.**—*n.* **deb″o-nair′ness.**

Deb-o-rah (dĕb′ō-rȧ), *n.* in the Bible, a prophetess who acted as judge of Israel and who helped to defeat Sisera, afterwards celebrating the victory in her song of triumph (Judges 4:4–14; 5:1–31).

de-bouch (dē-bōōsh′), *v.i.* **1**, to emerge or come out, as a river into a bay; **2**, to march out of a narrow pass or a wood into open ground; as, the regiment *debouched* into the open plain.—*n.* **de-bouch′ment.**

***dé-bris** (dā″brē′), [Fr.], *n.* [*pl.* débris], **1**, fragments; rubbish; **2**, loose pieces of rock at the base of a mountain; as, a landslide brings down tons of *débris.* Also, **de-bris′** (dĕ-brē′).

debt (dĕt), *n.* that which is due from one person to another; obligation.

debt-or (dĕt′ẽr), *n.* one who owes something to another; one who is under obligation to another: opp. of *creditor.*

***dé-but** (dā″bü′; dē-bū′), [Fr.], *n.* **1**, a first appearance in society, or before the public; as, a singer's *début;* **2**, any first attempt; beginning.

***dé-bu-tante** (dā″bü″täṅt′; dĕb″ū-tănt′), [Fr.], *n.* a young girl who makes a début, or first appearance in society, or in public.—*n.masc.* **dé″bu″tant′** (dā″bü″täṅ′; dĕb″ū-tănt′).

dec-a- (dĕk′ȧ-), a prefix or combining form from the Greek, meaning ten; as, *deca*gon; *deca*thlon. Also, **dek′a-.**

dec-ade (dĕk′ād), *n.* **1**, a group of ten; **2**, a period of ten consecutive years; as, the census is taken every *decade.* Also, *Rare,* **dec′ad** (dĕk′ăd).

de-ca-dence (dē-kā′dĕns; dĕk′ȧ-dĕns), *n.* **1**, decay; decline in quality or character; **2**, a lowering of standards in literature, art, etc. Also, **de-ca′den-cy.**

de-ca-dent (dē-kā′dĕnt; dĕk′ȧ-dĕnt), *adj.* **1**, decaying or falling into ruin; **2**, falling from a high standard, as of art:—*n.* one who has degenerated, as a writer.

dec-a-gon (dĕk′ȧ-gŏn), *n.* a plane figure having ten sides and ten angles.—*adj.* **de-cag′o-nal** (dē-kăg′ō-năl).

dec-a-gram (dĕk′ȧ-grăm), *n.* a metric weight of ten grams, or 0.3527 ounce. Also, **dec′a-gramme.**

dec-a-he-dron (dĕk″ȧ-hē′drŏn), *n.* [*pl.* decahedrons (-drŏnz); decahedra (-drȧ)], a solid figure having ten faces.—*adj.* **dec″a-he′dral.**

dec-a-li-ter (dĕk′ȧ-lē″tẽr), *n.* ten liters, the equivalent of 2.64 gallons: a metric measure of capacity. Also, **dec′a-li″tre.**

Dec-a-log (dĕk′ȧ-lŏg), *n.* **1**, the Ten Commandments; the moral law (Exodus 20:1–17); **2**, (usually, *decalog*), any set of authoritative moral principles. Also, **Dec′a-logue; dec′a-logue.**

dec-a-me-ter (dĕk′ȧ-mē″tẽr), *n.* a metric measure of ten meters, or about 32 feet 10 inches. Also, **dec′a-me″tre.**

de-camp (dē-kămp′), *v.i.* **1**, to break up camp; **2**, to steal away; **3**, to depart suddenly or secretly; go off or away. —*n.* **de-camp′ment.**

de-cant (dē-kănt′), *v.t.* to pour off gently, as from one vessel to another.—*n.* **de″can-ta′tion.**

de-cant-er (dē-kăn′tẽr), *n.* an ornamental glass bottle for holding wines, liquors, etc., for use on the table.

de-cap-i-tate (dē-kăp′ĭ-tāt), *v.t.* [*p.t.* and *p.p.* -tat″ed, *p.pr.* -tat″ing], to cut off the head of.—*n.* **de-cap″i-ta′tion.**

dec-a-pod (dĕk′ȧ-pŏd), *adj.* possessing five pairs of walking legs, as a lobster, or ten rays or arms, as certain mollusks; ten-footed:—*n.* **1**, any of an order of the Crustacea, including shrimps, lobsters, crabs, etc., with five pairs of walking legs, one pair of which bears claws; **2**, one of a suborder of mollusks similar to the octopus, cuttlefish, etc., but having two long tentacles, with suckers at the ends, besides the usual eight rays or arms; a ten-armed cephalopod.

de-car-bon-ize (dē-kär′bŏn-īz), *v.t.* [*p.t.* and *p.p.* -ized (-īzd), *p.pr.* -iz″ing], to deprive of carbon, as steel. Also, **de-car′bu-rize** (dē-kär′bū-rīz).

dec-are (dĕk′âr″; dĕk-âr′), *n.* a metric measure of surface containing ten ares, the equivalent of 0.2471 acre.

dec-a-stere (dĕk′ȧ-stēr), *n.* in the metric system, a measure of capacity containing ten cubic meters, the equivalent of 13.08 cubic yards.

dec-a-syl-la-ble (dĕk″ȧ-sĭl′ȧ-bl), *n.* a line of poetry having ten syllables.—*adj.* **dec″a-syl-lab′ic** (-sĭ-lăb′ĭk).

de-cath-lon (dē-kăth′lŏn), *n.* an athletic contest in which each contestant takes part in ten different events.

de-cay (dē-kā′), *v.i.* **1**, to rot; **2**, to decline or fail, as business; **3**, to lessen in numbers, health, etc.; as, his powers *decay:*—*n.* **1**, decline; gradual failure in mind or body; **2**, ruin; **3**, rottenness; corruption.

de-cease (dē-sēs′), *v.i.* [*p.t.* and *p.p.* -ceased′ (-sēst′), *p.pr.* -ceas′ing], to die:—*n.* death; the act of dying; as, the *decease* of a great man.—*p.adj.* **de-ceased′.**

de-ce-dent (dē-sē′dĕnt), *n.* in law, a deceased person.

de-ceit (dē-sēt′), *n.* fraud; cheat; deception; falsehood; double dealing.
Syn. delusion, guile, treachery, sham.

de-ceit-ful (dē-sēt′fo͝ol), *adj.* full of fraud and trickery; insincere; false. —*adv.* **de-ceit′ful-ly.**—*n.* **de-ceit′ful-ness.**
Syn. misleading, fallacious, fraudulent. (See deceptive.)—*Ant.* honest, open, sincere.

de-ceiv-a-ble (dē-sēv′ȧ-bl), *adj.* capable of being easily tricked; unwary.—*adv.* **de-ceiv′a-bly.**

de-ceive (dē-sēv′), *v.t.* [*p.t.* and *p.p.* -ceived′ (-sēvd′), *p.pr.* -ceiv′ing], **1**, to cheat; mislead or cause to err; **2**, to disappoint.—*n.* **de-ceiv′er.**
Syn. overreach, gull, dupe, cheat.

De-cem-ber (dē-sĕm′bẽr), *n.* the twelfth and last month of the year: so called because it was the tenth month of the Roman year.—*abbr.* **Dec.**

de-cem-vir (dē-sĕm′vẽr), *n.* [*pl.* decemvirs (-vẽrz); decemviri (-vĭ-rī)], one of ten Roman magistrates, esp. one of those who wrote the laws known as the Twelve Tables.—*adj.* **de-cem′vi-ral.**

de-cem-vi-rate (dē-sĕm′vĭ-rāt), *n.* **1**, a body of ten men joined in authority; **2**, their office, or term of office.

de-cen-cy (dē′sĕn-sĭ), *n.* [*pl.* decencies (-sĭz)], **1**, propriety; modesty; **2**, that which is modest or respectable.

de-cen-ni-al (dē-sĕn′ĭ-ăl), *adj.* consisting of ten years; occurring every ten years:—*n.* an anniversary recurring every tenth year.

de-cent (dē′sĕnt), *adj.* **1**, becoming; suitable; respectable; as, no *decent* clothes; **2**, modest; as, *decent* behavior; **3**, passable; good enough; as, a *decent* mark. —*adv.* **de′cent-ly.**—*n.* **de′cent-ness.**

de-cen-tral-ize (dē-sĕn′trȧl-īz), *v.t.* [*p.t.* and *p.p.* -ized (-īzd), *p.pr.* -iz″ing], to transfer from a central point to outlying points; esp., to distribute, as governmental authority, among communities. —*n.* **de-cen″tral-i-za′tion.**

de-cep-tion (dē-sĕp′shŭn), *n.* **1**, the act of tricking or cheating; **2**, the state of being cheated or misled; fraud.

de-cep-tive (dē-sĕp′tĭv), *adj.* tending to trick, cheat, or mislead.—*adv.* **de-cep′tive-ly.**—*n.* **de-cep′tive-ness.**
Syn. deceitful. *Deceptive* is applied only to things which cause error; as, a *deceptive* look. *Deceitful* is more commonly applied to persons, and emphasizes the idea of an intention to mislead or misrepresent; as, a *deceitful* companion; a *deceitful* answer.

dec-i- (dĕs′ĭ-), *prefix,* ten; also, esp. in the metric system of weights and measures, tenth, or a tenth part.

dec-i-are (dĕs′ĭ-âr″), *n.* in the metric system, a measure of surface equal to 10 square meters, or 11.96 square yards.

dec-i-bel (dĕs′ĭ-bĕl), *n.* in physics, the unit chiefly used for measuring differences in sound intensity.

de-cide (dē-sīd′), *v.t.* [*p.t.* and *p.p.* -cid′ed, *p.pr.* -cid′ing], **1**, to settle; determine; bring to an issue or conclusion; **2**, to cause (a person) to reach a conclusion; as, that trait *decides* me in his favor:—*v.i.* to give a judgment or decision; arbitrate; as, to *decide* between two debaters.

de-cid-ed (dē-sīd′ĕd), *p.adj.* **1**, definite, clear; as, that makes a *decided* difference; **2**, determined; resolute; as, a very *decided* man.—*n.* **de-cid′ed-ness.**

de-cid-ed-ly (dē-sīd′ĕd-lĭ), *adv.* positively; certainly.

de-cid-u-ous (dē-sĭd′ū-ŭs), *adj.* **1**, losing foliage or leaves every year; not evergreen; as, the maple is a *deciduous* tree; **2**, falling off at certain seasons, as antlers, wings of certain insects, etc.

dec-i-gram (dĕs′ĭ-grăm), *n.* a metric measure of weight equal to one tenth of a gram, or 1.5432 grains, troy. Also, **dec′i-gramme** (-grăm).

dec-i-li-ter (dĕs′ĭ-lē″tẽr), *n.* a metric measure of capacity equal to one tenth of a liter, or 3.38 fluid ounces. Also, **dec′i-li″tre** (-lē″tẽr).

de-cil-lion (dē-sĭl′yŭn), *n.* **1**, in France and the U. S., a number expressed by the figure one followed by 33 ciphers; **2**, in England, the figure one followed by 60 ciphers.—*adj.* and *n.* **de-cil′lionth.**

dec-i-mal (dĕs′ĭ-măl), *adj.* pertaining to, or based upon, the number ten: **decimal fraction**, a fraction having as its denominator ten or some power of ten: usually marked by a dot, called the *decimal point:* as,

.7 = $\frac{7}{10}$, and .07 = $\frac{7}{100}$, etc.: also called *decimal:*—*n.* a decimal fraction.—*v.t.* **dec′i-mal-ize.**

dec-i-mal-ly (dĕs′ĭ-măl-ĭ), *adv.* by decimals, or by tens or tenths.

dec-i-mate (dĕs′ĭ-māt), *v.t.* [*p.t.* and *p.p.* -mat″ed, *p.pr.* -mat″ing], **1,** to take a tenth of; **2,** to put to death, or punish, every tenth man in; as, to *decimate* a body of mutineers; **3,** to destroy a large part of, as an army in battle.—*n.* **dec″i-ma′tion.**

dec-i-me-ter (dĕs′ĭ-mē″tẽr), *n.* a metric measure of length equal to one tenth of a meter, the equivalent of 3.937 inches. Also, **dec′i-me″tre.**

de-ci-pher (dē-sī′fẽr), *v.t.* **1,** to translate (secret or unknown characters) into known terms; **2,** to discover or make out the meaning of, as something puzzling or hardly legible.—*adj.* **de-ci′pher-a-ble.**

de-ci-sion (dē-sĭzh′ŭn), *n.* **1,** the act of reaching a fixed opinion; **2,** the quality of being fixed and firm; determination; **3,** judgment; settlement; as, the *decision* of a court or of a case.

de-ci-sive (dē-sī′sĭv), *adj.* **1,** final; conclusive; as, a *decisive* victory; **2,** prompt; positive; determined; as, *decisive* action.—*adv.* **de-ci′sive-ly.**—*n.* **de-ci′sive-ness.**

dec-i-stere (dĕs′ĭ-stēr), *n.* in the metric system, a measure of capacity equal to one tenth of a cubic meter, the equivalent of 3.5314 cubic feet.

¹deck (dĕk), *n.* **1,** a platform serving as a floor in a ship, or the space between floors; **2,** a main surface of an airplane, esp. on a biplane; **3,** a pack of playing cards: **deck hand,** a common sailor.

²deck (dĕk), *v.t.* **1,** to put finery or ornamentation on; adorn: often with *out;* **2,** to cover with a deck; lay a deck on.
Syn. decorate, embellish, ornament, array.

deck-le-edged (dĕk′l-ĕjd″), *adj.* having edges untrimmed, and hence rough and irregular: said of paper.

de-claim (dē-klām′), *v.t.* to utter in rhetorical style; speak as an exercise in elocution:—*v.i.* **1,** to speak oratorically; **2,** to recite a selection as an exercise; as, the boy was asked to *declaim.*—*n.* **de-claim′er.**

dec-la-ma-tion (dĕk″lȧ-mā′shŭn), *n.* **1,** a speech delivered in public; **2,** the act of reciting; also, a selection recited from memory; **3,** a harangue.

de-clam-a-to-ry (dē-klăm′ȧ-tō-rĭ), *adj.* **1,** pertaining to, or characterized by, rhetorical speech; **2,** noisy in style; appealing to the emotions.

dec-la-ra-tion (dĕk″lȧ-rā′shŭn), *n.* **1,** the act of announcing or proclaiming; **2,** that which is announced: **Declaration of Independence,** the resolution, adopted July 4, 1776, by which the thirteen American colonies declared themselves politically independent of the British government.

de-clar-a-tive (dē-klăr′ȧ-tĭv), *adj.* making a statement or declaration; as, a *declarative* sentence.

de-clare (dē-klâr′), *v.t.* [*p.t.* and *p.p.* -clared′ (-klârd′), *p.pr.* -clar′ing], **1,** to make known; tell openly or publicly; proclaim formally; publish; **2,** to make a solemn affirmation of, before witnesses; **3,** to make a full statement of, as to goods, etc.:—*v.i.* to make a statement; avow; take sides: with *for* or *against.*—*adv.* **de-clar′ed-ly.**—*n.* **de-clar′er.** —*adj.* **de-clar′a-tory.**
Syn. announce, publish, proclaim. To *declare* is to state plainly or formally; as, to *declare* one's purpose; to *declare* war. To *announce* is to tell that which is not known, or not formally acknowledged; as, to *announce* a contest; to *announce* a marriage. To *publish* is to make known through some method that will reach everybody; as, to *publish* the news. To *proclaim* is to make known some event of consequence with great publicity; as, to *proclaim* a truce.—*Ant.* suppress, conceal.

de-clen-sion (dē-klĕn′shŭn), *n.* **1,** a descent; a sloping down; **2,** a falling off or away; **3,** decline; decay; **4,** in grammar, the inflection of nouns, pronouns, and adjectives for number, gender, and case; also, a group of such words declined alike; as, Latin nouns of the first *declension* end in *a.*—*adj.* **de-clen′sion-al.**

dec-li-na-tion (dĕk″lĭ-nā′shŭn), *n.* **1,** the act or state of bending, or moving, downward; **2,** degree of deviation; as, the *declination* of a magnetic needle from true north; **3,** slant from a given direction; **4,** decline; decay; **5,** the angular distance of a heavenly body from the celestial equator.

de-cline (dē-klīn′), *v.i.* [*p.t.* and *p.p.* -clined′ (-klīnd′), *p.pr.* -clin′ing], **1,** to bend or lean downward; droop; **2,** to draw to a close; become weak; **3,** to move from the right path; **4,** to refuse:—*v.t.* **1,** to refuse; as, to *decline* an invitation; **2,** to bend downward; depress; **3,** to inflect with declensional endings, as a noun, adjective, or pronoun:—*n.* **1,** a lessening; decay; **2,** a growing worse; **3,** the closing part of something; **4,** a wasting away with disease.—*adj.* **de-clin′a-ble.**

dec-li-nom-e-ter (dĕk″lĭ-nŏm′ē-tẽr), *n.* an instrument used for measuring the deviation of the magnetic needle from the true north.

de-cliv-i-ty (dē-klĭv′ĭ-tĭ), *n.* [*pl.* declivities (-tĭz)], **1,** a slope, or sloping direction; **2,** a surface sloping upward or downward.—*adj.* **de-cliv′i-tous.**

de-coct (dē-kŏkt′), *v.t.* to obtain the flavor, essence, or medicinal qualities of, by boiling; prepare by boiling.

de-coc-tion (dē-kŏk′shŭn), *n.* an extract or essence obtained by boiling down some substance.

***dé-col-le-té** (dā″kŏ″lĕ-tā′), [Fr.], *adj.* **1,** cut low in the neck so as to expose the neck and shoulders; as, a *décolleté* dress; **2,** wearing a low-necked dress.

de-com-pose (dē″kŏm-pōz′), *v.t.* [*p.t.* and *p.p.* -posed′ (-pōzd′), *p.pr.* -pos′ing], to separate into elementary parts; cause to decay:—*v.i.* to become separated into simpler compounds or elements; rot.—*adj.* **de″com-pos′a-ble.**

de-com-po-si-tion (dē-kŏm″pō-zĭsh′ŭn), *n.* **1,** the act of separating into simpler substances; as, *decomposition* of water produces oxygen and hydrogen; **2,** disintegration; a state of decay.

de-com-pound (dē″kŏm-pound′), *adj.* **1,** made by a mixing of mixtures; twice compounded; **2,** in botany, divided many times, as a leaf (see *leaf,* illus.).

dec-o-rate (dĕk′ō-rāt), *v.t.* [*p.t.* and *p.p.* -rat″ed, *p.pr.* -rat″ing], **1,** to ornament; as, to *decorate* a stage for an entertainment; **2,** to confer a badge of honor upon.

dec-o-ra-tion (dĕk″ō-rā′shŭn), *n.* **1,** the act of adorning; **2,** an ornament; **3,** a badge of honor.

Dec-o-ra-tion Day the day (in most States, May 30) on which the graves of those who fell in the Civil War and other wars of the United States are decorated: correctly called *Memorial Day.*

dec-o-ra-tive (dĕk′ō-rā-tĭv), *adj.* adorning; ornamental.—*adv.* **dec′o-ra-tive-ly.**—*n.* **dec′o-ra-tive-ness.**

dec-o-ra-tor (dĕk′ō-rā″tẽr), *n.* **1,** one who adorns or beautifies; **2,** a person whose business it is to do papering, painting, etc., in houses.

de-co-rous (dē-kō′rŭs; dĕk′ō-rŭs), *adj.* marked by propriety; decent; fit; proper; polite; as, *decorous* behavior.—*adv.* **de-co′rous-ly.**—*n.* **de-co′rous-ness.**

Syn. staid, sedate, demure, suitable.—*Ant.* unseemly, improper.

de-co-rum (dē-kō′rŭm), *n.* **1,** propriety and becomingness of language, dress, and conduct; suitableness; dignity; **2,** a fitting act.

de-coy (dē-koi′), *n.* **1,** a deceptive trick or snare; a lure; **2,** a piece of inclosed water into which wild fowl are induced to enter; **3,** the figure of a bird used to attract live birds within gunshot; **4,** a person who entices another into a position where he may be cheated: **decoy duck, 1,** a tame or imitation duck used to allure wild fowl; **2,** a person who entraps others:—*v.t.* to lead or draw into danger by a trick; entice.

de-crease (dē-krēs′), *v.i.* [*p.t.* and *p.p.* -creased′ (-krēst′), *p.pr.* -creas′ing], to grow less; diminish; dwindle; as, his income steadily *decreased;* abate; as, the storm *decreased* in violence:—*v.t.* to cause to grow less; as, to *decrease* the length of the working day:—*n.* (dē-krēs′; dē′krēs), **1,** gradual lessening or decay; **2,** the amount or degree of lessening.

Syn., v. diminish, lessen, dwindle. To *decrease* is to become less, esp. by an inner or natural process, or to make gradually less; as, the days *decrease* in length; the nurse *decreased* the dose. *Diminish* and *lessen* mean to become less in size, number, or quantity; as, the importance of royalty has *diminished;* responsibilities *lessen* with age. Both these words also have the meaning to make less; as, war *diminishes* the male population; the driver *lessened* his speed. To *dwindle* is to shrink or waste away, or to disappear gradually; as, his fortune *dwindled.*

de-cree (dē-krē′), *n.* **1,** an ordinance, law, or edict; **2,** a judicial decision; **3,** the award of an umpire or arbitrator:—*v.t.* [*p.t.* and *p.p.* -creed′ (-krēd′), *p.pr.* -cree′ing], to determine by a law, decision, etc.; ordain; assign:—*v.i.* to make a law, decision, etc.; determine.

Syn., v. dictate, command, order.

de-crep-it (dē-krĕp′ĭt), *adj.* weak with age or infirmity; wasted; feeble.

de-crep-i-tude (dē-krĕp′ĭ-tūd), *n.* the state of being feeble or infirm, as from old age.

de-cri-al (dē-krī′ăl), *n.* a crying down; loud condemnation.

de-cry (dē-krī′), *v.t.* [*p.t.* and *p. p.*-cried′ (-krīd′), *p.pr.* -cry′ing], to cry down; censure; disparage.—*n.* **de-cri′er.**

Syn. belittle, degrade, discredit.—*Ant.* overrate, praise, extol.

de-cum-bent (dē-kŭm′bĕnt), *adj.* lying down, esp. on the ground.

ded-i-cate (dĕd′ĭ-kāt), *v.t.* [*p.t.* and *p.p.* -cat″ed, *p.pr.* -cat″ing], **1,** to set apart by a solemn act or religious ceremony; as, to *dedicate* a church; **2,** to devote or set apart to some work or duty; as, to *dedicate* ourselves to peace; **3,** to inscribe, as a literary work.—*n.* **ded′i-ca″tor.**

Syn. devote, consecrate, offer, set, apportion.

ded-i-ca-tion (dĕd″ĭ-kā′shŭn), *n.* **1,** the act of devoting to a worthy purpose; as, the *dedication* of a church; **2,** an inscription or address expressing gratitude or respect for a patron or friend, prefixed to a literary or artistic work.—*adj.* **ded′i-ca-to-ry** (dĕd′ĭ-kȧ-tō-rĭ).

de-duce (dē-dūs′), *v.t.* [*p.t.* and *p.p.* -duced′ (-dūst′), *p.pr.* -duc′ing], to draw; gather by reasoning; derive; infer: with *from* or *out of.*—*adj.* **de-duc′i-ble.**

de-duct (dē-dŭkt′), *v.t.* to take away; subtract; as, *deduct* a dollar from the bill.—*adj.* **de-duct′i-ble.**

de-duc-tion (dē-dŭk′shŭn), *n.* **1,** the act or process of taking away; subtraction; also, that which is taken away; as, some stores make a *deduction* for cash payment; **2,** the drawing of conclusions from what is accepted; also, the conclusion itself; as, his *deduction* from the evidence was correct.

Syn. (see induction).

de-duc-tive (dē-dŭk′tĭv), *adj.* **1,** tending to take away; **2,** drawing a conclusion from what is accepted; as, *deductive* reasoning.—*adv.* **de-duc′tive-ly.**

deed (dēd), *n.* **1,** that which is done; an act; something done as contrasted with mere plans; **2,** a great achievement; **3,** a written paper for the transfer of land:—*v.t.* to convey by deed.

Syn., n. action, feat, performance.

deem (dēm), *v.t.* to think; believe; as, I *deem* it wise to call him back.

Syn. estimate, consider, suppose, conceive.

deep (dēp), *adj.* **1,** extending far down or back; **2,** penetrating; sagacious; **3,** difficult to understand; **4,** absorbed; involved; as, *deep* in study; **5,** grave in tone, or low in pitch; **6,** intense; heavy; as, a *deep* sleep; **7,** strongly colored; **8,** earnest; heartfelt:—*n.* **1,** that which extends far downward, as a great body of water or an abyss; **2,** the culmination; middle; as, the *deep* of night; **3,** an incomprehensible thing:—*adv.* profoundly.—*adv.* **deep′ly.**—*n.* **deep′ness.**

deep-en (dēp′n), *v.t.* **1,** to extend farther downward or backward; **2,** to make darker; **3,** to make more profound:—*v.i.* **1,** to extend farther down; **2,** to become more difficult; **3,** to become darker, as shadows.

deer (dēr), *n.* [*pl.* deer], any of many kinds of cud-chewing wild animals, having solid, branching antlers.—*n.* **deer′skin″.**

de-face (dē-fās′), *v.t.* [*p.t.* and *p.p.* -faced′ (-fāst′), *p.pr.* -fac′ing], to mar or destroy the surface of; spoil; as, chalk marks *deface* the wall of the house.—*n.* **de-fac′er.**

de-face-ment (dē-fās′mĕnt), *n.* injury to the appearance of something; disfiguration.

***de fac-to** (dē făk′tō), [Lat.], actually existing in fact; as, a *de facto* government: distinguished from *de jure.*

de-fal-cate (dē-făl′kāt), *v.i.* [*p.t.* and *p.p.* -cat″ed, *p.pr.* -cat″ing], to embezzle, or use for one's own purposes, money held in trust.—*n.* **def′al-ca″tor** (dĕf′ăl-kā″tẽr; dē′făl-kā″tẽr).

de-fal-ca-tion (dē″făl-kā′shŭn; dĕf′ăl-kā″shŭn), *n.* **1,** a shortage of funds caused by dishonesty; also, the dishonest use of trust funds; as, the bank lost money by the *defalcation* of the cashier; **2,** the money so lost.

def-a-ma-tion (dĕf″ȧ-mā′shŭn; dē″fȧ-), *n.* a malicious injuring of the good name or reputation of another; as, to accuse an honest man of stealing is a *defamation* of his character: called *slander* if spoken, *libel* if written.

de-fam-a-to-ry (dē-făm′ȧ-tō-rĭ), *adj.* slanderous; as, to spread *defamatory* reports about someone.

de-fame (dē-fām′), *v.t.* [*p.t.* and *p.p.* -famed′ (-fāmd′), *p.pr.* -fam′ing], **1,** to injure or destroy the good reputation of; speak maliciously of; **2,** to disgrace.—*n.* **de-fam′er.**

Syn. abuse, malign, slander, asperse.

de-fault (dē-fôlt′), *n.* neglect; failure in a contract; failure to appear at a time and place required: **in default of,** in case of failure of:—*v.t.* to make a failure in, as a payment, an appearance in court, etc.; neglect:—*v.i.* to fail to account for trust funds; fail to pay a debt, appear in court, etc.

Syn., *n.* lapse, forfeit, omission, absence, want, neglect, failure.

de-fault-er (dē-fôl'tẽr), *n.* **1**, one who fails in payment or performance; **2**, one who fails to make an honest accounting; **3**, a soldier who has broken a military regulation.

de-fea-sance (dē-fē'zăns), *n.* **1**, a causing to be null and void; **2**, a condition added to a contract, the performance of which annuls the contract.

de-fea-si-ble (dē-fē'zĭ-bl), *adj.* liable to be rendered void or annulled.

de-feat (dē-fēt'), *v.t.* **1**, to overthrow or vanquish; as, to *defeat* an enemy; **2**, to bring to naught; frustrate; as, to *defeat* a purpose:—*n.* **1**, the act of preventing or bringing to naught; **2**, overthrow, as of an army; **3**, the state of being conquered.

de-feat-ist (dē-fēt'ĭst), *n.* one who is accused of desiring the defeat of his country in war or who works toward that end in the hope that ultimate good may result.

def-e-cate (dĕf'ĕ-kāt), *v.t.* [*p.t.* and *p.p.* -cat″ed, *p.pr.* -cat″ing], to purify; remove worthless matter from:—*v.i.* **1**, to become free of impurities; **2**, to relieve oneself of excrement.—*n.* **def″e-ca'tion.**

de-fect (dē-fĕkt'), *n.* **1**, mental, moral, or physical imperfection; **2**, fault; error; **3**, lack of something necessary to completeness; want.

Syn. imperfection, flaw. (See blemish.)

de-fec-tion (dē-fĕk'shŭn), *n.* **1**, a falling away from duty or allegiance; desertion; **2**, failure.

de-fec-tive (dē-fĕk'tĭv), *adj.* **1**, having a blemish or flaw of any kind; incomplete; faulty; **2**, mentally deficient or subnormal; **3**, lacking some of the usual grammatical forms:—*n.* a person having a serious physical or mental defect.—*adv.* **de-fec'tive-ly.**—*n.* **de-fec'tive-ness.**

de-fend (dē-fĕnd'), *v.t.* **1**, to guard or protect from harm or violence; as, the navy *defends* our seacoast; **2**, to maintain or uphold, as one's legal rights, by force of argument or evidence; contest, as a suit.—*n.* **de-fend'er.**

Syn. guard, protect. To *defend* is to drive away an enemy who is actually assaulting; as, soldiers *defend* their country in time of war; he *defended* his home. To *guard* is to stand ready to ward off attack, to shield from threatened harm, or merely to keep in safety; as, soldiers *guard* their country in time of peace; we *guard* against disease; we *guard* valuable possessions. To *protect* is to shield from actual or possible harm; as, a hen *protects* her chicks; we *protect* ourselves from cold.

de-fend-ant (dē-fĕn'dănt), *n.* a person who is sued or one who is accused in a court of law:—*adj.* defending.

de-fense (dē-fĕns'), *n.* **1**, the act or state of guarding or being guarded; protection; **2**, one who or that which guards; **3**, vindication; esp., a plea or answer in court to a charge or a suit; **4**, the defendant's cause or counsel in a lawsuit. Also, **de-fence'.**—*adj.* **de-fense'less.**

Syn. excuse, plea, bulwark, rampart.

de-fen-si-ble (dē-fĕn'sĭ-bl), *adj.* **1**, capable of being protected; **2**, justifiable, as an act.

de-fen-sive (dē-fĕn'sĭv), *adj.* **1**, serving to guard or protect; **2**, carried on for protection; as, *defensive* warfare; **3**, in a condition of making defense:—*n.* the act, state, or means of defending; as, on the *defensive.*—*adv.* **de-fen'sive-ly.**

[1]**de-fer** (dē-fûr'), *v.t.* [*p.t.* and *p.p.* -ferred' (-fûrd'), *p.pr.* -fer'ring], to put off to a future time; delay; postpone; leave undone:—*v.i.* to procrastinate.

Syn. postpone, delay, procrastinate. These words agree in the idea of putting off. *Defer*, the most general term, implies putting off until some time in the future; as, to *defer* making a will. To *postpone* is to put off, usually to a stated time; as, we *postponed* the discussion until the next meeting. *Delay* also means to put off; as, she *delayed* her visit until fine weather; but it has in addition the meaning of retarding or hindering for a time; as, an accident *delayed* the express. To *procrastinate* is to put off habitually, from day to day; as, a good correspondent does not *procrastinate.*

[2]**de-fer** (dē-fûr'), *v.i.* [*p.t.* and *p.p.* -ferred' (-fûrd'), *p.pr.* -fer'ring], to yield; give in; as, I *defer* to you:—*v.t.* to refer; submit for decision.—*n.* **de-fer'rer.**

def-er-ence (dĕf'ẽr-ĕns), *n.* a yielding to the opinions or wishes of another; regard; courteous submission; respect.

def-er-en-tial (dĕf″ẽr-ĕn'shăl), *adj.* expressing regard for the wishes of another.—*adv.* **def″er-en'tial-ly.**

de-fer-ment (dē-fûr'mĕnt), *n.* the act of postponing; delay.

de-fi-ance (dē-fī'ăns), *n.* **1**, scornful disregard; challenge, as to a contest; **2**, refusal to obey.

de-fi-ant (dē-fī'ănt), *adj.* full of, or expressing, resistance or opposition; insolently disobedient.—*adv.* **de-fi'ant-ly.**

de-fi-cien-cy (dē-fĭsh'ĕn-sĭ), *n.* [*pl.* deficiencies (-sĭz)], the state of being incomplete; failure; also, deficit.

de-fi-cient (dē-fĭsh'ĕnt), *adj.* wanting; incomplete; defective.

Syn. short, inadequate, scanty, lacking.

def-i-cit (dĕf'ĭ-sĭt), *n.* a shortage, esp. of money, income, or resources compared with expenditures.

de-fi-er (dē-fī'ẽr), *n.* one who refuses to obey; as, a *defier* of the law.

[1]**de-file** (dē-fīl'), *v.t.* [*p.t.* and *p.p.* -filed' (-fīld'), *p.pr.* -fil'ing], **1**, to make foul or impure; desecrate; **2**, to corrupt.—*n.* **de-file'ment.**—*n.* **de-fil'er.**

Syn. soil, pollute, contaminate, violate.

[2]**de-file** (dē-fīl'), *v.i.* [*p.t.* and *p.p.* -filed' (-fīld'), *p.pr.* -fil'ing], to march off in a line or in files:—*n.* (dē-fīl'; dē'fīl), **1**, a long, narrow pass, as between mountains; **2**, a marching in line.

de-fine (dē-fīn'), *v.t.* [*p.t.* and *p.p.* -fined' (-fīnd'), *p.pr.* -fin'ing], **1**, to state the exact meaning of; explain; **2**, to fix the limits of.—*adj.* **de-fin'a-ble.**—*n.* **de-fin'er.**

Syn. fix, settle, limit. (See explain.)

def-i-nite (dĕf'ĭ-nĭt), *adj.* **1**, precise; exact; **2**, having fixed or distinct limits: **definite article**, the word *the:* so called because it limits or restricts the word it modifies.—*adv.* **def'i-nite-ly.**—*n.* **def'i-nite-ness.**

def-i-ni-tion (dĕf″ĭ-nĭsh'ŭn), *n.* **1**, the act of making clear; **2**, of a lens, the power to present a clear image; **3**, distinctness; **4**, a brief explanation of the exact meaning of a term, phrase, etc.

de-fin-i-tive (dē-fĭn'ĭ-tĭv), *adj.* **1**, positive; final; **2**, determining; limiting:—*n.* in grammar, a word used to limit the meaning of a noun.—*adv.* **de-fin'i-tive-ly.**—*n.* **de-fin'i-tive-ness.**

de-flate (dē-flāt'), *v.t.* [*p.t.* and *p.p.* -flat'ed, *p.pr.* -flat'ing], **1**, to release air or gas from, as a tire; **2**, to contract or reduce, as prices.—*n.* **de-fla'tion.**

de-flect (dē-flĕkt'), *v.t.* to cause to turn away, or bend, from a straight line, as a ray:—*v.i.* to swerve; bend or turn aside.—*adj.* **de-flec′tive.**

de-flec-tion (dē-flĕk′shŭn), *n.* a bending or turning aside, as a gun. Also, esp. in Great Britain, **de-flex′ion.**

de-flec-tor (dē-flĕk′tẽr), *n.* a plate or cone in a furnace or lamp to bring flames or gases into close contact, and thus increase the fire.

de-flow-er (dē-flou′ẽr), *v.t.* **1,** to deprive of flowers or bloom; **2,** to rob of beauty or grace; **3,** to ravish.

de-fo-li-ate (dē-fō′lĭ-āt), *v.t.* [*p.t.* and *p.p.* -at″ed, *p.pr.* -at″ing], to strip or deprive of leaves:—*adj.* (dē-fō′lĭ-āt), deprived of leaves.—*n.* **de-fo″li-a′tion.**

de-for-est (dē-fŏr′ĕst), *v.t.* to clear of trees; clear away or destroy the trees of.—*n.* **de-for″est-a′tion.**

de-form (dē-fôrm′), *v.t.* **1,** to render ugly or unshapely; disfigure; **2,** to mar; deface.—*p.adj.* **de-formed′.**—*n.* **def″or-ma′tion** (dĕf″ôr-mā′shŭn; dē″fôr-mā′shŭn).

de-form-i-ty (dē-fôr′mĭ-tĭ), *n.* [*pl.* deformities (-tĭz)], **1,** a part so formed as to disfigure or spoil the shape of something, esp. of the human body; **2,** the state of being misshapen; **3,** want of beauty.

de-fraud (dē-frôd′), *v.t.* to cheat or deceive; withhold wrongfully from (a person) what is due.—*n.* **de-fraud′er.**
Syn. overreach, trick, swindle, dupe.

de-fray (dē-frā′), *v.t.* to pay; settle; as, to *defray* the expenses of a journey.—*n.* **de-fray′er.**—*n.* **de-fray′ment.**
Syn. liquidate, discharge, satisfy.

de-fray-al (dē-frā′ăl), *n.* the act of paying expenses.

deft (dĕft), *adj.* skilful; dexterous; handy; clever.—*adv.* **deft′ly.**—*n.* **deft′ness.**
Syn. (see clever).

de-funct (dē-fŭngkt′), *adj.* dead; extinct:—*n.* **1,** a dead person; usually, one lately deceased; **2,** the dead collectively.

de-fy (dē-fī′), *v.t.* [*p.t.* and *p.p.* -fied′ (-fīd′), *p.pr.* -fy′ing], **1,** to challenge or provoke to strife; **2,** to act in contempt of; as, to *defy* the law; **3,** to resist successfully; as, his record *defies* criticism.

de-gen-er-a-cy (dē-jĕn′ẽr-ȧ-sĭ), *n.* **1,** the state of being degraded or worse than formerly; **2,** lowness of morals.

de-gen-er-ate (dē-jĕn′ẽr-āt), *v.i.* [*p.t.* and *p.p.* -at″ed, *p.pr.* -at″ing], to grow worse; decline; become inferior in goodness or quality; deteriorate:—*adj.* (dē-jĕn′ẽr-ăt), of a low grade of morals; as, *degenerate* times; degraded; as, *degenerate* offspring:—*n.* (dē-jĕn′ẽr-ăt), a person or organism that has become worse than its kind; a person of low morals.—*adv.* **de-gen′er-ate-ly.**—*n.* **de-gen′er-ate-ness.**

de-gen-er-a-tion (dē-jĕn″ẽr-ā′shŭn), *n.* the act, state, or process of growing physically, mentally, or morally worse; degeneracy; decline.

deg-lu-ti-tion (dĕg″lo͞o-tĭsh′ŭn; dē″glo͞o-), *n.* the act, process, or power of swallowing anything, as food.

deg-ra-da-tion (dĕg″rȧ-dā′shŭn), *n.* the act of lowering, or state of being lowered, in rank, morals, etc.; disgrace.
Syn. humiliation, dishonor, shame.—*Ant.* honor, exaltation, elevation.

de-grade (dē-grād′), *v.t.* [*p.t.* and *p.p.* -grad′ed, *p.pr.* -grad′ing], **1,** to reduce in grade or rank; deprive of honors, office, or dignity; as, to *degrade* a soldier to a lower rank; **2,** to lower physically or morally.—*p.adj.* **de-grad′ed.**

de-gree (dē-grē′), *n.* **1,** a step or grade in a series; **2,** rank in a society, as the Masons, or in life; **3,** a stage in progress; **4,** a remove in relationship; **5,** a title conferred in recognition of academic work, or special distinction; **6,** a relative amount, extent, quality; as, a good *degree* of skill; **7,** a unit for measuring temperature, as on a Fahrenheit or centigrade scale; **8,** a unit division or interval marked on a mathematical or scientific instrument, as for measuring angles; **9,** in algebra: **a,** of a term, rank as shown by the sum of the indices of the literal factors; as, x^2y^3z is of the sixth *degree;* **b,** of an equation, the rank as determined by that of the term having the highest degree; as, $x^2+2x+3=7$ is of the second *degree;* **10,** in geometry, the 360th part of the circumference of a circle; **11,** in grammar, one of three grades in the comparison of an adjective or adverb; **12,** in music, a line or a space on the staff, upon which notes may be placed; also, a tone of a scale: **by degrees,** gradually.
Syn. (see [1]rank).

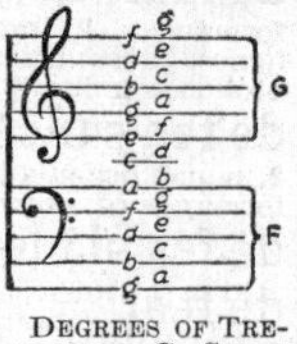

DEGREES OF TREBLE, OR G, STAFF AND BASS, OR F, STAFF.

de-hisce (dē-hĭs′), *v.i.* [*p.t.* and *p.p.* -hisced′ (-hĭst′), *p.pr.* -hisc′ing], to burst open; gape.

de-his-cence (dē-hĭs′ĕns), *n.* **1,** an opening wide; **2,** an opening to release or to discharge contents, as of a seed pod.—*adj.* **de-his′cent.**

de-horn (dē-hôrn′), *v.t.* to remove the horns from; as, to *dehorn* cattle.

de-i-fi-ca-tion (dē″ĭ-fĭ-kā′shŭn), *n.* **1,** the act of making a god of, or worshiping as a god; **2,** extravagant veneration.

de-i-fy (dē′ĭ-fī), *v.t.* [*p.t.* and *p.p.* -fied (-fīd), *p.pr.* -fy″ing], **1,** to praise or worship as a god; idolize; as, the druids *deified* the oak tree; **2,** to regard with extravagant affection or veneration.

deign (dān), *v.i.* to condescend; see fit; as, he did not *deign* to listen to our request:—*v.t.* to grant; condescend to give; as, he would *deign* us no reply.

de-ism (dē′ĭzm), *n.* **1,** a belief, founded on reason rather than on revelation or the authority of a church, in a personal God; **2,** belief in God as existing independently of the physical universe.—*n.* **de′ist.**—*adj.* **de-is′tic; de-is′ti-cal.**

de-i-ty (dē′ĭ-tĭ), *n.* [*pl.* deities (-tĭz)], **1,** a god, goddess, or person worshiped as a divine being; **2,** the character, nature, or attributes of God: **the Deity,** God; Jehovah.

de-ject (dē-jĕkt′), *v.t.* to depress the spirits of; dishearten; sadden.

de-ject-ed (dē-jĕk′tĕd), *p.adj.* cast down; low-spirited.—*adv.* **de-ject′ed-ly.**—*n.* **de-ject′ed-ness.**

de-jec-tion (dē-jĕk′shŭn), *n.* lowness of spirits; despondency.
Syn. gloom, discouragement, sadness.—*Ant.* elation, exaltation, happiness, glee.

***de ju-re** (dē jo͞o′rē), [Lat.], by right or lawful title; as, a government *de jure:* distinguished from *de facto.*

dek-a- (dĕk′ȧ-), a prefix or combining form meaning ten. See **dec′a-,** *Pfd. S.*

de-laine (dē-lān′), *n.* a light fabric made of wool, or of wool and cotton.

Del-a-ware (dĕl′ȧ-wâr), *n.* one of a tribe of American Indians, orig. inhabiting the region of the Delaware River.

de-lay (dē-lā′), *v.t.* to put off; postpone; make late; hinder for a time:—*v.i.* to act or proceed slowly:—*n.* postponement; detention; procrastination.—*n.* **de-lay′er.**
Syn., v. detain, check, retard. (See [1]defer.)—*Ant., v.* impel, accelerate, begin.

de-le (dē'lē), *v.t.* [*p.t.* and *p.p.* de'led (dē'lēd), *p.pr.* de'le-ing (dē'lē-ing)], to take out (a letter, etc.) in proof reading:—*n.* a mark [ϑ] indicating that a letter, etc., is to be deleted, or taken out.

de-lec-ta-ble (dē-lĕk'tȧ-bl), *adj.* pleasing; delightful; as, ice cream is *delectable* on a hot day.—*adv.* **de-lec'ta-bly.**—*n.* **de-lec'ta-ble-ness.**

de-lec-ta-tion (dē''lĕk-tā'shŭn), *n.* delight; pleasure.

del-e-gate (dĕl'ē-gāt), *n.* one sent to represent, and act for, others; as, the *delegates* to a convention:—*v.t.* (dĕl'ē-gāt), [*p.t.* and *p.p.* -gat''ed, *p.pr.* -gat''ing], **1,** to send as an agent, with authority to act; **2,** to intrust; as, the people *delegate* power to Congress.

Syn., *n.* agent, deputy, substitute.

del-e-ga-tion (dĕl''ē-gā'shŭn), *n.* **1,** the act of authorizing a person or persons to act for others; **2,** a body of persons chosen so to act; as, each state sends a *delegation* to the Republican convention.

de-lete (dē-lēt'), *v.t.* [*p.t.* and *p.p.* -let'ed, *p.pr.* -let'ing], to take out or blot out (a word or passage); erase; as, all references to the crime were *deleted* by the editor.

del-e-te-ri-ous (dĕl''ē-tē'rĭ-ŭs), *adj.* harmful, morally or physically; as, some drugs have a *deleterious* effect on the body.—*adv.* **del''e-te'ri-ous-ly.**—*n.* **del''e-te'ri-ous-ness.**

de-le-tion (dē-lē'shŭn), *n.* **1,** erasure; **2,** that which is blotted out.

delft-ware (dĕlft'wâr''), *n.* a kind of glazed earthenware, made first at Delft, in Holland: also called *delft; delf.*

de-lib-er-ate (dē-lĭb'ẽr-āt), *v.t.* [*p.t.* and *p.p.* -at''ed, *p.pr.* -at''ing], to reflect on; think upon; consider: as, he *deliberated* the matter before deciding:—*v.i.* to take counsel with oneself or others; as, the men elected to make laws are expected to *deliberate* before passing them:—*adj.* (dē-lĭb'ẽr-ȧt), **1,** circumspect; prudent; cautious; **2,** slow in determining or in acting; **3,** well-considered.—*adv.* **de-lib'er-ate-ly.**—*n.* **de-lib'er-ate-ness.**—*n.* **de-lib'er-a''tor.**

Syn., *v.* consider, meditate, ponder, debate.

de-lib-er-a-tion (dē-lĭb''ẽr-ā'shŭn), *n.* **1,** calm and careful consideration; **2,** slowness in action; **3,** discussion.

de-lib-er-a-tive (dē-lĭb'ẽr-ā-tĭv), *adj.* **1,** of or pertaining to discussion or debate; **2,** characterized by careful consideration.

del-i-ca-cy (dĕl'ĭ-kȧ-sĭ), *n.* [*pl.* delicacies (-sĭz)], **1,** the state or quality of being agreeable to the taste or other senses; **2,** a tidbit; dainty; **3,** grace, as of a sketch; **4,** sensitiveness; refinement; sensibility; **5,** consideration for the feelings of others; **6,** susceptibility to disease.

Syn. nicety, daintiness, tact, modesty.

del-i-cate (dĕl'ĭ-kȧt), *adj.* **1,** pleasing to the taste; as, a *delicate* flavor; **2,** tender; refined; as, *delicate* attentions; **3,** physically frail; as, a *delicate* child; **4,** sensitive, as to injury; **5,** sensitive to slight changes, as instruments; **6,** skilful; deft; as, a *delicate* touch; **7,** ticklish; as, a *delicate* matter.—*adv.* **del'i-cate-ly.**

Syn. frail, fragile. (See brittle.)

del-i-ca-tes-sen (dĕl''ĭ-kȧ-tĕs'ĕn), *n. pl.* **1,** prepared foods, as cooked meats, salads, preserves, and relishes; table delicacies; **2,** used as *sing.*, a place where these are sold.

de-li-cious (dē-lĭsh'ŭs), *adj.* highly pleasing to the mind or senses, esp. to the taste; exquisite.—*adv.* **de-li'cious-ly.**—*n.* **de-li'cious-ness.**

Syn. sweet, palatable, luscious.—*Ant.* nauseous, unpalatable, repulsive.

de-light (dē-līt'), *v.t.* to gratify or please greatly; charm:—*v.i.* to be highly gratified or pleased:—*n.* **1,** an extreme degree of pleasure; high satisfaction, joy; **2,** that which causes pleasure.

Syn., *n.* enjoyment, pleasure, happiness, ecstasy, gladness, rapture, bliss.—*Ant.*, *n.* unhappiness, misery, annoyance, agony.

de-light-ed (dē-līt'ĕd), *p.adj.* greatly pleased; gratified; charmed. —*adv.* **de-light'ed-ly.**

de-light-ful (dē-līt'fo͝ol), *adj.* affording enjoyment; pleasing; charming. —*adv.* **de-light'ful-ly.**—*n.* **de-light'ful-ness.**

de-light-some (dē-līt'sŭm), *adj.* affording keen enjoyment.—*adv.* **de-light'some-ly.**—*n.* **de-light'some-ness.**

De-li-lah (dē-lī'lȧ), *n.* in the Bible, a Philistine woman who betrayed Samson by cutting his long hair while he slept (Judges 16).

de-lim-it (dē-lĭm'ĭt), *v.t.* to mark out or fix the limits of, as territory.

de-lin-e-ate (dē-lĭn'ē-āt), *v.t.* [*p.t.* and *p.p.* -at''ed, *p.pr.* -at''ing], **1,** to mark out with lines; sketch; draw; **2,** to describe minutely and accurately in words. —*n.* **de-lin'e-a''tor.**

Syn. trace, depict, outline, portray.

de-lin-e-a-tion (dē-lĭn''ē-ā'shŭn), *n.* **1,** the act or art of picturing or describing; **2,** a sketch, description, etc.

de-lin-quen-cy (dē-lĭng'kwĕn-sĭ), *n.* [*pl.* delinquencies (-sĭz)], neglect of, or failure in, duty; a misdeed; fault.

de-lin-quent (dē-lĭng'kwĕnt), *adj.* falling short of duty:—*n.* **1,** one who neglects a duty; **2,** an offender; esp., a youthful offender.

Syn., *adj.* guilty, failing, faulty, remiss.

del-i-quesce (dĕl''ĭ-kwĕs'), *v.i.* [*p.t.* and *p.p.* -quesced' (-kwĕst'), *p.pr.* -quesc'ing], to dissolve gradually and become liquid by taking in moisture from the air, as certain salts.—*adj.* **del''i-ques'cent.**—*n.* **del''i-ques'cence.**

de-lir-i-ous (dē-lĭr'ĭ-ŭs), *adj.* **1,** raving, as from fever; wandering in mind; **2,** frantic with delight; wildly excited; as, *delirious* with joy.—*adv.* **de-lir'i-ous-ly.** —*n.* **de-lir'i-ous-ness.**

Syn. mad, crazed.

de-lir-i-um (dē-lĭr'ĭ-ŭm), *n.* **1,** a temporary mental disorder, often caused by fever, and marked by wandering speech and fancies; **2,** excitement; wild enthusiasm: **delirium tremens** (trē'mĕnz), a disease of the brain caused by drinking intoxicating liquors to excess.

de-liv-er (dē-lĭv'ẽr), *v.t.* **1,** to set free; save; **2,** to yield possession or control of; **3,** to carry and hand to an owner; **4,** to send forth vigorously, as a blow; **5,** to utter; as, to *deliver* a speech; **6,** to assist (a woman) in the birth of a child.—*n.* **de-liv'er-er.**

Syn. liberate, free, rescue.

de-liv-er-ance (dē-lĭv'ẽr-ăns), *n.* **1,** the act of setting free; rescue; release; **2,** a publicly expressed opinion.

de-liv-er-y (dē-lĭv'ẽr-ĭ), *n.* [*pl.* deliveries (-ĭz)], **1,** the act of releasing; a setting free; **2,** a surrender; transfer; **3,** manner of speaking; as, the orator had a splendid *delivery;* **4,** a distribution of letters, stock, etc.; **5,** the act or manner of pitching a ball; **6,** childbirth.

dell (dĕl), *n.* a small, narrow valley; ravine retired glen.

Del-phic (dĕl'fĭk), *adj.* **1,** pertaining to Delphi, to the famous sanctuary of Apollo with its priestess, or to the games celebrated there in honor of Apollo; 2, oracular.—*adj.* **Del'phi-an.**

del-ta (dĕl'tȧ), *n.* [*pl.* deltas (-tȧz)], **1**, the fourth letter [δ, Δ] of the Greek alphabet, approximately equivalent to English *d;* **2**, a fan-shaped deposit of sand or soil, formed at the mouth of a river; **3**, any triangular surface.

del-toid (dĕl'toid), *n.* **1**, a triangular muscle of the shoulder and upper part of the arm, used to lift the arm from the side; **2**, popularly, any of a variety of moths whose wings at rest form a triangle:—*adj.* **1**, having the shape of a delta; triangular, as a leaf (see *leaf*, illus.); **2**, designating, or pertaining to, the deltoid muscle.

de-lude (dē-lūd'), *v.t.* [*p.t.* and *p.p.* -lud'ed, *p.pr.* -lud'ing], to cheat; beguile; deceive; as, to *delude* oneself with false hopes.
Syn. dupe, trick, betray.

del-uge (dĕl'ūj), *n.* **1**, a heavy downpour or flood; **2**, a sudden and resistless calamity: **the Deluge**, the great flood of the time of Noah (Genesis 7):—*v.t.* [*p.t.* and *p.p.* -uged (-ūjd), *p.pr.* -ug-ing], **1**, to overflow; **2**, to overwhelm, as with a flood.

de-lu-sion (dē-lū'zhŭn), *n.* **1**, the act of deceiving, or the state of being deceived; **2**, a false idea, esp. if held persistently; as, he was under the *delusion* that all men were honest.
Syn. illusion. A *delusion* is the result of mental deception or of faulty reasoning; as, he was under the *delusion* that he was Cæsar; he had the *delusion* that he would soon become rich. *Illusion* implies faulty or mistaken perception of some actual object; as, a mirage is an optical *illusion*.

de-lu-sive (dē-lū'sĭv), *adj.* likely to mislead; deceptive.—*adj.* **de-lu'so-ry.**—*adv.* **de-lu'sive-ly.**—*n.* **de-lu'sive-ness.**

***de luxe** (dē lüks'), [Fr.], of unusually fine quality; luxurious; as, an edition *de luxe* of Shakespeare's plays.

delve (dĕlv), *v.t.* [*p.t.* and *p.p.* delved (dĕlvd), *p.pr.* delv'ing], *Archaic*, to dig:—*v.i.* **1**, to work with a spade; **2**, to make earnest search for knowledge; as, the scientist *delves* into the secrets of nature.—*n.* **delv'er.**

dem-a-gog (dĕm'ȧ-gŏg), *n.* **1**, a popular orator; leader of the rabble; **2**, an insincere political leader who seeks his own gain. Also, **dem'a-gogue.**

dem-a-gog-ic (dĕm"ȧ-gŏj'ĭk), *adj.* like, or pertaining to, an insincere leader. Also, **dem"a-gog'i-cal.**

dem-a-gog-ism (dĕm'ȧ-gŏg-ĭzm), *n.* **1**, insincere appeal to the masses; **2**, the principles of a demagog.

de-mand (dē-mȧnd'), *v.t.* **1**, to claim; exact; **2**, to question with authority; **3**, to require; have urgent need for; as, the letter *demands* an answer; **4**, in law, to summon:—*v.i.* to inquire by authority:—*n.* **1**, the act of claiming as due; **2**, an authoritative claim; an imperative request; **3**, the state of being sought after; as, coal is in great *demand*.—*n.* **de-mand'er.**

de-mar-ca-tion (dē"mär-kā'shŭn), *n.* the act of defining, or marking, bounds; a line of separation; as, the fence is the *demarcation* of the property. Also, **de"mar-ka'tion.**

1**de-mean** (dē-mēn'), *v.t.* to behave; conduct; carry: used with the reflexive pronoun.

2**de-mean** (dē-mēn'), *v.t. Colloq.*, to debase, lower, or degrade; as, to be rude is to *demean* oneself.

de-mean-or (dē-mēn'ẽr), *n.* behavior; bearing. Also, **de-mean'our.**

de-ment-ed (dē-mĕn'tĕd), *adj.* insane; mad; out of one's mind.

de-men-ti-a (dē-mĕn'shĭ-ȧ), *n.* unsoundness of mind; insanity, with loss of intellect, will, and memory.

de-mer-it (dē-mĕr'ĭt), *n.* **1**, an action or a deficiency which deserves blame; **2**, a mark for failure or misconduct.

de-mesne (dē-mān'; dē-mēn'), *n.* **1**, possession of land as one's own; **2**, a landed estate attached to a manor house. Also, **de-main'; de-maine'.**

De-me-ter (dē-mē'tẽr), *n.* in Greek mythology, the goddess of agriculture, fruitfulness, and marriage: identified with the Roman *Ceres*.

dem-i- (dĕm'ĭ-), *prefix*, **1**, half; as, *demi*semiquaver; **2**, less or smaller than usual; as, *demi*-tasse; inferior; as, *demi*god.

dem-i-god (dĕm'ĭ-gŏd"), *n.* an inferior god or one whose nature is partly divine; a hero.—*n.fem.* **dem'i-god"dess.**

dem-i-john (dĕm'ĭ-jŏn), *n.* a glass bottle with a small neck and large body, usually incased in wickerwork.

dem-i-monde (dĕm'ĭ-mŏnd; *Fr.* dē-mē"-môɴd'), *n.* collectively, women of ill repute.

de-mise (dē-mīz'), *n.* **1**, death, esp. of a royal personage; **2**, the conveyance or transfer of an estate by will or lease.—*v.t.* [*p.t.* and *p.p.* -mised' (-mīzd'), *p.pr.* mis'ing], to give or grant by will or lease:—*v.i.* to be bequeathed, as property by will.

dem-i-sem-i-qua-ver (dĕm"ĭ-sĕm'ĭ-kwā"vẽr), *n.* in music, a note equal in length to half a semiquaver; a thirty-second note.

***de-mi–tasse** (dē-mē'=täs'; dĕm'ĭ=tȧs"), [Fr.], *n.* **1**, half a cup; **2**, a small cup of, or for holding, black coffee.

de-mo-bi-lize (dē-mō'bĭ-līz; dē-mŏb'ĭ-līz), *v.t.* [*p.t.* and *p.p.* -lized (-līzd), *p.pr.* -liz"ing], **1**, to disband or dismiss, as troops; **2**, to change (an army or country) from a war footing to a peace footing.—*n.* **de-mo"bi-li-za'tion.**

de-moc-ra-cy (dē-mŏk'rȧ-sĭ), *n.* [*pl.* democracies (-sĭz)], **1**, government by the people; also, a community so governed; as, the United States is a *democracy;* **2**, practical or social equality as opposed to aristocracy; as, the world must be safe for *democracy:* **Democracy**, in the U. S., the Democratic party or its principles.

dem-o-crat (dĕm'ō-krăt), *n.* one who believes in and upholds the principles of popular government or social equality: **Democrat**, in the U. S., a member of the Democratic party.

dem-o-crat-ic (dĕm"ō-krăt'ĭk), *adj.* pertaining to democracy, or government by the people; believing in, or tending to, social equality: **Democratic party**, one of the great political groups in the U. S.: so named in 1828.—*adv.* **dem"o-crat'i-cal-ly.**

dem-oi-selle (dĕm"wä-zĕl'; *Fr.* dē-mwȧ"-zĕl'), *n.* a young unmarried woman; a damsel.

de-mol-ish (dē-mŏl'ĭsh), *v.t.* to pull down; reduce to ruins; destroy; annihilate.—*n.* **de-mol'ish-er.**—*n.* **de-mol'ish-ment.**
Syn. raze, ruin, overthrow. (See destroy.)

dem-o-li-tion (dĕm"ō-lĭsh'ŭn), *n.* the act or process of tearing down or destroying; destruction.

de-mon (dē'mŏn), *n.* **1**, an attendant spirit; inferior deity; **2**, an evil spirit; a devil; **3**, a very cruel person. Also, **dæ'mon.**—*adj.* **de-mon'ic.**

de-mon-e-tize (dē-mŏn'ē-tīz; dē-mŭn'-), *v.t.* [*p.t.* and *p.p.* -tized (-tīzd), *p.pr.* -tiz"ing], **1**, to deprive of value, as money; **2**, to withdraw from use as money;

as, the government will *demonetize* old, torn, paper money.—*n.* **de-mon″e-ti-za′tion.**

de-mo-ni-ac (dē-mō′nĭ-ăk), *n.* one thought to be possessed of an evil spirit; a lunatic or insane person:—*adj.* possessed by, or like, an evil spirit; devilish; frantic. Also, *adj.* **de″mo-ni′a-cal** (dē″mō-nī′ȧ-kăl).—*adv.* **de″mo-ni′a-cal-ly.**

de-mon-ism (dē′mŏn-ĭzm), *n.* belief in evil spirits or demons.

de-mon-ol-o-gy (dē″mŏn-ŏl′ō-jĭ), *n.* the study of ghosts or evil spirits.—*n.* **de″mon-ol′o-gist.**

de-mon-stra-ble (dē-mŏn′strȧ-bl), *adj.* capable of being shown or proved, as an assertion.—*adv.* **de-mon′stra-bly.**—*n.* **de-mon″stra-bil′i-ty.**

dem-on-strate (dĕm′ŏn-strāt; dē-mŏn′-strāt), *v.t.* [*p.t.* and *p.p.* -strat″ed, *p.pr.* -strat″ing], **1**, to prove beyond the possibility of a doubt; **2**, to teach by examples; illustrate; prove; **3**, to exhibit and explain, as a sweeper or an automobile.

dem-on-stra-tion (dĕm″ŏn-strā′shŭn), *n.* **1**, the act of showing or proving; **2**, a proof beyond the possibility of a doubt; **3**, manifestation; outward expression of feeling; **4**, a public exhibition of sympathy with some political or social movement; as, a party *demonstration;* **5**, the exhibition and description of specimens in showing or teaching something, esp. in anatomy; **6**, a show of military force.

Syn. certainty, conclusiveness, evidence, proof.—*Ant.* doubt, disproof.

de-mon-stra-tive (dē-mŏn′strȧ-tĭv), *adj.* **1**, having the power of showing or proving; **2**, in grammar, serving to point out; as, a *demonstrative* pronoun; **3**, showing the feelings, esp. affection, openly and strongly:—*n.* a pronoun that serves to point out the object to which it refers, as *this, that, these, those.*—*adv.* **de-mon′stra-tive-ly.**—*n.* **de-mon′stra-tive-ness.**

dem-on-stra-tor (dĕm′ŏn-strā″tẽr), *n.* **1**, one who proves, points out, or shows; **2**, a teacher of practical anatomy, or physical science.

de-mor-al-ize (dē-mŏr′ăl-īz), *v.t.* [*p.t.* and *p.p.* -ized (-īzd), *p.pr.* -iz″ing], **1**, to corrupt; **2**, to deprive of spirit or energy; throw into confusion; **3**, to disorganize.—*n.* **de-mor″al-i-za′tion.**

de-mount-a-ble (dē-moun′tȧ-bl), *adj.* capable of being taken down or removed; as, a *demountable* rim on an automobile wheel.

de-mul-cent (dē-mŭl′sĕnt), *adj.* softening; soothing:—*n.* a soothing and healing substance, as for a sore throat.

de-mur (dē-mûr′), *v.i.* [*p.t.* and *p.p.* -murred′ (-mûrd′), *p.pr.* -mur′ring], **1**, to hesitate; **2**, to raise objections:—*n.* **1**, an objection or exception; **2**, hesitation.

de-mure (dē-mūr′), *adj.* **1**, grave; sober; **2**, affectedly modest, as in manner.—*adv.* **de-mure′ly.**—*n.* **de-mure′ness.**

Syn. prim, sedate, coy, decorous.

de-mur-rage (dē-mûr′āj), *n.* **1**, the holding of a vessel in port, or of a freight car on a siding, beyond the time allowed for loading, unloading, etc.; **2**, the money paid by the freighter for such delay.

de-mur-rer (dē-mûr′ẽr), *n.* **1**, one who hesitates or objects; **2**, an objection on a point of law.

den (dĕn), *n.* **1**, a cavern; **2**, the cave of a wild beast; lair; **3**, *Colloq.*, a cozy, private room; **4**, a haunt of criminals.

de-na-ri-us (dē-nā′rĭ-ŭs), *n.* [*pl.* denarii (-ī)], in ancient Rome, a silver coin, the penny mentioned in the Bible; also, a gold coin, worth about $4.25.

de-na-tion-al-ize (dē-năsh′ŭn-ăl-īz), *v.t.* [*p.t.* and *p.p.* -ized (-īzd), *p.pr.* -iz″ing], **1**, to take away national rights or character from; **2**, to deprive of national significance and render local; as, to *denationalize* prohibition enforcement.—*n.* **de-na″tion-al-i-za′tion.**

de-nat-u-ral-ize (dē-năt′ū-răl-īz), *v.t.* [*p.t.* and *p.p.* -ized (-īzd), *p.pr.* -iz″ing], **1**, to make unnatural; **2**, to deprive of citizenship.

de-na-ture (dē-nā′tūr), *v.t.* [*p.t.* and *p.p.* -tured (-tūrd), *p.pr.* -tur-ing], to change the nature or character of; as, to *denature* alcohol in order to render it unfit to drink.—*p.adj.* **de-na′tured.**—*n.* **de-na″tur-a′-tion.**—*v.t.* **de-na′tur-ize.**

den-gue (dĕng′gā), *n.* an infectious, eruptive, painful disease of the tropics: also called *breakbone fever.*

de-ni-al (dē-nī′ăl), *n.* **1**, refusal to grant, believe, or admit; **2**, contradiction; as, the prisoner's *denial* of his guilt; **3**, refusal to acknowledge as having claims; as, *denial* of authority; **4**, restraint; as, *denial* of one's desires.

[1]**de-ni-er** (dē-nī′ẽr), *n.* one who refuses to grant, believe, or admit.

[2]**de-nier** (dē-nēr′), *n.* an ancient, small French coin of trifling value.

den-im (dĕn′ĭm), *n.* a coarse cotton material used for hangings, screens, etc.

den-i-zen (dĕn′ĭ-zĕn), *n.* **1**, an inhabitant; dweller; citizen; **2**, an alien, or foreigner, who has received papers admitting him to the rights and privileges of citizenship:—*v.t.* **1**, to admit to the rights of citizenship; **2**, to populate with citizens.

de-nom-i-nate (dē-nŏm′ĭ-nāt), *v.t.* [*p.t.* and *p.p.* -nat″ed, *p.pr.* -nat″ing], to designate, or give a name to:—*adj.* (dē-nŏm′ĭ-nāt), having a specific name: concrete; as, five cents is a *denominate* quantity.

de-nom-i-na-tion (dē-nŏm″ĭ-nā′shŭn), *n.* **1**, the act of designating or naming; **2**, a name; **3**, a class, division, or religious sect; **4**, a name for a certain class or unit in a series; as, in the U. S. we have coins of many *denominations.*

de-nom-i-na-tion-al (dē-nŏm″ĭ-nā′-shŭn-ăl), *adj.* pertaining to, or carried on by, a class or a religious sect.—*adv.* **de-nom″i-na′tion-al-ly.**—*n.* **de-nom″i-na′tion-al-ism.**

de-nom-i-na-tive (dē-nŏm′ĭ-nā-tĭv), *adj.* **1**, giving a name; **2**, derived from a noun or adjective; as, a *denominative* verb:—*n.* a denominative word.

de-nom-i-na-tor (dē-nŏm′ĭ-nā″tẽr), *n.* **1**, one who or that which gives a name to anything; **2**, that term of a fraction which, when placed below the line, indicates the number of equal parts into which a number is divided.

de-no-ta-tion (dē″nō-tā′shŭn), *n.* **1**, a plain marking out; a clear sign; indication; name; **2**, a meaning; esp., the precise meaning.

de-note (dē-nōt′), *v.t.* [*p.t.* and *p.p.* -not′ed, *p.pr.* -not′ing], **1**, to mean or signify; specif., to have as precise and literal meaning: distinguished from *connote;* **2**, to indicate; be a sign of; betoken; **3**, to mark out plainly, as by a sign.—*adj.* **de-not′a-ble.**

Syn. imply. (See connote.)

***dé-noue-ment** (dā″nōō″män′; dā-nōō′-män), [Fr.], *n.* **1**, the unraveling or solving of a plot or mystery; **2**, the outcome of a situation.

de-nounce (dē-nouns′), *v.t.* [*p.t.* and *p.p.* -nounced′ (-nounst′), *p.pr.* -nounc′ing], to threaten or accuse publicly; censure.—*n.* **de-nounce′ment.**

***de no-vo** (dē nō′vō), [Lat.], anew; afresh; from the start.

dense (dĕns), *adj.* 1, thick; heavy; as, a *dense* fog; compact; as, a *dense* crowd; 2, stupid; stolid; dull, as a person.—*adv.* **dense′ly.**—*n.* **dense′ness.**

den-si-ty (dĕn′sĭ-tĭ), *n.* [*pl.* densities (-tĭz)], 1, closeness or compactness, as of matter; 2, depth, as of shade; 3, ratio of mass to volume; 4, stupidity.

¹dent (dĕnt), *n.* a small hollow or depression:—*v.t.* to make a small hollow in:—*v.i.* to become hollowed in spots.

²dent (dĕnt), *n.* a tooth, as in a gear wheel, a comb, etc.

den-tal (dĕn′tăl), *adj.* 1, pertaining to the teeth; 2, pronounced by the aid of the teeth, as *t, d,* etc.:—*n.* a dental sound, as *t, d.*

den-tate (dĕn′tāt), *adj.* toothed; having indented edges; as, *dentate* leaves (see *leaf*, illus.). Also, **den′tat-ed.**

den-ti-form (dĕn′tĭ-fôrm), *adj.* having the shape of a tooth.

den-ti-frice (dĕn′tĭ-frĭs), *n.* a powder, liquid, or paste used for cleaning the teeth.

den-til (dĕn′tĭl), *n.* one of the small square blocks placed for ornament on the under side of cornices of roofs. Also, **den′tel.**

den-tine (dĕn′tĭn), *n.* the hard, dense tissue which forms the chief substance of a tooth (see *tooth*, illus.). Also, **den′tin.**—*adj.* **den′ti-nal.**

den-tist (dĕn′tĭst), *n.* one who practices dental surgery, as filling and extracting teeth.

den-tist-ry (dĕn′tĭs-trĭ), *n.* the art or science of treating or extracting the teeth; dental surgery.

den-ti-tion (dĕn-tĭsh′ŭn), *n.* 1, the process or period of cutting the teeth; 2, the arrangement of the teeth.

den-ture (dĕn′tŭr), *n.* an entire set of teeth, esp. of artificial teeth.

den-u-da-tion (dĕn″ū-dā′shŭn; dē″nū-dā′shŭn), *n.* the act of stripping or making bare.

de-nude (dē-nūd′), *v.t.* [*p.t.* and *p.p.* -nud′ed, *p.pr.* -nud′ing], 1, to make bare or naked; as, to *denude* one of clothing; 2, to lay bare (rocks) by the wearing action of water, frost, etc., upon the surface.

de-nun-ci-a-tion (dē-nŭn″sĭ-ā′shŭn; dē-nŭn″shĭ-ā′shŭn), *n.* public accusation with censure; a threat.

de-nun-ci-a-tor (dē-nŭn′shĭ-ā″tẽr; dē-nŭn′sĭ-ā″tẽr), *n.* one who censures or makes accusations publicly.

de-nun-ci-a-to-ry (dē-nŭn′shĭ-ȧ-tō-rĭ; dē-nŭn′sĭ-ȧ-tō-rĭ), *adj.* relating to, or containing, an accusation, censure, or threat.—*adj.* **de-nun′ci-a-tive.**

de-ny (dē-nī′), *v.t.* [*p.t.* and *p.p.* -nied′ (-nīd′), *p.pr.* -ny′ing], 1, to refuse to believe or admit; contradict; as, I *deny* his statement; 2, to withhold; refuse to grant; as, to *deny* help; 3, to disown; as, to *deny* his son; 4, to refuse to accept as real; as, to *deny* the existence of fairies.

Syn. gainsay, dispute, oppose, contest.

de-o-dor-ant (dē-ō′dẽr-ănt), *n.* something which takes away odor; a disinfectant.

de-o-dor-ize (dē-ō′dẽr-īz), *v.t.* [*p.t.* and *p.p.* -ized (-īzd), *p.pr.* -iz″ing], to disinfect; deprive of odor, or smell.—*n.* **de-o′-dor-iz″er** (-īz″ẽr).

de-ox-i-dize (dē-ŏk′sĭ-dīz), *v.t.* [*p.t.* and *p.p.* -dized (-dīzd), *p.pr.* -diz″ing], to free from oxygen; reduce (an oxide), as by heating with carbon, or in hydrogen gas.—*n.* **de-ox″i-di-za′tion.**—*n.* **de-ox′i-diz″er.**—*v.t.* **de-ox′i-date.**—*n.* **de-ox″i-da′tion.**

de-part (dē-pärt′), *v.i.* 1, to go or move away; leave; 2, to die; 3, to desist; deviate; as, to *depart* from virtue.

Syn. quit, decamp, retire, withdraw, vanish.

de-part-ment (dē-pärt′mĕnt), *n.* 1, a distinct division; 2, a separate room or office for business; 3, a branch of business, study, or science; 4, a division of government; as, the *Department* of State; 5, an administrative district, esp. in France.

de-part-men-tal (dē″pärt-mĕn′tăl), *adj.* 1, pertaining to a division; 2, governed by departments.

de-par-ture (dē-pär′tūr), *n.* 1, the act of leaving; a going away; 2, a change from an old to a new plan; 3, death.

de-pend (dē-pĕnd′), *v.i.* 1, to rely for support; as, the old man *depends* on his son; be conditioned; as, his answer *depends* on his point of view; 2, to hang down; dangle; 3, to trust or rely (on); as, pupils *depend* on their teachers for instruction.

de-pend-a-ble (dē-pĕn′dȧ-bl), *adj.* reliable; trustworthy; safe.—*n.* **de-pend′a-ble-ness.**—*adv.* **de-pend′a-bly.**

Syn. responsible, faithful.

de-pend-ence (dē-pĕn′dĕns), *n.* 1, the state of being influenced by, or subject to, another; reliance; trust; as, the *dependence* of a child on its father; 2, that on which one relies; 3, the state of needing aid; 4, the state of hanging down.

de-pend-en-cy (dē-pĕn′dĕn-sĭ), *n.* [*pl.* dependencies (-sĭz)], 1, the condition of relying on another; 2, a country under the control of another country.

de-pend-ent (dē-pĕn′dĕnt), *adj.* 1, hanging down; 2, relying on someone or something else for support; 3, conditional; as, his acts were *dependent* on his moods; 4, subordinate; as, a *dependent* clause:—*n.* 1, one who relies on another for support; 2, something which hangs down. Also, *n.* **de-pend′ant.**

de-pict (dē-pĭkt′), *v.t.* to portray; describe in words; as, the writer *depicted* the scene.—*n.* **de-pic′tion.**—*v.t.* and *n.* **de-pic′ture.**

dep-i-late (dĕp′ĭ-lāt), *v.t.* [*p.t.* and *p.p.* -lat″ed, *p.pr.* -lat″ing], to remove hair from.—*n.* **dep′i-la″tor.**

de-pil-a-to-ry (dē-pĭl′ȧ-tō-rĭ), *n.* [*pl.* depilatories (-rĭz)], a preparation for removing hair, as from the body:—*adj.* capable of removing hair.

de-plane (dē″plān′), *v.i.* [*p.t.* and *p.p.* -planed (-plānd′), *p.pr.* -plan′ing], to disembark from an airplane.

de-plete (dē-plēt′), *v.t.* [*p.t.* and *p.p.* -plet′ed, *p.pr.* -plet′ing], 1, to empty; as, to *deplete* the treasury; 2, to exhaust; as, his strength was *depleted;* 3, to relieve of congestion, as by drawing off blood.

de-ple-tion (dē-plē′shŭn), *n.* 1, the act of emptying; 2, exhaustion; as, the *depletion* of energy; 3, blood-letting.

de-plor-a-ble (dē-plōr′ȧ-bl), *adj.* sad; calamitous; grievous; as, a *deplorable* accident.—*adv.* **de-plor′a-bly.**

de-plore (dē-plōr′), *v.t.* [*p.t.* and *p.p.* -plored′ (-plōrd′), *p.pr.* -plor′ing], to lament; grieve for; as, to *deplore* the loss of a friend; *deplore* wrongdoing.

Syn. mourn, bewail, regret, bemoan.

de-ploy (dē-ploi′), *v.t.* to spread or open out, as a body of troops, in line of battle:—*v.i.* to extend the front line, as troops:—*n.* movement by which a body of troops is spread out in battle line.—*n.* **de-ploy′ment.**

de-po-nent (dē-pō′nĕnt), *adj.* having a passive form and an active meaning: used of certain Latin verbs:—*n.* 1, a deponent verb; 2, a witness who makes a sworn statement, usually in writing.

de-pop-u-late (dē-pŏp′ū-lāt), *v.t.* [*p.t.* and *p.p.* -lat″ed, *p.pr.* -lat″ing], to deprive of inhabitants or people. —*n.* **de-pop″u-la′tion.**

de-port (dē-pōrt′), *v.t.* **1**, to banish, as to another country; exile; remove; **2**, to behave (oneself): used reflexively.

de-por-ta-tion (dē″pōr-tā′shŭn; dĕp″-ŏr-), *n.* the act of taking, or state of being taken, forcibly into another country; specif., the sending to his own country of an alien living in, or seeking entrance into, another.

de-port-ment (dē-pōrt′mĕnt), *n.* conduct; behavior; demeanor.
Syn. bearing, carriage, manners.

de-pose (dē-pōz′), *v.t.* [*p.t.* and *p.p.* -posed′ (-pōzd′), *p.pr.* -pos′ing], **1**, to remove from a throne or other high station; deprive of office; **2**, to bear witness to:—*v.i.* to testify on oath.—*n.* **de-pos′al.**

de-pos-it (dē-pŏz′ĭt), *v.t.* **1**, to put or set down; place; **2**, to put in a bank, as money; intrust to another for security:—*n.* **1**, something committed to the care of another; a pledge; esp., money committed to a bank; **2**, something set or laid down; **3**, in chemistry, a sediment; settling.

de-pos-i-ta-ry (dē-pŏz′ĭ-tā-rĭ), *n.* [*pl.* depositaries (-rĭz)], **1**, (also, *depository*), one to whom something is intrusted; **2**, (usually, *depository*), a place where something is put for safe-keeping.

dep-o-si-tion (dĕp″ō-zĭsh′ŭn; dē″pō-), *n.* **1**, the act of putting down, placing in trust, etc.; **2**, a sediment; **3**, removal from a throne or office; **4**, in law, sworn testimony, obtained out of court by questioning a witness, called a *deponent*, and intended to be used as evidence.

de-pos-i-tor (dē-pŏz′ĭ-tẽr), *n.* one who puts down, or places in trust; specif., one who puts money in a bank.

de-pos-i-to-ry (dē-pŏz′ĭ-tō-rĭ), *n.* [*pl.* depositories (-rĭz)], **1**, (also, *depositary*), the place where anything is put for safe-keeping, as a bank; **2**, (usually, *depositary*), one intrusted with something; a guardian.

de-pot (dē′pō; dā′pō; dĕp′ō), *n.* **1**, a warehouse; **2**, a building for military stores, food, etc.; also, the headquarters of a regiment; **3**, in the U. S., a railway station.
Syn. (see station).

de-prave (dē-prāv′), *v.t.* [*p.t.* and *p.p.* -praved′ (-prāvd′), *p.pr.* -prav′ing], to make bad or corrupt.—*n.* **dep″ra-va′tion** (dĕp″rȧ-vā′shŭn; dē″prȧ-).
Syn. pervert, contaminate, pollute.—*Ant.* improve, elevate, redeem, save.

de-praved (dē-prāvd′), *p.adj.* morally debased; corrupt; made bad.
Syn. degenerate.—*Ant.* pure, good.

de-prav-i-ty (dē-prăv′ĭ-tĭ), *n.* [*pl.* depravities (-tĭz)], the state of being immoral or corrupt; wickedness.

dep-re-cate (dĕp′rē-kāt), *v.t.* [*p.t.* and *p.p.* -cat″ed, *p.pr.* -cat″ing], to disapprove strongly of; express regret for; as, the store manager *deprecates* the rudeness of the salesman to a customer.—*adv.* **dep′re-cat″ing-ly.**—*adj.* **dep′re-ca-tive.**

dep-re-ca-tion (dĕp″rē-kā′shŭn), *n.* the act of disapproving.

dep-re-ca-to-ry (dĕp′rē-kȧ-tō-rĭ), *adj.* **1**, apologetic; **2**, serving as a protest against something.

de-pre-ci-ate (dē-prē′shĭ-āt), *v.t.* [*p.t.* and *p.p.* -at″ed, *p.pr.* -at″ing], **1**, to lower the value or rate of; **2**, to speak slightingly of:—*v.i.* to fall in value; become of less worth; as, the property will *depreciate* in value if not kept in repair.—*adj.* **de-pre′ci-a-tive.**—*adj.* **de-pre′ci-a-to-ry.**

de-pre-ci-a-tion (dē-prē″shĭ-ā′shŭn), *n.* **1**, the act of lessening value or worth, as of property; **2**, a fall in value.

dep-re-date (dĕp′rē-dāt), *v.t.* and *v.i.* [*p.t.* and *p.p.* -dat″ed, *p.pr.* -dat″ing], to pillage; rob; ravage; plunder; lay waste.—*n.* **dep′re-da″tor.**

dep-re-da-tion (dĕp″rē-dā′shŭn), *n.* robbery; pillage; a destroying or laying waste.

de-press (dē-prĕs′), *v.t.* **1**, to press or thrust down; **2**, to sadden; dispirit; as, these cloudy days *depress* us all; **3**, to lower or cheapen; make dull, as trade. —*adj.* **de-pres′sive.**
Syn. discourage, dishearten.—*Ant.* elevate, encourage, lift, inspire.

de-pressed (dē-prĕst′), *p.adj.* **1**, cast down in spirits; **2**, lowered in position; **3**, flattened from above.

de-pres-sion (dē-prĕsh′ŭn), *n.* **1**, the act of making lower; **2**, the sinking or falling in of a surface; also, the hollow itself; **3**, low spirits; **4**, dulness of trade; as, the *depression* caused a panic.
Syn. gloom, sorrow, melancholy.

de-pres-sor (dē-prĕs′ẽr), *n.* **1**, one who or that which makes lower; **2**, a muscle that draws down an organ or part.

dep-ri-va-tion (dĕp″rĭ-vā′shŭn), *n.* the act of taking away; loss.

de-prive (dē-prīv′), *v.t.* [*p.t.* and *p.p.* -prived′ (-prīvd′), *p.pr.* -priv′ing], **1**, to take from; dispossess; as, to *deprive* him of his house; **2**, to debar; depose, as from office: with *of*.—*n.* **de-priv′al.**
Syn. strip, bereave, despoil, rob.

depth (dĕpth), *n.* **1**, the state or quality of being deep; distance below the surface, or from the observer in any direction; **2**, profoundness; extent of penetration; **3**, richness of tone or color; **4**, that which is deep; as, the ocean *depths*: **depth bomb**, in the World War, an effective contrivance arranged to explode at a certain depth under water, and thus destroy a submarine boat if in the vicinity: also called *depth charge*.

dep-u-ta-tion (dĕp″ū-tā′shŭn), *n.* **1**, the act of appointing, or giving power to, an agent; **2**, the person or persons so appointed to act; as, a *deputation* visited the governor.

de-pute (dē-pūt′), *v.t.* [*p.t.* and *p.p.* -put′ed, *p.pr.* -put′ing], **1**, to appoint as an agent or deputy; **2**, to send with authority to act on behalf of the principal.
Syn. commission, charge, intrust, delegate, authorize, accredit.

dep-u-tize (dĕp′ū-tīz), *v.t.* [*p.t.* and *p.p.* -tized (-tīzd), *p.pr.* -tiz″ing], to appoint as a deputy or agent.

dep-u-ty (dĕp′ū-tĭ), *n.* [*pl.* deputies (-tĭz)], one appointed to act for another; an agent; a delegate.

de-rail (dē-rāl′), *v.i.* to run off the rails:—*v.t.* to cause to leave, or run off, the rails; as, an open switch will *derail* a train. —*n.* **de-rail′ment.**

de-range (dē-rānj′), *v.t.* [*p.t.* and *p.p.* -ranged′ (-rānjd′), *p.pr.* -rang′ing], **1**, to disorder; confuse; disturb; **2**, to make insane.—*p.adj.* **de-ranged′.**

de-range-ment (dē-rānj′mĕnt), *n.* **1**, the act of putting out of order; also, a state of disorder; **2**, insanity.

der-by (dûr′bĭ; *Br.* där′bĭ), *n.* [*pl.* derbies (-bĭz)], a kind of stiff felt hat, with a dome-shaped crown and curved brim: **Derby**, a race, founded in 1780, for three-year-old horses, run annually at Epsom, England; hence, any of certain other races.

der-e-lict (dĕr′ē-lĭkt), *adj.* **1**, abandoned; adrift; **2**, negligent: unfaithful:—*n.* **1**, anything left, forsaken, or cast away intentionally, as at sea; as, the wrecked ship became a *derelict;* **2**, a social outcast.

der-e-lic-tion (dĕr″ē-lĭk′shŭn), *n.* **1**, neglect; omission, as of obligation or duty; **2**, abandonment.

de-ride (dē-rīd′), *v.t.* [*p.t.* and *p.p.* -rid′ed, *p.pr.* -rid′ing], to mock; laugh at:—*v.i.* to indulge in mockery, scorn, or ridicule.—*n.* **de-rid′er.**

de-rid-ing-ly (dē-rīd′ĭng-lĭ), *adv.* with mockery or scorn.

de-ris-i-ble (dē-rĭz′ĭ-bl), *adj.* open to scorn or ridicule.

de-ri-sion (dē-rĭzh′ŭn), *n.* **1**, the act of mocking; **2**, ridicule; scorn; contempt; **3**, that which is mocked.

Syn. disrespect, banter, mockery.—*Ant.* compliment, congratulation.

de-ri-sive (dē-rī′sĭv), *adj.* expressing ridicule or scorn.—*adj.* **de-ri′so-ry.** —*adv.* **de-ri′sive-ly.**—*n.* **de-ri′sive-ness.**

de-riv-a-ble (dē-rīv′ȧ-bl), *adj.* **1**, capable of being obtained from a source; as, the pleasure *derivable* from books; **2**, deducible, as from premises.

der-i-va-tion (dĕr″ĭ-vā′shŭn), *n.* **1**, the act of obtaining, or the condition of being obtained, from a definite source; **2**, the process of tracing a thing from its original source, esp. a word; as, the *derivation* of a word from the Latin; also, a brief statement of this; **3**, the source from which something is drawn.

Syn. origin, beginning, cause, root.

de-riv-a-tive (dē-rĭv′ȧ-tĭv), *adj.* obtained or taken from another; obtained from some other by a process of deduction; secondary:—*n.* **1**, a word formed from another; **2**, a modification of anything.

de-rive (dē-rīv′), *v.t.* [*p.t.* and *p.p.* -rived′ (-rīvd′), *p.pr.* -riv′ing], **1**, to draw from an original source; obtain by transmission or descent; **2**, to trace (a word) to its original root or stem; deduce; infer.

der-ma (dûr′mȧ), *n.* the true skin; also, skin in general. Also, **der′mis.**—*adj.* **der′mal.**—*adj.* **der′mic.**

der-ma-tol-o-gy (dûr″mȧ-tŏl′ō-jĭ), *n.* the science which treats of the skin and its diseases.—*n.* **der″ma-tol′o-gist.**—*adj.* **der″ma-to-log′i-cal.**

der-o-gate (dĕr′ō-gāt), *v.t.* [*p.t.* and *p.p.* -gat″ed, *p.pr.* -gat″ing], to detract from; lessen the value, etc., of; depreciate:—*v.i.* to take away; detract: with *from.* —*adj.* **de-rog′a-tive** (dē-rŏg′ȧ-tĭv).

der-o-ga-tion (dĕr″ō-gā′shŭn), *n.* the act of lessening in value; detraction; depreciation.

de-rog-a-to-ry (dē-rŏg′ȧ-tō-rĭ), *adj.* tending to degrade; belittling; disparaging.—*adv.* **de-rog′a-to-ri-ly.**

der-rick (dĕr′ĭk), *n.* a framework with ropes, gears, and pulleys, for lifting heavy weights.

der-ring do (dĕr′ĭng dōō″), *Archaic*, daring; valor; desperate courage; personal bravery.

der-rin-ger (dĕr′ĭn-jẽr), *n.* a pocket pistol with a short barrel of large caliber, effective at short range.

der-vish (dûr′vĭsh), *n.* a Mohammedan monk who professes extreme poverty, chastity, and humility.

des-cant (dĕs′kănt), *n.* **1**, a melody; a song with modulations; **2**, a discourse or series of remarks on one theme: —*v.i.* (dĕs-kănt′), to comment freely; talk in detail and at length.

de-scend (dē-sĕnd′), *v.i.* **1**, to go or come down from a higher to a lower position; **2**, to come or fall violently or in force; as, the army was ordered to *descend* upon the town; **3**, to be derived; come down in order of inheritance, or from one generation to another:—*v.i.* to go down or along.

de-scend-ant (dē-sĕn′dănt), *n.* one who is descended from a special ancestor; offspring; as, a *descendant* of the early Pilgrims:—*adj.* (preferably, *descendent*), **1**, coming down; falling; **2**, coming from an ancestor.

de-scent (dē-sĕnt′), *n.* **1**, change from a higher to a lower place; **2**, a sudden hostile invasion or attack; as, the *descent* of the enemy upon the coast; **3**, a coming from a common ancestor; birth; **4**, a downward slope; **5**, in music, a passage from a higher to a lower pitch.

Syn. declivity.—*Ant.* ascent, acclivity.

de-scribe (dē-skrīb′), *v.t.* [*p.t.* and *p.p.* -scribed′ (-skrībd′), *p.pr.* -scrib′ing], **1**, to give an account of; represent by words; set forth; **2**, to outline by drawing; as, to *describe* a square.—*n.* **de-scrib′er.**—*adj.* **de-scrib′a-ble.**

Syn. portray, illustrate, define. (See explain.)

de-scrip-tion (dē-skrĭp′shŭn), *n.* **1**, the act of giving an account of in words or writing; also, a picture in words; **2**, a class; sort; kind.

Syn. sketch, portrayal, relation, depiction.

de-scrip-tive (dē-skrĭp′tĭv), *adj.* tending, or serving, to picture in words.—*adv.* **de-scrip′tive-ly.**

de-scry (dē-skrī′), *v.t.* [*p.t.* and *p.p.* -scried′ (-skrīd′), *p.pr.* -scry′ing], to discover with the eye, esp. in the distance or through obscurity; discern.—*n.* **de-scri′er.**

des-e-crate (dĕs′ē-krāt), *v.t.* [*p.t.* and *p.p.* -crat″ed, *p.pr.* -crat″ing], to change from a sacred to a secular use; profane; as, to *desecrate* a holy place: opp. of *consecrate.*—*n.* **des′e-crat″er; des′e-cra″tor.**

des-e-cra-tion (dĕs″ē-krā′shŭn), *n.* the act of profanation; sacrilege; as, the *desecration* of a shrine.

[1]**de-sert** (dē-zûrt′), *v.t.* **1**, to forsake; abandon; **2**, to abandon (military service) without leave:—*v.i.* to run from duty; forsake a post.—*n.* **de-sert′er.**

Syn. leave, fail. (See abandon.)

[2]**de-sert** (dē-zûrt′), *n.*, often in *pl.*, a deserved reward or punishment.

Syn. due, worth, worthiness.

[3]**des-ert** (dĕz′ẽrt), *n.* **1**, a wilderness; solitude; esp., a vast expanse of dry, sandy waste; **2**, figuratively, anything unproductive or uninteresting:—*adj.* pertaining to a wilderness; waste; hence, figuratively, sterile.

de-ser-tion (dē-zûr′shŭn), *n.* **1**, the act of forsaking; a leaving of one's post; **2**, the state of being abandoned.

de-serve (dē-zûrv′), *v.t.* [*p.t.* and *p.p.* -served′ (-zûrvd′), *p.pr.* -serv′ing], to earn by service; be worthy of; merit: —*v.i.* to be worthy or deserving: usually with *well* or *ill.*—*n.* **de-serv′er.**

de-serv-ed-ly (dē-zûr′vĕd-lĭ), *adv.* justly; according to merit; as, he was *deservedly* punished.

de-serv-ing (dē-zûr′vĭng), *n.* worth; merit:—*p.adj.* worthy; as, a *deserving* student.—*adv.* **de-serv′ing-ly.**

des-ha-bille (dĕz″ȧ-bēl′), *n.* **1**, a loose, careless garment; **2**, the state of being partly or informally dressed. Also, **dis″ha-bille′**, *Pfd. S.*

des-ic-cate (dĕs′ĭ-kāt), *v.t.* [*p.t.* and *p.p.* -cat″ed, *p.pr.* -cat″ing], **1**, to dry thoroughly; dry up; **2**, to preserve by removing the moisture, as food:—*v.i.* to become dry.—*adj.* and *n.* **des′ic-ca-tive.**

des-ic-ca-tion (dĕs″ĭ-kā′shŭn), *n.* the act of drying; also, dryness.

des-ic-ca-tor (dĕs'ĭ-kā"tēr), *n.* an apparatus for drying foods, etc.

de-sid-er-a-tum (dē-sĭd"ēr-ā'tŭm), *n.* [*pl.* desiderata (-tȧ)], anything desired; a want, desire, or need generally felt and recognized.

de-sign (dē-zīn'), *v.t.* **1,** to draw, mark, or plan out, as a work of art; plan and draw in detail, as a house or bridge; **2,** to project; intend; set apart mentally; as, a nod *designed* to warn:—*v.i.* to make decorative plans or execute original work:—*n.* **1,** an outline; plan; drawing; **2,** project; intention; **3,** arrangement of details according to a plan.

Syn., n. delineation, sketch. (See plan.)

des-ig-nate (dĕs'ĭg-nāt; dĕz'ĭg-nāt), *v.t.* [*p.t.* and *p.p.* -nat"ed, *p.pr.* -nat"ing], **1,** to indicate by marks, lines, or a description, the limits of; point out; distinguish; **2,** to name; nominate; also, to indicate or set apart, as for a special purpose; **3,** to serve as a distinguishing or specifying modifier to; as, "dative" *designates* the case of the indirect object, or "dative case."—*adj.* **des'ig-na-tive.**—*n.* **des'ig-na"tor.**

des-ig-na-tion (dĕs"ĭg-nā'shŭn; dĕz"ĭg-), *n.* **1,** the act of naming or pointing out; indication; **2,** a distinctive mark or title; **3,** an appointment.

de-sign-ed-ly (dē-zīn'ĕd-lĭ), *adv.* intentionally; purposely.

de-sign-er (dē-zīn'ēr), *n.* **1,** one who makes plans or original sketches for decorations, works of art, etc.; **2,** a plotter; schemer.

de-sign-ing (dē-zīn'ĭng), *p.adj.* scheming; artful; cunning; wily:—*n.* **1,** the act or art of making sketches; **2,** the act of plotting.—*adv.* **de-sign'ing-ly.**

de-sir-a-bil-i-ty (dē-zīr"ȧ-bĭl'ĭ-tĭ), *n.* the state or quality of being pleasing or acceptable.—*n.* **de-sir'a-ble-ness.**

de-sir-a-ble (dē-zīr'ȧ-bl), *adj.* agreeable; pleasing.—*adv.* **de-sir'a-bly.**

Syn. advisable, acceptable, proper, beneficial, advantageous, profitable.—*Ant.* disagreeable, displeasing.

de-sire (dē-zīr'), *v.t.* [*p.t.* and *p.p.* -sired' (-zīrd'), *p.pr.* -sir'ing], **1,** to wish earnestly for; crave; **2,** to express a wish for; ask for; as, I *desire* that you go:—*n.* **1,** a longing for the possession of some object; an earnest wish; **2,** a petition or prayer; **3,** the object longed for; **4,** passion; lust.

Syn., n. wish, longing. Of the three words, *wish* is the most general; as, "if *wishes* were horses, beggars might ride"; a *wish* is often directed toward something that cannot be obtained; as, a *wish* for blue eyes. *Desire* expresses a stronger feeling and usually for something attainable; as, a *desire* to excel. *Longing* is a still stronger term; it implies something wished for which is far off but may come sometime; as, a *longing* for an education; a *longing* for home.

de-sir-ous (dē-zīr'ŭs), *adj.* full of a wish or longing; solicitous; anxious; as, he was *desirous* to please others.

de-sist (dē-zĭst'; dē-sĭst'), *v.i.* to cease; stop; as, *desist* from evil.

Syn. discontinue, quit, abstain.—*Ant.* continue, persist, persevere.

desk (dĕsk), *n.* **1,** a frame or table for reading or writing upon; **2,** a pulpit or public reading stand.

des-o-late (dĕs'ō-lāt), *v.t.* [*p.t.* and *p.p.* -lat"ed, *p.pr.* -lat"ing], **1,** to lay waste; **2,** to deprive of inhabitants; **3,** to overwhelm with sorrow; **4,** to forsake:—*adj.* (dĕs'ō-lāt), **1,** deprived of inhabitants; abandoned; **2,** in a condition of neglect or ruin; **3,** forlorn; miserable.—*adv.* **des'o-late-ly.**—*n.* **des'o-late-ness.**—*n.* **des'o-lat"er; des'o-la"tor.**

Syn., adj. lonely, forsaken, deserted, waste, bleak; bereaved.—*Ant., adj.* pleasant, comfortable, cheerful, bright, glad.

des-o-la-tion (dĕs"ō-lā'shŭn), *n.* **1,** the act of laying waste; **2,** the state of being laid waste or abandoned; **3,** a solitude; ruin; destruction; **4,** affliction; misery; melancholy.

Syn. unhappiness, sadness.—*Ant.* happiness, comfort, pleasure.

de-spair (dē-spâr'), *v.i.* to abandon all hope or expectation; become hopeless:—*n.* **1,** loss of hope or confidence; hopelessness; **2,** that which causes loss of hope or which is looked upon as hopeless.—*p.adj.* **de-spair'ing.**—*adv.* **de-spair'ing-ly.**

Syn., n. discouragement, desperation, despondency, dejection.

des-patch (dĕs-păch'), *v.t.* **1,** to send off quickly; **2,** to put to death; **3,** to finish quickly:—*n.* **1,** a sending off; **2,** death; **3,** speedy performance; celerity; promptness; **4,** a quick message, as a telegram; **5,** a government document sent to a minister abroad. Also, **dis-patch'**, *Pfd. S.*

des-patch-er (dĕs-păch'ēr), *n.* one who sends something off promptly or at the right time; as, a train *despatcher.* Also, **dis-patch'er,** *Pfd. S.*

des-per-a-do (dĕs"pēr-ā'dō), *n.* [*pl.* desperadoes; desperados (-dōz)], a bold and reckless criminal.

des-per-ate (dĕs'pēr-āt), *adj.* **1,** without regard to danger; reckless; **2,** proceeding from despair; furious; frantic; as, in this crisis they used *desperate* means; **3,** beyond hope or cure.—*adv.* **des'per-ate-ly.**—*n.* **des'per-ate-ness.**

des-per-a-tion (dĕs"pēr-ā'shŭn), *n.* the state of being without hope, and frantic; the recklessness of despair.

des-pi-ca-ble (dĕs'pĭ-kȧ-bl), *adj.* contemptible; mean; fit to be looked down upon.—*adv.* **des'pi-ca-bly.**—*n.* **des'pi-ca-ble-ness.**

de-spise (dē-spīz'), *v.t.* [*p.t.* and *p.p.* -spised' (-spīzd'), *p.pr.* -spis'ing], to look down upon; scorn; disdain.—*n.* **de-spis'er.**

Syn. abhor, disregard, spurn, slight.

de-spite (dē-spīt'), *n.* **1,** extreme contempt; malicious anger; scorn; hatred; **2,** an act of malice or hatred:—*v.t.* [*p.t.* and *p.p.* -spit'ed, *p.pr.* -spit'ing], to despise:—*prep.* notwithstanding.

de-spite-ful (dē-spīt'fo͝ol), *adj.* malicious; insulting; malignant.—*adv.* **de-spite'ful-ly.**—*n.* **de-spite'ful-ness.**

de-spoil (dē-spoil'), *v.t.* to rob; deprive of belongings.—*n.* **de-spoil'er.**

de-spond (dē-spŏnd'), *v.i.* to be cast down in spirits; be greatly depressed.—*p.adj.* **de-spond'ing.**—*adv.* **de-spond'ing-ly.**

de-spond-en-cy (dē-spŏn'dĕn-sĭ), *n.* absence of hope or courage; mental depression.—*n.* **de-spond'ence.**

de-spond-ent (dē-spŏn'dĕnt), *adj.* without hope; deeply depressed.—*adv.* **de-spond'ent-ly.**

Syn. hopeless, dejected, discouraged, blue.

des-pot (dĕs'pŏt), *n.* an absolute ruler; tyrant; as, Nero was a *despot.*

des-pot-ic (dĕs-pŏt'ĭk), *adj.* absolute in power; arbitrary; tyrannical. Also, **des-pot'i-cal.**—*adv.* **des-pot'i-cal-ly.**

des-pot-ism (dĕs'pŏt-ĭzm), *n.* **1,** absolute power or government; **2,** tyranny; any absolute control.

des-sert (dĕ-zûrt'), *n.* a course of fruits, nuts, or sweets, such as pastry or pudding, served last at dinner.

des-ti-na-tion (dĕs"tĭ-nā'shŭn), *n.* **1,** a purposed end or object;

ultimate or final design; goal; **2**, the stated end of a journey; **3**, the act of appointing for any purpose or end.

des-tine (dĕs′tĭn), *v.t.* [*p.t.* and *p.p.* -tined (-tĭnd), *p.pr.* -tin-ing], **1**, to appoint to any purpose or end; **2**, to settle the future use of; foreordain.

des-ti-ny (dĕs′tĭ-nĭ), *n.* [*pl.* destinies (-nĭz)], **1**, fate; inevitable or unavoidable necessity; **2**, lot; fortune.
Syn. decree, doom, end.

des-ti-tute (dĕs′tĭ-tūt), *adj.* **1**, without means; penniless; **2**, being wholly without something needed; lacking; as, *destitute* of courage.

des-ti-tu-tion (dĕs″tĭ-tū′shŭn), *n.* extreme poverty; want; lack.
Syn. indigence, penury. (See poverty.)

de-stroy (dē-stroi′), *v.t.* **1**, to pull down; overturn; lay waste; render desolate; **2**, to kill; put an end to; **3**, to render void; as, his acts *destroyed* his influence.
Syn. ruin, demolish. These words agree in the idea of breaking or tearing down. *Destroy* is the most general term, with the idea of unbuilding; as, the library was *destroyed* by fire. *Ruin* often means to bring about a state of total loss or uselessness; as, rain *ruined* her hat. To *demolish* is to pull or throw down; as, the building was *demolished* by the earthquake.

de-stroy-er (dē-stroi′ẽr), *n.* **1**, one who or that which spoils or puts an end to something; **2**, a war vessel for destroying torpedo boats or submarines.

de-struct-i-ble (dē-strŭk′tĭ-bl), *adj.* capable of being spoiled or laid waste.—*n.* **de-struct″i-bil′i-ty.**

de-struc-tion (dē-strŭk′shŭn), *n.* **1**, the act of ruining, or the state of being ruined; **2**, a cause of ruin.
Syn. desolation, downfall, havoc.

de-struc-tive (dē-strŭk′tĭv), *adj.* **1**, deadly; tending to, or causing, desolation; ruinous; hurtful; as, a *destructive* epidemic; a *destructive* fire; **2**, refuting without correcting; merely negative; as, *destructive* criticism: opp. of *constructive.*—*adv.* **de-struc′tive-ly.**—*n.* **de-struc′tive-ness.**
Syn. detrimental, noxious, injurious.

des-ue-tude (dĕs′wē-tūd), *n.* the passing into disuse, as of a custom, practice, or fashion; discontinuance.

des-ul-to-ry (dĕs′ŭl-tō-rĭ), *adj.* passing from one thing to another without order or method; aimless; erratic.—*adv.* **des′ul-to-ri-ly.**—*n.* **des′ul-to-ri-ness.**
Syn. rambling, discursive, loose, unmethodical, disconnected, fitful.—*Ant.* thorough, coherent, methodical.

de-tach (dē-tăch′), *v.t.* **1**, to separate; disconnect; **2**, to detail for a special purpose; as, to *detach* men to guard a pass.—*adj.* **de-tach′a-ble.**
Syn. sever, disjoin, disengage, abstract, disunite.—*Ant.* unite, connect, join.

de-tach-ment (dē-tăch′mĕnt), *n.* **1**, the act of separating; **2**, the thing separated; **3**, a body of troops, or certain ships, separated from the main body and sent on special service; **4**, absence of bias; as, to consider the case with *detachment;* **5**, absent-mindedness; aloofness; as, he was present, but his *detachment* was plain.

de-tail (dē-tāl′), *v.t.* **1**, to relate minutely; enumerate; **2**, to tell off for a given duty:—*n.* (dē-tāl′; dē′tāl), **1**, an item; **2**, a particular or minute account; **3**, a small detachment (of troops) for special service; **4**, in *pl.*, minute parts of a picture, statue, etc.

de-tain (dē-tān′), *v.t.* **1**, to hold back; restrain from departure; delay; **2**, to keep in custody.—*n.* **de-tain′ment.**

de-tain-er (dē-tān′ẽr), *n.* **1**, one who holds back; **2**, a writ for holding a person in custody or under arrest.

de-tect (dē-tĕkt′), *v.t.* to discover (something obscure); bring to light; expose; find out.—*adj.* **de-tect′a-ble; de-tect′i-ble.**—*n.* **de-tect′er.**

de-tec-tion (dē-tĕk′shŭn), *n.* the act of finding out, or its result.

de-tec-tive (dē-tĕk′tĭv), *n.* a person who investigates crimes and mysteries:—*adj.* **1**, employed, or skilled, in exposing or finding out; **2**, pertaining to detection.

de-tec-tor (dē-tĕk′tẽr), *n.* **1**, one who or that which finds out; a discoverer; **2**, a device for detecting: **crystal detector**, in radio, a special type of detector, consisting of a mineral with the property of allowing currents of electricity to pass in one direction more readily than in the other, together with a means of making electrical contact with its surface.

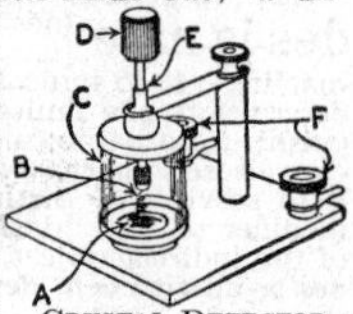

CRYSTAL DETECTOR
A, crystal; B, fine wire, or cat whisker; C, dust-proof glass container; D, adjusting handle; E, slip joint; F, binding post.

de-ten-tion (dē-tĕn′shŭn), *n.* **1**, the act of keeping back or withholding; **2**, confinement; restraint; **3**, delay.

de-ter (dē-tûr′), *v.t.* [*p.t.* and *p.p.* -terred′ (-tûrd′), *p.pr.* -ter′ring], to discourage, or hinder, as by fear; restrain; dishearten.

de-ter-gent (dē-tûr′jĕnt), *n.* a cleansing substance, as soap; a cleansing disinfectant for wounds, etc.:—*adj.* having cleansing qualities.

de-te-ri-o-rate (dē-tē′rĭ-ō-rāt), *v.t.* [*p.t.* and *p.p.* -rat″ed, *p.pr.* -rat″ing], to reduce to a lower quality or value:—*v.i.* to grow worse.—*n.* **de-te″ri-o-ra′tion.**

de-ter-mi-na-ble (dē-tûr′mĭ-nȧ-bl), *adj.* **1**, capable of being decided; **2**, capable of being found out.

de-ter-mi-nant (dē-tûr′mĭ-nănt), *adj.* causing a decision:—*n.* that which serves to settle, decide, or establish.

de-ter-mi-nate (dē-tûr′mĭ-nāt), *adj.* **1**, having definite or fixed limits; clearly defined; specific; **2**, positive; decisive; conclusive.—*adv.* **de-ter′mi-nate-ly.**—*n.* **de-ter′mi-nate-ness.**

de-ter-mi-na-tion (dē-tûr″mĭ-nā′shŭn), *n.* **1**, the act of deciding; **2**, the state of being firm in decisions; purpose; resolution; **3**, measurement, as of iron in ore.
Syn. firmness, decision, resolve.—*Ant.* hesitation, indecision, vacillation.

de-ter-mi-na-tive (dē-tûr′mĭ-nā-tĭv), *adj.* qualifying, limiting, or defining:—*n.* that which indicates the quality of something else.

de-ter-mine (dē-tûr′mĭn), *v.i.* [*p.t.* and *p.p.* -mined (-mĭnd), *p.pr.* -min-ing], **1**, to reach a decision; **2**, in law, to come to an end; expire:—*v.t.* **1**, to fix or settle the bounds of; **2**, to put an end to; settle, as a dispute; **3**, to restrict; **4**, to decide; resolve; **5**, to decree.—*n.* **de-ter′min-er.**

de-ter-mined (dē-tûr′mĭnd), *p.adj.* resolute; decided.—*adv.* **de-ter′mined-ly** (dē-tûr′mĭnd-lĭ; -mĭn-ĕd-lĭ).

de-ter-rent (dē-tĕr′ĕnt; dē-tûr′ĕnt), *adj.* serving, or tending, to prevent or hinder:—*n.* that which prevents; as, the fear of punishment is thought to be a *deterrent* from crime.

de-test (dē-tĕst′), *v.t.* to hate intensely; abhor; abominate; loathe.

de-test-a-ble (dē-tĕs′tȧ-bl), *adj.* worthy of being loathed; hateful. —*adv.* **de-test′a-bly.**—*n.* **de-test′a-ble-ness.**
Syn. odious, loathsome, abominable.—*Ant.* likable, attractive, pleasing.

de-tes-ta-tion (dē″tĕs-tā′shŭn; dĕt″ĕs-), *n.* **1,** extreme dislike or abhorrence; loathing; **2,** that which is abhorred.

de-throne (dē-thrōn′), *v.t.* [*p.t.* and *p.p.* -throned′ (-thrōnd′), *p.pr.* -thron′ing], to remove from a throne; deprive of authority or power.—*n.* **de-throne′ment.**

det-o-nate (dĕt′ō-nāt; dē′tō-nāt), *v.t.* [*p.t.* and *p.p.* -nat″ed, *p.pr.* -nat″ing], to cause to explode with a loud and sudden report, as a firecracker:—*v.i.* to explode loudly and suddenly.—*n.* **det″o-na′tion.**

det-o-na-tor (dĕt′ō-nā″tẽr), *n.* **1,** a substance that explodes a percussion cap; **2,** a device in a bomb that explodes the charge.

de-tour (dē-tŏŏr′), *n.* a roundabout way; esp., a path or road that leads around an obstruction in a main road; as, he made a *detour* to avoid an unsafe bridge.

de-tract (dē-trăkt′), *v.t.* **1,** to draw or take away; withdraw; subtract; **2,** to defame; disparage; as, he tries to *detract* his enemy:—*v.i.* to take away a part, esp. of reputation or credit: with *from.*—*adj.* **de-trac′tive.**
Syn. malign, disparage, slander.

de-trac-tion (dē-trăk′shŭn), *n.* depreciation; defamation; slander.

de-trac-tor (dē-trăk′tẽr), *n.* one who takes away something; esp., a slanderer or defamer.

de-train (dē-trān′), *v.t.* to discharge from a railroad train, as troops:—*v.i.* to leave a train, as troops.

det-ri-ment (dĕt′rĭ-mĕnt), *n.* **1,** that which injures or reduces in value; **2,** injury; damage; loss; harm.

det-ri-men-tal (dĕt″rĭ-mĕn′tăl), *adj.* injurious; hurtful; damaging.—*adv.* **det″ri-men′tal-ly.**

de-tri-tus (dē-trī′tŭs), *n.* **1,** accumulations arising from fragments of rocks broken or worn away; **2,** any débris; waste. —*adj.* **de-tri′tal.**

***de trop** (dē trō′), [Fr.], too much; hence, not wanted; unwelcome.

Deu-ca-li-on (dū-kā′lĭ-ŏn), *n.* in mythology, the husband of Pyrrha. These two survived the Deluge and peopled the earth once more.

¹deuce (dūs), *n.* **1,** a card or die bearing two spots; **2,** in lawn tennis, a score of forty on each side.

²deuce (dūs), *n.* **1,** the devil: chiefly as an exclamation, preceded by *the;* **2,** hence, mischief; damage; havoc; as, to play the *deuce* with one's plans.—*adj.* **deu′ced** (dū′sĕd; dūst).—*adv.* **deu′ced-ly** (dū′sĕd-lĭ).

Deu-ter-on-o-my (dū″tẽr-ŏn′ō-mĭ), *n.* the fifth book of the Old Testament, in which the law of Moses is stated a second time.—*abbr.* **Deut.**

dev-as-tate (dĕv′ȧs-tāt), *v.t.* [*p.t.* and *p.p.* -tat″ed, *p.pr.* -tat″ing], to lay waste; desolate; ravage; as, the fire *devastated* the town.—*n.* **dev′as-ta″tor.**

dev-as-ta-tion (dĕv″ȧs-tā′shŭn), *n.* a laying waste; destruction.

de-vel-op (dē-vĕl′ŏp), *v.t.* **1,** to unfold gradually; make known in detail; **2,** to make more complete; **3,** to cause to grow; **4,** to treat (a photographic plate or film) with chemicals so as to bring out the picture:—*v.i.* **1,** to advance from one stage to another; **2,** to become gradually apparent.
Syn. evolve, amplify, expand, enlarge.

de-vel-op-er (dē-vĕl′ŏp-ẽr), *n.* **1,** one that causes to grow or unfold gradually; **2,** a chemical mixture for bringing out the picture on plates, films, or prints.

de-vel-op-ment (dē-vĕl′ŏp-mĕnt), *n.* the act of unfolding; growth; expansion.—*adj.* **de-vel″op-men′tal.**

de-vi-ate (dē′vĭ-āt), *v.i.* [*p.t.* and *p.p.* -at″ed, *p.pr.* -at″ing], **1,** to turn aside; diverge; wander; **2,** to digress; as, to *deviate* from the argument:—*v.t.* to change the direction or position of.—*n.* **de′vi-a″tor.**—*n.* **de″vi-a′tion.**
Syn. swerve, deflect. (See wander.)

de-vice (dē-vīs′), *n.* **1,** a scheme; invention; trick; stratagem; **2,** a fanciful design or pattern; **3,** a heraldic emblem.
Syn. artifice, expedient, instrument.

dev-il (dĕv′l), *n.* **1,** (usually, *Devil*), the evil spirit; Satan: often used as an oath or expletive; **2,** a false god or demon; **3,** an excessively wicked person; **4,** an unfortunate person; as, the poor *devil* deserves pity; **5,** a daring or reckless person; **6,** an expletive; **7,** a printer's helper; **8,** any of various machines, as one for shredding rags in paper making:—*v.t.* [*p.t.* and *p.p.* dev′iled (-ld), *p.pr.* dev′il-ing], *Colloq.,* to plague, torment, or tease.—*n.* **dev′il-kin.**

dev-il-fish (dĕv′l-fĭsh″), *n.* **1,** any of various odd-shaped sea fishes, as the toadfish; **2,** the giant octopus.

dev-il-ish (dĕv′l-ĭsh), *adj.* diabolical; extremely wicked; infernal:—*adv. Colloq.,* excessively; extremely.—*adv.* **dev′il-ish-ly.**—*n.* **dev′il-ish-ness.**

dev-il-ment (dĕv′l-mĕnt), *n.* roguishness; mischief, often without evil intent; as, up to some *devilment.*

dev-il-ry (dĕv′l-rĭ), *n.* [*pl.* devilries (-rĭz)], wanton mischief; diabolical wickedness; spiteful pranks.

dev-il-try (dĕv′l-trĭ), *n.* [*pl.* deviltries (-trĭz)], wanton mischief; devilry: often used humorously.

de-vi-ous (dē′vĭ-ŭs), *adj.* **1,** indirect; rambling; circuitous or roundabout; **2,** straying from the way of right and duty.—*adv.* **de′vi-ous-ly.**—*n.* **de′vi-ous-ness.**

de-vis-a-ble (dē-vīz′ȧ-bl), *adj.* **1,** capable of being imagined or invented; **2,** capable of being given by will.

de-vise (dē-vīz′), *v.t.* [*p.t.* and *p.p.* -vised′ (-vīzd′), *p.pr.* -vis′ing], **1,** to imagine; scheme; contrive; concoct; **2,** to bequeath or give by will:—*v.i.* to plan; scheme:—*n.* **1,** a gift of real property by will; **2,** a will.—*n.* **de-vis′er.**—*n.* **de-vis′al.**
Syn., v. discover, invent.

dev-i-see (dĕv″ĭ-zē′; dē-vīz″ē′), *n.* the person to whom a bequest or gift by will has been made.

de-vi-sor (dē-vī′zŏr; dē-vī′zôr), *n.* one who bequeaths or gives by will.

de-vi-tal-ize (dē-vī′tăl-īz), *v.t.* [*p.t.* and *p.p.* -ized (-īzd), *p.pr.* -iz″ing], to deprive of life or power; destroy the vitality of; make lifeless.

de-void (dē-void′), *adj.* entirely without; lacking; as, *devoid* of sense.
Syn. void, wanting, unendowed, empty.

de-voir (dē-vwär′; dē-vwôr′; dĕv′wŏr), [Fr.], *n.,* usually in *pl.,* a service or duty owed; an act of courtesy or respect.

de-volve (dē-vŏlv′), *v.t.* [*p.t.* and *p.p.* -volved′ (-vŏlvd′), *p.pr.* -volv′ing], to hand on or down; pass or transfer from one to another; transmit; as, to *devolve* a duty upon another:—*v.i.* to be handed down or over; as, the duty *devolved* upon him.

de-vote (dē-vōt′), *v.t.* [*p.t.* and *p.p.* -vot′ed, *p.pr.* -vot′ing], **1,** to dedicate or consecrate; **2,** to doom; as, to *devote* to ruin; **3,** to give up wholly to; as, to *devote* a son to the church; apply (oneself) to some object.

de-vot-ed (dē-vōt′ĕd), *p.adj.* **1,** wholly given up to; attached; as, a *devoted* mother; **2,** dedicated; **3,** doomed.—*adv.* **de-vot′ed-ly.**—*n.* **de-vot′ed-ness.**

dev-o-tee (dĕv″ō-tē′), *n.* one entirely given up to a special interest; one zealous in religion; an enthusiast.

de-vo-tion (dē-vō′shŭn), *n.* **1,** the act of dedicating, or the state of being dedicated; **2,** strong affection; ardent love; as, the *devotion* of a mother; **3,** usually in *pl.*, religious worship; piety; prayer.

de-vo-tion-al (dē-vō′shŭn-ăl), *adj.* **1,** devout; **2,** expressing piety or worship; as, the meeting was opened with a *devotional* service.—*adv.* **de-vo′tion-al-ly.**

de-vour (dē-vour′), *v.t.* **1,** to swallow greedily or ravenously; **2,** to consume or destroy rapidly; annihilate; as, flames *devour* a building; **3,** to take in eagerly with ears or eyes; as, to *devour* the news.

de-vout (dē-vout′), *adj.* **1,** devoted to religious thoughts and exercises; **2,** expressing piety; as, *devout* exercises; **3,** sincere; earnest; as, a *devout* prayer.—*adv.* **de-vout′ly.**—*n.* **de-vout′ness.**

dew (dū), *n.* **1,** moisture from the atmosphere deposited in small drops; **2,** that which falls lightly and refreshingly.

dew-claw (dū′klô″), *n.* **1,** the little inner claw of a dog's foot; **2,** a false hoof, as of a deer.

dew-drop (dū′drŏp″), *n.* a small drop of moisture from the air.

dew-lap (dū′lăp″), *n.* the fold of skin that hangs from the neck of an ox, a cow, or a dog.

dew-y (dū′ĭ), *adj.* [*comp.* dew′i-er, *superl.* dew′i-est], moist with dew; looking as if covered with dew.—*n.* **dew′i-ness.**

dex-ter (dĕks′tẽr), *adj.* right; as, the *dexter* hand: applied in heraldry to the side of an escutcheon on the bearer's right, the beholder's left: opp. of *sinister* .

dex-ter-i-ty (dĕks-tĕr′ĭ-tĭ), *n.* skill with the hands; physical skill; mental or physical adroitness; cleverness.

Syn. aptitude, expertness, readiness, skill.

dex-ter-ous (dĕks′tẽr-ŭs), *adj.* skilful with the hands; possessing physical skill; quick, mentally or physically; adroit; clever; as, the game was won by a *dexterous* turn of the wrist. Also, **dex′trous.**—*adv.* **dex′ter-ous-ly.**—*n.* **dex′ter-ous-ness.**

Syn. deft, expert, handy. (See clever.)

dex-tral (dĕks′trăl), *adj.* pertaining to the right side or hand: opp. of *sinistral.*—*adv.* **dex′tral-ly.**—*n.* **dex-tral′i-ty.**

dex-trin (dĕks′trĭn), *adj.* a white substance closely related to starch: used as an adhesive, etc. Also, **dex′trine.**

dex-trose (dĕks′trōs), *n.* a simple variety of sugar found in most plants.

dey (dā), *n.* the former title of the governor of Algiers, in northern Africa, and of the chief of the Janizaries.

¹di- (dī-; dĭ-), *prefix,* **1,** two; twofold; double; as, *di*graph; *di*pterous: used in chemistry to indicate two atoms, radicals, groups, or equivalents; as, *di*oxide; **2,** a form of *dia-* used before a word beginning with a vowel.

²di- (dī-; dĭ-), *prefix,* apart; away; from; as, *di*vert; *di*late; *di*rect.

di-a- (dī′ȧ-), *prefix,* [before a vowel, *di-*], **1,** through; across; as, *dia*meter; *dia*phanous; **2,** apart; as, *dia*lysis; **3,** thoroughly; completely: used intensively; as, *dia*gnosis.

di-a-be-tes (dī″ȧ-bē′tēz), *n.* a disease of the kidneys.—*adj.* and *n.* **di″a-bet′ic** (dī″ȧ-bĕt′ĭk; dī″ȧ-bē′tĭk).

di-a-bol-ic (dī″ȧ-bŏl′ĭk), *adj.* devilish; outrageously wicked; impious. Also, **di″a-bol′i-cal.**—*adv.* **di″a-bol′i-cal-ly.**

di-a-crit-ic (dī″ȧ-krĭt′ĭk), *adj.* serving to separate or distinguish:—*n.* a mark used to distinguish the sounds of letters; a diacritical mark.

di-a-crit-i-cal (dī″ȧ-krĭt′ĭ-kăl), *adj.* serving to separate or distinguish, as a mark or sign: **diacritical mark,** a mark used to distinguish particular sounds of letters and to indicate their true pronunciation, as in ä, ō.—*adv.* **di″a-crit′i-cal-ly.**

di-a-dem (dī′ȧ-dĕm), *n.* **1,** a crown; tiara as, the *diadem* is the symbol of royalty; **2,** the power of royalty; sovereignty.

di-ær-e-sis (dī-ĕr′ē-sĭs; *Br.* dī-ē′rē-sĭs), *n.* [*pl.* diæreses (-sēz)], **1,** a mark [¨] over the second of two adjacent vowels to show that each has a separate sound in pronunciation, as in *coöperate, naïve;* **2** the division of a sound originally a diphthong into two vowels, as in *aëroplane, aërodrome.* Also, **di-er′e-sis.**

di-ag-nose (dī″ăg-nōs′; dī″ăg-nōz′), *v.t.* [*p.t.* and *p.p.* -nosed′ (-nōst′, -nōzd′), *p.pr.* -nos′ing], to determine the nature of, as a disease, by its general symptoms; as, the doctor was asked to *diagnose* the case.

di-ag-no-sis (dī″ăg-nō′sĭs), *n.* [*pl.* diagnoses (-sēz)], **1,** the recognition of a disease by its symptoms; **2,** any explanation based on an examination of facts.—*adj.* and *n.* **di″ag-nos′tic.**

di-ag-o-nal (dī-ăg′ō-năl), *adj.* **1,** slanting; oblique; **2,** having oblique lines; **3,** in geometry, extending from one angle to another not adjacent:—*n.* **1,** anything lying in an oblique direction; **2,** material having an oblique pattern; **3,** a straight line drawn from any angle of a polygon or polyhedron to any other angle not adjacent.—*adv.* **di-ag′o-nal-ly.**

DIAGONAL

di-a-gram (dī′ȧ-grăm), *n.* **1,** a geometrical figure; **2,** a mechanical plan; **3,** an outline, drawing, or figure; as, a *diagram* of rooms:—*v.t.* to illustrate by, or put in the form of, an outline or drawing; as, to *diagram* a house.

di-a-gram-mat-ic (dī″ȧ-grȧ-măt′ĭk), *adj.* pertaining to, or shown by, an outline or drawing. Also, **di″a-gram-mat′i-cal.**

di-al (dī′ăl), *n.* **1,** a flat surface on which a pointer casts a shadow in such a way as to show time by the sun; **2,** the face of a watch, clock, or the like; **3,** any plate on which a pointer marks revolutions, direction, pressure, or the like, as a miner's compass; **4,** in some telephones, a movable disk by means of which connections may be made without giving the number to a central operator:—*v.t.* **1,** to measure or indicate by a dial; **2,** to survey with a miner's compass; **3,** in telephoning, to call (a subscriber's number, or the like) by operating the movable dial.

di-a-lect (dī′ȧ-lĕkt), *n.* **1,** the peculiar manner in which a language is spoken in a province or district of a country; idiom; **2,** trade cant.—*abbr.* **dial.**—*adj.* **di″a-lec′tal.**

Syn. tongue, speech. (See language.)

di-a-lec-tic (dī″ȧ-lĕk′tĭk), *adj.* **1,** pertaining to the art of debate, **2,** pertaining to a peculiar style of speech: **dialectics,** *n.pl.* used as *sing.* **1,** the art of debating; **2,** logic; argumentation. Also, *adj.* **di″a-lec′ti-cal.**—*n.* **di″a-lec-ti′cian.**

di-a-log (dī′ȧ-lŏg), *n.* **1,** a conversation between two or more persons; **2,** a literary composition in which persons are represented as reasoning on, or discussing, a subject. Also, **di′a-logue.**

di-al-y-sis (dī-ăl′ĭ-sĭs), *n.* [*pl.* dialyses (-sēz)], **1**, separation; disorganization; **2**, in chemistry, a process by which a soluble substance, such as sugar, may be separated from a mixture of liquids containing colloids, such as albumin, gum, etc., by diffusion through a parchment or other membrane.

di-a-mag-net-ism (dī″ȧ-măg′nĕt-ĭzm), *n.* the property possessed by certain bodies when under the influence of magnetism, and freely suspended, of taking a position at right angles to the magnetic meridian.—*adj.* **di″a-mag-net′ic.**

di-am-e-ter (dī-ăm′ē-tẽr), *n.* **1**, a straight line through the center of a figure, dividing it in half; **2**, the length of a straight line through the center of a circle, sphere, etc.; as, the *diameter* of the earth is 7,926 miles; hence, thickness: **3**, the distance through the lower part of the shaft of a column.—*abbr.* **diam.**—*adj.* **di-am′e-tral.**

di-a-met-ri-cal (dī″ȧ-mĕt′rĭ-kăl), *adj.* **1**, pertaining to a diameter; **2**, directly opposite; as far apart as possible.—*adv.* **di″a-met′ri-cal-ly.**

di-a-mond (dī′ȧ-mŭnd), *n.* **1**, a brilliant, usually colorless, precious stone; crystallized carbon, the hardest known substance; **2**, a plane figure, with four equal straight lines, and two acute and two obtuse angles (see *quadrilateral*, illus.); **3**, a playing card stamped with red figures of this shape; **4**, a glass cutter's tool; **5**, in baseball, the space inside the lines connecting the bases; **6**, a very small size of type, nearly equivalent to 4½ point (see *type*):—*adj.* resembling, or made of, diamond.

Di-an-a (dī-ăn′ȧ; dī-ā′nȧ), *n.* in Roman mythology, goddess of the moon and of the hunt, twin sister of Apollo: identified with the Greek *Artemis.*

di-a-pa-son (dī″ȧ-pā′zŏn), *n.* **1**, the entire compass of a voice or instrument; **2**, harmony of voices or instruments; **3**, a recognized musical standard of pitch; **4**, the foundation stops of an organ.

di-a-per (dī′ȧ-pẽr), *n.* **1**, cotton or linen cloth woven in geometric patterns; **2**, a cloth for an infant's breech; **3**, a fabric decoration of one or more simple figures repeated:—*v.t.* to embroider; work or ornament in a geometric pattern.

di-aph-a-nous (dī-ăf′ȧ-nŭs), *adj.* gauzy; filmy; transparent; as, she wore a *diaphanous* garment.

di-a-phragm (dī′ȧ-frăm), *n.* **1**, any thin sheet or film that separates or divides; **2**, the muscular partition which divides the chest from the abdomen; **3**, the vibrating disk, as in a telephone; **4**, in a camera, optical instrument, etc., a perforated device for regulating the admission of light.—*adj.* **di″a-phrag-mat′ic** (-frăg-măt′ĭk).

di-a-rist (dī′ȧ-rĭst), *n.* one who keeps a record of daily events.

di-ar-rhe-a (dī″ȧ-rē′ȧ), *n.* a looseness of the bowels. Also, **di″ar-rhœ′a.**—*adj.* **di″ar-rhe′al.**—*adj.* **di″ar-rhet′ic.**

di-a-ry (dī′ȧ-rĭ), *n.* [*pl.* diaries (-rĭz)], **1**, a record of daily events; **2**, a book for daily memoranda.

di-a-stase (dī′ȧ-stās), *n.* a soluble white compound which acts as a ferment, formed in germinating grain and animal fluids, and having the property of converting starch into dextrin and sugar.

di-as-to-le (dī-ăs′tō-lē), *n.* **1**, the rhythmical expansion and dilatation of the heart, esp. of the ventricles, alternating with the systole, or contraction, with which it forms the pulse or heart beat; **2**, the lengthening of a syllable naturally short: opp. of *systole.*—*adj.* **di″as-tol′ic.**

di-a-ton-ic (dī″ȧ-tŏn′ĭk), *adj.* in music, designating a major or minor scale of eight tones, which divides the octave into seven intervals in any of the several standard ways.—*adv.* **di″a-ton′i-cal-ly.**

di-a-tribe (dī′ȧ-trīb), *n.* an abusive speech or discourse; bitter criticism.

dib-ble (dĭb′l), *n.* a pointed gardening tool for making holes in the earth:—*v.t.* [*p.t.* and *p.p.* -bled (-ld), *p.pr.* -bling], to plant with a dibble:—*v.i.* to dip bait gently into the water.

dice (dīs), *n.pl.* [*sing.* die (dī)], small cubes marked on the sides with one to six spots: used in games of chance:—*v.i.* [*p.t.* and *p.p.* diced (dīst), *p.pr.* dic′ing], to play with dice:—*v.t.* **1**, to decorate with woven patterns to resemble cubes; **2**, to cut into cubes or squares.—*n.* **dic′er.**

dic-ing (dīs′ĭng), *n.* **1**, gaming or playing with dice; **2**, ornamentation with squares or cubes.

dick-er (dĭk′ẽr), *v.i.* *U.S. Colloq.*, to barter or trade on a small scale; as, to *dicker* with a salesman over the price of eggs.

dick-ey (dĭk′ĭ), *n.* [*pl.* dickeys (-ĭz)], **1**, a small, separate shirt front; **2**, a seat at the back of a coach; **3**, a child's bib or pinafore; **4**, a small bird: also called *dickey bird.* Also, **dick′y** [*pl.* dickies (-ĭz)].

di-cot-y-le-don (dī-kŏt″ĭ-lē′dŭn), *n.* a plant having two cotyledons, or seed leaves.

dic-ta-phone (dĭk′tȧ-fōn), *n.* a trade name for an instrument like a phonograph, used to record what is later to be reproduced and taken down by a stenographer. Also, **dic′to-phone.**

dic-tate (dĭk′tāt), *v.t.* [*p.t.* and *p.p.* -tat-ed, *p.pr.* -tat-ing], **1**, to declare with authority; **2**, to express orally so that another may take down in writing; as, the business man *dictates* a letter to his stenographer:—*v.i.* to speak with final authority; prescribe:—*n.* **1**, an injunction; command; **2**, a controlling principle.

Syn., *v.* suggest, enjoin, order, command.

dic-ta-tion (dĭk-tā′shŭn), *n.* **1**, the act of speaking words to be written down; also, the words so spoken; **2**, authoritative utterance or command.

dic-ta-tor (dĭk-tā′tẽr), *n.* **1**, one who tells another what to write; **2**, one invested with absolute powers of government; **3**, in ancient Rome, a magistrate with supreme authority, appointed in times of emergency; **4**, one exercising similar authority in any sphere.—*n.* **dic-ta′tor-ship.**

dic-ta-to-ri-al (dĭk″tȧ-tō′rĭ-ăl), *adj.* pertaining to one who gives positive commands; overbearing; imperious.—*adv.* **dic″ta-to′ri-al-ly.**

Syn. domineering, arbitrary, tyrannical.

dic-tion (dĭk′shŭn), *n.* a manner of speaking or expression; choice of words; as, the *diction* of Robert Louis Stevenson.

Syn. vocabulary, phraseology, style. *Diction* is the term applied to the choice and use of words; as, Keats's *diction* is noted for its freshness and vividness. *Vocabulary* refers to the stock of words employed by a language, class, or individual; as, the *vocabulary* of a savage tribe is limited; the *vocabulary* of Shakespeare was exceptionally large. *Phraseology* emphasizes the grouping or arrangement of words and often refers to a characteristic use of these word groups; as, the *phraseology* of the Kentucky mountaineer. *Style* is a broader term than *diction* or *phraseology* and refers to a characteristic method of writing or speaking; as, Arnold's polished *style.* It also denotes a highly artistic method of expression; as, his works are interesting but lack *style.*

dic-tion-a-ry (dĭk′shŭn-ā-rĭ), *n.* [*pl.* dictionaries (-rĭz)], a book explaining the words of a language arranged alphabetically; a lexicon; vocabulary.

dic-to-graph (dĭk′tō-gråf), *n.* a form of telephone, the transmitter being connected with a phonograph, to record what is said in the room where it is placed: used by detectives. Also, **dic′ta-graph.**

dic-tum (dĭk′tŭm), *n.* [*pl.* dicta (-tȧ)], a positive opinion; a dogmatic or authoritative assertion; an aphorism.

did (dĭd), past tense of the transitive and intransitive verb *do.*

di-dac-tic (dĭ-dăk′tĭk; dī-), *adj.* pertaining to, or of the nature of, teaching; instructing; explanatory; as, a *didactic* poem. Also, **di-dac′ti-cal.**—*adv.* **di-dac′ti-cal-ly.**

di-dac-tics (dĭ-dăk′tĭks; dī-), *n.pl.* used as *sing.* the science or art of teaching or education; pedagogics.

di-do (dī′dō), *n.* [*pl.* didoes; didos (-dōz)], *Colloq.*, a caper; an extravagant action; antic.

Di-do (dī′dō), *n.* in classic legend, a Tyrian princess of Carthage, told of in Vergil's "Æneid."

didst (dĭdst), *Archaic*, second person singular, past tense, of the verb [1]*do.*

[1]**die** (dī), *v.i.* [*p.t.* and *p.p.* died (dīd), *p.pr.* dy′ing], **1,** to cease to live; expire; **2,** to perish; wither; **3,** to faint; languish; **4,** figuratively, to cease to exist; vanish.

Syn. depart, decline, decrease, wane, decay. —*Ant.* live, exist, flourish, increase, bloom.

[2]**die** (dī), *n.* [*pl.* dies (dīz)], **1,** a metal form used in stamping coins, medals, etc.; **2,** a tool used in cutting the threads of screws or bolts, etc.; **3,** a metal plate with holes for receiving a punch; also, a form of cutter, used in a press, for shaping leather, paper, sheet metal, or the like; **4,** [*pl.* dice (dīs)], a small cube used in gaming; also, the throwing of such a die; luck; chance: **the die is cast,** the decision is made, and cannot be recalled.

DIE for threading a pipe or bar, held in a frame, or stock.

di-er-e-sis (dī-ĕr′ĕ-sĭs; *Br.* dī-ē′rĕ-sĭs), *n.* [*pl.* diereses (-sēz)], **1,** a sign [¨] placed over the second of two separate vowels to show that each has a separate sound in pronunciation, as in *coöperate;* **2,** the division of a sound originally a diphthong into two syllables, as in *aërated.* Also, **di-ær′e-sis,** *Pfd. S.*

Die-sel en-gine (dē′zĕl), an internal-combustion oil engine of high efficiency: also called *Diesel motor.*

die-sink-er (dī′sĭngk″ẽr), *n.* a maker of dies.—*n.* **die′sink″ing.**

[1]**di-et** (dī′ĕt), *n.* **1,** a European parliamentary assembly; esp., one of the old German or Holy Roman Empire; **2,** an international congress.

[2]**di-et** (dī′ĕt), *n.* **1,** solid or liquid food; **2,** manner of living, with special reference to food; **3,** a prescribed course of food, intended as a health measure:—*v.t.* to regulate the eating and drinking of, as an invalid:—*v.i.* to eat or drink according to prescribed rules.—*n.* **di′et-er.**—*n.* **di′et-ist.**

Syn., n. fare, victuals. (See food.)

di-et-a-ry (dī′ĕt-ā-rĭ), *adj.* pertaining to the rules of proper food; as, the food for patients in a hospital is prepared in a *dietary* kitchen:—*n.* [*pl.* dietaries (-rĭz)], **1,** a certain fixed allowance of food; **2,** a system of regulating food.

di-e-tet-ic (dī″ĕ-tĕt′ĭk), *adj.* pertaining to diet: **dietetics,** *n.pl.* used as *sing.* that branch of hygiene relating to the healthful regulation of eating. Also, *adj.* **di″e-tet′i-cal.**—*adv.* **di″e-tet′i-cal-ly.**

di-et-ing (dī′ĕt-ĭng), *n.* the act of eating according to a strict rule.

di-e-ti-tian (dī″ĕ-tĭsh′ăn), *n.* one trained to plan meals with a proper proportion of various food elements.

dif- (dĭf-), *prefix,* apart; away: form of *dis-* before *f* in words of Latin derivation.

dif-fer (dĭf′ẽr), *v.i.* **1,** to be unlike; **2,** to disagree: dispute; quarrel.

dif-fer-ence (dĭf′ẽr-ĕns), *n.* **1,** the act or state of being unlike; distinction; **2,** controversy; quarrel; **3,** discrimination; as, to make a *difference* between synonyms.—*abbr.* **diff.**

Syn. distinction. *Difference* means the state or degree of being unlike or dissimilar; it applies to the things or persons compared; as, there was a great *difference* between the two sisters. *Distinction* refers to the recognition by the mind of such a difference or to its expression in words; as, we make a *distinction* between fear and cowardice.

dif-fer-ent (dĭf′ẽr-ĕnt), *adj.* unlike; distinct.—*adv.* **dif′fer-ent-ly.**

Syn. various, diverse.—*Ant.* alike.

dif-fer-en-tial (dĭf″ẽr-ĕn′shăl), *adj.* **1,** creating, pertaining to, or involving, a difference; **2,** pertaining to a differential: **differential calculus,** a branch of higher mathematics: **differential duty,** a customs tax imposed on certain merchandise at a higher rate under certain conditions of import than under others, as when goods from one country pay a higher duty than similar goods from another country: **differential gear,** a device in an automobile which allows one driving wheel to turn faster than another, as on a curve:—*n.* **1,** a difference in charge or cost; esp., a difference in railroad rates from one point to another by different routes; **2,** an infinitesimal difference between two values of a variable quantity; **3,** a differential gear.—*adv.* **dif″fer-en′tial-ly.**

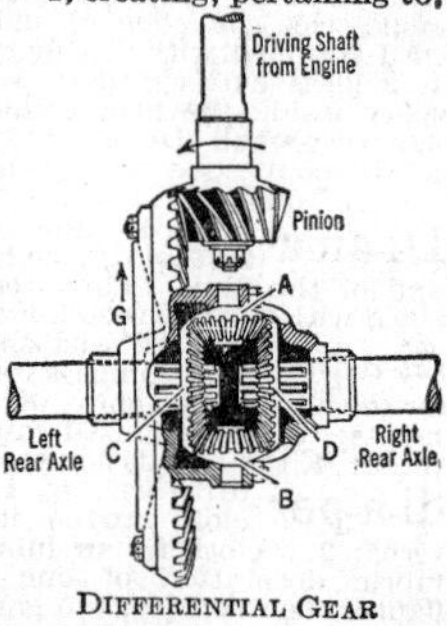

DIFFERENTIAL GEAR

A, B, gears rigidly attached to bevel gear, G, which is turned by pinion on driving shaft, but is not attached to left wheel axle. C, D, gears rigidly attached to left and right wheel axles. A and B, by rotating on their axles, permit wheel axles to turn at different rates when necessary.

dif-fer-en-ti-ate (dĭf″ẽr-ĕn′shĭ-āt), *v.t.* [*p.t.* and *p.p.* -at″ed, *p.pr.* -at″ing], **1,** to observe or state an unlikeness between; **2,** to mark (a person or thing) as unlike another; as, his genius *differentiates* him from his classmates:—*v.i.* to acquire a distinctive and separate character.

Syn. discriminate, distinguish, contrast.

dif-fer-en-ti-a-tion (dĭf″ẽr-ĕn″shĭ-ā′shŭn), *n.* **1,** the act of separating or classifying; specialization; **2,** the act of causing, observing, or marking out unlikenesses between things.

dif-fi-cult (dĭf′ĭ-kŭlt), *adj.* **1,** not easy; hard to do; **2,** not easily pleased or managed; as, a *difficult* customer.—*adv.* **dif′fi-cult-ly.** (See *Syn.* next page.)

Syn. intricate, involved, obscure. (See hard.)—*Ant.* easy, pleasant, simple.

dif-fi-cul-ty (dĭf′ĭ-kŭl-tĭ), *n.* [*pl.* difficulties (-tĭz)], **1**, the state of being hard or perplexing; **2**, something hard to do; **3**, a scruple; objection; **4**, a hindrance; impediment; **5**, in *pl.*, complication of affairs; embarrassment; perplexity.

dif-fi-dence (dĭf′ĭ-dĕns), *n.* lack of self-reliance; modest reserve; shyness; timidity.

dif-fi-dent (dĭf′ĭ-dĕnt), *adj.* lacking self-reliance; shy; modest.—*adv.* **dif′fi-dent-ly.**—*n.* **dif′fi-dent-ness.**

Syn. bashful, coy, demure. (See shy.)

dif-frac-tion (dĭ-frăk′shŭn), *n.* the turning aside or scattering of a ray of light when passing the edge of a body that will not admit light.

dif-fuse (dĭ-fūz′), *v.t.* and *v.i.* [*p.t.* and *p.p.* -fused′ (-fūzd′), *p.pr.* -fus′ing], **1**, to pour out and spread around; **2**, to scatter; circulate:—*adj.* (dĭ-fūs′), **1**, widely spread; **2**, wordy; as, a *diffuse* style of writing.—*adv.* **dif-fuse′ly** (dĭ-fūs′lĭ).—*n.* **dif-fuse′ness.**—*n.* **dif-fus′er** (dĭ-fūz′ẽr).

dif-fus-i-ble (dĭ-fūz′ĭ-bl), *adj.* capable of being poured out or spread.—*n.* **dif-fus″i-bil′i-ty.**

dif-fu-sion (dĭ-fū′zhŭn), *n.* **1**, the act of pouring out or spreading abroad; as, the *diffusion* of light; **2**, a mingling, as of gases or liquids.

dif-fu-sive (dĭ-fū′sĭv), *adj.* capable of being poured out; spreading every way; reaching far.—*adv.* **dif-fu′sive-ly.**—*n.* **dif-fu′sive-ness.**

dig (dĭg), *v.i.* [*p.t.* and *p.p.* dug (dŭg) or, *Archaic*, digged (dĭgd), *p.pr.* dig′ging], **1**, to work with a spade; cast up earth; **2**, *Colloq.*, to study hard; search in books for information: **dig in,** to make a hole or trench for protection against enemy fire:—*v.t.* **1**, to loosen or break up (ground) with a spade; **2**, to make, as a hole, by casting out earth; **3**, to bring up from underground; as, to *dig* potatoes; **4**, to thrust or force in; prepare a way for (oneself) by digging: with *into*:—*n.* **1**, a poke or thrust; **2**, *Colloq.*: **a**, a cutting or malicious remark; **b**, a plodding student.

di-gest (dī′jĕst), *n.* **1**, a systematic compilation of laws or court decisions; **2**, a classified arrangement of written or printed material; as, a literary *digest*:—*v.t.* (dĭ-jĕst′; dī-), **1**, to arrange methodically under proper heads or titles; classify; **2**, to think over and arrange in the mind; **3**, to dissolve or prepare (food), esp. in the stomach, for assimilation into the tissues of the body; **4**, to prepare by heat:—*v.i.* **1**, to be dissolved, esp. in the stomach, before assimilation, as food; **2**, to be prepared by heat.

di-gest-er (dĭ-jĕs′tẽr), *n.* a machine for dissolving out the essence of a substance by a suitably heated liquid.

di-gest-i-ble (dĭ-jĕs′tĭ-bl), *adj.* capable of being dissolved by the stomach or intestines for assimilation.—*adv.* **di-gest′i-bly.**—*n.* **di-gest″i-bil′i-ty.**

di-ges-tion (dĭ-jĕs′chŭn), *n.* **1**, the act of digesting; the conversion of food by the action of the gastric juices into forms that can be used by the body; **2**, mental or physical assimilation; as, the *digestion* of facts in the mind or of food in the stomach.

di-ges-tive (dĭ-jĕs′tĭv), *adj.* pertaining to the absorption of food by the body; as, the *digestive* organs.

dig-ger (dĭg′ẽr), *n.* **1**, one who works with a spade; **2**, an implement for turning up the soil; **3**, a plodder: **Digger,** a name of a class of California Indians who live chiefly on roots.

dig-ging (dĭg′ĭng), *n.* **1**, the act of excavating, or throwing up earth, as with a spade; **2**, in *pl.*: **a**, a locality where mining operations, esp. for gold, are carried on; **b**, *Slang*, locality; place of residence.

dig-it (dĭj′ĭt), *n.* **1**, a finger or toe; **2**, a measure of length (¾ inch); **3**, in astronomy, one twelfth of the diameter of the sun or moon; **4**, any one of the Arabic numerals.

dig-it-al (dĭj′ĭ-tăl), *adj.* pertaining to a digit, esp. to a finger or toe.

dig-i-ta-lis (dĭj″ĭ-tā′lĭs), *n.* **1**, any of several plants bearing spikes of finger-shaped flowers; esp., the foxglove; **2**, a drug made from the leaves of one species of digitalis and used as a heart stimulant.

dig-i-tate (dĭj′ĭ-tāt), *adj.* finger-shaped; as, *digitate* leaves.

dig-ni-fied (dĭg′nĭ-fīd), *p.adj.* lofty in manner; noble; stately.

dig-ni-fy (dĭg′nĭ-fī), *v.t.* [*p.t.* and *p.p.* -fied (-fīd), *p.pr.* -fy″ing], to exalt; confer honor upon; elevate.

Syn. invest, advance, promote, honor.—*Ant.* degrade, humble.

dig-ni-ta-ry (dĭg′nĭ-tă-rĭ), *n.* [*pl.* dignitaries (-rĭz)], one who holds a position of dignity or honor; esp., a high church official; as, an archbishop is a *dignitary*.

dig-ni-ty (dĭg′nĭ-tĭ), *n.* [*pl.* dignities (-tĭz)], **1**, nobleness; excellence; character which inspires or commands respect; **2**, stateliness of manner or style; **3**, high rank; **4**, an exalted office in church or state; **5**, an honor conferred.

di-graph (dī′grăf), *n.* the combination of two letters to represent one simple sound, as in *read*, *that*, *graph*.

di-gress (dĭ-grĕs′; dī-grĕs′), *v.i.* to turn aside; deviate from the main subject or line of argument; wander; as, a question caused the teacher to *digress*.

Syn. diverge, swerve. (See wander.)

di-gres-sion (dĭ-grĕsh′ŭn; dī-), *n.* **1**, the act of turning aside, as from the subject under discussion; **2**, in astronomy, the angular distance of the planets Mercury and Venus from the sun.

di-gres-sive (dĭ-grĕs′ĭv), *adj.* tending to turn aside or wander away—*adv.* **di-gres′sive-ly.**

di-he-dral (dī-hē′drăl), *adj.* **1**, having two plane faces or sides; **2**, in a kite, having wings which make an angle with each other; **3**, in airplanes, pertaining to wings the sides of which are bent slightly up or down.

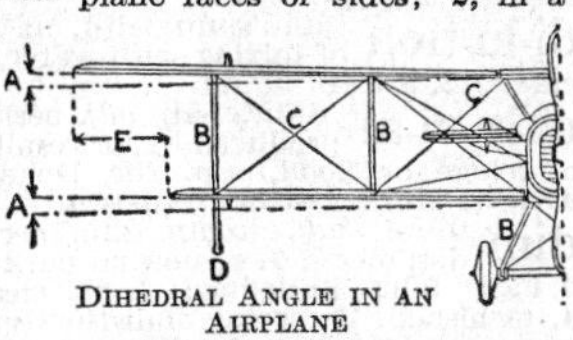

DIHEDRAL ANGLE IN AN AIRPLANE

A, A, dihedral angle of the upper and lower planes, respectively, the dotted lines being the horizontal, lateral axes of the planes; B, B, B, struts; C, C, guy wires; D, wing skid; E, overhang.

dike (dīk), *n.* **1**, an earthen bank along a ditch; a causeway; **2**, an embankment thrown up as a protection against the sea, or floods; as, the *dike* has been a great protection to Holland; **3**, in geology, a fissure in rock, filled with foreign matter, most commonly with igneous rock:—*v.t.* [*p.t.* and *p.p.* diked (dīkt), *p.pr.* dik′ing], **1**, to inclose or protect with an embankment; **2**, to drain by ditching. Also, **dyke.**

di-lap-i-date (dĭ-lăp′ĭ-dāt), *v.t.* [*p.t.* and *p.p.* -dat″ed, *p.pr.* -dat″ing], to bring into partial ruin by neglect:—*v.i.* to become ruined.—*p.adj.* **di-lap′i-dat″ed.**

di-lap-i-da-tion (dĭ-lăp″ĭ-dā′shŭn), *n.* partial ruin through neglect or misuse; as, the *dilapidation* of the deserted house.

dil-a-ta-tion (dĭl″*ȧ*-tā′shŭn; dī″l*ȧ*-), *n.* enlargement; expansion; as, *dilatation* of the heart.

di-late (dĭ-lāt′; dī-lāt′), *v.t.* [*p.t.* and *p.p.* -lat′ed, *p.pr.* -lat′ing], **1**, to enlarge or widen in all directions; **2**, to distend:—*v.i.* **1**, to be extended or enlarged; **2**, to speak fully and copiously; as, the explorer was glad to *dilate* on his experiences.—*n.* **di-lat′er.**—*n.* **di-la′tion.**—*adj.* **di-lat′a-ble.**
Syn. stretch, expand, swell, inflate.

di-la-tor (dĭ-lā′tẽr; dī-), *n.* **1**, one who or that which enlarges; **2**, a muscle that enlarges some opening of the body.

dil-a-to-ry (dĭl′*ȧ*-tō-rĭ), *adj.* causing, or tending to cause, delay; inactive.—*adv.* **dil′a-to-ri-ly.**—*n.* **dil′a-to-ri-ness.**
Syn. tardy, procrastinating, behindhand, lagging, dawdling.

di-lem-ma (dĭ-lĕm′*ȧ*; dī-lĕm′*ȧ*), *n.* an awkward situation; a difficult position or choice.

dil-et-tan-te (dĭl″ĕ-tăn′tē; dē″lĕt-tän′tā), *n.* [*pl.* dilettanti (-tē); dilettantes (-tēz)], **1**, one who pursues the fine arts, literature, or science, only for amusement; **2**, a dabbler. Also, **dil″et-tant′.**—*n.* **dil″et-tan′te-ism; dil″et-tant′ism.**

¹dil-i-gence (dĭl′ĭ-jĕns), *n.* industry; care; zeal; as, study with *diligence.*
Syn. heed, perseverance, application.—*Ant.* laziness, inattentiveness.

²dil-i-gence (dĭl′ĭ-jĕns; *Fr.* dē″lē″zhäns′), *n.* a stagecoach, esp. in France.

dil-i-gent (dĭl′ĭ-jĕnt), *adj.* **1**, industrious; persevering; **2**, performed with painstaking care; careful.—*adv.* **dil′i-gent-ly.**
Syn. persistent. (See busy.)

dill (dĭl), *n.* an herb of the carrot family, with aromatic seeds used as flavoring.

dil-ly-dal-ly (dĭl′ĭ-dăl″ĭ), *v.i.* [*p.t.* and *p.p.* -lied (-ĭd), *p.pr.* -ly-ing], *Colloq.*, to loiter; trifle; waver.

di-lute (dĭ-lūt′; dī-lūt′), *v.t.* and *v.i.* [*p.t.* and *p.p.* -lut′ed, *p.pr.* -lut′ing], to weaken by mixing with a fluid, esp. water:—*adj.* not concentrated; containing a large proportion of solvent; as, a *dilute* salt solution.—*p.adj.* **di-lut′ed.**

di-lu-tion (dĭ-lū′shŭn; dī-), *n.* **1**, the act of mixing with water, or weakening; **2**, a weak liquid.

di-lu-vi-al (dĭ-lū′vĭ-ăl), *adj.* pertaining to, produced by, or resulting from, a deluge or flood, esp. the Deluge. Also, **di-lu′vi-an.**—*n.* **di-lu′vi-an-ism.**

dim (dĭm), *adj.* [*comp.* dim′mer, *superl.* dim′mest], **1**, somewhat dark; obscure; **2**, hazy; faint; ill-defined; **3**, not clearly seen; **4**, tarnished; **5**, seeing indistinctly; as, *dim* eyes:—*v.t.* [*p.t.* and *p.p.* dimmed (dĭmd), *p.pr.* dim′ming], **1**, to render obscure or less distinct; **2**, to cloud; **3**, to tarnish; dull:—*v.i.* to become indistinct; fade.—*adv.* **dim′ly.**—*n.* **dim′ness.**

dime (dīm), *n.* a silver coin equal to one tenth of a dollar, or ten cents:—*adj.* of the value of ten cents: **dime novel,** a cheap, exciting story book.

di-men-sion (dĭ-mĕn′shŭn), *n.* **1**, measure in any one direction, as length, breadth, thickness; **2**, in *pl.:* **a**, size or extent of a body in these measurements; **b**, size; importance; scope.

di-men-sion-al (dĭ-mĕn′shŭn-ăl), *adj.* pertaining to size or extent; having length, breadth, etc.; as, a two-*dimensional* figure.

di-min-ish (dĭ-mĭn′ĭsh), *v.t.* **1**, to make less; reduce in bulk or amount; **2**, to weaken; impair; detract from:—*v.i.* to lessen; dwindle, as power or wealth.
Syn. contract, curtail. (See decrease.)

di-min-u-en-do (dĭ-mĭn″ū-ĕn′dō), *adj.* in music, gradually growing softer in sound.—*abbr.* **dim.; dimin.**

dim-i-nu-tion (dĭm″ĭ-nū′shŭn), *n.* **1**, the act of making less; reduction; **2**, the process of becoming less.

di-min-u-tive (dĭ-mĭn′ū-tĭv), *adj.* **1**, below the average size; little; **2**, contracted; narrow:—*n.* a word formed from another to express a smaller thing of the same kind; as, *lambkin*, a little *lamb.*—*adv.* **di-min′u-tive-ly.**—*n.* **di-min′u-tive-ness.**
Syn., adj. small, slight, insignificant.

dim-i-ty (dĭm′ĭ-tĭ), *n.* [*pl.* dimities (-tĭz)], a cotton material with raised ornamental stripes.

dim-mer (dĭm′ẽr), *n.* a device for regulating the brightness of a light.

dim-out (dĭm′out), *n.* a partial blackout; a dimming of lights.

dim-ple (dĭm′pl), *n.* a small dent or hollow, as in the cheek or chin; an indentation:—*v.i.* and *v.t.* [*p.t.* and *p.p.* -pled (-pld), *p.pr.* -pling], to form dimples (in).

din (dĭn), *n.* a continued and insistent noise:—*v.t.* [*p.t.* and *p.p.* dinned (dĭnd), *p.pr.* din′ning], to utter with insistent and confusing noise:—*v.i.* to make a clamor.

di-nar (dē-när′), *n.* the monetary unit of Yugoslavia, equivalent to 19.3 cents.

dine (dīn), *v.i.* [*p.t.* and *p.p.* dined (dīnd), *p.pr.* din′ing], to eat dinner:—*v.t.* to give a dinner for; feed.

din-er (dīn′ẽr), *n.* **1**, one who dines; **2**, a railroad car where meals are served.

din-ette (dī-nĕt′), *n.* an alcove or very small room, adjoining a kitchen or living room, and used as a dining room.

ding (dĭng), *v.i.* to make a noise like a bell:—*v.t. Colloq.*, to impress noisily.

ding-dong (dĭng′dŏng″), *n.* **1**, the sound of the strokes of a bell; **2**, monotonous repetition.

din-ghy (dĭng′gĭ), *n.* [*pl.* dinghies (-gĭz)], **1**, the smallest boat of a man-of-war; **2**, any of various East Indian boats; **3**, any of various kinds of small sailboat (see *ship*, illus.). Also, **din′gey** [*pl.* dingeys (-gĭz)].

din-gle (dĭng′gl), *n.* a cleft between hills; also, a secluded, wooded dell.

din-gle-dan-gle (dĭng′gl-dăng″gl), *adv.* so as to swing backward and forward; so as to hang loosely.

din-go (dĭng′gō), *n.* [*pl.* dingoes (-gōz)], the wild, foxlike dog of Australia.

DINGO (1/38)

din-gy (dĭn′jĭ), *adj.* [*comp.* din′gi-er, *superl.* din′gi-est], grimy; faded; dirty; as, the houses look *dingy* in a smoky city.—*adv.* **din′gi-ly.**—*n.* **din′gi-ness.**

din-ing car a railroad car in which meals are served; a diner.

din-ing room a room in which meals are served.

din-ner (dĭn′ẽr), *n.* **1**, the chief meal of the day; **2**, a formal party at which dinner is served.

di-no-saur (dī′nō-sôr), *n.* any of a great variety of large reptiles of prehistoric times.—*adj.* **di″no-sau′ri-an.**

dint (dĭnt), *n.* **1**, a mark left by a blow or pressure; a dent; **2**, force or power; as, by *dint* of much effort:—*v.t.* to dent.

di-oc-e-san (dī-ŏs′ē-săn; dī′ō-sē″săn), *adj.* of or pertaining to a diocese, or church district controlled by a bishop:—*n.* a bishop in charge of a diocese.

di-o-cese (dī′ō-sēs; dī′ō-sēs), *n.* the district in which a bishop has authority, called the bishop's see; a bishopric.

Di-o-me-des (dī″ō-mē′dēz), *n.* in mythology, **1**, a king of Argos, and a hero in the Trojan War: the bravest of the Greeks except Achilles; **2**, a Thracian king, the securing of whose man-eating mares was one of the labors of Hercules. Also, **Di′o-med** (dī′ō-mĕd).

Di-o-ny-sus (dī″ō-nī′sŭs), *n.* in Greek mythology, a son of Zeus, first worshiped as the god of vegetation, and later as the god and giver of the grape and of wine: identified with the Roman *Bacchus.*

di-op-tric (dī-ŏp′trĭk), *adj.* assisting vision by means of the refraction of light: used of lenses. Also, **di-op′tri-cal.**

Di-os-cu-ri (dī″ŏs-kū′rī), *n.pl.* in mythology, Castor and Pollux, twin sons of Zeus and Leda, brothers of Helen and Clytemnestra: regarded as patrons of warriors and of travelers. Also, **Di″os-ku′roi.**

di-ox-ide (dī-ŏk′sīd; dī-ŏk′sĭd), *n.* a compound of two atoms of oxygen and one of a metal or base. Also, **di-ox′id.**

dip (dĭp), *v.t.* [*p.t.* and *p.p.* dipped or dipt (dĭpt), *p.pr.* dip′ping], **1**, to plunge; put quickly into liquid and take out again; **2**, to scoop up with a ladle, spoon, bucket, etc.; **3**, to baptize by putting under water; **4**, to lower and raise quickly, as a flag:—*v.i.* **1**, to immerse oneself; **2**, to enter slightly into anything; as, to *dip* into a book; **3**, to slope downward; as, the road *dips;* **4**, to sink:—*n.* **1**, the act of putting into water temporarily; a short plunge; as, a *dip* in the ocean; **2**. something which is dipped; esp., a candle; **3**, a downward slope; **4**, in aviation, a quick descent followed by an ascent.

di-phos-gene (dī-fŏs′jēn), *n.* a poisonous gas, used in warfare.

diph-the-ri-a (dĭf-thē′rĭ-ȧ), *n.* an acute contagious disease of the throat.—*adj.* **diph″the-rit′ic** (dĭf″thē-rĭt′ĭk).

diph-thong (dĭf′thŏng), *n.* **1**, the union of two vowel sounds pronounced in one syllable, as in *out, oil;* **2**, two characters used to represent a single sound, as in *hear, both;* **3**, popularly, a ligature of two vowels, as in *æsthetic.*—*adj.* **diph-thon′gal** (-thŏng′găl).—*adv.* **diph-thon′gal-ly.**

di-plo-ma (dĭ-plō′mȧ), *n.* a document conferring some honor or degree; esp., a paper showing the completion of a course of study; as, the student receives a *diploma* on graduating from school.

di-plo-ma-cy (dĭ-plō′mȧ-sĭ), *n.* [*pl.* diplomacies (-sĭz)], **1**, the art or system of conducting negotiations or dealings between two states or nations; **2**, skill in conducting negotiations or social matters; tact: **dollar diplomacy**, diplomatic negotiations in the interests of monetary advantage.

dip-lo-mat (dĭp′lō-măt), *n.* **1**, a person skilled or employed in carrying on dealings between two nations; **2**, a tactful person.—*v.i.* **di-plo′ma-tize.**

dip-lo-mat-ic (dĭp″lō-măt′ĭk), *adj.* **1**, pertaining to the management of affairs between two nations; as, an ambassador is appointed to look after *diplomatic* business; **2**, characterized by special skill in the management of affairs; tactful; adroit.—*adv.* **dip″lo-mat′i-cal-ly.**

di-plo-ma-tist (dĭ-plō′mȧ-tĭst), *n.* **1**, one who is skilled in the art of managing affairs between nations; **2**, a tactful person.

dip-per (dĭp′ẽr), *n.* **1**, one who or that which dips, esp. a cup or ladle for water, or the like; **2**, any of various wrenlike birds with the habit of dipping the tail. also called *water ouzel:* **Dipper**, the group of seven stars in the constellation Ursa Major, arranged like a ladle: also called *Great Dipper:* **Little Dipper**, a group of stars in the constellation Ursa Minor, arranged in the form of a ladle with the North Star as the end of the handle.

dip-so-ma-ni-a (dĭp″sō-mā′nĭ-ȧ), *n.* an uncontrollable, often periodic, craving for alcoholic drinks.

dip-so-ma-ni-ac (dĭp″sō-mā′nĭ-ăk), *n.* one who suffers from an uncontrollable desire for strong drink:—*adj.* pertaining to dipsomania.

dip-ter-ous (dĭp′tẽr-ŭs), *adj.* having two wings, as the insects of the order (*Diptera*) which includes gnats, flies, etc.

dire (dīr), *adj.* dreadful; mournful; as, the *dire* news of an explosion.—*adv.* **dire′ly.**—*n.* **dire′ness.**

di-rect (dĭ-rĕkt′), *adj.* **1**, straight, as a road; **2**, open; straightforward; **3**, simple; plain; sincere; as, *direct* answers; **4**, lineally related; as, a *direct* descendant; **5**, in one direction only; as, a *direct* current: **direct primary**, in U. S. politics, an election held for the nomination of the candidates of each party by direct choice of the voters:—*v.t.* **1**, to aim or drive in a straight line; **2**, to guide or show; as, to *direct* him to the station; **3**, to regulate, as affairs; **4**, to instruct; **5**, to address, as a letter:—*v.i.* to act as a guide.—*n.* **di-rect′ness.**

Syn., v. order, manage, lead, command, dispose. (See conduct, govern.)

di-rec-tion (dĭ-rĕk′shŭn), *n.* **1**, the act of guiding or showing; **2**, aim; line of motion; **3**, address, as of a letter; **4**, a command; order.

Syn. course, tendency, way.

di-rect-ly (dĭ-rĕkt′lĭ), *adv.* **1**, in a straight line; **2**, immediately; soon; as, I will come *directly;* **3**, openly; honestly.

Syn. presently, straightway.

di-rec-tor (dĭ-rĕk′tẽr), *n.* **1**, one who guides or shows; esp., one appointed to transact the affairs of an organized body, as a club or concern; **2**, a spiritual guide or adviser.—*n. fem.* **di-rec′tress.**—*n.* **di-rec′tor-ship.**

di-rec-to-rate (dĭ-rĕk′tō-rāt), *n.* **1**, the office of a guide, manager, or adviser; **2**, a group of persons managing the affairs of an organized body.

di-rec-to-ri-al (dĭ-rĕk-tō′rĭ-ăl), pertaining to a director or directory.

di-rec-to-ry (dĭ-rĕk′tō-rĭ), *n.* [*pl.* directories (-rĭz)], **1**, an alphabetical list of names and addresses; **2**, a collection of rules:—*adj.* containing rules; guiding; commanding.

di-rec-trix (dĭ-rĕk′trĭks), *n.* [*pl.* directrices (-trĭ-sēz); directrixes (-trĭk-sĕz)], **1**, a woman who directs; a directress; **2**, in mathematics, a fixed line which determines a curve, or the motion of a point which describes a curve (see *parabola*, illus.).

dire-ful (dīr′fo͝ol), *adj.* dreadful; dismal; as, the *direful* news of the flood.—*adv.* **dire′ful-ly.**—*n.* **dire′ful-ness.**

dirge (dûrj), *n.* a funeral hymn; a song or tune expressing mourning.

dir-i-gi-ble (dĭr′ĭ-jĭ-bl), *adj.* capable of being guided or steered; as, a *dirigible* balloon:—*n.* a cigar-shaped balloon driven by motors and provided with a car for passengers.

dirk (dûrk), *n.* a dagger; esp., a dagger without a guard, used by the Scottish Highlanders.

dirt (dûrt), *n.* **1**, mud; filth; as, the streets are full of *dirt;* **2**, dust; garden earth.

dirt-y (dûr'tĭ) *adj.* [*comp.* dirt'i-er, *superl.* dirt'i-est], **1**, unclean; impure; **2**, soiled; dingy; **3**, muddy; of the weather, sleety; rainy; **4**, despicable; contemptible:—*v.t.* [*p.t.* and *p.p.* dirt'ied (-tĭd), *p.pr.* dirt'y-ing], to soil; sully; tarnish.—*n.* **dirt'i-ness.**—*adv.* **dirt'i-ly.**

dis- (dĭs-), *prefix*, expressing: **1**, removal; separation; as, *dis*tract; *dis*bar; **2**, negation; as, *dis*obliging; **3**, reversal: equivalent to *un-* or *not;* as, *dis*entangle; **4**, used intensively; as, *dis*annul. Also, **di-; dif-; de-.**

dis-a-bil-i-ty (dĭs″ȧ-bĭl'ĭ-tĭ), *n.* [*pl.* disabilities (-tĭz)], **1**, want of power; **2**, the state of being without ability.

Syn. inability. *Disability* implies a want of something necessary for the accomplishment of some purpose; it refers especially to some legal disqualification; as, a minor's *disability* as a voter. *Inability* suggests being unable to do something owing to lack of power within oneself; as, the *inability* of an infant to walk; his *inability* to work was due to old age.

dis-a-ble (dĭs-ā'bl), *v.t.* [*p.t.* and *p.p.* -bled (-bld), *p.pr.* -bling], **1**, to deprive of power; make unable; disqualify; **2**, to impair; incapacitate or render unable.—*p.adj.* **dis-a'bled.**—*n.* **dis-a'ble-ment.**

dis-a-buse (dĭs″ȧ-būz'), *v.t.* [*p.t.* and *p.p.* -bused' (-būzd'), *p.pr.* -bus'ing], to undeceive; set free from mistake; as, to *disabuse* oneself of a wrong idea.

dis-ad-van-tage (dĭs″ăd-vȧn'tăj), *n.* **1**, a hindrance; **2**, a cause of loss or injury; **3**, an unfavorable position; as, working at a *disadvantage;* **4**, loss; detriment; as, his sudden departure was a *disadvantage* to the campaign.

dis-ad-van-ta-geous (dĭs-ăd″văn-tā'jŭs), *adj.* unfavorable; likely to cause loss, injury, or failure.—*adv.* **dis-ad″van-ta'geous-ly.**

dis-af-fect (dĭs″ă-fĕkt'), *v.t.* **1**, to fill with discontent; **2**, to alienate or take the affections from; **3**, to disturb the functions of; disorder.

dis-af-fect-ed (dĭs″ă-fĕk'tĕd), *p.adj.* **1**, discontented; **2**, no longer friendly; out of sympathy; **3**, out of order; diseased; morbid.

dis-af-fec-tion (dĭs″ă-fĕk'shŭn), *n.* **1**, discontentment; **2**, disloyalty; ill will; hostility; **3**, disease.

Syn. discontent, dislike, unfriendliness.—*Ant.* loyalty, harmony, allegiance.

dis-a-gree (dĭs″ȧ-grē'), *v.i.* [*p.t.* and *p.p.* -greed' (-grēd'), *p.pr.* -gree'ing], **1**, to differ in opinion; **2**, to be unlike or unsuited; **3**, to be unfavorable or unsuitable.

dis-a-gree-a-ble (dĭs″ȧ-grē'ȧ-bl), *adj.* unpleasant; offensive; annoying; distasteful.—*adv.* **dis″a-gree'a-bly.**—*n.* **dis″a-gree'a-ble-ness.**

dis-a-gree-ment (dĭs″ȧ-grē'mĕnt), *n.* **1**, a difference of opinion; quarrel; **2**, lack of similarity or suitability; incongruity.

Syn. discord, dispute, dissension.

dis-al-low (dĭs″ă-lou'), *v.t.* to refuse to permit.—*n.* **dis″al-low'ance.**

dis-an-nul (dĭs″ă-nŭl'), *v.t.* [*p.t.* and *p.p.* -nulled' (-nŭld'), *p.pr.* -nul'ling], to cancel; make void, as a contract.—*n.* **dis″an-nul'ment.**

dis-ap-pear (dĭs″ă-pēr'), *v.i.* **1**, to pass from sight; vanish; **2**, to cease to exist; be lost.—*n.* **dis″ap-pear'ance.**

dis-ap-point (dĭs″ă-point'), *v.t.* **1**, to fail to gratify or fulfil the hope of; **2**, to frustrate, as a plan or purpose.

dis-ap-point-ed (dĭs″ă-poin'tĕd), *p.adj.* **1**, baffled; **2**, unhappy because of unfulfilled hope or defeated plans.—*adv.* **dis″ap-point'ed-ly.**

dis-ap-point-ment (dĭs″ă-point'mĕnt), *n.* **1**, defeat or failure of expectation; **2**, a state of depression caused by failure; **3**, that which causes failure of expectation.

Syn. humiliation, frustration, chagrin; discomposure.—*Ant.* fulfilment, attainment.

dis-ap-pro-ba-tion (dĭs-ăp″rō-bā'shŭn), *n.* failure to approve; blame; unfavorable opinion or judgment, as of one in authority.

dis-ap-prov-al (dĭs″ă-proov'ăl), *n.* unfavorable opinion; failure to approve; blame.

dis-ap-prove (dĭs″ă-proov'), *v.t.* [*p.t.* and *p.p.* -proved' (-proovd'), *p.pr.* -prov'ing], **1**, to fail to approve; condemn; blame; **2**, to refuse assent to:—*v.i.* to hold or express an unfavorable judgment.—*adv.* **dis″ap-prov'ing-ly.**

dis-arm (dĭs-ärm'), *v.t.* **1**, to deprive of weapons; **2**, to reduce to a peace footing, as an army; **3**, to render harmless

dis-ar-ma-ment (dĭs-är'mȧ-mĕnt), *n.* **1**, the act of depriving of weapons; **2**, the reduction of military and naval forces to a peace footing.

dis-ar-range (dĭs″ă-rānj'), *v.t.* [*p.t.* and *p.p.* -ranged' (-rānjd'), *p.pr.* -rang'ing], to put out of order; confuse.

dis-ar-ray (dĭs″ă-rā'), *v.t.* **1**, to strip; despoil; also, to undress; **2**, to overthrow; **3**, to throw into disorder; rout:—*n.* **1**, disordered or insufficient dress; **2**, confusion; disorder.

dis-as-ter (dĭz-ȧs'tẽr), *n.* a calamity; misfortune; a serious accident.

Syn. mishap, mischance, trouble, adversity.

dis-as-trous (dĭz-ȧs'trŭs), *adj.* unlucky; unfortunate; calamitous; attended with evil results.—*adv.* **dis-as'trous-ly.**

dis-a-vow (dĭs″ȧ-vou'), *v.t.* to deny; disclaim; disown.

dis-a-vow-al (dĭs″ȧ-vou'ăl), *n.* denial; rejection; as, he made a complete *disavowal* of responsibility.

dis-band (dĭs-bănd'), *v.t.* **1**, to dismiss from military service; **2**, to break up, as a society; scatter:—*v.i.* to be dispersed or broken up.—*n.* **dis-band'ment.**

dis-bar (dĭs-bär'), *v.t.* [*p.t.* and *p.p.* -barred' (-bärd'), *p.pr.* -bar'ring], to deprive (a lawyer) of the right to appear in court as an attorney.—*n.* **dis-bar'ment.**

dis-be-lief (dĭs″bē-lēf'), *n.* **1**, lack of belief or trust; **2**, denial of a creed.

Syn. unbelief. *Disbelief* implies a positive conviction that certain statements or principles are not true. *Unbelief* may mean merely an absence of all belief. In Biblical use, however, *unbelief* means a positive lack of faith that amounts to *disbelief*.

dis-be-lieve (dĭs″bē-lēv'), *v.t.* and *v.i.* [*p.t.* and *p.p.* -lieved' (-lēvd'), *p.pr.* -liev'ing], to refuse to believe; distrust.—*n.* **dis″be-liev'er.**

dis-bur-den (dĭs-bûr'dn), *v.t.* to remove a burden from; relieve of anything annoying or oppressive:—*v.i.* to ease one's mind.

dis-burse (dĭs-bûrs'), *v.t.* [*p.t.* and *p.p.* -bursed' (-bûrst'), *p.pr.* -burs'ing], to expend; pay out; as, the treasurer *disburses* the money.—*n.* **dis-burs'er.**

dis-burse-ment (dĭs-bûrs'mĕnt), *n.* money paid out.

disc (dĭsk), *n.* a flat, circular plate or anything resembling it. See **disk,** *Pfd. S.*

dis-card (dĭs-kärd'), *v.t.* **1**, to cast off or reject as useless; throw away; **2**, to cast aside (a card) as useless; also, to play (a card not of the suit led) when unable to follow suit:—*v.i.* in card playing, to throw out cards not required:—*n.* (dĭs-kärd'; dĭs'kärd), **1**, the act of discarding, as weak cards; **2**, that which is cast aside as worthless.

dis-cern (dĭ-zûrn'), *v.t.* **1**, to see as distinct from other objects; discriminate, as a difference in quality, kind, etc.; **2**, to distinguish mentally, or with the eye:—*v.i.* to make distinction.—*n.* **dis-cern'er.**
Syn. observe, recognize. (See perceive.)

dis-cern-i-ble (dĭ-zûr'nĭ-bl), *adj.* perceptible; capable of being seen.—*adv.* **dis-cern'i-bly.**

dis-cern-ing (dĭ-zûr'nĭng), *p.adj.* **1**, of keen sight; **2**, having good judgment.—*adv.* **dis-cern'ing-ly.**

dis-cern-ment (dĭ-zûrn'mĕnt), *n.* clearness in judgment; penetration; insight; discrimination.
Syn. sharpness, acuteness, shrewdness.

dis-charge (dĭs-chärj'), *v.t.* [*p.t.* and *p.p.* -charged' (-chärjd'), *p.pr.* -charg'ing], **1**, to free of a burden or responsibility; unload, as a ship; **2**, to remove, as a cargo or passengers; **3**, to send out; emit; **4**, to let fly, as an arrow; shoot, as a gun; **5**, to pay completely, as a debt; **6**, to send away as unnecessary or unsatisfactory, as a servant; **7**, to absolve; as, to *discharge* an accused person of a crime; **8**, to get rid of, as a burden, task, or responsibility; **9**, to perform, as a duty:—*v.i.* **1**, to get rid of any burden; **2**, to emit fluid:—*n.* **1**, an unloading or emitting; **2**, that which is unloaded; **3**, riddance of a burden, debt, accusation, or responsibility; **4**, the firing of a gun; **5**, dismissal, as of an employee; **6**, liberation; a legal release, as of a prisoner; also, the order granting it; **7**, the completion of a task or duty; **8**, something thrown out or emitted, as from a running sore; **9**, an electric current, esp. one of a brief or intermittent character.—*n.* **dis-charg'er.**
Syn., *v.* accomplish, achieve; liberate, release, dismiss.—*Ant.*, *v.* fail; confine, burden.

dis-ci-ple (dĭ-sī'pl), *n.* **1**, a pupil; **2**, one who believes the teaching of another; a follower.—*n.* **dis-ci'ple-ship.**

dis-ci-plin-a-ri-an (dĭs″ĭ-plĭn-ā'rĭ-ăn), *n.* one who believes in, or enforces, strict rules:—*adj.* pertaining to strict training or discipline.

dis-ci-plin-a-ry (dĭs'ĭ-plĭn-ā-rĭ), *adj.* pertaining to strict training; corrective.

dis-ci-pline (dĭs'ĭ-plĭn), *n.* **1**, strict and regular mental and moral training; **2**, development of character through trouble; **3**, obedience; **4**, punishment; **5**, regulation, as in many institutions; as, under strict *discipline*:—*v.t.* [*p.t.* and *p.p.* -plined (-plĭnd), *p.pr.* -plining], **1**, to train to obedience or efficiency; **2**, to regulate; **3**, to punish.—*adj.* **dis'ci-plin-a-ble.**—*n.* **dis'ci-plin-er.**—*adj.* **dis'ci-plin-al.**
Syn., *n.* order, strictness, training, drill.

dis-claim (dĭs-klām'), *v.t.* to disown; deny any connection with; as, he *disclaimed* any responsibility for the outbreak.
Syn. renounce, disavow, reject, repudiate.

dis-claim-er (dĭs-klām'ẽr), *n.* disavowal; denial.

dis-close (dĭs-klōz'), *v.t.* [*p.t.* and *p.p.* -closed' (-klōzd'), *p.pr.* -clos'ing], **1**, to uncover; bring to light; **2**, to make known; reveal.

dis-clo-sure (dĭs-klō'zhŭr), *n.* **1**, the act of revealing anything secret; **2**, the thing revealed or uncovered.

dis-coid (dĭs'koid), *adj.* disk-shaped; round and flat:—*n.* a flat, circular object.—*adj.* **dis-coi'dal.**

dis-col-or (dĭs-kŭl'ẽr), *v.t.* to change from the natural color; stain. Also, **dis-col'our.**—*n.* **dis-col″or-a'tion.**

dis-com-fit (dĭs-kŭm'fĭt), *v.t.* to frustrate; thwart; disconcert.
Syn. embarrass, confuse, abash.

dis-com-fi-ture (dĭs-kŭm'fĭ-tŭr), *n.* defeat; overthrow; disappointment; embarrassment.

dis-com-fort (dĭs-kŭm'fẽrt), *n.* **1**, want of ease; **2**, distress; as, the *discomfort* of traveling in hot weather:—*v.t.* to disturb; make uneasy.

dis-com-mode (dĭs″kŏ-mōd'), *v.t.* [*p.t.* and *p.p.* -mod'ed, *p.pr.* -mod'ing], to disturb; annoy; inconvenience.

dis-com-pose (dĭs″kŏm-pōz'), *v.t.* [*p.t.* and *p.p.* -posed' (-pōzd'), *p.pr.* -pos'ing], to disarrange; ruffle; agitate.

dis-com-po-sure (dĭs″kŏm-pō'zhŭr), *n.* agitation; unrest.

dis-con-cert (dĭs″kŏn-sûrt'), *v.t.* **1**, to disturb the composure or self-possession of; confuse; **2**, to frustrate.

dis-con-nect (dĭs″kŏ-nĕkt'), *v.t.* to disunite; unfasten; dissociate.—*n.* **dis″con-nec'tion.**

dis-con-nect-ed (dĭs″kŏ-nĕk'tĕd), *p.adj.* disjointed; separate; interrupted; desultory.—*adv.* **dis″con-nect'ed-ly.**—*n.* **dis″con-nect'ed-ness.**

dis-con-so-late (dĭs-kŏn'sŏ-lāt), *adj.* cheerless; hopeless; sad; as, *disconsolate* over the loss of a friend.—*adv.* **dis-con'so-late-ly.**—*n.* **dis-con″so-la'tion.**
Syn. dejected, forlorn, melancholy, sorrowful.—*Ant.* cheerful, optimistic, hopeful, gay.

dis-con-tent (dĭs″kŏn-tĕnt'), *n.* dissatisfaction; restlessness:—*v.t.* to displease.—*n.* **dis″con-tent'ment.**

dis-con-tent-ed (dĭs″kŏn-tĕn'tĕd), *p.adj.* not pleased with what one has; dissatisfied.—*adv.* **dis″con-tent'ed-ly.**—*n.* **dis″con-tent'ed-ness.**

dis-con-tin-u-ance (dĭs″kŏn-tĭn'ū-ăns), *n.* a stopping; a breaking off.
Syn. interruption, intermission, cessation.

dis-con-tin-ue (dĭs″kŏn-tĭn'ū), *v.t.* [*p.t.* and *p.p.* -ued (-ūd), *p.pr.* -u-ing], to stop; cease doing; put an end to; give up.—*n.* **dis″con-tin″u-a'tion.**

dis-con-tin-u-ous (dĭs″kŏn-tĭn'ū-ŭs), *adj.* intermittent; interrupted.—*adv.* **dis″con-tin'u-ous-ly.**—*n.* **dis-con″ti-nu'i-ty.**

dis-cord (dĭs'kôrd), *n.* **1**, disagreement; **2**, a confused noise; **3**, strife; dissension; **4**, in music, lack of harmony.—*n.* **dis-cord'ance.**
Syn. variance, difference, contention, clashing.—*Ant.* peace, harmony, accord, agreement.

dis-cord-ant (dĭs-kôr'dănt), *adj.* **1**, inharmonious; jarring; full of noise and strife; as, the *discordant* street noises; **2**, in music, out of harmony.

dis-count (dĭs'kount), *n.* **1**, a sum deducted or allowed for prompt payment of an account; **2**, a deduction from the usual price, made for some special reason; as, a clergyman's *discount*; **3**, a sum deducted, according to the current rate of interest, from the face value of a note or bill of exchange; **4**, the rate of interest so deducted:—*v.t.* (dĭs'kount; dĭs-kount'), **1**, to deduct (a sum) from for prompt payment; **2**, to advance money on, deducting a certain rate per cent; **3**, to count upon in advance; **4**, to allow for exaggeration in, as a story.—*adj.* **dis-count'a-ble.**

dis-coun-te-nance (dĭs-koun'tē-năns), *v.t.* [*p.t.* and *p.p.* -nanced (-nănst), *p.pr.* -nanc-ing], **1**, to disapprove of; **2**, to make ashamed.

dis-cour-age (dĭs-kŭr′āj), *v.t.* [*p.t.* and *p.p.* -aged (-ājd), *p.pr.* -ag-ing], **1**, to depress; lessen the enthusiasm or courage of; **2**, to dishearten; deter.

dis-cour-age-ment (dĭs-kŭr′āj-mĕnt), *n.* **1**, the act of depriving of confidence; **2**, that which destroys courage; **3**, the state of being without courage.
Syn. dejection, despair, hopelessness.

dis-course (dĭs-kōrs′), *n.* **1**, connected expression of ideas; **2**, conversation; **3**, a lecture, treatise, or sermon:—*v.i.* [*p.t.* and *p.p.* -coursed′ (-kōrst′), *p.pr.* -cours′ing], to talk or converse:—*v.t.* to utter; **as**, to *discourse* wisdom.

dis-cour-te-ous (dĭs-kûr′tē-ŭs), *adj.* impolite; rude; wanting in civility.—*adv.* **dis-cour′te-ous-ly.**
Syn. unmannerly, inconsiderate, blunt.

dis-cour-te-sy (dĭs-kûr′tē-sĭ), *n.* [*pl.* discourtesies (-sĭz)], rudeness; an unmannerly act.

dis-cov-er (dĭs-kŭv′ẽr), *v.t.* **1**, to bring to light; reveal; find (something previously unknown); **2**, to catch sight of.—*adj.* **dis-cov′er-a-ble.**—*n.* **dis-cov′er-er.**
Syn. invent, contrive. To *discover* is to find out that which we did not know as a certainty before, or that which we did not know existed at all; as, Columbus *discovered* America; doctors *discover* new methods of treating disease. To *invent* is to create something original, or to devise new means for doing things; as, Edison *invented* the phonograph; the boy *invented* a plan for carrying his books. To *contrive* is to find a way to do a thing or accomplish a purpose by a clever use or adaptation of the means at hand; as, Crusoe *contrived* a garment from a goatskin.

dis-cov-er-y (dĭs-kŭv′ẽr-ĭ), *n.* [*pl.* discoveries (-ĭz)], **1**, a bringing to light; **2**, a making known, **esp.** for the first time; **3**, disclosure.

dis-cred-it (dĭs-krĕd′ĭt), *n.* **1**, lack of belief; distrust; **2**, loss of reputation; dishonor:—*v.t.* **1**, to refuse to believe; **2**, to dishonor; take away reputation from; as, science *discredits* his theories.—*adj.* **dis-cred′it-a-ble.**—*adv.* **dis-cred′it-a-bly.**
Syn., v. depreciate, decry, disgrace.

dis-creet (dĭs-krēt′), *adj.* careful; prudent; as, a *discreet* answer; *discreet* behavior.—*adv.* **dis-creet′ly.**
Syn. cautious, judicious, wary. (See careful.)

dis-crep-an-cy (dĭs-krĕp′ăn-sĭ), *n.* [*pl.* discrepancies (-sĭz)], **1**, inconsistency; **2**, failure to agree or correspond; as, the man's accounts and the bank balance showed a *discrepancy*. Also, **dis-crep′ance.**
Syn. difference, variance, disparity.

dis-crep-ant (dĭs-krĕp′ănt; dĭs′krē-pănt), *adj.* discordant; inconsistent; out of agreement.

dis-crete (dĭs-krēt′; dĭs′krēt), *adj.* separate from others; distinct; not continuous; composed of distinct parts.—*adv.* **dis-crete′ly.**—*n.* **dis-crete′ness.**

dis-cre-tion (dĭs-krĕsh′ŭn), *n.* **1**, prudence; wise judgment; **2**, freedom to act; as, he has full *discretion.*—*adj.* **dis-cre′tion-al.**—*adj.* **dis-cre′tion-a-ry.**

dis-crim-i-nate (dĭs-krĭm′ĭ-nāt), *v.t.* [*p.t.* and *p.p.* -nat″ed, *p.pr.* -nat″ing], to distinguish; observe or mark the differences between; differentiate:—*v.i.* to make a difference or distinction.—*adv.* **dis-crim′i-nat″ing-ly.**—*adv.* **dis-crim′i-nate-ly.**
Syn., v. differentiate, discern. (See perceive.)

dis-crim-i-na-tion (dĭs-krĭm″ĭ-nā′shŭn), *n.* **1**, power of distinguishing; faculty of exact judgment; discernment; **2**, a difference in treatment, usually unfair; **3**, a discussion of nice distinctions, as in the meanings of synonyms.
Syn. acuteness, judgment, caution, insight.—*Ant.* dulness, stupidity, slowness.

dis-crim-i-na-tive (dĭs-krĭm′ĭ-nā-tĭv), *adj.* **1**, showing exact judgment; penetrating; acute; **2**, distinctively characteristic.

dis-cur-sive (dĭs-kûr′sĭv), *adj.* wandering from one thing to another; digressive; rambling.—*adv.* **dis-cur′sive-ly.**—*n.* **dis-cur′sive-ness.**

dis-cus (dĭs′kŭs), *n.* [*pl.* discuses (-ĕz); disci (dĭs′ī)], a heavy disk of metal or stone, thrown in athletic contests.

Discus Thrower of Myron

dis-cuss (dĭs-kŭs′), *v.t.* to debate; give reasons for and against; discourse upon; argue.

dis-cus-sion (dĭs-kŭsh′ŭn), *n.* **1**, argument; **2**, reasoned, detailed consideration of a point.

dis-dain (dĭs-dān′), *v.t.* to scorn; despise; look upon with contempt:—*n.* contempt; haughty dislike.

dis-dain-ful (dĭs-dān′fŏŏl), *adj.* contemptuous; scornful; as, a *disdainful* look or reply.—*adv.* **dis-dain′ful-ly.**
Syn. proud, lofty, arrogant.

dis-ease (dĭ-zēz′), *n.* disorder of mind or body; malady; illness:—*v.t.* [*p.t.* and *p.p.* -eased′ (-zēzd′), *p.pr.* -eas′ing], to cause disease in; derange.
Syn., n. sickness, illness. *Disease* is the general term for any departure from a state of health; it frequently suggests a more serious or long-continued state than either *sickness* or *illness;* as, leprosy is a foul and wasting *disease. Illness* and *sickness* mean practically the same thing; but *sickness* sometimes has the additional meaning of nausea or vomiting.

dis-em-bark (dĭs″ĕm-bärk′), *v.t.* and *v.i.* to remove from, or go ashore from, a vessel.—*n.* **dis-em″bar-ka′tion.**

dis-em-bar-rass (dĭs″ĕm-băr′ăs), *v.t.* to free from hindrances or entanglements; disengage.

dis-em-bod-y (dĭs″ĕm-bŏd′ĭ), *v.t.* [*p.t.* and *p.p.* -bod′ied (-ĭd), *p.pr.* -bod′y-ing], to set free from the body; divest of flesh; take physical existence from.—*n.* **dis″em-bod′i-ment.**

dis-em-bogue (dĭs″ĕm-bōg′), *v.t.* [*p.t.* and *p.p.* -bogued′ (-bōgd′), *p.pr.* -bo′guing], to pour forth or discharge at the mouth, as a river:—*v.i.* to be discharged; empty; flow out, as water from a river mouth.—*n.* **dis″em-bogue′ment.**

dis-em-bow-el (dĭs″ĕm-bou′ĕl), *v. t.* **1**, to deprive of bowels; **2**, to wound so that the bowels protrude.

dis-en-chant (dĭs″ĕn-chănt′), *v.t.* to set free from a charm, spell, or delusion.—*n.* **dis″en-chant′ment.**

dis-en-cum-ber (dĭs″ĕn-kŭm′bẽr), *v.t.* to free from burden or hindrance.—*n.* **dis″en-cum′brance.**

dis-en-gage (dĭs″ĕn-gāj′), *v.t.* [*p.t.* and *p.p.* -gaged′ (-gājd′), *p.pr.* -gag′ing], to release; disentangle; extricate; clear.—*n.* **dis″en-gage′ment.**

dis-en-tan-gle (dĭs″en-tăng′gl), *v.t.* [*p.t.* and *p.p.* -gled (-gld), *p.pr.* -gling], **1**, to unravel, as a skein; **2**, to rid of an entanglement or embarrassing connection; **3**, to clear; extricate; disengage.—*n.* **dis″en-tan′gle-ment.**

dis-es-tab-lish (dĭs″ĕs-tăb′lĭsh), *v.t.* **1**, to end the fixed existence or establishment of, **2**, to withdraw state support from, as from an established church.—*n.* **dis″es-tab′lish-ment.**

dis-fa-vor (dĭs-fā′vẽr), *n.* **1**, lack of regard or esteem; **2**, the state of not being well regarded:—*v.t.* to disapprove of. Also, **dis-fa′vour.**

dis-fig-ure (dĭs-fĭg′ūr), *v.t.* [*p.t.* and *p.p.* -ured (-ūrd), *p.pr.* -ur-ing], to mar; injure the shape, form, or beauty of; deform; as, the accident *disfigured* her.—*n.* **dis-fig′ure-ment.**—*n.* **dis-fig″u-ra′tion.**

dis-fran-chise (dĭs-frăn′chīz; dĭs-frăn′-chĭz), *v.t.* [*p.t.* and *p.p.* -chised (-chīzd; -chĭzd), *p.pr.* -chis-ing], to deprive of a political right, as the right to vote.

dis-gorge (dĭs-gôrj′), *v.t.* [*p.t.* and *p.p.* -gorged′ (-gôrjd′), *p.pr.* -gorg′-ing], **1**, to give up, as plunder; **2**, to force out of the mouth or stomach with violence:—*v.i.* **1**, to surrender what has been unlawfully obtained; **2**, to vomit.

dis-grace (dĭs-grās′), *n.* **1**, ignominy; shame; dishonor; **2**, the cause of shame:—*v.t.* [*p.t.* and *p.p.* -graced′ (-grāst′), *p.pr.* -grac′ing], **1**, to bring shame, reproach, or dishonor upon; **2**, to discharge with dishonor.

Syn., *n.* disrepute, odium, reproach.—*Ant.*, *n.* honor, fame, respect, favor.

dis-grace-ful (dĭs-grās′fo͝ol), *adj.* characterized by, or occasioning, dishonor; shameful.—*adv.* **dis-grace′ful-ly.**

dis-grun-tle (dĭs-grŭn′tl), *v.t.* [*p.t.* and *p.p.* -tled (-tld), *p.pr.* -tling], *Colloq.*, to make dissatisfied; put in bad humor; disappoint.

dis-guise (dĭs-gīz′), *v.t.* [*p.t.* and *p.p.* -guised′ (-gīzd′), *p.pr.* -guis′-ing], **1**, to conceal or change the appearance of, as by an unusual dress; **2**, to conceal or alter by a pretense; as, to *disguise* the handwriting:—*n.* **1**, a dress designed to conceal the identity of the wearer; **2**, concealment by assumed speech, manner, or appearance; a false pretense; **3**, that which serves to conceal; a cloak; a mask.—*adv.* **dis-guis′ed-ly.** —*n.* **dis-guis′er.**

Syn., *n.* pretext, simulation; *v.* (see conceal). —*Ant.*, *n.* reality, openness, candor.

dis-gust (dĭs-gŭst′), *n.* dislike; strong aversion:—*v.t.* **1**, to cause distaste or loathing in; **2**, to offend the taste or moral sense of.—*p.adj.* **dis-gust′ing.**—*adv.* **dis-gust′ing-ly.**—*adj.* **dis-gust′ful.**

Syn., *n.* distaste, loathing, abomination, abhorrence.

dish (dĭsh), *n.* **1**, a deep or shallow hollow vessel with a rimmed edge, used for serving food; **2**, food served in a dish; some special food; **3**, something like a dish:—*v.t.* **1**, to put into a dish for serving at table; **2**, to make concave, as a sheet of metal.

dis-ha-bille (dĭs″ȧ-bēl′; -bĭl′), *n.* **1**, a loose, careless garment; **2**, the state of being partly or informally dressed. Also, **des″ha-bille′** (dĕz″ȧ-bēl′).

dish-cloth (dĭsh′klôth″), *n.* a cloth used for washing dishes.

dis-heart-en (dĭs-här′tn), *v.t.* to discourage.

Syn. deject, abash, dispirit, depress.

di-shev-el (dĭ-shĕv′ĕl), *v.t.* **1**, to cause to hang negligently or loosely, as the hair; disarrange; **2**, to disorder, as the dress; **3**, to tousle; ruffle.

dis-hon-est (dĭs-ŏn′ĕst), *adj.* **1**, lacking in uprightness or fairness; as, a *dishonest* act; **2**, inclined to cheat or deceive; as, a *dishonest* man; **3**, false; as, a *dishonest* statement.—*adv.* **dis-hon′est-ly.**

dis-hon-es-ty (dĭs-ŏn′ĕs-tĭ), *n.* deceit; unfairness; lack of truth and uprightness; tendency to theft or fraud.

dis-hon-or (dĭs-ŏn′ẽr), *v.t.* **1**, to disgrace, bring shame upon the character of; **2**, to refuse, or fail, to pay (a bill or note):—*n.* **1**, disgrace; ignominy; shame; **2**, a dishonest act. Also, **dis-hon′our.**

Syn., *v.* degrade, humiliate, insult.

dis-hon-or-a-ble (dĭs-ŏn′ẽr-ȧ-bl), *adj.* **1**, discreditable: shameful; ignominious; as, *dishonorable* treatment; **2**, lacking in truth or uprightness; as, *dishonorable* conduct. Also, **dis-hon′our-a-ble.**—*adv.* **dis-hon′or-a-bly.**

dis-il-lu-sion (dĭs″ĭ-lū′zhŭn), *v.t.* to set free from a mistaken belief in the goodness, beauty, or value of some person or thing:—*n.* freedom from mistaken ideals; disenchantment.

dis-in-cli-na-tion (dĭs-ĭn″klĭ-nā′shŭn), *n.* lack of desire; unwillingness; distaste.

dis-in-cline (dĭs″ĭn-klīn′), *v.t.* [*p.t.* and *p.p.* -clined′ (-klīnd′), *p.pr.* -clin′ing], to make unwilling:—*v.i.* to be unwilling or indisposed.

dis-in-fect (dĭs″ĭn-fĕkt′), *v.t.* to cleanse from infection; purify of germs.—*n.* **dis″in-fec′tion.**—*n.* **dis″in-fec′tor.**

dis-in-fect-ant (dĭs″ĭn-fĕk′tănt), *n.* a substance which will destroy lower organisms that cause disease, or render them harmless; a germicide.

dis-in-gen-u-ous (dĭs″ĭn-jĕn′ū-ŭs), *adj.* **1**, not frank or candid; **2**, deceitful.—*adv.* **dis″in-gen′u-ous-ly.** —*n.* **dis″in-gen′u-ous-ness.**

dis-in-her-it (dĭs″ĭn-hĕr′ĭt), *v.t.* to deprive or cut off, as an heir, from property.—*n.* **dis″in-her′it-ance.**

dis-in-te-grate (dĭs-ĭn′tē-grāt), *v.t.* [*p.t.* and *p.p.* -grat″ed, *p.pr.* -grat″ing], to break up:—*v.i.* to fall to pieces.

dis-in-te-gra-tion (dĭs-ĭn″tē-grā′shŭn), *n.* **1**, a separating into fragments, or breaking up; **2**, the wearing down of rocks under the action of water, frost, ice, air, etc.

dis-in-ter (dĭs″ĭn-tûr′), *v.t.* [*p.t.* and *p.p.* -terred′ (-tûrd′), *p.pr.* -ter′ring], to dig up from a grave.—*n.* **dis″in-ter′ment.**

dis-in-ter-est-ed (dĭs-ĭn′tẽr-ĕs-tĕd), *adj.* not considering oneself; without a selfish motive.—*adv.* **dis-in′ter-est-ed-ly.**—*n.* **dis-in′ter-est-ed-ness.**

dis-join (dĭs-join′), *v.t.* **1**, to separate; break the union between; **2**, to prevent from uniting; keep apart:—*v.i.* to be parted or disconnected.

dis-joint (dĭs-joint′), *v.t.* **1**, in anatomy, to part at the joints; dislocate; **2**, to take apart, as a machine; **3**, to disturb the order of; render incoherent.

dis-junc-tive (dĭs-jŭngk′tĭv), *adj.* serving or tending to disconnect or separate:—*n.* a conjunction which connects two elements disjoined or contrasted in meaning, as *although*, *either*, *or*, etc.: opp. of *conjunctive*.—*adv.* **dis-junc′tive-ly.**

disk (dĭsk), *n.* **1**, a flat, circular plate, or anything resembling it; **2**, in botany, a flat, round growth or part, often composed of many small flowers, as the center of a daisy (see *composite*, illus.): **disk grinder**, a machine with disk-shaped wheels for sharpening tools (see illus. next page). Also, **disc.**

dis-like (dĭs-līk′), *n.* a strong feeling of aversion:—*v.t.* [*p.t.* and *p.p.* -liked′ (-līkt′), *p.pr.* -lik′ing], **1**, to regard with aversion; **2**, to be displeased with.

Syn., *n.* abhorrence, distaste, repugnance. —*Ant.*, *n.* affection, liking, affinity.

dis-lo-cate (dĭs'lō-kāt), *v.t.* [*p.t.* and *p.p.* -cat″ed, *p.pr.* -cat″ing], **1**, to put out of joint, as a bone; displace; **2**, to interrupt the continuation of.

dis-lo-ca-tion (dĭs″lō-kā'shŭn), *n.* **1**, the act of displacing or disjoining; **2**, the separation of the parts of a joint; **3**, in geology, a break in a layer of rock.

dis-lodge (dĭs-lŏj'), *v.t.* [*p.t.* and *p.p.* -lodged' (-lŏjd'), *p.pr.* -lodg'-ing], to remove; drive from a hiding place.—*n.* **dis-lodg'ment.**

dis-loy-al (dĭs-loi'ăl), *adj.* false to duty, government, or friends; faithless; disobedient.—*n.* **dis-loy'al-ty.**—*adv.* **dis-loy'al-ly.**

Syn. inconstant, traitorous, untrue.—*Ant.* true, faithful, loyal.

dis-mal (dĭz'măl), *adj.* **1**, gloomy; depressing; as, *dismal* weather; **2**, sorrowful, as a mood.—*adv.* **dis'mal-ly.**

dis-man-tle (dĭs-măn'tl), *v.t.* [*p.t.* and *p.p.* -tled (-tld), *p.pr.* -tling], **1**, to strip or deprive of furniture, equipment, means of defense, etc.; **2**, to demolish.—*n.* **dis-man'tle-ment.**

dis-mast (dĭs-måst'), *v.t.* to deprive of a mast; as, the ship was caught in a gale and *dismasted.*

dis-may (dĭs-mā'), *v.t.* **1**, to terrify; **2**, to dispirit; discourage:—*n.* **1**, loss of courage through fear; **2**, a condition of terror.

Syn., *v.* frighten, scare, dishearten.

dis-mem-ber (dĭs-mĕm'bẽr), *v.t.* **1**, to cut or tear limb from limb; **2**, to sever into parts and distribute; divide; **3**, to disjoint; dislocate.—*n.* **dis-mem'ber-ment.**

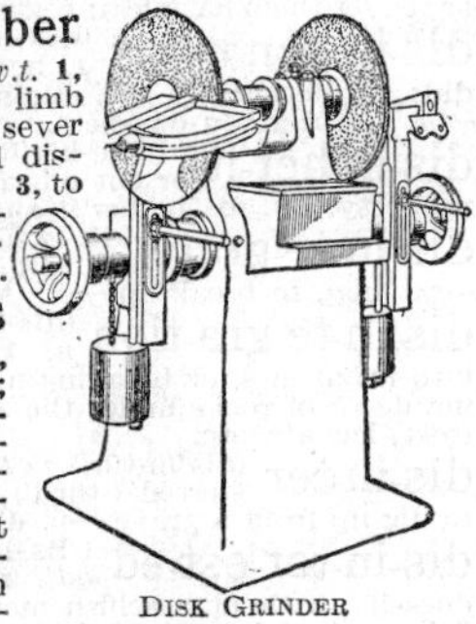
Disk Grinder

dis-miss (dĭs-mĭs'), *v.t.* **1**, to send away; permit to depart; **2**, to discharge from office or employment; **3**, to put away; as, to *dismiss* fear from one's mind.—*n.* **dis-mis'sion.**—*adj.* **dis-mis'sive.**

Syn. discard, banish.

dis-miss-al (dĭs-mĭs'ăl), *n.* **1**, the act of sending away; **2**, removal from office; also, a notice of such removal.

dis-mount (dĭs-mount'), *v.i.* to get off a horse, bicycle, etc.:—*v.t.* **1**, to take from a carriage, as a cannon; **2**, to unhorse; **3**, to take out of a setting, as a pearl.

dis-o-be-di-ence (dĭs″ō-bē'dĭ-ĕns), *n.* neglect to comply with an order or command.

dis-o-be-di-ent (dĭs″ō-bē'dĭ-ĕnt), *adj.* refusing or neglecting to carry out a command; not observant of duty or rules.—*adv.* **dis″o-be'di-ent-ly.**

dis-o-bey (dĭs″ō-bā'), *v.t.* to fail or refuse to carry out the orders of:—*v.i.* to refuse to carry out a command.

dis-o-blige (dĭs″ō-blīj'), *v.t.* [*p.t.* and *p.p.* -bliged' (-blījd'), *p.pr.* -blig'-ing], to refuse to accommodate.—*p.adj.* **dis″-o-blig'ing.**—*adv.* **dis″o-blig'ing-ly.**

dis-or-der (dĭs-ôr'dẽr), *n.* **1**, lack of system; irregularity; confusion; as, the earthquake caused great *disorder* in California. **2**, a riot; **3**, mental or physical disease:—*v.t.* **1**, to throw into confusion; disarrange; **2**, to derange in health of mind or body.—*p.adj.* **dis-or'dered.**

Syn., *n.* disturbance, tumult, clutter.—*Ant.*, *n.* order, method, regularity.

dis-or-der-ly (dĭs-ôr'dẽr-lĭ), *adj.* **1**, confused; **2**, turbulent; unruly; **3**, violating law and order; disreputable.—*n.* **dis-or'der-li-ness.**

dis-or-gan-ize (dĭs-ôr'găn-īz), *v.t.* [*p.t.* and *p.p.* -ized (-īzd), *p.pr.* -iz″ing], to destroy the regularity of; throw into confusion.—*n.* **dis-or″gan-i-za'tion.**—*n.* **dis-or'gan-iz″er.**

dis-own (dĭs-ōn'), *v.t.* **1**, to deny; reject; refuse to claim as one's own; as, his family *disowned* him; **2**, to renounce allegiance to; as, to *disown* one's country.

dis-par-age (dĭs-păr'āj), *v.t.* [*p.t.* and *p.p.* -aged (-ājd), *p.pr.* -ag-ing], **1**, to belittle; speak slightingly of; **2**, to bring discredit upon; dishonor.—*adv.* **dis-par'ag-ing-ly.**

Syn. depreciate, discredit, decry.

dis-par-age-ment (dĭs-păr'āj-mĕnt), *n.* **1**, the act of speaking slightingly of; depreciation; **2**, reproach; disgrace: often with *to.*

dis-pa-rate (dĭs'pȧ-rāt), *adj.* so unequal or unlike as to permit no comparison; totally different.—*adv.* **dis'pa-rate-ly.**—*n.* **dis'pa-rate-ness.**

dis-par-i-ty (dĭs-păr'ĭ-tĭ), *n.* [*pl.* disparities (-tĭz)], inequality; difference; disproportion; diversity.

dis-pas-sion-ate (dĭs-păsh'ŭn-āt), *adj.* free from passion; calm; impartial.—*adv.* **dis-pas'sion-ate-ly.**

dis-patch (dĭs-păch'), *v.t.* **1**, to send off; **2**, to finish quickly; **3**, to kill:—*n.* **1**, speedy performance; **2**, a sending off; **3**, death; **4**, a message sent with speed, as a telegram; **5**, a government document sent to a minister abroad. Also, **des-patch'.**

dis-patch-er (dĭs-păch'ẽr), *n.* one who or that which sends something off promptly or at the right time; as, a train *dispatcher.* Also, **des-patch'er.**

dis-pel (dĭs-pĕl'), *v.t.* [*p.t.* and *p.p.* -pelled' (-pĕld'), *p.pr.* -pel'ling], **1**, to drive away by, or as by, scattering; disperse; **2**, to cause to vanish; dissipate.

dis-pen-sa-ble (dĭs-pĕn'sȧ-bl), *adj.* **1**, capable of being administered; **2**, capable of being done without.

dis-pen-sa-ry (dĭs-pĕn'sȧ-rĭ), *n.* [*pl.* dispensaries (-rĭz)], **1**, a place where medicines are made up; **2**, an institution for providing the poor with medical advice and also with medicines.

dis-pen-sa-tion (dĭs″pĕn-sā'shŭn), *n.* **1**, the act of giving out in portions; **2**, that which is bestowed by a higher power; **3**, the suspending of a rule or law in some particular case; **4**, a license granted by the Pope, or by a bishop.

dis-pen-sa-to-ry (dĭs-pĕn'sȧ-tō-rĭ), *n.* [*pl.* dispensatories (-rĭz)], a book treating of the composition, effect, and preparation of medicines.

dis-pense (dĭs-pĕns'), *v.t.* [*p.t.* and *p.p.* -pensed' (-pĕnst'), *p.pr.* -pens'-ing], **1**, to deal out in portions; as, to *dispense* food; **2**, to carry out; enforce; as, to *dispense* justice:—*v.i.* to give special license: **dispense with**, to give up or go without; as, to *dispense with* the nurse.—*n.* **dis-pens'er.**

dis-perse (dĭs-pûrs'), *v.t.* [*p.t.* and *p.p.* -persed' (-pûrst'), *p.pr.* -pers'-ing], **1**, to scatter; **2**, to cause to vanish; as, the sun *disperses* the mist:—*v.i.* to separate; vanish out of sight; as, the crowd *dispersed.*

dis-per-sion (dĭs-pûr'shŭn), *n.* the act of scattering; the state of being scattered; as, the *dispersion* of a ray of light into rays of different colors when passed through a prism.—*adj.* **dis-per'sive.**

dis-pir-it (dĭs-pĭr'ĭt), *v.t.* to depress the spirits of; dishearten; discourage. —*p.adj.* **dis-pir'it-ed.**—*adv.* **dis-pir'it-ed-ly.**

dis-place (dĭs-plās'), *v.t.* [*p.t.* and *p.p.* -placed' (-plāst'), *p.pr.* -plac'-ing], **1**, to put out of place; change the arrangement of; **2**, to depose from office or dignity; as, to *displace* a dishonest official.

Syn. discharge, remove, disturb.

dis-place-ment (dĭs-plās'mĕnt), *n.* **1**, the act of putting out of place; **2**, removal from a usual position, or from an office; **3**, replacement of one thing by another; **4**, the weight of water, or of air, displaced by a solid body immersed in it; as, the *displacement* of a vessel or of an airship.

dis-play (dĭs-plā'), *v.t.* **1**, to spread out; unfold; **2**, to exhibit; show; **3**, in printing, to make prominent by large type:—*v.i.* to make a show of something:—*n.* **1**, an exhibit; **2**, a parade or show; as, the fashion *display* at the opera; **3**, in printing, the use of large type or special arrangement to attract attention.

Syn., *v.* open, expose, indicate.

dis-please (dĭs-plēz'), *v.t.* [*p.t.* and *p.p.* -pleased' (-plēzd'), *p.pr.* -pleas'-ing], **1**, to vex; annoy; **2**, to offend; **3**, to arouse a dislike in; excite aversion in.—*adj.* **dis-pleas'ing.**—*adv.* **dis-pleas'ing-ly.**

dis-pleas-ure (dĭs-plĕzh'ŭr), *n.* **1**, disapproval; vexation; indignation; **2**, distaste.

dis-port (dĭs-pōrt'), *v.t.* **1**, to amuse or divert: used reflexively; as, to *disport* oneself in the ocean; **2**, to display gaily.

dis-pos-al (dĭs-pōz'ăl), *n.* **1**, arrangement; as, the *disposal* of goods in a store; **2**, a giving over, as by gift, deed, contract, etc.; **3**, a riddance; as, the *disposal* of garbage; **4**, the right to give or control; as, money was at his *disposal*.

dis-pose (dĭs-pōz'), *v.t.* [*p.t.* and *p.p.* -posed' (-pōzd'), *p.pr.* -pos'ing], **1**, to place; arrange; **2**, to regulate or order; **3**, to direct or influence toward; incline; as, competition *disposes* a person to envy.

dis-po-si-tion (dĭs"pō-zĭsh'ŭn), *n.* **1**, the act of placing or arranging; **2**, order; arrangement; as, the *disposition* of property; **3**, inclination; as, a natural *disposition* to jealousy; **4**, temper or habit of mind; as, she has a cheerful *disposition*.

Syn. bent, humor. (See temperament.)

dis-pos-sess (dĭs"pŏ-zĕs'), *v.t.* to remove from ownership, esp. of land; eject.—*n.* **dis"pos-ses'sion.**

dis-proof (dĭs-prōōf'), *n.* evidence that a statement is untrue.

dis-pro-por-tion (dĭs"prō-pōr'shŭn), *n.* want of symmetry; lack of proper or suitable relation in form, size, importance, etc.—*adj.* **dis"pro-por'tion-al.**

dis-pro-por-tion-ate (dĭs"prō-pōr'-shŭn-āt), *adj.* lacking in symmetry or balance; out of proportion.—*adv.* **dis"pro-por'tion-ate-ly.**—*n.* **dis"pro-por'tion-ate-ness.**

dis-prove (dĭs-prōōv'), *v.t.* [*p.t.* -proved' (-prōōvd'), *p.p.* -proved' or, *Archaic*, -prov'en (-prōōv'n), *p.pr.* -prov'ing], to show to be untrue or unreasonable.

dis-pu-tant (dĭs'pū-tănt), *adj.* given to arguing:—*n.* a debater.

dis-pu-ta-tion (dĭs"pū-tā'shŭn), *n.* a debate; an argument; a verbal controversy; an altercation.

dis-pu-ta-tious (dĭs"pū-tā'shŭs), *adj.* contentious; inclined to argue or dispute; quarrelsome.

dis-pute (dĭs-pūt'), *v.i.* [*p.t.* and *p.p.* -put'ed, *p.pr.* -put'ing], to debate; argue; quarrel:—*v.t.* **1**, to contend for by words or actions; as, to *dispute* a prize; **2**, to express doubt of; controvert; contest; as, to *dispute* an election:—*n.* a contest in words; a quarrel.—*adj.* **dis'pu-ta-ble.**—*n.* **dis-put'er.**—*adj.* **dis-put'a-tive.**

Syn., *v.* wrangle, question; *n.* (see quarrel).—*Ant.*, *v.* accept, assent, consent, agree.

dis-qual-i-fy (dĭs-kwŏl'ĭ-fī), *v.t.* [*p.t.* and *p.p.* -fied (-fīd), *p.pr.* -fy"-ing], **1**, to make unfit; disable; **2**, to deprive of a right or privilege.—*n.* **dis-qual"i-fi-ca'tion.**

dis-qui-et (dĭs-kwī'ĕt), *v.t.* to make uneasy; worry:—*n.* a feeling of uneasiness; anxiety.—*n.* **dis-qui'e-tude.**

dis-qui-si-tion (dĭs"kwĭ-zĭsh'ŭn), *n.* a formal or elaborate discussion; dissertation.—*n.* **dis-quis'i-tor.**

dis-re-gard (dĭs"rē-gärd'), *v.t.* to fail to notice or give consideration to; slight; neglect:—*n.* lack of attention.—*adj.* **dis"re-gard'ful.**—*n.* **dis"re-gard'er.**

dis-re-pair (dĭs"rē-pâr'), *n.* the state of needing repair; dilapidation.

dis-rep-u-ta-ble (dĭs-rĕp'ū-tȧ-bl), *adj.* of bad character; low; disgraceful.—*adv.* **dis-rep'u-ta-bly.**

dis-re-pute (dĭs"rē-pūt'), *n.* lack or loss of good reputation.

dis-re-spect (dĭs"rē-spĕkt'), *n.* lack of proper courtesy toward elders or superiors; impoliteness.

dis-re-spect-ful (dĭs"rē-spĕkt'fōōl), *adj.* failing in proper courtesy, esp. to elders or superiors.—*adv.* **dis"re-spect'ful-ly.**

dis-robe (dĭs-rōb'), *v.t.* [*p.t.* and *p.p.* -robed' (-rōbd'), *p.pr.* -rob'ing], to remove clothes or covering from; uncover: —*v.i.* to undress.

dis-rupt (dĭs-rŭpt'), *v.t.* and *v.i.* to break apart; separate with violence. —*adj.* **dis-rup'tive.**—*n.* *Rare*, **dis-rup'ture.**

dis-rup-tion (dĭs-rŭp'shŭn), *n.* **1**, the act of rending or tearing apart; **2**, forcible separation or division.

dis-sat-is-fac-tion (dĭs-săt"ĭs-făk'-shŭn), *n.* discontent; lack of pleasure in that which one has.

dis-sat-is-fy (dĭs-săt'ĭs-fī), *v.t.* [*p.t.* and *p.p.* -fied (-fīd), *p.pr.* -fy"-ing], to cause displeasure to, as by lack of something; fail to content.

dis-sect (dĭ-sĕkt'), *v.t.* **1**, to cut in pieces in order to examine minutely; **2**, to examine point by point; analyze.

dis-sec-tion (dĭ-sĕk'shŭn), *n.* **1**, the act of cutting in pieces for critical examination; **2**, a plant or animal cut open to show its structure.

dis-sem-ble (dĭ-sĕm'bl), *v.t.* [*p.t.* and *p.p.* -bled (-bld), *p.pr.* -bling], **1**, to hide under a false appearance; as, to *dissemble* one's real intentions; **2**, to pretend not to notice:—*v.i.* to act the hypocrite; as, they *dissemble* and fawn in their efforts to gain favor.—*n.* **dis-sem'bler.**—*n.* **dis-sem'blance.**

Syn. feign, cover, mask, conceal.

dis-sem-i-nate (dĭ-sĕm'ĭ-nāt), *v.t.* [*p.t.* and *p.p.* -nat"ed, *p.pr.* -nat"ing], to scatter abroad, like seed; propagate, as opinions; diffuse.—*n.* **dis-sem"i-na'tion.**—*n.* **dis-sem'i-na"tor.**

Syn. spread, circulate, disperse.

dis-sen-sion (dĭ-sĕn'shŭn), *n.* strife; discord; angry disagreement; as, *dissension* between political parties.

Syn. contention, quarrel, wrangling.

dis-sent (dĭ-sĕnt'), *v.i.* to disagree in opinion: with *from*:—*n.* **1**, difference of opinion; **2**, refusal to be bound by

some established order, as the doctrine of a church or the customs of society.
Syn., v. quarrel, differ, vary.

dis-sent-er (dĭ-sĕn'tẽr), *n.* one who differs in opinion, esp. one who separates from the established church.

dis-ser-ta-tion (dĭs"ẽr-tā'shŭn), *n.* a lengthy, and usually formal, discourse; a learned treatise.

dis-sev-er (dĭ-sĕv'ẽr), *v.t.* to cut in two; separate.—*n.* **dis-sev'er-ance.**

dis-si-dence (dĭs'ĭ-dĕns), *n.* discord; disagreement in opinion.

dis-si-dent (dĭs'ĭ-dĕnt), *adj.* not agreeing or conforming:—*n.* one who disagrees or differs in opinion.

dis-sim-i-lar (dĭ-sĭm'ĭ-lȧr), *adj.* unlike; as, *dissimilar* tastes.—*adv.* **dis-sim'i-lar-ly.**—*n.* **dis-sim"i-lar'i-ty.**

dis-sim-u-late (dĭ-sĭm'ū-lāt), *v.i.* and *v.t.* [*p.t.* and *p.p.* -lat"ed, *p.pr.* -lat"ing], to dissemble; feign; pretend.—*adj.* **dis-sim'u-la-tive.**—*n.* **dis-sim'u-la"tor.**

dis-sim-u-la-tion (dĭ-sĭm"ū-lā'shŭn), *n.* hypocrisy; false pretense; deceit; deception.

dis-si-pate (dĭs'ĭ-pāt), *v.t.* [*p.t.* and *p.p.* -pat"ed, *p.pr.* -pat"ing], **1,** to scatter completely; drive in different directions; **2,** to squander; as, to *dissipate* a fortune:—*v.i.* **1,** to be scattered; vanish; **2,** to spend one's energies intemperately.

dis-si-pat-ed (dĭs'ĭ-pāt"ĕd), *p.adj.* **1,** scattered; dispersed; **2,** intemperate; morally loose.

dis-si-pa-tion (dĭs"ĭ-pā'shŭn), *n.* **1,** the act or state of being scattered or wasted; **2,** mental distraction; **3,** excess; intemperate living.

dis-so-ci-ate (dĭ-sō'shĭ-āt), *v.t.* [*p.t.* and *p.p.* -at"ed, *p.pr.* -at"ing], to separate; disconnect.—*n.* **dis-so"ci-a'tion.**

dis-so-lu-ble (dĭs'ō-lū-bl; dĭ-sŏl'ū-bl), *adj.* capable of being dissolved or of forming a solution; soluble.—*n.* **dis-sol"u-bil'i-ty.**

dis-so-lute (dĭs'ō-lūt), *adj.* morally loose; given to vice or dissipation.—*adv.* **dis'so-lute-ly.**—*n.* **dis'so-lute-ness.**
Syn. wild, wanton, licentious, profligate.—*Ant.* restrained, controlled, moral.

dis-so-lu-tion (dĭs"ō-lū'shŭn), *n.* **1,** the act of separating into parts; **2,** the separation of the soul from the body; death; **3,** disorganization.

dis-solv-a-ble (dĭ-zŏl'vȧ-bl), *adj.* capable of being absorbed into a liquid; capable of making a solution.

dis-solve (dĭ-zŏlv'), *v.t.* [*p.t.* and *p.p.* -solved' (-zŏlvd'), *p.pr.* -solv'-ing], **1,** to cause to be absorbed by a liquid; as, to *dissolve* salt in water; **2,** to separate into parts; **3,** to put an end to, as a partnership:—*v.i.* **1,** to be absorbed into a liquid; **2,** to disappear gradually; fade out of sight; as, the mists *dissolve.*

dis-so-nance (dĭs'ō-năns), *n.* a disagreeable mingling of sounds.

dis-so-nant (dĭs'ō-nănt), *adj.* harsh in sound; discordant; inharmonious.—*adv.* **dis'so-nant-ly.**

dis-suade (dĭ-swād'), *v.t.* [*p.t.* and *p.p.* -suad'ed, *p.pr.* -suad'ing], to advise or counsel against; divert by argument or persuasion from a purpose or action.

dis-sua-sion (dĭ-swā'zhŭn), *n.* advice against a purpose or action.

dis-sua-sive (dĭ-swā'sĭv), *adj.* tending to divert from a purpose or action:—*n.* an argument used to dissuade.

dis-syl-la-ble (dĭ-sĭl'ȧ-bl), *n.* a word of only two syllables.—*adj.* **dis"syl-lab'ic** (dĭs"ĭ-lăb'ĭk).

dis-taff (dĭs'tȧf), *n.* the staff from which flax or wool is drawn in spinning: **the distaff side,** the women of a family collectively.

dis-tal (dĭs'tăl), *adj.* away from the center or origin; as, the tip, or *distal* end, of a finger: opp. of *proximal.*

dis-tance (dĭs'tăns), *n.* **1,** the length of the straight line between two objects or points; **2,** remoteness of time, rank, relationship, or place; **3,** the interval between two notes; **4,** reserve of manner:—*v.t.* [*p.t.* and *p.p.* -tanced (-tănst), *v.pr.* -tanc-ing], **1,** to place remotely; **2,** to leave behind in a race.

dis-tant (dĭs'tănt), *adj.* **1,** so placed as to be (a stated distance) away or apart in time, space, etc.; as, a point two inches *distant* from another; **2,** remote; **3,** reserved; not cordial.
Syn. cold, aloof, unapproachable.

dis-taste (dĭs-tāst'), *n.* **1,** dislike of drink or food; **2,** aversion; disinclination; repugnance.

dis-taste-ful (dĭs-tāst'fo͝ol), *adj.* **1,** unpleasant to the taste; **2,** disagreeable; displeasing to the feelings.—*adv.* **dis-taste'ful-ly.**—*n.* **dis-taste'ful-ness.**
Syn. offensive, repugnant, nauseous.

[1]**dis-tem-per** (dĭs-tĕm'pẽr), *n.* **1,** ill humor; a bad state of mind; **2,** a disease of an animal body, esp. in brutes:—*v.t.* to disease; disorder.

[2]**dis-tem-per** (dĭs-tĕm'pẽr), *n.* **1,** a method of painting with colors mixed with white of egg or a similar binding medium; **2,** the paint so prepared, or the painting so made.

dis-tend (dĭs-tĕnd'), *v.t.* **1,** to stretch out in all directions; **2,** to expand:—*v.i.* to swell; enlarge.

dis-ten-tion (dĭs-tĕn'shŭn), *n.* a swelling out. Also, **dis-ten'sion.**

dis-tich (dĭs'tĭk), *n.* a couplet, or two lines of verse that make complete sense in themselves.

dis-til (dĭs-tĭl'), *v.i.* [*p.t.* and *p.p.* -tilled' (-tĭld'), *p.pr.* -till'ing], to fall in drops; flow gently; trickle forth:—*v.t.* **1,** to let fall in drops; **2,** to separate (a liquid) from a mixture by heating until it becomes a gas and then condensing the gas to a liquid; **3,** to subject (a mixture) to this process. Also, **dis-till'.**—*n.* **dis-till'er.**

dis-till-ate (dĭs-tĭl'ăt; dĭs'tĭ-lāt), *n.* the product obtained from a mixture by driving off, as by heat, a part of it in the form of a gas or vapor, and then condensing this.

dis-til-la-tion (dĭs"tĭ-lā'shŭn), *n.* **1,** the process of heating a mixture until one substance in it becomes a vapor, and then condensing this to a liquid again; **2,** the substance so obtained.

dis-till-er-y (dĭs-tĭl'ẽr-ĭ), *n.* [distilleries (-ĭz)], a place where liquids, esp. alcoholic liquors, are distilled, or produced by fermentation.

dis-tinct (dĭs-tĭngkt'), *adj.* **1,** separate; different; **2,** clear; as, a *distinct* view; **3,** carefully thought out; lucid; as, a *distinct* statement.—*n.* **dis-tinct'ness.**
Syn. obvious, evident, unconfused.

dis-tinc-tion (dĭs-tĭngk'shŭn), *n.* **1,** the act of noting clearly: **2,** difference; as, to make a *distinction* between moral and legal rights; **3,** the state of deserving special honor; eminence; superiority; as, Lincoln has the *distinction* of having given the slaves freedom; **4,** a title, office, or other mark of honor conferred for superiority.
Syn. (see difference).

dis-tinc-tive (dĭs-tĭngk'tĭv), *adj.* **1,** marking a difference; **2,** characteristic; as, a *distinctive* feature.—*adv.* **dis-tinc'tive-ly.**—*n.* **dis-tinc'tive-ness.**

dis-tinct-ly (dĭs-tĭngkt'lĭ), *adv.* clearly; plainly.

***dis-tin-gué** (dēs"tăṅ"gā'), [Fr.], *adj.* distinguished; polished.

dis-tin-guish (dĭs-tĭng'gwĭsh), *v.t.* **1,** to mark off from others; characterize; **2,** to recognize the special features of; **3,** to see clearly; as, to *distinguish* the ship on the horizon; **4,** to honor by a mark of preference:—*v.i.* to make a distinction: with *between.*—*adj.* **dis-tin'guish-a-ble.**

Syn. differentiate, discern. (See perceive.)

dis-tin-guished (dĭs-tĭng'gwĭsht), *p.adj.* superior in ability, achievement, or character.

Syn. famous, glorious, prominent, noted, illustrious.—*Ant.* unknown, obscure, ordinary.

dis-tort (dĭs-tôrt'), *v.t.* **1,** to twist from the natural shape or figure; pervert; **2,** to turn from the true meaning; misrepresent; as, to *distort* the truth.

dis-tor-tion (dĭs-tôr'shŭn), *n.* **1,** the act of twisting out of shape; **2,** a perversion; **3,** a deformity.

dis-tract (dĭs-trăkt'), *v.t.* **1,** to divert (attention) from one object to another; **2,** to confuse the mind of; bewilder; perplex; **3,** to drive mad; derange.—*adv.* **dis-tract'ed-ly.**—*adj.* **dis-trac'tive.**

dis-trac-tion (dĭs-trăk'shŭn), *n.* **1,** a drawing away of the attention from one object to another; **2,** that which diverts attention; **3,** bewilderment; mental confusion or distress; **4,** madness or frenzy.

Syn. disorder, disturbance, diversion, agitation.—*Ant.* tranquillity, poise.

dis-train (dĭs-trān'), *v.t.* in law, to seize as security for a debt; as, to *distrain* household furniture for rent:—*v.i.* to seize property for nonpayment of a debt: with *on* or *upon.*—*adj.* **dis-train'a-ble.**—*n.* **dis-train'or; dis-train'er.**

dis-traint (dĭs-trānt'), *n.* the act of seizing property, as goods and chattels, for nonpayment of debt.

***dis-trait** (dēs"trâ'), [Fr.], *adj.* absent-minded; wandering; distracted.

dis-traught (dĭs-trôt'), *adj.* bewildered or harassed; distracted.

dis-tress (dĭs-trĕs'), *v.t.* **1,** to inflict pain or suffering upon; grieve; **2,** to seize for debt:—*n.* **1,** physical or mental anguish; **2,** misfortune; **3,** the act of distraining or seizing for debt; **4,** goods taken by distraint.—*adj.* **dis-tress'ful.**

Syn., n. grief, pain, trouble, affliction.

dis-trib-ute (dĭs-trĭb'ūt), *v.t.* [*p.t.* and *p.p.* -ut-ed, *p.pr.* -ut-ing], **1,** to deal out or divide; allot; as, to *distribute* books to the soldiers; **2,** to classify; **3,** to spread.—*n.* **dis-trib'u-tor.**

Syn. share, dispense, assign, spread, apportion.—*Ant.* collect, keep, retain.

dis-tri-bu-tion (dĭs"trĭ-bū'shŭn), *n.* **1,** the act or manner of dealing out or dividing; apportionment; **2,** that which is apportioned; **3,** arrangement; classification.

dis-trib-u-tive (dĭs-trĭb'ū-tĭv), *adj.* **1,** apportioning or dealing out; as, *distributive* classes; **2,** in grammar, applying to a group of things individually; as, *any, each, both,* are *distributive* pronouns:—*n.* in grammar, a distributive word.—*adv.* **dis-trib'u-tive-ly.**—*n.* **dis-trib'u-tive-ness.**

dis-trict (dĭs'trĭkt), *n.* **1,** a section marked off within definite limits for administration; **2,** an indefinite region.

dis-trust (dĭs-trŭst'), *n.* **1,** want of confidence or reliance; **2,** suspicion:—*v.t.* **1,** to have no faith in; **2,** to doubt; suspect.

Syn., n. misgiving. (See doubt.)

dis-trust-ful (dĭs-trŭst'fo͝ol), *adj.* suspicious; lacking confidence.—*adv.* **dis-trust'ful-ly.**—*n.* **dis-trust'ful-ness.**

dis-turb (dĭs-tûrb'), *v.t.* **1,** to trouble; vex; **2,** to throw into confusion; agitate; **3,** to interfere with.—*n.* **dis-turb'er.**

Syn. derange, rouse, interrupt, confuse, annoy, worry.—*Ant.* pacify, quiet, soothe.

dis-turb-ance (dĭs-tûr'băns), *n.* **1,** any interruption of a settled order; **2,** confusion; **3,** mental agitation.

Syn. commotion, tumult, turmoil.

dis-un-ion (dĭs-ūn'yŭn), *n.* a breaking apart; division; rupture.

dis-u-nite (dĭs"ū-nīt'), *v.i.* and *v.t.* [*p.t.* and *p.p.* -nit'ed, *p.pr.* -nit'ing], **1,** to divide; **2,** to fall, or cause to fall, apart.

dis-use (dĭs-ūs'), *n.* **1,** a ceasing to use; **2,** neglect:—*v.t.* (dĭs-ūz'), [*p.t.* and *p.p.* -used' (-ūzd'), *p.pr.* -us'ing], to cease to use; neglect.

ditch (dĭch), *n.* a trench cut in the earth; a moat:—*v.i.* to make a trench:—*v.t.* **1,** to surround with a trench; **2,** to cause to run into a trench.—*n.* **ditch'er.**

dith-y-ramb (dĭth'ĭ-rămb; -răm), *n.* **1,** a choral hymn or poem in honor of Bacchus; **2,** a song or poem in a wild, exalted style.—*adj.* **dith"y-ram'bic.**

dit-to (dĭt'ō), *n.* [*pl.* dittos (-ōz)], **1,** the same thing as has been said before; **2,** *Colloq.,* a duplicate:—*adv.* as before; likewise.

dit-ty (dĭt'ĭ), *n.* [*pl.* ditties (-ĭz)], a little song; a short theme often repeated.

dit-ty-box (dĭt'ĭ-bŏks"), *n.* a small tin box in which sailors keep their personal possessions, such as shaving gear, etc.

di-u-ret-ic (dī"ū-rĕt'ĭk), *adj.* in medicine, promoting the secretion of urine:—*n.* a medicine that promotes the secretion of urine.

di-ur-nal (dī-ûr'năl), *adj.* **1,** pertaining to day or daylight; **2,** occurring every day; daily; **3,** active during the daytime, as many insects.—*adv.* **di-ur'nal-ly.**

Syn. (see daily).

***di-va** (dē'vä; dī'vȧ), [It.], *n.* [*pl.* dive (-vā); divas (-vȧz)], a prima donna; a female opera singer.

di-van (dĭ-văn'), *n.* **1,** a council of state, esp. in Turkey; **2,** an oriental council hall; **3,** a smoking room; café; **4,** (commonly, dī'văn), a low, cushioned sofa.

dive (dīv), *v.i.* [*p.t.* dived (dīvd) or, *Colloq.* or *Archaic,* dove (dōv), *p.p.* dived, *p.pr.* div'ing], **1,** to plunge headforemost into water; **2,** to make a plunging movement forward and down; **3,** to enter deeply into any subject or question:—*n.* **1,** a plunge headforemost into water; as, to take a high *dive* requires nerve; **2,** a low resort.—*n.* **div'er.**

di-verge (dĭ-vûrj'), *v.i.* [*p.t.* and *p.p.* -verged' (-vûrjd'), *p.pr.* -verg'ing], **1,** to spread out from one point: opp. of *converge;* **2,** to differ, as in thought; **3,** to differ from a standard or normal form.

di-ver-gence (dĭ-vûr'jĕns), *n.* **1,** a moving apart of two things starting from the same point; **2,** a deviation from a standard. Also, **di-ver'gen-cy.**

di-ver-gent (dĭ-vûr'jĕnt), *adj.* **1,** tending to move apart from the same starting point; **2,** deviating from a standard.

di-vers (dī'vẽrz), *adj.* various; sundry; several: used only with plurals; as, *divers* men.

di-verse (dĭ-vûrs'; dī'vẽrs), *adj.* essentially different; dissimilar; varied.—*adv.* **di-verse'ly.**

di-ver-si-fy (dĭ-vûr'sĭ-fī), *v.t.* [*p.t.* and *p.p.* -fied (-fīd), *p.pr.* -fy"ing], to make distinct; modify; give variety to.—*n.* **di-ver"si-fi-ca'tion.**

di-ver-sion (dĭ-vûr′shŭn), *n.* **1**, a turning aside from a set course; variation; **2**, hence, amusement; recreation; pastime.
Syn. sport, game, amusement, fun.

di-ver-si-ty (dĭ-vûr′sĭ-tĭ), *n.* [*pl.* diversities (-tĭz)], difference; variety.

di-vert (dĭ-vûrt′), *v.t.* **1**, to turn aside from any direction or course; draw away from; **2**, to entertain; amuse; **3**, to change the aim of; distract the attention of; as, to *divert* the mind of a crying child by a story.

Di-ves (dī′vēz), *n.* in the Bible, the rich man who, from hell, saw the beggar Lazarus in Abraham's bosom (Luke 16:19–31); hence, any rich, worldly man.

di-vest (dĭ-vĕst′), *v.t.* **1**, to strip or unclothe; **2**, to deprive; **3**, to despoil.

di-vide (dĭ-vīd′), *v.t.* [*p.t.* and *p.p.* -vid′ed, *p.pr.* -vid′ing], **1**, to cut into two or more parts; **2**, to separate; break up the union of; **3**, to cause to disagree; **4**, to share or distribute; as, to *divide* the money among them; **5**, in mathematics, to perform the operation of division (on or with):—*v.i.* **1**, to separate; **2**, to perform the operation of division with two numbers:—*n.* a watershed.

div-i-dend (dĭv′ĭ-dĕnd), *n.* **1**, a share of the profits of a public company or business; **2**, a number or quantity to be divided by another number or quantity.

di-vid-ers (dĭ-vīd′ẽrz), *n.pl.* an instrument used in mechanical drawing, for dividing lines, checking distances, etc.; compasses.

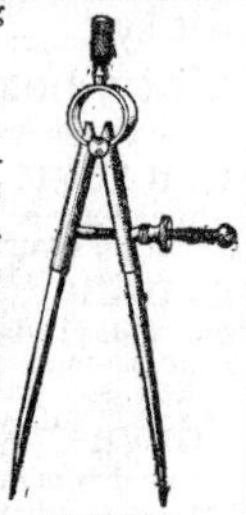
DIVIDERS

div-i-na-tion (dĭv″ĭ-nā′shŭn), *n.* **1**, the act of foreseeing or foretelling, or of guessing something hidden; **2**, a forecast; guess; augury.

¹di-vine (dĭ-vīn′), *adj.* **1**, of or pertaining to God; godlike; **2**, proceeding from God; **3**, sacred; holy; **4**, superhumanly excellent; **5**, pertaining to theology or divinity:—*n.* **1**, a theologian; **2**, a priest; clergyman.—*adv.* **di-vine′ly.**—*n.* **di-vine′ness.**
Syn., adj. heavenly, holy, celestial, superhuman, sacred.

²di-vine (dĭ-vīn′), *v.t.* [*p.t.* and *p.p.* -vined′ (-vīnd′), *p.pr.* -vin′ing], **1**, to foresee or foretell; **2**, to guess; perceive, as by reason or intuition:—*v.i.* **1**, to prophesy; **2**, to guess; conjecture.

di-vin-er (dĭ-vīn′ẽr), *n.* **1**, one who or that which foresees or foretells; **2**, a forked rod or branch, as of witch-hazel, which, when held loosely in the hand, is said to aid in finding hidden springs of water by dipping downward: also called *divining rod.*

div-ing bell a hollow chamber supplied with air, in which men may work under water (see *submarine*, illus.).

di-vin-i-ty (dĭ-vĭn′ĭ-tĭ), *n.* [*pl.* divinities (-tĭz)], **1**, the state or quality of being godlike; Godhead; **2**, a god; a deity; **3**, theology: **the Divinity**, God.

di-vis-i-ble (dĭ-vĭz′ĭ-bl), *adj.* **1**, capable of being separated into parts; **2**, in mathematics, capable of division without a remainder.—*adv.* **di-vis′i-bly.**—*n.* **di-vis′i-ble-ness.**—*n.* **di-vis″i-bil′i-ty.**

di-vi-sion (dĭ-vĭzh′ŭn), *n.* **1**, the act or state of being separated into parts; a partition; section; **2**, that which separates; a dividing line; **3**, discord; difference; as, the discussion caused *division* in the church; **4**, the separating of the members of a lawmaking or municipal assembly in order to take a vote; **5**, two or more army brigades under the command of a general officer; **6**, the process of finding how many times one number or quantity contains, or is contained in, another.—*adj.* **di-vi′sion-al.**
Syn. portion, share, piece. (See part.)

di-vi-sor (dĭ-vī′zẽr), *n.* the number or quantity by which another, the dividend, is divided.

di-vorce (dĭ-vōrs′), *n.* **1**, legal dissolution of the marriage contract; **2**, disunion:—*v.t.* [*p.t.* and *p.p.* -vorced′ (-vōrst′), *p.pr.* -vorc′ing], **1**, to dissolve the marriage contract between; **2**, to release from close union.—*n.* **di-vorce′ment.**—*n.* **di-vor″cee′.**

***di-vor-cé** (dē″vôr″sā′), [Fr.], *n.* a divorced man.—*n.fem.* ***di″-vor″cée′** (dē″vôr″sā′).

div-ot (dĭv′ŭt), *n.* in golf, a piece of turf cut from the sod by a stroke.

di-vulge (dĭ-vŭlj′), *v.t.* [*p.t.* and *p.p.* -vulged′ (-vŭljd′), *p.pr.* -vulg′ing], to make known (a secret); disclose; tell.
Syn. impart, reveal, tell.

Dix-ie (dĭk′sĭ), *n.* **1**, in the U. S., the Southern States; **2**, a favorite Southern song.

diz-en (dĭz′n; dī′zn), *v.t.* to deck out; bedizen; as, to *dizen* oneself with jewels.

diz-zy (dĭz′ĭ), *adj.* [*comp.* diz′zi-er, *superl.* diz′zi-est], giddy; also, causing giddiness; as, a *dizzy* height.—*adv.* **diz′zi-ly.**—*n.* **diz′zi-ness.**

¹do (do͞o), *v.t.* [*p.t.* did (dĭd), *p.p.* done (dŭn), *p.pr.* do′ing], **1**, to achieve; finish, as a task; carry out; perform; **2**, to produce by action; make ready; work out; as, he *did* six examples; **3**, to translate; as, *done* into English; **4**, to deal with in some way; as, to *do* up a parcel; put in order; arrange; as, the maid *does* the room; **5**, to employ, as effort; as, to *do* your best; **6**, to render; bestow; as, to *do* one a service; **7**, *Colloq.*, to suffice; be enough for; **8**, *Slang:* **a**, to swindle; **b**, to injure or kill; **c**, to serve (a term of imprisonment):—*v.i.* **1**, to act; behave; as, to *do* wisely; **2**, to work or strive; make an effort; as, *do* or die; **3**, to answer the purpose:—*substitute v.* used to replace a verb or verb construction and thereby avoid repetition; as, he talks just as his father *does.*—*adj.* **do′a-ble.**—*n.* **do′er.**
Syn. effect, accomplish, fulfil, transact.

²do (dō), *n.* the first in the series of syllables used in singing a diatonic scale.

do-cent (dō′sĕnt), *n.* **1**, one licensed to teach in a university, but not classed as a professor; **2**, an official who guides or lectures in a museum.

doc-ile (dŏs′ĭl; *Br.* dō′sīl), *adj.* easy to teach; tractable; easily managed; as, a gentle, *docile* pony.—*adv.* **doc′ile-ly.**
Syn. teachable, compliant, tame.—*Ant.* intractable, ungovernable, stubborn.

do-cil-i-ty (dō-sĭl′ĭ-tĭ), *n.* the quality of being gentle or easily managed.

¹dock (dŏk), *n.* any of several coarse weeds of the buckwheat family, with broad, red-veined leaves and reddish seeds.

²dock (dŏk), *n.* the place where a prisoner stays in court during trial.

³dock (dŏk), *n.* an artificial basin, or waterway for ships; sometimes, the piers inclosing the basin; a wharf: **dry dock**, a huge basin, often floating, into which a vessel can be taken and from which the water can be withdrawn, leaving the vessel exposed for repairs:—*v.t.* to bring to a pier and moor, as a ship:—*v.i.* to arrive at a pier.

⁴dock (dŏk), *n.* the stump of an animal's tail:—*v.t.* **1**, to cut off; **2**, to deduct from (wages, etc.); **3**, to penalize.

¹dock-age (dŏk′āj), *n.* reduction; deduction.

²dock-age (dŏk′āj), *n.* **1**, accommodation for the docking of vessels; **2**, money paid for the use of a dock.

dock-et (dŏk′ĕt), *v.t.* **1**, to mark (a paper) on the back, noting the title or contents; indorse; **2**, to record on a court or business calendar:—*n.* **1**, a directed label or ticket tied on goods; **2**, a summary of a larger writing; a digest; **3**, a list of cases for trial.

dock-yard (dŏk′yärd″), *n.* a place where ships are built and repaired, and naval stores are kept.

doc-tor (dŏk′tẽr), *n.* **1**, a licensed physician or surgeon; **2**, one holding the highest degree conferred by a university; **3**, formerly, a learned man:—*v.t.* **1**, *Colloq.*, to treat medically; **2**, *Slang*, to tamper with or give a false appearance to:—*v.i. Colloq.*, **1**, to practice medicine; **2**, to undergo medical treatment; take medicine.

doc-tor-ate (dŏk′tẽr-āt), *n.* the title, rank, or degree of doctor.

doc-tri-naire (dŏk″trĭ-nâr′), *n.* one who theorizes on political or other matters, disregarding practical considerations:—*adj.* visionary.

doc-trine (dŏk′trĭn), *n.* that which is taught; the principles, belief, or dogma of any church, sect, or party.—*adj.* **doc′tri-nal.**—*adv.* **doc′tri-nal-ly.**

doc-u-ment (dŏk′ū-mĕnt), *n.* a record; an official paper that gives information or evidence, as a deed.

doc-u-men-ta-ry (dŏk″ū-mĕn′tȧ-rĭ), *adj.* pertaining to, derived from, or consisting of, official papers.

[1]**dod-der** (dŏd′ẽr), *n.* a kind of parasitic flowering plant, leafless and with a threadlike stem, which attaches itself to other plants by small roots that absorb sap.

[2]**dod-der** (dŏd′ẽr), *v.i.* to shake; tremble; totter, as from weakness or age.

do-dec-a-gon (dō-dĕk′ȧ-gŏn), *n.* a plane figure or polygon with twelve sides and twelve angles.

do-dec-a-he-dron (dō″dĕk-ȧ-hē′drŏn), *n.* a solid bounded by twelve plane faces (see *solid*, illus.).

dodge (dŏj), *v.i.* [*p.t.* and *p.p.* dodged (dŏjd), *p.pr.* dodg′ing], **1**, to start aside and shift about; evade; avoid; **2**, to practice tricky devices:—*v.t.* to escape from by starting aside:—*n.* **1**, an act of evasion; **2**, a trick; a clever method.

dodg-er (dŏj′ẽr), *n.* **1**, one who jumps aside; **2**, a tricky fellow; **3**, a small handbill; **4**, an Indian-meal cake.

do-do (dō′dō), *n.* [*pl.* dodoes; dodos (-dōz)], a large, flightless bird, now extinct, with a strong, hooked bill.

doe (dō), *n.* the female of the deer, or of the antelope, rabbit, or hare.

does (dŭz), third person singular, present indicative active, of the verb [1]*do*.

doe-skin (dō′skĭn″), *n.* **1**, the skin of a doe, or female deer; **2**, a kind of fine woolen cloth with a smooth finish.

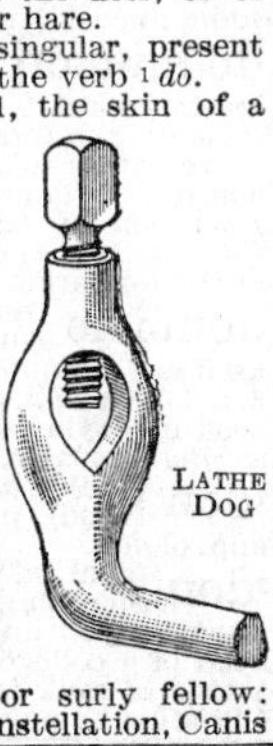

LATHE DOG

doff (dŏf), *v.t.* **1**, to take or put off, as clothes; remove (the hat) in saluting; **2**, to put away; abandon.

dog (dôg), *n.* **1**, any of a great variety of domesticated four-footed animals (genus *Canis*), some descended from the wolf, and others from some other wild ancestor related to the wolf; **2**, a male of the dog, fox, wolf, etc.; **3**, any of various mechanical devices for bracing or holding something, as a catch, stop, checking device, etc.; **4**, a worthless or surly fellow: **Great Dog**, in astronomy, a constellation, Canis Major, containing Sirius, the Dog Star, brightest of all fixed stars: **Lesser Dog**, a constellation, Canis Minor, east of Orion:—*v.t.* [*p.t.* and *p.p.* dogged (dôgd), *p.pr.* dog′ging], **1**, to follow as a hound follows; **2**, to worry, as if by dogs.—*adj.* **dog′gish.**

dog-cart (dôg′kärt″), *n.* a two-wheeled carriage with two transverse seats placed back to back.

dog days a very hot period in July and August, once thought to be due to the rising and setting of the Dog Star.

doge (dōj), *n.* the chief magistrate in the old republics of Venice and Genoa.

dog-fish (dôg′fĭsh″), *n.* any of several kinds of small shark, very destructive to some smaller fish.

dog-ged (dôg′ĕd), *adj.* stubborn; persistent.—*adv.* **dog′ged-ly.**

dog-ger (dôg′ẽr), *n.* a two-masted vessel with a broad beam, used in the cod and herring fisheries in the North Sea.

dog-ger-el (dôg′ẽr-ĕl), *n.* trivial verse, often senseless and poorly constructed:—*adj.* weak and absurd in construction: said of verse.

dog-ma (dôg′mȧ), *n.* [*pl.* dogmas (-mȧz); dogmata (-tȧ)], an established principle, creed, or doctrine, accepted as authoritative, esp. by the church.

dog-mat-ic (dôg-măt′ĭk), *adj.* **1**, pertaining to, or of the nature of, established doctrine; **2**, positive: **dogmatics**, *n.pl.* used as *sing.* doctrinal theology. Also, *adj.* **dog-mat′i-cal.**—*adv.* **dog-mat′i-cal-ly.**

Syn., *adj.* arrogant, imperious, dictatorial. —*Ant.*, *adj.* unassertive, considerate, gentle.

dog-ma-tism (dôg′mȧ-tĭzm), *n.* positive, authoritative assertion of opinion or doctrine; sometimes, unwarranted positiveness.—*n.* **dog′ma-tist**

dog-ma-tize (dôg′mȧ-tīz), *v.i.* [*p.t.* and *p.p.* -tized (-tīzd), *p.pr.* -tiz″ing], to make positive assertions, esp. without adducing proof in support:—*v.t.* to treat dogmatically.

dog–rose (dôg′-rōz″), *n.* a wild brier rose, common in English hedgerows.

dog's–ear (dôgz′-ēr″), *n.* the turned-down corner of a page in a book:—*v.t.* to turn down the corner of (a leaf in a book). Also, **dog′–ear″.**

Dog Star Sirius, the most brilliant fixed star in the heavens, a bright bluish white star in the constellation Canis Major, or the Great Dog.

dog tent a small, low, simply made tent without sides, open at the ends (see *tent*, illus.); a shelter tent.

dog-tooth vi-o-let (dôg′tōōth″), any of several herbs of the lily family, with two mottled leaves and a single lilylike flower, yellow, white, or purple.

dog-trot (dôg′trŏt″), *n.* a slow, easy run, like that of a dog.

dog-watch (dôg′wŏch″), *n.* one of two short watches on board ship, of two hours each, from four to six and six to eight in the afternoon.

dog-wood (dôg′wŏŏd″), *n.* any of several trees with hard, close-grained wood, bearing in spring white or pink blossoms.

doi-ly (doi′lĭ), *n.* [*pl.* doilies (-lĭz)], a small mat or napkin used on the table.

do-ings (dōō′ĭngz), *n.pl.* things done; acts; as, the day's *doings*.

doit (doit), *n.* **1**, orig., a small coin of the Netherlands, having little value; **2**, hence, a small thing; trifle.

dol-drums (dŏl′drŭmz), *n.pl.* **1**, the tropical regions: a sailor's term; **2**, hence, calm; dulness; depression of spirits; the dumps.

[1]dole (dōl), *n. Archaic*, woe; lamentation; sorrowing; grief.

[2]dole (dōl), *n.* that which is dealt out sparingly; a charitable gift of money or food; alms:—*v.t.* [*p.t.* and *p.p.* doled (dōld), *p.pr.* dol'ing], to deal out sparingly.

dole-ful (dōl'fŏŏl), *adj.* sad; dismal.—*adv.* **dole'ful-ly.**—*n.* **dole'ful-ness.**
Syn. dolorous, rueful, mournful, grievous, gloomy.—*Ant.* joyous, glad, merry, gay.

doll (dŏl), *n.* **1**, a girl's puppet or toy baby; **2**, a childish-featured girl or woman.

dol-lar (dŏl'ẽr), *n.* **1**, a silver coin used in the U. S. and Canada, equal to one hundred cents; **2**, a bank note, treasury note, etc., of the legal value of one hundred cents; **3**, any of various large silver coins, current in other countries; as, a Mexican dollar.

doll-y (dŏl'ĭ), *n.* [*pl.* dollies (-ĭz)], **1**, a little doll; **2**, any of various mechanical appliances, as a block used in driving piles, a machine for washing clothes, a contrivance for washing ore in mining, etc.

Doll-y Var-den (vär'dĕn), **1**, a woman's dress of light, bright-figured muslin, worn over a plain, bright-colored petticoat; **2**, a large hat for women, trimmed with numerous flowers.

dol-man (dŏl'măn), *n.* [*pl.* dolmans (-mănz)], **1**, a long outer garment with sleeves, worn by the Turks; **2**, a hussar's jacket; **3**, a woman's mantle with capelike sleeves.

dol-men (dŏl'mĕn), *n.* a monument and tomb, consisting of a large unhewn stone resting on two or more others.

do-lor (dō'lẽr), *n.* sorrow; pain; grief; lamentation; anguish.

dol-or-ous (dŏl'ẽr-ŭs), *adj.* sorrowful; full of grief.—*adv.* **dol'or-ous-ly.**
Syn. mournful, doleful, dismal, distressing.

dol-phin (dŏl'fĭn), *n.* any of various agile sea mammals, akin to the whales:

DOLPHIN (1/15)

also called *porpoise:* **dolphin striker,** a spar on a ship, extending downward from the end of the bowsprit (see *rigging,* illus.).

dolt (dōlt), *n.* a heavy, stupid fellow; a dunce; blockhead.—*adj.* **dolt'ish.**—*adv.* **dolt'ish-ly.**

dom (dŏm), *n.* **1**, a title of respect applied to gentlemen in Portugal and Brazil; in Portugal, formerly, a title of the king and members of the royal family; **2**, a title of certain dignitaries of the Roman Catholic Church.

-dom (-dŭm), *n. suffix,* used to form nouns expressing: **1**, rank, domain; as, duke*dom:* **2**, state or condition; as, martyr*dom;* **3**, a collection or group; as, official*dom.*

do-main (dō-mān'), *n.* **1**, right of possession; authority; **2**, landed property; **3**, range; scope.

dome (dōm), *n.* **1**, a large cupola; as, the *dome* of the Capitol at Washington; **2**, any domelike object; specif., the structure on a locomotive boiler, from which steam passes to the cylinders (see *locomotive,* illus.).

do-mes-tic (dō-mĕs'tĭk), *adj.* **1**, pertaining to the house or household affairs; private; homemade; **2**, staying at home; fond of home; **3**, pertaining to one's own country in distinction from foreign countries; **4**, of animals, tame; living with man: **domestic economy,** the art and science of managing household affairs; **domestic science:** —*n.* a household servant.

do-mes-ti-cate (dō-mĕs'tĭ-kāt), *v.t.* [*p.t.* and *p.p.* -cat″ed, *p.pr.* -cat″ing], **1**, to make suitable for a household; familiarize with home life; **2**, to tame; as, it is possible to *domesticate* some wild animals:—*v.i.* to become domestic; settle oneself at home.—*n.* **do-mes″ti-ca'tion.**

do-mes-tic-i-ty (dō″mĕs-tĭs'ĭ-tĭ), *n.* [*pl.* domesticities (-tĭz)], **1**, the state of being suited to home life; home-loving character; **2**, home life.

dom-i-cile (dŏm'ĭ-sĭl; *Br.* -sīl), *n.* a permanent place of abode; home; dwelling place:—*v.t.* [*p.t.* and *p.p.* -ciled (-sĭld; -sīld), *p.pr.* -cil-ing], to establish in a fixed residence; as, many aliens are *domiciled* in the United States. Also, **dom'i-cil.**

dom-i-cil-i-a-ry (dŏm″ĭ-sĭl'ĭ-ā-rĭ; -ĭ-ȧ-rĭ), *adj.* of or pertaining to a fixed residence or abode.

dom-i-nant (dŏm'ĭ-nănt), *adj.* **1**, exercising chief authority or control; ruling; predominant; **2**, of a musical scale, ascending: **dominant character,** in biology, a character which, if possessed by either of two parents, will appear in the offspring: opp. of *recessive character:*—*n.* in music, the fifth tone of an ascending diatonic scale. —*n.* **dom'i-nance.**
Syn., adj. governing, principal, preëminent.

dom-i-nate (dŏm'ĭ-nāt), *v.t.* [*p.t.* and *p.p.* -nat″ed, *p.pr.* -nat″ing], to govern or control; rule:—*v.i.* to exercise chief control; predominate.—*n.* **dom'i-na″tor.**—*adj.* **dom'i-na-tive.**

dom-i-na-tion (dŏm″ĭ-nā'shŭn), *n.* **1**, the act of controlling; **2**, absolute authority; power.

dom-i-neer (dŏm″ĭ-nēr'), *v.i.* to exercise authority arrogantly or tyrannically; bluster; swagger.

dom-i-neer-ing (dŏm″ĭ-nēr'ĭng), *p.adj.* masterful; tyrannical.
Syn. insolent, dogmatic, dictatorial.—*Ant.* meek, unassertive, submissive.

do-min-i-cal (dō-mĭn'ĭ-kăl), *adj.* pertaining to Christ as Lord, or to Sunday: **dominical letter,** one of the letters (A B C D E F G) used in the calendar of the Prayer Book to determine the date of Easter:—*n.* a dominical letter.

Do-min-i-can (dō-mĭn'ĭ-kăn), *adj.* pertaining to a religious order founded by St. Dominic in 1215:—*n.* a friar of that order.

dom-i-nie (dŏm'ĭ-nĭ; dō'mĭ-nĭ), *n.* **1**, a clergyman or minister, esp. of the Dutch Reformed Church: also, *domine* (dŏm'ĭ-nē; dō'mĭ-); **2**, a schoolmaster.

do-min-ion (dō-mĭn'yŭn), *n.* **1**, supreme authority or control; sovereignty; rule; **2**, independent right or possession; **3**, a territory or country with a high degree of local authority, but subject to the control of another government; as, the *Dominion* of Canada: **Dominion Day,** in Canada, July 1, celebrated as the anniversary of the formation of the Dominion.

dom-i-no (dŏm'ĭ-nō), *n.* [*pl.* dominos (-nōz)], **1**, a large, loose garment, used as a masquerade costume; **2**, a half mask; **3**, a flat, oblong, dotted piece of bone or wood used in playing a certain game; **4**, in *pl.* used as *sing.*, (usually, *dominoes* [-nōz]), the game.

[1]don (dŏn), (dŏnd) *v.t.* [*p.t.* and *p.p.* donned *p.pr.* don'ning], to put on: opp. of *doff.*

[2]don (dŏn), *n.* **1**, a title given commonly to Spanish gentlemen; **2**, a great person; **3**, at English universities, a fellow, tutor, or head of a college: **Don** [*fem.* Doña (dō'nyä)], a title of rank in Spain: used only before a Christian name.

do-nate (dō'nāt), *v.t.* [*p.t.* and *p.p.* -nat-ed, *p.pr.* -nat-ing], to give, esp. to some religious or charitable object; contribute; bestow.—*adj.* and *n.* **don'a-tive** (dŏn'ȧ-tĭv).—*n.* **do-na'tor** (dō-nā'tẽr; -tŏr).

do-na-tion (dō-nā'shŭn), *n.* a charitable gift; benefaction; present.
Syn. grant, offering, bestowal. (See gift.)

done (dŭn), past participle of the verb [1]*do:*—*p.adj.* **1**, completed; **2**, cooked sufficiently; **3**, *Colloq.:* **a**, thoroughly fatigued; seriously hurt or ill; **b**, cheated.

Don-go-la (dŏng'gō-lȧ), *adj.* designating a process for tanning goatskin to resemble kid.

don-jon (dŭn'jŭn; dŏn'jŏn), *n.* in a medieval castle, the massive chief tower, heavily fortified. Also, **dun'geon.**

Don Ju-an (dŏn jū'ăn; dōn hwän'), in Spanish legend, a profligate who kills the father of a lady he has wronged, visits his tomb and invites his statue to a feast, and is carried off to hell by the statue.

don-key (dŏng'kĭ), *n.* [*pl.* donkeys (-kĭz)], **1**, the ass; **2**, a stupid or obstinate fellow; a stubborn person.

don-na (dŏn'ȧ; dôn'nä), *n.* a lady; madam; mistress: **Donna**, in Italy, a title of respect, prefixed to a lady's Christian name; Mrs. or Miss.

don-nish (dŏn'ĭsh), *adj.* pertaining to, or like, a university don; pedantic.

do-nor (dō'nŏr), *n.* a giver; one who makes a donation or gift.

Don Quix-ote (dŏn kwĭk'sŏt; dōn kē-hō'tā), a quaint gentleman, hero of a famous Spanish satiric story of the 17th century by Cervantes.

don't (dōnt), colloquial contraction of *do not:* incorrectly used for *does not.*

doom (dōōm), *n.* **1**, judgment; sentence; **2**, destiny which cannot be changed; as, the judge pronounced the murderer's *doom;* **3**, ruin; **4**, the Last Judgment:—*v.t.* **1**, to pronounce condemnation upon; sentence to punishment; **2**, to pronounce as a penalty.
Syn., n. verdict, condemnation, lot.

dooms-day (dōōmz'dā″), *n.* the day of final and universal judgment; also, any day of judgment.

door (dōr), *n.* **1**, the gate or entrance of a house; a movable barrier, sliding or swinging on hinges, which opens and closes to allow or prevent entrance to a house, room, etc.; portal; **2**, a means of entrance.

door-keep-er (dōr'kēp″ẽr), *n.* one who guards an entrance.

door-way (dōr'wā″), *n.* the opening in which a door is hung.

dope (dōp), *n.* **1**, a thick liquid, as grease for making machinery run more easily; **2**, a varnish for the cloth of airplane wings; **3**, *Colloq.:* **a**, a drug that produces unconsciousness; **b**, advance information, esp. concerning race horses:—*v.t.* [*p.t.* and *p.p.* doped (dōpt), *p.pr.* dop'ing], *Colloq.*, **1**, to treat or affect with drugs; **2**, to gather from information; as, to *dope* out a story.

Dor-cas (dôr'kȧs), *n.* in the Bible, a woman who "was full of good works" and who made "coats and garments" (Acts 9 : 36-41): **Dorcas Society**, an organization of women who meet to sew for the poor.

Do-ri-an (dō'rĭ-ăn), *adj.* **1**, pertaining to, or characteristic of, Doris, a district of ancient Greece; **2**, simple; direct:—*n.* a member of the Doric race.

Dor-ic (dŏr'ĭk), *adj.* Dorian (which see): **Doric order**, the oldest and simplest of the orders of Greek architecture (see *column*, (illus.):—*n.* **1**, the broad, hard dialect or language of the Dorians; **2**, an unrefined, broad, or rustic dialect of English.

Dor-king (dôr'kĭng), *n.* one of a breed of heavy domestic fowls.

dor-mant (dôr'mănt), *adj.* **1**, sleeping; in temporary inaction; not used; as, a *dormant* title; **2**, in heraldry, lying down with the head on the paws.—*n.* **dor'man-cy.**
Syn. latent, unused, inactive, torpid.

dor-mer win-dow (dôr'mẽr), a window standing upright in a projection built out from a sloping roof; also, the projection: also called *dormer*.

dor-mi-to-ry (dôr'mĭ-tō-rĭ), *n.* [*pl.* dormitories (-rĭz)], a sleeping room, or a building containing sleeping rooms.

dor-mouse (dôr'mous″), *n.* [*pl.* dormice (-mīs″)], a small, hibernating, squirrel-like animal of the Old World.

dor-my (dôr'mĭ), *adj.* in golf, as many holes ahead of one's opponent as there are holes to play. Also, **dor'mie.**

dor-sal (dôr'săl), *adj.* pertaining to, or situated on or near, the back.

[1]**do-ry** (dō'rĭ), *n.* [*pl.* dories (-rĭz)], a deep flat-bottomed boat with a sharp prow and stern, much used by fishermen.

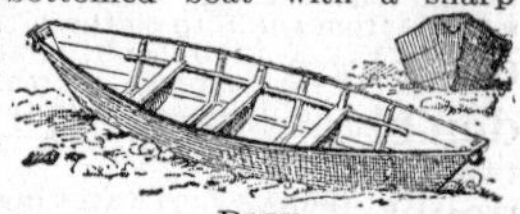

DORY

[2]**do-ry** (dō'rĭ), *n.* [*pl.* dories (-rĭz)], **1**, a European, bright-colored, edible sea fish, known in England as the *john dory;* **2**, a kind of pike found in the Great Lakes.

dose (dōs), *n.* **1**, the quantity of medicine to be taken at one time; **2**, anything unpleasant to have forced on one:—*v.t.* [*p.t.* and *p.p.* dosed (dōst), *p.pr.* dos'ing], to give medicine or anything unpleasant to.

dos-sier (dō-sēr'; dŏs'ĭ-ẽr), *n.* a bundle of papers relating to a given matter.

dost (dŭst), *Archaic*, second person singular, present indicative, of the verb [1]*do.*

[1]**dot** (dŏt), *n.* a very small spot or point, as the point over an *i* or *j;* a speck:—*v.t.* [*p.t.* and *p.p.* dot'ted, *p.pr.* dot'ting], to mark with small points or spots.

[2]**dot** (dŏt), *n.* a woman's fortune at marriage; dowry.—*adj.* **do'tal** (dō'tăl).

dot-age (dōt'ăj), *n.* **1**, the childishness of old age; senility; **2**, foolish or excessive affection.

do-tard (dō'tȧrd), *n.* **1**, one whose mind is impaired by age; **2**, one who is foolishly affectionate:—*adj.* imbecile; senile.

dote (dōt), *v.i.* [*p.t.* and *p.p.* dot'ed, *p.pr.* dot'ing], **1**, to show the feebleness of age; **2**, to feel excessive love: with *on* or *upon.*

doth (dŭth), *Archaic*, third person singular, present indicative, of the verb [1]*do.*

Dou-ay Bi-ble (dōō″ā'), an English translation of the Vulgate, made at Douay, France, by English Catholic refugees, about 1609, and the version commonly accepted by English-speaking Roman Catholics: also called *Douay Version.*

dou-ble (dŭb'l), *adj.* **1**, twofold; as, a *double* meaning; **2**, being in pairs; **3**, being twice as much; **4**, deceitful; insincere; **5**, folded over; **6**, in botany, having many petals: opp. of *single:* **double dagger,** a mark [‡] used to refer a reader to a note at the foot of the page:—*n.* **1**, twice the value; **2**, a duplicate; **3**, a turn made while running; hence, a trick:—*v.t.* [*p.t.* and *p.p.* -bled (-ld), *p.pr.* -bling], **1**, to make twice as large; **2**, to bend back upon itself; **3**, to be twice as much as; **4**, to pass around, as a cape of land; **5**, in bridge, to challenge (an opponent's bid), thus increasing his profit or loss in points scored:—*v.i.* **1**, to increase to twice as much; **2**, to return over the same course:—*adv.* by twos; in a pair.

dou-ble bass in music, an orchestral instrument shaped like a very large violin, the largest and deepest toned of the string group: also called *bass viol; contrabass* (see *musical instrument*, illus.).

dou-ble-deal-ing (dŭb'l=dēl'ĭng), *n.* dishonesty; the acting of two parts at once.—*n.* **dou'ble-deal'er.**

***dou-ble-en-ten-dre** (dōōbl''=äṅ"-täṅdr'), [Fr.], *n.* a word or phrase with two meanings, one often indelicate. Also, **dou'ble en"tente'.**

dou-ble en-try a method of bookkeeping in which two entries are made in the ledger for each transaction, one on the debit and one on the credit side.

dou-ble-faced (dŭb'l=fāst"), *adj.* playing two parts; insincere.

dou-ble-quick (dŭb'l=kwĭk"), *adj.* marching so fast as to be almost running:—*n.* such a step or march.

dou-blet (dŭb'lĕt), *n.* **1,** a duplicate; one of a pair; **2,** a couple; **3,** a close-fitting garment for men, worn in western Europe from the 15th to the 17th century.

dou-bloon (dŭb-lōōn'), *n.* an old Spanish gold coin, worth about $8.00.

dou-bly (dŭb'lĭ), *adv.* **1,** in twice the quantity or degree; **2,** in a double or twofold manner.

doubt (dout), *v.i.* to waver in opinion; hesitate:—*v.t.* **1,** to suspect; distrust; question; **2,** to fear:—*n.* **1,** uncertainty of mind; perplexity; apprehension; as, he was full of grave *doubt* as to her recovery; **2,** an uncertain state of affairs.—*n.* **doubt'er.**

Syn., n. question, distrust, suspicion, mistrust, uncertainty, indecision, misgiving, hesitation, scruple. *Doubt* implies a condition of unsettled opinion or a feeling of uncertainty; as, the statement raised a *doubt* in her mind. *Question* is active *doubt*, raised and expressed; as, that statement is open to *question*. *Distrust* means a want of proper confidence in others or in oneself; as, mutual *distrust* prevents friendship; her self-*distrust* made her work ineffective. *Suspicion* is *distrust* toward others, usually hostile, and based on insufficient evidence; as, she had a *suspicion* that he was a thief.

doubt-ful (dout'fōōl), *adj.* **1,** of uncertain result; **2,** vague; questionable; **3,** not definitely settled; undecided.—*adv.* **doubt'ful-ly.**

Syn. wavering, distrustful, suspicious.

doubt-less (dout'lĕs), *adj.* free from a feeling of uncertainty:—*adv.* assuredly; certainly; without doubt.—*adv.* **doubt'less-ly.**

douche (dōōsh), *n.* a spray of water for cleansing some part of the body.

dough (dō), *n.* **1,** a soft mixture of flour and other ingredients ready for baking; **2,** any such pasty mass.

dough-boy (dō'boi"), *n. Slang*, in the U. S. army, an infantry soldier.

dough-nut (dō'nŭt"), *n.* a small, sweetened cake fried in deep fat.

dough-ty (dou'tĭ), *adj.* [*comp.* dough'ti-er, *superl.* dough'ti-est], able; brave; strong; as, *doughty* knights.—*adv.* **dough'ti-ly.**—*n.* **dough'ti-ness.**

dough-y (dō'ĭ), *adj.* [*comp.* dough'i-er, *superl.* dough'i-est], **1,** soft like dough; **2,** flabby; pale; as, a *doughy* skin.

Dou-ma (dōō'mä), *n.* the former Russian legislature or parliament, created in 1905. See **Du'ma,** *Pfd. S.*

[1]**douse** (dous), *v.t.* [*p.t.* and *p.p.* doused (doust), *p.pr.* dous'ing], **1,** to plunge suddenly into a liquid; **2,** to drench by throwing water upon:—*v.i.* to fall suddenly into water. Also, **dowse.**

[2]**douse** (dous), *v.t.* [*p.t.* and *p.p.* doused (doust), *p.pr.* dous'ing], **1,** to strike (a sail); close (a porthole); **2,** *Slang*, to extinguish, as a light. Also, **dowse.**

[1]**dove** (dŭv), *n.* **1,** any one of numerous birds belonging to the same family as the pigeon; **2,** one who is pure and lovely: a term of endearment; **3,** the emblem of the Holy Spirit in Christian art and symbolism; **4,** an emblem of innocence and gentleness.

[2]**dove** (dōv), *Archaic* or *Colloq.*, past tense of the irregular verb *dive.*

dove-cot (dŭv'kŏt"), *n.* a small house or box raised above the ground, with nests for doves. Also, **dove'cote"** (-kōt").

dove-tail (dŭv'tāl"), *n.* in carpentry, an interlocking joint resembling a dove's tail spread out:—*v.t.* to fasten together by such a joint:—*v.i.* to fit closely and exactly.

dow-a-ger (dou'ȧ-jẽr), *n.* **1,** a widow who has inherited property or title from her husband; **2,** *Colloq.*, an elderly woman of dignified appearance.

dow-di-ly (dou'dĭ-lĭ), *adv.* in a shabby or untidy manner; carelessly.

dow-dy (dou'dĭ), *n.* [*pl.* dowdies (-dĭz)], a slatternly woman who wears soiled finery:—*adj.* [*comp.* dow'di-er, *superl.* dow'di-est], slovenly; ill-dressed.

dow-el (dou'ĕl), *n.* a pin to connect two pieces of wood or metal, or to prevent slipping, by being sunk in the edge or surface of each: also called *dowel pin*:—*v.t.* to fasten by such pins.

dow-er (dou'ẽr), *n.* **1,** that part of a deceased husband's real estate, usually a third, which the law gives to his widow to enjoy during her life; **2,** the property possessed by a woman at her marriage; dowry; **3,** one's natural talents:—*v.t.* to furnish with a dower or a dowry; endow.

[1]**down** (doun), *n.* **1,** the soft feathers of birds; **2,** any fluffy growth, as wool, soft hairs on a plant or on the face, etc.

[2]**down** (doun), *n.* **1,** in *pl.*: **a,** a turf-covered tract of rolling land used for pasture; **b,** banks or small rounded hills of sand; **2,** a dune.

[3]**down** (doun), *adv.* **1,** from a higher to a lower position or degree: opp. of *up;* at the lowest point; **2,** from an earlier to a later time or owner; as, heirlooms are handed *down;* **3,** at once, as if on the counter; as, to pay *down* for goods; **4,** to a heavier consistency; to a smaller size or bulk; as, to boil *down;* **5,** to lesser activity; as, to slow *down;* calm *down;* **6,** upon paper; as, to take *down* what the speaker says:—*adj.* **1,** descending; **2,** in golf, behind one's opponent; as, three *down;* **3,** dejected; downcast:—*prep.* from a higher to a lower point on; as, to row *down* the stream:—*v.t. Colloq.*, to subdue; as, to *down* a man in argument:—*n.* **1,** a descent; **2,** the duration of a play in football.

down-cast (doun'kȧst"), *adj.* **1,** directed downward; **2,** sad:—*n.* the ventilating shaft of a mine.

Syn., adj. downhearted, dispirited, dejected.

down-fall (doun'fôl"), *n.* **1,** a falling downward; **2,** a sudden fall from rank, fortune, or reputation; ruin; disgrace.—*adj.* **down'fall"en.**

down-heart-ed (doun'här"tĕd), *adj.* depressed; discouraged; dejected; in low spirits.—*adv.* **down"heart'ed-ly.**—*n.* **down"heart'ed-ness.**

down-hill (doun"hĭl'), *adv.* in a direction down a slope; downward:—*adj.* (doun'hĭl"), sloping; descending.

down-pour (doun'pōr"), *n.* a heavy and copious fall of rain.

down-right (doun'rīt"), *adj.* **1,** descending vertically; **2,** thorough;

complete; **3**, straight to the point; blunt:—*adv.* (preferably, doun″rīt′), **1**, in plain terms; **2**, utterly; extremely. —*adv.* **down′right″ly.**

down-stairs (doun″stârz′), *adv.* on a lower floor; below stairs:—*adj.* (doun′stârz″), below stairs; as, a *downstairs* hall; *downstairs* rooms.

down-trod-den (doun′trŏd″n), *adj.* oppressed; tyrannized over; held under by a stronger power.

down-ward (doun′wẽrd), *adj.* moving from a higher to a lower place, grade, or direction; descending:—*adv.* **1**, from a higher to a lower condition, state, or place; **2**, from an earlier time. Also, *adv.* **down′wards.**—*adv.* **down′ward-ly.**

down-y (doun′ĭ), *adj.* [*comp.* down′i-er, *superl.* down′i-est], **1**, covered with, or made of, soft feathers, hair, or wool; **2**, soft; **3**, *Slang*, in England, cunning; artful.

dow-ry (dou′rĭ), *n.* [*pl.* dowries (-rĭz)], **1**, the property a woman brings to a husband at marriage; **2**, an endowment; a gift.

¹dowse (dous), *v.t.* [*p.t.* and *p.p.* dowsed (doust), *p.pr.* dows′ing], **1**, to plunge into a liquid; **2**, to drench. See **¹douse**, *Pfd. S.*

²dowse (dous), *v.t.* [*p.t.* and *p.p.* dowsed (doust), *p.pr.* dows′ing], **1**, to strike (a sail); close (a porthole); **2**, *Slang*, to put out (the light). Also, **douse**, *Pfd. S.*

dox-ol-o-gy (dŏk-sŏl′ō-jĭ), *n.* [*pl.* doxologies (-jĭz)], a short hymn of praise to God, used in religious services.

doze (dōz), *v.i.* [*p.t.* and *p.p* dozed (dōzd), *p.pr.* doz′ing], to sleep lightly or fitfully:—*n.* a light sleep, or nap.—*n.* **doz′er.**

doz-en (dŭz′n), *n.* [*pl.* dozens (-nz); before nouns, dozen], twelve things of a kind, taken together.—*abbr.* **doz.**

¹drab (drăb), *n.* **1**, a slattern; **2**, a prostitute.

²drab (drăb), *n.* **1**, a dull brown or yellowish gray color; **2**, a thick woolen cloth of this color:—*adj.* **1**, of a dull brown or gray color; **2**, uninteresting.

drab-ble (drăb′l), *v.t.* [*p.t.* and *p.p.* -bled (-ld), *p.pr.* -bling], to make wet or dirty by dragging through mud or water:—*v.i.* **1**, to become wet or dirty: **2**, to fish with a long line and rod.

drachm (drăm), **1**, a drachma (which see); **2**, (preferably, *dram*), a small weight; **3**, (preferably, *dram*), a small drink.

drach-ma (drăk′mȧ), *n.* [*pl.* drachmas (-mȧz); drachmæ (-mē)], **1**, any of several small weights of ancient Greece; **2**, an ancient Greek coin weighing a drachma; also, a modern Greek coin worth 19.3 cents.

draft (drȧft), *n.* **1**, the act of drawing, or the thing drawn: used in many senses; **2**, a sketch or outline; **3**, a written order for the payment of money; also, a drawing upon a fund or stock; **4**, figuratively, a drawing upon any source of supply; a claim; as, a serious *draft* upon one's time; **5**, a method of recruiting soldiers by conscription; also, a contingent of new soldiers; **6**, the pulling of a load by beasts; also, a load; **7**, a quantity of fish obtained at one haul of the net; **8**, the depth of water from the surface to the level of the keel of a floating ship; **9**, a stream of air; **10**, a drink; **11**, an exhausting demand; **12**, an allowance deducted from the gross weight of goods, as for waste; **13**, in *pl.* used as *sing.*, (usually, *draughts*), in Great Britain, the game of checkers:—*v.t.* **1**, to sketch, write, or draw in outline; **2**, to select for military service; **3**, to draw off. Also, **draught.**—*adj.* **draft′y.**

drafts-man (drȧfts′măn), *n.* [*pl.* draftsmen (-mĕn)], **1**, one who makes plans, maps, designs, mechanical drawings, etc.; **2**, one who prepares writings or pleadings; **3**, (usually, *draughtsman*), one of the pieces used in the game of draughts, or checkers. Also, **draughts′man.**

drag (drăg), *v.t.* [*p.t.* and *p.p.* dragged (drăgd), *p.pr.* drag′ging], **1**, to pull by force or draw along slowly and heavily; **2**, to move with difficulty; **3**, to search the bottom of, as a stream; dredge; **4**, to harrow, as land; **5**, to continue tediously; **6**, to catch with a dragnet:—*v.i.* **1**, to trail along the ground; move heavily; **2**, to lag behind; also, to be protracted; be slow or uninteresting; **3**, to search with a grapnel or a dragnet:—*n.* **1**, the act of moving slowly along the ground; **2**, that which is so moved, as a net drawn along the bed of a stream, a sledge, etc.; **3**, a heavy harrow; also, a heavy frame used for smoothing roads; **4**, a coach drawn by four horses; **5**, anything which retards progress, as a brake on a vehicle; **6**, any obstruction to progress or pleasure; **7**, in aëronautics, the total resistance to the motion of an airplane offered by the air; **8**, *Slang*, influence; pull; as, he has a *drag* with the firm: **drag strut**, a stiffening rib of an airplane wing, designed to resist the drag, or fore-and-aft pressure caused by the air: **drag wire**, in an airplane, a wire designed to resist the drag (see *airplane*, illus.).

DRAG

drag-gle (drăg′l), *v.t.* [*p.t.* and *p.p.* -gled (-ld), *p.pr.* -gling], to wet or soil by drawing in the mud or along the ground:—*v.i.* to be drawn along the ground so as to become dirty or wet.

drag-net (drăg′nĕt″), *n.* a net for drawing along the bottom of a pond or stream, or along the ground, to catch fish or small game.

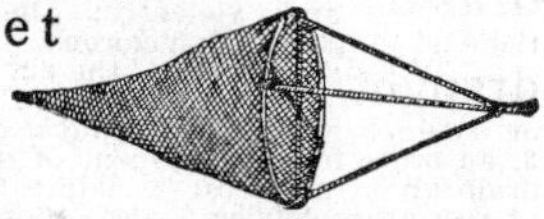
DRAGNET

drag-o-man (drăg′ō-măn), *n.* [*pl.* dragomans (-mănz)], in the East, an interpreter; a guide for travelers.

drag-on (drăg′ŭn), *n.* **1**, a very large, imaginary animal represented as a winged serpent or lizard; **2**, a fierce person.

drag-on-fly an insect with a long, slender body, large eyes, and four narrow, finely veined wings: in the U. S. often called *darning needle.*

drag-on-nade (drăg″ō-nād′), *n.*, usually in *pl.*, any form of punishment or persecution inflicted by soldiers. Also, **drag″o-nade′; drag″oon-ade′.**

dra-goon (drȧ-gōōn′), *n.* formerly, a soldier trained to serve either mounted or on foot; now, a cavalryman, or mounted soldier, heavily equipped.

drain (drān), *v.t.* **1**, to draw off gradually, as water; **2**, to empty, as a dish:—*v.i.* to become dry:—*n.* **1**, a channel or pipe for useless water; a sewer; **2**, the act of drawing off completely; **3**, a continual outpouring or demand, as of time, strength, etc.

drain-age (drān′āj), *n.* **1**, the manner in which the waters of a country pass off by its streams; **2**, a system of pipes or sewers for removing waste water from towns; **3**, that which is drained.

drake (drāk), *n.* the male of any kind of duck.

dram (drăm), *n.* **1**, one eighth of an ounce troy, and one sixteenth of an ounce avoirdupois; **2**, a small quantity of spirituous liquor. Also, **drachm** (drăm).

dra-ma (drä'mȧ), *n.* **1**, a prose or poetical composition telling a story of human life by means of the speech and action of the characters: usually intended to be acted on a stage; **2**, that branch of literary art concerned with the making of stage plays; **3**, real life so exciting as to seem like a play.

dra-mat-ic (drȧ-măt'ĭk), *adj.* **1**, pertaining to, or like, the drama; as, *dramatic* art; **2**, full of intense human interest. Also, **dra-mat'i-cal.**—*adv.* **dra-mat'i-cal-ly.**

dra-mat-ics (drȧ-măt'ĭks), *n.pl.* dramatic works or performances, esp. by amateurs, or the study of them.

***dra-ma-tis per-so-næ** (drăm'ȧ-tĭs pẽr-sō'nē), [Lat.], the characters or persons in a play.

dram-a-tist (drăm'ȧ-tĭst), *n.* a writer of plays; playwright.

dram-a-tize (drăm'ȧ-tīz), *v.t.* [*p.t.* and *p.p.* -tized (-tīzd), *p.pr.* -tiz″ing], to compose or write in the form of a play.—*n.* **dram″a-ti-za'tion.**

dram-shop (drăm'shŏp″), *n.* a barroom; a place where liquor is sold.

drank (drăngk), past tense and past participle of the verb *drink.*

drape (drāp), *v.t.* [*p.t.* and *p.p.* draped (drāpt), *p.pr.* drap'ing], **1**, to cover with cloth; **2**, to arrange in folds.

dra-per (drā'pẽr), *n.* a dealer in woolen or cotton cloth.

dra-per-y (drā'pẽr-ĭ), *n.* [*pl.* draperies (-ĭz)], fabrics used for garments or hangings; hence, hangings, curtains, or loose garments such as are represented in sculpture or painting.—*adj.* **dra'per-ied.**

dras-tic (drăs'tĭk), *adj.* **1**, acting rapidly and violently; as, a *drastic* remedy; **2**, powerful; vigorous.

draught (drȧft), *n.* **1**, the act of drawing, or the thing drawn; **2**, a sketch or outline; as, a rough *draught* of an essay; **3**, an order for the payment of money; **4**, a drain upon resources; a claim; **5**, a method of recruiting soldiers; also those recruited; **6**, the product of one haul, as of fish; **7**, the pulling of a load by beasts; also, a load; **8**, the depth required to float a vessel; **9**, an air current; **10**, a drink; **11**, an exhausting demand; **12**, an allowance deducted from the gross weight of goods, as for waste; **13**, in *pl.* used as sing., (sometimes, *drafts*), in Great Britain, the game of checkers:—*v.t.* **1**, to make an outline of; **2**, to select for military service; **3**, to draw off. Also, **draft**, *Pfd. S.*

draughts-man (drȧfts'măn), *n.* [*pl.* draughtsmen (-mĕn)], **1**, one who makes drawings; **2**, one who prepares writings or pleadings; **3**, one of the pieces used in playing draughts. Also, **drafts'-man**, *Pfd. S.* for senses 1 and 2.

drave (drāv), *Archaic*, past tense of the verb *drive.*

draw (drô), *v.t.* [*p.t.* drew (drōō), *p.p.* drawn (drôn), *p.pr.* draw'ing], **1**, to pull or haul along; drag; **2**, to pull out; haul up; **3**, to infer; deduce, as a conclusion; **4**, to extend or increase in length: with *out;* **5**, to extract or bring out, as a sword or cork; **6**, to obtain by chance; as, to *draw* a prize; **7**, to disembowel; as, to *draw* a fowl; **8**, to represent on paper with pen or pencil; **9**, to describe, by words; **10**, to write in legal form: often with *up;* **11**, to require to float in; as, the boat *draws* ten feet of water; **12**, to inhale; as, to *draw* a long breath; **13**, to attract, as attention or trade; **14**, to receive; as, to *draw* one's pay; **15**, to leave (a contest) without a decision; as, to *draw* a game; **16**, to take or get from a source; as, to *draw* inspiration; **17**, to obtain (money) from a bank:—*v.i.* **1**, to act as a pulling force; entice; **2**, to take, pull, or force something out; **3**, to move; as, to *draw* near; **4**, to be pulled; **5**, to practice the art of making designs or pictures; **6**, to write a formal demand for money, supplies, etc.; as, to *draw* on the bank; **7**, to allow a current of air to pass; as, the chimney *draws* well; **8**, to shrink; be contorted; **9**, to sink to a certain depth:—*n.* **1**, the act or result of drawing; **2**, a game or contest left undecided; **3**, the part of a drawbridge that moves to permit the passage of boats.

draw-back (drô'băk″), *n.* **1**, a loss of advantage; a hindrance; **2**, money paid back after having been collected.

draw-bridge (drô'brĭj″), *n.* a bridge which may be wholly or partially lifted up, let down, or drawn aside (see *bridge, postern,* illus.).

draw-ee (drô-ē'), *n.* one on whom an order, draft, etc., is drawn.

draw-er (drô'ẽr), *n.* **1**, one who draws; a draftsman; **2**, a sliding, boxlike arrangement for holding clothes, papers, etc.; **3**, one who issues a bill of exchange, an order to pay money, etc.; **4**, in *pl.*, an undergarment for the legs and lower part of the body.

draw-ing (drô'ĭng), *n.* **1**, the act of one who draws; **2**, a representation on a plane surface of the appearance of objects; **3**, a distribution of tickets in a lottery.

draw-ing knife a carpenter's tool consisting of a blade with a handle at each end (see *tool*, illus.).

draw-ing–room (drô'ĭng-rōōm″), *n.* **1**, a room for the reception of company; **2**, a reception of company, or the company there assembled.

drawl (drôl), *v.t.* and *v.i.* to speak in an affected, lazy manner:—*n.* a slow, lazy manner of speaking.

drawn (drôn), past participle of the irregular verb *draw:*—*p.adj.* **1**, left undecided; as, a *drawn* game; **2**, having the viscera removed, as a fowl: **drawn butter**, a sauce made of melted butter, flour, and water.

draw-tube (drô'tūb″), *n.* a tube which slides within the main tube of a microscope, and holds the eyepiece (see *microscope*, illus.).

dray (drā), *n.* a low, stoutly built cart, with removable sides, used for heavy loads.

dray-age (drā'āj), *n.* the use of a dray; also, the charge for using it.

dread (drĕd), *v.t.* **1**, to fear greatly; **2**, to look forward to with shrinking or fear:—*v.i.* to be in great fear:—*n.* **1**, imaginative terror; **2**, fear mingled with respect and awe:—*adj.* awful; solemn.

Syn., *n.* alarm, dismay. (See horror.)—*Ant.*, *n.* confidence, assurance, fearlessness.

dread-ful (drĕd'fōōl), *adj.* arousing fear or awe; as, a *dreadful* disaster.—*adv.* **dread'ful-ly.**—*n.* **dread'ful-ness.**

Syn. frightful, shocking, awful, horrible.

dread-nought (drĕd'nôt″), *n.* one of a class of heavily armored battleships.

dream (drēm), *n.* **1**, thoughts or other mental experiences occurring during sleep; **2**, something seen in the imagination; a state of abstraction or reverie; an idle fancy; as, a *dream* of greatness:—*v.t.* [*p.t.* and *p.p.* dreamed (drēmd) or dreamt (drĕmt), *p.pr.* dream'ing], **1**, to see or imagine in sleep; **2**, to see in the imagination, as possible future events:—*v.i.* **1**, to have a train of ideas in sleep; **2**, to imagine possible or impossible future events; **3,** to indulge in idle fancies. —*n.* **dream'er.**—*adj.* **dream'less.**

dream-land (drēm'lănd″), *n.* a lovely land seen in the imagination, waking or sleeping; the realm of fancies.

dreamt (drĕmt), past tense and past participle of the verb *dream.*

dream-y (drēm'ĭ), *adj.* [*comp.* dream'i-er, *superl.* dream'i-est], **1,** pertaining to, or full of, dreams; **2,** imaginative; not awake to realities; **3,** not clear; vague; **4,** soothing; soft, as music.—*adv.* **dream'i-ly.** —*n.* **dream'i-ness.**—*adj.* **dream'like.**

drear (drēr), *adj.* dismal or gloomy; sorrowful; as, a *drear* old age.

drear-y (drēr'ĭ), *adj.* [*comp.* drear'i-er, *superl.* drear'i-est], cheerless; gloomy; as, a *dreary* day; a *dreary* scene.—*adv.* **drear'i-ly.**—*n.* **drear'i-ness.**

[1]**dredge** (drĕj), *n.* a drag, or instrument used to bring up mud, etc., as from a river bottom:—*v.t.* [*p.t.* and *p.p.* dredged (drĕjd), *p.pr.* dredg'ing], **1,** to clean out and deepen, as a river channel; **2,** to collect or scoop with a dredge:—*v.i.* to use, or search with, a dredge. —*n.* [1]**dredg'er.**

DREDGE

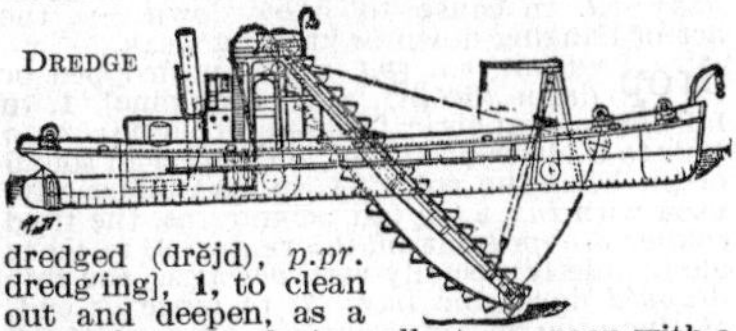

[2]**dredge** (drĕj), *n.* a box with perforated top used to sprinkle flour, etc.:—*v.t.* [*p.t.* and *p.p.* dredged (drĕjd), *p.pr.* dredg'ing], **1,** to sprinkle, as a roast, with flour; **2,** to sift (flour, sugar, etc.).—*n.* [2]**dredg'er.**

dregs (drĕgz), *n.pl.* **1,** the sediment of liquids; lees; **2,** worthless matter.

***Drei-bund** (drī'bo͝ont″), [Ger.], *n.* a triple alliance or union, esp. that made in 1882 by Germany, Austria-Hungary, and Italy.

drench (drĕnch), *v.t.* **1,** to wet thoroughly; soak; **2,** to give forcibly a dose to; as, to *drench* a horse:—*n.* **1,** a large drink or dose for an animal; **2,** a solution for drenching; **3,** a soaking rain.—*n.* **drench'er.**

Dres-den (drĕz'dĕn), *n.* a fine porcelain made near Dresden, Saxony:—*adj.* designating this porcelain.

dress (drĕs), *n.* **1,** covering for the body; clothing; elegant or fashionable attire; **2,** a woman's or a child's gown; **3,** the act of dressing:—*v.t.* **1,** to cover with, or as with, clothing; **2,** to adorn; deck out; **3,** to prepare or make ready; arrange; **4,** to prepare for the table, market, etc.; **5,** to curry or rub down, as a horse; **6,** to adjust to a straight line, as soldiers; **7,** to prune or trim; **8,** to treat or bind up, as a wound; **9,** to scold: usually with *down:*—*v.i.* **1,** to put on clothes; **2,** to form a line.
Syn., *n.* apparel, garments, costume, garb.

[1]**dress-er** (drĕs'ẽr), *n.* **1,** a chest of drawers with a mirror; a bureau; **2,** a closet to hold dishes, cooking utensils, etc.; **3,** a bench used when dressing meat.

[2]**dress-er** (drĕs'ẽr), *n.* **1,** one who adjusts clothing, as a valet, or who prepares or trims, as a window dresser; **2,** a surgeon's assistant.

dress-ing (drĕs'ĭng), *n.* **1,** the act of putting on clothes; **2,** material used in stiffening fabrics; **3,** the smoothing of the surface of stone or lumber; **4,** sauce or stuffing used in preparing a dish; as, a mayonnaise *dressing;* **5,** a reprimand; **6,** medicines, bandages, etc., applied to a wound; **7,** the preparation of mineral ores for the furnace; **8,** manure, gravel, etc., for a field or road: **dressing gown,** a loose-fitting gown, worn while dressing or resting.

dress-mak-ing (drĕs'māk″ĭng), *n.* the process or occupation of making women's gowns.—*n.* **dress'mak″er.**

dress-y (drĕs'ĭ), *adj.* [*comp.* dress'i-er, *superl.* dress'i-est], **1,** fond of clothes, esp. showy or elaborate ones; **2,** stylish.—*n.* **dress'i-ness.**

drew (dro͞o), past tense of the transitive and intransitive verb *draw.*

drib-ble (drĭb''l), *v.i.* [*p.t.* and *p.p.* -bled (-ld), *p.pr.* -bling], to fall in small drops; trickle:—*v.t.* **1,** to let fall in drops; give out in small portions; **2,** in soccer and hockey, to give slight kicks or shoves to (the ball); **3,** in basket ball, to bounce (the ball) rapidly along the floor:—*n.* a trickle of water.

drib-let (drĭb'lĕt), *n.* a small quantity; as, to give money in *driblets.*

dried (drīd), past tense and past participle of the verb *dry:*—*p.adj.* without moisture; evaporated: used esp. of fruits and preserved foods.

dri-er (drī'ẽr), *n.* **1,** one who or that which removes moisture, especially a substance added to paint, as turpentine; **2,** an apparatus for removing moisture. Also, **dry'er.**

drift (drĭft), *n.* **1,** the direction in which anything is driven; tendency; general meaning; as, the *drift* of a speech; **2,** a force which drives anything ahead; controlling influence; **3,** the act or state of being driven; **4,** that which is driven; as, a *drift* of snow; **5,** in geology, loose rocks, etc., brought a distance by ice, as in a glacier; **6,** the deviation of a ship or an airplaine from its course; **7,** the direction of a current: **drift angle,** the angle by which the actual course of an aircraft diverges from the way it points:—*v.t.* to drive along or heap up; as, the winds *drift* dry leaves into piles: —*v.i.* **1,** to be carried along by a current, or by circumstances; **2,** to gather together in heaps; pile up.—*n.* **drift'er.**
Syn., *n.* purpose, scope, aim.

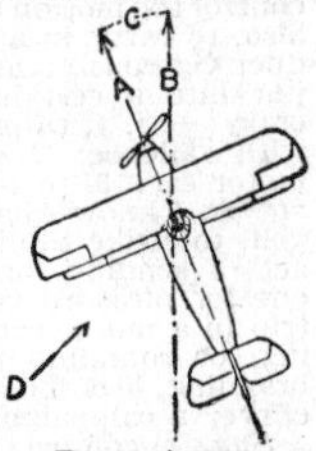

DRIFT ANGLE
A, direction in which airplane is pointed; B, actual direction of airplane's motion; D, direction of wind; C, drift angle.

drift-age (drĭft'āj), *n.* **1,** that which is driven along by a current of air or water; **2,** a turning aside, as of a ship, caused by currents.

drift-wood (drĭft'wo͝od″), *n.* floating wood cast ashore by water; hence, anything or anyone drifting aimlessly.

[1]**drill** (drĭl), *n.* **1,** a tool for boring holes: used of the bit, of the instrument that holds and turns the bit, or of the combination (see *tool,* illus.); **2,** a machine for sowing seeds in rows; **3,** military exercises; **4,** thorough training by means of frequent repetition:—*v.t.* **1,** to pierce with a boring tool; **2,** to bore (holes); **3,** to instruct thoroughly; train; **4,** to sow in rows; as, to *drill* oats.—*n.* **drill'er.**

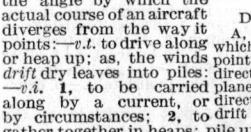

TWIST DRILL, showing narrow oil tubes (white) in lands (shaded), between grooves (white).

[2]**drill** (drĭl), *n.* a baboon of West Africa, similar to the mandrill.

drill-ing (drĭl'ĭng), *n.* a heavy, firm linen or cotton cloth, used for tents, etc.

dri-ly (drī′lĭ), *adv.* **1**, without moisture; **2**, sarcastically. See **dry′ly**, *Pfd. S.*

drink (drĭngk), *v.i.* [*p.t.* drank (drăngk) or, *Archaic*, drunk (drŭngk), *p.p.* drunk or, *Archaic*, drunk′en (drŭngk′n), *p.pr.* drink′ing], **1**, to swallow a liquid; **2**, to take alcoholic liquors habitually:—*v.t.* **1**, to swallow; suck in; **2**, to receive through the senses; as, the eye *drinks* in the beauty of the scene:—*n.* **1**, any liquid swallowed; **2**, as much liquor as can be taken at once; **3**, strong or intoxicating liquor; **4**, excessive taking of alcoholic liquors.—*adj.* **drink′a-ble.**—*n.* **drink′er.**

drip (drĭp), *v.i.* [*p.t.* and *p.p.* dripped or dript (drĭpt), *p.pr.* drip′ping], **1**, to fall in drops; as, the rain *drips* from the trees; **2**, to let fall drops:—*v.t.* to let fall in drops; as, the trees *drip* rain:—*n.* **1**, that which falls in drops; **2**, a projecting cornice shaped so as to throw off rain.

drip-ping (drĭp′ĭng), *n.* **1**, the act of falling in drops; **2**, that which falls in drops; **3**, the fat from roasted meat: **dripping pan**, a pan to receive the fat which falls in drops from roasting meat.

drip-stone (drĭp′stōn″), *n.* a projecting stone cornice or other horizontal piece, for throwing rain away from a wall.

drive (drīv), *v.t.* [*p.t.* drove (drōv) or, *Archaic*, drave (drāv), *p.p.* driv′en (drĭv′n), *p.pr.* driv′ing], **1**, to urge forward by force or threats; push forward forcibly; **2**, to control the motion of; steer, as an automobile; also, to carry in a driven vehicle; **3**, to conduct vigorously; as, to *drive* a business; **4**, to put into a certain state; as, to *drive* one crazy:—*v.i.* **1**, to press, or be moved, forward with violence; **2**, to travel in a carriage or motor car; **3**, to mean; intend to say: with *at;* as, I know what you are *driving* at; **4**, in golf, to strike the ball from a tee:—*n.* **1**, the act of sending forward; **2**, a road, usually one for pleasure vehicles; a driveway; **3**, a trip in a motor car or carriage; **4**, a gathering, or rounding together, as of cattle for branding, logs for floating, etc.; **5**, an urgent effort; a campaign.

Syn., *v.* compel, impel, repel, press, thrust.

driv-el (drĭv′l), *v.i.* **1**, to let saliva drip from the mouth; **2**, to come from the mouth like spittle; **3**, to be weak or foolish; talk or act like a fool:—*n.* **1**, saliva flowing from the mouth; **2**, idle, foolish talk.—*n.* **driv′el-er; driv′el-ler.**

driv-en (drĭv′n), past participle of the irregular verb *drive.*

driv-er (drīv′ẽr), *n.* **1**, one who forces something into motion; **2**, one who directs the motions of persons or things, as a chauffeur, a coachman, an overseer, etc.; **3**, in golf, a wooden-headed club for driving the ball from a tee; **4**, a part of a machine which imparts motion to another part.

drive-way (drīv′wā″), *n.* a road or way for animals or vehicles.

driv-ing wheel a wheel that passes on motion in a machine; esp., one of the large wheels of a locomotive.

driz-zle (drĭz′l), *v.i.* [*p.t.* and *p.p.* -zled (-ld), *p.pr.* -zling], to rain slightly or in fine, misty drops:—*n.* fine, misty rain.—*adj.* **driz′zly.**

droll (drōl), *adj.* queer; odd; amusing; as, a *droll* remark.

Syn. funny, laughable, comic, whimsical.

droll-er-y (drōl′ẽr-ĭ), *n.* [*pl.* drolleries (-ĭz)], jesting; humor; oddity; as, the company greatly enjoyed his *drollery.*

drom-e-da-ry (drŭm′ē-dā-rĭ; drŏm′-), *n.* [*pl.* dromedaries (-rĭz)], the Arabian, or one-humped, camel, noted for its speed (see illus. next column).

drone (drōn), *v.i.* [*p.t.* and *p.p.* droned (drōnd), *p.pr.* dron′ing], **1**, to utter a monotonous sound; **2**, to live in idleness; **3**, to move sluggishly:—*v.t.* to read or speak in a monotonous tone:—*n.* **1**, a dull, monotonous tone; as, the *drone* of bees; **2**, one of the pipes of a bagpipe; **3**, the male of the honeybee, which produces no honey; **4**, a lazy fellow; one who will not do his share.—*adj.* **dron′ish.**

ARABIAN DROMEDARY ($\frac{1}{100}$)

drool (drōōl), *v.i.* **1**, to run at the mouth; **2**, to speak foolishly.

droop (drōōp), *v.i.* **1**, to sink or hang down; **2**, to grow weak and faint or spiritless:—*v.t.* to cause to hang down:—*n.* the act of hanging down or growing weak.

drop (drŏp), *v.i.* [*p.t.* and *p.p.* dropped or dropt (drŏpt), *p.pr.* drop′ping], **1**, to fall in small spherical masses of liquid; **2**, to sink to a lower position; **3**, to lower in sound or pitch, as the voice; **4**, to visit informally: used with *in;* **5**, to fall behind: as, the tired soldier *dropped* out of the ranks; **6**, to move along quietly: usually with *down;* as, the ship *dropped* down the bay; **7**, to cease or end; as, there the matter *dropped:*—*v.t.* **1**, to let fall in, or as in, small drops; **2**, to have done with; dismiss; **3**, to lower or depress, as the eyes or the muzzle of a gun; **4**, to omit, as a letter; **5**, to fell with a blow or weapon; as, to *drop* a deer:—*n.* **1**, a small spherical mass of free liquid; **2**, anything that hangs like a small liquid mass, as an earring; **3**, any very small quantity, as a drink; **4**, a sudden descent, or fall; **5**, the depth to which, or the distance through which, one falls; as, a *drop* of fifty feet; **6**, whatever is arranged to fall; as, the *drop* in a gallows; the *drop*, or curtain, as in a theater: **drop kick**, in football, a play in which the ball is dropped and kicked at the instant of rebound from the ground: distinguished from *place kick* and *punt:* **drop shutter**, a device in a camera for making the exposure, composed of an opaque screen which drops down in front of the lens, the light passing through an opening in the screen.—*n.* **drop′per.**

drop-sy (drŏp′sĭ), *n.* an unnatural collection of watery, or serous, fluid in any cavity of the body or its tissues.—*adj.* **drop′si-cal.**—*adv.* **drop′si-cal-ly.**

drosh-ky (drŏsh′kĭ), *n.* [*pl.* droshkies (-kĭz)], a light four-wheeled carriage used in Russia. Also, **dros′ky.**

dross (drôs), *n.* **1**, the scum or refuse of melted metal; **2**, refuse; waste.

drought (drout), *n.* continued absence of rain or moisture; dryness. Also, **drouth** (drouth).—*adj.* **drought′y.**

[1]**drove** (drōv), past tense of the transitive and intransitive verb *drive.*

[2]**drove** (drōv), *n.* **1**, a herd of cattle or sheep driven in a body; **2**, a crowd of people, usually one in motion.

Syn. flock, shoal, multitude. (See herd.)

dro-ver (drō′vẽr), *n.* **1**, one who drives cattle to market; **2**, a buyer of, and dealer in, cattle.

drown (droun), *v.i.* to die by suffocation in water, or any liquid:—*v.t.* **1**, to suffocate in water; **2**, to overwhelm; flood.

drowse (drouz), *v.i.* [*p.t.* and *p.p.* drowsed (drouzd), *p.pr.* drows′ing], to be heavy with sleep:—*v.t.* to spend (time) in drowsing:—*n.* a light sleep.

drow-sy (drou′zĭ), *adj.* [*comp.* drow′si-er, *superl.* drow′si-est], sleepy; sluggish:—*adv.* **drow′si-ly.**—*n.* **drow′si-ness.**

drub (drŭb), *v.t.* [*p.t.* and *p.p.* drubbed (drŭbd), *p.pr.* drub′bing], to beat vigorously:—*n.* a thump.

drudge (drŭj), *v.i.* [*p.t.* and *p.p.* drudged (drŭjd), *p.pr.* drudg′ing], to labor hard at mean or disagreeable tasks; slave:—*n.* one employed in hard or slavish work.

drudg-er-y (drŭj′ẽr-ĭ), *n.* [*pl.* drudgeries (-ĭz)], hard, disagreeable, or servile work; unpleasant or monotonous labor.
Syn. toil. (See labor.)

drug (drŭg), *n.* **1**, a substance used in medicine, esp. a vegetable substance; **2**, specif., any of various habit-forming substances, such as opium; **3**, an unsalable article:—*v.t.* [*p.t.* and *p.p.* drugged (drŭgd), *p.pr.* drug′ging], **1**, to mix drugs with; **2**, to render stupid by a substance which deadens feeling.

drug-get (drŭg′ĕt), *n.* a coarse woolen fabric, used for floor covering.

drug-gist (drŭg′ĭst), *n.* a dealer in medicines and their ingredients.

dru-id (drōō′ĭd), *n.* a priest of the ancient religion of Britain and Gaul.—*adj.* **dru-id′ic; dru-id′i-cal.**

drum (drŭm), *n.* **1**, a musical instrument consisting of a hollow cylinder with vellum or dried skin stretched across the ends, and beaten with sticks; **2**, anything like a drum; **3**, the membrane or skin between the outer and the middle ear:—*v.i.* [*p.t.* and *p.p.* drummed (drŭmd), *p.pr.* drum′ming], **1**, to beat a drum; **2**, to beat rapidly with the fingers; make a noise like that of a beaten drum:—*v.t.* **1**, to beat on, or as on, the drum; **2**, to gather together, as customers: with *up;* **3**, to expel in disgrace, as from camp: with *out;* **4**, to din, or repeat constantly; as, to *drum* a complaint into one's ears.

DRUMS: 1, kettledrum; 2, tambourine; 3, side drum, or snare drum; 4, bass drum.

drum-head (drŭm′hĕd″), *n.* **1**, the vellum or skin stretched over one end of a drum; **2**, the top of a capstan or upright windlass.

drum-lin (drŭm′lĭn), *n.* a long, narrow hill or mound, formed of drift, or material deposited by a glacier.

drum ma-jor the leader of a band or drum corps.

drum-mer (drŭm′ẽr), *n.* **1**, one who plays a drum, as in an orchestra; **2**, *Colloq.*, a commercial traveler.

drum-stick (drŭm′stĭk″), *n.* **1**, the stick with which a drum is beaten; **2**, a clublike segment or joint of a fowl's leg.

drunk (drŭngk), past participle of *drink:*—*p.adj.* intoxicated.

drunk-ard (drŭngk′ẽrd), *n.* one frequently intoxicated; a sot.

drunk-en (drŭngk′n), *Archaic,* past participle of *drink:*—*p.adj.* intoxicated.—*adv.* **drunk′en-ly.**—*n.* **drunk′en-ness.**

drupe (drōōp), *n.* one of the characteristic types of fruit, consisting of a soft, pulpy body, inclosing a single, hard-shelled stone, or pit, with a kernel, as the peach.

dry (drī), *adj.* [*comp.* dri′er, *superl.* dri′est], **1**, free from moisture or wetness; **2**, not yielding juices; **3**, uninteresting; **4**, shrewdly humorous or quaint, as wit; **5**, in need of oil; as, *dry* bearings; **6**, without sweetness or fruity flavor; **7**, solid, as opposed to liquid; as, *dry* measure; **8**, *Colloq.:* **a**, thirsty; **b**, of a city, etc., forbidding the general sale of intoxicants:—*v.t.* [*p.t.* and *p.p.* dried (drīd), *p.pr.* dry′ing], **1**, to free from moisture or juice; **2**, to stop the flow of; parch:—*v.i.* to lose moisture:—*n.* [*pl.* drys (drīz)], *Colloq.*, a prohibitionist.—*n.* **dry′ness.**
Syn., adj. arid, parched; dull, insipid.

dry-ad (drī′ăd), *n.* in mythology, a nymph who lived in trees.—*adj.* **dry-ad′ic.**

dry-er (drī′ẽr), *n.* one who or that which removes moisture. See **dri′er**, *Pfd.S.*

dry goods woven fabrics, such as cloth, lace, ribbon, etc.

dry-ly (drī′lĭ), *adv.* **1**, without moisture; **2**, in an uninteresting manner; **3**, sarcastically. Also, **dri′ly.**

dry-salt (drī′=sôlt″), *v.t.* to cure by salting and drying, as meat.

du-al (dū′ăl), *adj.* expressing or composed of two; as, the United States Congress is a *dual* body:—*n.* in grammar, a form that denotes two persons or things: common in Greek, and formerly in English.

du-al-ism (dū′ăl-ĭzm), *n.* **1**, a twofold condition; **2**, the doctrine of two independent and separate natures in man, the spiritual and the bodily; **3**, the theory that there are in the universe two opposing principles, those of good and evil.—*n.* **du′al-ist.**—*adj.* **du″al-is′tic.**

du-al-i-ty (dū-ăl′ĭ-tĭ), *n.* [*pl.* dualities (-tĭz)], the state or quality of being twofold; division into two.

dub (dŭb), *v.t.* [*p.t.* and *p.p.* dubbed (dŭbd), *p.pr.* dub′bing], **1**, to bestow knighthood upon by striking the shoulder with a sword; **2**, to confer any rank, dignity, character, or name upon; **3**, to rub, dress, or smooth; as, to *dub* a stick of timber:—*n. Slang,* an awkward or stupid person.

du-bi-ous (dū′bĭ-ŭs), *adj.* **1**, doubtful; as, a *dubious* reply; **2**, of questionable character; as, a *dubious* transaction.—*adv.* **du′bi-ous-ly.**—*n.* **du′bi-ous-ness.**

du-cal (dū′kăl), *adj.* pertaining to a duke; as, a *ducal* crown.

duc-at (dŭk′ăt), *n.* **1**, formerly, a gold or silver European coin varying in value; **2**, in *pl.*, money in general; cash.

***du-ce** (dōō′chā), [It.], *n.* leader; guide: **il Duce** (ēl), the Leader: used of Benito Mussolini, leader of the Italian Fascisti.

duch-ess (dŭch′ĕs), *n.* the wife or widow of a duke; also, a woman sovereign of a duchy in her own right.

duch-y (dŭch′ĭ), *n.* [*pl.* duchies (-ĭz)], the territory or dominions of a duke.

[1]duck (dŭk), *n.* **1**, any of many flat-billed waterfowl with short legs and neck; **2**, the female of this species as distinguished from the male, or *drake;* **3**, *Colloq.*, a pet or favorite: **lame duck,** *Colloq.*, **1**, an inefficient or disabled person; **2**, a congressman not reëlected, but serving out his term.

[2]duck (dŭk), *v.t.* **1**, to plunge quickly and for an instant, as the head under water; also, to throw (a person) into the water; **2**, to bob or bow down; **3**, to avoid, by quickly bowing the head:—*v.i.* **1**, to take a quick dip in water; **2**, to move the head or body aside quickly; dodge:—*n.* **1**, a dip or quick plunge under water; **2**, a sudden lowering of the head; a cringing.—*n.* **duck′er.**

[3]duck (dŭk), *n.* **1**, a strong linen or cotton material; **2**, in *pl.*, *Colloq.*, sailors' trousers, or light clothes worn in hot weather.

duck-bill (dŭk′bĭl″), *n.* a small, egg-laying water mammal of Australia; the ornithorhynchus, or platypus.

duck-ing (dŭk′ĭng), *n.* **1,** the act of plunging under water; **2,** a thorough wetting; **3,** the sport of shooting wild ducks.

duck-ing stool a chair in which female scolds were formerly tied and plunged under water as a punishment.

duck-ling (dŭk′lĭng), *n.* **1,** a young duck; **2,** a favorite or pet.

duck mole a small, egg-laying water mammal of Australia; the ornithorhynchus, or platypus.

duct (dŭkt), *n.* a passage or tube by which a fluid is carried.—*adj.* **duct′less.**

duc-tile (dŭk′tĭl; *Br.* -tīl), *adj.* **1,** capable of being drawn out into threads or strands, as wire; **2,** easily led; yielding to persuasion or instruction; as, the mind of a small child is usually *ductile.*—*n.* **duc-til′i-ty.**

[1]dud (dŭd), *n.* **1,** *Colloq.*, an article of clothing; **2,** in *pl.*, clothes in general, esp. when old and shabby; small belongings.

[2]dud (dŭd), *n.* **1,** a shell or bomb that has failed to explode; **2,** *Colloq.*, a person who fails to make good.

dude (dūd), *n.* a dandy; an overdressed male.—*adj.* **dud′ish.**

dudg-eon (dŭj′ŭn), *n.* sullen anger; as, he went away in high *dudgeon.*

due (dū), *adj.* **1,** owed or owing; payable; **2,** suitable; proper; **3,** resulting from; **4,** expected; as, the train is *due* at five o'clock:—*adv.* exactly; directly; as, the ship sailed *due* west:—*n.* **1,** that which belongs or may be claimed as a right; that which is owed or required; a custom, toll, tribute, or fee; **2,** in *pl.*, an amount of money payable at stated intervals for membership in a club, etc.

Syn., adj. just, fair, right, sufficient.

due-bill (dū′bĭl″), *n.* a written acknowledgment of a debt, not made payable to the order of the creditor.

du-el (dū′ĕl), *n.* a fight, usually planned beforehand, between two persons with deadly weapons:—*v.i.* to fight in such a combat.—*n.* **du′el-ing; du′el-ling.**—*n.* **du′el-ist; du′el-list.**

du-en-na (dū-ĕn′ȧ), *n.* an elderly Spanish or Portuguese lady who acts as a guardian to a younger one; a chaperon.

du-et (dū-ĕt′), *n.* a musical composition for two performers. Also, ***du-et′to** (dōō-ĕt′tō).

duff (dŭf), *n.* **1,** pudding of flour, etc., boiled in a bag; **2,** decayed vegetable matter in forest ground.

duf-fel (dŭf′ĕl), *n.* **1,** a heavy woolen fabric; **2,** outfit; supplies, as for a camper: **duffel bag,** a bag for carrying camp equipment.

duff-er (dŭf′ẽr), *n.* a dull, stupid, inefficient person.

[1]dug (dŭg), past tense and past participle of the irregular verb *dig.*

[2]dug (dŭg), *n.* a teat or nipple: used of an animal.

du-gong (dōō′gŏng), *n.* a large, plant-eating sea mammal resembling the whale: also called *sea cow.*

dug-out (dŭg′out″), *n.* **1,** a canoe hollowed out from a log; **2,** a rough kind of shelter dug in the side of a hill or bank; **3,** in the World War, a cave dug to give shelter from gunfire, bombs, etc.

duke (dūk), *n.* **1,** one of the highest order of English nobility, ranking next below a royal prince; **2,** in some countries, the ruler of a duchy.—*n.fem.* **duch′ess** (dŭch′ĕs).

duke-dom (dūk′dŭm), *n.* the territory ruled by a duke; a duchy; also, the rank of a duke.

dul-cet (dŭl′sĕt), *adj.* sweet or pleasant to the ear; as, *dulcet* tones.

dul-ci-an-a (dŭl″sĭ-ăn′ȧ), *n.* a soft-toned organ stop.

dul-ci-mer (dŭl′sĭ-mẽr), *n.* a musical instrument with wire strings which are struck with light hammers.

dull (dŭl), *adj.* **1,** slow of understanding or action; stupid; **2,** without feeling or sensibility; **3,** not bright or clear to the eye; **4,** blunt; **5,** not brisk or active, as trade; **6,** wearisome; as, a *dull* story; **7,** cloudy, as weather:—*v.t.* **1,** to take away the sharpness of; **2,** to make stupid or heavy; **3,** to tarnish:—*v.i.* **1,** to become stupid; **2,** to become dull or blunt; **3,** to lose brightness.—*adv.* **dul′ly.**—*n.* **dul′ness; dull′ness.**

Syn., adj. depressing, gloomy, sad, dismal; commonplace. (See stupid.)—*Ant., adj.* bright, lively, clear, shining; unusual.

dull-ard (dŭl′ȧrd), *n.* a stupid person; blockhead:—*adj.* stupid.

dulse (dŭls), *n.* a coarse, reddish seaweed, used in Scotland, Iceland, and New England as a food.

du-ly (dū′lĭ), *adv.* in a fit and becoming manner; fitly; regularly.

Du-ma (dōō′mä), *n.* the former national legislature of Russia, created by the Czar in 1905 and discontinued at the revolution of 1917. Also, **Dou′ma.**

dumb (dŭm), *adj.* **1,** unable or unwilling to speak; silent; **2,** *Colloq.*, stupid; foolish.—*adv.* **dumb′ly.**—*n.* **dumb′ness.**

Syn. mute, still, speechless.

dumb-bell (dŭm′-bĕl″), *n.* **1,** one of a pair of weights, of wood or iron, used for muscular exercise; **2,** *Slang*, an ignorant or stupid person.

DUMB-BELL

dumb-wait-er (dŭm′-wāt′ẽr), *n.* **1,** a small elevator with shelves on which dishes or supplies are moved from one floor to another; **2,** a portable serving table.

dum-dum bul-let (dŭm′dŭm), a bullet partly cased in steel, the soft core of which spreads when it strikes, adding to the injury of the wound.

dum-found (dŭm″found′), *v.t.* to amaze; make dumb with surprise or fear. Also, **dumb″found′; dum″found′er.**

dum-my (dŭm′ĭ), *n.* [*pl.* dummies (-ĭz)], **1,** one who is mute or silent; **2,** a sham or make-believe; hence, a model or form for exhibiting clothing; **3,** an exposed hand at whist played by the opposite player when three persons are playing; **4,** one who appears to occupy a certain position without having real power; **5,** *Colloq.*, a stupid person:—*adj.* **1,** noiseless; **2,** sham; **3,** stupid; **4,** apparently acting for oneself, but really for another; as, a *dummy* director in a company.

[1]dump (dŭmp), *n.* **1,** a thick piece of lead formerly used as a counter in boys' games; **2,** anything short, heavy, or thick.

[2]dump (dŭmp), *v.t.* **1,** to throw down; esp., to unload without care from a vehicle; **2,** to unload (a cart) by tipping; **3,** to sell (stock or merchandise) in quantity regardless of the market price:—*n.* **1,** a place for throwing rubbish, etc.; **2,** a pit for the storage of military supplies; **3,** a boat or cart for carrying away rubbish.—*n.* **dump′er.**

dump-ling (dŭmp′lĭng), *n.* a pudding of paste or dough, often inclosing fruit or meat.

dumps (dŭmps), *n.pl.* discontent; sullenness; low spirits.—*adj.* **dump′ish.**

dump-y (dŭmp′ĭ), *adj.* [*comp.* dump′i-er, *superl.* dump′i-est], short and thick; stocky.—*n.* **dump′i-ness.**

[1]dun (dŭn), *adj.* of a dull brownish or grayish color:—*v.t.* [*p.t.* and *p.p.* dunned (dŭnd), *p.pr.* dun′ning], **1,** to make brown or gray in color; **2,** in New England, to cure, as fish, after salting, by covering with salt grass in a dark place.—*adj.* **dun'nish.**

²dun (dŭn), *n.* **1,** an urgent request, or demand, for the payment of a debt; **2,** one who demands his pay repeatedly:—*v.t.* [*p.t.* and *p.p.* dunned (dŭnd), *p.pr.* dun'-ning], to plague by insistent requests for payment:—*v.i.* to demand payment insistently.

dunce (dŭns), *n.* **1,** a dull, ignorant person; **2,** a backward student.

dun-der-head (dŭn'dẽr-hĕd″), *n.* a dunce; numskull; blockhead.—*adj.* **dun'der-head″ed.**

dune (dūn), *n.* a heap of drifted sand piled up on the seashore by the wind.

dung (dŭng), *n.* **1,** the waste material cast off through the bowels of animals; **2,** anything filthy:—*v.t.* to manure, as soil.

dun-geon (dŭn'jŭn), *n.* **1,** a dark underground cell; a prison; **2,** (usually, *donjon*), the principal defended part of an ancient castle.

dung-hill (dŭng'hĭl″), *n.* **1,** a heap of manure; **2,** anything mean or vile.

Dun-ker (dŭng'kẽr), *n.* one of a sect of German-American Baptists, formerly called *German Baptist Brethren,* now officially called *Church of the Brethren.* Also, **Dun'kard.**

dun-nage (dŭn'āj), *n.* **1,** loose wood, fagots, etc., stowed in the hold of a vessel to protect the cargo from injury; **2,** personal baggage: used by sailors.

dunn-ite (dŭn'īt), *n.* a powerful explosive for shells.

***du-o** (dōō'ō), [It.], *n.* [*pl.* duos (-ōz); dui (dōō'ē)], in music, a duet.

du-o-dec-i-mal (dū″ō-dĕs'ĭ-măl), *adj.* consisting of, or counting by, twelves or any power of twelve:—*n.* **1,** a twelfth power of anything; **2,** in *pl.*, a system of computing by twelves.

du-o-dec-i-mo (dū″ō-dĕs'ĭ-mō), *n.* [*pl.* duodecimos (-mōz)], **1,** in printing, a sheet of paper folded into twelve leaves: usually written *12mo;* **2,** a book made of such sheets:—*adj* **1,** folded to make twelve leaves to the sheet; **2,** made of sheets so folded.

du-o-de-num (dū″ō-dē'nŭm), *n.* [*pl.* duodena (-nȧ)], the first portion of the small intestine, immediately below the stomach.—*adj.* **du″o-de'nal.**

du-o-tone (dū'ō-tōn), *n.* a picture producing a two-tone effect in the same color.

dupe (dūp), *n.* **1,** one who is, or can be, easily tricked; **2,** a person who believes everything that he is told:—*v.t.* [*p.t.* and *p.p.* duped (dūpt), *p.pr.* dup'ing], to deceive by trickery; cheat.—*adj.* **dup'a-ble.**

du-ple (dū'pl), *adj.* **1,** double; **2,** in music, designating a measure with two beats, the first being accented; in double time.

du-plex (dū'plĕks), *adj.* **1,** double; compound; **2,** having two parts that work at the same time, as a machine with two cutters, a device for sending two telegraph messages over one wire at the same time, etc.:—*v.t.* to arrange (a telegraphic system) so that two messages can be sent in opposite directions at one time.

du-pli-cate (dū'plĭ-kāt), *v.t.* [*p.t.* and *p.p.* -cat″ed, *p.pr.* -cat″ing], to reproduce; make a copy or copies of:—*adj.* (dū'plĭ-kāt), **1,** corresponding exactly with another; twofold; **2,** double; growing in pairs: **duplicate bridge,** bridge in which the hands are preserved as dealt and played again by other players:—*n.* (dū'plĭ-kāt), facsimile; counterpart.—*n.* **du'pli-ca″tor.**

Syn., n. facsimile, copy, imitation, likeness, counterpart. The *duplicate* of an object is that which exactly corresponds to, and has the force, use, and appearance of, its counterpart; a *duplicate* of a signature is another signature made by the same person; two keys fitting the same lock are *duplicates.* A *facsimile* is an exact reproduction of an original; as, a *facsimile* of a letter. A *copy* is made from an original, but may not be exactly like it; as, a poor *copy* of a famous painting. An *imitation* is that which bears an outward resemblance to the thing imitated, and usually suggests the idea of inferiority; as, an *imitation* of oak; her pearls were good *imitations.*

du-pli-ca-tion (dū″plĭ-kā'shŭn), *n.* **1,** the act of reproducing or of making a copy; also, a copy so made; **2,** a fold; **3,** the act of making double.

du-plic-i-ty (dū-plĭs'ĭ-tĭ), *n.* [*pl.* duplicities (-tĭz)], double-dealing; deceit.

Syn. fraud, deception, deceitfulness, guile.

du-ra-bil-i-ty (dū″rȧ-bĭl'ĭ-tĭ), *n.* the state or quality of lasting or of wearing well; as, the *durability* of serge.

du-ra-ble (dū'rȧ-bl), *adj.* **1,** not perishing; permanent; lasting; **2,** resisting wear.—*adv.* **du'ra-bly.**—*n.* **du'ra-ble-ness.**

Syn. abiding, persistent. (See permanent.)

du-ra ma-ter (dū'rȧ mā'tẽr), the tough, outermost covering of the brain and spinal cord.

du-ra-men (dū-rā'mĕn), *n.* the tough heartwood of the trunk of a tree, beneath the sapwood, or alburnum.

dur-ance (dūr'ăns), *n.* imprisonment; confinement.

du-ra-tion (dū-rā'shŭn), *n.* continuance in time; as, the *duration* of the Civil War was about four years.

dur-bar (dûr'bär), *n.* **1,** in India, a hall of audience at a prince's court; **2,** in India, a state reception.

du-ress (dū'rĕs; dū-rĕs'), *n.* **1,** restraint of personal liberty by physical force; **2,** the illegal act of compelling a person by force to do something.

dur-ing (dūr'ĭng), *prep.* in the time of; at some period of.

durst (dûrst), an old form of the past tense of the verb *dare.*

du-rum (dū'rŭm), *n.* a hard wheat used in making macaroni.

dusk (dŭsk), *adj.* dim; shadowy:—*n.* **1,** the dim light at the beginning and end of daylight; **2,** shadow; gloom.

dusk-y (dŭs'kĭ), *adj.* [*comp.* dusk'i-er, *superl.* dusk'i-est], partly dark; tending to blackness; as, a *dusky* complexion.—*adv.* **dusk'i-ly.**—*n.* **dusk'i-ness.**

dust (dŭst), *n.* **1,** fine, dry particles of matter; a cloud or film of such fine particles; **2,** any fine powder; **3,** the particles into which a decaying body falls; **4,** pollen; **5,** a low condition:—*v.t.* **1,** to brush away dust from; **2,** to cover or sprinkle, as with powder; as, to *dust* a cake with sugar.

dust-er (dŭs'tẽr), *n.* **1,** one who dusts; **2,** a cloth, bunch of feathers, or the like, for dusting; **3,** a light, outer garment to protect clothing from the dust; **4,** a box, can, etc., having holes in the lid for sifting.

dust-pan (dŭst'păn″), *n.* a flat, shovel-like pan in which dust can be collected and removed.

dust-y (dŭs'tĭ), *adj.* [*comp.* dust'i-er, *superl.* dust'i-est], covered with dust.—*adv.* **dust'i-ly.**—*n.* **dust'i-ness.**

Dutch (dŭch), *adj.* pertaining to, or like, the people of the Netherlands, or their language:—*n.* **1,** the language of the Dutch; **2,** used as *pl.*, collectively, the inhabitants of the Netherlands, esp. Holland.

Dutch-man (dŭch'măn), *n.* [*pl.* Dutchmen (-mĕn)], **1,** a Hollander; 2, *Colloq.*, a German: **Dutchman's-breeches**, in the U. S., a woodland plant bearing delicate, creamy white flowers with long spurs, like a pair of breeches.—*n.fem.* **Dutch'wom″an.**

du-te-ous (dū'tē-ŭs), *adj.* fulfilling service owed; showing respect.—*adv.* **du'te-ous-ly.**—*n.* **du'te-ous-ness.**

du-ti-a-ble (dū'tĭ-*ȧ*-bl), *adj.* subject to payment of custom; as, to search at the port for *dutiable* articles.

du-ti-ful (dū'tĭ-fo͝ol), *adj.* **1**, acting upon a sense of responsibility; **2**, respectful; obedient to parents or superiors.—*adv.* **du'ti-ful-ly.**—*n.* **du'ti-ful-ness.**

Syn. compliant, duteous, docile.

du-ty (dū'tĭ), *n.* [*pl.* duties (-tĭz)], **1**, the respectful behavior due to parents or superiors; **2**, action required in a certain position; **3**, that which one is morally bound to do; **4**, a tax levied by the government on certain articles.

Syn. obligation, submission, requirement.

dwarf (dwôrf), *n.* [*pl.* dwarfs (dwôrfs)], a person, animal, or plant much below the average size:—*adj.* of smaller size or height than the average:—*v.t.* **1**, to hinder from growing to the natural size; **2**, to cause to look small by comparison:—*v.i.* to become stunted; grow smaller.—*adj.* **dwarf'ish.**

dwell (dwĕl), *v.i.* [*p.t.* and *p.p.* dwelt (dwĕlt) or dwelled (dwĕld), *p.pr.* dwell'ing], **1**, to reside for a length of time; **2**, to have a fixed place to live in; **3**, to continue; linger.—*n.* **dwell'er.**

Syn. stay, abide, sojourn, tarry, inhabit.

dwell-ing (dwĕl'ĭng), *n.* a house or place to live in; residence.

dwelt (dwĕlt), past tense and past participle of the verb *dwell.*

dwin-dle (dwĭn'dl), *v.i.* [*p.t.* and *p.p.* -dled (-dld), *p.pr.* -dling], to become gradually less; diminish; grow smaller.

Syn. (see decrease).

dye (dī), *v.t.* [*p.t.* and *p.p.* dyed (dīd), *p.pr.* dye'ing], to stain or color:—*v.i.* **1**, to follow the trade of a dyer; **2**, to give or take color in dyeing:—*n.* **1**, a coloring liquid or stain; **2**, a color produced by dyeing.—*n.* **dye'ing.**—*n.* **dy'er.**

dye-stuff (dī'stŭf″), *n.* any material that yields a dye; also, a dye.

dy-ing (dī'ĭng), present participle of the verb *die:*—*p.adj.* **1**, passing away from life; **2**, drawing to a close; **3**, at the time of, or connected with, death; as, his *dying* words:—*n.* the act of passing from life.

dyke (dīk), *n.* a bank of earth built as a barrier:—*v.t.* [*p.t.* and *p.p.* dyked (dīkt), *p.pr.* dyk'ing], to surround with such an embankment. See **dike**, *Pfd. S.*

dy-nam-ic (dī-năm'ĭk; dĭ-năm'ĭk), *adj.* **1**, pertaining to power or physical energy; **2**, pertaining to forces producing motion; **3**, active, as opposed to potential or static; **4**, energetic; forceful; as, a *dynamic* character: **dynamics**, *n.pl.* used as *sing.* **1**, the science which treats of forces and of their effects in producing motion; **2**, the different moving forces of any kind, physical or moral; also, the laws which govern them. Also, *adj.* **dy-nam'i-cal.**—*adv.* **dy-nam'i-cal-ly.**

dy-na-mite (dī'n*ȧ*-mīt; dĭn'*ȧ*-mīt), *n.* a highly explosive compound, used for blasting, etc.:—*v.t.* [*p.t.* and *p.p.* -mit″ed, *p.pr.* -mit″ing], to destroy by dynamite.—*n.* **dy'na-mit″er.**

ALTERNATING-CURRENT DYNAMO

dy-na-mo (dī'n*ȧ*-mō), *n.* [*pl.* dynamos (-mōz)], a machine which converts mechanical energy into an electric current.

dy-na-mo-e-lec-tric (dī″n*ȧ*-mō-ē-lĕk'trĭk; dĭn″*ȧ*-), *adj.* pertaining to the conversion of mechanical to electrical energy, or the reverse. Also, **dy″na-mo-e-lec'tri-cal.**

dy-na-mom-e-ter (dī″n*ȧ*-mŏm'ē-tẽr; dĭn″*ȧ*-mŏm'ē-tẽr), *n.* an apparatus for measuring force or power.—*n.* **dy″na-mom'e-try.**

dy-nas-tic (dī-năs'tĭk; dĭ-năs'tĭk), *adj.* pertaining to a line of rulers of a particular family. Also, **dy-nas'-ti-cal.**

dy-nas-ty (dī'n*ȧ*s-tĭ; dĭn'*ȧ*s-tĭ), *n.* [*pl.* dynasties (-tĭz)], **1**, a line or succession of sovereigns of a particular family; **2**, the length of time during which a certain family reigns.

dyne (dīn), *n.* a unit used in the measurement of force; the force which, acting upon a mass of one gram for one second, produces a speed of one centimeter per second: approximately equal to the force exerted upon a mass of a milligram by gravity.

dys- (dĭs-), *prefix*, [Gk.], bad, difficult, or painful; as, *dys*pepsia.

dys-en-ter-y (dĭs'ĕn-tẽr-ĭ), *n.* a disease of the bowels, characterized by a severe inflammation of the mucous membrane of the large intestine, attended with fever.—*adj.* **dys″en-ter'ic.**

dys-pep-si-a (dĭs-pĕp'sĭ-*ȧ*; dĭs-pĕp'sh*ȧ*), *n.* impairment of the power of digestion; indigestion.

dys-pep-tic (dĭs-pĕp'tĭk), *adj.* pertaining to, causing, or afflicted with, indigestion:—*n.* a person having chronic indigestion. Also, *adj.* **dys-pep'ti-cal.**

E

e- (ē-), *prefix*, out of, from; without: used before *b, d, g, h, l, m, n, r, v.* See [1]**ex-.**

each (ēch), *pron.* every one of a number considered separately:—*adj.* every (one) of two or more taken separately; as, *each* man is expected to do his duty.

ea-ger (ē'gẽr), *adj.* **1**, impetuous; enthusiastic; keenly desirous; as, *eager* to be off; **2**, energetic; spirited.—*adv.* **ea'ger-ly.**—*n.* **ea'ger-ness.**

Syn. ardent, fervent, impatient.—*Ant.* indifferent, unmoved, uninterested.

ea-gle (ē'gl), *n.* **1**, a bird of prey of the falcon family, noted for its strength, size, and keenness of vision; **2**, the ten-dollar gold piece, a coin of the U. S.; **3**, any seal or emblem bearing an eagle; esp., the military standard of ancient Rome: **Eagle**, in astronomy, the northern constellation Aquila.

ea-glet (ē'glĕt), *n.* a young eagle; as, the *eaglets* of some species do not grow their full plumage until the third or fourth year.

ea-gre (ē'gẽr; ā'gẽr), *n.* a high, swift tide in an estuary; a bore.

[1]**ear** (ēr), *n.* **1**, the entire organ of hearing; also, the outer, visible part of that organ; **2**, the sense of hearing; unusual ability to discern delicate sounds; as, she has an *ear*

for music; **3,** attention; heed; as, give *ear* to what I say; **4,** anything in the shape or position of an external ear, as the handle of a dish.

[2]**ear** (ēr), *n.* the spike of a cereal plant, containing the flowers or grains; as, an *ear* of corn:—*v.i.* to form ears, as grain.—*n.*[1]**ear'ing.**

ear-drum (ēr'drŭm″), *n.* **1,** the middle ear, or tympanum; **2,** popularly, a thin membrane, like the head of a drum, that closes the cavity of the middle ear.

[2]**ear-ing** (ēr'ĭng), *n.* a small rope for fastening the upper corner of a sail to a wooden bar.

earl (ûrl), *n.* a British nobleman next below a marquis.—*n.* **earl'dom** (-dŭm).

ear-ly (ûr'lĭ), *adj.* [*comp.* ear'li-er, *superl.* ear'li-est], **1,** being near the beginning, as of a day; **2,** before the usual time; in good time:—*adv.* at or near the beginning; soon; seasonably.—*n.* **ear'li-ness.**

ear-mark (ēr'märk″), *n.* a mark by which a person or thing may be known; as, the *earmark* of a student.

earn (ûrn), *v.t.* **1,** to gain as just pay for one's labor, service, etc.; **2,** to merit.

Syn. acquire, win, achieve. (See get.)

[1]**ear-nest** (ûr'nĕst), *adj.* **1,** zealous and direct of purpose; fervent; eager; **2,** proceeding from ardent feelings; **3,** important; serious; grave:—*n.* seriousness; serious intent: **in earnest, with sincere or serious intent.**—*adv.* **ear'nest-ly.**—*n.* **ear'nest-ness.**

Syn. solemn, intent, sincere, hearty, sedate. —*Ant.* trifling, gay, lively, joking.

[2]**ear-nest** (ûr'nĕst), *n.* **1,** money or a valuable article given to insure the fulfilment of a bargain; **2,** a promise of what will follow; a pledge.

earn-ings (ûr'nĭngz), *n.pl.* money or other compensation received for services; wages; reward.

ear-ring (ēr'rĭng″), *n.* an ornament for the ear: often consisting of a small hoop of gold passed through the lobe of the ear.

ear-shot (ēr'shŏt″), *n.* the distance within which the voice can be heard.

earth (ûrth), *n.* **1,** the globe on which we live, a planet which revolves about the sun (see *solar system,* illus.); **2,** the solid materials which compose the globe; **3,** ground; soil; **4,** worldly things or interests; as, the joys of *earth;* **5,** the inhabitants of the globe; as, the whole *earth* rejoiced; **6,** the hole of a burrowing animal; **7,** in electricity, a connection, as with the earth, for completing a circuit.

earth-en (ûr'thn), *adj.* made of earth or clay; as, an *earthen* jar.

earth-en-ware (ûr'thn-wâr″), *n.* vessels or other objects, usually inferior, made of baked clay.

earth-ly (ûrth'lĭ), *adj.* pertaining to this world or to the present life; material; as, *earthly* troubles.—*n.* **earth'li-ness.**

earth-quake (ûrth'kwāk″), *n.* a shaking or trembling of the ground produced by explosions beneath the surface or by a cracking of the rock foundation.

earth-ward (ûrth'wẽrd), *adv.* toward the earth. Also, **earth'wards.**

earth-work (ûrth'wûrk″), *n.* **1,** a cutting or an embankment made by removing or filling in with soil; **2,** a fortification made of clay, sand, gravel, etc.

earth-worm (ûrth'wûrm″), *n.* a common name for worms that live in damp ground; an angleworm.

earth-y (ûr'thĭ), *adj.* [*comp.* earth'i-er, *superl.* earth'i-est], **1,** composed of, or resembling, the soil; **2,** unrefined; coarse.—*n.* **earth'i-ness.**

ear trump-et a funnel-like device used by the deaf to collect and intensify sounds.

ear-wig (ēr'wĭg″), *n.* **1,** a well-known insect with a pair of curved forceps at its tail, formerly supposed to creep into the ear; **2,** any of several small centipedes.

ease (ēz), *n.* **1,** freedom from pain, disturbance, labor, or stiffness; hence, naturalness; as, *ease* of manner; **2,** quiet; repose:—*v.t.* [*p.t.* and *p.p.* eased (ēzd), *p.pr.* eas'ing], to free from pain, anxiety, trouble, or tension; give rest or relief to.—*adj.* **ease'ful.**

Syn., v. calm, alleviate, pacify, still, allay.

ea-sel (ē'zĕl), *n.* a frame or tripod, as for holding a blackboard or picture.

EASEL

ease-ment (ēz'mĕnt), *n.* **1,** that which gives rest or comfort; **2,** in law, any of several rights which one may have over another's land, as a right of way.

east (ēst), *n.* **1,** that part of the heavens where the sun is seen to rise; **2,** one of the four points of the compass; **3,** the part of the earth lying toward the sunrise: **East, 1,** the Orient and adjoining islands; **2,** the eastern part of the United States: **Far East,** the civilized countries of eastern Asia: **Near East,** the Mohammedan countries of southwestern Asia and Turkey in Europe:—*adj.* coming from the direction of the sunrise; lying on the right hand when one faces the north:—*adv.* in the direction of the sunrise.

East-er (ēs'tẽr), *n.* a festival of the Christian church to commemorate the resurrection of Jesus Christ.

east-er-ly (ēs'tẽr-lĭ), *adj.* **1,** toward the east; **2,** from the east, as a wind:—*adv.* in the direction of the east:—*n.* [*pl.* easterlies (-lĭz)], a wind blowing from the east.

east-ern (ēs'tẽrn), *adj.* pertaining to, situated toward, or lying in, the part of the earth toward the sunrise: **Eastern Church,** the Orthodox, Oriental, or Greek Christian Church: **Eastern Empire,** that part of the later Roman Empire which had its capital at Constantinople: **Eastern Hemisphere,** the hemisphere including Europe, Asia, and Africa: **Eastern question,** the problem of the politics of southeastern Europe.—*n.* **east'ern-er; East'ern-er.**

East-er-tide (ēs'tẽr-tīd″), *n.* the period directly following Easter, usually forty days, until Ascension Day.

east-ward (ēst'wẽrd), *adv.* and *adj.* toward, or in the direction of, the sunrise. Also, *adv.* **east'wards.**

eas-y (ēz'ĭ), *adj.* [*comp.* eas'i-er, *superl.* eas'i-est], **1,** free from constraint, trouble, or worry; as, an *easy* life; comfortable; as, an *easy* chair; **2,** not difficult; **3,** not burdensome; as, an *easy* task; **4,** moderate; **5,** not exacting; as, an *easy* teacher.—*adv.* **eas'i-ly.**—*n.* **eas'i-ness.**

Syn. untroubled, unconcerned.—*Ant.* disturbed, worried; hard, difficult.

eat (ēt), *v.t.* [*p.t.* ate (āt), *p.p.* eaten (ēt'n), *p.pr.* eat'ing], **1,** to chew and swallow, as food; **2,** to devour; consume; **3,** to corrode; waste or wear away; as, rust *eats* away the surface:—*v.i.* **1,** to take food; **2,** to become corroded.—*n.* **eat'er.**

eat-a-ble (ēt'ȧ-bl), *adj.* capable of being eaten:—*n.,* in *pl.,* things to eat.

***eau** (ō), [Fr.] *n.* [*pl.* eaux (ō)], water: used esp. in the names of perfumes, cordials, and the like: **eau de Cologne** (ō″ dē kō-lōn'), a toilet water made of alcohol and volatile oils.

eaves (ēvz), *n.pl.* the lower edges of the roof of a building, from which the rain drips (see *frame house,* illus.).

eaves-drop (ēvz'drŏp″), *v.i.* [*p.t.* and *p.p.* -dropped″(-drŏpt″), *p.pr.* -drop″ping], to listen secretly to the private conversation of others.—*n.* **eaves'drop″ping.** —*n.* **eaves'drop″per.**

ebb (ĕb), *n.* **1**, the flowing back of the tide; **2**, a decline: **ebb tide,** the receding tide; also, the point or time of lowest tide: opp. of *flood tide*:—*v.i.* **1**, to flow back or return, as the tide to the sea; **2**, to decline; decay.
Syn., *v.* recede, retire, subside.

eb-on (ĕb'ŭn), *adj.* made of, or like, ebony; very black.

eb-on-ite (ĕb'ŭn-īt), *n.* a hard, black rubber, used for buttons, combs, etc.

eb-on-ize (ĕb'ŭn-īz), *v.t.* [*p.t.* and *p.p.* -ized (-īzd), *p.pr.* -iz″ing], to make black like ebony.

eb-on-y (ĕb'ŭn-ĭ), *n.* [*pl.* ebonies (-ĭz)], a hard, heavy, durable, black-colored wood; also, the tree furnishing it:—*adj.* made of, or like, ebony; very black.

e-bul-lient (ē-bŭl'yĕnt), *adj.* **1**, in a boiling state; **2**, excited.

eb-ul-li-tion (ĕb″ŭ-lĭsh'ŭn), *n.* **1**, the act of boiling; bubbling; **2**, a sudden outburst of feeling; violent agitation.

ec- (ĕk-), *prefix,* meaning out: the form of *ex-* sometimes used before a consonant; as, *ec*centric; *ec*lectic.

é-car-té (ā″kär″tā'), *n.* a game of cards for two persons, played with 32 cards, from the seven up to the ace.

ec-cen-tric (ĕk-sĕn'trĭk), *adj.* **1**, out of center; **2**, not having the same center, as two circles, spheres, etc.: opp. of *concentric;* **3**, not perfectly circular, as an orbit; **4**, peculiar in manner or character; erratic; as, an *eccentric* person:—*n.* **1**, a circle or sphere not having the same center as another circle; **2**, one who or that which is erratic, irregular, or unusual; **3**, a circular disk mounted on an axis out of center, in such a way that the circular motion of the disk is changed to back-and-forth motion in an attached shaft.—*adv.* **ec-cen'tri-cal-ly.**
Syn., *adj.* odd, abnormal, strange. (See queer.)—*Ant.*, *adj.* regular, ordinary, normal.

ec-cen-tric-i-ty (ĕk″sĕn-trĭs'ĭ-tĭ), *n.* [*pl.* eccentricities (-tĭz)], a peculiarity of manner or character; oddity.

Ec-cle-si-as-tes (ĕ-klē″zĭ-ăs'tēz), *n.* a book of wisdom in the Old Testament.—*abbr.* **Eccl.**

ec-cle-si-as-tic (ĕ-klē″zĭ-ăs'tĭk), *adj.* pertaining to the church and its organization or government:—*n.* a person in holy orders; a clergyman. Also, *adj.* **ec-cle″si-as'ti-cal.**—*adv.* **ec-cle″si-as'ti-cal-ly.**

ec-cle-si-as-ti-cism (ĕ-klē″zĭ-ăs'tĭ-sĭzm), *n.* strong attachment to the forms, usages, organization, and privileges of the church.

ech-e-lon (ĕsh'ĕ-lŏn; ā″shĕ-lôn'), *n.* the arrangement of a body of troops in the form of steps; an arrangement of the vessels of a fleet in steplike formation:—*v.t.* and *v.i.* to form in such an arrangement.

ech-o (ĕk'ō), *n.* [*pl.* echoes (-ōz)], **1**, the repetition of a sound caused by the reflection of sound waves; **2**, the repeating of the words or opinions of others; **3**, one who copies his opinions and words from others:—*v.i.* to give back or repeat a sound:—*v.t.* to repeat the sound of; imitate.

é-clair (ā″klâr'), *n.* a small, oblong cake containing flavored cream or custard and covered with frosting.

é-clat (ā″klä'), *n.* renown; striking effect; splendor.

ec-lec-tic (ĕk-lĕk'tĭk), *adj.* **1**, selecting; choosing from various sources or systems; **2**, made up of choice, selected material:—*n.* one who selects from many sources, as a philosopher.

e-clipse (ē-klĭps'), *n.* **1**, the total or partial darkening of the light of the sun, moon, or other heavenly body caused by its entering the shadow of another body; **2**, an overshadowing; temporary failure:—*v.t.* [*p.t.* and *p.p.* e-clipsed' (-klĭpst'), *p.pr.* e-clips'ing], **1**, to darken or conceal, as one body by another; **2**, to outshine; surpass.

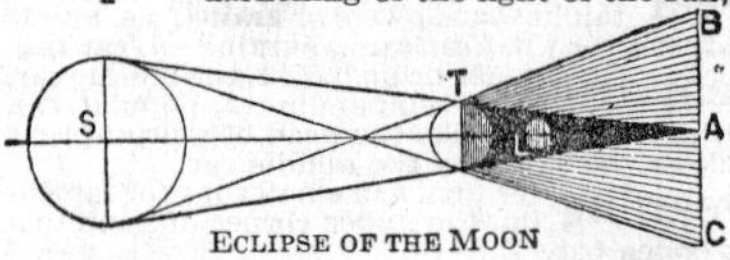

ECLIPSE OF THE MOON

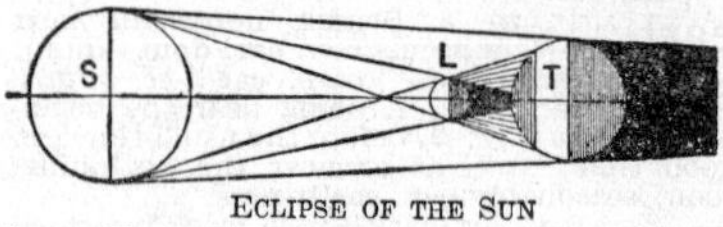

ECLIPSE OF THE SUN

S, sun; T, earth; L, moon; A, B, C, shadow of the earth.

e-clip-tic (ē-klĭp'tĭk), *n.* the great circle which is the apparent path of the sun, or real path of the earth in the heavens during a year:—*adj.* pertaining to the darkening of a heavenly body.

ec-logue (ĕk'lŏg), *n.* a poem about the country or about rural life; as, the *Eclogues* of Vergil.

e-co-nom-ic (ē″kō-nŏm'ĭk; ĕk″ō-), *adj.* **1**, frugal; saving; **2**, pertaining to the science of economics: **economic rent,** that part of the income from a piece of land due to its superiority in location, productivity, etc., over land which will barely pay a return to labor (wages) and invested capital (interest).

e-co-nom-i-cal (ē″kō-nŏm'ĭ-kăl; ĕk″ō-), *adj.* **1**, prudent in expenditure; frugal; saving; **2**, pertaining to economics.—*adv.* **e″co-nom'i-cal-ly.**
Syn. frugal, saving, sparing, thrifty, provident, prudent, chary. *Economical* describes the careful employment of money or other resources to the best advantage, whether on a large or a small scale; as, a good housekeeper, like a good government, is an *economical* manager. *Frugal* refers primarily to the use of food and suggests the idea of small cost; as, a *frugal* meal. *Saving* means merely avoiding unnecessary expenses. *Sparing* describes a reluctance to spend or use that with which one is sufficiently provided; as, he was *sparing* of his words. *Thrifty* emphasizes the determination to succeed through care in the spending of money.—*Ant.* extravagant, lavish, profuse, wasteful, prodigal.

e-co-nom-ics (ē″kō-nŏm'ĭks; ĕk″ō-), *n. pl.* used as *sing.* the science that treats of the production and use of wealth; political economy.

e-con-o-mist (ē-kŏn'ō-mĭst), *n.* **1**, one who is careful in the use of time, money, etc.; **2**, a student of economics.

e-con-o-mize (ē-kŏn'ō-mīz), *v.t.* [*p.t.* and *p.p.* -mized (-mīzd), *p.pr.* -miz″ing], to manage with care or frugality; treat savingly or sparingly:—*v.i.* to be careful in outlay; avoid waste and extravagance; as, to *economize* in housekeeping.

e-con-o-my (ē-kŏn'ō-mĭ), *n.* [*pl.* economies (-mĭz)], **1**, the regulation and management of means and resources; **2**, freedom from waste in the use of anything; thrift; **3**, any system of using or managing resources; organization.

é-cru (ā'kroo; ĕk'roo), *adj.* unbleached; having the pale brown color of raw silk, or of undyed linen.

ec-sta-sy (ĕk'stȧ-sĭ), *n.* [*pl.* ecstasies (-sĭz)], **1**, the state of being beside oneself; excessive joy; **2**, a mystic trance.
Syn. rapture, exaltation.

ec-stat-ic (ĕk-stăt'ĭk), *adj.* overpowering; rapturous; entrancing. Also, **ec-stat'i-cal.**—*adv.* **ec-stat'i-cal-ly.**

ec-u-men-i-cal (ĕk"ū-mĕn'ĭ-kăl), *adj.* general; universal; esp., pertaining to the Christian church throughout the world: said of certain councils of the church. Also, **œc"u-men'i-cal.**—*adj.* **ec"u-men'ic.**

ec-ze-ma (ĕk'zē-mȧ), *n.* a disease of the skin usually attended by the formation of scales and crusts, and by intense itching.

-ed (-ĕd; -d; -t), *v. suffix*, ending of the past tense and past participle of regular verbs; as, trust*ed*:—*adj. suffix*, possessed of, having the characteristics of, etc.: added to nouns; as, a wall*ed* garden.

Ed-da (ĕd'ȧ), *n.* either of two collections of the ancient literature of Iceland.

ed-dy (ĕd'ĭ), *n.* [*pl.* eddies (-ĭz)], a current of air or water running opposite to the main current, thus causing a circular motion; a small whirlpool:—*v.t.* and *v.i.* [*p.t.* and *p.p.* -died (-ĭd), *p.pr.* -dy-ing], to move with a circular motion; whirl.

e-del-weiss (ā'dĕl-vīs), *n.* a small, hardy herb native to the Alps, bearing thick white flowers.

E-den (ē'dn), *n.* **1**, the garden in which Adam and Eve were placed; **2**, any very delightful region or state; paradise.

e-den-tate (ē-dĕn'tāt), *adj.* **1**, without teeth; **2**, of a leaf, not having a toothed edge:—*n.* any toothless animal.

edge (ĕj), *n.* **1**, the thin, sharp, or cutting part of a knife or tool; **2**, extreme border; brink; margin; **3**, keenness: **edge tool,** any sharp tool, as a hatchet or chisel:—*v.t.* [*p.t.* and *p.p.* edged (ĕjd), *p.pr.* edg'ing], **1**, to make or put an edge upon; sharpen; **2**, to border; **3**, to make (one's) way along, little by little:—*v.i.* to move little by little; as, to *edge* one's way along.—*adj.* **edg'y.**
Syn., *n.* rim, brim, verge. (See border.)

edge-wise (ĕj'wīz"), *adv.* on, by, or with the edge; with the edge foremost. Also, **edge'ways".**

edg-ing (ĕj'ĭng), *n.* **1**, a border; an edge; **2**, the operation of shaping or ornamenting a border or edge.

ed-i-ble (ĕd'ĭ-bl), *adj.* fit to be used for food:—*n.*, usually in *pl.*, something fit to be eaten.

e-dict (ē'dĭkt), *n.* a public order issued by an official authority and having the force of a law; a decree.

ed-i-fi-ca-tion (ĕd"ĭ-fĭ-kā'shŭn), *n.* an improving of the mind, esp. in a moral or religious sense; instruction.

ed-i-fice (ĕd'ĭ-fĭs), *n.* a building, esp. of large size; structure.
Syn. (see building).

ed-i-fy (ĕd'ĭ-fī), *v.t.* [*p.t.* and *p.p.* -fied (-fīd), *p.pr.* -fy"ing], to instruct or benefit, esp. in religion or morals.

ed-it (ĕd'ĭt), *v.t.* **1**, to revise and prepare for publication; **2**, to direct, select, and adapt for publication; **3**, to direct the policies of, as a newspaper.

e-di-tion (ē-dĭsh'ŭn), *n.* **1**, the published form of a literary work; **2**, the number of copies of a book, magazine, or newspaper published at one time.

ed-i-tor (ĕd'ĭ-tẽr), *n.* **1**, one who superintends, revises, or prepares a literary work for publication; **2**, one who conducts a newspaper, magazine, etc.

ed-i-to-ri-al (ĕd"ĭ-tō'rĭ-ăl), *adj.* pertaining to an editor, or his duties:—*n.* a leading article in a paper, giving the editor's opinions.—*adv.* **ed"i-to'ri-al-ly.**

ed-u-cate (ĕd'ū-kāt), *v.t.* [*p.t.* and *p.p.* -cat"ed, *p.pr.* -cat"ing], to develop, improve, or train, either by study or by example, etc.; instruct.

ed-u-ca-tion (ĕd"ū-kā'shŭn), *n.* **1**, the training of the mental or moral powers; **2**, the knowledge and ability gained by such training.—*adj.* **ed"u-ca'tion-al.**
Syn. instruction, training, breeding, culture. *Education* is the usual word for schooling, gained either from teaching or from the experiences of life. *Instruction* emphasizes formal teaching. *Training* suggests exercises intended to form habits, not necessarily mental. *Breeding* means training in courtesy, esp. from example. *Culture* means refinement resulting from a sound training of mind and taste.

ed-u-ca-tor (ĕd'ū-kā'tẽr), *n.* **1**, one who teaches, develops, or trains others; **2**, one who is an authority in the theories and methods of teaching.

e-duce (ē-dūs'), *v.t.* [*p.t.* and *p.p.* e-duced' (-dūst'), *p.pr.* e-duc'ing], to draw out; evolve; infer.—*adj.* **e-duc'i-ble.**

e-duc-tion (ē-dŭk'shŭn), *n.* an inference or a conclusion.

-ee (-ē), *n. suffix*, one who receives, or is affected by, an action; as, pay*ee*.

eel (ēl), *n.* any of an order of slimy, snakelike fishes; as, slippery as an *eel*.

eel-grass (ēl'grȧs"), *n.* a sea plant with unusually long, narrow leaves.

eel-pout (ēl'pout"), *n.* **1**, any of a family of fishes, some of which bring forth young alive; **2**, the burbot.

e'en (ēn), *adv.* a short form of the adverb ²*even*:—*n.* a short form of ¹*even*; evening.

e'er (âr; ār), *adv.* a short form of *ever*: as, the sweetest song that *e'er* I heard.

ee-rie (ē'rĭ), *adj.* **1**, awe-inspiring; weird; **2**, stricken with fear. Also, **ee'ry.**—*adv.* **ee'ri-ly.**—*n.* **ee'ri-ness.**

ef- (ĕf-) *prefix*, a form of ¹*ex-*, which see, used before *f*; as, *ef*face.

ef-face (ĕ-fās'), *v.t.* [*p.t.* and *p.p.* -faced' (-fāst'), *p.pr.* -fac'ing], to erase; remove; wipe out.—*n.* **ef-face'ment.**
Syn. obliterate, expunge. (See erase.)

ef-fect (ĕ-fĕkt'), *v.t.* to accomplish; bring about; as, to *effect* a change in another's plans:—*n.* **1**, a resulting state or general impression made by some cause or agent; **2**, meaning; as, he wrote to this *effect*: **3**, working order; as, the rule went into *effect*; **4**, in *pl.*, movable goods; personal property.
Syn., *v.* perform, accomplish, achieve, execute. *Effect* and *perform* emphasize the process of getting a result. *Effect* often has the idea of opposition or difficulty to be conquered; as, Hamilton *effected* the adoption of the Constitution only with the greatest effort. *Perform* is the less familiar word for *do* and sometimes suggests long-continued effort; as, he tried to *perform* his whole duty. *Accomplish*, *achieve*, and *execute* put the emphasis on the result gained rather than on the process. *Accomplish* often has the idea of persistence or skill; as, he *accomplished* a great amount of reading during vacation. *Achieve* stresses the difficulty or greatness of the undertaking; as, to *achieve* independence. To *execute* is to secure a result, esp. formally or on a large scale; as, it is easier to make laws than to *execute* them; *execute* usually suggests carrying out the directions or plans of another; as, we must *execute* his orders.

ef-fec-tive (ĕ-fĕk'tĭv), *adj.* **1**, having the power to produce a result; efficient; **2**, producing an impression of beauty; impressive; striking; as, an *effective* picture:—*n.* a soldier fit for duty.—*adv.* **ef-fec'tive-ly.**—*n.* **ef-fec'tive-ness.**

Syn. effectual, efficient. *Effective* means producing a decided effect; as, an *effective* speech. *Effectual* means producing the particular effect desired; as, *effectual* remedies. Neither *effective* nor *effectual* is applied to persons. That is *efficient* which acts with an energy great enough to produce a desired result; as, an *efficient* heating plant; when applied to persons, it has the idea of general skill or ability; as, an *efficient* executive.

ef-fec-tu-al (ĕ-fĕk'tū-ăl), *adj.* producing, or having the ability to produce, a desired result.—*adv.* **ef-fec'tu-al-ly.**

Syn. efficient. (See effective.)

ef-fem-i-na-cy (ĕ-fĕm'ĭ-nȧ-sĭ), *n.* [*pl.* effeminacies (-sĭz)], the quality of being like a woman; weakness; lack of manliness or virility.

ef-fem-i-nate (ĕ-fĕm'ĭ-nāt), *v.t.* [*p.t.* and *p.p.* -nat"ed, *p.pr.* -nat"-ing], to make womanish; unman:—*v.i.* to become womanish:—*adj.* (ĕ-fĕm'ĭ-nȧt), having the qualities of a woman; unmanly.

ef-fen-di (ĕ-fĕn'dĭ), *n.* a Turkish title of respect, equivalent to sir.

ef-fer-ent (ĕf'ẽr-ĕnt), *adj.* conveying outward; as, an *efferent* nerve carries impulses away from a nerve center.

ef-fer-vesce (ĕf"ẽr-vĕs'), *v.i.* [*p.t.* and *p.p.* -vesced' (-vĕst'), *p.pr.* -vesc'ing], **1,** to bubble up; hiss; work, as new wine; **2,** to be lively or gay.

ef-fer-ves-cence (ĕf"ẽr-vĕs'ĕns), *n.* **1,** the state or condition of bubbling; **2,** uncontrollable excitement.

ef-fer-ves-cent (ĕf"ẽr-vĕs'ĕnt) *adj.* **1,** gently bubbling and hissing from the giving off of gas; **2,** gay.

ef-fete (ĕ-fēt'), *adj.* worn out, as a result of age; barren; exhausted; useless.

ef-fi-ca-cious (ĕf"ĭ-kā'shŭs), *adj.* producing, or capable of producing, a desired effect.—*adv.* **ef"fi-ca'cious-ly.**

Syn. powerful, sure, potent.

ef-fi-ca-cy (ĕf'ĭ-kȧ-sĭ), *n.* power to produce desired results: usually applied to remedies, plans, or the like.

Syn. energy, potency, strength.—*Ant.* powerlessness, futility, impotence.

ef-fi-cien-cy (ĕ-fĭsh'ĕn-sĭ), *n.* the quality of producing desired results with the least effort or expense; capability.

Syn. competency, ability, power.

ef-fi-cient (ĕ-fĭsh'ĕnt), *adj.* **1,** producing or causing desired effects; **2,** capable; competent; as, an *efficient* teacher. —*adv.* **ef-fi'cient-ly.**

Syn. fitted. (See effective.)

ef-fi-gy (ĕf'ĭ-jĭ), *n.* [*pl.* effigies (-jĭz)], an image or portrait, as a stuffed representation of a person, or a head on a medal.

ef-flo-resce (ĕf"lō-rĕs'), *v.i.* [*p.t.* and *p.p.* -resced' (-rĕst'), *p.pr.* -resc'ing], **1,** to blossom out; **2,** to become powdery, on being exposed to the air, by loss of water of crystallization, as washing soda.

ef-flo-res-cence (ĕf"lō-rĕs'ĕns), *n.* **1,** the time or state of flowering; the production of flowers; **2,** a rash on the skin; **3,** the change of certain chemical substances to fine powder when exposed to the air, caused by loss of water of crystallization. —*adj.* **ef"flo-res'cent.**

ef-flu-ence (ĕf'lo͞o-ĕns), *n.* an issuing or flowing out; also, something that flows out.—*n.* **ef'flu-en-cy.**

ef-flu-ent (ĕf'lo͞o-ĕnt), *adj.* flowing or issuing forth:—*n.* a stream which flows out of another stream or which forms the outlet of a lake.

ef-flu-vi-al (ĕ-flo͞o'vĭ-ăl), *adj.* pertaining to the invisible vapor that comes from decaying matter.

ef-flu-vi-um (ĕ-flo͞o'vĭ-ŭm), *n.* [*pl.* effluvia (-ȧ)], an invisible vapor or disagreeable odor from decaying matter.

ef-fort (ĕf'ŏrt; ĕf'ẽrt), *n.* **1,** severe exertion, physical or mental, made for a definite end; **2,** something produced by such exertion, as a literary production.

Syn. attempt, endeavor. *Effort* stresses the power or strength, physical or mental, put forth; as, by violent *efforts* he gained the shore. *Attempt* emphasizes the idea of trying to accomplish a definite end, and admits the possibility of failure; as, the *attempt* to fly across the sea. An *endeavor* is a continued or successive series of *efforts* or *attempts* directed steadily toward a general aim; as, constant *endeavor* in well-doing.

ef-front-er-y (ĕ-frŭn'tẽr-ĭ), *n.* [*pl.* effronteries (-ĭz)], impudence; boldness; shamelessness.

Syn. audacity, assurance.—*Ant.* diffidence.

ef-ful-gence (ĕ-fŭl'jĕns), *n.* a great luster, brightness, or splendor. —*adj.* **ef-ful'gent.**—*adv.* **ef-ful'gent-ly.**

ef-fu-sion (ĕ-fū'zhŭn), *n.* **1,** the act of pouring out, or shedding forth; **2,** an outpouring of thought or sentiment; **3,** the escape of a fluid from a vessel.

ef-fu-sive (ĕ-fū'sĭv), *adj.* **1,** pouring forth freely; **2,** gushing; expressing exaggerated feeling.—*adv.* **ef-fu'sive-ly.**—*n.* **ef-fu'sive-ness.**

eft (ĕft), *n.* **1,** in England, a newt; **2,** locally, any small lizard.

¹egg (ĕg), *n.* **1,** the female reproductive cell; a cell which may develop into a new individual, but usually only after it has united with a male, or sperm, cell; **2,** familiarly, the oval or roundish body laid by any of certain animals, as birds, fishes, and reptiles, esp. that laid by the domestic hen; **3,** an egg-shaped body or one used as an egg.

²egg (ĕg), *v.t.* to urge or incite: usually with *on.*

egg-nog (ĕg'nŏg'), *n.* a drink made of eggs, milk, and sugar, beaten and flavored, usually with nutmeg or vanilla.

egg-plant (ĕg'plănt"), *n.* a cultivated herb, with a large egg-shaped edible fruit, used as a vegetable.

e-gis (ē'jĭs), *n.* **1,** in mythology: **a,** the storm cloud around the thunderbolt of Zeus; **b,** the shield of Athena; **2,** any protecting power or shield. Also, æ'gis, *Pfd. S.*

eg-lan-tine (ĕg'lăn-tīn), *n.* the wild rose, dog-rose, or sweetbrier.

e-go (ē'gō; ĕg'ō), *n.* **1,** the self; **2,** one's sense of importance; **3,** in psychology, the individual as he feels himself to be a continuing conscious personality.

e-go-ism (ē'gō-ĭzm; ĕg'ō-ĭzm), *n.* **1,** the habit of being occupied with oneself; **2,** the theory that self-interest and the development of oneself are the chief end of life: opp. of *altruism;* **3,** egotism; constant talking about oneself.

Syn. (see egotism).

e-go-ist (ē'gō-ĭst; ĕg'ō-), *n.* **1,** one who thinks always of self; **2,** a supporter of the theory that self-interest is the basis of morality.—*adj.* **e"go-is'tic; e"go-is'ti-cal.**—*adv.* **e"go-is'ti-cal-ly.**

e-go-tism (ē'gō-tĭzm; ĕg'ō-), *n.* the habit of talking or writing too much about oneself; vanity.

Syn. egoism, vanity, self-esteem, conceit. *Egotism* means talking or writing unduly about oneself, a habit which is usually offensive. *Egoism* means being so engrossed in oneself that one ceases to think of others;

though selfish, it is not so offensive as the more conspicuous *egotism.*

e-go-tist (ē'gō-tĭst; ĕg'ō-), *n.* one who is vain and talks much of self.

e-go-tis-tic (ē″gō-tĭs'tĭk; ĕg″ō-), *adj.* characterized by too much thought of self; self-centered. Also, **e″go-tis'ti-cal.**—*adv.* **e″go-tis'ti-cal-ly.**

e-gre-gious (ē-grē'jŭs; -jĭ-ŭs), *adj.* unusual; extreme: usually in a bad sense; as, an *egregious* blunder.—*adv.* **e-gre'-gious-ly.**—*n.* **e-gre'gious-ness.**

e-gress (ē'grĕs), *n.* **1,** a departure or exit; **2,** a means of exit.—*n.* **e-gres'sion.**

e-gret (ē'grĕt; ĕg'rĕt), *n.* **1,** any of several large herons bearing, in the breeding season, long plumes drooping over the tail; **2,** (usually, *aigrette*), a showy plume for the head; an egret's plume.

E-gyp-tian (ē-jĭp'shăn), *adj.* of or pertaining to Egypt or its people:—*n.* **1,** a native of Egypt; **2,** the language of the ancient Egyptians.

eh (ā; ĕ), *interj.* what! an exclamation of doubt or inquiry.

ei-der (ī'dẽr), *n.* any of several large salt-water ducks, valued for their downy feathers: also called *eider duck.*

ei-der down the soft breast feathers of the eider duck, used in pillows, coverlets, or the like.

EIDER DUCK ($\frac{1}{16}$)

eight (āt), *adj.* composed of one more than seven:—*n.* **1,** the number consisting of seven plus one; **2,** a sign representing eight units, as 8 or viii; **3,** something having eight units as an essential characteristic, as the crew of a boat.

eight-een (ā'tēn″; ā″tēn'), *adj.* composed of eight plus ten:—*n.* **1,** the number consisting of seventeen and one; **2,** a sign representing eighteen units, as 18 or xviii.—*adj.* and *n.* **eight'eenth″.**

eight-een-mo (ā″tēn'mō″), *n.* [*pl.* eighteenmos (-mōz)], **1,** a sheet of paper folded into eighteen leaves: usually written *18mo;* **2,** a book made of such sheets, usually about 4 by 6½ inches in size:—*adj.* having eighteen leaves to the sheet.

eight-fold (āt'fōld″), *n.* a quantity eight times as great or as many:—*adj.* taken eight times:—*adv.* eight times.

eighth (ātth), *adj.* **1,** next in order after the seventh: the ordinal of eight; **2,** designating one of the eight equal parts of anything:—*n.* **1,** the quotient of one divided by eight; **2,** one of eight equal parts of anything; **3,** in music: **a,** a note (usually called *eighth note*) or rest having one eighth the time value of a whole note or rest; **b,** an octave.

eight-y (ā'tĭ), *adj.* eight times ten; four-score:—*n.* [*pl.* eighties (-tĭz)], **1,** the sum of eight tens; **2,** a sign representing eighty units, as 80 or lxxx.—*adj.* and *n.* **eight'i-eth.**

ei-kon (ī'kŏn), *n.* an image; esp., in the Eastern Church, a picture or mosaic of a sacred subject. See **i'con,** *Pfd. S.*

ei-ther (ē'*th*ẽr; ī'*th*ẽr), *adj.* **1,** one or the other of two; **2,** each; as, along *either* shore:—*pron.* one of two:—*conj.* in one of two cases: the correlative of *or;* as, *either* confess or die:—*adv.* also: used after a negative; as, he won't go, and she won't *either.*

e-jac-u-late (ē-jăk'ū-lāt), *v.t.* [*p.t.* and *p.p.* -lat″ed, *p.pr.* -lat″ing], to speak out suddenly or vehemently; as, to *ejaculate* a wish:—*v.i.* to exclaim suddenly.—*adj.* **e-jac'u-la-to-ry.**—*n.* **e-jac″u-la'tion.**

e-ject (ē-jĕkt'), *v.t.* to cast forth; dismiss from office; evict or turn out; as, to *eject* a tenant.—*adj.* **e-jec'tive.**—*n.* **e-jec'tor.**

e-jec-tion (ē-jĕk'shŭn), *n.* **1,** a driving forth; expulsion; **2,** that which has been expelled or ejected.

e-ject-ment (ē-jĕkt'mĕnt), *n.* **1,** the act of casting out; **2,** a legal action for the recovery of lands, houses, etc.

[1]**eke** (ēk), *adv.* and *conj. Archaic,* also; likewise; in addition.

[2]**eke** (ēk), *v.t.* [*p.t.* and *p.p.* eked (ēkt), *p.pr.* ek'ing], to piece out; supplement; esp., to contrive to make (a living) by one means or another: with *out.*

e-lab-o-rate (ē-lăb'ō-rāt), *v.t.* [*p.t.* and *p.p.* -rat″ed, *p.pr.* -rat″ing], to produce with labor; work out with great care; improve or refine with study or labor:—*adj.* (ē-lăb'ō-rĭt), highly finished; complicated.—*adv.* **e-lab'o-rate-ly.**—*adj.* **e-lab'o-ra-tive.**—*n.* **e-lab'o-rate-ness.**

e-lab-o-ra-tion (ē-lăb″ō-rā'shŭn), *n.* **1,** the act of producing or working out in detail and with care; **2,** that which has been so produced.

E-laine (ē-lān'), *n.* **1,** in Arthurian romance, "the lily maid of Astolat," who vainly loved Lancelot; **2,** any of several other ladies mentioned in Arthurian romance.

***é-lan** (ā″läN'), [Fr.], *n.* dash; ardor; enthusiasm; as, the soldiers went into the battle with great *élan.*

e-land (ē'lănd), *n.* a large South African antelope with twisted horns.

e-lapse (ē-lăps'), *v.i.* [*p.t.* and *p.p.* e-lapsed' (-lăpst'), *p.pr.* e-laps'ing], to slip or glide away; as, a long time has *elapsed.*

e-las-tic (ē-lăs'tĭk), *adj.* **1,** springing back; having the power of returning to its original form; rebounding; **2,** capable of extension; as, an *elastic* time limit; **3,** buoyant; able to recover; as, an *elastic* temperament:—*n.* a narrow woven cloth made in part of India rubber.—*adv.* **e-las'ti-cal-ly.**

e-las-tic-i-ty (ē″lăs-tĭs'ĭ-tĭ), *n.* **1,** the quality of being springy; **2,** the ability to recover from depression.

e-late (ē-lāt'), *v.t.* [*p.t.* and *p.p.* e-lat'ed, *p.pr.* e-lat'ing], to raise the spirits of; cause to feel happy or proud.—*p.adj.* **e-lat'ed.**

e-la-tion (ē-lā'shŭn), *n.* a happy state of mind; joyful excitement.

el-bow (ĕl'bō), *n.* **1,** the joint between the forearm and the upper arm; **2,** any object in the shape of the bent arm, as a pipe connection:—*v.t.* to jostle or push, as with the elbows:—*v.i.* to push one's way rudely.

eld (ĕld), *n. Archaic* or *Poetic,* **1,** old age; **2,** ancient times; antiquity.

[1]**eld-er** (ĕl'dẽr), *adj.* a comparative of *old:* older; prior in time, origin, or appointment; senior:—*n.* **1,** one older or superior in age, rank, or station; **2,** a leader or ruler of a tribe, family, or organization, as among the Jewish tribes of the Old Testament; **3,** in certain Protestant churches, esp. the Presbyterian, a governing officer.—*n.* **eld'er-ship.**

[2]**el-der** (ĕl'dẽr), *n.* **1,** any of several shrubs of the honeysuckle family, having flattened clusters of white or pink flowers, and dark berries; **2,** any of several plants resembling this shrub.

el-der-ber-ry (ĕl'dẽr-bĕr″ĭ), *n.* [*pl.* elderberries (-ĭz)], the purplish black fruit of the elder.

eld-er-ly (ĕl'dẽr-lĭ), *adj.* somewhat old; beyond middle age.

eld-est (ĕl'dĕst), *adj.* a superlative of *old:* oldest; first-born; as, the *eldest* son.

El Do-ra-do (ĕl dō-rä′dō), [*pl.* El Dorados (-dōz)], **1**, an imaginary country in South America, very rich in gold and precious stones; **2**, any place full of money-making opportunities.

e-lect (ē-lĕkt′), *v.t.* **1**, to choose for any office or use; **2**, to choose by ballot:—*adj.* **1**, chosen for office but not yet in charge; as, the president *elect;* **2**, taken in preference:—*n.* one favored or set apart: **the elect**, those divinely chosen for salvation.

Syn., v. choose, select, pick. *Elect* is the most formal of these words; it is used especially in connection with voting; as, to *elect* a governor. *Choose* is the most general term; it may imply deliberation or impulsiveness; as, to *choose* a profession; to *choose* at random. *Select* and *pick* alike have the idea of careful choice. *Select* suggests a number of possibilities with different claims for consideration. To *pick* is to *choose* with reference to fitness for a definite end; as, from among the applicants he *selected* the best ten, and from these one was finally *picked* for the position.

e-lec-tion (ē-lĕk′shŭn), *n.* **1**, the act of choosing or selecting; **2**, the act of choosing a person for some office, as by ballot; **3**, the selection by divine will of certain individuals for eternal salvation.

e-lec-tion-eer (ē-lĕk″shŭn-ēr′), *v.i.* to canvass for votes.

e-lec-tive (ē-lĕk′tĭv), *adj.* **1**, appointed or filled by choice, as an officer or office; **2**, optional, as a course of study; **3**, pertaining to the right of choice:—*n.* in the U. S., a course of study which a student may choose as opposed to one required.

e-lec-tor (ē-lĕk′tẽr), *n.* **1**, one lawfully qualified to vote; **2**, in the U. S., a member of the electoral college, a body of men chosen by the people every four years to elect the president and vice president; **3**, one of the group of German princes and bishops who chose the emperor of the Holy Roman Empire.—*adj.* **e-lec′to-ral** (ē-lĕk′tō-răl).

e-lec-to-ral col-lege in the U. S., a body of citizens chosen by the voters every four years to elect a president and vice president.

e-lec-to-rate (ē-lĕk′tō-rāt), *n.* **1**, the whole body of persons entitled to vote; **2**, formerly, the dignity or territory of one of the electoral princes of the Holy Roman Empire.

e-lec-tric (ē-lĕk′trĭk), *adj.* relating to, containing, generated by, or produced by, electricity: **electric eel**, any of several South American fishes having an eel-like body, and the power of giving an electric shock. Also, **e-lec′tri-cal.**—*adv.* **e-lec′tri-cal-ly.**

(1/30)
ELECTRIC EEL

e-lec-tri-cian (ē-lĕk-trĭsh′ăn), *n.* **1**, one who is skilled in the science of electricity; **2**, an inventor or maker of electrical appliances; one who repairs or installs electrical equipment.

e-lec-tric-i-ty (ē-lĕk-trĭs′ĭ-tĭ), *n.* **1**, an invisible agency producing light, heat, and other physical effects; **2**, the branch of physics dealing with this agency.

e-lec-tri-fi-ca-tion (ē-lĕk″trĭ-fĭ-kā′shŭn), *n.* **1**, the act of charging with electricity, or the state of being so charged; **2**, the process of installing electrical equipment.

e-lec-tri-fy (ē-lĕk′trĭ-fī), *v.t.* [*p.t.* and *p.p.* -fied (-fīd), *p.pr.* -fy″ing], **1**, to charge with, or act upon, by means of electricity; **2**, to fit for using electric power, as a railway; **3**, to thrill; startle.

e-lec-tro- (ē-lĕk′trō-), a combining form from the Greek, meaning, in English compounds, electric or electricity; as, *electro*magnet; *electro*graph.

e-lec-tro-cute (ē-lĕk′trō-kūt), *v.t.* [*p.t.* and *p.p.* -cut″ed, *p.pr.* -cut″ing], to kill by means of an electric current, as a criminal.—*n.* **e-lec″tro-cu′tion.**

e-lec-trode (ē-lĕk′trōd), *n.* either end or pole of an electric battery, a voltaic cell, a dynamo, or any source of electricity: when positive, called *anode;* when negative, called *cathode.*

e-lec-tro-dy-nam-ics (ē-lĕk″trō-dī-năm′ĭks; -dĭ-năm′ĭks), *n. pl.* used as *sing.* the science or study of electric currents and their action on one another, on themselves, and on magnets.

e-lec-tro-dy-na-mom-e-ter (ē-lĕk″-trō-dī″-nȧ-mŏm′ē-tẽr; -dĭn″ȧ-), *n.* an instrument for measuring the strength of an electric current.

e-lec-tro-graph (ē-lĕk′trō-grȧf), *n.* **1**, an electric device used in etching; **2**, a device for sending pictures, maps, etc., by electricity; **3**, a radiograph; **4**, a machine for preparing copper cylinders used in printing fabrics and wall papers.

e-lec-tro-ki-net-ics (ē-lĕk″trō-kī-nĕt′-ĭks; -kĭ-nĕt′ĭks), *n.pl.* used as *sing.* the science or study of electric currents: opp. of *electrostatics.*

e-lec-tro-lier (ē-lĕk″trō-lēr′), *n.* a fixture for holding electric lamps.

e-lec-trol-y-sis (ē-lĕk-trŏl′ĭ-sĭs), *n.* the separation of a compound into its several parts by electricity, as by running an electric current through a solution.

e-lec-tro-lyte (ē-lĕk′trō-līt), *n.* a substance which will conduct electricity, or becomes a conductor when in solution, and undergoes chemical decomposition when an electric current is passed through it.—*adj.* **e-lec″tro-lyt′ic** (-lĭt′ĭk).

e-lec-tro-mag-net (ē-lĕk″trō-măg′nĕt), *n.* a core of soft iron magnetized by electricity passing through a coil of wire around it.—*adj.* **e-lec″tro-mag-net′ic.**

ELECTRO-MAGNET

e-lec-tro-mag-net-ism (ē-lĕk″trō-măg′nĕt-ĭzm), *n.* **1**, magnetism produced by electric currents; **2**, the science treating of the development of magnetism by the electric current.

e-lec-tro-mo-tive (ē-lĕk″-trō-mō′tĭv), *adj.* **1**, producing an electric current; **2**, pertaining to an electric current or to electricity.

e-lec-tro-mo-tor (ē-lĕk″trō-mō′tẽr), *n.* **1**, an apparatus for using electricity to operate machinery; **2**, any apparatus for generating electricity.

e-lec-tron (ē-lĕk′trŏn), *n.* a minute negatively electrified particle charged with the smallest known quantity of electricity, and having a mass equal approximately to 1/1850 of that of a hydrogen atom; the atom of negative electricity; also, any electrified atom or portion of an atom: **electron tube**, a vacuum tube.—*adj.* **e-lec-tron′ic.**

e-lec-tron-ics (ē-lĕk-trŏn′ĭks), *n.pl.* used as *sing.* the science of the electron: applied in television, radar, etc.

e-lec-tro-plate (ē-lĕk′trō-plāt″), *v.t.* [*p.t.* and *p.p.* -plat″ed, *p.pr.*

-plat″ing], to cover with metal by means of an electric current:—*n.* an article thus coated: generally applied to silver plate.

e-lec-tro-scope (ē-lĕk′trō-skōp), *n.* an instrument for finding or observing the presence of an electric charge. —*adj.* **e-lec″tro-scop′ic.**

e-lec-tro-stat-ics (ē-lĕk″trō-stăt′ĭks), *n.pl.* used as *sing.* the science or study of static electricity.

e-lec-tro-type (ē-lĕk′trō-tīp), *n.* a metal copy of a surface, as of an engraved or etched plate, the face of set-up type, etc., made by depositing upon it by electrolysis a thin shell of metal, usually copper, and backing up this shell with type metal: used extensively in printing:—*v.t.* [*p.t.* and *p.p.* -typed (-tīpt), *p.pr.* -typ″ing], to make such a copy of.—*n.* **e-lec′tro-typ″er.**

el-ee-mos-y-na-ry (ĕl″ē-mŏs′ĭ-nā-rĭ; ĕl″ē-ē-), *adj.* **1,** pertaining to alms; **2,** devoted to charitable purposes; **3,** dependent upon charity:—*n.* [*pl.* eleemosynaries (-rĭz)], one who lives on alms.

el-e-gance (ĕl′ē-găns), *n.* **1,** beauty resulting from perfect propriety; studied refinement; **2,** anything essentially refined or in good taste. Also, **el′e-gan-cy.**

el-e-gant (ĕl′ē-gănt), *adj.* **1,** having grace, refinement, or beauty; **2,** characterized by a nice, and sometimes studied, sense of refinement.—*adv.* **el′e-gant-ly.**

e-le-gi-ac (ĕ-lē′jĭ-ăk; ĕl″ē-jī′ăk), *adj.* **1,** plaintive; mournful; **2,** written in the verse form used for classical elegies: —*n.* a song expressing sorrow; a funeral song.

el-e-gy (ĕl′ē-jĭ), *n.* [*pl.* elegies (-jĭz)], **1,** a mournful song or poem; dirge; **2,** a poem written in elegiac meter.

el-e-ment (ĕl′ē-mĕnt), *n.* **1,** a simple part of a more complicated whole; ingredient; **2,** a first or main principle; in ancient and medieval philosophy, one of the four main parts of the physical world—earth, fire, air, and water; now, one of the atmospheric forces; as, the *elements* rage; **3,** natural environment, or the life with which one is familiar; as, she is in her *element;* **4,** in chemistry, any one of about ninety substances which cannot be decomposed by ordinary means, as gold, oxygen, etc.

el-e-men-tal (ĕl″ē-mĕn′tăl), *adj.* **1,** relating to, or characteristic of, the natural world; **2,** pertaining to one of the four elements; **3,** hence, having to do with first principles; fundamental; essential; **4,** in chemistry, pertaining to one of the elementary chemical substances.—*adv.* **el″e-men′tal-ly.**

el-e-men-ta-ry (ĕl″ē-mĕn′tȧ-rĭ), *adj.* **1,** pertaining to first principles; introductory; as, an *elementary* education; **2,** in chemistry, never having been chemically decomposed by man.—*adv.* **el″e-men′ta-ri-ly.**—*n.* **el″e-men′ta-ri-ness.**

African Elephant ($\frac{1}{125}$)

el-e-phant (ĕl′ē-fănt), *n.* a large animal with a flexible snout, or trunk, and long, curved, ivory tusks.

el-e-phan-tine (ĕl″ē-făn′tĭn; -tīn), *adj.* **1,** unduly large; huge; unwieldy; clumsy; **2,** resembling an elephant.

El-eu-sin-i-an (ĕl″ū-sĭn′ĭ-ăn), *adj.* pertaining to the ancient city of Eleusis, near Athens: **Eleusinian mysteries,** religious ceremonies in honor of Demeter and Persephone, orig. held in secret at Eleusis, and later made a part of the state religion of Athens.

el-e-vate (ĕl′ē-vāt), *v.t.* [*p.t.* and *p.p.* -vat″ed, *p.pr.* -vat″ing], **1,** to raise from a lower to a higher position; **2,** to ennoble; **3,** to animate; inspire; raise by training or education.—*p.adj.* **el′e-vat″ed.**

Syn. promote, exalt, dignify.

el-e-va-tion (ĕl″ē-vā′shŭn), *n.* **1,** the act of raising, or the state of being raised; exaltation; **2,** a sketch plan of the front or principal side of a building; **3,** the height of a heavenly body above the horizon; **4,** a raised place; **5,** height above sea level.

el-e-va-tor (ĕl′ē-vā″tẽr), *n.* **1,** that which raises up or exalts; **2,** a hoisting machine or lift; a cage moving up and down in a shaft, to carry people or goods from one level to another; **3,** a warehouse for the storage of grain; **4,** a hinged horizontal wing or plane of an airplane, etc., for controlling its altitude or inclination (see *airplane, empennage,* illus.).

e-lev-en (ē-lĕv′n), *adj.* composed of one more than ten:—*n.* **1,** the number consisting of ten plus one; **2,** a sign representing eleven units, as 11 or xi; **3,** a team in cricket or football.—*adj.* and *n.* **e-lev′enth.**

elf (ĕlf), *n.* [*pl.* elves (ĕlvz)], **1,** in fairy tales, a tiny, mischievous sprite supposed to haunt hills and wild places; a dwarf; fairy; **2,** a fairylike child.

elf-in (ĕl′fĭn), *n.* **1,** a sprite; **2,** a sportive child; **3,** one of several delicate butterflies:—*adj.* pertaining to sprites or goblins.

elf-ish (ĕl′fĭsh), *adj.* resembling, or caused by, a sprite or goblin; impish; mischievous.—*adv.* **elf′ish-ly.**

elf-lock (ĕlf′lŏk″), *n.* a knot of hair twisted or tangled as if by fairies.

E-li (ē′lī), *n.* in the Bible, a judge and high priest of Israel, the teacher of Samuel (1 Samuel 1:9–17; 4:13–18).

e-lic-it (ē-lĭs′ĭt), *v.t.* to draw out; as, to *elicit* a reply.

e-lide (ē-līd′), *v.t.* [*p.t.* and *p.p.* e-lid′ed, *p.pr.* e-lid′ing], **1,** to slur over, or cut off, as a final vowel; **2,** to omit or ignore.

el-i-gi-ble (ĕl′ĭ-jĭ-bl), *adj.* capable of being, or fit to be, chosen; suitable: —*n.* one who meets the given requirements. —*adv.* **el′i-gi-bly.**—*n.* **el″i-gi-bil′i-ty.**

E-li-jah (ē-lī′jȧ), *n.* in the Bible, one of the greatest of the Hebrew prophets, told of in the books of First and Second Kings.

e-lim-i-nate (ē-lĭm′ĭ-nāt), *v.t.* [*p.t.* and *p.p.* -nat″ed, *p.pr.* -nat″ing], **1,** to leave out of consideration; **2,** to cast aside; **3,** to remove (an unknown quantity) from an equation.—*n.* **e-lim″i-na′tion.**

Syn. expel, eject, oust, dislodge, exclude.

E-li-sha (ē-lī′shȧ), *n.* in the Bible, a great Hebrew prophet, disciple and successor of Elijah, told of in the books of First and Second Kings.

e-li-sion (ē-lĭzh′ŭn), *n.* the cutting off of a vowel or syllable, usually for the sake of euphony, as *I'll* for *I will.*

***é-lite** (ā″lēt′), [Fr.], *n.* the best or choicest part, as of society or a profession.

e-lix-ir (ē-lĭk′sẽr), *n.* **1,** a sweetened preparation containing medicinal substances; **2,** an imaginary liquid for prolonging life indefinitely; also, one for changing baser metals, such as iron, into gold.

E-liz-a-be-than (ē-lĭz″ȧ-bē′thăn; ē-lĭz′ȧ-bĕth″ăn), *adj.* pertaining to the times of Queen Elizabeth, or the latter half of the 16th century; as, *Elizabethan* writers:—*n.* one who lived in that time.

elk (ĕlk), *n.* **1**, a large mammal of the deer family, with large, flattened antlers, closely akin to the American moose but slightly smaller, found in the northern regions of Europe and Asia: **2**, in North America, the wapiti (which see for illus.).

EUROPEAN ELK (def. 1) ($\frac{1}{80}$)

¹ell (ĕl), *n.* a lineal measure varying from 27 to 48 inches: formerly widely used in foreign countries.

²ell (ĕl), *n.* **1**, an addition to a house at right angles with the main structure; **2**, a right-angle joint, as of a pipe or tubing.

el-lipse (ĕ-lĭps′), *n.* the path of a point, the sum of whose distances from two given fixed points, called *foci*, is constant.

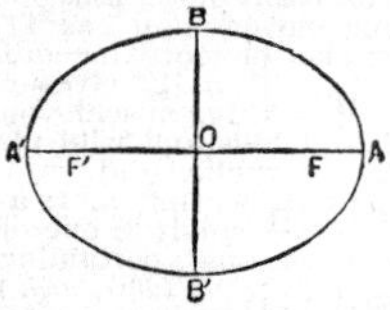

ELLIPSE
A′A, long axis; B′B, short axis; F′F, foci; O, center.

el-lip-sis (ĕ-lĭp′sĭs), *n.* [*pl.* ellipses (-sēz)], the omission of a word or words, the meaning of which is clearly enough implied to be understood.

el-lip-tic (ĕ-lĭp′tĭk), *adj.* **1**, relating to, or formed like, an ellipse; **2**, having a part omitted; defective. Also, **el-lip′ti-cal.**—*adv.* **el-lip′ti-cal-ly.**

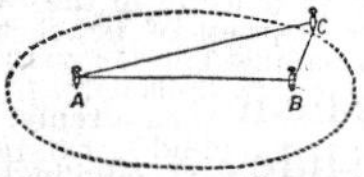

To draw an ellipse: A, B, fixed points; C, moving point; ABC, string.

elm (ĕlm), *n.* **1**, any of several large and graceful shade trees; **2**, the hard, tough wood obtained from these trees.

el-o-cu-tion (ĕl″ō-kū′shŭn), *n.* the art which teaches the proper use of voice and gesture in public speaking.—*adj.* **el″o-cu′tion-a-ry.**

el-o-cu-tion-ist (ĕl″ō-kū′shŭn-ĭst), *n.* one skilled in, or a teacher of, the art of public speaking.

E-lo-him (ĕ-lō′hĭm; ĕ-lō′hēm), *n.* one of the two Hebrew names for God.

e-lon-gate (ē-lŏng′gāt; ē′lŏng-gāt), *v.t.* [*p.t.* and *p.p.* -gat-ed, *p.pr.* -gat-ing], to stretch out; extend; lengthen:—*v.i.* to become longer.

e-lon-ga-tion (ē″lŏng-gā′shŭn), *n.* **1**, a lengthening; **2**, the angular distance of a celestial body from the sun.

e-lope (ē-lōp′), *v.i.* [*p.t.* and *p.p.* e-loped′ (-lōpt′), *p.pr.* e-lop′ing], **1**, to escape privately; **2**, to run away with a lover.—*n.* **e-lop′er.**—*n.* **e-lope′ment.**

el-o-quence (ĕl′ō-kwĕns), *n.* the art of speaking with ease and elegance; vivid and fluent expression of ideas.

el-o-quent (ĕl′ō-kwĕnt), *adj.* having the power of expressing strong emotion in vivid and appropriate speech; as, an *eloquent* preacher.—*adv.* **el′o-quent-ly.**

El-sa (ĕl′sȧ), *n.* the heroine of Richard Wagner's opera "Lohengrin."

else (ĕls), *adv.* besides; otherwise:—*adj.* and *pron.* other; as, somebody *else.*

else-where (ĕls′hwâr″), *adv.* in, at, or to, some other place; as, he is not here; you must look *elsewhere* for him.

e-lu-ci-date (ē-lū′sĭ-dāt), *v.t.* [*p.t.* and *p.p.* -dat″ed, *p.pr.* -dat″ing], to make clear; explain; illustrate; as, an experiment may *elucidate* a theory.

e-lude (ē-lūd′), *v.t.* [*p.t.* and *p.p.* e-lud′ed, *p.pr.* e-lud′ing], to avoid by deceit or cleverness; baffle; shun, as publicity.
Syn. evade, dodge, escape.

e-lu-sion (ē-lū′zhŭn), *n.* the act of escaping or avoiding; clever evasion.

e-lu-sive (ē-lū′sĭv), *adj.* **1**, tending to disappear or evade; slippery; **2**, hard to grasp mentally, as an idea.—*adv.* **e-lu′sive-ly.**—*n.* **e-lu′sive-ness.**

e-lu-so-ry (ē-lū′sō-rĭ), *adj.* likely to escape one's notice; evasive.

elves (ĕlvz), *n.* plural of *elf;* as, the old folk tales tell of *elves.*

elv-ish (ĕl′vĭsh), *adj.* **1**, like, or pertaining to, fairy sprites; **2**, mischievous.

E-ly-sian (ē-lĭzh′ăn; ē-lĭz′ĭ-ăn), *adj.* **1**, pertaining to paradise; **2**, full of the highest bliss or happiness: **Elysian fields,** the abode of the blessed after death.

E-ly-si-um (ē-lĭzh′ĭ-ŭm; ē-lĭz′ĭ-ŭm), *n.* **1**, in mythology, the abode of the blessed after death; **2**, any place of bliss.

el-y-trum (ĕl′ĭ-trŭm), *n.* [*pl.* elytra (-trȧ)], one of the hardened protective coverings, resembling a wing of a beetle.

em (ĕm), *n.* in printing, the square of any size of type, nearly equal to the size of an M, serving as a unit of measurement.

em- (ĕm-), *prefix,* form of *en-* when used before words beginning with *b, m,* or *p.*

e-ma-ci-ate (ē-mā′shĭ-āt), *v.t.* [*p.t.* and *p.p.* -at″ed, *p.pr.* -at″ing], to cause to become very thin:—*adj.* (ē-mā′shĭ-āt), very thin or lean.—*n.* **e-ma″ci-a′tion.**

em-a-nate (ĕm′ȧ-nāt), *v.i.* [*p.t.* and *p.p.* -nat″ed, *p.pr.* -nat″ing], to flow out, issue, or proceed, as from a source; as, light *emanates* from the sun.

em-a-na-tion (ĕm″ȧ-nā′shŭn), *n.* **1**, a flowing forth; **2**, that substance or agent which flows forth from a source; as, perfume is an *emanation* from the flower; **3**, any of several radioactive gases arising from the decomposition of radioactive substances, as radium.

e-man-ci-pate (ē-măn′sĭ-pāt), *v.t.* [*p.t.* and *p.p.* -pat″ed, *p.pr.* -pat″ing], to release from bondage; set free.—*n.* **e-man″ci-pa′tion.**—*n.* **e-man′ci-pa″tor.**
Syn. deliver, discharge, liberate.

e-mar-gi-nate (ē-mär′jĭ-nāt), *adj.* having a notched apex, as the clover leaf (see *leaf,* illus.).

e-mas-cu-late (ē-măs′kū-lāt), *v.t.* [*p.t.* and *p.p.* -lat″ed, *p.pr.* -lat″ing], to deprive of masculine strength.

em-balm (ĕm-bäm′), *v.t.* **1**, to preserve (a dead body) from decay by preservatives; **2**, to hold in memory, as kindnesses.—*n.* **em-balm′er.**

em-bank (ĕm-băngk′), *v.t.* to inclose with, or protect by, a ridge of earth.

em-bank-ment (ĕm-băngk′mĕnt), *n.* **1**, a ridge of earth, stones, etc., for protection or defense; **2**, the making of such a protection.

em-bar-go (ĕm-bär′gō), *n.* [*pl.* embargoes (-gōz)], **1**, a government act restraining vessels from leaving or entering a port, or stopping transportation by railway; **2**, any restraint on commerce by law.

em-bark (ĕm-bärk′), *v.t.* **1**, to put on board ship; **2**, to venture or invest, as money:—*v.i.* **1**, to go on board a vessel; **2**, to engage in any affair; as, to *embark* in a business.—*n.* **em″bar-ka′tion.**

em-bar-rass (ĕm-băr′ăs), *v.t.* **1**, to hinder; **2**, to disturb by money difficulties; as, lack of funds will *embarrass* the traveler; **3**, to perplex; confuse.

Syn. entangle, abash, confound, disconcert, trouble.—*Ant.* assist, assure, help, sustain.

em-bar-rass-ment (ĕm-băr′ăs-mĕnt), *n.* **1**, confusion of mind; **2**, financial difficulties; **3**, mortification.

em-bas-sa-dor (ĕm-băs′ȧ-dẽr), *n.* a government agent, of the highest diplomatic rank, sent by one country to another. See **am-bas′sa-dor**, *Pfd. S.*

em-bas-sy (ĕm′bȧ-sĭ), *n.* [*pl.* embassies (-sĭz)], **1**, the public function, mission, or official residence of an ambassador; **2**, a legation; an ambassador and his suite.

¹em-bat-tled (ĕm-băt′ld), *adj.* having, or provided with, battlements, or walls for defense.

²em-bat-tled (ĕm-băt′ld), *adj.* drawn up in fighting array.

em-bed (ĕm-bĕd′), *v.t.* [*p.t.* and *p.p.* -bed′ded, *p.pr.* -bed′ding,] to lay in, or as in, a bed; set in surrounding matter; as, to *embed* a thing in clay. Also, **im-bed′**.

em-bel-lish (ĕm-bĕl′ĭsh), *v.t.* **1**, to adorn; **2**, to add fanciful details to (a story).—*n.* **em-bel′lish-ment.**

Syn. ornament, decorate, bedeck.

em-ber (ĕm′bẽr), *n.* a small live coal smoldering in ashes.

em-ber days three days, Wednesday, Friday, and Saturday, set apart by the Roman Catholic and Anglican Churches for prayer and fasting in each of the four seasons of the church year.

em-bez-zle (ĕm-bĕz′l), *v.t.* [*p.t.* and *p.p.* -zled (-ld), *p.pr.* -zling], to steal (something intrusted to one's care); as, to *embezzle* a trust fund.—*n.* **em-bez′zler.**

em-bez-zle-ment (ĕm-bĕz′l-mĕnt), *n.* the dishonest appropriation of property intrusted to one's care.

em-bit-ter (ĕm-bĭt′ẽr), *v.t.* **1**, to make unhappy; **2**, to exasperate, or annoy exceedingly.

em-bla-zon (ĕm-blā′zn), *v.t.* **1**, to adorn with heraldic figures, such as the symbols on a coat of arms; decorate; **2**, to display brilliantly; **3**, to praise highly.—*n.* **em-bla′zon-er.**—*n.* **em-bla′zon-ment.**

em-bla-zon-ry (ĕm-blā′zn-rĭ), *n.* [*pl.* emblazonries (-rĭz)], **1**, the act or art of adorning with heraldic figures; **2**, heraldic decoration, as on coats of arms; **3**, any magnificent decoration.

em-blem (ĕm′blĕm), *n.* a symbol, or representation of an idea; as, a white robe is an *emblem* of purity.

Syn. symbol, token, sign. *Emblem* and *symbol* are often used interchangeably as figurative representations of ideas. An *emblem* is a device or object representing an idea by natural fitness or association; as, the thistle is the *emblem* of Scotland. A *symbol* may be a conventional representation agreed upon with or without natural fitness; as, algebraic *symbols;* the word suggests a deeper meaning than *emblem;* as, the cross is the *symbol* of Christianity. A *token* is something used as a reminder or guarantee; as, a *token* of friendship. *Sign* is the most general of these terms, and is often used interchangeably with any one of them; a *sign* may be a gesture or other significant movement; as, he gave a *sign* of approval; deaf-and-dumb *signs;* it may also indicate the existence or approach of something; as, the low clouds are a *sign* of rain; blushing is a *sign* of embarrassment.

em-blem-at-ic (ĕm″blĕm-ăt′ĭk), *adj.* symbolic. Also, **em″blem-at′i-cal.**—*adv.* **em″blem-at′i-cal-ly.**

em-bod-i-ment (ĕm-bŏd′ĭ-mĕnt), *n.* **1**, the act of uniting as a whole; **2**, a concrete expression, as of a purpose or quality; incarnation; as, she is the *embodiment* of virtue.

em-bod-y (ĕm-bŏd′ĭ), *v.t.* [*p.t.* and *p.p.* -bod′ied (-ĭd), *p.pr.* -bod′y-ing], **1**, to give bodily form to; **2**, to express in a concrete form; as, to *embody* thought in words; **3**, to collect into a united whole; as, to *embody* troops.

em-bold-en (ĕm-bōl′dn), *v.t.* to make brave; encourage.

Syn. inspirit, animate, cheer, stimulate.

***em-bon-point** (äṅ″bôṅ″pwâṅ′), [Fr.], *n.* bodily plumpness; slight corpulence; stoutness: often humorous.

em-bos-om (ĕm-bo͝oz′ŭm), *v.t.* **1**, to take into one's heart; **2**, to shelter.

em-boss (ĕm-bŏs′), *v.t.* to ornament with raised work; raise in relief from the surface.—*n.* **em-boss′er.**—*n.* **em-boss′ment.**

em-bow-er (ĕm-bou′ẽr), *v.t.* to cover with, or as with, a roof of flowers, vines, etc.; as, a cottage *embowered* with roses:—*v.i.* to rest, as under a roof of flowers. Also, **im-bow′er.**

em-brace (ĕm-brās′), *v.t.* [*p.t.* and *p.p.* -braced′ (-brāst′), *p.pr.* -brac′ing], **1**, to hold in the arms with affection; **2**, to receive with willingness; **3**, to include; inclose:—*v.i.* to join in an embrace:—*n.* the act of clasping in the arms; a hug.

em-bra-sure (ĕm-brā′zhūr), *n.* **1**, an opening in a wall or fort from which to fire guns; **2**, a window or door having its sides slanted on the inside.

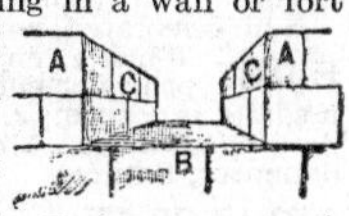

EMBRASURE: *A*, *A*, merlons; *B*, bottom; *C*, *C*, cheeks.

em-bro-cate (ĕm′brō-kāt), *v.t.* [*p.t.* and *p.p.* -cat″ed, *p.pr.* -cat″ing], to moisten and rub (an injured part of the body) with liniment.—*n.* **em″bro-ca′tion.**

em-broid-er (ĕm-broid′ẽr), *v.t.* **1**, to decorate or make beautiful with needlework; **2**, to embellish or exaggerate, as a story.—*n.* **em-broid′er-er.**

em-broid-er-y (ĕm-broid′ẽr-ĭ), *n.* [*pl.* embroideries (-ĭz)], ornamental work of gold, silver, silk, etc., done with the needle.

em-broil (ĕm-broil′), *v.t.* **1**, to disturb; confuse; **2**, to involve in contention.—*n.* **em-broil′ment.**

em-bry-o (ĕm′brĭ-ō), *n.* [*pl.* embryos (-ōz)], **1**, the young of an animal in the earliest stages, before birth or hatching; **2**, the first or undeveloped state of anything.

em-bry-ol-o-gy (ĕm″brĭ-ŏl′ō-jĭ), *n.* the study of the embryo, its formation and development.—*adj.* **em″bry-o-log′i-cal.**—*n.* **em″bry-ol′o-gist.**

em-bry-on-ic (ĕm″brĭ-ŏn′ĭk), *adj.* **1**, of or pertaining to an undeveloped organism; **2**, not fully developed.

e-mend (ē-mĕnd′), *v.t.* to alter or correct, as a text.—*adj.* **e-mend′a-ble.**

e-men-da-tion (ē″mĕn-dā′shŭn; ĕm″ĕn-dā′shŭn), *n.* the alteration or correction of a text, so as to give an improved reading.—*n.* **e′men-da″tor.**

em-er-ald (ĕm′ẽr-ăld), *n.* **1**, a precious stone of a rich, deep green color; **2**, a size of printer's type:—*adj.* of a color like that of the emerald.

e-merge (ē-mûrj′), *v.i.* [*p.t.* and *p.p.* e-merged′ (-mûrjd′), *p.pr.* e-merg′-

ing], to rise up or come forth from anything which conceals; become visible.

e-mer-gen-cy (ē-mûr′jĕn-sĭ), *n.* [*pl.* emergencies (-sĭz)], a sudden or unexpected happening; pressing necessity; crisis:—*adj.* pertaining to, or used in, a crisis requiring rapid action; as, an *emergency* brake.

e-mer-i-tus (ē-mĕr′ĭ-tŭs), *adj.* retired from service with honorary rank and title; as, a professor *emeritus.*

e-mer-sion (ē-mûr′shŭn), *n.* **1,** the act of coming forth or rising out of; **2,** in astronomy, the reappearance of a heavenly body after an eclipse.

em-er-y (ĕm′ẽr-ĭ), *n.* a very hard mineral substance, a form of alumina, used, when powdered, for grinding or polishing.

e-met-ic (ē-mĕt′ĭk), *adj.* inducing vomiting:—*n.* a medicine that induces vomiting, such as salt and water, soapsuds, etc.

em-i-grant (ĕm′ĭ-grănt), *n.* one who leaves his own country to settle in another:—*adj.* moving from one country to another; as, *emigrant* laborers.
Syn., n. (see im nigrant).

em-i-grate (ĕm′ĭ-grāt), *v.i.* [*p.t.* and *p.p.* -grat″ed, *p.pr.* -grat″ing], to leave one's own country in order to settle in another.—*n.* **em″i-gra′tion.**

em-i-nence (ĕm′ĭ-nĕns), *n.* **1,** that which is lofty; elevation; height; **2,** exalted rank, station, celebrity, or repute; as, to attain *eminence* in a profession: **Eminence,** a title of honor given to cardinals. Also, **em′i-nen-cy.**

em-i-nent (ĕm′ĭ-nĕnt), *adj.* **1,** elevated; **2,** high in office, rank, or reputation; distinguished.—*adv.* **em′i-nent-ly.**
Syn. celebrated, noted, renowned, famous.

e-mir (ē-mēr′; ē′mẽr), *n.* **1,** an Arabian prince or chieftain: used by Mohammedans as a title; **2,** a title given to persons descended from Mohammed through his daughter, Fatima.

em-is-sa-ry (ĕm′ĭ-sâ-rĭ), *n.* [*pl.* emissaries (-rĭz)], a person or agent sent on a mission, esp. of a secret nature.

e-mis-sion (ē-mĭsh′ŭn), *n.* **1,** the act of sending out; a throwing out; as, the *emission* of heat from a fire; **2,** the amount issued at one time, as of bank notes. —*adj.* **e-mis′sive.**

e-mit (ē-mĭt′), *v.t.* [*p.t.* and *p.p.* e-mit′ted *p.pr.* e-mit′ting], **1,** to send or give forth; throw out; **2,** to issue and send into circulation, as bank notes.

e-mol-lient (ē-mŏl′yĕnt; ē-mŏl′ĭ-ĕnt), *adj.* softening; lubricating:—*n.* a medicine that has a softening or soothing effect on the skin, or on an irritated internal surface.

e-mol-u-ment (ē-mŏl′ū-mĕnt), *n.* **1,** gain; profit; **2,** wages; salary.

e-mote (ē-mōt′), *v.i.* [*p.t.* and *p.p.* e-mot′ed, *p.pr.* e-mot′ing], to exhibit or feel emotion.

e-mo-tion (ē-mō′shŭn), *n.* **1,** mental agitation; **2,** any of the feelings of love, hate, joy, awe, grief, etc.
Syn. feeling, passion, sentiment.

e-mo-tion-al (ē-mō′shŭn-ăl), *adj.* **1,** excitable; easily agitated; **2,** tending to stir the feelings, as a book.—*adv.* **e-mo′tion-al-ly.**—*n.* **e-mo′tion-al-ism.**

em-pan-el (ĕm-păn′ĕl), *v.t.* to enter upon a list for jury duty. See **im-pan′el,** *Pfd. S.*

em-pen-nage (ĕm′pĕ-nāj; *Fr.* äṅ″pĕ-näzh′), *n.* **1,** a system of stabilizing planes placed at the rear of a dirigible (see illus. next column); **2,** the stationary stabilizing tail of an airplane.

em-per-or (ĕm′pẽr-ẽr), *n.* the sovereign or supreme ruler of an empire.

em-pha-sis (ĕm′fȧ-sĭs), *n.* [*pl.* emphases (-sēz)], **1,** a particular stress of the voice on a word or words in reading or speaking; **2,** in rhetoric, special force of language or thought.

em-pha-size (ĕm′fȧ-sīz), *v.t.* [*p.t.* and *p.p.* -sized (-sīzd), *p.pr.* -siz″ing], **1,** to pronounce clearly and positively; stress, as a word; **2,** to declare forcibly; as, she *emphasized* her denial.

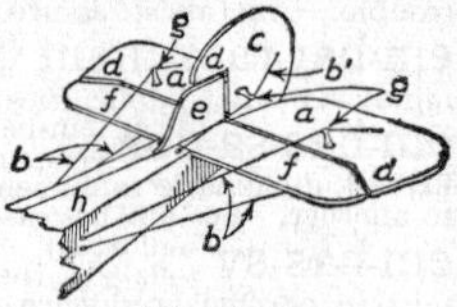

EMPENNAGE

a, a, elevators; *b, b,* control wires of elevators; *b′,* one of the control wires of rudder; *c,* rudder; *d, d, d,* balanced surfaces; *e,* fin; *f, f,* stabilizers; *g, g,* horns (matched by horns, not shown, on opposite surfaces); *h,* rear end of fuselage.

em-phat-ic (ĕm-făt′ĭk), *adj.* **1,** expressive; earnest; striking; **2,** marked by stress of voice.—*adv.* **em-phat′i-cal-ly.**

em-pire (ĕm′pīr), *n.* **1,** the region ruled over by an emperor; **2,** supreme power or dominion; imperial rule or sovereignty; hence, sway; control: **Empire,** *adj.* pertaining to the first French Empire (1804–15), set up by Napoleon I; as, *Empire* styles (see *furniture,* illus.).

em-pir-ic (ĕm-pĭr′ĭk), *n.* **1,** in medicine, one whose methods are based only on practical experience; **2,** hence, a quack doctor:—*adj.* based on, or guided by, experience; practiced from mere experience without accurate knowledge, esp. in medicine. Also, *adj.* **em-pir′i-cal.**—*adv.* **em-pir′i-cal-ly.**

em-pir-i-cism (ĕm-pĭr′ĭ-sĭzm), *n.* **1,** knowledge based on observation or practical experience; **2,** the practice of medicine without the usual theoretical medical training.—*n.* **em-pir′i-cist.**

em-place-ment (ĕm-plās′mĕnt), *n.* **1,** the position of guns within a fortification; **2,** a position built to hold a machine gun in trench warfare.

em-ploy (ĕm-ploi′), *v.t.* **1,** to give occupation to; keep busy; exercise; **2,** to make use of; **3,** to apply or devote to an object; as, to *employ* one's time in reading:—*n.* occupation.
Syn., v. use, hire. *Employ* and *use* as applied to things are often interchangeable. As applied to persons, *use* may suggest an advantage taken of weakness or inferiority; as, he *used* him to advance his own interests. *Employ* is a more dignified term than *hire,* for it emphasizes the idea of service to be rendered, while *hire* suggests the wages to be paid.

em-ploy-ee (ĕm-ploi-ē′), *n.* one who works for another for wages. Also, **em″ploy″é′** (ĕm-ploi-ā′; *Fr.* äṅ″plwȧ″yā′).

em-ploy-er (ĕm-ploi′ẽr), *n.* a person engaging or keeping others in paid service; one who employs.

em-ploy-ment (ĕm-ploi′mĕnt), *n.* **1,** the act of using, hiring, etc.; **2,** the state of being occupied, in service, etc.; **3,** business; occupation.
Syn. work, engagement, trade.

em-po-ri-um (ĕm-pō′rĭ-ŭm), *n.* [*pl.* emporiums (-ŭmz); emporia (-ȧ)], a commercial center or place of trade; popularly, a large shop or store.

em-pow-er (ĕm-pou′ẽr), *v.t.* **1,** to give authority to; authorize, as by law; **2,** to enable. Also, **im-pow′er.**

em-press (ĕm′prĕs), *n.* a woman who rules over an empire; also, the consort or widow of an emperor.

emp-ty (ĕmp′tĭ), *adj.* [*comp.* emp′ti-er, *superl.* emp′ti-est], **1**, containing nothing; **2**, vague; unsatisfactory; as, *empty* dreams; **3**, destitute of, or lacking in, force, knowledge, or sense; as, *empty* words; **4**, *Colloq.*, hungry; **5**, vacant, as a house:—*v.t.* [*p.t.* and *p.p.* -tied (-tĭd), *p.pr.* -ty-ing], **1**, to deprive of the contents; make vacant; **2**, to pour out:—*v.i.* to become empty; discharge itself.—*adv.* **emp′ti-ly.**—*n.* **emp′ti-ness.**

Syn., adj. vacant, blank. That is *empty* which contains nothing; that is *vacant* which, although now *empty*, has been, or is supposed to be, occupied. An *empty* house is bare of furniture; a *vacant* house has no one living in it. *Blank*, used especially of a surface, means free from writing or marks of any kind; as, a *blank* page. It may also mean confused or taken utterly by surprise; as, to look *blank*.

em-py-re-an (ĕm″pĭ-rē′ăn), *n.* the highest and purest region of heaven, in ancient times thought to be composed of pure fire:—*adj.* **1**, pertaining to highest heaven; celestial; **2**, composed of elemental fire.—*adj.* **em-pyr′e-al.**

e-mu (ē′mū), *n.* a large Australian bird resembling the ostrich. Also, **e′meu.**

Emu ($\frac{1}{80}$)

em-u-late (ĕm′ū-lāt), *v.t.* [*p.t.* and *p.p.* -lat″ed, *p.pr.* -lat″ing], **1**, to strive to equal or excel; as, to *emulate* the conduct of another; vie with; rival; **2**, to equal or match as a result of effort; as, try to *emulate* his example.—*adj.* **em′u-la-tive.**—*n.* **em′u-la″tor.**

em-u-la-tion (ĕm″ū-lā′shŭn), *n.* rivalry; competition; an effort to excel another in competition of any kind.

Syn. strife, opposition. (See rivalry.)

em-u-lous (ĕm′ū-lŭs), *adj.* desirous to excel.—*adv.* **em′u-lous-ly.**

e-mul-si-fy (ē-mŭl′sĭ-fī), *v.t.* [*p.t.* and *p.p.* -fied (-fīd), *p.pr.* -fy″ing], to make or form into an emulsion.

e-mul-sion (ē-mŭl′shŭn), *n.* a liquid mixture in which a fatty substance is suspended in minute globules; as, an *emulsion* of cod-liver oil; specif., a mixture used in preparing photographic dry plates.

en (ĕn), *n.* in printing, half an em: a unit of space on a line of type.

[1]en- (ĕn-), *prefix*, [*em-* before *b*, *m*, or *p*], **1**, in or into; as, *en*snare; *en*rage; **2**, on; as, *en*grave; **3**, to make; make into or like; as, *en*feeble; *en*rich; **4**, sometimes intensive; as, *en*cumber. Also, **in-.**

[2]en- (ĕn-), *prefix*, [*em-* before *b*, *m*, *p*, *ph*; *el-*, *er-* before *l*, *r*], in; on: in words of Greek derivation; as, *en*comium; *em*phasis; *el*lipse.

-en (-ĕn; -n), *n. suffix*, **1**, used to form certain plurals; as, ox*en*; **2**, used to form diminutives; as, maid*en*:—*v. suffix*, **1**, used to form the past participle of many irregular verbs; as, fall*en*; strick*en*; **2**, to make: added to nouns or adjectives; as, black*en*; height*en*:—*adj. suffix*, made of; composed of: added to nouns; as, wood*en*; gold*en*.

en-a-ble (ĕn-ā′bl), *v.t.* [*p.t.* and *p.p.* -bled (-bld), *p.pr.* -bling], to make capable; furnish with adequate or sufficient means or power; empower.

en-act (ĕn-ăkt′), *v.t.* **1**, to decree; make into law; **2**, to accomplish; **3**, to act the part of: **enacting clause**, the first clause in a legislative act, which usually begins *be it enacted*.—*n.* **en-ac′tor.**—*adj.* **en-ac′to-ry.**

en-act-ment (ĕn-ăkt′mĕnt), *n.* **1**, a statute or law; **2**, the process of the passing of a bill into law.

en-am-el (ĕn-ăm′ĕl), *n.* **1**, a hard, glassy substance used in coating the surface of metals or porcelain, and afterwards fired; **2**, anything covered with such a coat; **3**, a hard, glossy varnish; **4**, the dense, white outer coating of the teeth (see *tooth*, illus.):—*v.t.* **1**, to lay on, cover, or decorate with, enamel; **2**, to adorn with various hues:—*v.i.* to practice the art of enameling; decorate anything with enamel.—*n.* **en-am′el-er**; **en-am′el-ler.**

en-am-or (ĕn-ăm′ẽr), *v.t.* to inflame with love; charm. Also, **en-am′our.**

en-camp (ĕn-kămp′), *v.t.* and *v.i.* to settle, or be put, in temporary quarters consisting of tents or huts, as soldiers.

en-camp-ment (ĕn-kămp′mĕnt), *n.* a temporary resting place for an army or a company of travelers.

en-case (ĕn-kās′), *v.t.* [*p.t.* and *p.p.* -cased′ (-kāst′), *p.pr.* -cas′ing], to inclose in a box or other container. See **in-case′**, *Pfd.S.*

en-caus-tic (ĕn-kôs′tĭk), *adj.* designating, or pertaining to, a method of decorating in which the colors are set by heat, or burned in; as, *encaustic* pottery.

-ence (-ĕns), *n. suffix*, denoting, in general, act, quality, or state of, or the thing produced; as, diverg*ence*; emin*ence*.

en-chain (ĕn-chān′), *v.t.* **1**, to bind, as with fetters; confine; **2**, to hold tightly; captivate.

en-chant (ĕn-chȧnt′), *v.t.* **1**, to charm or subdue, as by spells or sorcery; **2**, to fill with delight.—*n.* **en-chant′ment.**

Syn. captivate, delight, enrapture, fascinate.

en-chant-er (ĕn-chȧn′tẽr), *n.* **1**, one who uses magic, sorcery, or witchcraft; **2**, one who charms or delights.—*n.fem.* **en-chant′ress.**

en-chant-ing (ĕn-chȧnt′ĭng), *p.adj.* charming; bewitching; delightful.—*adv.* **en-chant′ing-ly.**

en-chase (ĕn-chās′), *v.t.* [*p.t.* and *p.p.* -chased′ (-chāst′), *p.pr.* -chas′ing], **1**, to put in a setting, as a gem; incase; **2**, to embellish by inlaid or engraved work.

en-cir-cle (ĕn-sûr′kl), *v.t.* [*p.t.* and *p.p.* -cled (-kld), *p.pr.* -cling], to surround; encompass; embrace.

en-close (ĕn-klōz′), *v.t.* [*p.t.* and *p.p.* -closed′ (-klōzd′), *p.pr.* -clos′ing], **1**, to insert within; **2**, to surround with a barrier. See **in-close′**, *Pfd. S.*—*n.* **en-clo′sure.**

en-co-mi-um (ĕn-kō′mĭ-ŭm), *n.* formal praise or approbation; eulogy; laudation, as of a hero.

en-com-pass (ĕn-kŭm′pȧs), *v.t.* to surround; beset; as, *encompassed* by enemies.—*n.* **en-com′pass-ment.**

en-core (äṅ″kôr′; äng-kōr′), [Fr.], *adv.* once more; again:—*n.* (äṅ″kôr′; äng′-kōr), a repetition, as of a song, in response to a call by an audience:—*v.t.* (äng-kōr′; äng′-kōr), [*p.t.* and *p.p.* -cored′ (-kōrd′), *p.pr.* -cor′ing], to call for a repetition of (any part of a performance), esp. by applause.

en-coun-ter (ĕn-koun′tẽr), *v.t.* and *v.i.* **1**, to meet in conflict; **2**, to meet unexpectedly, as friends:—*n.* **1**, a sudden or accidental meeting; **2**, a conflict.

Syn., n. attack, engagement, battle, combat.

en-cour-age (ĕn-kŭr′ăj), *v.t.* [*p.t.* and *p.p.* -aged (-ăjd), *p.pr.* -aging], **1**, to help; foster; **2**, to inspire with courage; stimulate; as, to *encourage* a good cause.

Syn. hearten, cheer, support, inspirit.—*Ant.* discourage, dispirit, depress, dishearten.

en-cour-age-ment (ĕn-kŭr′ăj-mĕnt), *n.* **1**, the act of inspiring with confidence; **2**, that which incites to action or perseverance; an incentive.

en-cour-ag-ing (ĕn-kŭr′ă-jĭng), *p.adj.* **1**, giving hope; inspiring; 2, aiding; fostering; furthering.—*adv.* **en-cour'ag-ing-ly.**

Syn. hopeful, fortunate, promising.—*Ant.* hopeless, unfortunate.

en-croach (ĕn-krōch'), *v.i.* **1**, to infringe upon or restrict another's right; **2**, to enter, intrude, or trespass, upon the property of some other person: usually with *on* or *upon.*—*n.* **en-croach'ment.**

en-crust (ĕn-krŭst'), *v.t.* to cover with a hard coat. See **in-crust'**, *Pfd. S.*

en-cum-ber (ĕn-kŭm'bẽr), *v.t.* **1**, to impede or hinder; **2**, to clog; **3**, to load with debt; as, to *encumber* an estate with mortgages. Also, **in-cum'ber.**

Syn. burden, hamper.—*Ant.* relieve, help.

en-cum-brance (ĕn-kŭm'brăns), *n.* **1**, that which burdens; **2**, in law, a lien or liability attached to real property. Also, **in-cum'brance.**

Syn. load, burden, weight.

-en-cy (-ĕn'sĭ), *n. suffix*, denoting quality or state: alternative with *-ence.*

en-cyc-li-cal (ĕn-sĭk'lĭ-kăl; ĕn-sī'klĭ-kăl), *adj.* sent to all members of a class or community; intended for general circulation:—*n.* a circular letter sent by the Pope to the bishops, treating of topics of general church interest. Also, **en-cyc'lic.**

en-cy-clo-pe-di-a (ĕn-sī"klō-pē'dĭ-*ȧ*), *n.* a work outlining the entire circle of the arts and sciences; one or more volumes containing information on all branches of knowledge, topically arranged in alphabetical order. Also, **en-cy"clo-pæ'di-a.**

en-cy-clo-pe-dist (ĕn-sī"klō-pē'dĭst), *n.* a compiler of an encyclopedia; one whose studies embrace all branches of knowledge. Also, **en-cy"clo-pæ'-dist.**—*adj.* **en-cy"clo-pe'dic.**

end (ĕnd), *n.* **1**, the extreme limit or terminal point of anything; **2**, the termination of life; death; **3**, often in *pl.*, that which is left or remains; **4**, purpose in view; design; **5**, conclusion; issue; as, bring the discussion to an *end;* **6**, in football, a player stationed at the end of the line:—*v.t.* **1**, to finish; terminate; **2**, to destroy; put to death:—*v.i.* **1**, to come to a completion; **2**, to result; **3**, to die.

Syn., n. aim, object; *v.* (see [1]close).

en-dan-ger (ĕn-dān'jẽr), *v.t.* to expose to loss or injury; imperil.

en-dear (ĕn-dēr'), *v.t.* to make beloved; attach by ties of affection or love: with *to.*—*adv.* **en-dear'ing-ly.**

en-dear-ment (ĕn-dēr'mĕnt), *n.* **1**, an act or utterance that expresses affection; **2**, the state of being loved.

en-deav-or (ĕn-dĕv'ẽr), *v.i.* to strive for the attainment of some object; attempt:—*n.* an effort or attempt; mental or physical effort toward the attainment of some object. Also, **en-deav'our.**

Syn., v. try, essay, aim; *n.* (see effort).

en-dem-ic (ĕn-dĕm'ĭk), *adj.* peculiar to a nation, people, or locality: chiefly applied to diseases; as, goiter is *endemic* to certain localities. Also, **en-dem'i-cal.**

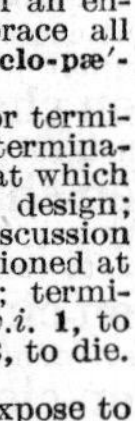

1/6 ENDIVE

end-ing (ĕn'dĭng), *n.* **1**, result; termination; **2**, in grammar, the final syllable or letter of a word; esp., an inflectional suffix.

en-dive (ĕn'dĭv; ĕn'dīv), *n.* an herb of the composite family, with curling leaves which are used as a salad.

end-less (ĕnd'lĕs), *adj.* **1**, enduring forever; **2**, having no termination; continuous because the ends are united.—*adv.* **end'less-ly.**—*n.* **end'less-ness.**

Syn. continual, incessant. (See eternal.)

en-do-gen (ĕn'dō-jĕn), *n.* one of a group of plants called *monocotyledons*, in which the vascular bundles are unevenly scattered through the stem: distinguished from *exogen.*—*adj.* **en-dog'e-nous** (-dŏj'ĕ-nŭs).

en-dorse (ĕn-dôrs'), *v.t.* [*p.t.* and *p.p.* -dorsed' (-dôrst'), *p.pr.* -dors'-ing], **1**, to approve; **2**, to write on the back of, as a check. Also, **in-dorse'**, *Pfd. S.*—*n.* **en-dorse'ment**—*n.* **en-dors'er.**—*n.* **en-dor-see'.**

en-dow (ĕn-dou'), *v.t.* **1**, to bestow a permanent fund or source of income upon; as, to *endow* a college; **2**, to equip or furnish with some gift; as, to be *endowed* with beauty, strength, or power.

en-dow-ment (ĕn-dou'mĕnt), *n.* **1**, property or a sum of money settled upon an institution or person, or devoted permanently to any cause; **2**, the act of making such a settlement; **3**, any talent or gift that a person possesses by nature.

Syn. aptitude, faculty, capacity, bent.—*Ant.* incapacity, lack.

en-due (ĕn-dū'), *v.t.* [*p.t.* and *p.p.* -dued' (-dūd'), *p.pr.* -du'ing], **1**, to put on, as clothes; **2**, to clothe; invest; furnish; as, to *endue* one with courage. Also, **in-due'.**

en-dur-a-ble (ĕn-dūr'*ȧ*-bl), *adj.* bearable.—*adv.* **en-dur'a-bly.**

en-dur-ance (ĕn-dūr'ăns), *n.* **1**, the power of sustaining without giving way; **2**, continuance (of time).

Syn. resignation, sufferance.

en-dure (ĕn-dūr'), *v.t.* [*p.t.* and *p.p.* -dured' (-dūrd'), *p.pr.* -dur'ing], **1**, to support without breaking or yielding; **2**, to bear with patience:—*v.i.* **1**, to remain firm, as under suffering; **2**, to remain in existence; last.

Syn. tolerate, abide, stand. (See [2]bear.)

en-dur-ing (ĕn-dūr'ĭng), *p.adj.* **1**, permanent; **2**, long-suffering.

Syn. fixed, unchanging. (See permanent.)

end-ways (ĕnd'wāz"), *adv.* **1**, on end; **2**, with the end forward or uppermost; **3**, lengthwise. Also, **end'wise".**

En-dym-i-on (ĕn-dĭm'ĭ-ŏn), *n.* in mythology, a beautiful shepherd, loved by Diana, endowed with eternal youth.

en-e-ma (ĕn'ē-m*ȧ*; ē-nē'm*ȧ*), *n.* [*pl.* enemas (-m*ȧ*z); enemata (ē-nĕm'-*ȧ*-t*ȧ*)], a liquid injected into the rectum.

en-e-my (ĕn'ē-mĭ), *n.* [*pl.* enemies (-mĭz)], **1**, one hostile to another; **2**, a foe; antagonist; a hostile army.

Syn. foe, opponent, adversary, antagonist. *Enemy* and *foe* are alike in the idea of intending injury; in private life, both suggest personal hatred, which is absent in military language; as, in war they were our *enemies*, but in peace, our friends. *Foe* is a more literary or poetic word than *enemy. Opponent* emphasizes the idea of resistance, but usually with no suggestion of hatred; as, our *opponents* opened the debate.

en-er-get-ic (ĕn"ẽr-jĕt'ĭk), *adj.* **1**, vigorous in action; forcible; **2**, full of life; active.—*adv.* **en"er-get'i-cal-ly.**

Syn. industrious, powerful, strenuous.—*Ant.* lazy, languid, lifeless.

en-er-gize (ĕn'ẽr-jīz), *v.t.* [*p.t.* and *p.p.* -gized (-jīzd), *p.pr.* -giz"ing], to lend power to:—*v.i.* to act vigorously.

en-er-gy (ĕn'ẽr-jĭ), *n.* [*pl.* energies (-jĭz)], capacity for work; power; force.

Syn. strength, vigor, might. (See power.)—*Ant.* lifelessness, languor.

en-er-vate (ĕn'ẽr-vāt; ē-nûr'vāt), *v.t.* [*p.t.* and *p.p.* -vat"ed, *p.pr.* -vat"-ing], to deprive of nerve, force, or vigor; weaken.—*n.* **en"er-va'tion.**—*n.* **en'er-va"tor.**

***en fa-mille** (äṅ" fȧ"mēy''), [Fr.], with one's family; at home; in domestic fashion; informally.

en-fee-ble (ĕn-fē'bl), *v.t.* [*p.t.* and *p.p.* -bled (-bld), *p.pr.* -bling], to weaken; destroy the force of; deprive of strength.—*n.* **en-fee'ble-ment.**

en-fi-lade (ĕn"fĭ-lād'), *n.* a firing along a line of works, a line of troops, or the like:—*v.t.* [*p.t.* and *p.p.* -lad'ed, *p.pr.* -lad'ing], to rake with gunfire from end to end.

en-fold (ĕn-fōld'), *v.t.* **1**, to envelop; **2**, to embrace. Also, **in-fold'**, *Pfd. S.*

en-force (ĕn-fōrs'), *v.t.* [*p.t.* and *p.p.* -forced' (-fōrst'), *p.pr.* -forc'ing], **1**, to urge with energy; **2**, to execute with vigor; **3**, to compel; **4**, to make clear or intelligible.—*adj.* **en-force'a-ble.**—*n.* **en-force'ment.**

en-fran-chise (ĕn-frăn'chīz; -chĭz), *v.t.* [*p.t.* and *p.p.* -chised (-chīzd; -chĭzd), *p.pr.* -chis-ing], **1**, to admit to the right to vote; **2**, to liberate; make free: said of a state, city, or corporation.—*n.* **en-fran'chise-ment.**

en-gage (ĕn-gāj'), *v.t.* [*p.t.* and *p.p.* -gaged (-gājd'), *p.pr.* -gag'ing], **1**, to pledge or bind by oath or contract; **2**, to betroth; **3**, to win; as, his smile *engages* everyone to him; **4**, in machinery, to come into gear with; **5**, to make liable for a debt; **6**, to secure for aid or employment; as, to *engage* a workman; **7**, to encounter in battle; **8**, to occupy the time or attention of; as, to *engage* one in conversation:—*v.i.* **1**, to promise, or assume an obligation; **2**, to occupy oneself; as, to *engage* in business; **3**, to enter a conflict; **4**, in machinery, to interlock.

en-gaged (ĕn-gājd'), *p.adj.* **1**, busy or occupied; **2**, affianced or betrothed; **3**, in machinery, geared together.

en-gage-ment (ĕn-gāj'mĕnt), *n.* **1**, betrothal; **2**, occupation; **3**, an appointment; obligation; **4**, in machinery, the state of being in gear; **5**, a battle between armies or fleets.
Syn. (see battle).

en-gag-ing (ĕn-gāj'ĭng), *p.adj.* winning; pleasing; as, an *engaging* manner.—*adv.* **en-gag'ing-ly.**

en-gen-der (ĕn-jĕn'dẽr), *v.t.* **1**, to beget; **2**, to cause; excite:—*v.i.* to come into existence.

en-gine (ĕn'jĭn), *n.* **1**, anything used to effect a purpose; **2**, a machine by which power is applied for the performance of work; **3**, an apparatus for converting some form of energy, as heat, into mechanical power, esp. a railway locomotive; **4**, a skilful mechanical contrivance.

en-gi-neer (ĕn"jĭ-nēr'), *n.* **1**, one who is skilled in the principles or practice of any branch of mechanical science; **2**, one who has charge of and manages an engine or a locomotive; **3**, one of a group trained in building bridges, roads, etc., for military use; **4**, one who carries through a scheme or undertaking:—*v.t.* **1**, to plan, lay out, or direct; **2**, to plan and execute the construction of (a road, canal, etc.).

en-gi-neer-ing (ĕn"jĭ-nēr'ĭng), *n.* **1**, the science and art of constructing and using machinery, or of designing and constructing public works; **2**, skilful or tactful management.

Eng-lish (ĭng'glĭsh), *adj.* belonging to, characteristic of, or pertaining to, England, its language, or its people:—*n.* **1**, the people of England or the language spoken by them; **2**, a size of printer's type, about equivalent to 14 point (see *type*).

Eng-lish horn an orchestral instrument of the wood-wind group (see *musical instrument*, illus.).

Eng-lish-man (ĭng'glĭsh-măn), *n.* [*pl.* Englishmen (-mĕn)], a citizen of England.—*n. fem.* **Eng'lish-wom"an.**

en-graft (ĕn-gråft'), *v.t.* **1**, to insert (a shoot) in a tree; **2**, to incorporate; **3**, to implant. See **in-graft'**, *Pfd.S.*

en-grail-ment (ĕn-grāl'mĕnt), *n.* a ring of dots or curves around the inner edge of the border on the flat side of a coin or medal.

en-grain (ĕn-grān'), *v.t.* **1**, to color in imitation of wood; **2**, (preferably, *ingrain*), to saturate or infuse deeply.

en-grave (ĕn-grāv'), *v.t.* [*p.t.* -graved' (-grāvd'), *p.p.* -graved' or -grav'en (-grāv'n), *p.pr.* -grav'ing], **1**, to cut or carve in sunken patterns; as, to *engrave* words on a monument; **2**, to impress deeply or indelibly; imprint; **3**, to cut (letters, etc.) on a metal plate, as for printing.—*n.* **en-grav'er.**

en-grav-ing (ĕn-grāv'ĭng), *n.* **1**, the act, process, or art of producing designs, cut by a tool or by acids, in metal, stone, or hard wood; **2**, a design so cut; **3**, an impression from an engraved plate; as, the *engraving* on visiting cards.

en-gross (ĕn-grōs'), *v.t.* **1**, to monopolize; occupy wholly; as, business *engrosses* his attention; **2**, to write in a large, distinct, round hand, as a public document.—*n.* **en-gross'er.**—*n.* **en-gross'ment.**
Syn. absorb, occupy, engage.

en-gulf (ĕn-gŭlf'), *v.t.* to swallow up, as in a deep hollow or whirlpool; plunge into a gulf. Also, **in-gulf'.**
Syn. absorb, submerge, bury.

en-hance (ĕn-håns'), *v.t.* [*p.t.* and *p.p.* -hanced' (-hånst'), *p.pr.* -hanc'ing], to increase or advance, as in attractiveness or value; intensify.—*n.* **en-hance'ment.**

E-nid (ē'nĭd), *n.* the faithful wife of Geraint, a Knight of the Round Table.

e-nig-ma (ē-nĭg'mȧ), *n.* **1**, a remark not easily understood; a riddle; **2**, anything that puzzles.
Syn. conundrum, puzzle, problem.

e-nig-mat-ic (ē"nĭg-măt'ĭk; ĕn"ĭg-), *adj.* obscure or puzzling. Also, **e"nig-mat'i-cal.**—*adv.* **e"nig-mat'i-cal-ly.**

en-join (ĕn-join'), *v.t.* **1**, to direct with authority; command, as a person; **2**, to prohibit or restrain by judicial order.
Syn. order, charge, admonish.—*Ant.* submit, yield, obey.

en-joy (ĕn-joi'), *v.t.* **1**, to feel or perceive with pleasure; **2**, to have the use or possession of.—*adj.* **en-joy'a-ble.**—*adv.* **en-joy'a-bly.**—*n.* **en-joy'er.**

en-joy-ment (ĕn-joi'mĕnt), *n.* **1**, pleasure; gratification; **2**, a source of joy or satisfaction.
Syn. satisfaction, comfort.—*Ant.* misery wretchedness, discomfort.

en-kin-dle (ĕn-kĭn'dl), *v.t.* [*p.t.* and *p.p.* -dled (-dld), *p.pr.* -dling], to set on fire; kindle; rouse.

en-lace (ĕn-lās'), *v.t.* [*p.t.* and *p.p.* -laced' (-lāst'), *p.pr.* -lac'ing], **1**, to cover or bind with lace or laces; **2**, to entangle.

en-large (ĕn-lärj'), *v.t.* [*p.t.* and *p.p.* -larged' (-lärjd'), *p.pr.* -larg'ing], **1**, to increase in quantity; extend in limits or dimensions; **2**, to extend to more purposes or uses:—*v.i.* to become larger; as, a plant *enlarges* with growth.
Syn. augment, broaden, expand. (See increase.)—*Ant.* diminish, reduce, decrease.

en-large-ment (ĕn-lärj'mĕnt), *n.* **1**, increase in size; **2**, a photograph reproduced in increased size.

en-light-en (ĕn-līt'n), *v.t.* to furnish with increased knowledge; elevate morally or spiritually.—*n.* **en-light'en-ment.**
Syn. illumine, instruct, inform.

en-list (ĕn-lĭst'), *v.t.* **1**, to enroll, as for military service; register; **2**, to win over, as for some cause:—*v.i.* **1**, to engage oneself for military service; **2**, to work for something enthusiastically.—*n.* **en-list'ment.**

en-liv-en (ĕn-lĭv'n), *v.t.* **1**, to make vigorous, active, or cheerful; **2**, to exhilarate; inspirit.
Syn. cheer, animate, inspire.—*Ant.* sadden, quiet, discourage, dampen.

***en masse** (äṅ" mäs'), [Fr.], collectively; all together.

en-mesh (ĕn-mĕsh'), *v.t.* to entangle, as in a net. Also, **im-mesh'; in-mesh'.**

en-mi-ty (ĕn'mĭ-tĭ), *n.* [*pl.* enmities (-tĭz)], animosity; hatred; hostility.
Syn. maliciousness, unfriendliness, contention.—*Ant.* friendliness, kindliness, affection.

en-no-ble (ĕ-nō'bl; ĕn-nō'bl), *v.t.* [*p.t.* and *p.p.* -bled (-bld), *p.pr.* -bling], **1**, to dignify; exalt; make famous or illustrious; **2**, to raise to the nobility.

en-nui (äṅ"nüē'; äng-nwē'), [Fr.], *n.* languor of mind; boredom; listlessness.

E-noch (ē'nŭk), *n.* in the Bible, **1**, a patriarch who "walked with God" (Genesis 5:24); **2**, son of Cain (Genesis 4:17).

e-nor-mi-ty (ē-nôr'mĭ-tĭ), *n.* [*pl.* enormities (-tĭz)], **1**, the state of being outrageous or extremely immoderate; **2**, an atrocity; a grave offense.

e-nor-mous (ē-nôr'mŭs), *adj.* very large; immense; greatly exceeding the normal size or number.—*adv.* **e-nor'mous-ly.**—*n.* **e-nor'mous-ness.**
Syn. huge, vast, immense, colossal. That is *enormous* which is far beyond the ordinary in size, number, or degree; the word suggests something extravagant, abnormal, or out of proportion; as, an *enormous* undertaking; *enormous* wealth. *Huge* usually refers to bulk; as, a *huge* beast. *Vast* ordinarily suggests extent; as, *vast* prairies. *Immense* means so great as to exceed ordinary measurements; as, great distances separate the *immense* audiences of the radio. *Colossal* suggests a person or thing of gigantic size; as, a *colossal* statue.

e-nough (ē-nŭf'), *adj.* sufficient:—*n.* a sufficiency:—*adv.* so as to be sufficient; sufficiently:—*interj.* stop!

e-now (ē-nou'), *adj., n.,* and *adv., Archaic* or *Poetic,* enough: as *adj.* or *adv.,* usually following the word it modifies.

en-plane (ĕn-plān'), *v.i.* [*p.t.* and *p.p.* -planed' (-plānd'), *p.pr.* -plan'ing], to get aboard an airplane, esp. at the start of a journey.

en-quire (ĕn-kwīr'), *v.i.* and *v.t.* [*p.t.* and *p.p.*-quired'(-kwīrd'), *p.pr.*-quir'ing], to ask for information (about). See **in-quire'**, *Pfd. S.*—*n.* **en-quir'er.**—*n.* **en-quir'y.**

en-rage (ĕn-rāj'), *v.t.* [*p.t.* and *p.p.* -raged' (-rājd'), *p.pr.* -rag'ing], to make intensely angry; provoke to fury.

***en rap-port** (äṅ" rȧ"pôr'), [Fr.], in sympathy; in accord.

en-rap-ture (ĕn-răp'tūr), *v.t.* [*p.t.* and *p.p.* -tured (-tūrd), *p.pr.* -tur-ing], to transport with delight; charm; captivate; enchant.
Syn. delight, fascinate, bewitch.

en-rich (ĕn-rĭch'), *v.t.* **1**, to increase the wealth of; **2**, to make fertile, as soil; improve; **3**, to adorn.—*n.* **en-rich'ment.**

en-roll (ĕn-rōl'), *v.t.* **1**, to insert or write down in a register; enlist; record; **2**, to write out a good copy of (a document); engross. Also, **en-rol'.**—*n.* **en-roll'ment.**

***en route** (äṅ" rōōt'), [Fr.], on the way; as, *en route* for Paris.

en-san-guine (ĕn-săng'gwĭn), *v.t.* [*p.t.* and *p.p.* -guined (-gwĭnd), *p.pr.* -guin-ing], to smear or cover with blood.

en-sconce (ĕn-skŏns'), *v.t.* [*p.t.* and *p.p.* -sconced' (-skŏnst'), *p.pr.* -sconc'ing], **1**, to fix securely or comfortably; **2**, to guard in a secret place.

***en-sem-ble** (äṅ"säṅbl'), [Fr.], *n.* the general appearance or effect; all the parts of a thing together.

en-shrine (ĕn-shrīn'), *v.t.* [*p.t.* and *p.p.* -shrined' (-shrīnd'), *p.pr.* -shrin'ing], to place on an altar or in a holy place; keep sacred.

en-shroud (ĕn-shroud'), *v.t.* to cover completely; conceal from view.

en-si-form (ĕn'sĭ-fôrm), *adj.* shaped like the blade of a sword.

en-sign (ĕn'sīn), *n.* **1**, a flag; **2**, a badge of authority; **3**, (also, ĕn'sĭn), in the U. S. navy, a commissioned officer of the lowest rank.—*n.* **en'sign-cy.**—*n.* **en'sign-ship.**

en-si-lage (ĕn'sĭ-lāj), *n.* **1**, fodder or vegetable produce stored in the green state in a silo; **2**, the process of preserving fodder.

en-slave (ĕn-slāv'), *v.t.* [*p.t.* and *p.p.* -slaved' (-slāvd'), *p.pr.* -slav'ing], to bring into bondage; deprive of moral liberty or power; as, to be *enslaved* by drink.

en-snare (ĕn-snâr'), *v.t.* [*p.t.* and *p.p.* -snared' (-snârd'), *p.pr.* snar'ing], to take in a trap. Also, **in-snare'**, *Pfd. S.*

en-sue (ĕn-sū'), *v.i.* [*p.t.* and *p.p.* -sued' (-sūd'), *p.pr.* -su'ing], to follow as a consequence; come afterward.

en-sure (ĕn-shōōr'), *v.t.* [*p.t.* and *p.p.* -sured' (-shōōrd'), *p.pr.* -sur'ing], **1**, to secure against loss or damage; **2**, to make sure or secure:—*v.i.* to undertake to give security against loss. See **in-sure'**, *Pfd. S.*

-ent (-ĕnt), *n. suffix,* attached to Latin verb stems to denote the doer of the action indicated by the stem; as, superintend*ent:*—*adj. suffix,* attached to Latin verb stems to form adjectives equivalent to present participles; as, persist*ent.*

en-tab-la-ture (ĕn-tăb'lȧ-tūr), *n.* that part of a structure supported by a colonnade which lies between the columns and the upper edge of the cornice, comprising the architrave, frieze, and cornice (cf. *architrave,* illus.).

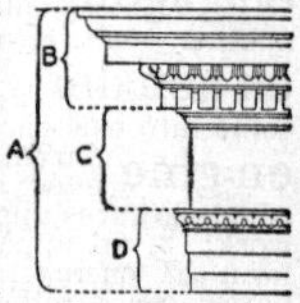

ENTABLATURE
A, entablature; B, cornice; C, frieze; D, architrave.

en-tail (ĕn-tāl'), *n.* **1**, an estate that may be left only to a particular heir or heirs; **2**, the act of so restricting the inheritance of property:—*v.t.* **1**, to leave, as money, land, or other property, to a succession of heirs, so that no one of them can give or will it away; **2**, to necessitate; require.—*n.* **en-tail'ment.**

en-tan-gle (ĕn-tăng'gl), *v.t.* [*p.t.* and *p.p.* -gled (-gld), *p.pr.* -gling], **1**, to involve in a snarl; **2**, to insnare; **3**, to perplex; bewilder.
Syn. embroil, twist, confuse.

en-tan-gle-ment (ĕn-tăng'gl-mĕnt), *n.* something that insnares; a complication; an obstruction.

***en-tente** (äṅ"täṅt'), [Fr.], *n.* an agreement or understanding: **Triple Entente**, the friendly understanding established among Great Britain, France, and Russia before the World War.

en-ter (ĕn'tẽr), *v.t.* **1**, to go or come into; penetrate; **2**, to set down in writing; as, the clerk *entered* the account in the journal; **3**, to join or become a member of; **4**, to go into or begin, as a business, etc.; **5**, to place on record, as a name in a contest:—*v.i.* **1**, to go or come in; **2**, to take part (in a discussion, agreement, etc.); sympathize: with *nto;* 3, to make a beginning, as in a business: with *into;* 4, to become a part: with *into;* 5, to come upon the stage, as an actor.

en-ter-ic (ĕn-tĕr′ĭk), *adj.* pertaining to the intestines.

en-ter-prise (ĕn′tĕr-prīz), *n.* 1, an undertaking of importance or risk; 2, boldness; energy and invention.
Syn. project, endeavor, venture, effort.

en-ter-pris-ing (ĕn′tĕr-prīz″ĭng), *adj.* ambitious; adventurous; energetic; progressive.

en-ter-tain (ĕn″tĕr-tān′), *v.t.* 1, to receive and treat hospitably; 2, to amuse; 3, to keep or harbor, as a grudge; 4, to take into consideration: as, to *entertain* a proposition:—*v.i.* to receive, or afford amusement for, guests.—*n.* **en″ter-tain′er.**

en-ter-tain-ing (ĕn″tĕr-tān′ĭng), *p.adj.* amusing; diverting; pleasing.—*adv.* **en″ter-tain′ing-ly.**

en-ter-tain-ment (ĕn″tĕr-tān′mĕnt), *n.* 1, the act of entertaining, or state of being entertained; esp., hospitality at table; a banquet; 2, a diverting or amusing performance; amusement.

en-thrall (ĕn-thrôl′), *v.t.* 1, to enslave; bring or hold under some compelling influence or power; 2, to charm. Also, **en-thral′; in-thrall′.**—*n.* **en-thrall′ment.**

en-throne (ĕn-thrōn′), *v.t.* [*p.t.* and *p.p.* -throned′ (-thrōnd′), *p.pr.* -thron′ing], to place on, or as on, a seat of power; invest or endow with royal power and authority. Also, **in-throne′.**

en-thu-si-asm (ĕn-thū′zĭ-ăzm), *n.* ardor of mind; intense interest, feeling, or emotion.—*n.* **en-thu′si-ast.**
Syn. devotion, earnestness, zeal, fervor.—*Ant.* indifference, coldness.

en-thu-si-as-tic (ĕn-thū″zĭ-ăs′tĭk), *adj.* ardent; zealous.—*adv.* **en-thu″si-as′ti-cal-ly.**

en-tice (ĕn-tīs′), *v.t.* [*p.t.* and *p.p.* -ticed′ (-tīst′), *p.pr.* -tic′ing], to allure; tempt.—*adv.* **en-tic′ing-ly.**—*n.* **en-tice′ment.**
Syn. decoy, coax, seduce.

en-tire (ĕn-tīr′), *adj.* 1, complete; whole; undivided or unbroken; 2, unqualified; as, *entire* approval:—*n.* the whole.

en-tire-ly (ĕn-tīr′lĭ), *adv.* 1, fully; completely; wholly; 2, solely.

en-tire-ty (ĕn-tīr′tĭ), *n.* [*pl.* entireties (-tĭz)], 1, completeness; 2, the whole; a complete thing.

en-ti-tle (ĕn-tī′tl), *v.t.* [*p.t.* and *p.p.* -tled (-tld), *p.pr.* -tling], 1, to give a name to; 2, to dignify by a name; 3, to give a right to. Also, **in-ti′tle.**

en-ti-ty (ĕn′tĭ-tĭ), *n.* [*pl.* entities (-tĭz)], being; existence; also, anything considered as having individual existence.

en-tomb (ĕn-tōōm′), *v.t.* to place in, or as in, a grave; bury.

en-tomb-ment (ĕn-tōōm′mĕnt), *n.* the act of placing in a grave; burial; interment.

en-to-mol-o-gy (ĕn″tō-mŏl′ō-jĭ), *n.* [*pl.* entomologies (-jĭz)], 1, that branch of zoölogy which treats of insects and their habits; 2, a book or treatise on this subject.—*adj.* **en″to-mo-log′i-cal.**—*n.* **en″to-mol′o-gist.**—*v.i.* **en″to-mol′o-gize.**

***en-tou-rage** (äṅ″tōō″räzh′), [Fr.], *n.* associates; retinue of attendants; surroundings.

en-trails (ĕn′trālz), *n.pl.* the intestines of animals; viscera.

en-train (ĕn-trān′), *v.t.* and *v.i.* to put or get aboard a train, as troops.

¹en-trance (ĕn′trăns), *n.* 1, the act of going or coming in; 2, a door, passage, etc., through which one enters a place; 3, permission to come in; 4, a fee paid for admission.
Syn. access, accession, admission; opening, portal, entry. (See admittance.)

²en-trance (ĕn-trȧns′), *v.t.* [*p.t.* and *p.p.* -tranced′ (-trȧnst′), *p.pr.* -tranc′ing], 1, to throw into a trance; 2, to put into a state of ecstasy; enrapture.—*adv.* **en-tranc′ing-ly.**

en-trap (ĕn-trăp′), *v.t.* [*p.t.* and *p.p.* -trapped′ (-trăpt′), *p.pr.* -trap′ping], to catch in, or as in, a trap; entangle.

en-treat (ĕn-trēt′), *v.t.* to solicit or ask earnestly; beseech. Also, **in-treat′.**
Syn. petition, importune, pray.

en-treat-y (ĕn-trēt′ĭ), *n.* [*pl.* entreaties (-ĭz)], an earnest petition or request; prayer.
Syn. supplication, solicitation, appeal.

en-trée (äṅ″trā′), *n.* 1, entrance; admission; the act of entering; 2, a dish served between the chief courses.

en-trench (ĕn-trĕnch′), *v.t.* to surround or defend, as with ditches:—*v.i.* to trespass. See **in-trench′**, *Pfd. S.*

en-trench-ment (ĕn-trĕnch′mĕnt), *n.* 1, a system of earthworks forming a battle line; 2, the state of being protected; 3, an infringement or encroachment. See **in-trench′ment**, *Pfd. S.*

***en-tre-pre-neur** (äṅtr′″prē-nûr′), [Fr.], *n.* an organizer; esp., one who, in producing commodities, organizes the enterprise and assumes the business risk: also called *undertaker.*

en-trust (ĕn-trŭst′), *v.t.* 1, to confide; as, to *entrust* certain funds to him; 2, to confide in trust to (a person); as, to *entrust* him with funds. Also, **in-trust′**, *Pfd. S.*

en-try (ĕn′trĭ), *n.* [*pl.* entries (-trĭz)], 1, the act of going or coming in; beginning; 2, a place for going in; a passage; 3, the act of writing an item in a list or record; the item written in; 4, the taking of rightful possession of land by setting foot on it; 5, the reporting of the arrival of a ship in port.

en-twine (ĕn-twīn′), *v.t.* [*p.t.* and *p.p.* -twined′ (-twīnd′), *p.pr.* -twin′ing], to wind around; twist together:—*v.i.* to become twisted together. Also, **in-twine′.**

en-twist (ĕn-twĭst′), *v.t.* to twine together, or in with.

e-nu-mer-ate (ē-nū′mĕr-āt), *v.t.* [*p.t.* and *p.p.* -at″ed, *p.pr.* -at″ing], to reckon or name singly; count.—*adj.* **e-nu′mer-a-tive.**—*n.* **e-nu′mer-a″tor.**
Syn. compute, calculate, estimate.

e-nu-mer-a-tion (ē-nū″mĕr-ā′shŭn), *n.* 1, the act of counting; a numbering; 2, a catalog; list.

e-nun-ci-ate (ē-nŭn′shĭ-āt; ē-nŭn′sĭ-āt), *v.t.* [*p.t.* and *p.p.* -at″ed, *p.pr.* -at″ing], 1, to declare; 2, to utter:—*v.i.* to speak; pronounce.—*n.* **e-nun′ci-a″tor.**

e-nun-ci-a-tion (ē-nŭn″sĭ-ā′shŭn; ē-nŭn″shĭ-ā′shŭn), *n.* 1, the act of declaring or pronouncing; 2, the manner of uttering vocal sounds; articulation; 3, a definite statement.

¹en-vel-op (ĕn-vĕl′ŭp), *v.t.* 1, to surround with, or as with, a wrapper; 2, to hide; cover.

en-ve-lope (ĕn′vĕ-lōp), *n.* 1, a paper wrapper, usually gummed, for safe conveyance of a letter by post, messenger, etc.; 2, any covering; wrapper. Also, **²en-vel′op** (ĕn-vĕl′ŏp; ĕn′vĕ-lōp).

en-vel-op-ment (ĕn-vĕl′ŭp-mĕnt), *n.* 1, the act of surrounding or covering on all sides; 2, anything that surrounds or conceals.

en-ven-om (ĕn-vĕn′ŭm), *v.t.* 1, to infuse poison into; 2, to embitter.

en-vi-a-ble (ĕn′vĭ-ȧ-bl), *adj.* exciting envy; awakening a wish for similar good fortune for oneself.—*adv.* **en′vi-a-bly.**

en-vi-ous (ĕn′vĭ-ŭs), *adj.* feeling, or characterized by, a desire to possess something belonging to another; as, an *envious* disposition.—*adv.* **en′vi-ous-ly.**

en-vi-ron (ĕn-vī′rŭn), *v.t.* to surround or inclose; encompass; hem in:—*n.*, in *pl.*, places near a town or city; suburbs.

en-vi-ron-ment (ĕn-vī′rŭn-mĕnt), *n.* **1,** the surroundings of one's life; conditions which influence character; as, a wholesome *environment;* **2,** the act of surrounding.—*adj.* **en-vi″ron-men′tal.**

en-voy (ĕn′voi), *n.* a government agent, next in rank to an ambassador; also, one sent on a special mission.

en-vy (ĕn′vĭ), *v.t.* [*p.t.* and *p.p.* -vied (-vĭd), *p.pr.* -vy-ing], **1,** to wish for (what is another's); **2,** to feel displeasure at (the excellence or prosperity of another); to begrudge; **3,** to feel displeasure at (a person) because of his excellence, prosperity, etc.:—*v.i.* to feel or exhibit covetousness:—*n.* [*pl.* envies (-vĭz)], **1,** ill will or displeasure felt because of the excellence or good fortune of another; **2,** a person or object exciting such feeling; as, her jewels were the *envy* of her rivals.

Syn., *n.* covetousness. (See jealousy.)

en-wrap (ĕn-răp′), *v.t.* [*p.t.* and *p.p.* -wrapped′ (-răpt′), *p.pr.* -wrap′-ping], **1,** to envelop in a wrapping; **2,** to engross. See **in-wrap′**, *Pfd. S.*

en-wreathe (ĕn-rēth′), *v.t.* [*p.t.* and *p.p.* -wreathed′ (-rēthd′), *p.pr.* -wreath′ing], to surround with, or as with, a garland. Also, **in-wreathe′**, *Pfd. S.*

en-zyme (ĕn′zīm), *n.* any of various complex substances, such as pepsin, found existing in both plant and animal life, and able to cause chemical action in other substances without taking direct part in the action. Also, **en′zym.**

E-o-cene (ē′ō-sēn), *adj.* in geology, pertaining to the earliest part of the Tertiary period, before the development of modern species:—*n.* the Eocene period.

E-o-li-an (ē-ō′lĭ-ăn), *adj.* pertaining to the winds: from *Æolus*, the god of the winds: **eolian harp,** an instrument played by a current of air. See **Æ-o′li-an**, *Pfd. S.*

e-o-lith-ic (ē″ō-lĭth′ĭk), *adj.* designating, or pertaining to, the geologic age which just preceded the old stone age.

e-on (ē′ŏn), *n.* a period of time too long to measure; an age. Also, **æ′on**, *Pfd. S.*

E-os (ē′ŏs), *n.* in Greek mythology, the goddess of the dawn: identified with the Roman *Aurora.*

ep-au-let (ĕp′ô-lĕt), *n.* an ornamental badge worn on the shoulder of a uniform. Also, **ep′au-lette.**

e-phah (ē′fȧ), *n.* an ancient Hebrew dry measure equal to a little more than a bushel. Also, **e′pha.**

e-phem-er-al (ē-fĕm′ẽr-ăl), *adj.* **1,** existing only for a day, as certain insects; **2,** short-lived.

Syn. fleeting, transient, transitory.

E-phe-sian (ē-fē′zhăn), *adj.* pertaining to Ephesus:—*n.* **1,** a citizen of Ephesus; **2,** in *pl.*, used as *sing.* (*abbr.* **Eph.**), the tenth book of the New Testament.

eph-od (ĕf′ŏd), *n.* a garment worn by the Jewish high priest in ancient times.

eph-or (ĕf′ŏr), *n.* [*pl.* ephors (-ŏrz); ephori (-ō-rī)], one of the five chief magistrates in ancient Sparta.

ep-i- (ĕp′ĭ-), [Gk.], *prefix*, [*ep-* before a vowel; as, *epode*; *eph-* before an aspirate; as, *eph*emeral], used with Greek stems, and usually meaning upon or over; as, *epi*dermis; *epi*glottis.

ep-ic (ĕp′ĭk), *n.* a long narrative poem of some heroic deed or event, written in a lofty style:—*adj.* **1,** designating, or pertaining to, a poem of this kind; **2,** grand; noble; heroic.

ep-i-cure (ĕp′ĭ-kūr), *n.* a person of luxurious tastes and habits; one fond of the delicacies of the table.

Ep-i-cu-re-an (ĕp″ĭ-kū-rē′ăn), *adj.* pertaining to the philosophy of Epicurus:—*n.* a follower of Epicurus: **epicurean,** *adj.* **1,** pursuing pleasure as a chief aim; **2,** devoted to the pleasures of the table:—*n.* an epicure.

ep-i-dem-ic (ĕp″ĭ-dĕm′ĭk), *adj.* attacking many at the same time: said of a disease:—*n.* **1,** a general attack of a disease throughout a locality; **2,** a widespread occurrence of anything.

ep-i-der-mis (ĕp″ĭ-dûr′mĭs), *n.* **1,** the cuticle or outer skin of an animal body; **2,** the outer coating of the leaf or bark of a plant.

ep-i-glot-tis (ĕp″ĭ-glŏt′ĭs), *n.* the leaf-shaped lid of cartilage which covers the larynx or upper part of the windpipe during the act of swallowing.

ep-i-gram (ĕp′ĭ-grăm), *n.* **1,** a verse or short poem with a witty point; **2,** a short phrase expressing a witty thought.

ep-i-gram-mat-ic (ĕp″ĭ-gră-măt′ĭk), *adj.* witty; pointed and concise. Also, **ep″i-gram-mat′i-cal.**

ep-i-graph (ĕp′ĭ-grăf), *n.* **1,** an inscription on a building, monument, or the like; **2,** a motto or quotation at the beginning of a book or chapter.

e-pig-ra-phy (ē-pĭg′rȧ-fĭ), *n.* **1,** inscriptions collectively; **2,** the study and interpretation of inscriptions.

ep-i-lep-sy (ĕp′ĭ-lĕp″sĭ), *n.* a chronic nervous disease often attended by loss of consciousness and convulsions.

ep-i-lep-tic (ĕp″ĭ-lĕp′tĭk), *adj.* pertaining to, or affected with, epilepsy:—*n.* one affected with epilepsy.

ep-i-log (ĕp′ĭ-lŏg), *n.* **1,** a poem or speech at the end of a play; **2,** the conclusion of a literary work. Also, **ep′i-logue.**

Ep-i-me-theus (ĕp″ĭ-mē′thūs; -thē-ŭs), *n.* in mythology, the slow-witted brother of Prometheus.

E-piph-a-ny (ē-pĭf′ȧ-nĭ), *n.* [*pl.* Epiphanies (-nĭz)], a church festival (January 6) commemorating the visit of the three wise men to Jesus at Bethlehem.

ep-i-phyte (ĕp′ĭ-fīt), *n.* a plant, as an air plant, attached above ground to another plant, but not drawing nourishment for development from it or from the ground.—*adj.* **ep″i-phyt′ic** (-fĭt′ĭk).

e-pis-co-pa-cy (ē-pĭs′kō-pȧ-sĭ), *n.* **1,** church government by bishops; **2,** bishops collectively; **3,** the state or rank of a bishop.

e-pis-co-pal (ē-pĭs′kō-păl), *adj.* **1,** pertaining to bishops; **2,** governed by a bishop: **Episcopal,** pertaining to the Protestant Episcopal Church.

E-pis-co-pa-li-an (ē-pĭs″kō-pā′lĭ-ăn), *adj.* pertaining to the Protestant Episcopal Church:—*n.* a member or supporter of that church.

e-pis-co-pate (ē-pĭs′kō-pȧt), *n.* **1,** the position and authority of a bishop; bishopric; **2,** a bishop's term of office; **3,** bishops collectively.

ep-i-sode (ĕp′ĭ-sōd), *n.* an incident or action standing by itself but more or less connected with a series of events; as, an *episode* of the war; an *episode* in a narrative.—*adj.* **ep″i-sod′ic; ep″i-sod′i-cal.**

e-pis-tle (ē-pĭs′l), *n.* a formal letter; a written communication: **Epistle,**

ne of the letters written by the apostles, and ecorded in the New Testament.

:-pis-to-la-ry (ē-pĭs'tō-lā-rĭ), *adj.* pertaining to letters; as, a 'raceful *epistolary* style.

:p-i-taph (ĕp'ĭ-tȧf), *n.* an inscription or writing on a tomb.

:p-i-tha-la-mi-um (ĕp″ĭ-thȧ-lā'mĭ-ŭm), *n.* [*pl.* epithalamiums (-ŭmz); epithalamia (-ȧ)], a song or oem in celebration of a marriage.

:p-i-thet (ĕp'ĭ-thĕt), *n.* an adjective expressing a quality; as, *rosy-fin-'ered* dawn; also, a descriptive title.

e-pit-o-me (ē-pĭt'ō-mē), *n.* [*pl.* epitomes (-mēz)], a brief statement of he contents of a literary work; a summary r summing up; an abridgment; synopsis.
Syn. syllabus, compendium, analysis.

e-pit-o-mize (ē-pĭt'ō-mīz), *v.t.* [*p.t.* and *p.p.* -mized (-mīzd), *p.pr.* -miz″ing], **1**, to make a brief outline of; **2**, to abridge; condense.

ep-i-zo-an (ĕp″ĭ-zō'ăn), *n.* an animal, as a flea or a louse, which lives as a parasite externally on another animal.

ep-i-zo-öt-ic (ĕp″ĭ-zō-ŏt'ĭk), *adj.* pertaining to a disease affecting many animals at one time: correlative of *epidemic*:—*n.* an epizoötic disease; esp., a form of influenza among horses.

ep-och (ĕp'ŏk; ē'pŏk), *n.* **1**, a point of time, marked by events of great importance, from which succeeding years are reckoned; as, the Civil War marks an important *epoch* in American history; **2**, a period filled with unusual events; an era.—*adj.* **ep'och-al.**

ep-ode (ĕp'ōd), *n.* an ancient form of lyric poem, in which a short verse follows a longer verse.

ep-si-lon (ĕp'sĭ-lŏn), *n.* the fifth letter (ε, E) of the Greek alphabet, nearly equivalent to English short *e*.

Ep-som salts (ĕp'sŭm), a white substance used in medicine, dyeing, finishing cotton goods, etc.

e-qua-ble (ē'kwȧ-bl; ĕk'wȧ-bl), *adj.* **1**, uniform; steady; regular; **2**, even and serene in temperament; tranquil. —*adv.* **e'qua-bly.**—*n.* **e″qua-bil'i-ty.**

e-qual (ē'kwăl), *adj.* **1**, of the same extent or magnitude; uniform; **2**, adequate; **3**, of the same rank, degree, or value; **4**, evenly balanced; **5**, just; equable:—*n.* a person or thing of the same value as another: —*v.t.* **1**, to have the same size, rank, or value with; **2**, to return a full equivalent for; **3**, to make equal.—*adv.* **e'qual-ly.**
Syn., adj. alike, commensurate, equitable.

e-qual-i-ty (ē-kwŏl'ĭ-tĭ), *n.* [*pl.* equalities (-tĭz)], the state of being the same in size, rank, value, etc.; uniformity.

e-qual-ize (ē'kwăl-īz), *v.t.* [*p.t.* and *p.p.* -ized (-īzd), *p.pr.* -iz″ing], **1**, to make the same in size, rank, value, etc.; **2**, to render uniform.—*n.* **e″qual-i-za'tion.**

e-qual-iz-er (ē'kwăl-īz″ẽr), *n.* **1**, one who or that which makes equal; an adjuster; **2**, a sliding panel which stabilizes an airplane laterally.

e-qua-nim-i-ty (ē″kwȧ-nĭm'ĭ-tĭ), *n.* evenness of temper or mind; calmness; composure.

e-quate (ē-kwāt'), *v.t.* [*p.t.* and *p.p.* e-quat'-ed, *p.pr.* e-quat'ing], **1**, to reduce to an average; **2**, to put into the form of an equation; make equal.

e-qua-tion (ē-kwā'shŭn; ē-kwā'zhŭn), *n.* **1**, the act of making, or the state of being, equal; **2**, a statement of equality between two quantities, the sign [=] being placed between them; **3**, a representation of a chemical reaction by symbols.

e-qua-tor (ē-kwā'tŏr), *n.* **1**, the imaginary circle round the earth, everywhere equally distant from the poles; **2**, a similar line dividing the sphere of the sky in two.—*adj.* **e″qua-to'ri-al.**

eq-uer-ry (ĕk'wẽr-ĭ; ē-kwĕr'ĭ), *n.* [*pl.* equerries (-ĭz)], an officer who is in attendance on a prince or nobleman, and has charge of his horses.

e-ques-tri-an (ē-kwĕs'trĭ-ăn), *adj.* **1**, pertaining to horses or horsemanship; performing with horses; **2**, mounted:—*n.* one skilled in horsemanship; a rider. —*n.fem.* **e-ques″tri-enne'.**

e-qui-an-gu-lar (ē″kwĭ-ăng'gū-lȧr), *adj.* having equal angles.

e-qui-dis-tant (ē″kwĭ-dĭs'tănt), *adj.* separated by equal distances.

e-qui-lat-er-al (ē″kwĭ-lăt'ẽr-ăl), *adj.* having all sides equal:—*n.* a figure with equal sides: **equilateral triangle,** a figure having three equal sides and three equal angles. —*adv.* **e″qui-lat'er-al-ly.**

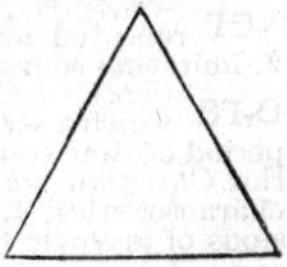
EQUILATERAL TRIANGLE

e-qui-li-brate (ē″kwĭ-lī'brāt), *v.t.* and *v.i.* [*p.t.* and *p.p.* -brat-ed, *p.pr.* -brat-ing], **1**, to balance; **2**, to counterpoise.—*n.* **e″qui-li-bra'tion.** —*n.* **e″qui-li'bra-tor.**

e-qui-lib-ri-um (ē″kwĭ-lĭb'rĭ-ŭm), *n.* [*pl.* equilibriums (-ŭmz); equilibria (-ȧ)], the state of balance; equipoise between opposing forces, actions, etc.

e-quine (ē'kwīn), *adj.* of, pertaining to, or like, a horse.

e-qui-noc-tial (ē″kwĭ-nŏk'shăl), *adj.* pertaining to the equinoxes:—*n.* **1**, the equator of the sky; **2**, a storm at the season of the equinox.—*adv.* **e″qui-noc'tial-ly.**

e-qui-nox (ē'kwĭ-nŏks), *n.* either of two times when the sun crosses the equator of the sky, making the days and nights of equal length, the *vernal equinox* occurring about March 21, and the *autumnal equinox* about September 22.

e-quip (ē-kwĭp'), *v.t.* [*p.t.* and *p.p.* e-quipped' (-kwĭpt'), e-quip'ping], **1**, to furnish or fit out for any service or undertaking; as, to *equip* an army for the field; **2**, to prepare mentally; as, to *equip* a boy with knowledge; **3**, to dress; as, to *equip* oneself for a walk.

eq-ui-page (ĕk'wĭ-pāj), *n.* **1**, the arms and outfit of an army, vessel, traveler, etc.; **2**, the carriage, horses, and liveried servants of a person of rank; a carriage of state; as, a royal *equipage*.

e-quip-ment (ē-kwĭp'mĕnt), *n.* **1**, all the necessary supplies for any particular service, as for fitting out offices, stores, armies, a fleet, a railway, a person, etc.; **2**, the act of fitting out, or the state of being fitted out, with supplies.

e-qui-poise (ē'kwĭ-poiz), *n.* **1**, equilibrium or balance; equality of weight; **2**, a counterbalancing weight or force.

e-qui-pon-der-ant (ē″kwĭ-pŏn'dẽr-ănt), *adj.* of the same weight.—*n.* **e″qui-pon'der-ance.**

eq-ui-ta-ble (ĕk'wĭ-tȧ-bl), *adj.* impartial; just; fair; honest.—*adv.* **eq'ui-ta-bly.**—*n.* **eq'ui-ta-ble-ness.**

eq-ui-ty (ĕk'wĭ-tĭ), *n.* [*pl.* equities (-tĭz)], **1**, justice; just regard to right or claim; **2**, the administration of law according to the spirit rather than the letter.

e-quiv-a-lence (ē-kwĭv'ȧ-lĕns), *n.* equality of value, quantity, or power. Also, **e-quiv'a-len-cy.**

e-quiv-a-lent (ē-kwĭv'ȧ-lĕnt), *adj.* equal in value or power; the same in significance or effect:—*n.* a thing of the same value, weight, power, effect, etc.

e-quiv-o-cal (ē-kwĭv'ō-kăl), *adj.* of a doubtful or double meaning; open to suspicion or doubt; uncertain. —*adv.* **e-quiv'o-cal-ly.**

Syn. dubious, doubtful, indefinite, obscure.

e-quiv-o-cate (ē-kwĭv'ō-kāt), *v.i.* [*p.t.* and *p.p.* -cat″ed, *p.pr.* -cat″ing], to speak with double meaning; evade the truth by speaking ambiguously.—*n.* **e-quiv″o-ca'tion.**—*n.* **e-quiv'o-ca″tor.**

Syn. quibble, shift. (See prevaricate.)

¹-er (-ẽr), *n. suffix,* denoting: **1,** one who occupies himself with (the idea of the word stem); as, astronom*er;* lawy*er;* **2,** an agent; as, lov*er;* mow*er;* **3,** an instrument; as, pok*er;* **4,** one living in; as, New York*er.*

²-er (-ẽr), *suffix,* forming the comparative degree of adjectives and adverbs; as, high*er.*

³-er (-ẽr), *suffix,* forming verbs: **1,** denoting repeated action; as, glimm*er;* wav*er;* **2,** imitating sounds; as, titt*er;* whisp*er.*

e-ra (ē'rȧ), *n.* **1,** the point of time from which a series of years is reckoned; **2,** a period of time starting from a given point; as, the Christian *era;* **3,** a period with notable characteristics; **4,** one of the seven great divisions of geologic time; as, the Cenozoic *era.*

e-rad-i-cate (ē-răd'ĭ-kāt), *v.t.* [*p.t.* and *p.p.* -cat″ed, *p.pr.* -cat″ing], to destroy completely; exterminate; wipe out; erase.—*adj.* **e-rad'i-ca-ble.**—*n.* **e-rad″i-ca'tion.**

e-rase (ē-rās'), *v.t.* [*p.t.* and *p.p.* e-rased' (-rāst'), *p.pr.* e-ras'ing], to rub or scrape out; efface.—*n.* **e-ra'sure** (ē-rā'zhũr).

Syn. cancel, efface, obliterate. To *erase* is to scratch out or otherwise remove by friction, usually in order to make space for something else; as, to *erase* a misspelled word. To *cancel* is literally to cross out by drawing lines across, to show that the inscription or passage is not to be used; as, to *cancel* a postage stamp. To *efface* is to make illegible, either by deliberate act or through the slower action of time; as, the epitaph had become *effaced.* To *obliterate* is to remove utterly all traces of; as, snow *obliterated* the tracks.

e-ras-er (ē-rās'ẽr), *n.* **1,** a device for rubbing out written marks; **2,** one who effaces marks by rubbing out.

Er-a-to (ĕr'ȧ-tō), *n.* in mythology, the Muse of lyric and love poetry.

ere (âr), *conj.* **1,** before; as, "the joys that came *ere* I was old"; **2,** rather than; as, I will fight *ere* I will submit:—*prep.* before.

Er-e-bus (ĕr'ē-bŭs), *n.* in mythology, a place of utter darkness through which the dead pass to Hades.

e-rect (ē-rĕkt'), *v.t.* **1,** to construct; build, as a house; **2,** to raise to an upright position; **3,** to institute; as, to *erect* a new government:—*adj.* **1,** upright; firmly uplifted; **2,** bold or unshaken.—*adj.* **e-rec'tive.** —*adv.* **e-rect'ly.**—*n.* **e-rect'ness.**—*n.* **e-rec'tor.**

e-rect-ile (ē-rĕk'tĭl), *adj.* capable of being raised upright.

e-rec-tion (ē-rĕk'shŭn), *n.* **1,** the act of raising a structure, such as a wall or building; also, the state of being constructed; **2,** the structure raised.

ere-long (âr″lông'), *adv.* before long; soon; shortly.

er-e-mite (ĕr'ē-mīt), *n.* a religious hermit; a recluse.

ere-while (âr″hwīl'), *adv. Archaic,* formerly. Also, **ere″whiles'.**

erg (ûrg), *n.* in physics, a unit of work; the work expended in overcoming a resistance of one dyne over a distance of one centimeter: also called *ergon.*

***er-go** (ûr'gō), [Lat.], *conj.* and *adv.* therefore; consequently; hence.

er-got (ûr'gŏt), *n.* a black, fungous growt on various grains, esp. on rye.

E-rin (ē'rĭn; ĕr'ĭn), *n.* Ireland: now use only in poetry.

E-rin-ys (ē-rĭn'ĭs; ē-rī'nĭs; ĕr-), *n.* [*p.* Erinyes (ē-rĭn ĭ-ēz)], in mytho ogy, any of the Greek Furies who relentlessl pursued and maddened unpunished criminals Also, **E-rin'nys.**

erl-king (ûrl'kĭng″), *n.* in mythology, a evil spirit, supposed to be esp malicious toward children.

er-mine (ûr'mĭn), *n.* **1,** any of severa weasel-like animals, much val ued for their fur; **2,** the fur itself; **3,** th dignity or office of a judge, the state robe o European judges being lined with ermine.

ern (ûrn), *n.* a northern sea eagle of the Ol World. Also, **erne.**

e-rode (ē-rōd'), *v.t.* [*p.t.* and *p.p.* e-rod'ed *p.pr.* e-rod'ing], to eat or wea away, as rocks by running water:—*v.i.* to dis integrate, as rocks.—*adj.* **e-ro'sive.**

E-ros (ē'rŏs), *n.* in Greek mythology, th god of love, son of Aphrodite: identi fied with the Roman *Cupid.*

e-ro-sion (ē-rō'zhŭn), *n.* the act of wearin away; gradual destruction o eating away: used esp. of the action of wate on rock or soil.

e-rot-ic (ē-rŏt'ĭk; ĕr-ŏt'ĭk), *adj.* pertaining to, or caused by, passionate love amorous:—*n.* a love poem or composition.

err (ûr), *v.i.* **1,** to go astray morally; **2,** to be mistaken; **3,** to blunder; as, to *err* in social usage.

er-rand (ĕr'ănd), *n.* **1,** a trip made to attend to some special business or to carry a message; **2,** the object for which the trip is made; a commission.

er-rant (ĕr'ănt), *adj.* **1,** roving; wandering in search of adventure; as, a knight-*errant;* hence, chivalric; **2,** wayward; as, *errant* thoughts.—*n.* **er'ran-cy.**

er-rant-ry (ĕr'ănt-rĭ), *n.* [*pl.* errantries (-rĭz)], the spirit and practice of roving in search of knightly adventure.

er-ra-ta (ĕ-rā'tȧ), *n.* plural of *erratum:* usually used of errors in printing.

er-rat-ic (ĕ-răt'ĭk), *adj.* **1,** having no fixed course; wandering; **2,** irregular; eccentric; queer.—*adv.* **er-rat'i-cal-ly.**

Syn. strange, odd. (See queer.)

er-ra-tum (ĕ-rā'tŭm), *n.* [*pl.* errata (-tȧ)], a mistake in printing or writing.

er-ro-ne-ous (ĕ-rō'nē-ŭs), *adj.* incorrect; mistaken; wrong.—*adv.* **er-ro'ne-ous-ly.**

er-ror (ĕr'ẽr), *n.* **1,** false belief; **2,** a mistake; an inaccuracy; **3,** a sin.

Syn. (see blunder).

Erse (ûrs), *adj.* pertaining to the Celts of Ireland and Scotland, or to their language; Gaelic:—*n.* the Gaelic language.

erst (ûrst), *adv. Archaic* or *Poetic,* **1,** at first; **2,** a long time ago; formerly.

erst-while (ûrst'hwīl″; ûrst″hwīl'), *adj. Archaic* or *Poetic,* of old:—*adv. Archaic* or *Poetic,* formerly; in times past.

e-ruct (ē-rŭkt'), *v.t.* and *v.i.* **1,** to eject violently, as wind or gas from the stomach; **2,** to belch, as a volcano. Also, **e-ruc'tate.**—*n.* **e″ruc-ta'tion.**

er-u-dite (ĕr'ōō-dīt), *adj.* learned; scholarly; well read—*adv.* **er'u-dite″ly.**—*n.* **er'u-dite″ness.**

er-u-di-tion (ĕr″ōō-dĭsh'ŭn), *n.* knowledge obtained by the study of books; learning in literature, history, etc.

e-rupt (ē-rŭpt'), *v.t.* and *v.i.* to burst forth, or cause to burst forth.

e-rup-tion (ē-rŭp'shŭn), *n.* **1,** a bursting out or forth, as of a volcano, war, or disease; **2**, that which bursts forth, as water from a geyser; **3**, a rash on the skin.

e-rup-tive (ē-rŭp'tĭv), *adj.* breaking out violently; bursting forth.

-er-y (-ẽr'ĭ), *n. suffix,* designating: **1**, place of business, storage, breeding, etc.; as, tann*ery;* hatch*ery;* **2**, qualities, conduct, practices, principles, etc.; as, snobb*ery;* rogu*ery;* trick*ery;* **3**, a class of goods; as, millin*ery;* **4**, art or employment; as, arch*ery;* **5**, state; condition; as, drudg*ery.* Also, **-ry.**

er-y-sip-e-las (ĕr″ĭ-sĭp'ē-lȧs), *n.* an infectious disease of the skin, accompanied by fever and inflammation.

E-sau (ē'sô), *n.* in the Bible, the son of Isaac and Rebekah, disinherited through the deceit of his younger brother Jacob (Genesis 25:25–34; 27:1–40).

es-ca-drille (ĕs″kȧ-drĭl'; *Fr.*ĕs″kȧ″drēy'), *n.* a squadron or fleet of airships; as, the Lafayette *escadrille.*

es-ca-lade (ĕs″kȧ-lād'), *n.* a scaling or climbing the walls of a fortified place by means of scaling ladders:—*v.t.* [*p.t.* and *p.p.* -lad'ed, *p.pr.* -lad'ing], to storm by means of scaling ladders.

es-ca-la-tor (ĕs'kȧ-lā″tẽr), *n.* a moving stairway.

es-cal-op (ĕs-kŏl'ŭp; ĕs-kăl'ŭp), *n.* **1**, a mollusk, or shellfish, having a ribbed shell with a wavy edge; also, its shell; **2**, a curved point in a wavy edge of lace, etc.:—*v.t.* **1**, to prepare (food) with bread crumbs, etc., and bake; **2**, to shape in curved points, as lace. Also, **es-cal'lop.** See **scal'lop,** *Pfd. S.*

es-ca-pade (ĕs″kȧ-pād'), *n.* **1**, the act of breaking loose from confinement; **2**, a foolish or reckless adventure.

es-cape (ĕs-kāp'), *v.t.* [*p.t.* and *p.p.* -caped' (-kāpt'), *p.pr.* -cap'ing], **1**, to flee from; get out of the way of, as a difficult task; **2**, to be unaffected by; as, he *escaped* contagion from the disease; **3**, to issue from, involuntarily; as, a sigh *escaped* him; **4**, to elude the notice or recollection of, as a name:—*v.i.* **1**, to get out of danger; also, to elude notice; **2**, to flow out; as, gas *escapes* from a leak; **3**, to slip away; as, to *escape* from memory:—*n.* **1**, a successful flight, as from prison; **2**, deliverance from harm; **3**, a place of issue; also, that which issues; leakage.

es-cape-ment (ĕs-kāp'mĕnt), *n.* a mechanical device for securing regularity of movement: used in clocks, watches, and motors.

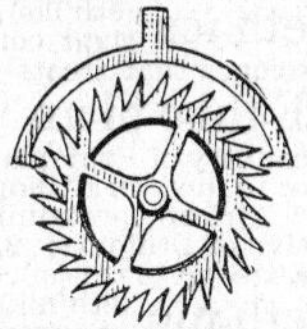

CLOCK ESCAPEMENT

es-carp (ĕs-kärp'), *v.t.* to give a steep slope to:—*n.* in fortification, the steep wall of a moat on the side next the rampart; also, any steep natural embankment (see *rampart, terreplein,* illus.).

es-carp-ment (ĕs-kärp'-mĕnt), *n.* **1**, a cliff; a steep side of a hill; **2**, ground cut to a steep slope about a fortress.

-esce (-ĕs), *v. suffix,* showing action just begun; as, efferv*esce;* conval*esce.*

-es-cent (-ĕs'ĕnt), *adj. suffix,* being or becoming; as, qui*escent;* efferv*escent;* coal*escent.*—*n. suffix,* **-es'cence.**

es-cheat (ĕs-chēt'), *v.t.* to take possession of (property to which there are no heirs):—*v.i.* to revert or go back to the crown, the lord of the manor, or the state, because there are no legal heirs:—*n.* land or tenements which fall to the crown, or lord of the manor, or, in the U. S., to the state, by forfeiture or failure of heirs.

es-chew (ĕs-chōō'), *v.t.* to shun; avoid; as, to *eschew* bad company.

es-cort (ĕs'kôrt), *n.* **1**, one or more persons, ships, etc., accompanying others as a mark of respect or means of protection; **2**, a gentleman accompanying a lady in public:—*v.t.* (ĕs-kôrt'), to accompany as escort.

es-cri-toire (ĕs″krĭ-twär'), *n.* a writing desk, or secretary.

es-cu-do (ĕs-kōō'dō), [Port.], *n.* [*pl.* escudos (-dōs)], a silver coin, the monetary unit of Portugal, equal to $1.08.

es-cu-lent (ĕs'kū-lĕnt), *adj.* eatable:—*n.* anything fit for food.

es-cutch-eon (ĕs-kŭch'ŭn), *n.* a shield showing the coat of arms of a family. Also, **scutch'eon.**

Es-dras (ĕz'drăs; ĕs'-), *n.* **1**, either of two books of the Old Testament (Ezra and Nehemiah) called, in the Douay Bible, *1* and *2 Esdras;* **2**, more commonly, either of two books of the Old Testament Apocrypha, not included in the Douay Bible.

Es-ki-mo (ĕs'kĭ-mō), *n.* [*pl.* Eskimos (-mōz)], one of a race of people inhabiting Labrador, Greenland, Alaska, and other arctic regions. Also, **Es'qui-mau.**

e-soph-a-gus (ē-sŏf'ȧ-gŭs), *n.* the gullet, or canal through which food and drink pass from the pharynx to the stomach. Also, **œ-soph'a-gus.**

es-o-ter-ic (ĕs″ō-tĕr'ĭk), *adj.* **1**, pertaining to doctrines or beliefs taught only to a select circle of followers; **2**, secret; confidential; profound: opp. of *exoteric.*

es-pe-cial (ĕs-pĕsh'ăl), *adj.* **1**, particular; chief; special; **2**, exceptional of its kind.—*adv.* **es-pe'cial-ly.**—*abbr.* **esp.**

Es-pe-ran-to (ĕs″pĕ-rän'tō), *n.* a language invented by L. L. Zamenhof, a Russian, and designed for use by people throughout the world.

es-pi-al (ĕs-pī'ăl), *n.* the action of a spy; secret watching; discovery.

es-pi-o-nage (ĕs'pĭ-ō-nāj; *Fr.* ĕs″pyô″-nȧzh'), *n.* **1**, the secret watching of another; **2**, employment of secret agents.

es-pla-nade (ĕs″plȧ-nād'), *n.* an open space or road, esp. by the water, for public use in walking or driving.

es-pouse (ĕs-pouz'), *v.t.* [*p.t.* and *p.p.* -poused' (-pouzd'), *p.pr.* -pous'ing], **1**, to promise, engage, or give in marriage; **2**, to wed; **3**, to adopt; advocate; defend, as a cause.—*n.* **es-pous'al.**

***es-prit** (ĕs″prē'), [Fr.], *n.* spirit; sprightly intelligence: ***esprit de corps,** (dē kôr'), a spirit binding together the members of an organization; comradeship.

es-py (ĕs-pī'), *v.t.* [*p.t.* and *p.p.* -pied' (-pīd'), *p.pr.* -py'ing], **1**, to see at a distance; **2**, to discover (something hidden).

Es-qui-mau (ĕs'kĭ-mō), *n.* [*pl.* Esquimaux (-mō; -mōz)], one of a race of people living in arctic regions. See **Es'ki-mo,** *Pfd. S.*

es-quire (ĕs-kwīr'), *n.* **1**, orig., the armor-bearer or attendant of a knight; **2**, a member of the English gentry ranking below a knight: **Esquire,** a title of courtesy, often written after a name.—*abbr.* **Esq.**

ess (ĕs), *n.* the letter S; also, sometimes, an object having the shape of an S.

-ess (-ĕs), *n. suffix,* forming feminine gender; as, prior*ess;* deacon*ess.*

es-say (ĕs'ā), *n.* **1**, a literary composition on some special subject; **2**, an attempt; experiment:—*v.t.* (ĕ-sā'), to attempt.

es-say-ist (ĕs'ā-ĭst), *n.* one who writes in prose, on various subjects.

es-sence (ĕs'ĕns), *n.* **1**, the alcoholic extract of a substance; as, *essence* of peppermint; **2**, a perfume; **3**, that which is the real character of a thing; the true substance of anything.

es-sen-tial (ĕ-sĕn′shăl), *adj.* **1**, pertaining to the real character of a thing; as, love is the *essential* element of Christianity; **2**, most important; indispensable; **3**, pure: **essential oil**, the volatile oil found naturally in plants, fruits, etc., to which the characteristic flavor or odor is due:—*n.* that which is a necessary element; a basic principle; as, the *essentials* of education.—*adv.* **es-sen′tial-ly.**—*n.* **es-sen″ti-al′i-ty** (-shĭ-ăl′ĭ-tĭ).

est (-ĕst), *suffix*, forming: **1**, the superlative degree of adjectives and adverbs; as, warm*est;* soon*est;* **2**, the second person singular, archaic or poetic form, of the present and past tenses indicative; as, thou sing*est*.

es-tab-lish (ĕs-tăb′lĭsh), *v.t.* **1**, to fix firmly; settle; **2**, to prove legally; **3**, to found, as an institution.
Syn. verify, substantiate.

es-tab-lish-ment (ĕs-tăb′lĭsh-mĕnt), *n.* **1**, the act of placing on a sure basis; settlement; **2**, something permanently placed, as a business institution.

***es-ta-mi-net** (ĕs″tȧ″mē″nā′), [Fr.], *n.* a café or coffeehouse in which smoking is permitted.

es-tate (ĕs-tāt′), *n.* **1**, condition of life; rank, position, or quality; as, a man of low *estate;* **2**, an order or class of people distinct politically or socially; **3**, property in land or buildings: used of large possessions; **4**, in law, property in general.

es-teem (ĕs-tēm′), *v.t.* **1**, to value highly; prize; **2**, to think; consider; as, to *esteem* it a privilege:—*n.* a favorable opinion; respect; regard.
Syn., v. favor, honor; *n.* (see regard).

Es-ther (ĕs′tẽr), *n.* in the Bible, a Jewess who delivered her people from the Persians; also, a book of the Old Testament relating her story.—*abbr.* **Esth.**

es-thete (ĕs′thēt), *n.* one possessing, or pretending to possess, an appreciation of art and culture. See **æs′thete,** *Pfd. S.*

es-thet-ic (ĕs-thĕt′ĭk), *adj.* pertaining to beauty or a love of beauty. Also, **æs-thet′ic,** *Pfd. S.*—*adv.* **es-thet′i-cal-ly.**

es-thet-ics (ĕs-thĕt′ĭks), *n.pl.* used as *sing.* the science of the beautiful in nature or art. Also, **æs-thet′ics,** *Pfd. S.*

es-ti-ma-ble (ĕs′tĭ-mȧ-bl), *adj.* **1**, worthy of respect or honor; deserving of esteem; **2**, calculable; as, *estimable* damage.—*adv.* **es′ti-ma-bly.**

es-ti-mate (ĕs′tĭ-māt), *v.t.* [*p.t.* and *p.p.* -mat″ed, *p.pr.* -mat″ing], **1**, to form an opinion of; **2**, to appraise; determine the value of; **3**, to calculate approximately, as the cost of a job:—*n.* (ĕs′tĭ-māt), **1**, a valuation of qualities; opinion; **2**, the computed or reckoned cost or value of anything; as, an *estimate* of the cost of a house; appraisement.
Syn., v. appreciate, value, rate.

es-ti-ma-tion (ĕs″tĭ-mā′shŭn), *n.* **1**, the act of calculating; **2**, calculation; appraisement; **3**, honor, respect, or esteem; favorable opinion.

es-trade (ĕs-träd′; ĕs-trād′), *n.* a slightly raised platform.

es-trange (ĕs-trānj′), *v.t.* [*p.t.* and *p.p.* -tranged′ (-trānjd′), *p.pr.* -trang′ing], **1**, to alienate the affections of; turn from kindness to indifference; **2**, to keep at a distance.—*n.* **es-trange′ment.**

es-tray (ĕs-trā′), *n.* **1**, a domestic animal that has strayed from its owner; **2**, anything wandering and unclaimed.

es-tu-a-ry (ĕs′tū-ā-rĭ), *n.* [*pl.* estuaries (-rĭz)], the wide mouth of a tidal river; a narrow inlet from the sea.

e-ta (ē′tȧ; ā′tȧ), *n.* the seventh letter of the Greek alphabet, corresponding in general to the English long *e*.

et-a-mine (ĕt′ȧ-mēn), *n.* a light woolen fabric resembling fine bunting. Also, **et′a-min.**

et cet-er-a (ĕt sĕt′ẽr-ȧ), and others (of the same kind); and so forth. Also, **et cæt′er-a.**—*abbr.* **etc.; &c.**

etch (ĕch), *v.t.* **1**, to engrave by biting out with an acid a design previously drawn upon a copperplate or the like with an etching needle; **2**, to subject to a process of incising with a pointed instrument:—*v.i.* to practice the art of etching.—*n.* **etch′ing.**

e-ter-nal (ē-tûr′năl), *adj.* **1**, without beginning or end; everlasting; **2**, incessant; never ceasing: **the Eternal,** God.
Syn. everlasting, endless, immortal. *Eternal*, when strictly used, describes that which, in its nature, is above time, having neither beginning nor end; as, the *eternal* God. *Everlasting*, while often interchangeable with *eternal*, refers always to time and rather to the future than to the past; it emphasizes the lack of interruption as well as of end; as, *everlasting* life after death; *everlasting* joy. *Endless* is sometimes used like *everlasting*, but it commonly describes more humble things; as, in mechanics, an *endless* belt; it is also used in the sense of incessant; as, *endless* discussions. *Immortal* emphasizes the idea of life that shall not cease, and often describes that which has its life only in men's memories; as, the *immortal* works of Milton.

e-ter-ni-ty (ē-tûr′nĭ-tĭ), *n.* [*pl.* eternities (-tĭz)], **1**, the state of being infinite and everlasting; **2**, indefinite time; time that seems endless; **3**, life after death.

e-ther (ē′thẽr), *n.* **1**, the upper, purer air; **2**, a liquid anæsthetic, the vapor of which, when inhaled, produces unconsciousness and insensibility to pain; also, any of various similar substances; **3**, in physics, a medium assumed to fill all space, by which the rays of light and heat are transmitted.

e-the-re-al (ē-thē′rē-ăl), *adj.* **1**, airy; light; exquisite; **2**, heavenly; spiritual.—*adv.* **e-the′re-al-ly.**

e-ther-ize (ē′thẽr-īz), *v.t.* [*p.t.* and *p.p.* -ized (-īzd), *p.pr.* -iz″ing], to make unconscious, or insensible, by the application of ether.—*n.* **e″ther-i-za′tion.**

eth-i-cal (ĕth′ĭ-kăl), *adj.* **1**, pertaining to the science of ethics; **2**, moral.—*adv.* **eth′i-cal-ly.**

eth-ics (ĕth′ĭks), *n.pl.* **1**, the principles of right conduct; **2**, used as *sing.*, the science that treats of right conduct.

E-thi-o-pi-an (ē″thĭ-ō′pĭ-ăn), *adj.* **1**, pertaining to the ancient country of Ethiopia, south of Egypt in Africa, or to modern Ethiopia, often called Abyssinia; **2**, African; pertaining to Negroes:—*n.* **1**, a native of Ethiopia; **2**, an African; a Negro.—*n.* **E′thi-op** (ē′thĭ-ŏp).—*adj.* and *n.* **E″thi-op′ic.**

eth-nic (ĕth′nĭk), *adj.* pertaining to races or peoples. Also, **eth′ni-cal.**—*adv.* **eth′ni-cal-ly.**

eth-nol-o-gy (ĕth-nŏl′ō-jĭ), *n.* the science that treats of races of men, their characteristics, etc.—*adj.* **eth″no-log′i-cal.**—*n.* **eth-nol′o-gist.**

eth-yl (ĕth′ĭl), *n.* the organic part of ordinary alcohol and ether, not found in the free state: **ethyl alcohol,** the ordinary alcohol of commerce, formed by the fermentation of sugar and used in alcoholic beverages, perfumery, etc., and as a solvent for gums and resins: **ethyl gasoline,** gasoline to which has been added a small amount of a lead compound to increase power and prevent knocking.

et-i-quette (ĕt′ĭ-kĕt), *n.* rules of conduct observed in polite society or in official intercourse; the forms of polite behavior demanded by good breeding.

E-trus-can (ē-trŭs′kăn), *adj.* pertaining to ancient Etruria, in Italy, its inhabitants, language, etc.:—*n.* an inhabitant of ancient Etruria; also, its language. Also, **E-tru′ri-an** (ē-trōō′rĭ-ăn).

-ette (-ĕt), *n. suffix,* in nouns borrowed from French since 17th century, forming: **1,** diminutives; as, statu*ette;* **2,** nouns originally diminutive, now not so regarded; as, etiqu*ette;* coqu*ette;* **3,** names of substances which are imitations; as, leather*ette.*

***é-tude** (ā″tüd′), [Fr.], *n.* [*pl.* études (ā″tüd′)], **1,** a study; **2,** in music, an exercise affording practice on some particular point of technique.

et-y-mo-log-i-cal (ĕt″ĭ-mō-lŏj′ĭ-kăl), *adj.* pertaining to the study of words.—*adv.* **et″y-mo-log′i-cal-ly.**

et-y-mol-o-gy (ĕt″ĭ-mŏl′ō-jĭ), *n.* [*pl.* etymologies (-jĭz)], a statement of the origin of a word and of its history, esp. a history of its successive forms and meanings; also, the science which treats of the origin and history of words.—*n.* **et″y-mol′o-gist.**

Et-zel (ĕt′sĕl), *n.* in the story of the Nibelungs, the king of the Huns, who married Kriemhild after the death of Siegfried: called *Atli* in the "Volsunga Saga."

eu- (ū-), [Gk.], *prefix,* meaning well or good; as, *eu*logy; *eu*phony.

eu-ca-lyp-tus (ū″kȧ-lĭp′tŭs), *n.* [*pl.* eucalypti (-tī)], any of various trees of the evergreen myrtle family; esp., the gum tree, many species of which furnish gum and a valuable medicine.

Eu-cha-rist (ū′kȧ-rĭst), *n.* **1,** the Holy Communion; the sacrament of the Lord's Supper; **2,** the consecrated elements, bread and wine, used in that sacrament.

eu-cha-ris-tic (ū″kȧ-rĭs′tĭk), *adj.* **1,** pertaining to the Eucharist, or Holy Communion; **2,** expressing thanksgiving. Also, **eu″cha-ris′ti-cal.**

eu-chre (ū′kẽr), *n.* **1,** a game of cards; **2,** failure to score in this game:—*v.t.* [*p.t.* and *p.p.* -chred (-kẽrd), *p.pr.* -chring (-krĭng)], **1,** to prevent (an opponent) in the game from scoring; **2,** *Slang,* to outwit.

eu-gen-ics (ū-jĕn′ĭks), *n.pl.* used as *sing.* the science of improving the human race through better heredity.

eu-lo-gist (ū′lō-jĭst), *n.* one who speaks in praise of another, esp. excessively.—*adj.* **eu″lo-gis′tic.**

eu-lo-gize (ū′lō-jīz), *v.t.* [*p.t.* and *p.p.* -gized (-jīzd), *p.pr.* -giz″ing], to praise highly; extol, as a deceased person.

eu-lo-gy (ū′lō-jĭ), *n.* [*pl.* eulogies (-jĭz)], high praise, either written or spoken, of the life or character of a person, usually deceased. Also, **eu-lo′gi-um.**

Eu-men-i-des (ū-mĕn′ĭ-dēz), *n.pl.* in mythology, the avenging Furies; the Erinyes.

eu-nuch (ū′nŭk), *n.* **1,** a man who has been castrated; **2,** a chamberlain or an attendant in a harem.

eu-pep-tic (ū-pĕp′tĭk), *adj.* **1,** pertaining to, having, or promoting, good digestion; **2,** easily digested.

eu-phe-mism (ū′fē-mĭzm), *n.* **1,** the use of a mild or pleasing expression in place of one that is plainer or more accurate but which might be offensive or embarrassing, as you *exaggerate* for you *lie;* **2,** the expression so used.—*adj.* **eu″phe-mis′tic.**—*n.* **eu′phe-mist.**

eu-pho-ni-ous (ū-fō′nĭ-ŭs), *adj.* pleasing or sweet in sound or tone; sounding well.—*adv.* **eu-pho′ni-ous-ly.**

eu-pho-ny (ū′fō-nĭ), *n.* [*pl.* euphonies (-nĭz)], pleasantness of sound or pronunciation.—*adj.* **eu-phon′ic.**

eu-phu-ism (ū′fū-ĭzm), *n.* an affected or high-flown style in writing or speaking.—*adj.* **eu″phu-is′tic.**

eu-re-ka (ū-rē′kȧ), [Gk.], *interj.* "I have found (it)!" an exclamation of triumph over a discovery or supposed discovery.

Eu-ro-pa (ū-rō′pȧ), *n.* in mythology, a Phœnician princess, beloved by Zeus, who, in the form of a white bull, carried her off on his back to Crete.

Eu-ro-pe-an (ū″rō-pē′ăn), *adj.* belonging or pertaining to Europe:—*n.* a native of Europe.

Eu-ryd-i-ce (ū-rĭd′ĭ-sē), *n.* in mythology, the wife of Orpheus, allowed after her death to return with him from Hades to the upper world, but snatched back to Hades because he turned to look at her on the way.

Eu-sta-chi-an tube (ū-stā′kĭ-ăn), the tube between the middle ear and the pharynx; the syrinx.

Eu-ter-pe (ū-tûr′pē), *n.* one of the nine Muses: the patron of music.

e-vac-u-ate (ē-văk′ū-āt), *v.t.* [*p.t.* and *p.p.* -at″ed, *p.pr.* -at″ing], **1,** to make void or empty; **2,** to abandon possession of, or withdraw from; vacate.

e-vac-u-a-tion (ē-văk″ū-ā′shŭn), *n.* **1,** the act of withdrawing or of voiding; **2,** that which is voided.

e-vade (ē-vād′), *v.t.* and *v.i.* [*p.t.* and *p.p.* e-vad′ed, *p.pr.* e-vad′ing], **1,** to escape; elude cleverly, or by some trick; as, to *evade* pursuers; **2,** to baffle or foil.
Syn. avoid. (See prevaricate.)

e-val-u-ate (ē-văl′ū-āt), *v.t.* [*p.t.* and *p.p.* -at′ed, *p.pr.* -at′ing], to place a value on; find the amount of.

ev-a-nes-cent (ĕv″ȧ-nĕs′ĕnt), *adj.* disappearing gradually from sight; vanishing; fleeting.—*n.* **ev″a-nes′cence.**

e-van-gel (ē-văn′jĕl), *n.* good news, esp. that of the gospel.

e-van-gel-i-cal (ē″văn-jĕl′ĭ-kăl; ĕv″ăn-), *adj.* **1,** pertaining to, or consistent with the teachings and ideals of, the four Gospels; **2,** maintaining the doctrines based by some Protestant theologies upon the Gospels; **3,** spiritually minded:—*n.* one who holds orthodox Protestant doctrines.—*adv.* **e″van-gel′i-cal-ly.**—*n.* **e″van-gel′i-cal-ism.**

e-van-gel-ism (ē-văn′jĕl-ĭzm), *n.* earnest effort for the spread of the gospel of Christ.—*adj.* **e-van″gel-is′tic.**

e-van-gel-ist (ē-văn′jĕl-ĭst), *n.* **1,** one of the four writers of the Gospels; **2,** one who spreads the gospel; esp., a traveling preacher.

e-van-gel-ize (ē-văn′jĕl-īz), *v.t.* [*p.t.* and *p.p.* -ized (-īzd), *p.pr.* -iz″ing], to teach the gospel to; convert to Christianity; as, to *evangelize* the heathen.

e-vap-o-rate (ē-văp′ō-rāt), *v.i.* [*p.t.* and *p.p.* -rat″ed, *p.pr.* -rat″ing], **1,** to disperse or pass off in vapor; **2,** to pass away without effect:—*v.t.* **1,** to convert into vapor; as, heat *evaporates* water; **2,** to dry by removing moisture from, as fruit; **3,** to concentrate by the removal of moisture, as milk.—*n.* **e-vap′o-ra″tor.**—*n.* **e-vap″o-ra′tion.**

e-va-sion (ē-vā′zhŭn), *n.* **1,** the act of eluding or getting out of the way; **2,** an artful escape; **3,** an excuse.

e-va-sive (ē-vā′sĭv), *adj.* tending or seeking to evade; elusive.—*adv.* **e-va′sive-ly.**—*n.* **e-va′sive-ness.**

eve (ēv), *n.* **1,** the evening before a church festival or saint's day: often a period of fasting; **2,** the period immediately before some important event; as, on the *eve* of departure; **3,** *Poetic,* evening.

Eve (ēv), *n.* in the Bible, the first created woman, wife of Adam.

[1]**e-ven** (ē'vn), *n. Poetic*, **1**, evening; **2**, the eve or time preceding any event.

[2]**e-ven** (ē'vn), *adj.* **1**, level; smooth; **2**, equal in quantity, size, number, etc.; uniform; **3**, on the same line; parallel; **4**, divisible by two without a remainder; **5**, impartial; fair; **6**, equally balanced; **7**, calm; unruffled; **8**, whole; exact; as, an *even* mile:—*v.i.* to be equal in any way:—*v.t.* **1**, to level or make smooth; **2**, to make equal:—*adv.* **1**, smoothly; regularly; **2**, precisely; just; as, *even* as I spoke; **3**, quite; so much as; as, I never *even* spoke; **4**, used to emphasize or imply comparison; as, clear *even* to a child.—*adv.* **e'ven-ly.**—*n.* **e'ven-ness.**

eve-ning (ēv'nĭng), *n.* **1**, the close of the day and beginning of the night; **2**, the latter part of life:—*adj.* pertaining to the later part of the day; as, the *evening* meal.

e-vent (ē-vĕnt'), *n.* **1**, an occurrence; incident; **2**, the result or outcome of an action; **3**, any single item in a program of sports or games.
Syn. issue, circumstance. (See result.)

e-vent-ful (ē-vĕnt'fool), *adj.* full of incidents or happenings; momentous.—*adv.* **e-vent'ful-ly.**—*n.* **e-vent'ful-ness.**

e-ven-tide (ē'vn-tīd"), *n. Poetic*, evening; as, the dusk of *eventide*.

e-ven-tu-al (ē-vĕn'tū-ăl), *adj.* **1**, happening as a result; depending on events; **2**, ultimate; final.—*adv.* **e-ven'tu-al-ly.**

e-ven-tu-al-i-ty (ē-vĕn"tū-ăl'ĭ-tĭ), *n.* [*pl.* eventualities (-tĭz)], a possible occurrence or happening.

e-ven-tu-ate (ē-vĕn'tū-āt), *v.i.* [*p.t.* and *p.p.* -at"ed, *p.pr.* -at"ing], to happen; turn out; result.

ev-er (ĕv'ẽr), *adv.* **1**, at any time; as, I do not know that I shall *ever* go; **2**, always; as, the poor are *ever* with us; **3**, in any degree; as, study as hard as *ever* you can.

ev-er-glade (ĕv'ẽr-glād), *n.* a low, swampy tract of land.

ev-er-green (ĕv'ẽr-grēn"), *n.* a tree or plant which remains green throughout the year, as the pine or cedar:—*adj.* always green or fresh.

ev-er-last-ing (ĕv"ẽr-làs'tĭng), *adj.* **1**, perpetual; endless; eternal; **2**, incessant; as, the *everlasting* noise:—*n.* **1**, any of various plants whose flowers retain their form and color when dried; **2**, eternity: **the Everlasting**, God.—*adv.* **ev"er-last'ing-ly.**
Syn., adj. permanent, unfailing, immortal, undying. (See eternal.)

ev-er-more (ĕv"ẽr-mōr'), *adv.* eternally; always; forever.

ev-er-y (ĕv'ẽr-ĭ; ĕv'rĭ), *adj.* all, taken one at a time; each; as, *every* man will do his duty; all possible; as, *every* kindness.

ev-er-y-bod-y (ĕv'ẽr-ĭ-bŏd"ĭ; ĕv'rĭ-bŏd"ĭ), *n.* every person.

ev-er-y-day (ĕv'ẽr-ĭ-dā"; ĕv"rĭ-dā'), *adj.* coming on each day; usual; commonplace; as, *everyday* matters.

ev-er-y-one (ĕv'ẽr-ĭ-wŭn"; ĕv'rĭ-wŭn"), *n.* everybody; as, *everyone* has his faults and virtues.

ev-er-y-thing (ĕv'ẽr-ĭ-thĭng"; ĕv'rĭ-thĭng"), *n.* all things; all that is concerned in a given matter.

ev-er-y-where (ĕv'ẽr-ĭ-hwâr"; ĕv'rĭ-hwâr"), *adv.* in all places or parts; as, they looked *everywhere*.

e-vict (ē-vĭkt'), *v.t.* to put out by force; expel, or dispossess by legal process; as, to *evict* a tenant.—*n.* **e-vic'tion.**

ev-i-dence (ĕv'ĭ-dĕns), *n.* proof; testimony:—*v.t.* [*p.t.* and *p.p.* -denced (-dĕnst), *p.pr.* -denc-ing], to prove; make evident or plain.
Syn., n. indication, certainty.

ev-i-dent (ĕv'ĭ-dĕnt), *adj.* clear to the eyes or mind.—*adv.* **ev'i-dent-ly.**
Syn. apparent, visible.—*Ant.* obscure, hidden, indistinct.

e-vil (ē'vl), *adj.* **1**, morally bad; wicked; sinful; **2**, hurtful; **3**, disastrous; **4**, of ill repute: **evil eye**, an influence for injury, superstitiously thought to be exerted by certain persons who cast hurtful glances:—*adv.* badly; harmfully:—*n.* **1**, conduct showing harmful intention; **2**, something that injures; **3**, sin.—*adv.* **e'vil-ly.**
Syn., n. harm, affliction; *adj.* (see bad).

e-vince (ē-vĭns'), *v.t.* [*p.t.* and *p.p.* e-vinced' (-vĭnst'), *p.pr.* e-vinc'ing], **1**, to manifest or make evident; **2**, to demonstrate, as a quality.—*adj.* **e-vin'ci-ble.**

e-vis-cer-ate (ē-vĭs'ẽr-āt), *v.t.* [*p.t.* and *p.p.* -at"ed, *p.pr.* -at"ing], **1**, to remove the bowels from; **2**, to deprive of characteristics or vital parts.

e-voke (ē-vōk'), *v.t.* [*p.t.* and *p.p.* e-voked' (-vōkt'), *p.pr.* e-vok'ing], to call forth; as, to *evoke* an answer.

ev-o-lu-tion (ĕv"ō-lū'shŭn; *Br.* ē"vō-), *n.* **1**, the act of unfolding or developing; as, the *evolution* of the plot of a story; **2**, the thing developed or evolved; **3**, ordered movement, as of troops in marching; **4**, a process in which something is set free, as a gas; **5**, in arithmetic or algebra, the process of extracting a root; **6**, the gradual development of higher forms of life from lower; also, the theory concerning this development.—*adj.* **ev"o-lu'tion-al.**—*adj.* **ev"o-lu'tion-a-ry.**—*n.* **ev"o-lu'tion-ist.**

e-volve (ē-vŏlv'), *v.t.* [*p.t.* and *p.p.* e-volved' (-vŏlvd'), *p.pr.* e-volv'ing], **1**, to develop; unfold; expand; **2**, to work out; **3**, to give forth; throw out:—*v.i.* to become developed or unfolded.

ewe (ū), *n.* a female sheep, or the female of any animal of the sheep family.

ew-er (ū'ẽr), *n.* a large water jug with a wide mouth, used esp. for the toilet.

[1]**ex-** (ĕks-), [Lat.], *prefix*, [*e-* before *b, d, g, h, l, m, n, r,* and *v; ef-* before *f; es-* in combining with French words], **1**, out; forth; outside; as, *ex*tract, *ex*cept, *ex*clude; **2**, removal or freedom from; as, *ex*patriation, *ex*oneration; **3**, beyond; in greater degree; as, *ex*cel, *ex*cess; **4**, thoroughly: used intensively; as, *ex*hort, *ex*asperate; **5**, (with a hyphen), formerly, but not now; as, *ex*-president.

[2]**ex-** (ĕks-), [Gk.], *prefix*, [*ec-* before consonants], used with Greek words and meaning out, from, away; as, *ex*odus; *ec*centric.

ex-ac-er-bate (ĕg-zăs'ẽr-bāt), *v.t.* [*p.t.* and *p.p.* -bat"ed, *p.pr.* -bat"ing], to make more bitter or sharp, as feelings or symptoms.—*n.* **ex-ac"er-ba'tion.**

ex-act (ĕg-zăkt'), *adj.* **1**, correct; precise; **2**, methodical; strict; particular:—*v.t.* **1**, to require or claim; **2**, to compel to be paid; extort.—*adv.* **ex-act'ly.**—*n.* **ex-act'ness.**
Syn., adj. (see correct).

ex-act-ing (ĕg-zăkt'ĭng), *p.adj.* **1**, making unreasonable demands, as a master; **2**, severe; arduous, as a task.

ex-ac-tion (ĕg-zăk'shŭn), *n.* **1**, the act of rigidly demanding; **2**, something demanded in excess of what is due.

ex-act-i-tude (ĕg-zăk'tĭ-tūd), *n.* the quality of being accurate.

ex-ag-ger-ate (ĕg-zăj'ẽr-āt), *v.t.* [*p.t.* and *p.p.* -at"ed, *p.pr.* -at"ing], **1**, to enlarge beyond truth or reason; overstate; **2**, to aggravate; **3**, to make of abnormal size, color, or the like, as in a picture.—*n.* **ex-ag'ger-a"tor.**—*adj.* **ex-ag'ger-a-tive.**

ex-ag-ger-at-ed (ĕg-zăj'ẽr-āt"ĕd), *p.adj.* enlarged or extended beyond truth or reason; overstated.

ex-ag-ger-a-tion (ĕg-zăj″ẽr-ā′shŭn), *n.* extravagant or untruthful representation; overstatement.

ex-alt (ĕg-zôlt′), *v.t.* **1**, to elevate in rank, station, or dignity; **2**, to raise on high; **3**, to glorify or extol; **4**, to inspire; elate.
Syn. ennoble, dignify, promote.

ex-al-ta-tion (ĕg″zôl-tā′shŭn), *n.* **1**, a raising or lifting up; hence, the act or state of being mentally or spiritually uplifted; **2**, a state of great dignity; **3**, a feeling of elation or pride; as, *exaltation* of spirit.

ex-am-i-na-tion (ĕg-zăm″ĭ-nā′shŭn), *n.* **1**, an investigation; a careful inquiry or inspection; **2**, a test of knowledge or fitness; esp., a written test; **3**, in law, a questioning, as of a witness.
Syn. analysis, search, scrutiny, trial.

ex-am-ine (ĕg-zăm′ĭn), *v.t.* [*p.t.* and *p.p.* -ined (-ĭnd), *p.pr.* -in-ing], **1**, to scrutinize or investigate carefully; **2**, in law, to question, as a witness; **3**, to test, orally or by papers, the knowledge, qualifications, etc., of, as a candidate for a degree or an office; **4**, to analyze; test.—*n.* **ex-am′in-er.**

ex-am-ple (ĕg-zăm′pl; ĕg-zȧm′pl), *n.* **1**, a pattern; a model or copy; **2**, an illustration of a rule or precept; **3**, a sample; specimen; **4**, a warning; as, his punishment was an *example* for the boys; **5**, a problem to be solved, as in arithmetic.
Syn. standard, type. (See specimen.)

ex-as-per-ate (ĕg-zăs′pẽr-āt), *v.t.* [*p.t.* and *p.p.* -at″ed, *p.pr.* -at″ing], **1**, to irritate exceedingly; enrage; **2**, to embitter; intensify.
Syn. annoy, provoke, inflame.

ex-as-per-a-tion (ĕg-zăs″pẽr-ā′shŭn), *n.* extreme irritation.

Ex-cal-i-bur (ĕks-kăl′ĭ-bŭr), *n.* in Arthurian romance, the sword of King Arthur. Also, **Ex-cal′i-bar.**

ex-ca-vate (ĕks′kȧ-vāt), *v.t.* [*p.t.* and *p.p.* -vat″ed, *p.pr.* -vat″ing], **1**, to dig or hollow out; scoop or cut into; **2**, to bring to light by digging; as, to *excavate* the ruins of ancient cities.—*n.* **ex″ca-va′tion.**

ex-ca-va-tor (ĕks′kȧ-vā″tẽr), *n.* **1**, that which digs or scoops, as a dredge; **2**, a person who digs, as in search of ancient relics, fossils, etc.

ex-ceed (ĕk-sēd′), *v.t.* **1**, to go beyond the limit or measure of; **2**, to excel:—*v.i.* **1**, to excel others; **2**, to go beyond bounds.

ex-ceed-ing (ĕk-sēd′ĭng), *p.adj.* very great; surpassing; extraordinary.—*adv.* **ex-ceed′ing-ly.**

ex-cel (ĕk-sĕl′), *v.i.* [*p.t.* and *p.p.* -celled′ (-sĕld′), *p.pr.* -cel′ling], to possess good qualities in a great degree; surpass others:—*v.t.* to surpass; outdo in comparison.

ex-cel-lence (ĕk′sĕ-lĕns), *n.* superior merit; worth; special virtue.
Syn. superiority, greatness, distinction.

ex-cel-len-cy (ĕk′sĕ-lĕn-sĭ), *n.* [*pl.* excellencies (-sĭz)], superior merit: **Excellency**, a title of honor of various high officials, as ambassadors, governors, etc.

ex-cel-lent (ĕk′sĕ-lĕnt), *adj.* **1**, of great value; **2**, highly useful or desirable; **3**, having great goodness or ability.—*adv.* **ex′cel-lent-ly.**
Syn. choice, select, superior, fine.

ex-cel-si-or (ĕk-sĕl′sĭ-ôr), *adj.* yet higher; ever upward: the motto of New York State:—*n.* a packing material made of long, fine wood shavings.

ex-cept (ĕk-sĕpt′), *v.t.* to leave out:—*v.i.* to object:—*prep.* omitting.

ex-cept-ing (ĕk-sĕpt′ĭng), *prep.* not including; except.

ex-cep-tion (ĕk-sĕp′shŭn), *n.* **1**, the act of omitting; exclusion; **2**, that which is not included; **3**, objection; disapproval: with *to;* as, to take *exception* to what was said; **4**, a formal objection to a ruling of a court made during a trial.

ex-cep-tion-a-ble (ĕk-sĕp′shŭn-ȧ-bl), *adj.* **1**, objectionable; open to criticism; **2**, liable to omission.
Syn. undesirable. (See exceptional.)

ex-cep-tion-al (ĕk-sĕp′shŭn-ăl), *adj.* unusual; uncommon; rare; extraordinary.—*adv.* **ex-cep′tion-al-ly.**
Syn. exceptionable, remarkable, signal, rare. *Exceptional* and *exceptionable* are often confused, but they have nothing in common. *Exceptional* means unusual or out of the ordinary, usually with the idea of superiority; as, *exceptional* ability. *Exceptionable* means objectionable or open to disapproval; as, the book is small but not otherwise *exceptionable.*

ex-cerpt (ĕk-sûrpt′), *v.t.* to take out or select, as a passage from a book; quote:—*n.* (ĕk′sûrpt; ĕk-sûrpt′), a selection or extract from a book or writing.

ex-cess (ĕk-sĕs′), *n.* **1**, an undue amount; **2**, the amount by which one thing is more than another; **3**, intemperance; **4**, an added charge, as for railway fare.
Syn. waste, dissipation, lavishness.

ex-ces-sive (ĕk-sĕs′ĭv), *adj.* extreme; unreasonable; immoderate.—*adv.* **ex-ces′sive-ly.**—*n.* **ex-ces′sive-ness.**

ex-change (ĕks-chānj′), *v.t.* [*p.t.* and *p.p.* -changed′ (-chānjd′), *p.pr.* -chang′ing], to give in return for something; barter:—*v.i.* to give one thing for another:—*n.* **1**, the act of giving one thing for another; barter; **2**, reciprocity, or the act of giving and receiving; as, an *exchange* of ideas; **3**, the act of substituting one thing for another; as, the *exchange* of red for green; **4**, a place where special business accounts are settled; as, a stock *exchange* (often, *'change*); **5**, a central office; as, a hotel *exchange;* **6**, the settling of accounts without the use of actual money, as by drafts, etc.; **7**, credit instruments, as bills of exchange; **8**, the act of securing currency of one country in return for that of another; also, the value of one currency in terms of another, or the difference in value between the two.—*adj.* **ex-change′a-ble.**

ex-cheq-uer (ĕks-chĕk′ẽr), *n.* **1**, a treasury; **2**, cash or funds: **Exchequer**, in Great Britain, the department of state having control of the revenue.

[1]**ex-cise** (ĕk-sīz′), *n.* a duty or tax levied on the manufacture, sale, or consumption of specified articles or commodities within a country.—*adj.* **ex-cis′a-ble.**

[2]**ex-cise** (ĕk-sīz′), *v.t.* [*p.t.* and *p.p.* -cised′ (-sīzd′), *p.pr.* -cis′ing], to cut out.

ex-cise-man (ĕk-sīz′măn), *n.* [*pl.* excisemen (-mĕn)], in Great Britain, one who collects certain taxes; a revenue officer.

ex-ci-sion (ĕk-sĭzh′ŭn), *n.* **1**, the act of cutting out or off; **2**, the state of being cut off; **3**, destruction; ruin.

ex-cit-a-ble (ĕk-sīt′ȧ-bl), *adj.* easily roused; irritable.—*n.* **ex-cit″a-bil′i-ty.**—*n.* **ex-cit′a-ble-ness.**
Syn. impetuous, fiery, passionate.

ex-cit-ant (ĕk-sīt′ănt), *n.* a stimulant:—*adj.* having a tendency to arouse; stimulating to the nerves.

ex-ci-ta-tion (ĕk″sĭ-tā′shŭn), *n.* **1**, the act of arousing; **2**, the state produced by stirring up or rousing.

ex-cite (ĕk-sīt′), *v.t.* [*p.t.* and *p.p.* -cit′ed, *p.pr.* -cit′ing], **1**, to animate; rouse; **2**, to encourage; **3**, to arouse mentally or emotionally.—*n.* **ex-cit′er.**
Syn. awaken, provoke, stir, impel.—*Ant.* lull, quiet, soothe.

ex-cit-ed (ĕk-sīt′ĕd), *p.adj.* aroused; provoked.—*adv.* **ex-cit′ed-ly.**

ex-cite-ment (ĕk-sīt′mĕnt), *n.* **1**, the condition of being stirred up; commotion; **2**, stimulation.

ex-cit-ing (ĕk-sīt′ĭng), *p.adj.* stirring; lively; as, an *exciting* adventure.

ex-claim (ĕks-klām′), *v.i.* and *v.t.* to cry out abruptly or passionately.

ex-cla-ma-tion (ĕks″klȧ-mā′shŭn), *n.* **1**, the act of crying out suddenly; **2**, an expression of surprise, pain, etc.; **3**, a mark [!] in writing or printing to denote emotion, surprise, etc.—*adj.* **ex-clam′a-to-ry** (ĕks-klăm′ȧ-tō-rĭ).

ex-clude (ĕks-klōōd′), *v.t.* [*p.t.* and *p.p.* -clud′ed, *p.pr.* -clud′ing], **1**, to shut out; hinder from entrance or admission; debar; **2**, to force out; reject.

Syn. expel, eject, eliminate.

ex-clu-sion (ĕks-klōō′zhŭn), *n.* **1**, the act of shutting out; **2**, the state of being debarred; **3**, omission; **4**, that which is shut out, rejected, or omitted.

ex-clu-sive (ĕks-klōō′sĭv), *adj.* **1**, shutting out; **2**, open to, or enjoyed only by, a privileged number; as, the *exclusive* use of a thing; **3**, limiting social relations; as, an *exclusive* assembly; **4**, including all except what is mentioned.—*adv.* **ex-clu′sive-ly.**

ex-com-mu-ni-cate (ĕks″kō-mū′nĭ-kāt), *v.t.* [*p.t.* and *p.p.* -cat″ed, *p.pr.* -cat″ing], **1**, to punish by cutting off from the membership and communion of the church; **2**, to expel from membership in any association or club.—*n.* **ex″com-mu″ni-ca′tion.**

ex-co-ri-ate (ĕks-kō′rĭ-āt), *v.t.* [*p.t.* and *p.p.* -at″ed, *p.pr.* -at″ing], to strip the skin from.—*n.* **ex-co″ri-a′tion.**

ex-cre-ment (ĕks′krē-mĕnt), *n.* waste matter discharged from an animal; dung; feces.—*adj.* **ex″cre-men′tal.**

ex-cres-cence (ĕks-krĕs′ĕns), *n.* an unnatural or disfiguring outgrowth, as a wart.

ex-cres-cent (ĕks-krĕs′ĕnt), *adj.* pertaining to an unnatural or useless growth; superfluous.

ex-cre-ta (ĕks-krē′tȧ), *n.pl.* useless matter eliminated or expelled from the body, as carbon dioxide, sweat, feces, etc.

ex-crete (ĕks-krēt′), *v.t.* [*p.t.* and *p.p.* -cret′ed, *p.pr.* -cret′ing], to throw off (waste matter) from the body:—*n.* (ĕks′krēt), that which is thrown off.—*n.* **ex-cre′tion.**—*adj.* **ex′cre-to-ry.**

ex-cru-ci-ate (ĕks-krōō′shĭ-āt), *v.t.* [*p.t.* and *p.p.* -at″ed, *p.pr.* -at″-ing], to put to torture; torment.—*p.adj.* **ex-cru′ci-at″ing.**—*adv.* **ex-cru′ci-at″ing-ly.**

ex-cru-ci-a-tion (ĕks-krōō″shĭ-ā′shŭn), *n.* agony; torture.

ex-cul-pate (ĕks-kŭl′pāt; ĕks′kŭl-pāt), *v.t.* [*p.t.* and *p.p.* -pat-ed, *p.pr.* -pat-ing], to clear from the imputation or charge of a fault; free from blame.—*n.* **ex″cul-pa′tion.**—*adj.* **ex-cul′pa-to-ry.**

Syn. acquit, absolve, release, exonerate.

ex-cur-sion (ĕks-kûr′shŭn; ĕks-kûr′zhŭn), *n.* **1**, a pleasure trip; **2**, a short or rapid tour; **3**, a turning aside from a subject or course.—*n.* **ex-cur′sion-ist.**

Syn. jaunt, ramble, expedition.

ex-cur-sive (ĕks-kûr′sĭv), *adj.* rambling; wandering; disconnected.

ex-cus-a-ble (ĕks-kūz′ȧ-bl), *adj.* worthy of being freed from blame or excused; pardonable; as, *excusable* delay. —*adv.* **ex-cus′a-bly.**

ex-cuse (ĕks-kūz′), *v.t.* [*p.t.* and *p.p.* -cused′ (-kūzd′), *p.pr.* -cus′ing], **1**, to pardon; **2**, to free from blame, obligation, or duty; **3**, to make an apology for; **4**, to justify:—*n.* (ĕks-kūs′), **1**, a plea offered to justify some fault or neglect of duty; an apology; **2**, a pretext or pretended reason.

Syn., n. apology. An *excuse* is an explanation which is intended at least partially to justify a fault by emphasizing the reason for the deed or omission that is regarded as wrong; as, his *excuse* was that he did not see the signal; he brought an *excuse* for absence on the next day. An *apology* is an expression of sorrow for what is wrong or appears to be wrong; as, the newspaper printed an *apology* for the error; an *apology* for apparent rudeness.

ex-e-cra-ble (ĕk′sē-krȧ-bl), *adj.* **1**, accursed; outrageous; **2**, very bad; of poor quality.—*adv.* **ex′e-cra-bly.**

ex-e-crate (ĕk′sē-krāt), *v.t.* [*p.t.* and *p.p.* -crat″ed, *p.pr.* -crat″ing], **1**, to curse; **2**, to detest; abhor; abominate.

ex-e-cra-tion (ĕk″sē-krā′shŭn), *n.* **1**, the act of cursing; **2**, an expression of utter detestation; a curse; imprecation; **3**, the thing cursed.

ex-e-cute (ĕk′sē-kūt), *v.t.* [*p.t.* and *p.p.* -cut″ed, *p.pr.* -cut″ing], **1**, to carry into effect; as, to *execute* a purpose or plan; **2**, to make valid or legal by signing or sealing; as, to *execute* a deed or lease; **3**, to put to death under sentence of the law; **4**, to perform, as a musical selection:—*v.i.* **1**, to perform any act or office; **2**, to play a piece of music; as, to *execute* with skill.—*n.* **ex′e-cut″er.**

Syn. enforce, manage. (See effect; kill.)

ex-e-cu-tion (ĕk″sē-kū′shŭn), *n.* **1**, performance; the act or manner of carrying anything into effect; completion; **2**, skill in performing on a musical instrument; **3**, the act of making a legal paper valid or good; **4**, capital punishment, or punishment by death; **5**, effective work or operation; esp., destruction; as, every shot did good *execution.*

ex-e-cu-tion-er (ĕk″sē-kū′shŭn-ẽr), *n.* one who puts to death condemned criminals.

ex-ec-u-tive (ĕg-zĕk′ū-tĭv; ĕk-sĕk′ū-tĭv), *adj.* **1**, pertaining to the carrying out of plans, orders, etc.; **2**, pertaining to that branch of government that administers the laws; **3**, skilful in carrying out plans: **Executive Mansion**, the residence at Washington of the President of the United States: popularly called *White House:*—*n.* **1**, an official or a body charged with carrying laws or policies into effect; as, the President is the chief *executive;* **2**, the administrative branch of a government.—*adj.* **ex-ec′u-to-ry.**

ex-ec-u-tor (ĕk′sē-kū″tẽr), *n.* **1**, one who carries something into effect; **2**, (ĕg-zĕk′ū-tẽr; ĕk-sĕk′-), a person appointed to see that the terms of a will are carried out.

ex-ec-u-trix (ĕg-zĕk′ū-trĭks; ĕk-sĕk′-), *n.* [*pl.* executrices (-trī′sēz); executrixes (-trĭk″sĕz)], a woman appointed to administer a will.

ex-e-ge-sis (ĕk″sē-jē′sĭs), *n.* [*pl.* exegeses (-sēz)], a critical explanation of a passage of literature, esp. of the Bible.

ex-e-get-ic (ĕk″sē-jĕt′ĭk), *adj.* expository; explanatory; interpretative: **exegetics**, *n.pl.* used as *sing.* the branch of theology which treats of the explaining of the Bible.

ex-em-plar (ĕg-zĕm′plȧr), *n.* **1**, something to be copied, or something serving as a model; **2**, an example or a pattern.

ex-em-pla-ry (ĕg′zĕm-plȧ-rĭ; ĕg-zĕm′plȧ-rĭ), *adj.* **1**, serving as a copy or model; commendable; as, the boy's conduct was *exemplary;* **2**, serving as a sample or an illustration.—*adv.* **ex′em-pla-ri-ly.**

ex-em-pli-fi-ca-tion (ĕg-zĕm″plĭ-fĭ-kā′shŭn), *n.* the making plain by example; illustration.

ex-em-pli-fy (ĕg-zĕm′plĭ-fī), *v.t.* [*p.t.* and *p.p.* -fied (-fīd), *p.pr.* -fy″-ing], to show by example; illustrate.—*n.* **ex-em″pli-fi-ca′tion.**

ex-empt (ĕg-zĕmpt′), *v.t.* to free from a due or obligation; release; as, to *exempt* clergymen from military service:—*adj.* free from a duty to which others are subject: with *from:*—*n.* a person thus set free.

ex-emp-tion (ĕg-zĕmp′shŭn), *n.* act of releasing, or state of being released, from some duty or obligation.
Syn. freedom, liberty, immunity.

ex-er-cise (ĕk′sẽr-sīz), *v.t.* [*p.t.* and *p.p.* -cised (-sīzd), *p.pr.* -cis″ing], **1**, to train by use; practice; **2**, to employ actively; **3**, to make anxious:—*v.i.* to undergo training:—*n.* **1**, bodily exertion; activity for the sake of mental or physical development; **2**, a lesson or example for practice; **3**, usually in *pl.*, the ceremony ending a course in school; as, graduating *exercises;* **4**, performance, as of a duty or an office.

ex-ert (ĕg-zûrt′), *v.t.* to put forth, as force or ability; use with an effort.

ex-er-tion (ĕg-zûr′shŭn), *n.* the active use of any power; effort.
Syn. exercise, work, endeavor.

***ex-e-unt** (ĕk′sē-ŭnt), [Lat.], [*sing.* *exit], they go out: a direction denoting that actors retire from the stage.

ex-ha-la-tion (ĕks″hȧ-lā′shŭn; ĕk″sȧ-lā′-shŭn), *n.* **1**, a breathing or a giving out; as, the *exhalation* of vapor from a swamp, or of perfume from a flower; **2**, that which is breathed or given out.

ex-hale (ĕks-hāl′; ĕgz-hāl′), *v.t.* [*p.t.* and *p.p.* -haled′ (-hāld′), *p.pr.* -hal′ing], **1**, to breathe forth; **2**, to cause to evaporate:—*v.i.* **1**, to rise in vapor; **2**, to breathe out.

ex-haust (ĕg-zôst′), *v.t.* **1**, to empty by drawing off the contents; drain; **2**, to weaken; wear out by exertion; **3**, to discuss or treat thoroughly; as, to *exhaust* a topic of conversation:—*n.* **1**, that which is drawn off, as steam from an engine; **2**, an apparatus for drawing off, as dust from a room.

ex-haust-i-ble (ĕg-zôs′tĭ-bl), *adj.* capable of being emptied or worn out.—*n.* **ex-haust″i-bil′i-ty.**

ex-haus-tion (ĕg-zôs′chŭn), *n.* **1**, the act of draining; **2**, the state or process of being drained; **3**, utter weariness.

ex-haus-tive (ĕg-zôs′tĭv), *adj.* **1**, tending to drain; **2**, complete; thorough; as, an *exhaustive* treatment of a subject.—*adv.* **ex-haus′tive-ly.**

ex-hib-it (ĕg-zĭb′ĭt), *v.t.* **1**, to present to view; **2**, to manifest publicly; present formally or officially:—*v.i.* to make a public exhibition:—*n.* **1**, an object or collection of objects offered for public view; as, an *exhibit* of paintings; **2**, in law, an article, paper, etc., marked to be used as evidence.—*n.* **ex-hib′i-tor.**

ex-hi-bi-tion (ĕk″sĭ-bĭsh′ŭn), *n.* **1**, the act of displaying for inspection; **2**, the thing or things displayed; **3**, a public show or demonstration.

ex-hil-a-rant (ĕg-zĭl′ȧ-rănt), *adj.* causing joy or pleasure; making lively:—*n.* that which enlivens.

ex-hil-a-rate (ĕg-zĭl′ȧ-rāt), *v.t.* [*p.t.* and *p.p.* -rat″ed, *p.pr.* -rat″ing], to make joyous; enliven; gladden.—*n.* **ex-hil″a-ra′tion.**

ex-hort (ĕg-zôrt′; ĕgz-hôrt′), *v.t.* and *v.i.* to incite or urge, by appeal or argument, to good deeds.—*n.* **ex-hort′er.**

ex-hor-ta-tion (ĕg″sôr-tā′shŭn), *n.* an effort to arouse or incite to that which is good; earnest appeal.—*adj.* **ex-hor′ta-tive.**—*adj.* **ex-hor′ta-to-ry.**

ex-hume (ĕks-hūm′), *v.t.* [*p.t.* and *p.p.* -humed′ (-hūmd′), *p.pr.* -hum′-ing], to disinter or dig up (something buried).—*n.* **ex″hu-ma′tion.**

ex-i-gen-cy (ĕk′sĭ-jĕn-sĭ), *n.* [*pl.* exigencies (-sĭz)], **1**, a time or situation that needs immediate attention; **2**, pressing necessity or demand; urgency; emergency. Also, **ex′i-gence.**
Syn. need, pressure, necessity.

ex-i-gent (ĕk′sĭ-jĕnt), *adj.* urgent; exacting; pressing; critical. Also, ***ex″i″geant′** (ĕg″zē″zhäɴ′).

ex-ig-u-ous (ĕg-zĭg′ū-ŭs; ĕk-sĭg′ū-ŭs), *adj.* scanty; meager.

ex-ile (ĕk′sīl), *v.t.* [*p.t.* and *p.p.* -iled (-sīld), *p.pr.* -il-ing], to banish, as from a native place:—*n.* **1**, the state of being banished; **2**, the state of living away from home or friends; **3**, a person expelled from his country.
Syn., *v.* (see banish).

ex-ist (ĕg-zĭst′), *v.i.* **1**, to have actual being; live; be; **2**, to continue in being; **3**, to occur; as, a situation *exists.*

ex-ist-ence (ĕg-zĭs′tĕns), *n.* **1**, the state of being; **2**, life; **3**, duration; **4**, reality; actuality.—*adj.* **ex-ist′ent.**

ex-it (ĕk′sĭt), *n.* **1**, the act of going out; **2**, a passage out; **3**, the departure of an actor from the stage: ***exit**, he (or she) goes out: a stage direction denoting that an actor leaves the stage: *pl.* ***exeunt** (ĕk′sē-ŭnt), they leave.

***ex li-bris** (ĕks lī′brĭs), [Lat.], from the books (of): an inscription used in the front of a book, with the owner's name; hence, a bookplate.

ex-o-dus (ĕk′sō-dŭs), *n.* a going out; departure: **Exodus**, **1**, the departure of the Jews from Egypt: with *the;* **2**, the second book of the Bible.—*abbr.* **Ex.; Exod.**

***ex of-fi-ci-o** (ĕks ō-fĭsh′ĭ-ō), [Lat.], by virtue or right of office and without other special authority.

ex-o-gen (ĕk′sō-jĕn), *n.* in a former classification, any of a class of seed-bearing plants, including most of our common trees, in whose stems a layer just under the bark forms annual rings of growing tissue: distinguished from *endogen.*—*adj.* **ex-og′e-nous.**

ex-on-er-ate (ĕg-zŏn′ẽr-āt), *v.t.* [*p.t.* and *p.p.* -at″ed, *p.pr.* -at″ing], to free from the imputation or charge of a fault; acquit; justify.—*n.* **ex-on″er-a′tion.**

ex-or-bi-tance (ĕg-zôr′bĭ-tăns), *n.* a going beyond due limits; excess. Also, **ex-or′bi-tan-cy.**

ex-or-bi-tant (ĕg-zôr′bĭ-tănt), *adj.* excessive; as, an *exorbitant* amount was charged.—*adv.* **ex-or′bi-tant-ly.**
Syn. immoderate, extravagant. (See dear.)

ex-or-cise (ĕk′sôr-sīz; ĕg-zôr′sīz), *v.t.* [*p.t.* and *p.p.* -cised (-sīzd), *p.pr.* -cis″ing], **1**, to expel (an evil spirit) by prayers or magical words; **2**, to deliver from evil spirits; **3**, to conjure or call up (a spirit). Also, **ex′or-cize.**—*n.* **ex′or-cis″er.**

ex-or-cism (ĕk′sôr-sĭzm), *n.* the act or process of expelling or conjuring evil spirits.—*n.* **ex′or-cist.**

ex-or-di-um (ĕg-zôr′dĭ-ŭm), *n.* [*pl.* exordiums (-ŭmz); exordia (-ȧ)], the opening part, as of a speech.

ex-o-ter-ic (ĕk″sō-tĕr′ĭk), *adj.* **1**, external; **2**, suitable for the general public; popular: opp. of *esoteric.*

ex-ot-ic (ĕg-zŏt′ĭk; ĕk-sŏt′ĭk), *adj.* foreign; strange; belonging, as a plant, to another part of the world:—*n.* anything not native to a place.

ex-pand (ĕks-pănd′), *v.t.* **1**, to spread or stretch out; unfold; **2**, to dilate; extend; as, to *expand* the chest; **3**, to enlarge upon, as a topic:—*v.i.* to increase in size.

ex-panse (ĕks-păns'), *n.* wide extent; uninterrupted stretch or area; as, an *expanse* of ocean or of sky.

ex-pan-si-ble (ĕks-păn'sĭ-bl), *adj.* capable of being spread, extended, or diffused.—*n.* **ex-pan"si-bil'i-ty.**

ex-pan-sion (ĕks-păn'shŭn), *n.* **1**, the act of spreading out; **2**, the state of being stretched out; **3**, increase in size or extent; enlargement.

ex-pan-sive (ĕks-păn'sĭv), *adj.* **1**, capable of being spread or stretched out; **2**, widely extended; large.—*adv.* **ex-pan'sive-ly.**—*n.* **ex-pan'sive-ness.**

***ex par-te** (ĕks pär'tē), literally, of the one part or side; hence, not disinterested: when used as attributive adjective, written *ex-parte;* as, an *ex-parte* hearing.

ex-pa-ti-ate (ĕks-pā'shĭ-āt), *v.i.* [*p.t.* and *p.p.* -at"ed, *p.pr.* -at"ing], to use many words in discussion; talk freely and at length.—*n.* **ex-pa"ti-a'tion.**

ex-pa-tri-ate (ĕks-pā'trĭ-āt), *v.t.* [*p.t.* and *p.p.* -at"ed, *p.pr.* -at"ing], to drive from one's native country:—*n.* (ĕks-pā'trĭ-āt), an exile.—*n.* **ex-pa"tri-a'tion.**

ex-pect (ĕks-pĕkt'), *v.t.* **1**, to look for, in thought, as likely to happen; **2**, to look for with confidence.

ex-pect-an-cy (ĕks-pĕk'tăn-sĭ), *n.* **1**, the act or state of looking forward to something; **2**, that which is looked forward to. Also, **ex-pect'ance.**

ex-pect-ant (ĕks-pĕk'tănt), *adj.* looking forward with confidence; prospective.—*adv.* **ex-pect'ant-ly.**

ex-pec-ta-tion (ĕks"pĕk-tā'shŭn), *n.* **1**, the act of looking forward to; anticipation; **2**, that which is expected; **3**, the prospect of future advancement.
Syn. hope, trust.—*Ant.* despair, doubt.

ex-pec-to-rant (ĕks-pĕk'tō-rănt), *adj.* promoting the discharge of mucus or other fluids from the lungs and throat:—*n.* a drug promoting such discharge.

ex-pec-to-rate (ĕks-pĕk'tō-rāt), *v.t.* [*p.t.* and *p.p.* -rat"ed, *p.pr.* -rat"ing], to throw off from the lungs by coughing or spitting; spit:—*v.i.* to discharge matter from the mouth, throat, and lungs.

ex-pec-to-ra-tion (ĕks-pĕk"tō-rā'shŭn), *n.* the act of spitting; also, the mucous matter which is ejected.

ex-pe-di-en-cy (ĕks-pē'dĭ-ĕn-sĭ), *n.* [*pl.* expediencies (-sĭz)], **1**, suitableness; fitness for a purpose; **2**, propriety; **3**, advisability. Also, **ex-pe'di-ence.**

ex-pe-di-ent (ĕks-pē'dĭ-ĕnt), *adj.* **1**, fit for a special purpose; **2**, proper:—*n.* **1**, that which acts as a means to an end; **2**, a device.—*adv.* **ex-pe'di-ent-ly.**
Syn., adj. practical, efficient, favorable.

ex-pe-dite (ĕks'pē-dīt), *v.t.* [*p.t.* and *p.p.* -dit"ed, *p.pr.* -dit"ing], **1**, to hasten; help forward; quicken; **2**, to carry out quickly; as, to *expedite* work.

ex-pe-di-tion (ĕks"pē-dĭsh'ŭn), *n.* **1**, haste; dispatch; promptness; **2**, a march, voyage, etc., by an army or a group of persons for some particular purpose; **3**, the body of persons engaged in such an enterprise.

ex-pe-di-tion-a-ry (ĕks"pē-dĭsh'ŭn-ā-rĭ), *adj.* pertaining to, or forming, a journey for a particular purpose; as, the American *Expeditionary* Forces.

ex-pe-di-tious (ĕks"pē-dĭsh'ŭs), *adj.* effective; speedy; as, *expeditious* work.—*adv.* **ex"pe-di'tious-ly.**—*n.* **ex"pe-di'tious-ness.**
Syn. efficient, energetic, quick, ready.—*Ant.* slow, unready, inefficient.

ex-pel (ĕks-pĕl'), *v.t.* [*p.t.* and *p.p.* -pelled' (-pĕld'), *p.pr.* -pel'ling], **1**, to drive away; force out; **2**, to send away by authority.
Syn. exile, eject, dismiss. (See banish.)

ex-pend (ĕks-pĕnd'), *v.t.* to lay out; pay out; spend; consume; as, to *expend* strength, time, or money.

ex-pend-i-ture (ĕks-pĕn'dĭ-tūr), *n.* **1**, a laying out, as of money, time, labor, etc.; **2**, that which is spent.

ex-pense (ĕks-pĕns'), *n.* **1**, the paying out of money; **2**, drain on resources; **3**, detriment or injury; as, he did it at the *expense* of his health; **4**, cost.

ex-pen-sive (ĕks-pĕn'sĭv), *adj.* costly; high-priced.—*adv.* **ex-pen'sive-ly.**—*n.* **ex-pen'sive-ness.**
Syn. exorbitant. (See dear.)

ex-pe-ri-ence (ĕks-pē'rĭ-ĕns), *n.* **1**, personal trial and practice; **2**, knowledge gained by practice and trial; **3**, something lived through:—*v.t.* [*p.t.* and *p.p.* -enced (-ĕnst), *p.pr.* -enc-ing], to come to know by personal trial or feeling; as, to *experience* hardships.—*p.adj.* **ex-pe'ri-enced.**

ex-per-i-ment (ĕks-pĕr'ĭ-mĕnt), *n.* **1**, a trial or operation to discover something previously unknown; **2**, a test by which something is confirmed or proved:—*v.i.* to make trials or tests to find out or confirm something.—*n.* **ex-per'i-ment-er.**
Syn., n. proof, examination. (See trial.)

ex-per-i-men-tal (ĕks-pĕr"ĭ-mĕn'tăl), *adj.* pertaining to, or founded on, trial; guided, or learned, by experience.—*adv.* **ex-per"i-men'tal-ly.**

ex-pert (ĕks-pûrt'), *adj.* skilful; adroit; dexterous:—*n.* (ĕks'pûrt), one who is skilled or thoroughly informed in any particular kind of knowledge or art; a specialist. —*adv.* **ex-pert'ly.**—*n.* **ex-pert'ness.**
Syn., adj. proficient, practiced. (See clever.)

ex-pi-ate (ĕks'pĭ-āt), *v.t.* [*p.t.* and *p.p.* -at"ed, *p.pr.* -at"ing], to atone or make amends for; as, to *expiate* a fault.

ex-pi-a-tion (ĕks"pĭ-ā'shŭn), *n.* **1**, the act of making satisfaction for an offense; **2**, atonement.

ex-pi-a-to-ry (ĕks'pĭ-ȧ-tō-rĭ), *adj.* having the power or nature of atonement; atoning.

ex-pire (ĕk-spīr'), *v.t.* [*p.t.* and *p.p.* -pired' (-spīrd'), *p.pr.* -pir'ing], to breathe out from the lungs:—*v.i.* **1**, to die; **2**, to come to an end; as, a leave of absence *expires.*—*n.* **ex"pi-ra'tion.**—*adj.* **ex-pir'a-to-ry.**

ex-plain (ĕks-plān'), *v.t.* **1**, to make intelligible or clear, **2**, to expound or interpret:—*v.i.* to give an explanation.—*adj.* **ex-plain'a-ble.**
Syn. define, describe. These words are alike in implying an attempt to make something clear. To *explain* is to make intelligible or to show the reason for, often by giving causes; as, to *explain* a difficult passage; he *explained* that his lameness was due to an accident. *Define* is less general than *explain;* it puts the emphasis on exactness; as, to *define* a word in a dictionary; he *defined* his policy. To *describe* is to set forth in words, often by supplying a mental picture; as, to *describe* a game.

ex-pla-na-tion (ĕks"plȧ-nā'shŭn), *n.* **1**, the act of making clear; **2**, interpretation; **3**, a mutual clearing up of a misunderstanding.

ex-plan-a-to-ry (ĕks-plăn'ȧ-tō-rĭ), *adj.* serving to make clear; as, an *explanatory* clause.

ex-ple-tive (ĕks'plē-tĭv), *n.* **1**, a word not necessary for the sense, inserted in a sentence for ornament or to fill up a verse; **2**, an oath:—*adj.* filling up; added or inserted for emphasis, or the like.

ex-pli-cate (ĕks'plĭ-kāt), *v.t.* [*p.t.* and *p.p.* -cat"ed, *p.pr.* -cat"ing], to make intelligible or clear; explain; tell the meaning of.—*n.* **ex″pli-ca′tion.**—*adj.* **ex′pli-ca-ble.**—*adj.* and *n.* **ex′pli-ca-tive.**

ex-plic-it (ĕks-plĭs′ĭt), *adj.* plain; definite. as, *explicit* instructions.—*adv.* **ex-plic′it-ly.**—*n.* **ex-plic′it-ness.**

ex-plode (ĕks-plōd′), *v.i.* [*p.t.* and *p.p.* -plod′ed, *p.pr.* -plod′ing], to burst with sudden noise and violence; collapse:—*v.t.* **1,** to cause to change violently from a solid to a gaseous state; **2,** to refute or disprove; as, to *explode* an idea or argument; **3,** to do away with; as, to *explode* a custom; **4,** to cause to burst.—*n.* **ex-plod′er.**

ex-ploit (ĕks-ploit′), *v.t.* **1,** to make use of for one's own profit; put to use selfishly; **2,** to make use of; work:—*n.* a remarkable deed or heroic act.—*n.* **ex-ploit′er.**
Syn., n. feat, achievement, performance.

ex-ploi-ta-tion (ĕks″ploi-tā′shŭn), *n.* **1,** the act of making use of or getting the value out of; **2,** the improvement of lands, working of mines, etc.; **3,** selfish use or employment, regardless of right.

ex-plo-ra-tion (ĕks″plō-rā′shŭn), *n.* **1,** the discovery and investigation of an unknown country; **2,** careful investigation or search, esp. geographical research; **3,** an examination, as of a wound.

ex-plore (ĕks-plōr′), *v.t.* [*p.t.* and *p.p.* -plored′ (-plōrd′), *p.pr.* -plor′ing], **1,** to search or examine thoroughly; **2,** to travel in or over (a country) to discover its characteristic features, resources, etc.—*adj.* **ex-plor′a-to-ry.**—*n.* **ex-plor′er.**

ex-plo-sion (ĕks-plō′zhŭn), *n.* **1,** the act of bursting from a solid to a gaseous state; **2,** a sudden bursting with a loud report; **3,** a sudden and violent outbreak, as of laughter, anger, or the like.

ex-plo-sive (ĕks-plō′sĭv), *adj.* **1,** likely to burst forth loudly and violently, or to cause to do so; **2,** pronounced with a slight expulsion of the breath, as the consonants *p, t, k,* etc.:—*n.* **1,** any substance that causes a loud and violent bursting forth, as gunpowder; **2,** an explosive consonant.—*adv.* **ex-plo′sive-ly.**—*n.* **ex-plo′sive-ness.**

ex-po-nent (ĕks-pō′nĕnt), *n.* **1,** a figure that shows how many times a quantity is to be used as a factor, as the figure 2 in a^2; **2,** one who explains or interprets the principles of something; as, an *exponent* of democracy.—*adj.* **ex″po-nen′tial.**

ex-port (ĕks-pōrt′; ĕks′pōrt), *v.t.* to send or carry out of a country, as merchandise:—*v.i.* to make a business of sending goods to a foreign country:—*n.* (ĕks′pōrt). **1,** usually in *pl.*, goods sold and sent to a foreign country; also, their amount or value; **2,** the act or business of sending goods to a foreign country to be sold.—*n.* **ex″por-ta′tion.**—*n.* **ex-port′er.**—*adj.* **ex-port′a-ble.**

ex-pose (ĕks-pōz′), *v.t.* [*p.t.* and *p.p.* -posed′ (-pōzd′), *p.pr.* -pos′ing], **1,** to lay open; reveal; **2,** to put forward for sale; **3,** to leave to the action of any force or circumstance; place in peril; **4,** to lay open to censure or ridicule; **5,** in photography, to subject (a film) to the action of light.
Syn. display, publish, exhibit.

***ex-po-sé** (ĕks″pō″zā′), [Fr.], *n.* **1,** a formal recital of the facts of a case; **2,** an undesired or undesirable exposure.

ex-po-si-tion (ĕks″pō-zĭsh′ŭn), *n.* **1,** an explanation or interpretation; **2,** an exhibition on a large scale; as, the San Francisco *Exposition* of 1915.

ex-pos-i-tor (ĕks-pŏz′ĭ-tẽr), *n.* one who expounds or interprets.

ex-pos-i-to-ry (ĕks-pŏz′ĭ-tō-rĭ), *adj.* serving to explain; tending to illustrate.—*adj.* **ex-pos′i-tive.**

***ex post fac-to** (ĕks pōst făk′tō), [Lat.], after the deed is done; judging a former state from a later point of view; as, the *ex post facto* working of a law.

ex-pos-tu-late (ĕks-pŏs′tū-lāt), *v.t.* [*p.t.* and *p.p.* -lat″ed, *p.pr.* -lat″ing], to reason earnestly or remonstrate.
Syn rebuke, reprimand, reprove.

ex-pos-tu-la-tion (ĕks-pŏs″tū-lā′shŭn), *n.* earnest pleading; kindly protest; remonstrance.

ex-po-sure (ĕks-pō′zhŭr), *n.* **1,** the act of revealing, as a crime; **2,** the state of being open or subject to attack; as, *exposure* to the weather or to contagion; **3,** situation; as, a southern *exposure;* **4,** the act of exposing, esp. in photography.

ex-pound (ĕks-pound′), *v.t.* to set forth, explain, or interpret; make clear.—*n.* **ex-pound′er.**

ex-press (ĕks-prĕs′), *adj.* **1,** plainly stated; definite; precise; **2,** pertaining to quick or direct conveyance; **3,** pertaining to the business of transporting goods rapidly; **express company,** an association or corporation engaged in the rapid transportation of goods or merchandise and providing special care, security, and quickness of delivery; **express train,** a fast railway train stopping only at principal stations.—*adv.* by express; quickly:—*n.* **1,** a person or vehicle that carries letters or packages rapidly; **2,** a fast railway train stopping only at principal stations; **3,** a parcel or dispatch carried by special messenger; **4,** a regular and systematic method of conveyance for passengers, mails, goods of small bulk, or the like; also, goods so forwarded:—*v.t.* **1,** to squeeze out; press; **2,** to make known in any way, esp. by language; utter; **3,** to show; reveal; **4,** to represent, as by a symbol; **5,** to send by quick and direct conveyance.—*adj.* **ex-press′i-ble.**

ex-press-age (ĕks-prĕs′āj), *n.* **1,** the charge made for carrying packages by express; **2,** the business of carrying packages by express.

ex-pres-sion (ĕks-prĕsh′ŭn), *n.* **1,** the act or power of representing anything; **2,** a saying; mode of speech; **3,** a change of the countenance; as, a peculiar *expression;* **4,** a modulation of the voice; **5,** the act of pressing or squeezing out.

ex-pres-sive (ĕks-prĕs′ĭv), *adj.* **1,** full of significance or importance; forcible; **2,** pertaining to, or displaying, expression; **3,** serving to point out.—*adv.* **ex-pres′sive-ly.**—*n.* **ex-pres′sive-ness.**

ex-press-ly (ĕks-prĕs′lĭ), *adv.* **1,** particularly; **2,** in direct terms.

ex-press-man (ĕks-prĕs′măn), *n.* [*pl.* expressmen (-mĕn)], one who is engaged in the business of transporting goods or merchandise by express.

ex-pul-sion (ĕks-pŭl′shŭn), *n.* a driving away; banishment; as, the *expulsion* of a student from college.

ex-pul-sive (ĕks-pŭl′sĭv), *adj.* serving to cast out or drive away.

ex-punge (ĕks-pŭnj′), *v.t.* [*p.t.* and *p.p.* -punged′ (-pŭnjd′), *p.pr.* -pung′ing], to blot or rub out; erase; efface.

ex-pur-gate (ĕks′pŭr-gāt; ĕks-pûr′gāt), *v.t.* [*p.t.* and *p.p.* -gat″ed, *p.pr.* -gat″ing], to remove (whatever is offensive to good taste or morality): said of books.—*n.* **ex″pur-ga′tion.**

ex-qui-site (ĕks′kwĭ-zĭt), *adj.* **1,** refined; delicate; **2,** nice; accurate; **3,** choice; excellent; **4,** highly finished; **5,** very intensely or sensitively felt; extreme:—*n.* a person very fastidious in dress; a dandy.—*adv.* **ex′qui-site-ly.**—*n.* **ex′qui-site-ness.**
Syn., adj. dainty, elegant, fine, rare.

ex-tant (ĕks'tănt), *adj.* in existence; not destroyed or lost; as, old prints or writings that are still *extant.*

ex-tem-po-ra-ne-ous (ĕks-tĕm″pō-rā'nē-ŭs), *adj.* 1, made without previous notes or study; as, an *extemporaneous* speech; 2, offhand; sudden. —*adv.* **ex-tem″po-ra'ne-ous-ly.**

ex-tem-po-ra-ry (ĕks-tĕm'pō-rā-rĭ), *adj.* 1, without notes or previous study; as, an *extemporary* speech; 2, made on the spur of the moment; sudden.

ex-tem-po-re (ĕks-tĕm'pō-rē), *adv.* without preparation; impromptu; as, to speak *extempore.*

ex-tem-po-rize (ĕks-tĕm'pō-rīz), *v.t.* [*p.t.* and *p.p.* -rized (-rīzd), *p.pr.* -riz″ing], to make, do, or compose, on the spur of the moment:—*v.i.* to make a speech without notes or previous study; improvise.

ex-tend (ĕks-tĕnd'), *v.t.* 1, to stretch out; 2, to enlarge; 3, to straighten out, as the arm; 4, to offer, as friendship:—*v.i.* to reach, in time or distance; be prolonged.
Syn. lengthen, widen. (See increase.)

ex-ten-si-ble (ĕks-tĕn'sĭ-bl), *adj.* capable of being made longer or wider. Also, **ex-ten'sile** (ĕks-tĕn'sĭl).

ex-ten-sion (ĕks-tĕn'shŭn), *n.* 1, the act of reaching or stretching out; 2, the state of being lengthened; enlargement; 3, an addition; 4, in physics, the property of a body by which it occupies space.

ex-ten-sive (ĕks-tĕn'sĭv), *adj.* wide; comprehensive; far-reaching; as, *extensive* business interests; an *extensive* view. —*adv.* **ex-ten'sive-ly.**—*n.* **ex-ten'sive-ness.**

ex-ten-sor (ĕks-tĕn'sŏr), *n.* a muscle that serves to straighten any part of the body, as an arm or finger: opp. of *flexor.*

ex-tent (ĕks-tĕnt'), *n.* the space or degree to which a thing is enlarged; size.

ex-ten-u-ate (ĕks-tĕn'ū-āt), *v.t.* [*p.t.* and *p.p.* -at″ed, *p.pr.* -at″ing], 1, to offer excuses for; lessen the blame for; as, he sought to *extenuate* his fault; 2, to diminish; soften.—*n.* **ex-ten″u-a'tion.**

ex-te-ri-or (ĕks-tē'rĭ-ĕr), *adj.* 1, outward; external; 2, coming, or acting, from without:—*n.* 1, that which is outside; 2, the outer surface; the outside: **exterior angle,** 1, an angle formed by a side of a polygon and the adjacent side produced; 2, one of the four outside angles AOB, BOC, DEG, GEH formed by a transversal cutting two parallels.

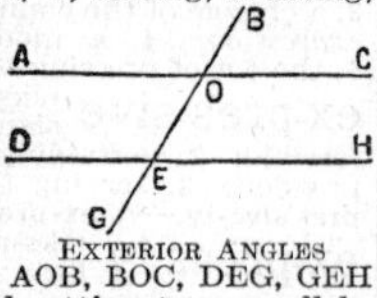

Exterior Angles

ex-ter-mi-nate (ĕks-tûr'mĭ-nāt), *v.t.* [*p.t.* and *p.p.* -nat″ed, *p.pr.* -nat″ing], to destroy utterly; root out.—*n.* **ex-ter'mi-na″tor.**—*adj.* **ex-ter'mi-na-tive.**
Syn. extirpate, eradicate.

ex-ter-mi-na-tion (ĕks-tûr″mĭ-nā'shŭn), *n.* a destroying wholly; complete destruction.

ex-ter-nal (ĕks-tûr'năl), *adj.* 1, outside; exterior; 2, foreign; 3, visible; 4, superficial:—*n.* 1, an outward part; 2, an outward form or ceremony.—*adv.* **ex-ter'nal-ly.**

ex-tinct (ĕks-tĭngkt'), *adj.* 1, put out; inactive, as a volcano; 2, of families, species, etc., having no surviving representatives; 3, no longer existing; obsolete.

ex-tinc-tion (ĕks-tĭngk'shŭn), *n.* 1, the act of putting out, or state of being put out; 2, complete destruction.

ex-tin-guish (ĕks-tĭng'gwĭsh), *v.t.* 1, to put out, as a light; 2, to end; destroy; 3, to eclipse; outshine.—*adj.* **ex-tin'guish-a-ble.**—*n.* **ex-tin'guish-ment.**

ex-tin-guish-er (ĕks-tĭng'gwĭsh-ĕr), *n.* 1, one who or that which puts out; 2, specif., a hollow cone for putting out a candlelight.

ex-tir-pate (ĕks'tĕr-pāt; ĕks-tûr'pāt), *v.t.* [*p.t.* and *p.p.* -pat″ed, *p.pr.* -pat″ing], to root out.—*n.* **ex'tir-pa″tor.**

ex-tir-pa-tion (ĕks″tĕr-pā'shŭn), *n.* a rooting out; destruction.

ex-tol (ĕks-tŏl'; ĕks-tōl'), *v.t.* [*p.t.* and *p.p.* -tolled' (-tŏld'; -tōld'), *p.pr.* -tol'ling], to praise highly; laud.—*n.* **ex-tol'ler.**—*n.* **ex-tol'ment; ex-toll'ment.**

ex-tort (ĕks-tôrt'), *v.t.* to obtain wrongfully; exact.—*n.* **ex-tort'er.**

ex-tor-tion (ĕks-tôr'shŭn), *n.* 1, the act of obtaining by force or threat; 2, unjust exaction, as of excessive interest; 3, that which has been exacted unlawfully.

ex-tor-tion-ate (ĕks-tôr'shŭn-āt), *adj.* oppressive; excessive; unjust; as, *extortionate* prices, taxes, or demands.—*adv.* **ex-tor'tion-ate-ly.**

ex-tor-tion-er (ĕks-tôr'shŭn-ĕr), *n.* one who demands more than is just or obtains it by unjust means.—*n.* **ex-tor'tion-ist.**

ex-tra (ĕks'trȧ), *adj.* 1, over and above what is ordinary or required; more than usual; 2, unusually good; better than usual:—*n.* something in addition to what is usual, as a copy of a newspaper issued in addition to the regular edition:—*adv.* exceptionally; as, *extra* fine silk.

ex-tra- (ĕks'trȧ-), *prefix,* used freely, with Lat. stems, meaning beyond; outside of; besides; as, *extra*judicial, beyond the jurisdiction of a court.

ex-tract (ĕks-trăkt'), *v.t.* 1, to obtain from a substance by some process; as, to *extract* perfume from flowers; 2, to pull out; as, to *extract* a tooth, 3, to get by effort; as, to *extract* money from a miser; 4, to select; as, to *extract* a passage from a book; 5, in mathematics, to calculate, as the root of a number:—*n.* (ĕks'trăkt), 1, that which has been obtained by some process; as, *extract* of beef; 2, a quotation.—*adj.* **ex-tract'a-ble.**

ex-trac-tion (ĕks-trăk'shŭn), *n.* 1, the act of drawing or taking out; 2, lineage; birth or descent.

ex-trac-tor (ĕks-trăk'tĕr), *n.* one who or that which takes out.

ex-tra-di-ta-ble (ĕks″trȧ-dī'tȧ-bl), *adj.* 1, liable to surrender to another authority; 2, making liable to such surrender; as, an *extraditable* offense.

ex-tra-dite (ĕks'trȧ-dīt), *v.t.* [*p.t.* and *p.p.* -dit″ed, *p.pr.* -dit″ing], 1, to surrender, as one accused of crime, to another country or state in which the crime was committed; 2, to secure such a surrender.

ex-tra-di-tion (ĕks″trȧ-dĭsh'ŭn), *n.* the surrender by a state of a person accused of a crime in another state.

ex-tra-dos (ĕks-trā'dŏs), *n.* the outer curve of an arch: opp. of *intrados.*

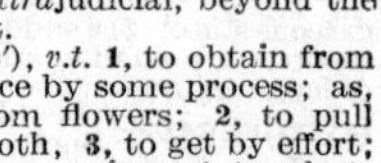

Extrados
A, extrados; B, intrados.

ex-tra-ne-ous (ĕks-trā'nē-ŭs), external; not essential.—*adv.* **ex-tra'ne-ous-ly.**—*n.* **ex-tra'ne-ous-ness.**

ex-traor-di-na-ry (ĕks-trôr'dĭ-nā-rĭ; ĕks″trȧ-ôr'dĭ-nā-rĭ), *adj.* 1, beyond or out of the usual course; unusual; 2, remarkable; rare; 3, special, as an envoy.—*adv.* **ex-traor'di-na-ri-ly.**

ex-trav-a-gance (ĕks-trăv'ȧ-găns), *n.* 1, excess in anything, esp. in spending money; 2, waste; profusion.

ex-trav-a-gant (ĕks-trăv′ȧ-gănt), *adj.* 1, exceeding reasonable limits; 2, wasteful; needlessly lavish in spending money; 3, exorbitant, as prices; 4, visionary; as, *extravagant* ideas.—*adv.* **ex-trav′a-gant-ly.**
Syn. immoderate, profuse, excessive.

ex-trav-a-gan-za (ĕks-trăv″ȧ-găn′zȧ), *n.* 1, something out of the ordinary; 2, a stage burlesque; 3, an irregular piece of music; 4, a wild flight of language or feeling.

ex-treme (ĕks-trēm′), *adj.* 1, of the highest degree; as, *extreme* old age; 2, farthest away; 3, most severe or strict; as, *extreme* measures; 4, last; final; 5, excessive; 6, advanced; radical; as, *extreme* ideas:—*n.* 1, the extremity; the very end; 2, the utmost degree of anything; 3, excess; as, to go to *extremes;* 4, the first or the last term of a proportion.—*adv.* **ex-treme′ly.**

ex-trem-ist (ĕks-trēm′ĭst), *n.* a supporter of very new and surprising, or very severe, views or measures.

ex-trem-i-ty (ĕks-trĕm′ĭ-tĭ), *n.* [*pl.* extremities (-tĭz)], 1, the utmost point or degree; remotest part; 2, the utmost violence, vigor, or necessity; also, end of life; 3, in *pl.*, the hands and feet.

ex-tri-cate (ĕks′trĭ-kāt), *v.t.* [*p.t.* and *p.p.* -cat″ed, *p.pr.* -cat″ing], to free from difficulties or perplexity; disentangle.—*adj.* **ex′tri-ca-ble.**—*n.* **ex″tri-ca′tion.**
Syn. release, disengage, relieve.

ex-trin-sic (ĕks-trĭn′sĭk), *adj.* external; not belonging or necessary to a thing; foreign.—*adv.* **ex-trin′si-cal-ly.**
Syn. extraneous, unessential, outward.

ex-tro-vert (ĕks′trō-vûrt), *n.* in psychology, one whose attention is habitually directed toward his environment; hence, a practical person, whose acts, emotions, and mental processes are influenced by external conditions rather than by introspection: opp. of *introvert.*—*n.* **ex″tro-ver′sion.**

ex-trude (ĕks-trōōd′), *v.t.* [*p.t.* and *p.p.* -trud′ed, *p.pr.* -trud′ing], to thrust or push out; expel.—*n.* **ex-tru′sion.**

ex-u-ber-ance (ĕgz-ū′bẽr-ăns), *n.* 1, an overflowing supply; 2, an example of this.—*n.* **ex-u′ber-an-cy.**

ex-u-ber-ant (ĕgz-ū′bẽr-ănt), *adj.* 1, copious; abundant; 2, abounding in good spirits.—*adv.* **ex-u′ber-ant-ly.**

ex-ude (ĕks-ūd′; ĕgz-ūd′), *v.t.* [*p.t.* and *p.p.* -ud′ed, *p.pr.* -ud′ing], to discharge gradually, as through pores:—*v.i.* to flow out slowly.—*n.* **ex″u-da′tion.**

ex-ult (ĕg-zŭlt′), *v.i.* to rejoice exceedingly; triumph.—*adv.* **ex-ult′ing-ly.**

ex-ult-ant (ĕg-zŭl′tănt), *adj.* rejoicing exceedingly or triumphantly; as, the *exultant* victors.—*adv.* **ex-ult′ant-ly.**

ex-ul-ta-tion (ĕk″sŭl-tā′shŭn; ĕg″zŭl-tā′shŭn), *n.* high spirits over success of any kind; triumphant joy.

eye (ī), *n.* 1, the organ of vision; 2, sight; power of observation or of appreciation; as, an *eye* for beauty; 3, look; gaze; 4, watch; oversight; as, to keep an *eye* on someone; 5, estimation; judgment; as, in the *eye* of the world; 6, that which resembles an eye, as of a needle, target, etc.:—*v.t.* [*p.t.* and *p.p.* eyed (īd), *p.pr.* ey′ing or eye′ing], to watch closely; scrutinize.—*adj.* **eye′less.**

eye-ball (ī′bôl″), *n.* the globe or ball of the eye.

eye-brow (ī′brou″), *n.* the bony ridge and fold of skin above either eye; esp., the hair on it.

eye-glass (ī′glȧs″), *n.* 1, a lens for the eyes; a monocle; 2, the glass of a telescope or microscope nearest the eye; 3, in *pl.*, a pair of lenses for the eyes held on the nose by a spring.

eye-lash (ī′lăsh″), *n.* 1, the fringe of hair that grows on the edge of the eyelid; 2, one of the hairs of this fringe.

eye-let (ī′lĕt), *n.* 1, a small hole to receive a lace or cord; 2, a ring of metal to strengthen such a hole.

eye-lid (ī′lĭd″), *n.* the movable structure which covers over and closes the eye.

eye-piece (ī′pēs″), *n.* the lens or system of lenses nearest the eye in a telescope or other optical instrument.

eye-serv-ant (ī′sûr″vănt), *n.* one who does his duty only when watched.—*n.* **eye′serv″er.**—*n.* **eye′serv″ice.**

eye-sight (ī′sīt″), *n.* 1, ability to see; 2, range of vision.

eye-sore (ī′sōr″), *n.* anything that offends or is disagreeable to the sight.

eye-splice (ī′-splīs″), *n.* a splice made by bending back and splicing a rope's end in such a way as to make a loop or eye (see *knot, splice,* illus.).

eye-tooth (ī′tōōth″), *n.* [*pl.* eyeteeth (-tēth″)], one of the two canine teeth in the upper jaw.

eye-wit-ness (ī′wĭt″nĕs; ī″wĭt′nĕs), *n.* 1, one who has seen an act; 2, one who testifies to what he has seen.

ey-rie (ē′rĭ; ā′rĭ); *n.* the nest of a bird of prey, as an eagle or a hawk. Also, **ae′ry; ey′ry.** See **ae′rie,** *Pfd. S.*

E-ze-ki-el (ē-zē′kĭ-ĕl; ē-zēk′yĕl), *n.* 1, one of the great Hebrew prophets; 2, the Old Testament book containing his prophecies. Also, in the Douay Bible, **E-ze′chi-el.**—*abbr.* **Ezek.**

Ez-ra (ĕz′rȧ), *n.* 1, a Hebrew scribe and priest; 2, the Old Testament book which concerns his life and teachings. Also, in the Douay Bible, **Es′dras.**

F

fa (fä), *n.* the fourth in the series of syllables used in singing a diatonic scale.

Fa-bi-an (fā′bĭ-ăn), *adj.* practicing a policy of delay: from Fabius's defeat of Hannibal by delay rather than by open battle.

fa-ble (fā′bl), *n.* 1, a fictitious story, esp. one intended to teach a useful or moral truth, in which, usually, animals talk and act like human beings; 2, a myth or legend; 3, a fictitious statement; specif., a lie:—*v.i.* [*p.t.* and *p.p.* -bled (-bld), *p.pr.* -bling], to write or tell stories of one's own invention; lie:—*v.t.* to pretend; tell of falsely.

fab-ric (făb′rĭk), *n.* 1, a framework; 2, the workmanship or texture of anything; 3, a woven or knitted material.

fab-ri-cate (făb′rĭ-kāt), *v.t.* [*p.t.* and *p.p.* -cat″ed, *p.pr.* -cat″ing], 1, to construct; form by manufacture or art; 2, to invent, as a tale; 3, to build by assembling standardized parts to form a whole, as ships.—*n.* **fab″ri-ca′tion.**—*n.* **fab′ri-ca″tor.**
Syn. frame, concoct, devise.

fab-u-list (făb′ū-lĭst), *n.* 1, a writer of stories or fables; 2, a falsifier.

fab-u-lous (făb′ū-lŭs), *adj.* 1, incredible; hard to believe; 2, mythical.—*adv.* **fab′u-lous-ly.**—*n.* **fab′u-lous-ness.**
Syn. legendary, astonishing, fictitious.—*Ant.* real, true, exact.

fa-çade (fȧ-säd′), *n.* the front of a building; esp., the main front.

face (fās), *n.* **1**, the fore part of the head; countenance; **2**, the principal side or surface of anything, as of a building, clock, tool, type, etc.; front; **3**, the physical aspect of a country; **4**, the value of a bond, note, etc., as specified in the paper itself; **5**, appearance; expression; **6**, reputation; as, to save his *face;* **7**, impudence; boldness; as, she had the *face* to go, uninvited; **8**, any one of the plane surfaces of a solid: **face card**, in a pack of playing cards, a card representing a king, queen, or jack: **face plate**, a disk attached to the live center, or revolving spindle, of a lathe, to which the work is often fastened (see *lathe*, illus.):—*v.t.* [*p.t.* and *p.p.* faced (fāst), *p.pr.* fac′ing], **1**, to turn toward; confront; **2**, to stand, be placed, or be situated, opposite; **3**, to oppose with confidence or boldness; **4**, to cover with an additional surface; **5**, to line near the edge, as the hem of a skirt; **6**, to cause to turn, as in a particular direction:—*v.i.* to turn the face; stand or front in any given direction.

fac-et (făs′ĕt), *n.* a small surface or face; one of the small plane surfaces which are cut or ground upon a gem:—*v.t.* to cut or work small faces upon; as, to *facet* a diamond.

fa-ce-tious (fȧ-sē′shŭs), *adj.* humorous; jocular.—*adv.* **fa-ce′tious-ly.** —*n.* **fa-ce′tious-ness.**

Syn. pleasant, jocose, laughable, funny, witty.—*Ant.* serious, grave, earnest.

fa-cial (fā′shăl), *adj.* pertaining to the face:—*n.* a massage of the face.

fac-ile (făs′ĭl), *adj.* **1**, not hard to do; easily done; **2**, ready or quick in doing; fluent.—*adv.* **fac′ile-ly.**—*n.* **fac′ile-ness.**

fa-cil-i-tate (fȧ-sĭl′ĭ-tāt), *v.t.* [*p.t.* and *p.p.* -tat″ed, *p.pr.* -tat″ing], to make easy or less difficult.

fa-cil-i-ty (fȧ-sĭl′ĭ-tĭ), *n.* [*pl.* facilities (-tĭz)], **1**, ease, as in speech or performance; **2**, skill in performance; dexterity; **3**, usually in *pl.*, the means by which any act may be more easily done.

fac-ing (fās′ĭng), *n.* **1**, a covering in front for ornamental or other purposes; **2**, a lining near the edge of a garment for ornament or protection; **3**, in *pl.*, the collars, cuffs, etc., of different color from the coat on a military uniform.

fac-sim-i-le (făk-sĭm′ĭ-lē), *n.* an exact reproduction or copy.

Syn. (see duplicate).

fact (făkt), *n.* **1**, a deed; act; as, before the *fact;* **2**, anything that actually happens; **3**, actuality; as, a matter of *fact;* **4**, a statement certainly and strictly true.

Syn. truth, certainty.—*Ant.* falsehood.

fac-tion (făk′shŭn), *n.* **1**, a group of persons, as in a state, who are working for a special end; **2**, a party in disloyal opposition; **3**, dissension.—*adj.* **fac′tion-al.**

Syn. cabal, gang, combination, clique.

fac-tious (făk′shŭs), *adj.* **1**, given to, or characterized by, a tendency to oppose; **2**, quarrelsome.—*adv.* **fac′tious-ly.**

fac-ti-tious (făk-tĭsh′ŭs), *adj.* artificial; sham; not natural.—*adv.* **fac-ti′tious-ly.**—*n.* **fac-ti′tious-ness.**

fac-tor (făk′tẽr), *n.* **1**, an agent; one who transacts business for another; **2**, one of two quantities (multiplier and multiplicand), or more, which, multiplied together, give a product; **3**, any of the elements which produce a result:—*v.t.* to resolve into mathematical factors.—*n.* **fac′tor-age.**

fac-to-ry (făk′tō-rĭ), *n.* [*pl.* factories (-rĭz)], **1**, a place where goods are made; a manufactory; **2**, a trading station.

fac-to-tum (făk-tō′tŭm), *n.* a person employed for, or in charge of, many small jobs; a handy man.

fac-tu-al (făk′tū-ăl), *adj.* pertaining to, or containing, facts; as, *factual* selections alternate with imaginative in the book.

fac-ul-ty (făk′ŭl-tĭ), *n.* [*pl.* faculties (-tĭz)], **1**, the power to act, mentally or physically; **2**, a power of the mind, as the memory, imagination, etc.; **3**, knack; readiness; skill obtained by practice; **4**, the professors and instructors, collectively, of a university, college, or school, or, specifically, of a single department of instruction; as, the *faculty* of theology.

Syn. aptitude, gift, capacity, leaning.—*Ant.* incompetency, incapacity.

fad (făd), *n.* a pet idea or hobby; also, a passing fashion.—*n.* **fad′dist.**

fade (fād), *v.i.* [*p.t.* and *p.p.* fad′ed, *p.pr.* fad′ing], **1**, to lose color or distinctness; **2**, to wither; droop, as flowers; **3**, to grow pale or weak, as persons.—*adj.* **fade′less.**

fæ-ces (fē′sēz), *n.pl.* excrement. See **fe′ces**, *Pfd. S.*—*adj.* **fæ′cal** (fē′kăl).

fag (făg), *v.i.* [*p.t.* and *p.p.* fagged (făgd), *p.pr.* fag′ging], to work hard; drudge for another: used esp. in English schools:—*v.t.* **1**, to tire out or exhaust; **2**, *Colloq.*, in English schools, to compel (a schoolboy) to drudge for another:—*n.* **1**, *Colloq.*, in England, one who drudges for another, as a schoolboy for one in a higher class; **2**, fatigue or weariness; drudgery; **3**, *Slang*, a cigarette.—*n.* **fag′ger.**

Syn., *v.* jade, weary, fatigue.

fag–end (făg′=ĕnd′), *n.* **1**, the latter or meaner part of anything; **2**, a frayed end, as of a piece of cloth, rope, etc.

fag-ot (făg′ŭt), *n.* **1**, a bundle of sticks bound together; **2**, a bundle of wrought iron or steel to be worked over:—*v.t.* to form into fagots. Also, **fag′got.**

Fah-ren-heit (făr′ĕn-hīt; fä′rĕn-), *adj.* designating, or pertaining to, a thermometric scale introduced by G. D. Fahrenheit:—*n.* the Fahrenheit scale, having 32° as the freezing point, and 212° as the boiling point, of water.—*abbr.* **Fahr.; F.**

fail (fāl), *v.i.* **1**, to fall short; be lacking; as, he just *failed* of an honor; **2**, not to succeed; as, he *failed* in his purpose; **3**, to prove false, as a prophecy; **4**, to become bankrupt; **5**, to lose strength; as, his spirits *fail:*—*v.t.* **1**, to be wanting to or insufficient for; as, time *fails* me; **2**, to forsake; as, the wind *failed* us; **3**, to leave undone: used with infinitives; as, he *failed* to appear:—*n.* failure; as, without *fail.*

Syn., *v.* droop; miscarry, disappoint.

fail-ing (fāl′ĭng), *n.* a fault; weakness; imperfection.

faille (fȧy′; fāl), [Fr.], *n.* a soft, dull silk used for dresses or trimmings, having a light grain, without gloss.

fail-ure (fāl′ūr), *n.* **1**, the act of falling short or lacking; **2**, lack of success; **3**, a deficiency; **4**, neglect; omission; **5**, bankruptcy; **6**, a loss of vigor; **7**, an unsuccessful person, effort, etc.

fain (fān), *adv.* willingly; gladly; as, I would *fain* do your pleasure:—*adj.* **1**, glad; **2**, willing; **3**, constrained; as, she was *fain* to keep silence.

faint (fānt), *v.i.* **1**, to lose consciousness; **2**, to lose hope and vigor; **3**, to grow dim:—*n.* a swoon:—*adj.* **1**, about to swoon; **2**, feeble; inadequate; as, a *faint* idea; **3**, timid; as, a *faint* heart; **4**, depressed; gloomy; **5**, not bright or vivid in color; not loud or clear.—*n.* **faint′ness.**—*adv.* **faint′ly.**

Syn., *adj.* indistinct, pale, vague.

faint–heart-ed (fānt′=härt″ĕd; fānt″=härt′ĕd), *adj.* lacking courage or boldness; cowardly.

[1]**fair** (fâr), *adj.* **1**, pleasing to the sight; **2**, hence, female; as, the *fair* sex;

3, not dark in color or complexion; blond; 4, without blemish; spotless; clean; as, *fair* fame; 5, not cloudy; fine: said of the weather; 6, giving promise; favorable; 7, moderately satisfactory; pretty good; 8, not partial; just: 9, according to regulations: as, a *fair* victory; 10, subject to lawful pursuit; as, *fair* game; 11, distinct; unobstructed; clear:—*n. Poetic*, womankind: with *the*:—*adv.* 1, in a manner courteously pleasant or agreeable; as, he spoke me *fair*; 2, honestly; justly; 3, according to rules; as, to play *fair*; 4, directly; as, he was struck *fair* in the face.—*adv.* **fair′ly.**—*n.* **fair′ness.**

Syn., adj. desirable, comely; unprejudiced.

²fair (fâr), *n.* 1, a gathering at a fixed time and place, for the sale or exhibition of farm products, etc., and often accompanied by entertainment, races, etc.; 2, a sale of useful and fancy goods, as for charity.

fair green in golf, the closely cut grass between the tees and the putting greens; the fairway.

fair–spo-ken (fâr′=spō″kĕn), *adj.* 1, using graceful, polite speech; 2, plausible.

fair-way (fâr′wā″), *n.* 1, the part of a road or river which is open to traffic; 2, in golf, a broad lane in which the grass is kept short.

fair-y (fâr′ĭ), *n.* [*pl.* fairies (-ĭz)], an imaginary, usually tiny, being of human form, supposed to interfere in human affairs for good or evil; fay; sprite:—*adj.* pertaining to, or like, fairies. Also, **fa′ër-y; fa′ër-ie.**

fair-y-land (fâr′ĭ-lănd″), *n.* 1, the supposed abode of fairies; 2, an enchanting and pleasant place.

faith (fāth), *n.* 1, belief; 2, trust in the honesty and truth of another; specif., trust in God; 3, fidelity; honesty; as, a man of good *faith;* 4, a promise or pledge; as, to keep *faith;* 5, any organized system of belief, religious or political; a creed.

Syn. conviction, doctrine.

faith-ful (fāth′fo͝ol), *adj.* 1, believing; 2, loyal, as a friend; 3, trustworthy, as a servant; 4, true; accurate; as, a *faithful* account.—*adv.* **faith′ful-ly.**—*n.* **faith′ful-ness.**

Syn. upright, constant, dependable, devoted.—*Ant.* faithless, treacherous.

faith-less (fāth′lĕs), *adj.* 1, not having belief, esp. in religion; 2, false to promises or allegiance; 3, false to duty or service.—*adv.* **faith′less-ly.**—*n.* **faith′less-ness.**

Syn. treacherous, inconstant, shifting.—*Ant.* faithful, loyal, dependable, true.

¹fake (fāk), *n.* a coil or turn of a rope:—*v.t.* [*p.t.* and *p.p.* faked (fākt), *p.pr.* fak′ing], to fold or coil, as a rope.

²fake (fāk), *v.t.* [*p.t.* and *p.p.* faked (fākt,) *p.pr.* fak′ing], *Slang,* 1, to make (an article, act, etc.) appear different from what it really is; falsify; 2, to do, make, etc., under false appearances; as, to *fake* the part of a benevolent stranger:—*v.i. Slang,* to assume a deceptive appearance; cheat:—*n. Slang,* any person, thing, or scheme made to appear different from what it is; a deception.—*n. Slang,* **fak′er-y.**

FAKIR

fak-er (fāk′ẽr), *n.* 1, one who deceives; a swindler; 2, a street vender.

fa-kir (fȧ-kēr′; fā′kẽr), *n.* a Mohammedan religious beggar, often a wonder worker. Also, **fa-keer′.**

fal-chion (fôl′chŭn; fôl′shŭn), *n.* a short, curved sword, with wide blade.

fal-con (fô′kn; fôl′kn), *n.* any of several hunting, hawklike birds, esp., one trained by man for hunting.

fal-con-er (fô′kn-ẽr), *n.* one who trains, or hunts with, falcons.

fal-con-ry (fô′kn-rĭ), *n.* 1, the art of training falcons to pursue other birds; 2, the sport of such hunting.

fal-de-ral (făl′dē-răl″; fäl′dē-räl″), *n.* 1, mere nonsense; 2, a refrain used in old songs. Also, **fol′de-rol″.**

fall (fôl), *v.i.* [*p.t.* fell (fĕl), *p.p.* fall′en (fôl′n), *p.pr.* fall′ing], 1, to drop freely from a higher to a lower place; 2, to be dropped or uttered, as remarks; 3, to extend downward; depend; droop, as a cloak; 4, to drop to the ground from an erect position; collapse; 5, to be taken captive, as a besieged city; be deposed from power, as a ministry, a leader; 6, to die; perish; as, to *fall* in battle; 7, to depart from dignified or moral behavior; be degraded; sin; 8, to decrease; abate; diminish in value, as prices; 9, to show dejection: said of the countenance; 10, to enter suddenly into a new condition; begin; as, he *fell* to cursing; 11, to slope, as land; sink; flow; 12, to come by chance or by inheritance; as, this part *falls* to me; 13, to happen; befall; occur; 14, to pass gradually or passively into some state or condition; as, to *fall* in love: **fall out,** 1, to quarrel; 2, to happen:—*n.* 1, the act or result of dropping from a higher to a lower place; 2, something which has dropped or descended; as, a heavy *fall* of rain; 3, a dropping down or casting off, as of leaves; 4, autumn; 5, often in *pl.*, a cascade; 6, ruin; death; overthrow, as of a city, country, etc.; loss of power or position, as of a leader; 7, the distance through which anything drops; also, a difference of levels; 8, decrease in price, value, etc.; 9, spiritual downfall; 10, slope; descent, as of land; 11, the rope that is pulled in hoisting with a tackle; as, a block and *fall:* **fall of man,** the change from perfection in man, due to the sins of Adam and Eve.

Syn., v. subside, decline.—*Ant., v.* rise, soar.

fal-la-cious (fă-lā′shŭs), *adj.* deceptive; misleading.—*adv.* **fal-la′cious-ly.**—*n.* **fal-la′cious-ness.**

fal-la-cy (făl′ȧ-sĭ), *n.* [*pl.* fallacies (-sĭz)], 1, a deceptive or false appearance; 2, an unsound method of reasoning; 3, a mistaken idea.

fall-en (fôl′n), *p.adj.* dropped; degraded; dead; lessened; decreased.

fall-ing star a meteor: also called *shooting star.*

fal-li-ble (făl′ĭ-bl), *adj.* 1, liable to err or fail; 2, liable to be wrong or to be deceived.—*n.* **fal″li-bil′i-ty.**

¹fal-low (făl′ō), *n.* 1, unseeded plowed land; 2, untilled land:—*adj.* 1, plowed but not cultivated; 2, untilled; also, neglected:—*v.t.* to make or keep fallow.

²fal-low (făl′ō), *adj.* of a pale yellow or yellowish brown color.

fal-low deer a kind of deer of yellowish brown color, with branched and recurved horns.

false (fôls), *adj.* 1, untrue; 2, dishonest; disloyal; 3, not well founded; unreliable; 4, artificial; spurious; fictitious: **false acacia,** the common locust, a tall, deciduous tree with weak thorns.—*adv.* **false′ly.**—*n.* **false′ness.**

Syn., adj. faithless; counterfeit.—*Ant., adj.* true, loyal; correct, genuine.

false-hood (fôls′ho͝od), *n.* 1, an untruth; a lie; misstatement with intention to deceive; 2, an inaccuracy.

Syn. deception, misrepresentation. (See ¹lie.)

fal-set-to (fôl-sĕt'ō), *n.* [*pl.* falsettos (-ōz)], **1**, a forced, shrill voice higher than one's natural range, esp. of a man; **2**, one who sings with such a voice:—*adj.* of the quality of falsetto.

fal-si-fi-ca-tion (fôl″sĭ-fĭ-kā'shŭn), *n.* **1**, the act or process of making false a statement, record, or the like; **2**, a counterfeit; **3**, a lie; **4**, a proof of falsity.

fal-si-fy (fôl'sĭ-fī), *v.t.* [*p.t.* and *p.p.* -fied (-fīd), *p.pr.* -fy″ing], **1**, to make false, as a record; **2**, to disprove; prove to be false; **3**, to counterfeit; forge:—*v.i.* to lie.—*n.* **fal'si-fi″er.**—*adj.* **fal″si-fi'a-ble.**

fal-si-ty (fôl'sĭ-tĭ), *n.* [*pl.* falsities (-tĭz)], **1**, the quality of being untrue or untrustworthy; **2**, an untruth.

Fal-staff-i-an (fôl-stăf'ĭ-ăn), *adj.* like Falstaff, the fat knight in Shakespeare's "Henry IV" and "Merry Wives of Windsor"; hence, boasting; coarsely or impudently jovial, etc.

fal-ter (fôl'tẽr), *v.t.* to utter in a weak, trembling manner:—*v.i.* **1**, to show moral or physical hesitancy; waver; tremble; **2**, to fail in utterance; stammer; as, his speech *falters.*—*adv.* **fal'ter-ing-ly.**

fame (fām), *n.* **1**, public report; rumor; **2**, celebrity; renown.—*adj.* **famed.**

Syn. reputation, honor, glory, notoriety.

fa-mil-iar (fȧ-mĭl'yȧr), *adj.* **1**, well acquainted, or intimate, with: of persons; **2**, well known: of things; **3**, taking liberties; as, he was too *familiar;* **4**, bold; impertinent:—*n.* **1**, an intimate friend; **2**, a spirit attending upon a wizard or a person: often called *familiar spirit.*—*adv.* **fa-mil'iar-ly.**

fa-mil-i-ar-i-ty (fȧ-mĭl″ĭ-ăr'ĭ-tĭ; fȧ-mĭl-yăr'ĭ-tĭ), *n.* [*pl.* familiarities (-tĭz)], **1**, intimacy; **2**, ease of conversation; **3**, freedom from ceremony or conventionality; liberty or freedom.

fa-mil-iar-ize (fȧ-mĭl'yȧr-īz), *v.t.* [*p.t.* and *p.p.* -ized (-īzd), *p.pr.* -iz″ing], **1**, to make well acquainted; as, he *familiarized* himself with every quarter of the city; **2**, to make well known.

fam-i-ly (făm'ĭ-lĭ), *n.* [*pl.* families (-lĭz)], **1**, a group of people made up of parents and their children; **2**, a group of persons under one roof; a household; **3**, a body of persons descended from a common ancestor; tribe; race; clan; **4**, noble lineage; **5**, a group of things with some common characteristics; **6**, in biology, a classification of plants or animals, larger than a genus but smaller than an order: **family marriage,** a marriage of which one or more children are born.

fam-ine (făm'ĭn), *n.* **1**, extreme scarcity of food; **2**, extreme dearth of some specified article; **3**, great hunger; starvation.

fam-ish (făm'ĭsh), *v.t.* and *v.i.* to starve; as, he was *famished.*

fa-mous (fā'mŭs), *adj.* renowned; celebrated.—*adv.* **fa'mous-ly.**

Syn. illustrious, eminent. (See notorious.)—*Ant.* unknown, obscure, infamous.

Electric Fan

¹fan (făn), *n.* **1**, an object with a handle, intended to cool the face by stirring the air; **2**, any instrument designed to exicte a current of air; **3**, anything like a fan in shape:—*v.t.* [*p.t.* and *p.p.* fanned (fănd), *p.pr.* fan'ning], **1**, to winnow, or separate, as chaff from grain; **2**, to drive a current of air upon; cool the face of; kindle (a flame); **3**, to rouse; excite; fire with passion; **4**, *Slang,* in baseball, to strike out: used of a pitcher:—*v.i.* **1**, to winnow; **2**, to wield a fan for the purpose of cooling the face, etc.; **3**, *Slang,* in baseball, to strike out.

²fan (făn), *n. Colloq.,* an enthusiast about a given sport, as baseball.

fa-nat-ic (fȧ-năt'ĭk), *n.* one who is wildly extravagant in his views, esp. on religious subjects:—*adj.* characterized by wild enthusiasm. Also, *adj.* **fa-nat'i-cal.**

fa-nat-i-cism (fȧ-năt'ĭ-sĭzm), *n.* extravagant or frenzied zeal, esp. on religious subjects; wild enthusiasm.

fan-cied (făn'sĭd), *p.adj.* imaginary; existing merely in the mind.

fan-ci-er (făn'sĭ-ẽr), *n.* one who breeds or sells animals or birds.

fan-ci-ful (făn'sĭ-fo͝ol), *adj.* **1**, led by imagination; unreal; **2**, whimsical; wild; as, *fanciful* ideas; **3**, curiously decorated or built.—*adv.* **fan'ci-ful-ly.**

Syn. fantastic, imaginative, visionary.

fan-cy (făn'sĭ), *v.t.* [*p.t.* and *p.p.* -cied (-sĭd), *p.pr.* -cy-ing], **1**, to imagine; **2**, to take a liking to; **3**, to suppose; guess:—*v.i.* to imagine something without proof or grounds for so doing; suppose:—*adj.* [*comp.* fan'ci-er, *superl.* fan'ci-est], **1**, ornamental; not plain; **2**, based on imagination; **3**, fantastic; capricious; **4**, above actual worth; as, a *fancy* price:—*n.* [*pl.* fancies (-sĭz)], **1**, imagination, esp. as applied to light matters; **2**, a fantastic notion; whim; delusion; **3**, liking, as for a person; **4**, a fad; hobby.

fan-cy–free (făn'sĭ-frē'), *adj.* **1**, not in love; **2**, free from care.

fan-dan-go (făn-dăng'gō), *n.* [*pl.* fandangos (-gōz)], **1**, a lively Spanish dance; **2**, a lively ball.

fane (fān), *n. Poetic,* a temple or church; a sanctuary.

fan-fare (făn'fâr″), *n.* **1**, a flourish of trumpets; **2**, noisy, showy parade.

fan-fa-ron-ade (făn″fȧ-rŏn-ād'), *n.* blustering talk or swagger.

fang (făng), *n.* **1**, the lower part of a tooth set in the socket; **2**, any long, sharp tooth, as a poison tooth of a serpent; **3**, a pointed tusk, claw, or talon.—*adj.* **fanged.**

fan-tail (făn'tāl″), *n.* a kind of pigeon having tail feathers spread out like a fan.—*adj.* **fan'–tailed″.**

fan–tan (făn'-tăn″), *n.* **1**, a Chinese gambling game played with coins or similar objects; **2**, a game with playing cards.

fan-ta-si-a (făn″tȧ-zē'ȧ; făn-tä'zĭ-ȧ), *n.* in music, a composition not restricted by the usual laws of form.

fan-tas-tic (făn-tăs'tĭk), *adj.* **1**, odd; whimsical; **2**, imaginary. Also, **fan-tas'ti-cal.**—*adv.* **fan-tas'ti-cal-ly.**

Syn. strange, absurd, fanciful.

fan-ta-sy (făn'tȧ-sĭ), *n.* [*pl.* fantasies (-sĭz)], **1**, the faculty of making mental images, esp. fanciful ones; **2**, the mental image so produced; **3**, a whimsical contrivance or notion; **4**, a work of literature showing extravagant fancy; **5**, in music, a fanciful composition; a fantasia; **6**, in psychology, mental imagery, usually pleasant, and sometimes recurring. Also, **phan'ta-sy.**

far (fär), *adj.* [*comp.* far'ther, *superl.* far'thest], **1**, situated remotely in time or space; as, a *far* country; **2**, more distant of two; as, the *far* end of the room; **3**, reaching to great distances; as, a *far* journey:—*adv.* **1**, at a distance more or less remote; **2**, to or from a great distance, position, or time; **3**, to a great extent; very much.

far–a-way (fär′=ȧ-wā″), *adj.* **1**, dreamy; absent-minded; as, a *far-away* look; **2**, remote.

farce (färs), *n.* **1**, a short comedy in which qualities and actions are much exaggerated; **2**, ridiculous or empty parade.

far-ci-cal (fär′sĭ-kăl), *adj.* pertaining to, or of the nature of, a ridiculous comedy; hence, ludicrous.—*adv.* **far′ci-cal-ly.**

fare (fâr), *v.i.* [*p.t.* and *p.p.* fared (fârd), *p.pr.* far′ing], **1**, to be in any state, either good or ill; as, how *fares* it? **2**, to journey; **3**, to happen; work out; **4**, to be entertained with food and drink:—*n.* **1**, the sum paid for a journey; **2**, a person conveyed for hire in a vehicle; **3**, food.

fare-well (fâr″wĕl′; fâr′wĕl″), *interj.* may you fare well or prosper; good-by:—*adj.* accompanying a parting:—*n.* an adieu; the act of departing.

far–fetched (fär′=fĕcht″; fär″=fĕcht′), *adj.* unnatural; unlikely; forced; as, a *far-fetched* story.

fa-ri-na (fȧ-rī′nȧ; fȧ-rē′nȧ), *n.* **1**, flour or meal obtained from the seeds of cereals, nuts, etc.; **2**, starch.

far-i-na-ceous (făr″ĭ-nā′shŭs), *adj.* **1**, consisting of, made from, or producing, flour or meal; **2**, like meal.

farm (färm), *n.* **1**, a single holding of tillable land with the buildings belonging to it; **2**, any other area for breeding or growing anything; as, a peach *farm*, an oyster *farm*: **farm club**, in sports, a team subsidized by a major league club to develop players:—*v.t.* to cultivate (land):—*v.i.* to operate a farm.—*n.* **farm′ing.**

farm-er (fär′mẽr), *n.* **1**, one who cultivates a portion of land; an agriculturist; **2**, one who collects revenues, taxes, etc., for a certain commission or rate.

farm-house (färm′hous″), *n.* the main dwelling house on a farm.

far-o (fâr′ō; fā′rō), *n.* a certain game at cards, popular in gambling resorts.

far-ra-go (fă-rā′gō), *n.* a medley; as, his tale was a *farrago* of nonsense.

far-ri-er (făr′ĭ-ẽr), *n.* **1**, one who shoes horses; **2**, a noncommissioned cavalry officer in charge of the horses.

far-ri-er-y (făr′ĭ-ẽr-ĭ), *n.* [*pl.* farrieries (-ĭz)], **1**, the art or business of a horseshoer; **2**, the shop of a horseshoer.

1far-row (făr′ō), *v.i.* and *v.t.* to give birth to (pigs):—*n.* a litter of pigs.

2far-row (făr′ō), *adj.* bearing no calf in a given year: said of a cow.

far-see-ing (fär′sē″ĭng; fär″sē′ĭng), *adj.* seeing far; having foresight.

far-sight-ed (fär′sīt″ĕd), *adj.* **1**, able to look ahead; of keen judgment; **2**, able to see distant objects most distinctly.—*n.* **far″sight′ed-ness.**

far-ther (fär′*th*ẽr), *adj.* comparative of *far:* **1**, more distant; **2**, additional:—*adv.* **1**, more remotely; **2**, moreover.

Syn. further. *Farther* is commonly restricted, esp. in American usage, to distance in space; as, I can go no *farther*. *Further* commonly refers to time, quantity, or degree; as, the trial cannot be *further* continued; a *further* rise in the barometer.

far-ther-most (fär′*th*ẽr-mōst), *adj.* most distant; farthest.

far-thest (fär′*th*ĕst), *adj.* superlative of *far:* most distant; most remote:—*adv.* to or at the greatest distance.

far-thing (fär′*th*ĭng), *n.* in Great Britain, a coin equal to one fourth of a penny: the smallest English coin.

far-thin-gale (fär′*th*ĭng-gāl), *n.* a hoop skirt formed of circles of whalebone, worn by women of the 16th and 17th centuries.

fas-ces (făs′ēz), *n.pl.* a bundle of rods containing an ax, carried before the magistrates of ancient Rome as a symbol of authority.—*adj.* **fas′ci-al.**

FASCES

fas-ci-cle (făs′ĭ-kl), *n.* a small bunch or bundle; a division of a printed work published in parts.—*adj.* **fas-cic′u-lar.**

fas-ci-nate (făs′ĭ-nāt), *v.t.* [*p.t.* and *p.p.* -nat″ed, *p.pr.* -nat″ing], **1**, to influence, as if by enchantment; charm; **2**, to allure; captivate; as, the subject *fascinates* him:—*v.i.* to exercise a captivating power.—*adv.* **fas′ci-nat″ing-ly.**—*n.* **fas′ci-na″tor.**

Syn. enrapture, bewitch, enchant, delight.

fas-ci-na-tion (făs″ĭ-nā′shŭn), *n.* **1**, the act of bewitching; **2**, the state of being bewitched; **3**, any invisible influence that overpowers the mind or will; **4**, attractiveness; charm.

fas-cine (fă-sēn′), *n.* a bundle of sticks bound together, used in building earthworks, dams, jetties, etc.

fas-cism (făsh′ĭzm), *n.* a strongly nationalistic political and economic movement, magnifying the rights of the state over those of the individual, in which both industry, though remaining largely under private ownership, and all administrative political units, are controlled by a strong central government.—*n.* and *adj.* **fas′cist.**

fash-ion (făsh′ŭn), *n.* **1**, the shape or form of anything; **2**, custom or usage, esp. in dress; **3**, the following of the rules of good society; method; general practice:—*v.t.* to mold, shape, or form.—*n.* **fash′ion-er.**

Syn., *n.* style, vogue. (See mode.)

fash-ion-a-ble (făsh′ŭn-ȧ-bl), *adj.* **1**, according to the prevailing mode; **2**, pertaining to polite society.—*adv.* **fash′ion-a-bly.**—*n.* **fash′ion-a-ble-ness.**

1fast (fȧst), *adj.* **1**, securely fixed; attached; stable; **2**, constant; faithful, as friends; **3**, profound, as sleep; **4**, not fading, as colors; **5**, rapid; able to move swiftly; **6**, more advanced than standard: said of timepieces; **7**, conducive to fast travel; as, a *fast* course; **8**, dissipated; as, *fast* society:—*adv.* **1**, fixedly; firmly; **2**, rapidly; **3**, dissipatedly; **4**, soundly; deeply; as, *fast* asleep.

Syn., *adj.* speedy, fleet, hurried, swift, brisk; lasting, secure. (See hasty.)—*Ant.*, *adj.* slow; movable, insecure.

2fast (fȧst), *v.i.* to take no food or take food sparingly, either from necessity or desire, or as a religious rite:—*n.* **1**, the doing without food as a religious duty; **2**, a period of going without food: **fast day**, a day set apart by civil or church authority for doing without food, or certain kinds of food, as a devotional rite.—*n.* **fast′ing.**

fas-ten (fȧs′n), *v.t.* **1**, to fix securely; make firm; bolt or bar; **2**, to keep fixed steadily, as the attention; **3**, to attach, as blame:—*v.i.* **1**, to take hold; **2**, to become attached.—*n.* **fas′ten-er.**

fas-ten-ing (fȧs′n-ĭng), *n.* **1**, the act of making secure; **2**, a bolt or clasp.

fas-tid-i-ous (făs-tĭd′ĭ-ŭs), *adj.* hard to please; finicking.—*adv.* **fas-tid′i-ous-ly.**—*n.* **fas-tid′i-ous-ness.**

fast-ness (fȧst′nĕs), *n.* **1**, the quality of being fast; **2**, a stronghold.

fat (făt), *adj.* [*comp.* fat′ter, *superl.* fat′test], **1**, plump; fleshy; **2**, greasy; **3**, unusually thick; broad; **4**, stupid; dull; **5**, prosperous; **6**, profitable, as a business; **7**, fertile, as land:—*n.* **1**, a semisolid, oily, yellow or white substance forming part of the tissue of animals; **2**, the best or richest of anything:—*v.t.* [*p.t.* and *p.p.* fat'ted, *p.pr.* fat'ting], to cause to gain flesh:—*v.i.* to become fleshy.

fa-tal (fā'tăl), *adj.* **1**, causing death or destruction; as, a *fatal* accident; **2**, fixed by fate; as, the *fatal* day.—*adv.* **fa'tal-ly.**
Syn. (see deadly).

fa-tal-ism (fā'tăl-ĭzm), *n.* **1**, the doctrine that all things are predetermined by fate and therefore happen regardless of one's efforts; **2**, submission to events as unavoidable.—*n.* **fa'tal-ist.**—*adj.* **fa″tal-is'tic.**

fa-tal-i-ty (fȧ-tăl'ĭ-tĭ), *n.* [*pl.* fatalities (-tĭz)], **1**, predetermined order or series of events; destiny; **2**, a calamity; an event involving death; **3**, tendency to peril; **4**, fatal power or influence.

***Fa-ta Mor-ga-na** (fä'tä môr-gä'nä), [It.], a medieval fairy, sister of King Arthur: ***fata morgana, 1**, a mirage sometimes seen near the straits of Messina, formerly ascribed to Morgana's power; **2**, figuratively, a fantastic conception.

fate (fāt), *n.* **1**, the power that determines events; destiny; **2**, one's predestined lot; **3**, the unalterable future: **the Fates**, in mythology, the three classic goddesses, Clotho, Lachesis, and Atropos, who were supposed to preside over the destinies of mankind.

fat-ed (fāt'ĕd), *adj.* decreed by fate; destined; doomed.

fate-ful (fāt'fo͝ol), *adj.* **1**, possessing fatal power or the power to kill; **2**, momentous; significant; **3**, prophetic.—*adv.* **fate'ful-ly.**—*n.* **fate'ful-ness.**

fa-ther (fä'*th*ẽr), *n.* **1**, a male parent or ancestor; **2**, one who stands in the relation of a father; **3**, an originator or founder; **4**, the official title of a dignitary, priest, or confessor of the Roman Catholic Church; **5**, an aged and reverend man or clergyman; **6**, any religious writer of the early Christian church: **Father**, or **the Father**, God, the Deity:—*v.t.* **1**, to beget or adopt, as a child; **2**, to assume authorship of or accept responsibility for; as, to *father* a bill in Congress.—*n.* **fa'ther-hood.**—*adj.* **fa'ther-less.**

fa-ther-in-law (fä'*th*ẽr-ĭn-lô″), *n.* [*pl.* fathers-in-law (fä'*th*ẽrz-)], the father of one's husband or wife.

fa-ther-land (fä'*th*ẽr-lănd″), *n.* one's native country.

fa-ther-ly (fä'*th*ẽr-lĭ), *adj.* kind and affectionate, like a father.—*n.* **fa'ther-li-ness.**

fath-om (făth'ŭm), *n.* a measure of length equal to six feet: used of the depth of water:—*v.t.* **1**, to measure by sounding; find the depth of; **2**, to get to the bottom of; comprehend; as, to *fathom* his meaning.—*adj.* **fath'om-a-ble.**

fath-om-less (făth'ŭm-lĕs), *adj.* **1**, so deep that it cannot be sounded; **2**, not possible to understand; as, a *fathomless* mystery.

fa-tigue (fȧ-tēg'), *n.* **1**, weariness resulting from labor; bodily or mental exhaustion; **2**, in mechanics, weakness resulting from age, strain, etc., as in metals: **fatigue duty**, the labor a soldier performs apart from the practice of arms:—*v.t.* [*p.t.* and *p.p.* -tigued' (-tēgd'), *p.pr.* -ti'guing (-tē'gĭng)], **1**, to weary with bodily or mental effort; tire; harass; **2**, in mechanics, to cause a condition of fatigue in (a metal, material, etc.).
Syn., *n.* lassitude, tiredness.—*Ant.*, *n.* freshness, strength, energy.

Fat-i-ma (făt'ĭ-mȧ; fä'tē-mä), *n.* **1**, in the "Arabian Nights," a certain woman magician; also, a queen of China; **2**, Bluebeard's last wife.

fat-ling (făt'lĭng), *n.* a young animal fattened for slaughter.

fat-ness (făt'nĕs), *n.* **1**, the quality or state of being stout; **2**, fertility or fruitfulness, as of soil.

fat-ten (făt'n), *v.t.* **1**, to make fat, or feed, for slaughter; **2**, to make fertile:—*v.i.* to grow plump.—*n.* **fat'ten-er.**

fat-ty (făt'ĭ), *adj.* [*comp.* fat'ti-er, *superl.* fat'ti-est], **1**, consisting largely of fat; **2**, greasy; oily.—*n.* **fat'ti-ness.**

fa-tu-i-ty (fȧ-tū'ĭ-tĭ), *n.* [*pl.* fatuities (-tĭz)], **1**, weakness of intellect; **2**, stupidity; **3**, unconscious and silly dulness.

fat-u-ous (făt'ū-ŭs), *adj.* weak in intellect; vain and silly.—*adv.* **fat'u-ous-ly.**—*n.* **fat'u-ous-ness.**

***fau-bourg** (fō″bo͞or'; fō'bo͞org), [Fr.], *n.* **1**, a suburb; **2**, a section of a city which originally was outside the city, as some parts of Paris.

fau-ces (fô'sēz), *n.pl.* the passage from the pharynx to the mouth, between the root of the tongue and the soft palate.—*adj.* **fau'cal** (-kăl).—*adj.* **fau'cial** (-shăl).

fau-cet (fô'sĕt), *n.* a device at the end of a pipe, for drawing liquids.

faugh (fô), *interj.* usually denoting contempt or disgust.

fault (fôlt), *n.* **1**, a slight offense; **2**, blemish; defect in character; **3**, the loss of scent by a hunting dog; **4**, a defective point in an electric circuit; **5**, an improper service in lawn tennis; **6**, in geology, a sliding displacement of rock structure along a fracture:—*v.t.* in geology, to produce a fracture in (rock) by a sliding displacement.
Syn., *n.* error, weakness, flaw, failing.

fault-find-er (fôlt'fīn″dẽr), *n.* **1**, a person who is always criticizing the acts of others; **2**, a mechanical device for locating faults in an electric current.

fault-less (fôlt'lĕs), *adj.* without imperfection or blemish; blameless.—*adv.* **fault'less-ly.**—*n.* **fault'less-ness.**

fault-y (fôl'tĭ), *adj.* [*comp.* fault'i-er, *superl.* fault'i-est], **1**, imperfect; defective; **2**, marked by faults of conduct.—*adv.* **fault'i-ly.**—*n.* **fault'i-ness.**

faun (fôn), *n.* a classic woodland deity or god, represented in human form, but with pointed ears, small horns, and a tail.

fau-na (fô'nȧ), *n.* [*pl.* faunas (-nȧz); faunæ (-nē)], the animals belonging to any particular region, or period of history.—*adj.* **fau'nal.**

FAUN

Faust (foust), *n.* the hero of various literary works, based on legends concerning a certain Doctor Faustus, a German magician of the 16th century, who sells his soul to the devil in return for worldly pleasures.

***faux pas** (fō″ pä'), [Fr.], [*pl.* faux pas (fō″ pä')], an error or slip, esp. in respect to good manners or propriety.

fa-vor (fā'vẽr), *n.* **1**, an act of kindness; patronage; **2**, approving regard; **3**, partiality; bias; as, he asked no *favor;* **4**, a small present, as at a party; also, a love token; a bunch of ribbons worn on some special occasion; **5**, *Archaic*, appearance, countenance; looks:—*v.t.* **1**, to regard with good will; approve; **2**, to show partiality to; **3**, to resemble (a person) in appearance; as, she *favors* her mother; **4**, to bear out; support, as an argument; **5**, to oblige; as, *favor* me with your attention. Also, **fa'vour.**—*n.* **fa'vor-er.**

fa-vor-a-ble (fā′vẽr-ȧ-bl), *adj.* convenient; advantageous; friendly; partial. Also, **fa′vour-a-ble.**—*adv.* **fa′vor-a-bly.**—*n.* **fa′vor-a-ble-ness.**

fa-vored (fā′vẽrd), *p.adj.* **1,** treated with partiality; **2,** having a special aspect; as, hard-*favored.* Also, **fa′voured.**

fa-vor-ite (fā′vẽr-ĭt), *n.* **1,** one who or that which is particularly esteemed; **2,** a person or animal considered to have the best chance of winning in a contest:—*adj.* preferred; esteemed. Also, **fa′vour-ite.**

fa-vor-it-ism (fā′vẽr-ĭt-ĭzm), *n.* the tendency to treat one person or class well in preference to others having equal claims; partiality. Also, **fa′vour-it-ism.**

¹fawn (fôn), *n.* a deer less than one year old:—*adj.* of a light, yellowish brown.

²fawn (fôn), *v.i.* **1,** to show pleasure or affection by crouching or cringing, as a dog; **2,** to flatter someone meanly; cringe: with *on* or *upon.*—*n.* **fawn′er.**
Syn. stoop, creep, grovel.

¹FAWN ($\frac{1}{40}$)

fay (fā), *n.* an elf; a fairy; an imaginary tiny being of human form.

faze (fāz), *v.t.* [*p.t.* and *p.p.* fazed (fāzd), *p.pr.* faz′ing], *Colloq.*, to worry; annoy; frighten; disturb. Also, **feaze; feeze.**

fe-al-ty (fē′ăl-tĭ), *n.* **1,** in the feudal period, the pledge of fidelity of vassal or tenant to his superior; **2,** loyalty; faithfulness.

fear (fēr), *n.* **1,** expectation of evil or danger; dread; anxiety; solicitude; **2,** reverence; as, the *fear* of God:—*v.t.* **1,** to regard with apprehension; dread; **2,** to revere:—*v.i.* to be in dread of something; feel anxiety.
Syn., n. timidity, timorousness. (See horror.)—*Ant., n.* boldness, courage, bravery.

fear-ful (fēr′fo͝ol), *adj.* **1,** affected with dread or anxiety; timorous; **2,** inspiring dread; **3,** filled with awe and reverence.—*adv.* **fear′ful-ly.**—*n.* **fear′ful-ness.**
Syn. shocking, terrible, frightful.

fear-less (fēr′lĕs), *adj.* without fear; bold; courageous; as, *fearless* explorers have discovered the north pole.—*adv.* **fear′less-ly.**—*n.* **fear′less-ness.**
Syn. brave, daring, valorous.

fear-some (fēr′sŭm), *adj.* dreadful; terrible; as, a *fearsome* journey.

fea-si-bil-i-ty (fē″zĭ-bĭl′ĭ-tĭ), *n.* practicability, as of a plan.

fea-si-ble (fē′zĭ-bl), *adj.* practicable; capable of being carried out; as, the plan that you suggest is not *feasible.*—*adv.* **fea′si-bly.**—*n.* **fea′si-ble-ness.**

feast (fēst), *n.* **1,** a costly repast, esp. in commemoration of some event; **2,** a festival, esp. of a church; **3,** anything affording pleasure to the taste or mind:—*v.t.* **1,** to entertain sumptuously; **2,** to delight:—*v.i.* to eat a sumptuous repast.
Syn., n. banquet, celebration, repast.

feat (fēt), *n.* **1,** a notable achievement; deed of valor; **2,** a difficult or striking act displaying courage, strength, skill, or cunning; as, a *feat* of juggling.
Syn. act, exploit, accomplishment.

feath-er (fĕth′ẽr), *n.* **1,** any of the light outgrowths from the skin that form the outer covering of a bird; a plume; **2,** kind or class; as, birds of a *feather;* **3,** something like a feather; esp., in mechanics, a flange for stiffening a casting, or a key such as fits into a keyway:—*v.t.* **1,** to ornament with feathers; **2,** to cover with, or as with, feathers; **3,** to turn the blade of (an oar) horizontally when leaving the water:—*v.i.* to become covered with feathers.—*p.adj.* **feath′ered.**

feath-er-brain (fĕth′ẽr-brān″), *n.* a giddy, silly, or weak-minded person.—*adj.* **feath′er-brained″.**

feath-er-weight (fĕth′ẽr-wāt″), *n.* **1,** in a handicap, the least weight that can be put on a race horse; **2,** any very light weight; an insignificant thing; esp., a person of very little importance.

feath-er-y (fĕth′ẽr-ĭ), *adj.* **1,** covered with, or as with, feathers; **2,** pertaining to feathers.—*n.* **feath′er-i-ness.**

fea-ture (fē′tūr), *n.* **1,** a striking attribute; a trait that arouses interest; **2,** a prominent element or item, as of a game or performance; **3,** any part of the face, such as the eyes, nose, chin, etc.; **4,** in *pl.*, the face:—*v.t.* [*p.t.* and *p.p.* -tured (-tūrd), *p.pr.* -turing], **1,** to picture; **2,** to give prominence to; as, to *feature* a story.—*p.adj.* **fea′tured.**
Syn., n. trait, mark. (See characteristic.)

fea-ture-less (fē′tūr-lĕs), *adj.* having no marked characteristic or feature; lacking in distinction.

feaze (fēz; fāz), *v.t.* [*p.t.* and *p.p.* feazed (fēzd; fāzd), *p.pr.* feaz′ing], *Colloq.*, to disturb; disconcert. Also, **faze,** *Pfd. S.*

feb-ri-fuge (fĕb′rĭ-fūj), *n.* a medicine that lessens or dispels fever.

fe-brile (fē′brĭl; fĕb′rĭl), *adj.* characteristic of, or indicating, fever.

Feb-ru-a-ry (fĕb′ro͞o-ā-rĭ), *n.* the second month.—*abbr.* **Feb.**

fe-cal (fē′kăl), *adj.* relating to animal excrement, dregs, or refuse. Also, **fæ′cal.**

fe-ces (fē′sēz), *n.pl.* **1,** animal excrement; **2,** dregs; sediment. Also, **fæ′ces.**

feck-less (fĕk′lĕs), *adj.* weak; without spirit; worthless.

fec-und (fĕk′ŭnd; fē′kŭnd), *adj.* fruitful; fertile; as, the *fecund* earth.

fec-un-date (fĕk′ŭn-dāt), *v.t.* [*p.t.* and *p.p.* -dat″ed, *p.pr.* -dat″ing], to fertilize; impregnate.—*n.* **fec″un-da′tion.**

fe-cun-di-ty (fē-kŭn′dĭ-tĭ), *n.* **1,** fruitfulness; **2,** fertility of invention; power of creating.

fed (fĕd), past tense and past participle of the verb *feed.*

fed-er-al (fĕd′ẽr-ăl), *adj.* **1,** pertaining to, constituting, or founded upon, a league or treaty; **2,** consisting of a union or compact between states; **3,** pertaining to the government of such a union; as, a *federal* constitution: **Federal, 1,** favoring the establishment of a strong central government; **2,** supporting the Union in the American Civil War; as, the *Federal* army: **Federal Reserve Bank,** any one of twelve district banks established in the United States in 1913 to centralize and coördinate the banking system: **Federal,** *n.* a supporter of the Union cause during the American Civil War.

Fed-er-al-ist (fĕd′ẽr-ăl-ĭst), *n.* **1,** before and immediately after the adoption of the U. S. constitution, an advocate of a strongly centralized government; **2,** a supporter of the Union in the American Civil War: **federalist,** an advocate of the federal system of national organization.

fed-er-al-ize (fĕd′ẽr-ăl-īz), *v.t.* [*p.t.* and *p.p.* -ized (-īzd), *p.pr.* -iz″ing], to bring together in a political union:—*v.i.* to unite under a central government.—*n.* **fed″er-al-i-za′tion.**

fed-er-ate (fĕd′ẽr-āt), *adj.* united by compact:—*v.t.* (fĕd′ẽr-āt), [*p.t.* and *p.p.* -at″ed, *p.pr.* -at″ing], to combine into a union:—*v.i.* to come into a union.—*n.* **fed″er-a′tion.**—*adj.* **fed′er-a-tive.**

fee (fē), *n.* **1,** payment for service rendered, esp. professional service; as, the doctor's *fee;* **2**, an inherited estate; **3**, under the feudal system, land held from a superior: also called *fief; feoff; feod; feud;* **4**, a charge for admission or membership; as, a club *fee;* **5**, a legal charge for a special privilege; as, a license *fee;* **6**, a tip: **fee simple**, an estate held by a person in his own right, without restrictions:—*v.t.* [*p.t.* and *p.p.* feed (fēd), *p.pr.* fee′ing], to pay or give a fee to.

Syn., *n.* remuneration. (See salary.)

fee-ble (fē′bl), *adj.* **1**, weak; wanting in physical strength; infirm; **2**, lacking in power or vigor; as, a *feeble* excuse.—*adv.* **fee′bly.**—*n.* **fee′ble-ness.**

Syn. slight, frail, decrepit.

fee-ble–mind-ed (fē′bl=mīn″dĕd), *adj.* **1**, seriously subnormal in intelligence; mentally deficient or defective; **2**, lacking in firmness; irresolute; vacillating.—*n.* **fee″ble–mind′ed-ness.**—*adv.* **fee″ble–mind′ed-ly.**

feed (fēd), *v.t.*[*p.t.* and *p.p.* fed (fĕd), *p.pr.* feed′ing], **1**, to give food to; nourish; **2**, to give as food; as, to *feed* oats to horses; **3**, to supply with necessaries; **4**, to furnish with materials; as, to *feed* a machine; **5**, to satisfy; as, to *feed* the imagination:—*v.i.* **1**, to eat; **2**, to subsist: with *on* or *upon;* **3**, to graze or pasture; **4**, to be satisfied, as with food:—*n.* **1**, a certain quantity of food given to animals at one time; **2**, fodder; pasturage; **3**, the material furnished to a machine; **4**, the motion which carries this into the machine; **5**, the mechanism causing this motion.

feed bag a bag containing grain, fastened to the head of an animal.

feed-er (fēd′ẽr), *n.* **1**, one who or that which feeds; esp., a person or device supplying material to a machine; **2**, a plant or animal that takes nourishment; **3**, that which nourishes or supplies the needs of, or increases the importance or value of, as a branch railroad; **4**, an electric wire supplying a current from a central station to a secondary center.

feel (fēl), *v.t.* [*p.t.* and *p.p.* felt (fĕlt), *p.pr.* feel′ing], **1**, to perceive through the skin, as by touch; hence, to perceive in any other way than by sight, hearing, taste, or smell; as, to *feel* hunger; **2**, to examine by touching; **3**, to be moved by; as, to *feel* her distress; **4**, reflexively, to be conscious of (oneself) as being in a special condition; as, to *feel* oneself about to faint; **5**, to think; be convinced of:—*v.i.* **1**, to have perception by touch; **2**, to be conscious of being (in some special condition); as, to *feel* tired; hence, to consider oneself to be; as, to *feel* insulted; **3**, to be stirred emotionally; **4**, to seem; as, it *feels* heavy; **5**, to grope:—*n.* **1**, the sense of touch; **2**, a quality perceived by touch; as, the *feel* of silk.

feel-er (fēl′ẽr), *n.* **1**, one who or that which feels; **2**, that part of an animal which serves as an organ of touch, as the antennæ of insects, etc.; **3**, a remark designed to draw forth the views of others.

feel-ing (fēl′ĭng), *n.* **1**, any of the senses of the skin; **2**, the act or state of perceiving by touch; **3**, a sensation received otherwise than through sight, hearing, taste, or smell; as, a *feeling* of hunger; **4**, emotion; as, *feeling* ran high; **5**, a belief or conviction; **6**, an animating spirit, as of a poem; **7**, in *pl.*, sensitiveness.—*adv.* **feel′ing-ly.**

feet (fēt), *n.* plural of *foot;* as, he is six *feet* tall.—*abbr.* **ft.**

feeze (fēz; fāz), *v.t.* [*p.t.* and *p.p.* feezed (fēzd; fāzd), *p.pr.* feez′ing], *Colloq.*, to disconcert; frighten. Also, **faze,** *Pfd. S.*

feign (fān), *v.t.* and *v.i.* to pretend; simulate; as, to *feign* illness.—*n.* **feign′er.**

Syn. sham, assume, affect.

feint (fānt), *n.* **1**, a pretense; mock attack, as in boxing or fencing; **2**, stratagem:—*v.i.* to make a sham, offensive movement.

feld-spar (fĕld′spär″), *n.* any of a group of crystalline minerals found in many common rocks. Also, **fel′spar″.**

fe-lic-i-tate (fē-lĭs′ĭ-tāt), *v.t.* [*p.t.* and *p.p.* -tat″ed, *p.pr.* -tat″ing], to congratulate.—*n.* **fe-lic″i-ta′tion.**

fe-lic-i-tous (fē-lĭs′ĭ-tŭs), *adj.* apt; delightful; neat; as, a *felicitous* compliment.—*adv.* **fe-lic′i-tous-ly.**

fe-lic-i-ty (fē-lĭs′ĭ-tĭ), *n.* [*pl.* felicities (-tĭz)], **1**, supreme happiness; blissfulness; hence, prosperity; **2**, appropriateness; also, a neat or well-chosen expression.

Syn. bliss, enjoyment, contentment.

fe-line (fē′līn), *adj.* **1**, pertaining to, or like, a cat; **2**, stealthy; treacherous:—*n.* one of the cat family.

[1]**fell** (fĕl), past tense of the irregular verb *fall,* which see.

[2]**fell** (fĕl), *n.* in the north of England, a moor; down; a rocky or barren hill.

[3]**fell** (fĕl), *n.* an animal's skin or hide; a fleece; also, unkempt hair.

[4]**fell** (fĕl), *v.t.* **1**, to cause to fall, as trees by cutting, or a man by a blow; **2**, to fold over and sew down flat, as seams:—*n.* **1**, the timber cut in a season; **2**, a seam made by felling.—*n.* **fell′er.**

[5]**fell** (fĕl), *adj.* cruel; destructive; barbarous; powerful.—*n.* **fell′ness.**

fel-lah (fĕl′ȧ), *n.* [*pl.* fellahs (-ȧz); fellahin; fellaheen (fĕl″ȧ-hēn′)], in Egypt and Syria, a peasant or laboring man.

fel-loe (fĕl′ō), *n.* the curved wooden rim of a wheel. See **fel′ly,** *Pfd. S.*

fel-low (fĕl′ō), *n.* **1**, a companion or associate; **2**, one of the same kind; as, a *fellow* in misery; **3**, one of a pair; as, a *fellow* to a glove; **4**, an individual: used familiarly; as, a jovial *fellow;* **5**, a member of a society, esp. of a learned body; **6**, a graduate member of a college who holds a fellowship; **7**, a member of a governing body of a college:—*adj.* associated or joined with; as, *fellow* members: **fellow feeling,** likeness of spirit; sympathy.

fel-low-ship (fĕl′ō-shĭp), *n.* **1**, association, esp. of a friendly kind; **2**, common interest, as in a society; **3**, in colleges and universities, an endowment for the support of a graduate student; also, a position, or title of honor, without money, conferred upon a graduate student.

Syn. companionship, comradeship.

fel-ly (fĕl′ĭ), *n.* [*pl.* fellies (-ĭz)], the outer, wooden rim of a wheel. Also, **fel′loe.**

[1]**fel-on** (fĕl′ŭn), *n.* **1**, one guilty of a serious crime; a wicked person; **2**, in law, one who has committed a felony (which see):—*adj.* malignant; wicked; murderous.

Syn., *n.* criminal, convict, evildoer.

[2]**fel-on** (fĕl′ŭn), *n.* a very painful abscess on a finger or toe, usually near the nail.

fe-lo-ni-ous (fē-lō′nĭ-ŭs), *adj.* **1**, wicked; villainous; **2**, in law, done with the intention of committing a crime.—*adv.* **fe-lo′ni-ous-ly.**

fel-o-ny (fĕl′ō-nĭ), *n.* [*pl.* felonies (-nĭz)], a serious crime, as treason, murder, etc., punishable by death or imprisonment.

fel-spar (fĕl′spär″), *n.* any of several crystalline minerals. Also, **feld′spar″,** *Pfd. S.*

[1]**felt** (fĕlt), past tense and perfect participle of the irregular verb *feel.*

[2]**felt** (fĕlt), *n.* **1**, a fabric made of wool, or of wool, hair, and fur, not woven but matted or forced together by pressure or by heat; **2**, material resembling felt:—*adj.* made of felt; as, a *felt* hat:—*v.t.* **1**, to mat together into felt; **2**, to cover with felt, or the like.

felt-ing (fĕlt′ĭng), *n.* **1,** the material of which felt is made; **2,** the process of making felt.

fe-male (fē′māl), *n.* **1,** an animal of the sex which produces eggs or bears young; **2,** a woman; **3,** the plant or flower which bears a pistil and receives the pollen of the male flower:—*adj.* designating, or pertaining to, that sex which produces young.

Syn., *adj.* feminine, womanly, womanish. *Female*, the opposite of *male*, applies to plants and animals as well as to human beings; it emphasizes the idea of sex, and is generally used in a somewhat scientific sense; as, a *female* fern; a doe is a *female* deer. *Feminine*, the opposite of *masculine*, stresses the characteristics of women; as, she was *feminine* in her love of pretty things; it frequently emphasizes less desirable qualities; as, *feminine* frivolity. *Womanly*, often contrasted with *girlish* or *manly*, also characterizes the qualities belonging to women, but the emphasis is laid on those that are desirable or, sometimes, belonging to maturity; as, *womanly* tenderness; *womanly* dignity. *Womanish*, the opposite of *mannish*, is generally applied, usually with contempt, to men who are like women in their ways; as, he shed *womanish* tears.

fem-i-nine (fĕm′ĭ-nĭn), *adj.* **1,** pertaining to, or like, women; **2,** delicate; tender; sensitive; **3,** wanting in manly traits; effeminate; **4,** in grammar, designating, or pertaining to, the gender to which nouns denoting females belong.—*adv.* **fem′i-nine-ly.** —*n.* **fem′i-nine-ness.**—*n.* **fem″i-nin′i-ty.**

Syn. womanly, womanish. (See female.)

***femme de cham-bre** (fȧm″ dẽ shäṅbr′′), [Fr.], a lady's maid; chambermaid.

fem-o-ral (fĕm′ō-răl), *adj.* relating to the thigh; as, the *femoral* artery.

fe-mur (fē′mŭr), *n.* [*pl.* femurs (-mŭrz); femora (fĕm′ō-rȧ)], the long bone from the hip to the knee.

FEMUR Greater (A) and lesser (B) trochanter.

fen (fĕn), *n.* **1,** low, flat, marshy land, covered with grass, etc.; **2,** a kind of mold or moss causing disease in hops.—*adj.* **fen′ny.**

fence (fĕns), *v.t.* [*p.t.* and *p.p.* fenced (fĕnst), *p.pr.* fenc′ing], **1,** to guard or protect; defend; **2,** to inclose or surround with a fence; fortify:—*v.i.* **1,** to practice the art of using swords or foils; **2,** to avoid making a direct reply:—*n.* **1,** the art of using the sword; **2,** defense; guard; **3,** a boundary consisting of boards, wire, etc.; inclosure; **4,** skill in debate.—*n.* **fenc′er.**

fen-ci-ble (fĕn′sĭ-bl), *adj.* capable of defense, or of being defended:—*n.* a soldier enlisted for home service.

fenc-ing (fĕn′sĭng), *n.* **1,** the art of using skilfully a foil or sword; **2,** materials used for making a fence; **3,** a collection of fences; guard; **4,** skilful debating.

fend (fĕnd), *v.t.* **1,** to ward off; **2,** to protect with a fender:—*v.i.* **1,** to act on the defensive; **2,** to provide a livelihood.

fend-er (fĕn′dẽr), *n.* **1,** a cushion of rope or a piece of wood hung over the side of a vessel to prevent injury by contact with a landing, wharf, etc.; **2,** a metal guard in front of a fireplace; **3,** a device attached to the front of a street car, locomotive, or the like, to prevent injury to people; **4,** in an automobile, a guard over a wheel; a mud guard.

Fe-ni-an (fē′nĭ-ăn), *n.* **1,** formerly, a member of an Irish secret society, whose purpose was home rule for Ireland; **2,** one of a legendary band of Irish heroes.

fen-nel (fĕn′ĕl), *n.* a fragrant plant of the carrot family, with yellow flowers.

feod (fūd), *n.* under the feudal system, land held by a vassal in return for service to a lord: also called *fee; feoff; fief.* Also, **feud,** *Pfd. S.*—*adj.* **feod′al.**

feoff (fĕf), *n.* a feod, or feud (which see): commonly written *fief.*

fer-ment (fûr′mĕnt), *n.* **1,** a substance that causes fermentation, as yeast, mold, etc.; **2,** fermentation; **3,** a commotion; as, he was in a *ferment* of anger:—*v.t.* **1,** to produce fermentation in; **2,** to excite:—*v.i.* **1,** to effervesce or bubble; **2,** to be in a state of fermentation; **3,** to be excited.

fer-men-ta-tion (fûr″mĕn-tā′shŭn), *n.* **1,** the decomposition produced in an organic substance, such as sugar, by the action of living organisms, such as yeast, bacteria, etc.; a working, as of yeast in liquor; **2,** excitement; agitation.

fern (fûrn), *n.* any of many flowerless plants with broad and feathery fronds or leaves.—*adj.* **fern′y.**

fern-er-y (fûr′nẽr-ĭ), *n.* [*pl.* ferneries (-ĭz)], a place where ferns are kept.

fe-ro-cious (fē-rō′shŭs), *adj.* savage; fierce; cruel.—*adv.* **fe-ro′cious-ly.**—*n.* **fe-ro′cious-ness.**

Syn. wild, barbarous, brutal, inhuman.

fe-roc-i-ty (fē-rŏs′ĭ-tĭ), *n.* [*pl.* ferocities (-tĭz)], savageness; cruelty.

fer-ret (fĕr′ĕt), *n.* a kind of weasel used to hunt rats and rabbits:—*v.t.* **1,** to drive out from a hiding place; search for with ferrets; **2,** to search perseveringly for: generally with *out;* as, to *ferret* out a gang of thieves:—*v.i.* to hunt with ferrets; search.—*n.* **fer′ret-er.**—*adj.* **fer′ret-y.**

fer-ri-age (fĕr′ĭ-āj), *n.* the act of conveying, or the money paid for conveyance, in a boat across a body of water.

fer-ric (fĕr′ĭk), *adj.* **1,** pertaining to, containing, or extracted from, iron; **2,** designating a compound in which the valence of iron is higher than in the ferrous compound; as, *ferric* oxide.

Fer-ris wheel (fĕr′ĭs), a power-driven amusement device consisting of a large, vertical wheel revolving on a fixed axle and having in its rim hanging cars for passengers.

fer-ro-type (fĕr′ō-tīp), *n.* a photograph made on a thin iron plate: usually called *tintype.*

fer-rous (fĕr′ŭs), *adj.* **1,** of, pertaining to, or obtained from, iron; **2,** designating a compound of iron in which iron has a valence of two. Also, **fer′re-ous.**

fer-ru-gi-nous (fĕ-ro͞o′jĭ-nŭs), *adj.* **1,** of the nature of, or containing, iron; **2,** resembling iron rust in color; brownish red; **3,** having an iron taste.

fer-rule (fĕr′o͞ol; fĕr′ĭl), *n.* a metal ring or cap placed at the end of a stick, tool handle, etc., to strengthen it; as, the *ferrule* of an umbrella.

fer-ry (fĕr′ĭ), *n.* [*pl.* ferries (-ĭz)], **1,** a passage, as across a river; **2,** a boat to carry passengers across a river; **3,** the place where such a boat lands its passengers:—*v.t.* and *v.i.* [*p.t.* and *p.p.* -ried (-ĭd), *p.pr.* -ry-ing], to convey or go, as across water, in a boat.

FERRYBOAT

fer-ry-boat (fĕr′ĭ-bōt″), *n.* a boat used for transportation across a comparatively narrow body of water.

fer-tile (fûr'tĭl; *Br.* -tīl), *adj.* **1,** producing abundantly; fruitful; reproductive; rich in resources or invention; **2,** capable of developing or reproducing.—*adv.* **fer'tile-ly.**
Syn. prolific, plenteous, productive.

fer-til-i-ty (fẽr-tĭl'ĭ-tĭ), *n.* [*pl.* fertilities (-tĭz)], the state of being fruitful; productiveness; also, inventiveness.

fer-ti-lize (fûr'tĭ-līz), *v.t.* [*p.t.* and *p.p.* -lized (-līzd), *p.pr.* -liz"ing], to make or render fruitful; as, to *fertilize* the soil.—*n.* **fer"ti-li-za'tion.**

fer-ti-liz-er (fûr'tĭ-līz"ẽr), *n.* any material put in or on the ground, which contains plant food.

fer-ule (fĕr'o͞ol; fĕr'ĭl), *n.* a rod or flat stick used in punishment:—*v.t.* [*p.t.* and *p.p.* -uled (-o͞old; -ĭld), *p.pr.* **-ul-ing**], to punish with such a stick.

fer-ven-cy (fûr'vĕn-sĭ), *n.* earnestness; ardor; as, the *fervency* of an address; *fervency* of prayer.
Syn. enthusiasm, eagerness, zeal, ecstasy.

fer-vent (fûr'vĕnt), *adj.* **1,** zealous; earnest; vehement; **2,** hot; glowing.—*adv.* **fer'vent-ly.**

fer-vid (fûr'vĭd), *adj.* **1,** burning; fiery; **2,** intense; eager; vehement.—*adv.* **fer'vid-ly.**—*n.* **fer'vid-ness.**
Syn. impetuous, earnest, passionate, zealous.

fer-vor (fûr'vẽr), *n.* **1,** intensity of feeling; zeal; as, patriotic *fervor;* **2,** heat.

fes-tal (fĕs'tăl), *adj.* pertaining to a feast or holiday; joyous; festive; hilarious; happy.—*adv.* **fes'tal-ly.**

fes-ter (fĕs'tẽr), *v.t.* **1,** to cause to ulcerate; **2,** to cause to rankle:—*v.i.* **1,** to become ulcerated or sore; generate pus; **2,** to rankle, as an insult:—*n.* **1,** a pus-forming sore; **2,** a rankling or festering.

fes-ti-val (fĕs'tĭ-văl), *n.* **1,** a joyful celebration in commemoration of some event, religious or civil; **2,** an entertainment of a special kind, often occurring at regular periods, as, the Handel *festival.*

fes-tive (fĕs'tĭv), *adj.* pertaining to a feast; gay; merry.—*adv.* **fes'tive-ly.**
Syn. joyful, festal, sportive, mirthful.

fes-tiv-i-ty (fĕs-tĭv'ĭ-tĭ), *n.* [*pl.* festivities (-tĭz)], **1,** social gaiety at an entertainment or feast; merrymaking; joyfulness; **2,** a celebration.

fes-toon (fĕs-to͞on'), *n.* **1,** a wreath or garland hung between two points; **2,** an architectural ornament of such form:—*v.t.* to decorate with, or form into, garlands.

fe-tal (fē'tăl), *adj.* pertaining to the fetus, or unborn young of an animal in its later stages; as, *fetal* life. Also, **fœ'tal.**

fetch (fĕch), *v.t.* **1,** to go after and bring; get; **2,** to attain by exertion; draw forth; heave, as a sigh; **3,** to be sold for; **4,** to cause to come; as, to *fetch* order out of chaos; **5,** to reach; arrive at by sailing: **fetch a compass,** on shipboard, to swing one's course about; make a detour:—*v.i.* on shipboard, to hold a course; as, to *fetch* to leeward:—*n.* the act of going and bringing.—*n.* **fetch'er.**
Syn., v. carry, transport. (See bring.)

fetch-ing (fĕch'ĭng), *adj. Colloq.,* pleasing; attractive; as, a *fetching* hat.

fête (fāt; *Fr.* fât), *n.* **1,** a festival or holiday; usually, an outdoor celebration; **2,** in France, the celebration of the day of the saint whose name one bears: observed like a birthday:—*v.t.* [*p.t.* and *p.p.* fêt'ed, *p.pr.* fêt'ing], to entertain or honor with festivities.

fet-id (fĕt'ĭd; fē'tĭd), *adj.* giving forth an offensive smell; stinking.
Syn. rotten, putrid, noxious.

fe-tish (fē'tĭsh; fĕt'ĭsh), *n.* **1,** among primitive peoples, any material object, as a stone, weapon, feather, etc., supposed to have magical power or to contain a spirit, and to give to its possessor power over such a deity; **2,** any object of unreasoning devotion. Also, **fe'tich.**—*n.* **fe'tish-ism.**—*n.* **fe'tish-ist.**

FETISHES

fet-lock (fĕt'lŏk), *n.* on a horse or similar animal, the tuft of hair just above the hoof, at the back of the foot.

fet-ter (fĕt'ẽr), *n.* **1,** a chain for the feet; **2,** a restraint; hindrance:—*v.t.* **1,** to place in bonds; **2,** to hinder; restrain.

fet-tle (fĕt'l), *n.* condition; repair; as, in fine *fettle.*

fe-tus (fē'tŭs), *n.* the unborn young of an animal in the later stages of development. Also, **fœ'tus** (fē'tŭs).

[1]**feud** (fūd), *n.* a quarrel, generally hereditary or of long standing, between clans or families.

[2]**feud** (fūd), *n.* under the feudal system, land held from a lord or landowner in return for service: also called *fee; feoff; fief.* Also, **feod.**—*adj.* **feu'da-ry.**

feu-dal (fū'dăl), *adj.* of or pertaining to a method of landholding in Europe during the Middle Ages, by which tenure of land was granted in return for service rendered: **feudal system,** a political and social system affecting almost every phase of life in Europe in the Middle Ages, whereby the land was divided into feuds, or fiefs, each held by the tenant, or vassal, as long as he rendered certain services to his superior lord, who might himself be a vassal, either of a higher nobleman or of the king.—*adv.* **feu'dal-ly.**

feu-dal-ism (fū'dăl-ĭzm), *n.* the feudal system; also, its laws and usages.—*n.* **feu'dal-ist.**—*adj.* **feu"dal-is'tic.**

feu-dal-ize (fū'dăl-īz), *v.t.* [*p.t.* and *p.p.* -ized (-īzd), *p.pr.* -iz"ing], to make conform to feudalism; as, the Normans *feudalized* England.—*n.* **feu"dal-i-za'tion.**

feu-da-to-ry (fū'dȧ-tō-rĭ), *n.* [*pl.* feudatories (-rĭz)], one holding land in return for service; a vassal:—*adj.* pertaining to the relation between a feudal vassal and his lord. Also, **feu'da-ry.**

fe-ver (fē'vẽr), *n.* **1,** any disease characterized by high temperature, quickened pulse, great weakness, etc.; a temperature of the human body exceeding 98.6 degrees Fahrenheit; **2,** extreme nervous excitement; as, a *fever* of anxiety:—*v.t.* to put into a fever.

fe-ver-few (fē'vẽr-fū), *n.* a perennial plant bearing small white flowers.

fe-ver-ish (fē'vẽr-ĭsh), *adj.* **1,** affected with, indicating, or causing, fever; **2,** restless; **3,** impatient; eager.—*adv.* **fe'ver-ish-ly.**—*n.* **fe'ver-ish-ness.**

few (fū), *adj.* not many; small in number.—*n.* **few'ness.**

fez (fĕz), *n.* [*pl.* fezzes (-ĕz)], a brimless felt hat, usually red, with a black tassel: worn esp. by Mohammedans.

FEZ

***fi-an-cé** (fē"äṅ"sā'), [Fr.], *n.* [*pl.*

fiancés (-sā')], a man engaged to be married.—*n.fem.* **fi″an″cée′** (fē″äṅ″sā′).

fi-as-co (fē-ȧs′kō), *n.* [*pl.* fiascoes; fiascos (-kōz)], **1**, orig., a long-necked flask, esp. one covered with wicker; **2**, a complete or ludicrous failure; as, the play was a *fiasco.*

fi-at (fī′ăt), *n.* an authoritative command; a decree: **fiat money**, paper currency made legal tender by law, or fiat, but not having its face value.

fib (fĭb), *n.* a petty falsehood:—*v.i.* [*p.t.* and *p.p.* fibbed (fĭbd), *p.pr.* fib′bing], to tell small untruths.—*n.* **fib′ber.**

fi-ber (fī′bẽr), *n.* **1**, a slender, threadlike filament; **2**, raw material which can be separated into threads for making up textile or woven fabrics; as, the *fiber* of hemp; **3**, fibrous structure; hence, quality of character; as, a man of tough *fiber.* Also, **fi′bre.**—*adj.* **fi′brous.**

fi-brin (fī′brĭn), *n.* a white substance formed when the blood is clotted.—*adj.* **fi′brin-ous.**

fi-broid (fī′broid), *adj.* fibrous in structure; fiberlike; as, a *fibroid* tissue.

fib-ster (fĭb′stẽr), *n.* a liar in a small way: used jocosely.

fib-u-la (fĭb′ū-lȧ), *n.* [*pl.* fibulæ (-lē)], the outer and smaller of the two bones of the lower leg (see *tibia*, illus.).—*adj.* **fib′u-lar.**

fich-u (fĭsh′ōō; *Fr.* fē″shü′), *n.* a light, three-cornered cape, usually made of muslin or lace, and worn over the shoulders.

fick-le (fĭk′l), *adj.* inconstant; changeable.—*n.* **fick′le-ness.**

Syn. capricious, freakish, whimsical, shifting.

fic-tile (fĭk′tĭl), *adj.* readily molded; plastic: used of pottery.

fic-tion (fĭk′shŭn), *n.* **1**, the act of feigning or inventing; **2**, that which is imagined, feigned, or invented; **3**, a literary production of the imagination in prose form, as a novel, romance, etc.—*adj.* **fic′tion-al.**

Syn. falsehood, fabrication, fable.

fic-ti-tious (fĭk-tĭsh′ŭs), *adj.* **1**, pertaining to, or of the nature of, fiction; **2**, false; unreal.—*adv.* **fic-ti′tious-ly.**

Syn. counterfeit, assumed, artificial.

fid (fĭd), *n.* **1**, an iron or wooden bar to support anything, as the topmast of a vessel; **2**, a large, tapering wooden or iron pin for opening the strands of a rope.

fid-dle (fĭd′l), *n.* **1**, *Colloq.*, a violin; **2**, a frame used on board ship to prevent articles from rolling off the table in stormy weather:—*v.i.* [*p.t.* and *p.p.* -dled (-ld), *p.pr.* -dling], **1**, to play the violin; **2**, to trifle; as, to *fiddle* at writing:—*v.t. Colloq.*, to play (a tune) on a violin: **to fiddle away**, to waste, as time.

fid-dle-dee-dee (fĭd″l-dē-dē′), *interj.* nonsense!—*n.* a piece of nonsense; an absurdity of any kind.

fid-dle-fad-dle (fĭd′l-făd″l), *n. Colloq.*, nonsense; trifling conversation:—*v.i.* [*p.t.* and *p.p.* -dled (-ld), *p.pr.* -dling], *Colloq.*, to talk nonsense; fuss.

fid-dler (fĭd′lẽr), *n.* **1**, a violinist; one who fiddles; **2**, a European sandpiper; **3**, a kind of burrowing crab of the Atlantic coast, having one claw much larger than the other: also called *fiddler crab.*

fid-dle-stick (fĭd′l-stĭk″), *n.* a bow for playing upon the violin: **fiddlesticks!** *interj.* nonsense!

fi-del-i-ty (fī-dĕl′ĭ-tĭ; fī-), *n.* [*pl.* fidelities (-tĭz)], integrity; faithfulness; honesty; loyalty; reliability.

Syn. allegiance, devotion, constancy.

fidg-et (fĭj′ĕt), *n.* **1**, one who is uneasy and restless; **2**, in *pl.*, nervous restlessness:—*v.t.* to make uneasy; worry:—*v.i.* to move about uneasily or restlessly.—*adj.* **fidg′et-y.**—*n.* **fidg′et-i-ness.**

fi-du-ci-a-ry (fĭ-dū′shĭ-ā-rĭ; -shȧ-rĭ), *n.* [*pl.* fiduciaries (-rĭz)], a trustee:—*adj.* **1**, pertaining to, or of the nature of, a trust; **2**, confident; unwavering.

fie (fī), *interj.* for shame! shame! as, *fie upon you!*

fief (fēf), *n.* under the feudal system, land held in return for service to a superior; also, the tenure of such land; as, lands held in *fief:* also called *fee; feod; feoff; feud.*

field (fēld), *n.* **1**, a piece of land inclosed for tillage or pasture; **2**, a plot of ground set aside for a special use; as, a cricket *field;* **3**, a region yielding some natural product; as, the oil *fields;* **4**, the site of a battle; **5**, a sphere of action; as, the *field* of research; **6**, a wide expanse; as, a *field* of ice; **7**, the space within which telescopic or microscopic objects are viewed; as, the *field* of vision; **8**, in physics, the space through which some influence is extended; as, the magnetic *field;* **9**, in sports, those who take part in a contest, considered together: **field artillery**, artillery so mounted as to be easily handled in active service: **field officer**, a military officer of the rank of major, lieutenant colonel, or colonel:—*v.t.* to catch or stop, and return from the field, as a ball at cricket or baseball:—*v.i.* to return such balls in baseball or cricket: act as fielder.

field day **1**, a military review; **2**, a day devoted to outdoor scientific research; **3**, a day set for a series of athletic contests; **4**, a gala day.

field-er (fēl′dẽr), in baseball or cricket, a player in the field on the side not at the bat, supposed to stop or catch balls.

field-fare (fēld′fâr″), *n.* a medium-sized thrush, native to Europe.

field glass a small portable telescope; a spyglass.

field mar-shal in some European countries, an officer of the highest military rank.

field mouse any of various wild mice that live in fields.

field-piece (fēld′pēs″), *n.* a cannon mounted on wheels.

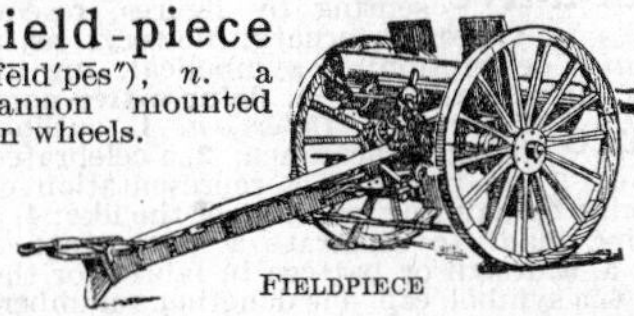

FIELDPIECE

field sports outdoor diversions, as hunting; specif., in athletic games, those events which do not take place on the running track, such as jumping.

field-work (fēld′wûrk″), *n.* a temporary defense, as an earthwork, thrown up by troops: **field work**, outdoor operations or observations, as surveying, exploring, natural history, etc.

fiend (fēnd), *n.* **1**, an evil spirit; a demon; one who is intensely malicious, wicked, or cruel; **2**, one who is the victim of a harmful practice; as, a drug *fiend.*

fiend-ish (fēnd′ĭsh), *adj.* savage; wicked; malicious; cruel.—*adv.* **fiend′ish-ly.**—*n.* **fiend′ish-ness.**

fierce (fērs), *adj.* **1**, furious; intense; violent, as a storm; **2**, uncontrolled in anger; merciless, as a man; **3**, eager; passionate.—*adv.* **fierce′ly.**—*n.* **fierce′ness.**

fi-er-y (fī′ẽr-ĭ; fīr′ĭ), *adj.* [*comp.* fi′er-i-er, *superl.* fi′er-i-est], **1**, like, pertaining to, or consisting of, fire; **2**, passionate; easily roused; **3**, fervent; ardent.—*adv.* **fi′er-i-ly.**

Syn. spirited, impetuous, fervid.

***fies-ta** (fyĕs′tä), [Sp.], *n.* a religious festival: holiday; saint's day.

fife (fīf), *n.* a shrill-toned musical instrument of the flute class:—*v.t.* [*p.t.* and *p.p.* fifed (fīft), *p.pr.* fif′ing], to play (a tune) on a fife:—*v.i.* to play the fife.—*n.* **fif′er.**

fif-teen (fĭf′tēn″; fĭf″tēn′), *adj.* consisting of five plus ten:—*n.* **1,** the number made up of ten and five; **2,** the sign representing it, as 15 or xv; **3,** the first point scored in lawn tennis.—*adj.* and *n.* **fif′teenth″.**

fifth (fĭfth), *adj.* **1,** next in order after the fourth: the ordinal of *five;* **2,** designating one of the five equal parts composing anything: **Fifth day,** Thursday: so named by the Society of Friends:—*n.* **1,** the quotient of one divided by five; **2,** one of the five equal parts composing anything; **3,** in music: **a,** an interval of three steps and a half step, as from C to G in the scale of C major; **b,** the fifth tone of a scale, counting up from the tonic; the dominant.—*adv.* **fifth′ly.**

fif-ty (fĭf′tĭ), *adj.* consisting of five times ten:—*n.* [*pl.* fifties (-tĭz)], **1,** the number which amounts to five times ten, or forty-nine plus one; **2,** the sign representing it, as 50 or l.—*adj.* and *n.* **fif′ti-eth.**

fig (fĭg), *n.* **1,** a small fruit tree native to southwestern Asia; **2,** the pear-shaped fruit of this tree; **3,** *Colloq.,* a trifle; as, I don't care a *fig.*

fight (fīt), *v.i.* [*p.t.* and *p.p.* fought (fôt), *p.pr.* fight′ing], **1,** to contend in battle or in arms; **2,** to strive for success against difficulty; as, to *fight* for a bill:—*v.t.* **1,** to war against; **2,** to strive for the mastery of; **3,** to manage in battle, as ships:—*n.* **1,** a combat; battle or engagement; contest; **2,** any strife or conflict; **3,** strength and willingness to struggle; as, full of *fight.*—*n.* **fight′er.**
Syn., v. contest, struggle; *n.* (see battle).

fig-ment (fĭg′mĕnt), *n.* an invention; fiction; something imagined.

fig-u-ra-tion (fĭg″ū-rā′shŭn), *n.* **1,** the act of marking with figures; emblematical representation; **2,** shape.

fig-ur-a-tive (fĭg′ūr-ȧ-tĭv), *adj.* **1,** representing by figures, resemblances, or types; **2,** ornate; flowery; as, a *figurative* description; **3,** symbolical; unreal.—*adv.* **fig′ur-a-tive-ly.**—*n.* **fig′ur-a-tive-ness.**

fig-ure (fĭg′ūr; *Br.* fĭg′ẽr), *n.* **1,** outline; shape; appearance; **2,** a celebrated person; **3,** an image or a representation of anything by painting, carving, or the like; **4,** a drawing made to illustrate a statement; a cut; **5,** a design or pattern in fabrics or the like; **6,** a symbol, esp. one denoting a number; **7,** a specific movement in a dance; **8,** the price or value of a thing; **9,** in rhetoric, the expression of ideas or thoughts in a fanciful manner; as, a *figure* of speech:—*v.t.* [*p.t.* and *p.p.* -ured (-ūrd), *p.pr.* -ur-ing], **1,** to form in any shape; **2,** to represent; **3,** to adorn with a pattern or design; **4,** to imagine; **5,** to compute:—*v.i.* **1,** to be prominent; as, to *figure* in politics; **2,** *Colloq.,* to calculate.
Syn., n. allegory, emblem, symbol, sign.

fig-ured (fĭg′ūrd), *p.adj.* **1,** covered with a design; as, *figured* cloth; **2,** in music, adorned with elaborate phrases.

fig-ure-head (fĭg′ūr-hĕd″), *n.* **1,** a carved image of a human or other shape placed at the prow of a ship; **2,** a person who is important in name but who has no real authority.

fig-wort (fĭg′wûrt″), *n.* a coarse herb with small flowers: used in medicine.

Fi-ji (fē′jē), *n.* one of the race native to the Fiji Islands.—*adj.* and *n.* **Fi′ji-an.**

fil-a-ment (fĭl′ȧ-mĕnt), *n.* a fine thread or threadlike fiber; specif., the threadlike stalk of a stamen, supporting the anther (see *flower,* ²*style,* illus.).—*adj.* **fil″a-men′ta-ry.**—*adj.* **fil″a-men′tous.**

fil-bert (fĭl′bẽrt), *n.* **1,** the hazel, a small tree bearing an edible nut; **2,** the nut.

filch (fĭlch), *v.t.* to pilfer or steal in a small way; rob of trifles.—*n.* **filch′er.**
Syn. thieve, crib, purloin.

¹file (fīl), *n.* **1,** a pointed wire, or any of various other devices, on or in which papers may be put; **2,** any collection of papers kept together and classified in some orderly way; as, a *file* of letters; **3,** a line of persons or things arranged one behind the other: opp. of *rank:*—*v.t.* [*p.t.* and *p.p.* filed (fīld), *p.pr.* fil′ing], to arrange or put away, as papers or the like, in orderly fashion; place on file:—*v.i.* to march in line, one person behind another.

²file (fīl), *n.* a roughened, hard steel tool used for smoothing or abrading (see *tool,* illus.):—*v.t.* [*p.t.* and *p.p.* filed (fīld), *p.pr.* fil′ing], to smooth or cut with a file; sharpen.

fil-ial (fĭl′yăl; fĭl′ĭ-ăl), *adj.* **1,** pertaining to a son or daughter; **2,** befitting a son or daughter in relation to a parent; as, *filial* obedience.—*adv.* **fil′ial-ly.**

fil-i-bus-ter (fĭl′ĭ-bŭs″tẽr), *n.* **1,** a freebooter or pirate; **2,** a lawless military adventurer who invades a foreign country to aid a revolution; **3,** a member of a lawmaking body who intentionally delays its action, esp. by much talking; also, an instance of such delay:—*v.i.* **1,** to act as a pirate; **2,** to delay legislation or lawmaking by irregular methods, as by wilfully prolonging a debate.—*n.* **fil″i-bus′ter-er.**

fil-i-gree (fĭl′ĭ-grē), *n.* **1,** ornamental work, resembling lace, in gold or silver wire; **2,** something delicate or ornamental, but not lasting:—*adj.* made of, or like, filigree.—*adj.* **fil′i-greed.**

fil-ing (fīl′ĭng), *n.,* usually in *pl.,* a fragment cut off by the action of a file.

Fil-i-pi-no (fĭl″ĭ-pē′nō), *n.* [*pl.* Filipinos (-nōz)], a native of the Philippine Islands.—*n.fem.* **Fil″i-pi′na.**

fill (fĭl), *v.t.* **1,** to make full; add or put into until level or complete, as a dish, crevice, cavity, etc.; **2,** to satisfy, as with food; **3,** to occupy completely; pervade; as, smoke *filled* the room; **4,** to perform, as duties, in the place of someone; **5,** to supply with an incumbent, as an office; **6,** to carry out, as a business order; **7,** to compound; as, the druggist *fills* a prescription:—*v.i.* **1,** to become full; **2,** to pour a glass or vessel full:—*n.* **1,** as much as produces complete satisfaction; a full supply; **2,** that which is used to fill; also, the place to be filled.

fill-er (fĭl′ẽr), *n.* **1,** one who or that which fills; **2,** something used in filling; specif., blank pages to be inserted into a notebook, or the like; **3,** a liquid compound for stopping up holes in wood before painting it; **4,** the tobacco used in the body of a cigar.

fil-let (fĭl′ĕt), *n.* **1,** a narrow band of metal, linen, silk, etc., worn around the forehead, for holding the hair; **2,** in cooking, a boneless lump of meat or fish served flat or rolled together and tied; **3,** a raised rim; a narrow ornament or molding; a plain line or band; **4,** in *pl.,* the loins of an animal, as of a horse:—*v.t.* **1,** to bind with a narrow band; **2,** to ornament with a rim or molding; **3,** to make into fillets, as meat or fish.

fill-ing (fĭl′ĭng), *n.* **1,** something that serves to fill up a vacant space or supplies a deficiency; **2,** in weaving, the woof.

fil-lip (fĭl′ĭp), *n.* **1,** a sudden, sharp jerk or stroke with the finger; **2,** some slight, sharp stimulus which reminds or arouses:—*v.t.* **1,** to snap with the finger; **2,** to arouse.

fil-li-peen (fĭl″ĭ-pēn′), *n.* a forfeit in a game. See **phil″o-pe′na,** *Pfd. S.*

fil-ly (fĭl′ĭ), *n.* [*pl.* fillies (-ĭz)], **1,** a young female horse; **2,** *Colloq.,* a lively girl.

film (fĭlm), *n.* **1**, a thin skin or filament; **2**, a haze or blur; **3**, a thin coating of chemicals, as upon a roll of celluloid, for receiving a photographic impression; also, the coated celluloid itself; **4**, a reel of celluloid upon which pictures are printed for motion pictures; also, a motion picture:—*v.t.* **1**, to cover with, or as with, a thin skin or layer; **2**, to make a motion picture of:—*v.i.* to become covered with a thin skin or layer.—*adj.* **film'y.**—*n.* **film'i-ness.**

fil-ter (fĭl'tẽr), *n.* **1**, any porous material, as sand, cloth, etc., used for clearing or purifying liquids by straining; **2**, an apparatus so used; a strainer:—*v.t.* to purify, as a liquid: —*v.i.* to pass or be strained through a filter.

filth (fĭlth), *n.* **1**, foul matter; dirt; **2**, anything dirty or morally impure; nastiness.

filth-y (fĭl'thĭ), *adj.* [*comp.* filth'i-er, *superl.* filth'i-est], **1**, foul; dirty; unclean morally or physically; **2**, low; contemptible. —*adv.* **filth'i-ly.**—*n.* **filth'i-ness.**
Syn. vile, obscene, nasty, impure.

fil-trate (fĭl'trāt), *n.* a liquid which has been strained through a filter:— *v.t.* [*p.t.* and *p.p.* -trat-ed, *p.pr.* -trat-ing], to purify, as a liquid, by passing through a filter or strainer.—*n.* **fil-tra'tion.**

fil-tra-tion plant a place where the water for a city or locality is purified and made fit to drink.

fin (fĭn), *n.* **1**, a winglike extension from the body of a fish that helps to move, balance, or steer it in the water; **2**, a small vertical or horizontal plane or wing on an airplane, to promote stability or steadiness (see *airplane*, illus.).—*adj.* **fin'less.**

fi-nal (fī'năl), *adj.* **1**, pertaining to the end; last; as, a *final* chapter; **2**, decisive; as, a *final* judgment or decree; **3**, relating to a purpose; as, in Latin, a *final* clause:—*n.* **1**, that which is last, or makes an end; **2**, the deciding heat of an athletic contest.
Syn., adj. (see last).

fi-na-le (fē-nä'lā), *n.* **1**, the last passage in a musical composition; **2**, the last act or scene of a performance; **3**, close; end.

fi-nal-i-ty (fī-năl'ĭ-tĭ), *n.* [*pl.* finalities (-tĭz)], **1**, the state of being fully settled; completeness; **2**, a decisive act.

fi-nal-ly (fī'năl-ĭ), *adv.* **1**, lastly; **2**, unalterably; completely; as, the business was *finally* settled.

fi-nance (fĭ-năns'; fī-năns'), *n.* **1**, the science of money credit; also, of government budgets; **2**, in *pl.*, the income of a government, society, or individual; as, the city *finances*:—*v.t.* [*p.t.* and *p.p.* -nanced' (-nănst'), *p.pr.* -nanc'ing], **1**, to manage, as the financial arrangement of; **2**, to provide the capital for.

fi-nan-cial (fĭ-năn'shăl), *adj.* pertaining to money; as, *financial* prosperity; *financial* distress.—*adv.* **fi-nan'cial-ly.**
Syn. fiscal, monetary, pecuniary.

fin-an-cier (fĭn″ăn-sēr'; fī-năn'sĭ-ẽr), *n.* **1**, one skilled in banking or money matters; **2**, one who conducts private or public money affairs.

fin-back (fĭn'băk″), *n.* a kind of whale having a large dorsal fin: also called *razorback.*

finch (fĭnch), *n.* any of various small song birds, as the chaffinch, canary, etc.

find (fīnd), *v.t.* [*p.t.* and *p.p.* found (found), *p.pr.* find'ing], **1**, to discover, esp. by chance; **2**, to obtain by searching; **3**, to learn by experiment; as, to *find* a principle in physics; **4**, to regain, as something lost; **5**, to supply, as tools; **6**, to arrive at, as a result. —*n.* the discovery of something valuable.

find-er (fīn'dẽr), *n.* **1**, one who or that which discovers; **2**, an extra lens on a camera to show the position of the picture to be taken; **3**, a small telescope attached to a larger one to locate something, as a star, to be examined by the larger instrument.

find-ing (fīnd'ĭng), *n.* **1**, discovery; **2**, the verdict of a jury, or court; **3**, in *pl.*, the tools, materials, etc., which a workman himself supplies.

¹fine (fīn), *n.* money paid in settlement or as a penalty; forfeiture: **in fine,** in conclusion:—*v.t.* [*p.t.* and *p.p.* fined (fīnd), *p.pr.* fin'ing], to punish by imposing a fine.

²fine (fīn), *adj.* **1**, pure; refined; as, *fine* gold; **2**, thin; as, a *fine* wire; **3**, keen; as, a *fine* edge; **4**, delicate; as, *fine* linen; **5**, excellent; as, a *fine* man; a *fine* day, etc.: **fine arts,** those arts which appeal chiefly to a sense of beauty, esp. painting, sculpture, and architecture:—*v.t.* and *v.i.* [*p.t.* and *p.p.* fined (fīnd), *p.pr.* fin'ing], to make or become finer, thinner, less coarse, etc.—*adv.* **fine'ly.**
Syn., adj. dainty, smooth, sensitive.—*Ant., adj.* coarse, unrefined, ugly.

fine-draw (fīn'drô″), *v.t.* [*p.t.* -drew″ (-drōō″), *p.p.* -drawn″ (-drôn″), *p.pr.* -draw″ing], **1**, to sew up neatly, as a tear in a garment; **2**, to draw out to extreme fineness, as copper wire.

fine-drawn (fīn'drôn″), *p.adj.* **1**, spun very fine; **2**, far-fetched.

fine-ness (fīn'nĕs), *n.* **1**, the proportion of pure metal contained in an alloy; **2**, freedom from foreign matter; purity.

fin-er-y (fīn'ẽr-ĭ), *n.* [*pl.* fineries (-ĭz)], personal adornment, as showy clothes, jewelry, etc.; outward show.

fine-spun (fīn'spŭn″), *adj.* **1**, drawn out or spun to extreme fineness; **2**, not practical; too subtle; as, *finespun* ideas.

fi-nesse (fĭ-nĕs'), *n.* **1**, artifice or trick; **2**, skill; dexterity; **3**, in the game of whist, an endeavor to take a trick with a lower card than that held by an opponent, while holding a higher card:—*v.i.* [*p.t.* and *p.p.* -nessed' (-nĕst'), *p.pr.* -ness'ing], to attempt to take a trick in this way.

fin-ger (fĭng'gẽr), *n.* **1**, one of the five terminal members of the hand; esp., one of the four digits as distinguished from the thumb; **2**, a finger's breadth or length; an eighth of a yard; **3**, any mechanical contrivance resembling a finger, as the pointer of a clock; **4**, a part of a glove into which a finger is inserted:—*v.t.* to handle; meddle with; steal:—*v.i.* to use the fingers in performing upon an instrument.—*n.* **fin'ger-er.**

fin-gered (fĭng'gẽrd), *p.adj.* **1**, having fingers; **2**, touched with the fingers; **3**, played with the fingers; **4**, marked to show how to use the fingers, as music.

fin-ger-ing (fĭng'gẽr-ĭng), *n.* **1**, the act of touching with the fingers; **2**, the manner of using the fingers, as on a piano or other musical instrument.

fin-ger-ling (fĭng'gẽr-lĭng), *n.* a young trout no bigger than a finger.

fin-ger-print (fĭng'gẽr-prĭnt″), *n.* an impression of the lines on the inner side of the last joint of a finger or thumb, used as a means of identification:—*v.t.* to make a fingerprint of.—*n.* **fin'ger-print″ing.**

fin-ger stall a covering for an injured finger.

fin-i-cal (fĭn'ĭ-kăl), *adj.* fastidious; too particular.—*adv.* **fin'i-cal-ly.**

fin-ick-ing (fĭn'ĭ-kĭng), *adj.* fussy or affectedly precise in trifles, as in dress, manners, etc. Also, **fin'ick-y; fin'i-kin.**

fin-ing (fīn'ĭng), *n.* **1**, the act or process of purifying or refining; **2**, clarification or clearing, as of a liquor.

fi-nis (fī'nĭs), *n.* the end: a word formerly placed at the end of a book.

fin-ish (fĭn'ĭsh), *v.t.* **1**, to bring to an end; complete; conclude; **2**, to make

perfect; polish, as furniture; 3, *Colloq.*, to kill or render powerless:—*v.i.* to come to an end; stop:—*n.* 1, the completion; end; 2, the final touches given to a work; 3, polish, as on furniture.—*n.* **fin'ish-er.**
Syn., v. perfect, terminate. (See close.)

fin-ished (fĭn'ĭsht), *p.adj.* 1, completed; ended; 2, worked out with minute care; as, a *finished* performance.

fi-nite (fī'nīt), *adj.* having limits; as, the *finite* mind of man: opp. of *infinite:* —*n.* that which is limited: with *the.*—*adv.* **fi'nite-ly.**—*n.* **fi'nite-ness.**

fin keel a downward projection shaped like the fin of a fish, attached to the keel of a yacht.

Finn (fĭn), *n.* a native of Finland.—*adj.* **Finn'ic.**—*adj.* and *n.* **Finn'ish.**

fin-nan had-die (fĭn'ăn hăd'ĭ), a smoked haddock. Also, **fin'nan had'dock.**

Fin-no–U-gric (fĭn"ō=ōō'grĭk), *adj.* pertaining to the Finns and Ugrians, or to their language, classed among the Ural-Altaic languages.

fin-ny (fĭn'ĭ), *adj.* 1, having fins; 2, resembling, containing, or abounding in, fish.—*adj.* **finned.**

fiord (fyôrd), *n.* a long, narrow inlet or arm of the sea between high rocks or banks. Also, **fjord.**

fir (fûr), *n.* any of various cone-bearing evergreen trees, prized for resin and timber, as the balsam fir (see *tree*, illus.), the red fir, etc.; also, the timber.—*adj.* **fir'ry.**

fire (fīr), *n.* 1, heat and light developed by combustion or burning; a spark; flash; 2, wood, coal, etc., burning; as, a hot *fire* in the stove; 3, a destructive burning; conflagration; 4, a discharge of firearms; 5, intensity of feeling; spirit; as, the *fire* of ambition; 6, light; brilliancy, as of a star or diamond; 7, severe trial and affliction, as if by burning: —*v.t.* [*p.t.* and *p.p.* fired (fīrd), *p.pr.* fir'ing], 1, to set on fire; inflame; kindle; 2, to bake, as porcelain; 3, to cause to explode; discharge, as a gun; 4, to illuminate; 5, to animate; excite; as, to *fire* troops with enthusiasm; 6, to stoke, as a locomotive:—*v.i.* 1, to become ignited; 2, to be inflamed; 3, to discharge, as firearms.—*adj.* **fire'less.**

fire-arm (fīr'ärm"), *n.* a weapon, as a rifle, revolver, etc., from which a charge is expelled by an explosive.

fire bal-loon 1, a balloon filled with hot air; 2, a balloon carrying fireworks which explode at a certain height.

fire box in a steam boiler, the place for the fire.

fire-brand (fīr'brănd"), *n.* 1, a piece of burning wood; 2, an incendiary, or one who fires buildings; 3, one who inflames the passions of others, as of a crowd.

fire brick a brick made of material that withstands great heat: used to line furnaces.

fire clay a kind of clay capable of resisting intense heat.

fire-crack-er (fīr'krăk"ẽr), *n.* a small paper cylinder filled with gunpowder and having a fuse: used to make a noise in times of celebration.

fire damp a gas formed in coal mines, which explodes when mixed with air and ignited.

fire-dog (fīr'dŏg"), *n.* an andiron or support for wood in a fireplace.

fire eat-er 1, a juggler who pretends to eat fire; 2, a defiantly uncompromising person; a fighting character.

fire en-gine a hand or steam engine for forcing water through a hose to put out a fire.

fire es-cape a kind of ladder, stairway, or other device for escaping from the upper parts of a burning building.

fire-fly (fīr'flī"), *n.* [*pl.* fireflies (-flīz")], any of various small beetles which emit light at night when flying.

fire i-rons the shovel, poker, and tongs used at an open fireplace.

fire-man (fīr'măn), *n.* [*pl.* firemen (-mĕn)], 1, one trained to put out fires; 2, one who tends fires; a stoker.

fire-place (fīr'plās"), *n.* the open recess under a chimney, in which a fire may be built; a hearth.

fire-proof (fīr'prōōf"), *adj.* made of material that resists fire; incapable of destruction by fire, as concrete structures: —*v.t.* to make proof against fire.

fire ship a ship filled with explosives, set afire and floated among the vessels of an enemy.

fire-side (fīr'sīd"), *n.* 1, the hearth; 2, the place of domestic comfort; the home:—*adj.* pertaining to the home.

fire trap a highly combustible building, or one with unsafe fire escapes.

fire wa-ter alcoholic spirits: the American Indian's name for strong drink.

fire-weed (fīr'wēd"), *n.* any of various plants, as the Jimson weed and willow-herb: found in burned clearings.

fire-wood (fīr'wŏŏd"), *n.* wood suitable for, or prepared for, fuel.

fire-works (fīr'wûrks"), *n.pl.* 1, devices made from a great variety of materials, which, when set on fire, produce figures in fire or a brilliant display of light, often in colors; 2, signals used at night.

fire wor-ship the worship of fire as a deity or god.

fir-ing (fīr'ĭng), *n.* 1, the act of discharging firearms; 2, the application of intense heat, as in baking; fuel.

fir-kin (fûr'kĭn), *n.* 1, a small wooden vessel for holding butter, lard, etc.; 2, a measure of capacity equal to one fourth of a barrel; nine gallons.

1**firm** (fûrm), *adj.* 1, hard; compact; solid; 2, stable; rigid; unyielding; immovable; as, a *firm* foundation for a structure; 3, steady and vigorous; as, a *firm* step; 4, enduring; steadfast; loyal; 5, resolute; positive; confident; as, a *firm* stand on some subject:—*v.t.* to compact; fix firmly.—*adv.* **firm'ly.**
Syn., adj. solid, stable. *Firm* applies to that which is steady under pressure; as, a *firm* foundation. *Solid* describes that which is hard and dense, substantial and unyielding; as, a *solid* block of marble. *Stable* suggests something which cannot be easily moved; as, a lighthouse must be a *stable* structure. All these terms are used figuratively; as, *firm* convictions; *solid* comfort; *stable* government.

2**firm** (fûrm), *n.* a partnership or association, of two or more persons, not a corporation, for doing business, each member being liable for all its debts.

fir-ma-ment (fûr'mȧ-mĕnt), *n.* the sky; the arch of the heavens.

fir-man (fûr'măn; fẽr-män'), *n.* a special edict, as of an oriental ruler.

first (fûrst), *adj.* 1, the ordinal of one; 2, foremost in place, rank, dignity, time, excellence, etc.; earliest; 3, most important; chief: **First day**, the name given to Sunday by the Society of Friends: **first mate**, in the merchant service, the officer next in rank below the captain:—*adv.* 1, before all others; 2, sooner:—*n.* the beginning.
Syn., adj. leading, principal, primary.

first–born (fûrst'=bôrn"), *n.* the earliest produced or born; the oldest direct descendant; hence, an heir.

first-class (fûrst′=klȧs″), *adj.* of the highest excellence, rank, or quality; as, *first-class* accommodations.

first fruits 1, the first gatherings of the produce of the season; 2, the first profits of any office or undertaking.

first-hand (fûrst′=hănd″), *adj.* obtained directly from the source, as from the producer or grower.

first-ling (fûrst′lĭng), *n.*, usually in *pl.*, the first-born; the first produced.

first-ly (fûrst′lĭ), *adv.* in the first place: occasionally used for the adverb *first*, as in numbering topics.

first-rate (fûrst′=rāt″), *adj.* of the highest excellence; having the highest quality or character:—*n.* a warship of the first class:—*adv. Colloq.*, excellently.

firth (fûrth), *n.* 1, the mouth of a tidal river; 2, an arm of the sea. Also, **frith.**

fis-cal (fĭs′kăl), *adj.* pertaining to the public treasury or revenue; financial:—*n.* in some countries, an attorney-general.

fish (fĭsh), *n.* [*pl.* fish; fishes (-ĕz)], 1, an animal, usually scaly, living in water, breathing through gills instead of lungs; 2, the flesh of fish used for food; 3, a machine for hoisting an anchor; 4, a piece of wood or metal fastened to another to strengthen it: **Fishes,** 1, the constellation Pisces; 2, the 12th sign of the zodiac (see *zodiac*, illus.):—*v.t.* 1, to search in quest of fish; 2, to catch (fish); 3, to seek for and bring to light; draw up:—*v.i.* 1, to try to catch fish; 2, to seek to gain or obtain something by trickery or indirect methods.

fish-er (fĭsh′ẽr), *n.* 1, one who fishes; 2, an animal of the weasel family.

fish-er-man (fĭsh′ẽr-măn), *n.* [*pl.* fishermen (-mĕn)], 1, one who catches fish as a sport or business; 2, a fishing smack or ship for catching fish.

fish-er-y (fĭsh′ẽr-ĭ), *n.* [*pl.* fisheries (-ĭz)], 1, the business of catching fish; 2, a fishing ground; 3, the right to fish at a particular time or ground.

fish-gig (fĭsh′gĭg″), *n.* a pronged staff for spearing fish. Also, **fiz′gig″.**

fish glue glue made from the skin and other waste parts of fish.

fish hawk the osprey, a large bird of prey which feeds on fish.

fish-hook (fĭsh′-hook″), *n.* a hook used for catching fish.

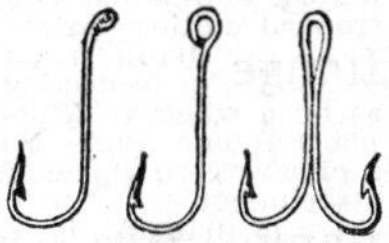

FISHHOOKS

fish-ing (fĭsh′ĭng), *n.* 1, the art, sport, or business of catching fish; 2, a fishing ground; 3, the operation of raising an anchor up to the gunwale of a vessel.

fish joint a pair of iron plates for uniting the ends of two railroad rails.

fish-mon-ger (fĭsh′mŭng″gẽr), *n.* one who sells fish.

fish-skin (fĭsh′skĭn″), *n.* a disease in which the skin becomes rough and scaly.

fish-wife (fĭsh′wīf″), *n.* [*pl.* fishwives (-wīvz″)], a woman who retails fish: also called *fishwoman.*

fish-y (fĭsh′ĭ), *adj.* [*comp.* fish′i-er, *superl.* fish′i-est], 1, pertaining to, consisting of, abounding in, or like, fish; 2, dull; vacant; 3, *Colloq.*, incredible or extravagant, as a story.—*n.* **fish′i-ness.**

fis-sion (fĭsh′ŭn), *n.* 1, the act of splitting or breaking up into parts; 2, cell division; the automatic dividing of a cell into two or more similar cells.

fis-sure (fĭsh′ûr), *n.* 1, a narrow opening; crack; 2, a cleft; as, a *fissure* in the earth:—*v.t.* [*p.t.* and *p.p.* -sured (-ûrd), *p.pr.* -sur-ing], to break or crack:—*v.i.* to cleave; separate in cracks.

fist (fĭst), *n.* the hand when closed or clenched; as, he struck him with his *fist.*

fist-ic (fĭs′tĭk), *adj.* pertaining to pugilism or boxing; as, a *fistic* battle.

fist-i-cuffs (fĭs′tĭ-kŭfs″), *n.pl.* a combat with the fists; boxing.

fis-tu-la (fĭs′tū-lȧ), *n.* [*pl.* fistulas (-lȧz); fistulæ (-lē)], 1, a reed; pipe; 2, a musical wind instrument; 3, an abnormal opening into one of the passages of the body, often accompanied by an ulcer.—*adj.* **fis′tu-lar.**

[1]fit (fĭt), *n.* 1, a convulsion; a sudden, violent attack, as of epilepsy, indigestion etc.: usually attended by unconsciousness; 2, a sudden impulse; as, a *fit* of ambition; an impulsive show of emotion; as, a *fit* of laughter.

[2]fit (fĭt), *adj.* [*comp.* fit′ter, *superl.* fit′test], 1, adapted or qualified; suitable; 2, convenient; proper; meet; 3, ready; prepared; properly trained; as, a *fit* baseball team; 4, *Colloq.*, in good condition; as, I feel very *fit* today:—*v.t.* [*p.t.* and *p.p.* fit′ted, *p.pr.* fit′ting], 1, to make suitable; adapt; 2, to accommodate with respect to size and shape; as, to *fit* a child with shoes; 3, to qualify; equip; prepare; as, to *fit* a field for corn; 4, to be properly suited or adjusted to; as, the shoes *fit* the child:—*v.i.* 1, to be adapted to one; as, his gloves *fit* well; 2, to be proper or suitable; be properly adjusted:—*n.* an adaptation of one thing to another; the suitability of a thing; as, the *fit* of a coat.—*adv.* **fit′ly.**—*n.* **fit′ness.**

Syn., adj. seemly, appropriate.—*Ant., adj.* unsuitable, improper, inappropriate.

fitch (fĭch), *n.* the European polecat; also, its fur. Also, **fitch′et; fitch′ew.**

fit-ful (fĭt′fo͝ol), *adj.* capricious; spasmodic, or occurring by fits and starts; changeable; as, a *fitful* mood.—*adv.* **fit′ful-ly.** —*n.* **fit′ful-ness.**

Syn. jerky, variable, irregular, impulsive.

fit-ter (fĭt′ẽr), *n.* 1, one who adjusts pipes, or puts the parts of a machine together; 2, one who tries on, adjusts, and shapes, as clothes.

fit-ting (fĭt′ĭng), *p.adj.* suitable; appropriate:—*n.*, in *pl.*, the necessary fixtures, equipment, etc., of a house or shop.

fitz (fĭts), *n. Obs.*, a son:—*prefix*, son of: used in Norman-French surnames, as *Fitz*herbert, esp. in the surnames of illegitimate sons of kings and princes.

five (fīv), *adj.* composed of one more than four: **Five Nations,** a confederacy of Iroquoian tribes, made up of the Mohawks, Onondagas, Cayugas, Oneidas, and Senecas, and later the Tuscaroras: also called *Iroquois:* —*n.* 1, the number consisting of four plus one; 2, a sign representing five units, as 5 or v.

five-fold (fīv′fōld″), *adj.* five times as much; multiplied by five.

fix (fĭks), *v.t.* 1, to make fast, secure, or stable; set or place permanently; adjust; 2, *Colloq.*, to put to rights or repair; 3, to hold firmly; as, to *fix* the attention of an audience:—*v.i.* to become solid or firm; become stable:—*n. Colloq.*, an awkward situation; a dilemma.—*adj.* **fix′a-ble.**

Syn., v. determine, establish, settle.

fix-a-tion (fĭk-sā′shŭn), *n.* 1, the act or process of making permanent; 2, the state of being permanent; 3, in chemistry, the process by which an element is combined in a stable compound so as to become available for commercial use; 4, in photography, the process of rendering permanent a negative or print.

fix-a-tive (fĭk′sȧ-tĭv), *n.* something that serves to make permanent, as colors in drawings or photographic impressions.

fixed (fĭkst), *p.adj.* **1**, firm; settled; permanent; stable; **2**, resolute; as, *fixed* ambition: **fixed star**, a star which seems to remain in the same position in the heavens.—*adv.* **fix'ed-ly.**—*n.* **fix'ed-ness.**

fix-ings (fĭks'ĭngz), *n.pl. Colloq.*, the things needed in any preparation; furnishings; ornaments.

fix-i-ty (fĭk'sĭ-tĭ), *n.* [*pl.* fixities (-tĭz)], stability; permanence; a state of being fastened.

fix-ture (fĭks'tûr), *n.* **1**, that which is firmly fastened; **2**, an article of furniture attached to a house and regarded as part of it; **3**, *Colloq.*, one who seems to be permanent in his position.

fizz (fĭz), *n.* **1**, a hissing noise; **2**, an effervescent or bubbling liquid, as soda water:—*v.i.* to make a hissing noise. Also, **fiz.**

fiz-zle (fĭz'l), *v.i.* [*p.t.* and *p.p.* -zled (-ld), *p.pr.* -zling], **1**, to make a hissing noise; **2**, to fail miserably:—*n.* **1**, a spluttering; hence, a state of restlessness; worry; **2**, a humiliating failure.

fjord (fyôrd), *n.* a narrow arm of the sea, with high rocky banks. Also, **fiord**, *Pfd. S.*

flab-ber-gast (flăb'ẽr-găst), *v.t. Colloq.*, to confound; astonish.

flab-by (flăb'ĭ), *adj.* [*comp.* flab'bi-er, *superl.* flab'bi-est], **1**, easily shaking or yielding to the touch; lacking muscle; **2**, mentally or physically feeble.—*adv.* **flab'-bi-ly.**—*n.* **flab'bi-ness.**

Syn. flaccid, limp, soft.—*Ant.* strong, stiff.

flac-cid (flăk'sĭd), *adj.* flabby; weak; limber; lacking firmness.—*adv.* **flac'cid-ly.**—*n.* **flac'cid-ness.**

flac-cid-i-ty (flăk-sĭd'ĭ-tĭ), *n.* flabby weakness; lack of stiffness.

¹flag (flăg), *n.* **1**, a piece of light cloth, usually bunting or silk, bearing some symbolic design, and chiefly used as an emblem or standard indicating nationality; **2**, in writing or printing music, one of the small diagonal strokes from the stem of a note which show it to be an eighth, sixteenth, etc.: also called *pennant* (see *note*, illus.):—*v.t.* [*p.t.* and *p.p.* flagged (flăgd), *p.pr.* flag'ging], **1**, to signal to, with a flag or light; **2**, to deck with flags.—*adj.* **¹flag'gy.**—*n.* **flag'pole".**

²flag (flăg), *v.i.* [*p.t.* and *p.p.* flagged (flăgd), *p.pr.* flag'ging], **1**, to hang loose; **2**, to become languid; move or act slowly.

Syn. droop, pine, languish, decline.

³flag (flăg), *n.* any of various plants having long, narrow leaves, and growing in swampy ground, esp. the iris and the sweet flag.—*adj.* **²flag'gy.**

⁴flag (flăg), *n.* **1**, a large, flat slab of stone suitable for pavements; a flagstone; also, any hard stone used for flags; **2**, in *pl.*, a pavement made of such slabs:—*v.t.* [*p.t.* and *p.p.* flagged (flăgd), *p.pr.* flag'ging], to pave with flat slabs of stone.

flag-el-lant (flăj'ĕ-lănt; flȧ-jĕl'ănt), *adj.* using a whip or scourge:—*n.* one who scourges himself as a religious duty.

flag-el-late (flăj'ĕ-lāt), *v.t.* [*p.t.* and *p.p.* -lat"ed, *p.pr.* -lat"ing], to whip:—*adj.* like a whiplash.—*n.* **flag"el-la'tion.**

flag-eo-let (flăj"ō-lĕt'; flăj"ō-lĕt), *n.* a small musical instrument of the flute class.

FLAGEOLET

¹flag-ging (flăg'ĭng), *n.* a pavement or walk of flagstones; also, flagstones collectively.

²flag-ging (flăg'ĭng), *p.adj.* weary; losing force; failing.

Syn. languid, drooping, languishing, pining.

fla-gi-tious (flȧ-jĭsh'ŭs), *adj.* **1**, atrocious; wicked; **2**, highly criminal.—*adv.* **fla-gi'tious-ly.**—*n.* **fla-gi'tious-ness.**

flag of-fi-cer an officer commanding a fleet, as an admiral.

flag-on (flăg'ŭn), *n.* a large drinking vessel with a narrow mouth and a handle.

fla-grant (flā'grănt), *adj.* openly wicked; heinous; notorious; as, a *flagrant* crime.—*n.* **fla'gran-cy.**—*adv.* **fla'grant-ly.**

flag-ship (flăg'shĭp"), *n.* the ship that leads a fleet, carries the commander, and flies his flag.

flag-staff (flăg'ståf"), *n.* [*pl.* flagstaffs (-ståfs"); flagstaves (-stāvz")], a pole or staff for a flag.

flag-stone (flăg'stōn"), *n.* a large, flat paving stone.

flail (flāl), *n.* a wooden instrument like a jointed pole, formerly used for threshing grain, as wheat, by hand.

FLAIL

flak (flăk), *n.* antiaircraft fire:—*adj.* pertaining to antiaircraft fire.

¹flake (flāk), *n.* a platform or rack, as for support or storage.

²flake (flāk), *n.* **1**, a small, thin, flat, scalelike fragment; as, a *flake* of ice; **2**, a flash of fire or light:—*v.i.* [*p.t.* and *p.p.* flaked (flākt), *p.pr.* flak'ing], to break off or separate into layers or thin fragments; scale or peel off.—*adj.* **flak'y.**—*n.* **flak'i-ness.**

flam-beau (flăm'bō), *n.* [*pl.* flambeaux (-bōz) or flambeaus (-bōz)], **1**, a flaming torch; **2**, a large, showy candlestick.

flam-boy-ant (flăm-boi'ănt), *adj.* **1**, showy, esp. when wanting in good taste; **2**, characterized by flamelike or waving curves, as the tracery of certain windows of Gothic architecture.—*adv.* **flam-boy'ant-ly.**

flame (flām), *n.* **1**, a burning gas or vapor; **2**, ardor of temper or passion; glow of imagination; **3**, *Colloq.*, a sweetheart:—*v.t.* [*p.t.* and *p.p.* flamed (flāmd), *p.pr.* flam'ing], **1**, to burn; singe; **2**, to excite:—*v.i.* to burst into flame; flare up, as in anger.—*adj.* **flam'y.**

Syn., *n.* and *v.* flare, flash, glare.

fla-men (flā'mĕn), *n.* [*pl.* flamens (-mĕnz); flamines (flăm'ĭ-nēz)], one of fifteen priests in ancient Rome, devoted to the service of a special deity or god.

fla-min-go (flȧ-mĭng'gō), *n.* [*pl.* flamingos; flamingoes (-gōz)], a long-legged, web-footed, brightly colored, tropical wading bird.

flange (flănj), *n.* a raised or projecting rim, as on a wheel to keep it in place upon a track, or on a pipe to give a place for attachment.

flank (flăngk), *n.* **1**, the fleshy part of an animal, between the ribs and hip (see *beef*, illus.); **2**, the side of an army, regiment, or building; **3**, that part of a fortification constructed to defend another:—*v.t.* **1**, to attack or go around the side of (an army); **2**, to guard on the flank:—*v.i.* to border or touch the side of a thing:—*adj.* pertaining to, or cut from, the flank.—*n.* **flank'er.**

FLAMINGO ($\frac{1}{26}$)

flan-nel (flăn'ĕl), *n.* **1**, a soft, loosely woven cloth, usually made of wool; **2**, in *pl.*, garments made of this material.

flan-nel-ette (flăn"ĕl-ĕt'), *n.* a soft cotton material resembling flannel. Also, **flan"nel-et'.**

flap (flăp), *n.* **1**, anything broad and flat hanging loosely, as the tail of a coat;

2, the motion or noise of anything broad and flat; 3, a slap:—*v.t.* [*p.t.* and *p.p.* flapped (flăpt), *p.pr.* flap'ping], 1, to strike with, or as with, a flap; 2, to move to and fro:—*v.i.* to move, as wings, with noise.

flap-jack (flăp'jăk″), *n.* a pancake or griddlecake: so called because of the way in which it is turned on the griddle.

flap-per (flăp'ẽr), *n.* 1, one who or that which waves loosely to and fro; 2, a young bird when first trying its wings; 3, *Colloq.*, a young girl in her teens.

flare (flâr), *n.* 1, a large, unsteady, glaring light; 2, a spreading outward or upward; 3, a signal; 4, gaudiness; showiness:—*v.i.* [*p.t.* and *p.p.* flared (flârd), *p.pr.* flar'ing], 1, to burn with a broad, unsteady light; 2, to spread outward or upward.—*adv.* **flar'ing-ly.**

Syn., *n.* and *v.* blaze, glare, flame, flash.

flash (flăsh), *n.* 1, a sudden, quick, fleeting blaze or light; as, a *flash* of lightning, or of a gun; 2, a sudden outburst, as of merriment, wit, or passion; 3, a very short period; an instant:—*v.t.* to cause to act, burst, or appear suddenly; as, to *flash* a light; to *flash* a look:—*v.i.* 1, to shine with a sudden, quick, fleeting blaze or light; 2, to appear suddenly, or to pass at great speed; as, the train *flashed* by:—*adj.* pertaining to thieves or their language; hence, cheap and gaudy.

Syn., *n.* flame, spark, gleam, blaze.

flash-ing (flăsh'ĭng), *n.* 1, any of various operations in glassmaking; 2, sheets of lead or other metal used to keep the joints and angles, as of roofs, water-tight:—*adj.* emitting bursts of light: **flashing point,** the temperature at which a mineral oil, when slowly heated, gives off vapor which will ignite with a flash upon the application of a flame: also called *flash point:* distinguished from *burning point*, at which the oil ignites.

Syn., *adj.* sparkling, glittering, gleaming.

flash light 1, a sudden brilliant light for taking photographs; also, the photograph so taken; 2, a light that comes and goes in flashes, as a signal; 3, a small electric lamp with a storage battery, to carry in the hand.—*adj.* **flash'-light″.**

flash-y (flăsh'ĭ), *adj.* [*comp.* flash'i-er, *superl.* flash'i-est], brilliant, but empty; gaudy; showy, but cheap in appearance.—*adv.* **flash'i-ly.**—*n.* **flash'i-ness.**

flask (flàsk), *n.* a narrow-necked bottle, made of glass, metal, or leather, for holding liquids, powder, etc.

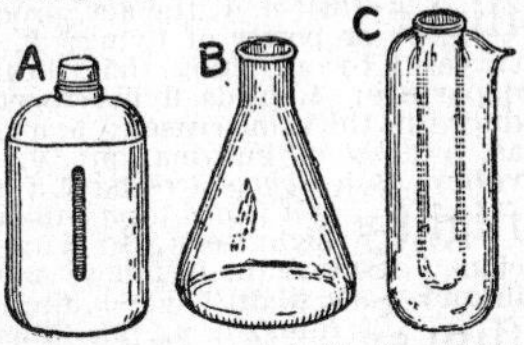

FLASKS: A, pocket; B, shaped for lateral shaking without spilling; C, vacuum, for holding liquid air.

[1]**flat** (flăt), *adj.* [*comp.* flat'ter, *superl.* flat'test], 1, having a plane, horizontal surface; level; 2, prostrate; ruined; 3, having breadth and smoothness, but little thickness; 4, unvarying; without discount; as, a *flat* rate; 5, monotonous; uninteresting; as, a *flat* speech; 6, tasteless; as, a *flat* drink; 7, unprofitable; as, a *flat* season in business; 8, wanting in brilliancy or in the prominence of important features; as, a *flat* painting; 9, deflated: said of pneumatic tires; 10, in music: a, below the true pitch; as, a *flat* note; b, lowered by a half step; as, B *flat:*—*adv.* 1, in a level or prostrate position; 2, exactly: said of numbers; as, his time was ten seconds *flat:*—*n.* 1, a surface free from unevenness; 2, a level or extended plain; a shallow or shoal; 3, the smooth, wide part of a thing; as, the *flat* of a sword; 4, in music, the sign [♭] which makes the staff degree on which it is placed or the letter name which it follows represent a half step lower; the pitch itself: **double flat,** in music, a sign [♭♭] indicating that the pitch of the notes of the staff is to be lowered two half steps:—*v.t.* and *v.i.* [*p.t.* and *p.p.* flat'ted, *p.pr.* flat'ting], to make or become flat; esp., in music, to lower or become lower in pitch, usually by a half step.—*adv.* **flat'ly.**—*n.* **flat'ness.**

Syn., *adj.* level. *Flat* stresses the absence of elevation, prominence, or curves; as, a *flat* roof. As applied to country, *flat* means without hills or valleys and therefore, usually, monotonous; as, a *flat* and uninteresting landscape. *Level* describes that which is without tilt or inclination; as, a *level* floor; a *level* plain.

[2]**flat** (flăt), *n.* a suite of rooms on one floor, usually planned for a single family and forming a complete residence; an apartment.

flat-fish (flăt'fĭsh″), *n.* a fish having a broad, flat, but thin, body, and both eyes on one side, as the flounder.

flat-i-ron (flăt'ī″ûrn), *n.* a heavy, usually wedge-shaped, iron utensil with a polished surface on its under side, used, when heated, for pressing or smoothing cloth.

flat-ten (flăt'n), *v.t.* 1, to make level or smooth; 2, to beat down; prostrate; 3, to sadden; depress; 4, to make dull, insipid, or tasteless; 5, in music, to lower in tone:—*v.i.* 1, to become even or level; 2, to become insipid.—*n.* **flat'ten-er.**

flat-ter (flăt'ẽr), *v.t.* 1, to please, or seek to please, by complimentary speech, usually insincere; 2, to praise too highly; 3, to encourage with false hopes or expectations:—*v.i.* to give false praise.—*n.* **flat'ter-er.**—*p.adj.* **flat'ter-ing.**—*adv.* **flat'ter-ing-ly.**

flat-ter-y (flăt'ẽr-ĭ), *n.* [*pl.* flatteries (-ĭz)], 1, insincere complimentary speech; 2, the act of one who flatters.

Syn. (see compliment).

flat-u-lence (flăt'ū-lĕns), *n.* 1, gas in the stomach or intestines; 2, emptiness; pretentiousness; conceit. Also, **flat'u-len-cy.**—*adj.* **flat'u-lent.**—*adv.* **flat'u-lent-ly.**

fla-tus (flā'tŭs), *n.* gas formed in the intestines, stomach, etc.

flat-ways (flăt'wāz″), *adv.* with the flat side up or foremost; not edgewise. Also, **flat'wise″.**

flat-worm (flăt'wûrm″), *n.* any of certain worms with flattened bodies: often parasitic.

flaunt (flänt; flônt), *v.t.* to display with unnecessary show:—*v.i.* 1, to make a gaudy display in dress; 2, to behave in a forward manner.—*adv.* **flaunt'ing-ly.**

Syn. wave, brandish, parade.

flau-tist (flô'tĭst), *n.* one who plays the flute: also called *flutist.*

fla-vor (flā'vẽr), *n.* 1, that quality which affects the sense of taste; as, a spicy *flavor* in a cake; 2, that quality which affects the sense of smell; as, the *flavor* of a perfume; 3, a flavoring substance, as vanilla; 4, a pervasive characteristic, as of a literary work:—*v.t.* to give a distinguishing characteristic to; as, to *flavor* an ice. Also, **fla'vour.**

Syn., *n.* relish, savor, taste.

fla-vor-ing (flā'vẽr-ĭng), *n.* an essence or extract for giving flavor. Also, **fla'vour-ing.**

[1]**flaw** (flô), *n.* a blemish; a weak spot; crack:—*v.t.* to make a flaw in; crack.—*adj.* **flaw'less.**—*adv.* **flaw'less-ly.**

Syn., *n.* (see blemish).

[2]**flaw** (flô), *n.* a sudden, sharp puff of wind.

flax (flăks), *n.* **1**, a slender plant with blue flowers, from the fiber of which linen is made; **2**, the fiber ready to be spun.

flax-en (flăk'sn), *adj.* resembling or made of flax; of a pale yellow color.

flax-seed (flăks'sēd"; flăk'sēd"), *n.* the seed of the flax, much used in medicine and for making linseed oil.

flay (flā), *v.t.* **1**, to strip off; skin; **2**, to torture.

flea (flē), *n.* any of various small, wingless, blood-sucking, jumping insects.

flea-bane (flē'bān"), *n.* any of several plants of the composite family, supposed to be useful for driving away fleas.

flea-bite (flē'bīt"), *n.* **1**, the bite of a flea; **2**, *Colloq.*: **a**, a trifling wound or trouble; **b**, a very small quantity.

fleck (flĕk), *n.* a streak or spot:—*v.t.* to streak or spot.

flec-tion (flĕk'shŭn), *n.* **1**, the act or process of bending; **2**, a curved or bent part; **3**, a grammatical variation for reasons of syntax; inflection; **4**, in anatomy, the bending of a limb toward the body: opp. of *extension*. Also, **flex'ion.**—*adj.* **flec'tion-al.**

fled (flĕd), past tense and past participle of the irregular verb *flee*.

fledge (flĕj), *v.i.* [*p.t.* and *p.p.* fledged (flĕjd), *p.pr.* fledg'ing], to have the full plumage or feathers necessary for flight:—*v.t.* to furnish with feathers ready for flight; as, the birds were *fledged*.

fledg-ling (flĕj'lĭng), *n.* a young bird just feathered out and able to fly. Also, **fledge'ling.**

flee (flē), *v.t.* [*p.t.* and *p.p.* fled (flĕd), *p.pr.* flee'ing], to run away from; avoid:—*v.i.* **1**, to run away; **2**, to disappear; vanish.
Syn. abscond, depart, shun.

fleece (flēs), *n.* **1**, the woolly coat of a sheep; also, all the wool shorn from a sheep at one time; **2**, anything resembling this coat of wool:—*v.t.* [*p.t.* and *p.p.* fleeced (flēst), *p.pr.* fleec'ing], **1**, to shear (a sheep) of the wool; **2**, to rob; strip.—*n.* **fleec'er.**

fleec-y (flēs'ĭ), *adj.* [*comp.* fleec'i-er, *superl.* fleec'i-est], like a sheep's coat of wool; white and fluffy; as, *fleecy* clouds.

fleer (flēr), *n.* mockery or derision:—*v.i.* to mock or sneer.—*adv.* **fleer'ing-ly.**

[1]**fleet** (flēt), *adj.* swift; nimble:—*v.i.* to pass or fly quickly.—*adv.* **fleet'ly.**—*n.* **fleet'ness.**—*p.adj.* **fleet'ing.**—*adv.* **fleet'ing-ly.**
Syn., adj. fast, speedy, quick.

[2]**fleet** (flēt), *n.* **1**, a number of vessels in a group, under one commander; **2**, the combined naval equipment of a nation.

[3]**fleet** (flēt), *n.* an inlet or river: obsolete except in place names: **the Fleet,** formerly, a London prison, used for debtors.

Flem-ing (flĕm'ĭng), *n.* a Belgian who speaks the Flemish tongue.

Flem-ish (flĕm'ĭsh), *adj.* pertaining to the Flemings or to Flanders:—*n.* the language of northern Belgium.

flesh (flĕsh), *n.* **1**, that part of an animal body beneath the skin, composed of soft, muscular tissue; **2**, animal food; **3**, pulp, as of fruit; **4**, the body: opp. of *soul;* **5**, present life; as, in the *flesh;* **6**, near relatives; kindred:—*v.t.* **1**, to satiate or glut; **2**, to feed dogs with meat so as to urge them to further exertion in hunting; **3**, to put weight on; fatten:—*v.i. Colloq.*, to get fat.

flesh fly a fly whose larvæ, called maggots, feed on flesh.

flesh-ly (flĕsh'lĭ), *adj.* pertaining to the body; corporeal; carnal:—*adv.* carnally.—*n.* **flesh'li-ness.**

flesh-pot (flĕsh'pŏt"), *n.* **1**, a vessel used for cooking meat; **2**, in *pl.*, plenty; physical ease and comfort.

flesh-y (flĕsh'ĭ), *adj.* [*comp.* flesh'i-er, *superl.* flesh'i-est], full of flesh; plump; corpulent; fat.—*n.* **flesh'i-ness.**

Fletch-er-ism (flĕch'ẽr-ĭzm), *n.* a system of diet in which the food is thoroughly chewed: from Horace Fletcher, its advocate.—*v.i.* **Fletch'er-ize.**

*__fleur–de–lis__ (flûr"=dē=lē'), [Fr.], *n.* [*pl.* fleurs=de=lis (flûr"=)], **1**, the emblem of French royalty; **2**, the iris. Also, ***fleur" de lys'** (lē'); **flow'er–de–luce'** (=dē=lūs').

FLEUR-DE-LIS

flew (flōō), past tense of the irregular verb *fly*.

flex (flĕks), *v.t.* to bend or curve by the muscles, as an arm.

flex-i-bil-i-ty (flĕk"sĭ-bĭl'ĭ-tĭ), *n.* the state or quality of being pliant.

flex-i-ble (flĕk'sĭ-bl), *adj.* **1**, easily bent; pliant; **2**, yielding to persuasion; **3**, adaptable; as, a *flexible* system.
Syn. pliable, limber, supple.—*Ant.* brittle, hard, inflexible, unyielding.

flex-ion (flĕk'shŭn), *n.* **1**, the act or process of bending; **2**, a curve; **3**, the grammatical variation of a word; inflection. See **flec'tion,** *Pfd. S.*—*adj.* **flex'ion-al.**

flex-or (flĕk'sŏr), *n.* a muscle that acts in bending a limb: opp. of *extensor*.

flex-ure (flĕk'shŭr; flĕks'ūr), *n.* **1**, the act of bending; **2**, the part bent; **3**, a curve or fold.

flib-ber-ti-gib-bet (flĭb'ẽr-tĭ-jĭb"ĕt), *n.* **1**, an imp; a restless, frivolous, or flighty person; **2**, formerly, a fiend; evil spirit.

flick (flĭk), *n.* a light, quick stroke, as with a whip:—*v.t.* to whip lightly.

[1]**flick-er** (flĭk'ẽr), *v.i.* **1**, to move with an unsteady and quick motion, as a flame in the wind; **2**, to flutter, as with the wings:—*n.* an unsteady light or movement; flutter.—*p.adj.* and *n.* **flick'er-ing.**
Syn., n. vibration, quiver.

[2]**flick-er** (flĭk'ẽr), *n.* the golden-winged woodpecker of North America: also called *yellow-hammer*.

fli-er (flī'ẽr), *n.* **1**, one who flies; **2**, one who flees; **3**, that part of a machine that moves rapidly; **4**, in *pl.*, a straight flight of steps; **5**, *Colloq.*: **a**, a speculative venture; **b**, something that moves very rapidly, as an express train; **c**, a handbill. See **fly'er,** *Pfd. S.*

flight (flīt), *n.* **1**, the act, process, manner, or power of flying; **2**, the distance traveled by anything that flies; **3**, a hasty departure; **4**, birds flying together, or produced in the same season; **5**, a soaring forth; as, a *flight* of imagination; **6**, a shower or volley; as, a *flight* of arrows; **7**, a series of steps.

flight-y (flīt'ĭ), *adj.* [*comp.* flight'i-er, *superl.* flight'i-est], **1**, changeful; capricious; extravagant in fancy; **2**, wild; mildly insane.—*adv.* **flight'i-ly.**—*n.* **flight'i-ness.**

flim-sy (flĭm'zĭ), *n.* [*pl.* flimsies (-zĭz)], a thin paper; also, reporters' copy:—*adj.* [*comp.* flim'si-er, *superl.* flim'si-est], **1**, thin; weak; **2**, ineffective; as, a *flimsy* argument.—*adv.* **flim'si-ly.**—*n.* **flim'si-ness.**
Syn., adj. feeble, frail, unsubstantial.

flinch (flĭnch), *v.i.* to shrink or draw back, as from pain, danger, etc.:—*n.* the act of drawing back from pain.
Syn., v. wince, start. To *flinch* is to draw back or fail to face, usually with the idea of weakness; as, he *flinched* from the torture. *Wince* is less strong than *flinch* and refers almost invariably to pain; as, he *winced* at the blow. *Start*, like the others, refers to a sudden movement, the cause of which, however, is not necessarily painful; as, he *started* at the sudden mention of his name.

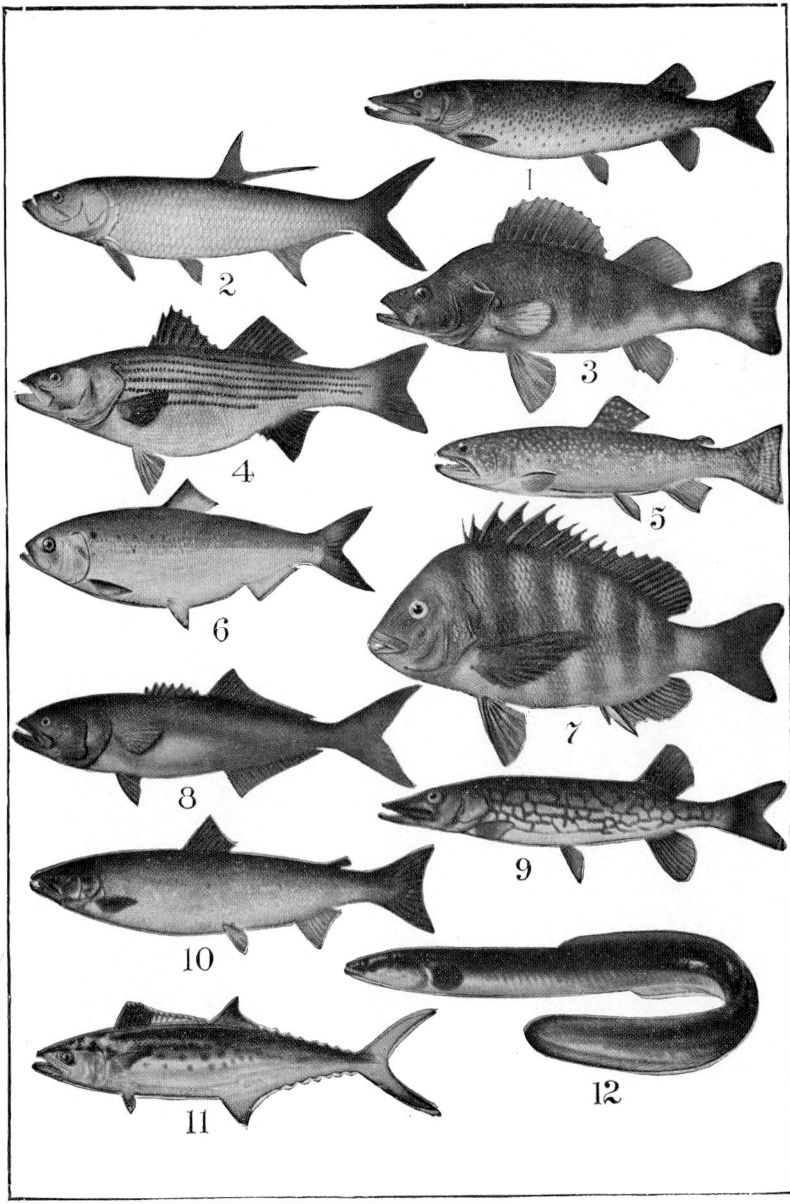

AMERICAN FRESH AND SALT WATER FISH

1. Muskellunge. 2. Tarpon. 3. Yellow perch. 4. Striped bass. 5. Brook trout. 6. Shad. 7. Sheepshead. 8. Blue fish. 9. Pickerel. 10. Land-locked salmon. 11. Spanish mackerel. 12. Common eel.

flin-ders (flĭn′dẽrz), *n.pl.* splinters; fragments; as, blown to *flinders.*

fling (flĭng), *v.t.* [*p.t.* and *p.p.* flung (flŭng), *p.pr.* fling′ing], **1**, to throw or hurl; drive by violence; scatter; **2**, to cast to the ground; **3**, to throw aside:—*v.i.* to rush about impatiently; flounce; as, to *fling* about the room:—*n.* **1**, the act of throwing or casting; **2**, a sneer or gibe; **3**, a period, usually brief, of unrestrained pleasure; **4**, a kind of dance.

flint (flĭnt), *n.* **1**, a very hard kind of quartz or rock which strikes fire with steel; **2**, anything hard like flint.

flint-lock (flĭnt′lŏk″), *n.* an old form of gun in which the powder was

FLINTLOCK

1, hammer with flint; 2, steel and powder pan.

ignited, or set on fire, by a spark from a stroke of flint on steel.

flint-y (flĭn′tĭ), *adj.* [*comp.* flint′i-er, *superl.* flint′i-est], **1**, composed of, or like, flint; hard; **2**, obdurate; cruel; as, a *flinty* heart.—*n.* **flint′i-ness.**

¹**flip** (flĭp), *n.* a short, quick stroke; a flick:—*v.t.* [*p.t.* and *p.p.* flipped (flĭpt), *p.pr.* flip′ping], to flick with the fingers; strike with a short, quick blow:—*v.i.* to move jerkily.

²**flip** (flĭp), *n.* a drink composed of ale, beer, or cider, sweetened, spiced, and heated.

flip-pan-cy (flĭp′ăn-sĭ), *n.* a trifling manner; pertness; as, the *flippancy* of her remarks displeased everybody.
Syn. levity, lightness.

flip-pant (flĭp′ănt), *adj.* **1**, impertinent; disrespectful; as, a *flippant* child; **2**, trifling, as an answer.—*adv.* **flip′pant-ly.**—*n.* **flip′pant-ness.**

flip-per (flĭp′ẽr), *n.* a broad fin, arm, or paddle used in swimming, as that of the whale, seal, or turtle.

flirt (flûrt), *v.t.* **1**, to move to and fro with a short, rapid action; **2**, to throw with a quick, elastic motion:—*v.i.* **1**, to move nimbly; **2**, to make love for mere amusement:—*n.* **1**, a coquette; one who plays at making love; **2**, a sudden jerk or toss.

flir-ta-tion (flẽr-tā′shŭn), *n.* a playing at love; a light love affair; as, merely a summer *flirtation.*—*adj.* **flir-ta′tious.**

flit (flĭt), *v.i.* [*p.t.* and *p.p.* flit′ted, *p.pr.* flit′ting], **1**, to pass lightly and swiftly along; fly away; **2**, to move suddenly about.

flitch (flĭch), *n.* the side of a hog salted and cured; as, a *flitch* of bacon.

flit-ter-mouse (flĭt′ẽr-mous″), *n.* [*pl.* flittermice (-mīs″)], a bat.

flit-ting (flĭt′ĭng), *n.* **1**, the act of flying or moving lightly and swiftly; a fluttering; **2**, a removal.

fliv-ver (flĭv′ẽr), *n. Slang*, **1**, a small, cheap automobile; **2**, a failure; fizzle.

float (flōt), *v.t.* **1**, to cause to be supported on the surface of a liquid or suspended in a volume of gas; **2**, to cover with water; flood; **3**, in plastering, to level off with a smooth implement; **4**, to launch or start, as a rumor, business, or scheme:—*v.i.* **1**, to be held up on the surface of a liquid or within a volume of gas; **2**, to move quietly or lightly; glide without apparent effort; **3**, to drift about; hover; move or be carried aimlessly:—*n.* **1**, anything that rests on the surface of a liquid, or supports something on a liquid, as a raft, a cork on a fishing line, or the like; **2**, a dray used for transporting heavy objects; **3**, a plasterer's tool for spreading and smoothing; **4**, a drag of timber, used for dressing the surface of a road or for hauling over plowed land; **5**, a low cart or platform on wheels, or a single group of objects or persons, exhibited in a procession or parade; **6**, in some water animals, as fishes, a sac or bladder filled with gas, to regulate the buoyancy of the body.

float-age (flōt′āj), *n.* **1**, things that rest on a liquid; **2**, the ability of anything to float. Also, **flo′tage**, *Pfd. S.*

float-er (flōt′ẽr), *n.* **1**, one who or that which floats; **2**, *Slang*, one who moves from place to place to repeat his vote.

float-ing (flōt′ĭng), *p.adj.* **1**, swimming or held up on the surface of a liquid; **2**, free to move about; circulating; **3**, not fixed or settled; **4**, not permanently invested, as funds; not funded, as debts.

floc-cu-lent (flŏk′ū-lĕnt), *adj.* **1**, of or pertaining to wool, or to soft flakes; **2**, resembling flakes, puffs, or shreds of wool; as, *flocculent* clouds.

¹**flock** (flŏk), *n.* **1**, a number of animals or birds of one kind keeping together; as, a *flock* of sheep or geese; **2**, a large number of persons together: used esp. of the members of a church; a congregation:—*v.i.* to come together in crowds; congregate.
Syn., n. (see herd).

²**flock** (flŏk), *n.* **1**, a tuft of wool; **2**, the fiberlike refuse of wool or rags, used for stuffing in upholstery; **3**, anything resembling light, tufted masses of wool.

floe (flō), *n.* a large mass of drifting ice from the polar ocean.

flog (flŏg), *v.t.* [*p.t.* and *p.p.* flogged (flŏgd), *p.pr.* flog′ging], **1**, to whip; punish; **2**, to lash (the water) with the line in angling.

flood (flŭd), *n.* **1**, a great flow of water; inundation; **2**, the rising, or inflowing, tide; **3**, *Poetic*, the sea; **4**, an abundant supply or outpouring of anything: **flood tide**, the rising tide; the point or time of highest tide: opp. of *ebb tide:* **the Flood**, the great deluge in the time of Noah (Genesis 7, 8):—*v.t.* to deluge; inundate; overflow.

flood-gate (flŭd′gāt″), *n.* a gate in a waterway, which when opened allows the water to escape when at a certain height; hence, any opportunity for a great outpouring; as, the *floodgate* of immigration.

flood-light (flŭd′līt″), *n.* a strong, diffused artificial light, used esp. on the stage and in making motion pictures.

floor (flōr), *n.* **1**, the bottom surface of a room or house; **2**, any similar surface; as, the *floor* of a bridge; the *floor* of the ocean; **3**, all the rooms on one level in a building; a story; **4**, the part of a legislative or lawmaking chamber occupied by the members; as, the *floor* of the Senate at Washington; **5**, the right to address an assembly; as, he has the *floor*:—*v.t.* **1**, to cover with a floor; **2**, to strike down; **3**, to put to silence.

floor-ing (flōr′ĭng), *n.* **1**, materials for floors; **2**, floors collectively.

floor-walk-er (flōr′wôk″ẽr), *n.* in the U. S., an overseer in the aisles of a large department store.

flop (flŏp), *v.t.* [*p.t.* and *p.p.* flopped (flŏpt), *p.pr.* flop′ping], to strike or drop heavily or with a jerk:—*v.i.* **1**, to throw oneself about; as, the fish *flops* in the boat; to flap, as the brim of a hat; **2**, to change over quickly, as from one group to another:—*n.* **1**, the act or sound of dropping suddenly and heavily; **2**, a sudden change of allegiance, as to a party.—*adj. Colloq.*, **flop′py.**

flo-ra (flō′rȧ), *n.* **1**, the native plants of a particular region or period of the earth's history; **2**, a description of such plants.

flo-ral (flō′răl), *adj.* pertaining to, resembling, or consisting of, flowers.

Flor-en-tine (flŏr′ĕn-tēn; flŏr′ĕn-tīn), *adj.* pertaining or belonging to Florence, Italy:—*n.* an inhabitant of Florence.

flo-res-cent (flō-rĕs′ĕnt), *adj.* blooming; in bloom.—*n.* **flo-res′cence.**

flo-ret (flō′rĕt), *n.* **1,** a little flower; **2,** one of the small flowers that form the head of a composite flower such as the daisy.

flo-ri-cul-ture (flō′rĭ-kŭl″tūr; flŏr′ĭ-kŭl″-tūr), *n.* the production and cultivation of flowers.—*adj.* **flo″ri-cul′-tur-al.**—*n.* **flo″ri-cul′tur-ist.**

flor-id (flŏr′ĭd), *adj.* **1,** bright in color; flushed; **2,** brilliant with decorations; **3,** covered with flowers.—*adv.* **flor′id-ly.** —*n.* **flo-rid′i-ty.**—*n.* **flor′id-ness.**

flor-in (flŏr′ĭn), *n.* **1,** orig., a gold coin of Florence; **2,** any of various European silver coins.

flo-rist (flō′rĭst; flŏr′ĭst), *n.* one who cultivates flowers for pleasure, or who raises or sells them for profit.

floss (flôs), *n.* **1,** waste silk fibers; **2,** the soft, downy, silken substance in certain husks: **floss silk,** an untwisted, soft silk, chiefly used in embroidery.—*adj.* **floss′y.**

flo-tage (flō′tāj), *n.* **1,** things that rest on the surface of a liquid, as driftwood; **2,** the ability of anything to float; buoyancy. Also, **float′age.**

flo-til-la (flō-tĭl′ȧ), *n.* **1,** a fleet of small vessels; **2,** a small fleet.

flot-sam (flŏt′săm), *n.* goods lost in shipwreck, and found floating.

[1]**flounce** (flouns), *n.* a piece of cloth sewed to a petticoat or the skirt of the dress, with the lower border loose and spreading; a deep ruffle:—*v.t.* [*p.t.* and *p.p.* flounced (flounst), *p.pr.* flounc′ing], to furnish or trim with deep ruffles.—*n.* **flounc′ing.**

[2]**flounce** (flouns), *n.* a sudden jerk or movement of the body, denoting impatience:—*v.i.* [*p.t.* and *p.p.* flounced (flounst), *p.pr.* flounc′ing], to move angrily and impatiently.

[1]**floun-der** (floun′dẽr), *v.i.* to struggle awkwardly; proceed with difficulty, as if hampered; get out of a difficult situation:—*n.* awkward struggling.

[2]**floun-der** (floun′dẽr), *n.* **1,** any of a large family of fishes, including the

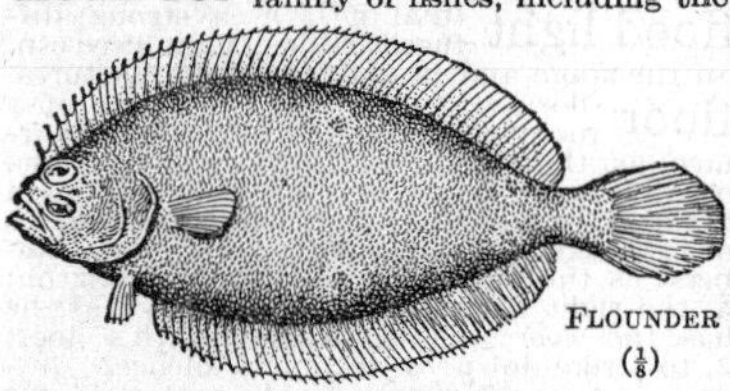

FLOUNDER ($\frac{1}{8}$)

halibut, having great flatness of body: also called *flatfish;* **2,** a shoemaker's tool used in molding boot fronts.

flour (flour), *n.* **1,** the fine meal of ground wheat or other grain; **2,** any fine, soft powder:—*v.t.* **1,** to grind into flour; **2,** to sprinkle flour upon.—*adj.* **flour′y.**

flour-ish (flŭr′ĭsh), *v.i.* **1,** to prosper or thrive; be vigorous; **2,** to wave about in a showy manner; **3,** to be flowery in language; **4,** to make ornamental lines with a pen; **5,** to boast or brag:—*v.t.* to swing about or brandish:—*n.* **1,** a figure formed by lines or strokes fancifully drawn; **2,** decoration; **3,** a musical passage intended for display; **4,** an elaborate trumpet call; **5,** ostentatious, showy parade; **6,** a waving about, as of a flag.

Syn., v. increase, grow, succeed; flaunt, parade.—*Ant., v.* decay, die, fall, droop.

flour-ish-ing (flŭr′ĭsh-ĭng), *p.adj.* thriving; vigorous; as, a *flourishing* business.—*adv.* **flour′ish-ing-ly.**

flout (flout), *v.t.* to insult; treat contemptuously:—*v.i.* to scoff; sneer:—*n.* an insult; contemptuous remark.—*adv.* **flout′-ing-ly.**—*n.* **flout′er.**

flow (flō), *v.i.* **1,** to run or spread; as, the river *flows* south; **2,** to glide; be uttered smoothly; **3,** to rise, as the tide; **4,** to melt; **5,** to issue forth; **6,** to hang freely, or sway; **7,** to abound; run over:—*n.* **1,** a current or stream; **2,** the quantity of fluid passing, as through a pipe, under given conditions; **3,** the rise of the tide; **4,** a marshy area which is inundated if the water is slightly raised.

flow-er (flou′ẽr), *n.* **1,** that part of a seed-bearing plant that contains the reproductive organs; a blossom; **2,** a plant cultivated for its blossoms; **3,** the choicest part of anything; as, the *flower* of a country's youth; **4,** an ornamental expression: **flowers of sulphur,** sulphur in the form of a powder, obtained by condensing sulphur vapor:—*v.i* to blossom:—*v.t.* to adorn with flowers or a floral design.—*adj.* **flow′er-less.**

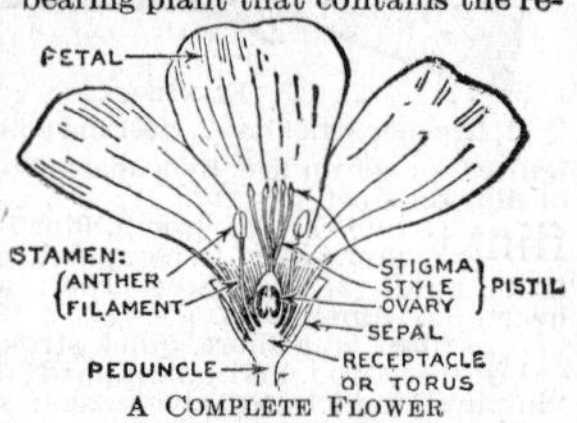

A COMPLETE FLOWER
Cut to show the floral parts

flow-er-de-luce (flou′ẽr-dē-lūs′), *n.* [*pl.* flowers-de-luce (-ẽrz-)], **1,** the floral emblem of French royalty; **2,** the iris. Also, **fleur″-de-lis′**, *Pfd.S.*

flow-er-et (flou′ẽr-ĕt), *n.* a little flower; a floret. Also, **flow′ret.**

flow-er-pot (flou′ẽr-pŏt″), *n.* a vessel containing earth in which to grow plants and flowers.

flow-er-y (flou′ẽr-ĭ), *adj.* **1,** abounding in, or adorned with, flowers; **2,** highly figurative or elaborate; as, *flowery* language.—*n.* **flow′er-i-ness.**

flow-ing (flō′ĭng), *p.adj.* **1,** moving or pouring forth, as a stream; **2,** copious; fluent; **3,** hanging loosely or swaying.—*adv.* **flow′ing-ly.**

Syn. easy, smooth, gliding.

flown (flōn), past participle of the transitive and intransitive verb *fly.*

flu (flōō), *n. Colloq.*, an infectious disease, often epidemic, characterized by inflammation of the air passages, muscular pains, headache, digestive disturbances, and prostration: a popular term for *influenza.*

fluc-tu-ate (flŭk′tū-āt), *v.i.* [*p.t.* and *p.p.* -at″ed, *p.pr.* -at″ing], **1,** to roll to and fro, as a wave; **2,** to rise and fall, as the stock market; **3,** to be undecided or wavering.—*n.* **fluc″tu-a′tion.**

Syn. waver, oscillate, vacillate, vibrate.

flue (flōō), *n.* **1,** a pipe or passage to convey away smoke, hot air, etc.; **2,** the opening in an organ pipe.

flu-en-cy (flōō′ĕn-sĭ), *n.* **1,** the quality of being eloquent; **2,** readiness and smoothness of speech; **3,** the quality of moving freely.

flu-ent (flōō′ĕnt), *adj.* **1,** possessing readiness and ease of speech; voluble; eloquent; **2,** moving freely.—*adv.* **flu′ent-ly.**

Syn. flowing, glib, lively, ready.

fluff (flŭf), *n.* light down or fur nap:—*v.t.* to spread out, as feathers.—*adj.* **fluff′y.**—*n.* **fluff′i-ness.**

flu-id (flōō′ĭd), *adj.* capable of flowing; liquid or gaseous: opp. of *solid:*—*n.* a substance which flows: **fluid dram,** a measure of capacity, equal to $\frac{1}{8}$ of a fluid ounce; about a teaspoonful; also written *fluidrachm* (flōō′ĭ-drăm″); *fluid drachm:* **fluid ounce,** a liquid measure of $\frac{1}{16}$ of a pint.—*n.* **flu-id′i-ty.**
Syn., n. liquid. Strictly, *fluid* means that which is flowing or moving; *liquid,* that which is melted; as, water in a river is a *fluid;* melted ice is a *liquid. Fluid* is the more general term: a *fluid* may be either liquid or gaseous; as, water, at an ordinary temperature, is both a *liquid* and a *fluid;* converted into steam, it is only a *fluid. Liquid* is the word applied to what we drink; as, milk is a *liquid;* a diet of *liquids.*

[1]**fluke** (flōōk), *n.* **1,** a flatfish: also called *flounder;* **2,** a parasitic, flattened worm causing a disease in sheep and other animals; **3,** a kind of kidney-shaped potato.

[2]**fluke** (flōōk), *n.* **1,** the flattened end of an arm of an anchor (see *anchor,* illus.); **2,** one of the broad lobes on the tail of a whale; **3,** the broad head of a harpoon.

[3]**fluke** (flōōk), *n. Slang,* **1,** a lucky stroke, as in some game; **2,** hence, a single victory or defeat, contrary to previous form or expectation.—*adj.* **fluk′y.**

flume (flōōm), *n.* **1,** an artificial channel for carrying water; **2,** a gap through which a torrent passes.

flum-mer-y (flŭm′ẽr-ĭ), *n.* [*pl.* flummeries (-ĭz)], **1,** a dish made of water-soaked oatmeal; **2,** a custard or blancmange; **3,** nonsense.

flung (flŭng), past tense and past participle of the verb *fling.*

flunk (flŭngk), *n. Slang,* a complete failure: —*v.i. Slang,* **1,** to fail completely; **2,** to retire through fear:—*v.t. Slang,* **1,** to fail in; **2** to give (a student) a grade of failure.

flunk-y (flŭngk′ĭ), *n.* [*pl.* flunkies (-ĭz)], **1,** a liveried servant: used contemptuously; **2,** a toady; snob. Also, **flunk′ey.**

flunk-y-ism (flŭngk′ĭ-ĭzm), *n.* the characteristics of a toady or snob. Also, **flunk′ey-ism.**

flu-or (flōō′ôr), *n.* calcium fluoride, a mineral occurring in crystalline form: a common name for *fluorite,* which see.

flu-o-res-cence (flōō″ō-rĕs′ĕns), *n.* **1,** the quality existing in certain substances of giving off, under the action of light, a color differing from their own; the property possessed by certain substances of becoming luminous under X rays or other forms of radiation; **2,** the light thus produced. —*v.i.* **flu″o-resce′.**—*adj.* **flu″o-res′cent.**

flu-or-ic (flōō-ŏr′ĭk), *adj.* pertaining to, or obtained from, fluorine.

flu-or-ide (flōō′ōr-īd; -ĭd), *n.* a salt of hydrofluoric acid.

flu-or-ine (flōō′ōr-ĭn; flōō′ōr-ēn), *n.* a pale, greenish yellow, gaseous element, similar to chlorine, but more active. Also, **flu′or-in.**

flu-or-ite (flōō′ōr-īt), *n.* a common mineral, calcium fluoride, used as a flux in the preparation of hydrofluoric acid, and for making lenses for scientific instruments: also called *fluor; fluor spar.*

flu-or-o-scope (flōō-ŏr′ō-skōp), *n.* a box adjustable to the eyes, used with X rays in making examinations of deep-seated parts of the body.

flu-or spar native fluoride of calcium; fluorite (which see).

flur-ry (flŭr′ĭ), *v.t.* [*p.t.* and *p.p.* -ried (-ĭd), *p.pr.* -ry-ing], to agitate, confuse, or bewilder:—*n.* [*pl.* flurries (-ĭz)], **1,** a sudden commotion or excitement; hurry; **2,** a sudden gust; as, a *flurry* of snowflakes.

[1]**flush** (flŭsh), *v.t.* **1,** to redden; cause to blush; **2,** to encourage; excite; thrill; **3,** to wash or cleanse by means of a strong flow of water:—*v.i.* **1,** to blush; glow; **2,** to become full of water:—*n.* **1,** a blush; glow; **2,** a sudden rush, as of water; **3,** a thrill; excitement:—*adj.* **1,** full; **2,** abundantly supplied, as with money; **3,** vigorous; **4,** even; level; as, nail the board *flush* with the corner: **flush deck,** a deck level from stem to stern:—*adv.* evenly (with the edge, as of a container).

[2]**flush** (flŭsh), *v.t.* to drive or startle from cover, as birds:—*v.i.* to rise or be startled from cover.

[3]**flush** (flŭsh), *n.* in certain card games, a hand of cards all of one suit.

flus-ter (flŭs′tẽr), *v.t.* **1,** to confuse or agitate; **2,** to hurry:—*n.* agitation or confusion; excitement.

flute (flōōt), *n.* **1,** a musical wind instrument furnished with finger holes and keys; **2,** a long channel or groove cut in the shaft of a column; **3,** a similar groove formed for decoration in wood, cloth, etc.:—*v.i.* [*p.t.* and *p.p.* flut′ed, *p.pr.* flut′ing], to play on, or as on, a flute:—*v.t.* to form parallel grooves in; decorate (wood, cloth, etc.) with grooves; as, to *flute* a ruffle.—*p.adj.* **flut′ed.**—*adj.* **flut′y.**

FLUTE

flut-ing (flōōt′ĭng), *n.* **1,** a channel or groove; **2,** work decorated with grooves; as, the *fluting* of a woman's ruffle; **3,** the act of sounding a flute; **4,** the act of making a flute-shaped groove.

flut-ist (flōōt′ĭst), *n.* a performer on the flute: also called *fluter; flautist.*

flut-ter (flŭt′ẽr), *v.i.* **1,** to flap the wings rapidly; **2,** to move rapidly and irregularly; **3,** to be in agitation or uncertainty:—*v.t.* **1,** to cause to move rapidly and irregularly; **2,** to throw into confusion:—*n.* **1,** a quick and irregular motion; vibration; **2,** a state of excitement or anxiety: **flutter wheel,** a water wheel placed at the bottom of a chute.—*n.* **flut′ter-er.**—*adv.* **flut′ter-ing-ly.**

flu-vi-al (flōō′vĭ-ăl), *adj.* pertaining to, growing or living in, or caused by, rivers.—*adj.* **flu′vi-a-tile** (flōō′vĭ-ȧ-tĭl).

flux (flŭks), *n.* **1,** any flow or issue of matter; **2,** the flow of the tide; **3,** a substance used in the working of ores to promote melting and to combine with impurities in the ore, as limestone in the blast furnace process for obtaining iron:—*v.t.* **1,** to fuse; melt; make fluid; **2,** to purge.

flux-ion (flŭk′shŭn), *n.* **1,** the act of flowing or melting; **2,** matter that flows.

fly (flī), *v.i.* [*p.t.* flew (flōō), *p.p.* flown (flōn), *p.pr.* fly′ing], **1,** to move through, or rise in, the air with wings; **2,** to pass swiftly; move rapidly; **3,** to go quickly through the air as if propelled by some driving impulse; **4,** to float in the air, as a flag; **5,** to run away; attempt to escape:—*v.t.* **1,** to avoid or shun; **2,** to cause to float in the air:—*n.* [*pl.* flies (flīz)], **1,** a two-winged insect of many kinds, including the common house fly; **2,** a hook in imitation of an insect: used in fishing; **3,** a piece of cloth stretched over a tent, forming an extra roof (see *tent,* illus.); **4,** a flap on a garment to cover a row of buttons; **5,** a disease in turnips; **6,** a hackney carriage; **7,** the horizontal dimension of a flag: opp. of *hoist;* **8,** in baseball, a ball batted so as to rise high in the air; also, the flight of a ball before it hits the ground; **9,** in *pl.,* space over a stage, with apparatus for handling scenery: **fly agaric,** a poisonous mushroom with a reddish cap.

fly-a-way (flī′ȧ-wā″), *adj.* flighty; not dependable:—*n.* a flighty person.

fly-blow (flī′blō″), *n.* the egg or larva of a fly:—*v.t.* [*p.t.* -blew″ (-blōō″), *p.p.* -blown″ (-blōn″), *p.pr.* -blow″ing], to lay eggs in (meat) as do flies; taint.

fly-catch-er (flī′kăch″ẽr), *n.* any of the small birds that catch insects while in the air, as the kingbird.

fly-er (flī′ẽr), *n.* **1**, one who or that which flies; specif., an aviator; **2**, one who flees; a fugitive; **3**, a swiftly moving part of a mechanism; **4**, one of a straight flight of steps; **5**, in *pl.*, a straight flight of steps; **6**, *Colloq.*: **a**, a speculative venture; as, a *flyer* in stocks; **b**, anything swiftly moving, as an express train; **c**, a handbill. Also, **fli′er.**

fly-ing (flī′ĭng), *p.adj.* **1**, capable of moving through the air with, or as if with, wings; as, a *flying* machine; **2**, moving rapidly and widely; as, a *flying* army; **3**, waving, as a flag; **4**, attached but projecting; as, a *flying* jib; **5**, brief; as, a *flying* visit.

fly-ing but-tress an arched brace against the wall of a building, resisting an outward thrust, as of the roof (see *buttress*, illus.).

fly-ing fish a fish with long, winglike fins that is able to remain in the air for a short time.

fly-ing frog any of several frogs of Borneo and the East Indies, living in trees, and capable of long, gliding leaps because of the membrane between their long toes (see *amphibian*, illus.).

fly-ing jib a sail beyond the jib or foremost sail of a ship.

fly-ing squir-rel a squirrel that makes very long, sailing leaps supported by folds of skin that stretch out between its fore and hind legs.

fly-leaf (flī′lēf″), *n.* [*pl.* flyleaves (-lēvz″)], a blank sheet at the beginning or at the end of a book.

fly-speck (flī′spĕk″), *n.* the spot made by the excrement of a house fly; hence, any insignificant speck:—*v.t.* to soil with flyspecks.

fly-wheel (flī′hwēl″), *n.* a heavy wheel in a machine to steady its motion.

foal (fōl), *n.* the young of a horse, ass, or camel:—*v.i.* to bring forth a foal.

foam (fōm), *n.* the white substance formed on a liquid by violent shaking or fermentation; froth:—*v.t.* to cause to foam:—*v.i.* **1**, to gather foam; **2**, to be enraged.

fob (fŏb), *n.* **1**, a small pocket, esp. for a watch; **2**, a short watch chain or ribbon.

fo-cal (fō′kăl), *adj.* pertaining to, or placed at, a focus or central point: **focal distance**, the distance between the center of a lens or mirror and the principal focus.

fo-cal-ize (fō′kăl-īz), *v.t.* [*p.t.* and *p.p.* -ized (-īzd), *p.pr.* -iz″ing], to bring to a center or central point, as light rays; focus.—*n.* **fo″cal-i-za′tion.**

fo-cus (fō′kŭs), *n.* [*pl.* focuses (-ĕz); foci (-sī)], **1**, the point where rays, as of light, meet, or from which they seem to diverge; **2**, the focal distance; **3**, a central point; also, a point the position of which determines a curve, as in a parabola or ellipse (see *parabola*, *ellipse*, illus.): **principal focus**, the point at which parallel rays, after striking a lens or mirror, converge, or from which they seem to diverge:—*v.t.* to centralize; concentrate.

fod-der (fŏd′ẽr), *n.* coarse food, as for cattle:—*v.t.* to feed with fodder.

foe (fō), *n.* **1**, a personal enemy; **2**, an enemy in war; **3**, an opposing or harmful factor; as, impure water is a *foe* to health.

Syn. (see enemy).

foe-man (fō′măn), *n.* [*pl.* foemen (-mĕn)], an adversary or enemy in war.

fœ-tus (fē′tŭs), *n.* the unborn young of vertebrates in the later stages of development. Also, **fe′tus**, *Pfd. S.*—*adj.* **fœ′tal.**

fog (fŏg), *n.* **1**, a cloud of condensed water vapor near the surface of the sea or land; **2**, bewilderment; **3**, in photography, a haze obscuring a developed plate: **fog bank**, a dense mass of fog, resting on the surface of the sea:—*v.i.* [*p.t.* and *p.p.* fogged (fŏgd), *p.pr.* fog′ging], to become clouded:—*v.t.* **1**, to cover with mist; **2**, to puzzle; **3**, to cloud (a photographic plate) by wrong exposure to light.

fog-gy (fŏg′ĭ), *adj.* [*comp.* fog′gi-er, *superl.* fog′gi-est], **1**, abounding in, or filled with, mist and vapor; **2**, bewildered; **3**, obscure.—*adv.* **fog′gi-ly.**—*n.* **fog′gi-ness.**

fog-horn (fŏg′hôrn″), *n.* a siren or horn for warning ships in a fog.

fo-gy (fō′gĭ), *n.* [*pl.* fogies (-gĭz)], a person of old-fashioned or eccentric habits and ideas. Also, **fo′gey; fo′gie.**—*n.* **fo′gy-ism.**—*adj.* **fo′gy-ish.**

foi-ble (foi′bl), *n.* **1**, a failing or minor defect in character; **2**, the weakest part of the blade in a sword.

[1]**foil** (foil), *n.* **1**, a lobe or leaflike space between cusps, as in a carved panel or in window tracery; **2**, a thin plate or sheet of metal, as on the back of a mirror; also, a paperlike sheet of metal used for wrapping; as, tin *foil;* **3**, anything that enhances by contrast.

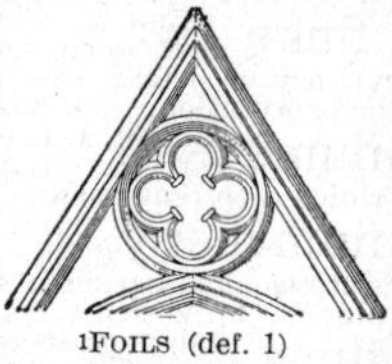

[1]FOILS (def. 1)

[2]**foil** (foil), *n.* a long, slender fencing weapon with a blunt point.

[3]**foil** (foil), *v.t.* **1**, to baffle or frustrate; defeat; **2**, in hunting, to run across and thus spoil (a scent) so as to baffle hounds:—*n.* the trail of an animal.

Syn., *v.* thwart, overthrow, outwit, frustrate.

foist (foist), *v.t.* **1**, to insert slyly: with *in* or *into;* as, to *foist* wrong words into a text; **2**, to pass off as genuine: with *on* or *upon.*

Fok-ker (fŏk′er), *n.* a type of powerful German monoplane.

[1]**fold** (fōld), *v.t.* **1**, to double; bend over (part of something); **2**, to inclose; wrap up; clasp:—*v.i.* to become closed by doubling up:—*n.* a part doubled over another; also, the hollow or crease made by folding.

[2]**fold** (fōld), *v.t.* to shut up in a pen or fold:—*n.* **1**, a pen for sheep; **2**, a flock of sheep; **3**, hence, the membership of a church.

-fold (-fōld), *suffix*, denoting multiplication; times; as, four*fold.*

fold-er (fōl′dẽr), *n.* **1**, one who or that which folds; **2**, a circular, map, or time-table on a folded sheet of paper.

fol-de-rol (fŏl′dē-rŏl″), *n.* **1**, mere nonsense; **2**, the refrain used in many old songs. Also, **fal′de-ral″**, *Pfd. S.*

fold-ing doors a pair of doors hung on opposite side posts and meeting in the middle.

fo-li-a-ceous (fō″lĭ-ā′shŭs), *adj.* resembling, or having, leaves.

fo-li-age (fō′lĭ-āj), *n.* **1**, leaves collectively; **2**, the artistic representation of leaves and flowers in decoration.

fo-li-ate (fō′lĭ-āt), *adj.* **1**, leafy; **2**, in the shape of a leaf; **3**, beaten into a leaf, as metal.—*adj.* **fo′li-at″ed.**

fo-li-a-tion (fō″lĭ-ā′shŭn), *n.* **1**, the act of leafing; **2**, the act or process of beating a metal into thin plates; **3**, ornamentation with leaflike tracery.

fo-li-o (fō′lĭ-ō; fōl′yō), *n.* [*pl.* folios (-ōz; -yōz)], **1**, a book of the largest size, formed of sheets of paper folded once; **2**, a page of manuscript or printed matter; **3**, the right- and left-hand pages of a ledger, etc.;

4, in legal documents, a fixed number of words of manuscript; 5, in Congressional reports, 100 words; 6, a case for music, etc.; 7, in printing, a page number:—*adj.* consisting of a sheet of paper folded once:—*v.t.* to number or arrange consecutively the pages of (a book).

folk (fōk), *n.* 1, a kindred tribe, race, or nation; 2, in *pl.*, *Colloq.*: a, people in general; b, one's relatives.

folk dance 1, a dance characteristic of some special race, usually of the peasants; 2, the music of such a dance.

folk-lore (fōk′lōr″), *n.* popular traditions, customs, beliefs, etc.

folk song a popular song or ballad, illustrative of the life of the people and the national or racial spirit.

folk tale a story or legend handed down in a certain race from its ancestors, and characteristic of that race.

fol-li-cle (fŏl′ĭ-kl), *n.* 1, a seed vessel; 2, a very small sac or gland.

fol-low (fŏl′ō), *v.t.* 1, to go or come after; pursue; 2, to succeed in order; 3, to support the opinions or cause of; 4, to imitate or conform to; 5, to watch or attend to closely; 6, to practice, as a profession:—*v.i.* 1, to go or come after another; 2, to result:—*n.* a particular stroke in billiards or croquet.

Syn., v. succeed, pursue, chase. These words are in some uses interchangeable. *Follow* is the most general term. *Succeed* suggests taking the place of one who or that which is ahead; it often refers to involuntary action; as, the prince *succeeded* his father. *Pursue*, like *follow*, may be applied to other than physical objects; as, he *pursued* the even tenor of his way. It may also, like *chase*, stress the will to catch up with some person or thing; as, he *pursued* the enemy. In *chase* the pursuit may be more eager and the distance between pursued and pursuer less than in *pursue*.

fol-low-er (fŏl′ō-ẽr), *n.* 1, one who goes after another; 2, a disciple, attendant, or dependent; 3, one of the same sect or party; 4, in mechanics, a piece which moves in a limited path, as between guides, or in contact with another piece, as a cam, from which it takes its motion.

Syn. adherent, retainer, pursuer, successor.

fol-low-ing (fŏl′ō-ĭng), *p.adj.* succeeding:—*n.* one's adherents.

fol-ly (fŏl′ĭ), *n.* [*pl.* follies (-ĭz)], 1, want of understanding; foolishness; 2, unbecoming conduct; 3, criminal weakness; sin; 4, any foolish undertaking.

Syn. silliness, senselessness, levity.

fo-ment (fō-mĕnt′), *v.t.* 1, to bathe with warm or medicated liquids; 2, to foster; excite; instigate.—*n.* **fo-ment′er.**

fo-men-ta-tion (fō″mĕn-tā′shŭn), *n.* 1, the act of applying warm or medicated liquids to a diseased part; 2, the liquids so applied; 3, encouragement.

fond (fŏnd), *adj.* 1, affectionate; also, foolishly indulgent; as, a *fond* parent; 2, cherished; as, a *fond* hope: **fond of**, partial to; feeling love for.—*adv.* **fond′ly.**—*n.* **fond′ness.**

Syn. enamored, ardent.—*Ant.* unfriendly, cold, undemonstrative.

fon-dant (fŏn′dănt; *Fr.* fôṅ″däṅ′), *n.* a creamy preparation of sugar, used as a basis in many candies.

fon-dle (fŏn′dl), *v.t.* [*p.t.* and *p.p.* -dled (-dld), *p.pr.* -dling], to caress; treat with tenderness; as, to *fondle* a pet.

fond-ling (fŏnd′lĭng), *n.* one who or that which is handled tenderly.

¹font (fŏnt), *n.* 1, a vessel to hold holy water, esp. for use in baptizing (see illus. next column); 2, a fountain or spring.

²font (fŏnt), *n.* a full assortment of one size and style of type. Also, *Br.*, **fount.**

food (fōōd), *n.* 1, nutriment; 2, material for eating; 3, that which nourishes or keeps active; as, *food* for thought.

Syn. diet. *Food* is the more general term. *Diet* means that portion of *food* and drink either taken daily or selected for a special purpose, usually on the prescription of a doctor; as, his *food*, consisting of meat without vegetables, formed an unwholesome *diet*.

BAPTISMAL FONT

fool (fōōl), *n.* 1, a person lacking in intelligence; an idiot; 2, in old times, a court jester; 3, one who acts in an unwise manner; 4, a victim or butt:—*v.t.* 1, to make a butt of; treat with contempt; 2, to disappoint; deceive:—*v.i.* to trifle.

fool-er-y (fōōl′ẽr-ĭ), *n.* [*pl.* fooleries (-ĭz)], habitual folly; absurd conduct.

fool-har-dy (fōōl′här″dĭ), *adj.* unwisely bold; regardless of consequences or results.—*adv.* **fool′har″di-ly.**—*n.* **fool′har″di-ness.**

Syn. venturesome, reckless, hasty, adventurous.—*Ant.* cautious, prudent, wary, careful.

fool-ing (fōōl′ĭng), *n.* senseless speech or conduct; banter; nonsense.

fool-ish (fōōl′ĭsh), *adj.* 1, acting without reason or judgment; 2, weak-minded; silly; 3, ridiculous; trifling; contemptible.—*adv.* **fool′ish-ly.**—*n.* **fool′ish-ness.**

Syn. simple, brainless, absurd, nonsensical.

fool-proof (fōōl′prōōf″), *adj.* 1, designed to prevent thoughtless persons from harming themselves; 2, simple or easy enough to be understood by anyone.

fools-cap (fōōlz′kăp″), *n.* 1, a hat adorned with bells and worn by court jesters; 2, a kind of paper, in sheets of about seventeen by fourteen inches, orig. watermarked with the jester's cap and bells.

foot (fŏŏt), *n.* [*pl.* feet (fēt)], 1, that part of the leg on which an animal walks or stands; 2, the lower part, base, foundation, or end of anything; 3, that part of a boot or stocking which receives the foot; 4, a measure equal to twelve inches; 5, foot soldiers; 6, a certain number of syllables constituting a metrical division of a line in verse:—*v.t.* 1, to add a foot to, as a stocking; 2, to add figures in (a column) and place the total at the bottom; 3, *Colloq.*, to pay; as, to *foot* the bill.

foot-ball (fŏŏt′bôl″), *n.* 1, any of several outdoor games in which two teams try to carry or kick an inflated ball to or across the opponents' goal; 2, the ball used.

foot-board (fŏŏt′bōrd″), *n.* 1, a board across the lower end of a bedstead; 2, a board or platform on which to stand or to brace the feet.

foot-bridge (fŏŏt′brĭj″), *n.* a bridge for pedestrians.

foot-fall (fŏŏt′fôl″), *n.* a footstep; the sound of a footstep.

foot-hill (fŏŏt′hĭl″), *n.* one of a range of low hills near the base of mountains; as, the *foothills* of the Rockies.

foot-hold (fŏŏt′hōld″), *n.* secure position; firm footing.

foot-ing (fŏŏt′ĭng), *n.* 1, ground or support for the feet; 2, tread; act of moving on foot, as in dancing or walking; 3, a firm or assured position; 4, state or condition; as, a friendly *footing*.

foot-lights (fŏŏt′līts″), *n.pl.* 1, the floor lights at the front of a theater stage; 2, the stage; the theater.

foot-man (fo͝ot′măn), *n.* [*pl.* footmen (-mĕn)], a servant who attends a carriage, waits on table, etc.

foot-note (fo͝ot′nōt″), *n.* an explanatory or illustrative statement placed at the bottom of a page.

foot-pad (fo͝ot′păd″), *n.* a highwayman who robs on foot.

foot-path (fo͝ot′pȧth″), *n.* a path for the use of people who are walking.

foot pound the unit of work, equal to that done in raising one pound vertically through a space of one foot.

foot-print (fo͝ot′prĭnt″), *n.* the mark made by a foot.

foot sol-dier a soldier who serves on foot; an infantryman.

foot-sore (fo͝ot′sōr″), *adj.* having sore feet, as from walking.

foot-stalk (fo͝ot′stôk″), *n.* the stem of a leaf or the stalk of a flower.

foot-step (fo͝ot′stĕp″), *n.* **1**, a footfall; **2**, the action of the foot in stepping; **3**, the sound of a step; **4**, the imprint or mark of a foot; track.

foot-stool (fo͝ot′sto͞ol″), *n.* a stool to rest the feet on.

foo-zle (fo͞o′zl), *v.t.* and *v.i.* [*p.t.* and *p.p.* -zled (-zld), *p.pr.* -zling], to bungle; do clumsily or awkwardly.

fop (fŏp), *n.* a man who is devoted to fine dress; a dandy.—*n.* **fop′per-y.**

Syn. dude, beau, coxcomb.

fop-pish (fŏp′ĭsh), *adj.* like a dandy in dress and manners.—*adv.* **fop′pish-ly.**—*n.* **fop′pish-ness.**

for (fôr), *prep.* **1**, in place of; **2**, as being; as, I took him *for* an honest man; **3**, in exchange against; as, two pencils *for* five cents; **4**, because of; as, he could not walk *for* weakness; **5**, because of lack of; as, we are pressed *for* time; **6**, for the sake of; as, *for* the love of God; **7**, in support of; as, he who is not *for* me is against me; **8**, in spite of; as, *for* all his money, he has no influence; **9**, to the number or amount of; as, a bill *for* five dollars; **10**, during; as, to stand *for* an hour; **11**, as regards; in consideration of; **12**, introducing the subject of an infinitive noun clause; as, it is right *for* me to do this:—*conj.* because; since; seeing that; owing to the fact that.

for- (fôr-), *prefix*, surviving in about a dozen common words, and meaning: **1**, off; apart; as, *for*get; **2**, prohibition; as, *for*fend; *for*bid; **3**, abstention or neglect; as, *for*bear; *for*sake; **4**, thoroughly; as, *for*lorn.

for-age (fŏr′āj), *n.* **1**, food for horses and cattle; **2**, a search for food or provisions for an army:—*v.i.* to go in search of provisions:—*v.t.* [*p.t.* and *p.p.* -aged (-ājd), *p.pr.* -ag-ing], **1**, to supply with provisions; **2**, to strip of provisions; ravage, as a land in war time.—*n.* **for′ag-er.**

for-as-much as (fôr″ăz-mŭch′),because; since; as, *forasmuch as* the time is short, we must go.

for-ay (fŏr′ā), *n.* in border warfare, a raid:—*v.t.* and *v.i.* to plunder or ravage.

for-bade (fôr-băd′), past tense of the irregular verb *forbid.* Also, **for-bad′.**

[1]**for-bear** (fôr-bâr′; fōr′bâr), *n.* an ancestor. Also, **fore′bear** (fōr′bâr).

[2]**for-bear** (fôr-bâr′), *v.t.* [*p.t.* -bore′ (-bōr′), *p.p.* -borne′ (-bōrn′), *p.pr.* -bear′ing], to abstain from; give up:—*v.i.* to restrain oneself; be patient.

for-bear-ance (fôr-bâr′ăns), *n.* **1**, patience; toleration; indulgence; **2**, self-command.

for-bid (fôr-bĭd′), *v.t.* [*p.t.* -bade′ or -bad′ (-băd′), *p.p.* -bid′den (-bĭd′n) or, *Archaic*, -bid′, *p.pr.* -bid′ding], **1**, to prohibit; command not to do; **2**, to oppose.

for-bid-ding (fôr-bĭd′ĭng), *p.adj.* repellent; disagreeable; as, a *forbidding* manner.—*adv.* **for-bid′ding-ly.**

for-bore (fôr-bōr′), past tense of the irregular verb [2]*forbear:* **forborne,** past participle of the irregular verb [2]*forbear.*

force (fōrs), *n.* **1**, active power; vigor; strength; energy; violence; **2**, power to produce conviction; persuasive power; **3**, meaning; special significance, as of a word or expression; **4**, troops; armament; a trained or organized body; **5**, unlawful violence to property or person; **6**, in physics, that which tends to produce motion, or a change of motion, in a body: **force pump,** a pump that delivers liquid through valves under pressure: distinguished from *lift pump* (see [1]*pump*, illus.):—*v.t.* [*p.t.* and *p.p.* forced (fōrst), *p.pr.* forc′ing], **1**, to compel; overpower by strength; **2**, to impel; push; **3**, to produce by unnatural or excessive effort; strain; **4**, to stimulate (plants) by artificial means.—*adj.* **force′less.**

Syn., *n.* compulsion, might. (See power.)

forced (fōrst), *p.adj.* **1**, compulsory; strained; as, a *forced* march; **2**, affected; as, a *forced* smile.—*adv.* **forc′ed-ly.**

force-ful (fōrs′fo͝ol), *adj.* having vigor; strong; powerful; as, a *forceful* speech.—*adv.* **force′ful-ly.**—*n.* **force′ful-ness.**

force-meat (fōrs′mēt″), *n.* meat finely chopped and highly seasoned, commonly used as a stuffing.

for-ceps (fôr′sĕps), *n.* [*pl.* forceps], pincers or pliers for seizing and extracting.

for-ci-ble (fōr′sĭ-bl), *adj.* **1**, having great mental or physical power; as, *forcible* speech; **2**, attained or done by compulsion; as, a *forcible* entry.—*adv.* **for′ci-bly.**

Syn. powerful, mighty, convincing.

ford (fōrd), *n.* a shallow part of a stream, etc., which can be crossed on foot by men or animals:—*v.t.* to wade through, or pass over without swimming.

[1]**fore** (fōr), *n.* the forward part:—*adj.* at or near the forward part:—*adv.* before; at or toward the bow of a ship: **fore and aft,** *Naut.*, lengthwise of the ship; from stem to stern: distinguished from *athwart.*

[2]**fore** (fōr), *interj.* in golf, a cry of warning to persons ahead.

fore- (fōr-), *prefix*, **1**, in front; as, *fore*runner; **2**, before or beforehand; as, *fore*tell; **3**, front part of; as, *fore*arm; **4**, near or at the front; as, *fore*most.

[1]**fore-arm** (fōr′ärm″), *n.* the arm between the wrist and the elbow.

[2]**fore-arm** (fōr-ärm′), *v.t.* to prepare beforehand for conflict.

fore-bode (fōr-bōd′), *v.i.* to presage evil; foresee:—*v.t.* to foretell (evil); have a presentiment of.—*n.* **fore-bod′er.**

Syn. portend, prophesy, betoken.

fore-bod-ing (fōr-bōd′ĭng), *n.* a feeling that evil is coming upon one; a presentiment of evil.

fore-cast (fōr′kȧst″), *n.* **1**, foresight; **2**, prediction, as of the weather:—*v.t.* (fōr-kȧst′), [*p.t.* and *p.p.* -cast′ or -cast′ed, *p.pr.* -cast′ing], to plan or calculate beforehand; foresee; predict; as, to *forecast* the weather:—*v.i.* to plan in advance.—*n.* **fore-cast′er.**

Syn., *n.* forethought, prophecy, estimate.

fore-cas-tle (fōr′kȧs-l; fōk′sl), *n.* the part of a vessel forward of the foremast, where the seamen eat and sleep.

fore-close (fōr-klōz′), *v.t.* [*p.t.* and *p.p.* -closed′ (-klōzd′), *p.pr.* -clos′ing], to cut off (a person) from the right of redeeming a mortgaged property; also, to enforce (a mortgage).—*n.* **fore-clo′sure.**

fore-doom (fōr-do͞om′), *v.t.* to doom beforehand; predestine to ruin.

fore-fa-ther (fōr′fä″*th*ẽr), *n.* a male ancestor, usually remote.

fore-fin-ger (fōr′fĭng″gẽr), *n.* the finger next to the thumb; the first or index finger.

fore-foot (fōr′fo͝ot″), *n.* [*pl.* forefeet (-fēt″)], one of the front feet of a quadruped, or four-footed animal.

fore-front (fōr′frŭnt″), *n.* the place farthest front; foremost place.

fore-gath-er (fōr-găth′ẽr), *v.i.* **1,** to assemble; **2,** to associate: followed by *with.* Also, **for-gath′er,** *Pfd. S.*

[1]**fore-go** (fōr-gō′), *v.t.* [*p.t.* -went′ (-wĕnt′), *p.p.* -gone′ (-gôn′), *p.pr.* -go′ing], to go before; precede.—*n.* **fore-go′er.**

[2]**fore-go** (fōr-gō′), *v.t.* [*p.t.* -went′ (-wĕnt′), *p.p.* -gone′ (-gôn′), *p.pr.* -go′ing], to do without; renounce. See **for-go′,** *Pfd. S.*

fore-gone (fōr-gôn′), *p.adj.* **1,** former; previous; **2,** determined in advance; as, a *foregone* conclusion.

fore-ground (fōr′ground″), *n.* that part of a landscape, picture, or scene near to the observer.

fore-hand (fōr′hănd″), *adj.* in tennis, designating a stroke made, in the case of a right-handed player, by holding the racket on the right side of the body, with the palm of the hand toward the ball.

fore-hand-ed (fōr′hănd″ĕd), *adj.* **1,** done in good season or beforehand; **2,** done with a view toward the future; thrifty.—*n.* **fore″hand′ed-ness.**

fore-head (fŏr′ĕd), *n.* the part of the face above the eyes; brow.

for-eign (fŏr′ĭn), *adj.* **1,** belonging to another nation or country; alien; **2,** belonging to other persons or things; **3,** inappropriate; as, those remarks are *foreign* to the spirit of the meeting.—*n.* **for′eign-ness.**

Syn. distant, extraneous, remote.

for-eign-er (fŏr′ĭn-ẽr), *n.* **1,** a citizen of a foreign country; **2,** an immigrant not admitted to citizenship.

fore-know (fōr-nō′), *v.t.* [*p.t.* -knew′ (-nū′), *p.p.* -known′ (-nōn′), *p.pr.* -know′ing], to be aware of in advance; know beforehand; as, we cannot *foreknow* the future.—*n.* **fore-knowl′edge.**

fore-land (fōr′lănd), *n.* a point of land projecting into the sea; headland.

fore-leg (fōr′lĕg″), *n.* one of the front legs of an animal, esp. of a mammal.

[1]**fore-lock** (fōr′lŏk″), *n.* a linchpin or wedge to hold a wheel or nut in place; a cotter pin.

[2]**fore-lock** (fōr′lŏk″), *n.* a lock of hair growing on the forehead.

fore-man (fōr′măn), *n.* [*pl.* foremen (-mĕn)], **1,** the spokesman of a jury; **2,** an overseer.—*n.fem.* **fore′wom″an.** —*n.* **fore′man-ship.**

fore-mast (fōr′mȧst), *n.* the mast nearest the bow or front of a vessel (see *rigging,* illus.).

fore-most (fōr′mōst), *adj.* chief; first; as, a matter of *foremost* interest.

fore-noon (fōr″no͞on′), *n.* the time between sunrise and midday; the morning; early part of the day.

fo-ren-sic (fō-rĕn′sĭk), *adj.* pertaining to, or used in, courts of justice or public debate; as, a *forensic* term.

fore-or-dain (fōr″ôr-dān′), *v.t.* to appoint beforehand; predestine; decree beforehand.—*n.* **fore″or-di-na′tion.**

fore-run (fōr-rŭn′), *v.t.* [*p.t.* -ran′ (-răn′), *p.p.* -run′, *p.pr.* -run′ning], **1,** to go before; precede; **2,** to announce.

fore-run-ner (fōr-rŭn′ẽr), *n.* **1,** a messenger sent before; herald; **2,** something that precedes a person or event.

fore-sail (fōr′sāl″; fōr′sl; fō′sl), *n.* **1,** on a square-rigged vessel or a schooner, the largest sail on the foremast (see *rigging,* illus.); **2,** on a sloop or a yawl, a sail carried on a forestay.

fore-see (fōr-sē′), *v.t.* [*p.t.* -saw′ (-sô′), *p.p.* -seen′ (-sēn′), *p.pr.* -see′ing], to have knowledge of or see beforehand; anticipate:—*v.i.* to show foresight.

fore-shad-ow (fōr-shăd′ō), *v.t.* to suggest beforehand.

fore-sheet (fōr′=shēt″), *n.* **1,** one of the clew ropes of a foresail; **2,** in *pl.,* the front part of an open boat.

fore-shore (fōr′shōr″), *n.* that part of a shore uncovered at low tide.

fore-short-en (fōr-shôr′tn), *v.t.* in drawing or painting, to shorten or make smaller, as objects, so that they will appear as they look when viewed from the front or obliquely; draw in perspective.

fore-show (fōr-shō′), *v.t.* [*p.t.* -showed′ (-shōd′), *p.p.* -shown′ (-shōn′) or -showed′, *p.pr.* -show′ing], **1,** to foretell; prophesy; **2,** to betoken.

fore-sight (fōr′sīt″), *n.* **1,** the power of seeing in advance; **2,** heedful thought for the future; prudence.

Syn. care, forethought, prevision.

fore-skin (fōr′skĭn″), *n.* the sheath of skin covering the end of the penis.

for-est (fŏr′ĕst), *n.* **1,** a large extent of ground covered with trees; woodland; **2,** an uncultivated tract of land, more or less covered with trees and undergrowth: —*adj.* pertaining to woodland; rustic; sylvan: —*v.t.* to cover with trees or woods.

fore-stall (fōr-stôl′), *v.t.* **1,** to hinder; prevent; frustrate; **2,** to get ahead of; anticipate.—*n.* **fore-stall′er.**

for-est-a-tion (fŏr″ĕs-tā′shŭn), *n.* **1,** the practical application of the science of caring for and cultivating trees; **2,** the extension of forest area.

fore-stay (fōr′stā″), *n.* a strong rope, usually of wire, reaching from the foremast head to the bow of a vessel to support the foremast (see *rigging,* illus.).

for-est-er (fŏr′ĕs-tẽr), *n.* **1,** one skilled in knowledge of trees and timber; **2,** an officer who has charge of a forest; **3,** an inhabitant of a forest or wild region.

fore-stick (fōr′stĭk″), *n.* in a wood fire, a stick laid in front of the backlog.

for-est-ry (fŏr′ĕst-rĭ), *n.* the science of caring for and cultivating trees in woodland, or of managing forests.

fore-taste (fōr-tāst′), *v.t.* [*p.t.* and *p.p.* -tast′ed, *p.pr.* -tast′ing], to enjoy before possessing:—*n.* (fōr′tāst″), a brief experience beforehand.

fore-tell (fōr-tĕl′), *v.t.* [*p.t.* and *p.p.* -told′ (-tōld′), *p.pr.* -tell′ing], to predict or prophesy:—*v.i.* to utter a prediction.

Syn. forecast, forebode, portend.

fore-thought (fōr′thôt″), *n.* **1,** a planning out beforehand; deliberate intention; **2,** heed for the future.

fore-to-ken (fōr′tō″kn), *n.* an omen:—*v.t.* (fōr-tō′kn), to give a sign of beforehand; foretell; forebode; as, the storm *foretokened* disaster to the ships.

fore-top (fōr′tŏp″), *n.* the platform at the head of a foremast.

fore-top-gal-lant (fōr″=tŏp-găl′ănt; fōr″=t′găl′ănt), *adj.* designating, or pertaining to, the mast or the sail next above the fore-topmast.

fore-top-mast (fōr″=tŏp′mȧst), *n.* a section of mast that is fastened to the foremast as an upward extension of it; a topmast fastened to a foremast (see *rigging,* illus.).

for-ev-er (fôr-ĕv′ẽr), *adv.* **1**, at all times; **2**, through eternity; perpetually.
Syn. endlessly, eternally, always.

for-ev-er-more (fôr-ĕv′ẽr-mōr), *adv.* for all eternity; forever.

fore-warn (fōr-wôrn′), *v.t.* to caution in advance; as, to *forewarn* a person of danger.—*n.* **fore-warn′ing.**

fore-word (fōr′wûrd″), *n.* a preface; introductory remark.

for-feit (fôr′fĭt), *n.* **1**, a fine or penalty; **2**, in *pl.*, a game in which losers perform some ludicrous task:—*v.t.* to lose, as a right or advantage, by neglect:—*adj.* alienated or lost.—*adj.* **for′feit-a-ble.**—*n.* **for′feit-er.**

for-fei-ture (fôr′fĭ-tûr), *n.* **1**, the act of losing possession; **2**, a fine; penalty; that which is forfeited.

for-fend (fôr-fĕnd′), *v.t.* to ward off; avert; prevent. Also, **fore-fend′.**

for-gath-er (fôr-găth′ẽr), *v.i.* **1**, to assemble; come together; **2**, to associate; with *with.* Also, **fore-gath′er.**

for-gave (fôr-gāv′), past tense of the irregular verb *forgive.*

[1]forge (fōrj; fôrj), *v.i.* [*p.t.* and *p.p.* forged (fōrjd; fôrjd), *p.pr.* forg′ing], to advance slowly or with difficulty: often used with *ahead.*

[2]forge (fōrj; fôrj), *v.t.* [*p.t.* and *p.p.* forged (fōrjd; fôrjd), *p.pr.* forg′ing], **1**, to shape or work (metal) while hot, under a hammer or press; **2**, to shape; form; invent; **3**, to counterfeit with intent to defraud, as a signature on a check, or the check itself:—*v.i.* to be guilty of counterfeiting with intent to defraud:—*n.* **1**, an open fire in which iron is heated by forced draft preparatory to shaping; as, a blacksmith's *forge;* a smithy; **2**, a shop for heating and working iron.
Syn., *v.* (see counterfeit).

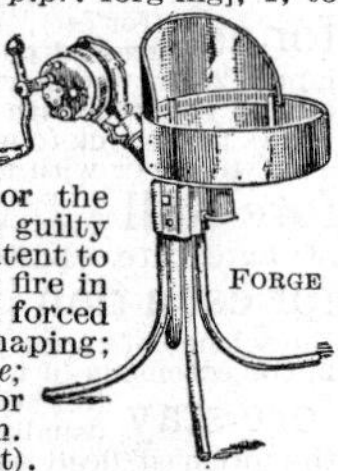
FORGE

forg-er (fōr′jẽr; fôr′jẽr), *n.* **1**, one who makes a false document in order to defraud; **2**, one who heats and shapes metal.

for-ger-y (fōr′jẽr-ĭ; fôr′jẽr-ĭ), *n.* [*pl.* forgeries (-ĭz)], **1**, the act of counterfeiting the handwriting of another with intent to defraud; **2**, a fraudulent article.

for-get (fôr-gĕt′), *v.t.* [*p.t.* -got′ (-gŏt′), *p.p.* -got′ten (-gŏt′n) or -got′, *p.pr.* -get′ting], **1**, to fail to retain in memory, or fail to recall; **2**, to cease to think of; **3**, to omit to take; **4**, to pass over without notice; **5**, to disregard:—*v.i.* to fail to remember.

for-get-ful (fôr-gĕt′fo͝ol), *adj.* **1**, apt not to remember; **2**, negligent.—*adv.* **for-get′ful-ly.**—*n.* **for-get′ful-ness.**

for-get–me–not (fôr-gĕt′=mē=nŏt″), *n.* [*pl.* forget-me-nots], any of various small plants with pale blue flowers.

forg-ing (fōr′jĭng; fôr′jĭng), *n.* metal shaped while hot by hammering.

for-giv-a-ble (fôr-gĭv′ȧ-bl), *adj.* worthy of being pardoned.

for-give (fôr-gĭv′), *v.t.* [*p.t.* -gave′ (-gāv′), *p.p.* -giv′en (-gĭv′n), *p.pr.* -giv′ing], **1**, to pardon, as a sin; **2**, to remit, as a debt; **3**, to cease to feel resentment toward (a person):—*v.i.* to display clemency or leniency.
Syn. condone, excuse, absolve, acquit.

for-give-ness (fôr-gĭv′nĕs), *n.* **1**, pardon; remission; as, *forgiveness* of sin; **2**, readiness to pardon.
Syn. leniency, forbearance, mercy.

for-giv-ing (fôr-gĭv′ĭng), *p.adj.* willing to excuse or pardon; lenient.—*adv.* **for-giv′ing-ly.**—*n.* **for-giv′ing-ness.**

for-go (fôr-gō′), *v.t* [*p.t.* -went′ (-wĕnt′), *p.p.* -gone′ (-gôn′), *p.pr.* -go′ing], to give up; deny oneself; renounce; abstain from. Also, **fore-go′.**—*n.* **for-go′er.**

for-got (fôr-gŏt′), past tense and past participle of *forget:* **forgotten,** past participle of *forget.*

fork (fôrk), *n.* **1**, an instrument with two or more prongs intended for picking up or holding something; **2**, anything resembling, or branching like, a fork; **3**, the angular opening or place of division caused by the branching of a road, river, or the like; **4**, one of the streams, roads, etc., at a fork:—*v.t.* **1**, to make in the shape of a fork; **2**, to raise, throw, or dig with a pronged tool:—*v.i.* to branch off.

forked (fôrkt; *Poetic*, fôr′kĕd), *adj.* **1**, having prongs; **2**, opening into two or more parts; **3**, zigzag; as, *forked* lightning.—*adv.* **fork′ed-ly.**—*n.* **fork′ed-ness.**

for-lorn (fôr-lôrn′), *adj.* **1**, abandoned; destitute; **2**, miserable; bereft; hopeless.—*adv.* **for-lorn′ly.**—*n.* **for-lorn′ness.**
Syn. forsaken, desolate, lone.

for-lorn hope **1**, a body of men detached for some service of great danger; **2**, a hopeless enterprise; **3**, a vain hope.

form (fôrm), *n.* **1**, the external or outward appearance or shape of anything; **2**, orderly arrangement; symmetry; **3**, pleasing appearance; beauty; **4**, determinate shape or structure; **5**, established practice or ritual; **6**, a mold or pattern; **7**, a long bench without a back; **8**, a class; **9**, one's state of fitness or condition; as, he was playing in good *form;* **10**, types, plates, etc., locked in a frame ready for printing; **11**, manner of doing something; style; conformity to standard:—*v.t.* **1**, to give shape to; create; **2**, to mold to a particular pattern; **3**, to imagine; **4**, to constitute; **5**, to devise; adjust:—*v.i.* to take shape.
Syn., *n.* observance, rite; figure, shape, fashion, semblance. (See ceremony.)

for-mal (fôr′măl), *adj.* **1**, according to custom or established rules; precise; ceremonious; conventional; essential; **2**, having the outward shape without the inward reality.—*adv.* **for′mal-ly.**
Syn. stiff, methodical, affected.

form-al-de-hyde (fôr-măl′dē-hīd), *n.* a gas used, largely in solution, as a preservative and disinfectant.

for-ma-lin (fôr′mȧ-lĭn), *n.* a solution of formaldehyde, used as a preservative, disinfectant, etc.: also called *formol.*

for-mal-ism (fôr′măl-ĭzm), *n.* **1**, exact observance of outward rites and customs, esp. in religious duties; **2**, stiffness of manners or behavior.—*n.* **for′mal-ist.**

for-mal-i-ty (fôr-măl′ĭ-tĭ), *n.* [*pl.* formalities (-tĭz)], **1**, strict adherence to external customs; ceremoniousness; **2**, any conventionally required act.
Syn. form, conventionality. (See ceremony.)

for-mal-ize (fôr′măl-īz), *v.t.* [*p.t.* and *p.p.* -ized (-īzd), *p.pr.* -iz″ing], **1**, to give shape to; **2**, to make stiff, precise, or ceremonious.

for-mat (fôr′măt; *Fr.* fôr″mȧ′), *n.* the whole style and size of a book, including the paper, type, and binding.

for-ma-tion (fôr-mā′shŭn), *n.* **1**, the act of molding or shaping; **2**, that which is shaped; **3**, a structure; **4**, in geology, a group of strata or rocks of similar origin or composition.

form-a-tive (fôr′mȧ-tĭv), *adj.* **1**, giving shape to; tending to mold; **2**, plastic or pliable:—*n.* **1**, a prefix or suffix; **2**, a word made by adding a prefix or suffix.

[1]form-er (fôr′mẽr), *n.* **1**, one who shapes or molds; **2**, that which gives shape, as a mold.

²for-mer (fôr′mẽr). *adj* 1, preceding in time or place; prior; 2, first of two mentioned.
Syn., previous, prior, foregoing.

for-mer-ly (fôr′mẽr-lĭ), *adv.* in past time; some time ago, as, modes of travel were *formerly* less convenient than now

for-mi-da-ble (fôr′mĭ-dȧ-bl), *adj.* 1, exciting dread; fearful; powerful; 2, hard to overcome or accomplish. —*adv.* **for′mi-da-bly.**—*n.* **for′mi-da-ble-ness.**
Syn. terrible, tremendous, alarming.—*Ant.* powerless, helpless, weak.

form-less (fôrm′lĕs), *adj.* without definite shape; lacking regularity of outline.—*adv.* **form′less-ly.**—*n.* **form′less-ness.**

for-mol (fôr′mōl; fôr′mŏl), *n.* a solution of formaldehyde: also called *formalin.*

for-mu-la (fôr′mū-lȧ), *n.* [*pl.* formulas (-lȧz); formulæ (-lē)], 1, a prescribed rule or model; 2, a group of symbols, expressing the composition of a chemical compound: 3, an orderly statement of faith or doctrine; 4, a prescription; a recipe; 5, the expression of a rule by algebraic symbols.

for-mu-la-ry (fôr′mū-lā-rĭ), *adj.* 1, stated by means of symbols; 2, set forth in orderly and prescribed manner:—*n.* [*pl.* formularies (-rĭz)], 1, a set form; 2, a collection or book of forms, as of prayers; ritual.

for-mu-late (fôr′mū-lāt), *v.t.* [*p.t.* and *p.p.* -lat″ed, *p.pr.* -lat″ing], to put into the terms of, or reduce to, a rule; state, in definite terms.—*n.* **for″mu-la′tion.**

for-ni-ca-tion (fôr″nĭ-kā′shŭn), *n.* unlawful sexual intercourse. esp. by one not married.—*n.* **for′ni-ca″tor.**

for-sake (fôr-sāk′), *v.t.* [*p.t.* -sook′ (-so͝ok′), *p.p.* -sak′en (-sāk′n), *p.pr.* -sak′ing], to leave; desert; abandon; depart from.
Syn. (see abandon).

For-set-i (fôr-sĕt′ē), *n.* in Norse mythology, the god of justice.

for-sooth (fôr-so͞oth′), *adv.* verily; in truth: usually ironical.

for-swear (fôr-swâr′). *v.i.* [*p.t.* -swore′ (-swōr′), *p.p* -sworn′ (-swōrn′), *p.pr.* -swear′ing], to take an oath falsely:—*v.t.* 1, to deny on oath; 2, to renounce earnestly.
Syn. reject, forgo, abjure, perjure.

for-syth-i-a (fôr-sĭth′ĭ-ȧ; fôr-sī′thĭ-ȧ), *n.* any of several ornamental shrubs bearing bright yellow flowers in early spring, before the leaves appear.

fort (fōrt), *n.* an inclosed fortified place; a castle; fortress.

for-ta-lice (fôr′tȧ-lĭs), *n.* a small fort or fortified place.

¹forte (fōrt), *n.* one's strong point, or special talent; as, his *forte* was music.

***²for-te** (fôr′tā), [It.], *adj.* and *adv.* loud: a term used in music.

forth (fōrth), *adv.* 1, onward in time, place, or order; forward; 2, out, as from concealment or seclusion.

forth-com-ing (fōrth′kŭm″ĭng; fōrth″kŭm′ĭng), *adj.* ready or about to appear:—*n.* (fōrth″kŭm′ĭng), a coming forth; an approach.

forth-right (fōrth″rīt′; fōrth′rīt″), *adv.* straightforward; at once.

forth-with (fōrth″wĭth′; fōrth″wĭth′), *adv.* immediately; directly; at once.

for-ti-fi-ca-tion (fôr″tĭ-fĭ-kā′shŭn), *n.* 1, the art or science of building defenses; 2, a military work erected for defense; 3, a strengthening; fortifying.
Syn. fort, citadel, stronghold.

for-ti-fy (fôr′tĭ-fī), *v.t.* [*p.t.* and *p.p.* -fied (-fīd), *p.pr.* -fy″ing], 1, to strengthen by military works; 2, to make strong; 3, to encourage or confirm:—*v.i.* to erect works of defense.—*n.* **for′ti-fi″er.**

***for-tis-si-mo** (fôr-tĭs′ĭ-mō), [It.], *adj.* and *adv.* very loud: a term used in music.

for-ti-tude (fôr′tĭ-tūd), *n.* spiritual strength to endure suffering or adversity with courage.
Syn. endurance, resolution, fearlessness.

fort-night (fôrt′nīt; fôrt′nĭt), *n.* a period of two weeks.

fort-night-ly (fôrt′nīt-lĭ), *adv.* once every fourteen days:—*adj.* coming or issued every fortnight.

for-tress (fôr′trĕs), *n.* a large place permanently fortified for defense, a castle; fort; stronghold.

for-tu-i-tous (fôr-tū′ĭ-tŭs), *adj.* happening by chance; accidental. —*adv.* **for-tu′i-tous-ly.**—*n.* **for-tu′i-tous-ness.**
Syn. incidental, random, occasional.—*Ant.* planned, foreseen, premeditated.

for-tu-i-ty (fôr-tū′ĭ-tĭ), *n.* [*pl.* fortuities (-tĭz)], 1. an accidental occurrence; 2, chance.

for-tu-nate (fôr′tū-nāt), *adj.* 1, happening by good fortune; 2, lucky; successful; as, a *fortunate* investment.—*adv.* **for′tu-nate-ly.**—*n.* **for′tu-nate-ness.**
Syn. happy, prosperous. (See lucky.)—*Ant.* unlucky, calamitous.

for-tune (fôr′tūn), *n.* 1, the good or ill that happens to mankind; chance; fate; 2, the personified power regarded as determining good or ill luck: 3, estate; wealth; possessions; 4, future destiny: as, to tell one's *fortune:* **fortune hunter**, one who seeks wealth, esp. through an advantageous marriage.
Syn. property, riches.—*Ant.* misfortune, poverty, loss.

for-ty (fôr′tĭ), *adj.* four times ten:—*n.* [*pl.* forties (-tĭz)], 1, the sum of four tens; 2, a sign denoting forty units, as 40 or xl: **Forty Thieves**, a band of robbers in the "Arabian Nights."—*n.* and *adj.* **for′ti-eth.**

fo-rum (fō′rŭm), *n.* [*pl.* forums (-rŭmz); fora (-rȧ)], 1, the public place of meeting in ancient Rome where the law courts, public offices, etc., were situated; 2, a place of public resort, or court of law; 3, a gathering for public discussion.

for-ward (fôr′wẽrd), *adv.* onward; in advance; toward the fore part: —*adj.* 1, situated near the front; 2, early in season or preparation; 3, ready; prompt; 4, eager; earnest; 5, pert; bold; impertinent:—*interj.* on!—*v.t.* 1, to help forward; hasten; 2, to transmit. Also, *adv.* **for′wards.**—*adv.* **for′ward-ly.**—*n.* **for′ward-er.**—*n.* **for′ward-ness.**
Syn., v. promote, further, facilitate.

fosse (fŏs), *n.* a moat or ditch, as about a fort (see *glacis*, illus.). Also, **foss.**

fos-sil (fŏs′ĭl), *n.* 1, an animal or plant, or any trace or impression of any animal or plant, of prehistoric times, imbedded or preserved in a rock deposit or in caves; 2, a person antiquated or old-fashioned in his ideas:—*adj.* pertaining to, of the nature of, or converted into, a fossil.

fos-sil-if-er-ous (fŏs″ĭl-ĭf′ẽr-ŭs), *adj.* containing fossils, or bodies changed into stone.

fos-sil-ize (fŏs′ĭl-īz), *v.t.* [*p.t.* and *p.p.* -ized (-īzd), *p.pr.* -iz″ing], 1, to petrify or turn to stone; 2, to render antiquated or old-fashioned:—*v.i.* 1, to become petrified; 2, to become old-fashioned: 3, to collect fossils.—*n.* **fos″sil-i-za′tion.**

fos-ter (fŏs′tẽr), *v.t.* 1, to nourish; nurse; rear up; 2, to support; cherish:—*adj.* giving, receiving, or sharing nurture or care, though not related by blood; as, *foster* mother; *foster* brother.—*n.* **fos′ter-er.**
Syn., v. promote, encourage.—*Ant., v.* discourage, neglect.

fought (fôt), past tense and past participle of the verb *fight*.

foul (foul), *adj.* **1**, offensive, morally or physically; dirty; impure; filthy; **2**, hateful; loathsome; disgraceful; **3**, of language, obscene; **4**, of sports, unfair; as, a *foul* blow; a *foul* ball; **5**, of the weather, cloudy and stormy; of the wind, contrary; **6**, thick with weeds, etc.; entangled, as an anchor; **7**, in printing, full of errors: said of proof; **8**, obstructed or impeded; as, to fall *foul* of the law:—*n.* **1**, an unfair play in football or other games; **2**, a wilful collision; **3**, in baseball, a ball struck by the batter which first strikes the ground outside of the base lines:—*v.t.* **1**, to make dirty; sully or defile; **2**, to come into collision with:—*v.i.* **1**, to become dirty; **2**, in baseball, to strike a foul ball; **3**, to collide; become entangled.—*adv.* **foul'ly.**—*n.* **foul'ness.**
Syn., adj. nasty, unclean, soiled.—*Ant., adj.* undefiled, pure, clean.

fou-lard (fōō-lärd'; *Fr.* fōō"lȧr'), *n.* **1**, a light silk, or silk and cotton, washable dress fabric; **2**, a silk handkerchief for wear around the neck or head.

¹found (found), past tense and past participle of the verb *find*:—*p.adj.* supplied with board, lodging, etc., usually in addition to money wages.

²found (found), *v.t.* **1**, to lay the basis of; build; **2**, to originate; establish, as a city, religion, or institution:—*v.i.* to be based; depend.—*n.* **¹found'ing.**

³found (found), *v.t.* to form, as a metal, by melting and then pouring into a mold; cast.—*n.* **¹found'er.**

foun-da-tion (foun-dā'shŭn), *n.* **1**, the basis or lowest part of a structure; groundwork; **2**, the principles or origin of anything; **3**, an endowment or gift of money to support an institution; **4**, the substance on which other parts are overlaid.

²found-er (foun'dẽr), *n.* **1**, one who lays the basis or originates; **2**, one who establishes, starts, or endows an institution, organization, etc.

³foun-der (foun'dẽr), *v.t.* **1**, to cause (a ship) to fill with water and sink; **2**, to disable or make lame: said of a horse:—*v.i.* **1**, to fill and sink; **2**, to go lame; **3**, to fall down; collapse.

²found-ing (found'ĭng), *n.* the method of making articles of cast iron, etc., by melting and pouring into a mold.

found-ling (found'lĭng), *n.* a child found after having been deserted by its unknown parents.

found-ry (foun'drĭ), *n.* [*pl.* foundries (-drĭz)], **1**, the place where metal casting is carried on; as, an iron *foundry*; **2**, the act or process of casting metals.

¹fount (fount), *n.* **1**, a spring of water; **2**, original source; origin.

²fount (fount), *n.* in printing, a complete assortment of one style and size of type. Also, **font**, *Pfd. S.*

foun-tain (foun'tĭn), *n.* **1**, a natural spring of water; **2**, the head or source of a river; **3**, an artificial jet or spout of water; **4**, a reservoir, as in a pen, containing a liquid to be drawn off as needed; **5**, the first cause or origin: **fountain pen**, a pen having a space in the holder for a supply of ink.

foun-tain-head (foun'tĭn-hĕd"), *n.* **1**, the spring from which a stream flows; **2**, the first source.

four (fōr), *adj.* consisting of one more than three:—*n.* **1**, the sum of three plus one; **2**, a sign representing four units, as 4 or iv; **3**, a four-oared boat, or its crew.

four-fold (fōr'fōld"), *n.* a quantity four times as great or as many:—*adj.* taken four times:—*adv.* four times.

four-foot-ed (fōr"=fŏŏt'ĕd), *adj.* having four feet, as a quadruped.

four-in-hand (fōr'=ĭn=hănd"), *n.* **1**, a coach drawn by four horses and driven by one person; **2**, a necktie worn tied in a knot so as to leave the ends hanging down in front:—*adj.* pertaining to such a coach or necktie.

four-score (fōr'skōr"), *adj.* four times twenty, or eighty:—*n.* eighty.

four-some (fōr'sŭm), *n.* in a game, as golf, a match in which two opponents play on each side.

four-square (fōr'skwâr"), *adj.* **1**, having four equal sides and four right angles; **2**, upright and honest:—*adv.* in a square form:—*n.* a figure having four equal sides and angles; a square.

four-teen (fōr'tēn"; fōr"tēn'), *adj.* consisting of four more than ten:—*n.* **1**, the number consisting of thirteen plus one; **2**, a sign representing fourteen units, as 14 or xiv.—*adj.* and *n.* **four'teenth".**

fourth (fōrth), *adj.* **1**, next in order after the third: the ordinal of *four*; **2**, designating one of the four equal parts of anything:—*n.* **1**, the quotient of one divided by four; **2**, one of four equal parts of anything; a quarter; **3**, in music, an interval of two steps and one half step: **fourth proportional**, the fourth term of a proportion, as *d* in the proportion $a : b :: c : d$.—*adv.* **fourth'ly.**

fowl (foul), *n.* a bird, esp. the common rooster or hen; poultry; also, birds collectively:—*v.i.* to catch or kill wild birds.

fowl-er (foul'ẽr), *n.* one who catches or kills wild birds for sport or food.

fowl-ing (foul'ĭng), *n.* the act or practice of catching or shooting wild birds.

fowl-ing piece a light gun used esp. for bird shooting.

fox (fŏks), *n.* **1**, any of several carnivorous animals of the dog family, noted for cunning; **2**, a sly, crafty person:—*v.t.* and *v.i.* to discolor; turn reddish brown, as the leaves of a book.—*n.fem.* **vix'en.**

fox brush the tail of a fox; as, the *fox brush* is the trophy of the chase.

foxed (fŏkst), *p.adj.* stained, as timber, or spotted a reddish brown, as books.

fox-glove (fŏks'glŭv), *n.* any of various plants of the figwort family, having showy, upright spikes of flowers.

fox grape any of several American wild grapes.

fox-hound (fŏks'hound"), *n.* one of a breed of medium-sized dogs used for fox-hunting.

fox ter-ri-er a small, intelligent dog used as a pet and for hunting.

fox trot a modern dance in two-four or four-four time.

fox-y (fŏk'sĭ), *adj.* [*comp.* fox'i-er, *superl.* fox'i-est], **1**, pertaining to, or like, a fox; **2**, cunning; crafty; **3**, reddish brown; **4**, discolored or stained.—*n.* **fox'i-ness.**

***foy-er** (fwȧ"yā'; foi'ẽr), [Fr.], *n.* the lobby or entrance hall of a theater, etc.

fra-cas (frā'kȧs; *Fr.* frȧ"kä'), *n.* a noisy quarrel; an uproar.

frac-tion (frăk'shŭn), *n.* **1**, a fragment; a part; **2**, in mathematics: **a**, a part, or an indicated number of equal parts, of unity, as ¼ or ⅝; **b**, an indicated quotient of one quantity, the *numerator*, divided by another, the *denominator*: called *simple* if both are whole numbers, as ¾; *compound* or *complex*, respectively, if one or both are fractional or mixed, as $\frac{1/3}{3}, \frac{1\frac{1}{4}}{2}$; *proper* if the numerator is less, or of lower degree, than the denominator, as ⅓, $a/(a^2+b)$; *improper* if the numerator is greater, or of higher degree, than the denominator, as

, $(a^2 + b)/a$: called *common* if both the numerator and denominator are expressed, as ⅞; *cimal*, if in decimal notation, without expression of the denominator, as 0.5.
Syn. portion, division. (See part.)

ac-tion-al (frăk′shŭn-ăl), *adj.* **1**, pertaining to a fraction; **2**, very small.—*adv.* **frac′tion-al-ly.**

ac-tious (frăk′shŭs), *adj.* unruly; cross; rebellious; as, a *fractious* child. —*adv.* **frac′tious-ly.**—*n.* **frac′tious-ness.**
Syn. touchy, testy, fretful.

ac-ture (frăk′tūr), *n.* **1**, the act of breaking; also, a break; **2**, a break in a part of the body, esp. a bone; **3**, the texture, as of a mineral, or of glass, shown by a fresh break:—*v.t.* and *v.i.* [*p.t.* and *p.p.* -tured (-tūrd), *p.pr.* -tur-ing], to break or crack.

ag-ile (frăj′ĭl; *Br.* frăj′īl), *adj.* easily broken; delicate; as, *fragile* china.
Syn. frail, frangible. (See brittle.)

ra-gil-i-ty (frȧ-jĭl′ĭ-tĭ), *n.* the state of being delicate or easily broken.

or a fitting reply; **3**, to adjust; adapt; as, his policy was *framed* for such an emergency; **4**, to surround or inclose, as a picture, with a stiff rim or edging; **5**, *Slang*, to accuse falsely of guilt: usually by forging evidence or corrupting officials, or both:—*n.* **1**, something constructed or made of parts fitted and joined together; **2**, that on which anything is held or stretched; **3**, any contrivance for inclosing or supporting something; **4**, shape; form; esp., a human form; **5**, temper; state, as of mind: **frame house**, a house built largely of wood, or around a wooden frame.—*n.* **fram′er.**
Syn., *v.* construct, mold, fashion.

frame-work (frām′wûrk″), *n.* **1**, that which incloses or supports; **2**, the basis for a more complete structure.

franc (frăngk), *n.* a French coin, and the unit of monetary value in France, equivalent to about four cents.

fran-chise (frăn′chīz; frăn′chĭz), *n.* **1**, liberty; freedom; **2**, the constitutional right of suffrage, or right to vote; **3**, a

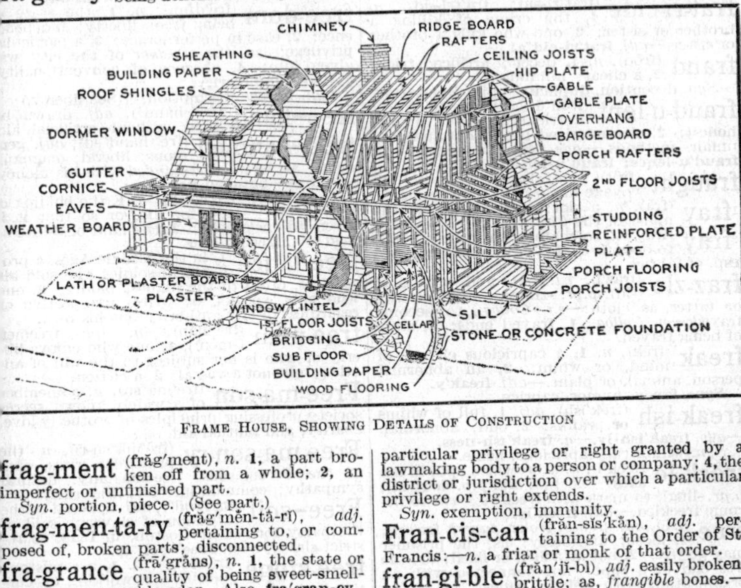

FRAME HOUSE, SHOWING DETAILS OF CONSTRUCTION

frag-ment (frăg′ment), *n.* **1**, a part broken off from a whole; **2**, an imperfect or unfinished part.
Syn. portion, piece. (See part.)

frag-men-ta-ry (frăg′mĕn-tā-rĭ), *adj.* pertaining to, or composed of, broken parts; disconnected.

fra-grance (frā′grăns), *n.* **1**, the state or quality of being sweet-smelling; **2**, an agreeable odor. Also, **fra′gran-cy.**

fra-grant (frā′grănt), *adj.* sweet-smelling; having a pleasing odor; as, a *fragrant* flower.—*adv.* **fra′grant-ly.**
Syn. perfumed, aromatic. (See odorous.)

[1]**frail** (frāl), *n.* **1**, a basket made of rushes: used esp. for figs, dates, or raisins; **2**, the quantity contained in such a basket.

[2]**frail** (frāl), *adj.* **1**, fragile or easily broken; brittle; **2**, weak, physically or morally; infirm.—*adv.* **frail′ly.**—*n.* **frail′ness.**
Syn. delicate, frangible. (See brittle.)

frail-ty (frāl′tĭ), *n.* [*pl.* frailties (-tĭz)], **1**, weakness, physical, mental, or moral; liability to be deceived or misled; **2**, a failing; a sin due to moral weakness.

frame (frām), *v.t.* [*p.t.* and *p.p.* framed (frāmd), *p.pr.* fram′ing], **1**, to fit (one thing) into another; put together; **2**, to invent; work up into form, as a constitution,

particular privilege or right granted by a lawmaking body to a person or company; **4**, the district or jurisdiction over which a particular privilege or right extends.
Syn. exemption, immunity.

Fran-cis-can (frăn-sĭs′kăn), *adj.* pertaining to the Order of St. Francis:—*n.* a friar or monk of that order.

fran-gi-ble (frăn′jĭ-bl), *adj.* easily broken; brittle; as, *frangible* bones.—*n.* **fran″gi-bil′i-ty.**

Frank (frăngk), *n.* a member of one of the Germanic tribes that established the Frankish empire in the third century A.D. —*adj.* and *n.* **Frank′ish.**

[1]**frank** (frăngk), *adj.* open or ingenuous; candid; outspoken.—*adv.* **frank′ly.** —*n.* **frank′ness.**
Syn. honest, plain, direct. (See open.)

[2]**frank** (frăngk), *n.* **1**, a signature that exempts mail matter from payment of postage; **2**, a letter or other mail matter privileged to go post-free; **3**, the privilege of using one's signature to send mail matter free:—*v.t.* **1**, to send post-free through the use of one's signature; **2**, to exempt.

frank-in-cense (frăngk′ĭn-sĕns), *n.* a fragrant resin from balsam trees, burned as incense.

frank-lin (frăngk′lĭn), *n.* **1**, formerly, in England, a substantial landholder of free but not noble birth; **2**, later, a small landowner.

fran-tic (frăn′tĭk), *adj.* violently distracted; wild.—*adv.* **fran′ti-cal-ly.**
Syn. furious, raving, frenzied.

***frap-pé** (frȧ″pā′), [Fr.], *adj.* chilled with ice:—*n.* a water ice.

fra-ter-nal (frȧ-tûr′năl), *adj.* **1**, pertaining to, or like, brothers; **2**, pertaining to a fraternity.—*adv.* **fra-ter′nal-ly.**—*n.* **fra-ter′nal-ism.**

fra-ter-ni-ty (frȧ-tûr′nĭ-tĭ), *n.* [*pl.* fraternities (-tĭz)], **1**, brotherly relationship; **2**, a body of men banded together by a common interest, as men of the same profession; **3**, a college secret society.

frat-er-nize (frăt′ẽr-nīz; frā′tẽr-), *v.i.* [*p.t.* and *p.p.* -nized (-nīzd), *p.pr.* -niz″ing], to associate or hold fellowship as brothers:—*v.t.* to bring into association as brothers.—*n.* **frat′er-niz″er.**

frat-ri-cide (frăt′rĭ-sīd; frā′trĭ-sīd), *n.* **1**, the crime of killing a brother or sister; **2**, one who kills a brother or sister.—*adj.* **frat′ri-cid″al.**

fraud (frôd), *n.* **1**, deceit; artifice; trick; **2**, a cheat; humbug.
Syn. deception, duplicity, guile, imposition.

fraud-u-lent (frôd′ū-lĕnt), *adj.* **1**, guilty of trickery; deceitful; dishonest; **2**, characterized by, or obtained by, unfair methods.—*adv.* **fraud′u-lent-ly.**—*n.* **fraud′u-lence; fraud′u-len-cy.**

fraught (frôt), *p.adj.* laden; full; as, the voyage was *fraught* with danger.

[1]fray (frā), *n.* a riot; quarrel; as, in the midst of the *fray.*

[2]fray (frā), *v.t.* to chafe or wear away:—*v.i.* to become chafed or raveled out: said esp. of fabrics.

fraz-zle (frăz′l), *v.t.* [*p.t.* and *p.p.* -zled (-ld), *p.pr.* -zling], *Colloq.*, to fray or tatter, as cloth:—*v.i. Colloq.*, to become frayed:—*n. Colloq.*, **1**, frayed ends; **2**, state of being frayed.

freak (frēk), *n.* **1**, a capricious change of mind, or whim; **2**, an abnormal person, animal, or plant.—*adj.* **freak′y.**
Syn., fancy, humor, caprice.

freak-ish (frēk′ĭsh), *adj.* **1**, full of whims or pranks; **2**, odd; abnormal.—*adv.* **freak′ish-ly.**—*n.* **freak′ish-ness.**
Syn. whimsical, capricious, fickle.

freck-le (frĕk′l), *n.* a brownish spot in the skin:—*v.t.* [*p.t.* and *p.p.* -led (-ld), *p.pr.* -ling], to mark with freckles:—*v.i.* to become freckled.—*adj.* **freck′ly.**

free (frē), *adj.* [*comp.* fre′er, *superl.* fre′est], **1**, loose; at liberty; as, the prisoner may go *free;* **2**, not attached or fixed; as, the *free* end of a rope; not connected with an organization with definite rules; as, a *free* church; **3**, not hampered; not influenced by other persons; as, a *free* choice; **4**, of literary style, versification, or the like, not according to the conventional rules of composition; of a translation, not literal; **5**, of conduct, spirited; also, familiar: often in the phrase, *free* and easy; **6**, lavish; generous; as, he was *free* with his praises; also, abundant; as, a *free* flow of blood; **7**, willing; voluntary; as, a *free* gift; **8**, allowable; permitted; as, it is *free* for him to go or stay; **9**, open or accessible to all comers; as, a *free* fight; a *free* port; **10**, clear of obstructions; open; as, *free* access; a *free* field; **11**, devoid, deprived: followed by *of;* as, *free* of impurities; **12**, released: followed by *from;* as, *free* from restraint; **13**, given without cost; as, a *free* ticket; **14**, in chemistry, of an element, not combined; **15**, not restrained by the regulations of a trade-union, or by artificial barrie set up by legislation; as, a *free* laborer; *fr* trade: **free silver**, free coinage of silv specif., free coinage of silver coins with leg tender value equal to a fixed fraction, as o sixteenth, of the value of coins containing t same weight of gold:—*v.t.* [*p.t.* and *p.p.* fre (frēd), *p.pr.* free′ing], **1**, to set at liberty; **2**, rid or exempt; clear: often with *of:*—*a* **1**, without money payment; **2**, without r straint.—*adv.* **free′ly.**—*n.* **free′ness.**
Syn., adj. unreserved, careless, unconcerne

free-board (frē′bōrd″), *n.* that part the side of a ship betwe the upper edge, or gunwale, and the water lin

free-boot-er (frē′bōōt″ẽr), *n.* one wh roves about for plunder pillage; a buccaneer; pirate.—*v.i.* **free′boot**

free–born (frē′-bôrn″), *adj.* not born bondage or slavery.

freed-man (frēd′măn), *n.* [*pl.* freedme (-mĕn)], a slave who has bee legally set free.—*n.fem.* **freed′wom″an.**

free-dom (frē′dŭm), *n.* **1**, the state o being free; liberty; independ ence; **2**, ease in performance; **3**, a particula privilege; as, the *freedom* of the city wa given him; **4**, absence of conventionality **5**, undue familiarity.
Syn. license, exemption. (See liberty.)

free–hand (frē′-hănd″), *adj.* drawn by hand without artificial aid

free–hand-ed (frē′-hănd″ĕd), *adj.* gen erous; liberal; magnani mous; as, he was *free-handed* with his money —*n.* **free″–hand′ed-ness.**

free-hold (frē′hōld″), *n.* **1**, the holding o land for life, or so that it is given to one's heirs; **2**, the land or estate so held.—*n.* **free′hold″er.**

free lance **1**, in the Middle Ages, a professional soldier who sold his services, often to the highest bidder; **2**, one who acts, speaks, or writes irrespective or regardless of any authority but his own.

free-man (frē′măn), *n.* [*pl.* freemen (-mĕn)], **1**, one who enjoys liberty or who is not subject to the will of another; one not a vassal; **2**, a citizen.

Free-ma-son (frē′mā″sn), *n.* a member of a widely known secret society professing principles of brotherly love, charity, and mutual aid.

Free-ma-son-ry (frē′mā″sn-rĭ), *n.* the principles, rites, etc., of the Freemasons: **freemasonry,** natural sympathy; common interest; fraternity.

Free–soil (frē′-soil″), *adj.* opposed to the extension of slavery: said of the party formed at Boston, in 1848, to restrict slavery.—*n.* **Free′–soil″er.**

free-stone (frē′stōn″), *n.* **1**, a sandstone suitable for working or cutting without splitting; **2**, a kind of peach.

free-think-er (frē′thĭngk″ẽr), *n.* one who forms his opinions independently, esp. in religious matters.—*adj.* and *n.* **free′think″ing.**

free trade trade with other countries, free from tariffs, customs duties, and other restrictions.

free-will (frē′wĭl″), *adj.* **1**, voluntary; **2**, holding the doctrine that man is free to exercise his will for good or evil.

freeze (frēz), *v.t.* [*p.t.* froze (frōz), *p.p.* fro′zen (frō′zn), *p.pr.* freez′ing], **1**, to harden with cold; **2**, to kill by cold:—*v.i.* **1**, to be hardened with cold; **2**, to be killed by cold; **3**, to be very cold; **4**, to adhere through cold; as, my hand *freezes* to the iron handle.

freez-er (frēz′ẽr), *n.* one who or that which freezes; esp., a machine that freezes cream or custard into ice cream.

reez-ing point the temperature at which a liquid begins change into a solid state: for water, 32° ahrenheit, 0° centigrade.

reight (frāt), *n.* **1**, the goods with which a vessel, car, etc., is loaded; cargo; , method of transporting bulky goods by ommon carriers, often slowly; **3**, the sum paid r charged for hauling goods:—*adj.* used for auling goods:—*v.t.* **1**, to load with goods for auling; **2**, to send (goods) by freight.
Syn., n. (see cargo).

reight-age (frāt′āj), *n.* **1**, transportation of goods, or the charge for t; **2**, cargo; lading.

reight-er (frāt′ẽr), *n.* **1**, one who loads a ship or car; shipper; **2**, a vessel for carrying a cargo, but no passengers.

French (frĕnch), *adj.* pertaining to France, its people, or language: **French leave**, departure without ceremony or notice; a hasty or secret departure:—*n.* **1**, the language of France; **2**, used as *pl.*, the people of France.

French horn an orchestral instrument of the brass group (see *musical instrument*, illus.).

French-man (frĕnch′măn), *n.* [*pl.* Frenchmen (-mĕn)], a native or inhabitant of France.—*n.fem.* **French′wom″an.**

fren-zy (frĕn′zĭ), *n.* [*pl.* frenzies (-zĭz)], violent agitation; temporary madness; fury:—*v.t.* [*p.t.* and *p.p.* -zied (-zĭd), *p.pr.* -zy-ing], to throw into a fury; render mad.—*p.adj.* **fren′zied.**
Syn., n. delirium, raving, wildness.

fre-quen-cy (frē′kwĕn-sĭ), *n.* [*pl.* frequencies (-sĭz)], **1**, the repeated occurrence of a thing at short intervals or periods; **2**, the number of cycles per second of an electric current produced by an alternating generator.—*n.* **fre′quence.**

fre-quent (frē′kwĕnt), *adj.* **1**, occurring often; **2**, habitual; as, a *frequent* visitor:—*v.t.* (frē-kwĕnt′), to resort to, or visit often or habitually.—*n.* **fre-quent′er.**
Syn., adj. usual, general.

fre-quent-ly (frē′kwĕnt-lĭ), *adv.* often; repeatedly.

fres-co (frĕs′kō), *n.* [*pl.* frescoes; frescos (-kōz)], **1**, a method of wall painting in water colors on fresh plaster; **2**, a picture made on plaster:—*v.t.* [*p.t.* and *p.p.* -coed (-kōd), *p.pr.* -co-ing], to decorate or paint in fresco.—*n.* **fres′co-er.**

fresh (frĕsh), *adj.* **1**, new; recent; unfaded; uninjured by time; **2**, in good condition; **3**, not forgotten; **4**, healthy; strong and active; not wearied; lively; brisk; **5**, pure and cool; refreshing; **6**, not salt, as water; **7**, *Slang*, forward; pert; **8**, inexperienced:—*n.* **1**, a spring; freshet; **2**, the union of fresh and salt water in a river.—*adv.* **fresh′ly.**—*n.* **fresh′ness.**
Syn., adj. vigorous, unused, sound.—*Ant., adj.* stale, old, withered, trite.

fresh-en (frĕsh′n), *v.t.* **1**, to make like new; also, to revive; **2**, to render less salt; **3**, to slacken (a rope) to relieve the part exposed to friction:—*v.i.* **1**, to become vigorous or strong, as a breeze; **2**, to brighten; **3**, to lose saltness.—*n.* **fresh′en-er.**

fresh-et (frĕsh′ĕt), *n.* a flood caused by melting snow or heavy rain.

fresh-man (frĕsh′măn), *n.* [*pl.* freshmen (-mĕn)], a college or high-school student in his or her first year.

fresh–wa-ter (frĕsh′-wô″tẽr), *adj.* **1**, pertaining to, living in, found in, or formed in, water that is not salt; **2**, accustomed to river navigation.

[1]**fret** (frĕt), *v.t.* [*p.t.* and *p.p.* fret′ted, *p.pr.* fret′ting], **1**, to wear away or injure by friction or by rubbing; **2**, to agitate; vex; irritate:—*v.i.* **1**, to be worn away by friction or corrosion; **2**, to be agitated; utter peevish complaints:—*n.* **1**, the act or process of fretting; erosion; **2**, irritation.

[2]**fret** (frĕt), *n.* **1**, an ornament formed by small bands or short lines crossing or meeting one another; **2**, perforated or interlaced ornamental work:—*v.t.* [*p.t.* and *p.p.* fret′ted, *p.pr.* fret′ting], **1**, to adorn with perforated or interlaced work; **2**, to ornament.

[3]**fret** (frĕt), *n.* a small ridge or bar on the finger board of certain stringed instruments, as the mandolin.

fret-ful (frĕt′fool), *adj.* peevish; irritable. —*adv.* **fret′ful-ly.**—*n.* **fret′ful-ness.**
Syn. testy, agitated.—*Ant.* serene, calm.

fret saw a long, narrow saw with fine teeth: used in cutting ornamental woodwork.

fret-work (frĕt′wûrk″), *n.* a kind of carved, raised, or open ornamental work.

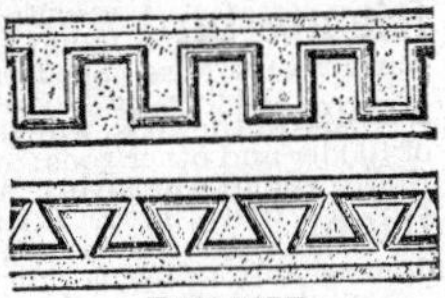
FRETWORK

Freud-i-an (froi′dĭ-ăn), *adj.* pertaining to the theories or practices of Sigmund Freud, an Austrian physician and psychiatrist; as, a *Freudian* analysis:—*n.* a believer in Freud's theories.

Frey (frā), *n.* in Norse mythology, one of the Vans, the god of love, peace, rain, sunshine, fruitfulness, and prosperity. Also, **Frey′r** (frā′r).

Frey-a (frā′ȧ), *n.* in Norse mythology, sister of Frey, goddess of love and beauty, also presiding over the regions of the dead: often confused with, and eventually superseding, *Frigg.* Also, **Frey′ja** (frā′yä).

fri-a-ble (frī′ȧ-bl), *adj.* readily crumbled or reduced to powder.—*n.* **fri′a-ble-ness.**—*n.* **fri″a-bil′i-ty.**

fri-ar (frī′ẽr), *n.* a brother, or member of certain religious orders, esp. a mendicant order; a monk.

fri-ar-y (frī′ẽr-ĭ), *n.* [*pl.* friaries (-ĭz)], an institution or brotherhood of friars.

fric-as-see (frĭk″ȧ-sē′), *n.* a dish of chicken, rabbit, or other meat cut into small pieces, stewed and fried, and served with gravy or sauce:—*v.t.* [*p.t.* and *p.p.* -seed′ (-sēd′), *p.pr.* -see′ing], to make into, or dress like, a fricassee.

fric-tion (frĭk′shŭn), *n.* **1**, the act of rubbing; **2**, in machinery, the resistance to relative motion of two or more surfaces in contact with each other; **3**, irritation caused by difference of opinion.—*adj.* **fric′tion-al.**—*adv.* **fric′tion-al-ly.**

Fri-day (frī′dā), *n.* the sixth day of the week: named from Frigg, the wife of Odin.—*abbr.* **Fri.**

fried (frīd), past tense and past participle of the verb [2]*fry.*

friend (frĕnd), *n.* **1**, one attached to another by affection, regard, or esteem; an intimate acquaintance; **2**, a supporter of a cause; **3**, an ally; **4**, used as a salutation or greeting: **Friend**, a member of the religious Society of Friends, or Quakers.

friend-less (frĕnd′lĕs), *adj.* without friends; unloved; forlorn.—*n.* **friend′less-ness.**

friend-ly (frĕnd′lĭ), *adj.* **1**, pertaining to a friend; **2**, having the qualities of a friend; **3**, ready to become acquainted; **4**, not hostile; amicable; affable; genial; **5**, convenient; favorable; as, a *friendly* breeze.—*n.* **friend′li-ness.**
Syn. sociable, companionable, cordial.

friend-ship (frĕnd′shĭp), *n.* **1**, intimacy united with affection or esteem; mutual attachment; **2**, good will.

[1]**frieze** (frēz), *n.* **1**, the part of an entablature supported by columns, below the cornice and above the architrave, usually ornamented (see *entablature*, illus.); **2**, any ornamental or sculptured band around a wall.

FRIEZE

[2]**frieze** (frēz), *n.* a coarse woolen cloth with a shaggy nap on one side: used for coats.

frig-ate (frĭg′āt), *n.* formerly, a fast, three-masted, square-rigged, war vessel carrying from 28 to 60 guns.

frig-ate bird a swift fish-eating sea bird found near land in the warmer seas: also called *man-of-war bird.*

Frigg (frĭg), *n.* in Norse mythology, queen of the gods, wife of Odin, and mother of Balder and other gods: often confused with *Freya*, goddess of love. Also, **Frig′ga.**

fright (frīt), *n.* **1**, a sudden and violent fear; alarm; **2**, a person whose dress or appearance is ridiculous.
Syn. dread, terror, dismay. (See horror.)

fright-en (frīt′n), *v.t.* to terrify; alarm suddenly; startle; as, the noise *frightened* the child.—*v.adj.* **fright′ened.**

fright-ful (frīt′fo͝ol), *adj.* terrible; dreadful; alarming; shocking; grotesque.—*adv.* **fright′ful-ly.**—*n.* **fright′ful-ness.**
Syn. fearful, dire, direful, terrific, horrible.

frig-id (frĭj′ĭd), *adj.* **1**, without warmth; wintry; **2**, cold in temperament; **3**, stiff; formal; dull: **frigid zone,** either of the areas about the earth's poles, extending 23°28′ toward the equator, or to the temperate zones.—*adv.* **frig′id-ly.**—*n.* **frig′id-ness.**

fri-gid-i-ty (frĭ-jĭd′ĭ-tĭ), *n.* the state of being very cold.

frill (frĭl), *n.* **1**, a plaited or crimped edging of fine linen on a garment, as a shirt front, etc.; ruffle; **2**, a growth, as of feathers or hair, about the neck of an animal; **3**, in *pl.*, *Colloq.*, affectation of manner; ornamentation of dress, etc.:—*v.t.* to make into, or ornament with, a ruffle.

fringe (frĭnj), *n.* **1**, an ornamental border of hanging cords, etc.; **2**, any border or edging like a fringe:—*v.t.* [*p.t.* and *p.p.* fringed (frĭnjd), *p.pr.* fring′ing], **1**, to border with, or as with, a fringe; **2**, to ravel, as cloth, to make a fringe.

frip-per-y (frĭp′ẽr-ĭ), *n.* [*pl.* fripperies (-ĭz)], **1**, old clothes or furniture; **2**, tawdry finery.

frisk (frĭsk), *v.i.* to gambol or dance in frolic:—*v.t. Slang,* to search (a person), esp. after arrest, for concealed articles; hence, to rob.—*n.* **frisk′er.**

frisk-y (frĭs′kĭ), *adj.* [*comp.* frisk′i-er, *superl.* frisk′i-est], lively in action; sprightly; gay; frolicsome.—*adv.* **frisk′i-ly.**—*n.* **frisk′i-ness.**

frith (frĭth), *n.* **1**, an inlet of the sea at the mouth of a river; **2**, a kind of weir or dam for capturing fish. Also, **firth.**

[1]**frit-ter** (frĭt′ẽr), *n.* a small cake made of batter, sometimes inclosing meat or fruit, and fried in deep fat.

[2]**frit-ter** (frĭt′ẽr), *n.* a small piece:—*v.t.* **1**, to cut or break into small pieces; **2**, to waste by degrees.

fri-vol-i-ty (frĭ-vŏl′ĭ-tĭ), *n.* [*pl.* frivolities (-tĭz)], **1**, a trifling thought or act; **2**, lightness of thought, speech, or act.

friv-o-lous (frĭv′ō-lŭs), *adj.* trifling; trivial; petty; of little importance.—*adv.* **friv′o-lous-ly.**—*n.* **friv′o-lous-ness.**

friz (frĭz), *v.t.* and *v.i.* [*p.t.* and *p.p.* frizzed (frĭzd), *p.pr.* friz′zing], **1**, to curl, as hair; form into little hard burs: said of the nap of cloth; **2**, to fry:—*n.* that which is curled, as hair. Also, **frizz.**—*adj.* **friz′zy.**

[1]**friz-zle** (frĭz′l), *v.t.* [*p.t.* and *p.p.* -zled (-ld), *p.pr.* -zling], to curl or friz:—*v.i.* to become curled or frizzed:—*n.* a crisped or curled lock of hair.—*adj.* **friz′zly.**—*n.* **friz′zle**r.

[2]**friz-zle** (frĭz′l), *v.t.* [*p.t.* and *p.p.* -zled (-ld), *p.pr.* -zling], to cook on hot coals:—*v.i.* to splutter in cooking.

fro (frō), *adv.* away from; backward or back: used only in the phrase *to and fro*, as, to swing to and *fro.*

frock (frŏk), *n.* **1**, a loose upper garment worn by children and women; dress; **2**, a monk's habit; **3**, a coarse outer garment worn by laborers, etc.; **4**, a coat worn by soldiers off duty; **5**, a frock coat:—*v.t.* to invest with the office of a monk or priest.

frock coat a close-fitting, double-breasted, straight-bodied coat for men, with wide skirts of the same length before and behind.

[1]**frog** (frŏg), *n.* a small, tailless amphibian with a smooth skin and webbed feet, notable for its swimming and jumping ability.

FROGS (1/3)

[2]**frog** (frŏg), *n.* **1**, a wedge-shaped, tender, horny growth in the middle of the sole of a horse's foot; **2**, a plate used to guide the wheels of a railroad car where one track crosses another, or at a switch.

[3]**frog** (frŏg), *n.* **1**, a spindle-shaped button that fits into a loop, used as a fastening for cloaks, mantles, etc.: also called *toggle;* **2**, an attachment at the belt for supporting a sword or bayonet.

frol-ic (frŏl′ĭk), *n.* **1**, a scene of merry-making or gaiety; **2**, a sportive outburst; wild prank:—*adj.* sportive; merry or gay:—*v.i.* [*p.t.* and *p.p.* -icked (-ĭkt), *p.pr.* -ick-ing], to make merry; gambol; play wild pranks.—*n.* **frol′ick-er.**

frol-ic-some (frŏl′ĭk-sŭm), *adj.* full of sport or gaiety; as, a *frolicsome* mood; a *frolicsome* child.—*adv.* **frol′ic-some-ly.**—*n.* **frol′ic-some-ness.**

from (frŏm), *prep.* meaning primarily out, out of, forth, away: used with words indicating: **1**, source or starting point; as, a letter *from* home; *from* morn till night; ten feet *from* the door; **2**, either of two named limits; as, *from* eight to a dozen persons; **3**, a person that is deprived; a thing out of which something is taken; as, candy taken *from* a child; an apple taken *from* the barrel; **4**, a reason or cause; as, weak *from* hunger; **5**, a thing distinguished or different; as, to tell real silk *from* imitation silk.

frond (frŏnd), *n.* the leaf of a fern, palm, or seaweed.—*adj.* **frond′ed.**

front (frŭnt), *n.* **1**, the forehead; **2**, the fore or foremost part of anything; **3**, position directly before something; van; the most prominent part; **4**, impudence; **5**, an expression of countenance, esp. when frank or bold; as, he kept up his *front;* **6**, a false shirt bosom:—*adj.* situated at the front:—*v.t.*

1, to stand, or be situated, opposite to; 2, to confront; meet:—*v.i.* to have the front turned in a particular direction.

front-age (frŭn′tāj), *n.* 1, the fore part of a building; also, the direction in which it faces; 2, the extent of a building or of land along a street or road; 3, the space lying between a building and a roadway.

fron-tal (frŭn′tăl; frŏn′tăl), *adj.* pertaining to the front or forehead:—*n.* 1, something worn on the forehead; 2, the bone forming the skeleton of the forehead (see *skull*, illus.); 3, a drapery, as before a church altar; a small pediment or ornament over a window or door.

fron-tier (frŏn′tēr; frŭn′tēr), *n.* 1, the boundary or limit of a country; 2, the most remote settled part of a country, facing an unexplored region:—*adj.* pertaining to, or situated near, the boundary of a country.

fron-tiers-man (frŏn′tērz-măn; frŭn′tērz-măn), *n.* [*pl.* frontiersmen (-mĕn)], 1, an inhabitant of the border section of a country, or of a newly settled region; 2, a pioneer.

fron-tis-piece (frŭn′tis-pēs; frŏn′-), *n.* an illustration facing the front page or title-page of a book.

accompanied by, frost; 2, frozen; hoary; 3, cold or distant in manner.—*adv.* **frost′i-ly.** —*n.* **frost′i-ness.**

froth (frôth), *n.* 1, the mass of bubbles formed on the surface of a liquid by agitation or fermentation; foam; 2, superficial or shallow knowledge:—*v.t.* 1, to cause to foam; 2, to give vent to, as foam:—*v.i.* to foam.

froth-y (frôth′ĭ), *adj.* [*comp.* froth′i-er, *superl.* froth′i-est], 1, full of, or composed of, foam or bubbles; 2, empty; frivolous or shallow, as talk; unsubstantial. —*adv.* **froth′i-ly.**—*n.* **froth′i-ness.**

fro-ward (frō′wẽrd), *adj.* wilful; disobedient; peevish; wayward; as, a *froward* heart; a *froward* child.—*adv.* **fro′ward-ly.**—*n.* **fro′ward-ness.**

Syn. intractable, ungovernable.—*Ant.* manageable, obedient, tractable.

frown (froun), *n.* a scowl; stern look; an expression showing dislike or disapproval:—*v.i.* 1, to contract the brows as a result of displeasure, etc.; scowl; lower; 2, to show disapproval by one's expression: with *upon*:—*v.t.* 1, to rebuke by a stern look; 2, to suppress by scowling.—*adv.* **frown′ing-ly.**

froze (frōz), past tense of the irregular verb *freeze*, which see.

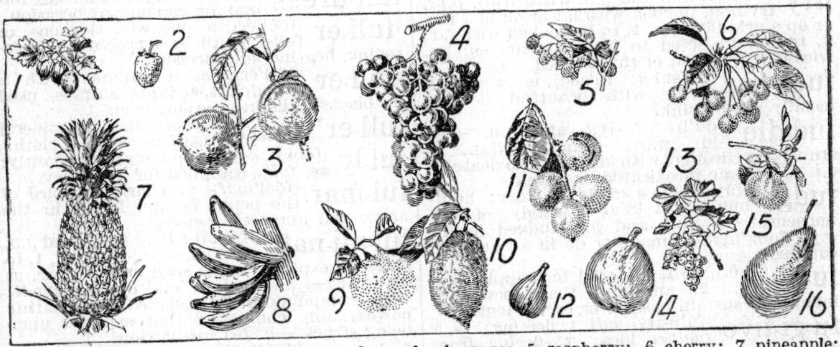

FRUIT: 1, gooseberry; 2, strawberry; 3, peach; 4, grape; 5, raspberry; 6, cherry; 7, pineapple; 8, banana; 9, orange; 10, lemon; 11, prune; 12, fig; 13, currant; 14, seckel pear; 15, mandarin orange; 16, Bartlett pear.

front-let (frŭnt′lĕt), *n.* 1, a fillet or band worn on the forehead; esp., a Jewish phylactery; 2, the forehead of a bird if marked by a special texture or color.

frosh (frŏsh), *n.* [Ger.], *Slang*, a freshman; a college student in his first year.

frost (frôst), *n.* 1, minute frozen particles of moisture; 2, the temperature of the atmosphere which causes the freezing of water; 3, *Slang*, an undertaking ending in failure:—*v.t.* 1, to cover with, or as with, hoarfrost; 2, to injure by frost; 3, to sharpen (horses' shoes) in cold weather; 4, to cover (a cake) with icing.

frost-bite (frôst′bīt″), *n.* a partially frozen condition of a part of the body: —*v.t.* [*p.t.* -bit″ (-bĭt″), *p.p.* -bit″ten (-bĭt″n), *p.pr.* -bit″ing], to nip with frost; freeze partially.—*p.adj.* **frost′bit″ten.**

frost-ed (frôs′tĕd; frôs′tĭd), *p.adj.* 1, covered with frost; 2, injured by severe cold; frostbitten; 3, covered with icing; 4, having a dull or translucent finish, as glass.

frost-ing (frôst′ĭng), *n.* 1, a preparation of fine sugar for covering cakes, etc.; 2, rough, powdered glass used in decorative work; 3, a dull finish, as for metal.

frost-y (frôs′tĭ), *adj.* [*comp.* frost′i-er, *superl.* frost′i-est], 1, producing, or

froz-en (frō′zn), past participle of *freeze*:—*p.adj.* 1, congealed; benumbed or killed with severe cold; 2, wanting in warmth of feeling or sympathy: **frozen credits,** assets which are of intrinsic value, but which at the moment cannot be used to raise cash.

fruc-ti-fy (frŭk′tĭ-fī), *v.t.* [*p.t.* and *p.p.* -fied (-fīd), *p.pr.* -fy″ing], to make productive; fertilize:—*v.i.* to bear fruit. —*n.* **fruc″ti-fi-ca′tion.**

fru-gal (frōō′găl), *adj.* 1, thrifty; economical, as a person; 2, sparingly used or supplied.—*adv.* **fru′gal-ly.**—*n.* **fru′gal-ness.**

Syn. provident, saving, sparing. (See economical.)—*Ant.* lavish, spendthrift, wasteful.

fru-gal-i-ty (frōō-găl′ĭ-tĭ), *n.* [*pl.* frugalities (-tĭz)], thrift; economy.

fruit (frōōt), *n.* 1, in general, a seed and all its enveloping parts; 2, the product of a tree or plant containing the seed and used for food; esp., any of certain such products, as the apple, peach, pear, etc., usually eaten raw; 3, product; offspring; 4, result or profit:—*v.i.* to produce fruit.

fruit-age (frōōt′āj), *n.* 1, fruit collectively, as of trees and plants; 2, the process of yielding fruit; 3, the results of action.

fruit-er-er (frōōt′ẽr-ẽr), *n.* one who deals in fruits of all kinds.

fruit-ful (frōōt′fōōl), *adj.* yielding fruit; productive; fertile; abundant.—*adv.* **fruit′ful-ly.**—*n.* **fruit′ful-ness.**

fru-i-tion (frōō-ĭsh′ŭn), *n.* **1,** the bearing of fruit; **2,** realization; as, the *fruition* of hopes.

fruit-less (frōōt′lĕs), *adj.* **1,** bearing, or having, no fruit; barren; unproductive; **2,** vain; unprofitable.—*adv.* **fruit′less-ly.**—*n.* **fruit′less-ness.**

fruit-y (frōōt′ĭ), *adj.* [*comp.* fruit′i-er, *superl.* fruit′i-est], full-flavored; rich; resembling fruit.

frump (frŭmp), *n. Colloq.,* a dowdy, quarrelsome, or vulgar woman.—*adj.* **frump′ish.**—*adj.* **frump′y.**

frus-trate (frŭs′trāt), *v.t.* [*p.t.* and *p.p.* -trat-ed, *p.pr.* -trat-ing], to defeat or disappoint; thwart or oppose; bring to nothing:—*adj.* brought to nothing; thwarted.—*n.* **frus-tra′tion.**

Syn., v. prevent, hinder, balk, baffle.

frus-tum (frŭs′tŭm), *n.* [*pl.* frustums (-tŭmz); frusta (-tȧ)], the remainder of a pyramid or cone when the top is cut off (see *cone,* illus.).

[1]**fry** (frī), *n.* [*pl.* fry], **1,** a young fish; **2,** a swarm of young fish or the like; **3,** a number of very small persons or objects.

[2]**fry** (frī), *v.t.* [*p.t.* and *p.p.* fried (frīd), *p.pr.* fry′ing], to cook with fat or oil in a pan or on a griddle:—*v.i.* **1,** to be cooked with fat; **2,** to be subjected to intense heat:—*n.* [*pl.* fries (frīz)], a dish of things fried.

fuch-si-a (fū′shĭ-ȧ; fū′shȧ), *n.* a garden plant with beautiful flowers, usually red or pink.

fud-dle (fŭd′l), *v.t.* [*p.t.* and *p.p.* -dled (-ld), *p.pr.* -dling], *Colloq.,* to stupefy or deaden with drink; intoxicate:—*v.i.* to become intoxicated or drunk.

fudge (fŭj), *n.* **1,** a made-up story; humbug; **2,** a kind of candy:—*interj.* nonsense!—*v.t.* [*p.t.* and *p.p.* fudged (fŭjd), *p.pr.* fudg′ing], to make or do in a bungling, careless manner.

fu-el (fū′ĕl), *n.* **1,** material for supplying a fire; **2,** anything that serves to inflame or sustain passion or excitement.

fu-gi-tive (fū′jĭ-tĭv), *adj.* **1,** fleeting; as, a *fugitive* idea; **2,** fleeing from danger, pursuit, or duty; as, a *fugitive* slave; **3,** wandering; vagabond; **4,** occasional; of temporary interest, as writings:—*n.* one who flees; a runaway or deserter; as, a *fugitive* from justice.—*adv.* **fu′gi-tive-ly.**

Syn., adj. escaping; transitory.

fugue (fūg), *n.* a musical composition in which the parts repeat at intervals the same subject or theme.—*n.* **fu′guist** (fū′gĭst).

-ful (-fōōl), *adj. suffix,* **1,** containing; characterized by; as, spite*ful;* grace*ful;* having the qualities of: added to nouns; as master*ful;* **2,** extremely: added to adjectives; as, dire*ful;* **3,** able to; likely to: added to verbs; as, forget*ful;* wake*ful:*—*n. suffix,* an amount that would fill: added to nouns; as, hand*ful;* cup*ful.*

NOTE: the plural of nouns ending in *-ful* is formed by adding *s* to the end of the suffix rather than to the noun to which the suffix is joined; as, cup*fuls.*

FULCRUM
A, lever; B, fulcrum; C, weight.

ful-crum (fŭl′krŭm), *n.* [*pl.* fulcrums (-krŭmz); fulcra (-krȧ)], the support on which a lever rests, often a wedge.

ful-fil (fōōl-fĭl′), *v.t.* [*p.t.* and *p.p.* -filled′ (-fĭld′), *p.pr.* -fill′ing], **1,** to complete or accomplish; **2,** to do; carry out (that which is promised, foretold, or expected); as, to *fulfil* a prophecy. Also, **ful-fill′.**—*n.* **ful-fill′er.**

Syn. effect, realize, satisfy.

ful-fil-ment (fōōl-fĭl′mĕnt), *n.* **1,** accomplishment; completion **2,** performance; as, the *fulfilment* of a promise Also, **ful-fill′ment.**

[1]**full** (fōōl), *v.t.* to scour and thicken, as cloth, in a mill:—*v.i.* to become thick by shrinking and pressing.

[2]**full** (fōōl), *adj.* **1,** filled; having no empty space; as, a *full* pail; **2,** well supplied; stored, as a cellar; saturated; satiated; **3,** rounded out; plump; **4,** expressing much; as, a *full* lecture; **5,** complete; filling the normal expectation; as, a *full* hour; a *full* orchestra; **6,** having material arranged in folds; as, a *full* skirt; **7,** clear; distinct; as, a *full* tone; **8,** *Colloq.,* intoxicated:—*n.* the highest state, extent, or measure; as, to enjoy something to the *full:*—*v.t.* to give fulness to; as, to *full* a skirt:—*adv.* completely; quite: used in composition, usually with a hyphen; as, *full*-armed; *full*-fledged.

full back in football, the player who, when his side has the ball, plays farthest back of the line of scrimmage.

full dress the dress required for any formal or ceremonial occasion.

[1]**full-er** (fōōl′ẽr), *n.* one who thickens, or fulls, cloth by a process of moistening, heating, and pressing.

[2]**full-er** (fōōl′ẽr), *n.* a hammer with a cylindrical striking surface, used by blacksmiths in grooving iron.

full-er's earth a soft, claylike mineral used in cleaning cloth.

ful-ly (fōōl′ĭ), *adv.* completely; abundantly; as, *fully* equipped for a journey.

ful-mar (fōōl′mȧr), *n.* a large sea bird of the petrel family, found in the arctic and antarctic regions.

ful-mi-nate (fŭl′mĭ-nāt), *v.t.* [*p.t.* and *p.p.* -nat″ed, *p.pr.* -nat″ing], **1,** to cause to explode; **2,** to send out or utter, as a threat:—*v.i.* to make a loud noise; explode:—*n.* a compound easily exploded: **fulminating powder,** any compound that explodes upon being struck.—*n.* **ful″mi-na′tion.**

ful-ness (fōōl′nĕs), *n.* **1,** completeness; abundance; **2,** the amount of folded material in a garment. Also, **full′ness.**

ful-some (fŭl′sŭm), *adj.* offensive from excess, as flattery; gross.—*adv.* **ful′some-ly.**—*n.* **ful′some-ness.**

Syn. coarse, sickening, rank.

fum-ble (fŭm′bl), *v.i.* [*p.t.* and *p.p.* -bled (-bld), *p.pr.* -bling], to grope or feel about in search; as, the boy began to *fumble* in his pockets:—*v.t.* to handle or manage awkwardly, as the ball in various games.—*n.* **fum′bler.**

fume (fūm), *n.* vapor or gas, esp. if offensive:—*v.i.* [*p.t.* and *p.p.* fumed (fūmd), *p.pr.* fum′ing], **1,** to send forth smoke; **2,** to complain angrily:—*v.t.* **1,** to subject to smoke or vapor; **2,** to give off (smoke, etc.).

fu-mi-gate (fū′mĭ-gāt), *v.t.* [*p.t.* and *p.p.* -gat″ed, *p.pr.* -gat″ing], **1,** to smoke; perfume; **2,** to disinfect or purify by the action of smoke or vapor.—*n.* **fu″mi-ga′tion.**—*n.* **fu′mi-ga″tor.**

fun (fŭn), *n.* pleasure; mirth; drollery; sport; amusement; play.

func-tion (fŭngk′shŭn), *n.* **1,** the act or performance of any duty, office, or business; **2,** faculty; power; **3,** the office of any organ, animal or vegetable; **4,** public or official ceremony; **5,** in mathematics, a quantity whose value depends on the value of another quantity; as, x^3 is a *function* of x; specif., **trigonometric function,** one of the six

REPRESENTATIVE PIECES OF PERIOD FURNITURE

1, Jacobean refectory table; 2, Chippendale chair; 3, Queen Anne chair; 4, American colonial highboy (Queen Anne period); 5, Heppelwhite chair; 6, colonial tall clock (Queen Anne period); 7, Adam chair; 8, colonial highboy (William and Mary period); 9, Jacobean chair with Spanish feet; 10, colonial corner cupboard (18th century); 11, Sheraton chair; 12, American Windsor comb-back chair; 13, American Empire chair; 14, Duncan Phyfe (American Empire) chair; 15, colonial ladder-back, rush-bottom chair; 16, Louis Quinze chair; 17, Carolean lounge; 18, Louis Seize chair.

possible ratios between the sides, in pairs, of the right triangle formed when a perpendicular is dropped from a point on one side of an angle to the other side: called *sine, cosine, tangent, cotangent, secant, cosecant* (for illus. see these terms):—*v.i.* to perform the duty or office for which a person or thing is intended.

func-tion-al (fŭngk′shŭn-ăl), *adj.* pertaining to a function or its performance, as by an agent or organ.

func-tion-a-ry (fŭngk′shŭn-ā-rĭ), *n.* [*pl.* functionaries (-rĭz)], one who holds an office; an official.

fund (fŭnd), *n.* **1,** a permanent supply of something; as, a *fund* of information; **2,** capital; money set apart for carrying out some object; **3,** a stock in reserve; **4,** in *pl.:* **a,** a permanent debt due by the government, on which interest is paid; **b,** securities; money; —*v.t.* to place in, or change into, a relatively permanent debt bearing interest.

fun-da-ment (fŭn′dȧ-mĕnt), *n.* the part of the body on which one sits; the buttocks; rump.

fun-da-men-tal (fŭn″dȧ-mĕn′tăl), *adj.* serving as a foundation or basis; essential; primary; as, the *fundamental* reasons for prohibition:—*n.* **1,** a primary or necessary principle; basis; **2,** the musical note on which a chord is formed.—*adv.* **fun″da-men′tal-ly.**

fund-ed (fŭn′dĕd; fŭn′dĭd), *p.adj.* existing in the form of a long-term debt bearing regular interest, and usually secured by bonds: opp. of *floating:* **funded debt,** that part of a public debt which is in the form of long-term bonds bearing regular interest.

fund-ing (fŭnd′ĭng), *n.* the act or process of turning short-term obligations into long-term debts bearing a fixed rate of interest; as, the *funding* of war loans.

fu-ner-al (fū′nĕr-ăl), *n.* **1,** the ceremony of burying a dead human body; **2,** the procession of mourners accompanying it:—*adj.* pertaining to, or fit for, a funeral.

fu-ne-re-al (fū-nē′rē-ăl), *adj.* **1,** suitable for a burial; **2,** mournful; sad.—*adv.* **fu-ne′re-al-ly.**

fun-gi-cide (fŭn′jĭ-sīd″), *n.* anything that kills fungous growths.

fun-gous (fŭng′gŭs), *adj.* **1,** pertaining to a fungus; **2,** growing up suddenly.

fun-gus (fŭng′gŭs), *n.* [*pl.* fungi (fŭn′jī); funguses (-ĕz)], one of the nongreen plants, including bacteria, molds, mushrooms, toadstools, etc., that feed upon organic matter.—*adj.* **fun′goid.**

funk (fŭngk), *n. Colloq.*, panic; fright:—*v.i. Colloq.*, to be in a state of cowardly fear; back out from fear:—*v.t. Colloq.*, **1,** to frighten; **2,** to shrink from.

fun-nel (fŭn′ĕl), *n.* **1,** a wide-mouthed vessel shaped like a cone and used for pouring liquids into small openings; **2,** the smokestack of a steamship or steam engine.

fun-ny (fŭn′ĭ), *adj.* [*comp.* fun′ni-er, *superl.* fun′ni-est], **1,** comical; droll; causing laughter; **2,** *Colloq.*, strange; odd; queer: **funny bone,** a point on the elbow on the side next the body.—*adv.* **fun′ni-ly.**

fur (fûr), *n.* **1,** the thick, soft hair of certain animals; **2,** a light coating on the tongue; **3,** the coating on the inside of a boiler; **4,** any light, fuzzy covering; **5,** in *pl.*, the dressed skins of fur-bearing animals, used for clothing: —*adj.* lined or trimmed with fur, or made of fur:—*v.t.* [*p.t.* and *p.p.* furred (fûrd), *p.pr.* fur′ring], **1,** to cover, line, or trim with fur; **2,** to level, as flooring, by inserting small strips of wood, called *furring*.—*p.adj.* **furred.**

fur-be-low (fûr′bĕ-lō), *n.* **1,** a ruffle, flounce, or the like used on women's clothing; **2,** showy ornamentation.

fur-bish (fûr′bĭsh), *v.t.* to make bright by rubbing or polishing.

fur-fur (fûr′fûr), *n.* [*pl.* furfures (-fū-rēz)], dandruff, or scales of skin that resemble particles of bran.

fu-ri-ous (fū′rĭ-ŭs), *adj.* **1,** very angry; mad; overcome with passion; **2,** moving violently, as a storm.—*adv.* **fu′ri-ous-ly.**—*n.* **fu′ri-ous-ness.**

Syn. violent, boisterous, vehement, fierce.—*Ant.* controlled, poised, serene, calm.

furl (fûrl), *v.t.* to roll up and fasten to something, as a sail, flag, etc.

fur-long (fûr′lŏng), *n.* one eighth of a mile; 40 rods; 220 yards.

fur-lough (fûr′lō), *n.* leave of absence; as, the soldier came home on a *furlough:*—*v.t.* to give leave of absence to.

fur-nace (fûr′nās), *n.* an inclosed structure where fuel is burned to make heat for any of various purposes.

fur-nish (fûr′nĭsh), *v.t.* **1,** to fit out or fit up with what is needed; **2,** to provide; give.—*n.* **fur′nish-er.**

fur-nish-ings (fûr′nĭsh-ĭngz), *n.pl.* **1,** the necessary fittings of a house; **2,** any necessary requirements.

fur-ni-ture (fûr′nĭ-tūr), *n.* the necessary fittings of a house, a ship, or a trade; outfit; esp., the movable articles of a house, as beds, chairs, etc.

fu-ror (fū′rôr), *n.* **1,** rage; **2,** a great outburst of excitement or enthusiasm. Also, ***fu-ro′re** (fōō-rō′rā; fū-rō′rē).

fur-ri-er (fûr′ĭ-ĕr), *n.* one who prepares or sells furs; a fur dresser.

fur-ring (fûr′ĭng), *n.* thin strips inserted under flooring to level it.

fur-row (fûr′ō), *n.* **1,** a trench made in the ground by a plow; also, the track of a ship; **2,** a groove; a wrinkle:—*v.t.* **1,** to plow; **2,** to make grooves or wrinkles in:—*v.i.* **1,** to plow; **2,** to become wrinkled.

fur-ry (fûr′ĭ), *adj.* [*comp.* fur′ri-er, *superl.* fur′ri-est], **1,** covered with, or made of, fur; as, a *furry* animal; **2,** like fur.

fur-ther (fûr′*th*ĕr), *adj.* comparative of *far:* **1,** more distant; **2,** additional:—*adv.* **1,** to a greater distance or degree; **2,** moreover; also:—*v.t.* to promote; help forward.

Syn., *v.* advance, aid, assist, foster, encourage; *adj.* (see farther).

fur-ther-ance (fûr′*th*ĕr-ăns), *n.* advancement; promotion; help.

fur-ther-more (fûr′*th*ĕr-mōr″), *adv.* besides; in addition.

fur-ther-most (fûr′*th*ĕr-mōst), *adj.* most distant; most remote.

fur-thest (fûr′*th*ĕst), *adj.* a superlative of *far:* most distant in time or degree:—*adv.* at the most remote time; to the greatest degree.

fur-tive (fûr′tĭv), *adj.* sly; secret; stealthy; as, *furtive* glances or actions.—*adv.* **fur′tive-ly.**—*n.* **fur′tive-ness.**

fu-ry (fū′rĭ), *n.* [*pl.* furies (-rĭz)], **1,** violent or very great temper; **2,** great violence; fierceness; **3,** an angry woman: **the Furies,** in mythology, the three goddesses of vengeance.

Syn. frenzy, rage, anger.

furze (fûrz), *n.* any of several spiny shrubs belonging to the pea family.

fus-cous (fŭs′kŭs), *adj.* grayish brown or black; somber; dark.

[1]**fuse** (fūz), *v.t.* [*p.t.* and *p.p.* fused (fūzd), *p.pr.* fus′ing], **1,** to melt, esp. by heat; make liquid; **2,** to join or blend by, or as by, melting:—*v.i.* **1,** to become melted, as by heat; **2,** to blend, as if melted. Also, **fuze.**

[2]**fuse** (fūz), *n.* **1,** a small tube filled with a material easily set on fire, or a cord saturated with such material, along which fire will run: used for exploding gunpowder,

etc.; **2**, a protective device in an electric circuit, usually a conductor which melts, thus breaking the circuit, when the current through it exceeds a safe strength. Also, **fuze**.

fu-see (fū-zē′), *n.* **1**, a kind of friction match that will burn in the wind; **2**, a signal consisting of colored lights, used on railroads. Also, **fu-zee′**.

fu-se-lage (fū′zĕ-lāj; *Fr.* fü″zē-làzh′), *n.* the body of an airplane, in which the pilot is seated and which contains the engine, controls, etc. (see *airplane*, illus.).

fu-sel oil (fū′zĕl), an oily, poisonous liquid obtained from grape, potato, or corn spirits: also called *fusel.*

fu-si-ble (fū′zĭ-bl), *adj.* capable of being melted; as, some metals are *fusible* at a lower temperature than are others. —*n.* **fu″si-bil′i-ty.**

fu-si-form (fū′zĭ-fôrm; fū′sĭ-fôrm), *adj.* spindle-shaped; tapering toward each end (see *root*, illus.).

fu-sil (fū′zĭl), *n.* the flintlock musket formerly in use.

fu-sil-eer (fū″zĭ-lēr′), *n.* **1**, formerly, a soldier armed with a fusil, or flintlock musket; **2**, in *pl.*, any of several British regiments. Also, **fu″sil-ier′**.

fu-sil-lade (fū″zĭ-lād′), *n.* the discharge of a large number of firearms at the same time or in quick succession:—*v.t.* [*p.t.* and *p.p.* -lad′ed, *p.pr.* -lad′ing], to shoot at with firearms in a volley or in quick succession.

fu-sion (fū′zhŭn), *n.* **1**, the act of melting, or state of being melted, together; as, the *fusion* of metals; **2**, the union or blending together of things; as, a *fusion* of parties.

fuss (fŭs), *n.* **1**, unnecessary or disturbing activity, esp. in small matters; disorderly bustling about; confusion; stir; **2**, a finicking person:—*v.i.* **1**, to worry; **2**, to be busy doing nothing:—*v.t. Colloq.*, to annoy.

fuss-y (fŭs′ĭ), *adj.* [*comp.* fuss′i-er, *superl.* fuss′i-est], **1**, worrying, or taking great trouble, about small matters; **2**, having much careful detail; requiring minute attention.—*adv.* **fuss′i-ly.**—*n.* **fuss′i-ness.**

fus-tian (fŭs′chăn), *n.* **1**, a kind of coarse twilled cotton cloth, as corduroy, velveteen, etc.; **2**, high-sounding speech; bombast:—*adj.* **1**, made of fustian; **2**, bombastic.

fus-tic (fŭs′tĭk), *n.* **1**, a West Indian tree used for yellow dye; **2**, the dye from this tree.

fust-y (fŭs′tĭ), *adj.* [*comp.* fust′i-er, *superl.* fust′i-est], **1**, moldy; musty; stuffy; **2**, antiquated; old-fashioned.—*n.* **fust′i-ness.**

fu-thorc (fōō′thôrk), *n.* the runic alphabet (see *rune*, illus.). Also, **fu′thork; fu′tharc; fu′thark.**

fu-tile (fū′tĭl; *Br.* fū′tīl), *adj.* **1**, ineffectual; useless; **2**, of no importance; worthless.—*adv.* **fu′tile-ly.**

Syn. trifling, trivial, frivolous.

fu-til-i-ty (fū-tĭl′ĭ-tĭ), *n.* [*pl.* futilities (-tĭz)], the quality of being useless; as, he soon saw the *futility* of argument.

fut-tock (fŭt′ŭk), *n.* one of the shaped sections which, placed end to end, form the heavy, curved rib of a wooden ship: **futtock plate**, in the rigging of a sailing vessel, a horizontal iron plate near the top of a lower mast, used to extend the topmast shrouds (see *rigging*, illus.) in bracing the topmast.

fu-ture (fū′tūr), *adj.* relating to time yet to come; about to take place:—*n.* **1**, time yet to come; **2**, the tense in grammar denoting time yet to come.

fu-tur-ism (fū′tūr-ĭzm), *n.* a movement in art, literature, and music, aiming at self-expression unhampered by tradition or conventional form.

fu-tur-ist (fū′tūr-ĭst), *n.* **1**, one whose main interests are in what is to come; **2**, an artist whose ideas and practice are extremely radical; a supporter of futurism; **3**, one who believes that certain Biblical prophecies are yet to be fulfilled.

fu-tu-ri-ty (fū-tū′rĭ-tĭ), *n.* [*pl.* futurities (-tĭz)], **1**, time to come; **2**, future events; posterity.

[1]**fuze** (fūz), *v.t.* and *v.i.* [*p.t.* and *p.p.* fuzed (fūzd), *p.pr.* fuz′ing], **1**, to melt, as by heat, **2**, to join or blend by, or as if by, melting. See [1]**fuse**, *Pfd. S.*

[2]**fuze** (fūz), *n.* **1**, a small tube or cord of inflammable material, along which fire will run to explode a charge, gunpowder, etc.; **2**, a protective device in an electric circuit. See [2]**fuse**, *Pfd. S.*

fuzz (fŭz), *n.* fine, minute particles of down, wool, etc.:—*v.i.* to fly off in small, fluffy pieces.

fuzz-y (fŭz′ĭ), *adj.* [*comp.* fuzz′i-er, *superl.* fuzz′i-est], covered with, or like, fuzz or down.—*n.* **fuzz′i-ness.**

-fy (-fī), *v. suffix*, to cause to be or form into; as, solidi*fy*; petri*fy*.

fyl-fot (fĭl′fŏt), *n.* a religious symbol or ornament, dating from very ancient times, consisting of a cross with arms of equal length, each having a projection at right angles: also called *swastika* and *gammadion* (see *swastika*, *cross*, illus.).

G

gab (găb), *n. Colloq.*, idle chatter; talkativeness:—*v.t.* [*p.t.* and *p.p.* gabbed (găbd), *p.pr.* gab′bing], *Colloq.*, to say in idle conversation:—*v.i. Colloq.*, to talk idly and much.

gab-ar-dine (găb″ẽr-dēn′; găb′ẽr-dēn), *n.* a kind of coat or cloak for rainy weather.

gab-ble (găb′l), *v.t.* [*p.t.* and *p.p.* -bled (-ld), *p.pr.* -bling], to say rapidly and senselessly:—*v.i.* **1**, to talk disconnectedly, or without real meaning or sense; **2**, to make a clatter of meaningless sounds, as a bird or animal:—*n.* rapid, meaningless sounds, as the cackling of geese.—*n.* **gab′bler.**

ga-bi-on (gā′bĭ-ŭn), *n.* a large wicker cylinder filled with earth: used for purposes of military defense, or in building dikes, or the like.

ga-ble (gā′bl), *n.* **1**, the triangular part of a wall of a building, between the slopes of a double-sloping roof; as, many old houses were built with the *gable* toward the street; **2**, the entire end wall of a building; **3**, a gablelike construction in a building: **gable end,** the end wall of a building having a gable: **gable plate,** a horizontal timber cutting across the studding of a gable end: **gable roof,** a roof, each end of which covers a gable.

GABLE (def. 3)

Ga-bri-el (gā′brĭ-ĕl), *n.* in the Bible, an angel sent as a herald of good tidings or comfort to man.

ga-by (gā′bĭ), *n.* [*pl.* gabies (-bĭz)], *Colloq.*, a silly, gaping person; a simpleton.

[1]gad (găd), *n.* **1,** *Colloq.*, a goad for driving cattle; **2,** a pointed tool for breaking or loosening ore:—*v.t.* [*p.t.* and *p.p.* gad′ded, *p.pr.* gad′ding], to loosen (ore) with a gad.

[2]gad (găd), *v.i.* [*p.t.* and *p.p.* gad′ded, *p.pr.* gad′ding], to go about without purpose; ramble.—*n.* **gad′der.**

[3]gad (găd), *interj.* an exclamation of surprise: a mild oath.

gad-a-bout (găd′ȧ-bout″), *Colloq.*, *n.* one who wanders continually with no apparent object in view.

gad-fly (găd′flī″), *n.* [*pl.* gadflies (-flīz″)], an insect that stings cattle.

gadg-et (găd′jĕt), *n.* an object or mechanical device, esp. if novel.

Gæ-a (jē′ȧ), *n.* in Greek mythology, a goddess personifying the earth, mother of *Cronus:* identified with the Roman *Tellus.*

Gael (gāl), *n.* **1,** formerly, a Scottish Highlander; **2,** now, any Celt of Irish, Scotch, or Manx stock.

Gael-ic (gāl′ĭk), *adj.* pertaining to the Celtic people of the Scottish Highlands, Ireland, and the Isle of Man, or to their language:—*n.* the language of the Gaels.

gaff (găf), *n.* **1,** a large hook on the end of a pole, used for landing salmon, etc.; **2,** the steel spur fastened to the leg of a gamecock; **3,** a spar branching out from the mast of a sailing vessel (see *rigging,* illus.):—*v.t.* to seize or land (a fish) with a large hook.

gaf-fer (găf′ẽr), *n.* a respectable and good old man, esp. a countryman: masculine of *gammer.*

gag (găg), *n.* **1,** something placed in the mouth to hinder speech, or to keep the mouth open; **2,** *Slang:* **a,** a practical joke; **b,** words added by an actor in a play:—*v.t.* [*p.t.* and *p.p.* gagged (găgd), *p.pr.* gag′ging], **1,** to stop the mouth; **2,** to silence by force or law:—*v.i.* to strain, as in the effort to vomit.

[1]gage (gāj), *n.* **1,** a promise or agreement; pledge; **2,** a pledge to appear to do battle: indicated by throwing down a glove; **3,** a challenge to fight; a glove, cap, or the like, thrown on the ground as such a challenge:—*v.t.* [*p.t.* and *p.p.* gaged (gājd), *p.pr.* gag′ing], *Obs.* or *Archaic,* **1,** to deposit as forfeit; **2,** to bet; wager.

[2]gage (gāj), *n.* any of several cultivated plums.

[3]gage (gāj), *n.* **1,** a standard of measure; **2,** an estimate or judgment; **3,** the distance between railway rails; **4,** any of various measuring instruments; **5,** the draft of a loaded vessel; **6,** the position of a vessel in relation to another vessel and the wind:—*v.t.* [*p.t.* and *p.p.* gaged (gājd), *p.pr.* gag′ing], **1,** to measure; **2,** to estimate; judge. See **gauge,** *Pfd. S.*—*n.* **gag′er.**

gai-e-ty (gā′ĕ-tĭ), *n.* [*pl.* gaieties (-tĭz)], **1,** the state or quality of being merry; pleasure; **2,** a performance of a merry nature; **3,** brilliancy, as of dress. Also, **gay′e-ty.**
Syn. merriment, sportiveness, fun.

gai-ly (gā′lĭ), *adv.* **1,** merrily; **2,** showily; as, to dress *gaily.* Also, **gay′ly.**

gain (gān), *n.* **1,** advantage; profit: opp. of *loss;* **2,** increase; as, a *gain* in weight:—*v.t.* **1,** to obtain, as profit or advantage; earn; **2,** to win; arrive at; as, he *gained* his point; **3,** to obtain through an increase; as, to *gain* ten pounds in weight:—*v.i.* **1,** to improve; increase; **2,** to advance; do better: often with *on* or *upon.*—*n.* **gain′er.**
Syn., n. benefit, winnings, earnings; *v.* (see get).—*Ant., n.* loss, privation, disadvantage.

gain-ful (gān′fo͝ol), *adj.* yielding profit; advantageous.—*adv.* **gain′ful-ly.**

gain-say (gān″sā′; gān′sā″), *v.t.* [*p.t.* and *p.p.* -said′ (-sĕd′), *p.pr.* -say′ing], to contradict; oppose.—*n.* **gain″say′er.**

gait (gāt), *n.* a manner of walking; as, a rapid *gait;* an awkward *gait.*

gai-ter (gā′tẽr), *n.* **1,** a covering of cloth for the ankle or entire lower leg, fitting over the top of the boot; **2,** in the U. S., a shoe with elastic strips at the sides.

ga-la (gā′lȧ), *n.* **1,** a festival; **2,** festive dress:—*adj.* festive; as, *gala* attire: **gala day,** a day of pleasure; a holiday.

Gal-a-had (găl′ȧ-hăd), *n.* in Arthurian legend, a knight of the Round Table, who was successful in his quest for the Holy Grail: the type of knightly purity.

Gal-a-te-a (găl″ȧ-tē′ȧ), *n.* in mythology, **1,** a sea nymph loved by the Cyclops Polyphemus; **2,** an ivory statue of a maiden, beautifully carved by Pygmalion, with which he fell in love and to which Aphrodite gave life: **galatea,** a high-grade cotton material, often striped.

Ga-la-tian (gȧ-lā′shăn), *n.* **1,** a native of Galatia, in ancient Asia Minor; **2,** in *pl.,* in the Bible, the Epistle addressed to the Galatians.—*abbr.* **Gal.**

Gal-ax-y (găl′ăk-sĭ), *n.* the Milky Way, a luminous band extending across the heavens, seen through the telescope to be composed of millions of stars: **galaxy,** [*pl.* galaxies (-sĭz)], a gathering of splendid persons or things; as, a *galaxy* of beautiful women.

gale (gāl), *n.* **1,** a strong wind; **2,** excitement; noisy merriment.

ga-le-na (gȧ-lē′nȧ), *n.* a lead ore; as, most of the lead used in the arts is obtained from *galena.*

[1]Gal-i-le-an (găl″ĭ-lē′ăn), *adj.* of or belonging to Galilee:—*n.* a native of Galilee: **the Galilean,** Jesus of Nazareth in Galilee. Also, **Gal″i-læ′an.**

[2]Gal-i-le-an (găl″ĭ-lē′ăn), *adj.* pertaining to Galileo (1564–1642), an Italian physicist and astronomer.

gal-i-pot (găl′ĭ-pŏt), *n.* a white resin obtained from certain pine trees; an impure turpentine. Also, **gal′li-pot.**

[1]gall (gôl), *n.* **1,** the bile, a bitter fluid secreted by the liver; **2,** the gall bladder; **3,** anything very bitter or distasteful to endure; **4,** evil feeling; rancor; **5,** in the U. S., *Slang,* pert assurance; insolence.

[2]gall (gôl), *n.* **1,** a sore on the skin caused by chafing; **2,** mental irritation or its cause:—*v.t.* **1,** to break or injure by rubbing, as the skin; render sore by friction; **2,** to vex; fret; harass; weary.—*p. adj.* **gall′ing.**

[3]gall (gôl), *n.* a swelling on plants, esp. on certain oaks; a gallnut (which see).

gal-lant (găl′ănt), *adj.* **1,** showy; gay; **2,** brave; high-spirited; chivalrous; as, a *gallant* knight; **3,** (gă-lănt′), showing elaborate courtesy and respect to women:—*n.* (gă-lănt′; găl′ănt), **1,** a young man of sprightly and gay manners; **2,** a beau; a man elaborately polite to women; as, the young *gallant* had excellent manners:—*v.t.* (gă-lănt′), to pay court to; accompany; escort.—*adv.* **gal′lant-ly; gal-lant′ly.**—*n.* **gal′lant-ness.**
Syn., adj. bold, courageous, intrepid, heroic.

gal-lant-ry (găl′ănt-rĭ), *n.* [*pl.* gallantries (-rĭz)], **1,** bravery; heroic courage; **2,** elaborate politeness; **3,** an instance of gallant conduct.

gall blad-der a pear-shaped sac which stores bile, attached to the liver in many vertebrates.

gal-le-on (găl′ē-ŭn), *n.* a large broad-beamed vessel of the 15th century and later (see illus. next page).

gal-ler-y (găl′ẽr-ĭ), *n.* [*pl.* galleries (-ĭz)], **1,** a long narrow hall, or place for walking; **2,** a platform projecting from the side and end walls of a theater, church, assembly room, etc., containing seats; **3,** the occupants of such seats; hence, the crowd; **4,** a building or room, used for exhibiting, as works of art, etc.; **5,** an underground passage for communication.—*adj.* **gal'ler-ied.**

gal-let (găl'ĕt), *n.* a small piece of stone chipped off by a hammer:—*v.t.* to fill (masonry joints) with chips of stone. —*n.* **gal'let-ing.**

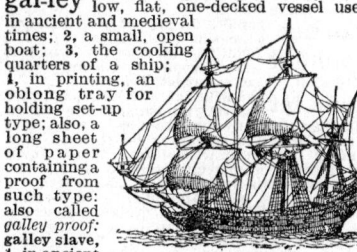

gal-ley (găl'ĭ), *n.* [*pl.* galleys (-ĭz)], **1,** a low, flat, one-decked vessel used in ancient and medieval times; **2,** a small, open boat; **3,** the cooking quarters of a ship; **4,** in printing, an oblong tray for holding set-up type; also, a long sheet of paper containing a proof from such type: also called *galley proof:* **galley slave, 1,** in ancient times, a slave compelled to row a galley; **2,** formerly, esp. in France, a convict condemned to hard labor, as at the oars on a state galley.

GALLEON

gall-fly (gôl'flī''), *n.* [*pl.* gallflies (-flīz'')], any of several insects that deposit their eggs on plants, causing a swelling of the plant tissue, called a *gall.*

Gal-lic (găl'ĭk), *adj.* pertaining to ancient Gaul, or modern France.

gal-lic ac-id an acid found in gallnuts, tea, etc.

Gal-li-can (găl'ĭ-kăn), *adj.* **1,** pertaining to Gaul, or France; **2,** pertaining to the Roman Catholic Church in France.

Gal-li-cism (găl'ĭ-sĭzm), *n.* a French manner of speech used in another language; a French idiom.

gal-li-na-ceous (găl''ĭ-nā'shŭs), *adj.* like, or belonging to, an order (*Gallinæ*) of birds which includes barnyard fowls, partridges, quail, etc.

[1]gal-li-pot (găl'ĭ-pŏt), *n.* a resinous juice from pines. *Pfd. S.,* **gal'i-pot.**

[2]gal-li-pot (găl'ĭ-pŏt), *n.* a smooth, glass-like, earthenware jar, used largely by druggists to hold medicines.

gal-li-um (găl'ĭ-ŭm), *n.* a rare metallic element, bluish white in color.

gal-li-vant (găl''ĭ-vănt'), *v.i.* **1,** to play the beau; **2,** to gad about.

gall-nut (gôl'nŭt''), *n.* a swelling produced on plants, esp. on the oak tree, by a substance injected with the eggs of the gallfly; a gall: also called *nutgall.*

gal-lon (găl'ŭn), *n.* **1,** a unit of liquid measure: the wine gallon, or standard gallon in the U. S., being equal to four quarts or 231 cubic inches, the imperial gallon in Great Britain to 277.274 cubic inches; **2,** sometimes, a unit of dry measure equal to one eighth of a bushel, or 268.8 cubic inches.

gal-loon (gă-lōōn'), *n.* a cotton, silk, worsted, or gold-lace trimming used for hats, shoes, uniforms, etc.

gal-lop (găl'ŭp), *n.* **1,** the rapid, forward, springing movement of a horse; **2,** the act of riding at this gait:—*v.i.* **1,** to run with leaps, like a horse; **2,** to ride a horse moving with a rapid forward spring; hasten:—*v.t.* to cause to move with a rapid springing gait.

gal-lows (găl'ōz; găl'ŭs), *n.* [*pl.* gallowses (-ōz-ĕz; -ŭs-ĕz)], **1,** a wooden structure consisting of two uprights with a crossbar on the top, used for hanging criminals; **2,** anything like such a framework.

gall-stone (gôl'stōn''), *n.* a lump of solid matter formed in the gall bladder, liver, or biliary passages.

gal-op (găl'ŭp; găl'ō), *n.* **1,** a lively dance; **2,** the music for it.

ga-lore (gȧ-lōr'), *adj.* very many; abundant; as, pretty girls *galore:*—*adv.* in great plenty.

ga-losh (gȧ-lŏsh'), *n.* in the U. S., any protective overshoe; esp., a high rubber overshoe with an outside cloth finish: also called *arctic.* Also, **go-losh'; go-loshe'.**

gal-van-ic (găl-văn'ĭk), *adj.* **1,** pertaining to electric currents, esp. those produced by chemical action; as, a *galvanic* battery; **2,** stimulating, as with an electric shock; as, the speech had a *galvanic* effect.

gal-va-nism (găl'vȧ-nĭzm), *n.* that branch of electric science which treats of electric currents, esp. those arising from chemical action.

gal-va-nize (găl'vȧ-nīz), *v.t.* [*p.t.* and *p.p.* -nized (-nīzd), *p.pr.* -niz''ing], **1,** to cover with gold, silver, zinc, etc., by means of electricity; **2,** to excite, as by an electric shock; **3,** to subject to the action of an electric current: **galvanized iron,** iron, often in thin sheets, coated with zinc to prevent it from rusting.—*n.* **gal''va-ni-za'tion.**

gal-va-nom-e-ter (găl''vȧ-nŏm'ē-tẽr), *n.* an instrument for measuring the intensity and direction of an electric current.—*n.* **gal''va-nom'e-try.**

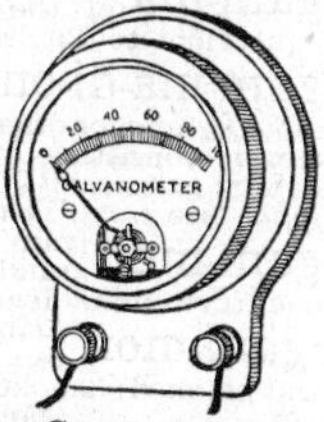

GALVANOMETER

gam-bit (găm'bĭt), *n.* an opening in chess in which a pawn, or other piece, is sacrificed intentionally.

gam-ble (găm'bl), *v.i.* [*p.t.* and *p.p.* -bled (-bld), *p.pr.* -bling], **1,** to play for money or a prize; **2,** to risk money on an event or a possible happening; **3,** to pursue a course in which danger or loss is likely to occur:—*v.t.* to squander by playing for stakes: often with *away:*—*n.* **1,** any game or act involving the risking of stakes; **2,** an act accompanied by risk of loss.—*n.* **gam'bler.**

Syn. wager, hazard, venture, stake.

gam-bling (găm'blĭng), *n.* **1,** the practice of wagering or playing for stakes; **2,** the action of one who gambles.

gam-boge (găm-bōj'; găm-bōōj'), *n.* a reddish yellow gum resin found in the Orient: used as a yellow pigment.

gam-bol (găm'bŏl), *n.* a dancing or skipping about for joy or sport; frolic:—*v.i.* to skip and dance about in play.

gam-brel (găm'brĕl), *n.* **1,** the hock joint of the hind leg of a horse; **2,** a bent stick, resembling a horse's leg, used by butchers; **3,** a ridged roof in which the slope on each side is broken by an obtuse angle: also called *gambrel roof.*

[1]game (gām), *n.* **1,** sport or amusement; fun; frolic; also, jest; as, to make *game* of a poor man; **2,** a contest carried on by rules, success depending upon strength, skill, luck, etc.; **3,** a single match at play; as, he won four *games* in the first set at tennis; **4,** the number of points to be scored in order to win; as, 61 points is the *game* in cribbage; **5,** a scheme, plan, or undertaking, sometimes not creditable; as, I've spoiled your little *game;* the *game* is up; **6,** wild animals, birds, or fish pursued by a hunter or fisherman; also, their flesh used for food; **7,** any object of pursuit: —*v.i.* [*p.t.* and *p.p.* gamed (gāmd), *p.pr.* gam'-ing], **1,** to play at any sport or diversion; **2,** to play for a stake or prize:—*adj.* **1**, pertaining to animals or birds hunted or taken for sport; **2**, *Colloq.*, ready; spirited; plucky.—*adv.* **game'ly.**—*n.* **game'ness.**

Syn., *n.* play, sport. *Game* stresses the idea of competition, usually under a set of rules; as, a *game* of tennis. *Play* is a general term for action or exercise, of the mind or body, taken for its own sake or for amusement; as, the children were at *play;* our work seemed only *play* to him. *Sport* is a wider term than *game*, for it includes the whole range of athletic or outdoor *games* or pastimes; as, tiger hunting is an exciting *sport.*

²game (gām), *adj. Slang*, lame or crooked; as, a *game* leg.

game-cock (gām'kŏk''), *n.* a cock bred and trained for fighting.

game-keep-er (gām'kēp''ẽr), *n.* one in charge of wild animals or birds that are to be protected or hunted.

game-some (gām'sŭm), *adj.* merry; gay; playful; ready to play.

game-ster (gām'stẽr), *n.* one who habitually plays for stakes or who wagers on the outcome of an event.

gam-in (găm'ĭn; *Fr.* gȧ''măṅ'), *n.* a neglected and impertinent street child.

gam-ing (gām'ĭng), *n.* the act of playing games for stakes; gambling.

gam-ma (găm'ȧ), *n.* the third letter [γ, Γ], of the Greek alphabet, nearly equivalent to English *g.*

gam-ma-di-on (gă-mā'dĭ-ŏn), *n.* [*pl.* gammadia (-ȧ)], a religious symbol or ornament, dating from ancient times, consisting of a cross formed of four capital gammas [卐]: also called *swastika* and *fylfot* (see *cross, swastika,* illus.).

gam-mer (găm'ẽr), *n.* an old woman; grandmother; esp., an old countrywoman: feminine of *gaffer.*

¹gam-mon (găm'ŭn), *n.* a leg or thigh; esp., the thigh of a hog salted and smoked; smoked ham.

²gam-mon (găm'ŭn), *n.* **1**, in backgammon, a victory in which the winner gets rid of all his men before the loser has thrown off a man; **2**, *Colloq.*, nonsense; humbug:—*v.t.* **1**, in backgammon, to beat by obtaining a gammon; **2**, to hoax.

gam-ut (găm'ŭt), *n.* **1**, the lines and spaces upon which musical notes are written or printed; **2**, the entire range of anything; as, the whole *gamut* of emotions.

gam-y (gām'ĭ), *adj.* [*comp.* gam'i-er, *superl.* gam'i-est], **1**, abounding in game; **2**, plucky; ready; spirited; **3**, having the flavor of game.

gan-der (găn'dẽr), *n.* **1**, a male goose; **2**, a simpleton.

gang (găng), *n.* **1**, a number of persons banded together for a particular purpose, as for political control or for crime; **2**, a group of laborers under one foreman; a number of a ship's company selected for special duty; a squad; **3**, an outfit; a set of tools arranged for use together: **gang plow**, a kind of plow having a number of plowshares arranged in series (see *plow*, illus.).

gan-gli-on (găng'glĭ-ŏn), *n.* [*pl.* ganglia (-ȧ); ganglions (-ŏnz)], **1**, a small collection of nerve-cell bodies and nerve fibers; **2**, a hard globular swelling on a tendon.

gang-plank (găng'plăngk''), *n.* a movable platform or bridge by which to enter or leave a ship; gangway.

gan-grene (găng'grēn), *n.* the mortification or decay of some part of a living body, caused by failure of the blood supply at that part:—*v.t.* [*p.t.* and *p.p.* -grened (-grēnd), *p.pr.* -gren''ing], to cause to mortify, as tissue:—*v.i.* to decay.—*adj.* **gan'gre-nous.**

gang-ster (găng'stẽr), *n.* one of a gang, as of criminals or politicians.

gang-way (găng'wā''), *n.* **1**, a narrow platform or bridge between a wharf and a ship; **2**, an opening in a ship's side, used as an entrance or exit, esp. for freight; **3**, a passage into or out of any place; **4**, a passageway between two rows of seats, as in a hall; **5**, the main level of a mine:—*interj.* room! make way!

gan-net (găn'ĕt), *n.* any of several large, fish-eating sea birds.

¹gant-let (gånt'lĕt; gănt'lĕt), *n.* a mailed glove, or one with a long wrist extension. See **¹gaunt'let**, *Pfd. S.*

²gant-let (gånt'lĕt; gănt'lĕt), *n.* **1**, a former military punishment in which an offender ran between two files of men who struck him with clubs as he passed; **2**, a similar torture practiced by Indians upon captives; **3**, figuratively, a series of tests, trials, or disagreeable events. Also, **gaunt'let.**

Gan-y-mede (găn'ĭ-mēd), *n.* in mythology, a Trojan lad, whom Zeus, in the guise of an eagle, carried to Olympus to be his cupbearer.

gaol (jāl), *n.* a place of confinement; prison. See **jail**, *Pfd. S.*—*n.* **gaol'er.**

gap (găp), *n.* **1**, an opening; cleft; passage; breach; **2**, a pass in a mountain ridge; **3**, in flying machines, the vertical distance between the upper and lower wings (see *airplane*, illus.).

gape (gāp; găp; gäp), *v.t.* [*p.t.* and *p.p.* gaped (gāpt; găpt; gäpt), *p.pr.* gap'ing], **1**, to open the mouth wide, as from drowsiness, wonder, etc.; yawn; **2**, to stare, as in amazement:—*n.* **1**, the act of opening the mouth and staring; **2**, a yawn; **3**, the opening between the jaws of birds or of fishes: **the gapes, 1**, a disease of poultry; **2**, a fit of yawning.—*n.* **gap'er.**

Syn., *v.* stare, gaze. *Gape* means to *stare* with open mouth, and hence expresses great surprise or stupid wonder; as, he *gaped* at the city crowds. *Stare* also expresses surprise; as, he *stared* at the apparition. *Gaze* and *stare* are alike in showing fixed attention; but in *stare* this is often impertinent or discourteous; as, he *stared* her out of countenance. *Gaze*, on the other hand, has the idea of respectful admiration or even rapture; as, we *gazed* at the beautiful yacht.

gar (gär), *n.* a long, slender, fish with a spearlike snout.

ga-rage (gȧ''räzh'; găr'ăj), [Fr.], *n.* a building in which automobiles are sheltered or repaired.

garb (gärb), *n.* dress; outside clothing; formerly, fashion:—*v.t.* to clothe.

gar-bage (gär'bāj), *n.* **1**, waste animal or vegetable matter from a kitchen, market, etc.; offal; **2**, anything worthless or filthy.

gar-ble (gär'bl), *v.t.* [*p.t.* and *p.p.* -bled (-bld), *p.pr.* -bling], to select such parts of as are wanted or may serve some particular, often unfair, purpose; mutilate; as, to *garble* a quotation.

***gar-çon** (gȧr''sôṅ'), [Fr.], *n.* [*pl.* garçons (-sôṅ')], **1**, a boy; **2**, a waiter.

gar-den (gär'dn), *n.* **1**, a piece of ground set apart for the cultivation of flowers, fruit, vegetables, etc.; **2**, a place specially delightful, rich, or fruitful:—*v.t.* and *v.i.* to cultivate, as a garden.—*n.* **gar'den-er.**—*n.* **gar'den-ing.**

gar-fish (gär'fĭsh''), *n.* any of several fishes with pikelike body and much elongated jaws, some species of which are valuable as food: also called *gar; gar pike.*

gar-gle (gär'gl), *n.* a medicinal liquid for washing the throat:—*v.t.* [*p.t.* and *p.p.* -gled (-gld), *p.pr.* -gling], to wash, as the throat, with a medicinal liquid, not swallowed, but kept in the throat by slowly expelling the breath:—*v.i.* to use a wash for the throat.

gar-goyle (gär'goil), *n.* in Gothic architecture, a projecting stone waterspout, often in the form of a grotesquely shaped man or animal.

gar-i-bal-di (găr″ĭ-băl'dĭ; gä″rĭ-bäl'dĭ), *n.* a loose, blouse-shaped shirt for women or children, usually red: named for the Italian patriot, Garibaldi.

gar-ish (gâr'ĭsh), *adj.* gaudy; dazzling; showy; as, she wore *garish* jewelry.—*adv.* **gar'ish-ly.**—*n.* **gar'ish-ness.**
Syn. glaring, flashy, striking.

gar-land (gär'lănd), *n.* **1,** a wreath made of flowers, branches, feathers, and sometimes of precious stones, to be worn on the head like a crown; as, the victor's *garland;* **2,** a collection of choice pieces of prose or poetry; an anthology; **3,** a kind of food bag used by sailors; **4,** in heraldry, a wreath of laurel, or oak leaves and acorns:—*v.t.* to deck or adorn with a wreath or chaplet.

gar-lic (gär'lĭk), *n.* a plant of the lily family, with a strong biting taste and an unpleasant odor; also, the bulb of this plant, used in cooking.—*adj.* **gar'lick-y.**

gar-ment (gär'mĕnt), *n.* **1,** any article of clothing; **2,** in *pl.*, clothing taken together as an outfit.

gar-ner (gär'nẽr), *n.* a building or place where grain is stored for safe-keeping; a granary:—*v.t.* to gather for safe-keeping; store, as in a granary; gather up.

gar-net (gär'nĕt), *n.* **1,** a precious or semi-precious stone of various colors, usually deep red; **2,** a deep red color.

gar-nish (gär'nĭsh), *n.* **1,** an ornament or decoration; **2,** something laid about food in a dish as a decoration:—*v.t.* **1,** to adorn; make beautiful; **2,** to decorate with something, as parsley, laid round a dish.
Syn., v. beautify, trim, deck, embellish.

gar-nish-ee (gär″nĭsh-ē'), *n.* the person in whose hands the property of another is attached pending the satisfaction of the claims of a third party:—*v.t.* [*p.t.* and *p.p.* -eed' (-ēd'), *p.pr.* -ee'ing], to attach (property) by law to pay a debt.—*n.* **gar'nish-er.**

gar-nish-ment (gär'nĭsh-mĕnt), *n.* **1,** the act of ornamenting or decorating; **2,** in law: **a,** a notice summoning a third party to appear in a suit; **b,** a proceeding to attach property of the defendant held by a third person called the garnishee, in order that such property may be applied to the claim of the plaintiff.

gar-ni-ture (gär'nĭ-tūr), *n.* a decoration; trimming, esp. of a dish.

gar-ret (găr'ĕt), *n.* the uppermost part of a house, beneath the roof; attic.

gar-ri-son (găr'ĭ-sn), *n.* **1,** a body of troops stationed in a fort; **2,** the place where such soldiers are stationed:—*v.t.* to furnish (a fortified place) with troops.

gar-rote (gă-rōt'; gă-rŏt'), *n.* formerly, in Spain, execution by strangling; also, the device used:—*v.t.* [*p.t.* and *p.p.* -rot'ed, *p.pr.* -rot'ing], to execute by strangling; seize by the throat so as to render helpless. Also, **gar-rotte'; ga-rotte'** (gă-rŏt').

gar-ru-li-ty (gă-rōō'lĭ-tĭ), *n.* talkativeness; as, the *garrulity* of old age.

gar-ru-lous (găr'ōō-lŭs), *adj.* talking much, esp. about things that are trivial.—*adv.* **gar'ru-lous-ly.**
Syn. talkative, glib, fluent, voluble.

gar-ter (gär'tẽr), *n.* a band by which a stocking is held up on the leg: **the Garter,** the insignia of the Order of the Garter, the highest order of British knighthood:—*v.t.* **1,** to bind or fasten with a band called a garter; **2,** to invest with the Order of the Garter.

gar-ter snake any of many small, harmless, yellow-striped snakes, common in America.

gas (găs), *n.* **1,** any completely elastic, airlike fluid tending to expand indefinitely; **2,** a mixture obtained from distilling soft coal, or by other means, and used to give light and heat; **3,** a mixture of nitrous oxide and oxygen, used as an anæsthetic, esp. by dentists: often called *laughing gas;* **4,** an airlike chemical, or mixture of chemicals, used in warfare to put the enemy out of action; as, tear *gas;* **5,** *Colloq.,* gasoline; **6,** *Slang,* empty, boastful talk: **natural gas,** a mixture of combustible gases found in the earth, as in western Pennsylvania, Kansas, etc.:—*v.t.* [*p.t.* and *p.p.* gassed (găst), *p.pr.* gas'sing], to cause to inhale poisonous gas:—*v.i. Slang,* to talk nonsense.

gas-con-ade (găs″kŏn-ād'), *n.* boastful, blustering, or bragging talk; as, the *gasconade* of the young soldier.

gas en-gine an internal-combustion engine; an engine in which the piston is driven by the explosion of a mixture of gas, esp. vaporized gasoline, and air, ignited within the engine cylinder, as by an electric spark plug (see also illus. next page).

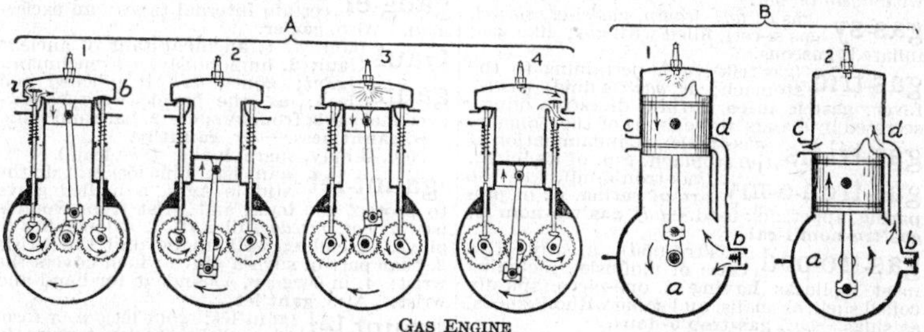

GAS ENGINE

A, four-cycle engine: *a,* intake valve; *b,* exhaust valve.—1, piston ready to start down, drawing in gas mixture at *a;* 2, piston ready to start up, compressing mixture; 3, spark, occurring at time of greatest compression, explodes gas mixture and forces piston down; 4, rising piston forces out spent exhaust gas at *b:* on next down stroke a fresh charge will be drawn in.

B, two-cycle engine.—1, at top of stroke: spark explodes compressed mixture in cylinder, and drives piston down, compressing in the closed crank case, *a,* gas mixture which has entered at *b* during up stroke; 2, at bottom of stroke: spent gases escape at *c;* fresh mixture, admitted from crank case at *d,* is deflected upward by baffle plate and is compressed ready for ignition as rising piston closes both *c* and *d.*

gas-e-ous (găs′ē-ŭs), *adj.* having the nature or form of gas.

gash (găsh), *n.* a deep or gaping cut or wound:—*v.t.* to cut deeply.

gas-i-fy (găs′ĭ-fī), *v.t.* [*p.t.* and *p.p.* -fied (-fīd), *p.pr.* -fy″ing], to convert into gas, as by heat or by chemical action:—*v.i.* to change into a gas.

GAS ENGINE

gas-ket (găs′kĕt), *n.* **1,** a flat, plaited cord by which furled sails are tied fast to a spar; **2,** hemp, etc., used for packing a piston or a sliding joint; **3,** a thin piece, as of rubber, placed between surfaces to make a tight joint.

gas-kin (găs′kĭn), *n.* **1,** that part of the hind leg of a horse or other quadruped between the hock and the stifle; **2,** in p.., *Dial.*, ..oose breeches.

gas man-tle a tubelike structure consisting of oxides of certain rare metals, which, when placed over a Bunsen gas flame, is heated to incandescence, thus giving out light.

gas mask a covering for the face to prevent the inhaling of poison gas: also called *gas helmet.*

gas-o-line (găs′ō-lēn; găs′ō-lĭn), *n.* a liquid easily set on fire, used for heating, cooking, etc., and for running engines, as of automobiles. Also, **gas′o-lene.**

GASOMETER

gas-om-e-ter (găs-ŏm′ē-tẽr), *n.* a large, round tank or reservoir for storing a large volume of gas.

gasp (gȧsp), *n.* a quick, painful effort to catch the breath:—*v.i.* to catch the breath with difficulty:—*v.t.* to breathe out in quick, painful breaths: with *away* or *out.*

gas-sy (găs′ĭ), *adj.* [*comp.* gas′si-er, *superl.* gas′si-est], filled with gas; like gas; inflated; gaseous.

gas-tric (găs′trĭk), *adj.* pertaining to the stomach; as, *gastric* fluid; *gastric* fever: **gastric juice,** a thin, digestive liquid, secreted by glands in the lining of the stomach.

gas-tri-tis (găs-trī′tĭs), *n.* inflammation of the stomach, esp. of its lining.

gas-tron-o-my (găs-trŏn′ō-mĭ), *n.* the art of eating, or of preparing, appetizing food.—*adj.* **gas″tro-nom′ic; gas″tro-nom′i-cal.**

gas-tro-pod (găs′trō-pŏd), *n.* any of a class of mollusks, including most mollusks having a one-piece, spirally coiled shell, as snails, and some without shells, as slugs.—*adj.* **gas-trop′o-dous.**

gate (gāt), *n.* **1,** an opening to allow entrance or passage; **2,** a frame or door which opens or closes such an entrance, esp. in a fence; **3,** a stately entrance to a city, castle, etc.; **4,** a valve or door to stop or permit a flow, as of water, in a pipe, mold, etc.; **5,** *Colloq.*, the sum of money paid for admission, as to a baseball game:—*v.t.* [*p.t.* and *p.p.* gat′ed, *p.pr.* gat′ing], in English universities, to punish by confining to the grounds.

gate-keep-er (gāt′kēp″ẽr), *n.* one in charge of an entrance.

gate-way (gāt′wā″), *n.* **1,** an entrance fitted with a frame or door; **2,** an approach.

gath-er (găth′ẽr), *v.t.* **1,** to assemble or bring together; collect; bring into one place; **2,** to pick up; glean; pluck; as, to *gather* a harvest; **3,** to summon; concentrate, as energies; **4,** to amass or gain, as a fortune; **5,** to pucker or plait; **6,** to infer:—*v.i.* **1,** to congregate; **2,** to generate pus, as an abscess; **3,** to increase; as, the storm *gathers:*—*n.* a series of folds in cloth, drawn together by a thread.—*n.* **gath′er-er.**

gath-er-ing (găth′ẽr-ĭng), *n.* **1,** the act of assembling or bringing together; **2,** an assemblage; **3,** a charitable contribution or gift; **4,** any sore filled with pus.

Gat-ling gun (găt′lĭng), a machine gun with many small, clustered barrels, which are discharged very rapidly.

gaud (gôd), *n.* a piece of worthless finery; ornament.

gaud-y (gôd′ĭ), *adj.* [*comp.* gaud′i-er, *superl.* gaud′i-est], showy; vulgarly gay or fine.—*adv.* **gaud′i-ly.**—*n.* **gaud′i-ness.**

Syn., flashy, tawdry, glittering.

gauge (gāj), *n.* **1,** any of various standards of measure, esp. of thickness or of the capacity of a barrel; **2,** an estimate or judgment, as of size or of a person's character; **3,** the distance between railway rails, standard gauge being 4 feet 8½ inches; **4,** any of various measuring or recording instruments or devices, as those for measuring rainfall, wind velocity, steam pressure, amount of water in a boiler, thickness or diameter of wire, etc.; **5,** a carpenter's tool for marking a line parallel with the edge of a board (see *tool,* illus.); **6,** a device on a cutting tool to regulate the size or depth of the cut; **7,** the depth to which a vessel, when loaded, sinks into the water; draft; **8,** the position of a vessel in relation to another vessel and the wind; **9,** in printing, a marked strip of metal or wood for measuring the length of a page, column, etc.; **10,** the part of a shingle, tile, etc., exposed to the weather; **11,** a row, or course, of shingles, tiles, etc.:—*v.t.* [*p.t.* and *p.p.* gauged (gājd), *p.pr.* gaug′ing], **1,** to measure by any of various measuring standards; **2,** to ascertain the contents or capacity of; **3,** to conform to a standard size or shape; **4,** to estimate. Also, **gage.**

gaug-er (gāj′ẽr), *n.* an officer who collects certain internal taxes; an exciseman. Also, **gag′er.**

Gaul (gôl), *n.* **1,** an inhabitant of ancient Gaul; **2,** humorously, a Frenchman.

gaunt (gänt; gônt), *adj.* **1,** pinched and lean; as, the people were hollow-eyed and *gaunt* from hunger; **2,** bare and grim.—*n.* **gaunt′ness.**—*adv.* **gaunt′ly.**

Syn. skinny, spare, lank. (See lean.)

[1]**gaunt-let** (gänt′lĕt; gônt′lĕt), *n.* **1,** in the Middle Ages, a mailed glove to protect the hand and wrist from wounds (see *armor, reredos,* illus.); **2,** a long, heavy glove, extending well up beyond the wrist; **3,** that part of such a glove which covers the wrist; **4,** in surgery, a bandage for hand and wrist. Also, **gant′let.**

[2]**gaunt-let** (gänt′lĕt; gônt′lĕt), *n.* a form of punishment or torture in which the culprit or victim was compelled to run between two lines of men, who beat him with rods, ropes, etc. See [2]**gant′let,** *Pfd. S.*

gauze (gôz), *n.* a thin, light, transparent silk or cotton fabric.—*adj.* **gauz′y.**

gave (gāv), past tense of the irregular verb *give.*

gav-el (găv′ĕl), *n.* a small mallet used by a presiding officer, as at a meeting.

ga-vi-al (gā′vĭ-ăl), *n.* the great crocodile of India.

ga-vot (gȧ-vŏt′; găv′ŏt), *n.* a lively, but dignified, French dance resembling the minuet; also, the music for it. Also, **ga-votte′**.

Ga-wain (gô′wān), *n.* a famous knight of romance, nephew of Arthur.

gawk (gôk), *n.* a simpleton; booby:—*v.i.* to stare stupidly.

gawk-y (gôk′ĭ), *adj.* [*comp.* gawk′i-er, *superl.* gawk′i-est], awkward; clumsy.—*adv.* **gawk′i-ly**.—*n.* **gawk′i-ness**.

gay (gā), *adj.* **1**, lively; merry; full of glee; cheerful; sportive; **2**, showy; bright-colored; **3**, addicted to pleasure; **4**, wanton.
Syn. sprightly, blithe, jovial. (See cheerful.)

gay-e-ty (gā′ĕ-tĭ), *n.* [*pl.* gayeties (-tĭz)], **1**, the state of being merry; **2**, a jolly performance or activity; **3**, brilliancy, as of dress. Also, **gai′e-ty**, *Pfd. S.*

gay-ly (gā′lĭ), *adv.* **1**, merrily; gleefully; **2**, showily. Also, **gai′ly**, *Pfd. S.*

gaze (gāz), *v.i.* [*p.t.* and *p.p.* gazed (gāzd), *p.pr.* gaz′ing], to look earnestly or eagerly:—*n.* a fixed look.—*n.* **gaz′er**.
Syn., v. stare, gawk, glare. (See gape.)

ga-zelle (gȧ-zĕl′), *n.* any of several small, swift antelopes of Africa and Asia, with large, soft, black eyes.

GAZELLES (1/40)

ga-zette (gȧ-zĕt′), *n.* **1**, an English government biweekly newspaper containing lists, official announcements, etc.; **2**, a newspaper:—*v.t.* [*p.t.* and *p.p.* -zet′ted, *p.pr.* -zet′ting], to publish in a list.—*abbr.* **gaz.**

gaz-et-teer (găz″ĕ-tēr′), *n.* **1**, a dictionary of geographical names; **2**, an official publisher of news.

G clef in music, the treble clef; a sign [𝄞] placed upon the treble staff in such a way that the central point of the lower curve falls upon the G line of the staff.

gear (gēr), *n.* **1**, a unit of machinery with some special purpose; as, the steering *gear;* **2**, armor and weapons; **3**, goods or other movable property; **4**, harness; **5**, apparatus; tackle; **6**, adjustment of parts to each other, as of wheels working on each other; as, out of *gear;* also, a gear wheel:—*v.t.* **1**, to put cogs or teeth on; **2**, to harness, as draft animals: **gear up, gear down,** to engage a gear wheel with (another) in such a way as to increase or decrease, respectively, the speed:—*v.i.* to be in, or come into, proper adjustment of parts.

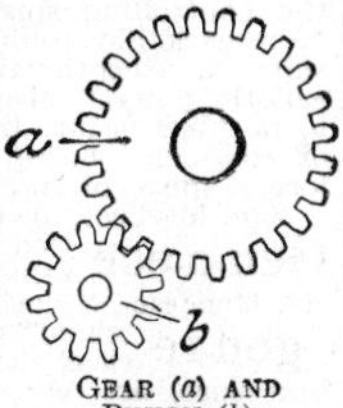

GEAR (*a*) AND PINION (*b*)
Power applied to *a*, gears *b* up; applied to *b*, gears *a* down.

gear-ing (gēr′ĭng), *n.* **1**, a train or series of parts for transmitting motion; **2**, ropes and tackle.

gear wheel a wheel with teeth, designed to fit with the cogs of another wheel, the thread of a screw, or the like; a pitch wheel. Also, *n.* **gear′wheel″**.

1gee (jē), *interj.* a command to oxen, horses, etc., to turn to the off side or from the driver: opp. of *haw*, which means to turn toward the driver.

2gee (jē), *interj. Colloq.*, an expression of amazement.

3gee (jē), *v.i.* [*p.t.* and *p.p.* geed (jēd), *p.pr.* gee′ing], *Colloq.*, to agree; harmonize.

geese (gēs), *n.* plural of the common noun *goose.*

gei-sha (gā′shȧ), *n.* [*pl.* geisha; geishas (-shȧz)], in Japan, a dancing girl; a professional entertainer.

gel (jĕl), *n.* a colloid solution in a semi-solid condition, as of gelatin when set.

gel-a-tin (jĕl′ȧ-tĭn), *n.* a substance extracted from bones, hoofs, connective tissue, etc.; animal jelly. Also, **gel′a-tine**.—*adj.* **ge-lat′i-nous** (jĕ-lăt′ĭ-nŭs).

geld (gĕld), *v.t.* [*p.t.* and *p.p.* geld′ed or gelt (gĕlt), *p.pr.* geld′ing], **1**, to deprive (a male) of reproductive power; castrate; **2**, to remove old comb from: used of a beehive.

geld-ing (gĕl′dĭng), *n.* a castrated horse or other animal.

gel-id (jĕl′ĭd), *adj.* frigid; frozen; very cold.—*n.* **ge-lid′i-ty**.

gem (jĕm), *n.* **1**, a precious stone; **2**, any perfect or rare object; **3**, a kind of light muffin:—*v.t.* [*p.t.* and *p.p.* gemmed (jĕmd), *p.pr.* gem′ming], to adorn with gems.

gem-i-nate (jĕm′ĭ-nāt), *adj.* growing in pairs; as, *geminate* leaves:—*v.t.* [*p.t.* and *p.p.* -nat″ed, *p.pr.* -nat″ing], to double:—*v.i.* to become double.

gem-i-na-tion (jĕm″ĭ-nā′shŭn), *n.* repetition; duplication; a doubling, as of a consonant.

Gem-i-ni (jĕm′ĭ-nī), *n.pl.* **1**, a northern constellation, containing the two bright stars, Castor and Pollux; the Twins; **2**, the third sign of the zodiac, entered by the sun about May 20 (see *zodiac*, illus.).

gem-ma (jĕm′ȧ), *n.* [*pl.* gemmæ (-ē)], **1**, a leaf bud; **2**, in mosses and other plants having no proper flowers, a budlike body capable of producing a new plant when detached; **3**, on some animals, a budlike growth that forms a new individual by a process called *gemmation*, or budding.

gem-mate (jĕm′āt), *adj.* having buds or reproducing by buds.

gem-ma-tion (jĕm-ā′shŭn), *n.* **1**, the act or process of forming a new individual by the formation of a small part capable of growing when separated from the parent, as in low animal forms; **2**, the period of bud opening; **3**, the arrangement of buds on a stalk or of leaves in the bud.

***gen-darme** (zhäṅ″därm′; jĕn-därm′), [Fr.], *n.* [*pl.* gendarmes (-därm′; -därmz′)], in France and Belgium, a policeman; one of the military police.

gen-darm-er-y (jĕn-där′mĕr-ĭ), *n.* in France or Belgium, a body of gendarmes or police. Also, ***gen″dar″me-rie′** (zhäṅ″där″mĕ-rē′).

gen-der (jĕn′dĕr), *n.* the grammatical distinction of sex, expressed by a suffix, a prefix, or by a different word.
Syn., sex. *Gender* is a grammatical distinction, which may or may not be based on actual sex; as, the German word for "girl" is of neuter *gender;* in English, there are three *genders:* masculine, feminine, and neuter. *Sex* names the character of being male or female, and applies only to living organisms.

gen-e-al-o-gist (jĕn″ĕ-ăl′ō-jĭst; jē″nĕ-), *n.* one skilled in tracing pedigrees or descent of persons or families.

gen-e-al-o-gy (jĕn″ĕ-ăl′ō-jĭ; jē″nĕ-ăl′ō-jĭ), *n.* [*pl.* genealogies (-jĭz)], **1**, the art or science of investigating descent; 2, a record of such descent; 3, descent; pedigree.—*adj.* **gen″e-a-log′i-cal** (jĕn″ē-ȧ-lŏj′ĭ-kăl).—*adv.* **gen″e-a-log′i-cal-ly.**

gen-e-ra (jĕn′ẽr-ȧ), *n.* plural of *genus:* used in the classification of certain plant and animal groups.

gen-er-al (jĕn′ẽr-ăl), *n.* 1, a general principle or condition: opp. of *particular;* 2, in the U. S. army: **a**, the commander in chief, under the President, of all the military forces; **b**, a shortened title of all officers above a colonel; as, brigadier *general;* **c**, the roll of a drum to summon troops:—*adj.* 1, relating to a whole genus, kind, class, order, or race; as, death is *general* to mankind; 2, not special or particular; as, in the *general* direction of west; 3, pertaining to the majority; as, in the interest of *general* prosperity; 4, usual; ordinary; as, the *general* procedure; 5, taken as a whole; as, the *general* situation; 6, senior; chief; as, postmaster *general.*

Syn., adj. universal, common. *General* describes that which belongs to all, or to nearly all, allowing for possible exceptions; as, she was a *general* favorite; there was *general* opposition to the proposal. That which is *universal* is subject to no exceptions; as, the experiences of birth and death are *universal. Common* describes that which is shared by many; as, *common* decency; the *common* lot. It may also describe that which, being without distinction, is vulgar; as, the *common* herd; the low thoughts of *common* minds.

gen-er-al-is-si-mo (jĕn″ẽr-ăl-ĭs′ĭ-mō), *n.* [*pl.* generalissimos (-mōz)], the commander in chief of the military forces of a country.

gen-er-al-i-ty (jĕn″ẽr-ăl′ĭ-tĭ), *n.* [*pl.* generalities (-tĭz)], 1, the state of not being limited or particularized; 2, the greatest part; majority; as, the *generality* of mankind is honest; 3, a statement true in a wide sense, but lacking application.

gen-er-al-i-za-tion (jĕn″ẽr-ăl-ĭ-zā′shŭn; -ī-zā′shŭn), *n.* the mental process or result of forming a statement or a conception covering everything within a given classification; an induction; a sweeping inference or conclusion.

gen-er-al-ize (jĕn′ẽr-ăl-īz), *v.t.* [*p.t.* and *p.p.* -ized (-īzd), *p.pr.* -iz″ing], 1, to reduce to, or arrange in, a class or classes; 2, to make large in scope or meaning; 3, to derive (a general rule) from particular instances:—*v.i.* 1, to discover a general rule from special instances; 2, to draw broad, general conclusions.—*n.* **gen′er-al-iz″er.**

gen-er-al-ly (jĕn′ẽr-ăl-ĭ), *adv.* 1, commonly; as a rule; 2, extensively; 3, without exact limitation.

gen-er-al of-fi-cer a member of the general staff of an army, commanding a body of troops, such as a brigade, division, corps, or army.

gen-er-al-ship (jĕn′ẽr-ăl-shĭp″), *n.* 1, the office, rank, or military skill of a chief or an army commander; 2, skilful tactics in leadership.

gen-er-ate (jĕn′ẽr-āt), *v.t.* [*p.t.* and *p.p.* -at″ed, *p.pr.* -at″ing], 1, to produce, as offspring; 2, to cause; originate, as steam from a boiler; 3, in mathematics, to trace out or form by motion; as, a moving point *generates* a line.

Syn. form, make, beget.

gen-er-a-tion (jĕn″ẽr-ā′shŭn), *n.* 1, the act or process of producing; 2, a single succession in natural descent; 3, people of the same period; 4, progeny.

gen-er-a-tive (jĕn′ẽr-ā-tĭv), *adj.* having the power to produce.

gen-er-a-tor (jĕn′ẽr-ā″tẽr), *n.* 1, one who or that which causes or produces; esp., an apparatus by which steam, electricity, or gas is produced; 2, in music, the principal tone of a chord.

ge-ner-ic (jē-nĕr′ĭk), *adj.* 1, pertaining to things of the same class: opp. of *specific;* 2, in biology, pertaining to a genus.—*adv.* **ge-ner′i-cal-ly.**

gen-er-os-i-ty (jĕn″ẽr-ŏs′ĭ-tĭ), *n.* [*pl.* generosities (-tĭz)], the quality of being liberal; magnanimity.

gen-er-ous (jĕn′ẽr-ŭs), *adj.* 1, characterized by liberality; munificent; bountiful; 2, broad-minded; honorable; 3, rich; abundant; strong; stimulating.—*adv.* **gen′er-ous-ly.**—*n.* **gen′er-ous-ness.**

Syn. liberal, beneficent, magnanimous.

gen-e-sis (jĕn′ē-sĭs), *n.* [*pl.* geneses (-sēz)], 1, the act or process of producing or originating; 2, the origin; beginning: **Genesis**, (*abbr.* **Gen.**), the first book of the Bible: so called because it tells of the supposed beginnings of the world and of men.

gen-et (jĕn′ĕt; jē-nĕt′), *n.* a small Spanish horse. Also, **jen′net**, *Pfd. S.*

ge-net-ic (jē-nĕt′ĭk), *adj.* pertaining to generation or origin: **genetics**, *n.pl.* used as *sing.* the science which deals with the origin and development of individuals or the evolution of species. Also, *adj.* **ge-net′i-cal.**

ge-ni-al (jē′nĭ-ăl; jēn′yăl), *adj.* 1, kindly and sympathetic; cordial; 2, contributing to cheerfulness and life; agreeably warm and cheerful.—*adv.* **ge′ni-al-ly.**

Syn. hearty, companionable, friendly.

ge-ni-al-i-ty (jē″nĭ-ăl′ĭ-tĭ; jēn-yăl′ĭ-tĭ), *n.* the quality of being kindly; cheerfulness; sympathetic warmth of disposition and manners.

ge-nie (jē′nĭ), *n.* [*pl.* genies (-nĭz) or, usually, genii (jē′nĭ-ī)], in Mohammedan mythology, a good or bad spirit that could take the form of an animal, giant, etc.; as, the *genie* of the lamp, in the story of Aladdin's lamp. Also, **jin-ni′; jin-nee′.**

ge-ni-i (jē′nĭ-ī), *n.* plural of *genius* or of *genie,* which see.

gen-i-tal (jĕn′ĭ-tăl), *adj.* pertaining to generation or to the sexual organs: **genitals**, *n.pl.* the sexual organs, esp. external: also, *genitalia* (jĕn″ĭ-tā′lĭ-ȧ).

gen-i-tive (jĕn′ĭ-tĭv), *adj.* designating, or pertaining to, a grammatical case used in Latin, Greek, and other inflected languages to express origin, possession, or relation:—*n.* the genitive case or a word in it.

gen-ius (jēn′yŭs; jē′nĭ-ŭs), *n.* [*pl.* geniuses (-ĕz)], 1, [*pl.* genii (-ī)], in Roman religion, a guardian spirit; 2, hence, the controlling spirit of a place or person; 3, remarkable ability for some special pursuit; 4, exceptional creative intellectual or artistic power; also, the one possessing it; 5, peculiar nature or quality, as of a nation or language; 6, [*pl.* genii], in Mohammedan lore, a spirit, often under magic control.

Syn. intellect, aptitude. (See talent.)

Gen-o-ese (jĕn″ō-ēz′; jĕn″ō-ēs′), *adj.* pertaining to Genoa, Italy:—*n.* [*pl.* Genoese], a native of Genoa.

***gen-re** (zhäṅr′), [Fr.], *n.* 1, a kind, sort, or class of anything; esp., a type in literature, art, etc.; 2, a style of painting representing everyday life and manners in a realistic way:—*adj.* presenting life in this way.

gens (jĕnz), *n.* [*pl.* gentes (jĕn′tēz)], 1, a clan regarded as a family group, including only those in a single line of descent; 2, in ancient Rome, a clan, or group of families of common stock.

gen-teel (jĕn-tēl′), *adj.* polite; well-bred, often used humorously or sarcastically.—*adv.* **gen-teel′ly.**

Syn. refined, polished. (See polite.)

gen-tian (jĕn′shăn), *n.* **1,** any of several herbs, usually bearing beautiful blue flowers; **2,** the root of the yellow gentian, used in medicine.

Gen-tile (jĕn′tīl), *n.* orig., one who is not a Jew; among Christians, one who is neither Christian nor Jew:—*adj.* of or pertaining to Gentile people.

gen-til-i-ty (jĕn-tĭl′ĭ-tĭ), *n.* [*pl.* gentilities (-tĭz)], good breeding; social rank and refinement.

gen-tle (jĕn′tl), *adj.* **1,** mild and refined in manner and disposition; kindly; **2,** moderate in action; **3,** peaceful; docile; **4,** not steep, as a slope; **5,** well-born; belonging to the gentry:—*n.* the larva or young of the flesh fly:—*v.t.* [*p.t.* and *p.p.* -tled (-tld), *p.pr.* -tling], to make docile, as a horse.—*n.* **gen′tle-ness.**—*adv.* **gen′tly.**
Syn., *adj.* placid, bland, tame.

gen-tle-folk (jĕn′tl-fōk″), *n.* persons of good family or breeding.

gen-tle-man (jĕn′tl-măn), *n.* [*pl.* gentlemen (-mĕn)], **1,** a well-bred and honorable man; **2,** in Great Britain, one who is entitled to bear a coat of arms; also, a person of independent income; **3,** in *pl.*, a term of politeness, as in addressing an assembly.—*n.fem.* **gen′tle-wom″an.**

gen-tle-man-ly (jĕn′tl-măn-lĭ), *adj.* polite and considerate in manner; well-trained socially.

gen-try (jĕn′trĭ), *n.* **1,** people of education and breeding; **2,** people of a particular class: usually contemptuous.

gen-u-flec-tion (jĕn″ū-flĕk′shŭn), *n.* the bending of the knee, as in worship. Also, **gen″u-flex′ion.**

gen-u-ine (jĕn′ū-ĭn), *adj.* **1,** real; unadulterated; pertaining to, or derived from, the original stock; **2,** sincere.—*adv.* **gen′u-ine-ly.**—*n.* **gen′-u-ine-ness.**
Syn. true, honest.—*Ant.* false, insincere.

ge-nus (jē′nŭs), *n.* [*pl.* genera (jĕn′ẽr-*ȧ*)], a group of plants or animals, next below the family and next above the species, having common characteristics; as, the lion, cat, and panther all belong to the same *genus*.

ge-o- (jē′ō-), a combining form from the Greek, meaning earth; as, *geo*logy.

ge-o-cen-tric (jē″ō-sĕn′trĭk), *adj.* having the earth as the center; viewed from the earth as a center.—*adv.* **ge″o-cen′tri-cal-ly.**

ge-o-des-ic (jē″ō-dĕs′ĭk), *adj.* pertaining to geodesy (which see): **geodesic line,** or **geodesic,** a line on a surface forming the shortest possible path between two points on the surface: with reference to the earth, often called *geodetic line:* **geodesics,** *n.pl.* used as *sing.* mathematics dealing with such lines.—*adj.* **ge″o-det′ic; ge″o-det′i-cal.**

ge-od-e-sy (jē-ŏd′ē-sĭ), *n.* the science of measuring large portions of the earth's surface; the determination of the earth's shape and size.

ge-og-ra-pher (jē-ŏg′rȧ-fẽr), *n.* one who is versed in, or a writer on, the science of the earth and its life.

ge-og-ra-phy (jē-ŏg′rȧ-fĭ), *n.* [*pl.* geographies (-fĭz)], **1,** the science that describes the surface of the earth, its division into continents, its climate, plants, animals, inhabitants and their distribution, industries, etc.; **2,** a treatise or book on this subject.—*adj.* **ge″o-graph′ic; ge″o-graph′i-cal.**—*adv.* **ge″o-graph′i-cal-ly.**

ge-ol-o-gist (jē-ŏl′ō-jĭst), *n.* one who knows the science of the structure of the earth.

ge-ol-o-gize (jē-ŏl′ō-jīz), *v.i.* [*p.t.* and *p.p.* -gized (-jīzd), *p.pr.* -giz″ing], to study the structure of the earth.

ge-ol-o-gy (jē-ŏl′ō-jĭ), *n.* [*pl.* geologies (-jĭz)], **1,** the science that investigates the structure of the earth and its successive physical changes; **2,** a treatise or book on this subject.—*adj.* **ge″o-log′ic; ge″o-log′i-cal.**—*adv.* **ge″o-log′i-cal-ly.**

ge-om-e-ter (jē-ŏm′ē-tẽr), *n.* one skilled in geometry; a geometrician.

ge-o-met-ric (jē″ō-mĕt′rĭk), *adj.* **1,** pertaining to geometry; **2,** characterized by straight lines, circles, angles, etc., in a regular design. Also, **ge″o-met′ri-cal.**—*adv.* **ge″o-met′ri-cal-ly.**

ge-om-e-tri-cian (jē-ŏm″ē-trĭsh′ăn), *n.* one who is skilled in that branch of mathematics called geometry.

ge-om-e-trid (jē-ŏm′ē-trĭd), *n.* any member of a family of moths, whose larvæ, known as measuring worms, are often injurious to trees; a measuring worm.

ge-om-e-try (jē-ŏm′ē-trĭ), *n.* [*pl.* geometries (-trĭz)], that branch of mathematics which treats of the properties and measurements of lines, angles, surfaces, and solids; also, a textbook or treatise on this subject.

Geor-gette crêpe (jôr-jĕt′), a dull-finished, sheer silk fabric, sometimes crinkly, used in making dresses and underwear: also called *georgette.*

Ge-raint (gē-rānt′), *n.* in old romances, one of King Arthur's knights.

ge-ra-ni-um (jē-rā′nĭ-ŭm), *n.* any of several plants, esp. certain species cultivated for their handsome flowers.

ger-fal-con (jûr′fô″kn; jûr′fôl″kn), *n.* any of various large northern falcons or hawks. Also, **gyr′fal″con.**

ger-kin (gûr′kĭn), *n.* a small cucumber used for pickling. Also, **gher′kin,** *Pfd. S.*

germ (jûrm), *n.* **1,** that from which anything springs; origin; as, the *germ* of war; **2,** the undeveloped beginning of an animal or plant; sprout; seed; **3,** a microbe, esp. one which may cause disease: **germ cell,** a cell which unites with another for reproduction, as the egg or the sperm.

Ger-man (jûr′măn), *adj.* pertaining to Germany, its people, or language; more generally, pertaining to the Teutonic peoples of central Europe:—*n.* **1,** a native of Germany; a member of the Teutonic race; **2,** the language of Germany: [1]**german,** a lively dance; cotillion.

[2]**ger-man** (jûr′măn), *adj.* of the same stock or parentage: used in combination; as, cousin-*german.*

ger-mane (jẽr-mān′; jûr′mān), *adj.* **1,** related; closely akin; **2,** relevant; appropriate; fitting.

Ger-man-ic (jẽr-măn′ĭk), *adj.* pertaining to Germany; Teutonic.

Ger-man-ism (jûr′măn-ĭzm), *n.* **1,** a German custom, idiom, or trait; **2,** love of German institutions.

ger-ma-ni-um (jẽr-mā′nĭ-ŭm), *n.* a rare, grayish white, metallic element, resembling tin in some respects.

Ger-man sil-ver a white alloy of zinc, nickel, and copper.

ger-mi-cide (jûr′mĭ-sīd), *n.* something used to destroy disease germs.—*adj.* **ger′mi-cid″al.**

ger-mi-cul-ture (jûr′mĭ-kŭl″tūr), *n.* the artificial cultivation of bacteria or germs for scientific study.

ger-mi-nal (jûr′mĭ-năl), *adj.* pertaining to a germ or seed bud.

ger-mi-nant (jûr′mĭ-nănt), *adj.* sprouting; gradually developing.

ger-mi-nate (jûr′mĭ-nāt), *v.i.* [*p.t.* and *p.p.* -nat″ed, *p.pr.* -nat″ing], to sprout or bud; begin to develop into a higher form:—*v.t.* to cause to develop; produce.

ger-mi-na-tion (jûr″mĭ-nā′shŭn), *n.* the process of sprouting.

germ-ule (jûr′mūl), *n.* a small germ; also a germ beginning to develop.

ger-ry-man-der (gĕr″ĭ-măn′dẽr), *v.t.* to divide, as a state, voting district, etc., so as to give an unfair advantage to a particular political party; garble: —*n.* the act or result of such division.

ger-und (jĕr′ŭnd), *n.* a verbal noun; as, *seeing* is *believing*.—*adj.* **ge-run′di-al.**

ge-run-dive (jē-rŭn′dĭv), *n.* in Latin, a verbal adjective with passive force, as *amandus*, lovable, to be loved: —*adj.* pertaining to the gerund; gerundial.

Ge-stalt psy-chol-o-gy (gē-shtält′), [Ger.], psychology which emphasizes the essential unity of any perception, rather than the elements of which it may appear to be composed.

ges-ta-tion (jĕs-tā′shŭn), *n.* pregnancy; the state of being with young.

ges-tic-u-late (jĕs-tĭk′ū-lāt), *v.i.* [*p.t.* and *p.p.* -lat″ed, *p.pr.* -lat″ing], to make expressive motions or gestures, as in speaking or in order to attract attention. —*n.* **ges-tic′u-la″tor.**—*adj.* **ges-tic′u-la-to-ry.** —*n.* **ges-tic″u-la′tion.**

ges-ture (jĕs′tūr), *n.* **1,** a movement of the face, body, or limbs, to express an idea, emotion, etc.; **2,** such movements collectively:—*v.i.* [*p.t.* and *p.p.* -tured (-tūrd), *p.pr.* -tur-ing], to make expressive motions.

Syn., n. attitude, action, posture.

get (gĕt), *v.t.* [*p.t.* got (gŏt), *p.p.* got or gotten (gŏt′n), *p.pr.* get′ting], **1,** to come to have; win; receive; **2,** to learn or find out; as, to *get* a lesson; to *get* an answer to an example; **3,** to beget: used now only of animals; **4,** to bring into some state; as, to *get* a machine started; to succeed in placing in or out of some position; as, to *get* the key into the keyhole; **5,** to prepare or eat (a meal); **6,** to persuade; as, to *get* her to go; **7,** to become infected with, as a disease; **8,** to cause to be done; as, to *get* a task accomplished; **9,** *Colloq.*, to catch or corner; as, to *get* someone in an argument; **10,** *Slang*, **1,** to understand; as, do you *get* me? **2,** to defeat, injure, or kill; as, I'll *get* you yet: **to have got,** *Colloq.*, **1,** to have; as, *I've got* a dime; **2,** to be obliged; as, *I've got* to go:—*v.i.* **1,** to bring, take, or put oneself; as, to *get* into clothes; to *get* off a train; **2,** to become; as, to *get* out of date; *get* well; **3,** *Colloq.*, to succeed; contrive; as, she *got* to go to the play: **get along,** to succeed (well or ill): **get out, 1,** to betake oneself off; **2,** of a secret, to become noised abroad: **get over,** to recover from; cease being affected by; as, he soon *got over* his fright: **get up,** to arise from bed.—*n.* **get′ter.**

Syn., v. gain, acquire, earn, attain, procure, win. To *get* is to come into possession of, with or without effort; as, to *get* a bargain, a cold, a lesson. To *gain* is to *get* by effort that which is an advantage; as, to *gain* promotion. *Acquire* has the sense of getting with the added idea of a long process; as, he *acquired* a knowledge of German. One *earns* that for which one works; as, to *earn* a living. One *attains* some lofty aim; as, to *attain* renown in some branch of learning. To *procure* is to obtain by search or payment; as, he *procured* a copy of a rare manuscript. To *win* is to get in competition, friendly or not, anything for which another is seeking; as, to *win* a scholarship.

Geth-sem-a-ne (gĕth-sĕm′ȧ-nē), *n.* **1,** in the Bible, a garden in which Christ was betrayed and arrested (Matthew 26:36); **2,** any agonizing crisis.

gew-gaw (gū′gô), *n.* a showy trifle; useless ornament; toy.

gey-ser (gī′sẽr; gī′zẽr), *n.* a hot spring which periodically throws forth jets of water, mud, etc.

ghast-ly (gȧst′lĭ), *adj.* [*comp.* ghast′li-er, *superl.* ghast′li-est], **1,** deathlike; pale; haggard; **2,** horrible; abhorrent; as, a *ghastly* crime.—*n.* **ghast′li-ness.**

Syn. pallid, wan; hideous, grim, shocking.

gher-kin (gûr′kĭn), *n.* a small cucumber used for pickling. Also, **ger′kin.**

ghet-to (gĕt′ō), *n.* [*pl.* ghetti (-tē); ghettos (-ōz)], the Jewish quarter in a city.

ghost (gōst), *n.* **1,** the spirit of a dead person; **2,** any apparition; **3,** the soul; as, to give up the *ghost;* **4,** a shadowy resemblance; as, the *ghost* of a smile: **Holy Ghost,** the Divine Spirit.—*adj.* **ghost′like″.**

Syn. specter, phantom.

ghost-ly (gōst′lĭ), *adj.* [*comp.* ghost′li-er, *superl.* ghost′li-est], **1,** pertaining to, or like, an apparition; spectral; **2,** *Archaic,* pertaining to religious matters; spiritual; as, *ghostly* counsel.—*n.* **ghost′li-ness.**

ghoul (gōōl), *n.* an imaginary evil being who robs graves and feeds on the flesh of the dead.—*adj.* **ghoul′ish.**—*adv.* **ghoul′ish-ly.**

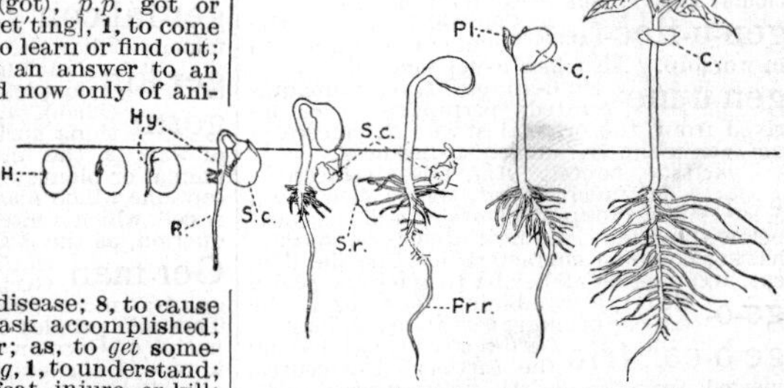

GERMINATION OF A LIMA BEAN

H., hilum; *Hy.*, hypocotyl; *R.*, radicle; *S.c.*, seed coat; *S.r.*, secondary root; *Pr.r.*, primary root; *Pl.*, plumule; *C.*, cotyledon, or seed leaf; *F.t.l.*, first true leaves.

gi-ant (jī′ănt), *n.* **1,** a man of great bulk or stature; **2,** one possessed of great physical or mental power; **3,** in mythology, one of a race of beings of immense size, who fought the gods; **4,** in fairy tales, an imaginary being of enormous size, as in "Jack the *Giant* Killer":—*adj.* like a person of great stature; huge.—*n.fem.* **gi′ant-ess.**

giaour (jour), *n.* in Mohammedan usage, one who does not believe in Islam; esp., a Christian.

gib-ber (jĭb′ẽr; gĭb′ẽr), *v.i.* and *v.t.* to speak rapidly and indistinctly; chatter.

gib-ber-ish (gĭb′ẽr-ĭsh), *n.* rapid, disconnected talk; unintelligible language:—*adj.* unmeaning.

gib-bet (jĭb′ĕt), *n.* a gallows:—*v.t.* **1,** to hang on a gallows; **2,** to expose to public scorn or ridicule.

gib-bon (gĭb′ŭn), *n.* any of several small apes of southeastern Asia.

gib-bous (gĭb′ŭs), *adj.* **1,** irregularly rounded; **2,** humpbacked; **3,** of the moon, nearly full; between full and half full. Also, **gib-bose′** (gĭ-bōs′).—*n.* **gib-bos′i-ty.**

gibe (jīb), *n.* a scoff; taunt; sneering or sarcastic expression:—*v.t.* [*p.t.* and *p.p.* gibed (jībd), *p.pr.* gib′ing], to sneer at; taunt:—*v.i.* to use taunts; cast reproaches; sneer; scoff. Also, **jibe.**—*n.* **gib′er.**
Syn., *v.* flout, mock, deride. (See jeer.)

gib-let (jĭb′lĕt), *n.*, usually in *pl.*, the heart, liver, gizzard, etc., of poultry.

gid-dy (gĭd′ĭ), *adj.* [*comp.* gid′di-er, *superl.* gid′di-est], **1,** having a confused, whirling sensation in the head; light-headed; dizzy; **2,** tending to produce giddiness; as, a *giddy* height; **3,** frivolous; fickle.—*adv.* **gid′di-ly.**—*n.* **gid′di-ness.**
Syn. unsteady, flighty, thoughtless.

Gid-e-on (gĭd′ē-ŭn), *n.* in the Bible, a judge of Israel who defeated the Midianites (Judges 6:11; 8:32).

gift (gĭft), *n.* **1,** something given or bestowed; present; donation; offering; benefaction; **2,** the power to bestow; as, the position is in his *gift;* **3,** natural talent; as, a *gift* for oratory: **gifted,** *adj.*, endowed by nature.
Syn. present, donation, gratuity. A *gift* is something bestowed without any idea of receiving anything in return. A *present* is usually a *gift* to a friend; as, he mailed his Christmas *presents.* A *donation* is a charitable *gift,* of large or small value, made to some cause or person; as, a *donation* to the church. A *gratuity* is a small sum given for some service, but always as a favor, not in payment of a charge; as, to give a *gratuity* to the waiter.

1gig (gĭg), *n.* **1,** a light, two-wheeled, open carriage drawn by one horse; **2,** a light ship's boat; **3,** a whirling object.

2gig (gĭg), *n.* a pronged spear for harpooning fish:—*v.i.* [*p.t.* and *p.p.* gigged (gĭgd), *p.pr.* gig′ging], to fish with such a spear:—*v.t.* to spear, as with a gig.

gi-gan-tic (jī-găn′tĭk), *adj.* huge; colossal; immense; tremendous; of extraordinary size.—*adv.* **gi-gan′ti-cal-ly.**
Syn. enormous, prodigious, vast.

gig-gle (gĭg′l), *n.* a nervous, silly laugh:—*v.i.* [*p.t.* and *p.p.* -gled (-ld), *p.pr.* -gling], to laugh in a nervous, foolish, tittering manner.—*n.* **gig′gler.**—*adj.* **gig′gly.**

gi-go-lo (zhĭg′ō-lō), *n.* [Fr.], [*pl.* gigolos (-lōz)], a man who acts, for pay, as dancing partner to women patrons of a café.

Gi-la mon-ster (hē′lȧ), a poisonous black-and-orange lizard of Arizona, New Mexico, and Mexico, reaching a length of 18 inches or more.

1gild (gĭld), *v.t.* [*p.t.* gild′ed, *p.p.* gilt (gĭlt) or gild′ed, *p.pr.* gild′ing], **1,** to overlay or wash with gold or something resembling it; **2,** to give a fair outward appearance to.

2gild (gĭld), *n.* **1,** a fraternity; **2,** a trade association. Also, **guild,** *Pfd. S.*

gild-ing (gĭld′ĭng), *n.* **1,** the process of overlaying or covering with gold or a substance resembling it; also, the substance so used; **2,** a fair outward appearance.

1gill (gĭl), *n.* **1,** a breathing organ of water animals, as fishes, lobsters, etc.; **2,** the fleshy flap that hangs below the beak of a fowl; wattle; **3,** one of the thin, leaflike structures on the under side of many mushrooms.

2gill (gĭl), *n.* a deep, narrow cleft through which a stream flows. Also, **ghyll.**

3gill (jĭl), *n.* a unit of liquid measure equal to one fourth of a pint.

4gill (jĭl), *n.* **1,** (also, *jill*), a girl; lass; sweetheart: used familiarly; **2,** the ground ivy.

gil-lie (gĭl′ĭ), *n.* [*pl.* gillies (-ĭz)], in Scotland, a manservant; esp., an attendant on a sportsman. Also, **gil′ly.**

gil-ly-flow-er (jĭl′ĭ-flou″ẽr), *n.* any of various cultivated garden plants, as the wallflower, stock, etc. Also, **gil′li-flow″er.**

gilt (gĭlt), past participle of the verb *gild:*—*p.adj.* covered with, or yellow like, gold:—*n.* **1,** gilding; **2,** a flashy exterior.

gim-bal (gĭm′băl; jĭm′-), *n.*, usually in *pl.*, one of two rings pivoted on axes at right angles, one ring within the other: used for suspending a mariner's compass, chronometer, etc., so that it will stay level.

gim-crack (jĭm′krăk″), *n.* a cheap, showy article; toy:—*adj.* showy, but useless.—*n.* **gim′crack″er-y.**

gim-let (gĭm′lĕt), *n.* a small boring tool with a pointed screw at the end:—*v.t.* to make a hole in with such a tool.

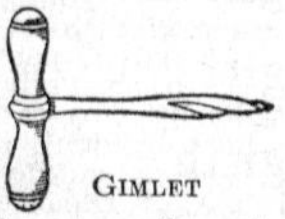
GIMLET

gimp (gĭmp), *n.* a kind of flat, laced twist or trimming interwoven with wire or cord:—*v.t.* to border with this trimming.

1gin (jĭn), *n.* an alcoholic liquor distilled from grain and juniper berries.

2gin (jĭn), *n.* **1,** a trap or snare; **2,** a machine for clearing cotton fibers from the seeds; a cotton gin; **3,** a portable hoisting device; **4,** a pile-driving machine:—*v.t.* [*p.t.* and *p.p.* ginned (jĭnd), *p.pr.* gin′ning], **1,** to catch in a trap; **2,** to clear (cotton) of seeds by a cotton gin.

gin-ger (jĭn′jẽr), *n.* **1,** any of various tropical herbs, esp. one cultivated for its pungent rootstock; **2,** its scraped and dried rootstock, used in cookery; **3,** *Colloq.*, courage; vim; snap: **ginger ale,** a nonalcoholic, effervescent drink flavored with ginger: also called *ginger beer; ginger pop.*

gin-ger-bread (jĭn′jẽr-brĕd″), *n.* **1,** a dark-colored cake made of flour, ginger, molasses, sugar, etc.; **2,** cheap, flimsy ornamentation, esp. on a house.

gin-ger-ly (jĭn′jẽr-lĭ), *adv.* cautiously; timidly:—*adj.* cautious; timid.

gin-ger-snap (jĭn′jẽr-snăp″), *n.* a thin and brittle molasses cooky flavored with ginger.

ging-ham (gĭng′ăm), *n.* a cotton dress cloth dyed in the yarn before weaving: often woven in stripes or checks.

gin-seng (jĭn′sĕng), *n.* **1,** any of several herbs, shrubs, and trees, esp. one with aromatic roots, native in China; **2,** the dried roots of this plant, used for medicinal purposes.

gip-sy (jĭp′sĭ), *n.* [*pl.* gipsies (-sĭz)], **1,** one of a wandering race, of Eastern, probably Hindu, origin; **2,** the language of the gypsies: also called *Romany;* **3,** an unconventional girl: **gipsy moth,** an insect highly destructive to tree foliage. See **gyp′sy,** *Pfd. S.*

gi-raffe (jĭ-răf′), *n.* an African animal with very long legs and neck.

GIRAFFES (1/150)

1gird (gûrd), *v.t.* [*p.t.* and *p.p.* girt (gûrt) or gird′ed, *p.pr.* gird′ing], **1,** to surround with a flexible band; bind; **2,** to encircle; **3,** to make ready; equip:—*n.* a girth.

2gird (gûrd), *v.t.* to jeer:—*v.i.* to sneer; gibe:—*n.* a taunt.

gird-er (gûr′dẽr), *n.* a main beam in a floor, supporting the joists.

gir-dle (gûr′dl), *n.* **1**, a belt for the waist; **2**, anything that surrounds like a belt:—*v.t.* [*p.t.* and *p.p.* -dled (-dld), *p.pr.* -dling], **1**, to bind with, or as with, a belt; **2**, to inclose; **3**, to kill or injure, as a tree, by making a cut in the bark around the trunk.

girl (gûrl), *n.* **1**, a female child; young unmarried woman; **2**, *Colloq.:* **a**, a servant; **b**, a sweetheart.—*n.* **girl′hood.**

girl-ish (gûrl′ĭsh), *adj.* like, or befitting, a young woman; as, *girlish* dress.—*adv.* **girl′ish-ly.**—*n.* **girl′ish-ness.**

girt (gûrt), past tense and past participle of the verb [1]*gird:*—*p.adj.* of a ship, held tight by two cables so as not to swing.

girth (gûrth), *n.* **1**, a band which secures a saddle on a horse (see *harness*, illus.); **2**, the circumference of a tree, animal, etc.; **3**, anything that binds or encircles.

gist (jĭst), *n.* the substance of a matter; main point; object.

give (gĭv), *v.t.* [*p.t.* gave (gāv), *p.p.* giv′en (gĭv′n), *p.pr.* giv′ing], **1**, to transfer from one's own possession to that of another; as, to *give* one a book to read; to *give* one's property to one's children; **2**, to bestow, as a present; donate; as, to *give* a library to the town; **3**, to offer or present for acceptance; as, to *give* a dinner; **4**, to deliver in return for an equivalent; pay; as, I *gave* three dollars for the book; **5**, to offer as due; as, *give* him credit; **6**, to yield: with *up;* as, to *give* up a claim; concede; as, to *give* a point in a game; **7**, to communicate, administer, or impart in any way; as, to *give* a message, inspiration, medicine, punishment, etc.; **8**, to utter, as a command or a cry; **9**, to produce; as, maple trees *give* sugar; the addition *gives* nine; **10**, to put forth, as effort, sound, light, etc.; as, the door *gave* a squeak:—*v.i.* **1**, to present gifts; bestow charity; **2**, to yield to pressure; as, the door began to *give;* **3**, to surrender; as, to *give* in; **4**, to be turned, or face, toward; as, the porch *gives* upon the lake:—*n.* a yielding to pressure.—*n.* **giv′er.**

Syn., v. bestow, grant, confer, offer. *Give* implies, in general, the act of making another the owner of something in one's possession; as, I *gave* the child a doll. Its use has been extended to cover the transfer or communication of things not considered gifts; as to *give* orders, medicine, reprimands. To *bestow* is to *give* something that is much needed; as, to *bestow* alms. To *grant* is to *give* in a formal way or with authority; as, the city *granted* the franchise; *grant* also implies conceding; as, the President *granted* the pardon. To *confer* is to *give* in a formal or gracious manner; as, a university *confers* degrees; he *confers* many favors. To *offer* is to bring forward for acceptance or rejection; as, he *offered* to go; to *offer* apologies.

giv-en (gĭv′n), *p.adj.* **1**, inclined; addicted: usually with *to;* as, *given* to lying; **2**, stated: **given name,** the Christian name, as distinguished from the surname.

giz-zard (gĭz′ẽrd), *n.* the second stomach of a fowl, in which the food is crushed and ground by means of pebbles that have been previously swallowed.

***gla-cé** (glȧ″sā′), [Fr.], *adj.* **1**, iced, cooled, or sugared; as, *glacé* nuts; **2**, having a glossy surface:—*n.* a thin, shiny silk.

gla-cial (glā′shăl), *adj.* **1**, pertaining to, consisting of, or caused by, ice; **2**, pertaining to glaciers: **glacial period,** a period when ice sheets covered great areas of the earth; the ice age.—*adv.* **gla′cial-ly.**

gla-ci-ate (glā′shĭ-āt), *v.t.* and *v.i.* [*p.t.* and *p.p.* -at″ed, *p.pr.* -at″ing], **1**, to freeze; **2**, to cover with an ice sheet; **3**, to alter or change by glacial action.—*n.* **gla″ci-a′tion.**

gla-cier (glā′shẽr; glăs′ĭ-ẽr), *n.* a vast collection of ice and snow which is formed among lofty mountains and moves slowly down the slopes and through the valleys until it melts or breaks off into icebergs.

gla-cis (glā′sĭs; glăs′ĭs), *n.* **1**, a gently sloping place; **2**, a gentle slope before a rampart, on which attackers are exposed to fire from the parapet: **glacis plate,** sloping armor on a warship to throw off hostile shot.

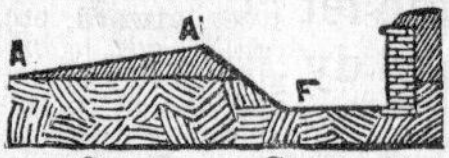

SECTION OF GLACIS
AA, glacis; F, fosse.

glad (glăd), *adj.* [*comp.* glad′der, *superl.* glad′dest], **1**, joyous; gay; **2**, expressive of joy; cheerful; satisfied; **3**, causing joy; as, *glad* news.—*adv.* **glad′ly.**—*n.* **glad′ness.**

Syn. joyful, pleased, delighted.—*Ant.* sad, disheartened, unhappy.

glad-den (glăd′n), *v.t.* to make happy:—*v.i.* to rejoice; become happy.

Syn. cheer, comfort, please.

glade (glād), *n.* an open space or passage in a wood or forest.

glad-i-a-tor (glăd′ĭ-ā″tẽr), *n.* in ancient Rome, a professional swordsman who fought in the arena with other men or with animals.—*adj.* **glad″i-a-to′ri-al.**

GLADIATORS

gla-di-o-lus (glȧ-dī′ō-lŭs; glăd″ĭ-ō′lŭs), *n.* [*pl.* gladioli (-ō-lī); gladioluses (-ō′lŭs-ĕz)], any of a number of plants of the iris family, with sword-shaped leaves and spikes of variously colored, showy flowers.

glad-some (glăd′sŭm), *adj.* joyous; gay; pleased; cheerful.

glair (glâr), *n.* **1**, the white of egg; also, any adhesive preparation made from it; **2**, any similar matter.—*adj.* **glair′y.**

glaive (glāv), *n.* **1**, a sword, esp. a broadsword; **2**, a halberd. Also, **glave.**

GLAIVE

glam-our (glăm′ẽr), *n.* **1**, witchery; spell; enchantment; **2**, the delusive charm or fascination of a person, place, or thing.—*adj.* **glam′or-ous.**

glance (glȧns), *n.* **1**, a sudden shoot of light; **2**, a quick passing look of the eye; a quick momentary view; **3**, a brief reference; allusion; **4**, a lustrous ore:—*v.i.* [*p.t.* and *p.p.* glanced (glȧnst), *p.pr.* glanc′ing], **1**, to shoot a sudden ray; **2**, to view with a quick movement of the eye; **3**, to allude in passing; **4**, to strike slantingly and fly off, as a blow:—*v.t.* **1**, to shoot suddenly or slantingly; **2**, to strike slantingly.

Syn. (see glimpse).

gland (glănd), *n.* in plants and animals, a cell or group of cells making and secreting or excreting some special substance; as, the salivary *glands.*—*adj.* **glan′du-lar.**

glan-ders (glăn′dẽrz), *n.pl.* a contagious disease in horses, marked by fever, swelling of the glands of the lower jaw, and a discharge of mucus from the nose.

glan-dule (glăn′dūl), *n.* a small gland or secreting organ.

glare (glâr), *n.* **1**, a bright, dazzling light; overpowering luster; **2**, a fierce, piercing look; **3**, in the U. S., a smooth, shining surface, as of ice:—*v.i.* [*p.t.* and *p.p.* glared (glârd), *p.pr.* glar′ing], **1**, to shine with a dazzling, overpowering light; **2**, to look with fierce, piercing eyes; **3**, to be excessively gaudy in dress or ornamentation:—*v.t.* to express with a fierce look.—*adj.* **glar′y.**

Syn., *n.* flame, flare, blaze.

glar-ing (glâr′ĭng), *p.adj.* **1**, evident; striking: used in a bad sense; as, a *glaring* error; **2**, having a fierce look, as eyes.

glass (glȧs), *n.* **1**, a very hard, brittle substance, usually transparent, made by fusing together some form of sand, soda, or potash, etc.; **2**, any substance of similar composition; **3**, an article made principally of glass, as a mirror, drinking utensil, etc.; **4**, the quantity of liquid contained in a drinking glass; **5**, any of certain instruments, as a telescope, microscope, etc., made partly or wholly of glass: **glasses**, spectacles; eyeglasses: **cut glass**, a hard glass shaped and ornamented by cutting or grinding: **ground glass**, glass roughened on the surface so as to destroy its transparency: **plate glass**, glass in large sheets, made by rolling and polishing.—*n.* **glass′ful.**—*n.* **glass′mak″ing.**

glass snake a harmless, legless lizard of various parts of the world, having a brittle tail that breaks like glass.

glass-ware (glȧs′wâr″), *n.* collectively, dishes or other glass articles.

glass-y (glȧs′ĭ), *adj.* [*comp.* glass′i-er, *superl.* glass′i-est], **1**, like glass in smoothness, transparency, etc.; **2**, staring without expression: said of the eye or look. —*adv.* **glass′i-ly.**—*n.* **glass′i-ness.**

glau-co-ma (glô-kō′mȧ), *n.* a disease of the eye marked by tension within the eyeball, and ending in blindness.

glau-cous (glô′kŭs), *adj.* **1**, sea-green; green tinted with bluish gray; **2**, covered with a bluish white bloom.

glave (glāv), *n.* **1**, a broadsword; **2**, a halberd. For illus. see **glaive**, *Pfd. S.*

glaze (glāz), *v.t.* [*p.t.* and *p.p.* glazed (glāzd), *p.pr.* glaz′ing], **1**, to furnish with glass; **2**, to overlay with a smooth or transparent substance, as pottery; **3**, to finish, as leather, with a glossy surface; **4**, to cover with a film, as the eye:—*v.i.* **1**, to become smooth, hard, and glossy on the surface; **2**, to become staring and without expression, as eyes:—*n.* **1**, the glassy coating of pottery; **2**, a fixed, filmy look, as in eyes.—*n.* **glaz′er.**

gla-zier (glā′zhẽr; glā′zĭ-ẽr), *n.* one whose trade is to set glass in windows.

glaz-ing (glāz′ĭng), *n.* **1**, a coating of glass or other smooth, transparent substance; **2**, the act of setting glass, or applying a coat of glass or other smooth, transparent substance; **3**, window panes collectively; **4**, a partly transparent color passed thinly over other colors to tone down their effect.

gleam (glēm), *n.* **1**, a brief flash of light; **2**, something resembling a flash of light; as, a *gleam* of hope:—*v.i.* to emit brightness; send out rays of light.

Syn., *n.* glimmer, glitter, beam, flash.

glean (glēn), *v.t.* **1**, to gather, as grain that the reapers have left; **2**, to strip, as a field, of what remains; **3**, to collect little by little, or piece by piece, as facts:—*v.i.* **1**, to gather grain left by reapers; **2**, to strip a field; **3**, to collect a little at a time.—*n.* **glean′er.**

glebe (glēb), *n.* **1**, ground or soil; **2**, land belonging to a parish church or assigned to a minister as part of his salary; **3**, in mining, a piece of land containing ore.

glee (glē), *n.* **1**, gaiety; mirth; entertainment; **2**, a musical composition for voices in harmony: **glee club**, a club organized to sing songs in harmony.—*adj.* **glee′some.**

Syn. merriment, joviality, joy.—*Ant.* sorrow, grief, dejection.

glee-ful (glē′fo͝ol), *adj.* merry; gay; as, *gleeful* children.—*adv.* **glee′ful-ly.**

glen (glĕn), *n.* a narrow valley; a quiet or secluded hollow between hills.

Glen-gar-ry (glĕn-găr′ĭ), *n.* [*pl.* Glengarries (-ĭz)], a kind of cap worn in the Scottish Highlands by men.

glib (glĭb), *adj.* [*comp.* glib′ber, *superl.* glib′best], voluble; flippant; fluent; as, a *glib* talker.—*adv.* **glib′ly.**—*n.* **glib′ness.**

glide (glīd), *n.* **1**, the act of moving along smoothly; **2**, in music, a slur; **3**, the movement of an airplane without any motor: —*v.i.* [*p.t.* and *p.p.* glid′ed, *p.pr.* glid′ing], **1**, to flow, or move along smoothly or noiselessly; **2**, in music, to slur; **3**, to move in an airplane under the influence of gravity only.

Syn., *v.* slip, slide.

glid-er (glīd′ẽr), *n.* **1**, one who or that which slides along smoothly; **2**, a form of aircraft similar to an airplane but without any motor.

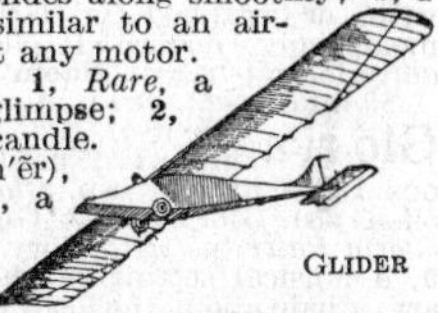

GLIDER

glim (glĭm), *n.* **1**, *Rare*, a glance; glimpse; **2**, *Slang*, a light or candle.

glim-mer (glĭm′ẽr), *n.* **1**, a faint, unsteady light; **2**, a glimpse; as, a *glimmer* of hope:—*v.i.* to shine or flare; flicker faintly and unsteadily.

Syn., *n.* gleam, flicker, glitter, glow.

glimpse (glĭmps), *n.* **1**, a passing appearance; **2**, a transient or temporary view:—*v.t.* [*p.t.* and *p.p.* glimpsed (glĭmpst), *p.pr.* glimps′ing], to catch a momentary view of:—*v.i.* to glance.

Syn., *n.* glance. A *glimpse* is a hurried and imperfect view; as, he caught a *glimpse* of the moon through the mist. A *glance* is a brief, casual, and sometimes indirect, look; as, he could not get the details at a *glance*.

glint (glĭnt), *n.* **1**, a gleam of light; **2**, a sly glance:—*v.i.* to gleam or flash out; —*v.t.* to reflect the sparkle of.

glis-ten (glĭs′n), *v.i.* to sparkle with light; shine; gleam:—*n.* a glitter.

glis-ter (glĭs′tẽr), *v.i.* to glitter; be bright: —*n.* a sparkle; luster.

glit-ter (glĭt′ẽr), *v.i.* **1**, to sparkle with light; gleam; flash; **2**, to be showy or attractive:—*n.* brilliancy; bright luster; sparkle.—*adj.* **glit′ter-y.**

Syn., *v.* glimmer, shine, glisten.

gloam-ing (glōm′ĭng), *n.* the twilight of early evening.

gloat (glōt), *v.i.* to gaze earnestly or rejoice triumphantly, usually with lustful or cruel greed or satisfaction.

glob-al (glō′băl), *adj.* **1**, spherical; round; **2**, gross; taken as a whole or in the lump; including all; as, *global* naval strength.

globe (glōb), *n.* **1**, a spherical body; ball; **2**, a sphere on which are represented the divisions of the earth (terrestrial *globe*), or the heavenly bodies (celestial *globe*); **3**, any more or less spherical vessel; as, a goldfish *globe*: **the globe**, the earth.

globe-fish (glōb′fĭsh″), *n.* any of various fishes that suck in water or air and distend the body to a globelike shape.

globe-flow-er (glōb′flou″ẽr), *n.* any of various plants of the crowfoot family, with large, showy flowers.

globe–trot-ter (glōb′-trŏt″ẽr), *n.* one who travels far and wide for sight-seeing, esp. frequently.

glo-bin (glō′bĭn), *n.* a substance obtainable from hæmoglobin, the coloring matter of the blood.

glo-bose (glō′bōs″; glō-bōs′), *adj.* spherical in shape. Also, **glo′bous.**

glob-u-lar (glŏb′ū-lȧr), *adj.* **1,** spherical in shape; **2,** composed of tiny spherical bodies. Also, **glob′u-lous.**

glob-ule (glŏb′ūl), *n.* a little spherical body; a small pill.

glom-er-ate (glŏm′ẽr-āt), *adj.* gathered into a roundish head or mass; conglomerate.—*n.* **glom″er-a′tion.**

¹gloom (glōōm), *n.* **1,** a partial darkness; obscurity; **2,** melancholy; depression; sullenness.
Syn. sadness, cheerlessness, dejection.—*Ant.* joy, brightness, optimism.

²gloom (glōōm), *v.i.* **1,** to look sullen; frown; be melancholy; **2,** to be or become cloudy or partially dark; present a dismal aspect:—*v.t.* **1,** to make dark; **2,** to depress or sadden; fill with despondency.

gloom-y (glōōm′ĭ), *adj.* [*comp.* gloom′i-er, *superl.* gloom′i-est], **1,** overspread with, or wrapped in, darkness; **2,** dismal; melancholy; dispirited; cheerless; morose.—*adv.* **gloom′i-ly.**—*n.* **gloom′i-ness.**
Syn. lowering, lurid, dim, dusky.

Glo-ri-a (glō′rĭ-ȧ), [Lat.], *n.* **1,** praise: the first word, used as a title, of various Latin hymns, esp. *Gloria in Excelsis* (ĭn ĕk-sĕl′sĭs), Glory be (to God) on High, and *Gloria Patri* (pä′trĭ), Glory be to the Father; **2,** a musical setting of these: **gloria, 1,** in art, a halo about the head of a saint or deity; **2,** a fabric of silk and wool, often used to cover umbrellas.

glo-ri-fy (glō′rĭ-fī), *v.t.* [*p.t.* and *p.p.* -fied (-fīd), *p.pr.* -fy″ing], **1,** to regard as worthy of high honor and dignity; **2,** to magnify and honor in worship; adore; **3,** to beautify; as, love *glorified* her face.—*n.* **glo′ri-fi″er.**—*n.* **glo″ri-fi-ca′tion.**
Syn. praise, elevate, exalt.

glo-ri-ous (glō′rĭ-ŭs), *adj.* **1,** full of honor; illustrious; celebrated; magnificent; exalted; **2,** *Colloq.*, splendid; inspiring admiration.—*adv.* **glo′ri-ous-ly.**

glo-ry (glō′rĭ), *n.* [*pl.* glories (-rĭz)], **1,** distinction; fame; honor; **2,** splendor; brightness; **3,** the beauty and splendor of the divine nature; **4,** the blessedness and brightness of heaven; **5,** a reason for pride; as, woman's *glory* is her hair; **6,** in art, a circle of light surrounding the head or person of a saint or deity; **7,** in *pl.*, qualities that result in honor:—*v.i.* [*p.t.* and *p.p.* -ried (-rĭd), *p.pr.* -ry-ing], to rejoice or exult: with *in.*
Syn., *n.* brilliance, grandeur.

¹gloss (glôs), *n.* **1,** a smooth, glistening luster; **2,** an insincere or deceptive appearance:—*v.t.* **1,** to make smooth and lustrous; give a superficial brilliance to; **2,** to cover up or mitigate, as faults, by plausible, insincere representation: often with *over.*

²gloss (glôs), *n.* an explanation or comment on some difficulty or obscurity in the text of a book; esp., such an explanation written in the margin or between the lines, sometimes intentionally misleading:—*v.t.* **1,** to furnish with notes or comments; **2,** to misrepresent (an author's words) by false interpretation:—*v.i.* to make comments on a text.

glos-sa-ry (glŏs′ȧ-rĭ), *n.* [*pl.* glossaries (-rĭz)], **1,** a collection of notes explaining a text; **2,** a dictionary of obsolete, difficult, uncommon, or technical words occurring in a certain book or in the works of a certain author.—*adj.* **glos-sa′ri-al.**

gloss-y (glôs′ĭ), *adj.* [*comp.* gloss′i-er, *superl.* gloss′i-est], **1,** having a shining, smooth surface; **2,** smooth and plausible.—*adv.* **gloss′i-ly.**—*n.* **gloss′i-ness.**

glot-tis (glŏt′ĭs), *n.* the small opening between the vocal cords in the larynx.—*adj.* **glot′tal.**

glove (glŭv), *n.* **1,** a covering for the hand with a separate covering for each finger; **2,** in *pl.*, boxing gloves:—*v.t.* [*p.t.* and *p.p.* gloved (glŭvd), *p.pr.* glov′ing], to cover with, or as with, a glove.

glov-er (glŭv′ẽr), *n.* a maker or seller of gloves.

glow (glō), *v.i.* **1,** to shine with intense heat; **2,** to radiate heat and light without flame; be incandescent; **3,** to be red; show brilliant color; **4,** to be warm or flushed; **5,** to be animated or inspired with passion, love, zeal, etc.:—*n.* **1,** intense or shining heat; incandescence; **2,** redness, or brightness of color; **3,** passion; ardor; **4,** warmth of body; as, in a *glow* of excitement.

glow-er (glou′ẽr), *v.i.* to stare threateningly or angrily; frown.

glow-worm (glō′wûrm″), *n.* any of various beetles which give out a phosphorescent light.

gloze (glōz), *v.t.* [*p.t.* and *p.p.* glozed (glōzd), *p.pr.* gloz′ing], to gloss over; make light of; as, to *gloze* sin; *gloze* a mistake.

glu-cose (glōō′kōs), *n.* **1,** a form of sugar existing in honey and most sweet fruits; **2,** commercial glucose, a syrup containing glucose and other substances.

glue (glōō), *n.* **1,** a sticky substance made by boiling to a jelly the skins, hoofs, etc., of animals; **2,** any sticky substance used as an adhesive:—*v.t.* [*p.t.* and *p.p.* glued (glōōd), *p.pr.* glu′ing], to unite or join with glue.—*adj.* **glu′ey.**

glum (glŭm), *adj.* [*comp.* glum′mer, *superl.* glum′mest], gloomy; moody; sullen; frowning; as, a *glum* expression.—*adv.* **glum′ly.**—*n.* **glum′ness.**
Syn. dismal, morose, dispirited.

glume (glōōm), *n.* the husk or chaffy scales of corn or grasses.

glut (glŭt), *n.* **1,** superabundance; **2,** an excess of supply over demand:—*v.t.* [*p.t.* and *p.p.* glut′ted, *p.pr.* glut′ting], **1,** to fill too full; **2,** to oversupply; as, to *glut* the market.
Syn., *v.* gorge, stuff, cram. (See satisfy.)

glu-ten (glōō′tĕn), *n.* the nutritious proteid found in wheat.

glu-ti-nous (glōō′tĭ-nŭs), *adj.* sticky; covered with sticky matter.

glu-ti-tion (glōō-tĭsh′ŭn), *n.* the act of swallowing.

glut-ton (glŭt′n), *n.* **1,** one who eats to excess; **2,** a small, flesh-eating and fur-bearing animal, akin to the mink and marten; the wolverene.

glut-ton-ize (glŭt′n-īz), *v.i.* [*p.t.* and *p.p.* -ized (-īzd), *p.pr.* -iz″ing], to overeat; eat to excess habitually.

glut-ton-ous (glŭt′n-ŭs), *adj.* eating to excess; given to overeating.—*adv.* **glut′ton-ous-ly.**

glut-ton-y (glŭt′n-ĭ), *n.* [*pl.* gluttonies (-ĭz)], the act or habit of eating to excess; voraciousness.

glyc-er-in (glĭs′ẽr-ĭn), *n.* a sweetish, colorless, sticky liquid obtained from oils, fat, etc.: used extensively in manufactures and in medicine. Also, **glyc′er-ine.**

gnarl (närl), *n.* a knot on the trunk or branch of a tree.—*adj.* **gnarl′y.**

gnarled (närld), *adj.* full of knots; distorted; as, an old, *gnarled* oak.

gnash (năsh), *v.t.* to strike together, as the teeth:—*v.i.* to grind the teeth in anger or in pain.

gnat (năt), *n.* any of several small, stinging or biting winged insects.

gnaw (nô), *v.t.* [*p.t.* gnawed (nôd), *p.p.* gnawed or gnawn (nôn), *p.pr.* gnaw′-ing], **1,** to bite off, or eat away, by degrees; **2,** to corrode; consume; hence, to torment; as, *gnawed* by remorse:—*v.i.* **1,** to bite repeatedly; **2,** to cause discomfort; torment.

gnaw-ing (nô′ĭng), *n.* a feeling of constant craving in the stomach; a fretting pain.

gneiss (nīs), *n.* a crystallized rock composed of quartz, mica, and feldspar.

¹gnome (nōm), *n.* **1,** one of a small, imaginary race of beings, who acted as guardians of the treasures hidden in mines, quarries, and secret places in the earth; **2,** a dwarf; a misshapen person.

²gnome (nōm), *n.* a pithy or instructive saying; a maxim.

gno-mic (nō′mĭk; nŏm′ĭk), *adj.* dealing in, or containing, pithy or instructive sayings; didactic. Also, **gno′mi-cal.**

gno-mon (nō′mŏn), *n.* anything that indicates the time of day by its shadow, as the arm of a sundial.

Gnos-ti-cism (nŏs′tĭ-sĭzm), *n.* an ancient system of philosophy, intermediate between Christianity and paganism.—*adj.* and *n.* **Gnos′tic.**

gnu (nōō; nū), *n.* any of several antelopes with a mane, a flowing tail, and curved horns, inhabiting Africa.

GNU (1/45)

go (gō), *v.i.* [*p.t.* went (wĕnt), *p.p.* gone (gôn), *p.pr.* go′ing], **1,** to move forward; move from one point to another; **2,** to move or remain in motion by mechanism; as, the clock *goes;* **3,** to depart; move away: opp. of *come;* **4,** to be abolished; as, slavery had to *go;* **5,** to be transferred by some process similar to movement; as, the estate *goes* to the heirs; the box *goes* by express; **6,** to become; pass into another condition; as, to *go* crazy; **7,** to continue in a specific state; as, to *go* hungry; **8,** to resort (to); as, to *go* to him for advice; **9,** to escape: with *let;* as, let me *go;* **10,** to be guided or led; as, to *go* by his example; **11,** to be appropriate; fit; as, such a course of action would hardly *go;* **12,** to extend; lead; as, the road *goes* to the city; tend toward a result; as, the plan will *go* far toward peace; **13,** to result; as, the election *goes* Republican; **14,** to be sold; as, the picture *goes* at ten dollars; **15,** to run; have a particular wording, tune, trend, or tenor; as, how does the first line *go?* **16,** to elapse: of time; **17,** to move about among people; as, he *goes* by the name of Smith; gold money *goes* anywhere; **18,** to belong; as, the dishes *go* in the pantry; **19,** to subject or put oneself to trouble or expense; **20,** in mathematics, to be contained; as, 3 *goes* into 9 three times: **going,** about (to); intending (to); as, he was *going* to insure his barn, when it burned: **go bail,** to act as surety (for):—*v.t. Colloq.,* **1,** to afford; as, I can't *go* the price; **2,** to bet; wager; as, I'll *go* you a box of candy; **3,** to endure; as, I can't *go* her chatter: **go better,** to exceed; surpass; outbid:—*n. Colloq.,* **1,** the fashion; style; rage; **2,** energy; enthusiasm; **3,** an agreement; as, it's a *go;* **4,** success; as, the venture was a *go.*—*n.* **go′er.**

goad (gōd), *n.* **1,** a pointed stick to urge on cattle; **2,** any necessity that causes one to act; as, hunger was the *goad* that made him work:—*v.t.* **1,** to urge on with, or as with, a spur; **2,** to stimulate; incite.

goal (gōl), *n.* **1,** the winning post, as at a race or at football; **2,** a play that scores by passing the ball between the posts, through a ring, etc., in a specified way; **3,** the end aimed at; **4,** the final purpose; desire or ambition.

goat (gōt), *n.* **1,** any of several hollow-horned, cud-chewing mammals bred as domestic animals, yielding milk, flesh, and hair; **2,** *Colloq.,* a butt of ridicule; a scapegoat; an unlucky person: **the Goat, 1,** Capricorn, a southern constellation; **2,** the tenth sign of the zodiac, entered by the sun at the winter solstice, about December 21 (see *zodiac,* illus.). —*adj.* **goat′ish.**—*n.* and *adj.* **goat′skin″.**

goat-ee (gō″tē′), *n.* a pointed beard, shaped like that of a goat, on the chin or lower lip of a man.

goat-herd (gōt′hûrd″), *n.* one who tends goats; a herder of goats.

¹gob (gŏb), *n.* **1,** *Colloq.,* a clot or lump of slimy substance; **2,** the refuse at the mouth of a coal mine.

²gob (gŏb), *n. Colloq.,* a sailor: a term used in the U. S. navy.

¹gob-ble (gŏb′l), *v.t.* [*p.t.* and *p.p.* -bled (-ld), *p.pr.* -bling], **1,** to swallow hastily or greedily; **2,** *Slang,* to seize greedily: —*v.i.* to eat greedily:—*n.* **1,** a greedy manner of eating; **2,** in golf, a quick, straight putting stroke into the hole.

²gob-ble (gŏb′l), *n.* the cry of a turkey cock:—*v.i.* [*p.t.* and *p.p.* -bled (-ld), *p.pr.* -bling], to utter this, or a like, cry.

gob-bler (gŏb′lẽr), *n.* a male turkey; a turkey cock.

Gob-e-lin (gŏb′ē-lĭn; *Fr.* gō″blăṅ′), *adj.* **1,** made in, or pertaining to, the Gobelin works in Paris; **2,** pertaining to, or imitating, the tapestry made there.

go–be-tween (gō′=bē-twēn″), *n.* an intermediary; agent.

gob-let (gŏb′lĕt), *n.* a drinking vessel with a stem and without a handle.

gob-lin (gŏb′lĭn), *n.* an evil, mischievous, misshapen spirit; gnome; fairy.

go-by (gō′bĭ), *n.* [*pl.* gobies (-bĭz)], any of several fishes, usually very small.

go–by (gō′=bī″), *n.* intentional neglect; as, to give him the *go-by.*

go-cart (gō′kärt″), *n.* **1,** a contrivance for teaching children to walk; **2,** a child's carriage; **3,** a light village cart.

god (gŏd), *n.* **1,** a being conceived of as possessing divine powers or attributes; **2,** an idol; **3,** a person or thing deified or honored to excess; **4,** an intelligence controlling the forces of good and evil: **God,** the Supreme Being; the Lord.

god-child (gŏd′chīld″), *n.* one for whom a person becomes sponsor at baptism, and who is therefore regarded as holding a religious relationship to the sponsor.

god-dess (gŏd′ĕs), *n.* **1,** a female deity or divinity; **2,** a woman of superior charms or excellence.

god-fa-ther (gŏd′fä″*th*ẽr), *n.* a man who acts as sponsor for a child at baptism:—*v.t.* to act as godfather to.—*n.fem.* **god′moth″er** (gŏd′mŭ*th*″ẽr).

god-head (gŏd′hĕd), *n.* the divine essence, nature, and attributes: **Godhead,** the Supreme Deity.

god-less (gŏd′lĕs), *adj.* without religion; impious.—*n.* **god′less-ness.**

god-like (gŏd′līk″), *adj.* **1,** like, or suitable for, a god or God; divine; **2,** the noblest possible.—*n.* **god′like″ness.**

god-ly (gŏd′lĭ), *adj.* pious; obedient to the commands of God.—*n.* **god′li-ness.**
Syn. righteous, holy, religious.

god-par-ent (gŏd′pâr″ĕnt), *n.* one acting as sponsor for a child at baptism; a godfather or godmother.

God's a-cre a churchyard; a consecrated burying ground.

god-send (gŏd′sĕnd″), *n.* unexpected assistance, help, or good fortune; something that seems to be sent by God.

god-ship (gŏd′shĭp), *n.* deity; the character or rank of a god.

god-son (gŏd′sŭn″), *n.* a male child for whom one has stood sponsor at baptism.—*n.fem.* **god′daugh″ter** (gŏd′dô″tẽr).

God-speed (gŏd′spēd″), *n.* success; a wish for a prosperous journey; as, I wish you *Godspeed.*

gof-fer (gŏf′ẽr), *v.t.* to form flutes in; crimp; as, to *goffer* a flounce.

gof-fer-ing (gŏf′ẽr-ĭng), *n.* **1,** fluting for frills, flounces, etc.; **2,** indented ornamentation on the edge of a book.

gog-gle (gŏg′l), *v.i.* [*p.t.* and *p.p.* -gled (-ld), *p.pr.* -gling], to strain or roll the eyes:—*adj.* staring; prominent:—*n.* **1,** a strained or affected rolling of the eyes; **2,** in *pl.,* a particular kind of spectacles for protecting the eyes from dust, excessive light, poison gas, etc.—*adj.* **gog′gle-eyed″.**

go-ing (gō′ĭng), *n.* **1,** departure, motion, etc.; **2,** the state of the roads; **3,** in *pl.,* conduct or habit of life.

goi-ter (goi′tẽr), *n.* a swelling of the thyroid glands, in the front and side of the neck. Also, **goi′tre.**—*adj.* **goi′trous.**

Gol-con-da (gŏl-kŏn′dȧ), *n.* a mine of wealth; as, California was a veritable *Golconda* to the adventurers of 1849.

gold (gōld), *n.* **1,** a precious metallic element of a bright yellow color when pure, very heavy, soft, malleable, and ductile, admirably fitted and widely used for coinage and jewelry; **2,** money; wealth; **3,** the color of gold; **4,** precious or pure quality; as, a voice of *gold:* **gold dust,** gold in fine particles.

gold-beat-er (gōld′bēt″ẽr), *n.* one who makes gold leaf for gilding.

gold-en (gōl′dn), *adj.* **1,** formed of, consisting of, abounding in, or like, gold; **2,** shining; bright like gold; **3,** most valuable, excellent: **golden age, 1,** in mythology, the imaginary time of perfect human happiness and innocence; **2,** the period of greatest glory in the civilization, history, literature, etc., of any country: **golden pheasant,** a handsome Chinese pheasant: **golden rule,** the principle of treating others as we wish them to treat us (Matthew 7:12).—*adv.* **gold′en-ly.**

Gold-en Fleece in mythology, a fleece of gold from a ram which carried Phrixus and his sister Helle away from their stepmother through the air: later hung in a grove at Colchis, guarded by a dragon, and taken, with Medea's help, by Jason.

gold-en-rod (gōl′dn-rŏd″), *n.* a tall autumn plant of the composite family, with heads of irregular clusters of small yellow flowers.

gold-filled (gōld′=fĭld″), *adj.* covered with a layer of gold considerably heavier than that applied in plating.

gold-finch (gōld′fĭnch″), *n.* **1,** a European finch with a patch of brilliant yellow on the wings; **2,** in the U. S., a finch having a lemon-yellow body and black wings.

gold-fish (gōld′fĭsh″), *n.* a gold- or orange-colored fresh-water fish of the carp family: often kept for decoration.

gold leaf sheets of gold beaten very thin: used in gilding.

gold mine **1,** a place where gold is mined; **2,** a source of great wealth.

gold-smith (gōld′smĭth″), *n.* a worker in gold, or dealer in gold plate.

golf (gŏlf; gŏf), *n.* a game played with a small, hard ball and club-headed sticks, the object being to drive the ball into a series of small holes with the fewest possible strokes:—*v.i.* to play the game of golf.—*n.* **golf′er.**

Gol-go-tha (gŏl′gō-thȧ), *n.* in the Bible, the place where Jesus was crucified (Matthew 27:33).

Go-li-ath (gō-lī′ăth), *n.* in the Bible, the Philistine giant killed by David with a stone from a sling (1 Samuel 17:4).

go-losh (gō-lŏsh′), *n.* an overshoe. Also, **go-loshe′.** See **ga-losh′,** *Pfd. S.*

Go-mor-rah (gō-mŏr′ȧ), *n.* in the Bible, a wicked city destroyed with Sodom by fire from heaven (Genesis 19:24). Also, **Go-mor′rha.**

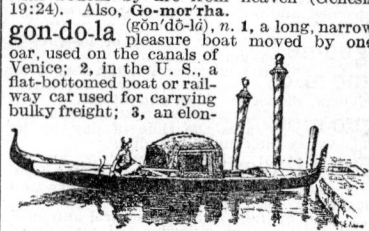

gon-do-la (gŏn′dō-lȧ), *n.* **1,** a long, narrow pleasure boat moved by one oar, used on the canals of Venice; **2,** in the U. S., a flat-bottomed boat or railway car used for carrying bulky freight; **3,** an elongated car attached to the under side of a dirigible balloon.

GONDOLA

gon-do-lier (gŏn″dō-lēr′), *n.* the rower of a gondola, or pleasure boat, used on the canals of Venice.

gone (gôn), past participle of the verb *go:*—*p.adj.* **1,** ruined; lost; **2,** faint or weak; **3,** departed; dead.—*n.* **gone′ness.**

gon-fa-lon (gŏn′fȧ-lŏn), *n.* **1,** a standard or ensign, usually with streamers, hung from a crossbar; **2,** any flag which hangs from a crossbar or frame instead of from the staff or the mast itself.

gong (gŏng), *n.* **1,** a disk or shallow bowl of metal producing a resonant note when struck with a padded mallet; **2,** any bell similar in shape and sound.

gon-or-rhe-a (gŏn″ō-rē′ȧ), *n.* a contagious and infectious inflammatory disease of the mucous membrane of the genital organs. Also, **gon″or-rhœ′a.**

good (good), *adj.* [*comp.* bet′ter, *superl.* best], **1,** adapted to the end in view; suited to its purpose; as, fish are *good* for food; sufficient; competent; as, a *good* physician; **2,** of satisfactory quality; giving pleasure; as, a *good* time; **3,** full or complete; as, the task requires a *good* hour; **4,** considerable; as, a *good* distance away; **5,** reliable; genuine; as, *good* money; **6,** virtuous; well-behaved; having excellent moral qualities; merciful; as, be *good* to her; **7,** favorable; beneficial; as, *good* weather; **8,** well-born; of high rank; as, to come of a *good* family; **9,** fertile; as, *good* soil:—*n.* **1,** that which is desirable; that which produces pleasure, satisfaction, or benefit; **2,** prosperity; benefit; advantage; **3,** that which is right; excellence: **goods, 1,** portable possessions, such as household furniture; **2,** textile fabric; **3,** merchandise; as, a dealer in leather *goods:*—*interj.* an expression of assent or pleasure.

Syn., adj. just, upright, righteous.—*Ant., adj.* bad, wicked.

good-by (good″=bī′), *n.* a farewell:—*interj.* farewell; a contraction of "God be with you." Also, **good″-bye′.**

Good Fri-day the Friday before Easter, kept as the anniversary of Christ's death upon the cross.

good hu-mor a cheery mood; a kindly temper.—*adj.* **good″-hu′mored.**—*adv.* **good″-hu′mored-ly.**

good-ly (good′lĭ), *adj.* [*comp.* good′li-er, *superl.* good′li-est], **1,** good-looking; noble; **2,** desirable; pleasant; **3,** of considerable size.—*n.* **good′li-ness.**

good-man (good′măn), *n.* [*pl.* goodmen (-mĕn)], *Archaic,* **1,** the head of a household; husband; **2,** a title of courtesy used for those not ranking as gentlemen: equivalent to *Master.*

good na-ture kindness of disposition; amiability.—*adj.* **good″-na′tured.**—*adv.* **good″-na′tured-ly.**

good-ness (good′nĕs), *n.* the state or quality of being good; virtue; kindness:—*interj.* expressing surprise, etc.

goods and chat-tels personal property, such as clothing, furniture, etc.; also, money, capital, livestock, etc., but not real estate.

good tem-per a disposition or spirit not easily provoked or irritated; habitual good nature.—*adj.* **good″-tem′pered.**—*adv.* **good″-tem′pered-ly.**

good-wife (good′wīf″), *n.* [*pl.* goodwives (-wīvz″)], the mistress of a house or an establishment.

good will **1,** benevolence; kindly feeling; **2,** hearty consent; **3,** the value a business has in trade and custom over and above its material property.

[1]**good-y** (good′ĭ), *n.* [*pl.* goodies (-ĭz)], *Colloq.,* **1,** a sweetmeat or bonbon; **2,** a person insincerely or weakly pious: often, *goody-goody*:—*adj. Colloq.,* affectedly or weakly pious; namby-pamby.

[2]**good-y** (good′ĭ), *n.* [*pl.* goodies (-ĭz)], *Archaic,* a woman of humble station: used formerly as a title; as, *Goody* Blake.

goose (goos), *n.* [*pl.* geese (gēs)], **1,** any of several web-footed, flat-billed birds larger than a duck but smaller than a swan; **2,** [*pl.* gooses (-ĕz)], a tailor's smoothing iron; **3,** a silly person; simpleton.

goose-ber-ry (gooz′bĕr-ĭ; goos′bĕr-ĭ), *n.* [*pl.* gooseberries (-ĭz)], **1,** a green berry similar to the currant, but larger and often prickly; **2,** the bush that bears it:—*adj.* made of gooseberries.

goose flesh a temporary roughness of the skin, like the skin of a plucked goose, produced by cold or fear: also called *goose skin.*

goose-foot (goos′foot″), *n.* [*pl.* goosefoots (-foots″)], any of various herbs, some of which have leaves shaped like a goose's foot; esp., the common pigweed, occasionally used as a potherb.

goose-neck (goos′nĕk″), *n.* anything curved like the neck of a goose, as a bar of iron connecting a mast with a spar, a piece of pipe, etc.

goose step a marching step used by German soldiers on parade, in which the legs are moved stiffly: so called by the English and Americans.

go-pher (gō′fẽr), *n.* **1,** any of several species of ground squirrels; **2,** any of several ratlike, burrowing rodents with cheek pouches; **3,** a burrowing land tortoise; **4,** a large, harmless, burrowing snake.

go-pher wood **1,** the unidentified wood of which Noah's ark was made (Genesis 6:14); **2,** a rare ornamental tree with yellowish wood, found in North Carolina, Kentucky, and Tennessee.

Gor-di-an knot (gôr′dĭ-ăn), **1,** in mythology, an intricate knot concerning which an oracle said that he who mastered it should master Asia, and which Alexander the Great cut through with a stroke of the sword; **2,** a problem requiring bold or daring measures to solve it.

[1]**gore** (gōr), *n.* blood; esp., thick or clotted blood.

[2]**gore** (gōr), *n.* **1,** a three-cornered piece of land; **2,** a three-cornered piece of cloth sewed or fitted into a dress, sail, etc.; **3,** one of the wedge-shaped pieces needed to make a dome-shaped object, as an umbrella, balloon, etc.:—*v.t.* [*p.t.* and *p.p.* gored (gōrd), *p.pr.* gor′ing], to insert three-cornered pieces into, as a garment, sail, etc.

[3]**gore** (gōr), *v.t.* [*p.t.* and *p.p.* gored (gōrd), *p.pr.* gor′ing], to pierce with, or as with, a horn; as, the bull *gored* him.

gorge (gôrj), *n.* **1,** that which is swallowed; **2,** the act of swallowing greedily; also, a very hearty meal; **3,** a filling or choking of a channel by an obstruction; as, an ice *gorge* in a river; **4,** a narrow passage between mountains or hills:—*v.t.* [*p.t.* and *p.p.* gorged (gôrjd), *p.pr.* gorg′ing], **1,** to swallow greedily or in large mouthfuls; satiate; glut; **2,** to choke up:—*v.i.* to eat greedily; stuff.

gor-geous (gôr′jŭs), *adj.* **1,** glittering in various colors; splendid; showy; **2,** inclined to magnificence.—*adv.* **gor′geous-ly.**—*n.* **gor′geous-ness.**
Syn. superb, grand.

gor-get (gôr′jĕt), *n.* **1,** a protective piece of armor for the throat or neck (see *armor,* illus.); **2,** a colored patch on the throat of certain birds.

Gor-gon (gôr′gŏn), *n.* in mythology, one of three frightful sisters with snakes on their heads instead of hair, one of whom, Medusa, was mortal, but was so terrible that anyone who beheld her was turned to stone: **gorgon,** an ugly or terrible woman.

go-ril-la (gō-rĭl′ȧ), *n.* an African manlike ape, some five feet in height, with very powerful limbs: the largest ape known.

gor-mand (gôr′mănd), *n.* **1,** a voracious eater; a glutton; **2,** an epicure. See **gour′mand,** *Pfd. S.*

gor-mand-ize (gôr′măn-dīz), *v.i.* [*p.t.* and *p.p.* -ized (-dīzd), *p.pr.* -iz″ing], to eat greedily or ravenously.—*n.* **gor′mand-iz″er.**

gorse (gôrs), *n.* any of several low, dense shrubs of the pea family; furze.

gor-y (gōr′ĭ), *adj.* [*comp.* gor′i-er, *superl.* gor′i-est], covered with blood; bloody.

gos-hawk (gŏs′hôk″), *n.* any of several fierce, short-winged hawks.

gos-ling (gŏz′lĭng), *n.* a young goose, covered with pale yellow down.

gos-pel (gŏs′pĕl), *n.* **1,** good news or tidings, esp. the announcement of the salvation of mankind by Jesus Christ; **2,** the general doctrines of the New Testament; **3,** something received as absolutely true; **4,** any doctrine earnestly advocated by its supporters: **Gospel, 1,** the history of the life and doctrines of Jesus Christ, contained in four books of the New Testament; **2,** one of these books; **3,** a selection from these in a church service:—*adj.* pertaining to the gospel.

gos-sa-mer (gŏs′ȧ-mẽr), *n.* **1,** a very fine spider's web which floats in the air; **2,** a very thin, soft, filmy, strong gauze; **3,** any thin, filmy material; **4,** an outer garment made of waterproof material:—*adj.* very thin; flimsy; gauzy.

gos-sip (gŏs′ĭp), *n.* **1,** familiar or idle talk; scandal; **2,** one who habitually talks of other people and their affairs:—*v.i.* to tell idle tales about others; tattle.—*n.* **gos′sip-er.**—*adj.* **gos′sip-y.**

gos-soon (gŏ-soon′), *n.* in Ireland, a boy; also, a boy servant.

got (gŏt), past tense and past participle of the irregular verb *get.*

Goth (gŏth), *n.* **1**, one of an ancient Teutonic tribe that overran the Roman Empire in the third and fourth centuries after Christ; **2**, a crude, inartistic, or savage person.

Goth-ic (gŏth'ĭk), *adj.* **1**, pertaining to the Goths or their language; **2**, pertaining to a style of architecture with high and pointed arches, steep roofs, and windows large in proportion to the wall space:—*n.* **1**, the language of the Goths; **2**, the pointed style of architecture; **3**, a variety of type.

got-ten (gŏt'n), past participle of the verb *get:* used esp. in the U. S.

Göt-ter-däm-mer-ung (gût″ẽr-dĕm'-ẽr-o͝ong), *n.* in German mythology, the twilight of the gods, or the time when the gods engage in the last great battle with their enemies and die.

gouge (gouj; go͞oj), *n.* **1**, a rounded hollow chisel for cutting grooves or holes; **2**, *Colloq.:* **a**, a groove or cavity made with, or as with, such a tool; **b**, a trick or fraud; also, one who tricks:—*v.t.* [*p.t.* and *p.p.* gouged (goujd; go͞ojd), *p.pr.* goug'ing], **1**, to scoop out with a gouge; **2**, *Colloq.*, to trick; overcharge.—*n.* **goug'er.**

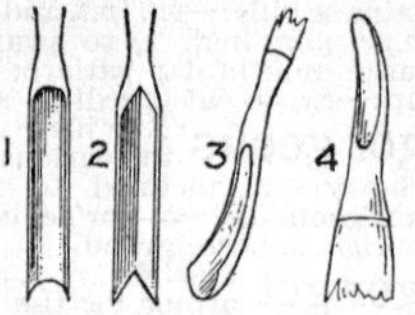

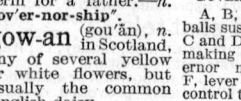

Gouges
1,2,3, carpenter's: 4, surgeon's.

gourd (gōrd; go͞ord), *n.* **1**, any of a number of fleshy, many-seeded fruits, such as the melon, pumpkin, cucumber, etc.; esp., an inedible variety whose dried shell serves for cups, dippers, etc.; **2**, a vessel made from such a fruit; **3**, the plant bearing the fruit.

gourde (go͞ord), *n.* **1**, the monetary unit of Haiti, formerly equivalent to $1.00, now to 20 cents; **2**, in Cuba, a silver dollar.

gour-mand (go͞or'mănd; *Fr.* go͞or″mäṅ'), *n.* **1**, a greedy eater; glutton; **2**, a judge of viands; epicure. Also, **gor'mand.**

*__gour-met__ (go͞or″mâ'), [Fr.], *n.* an epicure; one who is a good judge of things to eat and drink

gout (gout), *n.* a disease marked by painful swelling and inflammation of the joints or lower limbs, esp. of the great toe.—*adj.* **gout'y.**—*adv.* **gout'i-ly.**—*n.* **gout'i-ness.**

gov-ern (gŭv'ẽrn), *v.t.* **1**, to control by authority; regulate; **2**, to direct; manage; **3**, to steer; restrain; **4**, to require to be in a particular grammatical mood, case, etc.; as, a preposition *governs* a noun in the objective case:—*v.i.* to exercise authority; administer or execute the law.—*adj.* **gov'ern-a-ble.**—*p.adj.* **gov'ern-ing.**

Syn. control, direct, rule. To *govern* is to cause others to obey any power or authority; as, to *govern* the state. *Control* implies having another entirely under one's influence; as, he *controlled* the crowd by his eloquence. To *direct* is to point out a course of action and order it followed; as, the manager *directs* the policy of the company. *Rule* suggests governing with arbitrary power or influence.

gov-ern-ance (gŭv'ẽr-năns), *n.* rule; control; management.

gov-ern-ess (gŭv'ẽr-nĕs), *n.* a woman who teaches children and young people, esp. in their own home.

gov-ern-ment (gŭv'ẽrn-mĕnt). *n.* **1**, the act of administering or ruling; **2**, an established system of administration of public affairs; as, a democratic *government;* **3**, collectively, the body of officials in charge of the administration of the affairs of a state; **4**, a country or portion of a country governed.—*adj.* **gov″ern-men'tal.**

gov-er-nor (gŭv'ẽr-nẽr), *n.* **1**, a person or thing that controls, administers, or exercises large authority; **2**, in the U. S., the highest executive official in any State; **3**, in the British Empire, an official representing the crown in a dominion or dependency; **4**, a person appointed to administer affairs within a specified territory; **5**, any of several automatic devices for regulating the speed of an engine; **6**, *Slang,* anyone regarded as having authority: a term for a father.—*n.* **gov'er-nor-ship″.**

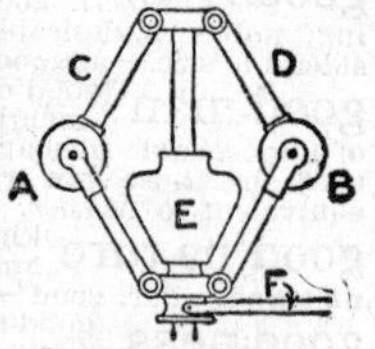

Governor (def. 5)
A, B, two centrifugal balls suspended on rods C and D; E, weight for making action of governor more sensitive; F, lever connected with control throttle valve.

gow-an (gou'ăn), *n.* in Scotland, any of several yellow or white flowers, but usually the common English daisy.

gowk (gōk; gouk), *n.* a clumsy or half-witted person; simpleton; gawk.

gown (goun), *n.* **1**, a woman's outer garment or dress; **2**, a long, loose robe worn by university and college students and by members of the learned professions; **3**, a dressing gown; nightgown; **4**, any loose, flowing outer garment.

gowns-man (gounz'măn), *n.* [*pl.* gownsmen (-mĕn)], one who wears a gown professionally; a student.

grab (grăb), *v.t.* and *v.i.* [*p.t.* and *p.p.* grabbed (grăbd), *p.pr.* grab'bing], to seize suddenly and forcibly; snatch:—*n.* a sudden and forcible seizure or grasp.

grace (grās), *n.* **1**, ease, elegance, or attractiveness in form, movement, attitude, language, etc.; **2**, favorable attitude; good will; as, he is in the good *graces* of his employer; **3**, excellence of character or disposition; any pleasing natural endowment; **4**, sense of propriety; as, he had the *grace* to apologize; **5**, a prayer before or after a meal, giving thanks and asking the divine blessing; **6**, something granted as a favor, rather than as a right; **7**, in religion: **a**, God's unmerited mercy toward mankind; **b**, the influence of God's spirit in the heart of a believer; **c**, any of the Christian virtues, as meekness, love, humility, temperance, faith, peace, etc.; a spiritual gift or attainment; **8**, a period of delay, usually three days, allowed in some states for payment of a note or draft after the date of maturity; **9**, in life insurance, a delay of payment of premium allowed for 30 days after date due: **grace note,** in music, a single, ornamental note immediately preceding and generally one degree above or below a harmony tone: **Grace,** a respectful title of address applied to a person of high rank, as an archbishop or duke: preceded by *your, his,* or *her:* **the Graces,** in mythology, three beautiful sister goddesses, givers of charm, elegance, and joyousness: **year of grace,** year since Christ; A. D.:—*v.t.* [*p.t.* and *p.p.* graced (grāst), *p.pr.* grac'ing], **1**, to adorn; decorate; **2**, to honor; dignify; favor.

grace-ful (grās'fo͝ol), *adj.* **1**, displaying beauty in form or action; elegant; **2**, felicitous in speech.—*adv.* **grace'ful-ly.**—*n.* **grace'ful-ness.**

grace-less (grās'lĕs), *adj.* lacking in good qualities; ill-mannered; awkward.—*adv.* **grace'less-ly.**—*n.* **grace'less-ness.**

gra-cious (grā'shŭs), *adj.* **1**, showing or bestowing goodness, kindness, or mercy; **2**, affable; polite; courteous.—*adv.* **gra'cious-ly.**—*n.* **gra'cious-ness.**

grack-le (grăk'l), *n.* **1**, any of various Old World birds of the starling family; **2**, in America, any of several blackbirds.

gra-date (grā'dāt), *v.t.* [*p.t.* and *p.p.* -dat-ed, *p.pr.* -dat-ing], **1**, to arrange (parts) in a whole, as colors in painting, so that they harmonize; **2**, to bring to a certain strength of concentration; as, to *gradate* a saline, or salt, solution:—*v.i.* to pass by small degrees from one grade to another.

gra-da-tion (grȧ-dā'shŭn), *n.* **1**, the act of arranging in order; also, the state of being so arranged; **2**, usually in *pl.*, a series of degrees in rank, size, etc.; **3**, any degree in such a series; **4**, in painting, a gradual blending of one tint into another.

grade (grād), *n.* **1**, a step or degree in rank, quality, order, etc.; **2**, in the U. S., one of the successive parts of the course in an elementary school, usually requiring a year for its completion: also, the pupils in it; **3**, in many schools and colleges, the mark or rating number given to a pupil for class work or an examination; **4**, the measure of slope of a road, railroad, surface, etc.; gradient; **5**, a stretch of a railway or highway which slopes; an incline or decline: **grade crossing, or crossing at grade,** a point at which a railroad track is crossed by another railroad track or by a highway on the same level at the point of crossing: **up to grade,** of sufficiently high quality: **to make the grade,** in automobiling, to ascend a steep place; hence, figuratively, to succeed in spite of obstacles; come up to standard:—*v.t.* [*p.t.* and *p.p.* grad'ed, *p.pr.* grad'ing], **1**, to level and prepare, as a lawn, a road, or a railway roadbed; **2**, to arrange in regular series:—*v.i.* to take (a specified) rank.

gra-di-ent (grā'dĭ-ĕnt), *n.* the incline of a railway or road:—*adj.* **1**, advancing by steps; **2**, fitted for walking, as the feet of certain birds.

grad-u-al (grăd'ū-ăl), *adj.* proceeding by degrees; step by step; regular and slow; as, he shows a *gradual* improvement:—*n.* **1**, in a church service, a response sung after the Epistle; **2**, an ancient book of responses used by the choir during Mass.—*adv.* **grad'u-al-ly.**—*n.* **grad'u-al-ness.**

Syn., *adj.* deliberate, moderate.—*Ant.*, *adj.* sudden, quick, immediate.

grad-u-ate (grăd'ū-ât), *n.* **1**, one on whom a degree or a diploma has been conferred; as, he is a *graduate* of Harvard University; **2**, a measuring glass accurately marked:—*v.t.* (grăd'ū-āt), [*p.t.* and *p.p.* -at″ed, *p.pr.* -at″ing], **1**, to mark with degrees; **2**, to arrange according to degrees of quality, color, heat, etc.; **3**, to confer a degree or diploma upon; as, he was *graduated* at Columbia:—*v.i.* **1**, to take or receive a college degree or a diploma; **2**, to change by degrees:—*adj.* (-ât), having been given a degree; pertaining to those upon whom degrees have been conferred; as, a *graduate* student; a *graduate* course.

grad-u-a-tion (grăd″ū-ā'shŭn), *n.* **1**, the act or occasion of conferring or receiving a college degree or the diploma of a school; **2**, regular progression; **3**, a marking into degrees or parts.

grad-u-a-tor (grăd'ū-ā″tẽr), *n.* an instrument for dividing lines or surfaces into minute parts, or one using it.

graft (grȧft), *n.* **1**, a small shoot of a tree inserted into another tree on which it continues to grow; **2**, the process or place of grafting; **3**, hence, something mixed with a foreign stock; **4**, *U. S. Colloq.*, the getting of money or position by underhand means or extortion; also, anything so gained:—*v.t.* **1**, to insert, as a shoot, in another tree; join so as to receive support from another thing; **2**, in surgery, to transplant (living tissue):—*v.i.* **1**, to practice grafting; **2**, *Colloq.*, to accept bribe money: **grafting knife,** a knife adapted for cutting twigs or vines for grafting.—*n.* **graft'er.**

GRAFTING KNIVES

Gra-ham flour (grā'-ȧm), whole or unsifted wheat flour.

grail (grāl), *n.* a dish or chalice: **Holy Grail,** the cup used by Christ at the Last Supper, said in some legends of the Middle Ages to have been preserved by Joseph of Arimathea, and taken by him to England, where it disappeared. Also, **graal** (grāl).

grain (grān), *n.* **1**, any very small, hard particle; as, a *grain* of sand; a small seed or kernel; **2**, a single seed of corn; the fruit of certain grasses which furnish the chief food of man, as corn, wheat, rye, oats, etc., or the plants themselves; **3**, any small particle or amount; **4**, a very small unit of weight, equal to $\frac{1}{7000}$ of a pound avoirdupois; **5**, the arrangement of particles or fibers in a body; as, the *grain* of wood; texture; **6**, in *pl.*, the refuse or dregs of malted barley:—*v.t.* **1**, to form into small particles; **2**, to paint in imitation of the grain of wood.—*adj.* **grain'y.**

grain-er (grān'ẽr), *n.* a tool for imitating the grain or texture of wood, or one who uses it.

grain-ing (grān'ĭng), *n.* the process of finishing material in imitation of the grain or texture of wood, leather, etc.

gram (grăm), *n.* a weight, the metric unit of mass; 15.43 grains troy: about the weight of $\frac{1}{5}$ teaspoonful of water. Also, **gramme.**—*abbr.* **g.; gr.**

-gram (-grăm), **1**, a suffix or combining form from the Greek, meaning a writing or something written; as, tele*gram;* **2**, in the metric system, a gram; as, kilo*gram.*

gra-mer-cy (grȧ-mûr'sĭ), *interj. Archaic,* great thanks; thank you.

gram-i-niv-o-rous (grăm″ĭ-nĭv'ō-rŭs), *adj.* feeding on grasses; grass-eating, as cattle.

gram-ma-log (grăm'ȧ-lŏg), *n.* in shorthand, a sign or mark for a whole word. Also, **gram'ma-logue.**

gram-mar (grăm'ẽr), *n.* **1**, the science that treats of the principles that govern the words of a language in their relation to each other; **2**, the art of speaking or writing a language according to these principles; **3**, a book on this science.

gram-ma-ri-an (grȧ-mā'rĭ-ăn), *n.* one who knows, writes on, or teaches, the science of language.

gram-mar school **1**, in the U. S., a graded school between the primary and the high, or junior high, school; **2**, in England, a school, preparatory for college, in which the classics and other higher subjects are taught.

gram-mat-i-cal (grȧ-măt'ĭ-kăl), *adj.* of or pertaining to, or in agreement with, grammar or its rules.—*adv.* **gram-mat'i-cal-ly.**

gram-o-phone (grăm'ō-fōn), *n.* an instrument for recording and reproducing sound.

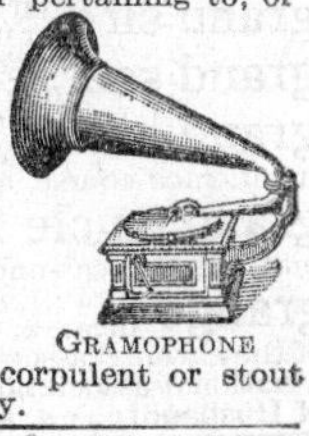
GRAMOPHONE

gram-pus (grăm'pŭs), *n.* **1**, one of the smaller whales: a sea mammal akin to the dolphins and porpoises; **2**, a corpulent or stout person who breathes loudly.

gran-a-ry (grăn′ȧ-rĭ), *n.* [*pl.* granaries (-rĭz)], **1**, a storehouse for grain; **2**, a country where grain is abundant.

grand (grănd), *adj.* **1**, large; majestic; **2**, high in dignity or power; illustrious; lofty in character; **3**, chief in importance; **4**, magnificent; splendid; **5**, complete; as, a *grand* total; **6**, in some compounds, belonging to the second generation; as, *grand*son; *grand*father; **7**, *Colloq.*, very good; as, a *grand* time; **8**, in law, chief; important; serious; as, *grand* larceny: opp. of *petit:* **grand piano**, a piano with a large, horizontal, triangular case: **grand tour**, a tour of Europe: —*n. Slang*, a thousand dollars.—*adv.* **grand′ly.**
Syn., *adj.* sublime, stately, dignified, noble, exalted, gorgeous, superb.

gran-dam (grăn′dăm), *n.* a grandmother; an ancestress; also, an old woman. Also, **gran′dame.**

grand-aunt (grănd′ȧnt″), *n.* the aunt of one's parent; a great-aunt.

grand-child (grănd′chīld″), *n.* the child of one's son or daughter.

grand-daugh-ter (grănd′dô″tẽr), *n.* the daughter of one's son or daughter; a female grandchild.

grand duke a duke ruling over a territory.—*fem.* **grand duch′ess.**

gran-dee (grăn-dē′), *n.* **1**, a Spanish or Portuguese nobleman of the highest rank; **2**, any man of high rank.

gran-deur (grăn′dūr), *n.* **1**, great power, rank, or eminence; **2**, splendor of surroundings; sublime beauty; **3**, social distinction and display; **4**, elevation of thought, sentiment, or demeanor.

grand-fa-ther (grănd′fä″*th*ẽr), *n.* the father of one's father or mother.—*adj.* **grand′fa″ther-ly.**

gran-dil-o-quent (grăn-dĭl′ō-kwĕnt), *adj.* characterized by a lofty or pompous style; bombastic.—*adv.* **gran-dil′o-quent-ly.**—*n.* **gran-dil′o-quence.**

gran-di-ose (grăn′dĭ-ōs), *adj.* impressive in reality or pretense.—*adv.* **gran′di-ose-ly.**—*n.* **gran″di-os′i-ty.**

grand ju-ry in England and the U. S., a group of duly appointed persons whose duty it is to inquire into crimes committed within its jurisdiction, and to indict for trial before a petit jury all persons against whom sufficient evidence is produced, and also, sometimes, to inquire into any public offense, as official corruption, nuisances, etc.

grand-ma (grănd′mä″; grăn′mä″), *n. Colloq.*, grandmother. Also, **grand′mam-ma″** (grănd′mȧ-mä″; -mä″mȧ).

grand-moth-er (grănd′mŭ*th*″ẽr), *n.* the mother of one's father or mother.—*adj.* **grand′moth″er-ly.**

grand op-er-a an elaborate and dignified musical drama.

grand-pa (grănd′pä″; grăn′pä″), *n. Colloq.*, grandfather. Also, **grand′-pa-pa″** (grănd′pȧ-pä″; -pä″pȧ).

grand-par-ent (grănd′pâr″ĕnt), *n.* a parent of one's parent.

grand-sire (grănd′sīr″), *n.* a grandfather or more remote male ancestor.

grand-son (grănd′sŭn″), *n.* the son of one's son or daughter.

grand stand the principal range of seats at any outdoor entertainment, race course, athletic field, etc.

grand-un-cle (grănd′ŭng″kl), *n.* the uncle of one's father or mother; a great-uncle.

grange (grānj), *n.* **1**, a farm with its buildings; **2**, in the U. S., a local lodge of the national association of farmers: **Grange**, a national association of farmers, the Patrons of Husbandry.—*n.* **grang′er.**

gran-ite (grăn′ĭt), *n.* a hard, crystalline rock composed of quartz, feldspar, and, usually, mica.

gran-ite ware a kind of enameled ironware, imitating granite.

gra-niv-o-rous (grȧ-nĭv′ō-rŭs), *adj.* eating grain or seeds.

gran-ny (grăn′ĭ), *n.* [*pl.* grannies (-ĭz)], **1**, a grandmother; an old woman; **2**, a fussy person. Also, **gran′nie.**

grant (grȧnt), *v.t.* **1**, to give or confer, esp. in response to a request; **2**, to admit as true; concede; **3**, to transfer the title of: —*n.* **1**, the act of conferring; **2**, the thing conferred, esp. a territory or right conferred by a government; **3**, in law, a transfer of property.
Syn., *v.* bestow, impart, yield, cede, allow, accord. (See give.)

gran-tee (grȧn-tē′), *n.* the person to whom property is transferred by law.

grant-or (grȧn′tŏr; grȧn-tôr′), *n.* one who transfers property by law.

gran-u-lar (grăn′ū-lȧr), *adj.* composed of, or like, grains or granules.

gran-u-late (grăn′ū-lāt), *v.t.* [*p.t.* and *p.p.* -lat″ed, *p.pr.* -lat″ing], **1**, to form into, or cover with, small grains or crystals; **2**, to roughen the surface of; as, *granulated* eyelids: **granulated sugar**, sugar which through refining has been whitened and made into small, separate grains; ordinary table sugar: distinguished from *confectioners' sugar* and *brown sugar:*—*v.i.* to become grainlike or form into crystals, as molasses.

gran-u-la-tion (grăn″ū-lā′shŭn), *n.* **1**, the act of forming into grains; **2**, specif., the formation in wounds of new tissue in the shape of grainlike masses.

gran-ule (grăn′ūl), *n.* a small grain or particle; as, a *granule* of sugar.

gran-u-lose (grăn′ū-lōs), *n.* the substance in starch grains capable of being formed into sugar during digestion.

grape (grāp), *n.* **1**, the smooth, round, edible fruit of the grapevine, growing in clusters and used for making wine and raisins; **2**, the grapevine; **3**, grapeshot.

grape-fruit (grāp′fro͞ot″), *n.* a citrous fruit, larger than an orange, having an acid pulp and a bitter-tasting rind.

grap-er-y (grāp′ẽr-ĭ), *n.* [*pl.* graperies (-ĭz)], a place for growing grapes.

grape-shot (grāp′shŏt″), *n.* a charge of shot of about the size of a grape, which scatters when fired.

grape-vine (grāp′vīn″), *n.* any of a large genus of the vine family, many being cultivated for their edible fruit.

graph (grȧf), *n.* **1**, a diagram or curve representing the successive values of a changing quantity; as, a *graph* showing the temperature hour by hour through a day; **2**, a line or diagram expressing a mathematical relation; as, the *graph* of an equation.

-graph (-grȧf), a combining form from the Greek, meaning something that writes or is written; as, tele*graph;* auto*graph.*

graph-ic (grăf′ĭk), *adj.* **1**, pertaining to the art of writing or delineating; **2**, illustrating by curves, diagrams, or pictures; **3**, vividly described; well delineated; lifelike: **graphic arts**, drawing, painting, and other fine arts which represent objects on a flat surface. Also, **graph′i-cal.**—*adv.* **graph′i-cal-ly.**
Syn. forcible, striking.—*Ant.* dull, ordinary.

graph-ite (grăf′īt), *n.* a kind of carbon used for lead pencils, etc.

graph-ol-o-gy (grăf-ŏl′ō-jĭ), *n.* the art or science of judging character from handwriting.

graph-o-phone (grăf′ō-fōn), *n.* a kind of phonograph, or machine for reproducing spoken sounds: a trade name.

-graph-y (-gräf-ĭ), a suffix or combining form from the Greek, meaning a writing or description: used in the names of sciences; as, geo*graphy*.

grap-nel (grăp′nĕl), *n.* **1**, a small anchor; **2**, heavy tongs used for lifting stone, ice, etc.

grap-ple (grăp′l), *v.t.* [*p.t.* and *p.p.* -pled (-ld), *p.pr.* -pling], to lay fast hold of:—*v.i.* to struggle or contend in a close fight:—*n.* **1**, a close fight; a close hold, as in wrestling; **2**, a mechanical device for taking hold of anything.

GRAPPLE

grasp (gråsp), *v.t.* **1**, to seize or catch at; hold by clasping or contracting; as, *grasp* the rope quickly; **2**, to take hold of mentally, or understand; as, to *grasp* the situation:—*v.i.* to endeavor to seize: with *at:* —*n.* **1**, a seizure of the hand; **2**, the power of seizure; hold; **3**, mental capacity.
Syn., *v.* clutch, clasp, grip, grab.—*Ant.*, *v.* lose, repel, relinquish.

grasp-ing (gråsp′ĭng), *p.adj.* avaricious; greedy of gain; close; miserly; as, he is *grasping* and selfish.—*adv.* **grasp′ing-ly.**

grass (grås), *n.* **1**, green herbage, on the leaves and stalks of which cattle feed; **2**, any plant of a very large family having hollow, jointed stalks, narrow leaves called blades, and seeds similar to those of grain; **3**, pasture: **grass widow**, a woman whose husband is divorced or otherwise separated from her:—*v.t.* **1**, to cover with turf or grass; **2**, to bleach, by exposure on grass; **3**, to pasture or graze:—*v.i.* to graze.

grass-hop-per (grås′hŏp″ẽr), *n.* any of many kinds of leaping and flying insects: also called *locust.*

grass-y (grås′ĭ), *adj.* [*comp.* grass′i-er, *superl.* grass′i-est], covered with, or like, grass.—*n.* **grass′i-ness.**

[1]**grate** (grāt), *v.t.* [*p.t.* and *p.p.* grat′ed, *p.pr.* grat′ing], **1**, to rub or wear into small particles by the friction of a rough body; grind down; **2**, to rub so as to produce a rasping sound; as, to *grate* metal on stone:—*v.i.* **1**, to produce a harsh noise by rubbing roughly; **2**, to produce mental irritation; sound discordantly; as, her manner *grates* on me; his voice *grates:*—*n.* the act or sound of grating.

[2]**grate** (grāt), *n.* **1**, a framework of horizontal iron bars to hold burning fuel, esp. coal; **2**, a partition made of bars, as in a window:—*v.t.* [*p.t.* and *p.p.* grat′ed, *p.pr.* grat′ing], to furnish with iron bars.

grate-ful (grāt′fo͝ol), *adj.* **1**, thankful; **2**, pleasurable; as, the cold air was *grateful* after the overheated room.—*adv.* **grate′ful-ly.**—*n.* **grate′ful-ness.**

grat-er (grāt′ẽr), *n.* one who or that which grates; a grating implement.

grat-i-fi-ca-tion (grăt″ĭ-fĭ-kā′shŭn), *n.* **1**, the act of pleasing; **2**, satisfaction; **3**, reward or recompense.
Syn. enjoyment, delight.

grat-i-fy (grăt′ĭ-fī), *v.t.* [*p.t.* and *p.p.* -fied (-fīd), *p.pr.* -fy″ing], to afford pleasure to; indulge; delight; humor.

[1]**grat-ing** (grāt′ĭng), *p.adj.* harsh; irritating to the ear.—*adv.* **grat′ing-ly.**

[2]**grat-ing** (grāt′ĭng), *n.* **1**, an open framework or lattice of parallel or crossed bars; **2**, a set of very fine parallel lines ruled on a polished surface: used in spectroscopic work.

gra-tis (grā′tĭs; grăt′ĭs), *adv.* without charge; out of favor or kindness; as, he gave me these flowers *gratis.*

grat-i-tude (grăt′ĭ-tūd), *n.* the state of being thankful; appreciation of favors received; response to kindness.

gra-tu-i-tous (grȧ-tū′ĭ-tŭs), *adj.* **1**, freely bestowed; voluntary; **2**, without provocation; as, a *gratuitous* insult; **3**, granted without merit or claim.—*adv.* **gra-tu′i-tous-ly.**—*n.* **gra-tu′i-tous-ness.**

gra-tu-i-ty (grȧ-tū′ĭ-tĭ), *n.* [*pl.* gratuities (-tĭz)], a donation or present.
Syn. bounty, boon. (See gift.)

gra-va-men (grȧ-vā′mĕn), *n.* [*pl.* gravamina (-văm′ĭ-nȧ); gravamens (-vā′mĕnz)], the substantial cause of an action at law.

[1]**grave** (grāv), *v.t.* [*p.t.* graved (grāvd), *p.p.* graved or grav′en (grāv′n), *p.pr.* grav′ing], **1**, to engrave; sculpture; **2**, to impress indelibly on, as the mind:—*n.* **1**, an excavation for the reception of a dead body; a place of burial; **2**, a place of great slaughter or mortality; **3**, figuratively, a place or occasion which proves the end or destruction of anything; as, the *grave* of his hopes.

[2]**grave** (grāv), *v.t.* [*p.t.* and *p.p.* graved (grāvd), *p.pr.* grav′ing], to clean (a ship's bottom) by scraping or burning off and covering with tar.

[3]**grave** (grāv), *adj.* **1**, important; needing serious consideration; **2**, solemn; dull in color; sedate; thoughtful; sober; **3**, low-pitched: used of an accent or its sign [\ ]:—*n.* a grave accent.—*adv.* **grave′ly.**
Syn., *adj.* serious, earnest, staid.—*Ant.*, *adj.* light-hearted, giddy, unimportant.

grave-clothes (grāv′klōthz″), *n.pl.* **1**, the garments in which a dead person is buried; **2**, a shroud.

grav-el (grăv′ĕl), *n.* **1**, fragments of rock coarser than sand, and frequently mixed with it; **2**, small, solid matter in the bladder and kidneys:—*v.t.* **1**, to cover with fragments of rock; **2**, to run aground on a beach: said of a vessel; **3**, to embarrass; **4**, to lame, as a horse, by a stone under the shoe.—*adj.* **grav′el-ly.**

grav-en (grāv′n), *p.adj.* cut; carved: **graven image**, an idol.

grav-er (grāv′ẽr), *n.* **1**, a cutting tool used by engravers and sculptors; **2**, an engraver or carver in stone.

grave-stone (grāv′stōn″), *n.* a stone, usually bearing an inscription, placed to mark a grave; tombstone.

grave-yard (grāv′yärd″), *n.* a burial place; cemetery.

grav-ing (grāv′ĭng), *n.* **1**, the act of engraving or incising; **2**, the clearing of the bottom of a ship.

grav-i-tate (grăv′ĭ-tāt), *v.i.* [*p.t.* and *p.p.* -tat″ed, *p.pr.* -tat″ing], **1**, to be acted upon or attracted by a force which draws all bodies in the universe toward one another; **2**, to be naturally attracted; as, office seekers *gravitate* toward those in authority.

grav-i-ta-tion (grăv″ĭ-tā′shŭn), *n.* the force which draws all bodies in the universe toward one another.—*adj.* **grav″i-ta′tion-al.**

grav-i-ty (grăv′ĭ-tĭ), *n.* [*pl.* gravities (-tĭz)], **1**, gravitation in relation to the earth; that force which tends to move all bodies toward the center of the earth; **2**, weight; importance; solemnity; **3**, the state of being serious or sedate; **4**, in music, lowness of a tone or note: **specific gravity**, the relative weight of any kind of matter as compared with the weight of an equal volume of some standard substance, as water or air; as, the *specific gravity* of gold is 19, meaning that gold is nineteen times as heavy as water.

gra-vy (grā′vĭ), *n.* [*pl.* gravies (-vĭz)], the fatty juice from roasting or frying meat, made into a dressing for food.

gray (grā), *adj.* **1**, of a color composed of white mixed with black; **2**, old;

mature: **gray matter**, 1, gray nerve tissue in the brain and spinal cord; 2, *Colloq.*, brains; intelligence:—*n.* a color resulting from mixing white and black:—*v.t.* to cause to whiten:—*v.i.* to be whitened, as with age. Also, **grey**.—*adj.* **gray'ish.**—*adv.* **gray'ly.**—*n.* **gray'ness.**

gray-beard (grā'bērd''), *n.* an old man; hence, a wise, experienced man; often said scornfully.—Also, **grey'beard''.**

gray-ling (grā'lĭng), *n.* any of several fresh-water fishes, allied to the trout. Also, **grey'ling.**

1**graze** (grāz), *v.t.* [*p.t.* and *p.p.* grazed (grāzd), *p.pr.* graz'ing], 1, to provide growing grass, herbage, etc., for; as, to *graze* cattle; 2, to eat grass or herbage from, as a pasture; 3, to tend, as cattle, while pasturing:—*v.i.* to eat grass; pasture.—*n.* **graz'er.**

2**graze** (grāz), *v.t.* and *v.i.* [*p.t.* and *p.p.* grazed (grāzd), *p.pr.* graz'ing], 1, to touch or rub lightly in passing; 2, to scratch or scrape slightly:—*n.* a slight rub; also, a rubbed place on a surface.

gra-zier (grā'zhẽr), *n.* one who pastures or breeds cattle for market.

grease (grēs), *n.* 1, soft animal fat; 2, any oily matter:—*v.t.* (grēs; grēz), [*p.t.* and *p.p.* greased (grēst; grēzd), *p.pr.* greas'ing], 1, to smear or rub with fat; 2, to cause to move easily by applying an oily substance.

greas-er (grēs'ẽr; grēz'ẽr), *n.* one who or that which oils or lubricates the operating parts of machinery.

greas-y (grēs'ĭ; grēz'ĭ), *adj.* [*comp.* greas'i-er, *superl.* greas'i-est], resembling, smeared, or spotted with, fat; oily.—*adv.* **greas'i-ly.**—*n.* **greas'i-ness.**

great (grāt), *adj.* 1, large in size, number, extent, etc.; vast: opp. of *small* or *little;* 2, of long duration; as, a *great* while after; 3, extreme; as, *great* ignorance; 4, important; weighty; as, *great* issues; 5, prominent; illustrious; 6, high-minded; noble; 7, marvelous; magnificent; 8, intimate, as a friend; 9, more remote in relationship by one generation; as, *great*-aunt: **Great War,** the war of 1914–18, which involved nearly all the great nations of the earth: also called *World War:*—*n.* noble or influential people collectively: with *the.*—*adv.* **great'ly.**—*n.* **great'ness.**
Syn., adj. big, huge, majestic, grand.

great–aunt (grāt'=ȧnt''), *n.* the sister of one's grandparent.

Great Bear in astronomy, a well-known northern constellation, Ursa Major, containing the seven bright stars forming the Dipper.

great-coat (grāt'kōt''), *n.* a heavy overcoat or topcoat.

great Dane one of a breed of very large, short-haired dogs.

great-est (grā'tĕst), *adj.* superlative of *great:* **greatest common divisor,** in arithmetic and algebra, the greatest factor common to two or more numbers.

great–grand-child (grāt''=grănd'-chīld''), *n.* the child of one's grandson or granddaughter.

great–grand-daugh-ter (grāt''=grănd'dô''-tẽr), *n.* the daughter of one's grandchild.

great–grand-fa-ther (grāt''=grănd'-fä''*th*ẽr), *n.* the father of one's grandfather or grandmother.

great–grand-moth-er (grāt''=grănd'-mŭ*th*''ẽr), *n.* the mother of one's grandparent.

great–grand-son (grāt''=grănd'sŭn''), *n.* the son of one's grandson or granddaughter.

great prim-er in printing, a large size of type, nearly equivalent to 18 point (see *type*).

Great Spir-it the Supreme Being: a name used by the Indians of North America.

great–un-cle (grāt'=ŭng''kl), *n.* the brother of one's grandfather or grandmother.

Great White Way the theater section of Broadway, New York: so called from the brightness of its lights at night.

1**greaves** (grēvz), *n.pl.* armor to protect the legs from the ankle to the knee (see *armor*, illus.).

2**greaves** (grēvz), *n.pl.* the sediment of melted tallow.

grebe (grēb), *n.* any of several four-toed, ducklike, expert diving birds, allied to the loon but smaller.

Gre-cian (grē'shăn), *adj.* pertaining to Greece; Greek:—*n.* 1, a native of Greece; a Greek; 2, a Greek scholar.

greed (grēd), *n.* 1, excessive hunger; 2, an unnatural desire or longing; avarice; as, a *greed* for gain.
Syn. cupidity, covetousness.

greed-y (grēd'ĭ), *adj.* [*comp.* greed'i-er, *superl.* greed'i-est], 1, too eager for food or drink; gluttonous; 2, eagerly desirous; covetous.—*adv.* **greed'i-ly.**—*n.* **greed'i-ness.**

Greek (grēk), *adj.* pertaining to, or like, Greece or the Greeks; Grecian: **Greek Church,** the church dominant in countries formerly composing the Eastern Roman Empire, as Yugoslavia, Rumania, and Bulgaria; the Eastern Church: **Greek cross,** a cross resembling a plus sign (see *cross*, illus.):—*n.* 1, a native of Greece; a Grecian; 2, the language of ancient and modern Greece.

green (grēn), *n.* 1, the color of growing grass or plants; a color between, or composed of, blue and yellow; 2, a grass plot or common; 3, a golf course, esp. the closely cut square of grass around any one of the holes; 4, in *pl.:* **a,** fresh or evergreen foliage cut for decorations; as, Christmas *greens;* **b,** spinach or similar vegetables:—*v.t.* and *v.i.* to make, or become, of the color of plants and grass:—*adj.* 1, having the color of, or covered with, growing grass or plants; of a color between, or composed of, blue and yellow; 2, fresh; flourishing; 3, unripe; immature, as fruit; 4, not seasoned, dried, or cured; 5, untrained; inexperienced.—*adj.* **green'ish.**—*adv.* **green'ly.**—*n.* **green'ness.**

green-back (grēn'băk''), *n.* any U. S. legal tender bank note or paper money with a green back.

green-er-y (grēn'ẽr-ĭ), *n.* [*pl.* greeneries (-ĭz)], 1, verdure; a verdant clump or mass of plants; 2, a place where green things are grown.

green-finch (grēn'fĭnch''), *n.* a common finch of Europe, having olive green and yellow feathers; the Texas sparrow.

green-gage (grēn'gāj''), *n.* a green-fleshed plum of fine flavor.

green-gro-cer (grēn'grō''sẽr), *n.* a retailer of fresh vegetables and fruit.—*n.* **green'gro''cer-y.**

green-horn (grēn'hôrn''), *n.* a simpleton; an inexperienced person.

green-house (grēn'hous''), *n.* a conservatory or glass house for the cultivation of tender flowers and plants.

green-ing (grēn'ĭng), *n.* 1, the act of turning green or becoming green; 2, any of several green-skinned apples.

green-room (grēn'ro͞om''), *n.* the actors' retiring room in a theater.

green-sward (grēn'swôrd''), *n.* turf well covered with grass.

green-wood (grēn'wo͝od''), *n.* a forest in full leaf.

[1]**greet** (grēt), *v.t.* **1**, to salute verbally; accost; welcome; receive in friendly fashion; **2**, to appear or be presented to; as, a sight *greeted* our eyes:—*v.i.* to exchange salutations.

[2]**greet** (grēt), *v.i.* in England and Scotland, to weep; mourn:—*n.* weeping.

greet-ing (grēt′ĭng), *n.* salutation; welcome; compliment.

gre-ga-ri-ous (grē-gā′rĭ-ŭs), *adj.* associating or going together in herds or companies.—*adv.* **gre-ga′ri-ous-ly.** —*n.* **gre-ga′ri-ous-ness.**

Gre-go-ri-an (grē-gō′rĭ-ăn), *adj.* pertaining to one named Gregory: **Gregorian calendar,** the system of reckoning time introduced by Pope Gregory XIII in 1582: now in use in all Christian countries, including Russia since 1918: **Gregorian chant,** one of a collection of psalm tones compiled by Pope Gregory I (the Great), about 590: an important part of the Roman Catholic ritual: also called *Gregorian tone.*

gre-nade (grē-nād′), *n.* **1**, an explosive shell fired by a fuse and usually thrown by hand; **2**, a flask or bottle containing chemicals to be thrown and burst, for putting out fires, scattering fumes, etc.: **rifle grenade,** a grenade fired from a rifle.

gren-a-dier (grĕn″*à*-dēr′), *n.* **1**, orig., a foot soldier of England who threw grenades; **2**, now, one of the British infantry regiment called *Grenadier Guards.*

[1]**gren-a-dine** (grĕn′*à*-dēn), *n.* a thin, gauzelike dress fabric of silk or silk and wool.

[2]**gren-a-dine** (grĕn′*à*-dēn), *n.* a dish of fillets of veal or poultry, trimmed and larded.

gres-so-ri-al (grĕ-sō′rĭ-ăl), *adj.* adapted for walking, as the feet of a barnyard fowl. Also, **gres-so′ri-ous.**

Gret-na Green (grĕt′n*à*), a village in Scotland just across the border, where, formerly, English runaway couples went to be married.

grew-some (grōō′sŭm), *adj.* repulsive. See **grue′some,** *Pfd. S.*

grey (grā), *adj.* **1**, of a color composed of white mixed with black; **2**, old:—*n.* a color resulting from mixing white with black: —*v.t.* to cause to whiten:—*v.i.* to become whitened, as with age. See **gray,** *Pfd. S.*— *adv.* **grey′ly.**—*n.* **grey′ness.**

grey-beard (grā′bērd″), *n.* an old man. Also, **gray′beard″,** *Pfd. S.*

grey-hound (grā′hound″), *n.* a slender, swift dog with keen sight: sometimes, incorrectly, *grayhound.*

grey-ling (grā′lĭng), *n.* an edible freshwater fish allied to the trout. Also, **gray′ling,** *Pfd. S.*

grid (grĭd), *n.* **1**, a grating of parallel bars; **2**, a gridiron; **3**, an electrode, or electric pole, placed between the filament and plate of an electron tube and controlling the current between plate and filament: **grid leak,** in radio, a resistance connected to the grid of an electron tube, usually in parallel with a blocking condenser, to lead off the grid charge.

grid-dle (grĭd′l), *n.* a metal plate used for cooking hot cakes.

grid-dle-cake (grĭd′l-kāk″), *n.* a thin batter cake, baked on a griddle; a flapjack.

gride (grīd), *v.t.* [*p.t.* and *p.p.* grid′ed, *p.pr.* grid′ing], to grind harshly; jar; grate:—*v.i.* to make a grinding sound; grate.

grid-i-ron (grĭd′ī″ûrn), *n.* **1**, a grated iron utensil for broiling meat or fish; **2**, a football field.

grief (grēf), *n.* **1**, sorrow on account of present or past trouble; **2**, that which causes sorrow or sadness; affliction; **3**, a mishap; as, to come to *grief.*
Syn. tribulation, suffering, woe.

griev-ance (grēv′ăns), *n.* **1**, a sense of wrong or oppression; **2**, a ground of complaint or cause of annoyance.
Syn. injury, wrong.

grieve (grēv), *v.t.* [*p.t.* and *p.p.* grieved (grēvd), *p.pr.* griev′ing], to cause to experience grief; afflict mentally:—*v.i.* to be in sorrow; lament; as, she *grieved* over her loss.
Syn. mourn, sorrow.

griev-ous (grēv′ŭs), *adj.* **1**, causing sadness or sorrow; **2**, hard to be borne; painful; oppressive; as, a *grievous* burden; **3**, atrocious, as a sin.—*adv.* **griev′ous-ly.**—*n.* **griev′ous-ness.**

grif-fin (grĭf′ĭn), *n.* **1**, a fabled animal with the body and legs of a lion, the wings and beak of an eagle, and with pricked ears; **2**, a careful watcher. Also, **grif′fon.**

GRIFFIN

grig (grĭg), *n.* a lively person; as, the clown was a merry *grig.*

grill (grĭl), *n.* **1**, a gridiron; also, a small portable stove for quick cooking; **2**, that which is broiled on a gridiron; **3**, a room in a hotel or restaurant, also called *grillroom,* where broiled meats, promptly served, are a specialty:—*v.t.* **1**, to broil; as, I am going to *grill* this meat; **2**, to subject to severe examination, as a criminal:— *v.i.* to undergo broiling; broil.

GRILLE

grille (grĭl), *n.* a grating, esp. one which is made of slender metal bars.

grim (grĭm), *adj.* [*comp.* grim′mer, *superl.* grim′mest], **1**, of a forbidding aspect; stern and surly; **2**, hideous; **3**, cruel; unyielding.—*adv.* **grim′ly.**—*n.* **grim′ness.**
Syn. relentless, terrible, fierce.—*Ant.* benign, merciful, kind.

gri-mace (grĭ-măs′), *n.* a twisting of the countenance; smirk; look of affectation:—*v.i.* [*p.t.* and *p.p.* -maced′ (-măst′), *p.pr.* -mac′ing], to make faces.

gri-mal-kin (grĭ-măl′kĭn; grĭ-môl′kĭn), *n.* an old female cat; also, a malicious old woman.

grime (grīm), *n.* foul matter; dirt deeply ingrained, or rubbed in:—*v.t.* [*p.t.* and *p.p.* grimed (grīmd), *p.pr.* grim′ing], to make dirty or grimy.

grim-y (grīm′ĭ), *adj.* [*comp.* grim′i-er, *superl.* grim′i-est], much soiled; with dirt ground in.—*adv.* **grim′i-ly.**—*n.* **grim′i-ness.**

grin (grĭn), *n.* the act of showing the teeth in laughter, scorn, pain, etc.; a broad smile:—*v.i.* [*p.t.* and *p.p.* grinned (grĭnd), *p.pr.* grin′ning], to show the teeth in laughter, scorn, or pain:—*v.t.* to express with a grin; as, he *grinned* his pleasure.

grind (grīnd), *v.t.* [*p.t.* and *p.p.* ground (ground), *p.pr.* grind′ing], **1**, to make into powder by friction; as, to *grind* flour; **2**, to sharpen or smooth by friction; as, to *grind* a knife; **3**, to grate or rub together, as the teeth; **4**, to oppress; harass; **5**, to turn the crank of, as a hand organ or the like:—*v.i.* **1**, to sharpen or polish something, or to make something into powder, by friction; **2**, to be grated or rubbed together; **3**, *Slang*, to study hard:—*n.* **1**, the act of sharpening, polishing, or making into powder; **2**, a grating or rubbing together; **3**, the turning of a crank; **4**, hard study, as for an examination; laborious and tedious work; **5**, wearisome routine; as, the daily *grind*; **6**, *Slang*, a student who studies laboriously.—*n.* **grind'er-y.**

grind-er (grīn'dẽr), *n.* **1**, that which sharpens or makes into powder, as a millstone; **2**, a molar tooth; **3**, a person who turns the crank of a machine.

grind-stone (grīnd'stōn''), *n.* a flat, circular stone turning on an axle: used for sharpening tools.

grip (grĭp), *n.* **1**, a grasp with the hand; a holding fast; **2**, that by which anything is held firmly; **3**, a particular mode of grasping the hand, as among Freemasons; **4**, a mechanical device for holding something; **5**, mental or physical mastery; as, he had a good *grip* on the situation; **6**, *Colloq.*, a valise; **7**, (also *grippe*), a disease like a bad cold with a fever; influenza:—*v.t.* [*p.t.* and *p.p.* gripped (grĭpt), *p.pr.* grip'ping], to grasp; seize:—*v.i.* to take fast hold.—*n.* **grip'per.**

gripe (grīp), *v.t.* [*p.t.* and *p.p.* griped (grīpt), *p.pr.* grip'ing], **1**, to hold with closed fingers; grasp; hold tightly; **2**, to cause pain in the bowels of; **3**, to seize; clutch; oppress; pinch:—*v.i.* to cause colic pains:—*Colloq.*, to find fault:—*n.* **1**, a clasping with the hand or arms; a twisting squeeze; **2**, a sharp intestinal pain; **3**, distress; oppression; **4**, in *pl.*, colic; **5**, *Colloq.*, an unpleasant mood.

grippe (grĭp), *n.* influenza; a feverish cold. Also, **grip**, *Pfd. S.*

grip-ping (grĭp'pĭng), *adj.* intense; holding one's interest strongly, as with books or music.

grip-sack (grĭp'săk''), *n. Colloq.*, in the U. S., a traveler's valise, or large hand bag: also called *grip*.

[1]gris-ly (grĭz'lĭ), *adj.* [*comp.* gris'li-er, *superl.* gris'li-est], terrible; wild; hideous.—*n.* **gris'li-ness.**

Syn. grim, gruesome, ghastly, horrible.

[2]gris-ly (grĭz'lĭ), *adj.* [*comp.* gris'li-er, *superl.* gris'li-est], somewhat gray. Also, **griz'zly**, *Pfd. S.*

grist (grĭst), *n.* **1**, grain for grinding; ground corn; **2**, provision or supply.

gris-tle (grĭs'l), *n.* cartilage; clear, elastic tissue.—*adj.* **gris'tly** (grĭs'lĭ).

grist-mill (grĭst'mĭl''), *n.* a mill for grinding grain.

grit (grĭt), *n.* **1**, rough, hard particles, as sand, etc.; **2**, a hard, coarse-grained sandstone; **3**, firmness of character; courage: —*v.i.* [*p.t.* and *p.p.* grit'ted, *p.pr.* grit'ting], to give forth a grating sound:—*v.t.* to grind; grate; as, to *grit* the teeth.

grits (grĭts), *n.pl.* a breakfast food of grain, esp. oats, wheat, or corn, hulled and sometimes coarsely ground.

grit-ty (grĭt'ĭ), *adj.* [*comp.* grit'ti-er, *superl.* grit'ti-est], **1**, containing, or like, sand; granular; **2**, plucky.—*n.* **grit'ti-ness.**

griz-zle (grĭz'l), *n.* a mixture of white and black; a gray color:—*v.t.* and *v.i.* [*p.t.* and *p.p.* -zled (-ld), *p.pr.* -zling], to turn gray.—*p.adj.* **griz'zled.**

griz-zly (grĭz'lĭ), *n.* [*pl.* grizzlies (-lĭz)], a large, fierce bear of North America: also called *grizzly bear*:—*adj.* [*comp.* griz'zli-er, *superl.* griz'zli-est], somewhat gray. Also, **gris'ly.**

groan (grōn), *n.* **1**, a low, deep sound uttered in pain or sorrow; **2**, a deep, rumbling sound expressive of disapprobation or ridicule; as, his speech was received with *groans* and hisses; **3**, a low, dismal sound, as of the wind:—*v.i.* **1**, to utter a deep sound of pain or sorrow; **2**, to creak; as, the door *groaned* on its hinges; **3**, to be oppressed; as, he *groaned* under heavy taxes: —*v.t.* to express by low, moaning sounds; as, he *groaned* out his wish.

groat (grōt; grôt), *n.* **1**, formerly, an English silver coin, in value four pence, or eight cents; **2**, any trifling sum.

groats (grōts; grôts), *n.pl.* oats or wheat hulled and crushed.

gro-cer (grō'sẽr), *n.* one who sells articles of food such as tea, sugar, etc.

gro-cer-y (grō'sẽr-ĭ), *n.* [*pl.* groceries (-ĭz)], **1**, in the U. S., a grocer's shop; **2**, in *pl.*, food supplies such as tea, sugar, coffee, spices, etc.

gro-ce-te-ri-a (grō''sē-tē'rĭ-ȧ), *n.* in the U. S., a grocery store where the customers pick out what they want and pay as they leave: a trade name.

grog (grŏg), *n.* an unsweetened mixture of spirits and water; spirituous liquor.

grog-gy (grŏg'ĭ), *adj.* [*comp.* grog'gi-er, *superl.* grog'gi-est], **1**, tipsy; **2**, moving with an unsteady gait; staggering as if dazed.—*n.* **grog'gi-ness.**

grog-ram (grŏg'răm), *n.* a coarse fabric of silk or mohair, or of silk and mohair, often stiffened by the use of gum: formerly called *grogran*.

grog-shop (grŏg'shŏp''), *n.* a saloon; barroom; drinking place.

groin (groin), *n.* **1**, the depressed part of the human body between the thigh and the belly; **2**, the curved ridge made by the intersection of two arches:—*v.t.* to build or form into such ridges; as, to *groin* a roof.

grom-met (grŏm'ĕt), *n.* **1**, a kind of metal eyelet in cloth, leather, etc.; **2**, a wad of rope, formerly used to hold a cannon ball in place; **3**, on shipboard, a ring formed of ropes. Also, **grom'et.**

groom (groom), *n.* **1**, a man or boy who has charge of horses; **2**, a man recently married or about to be married; **3**, one of several officers of a royal household:—*v.t.* **1**, to feed, curry, and brush, as a horse; **2**, to equip or dress; as, a well-*groomed* woman; **3**, to prepare; as, to *groom* a man for office.

grooms-man (groomz'măn), *n.* [*pl.* groomsmen (-mĕn)], one who attends a bridegroom; a best man.

groove (groov), *n.* **1**, a channel or furrow, esp. as cut by a tool; as, the plate sits in the *groove* on the rack; **2**, settled habit or routine:—*v.t.* [*p.t.* and *p.p.* grooved (groovd), *p.pr.* groov'ing], to form or cut a furrow in.

grope (grōp), *v.i.* [*p.t.* and *p.p.* groped (grōpt), *p.pr.* grop'ing], to feel one's way with the hands, as in the dark:—*v.t.* to search out, as in the dark, by feeling with the hands: used with *for*.—*n.* **grop'er.**

gros-beak (grōs'bēk''), *n.* any of various large-beaked song birds, related to the finches.

gros-grain (grō'grān''), *adj.* having a heavy cord, as silk:—*n.* a stout double-corded silk with little luster.

gross (grōs), *adj.* **1**, bulky; thick; coarse; **2**, rude; indelicate; **3**, flagrant; as, *gross* errors; **4**, heavy; corpulent; **5**, dull; dense; **6**, whole; total; as, *gross* income: distinguished from *net*:—*n.* **1**, twelve dozen; **2**, entire amount: often with *in* or *in the*; as, in the *gross*: **gross ton**, 2,240 pounds.—*adv.* **gross'ly.**—*n.* **gross'ness.**

Syn., *adj.* outrageous, unseemly, shameful.

grot (grŏt), *n. Poetic*, a grotto or cavern; a cave, natural or artificial.

gro-tesque (grō-tĕsk′), *n.* whimsical ornamentation, figures, or scenery; the incongruous or uncouth in art:—*adj.* fantastically or oddly formed; extravagant; whimsical; ridiculous.—*adv.* **gro-tesque′ly.**—*n.* **gro-tesque′ness.**
Syn., adj. bizarre, absurd, fanciful, comical.

grot-to (grŏt′ō), *n.* [*pl.* grottoes; grottos (-ōz)], a picturesque, natural or artificial cave or cavern in the earth.

grouch (grouch), *n. Slang,* **1,** a fit of ill temper; **2,** one who indulges in fits of ill temper:—*v.i. Slang,* to feel surly; complain.—*adj.* **grouch′y.**—*n.* **grouch′i-ness.**

[1]**ground** (ground), past tense and past participle of the verb *grind.*

[2]**ground** (ground), *n.* **1,** the earth or soil; **2,** the surface of a floor or pavement; **3,** land put to special use; as, hunting *ground;* **4,** distance or area on a surface; as, to gain *ground;* **5,** foundation; cause or reason; as, the *ground* for a belief; **6,** fundamental or preparatory part of an undertaking; as, to prepare the *ground;* **7,** in painting, a first surface coat of neutral color; also, a neutral background or undecorated part; **8,** in *pl.:* **a,** a country estate; lawns and gardens about a house; **b,** dregs or sediment, as of coffee; **9,** in electricity, the earth when employed as a return conductor; also, the contact of a conductor with the earth: **ground water,** water in the ground; esp., water near the surface, which may flow into a well or spring:—*v.t.* **1,** to fix firmly; establish; as, to *ground* a government on proper principles; **2,** to place or run in or on the earth; as, to *ground* a vessel on the beach; **3,** to teach the first principles to; as, to *ground* a pupil in Latin; **4,** in electricity, to connect, as a wire making part of a circuit, to the earth or other conductor by which the circuit can be completed:—*v.i.* to run on to land: said of vessels:—*adj.* **1,** fundamental; **2,** on or near the earth; as, *ground* ivy; *ground* floor.

ground floor that floor of a building which is built on or slightly above the ground.

ground hog a burrowing rodent akin to the beaver, rat, etc.

ground-less (ground′lĕs), *adj.* without foundation; without reason.

ground-ling (ground′lĭng), *n.* **1,** one who or that which lives on the earth or ground; **2,** a fish that keeps at the bottom of the water; **3,** formerly, a spectator who stood in the pit of a theater; hence, one of the crowd; a person of inferior tastes.

ground-nut (ground′nŭt″), *n.* **1,** any of various plants having seeds borne underground, as the peanut; **2,** the edible tuber of such a plant.

ground plan the floor plan of a building.

[1]**ground-sel** (ground′sĕl), *n.* a timber or beam used in a foundation; a doorsill. Also, **ground′sill.**

[2]**ground-sel** (ground′sĕl; *Colloq.,* ground′-sl), *n.* any of several weeds of the composite family, having yellow flowers.

ground swell a heavy rolling of the sea, caused by some disturbance, such as a storm or an earthquake.

ground-work (ground′wûrk″), *n.* foundation; fundamentals.

group (gro͞op), *n.* **1,** a small crowd or assemblage; a cluster; as, a *group* of houses; **2,** a collection of figures or objects forming an artistic whole; **3,** a division of organisms with certain characteristics; **4,** the chief division of a geological system; **5,** a number of persons holding common views; as, the radical *group:*—*v.t.* to form into a collection or class:—*v.i.* to combine into a class.

[1]**grouse** (grous), *n.* [*pl.* grouse], any of several rather large-bodied, dull-colored game birds allied to the partridges and pheasants.

[2]**grouse** (gro͞os), *v.i.* [*p.t.* and *p.p.* groused (gro͞ost), *p.pr.* grous′ing], *Slang,* to grumble in a good-natured way.

grout (grout), *n.* **1,** thin mortar or cement mixed with gravel, used for foundations and joints of masonry; **2,** a fine plaster for ceilings:—*v.t.* to surround or fill in with such cement.

grout-y (grout′ĭ), *adj. Slang,* cross; sulky; as, a *grouty* disposition.

grove (grōv), *n.* a small wood; a group of trees without undergrowth.

grov-el (grŏv′l), *v.i.* **1,** to lie prone; move with the body flat on the ground; **2,** to be mean or debased.—*n.* **grov′el-er**
Syn. crawl, cringe, fawn, sneak.

grow (grō), *v.t.* [*p.t.* grew (gro͞o), *p.p.* grown (grōn), *p.pr.* grow′ing], to produce by cultivation:—*v.i.* **1,** to increase by natural development; as, some children *grow* rapidly; **2,** to arise naturally; as, moss *grows* in damp places; **3,** to flourish; as, a well-tended business *grows;* **4,** to change by degrees; as, to *grow* quiet; **5,** to gain in favor: with *upon;* as, the book *grows* upon one; **6,** to adhere; as, to *grow* fast to the wall.—*n.* **grow′er.**

growl (groul), *n.* **1,** a deep, angry snarl, as made by a dog; **2,** an angry, muttered complaint:—*v.i.* **1,** to snarl like a dog; **2,** to find fault in a surly tone:—*v.t.* to say in an angry, muttering way.—*n.* **growl′er.**

grown (grōn), past participle of the irregular verb *grow:* **grown-up,** *adj.* mature: **grown-ups,** *n.pl.* adults.

growth (grōth), *n.* **1,** the progressive increase of animal or vegetable bodies; **2,** advancement; increase; **3,** that which is produced; result.

grub (grŭb), *v.t.* [*p.t.* and *p.p.* grubbed (grŭbd), *p.pr.* grub′bing], to dig up; root out of the ground, as stumps:—*v.i.* **1,** to dig in the earth; **2,** to drudge or toil; **3,** *Slang,* to eat:—*n.* **1,** the larva or egg of an insect; **2,** a slovenly person; **3,** a drudge; **4,** *Slang,* food.

grub-ber (grŭb′ẽr), *n.* one who or that which digs; esp., a machine or tool that works like an ax in digging up roots of trees, stumps, etc.

grub-bing hoe a mattock: a tool with a heavy metal head and a blade for digging into the ground.

grudge (grŭj), *n.* secret malice or ill will; as, to hold a *grudge:*—*v.t.* [*p.t.* and *p.p.* grudged (grŭjd), *p.pr.* grudg′ing], to envy the ownership of; grant with reluctance; begrudge; as, his enemy *grudged* him any word of praise.—*adv.* **grudg′ing-ly.**
Syn., n. spite, hatred. (See malice.)

gru-el (gro͞o′ĕl), *n.* a light, semisolid food made of oatmeal, etc., for invalids.

grue-some (gro͞o′sŭm), *adj.* horrible of aspect; ugly; frightful; as, a *gruesome* warning. Also, **grew′some.**—*adv.* **grue′some-ly.**—*n.* **grue′some-ness.**
Syn. ghastly, hideous, repulsive.

gruff (grŭf), *adj.* rough or surly; harsh; hoarse.—*adv.* **gruff′ly.**—*n.* **gruff′ness.**
Syn. blunt, rude, bearish.

grum-ble (grŭm′bl), *n.* **1,** a surly speech; **2,** a complaint:—*v.i.* and *v.t.* [*p.t.* and *p.p.* -bled (-bld), *p.pr.* -bling], to murmur discontentedly; growl.—*n.* **grum′-bler.**—*adv.* **grum′bling-ly.**

grump-y (grŭm′pĭ), *adj.* [*comp.* grump′i-er, *superl.* grump′i-est], surly; dissatisfied.—*adv.* **grump′i-ly.**—*n.* **grump′i-ness.**

Grun-dy, Mrs. (grŭn′dĭ), *n.* a prudish character symbolical of those who insist upon the strict proprieties.

grunt (grŭnt), *n.* **1**, the guttural noise of a hog: **2**, any of various edible marine fishes:—*v.t.* to utter with a guttural sound:—*v.i.* to make a noise like a hog.—*n.* **grunt'er.**

gua-no (gwä'nō), *n.* [*pl* guanos (-nōz)], the solidified excrement of sea fowls: used as a fertilizer.

guar-an-tee (găr"ăn-tē'), *n.* **1**, anything that assures the occurrence or maintenance of something; as, good will is a *guarantee* of peace; **2**, a solemn statement that something is as represented; as, he gave his *guarantee* that the stuff was all wool; **3**, in law: **a**, a promise made by a third person to secure the fulfilment of an agreement or the payment of a debt, etc., by another; **b**, one who becomes surety for the performance of another's promises; **c**, property pledged as security for the performance of promises:—*v.t.* [*p.t.* and *p.p.* -teed' (-tēd'), *p.pr.* -tee'ing], **1**, to make sure of, as a result; **2**, in law: **a**, to undertake that another shall perform a certain stipulation or agreement; warrant; **b**, to be responsible for.

guar-an-tor (găr'ăn-tôr"), *n.* one who becomes surety for the performance of obligations or promises of another.

guar-an-ty (găr'ăn-tĭ), *n.* [*pl.* guaranties (-tĭz)], **1**, an undertaking to answer for the payment of some debt, or the performance of some obligation, by another; a legal guarantee; **2**, property pledged as security for the performance of an agreement; surety:—*v.t.* [*p.t.* and *p.p.* -tied (-tĭd), *p.pr.* -ty-ing], **1**, to warrant; **2**, to be responsible for (the performance of another's obligation). Also, **guar"an-tee'.**

guard (gärd), *v.t.* **1**, to watch over or protect; preserve by caution; shield or defend; **2**, to prevent from escaping:—*v.i.* to watch; be cautious: with *against*:—*n.* **1**, security or defense against injury or attack; **2**, a state of watchfulness or caution; attention; as, be on *guard;* **3**, a position of defense in fencing; **4**, any contrivance or device for security; as, a mud *guard;* a *guard* on a sword hilt; **5**, a man or body of men employed for defense or control; **6**, in England, an official in charge of a train; conductor; **7**, in football, one of two players in the line, stationed one on each side of the center.

Syn., v. shelter, restrain. (See defend.)

guard-ed (gärd'ĕd), *p.adj.* **1**, defended; **2**, careful; cautious; as, a *guarded* answer; **3**, circumspect.—*adv.* **guard'-ed-ly.**—*n.* **guard'ed-ness.**

guard-house (gärd'hous"), *n.* **1**, a military jail; **2**, a house occupied by guards, as police or soldiers.

guard-i-an (gär'dĭ-ăn), *n.* **1**, one who legally has the care of the person or property of another; a warden; **2**, one who or that which protects anything, as from harm or attack:—*adj.* protecting.—*n.* **guard'i-an-ship".**

guard-room (gärd'rōōm"), *n.* **1**, the room occupied by a military guard during its term on duty; **2**, a place of imprisonment for soldiers.

guard ship a warship stationed at a port or harbor for its protection.

guards-man (gärdz'măn), *n.* [*pl.* guardsmen (-mĕn)], **1**, a man employed for defense or watching; **2**, an officer or soldier of any military body termed *Guards.*

gua-va (gwä'vȧ), *n.* a tree of South America, yielding a pear-shaped fruit from which a jelly is made.

gu-ber-na-to-ri-al (gū"bẽr-nȧ-tō'rĭ-ăl), *adj.* pertaining to a governor or to his office.

[1]**gud-geon** (gŭj'ŭn), *n.* **1**, a small, European fresh-water carp, easily caught and used as bait; **2**, a person easily imposed upon; **3**, anything easily secured.

[2]**gud-geon** (gŭj'ŭn), *n.* **1**, an iron pin or shaft on which a wheel revolves; **2**, a socket or ring receiving a pin that turns, as the ring or eye of a hinge.

Gud-run (gōōd'rōōn), *n.* **1**, in Norse mythology, the daughter of the king of the Nibelungs and wife of Sigurd, whom she took away from her rival, Brunhild, by a magic drink; **2**, in Teutonic mythology, a maiden who was carried off to Normandy, and rescued by her lover and her brother.

guer-don (gûr'dŭn), *n.* a reward for deeds of courage; recompense; merit.

Guern-sey (gûrn'zĭ), *adj.* designating a breed of dairy cattle from Guernsey, one of the Channel Islands:—*n.* an animal of this breed: **guernsey**, a close-fitting, knitted woolen shirt.

guer-ril-la (gĕ-rĭl'ȧ), *n.* one of an irregular force engaged in harassing an enemy in small bands:—*adj.* **1**, pertaining to, or consisting of, bandits or men engaged in irregular warfare; **2**, carrying on irregular warfare. Also, **gue-ril'la.**

guess (gĕs), *n.* **1**, a hasty or chance conclusion; an opinion formed without sufficient or real evidence; surmise; **2**, the act of forming such an opinion:—*v.t.* **1**, to hit upon, or judge of, at random; **2**, to solve by surmising, as a riddle; **3**, *Colloq.*, to believe or think:—*v.i.* to form an opinion without sound reason for it.—*n.* **guess'er.**

guess-work (gĕs'wûrk"), *n.* **1**, random opinion, formed without sufficient reason; **2**, the practice of guessing; also, guesses collectively.

guest (gĕst), *n.* **1**, one who is entertained at the house or table of another; a visitor; **2**, a lodger or boarder, as at a hotel.

guf-faw (gŭ-fô'), *n.* a rude or loud burst of coarse laughter.

guid-ance (gīd'ăns), *n.* direction; leadership; supervision.

guide (gīd), *n.* **1**, one who or that which directs; **2**, a conductor; director; that by which one directs his course; a guidebook; **3**, a standard; as, conscience is a good *guide;* **4**, a soldier who sets the pace and indicates the route for his detail:—*v.t.* [*p.t.* and *p.p.* guid'ed, *p.pr.* guid'ing], to lead or direct; influence; regulate; govern by counsel.—*adj.* **guid'a-ble.**—*n.* **guid'er.**

Syn., v. conduct, pilot.

guide-board (gīd'bōrd"), *n.* a board usually placed where roads meet or cross, with directions for travelers.

guide-book (gīd'bōōk"), *n.* a book of information for travelers.

guide-post (gīd'pōst"), *n.* a post which bears a board containing directions for travelers.

gui-don (gī'dŭn), *n.* a small flag serving as a standard for a single company of troops; also, the one who carries it.

guild (gĭld), *n.* **1**, a fraternity; **2**, a trade association. Also, **gild.**

guil-der (gĭl'dẽr), *n.* a Dutch silver coin, worth about 40 cents; a gulden.

guild-hall (gĭld'hôl"), *n.* the meeting place of a guild or an association.

guile (gīl), *n.* deceit; cunning; duplicity; fraud.—*adj.* **guile'ful.**—*adv.* **guile'-ful-ly.**—*n.* **guile'ful-ness.**

guile-less (gīl'lĕs), *adj.* free from guile; artless; innocent; frank.—*adv.* **guile'less-ly.**—*n.* **guile'less-ness.**

Syn. open, straightforward, honest.

guil-lo-tine (gĭl'ō-tēn), *n.* **1**, an apparatus for beheading a criminal by means of a heavy knife sliding in two upright grooves; **2**, a paper-cutting machine:—*v.t.*

(gĭl″lō-tēn′), [*p.t.* and *p.p.* -tined′ (-tēnd′), *p.pr.* -tin′ing], to behead with a guillotine.

guilt (gĭlt), *n.* the act or state of one who has sinned, or who is liable to a penalty for crime.—*adj.* **guilt′less.**

guilt-y (gĭl′tĭ), *adj.* [*comp.* guilt′i-er, *superl.* guilt′i-est], **1,** justly chargeable with, or responsible for, a crime; wicked; criminal; **2,** conscious of wrong; not innocent; as, a *guilty* look; a *guilty* feeling.—*adv.* **guilt′i-ly.**—*n.* **guilt′i-ness.**

Syn. culpable, sinful, delinquent.

guin-ea (gĭn′ĭ), *n.* a gold coin, formerly current in England, of the value of 21 shillings, or about $5.00.

guin-ea fowl a grayish blue bird with white spots, orig. from Guinea: also called *guinea* and *guinea hen.*

guin-ea pig a small, tame, South American rodent, usually white with spots of orange and black.

Guin-e-vere (gwĭn′ē-vēr), *n.* in Arthurian romances, the queen of King Arthur, whose guilty love for Lancelot brought destruction to the Round Table. Also, **Guin′e-ver** (gwĭn′ē-vẽr).

guise (gīz), *n.* external appearance; dress; manner; garb.

gui-tar (gĭ-tär′), *n.* a six-stringed instrument of the lute class, played with the fingers.

GUITAR

gulch (gŭlch), *n.* in the western U. S., a narrow, rocky valley; a gully.

gul-den (go͝ol′dĕn), *n.* **1,** the Dutch monetary unit, worth 40.2 cents; also, a silver coin of this value; **2,** the Austrian florin, worth 48.2 cents.

gulf (gŭlf), *n.* **1,** an arm of the sea extending into the land, larger in size than a bay; **2,** a deep place in the earth; an abyss; **3,** a whirlpool; **4,** an impassable chasm or separation.

Gulf Stream an important warm ocean current flowing out from the Gulf of Mexico, northward along the American coast, and across the Atlantic.

gulf-weed (gŭlf′wēd″), *n.* a floating seaweed, with round air vessels, found in the Gulf Stream.

[1]**gull** (gŭl), *n.* any of several web-footed sea birds, white, gray, or marked with black, as the herring gull; also, any of various allied sea birds, as the terns.

[2]**gull** (gŭl), *v.t.* to cheat; impose upon; outwit:—*n.* **1,** one easily deceived, as by a tale; a dupe; **2,** a trick; a cheat.

gul-let (gŭl′ĕt), *n.* **1,** the esophagus, or tube by which food and drink are carried from the mouth to the stomach; loosely, the throat; **2,** any similar channel.

gul-li-ble (gŭl′ĭ-bl), *adj.* capable of being easily deceived; credulous.—*n.* **gul″li-bil′i-ty.**

gul-ly (gŭl′ĭ), *n.* [*pl.* gullies (-ĭz)], a channel worn by water; narrow ravine:—*v.t.* [*p.t.* and *p.p.* -lied (-ĭd), *p.pr.* -ly-ing], to wear channels in, as by heavy rains.

gulp (gŭlp), *v.t.* to swallow eagerly or in large drafts:—*n.* **1,** the act of swallowing in large drafts; **2,** a large swallow.—*n.* **gulp′er.**

[2]**gum** (gŭm), *n.* the soft, fibrous tissue covering that part of the jawbones in which the teeth are embedded.

[1]**gum** (gŭm), *n.* **1,** a semitransparent vegetable substance that comes out of certain trees and shrubs and hardens on the surface; as, *gum* arabic; **2,** India rubber; **3,** in the U. S., a preparation of some cohesive substance, used for chewing; **4,** a gum tree; **5,** in *pl.*, *Colloq.*, overshoes:—*v.t.* [*p.t.* and *p.p.* gummed (gŭmd), *p.pr.* gum′ming], to smear or fasten with mucilage:—*v.i.* to become stiff or sticky.—*n.* **gum′mer.**

gum ar-a-bic (ăr′ȧ-bĭk), a gum obtained from certain species of acacia, used as an adhesive, in medicine, etc.

gum-bo (gŭm′bō), *n.* [*pl.* gumbos (-bōz)], **1,** a southern plant of the mallow family, bearing edible pods; the okra; **2,** a soup containing okra; **3,** in the western U. S., a kind of sticky prairie mud.

gum-boil (gŭm′boil″), *n.* a small abscess on the gums of the mouth.

gum-drop (gŭm′drŏp″), *n.* a candy made of vegetable gum or gelatin.

gum-my (gŭm′ĭ), *adj.* [*comp.* gum′mi-er, *superl.* gum′mi-est], like gum; covered or filled with a sticky substance; sticky.—*n.* **gum′mi-ness.**

gump-tion (gŭmp′shŭn), *n.* *Colloq.*, **1,** quickness of perception; common sense; **2,** energy; zest.

gum tree **1,** the black gum tree of the dogwood family; **2,** the sweet gum, a smaller tree of the witch-hazel family.

gun (gŭn), *n.* **1,** a weapon for discharging shot through a tube by the force of an explosive, as a rifle, pistol, or revolver; also, such a discharge as a salute or signal; **2,** any device resembling a gun:—*v.i.* [*p.t.* and *p.p.* gunned (gŭnd), *p.pr.* gun′ning], to shoot, or hunt, with such a weapon.

gun-boat (gŭn′bōt″), *n.* a warship of light draft, less in size than a cruiser.

gun-cot-ton (gŭn′kŏt″n), *n.* a highly explosive substance formed by the action of nitric and sulphuric acid upon cotton or a similar vegetable fiber.

gun-fire (gŭn′fīr″), *n.* the discharge of a gun or of guns.

gun-lock (gŭn′lŏk″), *n.* the mechanism of a gun by which a hammer is released and the charge exploded.

gun-man (gŭn′măn), *n.* [*pl.* gunmen (-mĕn)], a man armed with a gun; esp., an armed criminal who uses a gun in assault or robbery.

gun met-al a variety of bronze, formerly much used in making cannon: **gun-metal,** *adj.* of the color of this bronze.

gun-nel (gŭn′ĕl), *n.* the upper edge of the side of a ship or vessel. Also, **gun′wale,** *Pfd. S.*

gun-ner (gŭn′ẽr), *n.* one who uses a gun or artillery; also, an officer in the navy who has charge of the ordnance.

gun-ner-y (gŭn′ẽr-ĭ), *n.* the science of artillery, or the making and using of weapons of warfare.

gun-ning (gŭn′ĭng), *n.* the shooting of game with a gun.

gun-ny (gŭn′ĭ), *n.* [*pl.* gunnies (-ĭz)], a coarse sackcloth of jute or hemp.

gun-pow-der (gŭn′pou″dẽr), *n.* an explosive substance composed of sulphur, saltpeter, and charcoal.

gun-shot (gŭn′shŏt″), *n.* the range of a gun:—*adj.* made by a gun; as, a *gunshot* wound.

gun-smith (gŭn′smĭth″), *n.* an armorer, one who repairs firearms.

gun-stock (gŭn′stŏk″), *n.* the wooden part of a firearm, on which the barrel is mounted.

Gun-ther (go͝on′tẽr), *n.* in the "Nibelungenlied," a king of Burgundy.

gun-wale (gŭn′ĕl), *n.* the upper edge of the side of a ship. Also, **gun′nel.**

gur-gle (gûr′gl), *n.* a broken, bubbling sound:—*v.i.* [*p.t.* and *p.p.* -gled (-gld), *p.pr.* -gling], to make a murmuring or bubbling sound.

gur-nard (gûr′nȧrd), *n.* any of various marine fishes having an angular head covered with bony plates.

gush (gŭsh), *n.* **1,** a sudden and violent flow of a liquid from an inclosed space; **2,** *Colloq.*, a very great display of sentiment:—*v.i.* **1,** to issue with violence and rapidity; flow abundantly; **2,** *Colloq.*, to display affection and enthusiasm in a silly, demonstrative manner:—*v.t.* to send forth copiously.—*p.adj.* **gush′ing.**—*adv.* **gush′ing-ly.**

gush-er (gŭsh′ẽr), *n.* **1,** one who makes a display of sentiment; **2,** that which pours forth violently; **3,** an oil well that has a large natural flow.

gus-set (gŭs′ĕt), *n.* a small three-cornered piece of cloth inserted in a garment to strengthen or enlarge a part.

gust (gŭst), *n.* **1,** a sudden rush of wind, often accompanied by rain or snow; **2,** a violent outburst of passion.

gus-ta-to-ry (gŭs′tȧ-tō-rĭ), *adj.* pertaining to the sense of taste.

gus-to (gŭs′tō), *n.* zest; relish; fancy; as, to play with great *gusto.*
Syn. taste, liking, fondness.

gust-y (gŭs′tĭ), *adj.* [*comp.* **gust′i-er,** *superl.* **gust′i-est**], characterized by sudden blasts of wind; stormy.—*adv.* **gust′i-ly.**

gut (gŭt), *n.* **1,** the intestinal canal; **2,** catgut; **3,** a narrow channel or strait; **4,** in *pl.*, *Slang,* spunk; courage:—*v.t.* [*p.t.* and *p.p.* gut′ted, *p.pr.* gut′ting], **1,** to extract the entrails from; **2,** to plunder, or empty entirely; destroy the inside of; as, fire *gutted* his home.

gut-ta–per-cha (gŭt″ȧ-pûr′chȧ), *n.* a substance similar to rubber, made of the juice of a tree of the Malay Archipelago; also, the tree itself.

gut-ter (gŭt′ẽr), *n.* **1,** a trough under the eaves of a building to carry off rain water; **2,** a depression at the roadside to carry off surface water; **3,** any shallow trench:—*v.t.* to cut into, or furnish with, narrow channels:—*v.i.* to become channeled, as a flickering candle.

gut-tur-al (gŭt′ŭr-ăl), *adj.* pertaining to, or formed in, the throat:—*n.* a sound formed or modified in the throat, as that of *g* or *oo* in *goose.*—*adv.* **gut′tur-al-ly.**

[1]**guy** (gī), *n.* a rope, chain, wire, or the like, to secure or to keep steady; as, the *guy* of a tent pole:—*v.t.* to hold in place or keep steady with a guy, as a tent pole.

[2]**guy** (gī), *n.* **1,** a person of queer looks or dress; **2,** *Slang,* in the U. S., a fellow:—*v.t. Colloq.*, to ridicule.

guz-zle (gŭz′l), *v.i.* and *v.t.* [*p.t.* and *p.p.* -zled (-ld), *p.pr.* -zling], to eat or drink greedily and to excess.—*n.* **guz′zler.**

gybe (jīb), *v.i.* [*p.t.* and *p.p.* gybed (jībd), *p.pr.* gyb′ing], **1,** to shift or swing from one side of a vessel to the other, as a sail, when the vessel is running before the wind; **2,** to change course, as a vessel, so that the sail gybes:—*v.t.* to cause to gybe. Also, **jibe.**

gym-na-si-um (jĭm-nā′zĭ-ŭm), *n.* [*pl.* gymnasiums (-ŭmz); gymnasia (-ȧ)], **1,** a building where athletic exercises are practiced; **2,** (*Ger.* gĭm-nä′zĭ-o͞om), in Europe, a secondary or preparatory school; **3,** in ancient Greece, a place where athletic exercises, social intercourse, and learned discussions were carried on.

gym-nast (jĭm′năst), *n.* one who is expert in physical exercises.

gym-nas-tics (jĭm-năs′tĭks), *n.pl.* bodily exercises for developing the physical powers; athletic exercises as distinguished from competitive games and sports.—*adj.* **gym-nas′tic.**

gyn-e-col-o-gy (jĭn″ē-kŏl′ō-jĭ; jī″nē-), *n.* that branch of medical science which treats of the diseases of women. Also, **gyn″æ-col′o-gy.**—*n.* **gyn″e-col′o-gist.**

gyp-sum (jĭp′sŭm), *n.* calcium sulphate, found in a compact state as alabaster: used in making plaster of Paris and, when ground to a powder, as a fertilizer.

gyp-sy (jĭp′sĭ), *n.* [*pl.* gypsies (-sĭz)], **1,** one of a wandering, dark-skinned, dark-eyed race of Eastern, probably Hindu, origin; **2,** the language of the gypsies: also called *Romany;* **3,** a person of dark complexion; **4,** a wild, adventurous girl: **gypsy moth,** a European moth, accidentally introduced into eastern New England about 1869, very destructive to tree foliage. Also, **gip′sy.**

gy-ral (jī′răl), *adj.* rotary; moving in a whirling path or way.

gy-rate (jī′rāt), *v.i.* [*p.t.* and *p.p.* -rat-ed, *p.pr.* -rat-ing], to move in a spiral; revolve.—*n.* **gy-ra′tion.**—*adj.* **gy′ra-to-ry.**

gyr-fal-con (jûr′fô″kn; jûr′fôl″kn), *n.* any of various species of falcon inhabiting northern latitudes. Also, **ger′fal″con,** *Pfd. S.*

gy-ro-scope (jī′rō-skōp), *n.* an instrument consisting of a fly-wheel so mounted that its axis can move freely in one or more directions: used to illustrate the laws of rotation, and, practically, to stabilize monorail cars, airplanes, ships, etc.—*adj.* **gy″ro-scop′ic.**

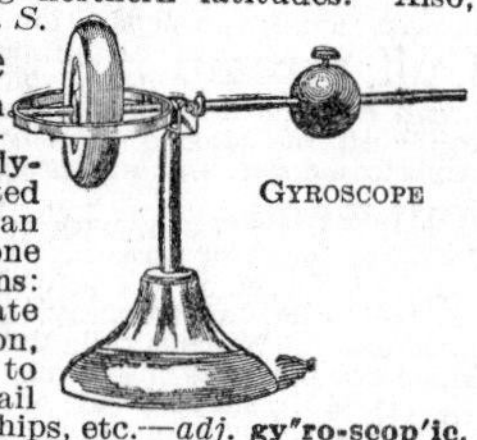

GYROSCOPE

gyve (jīv), *n.* a chain for the legs; a shackle:—*v.t.* [*p.t.* and *p.p.* gyved (jīvd), *p.pr.* gyv′ing], to fetter; chain; shackle.

H

ha (hä), *interj.* an exclamation expressing wonder, suspicion, doubt, mirth, joy, etc.

Ha-bak-kuk (hȧ-băk′ŭk; hăb′ȧ-kŭk), *n.* **1,** one of the Hebrew prophets; **2,** a book of the Old Testament recording his prophecies. Also, in the Douay Bible, **Hab′a-cuc.**—*abbr.* **Hab.**

ha-be-as cor-pus (hā′bē-ăs kôr′pŭs), a writ or order to produce a prisoner at a stated time to determine the justice of his detention.

hab-er-dash-er (hăb′ẽr-dăsh″ẽr), *n.* **1,** a dealer in small wares, as ribbons, laces, tapes, needles, etc.; **2,** in the U. S., a dealer in men's furnishings.

hab-er-dash-er-y (hăb′ẽr-dăsh″ẽr-ĭ), *n.* [*pl.* haberdasheries (-ĭz)], **1,** small supplies; notions; **2,** men's furnishings; **3,** a shop where such goods are sold.

hab-er-geon (hăb′ẽr-jŭn; hȧ-bûr′jŭn), *n.* a coat of metal covering the neck and shoulders.

ha-bil-i-ment (hȧ-bĭl′ĭ-mĕnt), *n.* **1,** an article of clothing; **2,** in *pl.*, dress in general.

hab-it (hăb′ĭt), *n.* **1,** an action so often repeated as to become a fixed characteristic; as, the *habit* of neatness; the drug *habit;* **2,** general condition or tendency; disposition; established custom; as, it is his *habit* to mock at religion; **3**, a woman's riding dress; **4**, the distinctive dress worn by members of a religious order:—*v.t.* to dress; clothe.

Syn., n. custom, routine, practice. *Habit* refers to an established tendency on the part of a person, caused by repetition; as, he has the *habit* of smoking. *Custom* implies an established manner of acting which a group as a whole follows; as, the *custom* of shaking hands. *Routine* relates to a regular round of happenings; as, office *routine* is often monotonous. *Practice* implies habitual manner of acting; as, it was his *practice* to rise early.

hab-it-a-ble (hăb'ĭt-ȧ-bl), *adj.* fit to live in comfortably.

hab-it-ant (hăb'ĭ-tănt), *n.* **1**, a dweller; permanent resident; **2**, (*Fr.* ȧ"bē"täṅ'), in Canada and Louisiana, a farmer of French descent.

hab-i-tat (hăb'ĭ-tăt), *n.* **1**, the natural abode of an animal or plant; **2**, the place where a person or thing is naturally or usually found.

hab-i-ta-tion (hăb"ĭ-tā'shŭn), *n.* **1**, a dwelling; **2**, the act of inhabiting or dwelling.

ha-bit-u-al (hȧ-bĭt'ū-ăl), *adj.* **1**, formed or acquired by use; **2**, customary; usual; regular; **3**, given to a (specified) practice; inveterate; as, a *habitual* coffee drinker.—*adv.* **ha-bit'u-al-ly.**

ha-bit-u-ate (hȧ-bĭt'ū-āt), *v.t.* [*p.t.* and *p.p.* -at"ed, *p.pr.* -at"ing], to make familiar by use or custom; accustom.

hab-i-tude (hăb'ĭ-tūd), *n.* **1**, customary manner; habit; **2**, native character; **3**, habitual association or familiarity.

ha-bit-u-é (hȧ-bĭt"ū-ā; *Fr.* ȧ"bē"tü-ā'), *n.* one who frequently visits a place, as a café or place of amusement.

ha-cien-da (ä-syĕn'dä; hä"sĭ-ĕn'dä), *n.* in Spanish America, a large plantation or ranch on which the owner resides; also, an establishment for raising stock, farm produce, etc.

1**hack** (hăk), *v.t.* **1**, to cut in notches; cut unevenly in pieces; **2**, to disfigure by cutting, crushing, or the like; injure by cutting; **3**, in football, to kick on the shins:—*v.i.* to give a short, dry cough:—*n.* **1**, a tool for cutting or notching, as a mattock; **2**, a gash made by a sharp instrument; **3**, *Colloq.*, a dry, broken cough; **4**, in sports, a kick in the shins.

2**hack** (hăk), *n.* **1**, a horse that may be hired for all sorts of labor; also, a saddle or carriage horse; **2**, a carriage which may be hired; **3**, one who hires out his services for pay, esp. in literary work; a drudge:—*v.t.* to wear out by frequent use; make stale.

3**hack** (hăk), *n.* **1**, a frame with slats or bars, as for drying fish; **2**, a row of bricks set out to dry after being molded; **3**, a board from which hawks are fed.

hack-ee (hăk'ē), *n.* the chipmunk or ground squirrel. Also, **hack'y.**

hack-le (hăk'l), *v.t.* [*p.t.* and *p.p.* -led (-ld), *p.pr.* -ling], **1**, to dress or comb, as flax or hemp; **2**, to tear into pieces; mangle in cutting:—*n.* **1**, an implement with sharp spikes for cleansing flax or hemp: also called *hatchel* or *heckle;* **2**, a long, narrow feather in the neck of a cock, used for making artificial flies for angling; **3**, a feather fly for angling.

hack-man (hăk'măn), *n.* [*pl.* hackmen (-mĕn)], the driver of a public hack or other carriage.

hack-ma-tack (hăk'mȧ-tăk"), *n.* a large, deciduous, cone-bearing tree; the tamarack, or American larch.

hack-ney (hăk'nĭ), *v.t.* **1**, to wear out by constant use; **2**, to make commonplace:—*adj.* **1**, let out for hire; **2**, common or trite:—*n.* [*pl.* hackneys (-nĭz)], **1**, a breed of horses, of average quality, used chiefly for riding or driving; **2**, a coach or hack kept for hire.

hack-ney coach in England, a licensed carriage.

hack-neyed (hăk'nĭd), *p.adj* **1**, worn out; trite; **2**, practiced.

hack saw a narrow, close-toothed saw, used for cutting metal (see *tool*, illus.). Also, *n.* **hack'saw".**

had (hăd), past tense of *have:* also used as an auxiliary in the past perfect tense: **I had rather,** I prefer to: **I had better** (go), it would be better for me (to go).

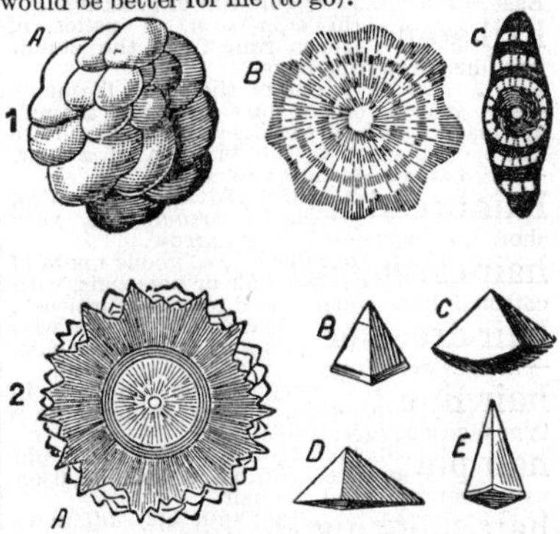

HAILSTONES

1: *A*, large hailstone, weighing over half an ounce; *B*, *C*, sections of hailstones.—2: *A*, section of hailstone with pyramids on surface; *B*, *C*, *D*, *E*, fragments of this hailstone, enlarged.

had-dock (hăd'ŭk), *n.* a North Atlantic food fish of the cod family.

Ha-des (hā'dēz), *n.* in mythology, **1**, the abode or state of the dead; **2**, the god of the underworld.

hæm-a-tite (hĕm'ȧ-tīt; hē'mȧ-), *n.* an ore of iron. *Pfd. S.*, **hem'a-tite.**

hæ-mo-glo-bin (hē"mō-glō'bĭn), *n.* the red coloring matter of the red blood corpuscles in vertebrates, having the property of combining with oxygen. Also, **he"mo-glo'bin.**

hæm-or-rhage (hĕm'ŏ-rāj), *n.* bleeding. *Pfd. S.*, **hem'or-rhage.**

hæm-or-rhoids (hĕm'ŏ-roidz), *n.pl.* painful swellings at the anus; piles. See **hem'or-rhoids**, *Pfd. S.*

haft (hăft), *n.* a handle of a tool, sword, or knife:—*v.t.* to furnish with a handle.

hag (hăg), *n.* **1**, a witch; **2**, an ugly old woman; **3**, an eel-like fish which bores into and kills other fishes.

Ha-gar (hā'gȧr), *n.* in the Bible, the maid of Abraham's wife, Sarah, whom he took as concubine and who bore **Ishmael** (Genesis 16).

Ha-gen (hä'gĕn), *n.* in the "Nibelungenlied," the murderer of Siegfried.

Hag-ga-i (hăg'ā-ī), *n.* a Hebrew prophet, or a book of the Old Testament in which his words are recorded. Also, in the Douay Bible, **Ag-ge'us** (ă-gē'ŭs).

hag-gard (hăg'ȧrd), *adj.* worn and anxious in appearance; lean and hollow-eyed; gaunt.—*n.* **hag'gard-ness.**

hag-gis (hăg'ĭs), *n.* a Scotch dish made of highly seasoned mutton.

hag-gle (hăg'l), *v.t.* [*p.t.* and *p.p.* -gled (-ld), *p.pr.* -gling], to cut roughly or hack; cut into small pieces; notch or cut in a rough way:—*v.i.* to dispute about trifles: —*n.* **1**, the act of hacking: **2**, a dispute about a trifle; a nagging, petty quarrel.

[1]hail (hāl), *n.* **1**, small pellets of ice precipitated from the sky; **2**, anything falling abundantly and with great force; as, a *hail* of shrapnel:—*v.t.* to pour down forcibly; as, to *hail* bullets:—*v.i.* to pour down hail.

[2]hail (hāl), *n.* a salutation; a hearty greeting:—*v.t.* to greet; salute; accost:—*v.i.* to call out greetings or the like; also, to be; come: with *from;* as, he *hails* from the East:—*interj.* an exclamation of greeting.

hail-stone (hāl'stōn''), *n.* a pellet of frozen rain from the clouds (see illus. preceding page).

hair (hâr), *n.* **1**, one of the small filaments growing out of the skin of any animal; **2**, a mass of such threadlike growth; **3**, minute fibers on plants; **4**, the breadth of a hair. —*adj.* **hair'y.**—*n.* **hair'i-ness.**

hair-breadth (hâr'brĕdth''), *n.* (also, *hair's breadth*), a very short distance:—*adj.* very narrow.

hair-cloth (hâr'klôth''), *n.* goods made of camel's hair or horsehair, with cotton or linen warp: used to cover furniture.

hair-dress-er (hâr'drĕs''ẽr), *n.* one who cuts and dresses the hair. —*n.* **hair'dress''ing.**

hair line **1**, a very slender line; **2**, in printing, a very thin line on a type face (see *type*, illus.).

hair-pin (hâr'pĭn''), *n.* a two-pronged pin of wire, celluloid, or the like, used by women to fasten the hair.

hair-split-ting (hâr'splĭt''ĭng), *adj.* making trivial or very small distinctions:—*n.* the act or habit of making trivial and fine distinctions.

hair-spring (hâr'sprĭng''), *n.* a very delicate spring to regulate the balance wheel of a timepiece.

hair trig-ger a trigger of a gun so adjusted that very slight pressure discharges the weapon.

Hai-ti-an (hā'tĭ-ăn), *adj.* pertaining to Haiti:—*n.* a native of Haiti.

hake (hāk), *n.* any of various fishes belonging to the cod family.

hal-berd (hăl'bẽrd), *n.* an ancient weapon consisting of a staff tipped with a bayonetlike point and an axlike edge, in various shapes, for cutting. Also, **hal'bert.**

hal-berd-ier (hăl''bẽr-dēr'), *n.* a foot soldier armed with a halberd.

hal-cy-on (hăl'sĭ-ŭn), *n.* **1**, a fabled bird, identified with the kingfisher; **2**, the kingfisher:—*adj.* peaceful; happy; calm: **halcyon days**, the fourteen days around the winter solstice, when, according to tradition, the weather is calm and peaceful because the halcyon is nesting on a floating island at sea; hence, a time of happiness and tranquillity.

[1]hale (hāl), *adj.* sound in body; robust; hearty.

[2]hale (hāl), *v.t.* [*p.t.* and *p.p.* haled (hāld), *p.pr.* hal'ing], to drag by violence.

half (häf), *n.* [*pl.* halves (hävz)], one of two equal parts:—*adv.* **1**, to the extent of a half; **2**, partially:—*adj.* **1**, forming a half; **2**, partial; incomplete.

half back in football, a player back of the scrimmage line, and between the quarter back and full back.

half blood **1**, one whose parents are of different races; **2**, relationship between persons who have only one parent in common.—*adj.* **half'-blood''ed.**

half-boot (häf'bōōt''), *n.* a boot which reaches above the ankle.

half-breed (häf'=brēd''), *n.* one of mixed breed; a half blood.

half broth-er a brother related through one common parent only.

half-caste (häf'=käst''), *n.* a person of an East Indian parent on one side and of a European on the other:—*adj.* of mixed European and Asiatic blood.

half cock the halfway position of a gun hammer, in which the trigger cannot be released.

half crown an English silver coin, worth about 60 cents.

half-heart-ed (häf'=härt''ĕd), *adj.* lacking in interest; not enthusiastic; timid; lukewarm.—*adv.* **half''-heart'ed-ly.**—*n.* **half''-heart'ed-ness.**

half hitch a kind of temporary knot (see *knot*, illus.).

half-mast (häf'=mäst''), *n.* the position of a flag midway of the staff, as an indication of death or distress.

half-moon (häf'=mōōn''), *n.* the moon when half its disk gives light; also, something shaped like a half-moon.

half-pen-ny (hā'pĕn-ĭ; häf'pĕn''ĭ), *n.* [*pl.* halfpence (hā'pĕns; häf'-pĕns''); halfpennies (hā'pĕn-ĭz; häf'pĕn''ĭz)], an English coin nearly equivalent to one cent.

half sis-ter a sister related through one common parent only.

half step **1**, in music, one of the smaller intervals of a diatonic scale, as between B and C or C and C sharp; **2**, in the U. S. army, a marching step of 15 inches.

half tone *n.* **1**, a photographic process of making plates for illustration; **2**, a picture so made; **3**, in music, a half step: **half-tone**, *adj.* designating, or pertaining to, the process of making half tones.

half-way (häf'wā''; häf''wā'), *adj.* situated in the middle:—*adv.* **1**, midway; **2**, partly; incompletely.

half-wit-ted (häf'=wĭt''ĕd), *adj.* mentally lacking.—*n.* **half'-wit''.**

hal-i-but (hăl'ĭ-bŭt; hŏl'ĭ-bŭt), *n.* the largest of the flatfish, highly prized for food. Also, **hol'i-but.**

hal-i-dom (hăl'ĭ-dŭm), *n.* *Archaic*, **1**, holiness; **2**, a holy relic.

hal-i-to-sis (hăl''ĭ-tō'sĭs), *n.* foul or unpleasant breath.

hall (hôl), *n.* **1**, in early times, the main living room of a castle; **2**, a large building or room for entertainments or the like; **3**, a court of justice; **4**, a university building used for residence, instruction, or the like; **5**, the passageway in a house; **6**, in England, the residence of a landed proprietor; a manor house; **7**, an English college dining room, or the dinner served there; **8**, in English universities, a lesser college, often unendowed.

hal-le-lu-jah (hăl''ē-lōō'yȧ), **1**, literally, in Hebrew, praise ye Jehovah; hence, an exclamation or song of praise to God; **2**, a musical composition having as its theme similar words of praise:—*interj.* an exclamation of praise to God:—*adj.* containing such praises. Also, **al''le-lu'ia; al''le-lu'iah; hal''le-lu'iah.**

hal-liard (hăl'yẽrd), *n.* a rope for hoisting and lowering a flag or sail. See **hal'yard**, *Pfd. S.*

hall mark *n.* **1**, a stamp used by English assay offices, attesting the quality of gold and silver articles; **2**, any mark or proof of genuineness.

hal-loo (hă-lōō'), *interj.* and *n.* a shout to attract attention, or to cheer or urge on:—*v.t.* to shout to; incite or cheer on, as dogs:—*v.i.* to cry out loudly. Also, **hal-lo'; hal-loa'**; *Pfd. S.*, **hol'lo.**

hal-low (hăl'ō), *v.t.* **1**, to consecrate; make holy; **2**, to set apart for holy or religious use; devote to sacred purposes.

Hal-low-een (hăl″ō-ēn′), *n.* the evening before All Saints' Day; evening of October 31. Also, **Hal″low-e'en′**.

hal-lu-ci-na-tion (hă-lū″sĭ-nā′shŭn), *n.* popularly, a false impression, or belief in something imaginary; a delusion, as the visions seen in a delirium.
Syn. illusion, perception, impression.

ha-lo (hā′lō), *n.* [*pl.* halos; haloes (-lōz)], **1**, a ring or circle of light around the sun or moon, caused by refraction; **2**, the bright ring represented in pictures as surrounding the heads of saints and other holy persons; **3**, the glory given by imagination to a person or thing highly prized.

¹halt (hôlt), *n.* a limp; lameness:—*adj.* crippled or lame:—*v.i.* **1**, to limp; **2**, to hesitate, as between two opinions.

²halt (hôlt), *n.* a stop in marching or progress:—*v.i.* to come to a stop; stand still:—*v.t.* to stop; bring to a stop.

hal-ter (hôl′tẽr), *n.* **1**, a rope for hanging criminals; **2**, a rope for leading or holding a horse:—*v.t.* to put on, or secure with, a rope of this kind.

halve (hȧv), *v.t.* [*p.t.* and *p.p.* halved (hȧvd), *p.pr.* halv′ing], **1**, to divide into two equal parts, as an apple; **2**, to fasten together, as timbers.

hal-yard (hăl′yẽrd), *n.* a rope or tackle for hoisting and lowering a sail, flag, or yard. Also, **hal′liard**.

¹ham (hăm), *n.* **1**, the hinder part of the thigh; the thigh and buttock; **2**, the thigh of an animal, esp. a pig; **3**, the region back of the knee joint.

²ham (hăm), *n.* in Anglo-Saxon times, a home, house, or village; also, an estate or manor together with its dependents: still used as a suffix in compounds; as, Buckingham; Birmingham.

³ham (hăm), *n.* [Cockney abbr. of *amateur* to *am*], a licensed amateur radio operator.

Ham (hăm), *n.* in the Bible, the second son of Noah (Genesis 10).

Ha-man (hā′măn), *n.* in the Bible, an enemy of the Jews, who plotted to hang his Jewish rival, Mordecai, but was himself hanged on the gallows he had constructed (Esther 3–7).

Ham-burg (hăm′bûrg; *Ger.* häm′bo͝orkh), *n.* **1**, a variety of European black grape; **2**, a breed of domestic fowl of various colors: **Hamburg steak**, finely chopped beef, seasoned and broiled or fried in cakes.

hame (hām), *n.* one of the curved bars on the collar to which the traces of a horse's harness are fastened (see *harness*, illus.).

Ham-ite (hăm′īt), *n.* **1**, a real or supposed descendant of Ham, the second son of Noah (Genesis 10); **2**, a member of the chief native race of northern Africa, as an Egyptian or a Berber.

Ham-it-ic (hăm-ĭt′ĭk), *adj.* pertaining to Ham or any of his supposed descendants, or to the languages of these peoples, esp. the ancient Egyptians.

ham-let (hăm′lĕt), *n.* a small village of only a few houses.

ham-mer (hăm′ẽr), *n.* **1**, an instrument with a handle and iron head, used for driving nails, beating metals, etc.; **2**, anything resembling this tool in its action or shape; **3**, one of the bones of the middle ear; the malleus; **4**, in field athletics, a weight attached to a flexible handle, hurled for distance:—*v.t.* **1**, to pound or beat with a heavy implement; **2**, to drive, as a nail, into place by pounding; **3**, to work hard at; as, to *hammer* out a plan; **4**, to drive, as an idea into a person's head:—*v.i.* **1**, to strike heavy blows; **2**, to make a noise like blows, as water in a pipe; **3**, to work hard.—*n.* **ham′mer-er**.

ham-mer-head (hăm′ẽr-hĕd″), *n.* any of various sharks with hammer-shaped heads.

ham-mock (hăm′ŭk), *n.* a swinging bed, as of network or canvas.

HAMMOCK

¹ham-per (hăm′pẽr), *n.* a large basket of wickerwork, used for carrying or containing clothes, food supplies, etc.

²ham-per (hăm′pẽr), *v.t.* **1**, to obstruct; impede; **2**, to embarrass; perplex; **3**, to put out of order; derange:—*n.* anything that hinders or impedes.

ham-shack-le (hăm′shăk″l), *v.t.* [*p.t.* and *p.p.* -led (-ld), *p.pr.* -ling], to fetter by fastening the head of an animal to one of its forelegs by a rope or strap; as, to *hamshackle* a horse.

ham-string (hăm′strĭng″), *v.t.* [*p.t.* and *p.p.* -strung″ (-strŭng″), *p.pr.* -string″ing], to cripple, as a horse, by cutting tendons above the hock in the hind leg; disable:—*n.* **1**, in man, one of the strong tendons at the back of the knee; **2**, in quadrupeds, the large tendon above and behind the hock in the hind leg.

hand (hănd), *n.* **1**, the divided lower part of the human arm, connected at the wrist and adapted for grasping; also, a similar formation on any of the limbs of the apes, or on the forelegs of certain other quadrupeds that grasp, as the opossum; **2**, something resembling this member in appearance or use; an index or pointer; as, the *hands* of a clock; **3**, a measure of four inches: used chiefly in measuring the height of horses; **4**, ability or skill; dexterity; knack; as, to try one's *hand* at something; **5**, direction; right or left side; **6**, possession; control; authority; as, to keep the mob in *hand;* **7**, agency in acting or promoting; as, lend a *hand;* **8**, penmanship; also, signature; **9**, an employee who labors with his hands; a member of a ship's crew; **10**, a player in a game of cards; also, the cards held by a player at each deal; a single round in a game; **11**, a pledge, esp. as given in betrothal or marriage; **12**, source from which a thing comes; as, at first *hand;* **13**, *Colloq.*, applause; as, give him a *hand;* **14**, in printing, a sign [☞] used to draw attention; a fist:—*v.t.* **1**, to give or transmit with, or as with, the hand; **2**, to lead or assist, as with the hand; **3**, to roll up and secure, as a sail; furl:—*adj.* belonging to, or used by, the hand.

hand-ball (hănd′bôl″), *n.* a game in which a ball is struck with the hands and kept bounding against a wall.

hand-bill (hănd′bĭl″), *n.* a printed sheet displayed for advertising purposes and distributed by hand.

hand-book (hănd′bo͝ok″), *n.* **1**, a small guidebook; a manual, or concise outline of some subject; **2**, a betting book.

hand-breadth (hănd′brĕdth″), *n.* a linear measure equal to the breadth of a hand, or about four inches.

hand-cuff (hănd′kŭf″), *n.* usually in *pl.*, a manacle or fetter confining the wrists; a ring, usually connected with another by a chain, used to fasten the wrists together:—*v.t.* to put fetters on.

hand-ful (hănd′fo͝ol), *n.* [*pl.* handfuls (-fo͝olz)], **1**, as much as a hand can hold; **2**, a small quantity; **3**, all that can be managed; **4**, a troublesome person or thing.

hand gre-nade **1**, a glass bottle containing chemicals for putting out a fire; **2**, an explosive shell to be thrown by the hand in battle.

hand-i-cap (hăn′dĭ-kăp), *n.* **1**, an extra weight or distance imposed on a superior contestant in a race; **2**, a hindrance; as, the young man's inability to speak well was a distinct *handicap*:—*v.t.* [*p.t.* and *p.p.* -capped (-kăpt), *p.pr.* -cap″ping], **1**, to hinder or retard; as, his inability to speak well *handicapped* him; **2**, to impose a disadvantage on, as on a contestant in a race.

hand-i-craft (hăn′dĭ-krȧft), *n.* **1**, the work or skill of a craftsman or mechanic; manual occupation; **2**, an art or a trade requiring great manual skill.—*n.* **hand′i-crafts″man.**

hand-i-ly (hăn′dĭ-lĭ), *adv.* in a handy or deft manner; skilfully; as, he used his tool *handily.*

hand-i-ness (hăn′dĭ-nĕs), *n.* the state or quality of being skilful or deft with the hands.

hand-i-work (hăn′dĭ-wûrk″), *n.* **1**, work done or produced by manual effort; **2**, anything done by personal effort; as, the result of her *handiwork.*

hand-ker-chief (hăng′kẽr-chĭf), *n.* **1**, a piece of cloth, usually square, for wiping the face, nose, etc.; **2**, a silk or cotton square for the neck.

han-dle (hăn′dl), *n.* **1**, that part of a tool, vessel, etc., grasped by the hand; **2**, an instrument to gain an end; as, this gives me a *handle* for interfering:—*v.t.* [*p.t.* and *p.p.* -dled (-dld), *p.pr.* -dling], **1**, to touch or feel with the hand; **2**, to manage; manipulate; **3**, to discourse on; **4**, to act toward or treat; **5**, to buy, sell, or invest in:—*v.i.* **1**, to use, or work with, the hands; **2**, to behave in a certain way when handled; as, the silk *handles* easily.

hand-made (hănd′mād″), *adj.* fashioned or made by hand.

hand-maid (hănd′mād″), *n.* a female servant or personal attendant. Also, *Archaic,* **hand′maid″en.**

hand or-gan a portable reed organ worked by a hand crank, played by street musicians.

hand-rail (hănd′rāl″), *n.* a railing used by the hand as a guide or support.

hand-saw (hănd′sô″), *n.* a carpenter's saw (see *tool,* illus.): called *ripsaw* if made to cut with the grain, *crosscut* if made to cut across the grain.

hand-sel (hănd′sĕl; hăn′sĕl), *n.* **1**, a pledge given or received as an indication of good will or to secure good luck, esp. in a new enterprise; **2**, pledge money; **3**, in Scotland, a gift to children or servants, formerly given on the first Monday of the year:—*v.t.* **1**, to give a pledge to; **2**, to use or do for the first time; **3**, to inaugurate; celebrate. Also, **han′sel.**

hand-some (hăn′sŭm), *adj.* **1**, pleasing to look upon; well formed; **2**, liberal; generous; **3**, ample, as an income. —*adv.* **hand′some-ly.**—*n.* **hand′some-ness.**
Syn. impressive, comely. (See beautiful.)

hand-spike (hănd′spīk″), *n.* a lever for moving heavy weights.

hand-writ-ing (hănd′rīt″ĭng), *n.* **1**, the style of penmanship peculiar to a person; **2**, matter written by hand.

hand-y (hăn′dĭ), *adj.* [*comp.* hand′i-er, *superl.* hand′i-est], **1**, dexterous; skilful; **2**, convenient; close beside; **3**, manageable; as, a *handy* skiff.

hang (hăng), *v.t.* [*p.t.* and *p.p.* hung (hŭng) or, *Archaic,* hanged (hăngd), *p.pr.* hang′ing] **1**, to attach to something above; suspend; **2**, to fasten to something so as to be movable, as a door; **3**, [*p.t.* and *p.p.* hanged (hăngd)], to suspend by the neck until dead; put to death on the gallows; **4**, to cause to droop; bow, as the head; **5**, to furnish with ornaments or drapery suspended or fastened to the walls; **6**, to adjust to the correct length; as, to *hang* a skirt; **7**, in the U. S., to cause to come to a deadlock, as a jury:—*v.i.* [*p.t.* and *p.p.* hung], **1**, to dangle; be suspended; **2**, to depend or swing on supports; **3**, to hover threateningly: with *over;* **4**, to be in a deadlock; **5**, to rest; depend: with *on;* **6**, [*p.t.* and *p.p.* hanged], to die by hanging:—*n.* **1**, the manner in which a thing hangs or balances; as, the *hang* of a garment; **2**, *Colloq.*: **a**, the manner of doing or using; knack; **b**, the general idea; as, the *hang* of a story.

han-gar (hăng′ẽr; häng′gär″), *n.* a shed for storing vehicles, esp. aircraft.

hang-bird (hăng′bûrd″), *n.* any of various birds that build hanging nests; esp., the oriole.

hang-dog (hăng′dôg″), *adj.* of degraded, ashamed, or sneaking appearance:—*n.* a sneak; a worthless fellow.

hang-er (hăng′ẽr), *n.* **1**, one who or that which hangs; **2**, that by which something is hung or suspended; **3**, a kind of cutlass, or short, curved sword.

hang-er–on (hăng′ẽr-ŏn′), *n.* [*pl.* hangers-on (-ẽrz-)], an unwelcome follower; a parasite.

hang-ing (hăng′ĭng), *p.adj.* **1**, suspended or dangling; **2**, suggesting or involving death, as a crime; **3**, jutting over; as, *hanging* gardens:—*n.* **1**, the act of putting to death by hanging; **2**, in *pl.*, the drapery for the walls, windows, or doors in a room.

hang-man (hăng′măn), *n.* [*pl.* hangmen (-mĕn)], a public officer who executes convicted criminals.

hang-nail (hăng′nāl″), *n.* a small piece of loose skin around a finger nail.

hank (hăngk), *n.* **1**, two or more skeins of thread, silk, wool, etc., fastened together; **2**, one of the wooden rings to which a fore-and-aft sail is bent; **3**, a withy or rope for fastening a gate:—*v.t.* to form into hanks.

han-ker (hăng′kẽr), *v.i.* to desire eagerly: with *after;* crave; as, to *hanker* after pleasure.—*p.adj.* **han′ker-ing.**

Han-o-ve-ri-an (hăn″ō-vē′rĭ-ăn), *adj.* **1**, pertaining to Hanover in Germany; **2**, pertaining to the German ducal house of Hanover; **3**, designating, or pertaining to, the dynasty of the British Empire:—*n.* a member of the House of Hanover.

hanse (hăns), *n.* **1**, a guild of merchants; **2**, the entrance fee to such a guild: **Hanse**, a league of merchants of various free cities of northern Germany, called the *Hanse towns,* formed about the middle of the 13th century to advance their commerce.

Han-se-at-ic (hăn″sē-ăt′ĭk), *adj.* pertaining to the Hanse towns or to the league formed by them: **Hanseatic League**, the league of Hanse towns.

han-sel (hăn′sĕl), *n.* a gift, token, or pledge: —*v.t.* **1**, to present or pledge with a handsel; **2**, to inaugurate. *Pfd. S.*, **hand′sel**.

han-som (hăn′sŭm), *n.* a two-wheeled, one-horse cab, with an outside driver's seat behind: also called *hansom cab.*

hap (hăp), *v.i.* [*p.t.* and *p.p.* happed (hăpt), *p.pr.* hap′ping], to happen; befall casually:—*n.* chance; a casual event.

hap-haz-ard (hăp′hăz″ȧrd), *n.* chance; accident; random:—*adv.* by chance:—*adj.* accidental.

hap-less (hăp′lĕs), *adj.* unfortunate; unlucky; unhappy; as, a *hapless* fate; the *hapless* Juliet.—*adv.* **hap′less-ly.**—*n.* **hap′less-ness.**

hap-ly (hăp′lĭ), *adv.* by chance, luck, or accident; perhaps; perchance.

hap-pen (hăp'n), *v.i.* **1,** to come by chance; **2,** to occur; come to pass.

hap-pi-ly (hăp'ĭ-lĭ), *adv.* **1,** successfully; **2,** by good fortune; luckily; **3,** in a contented manner or state; **4,** aptly; as, his speech was *happily* thought out.

hap-pi-ness (hăp'ĭ-nĕs), *n.* **1,** the state of being satisfied or glad; **2,** good fortune; good luck; prosperity; contentment; **3,** natural elegance of address; felicity, as of language.

Syn. joyfulness, bliss, delight, enjoyment.

hap-py (hăp'ĭ), *adj.* [*comp.* hap'pi-er, *superl.* hap'pi-est], **1,** enjoying pleasure or good; **2,** successful; prosperous; lucky; **3,** giving joy; **4,** apt; felicitous; as, a *happy* remark.

Syn. cheerful, blithe, merry, gay, contented. —*Ant.* unhappy, unfortunate.

hap-py-go-luck-y (hăp'ĭ=gō=lŭk'ĭ), *adj.* **1,** gay; lighthearted; **2,** trusting to chance; unreliable.

Haps-burg (hăps'bûrg; *Ger.* häps'-bo͝orkh), *n.* a German princely family to which have belonged rulers of Austria and Spain, and many emperors of the Holy Roman Empire.

ha-ra-ki-ri (hä'rä=kē'rē), *n.* formerly, in Japan, a method of suicide by ripping open the bowels, permitted by public opinion to nobles and military officers as a means of escape from public execution or official disgrace, and still occasionally practiced. Also, incorrectly, **ha'ri-ka'ri.**

ha-rangue (hȧ-răng'), *n.* a noisy, ranting, public speech:—*v.i.* [*p.t.* and *p.p.* -rangued' (-răngd'), *p.pr.* -rangu'ing (-răng'ĭng)], to deliver a harangue, ranting speech: —*v.t.* to address by a noisy speech.—*n.* **ha-rangu'er** (hȧ-răng'ẽr).

Syn., n. declamation. (See speech.)

har-ass (hăr'ăs), *v.t.* **1,** to annoy or vex; fatigue or weary with labor or importunity; **2,** to tire out and annoy (an enemy) by incessant petty attacks; **3,** to worry; tease; disturb; as, the merchant is *harassed* by many cares.—*n.* **har'ass-er.**—*n.* **har'ass-ment.**—*p.adj.* **har'ass-ing.**

Syn. fret, bother, pester, besiege.

har-bin-ger (här'bĭn-jẽr), *n.* a messenger; forerunner; as, the bluebird is the *harbinger* of spring:—*v.t.* to announce; foretell; usher in.

har-bor (här'bẽr), *n.* **1,** a port or haven for ships; **2,** any place of refuge or safety; formerly, an inn or lodging:—*v.t.* **1,** to shelter or protect; **2,** to cherish; indulge; as, to *harbor* resentment:—*v.i.* to find or take shelter. Also, **har'bour.**—*n.* **har'bor-age.**

Syn., n. shelter, security, refuge.

hard (härd), *adj.* **1,** compact and solid; firm; not easily pierced or broken: opp. of *soft;* **2,** unsympathetic; stern; unfeeling; unyielding; **3,** laborious; strenuous; fatiguing; as, *hard* tasks; **4,** cruel; oppressive; severe; as, a *hard* master; **5,** exacting; not easily complied with; as, *hard* rules; **6,** rough; coarse; wicked; hardened; as, a *hard* man; **7,** containing certain dissolved substances which interfere with the cleansing power of soap: used of water; **8,** thoroughgoing; strenuous; as, a *hard* rider: **hard coal,** anthracite:—*adv.* **1,** forcibly; laboriously; **2,** earnestly; diligently; **3,** tempestuously; vehemently; **4,** closely; near: mainly in the phrase *hard by;* **5,** roughly; **6,** to the utmost extent; **7,** so as to become firm and unyielding; as, the candy was *hard* set: often in compounds, as *hard*-boiled; **8,** with vexation, trouble, or sorrow; as, it has gone *hard* with us; **9,** securely; fast; firmly.—*n.* **hard'ness.**

Syn., adj. difficult, arduous, rigorous, exacting, trying, exhausting; unrelenting, callous. *Hard* is the more general word and describes any task requiring considerable effort, with the emphasis on physical exertion; as, a *hard* climb. *Difficult* stresses the idea of skill or cleverness, with or without physical effort; as, a *difficult* engineering feat.—*Ant., adj.* easy; soft, yielding; sympathetic, lenient.

hard-en (här'dn), *v.t.* **1,** to make firm or solid; **2,** to confirm in impudence or wickedness; **3,** to toughen; **4,** to accustom: —*v.i.* **1,** to become firm or solid; **2,** to become impudent or indifferent; **3,** to become hardy or robust.—*p.adj.* **hard'ened.**

hard-head-ed (härd'=hĕd"ĕd), *adj.* **1,** having shrewd judgment; keen; **2,** practical; not sentimental or theoretical; **3,** obstinate; persistent.

hard-heart-ed (härd'=härt"ĕd), *adj.* **1,** unfeeling; unsympathetic; **2,** cruel; merciless.—*adv.* **hard"-heart'ed-ly.**—*n.* **hard"-heart'ed-ness.**

har-di-hood (här'dĭ-ho͝od), *n.* **1,** impudence; **2,** physical endurance; **3,** bravery; pluck; resolution; **4,** foolhardy daring; boldness.

hard la-bor work imposed on some criminals as part of the punishment of a term of imprisonment.

hard-ly (härd'lĭ), *adv.* **1,** with difficulty; laboriously; **2,** scarcely, not fully or completely; as, the statement is *hardly* true; **3,** vigorously; severely.

hard-pan (härd'păn"), *n.* **1,** in mining, a bed or layer of gravel or sand; **2,** *Colloq.,* a solid foundation.

hard-ship (härd'shĭp), *n.* **1,** severe labor or want; **2,** oppression.

Syn. suffering, misfortune, adversity.

hard-tack (härd'=tăk"), *n.* a large, unsalted, solid biscuit used in the army and navy.

hard-ware (härd'wâr"), *n.* manufactured articles of metal, as cutlery, kitchen utensils, chains, hatchets, etc.

hard-wood (härd'wo͝od"), *n.* **1,** (also, *hard wood*), the wood from broad-leaved trees, as opposed to that from the conifers; also, any tree producing such wood; **2,** (properly, *hard wood*) any heavy, close-grained wood: opp. of *soft wood:*—*adj.* of or pertaining to hardwood.

har-dy (här'dĭ), *adj.* [*comp.* har'di-er, *superl.* har'di-est], **1,** robust; capable of bearing hardship; **2,** bold; **3,** able to survive wintry weather: used of plants:—*n.* a blacksmith's chisel with a square shank to fit into an anvil: **hardy hole,** a square hole in an anvil into which a hardy or chisel may be set.—*adv.* **har'di-ly.**—*n.* **har'di-ness.**

hare (hâr), *n.* a small, timid animal, larger than a rabbit, with a divided upper lip, long ears, and a short, fluffy tail.

hare-bell (hâr'bĕl"), *n.* a small, branching plant, having blue, bell-shaped flowers: in some places called *bluebell.*

hare-brained (hâr'brānd"), *adj.* wild; giddy; heedless rash.

hare-foot (hâr'fo͝ot"), *n.* **1,** a long, narrow foot; **2,** a fast runner.

hare-lip (hâr'lĭp"), *n.* a deformity in which the upper lip is divided in the middle, like a hare's lip.

ha-rem (hā'rĕm), *n.* **1,** the apartments of the women and children in a Mohammedan house; **2,** the wives and female relatives of a Mohammedan. Also, **ha-reem'.**

har-i-cot (hăr'ĭ-kō; hăr'ĭ-kŏt), *n.* **1,** a highly seasoned stew of meat and vegetables; **2,** the kidney bean, a climbing string bean (see illus. next page).

hark (härk), *v.i.* to listen: oftenest used in exclamation; as, *Hark!* listen **hark back, 1,** to retrace a course so as to get a fresh start; **2,** to return, as to a subject.

hark-en (här'kn), *v.i.* to listen, or heed what is said; as, *harken* to me. Also, **heark'en**, *Pfd. S.*

Har-le-quin (här'lē-kwĭn; här'lē-kĭn), *n.* the performer in a pantomime who wears party-colored, spangled garments: **harlequin**, *n.* a buffoon:—*adj.* **1**, fantastic or full of trickery; **2**, party-colored: —*v. i.* to make fun by playing tricks.

Haricot (def. 2)
a, flower; *b*, pod.

har-lot (här'lŏt), *n.* a woman of bad character or ill repute; a prostitute.

harm (härm), *n.* **1**, injury; damage; **2**, moral evil or wrongdoing:—*v.t.* to hurt, damage, or injure.
Syn., n. hurt, wrong, infliction. (See injury.)

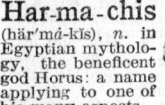

Har-ma-chis (här'mȧ-kĭs), *n.* in Egyptian mythology, the beneficent god Horus: a name applying to one of his many aspects.

harm-ful (härm'fo͝ol), *adj.* hurtful; injurious; mischievous.—*adv.* **harm'ful-ly.**—*n.* **harm'ful-ness.**

harm-less (härm'lĕs), *adj.* **1**, free from damage; not injurious; as, a *harmless* drug; **2**, innocent; as, a *harmless* child; **3**, without hurt; as, to escape *harmless.* —*adv.* **harm'less-ly.**—*n.* **harm'less-ness.**

har-mon-ic (här-mŏn'ĭk), *adj.* **1**, pertaining to, or producing, a right concord of sound; **2**, pertaining to harmony, as distinct from rhythm or melody; **3**, musical; concordant; **4**, pertaining to harmonics:—*n.* **1**, a wave or vibration, as of sound or electricity, having a frequency which is an exact multiple of a fundamental frequency; esp., an overtone having such a frequency; **2**, loosely, any overtone: **harmonics**, *pl.* used as *sing.* the science of musical sounds. Also, *adj.* **har-mon'i-cal.**—*adv.* **har-mon'i-cal-ly.**

har-mon-i-ca (här-mŏn'ĭ-kȧ), *n.* **1**, a musical instrument, the tones of which are produced by friction from a number of musical glasses filled to various heights with water; **2**, an oblong musical instrument consisting of a number of metal strips which are struck by a mallet; **3**, an instrument provided with metal reeds played by the mouth; a mouth organ: also called *harmonicon* [*pl.* harmonica].

har-mo-ni-ous (här-mō'nĭ-ŭs), *adj.* **1**, concordant; musical; **2**, symmetrical; **3**, adapted to each other; as, *harmonious* colors or sounds; **4**, agreeing in action and feeling; **5**, living in friendship; as, *harmonious* neighbors.—*adv.* **har-mo'ni-ous-ly.**—*n.* **har-mo'ni-ous-ness.**

har-mo-nist (här'mō-nĭst), *n.* **1**, one who is expert in musical science; **2**, one who points out parallel passages from different writings, esp. of the Gospels.

har-mo-ni-um (här-mō'nĭ-ŭm), *n.* a small reed organ; melodeon (see illus. next column).

har-mo-nize (här'mō-nīz), *v.t.* [*p.t.* and *p.p.* -nized (-nīzd), *p.pr.* -niz"ing], **1**, to arrange in musical harmony; **2**, to bring into agreement, as colors; **3**, to cause to agree; reconcile, as conflicting opinions:—*v.i.* **1**, to agree; correspond; **2**, to be in peace and friendship.—*n.* **har'mo-niz"er.**

har-mo-ny (här'mō-nĭ), *n.* [*pl.* harmonies (-nĭz)], **1**, careful adaptation of parts to one another, so as to form a connected whole; **2**, agreement in feeling, sentiment, or the like; as, perfect *harmony* in the home; **3**, a literary work showing the agreement between parallel or similar histories or passages; as, a *harmony* of the Gospels; **4**, in music: **a**, an agreeable combination of tones simultaneously heard; **b**, composition of music with reference to its chords; **c**, the science treating of this; **d**, the rendering, by the voice parts, of different agreeable tones at the same time: distinguished from *unison.*

Harmonium

Syn. conformity, concord. (See melody.)

har-ness (här'nĕs), *n.* [*pl.* harness (-nĕs); harnesses (-ĕz)], **1**, the working gear of a horse or other animal, used to attach it to a wagon, plow, or the like; **2**, the dress and armor of a knight or of his horse; **3**, any arrangement, as of straps, for performing some mechanical operation:—*v.t.* to put harness upon; formerly, to equip, as a knight.

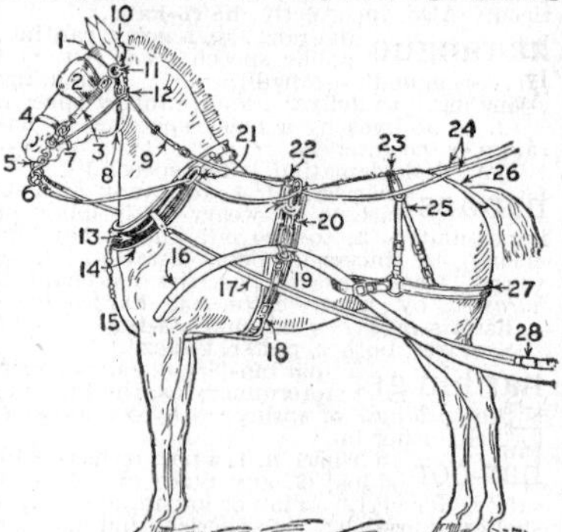

Harness

1–12, parts of the bridle: 1, brow band; 2, blinder; 3, cheek piece; 4, noseband; 5, bit; 6, curb; 7, curb strap; 8, throatlatch; 9, checkrein; 10, headstall; 11, cockade; 12, check ring; 13, collar; 14, collar pad; 15, martingale; 16, shaft; 17, trace; 18, girth, or bellyband; 19, shaft ring; 20, saddle; 21, ring on hame, for rein; 22, terret; 23, hip strap; 24, reins; 25, fork; 26, crupper; 27, breeching, attached to the shaft by the holdback; 28, trace buckle.

harp (härp), *n.* **1**, a stringed musical instrument of triangular shape, played with the fingers (see *musical instrument*, illus.); **2**, any object resembling a harp:—*v.i.* **1**, to play on such an instrument; **2**, to dwell unduly, tediously, or persistently on some particular subject: with *on* or *upon.*—*n.* **harp'er.**—*n.* **harp'ist.**

har-poon (här-po͞on'), *n.* a long spear having a line attached to the staff, for striking and killing whales or large fish: **harpoon gun**, a gun for throwing a harpoon (see illus. next page):—*v.t.* to strike with a harpoon.—*n.* **har-poon'er.**

harp-si-chord (härp′sĭ-kôrd), *n.* a harp-shaped, stringed instrument with a keyboard, in general use before the advent of the piano.

Har-py (här′pĭ), *n.* [*pl.* Harpies (-pĭz)], in mythology, one of three grasping and filthy winged monsters with a woman's face and body, and the wings, tail, and claws of a vulture: **harpy, 1,** an extortioner; **2,** a large, crested American eagle.

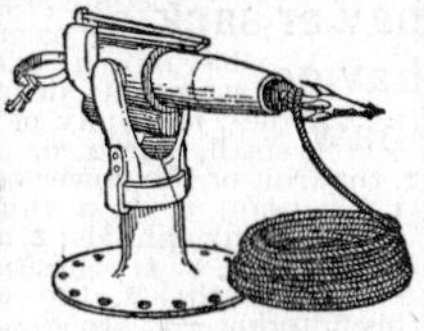

HARPOON GUN

har-que-bus (här′kwē-bŭs), *n.* an ancient gun having a matchlock: in use before the musket. Also, **har′que-buse; ar′que-bus.**—*n.* **har″que-bus-ier′.**

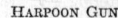

har-ri-dan (hăr′ĭ-dăn), *n.* **1,** a worn-out harlot; **2,** an ugly, shrewish old woman; a vixen; hag.

1**har-ri-er** (hăr′ĭ-ẽr), *n.* one of a breed of small dogs, similar to the hound, used for hunting hares.

2**har-ri-er** (hăr′ĭ-ẽr), *n.* **1,** one who or that which lays waste, ravages, or harries; **2,** any of various hawks or falcons.

har-row (hăr′ō), *n.* an agricultural or farming instrument having sharp iron or wooden teeth, for breaking up clods and casting earth upon sown land:—*v.t.* **1,** to drive a harrow over, as plowed land; **2,** to lacerate or torment; vex; as, to *harrow* the feelings.—*n.* **har′row-er.**

har-ry (hăr′ĭ), *v.t.* [*p.t.* and *p.p.* -ried (-ĭd), *p.pr.* -ry-ing], **1,** to plunder; lay waste; **2,** to annoy or vex; tease; harass.

harsh (härsh), *adj.* **1,** discordant; offensive to feelings or judgment; **2,** rough to the hearing, taste, or touch; **3,** austere; stern.—*adv.* **harsh′ly.**—*n.* **harsh′ness.**

Syn. strict, rigorous, severe, gruff.

hart (härt), *n.* the adult male of the red deer; a stag.

harte-beest (härt′bēst″; här′tē-bēst″), *n.* a large South African antelope or goat. Also, **hart′beest″.**

harts-horn (härts′hôrn″), *n.* **1,** a stag's horn or antler; **2,** a preparation of ammonia and sweet oil: so called because ammonia was formerly distilled from the horns of a deer; sal volatile.

har-um–scar-um (hâr′ŭm-skâr′ŭm), *adj. Colloq.*, wild; thoughtless; rash; giddy; reckless; untidy.

har-vest (här′vĕst), *n.* **1,** the season of reaping and gathering in grain and fruits; **2,** the gathering of a crop, as of grain or fruit; **3,** that which is gathered in: **harvest bug,** or **harvest tick,** any of various ticks in the larval form, having six legs, which burrow under the skin and cause itching (see illus. page 171): **harvest moon,** the full moon which occurs nearest the fall equinox, about September 22: **harvest mouse,** any of several field mice, which build their nests on stalks of grain:—*v.t.* to gather in, as corn.—*n.* **har′vest-er.**

har-vest home **1,** the gathering and bringing home of the harvest; **2,** an autumn festival after the harvest has been brought home; **3,** a church service of thanksgiving held during the season of the ingathering of crops; **4,** a song sung by the reapers, esp. at the harvest feast.

har-vest-man (här′vĕst-măn), *n.* [*pl.* harvestmen (-mĕn)], **1,** one who reaps; a harvester; **2,** an arachnid with a small body and very long, slender legs: commonly called *daddy longlegs.*

has (hăz), third person singular, present indicative, of the verb *have.*

hash (hăsh), *v.t.* **1,** to chop into small pieces, as meat; **2,** to jumble; botch:—*n.* **1,** something chopped in small pieces; esp., a dish of meat or vegetables chopped fine; **2,** any mixture; **3,** a botch.

hash-ish (hăsh′ēsh; hȧ-shēsh′), *n.* an Oriental narcotic drug made from Indian hemp. Also, **hash′eesh.**

hasp (hȧsp), *n.* a clasp folded over a staple and secured with a padlock:—*v.t.* to secure with a clasp and padlock.

has-sock (hăs′ŭk), *n.* **1,** a padded mat or cushion on which to kneel; **2,** a tuft of coarse grass.

hast (hăst), second person singular, present indicative, of the verb *have.*

has-tate (hăs′tāt), *adj.* **1,** shaped like a spear; **2,** in botany, triangular, with a spreading, pointed lobe at each side of the base: said of a leaf (see *leaf,* illus.).

haste (hāst), *n.* **1,** quickness of movement; celerity; speed; swiftness; **2,** undue, rash, or urgent speed:—*v.t.* and *v.i.* [*p.t.* and *p.p.* hast′ed, *p.pr.* hast′ing], to hurry.

has-ten (hās′n), *v.t.* **1,** to cause to hurry; urge forward; **2,** to dispatch; do quickly:—*v.i.* to move with speed; be quick.

Syn. accelerate, expedite, speed.

hast-y (hās′tĭ), *adj.* [*comp.* hast′i-er, *superl.* hast′i-est], **1,** rash; **2,** hurried; **3,** careless; superficial; as, *hasty* work; **4,** quick-tempered.—*adv.* **hast′i-ly.**—*n.* **hast′i-ness.**

Syn. speedy, quick, fast, rapid. *Hasty* implies hurried action, usually voluntary, under stress; as, a *hasty* decision. *Speedy* suggests absence of delay; as, a *speedy* approach. *Quick* suggests prompt and lively action, and is often used of intelligent response; as, a *quick* mind; a *quick* eye. *Fast* and *rapid* apply to swiftness of movement; as, a *fast* train; a *rapid* pulse.

hast-y pud-ding a pudding made by stirring Indian meal or, in England, flour, into boiling water; mush.

hat (hăt), *n.* **1,** a covering for the head, usually with a crown and brim; **2,** a cardinal's rank and dignity.

hat-band (hăt′bănd″), *n.* a band worn around the hat; specif., a black band worn thus as a sign of mourning.

1**hatch** (hăch), *n.* **1,** an opening in a deck, roof, floor, etc., often with a removable cover; hatchway; **2,** a cover for a hatchway; **3,** the lower half of a divided door, etc.

2**hatch** (hăch), *v.t.* **1,** to produce young from; as, to *hatch* eggs; **2,** to produce (young) from eggs; as, to *hatch* chickens; **3,** to plot or contrive:—*v.i.* **1,** to yield young, as eggs; **2,** to come forth from the egg, as a young chick:—*n.* **1,** the brood of young produced at one time; **2,** the act of producing young from eggs.—*n.* **hatch′er.**

3**hatch** (hăch), *n.* one of the system of fine crossed or parallel lines used in a drawing or engraving, as for shading:—*v.t.* to mark, engrave, or decorate with such lines.

hatch-el (hăch′ĕl), *v.t.* **1,** to dress or comb, as flax or hemp; **2,** to tease or vex:—*n.* a comb for dressing flax or hemp: also called *hackle* or *heckle.*

hatch-er-y (hăch′ẽr-ĭ), *n.* [*pl.* hatcheries (-ĭz)], a place where eggs, esp. those of fish, are artificially hatched.

hatch-et (hăch′ĕt), *n.* a small ax with a short handle, used with one hand: **to bury the hatchet,** to cease hostilities.

hatch-ing (hăch′ĭng), *n.* in a drawing or engraving, the fine parallel or crossed lines used for shading.

hatch-ment (hăch′mĕnt), *n.* a panel upon which the coat of arms of a deceased person is temporarily placed, as on a tomb or in a church.

hatch-way (hăch′wā″), *n.* an opening, as in the deck of a vessel, for passage below; a hatch.

hate (hāt), *v.t.* [*p.t.* and *p.p.* hat′ed, *p.pr.* hat′ing], **1**, to dislike intensely; abhor; detest; **2**, to dislike; as, I *hate* to ride:—*v.i.* to feel hatred:—*n.* detestation; thorough dislike.—*n.* **hat′er.**

hate-ful (hāt′fo͞ol), *adj.* **1**, showing deep dislike or abhorrence; as, a *hateful* spirit; **2**, deserving or causing hatred; abominable; as, *hateful* vices.—*adv.* **hate′ful-ly.**—*n.* **hate′ful-ness.**

Syn. odious, detestable, loathsome, abhorrent.—*Ant.* pleasing, lovable.

hath (hăth), *Archaic* or *Poetic*, third person singular, present indicative, of *have.*

ha-tred (hā′trĕd), *n.* bitter aversion; continued hostility of feeling.

Syn. enmity, animosity, rancor.

hat-ter (hăt′ẽr), *n.* a manufacturer of, or a dealer in, headgear.

hau-berk (hô′bẽrk), *n.* a coat of mail formed of steel rings.

haugh-ty (hô′tĭ), *adj.* [*comp.* haugh′ti-er, *superl.* haugh′ti-est], **1**, proud; disdainful; **2**, overbearing; contemptuous.—*adv.* **haugh′ti-ly.**—*n.* **haugh′ti-ness.**

Syn. arrogant, insolent.

haul (hôl), *v.t.* **1**, to pull or draw with force; **2**, to transport by drawing; **3**, to turn the course of (a ship), esp. closer to the wind:—*v.i.* **1**, to change the course of a ship; **2**, to shift: said of the wind; **3**, to pull:—*n.* **1**, a strong pull; **2**, a single draft of a net; **3**, the quantity of fish caught at one time; **4**, the distance over which anything is drawn.—*n.* **haul′age.**—*n.* **haul′er.**

haunch (hänch; hônch), *n.* **1**, of man, the hip and buttock; the hind part; **2**, of meats, the leg and loin taken together; a joint of venison or mutton; **3**, in architecture, the curved section of an arch.

haunt (hänt; hônt), *n.* **1**, a place of accustomed resort; as, the *haunt* of outlaws; **2**, *Colloq.*, a ghost:—*v.t.* **1**, to visit frequently or habitually; **2**, to trouble with frequent visits, as an apparition:—*v.i.* to remain or visit persistently or habitually.—*p.adj.* **haunt′ing.**—*n.* **haunt′er.**

haut-boy (hō′boi), *n.* a wind instrument of the reed class, similar in shape to a clarinet but with a double-reed mouthpiece; the oboe.

hau-teur (hō-tûr′), *n.* a haughty bearing or spirit; disdainful pride.

Ha-van-a (hȧ-văn′ȧ), *n.* a cigar made of Cuban tobacco. Also, **Ha-van′na; Ha-van′nah.**

have (hăv), *v.t.* [*present*, I have, thou hast, he has, we, you, they have; *p.t.* and *p.p.* had (hăd), *p.pr.* hav′ing], **1**, to hold; possess; **2**, to contain; include; as, the argument *has* good points; **3**, to get; obtain; as, most plants must *have* sunshine; **4**, to have knowledge of; understand; as, he *has* no Greek; **5**, to be obliged; be under necessity: with *to;* **6**, to harbor in mind; as, he *has* no ill will; **7**, to show or express, as a feeling or opinion; as, he *had* the kindness to come; **8**, to affirm; declare; as, rumor *has* it that . . .; **9**, in a general sense, to engage in; experience; suffer; enjoy; do with; as, to *have* a good time, a headache; **10**, to bear a given relation to; as, we *had* the shore on our lee; **11**, to be in control of; hold as or where desired; as, I *have* you where I want you; **12**, to cause to be (done or the like); as, I will *have* the damage repaired: also used when the effect of the action is involuntarily received; as, he *had* his leg broken:—*v.aux.* used with the past participle of a verb to form the present perfect, past perfect, and future perfect tenses; as, I *have* gone; I *had* gone; I *shall have* gone.

have-lock (hăv′lŏk), *n.* a white cover for a military cap, with a long rear flap as a protection from strong sunshine.

ha-ven (hā′vn), *n.* **1**, a sheltered anchorage for ships; **2**, a harbor; **3**, any place of shelter and safety.

hav-er-sack (hăv′ẽr-săk), *n.* a strong canvas bag for carrying rations.

hav-oc (hăv′ŏk), *n.* wide and general destruction; devastation; waste.

1**haw** (hô), *n.* **1**, any of several hawthorns, small, more or less thorny trees; **2**, the fruit or the flower of any of these trees.

2**haw** (hô), *n.* **1**, a third eyelid found in many animals; **2**, a disease of the haw.

3**haw** (hô), *n.* **1**, a hesitation or faltering in speech; **2**, the sound produced by this faltering:—*v.i.* to speak with interruption and hesitation; as, to hem and *haw.*

4**haw** (hô), *interj.* a sound made by a driver to direct his team to the left: opp. of *gee:*—*v.t.* and *v.i.* to turn toward the left.

Ha-wai-ian (hä-wī′yăn), *adj.* pertaining to Hawaii:—*n.* **1**, a native of Hawaii; **2**, the Hawaiian language.

haw-finch (hô′fĭnch″), *n.* a finch, the European grosbeak.

1**hawk** (hôk), *n.* **1**, any of several strong, swift-flying birds of prey related to the kites, eagles, and buzzards; **2**, any of several falcons, as the pigeon hawk and others; **3**, one who preys on others; a swindler:—*v.i.* to hunt wild birds or game with the assistance of hawks.—*p.adj.* and *n.* **hawk′ing.**

2**hawk** (hôk), *v.t.* to peddle; cry out (wares) for sale from place to place.

3**hawk** (hôk), *v.i.* to force phlegm from the throat by coughing; clear the throat with a grating noise:—*v.t.* to bring up noisily, as phlegm:—*n.* a noisy and forcible attempt to clear the throat.

1**hawk-er** (hôk′ẽr), *n.* one who breeds, trains, or hunts with, hawks.

2**hawk-er** (hôk′ẽr), *n.* one who cries and sells goods in the streets; a peddler.

hawk–eyed (hôk′=īd″), *adj.* sharp-sighted like a hawk.

hawk moth any of several large, stout-bodied, swift-flying moths.

hawk's–bill (hôks′=bĭl″), *n.* a sea turtle from which tortoise shell is obtained: so named from its curved upper jaw: also called *hawksbill turtle; hawk's-bill turtle.* Also, **hawks′bill″.**

hawk-weed (hôk′wēd″), *n.* any of various plants of the composite family, with yellow flowers.

hawse (hôz; hôs), *n.* **1**, that part of a ship's bow where the hawse holes are; **2**, the horizontal distance between a ship's bow and her anchor; **3**, a hawse hole: **hawse hole** (also, *hawsehole*), one of the holes in a ship's bow through which a hawser or an anchor chain passes.

haw-ser (hô′zẽr; hô′sẽr), *n.* a rope or cable used to tow or moor a vessel.

haw-thorn (hô′thôrn), *n.* any of many small, thorny trees bearing fragrant flowers and small red fruit (see *inflorescence*, illus.).

hay (hā), *n.* grass, clover, etc., cut and dried for fodder: **to make hay,** to cut, dry, and gather in grass for fodder:—*v.i.* to make hay.

hay-cock (hā′kŏk″), *n.* a cone-shaped pile of hay heaped up in the field.

hay fe-ver a catarrh, accompanied by sneezing, slight fever, and pains in the head, usually appearing in spring or late summer.

hay-mow (hā'mou″), *n.* **1**, a storing place for hay in a barn; also, the hay.

hay-rick (hā'rĭk″), *n.* a large pile of hay stacked in the open air.

hay-stack (hā'stăk″), *n.* a stack or pile of hay in the open air; a hayrick.

haz-ard (hăz'ȧrd), *n.* **1**, an old game of chance played with dice; **2**, chance; accident; **3**, risk; danger; **4**, in billiards, a stroke which puts the ball in the pocket; **5**, in golf, a bunker, water, ditch, or other obstruction:—*v.t.* **1**, to risk; subject to risk; **2**, to put forward (an opinion) as if uncertain; as, to *hazard* a guess.

haz-ard-ous (hăz'ȧr-dŭs), *adj.* risky; perilous; dangerous.

[1]**haze** (hāz), **1**, a slight fog or mist; **2**, confusion or dimness of sight; **3**, mental vagueness or bewilderment:—*v.t.* [*p.t.* and *p.p.* hazed (hāzd), *p.pr.* haz'ing], to be slightly foggy or misty; drizzle.

[2]**haze** (hāz), *v.t.* [*p.t.* and *p.p.* hazed (hāzd), *p.pr.* haz'ing], **1**, to subject to overwork or unpleasant tasks, esp. sailors; **2**, to play practical jokes upon; bully.—*n.* **haz'er.**

ha-zel (hā'zl), *n.* **1**, any of various shrubs or trees bearing a small, rounded, edible nut; **2**, the nut borne by this tree; filbert; **3**, a soft, reddish brown color:—*adj.* light reddish brown.—*n.* **ha'zel-nut″.**

ha-zy (hā'zĭ), *adj.* [*comp.* ha'zi-er, *superl.* ha'zi-est], **1**, misty; obscure; not clearly seen; **2**, vague; uncertain; as, a *hazy* idea.—*adv.* **ha'zi-ly.**—*n.* **ha'zi-ness.**

he (hē), *masc. pron.* of the third person [*nom.* he, *poss.* his (hĭz), *obj.* him (hĭm); *pl. nom.* they (*th*ā), *poss.* their (*th*âr), theirs (*th*ârz), *obj.* them (*th*ĕm)], **1**, a previously mentioned male, or object thought of as male; **2**, any man; anyone; as, *he* who runs may read:—*n.* [*pl.* hes (hēz)], a man or male.

head (hĕd), *n.* **1**, the uppermost part of the body in man, the fore part in most animals, attached to the neck, comprising the face, brain, ears, etc.; **2**, a part thought of as resembling, or near, the head, as the fore part of a hide (see *leather*, illus.); also, the top part of a plant, esp. when compact; as, a *head* of cabbage; specif., a rounded, compact form of bloom, as that of clover (see *inflorescence*, illus.); **3**, intelligence; wits; **4**, a person; as, the crowned *heads* of Europe; **5**, the front or foremost part of anything, as of a procession; hence, a leader; **6**, a place of honor or authority; preëminent position; **7**, the fore part, as of a vessel; **8**, the upper end of anything, as of a barrel, bed, drum, cane; **9**, a separate topic or subject; a title to a division of a discussion; **10**, origin or source, as of a river; **11**, often used as *pl.*, an individual; as, seven *head* of cattle; **12**, crisis or height; **13**, latent or reserve force; pressure, as of a stream; **14**, liberty; as, to give a horse his *head;* **15**, froth, as on liquor; **16**, in music, the oval mark attached to the stem of a note, which indicates the pitch (see *note*, illus.); **17**, a promontory, as of land:—*adj.* **1**, principal; chief; **2**, acting against, or meeting, the front; as, a *head* wind; **3**, placed at the front or top:—*v.t.* **1**, to lead; direct; **2**, to take the first place in; **3**, to get in front of; intercept; oppose: often with *off;* **4**, to supply with, or deprive of, a head:—*v.i.* **1**, to move in a given direction; **2**, to come to a climax: often with *up;* **3**, to form into a head.—*adj.* **head'-less.**—*n.* **head'ship.**

-head (-hĕd), *suffix*, used to form nouns of condition or character; as, God*head.*

head-ache (hĕd'āk″), *n.* pain in the head.—*adj.* **head'ach″y.**

head-dress (hĕd'drĕs″), *n.* **1**, a covering or ornament for the head; **2**, manner of wearing the hair.

head-er (hĕd'ẽr), *n.* **1**, a plunge or fall headforemost; **2**, one who puts heads on, as in pin making; **3**, a machine for making heads, as of nails, or for removing heads, as of grain; **4**, a brick or stone with its short face in front: opp. of *stretcher.*

head-first (hĕd″fûrst'), *adv.* **1**, headlong; headforemost; **2**, in rash, thoughtless haste.

head-fore-most (hĕd″fōr'mōst), *adv.* **1**, plunging headfirst; **2**, rashly; impetuously.

head-gear (hĕd'gēr″), *n.* anything worn upon the head.

head-ing (hĕd'ĭng), *n.* **1**, a title; **2**, material from which heads of casks or barrels are made; **3**, the strip on the edge of embroidery, by which it may be sewed to a garment; also, an edge of goods above a line of stitching; **4**, formation into a compact mass, as in certain plants.

head-land (hĕd'lănd), *n.* a promontory; cape.

head-light (hĕd'līt″), *n.* a bright lamp at the front of a locomotive or automobile (see *locomotive*, illus.).

head-line (hĕd'līn″), *n.* a line of type at the top of a page, chapter, or column, as of a newspaper.

head-long (hĕd'lông), *adv.* **1**, headforemost; with the head first; **2**, rashly:—*adj.* **1**, rash; violent; thoughtless; **3**, plunging headfirst.

head-piece (hĕd'pēs″), *n.* **1**, a covering or armor for the head; **2**, a design at the beginning of a chapter; **3**, *Colloq.:* **a**, the head; **b**, mental ability.

head-quar-ters (hĕd'kwôr'tẽrz), *n.* [*pl.* headquarters], **1**, the office or residence of a commanding officer; **2**, a central office from which orders are issued.

heads-man (hĕdz'măn), *n.* [*pl.* headsmen (-mĕn)], **1**, a public executioner; **2**, a leader; chief. Also, **head'man.**

head-stall (hĕd'stôl″), *n.* in a harness, the principal part of the bridle or halter, that fits about the horse's head.

head-stock (hĕd'stŏk″), *n.* a support for a rotating part; esp., in a lathe, the support of the chuck or live center that turns the work (see *lathe*, illus.).

head-stone (hĕd'stōn″), *n.* **1**, the corner piece in a foundation; **2**, a tombstone at the head of a grave.

head-strong (hĕd'strông), *adj.* ungovernable; self-willed.

Syn. perverse, determined. (See obstinate.)

head-wa-ters (hĕd'wô″tẽrz), *n.pl.* the upper waters of a stream.

head-way (hĕd'wā″), *n.* **1**, forward motion, as of a vessel; momentum; **2**, progress or success of any kind; **3**, the time between two trains, trolleys, etc., running in the same direction on the same track; **4**, clear space, as under a bridge; clearance.

head-y (hĕd'ĭ), *adj.* [*comp.* head'i-er, *superl.* head'i-est], **1**, precipitate; wilful; rash; ungovernable; **2**, intoxicating, as liquor.—*n.* **head'i-ness.**

heal (hēl), *v.t.* **1**, to restore to health; cure; **2**, to reconcile, as differences:—*v.i.* to become well or sound.—*n.* **heal'er.**

health (hĕlth), *n.* **1**, freedom from bodily pain or disease; **2**, vigor of mind; also, moral purity; **3**, a toast or pledge.

health-ful (hĕlth'fo͝ol), *adj.* **1**, promoting bodily welfare; wholesome; **2**, favorable; **3**, of sound health; healthy.—*adv.* **health'ful-ly.**—*n.* **health'ful-ness.**

Syn. sanitary, hygienic. (See healthy.)

health-y (hĕl'thĭ), *adj.* [*comp.* health'i-er, *superl.* health'i-est], **1**, in a sound or wholesome condition; as, a *healthy* mind in a *healthy* body is the greatest blessing of mankind; 2, contributing to bodily welfare.—*adv.* **health'i-ly.**—*n.* **health'i-ness.**

Syn. healthful. *Healthy* emphasizes the possession of health; as, a *healthy* person. *Healthful* implies the power to promote health; as, a *healthful* climate; *healthful* food. *Healthy* is often used in this sense also; as, *healthy* exercise.

heap (hēp), *n.* 1, a pile of things thrown together; 2, a large quantity:—*v.t.* 1, to form into a pile; 2, to bestow generously; 3, to fill to overflowing.

Syn., v. accumulate, amass.

hear (hēr), *v.t.* [*p.t.* and *p.p.* heard (hûrd), *p.pr.* hear'ing], 1, to perceive by the ear; 2, to attend or listen to; give heed to; 3, to receive information of by hearing, as news; 4, to obey; 5, to listen to regularly, as to a preacher or lecturer; 6, to carry on an examination of, as a suit at law:—*v.i.* 1, to have the sense of hearing; 2, to be told; 3, to listen; attend.—*n.* **hear'er.**

Syn. apprehend, learn. (See listen.)

hear-ing (hēr'ĭng), *n.* 1, the sense by which sound is perceived; 2, audience; 3, the distance over which sound may be heard; as, to be within *hearing;* 4, judicial or official investigation.

heark-en (här'kn), *v.i.* to listen; heed. Also, **hark'en.**

hear-say (hēr'sā''), *n.* rumor; gossip:—*adj.* secondhand; as, *hearsay* evidence is not accepted in a court of law.

hearse (hûrs), *n.* 1, formerly, a bier; 2, now, a wagon or other vehicle for carrying dead bodies to the grave:—*v.t.* [*p.t.* and *p.p.* hearsed (hûrst), *p.pr.* hears'ing], 1, to place in a hearse; 2, to bury.

heart (härt), *n.* 1, a hollow, muscular organ which maintains the circulation of the blood; 2, this organ considered as the seat of the affections and emotions; 3, tenderness; sympathy; 4, courage; spirit; energy; 5, one's secret thoughts; conscience; 6, the vital or chief part of anything; as, it is difficult to get to the *heart* of his dislike; 7, a conventional design representing a heart; 8, one of a suit of cards marked with this design in red; 9, in *pl.*, a certain game at cards.

heart-ache (härt'āk''), *n.* sorrow; grief; distress.

heart-bro-ken (härt'brō''kn), *adj.* in despair; inconsolable.

heart-burn (härt'bûrn''), *n.* 1, a burning sensation in the region of the stomach; 2, jealousy; discontent.—*n.* and *adj.* **heart'burn''ing.**

heart-en (här'tn), *v.t.* to give courage to; inspirit; animate or inspire.

heart-felt (härt'fĕlt''), *adj.* earnest; sincere; with deep emotion.

hearth (härth), *n.* 1, that part of a room where the fire is made; as, they gathered round the *hearth* on wintry evenings; 2, hence, the family circle.

hearth-stone (härth'stōn''), *n.* 1, a flat stone forming a hearth; 2, hence, the fireside or the home itself.

heart-less (härt'lĕs), *adj.* 1, without feeling or affection; 2, cruel; unsympathetic; 3, lacking in courage.—*adv.* **heart'less-ly.**—*n.* **heart'less-ness.**

heart-rend-ing (härt'=rĕn''dĭng), *adj.* causing extreme anguish or grief; as, *heart-rending* news.

hearts-ease (härts'ēz''), *n.* the pansy and some other species of violet. Also, **heart's'-ease''.**

heart-sick (härt'sĭk''), *adj.* distressed in mind; despondent.

heart-string (härt'strĭng''), *n.* 1, a tendon formerly believed to sustain the heart; 2, usually in *pl.*, the seat of the profoundest emotions or affections.

heart-whole (härt'=hōl''), *adj.* 1, having the heart's affections free; not in love; 2, sincere; 3, undaunted; fearless.

heart-wood (härt'wŏŏd''), *n.* in botany, the hard, tough, inner wood in a tree trunk; duramen.

heart-y (här'tĭ), *adj.* [*comp.* heart'i-er, *superl.* heart'i-est], 1, kind; sincere; warm; cordial; as, a *hearty* welcome; 2, vigorous; strong; as, he is hale and *hearty;* 3, healthful; abundant; as, I ate a *hearty* meal.—*adv.* **heart'i-ly.**—*n.* **heart'i-ness.**

Syn. earnest, ardent.

heat (hēt), *n.* 1, a form of energy due to vibration or motion of the molecules, or minute particles, of which a body is composed; 2, the sensation produced by a hot body; 3, high temperature: opp. of *cold;* as, the *heat* of summer; 4, the state of being hot; 5, effervescence or bubbling; 6, agitation of sudden or violent passion; ardor; vehemence; 7, redness or flush of the face; 8, a course at a race: **latent heat,** the heat necessary to change the state of a substance, as ice to water or water to ice, without changing its temperature: **heat lightning,** distant lightning without thunder:—*v.t.* 1, to make hot; 2, to excite with passion or desire; make feverish; animate:—*v.i.* 1, to become hot; 2, to become excited.

heat-er (hēt'ẽr), *n.* 1, one who or that which gives warmth; 2, a stove, furnace, or other appliance used to make a place warm, as a house, store, building, etc.

heath (hēth), *n.* 1, a tract of waste or level land covered with heather or other coarse vegetation, esp. in Great Britain; 2, heather or a similar evergreen shrub, such as the blueberry, huckleberry, or rhododendron.—*adj.* **heath'y.**

hea-then (hē'*th*n), *n.* [*pl.* heathen; sometimes, individually considered, heathens], 1, one who is ignorant of God; esp., popularly, one who is neither Jewish, Christian, nor Mohammedan; a pagan; idolater; 2, a rude, irreligious, uncultured person. —*v.t.* and *v.i.* **hea'then-ize.**

hea-then-dom (hē'*th*n-dŭm), *n.* 1, the state of being a pagan; 2, that part of the world inhabited by pagans; 3, heathen peoples collectively.

hea-then-ish (hē'*th*n-ĭsh), *adj.* 1, pertaining to, or like, a pagan; 2, rude; ignorant; uncultured; irreligious.—*adv.* **hea'then-ish-ly.**

hea-then-ism (hē'*th*n-ĭzm), *n.* 1, ignorance of the true God; 2, paganism; idolatry; 3, barbarous manners or morals; crudeness.

heath-er (hĕ*th*'ẽr), *n.* a small evergreen plant, often with rose-colored flowers: also called *heath.*—*adj.* **heath'er-y.**

heave (hēv), *v.t.* [*p.t.* and *p.p.* heaved (hēvd) or hove (hōv), *p.pr.* heav'ing], 1, to hoist or lift up with effort; 2, to force from the breast, as a sigh; 3, to cause to rise or swell; 4, to throw; 5, on shipboard, to draw or haul into a certain position, as an anchor:—*v.i.* 1, to be lifted up; 2, to swell; 3, to rise and fall alternately; 4, to struggle or toil; 5, to vomit; 6, on shipboard, to haul; push: with *at:*—*n.* 1, an effort or exertion upward; lift; 2, the act of throwing; 3, swell or rising; 4, struggle; 5, an effort to vomit.

heav-en (hĕv'n), *n.* 1, the abode of God and the blessed; 2, a state or condition of bliss; a sublime and exalted condition; 3, any place of supreme happiness: **the heavens,** the firmament or sky.

heav-en-ly (hĕv'n-lĭ), *adj.* 1, pertaining to, or like, the sky or visible

heavens; 2, pertaining to the abode of God; celestial; divine; 3, supremely excellent.—*n.* **heav'en-li-ness.**
Syn. sacred, blessed. (See celestial.)

heav-en-ward (hĕv'n-wẽrd), *adj.* pointed or directed toward heaven:—*adv.* in the direction of heaven. Also, *adv.*, **heav'en-wards.**

heav-er (hēv'ẽr), *n.* one who or that which lifts; esp., one who loads or unloads goods, coal, etc.

heaves (hēvz), *n.* a disease of horses, recognized by their difficult breathing, wheezing, peculiar cough, etc.

heav-y (hĕv'ĭ), *adj.* [*comp.* heav'i-er, *superl.* heav'i-est], 1, large in extent, quality, or effects; as, we had a *heavy* fall of snow; the store has a *heavy* trade; 2, ponderous; weighty; 3, oppressive; grievous; laborious; as, a *heavy* load; 4, grave; serious; 5, dejected; depressed; 6, dull; stupid; as, *heavy* reading; 7, powerful; loud, as a voice; 8, thick; coarse, as linen; 9, rough, as a road; 10, indigestible; as, that cake was *heavy.*—*adv.* **heav'i-ly.**—*n.* **heav'i-ness.**

heav-y-weight (hĕv'ĭ-wāt"), *n.* 1, a very heavy person; 2, a wrestler or boxer weighing over 175 pounds; 3, one whose moral force or business ability, etc., gives him great influence.

heb-dom-a-dal (hĕb-dŏm'ȧ-dăl), *adj.* 1, composed of seven days; 2, of weekly occurrence.

He-be (hē'bē), *n.* in mythology, the goddess of youth, possessing the power to restore youth, cupbearer to the gods, and wife of Hercules after his deification.

He-bra-ic (hē-brā'ĭk), *adj.* pertaining to the Hebrews or to the Jewish language or literature.

He-bra-ism (hē'brȧ-ĭzm), *n.* 1, a Hebrew phrase or custom; 2, a characteristic of the Hebrews.

He-bra-ist (hē'brȧ-ĭst), *n.* 1, one who is learned in the Hebrew language and literature; 2, a follower of Judaism.—*adj.* **He"bra-is'tic.**

He-brew (hē'broo͞), *adj.* pertaining to the Hebrews; Jewish:—*n.* 1, the Hebrew language; 2, a Jew; 3, in *pl.*, a book of the New Testament, the Epistle to the Hebrews.—*abbr.* **Heb.; Hebr.**

Hec-a-te (hĕk'ȧ-tē), *n.* 1, an ancient Grecian goddess supposed to have threefold power over the moon, earth, and the underworld; 2, later, the goddess of magic and witchcraft.

hec-a-tomb (hĕk'ȧ-tŏm; hĕk'ȧ-to͞om), *n.* 1, in ancient times, a sacrifice of a hundred oxen; 2, any great slaughter.

heck-le (hĕk'l), *n.* an instrument for cleaning flax; a hackle or hatchel:—*v.t.* [*p.t.* and *p.p.* -led (-ld), *p.pr.* -ling], 1, to comb or dress, as flax or hemp; hackle or hatchel; 2, to question severely or annoy with questions; as, the audience *heckled* the speaker.

hec-tare (hĕk'târ), *n.* in the metric system, a land measure equal to 100 ares, or 10,000 square meters, or 2,471 acres. Also, **hek'tare.**

hec-tic (hĕk'tĭk), *adj.* 1, constitutional; slow, but of long continuance, as the wasting of animal tissues; 2, consumptive; 3, hence, pertaining to the fever that accompanies tuberculosis; 4, *Colloq.*, exciting; feverish; as, we passed a *hectic* hour:—*n.* a fever accompanying tuberculosis, characterized by a bright pink spot or flush on the cheeks.

hec-to- (hĕk'tō-), a combining form from the Greek, meaning 100; as, *hecto*gram; *hecto*liter.

hec-to-gram (hĕk'tō-grăm), *n.* in the metric system, a weight equal to 100 grams, or 3.527 ounces avoirdupois. Also, **hec'to-gramme.**

hec-to-graph (hĕk'tō-grȧf), *n.* an apparatus for reproducing copies of a letter, drawing, etc.

hec-to-li-ter (hĕk'tō-lē"tẽr), *n.* in the metric system, a liquid measure equal to 100 liters, or 26.42 gallons; one tenth of a cubic meter. Also, **hec'to-li"tre.**

hec-to-me-ter (hĕk'tō-mē"tẽr), *n.* in the metric system, a measure of length equal to 100 meters, or 328 feet, 1 inch. Also, **hec'to-me"tre.**

Hec-tor (hĕk'tẽr), *n.* in Homer's "Iliad," the eldest son of Priam and Hecuba of Troy, husband of Andromache, and the greatest of the Trojan warriors: killed by Achilles with Athena's help.

hec-tor (hĕk'tẽr), *v.t.* 1, to bully; threaten; 2, to tease; irritate or provoke:—*v.i.* to bluster; swagger.

hec-to-stere (hĕk'tō-stēr), *n.* in the metric system, a cubic measure of length equal to 100 cubic meters, or 3,531.44 cubic feet.

Hec-u-ba (hĕk'ū-bȧ), *n.* in Homer's "Iliad," the wife of Priam, king of Troy, and mother of Hector.

hed-dle (hĕd'l), *n.* one of a series of cords or wires in the harness of a loom to regulate the warp threads:—*v.t.* [*p.t.* and *p.p.* -dled (-ld), *p.pr.* -dling], to draw (the thread) through the eye of the needle.

hedge (hĕj), *n.* 1, a fence of bushes or shrubs; 2, a barrier:—*v.t.* [*p.t.* and *p.p.* hedged (hĕjd), *p.pr.* hedg'ing], 1, to inclose with a border of bushes or shrubs; 2, to hinder; obstruct; 3, to hem in; encircle:—*v.i.* 1, to bet on both sides, so that the possibility of loss will be diminished; 2, to evade; skulk:—*adj.* mean; of the lowest class.

hedge-hog (hĕj'hŏg"), *n.* a small, insect-eating animal covered on the back with spines or prickles.

hedge-row (hĕj'rō"), *n.* a fence of small trees or shrubs.

heed (hēd), *v.t.* to regard with care; take notice of; mind; attend; regard:—*v.i.* to give attention:—*n.* careful attention.

heed-ful (hēd'fo͝ol), *adj.* 1, cautious; discreet; 2, watchful; attentive; as, she is *heedful* of my welfare.—*adv.* **heed'ful-ly.**—*n.* **heed'ful-ness.**

heed-less (hēd'lĕs), *adj.* careless; inattentive; neglectful.—*adv.* **heed'less-ly.**—*n.* **heed'less-ness.**
Syn. inconsiderate, unobserving.—*Ant.* cautious, thoughtful, prudent.

¹heel (hēl), *v.t.* to cause (a ship) to lean to one side:—*v.i.* to list: said of a ship.

²heel (hēl), *n.* 1, the hinder part of the foot; 2, the hinder part of a boot, shoe, or stocking; 3, anything shaped like, or resembling in position, the human heel; as, the *heel* of a scythe or golf club:—*v.t.* to furnish with a heel:—*v.i.* to tap with the heel, as in dancing.—*n.* **heel'ing.**

heel-er (hēl'ẽr), *n.* 1, one who follows close after another, as a political hanger-on; 2, one who heels shoes; 3, a fast runner.

¹heft (hĕft), *n. Colloq.*, 1, heaviness; weight; 2, the greater part or bulk; the gist of a thing:—*v.t. Colloq.*, 1, to try the weight of, as by lifting; 2, to lift:—*v.i. Colloq.*, to weigh.

²heft (hĕft), *n.* a haft or handle; the hilt of a sword, dagger, or the like.

he-gem-o-ny (hē-jĕm'ō-nĭ; hĕj'ē-mō-nĭ), *n.* [*pl.* hegemonies (-nĭz)], 1, leadership; 2, authority; powerful influence, esp. of one government over another.

heg-i-ra (hĕj'ĭ-rȧ; hē-jī'rȧ), *n.* 1, the flight of Mohammed from Mecca to Medina, A. D. 622; 2, a flight. Also, **hej'i-ra.**

heif-er (hĕf′ẽr), *n.* a young cow that has not yet calved.

heigh (hī; hā), *interj.* calling attention, or expressing jubilation, surprise, interrogation, or encouragement.

heigh–ho (hī′-hō″; hā′-hō″), *interj.* expressing languor, uneasiness, surprise, or joy.

height (hīt), *n.* **1,** extent from the base to the top; altitude; of man, stature; **2,** elevation; **3,** an eminence or hill; **4,** the highest point; top; summit; **5,** hence, high rank; distinction.

height-en (hīt′n), *v.t.* **1,** to raise; lift; elevate; **2,** to intensify; set off; increase; aggravate:—*v.i.* **1,** to rise in height; **2,** to increase.

Heim-dall (hām′däl), in Norse mythology, the vigilant, farseeing watchman of Asgard, the residence of the gods.

hei-nous (hā′nŭs), *adj.* hateful; extremely wicked; as, a *heinous* crime.—*adv.* **hei′nous-ly.**—*n.* **hei′nous-ness.**

Syn. odious, outrageous, atrocious.

heir (âr), *n.* one who succeeds another in the possession of property, title, office, mental gifts, etc.: **heir apparent,** one whose right to inherit property cannot be annulled if he outlives his ancestor: **heir presumptive,** one who will succeed as heir if his right is not voided by the birth of one nearer in succession.

heir-ess (âr′ĕs), *n.* a woman or girl who inherits, or is heir to, title or property; a female heir.

heir-loom (âr′lōōm″), *n.* **1,** any movable or personal property, which by its connection with an estate descends to posterity; **2,** any bit of personal property handed down in a family for generations.

held (hĕld), past tense and past participle of the verb *hold.*

Hel-en (hĕl′ĕn), *n.* in mythology, the beautiful daughter of Zeus and Leda, wife of Menelaus, king of Sparta, whose elopement with Paris caused the Trojan war.

he-li-a-cal (hē-lī′ȧ-kăl), *adj.* pertaining to the sun.

hel-i-cal (hĕl′ĭ-kăl), *adj.* pertaining to, or of the form of, the thread on a screw, or helix.—*adv.* **hel′i-cal-ly.**

Hel-i-con (hĕl′ĭ-kŏn), *n.* **1,** a mountain range in ancient Bœotia, Greece, believed by the Greeks to be frequented by Apollo and the Muses; **2,** hence, source of inspiration to poets: **helicon,** a brass wind instrument, similar to the bass tuba and often used in its place on marches (see *musical instrument,* illus.).

hel-i-cop-ter (hĕl″ĭ-kŏp′tẽr), *n.* a flying machine lifted and held up by horizontal propellers (see *aviation,* illus.).

he-li-o- (hē′lĭ-ō-), a prefix from the Greek, meaning sun; as, *helio*centric.

he-li-o-cen-tric (hē″lĭ-ō-sĕn′trĭk), *adj.* having the sun as a center. Also, **he″li-o-cen′tri-cal.**

he-li-o-graph (hē′lĭ-ō-gráf″), *n.* an apparatus for signaling by reflecting the sun's rays: used chiefly in military operations:—*v.t.* and *v.i.* to signal by means of such an instrument.—*adj.* **he″li-o-graph′ic.**—*n.* **he″li-og′ra-pher.**

he-li-om-e-ter (hē″lĭ-ŏm′ē-tẽr), *n.* an instrument for measuring small angular distances in the sky.

He-li-os (hē′lĭ-ŏs), *n.* in mythology, the sun god who drove his four-horse chariot across the sky.

he-li-o-stat (hē′lĭ-ō-stăt″), *n.* an instrument for signaling by means of a mirror moved by clockwork.

he-li-o-trope (hē′lĭ-ō-trōp), *n.* **1,** any of a group of plants including a sweet-scented, cultivated species bearing violet-colored flowers; **2,** a light purple color.

he-li-o-type (hē′lĭ-ō-tīp″), *n.* an impression from a photograph taken on a gelatin plate, later hardened for printing.

he-li-um (hē′lĭ-ŭm), *n.* a gaseous element found in some natural gases: used, because of its lightness and noninflammability, for balloons, dirigibles, etc.

he-lix (hē′lĭks; hĕl′ĭks), *n.* [*pl.* helices (hĕl′ĭ-sēz); helixes (hē′lĭk-sĕz; hĕl′ĭk-sĕz)], anything in the shape of the thread of a screw, or of a coiled spring.

hell (hĕl), *n.* **1,** the place of the dead or of departed souls; the grave; **2,** the place of punishment for the wicked after death; **3,** any place or condition of extreme misery or evil; **4,** a gambling house.—*adj.* **hell′ish.**

hell-ben-der (hĕl′bĕn″dẽr), *n.* a large aquatic salamander found commonly in the streams of the Ohio valley.

Hel-le (hĕl′ē), *n.* in mythology, the sister of Phrixus, with whom she was fleeing through the air on the ram with the Golden Fleece when she fell into the strait thereafter called the *Hellespont.*

hel-le-bore (hĕl′ē-bōr), *n.* **1,** any of several herbs of the crowfoot family; also, the powdered root of the plant, used for medicinal purposes; **2,** any of several similar plants having poisonous rootstocks; also, the powdered root of these plants.

Hel-lene (hĕl′ēn), *n.* [*pl.* Hellenes (-ēnz)], **1,** a person of the pure Greek race of the classical period; **2,** a modern Greek.

Hel-len-ic (hĕ-lĕn′ĭk; hĕ-lē′nĭk), *adj.* pertaining to, or characteristic of, the ancient Greeks, or Grecian art and literature.—*v.t.* and *v.i.* **Hel′len-ize.**

Hel-len-ism (hĕl′ĕn-ĭzm), *n.* **1,** a Greek manner of speech; **2,** Grecian culture and love of the beautiful in art

Hel-len-ist (hĕl′ĕn-ĭst), *n.* **1,** a Jew who spoke Greek in preference to Hebrew; **2,** one learned in Greek or devoted to the spirit of ancient Greece.

hell-gra-mite (hĕl′grȧ-mīt), *n.* the aquatic larva of a certain insect resembling a dragon fly: used as fish bait.

hel-lo (hĕ-lō′), *interj.* used as an informal greeting or to attract attention:—*v.i.* to call out:—*n.* [*pl.* hellos (-lōz′)], **1,** a salutation; greeting; **2,** (*Pfd. S., hollo*), a call.

1**helm** (hĕlm), *n.* **1,** the mechanism for steering a ship; **2,** a post of command, guidance, or government.

2**helm** (hĕlm), *n. Poetic,* a helmet:—*v.t.* to cover or equip with a helmet.

hel-met (hĕl′mĕt), *n.* **1,** metal or leather armor for the head; **2,** the hooded upper lip of a flower, as the snapdragon.

TRENCH HELMET

helms-man (hĕlmz′măn), *n.* [*pl.* helmsmen (-mĕn)], the person who steers a ship or boat; pilot.

Hel-ot (hĕl′ŏt; hē′lŏt), *n.* a slave in ancient Sparta: **helot,** any slave or serf.

help (hĕlp), *v.t.* **1,** to give assistance to; aid; support; sustain; succor; relieve; **2,** to avoid; prevent; as, I cannot *help* his going; **3,** to distribute food to at table; **4,** to cure:—*v.i.* to lend aid; be available or useful:—*n.* **1,** assistance; aid; support; succor; **2,** remedy; relief; **3,** that which forwards or promotes; **4,** a portion of food served at a meal; **5,** a hired servant; collectively, employees.—*n.* **help′er.**

Syn., v. aid, assist, succor. *Help* is the strongest word, and stresses the need of support; as, to *help* the poor: it is significant that the exclamations are God *help* me! and *help! help!* *Aid* implies less than *help;* to *aid* is merely to further another's efforts; as, to *aid* him to arise. To *assist* is to render some small service; as, he *assisted* the old lady to a chair. To *succor* is to give assistance to one in difficulties; as, to *succor* the besieged.

help-ful (hĕlp′fo͝ol), *adj.* giving aid; beneficial; useful.—*adv.* **help′ful-ly.** —*n.* **help′ful-ness.**

help-less (hĕlp′lĕs), *adj.* **1,** unable to do for oneself; feeble; dependent; **2,** beyond remedy; **3,** unable to help.—*adv.* **help′less-ly.**—*n.* **help′less-ness.**

help-mate (hĕlp′māt″), *n.* **1,** an assistant partner; **2,** a companion, esp. a wife. Also, **help′meet″.**

hel-ter–skel-ter (hĕl′tẽr-skĕl′tẽr), *adj.* and *adv.* in hurry and confusion; without definite purpose:—*n.* disorder; confused and hasty action.

helve (hĕlv), *n.* the handle of a tool, as an ax, hatchet, etc.

[1]hem (hĕm), *n.* the edge of a cloth turned back and sewed down to prevent fraying:—*v.t.* [*p.t.* and *p.p.* hemmed (hĕmd), *p.pr.* hem′ming], **1,** to fold over and sew down the edge of (a cloth or garment); **2,** to shut in; surround.

[2]hem (hĕm), *interj.* expressing doubt, or used to attract attention:—*n.* the utterance or sound of *hem*:—*v.i.* [*p.t.* and *p.p.* hemmed (hĕmd), *p.pr.* hem′ming], **1,** to utter the coughing sound, better expressed by *h′m;* **2,** to stammer or hesitate in speaking.

hem-a-tite (hĕm′ȧ-tīt; hē′mȧ-tīt), *n.* one of the most important of iron ores, red or black in color; native ferric oxide: also called *bloodstone.* Also, **hæm′a-tite.**

hem-i- (hĕm′ĭ-), a prefix, meaning half; as, *hemi*sphere.

hem-i-sphere (hĕm′ĭ-sfēr), *n.* **1,** a half sphere; **2,** half of the terrestrial globe; as, the Eastern or the Western *Hemisphere.*—*adj.* **hem″i-spher′ic** (hĕm″ĭ-sfĕr′ĭk); **hem″i-spher′i-cal.**

hem-lock (hĕm′lŏk), *n.* **1,** any of several evergreens of the pine family; also, the lumber from such a tree; **2,** any of several poisonous plants of the parsley family.

hem-mer (hĕm′ẽr), *n.* **1,** one who or that which hems; **2,** an attachment to a sewing machine for hemming.

he-mo-glo-bin (hē″mō-glō′bĭn), *n.* the coloring matter of the red blood corpuscles of vertebrates. See **hæ″mo-glo′bin,** *Pfd. S.*

hem-or-rhage (hĕm′ō-răj), *n.* bleeding from the lungs, arteries, veins, etc.; any copious flow of blood from blood vessels. Also, **hæm′or-rhage.**

hem-or-rhoids (hĕm′ō-roidz), *n. pl.* painful swellings of the veins of the mucous membranes of the rectum at the anus, often accompanied by bleeding: commonly called *piles.* Also, **hæm′or-rhoids.** —*adj.* **hem″or-rhoi′dal.**

hemp (hĕmp), *n.* an annual Asiatic herb, the tough fiber of which is used for cordage and various kinds of coarse linen; also, a related herb, the source of the drug and intoxicant called *hashish.*—*adj.* **hemp′en.**

hem-stitch (hĕm′stĭch″), *n.* a particular kind of ornamental stitching; also, a piece of sewing decorated or hemmed with this stitch:—*v.t.* to finish by this stitching.

hen (hĕn), *n.* the female of a bird, esp. of the domestic fowl.

hen-bane (hĕn′bān″), *n.* a poisonous, coarse, hairy, wild herb of the nightshade family, deadly to fowls.

hence (hĕns), *adv.* **1,** from this place, source, or time; as, a week *hence;* **2,** for this reason; as, *hence* you may go:—*interj.* begone!

hence-forth (hĕns″fōrth′; hĕns′fōrth″), *adv.* from this time on.

hench-man (hĕnch′măn), *n.* [*pl.* henchmen (-mĕn)], a political assistant; a trusted follower.

hen-na (hĕn′ȧ), *n.* **1,** an Oriental tree or shrub with lance-shaped leaves; **2,** a reddish brown dye and cosmetic made from its leaves; **3,** a reddish brown color.

hen-ner-y (hĕn′ẽr-ĭ), *n.* [*pl.* henneries (-ĭz)], **1,** a hen farm; **2,** a hen house or hen yard

hen-pecked (hĕn′pĕkt″), *adj.* governed by one's wife; domineered over.—*v.t.* **hen′peck″.**

hen-ry (hĕn′rĭ), *n.* [*pl.* henrys; henries (-rĭz)], a unit of measurement used in the science of electricity.

he-pat-ic (hē-păt′ĭk), *adj.* pertaining to the liver; as, *hepatic* disease.

he-pat-i-ca (hē-păt′ĭ-kȧ), *n.* [hepaticæ (-sē); hepaticas (-kȧz)], any of several plants of the crowfoot family, bearing pink, purple, or white flowers.

He-phæs-tus (hē-fĕs′tŭs), *n.* in Greek mythology, the god of fire and the forge: identified with the Roman *Vulcan.* Also, **He-phais′tos** (hē-fīs′tŏs).

Hep-pel-white (hĕp′ĕl-hwīt), *adj.* designating, or pertaining to, a style of English furniture of the 18th century developed by A. Heppelwhite and Company (see *furniture,* illus.).

hep-ta- (hĕp′tȧ-), a prefix or combining form from the Greek, meaning seven; as, *hepta*gon.

hep-ta-chord (hĕp′tȧ-kôrd), *n.* **1,** a series of seven notes; **2,** a seven-stringed musical instrument.

hep-ta-gon (hĕp′tȧ-gŏn), *n.* a plane figure having seven sides and seven angles.—*adj.* **hep-tag′o-nal** (hĕp-tăg′ō-năl).

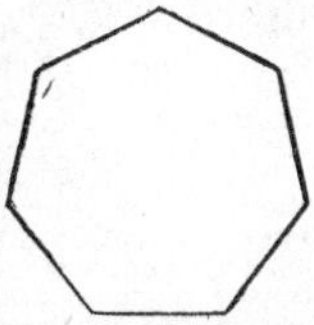

REGULAR HEPTAGON

hep-tarch-y (hĕp′-tär-kĭ), *n.* [*pl.* heptarchies (-kĭz)], a government by seven rulers, esp. the seven Anglo-Saxon kingdoms established in England in the ninth century.

her (hûr), *pron.* the singular objective and possessive case of *she.*

He-ra (hē′rȧ), *n.* in Greek mythology, wife and sister of Zeus, and goddess of marriage and maternity: identified with the Roman *Juno.* Also, **He′re** (hē′rē).

Her-a-cles (hĕr′ȧ-klēz), *n.* the most famous hero of classical antiquity, famed for his strength: generally called by the Roman name *Hercules,* which see. Also, **Her′a-kles.**—*adj.* **Her″a-cle′an.**

her-ald (hĕr′ăld), *n.* **1,** formerly, an official who proclaimed peace and war, bore messages from a sovereign to a commander, superintended coronations and other public ceremonial functions, etc.; **2,** in England, an official whose duty it is to grant, record, and blazon arms, trace pedigrees, etc.; **3,** a messenger; **4,** a forerunner:—*v.t.* to introduce; proclaim; usher in.

he-ral-dic (hē-răl′dĭk), *adj.* pertaining to those who design coats of arms; also, pertaining to the science that treats of making coats of arms.

her-ald-ry (hĕr′ăld-rĭ), *n.* [*pl.* heraldries (-rĭz)], **1,** the science that treats of armorial bearings or coats of arms, and of determining pedigrees, etc.; **2,** *Poetic,* a coat of arms.

herb (ûrb; hûrb), *n.* a plant with a soft and juicy stem that, after flowering, withers away; esp., one used for medicine, food, flavor, or the like.—*adj.* **herb'y.**

her-ba-ceous (hĕr-bā'shŭs), *adj.* pertaining to, or feeding upon, herbs, grasses, or certain small plants.

herb-age (ûr'băj; hûr'băj), *n.* **1**, grass or herbs collectively; **2**, pasturage for cattle; **3**, in law, the right of pasture on the lands of another.

herb-al (hûr'băl), *adj.* pertaining to herbs: —*n.* a book descriptive of plants.

herb-al-ist (hûr'băl-ĭst), *n.* **1**, orig., a botanist; **2**, later, a collector of, or dealer in, medicinal plants and dried herbs.

her-ba-ri-um (hĕr-bā'rĭ-ŭm), *n.* [*pl.* herbariums (-ŭmz); herbaria (-*ȧ*)], **1**, a collection of dried plants for purposes of study; **2**, a book, room, or building where such a collection is kept.

her-bif-er-ous (hĕr-bĭf'ĕr-ŭs), *adj.* producing grasses and various small plants: said of soil.

Her-biv-o-ra (hĕr-bĭv'ō-r*ȧ*), *n.pl.* in a former zoölogical classification, the group or division of animals that feed on grasses or vegetables, as distinct from the *Carnivora*, or flesh-eating animals.

her-biv-o-rous (hĕr-bĭv'ō-rŭs), *adj.* feeding on plants.

Her-cu-le-an (hĕr-kū'lē-ăn), *adj.* pertaining to Hercules, the hero of Grecian and Roman mythology, possessed of superhuman strength: **herculean**, **1**, of exceeding strength and power; **2**, huge; vast; **3**, very difficult; as, his *herculean* task.

Her-cu-les (hûr'kū-lēz), *n.* **1**, in classical mythology, a famous hero, son of Jupiter, (Zeus), noted for his great strength and for the twelve tasks imposed upon him; **2**, a large northern constellation. Also, **Her'a-cles; Her'a-kles.**

¹**herd** (hûrd), *n.* **1**, a collection of beasts or cattle feeding or traveling together; **2**, a rabble or crowd; mob; **3**, the ignorant and uncultured:—*v.i.* **1**, to flock together, as beasts; **2**, to crowd together; assemble:—*v.t.* to form, or crowd into, a flock or herd.

Syn., *n.* pack, flock, bevy, covey, school, shoal, drove, swarm. A *herd* is a group of the larger animals, feeding or traveling together; as, a *herd* of elephants; a *herd* of cattle. *Pack* is used to suggest animals hunting in company; as, a *pack* of dogs or of wolves. *Flock* is applied to the smaller domestic animals, such as sheep and goats, or to birds, feeding or flying together; as, a *flock* of wild geese. *Bevy* is used of birds, esp. quail, and of a lively group of girls or children. *Covey* is applied to birds, and is usually limited to a brood of partridges. *School* and *shoal* name large numbers of fish swimming in company. *Drove* denotes a *herd* or *flock* of animals, driven or traveling together. *Swarm* is applied to large numbers of small animals, esp. insects, as ants, bees, hornets, and particularly to insects in motion.

²**herd** (hûrd), *n. Archaic*, a herdsman: now, except in Scotland, usually in composition; as, cow*herd;* shep*herd:* also called *herder:*—*v.t.* to drive or tend, as cattle.

herds-man (hûrdz'măn), *n.* [*pl.* herdsmen (-mĕn)], one who owns or tends cattle: **Herdsman**, in astronomy, a northern constellation, Boötes.

here (hēr), *adv.* **1**, in this place; as, I live *here:* opp. of *there;* **2**, in this direction: as, come *here;* **3**, in the present life; **4**, on this occasion.

here-a-bout (hēr'*ȧ*-bout''), *adv.* in this locality. Also, **here'a-bouts''.**

here-aft-er (hēr-ȧf'tĕr), *adv.* **1**, after this; **2**, in the life to come:—*n.* **1**, the future; **2**, the life after death.

here-at (hēr-ăt'), *adv.* **1**, at this point; **2**, for this reason.

here-by (hēr-bī'), *adv.* by virtue of this: by means of this; as, you are *hereby* given the right to proceed.

he-red-i-ta-ble (hē-rĕd'ĭ-t*ȧ*-bl), *adj.* **1**, capable of being handed down from parent to child, as eye color; **2**, capable of being left to someone by will or received from another through inheritance.—*adv.* **he-red'i-ta-bly.**

he-red-i-ta-ry (hē-rĕd'ĭ-tā-rĭ), *adj.* **1**, passing from an ancestor to a descendant; **2**, holding title or possession by inheritance; as, a *hereditary* ruler; **3**, transmitted naturally from parent to child, or as a characteristic from one generation to another; as, a *hereditary* nose; **4**, pertaining to an inheritance.

he-red-i-ty (hē-rĕd'ĭ-tĭ), *n.* **1**, the transmission of physical or mental characteristics or qualities from parent to child; **2**, the tendency of an organism to reproduce the characteristics of ancestors.

here-in (hēr-ĭn'), *adv.* in this; as, you will find *herein* your reply.

here-of (hēr-ŏv'; hēr-ŏf'), *adv.* **1**, of this; about this; as, we will speak further *hereof;* **2**, from this; hence; as, *hereof* came many results.

here-on (hēr-ŏn'), *adv.* on this; hereupon; as, *hereon* he produced his proofs.

her-e-sy (hĕr'ē-sĭ), *n.* [*pl.* heresies (-sĭz)], an opinion or doctrine in opposition to views or opinions commonly accepted as true, as in religion, politics, literature, philosophy, etc.: used esp. when the opposing doctrine leads to division.

her-e-tic (hĕr'ē-tĭk), *n.* one who holds or maintains opinions contrary to customary views or prevailing religion.

he-ret-i-cal (hē-rĕt'ĭ-kăl), *adj.* pertaining to, or having the character of, doctrine contrary to accepted views; subversive of, or contrary to, orthodox or common belief.—*adv.* **he-ret'i-cal-ly.**

here-to (hēr-tōō'), *adv.* to this; to this point, end, place, time, or the like.

here-to-fore (hēr''tōō-fōr'), *adv.* previously; formerly; up to this time, hitherto.

here-un-to (hēr''ŭn-tōō'), *adv.* to this; up to the present; hereto.

here-up-on (hēr''ŭ-pŏn'), *adv.* on this; hereon; as, the meeting *hereupon* adjourned.

here-with (hēr-wĭ*th*'; hēr-wĭth'), *adv.* with this; as, I send *herewith* my check as agreed.

her-it-a-ble (hĕr'ĭt-*ȧ*-bl), *adj.* **1**, capable of being handed down by will; **2**, transmissible from one generation to another, as eye color; **3**, capable of receiving by inheritance.—*n.* **her''it-a-bil'i-ty.**

her-it-age (hĕr'ĭ-tāj), *n.* **1**, an estate that passes by descent; **2**, an inherited quality or characteristic; **3**, in the Bible, the people of God; Israel.

her-maph-ro-dite (hĕr-măf'rō-dīt), *n.* **1**, a plant or animal organism which combines the qualities of both sexes; **2**, a two-masted vessel on which the foremast is square-rigged and the mainmast fore-and-aft-rigged: also called *hermaphrodite brig* (see *ship*, illus.).—*adj.* **her-maph''ro-dit'ic.**

Her-mes (hûr'mēz), *n.* in Greek mythology, the god of eloquence, science, and good luck; the messenger of the gods: identified with the Roman *Mercury*.

her-met-ic (hĕr-mĕt'ĭk), *adj.* perfectly closed and air-tight. Also, **her-met'i-cal.**—*adv.* **her-met'i-cal-ly.**

her-mit (hûr′mĭt), *n.* one who retires from society and lives alone; a recluse: **hermit crab,** any of several crabs which live in empty shells, as of snails: **hermit thrush,** a bird of eastern North America, noted for its flutelike song.—*adj.* **her-mit′ic; her-mit′i-cal.**

her-mit-age (hûr′mĭ-tāj), *n.* the abode of a recluse, or of one who lives alone: **Hermitage,** a variety of red or white French wine.

her-ni-a (hûr′nĭ-*á*), *n.* [*pl.* hernias (-*á*z); herniæ (-ē)], a protrusion, or sticking out, of some part of the intestine, or of some other internal organ; a rupture.—*adj.* **her′ni-al.**

he-ro (hē′rō), *n.* [*pl.* heroes (-rōz)], **1,** a man of distinguished courage, moral or physical; **2,** the chief character in a play, novel, poem, etc.

He-ro (hē′rō), *n.* in mythology, a beautiful Thracian priestess of Aphrodite, whose lover, Leander, swam the Hellespont nightly to visit her, but was finally drowned and his corpse washed ashore, whereupon Hero cast herself into the sea.

he-ro-ic (hē-rō′ĭk), *adj.* **1,** having distinguished courage; brave; noble; fearless; **2,** producing men of great courage and noble deeds; **3,** in art, larger than life; **4,** venturesome; drastic; as, we must use *heroic* measures:—*n.* **1,** a poem dealing with heroes; **2,** in *pl.*, extravagant or bombastic language. Also, **he-ro′i-cal.**—*adv.* **he-ro′i-cal-ly.**

he-ro-ic age the age when the legendary great men of the Greeks and Romans, called the children of the gods, are supposed to have lived.

he-ro-ic verse a kind of verse particularly suited to lofty or heroic subjects; specif., in English, the iambic pentameter couplet or blank verse consisting of five iambic feet, each composed of an unaccented syllable followed by an accented one; as, The cur′few tolls′ the knell′ of part′ing day′.

he-ro-in (hē-rō′ĭn; hĕr′ō-ĭn), *n.* a white crystalline powder derived from morphine: a habit-forming drug, used to relieve pain or quiet the nerves.

her-o-ine (hĕr′ō-ĭn), *n.* **1,** a woman of distinguished courage, moral or physical; **2,** the leading female character in a play, novel, etc.

her-o-ism (hĕr′ō-ĭzm), *n.* **1,** high and noble courage; fearlessness; **2,** a heroic act.

her-on (hĕr′ŭn), *n.* any of several wading birds with long neck and legs, frequenting marshes and feeding on fish, frogs, and insects. Also, **hern.**

HERON

her-on-ry (hĕr′ŭn-rĭ), *n.* [*pl.* heronries (-rĭz)], a place where herons congregate and breed in large numbers.

her-pe-tol-o-gy (hûr″pē-tŏl′ō-jĭ), *n.* the study of the structure, habits, and classification of reptiles: a branch of zoölogy.—*n.* **her″pe-tol′o-gist.**

her-ring (hĕr′ĭng), *n.* a small, edible sea fish that lives in shallow water.

her-ring-bone (hĕr′ĭng-bōn″), *n.* **1,** a zigzag pattern, as of bricks or tiles; **2,** a kind of cross-stitch:—*v.t.* and *v.i.* [*p.t.* and *p.p.* -boned″ (-bōnd″), *p.pr.* -bon″ing], to work in such a stitch or pattern.

hers (hûrz), a possessive form of the personal pronoun *she*, used alone: **1,** as *adj.*, in the predicate; as, whose hat is it? it is *hers;* **2,** as *pron.;* as, which hat have you? I have *hers.*

her-self (hẽr-sĕlf′), *pron.* **1,** a reflexive form of *her;* as, she cut *herself;* **2,** an emphatic form of *she;* as, she did it *herself;* **3,** her normal or true self; as, she came to *herself;* she is not *herself.*

hes-i-tant (hĕz′ĭ-tănt), *adj.* slow in acting; irresolute; vacillating.—*adv.* **hes′i-tant-ly.**—*n.* **hes′i-tan-cy.**

hes-i-tate (hĕz′ĭ-tāt), *v.i.* [*p.t.* and *p.p.* -tat″ed, *p.pr.* -tat″ing], **1,** to be in suspense or uncertainty; **2,** to pause; **3,** to stammer; stutter.

Syn. falter, waver, delay, trifle, demur.

hes-i-ta-tion (hĕz″ĭ-tā′shŭn), *n.* **1,** a pause due to uncertainty; doubt; indecision; **2,** a faltering in speech; **3,** a halting movement in a dance.

Hes-pe-ri-an (hĕs-pē′rĭ-ăn), *adj.* **1,** western; **2,** in or of Hesperia, the name given by Greek poets to western lands; **3,** pertaining to the Hesperides; **4,** hence, glorious; as, "*Hesperian* curls."

Hes-per-i-des (hĕs-pĕr′ĭ-dēz), *n.pl.* in mythology, **1,** the nymphs who, with a dragon, guarded the golden apples of Hera; **2,** the garden where the apples were.

Hes-per-us (hĕs′pẽr-ŭs), *n.* the evening star. Also, *Poetic,* **Hes′per.**

Hes-sian (hĕsh′ăn), *n.* **1,** a native of Hesse, Germany; **2,** one of the mercenary soldiers employed by Great Britain in the American Revolution; **3,** any purchasable person; a hireling; **4,** in *pl.*, top-boots with tassels in front:—*adj.* relating to Hesse or its inhabitants.

het-er-o- (hĕt′ẽr-ō-), a combining form from the Greek, meaning other, different; as, *hetero*geneous: opp. of *homo-*.

het-er-o-dox (hĕt′ẽr-ō-dŏks), *adj.* contrary to, or differing from, an accepted doctrine or standard of faith, opinion, etc.; heretical: opp. of *orthodox.*—*n.* **het′er-o-dox″y.**

het-er-o-dyne (hĕt′ẽr-ō-dīn), *v.t.* [*p.t.* and *p.p.* -dyned (-dīnd), *p.pr.* -dyn″ing], **1,** in electricity, to superpose upon (a series of waves of a given frequency) a series of waves of slightly different frequency, producing beats; **2,** in radio signal reception, to produce beats with (an incoming wave signal) by generating local wave signals of slightly different frequency:—*adj.* in radio, designating, or pertaining to, such a method of receiving signals; as, *heterodyne* reception.

het-er-o-ge-ne-i-ty (hĕt″ẽr-ō-jē-nē′ĭ-tĭ), *n.* [*pl.* heterogeneities (-tĭz)], **1,** difference in kind; dissimilarity; **2,** the quality of being different.

het-er-o-ge-ne-ous (hĕt″ẽr-ō-jē′nē-ŭs), *adj.* **1,** opposite or dissimilar in character, quality, structure, etc.; not homogeneous; **2,** composed of parts of different kinds.

hew (hū), *v.t.* [*p.t.* hewed (hūd), *p.p.* hewn (hūn) or hewed, *p.pr.* hew′ing], **1,** to cut, as with an ax or other sharp instrument; hack; chop to pieces; **2,** to cut down, as trees; **3,** to cut into shape:—*v.i.* to strike, as with an ax.—*n.* **hew′er.**

hex (hĕks), *v.t. Dial.,* to bewitch; cast a spell upon:—*v.i. Dial.,* to practice the art of bewitching.

hex-a- (hĕk′s*á*-), a prefix meaning six; as, *hexa*chord, a six-stringed musical instrument. Also, **hex-.**

hex-a-gon (hĕk′s*á*-gŏn), *n.* a plane figure having six angles and six sides.—*adj.* **hex-ag′o-nal** (hĕk-săg′ō-năl).—*adv.* **hex-ag′o-nal-ly.**

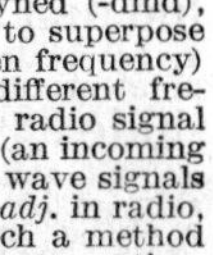

REGULAR HEXAGON

hex-a-he-dron (hĕk″s*á*-hē′drŏn), *n.* [*pl.* hexahedrons (-drŏnz); hexahedra (-dr*á*)], a solid bounded by six plane faces: **regular hexahedron,** a cube (see *solid,* illus.).

hex-am-e-ter (hĕk-săm′ē-tẽr), *n.* a poetic line consisting of six feet; as, This′ is the | for′est pri- | me′val. The | mur′muring | pines′ and the | hem′locks.

hey (hā), *interj.* an exclamation to express surprise, attract attention, etc.

¹hey-day (hā′dā″), *interj.* an exclamation of surprise, joy, welcome, etc.

²hey-day (hā′dā″), *n.* the time of greatest vigor and ardor; as, the *heyday* of youth; hence, happiness.

hi-a-tus (hī-ā′tŭs), *n.* [*pl.* hiatuses (-ĕz); hiatus], **1,** a break; vacancy; gap; **2,** a step lacking in a chain of proof; **3,** a space where something is wanting.

Hi-a-wa-tha (hī″ȧ-wô′thȧ), *n.* the hero of a poem by Longfellow, recounting the life and teachings of a legendary leader among the American Indians.

hi-ber-nal (hī-bûr′năl), *adj.* wintry; as, the *hibernal* sleep of the toad.

hi-ber-nate (hī′bẽr-nāt), *v.i.* [*p.t.* and *p.p.* -nat″ed, *p.pr.* -nat″ing], **1,** to pass the winter in a state of torpor or sleep, as do certain animals; **2,** hence, to remain inactive; **3,** to winter.—*n.* **hi″ber-na′tion.**

Hi-ber-ni-an (hī-bûr′nĭ-ăn), *adj.* pertaining to, or characteristic of, Hibernia, or Ireland:—*n.* a native of Hibernia, or Ireland.

hic-cup (hĭk′ŭp), *n.* a short, convulsive cough:—*v.i.* to utter a short, convulsive cough. Also, **hic′cough** (hĭk′ŭp).

hick-o-ry (hĭk′ō-rĭ), *n.* [*pl.* hickories (-rĭz)], **1,** an American nut-bearing tree of the walnut family; **2,** the nut of this tree; also, its wood.

hid (hĭd), past tense and past participle of ²*hide*:—*p.adj.* concealed; not known.

hi-dal-go (hĭ-dăl′gō), *n.* [*pl.* hidalgos (-gōz)], in Spain, a nobleman of the lowest rank.—*n.fem.* **hi-dal′ga.**

hid-den (hĭd′n), past tense and past participle of the verb ²*hide*:—*p.adj.* **1,** concealed; mysterious; not known; **2,** latent; dormant.

¹hide (hīd), *n.* the skin of an animal, either raw or tanned (see *leather*, illus.):—*v.t.* [*p.t.* and *p.p.* hid′ed, *p.pr.* hid′ing], **1,** to skin, as an animal; **2,** to cover with hide; **3,** *Colloq.*, to whip with a leather lash.

²hide (hīd), *v.t.* [*p.t.* hid (hĭd), *p.p.* hid′den (hĭd′n) or hid, *p.pr.* hid′ing], **1,** to conceal; put out of sight; **2,** to remove from danger; shelter; **3,** to keep hidden or secret; **4,** to obstruct, as a view:—*v.i.* to conceal oneself; also, to be concealed; keep oneself out of sight.

Syn. veil, cover. (See conceal.)—*Ant.* disclose, divulge, uncover, reveal.

³hide (hīd), *n.* in old English law, a measure of land varying from 80 to 120 acres.

hide-bound (hīd′bound″), *adj.* **1,** having the skin close or tight, as an animal; **2,** prejudiced; narrow-minded.

hid-e-ous (hĭd′ē-ŭs), *adj.* offensive to the sight, hearing, or taste; shocking; dreadful; horrible.—*adv.* **hid′e-ous-ly.** —*n.* **hid′e-ous-ness.**

Syn. grim, ghastly, frightful.

hie (hī), *v.t.* [*p.t.* and *p.p.* hied (hīd), *p.pr.* hy′ing or hie′ing], **1,** to cause to hasten; as, *hie* thee hence; **2,** to urge; incite:—*v.i.* to hasten; hurry.

hi-er-arch (hī′ẽr-ärk), *n.* **1,** the chief ruler of a religious body; **2,** the leader of an angelic host; **3,** in ancient Greece, an officer who had charge of offerings given in fulfilment of a religious vow.—*adj.* **hi″er-ar′chic; hi″er-ar′chi-cal.**

hi-er-arch-y (hī′ẽr-är″kĭ), *n.* [*pl.* hierarchies (-kĭz)], **1,** the clergy of a church in higher and lower ranks; priesthood; **2,** government by such a body; **3,** a rank of holy beings, as angels.

hi-er-at-ic (hī″ẽr-ăt′ĭk), *adj.* **1,** pertaining to priests; **2,** sacred; consecrated to sacred uses. Also, **hi″er-at′i-cal.**

hi-er-o-glyph (hī′ẽr-ō-glĭf″), *n.* a sacred character or symbol.

hi-er-o-glyph-ic (hī″ẽr-ō-glĭf′ĭk), *n.* **1,** a sacred character or symbol; **2,** a figure or picture denoting a sound or an idea; **3,** a secret symbol; **4,** in *pl.*, the picture writings of the ancient Egyptians, Mexicans, etc.; hence, any symbolic or illegible writing:—*adj.* **1,** pertaining to hieroglyphics; **2,** symbolic; **3,** illegible.

HIEROGLYPHICS

hig-gle (hĭg′l), *v.i.* [*p.t.* and *p.p.* -gled (-ld), *p.pr.* -gling], **1,** to carry provisions about for sale; **2,** to dispute about trifles.

hig-gle-dy–pig-gle-dy (hĭg′l-dĭ-pĭg′l-dĭ), *adj.* in confusion; topsy-turvy:—*adv.* in a confused manner:—*n.* confusion.

high (hī), *adj.* **1,** elevated in location, as a tree top; **2,** extending far upward, as a building or tree; **3,** having (a specified) elevation or extent; as, a foot *high;* **4,** exalted; noble; lofty in character; as, *high* art; **5,** extreme; as, *high* favor; **6,** containing a relatively large amount; as, wine *high* in alcohol; **7,** chief; head; as, *high* priest; **8,** well advanced toward fulness or completion; as, *high* noon; *high* tide; **9,** strong; violent; tempestuous; as, *high* winds; *high* passions; **10,** elated; lively; as, *high* spirits; **11,** of crime, grave; serious; **12,** haughty; boastful; as, *high* looks; **13,** of game, strongly scented; slightly tainted; **14,** expensive; costly; of prices, great; **15,** of voices, shrill; sharp; **16,** in music, of tones or pitch, made by relatively rapid vibrations: opp. of *low* or *deep;* **17,** in biology, with complex development: usually in the comparative; as, the *higher* animals: **high life, 1,** luxurious living; **2,** the manner of life of rich or aristocratic society: **High Mass,** a celebration of the Eucharist, usually at the high altar, accompanied by music: **high seas, 1,** the open sea or ocean; **2,** that part of the ocean more than three miles from the coast line, not within the territorial jurisdiction of any nation: **high treason,** a grave crime against the sovereign or state, considered as the highest civil offense: in the U. S., limited to making war against that country, adhering to a national enemy, or giving aid and comfort to such enemy:—*adv.* **1,** to a great altitude; **2,** to a great degree; **3,** at a great rate; **4,** luxuriously; **5,** in a shrill or loud pitch.—*adv.* **high′ly.**

high ball a drink of whisky diluted with soda water, or the like, and served in a high glass.

high-born (hī′bôrn″), *adj.* of noble birth or descent.

high-boy (hī′boi″), *n.* a high, spacious chest of drawers, mounted on long legs: distinguished from *lowboy*, which is usually of table height, with two long drawers (see *furniture*, illus.).

high–bred (hī′=brĕd″), *adj.* **1,** descended from a fine or pedigreed stock or race; **2,** having gentle manners and high ideals; cultivated.

High Church a party in the Anglican Church which emphasizes the importance of the historic doctrines and the maintenance of the ritual: **High–Church,** *adj.* designating this party, its doctrines, or its members.—*n.* **High″–Church′man.**

high-fa-lu-ting (hī″fȧ-lū′tĭng), *adj.* pompous; bombastic:—*n.* bombastic speech. Also, **high″fa-lu′tin.**

high–flown (hī′=flōn″), *adj.* **1,** proud; **2,** bombastic, as speech.

high-fly-er (hī′flī″ẽr; hī″flī′ẽr), *n.* **1,** a bird that flies high; **2,** one who is too ambitious; one who is extreme in his opinions, or ostentatious in his mode of living. Also, **high′fli″er.**

high–hand-ed (hī′=hăn″dĕd), *adj.* violent; arbitrary; oppressive; overbearing; as, *high-handed* interference.

high-land (hī′lănd), *n.* elevated or mountainous land: **Highlands,** the mountainous districts or regions, esp. of Scotland: **Highland fling,** a Scottish dance resembling the hornpipe.

high-land-er (hī′lăn-dẽr), *n.* a mountaineer: **Highlander,** a native of the Scotch Highlands.

high–mind-ed (hī′=mīnd″ĕd), *adj.* **1,** honorable; having high principles; **2,** haughty; arrogant.—*n.* **high″–mind′ed-ness.**

high-ness (hī′nĕs), *n.* the state or quality of being lofty: **Highness,** a title of honor applied to persons of royal or princely rank; as, His Royal *Highness.*

high–pres-sure (hī′=prĕsh″ūr), *adj.* **1,** having, or operated by, or suitable for, a relatively high pressure, as of steam in an engine or water in pipes; **2,** figuratively, strenuous; enthusiastic.

high priest a chief priest, esp. the principal priest of the Jewish hierarchy or council.

high-road (hī′rōd″), *n.* **1,** a chief or much traveled road; highway; **2,** an easy course or method.

high–spir-it-ed (hī′=spĭr″ĭt-ĕd), *adj.* **1,** having a lofty bearing; **2,** animated; fiery, as a horse.

high–strung (hī′=strŭng″), *adj.* **1,** extremely sensitive; nervous; easily excited, as a child; **2,** spirited; mettlesome, as a horse.

hight (hīt), *adj.* called or named; past participle of a verb not now in use: a form found only in poetry.

high–toned (hī′=tōnd″), *adj.* **1,** pitched in the upper range of musical or vocal sounds; **2,** aristocratic; dignified; fashionable: used sarcastically or humorously; **3,** having high principles; honorable.

high-way (hī′wā″), *n.* **1,** a main road; highroad; **2,** any public road.
Syn. thoroughfare. (See way.)

high-way-man (hī′wā″măn), *n.* [*pl.* highwaymen (-mĕn)], one who robs on the public road.

hi-jack-er (hī′jăk″ẽr), *n. U. S. Slang,* a robber; a bandit; esp., one who preys upon those engaged in bootlegging.

hike (hīk), *v.i.* [*p.t.* and *p.p.* hiked (hīkt), *p.pr.* hik′ing], *Colloq.,* to tramp; take a long walk; march:—*n.* a long walk or march.

hi-la-ri-ous (hī-lā′rĭ-ŭs; hĭ-lā′-), *adj.* merry; exhilarated; noisy; mirthful.—*adv.* **hi-la′ri-ous-ly.**

hi-lar-i-ty (hī-lăr′ĭ-tĭ; hĭ-), *n.* [*pl.* hilarities (-tĭz)], noisy merriment; exhilaration; jollity.

hill (hĭl), *n.* **1,** a natural elevation less than a mountain; **2,** a small mound or heap; as, an ant *hill;* a *hill* of beans:—*v.t.* to draw earth about (plants) in mounds, as potatoes; form into a mound.

hill-ock (hĭl′ŭk), *n.* a small hill or elevation; a mound; as, the cart jolted over one *hillock* after another.

hill-side (hĭl′sīd″), *n.* the slope of a hill; an incline or rise of land.

hill-y (hĭl′ĭ), *adj.* [*comp.* hill′i-er, *superl.* hill′i-est], abounding with hills; rugged; not level.—*n.* **hill′i-ness.**

hilt (hĭlt), *n.* a handle, esp. of a sword or dagger.

hi-lum (hī′lŭm), *n.* [*pl.* hila (-lȧ)], **1,** the scar on a seed marking the point of attachment to the parent plant (see *germination,* illus.); **2,** the nucleus of a grain of starch; **3,** the eye of a bean; **4,** in anatomy, the point where ducts, nerves, and blood vessels enter and leave a gland or other organ.

him (hĭm), *pron.* the objective case of *he;* as, they brought *him* home in triumph.

Hi-ma-la-yan (hĭ-mä′lȧ-yăn; sometimes, hĭm″ȧ-lā′yăn), *adj.* pertaining to the Himalayas, a very lofty range of mountains between Tibet and India.

him-self (hĭm-sĕlf′), *pron.* **1,** a reflexive form of *him;* as, he hurt *himself;* **2,** an emphatic form of *he;* as, he did it *himself;* **3,** his normal or true self; as, he came to *himself.*

¹hind (hīnd), *n.* **1,** the female of the red deer, esp. in and after the third year; **2,** any of several kinds of fishes.

²hind (hīnd), *n.* **1,** *Br.* or *Scot.,* a farm servant or steward; **2,** a peasant; rustic.

³hind (hīnd), *adj.* [*comp.* hind′er, *superl.* hind′most or hind′er-most], belonging or pertaining to the rear; found in the rear; as, the *hind* legs of an animal.

¹hind-er (hīn′dẽr), *adj.* pertaining to, or constituting, the back or rear.

²hin-der (hĭn′dẽr), *v.t.* to obstruct; impede; thwart; frustrate:—*v.i.* to impose obstructions; raise obstacles.
Syn. block, check, retard. (See prevent.) —*Ant.* further, help, push, promote.

Hin-di (hĭn′dē), *n.* the principal language spoken in northern India.

hind-most (hīnd′mōst), *adj.* farthest from the front; in the extreme rear; last. Also, **hind′er-most.**

hin-drance (hĭn′drăns), *n.* **1,** the act of hindering or state of being hindered; **2,** obstruction; anything that is in the way; as, stooping is a *hindrance* to deep breathing. Also, **hin′der-ance.**
Syn. impediment, encumbrance, obstacle.

Hin-du (hĭn′dōō; hĭn-dōō′), *n.* **1,** any native of India who believes in Hinduism; **2,** a native of Hindustan, belonging to the Aryan race:—*adj.* pertaining to the Hindus or to Hinduism. Also, **Hin′doo.**

Hin-du-ism (hĭn′dōō-ĭzm), *n.* the religious and social system of the Hindus. Also, **Hin′doo-ism**

Hin-du-sta-ni (hĭn″dōō-stä′nē), *n.* the chief language of the Mohammedans in India; Urdu: the common medium between Mohammedans and Hindus, also between Europeans and natives:—*adj.* of or pertaining to the Hindus, their country, or their language. Also, **Hin″doo-sta′ni.**

hinge (hĭnj), *n.* **1,** the joints or hooks on which a door, gate, lid, etc., turns or swings; **2,** the joint of an oyster or similar shell; **3,** that on which anything depends or turns:—*v.t.* [*p.t.* and *p.p.* hinged (hĭnjd), *p.pr.* hing′ing], to furnish with a hinge:—*v.i.* to turn or depend, as on a hinge; as, my future *hinges* upon the decision of one person.

hin-ny (hĭn′ĭ), *n.* [*pl.* hinnies (-ĭz)], the offspring of a stallion and a female ass: distinguished from *mule.*

hint (hĭnt), *v.t.* to suggest; mention casually:—*v.i.* to make an indirect suggestion:—*n.* an indirect suggestion; distant allusion.
Syn., v. imply, intimate, insinuate.

hin-ter-land (hĭn′tẽr-lănd″), *n.* territory back of a river or seacoast region; an inland region.

[1]**hip** (hĭp), *interj.* a signal used to organize a group into united action, as for a cheer; as, *hip, hip,* hurrah!

[2]**hip** (hĭp), *n.* **1**, the upper fleshy part of the thigh on each side of the pelvis; the thigh joint between the thigh and hip bones; haunch; **2**, the first joint of an insect's leg; **3**, the angle at the junction of two sloping sections of a roof: **hip bone**, a large irregular bone, part of the pelvis, forming the chief projection of the hip: **hip joint**, the joint connecting the hip bone with the thigh bone: **hip roof**, a roof which slopes from the ridge board to the eaves on all four sides:—*v.t.* [*p.t.* and *p.p.* hipped (hĭpt), *p.pr.* hip'ping], **1**, to injure the thigh joint of (an animal); **2**, to build with a hip, as a roof; **3**, in wrestling, to throw (one's adversary) over one's hip.

[3]**hip** (hĭp), *n.* in botany, the ripe fruit of the rose, esp. the wild rose.

hip-po-drome (hĭp'ō-drōm), *n.* **1**, an ancient Greek or Roman race course for chariots; **2**, a modern arena with seats for spectators; a circus.

hip-po-griff (hĭp'ō-grĭf), *n.* an imaginary winged monster, half horse, half griffin. Also, **hip'po-gryph.**

hip-po-pot-a-mus (hĭp″ō-pŏt'ȧ-mŭs), *n.* [*pl.* hippopotamuses (-ĕz); hippopotami (-mī)], a thick-skinned mammal of Africa, with short legs and massive body.

hir-cine (hûr'sĭn; hûr'sīn), *adj.* like a goat, esp. in odor; goatish.

hire (hīr), *v.t.* [*p.t.* and *p.p.* hired (hīrd), *p.pr.* hir'ing], **1**, to engage for temporary service at a certain price; employ, as a servant, for wages; **2**, to contract for the use of; lease; **3**, to grant temporary use of; as, to *hire* out a horse; **4**, to bribe:—*n.* **1**, the act of hiring; **2**, wages paid for personal service; **3**, recompense or consideration paid for the use of anything; **4**, a bribe.

Syn., *v.* procure, secure. (See employ.)

hire-ling (hīr'lĭng), *n.* one who serves for wages:—*adj.* mercenary.

hir-sute (hûr'sūt; hẽr-sūt'), *adj.* hairy; shaggy; as, a *hirsute* growth on the face.—*n.* **hir'sute-ness.**

his (hĭz), the possessive form of the personal pronoun *he*, used: **1**, as *adj.*: **a**, attributively; as, this is *his* hat; **b**, in the predicate; as, whose hat is it? it is *his;* **2**, as *pron.;* as, which hat have you? I have *his.*

His-pan-ic (hĭs-păn'ĭk), *adj.* pertaining to Hispania, or Spain.

hiss (hĭs), *n.* **1**, a noise made by forcing the breath between the tongue and upper teeth, and resembling that made by a serpent or goose; **2**, a similar sound expressing derision or disapproval:—*v.i.* to utter such a sound, esp. as expressing disapprobation or contempt; as, they *hissed* at what he said:—*v.t.* to condemn or express contempt for by such a sound; as, the audience *hissed* her.—*n.* **hiss'ing.**

hist (hĭst), *interj.* silence! hark! as, *hist!* What was that sound?

his-tol-o-gy (hĭs-tŏl'ō-jĭ), *n.* the science treating of the microscopic structure of animal and plant tissues.—*adj.* **his″to-log'i-cal.**—*n.* **his-tol'o-gist.**

his-to-ri-an (hĭs-tō'rĭ-ăn), *n.* one who writes of, or studies, the past.

his-tor-ic (hĭs-tŏr'ĭk), *adj.* **1**, of or pertaining to history; **2**, based upon, or true to, the facts of history; **3**, celebrated in history; famous; **4**, (usually, *historical*), in grammar, designating a tense used in telling of past events; as, the *historic* present is used for the past tense in vivid narrative. Also, **his-tor'i-cal.**—*adv.* **his-tor'i-cal-ly.**

his-to-ri-og-ra-pher (hĭs-tō″rĭ-ŏg'rȧ-fẽr), *n.* a writer appointed to study and write of past events, usually in a particular country.

his-to-ry (hĭs'tō-rĭ), *n.* [*pl.* histories (-rĭz)], **1**, a complete story; a narrative or tale of events; **2**, an account of past facts and events affecting one or more nations or peoples, arranged in the order of their occurrence; **3**, the branch of knowledge that studies and explains such facts; **4**, past facts or events in general, concerning some person, thing, nation, etc.

Syn. record, annals, chronicle. A *history* is a systematic account of public events, grouped in regard to importance, and selected, emphasized, and interpreted with attention to causes and consequences. A *record* may be a connected and uncritical narrative of facts, or it may be a piece of evidence preserved as document, monument, tablet, etc. *Annals* narrate events year by year. A *chronicle* relates events over a certain period, long or short. Both *annals* and *chronicles* present the events in order of time, but without interpretation.

his-tri-on-ic (hĭs″trĭ-ŏn'ĭk), *adj.* **1**, pertaining to actors or the stage; **2**, made for effect; showy: **histrionics**, —*n.pl.* used as *sing.* the art of theatrical representation; dramatics.

hit (hĭt), *v.t.* [*p.t.* and *p.p.* hit, *p.pr.* hit'ting], **1**, to strike; give a blow to; **2**, to wound the feelings of; affect; **3**, to touch (a mark); attain to; reach; **4**, to coincide with; suit; **5**, to meet with; find:—*v.i.* **1**, to clash or collide; **2**, to strike out; deliver a blow; **3**, to reach one's aim; succeed; as, to *hit* upon the result; **4**, *Colloq.*, to explode; as, to *hit* on all four cylinders:—*n.* **1**, a stroke or blow; **2**, success; as, the song was a great *hit;* **3**, repartee; as, his answer was a clever *hit;* **4**, in baseball, a ball so hit as to enable the batter to reach first base successfully.—*n.* **hit'ter.**

hitch (hĭch), *n.* **1**, a pulling or jerking upward; **2**, a sudden stop; an obstacle; **3**, a limp; **4**, an inconsistency, as in a story; **5**, on shipboard, a special kind of noose or knot, esp. for temporary fastening (see *knot*, illus.):—*v.i.* **1**, to become entangled or caught; **2**, to move by jerks; **3**, to strike the feet together, as horses; **4**, *Colloq.*, to agree; be consistent, as two stories or reports:—*v.t.* **1**, to fasten or tie; **2**, to pull up with a jerk.

hith-er (hĭ*th*'ẽr), *adv.* **1**, to this place; **2**, to this point or conclusion:—*adj.* on the side nearest to the speaker.

hith-er-to (hĭ*th*″ẽr-to͞o'; hĭ*th*'ẽr-to͞o″), *adv.* to this time; till now.

hith-er-ward (hĭ*th*'ẽr-wẽrd), *adv.* to this place; in this direction; hither. Also, **hith'er-wards.**

hive (hīv), *n.* **1**, a box or house for bees; **2**, a swarm of bees living in such a box; **3**, any place teeming with activity:—*v.i.* [*p.t.* and *p.p.* hived (hīvd), *p.pr.* hiv'ing], **1**, to enter a hive, as bees; **2**, to live together in swarms:—*v.t.* **1**, to gather or put into a hive; **2**, to harbor; store, as honey.

hives (hīvz), *n.pl.* nettle rash and similar diseases of the skin.

ho (hō), *interj.* **1**, (also, *whoa*), stop! hold! **2**, expressing delight, surprise, etc., or, when repeated, mockery; **3**, hollo! Also, **hoa.**

hoar (hōr), *adj.* **1**, white; **2**, gray with age; as, his locks were *hoar;* **3**, ancient.

hoard (hōrd), *n.* a store or treasure laid up secretly; a collection of things kept in reserve:—*v.i.* to lay up money; store goods; as, he *hoards* because it gives him pleasure:—*v.t.* to collect and lay up; store secretly; amass; accumulate; as, he *hoarded* his money for years.—*n.* **hoard'er.**

hoard-ing (hōr'dĭng), *n.* in England, a fence of rough boards inclosing a building site.

hoar-frost (hōr′frôst″), *n.* white particles of frozen dew or moisture.

hoar-hound (hōr′hound″), *n.* **1**, any of various plants of the mint family, esp. one used as a remedy for colds, coughs, etc.; **2**, an extract or candy flavored with this plant. See **hore′hound″**, *Pfd. S.*

hoarse (hōrs), *adj.* **1**, rasping; discordant, as a foghorn; **2**, rough and harsh, as the voice when affected by a cold.—*adv.* **hoarse′ly.**—*n.* **hoarse′ness.**

hoar-y (hōr′ĭ), *adj.* [*comp.* hoar′i-er, *superl.* hoar′i-est], **1**, white or gray, as hair from age; **2**, aged; ancient.—*n.* **hoar′i-ness.**

hoax (hōks), *n.* a sportive, deceptive trick; practical joke:—*v.t.* to take in, or delude, by a trick.

Syn., v. deceive, trick, cheat.

[1]**hob** (hŏb), *n.* **1**, a projection in a fireplace on which things are placed to be kept warm; **2**, the peg used as a target in some games, as quoits.

[2]**hob** (hŏb), *n.* an elf: **to play hob,** to work mischief; play tricks.

hob-ble (hŏb′l), *v.i.* [*p.t.* and *p.p.* -bled (-ld), *p.pr.* -bling], to walk with a limp or awkward step:—*v.t.* **1**, to make lame; **2**, to hamper, as by tying the legs of a horse:—*n.* **1**, a limping or awkward step; **2**, a clog.

hob-ble-de-hoy (hŏb′l-dē-hoi″), *n.* **1**, a lad between boyhood and manhood; **2**, a green, awkward youth.

hob-by (hŏb′ĭ), *n.* [*pl.* hobbies (-ĭz)], **1**, a hobbyhorse; **2**, one's particular, favorite pastime; a favorite pursuit.

hob-by-horse (hŏb′ĭ-hôrs″), *n.* **1**, a stick with a horse's head, on which children ride; **2**, a wooden rocking-horse; **3**, a wicker horse used by performers in old morris dances.

hob-gob-lin (hŏb′gŏb″lĭn), *n.* **1**, an impish elf; **2**, an evil sprite of frightful appearance; **3**, an alarming apparition: **Hobgoblin,** Robin Goodfellow, or Puck.

hob-nail (hŏb′nāl″), *n.* a short thick nail with a large head, used for protecting the soles of heavy boots.

hob-nob (hŏb′nŏb″), *v.i.* [*p.t.* and *p.p.* -nobbed″ (-nŏbd″), *p.pr.* -nob″-bing], to drink or talk familiarly (with); associate intimately together; as, some neighbors spend much of their time *hobnobbing.*

ho-bo (hō′bō), *n.* [*pl.* hobos; hoboes (-bōz)], an idle, shiftless vagrant; a tramp.—*n.* **ho′bo-ism.**

[1]**hock** (hŏk), *n.* **1**, a white or yellow German wine; **2**, any white Rhine wine.

[2]**hock** (hŏk), *n.* **1**, the joint in the hind leg of some animals, corresponding to the ankle in man; **2**, the back part of the knee joint:—*v.t.* to lame by cutting the tendons of the hamstring. Also, **hough** (hŏk).

[3]**hock** (hŏk), *v.t. Slang,* to pawn; pledge as security for a loan.

hock-ey (hŏk′ĭ), *n.* a game played with a ball or disk and with clubs curved at one end.

ho-cus (hō′kŭs), *v.t.* **1**, to cheat or trick; **2**, to stupefy or render insensible by means of drugged liquor in order to cheat; **3**, to adulterate:—*n.* drugged liquor.

ho-cus–po-cus (hō′kŭs=pō′kŭs), *n.* **1**, an incantation used by jugglers; **2**, a juggler's trick; **3**, a juggler; a cheat; **4**, nonsense; twaddle.

hod (hŏd), *n.* **1**, a wooden trough, fastened to a long handle, for carrying mortar or bricks; **2**, a coal scuttle.

hod-car-ri-er (hŏd′kăr″ĭ-ēr), *n.* a laborer who carries mortar and bricks; a hodman; hence, a common drudge.

hodge-podge (hŏj′pŏj″), *n.* **1**, a stew or broth of meat and vegetables; **2**, hence, a mixed mass of ingredients; a mixture; medley. Also, **hotch′potch″.**

hod-man (hŏd′măn), *n.* [*pl.* hodmen (-mĕn)], a mason's or bricklayer's helper; a hodcarrier.

hoe (hō), *n.* a farmer's tool for loosening soil, cutting weeds, etc.:—*v.t.* [*p.t.* and *p.p.* hoed (hōd), *p.pr.* hoe′ing], **1**, to cut or till with this tool; **2**, to clear from weeds:—*v.i.* to work with this tool.

hoe-cake (hō′kāk″), *n.* a kind of thin corn-meal bread.

hog (hŏg), *n.* **1**, a full-grown, domestic swine; **2**, any of various animals resembling this; **3**, a kind of rough broom used for scrubbing a ship's bottom under water; **4**, a grasping, gluttonous person; a coarse and disgusting person:—*v.t.* [*p.t.* and *p.p.* hogged (hŏgd), *p.pr.* hog′ging], **1**, to scrub (a ship's bottom) under water; **2**, to cut (a horse's hair) short; **3**, to take more than a fair share of.

hog-back (hŏg′băk″), *n.* **1**, an animal with back curved like a hog's; **2**, anything resembling a hog's back in form; **3**, a sharply crested, rocky or sandy ridge; any sharp, steep ridge.

hog-gish (hŏg′ĭsh), *adj.* **1**, gluttonous; coarsely selfish; **2**, filthy.

hogs-head (hŏgz′hĕd), *n.* **1**, a liquid measure of capacity equal to 52½ imperial gallons or 63 wine gallons; **2**, a large cask holding from 100 to 140 gallons.

Hoh-en-zol-lern (hō′ĕn-tsōl″ērn), *n.* the name of the princely family from which came the kings of Prussia after 1701, and the German emperors after 1871.

hoi-den (hoi′dn), *n.* a tomboy; romp:—*adj.* ill-mannered:—*v.i.* to romp roughly or indelicately. Also, **hoy′den,** *Pfd. S.*

***hoi pol-loi** (hoi″ pō-loi′), [Gk.], the crowd; the masses.

hoist (hoist), *v.t.* **1**, to lift with tackle; heave; **2**, to raise aloft, as a flag:—*n.* **1**, the act of lifting; **2**, the perpendicular dimension of a flag: opp. of *fly;* **3**, an apparatus for lifting goods from a lower to a higher floor; a tackle.

hoi-ty–toi-ty (hoi′tĭ=toi′tĭ), *interj.* an exclamation of surprise, rebuke, etc.:—*adj.* **1**, flighty; **2**, arrogant.

ho-key–po-key (hō′kĭ=pō′kĭ), *n. Colloq.,* a cheap kind of ice cream sold in the streets. Also, **ho′ky–po′ky.**

ho-kum (hō′kŭm), *n. Slang,* anything said, done, or used by an actor to cause approval or laughter; hence, empty talk.

[1]**hold** (hōld), *n.* the interior of a ship below deck, where the cargo is stored.

[2]**hold** (hōld), *v.t.* [*p.t.* held (hĕld), *p.p.* held or, *Archaic,* hold′en (hōl′dn), *p.pr.* hold′ing], **1**, to grasp and keep in the hand; clutch; **2**, to keep possession of; retain; keep; **3**, to possess; occupy, as an office; **4**, to keep (oneself) in a particular state; **5**, to restrain; hold in check; as, *hold* your tongue; **6**, to join together; combine; connect; **7**, to judge; consider; as, I *hold* him a model of culture; **8**, to entertain, believe, or accept, as an opinion; **9**, to have room or space for; contain; **10**, to observe; celebrate, as a festival; **11**, to call and conduct, as a meeting:—*v.i.* **1**, to keep a grasp on something; **2**, to cling; adhere; **3**, to stand good; remain firm and unbroken; be valid; as, this rule always *holds* good; **4**, to endure; continue; proceed; as, to *hold* to a given course of action; **5**, to hesitate; restrain oneself; refrain; **6**, to maintain an opinion:—*n.* **1**, the act of grasping or keeping; seizure; grasp; **2**, an embrace; **3**, support; **4**, a claim; ground or authority on which a thing is taken or kept; **5**, a fortified place; **6**, in law, a tenure or manner of holding prop-

erty: usually in compounds; as, free*hold;* copy*hold*, etc.; **7**, in music, a character placed over [⌒] or under [⌣] a note or rest to show that it is to be prolonged: also called *pause*.

hold-back (hōld'băk″), *n.* **1**, a check; hindrance; restraint; **2**, a part of the harness used in backing a carriage (see *harness*, illus.).

hold-er (hōl'dẽr), *n.* **1**, a container; **2**, a device by which something may be held in position; as, a cigar *holder;* **3**, a handle; **4**, a heavy cloth pad to protect the hand when grasping a hot article, as a flatiron; **5**, a possessor; **6**, an occupant; tenant; **7**, in law, one who holds, and is legally entitled to the payment of, a check, note, or bill.

hold-fast (hōld'fȧst″), *n.* **1**, a hook or support; **2**, something used to secure and keep in place something else, as a flat-headed nail, a catch, clamp, etc.

hold-ing (hōl'dĭng), *n.* **1**, property owned, as bonds, stocks, etc.; **2**, a farm or other estate rented from another; **3**, that which secures, binds, or influences.

hole (hōl), *n.* **1**, an opening in or through something; a cavity; **2**, a hollow place; pit; **3**, a perforation; **4**, the burrow of an animal; **5**, a mean habitation; **6**, a hiding place; **7**, *Colloq.*, a difficulty or dilemma; **8**, in golf: **a**, a cavity in the putting green into which is sunk a metal cup; **b**, the distance between such points.

hol-i-but (hŏl'ĭ-bŭt), *n.* a large flatfish. See **hal'i-but**, *Pfd. S.*

hol-i-day (hŏl'ĭ-dā), *n.* **1**, a day of gaiety and joy, as in celebration of some event; **2**, a day of freedom from labor; **3**, a day legally set aside by the government for suspension of business:—*adj.* pertaining to a festival; joyous; gay; as, in *holiday* dress.

ho-li-ness (hō'lĭ-nĕs), *n.* **1**, the state or quality of being free from sin; **2**, moral and spiritual purity; **3**, sacredness: **Holiness**, a title of the Pope.

Syn. sanctity, piety, righteousness.—*Ant.* impurity, impiety, unrighteousness.

hol-land (hŏl'ănd), *n.* fine unbleached linen, glazed or unglazed, used for window shades, children's garments, etc.: **Hollands**, a kind of gin.

hol-lo (hŏl'ō; hŏ-lō'), *v.t.* to shout to at a distance; incite, as hounds:—*v.i.* to shout out:—*n.* [*pl.* hollos (-ōz; -lōz')], a shout to attract attention; a greeting; hello:—*interj.* (hŏ-lō'), a cry to attract attention. Also, **hal-loo'; hel-lo'; hol'la; hul-lo'.**

hol-low (hŏl'ō), *n.* **1**, a cavity; pit; as, the *hollow* of a tree; **2**, a groove in moldings; **3**, space between hills or elevations; a valley:—*v.t.* to make hollow:—*v.i.* to become empty:—*adj.* **1**, having an empty space within: opp. of *solid;* **2**, sunken; **3**, superficial; unreal; insincere; **4**, deep or low: used of sound:—*adv. Colloq.*, completely: often with *all.*—*adv.* **hol'low-ly.**—*n.* **hol'low-ness.**

hol-ly (hŏl'ĭ), *n.* [*pl.* hollies (-ĭz)], **1**, a shrub or tree with glossy, prickly leaves and red berries, much used at Christmas time; **2**, the leaves and berries of this shrub.

hol-ly-hock (hŏl'ĭ-hŏk), *n.* a tall plant of the mallow family with large, decorative, varicolored flowers.

holm (hōm), *n.* **1**, low, flat land by the side of a river; **2**, a small island in a river.

holm oak an evergreen oak with tough, hard wood.

hol-o-caust (hŏl'ō-kôst), *n.* **1**, a sacrifice wholly consumed by fire; **2**, complete or total destruction, as by fire.

hol-ster (hōl'stẽr), *n.* a leather pistol case, carried at the belt.

holt (hōlt), *n.* a wooded hill; a group of trees; a grove; copse.

ho-ly (hō'lĭ), *adj.* [*comp.* ho'li-er, *superl.* ho'li-est], **1**, dedicated to the service of God; consecrated; **2**, pure; sinless:—*n.* [*pl.* holies (-lĭz)], a sacred thing: **holy of holies**, the innermost shrine of the Jewish tabernacle and temple, where the sacred relics were kept: **Holy Thursday**, the day before Good Friday: also called *Maundy Thursday.*—*adv.* **ho'li-ly.**

ho-ly day a day set aside as sacred, or to be observed with religious ceremonies. Also, **ho'ly-day″.**

Ho-ly Grail the cup used by Christ at the Last Supper, for a time miraculously preserved, but eventually lost.

Ho-ly Land Palestine, the ancient home of the Jews, and the birthplace of Christianity.

ho-ly-stone (hō'lĭ-stōn″), *n.* a large, flat sandstone used for scouring a ship's decks:—*v.t.* [*p.t.* and *p.p.* -stoned″ (-stōnd″), *p.pr.* -ston″ing], to scrub (a deck) with this stone:—*v.i.* to use a holystone.

hom-age (hŏm'āj), *n.* **1**, respect paid by external action; deference; reverence; honor; **2**, in feudal times, the ceremony by which a tenant or vassal promised fealty and service to his overlord.

Syn. allegiance, loyalty.

home (hōm), *n.* **1**, one's abode or residence; the dwelling place of a man and his family; **2**, a happy, congenial place of abode; **3**, fatherland; **4**, the locality where a plant or animal abounds; **5**, a benevolent or charitable institution; **6**, in various games, a goal:—*adj.* **1**, pertaining to one's abode or country; **2**, domestic; **3**, to the point designed; as, a *home* thrust: **home plate**, in baseball, the base at which the batsman stands to bat:—*adv.* **1**, to or at home; **2**, intimately; closely; as, the blow struck *home:*—*v.i.* [*p.t.* and *p.p.* homed (hōmd), *p.pr.* hom'ing], to return home, as pigeons.—*adj.* **home'less.**

home-like (hōm'līk″), *adj.* resembling a home; comfortable; cheerful; cozy; hospitable.—*n.* **home'like″ness.**

home-ly (hōm'lĭ), *adj.* [*comp.* home'li-er, *superl.* home'li-est], **1**, homelike; cozy; **2**, simple, as food; **3**, plain-featured; **4**, uncultured; crude.—*n.* **home'li-ness.**

home-made (hōm'mād″), *adj.* of household or domestic manufacture; as, *homemade* bread.

ho-me-o-path (hō'mē-ō-păth; hŏm'ē-), *n.* one who believes in, or practices, the system of curing disease known as homeopathy. Also, **ho'mœ-o-path.**

ho-me-o-path-ic (hō″mē-ō-păth'ĭk; hŏm″ē-), *adj.* **1**, pertaining to homeopathy, a system of treating disease: distinguished from *allopathic;* **2**, extremely small in quantity; as, a *homeopathic* dose of medicine. Also, **ho″mœ-o-path'ic.**

ho-me-op-a-thy (hō″mē-ŏp'ȧ-thĭ; hŏm″ē-), *n.* the system introduced by Hahnemann (1755–1843), which seeks to cure disease by giving, in minute quantities, medicines which would produce in a well person results similar to the symptoms of the disease treated: distinguished from *allopathy*, which see. Also, **ho″mœ-op'a-thy.**—*n.* **ho″me-op'a-thist.**

Ho-mer-ic (hō-mĕr'ĭk), *adj.* pertaining to the time and works of the Greek epic poet Homer.

home rule local self-government of a dependent country or province, esp. that form of government for Ireland.

home run in baseball, a run scored on a hit which enables the batter to circle the bases before the ball is returned to the plate; also, the hit.

home-sick (hōm'sĭk″), *adj.* longing for home.—*n.* **home'sick″ness.**

home-spun (hōm′spŭn″), *n.* **1**, cloth woven at home or made of yarn spun there, or an imitation of it; **2**, an unpolished rustic or countrified person:—*adj.* **1**, of domestic make; **2**, plain and homely.

home-stead (hōm′stĕd), *n.* a home; esp., the family home with the adjoining lands and buildings.

home-ward (hōm′wẽrd), *adj.* and *adv.* toward home or one's native land. Also, *adv.* **home′wards.**

hom-i-cide (hŏm′ĭ-sīd), *n.* **1**, the killing of a human being by another; **2**, one who kills another.—*adj.* **hom′i-cid″al.**

hom-i-let-ic (hŏm″ĭ-lĕt′ĭk), *adj.* **1**, pertaining to the composition of sermons; **2**, like a sermon: **homiletics,** *n.pl.* used as *sing.* in theology, the science or art of composing or delivering sermons.

hom-i-ly (hŏm′ĭ-lĭ), *n.* [*pl.* homilies (-lĭz)], **1**, a religious discourse or sermon delivered in public; **2**, a tedious moral discourse delivered in private.

hom-ing (hōm′ĭng), *p.adj.* easily finding the way home: **homing pigeon,** a messenger pigeon trained to find its way home from great distances.

hom-i-ny (hŏm′ĭ-nĭ), *n.* a cereal food made of Indian corn soaked so as to remove the hull, and coarsely ground.

ho-mo- (hō′mō-; hŏm′ō-), a combining form from the Greek, meaning same; as, *homo*geneity: opp. of *hetero-*.

ho-mo-ge-ne-i-ty (hō″mō-jē-nē′ĭ-tĭ; hŏm″ō-), *n.* identity; likeness, similarity; homogeneous quality.

ho-mo-ge-ne-ous (hō″mō-jē′nē-ŭs; hŏm″ō-), *adj.* uniform; of the same kind or nature; composed of similar elements: opp. of *heterogeneous.*

hom-o-graph (hŏm′ō-grăf; hō′mō-), *n.* one of two or more words identical in spelling but derived from different roots, and hence different in meaning, as *lie,* to prevaricate, and *lie,* to recline.

ho-mol-o-gous (hō-mŏl′ō-gŭs), *adj.* identical; exactly alike in structure, position, proportion, etc.

hom-o-lo-graph-ic (hŏm″ō-lō-grăf′ĭk), *adj.* pertaining to the drawing or representation of equal areas: **homolographic projection,** a drawing or map of the surface of the earth, made so that equal areas of the surface drawn are represented by equal areas on the drawing, and different continents or parts of them are given in proper proportion: also called *homolograph.*

ho-mol-o-gy (hō-mŏl′ō-jĭ), *n.* [*pl.* homologies (-jĭz)], likeness in general type of structure, as the relation between the leg and arm.

ho-mol-o-sine (hō-mŏl′ō-sīn″), *n.* a homolosine projection: **homolosine projection,** a drawing or map of the surface of the earth, made by a special method to show the continents with the least distortion.

hom-o-nym (hŏm′ō-nĭm; hō′mō-), *n.* a word like another in sound, but differing in spelling and meaning, as *pair, pare, pear; to, too, two; see, sea.*

hom-o-phone (hŏm′ō-fōn; hō′mō-fōn), *n.* **1**, a letter representing the same sound as another; **2**, a homonym.—*adj.* **ho-moph′o-nous** (hō-mŏf′ō-nŭs).

hone (hōn), *n.* a kind of fine whetstone for sharpening razors, etc.:—*v.t.* [*p.t.* and *p.p.* honed (hōnd), *p.pr.* hon′ing], to sharpen on such a whetstone.

hon-est (ŏn′ĕst), *adj.* **1**, upright; just; **2**, genuine; unadulterated; without fraud; as, *honest* weight; **3**, frank; open as to countenance.—*adv.* **hon′est-ly.**
Syn. trustworthy, candid, true.

hon-es-ty (ŏn′ĕs-tĭ), *n.* **1**, the quality of being free from deceit; **2**, fairness and truth; **3**, uprightness.
Syn. integrity, probity, sincerity.

hon-ey (hŭn′ĭ), *n.* **1**, a sweet, sticky, sirupy substance produced by bees from nectar which they collect from flowers; **2**, sweetness; **3**, darling or sweet one:—*v.t.* [*p.t.* and *p.p.* -eyed or -ied (-ĭd), *p.pr.* -ey-ing], **1**, to make sweet, as with honey; **2**, to talk to in an endearing or flattering manner:—*adj.* very sweet.

hon-ey-bee (hŭn′ĭ-bē″), *n.* the common hive bee which gathers nectar from flowers to make honey.

hon-ey-comb (hŭn′ĭ-kōm″), *n.* **1**, the structure of waxen six-sided cells made by bees for their home and storehouse; **2**, any similar structure: **honeycomb coil,** in radio communication, a form of concentrated inductance made by winding a coil of wire in lattice form:—*v.t.* and *v.i.* to fill, or become filled, with holes or cells like those of a honeycomb.

HONEYCOMB

hon-ey-dew (hŭn′ĭ-dū″), *n.* **1**, a sweet liquid deposited by aphids, or plant lice, upon the leaves of trees and plants; **2**, a variety of tobacco treated with molasses; **3**, a variety of melon.

hon-eyed (hŭn′ĭd), *p.adj.* **1**, covered, or filled, with honey; **2**, sweet; flattering; as, *honeyed* words. Also, **hon′ied.**

hon-ey lo-cust a large, thorny American tree of the pea family, having flowers and long, flat pods.

hon-ey-moon (hŭn′ĭ-mōōn″), *n.* the period spent together, often on a trip or tour, as a sort of holiday by a newly married couple before settling down to routine life; a wedding trip.

hon-ey-suck-le (hŭn′ĭ-sŭk″l), *n.* a climbing plant with tubular, fragrant flowers; esp., the woodbine.

honk (hŏngk), *n.* **1**, the call of a wild goose; **2**, any sound resembling this, as that of an automobile horn:—*v.i.* to make such a sound:—*v.t. Slang,* to sound; blow, as the horn of an automobile.

hon-or (ŏn′ẽr), *n.* **1**, respectful regard; high esteem; worship; reputation; fame; **2**, distinction; exalted rank; also, glory; credit; as, he is an *honor* to the family; **3**, uprightness; scorn of meanness, deceit, or unfairness; **4**, chastity, esp. of women; **5**, an outward mark of high esteem; **6**, a title used in addressing certain officials; **7**, one of the five highest trump cards in bridge; **8**, in *pl.*, distinguished standing in school or college; as, he graduated with *honors:*—*v.t.* **1**, to treat with respect, deference, or civility; **2**, to revere or worship; **3**, to bestow marks of esteem upon: followed by *with;* **4**, to accept and pay when due; as, the bank will *honor* my check. Also, **hon′our.**—*n.* **hon′or-er.**
Syn., n. respect, reverence, renown.

hon-or-a-ble (ŏn′ẽr-ȧ-bl), *adj.* **1**, worthy of esteem; illustrious; **2**, in accord with honor; as, *honorable* deeds; *honorable* defeat; **3**, distinguished in rank; **4**, high-minded; noble; upright; **5**, a title of distinction given to judges and other high officials. Also, **hon′our-a-ble.**—*adv.* **hon′or-a-bly.**—*n.* **hon′or-a-ble-ness.**
Syn. creditable, just, honest.

hon-o-ra-ri-um (ŏn″ō-rā′rĭ-ŭm), *n.* [*pl.* honoraria (-ȧ)], a fee paid to a professional man.

hon-or-a-ry (ŏn′ẽr-ā-rĭ), *adj.* **1**, done or conferred as a sign of high esteem; as, an *honorary* degree; **2**, possessing a title or position by courtesy, without giving service; as, an *honorary* president.

hooch (hōōch), *n. U. S. Slang,* intoxicating liquor. Also, **hootch.**

hood (hŏŏd), *n.* **1,** a soft wrapper or covering for the head; **2,** a head covering attached to a monk's or woman's cloak; **3,** something resembling such a head covering, as a folding cover for a carriage; **4,** a projecting cover above a hearth or range to carry off smoke; **5,** a bird's topknot; **6,** an expansible fold of skin on the neck of some snakes; **7,** a floral part shaped like a hood, as in a jack-in-the-pulpit; **8,** an ornamental fold hanging down the back of an academic gown, denoting a university degree:—*v.t.* to cover, or furnish with, or as with, a hood.—*p.adj.* **hood'ed.**

-hood (-hŏŏd), *suffix,* forming nouns from nouns and adjectives, meaning: **1,** state, quality, condition, or character of being; as, child*hood;* likeli*hood;* **2,** collective group or body; as, brother*hood;* **3,** example of; as, false*hood.*

hood-lum (hōōd'lŭm), *n. Colloq.,* a rowdy; street tough.

hoo-doo (hōō'dōō), *n. Colloq.,* a person or thing that causes ill luck:—*v.t. Colloq.,* to bring ill luck upon.

hood-wink (hŏŏd'wĭngk), *v.t.* **1,** to deceive; as, he *hoodwinked* everybody with his tale of misfortune; **2,** to blindfold.

hoof (hōōf), *n.* [*pl.* hoofs; rarely, hooves (hōōvz)], **1,** the horny substance covering the feet of certain animals, as horses; **2,** an animal with hoofs.—*adj.* **hoofed.**

hook (hŏŏk), *n.* **1,** a curved piece of metal, bone, etc., to hold or catch something; as, a crochet *hook;* **2,** an instrument for lopping or cutting, as a sickle; **3,** a cape or headland; as, the *Hook* of Holland; **4,** a sharp bend in a river; **5,** a snare; trap; **6,** in music, one of the short diagonal strokes from the stem of a note, which show it to be an eighth, sixteenth, etc.; a pennant (see *note,* illus.): **by hook or by crook,** by fair means or foul:—*v.t.* **1,** to catch with, or as with, a hook; **2,** to trap; ensnare; **3,** to gore or attack with the horns, as does a bull; **4,** in golf, to hit (the ball) so that it curves to the left: opp. of *slice;* **5,** *Slang,* to steal:—*v.i.* **1,** to bend into the shape of a hook; **2,** to become fastened to anything with a hook: with *on;* **3,** to attack with the horns.

hook-ah (hŏŏk'ȧ), *n.* a pipe with a long tube, for drawing tobacco smoke through water. Also, **hook'a.**

hooked (hŏŏkt; hŏŏk'ĕd), *p.adj.* **1,** curved like a hook; as, a *hooked* nose; **2,** made with a hook; as, a *hooked* rug.

hook-er (hŏŏk'ẽr), *n.* **1,** a fishing smack; **2,** a small Dutch vessel; **3,** any clumsy, ill-fitted, old craft.

hook-worm (hŏŏk'wûrm″), *n.* any of several large worms parasitic in the small intestines.

[1]**hoop** (hōōp), *n.* **1,** a circular band to hold together the staves of a cask, tub, or the like; **2,** the band of a finger ring; **3,** a large ring used by children at play; **4,** anything curved like such a ring, as a croquet wicket; **5,** in *pl.,* a hoop skirt:—*v.t.* to bind or secure with a curved band; encircle.

[2]**hoop** (hōōp), *n.* the cry made in whooping cough:—*v.i.* to utter this cry. Also, **whoop,** *Pfd. S.*

Hoo-sier (hōō'zhẽr), *n.* a citizen of the State of Indiana: a nickname.

hoot (hōōt), *n.* **1,** the cry of an owl; **2,** a sound like this cry; **3,** a shout of contempt:—*v.t.* to jeer or drive with contemptuous shouts:—*v.i.* **1,** to utter a sharp cry, as of an owl; **2,** to make a loud sound or whistle, as a steam boiler.

[1]**hop** (hŏp), *n.* **1,** a perennial vine whose ripened cones give a bitter flavor to malt liquors; **2,** in *pl.,* the dried, ripened cones of this plant, used in flavoring meat, making yeast, etc.:—*v.t.* [*p.t.* and *p.p.* hopped (hŏpt), *p.pr.* hop'ping], to flavor with these ripened cones: **hop clover,** any of several clovers; also, black medic, or nonesuch, one of the cloverlike plants called *shamrock* (see *shamrock,* illus.): **hop pillow,** a pillow or bag filled with dried hops, used to induce sleep.

[2]**hop** (hŏp), *v.t.* [*p.t.* and *p.p.* hopped (hŏpt), *p.pr.* hop'ping], **1,** to leap over on one leg; **2,** to make to jump:—*v.i.* **1,** to proceed by short leaps, using one leg only; **2,** to jump with both or all feet at once, as do frogs:—*n.* **1,** a short, brisk jump, esp. on one leg; **2.** *Colloq.,* an informal dance.

hope (hōp), *n.* **1,** the desire of good accompanied by expectation; anticipation; confidence; **2,** the source of hope; **3,** an object of desire:—*v.t.* [*p.t.* and *p.p.* hoped (hōpt), *p.pr.* hop'ing], **1,** to expect with confidence; **2,** to desire:—*v.i.* **1,** to cherish a desire for good; **2,** to trust confidently.

Syn., n. promise, reliance, trust.

hope-ful (hōp'fŏŏl), *adj.* **1,** full of confident expectation; as, he was *hopeful* that the war would soon end; **2,** promising success; as, *hopeful* prospects.—*adv.* **hope'-ful-ly.**—*n.* **hope'ful-ness.**

Syn. assured, confident, optimistic.—*Ant.* depressed, pessimistic, despairing.

hope-less (hōp'lĕs), *adj.* **1,** without expectation of good; despairing; as, *hopeless* grief; **2,** without promise of good; as, a *hopeless* situation.—*adv.* **hope'less-ly.**—*n.* **hope'less-ness.**

Syn. despondent, forlorn, cheerless.

hop-lite (hŏp'līt), *n.* in ancient Greece, a heavy-armed foot soldier.

hop-per (hŏp'ẽr), *n.* **1,** one who or that which makes short leaps or skips; **2,** a name for various leaping insects, as the grasshopper; **3,** a wooden trough through which grain passes into a mill; **4,** the mechanism in a piano for lifting the hammers; **5,** a receptacle for water, as for a water-closet.

hop-ple (hŏp'l), *n.* a fetter:—*v.t.* [*p.t.* and *p.p.* -pled (-ld), *p.pr.* -pling], to shackle or fetter; as, they *hoppled* the horses.

hop-scotch (hŏp'skŏch″), *n.* a child's game, in which a flat stone is driven by the foot while the player hops.

Ho-ra-ti-us Co-cles (hō-rā'shĭ-ŭs kō'-klēz; hō-rā'shŭs), in Roman legend, a famous hero who guarded the bridge over the Tiber and thus saved Rome.

horde (hōrd), *n.* **1,** a wandering tribe or clan dwelling in tents or wagons; **2,** a vast multitude:—*v.i.* [*p.t.* and *p.p.* hord'ed, *p.pr.* hord'ing], to live or act as in a horde.

hore-hound (hōr'hound″), *n.* **1,** any of various bitter, mint herbs, esp. a species brought into America from Europe, and used as a remedy for coughs and colds; **2,** a flavoring extract or confection made from this plant. Also, **hoar'hound″.**

ho-ri-zon (hō-rī'zŭn; hō-rī'zn), *n.* **1,** the line where the sky and earth or sea appear to meet; **2,** the limit of one's mental vision, experience, or interest.

hor-i-zon-tal (hŏr″ĭ-zŏn'tăl), *adj.* parallel to, or situated near, the line where earth meets sky; level: opp. of *vertical.*—*adv.* **hor'i-zon'tal-ly.**

hor-mone (hôr'mōn), *n.* a chemical substance carried by the blood from one organ of the body to another, and capable of exciting the latter to increased functional activity.

horn (hôrn), *n.* **1,** a hard and usually pointed projection, growing upon the head of certain animals, esp. cattle, goats, deer, etc.; **2,** the material of which animals' horns are composed, a thickened form of tissue; **3**, anything made of, or resembling, the horns of an animal, as one of the ends of the moon when in crescent form; **4**, a musical wind instrument; **5**, in an airplane, a projection on a rudder or similar surface, offering a leverage for the wire from the control lever (see *airplane, empennage*, illus.).—*adj.* **horn'less.**

horn-beam (hôrn'bēm″), *n.* a small tree of the birch family, with hard, tough white wood: also called *ironwood.*

horn-bill (hôrn'bĭl″), *n.* an Old World bird with a large bill bearing flat, hornlike protuberances.

horn-blende (hôrn'blĕnd″), *n.* a widely distributed dark green or black mineral composed chiefly of silica, magnesia, and lime.

horned (hôrnd; *Poetic* hôr'nĕd), *adj.* **1**, having horns; as, *horned* cattle; **2**, horn-shaped.

hor-net (hôr'nĕt; hôr'nĭt), *n.* any of several wasps which inflict a severe sting; esp., the yellow jacket.

horn-pipe (hôrn'pīp″), *n.* **1**, a lively dance, esp. popular with sailors; **2**, music for this dance; **3**, a musical wind instrument once much used in Wales.

horn-y (hôr'nĭ), *adj.* [*comp.* horn'i-er, *superl.* horn'i-est], **1**, hard like horn; **2**, made of horn; **3**, having horns.

hor-o-loge (hŏr'ō-lōj; hŏr'ō-lŏj), *n.* **1**, a timepiece of any kind, as a clock, watch, dial, etc.; **2**, a clock tower.

ho-rol-o-gy (hō-rŏl'ō-jĭ), *n.* the science or art of measuring time, or of making timepieces.

hor-o-scope (hŏr'ō-skōp), *n.* **1**, a representation of the heavens at any time, esp. at one's birth, from which astrologers profess to foretell the future; **2**, the diagram representing the twelve divisions of the heavens, used by astrologers.

hor-ri-ble (hŏr'ĭ-bl), *adj.* **1**, terrible; dreadful; shocking; **2**, *Colloq.*, disagreeable, as weather.—*adv.* **hor'ri-bly.**

Syn. awful, terrific, frightful, abominable.

hor-rid (hŏr'ĭd), *adj.* **1**, dreadful; terrible; hideous; obnoxious; **2**, *Colloq.*, gloomy.—*adv.* **hor'rid-ly.**—*n.* **hor'rid-ness.**

hor-ri-fy (hŏr'ĭ-fī), *v.t.* [*p.t.* and *p.p.* -fied (-fīd), *p.pr.* -fy″ing], to fill or strike with great fear, dread, terror, or repugnance.—*adj.* **hor-rif'ic.**

hor-ror (hŏr'ẽr), *n.* **1**, excessive fear accompanied with shuddering; extreme dread; **2**, great disgust; **3**, that which fills with dread or terror, as a great crime; **4**, in *pl.*, *Colloq.*, extreme dread or depression.

Syn. fear, fright, terror, dread, alarm, panic. *Horror* is *fear* mingled with abhorrence and aversion. *Fear* is the general term and describes the emotion aroused by danger, accompanied by the desire to escape from it. *Fright* and *terror* are extreme *fear; fright* is sudden, usually temporary; *terror* is violent and overpowering. *Dread* is very great *fear*, aroused by anticipation of evil. *Alarm* is an excited apprehension of danger. *Panic* is frantic, unreasoning *fear*, often experienced by large numbers.

horse (hôrs), *n.* **1**, a solid-hoofed quadruped, used for riding or drawing burdens; **2**, a male of the species; **3**, any of other members of the horse family, as the ass; **4**, cavalry; **5**, a framework or machine for the support of anything; **6**, in gymnastics, a padded and raised wooden block used for vaulting: **dark horse, 1**, in horse racing, a horse whose chances of success have not been considered by the public; **2**, in politics, an unforeseen competitor:—*v.t.* [*p.t.* and *p.p.* horsed (hôrst), *p.pr.* hors'ing], **1**, to mount on, or furnish with, a horse; **2**, to place astride:—*adj.* coarse or large of its kind: **horse sense,** practical common sense.—*adj.* **horse'less.**

horse-back (hôrs'băk″), *n.* the back of a horse:—*adv.* on horseback.

horse–chest-nut (hôrs'=chĕs'nŭt), *n.* a tree with large clusters of blossoms and large, nutlike seeds growing in burrs; also, the seed of this tree.

horse-fly (hôrs'flī″), *n.* [*pl.* horseflies (-flīz″)], any of several large flies that sting animals; a gadfly.

horse-hair (hôrs'hâr″), *n.* the hair of the mane or tail of a horse.

horse-hide (hôrs'hīd″), *n.* the hide of a horse, or leather made of it.

horse-man (hôrs'măn), *n.* [*pl.* horsemen (-mĕn)], **1**, a rider upon a horse; **2**, one clever at managing horses.—*n.fem.* **horse'wom″an.**—*n.* **horse'man-ship.**

horse-play (hôrs'plā″), *n.* coarse, rough, boisterous fun.

horse pow-er a unit of power equal to that required to raise 33,000 pounds one foot in one minute. Also, *n.* **horse'pow″er.**—*abbr.* **H. P.**

horse–rad-ish (hôrs'=răd″ĭsh), *n.* a plant of the mustard family, whose root is used as a relish.

horse-shoe (hôrs'shōō″), *n.* **1**, a U-shaped metal shoe to protect the hoof of a horse; **2**, anything roughly U-shaped.—*n.* **horse'sho″er.**

horse-tail (hôrs'tāl″), *n.* **1**, the tail of a horse; **2**, any of a family of low-growing, rushlike simple plants.

horse-whip (hôrs'hwĭp″), *n.* a long leather whip with a lash:—*v.t.* [*p.t.* and *p.p.* -whipped″ (-hwĭpt″), *p.pr.* -whip″ping], to flog with a heavy whip.

hors-y (hôr'sĭ), *adj.* [*comp.* hors'i-er, *superl.* hors'i-est], pertaining to horses; interested in horses.

hor-ta-to-ry (hôr'tȧ-tō-rĭ), *adj.* **1**, tending to rouse, encourage, or urge on; **2**, tending to give earnest advice.

hor-ti-cul-ture (hôr'tĭ-kŭl″tūr), *n.* the art or science of cultivating gardens or orchards.—*adj.* **hor″ti-cul'tur-al.**—*n.* **hor″ti-cul'tur-ist.**

Ho-rus (hō'rŭs), *n.* in Egyptian mythology, the sun god, or god of the day.

ho-san-na (hō-zăn'ȧ), *n.* and *interj.* an exclamation of praise to God.

hose (hōz), *n.* [*pl.* hose], **1**, a covering for the leg; a stocking; **2**, [*pl.* sometimes hoses (hōz'ĕz)], flexible tubing for carrying water.

Ho-se-a (hō-zē'ȧ), *n.* **1**, an ancient Hebrew prophet; **2**, the book of the Old Testament containing his teachings.—*abbr.* **Hos.**

ho-sier (hō'zhẽr), *n.* one who deals in stockings and other knit goods.

ho-sier-y (hō'zhẽr-ĭ), *n.* **1**, stockings, underclothing, etc.; **2**, a manufactory for such goods.

hos-pice (hŏs'pĭs; hŏs'pēs), *n.* **1**, a place of shelter for travelers; a refuge for the destitute or sick; **2**, a monastery, esp. in the Alps, that also serves as an inn.

hos-pi-ta-ble (hŏs'pĭ-tȧ-bl), *adj.* **1**, receiving and entertaining friends or strangers; kind and generous to guests and strangers; **2**, marked by, or indicating, such feeling.—*adv.* **hos'pi-ta-bly.**

hos-pi-tal (hŏs'pĭ-tăl), *n.* an institution for the medical and surgical treatment and care of the sick or wounded.

hos-pi-tal-i-ty (hŏs″pĭ-tăl'ĭ-tĭ), *n.* [*pl.* hospitalities (-tĭz)], the practice of entertaining friends and strangers with kindness and liberality.

[1]**host** (hōst), *n.* **1**, orig., a large army; **2**, a great number; throng.

[2]**host** (hōst), *n.* **1,** one who entertains another; **2,** a landlord; **3,** an organism that gives nourishment to a parasite.

Host (hōst), *n.* the consecrated bread or wafer of the Eucharist; also, the bread before consecration.

hos-tage (hŏs′tāj), *n.* **1,** a person who remains in the hands of another as a pledge for the fulfilment of certain conditions; **2,** any pledge.

hos-tel (hŏs′tĕl), *n.* formerly, an inn or hotel; hostelry.

hos-tel-ry (hŏs′tĕl-rĭ), *n.* [*pl.* hostelries (-rĭz)], formerly, an inn or lodging house; as, the Wayside Inn was a famous old *hostelry*.

host-ess (hōs′tĕs), *n.* **1,** a woman who receives and entertains guests; **2,** the mistress of an inn.

hos-tile (hŏs′tĭl; *Br.* hŏs′tīl), *adj.* **1,** belonging to an enemy; showing ill will or animosity; **2,** adverse; unfriendly:—*n.* an enemy; esp., an American Indian at war against the whites.—*adv.* **hos′tile-ly.**

hos-til-i-ty (hŏs-tĭl′ĭ-tĭ), *n.* [*pl.* hostilities (-tĭz)], **1,** the state of being opposed; **2,** antagonism; enmity; animosity; **3,** in *pl.*, acts of warfare.

hos-tler (hŏs′lẽr; ŏs′lẽr), *n.* **1,** one who takes care of horses at an inn or stable; **2,** one who takes charge of a railroad locomotive after a trip.

hot (hŏt), *adj.* [*comp.* hot′ter, *superl.* hot′test], **1,** having much heat; **2,** fiery; passionate; as, a *hot* temper; **3,** lustful; sensual; as, *hot* desire; **4,** pungent; acrid; as, a *hot* taste; **5,** fresh; strong; as, a *hot* scent; **6,** unendurable, as a situation; **7,** near to the object sought for, as in some games.—*adv.* **hot′ly.**—*n.* **hot′ness.**

hot-bed (hŏt′bĕd″), *n.* **1,** a bed of earth covered with glass and made artificially warm to force the growth of plants; **2,** hence, any place or condition that promotes growth or activity; as, a *hotbed* of treason.

hotch-potch (hŏch′pŏch″), *n.* **1,** a thick broth of meat and vegetables; **2,** a mixture. Also, **hodge′podge″.**

ho-tel (hō-tĕl′), *n.* a house for entertaining travelers or strangers; a superior inn or lodging house: ***hôtel** (ō″tĕl′), [Fr.], a public building; also, a private mansion.

hot-foot (hŏt′fo͝ot″), *adv. Colloq.*, in great haste; as, he set off *hotfoot.*

hot–head (hŏt′=hĕd″), *n.* an impetuous or fiery-tempered person.—*adj.* **hot′–head″ed.**

hot-house (hŏt′hous″), *n.* a glass house, heated for raising tender plants and for ripening fruits.

hot-spur (hŏt′spûr″), *n.* a rash, hasty, or hot-headed man:—*adj.* hot-headed; reckless; violent.

Hot-ten-tot (hŏt′n-tŏt), *n.* **1,** one of a savage South African race in Cape Colony; **2,** the language spoken by the Hottentots, characterized by a peculiar click; **3,** any uneducated and unrefined person.

hough (hŏk), *n.* **1,** the joint in the hind leg of some quadrupeds, corresponding to the ankle in man; **2,** the back of the knee joint. See [2]**hock,** *Pfd. S.*

hound (hound), *n.* **1,** a kind of domestic dog, with large, drooping ears, which hunts squirrels, rabbits, foxes, etc.; **2,** a despicable, mean fellow:—*v.t.* **1,** to chase with, or as if with, hunting dogs; **2,** to incite; set upon; **3,** to persecute; drive; nag.

hour (our), *n.* **1,** the 24th part of a day; 60 minutes; **2,** the time of day as marked by the clock; as, what is the *hour?* **3,** often in *pl.*, a particular or stated time; as, school *hours;* **4,** in *pl.*, in the Roman Catholic Church, prayers repeated at stated times: **Hours,** the book containing these prayers.—*adj.* and *adv.* **hour′ly.**

hour-glass (our′glȧs″), *n.* a device for measuring time by running sand through a narrow neck of a glass vessel.

HOUR-GLASS

hou-ri (ho͞o′rĭ; hou′rĭ), *n.* [*pl.* houris (-rĭz)], one of the dark-eyed nymphs or maidens of the Mohammedan paradise.

house (hous), *n.* **1,** a building for residence; place of abode; **2,** a building for some particular purpose; as, a work*house;* court*house;* hence, a shelter, as for animals; **3,** family or race, esp. if of high rank; **4,** one of the divisions of a lawmaking or church-governing body; **5,** a quorum of the members of such a body, or enough to transact business; **6,** a theater or its audience; **7,** a business firm or place of business; **8,** in astrology, the station of a planet in the heavens, or the twelfth part of the heavens; **9,** formerly, a square on a chessboard: **House of Commons,** the lower house of the British Parliament, consisting of elected representatives of the counties and boroughs: **House of Lords,** the upper house of the British Parliament, consisting of archbishops, bishops, and peers of the realm: **House of Representatives,** the lower and larger branch of the United States Congress, consisting of members elected in proportion to population: often called *the House:*—*v.t.* (houz), [*p.t.* and *p.p.* housed (houzd), *p.pr.* hous′ing], **1,** to shelter or lodge; **2,** to store, as goods; **3,** to secure; as, to *house* a yacht.—*v.i.* to hide; take shelter.

house boat a covered vessel fitted up as a floating residence.

house-break-er (hous′brāk″ẽr), *n.* one who breaks open and enters the dwelling of another with criminal intent.—*n.* **house′break″ing.**

house fly the common domestic fly, a two-winged insect with sucking mouth parts, breeding chiefly in manure and garbage, the larvæ being called *maggots.*

house-hold (hous′hōld), *n.* a group of persons living together; a family:—*adj.* pertaining to a family or home; domestic.—*n.* **house′hold″er.**

house-keep-ing (hous′kēp″ĭng), *n.* the management of domestic affairs:—*adj.* capable of being used in the management of a household; domestic.—*n.fem.* **house′keep″er.**

house-maid (hous′mād″), *n.* a girl hired to do housework, esp. chamber work, bed making, etc.

house-warm-ing (hous′wôr″mĭng), *n.* a feast celebrating entrance into a new house.

house-wife (hous′wīf″), *n.* **1,** [*pl.* housewives (-wīvz″)], the mistress of a home; one who manages domestic affairs; **2,** (hŭz′ĭf), a small case for sewing materials, particularly in the army.

house-work (hous′wûrk″), *n.* the work connected with housekeeping, as cooking, cleaning, etc.

[1]**hous-ing** (houz′ĭng), *n.* **1,** the act of giving shelter; **2,** that which gives shelter; hence, living conditions generally; **3,** a cavity designed to receive or contain some corresponding part; specif., a casing for gears or bearings, a mortise in a beam, or the like.

[2]**hous-ing** (houz′ĭng), *n.* **1,** a horse's saddlecloth; **2,** in *pl.*, the decorative trappings on a horse.

Hou-yhn-hnm (ho͞o-ĭn′m; hwĭn′m), *n.* one of the inhabitants of a land, described in Swift's "Gulliver's Travels," in which the dominant race is composed of horses, and a race of degraded human beings, or *Yahoos*, is subordinate to them.

hove (hōv), past tense and past participle of the irregular verb *heave*.

hov-el (hŏv′ĕl), *n.* a poor cottage, hut, or cabin:—*v.t.* to shelter in a hut.

hov-er (hŭv′ẽr), *v.i.* **1,** to flutter over or about; **2,** to stand in suspense or expectation; **3,** to move about or loiter uncertainly or anxiously.

how (hou), *adv.* **1,** in what manner or condition; **2,** to what degree, amount, or extent; **3,** with what reason, name, or meaning.

how-be-it (hou-bē′ĭt), *adv.* and *conj.* nevertheless; although; however.

how-dah (hou′dȧ), *n.* a seat for riding on an elephant or a camel, usually canopied and often richly decorated. Also, **hou′dah.**

HOWDAH

how-ev-er (hou″ĕv′ẽr), *adv.* in whatever manner or degree; at all events; in any case:—*conj.* notwithstanding; yet; nevertheless: often contracted to *howe'er.*

how-itz-er (hou′ĭt-sẽr), *n.* a short, light cannon, throwing shells at a higher angle of elevation than the ordinary cannon.

howl (houl), *n.* **1,** the prolonged cry of a dog or wolf; **2,** the cry of one in pain or distress; **3,** a loud shout of derision, as by a crowd:—*v.i.* **1,** to cry like a dog or wolf; **2,** to utter a prolonged cry of pain or distress; **3,** to roar, like the wind:—*v.t.* **1,** to cry down by clamor; **2,** to utter in a loud wailing tone.

howl-er (houl′ẽr), *n.* **1,** one who wails or cries loudly; **2,** any of several South American monkeys that climb trees and wail at night; **3,** *Slang,* anything excessive, as a bad blunder.

how-so-ev-er (hou″sō-ĕv′ẽr), *adv.* in whatsoever manner; however; in whatever degree.

[1]**hoy** (hoi), *n.* **1,** formerly, a small, one-masted, heavy coasting vessel; **2,** now, a heavy barge.

[2]**hoy** (hoi), *interj.* ho! hollo!:—*n.* on shipboard, a call or shout used in hailing.

hoy-den (hoi′dn), *n.* a rude, romping girl; a tomboy:—*adj.* rough; bold; ill-mannered:—*v.i.* to act in a rude, boisterous way. Also, **hoi′den.**

Hoyle (hoil), *n.* a book of rules for card games, orig. edited by Edmund Hoyle of England: **according to Hoyle,** adhering strictly to the rules in any game.

hub (hŭb), *n.* **1,** the central part of a wheel; nave; **2,** the peg at which quoits are thrown; **3,** a steel punch; **4,** the hilt of a weapon: **the Hub,** humorously, the city of Boston.

hub-bub (hŭb′ŭb), *n.* uproar; a loud confusion of voices; tumult.

huck-a-back (hŭk′ȧ-băk), *n.* a kind of linen or cotton cloth, used for toweling: also called *huck.*

huck-le-ber-ry (hŭk′l-bĕr″ĭ), *n.* [*pl.* huckleberries (-ĭz)], **1,** any of several low shrubs of the heath family, bearing an edible, berrylike fruit; **2,** in the Central States, a kind of blueberry, growing very tall; **3,** any of several shrubs related to these; also, the fruit of any huckleberry.

huck-ster (hŭk′stẽr), *n.* **1,** a peddler or hawker; one who retails small articles; **2,** a mean, tricky fellow:—*v.i.* **1,** to make petty bargains; **2,** to wrangle over:—*v.t.* to peddle; carry on petty dealings in.

hud-dle (hŭd′l), *v.t.* [*p.t.* and *p.p.* -dled (-ld), *p.pr.* -dling], **1,** to crowd together in a disorderly manner; collect closely; **2,** to place or perform in haste or disorder:—*v.i.* **1,** to come in a crowd or haste: with *on, up,* or *over;* **2,** to nestle together; **3,** to draw oneself up in a heap:—*n.* confusion; crowd.

hue (hū), *n.* **1,** color, as red; **2,** variety of color; as, red of a dark *hue.*
Syn. shade, dye. (See color.)

hue and cry **1,** a general outcry of alarm or pursuit; **2,** in law, the process of pursuing a felon, criminal, or wrongdoer; **3,** in England, an official gazette advertising crimes and criminals.

huff (hŭf), *n.* a fit of petulance or ill humor; sudden offense taken:—*v.t.* **1,** to puff or blow up; **2,** to treat with insolence; bully; **3,** to remove (a piece at checkers, when one's opponent fails to jump with it).—*adj.* **huff′ish.**

huff-y (hŭf′ĭ), *adj.* [*comp.* huff′i-er, *superl.* huff′i-est], **1,** arrogant; insolent; **2,** taking sudden offense; petulant.—*adv.* **huff′i-ly.**—*n.* **huff′i-ness.**

hug (hŭg), *n.* **1,** a close embrace; **2,** a particular grip in wrestling:—*v.t.* [*p.t.* and *p.p.* hugged (hŭgd), *p.pr.* hug′ging], **1,** to embrace closely; fondle; **2,** to hold fast to; **3,** to keep close to; as, to *hug* the coast.

huge (hūj), *adj.* **1,** vast; very large; **2,** great; as, the party was a *huge* success.—*adv.* **huge′ly.**—*n.* **huge′ness.**
Syn. bulky, colossal. (See enormous.)

hug-ger-mug-ger (hŭg′ẽr-mŭg″ẽr), *adj.* **1,** secret; **2,** confused:—*n.* **1,** secrecy; **2,** confusion:—*adv.* **1,** secretly; **2,** in confusion.

Hu-gue-not (hū′gē-nŏt), *n.* a French Protestant of the 16th and 17th centuries.—*adj.* **Hu″gue-not′ic.**

hulk (hŭlk), *n.* **1,** the body of a ship, esp. if old or unseaworthy; **2,** an old, clumsy vessel; **3,** any unwieldy object or person: **the hulks,** old mastless ships formerly used as convict prisons.

hulk-ing (hŭlk′ĭng), *adj.* unwieldy; bulky; as, a *hulking* fellow.

[1]**hull** (hŭl), *n.* the outer covering, as of various fruits, vegetables, and grains; the husk:—*v.t.* to shell, husk, or stem, as peas, corn, and berries.—*n.* **hull′er.**

[2]**hull** (hŭl), *n.* the body or frame of a vessel; as, a drifting, battered *hull.*

hul-la-ba-loo (hŭl″ȧ-bȧ-lōō′), *n.* clamor; uproar; noisy contention.

hul-lo (hŭ-lō′), *n.* and *interj.* [*pl.* hullos (-lōz′)], **1,** a call to attract attention; **2,** an informal salutation:—*v.i.* to call out or exclaim. See **hol′lo,** *Pfd. S.*

[1]**hum** (hŭm), *v.i.* [*p.t.* and *p.p.* hummed (hŭmd), *p.pr.* hum′ming], **1,** to make a sound without opening the lips, suggesting the sound of a prolonged *m;* **2,** to make a buzzing noise, as a bee in flight; drone; **3,** to sing with lips closed; **4,** to be in energetic motion or action; as, he made things *hum:*—*v.t.* **1,** to sing in a low undertone; **2,** to sing with the lips closed:—*n.* **1,** the noise made by bees and insects in flying; **2,** the act of making a low sound; **3,** a distant sound, as of machinery or people, or of airplanes in flight.

[2]**hum** (hŭm), *interj.* and *n.* a sound, followed by a pause, implying hesitation, surprise, doubt, etc.

hu-man (hū′măn), *adj.* **1,** pertaining to, or characteristic of, man or mankind; **2,** having the qualities of a man; neither divine nor brutish.—*n.* **hu′man-ness.**
Syn. (see humane).

hu-mane (hū-mān′), *adj.* **1,** having the feelings proper to man; benevolent; kind; compassionate; **2,** elevating or refining, as certain studies.—*adv.* **hu-mane′ly.**—*n.* **hu-mane′ness.**
Syn. human. *Humane* implies active

kindness and intention to prevent and relieve suffering of any kind; as, the *Humane* Society prevents cruelty. *Human* denotes pertaining to mankind; it often suggests a warmly sympathetic nature; as, a *human* point of view; or it may describe a forgivable weakness; as, his reply betrayed a *human* irritation.

hu-man-ism (hū′măn-ĭzm), *n.* **1,** the state of belonging to mankind, or of being human; **2,** interest in mankind; **3,** liberal education; the study of art and letters, esp. of the classics; **4,** a recent conception of religion which regards man as the chief consideration in religious thought.—*n.* **hu′man-ist.**—*adj.* **hu″man-is′tic.**

hu-man-i-ta-ri-an (hū-măn″ĭ-tā′rĭ-ăn), *n.* **1,** a philanthropist, or charitably inclined person; **2,** one who believes that the duty of man consists of acting rightly to others:—*adj.* **1,** philanthropic; benevolent; having broad human sympathies; **2,** holding, or believing in, the philosophy of love to mankind.—*n.* **hu-man″i-ta′ri-an-ism.**

hu-man-i-ty (hū-măn′ĭ-tĭ), *n.* [*pl.* humanities (-tĭz)], **1,** mankind; **2,** the state or quality of belonging to mankind; **3,** the nature which distinguishes man from other creatures; **4,** philanthropy, or charity toward others; kindness; **5,** in *pl.*, classical learning and literature, esp. the Latin and Greek classics; education.

hu-man-ize (hū′măn-īz), *v.t.* [*p.t.* and *p.p.* -ized (-īzd), *p.pr.* -iz″ing], **1,** to make like mankind; **2,** to make humane; refine or civilize:—*v.i.* to become human.

hu-man-kind (hū′măn-kīnd′), *n.* the race of mankind; humanity.

hu-man-ly (hū′măn-lĭ), *adv.* **1,** from a human viewpoint; **2,** after the manner of men; as, he was *humanly* fallible; **3,** within human power or knowledge; as, we will do whatever is *humanly* possible.

hum-ble (hŭm′bl), *adj.* **1,** having a low estimate of oneself; modest; meek; submissive; **2,** lowly in condition; mean; obscure; unassuming; as, they lived in a *humble* cottage by the sea:—*v.t.* [*p.t.* and *p.p.* -bled (-bld), *p.pr.* -bling], to make submissive; subdue; bring low; mortify; humiliate.—*n.* **hum′ble-ness.**—*adv.* **hum′bly.**

Syn., v. degrade, depress.

hum-ble-bee (hŭm′bl-bē″), *n.* a kind of large, hairy bee. Also, **bum′ble-bee″**, *U. S. Pfd. S.*

hum-ble pie orig., a pie made of the heart, liver, etc., of a deer, and intended for the servants' table: **to eat humble pie,** to make apologies; humiliate oneself; withdraw one's words.

hum-ble plant a tropical and greenhouse plant of the pea family, whose pinnate leaves fold their leaflets together at night or when touched; the sensitive plant.

hum-bug (hŭm′bŭg″), *n.* **1,** a fraud or imposition under fair pretenses; sham; **2,** a plausible deceiver; **3,** a spirit of trickery or deception:—*v.t.* [*p.t.* and *p.p.* -bugged″ (-bŭgd″), *p.pr.* -bug″ging], to impose upon; swindle.—*n.* **hum′bug″ger.**

hum-bug-ger-y (hŭm′bŭg″ẽr-ĭ), *n.* [*pl.* humbuggeries (-ĭz)], imposition or fraud; deception; quackery.

hum-drum (hŭm′drŭm″), *adj.* dull; monotonous; commonplace; as, a *humdrum* life:—*n.* monotony; sameness.

hu-mer-us (hū′mẽr-ŭs), *n.* [*pl.* humeri (-ī)], **1,** in man, the bone of the upper arm, from the shoulder to the elbow; **2,** a corresponding bone in the fore limb of other vertebrates.—*adj.* **hu′mer-al.**

hu-mid (hū′mĭd), *adj.* damp; moist; somewhat wet or watery; as, *humid* air.

hu-mid-i-ty (hū-mĭd′ĭ-tĭ), *n.* moisture: dampness, esp. of the air.

hu-mil-i-ate (hū-mĭl′ĭ-āt), *v.t.* [*p.t.* and *p.p.* -at″ed, *p.pr.* -at″ing], to humble; abase; put to shame.

Syn. mortify, disgrace, degrade.

hu-mil-i-a-tion (hū-mĭl″ĭ-ā′shŭn), *n.* **1,** the act of putting to shame; **2,** the state of being put to shame; chagrin; embarrassment; mortification.

hu-mil-i-ty (hū-mĭl′ĭ-tĭ), *n.* [*pl.* humilities (-tĭz)], **1,** the state or quality of being lowly in mind; modesty; meekness; **2,** subservience; submission; modest courtesy.

hum-ming bird any of several tiny birds noted for bright colors and for the habit of hovering about flowers moving their wings so rapidly as to make a humming noise in their flight.

hum-mock (hŭm′ŭk), *n.* **1,** a hillock or rounded mound; **2,** a similar ridge on an ice field.

hu-mor (hū′mẽr; ū′mẽr), *n.* **1,** a state of mind; mood; **2,** the mental capacity to perceive or express absurdities; **3,** any element in a situation that appeals to a sense of the incongruous; **4,** any fluid of the body, esp. of the eye:—*v.t.* **1,** to indulge; **2,** to adapt oneself to. Also, **hu′mour.**

Syn., n. disposition. (See wit.)

hu-mor-ist (hū′mẽr-ĭst), *n.* **1,** a droll or humorous person; one whose writing or conversation is characterized by a spirit of fun; **2,** an odd or erratic person.

hu-mor-ous (hū′mẽr-ŭs), *adj.* full of, or characterized by, mirth and fun; comical; diverting; witty; pleasant; merry; as, a *humorous* story; Mark Twain was a *humorous* writer.—*adv.* **hu′mor-ous-ly.**—*n.* **hu′mor-ous-ness.**

Syn. amusing, facetious, funny, whimsical.—*Ant.* serious, sad, sober, mournful.

hu-mor-some (hū′mẽr-sŭm), *adj.* **1,** peevish; full of moods; **2,** laughable; capricious; droll; witty.

hump (hŭmp), *n.* a protuberance or bulging, esp. that on the back of a camel, or that formed by a crooked back in man:—*v.t.* **1,** to make in such a shape; bend or curve, as the back; **2,** *Slang,* to exert (oneself).—*p.adj.* **humped.**

hump-back (hŭmp′băk″), *n.* **1,** one with a deformed back; a hunchback; **2,** a crooked back; **3,** a kind of whale.—*adj.* **hump′backed″.**

humph (h′m: pronounced without opening the lips, and with a very quick termination of the *m* sound), *interj.* an exclamation of doubt, surprise, or disgust:—*v.i.* (hŭmf), to utter such an exclamation.

Hump-ty Dump-ty (hŭmp′tĭ dŭmp′tĭ), the short, dumpy hero of a nursery rime, representing an egg: **humpty dumpty,** a short, dumpy person: **humpty-dumpty,** *adj.* characterized by short limbs and a round body.

hu-mus (hū′mŭs), *n.* that part of soil formed by the decay of animal and vegetable matter; vegetable mold.

Hun (hŭn), *n.* **1,** one of a warlike, wandering people of northern Asia, who, in the fifth century, overran and laid waste Europe; **2,** any savage invader; **3,** a destructive person; vandal.

hunch (hŭnch), *n.* **1,** a hump; **2,** a lump; **3,** a thrust with the fist or elbow; **4,** *Slang,* an instinctive feeling or conviction:—*v.t.* to bend or round (the back).

hunch-back (hŭnch′băk″), *n.* a crooked or hunched back, or a person with a crooked back.—*adj.* **hunch′backed″.**

hun-dred (hŭn′drĕd), *adj.* composed of ten times ten; five score:—*n.*

1, the number consisting of ten times ten; 2, a sign representing it, as 100 or C; 3, a division of an English county; 4, a township: so called in the State of Delaware.—*adj.* and *n.* **hun′dredth.**

hun-dred-weight (hŭn′drĕd-wāt″), *n.* the 20th part of a ton; 100 or 112 pounds avoirdupois.

hung (hŭng), past tense and past participle of the verb *hang.*

Hun-ga-ri-an (hŭng-gā′rĭ-ăn), *adj.* pertaining to Hungary or its people:—*n.* a native of Hungary.

hun-ger (hŭng′gẽr), *n.* 1, keenness of appetite; pain or uneasiness caused by want of food; 2, any strong desire:—*v.i.* 1, to feel the desire for food; 2, to have a longing or earnest desire for something.

hun-ger strike continued refusal to accept food, practiced to obtain a certain end, as release from prison, or publicity for a cause.

hun-gry (hŭng′grĭ), *adj.* [*comp.* hun′gri-er, *superl.* hun′gri-est], 1, having a keen appetite; feeling pain or uneasiness for want of food; 2, emaciated or thin; 3, eagerly desirous; 4, unfertile: said of land.—*adv.* **hun′gri-ly.**—*n.* **hun′gri-ness.**

hunk (hŭngk), *n. Colloq.*, a lump or large piece; as, a *hunk* of bread or meat.

hunks (hŭngks), *n.* a niggardly or mean fellow; a covetous man; miser.

hunt (hŭnt), *v.t.* 1, to pursue or chase, as game or wild animals; 2, to search through for something; 3, to persecute; hound; 4, to search after; as, to *hunt* gold:—*v.i.* 1, to follow the chase; 2, to seek:—*n.* 1, pursuit of game or wild animals; 2, a pack of hounds; 3, an association of huntsmen; 4, the district over which hounds pursue game; 5, a search.—*n.* **hunt′ing.**

Syn., *v.* seek, scour, track.

hunt-er (hŭn′tẽr), *n.* 1, one who pursues game; a huntsman; 2, a horse or hound trained for pursuing game; 3, one who searches for something; 4, a watch with a hinged metal cover protecting the face.

hunt-ing box a temporary residence for use during the hunting season; a hunting lodge.

hunt-ing case a watch case with a hinged metal cover to protect the crystal over the face.

hunt-ress (hŭn′trĕs), *n.* a woman who follows the chase; as, the goddess Diana was a *huntress.*

hunts-man (hŭnts′măn), *n.* [*pl.* huntsmen (-mĕn)], 1, one who pursues game; 2, one who manages a pack of hounds in a hunt.

hur-dle (hûr′dl), *n.* 1, a movable fence of interwoven twigs or branches, or of iron; 2, a fence or barrier to be leaped over in steeplechasing or in racing; 3, a rude frame on which criminals were formerly dragged to execution:—*v.t.* [*p.t.* and *p.p.* -dled (-dld), *p.pr.* -dling], 1, to cover or inclose with a fence or barrier; 2, to leap over, as the barriers in a hurdle race:—*v.i.* to make such a leap.—*n.* **hur′dler.**

HURDLE

hur-dy-gur-dy (hûr′dĭ-gûr″dĭ), *n.* [*pl.* hurdy-gurdies (-dĭz)], a musical instrument played by turning a crank; esp., a mechanical piano mounted on wheels and played on the street.

hurl (hûrl), *v.t.* 1, to throw with violence; drive forcibly; 2, to cast down; overthrow; 3, to utter with vehemence:—*v.i.* to rush:—*n.* 1, the act of throwing violently; 2, a cast; a violent throw.—*n.* **hurl′er.**

Syn., *v.* fling, cast, pitch.

hurl-y-burl-y (hûr′lĭ-bûr″lĭ), *n.* [*pl.* hurly-burlies (-lĭz)], tumult; commotion; uproar; racket.

Hu-ron (hū′rŏn), *n.* a member of an Iroquoian tribe of Indians, formerly living near Lakes Huron and Ontario.

hur-rah (hōō-rä′; hŭ-rä′), *interj.* expressing joy, triumph, applause, etc.:—*n.* a triumphant shout; a cheer:—*v.t.* to cheer:—*v.i.* to utter such a shout in applause, joy, etc. Also, **hur-ra′.**

hur-ri-cane (hŭr′ĭ-kān), *n.* a violent whirlwind; a gale of extreme violence, usually accompanied by thunder, lightning, and rain.

hur-ri-cane deck the topmost deck of a steamship.

hur-ried (hŭr′ĭd), *p.adj.* exhibiting, or characterized by, haste; hasty; as, a *hurried* meal.—*adv.* **hur′ried-ly.**

hur-ry (hŭr′ĭ), *v.t.* [*p.t.* and *p.p.* -ried (-rĭd), *p.pr.* -ry-ing], to impel to greater speed; hasten on:—*v.i.* to act or move with haste:—*n.* [*pl.* hurries (-ĭz)], haste; urgency; precipitation.

Syn., *v.* rush, quicken, dispatch, expedite.

hur-ry–scur-ry (hŭr′ĭ-skŭr″ĭ), *n.* [*pl.* hurry-scurries (-ĭz)], confused bustle:—*adv.* in disorderly haste:—*adj.* disorderly; hasty. Also, **hur′ry–skur″ry.**

hurt (hûrt), *v.t.* [*p.t.* and *p.p.* hurt, *p.pr.* hurt′ing], 1, to cause or inflict pain in; wound; 2, to grieve; 3, to injure; impair or damage:—*v.i.* 1, to be painful, as a sore; 2, to cause pain, as a blow or insult:—*n.* 1, a wound; injury; 2, damage; loss; 3, detriment; impairment of value.

hurt-ful (hûrt′fōōl), *adj.* injurious; harmful; as, *hurtful* exercise.—*adv.* **hurt′ful-ly.**—*n.* **hurt′ful-ness.**

Syn. noxious, pernicious, detrimental.

hur-tle (hûr′tl), *v.t.* [*p.t.* and *p.p.* -tled (-tld), *p.pr.* -tling], to move violently; impel forcibly:—*v.i.* 1, to clash; 2, to rush headlong; 3, to move with a clashing sound; clatter; resound.

hus-band (hŭz′bănd), *n.* a married man: correlative of *wife:*—*v.t.* to manage, direct, or use with economy; as, she will *husband* her money.

hus-band-man (hŭz′bănd-măn), *n.* [*pl.* husbandmen (-mĕn)], a tiller of the soil; farmer.

hus-band-ry (hŭz′bănd-rĭ), *n.* 1, agriculture; farming; 2, frugality.

Syn. cultivation, tillage.

hush (hŭsh), *interj.* be still! silence!—*n.* quietness; silence:—*v.t.* 1, to make silent; 2, to soothe; 3, to conceal, as scandal:—*v.i.* to keep quiet: **hush money,** a bribe, usually money, given to insure silence or secrecy.

husk (hŭsk), *n.* 1, the dry outer covering of certain fruits or seeds; 2, any rough and worthless outside covering:—*v.t.* to remove hulls from, as corn.—*n.* **husk′er.**

husk-ing bee a social gathering to assist in husking corn.

[1]**husk-y** (hŭs′kĭ), *adj.* [*comp.* husk′i-er, *superl.* husk′i-est], 1, consisting of, or like, husks, or dry hulls; worthless; 2, dry and harsh: said of the voice.—*adv.* **husk′i-ly.**—*n.* **husk′i-ness.**

[2]**hus-ky** (hŭs′kĭ), *adj. U. S. Colloq.*, strong; well-developed; powerful:—*n.* [*pl.* huskies (-kĭz)], *U. S. Colloq.*, a stalwart, well-developed man.

Hus-ky (hŭs′kĭ), *n.* [*pl.* Huskies (-kĭz)], 1, an Eskimo; 2, the language of the Eskimos: [3]**husky,** a powerful Eskimo dog used to draw sledges.

hus-sar (hōō-zär′), *n.* a light-armed cavalry soldier in European armies.

hus-sy (hŭz'ĭ), *n.* [*pl.* hussies (-ĭz)], **1,** a worthless woman; **2,** a saucy girl; a romp; **3,** (properly, *housewife*, which see), a small traveling case containing sewing materials. Also, **huz'zy.**

hus-tings (hŭs'tĭngz), *n.pl.*, usually used as *sing.*, **1,** formerly, the stand from which parliamentary candidates, when nominated, addressed the electors; **2,** now, a place where campaign speeches are made.

hus-tle (hŭs'l), *v.t.* [*p.t.* and *p.p.* -tled (-ld), *p.pr.* -tling], **1,** to push forward roughly; **2,** to jostle; crowd against; **3,** *Colloq.*, to cause to be done quickly; as, to *hustle* the work:—*v.i.* **1,** to jostle; crowd; **2,** *Colloq.*, to exhibit energy and alacrity; hurry.—*n.* **hus'tler.**

hut (hŭt), *n.* **1,** a small house or cabin; hovel; shanty; **2,** a temporary building for lodging troops.

FORMS OF HUT

hutch (hŭch), *n.* **1,** a bin, box, or chest in which things may be stored; as, a grain *hutch;* **2,** a coop or pen in which animals may be kept; as, a rabbit *hutch;* **3,** a mining trough for washing ore:—*v.t.* **1,** to store; **2,** to wash (ore) in a trough.

huz-za (hŭ-zä'; ho͞o-zä'), *interj.* expressing joy, triumph, or applause:—*n.* a shout of joy or triumph:—*v.i.* to utter such a shout. Also, **huz-zah'.**

hy-a-cinth (hī'*á*-sĭnth), *n.* **1,** any of several well-known plants of the lily family with stalks of bell-shaped flowers; also, one of its bulbs or flowers; **2,** a red or brownish mineral, used as a gem.

hy-a-cin-thine (hī"*á*-sĭn'thĭn), *adj.* **1,** pertaining to a reddish or brownish gem; **2,** pertaining to the hyacinth; **3,** sweet-scented; **4,** purplish blue; **5,** like Hyacinthus, the handsome youth who, according to Greek myth, was accidentally killed by Apollo and transformed into the hyacinth; **6,** hence, handsome; beautiful.

Hy-a-des (hī'*á*-dēz), *n.pl.* the five stars in the head of the constellation Taurus, supposed by the ancients to bring rain when they rose with the sun. Also, **Hy'ads.**

hy-æ-na (hī-ē'n*á*), *n.* a flesh-eating mammal, resembling both wolf and wildcat, of Africa and Asia. See **hy-e'na,** *Pfd.S.*

hy-brid (hī'brĭd), *n.* **1,** an animal or plant produced from the crossing of two distinct varieties or species; **2,** anything formed of diverse elements; specif., a compound word, the elements of which are derived from different languages; as, *cablegram:*—*adj.* **1,** produced from two classes; **2,** composed of incongruous elements, as a word.—*n.* **hy-brid'i-ty.**—*v.t.* **hy'brid-ize.**

Hy-dra (hī'dr*á*), *n.* **1,** in classical mythology, the sea serpent with nine heads, slain by Hercules, each of which on being cut off became two; **2,** a large southern constellation: **hydra,** [*pl.* hydras (-dr*á*z); hydræ (-drē)], **1,** any evil which, when grappled with, appears to become greater; **2,** any of several very small fresh-water polyps.

hy-dran-ge-a (hī-drăn'jē-*á*), *n.* any of many shrubs or small trees with large heads of showy flowers.

hy-drant (hī'drănt), *n.* a pipe with a valve and spout through which water may be drawn from the mains of water works; a fire plug or similar apparatus.

hy-drate (hī'drāt), *n.* a compound containing water:—*v.t.* [*p.t.* and *p.p.* -drat-ed, *p.pr.* -drat-ing], **1,** to combine or impregnate with water; **2,** to form into a hydrate.—*n.* **hy-dra'tion.**

hy-drau-lic (hī-drô'lĭk), *adj.* **1,** pertaining to fluids in motion; **2,** operated by water power; as, a *hydraulic* elevator; **3,** hardening in water; as, *hydraulic* cement: **hydraulic press,** a machine for compressing or lifting, in which the plunger is moved by water: **hydraulic ram,** a pumping device in which water, running by gravity through a straight pipe, attains such speed that when the end of the pipe is suddenly closed, some of the water is forced through a valve and up to a higher level: **hydraulics,** *n.pl.* used as *sing.* the science that deals with the action of liquids in motion.—*adv.* **hy-drau'li-cal-ly.**

hy-dro- (hī'drō-), a combining form from the Greek, meaning water; as, *hydro*gen; *hydro*meter; *hydro*plane.

hy-dro-air-plane (hī"drō-âr'plān"), *n.* an airplane so constructed that it can rise from, alight upon, or travel upon, the surface of water (see *aviation*, illus.). Also, **hy"dro-a'ër-o-plane".**

hy-dro-car-bon (hī"drō-kär'bŏn), *n.* one of a large class of compounds containing carbon and hydrogen, as acetylene, gasoline, etc.

hy-dro-chlo-ric (hī"drō-klō'rĭk), *adj.* pertaining to, or composed of, hydrogen and chlorine: **hydrochloric acid,** a colorless, suffocating, gaseous compound of hydrogen and chlorine: often used in solution in water, and called *muriatic acid.*

hy-dro-cy-an-ic (hī"drō-sī-ăn'ĭk), *adj.* composed of hydrogen and cyanogen: **hydrocyanic acid,** a colorless, poisonous liquid: also called *prussic acid.*

hy-dro-dy-nam-ic (hī"drō-dī-năm'ĭk), *adj.* pertaining to, or derived from, the pressure of fluids: **hydrodynamics,** *n.pl.* used as *sing.* the science that treats of the action and motion of fluids.

hy-dro-flu-or-ic (hī"drō-flo͞o-ŏr'ĭk), *adj.* composed of hydrogen and fluorine: **hydrofluoric acid,** a colorless, corrosive liquid, destructive to glass.

hy-dro-gen (hī'drō-jĕn), *n.* a colorless, gaseous, inflammable element, the lightest substance known: a constituent of water, all acids, and all organic compounds.—*adj.* **hy-drog'e-nous** (hī-drŏj'ē-nŭs).

hy-drog-ra-phy (hī-drŏg'r*á*-fĭ), *n.* the art of describing and mapping the surface waters of the earth, with reference to their depth, tides, etc.—*adj.* **hy"-dro-graph'ic.**—*n.* **hy-drog'ra-pher.**

hy-drom-e-ter (hī-drŏm'ē-tẽr), *n.* an instrument for determining the specific gravity, strength, etc., of fluids.—*adj.* **hy"dro-met'ric.**—*n.* **hy-drom'e-try.**

hy-drop-a-thy (hī-drŏp'*á*-thĭ), *n.* the water cure: the treatment of disease by frequent and copious use of water.—*adj.* **hy"dro-path'ic.**

hy-dro-pho-bi-a (hī"drō-fō'bĭ-*á*), *n.* an infectious disease of certain animals, esp. the dog, accompanied by convulsions and an unnatural dread of water; rabies: communicated to man usually by the bite of a dog so diseased.

hy-dro-phone (hī'drō-fōn), *n.* an instrument for detecting and analyzing sounds transmitted through water.

hy-dro-plane (hī'drō-plān), *n.* **1,** a motor boat with sloping bottom, which rises partly out of water when driven at high speed; **2,** erroneously, a hydro-airplane.

hy-dro-stat (hī'drō-stăt), *n.* **1,** an apparatus for the prevention of boiler explosions; **2,** an electrical contrivance for indicating or controlling the height of water in a reservoir or other receptacle.

hy-dro-stat-ic (hī"drō-stăt'ĭk), *adj.* pertaining to the pressure

āte, senāte, râre, căt, åsk, fär, ållow, sof*á*; ēve, ēvent, ĕll, writẽr, novĕl; nīne, pĭn; gō, ōbey, ôr, dôg, tŏp, cŏllide; ūnit, ūnite, ûrn, cŭt, focŭs; no͞on, fo͝ot; sour; coin;

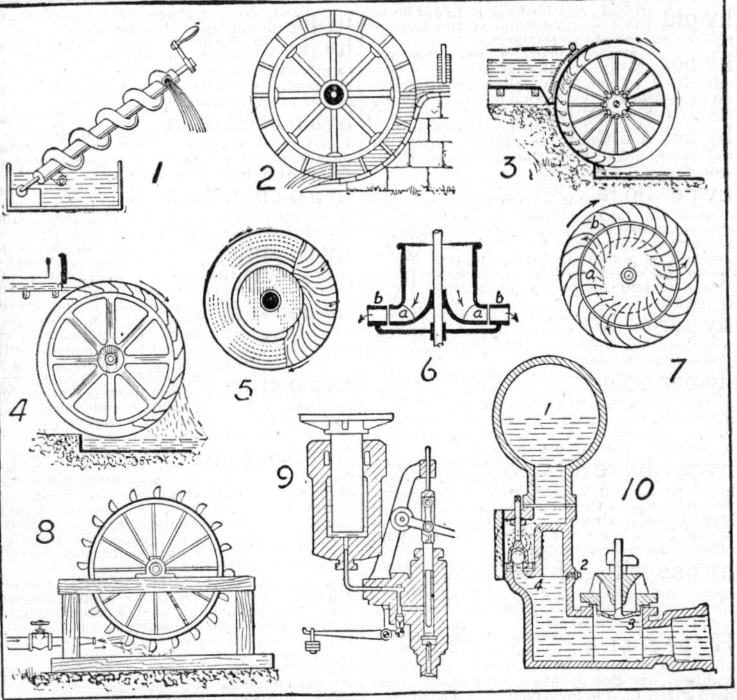

HYDRAULIC DEVICES

1, Archimedean screw; 2, breast wheel; 3, undershot wheel; 4, overshot wheel; 5, inward flow turbine wheel; 6, 7, vertical and horizontal sections of impulse turbine (*a*, central section, with fixed vanes which give moving water a certain direction outward; *b*, outer section, rotated by water); 8, Pelton wheel; 9, hand-power hydraulic press; 10, hydraulic ram (1, air chamber; 2, valve for admitting air as required; 3, discharge valve; 4, valve to delivery pipe).

and equilibrium of fluids: **hydrostatic press,** a powerful machine for compressing or lifting; a hydraulic press: **hydrostatics,** *n.pl.* used as *sing.* that branch of physics that treats of the pressure and equilibrium of fluids at rest.

hy-dro-ther-a-py (hī″drō-thĕr′*ȧ*-pĭ), *n.* treatment of disease by water; water cure; hydropathy.

hy-dro-ther-mal (hī″drō-thûr′măl), *adj.* pertaining to hot water and its action.

hy-drous (hī′drůs), *adj.* 1, watery; 2, in chemistry, containing water in combination, as in hydrates.

hy-drox-ide (hī-drŏk′sīd; -sĭd), *n.* a compound of an element with hydrogen and oxygen, but not regarded as containing water. Also, **hy-drox′id.**

hy-e-na (hī-ē′n*ȧ*), *n.* any of a family of flesh-eating mammals, resembling the wolf and wildcat in appearance and habits, native to Africa and Asia. Also, **hy-æ′na.**

Hy-ge-ia (hī-jē′y*ȧ*), *n.* in mythology, the daughter of Æsculapius, and goddess of health. Also, **Hy-ge′a** (-gē′*ȧ*); **Hy-gi′a** (-jī′*ȧ*).—*adj.* **Hy-ge′ian.**

hy-ge-ian (hī-jē′yăn), *adj.* pertaining to the preservation of health and the prevention of disease.

hy-gi-ene (hī′jĭ-ēn; hī′jēn), *n.* the science of health, its preservation, and the laws of sanitation.—*n.* **hy′gi-en-ist.**

hy-gi-en-ic (hī″jĭ-ĕn′ĭk), *adj.* 1, pertaining to health or the science of health; 2, healthful; sanitary.

hy-grom-e-ter (hī-grŏm′ē-tẽr), *n.* an instrument for measuring the variations of moisture in the atmosphere. —*n.* **hy-grom′e-try.**—*adj.* **hy″gro-met′ric.**

hy-gro-scope (hī′grō-skōp), *n.* an instrument which detects variations, without measuring them, in the moisture of the atmosphere.

Hy-men (hī′mĕn), *n.* the Greek god of marriage: **hymen,** marriage.

hy-me-ne-al (hī″mē-nē′ăl), *adj.* pertaining to marriage; nuptial: —*n.* a marriage song.

hymn (hĭm), *n.* a sacred song expressive of praise or adoration:—*v.t.* [*p.t.* and *p.p.* hymned (hĭmd), *p.pr.* hymn′ing (hĭm′ĭng; hĭm′nĭng)], to sing praises to:—*v.i.* to sing in praise.—*n.* **hym′nist** (hĭm′nĭst).

hym-nal (hĭm′năl), *n.* a collection of sacred songs for public worship.

hym-nol-o-gy (hĭm-nŏl′ō-jĭ), *n.* the study of hymns, or sacred songs, their origin, use, etc.—*n.* **hym-nol′o-gist.**

hy-oid (hī′oid), *adj.* U-shaped: **hyoid bone,** the U-shaped bone at the base of the tongue and above the larynx.

hy-per- (hī′pẽr-), *prefix,* **1,** over; beyond; **2,** abnormally great; as, *hyper*critical; **3,** in chemistry, indicating the highest in a series of oxygen compounds: generally abbreviated to *per-:* opp. of *hypo-*.

hy-per-a-cid-i-ty (hī″pẽr-ȧ-sĭd′ĭ-tĭ), *n.* a condition marked by too much acid, as in the secretions of the stomach or mouth.

hy-per-bo-la (hī-pûr′bō-lȧ), *n.* a plane curve such that the difference of the distances from any point thereon to two fixed points, or foci, is a constant: the curve formed by the intersection of two equal cones, placed vertex to vertex so that their axes form a straight line, by a plane parallel to the axes.

HYPERBOLA

hy-per-bo-le (hī-pûr′bō-lē), *n.* a figure of speech which expresses more than the truth; poetic exaggeration.

hy-per-bol-ic (hī″pẽr-bŏl′ĭk), *adj.* **1,** in literature, pertaining to, or containing, overstatements; exaggerated; **2,** in mathematics, belonging to, or of the nature of, a hyperbola. Also, **hy″per-bol′i-cal.**

hy-per-bo-re-an (hī″pẽr-bō′rē-ăn), *adj.* **1,** northern; most northern; arctic; **2,** very cold; frigid:—*n.* a person living in the far north, as an Eskimo: **Hyperborean,** a member of a fabled race of people living beyond the north wind, in a land of sunshine and eternal bliss.

hy-per-crit-i-cal (hī″pẽr-krĭt′ĭ-kăl), *adj.* **1,** too severe in judgment; too quick to find fault; **2,** excessively nice or exact; difficult to please; fastidious. —*adv.* **hy″per-crit′i-cal-ly.**

Hy-pe-ri-on (hī-pē′rĭ-ŏn; hī″pẽr-ī′ŏn), *n.* in mythology, a Titan, father of Helios (the sun god), Selene (the moon goddess), and Eos (goddess of the dawn): also used of *Helios,* and identified with *Apollo.*

hy-per-me-tro-pi-a (hī″pẽr-mē-trō′-pĭ-ȧ), *n.* farsightedness: opp. of *myopia.*—*adj.* **hy″per-me-trop′ic.**

hy-per-tro-phy (hī-pûr′trō-fĭ), *n.* abnormal or excessive growth of the body or part: opp. of *atrophy:*—*v.i.* [*p.t.* and *p.p.* -phied (-fĭd), *p.pr.* -phy-ing], to become excessively enlarged, as an organ.

hy-phen (hī′fĕn), *n.* a sign [-] used to join compound words, as *self-denial,* or to divide a word into syllables:—*v.t.* to join with, or separate by, such a mark.

hy-phen-ate (hī′fĕn-āt), *v.t.* [*p.t.* and *p.p.* -at″ed, *p.pr.* -at″ing], to insert a hyphen between the parts or syllables of (a word).

hyp-no-sis (hĭp-nō′sĭs), *n.* **1,** a state resembling sleep, in which the mind readily responds to external suggestion, **2,** a hypnotic trance; artificial sleep.

hyp-not-ic (hĭp-nŏt′ĭk), *adj.* pertaining to, or producing, artificial sleep: —*n.* **1,** a person who can be put into a trancelike sleep or hypnosis; **2,** a person in such a state; **3,** anything that produces sleep, as a drug.—*adv.* **hyp-not′i-cal-ly.**

hyp-no-tism (hĭp′nō-tĭzm), *n.* a method of causing a trancelike sleep, in which the mind readily responds to external influence.

hyp-no-tize (hĭp′nō-tīz), *v.t.* [*p.t.* and *p.p.* -tized (-tīzd), *p.pr.* -tiz″ing], to cause to fall into an artificial sleep, in which the mind readily responds to external direction. —*n.* **hyp′no-tiz″er.**—*adj.* **hyp′no-tiz″a-ble.**

hy-po (hī′pō), *n.* a coarse powder used esp. in photography; hyposulphite.

hy-po- (hī′pō-; hĭp′ō-), *prefix,* under; below; less than: in physiology, used to signify deficiency in functions of growth or development; in chemistry, indicating a compound lower in a series than another.

hyp-o-chon-dri-a (hĭp″ō-kŏn′drĭ-ȧ, hī″pō-kŏn′drĭ-ȧ), *n.* **1,** a mental disorder attended with extreme melancholy; **2,** the blues; low spirits; depression. Also, **hyp″o-chon-dri′a-sis.**

hyp-o-chon-dri-ac (hĭp″ō-kŏn′drĭ-ăk; hī″pō-), *n.* one who is affected with extreme melancholy:—*adj.* pertaining to, or affected with, melancholy.

hy-po-cot-yl (hī″pō-kŏt′ĭl; hĭp″ō-), *n.* in a germinating seed plant, that part of the axis, or stem, below the cotyledons (see *germination,* illus.).

hy-poc-ri-sy (hĭ-pŏk′rĭ-sĭ), *n.* [*pl.* hypocrisies (-sĭz)], a pretending to be what one is not; a putting on of an appearance of virtue which is not possessed.

Syn. pretense, sham, affectation, deception.

hyp-o-crite (hĭp′ō-krĭt), *n.* **1,** one who practices pretense or deception to gain his own ends; **2,** a pharisee.—*adj.* **hyp″o-crit′i-cal.**—*adv.* **hyp″o-crit′i-cal-ly.**

Syn. dissembler, impostor, cheat.

hy-po-der-mic (hī″pō-dûr′mĭk; hĭp″ō-), *adj.* **1,** pertaining to the parts under the skin; **2,** inserted under the skin: **hypodermic needle,** a hollow needle attached to a small pump, for injecting liquids under the skin:—*n.* a medicine thus injected.

hy-po-gas-tric (hī″pō-găs′trĭk; hĭp″ō-), *adj.* pertaining to the lower part of the abdomen.

hy-po-sul-phite (hī″pō-sŭl′fīt; hĭp″ō-), *n.* a white, coarsely crystalline compound, used in photography as a fixing agent, and in bleaching, tanning, etc.: popularly called *hypo.*

hy-pot-e-nuse (hī-pŏt′ē-nūs; hĭ-), *n.* the side of a right-angled triangle opposite the right angle. Also, **hy-poth′e-nuse** (hī-pŏth′ē-nūs, hĭ-).

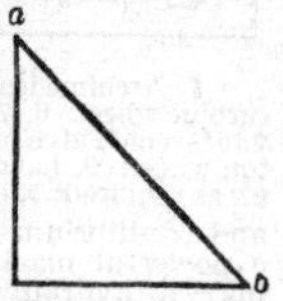

HYPOTENUSE (*ab*)

hy-poth-e-cate (hī-pŏth′ē-kāt, hĭ-), *v.t.* [*p.t.* and *p.p.* -cat″ed, *p.pr.* -cat″ing], to pledge (property) as security for a debt; mortgage.—*n.* **hy-poth″e-ca′tion.**—*n.* **hy-poth′e-ca″tor.**

hy-poth-e-sis (hī-pŏth′ē-sĭs, hĭ-), *n.* [*pl.* hypotheses (-sēz)], something assumed for the purpose of argument; a theory which may or may not prove to be true; supposition; conjecture.

hy-po-thet-ic (hī″pō-thĕt′ĭk; hĭp″ō-), *adj.* based on supposition, or on something assumed, conjectural. Also, **hy″po-thet′i-cal.**—*adv.* **hy″po-thet′i-cal-ly.**

hys-sop hĭs′ŭp), *n.* **1,** a fragrant medicinal herb of the mint family; also, its blue flowers; **2,** an unidentified plant mentioned in the Bible.

hys-te-ri-a (hĭs-tē′rĭ-ȧ), *n.* a nervous affection, esp. of women, marked by emotional excitement with lack of control, as in spasms of laughter or weeping.

hys-ter-i-cal (hĭs-tĕr′ĭ-kăl), *adj.* **1,** pertaining to, or affected by, a nervous disease marked by laughing and crying; **2,** violently emotional, uncontrolled. —*adv.* **hys-ter′i-cal-ly.**

hys-ter-ics (hĭs-tĕr′ĭks), *n.pl.* used as *sing.* a fit of nervous and uncontrolled laughing and crying.

I

I (ī), *pron.* of the first person [*nom.* **I**, *poss.* my (mī), mine (mīn), *obj.* me (mē); *pl. nom.* we (wē), *poss.* our (our), ours (ourz), *obj.* us (ŭs)], the pronoun by which the speaker or writer denotes himself.

I-a-go (ē-ä′gō), *n.* in Shakespeare's "Othello," a treacherous friend.

i-am-bic (ī-ăm′bĭk), *adj.* having a verse form in which each foot consists of a short or unaccented syllable followed by a long or accented syllable:—*n.* **1**, a metrical foot having a short syllable followed by a long one; **2**, a line or stanza composed in such meter; **3**, a satirical poem in verse composed of such metrical feet. Also, *n.* **i′amb.**

i-am-bus (ī-ăm′bŭs), *n.* [*pl.* iambi (-bī); iambuses (-ĕz)], a metrical foot consisting of a short or unaccented syllable followed by a long or accented one; an iambic.

-i-an (-ĭ-ăn), *suffix*, a variant of *-an* with euphonic *-i-*; as, barbar*ian*: **-iana**, a similar variant of *-ana*.

I-be-ri-an (ī-bē′rĭ-ăn), *adj.* of or pertaining to the Spanish-Portuguese peninsula, anciently called Iberia:—*n.* a member of the ancient race existing in the Iberian peninsula; also, the language of this race.

i-bex (ī′bĕks), *n.* [*pl.* ibexes (ī′bĕk-sĕz); ibices (ĭb′ĭ-sēz; ī′bĭ-)], any of a class of wild goats, having very large, recurved horns.

***i-bi-dem** (ĭ-bī′dĕm), *adv.* in the same place, as in a book, chapter, passage, etc.—*abbr.* **ib.; ibid.**

i-bis (ī′bĭs), *n.* any of several species of large wading bird, having a long, curved beak; esp., the species venerated by the ancient Egyptians.

-i-ble (-ĭ-bl), *adj. suffix*, capable of being: as, reduc*ible*. See **-a-ble.**

-ic (-ĭk), *adj. suffix*, **1**, made up of; as, trocha*ic*; **2**, like in nature or kind; as, angel*ic*; hypnot*ic*; **3**, of, pertaining to, or belonging to; as, Celt*ic*; rust*ic*; trag*ic*; **4**, patterning after or resembling; as, class*ic*; **5**, having to do with; as, publ*ic*; poet*ic*: domest*ic*; **6**, in chemistry, indicating a valence higher than that of the same element in a compound ending in *ous*; as, ferr*ic*; nitr*ic*:—*n. suffix*, used: **1**, in nouns derived from adjectives in *-ic*; as, mag*ic*; publ*ic*; **2**, in nouns adopted in English from certain Greek or Latin adjectives; as, mechan*ic*; log*ic*.

-i-cal (-ĭ-kăl), *adj. suffix*, forming a variation of many adjectives in *-ic*; as, class*ical*; poet*ical*.

Ic-a-rus (ĭk′ȧ-rŭs), *n.* in mythology, the young son of Dædalus (which see), who flew so high that the sun melted the wax of his wings and he fell into the sea.

ice (īs), *n.* **1**, frozen water; **2**, any substance resembling ice; as, menthol *ice*; **3**, frozen confection; as, water *ice*; **4**, the coating placed on cake; frosting:—*v.t.* [*p.t.* and *p.p.* iced (īst), *p.pr.* ic′ing], **1**, to change into a frozen state; freeze; **2**, to supply with ice; **3**, to cool by ice; **4**, to cover, as cake, by frosting.

-ice (-ĭs), *n. suffix*, quality or state of; as, serv*ice*; just*ice*; coward*ice*.

ice age the glacial epoch, or time when ice covered large areas of the world.

ice-berg (īs′bûrg″), *n.* a large mass of ice detached from a glacier, and floating in the sea.

ice boat **1**, a strong steamboat used to break a channel through a frozen river, lake, etc.; **2**, a boat mounted on runners and propelled on ice by sails.

ice cream *n.* flavored cream or custard, sweetened and frozen.

iced (īst), *p.adj.* **1**, covered with ice or made cold with ice; as, *iced* tea; **2**, covered with icing; as, *iced* cake.

ice field a very large sheet of floating ice: when smaller, called *ice floe.*

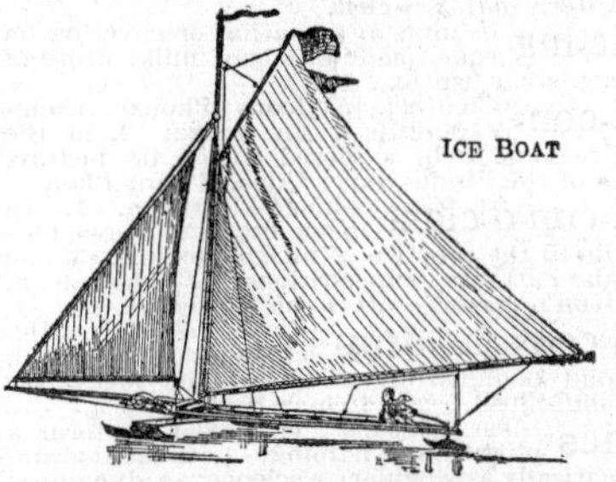

ICE BOAT

ice house a building in which ice is packed and stored for future use.

Ice-land-er (īs′lăn-dẽr), *n.* an inhabitant of Iceland.

Ice-lan-dic (īs-lăn′dĭk), *adj.* pertaining to Iceland, the Icelanders, or their language:—*n.* the language of the Icelanders, including, in its older stages, the language of the Norsemen: **Old Icelandic**, Old Norse.—*abbr.* **Icel.; Ice.**

ice pack **1**, a field of broken and drifting ice; **2**, a bag of cracked ice: used to reduce swellings, inflammation, or fever.

ich-neu-mon (ĭk-nū′mŏn), *n.* an Old World mongoose, a small, brave, dexterous mammal, weasel-like in form, which feeds on mice, rats, snakes, and other small animals: **ichneumon fly**, any of a large group of insects which lay their eggs in or upon the larvæ of other insects.

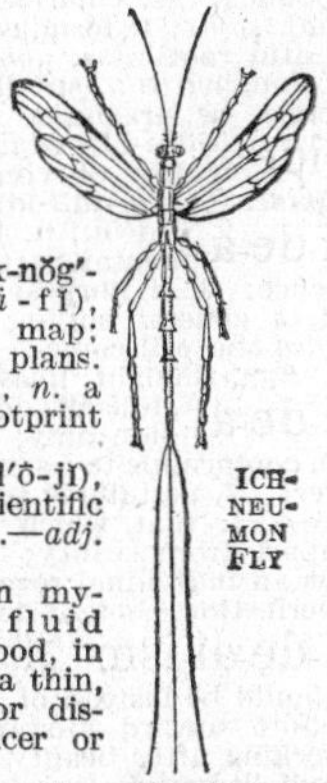

ICHNEUMON FLY

ich-nog-ra-phy (ĭk-nŏg′rȧ-fĭ), *n.* **1**, a ground plan; a map; **2**, the art of making such plans.

ich-no-lite (ĭk′nō-līt), *n.* a fossil footprint of a prehistoric animal.

ich-nol-o-gy (ĭk-nŏl′ō-jĭ), the scientific study of fossil footprints.—*adj.* **ich″no-log′i-cal.**

i-chor (ī′kôr), *n.* **1**, in mythology, the fluid which ran, instead of blood, in the veins of the gods; **2**, a thin, watery, acrid serum, or discharge, as from an ulcer or wound.—*adj.* **i′chor-ous.**

ich-thy-ic (ĭk′thĭ-ĭk), *adj.* pertaining to, or characteristic of, fishes.

ich-thy-o- (ĭk′thĭ-ō-), a combining form from the Greek, meaning fish; as, *ichthyo*logy; *ichthyo*sis.

ich-thy-og-ra-phy (ĭk″thĭ-ŏg′rȧ-fĭ), *n.* a treatise on fish.

ich-thy-o-lite (ĭk′thĭ-ō-līt″), a fossil of a fish, or of part of a fish.

ich-thy-ol-o-gy (ĭk″thĭ-ŏl′ō-jĭ), *n.* that branch of zoölogy which treats of fishes.—*n.* **ich″thy-ol′o-gist.**

ich-thy-o-sau-rus (ĭk″thĭ-ō-sô′rŭs), *n.* [*pl.* ichthyosauri (-rī)], any of a genus (*Ichthyosaurus*) of extinct reptiles with long jaws and fishlike body.

ich-thy-o-sis (ĭk″thĭ-ō′sĭs), *n.* a disease in which the skin becomes thick, rough, and scaly: also called *fishskin.*

i-ci-cle (ī′sĭ-kl), *n.* a tapering piece of ice formed by the freezing of dripping water.—*adj.* **i′ci-cled.**

ic-ing (īs′ĭng), *n.* a coating or covering on cake, made of sugar, milk, white of egg, etc.; frosting.

i-con (ī′kŏn), *n.* [*pl.* icons (ī′kŏnz); icones (ī′kō-nēz)], **1,** an image; **2,** in the Greek Church, a sacred image or picture, as of the Virgin Mary. Also, **ei′kon; i′kon.**

i-con-o-clast (ī-kŏn′ō-klăst), *n.* **1,** an image breaker; **2,** one hostile to the practice of image worship; **3,** one who attacks superstitions or shams.—*n.* **i-con′o-clasm.**—*adj.* **i-con″o-clas′tic.**

i-co-sa-he-dron (ī″kō-sȧ-hē′drŏn), *n.* [*pl.* icosahedra (-drȧ)], a solid bounded by twenty plane faces (see *solid,* illus.).—*adj.* **i″co-sa-he′dral.**

-ics (-ĭks), *n. suffix,* employed to form a plural noun naming: **1,** (treated grammatically as singular), a science; as, dynam*ics;* mechan*ics;* **2,** (usually construed as plural), a system; a group of practical matters or methods; as, tact*ics.*

ic-tus (ĭk′tŭs), *n.* **1,** a blow; stroke, as of paralysis; **2,** in prosody and music, rhythmical or metrical accent or stress placed upon a certain syllable of a word.

i-cy (ī′sĭ), *adj.* [*comp.* i′ci-er, *superl.* i′ci-est], **1,** pertaining to, resembling, or abounding in, ice; cold; **2,** chilling or frigid in manner; indifferent.—*adv.* **i′ci-ly.**—*n.* **i′ci-ness.**

-id (-ĭd), *n. suffix,* **1,** used in names of poems; as, Ǽne*id;* **2,** in zoölogy, a member of a (specified) class or family; as, arachn*id;* **3,** in chemistry (also, *-ide*), used in names of compounds, as, chlor*id:* chiefly in the U. S.:—*adj. suffix,* **1,** forming descriptive words from Latin roots, as, ac*id;* flu*id;* **2,** in zoölogy, belonging to a (specified) biological family or class; as, arachn*id.*

-ide (-ĭd; -īd), *suffix,* in chemistry, used in names of compounds; as, sulph*ide;* ox*ide.* Also, **-id** (-ĭd).

i-de-a (ī-dē′ȧ), *n.* **1,** a mental image; **2,** a mental pattern; standard of excellence; **3,** a purpose or plan; an intention; **4,** a general notion; belief; as, I have an *idea* she will come.

Syn. thought, imagination, fancy.

i-de-al (ī-dē′ăl), *adj.* **1,** existing in imagination only; visionary; impractical; **2,** conforming to a standard of perfection; perfect; **3,** pertaining to, or expressed by, ideas:—*n.* **1,** that which exists only as an idea, apart from reality; **2,** a mental conception or an individual regarded as the standard of perfection.—*adv.* **i-de′al-ly.**

i-de-al-ism (ī-dē′ăl-ĭzm), *n.* **1,** the tendency to see things as they should be instead of as they are; **2,** practical effort toward a standard of perfection; a seeking after beauty or excellence; **3,** in art and literature, purely imaginative treatment of subjects: opp. of *realism;* **4,** any of several systems of thought which hold that ideas are the only realities.

i-de-al-ist (ī-dē′ăl-ĭst), *n.* **1,** one who pursues perfection; **2,** one who holds the doctrine that all our knowledge of objects is a knowledge of ideas; **3,** one who views and treats a subject imaginatively rather than literally: opp. of *realist.*—*adj.* **i-de″al-is′tic.**—*adv.* **i-de″al-is′ti-cal-ly.**

i-de-al-i-ty (ī″dē-ăl′ĭ-tĭ), *n.* [*pl.* idealities (-tĭz)], **1,** the quality or state of existing in idea only; also, a thing so existing; **2,** the capacity to conceive mental images or ideas.

i-de-al-ize (ī-dē′ăl-īz), *v.t.* [*p.t.* and *p.p.* -ized (-īzd), *p.pr.* -iz″ing], **1,** to look upon as beautiful or good, regardless of fact; as, she *idealizes* her son; **2,** to see (something) as it should be, not as it is; **3,** to treat imaginatively, as a subject in art:—*v.i.* to see things in the light of perfection.—*n.* **i-de″al-i-za′tion.**

i-den-ti-cal (ī-dĕn′tĭ-kăl), *adj.* **1,** the very same; as, the *identical* spot; **2,** of different things, exactly alike; as, no two faces are *identical.*—*adv.* **i-den′ti-cal-ly.**

Syn. uniform. (See alike.)

i-den-ti-fy (ī-dĕn′tĭ-fī), *v.t.* [*p.t.* and *p.p.* -fied (-fīd), *p.pr.* -fy″ing], **1,** to make, consider, or treat as the same; **2,** to prove one's own, as stolen property; **3,** to aid in proof or recognition of, as a person.—*adj.* **i-den′ti-fi″a-ble.**—*n.* **i-den″ti-fi-ca′tion.**

i-den-ti-ty (ī-dĕn′tĭ-tĭ), *n.* [*pl.* identities (-tĭz)], **1,** essential or practical sameness; likeness; **2,** distinctive individuality; as, to establish one's *identity.*

i-de-o-gram (ĭ′dē-ō-grăm″; ĭd′ē-), *n.* **1,** a symbol, as in primitive picture writing, in which each object, action, or thought is expressed by a picture; **2,** any symbol standing for a word or idea, as 1, +, ×, etc. Also, **i′de-o-graph″.**

i-de-og-ra-phy (ī″dē-ŏg′rȧ-fĭ; ĭd′ē-), *n.* the study of symbols by which ideas are expressed.

ides (īdz), *n.pl.* in the ancient Roman calendar, the 15th of March, May, July, October, and the 13th of the other months.

id-i-o-cy (ĭd′ĭ-ō-sĭ), *n.* extreme mental weakness: usually due to incomplete development of the brain.

Syn. imbecility, stupidity, senselessness.

id-i-o-graph (ĭd′ĭ-ō-grăf″), *n.* a characteristic mark; trade-mark.

id-i-om (ĭd′ĭ-ŭm), *n.* **1,** the language of a people; also, the dialect of a group or section; as, the New England *idiom;* **2,** the peculiar genius or spirit of a language; **3,** an expression which, as a whole, has a meaning different from that of the joined meanings of its parts, as *hard put to it;* **4,** a method of expression peculiar to an individual.

id-i-o-mat-ic (ĭd″ĭ-ō-măt′ĭk), *adj.* **1,** peculiar to a language; colloquial; **2,** given to, or marked by, the use of expressions characteristic of a language; as, an *idiomatic* phrase. Also, **id″i-o-mat′i-cal.**—*adv.* **id″i-o-mat′i-cal-ly.**

id-i-o-syn-cra-sy (ĭd″ĭ-ō-sĭng′krȧ-sĭ), *n.* [*pl.* idiosyncrasies (-sĭz)], peculiarity of temperament; a characteristic peculiar to an individual, born of that individual's own particular bent; oddity.

id-i-ot (ĭd′ĭ-ŏt), *n.* **1,** one of weak mind; **2,** a foolish person; dunce.

id-i-ot-ic (ĭd″ĭ-ŏt′ĭk), *adj.* **1,** pertaining to, or like, an idiot; **2,** foolish. Also, **id″i-ot′i-cal.**—*adv.* **id″i-ot′i-cal-ly.**

i-dle (ī′dl), *adj.* **1,** empty; unoccupied; unused; as, *idle* servants; **2,** useless; futile; of no importance; as, an *idle* tale; **3,** lazy:—*v.i.* [*p.t.* and *p.p.* i′dled (-dld), *p.pr.* i′dling], **1,** to be inactive or without employment; **2,** to run slowly in neutral gear, as an automobile engine:—*v.t.* to spend or waste (time): usually with *away.*—*n.* **i′dle-ness.**

Syn., adj. indolent, lazy. *Idle* may suggest temporary or involuntary inactivity. To be *indolent* is to be averse to exertion, physical or mental, and fond of ease. *Lazy* implies either temporary or permanent unwillingness to work, and is used as a term of reproach.—*Ant., adj.* active, diligent.

i-dler (ī'dlẽr), *n.* one who wastes time in doing nothing; a lazy person.

i-dly (ī'dlĭ), *adv.* in an unoccupied or aimless manner; lazily; as, to wander *idly.*

i-dol (ī'dŏl), *n.* **1**, an image of a divinity or a god used as an object of worship; **2**, a person or thing greatly loved or adored.—*n.* **i'dol-ism.**

EGYPTIAN IDOL (The goddess Bast)

i-dol-a-ter (ī-dŏl'ȧ-tẽr), *n.* **1**, an idol worshiper; one who pays divine honors to images, talismans, etc.; **2**, one who loves a person or thing to excess; an ardent devotee; great admirer. —*n.fem.* **i-dol'a-tress.**

i-dol-a-trous (ī-dŏl'ȧ-trŭs), *adj.* **1**, pertaining to, or practicing, the worship of images; **2**, marked by undue reverence or excessive affection.

i-dol-a-try (ī-dŏl'ȧ-trĭ), *n.* [*pl.* idolatries (-trĭz)], **1**, the worship of images or any created object; **2**, very great veneration or love for any person or thing; undue reverence.

i-dol-ize (ī'dŏl-īz), *v.t.* [*p.t.* and *p.p.* -ized (-īzd), *p.pr.* -iz''ing], **1**, to worship, as an image regarded as a god; **2**, to love or admire to excess, as a hero. Also, **i'dol-ise.**

i-dyl (ī'dĭl), *n.* **1**, a short, pastoral poem; also, a description in verse or prose of a rustic scene, episode, etc.; **2**, an episode forming a suitable subject for an idyl; **3**, sometimes, a descriptive or narrative poem of greater length presenting simple, rural, or pastoral scenes. Also, **i'dyll.**

i-dyl-ist (ī'dĭl-ĭst), *n.* a writer, in poetry or prose, of incidents of rustic life. Also, **i'dyll-ist.**

i-dyl-lic (ī-dĭl'ĭk), *adj.* **1**, pertaining to, or of the nature of, short, pastoral scenes in prose or verse; **2**, pastoral; hence, pleasingly simple.

-ie (-ĭ), *n. dim. suffix*, esp. with Scotch words, implying affection; as, lass*ie*. See **¹-y.**

-ier (-ẽr), *n. suffix*, denoting an agent or one concerned with; as, financ*ier;* gondol*ier.*

if (ĭf), *conj.* **1**, on the condition that; as, *if* I let you have the book, you must read it carefully; supposing that; as, *if* I do go to New York, what is the best train to take? **2**, whether; as, he asked *if* he might go; **3**, although; as, *if* the answer is correct, the work is not neatly done; **4**, whenever; as, *if* I have any question, I will come to you:—*n.* the word *if;* hence, a supposition or condition; as, the *ifs* of life are many.

ig-loo (ĭg'lōō), *n.* an Eskimo dome-shaped house or hut, made of snow and blocks of ice. Also, **ig'lu.**

ig-ne-ous (ĭg'nē-ŭs), *adj.* **1**, pertaining to, consisting of, or resembling, fire; **2**, in geology, formed under intense heat; formed by volcanic action; as, *igneous* rocks.

***ig-nis fat-u-us** (ĭg'nĭs făt'ū-ŭs), [Lat.], [*pl.* ignes fatui (ĭg'nēz făt'ū-ī)], **1**, a strange light seen to flit above the ground in marshy places; will-o'-the-wisp; jack-o'-lantern; **2**, something that misleads, as a hope.

ig-nite (ĭg-nīt'), *v.t.* [*p.t.* and *p.p.* -nit'ed, *p.pr.* -nit'ing], **1**, to set on fire; **2**, to heat strongly:—*v.i.* **1**, to take fire; **2**, to glow with heat.—*adj.* **ig-nit'i-ble; ig-nit'a-ble.**

ig-nit-er (ĭg-nīt'ẽr), *n.* one who or that which kindles; esp., any of certain devices to explode charges.

ig-ni-tion (ĭg-nĭsh'ŭn), *n.* **1**, the act of setting on fire or kindling; **2**, the state of being set on fire; **3**, the means of producing fire; **4**, the device for exploding the charge in an internal-combustion engine.

ig-no-ble (ĭg-nō'bl), *adj.* **1**, of low birth or station; of no reputation; **2**, of mean character or quality; degraded; vile.—*n.* **ig-no'ble-ness.**—*adj.* **ig-no'bly.**

ig-no-min-i-ous (ĭg''nō-mĭn'ĭ-ŭs), *adj.* **1**, marked with dishonor or public disgrace; shameful; as, to sell a vote is *ignominious;* **2**, deserving disgrace; despicable; as, his conduct is *ignominious;* **3**, humiliating, as a punishment.

Syn. scandalous, infamous.

ig-no-min-y (ĭg'nō-mĭn-ĭ), *n.* [*pl.* ignominies (-ĭz)], **1**, loss of one's good name; public disgrace or dishonor; **2**, conduct deserving public disgrace.

Syn. shame, infamy, reproach.

ig-no-ra-mus (ĭg''nō-rā'mŭs), *n.* one without education or knowledge; a blockhead; dolt.

ig-no-rance (ĭg'nō-răns), *n.* the state of being uneducated or uninformed; lack or want of knowledge.

ig-no-rant (ĭg'nō-rănt), *adj.* **1**, lacking knowledge; uninstructed; **2**, unaware: with *of;* as, he was *ignorant* of the fact; **3**, displaying, marked by, or resulting from, lack of knowledge; as, an *ignorant* reply.—*adv.* **ig'no-rant-ly.**

Syn. illiterate, uneducated. *Ignorant* may imply lacking in education or knowledge, or it may mean uninformed on some specific subject: therefore, one may speak of an *ignorant* savage and also of a learned man who is *ignorant* of practical matters. *Illiterate* means lacking knowledge derived from reading, and, esp., unable to read or write. *Uneducated* means lacking systematic mental instruction or training.

ig-nore (ĭg-nōr'), *v.t.* [*p.t.* and *p.p.* -nored' (-nōrd'), *p. pr.* -nor'ing], **1**, to treat as unknown; disregard wilfully; fail to recognize; refuse to notice; **2**, in law, to throw out as false or unsupported by sufficient evidence, as a bill of indictment by a grand jury.

I-go-rot (ē''gō-rōt'), *n.* [*pl.* Igorot (-rōt'); Igorots (-rōts')], a member of one of the savage head-hunting tribes of Luzon in the Philippines. Also, **I''gor-ro'te** (ē''gŏr-rō'tā).

I-graine (ē-grān'; ē-grä'nē), *n.* in the Arthurian legends, the mother of King Arthur: also called *Ygerne.*

i-gua-na (ĭ-gwä'nȧ), *n.* any of several large lizards found in South and Central America, one species being used as food.

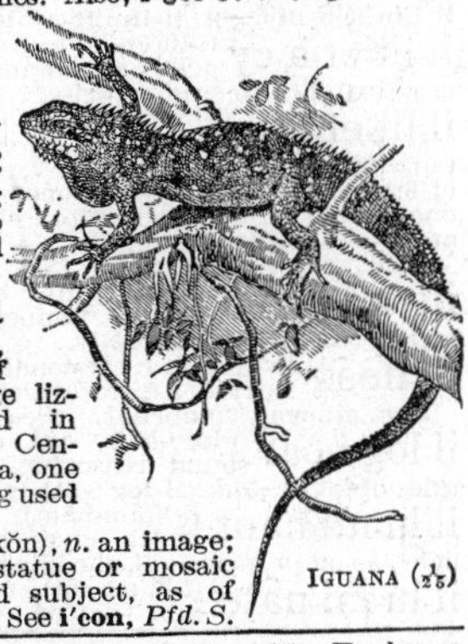

IGUANA ($\frac{1}{25}$)

i-kon (ī'kŏn), *n.* an image; a statue or mosaic of a sacred subject, as of the Virgin. See **i'con,** *Pfd. S.*

il- (ĭl-), *prefix*, a form of ¹*in-* or ²*in-*, used before words beginning with *l*.

-ile (-ĭl; -īl), *adj. suffix*, [sometimes, *-il*, as in civ*il*; sometimes changed to *-ble*, as in hum*ble*], of, like, or pertaining to; as, juven*ile*.

il-e-um (ĭl'ē-ŭm), *n.* the lower part of the small intestine.

i-lex (ī'lĕks), *n.* **1**, holly; **2**, a species of oak tree: commonly called *holm oak*.

Il-i-ad (ĭl'ĭ-ăd), *n.* a Greek epic poem in 24 books, written by Homer.

il-i-um (ĭl'ĭ-ŭm), *n.* [*pl.* ilia (-*á*)], either of the two broad, upper bones of the pelvis (see *pelvis*, illus.).—*adj.* **il'i-ac.**

ilk (ĭlk), *adj.* same: now rarely used except in the phrase *of that ilk*, of the same family, name, or estate.

ill (ĭl), *adj.* [*comp.* worse (wûrs), *superl.* worst (wûrst)], **1**, sick; diseased; as, the child is *ill;* **2**, morally bad; as, *ill* fame; **3**, harmful; **4**, faulty; unskilful; as, *ill* management; **5**, improper, as behavior; **6**, unfavorable; as, *ill* fortune; **7**, harsh; threatening; as, *ill* news; **8**, imperfect; as, *ill* success:—*n.* **1**, evil; the opposite of good; that which prevents happiness; **2**, something unfavorable or injurious; as, to work *ill* to one's neighbor; **3**, in *pl.*, misfortunes:—*adv.* **1**, badly; **2**, imperfectly; as, *ill* furnished; **3**, scarcely; as, he could *ill* afford it.
Syn., adj. indisposed, unwell.

ill–bred (ĭl'=brĕd''), *adj.* uncivil; rude; badly brought up; impolite.

il-le-gal (ĭ-lē'găl), *adj.* contrary to law; unlawful; illicit.—*adv.* **il-le'gal-ly.**—*n.* **il''le-gal'i-ty.**

il-leg-i-ble (ĭ-lĕj'ĭ-bl), *adj.* badly written; not to be read easily; undecipherable.—*adv.* **il-leg'i-bly.**—*n.* **il-leg''i-bil'i-ty.**—*n.* **il-leg'i-ble-ness.**

il-le-git-i-mate (ĭl''ē-jĭt'ĭ-māt), *adj.* **1**, born out of wedlock; **2**, unlawful; illegal; **3**, illogical; unsound; **4**, contrary to good usage; not genuine, as a word or expression.—*adv.* **il''le-git'i-mate-ly.**—*n.* **il''le-git'i-ma-cy.**

ill–fa-vored (ĭl'=fā'vẽrd), *adj.* **1**, ugly; **2**, offensive; unpleasant.

il-lib-er-al (ĭ-lĭb'ẽr-ăl), *adj.* **1**, without culture or education; **2**, not broad-minded; bigoted; **3**, stingy; ungenerous.—*adv.* **il-lib'er-al-ly.**—*n.* **il-lib''er-al'i-ty.**

il-lic-it (ĭ-lĭs'ĭt), *adj.* **1**, not authorized or allowed; illegal; as, *illicit* trade in drugs; **2**, not conforming to law; as, an *illicit* dealer.—*adv.* **il-lic'it-ly.**—*n.* **il-lic'it-ness.**

il-lim-it-a-ble (ĭ-lĭm'ĭt-*á*-bl), *adj.* immeasurable; vast.—*adv.* **il-lim'it-a-bly.**—*n.* **il-lim'it-a-ble-ness.**

il-lit-er-a-cy (ĭ-lĭt'ẽr-*á*-sĭ), *n.* [*pl.* illiteracies (-sĭz)], want of learning; esp., inability to read or write.

il-lit-er-ate (ĭ-lĭt'ẽr-āt), *adj.* **1**, unlearned; ignorant of letters or books; esp., unable to read or write; **2**, showing lack of learning:—*n.* one who is uneducated; esp., one unable to read and write.—*adv.* **il-lit'er-ate-ly.**—*n.* **il-lit'er-ate-ness.**
Syn., adj. uneducated. (See ignorant.)

ill–na-tured (ĭl'=nā'tūrd), *adj.* having a bad temper; spiteful; cross.—*adv.* **ill''–na'tured-ly.**

ill-ness (ĭl'nĕs), *n.* **1**, the condition of being sick; **2**, a disease; sickness.
Syn. ailment, complaint. (See disease.)

il-log-i-cal (ĭ-lŏj'ĭ-kăl), *adj.* contrary to sound reasoning, or to the rules of logic.—*adv.* **il-log'i-cal-ly.**

il-lu-mi-nant (ĭ-lū'mĭ-nănt), *n.* anything which gives or produces light, as oil or gas:—*adj.* shedding light.

il-lu-mi-nate (ĭ-lū'mĭ-nāt), *v.t.* [*p.t.* and *p.p.* -nat''ed, *p.pr.* -nat''ing], **1**, to give light to, as, they will *illuminate* the park with arc lights, **2**, to decorate with lights, in token of rejoicing; as, we *illuminate* the Christmas tree with colored electric lights: **3**, to enlighten, mentally or spiritually; make plain, as a difficult point; **4**, to adorn, as a manuscript, with small designs in colors and gold:—*v.i.* to display lights, as for a celebration.—*adj.* **ĭl-lu'mi-na-tive.**

il-lu-mi-na-tion (ĭ-lū''mĭ-nā'shŭn), *n.* **1**, the act of giving light to; also, the state of being lighted; esp., the decoration of houses or cities with lights; **2**, the amount of light given by a source of light; **3**, the art of adorning books or manuscripts; also, a design in a work so adorned; **4**, intellectual light; inspiration.

il-lu-mi-na-tor (ĭ-lū'mĭ-nā''tẽr), *n.* **1**, one who or that which gives light; **2**, one who adorns books, manuscripts, etc.; **3**, a condenser or reflector.

il-lu-mine (ĭ-lū'mĭn), *v.t.* [*p.t.* and *p.p.* -mined (-mĭnd), *p.pr.* -mining], to light; as, the moon *illumines* the night:—*v.i.* to be lighted.

il-lu-sion (ĭ-lū'zhŭn), *n.* **1**, a perception of an appearance, sound, or other object of sense, which does not correspond with reality; mistaken perception; as, an optical *illusion;* **2**, the state of being under a misconception; **3**, transparent tulle; delicate lace for veils.—*n.* **il-lu'sion-ist.**
Syn. fallacy, deception. (See delusion.)

il-lu-sive (ĭ-lū'sĭv), *adj.* misleading, deceptive; illusory.—*adv.* **il-lu'sive-ly.**—*n.* **il-lu'sive-ness.**

il-lu-so-ry (ĭ-lū'sō-rĭ), *adj.* **1**, causing deception; deceptive: **2**, of the nature of a misconception.
Syn. imaginary, visionary, deceiving, misleading.—*Ant.* actual, real, true.

il-lus-trate (ĭ-lŭs'trāt; ĭl'ŭs-trāt), *v.t.* [*p.t.* and *p.p.* -trat-ed, *p.pr.* -trating], **1**, to make clear or intelligible; explain by examples; **2**, to make plain by means of pictures; ornament with pictures; as, to *illustrate* a book.—*p.adj.* **il-lus'trat-ed.**

il-lus-tra-tion (ĭl''ŭs-trā'shŭn), *n.* **1**, the art of making plain by the use of examples, analogies, etc.; **2**, the act of adorning by pictures; **3**, that which makes clear, as a comparison or an example; **4**, that which adorns or decorates a text.

il-lus-tra-tive (ĭ-lŭs'trā-tĭv; ĭl'ŭs-trā-tĭv), *adj.* tending to explain or make clear; serving as an example.—*adv.* **il-lus'tra-tive-ly.**

il-lus-tra-tor (ĭl'ŭs-trā''tẽr; ĭ-lŭs'trā-tẽr), *n.* one who makes plain by example; esp., one who draws pictures, as for magazines, books, or newspapers.

il-lus-tri-ous (ĭ-lŭs'trĭ-ŭs), *adj.* distinguished by greatness; renowned; glorious; famous; honored.—*adv.* **il-lus'tri-ous-ly.**—*n.* **il-lus'tri-ous-ness.**
Syn. celebrated, eminent.

im- (ĭm-), *prefix*, a form of ¹*in-* or ²*in-*, used before words beginning with *b*, *m*, or *p*.

im-age (ĭm'āj), *n.* **1**, an imitation of any person or thing; a statue; bust; an idol; **2**, a counterpart; likeness; as, God created man in his own *image;* **3**, a mental picture, conception, or idea; as, it is easy to form an *image* of the scene you describe; **4**, a figure of speech; a simile or metaphor; **5**, a reflection of an object formed by rays of light; as, how I love to watch the *images* in the water:—*v.t.* [*p.t.* and *p.p.* -aged (-ājd), *p.pr.* -ag-ing], **1**, to form, or reflect, a likeness of; **2**, to represent to the mental vision; imagine; **3**, to describe well by words; **4**, to represent by a symbol; as, the cross *images* sacrifice.
Syn., n. representation, effigy.

im-age-ry (ĭm′ăj-rĭ), *n.* [*pl.* imageries (-rĭz)], **1**, imitations of objects taken collectively; **2**, mental pictures; imaginative work; as, the *imagery* of an artist; **3**, figures of speech as decoration in discourse.

im-ag-i-na-ble (ĭ-măj′ĭ-nȧ-bl), *adj.* capable of being pictured in the imagination, or conceived; as, the best nature *imaginable*.—*adv.* **im-ag′i-na-bly.**

im-ag-i-na-ry (ĭ-măj′ĭ-nā-rĭ), *adj.* existing only in the fancy; as, *imaginary* ills hurt as badly as real ones.
Syn. ideal, fanciful, illusory.

im-ag-i-na-tion (ĭ-măj″ĭ-nā′shŭn), *n.* **1**, the picture-forming power of the mind; the ability to create thoughts, ideas, or fancies; esp., the higher forms of this power exercised in art; the creative power; **2**, any product of this creative power; a conception or an idea; fanciful opinion; fancy; invention; **3**, the ability to appreciate a mental image created by another, esp. in art and literature.

im-ag-i-na-tive (ĭ-măj′ĭ-nā-tĭv), *adj.* proceeding from, exhibiting, or endowed with, the faculty of creating mental images; constructive; inventive; creative; fanciful.—*adv.* **im-ag′i-na-tive-ly.**—*n.* **im-ag′i-na-tive-ness.**

im-ag-ine (ĭ-măj′ĭn), *v.t.* [*p.t.* and *p.p.* -ined (-ĭnd), *p.pr.* -in-ing], **1**, to form a mental picture of; as, I shall describe the place and see if you can *imagine* the scene; conceive; as, can you *imagine* anyone taking that risk? **2**, to conjecture; think; **3**, to contrive; scheme:—*v.i.* **1**, to form a mental picture; fancy; as, the place is just as pretty as you *imagine;* **2**, to suppose; surmise.
Syn. deem, guess.—*Ant.* know, prove.

i-ma-go (ĭ-mā′gō), *n.* [*pl.* imagoes (-gōz); imagines (ĭ-măj′ĭ-nēz)], **1**, an image; **2**, in zoölogy, the last, or adult, stage of an insect's development.

im-be-cile (ĭm′bē-sĭl; *Br.* ĭm′bē-sēl; ĭm″-bē-sēl′), *adj.* **1**, feeble-minded; idiotic; **2**, marked by stupidity; as, an *imbecile* remark:—*n.* one of feeble mind.

im-be-cil-i-ty (ĭm″bē-sĭl′ĭ-tĭ), *n.* [*pl.* imbecilities (-tĭz)], **1**, mental weakness; also, an instance of mental weakness; **2**, silly folly or absurdity.
Syn. silliness, stupidity; senility, dotage.

im-bed (ĭm-bĕd′), *v.t.* [*p.t.* and *p.p.* -bed′-ded, *p.pr.* -bed′ding], to inclose in surrounding matter. See **em-bed′**, *Pfd. S.*

im-bibe (ĭm-bīb′), *v.t.* [*p.t.* and *p.p.* -bibed′ (-bībd′), *p.pr.* -bib′ing], **1**, to drink in; absorb, as if by drinking; **2**, to receive or absorb into the mind.—*n.* **im-bib′er.**—*n.* **im″bi-bi′tion** (ĭm″bĭ-bĭsh′ŭn).

im-bow-er (ĭm-bou′ẽr), *v.t.* to shelter or place in an arbor:—*v.i.* to rest in an arbor. See **em-bow′er**, *Pfd. S.*

im-bri-cate (ĭm′brĭ-kāt), *adj.* with the edges lapped over each other in regular order, as scales, shingles, or leaves in a bud. Also, **im′bri-cat″ed.**

im-bri-ca-tion (ĭm″brĭ-kā′shŭn), *n.* a regular overlapping of edges, as in scales, shingles, or the like.

im-bro-glio (ĭm-brōl′yō), *n.*[*pl.* imbroglios (-yōz)], an intricate state of affairs; perplexity; complicated plot.

im-brue (ĭm-brōō′), *v.t.* [*p.t.* and *p.p.* -brued′ (brōōd′), *p.pr.* -bru′ing], to wet or moisten; soak; drench, esp. in blood.

im-bue (ĭm-bū′), *v.t.* [*p.t.* and *p.p.* -bued′ (-būd′), *p.pr.* -bu′ing], **1**, to cause to absorb; tinge deeply; dye; **2**, to cause to become permeated; as, *imbued* with an idea.

im-i-ta-ble (ĭm′ĭ-tȧ-bl), *adj.* capable of being copied or patterned after.—*n.* **im″i-ta-bil′i-ty.**

im-i-tate (ĭm′ĭ-tāt), *v.t.* [*p.t.* and *p.p.* -tat″ed, *p.pr.* -tat″ing], **1**, to reproduce in form, color, qualities, conduct, and the like; **2**, to use as a model or pattern; take example by; as, the boy *imitates* his father's every act and word; **3**, to look like; as, paper doilies are made to *imitate* lace ones.
Syn. mimic, mock, ape. To *imitate* is to pattern after another, consciously or not. To *mimic* is to *imitate*, with the purpose of amusing others at the expense of the victim. To *mock* is to *imitate* in an insulting or jeering manner. To *ape* is to *imitate* outward appearances without reasoning, as a monkey would copy actions; as, to *ape* one's superiors.

im-i-ta-tion (ĭm″ĭ-tā′shŭn), *n.* **1**, the act of following, as a pattern or example, or of striving to copy; **2**, that which is made to resemble something:—*adj.* made as a copy of a superior object; not genuine; as, *imitation* lace.
Syn., *n.* likeness, copy. (See duplicate.)

im-i-ta-tive (ĭm′ĭ-tā-tĭv), *adj.* **1**, inclined to copy an original; as, a child is always *imitative;* **2**, formed after a model; hence, not genuine; counterfeit.—*adv.* **im′i-ta-tive-ly.**

im-i-ta-tor (ĭm′ĭ-tā″tẽr), *n.* one who copies or mimics others; also, a copier; counterfeiter; plagiarist.

im-mac-u-late (ĭ-măk′ū-lāt), *adj.* **1**, without blemish; unspotted; undefiled; pure; also, absolutely clean; **2**, without fault or error.—*adv.* **im-mac′u-late-ly.**—*n.* **im-mac′u-late-ness.**
Syn. unblemished, spotless, stainless.

im-ma-nent (ĭm′ȧ-nĕnt), *adj.* inherent; indwelling.—*n.* **im′ma-nence; im′ma-nen-cy.**

Im-man-u-el (ĭ-măn′ū-ĕl), *n.* literally, "God with us": a name of Christ (Isaiah 7:14; Matthew 1:23).

im-ma-te-ri-al (ĭm″ȧ-tē′rĭ-ăl), *adj.* **1**, not consisting of matter; spiritual; disembodied; **2**, unimportant; as, these details are *immaterial* to the plan.—*adv.* **im″ma-te′ri-al-ly.**—*n.* **im″ma-te″ri-al′i-ty.**
Syn. trifling, insignificant.

im-ma-ture (ĭm″ȧ-tūr′), *adj.* **1**, not ripe; not fully grown or developed; **2**, not finished or perfected; crude.—*adv.* **im″ma-ture′ly.**—*n.* **im″ma-tu′ri-ty.**

im-meas-ur-a-ble (ĭ-mĕzh′ŭr-ȧ-bl; ĭm-mĕzh′ŭr-ȧ-bl), *adj.* not capable of being reckoned in terms of length, breadth, etc.; limitless; vast.—*adv.* **im-meas′ur-a-bly.**—*n.* **im-meas″ur-a-bil′i-ty.**

im-me-di-ate (ĭ-mē′dĭ-āt), *adj.* **1**, directly related; next; close; as, one's *immediate* family; **2**, direct; acting without any agency or object coming between; as, the *immediate* causes of the war; **3**, not separated in time; urgent; as, *immediate* needs; **4**, not separated in space; in contact; **5**, perceived directly; as, an *immediate* inference; **6**, *Colloq.*, near at hand; as, the *immediate* neighborhood.—*adv.* **im-me′di-ate-ly.**

im-me-mo-ri-al (ĭm″ē-mō′rĭ-ăl), *adj.* extending beyond the reach of memory, record, or tradition; as, *immemorial* usage.—*adv.* **im″me-mo′ri-al-ly.**

im-mense (ĭ-mĕns′), *adj.* immeasurable; boundless; vast; very great or large.—*adv.* **im-mense′ly.**
Syn. huge, monstrous. (See enormous.)

im-men-si-ty (ĭ-mĕn′sĭ-tĭ), *n.* [*pl.* immensities (-tĭz)], **1**, the state or fact of being large; **2**, vastness.

im-men-su-ra-ble (ĭ-mĕn′shōō-rȧ-bl), *adj.* limitless; immeasurable.—*n.* **im-men″su-ra-bil′i-ty.**

im-merge (ĭ-mûrj′), *v.t.* [*p.t.* and *p.p.* -merged′ (-mûrjd′), *p.pr.*

-merg'ing], to plunge into or under anything, esp. into a fluid; immerse.

im-merse (ĭ-mûrs'), *v.t.* [*p.t.* and *p.p.* -mersed' (-mûrst'), *p.pr.* -mers'ing], **1**, to plunge into or under anything, esp. into a fluid; sink; dip; **2**, to plunge (a person), as into an occupation; absorb the attention of; **3**, to baptize by submerging entirely in water.—*p.adj.* **im-mersed'**.
Syn. immerge, submerge.

im-mer-sion (ĭ-mûr'shŭn), *n.* **1**, the act of plunging or the state of being plunged into a fluid; **2**, absorption, as in a task; **3**, baptism by submerging the whole person in water.

im-mesh (ĭ-mĕsh'), *v.t.* to entangle in a net. Also, **en-mesh'**, *Pfd. S.*

im-me-thod-i-cal (ĭm″ē-thŏd'ĭ-kăl; ĭm″mē-), *adj.* without method; unsystematic; irregular; confused.

im-mi-grant (ĭm'ĭ-grănt), *adj.* coming into a country as a settler:—*n.* one who comes into a country to settle.
Syn., *n.* emigrant. An *immigrant* is a person who is entering a land or country for the purpose of permanent residence. From the point of view of the country he is leaving, this same person is an *emigrant*.

im-mi-grate (ĭm'ĭ-grāt), *v.i.* [*p.t.* and *p.p.* -grat″ed, *p.pr.* -grat″ing], to come into a country as a permanent resident.—*n.* **im″mi-gra'tion.**

im-mi-nence (ĭm'ĭ-nĕns), *n.* **1**, the condition of being about to happen; **2**, that which impends, as evil or danger. Also, **im'mi-nen-cy**.

im-mi-nent (ĭm'ĭ-nĕnt), *adj.* threatening or about to fall or occur immediately: said esp. of misfortune or peril; as, *imminent* calamity.—*adv.* **im'mi-nent-ly.**
Syn. impending, perilous.

im-mo-bile (ĭ-mō'bĭl), *adj.* not movable; motionless; fixed; stable; stationary.—*n.* **im″mo-bil'i-ty.**

im-mod-er-ate (ĭ-mŏd'ẽr-ăt), *adj.* extreme; excessive; extravagant; intemperate.—*adv.* **im-mod'er-ate-ly.**—*n.* **im-mod″er-a'tion.**

im-mod-est (ĭ-mŏd'ĕst), *adj.* **1**, forward; brazen; **2**, wanting in decent restraint; **3**, impure in word or deed.—*adv.* **im-mod'est-ly.**
Syn. shameless, indecent.—*Ant.* modest, decent, pure, chaste, virtuous.

im-mod-es-ty (ĭ-mŏd'ĕs-tĭ), *n.* **1**, want of modesty, delicacy, or proper reserve; **2**, impudence; forwardness.

im-mo-late (ĭm'ō-lāt), *v.t.* [*p.t.* and *p.p.* -lat″ed, *p.pr.* -lat″ing], to offer, as a victim, in sacrifice; make a sacrifice of; as, to *immolate* ambition on the altar of duty.—*n.* **im″mo-la'tion.**—*n.* **im'mo-la″tor.**

im-mor-al (ĭ-mŏr'ăl), *adj.* **1**, contrary to conscience or the law of right as conceived by any group; wicked; vicious; **2**, specif., loose sexually.—*adv.* **im-mor'al-ly.**
Syn. bad, corrupt, depraved, sinful.

im-mo-ral-i-ty (ĭm″ō-răl'ĭ-tĭ), *n.* [*pl.* immoralities (-tĭz)], **1**, the state or quality of being wicked; lewdness; **2**, an evil act or practice.

im-mor-tal (ĭ-môr'tăl), *adj.* **1**, freed from the fate of death; divine; **2**, fitted to live through the ages; famous for all time; as, an *immortal* poem; **3**, marked by loftiness; heavenly; as, *immortal* yearnings:—*n.* **1**, one who never dies; **2**, one whose fame is undying or lasting; **3**, in *pl.*, in mythology, the gods.—*adv.* **im-mor'tal-ly.**
Syn., *adj.* everlasting. (See eternal.)

im-mor-tal-i-ty (ĭm″ôr-tăl'ĭ-tĭ), *n.* **1**, exemption from death; **2**, exemption from oblivion; everlasting fame.

im-mor-tal-ize (ĭ-môr'tăl-īz), *v.t.* [*p.t.* and *p.p.* -ized (-īzd), *p.pr.* -iz″ing], **1**, to give unending life to; **2**, to bestow lasting fame upon; as, Shakespeare's plays *immortalize* his name.

im-mor-telle (ĭm″ôr-tĕl'), *n.* any one of several flowers which may be dried without losing their form or color: commonly called *everlasting;* also, a wreath made of such flowers.

im-mov-a-ble (ĭ-mōōv'ȧ-bl), *adj.* **1**, incapable of being moved; fixed; **2**, steadfast; unchanging, as a state of mind; **3**, not emotionally sensitive; **4**, in law, not subject to removal, as lands:—*n.* **1**, that which cannot be moved; **2**, in *pl.*, in law, land, or things fixed to, or belonging to, land, as trees or buildings.—*n.* **im-mov″a-bil'i-ty.**—*n.* **im-mov'a-ble-ness.**—*adv.* **im-mov'a-bly.**

im-mune (ĭ-mūn'), *adj.* exempt; privileged; esp., protected against a disease; as, vaccination usually makes one *immune* from smallpox:—*n.* one who is not liable to take a disease by reason of having had it, by inoculation, or by natural resistance.

im-mu-ni-ty (ĭ-mū'nĭ-tĭ), *n.* [*pl.* immunities (-tĭz)], **1**, in law, freedom from any duty, office, or tax; **2**, freedom from natural or usual duties, evils, or misfortunes; **3**, usually in *pl.*, special privilege; as, the *immunities* of the rich; **4**, the state of freedom from any particular disease because of protection against it.

im-mun-ize (ĭ-mūn'īz; ĭm'ū-nīz), *v.t.* [*p.t.* and *p.p.* -ized (-īzd), *p.pr.* -iz″ing], **1**, to protect from the infection or contagion of a disease, as by inoculation; **2**, to render exempt, as from taxation.

im-mure (ĭ-mūr'), *v.t.* [*p.t.* and *p.p.* -mured' (-mūrd'), *p.pr.* -mur'ing], to inclose within walls; shut up in, or as in, prison; confine.

im-mu-ta-ble (ĭ-mū'tȧ-bl), *adj.* unchangeable; permanent.—*adv.* **im-mu'ta-bly.**—*n.* **im-mu″ta-bil'i-ty.**

imp (ĭmp), *n.* **1**, a young, little, or inferior devil; a hobgoblin; **2**, a pert or mischievous child.

im-pact (ĭm'păkt), *n.* a collision; a striking together of two objects; as, the *impact* of the two cars jarred the passengers.

im-pair (ĭm-pâr'), *v.t.* to make worse; lessen in quantity, excellence, value, or strength; weaken; harm; as, poor food *impairs* the health.—*n.* **im-pair'ment.**
Syn. injure, mar, diminish, decrease.

im-pale (ĭm-pāl'), *v.t.* [*p.t.* and *p.p.* -paled' (-pāld'), *p.pr.* -pal'ing], **1**, to pierce through with anything sharp; put to death by thrusting through and fixing with a sharp stake; **2**, to render helpless, as if fixed on a stake; also, to torment thus; as, to *impale* a criminal on his own words; **3**, in heraldry, to place side by side on a shield.—*n.* **im-pale'ment.**

im-pal-pa-ble (ĭm-păl'pȧ-bl), *adj.* **1**, not perceivable by touch; as, the air is full of *impalpable* particles of dust; **2**, not easily taken in by the mind; as, *impalpable* distinctions.—*n.* **im-pal″pa-bil'i-ty.**

im-pan-el (ĭm-păn'ĕl), *v.t.* **1**, to enter on a list for jury duty; enroll; **2**, to draw from the list and swear in (persons) to form a jury. Also, **em-pan'el.**

im-part (ĭm-pärt'), *v.t.* **1**, to bestow a share or portion of, as joy, one's thoughts, or the like; give; as, autumn *imparts* color to the trees; **2**, to communicate knowledge of; tell:—*v.i.* to give a share.
Syn. reveal, divulge, disclose.

im-par-tial (ĭm-pär'shăl), *adj.* not favoring one more than another; fair; just; as, a judge must be absolutely *impartial* in his decisions.—*adv.* **im-par'tial-ly.**

im-par-ti-al-i-ty (ĭm-pär″shĭ-ăl′ĭ-tĭ; ĭm″-pär-shăl′ĭ-tĭ), *n.* freedom from favoritism; fairness.

im-pass-a-ble (ĭm-pȧs′ȧ-bl), *adj.* **1**, not to be gone through or by; **2**, preventing passage; as, the way was blocked by an *impassable* barrier.—*adv.* **im-pass′a-bly.**—*n.* **im-pass′a-ble-ness.**

im-pas-si-ble (ĭm-păs′ĭ-bl), *adj.* **1**, not able to suffer; free from harm or pain; **2**, not to be moved to passion, sympathy, or any sign of emotion; apathetic; as, he met every trial with *impassible* courage. —*adv.* **im-pas′si-bly.**—*n.* **im-pas″si-bil′i-ty.**

im-pas-sion (ĭm-păsh′ŭn), *v.t.* to fill, or move, with strong feeling; excite: **impassioned**, showing strong emotional feeling; excited; as, an *impassioned* appeal.

im-pas-sive (ĭm-păs′ĭv), *adj.* not feeling or not showing pain, suffering, feeling, or emotion; hence, serene; calm; unimpressionable.—*adv.* **im-pas′sive-ly.**—*n.* **im-pas′sive-ness.**—*n.* **im″pas-siv′i-ty.**

im-pa-tience (ĭm-pā′shĕns), *n.* **1**, a feverish desire for results; as, her *impatience* ruined the cake; **2**, the state of being restless, irritable, or unwilling to wait.

im-pa-tient (ĭm-pā′shĕnt), *adj.* **1**, desiring quick results; restless because of pain, delay, opposition, control, or circumstances; intolerant; **2**, showing or expressing restlessness, irritability, or intolerance; eager.—*adv.* **im-pa′tient-ly.**
Syn. peevish, fretful, irritable; hasty.

im-peach (ĭm-pēch′), *v.t.* **1**, to call in question; challenge the truth or value of; as, to *impeach* the testimony of a witness or a document; **2**, to accuse of crime, esp. of official misconduct, before a court; as, to *impeach* the governor.—*adj.* **im-peach′a-ble.**

im-peach-ment (ĭm-pēch′mĕnt), *n.* **1**, a calling to account as to honesty of motive, truth of testimony, or the like; a discrediting; **2**, the calling to trial of a public officer for wrongdoing in office.

im-pec-ca-ble (ĭm-pĕk′ȧ-bl), *adj.* **1**, not liable to sin; **2**, faultless; perfect.—*n.* **im-pec″ca-bil′i-ty.**

im-pe-cu-ni-ous (ĭm″pē-kū′nĭ-ŭs), *adj.* without money; poor. —*n.* **im″pe-cu″ni-os′i-ty.**

im-ped-ance (ĭm-pēd′ăns), *n.* the apparent resistance of a circuit to the flow of an alternating current.

im-pede (ĭm-pēd′), *v.t.* [*p.t.* and *p.p.* -ped′ed, *p.pr.* -ped′ing], to obstruct; hinder; as, to *impede* progress.

im-ped-i-ment (ĭm-pĕd′ĭ-mĕnt), *n.* that which hinders or obstructs progress or activity; specif., an organic obstruction; as, an *impediment* in speech; a hindrance; obstacle; obstruction.
Syn. hindrance, barrier.

im-ped-i-men-ta (ĭm-pĕd″ĭ-mĕn′tȧ), *n.pl.* things which hinder progress; baggage, esp. military baggage.

im-pel (ĭm-pĕl′), *v.t.* [*p.t.* and *p.p.* -pelled′ (-pĕld′), *p.pr.* -pel′ling], to drive or urge forward or on; force or influence to any kind of motion or action; as, fear and remorse *impel* him to confess.—*n.* **im-pel′ler.**
Syn. actuate, induce, incite, instigate.—
Ant. retard, deter, discourage.

im-pend (ĭm-pĕnd′), *v.i.* to hang over something; be ready to fall; hence, as of events, to be at hand; threaten immediately.

im-pend-ing (ĭm-pĕn′dĭng), *p.adj.* **1**, overhanging; suspended so as to be about to fall; **2**, close at hand; as, *impending* ruin or disaster.
Syn. imminent, threatening.

im-pen-e-tra-bil-i-ty (ĭm-pĕn″ē-trȧ-bĭl′ĭ-tĭ), *n.* **1**, incapability of being pierced or entered; imperviousness; **2**, that property of matter by reason of which no two bodies can occupy the same space at the same time.

im-pen-e-tra-ble (ĭm-pĕn′ē-trȧ-bl), *adj.* **1**, not to be entered or pierced; not admitting entrance; **2**, not capable of being understood or comprehended; as, an *impenetrable* mystery; **3**, not touched by reason, sympathy, etc.; as, an *impenetrable* heart; **4**, having the property of matter by reason of which no two bodies can occupy the same space at the same time. —*adv.* **im-pen′e-tra-bly.**

im-pen-i-tence (ĭm-pĕn′ĭ-tĕns), *n.* failure to repent for wrong done. Also, **im-pen′i-ten-cy.**

im-pen-i-tent (ĭm-pĕn′ĭ-tĕnt), *adj.* not sorry for sin; unrepentant; as, an *impenitent* criminal:—*n.* one who finally neglects the duty of repentance; a hardened sinner.—*adv.* **im-pen′i-tent-ly.**

im-per-a-tive (ĭm-pĕr′ȧ-tĭv), *adj.* **1**, expressing command; authoritative; **2**, not to be avoided; as, an *imperative* necessity; **3**, in grammar, expressing command, entreaty, or exhortation; as, the *imperative* mood:—*n.* **1**, a command; an act or word that gives or expresses a command; **2**, the imperative mood.—*adv.* **im-per′a-tive-ly.**—*n.* **im-per′a-tive-ness.**
Syn., adj. urgent, obligatory.

im-per-cep-ti-ble (ĭm″pĕr-sĕp′tĭ-bl), *adj.* not capable of being perceived by the senses, or realized by the mind; hence, extremely small or brief; as, an almost *imperceptible* pause.—*adv.* **im″-per-cep′ti-bly.**—*n.* **im″per-cep″ti-bil′i-ty.**

im-per-fect (ĭm-pûr′fĕkt), *adj.* **1**, wanting in completeness, correctness, or excellence; wanting in some organ necessary to usual activity; incomplete; **2**, in grammar, designating that tense which indicates past action going on but not completed; as, he *was walking*:—*n.* the imperfect tense, or a word in it.—*adv.* **im-per′fect-ly.**—*n.* **im-per′fect-ness.**

im-per-fec-tion (ĭm″pĕr-fĕk′shŭn), *n.* **1**, incompleteness; faultiness; deficiency; **2**, a defect or blemish; failing; fault.
Syn. fault, vice, weakness.

im-pe-ri-al (ĭm-pē′rĭ-ăl), *adj.* **1**, pertaining to an empire or emperor; **2**, pertaining to a sovereign state as governing dependencies; **3**, pertaining to, or fit for, an emperor or sovereign; hence, domineering; imposing; **4**, designating, or pertaining to, the system of weights and measures legally established in Great Britian:—*n.* **1**, anything of unusual size or excellence, as a certain size of paper; **2**, the top of a carriage, esp. a diligence; **3**, a tuft of hair on a man's lower lip. —*n.* **im-pe′ri-al-ist.**—*adv.* **im-pe′ri-al-ly.**

im-pe-ri-al-ism (ĭm-pē′rĭ-ăl-ĭzm), *n.* **1**, the power or government of an emperor; **2**, the policy of the extension of the control or dominion of a nation, either by gaining new territory or by a close union of loosely connected parts.

im-pe-ri-al-is-tic (ĭm-pē″rĭ-ăl-ĭs′tĭk), *adj.* pertaining to, or favoring, the policy of extending the dominion of a nation.—*adv.* **im-pe″ri-al-is′ti-cal-ly.**

im-per-il (ĭm-pĕr′ĭl), *v.t.* to put in danger or jeopardy; endanger.

im-pe-ri-ous (ĭm-pē′rĭ-ŭs), *adj.* **1**, commanding; overbearing; **2**, urgent; imperative.—*adv.* **im-pe′ri-ous-ly.** —*n.* **im-pe′ri-ous-ness.**
Syn. domineering, authoritative, lordly.

im-per-ish-a-ble (ĭm-pĕr′ĭsh-ȧ-bl), *adj.* indestructible; not subject to decay; permanently enduring; undying; as, *imperishable* fame.—*adv.* **im-per'ish-a-bly.**—*n.* **im-per"ish-a-bil'i-ty.**

im-per-me-a-ble (ĭm-pûr'mē-*ȧ*-bl), *adj.* not permitting passage, as of a fluid through a substance; as, rubber is *impermeable* to water.—*adv.* **im-per'me-a-bly.**—*n.* **im-per"me-a-bil'i-ty.**

im-per-son-al (ĭm-pûr'sŭn-ăl), *adj.* **1,** not belonging or referring to a particular person; **2,** not existing as a separate person; as, most of us believe in an *impersonal* power called Luck; **3,** in grammar, designating verbs used either with no subject or with an indefinite one, always in the third person singular; as, *it snows; it seems*:—*n.* an impersonal verb.—*adv.* **im-per'son-al-ly.**

im-per-son-ate (ĭm-pûr'sŭn-āt), *v.t.* [*p.t.* and *p.p.* -at"ed, *p.pr.* -at"ing], **1,** to give the qualities of a person to; personify; **2,** to represent a person or character, esp. on the stage.—*n.* **im-per"son-a'tion.**

im-per-son-a-tor (ĭm-pûr'sŭn-ā"tẽr), *n.* one who represents persons or characters; an actor.

im-per-ti-nence (ĭm-pûr'tĭ-nĕns), *n.* **1,** that which has no relation to the matter in hand, as in speech or manners; **2,** lack of due respect for others in manners or speech; rudeness.

im-per-ti-nent (ĭm-pûr'tĭ-nĕnt), *adj.* **1,** of no relation to the matter in hand; **2,** rude; uncivil or offensive in behavior.—*adv.* **im-per'ti-nent-ly.**
Syn. impudent, disrespectful, pert.

im-per-turb-a-ble (ĭm"pẽr-tûr'b*ȧ*-bl), *adj.* not capable of being mentally disturbed or agitated; self-contained; calm; as, the child regarded the stranger with an *imperturbable* stare.—*adv.* **im"per-turb'a-bly.**—*n.* **im"per-turb"a-bil'i-ty.**

im-per-vi-ous (ĭm-pûr'vĭ-ŭs), *adj.* **1,** not permitting entrance or passage; impenetrable; as, cement should be *impervious* to water; **2,** not affected or influenced; as, *impervious* to argument.—*adv.* **im-per'vi-ous-ly.**—*n.* **im-per'vi-ous-ness.**

im-pe-ti-go (ĭm"pē-tī'gō), *n.* a skin disease characterized by pimples containing pus.—*adj.* **im"pe-tig'i-nous.**

im-pet-u-os-i-ty (ĭm-pĕt"ū-ŏs'ĭ-tĭ), *n.* [*pl.* impetuosities (-tĭz)], **1,** of physical things, sudden, violent energy of movement; **2,** of people or feelings, the quality which leads to action without thought or reflection; impulsiveness.

im-pet-u-ous (ĭm-pĕt'ū-ŭs), *adj.* **1,** of physical things, rushing with force and violence; as, an *impetuous* current; **2,** of people or feelings, acting with sudden energy; hasty and rash; passionate; as, an *impetuous* demand.—*adv.* **im-pet'u-ous-ly.**—*n.* **im-pet'u-ous-ness.**
Syn. violent, excitable, furious, vehement, impulsive.—*Ant.* calm, steady, deliberate.

im-pe-tus (ĭm'pē-tŭs), *n.* **1,** the force which any moving body possesses by reason of its motion and weight; momentum; **2,** any impulse; incentive.

im-pi-e-ty (ĭm-pī'ē-tĭ), *n.* [*pl.* impieties (-tĭz)], **1,** want of reverence for the Supreme Being; ungodliness; **2,** an act of irreverence or wickedness.

im-pinge (ĭm-pĭnj'), *v.i.* [*p.t.* and *p.p.* -pinged' (-pĭnjd'), *p.pr.* -ping'ing], **1,** to strike or dash; clash; come in collision: with *on, upon,* or *against;* as, sound waves *impinge* on the eardrum; **2,** to encroach: with *upon.*—*n.* **im-pinge'ment.**

im-pi-ous (ĭm'pĭ-ŭs), *adj.* wanting in reverence for God; irreligious; wicked; profane; as, *impious* thoughts.—*adv.* **im'pi-ous-ly.**—*n.* **im'pi-ous-ness.**

Syn. ungodly, irreverent.—*Ant.* devout, holy, reverent, godly.

imp-ish (ĭmp'ĭsh), *adj.* having the character of a mischievous little devil or urchin; as, *impish* behavior.—*adv.* **imp'ish-ly.**—*n.* **imp'ish-ness.**

im-pla-ca-ble (ĭm-plā'k*ȧ*-bl), *adj.* not to be pacified or appeased; constant in anger or enmity; relentless; as, an Indian is a loyal friend or an *implacable* enemy.—*n.* **im-pla'ca-ble-ness.**—*adv.* **im-pla'ca-bly.**—*n.* **im-pla"ca-bil'i-ty.**
Syn. merciless, pitiless.—*Ant.* forgiving, mild, gentle, placable.

im-plant (ĭm-plănt'), *v.t.* **1,** to set in deeply; cause to take root; **2,** to give a firm foothold to; instil; as, to *implant* a conviction.—*n.* **im"plan-ta'tion.**

im-ple-ment (ĭm'plē-mĕnt), *n.* **1,** that which supplies a want, or is a necessity to an end, esp. an instrument, tool, or utensil; **2,** in *pl.,* the equipment needed for a given project; as, the *implements* of war.

im-pli-cate (ĭm'plĭ-kāt), *v.t.* [*p.t.* and *p.p.* -cat"ed, *p.pr.* -cat"ing], **1,** to fold or twist together; entangle; **2,** to involve deeply; bring into connection with; as, the evidence *implicates* many in the plot.

im-pli-ca-tion (ĭm"plĭ-kā'shŭn), *n.* **1,** an entanglement; **2,** the act of implying, or the state of being implied; also, a meaning not expressed but understood; as, since he did not speak of the matter, the *implication* is that he knows nothing about it.

im-plic-it (ĭm-plĭs'ĭt), *adj.* **1,** to be understood, though not expressed; implied; as, *implicit* sympathy; **2,** trusting in the word or authority of another; blind; unreserved; as, *implicit* confidence.—*adv.* **im-plic'it-ly.**—*n.* **im-plic'it-ness.**
Syn. implied, tacit, virtual.

im-plied (ĭm-plīd'), *p.adj.* inferred though not expressed in words or actions; expressed indirectly.—*adv.* **im-pli'ed-ly** (ĭm-plī'ĕd-lĭ).

im-plore (ĭm-plōr'), *v.t.* [*p.t.* and *p.p.* -plored' (-plōrd'), *p.pr.* -plor'ing], to entreat earnestly and humbly; beg; pray; as, to *implore* God to have mercy:—*v.i.* to beg; supplicate.—*adv.* **im-plor'ing-ly.**
Syn. beseech, supplicate, plead.

im-ply (ĭm-plī'), *v.t.* [*p.t.* and *p.p.* -plied' (-plīd'), *p.pr.* -ply'ing], **1,** to mean or suggest (something not directly stated); as, your words *imply* distrust of him; involve as a consequence; as, wealth *implies* responsibility; **2,** to hint; insinuate.
Syn. denote, signify, intimate. (See infer.)

im-po-lite (ĭm"pō-līt'), *adj.* wanting in good manners; boorish; rude.—*adv.* **im"po-lite'ly.**—*n.* **im"-po-lite'ness.**

im-pol-i-tic (ĭm-pŏl'ĭ-tĭk), *adj.* **1,** of persons, unwise; indiscreet; imprudent; **2,** of actions, apt to endanger the result desired.—*adv.* **im-pol'i-tic-ly.**

im-pon-der-a-ble (ĭm-pŏn'dẽr-*ȧ*-bl), *adj.* without weight; very light.—*n.* **im-pon"der-a-bil'i-ty.**

[1]**im-port** (ĭm-pōrt'), *v.t.* **1,** to bring from without or from abroad, esp. for commercial purposes: opp. of *export*; **2,** to introduce, as bitterness into a debate:—*n.* (ĭm'pōrt), usually in *pl.,* an article brought from a foreign country; esp., merchandise intended for sale.—*n.* **im-port'er.**

[2]**im-port** (ĭm-pōrt'), *v.t.* **1,** to signify or imply; **2,** to be of consequence or concern to; affect significantly:—*v.i.* to have consequence:—*n.* (ĭm'pōrt), **1,** meaning; that which is implied; **2,** consequence.
Syn., n. sense, purport, weight.

im-por-tance (ĭm-pôr'tăns), *n.* **1,** the quality of being signifi-

cant, weighty, or momentous; **2**, social consequence; high position; **3**, pretentiousness.
Syn. significance, value, gravity, moment.

im-por-tant (ĭm-pôr′tănt), *adj.* **1**, of much consequence; bearing weight or significance; **2**, of high position; of social consequence; **3**, pretentious; pompous.—*adv.* **im-por′tant-ly.**
Syn. significant, valuable.—*Ant.* trifling.

im-por-ta-tion (ĭm″pōr-tā′shŭn), *n.* **1**, the act or practice of bringing merchandise into a country from abroad; **2**, that which is brought into a country from abroad, as merchandise, workmen, or fashions.

im-por-tu-nate (ĭm-pôr′tū-nāt), *adj.* unreasonable or troublesome in begging or asking; pressing; urgent.—*adv.* **im-por′tu-nate-ly.**

im-por-tune (ĭm″pôr-tūn′; ĭm-pôr′tŭn), *v.t.* [*p.t.* and *p.p.* -tuned′ (-tūnd′), *p.pr.* -tun′ing], to annoy with continual petitions or demands:—*v.i.* to beg persistently or urgently.
Syn. beseech, entreat, implore.

im-por-tu-ni-ty (ĭm-pôr-tū′nĭ-tĭ), *n.* [*pl.* importunities (-tĭz)], persistent demand; ceaseless asking or begging.

im-pose (ĭm-pōz′), *v.t.* [*p.t.* and *p.p.* -posed′ (-pōzd′), *p.pr.* -pos′ing], **1**, to place upon; as, to *impose* the hands in confirmation or ordination; **2**, to lay or inflict upon, as a burden, punishment, or charge; as, to *impose* taxes; **3**, to palm off deceitfully or fraudulently: with *upon;* **4**, to obtrude; intrude; as, to *impose* one's company on others; **5**, in printing, to arrange in order and lock up for printing, as forms, pages, etc.:—*v.i.* **1**, to place a burden upon; **2**, to take advantage; presume: with *upon;* as, to *impose* upon good nature; **3**, to take advantage through deception: with *upon.*—*n.* **im-pos′er.**

im-pos-ing (ĭm-pōz′ĭng), *p.adj.* commanding; stately; grand.—*adv.* **im-pos′ing-ly.**
Syn. striking, majestic, august, noble.

im-po-si-tion (ĭm″pō-zĭsh′ŭn), *n.* **1**, the act of imposing, as a burden; also, that which is imposed; **2**, in England, additional work required, as of a student, for punishment; **3**, a trick or fraud; **4**, a laying on of hands, as in ordination.

im-pos-si-bil-i-ty (ĭm-pŏs″ĭ-bĭl′ĭ-tĭ), *n.* [*pl.* impossibilities (-tĭz)], **1**, the state or fact of not being able to exist, be done, or happen; **2**, that which cannot exist or be done.

im-pos-si-ble (ĭm-pŏs′ĭ-bl), *adj.* **1**, not capable of occurring or being; **2**, hopeless; not to be done conveniently; as, it is *impossible* to meet you; **3**, *Colloq.*, utterly objectionable, as a person; outrageous, as a situation.—*adv.* **im-pos′si-bly.**

im-post (ĭm′pōst), *n.* a tax, tribute, or duty, esp. one levied by the government on goods brought into a country.

im-pos-tor (ĭm-pŏs′tẽr), *n.* one who deceives others by an assumed character or false pretensions; a swindler.

im-pos-ture (ĭm-pŏs′tūr), *n.* deception by false pretensions; fraud.

im-po-tence (ĭm′pō-tĕns), *n.* **1**, the state of being weak in body or mind; feebleness; as, *impotence* is often the result of old age; **2**, utter inability to accomplish a purpose. Also, **im′po-ten-cy.**
Syn. weakness, incapacity, infirmity, frailty.

im-po-tent (ĭm′pō-tĕnt), *adj.* wanting in physical, mental, or moral power; weak.—*adv.* **im′po-tent-ly.**
Syn. feeble, helpless, infirm.

im-pound (ĭm-pound′), *v.t.* **1**, to shut up in a pen, as stray cattle; confine; **2**, in law, to seize and hold.

im-pov-er-ish (ĭm-pŏv′ẽr-ĭsh), *v.t.* **1**, to make poor; **2**, to use up the strength, richness, or fertility of, as land.—*n.* **im-pov′er-ish-ment.**

im-pow-er (ĭm-pou′ẽr), *v.t.* **1**, to give authority to; authorize; **2**, to enable. Also, **em-pow′er**, *Pfd. S.*

im-prac-ti-ca-ble (ĭm-prăk′tĭ-kȧ-bl), *adj.* **1**, not to be effected by the means employed, or at command; **2**, not easily dealt with; unmanageable; **3**, impassable, as roads.—*adv.* **im-prac′ti-ca-bly.**—*n.* **im-prac′ti-ca-ble-ness.**—*n.* **im-prac″ti-ca-bil′i-ty.**

im-pre-cate (ĭm′prē-kāt), *v.t.* [*p.t.* and *p.p.* -cat″ed, *p.pr.* -cat″ing], to call down (an evil or a curse).

im-pre-ca-tion (ĭm″prē-kā′shŭn), *n.* a curse; also, the act of calling down evil upon anyone.

im-preg-na-ble (ĭm-prĕg′nȧ-bl), *adj.* **1**, not to be captured, as a fort; **2**, not to be overcome, as virtue.—*adv.* **im-preg′na-bly.**—*n.* **im-preg″na-bil′i-ty.**

im-preg-nate (ĭm-prĕg′nāt), *v.t.* [*p.t.* and *p.p.* -nat-ed, *p.pr.* -nat-ing], **1**, to make (a female) pregnant; make fertile, as land; **2**, to cause to be filled with; saturate, as wood with creosote; **3**, hence, to imbue, as with principles:—*adj.* (ĭm-prĕg′nāt), impregnated.—*n.* **im″preg-na′tion.**

im-pre-sa-ri-o (ĭm″prā-sä′rē-ō), *n.* [*pl.* impresarios (-ōz); impresari (-rē)], one who organizes, manages, or conducts an opera or concert company.

[1]**im-press** (ĭm-prĕs′), *v.t.* [*p.t.* and *p.p.* -pressed′ (-prĕst′), *p.pr.* -press′ing], **1**, to exert pressure upon; mark (a thing); as, she *impressed* the wax with her seal; **2**, to produce (a mark) by pressure on something; imprint; **3**, to affect or influence strongly; as, the speech *impressed* me deeply:—*n.* (ĭm′prĕs), **1**, a mark produced by pressure, as by a stamp; **2**, a distinguishing mark; characteristic.

[2]**im-press** (ĭm-prĕs′), *v.t.* [*p.t.* and *p.p.* -pressed′ (-prĕst′), *p.pr.* -press′ing], **1**, to compel to enter the public service, as soldiers or sailors; **2**, to seize for public service, as goods.—*n.* **im-press′ment.**

im-press-i-ble (ĭm-prĕs′ĭ-bl), *adj.* easily affected mentally; impressionable; sensitive; as, poetry appeals to *impressible* natures.—*n.* **im-press″i-bil′i-ty.**

im-pres-sion (ĭm-prĕsh′ŭn), *n.* **1**, the act of marking, or the state of being marked, stamped, or affected by outside influence; **2**, the mark made by a stamp or mold; as, the *impression* on a coin; **3**, the style or character formed by outside force or influence; **4**, an image in the mind caused by something outside it; the immediate effect produced upon the mind by sensation, emotion, or intellect; **5**, a vague notion, remembrance, or belief; as, the speech gave the audience the *impression* that the speaker was not interested in his subject; **6**, in printing, the act or result of pressing type, plates, etc., on paper; **7**, in publishing, the whole number of copies, as of a book, printed at one time.

im-pres-sion-a-ble (ĭm-prĕsh′ŭn-ȧ-bl), *adj.* capable of receiving effects from without or of being influenced by surroundings; as, an *impressionable* nature.—*n.* **im-pres″sion-a-bil′i-ty.**
Syn. susceptible, sensitive.

im-pres-sion-ism (ĭm-prĕsh′ŭn-ĭzm), *n.* in art or literature, a theory in which the underlying aim is to record the vividness and force of the first impression without elaborate detail.—*adj.* and *n.* **im-pres′sion-ist.**—*adj.* **im-pres″sion-is′tic.**

im-pres-sive (ĭm-prĕs′ĭv), *adj.* capable of producing an effect on

the intellect or feelings.—*adv.* **im-pres'sive-ly.** —*n.* **im-pres'sive-ness.**
Syn. stirring, exciting, moving.

im-press-ment (ĭm-prĕs'mĕnt), *n.* the act of impressing into public service or of seizing for public use.

im-prest (ĭm'prĕst), *n.* **1,** an advance of money to a person to enable him to carry out a specified piece of state business; **2,** formerly, advance pay of soldiers or sailors.

im-pri-ma-tur (ĭm"prĭ-mā'tûr), [Lat.], *n.* a license to print a book or pamphlet; hence, sanction in general.

im-print (ĭm-prĭnt'), *v.t.* **1,** to mark by pressure; **2,** to stamp, as letters and words on paper, by means of inked types; **3,** to impress deeply, as on the mind:—*n.* **1,** (ĭm'prĭnt), an impression, impress, or mark left by something; **2,** the publisher's or printer's name, usually with time and place of issue, on the title-page or at the end of a book.

im-pris-on (ĭm-prĭz'n), *v.i.* **1,** to put into a jail; detain in custody; **2,** to restrain or confine in any way.

im-pris-on-ment (ĭm-prĭz'n-mĕnt), *n.* **1,** the state of being shut in, or as in, jail; confinement; restraint; **2,** the act of shutting up in confinement.

im-prob-a-ble (ĭm-prŏb'ȧ-bl), *adj.* unlikely; not to be expected; not easily believed.—*adv.* **im-prob'a-bly.**—*n.* **im-prob"a-bil'i-ty.**

im-promp-tu (ĭm-prŏmp'tū), *adv.* without preparation; offhand; as, the minister spoke *impromptu:*—*adj.* said, made, or done on the spur of the moment; as, an *impromptu* address:—*n.* a speech or an effort made without preparation.

im-prop-er (ĭm-prŏp'ẽr), *adj.* **1,** not well adapted or suited to the purpose; **2,** not according to good manners; unseemly; unbecoming; indecent; **3,** not in accord with fact, truth, or reason; wrong; inaccurate: **improper fraction,** a fraction in which the numerator is greater than the denominator.—*adv.* **im-prop'er-ly.**

im-pro-pri-e-ty (ĭm"prō-prī'ē-tĭ), *n.* [*pl.* improprieties (-tĭz)], **1,** the quality of being improper; **2,** an act which is not in accord with usage or decency.

im-prove (ĭm-pro͞ov'), *v.t.* [*p.t.* and *p.p.* -proved' (-pro͞ovd'), *p.pr.* -prov'ing], **1,** to make better; as, to *improve* the mind; **2,** to use to advantage; as, to *improve* the opportunity:—*v.i.* **1,** to grow better, as in health; **2,** to make improvements: with *on* or *upon.*—*adj.* **im-prov'a-ble.**—*n.* **im-prov'er.**
Syn. amend, reform, rectify; use, employ.

im-prove-ment (ĭm-pro͞ov'mĕnt), *n.* **1,** advancement of anything to a better condition; **2,** usually in *pl.*, that by which the value of anything, esp. real estate, is increased.

im-prov-i-dent (ĭm-prŏv'ĭ-dĕnt), *adj.* lacking foresight; not providing for the future; as, the five foolish virgins in the old parable were *improvident.*—*adv.* **im-prov'i-dent-ly.**—*n.* **im-prov'i-dence.**
Syn. prodigal, wasteful, reckless.

im-prov-i-sa-tion (ĭm-prŏv"ĭ-sā'shŭn; ĭm-prŏv"ĭ-zā'shŭn), *n.* **1,** the act of composing poetry or music without preparation; **2,** an extemporaneous composition, as a poem or song.

im-pro-vise (ĭm"prō-vīz'), *v.t.* [*p.t.* and *p.p.* -vised' (-vīzd'), *p.pr.* -vis'ing], **1,** to compose without preparation or forethought, esp. verse or music; **2,** to make up on the spur of the moment, or for a special occasion; as, to *improvise* a fancy costume:—*v.i.* **1,** to compose without previous thought; **2,** to do a thing offhand.—*n.* **im"-pro-vis'er; im-prov'i-sa"tor.**

im-pru-dence (ĭm-pro͞o'dĕns), *n.* **1,** want of discretion; carelessness of consequences; inattention to one's interests; rashness; **2,** an act lacking caution, discretion, or foresight.

im-pru-dent (ĭm-pro͞o'dĕnt), *adj.* wanting caution or discretion; heedless of consequences; rash; reckless; as, it is *imprudent* to ride in a canoe if one cannot swim.—*adv.* **im-pru'dent-ly.**

im-pu-dence (ĭm'pū-dĕns), *n.* rudeness; forwardness; sauciness.
Syn. impertinence, insolence.

im-pu-dent (ĭm'pū-dĕnt), *adj.* pert; insolent; brazen; offensively forward; disrespectful; as, an *impudent* answer.—*adv.* **im'pu-dent-ly.**
Syn. saucy, impertinent, insulting.

im-pugn (ĭm-pūn'), *v.t.* to attack by arguments; question; attack as false.—*n.* **im-pugn'er.**

im-pulse (ĭm'pŭls), *n.* **1,** force communicated suddenly, causing motion; an impetus; **2,** the result of an impelling force; **3,** an urge to action arising from some external stimulus or state of mind; **4,** a sudden determination to act, not arising from careful thought; as, she spoke on the *impulse* of the moment: **impulse turbine,** a turbine wheel moved by the impact of water or other working fluid driven at high speed against the buckets or blades (see *hydraulic,* illus.).
Syn. incentive, incitement, motive.

im-pul-sion (ĭm-pŭl'shŭn), *n.* **1,** the act of driving forward, or the state of being driven forward; **2,** the sudden driving impact of a body in motion on another body; **3,** tendency to onward motion derived from a driving force; impetus; **4,** incitement to action, either external or mental.

im-pul-sive (ĭm-pŭl'sĭv), *adj.* **1,** having the power of urging forward; **2,** influenced by, or resulting from, some sudden moving force, either external or mental; as, *impulsive* movements; **3,** apt to be moved to action by sudden and momentary feeling; as, an *impulsive* person.—*adv.* **im-pul'sive-ly.**—*n.* **im-pul'sive-ness.**
Syn. rash, headlong, impetuous.

im-pu-ni-ty (ĭm-pū'nĭ-tĭ), *n.* freedom from punishment, injury, or loss; as, one cannot lie with *impunity.*

im-pure (ĭm-pūr'), *adj.* **1,** not clean; unwholesome; **2,** mixed with foreign or inferior substance; as, sugar mixed with sand is *impure* sugar; **3,** not virtuous in thought, word, or deed; **4,** unclean; unhallowed; **5,** not idiomatic; ungrammatical: said of a language or style.—*adv.* **im-pure'ly.** —*n.* **im-pure'ness.**

im-pu-ri-ty (ĭm-pū'rĭ-tĭ), *n.* [*pl.* impurities (-tĭz)], **1,** uncleanness; **2,** that which is, or tends to make, unclean.

im-put-a-ble (ĭm-pūt'ȧ-bl), *adj.* capable of being charged or ascribed; attributable; as, suicide is frequently *imputable* to insanity.—*adv.* **im-put'a-bly.**

im-pu-ta-tion (ĭm"pū-tā'shŭn), *n.* **1,** the act of laying a charge against someone; **2,** anything charged, esp. discredit; blame; reproach.
Syn. censure, charge, accusation.

im-pute (ĭm-pūt'), *v.t.* [*p.t.* and *p.p.* -put'ed, *p.pr.* -put'ing], **1,** to set to the account of; charge, attribute, or ascribe, as a fault; **2,** in theology, to attribute (sin or righteousness) as received from another. —*adj.* **im-put'a-tive.**—*n.* **im-put'er.**

in (ĭn), *prep.* **1,** within the bounds or limits of; as, lost *in* the woods; hurt *in* the hand; **2,** being surrounded by, as circumstances, interests, etc.; as, *in* business; *in* trouble; **3,** within, as a state, condition, occupation, or the like; as, still *in* death; *in* chains; *in* pain; **4**, within, as a period of time; during; as, *in* winter; **5**, after; as, return *in* two days; **6**, at the time of; as, *in* the beginning; **7**, in the person or case of; as, you have a friend *in* me; **8**, in the range of; as, *in* mathematics; within the capacity, thought, etc., of; as, it isn't *in* him to do that; **9**, made of; as, a figure *in* porcelain; expressed in; as, a play *in* French; **10**, on account of; as, to rejoice *in* youth; **11**, as a means of; as, *in* explanation, let me offer this; **12**, from among; as, nine times *in* ten: **in as much as, inasmuch as**, because; considering that:—*adv.* **1**, toward the inside; as, he went *in*; **2**, close by; at home; as, my master is *in*:—*adj.* **1**, incoming; inward; interior; **2**, in port; arrived; as, an *in* ship; **3**, *Slang*, the richer by; as, he was *in* five dollars:—*n.* **1**, in baseball, a ball pitched so as to curve toward a right-handed batter; **2**, in *pl.*: **a**, the political party in office; **b**, in baseball, the side at the bat: **ins and outs**, **1**, windings and turnings; **2**, vicissitudes; as, the *ins and outs* of life; **3**, the minute details of any procedure.

¹in- (ĭn-), *prefix*, [*il-* before *l*; *ir-* before *r*; *im-* before *b*, *m*, *p*; often *en-* in words coming from the French; as, *il*lusion, *ir*radiate, *im*bibe, *im*mense, *im*part, *en*rich], in; into; toward; within; on: also used intensively.

²in- (ĭn-), *prefix*, not; without; non-; un-; as, *in*audible; *in*active; *in*elastic: found, like ¹*in-*, in the forms *il-*, *-ir-*, and *im-*; as, *il*licit; *ir*regular; *im*mense.

-in (-ĭn), *suffix*, **1**, found in nouns and adjectives taken directly from Latin nouns and adjectives; as, orig*in*; mat*in*; Calv*in*; **2**, in chemistry, used in names of certain elements and of neutral compounds; as, fibr*in*: in elements, usually *-ine*; as, chlor*ine*.

in-a-bil-i-ty (ĭn″ȧ-bĭl′ĭ-tĭ), *n.* the state or condition of not having the power to do; lack of power; incapacity.
Syn. (see disability).—*Ant.* ability, power.

in-ac-ces-si-ble (ĭn″ăk-sĕs′ĭ-bl), *adj.* not easy to get to or into; not approachable; not obtainable.—*adv.* **in″ac-ces′si-bly**.—*n.* **in″ac-ces″si-bil′i-ty**.

in-ac-cu-ra-cy (ĭn-ăk′ū-rȧ-sĭ), *n.* [*pl.* inaccuracies (-sĭz)], **1**, the quality of being inexact; **2**, an error.

in-ac-cu-rate (ĭn-ăk′ū-rāt), *adj.* incorrect; not exact.—*adv.* **in-ac′cu-rate-ly**.—*n.* **in-ac′cu-rate-ness**.

in-ac-tion (ĭn-ăk′shŭn), *n.* **1**, lack of motion; **2**, the state of idleness.

in-ac-tive (ĭn-ăk′tĭv), *adj.* **1**, having no power to move; **2**, not inclined to move; sluggish; idle.—*n.* **in-ac′tive-ness**.—*adv.* **in-ac′tive-ly**.—*n.* **in″ac-tiv′i-ty**.

in-ad-e-quate (ĭn-ăd′ē-kwāt), *adj.* not equal to some demand; not sufficient.—*adv.* **in-ad′e-quate-ly**.—*n.* **in-ad′e-quate-ness**.—*n.* **in-ad′e-qua-cy**.

in-ad-mis-si-ble (ĭn″ăd-mĭs′ĭ-bl), *adj.* **1**, not to be granted as true; **2**, not to be admitted.—*adv.* **in″ad-mis′si-bly**.—*n.* **in″ad-mis″si-bil′i-ty**.

in-ad-vert-ence (ĭn″ăd-vûr′tĕns), *n.* **1**, want of attention; **2**, an oversight. Also, **in″ad-vert′en-cy**.

in-ad-vert-ent (ĭn″ăd-vûr′tĕnt), *adj.* **1**, inattentive; heedless; **2**, unintentional; unconscious; as, an *inadvertent* slight.—*adv.* **in″ad-vert′ent-ly**.
Syn. thoughtless.—*Ant.* thoughtful, careful.

in-al-ien-a-ble (ĭn-āl′yĕn-ȧ-bl), *adj.* incapable of being surrendered, or transferred to another; as, freedom of speech is man's *inalienable* right.—*adv.* **in-al′ien-a-bly**.—*n.* **in-al″ien-a-bil′i-ty**.

in-am-o-ra-ta (ĭn-ăm″ō-rä′tȧ), *n.* a woman in love or beloved.

in-ane (ĭn-ān′), *adj.* empty; silly; as, *inane* remarks.—*adv.* **in-ane′ly**.

in-an-i-mate (ĭn-ăn′ĭ-māt), *adj.* **1**, without life; **2**, dull; spiritless.—*adv.* **in-an′i-mate-ly**.—*n.* **in-an′i-mate-ness**.
Syn. apathetic, inert. (See dead.)

in-a-ni-tion (ĭn″ȧ-nĭsh′ŭn), *n.* emptiness; exhaustion from hunger.

in-an-i-ty (ĭn-ăn′ĭ-tĭ), *n.* [*pl.* inanities (-tĭz)], **1**, emptiness; senselessness; frivolity; **2**, in *pl.*, vain frivolities.

in-ap-pli-ca-ble (ĭn-ăp′lĭ-kȧ-bl), *adj.* **1**, not suitable or fit for some certain purpose or case; **2**, not bearing upon the case in hand.—*adv.* **in-ap′pli-ca-bly**.—*n.* **in-ap″pli-ca-bil′i-ty**.

in-ap-pre-ci-a-ble (ĭn″ă-prē′shĭ-ȧ-bl), *adj.* too small to be realized or perceived.—*adv.* **in″ap-pre′ci-a-bly**.

in-ap-pro-pri-ate (ĭn″ă-prō′prĭ-āt), *adj.* not suitable, fit, or proper.—*adv.* **in″ap-pro′pri-ate-ly**.—*n.* **in″ap-pro′pri-ate-ness**.

in-apt (ĭn-ăpt′), *adj.* not suitable; unfit.—*adv.* **in-apt′ly**.—*n.* **in-apt′ness**.

in-apt-i-tude (ĭn-ăp′tĭ-tūd), *n.* **1**, want of fitness; **2**, want of readiness; **3**, want of skill; unhandiness.

in-ar-tic-u-late (ĭn″är-tĭk′ū-lāt), *adj.* **1**, not uttered in the form of words, as the sounds uttered by animals; **2**, incapable of speech; as, he was *inarticulate* with rage; **3**, in zoölogy, not composed of segments united by joints.—*adv.* **in″ar-tic′u-late-ly**.—*n.* **in″ar-tic′u-late-ness**.

in-ar-tis-tic (ĭn″är-tĭs′tĭk), *adj.* **1**, not in accord with the principles of art; **2**, lacking appreciation of art; **3**, not graceful; not skilful. Also, **in″ar-tis′ti-cal**.—*adv.* **in″ar-tis′ti-cal-ly**.

in-as-much (ĭn″ăz-mŭch′), *adv.* in so far; to such a degree; because: with *as:* also written *in as much* (*as*).

in-at-ten-tion (ĭn″ă-tĕn′shŭn), *n.* heedlessness; failure to attend to a matter; lack of courteous regard.

in-at-ten-tive (ĭn″ă-tĕn′tĭv), *adj.* paying no heed to; negligent; heedless; thoughtless.—*adv.* **in″at-ten′tive-ly**.—*n.* **in″at-ten′tive-ness**.

in-au-di-ble (ĭn-ô′dĭ-bl), *adj.* incapable of being heard; not actually heard.—*adv.* **in-au′di-bly**.

in-au-gu-ral (ĭn-ô′gū-răl), *adj.* pertaining to the ceremonies accompanying the dedication of a public building, the formal installation of a person in an office, etc.:—*n.* an address made on such an occasion.

in-au-gu-rate (ĭn-ô′gū-rāt), *v.t.* [*p.t.* and *p.p.* -rat″ed, *p.pr.* -rat″ing], **1**, to admit or introduce into office with appropriate ceremonies; invest with office in a formal manner; **2**, to make a formal beginning of; as, to *inaugurate* a custom; begin, as a new policy; **3**, to celebrate the first public use of by some opening ceremony; dedicate, as a public building.—*n.* **in-au″gu-ra′tion**.

in-aus-pi-cious (ĭn″ôs-pĭsh′ŭs), *adj.* unfortunate; unlucky; unfavorable; as, an *inauspicious* sign.—*adv.* **in″aus-pi′cious-ly**.—*n.* **in″aus-pi′cious-ness**.

in-born (ĭn′bôrn″), *adj.* implanted by nature; innate.
Syn. inbred, natural, inherent.

in-bound (ĭn′bound″), *adj.* inward bound, as baggage or a steamer.

in-bred (ĭn′brĕd″), *p. adj.* **1**, born with one; natural; innate; **2**, (ĭn-brĕd′), born of closely related parents.

in-breed (ĭn-brēd′), *v.t.* [*p.t.* and *p.p.* -bred′ (-brĕd′), *p.pr.* -breed′ing], **1**, to produce or develop within; **2**, to mate animals closely related.—*n.* **in′breed″ing**.

In-ca (ĭng′kȧ), *n.* **1**, the Peruvian emperor, or a member of the royal race in Peru before the Spanish conquest; **2**, one of the tribe of Indians in Peru at that time.

in-cal-cu-la-ble (ĭn-kăl′kū-lȧ-bl), *adj.* **1**, beyond reckoning; beyond estimate; very great; **2**, uncertain; undependable.—*adv.* **in-cal′cu-la-bly.**

in-ca-les-cent (ĭn″kȧ-lĕs′ĕnt), *adj.* increasing in heat.

in-can-des-cence (ĭn″kăn-dĕs′ĕns), *n.* the condition of emitting light as a result of intense heat, as does the filament in an incandescent electric lamp.—Also, **in″can-des′cen-cy.**

in-can-des-cent (ĭn″kăn-dĕs′ĕnt), *adj.* glowing with heat; white with intense heat; hence, brilliant; shining; clear: **incandescent lamp**, a form of lamp in which the light is produced by a filament which is rendered luminous by its resistance to an electric current.

in-can-ta-tion (ĭn″kăn-tā′shŭn), *n.* **1**, the use of magical words, said or sung; as, the medicine men tried to cure by *incantation;* **2**, the words so used.

in-ca-pa-ble (ĭn-kā′pȧ-bl), *adj.* **1**, not having power or fitness for some specified action; as, *incapable* of understanding; **2**, not able to admit; as, *incapable* of improvement; **3**, not sufficiently wicked; as, *incapable* of murder; **4**, deficient in ordinary ability.—*n.* **in-ca′pa-ble-ness.**—*adv.* **in-ca′pa-bly.**—*n.* **in-ca″pa-bil′i-ty.**

Syn. incompetent, inadequate. (See unable.)—*Ant.* able, sufficient, qualified.

in-ca-pac-i-tate (ĭn″kȧ-păs′ĭ-tāt), *v.t.* [*p.t.* and *p.p.* -tat″ed, *p.pr.* -tat″ing], to deprive of ability or natural power; render powerless or unfit; disable; as, old age *incapacitates* one for hard labor.—*n.* **in″ca-pac″i-ta′tion.**

in-ca-pac-i-ty (ĭn″kȧ-păs′ĭ-tĭ), *n.* [*pl.* incapacities (-tĭz)], lack of power, physical or mental; disability.

Syn. inability, incompetency.—*Ant.* capacity, qualification, ability.

in-car-cer-ate (ĭn-kär′sẽr-āt), *v.t.* [*p.t.* and *p.p.* -at″ed, *p.pr.* -at″ing], to imprison; confine:—*adj.* imprisoned.—*n.* **in-car″cer-a′tion.**

in-car-na-dine (ĭn-kär′nȧ-dĭn), *v.t.* [*p.t.* and *p.p.* -dined (-dĭnd), *p.pr.* -din-ing], to dye crimson, red, pink, or flesh color:—*adj.* flesh-colored; pink; pale red; also, crimson, or blood red.

in-car-nate (ĭn-kär′nāt), *v.t.* [*p.t.* and *p.p.* -nat-ed, *p.pr.* -nat-ing], **1**, to clothe with flesh; embody in flesh; **2**, to express in concrete form; as, to *incarnate* his longings in poetry:—*adj.* (ĭn-kär′nāt), embodied in human form; personified.

in-car-na-tion (ĭn″kär-nā′shŭn), *n.* **1**, the act of clothing with or of assuming flesh; embodiment in human form; **2**, an actual form representing a principle, ideal, etc.; **3**, in theology, the taking upon himself of human nature by the Son of God.

in-case (ĭn-kās′), *v.t.* [*p.t.* and *p.p.* -cased′ (-kāst′), *p.pr.* -cas′ing], to inclose in a box or solid covering; surround with anything. Also, **en-case′.**—*n.* **in-case′ment.**

in-cau-tious (ĭn-kô′shŭs), *adj.* heedless; careless; unwary.—*adv.* **in-cau′tious-ly.**—*n.* **in-cau′tious-ness.**

Syn. indiscreet, thoughtless, rash.—*Ant.* discreet, cautious, prudent.

in-cen-di-a-rism (ĭn-sĕn′dĭ-ȧ-rĭzm), *n.* the act of one who, for evil purposes, sets fire to property.

in-cen-di-a-ry (ĭn-sĕn′dĭ-ā-rĭ), *adj.* **1**, pertaining to the malicious setting on fire of property; **2**, tending to excite sedition or violence; as, an *incendiary* speech:—*n.* [*pl.* incendiaries (-rĭz)], **1**, one who maliciously sets fire to the property of another; **2**, one who excites quarrels.

[1]in-cense (ĭn-sĕns′), *v.t.* [*p.t.* and *p.p.* -censed′ (-sĕnst′), *p.pr.* -cens′ing], **1**, to enrage; **2**, to inflame, as passion.

Syn. vex, exasperate, madden.

[2]in-cense (ĭn′sĕns), *n.* **1**, any material which gives off perfume when burned; **2**, the smoke or odor of such spices or gums when burned, as in religious rites; **3**, any pleasant odor or perfume, as of flowers; **4**, hence, anything offered in the way of homage, as flattery, applause, etc.

in-cen-tive (ĭn-sĕn′tĭv), *adj.* arousing to action; encouraging:—*n.* that which arouses to action; motive; as, real interest in a subject is an *incentive* to study.

Syn., n. stimulus, spur. (See impulse.)

in-cep-tion (ĭn-sĕp′shŭn), *n.* beginning; first stage; as, the movement was successful from its *inception.*

in-cep-tive (ĭn-sĕp′tĭv), *adj.* beginning; relating to a beginning:—*n.* in grammar, a word which by its form indicates the beginning of an action, as, in Latin, the verb *crescere;* an inchoative.

in-cer-ti-tude (ĭn-sûr′tĭ-tūd), *n.* doubt; lack of decision.

in-ces-sant (ĭn-sĕs′ănt), *adj.* unceasing; continuous; as, the *incessant* dropping of water will wear away a stone.—*adv.* **in-ces′sant-ly.**

Syn. ceaseless, continual, uninterrupted.

in-cest (ĭn′sĕst), *n.* sexual relationship between persons related within the degrees wherein marriage is forbidden by law.—*adj.* **in-ces′tu-ous.**

inch (ĭnch), *n.* **1**, a twelfth part of a foot; **2**, a small quantity or degree:—*v.i.* to move slowly.—*abbr.* **in.**

in-cho-ate (ĭn′kō-āt), *adj.* just begun; incomplete; as, an *inchoate* mass of matter.—*adv.* **in′cho-ate-ly.**

in-cho-a-tive (ĭn-kō′ȧ-tĭv), *adj.* **1**, incomplete; **2**, expressing or pertaining to a beginning:—*n.* a word which by its form expresses the beginning of an action.

in-ci-dence (ĭn′sĭ-dĕns), *n.* a falling upon or against something: **angle of incidence**, the angle between the line of direction of a ray and the perpendicular to the surface on which it falls.

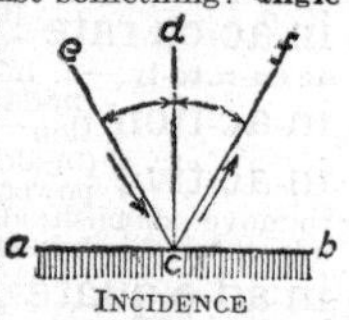

INCIDENCE
ecd, angle of incidence upon surface *ab;* *dcf*, angle of reflection.

in-ci-dent (ĭn′sĭ-dĕnt), *adj.* **1**, falling upon or against something; **2**, apt to occur; concerned: with *to;* as, the duties *incident* to his profession:—*n.* a chance happening; an episode; event.

in-ci-den-tal (ĭn″sĭ-dĕn′tăl), *adj.* casual; liable to happen unexpectedly; happening as a chance feature of something else; as, *incidental* expenses:—*n.* **1**, something casual or subordinate; **2**, in *pl.*, minor expenses.—*adv.* **in″ci-den′tal-ly.**

in-cin-er-ate (ĭn-sĭn′ẽr-āt), *v.t.* [*p.t.* and *p.p.* -at″ed, *p.pr.* -at″ing], to burn to ashes; consume by fire; as, to *incinerate* garbage.—*n.* **in-cin″er-a′tion.**

in-cin-er-a-tor (ĭn-sĭn′ẽr-ā″tẽr), *n.* a furnace or oven for burning substances to ashes, as garbage.

in-cip-i-ence (ĭn-sĭp′ĭ-ĕns), *n.* beginning. Also, **in-cip′i-en-cy.**

in-cip-i-ent (ĭn-sĭp′ĭ-ĕnt), *adj.* beginning; as, the *incipient* stage of a disease.—*adv.* **in-cip′i-ent-ly.**

in-cise (ĭn-sīz′), *v.t.* [*p.t.* and *p.p.* -cised′ (-sīzd′), *p.pr.* -cis′ing], to cut in; engrave; carve with a sharp instrument.

in-ci-sion (ĭn-sĭzh′ŭn), *n.* **1**, the act of cutting in or engraving; **2**, a cut made with a sharp instrument.

in-ci-sive (ĭn-sī′sĭv), *adj.* **1**, having the quality of cutting into; sharp; **2**, sarcastic; biting, as language.—*adv.* **in-ci′sive-ly.**—*n.* **in-ci′sive-ness.**

in-ci-sor (ĭn-sī′zẽr; ĭn-sī′sẽr), *n.* a cutting tooth; esp., a tooth in front of the canines.—*adj.* **in-ci′so-ry.**

in-ci-ta-tion (ĭn″sī-tā′shŭn), *n.* **1**, the act of urging; **2**, an incentive

in-cite (ĭn-sīt′), *v.t.* [*p.t.* and *p.p.* -cit′ed, *p.pr.* -cit′ing], to move to action; stir up; spur on; encourage.—*n.* **in-cit′er.**
Syn. instigate, excite, provoke, arouse, animate, stimulate, urge, impel.

in-cite-ment (ĭn-sīt′mĕnt), *n.* the act of inciting; a spurring on; also, that which goads or spurs on; incentive; impulse; encouragement; as, praise is often an *incitement* to further effort.
Syn. motive, stimulus, spur, inducement.

in-ci-vil-i-ty (ĭn″sĭ-vĭl′ĭ-tĭ), *n.* [*pl.* incivilities (-tĭz)], **1**, lack of courtesy; impoliteness; **2**, any uncivil act.
Syn. rudeness, discourtesy, disrespect.

in-clem-en-cy (ĭn-klĕm′ĕn-sĭ), *n.* [*pl.* inclemencies (-sĭz)], **1**, severity of weather; **2**, harshness of disposition.

in-clem-ent (ĭn-klĕm′ĕnt), *adj.* **1**, harsh; unmerciful; **2**, severe; stormy; as, *inclement* weather.

in-clin-a-ble (ĭn-klīn′ȧ-bl), *adj.* **1**, disposed favorably; as, *inclinable* to pity; **2**, having a tendency; **3**, capable of sloping.

in-cli-na-tion (ĭn″klĭ-nā′shŭn), *n.* **1**, a leaning; **2**, a turning aside from a given direction or position; **3**, a nod; as, a courteous *inclination* of the head; **4**, a tendency of the mind; disposition; bent; as, a natural *inclination* toward business; **5**, desire; preference; **6**, in geometry, the angle between two lines or planes.
Syn. bias, affection, attachment, wish, liking.—*Ant.* aversion, dislike, repulsion.

in-cline (ĭn-klīn′), *v.i.* [*p.t.* and *p.p.* -clined′ (-klīnd′), *p.pr.* -clin′ing], **1**, to turn from the given direction or position; lean; **2**, to bow; **3**, to have a mental bent or tendency; **4**, to have preference:—*v.t.* **1**, to cause to lean; direct; **2**, to bow; **3**, to give a tendency to; turn; dispose:—*n.* a slope; a sloping surface.
Syn., *v.* slant, tend, bend, bias.

in-clined (ĭn-klīnd′), *p.adj.* **1**, sloping; **2**, having a tendency; **3**, favorably disposed; **4**, in mathematics, forming any angle with some line or surface: **inclined plane**, one of the simple machines, or mechanical powers, consisting of a sloping surface forming any angle, except a right angle, with a horizontal plane (cf. *parbuckle*, illus.).

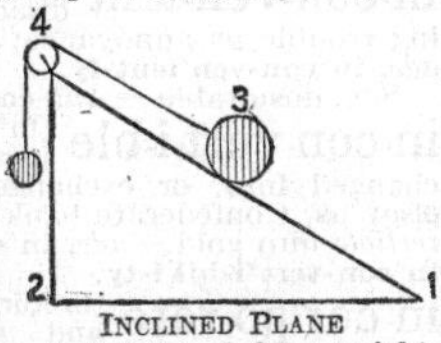

INCLINED PLANE
1–2, base; 3, large weight; 4, pulley or roller.

in-cli-nom-e-ter (ĭn″klĭ-nŏm′ē-tẽr), *n.* an instrument for measuring the inclination or slope of anything: used in surveying, on aircraft, etc.

in-close (ĭn-klōz′), *v.t.* [*p.t.* and *p.p.* -closed′ (-klōzd′), *p.pr.* -clos′ing], **1**, to shut in; surround; include within limits; **2**, to fold in with something, as a check in a letter. Also, **en-close′.**

in-clo-sure (ĭn-klō′zhŭr), *n.* **1** the act of shutting in, or state of being shut in; **2**, that which is surrounded; **3**, that which surrounds, as a fence; **4**, something included with a letter in an envelope, as a bill, check, etc. Also, **en-clo′sure.**

in-clude (ĭn-klōōd′), *v.t.* [*p.t.* and *p.p.* -clud′ed, *p.pr.* -clud′ing], **1**, to inclose; shut up within something; **2**, to contain as part of the whole.

in-clu-sion (ĭn-klōō′zhŭn), *n.* **1**, the act of inclosing or including; **2**, the state of being inclosed or contained.

in-clu-sive (ĭn-klōō′sĭv), *adj.* **1**, inclosing; containing; **2**, comprehensive; all-embracing; as, an *inclusive* survey; **3**, taking in extremes; as, from Monday to Saturday *inclusive:* that is, taking in both Monday and Saturday.—*adv.* **in-clu′sive-ly.**—*n.* **in-clu′sive-ness.**

in-cog-ni-to (ĭn-kŏg′nĭ-tō), *adv.* in disguise; under an assumed name; as, rulers often travel *incognito:*—*n.* [*pl.* incognitos (-tōz)], **1**, a great personage who travels under an assumed title; **2**, the assuming of a character to avoid recognition; disguise.—*n. fem.* **in-cog′ni-ta.**—*abbr.* **incog.**

in-co-her-ence (ĭn″kō-hēr′ĕns), *n.* **1**, looseness; **2**, want of connection in thought or language; inconsistency; as, the essay is marked by *incoherence* of thought; **3**, that which is marked by want of connection. Also, **in″co-her′en-cy.**

in-co-her-ent (ĭn″kō-hēr′ĕnt), *adj.* **1**, consisting of parts that do not cling together; as, particles of sand are *incoherent;* **2**, without logical connection; as, *incoherent* speech.—*adv.* **in″co-her′ent-ly.**

in-com-bus-ti-ble (ĭn″kŏm-bŭs′tĭ-bl), *adj.* incapable of being consumed by fire:—*n.* an unburnable substance.—*n.* **in″com-bus″ti-bil′i-ty.**

in-come (ĭn′kŭm), *n.* **1**, the amount, usually expressed in money, derived from labor, business, property, or capital; **2**, the yearly receipts of a person or business company: **income tax**, a tax levied upon yearly receipts or profits.

in-com-ing (ĭn′kŭm″ĭng), *adj.* **1**, coming in; as, the *incoming* mayor; **2**, accruing, as profits:—*n.* **1**, the act of coming in; **2**, that which comes in.—*n.* **in′com″er.**

in-com-men-su-ra-ble (ĭn″kŏ-mĕn′shōō-rȧ-bl), *adj.* **1**, having no common measure; **2**, in arithmetic, having no common divisor except one.—*n.* **in″com-men″su-ra-bil′i-ty.**

in-com-men-su-rate (ĭn″kŏ-mĕn′shōō-rāt), *adj.* **1**, having no common measure; **2**, not sufficient in measure; not great enough; as, his strength is *incommensurate* to the demands upon it.—*adv.* **in″com-men′su-rate-ly.**

in-com-mode (ĭn″kŏ-mōd′), *v.t.* [*p.t.* and *p.p.* -mod′ed, *p.pr.* -mod′ing] to inconvenience; trouble; disturb.
Syn. annoy, plague, molest, vex.

in-com-mo-di-ous (ĭn″kŏ-mō′dĭ-ŭs), *adj.* not giving comfort or advantage; inconvenient; as, *incommodious* apartments.—*n.* **in″com-mo′di-ous-ness.**—*adv.* **in″com-mo′di-ous-ly.**

in-com-mu-ni-ca-ble (ĭn″kŏ-mū′nĭ-kȧ-bl), *adj.* incapable of being shared or told; as, health and strength are *incommunicable* blessings.

in-com-mu-ni-ca-tive (ĭn″kŏ-mū′nĭ-kā-tĭv), *adj.* not given to speaking freely; reserved.

in-com-pa-ra-ble (ĭn-kŏm′pȧ-rȧ-bl), *adj.* **1**, not admitting of a statement of likenesses and differences; **2**, unequaled; peerless.—*adv.* **in-com'pa-ra-bly.**—*n.* **in-com'pa-ra-ble-ness.**

in-com-pat-i-bil-i-ty (ĭn″kŏm-păt″ĭ-bĭl′ĭ-tĭ), *n.* [*pl.* incompatibilities (-tĭz)], **1**, the state of being inharmonious or inconsistent; **2**, that which is incompatible.—*n.* **in″com-pat′i-ble-ness.**

in-com-pat-i-ble (ĭn″kŏm-păt′ĭ-bl), *adj.* incapable of being or acting together in harmony; as, health and filth are *incompatible:*—*n.*, in *pl.*, persons or things that do not agree.—*adv.* **in″com-pat′i-bly.**

in-com-pe-tence (ĭn-kŏm′pē-tĕns), *n.* inability, physical, mental, or moral; insufficiency. Also, **in-com′pe-ten-cy.**

Syn. incapacity, unfitness, inadequacy.

in-com-pe-tent (ĭn-kŏm′pē-tĕnt), *adj.* wanting ability; wanting fitness; inadmissible; as, a man who has any defect of body is considered *incompetent* to serve as a soldier:—*n.* one who is incapable of doing what is expected of him.

Syn., adj. incapable, unable, insufficient. —*Ant., adj.* sufficient, capable, qualified.

in-com-plete (ĭn″kŏm-plēt′), *adj.* **1**, not fully finished or developed; as, an *incomplete* story; **2**, not having all its parts; defective; imperfect; as, *incomplete* information.—*adv.* **in″com-plete′ly.**—*n.* **in″-com-plete′ness.**—*n.* **in″com-ple′tion.**

in-com-pre-hen-si-ble (ĭn-kŏm″prē-hĕn′sĭ-bl), *adj.* not to be understood or grasped by the mind; as, the vastness of the universe is *incomprehensible* to man; hence, infinite.—*adv.* **in-com″pre-hen′si-bly.**—*n.* **in-com″pre-hen″si-bil′i-ty.**

Syn. inconceivable, unintelligible, baffling.

in-com-press-i-ble (ĭn″kŏm-prĕs′ĭ-bl), *adj.* **1**, incapable of being reduced by pressure; **2**, resisting pressure.—*n.* **in″com-press″i-bil′i-ty.**

in-con-ceiv-a-ble (ĭn″kŏn-sēv′ȧ-bl), *adj.* incapable of being grasped by the mind or imagined; unbelievable.—*n.* **in″con-ceiv′a-ble-ness.**—*adv.* **in″con-ceiv′a-bly.**—*n.* **in″con-ceiv″a-bil′i-ty.**

in-con-clu-sive (ĭn″kŏn-klōō′sĭv), *adj.* **1**, leading to no definite result in evidence or argument; unconvincing, as an investigation; **2**, reaching no definite result in action; ineffective.—*adv.* **in″con-clu′sive-ly.**—*n.* **in″con-clu′sive-ness.**

in-con-gru-i-ty (ĭn″kŏn-grōō′ĭ-tĭ), *n.* [*pl.* incongruities (-tĭz)], want of fitness; unsuitableness of one thing to another; as, the *incongruity* of the fine building in the shabby little street.

in-con-gru-ous (ĭn-kŏng′grōō-ŭs), *adj.* disagreeing; unsuited to one another; inappropriate; as, laughter is *incongruous* at a funeral.—*adv.* **in-con′gru-ous-ly.**—*n.* **in-con′gru-ous-ness.**

Syn. conflicting, inconsistent.

in-con-se-quence (ĭn-kŏn′sē-kwĕns), *n.* **1**, the quality or state of being illogical; lack of proper sequence; irrelevancy; **2**, that which does not follow as a logical sequence.

in-con-se-quent (ĭn-kŏn′sē-kwĕnt), *adj.* **1**, not logically resulting from what has gone before; **2**, irrelevant; illogical; having nothing to do with the subject in hand; as, an *inconsequent* answer.

in-con-se-quen-tial (ĭn-kŏn″sē-kwĕn′shăl), *adj.* **1**, unrelated with the thing in hand; illogical; **2**, unimportant; of no consequence.

in-con-sid-er-a-ble (ĭn″kŏn-sĭd′ẽr-ȧ-bl), *adj.* not deserving consideration; trivial.—*adv.* **in″con-sid′er-a-bly.**—*n.* **in″con-sid′er-a-ble-ness.**

in-con-sid-er-ate (ĭn″kŏn-sĭd′ẽr-ȧt), *adj.* **1**, not properly considered; rash; **2**, not heeding the wishes, thoughts, or feelings of others; thoughtless.

Syn. negligent, heedless, careless.—*Ant.* considerate, thoughtful, careful.

in-con-sist-en-cy (ĭn″kŏn-sĭs′tĕn-sĭ), *n.* [*pl.* inconsistencies (-sĭz)], **1**, want of agreement, as between two stories of the same event; incongruity; **2**, the quality of being changeable; **3**, lack of harmony between practice and professed beliefs.

in-con-sist-ent (ĭn″kŏn-sĭs′tĕnt), *adj.* **1**, illogical; lacking agreement or uniformity; **2**, self-contradictory; as, the conduct of many Christians is *inconsistent* with their professed belief.—*adv.* **in″con-sist′ent-ly.**

Syn. incongruous, incompatible, conflicting.

in-con-sol-a-ble (ĭn″kŏn-sōl′ȧ-bl), *adj.* not to be comforted; disconsolate.—*adv.* **in″con-sol′a-bly.**

in-con-spic-u-ous (ĭn″kŏn-spĭk′ū-ŭs), *adj.* **1**, not easily perceived; so small as to escape notice; **2**, not attracting attention; as, *inconspicuous* dress shows good taste.—*adv.* **in″con-spic′u-ous-ly.**—*n.* **in″con-spic′u-ous-ness.**

in-con-stan-cy (ĭn-kŏn′stăn-sĭ), *n.* **1**, changeableness; fickleness; **2**, an instance of fickleness.

in-con-stant (ĭn-kŏn′stănt), *adj.* subject to change; unstable; variable; fickle.—*adv.* **in-con′stant-ly.**

Syn. changeable.—*Ant.* constant, faithful.

in-con-test-a-ble (ĭn″kŏn-tĕs′tȧ-bl), *adj.* not admitting of question or dispute.—*adv.* **in″con-test′a-bly.**

Syn. certain, unquestionable, undeniable. —*Ant.* doubtful, questionable.

in-con-ti-nence (ĭn-kŏn′tĭ-nĕns), *n.* lack of restraint, esp. in indulging the passions.

in-con-ti-nent (ĭn-kŏn′tĭ-nĕnt), *adj.* unrestrained; esp., not exercising control of the passions; impure:—*n.* an immoral person.—*adv.* **in-con′ti-nent-ly.**

in-con-tro-vert-i-ble (ĭn-kŏn″trō-vûr′tĭ-bl), *adj.* not open to debate; indisputable.—*adv.* **in-con″tro-vert′i-bly.**—*n.* **in-con″tro-vert″i-bil′i-ty.**

Syn. incontestable, certain, positive.

in-con-ven-ience (ĭn″kŏn-vēn′yĕns), *n.* **1**, troublesomeness; disadvantage; discomfort; **2**, that which causes trouble; a hindrance; annoyance or embarrassment:—*v.t.* [*p.t.* and *p.p.* -ienced (-yĕnst), *p.pr.* -ienc-ing], to put to trouble; annoy; molest.

in-con-ven-ient (ĭn″kŏn-vēn′yĕnt), *adj.* disadvantageous; giving trouble or annoyance; uncomfortable.—*adv.* **in″con-ven′ient-ly.**

Syn. unsuitable.—*Ant.* convenient, suitable.

in-con-vert-i-ble (ĭn″kŏn-vûr′tĭ-bl), *adj.* incapable of being changed into, or exchanged for, something else; as, Confederate bank notes were *inconvertible* into gold.—*adv.* **in″con-vert′i-bly.**—*n.* **in″con-vert″i-bil′i-ty.**

in-cor-po-rate (ĭn-kôr′pō-rāt), *v.t.* [*p.t.* and *p.p.* -rat″ed, *p.pr.* -rat″ing], **1**, to combine into one body; unite; specif., to form, as individuals, into a body with power to act legally or politically as one; as, to *incorporate* a manufacturing company; **2**, to embody; include; put in; as, to *incorporate* an idea in a written composition; **3**, to blend; mix, as one substance with another:—*v.i.* to unite with another body so as to form a part of it; be mingled or blended:—*adj.* (ĭn-kôr′pō-rȧt), **1**, closely united; united in one body; **2,** formed into, or united with others in, a corporation.

in-cor-po-ra-tion (ĭn-kôr″pō-rā′shŭn), *n.* **1,** the formation of a united body; combination or union; **2,** the formation of a corporation, or body of persons authorized by law to conduct a business under certain conditions; **3,** the body so formed: usually called *corporation.*

in-cor-po-ra-tor (ĭn-kôr′pō-rā″tẽr), *n.* **1,** one who embodies or unites; **2,** an original member or founder of a corporation, or the like.

in-cor-po-re-al (ĭn″kôr-pō′rē-ăl), *adj.* **1,** not made of matter; **2,** pertaining to spiritual beings or things.

in-cor-rect (ĭn″kŏ-rĕkt′), *adj.* **1,** not according to model or rule; faulty; **2,** not according to fact; inaccurate; **3,** not in accordance with morality or good manners; improper; as, *incorrect* behavior. —*adv.* **in″cor-rect′ly.**—*n.* **in″cor-rect′ness.**

in-cor-ri-gi-ble (ĭn-kŏr′ĭ-jĭ-bl), *adj.* bad beyond correction or reform; as, an *incorrigible* drinker or gambler:—*n.* one who is bad beyond correction. —*n.* **in-cor′ri-gi-ble-ness.**—*adv.* **in-cor′ri-gi-bly.**—*n.* **in-cor″ri-gi-bil′i-ty.**

in-cor-rupt (ĭn″kŏ-rŭpt′), *adj.* **1,** free from physical or moral spot; **2,** untainted; pure; honest.—*n.* **in″cor-rup′tion.**

in-cor-rupt-i-ble (ĭn″kŏ-rŭp′tĭ-bl), *adj.* **1,** incapable of physical corruption, or decay; **2,** not liable to moral contamination; esp., incapable of being bribed.—*adv.* **in″cor-rupt′i-bly.**—*n.* **in″cor-rupt′i-ble-ness.**—*n.* **in″cor-rupt″i-bil′i-ty.**

in-crease (ĭn-krēs′), *v.i.* [*p.t.* and *p.p.* -creased′ (-krēst′), *p.pr.* -creas′-ing], to become greater in any respect; multiply; grow:—*v.t.* to make greater in any respect; enlarge:—*n.* (ĭn′krēs), **1,** a growing larger; **2,** that which is added to the original stock, as profits or offspring.—*n.* **in-creas′er.** —*adv.* **in-creas′ing-ly.**

Syn., v. enlarge, extend. *Increase,* the general term, is applied to making bigger in number, quantity, or size, esp. by natural processes; as, nourishing food *increases* one's weight. To *enlarge* is to make the dimensions of width, length, or height greater; as, to *enlarge* a house. To *extend* is to make greater by stretching out to greater length, or into a greater space; as, to *extend* a boundary.—*Ant., v.* decrease, diminish, lessen.

in-cred-i-ble (ĭn-krĕd′ĭ-bl), *adj.* surpassing belief; hard to believe; unimaginable; unlikely.—*adv.* **in-cred′i-bly.**—*n.* **in-cred″i-bil′i-ty.**

in-cre-du-li-ty (ĭn″krē-dū′lĭ-tĭ), *n.* refusal or inability to believe; skepticism; lack of faith, as in a report.

Syn. unbelief, doubt, disbelief.

in-cred-u-lous (ĭn-krĕd′ū-lŭs), *adj.* **1,** indicating lack of belief; as, an *incredulous* expression; **2,** unbelieving; skeptical.—*adv.* **in-cred′u-lous-ly.**

in-cre-ment (ĭn′krē-mĕnt), *n.* **1,** increase; enlargement; **2,** that which is added; esp., a small addition.

in-cres-cent (ĭn-krĕs′ĕnt), *p.adj.* increasing; as, the *increscent* moon.

in-crim-i-nate (ĭn-krĭm′ĭ-nāt), *v.t.* [*p.t.* and *p.p.* -nat″ed, *p.pr.* -nat″ing], to accuse; implicate; charge with, or involve in, a crime.—*n.* **in-crim″i-na′tion.**

in-crust (ĭn-krŭst′), *v.t.* **1,** to cover with, or as with, a crust; coat; **2,** to overlay with a decorative covering, as with mosaics; inlay with mosaics. Also, **en-crust′.**

in-crus-ta-tion (ĭn″krŭs-tā′shŭn), *n.* **1,** the act of covering with a crust; **2,** a covering; **3,** an incrusted or inlaid object or substance; also, a covering or inlay, as of mosaic, attached to masonry.

in-cu-bate (ĭn′kū-bāt), *v.t.* [*p.t.* and *p.p.* -bat″ed, *p.pr.* -bat″ing], **1,** to sit upon in order to hatch (eggs); **2,** to keep, as bacteria, embryos, etc., under conditions favorable for development:—*v.i.* to sit on eggs; brood.—*n.* **in″cu-ba′tion.**

in-cu-ba-tor (ĭn′kū-bā″tẽr), *n.* **1,** an apparatus for hatching eggs; **2,** an apparatus for rearing prematurely born babies; **3,** an apparatus for maintaining cultures, as of bacteria, at the proper temperature.

in-cu-bus (ĭn′kū-bŭs), *n.* [*pl.* incubuses (-ĕz); incubi (-bī)], **1,** a nightmare; **2,** in the Middle Ages, a demon believed to lie heavily on persons in their sleep; **3,** any depressing weight or burden.

in-cul-cate (ĭn-kŭl′kāt; ĭn′kŭl-kāt), *v.t.* [*p.t.* and *p.p.* -cat-ed, *p.pr.* -cat-ing], to impress upon the mind by frequent warning or direction; as, to *inculcate* honesty.—*n.* **in″cul-ca′tion.**—*n.* **in-cul′ca-tor.**

in-cul-pate (ĭn-kŭl′pāt; ĭn′kŭl-pāt), *v.t.* [*p.t.* and *p.p.* -pat″ed, *p.pr.* -pat″ing], to accuse of wrongdoing; blame.—*n.* **in″cul-pa′tion.**—*adj.* **in-cul′pa-to-ry.**

in-cum-ben-cy (ĭn-kŭm′bĕn-sĭ), *n.* [*pl.* incumbencies (-sĭz)], **1,** the act or state of holding an office; **2,** full possession and exercise of any office; as, during the *incumbency* of the governor.

in-cum-bent (ĭn-kŭm′bĕnt), *adj.* **1,** exerting pressure; impending; **2,** imposed as a duty; obligatory; demanded; as, it is *incumbent* upon every good citizen to vote:—*n.* **1,** the holder of an office; **2,** a clergyman in possession of a parish.

in-cum-ber (ĭn-kŭm′bẽr), *v.t.* **1,** to impede; obstruct; **2,** to load with debt. See **en-cum′ber,** *Pfd. S.*

in-cum-brance (ĭn-kŭm′brăns), *n.* that which burdens or impedes. See **en-cum′brance,** *Pfd. S.*

in-cur (ĭn-kûr′), *v.t.* [*p.t.* and *p.p.* -curred′ (-kûrd′), *p.pr.* -cur′ring], **1,** to bring upon oneself, esp. by one's own action; as, to *incur* dislike; **2,** to contract, as a debt.

in-cur-a-ble (ĭn-kūr′ȧ-bl), *adj.* incapable of being healed; beyond the power of skill or medicine:—*n.* a person diseased beyond remedy.—*n.* **in-cur′a-ble-ness.** —*adv.* **in-cur′a-bly.**—*n.* **in-cur″a-bil′i-ty.**

in-cur-sion (ĭn-kûr′shŭn), *n.* an inroad; raid; invasion; as, an *incursion* into enemy territory.—*adj.* **in-cur′sive.**

in-cus (ĭng′kŭs), *n.* [*pl.* incudes (ĭn-kū′dēz)], a small, anvil-shaped bone, one of three in the middle ear.

Ind (ĭnd), *n. Poetic* and *Archaic,* India; as, the wealth of *Ind.*

in-debt-ed (ĭn-dĕt′ĕd), *adj.* **1,** owing money; **2,** being under obligation; owing gratitude.—*n.* **in-debt′ed-ness.**

in-de-cen-cy (ĭn-dē′sĕn-sĭ), *n.* [*pl.* indecencies (-sĭz)], **1,** want of delicacy, refinement, or good manners; **2,** that which is obscene or impure; **3,** a word or act offensive to modesty.

in-de-cent (ĭn-dē′sĕnt), *adj.* **1,** improper in language, behavior, etc.; immodest; indelicate; **2,** unfit to be heard or looked upon.—*adv.* **in-de′cent-ly.**

in-de-ci-sion (ĭn″dē-sĭzh′ŭn), *n.* mental wavering; hesitation.

in-de-ci-sive (ĭn″dē-sī′sĭv), *adj.* **1,** not bringing to a sure end; inconclusive; **2,** not positive; vacillating, as a person.—*adv.* **in″de-ci′sive-ly.**

in-de-clin-a-ble (ĭn″dē-klīn′ȧ-bl), *adj.* incapable of being varied by inflection; as, an *indeclinable* noun: —*n.* a word that cannot be inflected.

in-de-co-rous (ĭn″dē-kō′rŭs; ĭn-dĕk′ō-rŭs), *adj.* unsuitable or improper; against the accepted rule of good breeding or good manners.—*adv.* **in″de-co′rous-ly.**—*n.* **in″de-co′rous-ness.**

in-de-co-rum (ĭn″dē-kō′rŭm), *n.* violation of propriety or rules of conduct; a breach of etiquette or civility.

in-deed (ĭn-dēd′), *adv.* in fact; in truth; as, I was *indeed* surprised.

in-de-fat-i-ga-ble (ĭn″dē-făt′ĭ-gȧ-bl), *adj.* incapable of being wearied; untiring; unceasing in labor or effort, unflagging.—*adv.* **in″de-fat′i-ga-bly.**—*n.* **in″de-fat″i-ga-bil′i-ty.**

in-de-fea-si-ble (ĭn″dē-fē′zĭ-bl), *adj.* not to be annulled or made void, as a title, right, or claim.—*adv.* **in″de-fea′si-bly.**—*n.* **in″de-fea″si-bil′i-ty.**

in-de-fen-si-ble (ĭn″dē-fĕn′sĭ-bl), *adj.* incapable of being maintained or justified; as, an *indefensible* argument.—*n.* **in″de-fen′si-ble-ness.**—*adv.* **in″de-fen′si-bly.**—*n.* **in″de-fen″si-bil′i-ty.**

in-de-fin-a-ble (ĭn″dē-fīn′ȧ-bl), *adj.* incapable of being described exactly or explained clearly; as, an *indefinable* charm.—*n.* **in″de-fin′a-ble-ness.**—*adv.* **in″de-fin′a-bly.**

in-def-i-nite (ĭn-dĕf′ĭ-nĭt), *adj.* **1**, not exact; vague; uncertain; **2**, having no fixed limit, amount, or number; **3**, too large for measurement; **4**, in botany, too numerous or variable to be easily counted, as the stamens of certain flowers: **indefinite pronoun**, a pronoun not referring to a definite person or thing, as *some, any, each, another.*—*adv.* **in-def′i-nite-ly.**—*n.* **in-def′i-nite-ness.**
Syn. unsettled, unlimited; loose, lax.

in-del-i-ble (ĭn-dĕl′ĭ-bl), *adj.* not to be blotted out or forgotten; as, *indelible* ink; an *indelible* impression.—*adv.* **in-del′i-bly.**—*n.* **in-del″i-bil′i-ty.**

in-del-i-ca-cy (ĭn-dĕl′ĭ-kȧ-sĭ), *n.* [*pl.* indelicacies (-sĭz)], **1**, want of refinement; **2**, that which is offensive to modesty or refined taste.

in-del-i-cate (ĭn-dĕl′ĭ-kȧt), *adj.* lacking in refinement; offensive to modesty; coarse.—*adv.* **in-del′i-cate-ly.**

in-dem-ni-fi-ca-tion (ĭn-dĕm″nĭ-fĭ-kā′shŭn), *n.* **1**, the act of securing against loss or damage; **2**, repayment for loss, damage, or injury.
Syn. compensation, amends, redress.

in-dem-ni-fy (ĭn-dĕm′nĭ-fī), *v.t.* [*p.t.* and *p.p.* -fied (-fīd), *p.pr.* -fy″-ing], **1**, to protect or insure against loss or damage; **2**, to repay or compensate (a person) for loss or damage; also, to make good (a loss).

in-dem-ni-ty (ĭn-dĕm′nĭ-tĭ), *n.* [*pl.* indemnities (-tĭz)], **1**, security against loss, damage, or punishment; **2**, repayment for loss or injury.

1**in-dent** (ĭn-dĕnt′), *v.t.* **1**, to give a zigzag outline to; notch; **2**, to make formal agreement to, as in a bond, deed, articles of apprenticeship, or the like; **3**, in writing or printing, to begin (a line) with a blank space:—*n.* **1**, a notch in the border; **2**, a formal written agreement; **3**, a space at the beginning of a line in writing or printing.

2**in-dent** (ĭn-dĕnt′), *v.t.* to make a depression in; dent; stamp; press in.

in-den-ta-tion (ĭn″dĕn-tā′shŭn), *n.* **1**, a small hollow or depression, as from a blow; **2**, in writing or printing, a space left in a margin.

in-dent-ed (ĭn-dĕnt′ĕd), *p.adj.* **1**, notched on the edge or border like a row of teeth; zigzag; **2**, in writing or printing, having a space left in the margin; **3**, held by an agreement, as an apprentice.

in-den-tion (ĭn-dĕn′shŭn), *n.* **1**, in writing or printing, the act of leaving a space at the beginning of a line, or the space so left; **2**, a dent; an indenting.

in-den-ture (ĭn-dĕn′tûr), *n.* **1**, in writing or printing, a space left at the beginning of a line; **2**, a written agreement, formerly in duplicate, with the edges notched so as to correspond, esp. one binding an apprentice to service:—*v.t.* [*p.t.* and *p.p.* -tured (-tûrd), *p.pr.* -tur-ing], to bind by a written agreement, as an apprentice.

in-de-pend-ence (ĭn″dē-pĕn′dĕns), *n.* **1**, freedom from support or government by others; **2**, a sum of money sufficient for one's needs: **Independence Day**, July 4, the day on which, in 1776, the American Declaration of Independence was signed: observed in the U. S. as a holiday. Also, **in″de-pend′en-cy.**
Syn. exemption, immunity. (See liberty.)

in-de-pend-ent (ĭn″dē-pĕn′dĕnt), *adj.* **1**, not relying on, supported by, or governed by, another; **2**, having enough to live on; **3**, not easily influenced; unbiased; **4**, disinclined, through pride, to accept assistance:—*n.* one who in politics, art, literature, etc., acts or thinks for himself.—*adv.* **in″de-pend′ent-ly.**

in-de-scrib-a-ble (ĭn″dē-skrīb′ȧ-bl), *adj.* incapable of being portrayed in words; indefinite; vague; too wonderful or too bad to be described.

in-de-struct-i-ble (ĭn″dē-strŭk′tĭ-bl), *adj.* **1**, not capable of being broken up, ruined, destroyed, or demolished; **2**, durable; lasting.—*adv.* **in″de-struct′i-bly.**—*n.* **in″de-struct″i-bil′i-ty.**

in-de-ter-mi-na-ble (ĭn″dē-tûr′mĭ-nȧ-bl), *adj.* not to be known or exactly defined; without limit.

in-de-ter-mi-nate (ĭn″dē-tûr′mĭ-nāt), *adj.* **1**, not settled, or fixed; indefinite; vague; as, an *indeterminate* sentence for crime; **2**, in mathematics, having an indefinite number of values or solutions, as an equation.—*adv.* **in″de-ter′mi-nate-ly.**—*n.* **in″de-ter′mi-nate-ness.**

in-de-ter-mi-na-tion (ĭn″dē-tûr″mĭ-nā′shŭn), *n.* an unsettled, indecisive state of mind.

in-dex (ĭn′dĕks), *n.* [*pl.* indexes (-dĕk-sĕz; -sĭz); indices (-dĭ-sēz)], **1**, that which points out or indicates; **2**, the forefinger; **3**, a pointer, as the hand on a dial; **4**, a table of the contents of a book; **5**, in mathematics, a figure or letter placed above and to the right of another; as, 3 is the *index* in a^3; **6**, in printing, a fist [☞]: **Index**, a list of books which the Roman Catholic Church forbids its members to read: **index finger**, the forefinger: so called because used in pointing:—*v.t.* **1**, to provide with an alphabetical table of references; **2**, to indicate.

In-di-a (ĭn′dĭ-ȧ), *n.* a country occupying the central peninsula of southern Asia: **India ink**, a black pigment, from the Far East: properly sepia, now made of lampblack, gum, etc.: used for fine drawing, painting, etc.: **India paper**, **1**, a thin, absorbent paper used in making fine engravings; **2**, a strong, thin, opaque paper, used for printing books in which it is desired to avoid bulkiness.

In-di-a-man (ĭn′dĭ-ȧ-măn), *n.* [*pl.* Indiamen (-mĕn)], a large sailing vessel formerly employed in the India trade.

In-di-an (ĭn′dĭ-ăn), *adj.* **1**, pertaining to India, the East Indies, or the British Indian Empire, also to the West Indies or the American Indians; **2**, made of maize, or Indian corn; **3**, of a material, pattern, etc., made in India or by the American Indians:—*n.* **1**, an East Indian, West Indian, or, sometimes, a European who formerly lived in India; **2**, one of the first inhabitants of America, or a Red Indian.

In-di-an club a bottle-shaped club, swung by the hands in gymnastic exercises.

INDIAN CLUB

In-di-an corn an American cereal plant growing large yellow grains in ears; maize.

In-di-an file single file: the usual method of traveling among Indians or on a narrow trail.

In-di-an pipe a low, waxy white, sometimes reddish, fleshy herb, three to ten inches high, resembling a long-stemmed clay pipe: found in dense woods, often growing on decaying vegetation.

In-di-an sum-mer a period of mild, pleasant, usually hazy, weather occurring in the late fall in North America.

In-di-a rub-ber a gummy, elastic substance from the milky juice of certain tropical plants; caoutchouc; also, a piece of this substance, or some article made from it. Also, *n.* **in″di-a-rub′ber.**—*adj.* **In″di-a-rub′ber; in″di-a-rub′ber.**

in-di-cant (ĭn′dĭ-kănt), *adj.* serving to point out:—*n.* that which points out or indicates.

in-di-cate (ĭn′dĭ-kāt), *v.t.* [*p.t.* and *p.p.* -cat″ed, *p.pr.* -cat″ing], to point out; show; mark; suggest; hint; make known; as, signposts *indicate* which way to go.
Syn. betoken, signify, denote.

in-di-ca-tion (ĭn″dĭ-kā′shŭn), *n.* **1**, the act of showing or pointing out; **2**, that which points out; a token; evidence; sign; symptom; as, the expression of the face is often an *indication* of character.

in-dic-a-tive (ĭn-dĭk′ȧ-tĭv), *adj.* **1**, pointing out; as, cold hands are *indicative* of poor circulation of the blood; **2**, in grammar, designating, or pertaining to, that mood of the verb used to make an assertion or statement, or to ask a question:—*n.* the indicative mood.—*adv.* **in-dic′a-tive-ly.**

in-di-ca-tor (ĭn′dĭ-kā″tẽr), *n.* **1**, one who or that which points out; **2**, a device by which an effect is pointed out; as, the hands of a watch are *indicators* of the time; **3**, in chemistry, a substance, as litmus, used to show the condition of a solution.

in-di-ca-to-ry (ĭn′dĭ-kȧ-tō-rĭ), *adj.* serving to point out; as, the symptoms are *indicatory* of scarlet fever.

in-di-ces (ĭn′dĭ-sēz), *n.* Latin plural of *index.*

in-dict (ĭn-dīt′), *v.t.* to charge with a crime in due form of law; as, he was *indicted* for theft.—*n.* **in-dict′er; in-dict′or.**

in-dict-a-ble (ĭn-dīt′ȧ-bl), *adj.* **1**, liable to be indicted, or charged with a crime in due form of law; **2**, giving cause for indictment; as, an *indictable* offense.

in-dict-ment (ĭn-dīt′mĕnt), *n.* **1**, a written accusation against a prisoner presented by a grand jury to a court; **2**, the action of the grand jury in returning the case for trial; **3**, the legal document containing the accusation: also called *bill of indictment.*

In-dies (ĭn′dĭz), *n.pl.* India and the islands beyond; the East Indies; also, formerly, the West Indies.

in-dif-fer-ence (ĭn-dĭf′ẽr-ĕns), *n.* **1**, the state of being unconcerned; want of zeal or interest; **2**, unimportance; insignificance.
Syn. apathy, carelessness, listlessness, insensibility, unconcern, coldness.

in-dif-fer-ent (ĭn-dĭf′ẽr-ĕnt), *adj.* **1**, unconcerned; as, she was *indifferent* to her fate; **2**, unimportant; as, an *indifferent* matter; **3**, mediocre; as, *indifferent* work; **4**, impartial; as, *indifferent* to heat or cold.—*adv.* **in-dif′fer-ent-ly.**

in-di-gence (ĭn′dĭ-jĕns), *n.* the state of being destitute or very poor; poverty; want; as, *indigence* causes much suffering in the city slums. Also, **in′di-gen-cy.**
Syn. necessity, penury, destitution, privation, lack, deficiency. (See poverty.)

in-dig-e-nous (ĭn-dĭj′ē-nŭs), *adj.* born or produced in a country; not imported; native; as, cotton is *indigenous* to America.—*adv.* **in-dig′e-nous-ly.**—*n.* **in-dig′e-nous-ness.**
Syn. inborn, inherent, innate. (See native.)

in-di-gent (ĭn′dĭ-jĕnt), *adj.* destitute; needy; as, an *indigent* widow.

in-di-gest-i-ble (ĭn″dĭ-jĕs′tĭ-bl), *adj.* not easily assimilated or taken in, physically or mentally.—*adv.* **in″di-gest′i-bly.**—*n.* **in″di-gest″i-bil′i-ty.**

in-di-ges-tion (ĭn″dĭ-jĕs′chŭn), *n.* difficulty in converting, or inability to convert, food into such a form as can be assimilated by the system; dyspepsia.

in-dig-nant (ĭn-dĭg′nănt), *adj.* affected with anger or wrath because of unfair treatment; inflamed with mingled anger and scorn.—*adv.* **in-dig′nant-ly.**

in-dig-na-tion (ĭn″dĭg-nā′shŭn), *n.* anger at what is unworthy, unjust, dishonorable, or base; anger mingled with contempt or disgust.
Syn. wrath, ire, resentment, fury, rage.

in-dig-ni-ty (ĭn-dĭg′nĭ-tĭ), *n.* [*pl.* indignities (-tĭz)], an action intended to lower the self-respect of another; an insult.
Syn. affront, outrage, discourtesy, rudeness.
—*Ant.* honor, compliment, politeness.

in-di-go (ĭn′dĭ-gō), *n.* [*pl.* indigos; indigoes (-gōz)], **1**, a blue dye obtained from a substance found in the sap of various shrubs: now made synthetically; **2**, a deep violet blue, one of the primary colors.

in-di-rect (ĭn″dĭ-rĕkt′), *adj.* **1**, not straight or in a line; as, an *indirect* road; **2**, resulting, in a roundabout manner, from a cause; not reaching the end aimed at by the most straightforward method; **3**, not straightforward or fair.—*adv.* **in″di-rect′ly.**

in-di-rec-tion (ĭn″dĭ-rĕk′shŭn), *n.* roundabout means or methods.

in-dis-cern-i-ble (ĭn″dĭ-zûr′nĭ-bl), *adj.* incapable of being seen or perceived; not to be discovered.

in-dis-creet (ĭn″dĭs-krēt′), *adj.* imprudent; unwise; rash.—*adv.* **in″dis-creet′ly.**—*n.* **in″dis-creet′ness.**

in-dis-cre-tion (ĭn″dĭs-krĕsh′ŭn), *n.* **1**, rashness; imprudence; an unwise act; **2**, a blunder.

in-dis-crim-i-nate (ĭn″dĭs-krĭm′ĭ-nāt), *adj.* **1**, not choosing carefully; undistinguishing; **2**, confused; promiscuous; as, *indiscriminate* reading is unwise.—*adv.* **in″dis-crim′i-nate-ly.**—*n.* **in″dis-crim′i-nate-ness.**—*n.* **in″dis-crim″i-na′tion.**—*adj.* **in″dis-crim′i-na-tive.**

in-dis-pen-sa-ble (ĭn″dĭs-pĕn′sȧ-bl), *adj.* not to be done without; absolutely necessary.—*adv.* **in″dis-pen′sa-bly.**—*n.* **in″dis-pen″sa-bil′i-ty.**
Syn. essential, requisite.

in-dis-pose (ĭn″dĭs-pōz′), *v.t.* [*p.t.* and *p.p.* -posed′ (-pōzd′), *p.pr.* -pos′ing], **1**, to render unfit; disqualify; **2**, to make ill or not well; **3**, to make averse or unfavorable; disincline.—*p.adj.* **in″dis-posed′.**

in-dis-po-si-tion (ĭn-dĭs″pō-zĭsh′ŭn), *n.* **1**, slight illness; **2**, disinclination; unwillingness.
Syn. sickness, ailment, disease.

in-dis-pu-ta-ble (ĭn-dĭs′pū-tȧ-bl), *adj.* too evident to admit of debate or question; beyond question.—*adv.* **in-dis′pu-ta-bly.**—*n.* **in-dis″pu-ta-bil′i-ty.**
Syn. undeniable, certain, positive, sure.

in-dis-so-lu-ble (ĭn-dĭs′ō-lū-bl; ĭn″dĭ-sŏl′ū-bl), *adj.* **1,** not capable of being dissolved or broken up; indestructible; **2,** forever binding; as, an *indissoluble* agreement.—*adv.* **in-dis′so-lu-bly.**—*n.* **in-dis′so-lu-ble-ness.**—*n.* **in-dis″so-lu-bil′i-ty.**

in-dis-tinct (ĭn″dĭs-tĭngkt′), *adj.* **1,** not easily distinguishable by the senses or the mind; **2,** faint; undefined; indefinite; confused.—*adv.* **in″dis-tinct′ly.**

in-dis-tin-guish-a-ble (ĭn″dĭs-tĭng′gwĭsh-ȧ-bl), *adj.* **1,** incapable of being made out or discerned as separate and distinct; as, the twins are almost *indistinguishable;* **2,** imperceptible.—*adv.* **in″dis-tin′guish-a-bly.**

in-dite (ĭn-dīt′), *v.t.* [*p.t.* and *p.p.* -dit′ed, *p.pr.* -dit′ing], **1,** to compose; write; as, to *indite* a letter or an epistle; **2,** to express in formal style.—*n.* **in-dit′er.**

in-di-vid-u-al (ĭn″dĭ-vĭd′ū-ăl), *adj.* **1,** existing as a single and distinct thing or personality; **2,** pertaining to, or characteristic of, a single person or thing; **3,** of a peculiar or striking character; as, an *individual* style of speaking:—*n.* **1,** a single or separate person, animal, or thing; **2,** anything that cannot be divided without losing its identity.—*adv.* **in″di-vid′u-al-ly.**

in-di-vid-u-al-ism (ĭn″dĭ-vĭd′ū-ăl-ĭzm), *n.* **1,** egoism; the conduct of the individual in pursuing his own personal ends; **2,** selfishness; **3,** a social theory that favors the rights of the individual; **4,** a personal peculiarity.

in-di-vid-u-al-ist (ĭn″dĭ-vĭd′ū-ăl-ĭst), *n.* **1,** one who thinks or acts independently; **2,** one who believes in individualism.—*adj.* **in″di-vid″u-al-is′tic.**

in-di-vid-u-al-i-ty (ĭn″dĭ-vĭd″ū-ăl′ĭ-tĭ), *n.* [*pl.* individualities (-tĭz)], **1,** the condition of being separate and distinct; separate or distinct existence; **2,** the sum of the characteristics that distinguish a person or thing; **3,** an individual thing or person.

in-di-vid-u-al-ize (ĭn″dĭ-vĭd′ū-ăl-īz), *v.t.* [*p.t.* and *p.p.* -ized (-īzd), *p.pr.* -iz″ing], **1,** to make distinct in character; as, George Eliot strikingly *individualizes* the characters in her novels; **2,** to note particularly; select.

in-di-vis-i-ble (ĭn″dĭ-vĭz′ĭ-bl), *adj.* **1,** not separable into parts; **2,** not to be divided exactly, or without a remainder; as, 10 is *indivisible* by 4.—*adv.* **in″di-vis′i-bly.**—*n.* **in″di-vis″i-bil′i-ty.**

in-doc-tri-nate (ĭn-dŏk′trĭ-nāt), *v.t.* [*p.t.* and *p.p.* -nat″ed, *p.pr.* -nat″ing], to instruct in learning or doctrines.

In-do–Eu-ro-pe-an (ĭn″dō=ū″rō-pē′ăn), *adj.* designating, or pertaining to, a family of languages of India, western Asia, and Europe, and including Sanskrit, Persian, Greek, Latin, Italian, English, German, etc.: also called *Aryan* and *Indo-Germanic:*—*n.* a member of a race speaking one of these languages; loosely, an Aryan.

In-do–Ger-man-ic (ĭn″dō=jẽr-măn′ĭk), *adj.* pertaining to the linguistic family also known as *Aryan* or *Indo-European:*—*n.* a Caucasian who speaks one of the Aryan tongues, an Indo-European.

in-do-lence (ĭn′dō-lĕns), *n.* love of ease; objection to labor; laziness.

in-do-lent (ĭn′dō-lĕnt), *adj.* **1,** indulging in ease; lazy; **2,** causing little pain; as, an *indolent* ulcer.—*adv.* **in′do-lent-ly.**
Syn. slothful, sluggish. (See idle.)

in-dom-i-ta-ble (ĭn-dŏm′ĭ-tȧ-bl), *adj.* untamable; irrepressible; not to be conquered; as, he has an *indomitable* will.—*adv.* **in-dom′i-ta-bly.**

in-door (ĭn′dōr″), *adj.* **1,** of or pertaining to the interior of a building; **2,** living, belonging, or done, within doors.

in-doors (ĭn″dōrz′; ĭn′dōrz″), *adv.* inside or into the house.

in-dorse (ĭn-dôrs′), *v.t.* [*p.t.* and *p.p.* -dorsed′ (-dôrst′), *p.pr.* -dors′ing], **1,** to write (the name) on the back of, as a check, note, etc.; **2,** to approve, as a movement. Also, **en-dorse′.**—*adj.* **in-dors′a-ble.**

in-dor-see (ĭn″dôr-sē′), *n.* a person to whom a check, note, etc., is assigned, or made payable. Also, **en″dor-see′.**

in-dorse-ment (ĭn-dôrs′mĕnt), *n.* **1,** the act of writing on the back of a check, note, etc.; **2,** that which is so written; **3,** approval. Also, **en-dorse′ment.**

in-dors-er (ĭn-dôr′sẽr), *n.* one who indorses, or writes his name on the back of a check, note, etc.; a guarantor. Also, **en-dors′er; in-dor′sor.**

in-du-bi-ta-ble (ĭn-dū′bĭ-tȧ-bl), *adj.* too evident to be doubted; unquestionable.—*adv.* **in-du′bi-ta-bly.**
Syn. indisputable, certain, sure.

in-duce (ĭn-dūs′), *v.t.* [*p.t.* and *p.p.* -duced′ (-dūst′), *p.pr.* -duc′ing], **1,** to lead on; influence; prevail upon; as, no one can *induce* him to change his mind; **2,** to bring on; effect; cause; as, illness *induced* by exposure; **3,** in physics, to produce without contact, as an electric or magnetic effect; **4,** to arrive at (a conclusion) by reasoning from particular cases to general principles.—*adj.* **in-duc′i-ble.**
Syn. incite, impel, urge, move, persuade.

in-duce-ment (ĭn-dūs′mĕnt), *n.* that which causes action or influences conduct; motive; incentive.

in-duct (ĭn-dŭkt′), *v.t.* to introduce; place in an office; install.

in-duc-tance (ĭn-dŭk′tăns), *n.* **1,** the property of an electrical conductor or circuit by virtue of which an electromotive force is produced in it by the variation of an electric current; **2,** an electrical conductor, as wire, having this property.

in-duc-tion (ĭn-dŭk′shŭn), *n.* **1,** the introduction of a person into an office; **2,** in electricity: **a,** the production of an electric or magnetic effect by one body upon another without contact; **b,** an electric or magnetic condition produced in a body when placed in an electric or magnetic field; **3,** the process of reasoning from a part to a whole, or of arriving at a general conclusion from particular cases; also, the result so reached: **induction coil,** an electrical apparatus used for the production of induced currents of high potential.
Syn. deduction. *Induction* is the method of reasoning from a number of similar particular cases to the general principle relating them; *deduction*, from the general principle to the particular case. *Induction* is the method used in learning by experience: a child lifts a piece of iron, and finds it heavy; he lifts another, and another, and finds each heavy, and by *induction* reaches the conclusion that, in general, iron is heavy. The so-called laws of nature have all been formulated after a process of *induction.* Thus, Galileo dropped many bodies of different weights from the tower of Pisa, and observed that all fell with nearly the same speed, and by *induction* formulated the law that the weight of a body does not affect the speed with which it falls. *Deduction* is the method of applying a general law, already learned, to a special case. The child who has learned that iron is heavy

knows by *deduction*, when he sees any new object made of iron, that it will be heavy. The physicist familiar with Galileo's law knows also by *deduction*, that a feather will fall as fast as an iron ball; and when it does not do so, he suspects that the working of the law has been interfered with by the resistance of the air, and finds that in a vacuum they do actually fall at the same rate.

in-duc-tive (ĭn-dŭk′tĭv), *adj.* **1**, leading on; persuasive; **2**, reaching a general conclusion from particular instances: said of reasoning; **3**, producing an electrical or magnetic effect by nearness to a magnetized or electrified field: **inductive science**, any branch of science which allows and uses the method of experiment.—*adv.* **in-duc′tive-ly.**

in-duc-tiv-i-ty (ĭn″dŭk-tĭv′ĭ-tĭ), *n.* the property of a substance which determines its power to transmit electric or magnetic effects without contact.

in-duc-tor (ĭn-dŭk′tẽr), *n.* **1**, one who establishes another in an office or a benefice; **2**, a device in, or portion of, an apparatus which produces electric or magnetic effects without contact: **inductor compass**, a compass controlled by an inductor utilizing the magnetic field of the earth: also called *earth-inductor compass*.

in-due (ĭn-dū′), *v.t.* [*p.t.* and *p.p.* -dued′ (-dūd′), *p.pr.* -du′ing], **1**, to clothe; put on, as clothes; **2**, to furnish; as, to *indue* one with courage. Also, **en-due′**, *Pfd. S.*

in-dulge (ĭn-dŭlj′), *v.t.* [*p.t.* and *p.p.* -dulged′ (-dŭljd′), *p.pr.* -dulg′ing], **1**, to give way to; humor; **2**, to yield to:—*v.i.* to gratify oneself without restraint.

in-dul-gence (ĭn-dŭl′jĕns), *n.* **1**, the gratification or humoring of another; **2**, the act of yielding to or gratifying one's own desires; as, *indulgence* in laziness; **3**, in the Roman Catholic Church, remission of temporal punishment still due for sin after repentance and absolution.

in-dul-gent (ĭn-dŭl′jĕnt), *adj.* yielding to the humor, wishes, etc., of another; kind; lenient.—*adv.* **in-dul′gent-ly.**

in-du-rate (ĭn′dū-rāt), *v.i.* [*p.t.* and *p.p.* -rat″ed, *p.pr.* -rat″ing], to grow hard:—*v.t.* **1**, to make hard; as, heat *indurates* clay; **2**, to make unfeeling:—*adj.* (ĭn′dū-rāt), hardened.—*n.* **in″du-ra′tion.**

in-dus-tri-al (ĭn-dŭs′trĭ-ăl), *adj.* **1**, pertaining to, or of the nature of, industry, or productive enterprise; **2**, devoted to training for systematic labor; as, *industrial* courses of study; **3**, engaged in, or constituting, systematic labor; **4**, derived from, or engaged in, manufacturing on a large scale: **industrial insurance**, life insurance for small amounts, ranging from $15 to $500, with premiums payable weekly, intended to bring insurance within the reach of the poorer classes.—*adv.* **in-dus′tri-al-ly.**

in-dus-tri-al-ism (ĭn-dŭs′trĭ-ăl-ĭzm), *n.* a social system founded upon industrial activities, marked by machinery, large-scale production, etc.

in-dus-tri-ous (ĭn-dŭs′trĭ-ŭs), *adj.* diligent; hard-working; as, an *industrious* wife.—*adv.* **in-dus′tri-ous-ly.**

Syn. active, diligent. (See busy.)

in-dus-try (ĭn′dŭs-trĭ), *n.* [*pl.* industries (-trĭz)], **1**, steady attention to business or labor; **2**, all forms of economic activity; **3**, in a more limited sense, the productive occupations as distinguished from finance and commerce; **4**, a particular branch of work or trade; as, the cotton *industry*.

in-dwell (ĭn″dwĕl′), *v.t.* and *v.i.* [*p.t.* and *p.p.* -dwelt′ (-dwĕlt′) or -dwelled′ (-dwĕld′), *p.pr.* -dwell′ing], to abide in or within; inhabit.—*p.adj.* **in′dwell″ing.**

-ine (-ĭn; -īn; -ēn), *adj. suffix*, **1**, of, like, or pertaining to; as, mar*ine*; **2**, in zoölogy, belonging to a (specified) genus; as, can*ine*:—*n. suffix*, used in naming certain chemical compounds and elements; as, coca*ine*; chlor*ine*.

in-e-bri-ate (ĭn-ē′brĭ-āt), *v.t.* [*p.t.* and *p.p.* -at″ed, *p.pr.* -at″ing], **1**, to make drunk; intoxicate; **2**, to enliven beyond judgment; **3**, to stupefy:—*n.* (ĭn-ē′brĭ-āt), a drunkard:—*adj.* drunken.—*n.* **in-e″bri-a′tion.**

in-e-bri-e-ty (ĭn″ē-brī′ĕ-tĭ), *n.* intoxication; habitual drunkenness.

in-ed-i-ble (ĭn-ĕd′ĭ-bl), *adj.* not fit to be eaten.—*n.* **in-ed″i-bil′i-ty.**

in-ef-fa-ble (ĭn-ĕf′ȧ-bl), *adj.* **1**, unspeakable; inexpressible; **2**, too sacred for utterance or expression.—*adv.* **in-ef′fa-bly.**—*n.* **in-ef′fa-ble-ness.**

in-ef-face-a-ble (ĭn″ĕ-fās′ȧ-bl), *adj.* incapable of being blotted out or rubbed out.—*adv.* **in″ef-face′a-bly.**

in-ef-fec-tive (ĭn″ĕ-fĕk′tĭv), *adj.* not producing, or incapable of producing, the desired result; ineffectual.—*adv.* **in″ef-fec′tive-ly.**—*n.* **in″ef-fec′tive-ness.**

in-ef-fec-tu-al (ĭn″ĕ-fĕk′tū-ăl), *adj.* **1**, not producing the desired result; **2**, weak; unsuccessful; inefficient.—*adv.* **in″ef-fec′tu-al-ly.**—*n.* **in″ef-fec′tu-al-ness.**

Syn. vain, useless, ineffective.

in-ef-fi-ca-cious (ĭn-ĕf″ĭ-kā′shŭs), *adj.* not producing, or able to produce, the intended or desired result; powerless.—*adv.* **in-ef″fi-ca′cious-ly.**

in-ef-fi-ca-cy (ĭn-ĕf′ĭ-kȧ-sĭ), *n.* want of power to bring about the desired result; fruitlessness; ineffectualness.

in-ef-fi-cient (ĭn″ĕ-fĭsh′ĕnt), *adj.* **1**, not producing, or not capable of producing, the desired result; **2**, incapable; lacking in skill for an undertaking.—*adv.* **in″ef-fi′cient-ly.**—*n.* **in″ef-fi′cien-cy.**

in-e-las-tic (ĭn″ē-lăs′tĭk), *adj.* **1**, not capable, when stretched or compressed, of regaining the original form; **2**, rigid; **3**, hence, not adaptable.—*adv.* **in″e-las′ti-cal-ly.**

in-el-e-gance (ĭn-ĕl′ē-găns), *n.* want of any quality required by good taste; want of refinement in form or manner. Also, **in-el′e-gan-cy.**

in-el-e-gant (ĭn-ĕl′ē-gănt), *adj.* lacking in beauty, refinement, elegance, or good taste.—*adv.* **in-el′e-gant-ly.**

in-el-i-gi-ble (ĭn-ĕl′ĭ-jĭ-bl), *adj.* **1**, unworthy of choice; unsuitable; **2**, legally unfitted for choice or election; as, a foreign-born citizen of the United States is *ineligible* to the presidency.—*adv.* **in-el′i-gi-bly.**—*n.* **in-el″i-gi-bil′i-ty.**

in-ept (ĭn-ĕpt′), *adj.* **1**, not fit or suitable; **2**, foolish; absurd; **3**, clumsy; inefficient.—*adv.* **in-ept′ly.**—*n.* **in-ept′ness.**

in-ept-i-tude (ĭn-ĕp′tĭ-tūd), *n.* unfitness; unsuitability.

in-e-qual-i-ty (ĭn″ē-kwŏl′ĭ-tĭ), *n.* [*pl.* inequalities (-tĭz)], **1**, difference, esp. of rank, station, size, number, etc.; **2**, unevenness, as in surface; changeableness of condition; **3**, want of due proportion; uneven distribution; insufficiency.

in-eq-ui-ta-ble (ĭn-ĕk′wĭ-tȧ-bl), *adj.* not according to fairness or justice; unjust.—*adv.* **in-eq′ui-ta-bly.**

in-eq-ui-ty (ĭn-ĕk′wĭ-tĭ), *n.* [*pl.* inequities (-tĭz)], lack of fairness or justice.

in-e-rad-i-ca-ble (ĭn″ē-răd′ĭ-kȧ-bl), *adj.* incapable of being torn or rooted out.—*adv.* **in″e-rad′i-ca-bly.**

in-er-rant (ĭn-ĕr′ănt), *adj.* infallible; without error; free from mistakes.

in-ert (ĭn-ûrt′), *adj.* **1**, having no power of motion or action; as, an *inert* mass of rock; **2**, lifeless; sluggish; **3**, having no

active chemical or medicinal powers; as, an *inert* drug.—*adv.* **in-ert'ly.**—*n.* **in-ert'ness.**
Syn. passive, dead, dull, inactive.

in-er-ti-a (ĭn-ûr'shĭ-*ȧ*), *n.* **1**, tendency not to move; lack of activity; sluggishness; **2**, in physics, that property by virtue of which matter tends to remain at rest, if resting, or, if moving, to move uniformly in the same straight line unless it is acted upon by some outside force.

in-es-ti-ma-ble (ĭn-ĕs'tĭ-m*ȧ*-bl), *adj.* not to be measured; beyond measure or price; incalculable; invaluable; priceless.—*adv.* **in-es'ti-ma-bly.**

in-ev-i-ta-bil-i-ty (ĭn-ĕv″ĭ-t*ȧ*-bĭl'ĭ-tĭ), *n.* impossibility of being avoided; as, the *inevitability* of death.

in-ev-i-ta-ble (ĭn-ĕv'ĭ-t*ȧ*-bl), *adj.* not to be evaded; unavoidable; as, an *inevitable* accident.—*adv.* **in-ev'i-ta-bly.** —*n.* **in-ev'i-ta-ble-ness.**

in-ex-act (ĭn″ĕg-zăkt'), *adj.* not precise, correct, accurate, or punctual.—*adv.* **in″ex-act'ly.**—*n.* **in″ex-act'ness.**

in-ex-cus-a-ble (ĭn″ĕks-kūz'*ȧ*-bl), *adj.* not admitting of excuse or apology.—*adv.* **in″ex-cus'a-bly.**

in-ex-haust-i-ble (ĭn″ĕg-zôs'tĭ-bl), *adj.* **1**, not to be used up; unfailing; as, *inexhaustible* resources; **2**, of tireless power, vigor, or strength; unwearied. —*n.* **in″ex-haust'i-ble-ness.**—*adv.* **in″ex-haust'i-bly.**—*n.* **in″ex-haust″i-bil'i-ty.**

in-ex-o-ra-ble (ĭn-ĕk'sō-r*ȧ*-bl), *adj.* not to be moved by prayers; unyielding; unrelenting; as, an *inexorable* ruler.—*adv.* **in-ex'o-ra-bly.**—*n.* **in-ex'o-ra-ble-ness.**—*n.* **in-ex″o-ra-bil'i-ty.**

in-ex-pe-di-ent (ĭn″ĕks-pē'dĭ-ĕnt), *adj.* unsuitable to circumstances or conditions; not advisable; as, it is *inexpedient* to hurry.—*n.* **in″ex-pe'di-en-cy.**

in-ex-pen-sive (ĭn″ĕks-pĕn'sĭv), *adj.* cheap; costing little; as, *inexpensive* clothes; *inexpensive* pleasures.

in-ex-pe-ri-ence (ĭn″ĕks-pē'rĭ-ĕns), *n.* want of actual enjoyment, suffering, or personal contact with life; esp., lack of first-hand knowledge of any special type of work.—*adj.* **in″ex-pe'ri-enced.**

in-ex-pert (ĭn″ĕks-pûrt'), *adj.* unskilled; lacking the knowledge gained from practice.—*adv.* **in″ex-pert'ly.**

in-ex-pi-a-ble (ĭn-ĕks'pĭ-*ȧ*-bl), *adj.* **1**, not capable of being atoned for; as, an *inexpiable* crime; **2**, relentless.

in-ex-pli-ca-ble (ĭn-ĕks'plĭ-k*ȧ*-bl), *adj.* not capable of being explained, made plain, or understood; not to be interpreted or accounted for; as, shrouded in an *inexplicable* mystery.—*adv.* **in-ex'pli-ca-bly.**—*n.* **in-ex″pli-ca-bil'i-ty.**

in-ex-press-i-ble (ĭn″ĕks-prĕs'ĭ-bl), *adj.* incapable of being uttered or described.—*adj.* **in″ex-press'i-bly.**

in-ex-pres-sive (ĭn″ĕks-prĕs'ĭv), *adj.* **1**, lacking in expression or meaning; dull; as, an *inexpressive* face; **2**, not sufficient to convey meaning; as, an *inexpressive* phrase.—*adv.* **in″ex-pres'sive-ly.**

in-ex-ten-si-ble (ĭn″ĕks-tĕn'sĭ-bl), *adj.* incapable of being stretched; inelastic; as, *inextensible* fibers.—*adv.* **in″ex-ten'si-bly.**—*n.* **in″ex-ten″si-bil'i-ty.**

in-ex-tin-guish-a-ble (ĭn″ĕks-tĭng'gwĭsh-*ȧ*-bl), *adj.* unquenchable, as a fire; unslakable, as thirst.

in-ex-tri-ca-ble (ĭn-ĕks'trĭ-k*ȧ*-bl), *adj.* **1**, incapable of being untied or disentangled; as, an *inextricable* knot; **2**, hopelessly confused or obscure; unsolvable, as a mystery; **3**, intricate in design; elaborate, as a pattern.—*adv.* **in-ex'tri-ca-bly.**

in-fal-li-ble (ĭn-făl'ĭ-bl), *adj.* **1**, incapable of erring; unfailing; as, the predictions of the weather bureau are not *infallible;* **2**, not likely to mistake or disappoint; certain; as, an *infallible* judge of horses. —*adv.* **in-fal'li-bly.**—*n.* **in-fal″li-bil'i-ty.**

in-fa-mous (ĭn'f*ȧ*-mŭs), *adj.* **1**, having a very bad reputation; **2**, odious; scandalous; as, an *infamous* crime.—*adv.* **in'fa-mous-ly.**
Syn. shameful, detestable, disgraceful.

in-fa-my (ĭn'f*ȧ*-mĭ), *n.* [*pl.* infamies (-mĭz)], **1**, public disgrace; **2**, baseness or vileness; **3**, an odious act.
Syn. dishonor.—*Ant.* honor, respect.

in-fan-cy (ĭn'făn-sĭ), *n.* **1**, the state of being a babe in arms; early childhood; **2**, the first stage of anything; **3**, in law, the period of life from birth to the age of 21.

in-fant (ĭn'fănt), *n.* **1**, a young child; **2**, in law, a person who has not attained the age of twenty-one:—*adj.* **1**, pertaining to the earliest stages of childhood; **2**, pertaining to the legal period of minority.

in-fan-ta (ĭn-făn't*ȧ*), *n.* any daughter of the royal family of Spain: also used as a title.

in-fan-te (ĭn-făn'tā), *n.* any son of the royal family of Spain, except the eldest: also used as a title.

in-fan-ti-cide (ĭn-făn'tĭ-sīd), *n.* **1**, the murder of a newly born child; **2**, one who kills a newly born child.

in-fan-tile (ĭn'făn-tīl; ĭn'făn-tĭl), *adj.* pertaining to babies or the period of babyhood; childish: **infantile paralysis,** inflammation of the motor nerve cells of the spinal cord, an infectious form of which especially attacks children. Also, **in'fan-tine.**

in-fan-try (ĭn'făn-trĭ), *n.* a body of soldiers armed and equipped for service on foot.—*n.* **in'fan-try-man.**

in-fat-u-ate (ĭn-făt'ū-āt), *v.t.* [*p.t.* and *p.p.* -at″ed, *p.pr.* -at″ing], **1**, to lead into folly; **2**, to inspire with an extravagant admiration or passion.

in-fat-u-a-tion (ĭn-făt″ū-ā'shŭn), *n.* **1**, extravagant folly; **2**, a foolish and extravagant affection or passion.

in-fect (ĭn-fĕkt'), *v.t.* **1**, to contaminate; taint; **2**, to communicate a disease, mood, etc., to (a person); as, his gloominess *infected* everyone.

in-fec-tion (ĭn-fĕk'shŭn), *n.* **1**, the act or process of infecting, or the state of being infected; the communication of a condition of body or spirit to another; **2**, the communication of disease germs; **3**, that which depraves, as an evil influence; that which communicates disease; **4**, a disease communicated by germs in any manner: distinguished from *contagion*, which requires personal contact; an epidemic.

in-fec-tious (ĭn-fĕk'shŭs), *adj.* **1**, capable of communicating a condition, as disease, by spreading germs; **2**, corrupting; demoralizing; **3**, readily communicated or spread; as, *infectious* gaiety.—*adv.* **in-fec'tious-ly.**—*n.* **in-fec'tious-ness.**
Syn. communicable. (See contagious.)

in-fe-lic-i-tous (ĭn″fē-lĭs'ĭ-tŭs), *adj.* unfortunate; unhappy; ill-timed; inappropriate; as, an *infelicitous* remark.—*adv.* **in″fe-lic'i-tous-ly.**

in-fe-lic-i-ty (ĭn″fē-lĭs'ĭ-tĭ), *n.* [*pl.* infelicities (-tĭz)], **1**, misfortune; unhappiness; inappropriateness; **2**, an unfortunate or ill-timed act or expression.

in-fer (ĭn-fûr'), *v.t.* [*p.t.* and *p.p.* -ferred' (-fûrd'), *p.pr.* -fer'ring], **1**, to arrive at (a conclusion, etc.) by reasoning; as, from the study of Indian relics we *infer* that some tribes had highly developed arts; **2**, to lead to

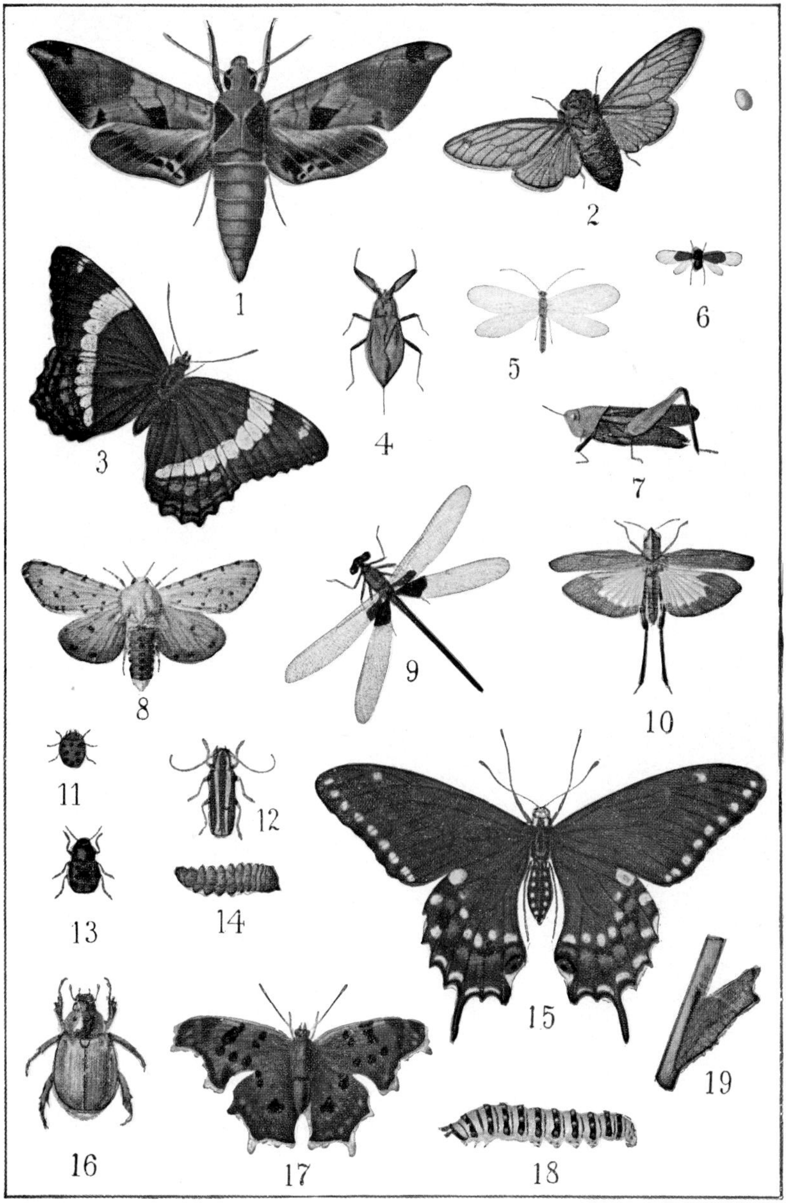

COMMON AMERICAN INSECTS

1. Sphinx moth. 2. Seventeen-year locust. 3. Admiral butterfly. 4. Giant water bug. 5. Aphis lion. 6. Plant louse or aphid. 7. Grasshopper. 8. Tiger moth. 9. Dragon fly. 10. Grasshopper, with wings spread. 11, 12, 13, 16. Beetles: 11. Lady "bird"; 12. Round-headed apple tree borer; 13. Leaf beetle. 14. Larva of No. 12. 15. Swallow-tail butterfly. 16. Scarab beetle. 17. Common butterfly. 18. Larva of No. 15. 19. Chrysalis of No. 15.

as a consequence; indicate; as, your haste *infers* your eagerness; **3**, *Colloq.*, to guess; suppose:—*v.i.* to conclude.

Syn. imply. To *infer* is to come to a conclusion. To *imply* is to suggest tangible grounds for reaching a conclusion. For example, from all that the newspapers *imply*, we *infer* that the case is closed.

in-fer-a-ble (ĭn-fûr′ȧ-bl), *adj.* capable of being arrived at by reasoning or deduction; deducible.

in-fer-ence (ĭn′fĕr-ĕns), *n.* **1**, the act of arriving at a conclusion by reasoning; **2**, a conclusion so reached.

in-fer-en-tial (ĭn″fĕr-ĕn′shăl), *adj.* having the nature of a conclusion arrived at by reasoning from known facts.—*adv.* **in″fer-en′tial-ly.**

in-fe-ri-or (ĭn-fē′rĭ-ẽr), *adj.* **1**, lower in place, rank, or value; secondary; **2**, mediocre; second-rate; **3**, in astronomy, having an orbit between those of the earth and the sun; as, *inferior* planets:—*n.* one who ranks below another.

in-fe-ri-or-i-ty (ĭn-fē″rĭ-ŏr′ĭ-tĭ), *n.* lower state or quality; as, *inferiority* of rank; mental *inferiority:* **inferiority complex**, an exaggerated sense of one's own inability or inadequacy, particularly in relation to other persons.

in-fer-nal (ĭn-fûr′năl), *adj.* **1**, pertaining to the regions of the dead; **2**, belonging to, or resembling, hell; hellish; **3**, fiendish; outrageous: **infernal machine**, an apparatus designed to destroy life and property.—*adv.* **in-fer′nal-ly.**

in-fer-no (ĭn-fûr′nō), *n.* [*pl.* infernos (-nōz)], **1**, the lower regions; hell; **2**, a scene so horrible as to resemble hell.

in-fer-tile (ĭn-fûr′tĭl; *Br.* ĭn-fûr′tīl), *adj.* lacking fruitfulness; barren.—*adv.* **in-fer′tile-ly.**—*n.* **in″fer-til′i-ty.**

in-fest (ĭn-fĕst′), *v.t.* to attack; overrun; beset or annoy constantly and in numbers; as, moths *infest* woolen materials.—*n.* **in″fes-ta′tion.**

Syn. molest, plague, harass.

in-fi-del (ĭn′fĭ-dĕl), *n.* **1**, one who rejects religion; a professed unbeliever in whatever religion is locally regarded as true, as, from the Turkish viewpoint, a non-Mohammedan; in Christian communities, a non-Christian; **2**, a renegade; **3**, in general, one who does not believe in something specified:—*adj.* **1**, unbelieving; heathen; **2**, pertaining to, or characteristic of, infidels.

Syn., n. freethinker, skeptic.

in-fi-del-i-ty (ĭn″fĭ-dĕl′ĭ-tĭ), *n.* [*pl.* infidelities (-tĭz)], **1**, disbelief in some religion, esp. in Christianity; **2**, the act of breaking a trust; disloyalty; **3**, adultery.

in-field (ĭn′fēld″), *n.* in baseball, the space within the base lines; also, the players there.—*n.* **in′field″er.**

in-fil-trate (ĭn-fĭl′trāt), *v.t.* and *v.i.* [*p.t.* and *p.p.* -trat-ed, *p.pr.* -trat-ing], to pass through pores or very small openings.—*n.* **in″fil-tra′tion.**

in-fi-nite (ĭn′fĭ-nĭt), *adj.* **1**, immeasurably great, as in power, knowledge, etc.; **2**, unlimited; endless: opp. of *finite;* **3**, in mathematics, having a value greater than any assignable value:—*n.* **1**, that which has no limit; **2**, in mathematics, an infinite quantity or magnitude: **the Infinite**, God; the Supreme Being.—*adv.* **in′fi-nite-ly.**—*n.* **in′fi-nite-ness.**

Syn., adj. boundless, endless, eternal.

in-fin-i-tes-i-mal (ĭn″fĭn-ĭ-tĕs′ĭ-măl), *adj.* **1**, immeasurably small; as, the weight of an insect's wing would be *infinitesimal;* **2**, in mathematics, having a value less than any assignable value.—*adv.* **in″fin-i-tes′i-mal-ly.**

in-fin-i-tive (ĭn-fĭn′ĭ-tĭv), *adj.* in grammar, not finite; not limited by person or number: applied to that verb form which merely expresses the general sense of the verb:—*n.* in grammar, the infinitive verb form: often with *to*, as *to sing, to be*, etc.

in-fin-i-tude (ĭn-fĭn′ĭ-tūd), *n.* **1**, the quality of being boundless or immeasurable; also, that which is boundless in space, number, etc.; **2**, a quantity too great to be counted.

in-fin-i-ty (ĭn-fĭn′ĭ-tĭ), *n.* [*pl.* infinities (-tĭz)], **1**, the state of being immeasurable; **2**, unlimited extent of time, space, or quantity; **3**, an extremely large quantity; in mathematics, an infinite quantity: represented by the symbol ∞.

in-firm (ĭn-fûrm′), *adj.* **1**, feeble in body or health; **2**, insecure; frail; **3**, weak; irresolute; **4**, uncertain.—*adv.* **in-firm′ly.**—*n.* **in-firm′ness.**

Syn. unsound, decrepit, precarious.

in-fir-ma-ry (ĭn-fûr′mȧ-rĭ), *n.* [*pl.* infirmaries (-rĭz)], a room or building for the treatment of the sick and injured, esp. in an institution, as a school.

in-fir-mi-ty (ĭn-fûr′mĭ-tĭ), *n.* [*pl.* infirmities (-tĭz)], **1**, the state of being weak or sick; **2**, weakness of body or of mind; illness; failing.

in-fix (ĭn-fĭks′), *v.t.* **1**, to fasten in, as by piercing; **2**, to implant; teach.

in-flame (ĭn-flām′), *v.t.* [*p.t.* and *p.p.* -flamed′ (-flāmd′), *p.pr.* -flam′ing], **1**, to set on fire; **2**, to fire with passion; **3**, to excite; provoke; **4**, to put into a state of redness, swelling, and pain; as, weeping *inflames* the eyes:—*v.i.* to become inflamed.

Syn. anger, enrage, incense, exasperate.

in-flam-ma-ble (ĭn-flăm′ȧ-bl), *adj.* **1**, easily set on fire; as, gasoline is an *inflammable* substance; **2**, easily excited; as, an *inflammable* temper.—*adv.* **inflam′ma-bly.**—*n.* **in-flam″ma-bil′i-ty.**

in-flam-ma-tion (ĭn″flă-mā′shŭn), *n.* **1**, the act of inflaming; **2**, a state of redness, heat, swelling, and pain in any part of the body.

in-flam-ma-to-ry (ĭn-flăm′ȧ-tō-rĭ), *adj.* **1**, tending to excite passion, tumult, or rebellion; **2**, tending to produce, or showing, inflammation.

in-flate (ĭn-flāt′), *v.t.* [*p.t.* and *p.p.* -flat′ed, *p.pr.* -flat′ing], **1**, to swell out with air or gas, as a balloon; **2**, to puff up; make proud; **3**, to expand or raise unduly, as prices:—*v.i.* to become swollen out, as with air or gas.—*adj.* **in-flat′a-ble.**—*n.* **in-flat′er; in-fla′tor.**—*n.* **in-fla′tion.**

in-flect (ĭn-flĕkt′), *v.t.* **1**, to bend; turn from a direct line; **2**, to vary the sound of, as the voice, by producing changes in pitch or tone; **3**, to vary the form of (a noun, verb, or adjective) so as to show changes in the person, number, case, etc.:—*v.i.* to undergo grammatical change of ending.

in-flec-tion (ĭn-flĕk′shŭn), *n.* **1**, the act of bending, or the state of being bent; **2**, the rise and fall in the voice; as, the soft *inflection* showed sympathy; **3**, the variations undergone by words to show case, number, gender, etc. Also, **in-flex′ion.**

in-flec-tion-al (ĭn-flĕk′shŭn-ăl), *adj.* in grammar, showing changes in form to denote changes in person, number, case, etc.; as, Latin is an *inflectional* language. Also, **in-flex′ion-al.**

in-flec-tive (ĭn-flĕk′tĭv), *adj.* **1**, capable of bending; **2**, having the forms showing changes in person, number, case, etc.; as, *inflective* languages.

in-flex-i-ble (ĭn-flĕk′sĭ-bl), *adj.* **1**, not to be bent; rigid; stiff; **2**, not to be moved by prayers; not to be varied or changed; unalterable; as, an *inflexible* determination.—*n.* **in-flex'i-ble-ness.**—*adv.* **in-flex'i-bly.**—*n.* **in-flex"i-bil'i-ty.**

Syn. unbending, rigorous; resolute.

in-flict (ĭn-flĭkt'), *v.t.* **1,** to cause by, or as if by, striking; cause to be suffered; **2,** to impose, as a punishment.—*n.* **in-flic'tion.**

in-flo-res-cence (ĭn"flō-rĕs'ĕns), *n.* **1,** the process of coming into flower; **2,** the arrangement of flowers on the stem; **3,** blossoms collectively; flower clusters.

of regular, customary, or legal form or ceremony; also, an instance of such lack.

in-form-ant (ĭn-fôr'mănt), *n.* one who gives news or knowledge.

in-for-ma-tion (ĭn"fôr-mā'shŭn), *n.* **1,** knowledge given or acquired; **2,** valuable or timely knowledge, esp. of facts; **3,** in law: **a,** a lawsuit brought on behalf of the government; **b,** a declaration made before a magistrate to cause him to issue a summons or warrant.

Syn. tidings, intelligence. (See news.)

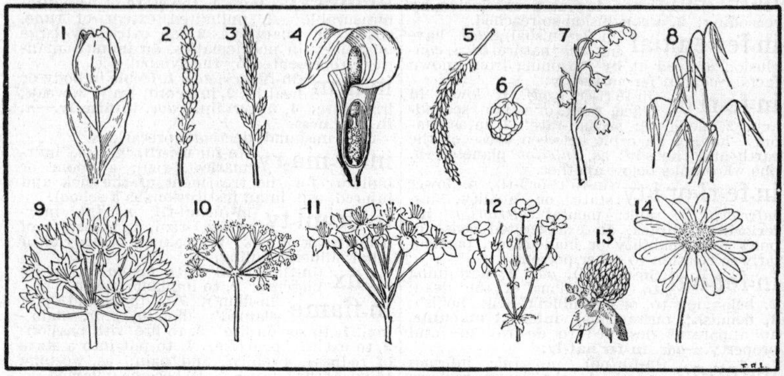

TYPES OF INFLORESCENCE

1, solitary (tulip); 2, spike (plantain); 3, compound spike (couch grass); 4, spadix (jack-in-the-pulpit); 5, ament, or catkin (birch); 6, cone, or strobile (hop); 7, raceme (lily of the valley); 8, panicle (oat); 9, umbel (African lily); 10, compound umbel (wild carrot); 11, corymb (hawthorn); 12, cyme (wild geranium); 13, head (clover); 14, composite head (daisy).

in-flow (ĭn'flō"), *n.* the act of running or flowing in; also, that which runs in.—*adj.* **in'flow"ing.**

in-flu-ence (ĭn'flo͞o-ĕns), *n.* **1,** energy or power tending to produce effects by indirect or invisible means; as, the *influence* of a good example; **2,** power arising from wealth or station; as, political *influence;* **3,** one who or that which exerts power:—*v.t.* [*p.t.* and *p.p.* -enced (-ĕnst), *p.pr.* -enc-ing], **1,** to have unseen power over, physically or mentally; as, to *influence* a community for good; **2,** to modify or change.

in-flu-en-tial (ĭn"flo͞o-ĕn'shăl), *adj.* having or exerting power; as, an *influential* citizen.—*adv.* **in"flu-en'tial-ly.**

in-flu-en-za (ĭn"flo͞o-ĕn'zȧ), *n.* an acute, infectious disease, frequently occurring in epidemic form, characterized by inflammation of the air passages, severe muscular pains, and headache: popularly called *flu.*

in-flux (ĭn'flŭks"), *n.* **1,** an inflow; a pouring in; **2,** the addition or continual incoming of persons or things; **3,** a point where a stream flows into another or into the sea.

in-fold (ĭn-fōld'), *v.t.* **1,** to wrap up or surround with folds; envelop; **2,** to hold in the arms; embrace. Also, **en-fold'.**

in-form (ĭn-fôrm'), *v.t.* **1,** to supply with knowledge; notify; tell; transmit knowledge to; **2,** to animate; inspire; as, the breath of life *informs* the clay:—*v.i.* to give information, esp. in accusation.

Syn. advise, notify, enlighten.

in-for-mal (ĭn-fôr'măl), *adj.* **1,** not according to custom or rule; irregular; **2,** without ceremony; unceremonious; as, an *informal* reception.—*adv.* **in-for'mal-ly.**

in-for-mal-i-ty (ĭn"fôr-măl'ĭ-tĭ), *n.* [*pl.* informalities (-tĭz)], want

in-form-a-tive (ĭn-fôr'mȧ-tĭv), *adj.* imparting knowledge.

in-form-er (ĭn-fôr'mẽr), *n.* **1,** one who informs a magistrate of a breaking of the law; **2,** one who gives information or news; a talebearer.

in-fra- (ĭn'frȧ-), *prefix,* beneath; below; as, *infra*costal: opp. of *supra-.*

in-fra-cos-tal (ĭn"frȧ-kŏs'tăl), *adj.* lying beneath or below the ribs.

in-frac-tion (ĭn-frăk'shŭn), *n.* the act of breaking, esp. a law.

in-fra–red (ĭn"frȧ=rĕd'), *adj.* designating, or pertaining to, the invisible light rays which fall outside the visible spectrum at the red end.

in-fre-quence (ĭn-frē'kwĕns), *n.* the state or fact of happening very seldom. Also, **in-fre'quen-cy.**

in-fre-quent (ĭn-frē'kwĕnt), *adj.* seldom occurring; as, *infrequent* visits; *infrequent* rains.—*adv.* **in-fre'quent-ly.**

in-fringe (ĭn-frĭnj'), *v.t.* [*p.t.* and *p.p.* -fringed' (-frĭnjd'), *p.pr.* -fring'-ing], to disregard or break, as a law; neglect to obey:—*v.i.* to encroach or trespass: followed by *on* or *upon;* as, to *infringe* upon a patent.—*n.* **in-fring'er.**

Syn. invade, intrude, transgress.

in-fringe-ment (ĭn-frĭnj'mĕnt), *n.* **1,** the act of breaking or neglecting a law; **2,** encroachment on a right, as by imitation of a patented article or the unlawful use of a trade name or trade-mark.

in-fu-ri-ate (ĭn-fū'rĭ-āt), *v.t.* [*p.t.* and *p.p.* -at"ed, *p.pr.* -at"ing], to enrage; madden.—*n.* **in-fu"ri-a'tion.**

in-fuse (ĭn-fūz'), *v.t.* [*p.t.* and *p.p.* -fused' (-fūzd'), *p.pr.* -fus'ing], **1,** to introduce, as by pouring; **2,** to fill; animate; as, to *infuse* a spirit of good will; **3**, to impart or teach gradually, as principles; **4**, to steep in water, as tea.—*n.* **in-fus′er.**

in-fu-si-ble (ĭn-fū′zĭ-bl), *adj.* incapable of being melted by heat.

in-fu-sion (ĭn-fū′zhŭn), *n.* **1**, a pouring in; something poured in or mingled; **2**, the imparting or teaching, as of ideas, good principles, etc.; **3**, the process of steeping a substance in water to extract something from it; also, the liquid so obtained; **4**, water containing dissolved organic matter.

-ing (-ĭng), *suffix*, used to form: **1**, the present participle; as, a walk*ing* delegate; **2**, certain types of verbal noun; as, the writ*ing* of books, or (gerund) writ*ing* books is hard; **3**, diminutives, patronymics, etc., as geld*ing*; farth*ing*.

in-gath-er-ing (ĭn′găth″ẽr-ĭng), *n.* the act of bringing in, esp. the harvest.—*n.* **in′gath″er-er.**

in-gen-ious (ĭn-jēn′yŭs), *adj.* **1**, having inventive skill; clever; as, an *ingenious* inventor; **2**, skilfully made; as, a speedometer is an *ingenious* device.—*adv.* **in-gen′ious-ly.**—*n.* **in-gen′ious-ness.**

in-gé-nue (ăṅ″zhā″nü′), [Fr.], *n.* [*pl.* ingénues (-nü′)], **1**, a frank, innocent, and unsophisticated girl or young woman; **2**, an actress who portrays such a character.

in-ge-nu-i-ty (ĭn″jē-nū′ĭ-tĭ), *n.* [*pl.* ingenuities (-tĭz)], **1**, cleverness in contriving or inventing; **2**, cleverness of design or execution; as, *ingenuity* of plot.

in-gen-u-ous (ĭn-jĕn′ū-ŭs), *adj.* frank; open; innocent; sincere; candid; as, an *ingenuous* child.—*adv.* **in-gen′u-ous-ly.**—*n.* **in-gen′u-ous-ness.**
Syn. unreserved, fair, plain.

in-gle (ĭng′gl), *n.* a fire or fireplace; a blaze; as, sit thee by the *ingle*.

in-gle-nook (ĭng′gl-no͝ok″), *n.* a chimney corner. Also, **in′gle nook.**

in-glo-ri-ous (ĭn-glō′rĭ-ŭs), *adj.* **1**, without fame; humble; **2**, disgraceful; shameful; as, an *inglorious* defeat.—*adv.* **in-glo′ri-ous-ly.**—*n.* **in-glo′ri-ous-ness.**

in-got (ĭng′gŏt; ĭn′-), *n.* a mass of metal cast into a mold.

in-graft (ĭn-grȧft′), *v.t.* **1**, to set (a scion) from one tree into another for propagation; **2**, to cause to undergo grafting, as a tree; **3**, figuratively, to incorporate; **4**, to implant, or cause to take root, as principles or ideas. Also, **en-graft′.**

in-grain (ĭn′grān″; ĭn-grān′), *v.t.* **1**, to dye in the fiber or before manufacture; **2**, to dye with any deep, lasting color; **3**, (also, *engrain*), to saturate or fix in deeply; as, *ingrained* vice:—*adj.* (ĭn′grān″), **1**, dyed before being manufactured; **2**, thoroughly worked in; deep-seated:—*n.* a carpet made of cotton and wool.—*p.adj.* **in′grained″.**

in-grate (ĭn′grāt), *adj.* not thankful:—*n.* one who is not thankful.

in-gra-ti-ate (ĭn-grā′shĭ-āt), *v.t.* [*p.t.* and *p.p.* -at″ed, *p.pr.* -at″ing], **1**, to bring (oneself) into the favor of another; as, he knew how to *ingratiate* himself with all; **2**, to secure good reception for: with *into*.

in-grat-i-tude (ĭn-grăt′ĭ-tūd), *n.* absence of thankfulness; insensibility to kindness; ungratefulness.

in-gre-di-ent (ĭn-grē′dĭ-ĕnt), *n.* a part of a compound or mixture; as, sugar is an *ingredient* of cake; an element.

in-gress (ĭn′grĕs), *n.* **1**, entrance; access; **2**, the place of entrance.

in-gulf (ĭn-gŭlf′), *v.t.* to swallow up; bury; overwhelm. See **en-gulf′**, *Pfd. S.*

in-hab-it (ĭn-hăb′ĭt), *v.t.* to dwell in; occupy, as a land or building:—*v.i. Archaic*, to dwell.—*adj.* **in-hab′it-a-ble.**

in-hab-it-ant (ĭn-hăb′ĭ-tănt), *n.* one who or that which occupies; a permanent resident in a place.

in-hab-it-ed (ĭn-hăb′ĭt-ĕd), *p. adj.* peopled; lived in; occupied.

in-hale (ĭn-hāl′), *v.t.* [*p.t.* and *p.p.* -haled′ (-hāld′), *p.pr.* -hal′ing], to draw into the lungs, as air, ether, or the like.—*n.* **in″ha-la′tion** (ĭn″hȧ-lā′shŭn).

in-hal-er (ĭn-hāl′ẽr), *n.* **1**, one who draws a breath into the lungs; **2**, an instrument through which a medicated vapor, or the like, is drawn into the lungs.

in-har-mo-ni-ous (ĭn″här-mō′nĭ-ŭs), *adj.* **1**, unmusical; disagreeing; as, *inharmonious* sounds; **2**, conflicting; not in accord; as, *inharmonious* views of life.—*adv.* **in″har-mo′ni-ous-ly.**

in-here (ĭn-hēr′), *v.i.* [*p.t.* and *p.p.* -hered′ (-hērd′), *p.pr.* -her′ing], to be fixed or exist in something else; be vested, as a right; as, responsibility *inheres* in citizenship.

in-her-ent (ĭn-hēr′ĕnt), *adj.* existing inseparably in something else; essential; inborn; as, fear of death is *inherent* in human nature.—*adv.* **in-her′ent-ly.**—*n.* **in-her′ence; in-her′en-cy.**
Syn. innate, inbred, native.

in-her-it (ĭn-hĕr′ĭt), *v.t.* **1**, to come into possession of, as property, from an ancestor by right of succession; **2**, to receive, as qualities, by nature from one's ancestors; receive by birth; **3**, to be heir to:—*v.i.* to come into possession of property, as the heir.—*adj.* **in-her′it-a-ble.**

in-her-it-ance (ĭn-hĕr′ĭ-tăns), *n.* **1**, the act of coming into a property, as an heir; **2**, property received by an heir; **3**, any immaterial possession inherited from previous generations; **4**, a possession or blessing, esp. one bestowed as a gift; **5**, in biology, the biologic process by which descendants possess or develop characters which were present in their ancestors.

in-her-i-tor (ĭn-hĕr′ĭ-tẽr), *n.* one who receives property or possessions from ancestors or others; an heir.—*n.fem.* **in-her′i-tress; in-her′i-trix.**

in-hib-it (ĭn-hĭb′ĭt), *v.t.* to restrain; hold in check; prevent.—*n.* **in″hi-bi′tion.**—*adj.* **in-hib′i-to-ry.**

in-hos-pi-ta-ble (ĭn-hŏs′pĭ-tȧ-bl), *adj.* **1**, not welcoming strangers or guests; **2**, affording no shelter; barren; cheerless; as, the Pilgrims landed on the *inhospitable* New England coast.—*adv.* **in-hos′pi-ta-bly.**—*n.* **in-hos′pi-ta-ble-ness.**

in-hos-pi-tal-i-ty (ĭn-hŏs″pĭ-tăl′ĭ-tĭ), *n.* **1**, the want of cordiality or desire to welcome strangers or guests; **2**, the lack of facilities for shelter or food, as in desert wastes.

in-hu-man (ĭn-hū′măn), *adj.* **1**, cruel; unfeeling; without kindly qualities; **2**, displaying a lack of human qualities; as, an *inhuman* brute; **3**, not like a human being in form.—*adv.* **in-hu′-man-ly.**
Syn. brutal, savage, barbarous, ruthless, merciless, ferocious, fierce.

in-hu-man-i-ty (ĭn″hū-măn′ĭ-tĭ), *n.* [*pl.* inhumanities (-tĭz)], **1**, the quality of being unfeeling or unkind; **2**, cruelty; **3**, an inhuman act.

in-im-i-cal (ĭn-ĭm′ĭ-kăl), *adj.* **1**, hostile; unfriendly; **2**, opposed; antagonistic; as, weariness of body is *inimical* to hard brain work.—*adv.* **in-im′i-cal-ly.**

in-im-i-ta-ble (ĭn-ĭm′ĭ-tȧ-bl), *adj.* matchless; impossible to imitate; as, an *inimitable* style.—*adv.* **in-im′i-ta-bly.**—*n.* **in-im″i-ta-bil′i-ty.**

in-iq-ui-tous (ĭn-ĭk′wĭ-tŭs), *adj.* wicked; grossly unjust; as, the

selling of slaves was an *iniquitous* practice.—*adv.* **in-iq'ui-tous-ly.**—*n.* **in-iq'ui-tous-ness.**
Syn. unrighteous, atrocious, criminal.—*Ant.* righteous, virtuous.

in-iq-ui-ty (ĭn-ĭk'wĭ-tĭ), *n.* [*pl.* iniquities (-tĭz)], **1,** wickedness; injustice; **2,** a wicked act; a sin or crime.

in-i-tial (ĭn-ĭsh'ăl), *adj.* **1,** placed at the beginning; **2,** marking, or pertaining to, the beginning:—*n.* **1,** a letter at the beginning of a word, paragraph, etc.; **2,** in *pl.*, the first letters of a person's name placed separately:—*v.t.* to mark, or sign, with an initial or initials.—*adv.* **in-i'tial-ly.**

in-i-ti-ate (ĭn-ĭsh'ĭ-āt), *v.t.* [*p.t.* and *p.p.* -at″ed, *p.pr.* -at″ing], **1,** to instruct in the first principles of anything; **2,** to set on foot; begin; introduce; as, to *initiate* a series of reforms; **3,** to introduce into a club, secret society, etc., by special teachings and ceremonies:—*adj.* (ĭn-ĭsh'ĭ-āt), **1,** introduced into a society; instructed, as in one's duties; **2,** beginning:—*n.* one who has been, or is about to be, initiated.—*n.* **in-i'ti-a″tor.**

in-i-ti-a-tion (ĭn-ĭsh″ĭ-ā'shŭn), *n.* **1,** the act of introducing into a club, society, business, literature, etc.; **2,** the rites, ceremonies, etc., with which one is made a member of a society or fraternity.

in-i-ti-a-tive (ĭn-ĭsh'ĭ-ȧ-tĭv), *adj.* introductory:—*n.* **1,** an introductory or first step; **2,** the power of originating something; the self-reliance or energy required to begin or dare new undertakings; **3,** the right or method by which a people may start a movement, as a reform, by demanding the required laws from their representative assembly: usually completed by the *referendum.*

in-i-ti-a-to-ry (ĭn-ĭsh'ĭ-ȧ-tō-rĭ), *adj.* **1,** introductory; as, the *initiatory* steps in an undertaking; **2,** serving to introduce or initiate, as into some society or some special knowledge.

in-ject (ĭn-jĕkt'), *v.t.* **1,** to drive or force in; introduce, as a liquid, by mechanical means; as, the doctor *injects* morphine; **2,** to introduce, as a remark.

in-jec-tion (ĭn-jĕk'shŭn), *n.* **1,** a forcing in; **2,** that which is forced in; **3,** in medicine, the act of forcing a liquid into some part, such as the rectum; also, the liquid so forced in; an enema; a hypodermic.

in-jec-tor (ĭn-jĕk'tẽr), *n.* one who or that which forces in, esp. an apparatus for injecting water into a steam boiler.

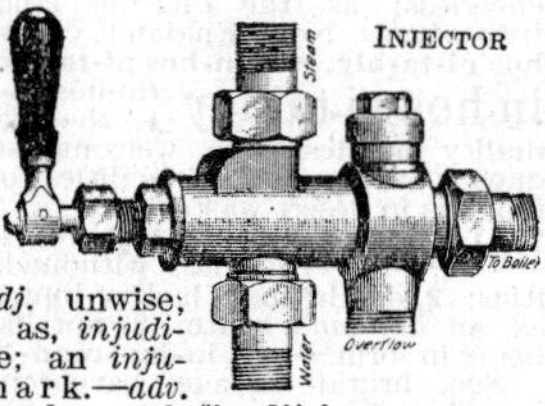

INJECTOR

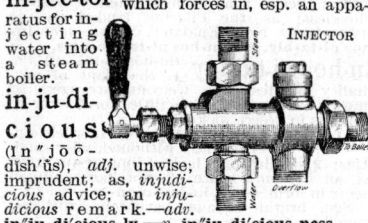

in-ju-di-cious (ĭn″jōō-dĭsh'ŭs), *adj.* unwise; imprudent; as, *injudicious* advice; an *injudicious* remark.—*adv.* **in″ju-di'cious-ly.**—*n.* **in″ju-di'cious-ness.**

in-junc-tion (ĭn-jŭngk'shŭn), *n.* **1,** the act of enjoining or commanding; **2,** that which is enjoined or commanded; order; precept; **3,** a legal paper to command or restrain certain proceedings.

in-jure (ĭn'jŏŏr), *v.t.* [*p.t.* and *p.p.* -jured (-jŏŏrd), *p.pr.* -jur-ing], to hurt; damage, physically or morally.—*n.* **in'jur-er.**
Syn. wrong, spoil, mar, sully.

in-ju-ri-ous (ĭn-jōō'rĭ-ŭs), *adj.* **1,** hurtful, physically or morally; harmful; **2,** abusive; malicious.—*adv.* **in-ju'ri-ous-ly.**—*n.* **in-ju'ri-ous-ness.**
Syn. baneful, noxious, detrimental.

in-ju-ry (ĭn'jōō-rĭ), *n.* [*pl.* injuries (-rĭz)], **1,** any hurt or harm, physical or moral; damage to one's person, property, rights, etc.; **2,** that which causes harm.
Syn. damage, harm, mischief. *Injury*, the general term, is applied to whatever affects one disadvantageously; as, an *injury* to the health, credit, or property. *Damage* means loss and diminished value; as, to insure against *damage* by fire. *Harm* is popularly used for *injury; harm* is usually done by a living agent, with or without intention; as, meddlers do more *harm* than good. *Mischief* also implies *injury* done by a living agent; the word often conveys the idea of minor annoyance of some kind; as, a moment's thoughtlessness may do much *mischief.*

in-jus-tice (ĭn-jŭs'tĭs), *n.* **1,** the quality of being unfair; disregard of another's rights; **2,** injury; wrong.
Syn. grievance, iniquity.—*Ant.* justice, equity, fairness.

ink (ĭngk), *n.* a colored fluid used for writing, printing, etc.; also, a sticky paste used for printing:—*v.t.* **1,** to spread ink upon; **2,** to color or blacken with such a fluid.

ink-horn (ĭngk'hôrn″), *n.* a small, portable receptacle, made of horn, wood, or other material, and formerly used for holding ink and, sometimes, pens, for writing.

ink-i-ness (ĭngk'ĭ-nĕs), *n.* **1,** the state of being covered with ink; **2,** blackness; as, the *inkiness* of the night.

ink-ling (ĭngk'lĭng), *n.* a slight knowledge; hint; suspicion; as, I had an *inkling* of the truth.

ink-stand (ĭngk'stănd″), *n.* **1,** a small receptacle for ink into which a pen may be dipped; **2,** a tray for holding pens, ink, and other articles used for writing.

ink-well (ĭngk'wĕl″), *n.* a cup for ink, fitted into a desk or an inkstand.

ink-y (ĭngk'ĭ), [*comp.* ink'i-er, *superl.* ink'i-est], consisting of, or like, ink; discolored with ink; black.

in-laid (ĭn-lăd'; ĭn'lăd″), *p. adj.* **1,** set into a surface in order to ornament it; as, ivory *inlaid* in ebony; **2,** ornamented with inlaid materials.

in-land (ĭn'lănd), *adj.* **1,** pertaining to, or situated in, the interior of a country; **2,** away from the sea; **3,** domestic; as, *inland* commerce:—*adv.* toward the interior; away from the coast or frontier:—*n.* (ĭn'lănd″), the interior of a country.

in-lay (ĭn-lā'), *v.t.* [*p.t.* and *p.p.* -laid' (-lăd'), *p.pr.* -lay'ing], to ornament (a surface) by setting in pieces of ivory, wood, metal, etc.:—*n.* (ĭn'lā″), materials for inlaying; also, the pattern so formed.

in-let (ĭn'lĕt), *n.* **1,** an entrance; **2,** a small bay or creek; **3,** a thing let or set in.

in-ly (ĭn'lĭ), *adv.* **1,** inwardly; in the innermost parts; **2,** cordially.

in-mate (ĭn'māt), *n.* **1,** a member of a family or body of persons living under one roof; **2,** one who is confined in a prison, lunatic asylum, or the like.

***in me-mo-ri-am** (mē-mō'rĭ-ăm), [Lat.], in memory (of): used in epitaphs, elegies, etc.

in-mesh (ĭn-mĕsh'), *v.t.* to ensnare in a net. Also, **en-mesh'**, *Pfd. S.*

in-most (ĭn'mōst), *adj.* furthest within; as, the *inmost* wish of my heart.

inn (ĭn), *n.* a house for the lodging and entertainment of travelers; tavern.

in-nate (ĭn'nāt; ĭn-nāt'), *adj.* inborn; native; natural; as, *innate* courtesy.—*adv.* **in'nate-ly.**—*n.* **in'nate-ness.**
Syn. inbred, inherent, original.

in-ner (ĭn'ẽr), *adj.* **1,** internal; interior; **2,** pertaining to the mind or soul;

3, in accordance with the true or real nature; as, the *inner* meaning of an act: **Inner Light,** in mystical religions, esp. Quakerism, a guiding enlightenment of the spirit of the individual through its direct contact with God.

in-ner-most (ĭn′ẽr-mōst), *adj.* farthest in from the outside; inmost.

in-ning (ĭn′ĭng), *n.* **1,** in baseball, cricket, etc., one of the divisions of the game during which a single side is at bat or each side in turn is at bat once; **2,** the period when a person or party is in power; **3,** in *pl.*, lands reclaimed from the sea, as swamps.

inn-keep-er (ĭn′kēp″ẽr), *n.* the proprietor, or lessee, of an inn.

in-no-cence (ĭn′ō-sĕns), *n.* **1,** freedom from guilt; purity; **2,** lack of acquaintance with evil; purity of thought and feeling; **3,** simplicity of heart; **4,** harmlessness; **5,** the bluet, or quaker-lady, a delicate meadow plant. Also, **in′no-cen-cy.**

in-no-cent (ĭn′ō-sĕnt), *adj.* **1,** free from guilt or wrongdoing; blameless; **2,** pure in heart and life; **3,** foolishly ignorant; **4,** without evil effect or intention; as, an *innocent* joke; **5,** devoid; as, *innocent* of humor; **6,** harmless; as, an *innocent* medicine:—*n.* **1,** one who is free from, or unacquainted with, sin; **2,** a simpleton.—*adv.* **in′no-cent-ly.**

Syn., adj. guiltless, sinless, inoffensive.—*Ant., adj.* guilty, sinful, wicked, unrighteous.

in-noc-u-ous (ĭ-nŏk′ū-ŭs), *adj.* harmless; safe; innocent; as, an *innocuous* dose.—*adv.* **in-noc′u-ous-ly.**—*n.* **in-noc′u-ous-ness.**

in-no-vate (ĭn′ō-vāt), *v.i.* [*p.t.* and *p.p.* -vat″ed, *p.pr.* -vat″ing], to make changes in something already established; introduce new things.—*n.* **in′no-va″tor.**

in-no-va-tion (ĭn″ō-vā′shŭn), *n.* **1,** the introduction of something new; **2,** a new custom, device, style, or the like.

in-nu-en-do (ĭn″ū-ĕn′dō), *n.* [*pl.* innuendoes (-dōz)], an insinuation; an indirect reference or allusion, usually suggesting something bad or derogatory.

in-nu-mer-a-ble (ĭ-nū′mẽr-*a*-bl; ĭn-nū′-), *adj.* incapable of being counted; as, *innumerable* stars.—*adv.* **in-nu′mer-a-bly.**—*n.* **in-nu″mer-a-bil′i-ty.**

in-oc-u-late (ĭn-ŏk′ū-lāt), *v.t.* [*p.t.* and *p.p.* -lat″ed, *p.pr.* -lat″ing], **1,** to produce a mild case of a disease in (a person), as by the insertion of germs in body tissues, to prevent future attacks; **2,** to inculcate, as harmful ideas, in the mind.

in-oc-u-la-tion (ĭn-ŏk″ū-lā′shŭn), *n.* **1,** the insertion of virus, or the poison of a disease, into body tissues, for the purpose of producing a mild form of the disease in order to ward off future attacks; **2,** inculcation, as of feelings, ideas, etc.

in-o-dor-ous (ĭn-ō′dẽr-ŭs), *adj.* without smell or scent; odorless.

in-of-fen-sive (ĭn″ō-fĕn′sĭv), *adj.* **1,** harmless; **2,** free from disagreeable or disgusting qualities.—*adv.* **in″of-fen′sive-ly.**—*n.* **in″of-fen′sive-ness.**

in-op-er-a-tive (ĭn-ŏp′ẽr-ȧ-tĭv), *adj.* **1,** not active; not capable of acting; **2,** producing no result.

in-op-por-tune (ĭn-ŏp″ŏr-tūn′), *adj.* not ready; not fit; unsuitable; unseasonable.—*adv.* **in-op″por-tune′ly.**—*n.* **in-op″por-tune′ness.**

in-or-di-nate (ĭn-ôr′dĭ-nȧt), *adj.* immoderate; excessive; unrestrained; as, *inordinate* vanity.—*adv.* **in-or′di-nate-ly.**—*n.* **in-or′di-nate-ness.**

Syn. intemperate, disorderly.

in-or-gan-ic (ĭn″ôr-găn′ĭk), *adj.* **1,** without organs; not having the characteristics of a member of the animal or vegetable kingdom; **2,** not formed from living substances; not produced by living organisms; as, rocks are *inorganic* substances: **inorganic chemistry,** that branch of chemistry which treats of substances not containing carbon.

in-quest (ĭn′kwĕst), *n.* **1,** an official inquiry, with the aid of a jury, into a special matter, as the cause of a sudden death; **2,** the body of men making such an inquiry.

in-qui-e-tude (ĭn-kwī′ē-tūd), *n.* **1,** a state of uneasiness or restlessness; **2,** in *pl.*, disturbing thoughts.

in-quire (ĭn-kwīr′), *v.t.* [*p.t.* and *p.p.* -quired′ (-kwīrd′), *p.pr.* -quir′ing], **1,** to seek for or after by questions; **2,** to make examination into: with *for, into, after, about:*—*v.i.* **1,** to ask a question; **2,** to make investigation. Also, **en-quire′.**—*n.* **in-quir′er.**

Syn. ask, question, interrogate.

in-quir-ing (ĭn-kwīr′ĭng), *p.adj.* given to asking questions or making investigations.—*adv.* **in-quir′ing-ly.**

in-quir-y (ĭn-kwīr′ĭ), *n.* [*pl.* inquiries (-ĭz)], **1,** the act of seeking information, knowledge, etc.; research; **2,** an investigation; **3,** a question. Also, **en-quir′y.**

Syn. examination, scrutiny, query.

in-qui-si-tion (ĭn″kwĭ-zĭsh′ŭn), *n.* **1,** inquiry; examination; **2,** an official inquiry in criminal matters, as by a coroner's jury: **Inquisition,** in the Roman Catholic Church, formerly, a court of inquiry dealing with heresy.—*adj.* **in″qui-si′tion-al.**

in-quis-i-tive (ĭn-kwĭz′ĭ-tĭv), *adj.* **1,** given to asking questions; curious; **2,** active in the pursuit of knowledge.—*adv.* **in-quis′i-tive-ly.**

in-quis-i-tor (ĭn-kwĭz′ĭ-tẽr), *n.* **1,** one who makes examinations or investigates; esp., one appointed by law to investigate, as a coroner; **2,** in the Roman Catholic Church, an officer of the Inquisition.

in-quis-i-to-ri-al (ĭn-kwĭz″ĭ-tō′rĭ-ăl), *adj.* **1,** pertaining to an investigator or to his office; **2,** making searching inquiry.—*adv.* **in-quis″i-to′ri-al-ly.**

in-road (ĭn′rōd), *n.* an invasion, esp. if sudden; a forcible entrance.

in-rush (ĭn′rŭsh″), *n.* an influx; a sudden invasion; as, an *inrush* of waters.

in-sane (ĭn-sān′), *adj.* **1,** mentally disordered; mad; deranged; crazy: now avoided in most scientific writing; **2,** very unreasonable; utterly senseless; **3,** intended for the mentally disordered; as, an *insane* asylum.—*adv.* **in-sane′ly.**—*n.* **in-sane′ness.**

in-san-i-ta-ry (ĭn-săn′ĭ-tā-rĭ), *adj.* not healthful; injurious to health; as, *insanitary* plumbing.

in-san-i-ty (ĭn-săn′ĭ-tĭ), *n.* **1,** disorder of mind or intellect; madness; **2,** extravagant folly, or an instance of it.

Syn. frenzy, delirium, mania.

in-sa-ti-a-ble (ĭn-sā′shĭ-*a*-bl; ĭn-sā′sh*a*-bl), *adj.* beyond gratification; immoderate; not to be satisfied; as, an *insatiable* appetite; an *insatiable* ambition.—*adv.* **in-sa′ti-a-bly.**—*n.* **in-sa′ti-a-ble-ness.**—*n.* **in-sa″ti-a-bil′i-ty.**

in-sa-ti-ate (ĭn-sā′shĭ-ȧt), *adj.* beyond gratification; not to be satisfied.—*adv.* **in-sa′ti-ate-ly.**

in-scribe (ĭn-skrīb′), *v.t.* [*p.t.* and *p.p.* -scribed′ (-skrībd′), *p.pr.* -scrib′ing], **1,** to write or engrave, as an inscription; **2,** to mark or engrave upon, as a tablet; **3,** to stamp deeply, as on the memory; **4,** to address formally; as, to *inscribe* a poem to a friend; **5,** in geometry, to draw, as a polygon, within a figure so that certain points of the figure drawn lie in the boundary of the original figure.—*n.* **in-scrib′er.**

in-scrip-tion (ĭn-skrĭp′shŭn), *n.* **1**, the act of writing or engraving, esp. in permanent form; also, anything so written or engraved, as on a monument, picture, coin, or the like; **2**, a brief dedication, as of a book, to a person; **3**, in archæology, writing cut in stone, metal, or the like, preserved from ancient times.—*adj.* **in-scrip′tive.**

in-scru-ta-ble (ĭn-skrōō′tȧ-bl), *adj.* not to be penetrated by inquiry or reason; not to be understood.—*adv.* **in-scru′ta-bly.**—*n.* **in-scru″ta-bil′i-ty.**

in-sect (ĭn′sĕkt), *n.* **1**, any of a numerous class (*Insecta*) of animals, including bugs, bees, flies, etc., having the body divided into three sections (head, thorax, abdomen), and three pairs of jointed legs; **2**, figuratively, a despicable person.

in-sec-ti-cide (ĭn-sĕk′tĭ-sīd), *n.* a substance, as a powder or solution, for killing bugs, flies, etc.

in-sec-ti-vore (ĭn-sĕk′tĭ-vōr), *n.* in zoölogy, any of an order (*Insectivora*) of mammals, comprising many small quadrupeds, as moles, shrews, hedgehogs, etc., that feed chiefly or entirely upon insects.—*adj.* **in″sec-tiv′o-rous.**

in-se-cure (ĭn″sē-kūr′), *adj.* **1**, not firm; unsafe; as, an *insecure* platform; **2**, not shielded or certainly protected from danger; not assured of safety.—*adv.* **in″se-cure′ly.**—*n.* **in″se-cu′ri-ty.**

in-sen-sate (ĭn-sĕn′sāt), *adj.* **1**, without feeling; soulless; mad; brutish; as, *insensate* rage; **2**, stupid; foolish; as, *insensate* fears; **3**, without sensation; lifeless.

in-sen-si-bil-i-ty (ĭn-sĕn″sĭ-bĭl′ĭ-tĭ), *n.* the quality or state of being incapable of physical or mental feeling.

in-sen-si-ble (ĭn-sĕn′sĭ-bl), *adj.* **1**, incapable of feeling; lacking the power to feel; **2**, by slow degrees; gradual; **3**, without feeling or emotion; indifferent; **4**, unconscious.—*adv.* **in-sen′si-bly.**

Syn. numb, unfeeling, impassive, dull.

in-sep-a-ra-ble (ĭn-sĕp′ȧ-rȧ-bl), *adj.* incapable of being divided or parted.—*adv.* **in-sep′a-ra-bly.**—*n.* **in-sep″a-ra-bil′i-ty.**

in-sert (ĭn-sûrt′), *v.t.* to place in or among other things; introduce into:—*n.* (ĭn′sûrt), that which is put in; inset.

in-ser-tion (ĭn-sûr′shŭn), *n.* **1**, the act of putting in; **2**, that which is put in, as a passage in a book; **3**, a band of lace or embroidery in a garment; **4**, the point at which a muscle is attached to the part that is to be moved: opp. of *origin*.

in-set (ĭn′sĕt), *n.* **1**, a leaf or leaves inserted in a newspaper, magazine, etc.; **2**, a smaller cut inserted within the border of a larger one:—*v.t.* (ĭn-sĕt′), [*p.t.* and *p.p.* -set′, *p.pr.* -set′ting], to put in; insert.

in-shore (ĭn′shōr″; ĭn″shōr′), *adv.* near or toward the coast or bank.

in-side (ĭn′sīd″), *adj.* **1**, interior; being within; **2**, *Colloq.*, secret; as, *inside* information:—*adv.* (ĭn″sīd′; ĭn′sīd″), within: **inside of**, *Colloq.*, within the space of:—*n.* (ĭn″sīd′), that which is within; inner part; contents:—*prep.* on the inner side of; within.

in-sid-er (ĭn″sīd′ẽr), *n.* one who is so situated as to be able to get reliable information not available to the public.

in-sid-i-ous (ĭn-sĭd′ĭ-ŭs), *adj.* treacherous; deceitful; operating secretly; as, an *insidious* disease.—*adv.* **in-sid′i-ous-ly.**—*n.* **in-sid′i-ous-ness.**

in-sight (ĭn′sīt″), *n.* **1**, penetration; mental vision; as, poetic *insight;* **2**, an understanding of the inner nature of things.

in-sig-ni-a (ĭn-sĭg′nĭ-ȧ), *n.pl.* [*sing.* insigne (-nē)], badges of honor or office; as, the crown and scepter were the ancient *insignia* of the power of a king; hence, distinguishing marks of any kind; as, the *insignia* of a profession or society.

in-sig-nif-i-cance (ĭn″sĭg-nĭf′ĭ-kăns), *n.* unimportance; triviality; pettiness. Also, **in″sig-nif′i-can-cy.**

in-sig-nif-i-cant (ĭn″sĭg-nĭf′ĭ-kănt), *adj.* **1**, without importance, force, influence, or meaning; **2**, trifling; mean; small.—*adv.* **in″sig-nif′i-cant-ly.**

Syn. petty, trivial, unimportant.

in-sin-cere (ĭn″sĭn-sēr′), *adj.* deceptive; false; not to be trusted; hypocritical.—*adv.* **in″sin-cere′ly.**

in-sin-cer-i-ty (ĭn″sĭn-sĕr′ĭ-tĭ), *n.* deception; lack of candor.

in-sin-u-ate (ĭn-sĭn′ū-āt), *v.t.* [*p.t.* and *p.p.* -at″ed, *p.pr.* -at″ing], **1**, to push, work, or introduce by slow, gentle, or artful means, as into the confidence or affections; **2**, to suggest or hint indirectly; as, do you mean to *insinuate* that I lie? **3**, to introduce, as by a winding motion; worm in.—*adj.* **in-sin′u-a-tive.**—*n.* **in-sin′u-a″tor.**

Syn. imply, intimate; infuse, instil.

in-sin-u-a-tion (ĭn-sĭn″ū-ā′shŭn), *n.* **1**, an indirect or sly hint; as, he slandered them more by *insinuations* than by direct statements; **2**, the act of hinting or suggesting slyly; **3**, a worming in, as into a crevice; **4**, ingratiation; also, a case of this.

in-sip-id (ĭn-sĭp′ĭd), *adj.* **1**, without flavor; tasteless; **2**, uninteresting; as, *insipid* conversation.—*adv.* **in-sip′id-ly.**—*n.* **in-sip′id-ness.**

Syn. dull, flat, stale; lifeless, unanimated. —*Ant.* tasty; bright, sparkling, lively.

in-si-pid-i-ty (ĭn″sĭ-pĭd′ĭ-tĭ), *n.* the quality of being tasteless or dull.

in-sist (ĭn-sĭst′), *v.i.* **1**, to urge or press a wish or command: with *on* or *upon;* **2**, to stand and refuse to give way; persist.

Syn. persist. *Insist* is used chiefly in a good sense, meaning to assert or demand a thing; its force is directed toward the action of others. *Persist* implies personal determination, or often obstinacy; it is used in a bad sense. He *persists* in his evil ways, but he *insists* that the children obey the laws.

in-sist-ence (ĭn-sĭs′tĕns), *n.* the act of persisting or holding fast; perseverance. Also, **in-sist′en-cy.**

in-sist-ent (ĭn-sĭs′tĕnt), *adj.* urgent; compelling attention; persistent.—*adv.* **in-sist′ent-ly.**

in-snare (ĭn-snâr′), *v.t.* [*p.t.* and *p.p.* -snared′ (-snârd′), *p.pr.* -snar′ing], to catch in a trap. Also, **en-snare′.**

in-so-bri-e-ty (ĭn″sō-brī′ĕ-tĭ), *n.* intemperance; drunkenness.

in-sole (ĭn′sōl″), *n.* **1**, the part of the sole inside a boot or shoe; **2**, a removable sole put inside a shoe.

in-so-lence (ĭn′sō-lĕns), *n.* contemptuous or haughty language or manner; offensive impertinence; impudence.

in-so-lent (ĭn′sō-lĕnt), *adj.* **1**, haughty or contemptuously offensive to others; **2**, insulting; rude.—*adv.* **in′so-lent-ly.**

Syn. saucy, pert, impertinent, abusive, impudent.—*Ant.* respectful, mannerly, mild.

in-sol-u-ble (ĭn-sŏl′ū-bl), *adj.* **1**, incapable of being dissolved; as, fat is *insoluble* in cold water; **2**, not to be explained; as, an *insoluble* mystery; **3**, of a debt, not capable of being paid off.—*n.* **in-sol′u-ble-ness.**—*n.* **in-sol″u-bil′i-ty.**

in-sol-ven-cy (ĭn-sŏl′vĕn-sĭ), *n.* [*pl.* insolvencies (-sĭz)], the state of being unable to pay debts; bankruptcy.

in-sol-vent (ĭn-sŏl′vĕnt), *adj.* **1**, unable to pay all debts; bankrupt;

2, pertaining to bankrupts:—*n*. one who cannot pay his debts; a bankrupt.

in-som-ni-a (ĭn-sŏm′nĭ-*ȧ*), *n*. sleeplessness; chronic wakefulness; as, *insomnia* is often caused by overwork.

in-so-much (ĭn″sō-mŭch′), *adv*. in such manner; to such a degree: usually followed by *that* or *as*.

in-spect (ĭn-spĕkt′), *v.t*. **1**, to examine closely and carefully, in order to find possible faults; investigate; as, to *inspect* all farms where milk is sold; **2**, to review officially, as troops.

in-spec-tion (ĭn-spĕk′shŭn), *n*. careful or critical examination.

in-spec-tor (ĭn-spĕk′tẽr), *n*. **1**, one who examines or oversees; **2**, an official who superintends some matter of public interest; **3**, a police officer ranking next below a superintendent.

in-spi-ra-tion (ĭn″spĭ-rā′shŭn), *n*. **1**, the act of drawing air into the lungs; **2**, the influence or impulse which causes creation in art, literature, music, etc.; **3**, the supernatural influence of the Holy Spirit, suggesting a message or a plan of action.—*adj*. **in″spi-ra′tion-al.**

in-spire (ĭn-spīr′), *v.t*. [*p.t*. and *p.p*. -spired′ (-spīrd′), *p.pr*. -spir′ing], **1**, to draw (air) into the lungs; **2**, to fill with ideas; as, to *inspire* a child with hatred of wrong; **3**, to control or guide by supernatural influence; as, God *inspired* the ancient prophets; **4**, to kindle, as an idea:—*v.i*. to draw air into the lungs.—*n*. **in-spir′er.**—*adj*. **in-spir′a-ble.**

Syn. animate, instil, enliven, impart, encourage.—*Ant*. dispirit, depress, discourage.

in-spired (ĭn-spīrd′), *p.adj*. **1**, affected by a supernatural influence; as, an *inspired* preacher; **2**, presented or suggested to the mind by someone else; as, an *inspired* speech.

in-spir-it (ĭn-spĭr′ĭt), *v.t*. to give life or vitality to; exhilarate; cheer.—*adv*. **in-spir′it-ing-ly.**

in-spis-sate (ĭn-spĭs′āt), *v.t*. [*p.t*. and *p.p*. -sat-ed, *p.pr*. -sat-ing], to thicken, as by evaporation:—*v.i*. to grow thick.—*n*. **in″spis-sa′tion.**

in-sta-bil-i-ty (ĭn″st*ȧ*-bĭl′ĭ-tĭ), *n*. [*pl*. instabilities (-tĭz)], want of firmness; inconstancy; fickleness.

Syn. mutability, changeableness.—*Ant*. constancy, steadiness, firmness.

in-stall (ĭn-stôl′), *v.t*. **1**, to establish with the usual ceremonies in an office or position; **2**, to put into condition for use; as, to *install* an electric lighting system.

in-stal-la-tion (ĭn″stô-lā′shŭn), *n*. **1**, the act of formally establishing in an office or position; **2**, the setting up in position for service, as machinery; **3**, the apparatus so set up.

in-stal-ment (ĭn-stôl′mĕnt), *n*. **1**, the act of establishing in a position or office; **2**, a part of a sum of money to be paid part by part at stated times; **3**, one of a number of parts of anything produced one part at a time; as, an *instalment* of a serial story. Also, **in-stall′ment.**

in-stance (ĭn′stăns), *v.t*. [*p.t*. and *p.p*. -stanced (-stănst), *p.pr*. -stanc-ing], to refer to, or offer as an example:—*n*. **1**, something offered as an illustration or example; **2**, a suggestion; request; as, a work begun at the *instance* of the publishers.

Syn., *n*. (see specimen).

in-stant (ĭn′stănt), *adj*. **1**, urgent; insistent; **2**, immediate; direct; **3**, imminent; **4**, of the present month: usually written *inst*.; as, yours of the fourth *inst*.:—*n*. **1**, a particular moment of time; **2**, a very small portion of time; a second.

in-stan-ta-ne-ous (ĭn″stăn-tā′nē-ŭs), *adj*. **1**, acting or occurring in a moment; **2**, at a given moment.—*adv*. **in″stan-ta′ne-ous-ly.**

in-stan-ter (ĭn-stăn′tẽr), *adv*. *Colloq*., immediately; without delay.

in-stant-ly (ĭn′stănt-lĭ), *adv*. at once; without delay:—*conj*. as soon as.

Syn., *adv*. directly, immediately.

in-state (ĭn-stāt′), *v.t*. [*p.t*. and *p.p*. -stat′ed, *p.pr*. -stat′ing], to put in office or rank; install.

in-stead (ĭn-stĕd′), *adv*. **1**, in room or place: followed by *of*; as, I will go *instead* of you; **2**, in place; as, do not take that chair, take this *instead*.

in-step (ĭn′stĕp), *n*. **1**, the arched fore part of the upper side of the human foot; **2**, part of the hind leg of a horse; **3**, a part, as of a stocking, covering the instep.

in-sti-gate (ĭn′stĭ-gāt), *v.t*. [*p.t*. and *p.p*. -gat″ed, *p.pr*. -gat″ing], to provoke or urge on: usually in a bad sense; as, to *instigate* one to murder.—*n*. **in″sti-ga′tion.**—*n*. **in′sti-ga″tor.**

Syn. impel, incite, stimulate, encourage.

in-still (ĭn-stĭl′), *v.t*. [*p.t*. and *p.p*. -stilled′ (-stĭld′), *p.pr*. -still′ing], **1**, to pour in by drops; **2**, to introduce gradually; as, to *instill* the principle of self-reliance. Also, **in-stil′.**—*n*. **in-still′ment; in-stil′ment.**

Syn. implant, inculcate, infuse.

in-stil-la-tion (ĭn″stĭ-lā′shŭn), *n*. **1**, act of pouring in drop by drop; also, that which is instilled; **2**, the act of infusing gradually, as ideas.

in-stinct (ĭn-stĭngkt′), *adj*. charged or filled with; as, creatures *instinct* with life:—*n*. (ĭn′stĭngkt), **1**, a natural impulse in animals; involuntary urge; **2**, a natural tendency; as, an *instinct* for direction.

in-stinc-tive (ĭn-stĭngk′tĭv), *adj*. acting or prompted by natural impulse; as, self-defense is *instinctive* in all creatures.—*adv*. **in-stinc′tive-ly.**

in-sti-tute (ĭn′stĭ-tūt), *v.t*. [*p.t*. and *p.p*. -tut″ed, *p.pr*. -tut″ing], **1**, to establish; set up; fix; originate; **2**, to set in operation; as, to *institute* a new custom:—*n*. **1**, an established law or principle; **2**, an institution or place of education; as, an *institute* of technology; **3**, a building devoted to the work of such an organization.

in-sti-tu-tion (ĭn″stĭ-tū′shŭn), *n*. **1**, the act of establishing; **2**, that which is established; as, church, home, and school are fundamental *institutions*; **3**, an organized body or society for promoting a particular object; **4**, the building for carrying on the work of such an organization.

in-sti-tu-tion-al (ĭn″stĭ-tū′shŭn-ăl), *adj*. **1**, of or pertaining to an establishment; **2**, established.

in-sti-tu-tor (ĭn′stĭ-tū″tẽr), *n*. a founder; one who establishes.

in-struct (ĭn-strŭkt′), *v.t*. **1**, to teach; educate; **2**, to furnish with orders or directions; **3**, to inform; advise; counsel.

Syn. direct, train. (See advise.)

in-struc-tion (ĭn-strŭk′shŭn), *n*. **1**, the act of teaching; **2**, knowledge imparted; **3**, in *pl*., orders or directions.

Syn. direction. (See education.)

in-struc-tion-al (ĭn-strŭk′shŭn-ăl), *adj*. **1**, pertaining to orders or teaching; **2**, conveying information.

in-struc-tive (ĭn-strŭk′tĭv), *adj*. tending to inform; giving knowledge.—*adv*. **in-struc′tive-ly.**

in-struc-tor (ĭn-strŭk′tẽr), *n*. **1**, one who gives knowledge; a teacher; **2**, in American colleges, a teacher ranking below a professor.—*n.fem*. **in-struc′tress.**

in-stru-ment (ĭn′strōō-mĕnt), *n.* **1**, that by which anything is accomplished; an agent; a means; **2**, a mechanical device; a tool; **3**, a mechanical contrivance for producing musical sounds; **4**, in law, a formal writing of any kind.

in-stru-men-tal (ĭn″strōō-mĕn′tăl), *adj.* **1**, helping to bring about some end; as, mountain air is often *instrumental* in restoring health; **2**, performed on, or composed for, a musical instrument or instruments.—*adv.* **in″stru-men′tal-ly.**

in-stru-men-tal-i-ty (ĭn″strōō-mĕn-tăl′ĭ-tĭ), *n.* [*pl.* instrumentalities (-tĭz)], an agency; a means.

in-stru-men-ta-tion (ĭn″strōō-mĕn-tā′shŭn), *n.* **1**, the arrangement of music for a number of instruments; **2**, the use of, or the method of using, a scientific or surgical instrument.

in-sub-or-di-nate (ĭn″sŭb-ôr′dĭ-nāt), *adj.* not submitting to authority; disobedient; mutinous; rebellious.—*adv.* **in″sub-or′di-nate-ly.**

in-sub-or-di-na-tion (ĭn″sŭb-ôr″dĭ-nā′shŭn), *n.* physical or mental resistance to authority.

in-sub-stan-tial (ĭn″sŭb-stăn′shăl), *adj.* not having solidity; frail; unreal; flimsy.—*adv.* **in″sub-stan′tial-ly.**

in-suf-fer-a-ble (ĭn-sŭf′ĕr-*ȧ*-bl), *adj.* not to be borne; as, *insufferable* conduct.—*adv.* **in-suf′fer-a-bly.**

in-suf-fi-cient (ĭn″sŭ-fĭsh′ĕnt), *adj.* deficient in quality, amount, power, etc.; inadequate.—*adv.* **in″suf-fi′cient-ly.**—*n.* **in″suf-fi′cien-cy.**

in-su-lar (ĭn′sū-l*ȧ*r), *adj.* **1**, pertaining to an island or to the inhabitants of an island, their customs, etc.; **2**, standing alone; narrow-minded; prejudiced.

in-su-lar-i-ty (ĭn″sū-lăr′ĭ-tĭ),*n.* **1**, the state of being an island; **2**, narrowness of opinions, ideas, associations, etc.

in-su-late (ĭn′sū-lāt), *v.t.* [*p.t.* and *p.p.* -lat″ed, *p.pr.* -lat″ing], **1**, to place alone, or in a separate situation; **2**, in physics, to separate by, or inclose in, a material that will not conduct electricity, heat, etc.

in-su-la-tion (ĭn″sū-lā′shŭn), *n.* **1**, the act of separating by, or inclosing in, materials that will not conduct heat, electricity, or sound; **2**, the state of being separated by such materials.

in-su-la-tor (ĭn′sū-lā″tĕr), *n.* **1**, one that insulates; **2**, a material that does not carry electricity, heat, or sound.

in-su-lin (ĭn′sū-lĭn), *n.* a preparation from certain parts of the pancreas of oxen, sheep, and the like, used in order to retard the formation of sugar in the blood of diabetic patients.

in-sult (ĭn′sŭlt), *n.* **1**, an affront or indignity; **2**, gross abuse in word or action:—*v.t.* (ĭn-sŭlt′), to treat with gross contempt, or abuse, by word or act.

Syn., *v.* affront, outrage, mock.

in-sult-ing (ĭn-sŭlt′ĭng), *p.adj.* containing, or intending, offense or affront.

in-su-per-a-ble (ĭn-sū′pĕr-*ȧ*-bl), *adj.* not to be overcome; as, *insuperable* difficulties.—*n.* **in-su′per-a-ble-ness.**—*adv.* **in-su′per-a-bly.**

in-sup-port-a-ble (ĭn″sŭ-pōr′t*ȧ*-bl), *adj.* not capable of being endured; insufferable.—*adv.* **in″sup-port′a-bly.**

in-sur-a-ble (ĭn-shōōr′*ȧ*-bl), *adj.* suitable or proper to be insured against loss, damage, etc.

in-sur-ance (ĭn-shōōr′ăns), *n.* **1**, a system of protection against the risk of individual loss, by distributing the burden of losses over a large number of individuals; **2**, a contract whereby, in consideration of a certain payment called a *premium*, one party agrees, in case of loss by fire, accident, death, etc., to pay the other party a stated sum of money; **3**, the sum paid for the insuring; the premium; **4**, the amount for which anything is insured.

in-sure (ĭn-shōōr′), *v.t.* [*p.t.* and *p.p.* -sured′ (-shōōrd′), *p.pr.* -sur′ing], **1**, to secure against loss or damage in return for the payment of a premium; **2**, to make sure or secure, as property, by the payment of a premium:—*v.i.* to contract to give security against loss or damage; underwrite. Also, **en-sure′.**—*n.* **in-sur′er; in-su′ror.**

in-sured (ĭn-shōōrd′), *n.* one secured by a contract of insurance.

in-sur-gence (ĭn-sûr′jĕns), *n.* a revolt; an uprising against authority or government; rebellion.

in-sur-gent (ĭn-sûr′jĕnt), *adj.* rising against authority:—*n.* a rebel: **Insurgent,** in the U. S., a member of a section of the Republican party which has advocated progressive policies.

Syn., *adj.* rebellious, mutinous.

in-sur-mount-a-ble (ĭn″sŭr-moun′t*ȧ*-bl), *adj.* insuperable; not to be overcome.—*adv.* **in″sur-mount′a-bly.**—*n.* **in″sur-mount″a-bil′i-ty.**

in-sur-rec-tion (ĭn″sŭ-rĕk′shŭn), *n.* active or open rebellion against authority; revolt.

Syn. mutiny, uprising. (See revolution.)

in-sur-rec-tion-a-ry (ĭn″sŭ-rĕk′shŭn-ā-rĭ), *adj.* pertaining to, or engaged in, active or open rebellion; as, *insurrectionary* ideas.

in-sur-rec-tion-ist (ĭn″sŭ-rĕk′shŭn-ĭst), *n.* one who takes part in a rebellion; an insurgent.

in-sus-cep-ti-ble (ĭn″sŭ-sĕp′tĭ-bl), *adj.* not easy to influence or impress.—*n.* **in″sus-cep″ti-bil′i-ty.**

in-tact (ĭn-tăkt′), *adj.* entire; uninjured; untouched, as by anything harmful.

in-tagl-io (ĭn-tăl′yō; *It.* ĕn-täl′yō), *n.* [*pl.* intaglios (-yōz); intagli (-yē)], **1**, a carved design or figure, as a die, in any hard material; **2**, a gem or stone having a design cut into the surface: opp. of *cameo;* **3**, the art of making intaglios: chiefly in the phrase *in intaglio;* **4**, a countersunk die for producing a design in relief: **intaglio printing,** printing from an engraved surface.

in-take (ĭn′tāk″), *n.* **1**, a thing taken in; also, a taking in, as of breath; **2**, the place where a fluid enters a pipe, channel, etc.; **3**, a narrowing, as in a stocking.

in-tan-gi-ble (ĭn-tăn′jĭ-bl), *adj.* incapable of being touched; hence, vague; not easily expressed or defined; as, the beauty of a poem is *intangible.*—*adv.* **in-tan′gi-bly.**—*n.* **in-tan″gi-bil′i-ty.**

in-te-ger (ĭn′tē-jĕr), *n.* **1**, an entity; **2**, a whole number, as 1, 2, 3, etc.

in-te-gral (ĭn′tē-grăl), *adj.* **1**, constituting a whole; complete; **2**, belonging to a whole number; **3**, necessary as a part:—*n.* a whole made up of parts.

in-te-grate (ĭn′tē-grāt), *v.t.* [*p.t.* and *p.p.* -grat″ed, *p.pr.* -grat″ing], **1**, to bring together the parts of; **2**, to give the sum total of:—*v.i.* to become complete or perfect.—*n.* **in″te-gra′tion.**

in-teg-ri-ty (ĭn-tĕg′rĭ-tĭ), *n.* **1**, uprightness; virtue; honesty; **2**, soundness; uninjured state; **3**, unbroken condition; completeness.

in-teg-u-ment (ĭn-tĕg′ū-mĕnt), *n.* a covering, as a skin or husk.

in-tel-lect (ĭn′tē-lĕkt), *n.* **1**, the powers of the mind that know and reason: distinguished from *feeling* and *will;* **2**, the power to reason, or think abstractly.

in-tel-lec-tu-al (ĭn″tĕ-lĕk′tū-ăl), *adj.* **1**, pertaining to, or performed by, the mind; **2**, endowed with powers of understanding above the ordinary; **3**, exercising the mind; as, *intellectual* pursuits:—*n.* a person of superior mentality; as, Bacon was an *intellectual.*—*adv.* **in″tel-lec′tu-al-ly.**

Syn., adj. intelligent, mental. *Intellectual* applies to whatever pertains to the intellect, as opposed to the emotions or to the physical body; it is also applied to persons. *Intelligent* describes those endowed with mind, and is applied to animals as well as human beings; it implies quickness, shrewdness, and comprehension. *Mental* is applied to whatever pertains to, or is done by, the mind; as, *mental* discipline; *mental* arithmetic.

in-tel-lec-tu-al-ism (ĭn″tĕ-lĕk′tū-ăl-ĭsm), *n.* **1**, the exercise of mental power; devotion to intellectual pursuits; **2**, the doctrine that all knowledge comes from pure reason.

in-tel-lec-tu-al-i-ty (ĭn″tĕ-lĕk″tū-ăl′ĭ-tĭ), *n.* [*pl.* intellectualities (-tĭz)], trained intelligence; the power of reasoning abstractly.

in-tel-li-gence (ĭn-tĕl′ĭ-jĕns), *n.* **1**, ability to learn, to profit by experience, or to acquire knowledge; comprehension; understanding; **2**, ability for reasoning and abstract thinking; intellect; **3**, ability to meet a new situation, to solve a problem, or to manage one's affairs effectively; common sense; **4**, that which possesses these abilities or powers of mind; as, the supreme *Intelligence;* **5**, information or news, particularly secret information, as that secured for government use during war time: **intelligence quotient**, a figure equal to 100 times the result of dividing the mental age rating given an individual in some intelligence test by his actual age in years, persons of sixteen years or older being considered to have an actual age of sixteen: generally abbreviated to *I. Q.:* **intelligence test**, any question, task, problem, or controlled situation used in measuring the degree of intelligence of persons or animals, or a series of such tests, used for classifying them.

Syn. tidings, report. (See news.)

in-tel-li-genc-er (ĭn-tĕl′ĭ-jĕn-sẽr), *n.* a person who conveys news or information; esp., a spy.

in-tel-li-gent (ĭn-tĕl′ĭ-jĕnt), *adj.* **1**, capable of purposeful mental activity, or of reasoning or learning by experience; **2**, showing comprehension; as, an *intelligent* answer.—*adv.* **in-tel′li-gent-ly.**

Syn. bright, knowing, sensible. (See intellectual.)—*Ant.* dull, stupid, ignorant.

in-tel-li-gent-si-a (ĭn-tĕl″ĭ-jĕnt′sĭ-ȧ), *n.* collectively, the educated or intellectual classes.

in-tel-li-gi-ble (ĭn-tĕl′ĭ-jĭ-bl), *adj.* capable of being understood; clear; as, an *intelligible* explanation.—*adv.* **in-tel′li-gi-bly.**—*n.* **in-tel″li-gi-bil′i-ty.**

Syn. obvious, plain, distinct.

in-tem-per-ance (ĭn-tĕm′pẽr-ăns), *n.* want of moderation or self-control; excess, esp. in the use of alcoholic liquors; intemperateness.

in-tem-per-ate (ĭn-tĕm′pẽr-ȧt), *adj.* **1**, characterized by want of moderation or self-control; **2**, severe; excessive; **3**, addicted to alcoholic liquors.—*adv.* **in-tem′per-ate-ly.**—*n.* **in-tem′per-ate-ness.**

Syn. immoderate, inordinate.—*Ant.* temperate, reasonable, moderate.

in-tend (ĭn-tĕnd′), *v.t.* **1**, to purpose; mean; as, we *intend* to win the war; **2**, to design (a thing) for some purpose.

in-tend-an-cy (ĭn-tĕn′dăn-sĭ), *n.* [*pl.* intendancies (-sĭz)], **1**, the duties or office of an intendant; also, a body of intendants; **2**, a territorial district in one of the Spanish American countries.

in-tend-ant (ĭn-tĕn′dănt), *n.* **1**, one who has direction of a public business; a superintendent; as, an *intendant* of a hospital; **2**, in Spanish American countries, an official in charge of a district.

in-tend-ed (ĭn-tĕn′dĕd), *adj.* **1**, purposed; as, the *intended* meaning of a remark; **2**, *Colloq.*, betrothed:—*n. Colloq.*, the person to whom one is engaged to be married.

in-tense (ĭn-tĕns′), *adj.* **1**, extreme in degree; excessive; **2**, intent; ardent; eager.—*adv.* **in-tense′ly.**—*n.* **in-tense′ness.**

Syn. earnest, vehement, fervid.

in-ten-si-fy (ĭn-tĕn′sĭ-fī), *v.t.* [*p.t.* and *p.p.* -fied (-fīd), *p.pr.* -fy″ing], to make greater in degree.—*n.* **in-ten′si-fi″er.**

Syn. aggravate, enhance, increase.

in-ten-sion (ĭn-tĕn′shŭn), *n.* **1**, determination; **2**, increase of energy.

in-ten-si-ty (ĭn-tĕn′sĭ-tĭ), *n.* [*pl.* intensities (-tĭz)], **1**, the state or quality of being extreme; extreme strength, force, or energy; as, he spoke with great *intensity;* **2**, degree or amount; as, the candle increased the *intensity* of the gloom.

in-ten-sive (ĭn-tĕn′sĭv), *adj.* **1**, increasing, or causing to increase, in degree or amount; **2**, of or pertaining to the degree of force, strength, depth, etc., of anything; **3**, deep and thorough rather than broad; as, *intensive* study of a short period of history; **4**, designating that method of agriculture which gets results by careful cultivation, usually of a relatively small area; **5**, in grammar, giving emphasis, as certain prefixes.—*adv.* **in-ten′sive-ly.**

in-tent (ĭn-tĕnt′), *adj.* having the mind closely fixed on a subject; diligent; intense:—*n.* **1**, purpose; aim; **2**, meaning.—*adv.* **in-tent′ly.**—*n.* **in-tent′ness.**

Syn., n. intention, purport. (See plan.)

in-ten-tion (ĭn-tĕn′shŭn), *n.* **1**, purpose; design; aim; as, his *intention* was good; **2**, meaning.

Syn. object, intent. (See plan.)

in-ten-tion-al (ĭn-tĕn′shŭn-ăl), *adj.* done on purpose; as, an *intentional* wrong.—*adv.* **in-ten′tion-al-ly.**

in-ter (ĭn-tûr′), *v.t.* [*p.t.* and *p.p.* -terred′ (-tûrd′), *p.pr.* -ter′ring], to bury.

in-ter- (ĭn′tẽr-), *prefix*, **1**, among; between; as, *inter*cede; *inter*costal; **2**, together; mutually; as, *inter*lock.

in-ter-act (ĭn″tẽr-ăkt′), *v.i.* to influence each other; have mutual effect.

in-ter-ac-tion (ĭn″tẽr-ăk′shŭn), *n.* the effect on one thing by another; mutual influence.

in-ter-breed (ĭn″tẽr-brēd′), *v.i.* and *v.t.* [*p.t.* and *p.p.* -bred′ (-brĕd′), *p.pr.* -breed′ing], to propagate by crossing different varieties, kinds, or stocks.

in-ter-ca-la-ry (ĭn-tûr′kȧ-lā-rĭ), *adj.* **1**, inserted in the calendar, as February 29 in leap year; **2**, of a year, having added days or an added month; **3**, interpolated.

in-ter-ca-late (ĭn-tûr′kȧ-lāt), *v.t.* [*p.t.* and *p.p.* -lat″ed, *p.pr.* -lat″ing], **1**, to insert, as a day, in the calendar; **2**, to interpolate.—*n.* **in-ter″ca-la′tion.**

in-ter-cede (ĭn″tẽr-sēd′), *v.i.* [*p.t.* and *p.p.* -ced′ed, *p.pr.* -ced′ing], **1**, to mediate as a friend between persons who are unfriendly; **2**, to plead for another.

in-ter-cel-lu-lar (ĭn″tẽr-sĕl′ū-lȧr), *adj.* lying between cells.

in-ter-cept (ĭn″tẽr-sĕpt′), *v.t.* **1**, to seize by the way, as a message; **2**, to obstruct, as a view; come in the way of; **3**, in mathematics, to include between two points or lines.—*n.* **in″ter-cep′tion.**

in-ter-ces-sion (ĭn″tẽr-sĕsh′ŭn), *n.* **1**, the act of trying to restore friendship between two who are separated by disagreement; mediation; **2**, the act of pleading in behalf of another.

in-ter-ces-sor (ĭn″tẽr-sĕs′ẽr), *n.* **1**, one who tries to restore friendly relations between two who are parted by differences; **2**, one who pleads for another.—*adj.* **in″ter-ces′so-ry.**

in-ter-change (ĭn″tẽr-chānj′), *v.t.* [*p.t.* and *p.p.* -changed′ (-chānjd′), *p.pr.* -chang′ing], **1**, to put one thing in the place of another; **2**, to vary; **3**, to exchange, as opinions, gifts, etc.:—*n.* (ĭn′tẽr-chānj″), **1**, the exchange of two things, one for the other; **2**, alternate sequence, as of seasons.

in-ter-change-a-ble (ĭn″tẽr-chān′jȧ-bl), *adj.* **1**, capable of being put in place of each other or substituted; **2**, capable of being exchanged.—*n.* **in″ter-change′a-ble-ness.**—*adv.* **in″ter-change′a-bly.**—*n.* **in″-ter-change″a-bil′i-ty.**

in-ter-col-le-gi-ate (ĭn″tẽr-kō-lē′jĭ-āt), *adj.* carried on, or existing, between colleges or universities.

in-ter-com-mu-ni-cate (ĭn″tẽr-kō-mū′nĭ-kāt), *v.t.* [*p.t.* and *p.p.* -cat″ed, *p.pr.* -cat″ing], to impart or convey mutually:—*v.i.* to communicate with one another.

in-ter-cos-tal (ĭn″tẽr-kŏs′tăl), *adj.* between the ribs; as, *intercostal* rheumatism or neuralgia.

in-ter-course (ĭn′tẽr-kōrs), *n.* connection, correspondence, or communication between individuals, nations, etc.; exchange; familiarity; fellowship.

in-ter-de-pend-ence (ĭn″tẽr-dē-pĕn′dĕns), *n.* the state of being mutually dependent; as, the *interdependence* of nations. Also, **in″ter-de-pend′en-cy.**—*adj.* **in″ter-de-pend′ent.**

in-ter-dict (ĭn″tẽr-dĭkt′), *v.t.* **1**, to restrain or forbid; **2**, to cut off from the spiritual services of the church:—*n.* (ĭn′-tẽr-dĭkt), **1**, a formal prohibition; **2**, in the Roman Catholic Church, an order from the Pope debarring a person or place from ecclesiastical privilege.—*n.* **in″ter-dic′tion.**

Syn., *v.* prohibit, inhibit, debar.

in-ter-est (ĭn′tẽr-ĕst), *n.* **1**, benefit; as, he acts for the public *interest;* **2**, that which concerns one, or the feeling that something concerns one; also, that which arouses such a feeling; as, suspense gives *interest* to a story; **3**, consideration for personal or selfish profit; **4**, personal influence over the action of others; as, he used his *interest* with the president; **5**, a share or part ownership in a business or other project; **6**, a sum paid for the use of money; **7**, in psychology, the tendency to give attention to an object, situation, or idea, in spite of distracting influences; **8**, in *pl.*, the persons concerned in some field of business or industry, taken collectively; as, the coal *interests:* **simple interest**, interest paid on the principal only, or the amount loaned: **compound interest**, interest paid on the sum of the principal and any interest due but not paid, such unpaid interest, as it falls due, being added to the principal:—*v.t.* **1**, to engage the attention of; arouse to curiosity, sympathy, or the like; **2**, to cause to take a share in; as, to *interest* oneself in politics; **3**, to produce an effect upon.

in-ter-est-ed (ĭn′tẽr-ĕs-tĕd), *p.adj.* **1**, having the feelings or emotions excited or held; **2**, concerned; **3**, having a share or a responsibility in.

in-ter-est-ing (ĭn′tẽr-ĕst-ĭng), *p.adj.* **1**, engaging the attention or curiosity; **2**, exciting the feelings or emotions.

in-ter-fere (ĭn″tẽr-fēr′), *v.i.* [*p.t.* and *p.p.* -fered′ (-fērd′), *p.pr.* -fer′ing], **1**, to enter into, or meddle in, the affairs of others; **2**, to come into collision; **3**, to strike the fetlock with the opposite hoof: said of a horse; **4**, in physics, to interact so as to modify the effect of one another, as sound waves, which, through interference, produce beats.

in-ter-fer-ence (ĭn″tẽr-fēr′ĕns), *n.* **1**, opposition; obstruction; objection or hindrance; **2**, the act of meddling in another person's affairs; **3**, in physics, the effect produced when two or more vibrations or trains of waves are superposed so as to strengthen or neutralize one another, producing, in the case of sound waves, beats; **4**, in radio, the overlapping or intermixing of electric waves from different sending stations, or from atmospheric or other disturbances, resulting in confusion at receiving stations.

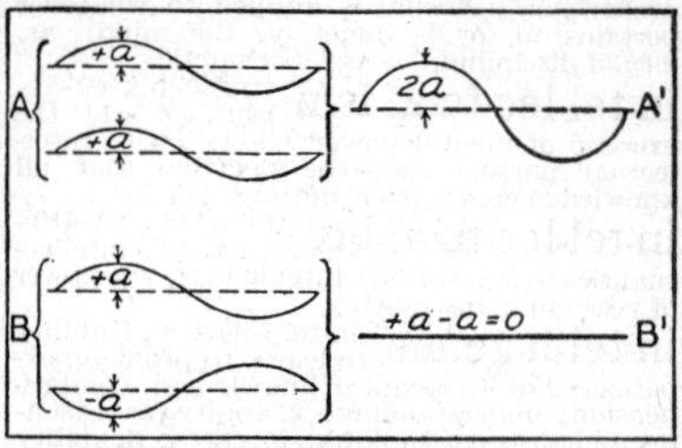

REËNFORCEMENT AND INTERFERENCE

In diagram A, a wave motion, as of sound, with amplitude *a*, is accompanied by another of the same amplitude vibrating with it (that is, in the same phase), producing by reënforcement the effect of a single wave motion A′ (equivalent to a sound of double intensity), with amplitude $a+a$, or $2a$.—In B, the wave motions vibrate against each other (that is, in opposite phase), producing by interference the effect, with amplitude $a-a$, or 0, shown by the straight line B′ (equivalent to silence).

in-ter-fuse (ĭn″tẽr-fūz′), *v.t.* [*p.t.* and *p.p.* -fused′ (-fūzd′), *p.pr.* -fus′ing], **1**, to cause to flow together; **2**, to cause to blend; **3**, to spread through; pervade.—*n.* **in″ter-fu′sion.**

in-ter-im (ĭn′tẽr-ĭm), *n.* intervening time or period:—*adj.* temporary.

in-te-ri-or (ĭn-tē′rĭ-ẽr), *adj.* **1**, inner; internal; **2**, far from the coast or frontier:—*n.* **1**, the inside, as of a building or room; **2**, the inland part of a country; **3**, the home affairs of a country; also, the government department dealing with them; as, the Secretary of the *Interior.*—*adv.* **in-te′ri-or-ly.**

in-ter-ject (ĭn″tẽr-jĕkt′), *v.t.* and *v.i.* to put in; insert; thrust in.

in-ter-jec-tion (ĭn″tẽr-jĕk′shŭn), *n.* **1**, an exclamation; **2**, the act of exclaiming; **3**, a word thrown in without grammatical connection to express sudden feeling, as *Alas!*—*adj.* **in″ter-jec′tion-al.**

in-ter-lace (ĭn″tẽr-lās′), *v.t.* and *v.i.* [*p.t.* and *p.p.* -laced′ (-lāst′), *p.pr.* -lac′ing], **1**, to join or unite by weaving or lacing together; **2**, to intersperse; intermingle.

in-ter-lard (ĭn″tẽr-lärd′), *v.t.* to mix; vary by mingling with something different; as, to *interlard* a speech with jests.

in-ter-leave (ĭn″tẽr-lēv′), *v.t.* [*p.t.* and *p.p.* -leaved′ (-lēvd′), *p.pr.* -leav′ing], to insert a leaf in; as, to *interleave* a book with illustrations.

¹in-ter-line (ĭn″tẽr-līn′), *v.t.* [*p.t.* and *p.p.* -lined′ (-līnd′), *p.pr.* -lin′ing], to write or insert between the lines of (anything written or printed).—*n.* **¹in″ter-lin′ing.**

²in-ter-line (ĭn″tẽr-līn′), *v.t.* [*p.t.* and *p.p.* -lined′ (-līnd′), *p.pr.* -lin′ing], to fit with an extra lining beneath the usual one: said of a garment.—*n.* **²in′ter-lin″ing.**

in-ter-lin-e-ar (ĭn″tẽr-lĭn′ē-ȧr), *adj.* **1,** written or printed between other lines, as a translation; **2,** having matter written or printed between lines.

in-ter-lock (ĭn″tẽr-lŏk′), *v.t.* and *v.i.* to fasten together by linking or engaging with one another.

in-ter-loc-u-tor (ĭn″tẽr-lŏk′ū-tẽr), *n.* **1,** one who takes part in a conversation; a questioner; an interpreter; **2,** in a minstrel troupe, the middleman, who questions the end men.

in-ter-loc-u-to-ry (ĭn″tẽr-lŏk′ū-tō-rĭ), *adj.* **1,** conversational; **2,** in law, not final; made or done during the process of an action.

in-ter-lope (ĭn″tẽr-lōp′), *v.i.* [*p.t.* and *p.p.* -loped′ (-lōpt′), *p.pr.* -lop′ing], to meddle; intrude where one is not wanted.

in-ter-lop-er (ĭn′tẽr-lōp″ẽr), *n.* one who interferes officiously; an intruder; as, an *interloper* in the family party.

in-ter-lude (ĭn′tẽr-lūd), *n.* **1,** a short entertainment given between acts of a play; **2,** a few bars of music played between the stanzas of a hymn, acts of an opera, etc.; **3,** a period of time between events.

in-ter-mar-riage (ĭn″tẽr-măr′ĭj), *n.* a joining in wedlock, as between two families.

in-ter-mar-ry (ĭn″tẽr-măr′ĭ), *v.i.* and *v.t.* [*p.t.* and *p.p.* -ried (-ĭd), *p.pr.* -ry-ing], to relate or become related by marriage between members: said of families.

in-ter-med-dle (ĭn″tẽr-mĕd′l), *v.i.* [*p.t.* and *p.p.* -dled (-ld), *p.pr.* -dling], to interfere in other people's affairs.—*n.* **in″ter-med′dler.**

in-ter-me-di-a-ry (ĭn″tẽr-mē′dĭ-ā-rĭ), *adj.* **1,** coming between; as, there is an *intermediary* time between election and installation in office; **2,** acting as a mediating agent:—*n.* [*pl.* intermediaries (-rĭz)], an agent; a deputy; means.

in-ter-me-di-ate (ĭn″tẽr-mē′dĭ-āt), *adj.* existing or lying in the middle; coming between:—*n.* **1,** that which lies between; **2,** a go-between.—*n.* **in″ter-me″di-a′tion.**—*adv.* **in″ter-me′di-ate-ly.**

in-ter-ment (ĭn-tûr′mĕnt), *n.* burial; as, *interment* in Westminster Abbey is a great honor.

in-ter-mez-zo (ĭn″tẽr-mĕd′zō), *n.* [*pl.* intermezzi (-zē)], **1,** in the drama, a light piece played between acts; **2,** in music, an interlude.

in-ter-mi-na-ble (ĭn-tûr′mĭ-nȧ-bl), *adj.* endless; boundless; immeasurable.—*adv.* **in-ter′mi-na-bly.**
Syn. infinite, limitless, eternal.

in-ter-min-gle (ĭn″tẽr-mĭng′gl), *v.t.* and *v.i.* [*p.t.* and *p.p.* -gled (-gld), *p.pr.* -gling], to mix together.

in-ter-mis-sion (ĭn″tẽr-mĭsh′ŭn), *n.* **1,** an interruption; a pause; short break; **2,** an interval of time between two parts, as acts of a play.

in-ter-mit (ĭn″tẽr-mĭt′), *v.t.* [*p.t.* and *p.p.* -mit′ted, *p.pr.*-mit′ting], to stop for a time; interrupt.—*n.* **in″ter-mit′tence.**

in-ter-mit-tent (ĭn″tẽr-mĭt′ĕnt), *adj.* occurring at intervals; periodic, as a fever.—*adv.* **in″ter-mit′tent-ly.**

in-ter-mix (ĭn″tẽr-mĭks′), *v.t.* to combine:—*v.i.* to become combined.

in-ter-mix-ture (ĭn″tẽr-mĭks′tūr), *n.* **1,** the act of mingling together; **2,** a mixture.

in-tern (ĭn-tûrn′), *v.t.* to confine within certain limits, as, in war time, ships in a neutral port; place under arrest:—*n.* (usually, *interne*), an inmate, as of a school; esp., a recently graduated physician or surgeon resident in a hospital.—*n.* **in-tern′ment.**

in-ter-nal (ĭn-tûr′năl), *adj.* **1,** belonging to the center; interior; inward; as, *internal* organs; **2,** not foreign; domestic; as, a country's *internal* problems; **3,** inherent; as, *internal* proof; **4,** to be taken inwardly: said of medicine.—*adv.* **in-ter′nal-ly.**

in-ter-nal com-bus-tion the process by which power is generated within an engine cylinder by the explosion of a mixture of air and a fuel, such as vaporized gasoline (see *gas engine*, illus.).—*adj.* **in-ter′nal–com-bus′tion.**

in-ter-na-tion-al (ĭn″tẽr-năsh′ŭn-ăl), *adj.* pertaining to, or carried on between, two or more nations or their people: **International,** pertaining to the International Workingmen's Association; also, a member of it: **Third International,** an international organization of communistic socialists, founded at Moscow in 1919.—*adv.* **in″ter-na′tion-al-ly.**—*v.t.* **in″ter-na′tion-al-ize.**

***In-ter-na-tio-nale** (ăṅ″târ″nä″syō″-năl′), [Fr.], *n.* a communistic hymn sung first by French socialists and, later, by others.

in-ter-na-tion-al-ism (ĭn″tẽr-năsh′ŭn-ăl-ĭzm), *n.* **1,** the fact or state of being attached by sentiment to more than one nation; **2,** organized action, as by the trade-unions of different countries, for the advancement of the working classes as a world group; **3,** the political philosophy which stresses the mutual dependence of all nations, and offers a theoretical foundation for world peace.—*n.* **in″ter-na′tion-al-ist.**

in-ter-ne-cine (ĭn″tẽr-nē′sĭn; ĭn″tẽr-nē′-sīn), *adj.* **1,** deadly; **2,** destructive of one another; as, *internecine* strife.

in-ter-pel-late (ĭn″tẽr-pĕl′āt), *v.t.* [*p.t.* and *p.p.* -lat-ed, *p.pr.* -lat-ing], to question formally, as an officer, in regard to his conduct.—*n.* **in″ter-pel-la′tion.**

in-ter-pen-e-trate (ĭn″tẽr-pĕn′ē-trāt), *v.t.* [*p.t.* and *p.p.* -trat″ed, *p.pr.* -trat″ing], to pass into all parts of, and throughout:—*v.i.* to pervade each other.—*n.* **in″ter-pen″e-tra′tion.**

in-ter-play (ĭn′tẽr-plā″), *n.* mutual action; interchange of action or influence; interaction, as of the parts of a machine.

in-ter-po-late (ĭn-tûr′pō-lāt), *v.t.* [*p.t.* and *p.p.* -lat″ed, *p.pr.* -lat″ing], **1,** to insert in a book or writing (new or unauthorized matter); **2,** to insert between other things or parts; **3,** to interpose.—*n.* **in-ter″po-la′tion.**—*n.* **in-ter′po-la″tor.**

in-ter-pose (ĭn″tẽr-pōz′), *v.t.* [*p.t.* and *p.p.* -posed′ (-pōzd′), *p.pr.* -pos′ing], **1,** to place between; **2,** to thrust in; put forth, in order to interfere; **3,** to introduce (a remark) into a conversation:—*v.i.* **1,** to mediate; **2,** to interrupt, **3,** to be between.
Syn. arbitrate; interfere, meddle.

in-ter-po-si-tion (ĭn″tẽr-pō-zĭsh′ŭn), *n.* **1,** the act of coming between, interrupting, or mediating; **2,** that which is thrust in or interjected.

in-ter-pret (ĭn-tûr′prĕt), *v.t.* **1,** to explain the meaning of; translate orally; as, to *interpret* a foreign language; **2,** to bring out the full meaning of, as a poem; **3,** to regard from one's own viewpoint; construe:—*v.i.* to act as a translator or interpreter.
Syn. construe, unfold, decipher.

in-ter-pre-ta-tion (ĭn-tûr″prē-tā′shŭn), *n.* **1**, the act of explaining the meaning of something; **2**, explanation; translation; **3**, the expression by an artist or actor of his conception of a subject, as of a landscape or a character.

in-ter-pre-ta-tive (ĭn-tûr′prē-tā-tĭv), *adj.* explanatory; intended or serving to explain or translate.

in-ter-pret-er (ĭn-tûr′prĕt-ẽr), *n.* **1**, one who explains or makes clear; **2**, one who translates orally the words of persons speaking in different languages.

in-ter-reg-num (ĭn″tẽr-rĕg′nŭm), *n.* **1**, the period between two reigns, governments, or ministries; **2**, a break in a continuous series of events.

in-ter-re-lat-ed (ĭn″tẽr-rē-lāt′ĕd), *adj.* having a connection between each other or among one another.

in-ter-ro-gate (ĭn-tĕr′ō-gāt), *v.t.* [*p.t.* and *p.p.* -gat″ed, *p.pr.* -gat″ing], to question; examine by asking questions:—*v.i.* to ask questions.
Syn. inquire, ask, search.

in-ter-ro-ga-tion (ĭn-tĕr″ō-gā′shŭn), *n.* **1**, the act of asking questions; **2**, a question; inquiry; **3**, a mark [?] denoting a question: also called *interrogation point* and *question mark.*

in-ter-rog-a-tive (ĭn″tĕ-rŏg′ȧ-tĭv), *adj.* denoting or containing a question or inquiry:—*n.* a word used in asking a question, as *why, where, who,* etc.—*adv.* **in″ter-rog′a-tive-ly.**

in-ter-ro-ga-tor (ĭn-tĕr′ō-gā″tẽr), *n.* one who asks questions.

in-ter-rog-a-to-ry (ĭn″tĕ-rŏg′ȧ-tō-rĭ), *adj.* containing, or expressing, a question:—*n.* [*pl.* interrogatories (-rĭz)], in law, a question or series of questions formally put in writing to a witness, to be used as evidence in a case.

in-ter-rupt (ĭn″tĕ-rŭpt′), *v.t.* **1**, to stop or hinder by breaking in upon; **2**, to obstruct; as, a rock *interrupts* the course of the stream; **3**, to cause to stop; end suddenly:—*v.i.* **1**, to break into a conversation or sentence; **2**, to interfere with an action.—*n.* **in″ter-rupt′er; in″ter-rup′tor.**

in-ter-rup-tion (ĭn″tĕ-rŭp′shŭn), *n.* **1**, the state of being broken in upon, or the act of breaking in upon something, as a conversation; **2**, a hindrance; something which blocks progress or breaks in upon speech, action, etc.; **3**, a sudden ceasing.

in-ter-sect (ĭn″tẽr-sĕkt′), *v.t.* to cut across; as, one street *intersects* another:—*v.i.* to cross each other.

in-ter-sec-tion (ĭn″tẽr-sĕk′shŭn), *n.* **1**, the act of dividing by cutting across; **2**, the place of crossing; **3**, the place where two lines or two surfaces cut each other; as, the *intersection* of two faces of a cube makes an edge.

in-ter-space (ĭn″tẽr-spās′), *v.t.* [*p.t.* and *p.p.* -spaced′ (-spāst′), *p.pr.* -spac′ing], **1**, to break up with intervals; **2**, to fill up intervals between:—*n.* (ĭn′tẽr-spās″), an interval or distance between objects.

in-ter-sperse (ĭn″tẽr-spûrs′), *v.t.* [*p.t.* and *p.p.* -spersed′ (-spûrst′), *p.pr.* -spers′ing], **1**, to vary by alternation or contrast; as, meadows *interspersed* with trees; **2**, to scatter about; as, to *intersperse* flowers in a garden.—*n.* **in″ter-sper′sion.**

in-ter-state (ĭn′tẽr-stāt″), *adj.* including, or existing between, different states or their inhabitants; as, *interstate* railways: **Interstate Commerce Commission,** a commission appointed by the President to investigate and regulate common carriers, as railroads, doing business between states, with a view of preventing unfair discrimination in rates, illegal combinations, etc.

in-ter-stel-lar (ĭn″tẽr-stĕl′ȧr), *adj.* pertaining to, or situated in, space between the stars.

in-ter-stice (ĭn-tûr′stĭs), *n.* [*pl.* interstices (-stĭ-sĕz)], a narrow space between things closely set; a crevice; chink; as, the *interstices* of a screen.—*adj.* **in″ter-sti′tial** (ĭn″tẽr-stĭsh′ăl).

in-ter-twine (ĭn″tẽr-twīn′), *v.t.* and *v.i.* [*p.t.* and *p.p.* -twined′ (-twīnd′), *p.pr.* -twin′ing], to twist with one another; wind or coil together.

in-ter-ur-ban (ĭn″tẽr-ûr′băn), *adj.* between or among cities or towns; as, an *interurban* railroad.

in-ter-val (ĭn′tẽr-văl), *n.* **1**, time intervening between two events; **2**, a space between objects; **3**, the difference in pitch between two tones.

in-ter-vene (ĭn″tẽr-vēn′), *v.i.* [*p.t.* and *p.p.* -vened′ (-vēnd′), *p.pr.* -ven′ing], **1**, to come in from outside, as an influence; come between; as, illness *intervened* to delay their trip; **2**, to occur in the meantime; elapse, as time; as, a month *intervened* between the events.—*n.* **in″ter-ven′er.**

in-ter-ven-tion (ĭn″tẽr-vĕn′shŭn), *n.* the act of coming between for any purpose; as, peace was brought about by the *intervention* of the League of Nations.

in-ter-view (ĭn′tẽr-vū), *v.t.* to question, esp. to obtain information for the press:—*n.* **1**, a personal conference or meeting; **2**, in journalism, the act of conversing with, or being questioned by, a reporter; also, the published account of such a conversation.—*n.* **in′ter-view″er.**

in-ter-weave (ĭn″tẽr-wēv′), *v.i.* and *v.t.* [*p.t.* -wove′ (-wōv′), *p.p.* -wov′en (-wō′vn) or -wove′, *p.pr.* -weav′ing], **1**, to twist together; **2**, to intermingle.

in-tes-ta-cy (ĭn-tĕs′tȧ-sĭ), *n.* the state of dying without a will.

in-tes-tate (ĭn-tĕs′tāt), *adj.* **1**, not having made a will; as, to die *intestate;* **2**, not lawfully bequeathed; as, an *intestate* piece of property:—*n.* one who dies without having made a valid will.

in-tes-ti-nal (ĭn-tĕs′tĭ-năl), *adj.* pertaining to, or found in, the bowels.—*adv.* **in-tes′ti-nal-ly.**

in-tes-tine (ĭn-tĕs′tĭn), *adj.* internal; not foreign; as, an *intestine* war:—*n.*, usually in *pl.*, the bowels.

in-thrall (ĭn-thrôl′), *v.t.* to enslave. See **en-thrall′**, *Pfd. S.*

in-throne (ĭn-thrōn′), *v.t.* [*p.t.* and *p.p.* -throned′ (-thrōnd′), *p.pr.* -thron′ing], to place on a seat of power; invest with royal power. Also, **en-throne′**, *Pfd. S.*

in-ti-ma-cy (ĭn′tĭ-mȧ-sĭ), *n.* [*pl.* intimacies (-sĭz)], close friendship.

in-ti-mate (ĭn′tĭ-măt), *adj.* **1**, close in friendship; well acquainted; familiar; confidential; **2**, pertaining to the inward nature of anything; as, *intimate* principles; **3**, resulting from close study; as, an *intimate* knowledge of art; **4**, closely combined; as, an *intimate* mixture:—*n.* a close friend:—*v.t.* (ĭn′tĭ-māt), [*p.t.* and *p.p.* -mat″ed, *p.pr.* -mat″ing], **1**, to suggest indirectly; **2**, to announce.—*adv.* **in′ti-mate-ly.**
Syn., v. hint, allude, insinuate, imply.

in-ti-ma-tion (ĭn″tĭ-mā′shŭn), *n.* **1**, the act of announcing; **2**, an indirect hint; **3**, a more formal announcement.

in-tim-i-date (ĭn-tĭm′ĭ-dāt), *v.t.* [*p.t.* and *p.p.* -dat″ed, *p.pr.* -dat″ing], to make afraid; overawe, esp. by threats.—*n.* **in-tim″i-da′tion.**—*n.* **in-tim′i-da″tor.**
Syn. dishearten, alarm, scare.

in-ti-tle (ĭn-tī'tl), *v.t.* [*p.t.* and *p.p.* -tled (-tld), *p.pr.* -tling], **1**, to give a name to; **2**, to dignify by a name; **3**, to give a right to. Also, **en-ti'tle**, *Pfd. S.*

in-to (ĭn'tōō), *prep.* **1**, to the inside of; as, come *into* the room; look *into* the matter; **2**, to the condition of; as, the rain later turned *into* snow; **3**, in mathematics: **a**, expressing division; as, 2 *into* 6 means 6 divided by 2; **b**, expressing multiplication; as, *x into y* means *x* times *y*, or *y* multiplied by *x*.

in-tol-er-a-ble (ĭn-tŏl'ẽr-ȧ-bl), *adj.* unbearable, as heat.—*n.* **in-tol'er-a-ble-ness.**—*adv.* **in-tol'er-a-bly.**
Syn. insupportable, insufferable.

in-tol-er-ance (ĭn-tŏl'ẽr-ăns), *n.* **1**, unwillingness to permit others to follow their own opinions and beliefs; as, religious *intolerance* has caused many wars; **2**, inability to bear or endure.

in-tol-er-ant (ĭn-tŏl'ẽr-ănt), *adj.* **1**, not allowing difference of opinion or belief to others, esp. in religious matters; **2**, unable to bear or endure: with *of.*—*adv.* **in-tol'er-ant-ly.**

in-to-nate (ĭn'tō-nāt), *v.t.* [*p.t.* and *p.p.* -nat″ed, *p.pr.* -nat″ing], to speak, read, or recite in a musical manner, as in reading the church service; intone.

in-to-na-tion (ĭn″tō-nā'shŭn), *n.* **1**, the modulation of the speaking voice; **2**, chanting or intoning.

in-tone (ĭn-tōn'), *v.t.* and *v.i.* [*p.t.* and *p.p.* -toned' (-tōnd'), *p.pr.* -ton'ing], to recite in a singing voice; chant; as, to *intone* a church service or psalm tune.

in-tox-i-cant (ĭn-tŏk'sĭ-kănt), *n.* **1**, that which makes drunk, as alcohol; **2**, anything that excites, as success.

in-tox-i-cate (ĭn-tŏk'sĭ-kāt), *v.t.* [*p.t.* and *p.p.* -cat″ed, *p.pr.* -cat″ing], **1**, to make drunk, as by alcoholic liquors; **2**, to excite exceedingly; as, pleasure *intoxicates* me; **3**, in medicine, to poison.—*p.adj.* **in-tox'i-cat″ed.**—*p.adj.* **in-tox'i-cat″ing.**

in-tox-i-ca-tion (ĭn-tŏk″sĭ-kā'shŭn), *n.* **1**, the act of making drunk; **2**, the state of being drunk; **3**, extreme excitement; **4**, in medicine, poisoning.

in-tra- (ĭn'trȧ-), *prefix*, within; inside; as, *intra*mural.

in-trac-ta-ble (ĭn-trăk'tȧ-bl), *adj.* **1**, unmanageable; as, an *intractable* horse; **2**, not easy to work; as, *intractable* metal.—*n.* **in-trac'ta-ble-ness.**—*adv.* **in-trac'ta-bly.**—*n.* **in-trac″ta-bil'i-ty.**
Syn. disobedient, perverse, unruly.

in-trac-tile (ĭn-trăk'tĭl), *adj.* incapable of being drawn out, as zinc.

in-tra-dos (ĭn-trā'dŏs), *n.* the under surface or curve of an arch or vault: opp. of *extrados* (see *extrados*, ¹*arch*, illus.).

in-tra-mu-ral (ĭn″trȧ-mū'răl), *adj.* entirely within the limits of a city, university, etc.; as, an *intramural* railway; the college has *intramural* sports.

in-tran-si-tive (ĭn-trăn'sĭ-tĭv), *adj.* in grammar, permitting of no object because not expressing action received: said of certain verbs, as he *sits;* he *laughed.*—*adv.* **in-tran'si-tive-ly.**

in-treat (ĭn-trēt'), *v.t.* to ask earnestly; supplicate. Also, **en-treat'**, *Pfd. S.*

in-trench (ĭn-trĕnch'), *v.t.* **1**, to make hollows or furrows in; **2**, to surround with a ditch:—*v.i.* to encroach; intrude; take possession; as, to *intrench* upon the rights of others. Also, **en-trench'.**

in-trench-ment (ĭn-trĕnch'mĕnt), *n.* **1**, a long, narrow ditch in the earth; **2**, in warfare, a defensive work consisting of ditches with a protecting wall of earth thrown up before them as a shield against gunfire; **3**, an infringement or encroachment, as upon rights. Also, **en-trench'ment.**

in-trep-id (ĭn-trĕp'ĭd), *adj.* bold; fearless; brave.—*adv.* **in-trep'id-ly.**
Syn. dauntless, courageous, heroic.

in-tre-pid-i-ty (ĭn″trē-pĭd'ĭ-tĭ), *n.* fearlessness; valor.

in-tri-ca-cy (ĭn'trĭ-kȧ-sĭ), *n.* [*pl.* intricacies (-sĭz)], **1**, the condition of being entangled or complicated; **2**, that which is entangled or involved.

in-tri-cate (ĭn'trĭ-kāt), *adj.* entangled; complicated; as, an *intricate* plot in a story.—*adv.* **in'tri-cate-ly.**
Syn. difficult, complex, obscure.

in-trigue (ĭn-trēg'), *v.i.* [*p.t.* and *p.p.* -trigued' (-trēgd'), *p.pr.* -tri'guing], **1**, to plot; **2**, to engage in secret love affairs:—*v.t.* to interest keenly:—*n.* (ĭn-trēg'; ĭn'trēg), **1**, a plot; **2**, a secret love affair.—*n.* **in-tri'guer.**
Syn., n. scheme, conspiracy, artifice, ruse.

in-trin-sic (ĭn-trĭn'sĭk), *adj.* pertaining to the very nature of a thing; as, *intrinsic* worth.—*adv.* **in-trin'si-cal-ly.**
Syn. true, genuine, native, natural, innate.

in-tro- (ĭn'trō-), *prefix*, in or into; as, *intro*duce; *intro*spection.

in-tro-duce (ĭn″trō-dūs'), *v.t.* [*p.t.* and *p.p.* -duced' (-dūst'), *p.pr.* -duc'ing], **1**, to conduct or bring in; **2**, to bring into use or notice, as a style; **3**, to bring into acquaintance, as one person to another; **4**, to put into something else, as lime into the soil; **5**, to present formally, as a resolution; **6**, to open, as a discussion.—*n.* **in″tro-duc'er.**

in-tro-duc-tion (ĭn″trō-dŭk'shŭn), *n.* **1**, the act of bringing into use, as a style; **2**, presentation, as of one person to another, a speaker to an audience, etc.; **3**, a preface, often long and explanatory.

in-tro-duc-to-ry (ĭn″trō-dŭk'tō-rĭ), *adj.* serving to bring into notice or use; preliminary.

in-tro-it (ĭn-trō'ĭt), *n.* that part of a church service sung before the celebration of the Eucharist.

in-tro-spect (ĭn″trō-spĕkt'), *v.t.* to look into or within; examine the interior of:—*v.i.* to examine one's thoughts.

in-tro-spec-tion (ĭn″trō-spĕk'shŭn), *n.* the act or process of examining one's own thoughts or feelings.

in-tro-spec-tive (ĭn″trō-spĕk'tĭv), *adj.* inclined to examine one's own thoughts and feelings.—*adv.* **in″tro-spec'tive-ly.**—*n.* **in″tro-spec'tive-ness.**

in-tro-vert (ĭn″trō-vûrt'), *v.i.* to look within:—*n.* (ĭn'trō-vûrt), in psychology, a person who habitually directs his attention to his own feelings, emotions, symptoms, etc.: opp. of *extrovert.*—*n.* **in″tro-ver'sion.**

in-trude (ĭn-trōōd'), *v.i.* [*p.t.* and *p.p.* -trud'ed, *p.pr.* -trud'ing], to come in without invitation or welcome:—*v.t.* to thrust or force in.—*n.* **in-trud'er.**

in-tru-sion (ĭn-trōō'zhŭn), *n.* the act of entering without invitation.

in-tru-sive (ĭn-trōō'sĭv), *adj.* **1**, inclined to enter without right or welcome; forward; **2**, forced or thrust in, as a foreign substance.—*adv.* **in-tru'sive-ly.**—*n.* **in-tru'sive-ness.**

in-trust (ĭn-trŭst'), *v.t.* **1**, to give into faithful keeping; confide; as, to *intrust* jewels to a bank; **2**, to place (someone) in charge; deliver in trust to; as, to *intrust* a bank with jewels. Also, **en-trust'.**

in-tu-i-tion (ĭn″tū-ĭsh'ŭn), *n.* **1**, knowledge based on insight rather than on reasoning; as, the child's *intuition* told him whom to trust; **2**, that which is known immediately or without reasoning.

in-tu-i-tion-al (ĭn″tū̇-ĭsh′ŭn-ăl), *adj.* pertaining to instinctive knowledge or insight.—*adv.* **in″tu-i′tion-al-ly.**

in-tu-i-tive (ĭn-tū̇′ĭ-tĭv), *adj.* **1**, known, or capable of being known, by the mind without reasoning; **2**, possessing, or acting by, instinctive knowledge or feeling; as, *intuitive* people.—*adv.* **in-tu′i-tive-ly.**—*n.* **in-tu′i-tive-ness.**

in-twine (ĭn-twīn′), *v.t.* and *v.i.* [*p.t.* and *p.p.* -twined′ (-twīnd′), *p.pr.* -twin′ing], to twist together. *Pfd.S.*, **en-twine′.**

in-un-date (ĭn′ŭn-dāt; ĭn-ŭn′-), *v.t.* [*p.t.* and *p.p.* -dat″ed, *p.pr.* -dat″ing], **1**, to fill to overflowing; flood; as, the overflowing of the Nile *inundates* the fertile fields of Egypt; **2**, to spread over; as, the army *inundated* the land.

in-un-da-tion (ĭn″ŭn-dā′shŭn), *n.* **1**, overflow; **2**, a superabundance.

in-ure (ĭn-ūr′), *v.t.* [*p.t.* and *p.p.* -ured′ (-ūrd′), *p.pr.* -ur′ing], to accustom; toughen; as, an outdoor life will *inure* one to hardships:—*v.i.* to come into use; take effect. —*p.adj.* **in-ured′.**

in-vade (ĭn-vād′), *v.t.* [*p.t.* and *p.p.* -vad′ed, *p.pr.* -vad′ing], to enter (a country) with a hostile army; enter upon; take possession of.—*n.* **in-vad′er.**

1**in-val-id** (ĭn-văl′ĭd), *adj.* **1**, of no force or authority, as a reason; **2**, in law, without legal force; as, an *invalid* claim.

2**in-va-lid** (ĭn′vȧ-lĭd; *Br.* ĭn″vȧ-lēd′), *n.* one who is weak or infirm in health:—*adj.* **1**, sick; enfeebled by ill health; **2**, adapted to the use of a sick person; as, an *invalid* chair:—*v.t.* **1**, to affect with sickness; make weak; **2**, to send away as sick; as, to *invalid* a man to his home.

in-val-i-date (ĭn-văl′ĭ-dāt), *v.t.* [*p.t.* and *p.p.* -dat″ed, *p.pr.* -dat″ing], to weaken or destroy the force or authority of; as, the last will made *invalidates* all others.—*n.* **in-val″i-da′tion.**
Syn. cancel, overthrow, nullify, annul.

in-va-lid-ism (ĭn′vȧ-lĭd-ĭzm), *n.* chronic illness or infirmity.

in-va-lid-i-ty (ĭn″vȧ-lĭd′ĭ-tĭ), *n.* [*pl.* invalidities (-tĭz)], want of legal force or argument.

in-val-u-a-ble (ĭn-văl′ū̇-ȧ-bl), *adj.* priceless; as, his services were *invaluable* to his firm.—*adv.* **in-val′u-a-bly.**

in-va-ri-a-ble (ĭn-vā′rĭ-ȧ-bl), *adj.* constant; uniform; unchanging; as, his *invariable* custom was to walk to his office.—*n.* **in-va′ri-a-ble-ness.**—*adv.* **in-va′ri-a-bly.**—*n.* **in-va″ri-a-bil′i-ty.**

in-va-sion (ĭn-vā′zhŭn), *n.* **1**, the act of entering a country with a hostile army; **2**, encroachment; infringement; **3**, an attack of anything injurious, as a disease. —*adj.* **in-va′sive.**

in-vec-tive (ĭn-vĕk′tĭv), *n.* violent denunciation; wordy abuse; as, the newspapers hurled *invectives* at the retiring cabinet officer:—*adj.* abusive.
Syn., *n.* reproach, vituperation, satire.

in-veigh (ĭn-vā′), *v.i.* to speak violently and bitterly; utter blame or reproach; as, a Congressman may *inveigh* against a proposed measure.—*n.* **in-veigh′er.**

in-vei-gle (ĭn-vē′gl), *v.t.* [*p.t.* and *p.p.* -gled (-gld), *p.pr.* -gling], to persuade, as by flattery; lure; cajole.—*n.* **in-vei′gle-ment.**—*n.* **in-vei′gler.**
Syn. allure, decoy, entice.

in-vent (ĭn-vĕnt′), *v.t.* **1**, to produce for the first time; originate, as a machine; **2**, to devise or contrive, as a tale.
Syn. frame. (See discover.)

in-ven-tion (ĭn-vĕn′shŭn), *n.* **1**, the act of originating; **2**, the thing originated, as a machine; **3**, the quality by which one creates or produces anything for the first time; **4**, the act of producing by the imagination; **5**, a falsehood; lie.

in-ven-tive (ĭn-vĕn′tĭv), *adj.* able to originate; clever at devising things, methods, or the like.—*adv.* **in-ven′tive-ly.**—*n.* **in-ven′tive-ness.**

in-ven-tor (ĭn-vĕn′tẽr), *n.* one who contrives or devises something new; as, Edison is America's greatest *inventor*.

in-ven-to-ry (ĭn′vĕn-tō̇-rĭ), *n.* [*pl.* inventories (-rĭz)], a catalog or list of goods, furniture, etc.; as, a merchant takes an *inventory* of his stock once a year:—*v.t.* to draw up such a list of, as goods in stock.

in-verse (ĭn-vûrs′; ĭn′vûrs), *adj.* opposite in tendency, direction, or effect; turned upside down; as, subtraction is the *inverse* operation of addition:—*n.* the direct opposite; the contrary.—*adv.* **in-verse′ly.**

in-ver-sion (ĭn-vûr′shŭn), *n.* **1**, the act of turning in the opposite direction, etc.; **2**, the state of being turned in the opposite direction, inside out, or upside down; **3**, any change of order or relative position.

in-vert (ĭn-vûrt′), *v.t.* **1**, to turn upside down, inside out, or in an opposite direction; **2**, to reverse, as in meaning or order.—*adj.* **in-vert′i-ble.**—*p.adj.* **in-vert′ed.**

in-ver-te-brate (ĭn-vûr′tē̇-brăt), *n.* an animal without a backbone:—*adj.* **1**, having no backbone; **2**, having no force of character; weak.

in-vest (ĭn-vĕst′), *v.t.* **1**, to array; dress; clothe; **2**, to place or lay out, as money at interest; **3**, to clothe, as with office, authority, or dignity; **4**, to surround; as, the armies *invest* the city:—*v.i.* to put money out for profit; as, to *invest* in oil stock.

in-ves-ti-gate (ĭn-vĕs′tĭ-gāt), *v.t.* [*p.t.* and *p.p.* -gat″ed, *p.pr.* -gat″ing], to make careful inquiry about; as, to *investigate* the cause of a disaster:—*v.i.* to pursue an inquiry.—*n.* **in-ves′ti-ga″tor.**

in-ves-ti-ga-tion (ĭn-vĕs″tĭ-gā′shŭn), *n.* careful examination, inquiry, or search; as, an official *investigation*.
Syn. inspection, scrutiny.

in-ves-ti-ture (ĭn-vĕs′tĭ-tūr), *n.* **1**, a garment or covering, esp. an official cloak; **2**, the receiving of the insignia of office; **3**, the act or right of giving possession or of installing in office.

in-vest-ment (ĭn-vĕst′mĕnt), *n.* **1**, the act of clothing with something, as the robes of office; **2**, that in which one is clothed; **3**, the act of laying out money for the sake of profit, or money so placed; also, that in which the money is placed; **4**, the act of besieging or blockading.

in-ves-tor (ĭn-vĕs′tẽr), *n.* one who puts out money for profit, esp. by buying stocks or bonds.

in-vet-er-a-cy (ĭn-vĕt′ẽr-ȧ-sĭ), *n.* the state of being firmly established, as a habit.

in-vet-er-ate (ĭn-vĕt′ẽr-ăt), *adj.* **1**, established a long time; deep-rooted; as, *inveterate* hatred; **2**, habitual; as, an *inveterate* smoker.—*adv.* **in-vet′er-ate-ly.**—*n.* **in-vet′er-ate-ness.**
Syn. confirmed, chronic.

in-vid-i-ous (ĭn-vĭd′ĭ-ŭs), *adj.* likely to provoke ill will or envy; unfairly partial; as, *invidious* discrimination.—*adv.* **in-vid′i-ous-ly.**—*n.* **in-vid′i-ous-ness.**
Syn. envious, hateful, odious.

in-vig-or-ate (ĭn-vĭg′ŏr-āt), *v.t.* [*p.t.* and *p.p.* -at″ed, *p.pr.* -at″ing], to give vitality to; strengthen; as, sea air *invigorates* the weak.—*n.* **in-vig″or-a′tion.**
Syn. brace, refresh, stimulate.

in-vin-ci-ble (ĭn-vĭn′sĭ-bl), *adj.* not to be overcome or subdued; unconquerable; as, *invincible* patience.—*adv.* **in-vin′ci-bly.**—*n.* **in-vin″ci-bil′i-ty.**

in-vi-o-la-ble (ĭn-vī′ō-lȧ-bl), *adj.* **1,** not to be profaned or injured, as a sanctuary; **2,** to be kept unbroken; as, an *inviolable* promise.—*adv.* **in-vi′o-la-bly.**—*n.* **in-vi″o-la-bil′i-ty.**

in-vi-o-late (ĭn-vī′ō-lāt), *adj.* **1,** uninjured; unbroken; **2,** pure. Also, **in-vi′o-lat″ed.**—*adv.* **in-vi′o-late-ly.**

in-vis-i-ble (ĭn-vĭz′ĭ-bl), *adj.* not capable of being seen; not visible under certain conditions: **invisible ink,** ink that remains invisible on the paper until exposed to the action of heat, strong light, etc.:—*n.* one who or that which cannot be seen: often used for the Deity.—*n.* **in-vis′i-ble-ness.** —*adv.* **in-vis′i-bly.**—*n.* **in-vis″i-bil′i-ty.**

in-vi-ta-tion (ĭn″vĭ-tā′shŭn), *n.* **1,** a request to a person to come to some place or to do something; **2,** the words or document by which the request is carried.

in-vite (ĭn-vīt′), *v.t.* [*p.t.* and *p.p.* -vit′ed, *p.pr.* -vit′ing], **1,** to request courteously to go to some place or to do some act; request the presence of; **2,** to tempt; attract; as, the title of the book *invites* the reader's interest; **3,** to give opportunity for; draw on; as, to *invite* disease through neglect.—*n.* **in-vit′er.**—*adv.* **in-vit′ing-ly.**
Syn. call, solicit.

in-vo-ca-tion (ĭn″vō-kā′shŭn), *n.* **1,** the act or form of addressing in prayer, esp. of calling for the help of God or a deity; **2,** the act of conjuring an evil spirit, or a formula so used; an incantation.

in-voice (ĭn′vois), *n.* **1,** a commercial paper or written document listing goods sent to a purchaser, with their prices, quantity, and charges; **2,** the goods mentioned in the document:—*v.t.* [*p.t.* and *p.p.* -voiced (-voist), *p.pr.* -voic-ing], to list on such a paper; include in such a list.

in-voke (ĭn-vōk′), *v.t.* [*p.t.* and *p.p.* -voked′ (-vōkt′), *p.pr.* -vok′ing], **1,** to address in prayer or supplication; as, to *invoke* a blessing; **2,** to ask solemnly or earnestly for (aid or protection); **3,** to conjure; appeal to by incantation; as, to *invoke* evil spirits.

in-vol-u-cel (ĭn-vŏl′ū-sĕl), *n.* in botany, a secondary involucre, usually of smaller size.

in-vo-lu-cre (ĭn′vō-lū″kẽr), *n.* a rosette of small leaves, sometimes resembling a calyx, situated below a flower or flower cluster, as in the dandelion and other composites (cf. *composite,* illus.).—*adj.* **in″vo-lu′cral.**

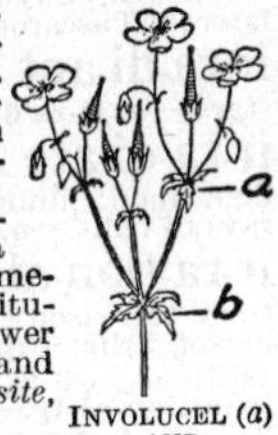

INVOLUCEL (*a*) AND INVOLUCRE (*b*)

in-vol-un-ta-ry (ĭn-vŏl′ŭn-tā-rĭ), *adj.* **1,** not under the control of the will; **2,** contrary to choice; **3,** unintentional.—*adv.* **in-vol′un-ta-ri-ly.**—*n.* **in-vol′un-ta-ri-ness.**

in-vo-lute (ĭn′vō-lūt), *adj.* **1,** folded or rolled inward, as certain leaves and flowers; **2,** coiled spirally, as some shells:—*n.* a curve traced by a point on a taut thread as it unwinds from, or winds upon, a fixed curve. Also, *adj.* **in′vo-lut″ed.**

in-vo-lu-tion (ĭn″vō-lū′shŭn), *n.* **1,** the act of folding or coiling in or round; also, that which folds in or round; **2,** that which is complicated; **3,** the return of an organ or tissue to its normal size after having been stretched or swelled out; **4,** the process of raising a mathematical quantity to a given power by multiplying it by itself; as, $3 \times 3 \times 3 \times 3 = 81$; hence, the *involution* of 3^4 gives 81.

in-volve (ĭn-vŏlv′), *v.t.* [*p.t.* and *p.p.* -volved′ (-vŏlvd′), *p.pr.* -volv′ing], **1,** to complicate; entangle; **2,** to surround; envelop; **3,** to implicate; draw in; as, to *involve* one in a quarrel; **4,** to produce as a consequence; as, to *involve* a loss of time; **5,** to multiply (a quantity) by itself any given number of times.—*n.* **in-volve′ment.**

in-vul-ner-a-ble (ĭn-vŭl′nẽr-ȧ-bl), *adj.* **1,** incapable of being wounded or injured; as, the Greek hero Achilles was *invulnerable* everywhere except in the heel; **2,** incapable of being answered or refuted; as, an *invulnerable* argument.—*adv.* **in-vul′ner-a-bly.**—*n.* **in-vul″ner-a-bil′i-ty.**

in-ward (ĭn′wẽrd), *adj.* **1,** situated within; as, the *inward* parts of a man; **2,** pertaining to the mind or soul; hence, private:—*adv.* toward the center or interior; as, to bend *inward.* Also, *adv.* **in′wards.**

in-ward-ly (ĭn′wẽrd-lĭ), *adv.* **1,** internally, esp. in the mind or feelings; secretly; **2,** toward the center or inside.

in-ward-ness (ĭn′wẽrd-nĕs), *n.* **1,** the inner meaning or purpose of a thing; its real nature; **2,** the quality of being internal; **3,** spirituality; **4,** intensity of feeling; earnestness.

in-weave (ĭn-wēv′), *v.t.* [*p.t.* -wove′ (-wōv′), *p.p.* -wov′en (-wō′vn) or -wove′, *p.pr.* -weav′ing], to twist or lace in or together; interlace.

in-wrap (ĭn-răp′), *v.t.* [*p.t.* and *p.p.* -wrapped′ (-răpt′), *p.pr.* -wrap′ping], **1,** to inclose by wrapping; **2,** to entangle, involve; **3,** to engross. Also, **en-wrap′.**

in-wreathe (ĭn-rēth′), *v.t.* [*p.t.* and *p.p.* -wreathed′ (-rēthd′), *p.pr.* -wreath′ing], to surround with, or as with, a garland. Also, **en-wreathe′.**

in-wrought (ĭn-rôt′; ĭn′rôt″), *adj.* **1,** worked in, as by embroidery; **2,** adorned with figures or patterns.

I-o (ī′ō), *n.* in mythology, a maiden beloved by Zeus, changed by Hera into a heifer.

i-o-dide (ī′ō-dīd; -dĭd), *n.* a compound containing iodine. Also, **i′o-did.**

i-o-dine (ī′ō-dīn; ī′ō-dĭn; -dēn), *n.* a blue-black, nonmetallic element found widely distributed in mineral springs, seaweeds, etc., its salts being largely used in medicine and photography. Also, **i′o-din.**

i-o-do-form (ī-ō′dō-fôrm; ī-ŏd′ō-fôrm), *n.* a yellow, crystalline powder, a compound of iodine.

i-on (ī′ŏn), *n.* **1,** one of the particles bearing electrical charges which transmit electric current through the air or other gases; **2,** a product of electrolytic decomposition liberated at one of the electrodes during the passage of the electric current, that formed at the positive electrode being called the *anion,* a negative *ion,* and that at the negative electrode, the *cation,* a positive *ion.*

-ion (-ŭn), *n. suffix,* denoting: **1,** action or the result of action; as, suspic*ion;* **2,** state or condition; as, deject*ion;* infect*ion.*

I-o-ni-an (ī-ō′nĭ-ăn), *adj.* pertaining to ancient Ionia, the western coast of Asia Minor, or its inhabitants; Ionic:—*n.* a member of the ancient Greek race which settled in Ionia and along the Mediterranean.

I-on-ic (ī-ŏn′ĭk), *adj.* pertaining to ancient Ionia, or the western coast of Asia Minor; Ionian: **Ionic order,** an order of classic architecture, characterized by the volute, or ram's-horn scroll, on its capital, or ornamental top (see illus. next page; see also *column,* illus.).

i-o-ni-um (ī-ō′nĭ-ŭm), *n.* a radioactive solid substance, from which radium is derived: produced by the decomposition of uranium.

i-o-ta (ī-ō′tȧ), *n.* **1,** the ninth and smallest letter [ι,I] of the Greek alphabet, corresponding to the English *i;* **2,** hence, a small or insignificant part or amount; jot.

I O U (ī ō ū), *n.* a duly signed but informal acknowledgment of a debt: **I. O. U.,** *abbr.* I owe you.

ip-e-cac (ĭp′ē-kăk), *n.* **1,** a creeping, shrubby plant of South America; also, its root; **2,** an extract of this root, used in medicine as an emetic and sometimes as a purgative: officially called *ipecacuanha* (ĭp″ē-kăk″-ū-ăn′ȧ).

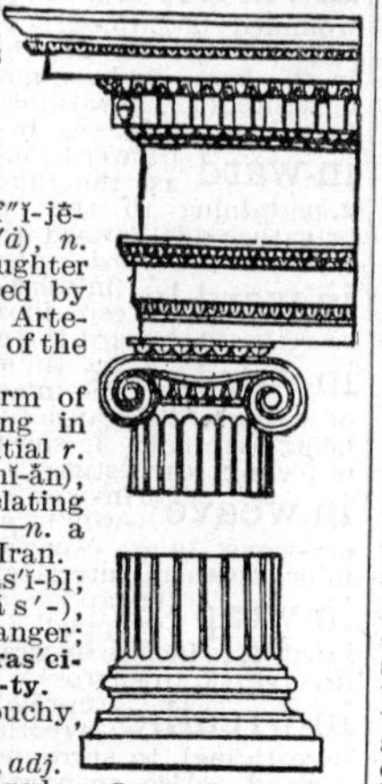
Ionic Column

Iph-i-ge-ni-a (ĭf″ĭ-jē-nī′ȧ), *n.* in mythology, a daughter of Agamemnon, offered by him as a sacrifice to Artemis, at the beginning of the Trojan War.

ir- (ĭr-), *prefix,* a form of [1]*in-*, [2]*in-*, meaning in or not, used before initial *r.*

I-ra-ni-an (ī-rā′nĭ-ăn), *adj.* relating to Persia, or Iran:—*n.* a native of Persia, or Iran.

i-ras-ci-ble (ī-răs′ĭ-bl; ĭ-răs′-), *adj.* easily excited to anger; hot-headed.—*adv.* **i-ras′ci-bly.**—*n.* **i-ras″ci-bil′i-ty.**
Syn. irritable, touchy, peevish, quarrelsome.

i-rate (ī-rāt′; ī′rāt), *adj.* angry; enraged; incensed.—*adv.* **i-rate′ly.**

ire (īr), *n.* anger; wrath; as, his *ire* was quickly aroused.—*adj.* **ire′ful.**

ir-i-des-cence (ĭr″ĭ-dĕs′ĕns), *n.* a shimmering or coming and going of colors like those of the rainbow.

ir-i-des-cent (ĭr″ĭ-dĕs′ĕnt), *adj.* having changing, shimmering, rainbowlike colors.—*adv.* **ir″i-des′cent-ly.**

i-rid-i-um (ī-rĭd′ĭ-ŭm), *n.* a rare element somewhat like platinum, used to harden alloys.

i-ris (ī′rĭs), *n.* [*pl.* irises (-ĕs; -ĭz); irides (ĭr′ĭ-dēz; ī′rĭ-)], **1,** the rainbow; **2,** the colored membrane of the eye, about the pupil; **3,** any of several plants with showy flowers; a flag.

I-rish (ī′rĭsh), *adj.* pertaining to Ireland, its inhabitants, or its language:—*n.* the native Celtic language of the Irish; Erse: Gaelic; also, English as spoken by the Irish: **the Irish,** collectively, the people of Ireland.

I-rish-ism (ī′rĭsh-ĭzm), *n.* an Irish peculiarity, esp. of speech.

I-rish-man (ī′rĭsh-măn), *n.* [*pl.* Irishmen (-mĕn)], a man of Irish birth.

irk (ûrk), *v.t.* to weary; annoy; as, the dull details of the business *irk* him.

irk-some (ûrk′sŭm), *adj.* tedious; wearisome; as, tasks may be *irksome.*—*adv.* **irk′some-ly.**—*n.* **irk′some-ness.**
Syn. tiresome, annoying, fatiguing.

i-ron (ī′ŭrn), *n.* **1,** a metallic element; the most common and useful of the metals: used commercially in many forms; as, *wrought iron,* soft, ductile, and of great toughness; *steel,* made by adding carbon and other elements, of great strength and hardness; *cast iron,* produced directly from the ore, hard and brittle; **2,** an instrument made of iron, esp. one to smooth clothes by heat; **3,** anything especially hard; **4,** firmness; rigidity; as, a man of *iron;* **5,** in golf, any of several clubs with an iron head; **6,** a preparation of iron used as a tonic; **7,** in *pl.,* chains or fetters for a prisoner:—*adj.* **1,** pertaining to, or made of, iron; **2,** resembling iron; hard; inflexible; harsh; as, an *iron* will:—*v.t.* **1,** to smooth with an iron; **2,** to furnish with iron; **3,** to fetter.

i-ron age **1,** the latest prehistoric age, characterized by the use of iron for weapons, tools, etc.; **2,** the last of the four ages of classic mythology.

i-ron-clad (ī′ŭrn-klăd″), *n.* a warship cased with iron or steel plates:—*adj.* **1,** covered, or protected, with iron plates; **2,** *Colloq.,* not to be evaded; as, an *ironclad* agreement.

i-ron-i-cal (ī-rŏn′ĭ-kăl), *adj.* **1,** expressing one thing and meaning the opposite; **2,** in the habit of using irony, or hidden sarcasm. Also, **i-ron′ic.**—*adv.* **i-ron′i-cal-ly.**—*n.* **i-ron′i-cal-ness.**

i-ron-side (ī′ŭrn-sīd″), *n.* **1,** a man of great strength or bravery; **2,** in *pl.* used as *sing.,* an armor-clad warship: **Ironsides,** Cromwell's cavalry: **Old Ironsides,** the U. S. frigate "Constitution."

i-ron-ware (ī′ŭrn-wâr″), *n.* hardware; articles made of iron.

i-ron-wood (ī′ŭrn-wo͝od″), *n.* in eastern North America, either of two trees of the birch family.

i-ron-work (ī′ŭrn-wûrk″), *n.* **1,** iron articles; **2,** usually in *pl.,* a place where iron is smelted and manufactured.

i-ro-ny (ī′rō-nĭ), *n.* **1,** hidden sarcasm; a mode of speech meaning the opposite of what is said; as, "to cry like a baby—that's a fine way for a man to act," said he with keen *irony;* **2,** pretended ignorance in argument: often called *Socratic irony;* **3,** an outcome the reverse of what would normally be expected; as, the *irony* of life.
Syn. satire, ridicule, raillery.

Ir-o-quois (ĭr″ō-kwoi′), *n.* [*pl.* Iroquois], a member of a powerful confederacy of American Indians, the Five Nations, formerly inhabiting central New York and comprising the Mohawk, Oneida, Onondaga, Cayuga, and Seneca tribes, and later the Tuscaroras.—*adj.* and *n.* **Ir″o-quoi′an.**

ir-ra-di-ant (ĭ-rā′dĭ-ănt), *adj.* giving forth rays of light; as, *irradiant* stars.—*n.* **ir-ra′di-ance.**

ir-ra-di-ate (ĭ-rā′dĭ-āt), *v.t.* [*p.t.* and *p.p.* -at″ed, *p.pr.* -at″ing], to shed light upon; illuminate; brighten:—*v.i.* to emit rays of light.—*n.* **ir-ra″di-a′tion.**

ir-ra-tion-al (ĭ-răsh′ŭn-ăl), *adj.* **1,** lacking reasoning powers; **2,** contrary to reason; **3,** in mathematics, not capable of being expressed in rational numbers; surd; as, $\sqrt{3}$ is an *irrational* number.—*adv.* **ir-ra′tion-al-ly.**—*n.* **ir-ra″tion-al′i-ty.**

ir-re-claim-a-ble (ĭr″ē-klām′ȧ-bl), *adj.* incapable of being recovered, amended, reformed, reclaimed, or restored.—*adv.* **ir″re-claim′a-bly.**

ir-rec-on-cil-a-ble (ĭ-rĕk″ŭn-sīl′ȧ-bl; ĭ-rĕk′ŭn-sīl″ȧ-bl), *adj.* not adjustable, as differences or quarrels; not in agreement, as actions and beliefs; hostile, as enemies:—*n.* one who refuses to accept compromises, as from political opponents; one who is discontented.—*n.* **ir-rec″on-cil′a-ble-ness.**—*adv.* **ir-rec″on-cil′a-bly.**

ir-re-cov-er-a-ble (ĭr″ē-kŭv′ẽr-ȧ-bl), *adj.* not capable of being regained.—*adv.* **ir″re-cov′er-a-bly.**

ir-re-deem-a-ble (ĭr″ē-dēm′ȧ-bl), *adj.* **1,** incapable of being bought back; **2,** not exchangeable for gold or silver: said of paper money; **3,** irreclaimable; thoroughly depraved.—*adv.* **ir″re-deem′a-bly.**

Ir-re-den-tist (ĭr″ē-dĕn′tĭst), *n.* in Italian politics, one of a party which favors incorporating into Italy neighboring regions largely Italian in population.

ir-re-du-ci-ble (ĭr″ē-dū′sĭ-bl), *adj.* **1,** incapable of being brought into a different condition or form; **2,** incapable of being diminished; **3,** not capable of being subdued; **4,** in mathematics, of a fraction, not capable of simplification through the cancellation of common factors in numerator and denominator.—*adv.* **ir″re-du′ci-bly.**

ir-ref-ra-ga-ble (ĭ-rĕf′rȧ-gȧ-bl), *adj.* undeniable; irrefutable; unanswerable.—*adv.* **ir-ref′ra-ga-bly.**

ir-re-fut-a-ble (ĭr″ē-fūt′ȧ-bl; ĭ-rĕf′ū-tȧ-bl), *adj.* incapable of being proved false or incorrect, as an argument; unanswerable.—*adv.* **ir″re-fut′a-bly.**

ir-reg-u-lar (ĭ-rĕg′ū-lẽr), *adj.* **1,** not straight or symmetrical; not uniform in shape, order, etc.; **2,** not according to rule or established method; abnormal.—*adv.* **ir-reg′u-lar-ly.**—*n.* **ir-reg″u-lar′i-ty.**

ir-rel-e-vant (ĭ-rĕl′ē-vănt), *adj.* not bearing upon the case; unrelated to the matter discussed.—*adv.* **ir-rel′e-vant-ly.**—*n.* **ir-rel′e-vance; ir-rel′e-van-cy.**

ir-re-li-gion (ĭr″ē-lĭj′ŭn), *n.* the state of being without, or hostile to, religion; ungodliness; impiety.

ir-re-li-gious (ĭr″ē-lĭj′ŭs), *adj.* **1,** lacking religion; **2,** profane.—*adv.* **ir″re-li′gious-ly.**—*n.* **ir″re-li′gious-ness.**

ir-re-me-di-a-ble (ĭr″ē-mē′dĭ-ȧ-bl), *adj.* not capable of being remedied.—*adv.* **ir″re-me′di-a-bly.**

ir-rep-a-ra-ble (ĭ-rĕp′ȧ-rȧ-bl), *adj.* not capable of being repaired or made good.—*adv.* **ir-rep′a-ra-bly.**

ir-re-press-i-ble (ĭr″ē-prĕs′ĭ-bl), *adj.* incapable of being subdued.—*n.* **ir″re-press′i-ble-ness.**—*adv.* **ir″re-press′i-bly.**—*n.* **ir″re-press″i-bil′i-ty.**

ir-re-proach-a-ble (ĭr″ē-prōch′ȧ-bl), *adj.* blameless; faultless; not to be discredited.—*n.* **ir″re-proach′a-ble-ness.**—*adv.* **ir″re-proach′a-bly.**

ir-re-sist-i-ble (ĭr″ē-zĭs′tĭ-bl), *adj.* incapable of being withstood; overpowering.—*adv.* **ir″re-sist′i-bly.**

ir-res-o-lute (ĭ-rĕz′ō-lūt), *adj.* undecided; wavering; not determined; changeable.—*adv.* **ir-res′o-lute-ly.**—*n.* **ir-res′o-lute-ness.**—*n.* **ir-res″o-lu′tion.**

ir-re-spec-tive (ĭr″ē-spĕk′tĭv), *adj.* independent; regardless: with *of;* as, citizens may vote, *irrespective* of race or color.—*adv.* **ir″re-spec′tive-ly.**

ir-re-spon-si-ble (ĭr″ē-spŏn′sĭ-bl), *adj.* **1,** not accountable; free from responsibility; **2,** not trustworthy.—*n.* **ir″re-spon′si-ble-ness.**—*adv.* **ir″re-spon′si-bly.**—*n.* **ir″re-spon″si-bil′i-ty.**

ir-re-triev-a-ble (ĭr″ē-trēv′ȧ-bl), *adj.* not recoverable; not to be made good.—*adv.* **ir″re-triev′a-bly.**

ir-rev-er-ence (ĭ-rĕv′ẽr-ĕns), *n.* **1,** lack of respect, esp. toward sacred things; **2,** a disrespectful act or speech.

ir-rev-er-ent (ĭ-rĕv′ẽr-ĕnt), *adj.* disrespectful; showing a want of respect or veneration, as for things held sacred.—*adv.* **ir-rev′er-ent-ly.**

ir-re-vers-i-ble (ĭr″ē-vûr′sĭ-bl), *adj.* incapable of being turned back or around.—*adv.* **ir″re-vers′i-bly.**

ir-rev-o-ca-ble (ĭ-rĕv′ō-kȧ-bl), *adj.* incapable of being recalled or undone; as, an *irrevocable* act.—*adv.* **ir-rev′o-ca-bly.**—*n.* **ir-rev″o-ca-bil′i-ty.**

ir-ri-gate (ĭr′ĭ-gāt), *v.t.* [*p.t.* and *p.p.* -gat″ed, *p.pr.* -gat″ing], to supply with water, as land under cultivation, by means of ditches, channels, etc.

ir-ri-ga-tion (ĭr″ĭ-gā′shŭn), *n.* the furnishing of a water supply, by ditches, canals, etc., to land under cultivation.

ir-ri-ta-ble (ĭr′ĭ-tȧ-bl), *adj.* **1,** easily provoked to anger; **2,** sensitive, as an organ of the body.—*n.* **ir′ri-ta-ble-ness.**—*adv.* **ir′ri-ta-bly.**—*n.* **ir″ri-ta-bil′i-ty.**

Syn. excitable, irascible, peevish, fretful.

ir-ri-tant (ĭr′ĭ-tănt), *adj.* causing sensitiveness or inflammation:—*n.* anything which causes sensitiveness or inflammation; as, rough clothing is an *irritant.*

ir-ri-tate (ĭr′ĭ-tāt), *v.t.* [*p.t.* and *p.p.* -tat″ed, *p.pr.* -tat″ing], to provoke or make angry; cause inflammation, redness, or pain in; as, a poor light *irritates* the eyes.

Syn. vex, annoy, aggravate, exasperate.

ir-ri-ta-tion (ĭr″ĭ-tā′shŭn), *n.* **1,** the act of exasperating; **2,** the state of being provoked or vexed; exasperation; impatience; **3,** the act of stimulating normally a muscle, organ, etc.; **4,** excessive sensitiveness, as of an organ.—*adj.* **ir′ri-ta-tive.**

ir-rup-tion (ĭ-rŭp′shŭn), *n.* **1,** a bursting or rushing in; **2,** sudden invasion.

ir-rup-tive (ĭ-rŭp′tĭv), *adj.* breaking or rushing in upon; tending to invade violently.

is (ĭz), third person singular, present indicative, of the verb *be.*

I-saac (ī′zȧk), *n.* in the Bible, a Hebrew patriarch; the son of Abraham and Sarah, father of Jacob and Esau.

I-sa-iah (ī-zā′yȧ; ī-zī′ȧ), *n.* **1,** in the Bible, a Hebrew prophet of the time of Hezekiah; **2,** a book of the Old Testament containing his preaching. Also, in the Douay Bible, **I-sa′ias.**

Is-car-i-ot (ĭs-kăr′ĭ-ŏt), *n.* the surname of Judas, who betrayed Christ into the hands of the Jews.

is-chi-um (ĭs′kĭ-ŭm), *n.* [*pl.* ischia (-ȧ)], the lowest of the three parts of the hip bone, which forms half of the pelvis: one of the bones on which the body rests when sitting (see *pelvis,* illus.).—*adj.* **is′chi-al.**

-ise (-īz), *v. suffix,* used, esp. in Great Britain, instead of *-ize.*

I-seult (ī-sōōlt′), *n.* **1,** in medieval romance, an Irish princess, wife of the king of Cornwall, called "the Beautiful," and beloved by Tristram: a figure in Tennyson's "Idylls of the King" and in Wagner's "Tristan und Isolde"; **2,** also, in some versions, the wife of Tristram, called "Iseult of Brittany" or "Iseult of the White Hands." Also, **I-solde′** (ĭ-sōld′).

1-ish (-ĭsh), *adj. suffix,* **1,** pertaining to: added to names of places or countries, as, Scott*ish;* **2,** of the nature of; like; esp., having the undesirable traits of: added to nouns; as, woman*ish;* **3,** somewhat: added to adjectives; as, black*ish.*

2-ish (-ĭsh), *suffix,* a termination of some verbs derived from the French; as, fin*ish;* furn*ish;* garn*ish.*

Ish-ma-el (ĭsh′mȧ-ĕl), *n.* **1,** in the Bible, the exiled son of Abraham and Hagar; **2,** hence, an outcast.

Ish-ma-el-ite (ĭsh′mȧ-ĕl-īt), *n.* **1,** a descendant of Ishmael; **2,** a social outcast.—*adj.* **Ish′ma-el-it″ish.**

i-sin-glass (ī′zĭng-glȧs), *n.* **1,** a white, semitransparent substance or gelatin prepared from the air bladders of the sturgeon, cod, etc.; **2,** sometimes, erroneously, mica, esp. when in thin sheets.

I-sis (ī′sĭs), *n.* the chief Egyptian female divinity, symbolical of fruitfulness.

Is-lam (ĭs′lȧm; ĭz′lȧm; ĭs-läm′), *n.* **1,** the Mohammedan religion; **2,** the whole body of Mohammedans and the countries they rule.—*n.* **Is′lam-ism.**

island (ī′lănd), *n.* **1**, a tract of land surrounded by water; **2**, anything resembling such a tract of land.

is-land-er (ī′lăn-dẽr), *n.* one born or living on an island.

isle (īl), *n.* an island: usually poetical; as, "the *isles* of Greece."

is-let (ī′lĕt), *n.* a small island; as, many *islets* compose the Lesser Antilles.

ism (ĭzm), *n.* a distinctive system or theory; fad; usually used slightingly.

-ism (-ĭzm), *n. suffix*, indicating: **1**, the action of; as, bapt*ism;* **2**, the state, condition, or quality of; as, mystic*ism;* hero*ism;* **3**, a system, doctrine, policy, etc., indicated by the first part of the word; as, liberal*ism;* Presbyterian*ism;* **4**, a characteristic or peculiarity, esp. in manner or language; as, American*ism;* **5**, a morbid condition induced by excessive use of; as, alcohol*ism.*

i-so- (ī′sō-), a combining form from the Greek, meaning equal; as, *iso*thermal.

i-so-bar (ī′sō-bär), *n.* on a map, a line connecting places of the same barometric pressure.—*adj.* **i″so-bar′ic** (-băr′ĭk).

i-so-late (ī′sō-lāt; ĭs′ō-), *v.t.* [*p.t.* and *p.p.* -lat″ed, *p.pr.* -lat″ing], **1**, to place alone; separate from others; as, to *isolate* contagious cases; **2**, in chemistry, to obtain in a pure or uncombined state.—*n.* **i″so-la′tion.**

Syn., *n.* solitude, separation, retirement.

I-solde (ĭ-sōld′), in medieval romance, **1**, an Irish princess beloved by Tristram; **2**, the faithful wife of Tristram. See **I-seult′**, *Pfd. S.*

i-sos-ce-les (ī-sŏs′ĕ-lēz), *adj.* having two equal sides, as a triangle.

i-so-therm (ī′sō-thûrm), *n.* a line on a map, connecting those places on the earth's surface having the same temperature at a given time.

i-so-ther-mal (ī″sō-thûr′măl), *adj.* having, or indicating, equal temperatures; pertaining to, or showing, lines, as a map or chart, indicating places at which the temperature at a given time, or usually, the mean annual temperature, is the same.

i-so-tope (ī′sō-tōp), *n.* one of two or more varieties of an element, identical as to chemical properties, but differing in atomic weight due to differences in the number of neutrons in the various nuclei.

Is-ra-el (ĭz′rā-ĕl), *n.* in the Bible, **1**, the Hebrew patriarch Jacob; **2**, the descendants of Jacob; the Jews; as, the children of *Israel;* **3**, the northern kingdom after the division of the Jews:—*n.* and *adj.* **Is′ra-el-ite.**

Is-rae-li (ĭz-rā′lĭ), *n.* a citizen of the modern state of Israel:—*adj.* pertaining to modern Israel or its people.

is-sue (ĭsh′ū), *n.* **1**, the act of passing or flowing out; **2**, a means of egress; an outlet or point of outlet, as of a river; **3**, that which is sent forth or produced, as a book, newspaper, etc.; esp., the entire number or amount sent out at one time; as, a government *issue* of bank notes; **4**, offspring; progeny; **5**, the final result; outcome; **6**, a point of contention; as, political *issues:*—*v.t.* [*p.t.* and *p.p.* -sued (-ūd), *p.pr.* -su-ing], **1**, to send out; discharge; **2**, to publish; send out officially; **3**, to provide, as the government or an employer, to those in service:—*v.i.* to come or pass forth; **2**, to arise, as from a source; flow; **3**, to come to an end; result: with *in;* **4**, to be sent out officially.—*n.* **is′su-ance.**

Syn., *n.* event, consequence. (See result.)

-ist (-ĭst), *n. suffix*, meaning: **1**, one who makes a practice of doing that which is expressed in the corresponding verb, usually ending in *-ize;* as, plagiar*ist;* moral*ist;* **2**, one who pursues some branch of art or science; as, art*ist;* alchem*ist;* humor*ist;* **3**, an adherent of some system, religion, political creed, etc.; as, Buddh*ist;* social*ist;* color*ist.*

isth-mi-an (ĭs′mĭ-ăn; ĭsth′-; ĭst′-), *adj.* pertaining to a neck of land which connects two larger bodies of land: **Isthmian games**, a series of athletic contests held on the Isthmus of Corinth, in ancient Greece, every two years:—*n.* one who lives on, or who was born on, an isthmus.

isth-mus (ĭs′mŭs; ĭsth′-; ĭst′-), *n.* a neck of land connecting two larger parts, or a peninsula, to the mainland.

it (ĭt), *neut. pron.* of third person [*nom.* it, *poss.* its (ĭts), *obj.* it; *pl. nom.* they (*th*ā), *poss.* their (*th*âr), theirs (*th*ârz), *obj.* them (*th*ĕm)], the thing or person in question; as, what is *it?* who is *it?*

I-tal-ian (ĭ-tăl′yăn), *adj.* pertaining to Italy, its people, or language:—*n.* **1**, a native of Italy; **2**, the language of Italy.

i-tal-ic (ĭ-tăl′ĭk), *adj.* denoting a slender, sloping kind of type [*italic*]: used for emphasis, etc.:—*n.*, usually in *pl.*, italic type.

i-tal-i-cize (ĭ-tăl′ĭ-sīz), *v.t.* [*p.t.* and *p.p.* -cized (-sīzd), *p.pr.* -ciz″ing], to print in italics:—*v.i.* to use italics.

itch (ĭch), *n.* **1**, a skin disease causing great irritation; **2**, a sensation of irritation in the skin; **3**, a constant and teasing desire for something:—*v.i.* **1**, to feel a particular uneasiness in the skin, causing a desire to scratch the part affected; **2**, to have a constant and teasing desire.—*n.* **itch′i-ness.**—*adj.* **itch′y.**

-ite (-īt; -ĭt), *n. suffix*, denoting: **1**, a follower, descendant, or inhabitant, of; as, Israel*ite;* Canaan*ite;* **2**, the name of commercial products; as, vulcan*ite;* **3**, fossil organisms; as, trilob*ite;* **4**, explosives; as, dyna*mite;* **5**, a part, segment, or joint of a body; **6**, in chemistry: **a.** a salt of an acid the name of which ends in *-ous;* as, phosph*ite;* nitr*ite;* **b.** any of certain saccharine substances; as, mann*ite;* **7**, certain rocks; as, gran*ite.*

i-tem (ī′tĕm), *n.* **1**, a separate article, entry, or particular; a sum entered in an account; **2**, a newspaper paragraph:—*adv.* also; likewise.

i-tem-ize (ī′tĕm-īz), *v.t.* [*p.t.* and *p.p.* -ized (-īzd), *p.pr.* -iz″ing], to state by separate entries; give particulars of; as, to *itemize* an account.—*n.* **i″tem-i-za′tion.**

it-er-ate (ĭt′ẽr-āt), *v.t.* [*p.t.* and *p.p.* -at″ed, *p.pr.* -at″ing], to utter a second time; repeat; as, to *iterate* a threat or command.—*n.* **it″er-a′tion.**

it-er-a-tive (ĭt′ẽr-ā-tĭv), *adj.* repeating: doing again and again; as, the *iterative* "Whoo, whoo, whoo" of the owl.

i-tin-er-a-cy (ī-tĭn′ẽr-ȧ-sĭ; ĭ-), *n.* the practice of passing from place to place, esp. with a specific purpose.

i-tin-er-an-cy (ī-tĭn′ẽr-ăn-sĭ; ĭ-), *n.* a passing from place to place, esp. in the discharge of some official duty, as by a judge, preacher, etc.

i-tin-er-ant (ī-tĭn′ẽr-ănt; ĭ-), *adj.* passing from place to place; as, an *itinerant* preacher or judge:—*n.* one who passes from place to place.

i-tin-er-a-ry (ī-tĭn′ẽr-ā-rĭ; ĭ-), *adj.* **1**, pertaining to traveling, a route, or a journey; **2**, traveling from place to place:—*n.* [*pl.* itineraries (-rĭz)], **1**, a traveler's guide or route book; also, a plan of an extended journey; **2**, a route; **3**, a record of a journey.

i-tin-er-ate (ī-tĭn′ẽr-āt; ĭ-), *v.i.* [*p.t.* and *p.p.* -at″ed, *p.pr.* -at″ing], to travel from place to place, usually for some definite purpose, as preaching.

-i-tis (-ī′tĭs), *n. suffix*, meaning inflammatory disease of; as, tonsil*itis*, bronch*itis.*

its (ĭts), *pron.* the possessive case of the pronoun *it;* as, the tree has lost *its* leaves.

it's (ĭts), a contraction of the two words *it is;* as, *it's* as broad as it is long.

it-self (ĭt-sĕlf′), *pron.* the intensive or reflexive form of *it;* as, he cared only for the work *itself*, and not for praise or money.

-ive (-ĭv), *adj. suffix*, relating to; of the nature of; as, act*ive;* fest*ive:* used also in nouns, which in reality are adjectives used substantively; as, nat*ive.*

I've (īv), a colloquial contraction of the two words *I have.*

i-vied (ī′vĭd), *adj.* covered with, or overgrown with, ivy; as, *ivied* walls.

i-vo-ry (ī′vō-rĭ), *n.* [*pl.* ivories (-rĭz)], **1**, the hard, white substance which forms the tusks of the elephant, walrus, etc.; **2**, ivory color; whiteness; **3**, a substance resembling ivory; **4**, an article, as a carving, made of ivory:—*adj.* made of, or like, ivory.

i-vo-ry nut the seed of a South American palm, from which vegetable ivory, used for buttons, is obtained.

i-vo-ry palm the palm yielding the ivory nut.

i-vy (ī′vĭ), *n.* [*pl.* ivies (ī′vĭz)], any of several clinging vines with ornamental leaves, as English ivy, Boston ivy, etc.

-ize (-īz), *v. suffix*, meaning: **1**, to subject or treat to the action denoted by the root; as, critic*ize;* **2**, to make or make like; as, fossil*ize;* human*ize;* **3**, to act like; treat after the manner or method of; as, Anglic*ize;* macadam*ize;* **4**, to treat or combine with; as, oxid*ize;* carbon*ize.* Also, **-ise.**

J

jab (jăb), *v.t.* and *v.i.* [*p.t.* and *p.p.* jabbed (jăbd), *p.pr.* jab′bing], to thrust suddenly with something pointed:—*n.* a sharp thrust.

jab-ber (jăb′ẽr), *v.i.* to talk rapidly and indistinctly; chatter; as, the monkeys *jabber* in the trees:—*v.t.* to utter unintelligibly:—*n.* incoherent or unintelligible talk.—*n.* **jab′ber-er.**

ja-bot (zhȧ′bō′), *n.* a lace frill on a woman's waist, or, formerly, on a man's shirt.

ja-cinth (jā′sĭnth; jăs′ĭnth), *n.* an orange gem. See **hy′a-cinth**, *Pfd. S.*

[1]**jack** (jăk), *n.* **1**, any one of several mechanical devices which may be considered to do the work of an assistant, servant, or the like; as, a boot*jack*, a roasting *jack* for turning meat on a spit, or a portable mechanism for lifting a great weight; **2**, the male of any of several animals, esp. the ass; **3**, any of several fish, esp. a small pike or pickerel; **4**, in cards, any one of the four knaves; **5**, a small flag, usually flown at the bowsprit of a vessel: when emblematic of union called *union jack* (which see for illus.); **6**, in *pl.*, the game of jackstones: **Jack**, **1**, a nickname for John; **2**, a young man: used with *Jill* to mean any youth and maid; **3**, a familiar term of address among laborers, sailors, etc.; hence, a sailor: often, *jack-tar:* **Jack-of-all-trades**, one who can do various kinds of work, often implying lack of skill in any line:—*v.t.* **1**, to raise or hoist by means of a jack, levers, blocks, or other mechanical devices: often with *up;* **2**, *Slang*, to incite to renewed effort: with *up.*

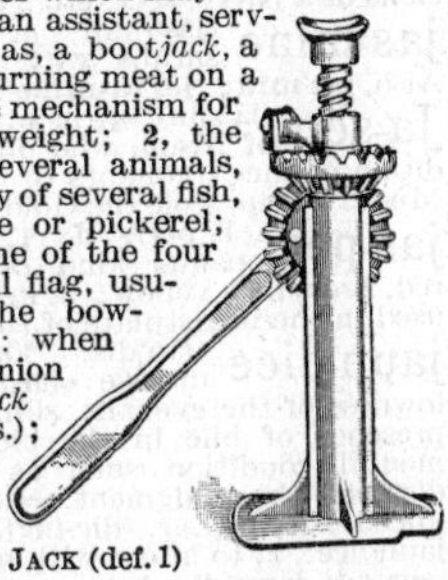
JACK (def. 1)

[2]**jack** (jăk), *n.* **1**, a defensive garment made of two interlined folds of leather; **2**, *Archaic:* **a**, a coat of mail; **b**, a leather or metal pitcher or canteen.

jack-al (jăk′ôl), *n.* **1**, any of several dog-like animals which hunt in packs; **2**, one who does base work for another.

jack-a-napes (jăk′ȧ-nāps″), *n.* an impertinent or conceited fellow.

jack-ass (jăk′ȧs″), *n.* **1**, the male ass; donkey; **2**, a blockhead.

jack boots large boots reaching above the knee. Also, *n.* **jack′boots″.**

jack-daw (jăk′dô″), *n.* a European bird of the crow family, which may be taught to imitate human speech.

jack-et (jăk′ĕt), *n.* **1**, a short, tailless coat; also, an outer covering put on like a coat, but not used as clothing; as, a cork *jacket* used as a life preserver; **2**, a covering for protection, insulation, etc.; as, a water *jacket* for cooling an engine:—*v.t.* to cover with, or as with, a jacket; protect by covering.

jack-in-the-pul-pit (jăk′-ĭn-*th*ē-pōōl′pĭt), *n.* an American plant of the arum family, bearing flowers on a fleshy axis covered by a hood.

jack-knife (jăk′nīf″), *n.* [*pl.* jackknives (-nīvz″)], a pocket knife larger and stronger than a penknife.

jack-o'-lan-tern (jăk′-ō-lăn″tẽrn), *n.* **1**, a hollow pumpkin cut to resemble a human face, having a light inside it; also, a lantern made to resemble this; **2**, a will-o'-the-wisp.

jack rab-bit any of several hares of western North America.

jack-stones (jăk′stōnz″), *n.pl.* **1**, a game played by picking up pebbles or metal pieces in various ways; **2**, the pieces used in the game.

jack-straws (jăk′strôz″), *n. pl.* **1**, a game in which light pieces of wood or metal are picked up with a hook or magnet; **2**, the pieces used in this game.

Ja-cob (jā′kŭb), *n.* a Hebrew patriarch, son of Isaac and Rebecca, ancestor of the twelve tribes of Israel: also called *Israel.*

Jac-o-be-an (jăk″ō-bē′ăn; jȧ-kō′bē-ăn), *adj.* pertaining to the times or reign of James I of England; specif., designating a style of architecture and design characteristic of that period (see *furniture*, illus.).

Jac-o-bin (jăk′ō-bĭn), *n.* **1**, a French friar of the Dominican order; **2**, one of a club of very extreme democrats during the French Revolution of 1789; **3**, hence, a violent extremist.—*adj.* **Jac″o-bin′ic.**

Jac-o-bite (jăk′ō-bīt), *n.* in English history, a supporter of James II or of his family.

jac-o-net (jăk′ō-nĕt), *n.* a fine, soft, white cotton material somewhat like cambric; nainsook. Also, **jac′co-net.**

[1]**jade** (jād), *n.* **1**, an inferior or worn-out horse; **2**, a vicious woman; **3**, a saucy young woman: used contemptuously or humorously:—*v.t.* [*p.t.* and *p.p.* jad′ed, *p.pr.* jad′ing], to tire by long-continued labor:—*v.i.* to become weary; flag.

Syn., *v.* exhaust, fatigue, weary.

[2]**jade** (jād), *n.* a hard, semiprecious stone, usually green.

jae-ger (yā′gẽr; jā′gẽr), *n.* any of several strong, long-winged birds closely resembling gulls, which rob gulls and other birds of their food; the skua.

[1]jag (jăg), *n.* a sharp, projecting point; a notch:—*v.t.* [*p.t.* and *p.p.* jagged (jăgd), *p.pr.* jag′ging], to cut into notches. Also, **jagg.**

[2]jag (jăg), *n.* **1,** *Colloq.*, a small load; **2,** *Slang*, a drinking spree.

Jag-an-nath (jŭg′ȧ-nät; jŭg′ȧ-nôt), *n.* the Hindu god Krishna, whose worship centers about the chief idol at Puri, in Orissa, before whose car it was formerly erroneously supposed that devotees cast themselves to death. Also, **Jag″an-na′tha; Jug′ger-naut.**

jag-ged (jăg′ĕd), *p.adj.* notched; irregular on the edge; cut or torn in points.—*adv.* **jag′ged-ly.**—*n.* **jag′ged-ness.**

jag-uar (jăg′wär; jȧ-gwär′), *n.* a fierce animal of South America, resembling the leopard, but larger and more powerful.

JAGUAR (1/35)

ja-had (jȧ-häd′), *n.* a Mohammedan holy war. See **ji-had′,** *Pfd. S.*

Jah-weh (yä′wĕ), *n.* Jehovah: a name of God. See **Yah′weh,** *Pfd. S.*

jail (jāl), *n.* a prison; esp., a place where persons guilty of minor offenses are confined. Also, *Br.*, **gaol** (jāl).

jail-bird (jāl′bûrd″), *n.* **1,** a convict; **2,** a habitual criminal; rogue.

jail-er (jāl′ẽr), *n.* one in charge of a jail. Also, **jail′or;** *Br.*, **gaol′er** (jāl′ẽr).

jal-ap (jăl′ăp), *n.* the dried root of a Mexican climbing plant from which a purgative extract or powder is made.

[1]jam (jăm), *v.t.* [*p.t.* and *p.p.* jammed (jămd), *p.pr.* jam′ming], **1,** to squeeze or crush; press in tightly; **2,** to block up:—*v.i.* to become tightly packed:—*n.* a collection of people or things crowded together.

[2]jam (jăm), *n.* a thick, sweet fruit preserve: often used on bread.

Ja-mai-can (jȧ-mā′kăn), *n.* a native or inhabitant of the island of Jamaica in the West Indies.

jamb (jăm), *n.* one of the sides of a doorway, window opening, or fireplace.

James (jāmz), *n.* in the Bible, **1,** the son of Zebedee, brother of John, one of the twelve apostles (Matthew 4:21); **2,** another apostle, the son of Alpheus (Matthew 10:3); **3,** a book in the New Testament.

jan-gle (jăng′gl), *v.i.* [*p.t.* and *p.p.* -gled (-gld), *p.pr.* -gling], **1,** to quarrel or wrangle; **2,** to gossip or chatter; **3,** to sound out of tune; as, the bells *jangle* on the ragman's cart:—*v.t.* to cause to jangle:—*n.* **1,** a discordant sound; **2,** a coarse quarrel.
Syn., v. conflict, disagree.

jan-i-tor (jăn′ĭ-tẽr), *n.* **1,** a doorkeeper; **2,** one who takes care of a building.—*n. fem.* **jan′i-tress.**

Jan-i-za-ry (jăn′ĭ-zā-rĭ), *n.* [*pl.* Janizaries (-rĭz)], **1,** a Turkish soldier; **2,** formerly, one of a body of infantry, acting as the standing army of the Turkish Empire and famous for fierce fighting. Also, **jan′i-za-ry; Jan′is-sa-ry; jan′is-sa-ry.**

Jan-u-a-ry (jăn′ū-ā-rĭ), *n.* the first month of the year, having 31 days: named for the god Janus.—*abbr.* **Jan.**

Ja-nus (jā′nŭs), *n.* an ancient Roman god, protector of doorways and gates, whose head had two faces on opposite sides: **Janus-faced,** *adj.* two-faced; deceitful.

ja-pan (jȧ-păn′), *n.* **1,** a hard, brilliant varnish for wood or metal; **2,** collectively, articles lacquered in the Japanese manner:—*v.t.* [*p.t.* and *p.p.* -panned′ (-pănd′), *p.pr.* -pan′ning], to coat with japan or similar varnish; make glossy, as with japan.

Jap-a-nese (jăp″ȧ-nēz′; -nēs′), *adj.* pertaining to Japan, or to its inhabitants or language: **Japanese beetle,** a small, bronze-green beetle, unintentionally brought to the neighborhood of Philadelphia in in 1916, and spreading with menacing rapidity: very destructive to vegetation:—*n.* **1,** a native of Japan; **2,** the language of Japan.

[1]jar (jär), *v.i.* [*p.t.* and *p.p.* jarred (järd), *p.pr.* jar′ring], **1,** to give out a harsh sound; be discordant; **2,** to shake; vibrate; **3,** to clash; disagree:—*v.t.* **1,** to make discordant; **2,** to cause to shake:—*n.* **1,** a harsh sound; discord; **2,** a sudden shake or quivering; **3,** a conflict of opinion.
Syn., v. jolt, quiver, disturb.

[2]jar (jär), *n.* a cylindrical broad-mouthed vessel of earthenware or glass: **Leyden jar** (lī′dĕn), a glass jar coated nearly to the top outside and inside with tin foil and used as an electrical condenser.

[3]jar (jär), *n.* a turn: obsolete except in *ajar; on the jar; on a jar.*

***jar-di-nière** (zhär″dē″nyâr′), [Fr.], *n.* an ornamental flower stand or container for a potted plant.

jar-gon (jär′gŏn), *n.* **1,** confused talk not to be understood; **2,** a mixture of two or more languages; **3,** the peculiar expressions of a party, sect, etc.; cant; lingo.

jas-mine (jăs′mĭn), *n.* any of various shrubs with fragrant flowers. Also, **jas′min; jes′sa-mine.**

Ja-son (jā′sŭn), *n.* in mythology, the son of Æson, who organized the expedition of the Argonauts to Colchis, and, with Medea's help, stole the Golden Fleece.

jas-per (jăs′pẽr), *n.* **1,** a many-shaded opaque kind of quartz, usually red, brown, or yellow; **2,** in the Bible, a stone used in the breastplate of the high priest.

jaun-dice (jän′dĭs; jôn′dĭs), *n.* **1,** a disease characterized by yellowness of the eyeballs, skin, etc., due to the presence of bile in the blood; **2,** hence, a mental condition such as jealousy, which distorts the judgment:—*v.t.* [*p.t.* and *p.p.* -diced (-dĭst), *p.pr.* -dic-ing], **1,** to affect with jaundice; **2,** to affect with envy or prejudice.—*p. adj.* **jaun′diced.**

jaunt (jänt; jônt), *n.* a short excursion or ramble:—*v.i.* to roam or ramble; take a short excursion or trip.
Syn., n. journey, trip, stroll, tour.

jaunt-ing car a vehicle used esp. in Ireland, with seats on which the passengers sit sidewise, back to back.

jaun-ty (jän′tĭ; jôn′tĭ), *adj.* [*comp.* jaun′ti-er, *superl.* jaun′ti-est], airy; gay; stylish; as, he has a *jaunty* air.—*adv.* **jaun′ti-ly.**—*n.* **jaun′ti-ness.**

Ja-va man (jä′vȧ), an apelike man part of whose fossil remains were found in Java.

jave-lin (jăv′-lĭn; jăv′ĕ-lĭn), *n.* a light spear intended to be hurled as a weapon.

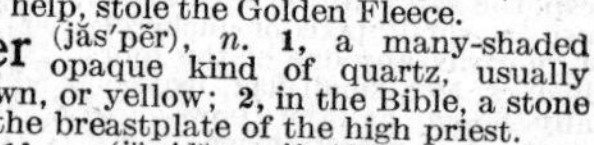

JAVELINS

jaw (jô), *n.* **1,** either of the bones of the mouth in which the teeth are fixed; **2,** anything that resembles an animal's jaw.—*adj.* **jaw′less.**

jaw-bone (jô′bōn″), *n.* a bone of the jaw; esp., a bone of the lower jaw.

jay (jā), *n.* any of several noisy, restless birds of Europe and America, akin to the crow, with bright, handsome feathers: **jaywalker**, *Slang*, a pedestrian who ignores regular street crossings or traffic signals.

jazz (jăz), *n. Colloq.*, ragtime music in loud tones and accompanied by novel musical effects, played on various instruments, as the banjo, mandolin, ukelele, saxophone, trombone, drum, piano, etc.

jeal-ous (jĕl′ŭs), *adj.* **1**, characterized by envy or suspicious fear; **2**, unwilling to have a rival, or fearful of a rival, in affection; **3**, intolerant of all but exclusive worship and love: said of God; **4**, anxiously suspicious or watchful; as, *jealous* of a good name.—*adv.* **jeal′ous-ly.**

jeal-ous-y (jĕl′ŭs-ĭ), *n.* [*pl.* jealousies (-ĭz)], **1**, envy; **2**, resentment toward, or fear of, a rival; **3**, insistence on exclusive affection; **4**, watchful care.

Syn. envy. *Jealousy* is an intense desire to keep what one has, combined with an anxious fear of losing it; it may be a watchfulness of one's rights, or a feeling of anger at another's intrusion on them. *Envy* is a base desire for what is possessed by another, felt toward a thing to which one has no right or claim.

jean (jēn; jān), *n.* **1**, a kind of twilled cotton cloth; **2**, in *pl.*, a garment of this cloth; as, overalls, or blue *jeans*.

jeep (jēp), *n.* a small automobile truck for four persons, used in the Army.

jeer (jēr), *v.t.* to sneer at; make loud fun of; ridicule:—*v.i.* to speak in a sneering or sarcastic manner:—*n.* a sneer; coarse ridicule.—*n.* **jeer′er.**

Syn., v. scoff, sneer, gibe, taunt. To *jeer* is to direct sarcastic and insulting words at a person. To *scoff* is to mock or deride serious or sacred things. To show contempt by facial expression or by derisive words is to *sneer*. To *gibe* is to utter ill-natured, usually reproachful, words, often disguised as fair speech. To *taunt* is to reproach a person to his face, often with sarcasm and contempt, esp. about conduct, an unfulfilled boast, or the like.

Je-ho-vah (jē-hō′vȧ), *n.* a form of the name of the Hebrew God, *Yahweh* (which see), thought by the Jews too sacred to utter.

je-hu (jē′hū), *n.* one fond of driving, esp. of fast driving: derived from the story of Jehu (2 Kings 9).

je-june (jē-jōōn′), *adj.* empty; dry; without interest; as, a *jejune* tale.

je-ju-num (jē-jōō′nŭm), *n.* [*pl.* jejuna (-nȧ)], the middle division of the small intestine.

Je-kyll, Dr., and Mr. Hyde (jēk′l, hīd), *n.* **1**, the two personalities, different phases of the same individual, who together form the hero of a tale by Stevenson; **2**, hence, any person having two distinct personalities, esp. an evil and a benevolent one.

jel-ly (jĕl′ĭ), *n.* [*pl.* jellies (-ĭz)], **1**, the stiffened juice of fruit, meat, etc., after boiling and cooling; **2**, any substance of similar semisolid consistency:—*v.i.* [*p.t.* and *p.p.* -lied (-ĭd), *p.pr.* -ly-ing], to become jelly:—*v.t.* to cause to become jelly.

jel-ly-fish (jĕl′ĭ-fĭsh″), *n.* any of several marine creatures without bones and with a jellylike body.

jen-net (jĕn′ĕt), *n.* a small Spanish horse. Also, **gen′et.**

jen-ny (jĕn′ĭ), *n.* [*pl.* jennies (-ĭz)], **1**, a machine for spinning; **2**, a female: often used before the name of an animal; as, the *jenny* wren; the *jenny* ass.

jeop-ard (jĕp′ard), *v.t.* to expose to loss or injury; jeopardize; risk; as, who would *jeopard* his life for nothing?

Syn. peril, endanger, hazard.

jeop-ard-ize (jĕp′ar-dīz), *v.t.* [*p.t.* and *p.p.* -ized (-dīzd), *p.pr.* -iz″ing], to endanger; expose to risk; as, to *jeopardize* one's chances.

jeop-ard-y (jĕp′ăr-dĭ), *n.* risk; peril; hazard; danger.

Jeph-thah (jĕf′thȧ), *n.* in the Bible, a judge in Israel who, in fulfilling a rash vow, sacrificed his only daughter (Judges 11:30–40).

jer-bo-a (jĕr-bō′ȧ), *n.* any of a family of ratlike, jumping rodents of the African desert.

JERBOA ($\frac{1}{10}$)

jer-e-mi-ad (jĕr″ē-mī′ăd), *n.* a lamentation; a tale of sorrow, disappointment, or complaint: so called in allusion to the "Lamentations of Jeremiah" in the Old Testament.

Jer-e-mi-ah (jĕr″ē-mī′ȧ), *n.* **1**, a great Hebrew prophet; **2**, a book of the Old Testament, containing his lamentations and prophecies. Also, in the Douay Bible, **Jer″e-mi′as.**—*abbr.* **Jer.**

¹jerk (jûrk), *v.t.* **1**, to give a quick pull, twist, or push to; **2**, to throw with a sudden, quick movement:—*v.i.* to move convulsively:—*n.* **1**, a sudden, quick pull, twist, push, or throw; **2**, a convulsive movement.

²jerk (jûrk), *v.t.* to cut (beef) into thin strips and dry in the sun:—*n.* beef so treated.

jer-kin (jûr′kĭn), *n.* a short, close-fitting coat, formerly worn by men.

jerk-y (jûr′kĭ), *adj.* [*comp.* jerk′i-er, *superl.* jerk′i-est], moving with quick starts and frequent stops.—*adv.* **jerk′i-ly.**

Jer-o-bo-am (jĕr″ō-bō′ăm), *n.* in the Bible, **1**, a Jewish leader who led the rebellion of the ten tribes and became the first king of the northern kingdom, Israel (1 Kings 11–14); **2**, a son of Joash, and king of Israel (2 Kings 13:13).

Jer-sey (jûr′zĭ), *adj.* **1**, pertaining to the island of Jersey, or to its breed of cattle; **2**, pertaining to New Jersey:—*n.* [*pl.* Jerseys (-zĭz)], one of a breed of dairy cows that originated in the island of Jersey: **jersey, 1**, a close-fitting upper garment of elastic wool or silk; **2**, a fine yarn wool.

jess (jĕs), *n.* a leathern strap fastened to the leg of a hawk and provided with a ring to which is attached the falconer's leash.

jes-sa-mine (jĕs′ȧ-mĭn), *n.* any of various shrubs with fragrant flowers. Also, **jas′min;** *Pfd. S.*, **jas′mine.**

Jes-se (jĕs′ē), *n.* in the Bible, a Hebrew of the time of Samuel and Saul, father of David (1 Samuel 16).

jest (jĕst), *n.* **1**, a joke; also, a taunt; jeer; **2**, the person or thing laughed at or jeered:—*v.i.* to joke; jeer; banter.

jest-er (jĕs′tĕr), *n.* **1**, one who makes jokes; **2**, in medieval times, a court fool.

Je-su (jē′sū; yā′sōō), *n. Poetic*, Jesus: used in direct address.

Jes-u-it (jĕz′ū-ĭt), *n.* a member of the Roman Catholic Society of Jesus, founded by Loyola, 1543.—*n.* **Jes′u-it-ism.**

Jes-u-it-ic (jĕz″ū-ĭt′ĭk), *adj.* pertaining to, or resembling, the Jesuits, or their practices.—Also, **Jes″u-it′i-cal; jes″u-it′i-cal.**

Je-sus (jē′zŭs), *n.* in the Bible, the Son of Mary: the founder of the Christian religion (Matthew 1 : 20–21): often called *Jesus of Nazareth* or *Jesus Christ*.

[1]jet (jĕt), *v.t.* [*p.t.* and *p.p.* jet′ted, *p.pr.* jet′ting], to spurt out:—*v.i.* **1**, to shoot or spout out; **2**, to jut out:—*n.* **1**, a stream of fluid issuing from an opening; as, the whale spouts a *jet* of water; **2**, a spout or nozzle for the issuing of a fluid; as, a gas *jet;* **3**, a jet airplane.

[2]jet (jĕt), *n.* **1**, a hard, black, mineral, akin to coal, used in making ornaments, buttons, etc.; **2**, the color of jet, a deep, glossy black:—*adj.* **1**, of jet; **2**, very black.—*adj.* **jet′ty.**

jet engine a reaction engine which takes in and compresses air to burn a liquid fuel, releasing the resultant gas through a controlled opening and thus providing thrust which may be used for propulsion.

jet plane an airplane driven by one or more jet engines.

jet-sam (jĕt′săm), *n.* goods thrown overboard to ease a ship in peril, esp. such goods when washed ashore.

jet-ti-son (jĕt′ĭ-sŭn), *n.* the throwing overboard of goods, esp. to ease a ship in time of peril:—*v.t.* to throw overboard to lighten a vessel in time of peril.

jet-ty (jĕt′ĭ), *n.* [*pl.* jetties (-ĭz)], **1**, a structure extending into the water, used as a pier, or wall, to protect a harbor or to direct currents; **2**, a projecting part of a building:—*v.i.* [*p.t.* and *p.p.* -tied (-ĭd), *p.pr.* -tying], to jut out or project.

***jeu d'es-prit** (zhû′ dĕs″prē′), [Fr.] literally, a play of mind; a witticism; a witty or brilliant remark.

Jew (jū; jōō), *n.* originally, a member of the tribe of Judah; racially, a Hebrew or Israelite; in religion, an adherent of the doctrines and rites of the Jews.—*adj.* **Jew′ish.**

jew-el (jū′ĕl; jōō′ĕl), *n.* **1**, a gem or precious stone, esp. one cut for use in personal adornment; **2**, a valuable ornament or trinket set with gems; **3**, a piece of precious stone used as a bearing in the works of a timepiece; **4**, anything of great value or dear to one:—*v.t.* **1**, to adorn with, or as with, gems; **2**, to fit, as the works of a timepiece, with pieces of precious stone for durable bearings.

jew-el-er (jū′ĕl-ẽr; jōō′-), *n.* one who makes or deals in valuable ornaments, gems, etc. Also, **jew′el-ler.**

jew-el-ry (jū′ĕl-rĭ; jōō′-), *n.* **1**, precious stones, ornaments of gold and silver, etc., taken collectively; **2**, the art or trade of a jeweler. Also, *Br.*, **jew′el-ler-y.**

jew-el-weed (jū′ĕl-wēd″; jōō′-), *n.* any of a genus of herbs of the balsam family; esp., either of two wild American species having spotted yellow or orange flowers and thin, silvery leaves, growing in damp, shady places: also called *touch-me-not.*

jew's–harp (jūz′-härp″; jōōz′-), *n.* a small, lyre-shaped musical instrument, with a thin, flexible metal tongue which, placed between the teeth and struck by the finger, gives forth tones. Also, **jews'′–harp″.**

JEW'S-HARP

Jez-e-bel (jĕz′ĕ-bĕl), *n.* **1**, in the Bible, the evil wife of Ahab, king of Israel (2 Kings 9 : 30); **2**, a bold or wicked woman.

[1]jib (jĭb), *n.* **1**, a three-cornered sail extending beyond the bow of a vessel (see *rigging*, illus.); **2**, the projecting arm or beam of a crane or lifting machine, from which the load is hung: **flying jib**, a sail set outside the jib, usually on an extension of the jib boom or bowsprit (see *rigging*, illus.). Also, **[1]jibb.**

[2]jib (jĭb), *v.t.* [*p.t.* and *p.p.* jibbed (jĭbd), *p.pr.* jib′bing], to move restlessly backward and sidewise, as a horse in harness; balk.

[3]jib (jĭb), *v.i.* [*p.t.* and *p.p.* jibbed (jĭbd); *p.pr.* jib′bing], to shift suddenly from one side of the boat to the other, as a sail or boom in tacking:—*v.t.* to shift from one side to the other; as, to *jib* a sail. Also, **[2]jibb.**

jib boom a spar on which the jib of a vessel is set.

[1]jibe (jīb), *v.i.* [*p.t.* and *p.p.* jibed (jībd), *p.pr.* jib′ing], **1**, to shift from one side of a vessel to the other, as a sail or boom; **2**, to change course, as a vessel, so that the sail shifts in this way:—*v.t.* to cause (a sail or boom) to shift in this way. Also, **gybe**, *Pfd. S.*

[2]jibe (jīb), *v.i.* [*p.t.* and *p.p.* jibed (jībd), *p.pr.* jib′ing], *Colloq.*, to harmonize, as two statements; agree.

[3]jibe (jīb), *n.* a scoff; taunt:—*v.t.* [*p.t.* and *p.p.* jibed (jībd), *p.pr.* jib′ing], to sneer at:—*v.i.* to scoff; sneer. See **gibe**, *Pfd. S.*

jif-fy (jĭf′ĭ), *n.* [*pl.* jiffies (-ĭz)], an instant; a moment; as, I will do it in a *jiffy.*

jig (jĭg), *n.* **1**, a quick, lively dance, or music for such a dance; **2**, a kind of fishhook:—*v.i.* [*p.t.* and *p.p.* jigged (jĭgd), *p.pr.* jig′ging], **1**, to dance a jig; **2**, to use a jig for fishing:—*v.t.* **1**, to jerk up and down; **2**, to dance, as a jig.

[1]jig-ger (jĭg′ẽr), *n.* **1**, one who jigs; **2**, any of various mechanical contrivances, esp. one for washing or separating ore; **3**, a small sail and tackle for yawl or canoe; **4**, in golf, a club with a narrow iron head with considerable loft, or slope: used for approach shots; **5**, a measure of 1½ fluid ounces: **jigger mast**, the after mast of a four-masted or a yawl-rigged vessel.

[2]jig-ger (jĭg′ẽr), *n.* **1**, a small flea of the West Indies and South America, which bites or burrows under the skin; **2**, a similar mite of the southern U. S. Also, **chig′re; chig′ger.** See **chig′oe**, *Pfd. S.*

jig-gle (jĭg′l), *v.t.* and *v.i.* [*p.t.* and *p.p.* -gled (-ld), *p.pr.* -gling], to move slightly and jerkily:—*n.* a slight, jerky movement.

jig saw a scroll saw; a saw with a very narrow blade held in a frame, used to cut along curved or irregular lines.

ji-had (jē-häd′), *n.* **1**, a holy war against the enemies of the Mohammedan faith; **2**, any bitter war for religion or principle. Also, **ja-had′** (jȧ-häd′).

jill (jĭl), *n.* **1**, (preferably, *gill*), a young woman; sweetheart; **2**, the female of a ferret or weasel.

jilt (jĭlt), *n.* a flirt:—*v.t.* to discard (a lover) after having encouraged him.

jim-my (jĭm′ĭ), *n.* [*pl.* jimmies (-ĭz)], a short crowbar used by burglars.—*v.t.* to force open with a jimmy.

Jim-son weed (jĭm′sn), a tall, coarse, poisonous weed, with white, trumpet-shaped flowers.

jin-gle (jĭng′gl), *n.* **1**, a sharp, tinkling, metallic sound; **2**, meaningless rime; **3**, a covered, two-wheeled car used in Australia and Ireland:—*v.i.* [*p.t.* and *p.p.* -gled (-gld), *p.pr.* -gling], to give a tinkling sound:—*v.t.* to cause to give a tinkling sound; as, he *jingled* the keys.

jin-go (jĭng′gō), *n.* [*pl.* jingoes (-gōz)], one who favors or supports a warlike policy in foreign affairs; one who boasts noisily of the prowess of his country: used in reproach: **by jingo**, a mild oath:—*adj.* characteristic of, or pertaining to, an aggressive foreign policy.—*n.* **jin′go-ism.**

jin-ni (jĭ-nē′), *n.* [*pl.* jinn (jĭn), often used as *sing.*], a supernatural being subject to magic control: often appearing in Oriental tales. Also, **jin-nee′; ge′nie.**

jin-rik-i-sha (jĭn-rĭk′ĭ-shä), *n.* a small, two-wheeled, Japanese carriage, drawn by one or more men. Also, **jin-rik′sha; jin-rick′sha; jin-rick′shaw.**

jit-ney (jĭt′nĭ), *n.* [*pl.* jitneys (-nĭz)], **1,** *Slang,* a five-cent piece; **2,** *Colloq.,* an automobile in which passengers are carried for a small fare:—*v.i. Colloq.,* **1,** to travel by short-distance automobile; **2,** to operate such a car.

jiu-jit-su (jōō′jĭt″sōō), *n.* a Japanese weaponless method of self-defense. Also, **jiu′jut″su** (jōō′jōōt″sōō). See **ju′jut″su,** *Pfd. S.*

jo (jō), *n.* [*pl.* joes (jōz)], in Scotland, a sweetheart of either sex.

job (jŏb), *n.* **1,** a piece of work, esp. of an odd or occasional kind; **2,** any scheme for making money or securing private advantage at the public expense; **3,** *Colloq.:* **a,** a business situation; employment; **b,** any event or circumstance; as, it is a bad *job:*—*v.t.* [*p.t.* and *p.p.* jobbed (jŏbd), *p.pr.* job′bing], **1,** to let out for hire; **2,** to buy up (goods) and retail (them):—*v.i.* **1,** to buy and sell, as a stockbroker; **2,** to do an occasional piece of work for wages; **3,** to work for one's own advantage under pretense of serving others.

Job (jōb), *n.* the hero of a book of the Old Testament, who patiently suffered much affliction; also, the book telling his story.

job-ber (jŏb′ẽr), *n.* **1,** a middleman; **2,** in England, one who acts as agent between stockbrokers; **3,** one who transacts public business for his own private interests; **4,** one who does odd pieces of work for hire.

job-ber-y (jŏb′ẽr-ĭ), *n.* [*pl.* jobberies (-ĭz)], low scheming for private advantage or political ends.

Jo-cas-ta (jō-kăs′tȧ), *n.* in Greek mythology, mother and wife of Œdipus.

jock-ey (jŏk′ĭ), *n.* [*pl.* jockeys (-ĭz)], **1,** one hired to ride a horse in a race; a groom; **2,** a dealer in horses; **3,** an unfair trader; a cheat:—*v.t.* **1,** to cheat or deceive; **2,** to jostle against and hinder by riding unfairly:—*v.i.* **1,** to cheat; be tricky; **2,** to seek to secure a fair advantage by maneuvering.

jo-cose (jō-kōs′), *adj.* full of jokes; sportive; humorous; merry; as, a *jocose* manner.—*adv.* **jo-cose′ly.**—*n.* **jo-cose′-ness.**—*n.* **jo-cos′i-ty.**

Syn. droll, playful, jocular, facetious, funny.

joc-u-lar (jŏk′ū-lȧr), *adj.* **1,** making jokes; **2,** done in joke.—*adv.* **joc′u-lar-ly.**—*n.* **joc″u-lar′i-ty.**

Syn. jocose, merry, blithe, sportive.

joc-und (jŏk′ŭnd; *Br.* jō′kŭnd), *adj.* jovial; sportive; gay.—*adv.* **joc′-und-ly.**—*n.* **jo-cun′di-ty** (jō-kŭn′dĭ-tĭ).

Jo-el (jō′ĕl), *n.* **1,** in the Bible, an ancient Hebrew prophet; **2,** a book of the Old Testament recording his preachings.

jog (jŏg), *v.t.* [*p.t.* and *p.p.* jogged (jŏgd), *p.pr.* jog′ging], **1,** to push or shake slightly, usually with the elbow or hand, by way of reminder; **2,** to arouse gently; as, to *jog* the memory:—*v.i.* to travel along with a slow, trotting motion:—*n.* **1,** a slight push or shake; **2,** a slow trot; **3,** a notch; an irregularity, as of line: **jog trot,** a slow, regular gait; hence, a dull routine; an easy-going way.

jog-gle (jŏg′l), *v.t.* [*p.t.* and *p.p.* -gled (-ld), *p.pr.* -gling], to shake slightly; nudge:—*v.i.* to totter:—*n.* a sudden shake.

John (jŏn), *n.* in the Bible, **1,** a son of Zebedee, one of the twelve apostles; **2,** the fourth Gospel; **3,** any of the three Epistles in the New Testament, ascribed to the apostle John: **John the Baptist,** a preacher of repentance who preceded Jesus (Matthew 3).

John Bull an Englishman; the English people personified.

john do-ry a brightly colored European food fish: also called *dory.*

john-ny-cake (jŏn′ĭ-kāk″), *n.* a flat cake of corn meal mixed with milk or water, eggs, etc., and baked.

join (join), *v.t.* **1,** to unite; connect; put or bring together; unite in marriage; **2,** to unite with; become a member of; as, to *join* a club; **3,** to engage in, with others; as, to *join* battle:—*v.i.* **1,** to be in contact; **2,** to become associated or united; come together as one:—*n.* a joint or union.

Syn., *v.* consolidate. (See combine.)—*Ant.,* *v.* separate, detach.

join-der (join′dẽr), *n.* in law, the joining of two or more causes of action.

join-er (join′ẽr), *n.* **1,** one who or that which joins; **2,** a skilled workman who finishes the inside woodwork for houses or who makes furniture; **3,** *Colloq.,* one who joins many societies; a good fellow.

join-er-y (join′ẽr-ĭ), *n.* skilled work in wood, as in making furniture.

joint (joint), *n.* **1,** the place where two or more things join; esp., the point where two bones of the body are joined; **2,** the part included between two joinings; as, a *joint* in a grass stem; **3,** an opening which divides rock masses into blocks; **4,** a large piece of meat cut for roasting; **5,** *Slang,* a low resort:—*adj.* **1,** united; combined; as, our *joint* efforts; **2,** used, held, or shared by two or more; as, *joint* property: **joint-stock company,** a company consisting of a number of persons doing business for gain, the shares owned by any member being transferable, and the shareholders individually liable for the debts of the company:—*v.t.* **1,** to form with joints; **2,** to prepare the edge, as of a board, to fit another; **3,** to cut, as meat, into pieces or joints.—*adv.* **joint′ly.**—*n.* **joint′er.**

join-ture (join′tūr), *n.* in law, a settlement accepted by a wife, by which, at her husband's death, she inherits certain specified property in place of her dower right:—*v.t.* [*p.t.* and *p.p.* -tured (-tūrd), *p.pr.* -turing], to settle property upon (a wife).

joist (joist), *n.* a horizontal timber to which floor boards or ceiling laths are fastened:—*v.t.* to furnish with joists.

joke (jōk), *n.* **1,** something said or done to cause mirth; jest; sport; **2,** a laughingstock:—*v.i.* [*p.t.* and *p.p.* joked (jōkt), *p.pr.* jok′ing], to jest:—*v.t.* to make fun of.

jok-er (jōk′ẽr), *n.* **1,** one who makes or tells humorous stories or plays pranks; **2,** an extra card used in certain card games, usually the highest trump.

jol-li-fi-ca-tion (jŏl″ĭ-fĭ-kā′shŭn), *n.* merrymaking; festivity.

jol-li-ty (jŏl′ĭ-tĭ), *n.* [*pl.* jollities (-tĭz)], the state of being merry, gay, or sportive; gaiety.

jol-ly (jŏl′ĭ), *adj.* [*comp.* jol′li-er, *superl.* jol′li-est], **1,** full of life and mirth; gay; **2,** causing mirth or gaiety:—*v.t.* [*p.t.* and *p.p.* -lied (-ĭd), *p.pr.* -ly-ing], *Slang,* to make good-humored fun of.

Syn., *adj.* merry, jovial. (See joyful.)

jol-ly–boat (jŏl′ĭ-bōt″), *n.* a ship's small boat, used for general or rough work: also called *jolly.*

jolt (jōlt), *v.t.* to shake by sudden jerks:—*v.i.* to have a jerky motion:—*n.* a sudden jerk or stop.—*n.* **jolt′er.**

Jo-nah (jō′nȧ), *n.* **1,** one of the minor Hebrew prophets; also, a book of the Old Testament which tells how Jonah was thrown overboard from a ship as being the cause of a perilous storm, and was swallowed by a great fish; **2,** hence, any person who brings ill luck or trouble. Also, in the Douay Bible, **Jo′nas.**

Jon-a-than (jŏn′ȧ-thăn), *n.* in the Bible, the son of King Saul and close friend of David (1 Samuel 18–20).

***jon-gleur** (zhôn″glûr′), *n.* in medieval times, a wandering minstrel.

jon-quil (jŏn'kwĭl; jŭng'kwĭl), *n.* a plant of the narcissus family, with yellow or white fragrant flowers, growing from bulbs. Also, **jon'quille.**

jo-rum (jō'rŭm), *n. Colloq.*, a large drinking bowl, or that which it contains.

Jos-eph (jō'zĕf), *n.* in the Bible, **1,** a Hebrew patriarch, the son of Jacob, sold into slavery in Egypt by his brothers (Genesis 37:28); **2,** the husband of Mary, mother of Jesus (Matthew 1:18–25); **3,** a man of Arimathea, who buried Jesus (Matthew 27:57–60).

Josh-u-a (jŏsh'ū-ȧ), *n.* **1,** in the Bible, the successor of Moses and leader of the Israelites in the conquest of Canaan; **2,** a book of the Old Testament, giving the history of this conquest.—*abbr.* **Josh.** Also, in the Douay Bible, **Jos'u-e** (jŏs'ū-ē).

joss (jŏs), *n.* a Chinese household divinity or idol: **joss house,** a Chinese temple: **joss stick,** a stick made of hardened paste of scented wood, burned esp. as incense.

jos-tle (jŏs'l), *v.t.* [*p.t.* and *p.p.* -tled (-ld), *p.pr.* -tling], to push against; run against and shake; elbow:—*n.* a collision, as of pedestrians; bumping; elbowing.

jot (jŏt), *v.t.* [*p.t.* and *p.p.* jot'ted, *p.pr.* jot'ting], to make a memorandum of: with *down:*—*n.* a tittle or very small particle; as, I don't care a *jot.*

jounce (jouns), *v.t.* and *v.i.* [*p.t.* and *p.p.* jounced (jounst), *p.pr.* jounc'ing], to shake up and down; jolt:—*n.* a jolt.

jour-nal (jûr'năl), *n.* **1,** a record of news or events; **2,** hence, a daily newspaper or other periodical; **3,** a diary; **4,** a book in which particular transactions are entered from the daybook; **5,** a ship's logbook.

jour-nal-ism (jûr'năl-ĭzm), *n.* the occupation of publishing, or writing for, newspapers or periodicals.

jour-nal-ist (jûr'năl-ĭst), *n.* an editor of, or contributor to, a newspaper.—*adj.* **jour"nal-is'tic.**

jour-nal-ize (jûr'năl-īz), *v.t.* [*p.t* and *p.p.* -ized (-īzd), *p.pr.* -iz"ing], to enter in a daybook or other record:—*v.i.* to keep a daily record or diary.

jour-ney (jûr'nĭ), *n.* [*pl.* journeys (-nĭz)], **1,** passage or expedition from one place to another; **2,** the time occupied or space covered in travel:—*v.i.* to travel from one place to another.—*n.* **jour'ney-er.**

Syn., n. tour, trip, excursion.

jour-ney-man (jûr'nĭ-măn), *n.* [*pl.* journeymen (-mĕn)], a mechanic who has served his apprenticeship or learned a trade, and who works, esp. by the day, for another.

joust (jŭst; jo͞ost), *n.* a combat with lances between two knights on horseback; esp., a mock combat in the lists, or inclosed field, as part of a tournament; as, the *jousts* at King Arthur's court:—*v.i.* to engage in such a combat. Also, [2]**just,** *Pfd. S.*—*n.* **joust'er.**

Jove (jōv), *n.* in mythology, Jupiter, the greatest of the gods.

jo-vi-al (jō'vĭ-ăl), *adj.* jolly; merry; as, he was always a *jovial* comrade.—*adv.* **jo'vi-al-ly.**—*n.* **jo"vi-al'i-ty.**

Syn. festive, gay. (See joyful.)

jowl (jōl; joul), *n.* **1,** the jaw or cheek; as, a heavy *jowl;* **2,** the head of a fish.

joy (joi), *n.* **1,** gaiety; gladness; **2,** that which causes gladness:—*v.i.* to rejoice or be glad; as, to *joy* in happiness.

Syn., n. pleasure, mirth, delight, happiness, enjoyment.—*Ant., n.* grief, gloom.

joy-ful (joi'fo͝ol), *adj.* full of, or causing, gladness; as, *joyful* days; *joyful* news.—*adv.* **joy'ful-ly.**—*n.* **joy'ful-ness.** (See *Syn.*, next column.)

Syn. joyous, jolly, jovial. That which is *joyful* inspires an emotion of extreme delight, and usually brings an outward expression; as, *joyful* news. That which is *joyous* springs from an innate quality; as, *joyous* laughter. *Jolly* and *jovial* suggest good-natured mirth; as, a *jolly* party; two *jovial* spirits.

joy-less (joi'lĕs), *adj.* without having or causing gladness; gloomy; despairing.—*adv.* **joy'less-ly.**—*n.* **joy'less-ness.**

joy-ous (joi'ŭs), *adj.* having or causing happiness; full of delight; glad. —*adv.* **joy'ous-ly.**—*n.* **joy'ous-ness.**

Syn. (see joyful).—*Ant.* sad, gloomy.

joy ride *Slang* or *Colloq.*, a ride in a motor car, taken with others for pleasure, esp. one taken secretly and accompanied by wildness and reckless driving.

joy stick the lever in an airplane which corresponds to the steering wheel of an automobile.

ju-bi-lant (jo͞o'bĭ-lănt), *adj.* **1,** uttering songs of triumph; **2,** shouting with joy; exultingly glad.—*adv.* **ju'bi-lant-ly.**

ju-bi-late (jo͞o'bĭ-lāt), *v.i.* [*p.t.* and *p.p.* -lat"ed, *p.pr.* -lat"ing], to utter triumphant rejoicing: **Jubilate,** (jū"bĭ-lā'tē; yo͞o"bē-lä'tā), *n.* **1,** the 100th Psalm: from its opening word in the Latin version; **2,** a musical setting for it used in certain churches; **3,** hence, any hymn of rejoicing.

ju-bi-la-tion (jo͞o"bĭ-lā'shŭn), *n.* a shouting for joy or triumph.

ju-bi-lee (jo͞o'bĭ-lē), *n.* **1,** a Jewish festival celebrated every fiftieth year, to commemorate the deliverance of the Israelites from Egyptian bondage; **2,** the fiftieth anniversary of any event; **3,** a year of special indulgence granted by the Pope every twenty-fifth year; **4,** hence, any occasion of rejoicing.

Ju-dah (jo͞o'dȧ), *n.* **1,** in the Bible, the son of Jacob and Leah; **2,** the powerful tribe descended from him, from which sprang the house of David; also, the district of southern Palestine in which the tribe lived, or the kingdom founded there.

Ju-da-ic (jo͞o-dā'ĭk), *adj.* pertaining to the Jews. Also, **Ju-da'i-cal.**

Ju-da-ism (jo͞o'dā-ĭzm), *n.* **1,** the religious ceremonies and doctrines of the Jews; **2,** conformity to Jewish rites, ceremonies, and customs.

Ju-da-ize (jo͞o'dā-īz), *v.i.* [*p.t.* and *p.p.* -ized (-īzd), *p.pr.* -iz"ing], to be converted to the ceremonies and doctrines of the Jews:—*v.t.* to convert to Judaism.

Ju-das (jo͞o'dȧs), *n.* in the Bible, the disciple who betrayed Jesus; hence, one who betrays another under pretense of friendship.

Jude (jo͞od), *n.* a book of the New Testament, containing the Epistle, or letter, written by Jude to the Christian believers.

Ju-de-an (jo͞o-dē'ăn), *adj.* pertaining to Judea, the land of Judah, a son of Jacob:—*n.* a Jew. Also, **Ju-dæ'an.**

judge (jŭj), *n.* **1,** the presiding official in a court of law, having authority to hear and decide civil and criminal cases, **2,** a person appointed to decide in a trial of skill, speed, etc., between two or more persons; **3,** one who has skill, knowledge, or experience to decide on the quality or value of anything; as, a *judge* of poetry; **4,** one of the chief rulers of the Israelites from the death of Joshua to the kingship of Saul: **Judges,** a book of the Old Testament, giving the history of the Jews during the time of the judges, from Joshua to Samuel:—*v.t.* [*p.t.* and *p.p.* judged (jŭjd), *p.pr.* judg'ing], **1,** to examine and pass sentence upon, as a law case; **2,** to estimate; criticize; as, we *judged* him unfairly; **3,** to rule; as, Samuel *judged* Israel:—*v.i.* **1,** to form an opinion or decision after careful consideration; **2**, to hear and determine a case and pass sentence; **3**, to consider; believe; **4**, to criticize, esp. adversely.—*n.* **judg'er.**—*n.* **judge'ship.**

Judge Ad-vo-cate an officer of the government in the trial by court-martial of an officer or soldier.

judg-ment (jŭj'mĕnt), *n.* **1**, the mental process by which we perceive differences and similarities; discrimination; **2**, the critical faculty; estimate; opinion; **3**, correct decision; discernment; good sense; as, a man of great *judgment;* **4**, the act of deciding or passing sentence; **5**, the decision of a court; **6**, God's attitude, as judge of man's actions; hence, calamity attributed to the anger of God: **the Judgment**, the final trial of mankind by God: also called *Last Judgment.* Also, **judge'ment.**

ju-di-ca-to-ry (jōō'dĭ-kȧ-tō-rĭ), *adj.* of or pertaining to the administration of justice:—*n.* [*pl.* judicatories (-rĭz)], **1**, a court of justice; **2**, that department of the government which administers justice.

ju-di-ca-ture (jōō'dĭ-kȧ-tūr), *n.* **1**, a court of justice; **2**, the power of doing justice by legal trial and judgment.

ju-di-cial (jōō-dĭsh'ăl), *adj.* **1**, pertaining to the administration of justice or to a judge; **2**, proceeding from, or inflicted by, a court of justice; **3**, impartial; **4**, functioning as a judge; involving judgment; as, a *judicial* decision.—*adv.* **ju-di'cial-ly.**

Syn. judicious. *Judicial* means pertaining to a court of justice or a judge; as, a *judicial* decision. *Judicious* means characterized by sound judgment; as, a *judicious* selection.

ju-di-ci-a-ry (jōō-dĭsh'ĭ-ā-rĭ), *n.* [*pl.* judiciaries (-rĭz)], **1**, judges collectively; **2**, that branch of a government concerned with the settlement of suits at law:—*adj.* pertaining to courts of justice; judicial.

ju-di-cious (jōō-dĭsh'ŭs), *adj.* prudent; wise; done with good judgment or discretion; as, a *judicious* choice.—*adv.* **ju-di'cious-ly.**—*n.* **ju-di'cious-ness.**

Syn. (see judicial).

jug (jŭg), *n.* **1**, a narrow-necked earthenware or metal vessel, usually with a handle, used to carry liquids; **2**, *Slang*, a prison or jail:—*v.t.* [*p.t.* and *p.p.* jugged (jŭgd), *p.pr.* jug'ging], to put into, or cook in, a jug.

Jug-ger-naut (jŭg'ĕr-nôt), *n.* **1**, (preferably, *Jagannath*), the Hindu god Krishna, or his idol: **2**, the idol dragged in yearly processions on a great car; **3**, anything demanding blind devotion and self-sacrifice, as a custom or institution: from the former belief that worshipers cast themselves to death before the car on which the idol of Jagannath was drawn.

jug-gle (jŭg'l), *v.t.* [*p.t.* and *p.p.* -gled (-ld), *p.pr.* -gling], **1**, to cheat by tricks; **2**, to perform tricks with:—*v.i.* **1**, to perform tricks by sleight of hand; **2**, to conjure:—*n.* **1**, a trick by sleight of hand; **2**, imposture.

jug-gler (jŭg'lĕr), *n.* **1**, a conjurer; one who is skilled in sleight-of-hand tricks; **2**, an impostor; deceiver.—*n.* **jug'gler-y.**

Ju-go-slav (yū'gō-släv″), *n.* a citizen of the Serb-Croat-Slovene State. Also, **Ju'go-Slav'.** See **Yu'go-slav″**, *Pfd. S.*

ju-gu-lar (jōō'gū-lȧr), *adj.* pertaining to the neck or throat: **jugular vein**, either of two large veins, lying on either side of the throat, which carry the blood from the head to the heart:—*n.* the jugular vein.

juice (jōōs), *n.* **1**, the fluid contents of plant or animal tissues; as, meat or fruit *juice;* **2**, essence; **3**, *Slang*, electric current.

juic-y (jōōs'ĭ), *adj.* [*comp.* juic'i-er, *superl.* juic'i-est], full of fluid; as, *juicy* fruit.—*adv.* **juic'i-ly.**—*n.* **juic'i-ness.**

ju-jube (jōō'jōōb), *n.* **1**, the edible fruit of any of various shrubs or trees of the Mediterranean region; **2**, a kind of lozenge or small tablet flavored with, or in imitation of, the jujube fruit.

ju-jut-su (jōō'jōōt″sōō), *n.* the Japanese art of wrestling, which opposes anatomical knowledge and skill to physical strength. Also, **jiu'jit″su.**

ju-lep (jōō'lĕp), *n.* **1**, a drink composed of brandy or whisky sweetened and flavored; **2**, a mixture of sugar and water in which medicine is given.

Jul-ian (jōōl'yăn), *adj.* pertaining to Julius Cæsar: **Julian calendar**, the calendar devised by Julius Cæsar in 46 B. C. to give a civil year of 365 days with one of 366 days every fourth year: often designated *Old Style* [*abbr.* O. S.]: replaced by the Gregorian calendar, often designated *New Style* [*abbr.* N. S.], in Roman Catholic countries in 1582, in the British Isles and colonies in 1752, in most of Russia in 1918, and in Greece in 1923.

***ju-lienne** (zhü″lyĕn'; jōō″lĭ-ĕn'), [Fr.], *n.* a clear meat soup, with chopped vegetables, esp. carrots: **julienne potatoes**, potatoes cut into long, very narrow strips and fried in deep fat.

Ju-li-et (jōō'lĭ-ĕt), *n.* the heroine of Shakespeare's "Romeo and Juliet," who, with her lover, Romeo, suffers tragic death.

Ju-ly (jōō-lī'), *n.* the seventh month of the year: so named from Julius Cæsar.

jum-ble (jŭm'bl), *n.* **1**, a confused mass, mixture, or collection; disorder; **2**, a kind of thin cake:—*v.t.* [*p.t.* and *p.p.* -bled (-bld), *p.pr.* -bling], to mix in a confused mass; throw together without order:—*v.i.* to mix or unite confusedly.

jum-bo (jŭm'bō), *n.* a huge person or animal: from the name (Jumbo) of the largest elephant ever in captivity.

jump (jŭmp), *n.* **1**, a spring or bound; hence, a sudden rise; **2**, the space covered by a jump; **3**, an unintended start or jerk:—*v.t.* **1**, to cause to spring or bound; **2**, to leap over or on; **3**, to take possession of (a mining claim) fraudulently:—*v.i.* to spring up or forward; start suddenly; rise, as prices.

jump-er (jŭm'pĕr), *n.* **1**, one who or that which jumps; **2**, a member of any of certain religious sects who practice dancing under religious excitement; **3**, a hooded fur jacket, worn in Arctic regions; **4**, a sort of blouse or loose jacket worn by workmen over their clothes as a protection; **5**, an outer blouse or jacket reaching to the hips.

jump spark in the ignition system of certain internal-combustion engines, the electric spark that is produced through an arc between permanently separated poles.

junc-tion (jŭngk'shŭn), *n.* **1**, the act of joining, or state of being joined; **2**, a point of union, as of two rivers.

junc-ture (jŭngk'tūr), *n.* **1**, the point at which two bodies are joined; joint; **2**, a union of events, esp. one causing a critical occasion or a crisis.

June (jōōn), *n.* the sixth month of the year, having 30 days: **June bug**, a reddish brown beetle that flies about at night in May and June: also called *June beetle.*

jun-gle (jŭng'gl), *n.* a close, tropical thicket of trees, bushes, etc.

jun-ior (jōōn'yĕr), *adj.* **1**, younger in years; as, John Smith, *Junior;* **2**, of lower standing; as, the *junior* partner in a firm; **3**, belonging to youth; **4**, later in date or occurrence; **5**, designating, or pertaining to, the next to the last year of a collegiate or high-school course: **junior college**, an institution offering, often in connection with studies of high-school rank, the equivalent of the first two years of collegiate work, and affording a basis for advanced professional specialization: **junior high school,** a school between the elementary school (first six grades) and the high school (last three grades), including the seventh, eighth, and ninth grades:—*n.* **1,** the younger; **2,** one of lower standing; **3,** in American colleges and high schools, a student in the next to the last year.—*n.* **jun-ior′i-ty** (jōōn-yŏr′ĭ-tĭ).

ju-ni-per (jōō′nĭ-pẽr), *n.* any of a genus of evergreen trees or shrubs of the pine family; esp., the red cedar.

[1]**junk** (jŭngk), *n.* **1,** old metal, glass, paper, etc., of small marketable value; hence, any jumble of almost worthless articles; **2,** pieces of cordage, cable, etc., used in making mats, for calking, etc.; **3,** hard, salt, ship beef; **4,** a chunk; lump.

[2]**junk** (jŭngk), *n.* a Chinese flat-bottomed vessel with a square bow and high stern, and from one to five masts, each in one piece.

CHINESE JUNK

Jun-ker (yŏŏng′-kẽr), *n.* a member of the aristocratic party in Prussia, which came into power in 1862. Also, **jun′ker.**—*n.* **jun′ker-ism.**

jun-ket (jŭng′kĕt), *n.* **1,** a preparation of curdled milk and cream; **2,** a kind of sweetmeat; **3,** an excursion; picnic:—*v.i.* to take part in an excursion or picnic.

Ju-no (jōō′nō), *n.* in Roman mythology, the goddess of marriage and childbirth, wife of Jupiter: identified with the Greek *Hera.*

jun-ta (jŭn′tȧ), *n.* an assembly or council for making laws; as, the Cuban *junta.*

jun-to (jŭn′tō), *n.* [*pl.* juntos (-tōz)], a number of men secretly combined for some purpose, esp. a political one.

Ju-pi-ter (jōō′pĭ-tẽr), *n.* **1,** in mythology, the god of the heavens: identified with the Greek *Zeus;* **2,** in the solar system, the largest and, except Venus, the brightest planet; the fifth planet in order of distance from the sun (see *solar system,* illus.).

ju-rid-i-cal (jōō-rĭd′ĭ-kăl), *adj.* pertaining to law or to the courts.

ju-ris-dic-tion (jōō″rĭs-dĭk′shŭn), *n.* **1,** the right to exercise legal authority; also, extent of power; as, the *jurisdiction* of a court or state; **2,** the district over which any authority extends.

Syn. dominion, power, right, control.

ju-ris-pru-dence (jōō″rĭs-prōō′dĕns), *n.* **1,** the science of law; **2,** the system of laws of a country.

ju-rist (jōō′rĭst), *n.* one skilled in the science of law.

ju-ror (jōō′rẽr), *n.* one who serves on a jury; a juryman.

ju-ry (jōō′rĭ), *n.* [*pl.* juries (-rĭz)], **1,** a body of persons, usually twelve in number, residents of the county having jurisdiction of the cases called before them, selected according to law and sworn to inquire into, or decide on, the evidence in a case of law before them: also called *petit jury;* **2,** a committee of experts selected to award prizes, adjudge the value of land, or the like: **grand jury,** a body of from 12 to 23 persons, residents of the county having jurisdiction of the cases called before them, chosen to inquire into bills of indictment to discover whether there is ground for formal criminal trial before a court.

ju-ry-man (jōō′rĭ-măn), *n.* [*pl.* jurymen (-mĕn)], a juror; one who serves on a jury.

ju-ry mast a temporary mast to replace one broken or carried away.

[1]**just** (jŭst), *adj.* **1,** according to divine or human laws; upright; **2,** giving to every man his due; faithful; equitable; **3,** based on reasonable grounds; as, a *just* opinion; **4,** exact; regular; fair; as, a *just* measure:—*adv.* **1,** exactly; without lack or excess; as, *just* right; **2,** but now; a moment ago; as, he has *just* gone; **3,** only; barely; as, *just* a little; **4,** *Colloq.*, perfectly; quite; as, *just* beautiful.—*adv.* **just′ly.**—*n.* **just′ness.**

Syn., adj. honest, honorable, true.

[2]**just** (jŭst), *n.* **1,** a combat with lances between knights on horseback; esp., a mock combat as part of a tournament; **2,** in *pl.,* a tournament:—*v.i.* to engage in a just. Also, **joust** (jŭst; jōōst).—*n.* **just′er.**

jus-tice (jŭs′tĭs), *n.* **1,** the principle or practice of dealing uprightly with others; **2,** absolute fairness; **3,** the rendering of due reward or punishment; **4,** legal authority; **5,** a judge: **justice of the peace,** in the U. S., an officer having duties widely varying in the several states, from the mere administering of oaths to the judging of minor cases and the holding of offenders charged with serious criminal offenses for trial by a superior court: **Justice,** a personification of justice, often shown blindfolded, holding a sword or scales.

Syn. equity, right, integrity, impartiality.

jus-ti-ci-a-ry (jŭs-tĭsh′ĭ-ȧ-rĭ), *n.* [*pl.* justiciaries (-rĭz)], (also, *justiciar*), formerly, in England, a judge:—*adj.* pertaining to law or to the work of the courts.

jus-ti-fi-a-ble (jŭs′tĭ-fī″ȧ-bl), *adj.* capable of being shown to be right; excusable; as, killing in self-defense is considered by law to be *justifiable.*—*n.* **jus′ti-fi″a-ble-ness.**—*adv.* **jus′ti-fi″a-bly.**

jus-ti-fi-ca-tion (jŭs″tĭ-fĭ-kā′shŭn), *n.* **1,** the act of showing a thing to be right or proper; **2,** an acceptable excuse; defense; **3,** vindication; exoneration.—*adj.* **jus′ti-fi-ca-to-ry.**

jus-ti-fy (jŭs′tĭ-fī), *v.t.* [*p.t.* and *p.p.* -fied (-fīd), *p.pr.* -fy″ing], **1,** to show or prove to be right; as, to *justify* the ways of God to men; **2,** to pronounce free from blame; **3,** in printing, to make even, as lines of type:—*v.i.* in printing, to make lines of type even by spacing properly.

Syn. vindicate, clear, absolve, defend, exonerate.—*Ant.* condemn, blame, censure.

jut (jŭt), *v.i.* [*p.t.* and *p.p.* jut′ted, *p.pr.* jut′ting], to project beyond the main body; stick out:—*n.* a projection.

jute (jōōt), *n.* the fiber of an East Indian plant used for ropes, bagging, etc.

Jute (jōōt), *n.* a member of a Low German tribe living in Jutland, some of whom, with the Angles and Saxons, settled in Britain during the fifth century.—*adj.* **Jut′ish.**

ju-ve-nes-cent (jōō″vē-nĕs′ĕnt), *adj.* becoming young again; rejuvenating.—*n.* **ju″ve-nes′cence.**

ju-ve-nile (jōō′vē-nĭl; *Br.* jōō′vē-nīl), *adj.* **1,** immature; youthful; **2,** characteristic of, or suitable to, youth; as, *juvenile* books:—*n.* **1,** a young person; **2,** a book for children.—*n.* **ju″ve-nil′i-ty.**

jux-ta (jŭks′tȧ-), *prefix,* near or alongside; as, *juxta*position.

jux-ta-po-si-tion (jŭks″tȧ-pō-zĭsh′ŭn), *n.* a placing or being placed close together or side by side; contiguity.

K

Ka-a-ba (kä′ȧ-bȧ; kä′bȧ), *n.* the shrine at Mecca, an object of pilgrimage, toward which all Mohammedans turn when praying. See **Ca′a-ba**, *Pfd. S.*

ka-di (kä′dĭ; kā′dĭ), *n.* [*pl.* kadis (-dĭz)], a Mohammedan judge. *Pfd. S.*, **ca′di.**

Ka-fir (kä′fẽr), *n.* **1**, a member of one of the negroid tribes of South Africa; **2**, a member of any of several tribes in northeastern Afghanistan; **3**, an infidel, or one who is not a Mohammedan. Also, **Kaf′fir** (kăf′ẽr).

kaf-tan (kăf′tăn; kȧf-tăn′), *n.* a kind of long-sleeved gown worn in Near Eastern countries. Also, **caf′tan**, *Pfd. S.*

kai-ser (kī′zẽr), *n.* **1**, emperor; **2**, the title of the former emperors of Germany and Austria.

kale (kāl), *n.* **1**, a cabbage with open, curled leaves; **2**, *Colloq.*, money. Also, **kail.**

ka-lei-do-scope (kȧ-lī′dō-skōp), *n.* an instrument containing small bits of colored glass, which, by an arrangement of mirrors, appear in a variety of beautiful patterns when turned around.—*adj.* **ka-lei″do-scop′ic.**

kal-en-dar (kăl′ĕn-dȧr), *n.* **1**, a system of dividing time into years, months, etc., so as to fix dates; **2**, a table or set of tables showing the divisions of a given year, with the days of the week on which dates fall. See **cal′en-dar**, *Pfd. S.*

ka-lif (kā′lĭf; kăl′ĭf), *n.* in Mohammedan countries, one having supreme civil and religious authority. Also, **ca′liph**, *Pfd. S.*

kal-so-mine (kăl′sō-mīn), *n.* a white or colored wash for coating walls, etc.:—*v.t.* [*p.t.* and *p.p.* -mined (-mīnd), *p.pr.* -min″ing], to coat with such a wash. Also, **cal′ci-mine**, *Pfd. S.*

Kan-a-ka (kăn′ȧ-kȧ; kȧ-năk′ȧ), *n.* **1**, a Hawaiian Islander; **2**, a South Sea Islander. Also, **Ka-nack′a.**

kan-ga-roo (kăng″gȧ-rōō′), *n.* an animal of Australia, having short forelegs, long, powerful hind legs with which it leaps, a long, strong tail, and an external pouch in which it carries its young.

KANGAROO ($\frac{1}{50}$)

ka-o-lin (kā′ō-lĭn; kä′-), *n.* a very pure white clay used to form the paste from which porcelain is made. Also, **ka′o-line.**

ka-pok (kä′pŏk), *n.* the mass of silky fibers within the seed pods of a certain tropical tree: used as a stuffing for mattresses, etc., and also woven into fabrics.

kap-pa (kăp′ȧ), *n.* [Gk.], the 10th letter of the Greek alphabet [κ, K], equivalent to English *k.*

ka-ra-kul (kä″rȧ-kōōl′; popularly, kăr′ȧ-kŭl), *n.* a valuable fur made from the pelt of the very young astrakhan, or curly-haired sheep of Asia. Also, **ca″ra-cul′.**

kar-at (kăr′ăt), *n.* **1**, a unit of weight, ⅕ of a gram; **2**, a 24th part: used in expressing the fineness of gold. See **car′at**, *Pfd. S.*

kat-a- (kăt′ȧ-), *prefix*, down; under; against. Also, **kath-; kat-.** See **cat′a-**, *Pfd. S.*

ka-ty-did (kā′tĭ-dĭd″), *n.* a large, green, tree insect which makes a shrill sound similar to the words "Katy did."

kay-ak (kī′ăk), *n.* a canoe used in Arctic America, made of sealskin and having a decklike covering laced about the paddler. Also, **kai′ak.**

ke-a (kā′ä; kē′ȧ), *n.* a large parrot of New Zealand, which sometimes kills sheep.

kedge (kĕj), *n.* a light anchor: also called *kedge anchor*:—*v.t.* [*p.t.* and *p.p.* kedged (kĕjd), *p.pr.* kedg′ing], to move (a vessel, raft, etc.) by carrying a small anchor out in a boat, dropping it overboard, and hauling the vessel up to it.

¹**keel** (kēl), *n.* **1**, the chief and lowest timber or steel plate of a vessel, extending from stem to stern along the bottom and supporting the whole frame; **2**, a ship; **3**, in an airship, the lowest and central part of the body of the machine, which helps to keep the balance; **4**, anything resembling a ship's keel:—*v.t.* to furnish with a keel:—*v.i.* to turn up the keel; turn over: **keel over**, *Colloq.*, to upset; fall suddenly.

²**keel** (kēl), *n.* a barge, esp. one used on the Tyne for carrying coal.

keel-haul (kēl′hôl″), *v.t.* **1**, to drag (a person) under water beneath the bottom of a ship from one side to the other: formerly a naval punishment; **2**, to rebuke sternly or abusively.

keel-son (kĕl′sŭn), *n.* a beam or timber bolted to the keel of a vessel to strengthen it. Also, **kel′son.**

¹**keen** (kēn), *adj.* **1**, sharp; cutting; as, a *keen* tool; piercing; bitter; as, a *keen* wind; *keen* sarcasm; **2**, acute; intelligent; discriminating; **3**, eager; ardent; as, a *keen* sportsman.—*adv.* **keen′ly.**—*n.* **keen′ness.**

Syn. penetrating, sagacious, shrewd.

²**keen** (kēn), *n.* a wailing lamentation for the dead:—*v.t.* and *v.i.* to lament (the dead) with a wail.

keep (kēp), *v.t.* [*p.t.* and *p.p.* kept (kĕpt), *p.pr.* keep′ing], **1**, to have the care of; defend; as, to *keep* a castle; **2**, to preserve; support; maintain; as, to *keep* servants; **3**, to conduct; carry on; manage; as, to *keep* a shop; *keep* house; **4**, to have and retain in use, ownership, or possession; as, whatever you find you may *keep*; **5**, to observe; fulfil; perform; as, to *keep* a holiday, or a promise; **6**, to reserve; hold in; detain; as, to *keep* a secret; to *keep* a boy after school; **7**, to have on hand or in stock, as for sale; as, to *keep* shoes; **8**, to cause to persist; as, to *keep* one's health; maintain or cause to continue in a specified condition; as, *keep* your hat on; **9**, to remain in; as, to *keep* one's room:—*v.i.* **1**, to remain or continue in any state or condition; as, to *keep* cheerful; **2**, to continue sweet, fresh, or unspoiled, as fruit; **3**, to continue in session:—*n.* **1**, means of, or provision for, maintenance; board; as, he worked for his *keep*; **2**, the stronghold of an ancient castle: **for keeps**, *Colloq.*, for the winner to retain what he wins; as, to play marbles *for keeps.*

Syn., v. (see celebrate).

keep-er (kēp′ẽr), *n.* one who keeps; esp., a person who has charge of prisoners, the mentally unsound, or animals.

keep-ing (kēp′ĭng), *n.* **1**, care; custody; charge; **2**, means of life; **3**, the condition of being fitting or becoming.

keep-sake (kēp′sāk″), *n.* something kept in memory of the giver.

keg (kĕg), *n.* a small, strong barrel, usually containing from five to ten gallons.

kelp (kĕlp), *n.* **1**, a large, brown seaweed; **2**, the ashes of seaweeds, from which iodine is obtained.

kel-pie (kĕl′pĭ), *n.* an evil water sprite, elf, or spirit, supposed to take the form of a horse, and to warn people who are to be drowned. Also, **kel'py.**

Kelt (kĕlt), *n.* a member of the Celtic branch of the Aryan race, which includes the ancient Gauls and Britons, the Gaelic Scotch, the Irish, the Bretons, and the Welsh. Also, **Celt** (sĕlt), *Pfd. S.*—*adj.* **Kelt'ic.**

kel-ter (kĕl'tẽr), *n. Colloq.*, proper order. See **kil'ter,** *Pfd. S.*

ken (kĕn), *n.* view; knowledge; comprehension:—*v.t.* and *v.i.* [*p.t.* and *p.p.* kenned (kĕnd), *p.pr.* ken'ning], *Scot.*, to know; understand; comprehend.

ken-nel (kĕn'ĕl), *n.* **1,** a house for a dog or dogs; also, a place where dogs are bred and reared; **2,** a pack of dogs; **3,** a vile lodging:—*v.t.* to confine in a kennel:—*v.i.* to live in a kennel.

ke-no (kē'nō), *n.* a game of chance, somewhat resembling lotto, played with numbered balls and cards.

ken-o-tron (kĕn'ō-trŏn), *n.* in radio, a vacuum tube containing a filament and plate, used as a rectifier of alternating current: a trade name.

kept (kĕpt), past tense and past participle of the irregular verb *keep.*

ke-ram-ic (kē-răm'ĭk), *adj.* pertaining to pottery: **keramics,** *n.pl.* used as *sing.* the art of making pottery. See **ce-ram'ic** (sē-răm'ĭk), *Pfd. S.*

kerb (kûrb), *n. Br.*, **1,** a border, as of stones, along a sidewalk or the like; **2.** the street as a market for buying or selling stocks:—*v.t. Br.*, to furnish with a curb. See **curb,** *Pfd. S.*—*n.* **kerb'ing.**—*n.* **kerb'stone".**

ker-chief (kûr'chĭf), *n.* **1,** a square of cloth worn by women on the head or about the neck; **2,** a handkerchief.

kerf (kûrf), *n.* the notch or slit made by cutting, as by a saw.

ker-mes (kûr'mēz), *n.* **1,** a scarlet dye consisting of the dried bodies of certain insects found esp. in countries bordering the Mediterranean; **2,** any of these insects; **3,** a Mediterranean dwarf oak on which the kermes insect lives.

ker-mis (kûr'mĭs), *n.* **1,** in the Netherlands, a periodical, outdoor fair; **2,** in the U. S., an indoor fair held for charity. Also, **ker'mess; kir'mess.**

¹kern (kûrn), *n.* a part of the printing face of a type which overhangs the body, as the long tail on an ornamental capital Q.

²kern (kûrn), *n.* **1,** a Celtic light-armed foot soldier; **2,** a peasant. Also, **kerne.**

ker-nel (kûr'nĕl), *n.* **1,** a grain or seed; the eatable substance of a nut or fruit stone; **2,** the nucleus of anything; as, the *kernel* of a plan:—*v.i.* to form kernels, as wheat.

ker-o-sene (kĕr'ō-sēn"), *n.* a light, colorless oil used in lamps and cooking stoves; a mixture of liquid hydrocarbons, distilled from petroleum, coal, etc.

KESTREL (1/8)

ker-sey (kûr'zĭ), *n.* [*pl.* kerseys (-zĭz)], a coarse, woolen cloth of light weight, often ribbed.

ker-sey-mere (kûr'zĭ-mēr), *n.* a fine, twilled woolen cloth. Also, **cas'si-mere.**

kes-trel (kĕs'trĕl), *n.* a small European falcon of reddish color.

¹ketch (kĕch), *n.* a small, fore-and-aft-rigged sailing vessel with relatively small mizzenmast located forward of the rudder post (see *ship,* illus.).

²ketch (kĕch), *n.* in Great Britain, a public executioner:—*v.t.* to hang.

ketch-up (kĕch'ŭp), *n.* a sauce prepared from tomatoes, mushrooms, spices, etc. Also, **cat'sup;** *Pfd. S.*, **catch'up.**

ket-tle (kĕt'l), *n.* **1,** a metal vessel for boiling liquids; a teakettle; **2,** a tin pail.

ket-tle-drum (kĕt'l-drŭm"), *n.* a drum made of a hollow hemisphere of copper or brass, with parchment stretched over the opening (see also *drum, musical instrument,* illus.).

KETTLEDRUM

¹key (kē), *n.* **1,** a metal instrument for moving the bolt of a lock; **2,** any of several instruments resembling a key; as, the *key* of a clock; **3,** a device which, when slipped into place, wedges, supports, or locks together different parts; as, a *key*stone; **4,** that which allows or hinders entrance or control; as, Gibraltar is the *key* to the Mediterranean; hence, that by means of which a difficulty is removed or something unintelligible explained; as, the *key* to a riddle, or to a code; **5,** in certain musical instruments, as the piano, in typewriters and similar devices, a lever by means of which the instrument is made to operate by the fingers; **6,** the general pitch or tone of the voice; as, men naturally speak in a lower *key* than women; also, tone of thought or expression; as, a poem in minor *key;* **7,** a device operated by the fingers for opening or closing an electric circuit; **8,** a straight piece of metal inserted into a slot called the *keyway,* so as to prevent a wheel from turning on a shaft; **9,** an arrangement or series of musical tones bearing a fixed relation to a given note, called the *keynote;* as, the *key* of G major:—*v.t.* **1,** to lock with a key; also, to provide with a key; **2,** in music, to regulate the pitch of; **3,** *Colloq.,* to make tense; stimulate: often with *up.*—*adj.* **key'less.**

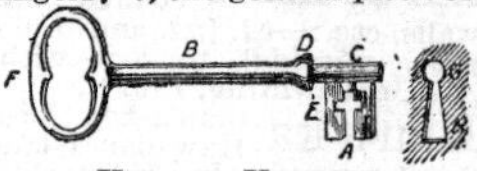

KEY AND KEYHOLE

A, main ward; B, stem; C, pin; D, collar; E, bit; F, bow; G, eye; H, slot.

²key (kē), *n.* a low, small reef or island; as, the Florida *keys.*

key-board (kē'bōrd"), *n.* **1,** the row of keys on a piano; **2,** the manual of an organ; **3,** the bank of keys of a typewriter, etc.

keyed (kēd), *p.adj.* **1,** having keys; **2,** tightly stretched, as a musical string; **3,** tuned, as a musical instrument; **4,** set to a stated key, as a tune; **5,** hence, in a state of tension: with *up;* as, *keyed* up by fear.

key-hole (kē'hōl"), *n.* a small opening in a door or lock for inserting a key.

key-note (kē'nōt"), *n.* **1,** the basic note in a system of musical notes; **2,** the ruling idea or principle; as, the *keynote* of her costume was simplicity.

key-stone (kē'stōn"), *n.* the stone at the topmost point of an arch which holds the whole structure in place (see *arch,* illus.; see also illus. next page): **Keystone State,** Pennsylvania.

kha-ki (kä′kē), *n.* **1**, a light, drab-colored cloth, used for uniforms; **2**, such uniforms collectively:—*adj.* olive drab in color.

kha-lif (kā′lĭf; kăl′ĭf), *n.* the sultan of Turkey. Also, **kha′liff**; see **ca′liph**, *Pfd.S.*

[1]**khan** (kän; kăn), *n.* **1**, a title applied to the princes who rule over certain semi-independent Asiatic states and to various officers and chiefs of lower rank; **2**, in Afghanistan, India, and Persia, a title of respect.

[2]**khan** (kän; kăn), *n* in the Orient, a public rest house, built around a courtyard.

khan-ate (kän′āt), *n.* a district ruled by a khan; also, the office of a khan.

khe-dive (kē-dēv′), *n.* formerly, the title of the Turkish viceroy of Egypt.

kib-itz-er (kĭb′ĭt-sēr), *n. Colloq.*, one who meddles in the affairs of others; esp., one who watches the play at a game, as of cards, without taking part as player.

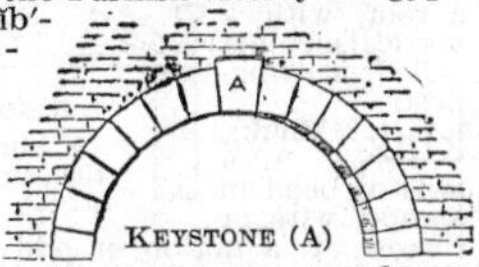

KEYSTONE (A)

kick (kĭk), *v.t.* **1**, to thrust at or strike with the foot; **2**, to push against in recoiling, as a firearm:—*v.i.* **1**, to strike out with the foot, esp. habitually; **2**, to spring back, as a firearm; **3**, *Slang*, to protest vigorously; grumble:—*n.* **1**, a blow with the foot; **2**, a spring backward, as of a gun; **3**, *Slang:* **a**, a vigorous objection or protest; **b**, thrill; as, to get a *kick* out of racing.—*n.* **kick′er**.

kick-shaw (kĭk′shô″), *n.* **1**, something fanciful or out of the way; a trifle; **2**, a light dish of food; a delicacy.

kid (kĭd), *n.* **1**, the young of the goat; also, its flesh; **2**, leather made from the skin of a kid or goat: used esp. for shoes and gloves; **3**, a young female deer; **4**, *Colloq.*, a child:—*adj.* **1**, made of leather called kid; **2**, *Slang*, youthful:—*v.t.* [*p.* and *p.p.* kid′ded, *p.pr.* kid′ding], *Slang*, to humbug; banter with:—*v.i. Slang*, to hoax.—*n.dim.* **kid′dy**.

kid-nap (kĭd′năp″), *v.t.* [*p.t.* and *p.p.* -naped (-năpt″) or -napped, *p.pr.* -nap″ing or -nap″ping], to steal or carry away (a human being, esp. a child).—*n.* **kid′nap″er; kid′nap″per**.

kid-ney (kĭd′nĭ), *n.* [*pl.* kidneys (-nĭz)], **1**, one of two glandular organs which secrete urine and so remove waste matter from the blood; **2**, temperament; disposition; sort or kind; as, a man of his *kidney:* **kidney bean**, **1**, a reddish brown bean shaped like a kidney; **2**, any of various other beans.

[1]**kill** (kĭl), *v.t.* **1**, to deprive (an animal or vegetable organism) of life; **2**, to deaden; weaken; consume; as, to *kill* one color with another; to *kill* time; **3**, to reject; discard; as, to *kill* an article or a play; **4**, in printing, to stop the publication of; mark as not to be used:—*v.i.* to destroy life:—*n.* **1**, in hunting, the act of killing; **2**, the animal killed, or the total amount of game taken.

Syn., *v.* execute, assassinate, murder. To *kill*, the general term, means to deprive of life in any way whatever. To *execute* is to *kill*, according to law, one legally sentenced to death. To *assassinate* is to *kill* by treacherous and violent assault. To *murder* is to *kill* unlawfully with premeditated malice.

[2]**kill** (kĭl), *n.* a creek or channel: archaic except in proper names, as Cats*kill*.

kill-deer (kĭl′dēr″), the ring plover of North America. Also, **kill′dee″**.

kiln (kĭl; kĭln), *n.* a furnace, oven, or pile for burning, drying, or hardening, as bricks:—*v.t.* to bake in such an oven.

kil-o (kĭl′ō), *n.* [*pl.* kilos (-ōz)], a kilogram (which see); about 2⅕ pounds.

kil-o- (kĭl′ō-), a combining form from the Greek, meaning 1000: used esp. in the metric system.

kil-o-cy-cle (kĭl′ō-sī″kl), in electricity, 1000 cycles per second: a unit used, esp. in radio, in giving the frequency of an alternating current or oscillation.

kil-o-gram (kĭl′ō-grăm), *n.* a metric measure of weight equal to 1000 grams, or 2.2046 (about 2⅕) pounds avoirdupois. Also, **kil′o-gramme** (-grăm).

kil-o-li-ter (kĭl′ō-lē″tẽr), *n.* a metric measure of capacity equal to 1000 liters, or one cubic meter: equivalent to 264.18 gallons. Also, **kil′o-li″tre** (-lē tẽr).

kil-o-me-ter (kĭl′ō-mē″tẽr), *n.* in the metric system, a measure of distance equal to 1000 meters: equivalent to 3280.8 feet or 0.62137 mile. Also, **kil′o-me″tre** (-tẽr).—*adj.* **kil″o-met′ric; kil″o-met′ri-cal.**

kil-o-watt (kĭl′ō-wŏt″), *n.* a unit of electrical power equal to 1000 watts: **kilowatt hour**, a commercial unit of electrical energy, equal to the work done by one kilowatt acting for one hour.

kilt (kĭlt), *n.* a short plaited petticoat worn by men of the Scottish Highlands; a skirt similarly made:—*v.t.* **1**, to form into broad, flat plaits; **2**, in Scotland, to tuck up (clothing) around the body.

kil-ter (kĭl′tẽr), *n. Colloq.*, proper order; good condition; as, out of *kilter;* in *kilter*. Also, **kel′ter**.

ki-mo-no (kĭ-mō′nō; kĭm′ō-nō), *n.* [*pl.* kimonos (-nōz)], **1**, the loose outer robe of the Japanese; **2**, a similar garment worn as a dressing gown by women of western nations.

[1]**kin** (kĭn), *n.* **1**, race; family; hence, kind; **2**, persons of the same race or family; kinsfolk; kindred; as, one's nearest *kin;* **3**, relationship:—*adj.* of the same ancestry or kind.—*n.* **kin′ship**.

[2]**kin** (kĭn), *n.* a Chinese lute having from five to twenty-five silk strings.

-kin (-kĭn), *suffix*, used to form diminutive nouns; as, lamb*kin;* Peter*kin*.

kind (kīnd), *adj.* **1**, indulgent; gracious; affectionate; sympathetic; **2**, mild; tractable; as, a *kind* horse:—*n.* **1**, a natural group of animals or plants; as, the cat *kind;* **2**, variety; sort; as, what *kind* of dress did she wear? **3**, nature; character; style; as, to differ in *kind*.

Syn., *n.* sort. *Kind* and *sort* are used interchangeably, but *sort* is often used to convey the idea of disparagement; as, that *sort* of thing is unpardonable. Avoid saying "that *kind* of *a* thing": omit the article *a*.

kin-der-gar-ten (kĭn′dẽr-gär″tĕn), *n.* a school for young children in which they are taught by object lessons, games, etc.—*n.* **kin′der-gart″ner**.

kind–heart-ed (kīnd′=härt″ĕd), *adj.* generous; sympathetic; charitable; full of good impulses.

kin-dle (kĭn′dl), *v.t.* [*p.t.* and *p.p.* -dled (-dld), *p.pr.* -dling], **1**, to set fire to; **2**, to inflame; inspire, as the passions; **3**, to brighten; as, enthusiasm *kindled* her face:—*v.i.* **1**, to catch fire; **2**, to become excited.—*n.* **kin′dler**.

kind-ling (kĭn′dlĭng), *n.* light, combustible material for starting a fire.

kind-ly (kīnd′lĭ), *adj.* [*comp.* kind′li-er, *superl.* kind′li-est], **1**, sympathetic; gracious; benevolent; **2**, agreeable; beneficial: said of surroundings:—*adv.* **1**, in a gracious manner; **2**, in a natural manner; as, willows take *kindly* to damp ground.—*n.* **kind′li-ness**.

Syn., *adj.* gentle, pleasant.—*Ant.*, *adj.* uncharitable, unkind, harsh.

kind-ness (kīnd′nĕs), *n.* **1,** the state or quality of being ready to do good to others; **2,** a helpful or gracious act.
Syn. gentleness, clemency, tenderness.—*Ant.* brutality, mercilessness, severity.

kin-dred (kĭn′drĕd), *adj.* **1,** of like nature or character; **2,** related by blood or marriage:—*n.* **1,** relationship, as by birth or marriage; **2,** persons so related.

kine (kīn), *n. Archaic,* plural of *cow:* cows; cattle; as, the home-bred *kine.*

kin-e-ma-col-or (kĭn′ē-mȧ-kŭl″ẽr), *n.* a process of producing motion pictures in colors: a trade name.

kin-e-mat-ics (kĭn″ē-măt′ĭks; kī″nē-), *n.pl.* used as *sing.* the science which treats of the motion of bodies and systems without regard to the causes.—*adj.* **kin″e-mat′ic; kin″e-mat′i-cal.**

ki-net-ic (kĭ-nĕt′ĭk; kī-), *adj.* pertaining to, or imparting, motion; active; as, the *kinetic* theory of gases: **kinetic energy,** the energy possessed by a moving body due to its motion: opp. of *potential energy:* **kinetics,** *n.pl.* used as *sing.* the science which treats of changes of motion as produced by unbalanced forces: distinguished from *statics.*

ki-ne-to-graph (kĭ-nē′tō-grȧf; kī-), *n.* **1,** a camera for taking photographs of moving objects; **2,** a lantern for projecting moving pictures on a screen.—*adj.* **ki-ne″to-graph′ic.**—*n.* **kin″e-tog′ra-pher.**

ki-ne-to-phone (kĭ-nē′tō-fōn; kī-), *n.* an instrument which combines sight and sound in motion pictures.

ki-ne-to-scope (kĭ-nē′tō-skōp; kī-), *n.* a machine which enables an observer to see, through slits in a revolving cylinder, a series of pictures inside the cylinder, receiving the impression of a moving object.

king (kĭng), *n.* **1,** a male sovereign or ruler; **2,** in chess, cards, etc., a piece or card representing a king; **3,** one who is specially distinguished in his class or kind; as, the *king* of beasts: **Kings,** either of two historical books in the Old Testament, recording the reigns of Jewish kings.—*adj.* **king′ly.**—*n.* **king′li-ness.**

King Ar-thur (är′thŭr), a legendary leader of the Celtic tribes in Britain, organizer of the Round Table and model of chivalry: the hero of many romances, as in Tennyson's "Idylls of the King."

king-bird (kĭng′bûrd″), *n.* any of several American flycatchers.

king-bolt (kĭng′bōlt″), *n.* a vertical bolt attaching the forward axle to the body of a vehicle or the truck to a railroad coach, and acting as a pivot in turning.

king crab any of several crabs, esp. one with a horseshoe-shaped anterior shell and a long spinelike tail; the horseshoe crab (see illus. page 171).

king-dom (kĭng′dŭm), *n.* **1,** the territory ruled by a king or queen; royal authority; **2,** any sphere of influence or activity; as, the *kingdom* of the mind; **3,** one of the classes into which all natural objects are divided; as, the animal, mineral, and vegetable *kingdoms.*

BELTED KINGFISHER ($\frac{1}{8}$)

king-fish-er (kĭng′fĭsh″ẽr), *n.* any of a family of long-billed, fish-eating birds having a harsh cry.

king–post (kĭng′-pōst″), *n.* **1,** in carpentry, an upright post or beam supporting the apex of a triangular truss, and resting on the center of a beam which forms the base of the triangle: used esp. in a truss, called *king truss,* formed by two rafters of a roof and the horizontal tiebeam: distinguished from *queen-post;* **2,** in an airplane, a similarly placed post bracing a wing (see *monoplane,* illus.).

king-ship (kĭng′shĭp), *n.* the state or position of a monarch.

king truss a braced structure supporting a roof, with a vertical member called a *king-post.*

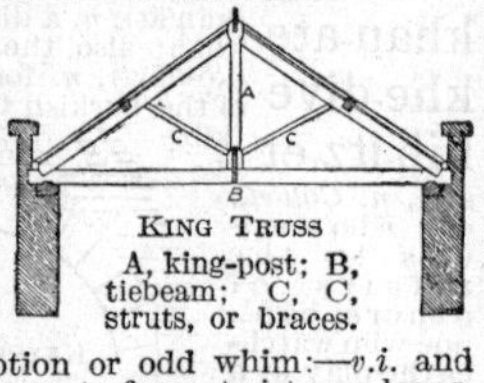

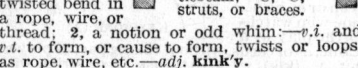

KING TRUSS
A, king-post; B, tiebeam; C, C, struts, or braces.

kink (kĭngk), *n.* **1,** a twisted bend in a rope, wire, or thread; **2,** a notion or odd whim:—*v.i.* and *v.t.* to form, or cause to form, twists or loops, as rope, wire, etc.—*adj.* **kink′y.**

kins-folk (kĭnz′fōk″), *n.* relatives; as, his *kinsfolk* came to his aid.

kins-man (kĭnz′măn), *n.* [*pl.* kinsmen (-mĕn)], one related by blood or marriage; a relative.—*n.fem.* **kins′wom″an.**

ki-osk (kē-ŏsk′), *n.* **1,** an Oriental open pavilion; **2,** a building of similar construction used as a news stand, etc.

kip (kĭp), *n.* the untanned skin of a young beast, as a calf, or leather made from it.

kip-per (kĭp′ẽr), *v.t.* to cure, as salmon, by cleaning, salting, and drying or smoking:—*n.* a salmon or herring that has been so cured.

Kir-ghiz (kĭr-gēz′), *n.* [*pl.* Kirghiz; Kirghizes (-ĕz)], a member of a wandering people allied to the Mongols in race and to the Tatars in speech, living in southwestern Siberia and the adjacent Chinese highlands. Also, **Kir-giz′; Kir-ghis′.**

kirk (kûrk), *n.* a church: **the Kirk,** the established church of Scotland.

kir-mess (kûr′mĕs), *n.* **1,** in Holland, a periodical, outdoor fair; **2,** in the U. S., an indoor fair held for charity. Also, **ker′mis,** *Pfd. S.*

kir-tle (kûr′tl), *n.* **1,** a woman's gown or dress; **2,** a man's tunic or coat.

kis-met (kĭs′mĕt), *n.* fate; destiny; as, there is no escape from *kismet.*

kiss (kĭs), *n.* a salute or caress with the lips; a slight touch:—*v.t.* to salute with the lips; touch slightly:—*v.i.* to salute each other with the lips; touch gently.—*n.* **kiss′er.**

¹kit (kĭt), *n.* **1,** a small wooden box or tub for packing mackerel, butter, or the like; **2,** an outfit of tools or articles for a special purpose: often including the box or bag holding them.

²kit (kĭt), *n.* a small, three-stringed violin, about sixteen inches long.

³kit (kĭt), *n.* a young cat; kitten; also, a cub of any member of the cat family.

⁴kit (kĭt), *n. Colloq.,* family; brood; as, the whole *kit* and crew of them.

kitch-en (kĭch′ĕn), *n.* **1,** a room or apartment where cooking is done; **2,** an establishment where food is cooked and sold: **kitchen police,** soldiers detailed for service in preparing and serving food.

kitch-en-ette (kĭch″ĕn-ĕt′), *n.* a small room or pantry for cooking.

kite (kīt), *n.* **1,** a bird of prey of the hawk family; **2,** a light frame of wood covered with paper or linen, for flying in the air; **3,** a light, lofty sail: **kite balloon,** an anchored balloon, so constructed as to take advantage, like a kite, of the lifting power of the wind, and used for observation purposes; an observation balloon.

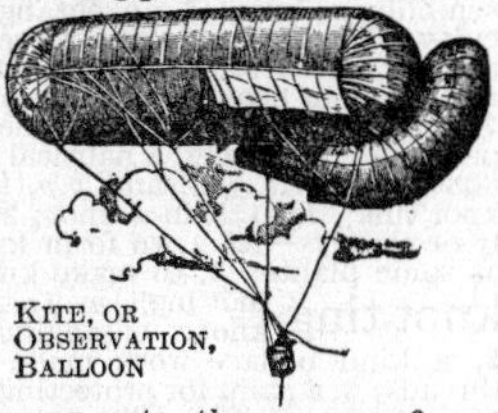

KITE, OR OBSERVATION, BALLOON

kith (kĭth), *n.* friends; neighbors: used only in the expression *kith and kin.*

kit-ten (kĭt'n), *n.* a young cat; the young of any animal of the cat family.—*adj.* **kit'ten-ish.**

Ki-wa-nis (kē-wä'nĭs), *n.* an international group of clubs of business and professional men, organized in 1915 for civic service and fraternity.—*n.* **Ki-wa'ni-an.**

ki-wi (kē'wĭ), *n.* a flightless night bird of New Zealand, which feeds chiefly on earthworms; an apteryx (which see for illus.).

klep-to-ma-ni-a (klĕp"tō-mā'nĭ-ȧ), *n.* a form of insanity showing itself in an irresistible impulse to steal. Also, **clep"to-ma'ni-a.**—*n.* **klep"to-ma'ni-ac.**

Kling-sor (klĭng'zôr), *n.* the chief enemy of the knights of the Grail, who, by his magic, attempts to corrupt the pure hero of Wagner's "Parsifal" and is destroyed on his failure to do so.

klip-spring-er (klĭp'sprĭng"ẽr), *n.* a small African antelope, noted for its coarse hair and its remarkable agility.

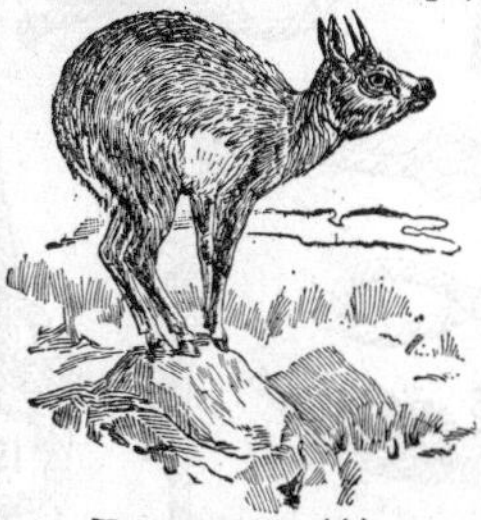

KLIPSPRINGER ($\frac{1}{30}$)

knack (năk), *n.* **1,** cleverness in performance; as, she could never acquire the *knack* of using a needle; **2,** an ingenious device; a clever contrivance.

knap-sack (năp'săk"), *n.* a leather or cloth bag carried on the back: used esp. by soldiers.

knave (nāv), *n.* **1,** a dishonest or deceitful person; **2,** a playing card with the figure of a soldier or servant upon it.

knav-er-y (nāv'ẽr-ĭ), *n.* [*pl.* knaveries (-ĭz)], dishonesty; fraud; deceit.

knav-ish (nāv'ĭsh), *adj.* dishonest; as, a *knavish* trick.—*adv.* **knav'ish-ly.** —*n.* **knav'ish-ness.**

knead (nēd), *v.t.* **1,** to work into a mass by pressing, usually with the hands, as dough; **2,** to operate upon in massage.—*n.* **knead'er.**

knee (nē), *n.* **1,** the joint between the lower leg and the thigh (see illus. next column); **2,** the part of a garment covering this joint; **3,** anything like a knee.

knee-cap (nē'kăp"), *n.* a flattened, triangular, movable bone on the fore part of the knee; the patella, or kneepan.

kneel (nēl), *v.i.* [*p.t.* and *p.p.* knelt (nĕlt) or kneeled (nēld), *p.pr.* kneel'ing], to bend down or rest upon the knees.

knee-pan (nē'păn"), *n.* the patella; the kneecap (which see).

knell (nĕl), *n.* the sound of a bell when struck, esp. a funeral bell; hence, a sign of coming evil:—*v.i.* to toll dolefully.

knelt (nĕlt), past tense of the irregular verb *kneel,* which see.

knew (nū), past tense of the irregular verb *know,* which see.

Knick-er-bock-er (nĭk'ẽr-bŏk"ẽr), *n.* a person descended from the original Dutch settlers of New York; also, any New Yorker: **knickerbockers,** wide breeches gathered in below the knee; now, a popular sports garment: also called *knickers.*

knick-knack (nĭk'năk"), *n.* a trifle; toy. Also, **nick'nack".**

knife (nīf), *n.* [*pl.* knives (nīvz)], **1,** a cutting instrument with a sharp-edged steel blade set in a handle; **2,** a sharp-edged blade in a machine:—*v.t.* [*p.t.* and *p.p.* knifed (nīft), *p.pr.* knif'ing], to stab with a knife.

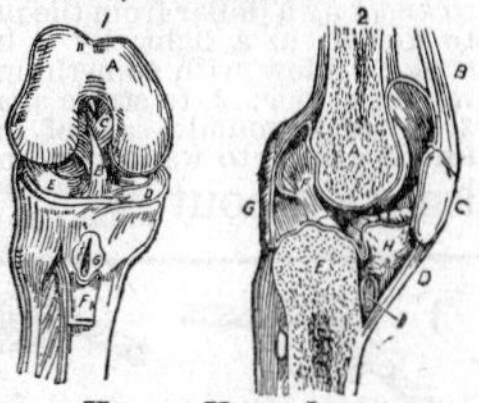

HUMAN KNEE JOINT

1, right knee from the front, showing ligaments: A, lower end of femur; B, anterior crucial ligament; C, posterior crucial ligament; D, interior semilunar cartilage; E, external cartilage; F, part of the ligament of the patella turned down; G, synovial bursa laid open beneath the ligature of the patella. 2, longitudinal section of the left knee: A, lower end of femur; B, tendon of extensor muscles of leg; C, patella; D, ligament of patella; E, head of tibia; F, anterior crucial ligament; G, posterior ligament; H, mass of fat projecting into the cavity of the joint below the patella; I, bursa.

knight (nīt), *n.* **1,** in Great Britain, one who holds rank next below a baronet, giving him the title *Sir;* **2,** in the Middle Ages, one of high birth, who, after serving as page and squire, was admitted by solemn ceremonies to the rank of knighthood; one who attended a lady or championed her cause in war or tournament; **3,** one of the pieces in chess: —*v.t.* to confer knighthood upon.

knight-er-rant (nīt'-ĕr'ănt), *n.* [*pl.* knights-errant], in the Middle Ages, a knight who went in search of adventure, to show his military prowess.—*n.* **knight'-er'rant-ry.**

knight-hood (nīt'hood), *n.* **1,** the character, rank, or dignity of a knight; **2,** knights collectively.

knight-ly (nīt'lĭ), *adj.* [*comp.* knight'li-er, *superl.* knight'li-est], **1,** chivalrous; brave; gentle and courteous; **2,** consisting of knights.—*n.* **knight'li-ness.**

Knight Tem-plar [*pl.* Knights Templars], **1,** a member of a powerful military order, founded about 1118 to protect pilgrims on the way to Jerusalem during the Crusades: suppressed in 1312; **2,** [*pl.* sometimes Knights Templar], a member of a branch of the Freemasons in the U. S., reputed to be based on the military order.

knit (nĭt), *v.t.* [*p.t.* and *p.p.* knit'ted or, chiefly *Archaic* or *Poetic,* knit, *p.pr.* knit'ting], **1,** to tie, unite, or draw together; **2,** to form, as a fabric, by looping or weaving thread or yarn on needles; **3,** to draw into wrinkles, as the brows:—*v.i.* **1,** to weave thread or yarn in loops on needles; **2,** to become closely joined or united; as, the broken limb *knitted* well.—*n.* **knit'ter.**

knit-ting (nĭt'ĭng), *n.* **1,** the work of a knitter; **2,** the netted fabric thus woven on long needles.

knives (nīvz), the irregular plural of the noun *knife,* which see.

knob (nŏb), *n.* **1,** the rounded handle of a door, etc.; **2,** a round swelling, mass, or lump; **3,** a rounded hill.

knob-by (nŏb'ĭ), *adj.* [*comp.* knob'bi-er, *superl.* knob'bi-est], full of humps or knolls; hilly; as, a *knobby* field or landscape.

knock (nŏk), *n.* a blow or stroke with something hard or heavy; rap:—*v.t.* **1,** to give a blow to; **2,** to bring in contact; as, to *knock* the head against a wall; **3,** *Slang,* to criticize harshly: **knock off,** *Colloq.,* **1,** to stop; as, to *knock off* work; **2,** to deduct; as, to *knock off* a dollar from the price: **knock out,** to defeat, in a fight, by a blow:—*v.i.* **1,** to strike a blow with something hard; esp., to rap on a door; **2,** to strike against something; **3,** to jar or pound: said of machinery parts: **knock about,** to wander in an aimless way.

knock-a-bout (nŏk'ȧ-bout"), *n.* **1,** a small yacht carrying a mainsail and jib and having a fin keel or centerboard (see *ship,* illus.); **2,** an article used for rough or everyday wear:—*adj.* characterized by roughness; suitable for rough or everyday usage.

knock-er (nŏk'ẽr), *n.* **1,** one who knocks; **2,** a loose handle attached to a door, to be used as a means of rapping.

knock-kneed (nŏk'=nēd"), *adj.* having the legs bent inward at the knees: opp. of *bow-legged.*

[1]**knoll** (nōl), *v.t. Archaic,* **1,** to ring slowly, as a bell for a funeral; **2,** to proclaim by tolling:—*n. Archaic,* a knell.

[2]**knoll** (nōl), *n.* a hilltop; a rounded hillock; a mound.

knop (nŏp) *n.* a knob or button; esp., a knoblike architectural ornament.

knot (nŏt), *n.* **1,** an interweaving or tying of thread, cord, etc.; **2,** anything resembling a knot; **3,** an entanglement; difficulty; **4,** a hard part in a piece of wood; the part of a tree where the branches shoot out; **5,** a group of people; **6,** a section of a log line; **7,** a unit of speed equal to one nautical mile per hour; **8,** loosely, a nautical mile, or about 6080 feet:—*v.t.* [*p.t.* and *p.p.* knot'ted, *p.pr.* knot'ting], **1,** to tie in a knot; **2,** to unite firmly or closely:—*v.i.* **1,** to form knots or joints, as some plants; **2,** to make knots for fringe.

knot-ting (nŏt'ĭng), *n.* **1,** the tying of a knot; entangling in a knot; **2,** a kind of lace work made with knotted threads; **3,** a paint for protecting metal.

knot-ty (nŏt'ĭ), *adj.* [*comp.* knot'ti-er, *superl.* knot'ti-est], **1,** full of knots; **2,** rugged; **3,** difficult; as, a *knotty* problem. —*n.* **knot'ti-ness.**

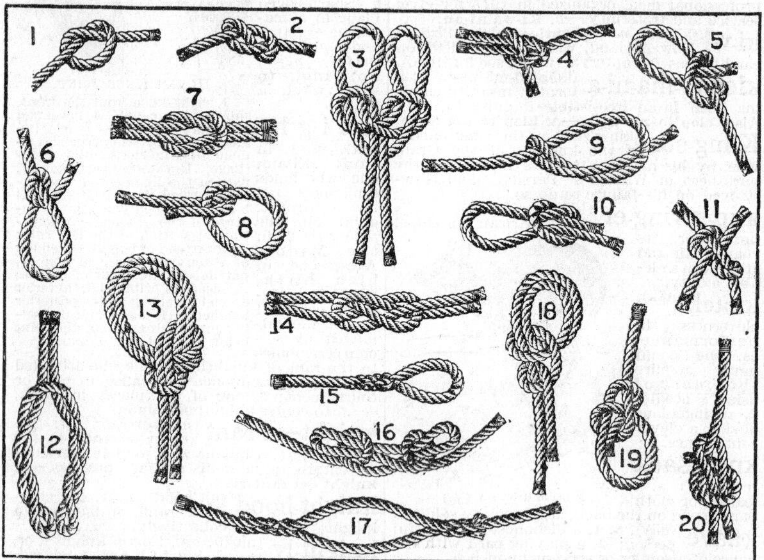

KNOTS, BENDS, AND HITCHES.—1, overhand knot; 2, figure eight; 3, Spanish bowline knot; 4, common, or sheet, bend; 5, studding-sail tack bend; 6, inside clinch; 7, square, or reef, knot; 8, half hitch; 9, timber hitch; 10, running knot; 11, clove hitch; 12, cat's-paw; 13, bowline knot on a bight; 14, double carrick bend; 15, eye-splice; 16, sheepshank; 17, cut splice; 18, fisherman's bend; 19, bowline knot, which will not slip and never pulls tight; 20, double sheet bend.

knout (nout; nōōt), *n.* a leathern whip, formerly used for the purpose of punishing criminals or serfs in Russia:—*v.t.* to punish by flogging.

know (nō), *v.t.* [*p.t.* knew (nū), *p.p.* known (nōn), *p.pr.* know'ing], **1,** to perceive with the mind; understand clearly; as, he *knows* right from wrong; **2,** to recognize; as, he *knew* the landscape; **3,** to be acquainted with; have experience of; as, to *know* Spanish; to *know* trouble:—*v.i.* to be informed; have certain knowledge:—*n. Slang,* knowledge; as, in the *know.*—*adj.* **know'a-ble.**—*n.* **know'er.**

know-ing (nō'ĭng), *p.adj.* **1,** having knowledge; intelligent; **2,** shrewd; as, a *knowing* look.—*adv.* **know'ing-ly.**

knowl-edge (nŏl'ĕj), *n.* **1,** clear perception of a truth or fact;

AMERICAN TREE LEAVES, FLOWERS AND FRUITS

1. Black oak. 2. White ash (7 leaflets more common than 5). 3. White oak. 4. White elm. 5. Magnolia. 6. Tulip tree. 7. Sycamore or Buttonwood. 8. White, or Silver maple. 9. Red cedar. 10. Sweet or Red gum

AMERICAN TREE LEAVES, FLOWERS AND FRUITS

1. White pine. 2. Shellbark hickory. 3. Red spruce. 4. Incense cedar. 5. Hemlock. 6. Black walnut. (Only 6 leaflets shown. They number from 13 to 23.) 7. Redwood. 8. Chestnut. 9. Cottonwood. 10. Red birch.

2, learning; 3, skill from practice; 4, information; notification; as, *knowledge* of the event has been made public.

Syn. wisdom. *Knowledge* may be the sum of what is known; as, every branch of *knowledge;* it may also be limited to the understanding of a single subject; as, a store of *knowledge;* a *knowledge* of chemistry. *Wisdom* is both ideal and practical; it combines *knowledge,* experience, and judgment; as, *wisdom* is *knowledge* digested by thought.

Know-Noth-ing (nō′=nŭth″ĭng), *n.* a member of a political party active in the U. S. in 1853 and for a few years following, which claimed that none but native Americans should hold office.

knuck-le (nŭk′l), *n.* 1, any of the joints of the fingers; 2, in cookery, the knee joint of a calf or pig:—*v.i.* [*p.t.* and *p.p.* -led (-ld), *p.pr.* -ling], 1, to bend the fingers; 2, to yield or submit: with *under;* 3, to apply oneself earnestly: with *down.*

knurl (nûrl), *n.* a hard knot or lump, as on a tree. Also, **knur.**—*adj.* **knurl′y.**

ko-bold (kō′bŏld), *n.* in old folk tales, a brownie or gnome.

ko-dak (kō′dăk), *n.* 1, a hand camera having the trade-mark name *Kodak;* 2, erroneously, any hand camera:—*v.t.* and *v.i.* to photograph with a kodak.—*n.* **ko′dak-er.**

Koh-i-noor (kō′hĭ-nŏŏr″; kō′ĭ-nŏŏr″), *n.* a famous large diamond, one of the British crown jewels.

ko-la (kō′lȧ), *n.* an African tree; also, its nut, containing caffeine: used for chewing, like tobacco, and in making a drink.

ko-peck (kō′pĕk), *n.* a Russian copper (formerly silver) coin worth about a half cent. Also, **co′peck; ko′pek.**

Ko-ran (kō-rän′; kō′răn), *n.* the sacred book of the Mohammedans, written in Arabic: also called *Alcoran.*

ko-sher (kō′shẽr), *adj.* lawful; clean according to Jewish law: used of food, esp. meat, or of shops where such meat is sold.

ko-tow (kō-tou′), *n.* a Chinese custom of kneeling and touching the ground with the forehead as a token of respect or worship:—*v.i.* to show deference by such an act; hence, to be obsequious. Also, **kow-tow′.**

kraal (kräl; krôl), *n.* 1, a South African village consisting of a group of huts surrounded by a defense of stakes; 2, a sheepfold, or cattle pen:—*v.t.* to inclose in a kraal.

kran (krän), *n.* a silver coin of Persia, formerly the monetary unit, worth about 7.6 cents: replaced in 1932 by the rial.

krem-lin (krĕm′lĭn), *n.* in Russia, a citadel or fortress: **Kremlin,** a large inclosure in Moscow, containing the palace of the former czar, churches, etc.

kreut-zer (kroit′sẽr), *n.* either of two copper coins, formerly current in Germany and Austria, worth about half a cent.

Kriem-hild (krēm′hĭlt), *n.* in the "Nibelungenlied," the sister of King Gunther, and the wife of Siegfried.

kris (krēs), *n.* a short Malay sword or dagger. See **creese,** *Pfd.S.*

Krish-na (krĭsh′nȧ), *n.* one of the forms of the Hindu god Vishnu.

Kriss Krin-gle (krĭs krĭng′gl), the good spirit of Christmas; hence, Santa Claus; St. Nicholas.

kro-na (krō′nȧ) *n.* [*pl.* kronor (-nŏr)], a Swedish silver coin, worth about 27 cents: also, by translation, called *crown.*

kro-ne (krō′nĕ), *n.* [*pl.* kroner (-nẽr)], 1, in Norway and Denmark, a silver coin, worth about 27 cents; 2, (krō′nĕ), [*pl.* kronen (-nĕn)], in Austria, a silver coin, formerly the monetary unit, normally worth about 20 cents: replaced in 1924 by the schilling, worth about 14 cents, as monetary unit; 3, in Germany, a gold coin worth about $2.40. Also, by translation, called *crown.*

kroon (krōn; krōōn), *n.* the monetary unit of Estonia, equivalent to 26.8 cents.

Ku-Klux (kū′=klŭks″), *n.* the Knights of the Ku-Klux Klan, a secret society in the southern U. S. after the Civil War, whose object was to regain white political control in the South: revived after the World War in many parts of the U. S., advocating the supremacy of native-born, white Protestants: also called *Ku-Klux Klan; Kuklux.*

***Kul-tur** (kōōl-tōōr′), [Ger.], *n.* a civilization; an organized system of life and education, esp. as exemplified by the German system before 1914.

ku-miss (kōō′mĭs), *n.* a fermented liquor made from mare's or camel's milk by Tatar tribes of central Asia; also, a similar drink made from cow's milk in western countries. Also, **ku′mys; kou′miss** (kōō′-).

kum-quat (kŭm′kwŏt), *n.* 1, a small, citrous fruit, used chiefly in preserves; 2, the tree bearing this fruit. Also, **cum′quat.**

Kun-dry (kōōn′drĭ), *n.* in Wagner's "Parsifal," a woman doomed to wander eternally for having laughed at Jesus.

Kurd (kōōrd), *n.* a member of a dark, fierce race in the undefined region of Kurdistan, eastern Turkey, and western Persia. Also, **Curd; Koord.**—*adj.* **Kurd′ish.**

Kym-ry (kĭm′rĭ), *n.pl.* the Welsh people, collectively. Also, **Kym′ri;** *Pfd.S.,* **Cym′ry.**—*adj.* **Kym′ric.**

L

la (lä), *n.* the sixth of the syllables used in singing a major or minor diatonic scale.

La-ban (lā′băn), *n.* in the Bible, the father of Leah and Rachel, wives of Jacob.

la-bel (lā′bĕl), *n.* 1, a small slip of paper, cloth, metal, etc., attached to anything, indicating its maker, contents, size, owner, destination, etc.; 2, hence, any distinguishing mark or characteristic; 3, in heraldry, a bar of special shape across a coat of arms, to indicate a first-born or only son:—*v.t.* 1, to mark with a label, as a garment; 2, to classify.

LABEL (def. 3)

la-bel-lum (lȧ-bĕl′ŭm), *n.* [*pl.* labella (-ȧ)], the lip, or lower petal, of an orchid; also, any liplike part.

la-bi-al (lā′bĭ-ăl), *adj.* 1, pertaining to the lips; as, a *labial* vein; 2, formed by the lips, as the consonants *b, m,* etc.:—*n.* a sound, or a letter representing a sound, formed by the lips, as *p, b, f, v, m.*—*adv.* **la′bi-al-ly.**

la-bi-ate (lā′bĭ-āt), *adj.* lipped; specif., having lips or liplike parts, as certain flowers, notably the lady's-slipper.

la-bor (lā′bẽr), *n.* 1, toil or exertion, physical or mental; 2, the whole class of workers, artisans, and others employed in the actual production of wealth, as distinguished from those who supply money or mental work; as, the relations between capital and *labor* are difficult to adjust; 3, a task; as, the twelve *labors* of Hercules; 4, the pangs and effort of bearing a child:—*v.i.* **1**, to use muscular strength; toil; **2**, to be hard pressed; move slowly and heavily; **3**, to strive; take pains; **4**, to pitch and roll heavily, as a ship in a storm; **5**, to suffer the pains of childbirth. Also, **la'bour.**

Syn., *n.* work, toil, drudgery. *Work*, the general word, means physical or mental effort directed to some purpose. *Labor* is hard, tiring *work*, more often physical than mental. *Toil* is exhausting *labor*. *Drudgery* is displeasing, often menial, *work;* though even light *work* may be *drudgery* to one who dislikes the task.—*Ant.*, *n.* idleness, ease, play.

lab-o-ra-to-ry (lăb'ō-rȧ-tō-rĭ), *n.* [*pl.* laboratories (-rĭz)], a place where scientific experiments and research are carried on, or where drugs, chemicals, etc., are made or tested for purity or strength.

La-bor Day in most states in the U. S., a day, usually the first Monday in September, set apart as a legal holiday. Also, **La'bour Day.**

la-bored (lā'bẽrd), *p.adj.* done with toil or care; not easy or natural; as, *labored* speech. Also, **la'boured.**

la-bor-er (lā'bẽr-ẽr), *n.* one who toils; one who does unskilled physical work for hire. Also, **la'bour-er.**

la-bo-ri-ous (lȧ-bō'rĭ-ŭs), *adj.* **1**, difficult; requiring toil; as, a *laborious* task; **2**, hard-working; as, a *laborious* mechanic.—*adv.* **la-bo'ri-ous-ly.**—*n.* **la-bo'ri-ous-ness.**

la-bor-ite (lā'bẽr-īt), *n.* one who supports the interests of the laboring class: **Laborite**, *Colloq.*, in Great Britain, a person belonging to the Labor party, a party which strives by political means to advance the interests of the working classes. Also, **la'bour-ite; La'bour-ite.**

la-bur-num (lȧ-bûr'nŭm), *n.* any of a genus (*Laburnum*) of poisonous, ornamental trees or shrubs, with pea-shaped yellow flowers.

Lab-y-rinth (lăb'ĭ-rĭnth), *n.* in mythology, the bewildering structure built for King Minos in Crete as a prison for the Minotaur and penetrated by Theseus: **labyrinth**, **1**, a series of passages winding in and out of one another; a maze; **2**, a confusing or puzzling state of things; **3**, the winding tubes of the inner ear.

LABYRINTH: Follow black line.

lab-y-rin-thine (lăb″ĭ-rĭn'thĭn), *adj.* intricate; perplexing.—*adj.* **lab″y-rin'thi-an; lab″y-rin'thic.**

[1]**lac** (lăk), *n.* in British India, the sum of 100,000, usually of rupees; hence, a very great number. Also, **lakh.**

[2]**lac** (lăk), *n.* a dark red, gummy substance deposited on certain trees by a scale insect: when melted and strained, called *shellac*, and used in sealing wax, dyes, varnishes, and lacquers.

lace (lās), *n.* **1**, an ornamental fabric of fine threads, as of linen, cotton, gold, etc., woven in a delicate open pattern; **2**, a cord passed through eyelets or other holes in order to bind or fasten:—*v.t.* [*p.t.* and *p.p.* laced (lāst), *p.pr.* lac'ing], **1**, to fasten with a cord; **2**, to adorn or trim, as with narrow braid, etc.; **3**, to weave or twine together; **4**, to lash.

Lac-e-dæ-mo-ni-an (lăs″ē-dē-mō'nĭ-ăn), *adj.* **1**, pertaining to the city or district of Lacedæmon, or Sparta, in Greece; **2**, Spartan:—*n.* a Spartan. Also, **Lac″e-de-mo'ni-an.**

lac-er-ate (lăs'ẽr-āt), *v.t.* [*p.t.* and *p.p.* -at″ed, *p.pr.* -at″ing], **1**, to tear or mangle, as flesh; **2**, to wound; also, to pain.

lac-er-a-tion (lăs″ẽr-ā'shŭn), *n.* **1**, the act of tearing or mangling; **2**, a jagged rent or wound; **3**, a harrowing or wounding, as of the feelings.

lace-wing (lās'wĭng″), *n.* any of various insects with delicately veined, lacelike wings and brilliant eyes.

Lach-e-sis (lăk'ē-sĭs), *n.* in mythology, that one of the three Fates who measured off the thread of life. The other two were Clotho and Atropos.

lach-ry-mal (lăk'rĭ-măl), *adj.* pertaining to tears. See **lac'ri-mal**, *Pfd. S.*

lach-ry-mose (lăk'rĭ-mōs), *adj.* tearful. See **lac'ri-mose,** *Pfd. S.*—*adv.* **lach'ry-mose-ly.**

lac-ing (lās'ĭng), *n.* **1**, a cord, string, braid, or the like, passed through eyelets to fasten something, or as a trimming; **2**, the act or method of fastening with such a cord.

lack (lăk), *v.t.* **1**, to be without; as, to *lack* common sense; **2**, to be in want of; need; as, to *lack* money:—*v.i.* **1**, to be wanting or absent; fail; as, proof is *lacking;* **2**, to have need; be short: with *of* or *in;* as, he *lacks* in wisdom:—*n.* want; deficiency; as, a *lack* of food.

Syn., *n.* need, scarcity, dearth, insufficiency.—*Ant.*, *n.* abundance, plenty, profusion.

lack-a-dai-si-cal (lăk″ȧ-dā'zĭ-kăl), *adj.* **1**, languidly sentimental; **2**, listless.—*adv.* **lack″a-dai'si-cal-ly.**

lack-er (lăk'ẽr), *n.* a varnish made by dissolving shellac in alcohol:—*v.t.* to cover with lacquer. See **lac'quer,** *Pfd. S.*

lack-ey (lăk'ĭ), *n.* [*pl.* lackeys (-ĭz)], an attendant of low rank; a footman:—*v.i.* and *v.t.* to act as attendant or servant (to). Also, **lac'quey.**

La-co-ni-an (lȧ-kō'nĭ-ăn), *adj.* of or pertaining to Laconia, a state in ancient Greece:—*n.* an inhabitant of Laconia.

la-con-ic (lȧ-kŏn'ĭk), *adj.* expressing much in few words; terse; concise: from the abrupt manner of the Laconians. Also, **la-con'i-cal.**—*adv.* **la-con'i-cal-ly.**

Syn. brief, short, pointed, pithy, succinct.—*Ant.* diffuse, wordy, verbose, long.

lac-quer (lăk'ẽr), *n.* **1**, a varnish consisting of shellac dissolved in alcohol, and used as a coating for brass, silver, etc., to prevent tarnishing; **2**, any of various varnishes made with resin, esp. one made from the sap of certain Oriental trees; **3**, Chinese or Japanese woodwork finished with lacquer and inlaid with gold, ivory, pearl, or the like:—*v.t.* to cover with lacquer. Also, **lack'er.**

lac-quey (lăk'ĭ), *n.* [*pl.* lacqueys (-ĭz)], a servile attendant:—*v.i.* and *v.t.* to act as servant (to). Also, **lack'ey,** *Pfd. S.*

lac-ri-mal (lăk'rĭ-măl), *adj.* pertaining to, or secreting, tears; as, *lacrimal* glands. Also, **lach'ry-mal; lac'ry-mal.**

lac-ri-mose (lăk'rĭ-mōs), *adj.* **1**, weeping easily; tearful; **2**, sad; mournful. Also, **lach'ry-mose.**—*adv.* **lac'ri-mose-ly.**

la-crosse (lȧ-krôs'), *n.* a field game played with a small ball and a netted bat or racket, called a *crosse*.

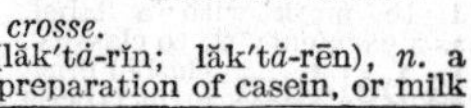

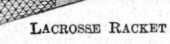

LACROSSE RACKET

lac-ta-rine (lăk'tȧ-rĭn; lăk'tȧ-rēn), *n.* a preparation of casein, or milk curds: used extensively in calico printing. Also, **lac'ta-rene.**

lac-ta-tion (lăk-tā'shŭn), *n.* the act or period of secreting milk or of suckling young.

lac-te-al (lăk'tē-ăl), *adj.* **1,** pertaining to, or like, milk; **2,** conveying the fluid called *chyle,* which contains fats from digested food, as ducts:—*n.* one of the lymphatic vessels of the small intestines, which take up and carry the chyle to the thoracic duct.

lac-tic (lăk'tĭk), *adj.* pertaining to, or derived from, milk; as, *lactic* acid.

lac-tom-e-ter (lăk-tŏm'ē-tẽr), *n.* an instrument for measuring the richness of milk.

lac-tose (lăk'tōs), *n.* a sugar contained in milk: also called *sugar of milk.*

la-cu-na (lȧ-kū'nȧ), *n.* [*pl.* lacunæ (-nē); lacunas (-nȧz)], **1,** a space from which something has been omitted, as in a manuscript; **2,** a small pit or hollow, such as is found in the substance of bone.

lad (lăd), *n.* a boy or youth; stripling; also, any male comrade.

lad-der (lăd'ẽr), *n.* **1,** a framework usually consisting of two side pieces connected by bars or crosspieces, called *rungs,* forming steps at suitable distances; **2,** figuratively, any means by which one climbs or ascends; as, the *ladder* of ambition: **ladder-back chair,** a chair with a straight back resembling the sides and rungs of a ladder (see *furniture,* illus.).

SCALING LADDER

lad-die (lăd'ĭ), *n. Scot.,* a lad; also, a boy sweetheart.

lade (lād), *v.t.* [*p.t.* lad'ed, *p.p.* lad'ed or lad'en (lād'n), *p.pr.* lad'ing], **1,** to load; put a burden on or in; **2,** to throw out or in with a scoop or dipper; bail; as, to *lade* water out of a tub.

lad-ing (lād'ĭng), *n.* **1,** the act of loading or of bailing; **2,** freight; cargo.

la-dle (lā'dl), *n.* a deep spoon or dipper for dipping out liquids:—*v.t.* [*p.t.* and *p.p.* -dled (-dld), *p.pr.* -dling], to dip up with a ladle.

la-dy (lā'dĭ), *n.* [*pl.* ladies (-dĭz)], **1,** a well-bred woman; a woman of good family or of high position in society; as, she was born a *lady;* **2,** a sweetheart or wife: **Lady, 1,** the title of the wife of a peer below the rank of duke, or of a knight or baronet; also, the title of the daughter of a duke, marquis, or earl; **2,** the Virgin Mary: with *Our.*

la-dy-bird (lā'dĭ-bûrd″), *n.* any of certain small, brightly colored beetles.

la-dy-bug (lā'dĭ-bŭg″), *n. Colloq.,* a small beetle; a ladybird.

La-dy Day in Catholic and Anglican churches, Annunciation, a feast day, March 25, commemorating the announcement to Mary of the coming birth of Jesus (Luke 1:28–38).

la-dy-like (lā'dĭ-līk″), *adj.* **1,** befitting a gentlewoman; courteous; **2,** suited to a woman; delicate; **3,** hence, unmanly.

la-dy-ship (lā'dĭ-shĭp), *n.* the rank of a lady: used with *her* or *your* in addressing one whose title is *Lady.*

la-dy's-slip-per (lā'dĭz-slĭp″ẽr), *n.* any of various orchids, the flowers of which somewhat resemble a slipper. Also, **la'dy-slip″per.**

lag (lăg), *v.i.* [*p.t.* and *p.p.* lagged (lăgd), *p.pr.* lag'ging], to move slowly; loiter; stay behind:—*n.* a falling behind in movement.—*n.* **lag'ger.**

lag bolt a bolt or screw with a square head: also called *lag screw.*

la-ger beer (lä'gẽr), a German brewed liquor which is stored for some months before use: also called *lager.*

lag-gard (lăg'ȧrd), *n.* a person who acts more slowly than he should; a loiterer; as, a *laggard* in love:—*adj.* backward; slow.—*adv.* **lag'gard-ly.**

lag-ging (lăg'ĭng), *n.* **1,** slow motion; the act of loitering; **2,** strips of wood or planks used to support an arch or the roof of a mine during construction.

la-goon (lȧ-gōōn'), *n.* **1,** a shallow lake, usually near to, and connected with, the sea; **2,** the shallow water inside a ring-shaped coral island, or atoll. Also, **la-gune'.**

la-ic (lā'ĭk), *adj.* pertaining to those who are not clergymen or members of some particular profession:—*n.* a layman.

laid (lād), past tense and past participle of the verb [3]*lay:* **laid paper,** paper marked with fine, parallel lines, or watermarked.

lain (lān), past participle of the intransitive verb [2]*lie.*

lair (lâr), *n.* the den or resting place of a wild beast; as, the lion's *lair.*

laird (lârd), *n. Scot.,* a lord; the master of a landed estate.

***lais-sez faire** (lâ″sā″ fâr'), [Fr.], a term meaning "let (people) do as they please": used, esp. in economics, of a policy of noninterference by the government with industry, conditions of labor, etc.

la-i-ty (lā'ĭ-tĭ), *n.* [*pl.* laities (-tĭz)], **1,** the people, as distinguished from the clergy; **2,** those outside any given profession.

[1]**lake** (lāk), *n.* a large body of water surrounded by land.

[2]**lake** (lăk), *n.* a purplish red coloring matter obtained from lac.

lakh (lăk), *n.* in British India, the sum of 100,000, usually of rupees; hence, a very great number. Also, **lac,** *Pfd. S.*

la-ma (lä'mȧ), *n.* a priest, monk, or nun of the branch of the Buddhist faith prevalent in Tibet and Mongolia.—*n.* **La'ma-ism.**

lamb (lăm), *n.* **1,** the young of the sheep; **2,** the flesh of such sheep; **3,** one who is gentle or innocent:—*v.i.* to bring forth lambs.

lamb-da (lăm'dȧ), *n.* the 11th letter of the Greek alphabet [λ, Λ], corresponding to English *l.*

lam-bent (lăm'bĕnt), *adj.* **1,** playing over the surface; flickering; touching lightly; as, a *lambent* flame; **2,** softly bright; as, the *lambent* light of stars.—*adv.* **lam'bent-ly.**—*n.* **lam'ben-cy.**

lamb-kin (lăm'kĭn), *n.* **1,** a little lamb; **2,** a tenderly cherished child.

lam-bre-quin (lăm'brē-kĭn; lăm'bẽr-), *n.* an ornamental drapery hanging from the upper part of a window or doorway, from the edge of a shelf, or the like.

lamb-skin (lăm'skĭn″), *n.* **1,** the skin of a lamb dressed with the fleece on, frequently colored; **2,** leather made from the skin of a lamb.

lame (lām), *adj.* **1,** crippled or disabled in the limbs; **2,** not sound or effective; as, a *lame* excuse:—*v.t.* [*p.t.* and *p.p.* lamed (lāmd), *p.pr.* lam'ing], to cripple or disable.—*adv.* **lame'ly.**—*n.* **lame'ness.**

la-mel-la (lȧ-mĕl'ȧ), *n.* [*pl.* lamellæ (-ē); lamellas (-ȧz)], a thin plate, sheet, or layer; a plate-shaped part.—*adj.* **la-mel'lar** (lȧ-mĕl'ȧr; lăm'ē-lȧr).

la-ment (lȧ-mĕnt'), *v.i.* and *v.t.* to express sorrow (for):—*n.* an expression of sorrow.—*p.adj.* **la-ment'ed.**

lam-en-ta-ble (lăm'ĕn-tȧ-bl), *adj.* **1,** mournful; as, a *lamentable* cry; **2,** regrettable; pitiable; as, a *lamentable* mistake.—*adv.* **lam'en-ta-bly.**
Syn. doleful, deplorable, sorrowful.

lam-en-ta-tion (lăm″ĕn-tā′shŭn), *n.* grief expressed aloud; outcry: **Lamentations,** a book of the Old Testament, attributed to Jeremiah.—*abbr.* **Lam.**

lam-i-na (lăm′ĭ-nȧ), *n.* [*pl.* laminæ (-nē); laminas (-nȧz)], **1,** a thin plate, layer, or scale, as of bone or rock; **2,** the blade of a foliage leaf or petal.—*adj.* **lam′i-nar.**

lam-i-nate (lăm′ĭ-nāt), *adj.* composed of, or arranged in, thin coats, scales, or layers:—*v.t.* (lăm′ĭ-nāt) [*p.t.* and *p.p.* -nat″ed, *p.pr.* -nat″ing], **1,** to roll, press, or divide into thin sheets, as metal; **2,** to build up with thin sheets or layers:—*v.i.* to separate into thin layers; also, to take the form of a thin sheet.—*p.adj.* **lam′i-nat″ed.**

lam-i-na-tion (lăm″ĭ-nā′shŭn), *n.* division into thin plates or sheets; also, a thin plate or scale.

lamp (lămp), *n.* **1,** a vessel in which oil, or the like, may be absorbed into a wick and ignited so as to produce light; **2,** hence, any device for producing artificial light.

Ancient Lamps

lamp-black (lămp′blăk″), *n.* a deep black pigment, or coloring matter, made by collecting the soot produced by burning oil, resin, gas, or the like: used in paints, printing ink, etc.

lam-poon (lăm-po͞on′), *n.* a written article holding a person up to ridicule and contempt; a personal satire:—*v.t.* to satirize in writing.—*n.* **lam-poon′er.**

lam-prey (lăm′prĭ), *n.* [*pl.* lampreys (-prĭz)], any of certain eel-like water animals, some being valued as food, having a large, circular, sucking mouth.

Lan-cas-tri-an (lăng-kăs′trĭ-ăn), *adj.* of or pertaining to the English royal house of Lancaster, of which Henry IV, V, and VI (1399–1461) reached the throne:—*n.* a member or follower of this family, esp. in its struggle with the house of York in the Wars of the Roses.

lance (lȧns), *n.* **1,** a long shaft of wood with a sharp steel head; **2,** a soldier equipped with a lance: **lance corporal,** an assistant to a corporal; a private soldier acting as corporal: **lance sergeant,** an acting sergeant:—*v.t.* [*p.t.* and *p.p.* lanced (lȧnst), *p.pr.* lanc′ing], **1,** to pierce with a lance; **2,** to cut open, as a boil, with a lancet, or surgeon's knife.

Lan-ce-lot (lȧn′sē-lŏt), *n.* the bravest, most generous, and handsomest of the knights of King Arthur's Round Table, and the lover of Guinevere.

lan-ce-o-late (lăn′sē-ō-lāt), *adj.* shaped like the head of a spear; tapering, as a leaf (see *leaf,* illus.).

lanc-er (lȧn′sẽr), *n.* **1,** a cavalry soldier armed with a long spear; **2,** in *pl.*, a kind of square dance arranged for four couples; also, the musical accompaniment.

lan-cet (lăn′sĕt), *n.* **1,** a small, two-edged surgical knife; **2,** a window with a sharply pointed arch.

lance-wood (lȧns′wo͝od″), *n.* a tough, elastic wood used in making bows and in cabinetwork, coach building, etc.; also, any tree yielding such wood.

land (lănd), *n.* **1,** the solid portion of the surface of the globe; **2,** a country or district; **3,** the people of a country; a nation; **4,** ground or soil, with reference to its location or use; as, farm *land;* **5,** in mechanics, the original level or face of a grooved or indented surface, as the surface between the spiral grooves of a drill or a rifle barrel (see [1]*drill,* Illus.):—*v.t.* **1,** to set on shore; as, to *land* passengers from a ship; **2,** to capture and bring to shore; as, to *land* a fish; **3,** to win; as, to *land* a prize; **4,** to put down after carrying; as, the train *landed* him at his destination:—*v.i.* **1,** to come or go ashore; **2,** to arrive at a dock, as a vessel; **3,** to come to the end of a course; get into a situation; as, he *landed* in jail; **4,** to alight; come to earth; as, the airplane *landed* in a swamp.

lan-dau (lăn′dô; lăn′dou), *n.* a four-wheeled covered carriage with a top in two sections which can be let down.

lan-dau-let (lăn″dô-lĕt′), *n.* **1,** a two-seated motor car with a divided top similar to that of a landau; **2,** a small landau (which see).

land-ed (lăn′dĕd), *p.adj.* **1,** possessing real estate; as, a *landed* proprietor; **2,** consisting of land; as, a *landed* estate.

land–grab-ber (lănd′=grăb″ẽr), *n.* **1** one who obtains public land by fraud; **2,** formerly, in Ireland, one who bought or occupied land from which another owner had been expelled.

land-hold-er (lănd′hōl″dẽr), *n.* an owner, holder, or occupier of property in the form of land.—*n.* **land′hold″ing.**

land-ing (lăn′dĭng), *n.* **1,** the act of going ashore or of coming to earth; **2,** a place, as a wharf, where passengers or goods may be loaded or discharged; **3,** a platform, as at the end of a flight of steps.

land-la-dy (lănd′lā″dĭ), *n.* [*pl.* landladies (-dĭz)], **1,** a woman who lets houses or rooms to tenants; the mistress of a boarding house or inn; **2,** the wife of a landlord.

land-locked (lănd′lŏkt″), *adj.* **1,** nearly surrounded by land; as, a *landlocked* bay; **2,** confined to fresh water by some barrier; as, *landlocked* fish.

land-lord (lănd′lôrd″), *n.* **1,** one who owns or leases buildings or lands; **2,** the keeper of a hotel or an inn.

land-lub-ber (lănd′lŭb″ẽr), *n.* **1,** one who has not been to sea: a sailor's term of ridicule; **2,** hence, anyone who is awkward on shipboard.

land-mark (lănd′märk″), *n.* **1,** an object that marks the boundary of a tract of land; **2,** a familiar or conspicuous object that serves as a guide to a locality; **3,** any fact or event that marks a turning point, or helps to recall other facts and events.

land-own-er (lănd′ōn″ẽr), *n.* a person who possesses land.

land–poor (lănd′=po͞or″), *adj.* possessing property in real estate, but having little or no income with which to maintain it and pay taxes on it.

land-scape (lănd′skāp), *n.* **1,** a section of country seen as one view; **2,** a picture representing a scene from nature.

land-slide (lănd′slīd″), *n.* **1,** the slipping of a mass of earth, stones, etc., down a steep slope; **2,** the material that slips down. Also, **land′slip″.**

lands-man (lăndz′măn), *n.* [*pl.* landsmen (-mĕn)], a person who lives on land: opp. of *seaman.*

Lands-thing (läns′tĭng″), *n.* the Upper House of the Danish Parliament, or Rigsdag.

land-ward (lănd′wẽrd), *adj.* facing or moving toward the shore:—*adv.* toward the shore. Also, *adv.* **land′wards.**

lane (lān), *n.* **1,** a narrow path, as between hedges, walls, etc.; **2,** a rural road or narrow street; any narrow way or track; **3,** one of the ocean courses fixed as routes for vessels going in the same direction.

lang-syne (lăng″sīn′), *adv. Scot.*, long since; long ago:—*n.* the days of long ago; old times.

lan·guage (lăng′gwĭj), *n.* **1**, human speech, spoken or written; **2**, the body of words and idioms used for the expression of ideas among members of a group or nation; as, the German *language;* **3**, a special style or expression peculiar to an individual or class; as, his *language* is poor; **4**, the words and phrases peculiar to a special field of knowledge; as, the *language* of physics; **5**, any means of expression; as, the *language* of signs.
Syn. speech, tongue, dialect. The *language* of a country is the vocabulary and way of using it prevalent in that country. *Speech* adds to this sense another, that of the power to utter articulate sounds. *Tongue* names the *language* or *speech* of some one country or race; as, English is our mother *tongue*. A *dialect* is a variation from the standard of literary form of a *language*, used in a certain district or class.

lan·guid (lăng′gwĭd), *adj.* **1**, wanting energy; weak; drooping; **2**, dull; listless.—*adv.* **lan′guid-ly.**—*n.* **lan′guid-ness.**
Syn. spiritless, lagging, sluggish, apathetic. —*Ant.* eager, vivid, vigorous, active.

lan·guish (lăng′gwĭsh), *v.i.* **1**, to become weak or spiritless; pine away; **2**, to show or affect a sentimental tenderness.

lan·guish·ing (lăng′gwĭsh-ĭng), *p.adj.* **1**, drooping; pining; **2**, sentimentally tender; as, *languishing* looks. —*adv.* **lan′guish-ing-ly.**

lan·guor (lăng′gẽr; lăng′gwẽr), *n.* **1**, listlessness; weariness of body and mind caused by exhaustion; **2**, dreamy indolence; **3**, slackness; dulness.—*adj.* **lan′guor-ous.**—*adv.* **lan′guor-ous-ly.**

lank (lăngk), *adj.* **1**, lean; shrunken; as, a *lank* figure; **2**, long and straight, as hair.—*n.* **lank′ness.**
Syn. gaunt, spare, bony. (See [2]lean.)

lank·y (lăngk′ĭ), *adj.* [*comp.* lank′i-er, *superl.* lank′i-est], tall and thin; loosely hung; as, a *lanky* figure.—*n.* **lank′i-ness.**

lan·o·lin (lăn′ō-lĭn), *n.* fat or grease from sheep's wool, used, when purified as the basis for ointments. Also, **lan′o-line.**

lan·tern (lăn′tẽrn), *n.* **1**, a transparent case containing and protecting a light; **2**, the room at the top of a lighthouse where the light is kept; **3**, a small tower on the roof of a building to admit light and air; a cupola.

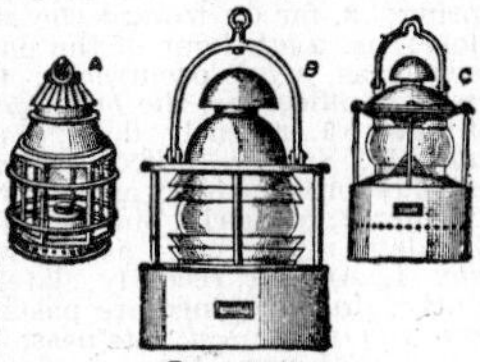

LANTERNS
A, post lantern; *B*, range light; *C*, riding light.

lan·tern-jawed (lăn′tẽrn-jôd″), *adj.* having a long, thin face.

lan·yard (lăn′yȧrd), *n.* **1**, a short line used for fastening the tackle of a ship; **2**, a strong cord used for firing a certain type of gun. Also, **lan′iard.**

La·oc·o·ön (lā-ŏk′ō-ŏn), *n.* in mythology, a priest of Apollo, who angered Athena by warning the Trojans against the wooden horse of the Greeks, and was destroyed, with his two sons, by two serpents summoned by her from the sea.

La·od·i·ce·an (lā-ŏd″ĭ-sē′ăn), *adj.* **1**, pertaining to Laodicea, a city of Asia Minor, where one of the early Christian churches was established; **2**, indifferent, or lukewarm, esp. in religion (Revelation 3:14–16):—*n.* **1**, an inhabitant of Laodicea; **2**, a lukewarm person.

[1]**lap** (lăp), *n.* **1**, the loose part of a garment which may be doubled over; **2**, the part of the body from the waist to the knees of a person when seated; also, the clothing that covers that part of the body; **3**, a place for supporting, sheltering, or rearing; **4**, the part of a thing, as a shingle, which lies partly upon another, so as to cover a strip along its edge; an overlapping part; also, the distance which one thing lies over another; as, a *lap* of two inches; **5**, one length of a course, esp. one which has to be passed over more than once in a race:—*v.t.* [*p.t.* and *p.p.* lapped (lăpt), *p.pr.* lap′ping], **1**, to lay or fold over, as cloth; **2**, to place over something else so as partly to cover it; as, to *lap* one shingle over another; **3**, to infold; surround: often figurative; as, *lapped* in luxury:—*v.i.* to lie partly over, or to project beyond, something.

[2]**lap** (lăp), *v.t.* [*p.t.* and *p.p.* lapped (lăpt), *p.pr.* lap′ping], **1**, to lick up with the tongue, as liquid; **2**, to wash or ripple against; as, the waves *lap* the shore:—*v.i.* **1**, to take up liquid with the tongue; **2**, to make a rippling sound, as waves:—*n.* the act or sound of lapping.

lap dog a small pet dog that may be held in the lap.

la·pel (lȧ-pĕl′), *n.* the part of a garment which is folded back; esp., the fold at each side of the front of a coat.

lap·ful (lăp′fo͝ol), *n.* [*pl.* lapfuls (-fo͝olz)], as much as can be held in the lap.

lap·i·da·ry (lăp′ĭ-dā-rĭ), *n.* [*pl.* lapidaries (-rĭz)], **1**, a skilled workman who cuts and sets precious stones; **2**, a dealer in, or collector of, gems:—*adj.* pertaining to stones, or to the act of cutting stones, esp. gems.

la·pis laz·u·li (lā′pĭs lăz′ū-lī), **1**, an opaque stone of a rich blue color; **2**, a deep blue color.

Lapp (lăp), *n.* **1**, an inhabitant of Lapland, an undefined region in the northern part of Scandinavia: also called *Laplander;* **2**, the language of Lapland.

lap·pet (lăp′ĕt), *n.* **1**, a loose flap, as on a headdress or garment; **2**, anything hanging loosely, as an ear lobe.

lapse (lăps), *v.i.* [*p.t.* and *p.p.* lapsed (lăpst), *p.pr.* laps′ing], **1**, to glide or slip slowly away; as, to *lapse* into unconsciousness; his interest *lapsed;* **2**, to commit a fault or fail in duty; slide or fall anew into sin; as, to *lapse* from good behavior; **3**, of an estate, right, etc., to revert to another because of the holder's negligence or failure to fulfil conditions; be or become void:—*n.* **1**, a gliding or passing away slowly; as, the *lapse* of time; **2**, a slight fault or mistake; a slip, as of memory, tongue, or pen; **3**, the ending of a claim, right, etc., through failure to assert or exercise it; **4**, a passing into ruin or disuse; as, the *lapse* of freedom of speech.—*p.adj.* **lapsed.**

lap·wing (lăp′wĭng″), *n.* a ploverlike bird of the Old World.

lar·board (lär′bōrd; lär′bẽrd), *n.* the left side of a ship as one faces the bow: now replaced by *port:*—*adj.* designating, or pertaining to, the left side of a ship.

lar·ce·ny (lär′sē-nĭ), *n.* [*pl.* larcenies (-nĭz)], the carrying away of another's property with the intention of defrauding the owner; theft: **grand larceny, petit** (or **petty**) **larceny,** theft of a relatively serious, or relatively unimportant, character, as defined by various statutes.—*adj.* **lar′ce-nous.**

larch (lärch), *n.* any of a genus of graceful trees of the pine family, having small cones and needlelike leaves that drop in the fall.

lard (lärd), *n.* a white, semisolid grease made from the fat of swine:—*v.t.* **1**, to cover with fat; **2**, to insert strips of bacon into before roasting; enrich; **3**, hence, to decorate; as, to *lard* a speech with compliments.

lard·er (lär′dẽr), *n.* **1**, a pantry; **2**, household provisions.

la-res (lā′rēz), *n.pl.* [*sing.* lar (lär); Eng. *pl.* lars (lärz)], among the ancient Romans, the spirits of ancestors considered as household gods.

large (lärj), *adj.* **1**, great in size; bulky; wide; extensive; as, *large* estates; **2**, comprehensive; broad in understanding or sympathy; as, a *large* mind: **at large, 1**, in full; as, to discuss a subject *at large;* **2**, free; as, the thief is *at large;* **3**, chosen to represent a whole state, district, etc.; as, a congressman *at large.* —*adv.* **large′ly.**—*n.* **large′ness.**

Syn. huge, ample, colossal, enormous, immense.—*Ant.* small, tiny, little, limited.

lar-gess (lär′jĕs), *n.* a generous gift or bounty; as, the king scattered *largess* as he rode along. Also, **lar′gesse.**

***lar-go** (lär′gō), [It.] *adj.* in music, slow:—*adv.* in music, slowly:—*n.* a musical composition of slow, dignified movement.

lar-i-at (lăr′ĭ-ăt), *n.* **1**, a rope, usually with a running noose, used for catching cattle; a lasso; **2**, a rope for tethering horses or cattle.

¹lark (lärk), *n.* **1**, any of various small European song birds, esp. the skylark; **2**, any of several similar American birds, as the meadow lark.

²lark (lärk), *n. Colloq.*, a lively or amusing adventure:—*v.i. Colloq.*, to frolic.

lark-spur (lärk′spûr), *n.* any of a genus of plants of the crowfoot family, with showy pink or blue flowers in spikes.

lar-va (lär′vȧ), *n.* [*pl.* larvæ (-vē)], the immature, often wormlike, form in which most insects hatch from the egg; also, the early form of any animal which changes in form as it develops; hence, an animal in this form, as a caterpillar or a tadpole.—*adj.* **lar′val.**

la-ryn-ge-al (lȧ-rĭn′jē-ăl; lăr″ĭn-jē′ăl), *adj.* pertaining to, or situated near, the larynx, or upper windpipe.

lar-yn-gi-tis (lăr″ĭn-jī′tĭs), *n.* inflammation of the larynx, or upper part of the windpipe: a form of sore throat. —*adj.* **lar″yn-git′ic** (lăr″ĭn-jĭt′ĭk).

lar-ynx (lăr′ĭngks), *n.* [*pl.* larynges (lȧ-rĭn′jēz)], an enlargement of the upper end of the windpipe, containing the vocal cords; the organ of voice. A cartilage on its front wall forms the Adam's apple.

las-car (lăs′kȧr; lăs-kär′), *n.* an East Indian native sailor, army servant, or artillery soldier.

las-civ-i-ous (lă-sĭv′ĭ-ŭs), *adj.* **1**, lewd; lustful; **2**, exciting lust.—*adv.* **las-civ′i-ous-ly.**—*n.* **las-civ′i-ous-ness.**

¹lash (lăsh), *v.t.* **1**, to strike or scourge, as with a whip; figuratively, to blame severely; as, to *lash* vice; **2**, to strike forcibly; as, the wind *lashed* the sails; **3**, to stir up by a strong emotional appeal; as, to *lash* an audience to fury:—*v.i.* **1**, to apply the whip; also, to rebuke severely; **2**, to rush, pour, or beat, as wind or rain:—*n.* **1**, the thong of a whip; **2**, a stroke with a whip or anything used like a whip, as sarcasm; **3**, one of the little hairs on the edge of an eyelid.—*n.* **lash′er.**

²lash (lăsh), *v.t.* to fasten or bind with a rope; as, *lashed* to the mast.

lash-ing (lăsh′ĭng), *n.* **1**, the act of lashing or of giving a sharp rebuke; also, a sharp reproof; as, a tongue *lashing;* **2**, the act of binding; also, a cord, rope, etc., used for binding.

lass (lȧs), *n. Scot.*, **1**, a girl; **2**, a sweetheart; **3**, a maidservant. Also, **las′sie.**

las-si-tude (lăs′ĭ-tūd), *n.* bodily or mental weariness; lack of energy.

las-so (lăs′ō), *n.* [*pl.* lassos (-ōz)], a rope, usually of hide, with a running noose, used for catching wild horses and cattle:—*v.t.* to catch with a noosed rope.—*n.* **las′so-er.**

¹last (lȧst), *n.* a wooden model of the foot on which shoes are shaped or fitted.

²last (lȧst), *adj.* superlative of *late:* **1**, coming after all others in time, place, order, or the like; **2**, next before the present; as, *last* week; **3**, authoritative; conclusive; as, the *last* word on style; **4**, least likely; least fitted; as, he is the *last* man to do the work:—*adv.* **1**, after all others; **2**, on the time or occasion next preceding the present; **3**, at the end; finally:—*n.* the end.

Syn., adj. latest, final. That is *last* which comes after all others or comes at the end; as, the *last* trolley; the *last* house on the street. *Last* is also used of that which is nearest the present time; as, *last* week; and of that which is most recent; as, his *last* trip. *Latest* differs from *last* as earliest differs from first; it is applied only to the order of time; the *latest* trolley may be also the *last* trolley, but an author's *latest* book may not be his *last* book. That is *final* which brings something to an end; a decision of the Supreme Court is *final.*

³last (lȧst), *v.i.* **1**, to continue in time; **2**, to be enough for a given time; hold out: often with indirect object; as, this will *last* me a week; **3**, to endure; wear well.

last-ing (lȧst′ĭng), *p.adj.* wearing well; permanent:—*n.* a fabric used for the uppers of women's shoes, for covering buttons, etc.—*adv.* **last′ing-ly.**—*n.* **last′ing-ness.**

last-ly (lȧst′lĭ), *adv.* finally; in conclusion; at the end.

lat (lăt), *n.* the monetary unit of Latvia, equivalent to 19.3 cents.

latch (lăch), *n.* a catch for a door or gate, often not requiring a key:—*v.t.* and *v.i.* to fasten with a catch.

latch-et (lăch′ĕt; lăch′ĭt), *n.* a shoe string; a strip of leather fastening a sandal.

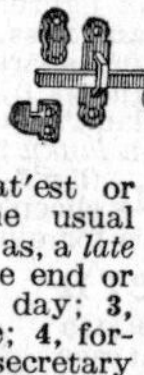
LATCH

late (lāt), *adj.* [*comp.* lat′er or lat′ter, *superl.* lat′est or last], **1**, coming after the usual time; tardy; long delayed; as, a *late* spring; **2**, far on toward the end or close; as, a *late* hour of the day; **3**, recent; as, a *late* occurrence; **4**, formerly in office; as, the *late* secretary of state; **5**, recently dead; as, the *late* Mr. Smith:—*adv.* **1**, after the usual or proper time; as, to arrive *late;* to get up *late;* **2**, formerly, but no longer; **3**, far into the day, night, etc.; as, to work early and *late;* **4**, *Archaic*, recently; lately: **of late**, recently; in the immediate past; as, I have not seen you *of late.*—*n.* **late′ness.**

Syn., adj. new; former. (See modern.)

la-teen sail (lă-tēn′), a three-cornered sail attached to a low mast.

LATEEN SAILS

late-ly (lāt′lĭ), *adv.* not long ago; recently; as, she has not been here *lately.*

la-ten-cy (lā′tĕn-sĭ), *n.* the state of being dormant, or present but not active or apparent.

la-tent (lā′tĕnt), *adj.* concealed; not visible; present, but not active; as, *latent* disease germs.—*adv.* **la′tent-ly.**

lat-er (lāt′ẽr), *adj.* comparative of *late:*—*adv.* after a lapse of time.

lat-er-al (lăt′ẽr-ăl), *adj.* pertaining to the side.—*adv.* **lat′er-al-ly.**

lat-est (lāt′ĕst), *adj.* superlative of *late:* pertaining to the most recent time; final:—*adv.* of the most recent occurrence.
Syn., adj. (see ²last).

la-tex (lā′tĕks), *n.* a milky juice secreted by certain plants, as the rubber tree.

lath (lȧth), *n.* a thin, narrow strip of wood nailed to the framework of a house to support the plaster:—*v.t.* to cover with such strips.—*n.* **¹lath′er.**

lathe (lā*th*), *n.* a machine by which articles of wood, metal, etc., are held and turned while being shaped and polished.

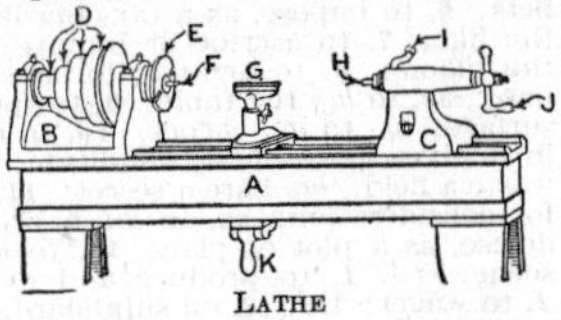

LATHE

A, bed; B, headstock; C, tailstock; D, cone-driving pulley; E, face plate; F, live center; G, tool rest; H, dead center; I, dead-center clamp handle; J, dead-center adjusting handle; K, cross slide clamp.

²lath-er (lăth′ẽr), *n.* **1,** froth made by moistened soap; **2,** foam made by sweat, as of a horse:—*v.t.* to cover with froth or foam:—*v.i.* to form foam or suds.—*n.* **lath′er-er.**—*adj.* **lath′er-y.**

lath-ing (lȧth′ĭng), *n.* the thin, narrow strips of wood on which plaster is laid in building; also, the act or process of putting them in place.

Lat-in (lăt′ĭn), *adj.* **1,** pertaining to Latium, a country of ancient Italy of which Rome was the capital, or to its inhabitants or language; **2,** designating, or pertaining to, the language of ancient Rome, or the races whose languages are derived from ancient Rome; as, the Italians are a *Latin* race: **Latin cross,** a cross like a plus sign with a lengthened lower limb (see *cross,* illus.): **Latin Quarter,** a section of Paris south of the Seine, populated largely by students:—*n.* **1,** a native of ancient Rome; **2,** the language of ancient Rome; **3,** one whose language is derived from the language of ancient Rome, as a Frenchman, Italian, Spaniard, etc.

Lat-in-ism (lăt′ĭn-ĭzm), *n.* an expression or idiom belonging peculiarly to the Latin language.

Lat-in-ist (lăt′ĭn-ĭst), *n.* one learned in Latin; a student of Latin.

Lat-in-ize (lăt′ĭn-īz), *v.t.* [*p.t.* and *p.p.* -ized (-īzd), *p.pr.* -iz″ing], **1,** to give Latin endings or characteristics to; **2,** to translate into Latin.

lat-i-tude (lăt′ĭ-tūd), *n.* **1,** distance on the earth's surface as measured by degrees north or south from the equator; **2,** breadth; extent; range; **3,** freedom from rules; **4,** a region or locality; as, a warm *latitude.*—*adj.* **lat″i-tu′di-nal.**

lat-i-tu-di-na-ri-an (lăt″ĭ-tū″dĭ-nā′rĭ-ăn), *adj.* liberal in thought or belief; not attached strictly to any particular belief or opinion, esp. in religious matters; allowing others their own beliefs; as, *latitudinarian* ministers:—*n.* one who holds liberal views, or who cares little about the external forms of creed, worship, or church government.

la-trine (lȧ-trēn′), *n.* a rough privy, usually with a wash room, in a camp.

lat-ter (lăt′ẽr), *adj.* comparative of *late:* **1,** being the second of two things already mentioned: opp. of *former;* **2,** more recent: **Latter-day Saint,** a Mormon.—*adv.* **lat′ter-ly.**

lat-tice (lăt′ĭs), *n.* crossed or interlaced openwork of metal or wood: hence, any door, window, gate, etc., made of such work:—*v.t.* [*p.t.* and *p.p.* -ticed (-ĭst), *p.pr.* -ticing], **1,** to arrange in a network; **2,** to furnish or cross with latticework.

lat-tice-work (lăt′ĭs-wûrk″), *n.* a grill made by crossing or interlacing strips of material.

laud (lôd), *v.t.* to praise highly:—*n.* praise; also, a song or hymn of praise.

laud-a-ble (lôd′ȧ-bl), *adj.* worthy of praise; commendable; as, a *laudable* effort.—*n.* **laud′a-ble-ness.**—*adv.* **laud′a-bly.**—*n.* **laud″a-bil′i-ty.**

lau-da-num (lô′dȧ-nŭm; lŏd′n-ŭm), *n.* a preparation of opium, a poisonous, narcotic drug.

lau-da-tion (lô-dā′shŭn), *n.* high praise; also, the act of praising.

laud-a-to-ry (lôd′ȧ-tō-rĭ), *adj.* pertaining to, or expressing, praise.

laugh (lȧf), *n.* an explosive sound, accompanied by peculiar movements of the face, expressive of mirth, ridicule, derision, or the like:—*v.i.* **1,** to express merriment by such a sound; **2,** to appear gay or pleasant; **3,** to jeer: with *at:*—*v.t.* **1,** to express or utter with laughter; **2,** to move or affect by merriment or ridicule; as, they *laughed* her out of her ill temper.—*n.* **laugh′er.**

laugh-a-ble (lȧf′ȧ-bl), *adj.* funny; mirth-provoking; ridiculous.—*n.* **laugh′a-ble-ness.**—*adv.* **laugh′a-bly.**
Syn. comical, droll, absurd. (See ludicrous.)

laugh-ing (lȧf′ĭng), *p.adj.* full of laughter; accompanied by gaiety: **laughing gas,** nitrous oxide gas, used as a light anæsthetic, esp. by dentists and surgeons.

laugh-ing-stock (lȧf′ĭng-stŏk″), *n.* an object of ridicule.

laugh-ter (lȧf′tẽr), *n.* convulsive sounds accompanied by characteristic facial movements, caused by merriment, amusement, derision, etc.

¹launch (länch; lônch), *v.t.* **1,** to move or cause to slide into the water, as a vessel; **2,** to start off, as an enterprise; **3,** to hurl; dart:—*v.i.* **1,** to put to sea; **2,** to plunge; **3,** to enter on a new career:—*n.* the sliding of a ship from the ways into the water.

²launch (länch; lônch), *n.* **1,** the largest boat of a man-of-war; **2,** a large, open pleasure boat, usually driven by motor.

laun-der (län′dẽr; lôn′-), *v.t.* to wash and iron, as clothes, linens, etc.:—*v.i.* to be washable; as, this silk *launders* well.—*n.* **laun′der-er.**

laun-dress (län′drĕs; lôn′-), *n.* a woman who washes and irons clothes.

laun-dry (län′drĭ; lôn′-), *n.* [*pl.* laundries (-drĭz)], **1,** an establishment where clothes are washed and ironed; **2,** the act of washing and ironing; **3,** *Colloq.,* articles sent to be washed.

Laun-fal (län′făl; lôn′-), *n.* in medieval romance, a knight of King Arthur's Round Table.

lau-re-ate (lô′rē-ăt), *adj.* decked or crowned with laurel; hence, worthy of honor: **poet laureate,** the official court poet of Great Britain:—*n.* **1,** one crowned or decked with laurel; **2,** a poet laureate.—*n.* **lau′re-ate-ship″.**

lau-rel (lô′rĕl; lŏr′ĕl), *n.* **1,** an evergreen shrub of southern Europe, used by the ancient Greeks as a symbol of fame and honor: also called *bay tree* and *sweet bay;* **2,** any of several shrubs resembling the true laurel; esp., the flowering mountain laurel; **3,** a crown or wreath of bay given as a prize or honor; hence, usually in *pl.,* the first prize; honor; distinction.—*adj.* **lau′reled; lau′relled.**

la-va (lä′vȧ), *n.* melted rock such as that which is thrown from a volcano.

lav-a-liere (lăv″ȧ-lēr′), *n.* a lady's flat, round, or oval pendant, and the chain on which it is worn around the neck. Also, **lav″a-lier′**; ***la″val″lière′** (lȧ″vȧ″lyâr′).

lav-a-to-ry (lăv′ȧ-tō-rĭ), *n.* [*pl.* lavatories (-rĭz)], **1,** a place for washing the hands and face; a retiring room; **2,** a basin for washing.

lave (lāv), *v.i.* [*p.t.* and *p.p.* laved (lāvd), *p.pr.* lav′ing], to bathe; wash oneself:—*v.t.* **1,** to wash; bathe; **2,** to flow or wash gently against, as the sea on a beach.

lav-en-der (lăv′ĕn-dẽr), *n.* **1,** a fragrant plant of the mint family; **2,** the perfume obtained from the plant; **3,** the pale lilac color of its flowers.

lav-ish (lăv′ĭsh), *adj.* **1,** extravagantly liberal or profuse; **2,** unrestrained: said of speech or action:—*v.t.* to expend or bestow liberally; squander; waste.—*n.* **lav′ish-er.**—*adv.* **lav′ish-ly.**—*n.* **lav′ish-ness.**

Syn., adj. immoderate, bountiful, excessive.

law (lô), *n.* **1,** a rule of action established by authority or custom; also, the whole body of such binding rules or customs; as, he was careless of social *law;* **2,** an act or enactment of a legislative, or lawmaking, body; **3,** judicial process; legal science; as, he studied *law;* **4,** the legal profession; as, he chose *law* as his career; **5,** trial by legal process; **6,** (usually, *Law*), the Mosaic system of rules; also, the part of the Scriptures containing it; **7,** in art, games, etc., recognized usage; rules of procedure; as, the *laws* of football; **8,** a scientific statement of the action and relation of things in nature, observed to be always the same under given conditions; as, the *law* of gravitation; an established principle: **common law,** the body of rules and principles of law not included in any legislative act, but carrying authority because of ancient custom and general acceptance: also called *unwritten law:* **statute law,** the body of laws included in specific legislative enactments.

Syn. edict, decree, regulation, code.

law-ful (lô′fo͝ol), *adj.* according to established rule or custom; just; as, *lawful* acts; rightful; as, *lawful* ownership of property.—*adv.* **law′ful-ly.**—*n.* **law′ful-ness.**

law-giv-er (lô′gĭv″ẽr), *n.* one who declares or enacts a law or code of laws, as Moses, Solon, and others.

law-less (lô′lĕs), *adj.* not obedient to, or controlled by, authority; unruly.—*adv.* **law′less-ly.**—*n.* **law′less-ness.**

law-mak-er (lô′māk″ẽr), *n.* one who makes, or helps to make, a law; a legislator.—*adj.* and *n.* **law′mak″ing.**

¹lawn (lôn), *n.* a thin, fine linen or cotton fabric for making dresses.

²lawn (lôn), *n.* **1,** a plot of grass kept closely mowed; **2,** *Poetic,* a glade.

lawn ten-nis an outdoor game played on a specially marked court with rackets, balls, and a net: in the U. S. commonly called *tennis.*

law-suit (lô′sūt″), *n.* an action in a court for the settlement of a claim or the enforcement of a right.

law-yer (lô′yẽr), *n.* one skilled in knowledge of law; a member of the legal profession.

lax (lăks), *adj.* **1,** not firm, tense, or rigid; flabby; **2,** loose; vague; weak; as, *lax* principles.—*adv.* **lax′ly.**—*n.* **lax′ness.**

lax-a-tive (lăk′sȧ-tĭv), *adj.* **1,** loosening: opp. of *astringent;* **2,** causing the bowels to move, as a medicine:—*n.* a medicine which causes the bowels to move.

lax-i-ty (lăk′sĭ-tĭ), *n.* the state or quality of being loose, negligent, or weak.

¹lay (lā), *n.* **1,** a lyric or ballad; as, *Lays* of Ancient Rome; **2,** any poem or song.

²lay (lā), *adj.* **1,** pertaining to, or done by, those outside the clergy; as, a *lay* sermon; **2,** not professional; as, the *lay* mind.

³lay (lā), *v.t.* [*p.t.* and *p.p.* laid (lād), *p.pr.* lay′ing], **1,** to cause to lie; place or put; as, to *lay* a card on the table; **2,** to bring or beat down; as, the blow *laid* him low; **3,** to settle; calm; as, to *lay* the dust; **4,** to bring forth and deposit, as an egg; **5,** to wager, as bets; **6,** to impose, as a tax, burden, duty, or the like; **7,** to ascribe or impute; as, to *lay* the blame; **8,** to arrange for a special purpose; as, to *lay* the table; **9,** to spread over a surface; as, to *lay* carpet; **10,** to cause to be in a given position or condition; as, to *lay* waste a field; *lay* bare a secret; **11,** to present for consideration; as, to *lay* a claim; **12,** to devise, as a plot or plan; **13,** to locate, as a scene:—*v.i.* **1,** to produce and deposit eggs; **2,** to wager; bet; **3,** on shipboard, to take up a position (as specified); as, to *lay* aft:—*n.* the manner or direction in which something lies; as, the *lay* of the land.

⁴lay (lā), past tense of the irregular verb *lie,* which see.

lay-er (lā′ẽr), *n.* **1,** one that lays; **2,** one thickness; a stratum, row, coating, or the like; as, a *layer* of earth; **3,** a runner, or long shoot, of a plant, which develops roots when partly covered with earth.

lay-ette (lā-ĕt′), *n.* an outfit of clothes, bedding, etc., for a new-born child.

lay fig-ure **1,** a jointed model of the human form upon which to hang drapery or costumes; **2,** hence, one subject to the will of another, esp. a person who, though in a position of authority, exerts no real power or influence.

lay-man (lā′măn), *n.* [*pl.* laymen (-mĕn)], **1,** a person not of the clergy; one of the laity; **2,** a person not belonging to a given profession; as, a *layman's* opinion of a painting may differ from that of an artist.

la-zar (lā′zȧr), *n.* a person, esp. a beggar, with a loathsome disease; a leper.

laz-a-ret-to (lăz″ȧ-rĕt′ō), *n.* [*pl.* lazarettos (-ōz)], a hospital for persons suffering with infectious or dangerous diseases, as smallpox. Also, **laz″a-ret′.**

Laz-a-rus (lăz′ȧ-rŭs), *n.* in the Bible, **1,** the brother of Mary and Martha, whom Christ raised from the dead (John 11); **2,** in one of the parables, a beggar who lay at a rich man's door (Luke 16).

la-zy (lā′zĭ), *adj.* [*comp.* la′zi-er, *superl.* la′zi-est], not inclined to action or work; idle; indolent.—*adv.* **la′zi-ly.**—*n.* **la′zi-ness.**

Syn. (see idle).

lea (lē), *n.* a meadow; a grassy field or pasture land.

leach (lēch), *v.t.* **1,** to cause (a liquid) to drip, or percolate, through some material; as, to *leach* water through wood ashes to obtain lye; **2,** to wash with water to extract the soluble substances; as, to *leach* bark; **3,** to extract by percolation; as, to *leach* lye from the ashes:—*v.i.* to be extracted or dissolved out by this process:—*n.* **1,** the substance through which a liquid is caused to drip in leaching, as wood ashes, or the substance dissolved from it, as lye; **2,** the vessel used in the process.

¹lead (lĕd), *n.* **1,** a soft, heavy, bluish gray metallic element; **2,** a weight attached to a rope for sounding depths at sea; **3,** a thin strip of metal for separating lines of type in printing; **4,** a stick of graphite or black carbon in a pencil:—*adj.* consisting wholly or partly of lead:—*v.t.* **1,** to cover, fit, or join with lead; **2,** in printing, to spread (lines of type) by the insertion of thin metal strips.

²lead (lēd), *v.t.* [*p.t.* and *p.p.* led (lĕd), *p.pr.* lead′ing], **1,** to conduct by the hand;

as, to *lead* a little child; **2**, to conduct or guide by going on in advance; **3**, to guide or conduct by advice or counsel; **4**, to have the direction or control of; as, to *lead* an army; **5**, to go or be ahead of; be first among; as, to *lead* one's class; **6**, to influence; induce; as, hunger *led* him to steal; **7**, to spend or pass; as, to *lead* an unhappy life; **8**, to play (a certain card) as the opening play of a trick:—*v.i.* **1**, to take the first place; **2**, to act as a guide, director, manager, etc.; **3**, to take a course; as, the path *leads* through the woods; **4**, to be capable of being led; as, the horse *leads* easily; **5**, to play the first card or domino:—*n.* **1**, guidance; **2**, first place or position; precedence; also, the measure of precedence; as, a *lead* of two yards; **3**, in games, the right to play first; also, the play thus made; **4**, something that may act as guide; **5**, the principal actor in a play, or his part.

lead bath (lĕd), a furnace in which the powdered ores of gold or silver are brought into mechanical contact with melted lead to form an alloy from which the precious metals may then be extracted.

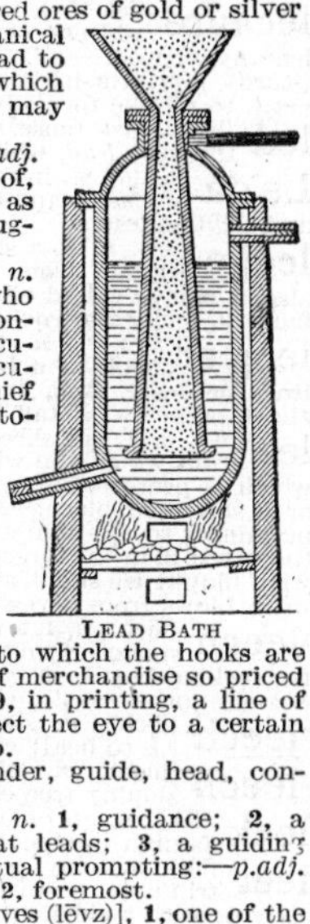
LEAD BATH

lead-en (lĕd'n), *adj.* **1**, made of, of the color of, or as heavy as, lead; **2**, sluggish; dull; spiritless.

lead-er (lēd'ẽr), *n.* **1**, one who guides, directs, or conducts; **2**, one who occupies, or is fitted to occupy, the first or chief place; **3**, the chief editorial article of a newspaper; **4**, a tendon; **5**, the foremost horse, when several are used to draw a vehicle; **6**, a pipe to carry off rain water from the roof of a house; **7**, a piece of catgut forming the end of a fishing line, to which the hooks are attached; **8**, a piece of merchandise so priced as to attract trade; **9**, in printing, a line of dots or dashes to direct the eye to a certain point.—*n.* **lead'er-ship.**

Syn. chief, commander, guide, head, conductor, director.

lead-ing (lēd'ĭng), *n.* **1**, guidance; **2**, a thing that leads; **3**, a guiding influence, esp. a spiritual prompting:—*p.adj.* **1**, guiding; directing; **2**, foremost.

leaf (lēf), *n.* [*pl.* leaves (lēvz)], **1**, one of the broad, thin, flat parts of a plant, variously shaped and usually borne on a stem; also, a petal; as, a rose *leaf* (see illus. page 407); **2**, a thinly beaten sheet; as, gold *leaf;* **3**, any of various thin, flat objects, esp. a single sheet of a book, a part of a folding table top, etc.:—*v.i.* to put forth foliage:—*v.t.* to turn the pages of (a book): usually with *through.*

leaf-age (lēf'āj), *n.* leaves collectively; foliage of trees, shrubs, etc.

leaf-let (lēf'lĕt), *n.* **1**, a small foliage leaf; **2**, a printed sheet or circular.

leaf-stalk (lēf'stôk″), *n.* the stem of a foliage leaf; the footstalk of a leaf; petiole.

leaf-y (lēf'ĭ), *adj.* [*comp.* leaf'i-er, *superl.* leaf'i-est], having, or abounding in, leaves; made of, or consisting of, leaves.

¹league (lēg), *n.* an agreement entered into by two or more persons, nations, or parties for their common good; also, the alliance so formed: **League of Nations**, an organization for the furtherance of international coöperation and the maintenance of peace among nations, established in 1919 largely through the efforts of Woodrow Wilson:—*v.t.* and *v.i.* [*p.t.* and *p.p.* leagued (lēgd), *p.pr.* lea'guing], to combine for mutual interests.

Syn., n. compact; union, coalition.

²league (lēg), *n.* a varying measure of distance, equal to about three miles.

Le-ah (lē'*ā*), *n.* in the Bible, the elder daughter of Laban, and first wife of Jacob.

leak (lēk), *n.* a hole, crack, or other opening, which accidentally lets anything, esp. a fluid, in or out: also used figuratively; as, a *leak* in the treasury:—*v.i.* to go in or out through, or as through, a hole, crack, or other outlet; of news, to become gradually known: with *out;* as, the scandal *leaked* out.

leak-age (lēk'āj), *n.* **1**, the passing in or out of anything through a hole or crack; **2**, the quantity that passes in or out; **3**, allowance for such loss.

leak-y (lēk'ĭ), *adj.* [*comp.* leak'i-er, *superl.* leak'i-est], **1**, allowing water or other fluid to pass in or out through holes; **2**, *Colloq.*, not able to keep a secret.—*n.* **leak'i-ness.**

leal (lēl), *adj. Scot.*, true-hearted; loyal; faithful.

¹lean (lēn), *v.i.* [*p.t.* and *p.p.* leaned (lēnd), sometimes leant (lĕnt), *p.pr.* lean'ing], **1**, to slant from an upright position; **2**, to bend over for support; as, to *lean* on a cane; **3**, to rely; as, to *lean* on one's friends for advice; **4**, to have a tendency; as, his opinions *lean* toward the popular side:—*v.t.* to place in a position not quite vertical:—*n.* the act, condition, or amount of inclining.

²lean (lēn), *adj.* **1**, thin; lacking in fat; as, a *lean* person or animal; *lean* meat; **2**, not productive; as, *lean* years; a *lean* harvest:—*n.* meat without fat.—*n.* **lean'ness.**

Syn., adj. thin, meager, spare, gaunt, lank. *Lean* is used of those whose lack of fat is natural and implies a healthy, often muscular, body. *Thin* may mean healthy but slender; it may also mean without fat as the result of illness, lack of proper food or rest, etc. *Meager* suggests a pinched and starved appearance. *Spare* adds to *lean* the idea of strength and sinew. *Gaunt* means bony and angular, sometimes hollow-eyed and haggard. *Lank* people may be either long and slender or shrunken and flabby.—*Ant., adj.* stout, fat, corpulent.

Le-an-der (lē-ăn'dẽr), *n.* in mythology, a youth who loved Hero, priestess of Aphrodite. He swam the Hellespont nightly to visit her, but was finally drowned, whereupon Hero cast herself into the sea.

lean–to (lēn'=tōō″), *n.* a building whose rafters rest against another building, as a shed built against a house; also, a crude shelter with a roof supported by poles.

leap (lēp), *v.t.* [*p.t.* and *p.p.* leaped (lēpt) or leapt (lĕpt), *p.pr.* leap'ing], **1**, to pass over by a bound or jump; as, to *leap* a ditch; **2**, to cause to jump or spring; as, to *leap* a horse over a hedge:—*v.i.* **1**, to jump or spring off the ground or from a high place; as, to *leap* down from a wall; **2**, to bound or move suddenly:—*n.* **1**, the act of passing over with a bound; also, a jump; spring; **2**, the space passed over in jumping.—*n.* **leap'er.**

leap-frog (lēp'frŏg″), *n.* a boy's game, in which one player stoops and another jumps over him.

leapt (lĕpt), a form of the past tense and past participle of the verb *leap.*

leap year a year of 366 days, in which February has 29 days. Century years exactly divisible by 400, and other years exactly divisible by 4, are leap years.

Lear (lēr), *n.* a king who, in Shakespeare's tragedy "King Lear," misjudges and disinherits his loving youngest daughter in favor of her false sisters, but is driven mad by their cruelty.

learn (lûrn), *v.t.* [*p.t.* and *p.p.* learned (lûrnd) or learnt (lûrnt), *p.pr.* learn'-ing], **1**, to acquire knowledge of, or skill in; as, to *learn* French; **2**, to ascertain; be informed about; as, I regret to *learn* of your illness; **3**, to memorize; as, to *learn* a poem:—*v.i.* to gain or receive knowledge or skill; as, to *learn* quickly.—*n.* **learn'er.**

learn-ed (lûr'nĕd), *p.adj.* having much knowledge; skilled; as, a *learned* professor or lawyer.—*adv.* **learn'ed-ly.**

learn-ing (lûrn'ĭng), *n.* **1**, the act or process of acquiring knowledge; **2**, knowledge or skill gained by study.
Syn. scholarship, erudition, lore.—*Ant.* ignorance, illiteracy.

lease (lēs), *n.* **1**, a written contract for the renting of land or buildings for a specified time; **2**, property so rented; **3**, the time for which property is rented:—*v.t.* [*p.t.* and *p.p.* leased (lēst), *p.pr.* leas'ing], **1**, to grant possession of, for a specified time, by a contract of lease; as, an owner *leases* a house to a tenant; **2**, to take possession of by lease; as, a tenant *leases* a house from the owner.

lease-hold (lēs'hōld''), *n.* **1**, the holding of property by contract of lease; **2**, property so held.—*n.* **lease'hold''er.**

leash (lēsh), *n.* **1**, a thong of leather or a long cord for holding a hawk or hound; **2**, in hunting, three creatures of one kind; as, a *leash* of dogs; hence, in general, three of a kind:—*v.t.* to tie or hold with a leash.

leas-ing (lēz'ĭng), *n.* *Archaic*, the act of lying; also, a lie or falsehood.

least (lēst), *adj.* superlative of *little:* smallest in degree, size, value, importance, etc.:—*adv.* in the lowest or smallest degree.

leath-er (lĕth'ẽr), *n.* the skin of an animal, tanned and prepared for use; also, anything made of, or like, the skin so prepared:—*v.t.* to cover or provide with leather.—*adj.* **leath'er-y.**

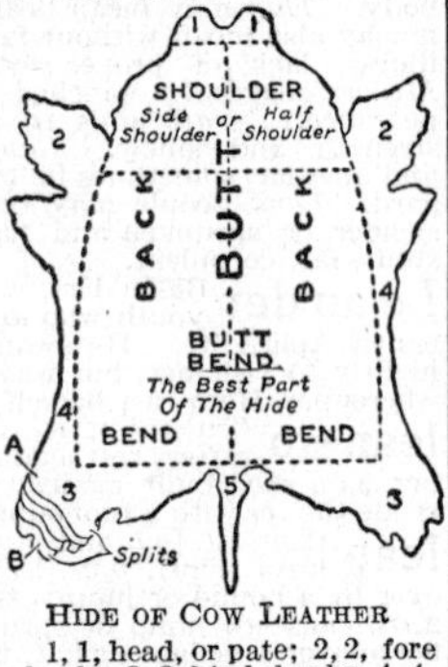

HIDE OF COW LEATHER
1, 1, head, or pate; 2, 2, fore shanks; 3, 3, hind shanks; 4, 4, belly; 5, tail: A, top grain split; B, flesh split.

leath-er-back (lĕth'ẽr-băk''), *n.* one of the largest known sea turtles, often weighing over 1,000 pounds.

leath-er-et (lĕth'ẽr-ĕt), *n.* a kind of imitation leather. Also, **leath''er-ette'.**

leath-ern (lĕth'ẽrn), *adj.* made of, or like, leather; leathery.

[1]**leave** (lēv), *v.t.* [*p.t.* and *p.p.* left (lĕft), *p.pr.* leav'ing], **1**, to fail to take; allow to remain behind; **2**, to allow to remain, or continue, in the same place or condition; as, the appeal *left* him cold; **3**, to depart from; forsake; **4**, to deliver; as, to *leave* cards; **5**, to cease from; as, *leave* your bickering; **6**, to give by legacy; **7**, to refer for decision; as, I *leave* the choice to you:—*v.i.* to go away; depart.
Syn. quit, desert. (See [2]let.)

[2]**leave** (lēv), *n.* **1**, a permission granted, **2**, permission for a short vacation; as from military service; also, the vacation thus permitted; **3**, departure; formal farewell.
Syn. freedom, license, allowance, liberty.

[3]**leave** (lēv), *v.i.* [*p.t.* and *p.p.* leaved (lēvd), *p.pr.* leav'ing], to put forth leaves.

leav-en (lĕv'n), *v.t.* **1**, to make light, as dough, by the addition of yeast or other substance that will cause fermentation; **2**, to touch with something which changes or modifies; mix; as, to *leaven* correction with a little praise:—*n.* **1**, a ferment mixed with a substance to render it light, as yeast with dough; **2**, any influence which, working silently and strongly, causes changes.

leav-ings (lēv'ĭngz), *n.pl.* what is left over; discarded remains.

lech-er-ous (lĕch'ẽr-ŭs), *adj.* lewd; lustful; sensual.—*adv.* **lech'er-ous-ly.**—*n.* **lech'er-y.**

lec-tern (lĕk'tẽrn), *n.* the reading desk of a church.

lec-ture (lĕk'tūr), *n.* **1**, a formal talk or address on any subject; **2**, a lengthy reproof:—*v.i.* [*p.t.* and *p.p.* -tured (-tūrd), *p.pr.* -tur-ing], to deliver a formal talk:—*v.t.* to rebuke formally.—*n.* **lec'tur-er.**

led (lĕd), past tense and past participle of the verb *lead*, which see.

Le-da (lē'dȧ), *n.* in mythology, the mother of Castor and Pollux, Helen of Troy, and Clytemnestra.

ledge (lĕj), *n.* **1**, a shelf or a shelflike projection from an upright surface; also, a rim or raised edge of a horizontal surface; **2**, a ridge of rock; reef.

ledg-er (lĕj'ẽr), *n.* the principal account book of a business house: **ledger line,** or **leger line,** in music, a short line above or below a staff to increase its scope.

lee (lē), *n.* **1**, the direction opposite to that from which the wind blows; **2**, the side which is protected from the wind; **3**, shelter or a sheltered place:—*adj.* **1**, designating, or pertaining to, the side which is protected from the wind; **2**, in the direction toward which the wind blows: **lee shore,** a shore toward which a wind blows from a vessel.

[1]**leech** (lēch), *n.* **1**, a worm furnished with a sucker, formerly used in medicine for sucking blood; **2**, one who gets all he can out of another:—*v.t.* to bleed with leeches.

[2]**leech** (lēch), *n.* *Archaic*, a physician:—*v.t.* to heal; cure.

[3]**leech** (lēch), *n.* the perpendicular or sloping free edge of a sail.

leek (lēk), *n.* an onionlike plant of the lily family, used as food or flavoring.

leer (lēr), *n.* a sly, sidelong look of malice, triumph, or evil desire:—*v.i.* to look slyly or with a sidelong or evil look.

lees (lēz), *n.pl.* the sediment at the bottom of a vessel containing liquor; dregs.

lee-ward (lē'wẽrd; lū'ẽrd), *adj.* pertaining to the lee, or the direction opposite to that from which the wind blows:—*adv.* toward the lee; down the wind from the observer:—*n.* the lee side.

lee-way (lē'wā''), *n.* **1**, the sidewise drift of a vessel caused by the wind; **2**, room for action or free play.

[1]**left** (lĕft), past tense and past participle of the verb *leave.*

[2]**left** (lĕft), *adj.* **1**, designating, or pertaining to, that side of the human body which, as one faces the sunrise, is toward the north: opp. of *right;* **2**, placed to the left side:—*n.* **1**, that which is on the left side; **2**, in a European parliament, the most liberal or radical party, often seated on the left.

left-hand (lĕft'-hănd''), *adj.* pertaining to, or situated on, the left side.

left-hand-ed (lĕft'-hănd''ĕd; lĕft'-hănd''-ĭd), *adj.* **1**, using the left

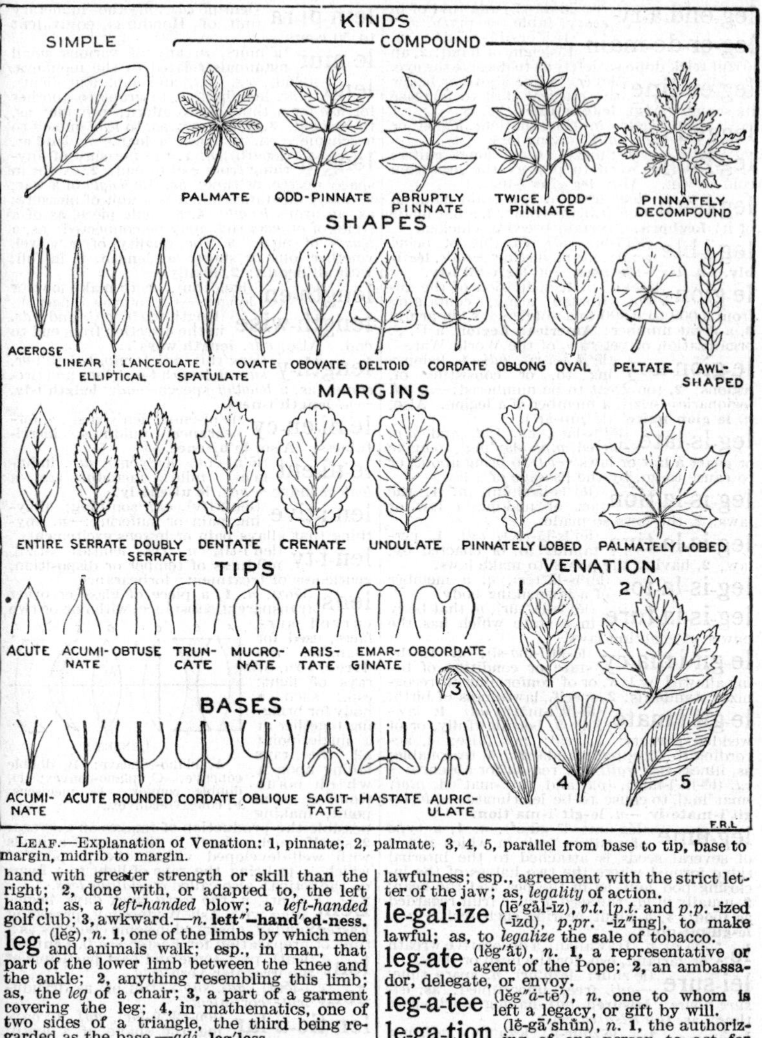

LEAF.—Explanation of Venation: 1, pinnate; 2, palmate; 3, 4, 5, parallel from base to tip, base to margin, midrib to margin.

hand with greater strength or skill than the right; 2, done with, or adapted to, the left hand; as, a *left-handed* blow; a *left-handed* golf club; 3, awkward.—*n.* **left"-hand'ed-ness.**

leg (lĕg), *n.* **1,** one of the limbs by which men and animals walk; esp., in man, that part of the lower limb between the knee and the ankle; **2,** anything resembling this limb; as, the *leg* of a chair; **3,** a part of a garment covering the leg; **4,** in mathematics, one of two sides of a triangle, the third being regarded as the base.—*adj.* **leg'less.**

leg-a-cy (lĕg'ȧ-sĭ), *n.* [*pl.* legacies (-sĭz)], **1,** a gift by will of money or property; bequest; **2,** anything that has come down from one's predecessors; as, a *legacy* of family pride.

le-gal (lē'găl), *adj.* **1,** pertaining to law; **2,** permitted or authorized by law; **3,** protected by law; as, *legal* rights: **legal tender,** money which by law is made suitable for the payment of a debt.—*adv.* **le'gal-ly.**

le-gal-i-ty (lē-găl'ĭ-tĭ), *n.* [*pl.* legalities (-tĭz)], conformity to law; lawfulness; esp., agreement with the strict letter of the law; as, *legality* of action.

le-gal-ize (lē'găl-īz), *v.t.* [*p.t.* and *p.p.* -ized (-īzd), *p.pr.* -iz"ing], to make lawful; as, to *legalize* the sale of tobacco.

leg-ate (lĕg'ăt), *n.* **1,** a representative or agent of the Pope; **2,** an ambassador, delegate, or envoy.

leg-a-tee (lĕg"ȧ-tē'), *n.* one to whom is left a legacy, or gift by will.

le-ga-tion (lē-gā'shŭn), *n.* **1,** the authorizing of one person to act for another; **2,** a diplomatic minister, esp. one not of the first rank, and his associates; **3,** the official residence of such a minister.

***le-ga-to** (lä-gä'tō), [It.], *adj.* and *adv.* in music, in a smooth, flowing manner, without breaks between notes.

leg-end (lĕj'ĕnd; lē'jĕnd), *n.* **1,** a romantic story handed down from the past, esp. one not verifiable, but connected with a person or event of authentic history; **2,** the words of a title or inscription, as on a coin.

leg-end-a-ry (lĕj′ĕn-dā-rĭ), *adj.* told of in story, fable, or myth.

leg-er-de-main (lĕj″ẽr-dē-măn′), *n.* **1,** sleight of hand; **2,** an artful trick done so deftly as to deceive the eye.

leg-er line (lĕj′ẽr), a line above or below the musical staff to increase its scope. Also, **ledg′er line,** *Pfd. S.*

legged (lĕgd; in combination, lĕg′ĕd or lĕgd), *adj.* having legs.

leg-gings (lĕg′ĭngz), *n.pl.* long gaiters worn to protect the legs from cold or wet. Also, **leg′gins** (-ĭnz).

leg-horn (lĕg′hôrn), *n.* **1,** a braid made of fine Italian straw; **2,** a hat made of it: **Leghorn,** a certain breed of chicken.

leg-i-ble (lĕj′ĭ-bl), *adj.* capable of being read; clear; distinct.—*adv.* **leg′i-bly.**—*n.* **leg′i-ble-ness.**—*n.* **leg″i-bil′i-ty.**

le-gion (lē′jŭn), *n.* **1,** a division of the ancient Roman army, containing from 3,000 to 6,000 foot soldiers; **2,** an army; **3,** a great number: **American Legion,** a U. S. organization of veterans of the World War.

le-gion-a-ry (lē′jŭn-ā-rĭ), *adj.* **1,** belonging to, or consisting of, legions; **2,** too great to be numbered:—*n.* [*pl.* legionaries (-rĭz)], a member of a legion. Also, *n.* **le″gion-naire′** (lē″jŭn-âr′).

leg-is-late (lĕj′ĭs-lāt), *v.i.* [*p.t.* and *p.p.* -lat″ed, *p.pr.* -lat″ing], to make or enact a law or laws:—*v.t.* to bring about, or to cause to go, by the passage of a law.

leg-is-la-tion (lĕj″ĭs-lā′shŭn), *n.* **1,** the act of making a law or laws; **2,** the laws so made.

leg-is-la-tive (lĕj′ĭs-lā-tĭv), *adj.* **1,** pertaining to, or enacted by, law; **2,** having the power to make laws.

leg-is-la-tor (lĕj′ĭs-lā″tẽr), *n.* a member of a lawmaking body.

leg-is-la-ture (lĕj′ĭs-lā″tūr), *n.* that body in a state which has the power of enacting laws.

le-git-i-ma-cy (lē-jĭt′ĭ-mȧ-sĭ), *n.* **1,** the state or condition of being allowed by law, or of conforming to recognized standards; **2,** specif., lawfulness of birth.

le-git-i-mate (lē-jĭt′ĭ-māt), *adj.* **1,** lawful; **2,** born lawfully, or of wedded parents; **3,** real; not false; **4,** according to accepted standards; **5,** reasonable; as, illness is a *legitimate* reason for absence:—*v.t.* (lē-jĭt′ĭ-māt), [*p.t.* and *p.p.* -mat″ed, *p.pr.* -mat″ing], to cause to be legitimate.—*adv.* **le-git′i-mate-ly.**—*n.* **le-git″i-ma′tion.**

leg-ume (lĕg′ūm; lē-gūm′), *n.* **1,** a type of podlike fruit in which a row of several seeds is attached to the internal ridge formed where the two halves of the inclosing pod join, as in the pea and the bean; **2,** usually in *pl.*, the seed of such fruit regarded as food; **3,** a plant bearing such fruit.—*adj.* **le-gu′mi-nous.**

le-i (lā′ē), *n.* [Hawaiian], a decorative wreath or garland, esp. for the head or neck.

lei-sure (lē′zhŭr; lĕzh′ūr), *n.* spare time:—*adj.* free; unoccupied; as, *leisure* hours: **leisured,** *adj.* having much spare time; as, the *leisured* class.

lei-sure-ly (lē′zhŭr-lĭ; lĕzh′ūr-), *adj.* not hasty; slow; deliberate:—*adv.* not hastily; deliberately.—*n.* **lei′sure-li-ness.**

lem-ming (lĕm′ĭng), *n.* any of several small, short-tailed, mouselike rodents of the arctic regions, with furry feet.

lem-on (lĕm′ŭn), *n.* **1,** an oval fruit with pale yellow skin and very acid juice; **2,** the tree, related to the orange, which bears this fruit; **3,** a pale yellow color:—*adj.* flavored with lemon, or colored like a lemon.

lem-on-ade (lĕm″ŭn-ād′), *n.* lemon juice and sweetened water: a drink.

lem-pi-ra (lĕm-pē′rȧ), *n.* the monetary unit of Honduras, equivalent to 50 cents.

le-mur (lē′mŭr), *n.* any of various small mammals related to the monkeys.

lend (lĕnd), *v.t.* [*p.t.* and *p.p.* lent (lĕnt), *p.pr.* lend′ing], **1,** to grant to another for use for a time; **2,** to afford; provide; as, to *lend* aid; **3,** to devote; as, to *lend* oneself to a scheme:—*v.i.* to make a loan.—*n.* **lend′er.**

length (lĕngth), *n.* **1,** the measure of anything from end to end; **2,** extent in space, degree, or time; as, the *length* of a war; **3,** a given distance taken as a unit of measure; as, an arm's *length;* **4,** a single piece, as of a series of objects that may be connected; as, a *length* of pipe; **5,** the quality of a vowel, whether long or short: **at length, 1,** in full; with all details; **2,** finally.

length-en (lĕng′thn), *v.t.* to make long or longer:—*v.i.* to grow longer.

length-wise (lĕngth′wīz″), *adj.* and *adv.* in the direction from end to end. Also, *adv.* **length′ways″.**

length-y (lĕng′thĭ), *adj.* [*comp.* length′i-er, *superl.* length′i-est], long and tiresome; as, a *lengthy* speech.—*adv.* **length′i-ly.**—*n.* **length′i-ness.**

le-ni-en-cy (lē′nĭ-ĕn-sĭ; lĕn′yĕn-sĭ), *n.* forbearance; mildness; mercifulness. Also, **le′ni-ence.**

le-ni-ent (lē′nĭ-ĕnt; lĕn′yĕnt), *adj.* indulgent; mild; merciful; as, a *lenient* judge.—*adv.* **le′ni-ent-ly.**

len-i-tive (lĕn′ĭ-tĭv), *adj.* soothing; allaying pain or suffering:—*n.* anything that allays pain or lessens excitement.

len-i-ty (lĕn′ĭ-tĭ), *n.* [*pl.* lenities (-tĭz)], mildness of temper or disposition; gentleness of treatment; forbearance.

lens (lĕnz), *n.* **1,** a piece of glass or other transparent substance, with one or two curved surfaces, used for changing the direction of rays of light; esp., such a body for bringing together at a single point all the rays falling upon it which issue from a given point, making possible the production of images on a screen; **2,** specif., such a body in the eyes of animals with well-developed vision, the purpose of which is to bring the rays of light to a focus on the retina: also called *crystalline lens.*

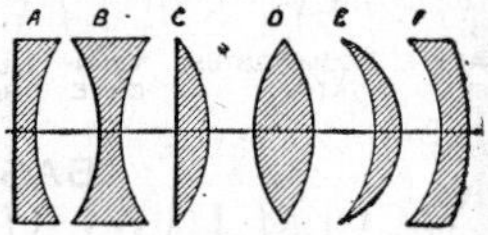

LENSES

A, plano-concave; B, double concave; C, plano-convex; D, double convex; E, meniscus; F, concavo-convex.

Lent (lĕnt), *n.* the forty week days, beginning with Ash Wednesday, preceding Easter Sunday, observed in some churches as a time of preparation for Easter.—*adj.* **Lent′en.**

lent (lĕnt), past tense and past participle of the irregular verb *lend.*

-lent (-lĕnt), *adj. suffix,* full of; as, fraudu*lent;* corpu*lent.*

len-tic-u-lar (lĕn-tĭk′ū-lȧr), *adj.* **1,** having the shape of a lentil; bulging, or convex, on both sides, as a reading glass; **2,** pertaining to a lens.

len-til (lĕn′tĭl), *n.* **1,** a food and fodder plant of the pea family, whose seeds are cooked as a vegetable or ground into meal; **2,** in *pl.*, the seeds of the plant used for food.

Le-o (lē′ō), *n.* **1,** a northern constellation, the Lion, containing the bright star Regulus; **2,** the fifth sign of the zodiac, entered by the sun about July 22 (see *zodiac*, illus.).

le-o-nine (lē′ō-nīn), *adj.* like a lion; hence, powerful; majestic.

leop-ard (lĕp′ẽrd), *n.* a large catlike beast of prey, with a beautiful spotted skin of yellow and black.—*n.fem.* **leop′ard-ess.**

lep-er (lĕp′ẽr), *n.* **1**, one suffering from leprosy, an infectious disease marked by ulcers and white scaly scabs; **2**, an outcast.

lep-ro-sy (lĕp′rō-sĭ), *n.* [*pl.* leprosies (-sĭz)], an infectious, loathsome skin disease, usually fatal, marked by ulcers and white scaly scabs.

lep-rous (lĕp′rŭs), *adj.* **1**, having the disease leprosy; hence, unclean; **2**, covered with white scales.

lese maj-es-ty (lēz), a crime against the government or sovereign; treason. Also, **leze maj′es-ty.**

le-sion (lē′zhŭn), *n.* injury; hurt; a change in a part of the body or in its functioning caused by injury or disease.

less (lĕs), *adj.* comparative of *little:* **1**, not so much; **2**, not so great in importance; as, *less* than the dust:—*prep.* made smaller by taking away; as, ten *less* seven:—*adv.* in a smaller or lower degree:—*n.* a smaller quantity; not so much.

-less (-lĕs), *adj. suffix,* without; free from; as, home*less;* worth*less;* daunt*less:*—*adv. suffix,* without; as, doubt*less.*

les-see (lĕs-ē′), *n.* a person to whom property is rented for a specified time, upon specified conditions, as by lease.

less-en (lĕs′n), *v.t.* **1**, to make smaller; reduce; **2**, to represent as less or less important than commonly supposed; disparage:—*v.i.* **1**, to grow smaller; **2**, to become less important or useful.

Syn. (see decrease).

less-er (lĕs′ẽr), *adj.* smaller; inferior; less; as, the *lesser* evil; the *lesser* value.

les-son (lĕs′n), *n.* **1**, that which is assigned to a pupil to learn as a single task; **2**, a lecture; the instruction given at one time; **3**, that which is learned or taught by experience, observation, etc.; **4**, a rebuke; **5**, a portion of scripture read at a church service; as, here endeth the first *lesson.*

les-sor (lĕs′ôr; lĕs-ôr′), *n.* one who rents or lets property to another.

lest (lĕst), *conj.* **1**, that . . . not; for fear that; as, take heed *lest* ye fall; **2**, that: used without *not* after expressions indicating fear; as, in dread *lest* the thief come.

¹let (lĕt), *n.* **1**, in lawn tennis, a ball which is served into the proper court, but touches the top of the net in passing; **2**, *Archaic,* interference; as, without *let* or hindrance.

²let (lĕt), *v.t.* [*p.t.* and *p.p.* let, *p.pr.* let′ting], **1**, to permit; allow; **2**, to grant to a tenant; lease; **3**, to give out; assign, as a contract:—*v.i.* to be hired or leased; as, the house *lets* for $50 a month: **let on, 1**, to pretend; as, I will *let on* to be sick; **2**, to give oneself away by revealing a fact; as, don't *let on* that you know me.

Syn. leave. To *let* is to permit or allow; as, I will *let* him go. *Leave* means to allow by not interfering; it is used with *to;* as, we *leave* our guests to follow their own wishes. Do not use *leave* without *to,* in the sense of *let:* we *left* him go, *leave* him come, are usages to be avoided.

-let (-lĕt), *n. suffix,* forming: **1**, diminutives; as, eag*let;* **2**, names of pieces of clothing; as, arm*let.*

le-thal (lē′thăl), *adj.* **1**, pertaining to death; **2**, deadly; fatal.

leth-ar-gy (lĕth′ȧr-jĭ), *n.* [*pl.* lethargies (-jĭz)], **1**, unhealthy drowsiness; unnaturally prolonged slumber; listlessness; **2**, a state of inaction or indifference; as, to awake a nation from *lethargy.*—*adj.* **le-thar′gic.**

Le-the (lē′thē), *n.* in mythology, an underworld stream whose waters, when drunk, produced forgetfulness.—*adj.* **Le-the′an.**

let-ter (lĕt′ẽr), *n.* **1**, a mark or character used to represent a sound; **2**, a written or printed communication; an epistle; **3**, the exact or word-for-word meaning; as, to keep the *letter* of the law; **4**, a document certifying certain privileges, authority, etc.; as, a *letter* of credit; **5**, in *pl.,* knowledge; learning; literature; as, great men of *letters:* **letters of marque (and reprisal)**, a government license to a person to engage in privateering; orig., a license to seize foreigners or their goods by way of reprisal or in retaliation: **letters patent,** written authority from a government to do some act or enjoy some privilege:—*v.t.* to mark with letters.—*p.adj.* **let′tered.**—*n.* **let′ter-ing.**

let-ter-gram (lĕt′ẽr-grăm), *n.* formerly, a relatively long telegram sent, by day or by night, at reduced rates because subject to possible delay in delivery: now called *day letter* or *night letter.*

let-ter-head (lĕt′ẽr-hĕd″), *n.* a sheet of writing paper with a printed or engraved heading; also, the heading.

let-ter-press (lĕt′ẽr-prĕs″), *n.* the text of a book, newspaper, etc., as distinguished from the illustrations.

let-tuce (lĕt′ĭs), *n.* a garden plant with tender, crisp leaves, which are used as a salad or garnish.

le-u (lĕ′o͞o) *n.* [*pl.* lei (lā)], the monetary unit of Rumania, worth .6 cent. Also, **ley.**

leu-co-cyte (lū′kō-sīt), *n.* a white blood corpuscle.

lev (lĕf), *n.* [*pl.* leva (lĕv′ȧ)], the monetary unit of Bulgaria, worth about .7 cent.

Le-vant (lē-vănt′), *n.* the Orient; esp., the Near East, or the countries about the eastern Mediterranean: **levant,** a fine kind of leather, ordinarily made of goatskin.

¹lev-ee (lĕv-ē′; lĕv′ē), *n.* **1**, in Great Britain, a reception held in the early afternoon by a sovereign or personage of high rank, for men; **2**, in the U. S., any general reception, esp. one at the White House.

²lev-ee (lĕv′ē; lĕv-ē′), *n.* **1**, a wall built along a river to keep it from overflowing its banks; **2**, a landing place or quay.

lev-el (lĕv′ĕl), *n.* **1**, an unbroken horizontal surface or line; **2**, equality of height; as, this position is on a *level* with that; **3**, a horizontal plane which represents the height of a certain position above the sea; as, at this *level* the air is rare; **4**, position above or below any standard; as, a high social *level;* **5**, an instrument used in carpentry and surveying to ascertain a horizontal line; a spirit level (see *tool,* illus.); **6**, a section of a canal between locks:—*adj.* **1**, having a flat, horizontal surface; **2**, exactly horizontal; **3**, equal to something else in height or importance; **4**, steady; judicious; well-balanced; as, a *level* head:—*adv.* in a horizontal direction:—*v.t.* **1**, to make smooth or flat in a horizontal plane; **2**, to bring into a horizontal position; **3**, to bring to the same plane or height as something else; specif., to bring to the level of the ground; raze; **4**, to point (a gun) in taking aim.—*n.* **lev′el-er; lev′el-ler.**—*n.* **lev′el-ness.**

Syn., adj. smooth. (See flat.)

le-ver (lē′vẽr; lĕv′ẽr), *n.* a bar, as of wood or iron, used to move a heavy object by placing one part of it against the object, bracing it against something fixed (the *fulcrum*), and lifting or pushing on another part.

le-ver-age (lē′vẽr-āj; lĕv′ẽr-āj), *n.* **1**, the action of a lever; **2**, the mechanical power gained by using a lever.

Le-vi (lē′vī), *n.* in the Bible, the third son of Jacob: ancestor of the Levites.

le-vi-a-than (lē-vī′ȧ-thăn), *n.* **1**, in the Bible, a water animal, real or imaginary, of enormous size; **2**, anything huge, as a whale or a very large ship.

lev-i-ta-tion (lĕv″ĭ-tā′shŭn), *n.* in spiritualism, the supposed suspension of heavy objects without support.

Le-vite (lē′vīt), *n.* **1**, in the Bible, an Israelite of the tribe of Levi; **2**, specif., one who assisted the priests in the rites of the tabernacle or temple.

Le-vit-i-cal (lē-vĭt′ĭ-kăl), *adj.* **1**, pertaining to the Levites; **2**, pertaining to the book of Leviticus.

Le-vit-i-cus (lē-vĭt′ĭ-kŭs), *n.* the third book of the Old Testament, containing the ceremonial laws administered by the priests and Levites.—*abbr.* **Lev.**

lev-i-ty (lĕv′ĭ-tĭ), *n.* [*pl.* levities (-tĭz)], lightness of disposition or conduct.

lev-y (lĕv′ĭ), *v.t.* [*p.t.* and *p.p.* lev′ied (-ĭd), *p.pr.* lev′y-ing], **1**, to raise or collect by compulsion, as an army or a tax; **2**, to wage (war):—*v.i.* to raise money by seizing property; as, to *levy* on household goods for unpaid rent:—*n.* [*pl.* levies (-ĭz)], **1**, the act of collecting or raising by compulsion, as money or men; **2**, the amount or number raised.

lewd (lūd), *adj.* sensual; impure; as, *lewd* talk.—*adv.* **lewd′ly.**—*n.* **lewd′ness.**

lex-i-cog-ra-pher (lĕk″sĭ-kŏg′rȧ-fẽr), *n.* one who edits or compiles a dictionary, or lexicon.

lex-i-cog-ra-phy (lĕk″sĭ-kŏg′rȧ-fĭ), *n.* the science, art, or occupation of editing or compiling dictionaries, or lexicons.—*adj.* **lex″i-co-graph′i-cal.**

lex-i-con (lĕk′sĭ-kŏn), *n.* a dictionary, esp. of Latin, Greek, or Hebrew.

leze maj-es-ty (lēz), a crime against the government or sovereign; treason. Also, **lese maj′es-ty**, *Pfd. S.*

li-a-bil-i-ty (lī″ȧ-bĭl′ĭ-tĭ), *n.* [*pl.* liabilities (-tĭz)], **1**, the state of being exposed to accident, danger, etc.; **2**, the state of being responsible for a loss, debt, etc.; **3**, that for which one is responsible; **4**, in *pl.*, debts; obligations: opp. of *assets*.

li-a-ble (lī′ȧ-bl), *adj.* **1**, exposed, as to damage, danger, expense, etc.; as, *liable* to misfortune; **2**, answerable; responsible.

Syn. accountable. (See apt.)

***li-ai-son** (lyā″zôɴ′), [Fr.], *n.* **1**, an improper intimacy between a man and a woman; **2**, communication between two points by means of officers in communication with both points through signals, radio, etc.

li-ar (lī′ẽr), *n.* one who intentionally tells an untruth; a prevaricator.

li-ba-tion (lī-bā′shŭn), *n.* **1**, the act of pouring out wine or other liquid in honor of a god; **2**, the liquid so poured out.

li-bel (lī′bĕl), *n.* **1**, a malicious written or printed statement tending to defame or to injure the reputation of another, or to hold him up to public ridicule; also, the act of publishing such a statement; **2**, in law, a written statement of a plaintiff, instituting a lawsuit and giving the causes of his action:—*v.t.* **1**, to publish a malicious, injurious statement against; defame; expose to public ridicule; **2**, in law, to bring a lawsuit against by filing a libel.—*n.* **li′bel-er; li′bel-ler.**

li-bel-ant (lī′bĕl-ănt), *n.* in law, one who brings a lawsuit by filing a libel. Also, **li′bel-lant.**

li-bel-ee (lī″bĕl-ē′), *n.* in law, one against whom a libel is filed in a lawsuit. Also, **li″bel-lee′.**

li-bel-ous (lī′bĕl-ŭs), *adj.* containing, or of the nature of, anything that maliciously defames; as, a *libelous* report. Also, **li′bel-lous.**—*adv.* **li′bel-ous-ly.**

lib-er-al (lĭb′ẽr-ăl), *adj.* **1**, generous; **2**, not narrowly restricted; as, a *liberal* education; **3**, abundant; plentiful; **4**, free from narrowness in ideas or doctrines; **5**, not literal; free, as a translation; **6**, progressive; not conservative: **liberal arts**, certain branches of learning such as literature, science, history, languages, philosophy, etc.:—*n.* one who believes in extension of freedom in political, social, religious, and other institutions: **Liberal**, a member of the party in England that advocates free trade, democratic reform, etc.—*adv.* **lib′er-al-ly.**—*n.* **lib′er-al-ism.**

lib-er-al-i-ty (lĭb″ẽr-ăl′ĭ-tĭ), *n.* [*pl.* liberalities (-tĭz)], **1**, the quality of being free and generous; **2**, mental breadth; freedom from prejudice; **3**, a gift; donation.

lib-er-ate (lĭb′ẽr-āt), *v.t.* [*p.t.* and *p.p.* -at″ed, *p.pr.* -at″ing], **1**, to set free from restraint or bondage; as, to *liberate* slaves; **2**, to free from combination, as a gas from a chemical compound.—*n.* **lib′er-a″tor.**—*n.* **lib″er-a′tion.**

Syn. release, emancipate, discharge.—*Ant.* confine, restrain, hold, bind.

lib-er-tine (lĭb′ẽr-tĭn), *n.* one who does not restrain his evil impulses, appetites, and desires:—*adj.* loose in morals.—*n.* **lib′er-tin-ism.**

lib-er-ty (lĭb′ẽr-tĭ), *n.* [*pl.* liberties (-tĭz)], **1**, freedom from despotic control or bondage; **2**, freedom to do as one pleases; **3**, an overstepping of the rules of propriety; undue freedom; **4**, a privilege or right granted by a sovereign power.

Syn. freedom, independence, license, immunity. *Liberty* and *freedom* are often interchanged, but *freedom* suggests the lack of restraint, *liberty* the removal of any previous restraint or control; as, *freedom* of the press or of conscience; to set a captive at *liberty*. *Independence* implies freedom from subjection or domination; as, the growing *independence* of women; the *independence* of the United States.

li-bid-i-nous (lĭ-bĭd′ĭ-nŭs), *adj.* having impure desires; lustful.

Li-bra (lī′brȧ), *n.* **1**, a southern constellation, the Scales: also called *Balance*; **2**, the seventh sign of the zodiac (see *zodiac*, illus.): **libra** (lē′brä), the monetary unit of Peru, equivalent to $4.87.

li-bra-ri-an (lī-brā′rĭ-ăn), *n.* one who has charge of a library.

li-bra-ry (lī′brā-rĭ), *n.* [*pl.* libraries (-rĭz)], **1**, a collection of books; **2**, a room or building where such a collection is kept.

li-bret-to (lĭ-brĕt′ō), *n.* [*pl.* librettos (-ōz); libretti (-tē)], a book containing the words of an opera, oratorio, or the like; also, the text itself.—*n.* **li-bret′tist.**

Lib-y-an (lĭb′ĭ-ăn), *adj.* pertaining to a region in northern Africa, called *Libya* by the ancient Greeks.

lice (līs), *n.* plural of the irregular noun *louse*, which see.

li-cense (lī′sĕns), *n.* **1**, authority to act as one sees fit; permission; leave; **2**, unrestrained liberty; abuse of freedom; **3**, legal permission to do something; as, a *license* to operate an automobile; **4**, intentional variation from fact or from a recognized rule, as by an artist or author for the sake of effect; as, poetic *license*:—*v.t.* [*p.t.* and *p.p.* -censed (-sĕnst), *p.pr.* -cens-ing], to grant permission to by law. Also, **li′cence.**

li-cen-ti-ate (lī-sĕn′shĭ-āt), *n.* one given authority to preach or to practice a profession.

li-cen-tious (lī-sĕn′shŭs), *adj.* sensual; unrestrained morally.—*adv.* **li-cen′tious-ly.**—*n.* **li-cen′tious-ness.**

li-chen (lī′kĕn), *n.* **1**, any of a group of low-growing plant formations composed of certain fungi growing close together with certain algæ: found on trees, fences, stones, etc.; **2**, a kind of inflammatory skin disease.—*adj.* **li′chen-ous.**

lich gate (lĭch), the roofed gate of a churchyard, under which a dead body is carried to the grave.

lick (lĭk), *v.t.* **1,** to pass the tongue over; lap up; **2,** of flames, to play over lightly; **3,** *Colloq.:* **a,** to whip; **b,** to conquer in fight: —*n.* **1,** the act of stroking with the tongue; **2,** *Colloq.*, a quick or careless stroke; hence, a small amount; as, not a *lick* of work; **3,** a place to which wild animals come for salt; a salt lick.

lic-o-rice (lĭk′ō-rĭs), *n.* **1,** a certain plant of the pea family, from the root of which is derived an extract, used esp. in cough medicines; **2,** the dried root of this plant; also, the extract. Also, **liq′uo-rice.**

lic-tor (lĭk′tŏr), *n.* a Roman official who attended the chief magistrates and carried as a badge of authority the fasces, a bundle of rods having among them an ax with the blade projecting.

lid (lĭd), *n.* **1,** a movable cover for an opening, as of a box; top; **2,** the cover of the eye; **3,** *Slang*, a hat.

[1]**lie** (lī), *n.* **1,** an untrue statement; falsehood; **2,** anything that misleads or is intended to mislead: **to give the lie to,** to accuse of falsehood:—*v.i.* [*p.t.* and *p.p.* lied (līd), *p.pr.* ly′ing], **1,** to speak a falsehood; **2,** to make false representations; as, figures never *lie.*

Syn., *n.* untruth, falsehood, mendacity. A *lie* is something untrue told with deliberate intent to deceive; an unwitting variation from the truth is not a *lie*, but a mistake. An *untruth* is something told which is contrary to fact; it may name a deliberate departure from the truth, or an inaccuracy resulting from misunderstanding. A *falsehood* is the utterance of something known to be untrue with intent to deceive. *Mendacity* is habitual, shameless lying.—*Ant.*, *n.* truth, fact, verity.

[2]**lie** (lī), *v.i.* [*p.t.* lay (lā), *p.p.* lain (lān), *p.pr.* ly′ing], **1,** to assume, or rest in, a reclining position: often with *down;* **2,** to be at rest, usually horizontally: used of things; **3,** to exist or be situated in a certain position or arrangement; as, the town *lies* yonder:—*n.* **1,** the way, position, or direction in which a thing lies; **2,** in golf, the position in which a ball in play comes to rest.

lief (lēf), *adv.* willingly; as, I had as *lief* go as stay.

liege (lēj), *adj.* **1,** having the right to devotion and service; sovereign; as, he reverenced his *liege* lady; **2,** bound to give service and devotion; **3,** loyal; faithful:—*n.* **1,** one bound to give service and devotion: also called *liege man*, or *liegeman;* **2,** a sovereign; a lord and master.

li-en (lē′ĕn; lēn), *n.* **1,** the right of a person having a claim against another to hold property of the other until the claim is paid, or to have the other's property seized and sold through legal proceedings to satisfy the claim; **2,** security for payment.

lieu (lū), *n.* place; room; stead: used in the phrase *in lieu of.*

lieu-ten-ant (lū-tĕn′ănt; *Br.* lĕf-tĕn′-), *n.* **1,** one who acts for a superior in his absence: also used in combination with the names of other ranks to indicate the next lower rank; as, *lieutenant* colonel; **2,** specif., in the army, an officer ranking next below a captain: **lieutenant governor,** an executive official next in rank to a governor, who is authorized to act for the governor in his absence, and who succeeds to the governorship if it becomes vacant during his term of office.—*n.* **lieu-ten′an-cy.**

life (līf), *n.* [*pl.* lives (līvz)], **1,** a certain quality or characteristic which distinguishes an animal or a plant from dead or inorganic matter; **also,** the state of being alive; living existence; vitality; **as,** to bring to *life* that which appears to be dead; **2,** a living person; as, but one *life* was saved from the wreck; **3,** living beings collectively; **as,** human *life;* animal *life;* **4,** the period between birth and death; as, all the years of a man's *life;* **5,** the period of usefulness or activity; as, the *life* of an automobile; **6,** manner of living; as, a *life* of pleasure; **7,** a biography; as, the *life* of Tennyson; **8,** animation; vivacity; as, to be full of *life;* to put *life* into an undertaking; **9,** the moving spirit; as, he was the *life* of the party: **life belt,** a belt, as of cork, to keep a person afloat in the water.

life-blood (līf′blŭd″), *n.* **1,** the blood necessary to life; **2,** any source or spring of vital strength.

life-boat (līf′bōt″), *n.* a boat for use in rescuing persons at sea.

life buoy a float, often a buoyant ring, to keep persons from sinking in the water until rescued.

life guard **1,** a body of troops for protecting a person of high rank; **2,** an attendant stationed on a beach to save bathers from drowning.

life in-sur-ance **1,** a method of financial protection in which a company, in consideration of certain periodic payments called *premiums*, agrees to pay a stated sum of money to the party designated at a stated time or at the death of the person insured; **2,** the amount to be so paid.

life-less (līf′lĕs), *adj.* **1,** without vitality; dead; **2,** wanting in energy; listless; dull.—*adv.* **life′less-ly.**—*n.* **life′less-ness.**

Syn. inanimate, spiritless. (See dead.)

life-like (līf′līk″), *adj.* like a living being or a real thing; natural; realistic.

life-long (līf′lŏng″), *adj.* enduring or remaining throughout life.

life pre-serv-er **1,** a device for keeping afloat a person who is in the water; **2,** a club or cane with a heavy metal head, for use as a weapon.

LIFE PRESERVER

life-time (līf′tīm″), *n.* the length of time that life lasts.

lift (lĭft), *v.t.* **1,** to raise to a higher point; place in a higher position; **2,** to exalt; support in the air; **3,** *Colloq.*, to steal:—*v.i.* **1,** to exert strength in raising; **2,** to rise, as fog:—*n.* **1,** the act of raising to a higher point; **2,** high position; as, the proud *lift* of her head; **3,** aid; help in raising or carrying; assistance; hence, a free ride along one's way; **4,** the height to which a thing is raised; **5,** in England, a machine for carrying up or down; an elevator; **6,** on shipboard, a rope connecting the ends of a yard with a masthead (see *rigging*, illus.): **lift pump,** a pump which lifts a liquid but does not force it out (see [1]*pump*, illus.): distinguished from *force pump.*—*n.* **lift′er.**

lig-a-ment (lĭg′ȧ-mĕnt), *n.* **1,** a tough, fibrous tissue connecting the ends of movable bones, or holding in place an organ of the body; **2,** hence, any bond or tie.

lig-a-ture (lĭg′ȧ-tūr), *n.* **1,** a thing which unites or binds, as a narrow bandage, a connecting part (see *saxophone*, illus.), or the like; **2,** in printing, a double character, or two or more letters united, as æ; **3,** in music, a curved line [⌒] connecting musical notes; also, the notes so connected: —*v.t.* [*p.t.* and *p.p.* -tured (-tūrd), *p.pr.* -turing], to bind with a narrow band.

[1]**light** (līt), *n.* **1,** the condition of illumination upon which sight depends: opp.

of *darkness;* as, the *light* of day; **2**, anything which illuminates, as the sun, a candle, etc.; **3**, the brightness so given out; **4**, appearance from a special point of view; as, to put the matter in a new *light;* **5**, clear mental vision or that which gives it; as, to throw *light* on a problem; **6**, a window, or a pane of glass in a window:—*adj.* **1**, clear; bright; not dark; **2**, pale in color; blond:—*v.t.* [*p.t.* and *p.p.* light′ed or lit (lĭt), *p.pr.* light′ing], **1**, to set fire to; **2**, to illuminate; **3**, to cause to give forth brightness; **4**, to furnish with, or guide by, a light:—*v.i.* **1**, to take fire; **2**, to become bright: usually followed by *up;* as, her face *lighted* up. —*n.* [1]**light′ness.**

[2]**light** (līt), *adj.* **1**, not heavy or dense; having little weight; **2**, not burdensome; easy; **3**, delicate; dainty; also, graceful; nimble; **4**, cheerful; gay; not serious; **5**, trifling; unimportant; also, unsteady; fickle; **6**, of bread, raised or leavened, as with yeast; **7**, of food, easy to digest; of wines, containing but little alcohol; **8**, not heavily equipped; as, *light* infantry:—*v.i.* [*p.t.* and *p.p.* light′ed or lit (lĭt), *p.pr.* light′ing], to come down; settle; alight: **light upon,** to come upon by chance; find.—*adv.* **light′ly.**—*n.* [2]**light′ness.**

Syn., adj. flippant, frivolous, inconstant.—*Ant., adj.* serious, earnest, constant.

[1]**light-en** (līt′n), *v.t.* to make clear or bright; illumine:—*v.i.* **1**, to become bright; **2**, to shine brightly in a flash, as in an electric storm.

[2]**light-en** (līt′n), *v.t.* **1**, to reduce in weight; make lighter; **2**, to gladden or brighten; cheer:—*v.i.* to become less heavy or burdensome.

[1]**light-er** (līt′ẽr), *n.* one who or that which illuminates or kindles; specif., a tightly twisted strip of paper or an electrical device for lighting cigarettes, gas, or the like.

[2]**light-er** (līt′ẽr), *n.* a large open barge used in loading and unloading vessels.

light-er-age (līt′ẽr-āj), *n.* **1**, the unloading of a cargo by large open barges; **2**, the charge made for such work.

light–fin-gered (līt′=fĭng″gẽrd), *adj.* pilfering; thievish.

light–foot-ed (līt′=fo͝ot″ĕd), *adj.* not heavy of step; nimble.

light–head-ed (līt′=hĕd″ĕd), *adj.* **1**, dizzy; also, delirious, as with fever; **2**, thoughtless; heedless.

light–heart-ed (līt′=härt″ĕd), *adj.* free from care; gay; cheerful; as, *light-hearted* laughter.—*adv.* **light″–heart′-ed-ly.**—*n.* **light″–heart′ed-ness.**

light-house (līt′hous″), *n.* a tower or other structure furnished with a light at the top to guide ships at sea.

STEEL LIGHTHOUSE

light-ning (līt′nĭng), *n.* a flash of electricity in the sky, usually accompanied by thunder: **lightning bug, 1**, a firefly; **2**, any insect that gives out a phosphorescent light while flying: **lightning rod,** a metal rod fastened on a building to protect it from lightning by receiving the electric discharge and carrying it to the earth.

light-ship (līt′shĭp″), *n.* a vessel with a light, moored at sea in a dangerous place to warn other ships.

light-some (līt′sŭm), *adj.* **1**, cheerful; lively; **2**, nimble.

light-weight (līt′wāt″), *n.* **1**, one who weighs less than the average; esp., a boxer weighing 130, but not 135, pounds; **2**, an unimportant person:—*adj.* **1**, below average in weight; **2**, of little account.

light year the distance traveled in one year by a wave of light, with a velocity of about 186,000 miles per second: a unit of distance, used in astronomy.

lig-ne-ous (lĭg′nē-ŭs), *adj.* composed of, or like, wood; woody.

lig-nite (lĭg′nīt), *n.* a soft, brownish black coal intermediate between peat and bituminous coal.—*adj.* **lig-nit′ic.**

lig-num–vi-tæ (lĭg′nŭm=vī′tē), *n.* the very heavy hard wood of certain South American, West Indian, and Australian trees; also, any of the trees.

lig-ule (lĭg′ūl), *n.* a thin, membranous part attached to a leaf where the blade joins the stem.

[1]**like** (līk), *adj.* **1**, similar; resembling; **2**, in a mood or condition for; as, I feel *like* reading; it looks *like* rain; **3**, characteristic of; as, that's just *like* a man:—*prep.* to the same extent; in the same manner; as, he dresses *like* his brother:—*adv. Colloq.*, probably; as, very *like* he'll come:—*conj.* (avoided by careful speakers), **1**, as; as, do *like* I do; **2**, as if; as, he acted *like* he was crazy:—*n.* that which is equal or similar to another; a copy.

[2]**like** (līk), *v.t.* [*p.t.* and *p.p.* liked (līkt), *p.pr.* lik′ing], **1**, to have a taste for; enjoy; find agreeable; **2**, to wish or want:—*v.i.* to choose; as, do as you *like:*—*n.*, in *pl.*, the things one enjoys or prefers.—*adj.* **lik′a-ble; like′a-ble.**

-like (-līk), *adj. suffix,* similar to; resembling: added freely to nouns, without a hyphen except after *l;* as, boy*like;* eel-*like.*

like-li-hood (līk′lĭ-ho͝od), *n.* **1**, probability; **2**, something that is likely to happen; **3**, evidence; indication.

like-ly (līk′lĭ), *adj.* [*comp.* like′li-er, *superl.* like′li-est], **1**, probable; credible; as, a *likely* story; **2**, suitable; as, *likely* behavior; **3**, favorable; promising; **4**, being such as to make probable; as, that is *likely* to happen:—*adv.* probably.

Syn., adj. probable. A *likely* event is one that in the circumstances would be expected to happen; a *likely* prophecy is such as might prove true. *Probable* is less emphatic than *likely;* a *probable* event, though more apt than not to happen, is nevertheless more in doubt than a *likely* event. (See apt.)—*Ant., adj.* doubtful, improbable, unlikely.

lik-en (līk′n), *v.t.* to compare; as, I will *liken* him unto a wise man.

like-ness (līk′nĕs), *n.* **1**, resemblance; similarity; **2**, a portrait; **3**, guise; external appearance.

like-wise (līk′wīz″), *adv.* in a similar manner; also:—*conj.* also; moreover.

lik-ing (līk′ĭng), *n.* **1**, fondness; inclination; desire; **2**, *Archaic,* good appearance.

li-lac (lī′lăk), *n.* **1**, a shrub with fragrant white or pinkish purple flowers; **2**, the pale purple color of the flowers.

lil-i-a-ceous (lĭl″ĭ-ā′shŭs), *adj.* **1**, pertaining to, or resembling, a lily; **2**, belonging to the lily family.

Lil-li-pu-tian (lĭl″ĭ-pū′shăn), *adj.* very small; like the tiny people of Lilliput, a country described in Swift's "Gulliver's Travels":—*n.* **1**, one of the tiny people of Lilliput; **2**, hence, any extremely small person; a dwarf.

lilt (lĭlt), *n.* **1**, a light or lively tune; a merry song; **2**, rhythmic movement; as, the *lilt* of verse:—*v.i.* and *v.t.* to sing lightly or gaily; as, to *lilt* and play; to *lilt* a song.

lil-y (lĭl′ĭ), *n.* [*pl.* lilies (-ĭz)], any of a genus (*Lilium*) of plants with bulblike root and handsome flowers; also, any of several plants or flowers resembling a lily: **lily of the valley**, a low-growing herb with fragrant, white, bell-shaped flowers (see *inflorescence*, illus.):—*adj.* **1**, like a lily; **2**, white; pale; **3**, pure; innocent.

Li-ma bean (lī′mȧ), any of various beans with flat seeds, prized as food.

¹limb (lĭm), *n.* **1**, a leg, an arm, or a wing; **2**, a main branch of a tree; **3**, any branchlike part; **4**, *Colloq.*, a roguish child:—*v.t.* to remove limbs from.—*adj.* **limb′less.**

²limb (lĭm), *n.* **1**, an edge or border, as of the moon's disk; **2**, a graduated circular scale in a leveling rod or an instrument for measuring angles (see *quadrant*, illus.).

limbed (lĭmd), *adj.* having legs, arms, branches, etc.: usually in combination; as, a long-*limbed* boy.

¹lim-ber (lĭm′bẽr), *n.* the fore part of a gun carriage:—*v.t.* to attach the limber to (a gun carriage).

²lim-ber (lĭm′bẽr), *adj.* **1**, flexible; **2**, supple; lithe:—*v.t.* and *v.i.* to make or become flexible or supple.—*n.* **lim′ber-ness.**

¹ LIMBER

lim-bo (lĭm′bō), *n.* **1**, a region thought of as lying between heaven and hell; **2**, a place of restraint, confinement, or oblivion.

Lim-burg cheese (lĭm′bûrg), a mild but strong-smelling cheese, orig. made in Limburg, Belgium: also called *Limburger cheese* and *Limburger*.

¹lime (līm), *n.* **1**, a white, earthlike substance obtained esp. by the action of heat upon limestone, marble, etc., and used in making cement, mortar, etc.: also called *quicklime;* **2**, a white powder made by treating quicklime with water: also called *slaked lime* or *slacked lime;* **3**, a sticky substance smeared on twigs to catch small birds: also called *birdlime:*—*v.t.* [*p.t.* and *p.p.* limed (līmd), *p.pr.* lim′ing], **1**, to apply lime to, as land; **2**, to catch, as birds, with birdlime.—*adj.* **lim′y.**

²lime (līm), *n.* a tree bearing a small, lemonlike fruit; also, the fruit.

³lime (līm), *n.* the linden tree, much used for shade and ornament.

lime-kiln (līm′kĭl″; līm′kĭln″), *n.* a furnace for the burning of limestone or shells, to obtain lime.

lime-light (līm′līt″), *n.* **1**, a brilliant, incandescent light produced by the action of a very hot flame upon lime: also called *calcium light;* **2**, the brilliant light upon the central figure or group on a stage; **3**, publicity; prominence; notoriety.

lim-er-ick (lĭm′ẽr-ĭk), *n.* a nonsense poem of five lines, of which lines 1, 2, and 5 rime, and lines 3 and 4 rime.

lime-stone (līm′stōn″), *n.* a rock containing carbonate of lime.

lim-it (lĭm′ĭt), *n.* **1**, a border or boundary; that which confines, ends, or checks; **2**, utmost extent or degree:—*v.t.* to confine within bounds; restrict.—*adj.* **lim′it-less.**

lim-i-ta-tion (lĭm″ĭ-tā′shŭn), *n.* **1**, the act of bounding or restricting; **2**, that which bounds or restrains; restriction.

lim-it-ed (lĭm′ĭt-ĕd), *p.adj.* **1**, restricted; circumscribed; **2**, of a government, controlled by constitutional provisions; as, a *limited* monarchy; **3**, of a corporation or partnership, having the liability of stockholders or partners restricted to the amount of their stock; **4**, of a train, accepting passengers only up to the number of places provided for them.

limn (lĭm), *v.t.* [*p.t.* and *p.p.* limned (lĭmd), *p.pr.* lim′ning (lĭm′nĭng; lĭm′ĭng)], **1**, to paint or draw; **2**, hence, to portray; depict.—*n.* **lim′ner** (lĭm′nẽr).

li-mou-sine (lĭm″o͝o-zēn′; lē″mo͞o-zēn′), *n.* a motor car having a closed body and a covered, outside, driver's seat.

¹limp (lĭmp), *n.* a lame, halting motion in walking:—*v.i.* to walk lamely.

²limp (lĭmp), *adj.* lacking stiffness, firmness, or strength; flabby.—*adv.* **limp′ly.**—*n.* **limp′ness.**

lim-pet (lĭm′pĕt; lĭm′pĭt), *n.* any of several shellfish with a cone-shaped shell, found sticking to rocks or timbers, and often used for food.

lim-pid (lĭm′pĭd), *adj.* transparent; sparklingly clear; as, a *limpid* stream.—*adv.* **lim′pid-ly.**—*n.* **lim′pid-ness.**

linch-pin (lĭnch′pĭn″), *n.* an iron pin put crosswise through the end of an axle to keep the wheel from coming off.

lin-den (lĭn′dĕn), *n.* any of a genus of large trees with heart-shaped leaves and small clusters of cream-colored flowers: also called *basswood; lime.*

¹line (līn), *n.* **1**, a mark drawn by pen or pencil; also, a wrinkle, as in the skin; crease; **2**, a strong, slender string or cord; **3**, a row; as, a *line* of trees; hence, harmony; accord; as, to bring voters into *line;* **4**, a boundary; as, to cross the *line* into Canada; hence, any limit; as, he drew the *line* at drinking; **5**, an imaginary circle on the globe; as, a *line* of latitude; specif., the equator: with *the;* **6**, a plan or method; as, follow this *line* of attack; **7**, a course of action, conduct, or thought; **8**, an industry or profession; a branch of commercial business; as, his *line* was drugs; also, a stock of goods of a specified kind; as, a *line* of perfumes; **9**, a row of printed or written letters or words; hence, a verse of poetry; **10**, family; descent; as, a *line* of kings; **11**, vehicles, cars, trains, ships, etc., making up a system of transportation; **12**, railroad tracks or route; as, the main *line* of the Erie; also, a wire in a telephone system; **13**, in geometry, that which has length, but no breadth or thickness; **14**, a row of defended positions; as, a trench in the front *line;* **15**, a row of soldiers marching abreast; **16**, in *pl.:* **a**, the words of a part in a play; **b**, a marriage certificate: **line telegraphy**, or **telephony**, telegraphy, or telephony, by means of wires: distinguished from *wireless telegraphy* and *radio:*—*v.t.* [*p.t.* and *p.p.* lined (līnd), *p.pr.* lin′ing], **1**, to draw lines upon; **2**, to place in a row side by side; **3**, to establish a row along; as, to *line* a path with roses:—*v.i.* to form a row.

²line (līn), *v.t.* [*p.t.* and *p.p.* lined (līnd), *p.pr.* lin′ing], **1**, to provide (a garment or the like) with an inside cover; **2**, to serve as the inside covering of; as, silk *lined* the coat.

lin-e-age (lĭn′ē-āj), *n.* **1**, direct descent from an ancestor; **2**, family; pedigree; as, a lady of high *lineage.*

lin-e-al (lĭn′ē-ăl), *adj.* **1**, composed of lines; **2**, in direct descent from an ancestor; as, the *lineal* descendants of David; **3**, hereditary.—*adv.* **lin′e-al-ly.**

lin-e-a-ment (lĭn′ē-ȧ-mĕnt), *n.*, usually in *pl.*, a feature or outline, esp. of the face; contour.

lin-e-ar (lĭn′ē-ẽr), *adj.* **1**, pertaining to, or composed of, lines; **2**, having length only; **3**, very narrow.

line-man (līn′măn), *n.* [*pl.* linemen (-mĕn)], **1**, a man who repairs electric wires; **2**, one who carries a tape, line, or chain in surveying.

lin-en (lĭn′ĕn; lĭn′ĭn), *n.* **1**, a cloth made of flax; **2**, collectively, articles made, or sometimes made, of this cloth, as tablecloths, napkins, towels, sheets, collars, cuffs, etc.:—*adj.* made of, or like, linen.

lin-er (lĭn′ẽr), *n.* a steamship belonging to a regular line of vessels.

-ling (-lĭng), *n. suffix*, **1**, one connected or related; as, nurs*ling;* **2**, forming diminutives; as, duck*ling:* often contemptuous.

lin-ger (lĭng′gẽr), *v.i.* **1**, to delay: be slow in going; **2**, to remain alive, though waning, suffering, dying, or the like.

***lin-ge-rie** (lăṅ″zhē-rē′), [Fr.] *n.* **1**, linen articles collectively; **2**, specif., women's undergarments of silk, linen, or cotton.

lin-go (lĭng′gō), *n.* [*pl.* lingoes (-gōz)], language; dialect: used generally in a humorous or contemptuous sense of an unfamiliar language or vocabulary.

lin-gua fran-ca (lĭng′gwȧ frăng′kȧ), a mixed dialect, as that used by western Europeans in their contact with Orientals.

lin-gual (lĭng′gwăl), *adj.* pertaining to, or formed by, the tongue or a special position of the tongue:—*n.* a sound formed by the tongue, as *l, r, th,* etc.

lin-guist (lĭng′gwĭst), *n.* one skilled in, or a student of, languages.

lin-guis-tic (lĭng-gwĭs′tĭk), *adj.* pertaining to the study and comparison of languages: **linguistics**, *n. pl.* used as *sing.* the science of languages, or the study of their origins, growth, and characteristics.

lin-i-ment (lĭn′ĭ-mĕnt), *n.* a liquid rubbed on the skin to soothe, relieve lameness, or stimulate.

lin-ing (lĭn′ĭng), *n.* an inside covering; also, the act of furnishing one.

[1]**link** (lĭngk), *n.* **1**, a single ring or division of a chain; specif., a single length in a surveyor's land measure, equal to 7.92 inches; **2**, anything that serves to connect the parts of a series; as, a *link* in a chain of evidence; **3**, a tie; connection:—*v.t.* and *v.i.* to connect, or be connected, by a link.

[2]**link** (lĭngk), *n.* a torch made of tow, or coarse flax, and pitch.

links (lĭngks), *n.pl.* **1**, *Scot.*, gently rolling land, as along the seashore; **2**, sometimes used as *sing.*, a golf course.

lin-net (lĭn′ĕt; lĭn′ĭt), *n.* a small singing bird common in the Old World.

li-no-le-um (lĭ-nō′lē-ŭm), *n.* a floor covering made of ground cork and linseed oil on a backing of burlap or felt.

lin-o-type (lĭn′ō-tīp″; lĭn′-), *n.* a typesetting machine, operated by keys similar to those of a typewriter, which casts each line of type in one piece.

lin-seed (lĭn′sēd″), *n.* the seed of flax: **linseed oil**, a pale yellow oil pressed from flaxseed, used in paint, linoleum, etc.

lin-sey–wool-sey (lĭn′zĭ-wo͝ol′zĭ; lĭn′-sĭ-wo͝ol′sĭ), *n.* a coarse cloth of linen and wool or of cotton and wool: also called *linsey.*

lint (lĭnt), *n.* ravelings from yarn or fabrics, or a soft down obtained by scraping linen: used for dressing wounds.

lin-tel (lĭn′tĕl), *n.* the horizontal top piece of a door frame or window frame.

li-on (lī′ŭn), *n.* **1**, a powerful, flesh-eating mammal of the cat family, found in the deserts of Africa and southern Asia; **2**, a celebrated person who is much sought after by

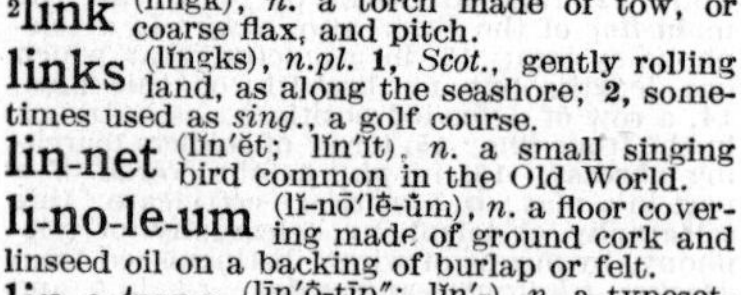

Rampant Salient Couchant Passant

THE LION AS DEPICTED IN HERALDIC DEVICES

society: **Lion, 1**, a constellation, Leo; **2**, the fifth sign of the zodiac (see *zodiac,* illus.); **3**, a member of a club affiliated with the Lions International, a group of clubs of business and professional men, organized for good fellowship and humanitarian service, esp. in the care of the blind.—*n. fem.* **li′on-ess.**

li-on-ize (lī′ŭn-īz), *v.t.* [*p.t.* and *p.p.* -ized (-īzd), *p.pr.* -iz″ing], to treat as a celebrity; pay very great attention to socially.

lip (lĭp), *n.* **1**, one of the two fleshy borders of the mouth; **2**, the flaring or folding edge of anything hollow:—*v.t.* [*p.t.* and *p.p.* lipped (lĭpt), *p.pr.* lip′ping], to touch with the lips; kiss:—*adj.* spoken but not felt; as, *lip* service.

liq-ue-fac-tion (lĭk″wē-făk′shŭn), *n.* **1**, the process of making a solid or gas into a liquid; **2**, the state of being melted.

liq-ue-fy (lĭk′wē-fī), *v.t.* [*p.t.* and *p.p.* -fied (-fīd), *p.pr.* -fy″ing], to change into a liquid:—*v.i.* to become liquid.

li-queur (lē″kûr′; lĭ-kûr′), [Fr.], *n.* a light alcoholic drink sweetened and variously flavored.

liq-uid (lĭk′wĭd), *adj.* **1**, not solid; freely flowing; **2**, clear; smooth in sound; as, a *liquid* melody; **3**, smooth or flowing, as the consonants *l* and *r*:—*n.* **1**, a substance that flows freely but does not expand indefinitely as does a gas; **2**, one of the consonants *l* or *r.* —*adv.* **liq′uid-ly.**—*n.* **li-quid′i-ty.**

Syn., n. (see fluid).

liq-uid air air which has been compressed and cooled to such a degree as to become liquid in form.

liq-ui-date (lĭk′wĭ-dāt), *v.t.* [*p.t.* and *p.p.* -dat″ed, *p.pr.* -dat″ing], **1**, to pay off or settle, as a debt, claim, mortgage, etc.; **2**, to arrange, as the affairs of a bankrupt: —*v.i.* to pay one's debts.—*n.* **liq″ui-da′tion.**

liq-uor (lĭk′ẽr), *n.* any substance that pours freely; esp., an alcoholic drink.

liq-uo-rice (lĭk′ō-rĭs), *n.* an herb of the pea family; also, its root, or an extract from it. See **lic′o-rice**, *Pfd. S.*

li-ra (lē′rä), *n.* [*pl.* lire (-rā)], **1**, an Italian silver coin, the monetary unit, normally worth 19.3 cents; **2**, a Turkish gold coin normally worth about $4.40.

lisle (līl), *n.* a fine, hard-twisted cotton thread, or a fabric woven from it.

lisp (lĭsp), *n.* the pronunciation of *s* or *z* nearly like *th;* hence, imperfect utterance:—*v.t.* and *v.i.* to speak with a lisp.

lis-som (lĭs′ŭm), *n.* limber; swift and light in motion. Also, **lis′some; lithe′some** (līth′sŭm).—*n.* **lis′some-ness.**

[1]**list** (lĭst), *n.* **1**, a series of names, items, etc., as in a memorandum; a catalog, roll, or register; **2**, an edge or selvage of cloth; **3**, a strip of cloth; **4**, in farming, a ridge thrown up along a furrow:—*v.t.* **1**, to catalog, register, or enroll; **2**, to cover with strips of cloth:—*v.i.* to enlist; go as a soldier.

[2]**list** (lĭst), *v.i.* [*p.t.* list′ed or list, *p.p.* list′ed, *p.pr.* list′ing], *Archaic*, to wish.

[3]**list** (lĭst), *v.i.* and *v.t.* to tilt or cause to tilt toward one side, as a ship:—*n.* a leaning to one side, as of a ship.

[4]**list** (lĭst), *v.i.* and *v.t.* to listen or hearken (to); attend.

lis-ten (lĭs′n), *v.i.* **1**, to attend closely, so as to hear: with *to;* **2**, to heed; obey: **listen in**, to listen to radio communications by means of a radio receiving set.—*n.* **lis′ten-er.**

Syn. hear. To *listen* is to make the effort to *hear*. To *hear* is to perceive by the ear, as a whistle or cry. We may *hear* without *listening*, and we may *listen* without *hearing*.

list-less (lĭst′lĕs), *adj.* lacking energy or interest; dull; languid; spiritless.—*adv.* **list′less-ly.**—*n.* **list′less-ness.**

lists (lĭsts), *n.pl.* the barriers of a field where tournaments were held; hence, the field itself, or any place of contest.

¹lit (lĭt), past tense and past participle of the verb ¹*light* or ²*light.* Also, **light'ed,** *Pfd. S.*

²lit (lĭt), *n.* the monetary unit of Lithuania, equivalent to ten cents. Also, **lit'as.**

lit-a-ny (lĭt'ȧ-nĭ), *n.* [*pl.* litanies (-nĭz)], a solemn form of prayer; esp., a series of responsive prayers in a church service.

li-ter (lē'tẽr), *n.* a metric unit of volume, equal to 1.0567 liquid quarts. Also, **li'tre.**

lit-er-a-cy (lĭt'ẽr-ȧ-sĭ), *n.* the state of being able to read and write.

lit-er-al (lĭt'ẽr-ăl), *adj.* **1,** following the given words; exact; as, a *literal* translation; **2,** precise; as, the *literal* truth; **3,** matter-of-fact; **4,** pertaining to, or consisting of, letters; as, a *literal* equation.—*adv.* **lit'er-al-ly.**—*n.* **lit'er-al-ness.**

lit-er-a-ry (lĭt'ẽr-ā-rĭ), *adj.* **1,** pertaining to, or appropriate to, literature or men of letters; **2,** having a knowledge of, or engaged in, literature.

lit-er-ate (lĭt'ẽr-ăt), *adj.* **1,** able to read and write; **2,** having a knowledge of letters or literature:—*n.* **1,** one who is able to read and write; **2,** a learned or educated person: opp. of *illiterate.*

***lit-e-ra-ti** (lĭt''ē-rä'tī), [Lat.], *n.pl.* men of letters; the literary class.

***lit-e-ra-tim** (lĭt''ē-rā'tĭm), [Lat.], *adv.* literally; exactly; precisely; without the change of a letter.

lit-er-a-ture (lĭt'ẽr-ȧ-tūr), *n.* **1,** the written or printed productions of a country or period, esp. those that are notable for beauty or force of style; **2,** the occupation of authors; **3,** the body of writing on a given subject; **4,** printed matter issued for a special purpose; as, campaign *literature.*

lith-arge (lĭth'ärj), *n.* lead monoxide, a yellowish red substance, sold in the form of flakes or powder: used in making glass, varnishes, etc.

lithe (līth), *adj.* bending easily; limber; gracefully supple; as, the dancer's *lithe* figure.—*adv.* **lithe'ly.**—*n.* **lithe'ness.**

lithe-some (līth'sŭm), *adj.* lithe; limber; nimble. Also, **lis'som; lis'some.**—*n.* **lithe'some-ness.**

lith-i-a (lĭth'ĭ-ȧ), *n.* a white crystalline substance, an oxide of lithium, found in various mineral waters.

lith-i-um (lĭth'ĭ-ŭm), *n.* a silver-white metallic element, the lightest known metal.

lith-o-graph (lĭth'ō-grăf), *n.* a picture or design, usually in colors, printed by a special process from a smooth, porous surface, as of stone:—*v.t.* to reproduce by this process.—*adj.* **lith''o-graph'ic.**

li-thog-ra-phy (lĭ-thŏg'rȧ-fĭ), *n.* the art or process of making lithographs.—*n.* **li-thog'ra-pher.**

lit-i-gant (lĭt'ĭ-gănt), *n.* one of the persons engaged in any given lawsuit:—*adj.* engaged in a lawsuit.

lit-i-gate (lĭt'ĭ-gāt), *v.t.* [*p.t.* and *p.p.* -gat''ed, *p.pr.* -gat''ing], to bring (a matter of dispute) to a court of law for settlement:—*v.i.* to engage in a lawsuit.

lit-i-ga-tion (lĭt''ĭ-gā'shŭn), *n.* the act or process of carrying on a lawsuit; also, a suit at law.

li-ti-gious (lĭ-tĭj'ŭs), *adj.* **1,** given to engaging in lawsuits; quarrelsome; **2,** pertaining to lawsuits.

lit-mus (lĭt'mŭs), *n.* a purplish blue dye, obtained from lichens, which is turned red by an acid and back to blue by an alkali.

lit-ter (lĭt'ẽr), *n.* **1,** a couch with a canopy, borne on men's shoulders by long shafts; **2,** a cot or stretcher for carrying a person lying down; **3,** straw, hay, etc., used as bedding for animals; **4,** odds and ends scattered about untidily; hence, a state of confusion or untidiness; **5,** the young, as of pigs, cats, etc., produced at one birth:—*v.t.* **1,** to supply with straw, etc., for bedding; **2,** to scatter about carelessly; **3,** to make untidy by scattering rubbish:—*v.i.* to bring forth young.

***lit-té-ra-teur** (lē''tā''rȧ''tûr'), [Fr.], *n.* a scholar; man of letters.

lit-tle (lĭt'l), *adj.* [*comp.* less or, *Dial.,* lit'tler, *superl.* least or, *Dial.,* lit'tlest], **1,** small in size, quantity, dignity, or importance; **2,** brief in time; **3,** young; **4,** petty; mean: **Little Bear,** a constellation in the form of a small dipper, the end star of the handle being the North Star: also called *Little Dipper; Ursa Minor:*—*adv.* **1,** in a small degree; not much; **2,** not at all: before such verbs as *know, think,* etc.; as, he *little* knows the result of his actions:—*n.* that which is small in size, quantity, etc.—*n.* **lit'tle-ness.**

lit-to-ral (lĭt'ō-răl), *adj.* pertaining to a shore:—*n.* land along a shore.

li-tur-gi-cal (lĭ-tûr'jĭ-kăl), *adj.* pertaining to divine service according to a set form; as, a *liturgical* form of worship.

lit-ur-gy (lĭt'ŭr-jĭ), *n.* [*pl.* liturgies (-jĭz)], a set form of service for public worship, as that in the Book of Common Prayer.

liv-a-ble (lĭv'ȧ-bl), *adj.* **1,** fit or agreeable to live in or with; **2,** endurable; as, such a life is hardly *livable.* Also, **live'a-ble.**

¹live (lĭv), *v.i.* [*p.t.* and *p.p.* lived (lĭvd), *p.pr.* liv'ing], **1,** to exist or have life; **2,** to pass life (in a certain manner); as, to *live* happily; **3,** to reside or dwell; as, to *live* in the woods; **4,** to get a livelihood; as, to *live* by farming; **5,** to subsist; as, to *live* on meat; **6,** to continue to have life; as, to *live* to be old; **7,** to survive; as, he *lived* through the ordeal:—*v.t.* to pass or spend; as, to *live* a happy life: **live down,** so to live as to refute or cause to be forgotten; as, to *live down* disgrace.

²live (līv), *adj.* **1,** having life; **2,** effective; specif., burning, as a coal; charged with electricity, as a wire; not exploded, as a shell; **3,** full of activity or interest, as a topic.

live-li-hood (līv'lĭ-hood), *n.* means of existence; regular support.
Syn. living, maintenance, subsistence.

live-long (lĭv'lông''), *adj.* **1,** long in passing; tedious; **2,** whole; entire; as, they toiled the *livelong* day.

live-ly (līv'lĭ), *adj.* [*comp.* live'li-er, *superl.* live'li-est], **1,** active; brisk; full of spirit; as, a *lively* disposition; **2,** vivid; as, a *lively* fancy; **3,** forcible; convincing; as, a *lively* impression.—*adv.* **live'li-ly.**—*n.* **live'li-ness.**
Syn. merry, sportive, sprightly, spirited.—*Ant.* sluggish, dull, inactive.

live oak any of various evergreen oaks of the southern and western U. S.

¹liv-er (lĭv'ẽr), *n.* one who exists, dwells, or spends time in some special way.

²liv-er (lĭv'ẽr), *n.* a large glandular organ in the upper part of the abdomen, which produces bile and causes important changes in certain food substances in the blood.

liv-er-ied (lĭv'ẽr-ĭd), *adj.* clothed in the peculiar dress used by any group of persons, esp. by servants.

liv-er-wort (lĭv'ẽr-wûrt''), *n.* **1,** any of a class of mosslike plants of very simple structure; **2,** the hepatica.

liv-er-y (lĭv'ẽr-ĭ), *n.* [*pl.* liveries (-ĭz)], **1,** a particular costume worn by servants or by any other special group of persons; **2,** the keeping and feeding of horses for compensation, or the hiring out of horses and vehicles; **3,** a stable where horses are boarded or hired out: also called *livery stable.*

liv-er-y-man (lĭv′ẽr-ĭ-măn), *n.* [*pl.* liverymen (-mĕn)], the keeper of a stable where horses are boarded or where horses and vehicles are hired out.

live stock domestic animals, as horses, cattle, sheep, or hogs, raised for market or for farm purposes (see illus.).

liv-id (lĭv′ĭd), *adj.* **1**, black and blue; discolored, as by a blow; **2**, ashy pale.

liv-ing (lĭv′ĭng), *p.adj.* **1**, having life; **2**, flowing, as a spring; **3**, vigorous; active; as, a *living* hope; **4**, producing life, action, or strength; as, *living* waters; **5**, true to life; as, a *living* image:—*n.* **1**, livelihood; also, mode of life; as, plain *living*; **2**, in England, a church appointment or office.

lix-iv-i-um (lĭk-sĭv′ĭ-ŭm), *n.* a solution resulting from draining water through a substance; esp., a solution of alkaline salts, as lye from wood ashes.

liz-ard (lĭz′ẽrd), *n.* any of various long, slender, usually scaly, reptiles, having four legs, each with five claw-bearing toes.

LIZARD (1/4)

lla-ma (lä′mȧ; *Span.* lyä′mä), *n.* a South American animal allied to the camel, but smaller and without a hump.

lla-no (lä′nō; *Span.* lyä′nō), *n.* [*pl.* llanos (-nōz; -nōs)], a broad, level, grassy plain, esp. in South America and Texas.

lo (lō), *interj.* behold! see! look! as, *lo!* the hero comes.

loach (lōch), *n.* a small, European, fresh-water fish of the carp family.

load (lōd), *v.t.* **1**, to put into or upon (a wagon, ship, animal, etc.) as much as can be carried; **2**, to put (the cargo) into or upon a vehicle, ship, etc.; **3**, to burden; weigh down; embarrass; **4**, to give to in great abundance; as, to *load* one with attentions; **5**, to put a cartridge into, as a gun; **6**, to weight fraudulently, as dice; adulterate, as silk:—*v.i.* **1**, to put the cartridge into a gun; **2**, to give or take on a load:—*n.* **1**, a burden; **2**, the mass or weight usually carried at one time; cargo; as, a *load* of coal; **3**, a mental burden; as, a *load* of care or suffering; **4**, the powder, bullet, etc., with which a gun is charged.—*n.* **load′er.**

Syn., n. pack, weight, encumbrance.

load-ed (lōd′ĕd), *p.adj.* **1**, laden; **2**, weighted, esp. fraudulently; as, *loaded* dice.

load-star (lōd′stär″), *n.* a guiding star; the polestar. See **lode′star″**, *Pfd. S.*

load-stone (lōd′stōn″), *n.* **1**, a magnetic oxide of iron; **2**, a natural magnet. Also, **lode′stone″.**

1**loaf** (lōf), *n.* [*pl.* loaves (lōvz)], **1**, a shaped mass of bread or cake; **2**, a shaped lump, as of sugar.

2**loaf** (lōf), *v.i.* to idle away time:—*v.t.* to pass (time) in idleness.—*n.* **loaf′er.**

loam (lōm), *n.* **1**, earth composed of clay and sand mixed; **2**, popularly, a rich soil of decayed vegetable matter, clay, and sand:—*v.t.* to cover with such soil.—*adj.* **loam′y.**

loan (lōn), *n.* **1**, a sum of money lent for a period, repayable with interest; **2**, something granted for temporary use:—*v.t.* and *v.i. Colloq.*, to lend.

loath (lōth), *adj.* unwilling; reluctant; as, I was *loath* to go. Also, **loth.**

Syn. indisposed, averse.—*Ant.* eager, desirous, willing, inclined.

loathe (lō*th*), *v.t.* [*p.t.* and *p.p.* loathed (lō*th*d), *p.pr.* loath′ing], to regard with extreme dislike or disgust; detest.

loath-ing (lō*th*′ĭng), *n.* disgust; nausea; aversion; abhorrence.

loath-some (lō*th*′sŭm), *adj.* causing disgust or abhorrence; detestable; as, a *loathsome* disease.—*adv.* **loath′some-ly.**—*n.* **loath′some-ness.**

Syn. revolting, disgusting, offensive, hateful.

loaves (lōvz), *n.* plural of *loaf;* as, five *loaves* of bread.

lo-bate (lō′bāt), *adj.* having rounded divisions or parts, as a leaf.

lob-by (lŏb′ĭ), *n.* [*pl.* lobbies (-ĭz)], **1**, a hall or waiting room; specif., that part of the assembly hall of a lawmaking body to which the public has access; **2**, in the U. S., persons who try to influence the votes of members of a lawmaking body:—*v.i.* [*p.t.* and *p.p.* -bied (-ĭd), *p.pr.* -by-ing], to try by personal influence to get the votes of members of a legislature or lawmaking body for a particular measure:—*v.t.* to try to get (a bill) passed by lobbying.—*n.* **lob′by-ist.**

lobe (lōb), *n.* any rounded projection or part, as of an organ or leaf; as, a *lobe* of the brain.—*adj.* **lobed.**

lo-be-li-a (lō-bē′lĭ-ȧ; lō-bēl′yȧ), *n.* any of a certain genus (*Lobelia*) of plants with beautiful red, blue, or white flowers of irregular shape.

lob-lol-ly (lŏb′lŏl″ĭ), *n.* [*pl.* loblollies (-ĭz)], a pine of the southern U. S.

lob-ster (lŏb′stẽr), *n.* **1**, any of various large, edible crustaceans, or shellfish, having a jointed tail, and two strong claws, or pincers (see *crustacean*, illus.); **2**, *Slang*, a cheap person.

lo-cal (lō′kăl), *adj.* **1**, pertaining to place; **2**, relating to, or characteristic of, a particular place; as, *local* customs: **local option**, a plan whereby the people of a district determine by vote whether some designated thing, as, formerly, the sale of alcoholic drinks, shall be allowed within that district:—*n. U. S. Colloq.*, **1**, a train stopping at small stations; an accommodation train; **2**, a branch of a labor union, consisting of members from one locality.—*adv.* **lo′cal-ly.**

lo-cal-ism (lō′kăl-ĭzm), *n.* **1**, a word, expression, or custom used in a particular region or place; **2**, attachment to a particular place.

lo-cal-i-ty (lō-kăl′ĭ-tĭ), *n.* [*pl.* localities (-tĭz)], **1**, a general region about a place; vicinity; **2**, restriction to a definite place.

Syn. neighborhood, district.

lo-cal-ize (lō′kăl-īz), *v.t.* [*p.t.* and *p.p.* -ized (-īzd), *p.pr.* -iz″ing], to limit to a particular place; as, quarantine attempts to *localize* disease.—*n.* **lo″cal-i-za′tion.**

lo-cate (lō′kāt), *v.t.* [*p.t.* and *p.p.* -cat-ed, *p.pr.* -cat-ing], **1**, to place in a particular spot; establish; **2**, to mark out and determine the position of, as a mining claim; **3**, to discover the position of; as, to *locate* the enemy:—*v.i. U. S. Colloq.*, to settle; take up one's residence.

lo-ca-tion (lō-kā′shŭn), *n.* **1**, the act of determining, settling, or finding; **2**, position or place; **3**, a piece of land marked out for a particular use; **4**, a site, outside a studio, on which a photoplay is filmed.

loc-a-tive (lŏk′ȧ-tĭv), *adj.* designating, or pertaining to, a case, esp. in Latin, denoting place where:—*n.* the locative case; also, a word in that case.

loch (lŏkh), *n. Scot.*, a lake; also, a bay or arm of the sea: in Ireland, usually *lough.*

1**lock** (lŏk), *n.* **1**, a tuft or small bunch, as of hair or silk; **2**, a ringlet of hair; **3**, in *pl.*, the hair.

2**lock** (lŏk), *n.* **1**, a device for fastening a door, trunk, safe, etc., so that it can be opened only by a special key or combina-

*Typical Judging Values**

4	Form	6
10	Quality	8
10	Action	4
1	Withers	0
3	Croup	4
1	Buttocks	2
2	Gaskins	3
4	Hocks	6

Driving Horse.—Tall; slender, sinewy legs, long from withers to knee and from hip to hock; narrow but deep chest; graceful neck; large windpipe.

Draft Horse.—Stocky; heavy; low-set; strong shoulders and hips; short, muscular legs; short neck, less erect than in driving horse; wide chest.

10	Weight	0
10	Form	5
12	Flesh	0
2	Neck	0
1	Ears	2
4	Shoulders	3
2	Forelegs	1
4	Chest	6
6	Ribs	3
8	Back	3
0	Udder, etc.	35

Beef Steer.—Body brick-shaped; bones well covered; flesh firm, smooth, and deep; neck and legs short, and legs wide apart.

Milk Cow.—Body pyramidal, with base at rear; hip bones prominent; tendency to gauntness; udder large; teats large and wide apart; veins on udder large.

6	Weight	6
10	Form	6
10	Quality	8
10	Condition	0
5	Shoulders	2
4	Chest	5
4	Ribs	3
6	Back	3
6	Loins	3
4	Rump	4
4	Thighs	3
5	Twist	3
12	Wool	40

Mutton Sheep.—Plump; flesh firm; low-built; wide back; well-spaced legs; long, coarse fleece.

Wool Sheep.—Thinner; wrinkled skin to provide large wool-growing surface; finer fleece.

10	Form	10
10	Quality	10
10	Flesh	6
8	Shoulders	6
4	Chest	5
8	Sides	8
9	Back	6
9	Loins	5
3	Belly	3
9	Hams	6

Lard Hog.—Chunky; fat; short, wide-spaced legs.

Bacon Hog.—Rangy; firm, lean flesh; long legs.

*On a score card the point values of all the characters listed usually total 100. Here are listed only the characters that emphasize the differences between the types contrasted.

Representative Types of Live Stock

tion of turns of a knob; **2**, an inclosure between gates in a canal or stream, used in raising or lowering boats from level to level; **3**, a mechanism for firing a gun; **4**, any of several holds in wrestling:—*v.t.* **1**, to fasten or secure with, or as with, a lock; **2**, to make firm by the linking or engaging of parts; **3**, to pass (a vessel) through a canal lock: **lock in** or **out**, to shut in or out of a given place by a lock: **lock up, 1**, to make secure with a lock, as a house; **2**, to confine, as a person:—*v.i.* **1**, to become fastened by a lock; as, the door *locks* from the inside; **2**, to become interlocked, as gears; **3**, to proceed by means of a canal lock.

lock-er (lŏk′ẽr), *n.* a drawer, closet, compartment, or chest secured by a lock; esp., a closet for individual use.

lock-et (lŏk′ĕt; lŏk′ĭt), *n.* a small gold or silver case, made to inclose a portrait or other small token, and to be worn on a necklace or chain.

lock-jaw (lŏk′jô″), *n.* a form of the disease tetanus, in which the lower jaw is drawn up and becomes fixed or locked.

lock-out (lŏk′out″), *n.* the refusal of an employer to continue to employ his labor force unless they accept his terms.

lock-smith (lŏk′smĭth″), *n.* a maker or repairer of locks.

lock step the step of men marching with exact rhythm in very close file.

lock stitch a sewing-machine stitch, made by the interlocking of two threads, which is not easily ripped.

lock-up (lŏk′ŭp″), *n.* a temporary prison for persons under arrest; a jail.

lo-co (lō′kō), *n.* [*pl.* locos (-kōz)], **1**, any of various poisonous American plants which cause a brain disease in animals: also called *loco weed;* **2,** the disease so caused:—*v.t.* **1,** to poison with loco; **2,** *Colloq.*, to make crazy.

lo-co-mo-tion (lō″kō-mō′shŭn), *n.* the act of moving, or the ability to move, from place to place.

lo-co-mo-tive (lō″kō-mō′tĭv), *adj.* **1,** pertaining to motion or travel from one place to another; **2,** pertaining to a machine that moves about under its own power; automotive:—*n.* an engine or motor for drawing railway cars (see illus. next page).

lo-co-mo-tor (lō″kō-mō′tŏr), *adj.* pertaining to motion from place to place: **locomotor ataxia** (*ȧ*-tăk′sĭ-*ȧ*), a disease of the nervous system, affecting muscular coördination, esp. in the legs.

lo-cus (lō′kŭs), *n.* [*pl.* loci (-sī)], **1,** a place; locality; **2,** in plane geometry, any line or surface containing all points which satisfy given conditions and only such points; as, a circumference is the *locus* of points in a plane equally distant from a given point.

lo-cust (lō′kŭst), *n.* **1,** any grasshopper; esp., any of certain migratory kinds of grasshopper destructive to vegetation; **2,** the cicada, or seventeen-year locust; **3,** any of several deciduous American trees; esp., the honey locust, or false acacia, with rough bark, thorny branches, and long pods.

lo-cu-tion (lō-kū′shŭn), *n.* a particular style of speech; phrase; idiom.

lode (lōd), *n.* **1,** any deposit of metallic ore containing gold, silver, etc., as in a vein or fissure; **2,** a fissure filled with ore.

lode-star (lōd′stär″), *n.* **1,** a guiding star; esp., the polestar, or North Star; **2,** hence, anything that strongly influences or attracts. Also, **load′star″.**

lode-stone (lōd′stōn″), *n.* **1,** a magnetic oxide of iron; **2,** a natural magnet. Also, **load′stone″**, *Pfd. S.*

lodge (lŏj), *v.t.* [*p.t.* and *p.p.* lodged (lŏjd), *p.pr.* lodg′ing], **1,** to furnish with a temporary dwelling; **2,** to deposit for safety; **3,** to settle, or bring to rest, in some spot; as, to *lodge* a stone on a ledge; **4,** to place before the proper authorities; as, to *lodge* information:—*v.i.* **1,** to live or reside for a time; have sleeping quarters; esp., to live in a rented room or rooms; **2,** to be deposited or fixed; as, seeds carried by the wind *lodge* in strange places; **3,** to fall down, as grain or trees beaten by a storm:—*n.* **1,** a small house; cottage; **2,** a steward's or gatekeeper's cottage on an estate; **3,** the den of a wild animal; **4,** the hut or wigwam of an American Indian; **5,** in some societies, the place where members of a local branch meet; also, the members collectively.

lodg-er (lŏj′ẽr), *n.* one who lives in a rented room or apartment in a house occupied by others.

lodg-ing (lŏj′ĭng), *n.* **1,** sleeping accommodation; as, board and *lodging;* **2,** temporary residence; **3,** in *pl.*, a room or rooms rented as living quarters.

lodg-ment (lŏj′mĕnt), *n.* **1,** the act of giving shelter, settling, or depositing; **2,** the state of being housed, settled, or deposited; **3,** a place in which to settle; as, the idea found *lodgment* in his brain; **4,** an accumulation or deposit of material, as of sand. Also, **lodge′ment.**

loft (lôft), *n.* **1,** a room directly beneath a roof; an attic; **2,** a floor or gallery raised above the main floor; as, an organ *loft* in a church; **3,** in the U. S., an upper floor in a warehouse; **4,** in golf: **a,** a slope on the face of a club to cause the ball to rise steeply when struck; **b,** a stroke made with such a club:—*v.t.* in golf, to strike (a ball) with a loft.

loft-y (lôf′tĭ), *adj.* [*comp.* loft′i-er, *superl.* loft′i-est], **1,** very high; **2,** dignified; proud; **3,** elevated in thought or language; as, *lofty* sentiments.—*adv.* **loft′i-ly.**—*n.* **loft′i-ness.**

Syn. noble, sublime, stately, majestic; haughty.—*Ant.* low, abject; humble, meek.

log (lŏg), *n.* **1,** a piece of timber in its natural state; **2,** a device for measuring the progress of a ship, consisting of a triangular piece of wood, the *log chip*, used as a float, attached to a line which is wound upon a reel; **3,** on shipboard, a log book (which see):—*v.t.* [*p.t.* and *p.p.* logged (lŏgd), *p.pr.* log′ging], **1,** to fell and cut into logs, as a tree; **2,** to fell and remove the timber on (a tract of woodland); **3,** to enter in the log book of a ship:—*v.i.* to cut or transport logs.

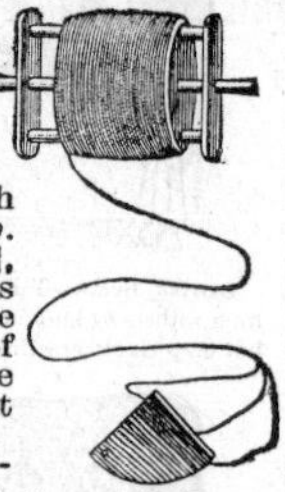

LOG: LOG LINE; LOG CHIP, AND LOG REEL

lo-gan-ber-ry (lō′găn-bĕr″ĭ), *n.* [*pl.* loganberries (-ĭz)], **1,** a plant obtained by crossing the red raspberry with a species of blackberry; **2,** the fruit of this plant.

log-a-rithm (lŏg′*ȧ*-rĭ*th*m; lŏg′*ȧ*-rĭthm), *n.* a figure representing the number of times a number called the *base* must be multiplied by itself to produce a given number; as, the *logarithm* of 1,000 to the base 10 is 3, since $10^3 = 1{,}000$.

log book a ship's diary, or journal, recording its progress, position, daily occurrences, and items of interest: also called *log.* Also, *n.* **log′book″.**

log-ger-head (lŏg′ẽr-hĕd″), *n.* **1,** a blockhead; numskull; **2,** a kind of large sea turtle: **to be at loggerheads,** to dispute or quarrel.

log-gia (lŏj′*ȧ*; lô′jĭ-*ȧ*; *It.* lôd′jä), *n.* [*pl.* loggias (lŏj′*ȧ*z; lô′jĭ-*ȧ*z); logge (lôd′jā)], a covered gallery or portico, with at least one side open to the air.

log-ic (lŏj′ĭk), *n.* **1,** the science or art of correct reasoning; also, a work on this science; **2,** accurate or sound reasoning.

log-i-cal (lŏj′ĭ-kăl), *adj.* **1,** pertaining to the science of reasoning; **2,** according to the rules of correct reasoning; **3,** reasonable; to be expected according to the laws of correct reasoning.—*adv.* **log′i-cal-ly.**

lo-gi-cian (lō-jĭsh′ăn), *n.* one skilled in the science of correct reasoning.

log-o-type (lŏg′ō-tīp), *n.* a single type containing two or more letters, or a syllable or word, as *fi, ffl.*

log-roll-ing (lŏg′rōl″ĭng), *n.* in politics, a combining to assist in furthering the schemes of one's associates in the expectation of receiving assistance in return.

log-wood (lŏg′wŏŏd″), *n.* the heartwood of a Central American tree, producing a deep red color much used in dyeing; also, the tree itself.

lo-gy (lō′gĭ), *adj.* [*comp.* lo′gi-er, *superl.* lo′gi-est], *U. S. Dial.*, heavy; lethargic.

Lo-hen-grin (lō′ĕn-grĭn), *n.* the hero of the German version of the legend of the knight of the swan, and of a music drama by Richard Wagner.

loin (loin), *n.* **1,** usually in *pl.*, that part of the body of an animal or man between the lowest rib and the hip bone; **2,** a special cut of meat from this part of an animal, as of beef or pork (see *beef*, illus.).

loi-ter (loi′tẽr), *v.t.* to spend idly, as time: with *away:*—*v.i.* to spend time idly; linger on the way; saunter.—*n.* **loi′ter-er.**

Lo-ki (lō′kē), *n.* in mythology, the Teutonic god of evil, inventor of constant trouble and mischief. Also, **Lo′ke.**

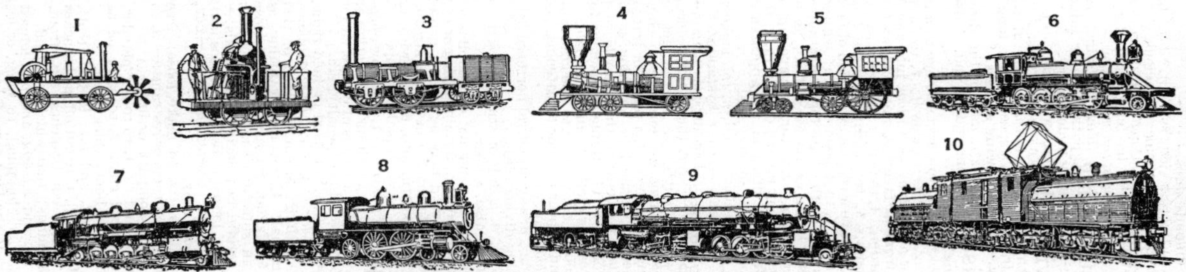

TYPES IN THE EVOLUTION OF THE AMERICAN LOCOMOTIVE

1, 1803: Oliver Evans's combination steam carriage and paddle-wheel boat; 2, 1831: Davis's "York"; 3, 1832: "Old Ironsides"; 4, 1842: locomotive with six drivers, the front four drivers connected in a flexible truck; 5, 1848: passenger locomotive; 6, 1876: consolidation type locomotive; 7, 1895: Atlantic type passenger locomotive; 8, 1893: Santa Fe type freight locomotive; 9, 1914: triplex freight locomotive, with twelve pairs of driving wheels: weight in working order, 850,000 pounds; 10, 1920: electric passenger locomotive.

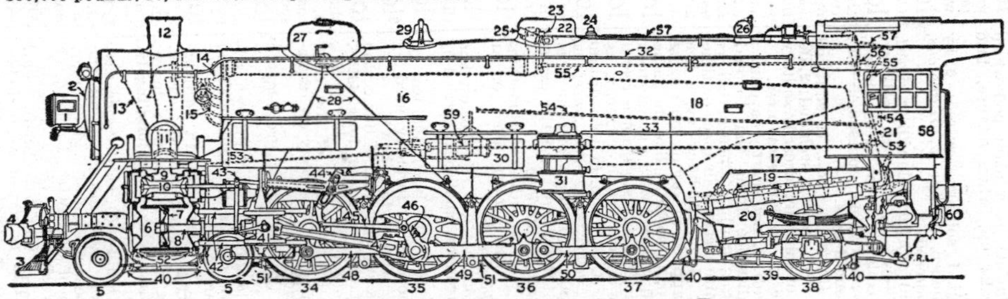

PARTS OF PASSENGER LOCOMOTIVE, MOUNTAIN TYPE

1, headlight; 2, smoke-box door; 3, pilot; 4, coupler; 5, truck wheels; 6, cylinders; 7, piston; 8, piston rod; 9, live-steam chamber; 10, steam-chest valve; 11, steam pipe; 12, smokestack; 13, smoke-box netting; 14, superheater; 15, superheater tubes; 16, boiler-tube space; 17, fire box; 18, combustion chamber; 19, grates; 20, ash pit; 21, fire door; 22, dome; 23, throttle valve; 24, safety valve; 25, whistle; 26, dynamo; 27, sand box; 28, sand pipes; 29, bell; 30, air drum; 31, air pump; 32, handrail; 33, running board; 34, front driving wheel; 35, main driving wheel; 36, intermediate driving wheel; 37, rear driving wheel; 38, rear truck wheel; 39, rear truck frame; 40, brake shoes; 41, crosshead; 42, crosshead guide bars; 43, combining lever in valve mechanism; 44, reversing link; 45, eccentric rod; 46, eccentric crank; 47, main connecting rod; 48, front driving rod; 49, main driving rod; 50, rear driving rod; 51, driver-brake beam; 52, cylinder cocks; 53, cylinder-cock operating rod; 54, power-reverse rod; 55, throttle lever; 56, water gauge; 57, whistle lever; 58, cab; 59, power-reverse cylinder; 60, tender coupling.

loll (lŏl), *v.i.* **1,** to lounge at ease; **2,** to hang out loosely, as the tongue:—*v.t.* **1,** to permit to hang out, as the tongue; **2,** to permit to rest lazily.

lol-li-pop (lŏl′ĭ-pŏp), *n.* a lump of hard candy on a stick. Also, **lol′ly-pop.**

Lom-bard (lŏm′bärd; lŭm′-), *n.* a member of a Teutonic tribe that invaded Italy and established the present Lombardy; also, a native of that region, or a descendant of the tribe.

lo-ment (lō′mĕnt), *n.* a plant pod which breaks up, when mature, into one-seeded cells.

lone (lōn), *adj.* **1,** solitary; retired; **2,** by itself; hence, lonely; **3,** *Humorous,* unmarried or widowed.

lone-ly (lōn′lĭ), *adj.* [*comp.* lone′li-er, *superl.* lone′li-est], **1,** deserted; solitary; without a companion; **2,** not often visited; **3,** depressed because alone; lonesome.—*adv.* **lone′li-ly.**—*n.* **lone′li-ness.**

lone-some (lōn′sŭm), *adj.* **1,** shut off from society; secluded; **2,** depressed because of solitude; drearily solitary. —*adv.* **lone′some-ly.**—*n.* **lone′some-ness.**

¹long (lông), *adj.* **1,** not short; covering a great distance from end to end; **2,** extended in time; not brief; hence, tedious; **3,** having a definite measure in space or time; as, a yard *long;* **4,** far-reaching; as, a *long* memory; **5,** as applied to any of the English vowels, *a, e, i, o, u,* sounded like its name; **6,** in finance, well supplied with a given stock, as a broker; also, holding stock for a rise in price:—*adv.* **1,** to a great length or extent; as, *long* drawn out; **2,** at, from, or to a distant time: with *after, before, hence, ago, since;* as, *long* before the war; **3,** during a long time; as, to wait *long;* **4,** throughout the entire extent or duration; as, all his life *long.*

²long (lông), *v.i.* to desire something eagerly: with *for* or *after,* or an infinitive; as, I *long* to go.

long-boat (lông′bōt″), *n.* the largest and strongest small boat carried by a merchant ship.

long bow a powerful bow, five feet or more long, formerly used by English archers. Also, *n.* **long′bow″.**

long cloth a superior kind of fine cotton fabric. Also, *n.* **long′cloth″.**

***lon-gé-ron** (lôn″zhā″rôn′; lŏn′jĕr-ŏn), [Fr.], *n.* one of the chief longitudinal members of the body of an airplane (see *airplane,* illus.).

lon-gev-i-ty (lŏn-jĕv′ĭ-tĭ), *n.* great length of life.

long-hand (lông′hănd″), *n.* ordinary handwriting, as distinguished from shorthand or typewriting.

long-head-ed (lông′=hĕd″ĕd), *adj.* farseeing; shrewd; clever.

long-ing (lông′ĭng), *n.* an earnest desire; craving; wish.—*adv.* **long′ing-ly.** *Syn.* aspiration. (See desire.)

lon-gi-tude (lŏn′jĭ-tūd), *n.* distance east or west measured by the angle between the meridian of a given point and the meridian of Greenwich, England, or the meridian of Washington, D. C.

lon-gi-tu-di-nal (lŏn″jĭ-tū′dĭ-năl), *adj.* **1,** pertaining to longitude or to length; **2,** running lengthwise.—*adv.* **lon″gi-tu′di-nal-ly.**

long-lived (lông′=lĭvd″), *adj.* **1,** lasting a long time; **2,** living to great age; as, elephants are *long-lived.*

long prim-er a size of type, nearly equivalent to 10 point, making 7.2 lines to an inch (see *type*).

long-shore-man (lông′shōr″măn), *n.* [*pl.* longshoremen (-mĕn)], one who works about wharves, esp. one who loads and unloads ships.

long-sight-ed (lông′=sīt″ĕd), *adj.* farseeing; sagacious.

long-stand-ing (lông′=stăn″dĭng), *adj.* having lasted for a long time; as, a *long-standing* grudge.

long-suf-fer-ing (lông′=sŭf′ĕr-ĭng), *adj.* patient under injury or offense:—*n.* patience under injury.

long-wind-ed (lông′=wĭn″dĕd), *adj.* **1,** speaking or writing at too great length; as, a *long-winded* speaker; **2,** tedious; long drawn out, as a speech.—*adv.* **long″-wind′ed-ly.**—*n.* **long″-wind′ed-ness.**

long-wise (lông′wīz″), *adv.* in the direction from end to end. Also, *Colloq.,* **long′ways″.**

look (lo͝ok), *v.i.* **1,** to direct the eye to anything, in order to view it; **2,** to direct the mind or attention; as, to *look* into a matter; **3,** to front or face; as, my windows *look* out on a garden; **4,** to expect: with *for;* as, to *look* for news; **5,** to appear; as, she *looks* happy; **6,** to have a certain expression of face; as, to *look* sad; **7,** to depend or turn: with *to;* as, citizens *look* to the state for protection:—*v.t.* **1,** to show by an expression of face; as, he *looked* his contempt; **2,** to turn the eyes upon; as, he *looked* the boy up and down:—*n.* **1,** the act of looking; **2,** often in *pl.,* appearance; **3,** expression of face:—*interj.* see!

look-er-on (lo͝ok″ĕr=ŏn′), *n.* [*pl.* lookers-on (-ĕrz=)], a bystander.

look-ing-glass (lo͝ok′ĭng=glȧs″), *n.* a mirror; that which reflects.

look-out (lo͝ok′out″), *n.* **1,** the act of watching for someone to come or something to happen; **2,** a place for watching; **3,** a person engaged in watching, as for fires; **4,** *Colloq.,* concern; as, that's my *lookout.*

¹loom (lo͞om), *n.* **1,** a frame or machine for weaving cloth; **2,** an oar handle.

²loom (lo͞om), *v.i.* to seem to rise gradually and appear huge or threatening; as, difficulties *loom* up.

¹loon (lo͞on), *n.* any of several northern fish-eating diving birds.

²loon (lo͞on), *n.* a dull or stupid person; a dunce; also, a boor.

loop (lo͞op), *n.* **1,** a folding or doubling of string, rope, etc., forming a ring or eye through which a cord may be run; a noose; **2,** a ring-shaped formation in a line, stream, road, etc.:—*v.t.* to form into, furnish with, or secure with, loops:—*v.i.* to make a loop.

loop-hole (lo͞op′hōl″), *n.* **1,** a narrow opening in a wall for observation or shooting through; **2,** a means of escape, as for evading a law, avoiding a penalty, etc.

loose (lo͞os), *adj.* **1,** not fixed or held tight; as, a *loose* tooth; *loose* ribbons; **2,** unbound, as hair; **3,** not confined or tied up, as an animal; **4,** not tightly fitting, as garments; **5,** vague; inexact; **6,** not close or compact in substance or texture, as soil; **7,** lax; not careful in principles or morals:—*v.t.* [*p.t.* and *p.p.* loosed (lo͞ost), *p.pr.* loos′ing], to set free; unbind; disengage; relax.—*adv.* **loose′ly.**—*n.* **loose′ness.**

loos-en (lo͞os′n), *v.t.* to make loose; free from tightness or restraint:—*v.i.* to become less tight, compact, or firm.

loot (lo͞ot), *v.t.* and *v.i.* **1,** to rob or plunder, as a captured city; **2,** to carry off as plunder; steal:—*n.* booty thus taken.

¹lop (lŏp), *v.t.* [*p.t.* and *p.p.* lopped (lŏpt), *p.pr.* lop′ping], **1,** to cut off, as branches from a tree; **2,** to cut branches, etc., from; trim:—*n.* trimmings; that which is cut off.

²lop (lŏp), *v.i.* and *v.t.* [*p.t.* and *p.p.* lopped (lŏpt), *p.pr.* lop′ping], to hang, or let hang, limply, as the long ears of a dog.

lope (lōp), *n.* a slow, easy, swinging gait, as of a horse:—*v.i.* [*p.t.* and *p.p.* loped (lōpt), *p.pr.* lop'ing], to move with such a gait.

lop-sid-ed (lŏp'sīd"ĕd), *n.* larger or heavier on one side than on the other; not symmetrical; poorly balanced.

lo-qua-cious (lō-kwā'shŭs), *adj.* talkative; chattering.—*adv.* **lo-qua'cious-ly.**—*n.* **lo-qua'cious-ness.**

lo-quac-i-ty (lō-kwăs'ĭ-tĭ), *n.* talkativeness; loquaciousness.

lord (lôrd), *n.* **1,** a ruler or governor; master; one who has supreme power; **2,** the owner of a manor; **3,** in Great Britain, a nobleman or one entitled by courtesy to be called *Lord:* **Lord,** in Great Britain, a title of honor given to noblemen, to certain officials, and to bishops and archbishops: **the Lord,** God: also, Jesus Christ:—*v.i.* to rule with absolute power: with *over:* **lord it,** to act as if possessed of absolute power.

lord-ling (lôrd'lĭng), *n.* a little or insignificant person of high rank.

lord-ly (lôrd'lĭ), *adj.* [*comp.* lord'li-er, *superl.* lord'li-est], **1,** suited to, or like, one of high rank; noble; **2,** proud; haughty.—*n.* **lord'li-ness.**

lord-ship (lôrd'shĭp), *n.* **1,** authority; control; **2,** the territory under the power of a lord; **3,** the rank of a lord; hence, a title or term of address for persons entitled to be called *Lord:* preceded by *his* or *your.*

Lord's Prayer the form of prayer given by Jesus to his disciples (Matthew 6:9–13).

Lord's Sup-per the sacrament held in memory of the last supper partaken of by Jesus before his crucifixion: also called *Communion; Eucharist.*

¹lore (lōr), *n.* knowledge; esp., the body of traditions and facts about a subject.

²lore (lōr), *n.* the space between the eye and bill of a bird.

Lo-re-lei (lō'rĕ-lī"; lŏr'ĕ-), *n.* in German folklore, a siren of the Rhine who lured sailors to destruction by her singing.

lor-gnette (lôr"nyĕt'), *n.* **1,** a long-handled opera glass; **2,** a pair of eyeglasses fixed to a handle.

lorn (lôrn), *adj.* forsaken; forlorn; desolate; lone.

lor-ry (lŏr'ĭ; lŭr'ĭ), *n.* [*pl.* lorries (-ĭz)], **1,** a long, four-wheeled wagon without sides; **2,** a miner's small cart with a drop bottom; **3,** in the army, a large, low autotruck.

lose (lo͞oz), *v.t.* [*p.t.* and *p.p.* lost (lôst), *p.pr.* los'ing], **1,** to be deprived of, or cease to have in possession; mislay; **2,** to wander from; as, to *lose* one's way; **3,** to waste; miss; as, to *lose* an opportunity; **4,** to fail to keep; as, to *lose* one's health; **5,** to fail to win; as, to *lose* a battle; **6,** to cause to be lost; as, illness *lost* him his job:—*v.i.* **1,** to experience loss; **2,** to fail of success; esp., to be defeated.—*n.* **los'er.**

loss (lôs), *n.* **1,** the state or fact of being lost or destroyed; as, the *loss* of a ship; also, usually in *pl.*, that which is lost; **2,** failure in the getting or keeping (of a job, a victory, a contract, a purse, a privilege, etc.); **3,** waste; as, a *loss* of gasoline; **4,** in business, the excess of expenses over receipts; **5,** in mechanics, energy or power wasted, as in friction; **6,** in *pl.*, the number of soldiers killed, wounded, or captured in battle.

Syn. disadvantage, damage, defeat, injury.

lost (lôst), *p.adj.* **1,** missing; parted with; **2,** not won; **3,** ruined; destroyed; hence, wasted; **4,** preoccupied; perplexed; as, *lost* in thought; **5,** not knowing where one is or how to proceed; as, *lost* in the woods; **6,** indifferent; insensible; as, *lost* to shame.

Lot (lŏt), *n.* in the Bible, Abraham's nephew, whose wife was turned into a pillar of salt because she looked back in her flight from Sodom (Genesis 19:26).

lot (lŏt), *n.* **1,** fortune; fate; as, the *lot* of man; **2,** a share; **3,** a method of deciding questions by drawing numbers, blocks, dice, etc.; as, to choose by *lot;* also, one of the objects so drawn; **4,** a portion or parcel; esp., a plot of land; **5,** *Colloq.*, a number of objects in a group; hence, often in *pl.*, a great quantity:—*v.t.* [*p.t.* and *p.p.* lot'ted, *p.pr.* lot'ting], **1,** to separate into lots; **2,** to assign.

loth (lōth), *adj.* reluctant; unwilling. Also, **loath,** *Pfd. S.*

Lo-tha-ri-o (lō-thā'rĭ-ō), *n.* [*pl.* Lotharios (-ōz)], a gay deceiver; esp., a deceiver of women: so called from a character in Rowe's play, "The Fair Penitent."

lo-tion (lō'shŭn), *n.* a medicated liquid for bathing the skin or an injury.

lot-ter-y (lŏt'ĕr-ĭ), *n.* [*pl.* lotteries (-ĭz)], a scheme for selling numbered tickets and giving a prize to the person holding a number drawn by lot; hence, any scheme whose outcome is a matter of chance.

lot-to (lŏt'ō), *n.* a parlor game played with 24 cards marked with numbered squares, and wooden disks numbered 1 to 100.

lo-tus (lō'tŭs), *n.* **1,** a plant of the water-lily family, esp. the sacred lotus of the ancient Nile; **2,** any of various trees and shrubs whose fruit was fabled to cause forgetfulness of care and create a state of dreamy indolence; **3,** any of a genus (*Lotus*) of plants of the pea family, with purple, yellow, or white flowers: **lotus–eater,** one who idles away his time in forgetful dreaming. Also, **lo'tos.**

loud (loud), *adj.* **1,** full, emphatic, or striking in sound; noisy; not subdued; **2,** *Colloq.*, showy in dress or manner; also, vivid or unpleasantly intense; as, *loud* color. —*adv.* **loud'ly.**—*n.* **loud'ness.**

Syn. clamorous, boisterous, turbulent, blusterous.—*Ant.* low, soft, noiseless.

loud–speak-er (loud'=spēk'ĕr), *n.* in radio, a telephone receiver with a horn or other sounding device by which vibrations as received may be reproduced as loud sounds.

lough (lŏkh), *n.* in Ireland, a lake; also, a bay: in Scotland, *loch.*

lounge (lounj), *v.i.* [*p.t.* and *p.p.* lounged (lounjd), *p.pr.* loung'ing], **1,** to move or act in a lazy manner; loll; **2,** to live lazily; loaf:—*n.* **1,** the act of lolling; a lazy motion or gait; **2,** a soft, low-backed couch with arms or a raised end (see *furniture,* illus.); **3,** a comfortable and informal parlor or waiting room in a hotel, club, etc.—*n.* **loung'er.**

lour (lour), *v.i.* **1,** to appear dark or threatening; **2,** to look angry:—*n.* a scowl. Also, **low'er,** *Pfd. S.*—*adj.* **lour'ing.**

louse (lous), *n.* [*pl.* lice (līs)], a small, flat, wingless insect living and feeding on the bodies of animals or men.

lous-y (louz'ĭ), *adj.* [*comp.* lous'i-er, *superl.* lous'i-est], **1,** infested with lice; **2,** mean; foul.

lout (lout), *n.* an awkward fellow; a clown; bumpkin.—*adj.* **lout'ish.**—*adv.* **lout'ish-ly.**—*n.* **lout'ish-ness.**

love (lŭv), *n.* **1,** a strong feeling of affection; fond and tender attachment; **2,** passionate devotion to one of the opposite sex; **3,** strong liking; as, *love* for music; **4,** the state of feeling kindly toward others and of desiring the welfare of all; as, in *love* and charity for all men; **5,** a sweetheart; **6,** in tennis scoring, zero:—*v.t.* [*p.t.* and *p.p.* loved (lŭvd), *p.pr.* lov'ing], **1,** to regard with strong affection; **2,** to delight in; as, to *love* dancing:—*v.i.* to be in love; have strong affection.—*adj.* **love'less.**—*adj.* **lov'a-ble.**—*n.* **lov'a-ble-ness.**—*adv.* **lov'a-bly.**

love bird any of several small parrots, which show especially marked affection for their mates.

love-lorn (lŭv'lôrn''), *adj.* deserted by, or longing for, one's love.

love-ly (lŭv'lĭ), *adj.* [*comp.* love'li-er, *superl.* love'li-est], **1**, causing affection or admiration; amiable; beautiful; **2**, *Colloq.*, inviting; delightful.—*n.* **love'li-ness.**

lov-er (lŭv'ẽr), *n.* **1**, one who loves; esp., a man who is in love; **2**, one deeply attached to anything; as, a *lover* of art; **3**, in *pl.*, a couple in love with each other.

lov-ing (lŭv'ĭng), *p.adj.* **1**, devoted; affectionate; **2**, expressing love: **loving cup**, a large ornamental drinking cup, having two or more handles by which it may be passed around.—*adv.* **lov'ing-ly.**

¹low (lō), *adj.* **1**, not high in elevation; **2**, below the normal level; as, *low* tide; *low* prices; **3**, deep in pitch; subdued, as sounds; **4**, near the horizon; as, the sun is *low;* **5**, lacking bodily or mental vigor; **6**, relatively small in amount, value, etc.; **7**, humble; **8**, unfavorable; as, a *low* opinion; **9**, vulgar: —*adv.* **1**, not on high; **2**, deeply; **3**, softly; quietly; **4**, at a small price; **5**, in humbleness, poverty, or disgrace.—*n.* **low'ness.**

Syn., *adj.* ignoble, commonplace, abject. —*Ant.*, *adj.* superior, noble.

²low (lō), *n.* the moo or soft call of cattle: —*v.i.* to call softly; moo, as cattle.

low-boy (lō'boi''), *n.* a chest of drawers usually of table height with two long drawers: distinguished from *highboy*, which is higher and has more drawers.

low-bred (lō'brĕd''), *adj.* **1**, born of humble or degraded parents; **2**, vulgar.

Low Church a party in the Anglican Church which is opposed to extreme ritual, form, and ceremony.

¹low-er (lō'ẽr), *v.t.* **1**, to lessen or bring down; reduce in price or value; **2**, to weaken; **3**, to let down; let fall by its own weight; **4**, to humble:—*v.i.* to become less high; sink; fall.

²low-er (lou'ẽr), *v.i.* **1**, to appear dark, gloomy, or threatening; **2**, to look angry; scowl:—*n.* a frown. Also, **lour.**

low-er case **1**, the lower part of a printer's type case, containing the small letters; **2**, letters which are not capitals.—*abbr.* **l. c.**—*adj.* and *v.t.* **low'er-case''.**

low-er-ing (lou'ẽr-ĭng), *p.adj.* overcast with clouds; threatening a storm; gloomy.—*adv.* **low'er-ing-ly.**

low-er-most (lō'ẽr-mōst), *adj.* lowest: opp. of *uppermost.*

low-ing (lō'ĭng), *n.* the mooing or soft calling of cattle:—*adj.* mooing.

low-land (lō'lănd), *adj.* pertaining to a low or level country:—*n.*, often in *pl.*, a low, level country.

low–lived (lō'=lĭvd''), *adj.* ill-bred; base in character and habits.

low-ly (lō'lĭ), *adj.* [*comp.* low'li-er, *superl.* low'li-est], **1**, low in rank or size; humble; modest; **2**, low in situation or development:—*adv.* **1**, modestly; **2**, in a low manner or position.—*n.* **low'li-ness.**

Low Mass Mass said without music, and by one priest.

low–necked (lō'=nĕkt''), *adj.* cut low at the top, as a dress.

low–spir-it-ed (lō'=spĭr'ĭt-ĕd), *adj.* depressed; downhearted.

loy-al (loi'ăl), *adj.* **1**, faithful, esp. to one's ruler or country; **2**, true to friend, promise, or duty; **3**, pertaining to, or showing, faithfulness.—*adv.* **loy'al-ly.**

loy-al-ist (loi'ăl-ist), *n.* one who supports the authority of his ruler or country, esp. in time of revolt.

loy-al-ty (loi'ăl-tĭ), *n.* [*pl.* loyalties (-tĭz)], faithfulness to country, friend, promise, duty, etc.; constancy; devotion.

Syn. fidelity, allegiance, trust.—*Ant.* disloyalty, perfidy, faithlessness.

loz-enge (lŏz'ĕnj; lŏz'ĭnj), *n.* **1**, a diamond-shaped figure with four equal sides (see *quadrilateral*, illus.); **2**, a sweetmeat; also, a cough drop.

lub-ber (lŭb'ẽr), *n.* **1**, an awkward, clumsy fellow; **2**, a raw or untrained sailor.—*adj.* and *adv.* **lub'ber-ly.**

lu-bri-cant (lū'brĭ-kănt), *n.* a substance for making anything smooth or slippery, as oil:—*adj.* making slippery.

lub-ri-cate (lū'brĭ-kāt), *v.t.* [*p.t.* and *p.p.* -cat''ed, *p.pr.* -cat''ing], **1**, to make smooth or slippery; **2**, to apply oil or grease to in order to reduce friction, as in gears.—*n.* **lu''bri-ca'tion.**

lu-bri-ca-tor (lū'brĭ-kā''tẽr), *n.* one who or that which makes slippery; esp., a device for oiling machinery.

lu-bric-i-ty (lū-brĭs'ĭ-tĭ), *n.* [*pl.* lubricities (-tĭz)], smoothness; slipperiness; hence, instability.

lu-cent (lū'sĕnt), *adj.* shining; bright; resplendent; clear.

lu-cern (lū-sûrn'), *n.* a plant of the pea family, with cloverlike leaves and flowers; alfalfa. Also, **lu-cerne'.**

lu-cid (lū'sĭd), *adj.* **1**, clear; readily understood; intelligible; as, a *lucid* explanation; **2**, pertaining to mental soundness or clarity; as, a *lucid* interval; **3**, shining; transparent; crystalline; as, a *lucid* stream of water.—*adv.* **lu'cid-ly.**—*n.* **lu'cid-ness.**

lu-cid-i-ty (lū-sĭd'ĭ-tĭ), *n.* the state or quality of being clear or intelligible; as, *lucidity* of thought.

lu-ci-fer (lū'sĭ-fẽr), *n.* a friction match: **Lucifer, 1**, Venus, when it appears as the morning star; **2**, Satan.

luck (lŭk), *n.* **1**, chance; fortune, either good or bad; **2**, good fortune; success.

luck-less (lŭk'lĕs), *adj.* unlucky; unfortunate; unfavorable.—*adv.* **luck'less-ly.**—*n.* **luck'less-ness.**

luck-y (lŭk'ĭ), *adj.* [*comp.* luck'i-er, *superl.* luck'i-est], **1**, having good fortune; **2**, successful; of good omen; **3**, producing good by chance.—*adv.* **luck'i-ly.**—*n.* **luck'i-ness.**

Syn. fortunate, favored, auspicious, successful. *Lucky* and *fortunate* are applied to those things that happen through favorable chance rather than the effort of those who benefit thereby. *Fortunate* is used of important or serious affairs; *lucky* is an everyday word. Both describe the timely, the unaccountable, the unexpected advantage; as, to have a *lucky* shot, day, escape; our meeting certain influential people was *fortunate;* the outcome of the enterprise was *fortunate.*—*Ant.* unfortunate, unlucky.

lu-cra-tive (lū'kră-tĭv), *adj.* profitable; producing wealth; as, he is engaged in a *lucrative* business.—*adv.* **lu'cra-tive-ly.**—*n.* **lu'cra-tive-ness.**

lu-cre (lū'kẽr; lōō'-), *n.* money; profits: used in an unfavorable sense.

lu-cu-brate (lū'kū-brāt), *v.i.* [*p.t.* and *p.p.* -brat''ed, *p.pr.* -brat''ing], **1**, to do mental work by artificial light; **2**, hence, to study or write laboriously.

lu-cu-bra-tion (lū''kū-brā'shŭn), *n.* close study; also, something produced by such study.

lu-di-crous (lū'dĭ-krŭs), *adj.* causing mirth; comical; droll.—*adv.* **lu'di-crous-ly.**—*n.* **lu'di-crous-ness.**

Syn. laughable, ridiculous, droll, absurd. That is *ludicrous* which is comical because of its exaggeration, inappropriateness, or absurdity. That is *laughable* which excites laughter or merriment, as a funny story. That is *ridiculous* which deserves to be made fun of. The *ludicrous* and the *ridiculous* both arouse scornful laughter, but the *ludicrous* excites a derisive, the *ridiculous* a contemptuous, mirth. The contrast between what we are and what we think we are is often *ludicrous;* the airs and affectations of conceited people make them *ridiculous.*—*Ant.* grave, serious, sensible.

luff (lŭf), *n.* **1**, the forward edge of a fore-and-aft sail; **2**, the broadest part of a ship's bow; **3**, the act of sailing closer to the wind:—*v.i.* to steer or sail nearer the wind.

¹lug (lŭg), *v.t.* [*p.t.* and *p.p.* lugged (lŭgd), *p.pr.* lug′ging], **1**, to pull or carry with effort; **2**, hence, to introduce, as a subject of conversation, in a forced manner: followed by *in:*—*v.i.* to move heavily or slowly; drag:—*n.* **1**, the act or effort of pulling or dragging along; **2**, in *pl.*, *Slang*, self-importance; airs.

²lug (lŭg), *n.* **1**, *Eng. Dial.* and *Scot.*, the ear; **2**, hence, any projection like an ear, esp. a handle or support; as, the *lug* of a kettle.

³lug (lŭg), *n.* a four-cornered sail on a slanting spar, or yard: also called *lugsail.*

lug-gage (lŭg′ĕj), *n.* a traveler's personal baggage: used chiefly in England.

lug-ger (lŭg′ẽr), *n.* a small vessel having two or three masts rigged with lugsails, or four-sided sails, fastened to spars hung obliquely to the masts.

lug-sail (lŭg′sāl″), *n.* a four-sided sail held out by a long spar or yard, which is slung obliquely to the mast.

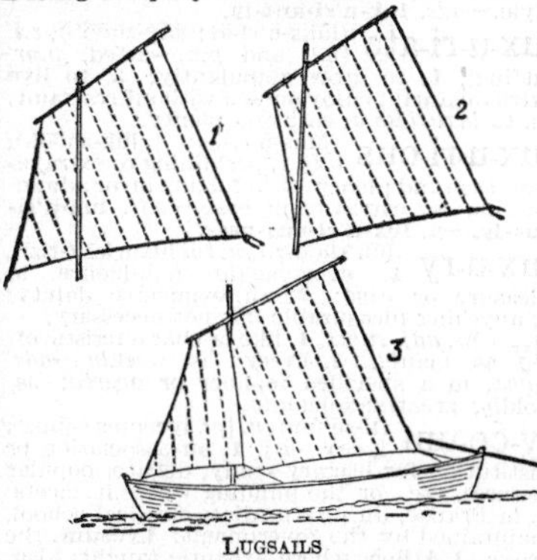

LUGSAILS
1, dipping lugsail; **2**, standing lugsail; **3**, split lugsail.

lu-gu-bri-ous (lū-gū′brĭ-ŭs), *adj.* mournful; sad; doleful; as, a *lugubrious* tone of voice.—*adv.* **lu-gu′bri-ous-ly.**—*n.* **lu-gu′bri-ous-ness.**

Luke (lūk), *n.* **1**, in the Bible, an early Christian disciple, a physician and a companion of the apostle Paul; **2**, the third book of the New Testament, containing Luke's account of Jesus.

luke-warm (lūk′wôrm″), *adj.* **1**, moderately warm; tepid; as, *lukewarm* tea; **2**, indifferent; as, *lukewarm* interest.—*adv.* **luke′warm″ly.**—*n.* **luke′warm″ness.**

lull (lŭl), *v.t.* to soothe to sleep; quiet:—*v.i.* to become calm:—*n.* a lessening of noise or violence; a calm lasting for a short time.

lull-a-by (lŭl′ȧ-bī″), *n.* [*pl.* lullabies (-bīz″)], a cradle song; a soothing refrain.

lum-ba-go (lŭm-bā′gō), *n.* rheumatism of the muscles of the lumbar region, or lower part of the back.

lum-bar (lŭm′bȧr), *adj.* pertaining to the loins, or lower part of the back; as, the *lumbar* vertebræ.

¹lum-ber (lŭm′bẽr), *n.* **1**, rubbish; **2**, forest timber sawed into boards:—*v.t.* **1**, to fill with rubbish; as, to *lumber* a room; **2**, to heap together in disorder:—*v.i.* in the U. S. and Canada, to cut down timber and prepare it for market.—*n.* **¹lum′ber-ing.**

²lum-ber (lŭm′bẽr), *v.i.* **1**, to move clumsily; **2**, to roll heavily along; rumble.—*n.* **lum′ber-er.**—*p.adj.* **²lum′ber-ing.**

lum-ber-man (lŭm′bẽr-măn), *n.* [*pl.* lumbermen (-mĕn)], a man engaged in cutting, or dealing in, forest timber.

lu-mi-na-ry (lū′mĭ-nȧ-rĭ), *n.* [*pl.* luminaries (-rĭz)], **1**, a body that gives light, esp. a heavenly body, as the sun; **2**, one who is a source of intellectual or spiritual light.

lu-mi-nif-er-ous (lū″mĭ-nĭf′ẽr-ŭs), *adj.* giving forth or carrying light; as, *luminiferous* ether.

lu-mi-nos-i-ty (lū″mĭ-nŏs′ĭ-tĭ), *n.* [*pl.* luminosities (-tĭz)], the quality of being bright or shining; also, a luminous or shining object.

lu-mi-nous (lū′mĭ-nŭs), *adj.* **1**, giving forth, or spreading, light; bright; as, *luminous* stars; *luminous* paint; **2**, clear; easily understood; intelligent; enlightening; as, a *luminous* statement.—*adv.* **lu′mi-nous-ly.**—*n.* **lu′mi-nous-ness.**

Syn. radiant, lustrous. (See bright.)

lump (lŭmp), *n.* **1**, a small, shapeless mass; as, a *lump* of clay; **2**, a swelling; **3**, a collection or lot taken as a whole; as, a *lump* of money; **4**, *Colloq.*, a stupid or slow-moving person: **lump sum,** a sum of several amounts not itemized; also, a sum of money paid at one time, rather than by instalments:—*v.t.* **1**, to unite in one body or amount; as, to *lump* expenses; **2**, to treat collectively; **3**, *Colloq.*, to put up with as best one can; as, if you don't like it, you can *lump* it:—*v.i.* to form into a mass or small masses; as, the paste *lumps.*

lump-ish (lŭmp′ĭsh), *adj.* gross; heavy; stupid; lethargic.—*adv.* **lump′ish-ly.**—*n.* **lump′ish-ness.**

lump-y (lŭm′pĭ), *adj.* [*comp.* lump′i-er, *superl.* lump′i-est], **1**, full of lumps; as, *lumpy* bread; **2**, choppy; as, a *lumpy* sea.

Lu-na (lū′nȧ), *n.* in mythology, the goddess of the moon and of the months.

lu-na-cy (lū′nȧ-sĭ), *n.* [*pl.* lunacies (-sĭz)], **1**, mental unsoundness; insanity; **2**, extreme foolishness.

lu-nar (lū′nȧr), *adj.* **1**, pertaining to the moon; **2**, resembling the moon; pale or crescent-shaped; **3**, *Obs.*, silver: **lunar caustic,** silver nitrate prepared for use in cauterizing, or burning, the skin. **lunar month,** the interval from one new moon to the next, approximately 29½ days: **lunar year,** a year of twelve lunar months, or about 355 days.

lu-nate (lū′nāt), *adj.* crescent-shaped; as, a *lunate* leaf. Also, **lu′nat-ed.**

lu-na-tic (lū′nȧ-tĭk), *adj.* **1**, affected with, or characteristic of, insanity; as, *lunatic* notions; **2**, pertaining to the insane; as, a *lunatic* asylum:—*n.* one who is insane.

lu-na-tion (lū-nā′shŭn), *n.* the period of time from one new moon to the next; a lunar month.

lunch (lŭnch), *n. Colloq.*, **1**, a light repast taken between meals; luncheon; also, any light meal, except breakfast; **2**, the food for such a meal:—*v.i.* to eat a lunch.

lunch-eon (lŭn′chŭn), *n.* **1**, food taken between meals; **2**, a light meal, esp. at noon; lunch; **3**, a midday meal served to guests.

lu-nette (lū-nĕt′), *n.* **1**, any of various objects suggesting a crescent or half-moon, as, in architecture, a semicircular window in a dome, the upper section of a wall at the end of a corridor with an arched or vaulted roof, or a picture painted in such a section; **2**, a corner or projecting section, shaped thus: jutting out from the main line of a rampart or defensive embankment; **3**, in *pl.*, spectacles.

lung (lŭng), *n.* in air-breathing vertebrates, one of two organs of breathing, in which the blood gives up water and carbon dioxide and receives oxygen.

lunge (lŭnj), *n.* **1**, a sudden thrust or pass with a fencing foil or with a sword; **2**, a sudden lurch; a leap forward:—*v.i.* [*p.t.* and *p.p.* lunged (lŭnjd), *p.pr.* lung'ing], **1**, to make a sudden thrust or pass in, or as in, fencing; **2**, to plunge forward.

lu-nu-la (lū'nū-lȧ), *n.* [*pl.* lunulæ (-lē)], anything crescent-shaped, as the white part of the finger nail near the base. Also, **lu'nule** (lū'nūl).—*adj.* **lu'nu-lar.**

¹lu-pine (lū'pīn), *adj.* like a wolf; fierce and eager to devour.

²lu-pine (lū'pĭn), *n.* **1**, a garden plant of the pea family with blue, pink, or white flowers; **2**, in *pl.*, its edible seeds.

¹lurch (lûrch), *n.* a sudden roll to one side, as of a ship; a swaying, staggering motion:—*v.i.* to roll or stagger suddenly.

²lurch (lûrch), *n.* **1**, in cribbage, the position of a loser who has pegged less than half the winning score; **2**, hence, a difficult or forlorn position: obsolete except in *left in the lurch.*

lurch-er (lûr'chẽr), *n.* **1**, one who lurks about; a spy; **2**, a petty thief; **3**, a crossbred dog noted for keenness of scent and sight, used esp. by poachers.

lure (lūr), *n.* **1**, anything used as a means of attracting by promising profit or pleasure; **2**, artificial bait; **3**, a device resembling a bird used by a falconer to recall the hawk:—*v.t.* [*p.t.* and *p.p.* lured (lūrd), *p.pr.* lur'ing], to attract by anything that promises profit or pleasure.

Syn., *v.* decoy, entice, tempt, seduce, coax.

lu-rid (lū'rĭd), *adj.* **1**, grayish yellow; wan; ghastly; pale; **2**, resembling flames seen through smoke; **3**, shockingly vivid, as a story.—*adv.* **lu'rid-ly.**—*n.* **lu'rid-ness.**

lurk (lûrk), *v.i.* **1**, to lie in wait; lie concealed or unnoticed; **2**, to move in a sneaking manner.

lus-cious (lŭsh'ŭs), *adj.* **1**, excessively sweet; **2**, delightful to the taste or sense.—*adv.* **lus'cious-ly.**—*n.* **lus'cious-ness.**

lush (lŭsh), *adj.* **1**, juicy; **2**, rich in growth or vegetation; as, *lush* meadows.

lust (lŭst), *n.* **1**, strong desire to possess and enjoy, usually in a bad sense; as, a *lust* for gold; **2**, sinful and impure desire:—*v.i.* **1**, to desire something strongly; **2**, to have impure desires: with *after.*—*adj.* **lust'ful.**

¹lus-ter (lŭs'tẽr), *n.* **1**, the quality of shining by reflected light; gloss; **2**, brightness; **3**, fame; glory; **4**, a chandelier ornamented with cut-glass pendants; **5**, a kind of cloth with a sheen; **6**, the reflecting power of the surface of a mineral as measured by the quality and brilliancy of the light reflected from it: **luster ware**, a kind of pottery with a metallic finish. Also, **lus'tre.**—*adj.* **lus'ter-less.**

lus-tral (lŭs'trăl), *adj.* pertaining to purification; as, *lustral* water.

lus-tra-tion (lŭs-trā'shŭn), *n.* a ceremony of purification.

lus-trous (lŭs'trŭs), *adj.* **1**, having a sheen or brightness; **2**, illustrious.

lus-trum (lŭs'trŭm), *n.* [*pl.* lustrums (-trŭmz); lustra (-trȧ)], **1**, a purification; **2**, the ceremonies of purification observed in ancient Rome every five years; **3**, a period of five years. Also, **²lus'ter.**

lust-y (lŭs'tĭ), *adj.* [*comp.* lust'i-er, *superl.* lust'i-est], robust; healthy; as, a *lusty* infant.—*adv.* **lust'i-ly.**—*n.* **lust'i-ness.**

¹lute (lūt), *n.* formerly, a stringed musical instrument with mandolin-shaped body and neck bent back at a sharp angle:—*v.t.* and *v.i.* [*p.t.* and *p.p.* lut'ed, *p.pr.* lut'ing], to play on the lute.

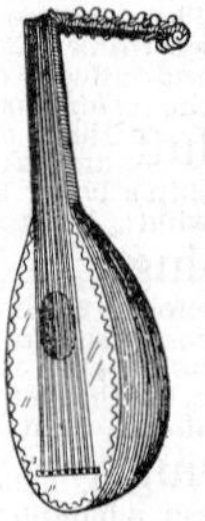

LUTE

²lute (lūt), *n.* a composition of clay, used for making joints tight, as in vessels, or for protecting them from the action of fire:—*v.t.* [*p.t.* and *p.p.* lut'ed, *p.pr.* lut'ing], to close up the cracks of with such a composition, as a vessel or retort.

Lu-ther-an (lū'thẽr-ăn), *adj.* **1**, pertaining to Martin Luther (1483–1546), the German reformer; **2**, designating, or pertaining to, the church founded by Luther:—*n.* a member of the Lutheran Church.—*n.* **Lu'ther-an-ism.**

lux (lŭks), *n.* [*pl.* lux; luxes (lŭk'sĕz)], in physics, a practical unit for the measurement of illuminating power.

lux-u-ri-ance (lŭks-ū'rĭ-ăns; lŭg-zhoo͞'-), *n.* abundant, vigorous growth. Also, **lux-u'ri-an-cy.**

lux-u-ri-ant (lŭks-ū'rĭ-ănt; lŭg-zhoo͞'-), *adj.* **1**, abundant and vigorous in growth, as plants, hair, etc.; **2**, fertile, as soil; **3**, profuse or elaborate, as a literary style.—*adv.* **lux-u'ri-ant-ly.**

lux-u-ri-ate (lŭks-ū'rĭ-āt; lŭg-zhoo͞'-), *v.i.* [*p.t.* and *p.p.* -at"ed, *p.pr.* -at"ing], **1**, to grow abundantly; **2**, to live extravagantly; enjoy oneself without restraint; as, to *luxuriate* in ease and plenty.

lux-u-ri-ous (lŭks-ū'rĭ-ŭs; lŭg-zhoo͞'-), *adj.* **1**, pertaining to extravagant ease and plenty; **2**, indulging in, or administering to, extravagant ease.—*adv.* **lux-u'ri-ous-ly.**—*n.* **lux-u'ri-ous-ness.**

lux-u-ry (lŭk'shoo͝-rĭ), *n.* [*pl.* luxuries (-rĭz)], **1**, extravagant indulgence in pleasure or ease; **2**, an expensive dainty; **3**, anything pleasurable but not necessary.

-ly (-lĭ), *adj. suffix*, **1**, like or characteristic of as, man*ly;* **2**, every; as, week*ly:*—*adv suffix*, in a specified manner or degree; as, bold*ly;* great*ly;* solemn*ly.*

ly-ce-um (lī-sē'ŭm), *n.* [*pl.* lyceums (-ŭmz); lycea (-ȧ)], **1**, an association or institution for literary study, debate, popular lectures, etc., or the building where it meets; **2**, in France, an intermediate classical school, maintained by the government: **Lyceum**, the grove at Athens where Aristotle taught; also, the school of philosophy which he founded.

lydd-ite (lĭd'īt), *n.* a powerful explosive for shells, chiefly picric acid.

Lyd-i-an (lĭd'ĭ-ăn), *adj.* **1**, pertaining to Lydia, an ancient province of Asia Minor, famed for its culture and wealth; **2**, hence, soft; effeminate; voluptuous.

lye (lī), *n.* an alkaline solution obtained by leaching, or dripping water through wood ashes; also, any strongly alkaline substance: sold commercially as white crystals or a white powder, usually caustic soda or caustic potash, and used in solution in washing, making soap, cleaning drain pipes, etc.

ly-ing (lī'ĭng), present participle and verbal noun from ¹*lie* or ²*lie.*

ly-ing-in (lī'ĭng-ĭn'), *n.* the period or state of confinement at childbirth.

lymph (lĭmf), *n.* a transparent, yellowish fluid in animal bodies, contained in certain vessels called *lymphatics*, and resembling diluted blood without the red corpuscles.

lym-phat-ic (lĭm-făt′ĭk), *adj.* **1**, pertaining to lymph; **2**, sluggish; phlegmatic:—*n.* one of the tiny tubes or vessels which carry lymph.

lynch (lĭnch), *v.t.* to kill or execute without legal trial, esp. through the agency of a mob: **lynch law**, punishment by private individuals without the usual legal formalities, as by a mob.—*n.* **lynch′er.**

lynx (lĭngks), *n.* any of a genus (*Lynx*) of large, fierce wild cats with short tail, tufted ears, and valuable fur.

lynx–eyed (lĭngks′=īd″), *adj.* keen-sighted; alert; watchful.

lyre (līr), *n.* a kind of harplike musical instrument, fabled to have been invented by Apollo or Hermes, and used by the ancients to accompany the voice: **Lyre** or **Lyra** (lī′rȧ), a small northern constellation containing the very brilliant star Vega.

lyre bird an Australian bird whose tail, when spread, suggests a lyre.

lyr-ic (lĭr′ĭk), *adj.* designating, or pertaining to, a poem with a songlike rhythm, and expressive of personal sentiment or emotion:—*n.* **1**, a lyric poem; **2**, in ancient Greece, a song or ode accompanied by the lyre; **3**, in music: **a**, a song of a character similar to that of a lyric poem; **b**, in a musical comedy, the words of any of the songs. Also, *adj.* **lyr′i-cal.**—*adv.* **lyr′i-cal-ly.**

lyr-ist (lĭr′ĭst; līr′ĭst), *n.* **1**, one who plays a lyre; **2**, a composer of lyrics, or poems that express the emotions.

M

ma (mä), *n.* contraction of *mamma:* a childish, often vulgar, form.

ma'am (mäm; măm), *n.* a colloquial contraction of *madam:* usually in direct address of inferiors to superiors.

Mac- (măk-), *prefix*, son of: used in Scotch or Irish names: often written *Mc* or *M′*.

mac-ad-am (măk-ăd′ăm), *n.* **1**, a pavement of crushed stone; **2**, crushed stone used for such a pavement.

mac-ad-am-ize (măk-ăd′ăm-īz), *v.t.* [*p.t.* and *p.p.* -ized (-īzd), *p.pr.* -iz″ing], to build or finish (a road) by covering with a compact layer of small broken stone, so as to form a smooth, hard, rounded surface.—*n.* **mac-ad″am-i-za′tion.**

mac-a-ro-ni (măk″ȧ-rō′nĭ), *n.* [*pl.* macaronis; macaronies (-nĭz)], **1**, a food consisting of long, thin tubes made of a paste composed chiefly of fine wheat flour; **2**, a dandy or dude of the 18th century.

mac-a-ron-ic (măk″ȧ-rŏn′ĭk), *adj.* designating, or pertaining to, a kind of writing in which words from several languages are used with humorous effect; as, *macaronic* verses; hence, confused; mixed.

mac-a-roon (măk″ȧ-rōōn′), *n.* a small cake made of flour, white of egg, crushed almonds, and sugar.

ma-caw (mȧ-kô′), *n.* a large and gaily colored parrot with a strong, hooked bill and a long tail.

Mac-beth (măk-bĕth′), *n.* king of Scotland (?-1057): hero of a tragedy of the same name by Shakespeare.

Mac-ca-be-an (măk″ȧ-bē′ăn), *adj.* of or pertaining to the Maccabees, a noted Jewish family, esp. to Judas Maccabeus, a hero in the struggle for Jewish independence in the second century B. C.

[1]**mace** (mās), *n.* **1**, a large and heavy staff of metal or topped with metal, often spiked, formerly used as a war club; **2**, a staff carried by or before an official as a symbol of authority; **3**, the person who bears such a staff.

[2]**mace** (mās), *n.* an aromatic spice consisting of the outermost of the two coverings of the nutmeg, usually ground.

Mac-e-do-ni-an (măs″ē-dō′nĭ-ăn), *adj.* pertaining to Macedonia, a district of northern Greece, a dominant nation under Alexander the Great:—*n.* a native or inhabitant of Macedonia.

mac-er-ate (măs′ẽr-āt), *v.t.* [*p.t.* and *p.p.* -at″ed, *p.pr.* -at″ing], **1**, to soften or separate the parts of by soaking in a fluid, as food in digestion; **2**, to cause to grow thin and weak.—*n.* **mac″er-a′tion.**

ma-che-te (mä-chā′tā), *n.* a large, heavy knife used in Cuba and South America for cutting sugar cane, brush, etc.

Mach-i-a-vel-li-an (măk″ĭ-ȧ-vĕl′ĭ-ăn; măk″ĭ-ȧ-vĕl′yăn), *adj.* pertaining to Machiavelli, the Florentine statesman, or to his principles of political deceit; hence, crafty; double-dealing.—*n.* **Mach″i-a-vel′li-an-ism; Mach″i-a-vel′lism.**

ma-chic-o-la-tion (mȧ-chĭk″ō-lā′shŭn; măch″ĭ-kō-lā′shŭn), *n.* **1**, an opening in a parapet through which missiles can be shot or hurled down upon an enemy; **2**, a parapet with such openings.

mach-i-nate (măk′ĭ-nāt), *v.t.* and *v.i.* [*p.t.* and *p.p.* -nat″ed, *p.pr.* -nat″ing], to plan, contrive, or plot, usually with evil intent.—*n.* **mach′i-na″tor.**

mach-i-na-tion (măk″ĭ-nā′shŭn), *n.* a hostile plot; a scheme to do evil; as, the *machinations* of traitors.

ma-chine (mȧ-shēn′), *n.* **1**, any contrivance to produce, increase, or regulate power or motion so as to do work; an engine; **2**, a light carriage or vehicle; **3**, an automobile; **4**, one who acts without purpose or at the bidding of another; **5**, a body of persons acting together for a common purpose; **6**, a political organization which controls the policies and activities of a party:—*v.t.* [*p.t.* and *p.p.* -chined′ (-shēnd′), *p.pr.* -chin′ing], to cut or make by a machine.

ma-chine gun a small, portable cannon capable of firing continuously and very rapidly a large number of bullets, usually operated by mechanism.

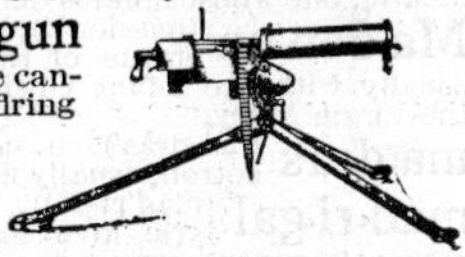

MACHINE GUN

ma-chin-er-y (mȧ-shēn′ẽr-ĭ), *n.* **1**, engines and other appliances collectively, or the parts of them; **2**, any means or combination by which something is kept in action or the result desired is obtained; as, the *machinery* of a political campaign.

ma-chin-ist (mȧ-shēn′ĭst), *n.* one who makes, repairs, or attends to, engines and other appliances, or is skilled in their design and principles.

mack-er-el (măk′ẽr-ĕl), *n.* [*pl.* mackerel], an edible fish, from twelve to eighteen inches in length, found in schools in the North Atlantic: **mackerel sky**, a sky covered with a mass of white flecks of cloud: so called from its resemblance to the marking of the fish, and thought to be a sign of storm.

mack-in-tosh (măk′ĭn-tŏsh), *n.* a waterproof overcoat.

mac-ro- (măk′rō-), a combining form from the Greek, meaning large, long; as, *macro*cosm: opp. of *micro-*.

mac-ro-cosm (măk′rō-kŏzm), *n.* the universe; the world at large, exterior to man: used in contrast to *microcosm*, or man.—*adj.* **mac″ro-cos′mic.**

ma-cron (mā′krŏn; măk′rŏn), *n.* a mark [¯] over a vowel to show that it is long in quantity, as in c*ā*me.

mad (măd), *adj.* [*comp.* mad′der, *superl.* mad′dest], **1,** mentally disordered or distracted; insane; **2,** rashly foolish; senseless; as, a *mad* undertaking; **3,** furious with rage or terror; **4,** rabid; as, a *mad* dog; **5,** *Colloq.*, greatly excited; as, *mad* with joy.—*adv.* **mad′ly.**—*n.* **mad′ness.**

Syn. crazy, delirious, violent, frantic, rash, infatuated.—*Ant.* sane, rational, reasonable.

mad-am (măd′ăm), *n.* [*pl.* mesdames (mā″dȧm′)], a complimentary title, or form of courteous address, to a lady.

***ma-dame** (mȧ″dȧm′; mȧ-dăm′; often, măd′ăm), [Fr.], *n.* [*pl.* mesdames (mā″dȧm′)], the French title for a married lady.—*abbr.* **Mme.** [*pl.* Mmes.].

mad-cap (măd′kăp″), *n.* a wild, thoughtless, or rattle-brained person:—*adj.* given to wild follies; recklessly adventurous; as, a *madcap* horseman.

mad-den (măd′n), *v.t.* and *v.i.* to make, or become, crazed or furious.

mad-der (măd′ẽr), *n.* **1,** a plant from the root of which a red dye is extracted; **2,** the dyestuff or pigment orig. made from this root: now made synthetically.

mad-ding (măd′ĭng), *adj.* raging; furious; wild; raving.

made (mād), past tense and past participle of *make:*—*p.adj.* **1,** artificially produced or formed; **2,** *Colloq.*, assured of success.

Ma-dei-ra (mȧ-dē′rȧ; mȧ-dā′rȧ), *n.* wine made on the island of Madeira.

***ma-de-moi-selle** (mȧd″mwȧ″zĕl′; măd″ẽ-mŏ-zĕl′; *Colloq.* mȧm″zĕl′), [Fr.], *n.* [*pl.* mesdemoiselles (mād″mwȧ″zĕl′)], Miss: a title of courtesy given by the French to an unmarried lady.—*abbr.* **Mlle.** [*pl.* Mlles.].

made-up (măd′=ŭp″), *adj.* not true; invented; artificial.

mad-man (măd′măn), *n.* [*pl.* madmen (-mĕn)], an insane man; a lunatic; one whose mind is deranged.

Ma-don-na (mȧ-dŏn′ȧ), *n.* **1,** a picture or statue of the Virgin Mary, usually with the infant Christ; **2,** in Italy, the Virgin Mary.

ma-dras (mȧ-drȧs′), *n.* a fabric of fine cotton, usually figured or corded.

mad-ri-gal (măd′rĭ-găl), *n.* **1,** a light, lyric love song; a pastoral poem; **2,** a part song unaccompanied by a musical instrument.

ma-du-ro (mȧ-do͞o′rō), *adj.* of full strength and color: said of cigars.

Mæ-ce-nas (mē-sē′năs), *n.* a patron, esp. of art and literature: from the name of the patron of Horace and Vergil.

Mael-strom (māl′strŏm), *n.* a celebrated whirlpool on the Norwegian coast: **maelstrom,** any destructive, irresistible, or widespread and harmful influence; as, the *maelstrom* of war.

mæ-nad (mē′năd), *n.* [*pl.* mænads (-nădz); mænades (mĕn′ȧ-dēz)], **1,** a nymph or bacchante attendant upon Dionysus, the Greek god of wine; **2,** any frantic woman.

ma-fi-a (mä′fē-ä), *n.* a Sicilian and Italian secret society, given to acts of lawlessness and violence. Also, **maf′fi-a.**

mag-a-zine (măg″ȧ-zēn′), *n.* **1,** a warehouse; **2,** a place for storing military supplies, as ammunition, etc.; **3,** the cartridge chamber of a gun; **4,** a literary or scientific publication, containing various articles, stories, etc., and issued at stated times.

mag-da-len (măg′dȧ-lĕn), *n.* a woman reformed from an evil and sinful life: from Mary Magdalen, said to be the repentant sinner forgiven by Christ (Luke 7:36–50). Also, **mag′da-lene.**

ma-gen-ta (mȧ-jĕn′tȧ), *n.* a red dye derived from coal tar; also, its peculiar shade of purplish red.

mag-got (măg′ŏt), *n.* **1,** the larva of an insect, such as the house fly, in its wormlike stage of development; esp., such a worm living in decaying flesh, food, etc.; a grub; **2,** a caprice; whim.—*adj.* **mag′got-y.**

Ma-gi (mā′jī), *n.pl.* [*sing.* Magus (mā′gŭs)], among the ancient Persians, the priestly and learned class; specif., the wise men of the East (Matthew 2:1–12).—*n.* and *adj.* **Ma′gi-an.**

mag-ic (măj′ĭk), *n.* **1,** the pretended art of exercising power over the hidden forces of nature or of working by the assistance of supernatural beings; sorcery; witchcraft; enchantment; **2,** sleight of hand; **3,** any hidden or secret power; as, the *magic* of beauty:—*adj.* **1,** pertaining to, produced by, or exercising, more than human power; **2,** having seemingly supernatural effect; **3,** enchanting: **magic lantern,** an optical instrument for throwing on a screen, in a darkened room, illuminated pictures enlarged by an arrangement of lenses; a stereopticon. Also, *adj.* **mag′i-cal.**—*adv.* **mag′i-cal-ly.**

Syn., *n.* witchery, charm.

ma-gi-cian (mȧ-jĭsh′ăn), *n.* **1,** one skilled in the pretended art of putting into action the power of spirits; a conjurer; sorcerer; **2,** one adept in sleight of hand.

mag-is-te-ri-al (măj″ĭs-tē′rĭ-ăl), *adj.* **1,** pertaining to, or suitable to, a master or magistrate; **2,** hence, commanding; having an air of authority; dictatorial; as, a *magisterial* air or tone.—*adv.* **mag″is-te′ri-al-ly.**—*n.* **mag″is-te′ri-al-ness.**

Syn. august, dignified, majestic, pompous.

mag-is-tra-cy (măj′ĭs-trȧ-sĭ), *n.* [*pl.* magistracies (-sĭz)], **1,** the office or dignity of a civil officer with public authority, or of a justice of the peace; **2,** civil officers, such as justices of the peace, collectively; **3,** the district of a magistrate.

mag-is-trate (măj′ĭs-trāt), *n.* a civil officer who has public authority; a local justice; as, a justice of the peace is a *magistrate.*—*adj.* **mag′is-tral.**

Mag-na Char-ta (măg′nȧ kär′tȧ), [Lat.], the Great Charter, forming the basis of English civil liberty, forced from King John of England by the barons at Runnymede, June 15, 1215. Also, **Mag′na Car′ta.**

mag-na-nim-i-ty (măg″nȧ-nĭm′ĭ-tĭ), *n.* [*pl.* magnanimities (-tĭz)], greatness of mind or soul; nobility; as, to forgive an enemy is an act of *magnanimity.*

mag-nan-i-mous (măg-năn′ĭ-mŭs), *adj.* great of mind; elevated in soul or feeling; generous; courageous; heroic.—*adv.* **mag-nan′i-mous-ly.**

Syn. unselfish, altruistic, lofty, benevolent, munificent, liberal.

mag-nate (măg′nāt), *n.* **1,** a person of rank or distinction; **2,** a man influential in a certain field of work or industry; as, a steel *magnate.*

mag-ne-si-a (măg-nē′zhĭ-ȧ; -zhȧ; măg-nē′shĭ-ȧ; -shȧ), *n.* a white, tasteless, earthy powder, used as a medicine.

mag-ne-si-um (măg-nē′zhĭ-ŭm; măg-nē′shĭ-ŭm), *n.* a silver-white metallic substance that burns with a brilliant light: used in alloys that combine strength with lightness, as in airplane construction, and in flash-light photography.

mag-net (măg′nĕt), *n.* **1**, the loadstone, a variety of ore having the property of attracting iron; also, a steel bar to which the power to attract iron has been artificially given; **2**, a person or thing that attracts.

mag-net-ic (măg-nĕt′ĭk), *adj.* **1**, pertaining to, exhibiting, or produced by, the magnet, or its power of attraction; **2**, hence, having the power to attract; as, a *magnetic* personality; **3**, pertaining to animal magnetism, or mesmerism: **magnetic needle,** a slim bar of steel, charged with the forces of attraction, which, swinging in a compass, indicates the earth's force of attraction, and hence, approximately, the north-and-south line.—*adv.* **mag-net′i-cal-ly.**

mag-net-ism (măg′nĕt-ĭzm), *n.* **1**, that property possessed by various bodies, as iron or steel, of attracting or repelling each other according to certain physical laws; **2**, the force to which this attraction is due; **3**, the science that treats of the laws of physical attraction and repulsion; **4**, personal attraction or charm: **animal magnetism,** mesmerism.

mag-net-ize (măg′nĕt-īz), *v.t.* [*p.t.* and *p.p.* -ized (-īzd), *p.pr.* -iz″ing], **1**, to give force of attraction to; to make a magnet of; **2**, to attract by personal influence; charm; **3**, to hypnotize; mesmerize. —*adj.* **mag′net-iz″a-ble.**—*n.* **mag″net-i-za′-tion.**—*n.* **mag′net-iz″er.**

mag-ne-to (măg-nē′tō; măg′nĕt-ō), *n.* [*pl.* magnetos (-tōz; -ōz)], a dynamo which generates the current for the ignition in certain internal-combustion engines, and which receives its driving force from the operation of the engine itself.

HIGH-TENSION MAGNETO

mag-net-o-e-lec-tric (măg′-nĕt-ō-ē-lĕk′trĭk; măg-nē′-tō-), *adj.* characterized by, or pertaining to, electricity developed by magnets. Also, **mag′net-o-e-lec′tri-cal.**

Mag-nif-i-cat (măg-nĭf′ĭ-kăt), *n.* the song of thanksgiving of the Virgin Mary at the Annunciation (Luke 1:46–55): used as a chant.

mag-nif-i-cence (măg-nĭf′ĭ-sĕns), *n.* grandeur of appearance; splendor; pomp; majesty.

mag-nif-i-cent (măg-nĭf′ĭ-sĕnt), *adj.* **1**, grand in appearance; splendid; pompous; sublime; **2**, noble; as, a *magnificent* idea.—*adv.* **mag-nif′i-cent-ly.**

mag-ni-fy (măg′nĭ-fī), *v.t.* [*p.t.* and *p.p.* -fied (-fīd), *p.pr.* -fy″ing], **1**, to make great or greater; cause to appear enlarged, as by a microscope; **2**, to exaggerate; as, to *magnify* one's importance:—*v.i.* to make greater the apparent size of an object by a lens.—*n.* **mag″ni-fi-ca′tion.**—*n.* **mag′ni-fi″er.**

mag-nil-o-quent (măg-nĭl′ō-kwĕnt), *adj.* pompous in style or speech; boastful; bombastic.—*adv.* **mag-nil′o-quent-ly.**—*n.* **mag-nil′o-quence.**

mag-ni-tude (măg′nĭ-tūd), *n.* **1**, comparative size or bulk; extent of dimensions (length, breadth, and thickness); **2**, greatness of size or importance; grandeur; **3**, in astronomy, the degree of brightness of a star.

Syn. mass, vastness, immensity.

mag-no-li-a (măg-nō′lĭ-ȧ), *n.* any of a genus (*Magnolia*) of ornamental trees, having aromatic bark, lustrous leaves, and large, fragrant flowers.

mag-pie (măg′pī), *n.* **1**, a chattering bird of the jay family; **2**, hence, one who talks continuously; a chatterer.

mag-uey (măg′wā; *Span.* mä-gā′ē), *n.* any of several species of agave yielding a fiber; esp., the century plant, or American aloe.

Mag-yar (mŏd′yŏr), *n.* **1**, one of the ruling race in Hungary; **2**, the language of that race:—*adj.* relating to that race or to its language.

ma-ha-ra-ja (mȧ-hä-rä′jȧ), *n.* a great prince among the Hindus. Also, **ma-ha-ra′jah.**

Mah-dist (mä′dĭst), *n.* among the Mohammedans, a follower of the Mahdi, or claimant for the position of leader of the faithful.—*n.* **Mah′dism.**

mahl-stick (mäl′stĭk″; môl′stĭk″), *n.* a stick used by painters as a rest to steady the hand while at work. Also, **maul′stick″**, *Pfd. S.*

ma-hog-a-ny (mȧ-hŏg′ȧ-nĭ), *n.* [*pl.* mahoganies (-nĭz)], a tree of tropical America yielding a beautiful, dark, reddish brown, hard wood, used for furniture; also, the wood: often imitated by staining cheaper woods a dark, reddish brown color.

Ma-hom-et-an (mȧ-hŏm′ĕt-ăn), *n.* a follower of Mahomet, or Mohammed, the founder of the religion that accepts Mohammed as the true prophet of God:—*adj.* of or pertaining to Mohammed, or the religion founded by him. Also, **Ma-hom′ed-an.** See **Mo-ham′med-an**, *Pfd. S.*

ma-hout (mȧ-hout′), *n.* in the East Indies, an elephant driver or keeper.

maid (mād), *n.* **1**, an unmarried girl or woman; a virgin; **2**, a female servant; domestic: **maid of honor, 1**, a noble lady, unmarried, who attends a queen; **2**, an unmarried young woman who acts as the bride's chief attendant at a wedding.

maid-en (mād′n), *n.* an unmarried girl or woman; a virgin:—*adj.* **1**, pertaining to, or like, a virgin; unmarried; as, a *maiden* lady; **2**, pure; unsoiled; as, *maiden* innocence; **3**, unused; untried; as, a *maiden* sword; **4**, earliest or first; as, a *maiden* trip.

maid-en-hair (mād′n-hâr″), *n.* a beautiful, delicate fern found in damp and shady woods.

maid-en-hood (mād′n-hŏŏd), *n.* **1**, the state of being a young, unmarried girl; **2**, virginity.

maid-en-ly (mād′n-lĭ), *adj.* like, or suitable to, a young girl; modest; gentle:—*adv.* in a manner suitable to a young girl; modestly.—*n.* **maid′en-li-ness.**

maid-serv-ant (mād′sûr″vănt), *n.* a woman servant.

¹mail (māl), *n.* **1**, defensive body armor of steel rings, net, or scales; hence, loosely, plate or other armor; **2**, the shell-like protective coat of some animals, as the turtle:—*v.t.* to clothe or cover with, or as with, armor.

²mail (māl), *n.* **1**, in the U. S., the letters and other matter, collectively, delivered by post; **2**, the government system for conveying letters, packages, etc.; **3**, the bag or bags for carrying letters, etc., sent by post; **4**, something that carries letters, etc., as a vehicle, boat, or person; **5**, *Obs.* or *Scot.*, a bag for use in traveling:—*v.t.* to post, or send by post; as, to *mail* a letter.

mail-a-ble (māl′ȧ-bl), *adj.* capable of being sent by post.

mailed (māld), *p.adj.* clad in, or covered by, armor.

maim (mām), *v.t.* to deprive of the use of a limb; cripple or disfigure:—*n.* an injury to the body by crippling or disfiguring: also called *mayhem.*

main (mān), *adj.* **1,** chief; principal; **2,** sheer; as, by *main* strength; **3,** leading; direct; **4,** connected with the mainmast of a ship; as, the *main* yard:—*n.* **1,** the ocean; **2,** strength; as, with might and *main;* **3,** the essential point; as, in the *main;* **4,** a principal conduit or pipe; as, a water *main.*

Syn., adj. first. (See chief.)

main-land (măn′lănd), *n.* a continent; a broad expanse of land, generally principal land as opposed to *island.*

main-ly (mān′lĭ), *adv.* principally; chiefly; for the most part.

main-mast (mān′mȧst), *n.* the chief mast of a ship (see *rigging,* illus.).

main-sail (mān′sāl″; mān′sl), *n.* the principal sail on the mainmast of a vessel (see *rigging,* illus.).

main-sheet (mān′shēt″), *n.* one of the ropes by which the mainsail is extended and fastened.

main-spring (mān′sprĭng″), *n.* **1,** the principal spring, or driving spring, in a mechanism, as a trigger or watch (see *trigger,* illus.); **2,** a chief motive or reason.

main-stay (mān′stā″), *n.* **1,** any of the large, strong ropes extending from the foot of the foremast to the platform about the head of the mainmast; **2,** hence, the principal dependence; chief support; as, the *mainstay* of the family.

main-tain (mān-tān′; mĕn-tān′), *v.t.* **1,** to support or bear the expense of; sustain, as a family; **2,** to keep possession of; as, to *maintain* one's hold; **3,** to affirm and defend by argument, as a claim; **4,** to continue in or with; keep up, as a war.—*adj.* **main-tain′a-ble.**—*n.* **main-tain′er.**

Syn. claim, allege, uphold. (See assert.)

main-te-nance (mān′tē-năns), *n.* **1,** the act of sustaining or defending; support; **2,** means of sustenance.

main-top (mān′tŏp″), *n.* a platform at the top of the mainmast.

main top-mast the next mast above the mainmast.

main top-gal-lant the mast, sail, or yard above the main topmast (see *rigging,* illus.).

main yard the spar on which the mainsail is extended.

maize (māz), *n.* Indian corn; field corn; also, the grain produced.

ma-jes-tic (mȧ-jĕs′tĭk), *adj.* having great dignity of person or appearance; stately; noble; sublime; regal. Also, **ma-jes′ti-cal.**—*adv.* **ma-jes′ti-cal-ly.**

Syn. royal, splendid, magnificent.

maj-es-ty (măj′ĕs-tĭ), *n.* [*pl.* majesties (-tĭz)], sovereignty; grandeur; nobility; sublimity: **Majesty,** a title given to a sovereign ruler; as, Your *Majesty.*

ma-jol-i-ca (mȧ-jŏl′ĭ-kȧ; mȧ-yŏl′ĭ-kȧ), *n.* a kind of decorative, glazed pottery with a richly adorned enameled surface. Also, **ma-iol′i-ca.**

ma-jor (mā′jẽr), *adj.* **1,** greater in number, extent, dignity, importance, or quality; as, the *major* part of a man's day is used for work; Isaiah was one of the *major* prophets; **2,** in music, greater by a half step than the minor; as, a *major* interval; also, characterized by major intervals; as, a *major* scale: —*n.* **1,** a military officer next in rank above a captain; **2,** in the U. S., a student's most important subject: **major general,** a military officer next in rank below a lieutenant general.

ma-jor-do-mo (mā″jẽr-dō′mō), *n.* [*pl.* major-domos (-mōz)], the chief steward of a great household.

ma-jor-i-ty (mȧ-jŏr′ĭ-tĭ), *n.* [*pl.* majorities (-tĭz)], **1,** the state of being greater; **2,** more than half of a total; the greater of two numbers making up a whole, or the greatest of several such numbers if it is more than half the whole; also, the difference between this number and the next smaller; **3,** the full legal age of 21 years; **4,** the office or rank of a major.

Syn. plurality. In U. S. politics, a candidate has a *majority* of votes if he receives more than half the votes cast, a *plurality* if he receives more votes than any other candidate, but still not more than half. *Majority* and *plurality* are measured by the difference between the votes for the leading candidate and those for his nearest rival. Thus if 10 votes are cast, divided 6, 3, 1, the winner has a *majority* of 3; if they are divided 4, 3, 3, the winner has a *plurality* of 1.

make (māk), *v.t.* [*p.t.* and *p.p.* made (mād), *p.pr.* mak′ing], **1,** to create; fashion; compose; frame; produce; bring about; **2,** to prepare for use; as, to *make* a garden; **3,** to obtain for oneself, as friends; **4,** to form, as plans; **5,** to compute to be; as, I *make* the amount fifty dollars; **6,** to amount to; as, three feet *make* a yard; **7,** to get; as, to *make* a fortune; also, to clear; net; as, to *make* five dollars; **8,** to raise to rank or dignity; as, his venture will *make* or break him; **9,** to score; as, we *made* ten points in the game; **10,** to arrive at, near, or in sight of; as, to *make* port; **11,** to become; as, a good son *makes* a good husband; **12,** to cause to be or become; as, to *make* him president; **13,** to cause to act in a certain manner; as, to *make* a child obey; **14,** to believe to be; as, he is not so clever as you *make* him; **15,** to perform; as, to *make* a gesture; carry on, as war; **16,** in electricity, to complete or close (a circuit): **make believe,** to pretend; sham; feign: **make out, 1,** to discern; perceive; **2,** to decipher; comprehend; **3,** to prove or represent; **4,** to fill out: **make up, 1,** to constitute; comprise; **2,** to form; name the members of (a committee); **3,** to bring together (a given sum); as, we *made up* our quota; **4,** to complete; **5,** to invent; fabricate, as a story; **6,** to finish (work not performed on time); **7,** to atone for; **8,** to reconcile (differences); **9,** to prepare the appearance, esp. the features, of (a person), as, for a stage rôle: **make up one's mind,** to decide; determine:—*v.i.* **1,** to tend or move; as, he *made* toward the goal; **2,** to have effect; as, the power that *makes* for righteousness; **3,** to put something into a specified condition; as, to *make* ready for a journey; **4,** to act in a specified manner; as, to *make* merry; **5,** to appear; increase, as ice; accumulate, as snow: **make up, 1,** to atone: with *for;* **2,** to become reconciled; **3,** to prepare or disguise one's appearance, as for stage impersonation; **4,** to approach; move forward:—*n.* **1,** shape; style; build; **2,** amount of output; **3,** brand; method or act of manufacture; as, this car is of a better *make* than mine; **4,** the completion of an electric circuit: **make and break,** in electricity, an automatic device for closing and opening a circuit: **make-and-break,** *adj.,* designating a spark made by breaking a circuit.

make-be-lieve (māk′=bē-lēv″), *n.* a pretense or sham, as a child's game of pretending something fancied is real:—*adj.* pretended; fictitious; false.

mak-er (māk′ẽr), *n.* **1,** one that fashions, composes, or produces; **2,** one who signs a promissory note: **Maker,** the Creator.

make-shift (māk′shĭft″), *n.* that which can be used for a time for lack of something better:—*adj.* capable of being used for a time; serving as a temporary tool, convenience, etc.; as, a *makeshift* bed.

make-up (māk′-ŭp″), *n.* **1**, the way in which the parts of anything are put together; **2**, the dress, paint, powder, etc., which an actor puts on for a part on the stage; **3**, the arrangement of type, articles, headlines, etc., in newspapers or printed matter.

mal- (măl-), *prefix,* meaning ill, bad, wrong; as, *mal*treat. Also, **mal′e-**.

Mal-a-chi (măl′ȧ-kī), *n.* **1**, an ancient Hebrew prophet; **2**, a book of the Old Testament believed to have been written by him. Also, in the Douay Bible, **Mal″a-chi′as** (-kī′ăs).—*abbr.* **Mal.**

mal-a-chite (măl′ȧ-kīt), *n.* green carbonate of copper: a valuable form of copper ore used in making ornaments.

mal-ad-min-is-ter (măl″ăd-mĭn′ĭs-tẽr), *v.t.* to manage or conduct badly:—*n.* **mal″ad-min″is-tra′tion.**

mal-a-droit (măl″ȧ-droit′), *adj.* unskilful; awkward; clumsy.—*adv.* **mal″a-droit′ly.**—*n.* **mal″a-droit′ness.**

mal-a-dy (măl′ȧ-dĭ), *n.* [*pl.* maladies (-dĭz)], a disease, esp. one deep-seated or lingering, mental or physical.

Mal-a-ga (măl′ȧ-gȧ), *n.* **1**, a variety of white wine; **2**, a sweet, white, firm-fleshed grape.

Mal-a-gas-y (măl″ȧ-găs′ĭ), *n.* [*pl.* Malagasy], **1**, a native of Madagascar; **2**, the language of Madagascar.

*__ma-laise__ (mȧ″lāz′; măl′āz), [Fr.], *n.* a vague feeling of uneasiness, often coming before an attack of illness.

mal-a-pert (măl′ȧ-pûrt), *adj.* pert; bold:—*n.* a bold, saucy person.

mal-a-prop-ism (măl′ȧ-prŏp-ĭzm), *n.* a ridiculous misuse of fine or pretentious words: from Mrs. Malaprop, in Sheridan's "The Rivals."

mal-ap-ro-pos (măl-ăp″rō-pō′), *adj.* out of place; coming at the wrong time; not appropriate or suitable:—*adv.* inappropriately.

ma-lar (mā′lȧr), *adj.* pertaining to the cheek or cheek bone.

ma-la-ri-a (mȧ-lā′rĭ-ȧ), *n.* **1**, harmful vapors from marshy land, supposed to produce fevers, etc.; **2**, a disease produced by a parasite deposited in the blood by the bite of certain mosquitoes; chills and fever.—*adj.* **ma-la′ri-al.**—*adj.* **ma-la′ri-ous.**

Ma-lay (mȧ-lā′; mā′lā), *n.* **1**, one of the race of brown men dominant in southeastern Asia and the islands off that coast; **2**, the language of these people:—*adj.* of or pertaining to the Malays or the region which they inhabit.—*adj.* **Ma-lay′an.**

Ma-lay-sian (mȧ-lā′shăn), *adj.* of or pertaining to the Malay Archipelago:—*n.* a Malay native.

mal-con-tent (măl′kŏn-tĕnt″), *adj.* discontented, esp. with established authority:—*n.* one who is discontented with the established order of things.

male (māl), *adj.* **1**, pertaining to the sex that begets young; **2**, consisting of men or boys; masculine; as, a *male* choir; **3**, in machinery, fitting into a corresponding hollow piece:—*n.* a human being of the sex that begets young; an animal or plant of such sex: opp. of *female.*—*n.* **male′ness.**

mal-e-dic-tion (măl″ē-dĭk′shŭn), *n.* **1**, a proclaiming of evil against anyone; curse; **2**, the act of speaking evil; **3**, the state of being slandered.

Syn. anathema, execration, imprecation.—*Ant.* benediction, blessing.

mal-e-fac-tor (măl″ē-făk′tẽr), *n.* a wrongdoer; a criminal; culprit; felon.—*n.* **mal″e-fac′tion.**

ma-lev-o-lence (mȧ-lĕv′ō-lĕns), *n.* spitefulness; ill will; intent to do injury to others.

ma-lev-o-lent (mȧ-lĕv′ō-lĕnt), *adj.* malicious; spiteful; disposed to injure others.—*adv.* **ma-lev′o-lent-ly.**

mal-fea-sance (măl-fē′zăns), *n.* **1**, an illegal act; evil deed; **2**, wrongdoing by a public official.

mal-for-ma-tion (măl″fôr-mā′shŭn), *n.* faulty or abnormal structure of any body or part of a body; as, a clubfoot is a *malformation.*

mal-ice (măl′ĭs), *n.* **1**, evil intention to injure others; deliberate mischief; spite; **2**, in law, a state of mind shown by intention to perform an unlawful act or deed.

Syn. spite, grudge, resentment, rancor, hostility, ill will, revenge, animosity, pique. *Malice* loves to injure because of its very nature and needs no provocation; as, his eyes shone with *malice. Spite* is a mean desire to thwart or hurt others in petty or trifling ways. *Grudge* and *resentment* are born of anger over personal injury; a *grudge* is *ill will* nursed in a bitter heart, and ready to act on opportunity; as, I have long held a *grudge* against him. *Resentment* is a sullen anger continued by brooding over its cause. *Rancor* is *spite* mixed with *malice* to make a deep-rooted bitterness; as, an unholy *rancor* soured their hearts.—*Ant.* benignity, kindness, favor, good will.

ma-li-cious (mȧ-lĭsh′ŭs), *adj.* **1**, bearing ill will; influenced by hatred or spite; **2**, indulging in deliberate mischief; as, a *malicious* person; **3**, arising from ill will; as, a *malicious* act.—*adv.* **ma-li′cious-ly.**—*n.* **ma-li′cious-ness.**

ma-lign (mȧ-līn′), *v.t.* to speak evil of with spite or ill will; slander; as, to *malign* the character of another:—*adj.* **1**, evil in disposition; slanderous; **2**, tending to injure; baleful; as, *malign* influences.—*n.* **ma-lign′er.**—*adv.* **ma-lign′ly.**

Syn. revile, vilify, abuse, asperse.

ma-lig-nan-cy (mȧ-lĭg′năn-sĭ), *n.* **1**, the state of being disposed to do harm; **2**, in medicine, the virulence of a disease which threatens to produce death.

ma-lig-nant (mȧ-lĭg′nănt), *adj.* **1**, malicious; having extreme, active enmity toward anyone; intending or bringing about evil; **2**, of disease, tending to cause death; virulent.—*adv.* **ma-lig′nant-ly.**

ma-lig-ni-ty (mȧ-lĭg′nĭ-tĭ), *n.* [*pl.* malignities (-tĭz)], **1**, the state of being disposed to do evil to others; malice; **2**, an evil act or event; **3**, deadly quality; as, the *malignity* of cancer.

ma-lin-ger (mȧ-lĭng′gẽr), *v.i.* to pretend illness in order to escape duty, esp. military duty.—*n.* **ma-lin′ger-er.**

mal-i-son (măl′ĭ-zn; măl′ĭ-sn), *n.* a curse; malediction.

mall (môl), *n.* **1**, (preferably, *maul*), a large, heavy, wooden mallet used in the game of pall-mall; **2**, a public walk shaded by trees:—*v.t.* (preferably, *maul*), to bruise roughly.

mal-lard (măl′ȧrd), *n.* a species of large wild duck, esp. the male; commonly, any wild duck.

mal-le-a-ble (măl′ē-ȧ-bl), *adj.* capable of being extended by hammering or rolling; as, gold is the most *malleable* of all metals.—*n.* **mal″le-a-bil′i-ty.**

mal-le-o-lus (mă-lē′ō-lŭs), *n.* [*pl.* malleoli (-lī)], either of the two rounded projections at each ankle joint (see *tibia,* illus.).

mal-let (măl'ĕt), *n.* **1**, a short-handled hammer used for driving a tool; **2**, the long-handled implement, hammerlike at one end, used to drive the balls in croquet or polo.

MALLET

mal-le-us (măl'ē-ŭs), *n.* [*pl.* mallei (-ī)], one of the three small bones in the middle ear: also called *hammer.*

mal-low (măl'ō), *n.* a plant having pink, purple, white, or yellow, cup-shaped flowers.

malm-sey (mäm'zĭ), *n.* **1**, a rich variety of grape; **2**, a full-flavored, sweet wine. Also, **mal'voi-sie.**

mal-nu-tri-tion (măl″nū-trĭsh'ŭn), *n.* insufficient nourishment, either on account of actual lack of food or faulty digestive processes.

mal-o-dor-ous (măl-ō'dẽr-ŭs), *adj.* having a disagreeable smell; objectionable in odor.—*adv.* **mal-o'dor-ous-ly.**

mal-prac-tice (măl-prăk'tĭs), *n.* **1**, the treatment of a case by a surgeon or physician in a manner contrary to accepted rules and with harmful results to the patient; **2**, the conduct of any profession in an illegal or wrong way.

malt (môlt), *n.* barley or other grain sprouted by being soaked in water, and dried for brewing:—*v.i.* to ferment, or change into malt: said of grain:—*v.t.* to make into, or with, malt, or fermented grain:—*adj.* made with such fermented grain; as, beer and ale are *malt* liquors.—*adj.* **malt'y.**

Mal-tese (môl-tēz'; -tēs'; môl-), *adj.* pertaining to Malta, an island in the Mediterranean: **Maltese cat,** a tame cat with soft, slate-gray fur: **Maltese cross,** a cross somewhat like a cross pattée (see *cross,* illus.), but with the arms indented across the ends like a fish's tail:—*n.* [*pl.* Maltese], **1**, a native of Malta; **2**, the language of Malta.

mal-treat (măl-trēt'), *v.t.* to treat ill or unkindly.—*n.* **mal-treat'ment.**

mal-ver-sa-tion (măl″vẽr-sā'shŭn), *n.* evil behavior; esp., misconduct in public office.

mal-voi-sie (măl'vwȧ-zē; -vȧ-), *n.* **1**, a variety of grape; **2**, a strong, sweet wine. Also, **malm'sey,** *Pfd. S.*

Mam-e-luke (măm'ē-lūk), *n.* one of a corps of mounted soldiers, orig. slaves, which dominated Egypt in the 13th century: **mameluke,** a Turkish slave.

[1]**mam-ma** (mȧ-mä'; mä'mȧ), *n.* mother: a familiar or childish name. Also, **ma-ma'.**

[2]**mam-ma** (măm'ȧ), *n.* [*pl.* mammæ (-ē)], a glandular organ secreting milk, found in all animals that suckle their young.

mam-mal (măm'ăl), *n.* a member of the highest class of animals, which feed their young by means of milk glands.

Mam-ma-li-a (mă-mā'lĭ-ȧ), *n.pl.* the highest class of animals, which feed their young with milk from the breast.—*adj.* **mam-ma'li-an.**

mam-ma-ry (măm'ȧ-rĭ), *adj.* of or pertaining to the breasts, or mammæ; as, the *mammary* glands.

mam-mon (măm'ŭn), *n.* **1**, wealth; worldly gain; **2**, greed for riches: **Mammon,** greed: personified as a god.—*n.* **mam'mon-ism.**

mam-moth (măm'ŏth), *n.* a huge, hairy-skinned elephant no longer in existence (see illus. next column):—*adj.* gigantic; immense.

mam-my (măm'ĭ), *n.* [*pl.* mammies (-ĭz)], **1**, mother: a childish name; **2**, in the South, a negro servant or nurse who cares for white children.

man (măn), *n.* [*pl.* men (mĕn)], **1**, a human being; also, the human race; **2**, an adult male of the human species; **3**, anyone: with *a;* **4**, a male servant; valet; **5**, one possessed of manly qualities in a high degree; **6**, a husband: used in *man and wife* and, vulgarly, in *her man, my man,* etc.; **7**, one of the pieces in chess, checkers, or similar games; also, a player in a game, whether male or female; **8**, manly quality; manliness: **to a man,** none being excepted: **man in the street,** an average or ordinary man:—*v.t.* [*p.t.* and *p.p.* manned (mănd), *p.pr.* man'ning], **1**, to furnish with men; **2**, to supply with strength.

SKELETON OF MAMMOTH ($\frac{1}{180}$)

man-a-cle (măn'ȧ-kl), *n.*, usually in *pl.*, a handcuff; a fetter:—*v.t.* [*p.t.* and *p.p.* -cled (-kld), *p.pr.* -cling], to place handcuffs upon; put into chains.

man-age (măn'āj), *v.t.* [*p.t.* and *p.p.* -aged (-ājd), *p.pr.* -ag-ing], **1**, to conduct or carry on; **2**, to govern; make obedient; control; **3**, to bring about by ingenious devices; contrive:—*v.i.* **1**, to conduct or direct affairs; **2**, to make use of one's means in a thrifty fashion.

Syn. control, direct, regulate, superintend, engineer, supervise. (See conduct.)

man-age-a-ble (măn'āj-ȧ-bl), *adj.* easily conducted or controlled; obedient; controllable; subject to guidance.—*adv.* **man'age-a-bly.**—*n.* **man'age-a-ble-ness.**—*n.* **man″age-a-bil'i-ty.**

man-age-ment (măn'āj-mĕnt), *n.* **1**, the act or art of conducting or controlling; administration; control; **2**, skill in direction; **3**, those collectively who are responsible for the direction of an enterprise or business.

Syn. superintendence, conduct, care, charge direction, economy, regulation, guidance.

man-ag-er (măn'ā-jẽr), *n.* **1**, one who directs or conducts anything; **2**, a person who conducts business or household affairs with skill and economy.—*adj.* **man″a-ge'ri-al.**

man-a-tee (măn″ȧ-tē'), *n.* any of several sea mammals resembling, but smaller than, a whale.

Man-chu (măn-chōō'), *n.* **1**, a member of the native Mongolian race of Manchuria, which conquered China in 1644; **2**, the language of the Manchus:—*adj.* pertaining to Manchuria or to its inhabitants. —*n.* and *adj.* **Man-chu'ri-an.**

man-da-mus (măn-dā'mŭs), *n.* a written paper given out by a superior court directing the person, corporation, or inferior court to whom it is addressed to perform some public duty or act.

man-da-rin (măn'dȧ-rĭn; măn″dȧ-rēn'), *n.* **1**, in China, an official of one of nine classes, which are distinguished by a particular kind of button worn on the cap; **2**, a variety of orange: **Mandarin,** the Chinese dialect in use by the official classes; loosely, the chief Chinese dialect.

man-date (măn'dāt), *n.* **1**, an order; command; an official charge or injunction; **2**, the control and supervision of a small, weak country by a great power.

man-da-to-ry (măn'dȧ-tō-rĭ), *adj.* **1**, containing, or pertaining to, an official command; expressing a command; **2**, carrying authority; obligatory:—*n.* [*pl.* mandatories (-rĭz)], **1**, an attorney or agent who acts for another; **2**, a nation or state chosen to govern or administer a colony, or certain territory. Also, *n.* **man'da-ta-ry.**

man-di-ble (măn'dĭ-bl), *n.* **1**, the bone of the lower jaw, esp. if in one piece; **2**, in birds, either jaw.

man-do-lin (măn'dō-lĭn), *n.* a musical instrument which has a pear-shaped sound box, a neck with frets, and metal strings arranged in pairs (see *musical instrument*, illus.). Also, **man'do-line.**

man-drake (măn'drāk), *n.* **1**, a plant of the nightshade family with a very large, forked root and a white or purple flower; **2**, in the U. S., the May apple, a low-growing herb with a white blossom.

man-drel (măn'drĕl), *n.* **1**, the part of a lathe on which the work to be turned is placed; **2**, the revolving axle of a circular saw. Also, **man'dril.**

man-drill (măn'drĭl), *n.* the blue-faced baboon of Africa.

mane (mān), *n.* **1**, the long hair on the upper side of or about the neck of certain animals, as the horse and the lion; **2**, a line of stubble left by mowers.—*adj.* **maned.** —*adj.* **mane'less.**

ma-nège (mȧ″nâzh′), *n.* **1**, a riding academy; a school where horsemanship is taught; **2**, the art of training, riding, or driving horses. Also, **ma-nege′** (mȧ-nĕzh′).

ma-nes (mā'nēz), *n.pl.* among the ancient Romans, the spirits of the dead and the gods of the lower regions.

ma-neu-ver (mȧ-nōō'vẽr; mȧ-nū'vẽr), *n.* **1**, swift and skilful management or operation in military or naval affairs; **2**, an artful device or proceeding; a stratagem; skilful management:—*v.i.* **1**, to perform certain movements with troops or war vessels; **2**, to manage with art and skill:—*v.t.* **1**, to cause to make certain movements, as troops or vessels; **2**, to handle skilfully; manage with dexterity; **3**, to make, move, or put into certain positions, by skilful management. Also, **ma-neu'vre, ma-nœu'vre** [*p.t.* and *p.p.* -vred (-vẽrd), *p.pr.* -vring]; **ma-nœu'ver.**

man-ful (măn'fōōl), *adj.* courageous; bravely determined.—*adv.* **man'ful-ly.**—*n.* **man'ful-ness.**

Syn. noble, brave, manly, manlike, mannish. *Manly* implies the possession of such qualities as befit a man, as courage, endurance, hardiness; as, a *manly* fellow. *Manlike* describes the appearance and the qualities, esp. the finer ones, that distinguish a man; as, *manlike* determination. *Manful* stresses the fighting qualities, the bravery and resolution characteristic of men; as, a *manful* spirit. *Mannish* describes those who ape the fashions or manners of men; as, a *mannish* girl.

man-ga-nese (măng″gȧ-nēs′; măng'gȧ-nēz), *n.* a hard, brittle, metallic substance, of a grayish color tinged with red: used in making paint, glass, etc.

mange (mānj), *n.* a contagious skin disease of dogs, cattle, etc.: caused by parasitic mites and sometimes affecting man.

man-gel-wur-zel (măng'gl=wûr″zl), *n.* a large, coarse variety of beet, cultivated as a cattle fodder.

man-ger (mān'jẽr), *n.* a feeding trough for horses or cattle.

¹man-gle (măng'gl), *n.* a machine for ironing cloth, esp. damp linen, between rollers:—*v.t.* [*p.t.* and *p.p.* -gled (-gld), *p.pr.* -gling], to iron in a mangle, as cloth, sheets, etc.—*n.* **¹man'gler.**

²man-gle (măng'gl), *v.t.* [*p.t.* and *p.p.* -gled (-gld), *p.pr.* -gling], **1**, to cut to pieces; maim; mutilate by cutting or hacking; **2**, to spoil in the performing or making; make a botch of.—*n.* **²man'gler.**

man-go (măng'gō), *n.* [*pl.* mangoes; mangos (-gōz)], **1**, a tropical tree bearing a fruit of oblong shape, yellowish color, thick rind, and juicy pulp; **2**, the fruit.

man-grove (măng'grōv), *n.* an East and West Indian tree yielding a bark used in tanning, and having branches which take root and cause the tree to spread in a thick mass over large areas.

man-gy (mān'jĭ), *adj.* [*comp.* man'gi-er, *superl.* man'gi-est], **1**, suffering or afflicted with a contagious skin disease, as dogs and cattle; **2**, shabby; squalid; neglected.—*n.* **man'gi-ness.**

man-hole (măn'hōl″), *n.* an opening by which a workman may enter a tank, sewer, or the like.

man-hood (măn'hŏŏd), *n.* **1**, the state of being a man; man's estate; **2**, men collectively; as, the *manhood* of the United States; **3**, the qualities belonging to a man; courage.

ma-ni-a (mā'nĭ-ȧ), *n.* violent insanity; intense excitement; also, excessive or unreasonable desire or enthusiasm; as, some people have a *mania* for collecting.

Syn. frenzy, madness, lunacy.

ma-ni-ac (mā'nĭ-ăk), *adj.* affected with insanity; raving; frantic:—*n.* a madman. Also, *adj.* **ma-ni'a-cal** (mȧ-nī'ȧ-kăl).—*adv.* **ma-ni'a-cal-ly.**

man-i-cure (măn'ĭ-kūr), *n.* **1**, the care of the hands, nails, etc.; **2**, one whose business it is to care for the hands and nails:—*v.i.* and *v.t.* to care for the hands and nails (of).—*n.* **man'i-cur″ist.**

man-i-fest (măn'ĭ-fĕst), *adj.* clear; plain; apparent to the sight or understanding:—*v.t.* **1**, to make clear; place beyond the possibility of misunderstanding; prove; **2**, to show the list of, as a cargo:—*n.* the list of a cargo to be shown to the customhouse officials; an invoice.—*adv.* **man'i-fest-ly.**

Syn., adj. evident, open, visible, unmistakable, overt, obvious, patent; *v.* demonstrate, reveal, display.—*Ant., adj.* hidden.

man-i-fes-ta-tion (măn″ĭ-fĕs-tā'shŭn), *n.* **1**, a public display, either for showing feeling or gaining attention; **2**, a revealing or disclosure; the act of making plain.

man-i-fes-to (măn″ĭ-fĕs'tō), *n.* [*pl.* manifestoes (-tōz)], a public declaration, as on the part of an official or a state, concerning political measures or intentions.

man-i-fold (măn'ĭ-fōld), *adj.* **1**, various in kind or quality; numerous; **2**, comprehensive:—*v.t.* to make many copies of by means of a duplicating machine:—*n.* **1**, a copy made by a duplicating machine; **2**, a pipe having two or more lateral outlets, used for connecting one pipe with others. —*adv.* **man'i-fold″ly.**—*n.* **man'i-fold″ness.**

Syn., adj. several, sundry, divers.

man-i-kin (măn'ĭ-kĭn), *n.* **1**, a dwarf; little man; **2**, a model of the human body for study of the organs. Also, **man'a-kin; man'ni-kin.**

Ma-nil-a (mȧ-nĭl'ȧ), *n.* **1**, a kind of cigar manufactured at Manila in the Philippine Islands; **2**, a hemp used for ropes, paper, etc., made from the fibers of a Philippine tree related to the banana; **3**, a strong paper made from these fibers. Also, **ma-nil'a; Ma-nil'la; ma-nil'la.**

man-i-oc (măn'ĭ-ŏk; mā'nĭ-ŏk), *n.* **1**, any of several tropical plants from the roots of which tapioca and starch are made; cassava; **2**, the starch.

ma-nip-u-late (mȧ-nĭp'ū-lāt), *v.t.* [*p.t.* and *p.p.* -lat″ed, *p.pr.* -lat″ing], **1**, to operate or work skilfully by means of the hands, as tools; **2**, to treat; influence artfully; control the action of, by skilful management; **3**, to falsify, as books in bookkeeping:—*v.i.* to use the hands, esp. in scientific operations or mechanical processes.

ma-nip-u-la-tion (mȧ-nĭp″ū-lā′shŭn), *n.* **1**, the act or process of operating or working skilfully with the hands; **2**, falsification, as of books, accounts, etc.; **3**, skilful management, as of a boat or machine.—*n.* **ma-nip′u-la″tor.**

ma-nip-u-la-tive (mȧ-nĭp′ū-lā-tĭv), *adj.* pertaining to, or performed by, skilful use of the hands; managing skilfully.—*adj.* **ma-nip′u-la-to-ry.**

man-i-to (măn′ĭ-tō), *n.* among certain North American Indians, a spirit of good or evil regarded with reverence; the Great Spirit. Also, **man′i-tou; man′i-tu.**

man-kind (măn″kīnd′), *n.* **1**, the human race; **2**, (măn′kīnd″), men, distinguished from women.

man-like (măn′līk″), *adj.* like, or suitable to, a man; manly.
Syn. masculine, mannish. (See manful.)

man-li-ness (măn′lĭ-nĕs), *n.* the state or quality of possessing manly virtues, as strength and courage.

man-ly (măn′lĭ), *adj.* [*comp.* man′li-er, *superl.* man′li-est], having the qualities befitting a man; courageous; noble; dignified; resolute:—*adv.* like a man.
Syn., adj. masculine, vigorous, frank, brave, heroic, intrepid, determined. (See manful.)

man-na (măn′ȧ), *n.* **1**, the food miraculously supplied to the Israelites during their 40 years' wandering in the wilderness (Exodus 16:15); hence, spiritual nourishment; **2**, the sweet juice from certain kinds of ash of southern Europe, used in medicine as a mild laxative.

man-ner (măn′ẽr), *n.* **1**, method; mode of action; **2**, habit; way of acting; custom; **3**, sort; kind; species; **4**, aspect; style; fashion; **5**, in *pl.*: **a**, morals; behavior; politeness; **b**, rules of conduct; practices of society.—*adj.* **man′nered.**
Syn. way, air, look, appearance, demeanor, address, system, mode.

man-ner-ism (măn′ẽr-ĭzm), *n.* a peculiarity of style, action, or bearing, esp. if strained or affected.

man-ner-less (măn′ẽr-lĕs), *adj.* impolite; lacking in respect.

man-ner-ly (măn′ẽr-lĭ), *adj.* polite; respectful:—*adv.* politely; respectfully.—*n.* **man′ner-li-ness.**

man-nish (măn′ĭsh), *adj.* masculine; characteristic of a man.—*adv.* **man′nish-ly.**—*n.* **man′nish-ness.**
Syn. (see manful).

man-nite (măn′īt), *n.* a white crystalline substance found in the larch and other plants: also called *manna sugar.*

ma-nœu-ver (mȧ-nōō′vẽr; mȧ-nū′vẽr), *n.* **1**, swift and skilful management, as in war; **2**, artful device; stratagem:—*v.t.* **1**, to handle (troops or ships) skilfully; **2**, to manage with dexterity:—*v.i.* to manage with art and skill; scheme. Also, **ma-nœu′vre.** See **ma-neu′ver**, *Pfd. S.*
Syn., n. trick, artifice, intrigue.

man-of-war (măn″=ŏv=wôr′), *n.* [*pl.* men-of-war (mĕn″=)], a large ship of war; an armed vessel belonging to a navy of recognized status: **man-of-war bird,** a large, rapacious sea bird; a frigate bird.

man-or (măn′ẽr), *n.* **1**, in England, the district over which a lord held authority, orig. with feudal obligations to the king; **2**, in America, a tract of land occupied by tenants who pay rent to the owner: **manor house,** the dwelling of the owner of the manor. —*adj.* **ma-no′ri-al** (mȧ-nō′rĭ-ăl).

man-sard roof (măn′särd), a roof which has on all sides two slopes, the lower being steeper than the upper.

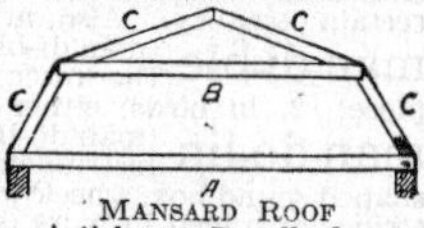

MANSARD ROOF
A, tiebeam; B, collar beam; C, C, C, C, rafters.

manse (măns), *n.* the home of a Presbyterian minister, esp. in Scotland; a parsonage; the residence of a minister.

man-serv-ant (măn′sûr″vănt), *n.* [*pl.* menservants (mĕn′sûr″-vănts)], a male servant.

man-sion (măn′shŭn), *n.* a large dwelling house; stately residence.

man-slaugh-ter (măn′slô″tẽr), *n.* the unlawful killing of a human being by another or others, but without malice aforethought.

man-teau (măn′tō; *Fr.* mäṅ″tō′), *n.* [*pl.* manteaus (-tōz); manteaux (-tō′)], **1**, a cloak worn by women; **2**, formerly, a loose gown opening in front; mantua.

man-tel (măn′tl), *n.* a narrow, ornamental shelf projecting above a fireplace: also called *mantelpiece.*

man-tel-et (măn′tl-ĕt), *n.* **1**, a bullet-proof shelter, formerly movable, to protect besiegers, gunners, etc.; **2**, a short cloak or cape.

man-til-la (măn-tĭl′ȧ), *n.* **1**, a lady's light cloak or hood; **2**, a lace veil worn over the head by women in Mexico, Spain, Italy, etc.

man-tis (măn′tĭs), *n.* [*pl.* mantes (-tēz)], an insect allied to the grasshopper, noted for taking a position with its front legs folded as if praying, commonly called *praying mantis.*

man-tle (măn′tl), *n.* **1**, a loose cloak or cape; also, anything resembling a cloak; as, a *mantle* of flowers; **2**, the outside fold of the skin of the body of the clam and other shellfish; **3**, a conelike network of material that will not burn, but which fits like a cap over a flame and gives light by glowing at high temperature:—*v.t.* [*p.t.* and *p.p.* -tled (-tld), *p.pr.* -tling], to cover with, or as with, a cloak:—*v.i.* **1**, to become covered; as, her face *mantled* with blushes; **2**, to take on a coating; as, the pool *mantles* with scum.

man-tu-a (măn′tū-ȧ), *n.* in the 17th and 18th centuries, a woman's loose gown or cloak, esp. one having an open front: **mantuamaker,** formerly, a dressmaker.

man-u-al (măn′ū-ăl), *adj.* pertaining to, or done by, the hands:—*n.* **1**, a small book; a handbook; **2**, in military usage, an exercise in the handling of a weapon, done in a prescribed way; as, a *manual* of arms; **3**, on an organ, a keyboard for the hand; as, an organ of two *manuals.*

man-u-fac-to-ry (măn″ū-făk′tō-rĭ), *n.* [*pl.* manufactories (-rĭz)], a place where goods are made from raw materials, esp. on a large scale; a factory.

man-u-fac-ture (măn″ū-făk′tūr; măn″-ū-făk′chōōr), *v.t.* [*p.t.* and *p.p.* -tured (-tūrd; -chōōrd), *p.pr.* -turing], **1**, to make, as shoes, paper, etc., from raw materials; produce by varied processes; **2**, to work into a more useful form, as wool or cotton:—*v.i.* to be occupied in the making of goods from raw materials:—*n.* **1**, the making, usually on a large scale, of articles by hand, machinery, or a combination of processes; **2**, anything made from raw material by these processes; also, such articles collectively. —*n.* **man″u-fac′tur-er.**

man-u-mis-sion (măn″ū-mĭsh′ŭn), *n.* **1**, the act of freeing from slavery; liberation; **2**, the state of being freed from slavery.

man-u-mit (măn″ū-mĭt′), *v.t.* [*p.t.* and *p.p.* -mit′ted, *p.pr.* -mit′ting], to set free from slavery.

ma-nure (mȧ-nūr′), *n.* any fertilizing substance used for enriching the soil:—*v.t.* [*p.t.* and *p.p.* -nured′ (-nūrd′), *p.pr.* -nur′ing], to enrich, as a field or garden, with fertilizing substances.

man-u-script (măn′ū-skrĭpt), *adj.* written by hand:—*n.* **1**, a book or paper written by hand; **2**, esp., an author's copy of his work, in handwriting or in typewriting; **3**, writing, as opposed to printing.—*abbr.* **MS.**; **ms.** [*pl.* MSS.; mss.].

Manx (măngks), *adj.* relating to the Isle of Man, to its people, or to the old language of the island:—*n.* [*pl.* Manx], **1**, a native of the Isle of Man; **2**, the Manx language.—*n.* **Manx′man.**

man-y (mĕn′ĭ), *adj.* [*comp.* more, *superl.* most], numerous; consisting of a great number:—*n.* a great number; multitude; crowd.

Ma-o-ri (mä′ō-rĭ; *Colloq.* mou′rĭ), *adj.* pertaining to the Maoris, or natives of New Zealand, or to their language:—*n.* [*pl.* Maoris (-rĭz)], a native of New Zealand, or its language.

map (măp), *n.* **1**, a representation, on a flat surface, of the earth or some portion of it; **2**, a chart of the heavens:—*v.t.* [*p.t.* and *p.p.* mapped (măpt), *p.pr.* map′ping], **1**, to picture or lay down in a chart; describe clearly; **2**, to plan in detail: usually with *out;* as, to *map* out a journey into Egypt.
Syn., n. (see chart).

ma-ple (mā′pl), *n.* any of several well-known trees, valued for their shade, for their wood, and, in some species, for their sap, which is used for making sugar and sirup.

mar (mär), *v.t.* [*p.t.* and *p.p.* marred (märd), *p.pr.* mar′ring], **1**, to disfigure; damage; as, to *mar* a painting; **2**, to injure; impair; as, to *mar* one's success.
Syn. spoil, ruin.

mar-a-bou (măr′ȧ-bōō), *n.* any of several Old World storks, esp. the African species whose soft wing or tail feathers are used for dress trimming and for apparel; also, the feathers so used.

mar-a-schi-no (măr″ȧ-skē′nō), *n.* a delicate alcoholic cordial distilled from cherries.

ma-ras-mus (mȧ-răz′mŭs), *n.* a gradual wasting away of the body; emaciation: usually a disease of small children.—*adj.* **ma-ras′mic.**

Mar-a-thon (măr′ȧ-thŏn), *n.* a long-distance foot race: so called from the runner who carried to Athens the news of the victory of Marathon.

ma-raud (mȧ-rôd′), *v.i.* to plunder; rove in search of plunder; as, wild beasts *maraud* at night.—*n.* **ma-raud′er.**

mar-ble (mär′bl), *n.* **1**, a hard limestone of various colors, capable of taking a fine polish; **2**, anything like such stone in hardness, smoothness, or coldness; **3**, a sculptured piece of such stone; **4**, a small stone or glass ball used as a child's plaything; **5**, in *pl.:* **a**, the game played with these balls; **b**, a collection of sculpture in marble:—*adj.* made of, or like, marble; cold; hard; unfeeling:—*v.t.* [*p.t.* and *p.p.* -bled (-bld), *p.pr.* -bling], to stain or vein like marble.—*p.adj.* **mar′bled.**—*adj.* **mar′bly.**

¹march (märch), *n.* a frontier boundary; borderland.

²march (märch), *n.* **1**, a regular, measured step or walk, esp. of soldiers; **2**, the distance passed over in walking in such a manner from one place to another; **3**, steady onward movement; as, the *march* of the years; **4**, a musical composition to be played as troops march:—*v.t.* to cause to move in a regular, measured walk, as troops:—*v.i.* to move with regular steps, or in military form.
Syn., v. tramp, tread, walk, step.

March (märch), *n.* the third month of the year, having 31 days.—*abbr.* **Mar.**

mar-chion-ess (mär′shŭn-ĕs), *n.* the wife or widow of a marquis; a lady of the rank of a marquis.

mar-co-ni-gram (mär-kō′nĭ-grăm), *n.* a message sent or received by Marconi wireless telegraphy.

mar-co-ni-graph (mär-kō′nĭ-grȧf), *n.* the apparatus used to send a message in Marconi wireless telegraphy.

Mar-di gras (mär″dē grä′), Shrove Tuesday; the Tuesday before Ash Wednesday; the last day before Lent, celebrated in some cities, as Rome, Paris, or New Orleans, with great merriment.

mare (mâr), *n.* the female of the horse, and other equine animals: **to ride Shanks's mare,** to go afoot; walk.

mare's-nest (mârz′-nĕst″), *n.* some discovery which at first seems to be wonderful but which proves to be a cheat or imaginary.

mar-ga-rine (mär′gȧ-rēn; mär′gȧ-rĭn), *n.* artificial butter; oleomargarine, a butter substitute made from animal or vegetable fats.

mar-gin (mär′jĭn), *n.* **1**, a border; an edge; **2**, the unprinted edge of a page; **3**, a limit; **4**, an amount in reserve, as of money or time; as, he allowed a *margin* of an hour to catch the train; **5**, money, stock certificates, etc., given to a broker to secure him from loss in advancing funds for an investment; as, to buy on a *margin:*—*v.t.* **1**, to furnish with an edge or a border; **2**, to enter, as notes, upon the edge of a page.
Syn., n. rim, brink, verge. (See border.)

mar-gin-al (mär′jĭ-năl), *adj.* pertaining to, or placed on, the edge or border; as, a *marginal* design.

mar-grave (mär′grāv), *n.* the English form of *Markgraf,* a German hereditary title of nobility equivalent to *marquis.*—*n.fem.* **mar′gra-vine** (mär′grȧ-vēn).

mar-gra-vi-ate (mär-grā′vĭ-āt), *n.* the district presided over by, or the jurisdiction of, a margrave, or German marquis. Also, **mar′gra-vate.**

mar-gue-rite (mär′gē-rēt; mär″gē-rēt′), *n.* the oxeye daisy; more commonly, the garden and greenhouse daisy.

mar-i-gold (măr′ĭ-gōld), *n.* any of several herbs of the aster family with showy yellow flowers; also, the flower.

ma-rine (mȧ-rēn′), *adj.* **1**, pertaining to, living in, or formed by, the sea; as, *marine* plants and animals; **2**, naval; relating to commerce at sea; near the sea; used at sea:—*n.* **1**, a soldier who serves on a warship; **2**, the navy of a nation; also, the executive department dealing with naval affairs; **3**, the collective shipping of a country; **4**, a picture of a sea scene.
Syn., adj. (see maritime).

mar-i-ner (măr′ĭ-nẽr), *n.* a sailor or seaman; one of the crew.

mar-i-o-nette (măr″ĭ-ō-nĕt′), *n.* an image in human form moved by strings or by the hand, as in a puppet show.

mar-i-tal (măr′ĭ-tăl), *adj.* **1**, concerning, or belonging to, a husband; as, *marital* devotion; **2**, pertaining to marriage.

mar-i-time (măr′ĭ-tĭm; -tīm), *adj.* **1**, pertaining to, connected with, o bordering upon, the sea; **2**, relating to sea trade; as, the *maritime* power of England.

Syn. marine, naval, nautical. *Marine* describes that which belongs to, or is produced by, the sea, or which is for use at sea; as, *marine* animals; a *marine* engineer; a *marine* compass. *Maritime* is applied to places bordering on the sea; as, *maritime* states; or things connected with the sea; as, *maritime* law. *Naval* refers sometimes to ships as used in commerce, but usually to a navy or that branch of government which directs a navy. *Nautical* refers to sailors or the art of navigation; as, a *nautical* chart or almanac.

mar-jo-ram (mär′jō-răm), *n.* any of several plants of the mint family, esp. sweet marjoram: used as flavoring.

¹mark (märk), *n.* **1**, the target at which one aims, as in shooting; an aim or goal; **2**, a visible imprint, as a line, scratch, written word, or the like; as, an ink *mark;* **3**, a sign by which anything is known, as a label or trademark; **4**, a trait; symptom; distinguishing feature; as, a *mark* of intelligence; **5**, a character made by one who cannot write his name; **6**, a written or printed symbol; as, an exclamation *mark;* **7**, a figure or letter indicating a student's grade; **8**, high position; distinction; as, men of *mark;* **9**, a boundary or limit; a set standard; as, to fall below the *mark;* **10**, a line, object, or the like, serving to indicate position; **11**, in medieval England and Germany, the tract of land about a village; a political district; **12**, on the sounding line of a ship, any of certain bits of leather, bunting, or the like, to indicate various depths in fathoms; **13**, *Slang*, one easily deceived or misled: usually, *easy mark:*—*v.t.* **1**, to furnish with an identifying sign; **2**, to characterize; identify or indicate, as by a sign; as, faith and courage *mark* the leader; **3**, to single out or select, as by a sign; destine; **4**, to notice; observe; **5**, to rank or grade, as examination papers; **6**, to set apart, as by a boundary: usually with *off* or *out;* as, to *mark* out a tennis court; **7**, to keep account of, as the points in a game; **8**, to put a price upon; supply with a tag indicating price:—*v.i.* **1**, to notice; consider; observe critically; **2**, to make a mark; **3**, to keep score, as in a game.—*n.* **mark′er**.—*p.adj.* **marked**—*adv.* **mark′ed-ly**.

²mark (märk), *n.* a German coin normally worth 23.8 cents; also, the gold monetary unit of Germany.

Mark (märk), *n.* the second book of the New Testament, the Gospel thought to have been written by the evangelist John Mark, a nephew of Peter.

mar-ket (mär′kĕt; -kĭt), *n.* **1**, a public or private place for the sale or purchase of provisions; **2**, a region or country where anything can be sold; as, American manufactures find a ready *market;* **3**, the state of trade as shown by rate or price; as, a dull *market:*—*v.i.* to deal in a public place where provisions are exposed for sale; buy or sell goods or provisions:—*v.t.* to offer for sale, or to sell, in a public place.—*n.* **mar′ket-er**.

mar-ket-a-ble (mär′kĕt-ȧ-bl), *adj.* **1**, fit or suitable to be offered for sale; in demand; **2**, current in markets; as, *marketable* prices.—*n.* **mar″ket-a-bil′i-ty**.

mark-ka (märk′kä), *n.* the monetary unit of Finland, worth about 2½ cents.

marks-man (märks′măn), *n.* [*pl.* marksmen (-mĕn)], one skilled in shooting.—*n.* **marks′man-ship**.

¹marl (märl), *n.* earth containing calcium mixed with clay and carbonate of lime, used as a manure:—*v.t.* to fertilize with marl.

mar-line (mär′lĭn), *n.* a two-stranded cord used for winding around ropes, esp. on ships.—*v.i.* **²marl**.

mar-line-spike (mär′lĭn-spīk″), *n.* a pointed piece of iron used for opening the strands of a rope in splicing, or uniting two ropes by interweaving the strands. Also, **mar′lin-spike″**.

mar-ma-lade (mär′mȧ-lād), *n.* a thick preserve made of oranges or other fruits boiled together with sugar.

mar-mo-re-al (mär-mō′rē-ăl), *adj.* pertaining to, like, or made of, marble. Also, **mar-mo′re-an**.

mar-mo-set (mär′mō-zĕt″), *n.* a small South American monkey.

mar-mot (mär′mŏt), *n.* a small, coarse-furred, stout-bodied animal akin to the rat and squirrel.

¹ma-roon (mȧ-rōōn′), *n.* **1**, formerly, a runaway slave in the West Indies, or the descendant of such a person, living in the open; **2**, one who is left alone or abandoned on an island or lonely coast:—*v.t.* to place and leave alone on a desert island.

²ma-roon (mȧ-rōōn′), *n.* a dark, brownish red color:—*adj.* of a dark, brownish red color.

mar-plot (mär′plŏt″), *n.* one who spoils or hinders some plan or plot by meddling interference.

marque (märk), *n.* a license granted by a state to a private vessel to attack and capture the ships of another nation: no longer used except in the expression *letters of marque*, the official papers giving authority to private owners to make seizures.

mar-quee (mär-kē′), *n.* **1**, a large field tent: often used for outdoor entertainment; **2**, an awning raised as a temporary shelter, as from the curb to the door of a church.

mar-quet-ry (mär′kĕt-rĭ), *n.* inlaid work, as in furniture or floors.

mar-quis (mär′kwĭs), *n.* a nobleman ranking next below a duke and next above an earl or count. Also, **mar′quess**.

mar-quis-ate (mär′kwĭs-āt), *n.* the office, title, or dignity of, or territory governed by, a marquis, or margrave.

mar-quise (mär-kēz′), *n.* the wife or widow of a French marquis, a woman of similar position in the British peerage being called *marchioness*.

mar-riage (măr′ĭj), *n.* **1**, the act of legally uniting a man and woman in wedlock; the wedding ceremony; **2**, the state of being wedded; the relation existing between husband and wife.—*adj.* **mar′riage-a-ble**.

Syn. matrimony, wedlock, wedding, nuptials. *Marriage* is the common name for the relationship of husband and wife, and is used chiefly of the act or ceremony of joining two persons. *Matrimony* is a somewhat formal word naming the married state. *Wedlock* is a poetical or legal name for the married state; as, to be born in *wedlock*. *Wedding* may name the ceremony of *marriage*, or the *marriage* together with the festivities that accompany it. *Nuptials* is a more formal and less familiar word for *wedding*.

mar-ried (măr′ĭd), *p.adj.* **1**, united in wedlock; wedded; **2**, pertaining to matrimony; as, *married* duties.

mar-row (măr′ō), *n.* **1**, the oily tissue which fills the open canals of bones; **2**, hence, the real meaning or significance of anything: **vegetable marrow**, a kind of squash.—*adj.* **mar′row-y**.

mar-row-bone (măr′ō-bōn″), *n.* a bone containing marrow, esp. in sufficient quantity to be used in cookery.

mar-row-fat (măr′ō-făt″), *n.* a late, large variety of pea.

¹mar-ry (măr′ĭ), *v.t.* [*p.t.* and *p.p.* -ried (-ĭd), *p.pr.* -ry-ing], **1**, to unite as husband and wife; **2**, to take in marriage; wed;

3, to dispose of in wedlock; as, to *marry* off a daughter; 4, to bring together in close union; wed:—*v.i.* to enter into the state of wedlock.

²mar-ry (măr'ĭ), *interj. Archaic*, indeed! forsooth! a mild oath expressing surprise or assent.

Mars (märz), *n.* 1, the Roman god of war: identified with the Greek *Ares;* 2, one of the planets, notable for the redness of its light (see *solar system*, illus.).

Mar-se-illaise (mär″sĕ-lāz′; *Fr.* mȧr″-sâ″yâz′), *n.* the national anthem of the Republic of France: composed by an army officer, Rouget de l'Isle, 1792.

mar-seilles (mär-sālz′), *n.* a ribbed or striped double cotton fabric.

marsh (märsh), *n.* a swampy tract of land; a fen; morass.

mar-shal (mär′shăl), *n.* 1, an official of high rank who superintends and regulates ceremonies; 2, an official of lower rank than a herald, but having similar duties; 3, in the French army, the highest military officer: also called *field marshal;* 4, one who arranges and regulates order, rank, etc., in a public ceremony; 5, one who has certain police duties; a sheriff:—*v.t.* 1, to arrange or dispose in order, as facts or military forces; 2, to lead; guide; as, he *marshaled* us into the hall.—*n.* **mar′shal-ship.**—*n.* **mar′shal-cy.**

marsh mal-low 1, a perennial wild herb of the mallow family; 2, (often, *marshmallow*), a confection made from the root of this herb.

marsh-y (mär′shĭ), *adj.* [*comp.* marsh′i-er, *superl.* marsh′i-est], 1, swampy; 2, growing in, like, or pertaining to, a swamp or fen.—*n.* **marsh′i-ness.**

mar-su-pi-al (mär-sū′pĭ-ăl), *adj.* having a pouch: used of a class of animals that carry their young in a marsupium, or pouch:—*n.* one of these animals, as the opossum or kangaroo.

mar-su-pi-um (mär-sū′pĭ-ŭm), *n.* [*pl.* marsupia (-ȧ)], in female marsupials, such as the kangaroo or wallaby, an outside pouch on the abdomen for carrying the immature young.

Mar-sy-as (mär′sĭ-ăs), *n.* in mythology, a Phrygian satyr and flute player who, challenging Apollo to a musical contest, was defeated, and punished for his presumption by being flayed alive.

mart (märt), *n.* a place of public purchase and sale:—*v.t.* and *v.i.* to market.

mar-ten (mär′tĕn), *n.* 1, a small animal of the weasel family; 2, the valuable fur of the animal.

MARTEN (1/20)

Mar-tha (mär′thȧ), *n.* in the Bible, the sister of Lazarus and Mary, and friend of Jesus (Luke 10:39; John 11).

mar-tial (mär′shăl), *adj.* 1, pertaining to, or suited to, war or warriors; 2, military; as, *martial* music stirs the blood: **martial law**, a set of laws enforced by the military power and used in governing citizens in time of war, insurrection, etc.; as, a conquered city or country is usually put under *martial law* until a permanent government can be established.—*adv.* **mar′tial-ly.**

Syn. warlike, soldierly.

Mar-tian (mär′shăn), *n.* an inhabitant of Mars:—*adj.* pertaining to the planet Mars, or to Mars, the god of war.

mar-tin (mär′tĭn), *n.* a kind of small swallow.

mar-ti-net (mär″tĭ-nĕt′; mär′tĭ-nĕt″), *n.* one who requires and sternly enforces strict obedience in all details; an unusually strict or severe disciplinarian.

mar-tin-gale (mär′tĭn-gāl; mär′tĭng-gāl), *n.* 1, a broad strap passing from the girth of a horse's harness between its forelegs, to the reins or collar (see *harness*, illus.); 2, a rope or chain used to stay the end of the jib boom (see *rigging*, illus.). Also, **mar′tin-gal.**

Mar-tin-mas (mär′tĭn-mȧs), *n.* a feast day held in honor of Saint Martin, November 11.

mar-tyr (mär′tẽr), *n.* 1, one who dies for a faith, cause, or principle; 2, one who suffers keenly, esp. for a cause or principle:—*v.t.* 1, to put to death for loyalty to some belief, esp. Christianity; 2, to persecute; torture; torment; destroy.

mar-tyr-dom (mär′tẽr-dŭm), *n.* death or suffering for the sake of a faith, cause, or principle.

mar-tyr-ol-o-gy (mär″tẽr-ŏl′ō-jĭ), *n.* [*pl.* martyrologies (-jĭz)], a register or history of martyrs, or those who have suffered and died for a faith or a cause.

mar-vel (mär′vĕl), *n.* something extraordinary and astonishing; a wonder:—*v.i.* to be struck with astonishment.

mar-vel-ous (mär′vĕl-ŭs), *adj.* causing wonder; scarcely to be believed; incredible. Also, **mar′vel-lous.**—*adv.* **mar′vel-ous-ly.**—*n.* **mar′vel-ous-ness.**

Marx-i-an (märk′sĭ-ăn), *adj.* of or pertaining to Karl Marx (1818–83), a German socialist, or his theories.

Ma-ry (mā′rĭ; mâr′ĭ), *n.* 1, in the Bible, the mother of Jesus: also called *the Virgin Mary;* 2, Mary of Bethany, the sister of Lazarus and Martha, and a friend of Jesus (Luke 10:39; John 11); 3, Mary of Magdala, or Mary Magdalen, healed by Jesus of seven devils (Luke 8:2; John 20:1–18).

mas-cot (măs′kŏt), *n.* a person or thing that is supposed to bring good luck; as, a little yellow dog was the *mascot* of the baseball team. Also, **mas′cotte.**

mas-cu-line (măs′kū-lĭn), *adj.* 1, pertaining to, having the qualities of, or suitable for, a man; manly; powerful; virile; 2, coarse; mannish: said of a woman; 3, in grammar, designating the gender of words that denote males, and of other words classed with them.

mas-cu-lin-i-ty (măs″kū-lĭn′ĭ-tĭ), *n.* the quality of being manlike.

mash (măsh), *n.* 1, a soft or pulpy mass; 2, a warm mixture of bran and water for horses or other animals; 3, bruised malt, or meal, soaked in hot water for making beer, etc.:—*v.t.* 1, to mix with hot water, as malt, in brewing; 2, to change into a soft, pulpy state; crush.—*n.* **mash′er.**

mash-ie (măsh′ĭ), *n.* [*pl.* mashies (-ĭz)], an iron-headed golf club similar to the niblick. Also, **mash′y.**

mask (mȧsk), *n.* 1, a full or partial cover for the face in order to disguise or protect it; as, a gas *mask;* 2, that which disguises or conceals: a pretense; as, under the *mask* of friendliness he hid his evil plans; 3, (usually, *masque*), an old form of play, in which the actors wore masks, or face coverings; also, the text for such a play; 4, (also, *masque*), a masquerade:—*v.t.* 1, to conceal with, or as with, a mask; 2, to cover or hold in check, as troops about to launch a surprise attack:—*v.i.* to take part in a masquerade; be disguised.—*n.* **mask′er.**

masked (mȧskt), *p.adj.* 1, wearing or using a cover over the face; 2, concealed; disguised; hidden.

ma-son (mā′sn), *n.* a builder in stone or brick; a layer of brick: **Mason,** a member of the society of Freemasons.

Ma-son and Dix-on's Line (dĭk′-snz), the southern boundary of Pennsylvania: so called from two English surveyors who laid it out, and notable as part of the boundary line between the free and the slave states.

Ma-son-ic (mȧ-sŏn′ĭk), *adj.* relating to Freemasons or to their rites.

ma-son-ry (mā′sn-rĭ), *n.* [*pl.* masonries (-rĭz)], **1,** the art or occupation of a builder in stone; **2,** a structure made by builders in stone; stonework: **Masonry,** Freemasonry: the institutions and practices of an ancient and secret association or fraternity.

masque (mȧsk), *n.* **1,** a masquerade; **2,** a short play, orig. acted as entertainment at a great castle. Also, **mask.**

mas-quer-ade (mȧs″kẽr-ād′), *n.* **1,** a ball or festive gathering where masks are worn; **2,** an acting or living under false pretenses; **3,** a disguise:—*v.t.* [*p.t.* and *p.p.* -ad′ed, *p.pr.* -ad′ing], to cover with a mask or disguise:—*v.i.* **1,** to take part in a ball where the persons present are disguised; **2,** to take the part or character of another for amusement or deceit; **3,** to make a false appearance.—*n.* **mas″quer-ad′er.**

mass (mȧs), *n.* **1,** a quantity of matter or an aggregation of things united into one body; **2,** a large quantity or number; as, a *mass* of corrections; **3,** bulk; size; **4,** the main part: **the masses,** the common people:—*v.t.* to collect into a lump or body; arrange in close relation; as, to *mass* shrubbery:—*v.i.* to make, form, or gather into a lump or group.

Syn., n. amount, total, agglomeration, body.

Mass (mȧs), *n.* **1,** in liturgical churches, the celebration of the Holy Communion, or Eucharist; **2,** the musical setting for the words of the eucharistic service: **High Mass,** celebration of the Eucharist at the high altar, with music and incense: **Low Mass,** celebration of the Eucharist by one priest, without music or incense.

mas-sa-cre (măs′ȧ-kẽr), *n.* the killing of many people with violence and cruelty; wholesale slaughter or murder of people who cannot offer resistance:—*v.t.* [*p.t.* and *p.p.* -cred (-kẽrd), *p.pr.* -cring], to slaughter in such a manner.—*n.* **mas′sa-crer.**

mas-sage (mȧ-säzh′), *n.* a method of remedial treatment by rubbing or kneading the body:—*v.t.* [*p.t.* and *p.p.* -saged′ (-säzhd′), *p.pr.* -sag′ing], to treat by rubbing and kneading.

mas-seur (mȧ″sûr′), *n.* [*pl.* masseurs (-sûrz′; *Fr.* -sûr′)], one who performs the operation of massage, a method of treating the body, for purposes of health, by rubbing and kneading with the hands; one who massages.—*n.fem.* **mas″seuse′** (mȧ″-söz′), [*pl.* masseuses (mȧ″söz′)].

mas-si-cot (măs′ĭ-kŏt), *n.* a yellow compound of oxygen and lead, used in paints as a pigment and drier.

mas-sif (măs′ĭf; *Fr.* mä″sēf′), *n.* **1,** a thickly wooded hill, or the like, shutting out a view beyond; **2,** the high ground around a higher central point; as, the *massif* of Mont Blanc.

mas-sive (mȧs′ĭv), *adj.* **1,** weighty; heavy; bulky; **2,** hence, imposing; impressive; **3,** imperfectly and irregularly formed: used in speaking of minerals.—*adv.* **mas′sive-ly.**—*n.* **mas′sive-ness.**

Syn. ponderous, unwieldy, solid, substantial.—*Ant.* flimsy, unsubstantial, light, frail.

mass meet-ing a general assembly of people for the discussion of some question of public interest.

mass-y (mȧs′ĭ), *adj.* [*comp.* mass′i-er, *superl.* mass′i-est], weighty; heavy; bulky; ponderous.—*n.* **mass′i-ness.**

[1]mast (mȧst), *n.* **1,** a spar; a long, round iron tube or piece of timber placed upright in a vessel to support the sails; **2,** any upright pole, as the main post of a derrick: **before the mast,** as a common sailor: since living quarters of common sailors were formerly forward.—*adj.* **mast′less.**

[2]mast (mȧst), *n.* nuts, as of the oak, beech, chestnut, etc., esp. when used as fodder for swine.

mas-ter (mȧs′tẽr), *n.* **1,** a male person who rules or commands persons or things; a director; employer; owner; **2,** the head of a household, college, school, etc.; **3,** an expert; as, a *master* at science; hence, a skilled workman; craftsman; **4,** a winner in a contest; **5,** a great artist; **6,** the commander of a merchant vessel: **Master, 1,** a person holding an advanced university degree; **2,** in law, an officer appointed to assist the judge; **3,** used as a title before the names of boys:—*adj.* exercising control; chief; skilled:—*v.t.* to subdue or overcome; as, to *master* a task.

mas-ter-ful (mȧs′tẽr-fo͝ol), *adj.* **1,** showing power or control; as, a *masterful* speaker; **2,** inclined to be domineering.—*adv.* **mas′ter-ful-ly.**

mas-ter key a key that will open several different locks.

mas-ter-ly (mȧs′tẽr-lĭ), *adj.* characteristic of a chief or expert:—*adv.* in the manner of, or with the skill of, a chief or expert.—*n.* **mas′ter-li-ness.**

mas-ter-piece (mȧs′tẽr-pēs″), *n.* **1,** a thing which surpasses in excellence everything else done by the maker; **2,** anything made with extraordinary skill.

mas-ter-ship (mȧs′tẽr-shĭp), *n.* **1,** the dignity of a chief; **2,** control; dominion; mastery; **3,** expert skill.

mas-ter-y (mȧs′tẽr-ĭ), *n.* [*pl.* masteries (-ĭz)], **1,** dominion; **2,** superiority or triumph, as in a contest; **3,** skill.

Syn. rule, sway, ascendancy, supremacy.

mast-head (mȧst′hĕd″), *n.* the top of a mast:—*v.t.* to send to the mast top as a punishment on shipboard.

mas-ti-cate (măs′tĭ-kāt), *v.t.* [*p.t.* and *p.p.* -cat″ed, *p.pr.* -cat″ing], to grind with the teeth; chew.—*n.* **mas′ti-ca″tor.**—*adj* **mas′ti-ca-to-ry.**

mas-ti-ca-tion (măs″tĭ-kā′shŭn), *n.* the act of grinding with the teeth; a chewing; as, *mastication* of food.

mas-tiff (mȧs′tĭf), *n.* one of a breed of large, courageous, powerful dogs, valued chiefly as watchdogs.

mas-to-don (măs′tō-dŏn), *n.* any of several species of very large, extinct elephants.

MASTODON: A, mastodon, restored; B, a molar tooth; C, side view of skull.

mas-toid (măs′toid), *adj.* **1,** nipple-shaped; **2,** in animal bodies, designating, or pertaining to, a projection, or process, of the temporal bone of the skull behind the ear:—*n.* the mastoid bone (see *skull,* illus.).—*adj.* **mas-toi′dal.**

mas-toid-i-tis (măs″toid-ī′tĭs), *n.* a disease caused by an abscess formed inside the mastoid bone, near the brain.

[1]**mat** (măt), *n.* **1**, a flat piece of coarse woven fabric, made of straw, grass, or the like, and used as a floor covering or for wiping the feet at the door; also, an ornamental article on which to place things at table; **2**, anything thickly overgrown or entangled, as weeds:—*v.t.* [*p.t.* and *p.p.* mat′ted, *p.pr.* mat′ting], to mass, knot, or twist together:—*v.i.* to become tangled.

[2]**mat** (măt), *adj.* dull, lusterless, but uniform: said of a surface and of colors:—*n.* **1**, a border for a picture; **2**, (also, *matte*), a dull finish on a gilded or painted surface; in painting, a dull surface of paint spread evenly.

mat-a-dor (măt′ȧ-dōr; măt′ȧ-dôr), *n.* the man chosen to kill the bull in a bullfight. Also, **mat′a-dore.**

[1]**match** (măch), *n.* **1**, anything which agrees with, or is exactly like, another thing; **2**, an equal; as, he met his *match;* **3**, a game or contest; **4**, marriage; **5**, one to be gained in marriage: **match play,** in golf, a competition in which the score is counted by the number of holes won:—*v.t.* **1**, to marry; **2**, to compete with successfully; **3**, to bring an equal against; as, none *matched* his good fortune; **4**, to get a counterpart of, or the equal of:—*v.i.* **1**, to mate; **2**, to agree with, or be like, each other.

[2]**match** (măch), *n.* **1**, a slender piece of wood tipped with material that is easily ignited by friction: now almost universally used for starting fires; **2**, a fuse.—*n.* [1]**match′mak″er.**—*n.* [1]**match′mak″ing.**

match-less (măch′lĕs), *adj.* not capable of being equaled; peerless.

match-lock (măch′lŏk″), *n.* an old kind of musket set off by a match.

[2]**match-mak-er** (măch′māk″ẽr), *n.* one who seeks to arrange marriages for others.—*adj.* and *n.* [2]**match′-mak″ing.**

mate (māt), *n.* **1**, a companion or associate; an equal; **2**, the male or female of a pair of animals for breeding; **3**, a ship's officer ranking below the captain:—*v.t.* [*p.t.* and *p.p.* mat′ed, *p.pr.* mat′ing], **1**, to match; equal; **2**, to marry; of animals, to pair:—*v.i.* to be coupled or united.—*n.* and *p.adj.* **mat′ing.**

ma-té (mä′tā; măt′ā), *n.* a tea made of the dried leaves of Brazilian holly, much used in South America. Also, **ma′te.**

ma-te-ri-al (mȧ-tē′rĭ-ăl), *adj.* **1**, consisting of matter or substance; not spiritual; **2**, pertaining to bodily wants; as, the *material* needs of the poor; **3**, important; as, it is not *material* to me what you do:—*n.* the substance of which anything is made.—*n.* **ma-te″ri-al′i-ty.**

Syn., adj. bodily, physical, temporal.—*Ant., adj.* spiritual, unsubstantial.

ma-te-ri-al-ism (mȧ-tē′rĭ-ăl-ĭzm), *n.* **1**, the doctrine that all the facts of life are the result of the nature, action, etc., of substance or matter; **2**, the tendency to give too much importance to physical well-being and comfort, and too little to spiritual and intellectual life.

ma-te-ri-al-ist (mȧ-tē′rĭ-ăl-ĭst), *n.* **1**, one who holds the doctrine that the universe consists of substance or matter without spirit; **2**, one who is absorbed in bodily things to the exclusion of spiritual interests.—*adj.* **ma-te″ri-al-is′tic.**

ma-te-ri-al-ize (mȧ-tē′rĭ-ăl-īz), *v.t.* [*p.t.* and *p.p.* -ized (-īzd), *p.pr.* -iz″ing], **1**, to make capable of being seen, heard, or felt; **2**, to express through outward objects; as, to *materialize* ambition; **3**, to give bodily form to:—*v.i.* to become a fact.—*n.* **ma-te″ri-al-i-za′tion.**

ma-te-ri-al-ly (mȧ-tē′rĭ-ăl-ĭ), *adv.* **1**, with respect to body or substance; **2**, actually; to a great degree; as, his gift helped our plans *materially.*

ma-te-ri-a med-i-ca (mȧ-tē′rĭ-ȧ mĕd′ĭ-kȧ), **1**, the various substances used as remedies in medicine; **2**, the science of remedies.

ma-ter-nal (mȧ-tûr′năl), *adj.* **1**, motherly; peculiar to motherhood; **2**, coming through the relationship of one's mother; derived from a mother; as, a *maternal* uncle.—*adv.* **ma-ter′nal-ly.**

ma-ter-ni-ty (mȧ-tûr′nĭ-tĭ), *n.* [*pl.* maternities (-tĭz)], the state of being a mother; motherhood: **maternity hospital** or **ward**, a hospital, or a ward in a hospital, for the care of women in childbirth.

math-e-mat-i-cal (măth″ē-măt′ĭ-kăl), *adj.* **1**, pertaining to, or performed by, mathematics, or the science of quantities; **2**, exact; precise; accurate.—*adv.* **math″e-mat′i-cal-ly.**

math-e-ma-ti-cian (măth″ē-mȧ-tĭsh′ăn), *n.* one skilled in mathematics, or the science of quantities.

math-e-mat-ics (măth″ē-măt′ĭks), *n. pl.* used as *sing.* the science that treats of quantities and magnitudes, by the use of symbols, and the measuring, relations, and properties of such quantities and magnitudes.

mat-in (măt′ĭn), *adj.* pertaining to the morning or to morning prayer:—*n.*, in *pl.*, morning prayer.—*adj.* **mat′in-al.**

mat-i-née (măt″ĭ-nā′), *n.* a reception or musicale held in the daytime; esp., a dramatic performance taking place in the afternoon.

mat-ri-ces (măt′rĭ-sēz; mȧ-trī′sēz), *n.* plural of *matrix*, which see.

mat-ri-cide (măt′rĭ-sīd; mā′trĭ-sīd), *n.* **1**, the murder of a mother by her son or daughter; **2**, one who murders his mother.—*adj.* **mat′ri-cid″al.**

ma-tric-u-late (mȧ-trĭk′ū-lāt), *v.t.* [*p.t.* and *p.p.* -lat″ed, *p.pr.* -lat″ing], to admit to the membership of a college or university by entering one's name in a register:—*v.i.* to be admitted as a student, as in a college or university.

ma-tric-u-la-tion (mȧ-trĭk″ū-lā′shŭn), *n.* the act of registering and being admitted as a student, as in a college or university.

mat-ri-mo-ni-al (măt″rĭ-mō′nĭ-ăl), *adj.* pertaining to marriage; nuptial.—*adv.* **mat″ri-mo′ni-al-ly.**

mat-ri-mo-ny (măt′rĭ-mō-nĭ), *n.* [*pl.* matrimonies (-nĭz)], marriage.

Syn. (see marriage).

ma-trix (mā′trĭks), *n.* [*pl.* matrices (măt′rĭ-sēz; mȧ-trī′sēz)], **1**, that which gives form, origin, or foundation to anything inclosed or embedded in it; **2**, a die or mold, as for the face of type, for linotype, or for a monotype typesetting machine; **3**, the rock in which a fossil or mineral is embedded; **4**, *Archaic,* the womb.

ma-tron (mā′trŭn), *n.* **1**, a married woman, esp. one who has borne children; a wife or a widow; **2**, the woman who superintends the housekeeping in a hospital or other institution.—*adj.* **ma′tron-al.**

ma-tron-ly (mā′trŭn-lĭ), *adj.* like a married woman; sedate; as, elderly women wear *matronly* clothes:—*adv.* like a married woman; sedately.

mat-ro-nym-ic (măt″rō-nĭm′ĭk), *n.* a man's or woman's name taken from that of a mother:—*adj.* pertaining to such a name. See **me″tro-nym′ic**, *Pfd. S.*

mat-ted (măt′ĕd), *p.adj.* **1**, covered with a mat or mats; **2**, closely tangled together, as hair.

mat-ter (măt′ẽr), *n.* **1**, that which occupies space, and of which any material body is composed; substance: opp. of *spirit; mind;* **2**, the material of which anything is made; as, solid *matter;* coloring *matter;* **3**, a thing of importance; business; as, the *matter* needs prompt attention; **4**, an indefinite amount; as, a *matter* of $1,000; **5**, a cause of difficulty; as, what is the *matter?* **6**, pus; **7**, set-up type for a printer:—*v.i.* **1**, to be of importance; signify; **2**, to form pus; maturate.

mat-ter-of-fact (măt′ẽr-ŏv-făkt′), *adj.* sticking to real things; literal; not imaginative; commonplace.

Mat-thew (măth′ū), *n.* the first book of the New Testament, the Gospel thought to have been written by Matthew, one of the twelve apostles.—*abbr.* **Matt.**

mat-ting (măt′ĭng), *n.* a kind of carpeting, usually made of woven straw.

mat-tock (măt′ŭk), *n.* a pickax having one of its ends flat.

mat-tress (măt′rĕs), *n.* a quilted hair- or straw-stuffed sack, used as a soft pad for a bed.

mat-u-rate (măt′ū-rāt), *v.i.* [*p.t.* and *p.p.* -rat″ed, *p.pr.* -rat″ing], **1**, to ripen; **2**, to form pus:—*v.t.* to cause to generate pus; bring (an abscess) to a head.—*n.* **mat″u-ra′tion.**—*adj.* **ma-tur′a-tive.**

ma-ture (mȧ-tūr′), *v.i.* [*p.t.* and *p.p.* -tured′ (-tūrd′), *p.pr.* -tur′ing], to become ripe:—*v.t.* to bring or hasten to full growth:—*adj.* **1**, ripe; full-grown; completely developed; as, *mature* fruit; **2**, perfected; ready for use, as a plan.—*adv.* **ma-ture′ly.**

Syn., adj. developed, prime. (See mellow.)

ma-tu-ri-ty (mȧ-tū′rĭ-tĭ), *n.* [*pl.* maturities (-tĭz)], **1**, the state or quality of being full-grown; ripeness; full development; as, the higher animals reach *maturity* much more slowly than the lower animals; **2**, a coming due: said of a note.

ma-tu-ti-nal (mȧ-tū′tĭ-năl; măt″ū-tī′năl), *adj.* of, pertaining to, or occurring in, the morning; early.

maud-lin (môd′lĭn), *adj.* **1**, easily moved to tears; weakly and foolishly sentimental; **2**, drunkenly silly.

mau-ger (mô′gẽr), *prep. Archaic,* in spite of; as, *mauger* all my pride. Also, **mau′gre.**

maul (môl), *n.* a large wooden hammer:—*v.t.* to wound or bruise in a rough manner. Also, **mall.**—*n.* **maul′er.**

maul-stick (môl′stĭk″), *n.* a stick used by painters as a rest to steady the hand while painting. Also, **mahl′stick″.**

maun-der (môn′dẽr; män′dẽr), *v.t.* to utter without meaning or connection:—*v.i.* **1**, to talk foolishly or indistinctly; grumble; **2**, to wander aimlessly.

Maun-dy Thurs-day (môn′dĭ), the day before Good Friday; the Thursday before Easter.

mau-ser (mou′zẽr), *n.* a repeating rifle of high power, a shot from which carries a long distance.

mau-so-le-um (mô″sŏ-lē′ŭm), *n.* [*pl.* mausoleums (-ŭmz); mausolea (-ȧ)], a stately tomb or monument: named from that of Mausolus, King of Caria, erected by his widow Artemisia; as, Grant's tomb is a handsome *mausoleum.*

mauve (mōv), *n.* a soft lilac or purple color or dye, derived from coal tar.

ma-vis (mā′vĭs), *n.* the European song thrush.

maw (mô), *n.* **1**, the stomach, or the mouth and throat, of an animal; **2**, in birds, the craw or crop.

mawk-ish (môk′ĭsh), *adj.* **1**, causing disgust or loathing; **2**, maudlin; foolishly sentimental; as, *mawkish* love stories.—*adv.* **mawk′ish-ly.**—*n.* **mawk′ish-ness.**

max-il-la (măk-sĭl′ȧ), *n.* [*pl.* maxillæ (-ē)], **1**, one of the jawbones, esp. the upper jawbone; **2**, one of the mouth parts of insects, shellfish, etc.

max-il-la-ry (măk′sĭ-lā-rĭ), *adj.* pertaining to, or situated near, the jaw:—*n.* [*pl.* maxillaries (-rĭz)], one of the jawbones, esp. the upper jawbone.

max-im (măk′sĭm), *n.* an established principle or truth; a proverb; a well-known saying; as, the old *maxim,* "Waste not, want not," is full of truth.

Syn. adage, saying, byword, saw.

Max-im gun an automatic machine gun: named after its inventor, Hiram S. Maxim.

max-im-ite (măk′sĭm-īt), *n.* a high explosive, used as a bursting charge for armor-piercing projectiles: named for its inventor, Hudson Maxim.

max-i-mum (măk′sĭ-mŭm), *n.* [*pl.* maxima (-mȧ); maximums (-mŭmz)], the greatest number, quantity, or degree possible; as, a *maximum* of good result: opp. of *minimum:*—*adj.* **1**, greatest in quantity or highest in degree; **2**, highest allowed by law; as, the *maximum* price for copper.

may (mā), *v.aux.* followed by infinitive without *to* [*p.t.* might (mīt)], **1**, to be allowed; be free; be permitted; as, you *may* look; **2**, to be possible; be likely, but not certain; **3**, expressing the earnest desire, or wish, of the speaker; as, *may* the report prove untrue; **4**, to be able; have power: more precisely expressed by *can.*

Syn. can. *Can* expresses the ability to do; *may* expresses permission; as, I shall go if I *can* (that is, if I am able to); I shall go if I *may* (that is, if I am permitted to). Hence, in asking permission, one should not say "*can* I go?" but "*may* I go?"

May (mā), *n.* **1**, the fifth month of the year, containing 31 days; **2**, youth, or the springtime of existence:—*v.i.* to celebrate the first day of May, as by gathering flowers: **may,** *n.* the hawthorn or a similar plant blooming in the spring.

May ap-ple an American plant of the barberry family, or its edible fruit: also called *mandrake.*

may-be (mā′bē), *adv.* it may happen that; perhaps; possibly.

May Day the first day of May: often celebrated by outdoor festivities, such as dancing about a garlanded Maypole or crowning a May queen.

May-fair (mā′fâr″), *n.* **1**, the section of London where the aristocracy lives; **2**, hence, the best London society.

May-flow-er (mā′flou″ẽr), *n.* **1**, any of several plants flowering in May or early spring, as the arbutus; **2**, the vessel that brought the Pilgrims from England to the New World in 1620.

may-hem (mā′hĕm), *n.* the offense of disabling a person by injuring any of his members: also called *maim.*

May-ing (mā′ĭng), *n.* the celebration of May Day by gathering flowers or by appropriate festivities. Also, **may′ing.**

may-on-naise (mā″ŏ-nāz′; *Fr.* mȧ″yŏ″-nâz′), *n.* a sauce or salad dressing of the raw yolks of eggs, olive oil, and seasoning.

may-or (mā′ẽr; mâr), *n.* the chief magistrate of a city or borough.

may-or-al-ty (mā′ŏr-ăl-tĭ), *n.* [*pl.* mayoralties (-tĭz)], the office, or term of office, of a mayor, or chief magistrate of a city; as, a candidate for the *mayoralty.*

May-pole (mā'pōl″), *n.* a pole decorated with flowers and ribbons around which May Day celebrations are held.

May-tide (mā'tīd″), *n.* the month of May. Also, **May'time″.**

may-weed (mā'wēd″), *n.* a pungent plant of the aster family, with white and yellow daisylike flowers.

maze (māz), *n.* **1,** bewilderment; perplexity; confusion of mind; **2,** a confusing tangle; a network, as of passages.

ma-zur-ka (mȧ-zûr'kȧ; mȧ-zōōr'kȧ), *n.* **1,** a lively Polish dance; **2,** music for such a dance. Also, **ma-zour'ka.**

ma-zy (mā'zĭ), *adj.* [*comp.* ma'zi-er, *superl.* ma'zi-est], hard to unravel or to trace out; bewildering; winding.—*adv.* **ma'zi-ly.**—*n.* **ma'zi-ness.**

me (mē), *pron.* the objective case of *I*, the pronoun of the first person.

[1]**mead** (mēd), *n.* **1,** a liquor of the Middle Ages, made by fermenting honey and water; **2,** a beverage made of sirup of sarsaparilla and carbonated water.

[2]**mead** (mēd), *n. Poetic,* a grassy field; meadow; lea.

mead-ow (mĕd'ō), *n.* **1,** a tract of rich pasture land; **2,** land from which hay is obtained; **3,** often in *pl.*, low, grassy land by the banks of streams.

mead-ow lark an American song bird allied to the blackbird, with a yellow breast marked with black.

mea-ger (mē'gẽr), *adj.* **1,** lacking in flesh; lean; gaunt; as, her *meager* frame; **2,** lacking in fertility, richness, or strength; scanty; as, a *meager* harvest. Also, **mea'gre.**—*adv.* **mea'ger-ly.**—*n.* **mea'ger-ness.**

Syn. poor, lank. (See lean.)

[1]**meal** (mēl), *n.* **1,** the edible part of grain coarsely ground; **2,** unsifted flour made from corn or wheat.

[2]**meal** (mēl), *n.* a repast; an occasion of taking food; also, the food so taken.

meal-time (mēl'tīm″), *n.* the hour fixed for a meal.

meal-y (mēl'ĭ), *adj.* [*comp.* meal'i-er, *superl.* meal'i-est], **1,** consisting of, sprinkled with, or like, coarsely ground grain; **2,** dry and soft; as, *mealy* potatoes.

meal-y–mouthed (mēl'ĭ-mou*th*d″; -moutht″), *adj.* using soft words; unwilling to use plain words.

[1]**mean** (mēn), *v.t.* [*p.t.* and *p.p.* meant (mĕnt), *p.pr.* mean'ing], **1,** to intend or determine upon; as, he *means* mischief; to design; purpose; as, he *meant* it as a jest; **2,** to convey, or be intended to convey, the significance of; signify; denote; as, charity *means* love; designate; as, she *means* me:—*v.i.* to be disposed; as, to *mean* well or ill.

[2]**mean** (mēn), *adj.* **1,** lacking in distinction; humble; plebeian; **2,** lacking in intelligence; inefficient; ordinary; **3,** lacking in dignity; ignoble; insignificant; **4,** lacking in generosity; stingy; sordid; **5,** lacking in honor; base; as, a *mean* motive; **6,** *Colloq.*, petty and malicious; disobliging; disagreeable. —*adv.* **mean'ly.**—*n.* **mean'ness.**

Syn. abject, vile, degraded, pitiful.

[3]**mean** (mēn), *adj.* **1,** in an intermediate position; between two extremes; **2,** average; medium as to quality, degree, or bulk:—*n.* **1,** a condition, quality, course of action, or the like, which is near the middle point between two extremes; **2,** hence, absence of excess; moderation; **3,** in mathematics: **a,** a quantity intermediate between the extremes of a set of quantities; **b,** one of the two middle terms in a proportion; **c,** an average; a sum computed by dividing the sum of a number of quantities by their number: known as the *arithmetic mean:* **4,** in *pl.:* **a,** used as *sing.*, instrumentality; agency; as a *means* to an end; **b,** wealth; property.

Syn., adj. average. As here compared, *mean* describes a condition intermediate between two opposite extremes, as in size or quality; as, the *mean* height or quality. *Average* refers to a usual, prevalent standard, and hence describes the general quality of something; as, *average* attendance.

me-an-der (mē-ăn'dẽr), *v.t.* and *v.i.* to wind or flow round, as a river; wander aimlessly or without purpose:—*n.*, usually in *pl.*, a winding, as of a stream.—*adj.* **me-an'drous.**

mean-ing (mēn'ĭng), *p.adj.* expressive; full of significance; as, a *meaning* glance:—*n.* **1,** object; aim; intention; as, the *meaning* of her visit; **2,** that which is signified; as, the *meaning* of a word.—*adj.* **mean'ing-less.**—*adv.* **mean'ing-ly.**

Syn., n. signification, import, sense, purport.

meant (mĕnt), past tense and past participle of the verb *mean.*

mean-time (mēn'tīm″), *adv.* **1,** in the time between two occasions; **2,** at the same time:—*n.* the intervening time. —*adv.* and *n.* **mean'while″.**

mea-sles (mē'zlz), *n.pl.* used as *sing.* **1,** an easily spread disease, esp. of children, marked by fever and small red spots on the skin; **2,** a disease of swine and cattle caused by tapeworm larvæ.

mea-sly (mē'zlĭ), *adj.* **1,** infected with the disease called measles; **2,** infected with tapeworm larvæ: said of meat; **3,** *Slang,* slight; contemptible.

meas-ur-a-ble (mĕzh'ūr-ȧ-bl), *adj.* **1,** capable of being estimated or computed; **2,** of limited amount; moderate. —*adv.* **meas'ur-a-bly.**

meas-ure (mĕzh'ūr), *n.* **1,** the standard by which the volume or extent of anything is compared; as, the light given by a candle is the *measure* by which the power of other light is calculated; **2,** size or quantity, determined by the rule or standard; **3,** hence, any standard of judgment, criticism, or comparison; **4,** a divisor leaving no remainder; as, five is a common *measure* of ten and fifteen; **5,** an instrument or vessel for finding length, quantity, etc.; as, a yard or a quart *measure;* **6,** a system of fixing quantities; as, dry *measure;* **7,** musical time; also meter in poetry; **8,** a law or a legislative bill; **9,** a method or step; **10,** in *pl.*, layers of rock or soil or deposits of minerals:—*v.t.* [*p.t.* and *p.p.* -ured (-ūrd), *p.pr.* -ur-ing], **1,** to find out the extent, size, or volume of; hence, to estimate; **2,** to allot; give out by a rule; as, to *measure* out rations; **3,** to determine by rule or standard; regulate; as, to *measure* one's words or conduct:—*v.i.* **1,** to take dimensions; **2,** to extend or be of a given length; as, the room *measures* fifteen feet.—*abbr.* **meas.**—*n.* **meas'ur-er.**

meas-ured (mĕzh'ūrd), *p.adj.* **1,** determined by a standard; **2,** regular; steady; as, the soldiers march with *measured* tread; **3,** resulting from thought; as, *measured* words.—*adv.* **meas'ured-ly.**

meas-ure-less (mĕzh'ūr-lĕs), *adj.* unlimited; vast; immense; of a size too large to be found out.

meas-ure-ment (mĕzh'ūr-mĕnt), *n.* **1,** the act of finding the size, quantity, amount, etc., by some standard; **2,** size or quantity determined by such standard; length; area; **3,** a system of standards or units for comparison.

meas-ur-ing worm any of numerous caterpillars, the larvæ of the geometrid moths, which progress by humping the body into a loop and then extending the head end: also called *measurer.*

meat (mēt), *n.* **1**, animal flesh used as food; **2**, food in general; victuals: **meat grinder**, a kitchen utensil for rapidly cutting or grinding meat and vegetables into small pieces.

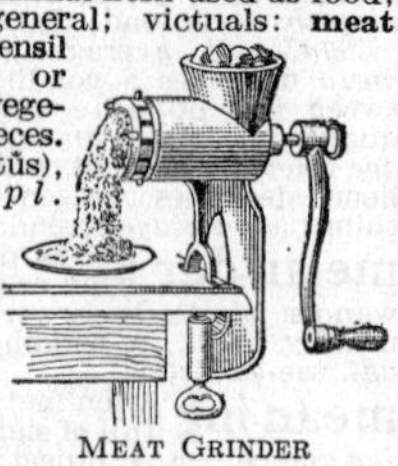

MEAT GRINDER

me-a-tus (mē-ā′tŭs), *n.* [*pl.* meatuses (-ĕz); meatus (-tūs)], in anatomy, a natural passage or canal, or the opening of a duct.

meat-y (mēt′ĭ), *adj.* [*comp.* meat′i-er, *superl.* meat′i-est], resembling meat; hence, full of substance; pithy.

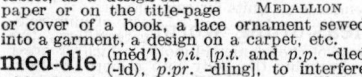

me-chan-ic (mē-kăn′ĭk), *n.* **1**, a skilled workman, esp. one who understands the construction and use of machinery; **2**, one who works as if he were a machine: **mechanics**, *pl.* used as *sing.* the science of the laws of matter and motion; esp., the science of machinery:—*adj.* **1**, of or pertaining to a workman, esp. one with knowledge of machinery; involving skill with the hands; **2**, relating to machinery; as, *mechanic* arts.

me-chan-i-cal (mē-kăn′ĭ-kăl), *adj.* **1**, pertaining to the laws of matter and motion; **2**, pertaining to, or produced by, machines or machinery; as, *mechanical* toys; **3**, done without thought, as if from habit; as, a *mechanical* smile.—*adv.* **me-chan′i-cal-ly.**—*n.* **me-chan′i-cal-ness.**

me-chan-i-cal pow-er any of several instruments which convert a smaller force acting through a greater space into a greater force acting through a lesser space, as the lever, inclined plane, wheel and axle, screw, pulley, and wedge.

mech-a-ni-cian (mĕk″ȧ-nĭsh′ăn), *n.* one skilled in the laws of matter and motion, or in the actual construction of machinery; a machinist.

me-chan-ic's li-en a legal claim upon property in compensation for labor or material spent on it.

mech-a-nism (mĕk′ȧ-nĭzm), *n.* **1**, the relative arrangement of the working parts of an engine, machine, or of anything resembling a machine; **2**, the construction of the works; as, the *mechanism* of a watch is most delicate; also, the operation or action of the parts.

Mech-lin (mĕk′lĭn), *n.* a beautiful and very delicate kind of lace, made at Mechlin, Belgium.

med-al (mĕd′ăl), *n.* **1**, a coin-shaped piece of metal marked with a design or with words to commemorate some event, distinguished person, etc.; **2**, such a metal disk given as a reward: **medal play**, in golf, a competition in which the score is counted by the total number of strokes made.

med-al-ist (mĕd′ăl-ĭst), *n.* **1**, one who designs or makes medals; **2**, the winner of a medal. Also, **med′al-list.**

me-dal-lion (mē-dăl′yŭn), *n.* **1**, a large antique medal; **2**, a framed decorative tablet or panel bearing a figure or design drawn, sculptured, or engraved; **3**, anything resembling such a tablet, as a design on wall paper or on the title-page or cover of a book, a lace ornament sewed into a garment, a design on a carpet, etc.

MEDALLION

med-dle (mĕd′l), *v.i.* [*p.t.* and *p.p.* -dled (-ld), *p.pr.* -dling], to interfere with what does not concern one.—*n.* **med′dler.**

med-dle-some (mĕd′l-sŭm), *adj.* apt to interfere in the affairs of others; officious.—*adv.* **med′dle-some-ly.**—*n.* **med′dle-some-ness.**

Mede (mēd), *n.* a native of ancient Media, situated in what is now northwestern Persia.—*adj.* and *n.* **Me′di-an.**

Me-de-a (mē-dē′ȧ), *n.* in mythology, a sorceress of Colchis, who helped Jason win the Golden Fleece, and who, after he had deserted her, destroyed her children and her rival.

me-di-al (mē′dĭ-ăl), *adj.* **1**, pertaining to the middle; **2**, average; ordinary.—*adv.* **me′di-al-ly.**

me-di-an (mē′dĭ-ăn), *adj.* pertaining to, or connected with, the middle of anything; as, the *median* vein of a leaf.

me-di-ate (mē′dĭ-āt), *v.i.* [*p.t.* and *p.p.* -at″ed, *p.pr.* -at″ing], to interpose between those who are openly disagreeing, so as to bring about friendly relations:—*v.t.* to bring about by interposing between enemies or opponents; as, to *mediate* a peace:—*adj.* (mē′dĭ-āt), not direct; acting by or through an agency.—*adv.* **me′di-ate-ly.**

me-di-a-tion (mē″dĭ-ā′shŭn), *n.* **1**, the act of trying to bring about friendly relations; **2**, reconciliation; intercession; intervention.

me-di-a-tor (mē′dĭ-ā″tẽr), *n.* one who tries to bring about friendly relations between those (persons, nations, etc.) who are openly disagreeing; as, the *mediator* between Japan and Russia.

me-di-a-to-ry (mē′dĭ-ȧ-tō-rĭ), *adj.* pertaining to, or having the nature of, a peacemaker or peacemaking.—*adj.* **me″di-a-to′ri-al.**

med-ic (mĕd′ĭk), *n.* any of various clover-like plants of the pea family, as alfalfa: **black medic**, nonesuch, a common, annual trailing plant (see *shamrock*, illus.).

med-i-ca-ble (mĕd′ĭ-kȧ-bl), *adj.* curable; in a condition to be helped or cured by medicine.

med-i-cal (mĕd′ĭ-kăl), *adj.* pertaining to, or connected with, the science or art of medicine, or the treatment of disease: **medical corps**, the branch of an army which is in charge of those who are sick and wounded.—*adv.* **med′i-cal-ly.**

me-dic-a-ment (mē-dĭk′ȧ-mĕnt; mĕd′ĭ-kȧ-), *n.* **1**, anything used for healing diseases or wounds; **2**, anything that heals or cures.

med-i-cate (mĕd′ĭ-kāt), *v.t.* [*p.t.* and *p.p.* -cat″ed, *p.pr.* -cat″ing], **1**, to treat with any curative or healing substance; **2**, to fill with any such substance; as, to *medicate* cotton; **3**, to cure.—*n.* **med″i-ca′tion.**

Med-i-ce-an (mĕd″ĭ-sē′ăn), *adj.* of or pertaining to the Medici, a wealthy and powerful Florentine family of the 14th, 15th, and 16th centuries, liberal patrons of the arts.

me-dic-i-nal (mē-dĭs′ĭ-năl), *adj.* having the properties of, or used in, any curative substance; healing; as, *medicinal* springs.—*adv.* **me-dic′i-nal-ly.**

med-i-cine (mĕd′ĭ-sĭn; *Br.* mĕd′sn), *n.* **1**, the science which relates to the prevention, treatment, and cure of disease; **2**, a substance or preparation for the cure of disease: **medicine man**, among primitive peoples, as the North American Indians, one who professes to drive away evil spirits or disease by magical arts or spells.

me-di-e-val (mē″dĭ-ē′văl; mĕd″ĭ-ē′văl), *adj.* **1**, pertaining to, or characteristic of, the Middle Ages, a period extending approximately from the fifth to the sixteenth centuries after Christ; **2**, specif., not modern; out of date. Also, **me″di-æ′val.**—*adv.* **me″di-e′val-ly.**

me-di-o-cre (mē′dĭ-ō″kẽr), *adj.* of medium excellence; ordinary; of a medium quality; commonplace.

me-di-oc-ri-ty (mē″dĭ-ŏk′rĭ-tĭ), *n.* [*pl.* mediocrities (-tĭz)], **1**, the quality of being ordinary or commonplace; **2**, a person of average ability.

med-i-tate (mĕd′ĭ-tāt), *v.i.* [*p.t.* and *p.p.* -tat″ed, *p.pr.* -tat″ing], to muse or think deeply; contemplate:—*v.t.* **1**, to think or muse upon; **2**, to design; purpose; plan.

med-i-ta-tion (mĕd″ĭ-tā′shŭn), *n.* the act of thinking long and deeply, esp. such thought as a part of one's prayers or devotions.

med-i-ta-tive (mĕd′ĭ-tā-tĭv), *adj.* devoted to, or disposed to, long and serious thought.—*adv.* **med′i-ta-tive-ly.**—*n.* **med′i-ta-tive-ness.**

Med-i-ter-ra-ne-an (mĕd″ĭ-tẽr-ā′nē-ăn), *adj.* designating, or pertaining to, an arm of the Atlantic Ocean which separates Europe from Africa: **mediterranean**, landlocked; inclosed by land.

me-di-um (mē′dĭ-ŭm), *n.* [*pl.* mediums (-ŭmz); media (-*ȧ*)], **1**, the mean; that which comes between or in the middle; **2**, agency; as, the newspaper is a great advertising *medium;* **3**, the space or substance in which bodies exist or move; as, water is the only *medium* in which fish can live; **4**, a size of paper eighteen by twenty-three inches; **5**, a person who claims to deliver messages from the spirit world to earth; **6**, the liquid with which dry paints are mixed in preparing them for use; **7**, the material used to produce a work of art; as, charcoal is a good *medium* for a sketch:—*adj.* having a middle position; halfway between two things.

Syn., *n.* organ, channel, instrument, means.

med-lar (mĕd′lȧr), *n.* a small European tree of the apple family, with an edible fruit; also, the fruit.

med-ley (mĕd′lĭ), *n.* [*pl.* medleys (-lĭz)], **1**, a mixture or confused mass; **2**, in music, a composition made up of passages selected from different songs or pieces, arranged as a continuous composition.

Syn. variety, diversity, jumble, miscellany.

me-dul-la (mē-dŭl′*ȧ*), *n.* **1**, the marrow of bones; **2**, the pith of plants: **medulla oblongata** (ŏb″lŏng-gā′t*ȧ*), that part of the brain which is lowest and a continuation of the spinal cord: also called *medulla.*

med-ul-la-ry (mĕd′ū-lā-rĭ; mē-dŭl′*ȧ*-rĭ), *adj.* pertaining to, or consisting of, marrow, or medulla: **medullary ray**, in the stems of many plants, one of the plates of dense tissue extending from the center to the bark: the cause of the silver grain in quartered oak.

me-du-sa (mē-dū′s*ȧ*), *n.* [*pl.* medusæ (-sē)], the sea nettle or jellyfish: **Medusa**, in classical mythology, one of the three Gorgons, whose fine hair was changed into snakes, and whose glance changed all who looked on her into stone.

meed (mēd), *n.* reward; that which is given in consideration of merit.

meek (mēk), *adj.* **1**, mild of temper; patient; gentle; **2**, easily imposed upon; spiritless; **3**, modest; humble.—*adv.* **meek′ly.**—*n.* **meek′ness.**

meer-schaum (mēr′shôm; mēr′shŭm), *n.* **1**, a white, claylike substance from which pipe bowls are made; **2**, a pipe of this material.

¹meet (mēt), *v.t.* [*p.t.* and *p.p.* met (mĕt), *p.pr.* meet′ing], **1**, to come up to or approach from a different direction; **2**, to come face to face with; **3**, to come into contact with; intersect; as, a line *meets* a circumference; **4**, to oppose in a battle, contest, duel, or the like; **5**, to be introduced to; **6**, to experience; encounter; **7**, to be perceived by; as, to *meet* the eye; **8**, to conform to, as a requirement; **9**, to refute, as an argument:—*v.i.* **1**, to come together in one place; assemble; **2**, to come in contact with another; **3**, to unite; **4**, to contend; conflict:—*n.* a gathering or assemblage for some definite purpose; also, the place of meeting, or those who gather there.

²meet (mēt), *adj.* suitable; fitting; proper; appropriate; convenient; adapted.

meet-ing (mēt′ĭng), *n.* **1**, a coming together of persons or things; **2**, an assembly; **3**, a gathering for a special purpose, as for a religious service; **4**, a junction or union, as of roads.

meet-ing-house (mēt′ĭng-hous″), *n.* a building for public worship, esp. one used by Friends.

meg-a- (mĕg′*ȧ*-), a prefix or combining form from the Greek, meaning great; as, *mega*lith; *mega*phone.

meg-a-lith (mĕg′*ȧ*-lĭth), *n.* a huge stone or boulder used in making certain prehistoric monuments.

meg-a-lo-ma-ni-a (mĕg″*ȧ*-lō-mā′nĭ-*ȧ*), *n.* a craze or passion for fame or personal greatness.

meg-a-phone (mĕg′*ȧ*-fōn), *n.* a conical, trumpetlike device, enabling the voice to be carried for a long distance.

meg-a-the-ri-um (mĕg″*ȧ*-thē′rĭ-ŭm), *n.* a very large, slothlike animal living ages ago, the bones of which have been discovered in South America.

me-grim (mē′grĭm), *n.* **1**, (preferably, *migraine*), a nervous headache; **2**, in *pl.*, depression; low spirits; despondency.

Meis-ter-sing-er (mīs′tẽr-sĭng″ẽr; *Ger.* -zĭng″ẽr), *n.* [*pl.* Meistersinger], a member of a guild of musicians, chiefly workingmen, which originated in Germany in the 14th century and flourished particularly in the 16th century, maintained for the cultivation of poetry and music: the successors of the *minnesingers.*

mel-an-cho-li-a (mĕl″ăn-kō′lĭ-*ȧ*), *n.* a mental disorder marked by great depression of spirits.

mel-an-chol-ic (mĕl″ăn-kŏl′ĭk; mĕl′ăn-kŏl″ĭk), *adj.* affected with depression of spirits; downcast; sad; dejected.—*adv.* **mel″an-chol′i-cal-ly.**

mel-an-chol-y (mĕl′ăn-kŏl-ĭ), *n.* [*pl.* melancholies (-ĭz)], dejection; depression of spirits:—*adj.* dejected.

Syn., *adj.* dispirited, dreamy, sad, mournful.

***mé-lange** (mā″läṅzh′), [Fr.], *n.* a confused mixture; medley.

mel-a-nite (mĕl′*ȧ*-nīt), *n.* a garnet of velvety black color.

***mê-lée** (mâ″lā′), [Fr.], *n.* a hand-to-hand conflict; scuffle; scrimmage.

mel-i-nite (mĕl′ĭ-nīt), *n.* a powerful explosive, used for charging shells.

mel-io-rate (mēl′yō-rāt), *v.t.* [*p.t.* and *p.p.* -rat″ed, *p.pr.* -rat″ing], to improve or make better; make more bearable:—*v.i.* to grow better; improve.—*adj.* **mel′io-ra-tive.**—*n.* **mel″io-ra′tion.**

mel-lif-lu-ence (mĕ-lĭf′lo͞o-ĕns), *n.* the quality of being smooth, sweet, and honeylike.—*adj.* **mel-lif′lu-ent.**

mel-lif-lu-ous (mĕ-lĭf′lo͞o-ŭs), *adj.* flowing with, or as with, honey; smooth and sweet; honeyed.—*adv.* **mel-lif′lu-ous-ly.**

mel-low (mĕl′ō), *adj.* **1**, fully ripe; **2**, not hard, harsh, or stiff; delicate, as a color; **3**, made sweet or gentle, as by age or maturity; **4**, *Colloq.*, genial; partly tipsy:—

v.t. and *v.i.* to make or become ripe or gentle. —*n.* **mel'low-ness.**

Syn., adj. mature, ripe, soft. That is *mature* which is fully developed; as, a *mature* mind. That is *ripe* which is ready to be harvested, gathered, or used; as, *ripe* grain; *ripe* for mischief. That is *mellow* which is soft, juicy, and sweet in its ripeness. *Mellow* may also describe that which has been made wise, gentle, or sweet by maturity; as, *mellow* judgment; *mellow* age; *mellow* wine.—*Ant., adj.* immature, green, hard, unripe, bitter.

me-lo-de-on (mē-lō'dē-ŭn), *n.* a small reed organ, supplied with air by bellows worked by treadles.

me-lo-di-ous (mē-lō'dĭ-ŭs), *adj.* full of, or produced by, a sweet succession of sounds; musical.—*adv.* **me-lo'di-ous-ly.**—*n.* **me-lo'di-ous-ness.**

Syn. tuneful, dulcet, sweet, harmonious, pleasing.—*Ant.* discordant, jarring.

mel-o-dist (mĕl'ō-dĭst), *n.* a composer or singer of tuneful music.

mel-o-dra-ma (mĕl″ō-drä'mȧ; mĕl'ō-drä″mȧ), *n.* **1,** a highly sensational or romantic play which ends happily; **2,** hence, romantic or sensational behavior.

mel-o-dra-mat-ic (mĕl″ō-drȧ-măt'ĭk), *adj.* **1,** pertaining to, or of the nature of, romantic or sensational plays; **2,** highly sensational or emotional.—*adv.* **mel″o-dra-mat'i-cal-ly.**

mel-o-dy (mĕl'ō-dĭ), *n.* [*pl.* melodies (-dĭz)], **1,** the arrangement of different musical sounds for a single voice or part; **2,** a tune or an air in harmonized music; **3,** an agreeable succession of single tones, making a pleasing musical composition.—*adj.* **me-lod'ic.**—*v.t.* and *v.i.* **mel'o-dize.**

Syn. harmony. A *melody* is an arrangement of single notes in succession, serving to express a musical idea. *Harmony* names a combination of notes of different pitch produced at the same time to form a chord.

mel-on (mĕl'ŭn), *n.* **1,** a plant of the gourd family; also, its edible fruit; muskmelon; **2,** the watermelon.

Mel-pom-e-ne (mĕl-pŏm'ē-nē), *n.* in mythology, that one of the nine Muses who presided over tragedy.

melt (mĕlt), *v.t.* and *v.i.* [*p.t.* melt'ed, *p.p.* melt'ed or, *Archaic,* molt'en (mōl'tn), *p.pr.* melt'ing], **1,** to change from a solid to a liquid state, often by heat; as, ice *melts;* **2,** to dissolve; blend, as sugar; **3,** to soften to love and tenderness; as, to *melt* anger; **4,** to dwindle; waste; as, his money *melted* away.

mem-ber (mĕm'bẽr), *n.* **1,** a limb or organ, as of the body; hence, a necessary part of anything; **2,** one of an association or community; as, a club *member.*

mem-ber-ship (mĕm'bẽr-shĭp), *n.* **1,** the state of being one of an association or community; **2,** the persons belonging to an organization, collectively; as, the *membership* of the United States Senate.

mem-brane (mĕm'brān), *n.* a thin fold or layer of animal or vegetable tissue, covering some part or organ.

mem-bra-nous (mĕm'brȧ-nŭs), *adj.* pertaining to, consisting of, or like, a membrane, or layer of tissue covering some part or organ.

me-men-to (mē-mĕn'tō), *n.* [*pl.* mementos; mementoes (-tōz)], a souvenir; memorial.

Mem-non (mĕm'nŏn), *n.* in mythology, the son of Tithonus and Eos, king of the Ethiopians, slain by Achilles in the Trojan War: **Singing Memnon,** one of two colossal statues of Amenophis III, later taken as statues of Memnon, fabled to emit harplike music at sunrise.

mem-oir (mĕm'wŏr; -wär; mēm'-), *n.* **1,** a record of something considered noteworthy, as an address to, or a record of the transactions of, a learned or scientific society; **2,** a memorial to, or biography of, an individual; **3,** in *pl.,* a history written from personal experience and knowledge.

mem-o-ra-bil-i-a (mĕm″ō-rȧ-bĭl'ĭ-ȧ), *n.pl.* **1,** things worthy of remembrance or record; **2,** the record that is kept of such things.

mem-o-ra-ble (mĕm'ō-rȧ-bl), *adj.* worthy of remembrance; remarkable; notable.—*adv.* **mem'o-ra-bly.**

Syn. signal, marked, noteworthy.

mem-o-ran-dum (mĕm″ō-răn'dŭm), *n.* [*pl.* memorandums (-dŭmz); memoranda (-dȧ)], **1,** a note or outline to help one to remember; a brief record of something to be remembered; **2,** in diplomacy, an informal outline or statement of the subject under discussion.

me-mo-ri-al (mē-mō'rĭ-ăl), *adj.* in remembrance; sacred to the memory of a deceased person, or of some event:—*n.* **1,** a thing intended to keep in mind an event, a place, or a person, as a monument; **2,** an informal diplomatic paper; **3,** a written statement of facts addressed to a government, a public body, etc.: **Memorial Day,** in various states of the U. S., a day, May 30, appointed by law for observing the memory of those who died for the Union in the Civil War: often called *Decoration Day.* A similar day is observed by the Southern States on various dates.—*n.* **me-mo'ri-al-ist.**

me-mo-ri-al-ize (mē-mō'rĭ-ăl-īz), *v.t.* [*p.t.* and *p.p.* -ized (-īzd), *p.pr.* -iz″ing], **1,** to request something from (a government or the like), by sending a written statement of facts; **2,** to commemorate.—*n.* **me-mo″ri-al-i-za'tion.**

mem-o-rize (mĕm'ō-rīz), *v.t.* [*p.t.* and *p.p.* -rized (-rīzd), *p.pr.* -riz″ing], **1,** to keep in remembrance; **2,** to learn by heart; as, to *memorize* poetry.

mem-o-ry (mĕm'ō-rĭ), *n.* [*pl.* memories (-rĭz)], **1,** that faculty of the mind by which it keeps the knowledge of occurrences, facts, thoughts, etc., which are a part of the past, and recalls them; **2,** a particular experience or period remembered; as, he was lost in *memories* of his youth; **3,** the range of time within which past happenings are remembered; as, within the *memory* of the oldest inhabitant; **4,** the subject of remembrance; as, his youthful ideals were but *memories* to him.

Syn. remembrance, recollection, reminiscence. *Memory* is the faculty of retaining or reproducing past images, impressions, or thoughts. *Remembrance* suggests the state of being recalled, or the act of keeping in mind. *Recollection* is remembering by act of will, or the conscious effort to recall. *Reminiscence* implies the recalling of events or experiences in which one has had a part.—*Ant.* forgetfulness, oblivion.

men (mĕn), *n.* plural of *man;* as, "all *men* are created free and equal."

men-ace (mĕn'ās), *n.* **1,** a danger or evil; **2,** a threat:—*v.t.* [*p.t.* and *p.p.* -aced (-āst), *p.pr.* -ac-ing], to express the intention of inflicting evil upon:—*v.i.* to act in a threatening manner.—*adv.* **men'ac-ing-ly.**

Syn., v. (see threaten).

mé-nage (mā″nȧzh'), *n.* **1,** a household; **2,** household management. Also, **me-nage'** (mē-näzh').

me-nag-er-ie (mē-năj'ẽr-ĭ; mē-năzh'ẽr-ĭ), *n.* **1,** a place where wild animals are kept; **2,** a collection of wild or trained animals for exhibition.

mend (mĕnd), *v.t.* **1**, to repair (that which is broken or worn); **2**, to make better; correct; reform:—*v.i.* to grow better; improve.—*n.* **mend′er.**
Syn. amend, better, rectify.

men-da-cious (mĕn-dā′shŭs), *adj.* **1**, given to falsehood; as, a *mendacious* person; **2**, lying; false, as a statement.—*adv.* **men-da′cious-ly.**

men-dac-i-ty (mĕn-dăs′ĭ-tĭ), *n.* [*pl.* mendacities (-tĭz)], falsehood; habitual lying; also, a lie.
Syn. deceit, untruth. (See lie.)

men-di-can-cy (mĕn′dĭ-kăn-sĭ), *n.* **1**, the state of being a beggar; **2**, the act of begging. Also, **men-dic′i-ty.**

men-di-cant (mĕn′dĭ-kănt), *n.* a beggar; specif., a begging friar:—*adj.* practicing begging; as, *mendicant* friars.

Men-e-la-us (mĕn″ĕ-lā′ŭs), *n.* in Greek mythology, brother of Agamemnon, and husband of Helen.

men-ha-den (mĕn-hā′dn), *n.* a sea fish of the herring family, used for bait and fertilizer.

me-ni-al (mē′nĭ-ăl; mēn′yăl), *n.* **1**, a domestic servant; **2**, one who performs servile or slavelike work:—*adj.* **1**, pertaining to servants in a household; **2**, mean; slavish; servile; sordid.—*adv.* **me′ni-al-ly.**

me-nin-ges (mē-nĭn′jēz), *n.pl.* the three membranes that inclose the brain and spinal cord.

men-in-gi-tis (mĕn″ĭn-jī′tĭs), *n.* a disease in which the membranes inclosing the brain and the spinal cord become inflamed; as, spinal *meningitis.*

me-nis-cus (mē-nĭs′kŭs), *n.* [*pl.* menisci (-nĭs′ī); meniscuses (-kŭs-ĕz)], **1**, a crescent-shaped body; **2**, a lens one surface of which is concave and the other convex (see *lens,* illus.).

men-ses (mĕn′sēz), *n.pl.* the monthly discharge in women; menstruation.

Men-she-vi-ki (mĕn″shĕ-vē-kē′; -vē′-kē), *n.pl.* [*sing.* Menshevik (-vĕk′)], a Russian political party representing the moderate wing of the Socialists.—*n.* **Men′she-vism.**—*adj.* **Men′she-vist.**

men-stru-ate (mĕn′strōō-āt), *v.i.* [*p.t.* and *p.p.* -at″ed, *p.pr.* -at″ing], to discharge the menses, or menstrual flow.—*adj.* **men′stru-al.**—*n.* **men″stru-a′tion.**

men-su-ra-ble (mĕn′shōō-rȧ-bl), *adj.* measurable.

men-su-ra-tion (mĕn″shōō-rā′shŭn), *n.* **1**, the act or process of measuring; **2**, that branch of mathematics concerned with finding the length of lines, areas of surfaces, and volumes of solids.

-ment (-mĕnt), *n. suffix,* signifying: **1**, the act or fact of doing something; as, enforce*ment;* infringe*ment;* **2**, the condition or state resulting from an act; as, excite*ment;* retire*ment;* **3**, means or instrument; as, adorn*ment;* tegu*ment;* **4**, a concrete result or outcome of an action; as, attach*ment;* pave*ment.*

men-tal (mĕn′tăl), *adj.* pertaining to the mind; intellectual; as, *mental* exercise.—*adv.* **men′tal-ly.**
Syn. (see intellectual).

men-tal-i-ty (mĕn-tăl′ĭ-tĭ), *n.* [*pl.* mentalities (-tĭz)], quality or amount of mental power or intellectual ability.

men-thol (mĕn′thōl; mĕn′thŏl), *n.* a substance with a mintlike, pungent odor, obtained from oil of peppermint: used to dull pain, esp. in neuralgia.

men-tion (mĕn′shŭn), *n.* a brief notice; light or chance remark:—*v.t.* to speak briefly of; name; refer to.
Syn., v. tell, communicate, impart, divulge, reveal, disclose, intimate.

men-tion-a-ble (mĕn′shŭn-ȧ-bl), *adj.* fit to be spoken of.

Men-tor (mĕn′tŏr), *n.* in mythology, the friend and tutor of Ulysses: **mentor,** a wise and faithful adviser.

men-u (mĕn′ū; mā′nū; *Fr.* mĕ-nü′), *n.* a bill of fare; a list of the dishes served at a meal; also, the dishes served.

Meph-is-toph-e-les (mĕf″ĭs-tŏf′ĕ-lēz), *n.* **1**, in medieval legend, a demon or familiar spirit, to whom Faust sold his soul; **2**, a fiendish, crafty person.

mer-can-tile (mûr′kăn-tĭl; mûr′kăn-tīl), *adj.* having to do with, or engaged in, trade; pertaining to merchants.

mer-ce-na-ry (mûr′sĕ-nā-rĭ), *n.* [*pl.* mercenaries (-rĭz)], a soldier hired into foreign service:—*adj.* **1**, serving only for pay or reward; eager to gain money; **2**, resulting from greed; as, a *mercenary* crime.—*adv.* **mer′ce-na-ri-ly.**—*n.* **mer′ce-na-ri-ness.**

mer-cer (mûr′sẽr), *n.* a dealer in woven fabrics, as silks and woolens.

mer-cer-ize (mûr′sẽr-īz), *v.t.* [*p.t.* and *p.p.* -ized (-īzd), *p.pr.* -iz″-ing], to treat (a cotton fabric) in such a way that the fabric is strengthened, made more receptive of dyes, and given a silken sheen.

mer-chan-dise (mûr′chăn-dīz), *n.* goods, wares, or articles bought and sold; commodities.

mer-chant (mûr′chănt), *n.* **1**, one who carries on trade on a large scale, esp. with foreign countries; **2**, a shopkeeper:—*adj.* pertaining to, or employed in, trade; mercantile: **merchant marine,** that part of the shipping of a country that is engaged in trade.—*adj.* **mer′chant-a-ble.**

mer-chant-man (mûr′chănt-măn), *n.* [*pl.* merchantmen (-mĕn)], a trading vessel.

mer-ci-ful (mûr′sĭ-fo͝ol), *adj.* full of, or exercising, leniency or compassion; tender-hearted; full of pity.—*adv.* **mer′ci-ful-ly.**—*n.* **mer′ci-ful-ness.**

mer-ci-less (mûr′sĭ-lĕs), *adj.* without pity; unfeeling; cruel.—*adv.* **mer′ci-less-ly.**—*n.* **mer′ci-less-ness.**
Syn. hard-hearted, pitiless, remorseless, unrelenting.—*Ant.* merciful, kind, humane.

mer-cu-ri-al (mẽr-kū′rĭ-ăl), *adj.* **1**, having the qualities attributed to the god Mercury; hence, active; fickle; light-hearted; **2**, pertaining to, made of, or caused by, mercury, or quicksilver.

mer-cu-ry (mûr′kū-rĭ), *n.* quicksilver; a heavy, liquid, metallic substance, used in thermometers and for other scientific purposes: **mercury arc,** an electric arc sent through mercury vapor in a vacuum tube: **Mercury, 1**, the planet nearest to the sun (see *solar system,* illus.); **2**, [*pl.* Mercuries (-rĭz)], in Roman mythology, the god of gain and the messenger of the gods: identified with the Greek *Hermes.*—*adj.* **mer-cu′ric.**—*adj.* **mer′cu-rous** (mûr′kū-rŭs; mẽr-kū′rŭs).

mer-cy (mûr′sĭ), *n.* [*pl.* mercies (-sĭz)], **1**, willingness to forgive, spare, or pity; forbearance; **2**, pity; kindness; mildness; **3**, hence, an act of forbearance or favor.
Syn. benevolence, clemency, forgiveness, pardon, leniency.—*Ant.* cruelty, severity.

[1]**mere** (mēr), *n.* **1**, a shallow lake or pool; **2**, a marsh.

[2]**mere** (mēr), *adj.* [*superl.* mer′est], nothing but; no more than; this only; as, a *mere* child could do it.

mere-ly (mēr′lĭ), *adv.* simply; purely; only; not otherwise than.

mer-e-tri-cious (mĕr″ĕ-trĭsh′ŭs), *adj.* attracting by false show; tawdry; deceitfully alluring.—*adv.* **mer″e-tri′cious-ly.**—*n.* **mer″e-tri′cious-ness.**

mer-gan-ser (mẽr-găn′sẽr), *n.* any of several fish-eating ducks with a long bill bearing toothlike notches.

merge (mûrj), *v.t.* [*p.t.* and *p.p.* merged (mûrjd), *p.pr.* merg′ing], to absorb or swallow up:—*v.i.* to be swallowed up or lost in something else.
Syn. unite, blend, join. (See mix.)

merg-er (mûr′jẽr), *n.* **1**, the legal combination of two estates; **2**, the placing of two or more business corporations under the control of a single body.

me-rid-i-an (mē-rĭd′ĭ-ăn), *adj.* **1**, pertaining to the highest point reached by a heavenly body; **2**, pertaining to midday; **3**, pertaining to the point of greatest success or vigor; culminating:—*n.* **1**, the highest point reached by a heavenly body; **2**, the highest point, as of success, prosperity, and the like; **3**, an imaginary circle around the earth in a north-and-south direction, passing through the poles; also, a similar circle on the celestial sphere passing through the poles and the zenith.—*adj.* **me-rid′i-o-nal.**

me-ringue (mẽ-răng′; *Fr.* mẽ-râṅg′), *n.* an icing or garnish; also, a small cake, made chiefly of beaten white of egg and sugar.

me-ri-no (mẽ-rē′nō), *n.* [*pl.* merinos (-nōz)], **1**, a certain breed of sheep with fine wool; **2**, wool of such sheep; **3**, cloth or yarn made from this wool:—*adj.* pertaining to, or made of, the wool of such sheep.

mer-it (mĕr′ĭt), *n.* **1**, excellence; worth; **2**, the quality or state of deserving; as, treat him according to his *merit;* **3**, deserved reward; **4**, in *pl.*, essential circumstances; as, it was hard to discover the real *merits* of the case:—*v.t.* to earn; be entitled to; be deserving of; as, to *merit* punishment.

mer-i-to-ri-ous (mĕr″ĭ-tō′rĭ-ŭs), *adj.* having worth or excellence; deserving of reward or praise.—*adv.* **mer″i-to′ri-ous-ly.**—*n.* **mer″i-to′ri-ous-ness.**

merl (mûrl), *n.* the European blackbird. Also, **merle.**

Mer-lin (mûr′lĭn), *n.* in medieval romances, a famous bard, magician, and seer at the court of King Arthur.

mer-lon (mûr′lŏn), *n.* one of the solid intervals between two openings in a battlement (see *embrasure*, illus.).

mer-maid (mûr′mād), *n.* a creature, said in fable and fairy tale to live in the sea, having the body of a woman and the tail of a fish.—*n. masc.* **mer′man.**

mer-ri-ment (mĕr′ĭ-mĕnt), *n.* mirth; fun; frolic; gaiety.

mer-ry (mĕr′ĭ), *adj.* [*comp.* mer′ri-er, *superl.* mer′ri-est], full of mirth and good humor; gay; jolly; pleasant.—*adv.* **mer′ri-ly.** —*n.* **mer′ri-ness.**
Syn. cheerful, mirthful, joyous, sprightly, jovial, blithe, sportive.—*Ant.* sad, dispirited, cheerless, downcast, melancholy.

mer-ry–an-drew (mĕr″ĭ=ăn′drōō), *n.* one whose business is to make sport for others; a clown.

mer-ry–go–round (mĕr′ĭ=gō=round″), *n.* **1**, an amusement device consisting of a revolving circular floor fitted with wooden horses or seats, on which persons ride; **2**, figuratively, a whirl of gaiety.

mer-ry-mak-ing (mĕr′ĭ-māk″ĭng), *n.* festivity:—*adj.* festive; gay.—*n.* **mer′ry-mak″er.**

mer-ry-thought (mĕr′ĭ-thôt″), *n.* the wishbone of a fowl.

me-sa (mā′sä), *n.* a table-land or plateau with steep or sloping sides.

***mé-sal-liance** (mā″zȧl″yäṅs′), [Fr.], *n.* a marriage with one of lower social position. Also, **mis″al-li′ance.**

***mes-dames** (mā″dȧm′), [Fr.], *n.* plural of *madam* and *madame:* a term of address.—*abbr.* **Mmes.**

***mes-de-moi-selles** (mād″mwȧ″-zĕl′), [Fr.], *n.* plural of *mademoiselle.*—*abbr.* **Mlles.**

me-seems (mē-sēmz′), *v. impersonal, Archaic,* it seems to me.

mesh (mĕsh), *n.* **1**, one of the openings of a net; as, a veil of coarse or fine *mesh;* **2**, a network; **3**, in machinery, the engagement of gear teeth:—*v.t.* and *v.i.* **1**, to catch or entangle in, or as in, the openings of a net; **2**, in machinery, to engage: said of gear teeth.

Me-shach (mē′shăk), *n.* in the Bible, a Jewish captive in Babylon who, with Shadrach and Abednego, survived the fiery furnace (Daniel 3).

mes-mer-ic (mĕz-mĕr′ĭk), *adj.* **1**, pertaining to, or produced by, mesmerism; hypnotic; **2**, hence, strongly attractive; fascinating.

mes-mer-ism (mĕz′mẽr-ĭzm), *n.* **1**, the producing of an unnatural state of the nervous system resembling sleep, in which the sensations and actions of the subject are easily influenced by suggestion; hypnotism; animal magnetism; **2**, personal attraction.—*n.* **mes′mer-ist.**

mes-mer-ize (mĕz′mẽr-īz), *v.t.* [*p.t.* and *p.p.* -ized (-īzd), *p.pr.* -iz″ing], **1**, to send into a hypnotic trance; hypnotize; **2**, hence, to influence strongly; charm.—*n.* **mes′mer-iz″er.**

Mes-o-zo-ic (mĕs″ō-zō′ĭk), *adj.* in geology, designating, or pertaining to, the era of the earliest birds and the great reptiles, immediately following the Paleozoic.

mes-quite (mĕs-kēt′; mĕs′kēt), *n.* a shrub found in the southwestern U. S. and Mexico, having fragrant flowers and sugary pods, used as food or fodder.

mess (mĕs), *n.* **1**, a number of persons who take their meals together, esp. soldiers or sailors; **2**, in the army and navy, any meal; **3**, *Colloq.*, enough for one meal; as, he caught a *mess* of fish; **4**, a state of dirt or confusion; a muddle; a botch: **mess kit**, a soldier's canvas bag containing a compact set of simple cooking utensils:—*v.t.* **1**, to provide food for; **2**, *Colloq.*, to muddle; as, he *messed* the job; **3**, to soil:—*v.i.* **1**, to eat together; **2**, to potter; trifle; **3**, to muddle.

mes-sage (mĕs′ăj), *n.* a communication, written or sent by word of mouth, from one person to another.

mes-sen-ger (mĕs′ĕn-jẽr), *n.* **1**, one who carries a message; also, one who does errands or carries communications; **2**, a herald or bringer of news.

Mes-si-ah (mẽ-sī′ȧ), *n.* Christ, the Anointed One; the expected king and deliverer of the Hebrews. Also, **Mes-si′as.**—*adj.* **Mes″si-an′ic.**

mes-sieurs (mĕs′yẽrz; *Fr.* mā″syö′), *n.* **1**, plural of *monsieur;* sirs; gentlemen; **2**, sometimes, plural of *Mister:* usually abbreviated.—*abbr.* **Messrs.** (mĕs′rz).

mess-mate (mĕs′māt″), *n.* a person, esp. a fellow soldier or sailor, with whom one is associated at meals; hence, a friend or companion.

mes-suage (mĕs′wăj), *n.* in law, a dwelling house, with its outbuildings and its lands.

mess-y (mĕs′ĭ), *adj.* [*comp.* mess′i-er, *superl.* mess′i-est], disorderly; soiled; botched.—*n.* **mess′i-ness.**

mes-ti-zo (mĕs-tē′zō), *n.* [*pl.* mestizos (-zōz)], [Span.], one of mixed blood, esp. of Spanish and Indian blood.

met (mĕt), past tense and past participle of the verb *meet.*

me-tab-o-lism (mē-tăb′ō-lĭzm), *n.* the process by which living cells in plants and animals are continually worn out by use and build themselves up again by means of food.—*adj.* **met″a-bol′ic.**

met-al (mĕt′ăl), *n.* **1,** any of a class of heavy, lustrous substances, as gold, silver, iron, lead, copper, etc., capable of being drawn into fine threads or beaten or hammered into thin plates, of being melted by heat, and of carrying electricity; also, a mixture of these substances; **2,** material; substance; **3,** molten glass; **4,** in *pl.*, *Colloq.*, the rails of a railroad:—*v.t.* [*p.t.* and *p.p.* -aled (-ăld), *p.pr.* -al-ing], to cover with metal.

me-tal-lic (mē-tăl′ĭk), *adj.* **1,** pertaining to, consisting of, or like, gold, silver, iron, copper, or other metals; as, a *metallic* dish; **2,** having qualities suggestive of a metal; as, a *metallic* sound.

met-al-lif-er-ous (mĕt″ăl-ĭf′ẽr-ŭs), *adj.* yielding or containing metal; as, *metalliferous* ore; also, yielding metallic ores; as, a *metalliferous* region.

met-al-lur-gy (mĕt′ăl-ûr″jĭ), *n.* the art or science of preparing metals, such as gold, silver, iron, copper, lead, etc., for use by separating them from the materials in which they are found in the mines; also, further treatment of them for special uses, as with iron.—*adj.* **met″al-lur′gic; met″al-lur′gi-cal.**—*n.* **met′al-lur″gist.**

met-a-mor-phism (mĕt″ȧ-môr′fĭzm), *n.* **1,** change of form, shape, or structure; hence, the process by which rocks are changed under the influence of heat, pressure, chemical action, etc., as limestone to marble; **2,** metamorphosis (which see).—*adj.* **met″a-mor′phic.**

met-a-mor-phose (mĕt″ȧ-môr′fōz; mĕt″ȧ-môr′fōs), *v.t.* [*p.t.* and *p.p.* -phosed (-fōzd; -fōst), *p.pr.* -phos-ing], to change into a different form.

met-a-mor-pho-sis (mĕt″ȧ-môr′fō-sĭs), *n.* [*pl.* metamorphoses (-sēz)], change of form, shape, or structure; transformation; esp., the striking change in form and habits of certain organisms, as from a chrysalis into a butterfly.

met-a-phor (mĕt′ȧ-fŏr), *n.* a figure of speech by which an expression applying literally to one concept is applied figuratively to another to suggest some similarity between them; as, a *rain* of bullets; we *rack* our brains.—*adj.* **met″a-phor′ic; met″a-phor′i-cal.**—*adv.* **met″a-phor′i-cal-ly.**

met-a-phys-i-cal (mĕt″ȧ-fĭz′ĭ-kăl), *adj.* **1,** pertaining to, or according to the rules of, abstract philosophy; abstruse; difficult to understand; **2,** beyond the material world; as, *metaphysical* ideals or theories.—*adv.* **met″a-phys′i-cal-ly.**

met-a-phy-si-cian (mĕt″ȧ-fĭ-zĭsh′ăn), *n.* one skilled in abstruse knowledge or philosophical thought.

met-a-phys-ics (mĕt″ȧ-fĭz′ĭks), *n. pl.* used as *sing.* that branch of knowledge which deals with the nature, character, and causes of being, the existence of God, etc.; the study of those things which relate to the mental as distinguished from the physical; philosophy.

met-a-tar-sus (mĕt″ȧ-tär′sŭs), *n.* [*pl.* metatarsi (-sī)], that part of the lower or hinder limb between the ankle and toes, consisting, in man, of five long bones in the foot.—*adj.* and *n.* **met″a-tar′sal.**

mete (mēt), *v.t.* [*p.t.* and *p.p.* met′ed, *p.pr.* met′ing], to give out by measure; allot; divide in just proportion.

me-temp-sy-cho-sis (mē-tĕmp″sĭ-kō′sĭs), *n.* [*pl.* metempsychoses (-sēz)], the passage of the soul of man or animal from one body to another after death; transmigration of souls: believed in by the ancient Egyptians and other Eastern peoples and still held to in India.

me-te-or (mē′tē-ŏr), *n.* **1,** a mass of matter from space that glows as it travels through the earth's atmosphere, as a falling or shooting star; **2,** hence, anything that dazzles or excites wonder for the moment.

me-te-or-ic (mē″tē-ŏr′ĭk), *adj.* **1,** pertaining to, formed of, or like, a shooting star; **2,** hence, swift; dazzling.

me-te-or-ite (mē′tē-ŏr-īt″), *n.* a body, usually of iron, which has fallen upon the earth from outer space.

me-te-or-oid (mē′tē-ŏr-oid″), *n.* a small solid body of matter in space, that becomes a meteor when it encounters the earth's atmosphere.

me-te-or-ol-o-gist (mē″tē-ŏr-ŏl′ō-jĭst), *n.* one who is skilled in the science of the atmosphere.

me-te-or-ol-o-gy (mē″tē-ŏr-ŏl′ō-jĭ), *n.* the science of the atmosphere and its various changes of heat and moisture, its winds, storms, etc.—*adj.* **me″te-or-o-log′ic; me″te-or-o-log′i-cal.**

[1]**me-ter** (mē′tẽr), *n.* **1,** the measured arrangement, in a line of verse, of groups of syllables having a time unit and a regular beat; rhythm; also, a specific arrangement of metrical groups; as, iambic *meter;* **2,** that part of musical composition or structure which depends on time values:—*v.t.* to compose or arrange in metrical form. Also, **me′tre** [*p.t.* and *p.p.* -tred (-tẽrd), *p.pr.* -tring].

[2]**me-ter** (mē′tẽr), *n.* **1,** a person who measures: usually an official; **2,** an instrument, generally automatic, for measuring and recording the passage of liquids, gases, or electric current:—*v.t.* to measure with such an instrument.

[3]**me-ter** (mē′tẽr), *n.* the standard unit of length in the metric system, equal to 39.37+inches. Also, **me′tre.**—*abbr.* **m.**

meth-an-ol (mĕth′ăn-ōl; ŏl), *n.* wood, or methyl, alcohol.

me-theg-lin (mē-thĕg′lĭn), *n.* an old-fashioned fermented drink, made of honey and water.

me-thinks (mē-thĭngks′), *v. impersonal* [*p.t.* -thought′ (-thôt′)], *Archaic* or *Poetic,* it appears or seems to me.

meth-od (mĕth′ŭd), *n.* **1,** a regular arrangement of things; system; as, he has *method* in his study; **2,** the use of a definite plan; as, a *method* of teaching.

Syn. manner, mode, process, order, rule.

me-thod-i-cal (mē-thŏd′ĭ-kăl), *adj.* **1,** arranged with regard to order; **2,** devoted to order; systematic. Also, **me-thod′ic.**—*adv.* **me-thod′i-cal-ly.**

Meth-od-ist (mĕth′ŭd-ĭst), *n.* a member of a religious denomination founded by John Wesley:—*adj.* pertaining to this sect.—*adj.* **Meth″od-is′tic; Meth″od-is′ti-cal.**—*n.* **Meth′od-ism.**

meth-od-ize (mĕth′ŭd-īz), *v.t.* [*p.t.* and *p.p.* -ized (-īzd), *p.pr.* -iz″ing], to set in order; make systematic.

Me-thu-se-lah (mē-thū′sē-lȧ), *n.* in the Bible, the longest-lived of the patriarchs, 969 years old (Genesis 5:27).

meth-yl (mĕth′ĭl), *n.* a group of hydrogen and carbon atoms, which forms the important part of methyl alcohol, or wood alcohol, and of many other substances.

me-tic-u-lous (mē-tĭk′ū-lŭs), *adj.* **1,** too careful of small details; very particular; **2,** orig., timorous; timid.—*adv.* **me-tic′u-lous-ly.**—*n.* **me-tic′u-lous-ness.**

***mé-tier** (mā″tyā′), [Fr.], *n.* profession; trade; business; line of work.

me-ton-y-my (mē-tŏn'ĭ-mĭ), *n.* a figure of speech in which a word is used in place of another which it suggests by association, as the name of a part for that of the whole (as, he employs two hundred *hands*), or the container for the thing contained (as, the *kettle* boils).

met-o-pe (mĕt'ō-pē), *n.* one of the square tablets, plain or sculptured, between two triglyphs in a Doric frieze.

[1]me-tre (mē'tẽr), *n.* **1,** a regular arrangement of syllables in verse; rhythm; poetical measure; **2,** in music, that part of musical structure which depends upon time values. See **[1]me'ter,** *Pfd. S.*

[2]me-tre (mē'tẽr), *n.* the standard unit of length in the metric system, equal to 39.37+ inches. Also, **me-ter,** *Pfd. S.*

met-ric (mĕt'rĭk), *adj.* pertaining to measurement, measure, or rhythm, or to the metric system: **metric system,** a decimal system of weights and measures based on the *meter* (39.37 inches), legalized in the U. S. in 1866. Also, **met'ri-cal.**—*adv.* **met'ri-cal-ly.**

met-ro-graph (mĕt'rō-gråf), *n.* an apparatus for measuring and recording the distance run by a locomotive, and the number and time of its stops.

met-ro-nome (mĕt'rō-nōm), *n.* an instrument which beats time by means of a short pendulum: often used in practicing music. —*adj.* **met"ro-nom'ic.**

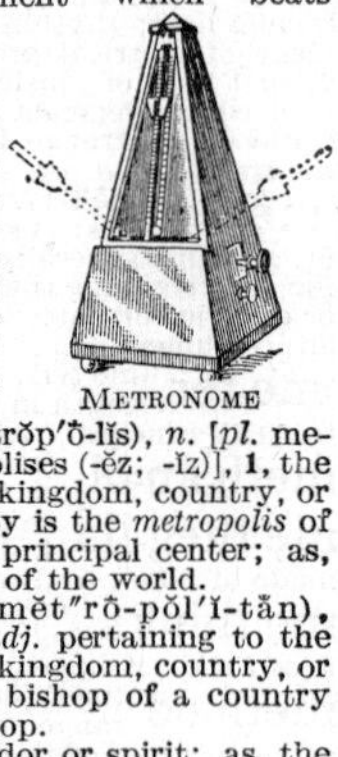

METRONOME

me-tro-nym-ic (mē"trō-nĭm'ĭk; mĕt"-rō-), *adj.* designating, or pertaining to, a name derived from that of the mother or a female ancestor: opp. of *patronymic:* —*n.* a metronymic name. Also, **mat"ro-nym'ic.**

me-trop-o-lis (mē-trŏp'ō-lĭs), *n.* [*pl.* metropolises (-ĕz; -ĭz)], **1,** the chief city or capital of a kingdom, country, or state; as, New York City is the *metropolis* of the United States; **2,** a principal center; as, London is the *metropolis* of the world.

met-ro-pol-i-tan (mĕt"rō-pŏl'ĭ-tăn), *adj.* pertaining to the chief city or capital of a kingdom, country, or state:—*n.* the presiding bishop of a country or province; an archbishop.

met-tle (mĕt'l), *n.* ardor or spirit; as, the danger tried his *mettle.*

met-tle-some (mĕt'l-sŭm), *adj.* high-spirited; fiery.

[1]mew (mū), *n.* a gull; esp., the common European gull.

[2]mew (mū), *n.* **1,** a cage for confining hawks or fowls; **2,** imprisonment; concealment; also, a hiding place; den; **3,** in *pl.:* **a,** orig., the royal stables in London, on the site of the old hawks' mews; **b,** a stable, or group of stables, around a court:—*v.t.* to confine or inclose, as in a cage.

[3]mew (mū), *n.* the cry of a cat:—*v.i.* to utter a sound or cry resembling *mew.*

mewl (mūl), *v.i.* to whimper like a young child:—*n.* the cry of a baby.

Mex-i-can (mĕk'sĭ-kăn), *adj.* pertaining to Mexico or its people, language, or customs:—*n.* **1,** a native of Mexico; **2,** the language of Mexico.

mez-za-nine (mĕz'ȧ-nĭn; mĕz'ȧ-nēn), *n.* a low story in a building, between two higher ones, often in the form of a gallery: also called *mezzanine floor.*

***mez-zo** (mĕd'zō), [It.], *adj.* in music, middle; half; not extreme; moderate; as, *mezzo*-soprano.

mez-zo-so-pra-no (mĕd'zō=sō-prä'-nō), *n.* **1,** a voice of rich quality between soprano and contralto; **2,** a person with such a voice.

mez-zo-tint (mĕd'zō-tĭnt; mĕz'ō-tĭnt), *n.* a variety of copper engraving. Also, **mez"zo-tin'to.**

mi (mē), *n.* in music, the third tone of any diatonic scale, as E in the scale of C major.

mi-aow (mĭ-ou'), *n.* the cry of a cat:—*v.i.* to cry like a cat. Also, **mi-aou'.**

mi-as-ma (mī-ăz'mȧ), *n.* [*pl.* miasmata (-tȧ); miasmas (-mȧz)], a harmful vapor in the air: formerly applied to malaria, which was supposed to be caused by mists arising from swampy ground.—*adj.* **mi-as'mal.**—*adj.* **mi"as-mat'ic.**

mi-ca (mī'kȧ), *n.* any of a large group of minerals easily separated into thin, transparent plates which are used in lanterns, stove doors, etc.: often incorrectly called *isinglass.*—*adj.* **mi-ca'ce-ous.**

Mi-cah (mī'kȧ), *n.* **1,** an ancient Hebrew prophet; **2,** a book of the Old Testament, containing his prophecies. Also, in the Douay Bible, **Mi-che'as.**

mice (mīs), *n.* plural of the irregular noun *mouse,* which see.

Mi-chael (mī'kĕl), *n.* in the Bible, one of the archangels, leader of a host of angels which warred against Satan and his hosts (Revelations 12:7–9).

Mich-ael-mas (mĭk'ĕl-mȧs), *n.* September 29, a feast day in honor of St. Michael.

mi-cro- (mī'krō-), a combining form from the Greek, meaning small, little, insignificant; as, *micro*cosm: opp. of *macro-.*

mi-crobe (mī'krōb), *n.* a living thing so tiny as to be seen only under the microscope; esp., a germ carrying disease. —*adj.* **mi-cro'bic.**—*adj.* **mi-cro'bi-al.**

mi-cro-cosm (mī'krō-kŏzm), *n.* **1,** a little world; a world in miniature; **2,** hence, man, as opposed to the great universe about him: opp. of *macrocosm.* —*adj.* **mi"cro-cos'mic.**

mi-cro-film (mī'krō-fĭlm), *n.* a photographic film for small photographs, often used to preserve copies of documents, records, pictures, etc.

mi-crom-e-ter (mī-krŏm'ē-tẽr), *n.* an instrument for measuring very small distances: often used in connection with a microscope or telescope: **micrometer caliper,** a gauge, with a fine screw, for making accurate measurements.

MICROMETER CALIPER

mi-cro-ör-gan-ism (mī"krō-ôr'găn-ĭzm), *n.* a very tiny organism; a bacterium; microbe.

mi-cro-phone (mī'krō-fōn), *n.* an instrument for making feeble sounds louder, as in the telephone or radio.

mi-cro-pho-tog-ra-phy (mī"krō-fō-tŏg'rȧ-fĭ), *n.* the art of making an exceedingly small photograph of an object; also, the art of making a photograph of a minute object, with the aid of a microscope.—*n.* **mi"cro-pho'to-graph.**

mi-cro-scope (mī'krō-skōp), *n.* an optical instrument for making very tiny objects appear larger, so that they may be seen and studied; a powerful magnifying glass (see illus. next page).

mi-cro-scop-ic (mī"krō-skŏp'ĭk), *adj.* **1,** pertaining to, seen, or discovered by, a magnifying glass; **2,** very small; invisible without a microscope. Also, **mi″cro-scop′i-cal.**—*adv.* **mi″cro-scop′i-cal-ly.**

mi-cros-co-pist (mī-krŏs′kō-pĭst; mī′-krō-skō″pĭst), *n.* one skilled in the use of a microscope, or the study of objects through the microscope.

mi-cros-co-py (mī-krŏs′kō-pĭ; mī′krō-skō″pĭ), *n.* the use or study of the microscope.

mid (mĭd), *adj.* [*superl.* mid′most], middle: usually in combination; as, *mid*winter: —*prep.* amid; among.

Mi-das (mī′dȧs), *n.* in mythology, a Phrygian king to whom was granted the power to change everything he touched into gold, but who begged release when his food and his daughter were turned into gold.

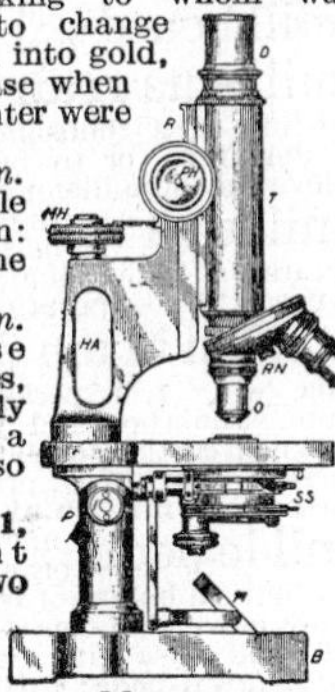

MICROSCOPE

D, drawtube; *T*, body tube; *R*, rack; *PH*, pinion head; *MH*, micrometer head; *HA*, handle arm; *RN*, revolving nose piece; *O*, objective: *S*, stage; *SS*, substage; *P*, inclination pillar; *I*, inclination joint; *M*, mirror; *B*, base.

mid-day (mĭd′dā″), *n.* the middle hours of the day; noon: —*adj.* at noon; as, the *midday* meal.

mid-den (mĭd′n), *n.* a refuse heap containing bones, implements, etc., usually marking the site of a primitive dwelling: also called *kitchen midden.*

mid-dle (mĭd′l), *n.* **1,** the point equally distant from two given points or extremes; central part; **2,** that which is between:—*adj.* **1,** equally distant from the extremes; halfway between two given points; mean; medial; **2,** intervening.

mid-dle-aged (mĭd′l-ājd″), *adj.* neither young nor old: said of a person from about 40 to about 60 years old.

Mid-dle Ages the period between the fifth and fifteenth centuries after Christ.—*adj.* **Mid′dle-Age″.**

mid-dle-man (mĭd′l-măn), *n.* [*pl.* middlemen (-mĕn)], **1,** one who acts as agent between two people or groups of people; a broker; one who buys at wholesale and sells at retail; **2,** an interlocutor.

mid-dling (mĭd′lĭng), *adj.* of moderate rank, size, or quality; neither good nor bad; mediocre:—*n.*, in *pl.*, a mixture of coarse-ground wheat flour and fine bran.

mid-dy (mĭd′ĭ), *n.* [*pl.* middies (-ĭz)], *Colloq.*, a midshipman, or naval cadet: **middy blouse,** a kind of shirt or waist, worn esp. by women, having a sailor collar, and reaching unconfined to the hips: also called *middy.*

Mid-gard (mĭd′gärd), *n.* in Teutonic mythology, one of the nine worlds composing the universe: the earth, midway between heaven and hell; the dwelling place of men. Also, **Mid′garth.**

midge (mĭj), *n.* **1,** a very small fly; very tiny gnat; **2,** a dwarf.

midg-et (mĭj′ĕt), *n.* **1,** a small dwarf; **2,** a little and active child.

Mid-i-an-ite (mĭd′ĭ-ăn-īt), *n.* in the Bible, a member of a nomadic tribe hostile to the Israelites (Judges 6–7).

mid-land (mĭd′lănd), *adj.* inland; in the central part of a country:—*n.*, in *pl.*, the interior of a country.

mid-night (mĭd′nīt″), *n.* **1,** the middle of the night; twelve o'clock at night; **2,** intense darkness:—*adj.* pertaining to the middle of the night.

mid-rib (mĭd′rĭb″), *n.* in botany, the central vein of a leaf (see *leaf*, illus.).

mid-riff (mĭd′rĭf), *n.* the muscular partition separating the cavity of the chest from the abdomen; diaphragm.

mid-ship-man (mĭd′shĭp″măn), *n.* [*pl.* midshipmen (-mĕn)], **1,** a naval cadet, or youth in training for a naval officer's commission; one whose rank is next below that of ensign; **2,** a petty officer in the British navy.

midst (mĭdst), *n.* the middle; the central place:—*prep.* amidst.

mid-sum-mer (mĭd′sŭm″ẽr; mĭd″sŭm′ẽr), *n.* the period about June 21, or the longest day of summer:—*adj.* in the middle of summer.

mid-way (mĭd′wā″; mĭd″wā′), *adj.* and *adv.* halfway:—*n.* (mĭd′wā″), the amusement section of an exposition or fair.

mid-wife (mĭd′wīf″), *n.* [*pl.* midwives (-wīvz″)], a woman who assists women at childbirth.

mid-wife-ry (mĭd′wīf″rĭ; mĭd′wĭf-rĭ), *n.* the act, art, or practice of assisting at childbirth.

mid-win-ter (mĭd′wĭn″tẽr; mĭd″wĭn′tẽr), *n.* the period about December 21, or the shortest day of winter:—*adj.* in the middle of winter.—*adj.* **mid″win′try.**

mien (mēn), *n.* outward appearance; air; look; manner; aspect.

miff (mĭf), *v.t. Colloq.*, to cause to be vexed: —*n.* a slight vexation.—*adj.* **miff′y.**

¹might (mīt), past tense of the irregular verb *may.*

²might (mīt), *n.* force or power of body, mind, or action; superior strength.

might-y (mīt′ĭ), *adj.* [*comp.* might′i-er, *superl.* might′i-est], **1,** powerful; strong; having influence; **2,** wonderful; huge: —*adv. Colloq.*, very or exceedingly.—*adv.* **might′i-ly.**—*n.* **might′i-ness.**

mi-gnon-ette (mĭn″yŭn-ĕt′), *n.* a fragrant garden plant with greenish white flowers.

mi-graine (mĭ-grān′; mī′grān), *n.* a headache, usually affecting one side of the head only, and usually accompanied by nausea. Also, **me′grim.**

mi-grant (mī′grănt), *adj.* moving from place to place; roving:—*n.* a wanderer; rover.

mi-grate (mī′grāt), *v.i.* [*p.t.* and *p.p.* -grat-ed, *p.pr.* -grat-ing], **1,** to move from one country to another for permanent residence; **2,** to go regularly from one climate or region to another at certain times of the year, as many birds.

mi-gra-tion (mī-grā′shŭn), *n.* **1,** a moving from one place to another; a change of residence from one country to another; **2,** the groups of individuals making such a movement.

mi-gra-to-ry (mī′grȧ-tō-rĭ), *adj.* removing or passing from one place to another; esp., moving habitually from one climate or region to another; as, *migratory* birds; roving, as tribes.

Syn. strolling, wandering, vagrant.

mi-ka-do (mĭ-kä′dō), *n.* the Emperor of Japan: a popular title.

milch (mĭlch), *adj.* yielding milk; giving milk; as, a *milch* cow.

mild (mīld), *adj.* **1,** gentle in temper and disposition; kind; calm; **2,** moderate in quality or degree; not sharp, sour, severe, or bitter.—*adv.* **mild′ly.**—*n.* **mild′ness.**

mil-dew (mĭl′dū), *n.* **1,** any of several tiny growths of the nature of fungi, found on plants or other substances, by which it is nourished; 2, a disease of plants produced by this growth; 3, spots of mold on cloth, etc., caused, when damp, by this growth:—*v.t.* to affect with mildew:—*v.i.* to be affected with mildew.—*adj.* **mil'dew-y.**

mile (mīl), *n.* a measure of length varying in different countries; specif., a statute mile: **nautical** (or **geographical**) **mile,** a knot; in the U. S., 6,080.27 feet; in Great Britain, 6,080 feet: **square mile,** 640 acres: **statute mile,** in the U. S. and Great Britain, 5,280 feet.

mile-age (mīl'āj), *n.* 1, an allowance for traveling expenses of so much per mile; 2, length in miles; 3, on railroads, a charge per mile: **mileage book,** a book of coupons bought for a certain sum and allowing the possessor to travel a given number of miles on a railroad.

mile-post (mīl'pōst"), *n.* a signboard, usually at a crossroads, stating the distance in miles to certain points.

mile-stone (mīl'stōn"), *n.* a stone marker indicating the distance in miles from one point to another; also, one of a series of posts, set at intervals of a mile, along a railroad track, to tell the distance in miles to a given point.

mil-i-tan-cy (mĭl'ĭ-tăn-sĭ), *n.* 1, warfare; 2, a warlike spirit or policy.

mil-i-tant (mĭl'ĭ-tănt), *adj.* warlike; fighting:—*n.* one who fights; one who uses warlike methods in aid of a cause; as, *militant* suffragists.

mil-i-ta-rism (mĭl'ĭ-tă-rĭzm), *n.* 1, a disposition to uphold the nation's power by means of a strong army and navy; 2, a warlike policy; readiness to fight with little cause; as, *militarism* leads to war.

mil-i-ta-rist (mĭl'ĭ-tă-rĭst), *n.* 1, one who believes in war and warlike policy; 2, an expert in military affairs.—*adj.* **mil"i-ta-ris'tic.**

mil-i-ta-ry (mĭl'ĭ-tă-rĭ), *adj.* 1, pertaining to soldiers or to arms; warlike; 2, performed by soldiers; as, a *military* election. opp. of *civil:* **military police,** a branch of the army, whose duty it is to preserve order, protect the inhabitants of an occupied or invaded district, care for prisoners of war, and arrest soldiers guilty of misconduct:—*n.* soldiers collectively; army; troops.

mil-i-tate (mĭl'ĭ-tāt), *v.i.* [*p.t.* and *p.p.* -tat"ed, *p.pr.* -tat"ing], 1, to have force, as in an argument: with *against;* as, the testimony *militates* against the prisoner 2, to wage war; contend.

mi-li-tia (mĭ-lĭsh'ȧ), *n.* a body of citizens enrolled and trained for the defense of a state, or nation.—*n.* **mi-li'tia-man.**

milk (mĭlk), *n.* 1, a white fluid produced by the mammary glands of females among the higher animals for the nourishment of their young; esp., the milk of the cow, largely used as food; 2, the white juice of certain plants:—*v.t.* to draw milk from; supply with milk.—*n.* **milk'er.**—*n.* **milk'maid".** —*n.* **milk'man.**

milk-sop (mĭlk'sŏp"), *n.* an effeminate, weak man.

milk tooth one of the first set of teeth in the young of the higher animals; a baby tooth.

milk-weed (mĭlk'wēd"), *n.* any of a family of wild plants whose juice is white like milk.

milk-y (mĭl'kĭ), *adj.* [*comp.* milk'i-er, *superl.* milk'i-est], 1, containing, or like, milk; 2, giving milk; 3, very mild.

Milk-y Way a broad band of pale light across the heavens, visible at night, and consisting of countless stars.

[1]**mill** (mĭl), *n.* the thousandth part of a do'lar; $\frac{1}{10}$ of one cent.

[2]**mill** (mĭl), *n.* 1, a building equipped with machinery to grind grain; 2, any machine for grinding solid substances, as coffee, pepper, etc., or for extracting juice or sap; as, a cider *mill;* 3, a manufacturing plant; as, a steel *mill;* paper *mill;* 4, *Slang,* a pugilistic encounter; hence, any wearing or exhausting experience:—*v.t.* 1, to subject to any operation like that performed by a mill; grind very fine, as grain; cut or saw (timber); crush (ore), etc.; 2, to make a raised border around the edges of (a coin); 3, in the U. S., to cause to move in circles: said of cattle:—*v.i.* to move in circles, as cattle.

mill-board (mĭl'bōrd"), *n.* a kind of thick pasteboard.

mil-le-na-ri-an (mĭl"ē-nā'rĭ-ăn), *adj.* 1, pertaining to, or consisting of, a thousand; 2, pertaining to the millennium, or to believers in it:—*n.* a believer in the millennium.

mil-le-na-ry (mĭl'ē-nā-rĭ), *n.* [*pl.* millenaries (-rĭz)], 1, a thousand years; a millennium; 2, a thousandth anniversary:—*adj.* pertaining to a thousand.

mil-len-ni-um (mĭ-lĕn'ĭ-ŭm), *n.* [*pl.* millenniums (-ŭmz); millennia (-ȧ)], 1, a period of a thousand years; esp., the thousand years when Christ will reign on earth (Revelation 20:1-4); 2, hence, a period of great joy, prosperity, and righteousness.—*adj.* **mil-len'ni-al.**

mil-le-pede (mĭl'ē-pēd), *n.* 1, any of an order of myriapods having cylindrical bodies of from 25 to 100 segments, most of which have two pairs of legs; 2, a kind of wood louse with many legs. Also, **mil'le-ped; mil'li-pede; mil'li-ped.**

mil-le-pore (mĭl'ē-pōr), *n.* any of various small, coral-forming animals having a skeleton with a smooth, finely perforated surface.

mill-er (mĭl'ẽr), *n.* 1, one who owns or works a flour mill; 2, any moth whose wings look as if powdered with flour.

mil-let (mĭl'ĕt), *n.* 1, a grain-bearing grass, widely used as food for man and birds: in the U. S. also cut for hay; 2, its seed.

mil-li- (mĭl'ĭ-), a prefix from the Latin, used, esp. in the metric system, to indicate the 1000th part (of a designated unit); as, *milli*gram (the 1000th part of a gram); *milli*liter (equivalent to a cubic centimeter); *milli*meter (equivalent to about $\frac{1}{25}$ of an inch); *milli*ampere, etc.

mil-li-am-meter (mĭl"ĭ-ăm'ē-tẽr), *n.* an instrument for measuring milliamperes.

mil-li-ard (mĭl'ĭ-ärd; *Fr.* mĭl'yärd), *n.* one thousand millions; a billion.

***mil-lier** (mē"lyā'), [Fr.] *n.* a metric ton; one thousand kilograms, or 2,204.6 pounds, avoirdupois.

Mil-li-kan rays (mĭl'ĭ-kăn), radiations similar to X rays, but of greater penetrating power; cosmic rays.

mil-line (mĭl"lĭn'), *n.* a unit of measurement used in determining advertising cost: the equivalent of one agate line in one million copies.

mil-li-ner (mĭl'ĭ-nẽr), *n.* one who deals in, makes, or trims women's bonnets, hats, headdresses, etc.

mil-li-ner-y (mĭl'ĭ-nẽr-ĭ), *n.* [*pl.* millineries (-ĭz)], 1, such articles as women's hats, bonnets, etc.; 2, the business of making and selling hats.

mill-ing (mĭl'ĭng), *n.* 1, the act of passing something through a mill or similar machine; 2, hence, the manufacture of cereal foods from grain; 3, the thickened or roughened rim of a coin or surface of a screw; also, the process of making such an edge or surface: **milling machine**, an apparatus for notching the edges of coins, cutting screw heads, etc.

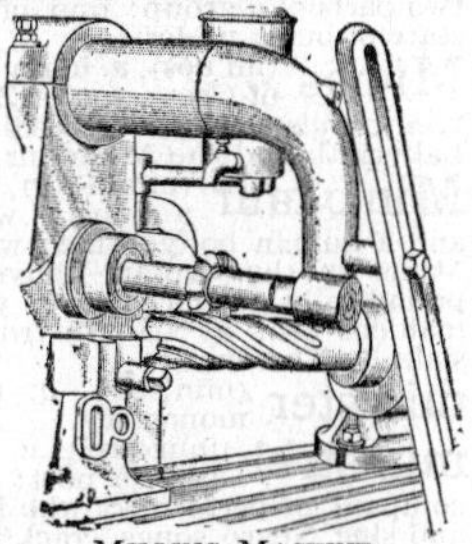

MILLING MACHINE
Cutting a spiral channel in a twist drill.

mil-lion (mĭl′yŭn), *n.* **1**, ten hundred thousand: written 1,000,000; **2**, an indefinitely large number; as, a *million* flies.—*n.* and *adj.* **mil′lionth.**

mil-lion-aire (mĭl″yŭn-âr′), *n.* **1**, one who has a million dollars; **2**, a very rich person. Also, **mil″lion-naire′.**

mill race a stream or canal of water with a current that drives a mill.

mil-reis (mĭl′rās; -rēs), [Port.], *n.* Brazilian monetary unit, replaced by the *cruzeiro;* worth about five cents.

mill-stone (mĭl′stōn″), *n.* one of two flat, circular stones used for grinding grain in a mill.

mill wheel a large wheel, moved by a current of water, which drives a mill; a water wheel

mill-wright (mĭl′rīt″), *n.* one who builds mills or installs their machinery.—*n.* **mill′wright″ing.**

milt (mĭlt), *n.* **1**, the male reproductive glands of a fish when filled with secretion; also, the secretion; **2**, locally, the spleen in mammals:—*v.t.* to make fertile (the egg, or roe, of a female fish).—*n.* **milt′er.**

mime (mīm), *n.* **1**, a kind of drama among the Greeks and Romans, in which real persons and events were represented in a laughable manner; **2**, an actor in such a drama:—*v.i.* and *v.t.* [*p.t.* and *p.p.* mimed (mīmd), *p.pr.* mim′ing], **1**, to play (a part), usually without speaking; **2**, to imitate.

mim-e-o-graph (mĭm′ē-ō-grȧf″), *n.* an apparatus for making copies of written, or typewritten, matter by means of stencils and an ink roller:—*v.t.* to copy by such an apparatus.

mi-met-ic (mĭ-mĕt′ĭk; mī-mĕt′ĭk), *adj.* **1**, inclined to imitate; gifted as a mimic; **2**, pertaining to imitation.

mim-ic (mĭm′ĭk), *n.* one who imitates, esp. to make fun of the person or thing imitated:—*v.t.* [*p.t.* and *p.p.* -icked (-ĭkt), *p.pr.* -ick-ing], **1**, to imitate, or ridicule by imitation; **2**, to make an imitation of; as, clouds *mimic* the land:—*adj.* **1**, inclined to imitate; imitative; **2**, mock; copying, usually in smaller form. Also, *adj.* **mim′i-cal.**—*n.* **mim′ick-er.**
Syn., v. ape, mock, copy. (See imitate.)

mim-ic-ry (mĭm′ĭk-rĭ), *n.* [*pl.* mimicries (-rĭz)], **1**, the practice of one who imitates; ridiculous imitation for sport or for the purpose of making fun of another; **2**, close outward likeness; as, certain insects are saved from destruction by their *mimicry* of the twigs or leaves on which they rest.

mi-mo-sa (mĭ-mō′sȧ; mī-mō′sȧ; -zȧ), *n.* any of a genus of herbs, shrubs, or trees of the pea family, growing in warm regions, esp. the sensitive plant.

min-a-ret (mĭn′ȧ-rĕt), *n.* a tall, slender tower attached to a Mohammedan place of worship, surrounded by several balconies from which the call to prayer is made (see ill s. ne t column).

mina-to-ry (mĭn′ȧ-tō-rĭ), *adj.* threatening; menacing.

mince (mĭns), *v.t.* [*p.t.* and *p.p.* minced (mĭnst), *p.pr.* minc′ing], **1**, to cut or chop into very small pieces; **2**, to tell in part or by degrees; make less in importance; as, don't *mince* matters; **3**, to pronounce or speak with assumed elegance or daintiness:—*v.i.* **1**, to talk with assumed elegance; **2**, to walk with short steps or in a prim manner.

mince-meat (mĭns′mēt″), *n.* **1**, meat chopped very fine, and mixed with suet, raisins, lemon peel, etc.; **2**, hence, anything chopped very fine.

minc-ing (mĭn′sĭng), *p.adj.* **1**, with assumed elegance; affected; **2**, walking primly.—*adv.* **minc′ing-ly.**

mind (mīnd), *n.* **1**, the seat of consciousness, thought, opinion, and feeling; **2**, the power of remembering; **3**, the intellect; **4**, the choosing and willing of one's actions; **5**, in psychology, the entire mental experience, connected with the action of the brain and nervous system:—*v.t.* **1**, to pay attention to; as, *mind* your step; **2**, to be troubled by; as, to *mind* the heat; **3**, to obey; as, *mind* your parents; **4**, to watch; as, to *mind* the baby:—*v.i.* **1**, to be troubled; feel annoyance; **2**, to obey; **3**, to be careful.

MINARET

mind-ed (mīn′dĕd), *p.adj.* disposed or inclined; as, he was *minded* to retort, but remained silent.

mind-ful (mīnd′fo͝ol), *adj.* keeping in one's thought; regardful; as, the Lord is *mindful* of his own.—*adv.* **mind′ful-ly**—*n.* **mind′ful-ness.**
Syn. heedful, thoughtful, careful.

¹mine (mīn), *n.* **1**, in mining, an excavation from which minerals, precious stones, etc., are dug out; **2**, hence, an inexhaustible supply of anything, or a source of great wealth; **3**, a cavity, at the end of a tunnel run under an enemy's trench or fortification, in which is fired a charge of high explosive; also, an explosive device, on or near the surface of the water, fired by contact with a passing vessel, or by electricity, as from a fort: **mine sweeper,** a vessel used in finding submarine or floating mines and removing or exploding them:—*v.t.* [*p.t.* and *p.p.* mined (mīnd), *p.pr.* min′ing], **1**, to make or get by digging underground; as, to *mine* coal; **2**, to dig into, as for ore or metals; **3**, to destroy slowly or secretly; undermine; **4**, to place explosives under (an enemy's work); moor submerged explosives in (a harbor, river, ocean lane, or the like):—*v.i.* **1**, to carry on the work of digging for metals, etc.; **2**, to burrow; **3**, to lay explosives, as under an enemy's work or in a harbor.

²mine (mīn), a possessive form of the personal pronoun *I*, used: **1**, alone: **a**, as *adj.*, in the predicate; as, whose hat is this? it is *mine:* **b**, as *pron.;* as, which one is this? it is *mine;* **2**, *Archaic* or *Poetic*, as an attributive adjective before initial vowel or *h;* as, *mine* eyes; *mine* host.

min-er (mīn′ẽr), *n.* **1**, one who works in a mine; **2**, one who lays mines.

min-er-al (mĭn′ẽr-ăl), *n.* **1**, any substance not animal or vegetable; **2**, any chemical substance resulting naturally from inorganic processes; **3**, ore:—*adj.* pertaining to, consisting of, or mingled with, a substance not animal or vegetable; as, *mineral* kingdom; *mineral* ore; *mineral* water.

min-er-al-o-gist (mĭn″ẽr-ăl′ō-jĭst), *n.* one skilled, or well informed, in the science of minerals.

min-er-al-o-gy (mĭn″ẽr-ăl′ō-jĭ), *n.* [*pl.* mineralogies (-jĭz)], **1**, the science of minerals; **2**, a written work or treatise on minerals.—*adj.* **min″er-al-og′i-cal.**

Mi-ner-va (mĭ-nûr′vȧ), *n.* in mythology, the Roman goddess of wisdom: identified with the Greek *Athena.*

min-gle (mĭng′gl), *v.t.* [*p.t.* and *p.p.* -gled (-gld), *p.pr.* -gling], **1**, to combine by mixing; blend; **2**, to associate; **3**, to prepare by mixing; concoct:—*v.i.* to mix or blend.
Syn. unite, join, merge. (See mix.)

min-i-a-ture (mĭn′ĭ-ȧ-tūr), *n.* a very small painting, esp. a portrait on ivory:—*adj.* done on a very small scale; minute.

min-im (mĭn′ĭm), *n.* **1**, the smallest liquid measure; a single drop; **2**, in music, a half note.—*adj.* **min′i-mal.**

min-i-mize (mĭn′ĭ-mīz), *v.t.* [*p.t.* and *p.p.* -mized (-mīzd), *p.pr.* -miz″-ing], to reduce to, or estimate at, the smallest degree, part, or proportion; as, do not *minimize* the danger.

min-i-mum (mĭn′ĭ-mŭm), *n.* [*pl.* minima (-mȧ); minimums (-mŭmz)], **1**, the least quantity possible or allowable: opp. of *maximum;* **2**, the lowest point reached or recorded, as of temperature:—*adj.* lowest; least possible or allowable.

min-ing (mīn′ĭng), *p.adj.* pertaining to the excavating of metals, ores, precious stones, or the like, or to the laying of explosives:—*n.* the act of making or working mines for digging metals, or of laying military mines.

min-ion (mĭn′yŭn), *n.* in printing, a size of type, nearly equivalent to 7 point (see *type*).

min-is-ter (mĭn′ĭs-tẽr), *n.* **1**, one intrusted by the head of a government with the direction of affairs of state; **2**, an agent sent as a representative to a foreign government; **3**, a clergyman, priest, or pastor of a church, authorized to preach and administer the sacraments:—*v.i.* **1**, to serve; act as an attendant or servant; **2**, to give aid by doing helpful things; as, she *ministered* to the child's needs; **3**, to serve as pastor of a church.

min-is-te-ri-al-ist (mĭn″ĭs-tē′rĭ-ăl-ĭst), *n.* a supporter of government officials, and hence of their party.

min-is-tra-tion (mĭn″ĭs-trā′shŭn), *n.* **1**, the act of serving or ministering; **2**, service; ministry.

min-is-try (mĭn′ĭs-trĭ), *n.* [*pl.* ministries (-trĭz)], **1**, the act of serving; **2**, the service of one who preaches a religion; pastorate; **3**, the office or duties of an officer of state; **4**, the clergy or the officers of state collectively; **5**, the term of service of an officer of state or of a clergyman.

min-i-ver (mĭn′ĭ-vẽr), *n.* **1**, any soft white fur; **2**, an ermine in its white winter fur. Also, **min′e-ver.**

mink (mĭngk), *n.* **1**, an animal somewhat like the weasel; **2**, its brown fur.

min-ne-sing-er (mĭn′ē-sĭng″ẽr), *n.* in the 12th to the 14th century, one of a class of German poets and musicians of noble birth, predecessors of the Meistersingers, who accompanied their own songs, usually with a lute. Also, **Min′ne-sing″er.**

min-now (mĭn′ō), *n.* **1**, a small, freshwater fish of the carp family; **2**, locally, any of several small fishes; also, the young of any of several larger fishes.

mi-nor (mī′nẽr), *n.* **1**, a person who is under full legal age; **2**, in the U. S., a subject next in importance to a student's major subject:—*adj.* **1**, smaller; less; unimportant; **2**, in music, less by half a step than the corresponding major interval; hence, designating a scale in which such intervals occur.

mi-nor-i-ty (mĭ-nŏr′ĭ-tĭ), *n.* [*pl.* minorities (-tĭz)], **1**, the smaller of two parts of a group: opp. of *majority;* **2**, the state of being under age.

Mi-nos (mī′nŏs), *n.* in mythology, **1**, a king of Crete, son of Zeus and Europa; **2**, a grandson of the preceding, owner of the Labyrinth and the Minotaur.

Min-o-taur (mĭn′ō-tôr), *n.* in mythology, a monster with a bull's head and a human body, which was kept by King Minos in the Cretan Labyrinth and which periodically devoured seven youths and seven maidens sent as tribute from Athens, until slain by Theseus.

min-ster (mĭn′stẽr), *n.* the church of a monastery.

min-strel (mĭn′strĕl), *n.* **1**, in the Middle Ages, a poet; **2**, now, one of a company of performers who black their faces, and sing Negro songs, crack jokes, and dance.

min-strel-sy (mĭn′strĕl-sĭ), *n.* [*pl.* minstrelsies (-sĭz)], **1**, the art or occupation of those who play or sing ballads, songs, etc.; **2**, such performers collectively; **3**, ballads or lyrics collectively.

[1]**mint** (mĭnt), *n.* any of a large family of aromatic-leaved herbs, esp. those extensively used as flavoring.

[2]**mint** (mĭnt), *n.* **1**, a place where money is coined under government authority and supervision; **2**, an abundant supply; a vast amount, as of money; **3**, figuratively, the source or place of manufacture:—*v.t.* **1**, to coin or stamp (money); **2**, to invent; make.

mint-age (mĭn′tăj), *n.* **1**, coinage; **2**, the cost of coining gold or silver; **3**, the stamp impressed upon a coin.

min-u-end (mĭn′ū-ĕnd), *n.* that number from which another number is to be subtracted.

min-u-et (mĭn″ū-ĕt′; mĭn′ū-ĕt), *n.* **1**, a slow, graceful square dance; **2**, the music for such a dance.

mi-nus (mī′nŭs), *n.* the sign [−] **indicating** subtraction: also called *minus sign:* —*adj.* **1**, less; decreased by; **2**, *Colloq.*, lacking.

[1]**min-ute** (mĭn′ĭt), *n.* **1**, the sixtieth part of an hour or a degree; a moment; **2**, an official note; a memorandum; **3**, in *pl.*, the official record made of the proceedings of a meeting: **minute hand**, the longer hand of a timepiece, which makes a complete circuit of the dial once an hour and marks the minutes.

[2]**mi-nute** (mĭ-nūt′; mī-nūt′), *adj.* **1**, very small; **2**, precise; **3**, trifling. —*adv.* **mi-nute′ly.**—*n.* **mi-nute′ness.**

min-ute-man (mĭn′ĭt-măn), *n.* [*pl.* minutemen (-mĕn)], in the American Revolution, a citizen ready to take arms at a minute's notice.

mi-nu-ti-æ (mĭ-nū′shĭ-ē), *n.pl.* smaller or less important particulars; minute or trivial details.

minx (mĭngks), *n.* a bold or saucy girl: used playfully.

mir (mēr), *n.* the village commune or civil community of the Russian peasants.

mir-a-cle (mĭr′ȧ-kl), *n.* an act or happening in the material or physical sphere that apparently departs from the laws of nature or goes beyond what is known concerning these laws; a wonder; a marvel: **miracle play**, a medieval dramatic representation of events related in the Bible.

mi-rac-u-lous (mĭ-răk′ū-lŭs), *adj.* **1**, wonderful; **2**, happening contrary to the known laws of nature; **3**, able to perform, or performing, great wonders, or the supernatural.—*adv.* **mi-rac′u-lous-ly.** —*n.* **mi-rac′u-lous-ness.**

mi-rage (mē-räzh′), *n.* a misleading effect presented to the eye on oceans, deserts, or plains, by which the inverted images of distant objects are seen, the objects so reflected being frequently quite out of sight.

mire (mīr), *n.* deep mud; wet earth; slush; dirt:—*v.t.* and *v.i.* [*p.t.* and *p.p.* mired (mīrd), *p.pr.* mir'ing], **1**, to soil with mud; **2**, to sink in mud.

mir-ror (mĭr'ẽr), *n.* **1**, a looking-glass; any substance that reflects images; **2**, that which gives a true likeness; hence, a pattern:—*v.t.* to reflect, as in a mirror.

mirth (mûrth), *n.* noisy gaiety; social merriment; jollity.

mirth-ful (mûrth'fool), *adj.* merry; festive; jolly.—*adv.* **mirth'ful-ly.** —*n.* **mirth'ful-ness.**

mirth-less (mûrth'lĕs), *adj.* without glee; without gladness or gaiety. —*adv.* **mirth'less-ly.**

mir-y (mīr'ĭ), *adj.* [*comp.* mir'i-er, *superl.* mir'i-est], **1**, covered with deep mud; hence, dirty; **2**, like mud.—*n.* **mir'i-ness.**

mir-za (mẽr'zä), *n.* a Persian title meaning prince.

mis- (mĭs-), *prefix*, meaning bad(ly), wrong(ly), ill, amiss; as, *mis*conduct.

mis-ad-ven-ture (mĭs"ăd-vĕn'tūr), *n.* an unlucky accident; a misfortune; mishap; disaster.

mis-al-li-ance (mĭs"ȧ-lī'ăns), *n.* an improper or undesirable union by marriage, esp. with one of lower social standing. Also, ***mé"sal"liance'.**

mis-an-thrope (mĭs'ăn-thrōp), *n.* one who hates or distrusts mankind. Also, **mis-an'thro-pist.**—*adj.* **mis"-an-throp'ic; mis"an-throp'i-cal.**—*adv.* **mis"-an-throp'i-cal-ly.**—*n.* **mis-an'thro-py.**

mis-ap-pre-hend (mĭs-ăp"rē-hĕnd'), *v.t.* to fail to understand.—*n.* **mis-ap"pre-hen'sion.**

mis-ap-pro-pri-ate (mĭs"ȧ-prō'prĭ-āt), *v.t.* [*p.t.* and *p.p.* -at"ed, *p.pr.* -at"ing], **1**, to apply to a wrong use or purpose, as money; **2**, *Colloq.*, to steal. —*n.* **mis"ap-pro"pri-a'tion.**

mis-be-have (mĭs"bē-hāv'), *v.i.* [*p.t.* and *p.p.* -haved' (-hāvd'), *p.pr.* -hav'ing], to act in a wrong or improper fashion.—*n.* **mis"be-hav'ior; mis"be-hav'iour.**

mis-cal-cu-late (mĭs-kăl'kū-lāt), *v.t.* [*p.t.* and *p.p.* -lat"ed, *p.pr.* -lat"ing], to make a mistake in; misjudge: —*v.i.* to make an error in judgment or foresight.—*n.* **mis-cal"cu-la'tion.**

mis-call (mĭs-kôl'), *v.t.* **1**, to name incorrectly; **2**, *Dial.*, to heap abuse upon; revile; slander.

mis-car-riage (mĭs-kăr'ĭj), *n.* **1**, failure; mismanagement; **2**, a premature birth; abortion.

mis-car-ry (mĭs-kăr'ĭ), *v.i.* [*p.t.* and *p.p.* -ried (-ĭd), *p.pr.* -ry-ing], **1**, to go wrong; **2**, to be unsuccessful.

mis-ce-ge-na-tion (mĭs"ē-jē-nā'shŭn), *n.* **1**, marriage between persons of different races; **2**, specif., interbreeding of whites and negroes.

mis-cel-la-ne-ous (mĭs"ĕ-lā'nē-ŭs), *adj.* **1**, consisting of several kinds mixed together; **2**, many-sided; consisting of various qualities.—*adv.* **mis"cel-la'ne-ous-ly.**—*n.* **mis"cel-la'ne-ous-ness.**

mis-cel-la-ny (mĭs'ĕ-lā-nĭ), *n.* [*pl.* miscellanies (-nĭz)], **1**, a mixture of various kinds; **2**, a book containing a variety of literary compositions.

mis-chance (mĭs-chåns'), *n.* misfortune; mishap.

mis-chief (mĭs'chĭf), *n.* **1**, harm; injury; damage; misfortune; **2**, a source of vexation; **3**, a tendency to vex or annoy.

Syn. evil, ill, prank. (See injury.)

mis-chie-vous (mĭs'chĭ-vŭs), *adj.* **1**, producing injury or damage; hurtful; **2**, full of pranks; causing annoyance or trouble to others.—*adv.* **mis'chie-vous-ly.**—*n.* **mis'chie-vous-ness.**

mis-con-ceive (mĭs"kŏn-sēv'), *v.t.* and *v.i.* [*p.t.* and *p.p.* -ceived' (-sēvd'), *p.pr.* -ceiv'ing], to judge wrongly; mistake; misunderstand; misjudge.

mis-con-cep-tion (mĭs"kŏn-sĕp'shŭn), *n.* false opinion; misunderstanding; mistake.

mis-con-duct (mĭs-kŏn'dŭkt), *n.* improper or wrong behavior: —*v.t.* (mĭs"kŏn-dŭkt'), **1**, to manage or handle badly; **2**, to lead amiss.

mis-con-strue (mĭs-kŏn'stroo; mĭs"-kŏn-stroo'), *v.t.* [*p.t.* and *p.p.* -strued (-strood), *p.pr.* -stru-ing], to get the wrong meaning from; misinterpret.—*n.* **mis"con-struc'tion.**

mis-cre-ant (mĭs'krē-ănt), *n.* a villain; vile wretch; rascal:—*adj.* unscrupulous; villainous.

Syn., *n.* ruffian, scoundrel, wrongdoer.

mis-date (mĭs-dāt'), *v.t.* [*p.t.* and *p.p.* -dat'ed, *p.pr.* -dat'ing], to affix the wrong day, month, or year to.

mis-deal (mĭs-dēl'), *v.t.* and *v.i.* to apportion wrongly, as cards:—*n.* a wrong distribution of cards.

mis-deed (mĭs-dēd'), *n.* a wrong act; a crime; transgression.

mis-de-mean (mĭs"dē-mēn'), *v.t.* and *v.i.* to behave improperly; conduct (oneself) badly.

mis-de-mean-or (mĭs"dē-mēn'ẽr), *n.* ill conduct; a fault or transgression; a crime of only moderate seriousness. Also, **mis"de-mean'our.**

mis-di-rect (mĭs"dĭ-rĕkt'), *v.t.* **1**, to give false or incorrect instructions to; **2**, to place a wrong address on, as a letter; **3**, to apply wrongly, as one's talents. —*n.* **mis"di-rec'tion.**

mis-doubt (mĭs-dout'), *v.t.* and *v.i.* to suspect:—*n.* suspicion.

mi-ser (mī'zẽr), *n.* a man who is interested in nothing except heaping up money; a covetous person.

mis-er-a-ble (mĭz'ẽr-ȧ-bl), *adj.* **1**, wretched; very unhappy; **2**, worthless; very mean or poor in quality.—*adv.* **mis'er-a-bly.**—*n.* **mis'er-a-ble-ness.**

Syn. distressed, afflicted, forlorn.—*Ant.* happy, contented, worthy.

Mis-e-re-re (mĭz"ē-rē'rē), *n.* **1**, the 51st Psalm; **2**, a musical setting of this Psalm: **miserere**, a prayer for mercy.

mi-ser-ly (mī'zẽr-lĭ), *adj.* **1**, of the disposition of, or like, one who hoards money; stingy; grasping; as, a *miserly* money lender; **2**, saving.—*n.* **mi'ser-li-ness.**

mis-er-y (mĭz'ẽr-ĭ), *n.* [*pl.* miseries (-ĭz)], extreme pain, distress, or misfortune; great unhappiness.

Syn. wretchedness, destitution, privation, beggary, anguish, suffering.—*Ant.* happiness, health, comfort.

mis-fit (mĭs-fĭt'), *n.* **1**, clothing which does not fit; **2**, *Colloq.*, a person in a position for which he is unfitted.

mis-for-tune (mĭs-fôr'tūn), *n.* adversity; bad luck; mischance.

mis-give (mĭs-gĭv'), *v.t.* [*p.t.* -gave' (-gāv'), *p.p.* -giv'en (-gĭv'n), *p.pr.* -giv'ing], to cause to fail in confidence or courage; make fearful; as, my heart *misgives* me.

mis-giv-ing (mĭs-gĭv'ĭng), *n.* a feeling of doubt or apprehension; lack of confidence; uncertainty.

mis-gov-ern (mĭs-gŭv'ẽrn), *v.t.* to rule inefficiently or badly; mis-manage; direct ill, as a business venture or a career.—*n.* **mis-gov'ern-ment.**

mis-guide (mĭs-gīd'), *v.t.* [*p.t.* and *p.p.* -guid'ed, *p.pr.* -guid'ing], to mislead; guide wrongly.

mis-guid-ed (mĭs-gīd'ĕd), *p.adj.* **1,** in error; wrong in opinion or act; **2,** under a wrong influence, as youth.

mis-hap (mĭs-hăp'), *n.* ill fortune; an unlucky accident.

mis-in-form (mĭs"ĭn-fôrm'), *v.t.* and *v.i.* to tell news or facts wrongly (to); make false statements (to).—*n.* **mis"-in-form'er.**—*n.* **mis-in"for-ma'tion.**

mis-in-ter-pret (mĭs"ĭn-tûr'prĕt), *v.t.* **1,** to misunderstand; mistake; **2,** to give a wrong explanation of.—*n.* **mis"in-ter"pre-ta'tion.**

mis-judge (mĭs-jŭj'), *v.t.* [*p.t.* and *p.p.* -judged' (-jŭjd'), *p.pr.* -judg'ing], to form a wrong or unjust opinion of:—*v.i.* to be mistaken in opinion.—*n.* **mis-judg'ment; mis-judge'ment.**

mis-lay (mĭs-lā'), *v.t.* [*p.t.* and *p.p.* -laid' (-lād'), *p.pr.* -lay'ing], to lose temporarily; put in the wrong place.

mis-lead (mĭs-lēd'), *v.t.* **1,** to deceive; delude; misguide; **2,** to conduct in the wrong way.—*p.adj.* **mis-lead'ing.**

mis-man-age (mĭs-măn'āj), *v.t.* and *v.i.* [*p.t.* and *p.p.* -aged (-ājd), *p.pr.* -ag-ing], to direct badly.—*n.* **mis-man'age-ment.**—*n.* **mis-man'ag-er.**

mis-no-mer (mĭs-nō'mẽr), *n.* a wrong naming or name.

mi-sog-y-ny (mĭ-sŏj'ĭ-nĭ; mī-), *n.* hatred of women.—*n.* **mi-sog'y-nist.**

mis-place (mĭs-plās'), *v.t.* [*p.t.* and *p.p.* -placed' (-plāst'), *p.pr.* -plac'ing], **1,** to put in a wrong place; **2,** to bestow on an improper or undeserving object; as, to *misplace* one's affections.—*n.* **mis-place'ment.**

mis-print (mĭs-prĭnt'), *v.t.* to print wrongly:—*n.* a mistake in type.

mis-pri-sion (mĭs-prĭzh'ŭn), *n.* in law, a grave offense, not so serious as to be punishable by death, but bordering upon it; high misdemeanor: **misprision of felony,** the hiding of a crime by one who knows of it but has had nothing to do with it.

mis-pro-nounce (mĭs"prō-nouns'), *v.t.* and *v.i.* [*p.t.* and *p.p.* -nounced' (-nounst'), *p.pr.* -nounc'ing], to speak with a wrong sound or accent, as a word.—*n.* **mis"pro-nun"ci-a'tion.**

mis-rep-re-sent (mĭs-rĕp"rē-zĕnt'), *v.t.* and *v.i.* to report incorrectly, either wilfully or through carelessness.—*n.* **mis-rep"re-sen-ta'tion.**

mis-rule (mĭs-ro͞ol'), *v.t.* [*p.t.* and *p.p.* -ruled' (-ro͞old'), *p.pr.* -rul'ing], to govern badly:—*n.* bad government; tumult.

[1]miss (mĭs), *v.t.* **1,** to fail to hit; as, to *miss* the mark; **2,** to feel the need or absence of; as, he *misses* his mother; **3,** to omit or pass by; fail to observe; as, he never *misses* church; **4,** to escape by good luck; as, he just *missed* being seriously injured:—*v.i.* **1,** to fail to make a hit; **2,** to fail; **3,** to fail to secure, attain, do, etc.: with *of* or *in*:—*n.* failure to hit, reach, see, or obtain.

Syn., *v.* overlook, lose, omit, escape, fail.

[2]miss (mĭs), *n.* [*pl.* misses], a young girl: **Miss,** [*pl.* Misses, preceded by *the*, with following name in *sing.*; as, the *Misses* Smith], a title used before the name of a girl or an unmarried woman.

mis-sal (mĭs'ăl), *n.* **1,** the book containing the order of service for the Roman Catholic Mass; **2,** hence, loosely, a book of devotions or prayers.

mis-shap-en (mĭs-shāp'n), *adj.* distorted; deformed; ill-favored

mis-sile (mĭs'ĭl), *n.* a weapon or thing thrown, or made to be thrown, to injure another; a projectile.

miss-ing (mĭs'ĭng), *p.adj.* lost; wanting; absent.

mis-sion (mĭsh'ŭn), *n.* **1,** the act of sending, or state of being sent, with certain powers, to do some special service; **2,** a business or duty on which one is sent; **3,** a calling, esp. to preach and spread a religion; **4,** a series of special religious services; **5,** an organization for doing religious and charitable work, esp. one dependent on one or more churches; as, a rescue *mission*; **6,** a body of people sent to perform a special work, as envoys or delegates; **7,** a body of persons spreading a religion in a foreign land; also, their organization and residence; **8,** in *pl.*, the organized work of spreading religion.

mis-sion-a-ry (mĭsh'ŭn-ā-rĭ), *n.* [*pl.* missionaries (-rĭz)], a person who is sent to spread the knowledge of a religion and convert people to it, esp. in foreign lands:—*adj.* pertaining to missions or to missionaries; as, *missionary* service.

mis-sive (mĭs'ĭv), *n.* a letter or message:—*adj.* sent specially.

mis-spell (mĭs-spĕl'), *v.t.* to spell incorrectly.

mis-state (mĭs-stāt'), *v.t.* [*p.t.* and *p.p.* -stat'ed, *p.pr.* -stat'ing], to state falsely or incorrectly; declare inaccurately; misrepresent.—*n.* **mis-state'ment.**

mist (mĭst), *n.* **1,** visible watery vapor in the atmosphere, at or near the earth's surface; fog; **2,** anything that dims the sight:—*v.i.* to rain in very fine drops.

mis-tak-a-ble (mĭs-tāk'ȧ-bl), *adj.* liable to be misunderstood.

mis-take (mĭs-tāk'), *v.t.* [*p.t.* -took' (-to͝ok'), *p.p.* -tak'en (-tāk'n), *p.pr.* -tak'ing], **1,** to misunderstand; misconstrue; **2,** to put wrongly in place of another person or thing; as, he *mistook* her for her sister:—*v.i.* to err in judgment or opinion:—*n.* an error in judgment; fault; misunderstanding.

Syn., *n.* oversight. (See blunder.)

mis-tak-en (mĭs-tāk'n), *p.adj.* **1,** incorrect; wrong; as, a *mistaken* idea; **2,** wrong in judgment; as, he is *mistaken*; **3,** misunderstood; as, a *mistaken* meaning.—*adv.* **mis-tak'en-ly.**

Mis-ter (mĭs'tẽr), *n.* [*pl.* Messrs. (mĕs'rz)], Master: a title used before a man's name: usually written *Mr.*

mis-tle-toe (mĭs'l-tō; mĭz'l-tō), *n.* an evergreen plant which grows and feeds on apple trees, oak trees, etc.

mis-trans-late (mĭs"trăns-lāt'), *v.t.* [*p.t.* and *p.p.* -lat'ed, *p.pr.* -lat'ing], to translate incorrectly, as a passage.—*n.* **mis"trans-la'tion.**

mis-tress (mĭs'trĕs), *n.* **1,** a woman who has authority or who governs; the female head of a family, school, etc.; **2,** a woman well skilled in anything; **3,** a woman courted and beloved; a sweetheart; **4,** a female paramour: **Mistress,** a title formerly used before the name of a woman, married or unmarried: now *Mrs.* (mĭs'ĭs; mĭs'ĭz) for married women, and *Miss* for unmarried women.

mis-tri-al (mĭs-trī'ăl), *n.* a court trial which is worth nothing because of some error in the course of it.

mis-trust (mĭs-trŭst'), *n.* lack of confidence:—*v.t.* and *v.i.* **1,** to doubt; suspect; **2,** to surmise; apprehend.—*adj.* **mis-trust'ful.**

Syn., *n.* doubt, uncertainty, suspicion.

mist-y (mĭs'tĭ), *adj.* [*comp.* mist'i-er, *superl.* mist'i-est], **1,** characterized by, or hidden by, watery vapor; **2,** dim; obscure; clouded.—*adv.* **mist'i-ly.**—*n.* **mist'i-ness.**

mis-un-der-stand (mĭs″ŭn-dẽr-stănd′; mĭs-ŭn″-), *v.t.* and .i. [*p.t.* and *p.p.* -stood′ (-stŏŏd′), *p.pr.* stand′ing], to take in a wrong sense; get he wrong idea of; misconstrue.

mis-un-der-stand-ing (mĭs″ŭn-dẽr-stănd′ĭng), *n.* 1, disagreement; a quarrel; **2,** a mistake as to neaning or motive.

mis-use (mĭs-ūs′), *n.* **1,** wrong use; **2,** abuse:—*v.t.* (mĭs-ūz′), [*p.t.* and *p.p.* -used′ (-ūzd′), *p.pr.* -us′ing], to use wrongly.

mite (mīt), *n.* a very tiny insect infesting plants, stored goods, and the like.

mite (mīt), *n.* **1,** a small coin used in Palestine; as, the widow's *mite* (Mark 12:42); hence, any small contribution; **2,** *Colloq.*, a very small object; a small child.

mi-ter (mī′tẽr), *n.* **1,** a kind of crown, in two sections, worn by archbishops, bishops, and sometimes by abbots, on special occasions; **2,** the dignity or office of a bishop; **3,** a slanting junction at the corners, as in moldings, laces, etc.: **miter square,** an instrument having two blades at an angle of 45 degrees:—*v.t.* **1,** to place a bishop's crown on; hence, to raise to the office of a bishop; **2,** to adorn with such a crown; **3,** to join on a slanting line at a corner. Also, **mi′tre** [*p.t.* and *p.p.* -tred (-tẽrd), *p.pr.* -tring].—*adj.* **mi′tral.**

MITER SQUARE

mit-i-gate (mĭt′ĭ-gāt), *v.t.* [*p.t.* and *p.p.* -gat″ed, *p.pr.* -gat″ing], to render less severe or painful; soften; as, time *mitigates* grief.—*adj.* **mit′i-ga-tive.**—*n.* **mit′i-ga″tor.**—*n.* **mit″i-ga′tion.**

Syn. relieve, diminish, abate.

***mi-tra-illeuse** (mē″trȧ″yöz′), [Fr.], *n.* a machine gun.

mitt (mĭt), *n.* **1,** a kind of glove, often of lace or net, without fingers or with half fingers; **2,** a glove with a thick protective pad over the palm, used in baseball.

mit-ten (mĭt′ĕn), *n.* a winter glove covering the four fingers together and the thumb separately.

mit-ti-mus (mĭt′ĭ-mŭs), *n.* a warrant which commits to prison.

mix (mĭks), *v.t.* [*p.t.* and *p.p.* mixed or mixt (mĭkst), *p.pr.* mix′ing], to unite or blend into one mass or compound; join:—*v.i.* to become united in a compound:—*n.* **1,** a confused mass of several elements; **2,** *Colloq.*, a muddle.

Syn., v. compound, mingle, unite, blend, merge. To *mix* is to unite two or more substances so that they become as one; as, to *mix* the ingredients of a cake. To *mingle* is to join, as one substance or color with another, so that the two elements joined are distinguishable; as, people received the news with *mingled* joy and pain. To *unite* is to bring together or to make one; as, to *unite* broken parts with cement. To *blend* is to mix elements or parts into a whole in which they are inseparable and cannot be distinguished; as, to *blend* colors. To *merge* is to lose identity in the whole; as, several companies are *merged* to form one.—*Ant., v.* separate, divide, sever, split, part, scatter.

mix-ture (mĭks′tũr), *n.* **1,** the state of being blended or mingled; **2,** a compound or mass formed by putting two or more things together.

miz-zen (mĭz′n), *n.* **1,** the hindmost mast on a two- or three-masted vessel: also called *mizzenmast;* **2,** a sail attached to the mizzenmast (see *rigging,* illus.).

miz-zle (mĭz′l), *v.t.* [*p.t.* and *p.p.* -zled (-ld), *p.pr.* -zling], to rain in very tiny drops:—*n.* fine rain.

mne-mon-ic (nē-mŏn′ĭk), *adj.* aiding the memory: **mnemonics,** *n.pl.* used as *sing.* **1,** the science of aiding the memory; **2,** a system for improving the memory.

moan (mōn), *v.i.* to utter a low sound from, or as from, pain or sorrow:—*v.t.* to utter in a low wail:—*n.* a low, prolonged sound expressing sorrow or pain; hence, any similar sound; as, the *moan* of the wind.

moat (mōt), *n.* a deep ditch as part of the fortification around a fortress or castle, usually containing water (see *rampart, terreplein,* illus.):—*v.t.* to surround with a moat.

mob (mŏb), *n.* **1,** the common people; **2,** a rude, disorderly crowd; rabble:—*v.t.* [*p.t.* and *p.p.* mobbed (mŏbd), *p.pr.* mob′bing], to attack in a disorderly crowd; crowd about and annoy.—*adj.* **mob′bish.**

Syn., n. multitude. (See throng.)

mo-bile (mō′bĭl; mō′bēl), *adj.* **1,** easily moved; as, *mobile* troops; **2,** flowing freely, as some liquids; **3,** easily changing in expression under emotion; changeable; as, a *mobile* face.—*n.* **mo-bil′i-ty.**

mo-bi-lize (mō′bĭ-līz; mŏb′ĭ-līz), *v.t.* [*p.t.* and *p.p.* -lized (-līzd), *p.pr.* -liz″ing], to call (troops) into active service:—*v.i.* to gather, as troops, and prepare for active service.—*n.* **mo″bi-li-za′tion.**

moc-ca-sin (mŏk′ȧ-sĭn), *n.* **1,** a deerskin sandal or shoe worn by the North American Indians; **2,** any of several poisonous American snakes, esp. the water moccasin; **3,** a kind of wild orchid.

Mo-cha (mō′kȧ), *n.* a kind of coffee from Mocha, a seaport of Arabia.

mock (mŏk), *v.t.* **1,** to ridicule; imitate in sport or contempt; **2,** to disappoint the hopes of; tantalize:—*n.* **1,** ridicule; **2,** a scornful jest; **3,** an object of ridicule:—*adj.* false; counterfeit: **mock orange,** the syringa; any of a genus of flowering shrubs with white or cream-colored blossoms.—*n.* **mock′er.**

Syn. v. ape, mimic. (See imitate.)

mock-er-y (mŏk′ẽr-ĭ), *n.* [*pl.* mockeries (-ĭz)], **1,** the act of making fun of a person or thing; **2,** derision; ridicule; **3,** impertinent imitation; **4,** an empty sham.

mock-ing (mŏk′ĭng), *p.adj.* scornful; mimicking.—*adv.* **mock′ing-ly.**

mock-ing bird an American thrush, about the size of a robin, noted for imitating the calls of other birds.

mod-al (mōd′ăl), *adj.* **1,** pertaining to a manner or form; **2,** in grammar, pertaining to the manner in which a verb expresses action: that is, whether it expresses fact, possibility, command, etc.; as, the verbs *should, would, may, must, can, ought* are used as *modal* auxiliaries.

mode (mōd), *n.* **1,** form; **2,** custom; fashion; manner; **3,** in grammar, a certain change in the form of a verb: also, *mood,* which see.

Syn. fashion, style. *Mode* names the general fashion, esp. of a particular time; as, her wedding dress was in the *mode* of the Civil War. *Fashion* is the general term for current custom or usage, esp. in polite society; as, bright colors are the *fashion.* *Style* suggests an approved fashion and often signifies a certain distinction in one's manner of conforming to it; as, her hat was in the Parisian *style.*

mod-el (mŏd′ĕl), *n.* **1,** a pattern of something to be made, copied, or imitated; a standard copy; **2,** a small-sized representation of something to be made, as an engine or building; **3,** a person who poses for a painter or sculptor; **4,** a woman who tries on costumes so that customers may see their effect:—*v.t.* to form after a pattern, esp. in clay:—*v.i.* to practice shaping objects out of clay; make designs:—*adj.* **1,** serving as a pattern; 2, worthy of being imitated.—*n.* **mod′el-er; mod′el-ler.**

Syn., *n.* design, mold, standard.

mod-el-ing (mŏd′ĕl-ĭng), *n.* the act or art of making a pattern, esp. of a work of art in clay or similar material. Also, **mod′el-ling.**

mod-er-ate (mŏd′ẽr-āt), *v.t.* [*p.t.* and *p.p.* -at″ed, *p.pr.* -at″ing], **1**, to keep within bounds; make less violent, intense, or extreme; as, to *moderate* rage, heat, etc.; **2**, to preside over, as a meeting:—*v.i.* **1**, to become less violent or intense; **2**, to act as presiding officer:—*adj.* (mŏd′ẽr-ȧt), **1**, kept within bounds; not extreme or excessive; calm; reasonable; mild; **2**, limited; mediocre.—*adv.* **mod′er-ate-ly.**—*n.* **mod′er-ate-ness.**

Syn., *adj.* temperate, gentle.—*Ant.*, *adj.* intemperate, unrestrained.

mod-er-a-tion (mŏd″ẽr-ā′shŭn), *n.* **1**, the act of keeping within bounds; **2**, freedom from excess; calmness of mind, speech, or action.

mod-er-a-tor (mŏd′ẽr-ā″tẽr), *n.* **1**, one who or that which regulates or restrains; as, courtesy is a *moderator* of conduct; **2**, a presiding officer, as at a town meeting, debate, or the like.

mod-ern (mŏd′ẽrn), *adj.* pertaining to the present time; recent:—*n.* a person of recent and present times; also, one who is up-to-date in his views or manners.

Syn., *adj.* new, recent, late. *Modern* refers to the present period in contrast with times quite remote; as, a *modern* invention. That is *new* which has not existed before or long; as, a *new* recipe. *Recent* is applied to things that have happened in the near past; as, a *recent* discovery. *Late* is like *recent* in applying to that just past; as, of *late* years; but it is esp. used in the sense of formerly but not now; as, the *late* president; and also in the sense of lately deceased; as, her *late* husband.

mod-ern-ism (mŏd′ẽr-nĭzm), *n.* a thing of recent date, esp. a usage, method, or characteristic of present times: **Modernism,** a religious movement based on modern scholarship.—*n.* **mod′ern-ist.**

mod-ern-ize (mŏd′ẽr-nīz), *v.t.* [*p.t.* and *p.p.* -ized (-nīzd), *p.pr.* -iz″ing], to make like present usage, taste, or speech. Also, **mod′ern-ise.**

mod-est (mŏd′ĕst), *adj.* **1**, held back by a sense of what is fit and proper; **2**, retiring; as, the *modest* violet; **3**, not excessive or extreme; as, his ambition was a *modest* one; **4**, chaste.—*adv.* **mod′est-ly.**

Syn. virtuous, bashful, reserved. (See shy.)

mod-es-ty (mŏd′ĕs-tĭ), *n.* **1**, regard for what is proper in behavior or manner; **2**, reserve concerning one's own powers; lack of conceit; **3**, freedom from what is extreme; moderation; as, *modesty* in dress.

Syn. bashfulness, shyness, humility.—*Ant.* forwardness, boldness.

mod-i-cum (mŏd′ĭ-kŭm), *n.* a little; a small quantity.

mod-i-fi-ca-tion (mŏd″ĭ-fĭ-kā′shŭn), *n.* **1**, a slight change in form; as, a *modification* of the house plans; **2**, a slight reduction; qualification; abatement.

mod-i-fy (mŏd′ĭ-fī), *v.t.* [*p.t.* and *p.p.* -fied (-fīd), *p.pr.* -fy″ing], **1**, to change slightly in form; **2**, to limit; reduce; **3**, in grammar, to qualify or limit; as, adjectives *modify* nouns.

Syn. alter, soften, change. (See qualify.)

mod-ish (mōd′ĭsh), *adj.* fashionable; stylish; as, a *modish* young lady.—*adv.* **mod′ish-ly.**—*n.* **mod′ish-ness.**

mo-diste (mō″dēst′), *n.* a fashionable dressmaker or dealer in women's apparel; a milliner.

mod-u-late (mŏd′ū-lāt), *v.t.* [*p.t.* and *p.p.* -lat″ed, *p.pr.* -lat″ing], **1**, to vary the sound of; as, to *modulate* the voice; **2**, to tone down:—*v.i.* in music, to pass from one key to a related key.

mod-u-la-tion (mŏd″ū-lā′shŭn), *n.* the act of varying the sound of; a toning down, as of the voice.

mod-u-la-tor (mŏd′ū-lā″tẽr), *n.* in electricity, a device for periodically or intermittently varying the amplitude of an alternating current.

Mo-gul (mō-gŭl′), *n.* **1**, a person of the Mongolian race; esp., one of the Mongols who conquered India in the 16th century; **2**, the ruler of their empire: called the *Great Mogul;* **3**, (also, *mogul*), any imposing personage:—*adj.* pertaining to the Mongols, their language, or customs.

mo-hair (mō′hâr″), *n.* **1**, a woven material made from the hair of the Angora goat; **2**, an imitation of such a material.

Mo-ham-med-an (mō-hăm′ĕd-ăn), *n.* a follower of Mohammed (about A. D. 570–632), or of the religion founded by him which claims that Mohammed was the greatest prophet of God:—*adj.* pertaining to Mohammed, or to Mohammedanism. Also, **Ma-hom′et-an; Ma-hom′ed-an.**—*n.* **Mo-ham′med-an-ism.**

Mo-hawk (mō′hôk), *n.* **1**, one of a tribe of American Indians formerly occupying the valley of the Mohawk River in New York; **2**, one of certain ruffians who, during the 17th and 18th centuries, annoyed persons in the streets of London, esp. at night.

Mo-hi-can (mō-hē′kăn), *n.* one of a tribe of American Indians formerly living in Connecticut and New York.

moi-e-ty (moi′ē-tĭ), *n.* [*pl.* moieties (-tĭz)], **1**, a half; **2**, a small portion.

moil (moil), *n.* **1**, drudgery; **2**, confusion; vexation; **3**, a spot or deflement:—*v.t.* to soil:—*v.i.* to be tired; toil; drudge; labor.

moire (mwär; mōr), *n.* a watered silk or mohair fabric.

moi-ré (mwä″rā′; mō′rā), [Fr.], *adj.* **1**, watered, as silk; **2**, having a clouded finish like watered silk, as a metal:—*v.t.* [*p.t.* and *p.p.* -réed′ (-rād′), *p.pr.* -ré′ing], to give a watered appearance to.

moist (moist), *adj.* **1**, containing water or other liquid; damp; **2**, tearful; as, *moist* eyes.—*n.* **moist′ness.**

Syn. dank, wet, damp. *Moist* applies to that which is but slightly wet; as, a *moist* sponge. *Dank* describes that which is unpleasantly damp; as, a *dank* cave. That is *wet* which consists of, or contains, liquid; as, a *wet* rag. *Damp* usually implies unpleasant or disagreeable moisture; as, *damp* air.

mois-ten (mois′n), *v.t.* and *v.i.* to make, or become, damp or slightly wet.

mois-ture (mois′tŭr), *n.* **1**, a moderate degree of dampness; **2**, water, or other liquid, in small quantity.

mo-lar (mō′lȧr), *n.* a double tooth, or grinder:—*adj.* used for grinding.

mo-las-ses (mō-lăs′ĕz), *n.* [*pl.* molasses], the dark-colored, sticky sirup obtained as a by-product in the making of sugar: used in cookery.

[1]**mold** (mōld), *n.* **1**, fine, soft soil, rich in decayed matter; **2**, matter; material; **3**, *Obs.*, the earth; hence, a grave:—*v.t.* to cover with soft, rich earth. Also, **mould.**

[2]**mold** (mōld), *n.* **1**, a form, as of sand or metal, in which anything is cast or shaped; **2**, the shape in which a thing is cast; form; **3**, that after which a thing is patterned; **4**, kind; character; **5**, bodily form:—*v.t.* **1**, to fashion in, or as in, a form, matrix, or the like; **2**, to decorate with an ornamental strip; **3**, to

shape into a mass of the desired consistency; knead, as dough. Also, **mould.**—*n.* **mold'er.** —*adj.* **mold'a-ble.**

Syn., *v.* frame, shape, model, ornament.

[3]**mold** (mōld), *n.* any of many fungi which grow chiefly on dead organic matter, spreading by means of tiny spores and forming dense, feltlike mats:—*v.t.* to cover with mold; cause to become moldy:—*v.i.* to become covered with mold. Also, **mould.**

mold-er (mōl'dẽr), *v.i.* and *v.t.* to crumble, or cause to crumble, away; waste away by degrees. Also, **mould'er.**

mold-ing (mōld'ĭng), *n.* **1,** the act of shaping in a form; **2,** anything made in or by a mold or form; **3,** an ornamental strip used on a wall, picture frame, etc. Also, **mould'ing.**

mold-y (mōl'dĭ), *adj.* [*comp.* mold'i-er, *superl.* mold'i-est], covered with, or containing, a musty growth; musty. Also, **mould'y.**—*n.* **mold'i-ness.**

[1]**mole** (mōl), *n.* a dark-colored spot or growth on the skin.

[2]**mole** (mōl), *n.* any of several grayish brown mammals with soft fur, rudimentary eyes, and broad feet with which they dig long underground furrows.

[3]**mole** (mōl), *n.* a massive breakwater, as at the mouth of a harbor.

Mo-lech (mō'lĕk), *n.* the fire god of the ancient Phœnicians, to whom human sacrifices, esp. first-born children, were offered. Also, **Mo'loch,** *Pfd. S.*

mo-lec-u-lar (mō-lĕk'ū-lȧr), *adj.* pertaining to, consisting of, produced by, or existing between, molecules.

mol-e-cule (mŏl'ē-kūl; mō'lē-kūl), *n.* **1,** the smallest quantity of any substance which can exist separately, and still retain the characteristics of the substance; a group of atoms acting as a physical unit; **2,** hence, any minute particle.

mole-hill (mōl'hĭl''), *n.* **1,** a little mound made by the burrowing of a mole; **2,** a small hindrance or difficulty.

mole-skin (mōl'skĭn''), *n.* **1,** the fur of the mole, a small burrowing animal; **2,** a cloth with a soft surface supposed to resemble a mole's fur; **3,** in *pl.*, a garment of this cloth, esp. trousers.

mo-lest (mō-lĕst'), *v.t.* to interfere with; trouble; disturb maliciously or without cause.—*n.* **mo-lest'er.**

Syn. plague, vex, pester.

mo-les-ta-tion (mō''lĕs-tā'shŭn; mŏl''-ĕs-tā'shŭn), *n.* **1,** the act of annoying, interfering with, or troubling; hostile interference; **2,** the state of being annoyed or disturbed.

mol-li-fy (mŏl'ĭ-fī), *v.t.* [*p.t.* and *p.p.* -fied (-fīd), *p.pr.* -fy''ing], **1,** to calm; soften; **2,** to make less severe, violent, or hard. —*n.* **mol'li-fi''er.**—*n.* **mol''li-fi-ca'tion.**

mol-lusk (mŏl'ŭsk), *n.* any of a phylum (*Mollusca*) of animals with soft, fleshy bodies, usually covered with shells containing lime, including the limpets, snails, oysters, cuttlefish, etc.—*adj.* **mol-lus'cous.**

mol-ly-cod-dle (mŏl'ĭ-kŏd''l), *n. Slang,* one who is too careful of himself; a milksop; an effeminate male.

Mo-loch (mō'lŏk), *n.* the fire god of the ancient Phœnicians, to whom human sacrifices, esp. first-born children, were offered. Also, **Mo'lech.**

molt (mōlt), *v.i.* to cast the hair, feathers, skin, etc.:—*v.t.* to shed, as the skin, hair, horns, etc.:—*n.* the shedding of hair, feathers, etc., or the season when such shedding takes place. Also, **moult.**

mol-ten (mōl'tn), *p.adj.* **1,** melted; **2,** cast of melted metal.

mo-lyb-de-num (mō-lĭb'dē-nŭm; mŏl''-ĭb-dē'nŭm), *n.* a hard, silvery white, metallic element, chiefly used in the manufacture of steel.

mo-ment (mō'mĕnt), *n.* **1,** a portion of time; an instant; **2,** the present time; **3,** importance; as, affairs of great *moment;* **4,** tendency, as of a force or velocity, to cause motion around a central point.

Syn. weight, consequence, significance.

mo-men-ta-ry (mō'mĕn-tā-rĭ), *adj.* lasting only for, or done in, an instant; transitory.—*adv.* **mo'men-ta-ri-ly.**—*n.* **mo'men-ta-ri-ness.**

Syn. passing, transient, fugitive.

mo-men-tous (mō-mĕn'tŭs), *adj.* very important; of great consequence; as a decision.—*n.* **mo-men'tous-ness.**

mo-men-tum (mō-mĕn'tŭm), *n.* **1,** in mechanics, the quantity of motion in a moving body as measured by the product of its mass and velocity; **2,** popularly, impetus due to motion; as, a body gathers *momentum* as it moves.

mon-ad (mŏn'ăd; mō'năd), *n.* **1,** a unit of matter; an atom; also, an individual; **2,** one of the smallest and simplest of living creatures, supporting life in water; **3,** formerly, a simple organism or cell.—*adj.* **mo-nad'ic.**—*n.* **mon'ad-ism.**

mon-arch (mŏn'ȧrk), *n.* **1,** a supreme ruler; sovereign; **2,** the chief of its class or kind:—*adj.* supreme.—*adj.* **mo-nar'chal; mo-nar'chi-al.**

mo-nar-chic (mō-när'kĭk), *adj.* pertaining to a king or an emperor or to the government of a king or an emperor. Also, **mo-nar'chi-cal.**

mon-arch-ist (mŏn'ȧr-kĭst), *n.* one who believes in, or supports, a government whose power is possessed by a king, emperor, etc.—*n.* **mon'arch-ism.**

mon-arch-y (mŏn'ȧr-kĭ), *n.* [*pl.* monarchies (-kĭz)], **1,** government in which the supreme power is possessed by a king or emperor; **2,** a kingdom; an empire.

mon-as-ter-y (mŏn'ăs-tĕr-ĭ), *n.* [*pl.* monasteries (-ĭz)], a home to which men retire under vows to devote their lives to religion.—*adj.* **mon''as-te'ri-al.**

Syn. cloister, abbey, convent.

mo-nas-tic (mō-năs'tĭk), *adj.* **1,** pertaining to religious houses called monasteries, or to monks and their rules or their manner of life; **2,** withdrawn; secluded for religious study. Also, **mo-nas'ti-cal.**—*adv.* **mo-nas'ti-cal-ly.**—*n.* **mo-nas'ti-cism.**

Mon-day (mŭn'dā), *n.* the second day of the week.—*abbr.* **Mon.**

mon-e-ta-ry (mŏn'ē-tā-rĭ; mŭn'-), *adj.* **1,** of or pertaining to money; **2,** pecuniary; as, a *monetary* claim.

mon-e-tize (mŏn'ē-tīz; mŭn'-), *v.t.* [*p.t.* and *p.p.* -tized (-tīzd), *p.pr.* -tiz''ing], **1,** to convert into money; **2,** to give a standard value to, as money; as, to *monetize* silver.—*n.* **mon''e-ti-za'tion.**

mon-ey (mŭn'ĭ), *n.* [*pl.* moneys (-ĭz)], **1,** coin; gold, silver, or other metal stamped by legal authority, and used as a means of exchange; **2,** anything, as bank notes, checks, drafts, etc., used as a means of exchange; **3,** wealth: **money of account,** a basis of exchange, used in accounts, but not necessarily represented by a coin, as the mill: **money order,** an order, usually sold by a post office, authorizing the payment of a stated amount of money to the holder.

Syn. cash, currency, bullion.

mon-eyed (mŭn'ĭd), *adj.* possessed of money; wealthy.

mon-ger (mŭng'gẽr), *n.* a dealer: used in combination; as, fish*monger.*

Mon-gol (mŏng'gŏl), *adj.* pertaining to Mongolia, in Asia, to its people, or to the yellow race:—*n.* **1,** a native of Mongolia; **2,** a member of the yellow race; **3,** the Mongolian language.

Mon-go-li-an (mŏng-gō'lĭ-ăn), *adj.* **1,** designating, or pertaining to, the yellow race of Asia, including the Chinese, Tatars, etc.; **2,** pertaining to Mongolia, its natives, or their language:—*n.* one of the yellow race.—*adj.* and *n.* **Mon-gol'ic.**

mon-goose (mŏng'gōōs), *n.* [*pl.* mongooses (-ĕz)], a small mammal of India, which kills poisonous snakes.

mon-grel (mŭng'grĕl; mŏng'grĕl), *adj.* **1,** of a mixed breed or kind; **2,** of mixed origin: used esp. of a language or word:—*n.* an animal of mixed breed or kind.

mo-ni-tion (mō-nĭsh'ŭn), *n.* **1,** a caution; warning; **2,** a formal notice.

mon-i-tor (mŏn'ĭ-tẽr), *n.* **1,** one who warns or advises; **2,** a senior pupil selected to instruct or oversee the younger ones; **3,** an ironclad warship, having low sides and one or more turrets mounted with guns; **4,** a kind of large lizard.—*n.fem.* **mon'i-tress.**

mon-i-to-ri-al (mŏn″ĭ-tō'rĭ-ăl), *adj.* pertaining to, or performed by, an adviser or guide.

mon-i-to-ry (mŏn'ĭ-tō-rĭ), *adj.* giving warning or advice.

monk (mŭngk), *n.* a man who devotes himself to a religious life and lives with others bound as he is by vows.—*adj.* **monk'ish.**

monk-er-y (mŭngk'ẽr-ĭ), *n.* the life, practices, vows, and customs of monks: used usually in reproach.

mon-key (mŭng'kĭ), *n.* [*pl.* monkeys (-kĭz)], **1,** in the broadest sense, any one of the highest order of animals below man; in the narrower sense, one of the smaller, long-tailed forms differing from the larger, nearly tailless forms, called apes; **2,** any of various mechanical contrivances, as the falling block in a pile driver: **monkey bread,** the large, acid fruit of the baobab, used by monkeys as food: **monkey gaff,** a spar attached to the mizzenmast for displaying signals (see *rigging,* illus.): **monkey jacket,** a short, closely fitting, thick coat worn by sailors.

mon-key wrench a tool with an adjustable jaw, for turning a nut, bolt, etc. (see *tool,* illus.).

monks-hood (mŭngks'hŏŏd″), *n.* wolfsbane, or aconite, a plant of the crowfoot family.

mon-o- (mŏn'ō-), [*mon-* before a vowel], a prefix or combining form from the Greek, meaning one or single; as, *mono*xide; *mono*plane; *mon*arch.

mon-o-chrome (mŏn'ō-krōm), *n.* a painting in one color or in different shades of the same color.

mon-o-cle (mŏn'ō-kl), *n.* an eyeglass for one eye.

mon-o-cot-y-le-don (mŏn″ō-kŏt″ĭ-lē'dŭn), *n.* a seed plant having a single cotyledon, or seed leaf.

mo-noc-u-lar (mō-nŏk'ū-lȧr; mŏn-ŏk'-), *adj.* **1,** fitted for use of one eye; **2,** using only one eye; one-eyed.

mon-o-dy (mŏn'ō-dĭ), *n.* [*pl.* monodies (-dĭz)], a mournful poem or song for one voice; a lament.—*n.* **mon'o-dist.**

mo-nog-a-my (mō-nŏg'ȧ-mĭ), *n.* **1,** marriage with only one wife or one husband at a time; **2,** in zoölogy, the habit of pairing with a single mate.—*adj.* **mo-nog'a-mous.**—*adj.* **mon″o-gam'ic.**—*n.* **mo-nog'a-mist.**

mon-o-gram (mŏn'ō-grăm), *n.* a character formed by the interweaving of two or more letters.

mon-o-graph (mŏn'ō-grȧf), *n.* a paper written on one particular subject or some branch of it.

mon-o-lith (mŏn'ō-lĭth), *n.* **1,** a pillar or column formed of a single stone; **2,** a building material which is both fireproof and waterproof, and is used esp. for floors.—*adj.* **mon″o-lith'ic.**

mon-o-log (mŏn'ō-lŏg), *n.* **1,** a dramatic scene in which only one person speaks; **2,** a lengthy speech by one person. Also, **mon'o-logue.**—*n.* **mo-nol'o-gist.**

mon-o-ma-ni-a (mŏn″ō-mā'nĭ-ȧ), *n.* **1,** insanity in regard to a single subject or class of subjects; **2,** a craze; the immoderate following of one idea or hobby.—*n.* and *adj.* **mon″o-ma'ni-ac.**

mon-o-met-al-lism (mŏn″ō-mĕt'ăl-ĭzm), *n.* **1,** the use of one metal only as the standard of value of money; **2,** the theory of such a standard.

mo-no-mi-al (mō-nō'mĭ-ăl), *adj.* in algebra, consisting of a single term:—*n.* an expression containing one term.

mon-o-plane (mŏn'ō-plăn), *n.* a flying machine whose main sup-

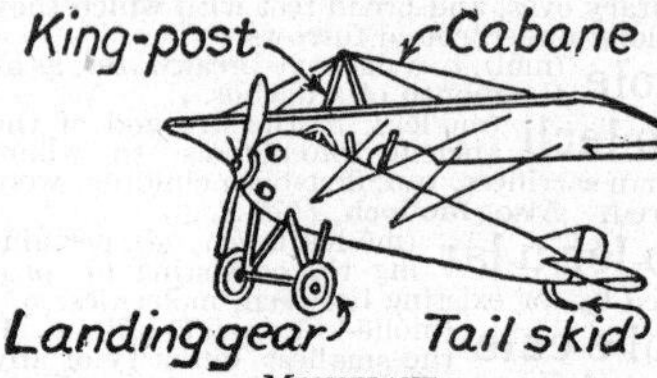

MONOPLANE

porting surface is a single wing on each side of the body: distinguished from *biplane.*

mo-nop-o-list (mō-nŏp'ō-lĭst), *n.* one who, alone, or in connection with others, takes complete possession or control of any interest, or any branch of trade, commerce, transportation, or production.—*adj.* **mo-nop″o-lis'tic.**

mo-nop-o-lize (mō-nŏp'ō-līz), *v.t.* [*p.t.* and *p.p.* -lized (-līzd), *p.pr.* -liz″ing], **1,** to gain possession of so as to be the only producer or trader in; **2,** to take the whole of; gain exclusive possession of; as, to *monopolize* the attention of another. Also, **mo-nop'o-lise.**—*n.* **mo-nop″o-li-za'tion.**

mo-nop-o-ly (mō-nŏp'ō-lĭ), *n.* [*pl.* monopolies (-lĭz)], **1,** the exclusive control of any industry: as, the government has a *monopoly* of the postal business in the U. S.; **2,** a company that possesses such control; **3,** the sole possession of anything.

mon-o-rail (mŏn'ō-rāl″), *n.* in a railway system, a single rail on which cars are run: also used for a hanging car.

mon-o-syl-lab-ic (mŏn″ō-sĭ-lăb'ĭk), *adj.* **1,** not divided, as a word, in pronouncing; **2,** composed of one-syllabled words, or those that are not divided into parts in pronouncing.

mon-o-syl-la-ble (mŏn'ō-sĭl″ȧ-bl), *n.* a word of one syllable, not divided into parts in being pronounced.

mon-o-the-ism (mŏn'ō-thē-ĭzm), *n.* the doctrine of, or belief in, the existence of but one God.—*n.* **mon'o-the-ist.**—*adj.* **mon″o-the-is'tic.**

mon-o-tone (mŏn'ō-tōn), *n.* **1,** a recitation on a single note or key; **2,** lack of variety in style of a written composition; **3,** sameness of color:—*v.t.* [*p.t.* and *p.p.* -toned (-tōnd), *p.pr.* -ton″ing], to recite, as prayers, on a single note; intone; chant.

mo-not-o-nous (mō-nŏt′ō-nŭs), *adj.* continued in the same tone or manner; wearisome; tedious; without variety.—*n.* **mo-not′o-nous-ness.**—*adv.* **mo-not′o-nous-ly.**

mo-not-o-ny (mō-nŏt′ō-nĭ), *n.* **1**, dull sameness of tone; **2**, unvarying or tiresome sameness.

mon-o-type (mŏn′ō-tīp), *n.* a typesetting machine that casts single letters, instead of words and lines.

mon-ox-ide (mŏn-ŏk′sīd; -sĭd), *n.* in chemistry, a compound in which each molecule contains a single atom of oxygen: **carbon monoxide**, a colorless, odorless gas, very poisonous, resulting from the incomplete combustion of carbon, as in gasoline engines of automobiles. Also, **mon-ox′id.**

Mon-roe Doc-trine (mŏn-rō′), a principle announced by President Monroe in 1823, by which the United States insisted that no European nation should intervene in, or increase its holdings on, either American continent.

Mon-sei-gneur (mô̂n″sâ″nyûr′; mŏn-sĕn′yẽr), [Fr.], *n.* [*pl.* Messeigneurs (mā″sâ″nyûr′; mĕ-sĕn′yẽrz)], my lord: a title given in France to church dignitaries and, formerly, to the higher nobility: used before title or rank; as, *Monseigneur* the Prince.—*abbr.* **Mgr.; Monsig.**

***mon-sieur** (msyö′), [Fr.], *n.* [*pl.* messieurs (mā″syö′)], a French title of courtesy, equivalent to *Sir* or *Mr.*: capitalized when used with a proper name.—*abbr.* **M.; Mons.** [*pl.* **MM.; Messrs.**]

mon-si-gnor (mŏn-sē′nyôr; *It.* mōn″sē-nyōr′), *n.* [*pl.* monsignori (mōn″sē-nyō′rē)], my lord: a title of honor conferred by the Pope.—*abbr.* **Mgr.; Monsig.**

mon-soon (mŏn-sōōn′), *n.* **1**, a wind, esp. in the Indian Ocean, blowing from the southwest from May to September, and from the northeast during the other part of the year; **2**, the rainy season that accompanies the former.

mon-ster (mŏn′stẽr), *n.* **1**, any animal or thing out of the usual course of nature; **2**, something very huge or remarkably deformed or hideous; **3**, a person remarkable for extreme wickedness, cruelty, or ugliness:—*adj.* of unusual size.

mon-strance (mŏn′străns), *n.* one of the altar vessels in the Roman Catholic Church.

mon-stros-i-ty (mŏn-strŏs′ĭ-tĭ), *n.* [*pl.* monstrosities (-tĭz)], **1**, the state or quality of being deformed or hideous or extremely unusual; **2**, anything unnaturally huge, hideous, or deformed.

mon-strous (mŏn′strŭs), *adj.* **1**, out of the common course of nature; **2**, enormous; huge; as, a *monstrous* fire; **3**, horrible; hideous; causing disgust; as, *monstrous* cruelty.—*adv.* **mon′strous-ly.**
Syn. shocking, dreadful, hateful, immense.
—*Ant.* small, ordinary, attractive.

mon-te (mŏn′tā; mōn′tā), [Sp.], *n.* a Spanish gambling game played with dice or a Spanish deck of forty cards.

Mon-tes-so-ri meth-od (mŏn″tĕs-sō′rē; mōn″-), a system of training and instruction for small children, in which emphasis is placed upon freedom for physical activity, individual instruction, and the early development of various activities, as that of writing: developed by Maria Montessori, Italian educator.

month (mŭnth), *n.* one of the twelve parts into which the year is divided, each containing about four weeks, or 28 to 31 days.

month-ly (mŭnth′lĭ), *adj.* **1**, continued for a month; as, the *monthly* course of the moon around the earth; **2**, performed, happening, or published once a month; as, a *monthly* bill; a *monthly* magazine:—*adv.* once each month; as, the magazine is issued *monthly*:—*n.* [*pl.* monthlies (-lĭz)], a magazine or periodical published each month.

mon-u-ment (mŏn′ū-mĕnt), *n.* **1**, anything that keeps alive the memory of a person or event, as a pillar, a statue, an arch, a tomb, etc.; **2**, any act or production which serves as a memorial of a person or an event.
Syn. memorial, record, cenotaph.

mon-u-men-tal (mŏn″ū-mĕn′tăl), *adj.* **1**, serving to keep alive the memory of a person or event, as a statue; **2**, like a monument; huge; lasting; as, Milton's "Paradise Lost" is a *monumental* work. —*adv.* **mon″u-men′tal-ly.**

moo (mōō), *n.* the lowing of a cow:—*v.i.* to utter the call characteristic of a cow, or make a noise like it; low.

[1]**mood** (mōōd), *n.* in grammar, any one of the verb forms used to suggest how the action or state is considered; as, the indicative *mood* (the boy *was* ready); the subjunctive *mood* (if the boy *were* ready); the imperative *mood* (boy, *be* ready). Also, **mode.**

[2]**mood** (mōōd), *n.* the state or temper of mind; humor; as, in pensive *mood.*
Syn. disposition, vein.

mood-y (mōōd′ĭ), *adj.* [*comp.* mood′i-er, *superl.* mood′i-est], **1**, absent-minded; out of temper; gloomy; **2**, given to changes in the state of mind or temper.—*adv.* **mood′i-ly.**—*n.* **mood′i-ness.**

moon (mōōn), *n.* **1**, the heavenly body that revolves round the earth; **2**, a heavenly body that revolves about any planet; **3**, a month; as, it is many *moons* since he went away; **4**, anything shaped like a moon: —*v.i.* to wander and look about in an absent-minded and listless manner.—*adj.* **moon′y.**

moon-beam (mōōn′bēm″), *n.* a ray of light from the moon.

moon-light (mōōn′līt″), *n.* the light given by the moon:—*adj.* **1**, lighted by the moon; **2**, occurring by moonlight; as, a *moonlight* sail.—*adj.* **moon′lit″.**

moon-sail (mōōn′sāl″), *n.* a light sail carried above the skysail.

moon-shine (mōōn′shīn″), *n.* **1**, moonlight; **2**, empty show; **3**, *Colloq.*, liquor, as whisky, smuggled or made against the law.

moon-shin-er (mōōn′shīn″ẽr), *n. Colloq.*, one who makes, or trades in, alcoholic drinks against the law.

moon-stone (mōōn′stōn″), *n.* any kind of translucent feldspar which shows delicate opal tints and is beautiful enough to be used as a gem.

moon-struck (mōōn′strŭk″), *adj.* having an unbalanced mind through the supposed influence of the moon.

[1]**moor** (mōōr), *n.* a broad tract of waste land, covered with heather.

[2]**moor** (mōōr), *v.t.* to secure in a particular place by a cable or anchor; as, they *moor* the ship:—*v.i.* to be secured in such a way; as, the ships *moor* in the harbor.

Moor (mōōr), *n.* **1**, a native of Morocco; **2**, a Mohammedan; esp., one of the Saracens who invaded Spain.

moor-age (mōōr′āj), *n.* a place for anchoring or fastening a vessel.

moor cock the male of the red grouse: also called *moor fowl.*

moor-ing (mōōr′ĭng), *n.* **1**, the act of fastening a vessel to a particular place; **2**, the cables, anchors, etc., by which a vessel is fastened; **3**, in *pl.*, the place where a vessel is anchored.

moor-ish (mo͞or′ĭsh), *adj.* resembling, or growing on, a heath; marshy; as, *moorish* soil.

Moor-ish (mo͞or′ĭsh), *adj.* pertaining to, or in the style of, the Moors.

moor-land (mo͞or′lănd), *n.* waste land covered with heather.

moose (mo͞os), *n.* [*pl.* moose], a large North American deer resembling the European elk.

Moose ($\frac{1}{100}$)

moot (mo͞ot), *v.t.* to propose for discussion:—*n.* discussion of a mock law case for practice:—*adj.* open to discussion; as, a *moot* question: **moot court**, a mock court held by students for practice in legal procedure.

mop (mŏp), *n.* **1**, a bundle of cloth, rags, etc., fastened to the end of a long handle: used for washing floors; **2**, a similar, loose, tangled bunch; as, a *mop* of hair:—*v.t.* [*p.t.* and *p.p.* mopped (mŏpt), *p.pr.* mop′ping], to rub, dry, or remove with a mop.

mope (mōp), *n.* one who is dull or out of spirits:—*v.i.* [*p.t.* and *p.p.* moped (mōpt), *p.pr.* mop′ing], to be silent or dull.

mo-quette (mō-kĕt′), *n.* a woolen material with a thick, velvety nap.

mo-raine (mō-rān′), *n.* a ridge or heap of rocks and gravel deposited at the edges and base of a glacier.

mor-al (mŏr′ăl), *n.* **1**, the lesson taught by a fable or story; **2**, in *pl.*, conduct; behavior:—*adj.* **1**, referring to man's idea of what is right and wrong; ethical; as, *moral* courage; **2**, governed by good conduct; chaste; as, a *moral* way of living; **3**, able to be influenced by a sense of right; as, a *moral* race of people; **4**, according to reason or probability; as, a *moral* certainty; **5**, teaching a pious lesson; as, a *moral* book; **6**, the same as; virtual; as, a *moral* victory: **moral philosophy**, the science and study of right and wrong.—*adv.* **mor′al-ly.**

mo-rale (mō-răl′; mō-räl′), *n.* the moral or mental state which makes men capable of endurance and of showing courage in the presence of discouragement or danger; as, the *morale* of an army.

mo-ral-i-ty (mō-răl′ĭ-tĭ), *n.* [*pl.* moralities (-tĭz)], **1**, the teaching or practice of the duties of life; **2**, righteousness; virtue; **3**, formerly, a kind of play intended to teach a lesson, and representing such characters as Faith, Love, and the like.

mor-al-ize (mŏr′ăl-īz), *v.t.* [*p.t.* and *p.p.* -ized (-īzd), *p.pr.* -iz″ing], **1**, to apply or explain in a way that teaches a lesson; as, to *moralize* a story; **2**, to make virtuous; as, to *moralize* the natives:—*v.i.* to talk at length about right and wrong, duty, goodness, truth, or the like.—*n.* **mor′al-iz″er.** —*n.* **mor″al-i-za′tion.**

mo-rass (mō-răs′), *n.* a swamp; tract of wet ground; bog.

mor-a-to-ri-um (mŏr″ȧ-tō′rĭ-ŭm), *n.* [*pl.* moratoria (-ȧ)], a period established by law, during which a debtor, usually a government, may suspend payment of obligations; also, the law itself.

Mo-ra-vi-an (mō-rā′vĭ-ăn), *n.* **1**, a native of Moravia; **2**, the Slavic dialect spoken in Moravia; **3**, a member of the sect of United Brethren:—*adj.* **1**, pertaining to Moravia or to its language or people; **2**, pertaining to the sect of United Brethren.

mor-bid (môr′bĭd), *adj.* **1**, pertaining to, or caused by, disease; **2**, sickly; unhealthy; hence, mentally gloomy or unwholesome.—*adv.* **mor′bid-ly.**—*n.* **mor-bid′-i-ty.**—*n.* **mor′bid-ness.**
Syn. unsound, diseased, corrupt.

mor-dant (môr′dănt), *n.* **1**, a substance that serves to fix certain colors in dyeing; **2**, a substance to make gold leaf stick; **3**, a substance that eats into a surface: —*adj.* **1**, having power to fix colors; **2**, sarcastic; biting; keen.

Mor-de-cai (môr′dē-kī; môr″dē-kā′ī), *n.* in the Bible, the cousin and foster father of Esther, who, by his warning, enabled her to save the Jews from being destroyed by Haman (Esther 2: 5–7).

more (mōr), *adj.* comparative of *many* and *much:* **1**, greater in number, quality, extent, etc.; **2**, additional; longer:—*adv.* **1**, to a greater degree, etc.; **2**, again; as, we shall not see her *more;* **3**, besides:—*n.* **1**, a greater quantity, number, etc.; **2**, something further or additional.

mo-reen (mō-rēn′), *n.* a stout, woolen fabric, often watered or figured.

more-o-ver (mōr-ō′vẽr), *adv.* besides; further; also.

mor-ga-nat-ic (môr″gȧ-năt′ĭk), *adj.* designating, or pertaining to, the marriage of a man of royal or other high rank with a woman of lower degree, whose children cannot inherit their father's rank.

morgue (môrg), *n.* a place where the bodies of persons found dead are left until recognized and claimed.

mor-i-bund (môr′ĭ-bŭnd), *adj.* in a dying condition.

mo-ri-on (mō′rĭ-ŏn), *n.* an open helmet somewhat like a hat.

Mo-ris-co (mō-rĭs′kō), *n.* [*pl.* Moriscos; Moriscoes (-kōz)], **1**, a Moor, usually a Christianized Moor, living in Spain after the Moorish power there was overthrown; **2**, the language of the Moriscos; **3**, Moorish ornamentation or architecture.

Mor-mon (môr′mŭn), *n.* a member of the sect, also called *Latter-day Saints*, founded in 1830 by Joseph Smith, who declared that he had found in the U. S. the "Book of Mormon," which, it is claimed, is a sacred history of the ancient inhabitants of America:—*adj.* designating, or pertaining to, this sect.—*n.* **Mor′mon-ism.**

morn (môrn), *n. Poetic,* morning; dawn; daybreak.

morn-ing (môr′nĭng), *n.* **1**, the early part of the day; **2**, any early part; as, the *morning* of life:—*adj.* pertaining to, occurring, or performed in, the early part of the day, or before noon.

morn-ing-glo-ry (môr′nĭng-glō″rĭ), *n.* [*pl.* morning-glories (-rĭz)], a twining plant with heart-shaped leaves and funnel-shaped flowers, blue, pink, or white in color.

Mo-ro (mō′rō), *n.* [*pl.* Moros (-rōz)], **1**, a native Mohammedan inhabitant of the southern Philippines; **2**, the language of the Moros, including many dialects.

mo-roc-co (mō-rŏk′ō), *n.* [*pl.* moroccos (-ōz)], a kind of fine-grained leather of goatskin or sheepskin: used for binding books: so called because first prepared in Morocco, Africa.

mo-ron (mō′rŏn), *n.* **1**, a person who is mentally deficient, but whose mental development is only slightly subnormal; **2**, *Colloq.*, a stupid person.—*n.* **mo′ron-ism.**

mo-rose (mō-rōs′), *adj.* sullen; surly; ill-tempered; gloomy; as, a *morose* look.—*adv.* **mo-rose′ly.**—*n.* **mo-rose′ness.**
Syn. sulky, fretful, crabbed.

Mor-pheus (môr′fūs; môr′fē-ŭs), *n.* in mythology, the god of dreams and of sleep.—*adj.* **Mor′phe-an.**

mor-phi-a (môr′fĭ-ȧ), *n.* in chemistry, morphine, a narcotic drug derived from opium.

mor-phine (môr′fĭn; môr′fēn), *n.* a substance found in opium, which has the power to deaden feeling and produce sleep. Also, **mor′phin.**

mor-phin-ism (môr′fĭn-ĭzm), *n.* a diseased state caused by the habitual use of morphine, a narcotic drug obtained from opium.

mor-phol-o-gy (môr-fŏl′ō-jĭ), *n.* that branch of science which deals with the form and structure of plants and animals.—*adj.* **mor″pho-log′i-cal.**

mor-ris (mŏr′ĭs), *n.* an Old English pastoral dance with tambourines, bells, etc., supposed to be of Moorish origin: also called *morris dance*. Also, **mor′rice.**

mor-row (mŏr′ō), *n.* **1,** the next day after any day specially mentioned; **2,** tomorrow; **3,** formerly, morning; as, good *morrow*, friend.

morse (môrs), *n.* a clasp for fastening a long circular garment or cloak worn on special occasions by a priest; a pectoral.

Morse (môrs), *adj.* designating, or pertaining to, the system of telegraphy developed by Samuel F. B. Morse (1791-1872): **Morse alphabet** or **code**, a system of telegraphic signals invented by S. F. B. Morse, consisting of groups of shorter and longer marks, sounds, or flashes, called *dots* and *dashes*, representing the various letters of the alphabet, numerals, etc. (see page 934):—*n. Colloq.*, the Morse alphabet or code.

mor-sel (môr′sĕl), *n.* **1,** a bite; mouthful; **2,** a small amount of anything.

mort (môrt), *n.* a note or notes sounded on a hunting horn to announce that the game has been killed.

mor-tal (môr′tăl), *n.* a human being; man, as subject to death:—*adj.* **1,** subject to death; as, *mortal* man; **2,** causing death; as, a *mortal* wound or illness; **3,** punishable with death; as, a *mortal* sin; **4,** filled with desire to kill; as, a *mortal* enemy; **5,** violent; extreme; as, *mortal* fear; **6,** pertaining to human beings; as, *mortal* greatness.—*adv.* **mor′tal-ly.**

Syn., adj. fatal, human. (See deadly.)

mor-tal-i-ty (môr-tăl′ĭ-tĭ), *n.* [*pl.* mortalities (-tĭz)], **1,** the condition of being subject to death; **2,** the quality of causing death; as, a disease of high *mortality;* **3,** number of deaths in proportion to the population.

mor-tar (môr′tẽr), *n.* **1,** a vessel in which substances are pounded with an implement called a pestle, chiefly used in making medicines; **2,** a short cannon used for throwing shells high upward, so as to drop from above on to the object aimed at; **3,** a building cement of lime, sand, and water: **mortar board, 1,** a flat, square board supported by a handle, for holding mortar; **2,** *Colloq.*, a scholar's flat-topped cap:—*v.t.* to plaster or secure with building cement.

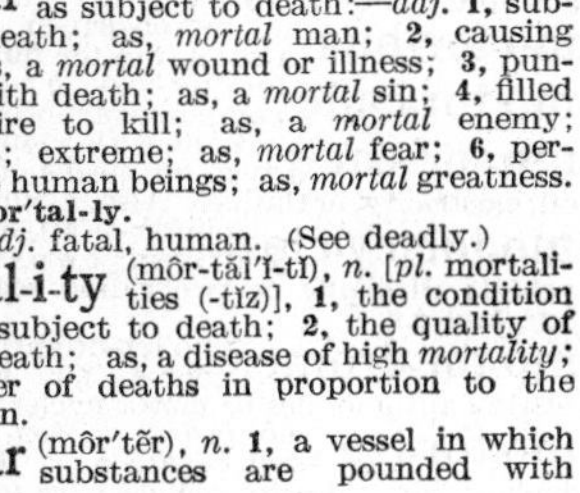

MORTARS

Mortar and Pestle

Siege Mortar

mort-gage (môr′gāj), *n.* a giving over of property, as security for the payment of a debt, to become void when the debt is paid; as, a *mortgage* on a house; also, the legal paper making such a pledge of property:—*v.t.* [*p.t.* and *p.p.* -gaged (-gājd), *p.pr.* -gag-ing], to make over (property) as security to one to whom a debt is owed; pledge.

mort-ga-gee (môr″gȧ-jē′), *n.* the person who is secured against loss by the mortgaged property.

mort-ga-gor (môr″gȧ-jôr′; môr′gȧ-jẽr), *n.* the person who gives property as security. Also, **mort′gag-er.**

mor-ti-cian (môr-tĭsh′ăn), *n.* an undertaker; one who prepares the dead for burial and conducts funerals.

mor-ti-fi-ca-tion (môr″tĭ-fĭ-kā′shŭn), *n.* **1,** the act of humbling or depressing; **2,** the death of one part of an animal body while the rest continues to live; gangrene; **3,** the subduing of the passions and appetites by self-denial; **4,** humiliation, or its cause; vexation.

mor-ti-fy (môr′tĭ-fī), *v.t.* [*p.t.* and *p.p.* -fied (-fīd), *p.pr.* -fy″ing], **1,** to subdue by self-denial; as, to *mortify* the appetites; **2,** to humble; humiliate; depress; **3,** to cause (a part of the body) to decay, or undergo gangrene:—*v.i.* to lose all living functions, as an injured part of the body; be affected with gangrene.—*n.* **mor′ti-fi″er.**

mor-tise (môr′tĭs), *n.* a hole or space hollowed out, as in a timber, into which is fitted a corresponding part called a *tenon:*—*v.t.* [*p.t.* and *p.p.* -tised (-tĭst), *p.pr.* -tis-ing], to join, by putting a projecting part into a hole made to fit. Also, **mor′tice.**

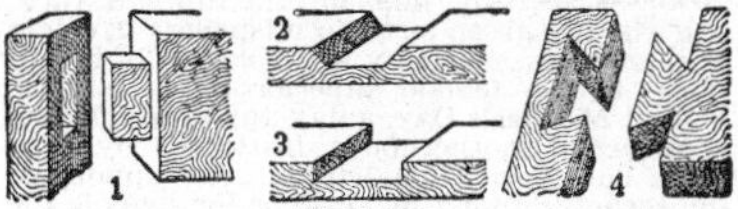

MORTISES

1, mortise and tenon; 2, bevel mortise; 3, right-angled mortise; 4, dovetail mortise and tenon.

mort-main (môrt′mān″), *n.* possession of lands or tenements by a corporation, esp. by a church corporation.

mor-tu-a-ry (môr′tū-ā-rĭ), *n.* [*pl.* mortuaries (-rĭz)], a building for the dead awaiting burial:—*adj.* pertaining to the burial of the dead.

mo-sa-ic (mō-zā′ĭk), *n.* a design made of small pieces of glass, stone, etc., of various colors, inlaid in a ground of stucco or metal; also, a piece of work so made:—*adj.* pertaining to, or consisting of, such work.

Mo-sa-ic (mō-zā′ĭk), *adj.* pertaining to Moses, to the laws, institutions, etc., given through him, or to his writings.

Mo-selle (mō-zĕl′), *n.* a mild white wine made in the valley of the Moselle, a river of northeastern France.

Mo-ses (mō′zĕz), *n.* **1,** the great prophet and lawgiver of the Israelites, who led them out of Egypt; **2,** hence, any great leader; **3,** a meek man (Numbers 12:3).

Mos-lem (mŏz′lĕm; mŏs′lĕm), *n.* a follower of the religion founded by Mohammed; a Mohammedan: also called *Mussulman:*—*adj.* pertaining to Mohammedans, or a people who believe that Mohammed was the latest and greatest prophet of God.

mosque (mŏsk), *n.* a Mohammedan temple. Also, **mosk.**

mos-qui-to (mŏs-kē′tō), *n.* [*pl.* mosquitoes (-tōz)], any of a family of two-winged insects, the females of which puncture the skin of men and animals, some species depositing disease germs, as of malaria.

moss (môs), *n.* **1**, any of several low-growing, small-leaved plants reproducing by spores rather than seeds; **2**, any of several lichens; as, Iceland *moss;* **3**, erroneously, any of several tiny plants found on trees, rocks, etc.; **4**, a soft, peaty swamp.

moss-y (môs'ĭ), *adj.* [*comp.* moss'i-er, *superl.* moss'i-est], covered with, or resembling, moss.—*n.* **moss'i-ness.**

most (mōst), *adj.* superlative of *many* or *much:* greatest in number, quantity, or degree:—*n.* the greatest number, part, quality, or value:—*adv.* in the greatest degree.

-most (-mōst), *adj. suffix,* used to form adjectives in the superlative degree; as, in*most;* fore*most.*

most-ly (mōst'lĭ), *adv.* for the most part; usually.

mot (mō), *n.* [*pl.* mots (mōz)], a witty saying; a bon mot.

¹mote (mōt), *n.* formerly, an Anglo-Saxon assembly or assembly place.

²mote (mōt), *n.* a very small particle; a speck.

³mote (mōt), *v.aux. Archaic,* might; sometimes, may; as, so *mote* it be.

moth (môth), *n.* [*pl.* moths (môthz)], a four-winged insect somewhat like the butterfly, but flying chiefly at night; esp., one of a species which feeds upon cloth, fur, etc.

moth–eat-en (môth'=ēt"n), *adj.* damaged by moths; having holes made by moths, as cloth; hence, shabby.

¹moth-er (mŭth'ẽr), *n.* **1**, a female parent, esp. one of the human race; one who has given birth to offspring; **2**, origin or source; as, necessity is the *mother* of invention; **3**, the female superior of a religious house: **Mother's Day,** a day appointed for the honoring of motherhood: instituted by Miss Anna Jarvis, of Philadelphia, who appointed the second Sunday in May, or for schools the second Friday, as the day, and designated the carnation as the emblem:—*adj.* **1**, native; as, one's *mother* tongue; **2**, female; as, a *mother* cat:—*v.t.* to act as a mother to, or to adopt as a son or daughter.

²moth-er (mŭth'ẽr), *n.* a thick, slimy substance or film in liquids, as in vinegar when it is fermenting.

Moth-er Goose the pen name of the compiler of a collection of well-known, simple nursery rimes.

moth-er-hood (mŭth'ẽr-ho͝od), *n.* the state of being a mother.

moth-er–in–law (mŭth'ẽr=ĭn=lô"), *n.* [*pl.* mothers-in-law (-ẽrz=)], the mother of one's husband or wife.

moth-er-less (mŭth'ẽr-lĕs), *adj.* without a mother living.

moth-er-ly (mŭth'ẽr-lĭ), *adj.* tender and kind like a mother.

moth-er–of–pearl (mŭth"ẽr=ŏv=pûrl'), *n.* the hard, lustrous lining of any of various shells.

moth-er wit natural good sense or wit; innate intelligence.

moth-y (môth'ĭ), *adj.* [*comp.* moth'i-er, *superl.* moth'i-est], full of insects that feed on cloth or fur; moth-eaten.

***mo-tif** (mō"tēf'), [Fr.], *n.* **1**, the central and controlling idea of a work of art or literature; **2**, in music, a phrase or passage which is repeated many times with variations. Also, **mo'tive.**

mo-tion (mō'shŭn), *n.* **1**, the act, process, or state of changing place; action, as opposed to rest; **2**, a gesture; **3**, impulse or desire; as, they did it of their own *motion;* **4**, a formal proposal made in a meeting; as, a *motion* to adjourn:—*v.i.* to make a movement or gesture full of meaning; as, I *motioned* to him:—*v.t.* to guide or invite by a gesture; as, to *motion* someone forward.—*adj.* **mo'tion-less.**
Syn., n. proposition, proposal, movement.

mo-tion pic-ture a series of action pictures, taken by a special machine; when thrown rapidly on a screen, they form a continous reproduction of the action: also called *moving picture.*

mo-ti-vate (mō'tĭ-vāt), *v.t.* [*p.t.* and *p.p.* -vat"ed, *p.pr.* -vat"ing], to act as an impulse or incentive for; give a motive for.—*n.* **mo"ti-va'tion.**

mo-tive (mō'tĭv), *n.* **1**, that which urges to action; inducement; as, love of country is the *motive* that sends many men to war; **2**, (also, *motif*), in art, a leading idea; **3**, (also, *motif*), in music, a passage which is repeated many times with variations:—*adj.* causing action; as, the *motive* power in the locomotive: **motive power, 1**, a natural agent, as wind, water, steam, electricity, used to produce action in a machine; **2**, any compelling force.
Syn., n. reason, object. (See cause.)

mot-ley (mŏt'lĭ), *adj.* **1**, consisting of different colors; **2**, wearing particolored clothing; as, a *motley* fool; **3**, composed of different kinds; as, a *motley* crowd.

mo-tor (mō'tẽr), *n.* **1**, that which produces action or power; **2**, esp., a machine which changes other forms of energy into motion; as, an electric *motor*; **3**, an automobile:—*adj.* imparting action; as, *motor* nerves:—*v.i.* to travel by automobile.—*n.* **mo'tor-ist.**

ELECTRIC MOTOR

mo-tor-boat a boat moved by a gasoline engine or by any other small engine.

mo-tor-bus a motor-driven omnibus. Also, *n.* **mo'tor bus".**

mo-tor-cade (mō"tẽr-kād'), *n.* a procession composed of motor vehicles.

mo-tor car a vehicle with a small engine driven by means of gasoline, oil, electricity, or the like. Also, *n.* **mo'tor-car".**

mo-tor-cy-cle (mō'tẽr-sī"kl), *n.* a motor-driven, two-wheeled vehicle with one or two riding seats.—Also *adj.* and *v.i.*

mo-tor-drome (mō'tẽr-drōm"), *n.* a course for racing or testing automobiles or motor cycles.

mo-tor-ize (mō'tẽr-īz), *v.t.* [*p.t.* and *p.p.* -ized (-īzd), *p.pr.* -iz"ing], to replace (horse-drawn vehicles), or equip, with motor-driven vehicles.—*n.* **mo"tor-i-za'tion.**

mo-tor-man (mō'tẽr-măn), *n.* [*pl.* motormen (-mĕn)], one who drives a motor, esp. an electric car on a street railway.

mo-tor truck a heavy, motor-driven van for carrying bulky loads or freight. Also, *n.* **mo'tor–truck".**

mot-tle (mŏt'l), *v.t.* [*p.t.* and *p.p.*- tled (-ld), *p.pr.* -tling], to mark with spots of various colors.

mot-to (mŏt'ō), *n.* [*pl.* mottoes (-ōz)], a word, phrase, or brief sentence suggesting some guiding principle, used as an inscription, a slogan, or the like.
Syn. saying, adage, maxim.

mou-jik (mo͞o-zhĭk'; mo͞o'-), *n.* a Russian peasant. See **mu-zhik',** *Pfd. S.*

¹mould (mōld), *n.* **1**, a soft, rich soil; **2**, earthy material:—*v.t.* to cover with earth. See **¹mold,** *Pfd. S.*

²**mould** (mōld), *n.* **1**, a hollow form, as of sand or metal, used in casting; **2**, form; shape; **3**, that after which a thing is patterned; **4**, character; **5**, bodily form:—*v.t.* **1**, to fashion in a form, matrix, or the like; **2**, to cast or form according to a pattern. See ²**mold**, *Pfd. S.*—*adj.* **mould'a-ble.**

³**mould** (mōld), *n.* any of many fungi growing on damp or decaying matter:—*v.t.* to cover, or cause to spoil, with a musty growth:—*v.i.* to become spoiled. See ³**mold**, *Pfd. S.*

mould-er (mōl'dẽr), *v.t.* to cause to crumble away:—*v.i.* to crumble by natural decay; disintegrate. Also, **mold'er**, *Pfd. S.*

mould-ing (mōl'dĭng), *n.* **1**, the act of shaping; **2**, anything cast in a form; **3**, an ornamental strip or cornice. See **mold'ing**, *Pfd. S.*

mould-y (mōl'dĭ), *adj.* [*comp.* mould'i-er, *superl.* mould'i-est], covered with, or spoiled by, mould. Also, **mold'y**, *Pfd. S.*

moult (mōlt), *v.i.* to shed or cast off the hair, feathers, or outer layer of skin:—*v.t.* to shed and renew, as feathers:—*n.* the act or season of moulting. Also, **molt**, *Pfd. S.*

¹**mound** (mound), *n.* an artificial bank of earth or stone, esp. one formed over a grave as a monument; a rampart:—*v.t.* to furnish, or fortify, with a bank of earth, stones, etc.; heap up into a ridge or hillock.

²**mound** (mound), *n.* a small jeweled globe topped by a cross: used as an emblem of empire, as in the regalia of a king.

¹**mount** (mount), *n.* a hill or mountain; a rocky mass or elevation rising above the level of the surrounding land.

²**mount** (mount), *n.* **1**, the act or method of getting up, as on a wall or bicycle; **2**, that which acts as a support, as for a picture, gun, or the like; **3**, a horse:—*v.t.* **1**, to ascend, or get up on, as a mountain, a horse, or the like; **2**, to raise up; as, to *mount* the statue on a block; **3**, to prepare for use or exhibition, as a photograph, an insect, or the like; **4**, to furnish with horses; as, to *mount* the party; **5**, to furnish with necessary scenery, costumes, and the like, as a play; **6**, to be armed with; as, the battery *mounts* twelve guns:—*v.i.* **1**, to rise, tower, or increase; as, debts *mount* fast: often with *up;* **2**, to get up on something, as a horse, etc.
Syn., *v.* arise, soar, scale, elevate, climb.

moun-tain (moun'tĭn), *n.* **1**, a large mass of rock or earth rising high above the level of the surrounding country; **2**, anything very large.

moun-tain-eer (moun″tĭ-nēr'), *n.* one who dwells among, or climbs, mountains:—*v.i.* to climb mountains.

moun-tain li-on the cougar, or American panther.

moun-tain-ous (moun'tĭ-nŭs), *adj.* **1**, full of great elevations of land; **2**, large, like a mountain.

moun-te-bank (moun'tē-băngk), *n.* **1**, one who publicly sells remedies which he pretends will cure diseases; **2**, a boastful pretender.

mount-ed (moun'tĕd), *p.adj.* **1**, seated or serving on horseback; as, *mounted* police; **2**, raised on a suitable support; **3**, fixed on or in something.

mount-ing (mount'ĭng), *n.* **1**, the act of getting on a horse; **2**, the act of preparing for use or exhibition, as a photograph; **3**, the thing on or in which anything is set, as a jewel; **4**, the ornamentation on guns, harness, etc.; **5**, the assembling of parts, as of a machine.

mourn (mōrn), *v.i.* and *v.t.* to grieve or sorrow (for); bemoan; lament.

mourn-er (mōr'nẽr), *n.* one who grieves; also, one who attends a funeral.

mourn-ful (mōrn'fo͝ol), *adj.* causing, or expressing, sorrow; doleful; as, *mournful* news; a *mournful* face.—*adv.* **mourn'ful-ly.**—*n.* **mourn'ful-ness.**
Syn. sad, grievous.—*Ant.* happy, gay, glad.

mourn-ing (mōrn'ĭng), *n.* **1**, the expression of grief; lamentation; **2**, a special garb, such as black clothes, worn as a sign of grief for one who has died.

mouse (mous), *n.* [*pl.* mice (mīs)], a small animal with teeth formed for gnawing, that infests houses, granaries, etc.; —*v.i.* (mouz), [*p.t.* and *p.p.* moused (mouzd), *p.pr.* mous'ing], **1**, to watch for or catch mice, as a cat; **2**, to watch for something in a sly manner; pry curiously; as, he *moused* about the house:—*v.t.* to tear, as a cat tears a mouse.—*n.* **mous'er.**

mous-tache (mŭs-tȧsh'; mo͞os-tȧsh'), *n.* the hair growing on the upper lip. See **mus-tache'**, *Pfd. S.*

mouth (mouth), *n.* [*pl.* mouths (mouthz)], **1**, the opening in the head of an animal through which it receives food and utters sounds; **2**, an opening through which to go in or out; as, the *mouth* of a cave; **3**, an opening for putting anything in or out; as, the *mouth* of a bottle; **4**, a grimace; as, to make a *mouth:*—*v.t.* (mouth), **1**, to utter with a swelling or pompous voice; also, to mumble; **2**, to seize in the mouth; as, a dog *mouths* a bone:—*v.i.* **1**, to make faces; grimace; **2**, to declaim or rant.—*n.* **mouth'er.**

mouth-ful (mouth'fo͞ol), *n.* [*pl.* mouthfuls (-fo͞olz)], **1**, as much as can be, or is usually, put into the mouth at one time; **2**, a small quantity.

mouth or-gan a small musical instrument held horizontally against the lips and played by blowing directly into it; a harmonica.

mouth-piece (mouth'pēs″), *n.* **1**, something forming or used as a mouth; **2**, that part of an instrument which is held in, or applied to, the mouth; **3**, one who speaks for others; as, he was their *mouthpiece.*

mov-a-ble (mo͞ov'ȧ-bl), *adj.* **1**, capable of being changed or carried from one place or position to another; **2**, changing from one time to another; as, Easter is a *movable* feast: **movable feasts**, certain church festivals, the dates of which are determined by Easter:—*n.*, in *pl.*, goods, wares, or furniture that can be carried from place to place. Also, **move'a-ble.**—*n.* **mov'a-ble-ness.**—*adv.* **mov'a-bly.**—*n.* **mov″a-bil'i-ty.**

move (mo͞ov), *v.t.* [*p.t.* and *p.p.* moved (mo͞ovd), *p.pr.* mov'ing], **1**, to change from place to place; as, to *move* a table; **2**, to set in motion; as, the breeze *moves* the grass; **3**, to cause to act; impel; stir; as, his crimes *move* us to protest; **4**, to put before a meeting for a vote; as, I *move* we accept the invitation; **5**, to cause (the bowels) to operate:—*v.i.* **1**, to change place or position; figuratively, to advance; **2**, to change one's residence; **3**, to take action; as, to *move* in this affair; **4**, to engage in activities; as, to *move* in society; **5**, to make an application: with *for:*—*n.* **1**, the act of changing place or position; **2**, an act in the executing of a plan; **3**, a scheme; **4**, a change of residence.—*n.* **mov'er.**
Syn., *v.* induce, persuade, propel, actuate, instigate, incite, goad, influence, convey.

move-ment (mo͞ov'mĕnt), *n.* **1**, the act of changing place; **2**, any change of place or position; **3**, a series of acts and events which progress toward a desired end or aim; as, the temperance *movement;* **4**, the delicate mechanism of a watch or clock; **5**, any single part in a musical composition;

6, the rate of speed most suitable for interpreting a given musical composition; 7, the act of ejecting waste matter from the body through the bowels; also, the matter so ejected.

mov-ie (mo͞ov'ĭ), *n.*, often in *pl.*, *Colloq.*, a motion picture or a motion-picture theater; a cinema.

mov-ing (mo͞ov'ĭng), *p.adj.* 1, changing place or position; as, a *moving* shadow; 2, causing action; 3, stirring the feelings or affections; pathetic:—*n.* 1, movement; 2, the act of changing one's residence.
Syn., *adj.* impressive, exciting, touching.

mov-ing pic-ture a series of pictures of persons and things in action, taken by a special machine and thrown on a screen in such rapid succession as to form a continuous picture reproducing the action: preferably called *motion picture.*

¹mow (mō), *v.t.* [*p.t.* mowed (mōd), *p.p.* mowed or mown (mōn), *p.pr.* mow'ing], 1, to cut down with, or as with, a scythe or a machine; 2, to cut grass from:—*v.i.* to cut grass, etc., as with a scythe.—*n.* **mow'er.**

²mow (mou), *n.* 1, a heap of hay, etc., stowed in a barn; 2, the compartment in a barn where hay or grain is stowed:—*v.t.* to stow in a special place in a barn.

mpret (mprĕt), *n.* the title of the ruler of Albania.

Mr. (mĭs'tẽr), [*pl.* Messrs. (mĕs'rz)], the abbreviated form of the title *Mister.*

Mrs. (mĭs'ĭs; -ĭz), an abbreviated form of the title *Mistress.*

mu (mū), *n.* the 12th letter of the Greek alphabet [μ, M], approximately equivalent to English *m.*

much (mŭch), *adj.* [*comp.* more, *superl.* most], 1, great in quantity or amount; as, *much* wealth; 2, long in duration; as, *much* time:—*adv.* 1, to a great degree or extent; as, to be *much* obliged; 2, nearly; as, *much* of a size:—*n.* 1, a great quantity; 2, something considerable or unusual.

mu-ci-lage (mū'sĭ-lāj), *n.* 1, a gummy substance in certain plants; 2, a gummy fluid used to stick things together. —*adj.* **mu″ci-lag'i-nous** (mū″sĭ-lăj'ĭ-nŭs).

muck (mŭk), *n.* 1, moist manure; 2, a mixture of rich earth and decayed matter, used as a fertilizer; 3, anything filthy or vile:—*v.t.* 1, to manure; enrich, as soil; 2, to soil with filth.—*adj.* **muck'y.**

muck-rake (mŭk'rāk″), *v.i.* [*p.t.* and *p.p.* -raked″ (-rākt″), *p.pr.* -rak″ing], to seek for and expose wrongdoing on the part of public men.—*n.* **muck'rak″er.**

muck-worm (mŭk'wûrm″), *n.* 1, a grub bred in manure; 2, a miser.

mu-cous (mū'kŭs), *adj.* pertaining to, resembling, or producing, mucus: **mucous membrane**, the moist lining of the cavities and canals communicating with the exterior of the human body.

mu-cro-nate (mū'krō-nāt), *adj.* ending abruptly in a sharp point, as a leaf or feather (see *leaf*, illus.).

mu-cus (mū'kŭs), *n.* 1, the ropy, sticky fluid given off by the glands of the mucous membrane (which see); 2, in botany, a gummy substance found in certain plants.

mud (mŭd), *n.* soft, wet earth; mire:—*v.t.* [*p.t.* and *p.p.* mud'ded, *p.pr.* mud'ding], to soil with soft, wet earth.

mud-dle (mŭd'l), *n.* 1, a confused state; 2, mental dulness or confusion: —*v.t.* [*p.t.* and *p.p.* -dled (-ld), *p.pr.* -dling], 1, to make a mess of; as, to *muddle* his work; 2, to confuse or stupefy; make partially drunk: —*v.i.* to act in a confused or stupid way.

mud-dy (mŭd'ĭ), *adj.* [*comp.* mud'di-er, *superl.* mud'di-est], 1, full of, or covered with, soft, wet earth; as, a *muddy* stream; *muddy* roads; 2, clouded; confused; as, *muddy* ideas:—*v.t.* to make dirty; befoul. —*adv.* **mud'di-ly.**—*n.* **mud'di-ness.**

mud-sill (mŭd'sĭl″), *n.* the foundation timber of a building or other structure placed on the ground.

mu-ez-zin (mū-ĕz'ĭn), *n.* a Mohammedan public crier, who, from the tower of a mosque, calls the people to prayer.

¹muff (mŭf), *n.* a warm, soft cover, as of fur, usually tube-shaped, into which the hands may be thrust for warmth.

²muff (mŭf), *n.* 1, in baseball or cricket, failure to keep hold of a ball; 2, *Colloq.*, a spiritless person:—*v.t.* and *v.i.* to handle clumsily; fail to hold (a ball); fumble; bungle.

muf-fin (mŭf'ĭn), *n.* a soft light, unsweetened cake, usually served hot.

muf-fle (mŭf'l), *v.t.* [*p.t.* and *p.p.* -fled (-ld), *p.pr.* -fling], 1, to wrap up closely and warmly; as, to *muffle* the hands; 2, to keep from seeing, hearing, or speaking by wrapping up the head; 3, to cover up so as to deaden the sound of; as, to *muffle* a bell:—*v.i.* to speak indistinctly:—*n.* anything used as a wrap or covering to deaden sound.

muf-fler (mŭf'lẽr), *n.* 1, a scarf for the throat, or for wrapping around the head, throat, and ears; 2, any of various devices for deadening noise, as in an automobile exhaust (see *automobile*, illus.).

muf-ti (mŭf'tĭ), *n.* [*pl.* muftis (-tĭz)], civilian dress when worn by an officer of the army or navy.

mug (mŭg), *n.* 1, an earthenware or metallic drinking vessel with a handle; 2, the quantity that it will contain.

mug-gy (mŭg'ĭ), *adj.* [*comp.* mug'gi-er, *superl.* mug'gi-est], 1, warm, damp, and close; as, a *muggy* day; 2, moldy, as hay.—*n.* **mug'gi-ness.**

mug-wump (mŭg'wŭmp″), *n.* a voter who belongs to one party, but who claims the right to vote with another, if he prefers the candidate of the latter.

mu-lat-to (mū-lăt'ō), *n.* [*pl.* mulattoes (-ōz)], the offspring of a negro and a white person.

mul-ber-ry (mŭl'bẽr-ĭ), *n.* [*pl.* mulberries (-ĭz)], 1, any of a group of trees bearing a dark, sweet berry; 2, the fruit of such a tree; 3, a dark purple color.

mulch (mŭlch; mŭlsh), *n.* a layer of dried leaves, straw, sawdust, or the like, used to protect the roots of trees and plants: —*v.t.* to cover or protect with a mulch.

mulct (mŭlkt), *v.t.* to punish with a fine; hence, to take something from (a person) unjustly; defraud:—*n.* a fine.

mule (mūl), *n.* 1, the offspring of a male ass and a mare: distinguished from *hinny;* 2, a machine for spinning cotton; 3, *Colloq.*, a very stubborn person.

mu-le-teer (mū″lĕ-tēr'), *n.* a driver of a mule or mules.

mul-ish (mūl'ĭsh), *adj.* like a mule; obstinate; stubborn.—*adv.* **mul'ish-ly.** —*n.* **mul'ish-ness.**

¹mull (mŭl), *n.* a very thin, fine muslin, used for draperies and light dresses.

²mull (mŭl), *v.i.* *U. S. Colloq.*, to cogitate or ponder: usually with *over.*

mul-lah (mo͞ol'ȧ; mŭl'ȧ), *n.* among the Mohammedans, a title given to scholars and religious teachers.

mul-lein (mŭl'ĭn), *n.* a coarse plant having large leaves and flowers in close spikes. Also, **mul'len.**

mull-er (mŭl'ẽr), *n.* a pestle and a flat slab used for grinding paints or drugs.

mul-let (mŭl'ĕt), *n.* a fish found in both fresh and salt water, and much valued for food.

mul-lion (mŭl'yŭn), *n.* an upright bar or division between the panes of a window, screen, etc.:—*v.t.* to furnish with, or divide by, upright bars.

mul-ti- (mŭl'tĭ-), a prefix or combining form from the Latin, meaning many, much; as, *multi*form; *multi*graph.

mul-ti-fa-ri-ous (mŭl"tĭ-fā'rĭ-ŭs), *adj.* having much variety; manifold; diverse.—*adv.* **mul"ti-fa'ri-ous-ly.** —*n.* **mul"ti-fa'ri-ous-ness.**

mul-ti-form (mŭl'tĭ-fôrm), *adj.* having many different forms or shapes.—*n.* **mul"ti-for'mi-ty.**

mul-ti-graph (mŭl'tĭ-grȧf), *n.* a machine that both sets type and prints; a rotary typesetting and printing machine: a trade name.

mul-ti-ple (mŭl'tĭ-pl), *n.* a number or quantity which contains another an exact number of times; as, 12 is a *multiple* of 4:—*adj.* **1,** consisting of many parts; many; as, *multiple* injuries; **2,** repeated many times.

mul-ti-plex (mŭl'tĭ-plĕks), *adj.* **1,** made up of many parts; **2,** repeated many times; **3,** capable of bearing messages in opposite directions at the same time; as, a *multiplex* telegraph wire.

mul-ti-pli-cand (mŭl"tĭ-plĭ-kănd'; mŭl'-tĭ-plĭ-kănd"), *n.* the number or quantity to be multiplied by another.

mul-ti-pli-cate (mŭl'tĭ-plĭ-kāt), *adj.* consisting of many; manifold:—*adj.* **mul'ti-pli-ca-tive.**

mul-ti-pli-ca-tion (mŭl"tĭ-plĭ-kā'shŭn), *n.* **1,** the act or process of increasing in number or quantity; **2,** the rule or operation by which any given number or quantity (the multiplicand) is increased to a given number of times its value.

mul-ti-plic-i-ty (mŭl"tĭ-plĭs'ĭ-tĭ), *n.* [*pl.* multiplicities (-tĭz)], a great number; as, a *multiplicity* of duties.

mul-ti-pli-er (mŭl'tĭ-plī"ẽr), *n.* **1,** one who or that which increases; **2,** the number or quantity which shows how many times another is to be repeated or increased.

mul-ti-ply (mŭl'tĭ-plī), *v.t.* [*p.t.* and *p.p.* -plied (-plīd), *p.pr.* -ply"ing], **1,** to cause to increase in number or quantity; **2,** to make more by natural production, or addition; as, peace *multiplies* the population; **3,** to repeat (any given number or quantity) a given number of times:—*v.i.* to increase in number or extent; as, rabbits *multiply* very fast.

mul-ti-tude (mŭl'tĭ-tūd), *n.* **1,** a great number; crowd; **2,** people in general; as, the *multitude* came to hear him.
Syn. throng, host, mob, swarm.

mul-ti-tu-di-nous (mŭl"tĭ-tū'dĭ-nŭs), *adj.* consisting of a great number; very numerous.—*adv.* **mul"ti-tu'di-nous-ly.**—*n.* **mul"ti-tu'di-nous-ness.**

mum (mŭm), *adj.* silent:—*interj.* be silent! —*v.i.* [*p.t.* and *p.p.* mummed (mŭmd), *p.pr.* mum'ming], to wear a fantastic costume for sport, as at Christmas. Also, *v.i.* **mumm.**

mum-ble (mŭm'bl), *v.t.* and *v.i.* [*p.t.* and *p.p.* -bled (-bld), *p.pr.* -bling], **1,** to mutter or speak indistinctly; **2,** to chew gently with closed lips:—*n.* a mutter.

Mum-bo Jum-bo (mŭm'bō jŭm'bō), a West African idol, or object of superstitious worship or dread: **mumbo jumbo,** any vulgar superstition.

mumm (mŭm), *v.i.* to disguise oneself for sport. See **mum,** *Pfd. S.*

mum-mer (mŭm'ẽr), *n.* one who makes sport in disguise; a masker.

mum-mer-y (mŭm'ẽr-ĭ), *n.* [*pl.* mummeries (-ĭz)], **1,** masquerading; a frolic in disguise; **2,** ceremonies or performances regarded as ridiculous or insincere.

mum-mi-fy (mŭm'ĭ-fī), *v.t.* [*p.t.* and *p.p.* -fied (-fīd), *p.pr.* -fy"ing], to preserve (a corpse) by a drying process.

mum-my (mŭm'ĭ), *n.* [*pl.* mummies (-ĭz)], **1,** a dead body embalmed by a drying process, after the manner of the ancient Egyptians; **2,** a rich brown color.

[1]**mump** (mŭmp), *v.i.* **1,** to move the lips with the mouth nearly closed; **2,** to mutter; mumble; **3,** to be sulky; sulk: —*v.t.* **1,** to work, as food, with the mouth; **2,** to utter indistinctly.

[2]**mump** (mŭmp), *v.i.* to play the beggar: —*v.t.* to cheat; impose upon.

mumps (mŭmps), *n.pl.* used as *sing.* **1,** a contagious disease marked by inflammation and painful swelling of the salivary glands, esp. of the parotid, below and in front of the ear; **2,** the sulks.

munch (mŭnch), *v.t.* to chew with a crunching noise, as does a horse: —*v.i.* to grind with the teeth.—*n.* **munch'er.**

mun-dane (mŭn'dān), *adj.* pertaining to the world; as, this *mundane* sphere; worldly; as, *mundane* pleasures.

mu-nic-i-pal (mū-nĭs'ĭ-păl), *adj.* pertaining to a city or town, or to its local self-government.—*adv.* **mu-nic'i-pal-ly.**

mu-nic-i-pal-i-ty (mū-nĭs"ĭ-păl'ĭ-tĭ), *n.* [*pl.* municipalities (-tĭz)], a town, city, or borough having powers of local self-government.

mu-nif-i-cence (mū-nĭf'ĭ-sĕns), *n.* the quality or state of being bountiful; liberality.

mu-nif-i-cent (mū-nĭf'ĭ-sĕnt), *adj.* marked by great liberality in giving; bountiful; as, a *munificent* gift.—*adv.* **mu-nif'i-cent-ly.**
Syn. large, vast, princely, lavish.

mu-ni-ment (mū'nĭ-mĕnt), *n.* **1,** that which supports or defends; **2,** in *pl.*, title deeds, records, or other papers by which the title to property may be defended.

mu-ni-tion (mū-nĭsh'ŭn), *n.*, usually in *pl.*, ammunition and military stores or material.

mu-ral (mū'răl), *adj.* pertaining to, resembling, or on the surface of, a wall; as, *mural* paintings:—*n.* a wall painting.

mur-der (mûr'dẽr), *n.* the offense of unlawfully killing a human being with definite purpose formed beforehand:—*v.t.* **1,** to kill with deliberate malice; **2,** to destroy; **3,** to spoil.
Syn.,v. assassinate, slay, massacre. (See kill.)

mur-der-er (mûr'dẽr-ẽr), *n.* one who is guilty of killing another unlawfully.—*n.fem.* **mur'der-ess.**

mur-der-ous (mûr'dẽr-ŭs), *adj.* **1,** pertaining to, guilty of, or causing, the unlawful killing of another; **2,** brutal; bloodthirsty.—*adv.* **mur'der-ous-ly.** —*n.* **mur'der-ous-ness.**

mu-ri-at-ic (mū"rĭ-ăt'ĭk), *adj.* hydrochloric: the popular term: **muriatic acid,** a solution in water of hydrochloric acid, a yellowish, gaseous, corrosive compound of equal parts, atom for atom, of hydrogen and chlorine: the commercial term.

murk (mûrk), *n.* darkness; gloom; obscurity:—*adj.* dark.

murk-y (mûr'kĭ), *adj.* [*comp.* murk'i-er, *superl.* murk'i-est], dark; gloomy; obscure.—*adv.* **murk'i-ly.**—*n.* **murk'i-ness.**

mur-mur (mûr'mûr), *n.* **1,** a low, indistinct sound, as of a running stream; **2,** a complaint in a low, muttering tone; grumble:—*v.i.* **1,** to make a low, continued noise like the hum of bees; speak in a low voice; **2,** to mutter in discontent; grumble:—*v.t.* to utter complainingly or in a low voice; grumble.—*n.* **mur'mur-er.**

Syn., v. growl, mutter, whine.

mur-rain (mŭr'ĭn), *n.* an infectious and fatal disease among cattle.

mus-cat (mŭs'kăt), *n.* **1**, any of several kinds of musk-flavored European grapes; **2**, the wine made from them.

mus-ca-tel (mŭs"kȧ-tĕl'; mŭs'kȧ-tĕl), *n.* **1**, a variety of rich wine: also called *muscadine;* **2**, the muscat grape; **3**, a sweet, fragrant pear. Also, **mus"ca-del'.**

mus-cle (mŭs'l), *n.* **1**, an organ of fiberlike tissue which is capable of being contracted and expanded, thus producing movement in an animal body; **2**, *Colloq.*, bodily strength or power.

Mus-co-vite (mŭs'kō-vīt), *n.* a Russian: —*adj.* Russian: from *Muscovy*, the ancient name of Russia.

mus-cu-lar (mŭs'kū-lȧr), *adj.* **1**, pertaining to, consisting of, or performed by, muscles; **2**, strong; vigorous.—*n.* **mus"cu-lar'i-ty.**—*n.* **mus'cu-la-ture.**

muse (mūz), *v.i.* [*p.t.* and *p.p.* mused (mūzd), *p.pr.* mus'ing], **1**, to meditate in silence; think deeply; **2**, to be absent-minded:—*v.t. Rare*, to think deeply about:—*n.* deep thought; meditation.

Syn., v. consider, reflect, ponder, meditate.

Muse (mūz), *n.* in mythology, any of the nine goddesses who presided over the arts and sciences: Calliope (the chief, Muse of poetic inspiration, eloquence, and epic poetry), Clio (history), Erato (erotic poetry), Euterpe (music and lyric poetry), Melpomene (tragedy), Polyhymnia (the stately hymn), Terpsichore (choral dancing), Thalia (comedy), Urania (astronomy): **muse**, the inspiring force of poetry; poetic inspiration; as, to invoke the *muse.*

mu-se-um (mū-zē'ŭm), *n.* **1**, a collection of natural, scientific, or literary curiosities, or of works of art; **2**, the building containing such a collection.

mush (mŭsh), *n.* **1**, a kind of porridge of boiled Indian corn meal; **2**, any mixture, soft and thick, like it.

mush-room (mŭsh'rōōm), *n.* **1**, an edible fungus, or plant without leaves or flowers, often flat, spherical, or shaped somewhat like an umbrella, and growing very quickly in a moist, dark place; also, any of various forms of fungi, some of which are poisonous; **2**, anything like this fungus in quickness of growth; an upstart: —*adj.* **1**, made from mushrooms; **2**, like mushrooms in quickness of growth, upstart.

Mushrooms

mush-y (mŭsh'ĭ), *adj.* [*comp.* mush'i-er, *superl.* mush'i-est], **1**, mushlike; soft and yielding; **2**, weakly sentimental.

mu-sic (mū'zĭk), *n.* **1**, the art or science of making pleasing or harmonious combinations of sound tones; **2**, harmony or melody; **3**, a musical composition; also, such a composition written or printed.

mu-si-cal (mū'zĭ-kăl), *adj.* **1**, pertaining to, producing, or full of, harmony or melody; melodious; **2**, having a talent or fondness for music: **musical comedy**, a light, amusing play with songs, choruses, dancing, etc.—*adv.* **mu'si-cal-ly.**

Syn. tuneful, dulcet, sweet, harmonious.

mu-si-cale (mū"zĭ-kăl'), *n.* a private musical entertainment.

mu-si-cal in-stru-ment any of a large variety of devices for producing musical sounds, as the piano, violin, bugle, drum, and the like.

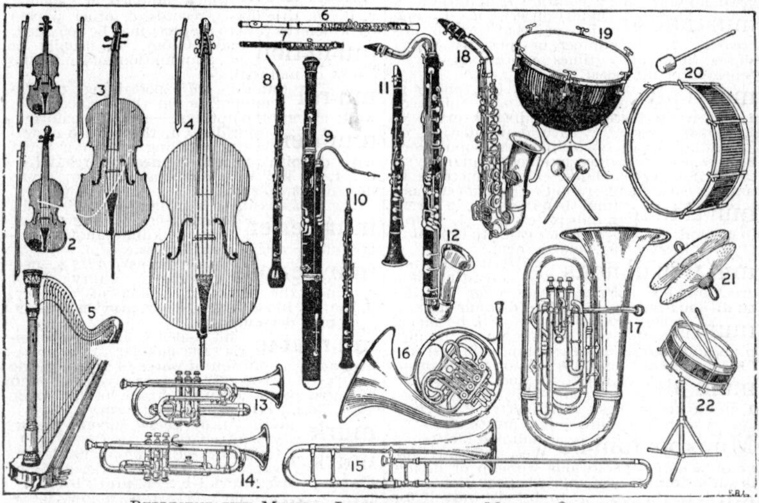

Representative Musical Instruments of a Modern Orchestra

1–4, stringed instruments played with a bow (1, violin; 2, viola; 3, violoncello; 4, contrabass); 5, harp; 6–12, wood-wind instruments (6, flute; 7, piccolo; 8, English horn; 9, bassoon; 10, oboe; 11, clarinet; 12, bass clarinet); 13–17, brass-wind instruments (13, cornet, 14, trumpet; 15, trombone; 16, French horn; 17, bass tuba); 18, saxophone; 19–22, percussion instruments (19, kettledrum; 20, bass drum; 21, cymbals; 22, snare drum).

mu-si-cian (mū-zĭsh′ăn), *n.* one skilled in the science of music, as composer, critic, or conductor; also, one who sings or who plays on a musical instrument, esp. as a profession.

mus-ing (mūz′ĭng), *n.* deep thought:—*p.adj.* engaged in deep thought; dreamy; meditative.—*adv.* **mus′ing-ly.**

musk (mŭsk), *n.* **1**, a strong-scented substance obtained from the male musk deer, or an imitation of it: used in many perfumes; **2**, the odor of this substance or something resembling it.—*adj.* **musk′y.**

musk deer a small, hornless deer of Central Asia, which yields a substance called *musk.*

1/15
MUSK DEER

mus-kel-lunge (mŭs′kĕ-lŭnj; mŭs″kĕ-lŭnj′), *n.* a large pike of the Great Lakes, sometimes weighing 60 to 80 pounds and much valued as food. Also, **mus′kal-longe.**

mus-ket (mŭs′kĕt), *n.* a small gun formerly carried by foot soldiers.

mus-ket-eer (mŭs″kĕt-ēr′), *n.* a foot soldier armed with a musket, or small gun.

mus-ket-ry (mŭs′kĕt-rĭ), *n.* **1**, the fire of small arms, or the art of firing such arms; **2**, muskets collectively; **3**, troops bearing muskets.

musk-mel-on (mŭsk′mĕl″ŭn), *n.* the gourdlike, juicy fruit of a trailing vine; also, the plant.

musk ox an Arctic, hoofed animal with curving horns: so called because musk is obtained from one of its glands.

musk-rat (mŭsk′răt″), *n.* a valuable fur-bearing animal of North America, having teeth formed for gnawing, and living in the water, through which it swims by means of its flat, scaly tail and webbed hind feet: so called because of its musky odor.

mus-lin (mŭz′lĭn), *n.* a cotton cloth, either fine and thin or stout and heavy in quality:—*adj.* made of such cotton cloth.

muss (mŭs), *n. U. S. Colloq.*, **1**, confusion; disorder; **2**, a squabble:—*v.t. Colloq.*, to disorder, as clothing; wrinkle; also, to soil.

mus-sel (mŭs′l), *n.* an edible shellfish of both fresh and salt water.

Mus-sul-man (mŭs′ŭl-măn), *n.* [*pl.* Mussulmans (-mănz)], a Mohammedan, or believer in Mohammedanism, which teaches that Mohammed was the greatest prophet of God: also called *Moslem.*

muss-y (mŭs′ĭ), *adj.* [*comp.* muss′i-er, *superl.* muss′i-est], *Colloq.*, disordered; disarranged; soiled.

[1]**must** (mŭst), *n.* grape juice, pressed from the grapes but not fermented.

[2]**must** (mŭst), *v.t.* and *v.i.* to make, or become, moldy and sour:—*n.* moldiness; mold.

[3]**must** (mŭst), *v. aux.* [used without inflection], **1**, to be obliged or compelled; as, he *must* go; **2**, to be logically necessary; as, this *must* be what he means.

Syn. (see ought).

mus-tache (mŭs-tȧsh′), *n.* hair growing on a man's upper lip; also, similar hair or bristles growing near the mouth of an animal. Also, **mous-tache′; mus-ta′chio.**

mus-tang (mŭs′tăng), *n.* the small, hardy, half-wild horse of the prairies and pampas of America.

mus-tard (mŭs′tȧrd), *n.* a plant, from the tiny seeds of which a seasoning is made; also, the powdered seasoning made from the seed: **mustard gas,** a poisonous, highly irritating substance used in shells in chemical warfare, as in the World War, and producing severe burns and inflammation.

mus-ter (mŭs′tẽr), *n.* **1**, an assembly of troops for review or active service; **2**, a list of troops assembled; **3**, an assemblage; collection:—*v.t.* **1**, to assemble, esp. troops for review or active service; **2**, to collect and show; as, to *muster* one's courage: **muster in,** to enlist, as troops or recruits: **muster out,** to assemble (troops that have been in service) for final payment and discharge:—*v.i.* to meet in one place.

mus-ty (mŭs′tĭ), *adj.* [*comp.* mus′ti-er, *superl.* mus′ti-est], **1**, spoiled with damp; moldy; **2**, spoiled by age; stale or sour.—*adv.* **mus′ti-ly.**—*n.* **mus′ti-ness.**

mu-ta-ble (mū′tȧ-bl), *adj.* **1**, easily and frequently changed; **2**, fickle; unstable.—*adv.* **mu′ta-bly.**—*n.* **mu″ta-bil′i-ty.**

Syn. changeable, undependable, unsteady.

mu-ta-tion (mū-tā′shŭn), *n.* alteration; change; variation.

mute (mūt), *adj.* **1**, silent; speechless; **2**, incapable of speech; dumb; **3**, not pronounced or sounded, as the *e* in *mute:* also, pronounced with complete closure of the voice passage, as *p, b, t, d, k, g:*—*n.* **1**, one who cannot speak or who remains silent; **2**, a mute letter or sound; **3**, a contrivance to deaden or soften the sound of a musical instrument.—*adv.* **mute′ly.**—*n.* **mute′ness.**

mu-ti-late (mū′tĭ-lāt), *v.t.* [*p.t.* and *p.p.* -lat″ed, *p.pr.* -lat″ing], **1**, to cut off a limb or necessary part of; maim; **2**, to render incomplete or imperfect, as a document.—*n.* **mu″ti-la′tion.**—*n.* **mu′ti-la″tor.**

Syn. cripple, disfigure.

mu-ti-neer (mū″tĭ-nēr′), *n.* one who is guilty of rebellion against authority:—*v.i.* to rebel against authority.

mu-ti-nous (mū′tĭ-nŭs), *adj.* disposed to, or guilty of, active rebellion against authority; disobedient.—*adv.* **mu′ti-nous-ly.**—*n.* **mu′ti-nous-ness.**

Syn. insurgent, tumultuous, turbulent, riotous.—*Ant.* obedient, submissive.

mu-ti-ny (mū′tĭ-nĭ), *n.* [*pl.* mutinies(-nĭz)], rebellion against authority, esp. of soldiers or sailors against their officers:—*v.i.* [*p.t.* and *p.p.* -nied (-nĭd), *p.pr.* -ny-ing], to rise against established authority; rebel.

Syn., n. riot, revolt. (See revolution.)

mut-ter (mŭt′ẽr), *n.* indistinct utterance; a murmur; a grumble:—*v.i.* **1**, to utter words in a low voice with lips almost closed; murmur; **2**, to sound with low, rumbling noises, as thunder:—*v.t.* to utter low and indistinctly.—*n.* **mut′ter-er.**—*n.* **mut′ter-ing.**

mut-ton (mŭt′n), *n.* the flesh of sheep, used as food.

mu-tu-al (mū′tū-ăl), *adj.* **1**, interchanged; given and received; as, *mutual* esteem; **2**, joint; common; as, *mutual* interests.—*adv.* **mu′tu-al-ly.**

Syn. common. That is *mutual* which is felt by each toward the other; as, *mutual* love; or that which is done by each toward the other; as, *mutual* aid; or, sometimes, that which is experienced in common; as, *mutual* misery. The use of *mutual* in the expression, "our *mutual* friend," is sometimes frowned upon, though approved by many good writers. That is *common* which belongs to, or is done by, or shared alike with, more than one; as, *common* consent; *common* property.

mu-tu-al-i-ty (mū″tū-ăl′ĭ-tĭ), *n.* [*pl.* mutualities (-tĭz)], interchange; interdependence; reciprocity.

mu-zhik (mōō-zhĭk′; mōō′zhĭk), *n.* **1**, a Russian peasant; **2**, a woman's loose fur cape. Also, **mu-jik′; mou-jik′.**

muz-zle (mŭz′l), *n.* **1**, the projecting mouth, lips, and nose of an animal; snout; **2**, the mouth of a gun; **3**, a fastening or cover for the mouth of a dog or horse to prevent biting:—*v.t.* [*p.t.* and *p.p.* -zled (-ld), *p.pr.* -zling], **1**, to secure the mouth of with a fastening or cover; **2**, figuratively, to prevent from talking; silence; as, to *muzzle* the press.

my (mī), *poss. adj.* of or belonging to me; as, it is *my* turn.

my-col-o-gy (mī-kŏl′ō-jĭ), *n.* the science or study of fungi.—*adj.* **my″co-log′ic.**—*n.* **my-col′o-gist.**

Myn-heer (mīn-hār′; mĭn-hēr′), *n.* a Dutch title of courtesy, equivalent to *Sir* or *Mr.*

my-o-pi-a (mī-ō′pĭ-ȧ), *n.* nearsightedness. Also, **my′o-py.**—*adj.* **my-op′ic.**

myr-i-ad (mĭr′ĭ-ăd), *n.* ten thousand; hence, a very large number; as, the sky at night is covered with *myriads* of stars:—*adj.* innumerable.

myr-i-a-pod (mĭr′ĭ-ȧ-pŏd″), *n.* any of a subclass (*Myriapoda*) of the arthropods, or group including the centipedes, spiders, insects, crabs, etc., distinguished by a body made up of similar segments ranging from ten to two hundred or more, each segment, except the first and last, bearing jointed legs.—*adj.* and *n.* **myr″i-ap′o-dan.**

myr-mi-don (mûr′mĭ-dŏn), *n.* a brutal or unprincipled subordinate officer who carries out all the orders of a superior without protest or pity: so called from the Myrmidons, warriors who unquestioningly followed Achilles in the Trojan War and carried out his orders.

myrrh (mûr), *n.* a yellowish brown, gummy substance with a spicy fragrance and a bitter taste, obtained from a shrub growing in Arabia and Abyssinia: used in medicine and perfumery; also, the shrub.

myr-tle (mûr′tl), *n.* **1**, a fragrant evergreen shrub; **2**, the periwinkle.

my-self (mī-sĕlf′), *pron.* [*pl.* ourselves (our-sĕlvz′)], I or me in person: an emphatic form; as, I *myself* am here.

mys-te-ri-ous (mĭs-tē′rĭ-ŭs), *adj.* not clear to the understanding; obscure; unexplained; as, he had a *mysterious* look.—*adv.* **mys-te′ri-ous-ly.**—*n.* **mys-te′ri-ous-ness.**

Syn. dark, hidden, secret, dim.

mys-ter-y (mĭs′tẽr-ĭ), *n.* [*pl.* mysteries (-ĭz)], **1**, something secret, hidden, or unexplained; **2**, that which is beyond human understanding; **3**, in *pl.*, among the ancients, sacred rites and ceremonies to which only certain persons were admitted: **mystery play**, a Biblical drama, or miracle play, of the Middle Ages.

mys-tic (mĭs′tĭk), *n.* a believer in direct communion with God:—*adj.* **1**, beyond human understanding; **2**, involving some secret meaning; **3**, hidden. Also, *adj.* **mys′ti-cal.**—*adv.* **mys′ti-cal-ly.**—*n.* **mys′ti-cal-ness.**

mys-ti-cism (mĭs′tĭ-sĭzm), *n.* **1**, the quality of being beyond human understanding; as, *mysticism* is independent of reason; **2**, the doctrine that man may have a more direct communion with God through meditation than is gained by mere understanding and thought.

mys-ti-fi-ca-tion (mĭs″tĭ-fĭ-kā′shŭn), *n.* **1**, the act of perplexing or puzzling; a trick; **2**, the state of being perplexed or puzzled.

mys-ti-fy (mĭs′tĭ-fī), *v.t.* [*p.t.* and *p.p.* -fied (-fīd), *p.pr.* -fy″ing], **1**, to involve in secrecy; obscure; as, he *mystifies* the facts; **2**, to bewilder; puzzle; as, his acts *mystify* me.

Syn. baffle, confuse. (See perplex.)

myth (mĭth), *n.* **1**, a legend; a traditional story, often founded on some fact of nature, or on an event in the early existence of a people, and embodying some religious belief, idea of the world, of nature, or of the gods, etc., of that people; **2**, an imaginary person, thing, or event.

myth-i-cal (mĭth′ĭ-kăl), *adj.* **1**, pertaining to, or described in, a myth; as, Cadmus is a *mythical* person; **2**, imaginary; fictitious; false; as, those are *mythical* reasons. Also, **myth′ic.**—*adv.* **myth′i-cal-ly.**

myth-o-log-i-cal (mĭth″ō-lŏj′ĭ-kăl), *adj.* pertaining to the tales and legends in which are embodied the beliefs of a people as to their origin, gods, etc.—*adv.* **myth″o-log′i-cal-ly.**

my-thol-o-gy (mĭ-thŏl′ō-jĭ), *n.* [*pl.* mythologies (-jĭz)], **1**, the collected body of the legends of a people, in which are recorded their beliefs concerning their origin, gods, heroes, etc.; **2**, the science of such legends; **3**, a book about them.—*abbr.* **myth.**—*n.* **my-thol′o-gist.**

N

nab (năb), *v.t.* [*p.t.* and *p.p.* nabbed (năbd), *p.pr.* nab′bing], *Colloq.*, to catch or seize unexpectedly.

na-bob (nā′bŏb), *n.* **1**, a native governor of a province in India under the Mogul empire; **2**, any very rich man.

na-celle (nȧ-sĕl′), *n.* a basket, cabin, or other inclosure for carrying passengers or motors on an aircraft.

na-cre (nā′kẽr), *n.* mother-of-pearl.—*adj.* **na′cre-ous.**

na-dir (nā′dẽr), *n.* **1**, that part of the heavens directly beneath the place where one stands, and opposite to the zenith; **2**, the lowest point.

¹nag (năg), *n.* a small horse; hence, any horse, esp. when worn out.

²nag (năg), *v.t.* [*p.t.* and *p.p.* nagged (năgd), *p.pr.* nag′ging], **1**, to find fault with continually; **2**, to urge:—*v.i.* to scold or urge constantly.—*p.adj.* **nag′ging.**—*adj.* **nag′gy.**

Na-hum (nā′hŭm), *n.* **1**, in the Bible, a Hebrew prophet; **2**, a book of the Old Testament containing his prophecies.

na-iad (nā′yăd; nī′ăd), *n.* [*pl.* naiads; naiades (nā′yȧ-dēz; nī′ȧ-)], in mythology, one of the water nymphs, supposed to live in fountains, rivers, lakes, etc.

nail (nāl), *n.* **1**, the horny substance at the ends of the fingers and toes; also, the claw of a bird or other animal; **2**, a measure two and one fourth inches long; **3**, a pointed piece of metal, furnished with a head, and used for driving into woodwork:—*v.t.* **1**, to fasten with such a piece of metal; **2**, to secure or make certain; clinch, as an argument; **3**, to expose; as, to *nail* a lie.

nain-sook (nān′sōōk; năn′-), *n.* a fine, soft muslin, plain or striped.

na-ïve (nä-ēv′), *adj.* artless; frank; simple; as, *naïve* manners; a *naïve* person. Also, **na-ïf′** (nä-ēf′).—*adv.* **na-ïve′ly.**

***na-ïve-té** (nȧ″ēv″tā′), [Fr.], *n.* natural, unaffected frankness or simplicity in speech or action.

na-ked (nā′kĕd), *adj.* **1**, unclothed; bare; **2**, unarmed; defenseless; **3**, exposed to view; clear; obvious; **4**, plain; without addition or ornament; as, the *naked* truth; **5**, without means; destitute; **6**, without glasses; as, to see with the *naked* eye.—*adv.* **na′ked-ly.**—*n.* **na′ked-ness.**

nam-by–pam-by (năm′bĭ-păm″bĭ), *n.* that which is weakly sentimental, or affectedly pretty or nice:—*adj.* weakly sentimental in writing or talk; affectedly nice or pretty.

name (nām), *n.* **1**, the term or title by which a person or thing is called or known; **2**, designation; **3**, character; reputation; fame; **4**, something having no real existence; as, truth has become a *name*:—*v.t.* [*p.t.* and *p.p.* named (nāmd), *p.pr.* nam′ing], **1**, to give a special term or title to; **2**, to appoint for a special purpose; specify; as, to *name* the day; **3**, to mention by a special term or title.—*adj.* **name′less.**—*adj.* **nam′a-ble; name′a-ble.**

Syn., *n.* appellation, epithet, denomination.

name-ly (nām′lĭ), *adv.* that is to say; to wit; to state more particularly

name-sake (nām′sāk″), *n.* **1**, one having the same name as another; **2**, one called after another

nan-keen (năn-kēn′), *n.* a brownish yellow cotton cloth, formerly brought from China. Also, **nan-kin′.**

Na-o-mi (nā′ō-mĭ; nā-ō′mĭ; -mī), *n.* in the Bible, Ruth's mother-in-law (Ruth 1–4).

¹nap (năp), *v.i.* [*p.t.* and *p.p.* napped (năpt), *p.pr.* nap′ping], to take a short slumber; doze; hence, to be off one's guard:—*n.* a short slumber; doze.

²nap (năp), *n.* **1**, the short, projecting hairs or fibers forming the surface of some materials, such as broadcloth; the pile, as of velvet; **2**, the downy covering of some plants.—*adj.* **nap′py.**

nape (nāp), *n.* in man or animals, the back of the neck.

na-per-y (nā′pēr-ĭ), *n.* household linen, esp. linen used for the table.

naph-tha (năf′thȧ), *n.* any of several clear, volatile, oily liquids obtained from petroleum, coal tar, etc., esp. one classed between gasoline and benzine.

na-pi-form (nā′pĭ-fôrm), *adj.* turnip-shaped; large above and tapering below: said of roots (see *root*, illus.).

nap-kin (năp′kĭn), *n.* a small cloth, usually of linen, used at table for wiping the fingers or lips.

na-po-le-on (nȧ-pō′lē-ŏn), *n.* **1**, a gold coin formerly used in France; **2**, a certain card game; six-handed euchre.

Na-po-le-on-ic (nȧ-pō″lē-ŏn′ĭk), *adj.* pertaining to, or resembling, Napoleon Bonaparte (1769–1821).

Nar-cis-sus (när-sĭs′ŭs), *n.* in mythology, a youth who was doomed to pine away for love of his own image, until finally changed into a flower: **narcissus,** [*pl.* narcissuses (-ĕz); narcissi (-ī)], any of a genus of plants including the jonquil and daffodil, growing from bulbs, and bearing handsome flowers.

nar-cot-ic (när-kŏt′ĭk), *n.* a medicine which relieves pain and produces sleep, or, in large doses, stupor or insensibility:—*adj.* producing stupor or sleep.

nard (närd), *n.* an aromatic herb, spikenard, or a fragrant ointment made from it.

na-res (nā′rēz), *n.pl.* [*sing.* naris (-rĭs)], the nostrils: the nasal openings.

nar-rate (nă-rāt′), *v.t.* [*p.t.* and *p.p.* -rat′ed, *p.pr.* -rat′ing], to tell; recite; give an account of; relate, as a story.—*n.* **nar-ra′tor.**

Syn. recount, report, describe, rehearse.

nar-ra-tion (nă-rā′shŭn), *n.* **1**, the act of telling of events in the order of their happening; **2**, an account or story.

nar-ra-tive (năr′ȧ-tĭv), *n.* **1**, the art of story-telling; **2**, the recital of a story or event; **3**, a story or tale:—*adj.* pertaining to, or of the nature of, story-telling.

Syn., *n.* account, narration, relation.

nar-row (năr′ō), *adj.* **1**, of little breadth or width; as, a *narrow* lane; a *narrow* space; **2**, limited; straitened; as, *narrow* circumstances; **3**, lacking breadth or broadness of view; as, a *narrow* mind; *narrow* opinions; **4**, close; near; as, a *narrow* escape; a *narrow* majority:—*v.t.* **1**, to lessen the breadth or extent of; confine or contract; **2**, to make less liberal; restrict:—*v.i.* to become less broad:—*n.*, usually in *pl.*, a strait, or narrow passage between two bodies of water.—*n.* **nar′row-ness.**

nar-row-ly (năr′ō-lĭ), *adv.* **1**, by a slight margin; barely; **2**, with close scrutiny; carefully; **3**, intolerantly.

nar-row–mind-ed (năr′ō-mīnd″ĕd), *adj.* without breadth of view or opinion; intolerant; prejudiced; bigoted.

nar-whal (när′hwȧl), *n.* a sea mammal related to the whale, with a large, twisted tusk: valued in commerce for its oil and ivory. Also, **nar′wal; nar′whale.**

NARWHAL ($\frac{1}{150}$)

na-sal (nā′zăl), *adj.* pertaining to, affected by, or pronounced through, the nose:—*n.* a sound pronounced through the nose, as *m*, *n*, *ng*.—*n.* **na-sal′i-ty.**—*adv.* **na′sal-ly.**

nas-cent (năs′ĕnt), *adj.* **1**, beginning to exist or grow; **2**, in chemistry, just set free: applied to an element at the instant of its liberation from a compound.

nas-tur-tium (năs-tûr′shŭm; năs-tûr′-shĭ-ŭm), *n.* any of a genus of plants of the mustard family, having red and yellow flowers.

nas-ty (nȧs′tĭ), *adj.* [*comp.* nas′ti-er, *superl.* nas′ti-est], **1**, dirty; filthy; **2**, disgusting to taste or smell; as, *nasty* medicine; **3**, obscene; indecent; **4**, troublesome; as, a *nasty* cut; **5**, *Colloq.*: **a**, ill-natured; mean; **b**, unpleasant; as, a *nasty* day.—*adv.* **nas′ti-ly.**—*n.* **nas′ti-ness.**

Syn. unclean, indecent, impure.

na-tal (nā′tăl), *adj.* **1**, pertaining to one's birth or birthday; **2**, native.

na-ta-to-ri-al (nā″tȧ-tō′rĭ-ăl), *adj.* pertaining to, or adapted for, swimming; as, *natatorial* skill.—*adj.* **na′ta-to-ry.**—*n.* **na″ta-to′ri-um.**

na-tion (nā′shŭn), *n.* **1**, the people of one country united under the same government; **2**, a race of people having the same religion, language, history, etc.

Syn. people, tribe. *Nation* denotes a race united under the same government, and having the same religion, language, and history; as, the French *nation*. *People* is used of any group of individuals regarded as a unit; as, the American *people;* it often suggests the idea of the ruled in contrast to the rulers; as, unjust taxes infuriate the *people*. *Tribe* contains the idea of a common descent, and is chiefly used of primitive *peoples;* as, the twelve *tribes* of Israel.

na-tion-al (năsh'ŭn-ăl), *adj.* **1,** pertaining to a united people as a whole: opp. of *local;* **2,** peculiar to, or characteristic of, a particular nation; as, a *national* trait; **3,** public; as, the *national* debt: **national bank,** in the U. S., a corporation with a national charter, empowered to issue bank notes, affiliated with the Federal Reserve System and subject to the Federal Reserve Board: **National Guard,** the organized militia of the several States of the United States: summoned in emergencies.—*adv.* **na'tion-al-ly.**

na-tion-al-ism (năsh'ŭn-ăl-ĭzm), *n.* **1,** patriotic feeling, efforts, or principles; devotion to the interests or glory of one's own country; **2,** demand for national independence; **3,** an idiom, trait, or custom peculiar to any nation.—*n.* **na'-tion-al-ist.**—*adj.* **na"tion-al-is'tic.**

na-tion-al-i-ty (năsh"ŭn-ăl'ĭ-tĭ), *n.* [*pl.* nationalities (-tĭz)], **1,** the state of being, or belonging to, a united people or country; **2,** character or traits of the people of a country as a whole; **3,** patriotism; **4,** a people united by customs, institutions, etc.

na-tion-al-ize (năsh'ŭn-ăl-īz), *v.t.* [*p.t.* and *p.p.* -ized (-īzd), *p.pr.* -iz"ing], **1,** to admit to the rights and privileges of citizenship in a nation; **2,** to make a united country of; **3,** to put under the control of the government of a country, as mines.—*n.* **na"tion-al-i-za'tion.**—*n.* **na'tion-al-iz"er.**

na-tive (nā'tĭv), *adj.* **1,** pertaining to one's birth or to the place of one's birth; as, one's *native* land; **2,** born or produced in, or belonging to, a country; as, the *native* population; *native* plants; **3,** peculiar to those born in a certain region; as, *native* customs; **4,** produced by nature; not artificial; as, *native* copper; **5,** inborn; not acquired; natural; as, *native* charm:—*n.* one that is born, or that which is produced, in a certain country or place.—*adv.* **na'tive-ly.**

Syn., adj. natural, indigenous. *Native* is used to describe what is inborn or inherent, in contrast to what is acquired or cultivated; it also describes whatever belongs to one by birth; as, one's *native* town. *Natural* suggests that which exists in one's nature, as opposed to the artificial; unlike *native,* it does not always apply to desirable traits; as, *natural* clumsiness. *Indigenous* is applied to whatever belongs naturally to a soil, country, or climate; as, fruits *indigenous* to America.

na-tiv-ism (nā'tĭv-ĭzm), *n.* **1,** the practice of favoring native-born citizens rather than immigrants; **2,** the doctrine that the mind receives impressions from an internal rather than an external source.

na-tiv-i-ty (nȧ-tĭv'ĭ-tĭ), *n.* [*pl.* nativities (-tĭz)], **1,** birth; **2,** the time, place, and manner of birth: **Nativity,** the birth of Christ.

nat-ty (năt'ĭ), *adj.* [*comp.* nat'ti-er, *superl.* nat'ti-est], tidy; neat; smart; trim.—*adv.* **nat'ti-ly.**—*n.* **nat'ti-ness.**

nat-u-ral (năt'ū-răl), *adj.* **1,** pertaining to one's nature; innate; inborn; as, *natural* gifts; **2,** occurring in the ordinary course of things; as, a *natural* result; **3,** true to life; as, a *natural* likeness; **4,** produced by nature; as, a *natural* bridge; **5,** related by birth, but not legitimate; as, a *natural* son; **6,** in accordance with the kindly characteristics of human kind; as, the *natural* affections; **7,** relating to the physical universe, or to a particular branch of nature; **8,** in music, written without sharps or flats; as, the *natural* scale of C: **natural science,** organized knowledge concerning the physical universe: often called *science:*—*n.* in music, a sign [♮] used to remove the effect of a preceding sharp or flat; also, the note so affected.—*adv.* **nat'u-ral-ly.**—*n.* **nat'u-ral-ness.**

Syn., adj. inherent, inbred. (See native.)

nat-u-ral his-to-ry the study of plants, minerals, and natural objects in general; esp., now, animals, with relation to their life, habits, etc.

nat-u-ral-ism (năt'ū-răl-ĭzm), *n.* **1,** an uncivilized condition; **2,** in literature and art, a careful following or representation of things as they really are.

nat-u-ral-ist (năt'ū-răl-ĭst), *n.* **1,** one who has made a special study of natural objects, as plants, minerals, and, esp., animals; **2,** one who practices or teaches realism.—*adj.* **nat"u-ral-is'tic.**

nat-u-ral-i-za-tion (năt"ū-răl-ĭ-zā'-shŭn), *n.* **1,** the act of legally granting a foreigner the rights and privileges of a citizen born in the country; **2,** a growing accustomed to new conditions.

nat-u-ral-ize (năt'ū-răl-īz), *v.t.* [*p.t.* and *p.p.* -ized (-īzd), *p.pr.* -iz"ing], **1,** to grant to (a foreigner) the privileges of a citizen or subject born in the country; **2,** to accept or adopt, as a foreign word, custom, etc.; **3,** to acclimatize, as a plant.

nat-u-ral se-lec-tion the process of nature by which the plants and animals best fitted to their surroundings tend to survive and perpetuate the variations or peculiarities that enabled them to survive.

na-ture (nā'tūr; nā'chōōr), *n.* **1,** that which is the source or essence of life; the forces that create; as, the laws of *nature;* **2,** the universe; **3,** original or essential qualities; **4,** kind; as, everything of this *nature;* **5,** man's primitive condition, unregulated by social laws; as, a state of *nature;* **6,** physical constitution; vital forces; **7,** personal or individual character or disposition; as, a generous *nature.*

naught (nôt), *n.* **1,** nothing; **2,** a cipher; the character [0]:—*adj.* of no account.

naugh-ty (nô'tĭ), *adj.* [*comp.* naugh'ti-er, *superl.* naugh'ti-est], bad; wayward; mischievous; disobedient.—*adv.* **naugh'-ti-ly.**—*n.* **naugh'ti-ness.**

Syn. wicked, perverse. (See bad.)

nau-se-a (nô'shē-ȧ; nô'sē-ȧ), *n.* **1,** sickness of the stomach, with a desire to vomit, as in seasickness; **2,** loathing; disgust.

nau-se-ate (nô'shē-āt; nô'sē-āt), *v.t.* [*p.t.* and *p.p.* -at"ed, *p.pr.* -at"ing], **1,** to affect with sickness of the stomach or with strong disgust; sicken; **2,** to loathe:—*v.i.* to be inclined to vomit; feel disgust.

nau-seous (nô'shŭs; nô'shē-ŭs), *adj.* **1,** causing sickness of the stomach; **2,** loathsome; abhorrent.—*adv.* **nau'seous-ly.**—*n.* **nau'seous-ness.**

Nau-sic-a-ä (nô-sĭk'ā-ȧ; nou-), *n.* in Homer's "Odyssey," a princess who befriends Odysseus.

nautch (nôch), *n.* in India, a kind of entertainment in which trained girl dancers perform.

nau-ti-cal (nô'tĭ-kăl), *adj.* pertaining to ships, sailors, or navigation; maritime: **nautical mile,** 6,080.2 feet (in British usage, 6,080 feet): also called *geographical mile.*—*adv.* **nau'ti-cal-ly.**

Syn. marine, naval. (See maritime.)

nau-ti-lus (nô'tĭ-lŭs), *n.* [*pl.* nautiluses (-ĕz); nautili (-lī)], **1,** any of several mollusks with a spiral shell, of the South Pacific and Indian oceans; **2,** a small marine mollusk related to the octopus: also called *paper nautilus.*

Nav-a-ho (năv'ȧ-hō), *n.* [*pl.* Navahos; Navahoes (-hōz)], a member of a tribe of North American Indians of Arizona and New Mexico. Also, **Nav'a-jo** (năv'ȧ-hō).

na-val (nā'văl), *adj.* of or pertaining to war vessels or a navy.

Syn. marine, nautical. (See maritime.)

¹nave (nāv), *n.* the main body of a church, from the choir to the main entrances, exclusive of the aisles.

²nave (nāv), *n.* the hub or center of a wheel, in which the spokes are fixed.

na-vel (nā'vl), *n.* the depression or knob in the center of the lower part of the abdomen, or belly; the umbilicus: **navel orange**, a kind of orange, usually seedless, having a navel-like depression in the rind.

na-vic-u-lar (nȧ-vĭk'ū-lȧr), *adj.* **1**, of or pertaining to a boat; **2**, boat-shaped:—*n.* **1**, a bone on the thumb side of the human wrist, or a corresponding bone in the ankle; the scaphoid bone; **2**, a bone at the back of a horse's foot just above the hoof.

nav-i-ga-ble (năv'ĭ-gȧ-bl), *adj.* **1**, capable of being traveled over by a boat or an airplane; **2**, capable of being steered; as, a *navigable* balloon.—*n.* **nav"i-ga-bil'i-ty.**—*n.* **nav'i-ga-ble-ness.**

nav-i-gate (năv'ĭ-gāt), *v.i.* [*p.t.* and *p.p.* -gat"ed, *p.pr.* -gat"ing], **1**, to travel by water or air; **2**, to sail or direct a ship or an airplane:—*v.t.* **1**, to pass over water in a ship, or through the air in an airplane; **2**, to steer or manage a ship in sailing, or an airplane in flying.

nav-i-ga-tion (năv"ĭ-gā'shŭn), *n.* **1**, the act of traveling by water or in the air; **2**, the act or the science of managing a ship or an airplane.

nav-i-ga-tor (năv'ĭ-gā"tēr), *n.* one who travels in ships or airplanes, or one skilled in managing ships or airplanes.

na-vy (nā'vĭ), *n.* [*pl.* navies (-vĭz)], **1**, the warships of a nation; **2**, the sea war force of a nation, including ships, shipyards, shops, officers, men, etc.; **3**, a fleet, as of merchant ships: **navy blue**, a dark blue color, used in naval uniforms: **navy yard**, a place where warships are built or repaired.

nay (nā), *adv.* **1**, no; **2**, not only so, but: introducing a more explicit or emphatic statement; as, I suspect, *nay*, I know that he has gone:—*n.* **1**, a refusal or denial; **2**, a negative vote or reply; also, a negative voter.

Naz-a-rene (năz"ȧ-rēn'), *n.* **1**, a native of Nazareth: applied to Jesus Christ, and, as a term of contempt, to his followers and to the early Christians; **2**, a member of an early sect of Jewish Christians.

Naz-a-rite (năz'ȧ-rīt), *n.* **1**, a Jew bound by a religious vow to a life of purity (Numbers 6); **2**, a Nazarene; native of Nazareth. Also, **Naz'i-rite.**

Na-zi (nä'tsē; nä'zĭ; nă'zĭ), *n.* [*pl.* Nazis (-tsēz; -zĭz)], a member of the National Socialist German Workers' party, formed under the leadership of Adolf Hitler.

Ne-an-der-thal man (nā-än'dēr-täl"), an extinct race of men, of the old stone age, who dwelt in caves, and used fire and rude stone implements.

neaped (nēpt), *adj.* left aground by the tide: said of a ship or boat.

Ne-a-pol-i-tan (nē"ȧ-pŏl'ĭ-tăn), *adj.* pertaining to the city or people of Naples, in Italy:—*n.* a native of, or resident in, Naples.

neap tide (nēp), the tide which occurs somewhat after the beginning of the first or the third quarter of the moon, in which the rise and fall are of relatively small range: opp. of *spring tide* (see *tide*, illus.).

near (nēr), *adj.* **1**, not far distant in time, place, or degree; close; **2**, intimate; dear; as, *near* to my heart; **3**, narrow; barely missing; as, a *near* escape; **4**, closely related, esp. by blood; **5**, situated on the left: used of vehicles or animals, because in this location close to one who leads horses with the right hand: opp. of *off;* as, the *near* horse; **6**, direct or quick; as, to go by the *near* way; **7**, mean or stingy; **8**, *Colloq.*, almost equal to; as, a *near* riot:—*adv.* **1**, not distant in time, place, or degree; **2**, almost; approximately; **3**, closely:—*prep.* close to or upon:—*v.t.* to approach:—*v.i.* to come close.—*adj.* **near'ish.**—*n.* **near'ness.**

near–by (nēr'=bī"), *adj. Colloq.*, not far off; neighboring; adjacent:—*adv.* and *prep.* (preferably, *near by*), near.

near-ly (nēr'lĭ), *adv.* **1**, almost; all but; as, *nearly* frozen; **2**, not far off; **3**, stingily; **4**, closely; as, *nearly* related.

near-sight-ed (nēr'sīt"ĕd), *adj.* seeing with distinctness at a short distance only.—*adv.* **near"sight'ed-ly.**—*n.* **near"sight'ed-ness.**

¹neat (nēt), *adj.* **1**, tidy; trim; **2**, simple and elegant; **3**, not adulterated; as, *neat* liquor; **4**, adroit; as, a *neat* reply; **5**, with all deductions and charges made; net.—*adv.* **neat'ly.**—*n.* **neat'ness.**

Syn. prim, orderly.—*Ant.* untidy, disorderly.

²neat (nēt), *n.* cattle, as oxen and cows, as distinguished from horses, sheep, and goats:—*adj.* designating such cattle.

neat-herd (nēt'hûrd"), *n.* one who takes care of neat cattle; a cowherd.

neat's–foot oil (nēts'=fo͝ot"), a pale yellow oil obtained from the feet and shin bones of neat cattle: used for fine lubrication and for dressing leather.

neb (nĕb), *n.* **1**, a beak, as of a bird; **2**, a snout; **3**, the pointed end of a thing.

Neb-u-chad-rez-zar (nĕb"ū-kăd-rĕz'ȧr), *n.* in the Bible, a king of Babylon (604–561 B. C.), who enslaved the Jews: in the Authorized Version written *Nebuchadnezzar* (2 Kings 24, 25).

neb-u-la (nĕb'ū-lȧ), *n.* [*pl.* nebulæ (-lē)], a luminous, cloudlike formation in the heavens, consisting either of a mass of luminous gas or of a cluster of stars too far off to be distinguishable.

neb-u-lar (nĕb'ū-lȧr), *adj.* **1**, pertaining to a nebula; **2**, cloudy; hazy: **nebular hypothesis**, in astronomy, the theory that the solar system was formed from a nebula, which, as it revolved, threw off rings which condensed to form the planets.

neb-u-lous (nĕb'ū-lŭs), *adj.* **1**, pertaining to, or like, a nebula; **2**, cloudy; hazy; indistinct; vague; **3**, perplexed.—*n.* **neb'u-lous-ness.**—*n.* **neb"u-los'i-ty.**

nec-es-sa-ry (nĕs'ĕ-sĕr"ĭ), *adj.* **1**, existing from the nature of the case; as, a *necessary* conclusion; **2**, not to be done without; essential; indispensable; as, food is *necessary* to life; **3**, unavoidable; inevitable; as, the *necessary* result of an act; **4**, acting under obligation or compulsion: opp. of *free:*—*n.*, usually in *pl.*, [*pl.* necessaries (-rĭz)], an indispensable thing.—*adv.* **nec'es-sa-ri-ly.**

Syn., adj. needful, requisite.

ne-ces-si-tate (nē-sĕs'ĭ-tāt), *v.t.* [*p.t.* and *p.p.*-tat"ed, *p.pr.*-tat"ing], **1**, to imply as a condition or result; **2**, to make unavoidable; **3**, to compel; oblige; demand.

ne-ces-si-tous (nē-sĕs'ĭ-tŭs), *adj.* very poor; destitute; needy.

ne-ces-si-ty (nē-sĕs'ĭ-tĭ), *n.* [*pl.* necessities (-tĭz)], **1**, the state or quality of being indispensable, inevitable, or obligatory; **2**, that which is necessary; a requisite; **3**, extreme poverty; **4**, in *pl.*, the things needed for a decent living.

Syn. indigence, want. (See need.)

neck (nĕk), *n.* **1**, that part of the body connecting the head with the trunk; **2**, a long, extended part of an object, esp. if near one end; as, the *neck* of a bottle; **3**, a narrow stretch of land or water; an isthmus or strait; **4**, the part of a garment which fits around the neck; collar.—*v.i.* *Slang*, to pet, caress, or fondle a person of the opposite sex; spoon.

neck-cloth (nĕk′klŏth″), *n.* formerly, a cloth band worn around the neck for protection or ornament, like a stock or a broad necktie with long ends.

neck-er-chief (nĕk′ẽr-chĭf), *n.* formerly, a piece of cloth worn about the neck for protection or ornament; a scarf or muffler.

neck-lace (nĕk′lās), *n.* a decorative chain, as of gold, or a string of beads, jewels, etc., worn around the neck.

neck-tie (nĕk′tī″), *n.* **1**, a narrow scarf or band of silk, fine linen, etc., worn around the neck and shirt collar, tied in front; **2**, a bow worn at the front of the neck.

neck-wear (nĕk′wâr″), *n.* collectively, articles of clothing worn about the neck; specif., neckties, cravats, etc.; also, collars, scarfs, mufflers, etc.

nec-ro- (nĕk′rō-), a combining form from the Greek, meaning dead person; as, *necro*logy; *necro*polis.

nec-rol-o-gy (nĕk-rŏl′ō-jĭ), *n.* [*pl.* necrologies (-jĭz)], **1**, a list of persons who have died; **2**, a death notice; obituary.

nec-ro-man-cer (nĕk′rō-măn″sẽr), *n.* **1**, one who claims to be able to foretell the future by communicating with the spirits of the dead; **2**, a conjurer.

nec-rop-o-lis (nĕk-rŏp′ō-lĭs), *n.* [*pl.* necropolises (-ĕz); necropoleis (-līs)], a cemetery or graveyard.

nec-ro-sis (nĕk-rō′sĭs), *n.* **1**, mortification, or decay and death of part of the body, esp. of a bone; **2**, a disease in plants, marked by small black spots that show decay.

nec-tar (nĕk′tȧr), *n.* **1**, in mythology, the wine of the gods; **2**, any delicious beverage; **3**, the honey of plants.

nec-tar-ine (nĕk′tȧr-ĭn; nĕk″tȧr-ēn′), *n.* a kind of peach with a smooth skin and firm pulp.

nec-ta-ry (nĕk′tȧ-rĭ), *n.* [*pl.* nectaries (-rĭz)], in plants, a gland that secretes nectar.

***née** (nā), [Fr.], *p.adj.* born: often placed before the maiden name of a married woman; as, Mrs. Smith, *née* Brown.

need (nēd), *n.* **1**, lack of anything desired or useful; **2**, necessity; urgent want; **3**, poverty:—*v.t.* to be in want of; require; have use for:—*v.i.* **1**, to be in poverty or want; **2**, to be necessary; as, it *needs* to be done; **3**, to be under obligation; as, he *need* not go.

Syn., *n.* necessity, want. *Need* is a state of affairs requiring something, or it may be the thing required. *Necessity* is more urgent than *need;* as, one may be in *need* of diversion but he must have the *necessities* of life. *Want* simply denotes the absolute lack of something; as, one who is in *want* of friends obviously has none. (See poverty.)

need-ful (nēd′fo͝ol), *adj.* necessary; needy; required.—*adv.* **need′ful-ly.**

nee-dle (nē′dl), *n.* **1**, a small, sharp-pointed steel instrument furnished with an eye to hold thread; **2**, a thin, straight rod used in knitting or, when hooked at the end, for crocheting; **3**, anything sharply pointed like a needle; **4**, the magnetic needle: **needle valve,** a valve in which a slender rod, or needle, with a cone-shaped end, fits into a funnel-shaped seat: used esp. for the accurate control of the flow of a fluid.

nee-dle-ful (nē′dl-fo͝ol), *n.* [*pl.* needlefuls (-fo͝olz)], the length of thread that can be used in a needle at one time.

need-less (nēd′lĕs), *adj.* unnecessary; useless; not needed.—*adv.* **need′-less-ly.**—*n.* **need′less-ness.**

nee-dle-wom-an (nē′dl-wo͝om″ăn), *n.* [*pl.* needlewomen (-wĭm″ĕn)], a seamstress; a woman who sews.

nee-dle-work (nē′dl-wûrk″), *n.* **1**, hand sewing; embroidery done by hand; **2**, the occupation of sewing.

needs (nēdz), *adv.* necessarily; of necessity; as, he *needs* must come.

need-y (nēd′ĭ), *adj.* [*comp.* need′i-er, *superl.* need′i-est], very poor; poverty-stricken.—*n.* **need′i-ness.**

ne'er (nâr; năr), *adv.* contraction of *never:* used chiefly in poetry.

ne-fa-ri-ous (nē-fā′rĭ-ŭs), *adj.* extremely wicked; vile; infamous; as, *nefarious* conduct.—*adv.* **ne-fa′ri-ous-ly.**—*n.* **ne-fa′ri-ous-ness.**

ne-ga-tion (nē-gā′shŭn), *n.* **1**, denial: opp. of *affirmation;* **2**, absence of positive qualities.

neg-a-tive (nĕg′ȧ-tĭv), *adj.* **1**, expressing or implying refusal or denial: opp. of *affirmative;* as, a *negative* reply; **2**, lacking positive qualities; as, a *negative* personality; **3**, having the power of veto; as, a *negative* voice in a legislative matter; **4**, designating the kind of electric charge that is produced by friction on resin: opp. of *positive;* **5**, in electricity, designating the plate in the cell which is not positive; **6**, in mathematics, designating a quantity to be subtracted; minus; **7**, in photography, showing the relations of light and shade of the original reversed:—*n.* **1**, a refusal or denial; **2**, the side of a question which denies what the opposite side affirms; as, to support the *negative* in a debate; **3**, the right of veto; **4**, in mathematics, a quantity to be subtracted, or less than zero; also, the symbol denoting the quantity; **5**, in electricity, the plate in the cell which is not positive; **6**, a picture in which the relations of light and shade of the original are reversed, from which the positive picture is printed; **7**, a word or particle expressing denial, as *no, not, neither:* **double negative,** in grammar, two negative words or particles within the same construction, in modern English destroying the force of the original negative; as, *not un*known, or, incorrectly, he had*n't no* money:—*v.t.* [*p.t.* and *p.p.* -tived (-tĭvd), *p.pr.* -tiv-ing], **1**, to deny the truth of; contradict; **2**, to refuse assent to; **3**, to prove to be false, as a hypothesis; **4**, to dismiss or reject by vote; veto; **5**, to counteract.—*adv.* **neg′a-tive-ly.**

neg-lect (nĕg-lĕkt′), *n.* **1**, omission to do that which should be done; **2**, habitual lack of attention; disregard; **3**, carelessness:—*v.t.* **1**, to omit to do, by carelessness or design; as, to *neglect* a duty; **2**, to slight; disregard; as, to *neglect* a point in reasoning; **3**, to leave uncared for; as, to *neglect* a child.—*n.* **neg-lect′er.**

Syn., *n.* negligence. *Neglect* and *negligence* are often used interchangeably to name the act of omitting something that should have been done. *Negligence* ordinarily denotes the habit of *neglect;* however, not *negligence* but *neglect* is used in regard to duty, business, studies, and health.

neg-lect-ful (nĕg-lĕkt′fo͝ol), *adj.* **1**, indicating or showing disregard; **2**, careless; negligent.—*adv.* **neg-lect′ful-ly.**

neg-li-gee (nĕg″lĭ-zhā′; nĕg′lĭ-zhā″), *n.* **1**, a loosely fitting dress or gown; **2**, easy and unceremonious dress in general:—*adj.* carelessly attired. Also, ***né″gli″gé′** (nā″glē″zhā′).

neg-li-gence (nĕg′lĭ-jĕns), *n.* **1**, the habit of not doing that which

should be done; **2**, carelessness; thoughtlessness; as, the accident was due to *negligence;* **3**, disregard of appearance, manner, or style.
Syn. heedlessness, remissness. (See neglect.)

neg-li-gent (nĕg′lĭ-jĕnt), *adj.* **1**, inclined to leave undone what should be done; **2**, careless; heedless; showing lack of attention.—*adv.* **neg′li-gent-ly.**
Syn. thoughtless, neglectful, remiss, lax.

neg-li-gi-ble (nĕg′lĭ-jĭ-bl), *adj.* capable of being disregarded; of little account or value; as, the loss was *negligible.*

ne-go-ti-a-ble (nē-gō′shĭ-ȧ-bl), *adj.* capable of being transferred or exchanged; as, a *negotiable* note: **negotiable paper**, notes, bills, and drafts which may be transferred by indorsement or assignment.—*n.* **ne-go″ti-a-bil′i-ty.**

ne-go-ti-ate (nē-gō′shĭ-āt), *v.t.* [*p.t.* and *p.p.* -at″ed, *p.pr.* -at″ing], **1**, to sell, as commercial paper or securities; **2**, to put through (any business); **3**, to conclude by treaty, bargain, or agreement; as, to *negotiate* peace; **4**, *Colloq.*, to surmount with success, as an obstacle or difficulty:—*v.i.* to treat with others in political or business affairs.—*n.* **ne-go′ti-a″tor.**

ne-go-ti-a-tion (nē-gō″shĭ-ā′shŭn), *n.* **1**, the act of transacting business, or of arranging some agreement; **2**, the discussion of a treaty; **3**, the putting into circulation of a note, draft, etc., that may be bought and sold.—*adj.* **ne-go′ti-a-to-ry.**

Ne-gri-to (nē-grē′tō), *n.* [*pl.* Negritos; Negritoes (-tōz)], a member of any of the dwarflike Negroid races of Polynesia; an Asiatic Pygmy.

Ne-gro (nē′grō), *n.* [*pl.* Negroes (-grōz)] **1**, a member of the typical African branch of the Ethiopian race, characterized by black or very dark skin; **2**, loosely, a member of any of the black African races: **negro** a black man, esp. one who has some Negro blood:—**Negro**, *adj.* pertaining to Negroes: **negro**, like, or pertaining to, a negro; black.

Ne-groid (nē′groid), *adj.* resembling the Negroes in appearance, racial characteristics, etc.: also written *negroid:*—*n.* a member of a race having Negro blood or characteristics.

ne-gus (nē′gŭs), *n.* a beverage or drink made of hot water, wine, and lemon juice, sweetened and spiced.

Ne-gus (nē′gŭs), *n.* king: the title of the ruler of Ethiopia, or Abyssinia.

Ne-he-mi-ah (nē″hē-mī′ȧ), *n.* **1**, an ancient Hebrew leader, statesman, and historian; **2**, an Old Testament book describing his rebuilding of Jerusalem: called, in the Douay Bible, *2 Esdras.*—*abbr.* **Neh.**

neigh (nā), *n.* the cry of a horse; a whinny: —*v.i.* to utter the call of a horse.

neigh-bor (nā′bẽr), *n.* **1**, one who dwells near another; **2**, a person or thing that is near another:—*adj.* near; bordering:—*v.t.* **1**, to adjoin; **2**, to live or be near to:—*v.i.* to be friendly. Also, **neigh′bour.**

neigh-bor-hood (nā′bẽr-ho͝od), *n.* **1**, the region near; vicinity; **2**, the state of being or of living near; **3**, all the people living near one another; **4**, a district with regard to its characteristics; as, a fashionable *neighborhood.* Also, **neigh′bour-hood.**

neigh-bor-ing (nā′bẽr-ĭng), *adj.* living or being near; adjoining; adjacent. Also, **neigh′bour-ing.**

neigh-bor-ly (nā′bẽr-lĭ), *adj.* **1**, like, or appropriate to, those who live near one another; **2**, social; friendly:—*adv.* in a friendly manner. Also, **neigh′bour-ly.**—*n.* **neigh′bor-li-ness.**

nei-ther (nē′*th*ẽr; nī′*th*ẽr), *pron.* not the one nor the other; as, I want *neither* of the books:—*adj.* not either; as, *neither* book will do:—*conj.* **1**, not either; not (one or the other): often with *nor;* as, *neither* the book nor the paper; **2**, and . . . not; nor; nor yet; as, I know not, *neither* can I guess.

Nem-e-sis (nĕm′ē-sĭs), *n.* in mythology, the goddess of revenge: **nemesis**, justice, esp. retribution, allotted to every man according to his deeds.

ne-o- (nē′ō-), a combining form from the Greek, meaning new or recent; as *neo*lithic; *neo*logy.

ne-o-lith-ic (nē″ō-lĭth′ĭk), *adj.* pertaining to, or like, the late stone age, in which polished stone implements were used, and agriculture and the domestication of animals were started.

ne-ol-o-gism (nē-ŏl′ō-jĭzm), *n.* **1**, a new word or phrase introduced into a language; a newly coined word; **2**, the use of such a word or phrase.

ne-ol-o-gy (nē-ŏl′ō-jĭ), *n.* [*pl.* neologies (-jĭz)], **1**, the use of a new word or phrase, or new meaning of a word; **2**, the new word, phrase, or meaning; **3**, a new theory or doctrine; **4**, specif., in theology, rationalism.—*n.* **ne-ol′o-gist.**

ne-o-phyte (nē′ō-fīt), *n.* **1**, a novice; a beginner; **2**, one recently baptized; a convert.

nep (nĕp), *n.* catnip, a strong-scented herb which cats like to eat.

ne-pen-the (nē-pĕn′thē), *n.* a drug supposed by the ancient Greeks to cause forgetfulness of pain and sorrow.

neph-ew (nĕf′ū; nĕv′ū), *n.* the son of one's brother or sister.

ne-phri-tis (nē-frī′tĭs; nĕf-rī′tĭs), *n.* inflammation or disease of the kidneys; specif., Bright's disease.

nep-o-tism (nĕp′ō-tĭzm), *n.* **1**, favoritism or partiality to nephews and other relatives; **2**, patronage or preference, esp. in the case of those holding office, shown because of relationship:—*adj.* **ne-pot′ic.**

Nep-tune (nĕp′tūn), *n.* **1**, in Roman mythology, the god of the sea, son of Saturn: identified with the Greek *Poseidon;* **2**, in astronomy, one of the outermost planets of the solar system (see *solar system*, illus.).—*adj.* **Nep-tu′ni-an.**

Ne-re-id (nē′rē-ĭd), *n.* in mythology, any of the fifty daughters of the sea god Nereus, who attended Poseidon as sea nymphs: **nereid**, a sea nymph, or imaginary maiden dwelling in the sea, having the head and body of a woman and the tail of a fish.

nerve (nûrv), *n.* **1**, one of the cordlike fibers which serve as a means of communication between the brain and all parts of the body; **2**, bodily or mental strength or control; coolness; **3**, the strong vein of a leaf:—*v.t.* [*p.t.* and *p.p.* nerved (nûrvd), *p.pr.* nerv′ing], to fill with vigor, strength, or courage.

nerve-less (nûrv′lĕs), *adj.* **1**, having no strength, courage, or vigor; weak; **2**, without nerves.—*adv.* **nerve′less-ly.**

nerv-ine (nûr′vēn; nûr′vīn), *n.* any tonic for the nerves:—*adj.* affecting or quieting the nerves.

nerv-ous (nûr′vŭs), *adj.* **1**, pertaining to, or made of, nerves; **2**, having weak nerves; easily excited; timid; as, she is *nervous* in the dark; **3**, forceful; vigorous; as, a *nervous* literary style; **4**, restless or uneasy.—*adv.* **nerv′ous-ly.**—*n.* **nerv′ous-ness.**

nes-ci-ence (nĕsh′ĭ-ĕns; nĕsh′ĕns), *n.* the state of ignorance; lack of knowledge.—*adj.* **nes′ci-ent.**

-ness (-nĕs), *n. suffix*, the quality or state of being: used with adjectives; as, sick*ness;* good*ness.*

nest (nĕst), *n.* **1,** the bed or dwelling made or chosen by a bird for the hatching of its eggs and the rearing of its young; **2,** a hatching place for insects, turtles, etc.; as, a hornets' *nest;* **3,** a cozy retreat or residence; **4,** the haunt of anything bad, or those who gather there; as, a *nest* of thieves; **5,** a number of boxes, bowls, etc., one fitting inside another: —*v.i.* to build and occupy a nest:—*v.t* **1,** to place in a nest; **2,** to build a nest for.

nest egg **1,** an egg left in a nest to keep the hen from leaving it, and to cause her to lay more eggs in the same place; **2,** money laid by with intention of adding to it; as, the *nest egg* of a fortune.

nes-tle (nĕs'l), *v.i.* [*p.t.* and *p.p.* -tled (-ld), *p.pr.* -tling], **1,** to make and use a nest; **2,** to lie close and snug; as, a child *nestles* in its mother's arms:—*v.t.* **1,** to cherish or cuddle; **2,** to shelter.

nest-ling (nĕst'lĭng; nĕs'lĭng), *n.* a young bird recently hatched and not yet able to fly:—*adj.* recently hatched.

Nes-tor (nĕs'tŏr), *n.* **1,** in mythology, a Greek king of Pylos, famed for his wisdom, who, as an old man, fought with the Greeks at Troy; **2,** hence, a wise old man.

[1]**net** (nĕt), *n.* **1,** a fabric made of twine knotted into meshes, used for catching birds, fish, etc.; **2,** a fine, openwork fabric, very often of silk, used for bridal veils, laces, etc.; **3,** any of various other meshed fabrics used for covering, protecting, or confining something; as, a *net* for the hair; **4,** that which entraps; entanglement; snare; as, a *net* spread to capture a criminal; **5,** a dragnet: —*adj.* of or like net or netting; as, a *net* dress: —*v.t.* [*p.t.* and *p.p.* net'ted, *p.pr.* net'ting], **1,** to make into a net or network; **2,** to catch in a net; hence, to entrap by clever stratagem; snare; **3,** to cover or protect with, or as with, a net:—*v.i.* **1,** to make nets or network; **2,** to use nets in fishing, hunting game, etc.

[2]**net** (nĕt), *adj.* remaining after deducting all necessary expenses; as, *net* gain; also, excluding all waste, refuse, etc.; as, *net* weight: distinguished from *gross:* **net ton,** 2,000 lbs. avoirdupois:—*v.t.* [*p.t.* and *p.p.* net'ted, *p.pr.* net'ting], to earn as clear profit; as, the deal *netted* $2,000.

neth-er (nĕth'ẽr), *adj.* **1,** situated below; lying beneath; lower; as, *nether* garments; **2,** pertaining to the regions below the heavens or the earth; as, the *nether* regions: opp. of *upper:* **nether world,** the underworld, esp. as a place of punishment.

neth-er-most (nĕth'ẽr-mōst), *adj.* lowest; farthest down.

net-ting (nĕt'ĭng), **1,** the act or method of making nets; **2,** a fabric made of twine knotted into meshes; as, fish *netting;* **3,** any of several types of openwork fabric; as, mosquito *netting;* **4,** a fabric of crossed wires, as for fences; **5,** network; any system of crossed lines; **6,** the use of nets, as in fishing.

net-tle (nĕt'l), *n.* any of various plants having prickles or stinging hairs: —*v.t.* [*p.t.* and *p.p.* -tled (-ld), *p.pr.* -tling], **1,** to sting, as with nettles; **2,** hence, to provoke; irritate; vex.

net-tle rash an eruption on the skin resembling the effects of a nettle sting; hives.

net-work (nĕt'wûrk''), *n.* **1,** an openwork fabric made by the interlaced threads of any material; **2,** the process of making this fabric; **3,** any system of crossed lines; as, a *network* of railroad tracks.

neu-ral (nū'răl), *adj.* pertaining to the nerves or to the nervous system.

neu-ral-gi-a (nū-răl'jĭ-ȧ), *n.* acute and intermittent pain along the course of a nerve.—*adj.* **neu-ral'gic.**

neu-ras-the-ni-a (nū''răs-thē'nĭ-ȧ; nū-răs''thē-nĭ'ȧ), *n.* nerve exhaustion or prostration: a disorder marked by extreme fatigue.—*adj.* and *n.* **neu''ras-then'ic.**

neu-ri-tis (nū-rī'tĭs), *n.* inflammation of a nerve or nerves; as, optic *neuritis.*—*adj.* **neu-rit'ic.**

neu-rol-o-gy (nū-rŏl'ō-jĭ), *n.* the science of the nervous system.

neu-ron (nū'rŏn), *n.* [*pl.* neura (-rȧ); neurons (-rŏnz)], a nerve cell with all its extensions and processes, regarded as the structural unit of a nervous system. Also, **neu'rone** (nū'rōn).

neu-ro-path (nū'rō-păth), *n.* a physician who believes that most diseases are of nervous origin.

neu-rop-a-thy (nū-rŏp'ȧ-thĭ), *n.* any disease or derangement of the nervous system.—*adj.* **neu''ro-path'ic.**

neu-ro-sis (nū-rō'sĭs), *n.* [*pl.* neuroses (-sēz)], a functional disturbance accompanied by disorder of the nervous system, not traceable to any physical cause.

neu-rot-ic (nū-rŏt'ĭk), *adj.* **1,** pertaining to the nerves or to the nervous system; affecting the nerves; as, a *neurotic* remedy; **2,** affected with a marked nervous disorder:—*n.* a person with a nervous disease.

neu-ter (nū'tẽr), *adj.* **1,** in grammar: **a,** neither masculine nor feminine in gender; **b,** neither active nor passive; intransitive; as, a *neuter* verb; **2,** in biology: **a,** having no sex, as certain plants; **b,** without fully developed sex organs in adult life; as, *neuter* bees:—*n.* **1,** a word pertaining to something neither masculine nor feminine; also, an intransitive verb neither active nor passive; **2,** a plant or insect which does not develop sex organs.

neu-tral (nū'trăl), *adj.* **1,** unbiased; indifferent; **2,** taking no part on either side in a contest; as, a *neutral* nation; **3,** pertaining to a nation not taking sides; as, *neutral* ships; **4,** neither good nor bad; of no decided color or characteristics; **5,** neither acid nor alkaline: said of chemical salts:—*n.* one who or that which does not take sides in a dispute or conflict.—*adv.* **neu'tral-ly.**

neu-tral-i-ty (nū-trăl'ĭ-tĭ), *n.* [*pl.* neutralities (-tĭz)], **1,** the state of not taking sides; **2,** the state of being neither one thing nor the other; indifference.

neu-tral-ize (nū'trăl-īz), *v.t.* [*p.t.* and *p.p.* -ized (-īzd), *p.pr.* -iz''ing], **1,** to render inactive; make of no effect; counteract; as, to *neutralize* the effects of a poison; **2,** to declare by treaty to be free from taking sides, as a small nation; **3,** to destroy the characteristics of (a substance) by chemical combination; as, to *neutralize* an acid.—*n.* **neu''tral-i-za'tion.**—*n.* **neu'tral-iz''er.**

neu-tro-dyne (nū'trō-dīn), *n.* **1,** an arrangement, as of small condensers, for controlling oscillation in a radio receiving set; **2,** a receiver employing this arrangement.

nev-er (nĕv'ẽr), *adv.* **1,** not ever; not at any time; **2,** in no degree; under no condition: used for emphasis; as, *never* fear.

nev-er-more (nĕv''ẽr-mōr'), *adv.* not ever again; at no future time.

nev-er-the-less (nĕv''ẽr-*thē*-lĕs'), *adv.* and *conj.* notwithstanding: in spite of that; yet; however; still.

new (nū), *adj.* **1,** recent in origin or development; modern; novel; as, *new* art; the *new* woman; **2,** lately made, produced, invented, or discovered; as, *new* wine; a *new* novel; **3,** changed in character, health, etc.; as, I feel like a *new* man; **4,** beginning afresh; recurring anew; as, a *new* year; a *new* start in

li'e:—*adv.* newly; recently; as, a field of *new-mown* hay.—*adv.* **new'ly.**—*n.* **new'ness.**
Syn., adj. late. (See modern.)

new-com-er (nū'kŭm″ẽr), *n.* one who has lately arrived.

new-el (nū'ĕl), *n.* **1,** in a winding staircase, the central upright pillar around which the steps turn; **2,** the post at the foot of a stairway.

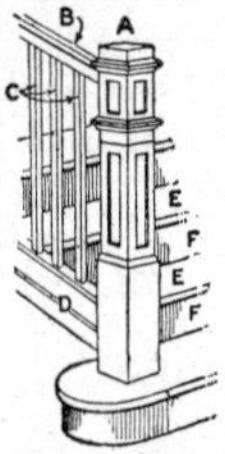

NEWEL POST
A, newel post; B, handrail; C, balusters; D, outside string; E, E, treads; F, F, risers.

new-fan-gled (nū″făng'-gld; nū'-făng″gld), *adj.* **1,** new-fashioned; recently made; novel: usually said in disfavor of a thing; as, *newfangled* ideas or notions; **2,** inclined to new theories, fashions, etc.

new–fash-ioned (nū″-făsh'-ŭnd; nū'-făsh″ŭnd), *adj.* of a recent style; up-to-date in fashion; modern.

New-found-land (nū-found'-lănd; nū'-fŭnd-lănd″), *adj.* pertaining to Newfoundland, an island and British dominion at the mouth of the Saint Lawrence: **Newfoundland dog,** a breed of large, shaggy, intelligent dog, orig. from Newfoundland:—*n.* (usually, nū'fŭnd-lănd″), a Newfoundland dog.

news (nūz), *n. pl.* used as *sing.* recent tidings; fresh information; hence, recent events.
Syn. information, intelligence, tidings. *News* is the general term and means knowledge or report of recent events. *Information* is specific knowledge; it may be a fact sought for some specific purpose, or it may be, if recent, *news. Intelligence* is *news* or *information* formally made known. *Tidings,* now chiefly a literary word, is a piece of *news;* as, to bring glad *tidings.*

news-boy (nūz'boi″), *n.* a boy who delivers or sells newspapers.

news-mon-ger (nūz'mŭng″gẽr), *n.* a tattler; gossip.

news-pa-per (nūz'pā″pẽr), *n.* a paper published periodically, usually daily or weekly, containing the most recent news, photographs, etc.

New Style the Gregorian or present style of reckoning the calendar, which differs from the Julian or *Old Style* by the omission of leap year in the century years (1700, 1800, etc.), except when they are evenly divisible by 400.

news-y (nūz'ĭ), *adj.* [*comp.* news'i-er, *superl.* news'i-est], *Colloq.*, **1,** containing, or conveying, much news; gossipy; **2,** inquisitive; curious; prying.

newt (nūt), *n.* any of several small, harmless salamanders found in water or damp places, erroneously called *lizards.*

New Tes-ta-ment the second of the two great divisions of the Bible, containing the Gospels and writings based thereon.—*abbr.* **New Test.; N. T.**

New Thought a system of religious philosophy which affirms the power of mind and spirit to control and direct material conditions, and to rise above material pain and anxiety.

New World the Western Hemisphere, containing the continents of North and South America.

new year **1,** the year following the one which will soon end; also, the year just beginning; **2,** the first week of a new year: **new-year,** *adj.* pertaining to a new year: **New Year,** the first day of January, usually celebrated as a legal holiday: also called *New Year's Day:* **New-Year,** *adj.* pertaining to the first of January or to the year then beginning.

next (nĕkst), *adj.* superlative of *nigh:* nearest in time, place, degree, or rank; immediately following; as, the *next* day; the *next* street; the *next* quality; *next* in order:—*adv.* immediately succeeding; in the nearest time, place, or order; as, you go *next:* **next of kin,** nearest relative.

Nez Per-cé (nā″ pâr″sā'), one of a tribe of American Indians, orig. inhabiting Idaho, Oregon, and Washington.

nib (nĭb), *n.* **1,** a bird's beak or bill; **2,** the point of anything, esp. of a pen; **3,** a sharp point or prong.

nib-ble (nĭb'l), *n.* **1,** the act of biting off little bits; **2,** a small bite:—*v.i.* [*p.t.* and *p.p.* -bled (-ld), *p.pr.* -bling], to bite a little at a time; as, the child merely *nibbles:*—*v.t.* to continue to bite at gently and quickly; as, a fish *nibbles* bait.—*n.* **nib'bler.**

Ni-be-lung (nē'bĕ-lo͝ong), *n.* in Teutonic mythology, **1,** one of the children of the mist, a race of dwarfs, possessors of a treasure, conquered by Siegfried; **2,** any of the race of kings who took from Siegfried the treasure known as the hoard of the Nibelungs.

Ni-be-lung-en-lied (nē'bĕ-lo͝ong″ĕn-lēt″), *n.* a famous medieval German epic, telling of Siegfried's adventures in the land of the Nibelungs: partly paralleled by the "Volsunga Saga."

nib-lick (nĭb'lĭk), *n.* in golf, a heavy, iron-headed club having a slanting face: used when the ball lies in bad places.

Nic-a-ra-guan (nĭk″ȧ-rä'gwăn), *adj.* pertaining to Nicaragua, a republic of Central America:—*n.* a native of Nicaragua.

nice (nīs), *adj.* **1,** precise; acute; accurate; as, *nice* judgment; a *nice* piece of work; **2,** fine; delicate; as, a *nice* discrimination; a *nice* ear for music; **3,** fastidious; too particular; **4,** delicate; refined; as, to be *nice* in one's habits or dress; **5,** *Colloq.*, socially agreeable; pleasant; as, *nice* manners; *nice* people.—*adv.* **nice'ly.**—*n.* **nice'ness.**

Ni-cene (nī'sēn; nī-sēn'), *adj.* **1,** pertaining to Nicæa, where was held the first great church council, in the fourth century; **2,** denoting the creed of Christian belief adopted by that council.

ni-ce-ty (nī'sĕ-tĭ), *n.* [*pl.* niceties (-tĭz)], **1,** a very small distinction, detail, or point; as, the *niceties* of a debate; **2,** demanding delicate management; as, the *nicety* of a situation; **3,** fastidious delicacy; subtlety; precision; as, *nicety* of decision; *nicety* of measurement; **4,** fastidiousness.

niche (nĭch), *n.* **1,** a recess or hollow in a wall, as for a statue; **2,** a condition or position especially suitable to a person or thing:—*v.t.* [*p.t.* and *p.p.* niched (nĭcht), *p.pr.* nich'ing], to put in a recess in a wall, as a statue.

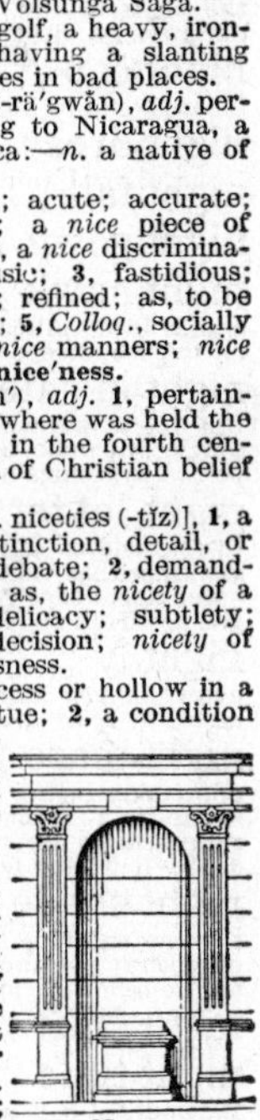
NICHE

nick (nĭk), *n.* **1,** a notch; slit; **2,** a broken place in any edge or surface; as, a *nick* in the table; **3,** exact or critical point (of time); as, he arrived in the *nick* of time:—*v.t.* **1,** to cut notches in; **2,** to hit or grasp at the lucky moment.

Nick (nĭk), *n.* the Devil; Satan: usually called *Old Nick.*

nick-el (nĭk'l), *n.* **1,** a hard, white, metallic element; **2,** in the U. S., a five-cent coin, made of nickel and copper.

nick-el sil-ver a strong, hard alloy of nickel, copper, and zinc: also called *German silver*.

nick-nack (nĭk'năk″), *n.* a toy; trinket. Also, **knick'knack″**, *Pfd. S.*

nick-name (nĭk'nām″), *n.* a familiar form of a given name, or a wholly new name given in derision, sport or familiarity:—*v.t.* [*p.t.* and *p.p.* -named″ (-nāmd″), *p.pr.* -nam″ing], to give a nickname to; call by a contemptuous name.

nic-o-tine (nĭk'ō-tĭn; nĭk'ō-tēn), *n.* a poison contained in tobacco: used in insecticides. Also, **nic'o-tin.**

niece (nēs), *n.* the daughter of one's brother or sister.

nig-gard (nĭg'ȧrd), *n.* a stingy person; a miser:—*adj.* miserly; stingy.

nig-gard-ly (nĭg'ȧrd-lĭ), *adj.* **1,** stingy; miserly; as, a *niggardly* person; **2,** scanty, as a meal:—*adv.* stingily; miserly; scantily; meanly.—*n.* **nig'gard-li-ness.**

nigh (nī), *adj.* [*comp.* **nigh'er,** *superl.* **nigh'est** or next], **1,** near in time or place; as, the hour of his triumph is *nigh;* **2,** closely related by blood or friendship; as, *nigh* relatives; **3,** on the left; as, the *nigh* horse:—*adv.* **1,** near in time or place; **2,** almost; as, he was *nigh* starved:—*prep.* near to; not remote or distant from; as, the well was *nigh* the house.

night (nīt), *n.* **1,** the time from sunset to sunrise; **2,** the period of darkness; the close of the day; **3,** mental or moral darkness; **4,** death; old age.

night-cap (nīt'kăp″), *n.* **1,** a head covering worn in bed; **2,** *Colloq.*, a drink before going to bed.

night-dress (nīt'drĕs″), *n.* a garment worn in bed; a nightgown.

night-fall (nīt'fôl″), *n.* the coming of darkness at evening.

night-gown (nīt'goun″), *n.* a loose garment worn in bed.

night-hawk (nīt'hôk″), *n.* **1,** any of a genus of American insect-eating birds allied to the whippoorwill; **2,** a person who keeps late hours.

night-in-gale (nīt'ĭng-gāl; nīt'ĭn-), *n.* **1,** any of several small Old World thrushes noted for the melodious song of the male, heard oftenest at night; **2,** a person who sings beautifully.

night let-ter a telegram with a minimum charge for 50 words, accepted for sending during the night on the understanding that regular telegrams take precedence, and hence sent at a lower rate: distinguished from *day letter*.

night-ly (nīt'lĭ), *adj.* **1,** pertaining to, or occurring at, night; **2,** occurring every night:—*adv.* night by night; every night; at or by night.

night-mare (nīt'mâr″), *n.* **1,** a distressing dream accompanied with oppression in the chest and a feeling of helplessness; **2,** formerly, in folklore, a monster supposed to oppress people in their sleep; **3,** any haunting fear.

night-shade (nīt'shād″), *n.* any of a genus of plants including the potato plant and the eggplant; esp., any of several poisonous or medicinal species, as the common nightshade and the bittersweet.

night-shirt (nīt'shûrt″), *n.* a man's or boy's garment worn in bed.

night-time (nīt'tīm″), *n.* **1,** the period between dusk and dawn; the hours of darkness; **2,** darkness.

night-walk-er (nīt'wôk″ẽr), *n.* **1,** a person who is abroad at night for an evil purpose; **2,** a kind of earthworm.

ni-hil-ism (nī'hĭ-lĭzm), *n.* **1,** the doctrine that nothing can really be known, because nothing exists; **2,** nothingness: **Nihilism, 1,** a socialist movement in Russia to destroy existing institutions and found an order of things with equal rights of land and property; **2,** violent revolutionism; anarchism.—*n.* **ni'hil-ist.**—*adj.* **ni″hil-is'tic.**

nil (nĭl), *n.* **1,** nothing; **2,** a thing of no account.

nim-ble (nĭm'bl), *adj.* **1,** active; alert; as, a *nimble* mind; **2,** lively; as *nimble* feet.—*n.* **nim'ble-ness.**—*adv.* **nim'bly.**

nim-bus (nĭm'bŭs), *n.* [*pl.* nimbi (-bī); nimbuses (-ĕz)], **1,** the halo or cloud of light represented in pictures as surrounding the heads of divinities, saints, and sovereigns; **2,** a heavy rain cloud.

Nim-rod (nĭm'rŏd), *n.* in the Bible, a great hunter and ruler (Genesis 10:8, 9); hence, a hunter.

nine (nīn), *adj.* composed of one more than eight:—*n.* **1,** the number consisting of eight plus one; **2,** a sign representing nine units, as 9 or ix.—*adj.* and *n.* **ninth.**

nine-fold (nīn'fōld″), *adj.* nine times as many or as great:—*adv.* up to nine times as many or as great.

nine-pins (nīn'pĭnz″), *n.pl.* used as *sing.* a game which consists in bowling a ball at nine wooden pins set up at one end of a bowling alley.

nine-teen (nīn'tēn″; nīn″tēn'), *adj.* composed of ten more than nine:—*n.* **1,** the sum of eighteen and one; **2,** a sign representing nineteen units, as 19 or xix. —*adj.* and *n.* **nine'teenth″.**

nine-ty (nīn'tĭ), *adj.* composed of one more than eighty-nine:—*n.* [*pl.* nineties (-tĭz)], **1,** the number consisting of eighty-nine plus one; **2,** a sign representing ninety units, as 90 or xc.—*adj.* and *n.* **nine'ti-eth.**

nin-ny (nĭn'ĭ), *n.* [*pl.* ninnies (-ĭz)], a foolish person; simpleton; dunce.

Ni-o-be (nī'ō-bē), *n.* a Grecian mother whose fourteen children were slain by Apollo and Artemis, because she in her pride compared herself with their mother who had only two children: changed by Zeus into a stone which in summer shed tears.

¹nip (nĭp), *v.t.* [*p.t.* and *p.p.* nipped (nĭpt), *p.pr.* nip'ping], **1,** to pinch; **2,** to cut off the end of; clip; **3,** to check; restrain; as, to *nip* a thing in the bud; **4,** to blight; blast; destroy, as by frost:—*n.* **1,** a pinch, as with the nails or teeth; a bite; **2,** a blast or blight, as by cold; **3,** a sharp retort; sarcasm; **4,** a very small quantity; as, a *nip* of salt: **nip and tuck,** an expression indicating approximate equality, as in a contest.

²nip (nĭp), *n.* a small drink or draft of spirits, esp. one taken frequently:—*v.i.* [*p.t.* and *p.p.* nipped (nĭpt), *p.pr.* nip'ping], to take a nip, esp. of some alcoholic liquor.

nip-per (nĭp'ẽr), *n.* **1,** one who or that which pinches or cuts off; **2,** the large claw of a crab or lobster; **3,** a horse's incisor tooth; **4,** in *pl.*, any of various tools with jaws; forceps; tongs (see *tool*, illus.).

nip-ple (nĭp'l), *n.* **1,** that part of a female animal's breast through which milk is drawn; a teat; **2,** the mouthpiece of a nursing bottle; **3,** any of various devices resembling a nipple.

Nir-va-na (nẽr-vä'nȧ; nẽr-), *n.* in Buddhism, the highest religious state, when all desire for existence is destroyed, and the soul becomes one with its Creator.

Ni-sei (nē'sā'), *n. sing.* and *pl.*, a child of Japanese parents, born outside Japan.

nit (nĭt), *n.* **1,** the egg of any small insect, such as a louse; **2,** the young insect.

ni-ter (nī'tẽr), *n.* a white crystalline salt; potassium nitrate or saltpeter: **sweet**

spirits of niter, an alcoholic solution of ethyl nitrite used as a sedative: often called *niter.* Also, **ni'tre.**

ni-ton (nī'tŏn), *n.* radon, a gaseous radium emanation, sometimes considered an element, which confers radioactive properties on substances exposed to it.

ni-trate (nī'trāt), *n.* **1,** a salt of nitric acid; **2,** potassium or sodium nitrate, extensively used as a fertilizer: **nitrate of silver,** a white crystalline salt used in photography and for cauterizing, or burning the flesh; lunar caustic.—*n.* **ni-tra'tion.**

ni-tric (nī'trĭk), *adj.* **1,** pertaining to, or containing, nitrogen; **2,** designating compounds containing more oxygen than those designated by *nitrous:* **nitric acid,** a powerful acid which contains nitrogen, hydrogen, and oxygen, and which is used in the arts and in manufacturing processes.

ni-trite (nī'trīt), *n.* a salt of nitrous acid, which contains a smaller amount of oxygen than a nitrate.

ni-tro-ben-zene (nī″trō-bĕn'zēn; nī″-trō-bĕn-zēn'), *n.* a yellow, oily liquid formed by the action of nitric acid on benzene.

ni-tro-gen (nī'trō-jĕn), *n.* a colorless, odorless, tasteless, inert, gaseous element which forms four fifths of the volume of the atmosphere, and is the basis of nitric acid: occurring in combination in all animal and vegetable tissue and as a constituent of soils: **nitrogen fixation,** the process of combining the nitrogen of the atmosphere into any of various fixed, or stable, chemical compounds that may be used for the manufacture of explosives, fertilizers, etc.: **nitrogen monoxide,** nitrous oxide, or laughing gas.

ni-trog-e-nous (nī-trŏj'ē-nŭs), *adj.* pertaining to, or containing, the gas nitrogen; esp., designating any of many compounds, generally organic, in which nitrogen is an important constituent, as urea, proteins, etc.: **nitrogenous foods,** foods containing some form of proteid, a class of substances composed mainly of nitrogen, carbon, hydrogen, oxygen, and sulphur, found esp. in lean meats, egg albumen, milk, and, in smaller quantities, in all vegetables and grains.

ni-tro-glyc-er-in (nī″trō-glĭs'ēr-ĭn), *n.* a highly explosive, oily liquid, prepared by the action of nitric and sulphuric acids upon glycerin. Also, **ni″tro-glyc'er-ine.**

ni-trous (nī'trŭs), *adj.* **1,** resembling, obtained from, or soaked with, niter, or saltpeter; **2,** designating compounds containing less oxygen than those designated by *nitric:* **nitrous acid,** the acid from which nitrites are formed: **nitrous oxide,** a gas used as an anæsthetic; laughing gas.

nix (nĭks), *n.* [*pl.* nixes (nĭk'sĕz; nĭk'sĭz)], in mythology, a water elf or fairy, beneficent or mischievous, similar to the kelpie in Scotch folklore.—*n.fem.* **nix'ie.**

Njorth (nyôrth), *n.* in Norse mythology, one of the Vans, or gods who were protectors of trade.

¹no (nō), *n.* **1,** [*pl.* no's (nōz)], a reply of denial or refusal; as, an emphatic *no;* also, a negative vote; **2,** [*pl.* noes (nōz)], in *pl.*, the voters in the negative.

²no (nō), *adv.* **1,** nay; not so; as, *No,* I cannot go: opp. of *yes;* **2,** not any; not at all; as, he is *no* better, *no* worse; **3,** not; as, whether or *no.*

No-ah (nō'ȧ), *n.* in the Bible, the Hebrew patriarch who built the ark: **Noah's Ark, 1,** the ark built by Noah, in which his family and animals lived to escape the great flood (Genesis 6–9); **2,** a child's toy ark with its people and animals.

No-bel priz-es (nō-bĕl'), five money prizes, averaging about $40,000 each, founded by Alfred B. Nobel (1833–96), a Swedish chemist, the originator of dynamite, to be given annually to those who have done most in the fields of science (physics, chemistry, medicine or physiology), literature, and the maintenance of peace.

no-bil-i-ty (nō-bĭl'ĭ-tĭ), *n.* [*pl.* nobilities (-tĭz)], **1,** the state or quality of being lofty, excellent, or worthy; **2,** those who possess the characteristics of nobleness; **3,** high birth or rank as denoted by a title; **4,** dignity of character; greatness; **5,** the body of persons of rank and title, above the common people; as, the *nobility* of Europe.

Syn. aristocracy, peerage.

no-ble (nō'bl), *adj.* **1,** high in excellence or worth; illustrious; as, a *noble* character; **2,** high in rank; of ancient lineage or descent; as, *noble* birth; **3,** stately in appearance; grand; as, *noble* architecture:—*n.* **1,** a peer or person of high rank and title; **2,** formerly, an English gold coin or a Scotch silver coin.—*n.* **no'ble-ness.**—*adv.* **no'bly.**

Syn., adj. elevated, lofty, magnificent.—*Ant., adj.* insignificant, obscure.

no-ble-man (nō'bl-măn), *n.* [*pl.* noblemen (-mĕn)], a man of rank above that of a commoner; peer.—*n.fem.* **no'ble-wom″an.**

no-bod-y (nō'bŏd-ĭ), *n.* [*pl.* nobodies (-ĭz)], **1,** no one; **2,** a person of no importance or influence.

noc-turn (nŏk'tûrn), *n.* **1,** a Roman Catholic Church service held at daybreak; **2,** in music, a nocturne (which see).

noc-tur-nal (nŏk-tûr'năl), *adj.* **1,** pertaining to, or done or happening at, night; as, a *nocturnal* visit; **2,** active or seeking food at night; as, *nocturnal* insects or birds.—*adv.* **noc-tur'nal-ly.**

noc-turne (nŏk'tûrn; nŏk-tûrn'), *n.* **1,** a picture of a night scene; **2,** a quiet, dreamy song without words.

nod (nŏd), *n.* **1,** the act of bowing the head; **2,** a quick inclination of the head; **3,** inclining the head as a sign of authority; as, at the ruler's *nod;* **4,** a hanging downward or bending forward, as of the top of a tree, flowers, etc.:—*v.t.* [*p.t.* and *p.p.* nod'ded, *p.pr.* nod'ding], **1,** to signify by a quick inclination of the head; **2,** to incline or bend with a quick movement:—*v.i.* **1,** to incline or bend the top with a quick, forward motion; as, flowers *nod* in the breeze; **2,** to bend the head in token of assent or as a salute; **3,** to be drowsy; bend the head forward sleepily.—*n.* **nod'der.**

nod-al (nōd'ăl), *adj.* of, pertaining to, or like, a node or nodes.

nod-dle (nŏd'l), *n. Colloq.*, the head: used in contempt.

node (nōd), *n.* **1,** a knot; knob; swelling; **2,** a hard swelling on a tendon or bone; **3,** the point on the stem of a plant from which a leaf springs; **4,** one of the two points at which the orbit of a planet intersects the ecliptic.—*adj.* **no'dose.**—*n.* **no-dos'i-ty.**

nod-ule (nŏd'ūl), *n.* a little knot, or irregular, rounded lump.—*adj.* **nod'u-lar.**—*adj.* **nod'u-lose.**

no-el (nō-ĕl'; nō'ĕl), *n.* a shout of joy at Christmas time; hence, a Christmas carol: **Noel,** *Obs.*, Christmas. Also, **no-ël'.**

nog-gin (nŏg'ĭn), *n.* **1,** a small cup or mug; **2,** a liquid measure equal to one gill.

noise (noiz), *n.* **1,** sound, esp. when confused or disagreeable; **2,** clamor; outcry; loud discussion:—*v.t.* [*p.t.* and *p.p.* noised (noizd), *p.pr.* nois'ing], to spread by rumor; as, they *noise* their affairs abroad.

Syn., n. sound, clamor, uproar, tumult. *Sound* is the general term for what is or may be heard. A *sound* may be pleasant or unpleasant; a *noise* is discordant. *Clamor, uproar,* and *tumult* all name louder varieties of *noise.*

noise-less (noiz'lĕs), *adj.* silent; making no sound.—*adv.* **noise'less-ly.** —*n.* **noise'less-ness.**

noi-some (noi'sŭm), *adj.* **1,** injurious to health; harmful; as, *noisome* vapors; **2,** offensive; disgusting; as, *noisome* odors.—*adv.* **noi'some-ly.**—*n.* **noi'some-ness.**
Syn. noxious, destructive—*Ant.* healthful.

nois-y (noiz'ĭ), *adj.* [*comp.* nois'i-er, *superl.* nois'i-est], **1,** full of loud, confused, disagreeable sounds; as, a *noisy* city; **2,** making, or given to making, an outcry or uproar; clamorous; as, a *noisy* crowd; **3,** *Colloq.,* conspicuous; showy; as, *noisy* colors.—*adv.* **nois'i-ly.**—*n.* **nois'i-ness.**

nom-ad (nŏm'ăd; nō'măd), *n.* one of an unsettled tribe of people who wander about in search of game, pasture, etc.:—*adj.* wandering; roving.—*adj.* **no-mad'ic.**

no-men-cla-ture (nō'mĕn-klā″tūr), *n.* the collection of words and terms, or the system of naming, used in any art or science, as chemistry or botany.

nom-i-nal (nŏm'ĭ-năl), *adj.* **1,** pertaining to, or consisting of, a name or names; as, a *nominal* list; **2,** existing in name only; as, *nominal* power.—*adv.* **nom'i-nal-ly.**

nom-i-nate (nŏm'ĭ-nāt), *v.t.* [*p.t.* and *p.p.* -nat″ed, *p.pr.* -nat″ing], to propose or name for an office; as, to *nominate* a candidate for election.—*n.* **nom'i-na″tor.**

nom-i-na-tion (nŏm″ĭ-nā'shŭn), *n.* **1,** the act of naming for office; **2,** the state of being named for office.

nom-i-na-tive (nŏm'ĭ-nȧ-tĭv), *adj.* designating, or pertaining to the case of the subject of a finite verb:—*n.* **1,** the case of the subject of a finite verb; the nominative case; **2,** a word in this case.

nom-i-nee (nŏm″ĭ-nē'), *n.* one who is named or proposed for an office or duty; as, the *nominee* for president.

non- (nŏn-), *prefix,* having the general meaning *not;* as, *non*combatant; *non*resident.

non-age (nŏn'āj; nō'nāj), *n.* minority, or the period before one is legally old enough to look after one's own property; usually, the first twenty-one years of life.

non-a-ge-na-ri-an (nŏn″ȧ-jē-nā'rĭ-ăn), *n.* a person of from 90 to 100 years of age:—*adj.* between the ages of 90 and 100 years.

non-a-gon (nŏn'ȧ-gŏn), *n.* in geometry, a plane figure with nine sides and nine angles.

nonce (nŏns), *n.* the present occasion or time; as, this will do for the *nonce.*

non-cha-lance (nŏn'shȧ-lȧns; *Fr.* nôṅ″-shȧ″läṅs'), *n.* lack of interest or enthusiasm; carelessness; indifference. —*adj.* **non'cha-lant.**—*adv.* **non'cha-lant-ly.**

non-com-bat-ant (nŏn-kŏm'băt-ănt; nŏn-kŭm'-), *n.* **1,** one connected with any army or navy whose duties do not include fighting, as a surgeon or nurse; **2,** one not in the army or navy in time of war, as a person physically unfit.

non-com-mis-sioned (nŏn″kŏ-mĭsh'-ŭnd), *adj.* not having a certificate to engage in a service: **noncommissioned officer,** an enlisted man who has risen to the rank of sergeant or corporal.

non-com-mit-tal (nŏn″kŏ-mĭt'ăl), *adj.* not revealing one's opinion or purpose; as, his answer was wholly *noncommittal.*—*adv.* **non″com-mit'tal-ly.**

non-con-duc-tor (nŏn″kŏn-dŭk'tẽr), *n.* any substance through which heat, light, electricity, etc., will not pass readily; an insulator.

non-con-form-i-ty (nŏn″kŏn-fôr'mĭ-tĭ), *n.* failure or refusal to make one's conduct or opinion fit those prevailing generally: used esp. of lack of agreement with established church beliefs or doctrines, orig. those of the Church of England. —*n.* **non″con-form'ist.**

non-co-öp-er-a-tion (nŏn″kō-ŏp″ẽr-ā'-shŭn), *n.* refusal to work with others; esp., the refusal of the followers of M. Gandhi to support the British government in India.

non-de-script (nŏn'dē-skrĭpt), *n.* a person or thing that cannot be easily described or classed:—*adj.* not easily described; odd; of no particular character.

none (nŭn), *pron.* **1,** not any; as, I will have *none* of it; **2,** not one; no one: used as *sing.* or *pl.;* as, *none* of them came: —*adv.* in no respect; not at all.

non-en-ti-ty (nŏn-ĕn'tĭ-tĭ), *n.* [*pl.* nonentities (-tĭz)], **1,** the state of not existing; **2,** a thing not existing; **3,** a person of no importance or influence.

nones (nōnz), *n.pl.* in the Roman calendar, the ninth day before the ides.

non-es-sen-tial (nŏn″ĕ-sĕn'shăl), *adj.* **1,** of little importance; **2,** not necessary to life; as, *nonessential* industries:—*n.* a thing or person of little importance.

none-such (nŭn'sŭch″), *n.* **1,** a person or object that has no equal; a paragon; **2,** a common, annual plant of the pea family, with trailing branches and yellow flowers: also called *black medic.*

non-met-al (nŏn'mĕt″ăl; nŏn-mĕt'ăl), *n.* an element without metallic properties, as sulphur, carbon, oxygen, etc.—*adj.* **non″me-tal'lic.**

non-pa-reil (nŏn″pȧ-rĕl'), *adj.* without an equal; peerless:—*n.* **1,** a person or thing of unequaled excellence; **2,** a finch of the southern U. S.; **3,** a small size of type, equivalent to 6 point (see *type*).

non-plus (nŏn'plŭs), *v.t.* [*p.t.* and *p.p.* -plused or -plussed (-plŭst), *p.pr.* -plus-ing or plus-sing], to throw into complete perplexity; bring to a standstill:—*n.* inability to say or do more.

non-res-i-dent (nŏn-rĕz'ĭ-dĕnt), *n.* **1,** one who does not live in a particular place; **2,** one who does not reside on his own estate, in his proper business location, or the like:—*adj.* **1,** not living in a particular place; **2,** not residing where one's official duties lie.—*n.* **non-res'i-dence.**

non-re-sist-ant (nŏn″rē-zĭs'tănt), *adj.* not opposing attack: —*n.* one who does not believe in using force to defend himself.—*n.* **non″re-sist'ance.**

non-sense (nŏn'sĕns), *n.* **1,** a thing without sense; language without meaning; **2,** *Colloq.,* things of little worth or importance; trifles:—*interj.* absurd.—*adj.* **non-sen'si-cal.**—*adv.* **non-sen'si-cal-ly.**
Syn., n. foolishness, folly, absurdity.

non-stop (nŏn″stŏp'), *adj.* without a stop from start to finish.

non-suit (nŏn'sūt″), *n.* the withdrawal of a suit during trial, either voluntarily or by judgment of the court, on discovery of error or defect in the case:—*v.t.* to dismiss (a case), esp. for lack of evidence.

non-un-ion (nŏn-ūn'yŭn), *adj.* **1,** not belonging to a trade-union; as, to employ *nonunion* laborers; **2,** not favoring trade-unions; as, a *nonunion* factory.—*n.* **non-un'ion-ism.**—*n.* **non-un'ion-ist.**

[1]**noo-dle** (nōō'dl), *n.* *Colloq.,* **1,** a simpleton; dunce; **2,** the head; noddle.

[2]**noo-dle** (nōō'dl), *n.* a narrow strip of dried dough, resembling macaroni in appearance, used chiefly in soups.

nook (no͝ok), *n.* **1**, a small recess or secluded retreat; **2**, a corner, as between walls.

noon (no͞on), *n.* **1**, the middle of the day; twelve o'clock; **2**, height or time of greatest brilliancy or power; as, the *noon* of life:—*adj.* pertaining to midday.

noon-day (no͞on'dā''), *n.* the middle of the day:—*adj.* pertaining to midday.

noon-time (no͞on'tīm''), *n.* noon; midday:—*adj.* pertaining to noon. —*adj.* and *n.* **noon'tide''**.

noose (no͞os), *n.* **1**, a slipknot which binds the closer the more tightly it is drawn; **2**, any snare:—*v.t.* [*p.t.* and *p.p.* noosed (no͞ost), *p.pr.* noos'ing], to catch or tie in a slipknot, as wild horses; insnare.

nor (nôr), *conj.* and not: a negative connective used after the negatives *neither* and *not* to continue or complete their meaning.

no-ri-a (nō'rĭ-ȧ), *n.* a device for raising water, as a wheel and chain carrying buckets, used in various Mediterranean countries and in China.

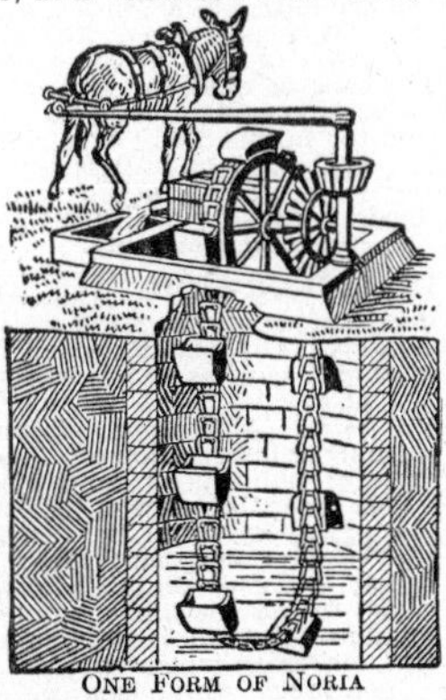

One Form of Noria

norm (nôrm), *n.* a rule or standard; model; pattern; type.

nor-mal (nôr'măl), *adj.* according to rule; perpendicular; regular; natural; serving as a standard or model: **normal school**, **1**, a school for the training of teachers, esp. for elementary schools; **2**, a school in which the methods of instruction are intended to serve as a model of good teaching:—*n.* **1**, the usual or ordinary condition, quantity, etc. **2**, in geometry, a line perpendicular to a given line or surface.—*adv.* **nor'mal-ly.**—*n.* **nor-mal'i-ty.**

Syn., *adj.* usual, ordinary, typical.

nor-mal-cy (nôr'măl-sĭ), *n.* **1**, the state or quality of conforming to the ordinary and established standard, rule, or principle; normality; **2**, the state of business in time of peace and average prosperity.

Nor-man (nôr'măn), *n.* a native or inhabitant of Normandy, in France; **orig.**, a Northman, or Scandinavian:—*adj.* pertaining to Normandy, the Normans, or to a style of architecture introduced into England by the Normans, and marked by massive square towers and rounded arches: **Norman-French**, the French language as spoken by the Normans who settled in England in the 11th century.

Norn (nôrn), *n.* in Norse mythology, any one of the three Fates, who possessed absolute power over the destinies of gods and men; similar to the Greek Fates.

Norse (nôrs), *adj.* pertaining to the country, people, and language of Scandinavia, esp. ancient Scandinavia:—*n.* **1**, the ancient Norse language, spoken in Scandinavia and Iceland: also called *Old Norse; Old Icelandic;* **2**, [*pl.* Norse], a Norseman.

Norse-man (nôrs'măn), *n.* [*pl.* Norsemen (-mĕn)], a Northman; a Scandinavian of ancient times.

north (nôrth), *n.* **1**, one of the four points of the compass; the point opposite to the south, or to the left of a person facing the sunrise; **2**, a section of country lying north of another; as, the *north* of Europe: **North**, that part of the United States lying generally north of the Ohio River and the southern boundary line of Pennsylvania:—*adj.* pertaining to, situated in, or coming from, the north; as, a *north* wind: **north pole**, the northern end of the earth's axis: **North Star**, the star toward which the north pole points:—*adv.* to the north; as, walk *north* one block.

north-east (nôrth''ēst'), *n.* **1**, the point of the compass halfway between north and east; **2**, country lying in the direction of that point:—*adj.* pertaining to, situated in, or coming from, the northeast:—*adv.* toward the northeast.—*adj.* and *adv.* **north''-east'er-ly.**—*adj.* **north''east'ern.**—*adv.* **north''-east'ward.**—*abbr.* **N. E.**

north-east-er (nôrth''ēs'tẽr), *n.* a violent storm from the northeast.

north-er (nôr'*th*ẽr), *n.* a strong, cold wind from the north, esp. such a wind in Texas and the Gulf of Mexico.

north-er-ly (nôr'*th*ẽr-lĭ), *adj.* pertaining to, situated in, or coming from, the north:—*adv.* toward the north.

north-ern (nôr'*th*ẽrn), *adj.* in, from, or toward, the north; as, a *northern* course: **northern lights**, the aurora borealis, or streams of light seen in the sky at night, due probably to electrical discharges in the upper air: best seen in the arctic regions: **Northern**, pertaining to that part of the U. S. north of Mason and Dixon's line: **Northern Hemisphere**, that part of the earth's surface between the equator and the north pole.

north-ern-er (nôr'*th*ẽr-nẽr), *n.* a person living in, or coming from, the north: **Northerner**, a person living in, or coming from, the part of the U. S. north of Mason and Dixon's line: opp. of *Southerner*.

North-man (nôrth'măn), *n.* [*pl.* Northmen (-mĕn)], a Scandinavian of ancient times; a Norseman.

North-um-bri-an (nôr-thŭm'brĭ-ăn), *adj.* pertaining to the ancient kingdom of Northumbria, or to the modern county of Northumberland in England.—*n.* a native or inhabitant of ancient Northumbria, or of the modern county of Northumberland; also, the dialects spoken there.

north-ward (nôrth'wẽrd), *adj.* and *adv.* to or toward the north; leading to the north. Also, *adv.* **north'wards.** —*adj.* and *adv.* **north'ward-ly.**

north-west (nôrth''wĕst'), *n.* **1**, the point of the compass halfway between north and west; **2**, country lying in the direction of that point:—*adj.* pertaining to, situated in, or coming from, the northwest:—*adv.* toward the northwest.—*adj.* and *adv.* **north''west'er-ly.**—*adj.* **north''west'ern.** —*adv.* **north''west'ward.**—*abbr.* **N. W.**

north-west-er (nôrth''wĕs'tẽr), *n.* a strong wind or storm from the northwest.

Nor-we-gian (nôr-wē'jăn, nôr-wē'jĭ-ăn), *n.* a native of Norway; also, its language:—*adj.* pertaining to Norway, its language, or people.

nose (nōz), *n.* **1**, in man or other animals, that part of the face or head containing the nostrils and olfactory nerves; **2**, the organ of smell; **3**, the sense of smell; **4**, anything like a nose, as a spout:—*v.t.* [*p.t.* and *p.p.* nosed (nōzd), *p.pr.* nos'ing], **1**, to smell or scent; **2**, to rub or push with the nose or front; as, horses *nose* each other; the boat *nosed* its way through the jam:—*v.i.* **1**, to smell or scent; **2**, to pry curiously.

nose-band (nōz′bănd″), *n.* on a bridle, the strap which passes over the horse's nose (see *harness*, illus.).

nose-cap (nōz′kăp″), *n.* **1,** a metal cap on a projectile; **2,** a metal cap used to strengthen the extreme forward end of a dirigible: a bow cap.

nose dive a maneuver in which an airplane dives rapidly downward.

nose-gay (nōz′gā″), *n.* a bouquet or bunch of flowers.

nos-ing (nōz′ĭng), *n.* the part of the tread of a step which projects over the riser, or vertical piece (see *step*, illus.).

nos-tal-gi-a (nŏs-tăl′jĭ-*ȧ*), *n.* homesickness; esp., the longing for home which causes acute illness.

nos-tril (nŏs′trĭl), *n.* one of the two external openings in the nose.

nos-trum (nŏs′trŭm), *n.* **1,** a quack medicine; **2,** a pet scheme or remedy for some evil condition.

not (nŏt), *adv.* an adverbial particle expressive of negation, denial, prohibition, or refusal; as, he will *not* go.

no-ta-bil-i-ty (nō″t*ȧ*-bĭl′ĭ-tĭ), *n.* [*pl.* notabilities (-tĭz)], **1,** a person of distinction or importance; **2,** the quality of being important or out of the ordinary.

no-ta-ble (nō′t*ȧ*-bl), *adj.* **1,** worthy of attention; memorable; as, a *notable* event; **2,** notorious; **3,** remarkable; **4,** distinguished; eminent:—*n.* a person or thing of distinction.—*n.* **no′ta-ble-ness.**—*adv.* **no′ta-bly.**

Syn., *adj.* noted, rare, signal, striking.—*Ant.*, *adj.* obscure, usual, ordinary.

no-ta-ri-al (nō-tā′rĭ-ăl), *adj.* pertaining to, or done by, a notary.

no-ta-ry (nō′t*ȧ*-rĭ), *n.* [*pl.* notaries (-rĭz)], an official permitted by law to attest or certify deeds and contracts, administer oaths, etc.: also called *notary public* [*pl.* notaries public].

no-ta-tion (nō-tā′shŭn), *n.* **1,** the act or practice of recording by marks or symbols; **2,** a system of signs or symbols used in place of language, for brevity or clearness; esp., the system of numbers, letters, and signs used in arithmetic and algebra, and the signs used in writing or printing music.

notch (nŏch), *n.* **1,** a small nick or V-shaped cut, as in a stick; **2,** *Colloq.*, a narrow pass through mountains:—*v.t.* **1,** to nick or cut into small hollows; **2,** to tally, record, or keep count of, by nicks.

note (nōt), *n.* **1,** a brief memorandum to assist the memory; **2,** a brief explanatory comment; annotation; as, the *notes* make the text clearer; **3,** a short, informal letter; **4,** a formal official or diplomatic communication; **5,** characteristic quality; as, a *note* of languor in the voice; **6,** reputation; fame; distinction; as, a family of *note;* **7,** observance; heed; attention; as, a matter worthy of *note;* **8,** a cry, song, or call, as of a bird; **9,** in music, a written sign or character representing the pitch and relative length of a tone; also, a single tone itself, as made by a musical instrument or the voice; **10,** a legal paper acknowledging a debt and promising payment; as, a promissory *note;* a bank *note:*—*v.t.* [*p.t.* and *p.p.* not′ed, *p.pr.* not′ing], **1,** to make a memorandum of; **2,** to make mention of; **3,** to observe; notice; as, he *noted* her beauty; **4,** to set down in musical notation.—*n.* **not′er.**

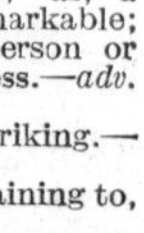

EIGHTH NOTE

a, flag, hook, or pennant; *b*, stem; *c*, head.

note-book (nōt′bo͝ok″), *n.* a book in which memoranda are made; esp., a student's book for lecture notes, etc.

not-ed (nōt′ĕd), *p.adj.* well known; celebrated; as, a *noted* musician.—*adv.* **not′ed-ly.**—*n.* **not′ed-ness.**

Syn. distinguished. (See notorious.)

note-wor-thy (nōt′wûr″thĭ), *adj.* worthy of notice; remarkable.—*adv.* **note′wor″thi-ly.**—*n.* **note′wor″thi-ness.**

noth-ing (nŭth′ĭng), *n.* **1,** not anything; as, I have *nothing* to say; **2,** a thing of no value, use, or importance; as, the story is a mere *nothing;* **3,** a nobody; **4,** in mathematics, absence of magnitude or quantity; a cipher; zero:—*adv.* in no degree; not at all; as, he was *nothing* loath.

noth-ing-ness (nŭth′ĭng-nĕs), *n.* **1,** nonexistence; **2,** worthlessness; unimportance; **3,** a nonentity.

no-tice (nō′tĭs), *n.* **1,** a taking heed; attention; observation; as, to take *notice* of what passes before one; **2,** information; warning; as, he received *notice* to vacate the building; **3,** a printed announcement or sign; as, a *notice* of a death; **4,** press criticism:—*v.t.* [*p.t.* and *p.p.* -ticed (-tĭst), *p.pr.* -tic-ing], **1,** to see or observe; regard; **2,** to make remarks upon; **3,** *Colloq.*, to pay polite attention to; as, she didn't even *notice* me.

no-tice-a-ble (nō′tĭs-*ȧ*-bl), *adj.* **1,** capable of being observed or noticed; **2,** conspicuous; likely to attract attention.—*adv.* **no′tice-a-bly.**

no-ti-fi-ca-tion (nō″tĭ-fĭ-kā′shŭn), *n.* **1,** the act of giving warning or information; **2,** the warning or information given; **3,** the document by which information is sent, as an advertisement.

no-ti-fy (nō′tĭ-fī), *v.t.* [*p.t.* and *p.p.* -fied (-fīd), *p.pr.* -fy″ing], **1,** to give warning or information to; **2,** to make known; declare; publish.—*n.* **no′ti-fi″er.**

Syn. acquaint, inform, advise.

no-tion (nō′shŭn), *n.* **1,** a general mental conception; idea; **2,** a theory or belief; **3,** *Colloq.*, an inclination; as, to have a *notion* to do something; **4,** in *pl.*, *U. S. Colloq.*, small useful articles, such as pins, thread, etc.; also, clever contrivances.

Syn. fancy, whim, caprice.

no-tion-al (nō′shŭn-ăl), *adj.* **1,** pertaining to, or conveying, an idea or fancy; **2,** given to whims or hobbies.

Syn. fanciful, whimsical, capricious, changeable.—*Ant.* steady, constant, practical.

no-to-ri-e-ty (nō″tō-rī′ĕ-tĭ), *n.* [*pl.* notorieties (-tĭz)], **1,** the state of being well known, esp. in an undesirable sense; **2,** one who or that which is well known.

no-to-ri-ous (nō-tō′rĭ-ŭs), *adj.* commonly known: usually in a bad sense; as, a *notorious* criminal.—*adv.* **no-to′ri-ous-ly.**—*n.* **no-to′ri-ous-ness.**

Syn. noted, famous. *Notorious* is used to mean generally known in an unfavorable sense; as, a *notorious* liar. *Noted* means widely known, and is used in both the good and bad senses; as, a *noted* preacher and a *noted* gambler. *Famous* means widely known in a good sense: as, a *famous* doctor.

not-with-stand-ing (nŏt″wĭ*th*-stăn′dĭng), *prep.* in spite of:—*conj.* yet; although:—*adv.* nevertheless, however.

nou-gat (no͞o′găt; no͞o″gȧ′), *n.* [*pl.* nougats (-găts; -gȧ′)], a pasty confection containing almonds and sometimes candied fruits: usually flavored with honey.

nought (nôt), *n.* **1,** a person or thing of no importance; **2,** in arithmetic, zero; a cipher; a naught.

noun (noun), *n.* a word used to name a person or thing; a substantive.

nour-ish (nûr′ĭsh), *v.t.* **1,** to feed (a plant or animal) with the material

necessary to repair waste and promote growth and development; **2**, to foster; as, to *nourish* hatred; **3**, to educate:—*v.i.* to be nutritious; as, good food *nourishes*.—*n.* **nour'ish-ment.**
Syn. nurture, feed, cherish, sustain.

***nou-veau riche** (no͞o″vō'rĕsh'), [Fr.], [*pl.* nouveaux riches (no͞o″vō' rĕsh')], a person who has lately become wealthy: often suggesting vulgarity.

¹nov-el (nŏv'ĕl), *adj.* **1**, modern; unknown formerly; of recent origin or introduction; as, a *novel* plan; **2**, new or unusual.

²nov-el (nŏv'ĕl), *n.* a piece of narrative prose fiction, of considerable length, involving a plot of more or less intricacy, and supposedly presenting a picture true to life.—*n.* **nov'el-ist.**

nov-el-ette (nŏv″ĕl-ĕt'), *n.* a short fictional story, with characters and events representing real life; a short novel.

nov-el-ty (nŏv'ĕl-tĭ), *n.* [*pl.* novelties (-tĭz)], **1**, freshness; newness; as, the *novelty* of an idea or an experience; **2**, something new; a change or innovation; **3**, in *pl.*, new articles, usually of small value.

No-vem-ber (nō-vĕm'bẽr), *n.* the eleventh month of the year, containing thirty days.—*abbr.* **Nov.**

nov-ice (nŏv'ĭs), *n.* **1**, a beginner in any business, profession, or calling; **2**, a monk or nun who has entered a religious house, but has not yet taken the vows.

no-vi-ti-ate (nō-vĭsh'ĭ-ăt), *n.* **1**, the state of being a beginner; **2**, the time during which fitness for any position is being tested; **3**, a novice. Also, **no-vi'ci-ate.**

now (nou), *adv.* **1**, at the present time; as, the danger is *now* over; **2**, a short while ago; quite recently; as, he left just *now;* **3**, immediately; at once; as, I am going *now;* **4**, under the present circumstances; as, *now* what will you do?—*conj.* **1**, since; now that; as, I need not stay, *now* you are here; **2**, used as a mark of transition; as, *now* what do you mean?—*n.* the present moment; as, *now* is the time to do it.

now-a-days (nou'ȧ-dāz″), *adv.* at the present time or age.

no-way (nō'wā″), *adv.* in no manner or degree; not at all. Also, **no'ways″.**

no-where (nō'hwâr″), *adv.* not in, at, or to, any place.

no-wise (nō'wīz″), *adv.* not in any manner or degree; noway.

nox-ious (nŏk'shŭs), *adj.* harmful; injurious; deadly; as, *noxious* gases.—*adv.* **nox'ious-ly.**—*n.* **nox'ious-ness.**
Syn. hurtful, noisome, destructive.

noz-zle (nŏz'l), *n.* **1**, a projecting mouthpiece or spout; as, the *nozzle* of a hose; **2**, an inlet or outlet pipe in a locomotive.

nu (nū; nü), *n.* the 13th letter of the Greek alphabet [ν, N], corresponding in general to the English *n.*

***nu-ance** (nü″äṅs'), [Fr.], *n.* [*pl.* nuances (nü″äṅs')], a delicate shading, as of color, tone, meaning, or expression.

nub-bin (nŭb'ĭn), *n.* *U. S. Colloq.*, an imperfect ear of corn.

nu-cle-ar (nū'klē-ẽr), *adj.* of or pertaining to a nucleus: **nuclear fission**, an atomic disintegration in which a heavy nucleus splits into two nuclei of nearly comparable, medium atomic weights: **nuclear physics**, the branch of physics which deals with the structure of the atom and the behavior of its parts.

nu-cle-ate (nū'klē-āt), *adj.* having a center about which matter gathers:—*v.t.* and *v.i.* (nū'klē-āt), [*p.t.* and *p.p.* -at″ed, *p.pr.* -at″ing], to gather into or around a center, or nucleus.

nu-cle-o-lus (nū-klē'ō-lŭs), *n*, [*pl.* nucleoli (-lī)], in biology, a very small, well-defined body found within the nucleus of most cells.

nu-cle-on-ics (nū″klē-ŏn'ĭks), *n.* the science of the atomic nucleus.

nu-cle-us (nū'klē-ŭs), *n.* [*pl.* nuclei (-klē-ī); nucleuses (-ĕz)], **1**, a kernel; a central part about which matter collects; **2**, anything that serves as the center of growth or development; as, the *nucleus* of a government; **3**, in biology, the central, or denser, mass of protoplasm in a cell, regarded as essential to growth, reproduction, and heredity; **4**, the central, positively charged, portion of an atom.

nude (nūd), *adj.* **1**, bare; naked; **2**, in law, designating a contract that is without consideration and hence, usually, void:—*n.* in art, a naked human figure; also, the state of being undraped.—*adv.* **nude'ly.**—*n.* **nude'ness.**

nudge (nŭj), *v.t.* [*p.t.* and *p.p.* nudged (nŭjd), *p.pr.* nudg'ing], to touch or push gently:—*n.* a gentle touch or poke.

nud-ist (nū'dĭst), *n.* a person, or one of a society, advocating and practicing nudity in the interest of health and morality.

nu-di-ty (nū'dĭ-tĭ), *n.* [*pl.* nudities (-tĭz)], the state of being naked; nakedness; also, a naked part.

nu-ga-to-ry (nū'gȧ-tō-rĭ), *adj.* **1**, trifling; **2**, invalid, as in law.

nug-get (nŭg'ĕt), *n.* a lump of precious metal, as gold, in the natural state.

nui-sance (nū'săns), *n.* anything offensive, injurious, or annoying.

null (nŭl), *adj.* **1**, of no legal force; invalid; as, the law was *null* and void; **2**, of no value; **3**, having no existence.

nul-li-fi-ca-tion (nŭl″ĭ-fĭ-kā'shŭn), *n.* the act of rendering, or the state of being, invalid or void.

nul-li-fy (nŭl'ĭ-fī), *v.t.* [*p.t.* and *p.p.* -fied (-fīd), *p.pr.* -fy″ing], **1**, to deprive of effect or legal force; as, to *nullify* a decision or a law; **2**, to destroy.—*n.* **nul'li-fi″er.**
Syn. invalidate, repeal, quash, cancel.

nul-li-ty (nŭl'ĭ-tĭ), *n.* [*pl.* nullities (-tĭz)], **1**, the state of being without force; insignificance; **2**, that which is null.

numb (nŭm), *adj.* deprived of sensation or motion; torpid; dulled:—*v.t.* to deprive of sensation; benumb, as by cold.—*adv.* **numb'ly.**—*n.* **numb'ness.**

num-ber (nŭm'bẽr), *n.* **1**, a total of units; **2**, the symbol representing this total; **3**, a numeral; as, the *number* following 10 is 11: also called *cardinal number;* **4**, often in *pl.*, a considerable collection; as, *numbers* of people were present; **5**, one of a series; as, the October *number* of a magazine; **6**, in *pl.*, the science of arithmetic; **7**, usually in *pl.*, poetry; verses; **8**, in grammar, the characteristic of a word form whereby it refers either to one or to more than one; also, the state or condition of so referring; as, *man* is in the singular *number;* *men* is in the plural *number:* **Numbers** (*abbr.* **Num.**), the fourth book of the Old Testament:—*v.t.* **1**, to count; **2**, to put a number on; **3**, to amount to; **4**, to include; **5**, to limit the number of.

num-ber-less (nŭm'bẽr-lĕs), *adj.* **1**, having no number; **2**, countless; innumerable; very many.

nu-mer-a-ble (nū'mẽr-ȧ-bl), *adj*, capable of being counted.

nu-mer-al (nū'mẽr-ăl), *adj.* pertaining to, consisting of, or denoting, number:—*n.* **1**, a word expressing a number; **2**, a sign or figure used to express a number.

nu-mer-a-ry (nū'mẽr-ā-rĭ), *adj.* pertaining to numbers; numerical.

nu-mer-ate (nū'mẽr-āt), *v.t.* [*p.t.* and *p.p.* -at″ed, *p.pr.* -at″ing], **1**, to count or number, as by a census; **2**, to point off and read (several figures) as one number.

nu-mer-a-tion (nū″mẽr-ā′shŭn), *n.* **1,** the method, process, or act of counting or numbering; **2,** the act or method of reading numbers.

nu-mer-a-tor (nū′mẽr-ā″tẽr), *n.* **1,** one that counts or numbers; **2,** in fractions, the number above the line, which shows how many of the equal fractional parts of a unit are taken.

nu-mer-i-cal (nū-mĕr′ĭ-kăl), *adj.* **1,** pertaining to numbers; **2,** expressed in numbers; as, a *numerical* equation. —*adv.* **nu-mer′i-cal-ly.**

nu-mer-ous (nū′mẽr-ŭs), *adj.* **1,** consisting of a great number; as, there was a *numerous* crowd; **2,** many; as, there are *numerous* reasons for this.—*adv.* **nu′mer-ous-ly.**—*n.* **nu′mer-ous-ness.**

nu-mis-mat-ic (nū″mĭz-măt′ĭk; nū″-mĭs-), *adj.* pertaining to, or consisting of, coins or medals: **numismatics,** *n. pl.* used as *sing.* the science and study of coins and medals, with reference to history.

nu-mis-ma-tist (nū-mĭz′mȧ-tĭst; nū-mĭs′-), *n.* one who collects and studies coins and medals.

num-skull (nŭm′skŭl″), *n.* a blockhead; dunce; stupid fellow.

nun (nŭn), *n.* **1,** a woman living in a convent and devoted to a religious life under a vow of poverty and obedience to a superior; **2,** a variety of pigeon; **3,** the blue titmouse.

nun-ci-o (nŭn′shĭ-ō), *n.* [*pl.* nuncios (-ōz)], **1,** a permanent ambassador or agent of the Pope, esp. at a foreign court; **2,** *Rare,* any messenger.

nun-ner-y (nŭn′ẽr-ĭ), *n.* [*pl.* nunneries (-ĭz)], a convent for nuns.

nup-tial (nŭp′shăl), *adj.* of or pertaining to marriage:—*n.,* in *pl.,* a marriage; marriage ceremony.

Syn., n. wedding. (See marriage.)

nurse (nûrs), *n.* **1,** one who cares for a young child or children; **2,** one who takes care of the sick or infirm; **3,** one who or that which protects or fosters: **graduate nurse,** a nurse who has been trained and graduated by some institution: **practical nurse,** one who has attained a certain skill in ordinary nursing, through practice, but has not completed a systematic course of instruction: **trained nurse,** a graduate nurse:—*v.t.* [*p.t.* and *p.p.* nursed (nûrst), *p.pr.* nurs′ing], **1,** to suckle or feed (an infant) at the breast; **2,** to rear; bring up; **3,** to care for or wait upon in sickness; **4,** to promote growth or vigor in; develop; **5,** to encourage; cherish; foster, as a grudge:—*v.i.* **1,** to suckle; **2,** to take the breast: said of an infant; **3,** to care for the sick or infirm.—*n.* **nurse′maid″.**

nurs-er-y (nûr′sẽr-ĭ), *n.* [*pl.* nurseries (-ĭz)], **1,** an apartment for young children; **2,** a place or garden for raising young plants; **3,** a trough for rearing young fish.

nurs-er-y-man (nûr′sẽr-ĭ-măn), *n.* [*pl.* nurserymen (-mĕn)], one whose business is the starting and raising of young plants for sale.

nurs-ling (nûrs′lĭng), *n.* **1,** an infant; a child; **2,** anything that is tenderly fostered and protected.

nur-ture (nûr′tūr), *n.* **1,** food; nourishment; **2,** the act or process of feeding or promoting growth; education; training:—*v.t.* [*p.t.* and *p.p.* -tured (-tūrd), *p.pr.* -tur-ing], **1,** to bring up; educate; **2,** to nourish.

nut (nŭt), *n.* **1,** the dry fruit of certain trees, as the oak, hazel, hickory, beech, etc., consisting of a kernel, or seed, inclosed in a hard, woody, or leathery shell; **2,** the kernel itself; **3,** a perforated block, usually of metal, having an internal screw thread, as for securing or adjusting a bolt; **4,** a problem; also, a person or thing hard to deal with or outwit; **5,** in the violin and similar instruments, a piece of ebony or the like, supporting the strings at the upper end of the finger board; **6,** *Slang:* **a,** an insane person; also, a queer or foolish person; **b,** the head.

nut-crack-er (nŭt′krăk″ẽr), *n.* **1,** an implement for cracking nuts; **2,** a bird that feeds on nuts, seeds, etc.

nut-gall (nŭt′gôl″), *n.* a nutlike swelling or excrescence on plants, esp. one on the oak, due to insects or to a parasitic fungus: also called *gall; gallnut.*

nut-hatch (nŭt′hăch″), *n.* any of several small, related birds that creep on tree trunks.

nut-meg (nŭt′mĕg), *n.* the hard, aromatic kernel of the fruit of an East Indian tree: used as spice; also, the tree.

nu-tri-ent (nū′trĭ-ĕnt), *n.* anything, as an article of food, that nourishes or promotes growth:—*adj.* nutritious or promoting growth; nourishing.

nu-tri-ment (nū′trĭ-mĕnt), *n.* that which provides nourishment; food.

nu-tri-tion (nū-trĭsh′ŭn), *n.* **1,** the processes by which an animal or plant uses food to repair wasted tissues and promote growth and development; **2,** that which nourishes; food.—*adj.* **nu-tri′tion-al.**

nu-tri-tious (nū-trĭsh′ŭs), *adj.* promoting growth and repair of the body; nourishing.—*adv.* **nu-tri′tious-ly.**—*n.* **nu-tri′tious-ness.**

nu-tri-tive (nū′trĭ-tĭv), *adj.* **1,** having qualities that nourish and repair; nourishing; **2,** pertaining to the process of growth and repair in the body.—*adv.* **nu′tri-tive-ly.**

nut-ting (nŭt′ĭng), *n.* the act of gathering or searching for nuts.

nut-ty (nŭt′ĭ), *adj.* [*comp.* nut′ti-er, *superl.* nut′ti-est], abounding in, or tasting like, nuts; also, full of flavor.

nux vom-i-ca (nŭks vŏm′ĭ-kȧ), **1,** the seed of an East Indian tree, which yields the deadly poison strychnine; also, the tree; **2,** the medicine made from this seed and used as a stimulant.

nymph (nĭmf), *n.* **1,** in mythology, a lesser goddess of nature, living in the mountains, woods, streams, etc.; **2,** an attractive, handsome young woman.—*adj.* **nymph′al.**

O

O (ō), *interj.* **1,** expressing wonder, fear, pain, etc.: preferably, *oh,* except when not set off by punctuation; as, *O* dear me; *oh,* it's you; **2,** used before an expression of address; as, I will praise thee, *O* God; **3,** used before an imperative verb; as, *O* tarry. Also, **oh.**

o′ (ō; ŏ), *prep. Colloq.* or *Dial.,* of; also, on; as, ten *o′*clock: **O′,** in certain Irish names, indicating noble ancestry; as, *O′*Neill.

oaf (ōf), *n.* **1,** orig., a deformed child said to have been left by fairies in place of a pretty child; a changeling; **2,** a misshapen or foolish child; an idiot.—*adj.* **oaf′ish.**

oak (ōk), *n.* **1,** any of many timber-yielding trees noted for their peculiar fruit, the acorn; **2,** the wood of this tree; **3,** any of several plants resembling the oak in foliage; as, the poison *oak.*

oak ap-ple an abnormal growth on the leaves or young branches of the oak, caused by the sting of certain insects.

oak-en (ōk'n), *adj.* made of, or consisting of, oak or oaks; as, an *oaken* bucket.

oa-kum (ō'kŭm), *n.* loose hemp fiber obtained by untwisting old ropes: used for stopping leaks, calking boats, etc.

oar (ōr), *n.* **1,** a light pole with a broad, flat or spoon-shaped blade at one end, used for rowing or steering a boat; **2,** one who rows a boat:—*v.t.* to row.

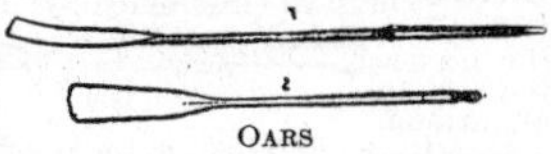

OARS
1, spoon racing oar; 2, flat-bladed oar.

oar-lock (ōr'lŏk″), *n.* a U-shaped ring in which the oar rests in rowing a boat; a rowlock.

oars-man (ōrz'măn), *n.* [*pl.* oarsmen (-mĕn)], one who is skilled in rowing a boat.

o-a-sis (ō-ā'sĭs; ō'ȧ-sĭs), *n.* [*pl.* oases (-sēz)], a fertile place in a barren desert.

oat (ōt), *n.*, a hardy cereal plant; also, usually in *pl.*, its seed, a grain used as food, esp. for horses.

oat-en (ōt'n), *adj.* **1,** made of oats or oatmeal; **2,** made of oat straw.

oath (ōth), *n.* [*pl.* oaths (ōthz)], **1,** a solemn declaration that one speaks the truth, with an appeal to God as witness; **2,** a profane use of the name of God or of any sacred thing.

oat-meal (ōt'mēl″), *n.* **1,** meal made from oats; **2,** porridge or pudding made from the meal.

ob- (ŏb-), *prefix,* [*oc-* before *c; of-* before *f; op-* before *p;* as, *oc*cur, *of*fer, *op*press], occurring in words already compounded in Latin, and indicating: **1,** meeting, contact, or direction; as, *ob*trude; **2,** opposition or hindrance; as, *ob*stacle; **3,** completeness; as, *ob*tain; **4,** reverse direction; as, *ob*ovate.

O-ba-di-ah (ō″bȧ-dī'ȧ), *n.* **1,** in the Bible, a Hebrew minor prophet; **2,** a book of the Old Testament recording his prophecies. Also, in the Douay Bible, **Abdi'as.**—*abbr.* **Obad.**

ob-bli-ga-to (ŏb″blē-gä'tō), *n.* [*pl.* obbligati (-tē)], in music, an accompaniment which is important in itself, and is played by a single instrument.

ob-cor-date (ŏb-kôr'dāt), *adj.* in botany, heart-shaped, as a leaf, with the pointed end at the stem (see *leaf*, illus.).

ob-du-ra-cy (ŏb'dū-rȧ-sĭ; ŏb-dū'rȧ-sĭ), *n.* **1,** extreme hardness of heart; **2,** obstinacy; stubbornness.

ob-du-rate (ŏb'dū-rāt; ŏb-dū'rāt), *adj.* **1,** not to be moved by appeals to the feelings; **2,** hardened in heart or feelings, esp. against moral influence; **3,** obstinate.—*adv.* **ob'du-rate-ly.**

Syn. hard, callous, unfeeling, insensible.—*Ant.* yielding, submissive, obedient.

o-be-di-ence (ō-bē'dĭ-ĕns), *n.* the act or state of yielding willingly to control by others; submission to authority.

o-be-di-ent (ō-bē'dĭ-ĕnt), *adj.* willing to do as one is bidden; submissive to authority; dutifully yielding.—*adv.* **o-be'di-ent-ly.**

Syn. compliant, respectful, docile, tractable.—*Ant.* disobedient, insubordinate.

o-bei-sance (ō-bā'săns; ō-bē'-), *n.* a bow or bend of the knee as an expression of obedience or respect.

ob-e-lisk (ŏb'ē-lĭsk), **1,** *n.* a lofty, four-sided stone pillar shaped at the top like a pyramid (see illus. next column); **2,** a reference mark [†]: also called *dagger* and *obelus.*

ob-e-lus (ŏb'ē-lŭs), *n.* [*pl.* obeli (-lī)], **1,** a mark [— or ÷] used in old manuscripts to indicate a doubtful reading; **2,** in modern books, a mark of reference [†]: usually called *dagger* or *obelisk.*

O-ber-on (ō'bẽr-ŏn; ŏb'ẽr-ŏn), *n.* in medieval folklore, and in Shakespeare's "Midsummer Night's Dream," the king of the fairies and husband of Titania.

OBELISK

o-bese (ō-bēs'), *adj.* very fat; esp., unhealthily fat; corpulent; fleshy; as, an *obese* man.—*n.* **o-bese'ness.**

o-bes-i-ty (ō-bēs'ĭ-tĭ), *n.* excessive fatness, esp. when unhealthy.

o-bey (ō-bā'), *v.t.* **1,** to submit to the rule or authority of; as, to *obey* the commandments; **2,** to comply with the orders or instructions of; as, to *obey* parents; **3,** to respond to direction or control of; as, a horse *obeys* the rein:—*v.i.* to yield; do as bidden.

ob-fus-cate (ŏb-fŭs'kāt), *v.t.* [*p.t.* and *p.p.* -cat-ed, *p.pr.* -cat-ing], to bewilder; perplex; confuse the mind of.

¹o-bi (ō'bĭ), *n.* **1,** orig., a system of secret sorcery; **2,** a charm; fetish.

²o-bi (ō'bĭ), *n.* a kind of wide sash with a large bow behind, worn by the Japanese.

OBI

o-bit-u-a-ry (ō-bĭt'ū-ā-rĭ), *n.* [*pl.* obituaries (-rĭz)], a printed notice of a death; also, a brief account of the life of a person just deceased:—*adj.* pertaining to the death of a person; as, an *obituary* notice.

¹ob-ject (ŏb-jĕkt'), *v.t.* to urge as a reason in opposition to a plan, proposal, etc.:—*v.i.* **1,** to offer opposition: usually with *to;* **2,** to feel or express disapproval; view with disfavor; disapprove.—*n.* **ob-jec'tor.**

²ob-ject (ŏb'jĕkt), *n.* **1,** anything that can be perceived by the senses; **2,** anything presented to the mind; anything perceived or thought of; **3,** a person or thing affected by an action, or arousing feeling; as, an *object* of charity; an *object* of hatred; **4,** a motive; end; aim; **5,** a word, phrase, or clause that receives the action of the verb and completes the predicate; as, in the sentence "he gave me my hat," "hat" is the *direct*, and "me" the *indirect, object:* opp. of *subject:* **object glass,** the lens of a microscope or telescope nearest to the object to be observed and forming the image: also called *objective.*

Syn. intention, purpose, design.

ob-jec-tion (ŏb-jĕk'shŭn), *n.* **1,** a feeling of opposition or of finding fault, or an expression of this feeling; **2,** a reason against anything; opposition.

ob-jec-tion-a-ble (ŏb-jĕk'shŭn-ȧ-bl), *adj.* **1,** liable or open to opposition; **2,** arousing disapproval; undesirable; unpleasant.—*adv.* **ob-jec'tion-a-bly.**—*n.* **ob-jec'tion-a-ble-ness.**

ob-jec-tive (ŏb-jĕk'tĭv), *n.* **1,** the end or goal toward which any action is directed; an aim; **2,** that which exists independently of the mind; an outward fact as opposed to thought and feeling; **3,** in grammar, the case of a word governed by a transitive active verb or a preposition; also, the word so governed; **4,** the lens of a microscope or telescope nearest to the object observed; an object glass (see *microscope*, illus.):—*adj.* **1**, serving as an end or goal of action or feeling; as, the *objective* point of military operations; **2**, belonging to a material thing; being outside of the mind: opp. of *subjective;* **3**, dealing with outward facts and realities rather than with thoughts or feelings; **4**, in grammar, designating the case which follows, and is governed by, a transitive active verb or a preposition.—*adv.* **ob-jec′tive-ly.**—*n.* **ob-jec′tive-ness.**—*n.* **ob″jec-tiv′i-ty.**

ob-jur-gate (ŏb-jûr′gāt; ŏb′jûr-gāt), *v.t.* [*p.t.* and *p.p.* -gat-ed, *p.pr.* -gat-ing], to chide, reprove, censure, or rebuke. —*n.* **ob″jur-ga′tion.**—*adj.* **ob-jur′ga-to-ry.**

ob-late (ŏb′lāt; ŏb-lāt′), *adj.* **1**, depressed or flattened at the poles, as the earth; orange-shaped: opp. of *prolate* (see *prolate*, illus.); **2**, in the Roman Catholic Church, consecrated to sacred purposes or to a religious life or vocation.—*n.* **ob-late′ness.**

ob-la-tion (ŏb-lā′shŭn), *n.* **1**, the act of making an offering or sacrifice to God or to the gods; **2**, anything presented as a religious sacrifice.

ob-li-gate (ŏb′lĭ-gāt), *v.t.* [*p.t.* and *p.p.* -gat″ed, *p.pr.* -gat″ing], to bind legally or morally by contract or treaty, or by a sense of duty or a promise.

ob-li-ga-tion (ŏb″lĭ-gā′shŭn), *n.* **1**, the binding power of a vow, promise, contract, or sense of duty; **2**, any duty imposed by law, by propriety, etc.; **3**, the state of being bound to perform some duty or do something burdensome; **4**, a written deed or bond by which one binds himself under penalty to do a thing; a contract.

ob-li-ga-to-ry (ŏb′lĭ-gȧ-tō-rĭ; ŏb-lĭg′ȧ-tō-rĭ), *adj.* morally or legally binding; imposed by law, duty, etc.: often followed by *on* or *upon.*

o-blige (ō-blīj′), *v.t.* [*p.t.* and *p.p.* o-bliged′ (ō-blījd′), *p.pr.* o-blig′ing], **1**, to compel by force, morally, legally, or physically; **2**, to bind by some favor or kindness; **3**, to render a favor to; gratify.—*n.* **o-blig′er.**

o-blig-ing (ō-blīj′ĭng), *p.adj.* willing to do favors; civil or courteous; kindly; accommodating; as, an *obliging* neighbor.—*adv.* **o-blig′ing-ly.**—*n.* **o-blig′ing-ness.**

ob-lique (ŏb-lēk′; ŏb-līk′), *adj.* **1**, neither horizontal nor vertical; slanting; **2**, not direct or straightforward; evasive; indirect: **oblique angle,** an acute or obtuse angle (see [1]*angle*, illus.): **oblique case,** in grammar, any case other than the nominative or vocative:—*v.i.* [*p.t.* and *p.p.* -liqued′ (-lēkt′; -līkt′), *p.pr.* -li′quing], **1**, to slant; **2**, to march in a slanting direction.—*adv.* **ob-lique′ly.**—*n.* **ob-lique′ness.**

ob-liq-ui-ty (ŏb-lĭk′wĭ-tĭ), *n.* [*pl.* obliquities (-tĭz)], **1**, the quality possessed by lines which are neither parallel nor at right angles; **2**, divergence from a vertical or a horizontal position; **3**, moral error.

ob-lit-er-ate (ŏb-lĭt′ẽr-āt), *v.t.* [*p.t.* and *p.p.* -at″ed, *p.pr.* -at″ing], **1**, to erase or blot out; as, to *obliterate* a mark; **2**, to destroy by the effects of time or exposure. —*n.* **ob-lit″er-a′tion.**

Syn. expunge, cancel, efface. (See erase.)

ob-liv-i-on (ŏb-lĭv′ĭ-ŭn), *n.* the state of being blotted out from memory; forgetfulness.

ob-liv-i-ous (ŏb-lĭv′ĭ-ŭs), *adj.* **1**, lost in thought; **2**, forgetful.—*adv.* **ob-liv′i-ous-ly.**—*n.* **ob-liv′i-ous-ness.**

ob-long (ŏb′lŏng), *adj.* longer than broad; as, an *oblong* box:—*n.* a rectangle longer than it is broad.

ob-lo-quy (ŏb′lō-kwĭ), *n.* [*pl.* obloquies (-kwĭz)], **1**, abusive or contemptuous language spoken to or about a person; reproach; censure; slander; **2**, the state of being in disgrace.

Syn. shame, scandal, dishonor, infamy.—*Ant.* honor, credit, renown, glory.

ob-nox-ious (ŏb-nŏk′shŭs), *adj.* hateful; offensive; unpopular.—*adv.* **ob-nox′ious-ly.**—*n.* **ob-nox′ious-ness.**

Syn. unpleasant, odious, repugnant.

o-boe (ō′boi; ō′bō-ā), *n.* **1**, a wood-wind musical instrument of high, plaintive tone; the hautboy; **2**, an organ stop.

OBOE

ob-o-lus (ŏb′ō-lŭs), *n.* [*pl.* oboli (-lī)], **1**, an ancient Greek coin worth about four cents; also, a weight of ancient Athens equal to one sixth of a drachma; **2**, a small European coin of varying weight.

ob-o-vate (ŏb-ō′vāt), *adj.* having the broad end upward or toward the apex: said of a leaf (see *leaf*, illus.).

ob-scene (ŏb-sēn′), *adj.* offensive to modesty; impure in language or action; indecent; filthy.—*adv.* **ob-scene′ly.** —*n.* **ob-scene′ness.**—*n.* **ob-scen′i-ty.**

ob-scur-ant-ism (ŏb-skūr′ăn-tĭzm), *n.* opposition to the advancement or spreading of knowledge or learning.—*n.* **ob-scur′ant-ist.**

ob-scure (ŏb-skūr′), *adj.* **1**, without clearness or distinctness; as, an *obscure* view; *obscure* objects; **2**, shadowy; dim; dark; as, an *obscure* room; **3**, not easily understood; as, an *obscure* meaning; **4**, illegible; as, faint or *obscure* writing; **5**, remote; unknown; as, he lived in an *obscure* little village; **6**, secluded; humble; as, he occupied an *obscure* position:—*v.t.* [*p.t.* and *p.p.* -scured′ (-skūrd′), *p.pr.* -scur′ing], **1**, to darken or hide from view; as, clouds *obscure* the sun; **2**, to disguise or render less intelligible; as, to *obscure* one's meaning.—*adv.* **ob-scure′ly.**—*n.* **ob-scure′ness.**

Syn., adj. indistinct, vague, hidden.

ob-scu-ri-ty (ŏb-skū′rĭ-tĭ), *n.* [*pl.* obscurities (-tĭz)], **1**, dimness or indistinctness of a place or object; **2**, lack of clearness of thought or expression; **3**, the state or fact of being unknown.

ob-se-quies (ŏb′sē-kwĭz), *n.pl.* funeral rites or ceremonies.

ob-se-qui-ous (ŏb-sē′kwĭ-ŭs), *adj.* meanly submissive to the will of another; servile; fawning.—*adv.* **ob-se′qui-ous-ly.**—*n.* **ob-se′qui-ous-ness.**

ob-serv-a-ble (ŏb-zûr′vȧ-bl), *adj.* **1**, capable of being seen or noticed; **2**, worthy of, or attracting, attention; remarkable; **3**, noticeable; **4**, usual; necessary.—*adv.* **ob-serv′a-bly.**

ob-serv-ance (ŏb-zûr′văns), *n.* **1**, the act of keeping, or of paying attention to, laws or customs; as, the *observance* of the Sabbath; **2**, an act, as a ceremony, performed in token of worship or respect; **3**, occasionally, attention; heed.

ob-serv-ant (ŏb-zûr′vănt), *adj.* **1**, quick to notice; attentive; **2**, watchful; mindful of duties or authority.

ob-ser-va-tion (ŏb″zẽr-vā′shŭn), *n.* **1**, the act, power, or habit of seeing and noting; thorough, careful notice; **2**, that which is noticed or learned; **3**, a remark, judgment, or conclusion based on something noticed: **observation balloon,** a captive balloon, esp. one from which to watch the movements of an enemy (see *kite balloon*, illus.): **observation car,** in the U. S., a railway car arranged so as to give passengers an unobstructed view: **observation post,** in warfare, a position, usually near the front line, for observing the enemy, watching the effect of gunfire, etc.—*adj.* **ob″ser-va′tion-al.**

ob-serv-a-to-ry (ŏb-zûr′vȧ-tō-rĭ); *n.* [*pl.* observatories (-rĭz)], **1**, a building fitted up with telescopes, etc., for studying the heavens; **2**, a tower or other high place built to give an extensive view.

ob-serve (ŏb-zûrv′), *v.t.* [*p.t.* and *p.p.* -served′ (-zûrvd′), *p.pr.* -serv′-ing], **1**, to take notice of; **2**, to watch closely; **3**, to keep or celebrate; **4**, to remark; **5**, to comply with; as, to *observe* the social conventions:—*v.i.* **1**, to take notice; **2**, to comment.—*n.* **ob-serv′er.**

Syn. commemorate. (See celebrate.)

ob-serv-ing (ŏb-zûrv′ĭng), *p.adj.* attentive.—*adv.* **ob-serv′ing-ly.**

ob-sess (ŏb-sĕs′), *v.t.* to beset or rule; as, the idea *obsessed* him.

ob-ses-sion (ŏb-sĕsh′ŭn), *n.* **1**, the state of being ruled by one idea; **2**, a fixed idea not to be driven from one's mind.

ob-sid-i-an (ŏb-sĭd′ĭ-ăn), *n.* a kind of dark, glassy, volcanic rock.

ob-so-les-cent (ŏb″sō-lĕs′ĕnt), *adj.* passing out of use; as, an *obsolescent* word.—*n.* **ob″so-les′cence.**

ob-so-lete (ŏb′sō-lēt), *adj.* **1**, gone out of use; as, *obsolete* firearms; no longer practiced or accepted; as, an *obsolete* custom; **2**, old.—*n.* **ob′so-lete-ness.**

Syn. antique, ancient, antiquated.—*Ant.* new, modern, recent.

ob-sta-cle (ŏb′stȧ-kl), *n.* that which hinders or stands in the way; an obstruction; impediment; a hindrance.

ob-stet-ric (ŏb-stĕt′rĭk), *adj.* pertaining to childbirth or to the medical treatment of it. Also, **ob-stet′ri-cal.**

ob-ste-tri-cian (ŏb″stē-trĭsh′ăn), *n.* a physician skilled in the branch of medical science relating to, or concerned with, childbirth.

ob-stet-rics (ŏb-stĕt′rĭks), *n.pl.* used as *sing.* **1**, the branch of medical science relating to childbirth or to the management and medical treatment of pregnancy and labor; **2**, midwifery.

ob-sti-na-cy (ŏb′stĭ-nȧ-sĭ), *n.* [*pl.* obstinacies (-sĭz)], **1**, stubborn and unreasonable determination to have one's own way; stubbornness; **2**, unyielding resistance to remedy; as, the *obstinacy* of a fever.

ob-sti-nate (ŏb′stĭ-nāt), *adj.* **1**, not yielding to argument, persuasion, or entreaty; headstrong; adhering to one's opinion or purpose; stubborn; **2**, not yielding to treatment, as a disease.—*adv.* **ob′sti-nate-ly.**

Syn. headstrong, stubborn. *Obstinate* is used of one who holds to his own opinions in spite of appeals, reason, and persuasion. *Headstrong* is applied to one who is violent and impetuous in pursuing his purpose. *Stubborn* implies an unyielding or a refractory quality in things or persons; it suggests an innate characteristic, whereas to be *obstinate* is usually a matter of the will.

ob-strep-er-ous (ŏb-strĕp′ẽr-ŭs), *adj.* clamorous; noisy; turbulent; as, an *obstreperous* person.—*adv.* **ob-strep′er-ous-ly.**—*n.* **ob-strep′er-ous-ness.**

ob-struct (ŏb-strŭkt′), *v.t.* **1**, to block up or close so as to prevent passage; as, a great pile of stones *obstructs* the road; **2**, to impede, or prevent from progress; as, to *obstruct* work; to *obstruct* travel; **3**, to be in the way of, or cut off from, sight; as, to *obstruct* the light; to *obstruct* the view.—*n.* **ob-struct′er; ob-struc′tor.**

Syn. bar, check, retard, hinder. (See prevent.)—*Ant.* help, promote, further.

ob-struc-tion (ŏb-strŭk′shŭn), *n.* anything that stops, closes, or bars the way; that which prevents progress or hinders; an obstacle or barrier.

ob-struc-tion-ist (ŏb-strŭk′shŭn-ĭst), *n.* one who hinders progress; esp., a member of a legislative body who uses its rules to hinder legislation.

ob-struc-tive (ŏb-strŭk′tĭv), *adj.* serving or tending to stop or to hinder progress.—*adv.* **ob-struc′tive-ly.**

ob-tain (ŏb-tān′), *v.t.* to get possession of; gain; acquire; as, to *obtain* knowledge:—*v.i.* to be established in practice or use; prevail or be in fashion; as, widely different customs *obtain* in different countries.—*adj.* **ob-tain′a-ble.**—*n.* **ob-tain′ment.**

Syn. achieve, secure, earn, attain.

ob-trude (ŏb-trōōd′), *v.t.* [*p.t.* and *p.p.* -trud′ed, *p.pr.* -trud′ing], **1**, to thrust into a place boldly or thoughtlessly; **2**, to urge or offer with unreasonable persistence:—*v.i.* to force oneself upon others; intrude.—*n.* **ob-trud′er.**

ob-tru-sive (ŏb-trōō′sĭv), *adj.* inclined to push oneself into undue prominence; intrusive.—*adv.* **ob-tru′sive-ly.**—*n.* **ob-tru′sive-ness.**—*n.* **ob-tru′sion.**

ob-tuse (ŏb-tūs′), *adj.* **1**, not pointed or acute; as, an *obtuse* angle (see also *angle*, illus.); **2**, dull; stupid; as, an *obtuse* person.—*adv.* **ob-tuse′ly.**—*n.* **ob-tuse′ness.**

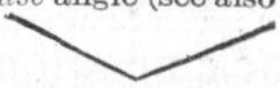

Obtuse Angle

ob-verse (ŏb′vûrs), *n.* the front surface of anything; the side of a coin or medal having the principal design upon it: opp. of *reverse:*—*adj.* **1**, (ŏb-vûrs′; ŏb′vûrs), facing the observer; **2**, narrower at the base than at the top: said of a leaf.—*adv.* **ob-verse′ly.**

ob-vi-ate (ŏb′vĭ-āt), *v.t.* [*p.t.* and *p.p.* -at″ed, *p.pr.* -at″ing], to remove, or clear away beforehand, as difficulties or objections.—*n.* **ob″vi-a′tion.**

ob-vi-ous (ŏb′vĭ-ŭs), *adj.* easily understood or seen; evident; plain; as, the effect is *obvious.*—*adv.* **ob′vi-ous-ly.**—*n.* **ob′vi-ous-ness.**

Syn. apparent, clear, manifest.

oc-a-ri-na (ŏk″ȧ-rē′nȧ), *n.* a small musical instrument, giving soft, pleasing sounds: usually made of terra cotta, with a mouthpiece and finger holes.

Ocarina

oc-ca-sion (ŏ-kā′zhŭn), *n.* **1**, a particular event or celebration; as, it was an unusual *occasion;* **2**, occurrence; as, on the *occasion* of her last visit; **3**, a state or position of affairs leading to unexpected results; incidental cause; as, his carelessness was the *occasion* of the whole trouble; **4**, need; as, having *occasion* to buy food; **5**, chance or opportunity; as, he seized the *occasion* to speak his mind; **6**, justification; reason; as, no *occasion* for anger:—*v.t.* to cause; give rise to.

Syn., n. necessity, exigency. (See cause.)

oc-ca-sion-al (ŏ-kā′zhŭn-ăl), *adj.* **1**, incidental or casual; as, *occasional* remarks; **2**, happening now and then, but not regularly; as, an *occasional* visit; **3**, referring to some especial happening; as, an *occasional* poem.—*adv.* **oc-ca′sion-al-ly.**

oc-ci-dent (ŏk′sĭ-dĕnt), *n.* the west: opp. of *orient* or *east:* **Occident,** the countries west of Asia and the former Turkish dominions: now applied to western Europe and the Western Hemisphere: opp. of *Orient.*

oc-ci-den-tal (ŏk″sĭ-dĕn′tăl), *adj.* pertaining to the west: opp. of *oriental:* **Occidental,** of or pertaining to the Occident, or countries west of Asia:—*n.* a native of a western region or country: **Occidental,** a native of the Occident.

oc-cip-i-tal (ŏk-sĭp′ĭ-tăl), *adj.* designating, or pertaining to, the lower back bone of the skull (see *skull*, illus.):—*n.* the occipital bone, or occiput.

oc-ci-put (ŏk′sĭ-pŭt), *n.* the back part of the skull or head.

oc-clude (ŏ-klōōd′), *v.t.* [*p.t.* and *p.p.* -clud′ed, *p.pr.* -clud′ing], **1**, to absorb: used in chemistry of certain metals which absorb gases; **2**, to shut up or out; close, as pores.—*n.* **oc-clu′sion.**

oc-cult (ŏ-kŭlt′), *adj.* **1**, hidden; concealed; secret; invisible; **2**, hence, supernatural.—*adv.* **oc-cult′ly.**

oc-cul-ta-tion (ŏk″ŭl-tā′shŭn), *n.* a concealment; esp., a hiding from view of one heavenly body by another, as an eclipse of a planet or star by the moon.

oc-cult-ism (ŏ-kŭl′tĭzm), *n.* a belief in, or an inquiring into, the mysterious or supernatural; also, doctrines or practices based on such belief.

oc-cu-pan-cy (ŏk′ū-păn-sĭ), *n.* **1**, the act of dwelling in, or holding in possession, a house or the like; **2**, the time during which anything, as a house, is occupied.

oc-cu-pant (ŏk′ū-pănt), *n.* one who dwells in, has possession of, or holds in use, a house, property, etc.

oc-cu-pa-tion (ŏk″ū-pā′shŭn), *n.* **1**, the act of holding in possession, or of dwelling in something; **2**, the time during which a property or position is held; **3**, one's regular business, employment, or calling; **4**, the state of being busy.

oc-cu-py (ŏk′ū-pī), *v.t.* [*p.t.* and *p.p.* -pied (-pīd), *p.pr.* -py″ing], **1**, to take possession of; **2**, to dwell in; as, to *occupy* a room; **3**, to fill or cover the time or space of; as, studies *occupy* her day; the building *occupies* a block; **4**, to employ; busy; as, to *occupy* oneself with work.—*n.* **oc′cu-pi″er.**

oc-cur (ŏ-kûr′), *v.i.* [*p.t.* and *p.p.* -curred′ (-kûrd′), *p.pr.* -cur′ring], **1**, to happen or take place; as, the same mistake must not *occur* again; **2**, to be found; exist; as, such plants *occur* in Africa; **3**, to come to the mind; as, did it *occur* to you to go?

oc-cur-rence (ŏ-kŭr′ĕns), *n.* a happening; event; incident.

o-cean (ō′shăn), *n.* **1**, the vast body of salt water covering more than three fifths of the globe, and averaging about 13,000 feet in depth; also, any one of its five chief divisions; as, the Atlantic *Ocean;* **2**, usually in *pl.*, an immense expanse or amount; as, *oceans* of time.

o-ce-an-ic (ō″shē-ăn′ĭk), *adj.* of or pertaining to the ocean.

o-ce-lot (ō′sē-lŏt), *n.* a leopardlike cat, yellowish or reddish gray with markings of black, found in both North and South America.

OCELOT (1/30)

o-cher (ō′kẽr), *n.* any of several earthy varieties of iron ore used as pigments; as, yellow *ocher.* Also, **o′chre** (-kẽr).—*adj.* **o′cher-ous; o′chre-ous** (ō′kẽr-ŭs).

o′-clock (ō-klŏk′), *adv.* contraction for *of the clock*, or according to the clock.

oc-ta- (ŏk′tȧ-), *prefix*, eight; as, *octa*gon; *octa*hedron. Also, **oct-; oc′ti-; oc′to-.**

oc-ta-gon (ŏk′tȧ-gŏn), *n.* a plane figure of eight sides and eight angles.—*adj.* **oc-tag′o-nal.**

OCTAGON Inscribed in a circle.

oc-ta-he-dron (ŏk″tȧ-hē′drŏn), *n.* [*pl* octahedrons (-drŏnz); octahedra (-drȧ)], a solid figure having eight plane faces (see *solid*, illus.).—*adj.* **oc″ta-he′dral.**

oc-tane (ŏk′tān), *n.* one of the substances composing gasoline, very volatile, and hence used as a standard in rating gasoline.

oc-tan-gu-lar (ŏk-tăng′gū-lȧr), *adj.* having eight angles; octagonal.

oc-tave (ŏk′tāv), *n.* **1**, in music: **a**, an interval of twelve half steps, as from C in the scale to the C next above or below; **b**, the series of tones in a scale in such an interval; **c**, the eighth note in a diatonic scale; **2**, the eighth day after a church festival, the day of the festival itself being counted as first:—*adj.* consisting of eight.

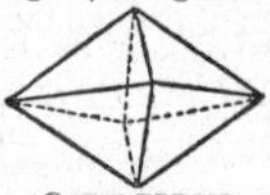

OCTAHEDRON

oc-ta-vo (ŏk-tā′vō; ŏk-tä′-), *n.* [*pl.* octavos (-vōz)], **1**, in printing, a sheet of paper folded three times, making eight leaves or sixteen pages; **2**, a book made of such sheets:—*adj.* **1**, folded to make eight leaves to the sheet: said of paper; **2**, made of sheets so folded: said of a book.—*abbr.* **8vo.**

oc-tet (ŏk-tĕt′), *n.* **1**, a musical composition with eight parts for voices or instruments; **2**, the performers of such a composition.

oc-til-lion (ŏk-tĭl′yŭn), *n.* in French and American numeration, the number one followed by 27 ciphers; in English numeration, one followed by 48 ciphers.

Oc-to-ber (ŏk-tō′bẽr), *n.* the tenth month of the year.—*abbr.* **Oct.**

oc-to-ge-na-ri-an (ŏk″tō-jē-nā′rĭ-ăn), *n.* one who is between 80 and 90 years old:—*adj.* between 80 and 90 years old; also, 80 years old.—*adj.* **oc-tog′e-na-ry** (ŏk-tŏj′ē-nă-rĭ).

oc-to-pus (ŏk′tō-pŭs; ŏk-tō′pŭs), *n.* [*pl.* octopuses (-ĕz); octopi (-pī)], **1**, any of a genus of sea mollusks related to the cuttlefishes, having eight arms provided with suckers; **2**, hence, any organization with many branches, reaching out to do injury.

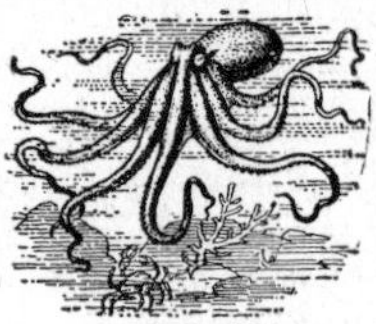

OCTOPUS (1/30)

oc-to-roon (ŏk″tō-rōōn′), *n.* a person who by descent is seven-eighths white and one-eighth Negro; the child of a white person and a quadroon, or a person who is one-fourth Negro.

oc-tu-ple (ŏk′tū-pl), *adj.* eightfold; consisting of eight parts:—*n.* the product of multiplying by eight:—*v.t.* [*p.t.* and *p.p.* -pled (-pld), *p.pr.* -pling], to multiply by eight:—*v.i.* to become eightfold.

oc-u-lar (ŏk′ū-lȧr), *adj.* **1**, pertaining to the eye or to eyesight; **2**, depending on, or seen by, the eye; visual.

oc-u-list (ŏk′ū-lĭst), *n.* one who is skilled in the treatment of eye diseases.

o-da-lisque (ō′dȧ-lĭsk), *n.* a woman slave in a harem. Also, **o′da-lisk.**

odd (ŏd), *adj.* **1**, not paired or matched with another; as, an *odd* glove; **2**, not even; not exactly divisible by two; as, seven is an *odd* number; **3**, left over after equal division; extra; as, you may have the *odd* one; **4**, unusual; as, an *odd* occurrence; **5**, eccentric; as, an *odd* person; **6**, occasional; as, *odd* jobs; **7**, not occupied; as, *odd* moments: **50 odd, 500 odd,** between 50 and 60, or between 500 and 600.—*adv.* **odd′ly.**—*n.* **odd′ness.**

Syn. strange, grotesque, fantastic. (See queer.)—*Ant.* ordinary, usual, normal.

odd-i-ty (ŏd'ĭ-tĭ), *n.* [*pl.* oddities (-tĭz)], **1,** a person, thing, or quality, that is peculiar; **2,** strangeness; eccentricity.

odd-pin-nate (ŏd'-pĭn'āt), *adj.* of leaves, having leaflets on each side of a midrib and a single leaflet at the end of the midrib (see *leaf,* illus.).

odds (ŏdz), *n.pl.* **1,** inequality; **2,** advantage; superiority; excess in favor of one as compared with another; as, the *odds* are in her favor; **3,** probability; **4,** a more than even wager; as, the *odds* on a certain horse; **5,** disagreement; quarrel; as, to be at *odds* with a person: **odds and ends,** remnants.

ode (ōd), *n.* a short poem expressing noble sentiments in a dignified style.

O-din (ō'dĭn), *n.* in Norse mythology, the chief of the gods: identified with the German *Woden.*

o-di-ous (ō'dĭ-ŭs), *adj.* deserving of, or calling forth, hatred or abhorrence; offensive; unpopular; as, his conduct was *odious.*—*adv.* **o'di-ous-ly.**—*n.* **o'di-ous-ness.**

Syn. detestable, disagreeable, hateful.

o-di-um (ō'dĭ-ŭm), *n.* **1,** hatred; abhorrence; **2,** blame; reproach attached to a person or action; discredit.

o-dom-e-ter (ō-dŏm'ē-tẽr), *n.* an instrument attached to the wheel of a vehicle for measuring the distance traveled.

o-dor (ō'dẽr), *n.* **1,** a scent; smell, whether pleasant or offensive; **2,** estimation or repute; as, to be in bad *odor.* Also, **o'dour.**

o-dor-if-er-ous (ō"dẽr-ĭf'ẽr-ŭs), *adj.* diffusing or giving out fragrance; as, *odoriferous* spices.

Syn. fragrant, aromatic, odorous.

o-dor-less (ō'dẽr-lĕs), *adj.* without smell, whether pleasant or offensive.

o-dor-ous (ō'dẽr-ŭs), *adj.* giving out an odor or scent; fragrant.—*adv.* **o'dor-ous-ly.**—*n.* **o'dor-ous-ness.**

Syn. fragrant, aromatic. *Odorous* describes anything that sends out a scent, and may mean a pleasant or a disagreeable odor. *Fragrant* is used of that which is sweet-scented; as, *fragrant* roses. *Aromatic* means spicy and pungent, as coffee, pine trees, or cinnamon.

O-dys-seus (ō-dĭs'ūs; ō-dĭs'ē-ŭs), *n.* in Greek mythology, a famous king of Ithaca, the wisest, shrewdest, and most eloquent of the Greek chiefs who fought against Troy, and hero of Homer's "Odyssey": called by the Romans *Ulysses.*

Od-ys-sey (ŏd'ĭ-sĭ), *n.* **1,** a Greek epic poem, attributed to Homer, describing the ten years' wanderings of Odysseus from Troy to Ithaca; **2,** any long and adventurous journey.

œc-u-men-i-cal (ĕk"ū-mĕn'ĭ-kăl), *adj.* pertaining to the entire inhabited world, or to the entire Christian church. Also, **œc"u-men'ic.** See **ec"u-men'i-cal,** *Pfd S.*

Œd-i-pus (ĕd'ĭ-pŭs; ē'dĭp-ŭs), *n.* in mythology, the unfortunate son of Laius and Jocasta of Thebes in Greece, who unwittingly fulfilled the prophecy of an oracle at his birth by killing his father and marrying his mother: famous as the solver of the riddle of the Sphinx.

o'er (ōr), *prep.* and *adv.* over; as, *o'er* hill and dale: used chiefly in poetry.

œ-soph-a-gus (ē-sŏf'ȧ-gŭs), *n.* the tube that leads from the pharynx to the stomach; the gullet. Also, **e-soph'a-gus,** *Pfd. S.*

of (ŏv; unaccented, ŏv), *prep.* **1,** from: denoting removal, origin, etc.; as, to cure *of* a fever; born *of* a line of kings; **2,** out of; as a result of; as, he did it *of* necessity; **3,** about; concerning; as, talk *of* success; news *of* a victory; **4,** in; as, quick *of* speech; **5,** belonging or related to, or connected with; as, the palace *of* the king; **6,** containing, having, consisting of, etc.; as, a glass *of* milk; a man *of* brains; **7,** on: during: now used only in the phrases *of late, of old,* etc.

off (ôf), *adj.* **1,** most distant; on the farther side; hence, right, since the regular position of a driver, esp. on foot, is on the left; as, the *off* horse of a team: opp. of *near;* **2,** unlucky; unfit; as, this is an *off* day for him:—*adv.* [often used in the predicate like an *adj.;* as, turn the gas *off;* it is *off*], **1,** away, so as not to be on, against, near, etc.; as, take *off* your hat; he stood afar *off;* hence, started; as, the runners are *off;* **2,** wrong; mistaken; as, he is *off* in his estimate; **3,** given up; abandoned; as, all arrangements are *off;* **4,** out of order; not functioning; as, the electricity is *off;* **5,** provided for; conditioned, esp. in health or wealth; as, well *off:* **off and on,** intermittently:—*prep.* **1,** not on; away from; as, the cover is *off* my book; take the bowl *off* the shelf; **2,** *Colloq.,* not in condition for; as, *off* one's feed; **3,** distant from; as, a mile *off* shore: **off side,** in advance of the line or play; specif., in football, in the position of a player when the ball has last been touched by one of his own side behind him:—*interj.* begone! away!

of-fal (ŏf'ăl), *n.* **1,** refuse or garbage; **2,** waste meat; as, the *offal* of a butchered animal; **3,** anything thrown away as worthless.

off-cast (ôf'kȧst"), *adj.* thrown aside; cast off:—*n.* anyone or anything thrown aside or cast off.

off-col-or (ôf'-kŭl"ẽr), *adj.* **1,** not of a natural or satisfactory color; as, the jewel is *off-color;* **2,** *Colloq.,* slightly improper or indecent; as, an *off-color* remark.

of-fend (ŏ-fĕnd'), *v.t.* to displease or make angry; vex or annoy:—*v.i.* **1,** to transgress; sin; as, to *offend* against the law, **2,** to do anything displeasing; as, in what way have I *offended?*—*n.* **of-fend'er.**

of-fense (ŏ-fĕns'), *n.* **1,** a sin, wrong, crime, or misdemeanor; **2,** the act of offering an injury or affront, or the state of being injured, affronted, or displeased; **3,** an attack or assault. Also, **of-fence'.**—*adj.* **of-fense'less.**

Syn. affront, misdeed, transgression, trespass.

of-fen-sive (ŏ-fĕn'sĭv), *adj.* **1,** causing displeasure; annoying; as, *offensive* actions; **2,** disagreeable; as, an *offensive* odor; **3,** used in attack; as, *offensive* weapons:—*n.* an aggressive method or attitude.—*adv.* **of-fen'sive-ly.**—*n.* **of-fen'sive-ness.**

Syn., adj. obnoxious, insolent hateful.—*Ant., adj.* pleasing, agreeable, inoffensive.

of-fer (ŏf'ẽr), *n.* **1,** a proposal; **2,** a price bid; proffer; **3,** an attempt or endeavor; as, to make an *offer* of resistance:—*v.t.* **1,** to present for acceptance or refusal; as, to *offer* money; **2,** proffer; as, to *offer* help or advice; **3,** to propose; as, to *offer* a plan; **4,** to present in worship or sacrifice; as, to *offer* a prayer; **5,** to bid as a price; as, how much am I *offered?* **6,** to attempt to make or give; as, to *offer* resistance:—*v.i.* to present itself; appear; arise; as, a favorable opportunity soon *offered.*—*n.* **of'fer-er.**

Syn., v. extend, tender. (See give.)

of-fer-ing (ŏf'ẽr-ĭng), *n.* **1,** the act of making a proffer or proposal; **2,** that which is proffered or given; a gift; a sacrifice.

of-fer-to-ry (ŏf'ẽr-tō-rĭ), *n.* [*pl.* offertories (-rĭz)], **1,** that part of the Mass or church service at which the money offering is made; **2,** a vocal or organ selection rendered at this time; **3,** the money offering made at this time.

off-hand (ôf'hănd"), *adj.* **1,** done without preparation; as, an *offhand* speech; **2**, informal; as, an *offhand* manner:—*adv.* (ôf″hănd′), without preparation.

of-fice (ôf′ĭs), *n.* **1**, a position of trust or authority; as, the *office* of President; **2**, a function; as, the *office* of the ears is to hear; **3**, a religious ceremony or rite; as, the *office* of marriage; **4**, a duty or service; as, an *office* of kindness; **5**, a place for the transaction of business; as, a doctor's *office;* an express *office;* **6**, in *pl.*, in England, the part of a house where servants perform their duties.

of-fi-cer (ôf′ĭ-sẽr), *n.* one authorized to do a given public duty, or the administrative duties of an organization:—*v.t.* **1**, to furnish with officers; **2**, to command.

of-fi-cial (ō-fĭsh′ăl), *n.* one who holds a public position; also, one authorized to perform duties of trust or administration:—*adj.* **1**, pertaining to an office or public duty; **2**, derived from the proper authority; authorized; authoritative.—*adv.* **of-fi′cial-ly.** —*n.* **of-fi′cial-dom.**

of-fi-cial-ism (ō-fĭsh′ăl-ĭzm), *n.* government by established system; also, close observance of routine.

of-fi-ci-ate (ō-fĭsh′ĭ-āt), *v.i.* [*p.t.* and *p.p.* -at″ed, *p.pr.* -at″ing], **1**, to perform the duties of a divine service; **2**, to act in a public service or duty.

of-fic-i-nal (ō-fĭs′ĭ-năl; ŏf″ĭ-sī′năl), *adj.* kept on hand by apothecaries:—*n.* any herb or drug ready for sale.

of-fi-cious (ō-fĭsh′ŭs), *adj.* too bold in offering services; meddling.—*adv.* **of-fi′cious-ly.**—*n.* **of-fi′cious-ness.**
Syn. intrusive, obtrusive, meddlesome.

off-ing (ôf′ĭng), *n.* the open sea, visible from shore but beyond the anchoring ground.

off-ish (ôf′ĭsh), *adj.* reserved; inclined to hold oneself aloof.

off-scour-ing (ôf′skour″ĭng), *n.*, usually in *pl.*, refuse or cast-off filth.

off-set (ôf′sĕt″), *n.* **1**, that which develops from, or is set off from, something; **2**, a young shoot or branch that takes root at the tip; **3**, a spur or branch from a chain of mountains; **4**, a sharp curve, as in a pipe, to avoid an obstacle; **5**, anything set off as an equivalent or a compensation for something else; **6**, in surveying, a perpendicular let fall from the main line to an outlying point; **7**, in printing, an ink stain, transferred from a freshly printed surface to the back of the next sheet; **8**, in architecture, a ledge on the face of a wall, made by the difference in thickness of two parts of the wall:—*v.t.* (ôf″sĕt′; ôf′sĕt″), [*p.t.* and *p.p.* -set′, *p.pr.* -set′ting], **1**, to balance; compensate for; **2**, to terrace:—*v.i.* **1**, to form an offset; **2**, in printing, to transfer a stain.

off-shoot (ôf′shōōt″), *n.* a branch of a family, race, stem, etc.; a scion.

off-shore (ôf′shōr″), *adj.* **1**, moving toward the sea; **2**, pertaining to the sea at a distance, usually of three miles or more, from the shore:—*adv.* (ôf″shōr′), away from, or at some distance from, the shore.

off-spring (ôf′sprĭng″), *n.* **1**, a child or children; **2**, a descendant or descendants; issue; **3**, result; outcome.

of-ten (ôf′n), *adv.* many times; frequently. Also, *Poetic*, **oft.**

of-ten-times (ôf′n-tīmz″), *adv.* often. Also, *Poetic*, **oft′times″.**

o-gle (ō′gl), *v.t.* [*p.t.* and *p.p.* o′gled (-gld), *p.pr.* o′gling], to look at with admiring or too familiar glances:—*n.* an admiring or too familiar look; a side glance.

o-gre (ō′gẽr), *n.* **1**, an imaginary man-eating monster; **2**, a cruel or hideous person.—*n.fem.* **o′gress.**—*adj.* **o′gre-ish; o′grish.**

oh (ō), *interj.* **1**, an exclamation of wonder, sorrow, shame, pain, or anxiety; **2**, (preferably, *O*), a word used in earnest address, as in prayer:—*n.* [*pl.* oh's; ohs (ōz)], an exclamation of wonder, sorrow, shame, etc.; as, full of *oh's.* Also, **O.**

ohm (ōm), *n.* a unit of measurement in electrical science, used in calculating the resistance of a circuit.

-oid (-oid), *suffix*, denoting like, in the form of, or resembling.

oil (oil), *n.* **1**, a greasy or unctuous liquid, insoluble in water, but generally soluble in alcohol or ether, inflammable and burning with a luminous, smoky flame, including: *essential oils*, obtained from various leaves, fruits, flowers, etc., and used in flavoring extracts, perfumes, etc.; as, *oil* of clove; *mineral oils*, esp. *petroleum*, or *rock oil*, derived from natural mineral deposits in rock strata, and used for fuel, and for the production of gasoline, kerosene, lubricating oils, paraffin, etc.; and *fixed* or *fatty oils*, derived from animal or vegetable substances, greasy, and used with caustic alkalies in making soap; **2**, any substance of a mobile, unctuous character; as, *oil* of vitriol; **3**, in art: **a**, a pigment mixed for use with oil: called *oil color* or *oil paint;* **b**, a picture painted with this material; **c**, in *pl.*, oil colors used in painting: **oil of vitriol**, sulphuric acid: the commercial name:—*v.t.* **1**, to lubricate with oil; **2**, to anoint.

oil cake a mass of compressed seeds or vegetable substance remaining after oil has been extracted: often fed to cattle.

oil-cloth (oil′klŏth″), *n.* coarse cloth coated with oil or oil paint, used for covering floors, shelves, tables, etc.

O-ï-leus (ō-ī′lūs), *n.* king of Locris, one of the Argonauts.

oil-skin (oil′-skĭn″), *n.* **1**, cloth made waterproof by having been treated with oil; **2**, in *pl.*, waterproof clothing made of such cloth.

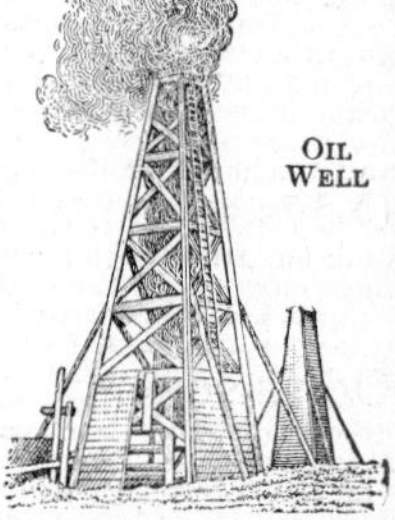

OIL WELL

oil-stone (oil′stōn″), *n.* a fine-grained stone, moistened with oil, used as a whetstone for sharpening edged tools, as knives.

oil well a well for petroleum, made by boring into rock, and from which the crude oil is pumped.

oil-y (oil′ĭ), *adj.* [*comp.* oil′i-er, *superl.* oil′i-est], **1**, containing, or like, oil; greasy; **2**, smooth in speech or manner; smooth-tongued; fawning; as, *oily* remarks; an *oily* tongue.—*adv.* **oil′i-ly.**—*n.* **oil′i-ness.**

oint-ment (oint′mĕnt), *n.* a fatty preparation of about the consistency of butter, having medicinal qualities, and applied to wounds or injured parts.

O-jib-wa (ō-jĭb′wā), *n.* one of a tribe of American Indians, formerly living near Lake Superior. Also, **O-jib′way.**

O. K. *abbr. Colloq.*, correct or in order; approved:—*v.t.* [*p.t.* and *p.p.* O. K'd, *p.pr.* O. K'ing], to mark as O. K. Also, **OK;** *Rare*, **o″kay′; o′keh″.**

o-ka-pi (ō-kä′pē), *n.* a giraffelike mammal of central Africa (see illus. next page).

o-kie (ō′kĭ), *n.* in the southwestern United States, an itinerant harvest worker.

o-kra (ō′krȧ; ŏk′rȧ), *n.* a West Indian plant, the pods of which are used as vegetables, in soups, and in a dish called *gumbo.*

-ol (-ōl; -ŏl), *suffix*, **1**, a termination denoting an oil or an oil derivative; as, benz*ol;* **2**, a termination denoting an alcohol or a phenol; as, methan*ol*.

OKAPI ($\frac{1}{60}$)

old (ōld), *adj.* [*comp.* old'er or eld'er, *superl.* old'est or eld'-est], **1**, having existed or lived many years; aged; as, an *old* oak; an *old* man; **2**, having an appearance of age; as, an *old* face; **3**, having reached a certain age; as, twenty-one years *old;* **4**, decayed by time; as, an *old* ruin; ancient; **5**, out of date; as, *old* customs; *old* coins; **6**, long used; not new; as, *old* shoes; **7**, long practiced; as, *old* habits; **8**, belonging to the past; as, one's *old* home; **9**, *Colloq.*, familiar and dear; as, *Old* Glory; **10**, long experienced; as, he is an *old* hand at that work:—*n.* former times; as, in days of *old*.—*n.* **old'ness.**

Syn., *adj.* antique, antiquated, venerable.

Old (ōld), *adj.* ancient: used specif. of various languages in the earliest stage of their development preserved to us: **Old English,** the language spoken in England from the 5th to the 12th centuries, by the Anglo-Saxons: also called *Anglo-Saxon:* **Old French,** the language spoken in France from about 900 to about 1600: **Old High German,** the language spoken in southern Germany from 750 to 1150: the forerunner of modern literary German: **Old Icelandic,** Old Norse (which see): **Old Low German,** the language spoken in northern Germany and the Netherlands from 750 to 1150: also called *Old Saxon:* **Old Norse,** the language of Norway, Denmark, and Iceland from about 700 to 1300: also called *Old Icelandic:* **Old Saxon,** Old Low German (which see).

old-en (ōl'dn), *adj.* ancient; bygone; as, in *olden* times.

old–fash-ioned (ōld''=făsh'ŭnd), **1**, *adj.* having or adhering to old ideas or customs; as, an *old-fashioned* person; **2**, having the feelings or tastes of an older person; as, an *old-fashioned* child; **3**, out of style; as, an *old-fashioned* coat.

Syn. quaint, obsolete.—*Ant.* modern, new.

Old Glo-ry the flag of the United States: a familiar term of affection.

old maid **1**, a middle-aged or elderly unmarried woman; **2**, a precise, crotchety person; **3**, a certain game of cards.

old-ster (ōld'stẽr), *n.* **1**, *Colloq.*, one who is no longer a youngster; **2**, a British midshipman of four years' service.

Old Style the old mode of reckoning time according to the Julian calendar.

Old Tes-ta-ment the first of the two main divisions of the canonical books of the Bible.

old–world (ōld'=wûrld''), *adj.* **1**, of or pertaining to ancient times; **2**, (usually, *Old World*), pertaining to the Eastern Hemisphere.

o-le-ag-i-nous (ō''lē-ăj'ĭ-nŭs), *adj.* **1**, having greasy qualities; oily; **2**, sleek or smooth in appearance, voice, or manner; fawning.—*n.* **o''le-ag'i-nous-ness.**

o-le-an-der (ō''lē-ăn'dẽr), *n.* an evergreen shrub with handsome, fragrant, red or white flowers, every part of the plant being poisonous.

o-le-as-ter (ō''lē-ăs'tẽr), *n.* **1**, a shrub of southern Europe, with yellow flowers and a bitter, olivelike fruit; **2**, the true wild olive; a wild variety of the olive.

o-le-o-mar-ga-rine (ō''lē-ō-mär'gȧ-rēn; -rĭn; *Colloq.* ō''lē-ō-mär'jẽr-ēn), *n.* a waxy, solid fat, extracted from animal fats and used for butter: also called *oleo* (ō'lē-ō). Also, **o''le-o-mar'ga-rin.**

o-le-o-res-in (ō''lē-ō-rĕz'ĭn), *n.* **1**, a natural mixture of resins and volatile essential oils: usually called *balsam;* **2**, a liquid extract made up of an essential oil holding resin in solution.

ol-fac-to-ry (ŏl-făk'tō-rĭ), *adj.* pertaining to, or used in, smelling; as, an *olfactory* nerve:—*n.*, usually in *pl.*, [*pl.* olfactories (-rĭz)], the organ or sense of smell.

ol-i-garch (ŏl'ĭ-gärk), *n.* one of the rulers in a government that is controlled by a few persons.

ol-i-gar-chy (ŏl'ĭ-gär''kĭ), *n.* [*pl.* oligarchies (-kĭz)], **1**, government in which the supreme power is in the hands of a few; **2**, a state so governed; **3**, the few who rule.—*adj.* **ol''i-gar'chic; ol''i-gar'chi-cal.**

ol-ive (ŏl'ĭv), *n.* **1**, any of a genus (*Olea*) of trees and shrubs; esp., an Old World evergreen tree cultivated for its oily fruit; **2**, the fruit of this tree; **3**, a dull brownish or yellowish green color; **4**, an olive branch:—*adj.* **1**, pertaining to, or like, the olive; **2**, of a dull brownish or yellowish green color; **3**, tawny: said of the complexion: **olive branch,** a branch of the olive tree, considered as the emblem of peace.

Ol-i-ver (ŏl'ĭ-vẽr), *n.* one of the knights of Charlemagne's court, celebrated in legend as the friend of Roland.

ol-iv-ine (ŏl'ĭ-vĭn; ŏl'ĭ-vēn), *n.* a transparent or translucent olive-green variety of chrysolite.

ol-o-gy (ŏl'ō-jĭ), *n.* [*pl.* ologies (-jĭz)], *Humorous,* a branch of learning.

-ol-o-gy (-ŏl'ō-jĭ), *n. suffix,* a science or branch of learning; as, ge*ology*.

O-lym-pi-ad (ō-lĭm'pĭ-ăd), *n.* in ancient Greece, the period of four years between two celebrations of the Olympic games: a standard used to reckon time from the first Olympiad, which began 776 B. C.

O-lym-pic (ō-lĭm'pĭk), *adj.* **1**, pertaining to Olympia in Elis, Greece, where games were celebrated every four years in honor of Zeus; **2**, in mythology, pertaining to Mount Olympus, in Thessaly, the home of the gods: **Olympic games, 1**, the athletic games and races of ancient Greece, celebrated every four years in honor of the god Zeus; **2**, a modern revival of these games, first held at Athens in 1896.

O-lym-pus (ō-lĭm'pŭs), *n.* the mountain in Thessaly where the gods of the ancient Greeks were supposed to dwell; hence, the sky; heaven.—*adj.* **O-lym'pi-an.**

O-ma-ha (ō'mȧ-hô''), *n.* a member of a tribe of American Indians, formerly living in what is now Nebraska.

o-me-ga (ō-mē'gȧ; ō'mĕ-gȧ; ō-mĕg'ȧ), *n.* **1**, the last letter of the Greek alphabet [ω, Ω], equivalent to the English long *o;* **2**, hence, the last; end.

om-e-let (ŏm'ĕ-lĕt; ŏm'lĕt), *n.* eggs and milk, with, sometimes, other ingredients, beaten together and browned in a pan. Also, **om'e-lette.**

o-men (ō'mĕn), *n.* a prophetic sign of some future event; augury:—*v.t.* to foretell by signs; predict.

o-men-tum (ō-mĕn'tŭm), *n.* [*pl.* omenta (-tȧ)], a free fold of the peritoneum or membrane that lines the abdominal cavity, connecting the stomach with the spleen, large intestine, and liver.

o-mer (ō'mẽr), *n.* in the Bible, a Hebrew dry measure, one tenth of an ephah, or rather more than a bushel (Exodus 16:36).

om-i-cron (ŏm′ĭ-krŏn; ō-mī′krŏn; ŏm″ĭ-krŏn′), *n.* the 15th letter of the Greek alphabet [*o*, O], corresponding in general to the English short *o*.

om-i-nous (ŏm′ĭ-nŭs), *adj.* foreboding evil; threatening.—*adv.* **om′i-nous-ly.**—*n.* **om′i-nous-ness.**

o-mis-sion (ō-mĭsh′ŭn), *n.* **1,** neglect or failure to do something required; **2,** something left out.

o-mit (ō-mĭt′), *v.t.* [*p.t.* and p.p. o-mit′ted, *p.pr.* o-mit′ting], **1,** to leave out; as, to *omit* the address; **2,** to neglect, as a task.

om-ni-bus (ŏm′nĭ-bŭs), *n.* a large four-wheeled public vehicle for passenger traffic over a fixed route:—*adj.* including many different subjects or cases; as, in lawmaking, an *omnibus* bill.

om-ni-graph (ŏm′nĭ-grȧf), *n.* an instrument designed for teaching telegraphy: a trade name.

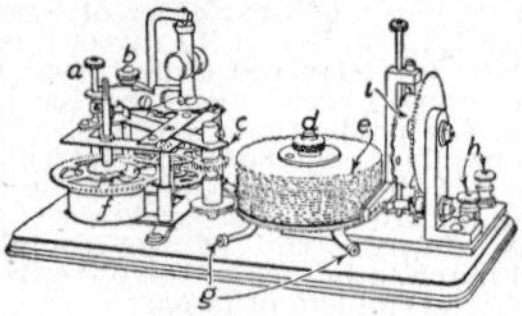

OMNIGRAPH

a, screw for adjusting speed; *b*, lever to start or stop spring motor; *c*, lever to disconnect motor from transmitter; *d*, thumbscrew for changing dial, *e*; *f*, spring; *g*, message changers; *h*, binding posts; *i*, dial changing wheel.

om-nip-o-tence (ŏm-nĭp′ō-tĕns), *n.* unlimited power: **Omnipotence,** God, the all-powerful.

om-nip-o-tent (ŏm-nĭp′ō-tĕnt), *adj.* having unlimited power; as, the *omnipotent* God: **the Omnipotent,** God, the all-powerful.—*adv.* **om-nip′o-tent-ly.**

om-ni-pres-ence (ŏm″nĭ-prĕz′ĕns), *n.* universal presence, or the quality of being present everywhere at once; as, the *omnipresence* of God.

om-ni-pres-ent (ŏm″nĭ-prĕz′ĕnt), *adj.* present everywhere at the same time: used esp. of God.

om-nis-cience (ŏm-nĭsh′ĕns), *n.* unlimited knowledge: **Omniscience,** God, the all-knowing.

om-nis-cient (ŏm-nĭsh′ĕnt), *adj.* knowing all; infinitely wise; as, the *omniscient* God.—*adv.* **om-nis′cient-ly.**

om-niv-o-rous (ŏm-nĭv′ō-rŭs), *adj.* **1,** feeding upon both animal and vegetable food; as, *omnivorous* animals; **2,** all-devouring; as, an *omnivorous* reader.—*adv.* **om-niv′o-rous-ly.**—*n.* **om-niv′o-rous-ness.**

on (ŏn), *prep.* **1,** upon; supported by; as, to sit *on* a chair; **2,** in contact with the upper surface of; as, we live *on* the earth; **3,** covering; as, shoes *on* one's feet; **4,** along or by; as, Paris is *on* the Seine; **5,** in the act or state of; as, *on* a journey; *on* fire; **6,** toward; as, he looked *on* her as his guide; have pity *on* the needy; **7,** forming part of; as, *on* the committee; **8,** showing the relation of following after; as, they are *on* his trail; **9,** in the direction of; as, the door opens *on* a lawn; **10,** about; concerning; as, an address *on* peace; **11,** at the time of; as, *on* June first; **12,** against or hanging from; as, a picture *on* the wall; **13,** denoting cause or basis; as, *on* purpose; to go *on* business; *on* my honor; **14,** denoting the instrument of an action; as, to play *on* the harp; **15,** upon the event of; as, she saw him *on* his arrival:—*adv.* **1,** forward; as, to go *on*; **2,** in or into a position to cover, support, etc.; as, put *on* your coat; **3,** in or into action or use; as, to turn *on* the gas; **4,** in progress; as, a fight is *on*.

once (wŭns), *adv.* **1,** at one time; formerly; as, *once* upon a time; this was *once* my home; **2,** one time only; as, read it over *once*; **3,** at any time; ever; as, if *once* they lose heart, their cause will be lost:—*n.* one time: **at once, 1,** together; as, all talk *at once*; **2,** immediately; as, do it *at once*.

one (wŭn), *adj.* **1,** composed of a single unit, being, or object; individual; **2,** a certain; as, *one* Henry; **3,** single in number; united; as, they answered with *one* voice; **4,** the same: **one day,** on an unspecified day in the past or future; sometime:—*n.* [*pl.* ones (wŭnz)], **1,** the first number used in counting by units; also, its symbol, as 1 or i; **2,** a single person or thing:—*pron.* a certain person or thing considered indefinitely; anybody; as, *one* must live: **one another,** each one the other: used as a reciprocal pronoun referring to more than two.—*n.* **one′ness.**

O-nei-da (ō-nī′dȧ), *n.* one of a tribe of American Indians, orig. inhabiting what is now central New York.

on-er-ous (ŏn′ẽr-ŭs), *adj.* burdensome; weighty; as, an *onerous* duty.—*adv.* **on′er-ous-ly.**—*n.* **on′er-ous-ness.**
Syn. arduous, difficult, oppressive.

one-self (wŭn″sĕlf′), *pron.* an emphatic and reflexive form of the indefinite pronoun *one*; one's self.

one–sid-ed (wŭn′=sīd″ĕd), *adj.* **1,** having, or appearing on, only one side; **2,** giving more prominence or greater development to one side; **3,** hence, uneven; partial; unfair; **4,** having leaves on only one side of the stem.—*adv.* **one″–sid′ed-ly.**

one–step (wŭn′=stĕp″), *n.* a modern dance of quick movement, in two-four time.

on-ion (ŭn′yŭn), *n.* **1,** a plant of the lily family, having a strong-smelling edible bulb; **2,** the bulb of the plant.

on-ly (ōn′lĭ), *adj.* **1,** sole; single; as, the *only* man there; **2,** one and no more;—*adv.* **1,** singly; **2,** merely:—*conj.* except; but: often with *that*.

on-o-mat-o-pœ-ia (ŏn″ō-măt″ō-pē′yȧ; ō-nŏm″ȧ-tō-pē′yȧ), *n.* **1,** the formation or use of words in imitation of natural sounds, as *rumble, hiss, buzz, murmur*; **2,** a word so formed.

On-on-da-ga (ŏn″ŏn-dä′gȧ), *n.* a member of a tribe of North American Indians, formerly living in what is now New York and Ontario.

on-rush (ŏn′rŭsh″), *n.* an onset; a rushing on; an assault.

on-set (ŏn′sĕt″), *n.* an assault; attack; as, the *onset* was furious.

on-slaught (ŏn′slôt″), *n.* a furious attack or assault.

on-to (ŏn′tōō), *prep.* upon the top of: usually considered a colloquialism.

on-tol-o-gy (ŏn-tŏl′ō-jĭ), *n.* that branch of metaphysics dealing with the nature and characteristics of being; the philosophical analysis of reality or existence.—*adj.* **on″to-log′i-cal.**—*n.* **on-tol′o-gist.**

o-nus (ō′nŭs), *n.* a burden; duty; obligation; responsibility.

on-ward (ŏn′wẽrd), *adj.* advancing; forward; as, the *onward* march of troops:—*adv.* toward the desired end; forward; as, to move *onward*. Also, *adv.* **on′wards.**

on-yx (ŏn′ĭks; ō′nĭks), *n.* a kind of quartz consisting of layers of various colors, such as brown, black, red, white.

o-ö- (ō′ō-), *prefix*, a combining form from the Greek, meaning egg; as, *oölogy*.

o-ö-lite (ō′ō-līt), *n.* a granular form of limestone resembling fish roe.

o-öl-o-gy (ō-ŏl′ō-jĭ), *n.* that branch of ornithology that treats of birds' eggs.—*adj.* **o″ö-log′i-cal.**

oo-mi-ak (o͞o′mĭ-ăk), *n.* an Eskimo open boat, driven by paddles, and made of skins drawn over a framework of wood. Also, **u′mi-ak.**

OOMIAK

[1]**ooze** (o͞oz), *n.* **1,** soft, slimy mud; **2,** a bog or marsh; **3,** a soft material, largely composed of the chalky shells of minute marine animals, occurring in great deposits on the ocean floor, esp. in its deeper parts.

[2]**ooze** (o͞oz), *n.* **1,** a gentle or imperceptible flow, as of a stream through sedges or sweat from pores; **2,** a tanning infusion made of oak bark, sumac, etc.:—*adj.* tanned by forced permeation with ooze and finished on the flesh side, as certain pliant leathers with a fine-grain, velvety surface; as, *ooze* calf:—*v.i.* [*p.t.* and *p.p.* oozed (o͞ozd), *p.pr.* ooz′ing], **1,** to flow gently; exude; **2,** to leak out gradually, as news:—*v.t.* to discharge or give out slowly.—*adj.* **oo′zy.**

o-pac-i-ty (ō-păs′ĭ-tĭ), *n.* **1,** the quality of not allowing light to pass through; opaqueness; **2,** cloudiness; darkness.

o-pal (ō′păl), *n.* a precious stone, translucent and lustrous, showing a play of various and delicate colors.

o-pal-es-cent (ō″păl-ĕs′ĕnt), *adj.* showing a play of delicate colors, like an opal.—*n.* **o″pal-es′cence.**

o-pal-ine (ō′păl-ĭn; ō′păl-īn), *adj.* having a play of delicate colors; iridescent, as the wings of certain insects.

o-paque (ō-pāk′), *adj.* **1,** not allowing light to pass through; dark; not transparent; **2,** having no luster or brightness: said of some colors:—*n.* that which will not allow light to pass.—*adv.* **o-paque′ly.**—*n.* **o-paque′ness.**

ope (ōp), *v.t.* [*p.t.* and *p.p.* oped (ōpt), *p.pr.* op′ing], *Poetic*, to open:—*adj.* open.

o-pen (ō′pn), *adj.* **1,** not shut; unclosed; **2,** unsealed or unstopped, as a letter or a bottle; **3,** uncovered or exposed; as, an *open* boat; **4,** not obstructed; as, a river *open* to navigation; **5,** clear of trees; as, *open* country; **6,** unfilled; unoccupied; disengaged; as, the position is still *open;* **7,** undecided; as, an *open* question; **8,** not settled or balanced; as, the account was left *open* for final receipts; **9,** not surrounded by walls, shores, etc.; as, the *open* sea; **10,** not frozen; free from ice and snow; as, an *open* winter; **11,** unfolded or spread out; as, an *open* newspaper; **12,** not hidden; in plain view; as, an *open* scandal; *open* lawlessness; unreserved; as, an *open* criticism; **13,** public; free for all; as, an *open* meeting; *open* competition; **14,** ready to hear or to receive suggestion; as, an *open* mind; **15,** generous; as, to give with an *open* hand; **16,** frank; sincere; as, an *open* countenance; **17,** having spaces, gaps, or holes, as certain needlework; **18,** at sea, not foggy or misty; **19,** of vowel and consonant sounds, uttered with relatively unclosed position of the speaking parts specially concerned: opp. of *close;* as, the vowel sound of *see* is close, of *saw* is *open;* *p* is close, *f* is *open;* **20,** of syllables, not ending with a consonant, as in *go, ba-by:* opp. of *close,* as in *gaunt-let:*—*v.t.* **1,** to unclose or unlock, as a window or door; **2,** to spread out, as a fan; **3,** to break the seal of or untie, as an envelope or package; **4,** to remove obstructions from; as, to *open* a road; **5,** to begin; as, to *open* the discussion; **6,** to put into operation; as, to *open* a store; **7,** to reveal; expose; as, to *open* one's mind to a friend; **8,** to pierce or make a hole in; **9,** to offer for settlement, use, etc.; as, to *open* undeveloped land; **10,** *Archaic,* to give light or knowledge to; as, he *opened* their understanding:—*v.i.* **1,** to unclose itself; **2,** to commence; **3,** to lead; give; as, the door *opens* into the hall; **4,** to expand; develop; **5,** to become more clearly visible:—*n.* any wide space, clear of trees, buildings, etc.; outdoors: with *the.*—*adv.* **o′pen-ly.**—*n.* **o′pen-ness.**—*n.* **o′pen-er.**

Syn., adj. frank, candid, artless. *Open* denotes plain, straightforward, and aboveboard; as, an *open* countenance; an *open* nature. *Frank* and *candid* imply sincere and impartial, true, and perhaps a little blunt; as, a *frank* reply; a *candid* criticism. *Artless* means naïve and guileless; as, an *artless* child.

o-pen-hand-ed (ō′pn=hănd″ĕd), *adj.* generous; liberal.

o-pen-heart-ed (ō′pn=härt″ĕd), *adj.* frank; sincere; candid.

o-pen-ing (ō′pn-ĭng; ōp′nĭng), *n.* **1,** an aperture, or a hole; as, an *opening* in a fence; **2,** a space in a woods where there are few trees and little undergrowth; **3,** the first steps; beginning; as, the *opening* of a trial; **4,** an opportunity or a chance:—*adj.* first in order.

o-pen ses-a-me an unfailing means of entrance or access: from the magic words which opened the robbers' cave in the story of Ali Baba.

o-pen shop a shop or factory that employs both union and nonunion labor: opp. of *closed shop,* which employs one kind only, usually union labor.

o-pen-work (ō′pn-wûrk″), *n.* carving, metal work, embroidery, etc., so made that it shows open spaces.

op-er-a (ŏp′ẽr-*ȧ*), *n.* **1,** a drama, with scenery, costumes, and acting, in which music is the most conspicuous feature, and with an orchestral accompaniment; esp., grand opera; **2,** the score of such a drama; **3,** the representation of such a drama; also, the theater in which it is performed: **grand opera,** a serious opera, usually ending tragically, the entire text of which is sung: **comic opera,** a light opera with catchy music and an amusing, farcical plot with a happy ending, with or without spoken parts: distinguished from *musical comedy.*

op-er-a glass a small telescope made for both eyes and used in the theater, etc.: also called *opera glasses.*

op-er-ate (ŏp′ẽr-āt), *v.i.* [*p.t.* and *p.p.* -at″ed, *p.pr.* -at″ing], **1,** to work; act; **2,** to produce a certain effect; **3,** to perform a surgical action upon the body:—*v.t.* **1,** to cause to perform certain work; as, to *operate* a machine; **2,** to manage; direct; conduct; as, to *operate* a coal mine.

op-er-at-ic (ŏp″ẽr-ăt′ĭk), *adj.* pertaining to, suitable for, or like, opera.

op-er-a-tion (ŏp″ẽr-ā′shŭn), *n.* **1,** the act or way of working; **2,** regular action; as, the machine is in *operation;* **3,** an agency; as, by *operation* of the law of gravitation, the building fell; **4,** a surgical treatment upon the living body, usually understood to involve the cutting of tissues; **5,** a series of movements of an army or fleet; as, a naval *operation;* **6,** in mathematics, the process of producing a change in the form or value of a quantity.

op-er-a-tive (ŏp′ẽr-ā-tĭv), *adj.* **1,** having the power of acting; **2,** having effect; as, an *operative* law; **3,** vigorous; efficient; **4,** concerned with physical work, either with the hands or with machinery; as, an *operative* art:—*n.* an artisan or skilled workman; as, an *operative* in a spinning mill.

op-er-a-tor (ŏp′ẽr-ā″tẽr), *n.* **1**, one who or that which works or acts; **2**, one who is employed in a telephone exchange to make connections between lines; **3**, one who runs a machine, as in a factory; **4**, a broker, or one who acts for others; as, a coal *operator;* **5**, a surgeon.

op-er-et-ta (ŏp″ẽr-ĕt′*ȧ*), *n.* a short musical drama, usually of a light and humorous character.

oph-thal-mi-a (ŏf-thăl′mĭ-*ȧ*), *n.* inflammation of the eye.

oph-thal-mic (ŏf-thăl′mĭk), *adj.* **1**, pertaining to the eye; ocular; **2**, afflicted with ophthalmia.

oph-thal-mol-o-gy (ŏf″thăl-mŏl′ō-jĭ), *n.* that branch of medical science which treats of the functions, structure, and diseases of the eye.

oph-thal-mo-scope (ŏf-thăl′mō-skōp), *n.* an instrument for examining the inside of the eye.

o-pi-ate (ō′pĭ-āt), *n.* **1**, a medicine containing, or made from, opium, that causes sleep, as laudanum; **2**, anything that soothes:—*adj.* soothing; inducing sleep or quiet.

o-pine (ō-pīn′), *v.t.* [*p.t.* and *p.p.* -pined′ (-pīnd′), *p.pr.* -pin′ing], to think; suppose; as, I *opine* that this is the case:—*v.i.* to conjecture; guess.

o-pin-ion (ō-pĭn′yŭn), *n.* **1**, belief; what one thinks about any subject; as, that is my *opinion;* **2**, usually in *pl.*, a judgment formed after careful consideration; **3**, the statement of the law bearing upon a case; as, an *opinion* handed down by a judge; **4**, estimation; as, I have a good *opinion* of him.
Syn. notion, view, idea, sentiment.

o-pin-ion-at-ed (ō-pĭn′yŭn-āt″ĕd), *adj.* firm or obstinate in one's ideas or beliefs; stubborn.

o-pi-um (ō′pĭ-ŭm), *n.* a powerful sleep-producing drug obtained from a certain species of poppy.

o-pos-sum (ō-pŏs′ŭm), *n.* a small American animal which, if captured or in danger, pretends to be dead: **to play 'possum**, to feign unconsciousness.

OPOSSUM (1/18)

op-po-nent (ŏ-pō′nĕnt), *n.* one who takes or supports the opposite side, as in argument or debate:—*adj.* **1**, acting in opposition; **2**, opposite.
Syn., *n.* adversary, antagonist. (See enemy.)

op-por-tune (ŏp″ŏr-tūn′; ŏp′ŏr-tūn), *adj.* well-timed; seasonable; convenient; suitable.—*adv.* **op″por-tune′ly.**—*n.* **op″por-tune′ness.**

op-por-tu-nism (ŏp″ŏr-tū′nĭzm), *n.* **1**, quickness to grasp favorable chances; **2**, a taking advantage of circumstances to gain one's ends regardless of consequences or principles, esp. in politics.

op-por-tu-nist (ŏp″ŏr-tū′nĭst), *n.* **1**, one who takes advantage of circumstances to promote or push forward his own interest or the political interests of his party; **2**, one who waits for a suitable time before trying to act upon his beliefs; **3**, one who alters his principles to suit an occasion.

op-por-tu-ni-ty (ŏp″ŏr-tū′nĭ-tĭ), *n.* [*pl.* opportunities (-tĭz)], **1**, convenient time or occasion; **2**, chance; **3**, a favorable opening, as in business.

op-pos-a-ble (ŏ-pōz′*ȧ*-bl), *adj.* **1**, capable of being resisted; **2**, capable of being placed in front of, or over against, something else; as, the thumb is *opposable* to the fingers of the hand.

op-pose (ŏ-pōz′), *v.t.* [*p.t.* and *p.p.* -posed′ (-pōzd′), *p.pr.* -pos′ing], **1**, to speak or act against; **2**, to resist; **3**, to set up as an obstacle.—*n.* **op-pos′er.**
Syn. withstand, thwart, obstruct, prevent.
—*Ant.* further, promote, foster, advance.

op-po-site (ŏp′ō-zĭt), *adj.* **1**, placed or standing in front of or over against; as, the *opposite* side of the street; the houses were *opposite* to each other; **2**, contrary; as, in an *opposite* direction; **3**, antagonistic; very different; as, *opposite* opinions:—*n.* that which is contrary or in marked contrast.—*abbr.* **opp.**—*adv.* **op′po-site-ly.**—*n.* **op′po-site-ness.**
Syn., *adj.* contrary, contradictory. *Opposite* is used of things diametrically different; as, *opposite* sides of the street; *opposite* poles of a magnet. *Contrary* indicates a difference in the nature of anything, and is used to suggest conflict; as, I had *contrary* feelings when I read the news. *Contradictory* implies a condition of direct opposition; as, *contradictory* accounts of an event.

op-po-si-tion (ŏp″ō-zĭsh′ŭn), *n.* **1**, the act of resisting or checking; **2**, the state of being resisted or checked; **3**, the relation of two heavenly bodies to each other when their longitudes differ by 180 degrees; **4**, the political party that does not support the party in power: with *the.*

op-po-si-tion-ist (ŏp″ō-zĭsh′ŭn-ĭst), *n.* a member of the political party that does not support an administration or government.

op-press (ŏ-prĕs′), *v.t.* **1**, to burden· crush by hardships or severity; as, to *oppress* the poor; **2**, to weigh heavily upon; as, anxiety and care *oppressed* him; **3**, to tyrannize over.—*n.* **op-pres′sor.**

op-pres-sion (ŏ-prĕsh′ŭn), *n.* **1**, the act of burdening; **2**, the state of being burdened; hardship; **3**, injustice; **4**, weariness; listlessness.

op-pres-sive (ŏ-prĕs′ĭv), *adj.* **1**, unreasonably burdensome; as, *oppressive* laws; **2**, unjustly severe; tyrannical; as, an *oppressive* ruler; **3**, overpowering; as, the *oppressive* air of a closed room; **4**, causing uneasiness; as, *oppressive* formality.—*adv.* **op-pres′sive-ly.**—*n.* **op-pres′sive-ness.**

op-pro-bri-ous (ŏ-prō′brĭ-ŭs), *adj.* **1**, expressing disrespectful reproach or contemptuous abuse; as, *opprobrious* words; **2**, disgraceful, as conduct.—*adv.* **op-pro′bri-ous-ly.**—*n.* **op-pro′bri-ous-ness.**
Syn. insulting, abusive, offensive.

op-pro-bri-um (ŏ-prō′brĭ-ŭm), *n.* **1**, abusive or insulting language; **2**, disgrace; shame.

op-pugn (ŏ-pūn′), *v.t.* **1**, to dispute with; contend against; oppose; resist; **2**, to attack with argument.

op-ta-tive (ŏp′t*ȧ*-tĭv), *adj.* expressing wish or desire:—*n.* in verbs, the mood that expresses a wish or desire; also, a verb in this mood.

op-tic (ŏp′tĭk), *adj.* **1**, pertaining to the eye or vision; ocular; as, the *optic* nerve; **2**, optical: **optic nerve**, the nerve running from the eye to the optic centers of the brain:—*n.* the eye.

op-ti-cal (ŏp′tĭ-kăl), *adj.* **1**, pertaining to the science of light and vision; as, *optical* instruments; **2**, pertaining to the eyesight.—*adv.* **op′ti-cal-ly.**

op-ti-cian (ŏp-tĭsh′ăn), *n.* one who makes or sells eyeglasses, lenses, and instruments used in the study of light, vision, and sight.

op-tics (ŏp'tĭks), *n.pl.* used as *sing.* that branch of physics which treats of light and its properties, of the laws of vision, and of the construction of optical instruments, as microscopes, telescopes, etc.

op-ti-mism (ŏp'tĭ-mĭzm), *n.* **1**, the cheerful belief that everything in nature and history happens for the best; **2**, the inclination to look on the best side of things: opp. of *pessimism.*

op-ti-mist (ŏp'tĭ-mĭst), *n.* a person of hopeful and confident disposition; one who looks on the bright side of things: opp. of *pessimist.*

op-ti-mis-tic (ŏp"tĭ-mĭs'tĭk), *adj.* hopeful; inclined to look upon the best side of things. Also, **op"ti-mis'ti-cal.** —*adv.* **op"ti-mis'ti-cal-ly.**
Syn. cheerful, confident, sanguine.

op-tion (ŏp'shŭn), *n.* **1**, the right or power of choosing; as, you have the *option* of taking it or leaving it; **2**, the act of choosing; choice; **3**, that which can be or is chosen; **4**, a right, usually purchased, to buy or sell securities, land, or staple commodities at a specified price, within a specified time.
Syn. preference, alternative.

op-tion-al (ŏp'shŭn-ăl), *adj.* left to one's wish or choice:—*n.* a study which may be taken or not, as one chooses; an elective.—*adv.* **op'tion-al-ly.**

op-tom-e-try (ŏp-tŏm'ē-trĭ), *n.* the measurement of the powers of vision, and the fitting of glasses to correct visual defects.—*n.* **op-tom'e-trist.**

op-u-lence (ŏp'ū-lĕns), *n.* great riches; wealth. Also, **op'u-len-cy.**

op-u-lent (ŏp'ū-lĕnt), *adj.* **1**, wealthy; rich; as, an *opulent* merchant; **2**, abundant; luxuriant.

*__o-pus__ (ō'pŭs), [Lat.], *n.* [*pl.* opera (ŏp'ē-rȧ)], in music, a work; composition.

or (ôr), *conj.* **1**, otherwise; either; else; as, you may take this book *or* that one; **2**, also; in other words; as, a triangle, *or* figure with three sides.

-or (-ôr; -ẽr), *n. suffix,* **1**, denoting state or quality; as, fav*or;* splend*or;* hon*or:* in British usage spelled *-our;* **2**, denoting agent or instrument; as, doct*or;* sail*or;* extens*or:* sometimes changed to *-er;* as, labor*er.*

or-a-cle (ŏr'ȧ-kl), *n.* **1**, among the ancients, the reply of a deity or god, through an inspired priest, to some inquiry; **2**, the deity who gave the answer; **3**, the place where a deity might be consulted; **4**, the holy of holies in the Jewish temple; **5**, instruction given by God through his prophets; as, the divine *oracle;* **6**, a prophet or person of great wisdom and inspiration.

o-rac-u-lar (ō-răk'ū-lȧr), *adj.* **1**, of the nature of a prophecy; **2**, having the quality of authority or solemnity; **3**, having the power to utter wise sayings or prophecies; **4**, ambiguous, or having two possible meanings.—*adv.* **o-rac'u-lar-ly.**—*n.* **o-rac'u-lar-ness.**

o-ral (ō'răl), *adj.* **1**, uttered by the mouth; spoken; as, an *oral* statement; **2**, pertaining to, or situated near, the mouth; as, the *oral* cavity.—*adv.* **o'ral-ly.**

or-ange (ŏr'ĕnj; ŏr'ĭnj), *n.* **1**, an evergreen tree with fragrant white flowers and a deep golden-colored and juicy fruit; **2**, the fruit itself; **3**, the golden or reddish yellow color of the rind of such fruit:—*adj.* **1**, pertaining to such fruit; **2**, of a deep golden or reddish yellow color.

or-ange-ade (ŏr"ĕnj-ād'; ŏr"ĭnj-), *n.* a cooling drink made from orange juice and water.

Or-ange-man (ŏr'ĕnj-măn; ŏr'ĭnj-), *n.* [*pl.* Orangemen (-mĕn)], a member of a secret society of Irish Protestants, named from William III, Prince of Orange and King of England, whose cause the Irish Protestants supported in 1688.

or-ange-ry (ŏr'ĕnj-rĭ; ŏr'ĭnj-), *n.* [*pl.* orangeries (-rĭz)], a sheltered place for growing oranges; an orange grove.

o-rang-u-tan (ō-răng'=ōō-tăn"; ō'răng=ōō'tăn), *n.* a large, manlike ape of Borneo and Sumatra. Also, **o-rang'-ou-tang".**

o-ra-tion (ō-rā'shŭn), *n.* a formal and dignified public speech delivered on a special occasion; as, a funeral *oration.*
Syn. address. (See speech.)

or-a-tor (ŏr'ȧ-tẽr), *n.* **1**, one who makes an eloquent and dignified speech upon an occasion of special importance; **2**, a public speaker noted for skill and power.

or-a-tor-i-cal (ŏr"ȧ-tŏr'ĭ-kăl), *adj.* pertaining to, or suitable to, a skilful public speaker or to eloquent and dignified public speaking; as, *oratorical* gestures.—*adv.* **or"a-tor'i-cal-ly.**

or-a-to-ri-o (ŏr"ȧ-tō'rĭ-ō), *n.* [*pl.* oratorios (-ōz)], a dramatic dialog in music, usually on a sacred theme, sung with orchestral accompaniment, but without action, scenery, or costume.

[1]**or-a-to-ry** (ŏr'ȧ-tō-rĭ), *n.* the art of speaking well in public; eloquence or skill in public speaking.

[2]**or-a-to-ry** (ŏr'ȧ-tō-rĭ), *n.* [*pl.* oratories (-rĭz)], a small chapel, esp. one for private devotion.

orb (ôrb), *n.* **1**, a globe; **2**, a sphere, esp. one of the heavenly bodies, as the moon; **3**, the eye or eyeball:—*v.t.* **1**, to form into a circle; **2**, to encircle.

orbed (ôrbd), *adj.* **1**, round; as, the *orbed* moon; **2**, encircled; as, *orbed* with light; **3**, having eyes.

or-bit (ôr'bĭt), *n.* **1**, the bony cavity which contains the eye; **2**, the course followed by a heavenly body; as, the *orbit* of a planet.—*adj.* **or'bit-al.**

or-chard (ôr'chẽrd), *n.* a plantation of fruit trees, as apple, pear, or peach trees; also, the trees collectively.

or-ches-tra (ôr'kĕs-trȧ), *n.* **1**, in a modern theater or opera house, the place occupied by the instrumental musicians; **2**, the body of musicians; **3**, the collection of instruments, principally of the viol class, on which they play; **4**, the forward part or all of the main floor of a theater.

or-ches-tral (ôr-kĕs'trăl; ôr'kĕs-trăl), *adj.* pertaining to, suited to, or performed by, an orchestra or its instruments (cf. *musical instrument,* illus.).

or-ches-tra-tion (ôr"kĕs-trā'shŭn), *n.* the arrangement of a musical score so that it can be played by orchestral instruments.

or-chid (ôr'kĭd), *n.* **1**, any of a large family of plants bearing beautiful, showy, or often grotesque, blossoms; **2**, the blossom of any of these plants, as the lady's-slipper.

or-chis (ôr'kĭs), *n.* a small American wood plant, having two glossy leaves and a raceme of magenta-pink and white flowers.

or-dain (ŏr-dān'), *v.t.* **1**, to appoint or set apart for some special work; as, to *ordain* a minister or priest; **2**, to regulate by law; decree; **3**, to destine; as, fate *ordains* our destiny.—*n.* **or-dain'er.**

or-de-al (ŏr'dē-ăl; ôr'dēl), *n.* **1**, an ancient method of trial by fire, water, combat, etc., to determine the guilt or innocence of an accused person; **2**, hence, a severe trial or test.

or-der (ôr'dẽr), *n.* **1**, orig., a row, rank, or line; sequence; **2**, a rank, degree, or class in the social scale; as, the *order* of nobility; **3,** a group of persons united in a fraternal or monastic society; as, a Masonic *order;* the Franciscan *order;* **4,** a group of persons united by the common possession of some sign of merit or dignity; as, the *Order* of the Legion of Honor; the *Order* of the Garter; also, the badge of distinction worn by a member of the group; **5,** a regular or settled method of action; established custom; as, in worship, an *order* of service; in a meeting, the *order* of business; **6,** a regular or harmonious placing of the parts of a whole, as the phrases in a sentence, or the furniture in a room; **7,** command or authority; as, by *order* of the governor; **8,** a rule or law; as, an army *order;* **9,** public quiet or observance of law; as, *order* in the streets; **10,** working condition; as, the engine was out of *order;* **11,** the rank or degree of a clergyman or priest, as deacon, priest, bishop, etc.; **12,** usually in *pl.,* in ritualistic churches, the rite of ordination to the office of clergyman; as, to take *orders,* or enter the ministry; **13,** in botany and zoölogy, a group next larger than the family and smaller than the class; **14,** in mathematics, the degree of a mathematical expression; **15,** a type of architectural style, best seen in the column; as, the Doric *order* (see *column,* illus.): **in order to,** for the purpose of: **in order that,** so that: used as a conjunction introducing a clause of purpose:—*v.t.* **1,** to regulate or manage; direct; **2,** to instruct with authority; **3,** to give directions for the purchase of:—*v.i.* to give a command or direction; supervise.

Syn., n. division. (See rank.)

or-der-ly (ôr'dẽr-lĭ), *adj.* **1,** regular; as, an *orderly* arrangement; **2,** methodical; systematic; as, an *orderly* worker; **3,** carefully arranged, as a room; neat; **4,** well conducted or regulated; as, an *orderly* meeting; **5,** performed carefully and methodically; as, the task was done in an *orderly* manner; **6,** peaceable; as, an *orderly* crowd; **7,** charged, on military duty, with the carrying of commands; as, an *orderly* officer:—*adv.* properly:—*n.* [*pl.* orderlies (-lĭz)], **1,** a soldier who attends upon an officer to carry his orders; as, the colonel's *orderly;* **2,** a man who acts as general attendant in a hospital: **orderly sergeant, orderly corporal,** non-commissioned officers who carry commands.—*n.* **or'der-li-ness.**

or-di-nal (ôr'dĭ-năl), *n.* **1,** a number showing succession in a series; as, *first, second, third* are *ordinals:* distinguished from *cardinal;* **2,** (also, *Ordinal*), a book containing certain church forms and services:—*adj.* **1,** noting succession in a series; as, the *ordinal* numbers are first, second, etc.; **2,** belonging to a class, as of plants, animals, etc.

or-di-nance (ôr'dĭ-năns), *n.* **1,** that which God or fate has decreed; **2,** an established rule, rite, or law; as, a city *ordinance;* **3,** a religious rite or ceremony.

or-di-na-ry (ôr'dĭ-nā-rĭ), *adj.* **1,** according to established custom or rule; **2,** usual; **3,** commonplace:—*n.* [*pl.* ordinaries (-rĭz)], **1,** one who has jurisdiction in his own right, as a bishop or certain judges; **2,** a customary or appointed form; **3,** a meal served at a fixed time; a table d'hote; **4,** a place where such a meal is served.—*adv.* **or'di-na-ri-ly.**

Syn., adj. regular, common, normal, average.

or-di-na-tion (ôr"dĭ-nā'shŭn), *n.* admission to the Christian ministry; as, the *ordination* of a minister.

ord-nance (ôrd'năns), *n.* **1,** the heavy guns used in warfare; **2,** military supplies; also, the department having charge of them.

or-dure (ôr'dûr), *n.* **1,** excrement; dung; filth; **2,** obscenity; foul language.

ore (ōr), *n.* a metal-bearing mineral or rock, esp. one containing sufficient metal to be commercially valuable.

or-gan (ôr'găn), *n.* **1,** a part of an animal or plant fitted to perform some special duty; as, the *organ* of sight; **2,** a means of making known the opinions or official acts of a person or party, as a newspaper; **3,** a means by which an action is performed; as, courts are the *organs* of justice; **4,** a large musical wind instrument with pipes or reeds, sounded by compressed air from bellows, and played by means of keys; also, a smaller instrument operated by pedals or a crank.

or-gan-die (ôr'găn-dĭ), *n.* a fine, transparent, muslin dress goods, often with delicate patterns. Also, **or'gan-dy.**

or-gan-ic (ôr-găn'ĭk), *adj.* **1,** pertaining to, of the nature of, or affecting, some organ of the body; as, an *organic* disease; **2,** pertaining to, or derived from, anything that has life in itself; as, fossils are remains of *organic* bodies; **3,** constitutional; inherent; as, an *organic* fault; **4,** containing carbon as an essential ingredient, as a compound; **5,** systematized: **organic chemistry,** the chemistry of carbon compounds. Also, **or-gan'i-cal.**—*adv.* **or-gan'i-cal-ly.**

or-gan-ism (ôr'găn-ĭzm), *n.* **1,** anything that has life in itself; **2,** a body composed of parts performing special duties, but mutually dependent; **3,** anything like such a body; as, the social *organism.*

or-gan-ist (ôr'găn-ĭst), *n.* a player on the musical instrument, the organ.

or-gan-i-za-tion (ôr"găn-ĭ-zā'shŭn), *n.* **1,** the parts of an animal or a plant, regarded as a whole, acting or working together; as, the *organization* of a fish; **2,** any body consisting of parts mutually dependent but each having a special duty; as, the educational *organization* of the country; **3,** a body of persons united for some end or work; as, a church *organization;* **4,** the act of forming a union to work together for a common end; as, the *organization* of a club.

or-gan-ize (ôr'găn-īz), *v.t.* [*p.t.* and *p.p.* -ized (-īzd), *p.pr.* -iz"ing], **1,** to give life or being to; as, to *organize* a rebellion; **2,** to cause to unite and work together in orderly fashion; as, to *organize* forces for a campaign; **3,** in biology, to form into a living being, or living tissue.—*n.* **or'gan-iz"er.**

or-gy (ôr'jĭ), *n.* [*pl.* orgies (-jĭz)], **1,** among the Greeks and Romans, a secret rite or celebration in honor of a god, esp. Bacchus; **2,** a wild, drunken revel.

o-ri-bi (ŏr'ĭ-bĭ), *n.* a small South African antelope with slender, ringed horns. Also, **ou're-bi,** *Pfd. S.*

o-ri-el (ō'rĭ-ĕl), *n.* a large bay window which rests on brackets.

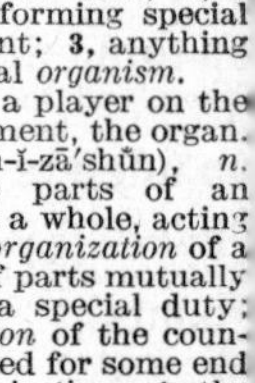

ORIEL WINDOW

o-ri-ent (ō'rĭ-ĕnt), *adj.* **1,** rising, like the sun; **2,** pertaining to, or coming from, the east; **3,** like the sunrise; bright; **4,** clear; translucent; as, *orient* pearls:—*v.t.* **1,** to set facing the east; **2,** to find the position of, in relation to the east; **3,** to find the bearings of, as in surveying; **4,** to set right in relation to some fixed rule or principle:—*n.* the east: opp. of *occident,* or *west:* **Orient,** *n.* the East; the countries of Asia, esp. the Far East; also, the countries near the eastern Mediterranean or the Near East: opp. of *Occident.*

o-ri-en-tal (ō"rĭ-ĕn'tăl), *adj.* **1,** pertaining to the east; **2,** (usually, *Oriental*), pertaining to, or characteristic of, the Orient; as, an *oriental* rug:—*n.* (usually,

Oriental), a native of one of the countries east of Europe, esp. a member of a native race; an Asiatic.—*adv.* **o″ri-en′tal-ly.**

O-ri-en-tal-ism (ō″rĭ-ĕn′tăl-ĭzm), *n.* **1,** an expression, trait, or custom peculiar to the East; **2,** knowledge of Eastern history, languages, and literature. Also, **o″ri-en′tal-ism.**

O-ri-en-tal-ist (ō″rĭ-ĕn′tăl-ĭst), *n.* one who knows well the history, language, and literature of the East.

o-ri-en-tate (ō′rĭ-ĕn-tāt″; ō″rĭ-ĕn′tāt), *v.t.* [*p.t.* and *p.p.* -tat″ed, *p.pr.* -tat″ing], **1,** to place so as to face the east; **2,** to determine the position of, with reference to the east:—*v.i.* to face the east.

o-ri-en-ta-tion (ō″rĭ-ĕn-tā′shŭn), *n.* **1,** the finding of the east point so as to get one's bearings; **2,** the act of facing toward the east in worship; **3,** the placing of an object with respect to certain fixed points of direction; also, the position so determined; **4,** the placing of a church so that the altar shall be at the east end; **5,** the faculty possessed by certain birds of finding their way home from distant places; **6,** the faculty of plants and animals to direct their parts in response to external stimuli; **7,** the ability to find and hold the right mental attitude toward a subject.

or-i-fice (ŏr′ĭ-fĭs), *n.* a mouth or opening into a cavity or tube; a vent.

or-i-flamme (ŏr′ĭ-flăm), *n.* **1,** the ancient royal standard of France, a red flag split at one end and forming flame-shaped streamers; **2,** any symbol of glory. Also, **or′i-flamb** (ŏr′ĭ-flăm).

or-i-gin (ŏr′ĭ-jĭn), *n.* **1,** a beginning; birth; source; **2,** parentage; **3,** cause; **4,** derivation, as of a word; **5,** in anatomy, the end of a muscle attached to a part which does not move: opp. of *insertion.*

Syn. root, commencement, inception.

o-rig-i-nal (ō-rĭj′ĭ-năl), *adj.* **1,** of or pertaining to the beginning or origin; **2,** first in existence or order; primary; as, an *original* edition of a book; **3,** not copied; as, an *original* painting; **4,** able to create or invent that which is new; as, an *original* writer: **original sin,** in theology, innate depravity, considered as mankind's heritage from Adam:—*n.* **1,** that from which anything is copied; **2,** the language in which a translated work was written; **3,** an unusual person.—*adv.* **o-rig′i-nal-ly.**

Syn., adj. primitive, novel, fresh.

o-rig-i-nal-i-ty (ō-rĭj″ĭ-năl′ĭ-tĭ), *n.* **1,** the ability to create or make something new; as, the *originality* of an inventor; **2,** the quality of being new or novel.

o-rig-i-nate (ō-rĭj′ĭ-nāt), *v.t.* [*p.t.* and *p.p.* -nat″ed, *p.pr.* -nat″ing], to bring into existence; invent; create:—*v.i.* to begin to exist; rise or spring from a source.—*n.* **o-rig″i-na′tion.**—*n.* **o-rig′i-na″tor.**

o-ri-ole (ō′rĭ-ōl), *n.* **1,** any of various black-and-yellow birds which build hanging nests, esp. the golden oriole of Europe; **2,** any of certain American black-and-orange birds, which build hanging nests.

O-ri-on (ō-rī′ŏn), *n.* **1,** in mythology, a Greek hunter beloved by Artemis (Diana), who accidentally killed him and in sorrow placed him and his dog Sirius among the constellations; **2,** in astronomy, a large constellation near the celestial equator, noted for its group of three bright stars in a line.

or-i-son (ŏr′ĭ-zŭn), *n. Archaic,* a prayer; devotions.

or-na-ment (ôr′nȧ-mĕnt), *n.* **1,** anything that adorns or beautifies; **2,** decoration; ornaments collectively:—*v.t.* (ôr′nȧ-mĕnt; ôr″nȧ-mĕnt′), to adorn; bedeck.

or-na-men-tal (ôr″nȧ-mĕn′tăl), *adj.* serving to adorn or decorate.—*adv.* **or″na-men′tal-ly.**

or-na-men-ta-tion (ôr″nȧ-mĕn-tā′shŭn), *n.* decoration; trimming; adornment.

or-nate (ŏr-nāt′; ôr′nāt), *adj.* **1,** much adorned or decorated; **2,** of literature, embellished; often, showy; as, an *ornate* style.—*adv.* **or-nate′ly.**—*n.* **or-nate′ness.**

or-ni-tho-log-i-cal (ôr″nĭ-thō-lŏj′ĭ-kăl), *adj.* pertaining to the scientific study of birds.

or-ni-thol-o-gy (ôr″nĭ-thŏl′ō-jĭ), *n.* the scientific study of birds and their habits.—*n.* **or″ni-thol′o-gist.**

or-ni-tho-rhyn-chus (ôr″nĭ-thō-rĭng′kŭs; ŏr-nī″-), *n.* an Australian egg-laying mammal, with a bill like a duck; a duckbill, or platypus.

o-ro-tund (ō′rō-tŭnd; ŏr′ō-tŭnd), *adj.* **1,** having a full, clear, musical quality: said of the voice or manner of utterance; **2,** imposing; pompous.

or-phan (ôr′făn), *n.* a child who has lost one or, more commonly, both parents by death:—*adj.* being without parents, because of their death:—*v.t.* to deprive of a parent or parents.

or-phan-age (ôr′făn-āj), *n.* **1,** the state of being without parents; **2,** an institution for orphans.

Or-phe-an (ŏr-fē′ăn), *adj.* pertaining to Orpheus; hence, melodious.

Or-pheus (ôr′fūs; ôr′fē-ŭs), *n.* in mythology, a Thracian poet and musician, who, with his lyre, could draw to himself beasts, rocks, and trees.

Or-phic (ôr′fĭk), *adj.* **1,** pertaining to Orpheus; hence, melodious; enchanting; **2,** mysterious; oracular.

or-rer-y (ŏr′ẽr-ĭ), *n.* [*pl.* orreries (-ĭz)], a contrivance showing the relative motions of the solar system by means of balls moved by wheels and clockwork: also called *planetarium.*

or-ris (ŏr′ĭs), *n.* the iris, a plant, the dried and finely ground roots of which are used as a perfume or sachet powder, called *orris root.* Also, **or′rice.**

or-tho-dox (ôr′thō-dŏks), *adj.* **1,** holding what is regarded as the conservative opinion, esp. in regard to religion; **2,** approved; accepted; **3,** in agreement with the Scriptures as interpreted by a given church authority: opp. of *heterodox.*

or-tho-dox-y (ôr′thō-dŏk″sĭ), *n.* [*pl.* orthodoxies (-sĭz)], a holding to, or a following of, the accepted or common belief or opinion, esp. a religious doctrine.

or-tho-ë-py (ôr′thō-ē-pĭ; ŏr-thō′ē-pĭ), *n.* **1,** the art of correct pronunciation; **2,** that branch of grammar which treats of pronunciation.—*n.* **or′tho-ë-pist.**—*adj.* **or″tho-ëp′ic; or″tho-ëp′i-cal.**

or-thog-ra-pher (ŏr-thŏg′rȧ-fẽr), *n.* **1,** one who knows thoroughly the principles of spelling; **2,** one who spells correctly. Also, **or-thog′ra-phist.**

or-tho-graph-ic (ôr″thō-grăf′ĭk), *adj.* **1,** pertaining to correct spelling; **2,** in geometry, pertaining to right angles, or to straight lines. Also, **or″tho-graph′i-cal.**—*adv.* **or″tho-graph′i-cal-ly.**

or-thog-ra-phy (ŏr-thŏg′rȧ-fĭ), *n.* [*pl.* orthographies (-fĭz)], the art of spelling words correctly; also, the standard way of grouping letters to form words.

or-thol-o-gy (ôr-thŏl′ō-jĭ), *n.* the art of using words correctly.—*adj.* **or″tho-log′i-cal.**—*n.* **or″tho-lo′gi-an.**

or-tho-pe-dics (ôr″thō-pē′dĭks), *n.pl.* used as *sing.* **1,** the prevention or treatment of deformities, esp. in young children; **2**, a branch of plastic surgery connected with the treatment of deformities. Also, **or″tho-pæ′dics.**—*adj.* **or″tho-pe′dic.**

or-to-lan (ôr′tō-lăn), *n.* **1**, a European and African species of bunting, much prized for its flesh; **2**, in the U. S., the bobolink.

ORTOLAN ($\frac{1}{7}$)

-o-ry (-ō-rĭ), *n. suffix*, where; place for: added to Latin roots; as, fact*ory;* labora*tory:*—*adj. suffix*, pertaining to; characterized by: added to Latin roots; as, obligat*ory.*

o-ryx (ō′rĭks; ŏr′ĭks), *n.* any of a genus (*Oryx*) of African antelopes with long, almost straight, horns.

O-sage (ō-sāj′; ō′sāj), *n.* one of a tribe of American Indians, orig. inhabiting the region of the Arkansas and Osage rivers: **Osage orange,** (ō′sāj), an ornamental American tree with glossy leaves and fruit resembling the orange, but inedible.

os-cil-late (ŏs′ĭ-lāt), *v.i.* [*p.t.* and *p.p.* -lat″ed, *p.pr.* -lat″ing], **1**, to swing backward and forward, as the pendulum of a clock; vibrate; **2**, to pass back and forth from one state to another:—*v.t.* to cause to swing back and forth.

os-cil-la-tion (ŏs″ĭ-lā′shŭn), *n.* **1**, a swinging backward and forward, as of a pendulum; vibration; **2**, a wavering, as in forming an opinion.

os-cil-la-tor (ŏs′ĭ-lā″tẽr), *n.* **1**, one who or that which moves backward and forward like a pendulum; **2**, a device for producing electric vibrations, esp. in a wireless telegraph system.—*adj.* **os′cil-la-to-ry.**

os-cu-late (ŏs′kū-lāt), *v.t.* [*p.t.* and *p.p.* -lat″ed, *p.pr.* -lat″ing], to kiss:—*v.i.* to kiss one another.—*n.* **os″cu-la′tion.**—*adj.* **os′cu-la-to-ry.**

-ose (-ōs), *adj. suffix*, like; full of; as, ver*bose:*—*n. suffix*, in chemistry, used to form the names of the various carbohydrates related to glucose; as, cellul*ose;* dextr*ose.*

O-see (ō′zē; ō′sē), *n.* Hosea, the Hebrew prophet or the book of the Old Testament: so called in the Douay Bible.

o-sier (ō′zhẽr), *n.* **1**, a willow, the twigs of which are used in basket making; **2**, a similar plant of another family, as the American dogwood:—*adj.* made of, or consisting of, willow twigs.

O-si-ris (ō-sī′rĭs), *n.* in Egyptian mythology, the chief god of the underworld, brother and husband of Isis.

-o-sis (-ō′sĭs), *n. suffix*, condition, state, process, etc.; as, halit*osis.*

Os-man-li (ŏs-măn′lĭ), *n.* [*pl.* Osmanlis (-lĭz)], **1**, an Ottoman Turk; **2**, the language spoken by the Ottoman Turks:—*adj.* pertaining to Turkey or only to the Ottoman Turks.

os-prey (ŏs′prā), *n.* a large, brown-and-white hawk that feeds on fish: also called *ossifrage.*

OSPREY ($\frac{1}{20}$)

Os-sa (ŏs′ȧ), *n.* in mythology, a mountain in Thessaly. The giants, by piling Pelion on Ossa, or, in some stories, Ossa on Pelion, hoped to reach the abode of the gods.

os-se-ous (ŏs′ē-ŭs), *adj.* consisting of, like, or capable of forming, bone or bonelike substance; bony.

os-si-fi-ca-tion (ŏs″ĭ-fĭ-kā′shŭn), *n.* **1**, the changing of soft animal tissue into bone; **2**, that which has become hardened or changed into bone.

os-si-fy (ŏs′ĭ-fī), *v.t.* [*p.t.* and *p.p.* -fied (-fīd), *p.pr.* -fy″ing], to convert or change into bone or into a bonelike substance; harden:—*v.i.* to become bone.

os-ten-si-ble (ŏs-tĕn′sĭ-bl), *adj.* seeming; pretended; apparent; as, an *ostensible* reason.—*adv.* **os-ten′si-bly.**

os-ten-ta-tion (ŏs″tĕn-tā′shŭn), *n.* unnecessary show or parade; ambitious or vain display.

os-ten-ta-tious (ŏs″tĕn-tā′shŭs), *adj.* fond of show; intended for vain display; showy; gaudy; as, *ostentatious* jewelry.—*adv.* **os″ten-ta′tious-ly.**

os-te-ol-o-gy (ŏs″tē-ŏl′ō-jĭ), *n.* the scientific study of the bones of vertebrate animals, or those that have a backbone.—*n.* **os″te-ol′o-gist.**

os-te-o-path (ŏs′tē-ō-păth), *n.* one who practices osteopathy.—*n.* **os″te-op′a-thist.**—*adj.* **os″te-o-path′ic.**

os-te-op-a-thy (ŏs″tē-ŏp′ȧ-thĭ), *n.* a system of medicine which, while recognizing the value of surgery and other special branches of therapy, teaches that structural derangement, esp. of the spinal column, is the chief cause of disease, and in healing lays stress on restoring normal structural position by manipulation.

ost-ler (ŏs′lẽr), *n.* a man who attends to horses at an inn; a stableman. See **hos′tler,** *Pfd. S.*

os-tra-cism (ŏs′trȧ-sĭzm), *n.* **1**, in ancient Greece, temporary banishment for a period of five to ten years by popular vote; **2**, exclusion from favor by general consent; as, *ostracism* by society.

os-tra-cize (ŏs′trȧ-sīz), *v.t.* [*p.t.* and *p.p.* -cized (-sīzd), *p.pr.* -ciz″ing], **1**, among the ancient Greeks, to banish or drive out by popular vote; **2**, to put out of public or private favor; as, he was *ostracized* from good society.

os-trich (ŏs′trĭch), *n.* a swiftly running African bird, incapable of flight, the largest bird known: valued for its feathers.

OSTRICH ($\frac{1}{80}$)

Os-tro-goth (ŏs′trō-gŏth), *n.* a member of the tribe of East Goths who overran the Roman Empire in the fifth and sixth centuries: distinguished from *West Goth* or *Visigoth.* —*adj.* **Os″tro-goth′ic.**

O-thel-lo (ō-thĕl′ō), *n.* in Shakespeare's "Othello," a Moor of Venice, of great military prowess, who, in a fit of jealousy, smothered his wife, Desdemona, and later killed himself.

oth-er (ŭth′ẽr), *adj.* **1**, not the same; different; as, I have *other* matters to attend to; **2**, additional; more; as, I have *other* sisters; **3**, opposite; as, the *other* side of the street; **4**, second; as, every *other* line: **the other world,** the world to come; the world of those who have died:—*adv.* otherwise; as, she could not do *other* than help him:—*pron.* **1**, the opposite one of two; as, one or the *other* of you must do it; **2**, a different person or thing:—*conj.* or; either.

oth-er-wise (ŭth′ẽr-wīz″), *adv.* **1**, in a different way; differently;

as, he could not do *otherwise;* **2,** in different conditions or respects; as, I know him professionally, but not *otherwise:—conj.* else:—*adj.* different.

ot-tar (ŏt′ȧr), *n.* the fragrant oil extracted from the petals of flowers, esp. roses: used in perfumery. Also, **ot′to;** *Pfd. S.*, **at′tar.**

ot-ter (ŏt′ẽr), *n.* a fish-eating animal of the weasel family, living in the water and valued for its fur.

Ot-to-man (ŏt′ō-măn), *adj.* pertaining to the Turks:—*n.* [*pl.* Ottomans (-mănz)], a Turk: **ottoman, 1,** a cushioned seat, somewhat like those used in Turkey; **2,** a movable cushioned foot rest.

***ou-bli-ette** (ōō″blē-ĕt′) [Fr.], *n.* in ancient castles, a dungeon, commonly with an entrance only through the ceiling; also, a secret pit in a dungeon floor.

ouch (ouch), *interj.* an exclamation signifying sudden pain.

1ought (ôt), *v.aux.* [no other form found], **1,** *Obs.*, owed: the past tense or past participle of *owe;* **2,** expressing obligation, fitness, necessity, duty, or probability: followed by infinitive; as, I *ought* to do it.

Syn. must, should. *Ought* expresses moral obligation; as, we *ought* to tell the truth; it may also express strong probability; as, the message *ought* to reach him soon. *Must* denotes compulsion, physical or moral; as, one *must* get enough sleep; you *must* obey your parents. *Should* expresses duty or necessity, but is milder than *ought;* as, you *should* be more careful.

2ought (ôt), *n.* **1,** anything; any part; **2,** in arithmetic, a cipher; hence, nothing:—*adv.* to any extent; at all. Also, **aught,** *Pfd.S.*

1ounce (ouns), *n.* **1,** a weight of $\frac{1}{16}$ of a pound avoirdupois; $\frac{1}{12}$ of a pound troy, or apothecaries' weight; **2,** figuratively, any small quantity; as, an *ounce* of prevention is worth a pound of cure.

2ounce (ouns), **1,** a handsome leopardlike animal of central Asia; **2,** in America, any similar animal, as the jaguar.

our (our), *poss. pron.* and *adj.* of or pertaining to us; as, *our* school; on *our* behalf.

-our (-ôr; ẽr), *n. suffix,* denoting state or quality; as, fa*vour;* hon*our.* *Pfd. S.*, **-or.**

ou-re-bi (ōō′rā-bē), *n.* a small South African antelope with slender, ringed horns. Also, **or′i-bi.**

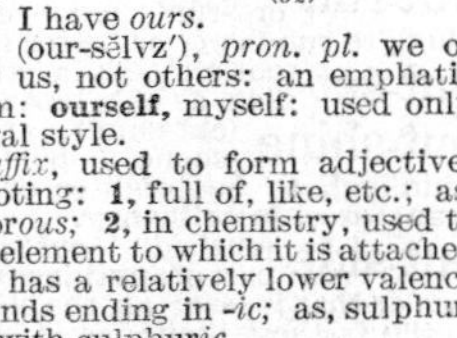
OUREBI ($\frac{1}{32}$)

ours (ourz), a possessive form of the personal pronoun *we*, used alone: **1,** as *adj.*, in the predicate; as, whose cat is that? it is *ours;* **2,** as *pron.;* as, whose book have you? I have *ours.*

our-selves (our-sĕlvz′), *pron. pl.* we or us, not others: an emphatic or reflexive form: **ourself,** myself: used only in formal or regal style.

-ous (-ŭs), *suffix,* used to form adjectives and denoting: **1,** full of, like, etc.; as, poison*ous;* amor*ous;* **2,** in chemistry, used to denote that the element to which it is attached in a compound has a relatively lower valence than in compounds ending in *-ic;* as, sulphur*ous* contrasted with sulphur*ic.*

ou-sel (ōō′zl), *n.* the European blackbird. See **ou′zel,** *Pfd. S.*

oust (oust), *v.t.* to eject or turn out; as, to *oust* a person from a position.

out (out), *adv.* [but often used in the predicate like an *adj.;* as, the stars are *out*], **1,** outside; not within doors; as, stay *out* in the fresh air; **2,** abroad; away; forth; as, to go *out* to India; **3,** from a given condition (to another); as, a light is turned *out;* the butterfly comes *out;* **4,** in baseball, not at the bat, as a side; also, dismissed, or retired from running or batting, as a runner or a side; **5,** from one's own use or possession to another's; as, he lends his money *out;* **6,** so as to clear of obstruction or refuse; as, to sweep *out* a room; **7,** without restraint; loudly; as, to speak *out;* **8,** to a conclusion or an end; as, to burn *out;* hear me *out;* **9,** idle; without occupation; on strike; as, the mill workers are *out;* **10,** out of pocket; minus; as, *out* five dollars; **11,** in error; wrong; as, your figures are *out;* **12,** not in fashion; as, low heels are *out;* **13,** disclosed; made known; as, the secret is *out:* **out of sorts,** indisposed; dissatisfied:—*adj.* **1,** outer; **2,** outlying; **3,** in baseball or cricket, fielding, or not having an inning: said of a team or a side; **4,** unusual; abnormal; as, an *out* size:—*interj.* begone!—*n.* **1,** usually in *pl.*, one who is not in office; **2,** an outer nook or corner; as, the ins and *outs* of a garden; **3,** in *pl.*, the side in a baseball game not having its inning: opp. of *ins:* **on the outs, at outs,** not friendly:—*v.t.* to expel; dispossess:—*v.i. Colloq.*, to go out.

out- (out-), *prefix,* used with many self-explaining compounds and denoting: **1,** more than; exceeding; as, *out*bid; **2,** outside; some distance away; as, *out*house; **3,** out; away; as, *out*bound.

out and out thoroughly; completely.—*adj.* **out″-and-out′.**

out-bid (out-bĭd′), *v.t.* [*p.t.* -bade′ (-băd′) or -bid′, *p.p.* -bid′den (-bĭd′n) or -bid′, *p.pr.* -bid′ding], to exceed in bidding.

out-bound (out′bound″), *adj.* outward bound; leaving a port, railway terminal, or the like.

out-break (out′brāk″), *n.* **1,** a sudden bursting forth, as of an epidemic; **2,** a revolt; riot.

out-build-ing (out′bĭl″dĭng), *n.* a structure apart from, but belonging to and used by, the main house, as a barn, shed, etc.

out-burst (out′bûrst″), *n.* a breaking forth; an outbreak.

out-cast (out′kȧst″), *n.* one who is driven forth or exiled, esp. socially; a vagabond; exile:—*adj.* driven forth; rejected; forlorn; degraded.

out-class (out-klȧs′), *v.t.* to surpass or excel in quality, skill, etc.

out-come (out′kŭm″), *n.* the result or consequence of an act.

out-crop (out′krŏp″), *n.* the coming out of strata, or layers, as of rock, to the surface of the ground:—*v.i.* [*p.t.* and *p.p.* -cropped″ (-krŏpt″), *p.pr.* -crop″ping], to come out to the surface of the ground.

out-cry (out′krī″), *n.* [*pl.* outcries (-krīz″)], clamor; uproar; confused noise.

out-curve (out′kûrv″), *n.* **1,** something that curves outward; **2,** in baseball, a pitched ball that curves away from a (right-handed) batter.

out-dis-tance (out-dĭs′tăns), *v.t.* [*p.t.* and *p.p.* -tanced (-tănst), *p.pr.* -tanc-ing], to outstrip; excel in speed.

out-do (out-dōō′), *v.t.* [*p.t.* -did′ (-dĭd′), *p.p.* -done′ (-dŭn′), *p.pr.* -do′ing], to surpass; excel; as, he tried to *outdo* his opponents.

out-door (out′dōr″), *adj.* not inside the walls of a building; in the open air.

out-doors (out″dōrz′), *n.* the world outside the walls of a dwelling:—*adv.* (out″dōrz′; out′dōrz″), not inside a dwelling; in or into the open air.

out-er (out′ẽr), *adj.* being on the outside: opp. of *inner.*

out-er-most (out'ẽr-mōst), *adv.* farthest on the outside; outmost.

out-face (out-fās'), *v.t.* [*p.t.* and *p.p.* -faced' (-fāst'), *p.pr.* -fac'ing], to stare (one) out of countenance; defy.

out-field (out'fēld"), *n.* **1**, the part of a baseball ground beyond the diamond; **2**, the players outside the diamond.—*n.* **out'field"er.**

out-fit (out'fĭt), *n.* all the articles necessary for any undertaking; as, the *outfit* for a journey or expedition; a bride's *outfit*:—*v.t.* and *v.i.* [*p.t.* and *p.p.* -fit"ted, *p.pr.* -fit"-ting], to furnish with everything necessary for an undertaking.—*n.* **out'fit"ter.**

out-flank (out-flăngk'), *v.t.* **1**, to go or pass around the sides of; **2**, to get the better of (an enemy) by passing troops around the end of the opposing line.

out-flow (out'flō"), *n.* a flowing out; an effusion; emanation.

out-gen-er-al (out-jĕn'ẽr-ăl), *v.t.* to excel in management; esp., to surpass in military skill.

out-go (out'gō"), *n.* [*pl.* outgoes (-gōz")], that which goes out; that which is paid out; outlay; as, the *outgo* was greater than the income:—*v.t.* (out-gō'), [*p.t.* -went' (-wĕnt'), *p.p.* -gone' (-gôn'), *p.pr.* -go'ing], to go beyond; surpass; excel.

out-go-ing (out'gō"ĭng), *adj.* leaving; departing; as, *outgoing* baggage:—*n.* **1**, departure; **2**, in *pl.*, expenses.

out-grow (out-grō'), *v.t.* [*p.t.* -grew' (-grōō'), *p.p.* -grown' (-grōn'), *p.pr.* -grow'ing], **1**, to excel in growing; as, weeds *outgrow* crops; **2**, to grow away from; as, to *outgrow* a habit; **3**, to become too big for; as, to *outgrow* clothes.

out-growth (out'grōth"), *n.* anything that grows out of, or proceeds from, anything else; a result.

out-Her-od (out=hĕr'ŭd), *v.t.* to exceed the cruelty or violence of (Herod the Great); hence, to surpass in any extreme, as of evil.

out-house (out'hous"), *n.* an outbuilding; a building belonging to, but separate from, a main house, as a barn or shed.

out-ing (out'ĭng), *n.* a short excursion or pleasure trip.

out-land-er (out'lăn-dẽr), *n.* one who is not a native; a foreigner.

out-land-ish (out-lăn'dĭsh), *adj.* **1**, strange; unfamiliar; uncouth; as, *outlandish* conduct or dress; **2**, far away.—*adv.* **out-land'ish-ly.**—*n.* **out-land'ish-ness.**

out-last (out-låst'), *v.t.* to last longer than; surpass in duration; outlive.

out-law (out'lô"), *n.* **1**, one who is deprived of legal rights and protection; esp., a dangerous criminal sought dead or alive; **2**, one who flees from justice:—*v.t.* **1**, to deprive of legal benefits and protection, as a dangerous criminal; **2**, to remove from legal control; as, to *outlaw* a claim.—*n.* **out'law"ry.**

out-lay (out'lā"), *n.* that which is spent, either money or effort, in any undertaking; expenditure.

out-let (out'lĕt), *n.* **1**, a means of passing out; **2**, a market, as for products.

out-line (out'līn"), *n.* **1**, the line that shows the outer limits or shape of a figure; **2**, in drawing, a sketch which shows the shape of figures without light and shade; **3**, in writing or speaking, a first draft or sketch in words; as, an *outline* of a lecture; **4**, in *pl.*, chief features:—*v.t.* [*p.t.* and *p.p.* -lined" (-līnd"), *p.pr.* -lin"ing], **1**, to draw the limiting edge of; **2**, to state the plan of in words.

out-live (out-lĭv'), *v.t.* [*p.t.* and *p.p.* -lived' (-lĭvd'), *p.pr.* -liv'ing], to be in existence longer than; survive.

out-look (out'lŏŏk"), *n.* **1**, a view, as seen by one who looks from a window or other opening; **2**, the present state or future prospect of things; as, a favorable *outlook;* **3**, foresight; **4**, a place where watch is kept; a watchtower; lookout; **5**, vigilance.

out-ly-ing (out'lī"ĭng), *adj.* being distant from the center, or main body; remote; detached; unrelated.

out-most (out'mōst), *adv.* farthest outside; outermost.

out-num-ber (out-nŭm'bẽr), *v.t.* to be more than, in number.

out–of–door (out'=ŏv=dōr'), *adj.* outside a dwelling; in the open air; outdoor. Also, **out'–of–doors'.**

out–pa-tient (out'=pā"shĕnt), *n.* a person who goes to a hospital for treatment but does not remain there.

out-port (out'pōrt"), *n.* a harbor at some distance from the chief port.

out-post (out'pōst"), *n.* **1**, a soldier or body of troops stationed at a distance from the main army to guard against surprise; **2**, the position so occupied.

out-pour (out-pōr'), *v.t.* and *v.i.* to pour out; send out (in) a stream.

out-put (out'pŏŏt"), *n.* **1**, quantity produced, as from a mine or mill; the yield; **2**, the quantity which a man, machine, etc., produces in a given time.

out-rage (out'rāj), *n.* gross insult or injury; a cruel or violent act:—*v.t.* [*p.t.* and *p.p.* -raged (-rājd), *p.pr.* -rag-ing], **1**, to abuse violently; injure grievously; **2**, to assault by violence; rape.

Syn., *n.* abuse, violence, affront.

out-ra-geous (out-rā'jŭs), *adj.* violent; atrocious; excessive; without regard for decency; shocking; as, his conduct was *outrageous*.—*adv.* **out-ra'geous-ly.**—*n.* **out-ra'geous-ness.**

out-rank (out-răngk'), *v.t.* to exceed in rank; come before in grade.

***ou-tré** (ōō"trā'), [Fr.], *adj.* extremely odd; exaggerated.

out-ride (out-rīd'), *v.t.* [*p.t.* -rode' (-rōd'), *p.p.* -rid'den (-rĭd'n), *p.pr.* -rid'ing], to ride better or faster than:—*v.i.* to ride as an attendant beside a carriage.

out-rid-er (out'rīd"ẽr), *n.* a servant on horseback who rides in advance of, or beside, a carriage.

out-rig-ger (out'rĭg"ẽr), *n.* **1**, on a ship, a projecting spar or beam for extending sails or ropes; **2**, a boat with attachments at the sides to keep it from upsetting; also, such an attachment; **3**, a projecting bracket supporting a rowlock to give leverage to the oar, as in a racing shell.

out-right (out"rīt'; out'rīt"), *adv.* **1**, completely; **2**, at once; immediately, **3**, straightforwardly:—*adj.* (out'rīt"), downright; straightforward.

out-run (out-rŭn'), *v.t.* [*p.t.* -ran' (-răn') or -run', *p.p.* -run', *p.pr.* -run'ning], to run faster or better than; outstrip.

out-set (out'sĕt"), *n.* a start; the beginning, as of a business or journey.

out-shine (out-shīn'), *v.t.* [*p.t.* and *p.p.* -shone' (-shōn'; -shŏn'), *p.pr.* -shin'ing], to be brighter or more splendid than; excel in brilliancy.

out-side (out"sīd'; out'sīd"), *n.* **1**, the part of anything that is on the surface or that is seen; as, the *outside* of a house; **2**, the farthest limit; as, I shall return in a week, at the *outside*:—*adj.* (out'sīd"), **1**, pertaining to, or situated upon, the surface or outside; external or exterior; **2**, reaching the limit; **3**, having no part in:—*adv.* beyond the border; without:—*prep.* beyond the limit of; out of; without.

out-sid-er (out″sīd′ẽr), *n.* one that does not belong to a given party, company, etc.; a trespasser.

out-skirt (out′skûrt″), *n.*, usually in *pl.*, the outer edge, or border, as of a town or forest.

out-spo-ken (out′spō″kn; out″spō′kn), *adj.* candid; free or bold of speech; frank; as, he was very *outspoken.* —*adv.* **out″spo′ken-ly.**—*n.* **out″spo′ken-ness.**

out-stand-ing (out-stănd′ĭng), *adj.* **1,** prominent; conspicuous, as a person; **2,** unpaid, as debts.

out-stretch (out-strĕch′), *v.t.* to stretch out; reach out toward something; extend: usually in the past participle.

out-strip (out-strĭp′), *v.t.* [*p.t.* and *p.p.* -stripped′ (-strĭpt′), *p.pr.* -strip′-ping], **1,** to go faster than; **2,** to excel; exceed.

out-ward (out′wẽrd), *adj.* **1,** pertaining to the exterior of an object; exterior; outside; external; outer; visible; as, *outward* appearance; hence, superficial; **2,** moving out from the shore; as, the *outward* course of a ship:—*adv.* **1,** away from an inner place; on the surface; toward the outside; **2,** externally; apparently. Also, *adv.* **out′-wards.**—*adv.* **out′ward-ly.**

out-wear (out-wâr′), *v.t.* [*p.t.* -wore′ (-wōr′), *p.p.* -worn′ (-wōrn′), *p.pr.* -wear′ing], **1,** to last longer than; as, one pair of these shoes will *outwear* two pairs of those; **2,** to outlive; outgrow.

out-weigh (out-wā′), *v.t.* to surpass in weight, value, etc.

out-wit (out-wĭt′), *v.t.* [*p.t.* and *p.p.* -wit′-ted, *p.pr.* -wit′ting], to defeat, or get the better of, by superior skill or cunning; as, to *outwit* an enemy.

Syn. foil, baffle, circumvent, thwart.

out-work (out′wûrk″), *n.* a defense or protection built beyond the main body of a fort; hence, any defense.

out-worn (out-wōrn′), past participle of the irregular verb *outwear.*

ou-zel (ōō′zl), *n.* **1,** a small European blackbird; **2,** any of several kinds of small thrushlike birds, as the ring ouzel, water ouzel, etc. Also, **ou′sel.**

o-va (ō′vȧ), *n.* plural of *ovum:* egg cells; eggs.

o-val (ō′văl), *adj.* **1,** shaped like an egg; **2,** shaped almost like an ellipse:—*n.* anything egg-shaped.

o-va-ry (ō′vȧ-rĭ), *n.* [*pl.* ovaries (-rĭz)], **1,** the organ in a female animal in which the ova, or egg cells, are formed; **2,** in a flower, the lower part of the pistil, where the seeds form (see *flower,* [2]*style,* illus.).—*adj.* **o-va′ri-an.**

o-vate (ō′vāt), *adj.* having the base broader in shape than the apex: said of a leaf (see *leaf,* illus.).

o-va-tion (ō-vā′shŭn), *n.* applause and admiration for a hero or favorite; a noisy demonstration of public esteem; as, the flyers received a tremendous *ovation.*

ov-en (ŭv′n), *n.* an inclosed chamber for baking, heating, or drying, esp. one connected with a stove or range.

ov-en-bird (ŭv′n-bûrd″), *n.* a warbler with olive-green back and mottled white under parts, its arched nest of dry leaves, built on the ground, resembling an old-fashioned oven.

o-ver (ō′vẽr), *prep.* **1,** above in position, authority, dignity, excellence, or value; **2,** across; as, to jump *over* a ditch; **3,** covering; upon; as, to wear a cape *over* the shoulders; **4,** more than; as, he spent *over* ten dollars; **5,** during; throughout; as, to stay *over* the week-end; **6,** back and forth upon; as, to wander *over* the plains:—*adv.* **1,** from beginning to end; as, to talk the matter *over;* **2,** from one to another; as, to make *over* property; from one side to the other; as, to go *over* to the enemy; **3,** in excess; in addition; as, all that is left *over;* **4,** so as to bring the opposite side up; as, to turn a coin *over;* so as to be upright no longer; as, to topple *over;* **5,** from end to end; throughout; as, a landscape dotted *over* with trees; **6,** once again; as, I will do it *over;* **7,** across the top; as, he came to a wall and jumped *over;* **8,** at an end; as, it is all *over:*—*adj.* (chiefly in composition), **1,** upper; covering; as, an *over*coat; **2,** higher; superior; as, an *over*lord.

o-ver- (ō′vẽr-), *prefix,* used in many self-explaining words, to denote: **1,** excess; as, *over*capitalize; *over*due; **2,** outer or upper position; as, *over*dress; *over*lord; **3,** motion from one side to the other; from edge to edge; across the brim, etc.; as, *over*step; *over*lap; **4,** motion passing beyond; as, *over*shoot; **5,** completeness; as, *over*joyed.

o-ver-all (ō′vẽr-ôl″), *n.* **1,** a garment entirely covering other garments; **2,** in *pl.,* loose trousers worn over other trousers to protect them from soil, dirt, etc.

o-ver-awe (ō″vẽr-ô′), *v.t.* [*p.t.* and *p.p.* -awed′ (-ôd′), *p.pr.* -aw′ing], to subdue by reverential fear or dread.

o-ver-bal-ance (ō″vẽr-băl′ăns), *v.t.* [*p.t.* and *p.p.* -anced (-ănst), *p.pr.* -anc-ing], **1,** to exceed in weight or influence; **2,** to upset the balance of:—*v.i.* to lose balance and fall:—*n.* a surplus in weight, value, etc.; an excess.

o-ver-bear (ō″vẽr-bâr′), *v.t.* [*p.t.* -bore′ (-bōr′), *p.p.* -borne′ (-bōrn′), *p.pr.* -bear′ing], **1,** to bear down, as by greater weight or force; **2,** to overcome; domineer over:—*v.i.* to produce young or fruit too freely.—*p.adj.* **o″ver-bear′ing.**

o-ver-board (ō′vẽr-bōrd″), *adv.* over the side of a ship or boat.

o-ver-bur-den (ō″vẽr-bûr′dn), *v.t.* to load with too heavy a weight; oppress with work, anxiety, etc.

o-ver-cap-i-tal-ize (ō″vẽr-kăp′ĭ-tăl-īz), *v.t.* [*p.t.* and *p.p.* -ized (-īzd), *p.pr.* -iz″ing], to issue (capital stock) out of proportion to the earning capacity or investment worth of a corporation.

o-ver-cast (ō″vẽr-kȧst′), *v.t.* [*p.t.* and *p.p.* -cast′, *p.pr.* -cast′ing], **1,** to cover over; **2,** to cloud; darken; **3,** (ō′vẽr-kȧst″), to sew over and over; take long, loose stitches over (the raw edges of a seam).

o-ver-charge (ō″vẽr-chärj′), *v.t.* [*p.t.* and *p.p.* -charged′ (-chärjd′), *p.pr.* -charg′ing], **1,** to fill or load too heavily, as a gun; **2,** to ask too high a price from or for:—*n.* (ō′vẽr-chärj″), **1,** too heavy a load, as in a firearm; **2,** too high a price.

o-ver-coat (ō′vẽr-kōt″), *n.* an out-of-door coat; a topcoat.

o-ver-come (ō″vẽr-kŭm′), *v.t.* [*p.t.* -came′ (-kām′), *p.p.* -come′, *p.pr.* -com′ing], to get the better of; conquer; hence, to make helpless:—*v.i.* to be victorious.

o-ver-crowd-ed (ō″vẽr-kroud′ĕd), *adj.* excessively crowded; congested; as, *overcrowded* tenements.

o-ver-do (ō″vẽr-dōō′), *v.t.* [*p.t.* -did′ (-dĭd′), *p.p.* -done′ (-dŭn′), *p.pr.* -do′ing], **1,** to go too far in doing; exaggerate; carry to excess; **2,** to weary by overwork; **3,** to cook too long:—*v.i.* to go beyond one's strength; exert oneself too much.

o-ver-dose (ō′vẽr-dōs″), *n.* a dose larger than the prescribed amount:—*v.t.* (ō″vẽr-dōs′), [*p.t.* and *p.p.* -dosed′ (-dōst′), *p.pr.* -dos′ing], to give too large a dose to.

o-ver-draw (ō″vẽr-drô′), *v.t.* [*p.t.* -drew′ (-drōō′), *p.p.* -drawn′ (-drôn′), *p.pr.* -draw'ing], **1**, to exaggerate; **2**, in banking, to make drafts or checks upon (an account) for a greater amount than the money on deposit in the bank.

o-ver-dress (ō″vẽr-drĕs′), *v.t.* to bedeck or array to excess; put too many adornments on:—*n.* (ō′vẽr-drĕs″), a tunic worn over a foundation dress.

o-ver-due (ō′vẽr-dū″; ō″vẽr-dū′), *adj.* **1**, unpaid at the time for payment; **2**, not present, or not occurring, at the proper time; as, the train is *overdue*.

o-ver-eat (ō″vẽr-ēt′), *v.i.* [*p.t.* -ate′ (-āt′), *p.p.* -eat′en (-ēt′n), *p.pr.* -eat′ing], to eat more than is necessary to satisfy hunger; gormandize.

o-ver-flow (ō′vẽr-flō″), *n.* **1**, the spreading of water or other liquid beyond its proper limits; **2**, that which goes beyond its proper limits; **3**, an outlet for something to spread or pour into:—*v.t.* (ō″vẽr-flō′), to flood; cover with liquid:—*v.i.* to pass the limits; be more than full.

o-ver-grown (ō′vẽr-grōn″; ō″vẽr-grōn′), *adj.* **1**, covered with too much herbage, etc.; as, a field *overgrown* with weeds; **2**, grown too large; too big for one's age.

o-ver-hand (ō′vẽr-hănd″), *adj.* **1**, down from above; as, an *overhand* blow; **2**, grasping with the hand over the object; **3**, in baseball, cricket, etc., thrown or bowled with the arm swung above the shoulder; **4**, designating a certain kind of knot (see *knot*, illus.):—*adv.* (ō′vẽr-hănd″; ō″vẽr-hănd′), so that the palm is down, or turned in toward the body; as, to catch a ball *overhand*.

o-ver-hang (ō″vẽr-hăng′), *v.t.* and *v.i.* [*p.t.* and *p.p.* -hung′(-hŭng′), *p.pr.* -hang′ing], to project above:—*n.* (ō′vẽr-hăng″), a projection or jut above something; specif., the part of a roof that projects over a gable end (see *frame house*, illus.), or, in an airplane, of the upper wing beyond the lower (see *dihedral*, illus.).

o-ver-haul (ō″vẽr-hôl′), *v.t.* **1**, to examine thoroughly for the purpose of making repairs; **2**, to overtake; gain upon.

o-ver-head (ō″vẽr-hĕd′), *adv.* over one's head; above; on an upper floor; on high:—*adj.* (ō′vẽr-hĕd″), situated above; passing through the air; pertaining to what is above or aloft: **overhead charges**, or **overhead**, **1**, those expenses incurred in running a business which do not include the cost of materials, labor, and other direct agents of production, but which cover indirect costs, such as rent, interest, insurance, heating, advertising, etc.; **2**, the general costs of running a business.

o-ver-hear (ō″vẽr-hēr′), *v.t.* [*p.t.* and *p.p.* -heard′ (-hûrd′), *p.pr.* -hear′ing], to hear (something or someone) either as an eavesdropper or unintentionally.

o-ver-heat (ō″vẽr-hēt′), *v.t.* to make too hot; heat to excess.

o-ver-joy (ō″vẽr-joi′), *v.t.* to gladden excessively; transport with joy.

o-ver-land (ō′vẽr-lănd″), *adj.* and *adv.* across the land rather than the sea; as, an *overland* journey.

o-ver-lap (ō″vẽr-lăp′), *v.t.* [*p.t.* and *p.p.* -lapped′ (-lăpt′), *p.pr.* -lap′ping], **1**, to rest upon and extend over the edge of (a flat surface); lie so as partly to cover; **2**, to lay so as to cover the edge of something, as shingles:—*v.i.* **1**, to be superimposed in part; **2**, to involve duplication; as, their fields of influence *overlapped*:—*n.* (ō′vẽr-lăp″), **1**, the extension, or amount of extension, of one thing over the edge of another; **2**, that which covers or laps over something.

o-ver-lay (ō″vẽr-lā′), *v.t.* [*p.t.* and *p.p.* -laid′ (-lād′), *p.pr.* -lay′ing], to spread above or across, as a cover or layer:—*n.* a thin sheet of paper, used in printing, to make the impression heavier.

o-ver-lie (ō″vẽr-lī′), *v.t.* [*p.t.* -lay′ (-lā′), *p.p.* -lain′ (-lān′), *p.pr.* -ly″ing], **1**, to lie over or on; **2**, to smother by lying on, as an infant.

o-ver-look (ō″vẽr-lo͝ok′), *v.t.* **1**, to look down on from above; **2**, to inspect; watch over; **3**, to fail to notice; pass over, as without punishment.

o-ver-lord (ō′vẽr-lôrd″), *n.* one who is supreme over others.

o-ver-match (ō″vẽr-măch′), *v.t.* to be too strong for; defeat.

o-ver-much (ō′vẽr-mŭch″; ō″vẽr-mŭch′), *adj.* too great:—*n.* too large an amount:—*adv.* (ō″vẽr-mŭch′), too greatly.

o-ver-night (ō″vẽr-nīt′), *adv.* on or during the previous night:—*adj.* (ō′vẽr-nīt″), **1**, pertaining to the previous evening; **2**, pertaining to a stay of one night; as, an *overnight* bag.

o-ver-plus (ō′vẽr-plŭs), *n.* excess; surplus; that which remains.

o-ver-pow-er (ō″vẽr-pou′ẽr), *v.t.* **1**, to crush by superior force; **2**, to affect greatly.—*p.adj.* **o″ver-pow′er-ing.**

o-ver-pro-duc-tion (ō″vẽr-prō-dŭk′shŭn), *n.* **1**, a raising or making of more than is needed; **2**, supply in excess of what can be sold with profit.

o-ver-rate (ō″vẽr-rāt′), *v.t.* [*p.t.* and *p.p.* -rat′ed, *p.pr.* -rat′ing], to set too high a value upon.

o-ver-reach (ō″vẽr-rēch′), *v.t.* **1**, to reach above or beyond; **2**, to miss by attempting too much; defeat (oneself) by doing too much; **3**, to get the better of by trickery; cheat:—*v.i.* to reach too far.
Syn. baffle, outwit, circumvent.

o-ver-ride (ō″vẽr-rīd′), *v.t.* [*p.t.* -rode′ (-rōd′), *p.p.* -rid′den (-rĭd′n), *p.pr.* -rid′ing], **1**, to trample down; **2**, to set aside tyrannically; as, to *override* a decision; **3**, to disregard the rights or wishes of; **4**, to ride (a horse) to exhaustion.

o-ver-rule (ō″vẽr-ro͞ol′), *v.t.* [*p.t.* and *p.p.* -ruled′ (-ro͞old′), *p.pr.* -rul′ing], **1**, in law, to decide against; as, to *overrule* an objection; **2**, to cause to change an intention, decision, etc.:—*v.i.* to control others by influence, character, etc.

o-ver-run (ō″vẽr-rŭn′), *v.t.* [*p.t.* -ran′ (-răn′), *p.p.* -run′, *p.pr.* -run′ning], **1**, to grow or spread over in great quantity or numbers; **2**, to invade; infest; **3**, in baseball, to go beyond, as a base; **4**, in printing, to carry over, as type, to another line; change the arrangement of by a change of lines:—*v.i.* to spread, flow, or extend over something or beyond the limits of something.

o-ver-sea (ō′vẽr-sē′), *adv.* (also, *overseas*), across the ocean; abroad: **oversea** (ō′vẽr=sē″), *adj.* across the sea; foreign.

o-ver-see (ō″vẽr-sē′), *v.t.* [*p.t.* -saw′ (-sô′), *p.p.* -seen′ (-sēn′), *p.pr.* -see′ing], **1**, to inspect; **2**, to superintend.

o-ver-se-er (ō′vẽr-sē′ẽr; ō′vẽr-sē″ẽr), *n.* **1**, the superintendent of some department of a business; **2**, one who looks over or inspects the work of laborers.

o-ver-shad-ow (ō″vẽr-shăd′ō), *v.t.* **1**, to throw a shade over; darken; **2**, to be more important than.

o-ver-shoe (ō′vẽr-sho͞o″), *n.* a waterproof shoe, worn over another.

o-ver-shoot (ō″vẽr-sho͞ot′), *v.t.* [*p.t.* and *p.p.* -shot′ (-shŏt′), *p.pr.* -shoot′ing], to shoot beyond:—*v.i.* **1**, to shoot beyond the mark; **2**, to shoot too far.

o-ver-shot (ō′vẽr-shŏt″), *p.adj.* **1**, with the upper jaw protruding over the lower; **2**, operated by water flowing over the top: **overshot wheel**, a water wheel which is driven by the weight and motion of the water flowing over its top.

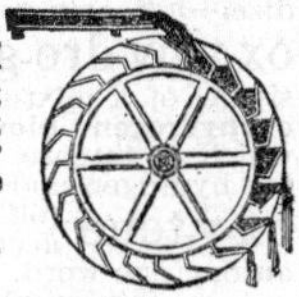

OVERSHOT WHEEL

o-ver-sight (ō′vẽr-sīt″), *n.* **1**, watchful care; management; **2**, failure to see or observe; **3**, something not seen or observed; **4**, a mistake due to inattention.
Syn. charge, supervision, direction, guidance.

o-ver-state (ō″vẽr-stāt′), *v.t.* [*p.t.* and *p.p.* -stat′ed, *p.pr.* -stat′ing], to put into too strong terms; exaggerate; express too forcefully.—*n.* **o″ver-state′ment.**

o-ver-step (ō″vẽr-stĕp′), *v.i.* [*p.t.* and *p.p.* -stepped′ (-stĕpt′), *p.pr.* -step′ping], to go too far:—*v.t.* to go beyond, as a rule, boundary, etc.; transgress.

o-ver-sub-scribe (ō″vẽr-sŭb-skrīb′), *v.t.* [*p.t.* and *p.p.* -scribed′ (-skrībd′), *p.pr.* -scrib′ing], to promise to buy a larger amount of (stock or bonds) than is offered for sale.—*n.* **o″ver-sub-scrip′tion.**

o-vert (ō′vẽrt), *adj.* **1**, publicly seen or known; **2**, in law, done with criminal intent; as, an *overt* act.—*adv.* **o′vert-ly.**

o-ver-take (ō″vẽr-tāk′), *v.t.* [*p.t.* -took′ (-tŏŏk′), *p.p.* -tak′en (-tāk′n), *p.pr.* -tak′ing], **1**, to catch up with; **2**, to take by surprise; as, a storm *overtook* us.

o-ver-throw (ō″vẽr-thrō′), *v.t.* [*p.t.* -threw′ (-thrōō′), *p.p.* -thrown′ (-thrōn′), *p.pr.* -throw′ing], **1**, to turn upside down; **2**, to defeat; destroy:—*n.* (ō′vẽr-thrō″), ruin; defeat.

o-ver-time (ō′vẽr-tīm″), *n.* hours of work beyond the regular hours:—*adj.* and *adv.* after the regular hours.

o-ver-tone (ō′vẽr-tōn″), *n.* in music, a harmonic or partial tone; any of the higher, secondary tones attending the production of the basic, or fundamental, tone of a sounding body, as a stretched string:—*v.t.* (ō″vẽr-tōn′), [*p.t.* and *p.p.* -toned′ (-tōnd′), *p.pr.* -ton′ing], in photography, to give too much tone to.

o-ver-top (ō″vẽr-tŏp′), *v.t.* [*p.t.* and *p.p.* -topped′ (-tŏpt′), *p.pr.* -top′ping], **1**, to be higher than; tower above; **2**, to surpass; obscure.

o-ver-ture (ō′vẽr-tūr), *n.* **1**, an offer or proposal; opening of negotiations; as, an *overture* of peace; **2**, a piece of music played by the orchestra before the commencement of an opera.

o-ver-turn (ō″vẽr-tûrn′), *v.t.* **1**, to conquer; **2**, to cause to upset; throw from a firm position:—*v.i.* to upset:—*n.* (ō′vẽr-tûrn″), **1**, the act of overthrowing or upsetting; **2**, the state of being overthrown or upset.

o-ver-ween-ing (ō″vẽr-wēn′ĭng), *adj.* conceited; too self-confident; arrogant.—*adv.* **o″ver-ween′ing-ly.**

o-ver-whelm (ō″vẽr-hwĕlm′), *v.t.* **1**, to cover completely; swallow up, as by a flood; **2**, to crush utterly; oppress beyond bearing; as, to *overwhelm* a person by harsh criticism.—*p.adj.* **o″ver-whelm′ing.**—*adv.* **o″ver-whelm′ing-ly.**

o-ver-work (ō″vẽr-wûrk′), *v.t.* to impose too much labor upon; as, to *overwork* a servant:—*v.i.* to labor too hard or beyond one's strength:—*n.* (ō′vẽr-wûrk″; ō″vẽr-wûrk′), **1**, exertion beyond one's strength; **2**, work in excess of a certain amount.

o-ver-wrought (ō′vẽr-rôt″; ō″vẽr-rôt′), *adj.* **1**, greatly excited; as, *overwrought* nerves; **2**, made to work to excess; **3**, too elaborate, as embroidery.

o-vi-form (ō′vĭ-fôrm), *adj.* shaped like an egg; as, an *oviform* vase.

o-vip-a-rous (ō-vĭp′ȧ-rŭs), *adj.* producing offspring from eggs which hatch outside the body, as the birds: opp. of *viviparous*.—*n.* **o″vi-par′i-ty.**

o-vi-pos-i-tor (ō″vĭ-pŏz′ĭ-tẽr), *n.* the organ for depositing eggs, found in the females of many insects, as the grasshopper and cricket.

o-void (ō′void), *n.* an egg-shaped body:—*adj.* egg-shaped. Also, *adj.* **o-voi′dal.**

o-vule (ō′vūl), *n.* **1**, the spore case of a seed plant, in which develop the egg and surrounding structures which form the seed (see [2]*style*, illus.); **2**, an immature seed.

o-vum (ō′vŭm), *n.* [*pl.* ova (ō′vȧ)], **1**, the female germ cell; an egg; **2**, in architecture, an egg-shaped ornament.

owe (ō), *v.t.* [*p.t.* and *p.p.* owed (ōd), *p.pr.* ow′ing], **1**, to be obliged to pay; as, to *owe* an apology; **2**, to be obliged or indebted for:—*v.i.* to be in debt: often with *to.*

ow-ing (ō′ĭng), *p.adj.* **1**, due as a debt; **2**, ascribable to as a result: with *to;* as, his success was *owing* to his honesty.

owl (oul), *n.* a bird that flies at night, known for its large head and eyes and for its hoot.—*adj.* **owl′ish.**

OWL ($\frac{1}{12}$)

owl-et (oul′ĕt), *n.* **1**, a young owl; **2**, a certain small owl of Europe.

own (ōn), *adj.* **1**, belonging to oneself or itself; **2**, peculiar or private: used with a possessive; as, my *own* affair:—*v.t.* **1**, to possess or hold by right; **2**, to admit or acknowledge, as a fault:—*v.i.* to confess: followed by *to.*

own-er (ōn′ẽr), *n.* one who has or possesses; a proprietor.

own-er-ship (ōn′ẽr-shĭp), *n.* sole right of possession; proprietorship; as, the *ownership* of land.

ox (ŏks), *n.* [*pl.* oxen (ŏk′sn)], the male animal of a domestic species of mammals, used as a beast of burden.

ox-al-ic ac-id (ŏk-săl′ĭk), a poisonous compound obtained from many vegetable substances, and used in bleaching, removing stains, etc.

ox-a-lis (ŏk′sȧ-lĭs), *n.* any of a widely distributed genus (*Oxalis*) of wood sorrels having small yellow, white, pink, or purple flowers.

ox-bow (ŏks′bō″), *n.* **1**, a U-shaped piece of wood in an ox yoke which forms a collar for the ox's neck; **2**, in the U. S., a U-shaped or S-shaped bend in a river.

ox-eye (ŏks′ī″), *n.* **1**, any of various plants of the composite family, such as the common daisy, often called *oxeye daisy;* **2**, any of a number of birds, including the titmouse and the least sandpiper.

Ox-ford (ŏks′fẽrd), *n.* a low, laced shoe, tying over the instep.

ox-i-da-tion (ŏk″sĭ-dā′shŭn), *n.* the process of combining with oxygen, as in burning or the formation of iron rust.

ox-ide (ŏk′sīd; ŏk′sĭd), *n.* a compound of oxygen and another element; as, *oxide* of iron. Also, **ox′id.**

ox-i-dize (ŏk′sĭ-dīz), *v.t.* [*p.t.* and *p.p.* -dized (-dīzd), *p.pr.* -diz″ing], to cause to combine with oxygen:—*v.i.* to combine with oxygen. Also, **ox′i-dise.**—*n.* **ox′i-diz″er.**

ox-lip (ŏks′lĭp″), *n.* a variety of primrose, much like the cowslip.

Ox-o-ni-an (ŏk-sō′nĭ-ăn), *adj.* pertaining to Oxford, England:—*n.* a student or graduate of Oxford University.

ox-y-a-cet-y-lene (ŏk″sĭ-ȧ-sĕt′ĭ-lēn), *adj.* of, pertaining to, or consisting of, a mixture of oxygen and acetylene: **oxyacetylene burner** or **torch**, an instrument burning a mixture of oxygen and acetylene to produce an intensely hot flame: used for the cutting and welding of metals.

ox-y-gen (ŏk′sĭ-jĕn), *n.* an active, colorless, odorless, gaseous element, essential to all vegetable and animal life, occurring as a constituent of water and of most animal and vegetable products, acids, bases, and salts: **oxygen tent**, a tentlike covering for the head and shoulders, within which the air can be enriched with oxygen.

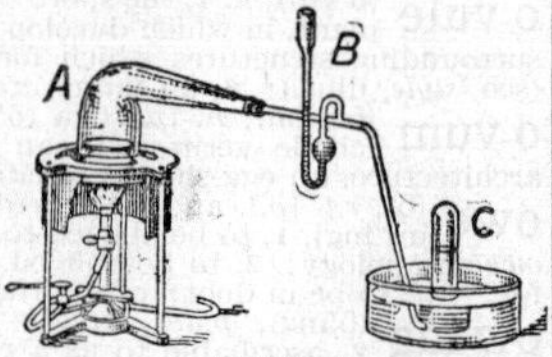

OXYGEN

Apparatus for the preparation of oxygen by heating chlorate of potassium: *A*, retort containing the chlorate; *B*, safety tube; *C*, test tube in which the gas is collected.

ox-y-gen-ate (ŏk′sĭ-jĕn-āt), *v.t.* [*p.t.* and *p.p.* -at″ed, *p.pr.* -at″ing], to oxygenize: oxidize.—*n.* **ox″y-gen-a′tion.**

ox-y-gen-ize (ŏk′sĭ-jĕn-īz), *v.t.* [*p.t.* and *p.p.* -ized (-īzd), *p.pr.* -iz″ing], to mix or combine with oxygen; oxidize.—*adj.* **ox′y-gen-iz″a-ble.**

ox-y-hy-dro-gen (ŏk″sĭ-hī′drō-jĕn), *adj.* pertaining to, or consisting of, a mixture of oxygen and hydrogen: **oxyhydrogen blowpipe**, an instrument by which an intense heat is produced by burning hydrogen and oxygen.

ox-y-tone (ŏk′sĭ-tōn), *adj.* having an acute accent on the last syllable:—*n.* an oxytone word.

o-yer (ō′yẽr; oi′ẽr), *n.* in law, a hearing or trial of legal cases or causes.

o-yer and ter-mi-ner (tûr′mĭ-nẽr), **1**, a higher criminal court; **2**, in England, a court composed of two or more judges, for the trial of cases of treason, felony, and misdemeanor.

o-yez (ō′yĕs″), *interj.* the introductory cry of an official or public crier demanding silence in a court room: usually repeated three times. Also, **o′yes″.**

oys-ter (ois′tẽr), *n.* **1**, any of a family of edible sea mollusks having two unequal hinged shells; **2**, any of several other bivalve mollusks, as the pearl oyster; **3**, the small oyster-shaped piece of dark meat, found in the back of a fowl.

oys-ter plant a plant whose root, when cooked, has a flavor suggesting that of oysters; salsify.

o-zone (ō′zōn), *n.* a colorless gas regarded as a form of oxygen: used in bleaching and in purifying water.

P

pab-u-lum (păb′ū-lŭm), *n.* **1**, food; nourishment; **2**, food for thought; as, mental *pabulum.*

pace (pās), *n.* **1**, a step; the space covered by a step in walking; hence, about 30 inches; **2**, gait, or manner of moving, such as a trot, gallop, etc.; **3**, a certain swaying gait of a horse; **4**, rate of speed; as, to keep up the *pace*:—*v.t.* [*p.t.* and *p.p.* paced (pāst), *p.pr.* pac′ing], **1**, to measure by steps; **2**, to walk over with long, even steps; **3**, to train to go at a certain gait:—*v.i.* **1**, to walk with long, regular steps, as in measuring; **2**, to go at a swaying gait, as a horse.

pac-er (pās′ẽr), *n.* **1**, one who moves with measured steps; **2**, a horse with a swaying gait called a pace, in which the legs on each side move together.

pa-cha (pȧ-shä′; pȧsh′ä), *n.* the title used in Turkey for officers of high rank. See **pa-sha′**, *Pfd. S.*

pa-chi-si (pä-chē′sĭ; -zĭ), *n.* a four-handed game of East Indian origin, played with pieces moved according to a throw of dice. Also, **par-che′si; par-chi′si.**

pach-y-derm (păk′ĭ-dûrm), *n.* **1**, one of a group of thick-skinned animals, such as the elephant, rhinoceros, etc.; **2**, humorously, a person lacking sensitiveness. —*adj.* **pach″y-der′ma-tous.**

pa-cif-ic (pȧ-sĭf′ĭk), *adj.* **1**, peacemaking; peaceable; mild; as, *pacific* words; **2**, peaceful; tranquil: **Pacific Ocean**, the ocean west of America and east of Asia and Australia: so called because of the calmness of its surface. Also, **pa-cif′i-cal.**—*adv.* **pa-cif′i-cal-ly.**

Syn. calm, gentle, still, smooth.—*Ant.* stormy, quarrelsome, contentious.

pa-cif-i-cate (pȧ-sĭf′ĭ-kāt), *v.t.* [*p.t.* and *p.p.* -cat″ed, *p.pr.* -cat″ing], to pacify; appease; soothe.—*n.* **pa-cif′i-ca″-tor.**—*adj.* **pa-cif′i-ca-to-ry.**

pac-i-fi-ca-tion (păs″ĭ-fĭ-kā′shŭn; pȧ-sĭf″ĭ-kā′shŭn), *n.* **1**, the act of bringing about peace; **2**, the arrangement of terms of peace, or the terms so arranged; reconciliation.

pac-i-fist (păs′ĭ-fĭst), *n.* one who opposes war as wrong, and who believes in, and works for, peace between the nations; a peacemaker: opp. of *militarist.*—*n.* **pac′i-fism.**

pac-i-fy (păs′ĭ-fī), *v.t.* [*p.t.* and *p.p.* -fied (-fīd), *p.pr.* -fy″ing], **1**, to calm or appease; as, to *pacify* an angry man; **2**, to free from war or violence; restore to quiet. —*n.* **pac′i-fi″er.**

Syn. soothe, compose, allay, tranquilize.—*Ant.* excite, disturb, irritate, provoke.

pack (păk), *n.* **1**, a large bundle tied up for carrying, esp. on the back; a load; burden, esp. for carrying on an animal's back; **2**, a collection or quantity; as, a *pack* of worries; **3**, a full set of things; as, a *pack* of playing cards; **4**, a number of animals associated together for hunting, etc.; as, a *pack* of hounds; **5**, a gang; as, a *pack* of thieves; **6**, a number of floating cakes of ice driven close together; **7**, a therapeutic measure in which the patient is wrapped in hot or cold wet cloths: **pack animal**, an animal used for carrying loads, as of food, ore, etc.:—*v.t.* **1**, to stow away, arrange compactly, or press into a bundle; as, to *pack* clothes for a trip; **2**, to fill (a receptacle) entirely; as, to *pack* a trunk; *pack* a freight car with crates; **3**, to crowd together; as, to *pack* people in a room; **4**, to press into a hard mass; as, to *pack* earth; **5**, to dismiss or discharge: with *off*; as, to *pack* off a servant; **6**, to carry on the back; as, to *pack* a load of gravel by mule train; **7**, *Slang*, in the western U. S., to carry loaded:

said of guns; as, the cowboy *packed* two pistols; **8**, to fill in, as a joint, so as to make water- or air-tight:—*v.i.* **1**, to press or crowd together into a hard mass; as, ice *packs* together; **2**, to stow things for safety or carrying; **3**, to admit of being stowed; as, these articles *pack* well; **4**, to depart or remove in haste: usually with *off*.

Syn., *n.* drove, flock. (See herd.)

pack-age (păk′ăj), *n.* **1**, a bundle or bale of goods; a parcel; packet; **2**, the act or process of stowing for safe-keeping or transportation.

Syn. (see bundle).

pack-er (păk′ẽr), **1**, one who or that which stows things for safety in carrying; **2**, in the U. S., one who prepares and packs provisions in large quantities for preservation or for the market.

pack-et (păk′ĕt), *n.* **1**, a small bundle or parcel; **2**, a vessel sailing between two or more ports at regular periods, and carrying passengers, mail, and merchandise.

pack-ing (păk′ĭng), *n.* **1**, the act of one who packs; **2**, straw, paper, or other material used in stowing goods for carrying; **3**, material used to fill small spaces.

pack-sad-dle (păk′săd″l), *n.* a saddle so constructed as to hold a load on a pack animal.

pack-thread (păk′thrĕd″), *n.* strong twine used to tie bundles.

pact (păkt), *n.* an agreement or contract: usually not to be enforced by law.

¹pad (păd), *n.* a slow-paced horse:—*v.i.* [*p.t.* and *p.p.* pad′ded, *p.pr.* pad′ding], to walk slowly and heavily.

²pad (păd), *n.* **1**, a soft cushion used to fill a hollow space, lessen pressure or friction, protect from blows, etc.; **2**, a cushionlike part of anything, as the under part of the toes of some animals; **3**, a block of sheets of paper for writing or drawing; **4**, in the U. S., the floating leaf of certain water plants:—*v.t.* [*v.t.* and *p.p.* pad′ded, *p.pr.* pad′ding], **1**, to stuff, or line thickly, as a coat; **2**, to increase in size by adding unnecessary material; as, to *pad* a story: **padded cell,** in a hospital for the insane, a room with padded walls, to prevent violent patients from injuring themselves.

pad-ding (păd′ĭng), *n.* **1**, a material used for stuffing; **2**, useless or unnecessary matter used for filling space, as in a newspaper or magazine article.

¹pad-dle (păd′l), *v.i.* [*p.t.* and *p.p.* -dled (-ld), *p.pr.* -dling], **1**, to move a canoe or rowboat by means of a short oar without a rowlock; **2**, to row slowly:—*v.t.* **1**, to propel or move with a short oar without a rowlock; **2**, to spank:—*n.* **1**, a short oar with a broad blade at one or both ends, used without a rowlock; **2**, a short, broad-bladed instrument used for stirring, mixing, etc.; **3**, one of the broad boards of a water wheel or of the paddle wheel of a steamboat.—*n.* **pad′dler.**

²pad-dle (păd′l), *v.i.* [*p.t.* and *p.p.* -dled (-ld), *p.pr.* -dling], to move about, play, or wade, in shallow water.

pad-dle wheel a wheel for moving a boat, having broad boards arranged like spokes around its rim.

¹pad-dock (păd′ŭk), *n.* formerly, a large toad or frog.

²pad-dock (păd′ŭk), *n.* **1**, a small field for pasture; **2**, a stable yard where horses are exercised; **3**, at a race course, an inclosure in which horses are saddled and gently exercised before a race.

pad-dy (păd′ĭ), *n.* rice in the husk; also, rice generally.

Pad-dy (păd′ĭ), *n.* [*pl.* Paddies (-ĭz)], an Irishman: the most general Irish nickname, from Patrick.

pad-lock (păd′lŏk″), *n.* a portable lock with a jointed link to pass through a staple or eye:—*v.t.* to fasten with, or as with, such a lock.

***pa-dre** (pä′drā), [Span., Port., and It.], *n.* [*pl.* *Span.* and *Port.* padres (-drās); *It.* padri (-drē)], father: the Spanish and Italian title for a priest or monk.

***pa-dro-ne** (pä-drō′nā), [It.], *n.* [*pl.* padrones (-nāz); *It.* padroni (-nē)], **1**, a person, usually an Italian, who employs street musicians and child beggars; **2**, in Italy, a master; a proprietor, as of an inn; **3**, an Italian contractor for labor.

pæ-an (pē′ăn), *n.* a loud, joyous song of praise or triumph. Also, **pe′an.**

pa-gan (pā′găn), *n.* **1**, a heathen; an idolater; **2**, a person having no religious beliefs:—*adj.* **1**, heathen; idolatrous; **2**, irreligious.—*n.* **pa′gan-ism.**

¹page (pāj), *n.* **1**, in the days of chivalry, a boy, usually of high birth, attending on a person of distinction as the first stage in the process of his training toward knighthood; **2**, a serving boy in livery or uniform; **3**, a male attendant on a legislative, or lawmaking, body:—*v.t.* [*p.t.* and *p.p.* paged (pājd), *p.pr.* pag′ing], **1**, to attend as a page; **2**, *U. S. Colloq.*, to call for or summon by a page.

²page (pāj), *n.* **1**, one side of a leaf, as of a book; also, the type for printing such a side; **2**, any record or writing; as, the *page* of history:—*v.t.* [*p.t.* and *p.p.* paged (pājd), *p.pr.* pag′ing], to mark or number in pages.

pag-eant (păj′ĕnt; pā′jĕnt), *n.* **1**, a brilliant or stately display or procession; a series of scenes acted in costume, for public entertainment; **2**, empty show; mere display.—*n.* **pag′eant-ry.**

pag-i-na-tion (păj″ĭ-nā′shŭn), *n.* **1**, the act, method, or system of numbering the pages of a book; **2**, the sequence of page numbers in a book or the like.

pa-go-da (pȧ-gō′dȧ), *n.* in the Far East, a temple built like a pyramidal tower with many stories.

PAGODA

paid (pād), past tense and past participle of the verb *pay*.

pail (pāl), *n.* an open vessel of wood or metal with a curved handle: used for carrying liquids; a bucket.

pail-ful (pāl′fo͝ol), *n.* [*pl.* pailfuls (-fo͝olz)], as much as a pail will hold.

pail-lasse (păl-yăs′), *n.* a mattress filled with straw or other cheap material.

pain (pān), *n.* **1**, orig., penalty: now rare, except in such phrases as *on pain of death;* **2**, distress of body or mind; **3**, in *pl.*, diligent effort; as, he took great *pains* with his work:—*v.t.* **1**, to cause bodily suffering to; **2**, to make uneasy; grieve.—*p.adj.* **pained.**

Syn., *n.* suffering, pang, affliction, agony.—*Ant.*, *n.* comfort, pleasure, ease.

pain-ful (pān′fo͝ol), *adj.* **1**, full of, or causing, distress of body or mind; distressing; as, a *painful* illness; a *painful* duty; **2**, difficult; as, a *painful* task.—*adv.* **pain′ful-ly.**—*n.* **pain′ful-ness.**

pain-less (pān′lĕs), *adj.* free from distress or hurt; as, a *painless* operation.—*adv.* **pain′less-ly.**—*n.* **pain′less-ness.**

pains-tak-ing (pānz′tāk″ĭng), *adj.* using great effort; taking much trouble; careful.—*adv.* **pains′tak″ing-ly.**

paint (pānt), *v.t.* **1,** to portray in colors; as, to *paint* a portrait; **2,** to describe in words; as, to *paint* the joys of heaven; **3,** to decorate by the use of paint; **4,** to coat or cover with color; as, to *paint* a house:—*v.i.* **1,** to practice the art of making pictures with color; **2,** to use artificial color on the face:—*n.* **1,** a coloring substance or pigment or a preparation of this, as with oil or water; **2,** cosmetic rouge.—*p.adj.* **paint′ed.**

¹paint-er (pān′tẽr), *n.* **1,** one whose occupation is to cover surfaces with paint; as, a house *painter;* **2,** one who paints pictures; an artist: **painter's colic,** a disease caused by poisoning from the lead used in paint.

²paint-er (pān′tẽr), *n.* a rope attached to the bow of a boat for fastening it.

³paint-er (pān′tẽr), *n. U. S. Dial.,* the puma, or American panther.

paint-ing (pānt′ĭng), *n.* **1,** the act, art, or occupation of laying on colors with a brush; **2,** the art of showing objects on a surface by means of colors; **3,** a picture in colors; **4,** a vivid, clear description in words.

pair (pâr), *n.* **1,** two things of a kind, similar in form, intended to be used together, or corresponding to each other in some way; as, a *pair* of eyes, horses, or shoes; **2,** a single thing composed of two like parts; as, a *pair* of scissors; **3,** a married couple; **4,** any couple or brace; as, a *pair* of ducks; **5,** two members of different parties, as in a legislative body, who agree that neither will vote on a given motion; **6,** a set: now used only in a *pair* of stairs:—*v.t.* to join in couples; mate:—*v.i.* **1,** to come together in couples; as, to *pair* off in a dance; **2,** to match; form a pair, or couple.

pa-ja-ma (pȧ-jä′mȧ), *n.* **1,** an Oriental garment, consisting of loose silk or cotton trousers; **2,** in *pl.,* a sleeping suit consisting of a loose coat and trousers. Also, **py-ja′ma,** *Pfd. S.*

pal (păl), *n. Slang,* an intimate friend; chum; mate.

pal-ace (păl′ās), *n.* **1,** the official residence of a king or other ruler, or of an archbishop or bishop; **2,** a magnificent house.

pal-a-din (păl′ȧ-dĭn), *n.* **1,** a knight, esp. one of the knights of Charlemagne; **2,** hence, a notable champion.

pa-læ-o- (pā′lē-ō-; păl′ē-ō-), a combining form from the Greek, meaning old; as, *palæo*lithic. Also, **pa′le-o-,** *Pfd. S.*

pa-læ-o-lith-ic (pā″lē-ō-lĭth′ĭk; păl″ē-), *adj.* pertaining to the old stone age, or earliest period of human development. Also, **pa″le-o-lith′ic,** *Pfd. S.*

pa-læ-on-tol-o-gy (pā″lē-ŏn-tŏl′ō-jĭ; păl″ē-), *n.* that branch of geology which treats of the fossil remains of animals and plants. Also, **pa″le-on-tol′o-gy,** *Pfd. S.*—*n.* **pa″læ-on-tol′o-gist.**

Pa-læ-o-zo-ic (pā″lē-ō-zō′ĭk; păl″ē-), *adj.* pertaining to the geological era once supposed to mark the beginning of life:—*n.* the geological division just before the Mesozoic, or Age of Reptiles. Also, **Pa″le-o-zo′ic,** *Pfd. S.*

pa-læs-tra (pȧ-lĕs′trȧ), *n.* [*pl.* palæstræ (-trē); palæstras (-trȧz)], in ancient Greece, a school for wrestling or gymnastic exercises. Also, **pa-les′tra.**

pal-an-quin (păl″ăn-kēn′), *n.* in India and China, a covered carriage for one passenger, carried on the shoulders of men. Also, **pal″an-keen′.**

pal-at-a-ble (păl′ăt-ȧ-bl), *adj.* agreeable to the taste; pleasing.—*n.* **pal′at-a-ble-ness.**—*adv.* **pal′at-a-bly.**

pal-a-tal (păl′ȧ-tăl), *adj.* **1,** of or pertaining to the roof of the mouth; **2,** designating various sounds formed between the tongue and the roof of the mouth, as the consonant *k* in *keen,* the vowels *ē* and *ĭ,* the *y* in *yes,* etc.:—*n.* a palatal sound.

pal-ate (păl′āt), *n.* **1,** the roof of the mouth in vertebrate animals; **2,** the sense of taste; also, figuratively, mental liking: **hard palate,** the bony front part of the roof of the mouth: **soft palate,** the fleshy back part of the roof of the mouth: often, but incorrectly, the uvula.

pa-la-tial (pȧ-lā′shăl), *adj.* pertaining to, or suitable to, a palace; stately; magnificent.—*adv.* **pa-la′tial-ly.**

pa-lat-i-nate (pȧ-lăt′ĭ-nāt), *n.* a province ruled over by an earl, count, etc., having certain royal privileges.

pal-a-tine (păl′ȧ-tīn; păl′ȧ-tĭn), *adj.* clothed with, or given, certain royal privileges or rights; as, an elector *palatine:*—*n.* a count, earl, etc., who is given such privileges.

pa-la-ver (pȧ-lä′vẽr; pȧ-lăv′ẽr), *n.* **1,** in Africa, a parley with natives; **2,** deceitful or idle talk; chatter:—*v.i.* **1,** to talk in a deceitful way; **2,** to talk idly; chatter.

¹pale (pāl), *adj.* **1,** wan; wanting in color; **2,** of a faint luster or brightness:—*v.i.* [*p.t.* and *p.p.* paled (pāld), *p.pr.* pal′ing], to turn white, or lose color:—*v.t.* to render wan.—*adv.* **pale′ly.**—*n.* **pale′ness.**

Syn., adj. pallid, ashen, bloodless, ghastly.

²pale (pāl), *n.* **1,** a narrow board, placed vertically, used in fencing; a pointed stake; **2,** a fence of such stakes inclosing a space; hence, a limit; **3,** a district or territory within bounds; a restricted locality:—*v.t.* [*p.t.* and *p.p.* paled (pāld), *p.pr.* pal′ing], to inclose or fence with pales.

pale-face (pāl′fās″), *n.* a white person: a name for the white man, attributed to the American Indians.

pa-le-o- (pā′lē-ō-; păl′ē-ō-), a combining form from the Greek, meaning old; as, *paleo*lithic. Also, **pa′læ-o-.**

pa-le-o-lith-ic (pā″lē-ō-lĭth′ĭk; păl″ē-), *adj.* pertaining to the old stone age, or earliest period of human development. Also, **pa″læ-o-lith′ic.**

pa-le-on-tol-o-gy (pā″lē-ŏn-tŏl′ō-jĭ; păl″ē-), *n.* that branch of geology which treats of life in past geological periods, as shown by fossil or stonelike remains of animals and plants. Also, **pa″læ-on-tol′o-gy.**—*n.* **pa″le-on-tol′o-gist.**

Pa-le-o-zo-ic (pā″lē-ō-zō′ĭk; păl″ē-), *adj.* in geology, designating, or pertaining to, the era during which it was once supposed the earliest forms of life existed:—*n.* the geological era just before the Mesozoic, or Age of Reptiles. Also, **Pa″læ-o-zo′ic.**

pa-les-tra (pȧ-lĕs′trȧ), *n.* [*pl.* palestræ (-trē); palestras (-trȧz)], in ancient Greece, a school for wrestling or gymnastic exercises. Also, **pa-læs′tra,** *Pfd. S.*

pal-e-tot (păl′ē-tō; păl′-tō), *n.* a kind of loose cloak or coat, worn by men and women.

pal-ette (păl′ĕt), *n.* a thin, oval, wood or porcelain plate with a hole for the thumb, used by artists for mixing and holding colors.

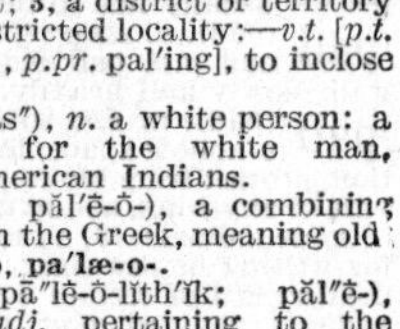

PALETTE

pal-frey (pôl′frĭ; păl′frĭ), *n.* a saddle horse, esp. a small one for a lady's use; as, she rode a snowy *palfrey.*

pal-imp-sest (păl′ĭmp-sĕst), *n.* a parchment manuscript which, after the writing upon it has been partially erased, is used again, the former writing being more or less visible.

pal-ing (pāl′ĭng), *n.* **1**, a fence made of narrow upright boards, usually pointed at the top; **2**, one of the strips of wood used for making a fence; a picket.

pal-in-gen-e-sis (păl″ĭn-jĕn′ē-sĭs), *n.* **1**, new or second birth; **2**, metamorphosis, the change in form and structure of an insect during its development.

pal-i-sade (păl″ĭ-sād′), *n.* **1**, a fence or fort formed of pointed stakes driven into the ground; **2**, in *pl.*, a long line of cliffs, usually along a river:—*v.t.* [*p.t.* and *p.p.* -sad′ed, *p.pr.* -sad′ing], to inclose or fortify with stakes.

[1]**pall** (pôl), *n.* a covering for a coffin, hearse, or tomb; hence, any heavy, deep covering; as, a *pall* of smoke:—*v.t.* to cover with, or as with, a pall.

[2]**pall** (pôl), *v.i.* to become distasteful or wearisome; lose power to interest: usually with *on:*—*v.t.* to satiate.

[1]**pal-la-di-um** (pă-lā′dĭ-ŭm), *n.* [*pl.* palladia (-*ȧ*)], in mythology, any statue of Pallas Athena, esp. (usually, *Palladium*) the statue at Troy, said to have fallen from heaven and to be necessary to the safety of the city; hence, any safeguard.

[2]**pal-la-di-um** (pă-lā′dĭ-ŭm), *n.* a rare silver-white metal of the platinum group, notable for its power of absorbing gases.

Pal-las (păl′*ȧ*s), *n.* **1**, one of the many small planets or asteroids whose orbits lie between Jupiter and Mars; **2**, in mythology, a name often prefixed to that of Athena, the goddess of wisdom.

pall-bear-er (pôl′bâr″ẽr), *n.* one of the persons who carry or attend a coffin at a funeral.

[1]**pal-let** (păl′ĕt), *n.* any of various tools or devices, as a wooden, shovel-like tool used in making pottery, a pawl that regulates the movement of a ratchet wheel, etc.

[2]**pal-let** (păl′ĕt), *n.* a small, rough bed, as of straw.

pal-li-ate (păl′ĭ-āt), *v.t.* [*p.t.* and *p.p.* -at″ed, *p.pr.* -at″ing], **1**, to excuse or cause to appear less wrong; as, to *palliate* a fault; **2**, to lessen or abate the severity or painfulness of; as, to *palliate* disease.—*n.* **pal″li-a′tion.**
Syn. soften, mitigate, extenuate.

pal-li-a-tive (păl′ĭ-*ȧ*-tĭv), *adj.* **1**, tending to excuse or cover over; as, *palliative* circumstances; **2**, serving to relieve without curing:—*n.* that which serves to excuse guilt or to lessen disease or pain.

pal-lid (păl′ĭd), *adj.* pale; wan; lacking in color; as, a *pallid* face.—*adv.* **pal′lid-ly.**—*n.* **pal′lid-ness.**
Syn. ghastly, bloodless, ashen.

pall–mall (pĕl″=mĕl′), *n.* **1**, a game formerly played with a ball which was driven through an iron ring by a mallet; **2**, a court or alley for playing the game: **Pall Mall** (also, păl″ măl′), a street in London famous for its clubs: formerly a pall-mall alley.

pal-lor (păl′ŏr), *n.* lack of color, as in the face; paleness.

[1]**palm** (päm), *n.* **1**, the hollow, hairless, inner surface of the human hand; **2**, a measure of length varying from three to four inches:—*v.t.* **1**, to conceal in the closed hand, as in the performance of a sleight-of-hand trick; **2**, hence, to pass by fraud or trickery: with *off;* as, to *palm* off inferior goods.

[2]**palm** (päm), *n.* **1**, any of various species of tropical trees, characterized by large, heavy leaves generally radiating from the summit of a slender trunk from which no large branches grow (see illus. next column); **2**, a leaf of the tree, used as an emblem of victory; **3**, hence, victory; superiority.

pal-mate (păl′māt), *adj.* **1**, like a hand with fingers spread; as, *palmate* antlers; **2**, having the digits joined by a web, as certain birds; web-footed; **3**, in botany, having several leaflets diverging from a central point, as in the horse-chestnut tree (see *leaf*, illus.). Also, **pal′mat-ed.**—*adv.* **pal′mate-ly.**—*n.* **pal-ma′tion.**

palm-er (päm′ẽr), *n.* a pilgrim to the Holy Land who carried a palm branch as a token or sign of his pilgrimage.

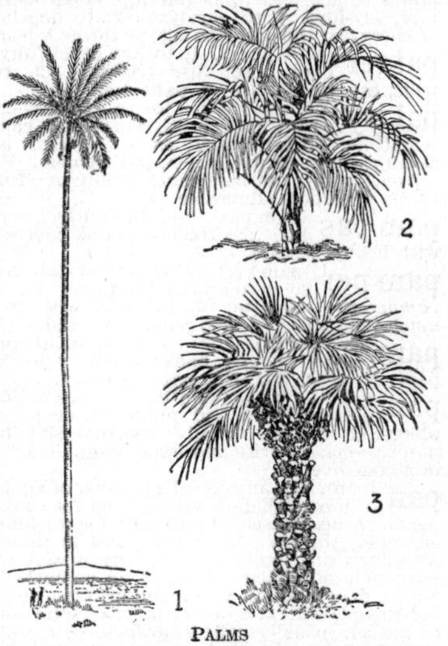

Palms
1, wax palm; 2, feather palm; 3, Chinese hemp.

palm-er worm **1**, any one of a number of kinds of destructive caterpillar; **2**, specif., a brownish green caterpillar which feeds on apple leaves and fruit.

pal-met-to (păl-mĕt′ō), *n.* [*pl.* palmettos; palmettoes (-ōz)], a kind of palm tree with fan-shaped leaves, growing in the West Indies and the southern part of the U. S.; the cabbage palm.

palm-ist (päm′ĭst; păl′mĭst), *n.* one who claims to tell fortunes or read character from the lines inside the hand.

palm-is-try (päm′ĭs-trĭ; păl′mĭs-trĭ), *n.* the pretended art of reading character or foretelling the future by the lines and marks on the inside of a person's hand.

Palm Sun-day the Sunday next before Easter: so called in allusion to Christ's entry into Jerusalem, when palm branches were strewn before him

palm-y (päm′ĭ), *adj.* [*comp.* palm′i-er, *superl.* palm′i-est], **1**, abounding in palm trees; as, a *palmy* land; **2**, flourishing; prosperous; as, *palmy* days.

palp (pălp), *n.* a feeler or organ of touch or taste, connected with a mouth part, as in certain insects and crustaceans. Also, **pal′pus** [*pl.* palpi (-pī)].

pal-pa-ble (păl′p*ȧ*-bl), *adj.* **1**, capable of being touched or felt; as, a *palpable* substance; **2**, easily seen; noticeable; plain; as, a *palpable* wrong.—*n.* **pal′pa-ble-ness.**—*adv.* **pal′pa-bly.**—*n.* **pal″pa-bil′i-ty.**
Syn. manifest, obvious, apparent, evident.

pal-pi-tate (păl'pĭ-tāt), *v.i.* [*p.t.* and *v.p.* -tat"ed, *p.pr.* -tat"ing], to beat or throb rapidly, as the heart; flutter.

pal-pi-ta-tion (păl"pĭ-tā'shŭn), *n.* **1**, too rapid beating or throbbing of the heart; **2**, a fluttering movement.

pal-sied (pôl'zĭd), *p.adj.* paralyzed; shaky; tottering.

pal-sy (pôl'zĭ), *n.* [*pl.* palsies (-zĭz)], **1**, paralysis, or loss of motion or of feeling in any part of the body; **2**, loss of power to act:—*v.t.* [*p.t.* and *p.p.* -sied (-zĭd), *p.pr.* -sy-ing], **1**, to paralyze; **2**, to deprive of energy or the power to act, as through fear.

pal-ter (pôl'tẽr), *v.i.* **1**, to act deceitfully; play false; use trickery; **2**, to trifle, esp. in speech.—*n.* **pal'ter-er.**

pal-try (pôl'trĭ), *adj.* [*comp.* pal'tri-er, *superl.* pal'tri-est], worthless; contemptible; pitiful; small; as, a *paltry* gift to charity.—*adv.* **pal'tri-ly.**—*n.* **pal'tri-ness.**
Syn. petty, insignificant, trifling.—*Ant.* noble, generous, admirable.

pam-pas (păm'pȧz), *n.pl.* in South America, vast treeless plains covered with heavy pasture.

pam-per (păm'pẽr), *v.t.* **1**, to treat daintily so as to gratify the taste; as, to *pamper* the appetite; **2**, to treat with too much indulgence; as, to *pamper* a child.

pam-phlet (păm'flĕt), *n.* **1**, a small unbound book, usually with a paper cover; **2**, a brief treatise or essay.

pam-phlet-eer (păm"flĕt-ẽr'), *n.* a writer and publisher of pamphlets or essays, usually controversial in nature:—*v.i.* to write and issue pamphlets, as in a controversy.

pan (păn), *n.* **1**, any one of a number of kinds of broad, shallow vessel, used for cooking and other household purposes, for washing out gold, tin, etc., in mining, and in many manufacturing processes; **2**, any vessel or receptacle of similar shape; **3**, in a flintlock gun, a depression in which the priming powder was placed; **4**, a bed or layer of solid soil or gravel: usually called *hardpan*:—*v.t.* [*p.t.* and *p.p.* panned (pănd), *p.pr.* pan'ning], to cook or wash in a shallow vessel; as, to *pan* oysters; *pan* gravel for gold:—*v.i.* in mining, to yield gold; also, to appear in the pan, as gold: with *out:* **pan out**, *Colloq.*, to turn out successfully or well; also, to turn out (in a specified way).

Pan (păn), *n.* in Greek mythology, the god of flocks and herds and of the woods, represented as having a goat's legs, ears, and horns: identified with the Roman god *Faunus.*

pan- (păn-), a combining form from the Greek, meaning all; as, *panacea; pantheon.* Also, **pan'to-.**

pan-a-ce-a (păn"ȧ-sē'ȧ), *n.* a remedy or medicine for all ills.

Pan-a-ma (păn"ȧ-mä'), *n.* a hat of excellent quality and texture, made in South and Central America of the hand-plaited, young leaves of the palm tree: called in full *Panama hat.* Also, **pan"a-ma'.**

Pan–A-mer-i-can (păn"-ȧ-mĕr'ĭ-kăn), *adj.* pertaining to both North and South America or to all Americans: **Pan–American Union**, an association of the 21 American republics, for promoting commercial and political coöperation.—*n.* **Pan"–A-mer'i-can-ism.**

pan-cake (păn'kāk"), *n.* a thin cake made of batter, baked on a griddle.

pan-cre-as (păng'krē-ăs; păn'krē-ăs), *n.* a large fleshy gland, under and behind the stomach, producing a juice that helps digestion.—*adj.* **pan"cre-at'ic.**

Pan-de-an (păn-dē'ăn), *adj.* pertaining to Pan, the god of flocks and pastures and of the wild life of the forests: **Pandean pipes**, *n.pl.* a simple musical wind instrument made of hollow reeds: also called *Panpipe; Panpipes; Pan's pipe.*

Pan-de-mo-ni-um (păn"dē-mō'nĭ-ŭm), *n.* the abode of demons or the council chamber of the infernal regions: **pandemonium**, **1**, a place or abode of general disorder; **2**, wild uproar.

pan-der (păn'dẽr), *v.i.* to contribute to the satisfying of the unworthy desires of others:—*n.* one who so contributes.

Pan-do-ra (păn-dō'rȧ), *n.* in mythology, the first mortal woman, induced by curiosity to open a certain box, thus letting out into the world all evils and diseases.

pane (pān), *n.* a square or oblong section or panel of a wall, door, etc., esp. of glass in a window or door.

pan-e-gyr-ic (păn"ē-jĭr'ĭk), *n.* praise formally written or spoken in honor of some person or event; any high praise.—*adj.***pan"e-gyr'i-cal.**—*n.***pan'e-gyr"ist.**
Syn. laudation, eulogy.

pan-el (păn'ĕl), *n.* **1**, a division or section of a wall or ceiling; **2**, a piece of board, the edges of which are put in a frame; as, the *panel* of a door; **3**, a thin board on which a picture is painted; also, the picture itself; **4**, a strip of material of different kind or color put lengthwise in a skirt; **5**, a list of persons summoned to serve as jurors; also, the whole jury; **6**, the segment of an airplane wing:—*v.t.* to form, fit, or decorate with strips or sections of different kind, color, or design.—*n.* **pan'el-ing.**

pang (păng), *n.* a violent, sudden pain either mental or physical.

Pan-hel-len-ic (păn"hĕ-lĕn'ĭk; păn"hĕ-lē'nĭk), *adj.* of or pertaining to all the Greeks; esp., designating a movement for uniting all Greeks into one political body.

¹pan-ic (păn'ĭk), *adj.* like, or due to, sudden, extreme, and unreasoning fright: with reference to the god Pan as the supposed cause of such fright: **Panic**, of or pertaining to Pan, the god of flocks and pastures:—*n.* **1**, extreme and sudden fright, orig. supposed to be caused by the god Pan, affecting an individual, or, more usually, a group of persons or animals; **2**, a sudden general condition of distrust in financial and commercial quarters, marked by the sudden attempt to withdraw deposits from banks, the selling of property, and the demand for immediate payment of loans.—*adj.* **pan'ick-y.**
Syn., n. fear, terror, alarm. (See horror.)

²pan-ic (păn'ĭk), *n.* any of a large genus of North American grasses: also called *panic grass.*

pan-i-cle (păn'ĭ-kl), *n.* a compound raceme; commonly, any conical, irregularly branched flower cluster, as in the lilac (cf. *inflorescence*, illus.).

pan-ic–strick-en (păn'ĭk-strĭk"n), *adj.* filled with overwhelming fear. Also, **pan'ic–struck".**

pan-nier (păn'yẽr; păn'ĭ-ẽr), *n.* **1**, a bread basket; **2**, one of two baskets suspended across the back of a horse for carrying market produce; **3**, a kind of framework to enlarge a woman's skirts at the hips.

pan-o-ply (păn'ō-plĭ), *n.* [*pl.* panoplies (-plĭz)], **1**, a complete suit of armor; **2**, hence, anything covering completely or splendidly.—*adj.* **pan'o-plied.**

pan-o-ra-ma (păn"ō-rä'mȧ), *n.* **1**, a picture giving a view in every direction, seen from a central standpoint; **2**, a picture seen part at a time in several scenes, unrolled and made to pass before the spectator; **3**, an entire, or complete, view of a region; **4**, a scene that moves constantly before one, as from the window of a moving train; **5**, a mental picture of events.

pan-o-ram-ic (păn″ō-răm′ĭk), *adj.* **1**, presenting a complete and extended view in all directions; **2**, passing before the eyes in a series of pictures. Also **pan″o-ram′i-cal.**—*adv.* **pan″o-ram′i-cal-ly.**

Pan-pipe (păn′pīp″), *n.* a kind of simple wind instrument composed of hollow reeds or pipes, of graduated lengths, bound together and played by blowing across the upper edges: also called *Panpipes; Pan's pipe; Pandean pipes.*

Pan-slav-ism (păn-släv′ĭzm; păn-slăv′ĭzm), *n.* a Russian movement for the political union of all the Slavic races.—*adj.* **Pan-slav′ic.**

pan-sy (păn′zĭ), *n.* [*pl.* pansies (-zĭz)], a kind of cultivated violet; heartsease.

pant (pȧnt; pănt), *v.i.* **1**, to breathe rapidly; as, to *pant* like a dog; **2**, to desire earnestly: with *for* or *after:*—*v.t.* to utter with a gasp; as, he *panted* forth the message:—*n.* a short, rapid breath; also, a throb.

pan-ta-lets (păn″tȧ-lĕts′), *n.pl.* long, frilled drawers formerly worn by women and girls. Also, **pan″ta-lettes′.**

pan-ta-loon (păn″tȧ-lo͞on′), *n.* **1**, a buffoon or foolish character in pantomime; **2**, in *pl.*, trousers.

pan-the-ism (păn′thē-ĭzm), *n.* the doctrine that God and nature are one.—*adj.* **pan″the-is′tic; pan″the-is′ti-cal.**—*n.* **pan′the-ist.**

pan-the-on (păn′thē-ŏn; păn-thē′ŏn), *n.* **1**, a temple dedicated to all the gods; **2**, a building where rest the famous dead of a nation: **Pantheon,** a circular temple in ancient Rome, now used as a Christian church.

pan-ther (păn′thẽr), *n.* **1**, a large, American species of wild cat: also called *cougar, puma, mountain lion, catamount,* and *painter;* **2**, less frequently, the jaguar.

pan-tile (păn′tīl″), *n.* a doubly curved roofing tile.

pan-to- (păn′tō-), a combining form from the Greek, meaning *all;* as, *pantograph.* Also, **pan-.**

pan-to-graph (păn′tō-grȧf), *n.* an instrument for copying drawings, designs, etc., on an enlarged or reduced scale. Also, **pan′ta-graph.**—*adj.* **pan″to-graph′ic.**—*n.* **pan-tog′ra-phy.**

pan-to-mime (păn′tō-mīm), *n.* **1**, a series of actions that express meaning without spoken words; as, he replied in *pantomime;* **2**, a play in which there is no talking.—*adj.* **pan″to-mim′ic; pan″to-mim′i-cal.**

pan-try (păn′trĭ), *n.* [*pl.* pantries (-trĭz)], **1**, a room for bread and other food; **2**, a small room from which food is served.

pants (pănts), *n.pl. Colloq.*, trousers; pantaloons; rarely, drawers.

Pan-za, San-cho (săng′kō păn′zȧ; sän′chō pän′thä), *n.* in Cervantes's "Don Quixote," Don Quixote's squire, an ignorant but shrewd peasant.

¹pap (păp), *n.* **1**, soft food for infants; **2**, pulp of fruits.—*adj.* **pap′py.**

²pap (păp), *n. Archaic,* **1**, a nipple; teat; **2**, something like a nipple, as a small hill.

pa-pa (pȧ-pä′; pä′pȧ), *n.* father: a child's term of address.

pa-pa-cy (pā′pȧ-sĭ), *n.* **1**, the office, dignity, or authority, of the Pope; **2**, the popes collectively; **3**, the Roman Catholic system of church government.

pa-pal (pā′păl), *adj.* of or pertaining to the Pope, or to the Roman Catholic Church; as, *papal* authority: **papal cross,** a cross like a plus sign with two additional, shorter cross bars (see *cross,* illus.).

pa-paw (pȧ-pô′; pô′pô″), *n.* **1**, a tree of the central and southern U. S.; also, the sweet, yellowish, pulpy fruit; **2**, the papaya; also, its fruit. Also, **paw′paw″.**

pa-pa-ya (pä-pä′yä), *n.* the edible fruit of a certain tropical tree; also, the tree itself; the papaw.

pa-per (pā′pẽr), *n.* **1**, a material made of finely divided fibers, commonly in the form of a thin, smooth, flexible sheet, used for writing, printing, and various other purposes; **2**, a piece or sheet of this material; **3**, a packet wrapped in this material; as, a *paper* of needles; **4**, a newspaper or journal; **5**, an essay or special article; **6**, a legal or commercial document; **7**, bank notes or bills of exchange: called *commercial paper;* **8**, a decorative covering for interior walls of houses; **9**, in *pl.*, in the theater, free tickets of admission, collectively; also, the persons, collectively, admitted by these tickets: **brown paper,** paper made from jute, hemp, or wood pulp, and used for wrapping: **carbon paper,** thin paper coated with a preparation of pigment, for making duplicate copies of letters, manuscripts, etc.: **crêpe paper,** paper pressed into slight ridges so as to resemble crêpe: **tissue paper.** a very thin paper of fine, soft texture: **wax paper,** thin paper made slightly waterproof with wax or paraffin:—*adj.* **1**, made of, or like, paper; thin; **2**, existing only on paper:—*v.t.* **1**, to cover with paper; **2**, to fill (a theater) by issuing passes.—*adj.* **pa′per-y.**

pa-per hang-er a person who puts wall paper on interior walls, ceilings, etc., of buildings.

pa-per knife an instrument with a flat blade for cutting the pages of books, etc.: also called *paper cutter.*

pa-per mon-ey notes issued by a government, a bank, etc., and good as legal tender; any paper security used as a substitute for coin.

pa-pier–mâ-ché (pȧ″pyā′=mä″shā′; pȧ′pyā=mä′shā), *n.* a hard, strong material made of paper pulp mixed with glue, casein, etc., and molded into various shapes, as buckets, etc.

pa-pil-la (pȧ-pĭl′ȧ), *n.* [*pl.* papillæ (-ē)], a very small projection like a nipple, esp. one of those on the tongue.—*adj.* **pap′il-la-ry** (păp′ĭ-lā-rĭ; pȧ-pĭl′ȧ-rĭ).

pa-pist (pā′pĭst), *n.* an adherent of the Church of Rome; a Roman Catholic: often used scornfully.—*adj.* **pa-pis′tic; pa-pis′ti-cal.**—*n.* **pa′pist-ry.**

pa-poose (pȧ-po͞os′), *n.* a young child of North American Indian parents.

pap-pus (păp′ŭs), *n.* [*pl.* pappi (-ī)], a downy tuft or appendage crowning the fruit in certain seed plants, as in thistles.—*adj.* **pap′pose.**

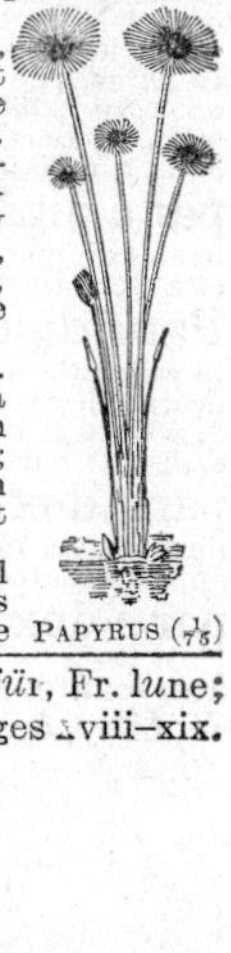

PAPYRUS ($\frac{1}{75}$)

pa-pri-ka (pä′prē-kä), *n.* **1**, the dried ripe fruit of various kinds of peppers; **2**, the red, pungent relish made from it.

Pap-u-an (păp′ū-ăn; păp′o͞o-ăn), *adj.* of or pertaining to Papua, or New Guinea:—*n.* a native of Papua, or New Guinea; also, generally, a member of any of the native races of Oceania.

pa-py-rus (pȧ-pī′rŭs), *n. pl.* papyri (-rī)], **1**, a kind of Egyptian reed from which the ancients made paper; **2**, the paper made from the pith of this plant; **3**, a manuscript or writing on papyrus.

par (pär), *n.* **1**, full or normal value; as, the stock is below *par;* **2**, equality; as, the man is not on a *par* with his associates; **3**, the rate of exchange at which the money unit of one country may be exchanged for an equivalent weight of the precious metal of the money unit of another country; as, the *par* of the English gold sovereign is $4.8665 in American money, the sovereign containing 4.8665 times as much gold by weight as the dollar; **4**, the established standard from which to measure quality of goods or value of money or property; **5**, in golf, the perfect score estimated for each hole from its length, the club required for each stroke, and the standard perfect performance of each club used.

par-a- (păr′ȧ-), *prefix*, orig. meaning beyond, against, near by, alongside, but often having a hardly identifiable force; as, *para*llel.

par-a-ble (păr′ȧ-bl), *n.* a short story to illustrate and enforce moral or religious truth.

pa-rab-o-la (pȧ-răb′ō-lȧ), *n.* a plane curve every point of which is equally distant from a point called the *focus* and a straight line called the *directrix:* the curve formed by the intersection of a cone with a plane parallel to its side.—*adj.* [1]**par″a-bol′ic.**

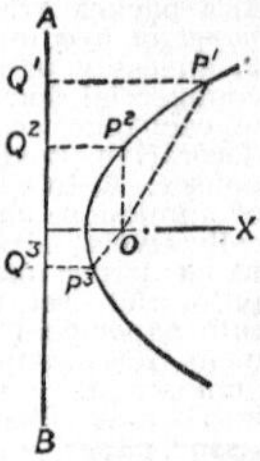

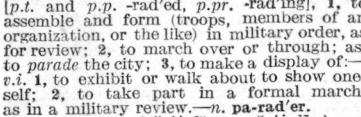

PARABOLA: O, focus; AB, directrix; OX, axis; P^1, P^2, P^3, points on the parabola. $P^1Q^1 = P^1O$, $P^2Q^2 = P^2O$, etc.

[2]**par-a-bol-ic** (păr″ȧ-bŏl′ĭk), *adj.* allegorical, or of the nature of a parable; as, a *parabolic* story. Also, **par″a-bol′i-cal.**

par-a-chute (păr′ȧ-shōōt), *n.* an umbrella-shaped apparatus used in descending from a balloon or airplane, as in emergencies or test flights.

PARACHUTE

pa-rade (pȧ-rād′), *n.* **1**, pompous display; as, a *parade* of wealth; **2**, a military display, or review of troops; **3**, a place of assembly for exercising and inspecting troops; **4**, a formal march or procession; as, a circus *parade;* **5**, a promenade or public place for walking; **6**, the level plain or area inside a rampart, or a roadway or boulevard along the rampart, on the original level (see *rampart, terreplein,* illus.):—*v.t.* [*p.t.* and *p.p.* -rad′ed, *p.pr.* -rad′ing], **1**, to assemble and form (troops, members of an organization, or the like) in military order, as for review; **2**, to march over or through; as, to *parade* the city; **3**, to make a display of:—*v.i.* **1**, to exhibit or walk about to show oneself; **2**, to take part in a formal march, as in a military review.—*n.* **pa-rad′er.**

par-a-digm (păr′ȧ-dĭm; păr′ȧ-dīm), *n.* **1**, an example or a model; **2**, an example of the declension or conjugation of a word to show all its forms.

Par-a-dise (păr′ȧ-dīs), *n.* the garden of Eden: **paradise**, **1**, the place in which the souls of the righteous abide after death; heaven; **2**, any place of happiness; **3**, a state of bliss.—*adj.* **par″a-dis′i-ac** (păr″ȧ-dĭs′ĭ-ăk); **par″a-di-si′a-cal** (păr″ȧ-dĭ-sī′ȧ-kăl).

par-a-dox (păr′ȧ-dŏks), *n.* **1**, something which seems absurd or unbelievable, yet may be true; **2**, a statement that appears contradictory.

par-a-dox-i-cal (păr″ȧ-dŏk′sĭ-kăl), *adj.* seemingly contradictory, but possibly true.—*adv.* **par″a-dox′i-cal-ly.**—*n.* **par″a-dox′i-cal-ness.**

par-af-fin (păr′ă-fĭn), *n.* an inflammable substance obtained by the distillation of wood, coal, etc., and from crude petroleum. Also, **par′af-fine** (păr′ȧ-fĭn; -fēn).

par-a-gon (păr′ȧ-gŏn), *n.* something of extraordinary excellence; a model of perfection; as, a *paragon* of virtue.

par-a-graph (păr′ȧ-grȧf), *n.* **1**, a small, definite section of a piece of writing, dealing with one topic; a short passage; **2**, a reference mark [¶] indicating the need of subdivision, as in copy; **3**, an item in a newspaper, magazine, etc.:—*v.t.* **1**, to arrange or divide into definite sections; **2**, to write a brief passage about.

par-a-keet (păr′ȧ-kĕt), *n.* any of several parrots. See **par′ra-keet**, *Pfd.S.*

Par-a-li-pom-e-non (păr″ȧ-lĭ-pŏm′ē-nŏn), *n.* literally, (book) of things omitted: used as a title of either of two books in the Douay Bible, corresponding to the Books of Chronicles.

par-al-lax (păr′ă-lăks), *n.* **1**, the apparent shifting of an object caused by change in the position of the observer; **2**, the apparent displacement of a heavenly body as seen by an observer from two different positions.—*adj.* **par″al-lac′tic.**

par-al-lel (păr′ă-lĕl), *adj.* **1**, equally distant from each other at all points; as, *parallel* lines; **2**, having the same course; **3**, similar; corresponding: **parallel circuit**, a circuit composed of two or more conductors, such as lamps, with corresponding terminals joined so that a current will divide, part passing through each conductor: opp. of *series circuit:*—*n.* **1**, a line or plane equally distant at all points from another line or plane; **2**, one of the parallel lines drawn on the surface of the earth, which indicate degrees of latitude: distinguished from *meridian;* **3**, in printing, a reference mark [‖] calling attention to a footnote; **4**, a person or thing closely resembling another; **5**, a presentation of resemblance; as, to draw a *parallel* between Alexander and Napoleon:—*v.t.* **1**, to state the likeness of; **2**, to be parallel with; **3**, to correspond to; **4**, to find a match for; equal.—*n.* **par′al-lel-ism.**

par-al-lel-e-pi-ped (păr″ă-lĕl″ē-pī′pĕd; -pĭp′ĕd; -lĕl-ĕp′ĭ-pĕd), *n.* a solid bounded by six parallelograms of which the opposite pairs are equal and parallel (see *solid*, illus.). Also, **par″al-lel″e-pip′e-don; par″al-lel″o-pi′ped.**

par-al-lel-o-gram (păr″ă-lĕl′ō-grăm), *n.* a four-sided, plane figure whose opposite sides are equal and parallel (see *quadrilateral*, illus.).

pa-ral-y-sis (pȧ-răl′ĭ-sĭs), *n.* [*pl.* paralyses (-sēz)], loss or diminution of the powers of feeling or of motion in one or more parts of the body; palsy.

par-a-lyt-ic (păr″ȧ-lĭt′ĭk), *adj.* pertaining to, affected by, or inclined to, paralysis:—*n.* one who is affected by paralysis.

par-a-lyze (păr′ȧ-līz), *v.t.* [*p.t.* and *p.p.* -lyzed (-līzd), *p.pr.* -lyz″ing], **1**, to affect with paralysis in any part; **2**, to unnerve; render useless or ineffective.—*n.* **par″a-ly-za′tion.**—*n.* **par′a-lyz″er.**

par-a-mount (păr′ȧ-mount), *adj.* above all others; supreme; chief; as, of *paramount* importance.

Syn. dominant, superior, **principal**, **foremost.**—*Ant.* minor, secondary.

par-a-mour (păr′ȧ-mōōr), *n.* one who unlawfully takes the place of a husband or wife.

par-a-noi-a (păr″ȧ-noi′ȧ), *n.* a chronic form of insanity marked by fixed delusions, or false beliefs, as of persecution.—*adj.* **par″a-noi′ac.**

par-a-pet (păr′ȧ-pĕt), *n.* **1,** a wall at the edge of a roof, platform, etc.; **2,** in fortification, a permanent wall to protect troops from the fire of an enemy; specif., a rampart of earth, sandbags, etc., built upon the front wall of a trench (see *rampart, terreplein,* illus.).

PARAPETS OF BRIDGE

par-a-pher-na-li-a (păr″ȧ-fẽr-nā′lĭ-ȧ), *n.pl.* **1,** personal belongings; **2,** ornaments of dress; **3,** articles of equipment; as, the *paraphernalia* of a circus.

par-a-phrase (păr′ȧ-frāz), *n.* **1,** a free translation or explanation of a text, etc., giving the meaning in another form; **2,** a hymn based on some Scriptural passage:—*v.t.* [*p.t.* and *p.p.* -phrased (-frāzd), *p.pr.* -phras″ing], to make a free translation of; explain in one's own words:—*v.i.* to make a free translation; put something into one's own words.—*n.* **par″a-phras′tic.**

par-a-site (păr′ȧ-sīt), *n.* **1,** a hanger-on; one who lives at others' expense, doing no work himself; **2,** an animal or plant which lives on or within another at the latter's expense, as lice, disease germs, and the various blights.—*adj.* **par″a-sit′ic; par″a-sit′i-cal.**

par-a-sol (păr′ȧ-sŏl″; păr″ȧ-sŏl′), *n.* a lady's sunshade.

par-a-troops (păr′ȧ-tro͞ops), *n.pl.* troops dropped upon a field of action by parachute.

par-a-vane (păr′ȧ-vān), *n.* a device towed from the bow of a vessel, shaped like a torpedo equipped with projecting fins, and used to destroy floating mines.

par-boil (pär′boil″), *v.t.* **1,** to cook partially by boiling; **2,** figuratively, to subject to extreme heat.

par-buck-le (pär′bŭk″l), *n.* **1,** a device for hauling up or lowering a heavy object by passing the middle of a rope around a stationary fastening and its two ends under and over the object; **2,** a sling made by passing both ends of a rope through its bight.

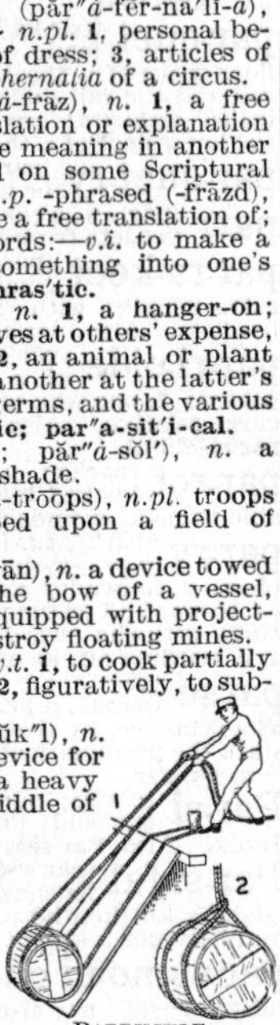

PARBUCKLE

1, for rolling an object up or down an incline; 2, for raising an object in dead lift.

par-cel (pär′sĕl), *n.* **1,** a small bundle or package; **2,** a separate, distinct part; as, a *parcel* of land; **3,** an indefinite number; as, a *parcel* of scamps:—*v.t.* **1,** to do up in a small bundle; **2,** to divide into parts.

Syn., n. packet. (See bundle.)

par-cel post a government system of carrying packages by mail, charging at postal rates.

parch (pärch), *v.t.* **1,** to scorch; burn slightly; as, to *parch* corn; **2,** to dry with heat; as, the sun *parches* the grass:—*v.i.* to become dry and hot; as, the tongue *parches* for want of water.

par-che-si (pär-chē′sĭ; pär-chē′-zĭ), *n.* a four-handed game played on a board with counters. See **pa-chi′si,** *Pfd. S.*

parch-ment (pärch′mĕnt), *n.* **1,** the skin of a sheep, goat, etc., dressed and prepared for writing purposes; **2,** a deed or document on such a prepared skin:—*adj.* made of, or like, parchment.

¹**pard** (pärd), *n.* a leopard or panther: a poetical term.

²**pard** (pärd), *n. U. S. Slang,* partner; as, he was my *pard* in the old mining days.

par-don (pär′dŭn; pär′dn), *v.t.* **1,** to free from penalty; as, to *pardon* an offender; **2,** to forgive; as, to *pardon* an offense; **3,** to overlook; excuse; as, *pardon* my mistake:—*n.* **1,** forgiveness; **2,** polite indulgence; as, I beg your *pardon;* **3,** release from punishment; **4,** an official act setting one free from penalty.—*adj.* **par′don-a-ble.**—*adv.* **par′don-a-bly.**—*n.* **par′don-er.**

pare (pâr), *v.t.* [*p.t.* and *p.p.* pared (pârd), *p.pr.* par′ing], **1,** to cut or shave off the outside or ends of; as, to *pare* an apple; **2,** to cut away little by little; lessen, as profits; **3,** to remove by cutting off from a surface; as, to *pare* off a rind.—*n.* **par′er.**

par-e-gor-ic (păr″ē-gŏr′ĭk), *n.* a medicine obtained from opium and used to ease pain or relieve suffering.

pa-ren-chy-ma (pȧ-rĕng′kĭ-mȧ), *n.* **1,** the tissue making up glandular organs; **2,** tissue such as the pith in plants or the pulp of fruits.

par-ent (pâr′ĕnt), *n.* **1,** a father or mother; **2,** the source of any living thing; **3,** that which causes; occasion.—*adj.* **pa-ren′tal.**—*adv.* **pa-ren′tal-ly.**—*n.* **par′ent-hood.**

par-ent-age (pâr′ĕn-tāj), *n.* **1,** fatherhood or motherhood; **2,** birth or descent; origin; as, of noble *parentage.*

pa-ren-the-sis (pȧ-rĕn′thē-sĭs), *n.* [*pl.* parentheses (-sēz)], **1,** an explanatory or qualifying word or clause put in a sentence which is grammatically complete without it: indicated by the marks ( ); **2,** either or both of the marks ( ).

par-en-thet-i-cal (păr″ĕn-thĕt′ĭ-kăl), *adj.* **1,** introduced by way of explanation; **2,** filled with, or given to, inserted explanations. Also, **par″en-thet′ic.**—*adv.* **par″en-thet′i-cal-ly.**

par-e-sis (păr′ē-sĭs; pȧ-rē′sĭs), *n.* **1,** a chronic disease of the brain, marked by loss of mental and physical power: called in full *general paresis:* **2,** partial paralysis.—*adj.* **pa-ret′ic** (pȧ-rĕt′ĭk; -rē′tĭk).

***par ex-cel-lence** (pär″ĕk″sĕ″läns′), [Fr.], beyond comparison; superior.

par-he-li-on (pär-hē′lĭ-ŏn), *n.* [*pl.* parhelia (-ȧ)], a mock sun, or bright light, often seen near the sun and sometimes opposite to it.

pa-ri-ah (pä′rĭ-ȧ; pâr′ĭ-ȧ), *n.* **1,** a member of one of the low castes of Hindus; **2,** an outcast; one despised by society.

pa-ri-e-tal (pȧ-rī′ē-tăl), *adj.* of or pertaining to the walls of an organ or cavity; specif., designating two bones, called *parietal bones,* which form a part of the top and sides of the skull in mammals (see *skull,* illus.), or the lobes of the brain lying beneath them.

par-ing (pâr′ĭng), *n.* **1,** a cutting off of the surface or edge; **2,** the part cut off; as, potato *parings.*

¹**Par-is** (păr′ĭs), *n.* in mythology, the handsome son of Priam, king of Troy, whose abduction of Helen, wife of Menelaus, king of Sparta, precipitated the Trojan War.

²**Par-is** (păr′ĭs), *n.* the capital city of France: **paris green,** an emerald-green pigment, used also as an insecticide for fruit trees, etc.—*adj.* and *n.* **Pa-ri′sian.**

par-ish (păr′ĭsh), *n.* **1,** orig., an ecclesiastical or church district under the particular charge of one priest, clergyman, or minister; **2,** in England, a civil district looking after its own education, charity, etc.; **3,** a congregation; also, the locality covered by its activities; **4**, in Louisiana, a civil division, the equivalent of a county:—*adj.* pertaining to, or maintained by, a church, congregation, or district.—*adj.* **pa-rish'ion-al.**

pa-rish-ion-er (pȧ-rĭsh'ŭn-ẽr), *n.* **1**, one who belongs to a given church district or parish; **2**, a member of a congregation.

par-i-ty (păr'ĭ-tĭ), *n.* **1**, a like state or degree; equality; likeness; **2**, equal value of different kinds of currency, for purchasing purposes; **3**, equality in value of the currency or products of two countries.

park (pärk), *n.* **1**, a tract of ground used as a public place for recreation or pleasure; **2**, a large extent of woods and fields attached to a country house; **3**, the train of artillery belonging to an army; an artillery encampment:—*v.t.* **1**, to inclose, as in a park; **2**, to collect and station in order; as, to *park* artillery; **3**, to place and leave for a time; as, to *park* automobiles.

par-lance (pär'lăns), *n.* conversation; talk; language.

par-ley (pär'lĭ), *n.* [*pl.* parleys (-lĭz)], a conference, esp. one with an enemy: —*v.i.* to hold a conference, esp. with an enemy with a view to peace.

par-lia-ment (pär'lĭ-mĕnt), *n.* a general council; a meeting of the people or their representatives to consider or legislate on matters of common interest: **Parliament, 1**, the supreme lawmaking body of Great Britain, consisting of the House of Lords and the House of Commons; **2**, a similar assembly in certain other countries.

par-lia-men-ta-ri-an (pär″lĭ-mĕn-tā'-rĭ-ăn), *n.* one who is versed in the laws and usages of lawmaking or deliberative bodies.

par-lia-men-ta-ry (pär″lĭ-mĕn'tȧ-rĭ), *adj.* **1**, according to the rules and customs of public assemblies; as, *parliamentary* order; **2**, decreed or enacted by a parliament.

par-lor (pär'lẽr), *n.* **1**, a room for conversation, reception of guests, etc.; **2**, in England, a family sitting room; **3**, in the U. S., a shop furnished with some pretensions to elegance; as, a beauty *parlor.* Also, **par'lour.**

par-lous (pär'lŭs), *adj.* **1**, *Archaic,* perilous; **2**, *Colloq.,* dangerously clever; hence, shrewd; exciting; as, *parlous* times:—*adv.* extremely; tremendously.

Par-nas-sus (pär-năs'ŭs), *n.* **1**, in mythology, a mountain in Greece, sacred to Apollo and the Muses; **2**, figuratively, a center of poetic and artistic activity.—*adj.* **Par-nas'si-an.**

pa-ro-chi-al (pȧ-rō'kĭ-ăl), *adj.* **1**, of or pertaining to a parish, or church district; as, a *parochial* school; **2**, narrow; local.—*n.* **pa-ro'chi-al-ism.**

par-o-dy (păr'ō-dĭ), *n.* [*pl.* parodies (-dĭz)], an imitation of a serious writing, as a poem or song, written in a humorous manner; a burlesque imitation:—*v.t.* [*p.t.* and *p.p.* -died (-dĭd), *p.pr.* -dy-ing], to write a humorous imitation of.—*n.* **par'o-dist.**

Syn., n. caricature, burlesque. A *parody* is a written imitation of some serious work of which it retains the style, but alters the subject matter to produce a ludicrous effect. A *caricature* may be literary or pictorial; it exaggerates certain distinguishing traits of the original in order to ridicule it. A *burlesque* may be written or acted; it achieves an absurd effect by treating a serious subject lightly, or a trifling subject seriously, and may either be based on some play, poem, etc., or be independent as to subject.

pa-role (pȧ-rōl'), *n.* **1**, a word of honor; esp., a promise given by a prisoner of war that in return for conditional freedom he will not try to escape; also, the condition of being on parole; **2**, a special password used by officers in a camp or garrison:—*v.t.* [*p.t.* and *p.p.* -roled' (-rōld'), *p.pr.* -rol'ing], to release (a prisoner) on his word of honor to observe certain conditions.

pa-rot-id (pȧ-rŏt'ĭd), *n.* one of the salivary glands below and in front of the ear:—*adj.* pertaining to, or situated near, this salivary gland; as, the *parotid* nerves.

par-ox-ysm (păr'ŏk-sĭzm), *n.* **1**, a spasm, or fit of acute pain recurring at intervals; **2**, a sudden outburst of emotion; a fit of any kind; as, a *paroxysm* of rage.—*adj.* **par″ox-ys'mal.**

par-quet (pär-kā'; pär-kĕt'), *n.* **1**, flooring made of wooden inlay; **2**, the floor space of a theater between the orchestra rail and the rail under the balcony line: also called *orchestra:* **parquet circle**, the part of the lower floor of a theater under the balcony.

par-quet-ry (pär'kĕt-rĭ), *n.* wooden inlay or mosaic work for floors.

parr (pär), *n.* a young salmon that has not yet left fresh water for the sea.

par-ra-keet (păr'ȧ-kēt), *n.* any of several small, slender-bodied parrots, usually with long and pointed tail feathers. Also, **par'a-keet.**

par-ri-cide (păr'ĭ-sīd), *n.* **1**, the murder of a close relative, esp. a parent; **2**, one who murders a parent or other close relative. Also called *patricide.*—*adj.* **par'ri-cid″al.**

par-rot (păr'ŭt), *n.* a tropical bird with a hooked bill and brilliant feathers, able to make sounds resembling words.

par-ry (păr'ĭ), *v.t.* [*p.t.* and *p.p.* -ried (-ĭd), *p.pr.* -ry-ing], **1**, to ward off, as a blow; **2**, to evade; as, to *parry* a question:—*v.i.* to ward off or turn something aside; as, to *parry* with the sword:—*n.* [*pl.* parries (-ĭz)], **1**, a warding off, as of a blow; **2**, evasion.

parse (pärs), *v.t.* [*p.t.* and *p.p.* parsed (pärst), *p.pr.* pars'ing], **1**, to analyze, as a sentence, by the rules of grammar; **2**, to state the grammatical relations of, as a word. —*n.* **pars'er.**

Par-si (pär'sē; pär-sē'), *n.* a descendant of the old Persians, now living in India. Also, **Par'see.**—*n.* **Par'si-ism.**

Par-si-fal (pär'sĭ-fäl), *n.* in the Holy Grail legends, and in Wagner's "Parsifal," a knight who recovers the sacred spear and becomes a knight of the Holy Grail.

par-si-mo-ni-ous (pär″sĭ-mō'nĭ-ŭs), *adj.* close; stingy; miserly.—*adv.* **par″si-mo'ni-ous-ly.**

Syn. niggardly, grasping, avaricious.

par-si-mo-ny (pär'sĭ-mō-nĭ), *n.* stinginess; extreme and unnecessary economy; closeness.

pars-ley (pärs'lĭ), *n.* a garden plant, the leaves of which are used as a garnish and for flavoring.

pars-nip (pärs'nĭp), *n.* a plant with an edible carrotlike root.

par-son (pär'sn), *n.* **1**, a clergyman in charge of a parish; **2**, *Colloq.,* any minister or preacher.

par-son-age (pär'sn-āj), *n.* the residence of a minister in charge of a parish, esp. when belonging to the church.

part (pärt), *n.* **1**, something less than the whole; as, *part* of a pear; a piece, section, or division; an individual portion; **2**, a share in action, duty, or responsibility; as, to do one's *part;* **3**, an essential member or organ; as, *part* of the body; **4**, a side or party; as, they took his *part;* **5**, concern or interest; as, he had no *part* in the business; **6**, a character assigned to an actor in a play; as, Irving chose the *part* of Shylock; also, the words spoken by that character; **7**, a division of the hair; **8**, in *pl.:* **a**, a quarter; region; as, they live in these *parts;* **b**, ability or talent; as, a man of fine *parts;* **9**, in music: **a**, one of the melodies in a harmony; **b**, one of the voices or instruments, which, in combination, form a concerted piece; **c**, the written score for one of the melodies, voices, or instruments; **10**, one of a given number of equal quantities into which a number, quantity, or object may be divided; as, three is the third *part* of nine:—*v.t.* **1**, to divide into two or more pieces or portions; divide for the purpose of analysis; hence, to examine critically and closely; **2**, to disunite; force to go apart; **3**, to separate; as, to *part* the fighters; **4**, in chemistry, to separate, as the metals in an ore:—*v.i.* **1**, to be separated or divided; as, the crowd *parted* to let us pass; **2**, to separate; withdraw; as, they *parted* from us; **3**, *Rare*, to go away; hence, to die: **part with**, to give up.

Syn., *n.* portion, division, fraction, piece, fragment. *Part*, the general term, denotes some, but not all, of a thing or things, whether separated from the whole or considered as separated; as, the *parts* of the human body. A *portion* is a *part* of a whole, viewed as assigned to one person; as, the widow's *portion* of the estate. A *division* is a certain *part* of a whole, esp. as viewed by one who is dividing or distributing it; as, geographical *divisions; division* of labor. A *fraction* is one or more of several equal *parts* composing anything; loosely, it is any *part* or *portion*. *Piece* and *fragment* suggest *parts* cut or broken off; as, a *piece* of bread; a *fragment* of glass.

par-take (pär-tāk'; pȧr-), *v.i.* [*p.t.* -took' (-to͝ok'), *p.p.* tak'en (-tāk'n), *p.pr.* -tak'ing], **1**, to have or receive a portion or share in common with others; **2**, to take a portion: with *of;* as, to *partake* of food:—*v.t.* to receive a share in.—*n.* **par-tak'er.**

par-terre (pär-târ'), *n.* **1**, a series of flower beds arranged ornamentally, with spaces of gravel or turf between; **2**, in the U. S., that part of the floor of a theater under the galleries: also called *parquet circle.*

Par-the-non (pär'thē-nŏn), *n.* the temple of Athena at Athens.

Par-thi-an (pär'thĭ-ăn), *adj.* of or pertaining to Parthia, an ancient division of Persia: **Parthian shot,** a parting shot: in allusion to a Parthian custom by which the cavalry would turn their horses as if about to retreat, and then discharge their arrows at the enemy:—*n.* a native of Parthia.

par-tial (pär'shăl), *adj.* **1**, inclined to favor one side or party; **2**, having a liking (for); as, she is *partial* to candy; **3**, not entire; incomplete: **partial tones,** the secondary tones contained in practically every musical sound: also called *overtones.*—*adv.* **par'tial-ly.**

par-ti-al-i-ty (pär"shĭ-ăl'ĭ-tĭ; pär"shăl'-), *n.* **1**, the state or quality of being biased or unfair; **2**, a strong liking.

par-tic-i-pant (pär-tĭs'ĭ-pănt; pȧr-), *adj.* sharing:—*n.* one who takes part; as, a *participant* in the game.

par-tic-i-pate (pär-tĭs'ĭ-pāt; pȧr-), *v.i.* [*p.t.* and *p.p.* -pat"ed, *p.pr.* -pat"ing], to share in common with others; take part:—*v.t.* to have a share of; take part in.—*n.* **par-tic'i-pa"tor.**—*n.* **par-tic"i-pa'tion.**

par-ti-ci-ple (pär'tĭ-sĭ-pl), *n.* a part of a verb which orig. had the force of an adjective, but in some uses is no longer felt as such, as *looking, painted, drawn.*—*adj.* **par"ti-cip'i-al.**—*adv.* **par"ti-cip'i-al-ly.**

par-ti-cle (pär'tĭ-kl), *n.* **1**, a very small piece; a bit; as, a *particle* of dust; **2**, the smallest possible amount of anything; as, not a *particle* of courage; **3**, in grammar, a short, subordinate part of speech, as a conjunction or a preposition.

par-ti-col-ored (pär'tĭ-kŭl"ẽrd), *adj.* having many and varied colors, as a flower. Also, **par'ti-col"-oured;** *Pfd. S.*, **par'ty-col"ored.**

par-tic-u-lar (pär-tĭk'ū-lȧr; pȧr-), *adj.* **1**, distinct from others; as, a *particular* person or thing; **2**, peculiar or special; as, of *particular* importance; **3**, exact; as, *particular* in speech:—*n.* **1**, one that is distinct from others; an individual; **2**, a single case; a detail.—*adv.* **par-tic'u-lar-ly.**

Syn., *adj.* precise; singular, unusual.

par-tic-u-lar-i-ty (pär-tĭk"ū-lăr'ĭ-tĭ; pȧr-), *n.* [*pl.* particularities (-tĭz)], **1**, strict attention to detail; **2**, fastidiousness; **3**, individuality.

par-tic-u-lar-ize (pär-tĭk'ū-lȧr-īz; pȧr-), *v.t.* [*p.t.* and *p.p.* -ized (-īzd), *p.pr.* -iz"ing], **1**, to give the details of; **2**, to give special mention to:—*v.i.* to be attentive to single things or details.

part-ing (pär'tĭng), *p.adj.* **1**, taking leave; hence, dying; as, a *parting* soul; **2**, given when taking leave; as, a *parting* gift:—*n.* **1**, division; **2**, the place of division; **3**, a taking leave; as, the *parting* of friends.

[1]**par-ti-san** (pär'tĭ-zăn), *n.* a devoted, sometimes prejudiced, follower, esp. of a political cause or faction:—*adj.* pertaining to, or strongly in favor of, a person, cause, or faction, esp. a political party or faction; as, *partisan* politics. Also, [1]**par'ti-zan.**—*n.* **par'ti-san-ship".**

[2]**par-ti-san** (pär'tĭ-zăn), *n.* formerly, a long-handled, steel-pointed weapon; a kind of pike. Also, [2]**par'ti-zan.**

par-ti-tion (pär-tĭsh'ŭn; pȧr-), *n.* **1**, the act of dividing or state of being divided; separation; **2**, a dividing wall within a building; **3**, a section or division:—*v.t.* **1**, to divide into shares; as, to *partition* an estate or a country; **2**, to divide by walls.

par-ti-tive (pär'tĭ-tĭv), *adj.* **1**, serving to divide into parts; **2**, in grammar, denoting a part; as, a *partitive* genitive:—*n.* a word that denotes a part or expresses partition or division.—*adv.* **par'ti-tive-ly.**

part-ly (pärt'lĭ), *adv.* in part; not wholly; to some extent.

part-ner (pärt'nẽr), *n.* **1**, one who is associated with another or others in some coöperative connection for mutual benefit or united action, as in a business, etc.; **2**, in games, one who plays with another against opponents; **3**, one who dances with another; **4**, a husband or wife.

Syn. colleague, confederate. (See ally.)

part-ner-ship (pärt'nẽr-shĭp), *n.* **1**, the state of being associated for a common purpose; **2**, joint interest or ownership; **3**, the union of two or more persons in the same business or profession; **4**, in law, the relation between two or more persons who have contracted to do business together and share the profits; also, the contract establishing this relationship.

par-took (pär-to͝ok'; pȧr-), past tense of the verb *partake.*

par-tridge (pär'trĭj), *n.* **1**, in the Old World, any of various game birds allied to the quails and pheasants; **2**, locally, esp. in America, any of a number of similar game birds, as the bobwhite, quail, and ruffed grouse: **partridge berry,** an American trailing evergreen plant bearing a bright red berry; also, the berry.

par-tu-ri-tion (pär"tū-rĭsh'ŭn), *n.* the act of bringing forth young; childbirth.—*adj.* **par-tu'ri-ent.**

par-ty (pär'tĭ), *n.* [*pl.* parties (-tĭz)], **1**, a number of persons united for a particular purpose; faction; as, a political *party;* **2**, one of the sections into which any social group divides in opinion on a public question; **3**, one concerned in an affair, cause, or side; as, a *party* to a suit; **4**, a small body of troops sent to perform some special service; as, a scouting *party;* **5**, a social gathering assembled by invitation; a select company; as, a dinner *party:* **party line, 1**, a line defining the boundary between pieces of land belonging to different persons; **2**, a telephone circuit serving more than one subscriber: also called *party wire:* **party wall**, a wall erected on a party line, for the use of both parties.

par-ty–col-ored (pär′tĭ=kŭl″ẽrd), *adj.* having various colors; as, a *party-colored* flower. Also, **par′ty–col″oured; par′ti–col″ored.**

par-ve-nu (pär′vē-nū″; *Fr.* pȧr″vē-nü′), *n.* [*pl.* parvenus (-nūz″; *Fr.* -nü′)], one who has recently risen, because of his wealth, to a position above that in which he was born; an upstart.—*n. fem.* **par′ve-nue″** [*pl.* parvenues (-nūz″; *Fr.* -nü′)].

pas-chal (păs′kăl), *adj.* pertaining to the feast of the Passover, or to Easter; as, the *paschal* lamb.

pa-sha (pȧ-shä′; pȧsh′ä), *n.* in Turkey, a civil or military official of high rank: also used, after a name, as an honorary title. Also, **pa-cha′**.

pa-sha-lic (pȧ-shä′lĭk), *n.* the authority, or the territory under the control or jurisdiction, of a pasha.

pas-quin-ade (păs″kwĭ-nād′), *n.* a sarcastic political or personal squib posted in a public place.

pass (pȧs), *v.i.* [*p.t.* passed (pȧst), or, *Rare,* past (pȧst), *p.p.* passed or past, *p.pr.* pass′ing], **1**, to go from one place or condition to another; move along; as, the parade *passes* down the street; **2**, to move from one to another; be exchanged; circulate freely, as money; **3**, to elapse or go by; as, the night *passed;* **4**, to make or force one's way; as, to *pass* through a crowd; **5**, to go unnoticed; as, his action *passed* without rebuke; **6**, to be enacted; as, the law was finally *passed;* **7**, to depart; die; **8**, to go through a test with success; **9**, to give a decision as to the quality or validity of something: with *on* or *upon;* **10**, in cards, to relinquish the right or opportunity of playing or bidding; **11**, in fencing, to make a thrust; **12**, in law, to be conveyed to another by will or other document: used of property:—*v.t.* **1**, to go by, through, beyond, etc.; as, to *pass* the house; **2**, to cause or allow to go; hand; as, to *pass* the butter; also, to convey to another; cause to circulate; as, to *pass* bad money; **3**, to spend; as, to *pass* the day; **4**, to exceed; as, it *passes* belief; **5**, to give as a judgment; as, to *pass* sentence; **6**, to utter or pronounce; as, to *pass* an opinion; **7**, to give legal status to, as a bill or law; approve, as a candidate; **8**, to void from the body, as urine or excrement; **9**, to omit, as a dividend; **10**, *Rare,* to promise:—*n.* **1**, a narrow passage, avenue, or entrance; defile; as, a *pass* in the mountains; **2**, a permit allowing free admission or passage; as, a railway *pass;* **3**, a state of extremity; as, matters have come to a dreadful *pass;* **4**, a quick movement, as of a card or other object, by sleight of hand; **5**, a movement of the hand, as by a mesmerist; **6**, in fencing, a thrust.—*n.* **pass′er.**

pass-a-ble (pȧs′ȧ-bl), *adj.* **1**, capable of being traveled; as, a *passable* road; **2**, not open to great objection; fairly good; as, a book in a *passable* condition; **3**, capable of being circulated; as, American money is *passable* in Canada.—*adv.* **pass′a-bly.**

pas-sage (păs′ĭj), *n.* **1**, the act of going from one place or condition to another; **2**, course or progress; as, the *passage* of time; **3**, a journey, esp. a voyage; as, a stormy *passage;* **4**, a way by which one passes; a hall or corridor; **5**, the right to go; as, a free *passage;* **6**, legal enactment; as, the *passage* of a law; **7**, a single clause or portion of a book; **8**, migratory habits; as, birds of *passage;* **9**, a conflict; as, a *passage* at arms.

pas-sage-way (păs′ĭj-wā″), *n.* a hall, corridor, or alley.

pas-sant (păs′ănt), *adj.* in heraldry, applied to an animal walking and facing toward the dexter side, with the right, front paw raised (see *lion,* illus.).

pass book **1**, a customer's book in which a storekeeper enters the list of goods bought on credit; **2**, a depositor's bank book, containing a record of his deposits.

***pas-sé** (pä″sā′), [Fr.], *adj.* past; out of date; faded.—*adj. fem.* **pas″sée′**.

passe-men-terie (pȧs-mĕn′trĭ; *Fr.* päs″mäṅ″trē′), *n.* dress trimmings, as of braid or silk embroidery.

pas-sen-ger (păs′ĕn-jẽr), *n.* **1**, one who travels, usually at a stated fare, in or on a conveyance, as a boat, train, etc.; **2**, formerly, a traveler or wayfarer.

***passe par-tout** (päs″ pȧr″to͞o′), [Fr.], **1**, a flat surface of cardboard, wood, etc., with a space cut out in its center so as to make a frame for a picture; **2**, a kind of picture frame in which the glass is held to the cardboard back by strips of gummed tape at the edges.

pass-er–by (pȧs′ẽr=bī′), *n.* [*pl.* passers-by (-ẽrz=)], one who goes past; one who goes by or near.

pas-ser-ine (păs′ẽr-ĭn; -īn), *adj.* **1**, designating, or pertaining to, a very large order (*Passeres*) of birds, the perching birds, including more than half of all the birds, among them the song birds, ranging in size from the titmouse to the crow; **2**, sparrowlike:—*n.* a member of this order.

pass-ing (pȧs′ĭng), *adj.* **1**, going by, beyond, or through; as, a *passing* car; **2**, departing; as, the *passing* hour; **3**, casual; as, a *passing* comment:—*n.* **1**, the act of going by; departure; as, the *passing* of summer; **2**, a way or means of passing; ford.

pas-sion (păsh′ŭn), *n.* **1**, a fit of violent anger; as, he flew into a *passion;* **2**, intense feeling or excitement; **3**, sexual excitement; **4**, love; ardor; intense desire or feeling; as, a *passion* for music; **5**, in *pl.,* the emotions collectively: **Passion**, the sufferings of Christ in his last agonies.

pas-sion-ate (păsh′ŭn-ȧt), *adj.* **1**, capable of intense feeling; excitable; as, a *passionate* nature; **2**, ardent; as, a *passionate* desire; **3**, amorous.—*adv.* **pas′sion-ate-ly.**—*n.* **pas′sion-ate-ness.**

pas-sion flow-er a plant so named because its flower suggests the symbols of Christ's death.

pas-sion-less (păsh′ŭn-lĕs), *adj.* displaying no anger, intense love, ardor, etc.; tranquil; unmoved.

Pas-sion play a play showing certain scenes of the suffering and death of Christ, and given every ten years at Oberammergau, Bavaria.

Pas-sion Sun-day the second Sunday before Easter.

pas-sive (păs′ĭv), *adj.* **1**, suffering without resisting; **2**, not acting but acted upon; as, a *passive* disposition; **3**, in grammar, indicating that form of the transitive verb which carries the idea that the subject is acted upon: opp. of *active;* **4**, not having, or not using, motive power; as, a *passive* balloon or airplane.—*adv.* **pas′sive-ly.**—*n.* **pas′sive-ness.**—*n.* **pas-siv′i-ty.**

pass-key (pȧs′=kē″), *n.* **1**, a master key, which will open all of a certain set of locks whose regular keys are not interchangeable; **2**, a key for opening more than one lock; **3**, a private key.

Pass-o-ver (pȧs′ō″vẽr), *n.* a Jewish feast commemorating the passing of the destroying angel over the houses of the Israelites when he slew the first-born of the Egyptians (Exodus 12).

pass-port (pȧs′pōrt), *n.* **1**, an official paper giving one permission to travel in a foreign country; **2**, anything that opens the way to success.

pass-word (pȧs′wûrd″), *n.* a word by means of which friends are known from strangers or enemies and are permitted to enter or pass; a watchword; as, the *password* of a lodge.

past (pȧst), *p.adj.* **1**, having formerly been; as, the *past* generation; **2**, just gone by; last; as, the *past* hour; **3**, in grammar, referring to time gone by; as, the *past* tense; **4**, in various societies and lodges, having served at a former time; **5**, thoroughly adept; as, he is a *past* master in the art of dancing:—*n.* **1**, the time gone by; as, memories of the *past;* **2**, previous life or history; as, we knew nothing of his *past;* **3**, in grammar, the past tense:—*adv.* by; beyond; as, he just walked *past:*—*prep.* beyond in time; after; as, it is *past* his time; he is *past* cure.

paste (pāst), *n.* **1**, a sticky mixture, often of flour and water, used for joining things together; **2**, dough prepared for pies, etc.; **3**, a preparation, as of fish, nuts, etc., finely ground and reduced to a creamy consistency; also, a jellylike confection; as, Turkish *paste;* **4**, a composition or mixture used for making artificial gems:—*v.t.* [*p.t.* and *p.p.* past′ed, *p.pr.* past′ing], **1**, to fasten with a sticky mixture; as, to *paste* together sheets of paper; **2**, to cover by, or as by, pasting.

paste-board (pāst′bōrd″), *n.* thick, stiff material made by compressing paper pulp.

pas-tel (păs′tĕl; păs-tĕl′), *n.* **1**, a kind of crayon made by mixing ground paints with gum water; also, the mixture from which the crayon is made; **2**, a picture drawn with such crayon:—*adj.* light and soft in tint; as, a *pastel* shade of green.—*n.* **pas′tel-ist.**

past-er (pās′tẽr), *n.* **1**, a strip of gummed paper, often with printed matter on it, to be pasted over something; **2**, one who applies paste.

pas-tern (păs′tẽrn), *n.* **1**, that part of a horse's foot between the fetlock and the foot bone; **2**, a shackle for a horse's foot, as while in pasture.

pas-teur-ize (pȧs′tẽr-īz; pȧs-tûr′īz), *v.t.* [*p.t.* and *p.p.* -ized (-īzd), *p.pr.* -iz″ing], to treat (milk or fermented liquids) by exposing to a temperature of 140° F. for 30 minutes: applied esp. to milk, which is thus partly sterilized with a minimum of harm to its nutritive value.—*n.* **pas″teur-i-za′tion.**

pas-til (păs′tĭl), *n.* **1**, a small mass of aromatic, or sweet-smelling, substances, burnt slowly to fumigate sick rooms, etc.; **2**, a kind of lozenge. Also, **pas-tille′** (păs-tēl′).

pas-time (pȧs′tīm″), *n.* diversion; sport; amusement; occupation that fills time agreeably.

pas-tor (pȧs′tẽr), *n.* a minister in charge of a church and congregation.

pas-tor-al (pȧs′tŏr-ăl), *adj.* **1**, pertaining to the duties of a minister; as, *pastoral* duties; **2**, pertaining to shepherds or to rural life or scenes:—*n.* **1**, a poem showing happenings in a country life; **2**, a picture showing rural life or scenes.—*adv.* **pas′tor-al-ly.**

pas-tor-ate (pȧs′tŏr-āt), *n.* **1**, the office or parish of a clergyman; **2**, the time during which a minister holds one charge; **3**, the body of ministers serving a locality.

pas-try (pās′trĭ), *n.* [*pl.* pastries (-trĭz)], desserts, as pies, tarts, etc., made with a rich crust of shortened paste.

pas-tur-age (pȧs′tūr-āj), *n.* **1**, feed for cattle, as grass; **2**, land used for feeding cattle; pasture.

pas-ture (pȧs′tūr), *n.* land or grass on which cattle feed:—*v.t.* [*p.t.* and *p.p.* -tured (-tūrd), *p.pr.* -tur-ing], to supply with grass or pasture:—*v.i.* to graze.

[1]**past-y** (pās′tĭ), *adj.* [*comp.* past′i-er, *superl.* past′i-est], covered with paste; also, like paste, as in color; as, a *pasty* complexion.—*n.* **past′i-ness.**

[2]**past-y** (pās′tĭ), *n.* [*pl.* pasties (-tĭz)], a pie, usually of highly seasoned meat, covered with crust.

[1]**pat** (păt), *n.* **1**, a light, quick blow with the hand; **2**, a small, shaped lump, as of butter; **3**, a light sound or tap:—*v.t.* [*p.t.* and *p.p.* pat′ted, *p.pr.* pat′ting], to strike gently with a flat surface, or, esp., with the hand or fingers; stroke gently.

[2]**pat** (păt), *adj.* [*comp.* pat′ter, *superl.* pat′test], apt; fitting:—*adv.* aptly; readily.—*n.* **pat′ness.**—*adv.* **pat′ly.**

Pat-a-go-ni-an (păt″ȧ-gō′nĭ-ăn), *adj.* pertaining to Patagonia, a region in South America divided between Chile and Argentina:—*n.* a native of this region; esp., one of the aboriginal Indians, the tallest known race.

patch (păch), *n.* **1**, a piece of material, as cloth or metal, put on to cover a hole, to shield, strengthen, or the like; **2**, a small plot of ground; also, a small piece of anything; **3**, a small piece of black court plaster applied to the skin to beautify it by contrast:—*v.t.* **1**, to mend or strengthen by putting on an extra piece of material; **2**, to mend clumsily; **3**, to piece together; as, to *patch* up a quarrel.—*n.* **patch′er.**—*adj.* **patch′y.**

patch-work (păch′wûrk″), *n.* **1**, a fabric made of pieces of cloth sewed together, esp. pieces of various colors; **2**, hence, a jumble; work carelessly done.

pate (pāt), *n.* **1**, the head; crown of the head; as, a boy with an empty *pate;* **2**, the hide on or near the head of a cow (see *leather*, illus.).

pa-tel-la (pȧ-tĕl′ȧ), *n.* [*pl.* patellæ (-ē)], the kneecap, or kneepan; the flat, movable bone forming the front of the knee joint (see *knee*, illus.).—*adj.* **pa-tel′lar.**

pat-en (păt′ĕn), *n.* the plate used for the bread in the Communion service.

pat-ent (păt′ĕnt; pā′tĕnt), *adj.* **1**, (usually pā′tĕnt), apparent; evident; plain; as, the truth was *patent* to all; **2**, (usually pā′tĕnt), open to public view: said esp. of an official paper which grants a privilege; as, letters *patent;* **3**, secured by government protection; as, a *patent* lock: **patent medicine**, *Colloq.*, a remedy, the name of which is copyrighted for commercial purposes:—*n.* **1**, a right or privilege granted by the government, as the sole right to make, use, or sell an invention for a certain number of years; **2**, the official paper granting this right; **3**, the thing that is so protected; **4**, a grant of land by a government; also, the land so granted, and the official document certifying it:—*v.t.* to grant or secure the sole right to.—*adj.* **pat′ent-a-ble.**—*adv.* **pa′tent-ly** (pā′tĕnt-lĭ).

Syn., adj. manifest, clear, obvious.

pat-ent-ee (păt″ĕn-tē′; pā″tĕn-tē′), *n.* a person or inventor who has secured from the government the sole right to make, use, or dispose of, an invention.

pat-ent leath-er a leather with a hard, glossy, usually black, surface: used for boots, shoes, etc.

pa-ter-fa-mil-i-as (pā″tẽr-fȧ-mĭl′ĭ-ăs), *n.* [*pl.* patresfamilias (pā″trēz-)], the father of a family; also, the male head of a household.

pa-ter-nal (pȧ-tûr′năl), *adj.* **1,** pertaining to, or like, a father; **2,** received from a father; **3,** related through the father; as, a *paternal* uncle.—*adv.* **pa-ter′nal-ly.**

pa-ter-nal-ism (pȧ-tûr′năl-ĭzm), *n.* a principle of government whereby the relationship between the government and the governed is like that between a father and his children.

pa-ter-ni-ty (pȧ-tûr′nĭ-tĭ), *n.* **1,** fatherhood; **2,** male parentage; as, the *paternity* of a child; **3,** authorship.

pa-ter-nos-ter (pā′tẽr-nŏs″tẽr; păt′ẽr-nŏs″tẽr), *n.* **1,** the Lord's Prayer; **2,** any formula used as a prayer; **3,** every eleventh bead in a rosary, showing the Lord's Prayer must be said; **4,** a rosary.

path (påth), *n.* [*pl.* paths (på*th*z)], **1,** a road; footpath; **2,** a track; **3,** a course of conduct or action.

pa-thet-ic (pȧ-thĕt′ĭk), *adj.* arousing sorrow and pity; as, a *pathetic* appearance; her grief was *pathetic.* Also, **pa-thet′i-cal.**—*adv.* **pa-thet′i-cal-ly.**

path-find-er (påth′fīn″dẽr), *n.* an explorer in an unknown country; a pioneer in unknown territory.

path-less (påth′lĕs), *adj.* without a beaten way; untrodden; trackless; as, the *pathless* forest.

path-o-gen-ic (păth″ō-jĕn′ĭk), *adj.* causing disease; also, pertaining to the causing of disease.

path-o-log-i-cal (păth″ō-lŏj′ĭ-kăl), *adj.* **1,** pertaining to the science of disease; **2,** due to disease; as, her depression is *pathological.* Also, **path″o-log′ic.** —*adv.* **path″o-log′i-cal-ly.**

pa-thol-o-gist (pȧ-thŏl′ō-jĭst), *n.* one skilled in pathology, or the science treating of diseases.

pa-thol-o-gy (pȧ-thŏl′ō-jĭ), *n.* [*pl.* pathologies (-jĭz)], **1,** the science that treats of diseases; **2,** the physical condition of an organ, or other part of the body, caused by disease.

pa-thos (pā′thŏs), *n.* that quality in an experience which excites sympathy and pity.

path-way (påth′wā″), *n.* **1,** a narrow footpath; **2,** any course or road.

pa-tience (pā′shĕns), *n.* **1,** the quality of suffering without complaint; meekness; **2,** endurance and perseverance; **3,** forbearance; **4,** the power to wait calmly.
Syn. composure, resignation, calmness.—
Ant. impatience, peevishness, intolerance.

pa-tient (pā′shĕnt), *adj.* **1,** suffering pain, hardship, affliction, insult, etc., with meekness; **2,** forbearing; **3,** untiring in labor; **4,** persevering; as, a *patient* worker; **5,** waiting with calmness:—*n.* one under the care of a doctor.—*adv.* **pa′tient-ly.**

***pa-tio** (pät′yō), [Span.], *n.* a courtyard within a house or other building.

pa-tois (pȧ″twä′; păt′wä), [Fr.], *n.* the language of uneducated people, used in a given locality; a dialect; as, the *patois* of the French Canadians.

pa-tri-arch (pā′trĭ-ärk), *n.* **1,** the founder or head of a family or tribe; esp., one of the early ancestors of the Jews, as Jacob; **2,** an aged and venerable man; **3,** in the Greek Church, a bishop of the highest rank.

pa-tri-ar-chal (pā″trĭ-är′kăl), *adj.* pertaining to a patriarch:

patriarchal cross, a cross emblematic of patriarchs and archbishops (see *cross,* illus.).

pa-tri-cian (pȧ-trĭsh′ăn), *n.* **1,** a member of the ancient Roman aristocracy: contrasted with *plebeian;* **2,** any person of noble or high birth:—*adj.* **1,** pertaining to the ancient Roman aristocracy; **2,** noble.

pat-ri-cide (păt′rĭ-sīd), *n.* **1,** the killing of a father; **2,** one who murders his father; a parricide.

pat-ri-mo-ny (păt′rĭ-mō-nĭ), *n.* [*pl.* patrimonies (-nĭz)], **1,** property inherited from a father or other ancestor; **2,** property settled upon a religious institution for its support.—*adj.* **pat″ri-mo′ni-al.**

pa-tri-ot (pā′trĭ-ŏt; păt′rĭ-ŏt), *n.* one who loves and supports his government or native country.

pa-tri-ot-ic (pā″trĭ-ŏt′ĭk; păt″rĭ-), *adj.* characterized or influenced by love of one's own country; as, a *patriotic* leader.—*adv.* **pa″tri-ot′i-cal-ly.**

pa-tri-ot-ism (pā′trĭ-ŏt-ĭzm), *n.* love of one's country.

pa-tris-tic (pȧ-trĭs′tĭk), *adj.* pertaining to the early historians of the Christian church, called the Fathers, or to their writings or doctrines. Also, **pa-tris′ti-cal.**

Pa-tro-clus (pȧ-trō′klŭs), *n.* a Greek hero of the Trojan War, who, while wearing the armor of his friend Achilles, was mistaken for him by Hector and slain in combat.

pa-trol (pȧ-trōl′), *n.* **1,** a guard; policeman; **2,** the act of going the rounds of a district in order to protect it; **3,** a small body of soldiers on guard duty; **4,** in the World War, a group of soldiers sent out at night to approach the enemy's trenches in search of information:—*v.t.* [*p.t.* and *p.p.* -trolled′ (-trōld′), *p.pr.* -trol′ling], **1,** to go or walk round in order to protect; as, a policeman *patrols* his beat; **2,** to act as guard to (a camp or entrenchment):—*v.i.* to go round a district in order to protect it.

pa-trol-man (pȧ-trōl′măn), *n.* [*pl.* patrolmen (-mĕn)], a policeman or watchman whose duty it is to go round a certain beat in order to protect it.

pa-tron (pā′trŭn), *n.* **1,** a guardian or protector; **2,** an upholder or supporter; as, a *patron* of music; **3,** in business, a regular customer; **4,** a man who lends his support to a social or charitable event:—*adj.* aiding, or acting as guardian; as, *patron* saints. —*n.fem.* **pa′tron-ess** (pā′trŭn-ĕs; păt′rŭn-ĕs).

pat-ron-age (păt′rŭn-āj; pā′trŭn-āj), *n.* **1,** special support; guardianship or protection; **2,** the act of buying goods regularly at one store.

pat-ron-ize (păt′rŭn-īz; pā′trŭn-īz), *v.t.* [*p.t.* and *p.p.* -ized (-īzd), *p.pr.* -iz″ing], **1,** to act as guardian or benefactor toward; support or protect; **2,** to treat with condescension; favor; **3,** *Colloq.,* to frequent or deal with regularly as a customer; as, to *patronize* a store.—*n.* **pat′ron-iz″er.**—*p. adj.* **pat′ron-iz″ing.**—*adv.* **pat′ron-iz″ing-ly.**

pat-ro-nym-ic (păt″rō-nĭm′ĭk), *adj.* formed from the name of an ancestor:—*n.* a name coming from an ancestor; the family name.

pa-troon (pȧ-trōōn′), *n.* one who received a large tract of land under the old Dutch governments of New York and New Jersey.

pat-tée (pȧ″tā′; păt′ē), [Fr.], *adj.* in heraldry, designating a certain kind of cross (see *cross,* illus.). Also, **pat′té.**

pat-ten (păt′ĕn), *n.* **1,** a wooden shoe with a thick sole; also, such a shoe with an iron ring under the sole to raise the foot from the ground, formerly worn by women as a protection against damp; a clog; 2, the base of a column.

¹pat-ter (păt'ẽr), *v.i.* 1, to mumble or mutter something over and over rapidly, esp. a prayer; 2, *Slang*, to talk glibly:—*v.t.* to mumble indistinctly; as, to *patter* one's prayers:—*n.* 1, rapid, cheap, fluent talk; 2, *Colloq.*: a, idle talk or gossip; b, lingo spoken by thieves, beggars, etc.; c, dialect; d, rapid speech, sometimes set to music.

²pat-ter (păt'ẽr), *n.* a quick succession of light sounds:—*v.i.* 1, to run with quick, short steps; 2, to strike with a quick succession of light sounds; as, the rain *patters* on the window.

pat-tern (păt'ẽrn), *n.* 1, a model, sample, or specimen; 2, anything cut out or formed into a shape to be copied; 3, a design or figure; as, the *pattern* of a carpet; 4, a piece of material sufficient for a garment; as, a dress *pattern*:—*v.t.* 1, to make in imitation of; copy: with *after*, *from*, or *by*; as, to *pattern* a dress after a model; 2, to decorate, as with a design:—*v.i.* to follow an example; as, you would do well to *pattern* by him.

pat-ty (păt'ĭ), *n.* [*pl.* patties (-ĭz)], a small, cup-shaped shell of pastry, holding meat, oysters, or the like; as, a chicken *patty*.

pau-ci-ty (pô'sĭ-tĭ), *n.* [*pl.* paucities (-tĭz)], smallness of number or quantity.

Paul (pôl), *n.* a Jew of Tarsus who became an apostle of Christ and whose epistles, or letters, to the Gentiles are contained in several books of the New Testament: orig. known as *Saul*.—*adj.* **Paul'ine.**

paul-dron (pôl'drŭn), *n.* a piece of plate armor used to protect the shoulder (see *armor*, *reredos*, illus.).

paunch (pänch; pônch), *n.* the abdomen; the belly and its contents.

pau-per (pô'pẽr), *n.* a very poor person, esp. one who is supported by the public or by charity.—*n.* **pau'per-ism.**

pau-per-ize (pô'pẽr-īz), *v.t.* [*p.t.* and *p.p.* -ized (-īzd), *p.pr.* -iz"ing], 1, to reduce to extreme poverty; 2, to accustom (a person) to receive support from the public; as, charity tends to *pauperize* the poor.

pause (pôz), *n.* 1, a temporary stop or rest; a brief ceasing of action; interruption; 2, hesitation; 3, a break in speaking; 4, a break in writing indicated by a punctuation mark; 5, a mark in music over or under a note or rest to show that it is to be prolonged: also called *hold*:—*v.i.* [*p.t.* and *p.p.* paused (pôzd), *p.pr.* paus'ing], to make a short stop; wait; hesitate: often with *on* or *upon*.

pave (pāv), *v.t.* [*p.t.* and *p.p.* paved (pāvd), *p.pr.* pav'ing], 1, to cover or lay with stones, bricks, etc.; as, to *pave* a street; 2, to make smooth or easy; as, to *pave* the way for another.—*n.* **pav'er.**

pave-ment (pāv'mĕnt), *n.* 1, a roadway or floor covered or laid with stone, brick, tile, etc.; 2, a sidewalk; 3, a prepared surface, as of stones, concrete, or the like, used in covering a road, pathway, or floor.

pa-vil-ion (pȧ-vĭl'yŭn), *n.* 1, an ornamental, dome-shaped building; as, a garden *pavilion*; 2, a large tent; 3, a temporary open building for shelter, entertainment, etc.; 4, a decorative part of a large building, extending out from the main part or rising above it.

pav-ing (pāv'ĭng), *n.* 1, construction of a pavement; 2, material for a pavement, as of a floor, street, etc.

paw (pô), *n.* 1, the foot of a four-footed animal with claws; 2, *Slang*, the hand:—*v.t.* 1, to touch or scrape with the forefoot; as, a horse *paws* the ground; 2, *Colloq.*, to handle awkwardly or coarsely; as, to *paw* things over:—*v.i.* 1, to scrape or touch something with the forefoot; as, the dog *pawed* at his meat; 2, *Colloq.*, to handle a thing awkwardly; grope clumsily.

pawl (pôl), *n.* a short bar or bolt on a machine, made to fall into notches in another part, as a wheel, in order to prevent it from turning back (see *capstan*, illus.).

¹pawn (pôn), *n.* 1, something given or deposited as security for the payment of a debt or return of a loan; 2, the state of being so pledged; as, my watch is in *pawn*:—*v.t.* to give as security for a loan.—*adj.* **pawn'a-ble.**—*n.* **pawn'er.**

²pawn (pôn), *n.* in chess, a piece of lowest value; in checkers, a counter.

pawn-bro-ker (pôn'brō"kẽr), *n.* one whose business it is to lend money on goods left with him.

Paw-nee (pô-nē'), *n.* one of a tribe of American Indians, orig. inhabiting the region of the Arkansas River in what is now Nebraska and Kansas.

pawn-shop (pôn'shŏp"), *n.* a shop where money is lent on goods deposited as security.

paw-paw (pô'pô"), *n.* the papaw or the papaya, tropical American trees bearing an edible fruit. See **pa-paw'**, *Pfd. S.*

¹pay (pā), *v.t.* [*p.t.* and *p.p.* paid (pād), or, in sense 5, payed (pād), *p.pr.* pay'ing], 1, to satisfy the claims of; recompense; as, to *pay* workmen; 2, to discharge, as a debt, by giving what is required; 3, to be profitable to; as, it will *pay* you to study; 4, to give without any sense of obligation; as, to *pay* a compliment; 5, to pass or slide out with the hands, as a rope or cable: with *out* or *away*:—*v.i.* 1, to make recompense; discharge a debt; as, he always *pays* promptly; 2, to make suitable return for effort; be worth while; as, the business *pays* well:—*n.* 1, money given for service done, for goods, etc.; 2, a person viewed from the standpoint of his ability or willingness to discharge his debts; as, he is good *pay*.—*n.* **pay'er.**

Syn., *n.* (see salary).

²pay (pā), *v.t.* [*p.t.* and *p.p.* payed (pād), *p.pr.* pay'ing], on shipboard, to smear with tar, pitch, etc.

pay-a-ble (pā'ȧ-bl), *adj.* 1, due, as a bill; 2, requiring payment; 3, profitable; as, a *payable* business.

pay-ee (pā-ē'), *n.* one to whom money is, is to be, or has been, paid.

pay-mas-ter (pā'mȧs"tẽr), *n.* one who gives out money for wages; esp., an officer in the army or navy whose duty it is to pay the officers and men.

pay-ment (pā'mĕnt), *n.* 1, the act of giving money for wages, a debt, etc.; 2, that which is given in discharge of a debt, duty, etc.; recompense.

pay-nim (pā'nĭm), *adj.* formerly, heathen; pagan:—*n.* formerly, a pagan; a Moslem; also, the heathen world.

pea (pē), *n.* [*pl.* peas; pease (pēz)], 1, a pod-bearing vine of the bean family, widely cultivated as a vegetable; 2, its edible seed.

peace (pēs), *n.* 1, a state of rest or calm; quiet; 2, freedom from war or disorder; 3, friendly relations, as between nations.

peace-a-ble (pēs'ȧ-bl), *adj.* 1, not quarrelsome; 2, calm; quiet.—*n.* **peace'a-ble-ness.**—*adv.* **peace'a-bly.**

peace-ful (pēs'fo͝ol), *adj.* 1, free from war or commotion; 2, mild; calm; undisturbed; quiet; as, a *peaceful* evening.—*adv.* **peace'ful-ly.**—*n.* **peace'ful-ness.**

Syn. tranquil, peaceable. (See calm.)

peace-mak-er (pēs'māk"ẽr), *n.* one who restores friendly feeling between two unfriendly parties; a mediator.—*adj.* and *n.* **peace'mak"ing.**

peach (pēch), *n.* **1**, a well-known orchard tree; **2**, its fleshy, juicy fruit.

pea-cock (pē′kŏk″), *n.* the male bird of the peafowl, noted for its long, handsome tail coverts, commonly called tail feathers, marked with iridescent, eyelike spots.—*n. fem.* **pea′hen″.**

PEACOCKS ($\frac{1}{32}$)

pea-fowl (pē′foul″), *n.* a large domestic fowl, with vivid greenish blue plumage; a peacock or a peahen.

pea-jack-et (pē′-jăk″ĕt), *n.* a loose, double-breasted coat of thick woolen cloth, worn by sailors.

[1]peak (pēk), *n.* **1**, the sharp-pointed summit of a mountain or hill; **2**, a mountain standing alone; **3**, a pointed end of anything; as, the *peak* of a roof; **4**, the visor of a cap; **5**, the period of maximum intensity, or the maximum itself as shown on a graph or curve, as of traffic, demand, load, etc.: also called *peak load;* **6**, the crest, or maximum value, of an alternating electric current or voltage; **7**, the upper outer corner of a sail, extended by a gaff; **8**, the narrow part, fore or aft, of a vessel's hull.

[2]peak (pēk), *v.i. Obs.*, to grow pale and wan; as, dwindle, *peak*, and pine.

[3]peak (pēk), *v.t.* on shipboard, to raise in a vertical direction, as a yard, gaff, etc.

[1]peaked (pēkt), *adj.* pointed; as, a *peaked* roof; projecting; as, a *peaked* cap.

[2]peak-ed (pēk′ĕd), *adj. Colloq.*, **1**, sharp-featured; **2**, thin; wan.

peal (pēl), *n.* **1**, a loud, long sound, as of thunder, bells, etc.; **2**, a set of bells, or the changes rung on them:—*v.i.* to give forth loud sounds, as a bell or organ:—*v.t.* to cause to sound loudly; as, to *peal* a bell.

pe-an (pē′ăn), *n.* a joyous song of praise or triumph. Also, **pæ′an,** *Pfd. S.*

pea-nut (pē′nŭt), *n.* **1**, a tropical plant of the pea family; **2**, the fruit of this plant: also called *groundnut.*

pear (pâr), *n.* **1**, an orchard tree related to the apple; **2**, its fleshy, edible fruit.

pearl (pûrl), *n.* **1**, a small rounded mass of lustrous, satiny substance, creamy or silvery white to black in color, valued as a gem: found within the shells of some shellfish, esp. certain oysters, where it is produced by the covering up of some small foreign body, as a grain of sand, with a substance resembling mother-of-pearl; **2**, anything like such a gem in form or value; **3**, a pale, grayish white color; **4**, an imitation of the gem; **5**, mother-of-pearl; **6**, in printing, a size of type, 5 point (see *type*): **baroque pearl,** a pearl of irregular form: **mother-of-pearl,** the lining of the shell of various mollusks, delicately tinted and lustrous: also called *nacre:*—*v.t.* to set, or adorn, with pearls:—*v.i.* to fish for pearls.

pearl-ash (pûrl′ăsh″), *n.* crude potash with the impurities taken out, used in glass and soap manufacture.

pearl-y (pûr′lĭ), *adj.* [*comp.* pearl′i-er, *superl.* pearl′i-est], **1**, having a soft, grayish white color or luster; **2**, hence, lustrous; as, *pearly* teeth.—*n.* **pearl′i-ness.**

peart (pĭrt), *adj. Colloq.*, in good spirits. Also, **pert,** *Pfd. S.*—*adv.* **peart′ly.**

peas-ant (pĕz′ănt), *n.* in Europe, a rustic of low social rank; esp., a farm laborer or a petty farmer:—*adj.* rude; rustic; as, *peasant* manners.

peas-ant-ry (pĕz′ănt-rĭ), *n.* rustics, countrymen, or farmers of low rank, collectively.

peas-cod (pēz′kŏd″) *n.* the covering of the pea seed; a pea pod.

pease (pēz), *n.pl.* peas collectively: now generally written *peas.*

peat (pēt), *n.* a substance, valuable as a fuel, formed of partly decayed vegetable matter and found principally in swamps and marshy places.—*adj.* **peat′y.**

pea-vey (pē′vĭ), *n.* [*pl.* peaveys (-vĭz)], an iron-pointed lever with a movable iron hook near the end: used in lumbering. Also, **pea′vy** [*pl.* peavies (-vĭz)].

peb-ble (pĕb′l), *n.* **1**, a small, roundish stone, worn smooth, as by water; **2**, transparent or clear rock crystal used for lenses in spectacles:—*v.t.* [*p.t.* and *p.p.* -bled (-ld), *p.pr.* -bling], to grain (leather) so as to produce an uneven surface.

peb-bly (pĕb′lĭ), *adj.* **1**, full of pebbles; **2**, having a pebbled surface.

pe-can (pē-kăn′; pē-kän′), *n.* **1**, a kind of hickory tree of the southern U. S.; **2**, its thin-shelled nut.

pec-ca-dil-lo (pĕk″ȧ-dĭl′ō), *n.* [*pl.* peccadillos; peccadilloes (-ōz)], a trifling fault or slight offense.

pec-ca-ry (pĕk′ȧ-rĭ), *n.* [*pl.* peccaries (-rĭz)], any of several species of hoglike animals native to tropical America.

[1]peck (pĕk), *n.* **1**, in dry measure, one quarter of a bushel; eight quarts; also, a vessel for measuring out a peck; **2**, a lot; a great deal; as, a *peck* of trouble.

[2]peck (pĕk), *v.t.* **1**, to strike with the beak, as does a bird; **2**, to strike with a pointed instrument, as a pick; **3**, to pick up with the beak; as, the hen *pecks* corn; **4**, to eat sparingly; as, she *pecks* her food:—*v.i.* **1**, to make strokes with the beak or a sharp instrument; **2**, to pick up food with the beak:—*n.* **1**, a quick, sharp stroke, as with the beak; **2**, a mark made by a blow with a sharp point; **3**, *Slang*, a quick, light kiss.

peck-er (pĕk′ẽr), *n.* **1**, one that pecks, or picks; esp., a bird that picks holes in trees, such as the woodpecker; **2**, a pick, pickax, or other tool for making holes.

Peck-sniff (pĕk′snĭf), *n.* a hypocritical character in Dickens's "Martin Chuzzlewit."—*adj.* **Peck-sniff′i-an.**

pec-to-ral (pĕk′tō̆-răl), *adj.* pertaining to, good for, or worn on, the chest; as, a *pectoral* muscle; a *pectoral* remedy; a *pectoral* ornament:—*n.* **1**, an ornament worn on the breast, as the breastplate formerly worn by the Jewish high priest; **2**, a medicine for chest complaints.

pec-u-late (pĕk′ū-lāt), *v.t.* and *v.i.* [*p.t.* and *p.p.* -lat″ed, *p.pr.* -lat″ing], to steal; embezzle.—*n.* **pec′u-la″tor.**

pec-u-la-tion (pĕk″ū-lā′shŭn), *n.* theft, as of money; embezzlement.

pe-cul-iar (pē-kūl′yẽr), *adj.* **1**, one's own; not owned in common; as, my *peculiar* property; **2**, not like anything else; individual; as, her style of dress is *peculiar* to her; **3**, strange; queer.—*adv.* **pe-cul′iar-ly.**

Syn. singular, odd, unusual, rare.

pe-cu-li-ar-i-ty (pē-kū″lĭ-ăr′ĭ-tĭ), *n.* [*pl.* peculiarities (-tĭz)], **1**, something which marks a person or thing as being different from others; **2**, the state or quality of being different from others; **3**, an unusual or odd trait; queerness.

pe-cu-ni-a-ry (pē-kū′nĭ-ā-rĭ), *adj.* relating to money; as, *pecuniary* losses.—*adv.* **pe-cu′ni-a-ri-ly.**

Syn. monetary, fiscal, financial.

ped-a-gog (pĕd′ȧ-gŏg), *n.* a teacher of children; a schoolmaster, esp. if conceited and narrow-minded. Also, **ped′a-gogue.**—*n.* **ped′a-gog″ism.**

ped-a-gog-ic (pĕd″ȧ-gŏj′ĭk), *adj.* pertaining to a teacher or to teaching: **pedagogics,** *n.pl.* used as *sing.* the science of teaching. Also, *adj.* **ped″a-gog′i-cal.**

ped-a-go-gy (pĕd′ȧ-gō″jĭ; pĕd′ȧ-gŏj″ĭ), *n.* [*pl.* pedagogies (-jĭz)], **1,** the science or art of teaching; **2,** instruction and training; discipline.

ped-al (pĕd′ăl; pē′dăl), *adj.* **1,** pertaining to a foot or feet; as, *pedal* digits, or toes; **2,** pertaining to, or operated by, a foot lever or treadle; as, a *pedal* note in organ music:—*n.* (pĕd′ăl), **1,** the treadle, as of a bicycle; **2,** a lever attached to a musical instrument and moved by the foot, to lessen or swell the tone:—*v.t.* and *v.i.* to operate by means of treadles.

ped-ant (pĕd′ănt), *n.* one who makes a needless display of his learning or who overvalues mere knowledge.—*adj.* **pe-dan′tic.**—*adv.* **pe-dan′ti-cal-ly.**

ped-ant-ry (pĕd′ănt-rĭ), *n.* [*pl.* pedantries (-rĭz)], **1,** conceited and needless display of learning; **2,** the habit of mind that overvalues, and insists upon emphasizing, trifling details of learning.

ped-dle (pĕd′l), *v.i.* [*p.t.* and *p.p.* -dled (-ld), *p.pr.* -dling], **1,** to travel about selling small wares; **2,** to do a small business; **3,** to be busy about trifles:—*v.t.* **1,** to sell in small quantities from house to house; hawk; **2,** to deal out little by little.

ped-dler (pĕd′lẽr), *n.* one who travels about selling small articles; a hawker. Also, **ped′lar; ped′ler.**

ped-es-tal (pĕd′ĕs-tăl), *n.* the base of a column, statue, vase, etc.; hence, any support.

PEDESTAL
B, base; *C*, cornice; *D*, dado.

pe-des-tri-an (pē-dĕs′trĭ-ăn), *adj.* **1,** going on foot; walking; **2,** pertaining to walking; hence, slow-moving; dull:—*n.* **1,** one who journeys on foot; **2,** one who walks as a feat or an athletic performance—*n.* **pe-des′tri-an-ism.**

ped-i-cel (pĕd′ĭ-sĕl), *n.* **1,** in botany: **a,** a secondary flower stalk branching from the main flower stalk, or peduncle, and bearing one flower, as in the geranium; **b,** any slender supporting stalk; **2,** in zoölogy, a slender, stalklike support or stem; a peduncle. Also, **ped′i-cle** (pĕd′ĭ-kl).

ped-i-gree (pĕd′ĭ-grē), *n.* recorded ancestry or line of descent; family history; as, the *pedigree* of a horse; hence, notable ancestry.—*adj.* **ped′i-greed.**

ped-i-ment (pĕd′ĭ-mĕnt), *n.* orig., an ornamented triangular space, or low gable, over the front of a building; hence, any like decoration over a door, window, or the like.—*adj.* **ped″i-men′tal.**

pe-dom-e-ter (pē-dŏm′ē-tẽr), *n.* a watch-shaped instrument for measuring the distance covered in walking.

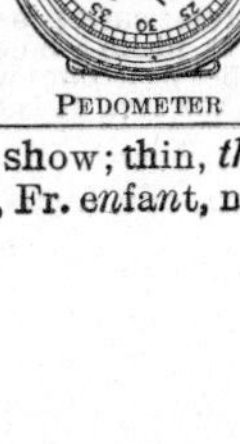

PEDOMETER

pe-dun-cle (pē-dŭng′kl), *n.* **1,** a primary flower stalk, which may bear a solitary flower, as that of the Easter lily, or a cluster of flowers, as that of the lily of the valley, cherry, geranium, etc.; **2,** in zoölogy, a stalklike process.—*adj.* **pe-dun′cu-lar.**—*adj.* **pe-dun′cu-late.**

peek (pēk), *v.i.* to look slyly through a crevice or crack; peep:—*n.* a peep.

¹peel (pēl), *v.t.* **1,** to strip off an outer covering from, as a husk from corn; **2,** to strip off, as bark or rind:—*v.i.* **1,** to come off; as, the bark of the tree *peels* easily; **2,** to lose an outer covering:—*n.* skin or rind.

²peel (pēl), *n.* a baker's long, flat, wooden shovel for reaching into the oven.

¹peep (pēp), *v.i.* to chirp; cry, as a young bird:—*n.* the cry of a young bird, chicken, etc.; chirp; squeak.

²peep (pēp), *v.i.* **1,** to look through a crack or from a hiding place; look slyly; **2,** to begin to appear, as the rising sun:—*n.* **1,** a quick, furtive look; **2,** a glimpse; **3,** first appearance, as of the sun or dawn.

peep-er (pēp′ẽr), *n.* one that peeps, or chirps; esp., a young frog that makes a cheeping noise in the spring.

¹peer (pēr), *n.* **1,** one of the same rank; an equal before the law; as, to be tried before one's *peers;* also, any equal or associate; **2,** a nobleman; **3,** a member of the British House of Lords.

²peer (pēr), *v.i.* **1,** to look closely; **2,** in poetry, to show the head or face; appear; as, violets *peer* through the leaves.

peer-age (pēr′ăj), *n.* **1,** the rank or dignity of a nobleman; **2,** the whole body of noblemen; **3,** a book containing information about the nobility.

peer-ess (pēr′ĕs), *n.* **1,** the wife of a nobleman; **2,** a lady of noble rank.

peer-less (pēr′lĕs), *adj.* without an equal; matchless; as, *peerless* courage.—*adv.* **peer′less-ly.**—*n.* **peer′less-ness.**

peeve (pēv), *v.t.* [*p.t.* and *p.p.* peeved (pēvd), *p.pr.* peev′ing], *Colloq.*, to vex; irritate; exasperate:—*v.i. Colloq.*, to become childishly fretful or ill-tempered; be vexed:—*n. Colloq.*, vexation.

pee-vish (pē′vĭsh), *adj.* childishly fretful; hard to please; as, a *peevish* disposition.—*adv.* **pee′vish-ly.**—*n.* **pee′vish-ness.**
Syn.: irritable, petulant, testy, cross.—*Ant.* placid, gentle, patient.

peg (pĕg), *n.* **1,** a pointed wooden pin used as a fastening; as, a shoe *peg;* a tent *peg;* **2,** a piece of wood serving as a nail; as, to hang one's coat on a *peg;* **3,** a fact or reason upon which an argument depends; **4,** a drink of whisky, or brandy, and soda:—*v.t.* [*p.t.* and *p.p.* pegged (pĕgd), *p.pr.* peg′ging], **1,** to fasten with small wooden pins; as, to *peg* shoes; **2,** to mark by driving in small stakes of wood; as, to *peg* out a mining claim:—*v.i.* to work steadily; as, to *peg* away at one's lessons.

Peg-a-sus (pĕg′ȧ-sŭs), *n.* **1,** in mythology, a winged horse caught and tamed by Minerva, presented by her to the Muses, and used by Bellerophon in overcoming the Chimera: a symbol of the flight of poetic imagination; **2,** a large, northern constellation, its three brightest stars forming, with one star from the constellation Andromeda, the square of Pegasus.

peg top a pear-shaped, wooden spinning top with a sharp metal point.—*adj.* **peg′-top″.**

pel-age (pĕl′ăj), *n.* the hair, wool, or fur covering a mammal: corresponding to the *plumage* of a bird.

pe-lag-ic (pē-lăj′ĭk), *adj.* pertaining to, or living in, the ocean, esp. on the surface, far from land; as, *pelagic* fish.

pel-er-ine (pĕl′ẽr-ĭn; pĕl″ẽr-ēn′), *n.* a woman's cape, often of fur, longer in the back than in the front.

Pe-leus (pē′lūs), *n.* in mythology, king of the Myrmidons; father of Achilles.

pelf (pĕlf), *n.* **1**, stolen property; **2**, money; wealth: used contemptuously.

pel-i-can (pĕl′ĭ-kăn), *n.* a large water bird with a huge bill, and a large pouch on the throat for storing food.

Pe-li-on (pē′lĭ-ŏn), *n.* in mythology, a mountain in Thessaly, which the Titans tried to combine with Ossa so as to scale Olympus, abode of the gods (see *Ossa*).

PELICANS (1/40)

pe-lisse (pĕ-lēs′), *n.* a woman's long cloak, orig. fur-lined or made entirely of fur.

pel-lag-ra (pĕ-lăg′rȧ; pĕ-lā′grȧ), *n.* a skin disease which seriously disturbs the digestive and nervous systems and frequently results in insanity.

Pel-le-as (pĕl′ē-ăs), *n.* a knight of King Arthur's Round Table, hero of one of Tennyson's "Idylls of the King."

pel-let (pĕl′ĕt), *n.* a little ball, often of food or medicine; a pill.

pel-li-cle (pĕl′ĭ-kl), *n.* a very thin skin or film.

pell–mell (pĕl″=mĕl′), *adv.* **1**, in a disorderly manner; **2**, headlong; as, they rushed out *pell-mell*. Also, **pell″mell′**.

pel-lu-cid (pĕ-lū′sĭd), *adj.* **1**, perfectly clear; as, a *pellucid* stream; **2**, easily understood; as, *pellucid* thought.

Pel-o-pon-ne-sian (pĕl″ō-pŏ-nē′shăn; -zhăn), *adj.* of or pertaining to the southern peninsula of Greece, known to the ancient Greeks as the Peloponnesus, but now called Morea.

¹pelt (pĕlt), *n.* a raw hide; the undressed skin of a fur-bearing animal.

²pelt (pĕlt), *v.t.* **1**, to strike by throwing missiles at; **2**, to hurl:—*v.i.* **1**, to strike repeated blows with something thrown; **2**, to beat down heavily, as rain or hail:—*n.* a blow from something thrown.

pel-tate (pĕl′tāt), *adj.* shield-shaped and attached to the stalk on the lower surface near the center: said of leaves, as in the nasturtium (see *leaf*, illus.).

Pel-ton wheel (pĕl′tŭn), a water wheel in which jets of water at high speed are played into cup-shaped buckets on the rim of the wheel (see *hydraulic*, illus.).

pelt-ry (pĕl′trĭ), *n.* [*pl.* peltries (-trĭz)], **1**, skins or furs collectively; **2**, a pelt, or skin.

pel-vis (pĕl′vĭs), *n.* [*pl.* pelves (-vēz)], in anatomy, the bony, basin-shaped structure which supports the spinal column and the lower abdomen and to which the lower limbs are attached.—*adj.* **pel′vic.**

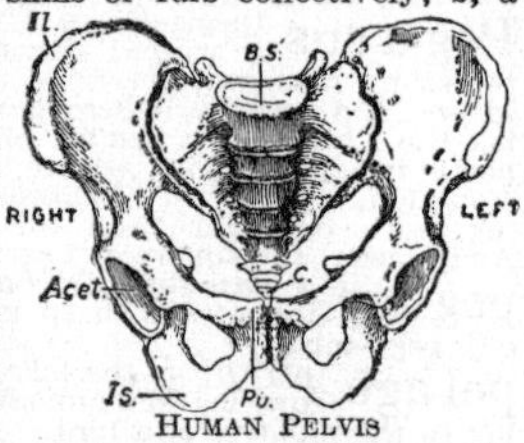

HUMAN PELVIS

B.S., upper base of sacrum; *Il.*, ilium; *Acet.*, acetabulum, or cup to receive upper end of femur; *Is.*, ischium; *Pu.*, pubis; *C.*, coccyx.

pem-mi-can (pĕm′ĭ-kăn), *n.* a food made of lean meat, with fat and, sometimes, fruit, dried, pounded, and pressed into cakes.

¹pen (pĕn), *n.* a small inclosure, chiefly for confining animals; a coop; as, a pig-*pen;* also, sometimes, the animals confined in the inclosure:—*v.t.* [*p.t.* and *p.p.* penned (pĕnd) or pent (pĕnt), *p.pr.* pen′ning], to shut up or confine, as in a small inclosure.

²pen (pĕn), *n.* **1**, a quill or feather; **2**, an instrument for writing with ink, orig. a quill; now, ordinarily, a split point of gold or steel to be fitted in a holder; also, the holder and the point together; **3**, a style of writing; **4**, an author; **5**, writing in general:—*v.t.* [*p.t.* and *p.p.* penned (pĕnd), *p.pr.* pen′ning], to write; compose and put on paper.

pe-nal (pē′năl), *adj.* pertaining to, or liable to, punishment; as, the *penal* laws.

pe-nal-ize (pē′năl-īz), *v.t.* [*p.t.* and *p.p.* -ized (-īzd), *p.pr.* -iz″ing], **1**, to inflict punishment upon; **2**, to make subject to punishment.

pen-al-ty (pĕn′ăl-tĭ), *n.* [*pl.* penalties (-tĭz)], **1**, legal punishment for breaking the law, consisting of fine, imprisonment, or death; **2**, a fine or forfeit; **3**, suffering or punishment coming as the result of any wrongdoing or condition.

pen-ance (pĕn′ăns), *n.* **1**, self-imposed suffering showing sorrow for wrongdoing; **2**, in the Roman Catholic Church, the sacrament by which sins are pardoned after confession and reparation; also, the act or discipline imposed by the priest as an expression of repentance.

pe-na-tes (pē-nā′tēz), *n.pl.* the household gods of the ancient Romans, worshiped in conjunction with the *lares*, or deified spirits of ancestors.

pence (pĕns), *n.* plural of *penny*, expressing total amount of money: distinct from *pennies*, which indicates separate coins.

***pen-chant** (päṅ″shäṅ′; pĕn′chănt), [Fr.], *n.* a strong leaning or taste; as, she has a *penchant* for music.

pen-cil (pĕn′sĭl), *n.* **1**, a small, fine brush used by artists; **2**, a pointed instrument of black lead, colored chalk, etc., often inclosed in wood, and used for writing, drawing, etc.; **3**, a crayon of caustic, rouge, or the like:—*v.t.* to write, sketch, paint, or mark with, or as with, a pencil.—*p.adj.* **pen′ciled.**

pend-ant (pĕn′dănt), *n.* **1**, anything hanging for ornamentation; **2**, an earring or locket.

pend-ent (pĕn′dĕnt), *adj.* **1**, hanging; swinging; **2**, jutting over; as, a *pendent* rock; **3**, undetermined; in suspense.

pend-ing (pĕnd′ĭng), *adj.* not yet finished or decided; as, a *pending* trial:—*prep.* during the continuance of; awaiting.

pen-drag-on (pĕn-drăg′ŭn), *n.* the supreme leader: a title conferred on chiefs in ancient Britain.

pen-du-lous (pĕn′dū-lŭs), *adj.* hanging so as to swing; swaying.—*adv.* **pen′du-lous-ly.**—*n.* **pen′du-lous-ness.**

pen-du-lum (pĕn′dū-lŭm), *n.* a body suspended from a fixed point so that it is free to swing to and fro; as, the *pendulum* of a clock.

Pe-nel-o-pe (pē-nĕl′ō-pē), *n.* in mythology, the wife of Odysseus (Ulysses) of Ithaca: noted for her faithfulness during her husband's long absence after the Trojan War.

pen-e-tra-ble (pĕn′ē-trȧ-bl), *adj.* capable of being entered or pierced by another body.—*n.* **pen″e-tra-bil′i-ty.**

pen-e-trate (pĕn′ē-trāt), *v.t.* [*p.t.* and *p.p.* -trat″ed, *p.pr.* -trat″ing], **1**, to pierce; enter; as, light *penetrates* darkness; **2**, to make a hole through; perforate; as, a bullet *penetrates* wood; **3**, to make a way into; as, the idea at last *penetrated* his intelligence;

4, to affect deeply; 5, to reach the interior of; 6, to understand; 7, to pervade:—*v.i.* 1, to pass or pierce into something; 2, to affect the feelings deeply.—*adj.* **pen'e-tra″tive.**—*n.* **pen″e-tra'tion.**

pen-e-trat-ing (pĕn'ē-trāt″ĭng), *p.adj.* 1, piercing; sharp; acute; 2, discerning; knowing.

pen-gö (pĕn'gö), *n.* [*pl.* pengö], a silver coin and the monetary unit of Hungary, equivalent to about 30 cents.

pen-guin (pĕn'gwĭn; pĕng'gwĭn), *n.* any of several large antarctic sea birds, unable to fly.

pen-i-cil-lin (pĕn″ĭ-sĭl'ĭn), *n.* a substance produced by a common mold (usually of bread) which arrests the growth of several disease-producing microorganisms; non-toxic and effective in the treatment of such infections as pneumonia and gonorrhea.

pen-in-su-la (pĕn-ĭn'sū-lȧ), *n.* a point of land extending out from the mainland.—*adj.* **pen-in'su-lar.**

pe-nis (pē'nĭs), *n.* [*pl.* penises (-ĕz); penes (-nēz)], the male genital organ.

pen-i-tence (pĕn'ĭ-tĕns), *n.* sorrow, or the state of being sorry, for sin.

pen-i-tent (pĕn'ĭ-tĕnt), *adj.* sorry; repentant:—*n.* 1, one who is repentant, or sorry for sin; 2, one who has confessed sin and is doing penance under the direction of a confessor.—*adv.* **pen'i-tent-ly.**

pen-i-ten-tial (pĕn″ĭ-tĕn'shăl), *adj.* pertaining to penitence or to penance; as, *penitential* psalms.

pen-i-ten-tia-ry (pĕn″ĭ-tĕn'shȧ-rĭ), *adj.* 1, pertaining to penance; 2, pertaining to systems of punishment for wrongdoing; 3, making the offender liable to imprisonment:—*n.* [*pl.* penitentiaries (-rĭz)], a house of correction; esp., a state prison.

pen-knife (pĕn'nīf″), *n.* [*pl.* penknives (-nīvz″)], a small pocketknife: used formerly for sharpening quill pens.

pen-man (pĕn'măn), *n.* [*pl.* penmen (-mĕn)], 1, a person considered with regard to his handwriting; as, a good *penman*; 2, one who teaches handwriting.

pen-man-ship (pĕn'măn-shĭp), *n.* 1, the art of handwriting; 2, style of writing; as, unusual *penmanship.*

pen name a name adopted by an author; a pseudonym.

pen-nant (pĕn'ănt), *n.* 1, a long, narrow flag; as, a naval *pennant*; 2, any small flag used for various purposes; as, a college *pennant*; 3, in music, a hook; one of the small strokes from the stem of a note which indicate its time value (see *note*, illus.).

pen-ni-less (pĕn'ĭ-lĕs), *adj.* without money; very poor.

pen-non (pĕn'ŭn), *n.* 1, a small swallow-tailed or triangular flag or streamer, formerly borne by a knight on his lance; 2, any flag or banner.

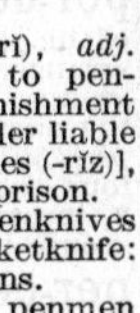
PENNON

pen-ny (pĕn'ĭ), *n.* [*pl.* pennies (-ĭz) denoting number of coins; pence (pĕns), denoting amount in value]. 1, in England, a coin, formerly copper, now bronze, equal to one twelfth of a shilling, or about two cents of U. S. money; 2, any insignificant amount of money; as, with not a *penny:* 3, *U.S. Colloq.*, a cent (which see): **-penny**, orig., designating, with a numeral, the price of nails as (so many) pence per 100; now arbitrarily designating their size, as follows [line 1, size number (2d = twopenny, etc.); line 2, length in inches; line 3, number of nails per pound]:

2d	4d	6d	8d	10d	12d	16d	20d	30d	40d	60d
1	1½	2	2½	3	3¼	3½	4	4½	5	6
876	316	181	106	69	63	49	31	24	18	11

pen-ny-roy-al (pĕn″ĭ-roi'ăl), *n.* a fragrant herb of the mint family, found in old pastures.

pen-ny-weight (pĕn'ĭ-wāt″), *n.* a Troy weight equal to 24 grains, or $\frac{1}{20}$ of an ounce Troy.

pen-ny–wise (pĕn'ĭ-wīz″), *adj.* saving in small affairs only; as, *penny-wise* and pound-foolish. Also, **pen'ny wise.**

pen-ny-worth (pĕn'ĭ-wûrth″), *n.* 1, the amount that a penny will buy; 2, a small amount.

pe-nol-o-gy (pē-nŏl'ō-jĭ), *n.* the scientific study of punishments for crime, of prison management, etc.—*adj.* **pe″no-log'i-cal** (pē″nō-lŏj'ĭ-kăl; pĕn″ō-).

pen-sile (pĕn'sĭl), *adj.* 1, hanging and swaying, as an oriole's nest; 2, having a hanging nest.

pen-sion (pĕn'shŭn), *n.* 1, a certain sum paid regularly by a government, employer, or corporation, in return for past services; as, a *pension* paid by the government to ex-soldiers; 2, such an allowance paid to artists, scientists, etc., who work for the public benefit; 3, (păṅ″syôṅ'), in Europe, a boarding house or boarding school:—*v.t.* to grant a regular allowance of money to.

pen-sion-a-ry (pĕn'shŭn-ā-rĭ), *adj.* depending for support upon an allowance made because of past services or through bounty:—*n.* [*pl.* pensionaries (-rĭz)], one who depends on such an allowance.

pen-sion-er (pĕn'shŭn-ẽr), *n.* one who receives a regular allowance because of past services or through the bounty of another.

pen-sive (pĕn'sĭv), *adj.* sadly thoughtful; musing; as, a *pensive* mood.—*adv.* **pen'sive-ly.**—*n.* **pen'sive-ness.**

Syn. meditative, reflective, dreamy.

pent (pĕnt), *p.adj.* shut up; closely confined: often with *up;* as, *pent-up* rage.

pen-ta- (pĕn'tȧ-), a combining form from the Greek, meaning five; as, *penta*gon; *penta*meter.

pen-ta-gon (pĕn'tȧ-gŏn), *n.* a plane figure of five sides and five angles.—*adj.* **pen-tag'o-nal.**

REGULAR PENTAGON

pen-tam-e-ter (pĕn-tăm'ē-tẽr), *n.* a verse, or line of poetry, consisting of five metrical feet:—*adj.* having five metrical feet.

Pen-ta-teuch (pĕn'tȧ-tūk), *n.* the first five books of the Old Testament.

pen-tath-lon (pĕn-tăth'lŏn), *n.* in the ancient or modern Olympic games, an athletic contest of five events.

Pen-te-cost (pĕn'tē-kŏst), *n.* 1, a Jewish festival kept the fiftieth day after the second day of the Passover; 2, the Christian feast of Whitsunday, celebrating the descent of the Holy Ghost upon the disciples (Acts 2: 1-4).—*adj.* **Pen″te-cos'tal.**

pent-house (pĕnt'hous″), *n.* 1, a shed or a slanting roof projecting from a main wall or building; 2, a small, slanting roof, as over a door or window.

pe-nult (pē'nŭlt; pē-nŭlt'), *n.* the last syllable but one. Also, **pe-nul'ti-ma.**

pe-nul-ti-mate (pē-nŭl'tĭ-māt), *adj.* last but one; as, a *penultimate* syllable:—*n.* the penult, or the next to the last syllable of a word.

pe-num-bra (pē-nŭm'brȧ), *n.* a partial shadow on the outside of a complete shadow, as in an eclipse, or at the edge of a sun spot (see *umbra*, illus.).

pe-nu-ri-ous (pē-nū'rĭ-ŭs), *adj.* 1, miserly; 2, poor; scanty.—*adv.* **pe-nu'ri-ous-ly.**—*n.* **pe-nu'ri-ous-ness.**

pen-u-ry (pĕn′ū-rĭ), *n.* want of the necessities of life; extreme poverty.
Syn. need, privation, destitution.

pe-on (pē′ŏn), *n.* **1**, in Spanish America and in the southern U. S., a laborer, esp. one who is forced to work for a creditor to pay a debt; **2**, in India, a native foot soldier; also, a native constable.

pe-on-age (pē′ŏn-āj), *n.* a system of contract labor, by which gangs of workmen are rented to employers.

pe-o-ny (pē′ō-nĭ), *n.* [*pl.* peonies (-nĭz)], **1**, a plant of the crowfoot family with handsome flowers; **2**, the flower of the plant.

peo-ple (pē′pl), *n.* **1**, [*pl.* peoples (-plz)], a body of persons united into a community, race, tribe, nation, etc.; as, the American *people;* the *peoples* of Europe; **2**, used as *pl.:* **a**, inhabitants; population; as, we, the *people* of the United States; **b**, the public; esp., the populace or masses; **c**, persons; as, only three *people* came; **d**, *Colloq.*, relatives; as, my own *people:*—*v.t.* [*p.t.* and *p.p.* -pled (-pld), *p.pr.* -pling], to fill with inhabitants; as, to *people* a country.
Syn., n. multitude. (See nation.)

pep-per (pĕp′ẽr), *n.* **1**, a hot spice made of the ground seeds of any of various East Indian plants; also, one of the plants producing the spice; **2**, capsicum, or red pepper; specif., a garden plant bearing podlike fruit, the rind of which is mild:—*v.t.* **1**, to season with pepper; **2**, to sprinkle thickly; **3**, to shower objects upon; as, to *pepper* with shot.

pep-per-corn (pĕp′ẽr-kôrn″), *n.* **1**, the small berry of the pepper plant; **2**, anything small or trifling.

pep-per-grass (pĕp′ẽr-gràs″), *n.* a pungent herb of the mustard family; esp., wild peppergrass and garden cress.

pep-per-mint (pĕp′ẽr-mĭnt), *n.* **1**, a pungent herb of the mint family; **2**, the oil prepared from it; **3**, a lozenge flavored with this oil.

pep-per-y (pĕp′ẽr-ĭ), *adj.* **1**, fiery; pungent or sharp; as, a *peppery* dish; **2**, irritable; as, a *peppery* temper.

pep-sin (pĕp′sĭn), *n.* **1**, a ferment formed in the gastric juice of the stomach; **2**, a preparation of this substance, used in medicine to aid digestion. Also, **pep′sine**.

pep-tic (pĕp′tĭk), *adj.* **1**, pertaining to digestion; **2**, pertaining to pepsin.

pep-tone (pĕp′tōn), *n.* any of a class of substances formed by the action of pepsin upon albuminous matter in food.

pep-to-nize (pĕp′tō-nīz), *v.t.* [*p.t.* and *p.p.* -nized (-nīzd), *p.pr.* -niz″ing], **1**, to change into peptones; **2**, to treat, as certain food products, with pepsin, so as to aid digestion.—*n.* **pep″to-ni-za′tion**.

per (pûr), *prep.* in Latin phrases, and in colloquial use, meaning: **1**, through; by means of; by; as, *per* bearer; **2**, for each; as, two dollars *per* man: **per annum**, by the year; yearly: **per diem**, by the day; daily: **per mensem**, by the month: **per se**, by or in itself.

per- (pûr-; pẽr-), *prefix*, **1**, through; over the whole extent of; as, *per*vade; **2**, very thoroughly; as, *per*fervid; *per*turb; **3**, to destruction; bad; as, *per*dition; **4**, in chemistry, denoting the higher degree of valence, or the highest degree of combination in similar compounds; as, iron *per*oxide.

per-ad-ven-ture (pẽr″ăd-vĕn′tūr; pûr″-), *conj.* supposing; if:—*adv. Archaic*, perhaps:—*n.* doubt; question; as, proved beyond *peradventure*.

per-am-bu-late (pẽr-ăm′bū-lāt), *v.t.* [*p.t.* and *p.p.* -lat″ed, *p.pr.* -lat″ing], to walk through or over, esp. to inspect or oversee:—*v.i.* to walk or stroll about.—*n.* **per-am″bu-la′tion**.

per-am-bu-la-tor (pẽr-ăm′bū-lā″tẽr), *n.* **1**, a baby carriage; **2**, an instrument for measuring distances traveled over.

per-cale (pẽr-kāl′; pẽr″kȧl′), *n.* a fine cotton fabric with a linen finish, often with a printed pattern.

per-ceive (pẽr-sēv′), *v.t.* [*p.t.* and *p.p.* -ceived′ (-sēvd′), *p.pr.* -ceiv′ing], **1**, to obtain knowledge of by the senses; see, hear, feel, taste, or smell; **2**, to understand; as, to *perceive* the point of an argument.—*n.* **per-ceiv′er**.—*adj.* **per-ceiv′a-ble**.
Syn. discern, distinguish, discriminate. To *perceive* is to become aware of a thing through the mind or senses; as, he *perceived* the meaning. To *discern* is to make out by an effort of the eye or mind; as, they *discerned* the lights of a distant shore. To *distinguish* is to note differences between objects by some outward sign; as, the Arab is *distinguished* from the Turk by his costume. To *discriminate* is to note differences, and to judge accordingly; as, to *discriminate* between true and false friends.

per cent by the hundred; in each hundred; as, five *per cent* means five hundredths. Also, **per cent.; per cen′tum.**

per-cent-age (pẽr-sĕn′tāj), *n.* **1**, a given number of parts or individuals in each hundred; a rate per cent; loosely, any portion of a whole; **2**, the duty, interest, etc., on a hundred; **3**, that part of arithmetic which deals with computing interest, etc.

per-cent-ile (pẽr-sĕn′tĭl; -tīl), *adj.* designating, or pertaining to, any of the points which divide a series of quantities arranged in order of magnitude into 100 groups, each containing the same number of the quantities; as, the 25th, 50th, and 75th *percentile* points will divide the quantities into four equal groups:—*n.* **1**, a percentile point; **2**, incorrectly, but commonly, any of the 100 groups between consecutive percentile points.

per-cept (pûr′sĕpt), *n.* a mental impression, the counterpart in consciousness of an object of sense.

per-cep-ti-ble (pẽr-sĕp′tĭ-bl), *adj.* capable of being known by the senses; evident.—*adv.* **per-cep′ti-bly.**—*n.* **per-cep″ti-bil′i-ty.**

per-cep-tion (pẽr-sĕp′shŭn), *n.* **1**, the act of becoming, or ability to become, aware of something; observation; **2**, mental apprehension; understanding; **3**, a mental impression; percept (which see); **4**, the mental action involved in perceiving.

per-cep-tive (pẽr-sĕp′tĭv), *adj.* pertaining to, or exercising, perception, or sensory knowledge.—*adv.* **per-cep′tive-ly.**—*n.* **per-cep′tive-ness.**—*n.* **per″cep-tiv′i-ty.**

[1]**perch** (pûrch), *n.* any of several small, edible, spiny-finned, fresh-water fishes.

[2]**perch** (pûrch), *n.* **1**, a measure of length equal to 5½ yards, or a surface measure equal to 30¼ square yards: also called *rod*, and sometimes *pole;* **2**, anything, as a rod or pole, on which birds sit or roost; **3**, any high seat:—*v.i.* and *v.t.* to sit or place on a high seat or roost.—*n.* **perch′er**.

per-chance (pẽr-chȧns′), *adv.* **1**, perhaps; maybe; **2**, by chance.

per-cip-i-ent (pẽr-sĭp′ĭ-ĕnt), *adj.* having the power to know through the senses.—*n.* **per-cip′i-ence.**

Per-ci-vale (pûr′sĭ-văl), *n.* in the Arthurian legends, one of the few knights of the Round Table permitted to see the Holy Grail. Also, **Per′ci-val; Per′ce-val.**

per-co-late (pûr′kō-lāt), *v.i.* and *v.t.* [*p.t.* and *p.p.* -lat″ed, *p.pr.* -lat″ing], to pass or cause to pass through very small spaces, as water through sand, ground coffee, or the like.—*n.* **per″co-la′tion.**

per-co-la-tor (pûr′kō-lā″tẽr), *n.* **1,** a cylindrical or slightly conical vessel for holding a substance through which a liquid is to be percolated; **2,** esp., a coffeepot or urn in which coffee is made by the filtering of heated water through ground coffee.

per-cus-sion (pẽr-kŭsh′ŭn), *n.* **1,** a violent collision, or meeting; **2,** the shock produced by the violent meeting of bodies; **3,** the striking of the hammer of a gun upon the cap containing powder; **4,** the impression of sound on the ear; **5,** the medical examination of a part of the body by striking it with sharp taps so as to determine its condition by the sound produced: **percussion cap,** in a rifle or revolver, a small copper cup attached to the cartridge and containing powder which, when the hammer strikes the cap, explodes and discharges the gun: **percussion instrument,** a musical instrument which produces its sound by being struck, as the drum, cymbal, or xylophone (see *musical instrument,* illus.).—*adj.* **per-cus′sive.**

per-di-tion (pẽr-dĭsh′ŭn), *n.* total destruction; ruin; utter loss of the soul or of hopes of heaven.

per-e-gri-nate (pĕr′ē-grĭ-nāt), *v.i.* and *v.t.* [*p.t.* and *p.p.* -nat″ed, *p.pr.* -nat″ing], to journey (through or over); travel.—*n.* **per′e-gri-na″tor.**

per-e-gri-na-tion (pĕr″ē-grĭ-nā′shŭn), *n.* the act of traveling about; a wandering from place to place.

per-emp-to-ry (pĕr′ĕmp-tō-rĭ; pĕr-ĕmp′-) *adj.* **1,** positive; final; allowing no discussion; as, a *peremptory* command; **2,** stubborn; dictatorial.—*adv.* **per′emp-to-ri-ly.**—*n.* **per′emp-to-ri-ness.**

per-en-ni-al (pĕr-ĕn′ĭ-ăl), *adj.* **1,** lasting throughout the year; as, a *perennial* summer; **2,** lasting more than two years; as, *perennial* plants; **3,** enduring; as, *perennial* youth:—*n.* a plant that lives over from year to year.—*adv.* **per-en′ni-al-ly.**

per-fect (pûr′fĕkt), *adj.* **1,** complete; finished; whole; **2,** without defect or blemish; lacking nothing; exact; as, a *perfect* likeness; **3,** of the highest type of excellence, esp. in moral character; blameless; **4,** fully skilled or accomplished; as, *perfect* technique; **5,** having both stamens and pistil: said of flowers; **6,** *Colloq.,* utter; entire; as, a *perfect* stranger: **present perfect tense,** that tense of verbs which signifies: **1,** action just completed; as, I *have done* the deed; **2,** action completed at or before the present, with emphasis on action rather than time; as, of the three brothers, one *has died;* **3,** action begun in the past, which continues, in fact or result, into the present; as, I *have lived* here ten years: **past perfect tense,** that tense of verbs which signifies action completed before a stated past time; as, they *had gone* before we arrived: **future perfect tense,** that tense of verbs which signifies action completed at a specified future time; as, by tonight I *shall have done* the job:—*n.* in grammar, the present perfect tense:—*v.t.* (pûr′fĕkt; pẽr-fĕkt′), **1,** to complete or finish; **2,** to bring to final excellence; **3,** to instruct, train, or inform so as to make faultless or complete by skill.—*adj.* **per-fec′tive.**—*adv.* **per′fect-ly.**—*n.* **per′fect-er.**—*n.* **per′fect-ness.**—*adj.* **per-fect′i-ble.**

per-fec-tion (pẽr-fĕk′shŭn), *n.* **1,** the state of being without fault or blemish; completeness; **2,** one who or that which is faultless; **3,** supreme excellence.

per-fer-vid (pẽr-fûr′vĭd), *adj.* very fervid; ardent; exceedingly zealous.

per-fid-i-ous (pẽr-fĭd′ĭ-ŭs), *adj.* treacherous; faithless; disloyal; as, a *perfidious* friend.—*adv.* **per-fid′i-ous-ly.**
Syn. deceitful, traitorous.

per-fi-dy (pûr′fĭ-dĭ), *n.* [*pl.* perfidies (-dĭz)], treachery; breach of faith.

per-fo-rate (pûr′fō-rāt), *v.t.* [*p.t.* and *p.p.* -rat″ed, *p.pr.* -rat″ing], to pierce through; make a hole through.—*n.* **per′fo-ra″tor.**—*p.adj.* **per′fo-rat″ed.**

per-fo-ra-tion (pûr″fō-rā′shŭn), *n.* **1,** the act of piercing through; **2,** a hole bored or punched, esp. in paper.

per-force (pẽr-fōrs′), *adv.* by force; by or of necessity.

per-form (pẽr-fôrm′), *v.t.* **1,** to do or carry out; execute; achieve; as, to *perform* an operation; **2,** to discharge or fulfil; as, to *perform* a duty; **3,** to represent, render, or portray; as, to *perform* a part in a play:—*v.i.* **1,** to act a part; as, to *perform* on the stage; **2,** to exhibit skill in public; as, to *perform* on the piano.—*n.* **per-form′er.**
Syn. accomplish, transact. (See effect.)

per-form-ance (pẽr-fôr′măns), *n.* **1,** the carrying out of something; completion; as, the *performance* of an undertaking; **2,** a thing done; deed or feat; **3,** a public exhibition, esp. on the stage.

per-fume (pẽr-fūm′), *v.t.* [*p.t.* and *p.p.* -fumed′ (-fūmd′), *p.pr.* -fum′ing], to fill with a pleasant odor; scent:—*n.* (pûr′fūm; pẽr-fūm′), **1,** a pleasing scent, as of flowers, incense, etc.; fragrance; **2,** a mixture prepared to give out a pleasing odor.

per-fum-er (pẽr-fūm′ẽr), *n.* **1,** one who perfumes; **2,** one whose trade it is to make and sell perfumes, scented soaps, powders, and the like.

per-fum-er-y (pẽr-fūm′ẽr-ĭ), *n.* [*pl.* perfumeries (-ĭz)], **1,** perfumes in general; also, the place where perfumes are made; **2,** *Colloq.,* a perfume.

per-func-to-ry (pẽr-fŭngk′tō-rĭ), *adj.* characterized by a half-hearted manner, without interest; careless.—*adv.* **per-func′to-ri-ly.**—*n.* **per-func′to-ri-ness.**

per-go-la (pûr′gō-lȧ), *n.* a latticework covering a walk or veranda and used as a trellis for climbing plants; an arbor.

per-haps (pẽr-hăps′), *adv.* possibly; perchance; maybe.

pe-ri (pē′rĭ), *n.* in Persian mythology, a fairy or elf, descended from the disobedient angels, and barred out of Paradise.

per-i- (pĕr′ĭ-), *prefix,* around; about; inclosing; surrounding.

per-i-anth (pĕr′ĭ-ănth), *n.* the calyx and corolla of a flower, taken together; floral envelope.

per-i-car-di-tis (pĕr″ĭ-kär-dī′tĭs), *n.* inflammation of the membrane that surrounds the heart.

per-i-car-di-um (pĕr″ĭ-kär′dĭ-ŭm), *n.* [*pl.* pericardia (-ȧ)], the membrane that surrounds the heart.—*adj.* **per″i-car′di-ac; per″i-car′di-al.**

per-i-carp (pĕr′ĭ-kärp), *n.* in botany, the layers forming the wall of a fruit; the ripened walls of the ovary.

per-i-cra-ni-um (pĕr″ĭ-krā′nĭ-ŭm), *n.* [*pl.* pericrania (-ȧ)], the fibrous membrane that covers the skull.

per-i-gee (pĕr′ĭ-jē), *n.* that point in the moon's orbit, or path, where it is nearest the earth: opp. of *apogee.*

per-i-he-li-on (pĕr″ĭ-hē′lĭ-ŏn), *n.* [*pl.* perihelia (-ȧ)], that point in the orbit, or path, of a planet or comet when it is nearest the sun: opp. of *aphelion.*

per-il (pĕr′ĭl), *n.* exposure to injury; danger; risk; as, he was in great *peril:*—*v.t.* to expose to danger or risk.
Syn., n. hazard, jeopardy. (See danger.)

per-il-ous (pĕr′ĭ-lŭs), *adj.* full of danger; dangerous; involving risk.—*adv.* **per′il-ous-ly.**—*n.* **per′il-ous-ness.**

per-im-e-ter (pĕr-ĭm'ē-tẽr), *n.* the outer boundary of a plane surface, as the circumference of a circle; also, the measure of this boundary.

per-i-ne-um (pĕr"ĭ-nē'ŭm), *n.* [*pl.* perinea (-*ȧ*)], the area between the anus and the genital organs.

pe-ri-od (pē'rĭ-ŏd), *n.* **1**, a definite portion of time, the beginning and end of which are fixed; **2**, any space of time; an indefinite part of a continued series of events; as, the critical *period* of American history; **3**, the concluding point of a cycle of events or of a specified length of time; **4**, a dot [.] used as a mark of punctuation, as at the end of a complete declarative sentence, or after an abbreviation; **5**, usually in *pl.*, the menses; **6**, the time of one revolution of a planet, satellite, or comet; **7**, in geology, a time division next in importance to an era; **8**, a complete sentence; specif., a sentence in which the completeness of the thought is purposely withheld until the end; **9**, in *pl.*, flowing or rhetorical sentences; **10**, a full pause at the end of a complete sentence: **period furniture**, furniture showing the characteristics of a given period or of a given maker or designer.

pe-ri-od-ic (pē"rĭ-ŏd'ĭk), *adj.* **1**, pertaining to a definite round of time; **2**, occurring or recurring at definite intervals, as day and night or the revolution of a heavenly body; **3**, designating a sentence structure which obtains its effect by withholding till the end that which completes the thought.

pe-ri-od-i-cal (pē"rĭ-ŏd'ĭ-kăl), *adj.* **1**, periodic; **2**, designating, or pertaining to, a magazine, journal, or the like, published or appearing at regular stated intervals of more than a day:—*n.* a magazine, journal, or the like, published at intervals of more than a day.—*adv.* **pe"ri-od'i-cal-ly.**

pe-ri-o-dic-i-ty (pē"rĭ-ō-dĭs'ĭ-tĭ), *n.* [*pl.* periodicities (-tĭz)], the state or quality of occurring regularly.

per-i-os-te-um (pĕr"ĭ-ŏs'tē-ŭm), *n.* [*pl.* periostea (-*ȧ*)], the membrane which covers the bones except at the joints.—*adj.* **per"i-os'te-al.**

Per-i-pa-tet-ic (pĕr"ĭ-pȧ-tĕt'ĭk), *n.* a disciple of Aristotle, who taught his disciples while he walked about the Lyceum:—*adj.* pertaining to the philosophy of Aristotle: **peripatetic**, walking about.

pe-riph-er-y (pē-rĭf'ẽr-ĭ), *n.* [*pl.* peripheries (-ĭz)], **1**, the circumference of a circle, ellipse, or similar figure; **2**, the outside surface of a rounded solid, as a sphere.—*adj.* **pe-riph'er-al.**

pe-riph-ra-sis (pē-rĭf'rȧ-sĭs), *n.* [*pl.* periphrases (-sēz)], a roundabout way of saying a thing; circumlocution; also, wordiness as a habit. Also, **per'i-phrase.**

per-i-phras-tic (pĕr"ĭ-frăs'tĭk), *adj.* **1**, roundabout; **2**, expressed in more words than are necessary. Also, **per"i-phras'ti-cal.**—*adv.* **per"i-phras'ti-cal-ly.**

per-i-scope (pĕr'ĭ-skōp), *n.* **1**, an instrument consisting of a revolving prism capable of reflecting light from any quarter down an upright tube: used as an outlook over the water for guiding submarine boats when submerged; **2**, in trench warfare, a similar instrument projecting above the parapet of a trench and used as an outlook.

per-ish (pĕr'ĭsh), *v.i.* **1**, to lose life or vitality; decay or die: **2**, to be destroyed or come to nothing.

per-ish-a-ble (pĕr'ĭsh-*ȧ*-bl), *adj.* liable to decay, injury, or death; easily spoiled; as, *perishable* food.—*adv.* **per'ish-a-bly.**—*n.* **per'ish-a-ble-ness.**

per-i-stal-sis (pĕr"ĭ-stăl'sĭs), *n.* a wavelike, involuntary, muscular contraction occurring in some tubular structures, esp. the alimentary canal, which propels the contents onward.—*adj.* **per"i-stal'tic.**

per-i-style (pĕr'ĭ-stīl), *n.* a row of columns surrounding a building or an open court and supporting a roof or cornice; also, the space so inclosed.

per-i-to-ne-um (pĕr"ĭ-tō-nē'ŭm), *n.* [*pl.* peritonea (-*ȧ*)], the thin membrane which lines the abdomen and covers the organs in it.—*adj.* **per"i-to-ne'al.**

per-i-to-ni-tis (pĕr"ĭ-tō-nī'tĭs), *n.* inflammation of the peritoneum, or membrane which lines the abdomen.

per-i-wig (pĕr'ĭ-wĭg), *n.* a headdress of false hair, formerly worn by men as an ornament and still worn by British barristers and judges as part of the official costume; a wig; peruke.

[1]**per-i-win-kle** (pĕr'ĭ-wĭng"kl), *n.* any of several creeping evergreen plants; esp., the common myrtle, a creeping herb with oval, shiny, dark green leaves, and blue, or sometimes white, flowers.

[2]**per-i-win-kle** (pĕr'ĭ-wĭng"kl), *n.* any of various snails, esp. an edible European species introduced along the Atlantic shores of North America.

per-jure (pûr'jŭr), *v.t.* [*p.t.* and *p.p.* -jured (-jŭrd), *p.pr.* -jur-ing], to cause to swear falsely, or to break a vow; as, to *perjure* oneself.—*n.* **per'jur-er.**

per-ju-ry (pûr'jŭ-rĭ), *n.* [*pl.* perjuries (-rĭz)], **1**, the wilful breaking of an oath or solemn promise; **2**, the wilful giving, under oath, of false testimony.

perk (pûrk), *v.t.* to make trim or neat:—*v.i.* **1**, to hold up the head saucily; **2**, to become brisk or jaunty: followed by *up.*

perk-y (pûr'kĭ), *adj.* [*comp.* perk'i-er, *superl.* perk'i-est], pert; lively; jaunty; airy.—*adv.* **perk'i-ly.**—*n.* **perk'i-ness.**

per-ma-nence (pûr'mȧ-nĕns), *n.* the state or quality of being fixed or lasting; unlikelihood of change.

per-ma-nen-cy (pûr'mȧ-nĕn-sĭ), *n.* [*pl.* permanencies (-sĭz)], **1**, the state or quality of being fixed or lasting; **2**, a thing that is lasting.

per-ma-nent (pûr'mȧ-nĕnt), *adj.* lasting; durable; continuing in the same state.—*adv.* **per'ma-nent-ly.**

Syn. durable, enduring. *Permanent* is applied to that which is not temporary, not subject to change, and is supposed to continue until the end; as, *permanent* institutions. *Durable* is used entirely in a material sense to suggest the wearing or lasting qualities of things; as, *durable* ginghams. *Enduring* refers to the quality of wearing well or lasting long, and also that of suffering patiently; as, oak is an *enduring* wood; *enduring* patience.

per-man-ga-nate (pẽr-măng'gȧ-nāt), *n.* a dark purple crystalline salt with marked oxidizing properties: used as an antiseptic and in tanning.

per-me-a-ble (pûr'mē-*ȧ*-bl), *adj.* capable of allowing fluids to pass through or into; as, sand is *permeable* to water.—*n.* **per"me-a-bil'i-ty.**

per-me-ate (pûr'mē-āt), *v.t.* [*p.t.* and *p.p.* -at"ed, *p.pr.* -at"ing], **1**, to pass through the pores or crevices of; as, water *permeates* sand; **2**, to spread through or mingle with; pervade; as, the perfume of flowers *permeates* the air.—*n.* **per"me-a'tion.**

per-mis-si-ble (pẽr-mĭs'ĭ-bl), *adj.* tolerable; allowable.

per-mis-sion (pẽr-mĭsh'ŭn), *n.* **1**, the act of allowing; **2**, consent; leave; as, he was given *permission* to speak.

Syn. license, sufferance, authority, allowance.—*Ant.* refusal, denial, prohibition.

per-mis-sive (pẽr-mĭs′ĭv), *adj.* giving consent; not forbidding.

per-mit (pẽr-mĭt′), *v.t.* [*p.t.* and *p.p.* -mit′ted, *p.pr.* -mit′ting], **1,** to allow by not trying to prevent; tolerate; as, to *permit* smoking; **2,** to authorize:—*v.i.* to give consent; allow; as, if the weather *permits*, I shall go:—*n.* (pûr′mĭt), a written warrant, or leave, to do something.
Syn., *v.* suffer, endure. (See allow.)

per-mu-ta-tion (pûr″mū-tā′shŭn), *n.* **1,** the exchange of one thing for another; **2,** any of the ways in which a number of objects, letters, etc., may be arranged; as, the letters *a*, *b*, *c*, taken two at a time, have six *permutations: ab, ac, ba, bc, ca, cb.*

per-ni-cious (pẽr-nĭsh′ŭs), *adj.* highly injurious or hurtful; destructive; as, foul air is *pernicious* to health.—*adv.* **per-ni′cious-ly.**—*n.* **per-ni′cious-ness.**
Syn. harmful, baneful, deadly, ruinous.—*Ant.* beneficial, wholesome.

per-nick-et-y (pẽr-nĭk′ĕt-ĭ), *adj. Colloq.*, attentive to trifles; fussily particular; fastidious.

per-o-rate (pĕr′ō-rāt), *v.i.* [*p.t.* and *p.p.* -rat″ed, *p.pr.* -rat″ing], **1,** to discourse at length; make a long speech; **2,** to sum up a speech in conclusion.—*n.* **per″o-ra′tion.**

per-ox-ide (pẽr-ŏk′sīd; pẽr-ŏk′sĭd), *n.* the oxide, or compound of oxygen with another element, which contains a larger proportion of oxygen than another oxide of the same element; esp., peroxide of hydrogen, used in a solution of water as an antiseptic and in bleaching. Also, **per-ox′id.**

per-pen-dic-u-lar (pûr″pĕn-dĭk′ū-lẽr), *adj.* **1,** at right angles to a given line or surface; **2,** perfectly upright:—*n.* **1,** an upright line; **2,** a line or plane at right angles to another.—*adv.* **per″pen-dic′u-lar-ly.**—*n.* **per″pen-dic″u-lar′i-ty.**

per-pe-trate (pûr′pē-trāt), *v.t.* [*p.t.* and *p.p.* -trat″ed, *p.pr.* -trat″ing], to do; perform: usually in a bad sense; as, to *perpetrate* a crime.—*n.* **per″pe-tra′tion.**—*n.* **per′pe-tra″tor.**

per-pet-u-al (pẽr-pĕt′ū-ăl), *adj.* never-ceasing; continuous; endless; everlasting.—*adv.* **per-pet′u-al-ly.**
Syn. incessant, eternal, enduring.

per-pet-u-ate (pẽr-pĕt′ū-āt), *v.t.* [*p.t.* and *p.p.* -at″ed, *p.pr.* -at″ing], to make everlasting; as, to *perpetuate* the memory of a hero.—*n.* **per-pet″u-a′tion.**

per-pe-tu-i-ty (pûr″pē-tū′ĭ-tĭ), *n.* [*pl.* perpetuities (-tĭz)], **1,** the state of being everlasting; **2,** endless time; **3,** something that lasts forever.

per-plex (pẽr-plĕks′), *v.t.* **1,** to make (something) hard to understand; confuse; **2,** to make (a person) anxious; puzzle; distract; embarrass.—*p.adj.* **per-plexed′.**
Syn. puzzle, confuse, bewilder, mystify. To *perplex* is to cause a state of mental uncertainty and indecision resulting in doubt as to what to do, think, or say; as, contradictory directions *perplex*. To *puzzle* is to bring the mind to a halt by something complicated or incomprehensible; difficulties and mysteries *puzzle*. To *confuse* a person is to throw his mental processes into disorder so that he cannot think clearly or remember correctly; as, the witness was *confused*. To *bewilder* is to daze but not to *confuse* the mind; as, winding paths *bewilder* a stranger. To *mystify* is to *bewilder* purposely; as, magicians *mystify* audiences.

per-plex-i-ty (pẽr-plĕk′sĭ-tĭ), *n.* [*pl.* perplexities (-tĭz)], **1,** the state of being anxious, confused, doubtful, or puzzled; embarrassment; **2,** that which puzzles or confuses.
Syn. confusion, bewilderment, doubt.

per-qui-site (pûr′kwĭ-zĭt), *n.* a gain or profit in addition to regular wages or salary; a customary gratuity.

per-ry (pĕr′ĭ), *n.* pear cider: made from the fermented juice of pears.

per-se-cute (pûr′sē-kūt), *v.t.* [*p.t.* and *p.p.* -cut″ed, *p.pr.* -cut″ing], to pursue in order to injure or afflict; harass or treat cruelly, esp. because of religious opinions; annoy; vex.—*n.* **per′se-cu″tor.**

per-se-cu-tion (pûr″sē-kū′shŭn), *n.* **1,** the continued infliction of unjust pain or punishment; specif., a period of oppression because of religious beliefs; **2,** the state of being unjustly or annoyingly treated; also, repeated injury of any kind.

Per-seph-o-ne (pẽr-sĕf′ō-nē), *n.* in Greek mythology, the daughter of Demeter by Zeus, wife of Pluto, and queen of the lower world: called by the Romans *Proserpina* or *Proserpine.*

Per-seus (pûr′sūs; pûr′sē-ŭs), *n.* **1,** in mythology, the Greek hero who slew the Gorgon Medusa, and saved Andromeda; **2,** a northern constellation.

per-se-ver-ance (pûr″sē-vēr′ăns), *n.* constant effort, esp. under handicap; steadfastness; pertinacity.
Syn. application, persistence.

per-se-vere (pûr′sē-vēr′), *v.i.* [*p.t.* and *p.p.* -vered′ (-vērd′), *p.pr.* -ver′ing], to persist in any enterprise or business undertaken; continue steadfastly.—*p.adj.* **per″se-ver′ing.**—*adv.* **per″se-ver′ing-ly.**

Per-sian (pûr′shăn; pûr′zhăn), *adj.* of or pertaining to Persia, its people, or its language:—*n.* **1,** a native of Persia; **2,** the language of Persia; **3,** a fine silk material, often figured.

per-si-flage (pĕr″sē-fläzh′; pûr′sĭ-fläzh), *n.* a flippant or thoughtless style of talking or writing; banter.

per-sim-mon (pẽr-sĭm′ŭn), *n.* **1,** a tree with a pulpy fruit palatable only after frost; **2,** the fruit of the tree.

per-sist (pẽr-sĭst′), *v.i.* **1,** to continue steadily in any course commenced; persevere; **2,** to continue fixed; endure; as, kinky hair *persists* in certain races.
Syn. stay, remain. (See insist.)

per-sist-ence (pẽr-sĭs′tĕns), *n.* **1,** perseverance; continuous effort; as, the inventor's *persistence* was crowned with success; **2,** obstinacy; **3,** lasting quality; endurance. Also, **per-sist′en-cy.**

per-sist-ent (pẽr-sĭs′tĕnt), *adj.* **1,** continuing; constant; persevering; as, a *persistent* worker; **2,** not falling off; as, a *persistent* rain.—*adv.* **per-sist′ent-ly.**

per-son (pûr′sŭn; pûr′sn), *n.* **1,** a human being as distinguished from a thing or an animal; an individual; **2,** one's actual self; personality; **3,** the body of a human being; bodily appearance; **4,** in grammar, a certain relation existing between a verb and its subject, called *first, second,* or *third person* according as the subject is the speaker, the person spoken to, or the person or thing spoken of: seen in English esp. in the personal pronouns, as *I*, *you*, *he*, and the corresponding verbal inflections; **5,** an inflectional form, as of a pronoun or verb, exhibiting this grammatical relation; **6,** the quality of a word said to exhibit this relation; as, verbs and pronouns have *person.*

per-son-a-ble (pûr′sŭn-ȧ-bl), *adj.* attractive in form and figure; handsome; graceful.

per-son-age (pûr′sŭn-āj), *n.* **1,** a person; esp., a man or woman of distinction; **2,** a part or character in a play.

per-son-al (pûr′sŭn-ăl), *adj.* **1,** relating to, or peculiar to, an individual and his private affairs; as, *personal* business; 2, pertaining to the outward appearance or looks; as, *personal* beauty; 3, done by oneself; as, a *personal* greeting; 4, relating to one's character or conduct, often unkindly; as, *personal* remarks; 5, movable; as, *personal* property; 6, in grammar, designating any of the pronouns *I, you, he, she, it.* or their plurals or other forms.—*adv.* **per'son-al-ly.**

per-son-al-i-ty (pûr"sŭn-ăl'ĭ-tĭ), *n.* [*pl.* personalities (-tĭz)], 1, the sum of one's qualities of body, mind, and character; 2, that which makes one human being different from another; individuality; 3, an individual with some noteworthy quality or qualities; 4, an offensive remark made about a person, his character, or condition.

per-son-al-ty (pûr'sŭn-ăl-tĭ), *n.* [*pl.* personalties (-tĭz)], property other than land or buildings; all kinds of movable property, as stocks, bonds, clothing, furniture, etc.; opp. of *realty.*

per-son-ate (pûr'sŭn-āt), *v.t.* [*p.t.* and *p.p.* -at"ed, *p.pr.* -at"ing], to act the part of; pretend to be, esp. with dishonest intent; represent falsely.—*n.* **per"son-a'tion.**—*n.* **per'son-a"tor.**

per-son-i-fi-ca-tion (pĕr-sŏn"ĭ-fĭ-kā'shŭn), *n.* 1, a striking example of some special quality; as, she is the *personification* of neatness; 2, the act of regarding as a person; 3, a figure of speech that gives to things or abstract ideas the qualities of human beings.

per-son-i-fy (pĕr-sŏn'ĭ-fī), *v.t.* [*p.t.* and *p.p.* -fied (-fīd), *p.pr.* -fy"ing], 1, to treat or regard as a person; attribute life to (things without life); 2, to be a striking example of; as, caution *personified.*

per-son-nel (pûr"sŏ-nĕl'; *Fr.* pâr"sŏ"nĕl'), *n.* the persons employed in any business or public service:—*adj.* pertaining to a personnel: **personnel work,** welfare work among employees.

per-spec-tive (pĕr-spĕk'tĭv), *adj.* pertaining to, or in accordance with, the art of showing, on a surface, objects as they actually appear to the eye:—*n.* 1, the art of representing objects, on a plane surface, in three dimensions, as they appear to the eye; hence, the effect of distance on the appearance of objects; 2, figuratively, a far-reaching mental view, in which things appear in proper relation to one another; 3, right proportion.—*adv.* **per-spec'tive-ly.**

per-spi-ca-cious (pûr"spĭ-kā'shŭs), *adj.* mentally acute or keen; mentally quick-sighted.—*adv.* **per"spi-ca'cious-ly.**

Syn. astute, shrewd, sagacious.

per-spi-cac-i-ty (pûr"spĭ-kăs'ĭ-tĭ), *n.* keenness or quickness of sight and brain; mental clear-sightedness.

per-spi-cu-i-ty (pûr"spĭ-kū'ĭ-tĭ), *n.* clearness of thought or expression; lucidity; explicitness.

per-spic-u-ous (pĕr-spĭk'ū-ŭs), *adj.* clear to the understanding; plainly expressed; easily understood.—*adv.* **per-spic'u-ous-ly.**

per-spi-ra-tion (pûr"spĭ-rā'shŭn), *n.* 1, sweat, or the fluid secreted by the sweat glands of the skin; 2, the act or process of secreting and giving off fluid through the pores of the skin.

per-spire (pĕr-spīr'), *v.t.* and *v.i.* [*p.t.* and *p.p.* -spired' (-spīrd'), *p.pr.* -spir'ing], to sweat; pass off (fluid) through the pores of the skin.—*adj.* **per-spir'a-to-ry.**

per-suade (pĕr-swād'), *v.t.* [*p.t.* and *p.p.* -suad'ed, *p.pr.* -suad'ing], to influence by argument, advice, entreaty, etc.; induce; prevail upon; convince; as, to *persuade* a person to believe something.—*adj.* **per-suad'a-ble.**—*n.* **per-suad'er.**

Syn. allure, entice. (See convince.)

per-sua-si-ble (pĕr-swā'sĭ-bl), *adj.* capable of being influenced by advice or entreaty; open to conviction.—*n.* **per-sua"si-bil'i-ty.**

per-sua-sion (pĕr-swā'zhŭn), *n.* 1, the act or art of influencing, or the state of being influenced, by argument or entreaty; 2, a conviction; a belief, generally religious or political.

per-sua-sive (pĕr-swā'sĭv), *adj.* having power to convince or influence; as, a *persuasive* argument; influencing the will or passion:—*n.* an inducement.—*adv.* **per-sua'sive-ly.**—*n.* **per-sua'sive-ness.**

pert (pûrt), *adj.* saucy; bold. Also, *Colloq.,* **peart.**—*adv.* **pert'ly.**—*n.* **pert'ness.**

per-tain (pĕr-tān'), *v.i.* 1, to belong, as a quality, duty, etc.; as, joy *pertains* to youth; 2, to relate or refer to something; as, the telegram *pertains* to business.

per-ti-na-cious (pûr"tĭ-nā'shŭs), *adj.* unyielding; obstinate; resolute; holding stubbornly to any opinion or design; as, a *pertinacious* solicitor.—*adv.* **per"ti-na'cious-ly.**—*n.* **per"ti-na'cious-ness.**

Syn. stubborn, inflexible, persistent, determined.—*Ant.* yielding, pliable, tractable.

per-ti-nac-i-ty (pûr"tĭ-năs'ĭ-tĭ), *n.* the quality or state of holding stubbornly to a purpose; unyielding perseverance; obstinacy.

per-ti-nence (pûr'tĭ-nĕns), *n.* suitableness. Also, **per'ti-nen-cy**

per-ti-nent (pûr'tĭ-nĕnt), *adj.* fitting or appropriate; to the point belonging to; as, these remarks are *pertinent* to the subject.—*adv.* **per'ti-nent-ly.**

Syn. timely, suitable, applicable, relevant.

per-turb (pĕr-tûrb'), *v.t.* to agitate; disturb greatly; disquiet.

per-tur-ba-tion (pûr"tŭr-bā'shŭn), *n.* 1, mental disorder; disquiet of mind; 2, irregular or violent variation.

pe-ruke (pĕ-rōōk'), *n.* a wig, sometimes made to look like a natural head of hair; a periwig.

pe-rus-al (pĕ-rōōz'ăl), *n.* the act of reading carefully and with attention, as, the *perusal* of a book.

pe-ruse (pĕ-rōōz'), *v.t.* [*p.t.* and *p.p.* -rused' (-rōōzd'), *p.pr.* -rus'ing], to read with care and attention; as, to *peruse* a letter.

Pe-ru-vi-an (pĕ-rōō'vĭ-ăn), *adj.* of or pertaining to Peru:—*n.* 1, a native of Peru; 2, the language of Peru: **Peruvian bark,** cinchona, the bark of any of several South American trees, from which the drug quinine is obtained.

per-vade (pĕr-vād'), *v.t.* [*p.t.* and *p.p.* -vad'ed, *p.pr.* -vad'ing], to pass or spread through every part of; as, a perfume *pervades* the air; content *pervades* the country.

per-va-sion (pĕr-vā'zhŭn), *n.* 1, the act of going through or spreading all over; 2, the state of being permeated.

per-va-sive (pĕr-vā'sĭv), *adj.* tending to pass through or fill every part of; as, a *pervasive* odor.—*adv.* **per-va'sive-ly.**—*n.* **per-va'sive-ness.**

per-verse (pĕr-vûrs'), *adj.* 1, wilfully wrong; set against doing right, 2, obstinate; 3, wayward, as a child.—*adv.* **perverse'ly.**—*n.* **per-verse'ness.**—*adj.* **per-ver'sive.**

Syn. contrary, fractious, headstrong, wilful.

per-ver-sion (pĕr-vûr'shŭn), *n.* 1, a turning from the true meaning or proper purpose; the misuse of a good thing; 2, a false form of something.

per-ver-si-ty (pĕr-vûr'sĭ-tĭ), *n.* [*pl.* perversities (-tĭz)], 1, wilful refusal to do right; **2,** disposition to be contrary; stubbornness.

per-vert (pẽr-vûrt′), *v.t.* **1,** to turn from the true end or proper purpose; misuse; mislead; **2,** to give a wrong meaning to purposely:—*n.* (pûr′vẽrt), one who has turned from right to wrong.—*p.adj.* **per-vert′ed.**—*adj.* **per-vert′i-ble.**

per-vi-ous (pûr′vĭ-ŭs), *adj.* **1,** admitting passage of another substance, as a fluid; as, a *pervious* soil; **2,** capable of listening to reason, or of accepting new ideas. —*n.* **per′vi-ous-ness.**

pe-se-ta (pĕ-sā′tä), [Span.], *n.* a silver coin and the monetary unit of Spain, equivalent to 19.3 cents.

pes-ky (pĕs′kĭ), *adj.* [*comp.* pes′ki-er, *superl.* pes′ki-est], troublesome; annoying.

pe-so (pā′sō), *n.* [*pl.* pesos (-sōz; -sōs)], **1,** the old Spanish dollar, or piece of eight; **2,** the monetary unit in Mexico (the Mexican dollar) and in the Philippines, worth 50 cents; **3,** the monetary unit in Argentine, Colombia, Cuba, Uruguay, and Paraguay (about $1.00), and in Chile (about 12 cents).

pes-si-mism (pĕs′ĭ-mĭzm), *n.* **1,** the philosophical belief that the world is bad rather than good; **2,** a habit of looking on the dark side of life or of expecting failure: opp. of *optimism.*

pes-si-mist (pĕs′ĭ-mĭst), *n.* one who looks on the worst side of things.

pes-si-mis-tic (pĕs″ĭ-mĭs′tĭk), *adj.* pertaining to, or marked by, the belief that the world is bad rather than good; gloomy.—*adv.* **pes″si-mis′ti-cal-ly.**

pest (pĕst), *n.* **1,** a widespread, fatal, contagious disease, as smallpox; a plague; **2,** anything very mischievous or injurious.

pes-ter (pĕs′tẽr), *v.t.* to annoy; bother; tease; irritate with little vexations.—*n.* **pes′ter-er.**

pest-house (pĕst′hous″), *n.* a house or hospital for infectious or contagious diseases; an isolation ward.

pes-tif-er-ous (pĕs-tĭf′ẽr-ŭs), *adj.* **1,** carrying disease; **2,** mischievous; injurious.—*adv.* **pes-tif′er-ous-ly.**

pes-ti-lence (pĕs′tĭ-lĕns, *n.* a widespread, infectious, fatal disease; esp., the bubonic plague.

pes-ti-lent (pĕs′tĭ-lĕnt), *adj.* **1,** poisonous; deadly; **2,** bad for health, morals, or society; **3,** making mischief; vexatious.—*adv.* **pes′ti-lent-ly.**

pes-ti-len-tial (pĕs″tĭ-lĕn′shăl), *adj.* **1,** pertaining to, or causing, a contagious disease, like smallpox; **2,** wicked; destructive to morals.

pes-tle (pĕs′l), *n.* a tool for pounding substances in a mortar, or druggist's mixing bowl (see *mortar*, illus.):—*v.t.* and *v.i.* [*p.t.* and *p.p.* -tled (-ld), *p.pr.* -tling], to pound with a pestle in a mortar.

¹pet (pĕt), *n.* **1,** a tame animal, kept, treated kindly, and played with; **2,** a person treated with special affection; a favorite:—*adj.* **1,** favorite; **2,** accustomed to fondling and indulgence:—*v.t.* [*p.t.* and *p.p.* pet′ted, *p.pr.* pet′ting], to fondle or indulge.

²pet (pĕt), *n.* a sudden fit of peevishness or ill humor.

pet-al (pĕt′ăl), *n.* one of the leaves, usually bright-colored, of a flower's corolla. —*adj.* **pet′aled; pet′alled.**

pet-al-oid (pĕt′ăl-oid), *adj.* resembling a petal in form or texture.

pe-tard (pē-tärd′), *n.* formerly, a bell-shaped case containing explosives, used to break walls, burst open gates, etc.

Pe-ter (pē′tẽr), *n.* **1,** in the Bible, one of the twelve apostles: also called *Simon* and *Simon Peter;* **2,** either of two books of the New Testament, traditionally containing his epistles, or letters.

pe-ter (pē′tẽr), *v.i.* to thin out or fail, as a vein of coal; diminish or lessen: usually with *out.*

pet-i-ole (pĕt′ĭ-ōl), *n.* **1,** the slender stem that bears the broad part of a leaf; a leafstalk; **2,** in zoölogy, a stalk, or slender part that joins two larger parts of an insect body, as in ants, wasps, etc.—*adj.* **pet′i-o-lar.**—*adj.* **pet′i-o-late.**

pet-it (pĕt′ĭ; *Fr.* pē-tē′), *adj.* small, insignificant, mean, or inferior: used now only in law; as, *petit* larceny: **petit jury,** (also, *petty jury*), a trial jury as distinguished from a grand jury.

***pe-tite** (pē-tēt′), [Fr.], *adj.* having a small, trim figure: said of a woman.

pe-ti-tion (pē-tĭsh′ŭn), *n.* **1,** an earnest request or prayer; **2,** a formal request from an inferior to a superior; **3,** a document containing a request supported by many signatures:—*v.t.* **1,** to present a formal request to; **2,** to solicit or ask for earnestly; entreat; pray.—*adj.* **pe-ti′tion-a-ry.**—*n.* **pe-ti′tion-er.**

pet-rel (pĕt′rĕl), *n.* a strong-winged sea bird which flies far from the land.

pet-ri-fac-tion (pĕt″rĭ-făk′shŭn), *n.* **1,** the process of changing animal or vegetable substance into stone; **2,** an animal or vegetable body changed into stone; a fossil; **3,** the state of being benumbed, as with fear.—*n.* **pet″ri-fi-ca′tion.**—*adj.* **pet″ri-fac′tive.**

pet-ri-fy (pĕt′rĭ-fī), *v.t.* [*p.t.* and *p.p.* -fied (-fīd), *p.pr.* -fy″ing], **1,** to change into stone; **2,** to fix in silent amazement or fear, as at the approach of danger:—*v.i.* to become stone or of a stony hardness.

pe-trog-ra-phy (pē-trŏg′rȧ-fĭ), *n.* the scientific study or description of rocks as to their structure, formation, and classification.—*n.* **pe-trog′ra-pher.**—*adj.* **pet″ro-graph′ic** (pĕt″rō-grăf′ĭk); **pet″ro-graph′i-cal.**

pet-rol (pĕt′rōl; pĕt′rŏl; pē-trōl′), *n.* in Europe, gasoline: short for *petroleum.*

pe-tro-le-um (pē-trō′lē-ŭm), *n.* an inflammable, dark yellowish brown liquid issuing from certain rocks, pumped from the earth, or distilled from oil shale; rock, mineral, or crude oil: extensively used for fuel and the source of benzine, kerosene, paraffin oil, gasoline, etc.

pe-trol-o-gy (pē-trŏl′ō-jĭ), *n.* the scientific study of rocks; petrography. —*adj.* **pet″ro-log′ic** (pĕt″rō-lŏj′ĭk); **pet″ro-log′i-cal.**—*n.* **pe-trol′o-gist.**

pet-ti-coat (pĕt′ĭ-kōt), *n.* **1,** a loose underskirt worn by women and girls; **2,** *Slang,* a woman.

pet-ti-fog (pĕt′ĭ-fŏg), *v.i.* [*p.t.* and *p.p.* -fogged (-fŏgd), *p.pr.* -fog″ging], to practice law in small or mean cases, esp. by sharp practice or unethical methods.—*n.* **pet′ti-fog″ger.**

pet-tish (pĕt′ĭsh), *adj.* fretful; cross.—*adv.* **pet′tish-ly.**—*n.* **pet′tish-ness.**

pet-ty (pĕt′ĭ), *adj.* [*comp.* pet′ti-er, *superl.* pet′ti-est], **1,** having little worth; trifling; unimportant; as, a *petty* quarrel; **2,** not serious; as, a *petty* offense; **3,** occupied with trivial things; as, *petty* criticisms: **petty cash,** small sums of money received or paid out: **petty jury,** a trial jury; a petit jury (see *petit*): **petty officer,** a naval officer of similar rank to a sergeant or corporal in the army.—*adv.* **pet′ti-ly.**—*n.* **pet′ti-ness.**

Syn. trivial, insignificant, small.—*Ant.* important, weighty, big.

pet-u-lance (pĕt′ū-lăns), *n.* impatience; fretfulness; snappishness. Also, **pet′u-lan-cy.**

pet-u-lant (pĕt′ū-lănt), *adj.* fretful; cross; impatient.—*adv.* **pet′u-lant-ly.**

pe-tu-ni-a (pē-tū′nĭ-ȧ), *n.* a plant of the nightshade family, with beautiful funnel-shaped flowers.

PETUNIA ($\frac{1}{5}$)

pew (pū), *n.* one of the long, fixed benches in a church, sometimes inclosed.

pe-wee (pē′wē), *n.* **1,** a small, olive-green bird, so named from its note: also called *wood pewee;* **2,** the phœbe.

pe-wit (pē′wĭt; pū′ĭt), *n.* **1,** the lapwing; **2,** the black-headed, or laughing, gull; **3,** a phœbe, or pewee: so called from its cry.

pew-ter (pū′tẽr), *n.* **1,** a lustrous metal made of tin and lead, or of tin and some other metal, as copper, bismuth, antimony, etc.; **2,** dishes or utensils made of this metal:—*adj.* made of pewter.

pfen-nig (pfĕn′ĭg), *n.* [*pl.* pfennigs (-ĭgz); *Ger.* pfennige (-ĭ-gē)], a small copper coin of Germany, worth about ¼ cent.

Pha-ë-thon (fā′ē-thŏn), *n.* in mythology, the son of Helios, the sun god, who, attempting one day to drive the sun chariot, was struck down by a thunderbolt lest he burn up the earth. Also, **Pha′ë-ton.**

pha-ë-ton (fā′ē-tŏn), *n.* a light, open, four-wheeled carriage.

phag-o-cite (făg′ō-sīt), *n.* a white blood corpuscle.

pha-lan-ger (fȧ-lăn′jẽr), *n.* any of several small Australian marsupials, or pouched animals.

pha-lan-ges (fȧ-lăn′jēz), *n.pl.* [*sing.* phalanx], the small bones of the fingers and toes.

pha-lanx (fā′lăngks; făl′ăngks), *n.* [*pl.* phalanxes (-lăngk-sĕz); phalanges (fȧ-lăn′jēz)], **1,** among the ancient Greeks, a company of heavy-armed soldiers drawn up in close rank; **2,** hence, any compact body of persons, animals, or things; **3,** [*pl.* phalanges], a bone of a finger or a toe.

phan-tasm (făn′tăzm), *n.* **1,** a vision; ghost; **2,** a supposed appearance of an absent person.—*adj.* **phan-tas′mal.**

phan-tas-ma-go-ri-a (făn-tăz″mȧ-gō′rĭ-ȧ), *n.* **1,** a fastastic magic-lantern show; **2,** a changing group of figures, seen as if in a dream.

phan-ta-sy (făn′tȧ-sĭ), *n.* [*pl.* phantasies (-sĭz)], **1,** the power to create visionary mental images; **2,** the mental image so created; a fancy. See **fan′ta-sy,** *Pfd. S.*

phan-tom (făn′tŭm), *n.* **1,** an apparition; spirit; **2,** something having appearance without substance; a hallucination:—*adj.* ghostlike; illusive.

Pha-raoh (fā′rō; fā′rā-ō), *n.* **1,** in ancient Egypt, a king: a descriptive term or title; **2,** in the Bible, the name of many of the kings of Egypt.

Phar-i-sa-ic (făr″ĭ-sā′ĭk), *adj.* pertaining to, or like, the Pharisees, a sect of the ancient Jews: **pharisaic,** pretending to be religious without really being so; self-righteous; hypocritical. Also, **Phar″i-sa′i-cal; phar″i-sa′i-cal.**

Phar-i-sa-ism (făr′ĭ-sā-ĭzm), *n.* the doctrines and practices of the Pharisees: **pharisaism,** pretense of religion; self-righteousness; hypocrisy.

Phar-i-see (făr′ĭ-sē), *n.* one of a religious sect among the ancient Jews which paid strict regard to outward observance of the law: **pharisee,** one who observes the form rather than the spirit of religion.

phar-ma-ceu-tics (fär″mȧ-sū′tĭks), *n.pl.* used as *sing.* the science of preparing drugs, as for medicine.—*adj.* **phar″ma-ceu′tic; phar″ma-ceu′ti-cal.**—*n.* **phar″ma-ceu′tist.**

phar-ma-cist (fär′mȧ-sĭst), *n.* one skilled in drugs or in the preparation of medicines; a druggist.

phar-ma-co-pœ-ia (fär″mȧ-kō-pē′yȧ), *n.* **1,** an official book describing drugs and medicines; **2,** a stock or collection of drugs.

phar-ma-cy (fär′mȧ-sĭ), *n.* [*pl.* pharmacies (-sĭz)], **1,** the art of preparing medicines; **2,** a drug store.

pha-ros (fā′rŏs), *n.* a lighthouse; beacon; watchtower.

phar-yn-gi-tis (făr″ĭn-jī′tĭs), *n.* inflammation of the pharynx, or cavity between the upper end of the windpipe and the mouth: a form of what is popularly called *sore throat.*

phar-ynx (făr′ĭngks), *n.* [*pl.* pharynges (fȧ-rĭn′jēz)], a cavity or passage behind the nose, mouth, and larynx, or upper part of the windpipe.—*adj.* **pha-ryn′ge-al** (fȧ-rĭn′jē-ăl; făr″ĭn-jē′ăl).

phase (fāz), *n.* **1,** any particular aspect or appearance; as, a *phase* of the moon; **2,** any of the changing appearances that an object may assume; **3,** one side of a subject.

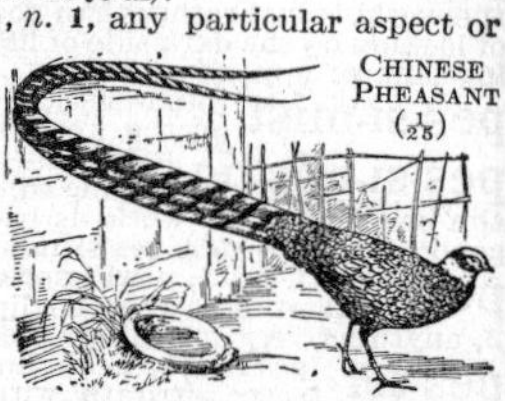

CHINESE PHEASANT ($\frac{1}{25}$)

pheas-ant (fĕz′ănt), *n.* a large game bird with brilliant feathers.

phe-nac-e-tin (fē-năs′-ē-tĭn), *n.* a white crystalline compound used in medicine as a remedy for fever.

Phe-ni-cian (fē-nĭsh′ăn), *adj.* pertaining to ancient Phœnicia, or its people or language:—*n.* **1,** one of the people of Phœnicia or its colonies; **2,** the language of Phœnicia. Also, **Phœ-ni′cian,** *Pfd. S.*

Phe-nix (fē′nĭks), *n.* an imaginary bird which, after living 500 years, is burned and rises again from its own ashes: an emblem of immortality. See **Phœ′nix,** *Pfd. S.*

phe-nol (fē′nōl; fē′nŏl), *n.* carbolic acid, a substance obtained from coal tar.

phe-nom-e-nal (fē-nŏm′ē-năl), *adj.* **1,** pertaining to, or of the nature of, a phenomenon; extraordinary; **2,** in philosophy, pertaining to the appearance of things, rather than to the things themselves.

phe-nom-e-non (fē-nŏm′ē-nŏn), *n.* [*pl.* phenomena (-nȧ)], **1,** any natural fact or event that can be seen; **2,** something uncommon, as snow in summer; **3,** in philosophy, the appearance of a thing as distinguished from the thing in itself.

phi (fī; fē), *n.* the **21st** letter of the Greek alphabet [ϕ, Φ], equivalent to *phi* or *f.*

phi-al (fī′ăl), *n.* a small glass bottle or vessel; a vial.

phi-lan-der (fĭ-lăn′dẽr), *v.i.* to make light love; flirt.—*n.* **phi-lan′der-er.**

phil-an-throp-ic (fĭl″ăn-thrŏp′ĭk), *adj.* loving mankind; benevolent; kind; humane. Also, **phil″an-throp′i-cal.**—*adv.* **phil″an-throp′i-cal-ly.**

phi-lan-thro-pist (fĭ-lăn′thrō-pĭst), *n.* one who loves and seeks to benefit mankind, esp. one who uses his wealth for this purpose.

phi-lan-thro-py (fĭ-lăn′thrō-pĭ), *n.* [*pl.* philanthropies (-pĭz)],

1, love of mankind; desire to do good to men; benevolence; 2, a benevolent act or agency. *Syn.* charity, beneficence.

phi-lat-e-ly (fĭ-lăt′ē-lĭ), *n.* the collecting and study of postage stamps. —*adj.* **phil″a-tel′ic.**—*n.* **phi-lat′e-list.**

Phi-le-mon (fĭ-lē′mŏn), *n.* a book of the New Testament, containing the epistle, or letter, of Paul, the apostle, to Philemon, a convert to the Christian faith.

phil-har-mon-ic (fĭl″här-mŏn′ĭk), *adj.* loving harmony; fond of music; as, the *Philharmonic Society.*

Phil-ip (fĭl′ĭp), *n.* in the Bible, 1, one of the twelve apostles (John 1: 43, 44); 2, a deacon and preacher of the early church (Acts 6:5; 8:5, 26).

Phi-lip-pi-an (fĭ-lĭp′ĭ-ăn), *adj.* of or pertaining to the city of Philippi, in ancient Macedonia:—*n.* 1, a citizen or inhabitant of that city; 2, in *pl.*, a book of the New Testament, containing the letter of Paul to the church at Philippi.—*abbr.* **Phil.**

phi-lip-pic (fĭ-lĭp′ĭk), *n.* an abusive or angry speech: so called from the three speeches of Demosthenes against Philip of Macedon.

Phil-ip-pine (fĭl′ĭ-pĭn; fĭl′ĭ-pēn), *adj.* of or pertaining to the Philippine Islands, in the Pacific Ocean, or to the inhabitants of these islands.

Phi-lis-tine (fĭ-lĭs′tĭn; fĭl′ĭs-tĭn), *n.* 1, an ancient inhabitant of the southwestern coast of Palestine; 2, an uncultured person or one of narrow views; one who cares more for material than for intellectual interests:—*adj.* 1, pertaining to, or like, the Philistines; 2, narrow-minded; uncultured.—*n.* **Phi-lis′tin-ism.**

phi-lo- (fĭ′lō-; fĭl′ō-), a combining form from the Greek, meaning love, loving; as, *philo*sophy. Also, **phil-.**

phil-o-log-i-cal (fĭl″ō-lŏj′ĭ-kăl), *adj.* pertaining to the scientific or historic study of language.

phi-lol-o-gy (fĭ-lŏl′ō-jĭ), *n.* the scientific and historic study of the origin, development, relationships, etc., of language.—*n.* **phi-lol′o-gist.**

phil-o-mel (fĭl′ō-mĕl), *n.* the nightingale: a poetic name.

phil-o-pe-na (fĭl″ō-pē′nȧ), *n.* 1, a game played in various ways, usually with the understanding that a forfeit of some kind is to be paid by the one who first fails to fulfil a given requirement; 2, the forfeit, usually a gift. Also, **fil″li-peen′.**

phil-o-pro-gen-i-tive-ness (fĭl″ō-prō-jĕn′ĭ-tĭv-nĕs), *n.* love of offspring; also, instinctive love of children in general.

phi-los-o-pher (fĭ-lŏs′ō-fẽr), *n.* 1, a student of the principles that explain or govern facts and events; 2, one who keeps calm under trying conditions; also, a person of judgment and practical wisdom: **philosophers' stone,** an imaginary stone thought to have the property of transmuting baser metals into gold or silver: one of the main objects of the alchemists' search.

phil-o-soph-ic (fĭl″ō-sŏf′ĭk), *adj.* 1, pertaining to philosophy, 2, wise, calm; thoughtful. Also, **phil″o-soph′i-cal.**—*adv.* **phil″o-soph′i-cal-ly.**

phi-los-o-phize (fĭ-lŏs′ō-fīz), *v.i.* [*p.t.* and *p.p.* -phized (-fīzd), *p.pr.* -phiz″ing], to reason about, or seek the causes or nature of, facts, events, conduct, etc. —*n.* **phi-los′o-phiz″er.**

phi-los-o-phy (fĭ-lŏs′ō-fĭ), *n.* [*pl.* philosophies (-fĭz)], 1, the study and knowledge of the principles that cause, control, or explain facts and events, 2, the calmness of temper and practical wisdom that come from knowledge; 3, a system of general beliefs; as, her *philosophy* of life.

phil-ter (fĭl′tẽr), *n.* 1, a charm or potion supposed to have the power to excite love; 2, hence, any potion used for magic purposes. Also, **phil′tre.**

Phin-ti-as (fĭn′tĭ-ăs), *n.* in mythology, the friend of Damon: usually called *Pythias,* which see.

phle-bot-o-my (flē-bŏt′ō-mĭ), *n.* the act or practice of opening a vein to let blood.—*v.t.* **phle-bot′o-mize.**

Phleg-e-thon (flĕg′ē-thŏn; flĕj′-), *n.* in mythology, the river of fire in the lower world.

phlegm (flĕm), *n.* 1, thick, stringy mucus discharged from the throat; 2, heaviness of disposition; coldness; calmness.

phleg-mat-ic (flĕg-măt′ĭk), *adj.* sluggish; dull; not easily excited; cool; as, a *phlegmatic* temperament. Also, **phleg-mat′i-cal.**—*adv.* **phleg-mat′i-cal-ly.**

phlo-ëm (flō′ĕm), *n.* in higher plants, that portion of a vascular bundle having thin-walled cells, and devoted to food carrying: distinguished from *xylem.*

phlox (flŏks), *n.* any of a genus (*Phlox*) of herbs bearing bright-colored flowers.

pho-bi-a (fō′bĭ-ȧ), *n.* a morbid fear or dread: often used as a suffix.

phœ-be (fē′bē), *n.* any of several small American birds; esp., a bird slightly larger than the song sparrow, with a plaintive note: also called *pewee* and *pewit.*

Phœ-be (fē′bē), *n.* 1, in Greek mythology, Artemis, twin sister of Phœbus Apollo and goddess of the moon and of the chase: called by the Romans *Diana;* 2, *Poetic,* the moon. Also, **Phe′be.**

Phœ-bus (fē′bŭs), *n.* 1, in mythology, Apollo: called *Phœbus Apollo* when regarded as the sun god; 2, *Poetic,* the sun.

Phœ-ni-cian (fē-nĭsh′ăn), *adj.* pertaining to ancient Phœnicia in Syria, or to its people or their language: —*n.* 1, an inhabitant of Phœnicia or its colonies; 2, the language of the people of Phœnicia. Also, **Phe-ni′cian.**

Phœ-nix (fē′nĭks), *n.* an imaginary bird, said to live 500 years in the desert of Arabia, and, after being consumed by fire, to rise again, fresh and beautiful, from its own ashes; hence, an emblem of immortality. Also, **Phe′nix.**

phone (fōn), *n. Colloq.,* a telephone:—*v.t.* and *v.i.* [*p.t.* and *p.p.* phoned (fōnd), *p.pr.* phon′ing], *Colloq.,* to telephone.

pho-net-ic (fō-nĕt′ĭk), *adj.* 1, pertaining to the voice or to speech sounds; 2, representing the simple speech sounds; as, *phonetic* spelling: **phonetics,** *n.pl.* used as *sing.* the science of speech sounds, and of the symbols that stand for them. Also, *adj.* **pho-net′i-cal.**—*adv.* **pho-net′i-cal-ly.**

pho-ne-ti-cian (fō″nē-tĭsh′ăn), *n.* one skilled in the science of speech sounds and their symbols.

phon-ic (fŏn′ĭk; fō′nĭk), *adj.* 1, pertaining to sound, esp. as used in speech; phonetic; 2, uttered with the voice: **phonics,** *n.pl.* used as *sing.* the science of sound, esp. as used in speech; phonetics.

pho-no-cin-e-mat-o-graph (fō″nō-sĭn″ē-măt′ō-grȧf), *n.* a device for presenting motion pictures and a corresponding phonographic dialog at the same time: also called *kinetophone* (see illus. next page).

pho-no-gram (fō′nō-grăm), *n.* 1, the record of sound produced by a phonograph; 2, a written character representing a certain sound.

pho-no-graph (fō'nō-grȧf), *n.* **1**, formerly, a letter or character indicating a distinct spoken sound: **2**, an instrument to record and reproduce accurately speech, music, or other sounds.

pho-no-graph-ic (fō"nō-grăf'ĭk), *adj.* **1**, pertaining to, or representing, sounds; **2**, pertaining to a phonograph or phonography. Also, **pho"no-graph'i-cal.**—*adv.* **pho"no-graph'i-cal-ly.**

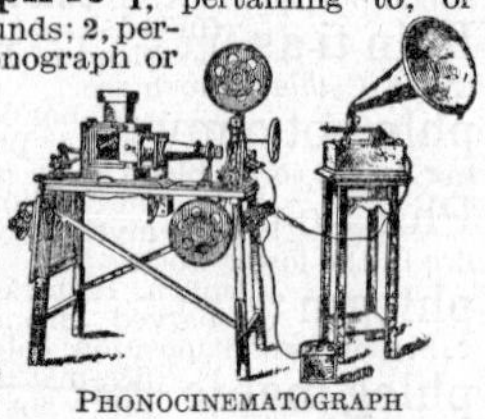

PHONOCINEMATOGRAPH

pho-nog-ra-phy (fō-nŏg'-rȧ-fĭ), *n.* **1**, a description of sounds uttered by the human voice; **2**, a system of shorthand, by which every sound is represented by a separate character or mark.

pho-nol-o-gy (fō-nŏl'ō-jĭ), *n.* **1**, the science of speech sounds, together with their history and the theory of their changes; **2**, that section of grammar which treats of the sounds and sound changes of a language.—*adj.* **pho"no-log'ic; pho"no-log'i-cal.**—*n.* **pho-nol'o-gist.**

pho-ny (fō'nĭ), *adj. Slang*, counterfeit; as, *phony* money.

phos-gene (fŏs'jēn), *n.* a colorless gas with the odor of musty hay: used in warfare as a poison gas. Also, **phos'gen.**

phos-phate (fŏs'fāt), *n.* **1**, a salt of phosphoric acid; **2**, any of various mineral substances consisting of salts of the acids of phosphorus: **phosphate rock**, any of several mineral phosphates that can be used as sources of fertilizer.

phos-phite (fŏs'fīt), *n.* a salt of phosphorous acid.

Phos-phor (fŏs'fŏr), *n.* the morning star, esp. the planet Venus; Lucifer.

phos-phor-esce (fŏs"fŏr-ĕs'), *v.i.* [*p.t.* and *p.p.* -esced' (-ĕst'), *p.pr.* -esc'ing], to give off light without heat or combustion, as does the element phosphorus.

phos-phor-es-cence (fŏs"fŏr-ĕs'ĕns), *n.* **1**, the giving out of light without heat by certain bodies, such as phosphorus, decaying wood, and some insects and marine animals; **2**, the property of thus giving out light; **3**, the light thus given out.—*adj.* **phos"phor-es'cent.**

phos-phor-us (fŏs'fŏr-ŭs), *n.* a nonmetallic element, a yellowish, waxy, poisonous substance with an unpleasant odor, luminous and highly inflammable: used in rat poison, match tips, etc.—*adj.* **phos-phor'ic.**—*adj.* **phos'phor-ous.**

phos-phu-ret-ed (fŏs'fū-rĕt"ĕd), *adj.* mixed or combined with phosphorus. Also, **phos'phu-ret"ted.**

pho-to (fō'tō), *n. Colloq.*, a photograph: a popular abbreviation.

pho-to–en-grav-ing (fō"tō-ĕn-grāv'-ĭng), *n.* **1**, a process by which a photograph is reproduced in relief upon a metal plate, for printing; **2**, a picture printed from such a plate.

pho-to-gen-ic (fō"tō-jĕn'ĭk), *adj.* having such form and color as to photograph effectively.

pho-to-graph (fō'tō-grȧf), *v.t.* to take a picture of, by exposing a sensitized plate or film to the action of light:—*n.* a picture so made.

pho-to-graph-ic (fō"tō-grăf'ĭk), *adj.* **1**, pertaining to, or made by, the exposure of a sensitized plate or film to the action of light; **2**, reproducing life or nature in all its details; as, a *photographic* style of painting.—*adv.* **pho"to-graph'i-cal-ly.**

pho-tog-ra-phy (fō-tŏg'rȧ-fĭ), *n.* the art or process of making pictures by the action of light on plates or films, sensitized, or coated with certain chemicals.—*n.* **pho-tog'ra-pher.**

pho-to-gra-vure (fō"tō-grȧ-vūr'; fō"tō-grā'vūr), *n.* **1**, any one of several processes for printing pictures from an intaglio plate prepared by photographic methods; **2**, a picture so printed.

pho-to-lith-o-graph (fō"tō-lĭth'ō-grȧf), *n.* a picture, often in colors, printed from a smooth, flat, porous surface of stone or other material, of a design which has been transferred to the surface by means of photography.—*n.* **pho"to-li-thog'ra-phy.**—*adj.* **pho"to-lith"o-graph'ic.**

pho-to-me-chan-i-cal (fō"tō-mē-kăn'ĭ-kăl), *adj.* pertaining to the mechanical printing of pictures from plates made photographically.

pho-tom-e-ter (fō-tŏm'ē-tẽr), *n.* an instrument by which the intensity of light is measured.—*n.* **pho-tom'e-try.**—*adj.* **pho"to-met'ric.**

pho-to-phone (fō'tō-fōn), *n.* an instrument for communicating sounds by means of light.

pho-to-play (fō'tō-plā"), *n.* a motion-picture play; a play for exhibition by motion pictures.—*n.* **pho'to-play"er.**—*n.* **pho"to-play'wright".**

pho-to-sphere (fō'tō-sfēr), *n.* the luminous, incandescent surface of the sun as seen from the earth.

pho-to-stat (fō'tō-stăt), *n.* a camera used for photographing maps, manuscripts, etc., directly upon the surface of prepared paper; also, a photograph so made:—*v.t.* [*p.t.* and *p.p.* -stat"ed, *p.pr.* -stat"ing], to reproduce with a photostat.—*adj.* **pho"to-stat'ic.**

pho-to-type (fō'tō-tīp), *n.* **1**, a block on whose surface a photograph is reproduced in such a way that pictures may be printed from it; **2**, the process of preparing such a block; **3**, a picture made from it.

phrase (frāz), *n.* **1**, in grammar, a group of related words not containing a subject and a predicate; **2**, any brief, pithy expression containing a single idea; **3**, a characteristic style or manner of speech:—*v.t.* [*p.t.* and *p.p.* phrased (frāzd), *p.pr.* phras'ing], to put into words, esp. into suitable words.

phra-se-ol-o-gy (frā"zē-ŏl'ō-jĭ), *n.* style or manner of expression. *Syn.* language, vocabulary. (See diction.)

phren-o-log-i-cal (frĕn"ō-lŏj'ĭ-kăl), *adj.* pertaining to the theory that qualities of mind and character are shown by the shape of the head.

phre-nol-o-gy (frē-nŏl'ō-jĭ), *n.* a system of character reading based on the theory that the qualities of the mind and character are shown by the form of the skull.—*n.* **phre-nol'o-gist.**

Phrix-us (frĭk'sŭs), *n.* in mythology, a Grecian prince who, condemned to be sacrificed to Zeus, rode away through the air with his sister, Helle, on the ram which bore the Golden Fleece, Helle, however, falling off the ram into the Hellespont.

Phryg-i-an (frĭj'ĭ-ăn), *adj.* pertaining to Phrygia, an ancient country in Asia Minor, or to its people:—*n.* **1**, an inhabitant of Phrygia; **2**, the language of Phrygia.

phthis-ic (tĭz'ĭk), *n.* **1**, (also, *phthisis*), a wasting of the tissues; esp., tuberculosis or consumption; **2**, a person affected with phthisis.—*adj.* **phthis'i-cal.**

phthi-sis (thī′sĭs), *n.* **1**, a wasting away of the body or its parts; **2**, esp., tuberculosis of the lungs; consumption. Also, **phthis′ic** (tĭz′ĭk).

phy-lac-ter-y (fĭ-lăk′tẽr-ĭ), *n.* [*pl.* phylacteries (-ĭz)], a small square box containing a thin strip of parchment upon which certain texts from the law are inscribed: worn, during prayer, by pious Jews, upon the forehead and left wrist.

phy-lum (fī′lŭm), *n.* [*pl.* phyla (-lȧ)], **1**, in zoölogy, one of the large fundamental divisions of the animal kingdom, as that including the vertebrates or the mollusks; **2**, in botany, a similar division of plants.

phys-ic (fĭz′ĭk), *n.* **1**, the science of medicine, or the art of healing; **2**, medicine in general; **3**, a cathartic:—*v.t.* [*p.t.* and *p.p.* -icked (-ĭkt), *p.pr.* -ick-ing], to give medicine, esp. a cathartic, to; purge.

phys-i-cal (fĭz′ĭ-kăl), *adj.* **1**, relating to nature or natural science; **2**, material as opposed to moral or spiritual; **3**, pertaining to the body; as, *physical* weakness.—*adv.* **phys′i-cal-ly.**

phy-si-cian (fĭ-zĭsh′ăn), *n.* one skilled in the art of healing and legally qualified to treat disease; a doctor of medicine.

phys-i-cist (fĭz′ĭ-sĭst), *n.* a student or specialist in physics.

phys-ics (fĭz′ĭks), *n.pl.* used as *sing.* the science which treats of matter and energy, including the study of mechanics, heat, light, sound, electricity, etc.

phys-i-og-no-my (fĭz″ĭ-ŏg′nō-mĭ), *n.* [*pl.* physiognomies(-mĭz)], **1**, the art of reading in the face the qualities of the mind; **2**, the face as expressive of character; **3**, outward appearance or aspect; expression.—*n.* **phys″i-og′no-mist.**

phys-i-og-ra-phy (fĭz″ĭ-ŏg′rȧ-fĭ), *n.* physical geography, esp. that part which treats of the land.

phys-i-o-log-i-cal (fĭz″ĭ-ō-lŏj′ĭ-kăl), *adj.* pertaining to physiology, esp. that part which treats of the functions of the human body. Also, **phys″i-o-log′ic.** —*adv.* **phys″i-o-log′i-cal-ly.**

phys-i-ol-o-gy (fĭz″ĭ-ŏl′ō-jĭ), *n.* [*pl.* physiologies (-jĭz)], **1**, the science that treats of the life processes of plants and animals; **2**, in common use, that part of biology which treats of the work of the organs and tissues in the human body.—*n.* **phys″i-ol′o-gist.**

phy-sique (fĭ-zēk′), *n.* the formation of the body; constitution; appearance; as, a man of powerful *physique.*

[1]**pi** (pī; pē), *n.* **1**, the 16th letter in the Greek alphabet [π, Π], corresponding in general to English *p;* **2**, the number (3.14159+) by which the diameter of a circle must be multiplied in order to find the circumference: indicated by the Greek letter pi [π].

[2]**pi** (pī), *n.* jumbled printing type:—*v.t.* [*p.t.* and *p.p.* pied (pīd), *p.pr.* pie′ing], to jumble, as type. Also, **pie.**

pi-a ma-ter (pī′ȧ mā′tẽr), a delicate membrane, innermost of three that cover the brain and spinal cord.

***pi-a-nis-si-mo** (pē″ȧ-nĭs′ĭ-mō; pyä-nēs′sē-mō), [It.], *adv.* very softly: a musical direction.—*abbr.* **pp.**

pi-an-ist (pĭ-ăn′ĭst; pē′ȧ-nĭst), *n.* a performer on the piano.

*[1]**pia-no** (pyä′nō), [It.], *adv.* softly: a musical direction.—*abbr.* **p.**

[2]**pi-an-o** (pĭ-ăn′ō), *n.* [*pl.* pianos (-ōz)], a large, modern musical instrument, the tones of which come from steel wires of graduated length stretched on a harp-shaped frame and struck by hammers operated from a keyboard: occurring in three varieties: the *grand,* in which the frame is horizontal and the short side parallel with the keyboard; the *upright,* in which the frame is vertical; and the *square,* in which the frame is horizontal and the long side parallel with the keyboard.

pi-an-o-for-te (pĭ-ăn″ō-fōr′tā; pĭ-ăn″ō-fōrt′), *n.* a musical instrument, played by means of keys; a piano.

pi-a-no-la (pē″ȧ-nō′lȧ), *n.* a mechanical apparatus for playing a piano.

pi-as-ter (pĭ-ăs′tẽr), *n.* a coin current in Turkey, Egypt, Spain, etc., worth about five cents. Also, **pi-as′tre.**

pi-az-za (pĭ-ăz′ȧ; *It.* pyät′sä), *n.* **1**, in Italy, an open square surrounded by buildings or columns; **2**, a walk under a pillared roof, along the outside of a building; **3**, in the U. S., a veranda.

pi-broch (pē′brŏkh), *n.* **1**, the wild, warlike music of the Scottish bagpipes; **2**, a bagpipe.

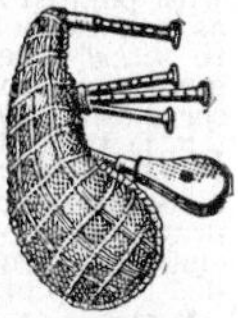
PIBROCH

pi-ca (pī′kȧ), *n.* in printing, a large size of type; 12 point (see *type*).

pic-a-dor (pĭk″ȧ-dōr′), *n.* a horseman who, in a bullfight, incites the bull by pricking it with a lance.

pic-a-resque (pĭk″ȧ-rĕsk′), *adj.* **1**, pertaining to rascals or vagabonds; **2**, having a rogue as hero: said of a kind of fiction.

pic-a-roon (pĭk″ȧ-ro͞on′), *n.* **1**, a pirate; rogue; **2**, a pirate ship.

pic-a-yune (pĭk″ȧ-yo͞on′), *n.* **1**, a small silver coin equal to 6¼ cents, formerly used in the U. S.; **2**, *Colloq.*, a trifle; little bit; as, it is not worth a *picayune.*

Pic-ca-dil-ly (pĭk″ȧ-dĭl′ĭ; pĭk′ȧ-dĭl″ĭ), *n.* a street in London famous for its clubs and shops.

pic-ca-lil-li (pĭk′ȧ-lĭl″ĭ), *n.* a pickle, or relish, made of finely chopped vegetables and hot spices.

pic-co-lo (pĭk′ō-lō), *n.* [*pl.* piccolos (-lōz)], a small, flute-shaped instrument with notes an octave higher than the ordinary flute (see *musical instrument,* illus.).

[1]**pick** (pĭk), *n.* **1**, a heavy tool for breaking earth or rock, consisting of an iron bar sharpened at the ends, with a wooden handle set at right angles to it in the middle; **2**, any of various sharp-pointed instruments.

[2]**pick** (pĭk), *v.t.* **1**, to strike or break with a sharp instrument, or with the beak; pierce or peck; as, to *pick* a hole; **2**, to open by a sharp instrument; as, to *pick* a lock; **3**, to lift: often used with *up;* as, to *pick* up something fallen; **4**, to pluck or gather; as, to *pick* berries; **5**, to separate with the fingers; as, to *pick* rags; **6**, to clean of something; pluck; as, to *pick* a chicken; **7**, to eat fastidiously or in small bits; **8**, to choose or select; as, to *pick* the best one; **9**, hence, to bring about by choice or intention; as, to *pick* a quarrel; **10**, to rob; as, to *pick* a pocket; **11**, to pull or twitch the strings of; as, to *pick* a banjo:—*v.i.* **1**, to eat slowly and daintily; **2**, to pilfer; as, to *pick* and steal; **3**, *Slang,* to find fault; nag:—*n.* **1**, a stroke, as with a sharp point; **2**, the act of choosing; **3**, choice; as, take your *pick;* **4**, the best of anything; as, the *pick* of the lot.—*n.* **pick′er.**—*n.* **pick′ing.**

Syn., *v.* cull, collect. (See elect.)

pick-a-back (pĭk′ȧ-băk″), *adv.* on the shoulders like a pack; as, to carry a child *pickaback:* **pickaback plane,** an airplane carried aloft by a larger plane for easier launching.

pick-a-nin-ny (pĭk′ȧ-nĭn″ĭ), *n.* [*pl.* pickaninnies (-ĭz)], a negro baby or child. Also, **pic′ca-nin″ny.**

pick-ax (pĭk′ăks″), *n.* a hand tool for digging, having a heavy iron head pointed at the ends, or pointed at one end and broad at the other. Also, **pick′axe″**.

pick-er-el (pĭk′ĕr-ĕl), *n.* any of several fresh-water fishes of the pike family; sometimes, the pike: **pickerel weed**, a water plant, with blue flowers and heart-shaped leaves, that grows in shallow water.

pick-et (pĭk′ĕt), *n.* **1**, an upright pointed stake, used in making fences, for fastening a horse, etc.; **2**, a military guard, consisting of not more than half a company, stationed at a given place to prevent surprise by an enemy; **3**, one or more persons appointed by a labor union to watch a factory, shop, etc., where nonunion men are employed during a strike; **4**, hence, any person or persons appointed by an organization to watch at a given place for any purpose:—*v.t.* **1**, to fence with pointed stakes; **2**, to fasten to a stake; as, to *picket* a horse; **3**, to watch or guard; as, to *picket* a certain position; **4**, to place on guard; as, to *picket* men for duty:—*v.i.* to serve as a picket.

pick-le (pĭk′l), *n.* **1**, brine, or a mixture of salt and water, used for preserving food; also, vinegar; **2**, vegetables, fruit, etc., preserved in brine or in vinegar; **3**, *Colloq.*, an embarrassment; difficulty:—*v.t.* [*p.t.* and *p.p.* -led (-ld), *p.pr.* -ling], to preserve in pickle.

pick-pock-et (pĭk′pŏk″ĕt), *n.* one who steals from another's pocket.

pic-nic (pĭk′nĭk), *n.* a short trip, as into the country, by a pleasure party carrying its own food:—*v.i.* [*p.t.* and *p.p.* -nicked (-nĭkt), *p.pr.* -nick-ing], to go on, or hold, an outdoor pleasure party.—*n.* **pic′nick-er.**

pi-cot (pē″kō′), *n.* one of the small projecting loops forming the edge of certain laces, ribbons, etc.:—*v.t.* [*p.t.* and *p.p.* -coted′ (-kōd′), *p.pr.* -cot′ing], to finish or edge with picots, as ribbon.

pic-ric ac-id (pĭk′rĭk), a pale yellowish crystalline compound with an intensely bitter taste, forming a brilliant yellow solution: chiefly used as an explosive.

Pict (pĭkt), *n.* one of an ancient, probably Celtic, race of the Scotch Highlands, who united with the Scots in the ninth century.

pic-to-graph (pĭk′tō-grȧf), *n.* **1**, a primitive drawing or crude figure which served to express an idea; **2**, a hieroglyphic; **3**, a specimen of the picture writing of certain ancient peoples.

pic-to-ri-al (pĭk-tō′rĭ-ăl), *adj.* **1**, pertaining to, shown by, or containing, pictures; as, a *pictorial* magazine; **2**, vividly described.—*adv.* **pic-to′ri-al-ly.**

pic-ture (pĭk′tūr), *n.* **1**, a painting, drawing, or photograph, of a person, object, scene, or incident; **2**, a likeness or image; as, she is the *picture* of her mother; **3**, a vivid portrayal in words or by the imagination; as, a *picture* of future happiness; **4**, bodily representation; as, he was the *picture* of despair; **5**, *Colloq.*, a motion picture:—*v.t.* [*p.t.* and *p.p.* -tured (-tūrd), *p.pr.* -turing], **1**, to represent in a painting, drawing, etc.; **2**, to describe vividly in words; **3**, to form a mental image of; imagine.

pic-tur-esque (pĭk″tūr-ĕsk′), *adj.* **1**, giving a vivid impression, as a picture does; graphic, as language; **2**, suitable to be drawn or painted as a picture; as, a *picturesque* cottage; **3**, having wild or rugged beauty; romantic; as, *picturesque* scenery.—*adv.* **pic″tur-esque′ly.**—*n.* **pic″tur-esque′ness.**

pidg-in Eng-lish (pĭj′ĭn; pĭj′ŭn), a form of English based on Chinese syntax, used in the Orient by the Chinese in their commercial dealings with foreigners. Also, **pi′geon Eng′lish.**

¹pie (pī), *n.* a made dish consisting of meat, fruit, or the like, baked between two layers of pastry or on one lower crust.

²pie (pī), *n.* the magpie, a black-and-white member of the crow family.

³pie (pī), *n.* printer's type confusedly mixed:—*v.t.* [*p.t.* and *p.p.* pied (pīd), *p.pr.* pie′ing], to jumble, as type. Also, **pi**, *Pfd. S.*

pie-bald (pī′bôld″), *adj.* having patches of different colors, esp. black and white or brown and white; as, a *piebald* horse.

piece (pēs), *n.* **1**, a part of anything; a fragment; as, a *piece* of bread; a plot or division; as, a *piece* of land; **2**, a certain quantity regarded as a unit in manufacture; as, muslin comes at twelve yards to the *piece;* **3**, a separate instance, example, or performance; as, a bad *piece* of business; **4**, a single object of a group; as, each *piece* in the set; **5**, a single, distinct, literary or artistic composition; as, a *piece* of music; **6**, the amount of work done as a distinct job; as, the work is paid for by the *piece;* **7**, a coin; as, a five-cent *piece;* **8**, a gun; as, a field*piece;* fowling *piece;* **9**, one of the counters or men with which chess, checkers, and similar games are played: **piece of eight**, the Spanish dollar, equal to eight reals:—*v.t.* [*p.t.* and *p.p.* pieced (pēst), *p.pr.* piec′ing], **1**, to enlarge or mend by adding material; as, to *piece* a skirt; **2**, to make by joining sections together; as, to *piece* a quilt:—*v.i.* to fit or join.

Syn., *n.* portion, section. (See part.)

piece-meal (pēs′mēl″), *adj.* made of small portions or parts; fragmentary:—*adv.* **1**, in portions or parts; **2**, by degrees; gradually.

piece-work (pēs′wûrk″), *n.* work measured and paid for by the piece: distinguished from *timework*, or work paid for by the hour, day, etc.—*n.* **piece′work″er.**

pied (pīd), *adj.* many-colored or spotted; piebald.

pied-mont (pēd′mŏnt), *adj.* at, or formed at, the base of mountains; as, a *piedmont* plain:—*n.* a piedmont district.

pie-plant (pī′plănt″), *n.* in the U. S., the garden rhubarb.

pier (pēr), *n.* **1**, a mass of masonry supporting one end of an arch, bridge, etc. (see ¹*arch*, illus.); **2**, a similar support, as of iron or timbers, in the structure of a bridge or building; **3**, a projecting part of a wall, such as a buttress; **4**, a portion of the wall of a room between two windows; **5**, a mole, wharf, or dock, or any structure built out over the water, as for a promenade.

pierce (pērs), *v.t.* [*p.t.* and *p.p.* pierced (pērst), *p.pr.* pierc′ing], **1**, to run into or through, esp. with a pointed instrument; **2**, to affect deeply; as, to *pierce* the heart with sorrow; **3**, to force a way through; as, the bullet *pierced* his side; to *pierce* the lines of the enemy; **4**, to see through mentally; solve, as a mystery:—*v.i.* to enter; penetrate.

pierc-ing (pēr′sĭng), *p.adj.* penetrating; sharp; as, a *piercing* look.

pier glass a large high mirror, esp. one between windows.

pi-e-tism (pī′ē-tĭzm), *n.* a devotional, rather than an intellectual or practical, type of religious experience: **Pietism**, a reform movement in the Lutheran Church in the latter part of the 17th century.—*n.* **pi′e-tist.**—*adj.* **pi″e-tis′tic; pi″e-tis′ti-cal.**

pi-e-ty (pī′ē-tĭ), *n.* [*pl.* pieties (-tĭz)], **1**, deep devotion to religion; godliness; **2**, reverence for, and observance of duty toward, God; **3**, honor and obedience to parents; as, filial *piety*.

pig (pĭg), *n.* **1**, a two-toed, hoofed, domesticated mammal; a swine, esp. a young one; **2**, *Colloq.*, a greedy or selfish person;

3, an oblong mass of metal, as of iron, formed by running into molds when melted:—*v.i.* [*p.t.* and *p.p.* pigged (pĭgd), *p.pr.* pig ging], to bring forth, or to act like, swine.

pi-geon (pĭj'ŭn), *n.* any of numerous well-known birds with short, stocky body, short legs, and long wings.

pi-geon-hole (pĭj'ŭn-hōl''), *n.* **1**, a hole for pigeons; **2**, a small, open, boxlike space in a desk, case, etc., for documents, letters, or the like:—*v.t.* [*p.t.* and *p.p.* -holed'' (-hōld''), *p.pr.* -hol''ing], **1**, to place, as letters, in such a boxlike space; **2**, to lay aside and forget; shelve.

pi-geon-toed (pĭj'ŭn-tōd''), *adj.* having the toes turned in.

pi-geon-wing (pĭj'ŭn-wĭng''), *n.* a dancing step in which the dancer jumps, striking his heels together.

pig-ger-y (pĭg'ẽr-ĭ), *n.* [*pl.* piggeries (-ĭz)], a place for keeping or raising pigs; a pigsty.

pig-gin (pĭg'ĭn), *n.* a small wooden vessel, as a pail or tub, having a stave extended upward as a handle.

pig-gish (pĭg'ĭsh), *adj.* piglike; hence, obstinate, greedy, or dirty.—*adv.* **pig'gish-ly.**—*n.* **pig'gish-ness.**

pig-head-ed (pĭg'-hĕd''ĕd), *adj.* stupidly obstinate or stubborn.

pig i-ron iron from the blast furnace, cast into rough, troughlike molds, or pigs: also called *pig.*

pig-ment (pĭg'mĕnt), *n.* **1**, any substance used to impart color; specif., an insoluble, dry, coloring matter, which, when mixed with a suitable medium, forms paint; **2**, the coloring matter in animals and plants, as in a tissue.—*adj.* **pig'men-ta-ry.**—*n.* **pig''men-ta'tion.**

Pig-my (pĭg'mĭ), *n.* [*pl.* Pigmies (-mĭz)], **1**, in classical antiquity, one of a race of drawfs; **2**, one of a race of very small Africans: **pigmy, 1**, a dwarf; **2**, any extremely small or insignificant person:—*adj.* dwarfish; very small. Also, **Pyg'my,** *Pfd. S.*

pig-nut (pĭg'nŭt''), *n.* **1**, the thin-shelled nut of a species of hickory, tasting first sweet, then bitter; also, the tree; **2**, a nut that grows in the ground.

pig-pen (pĭg'pĕn''), *n.* a pigsty; an inclosure in which pigs are kept.

pig-skin (pĭg'skĭn''), *n.* **1**, leather made from the hide of a pig; **2**, the hide itself; **3**, *Colloq.*: **a**, a football; **b**, in England, a saddle.

pig-sty (pĭg'stī''), *n.* [*pl.* pigsties (-stīz'')], a pen for pigs; a piggery.

pig-tail (pĭg'tāl''), *n.* **1**, hair twisted into a braid, usually hanging down from the back of the head; **2**, a long twist of tobacco.

pig-weed (pĭg'wēd''), *n.* **1**, any of a genus of plants of the goosefoot family, esp. the common goosefoot; **2**, locally, the common garden purslane.

1pike (pīk), *n.* **1**, formerly, a weapon consisting of a long wooden shaft with a spearhead at one end; **2**, a sharp, central spike or point, as in a shield.

2pike (pīk), *n.* any of certain voracious fresh-water fish with a pointed head, as the pickerel and muskellunge.

3pike (pīk), *n.* **1**, a road on which a charge is made for driving; a turnpike or toll road; **2**, any main road; **3**, a place where the toll is paid.

pik-ed (pīk'ĕd; pīkt), *adj.* having a sharp point; peaked.

pik-er (pīk'ẽr), *n. Slang,* one who bets cautiously or for small amounts.

pike-staff (pīk'stȧf''), *n.* a pole or shaft with a spike at the end, as carried by mountaineers to keep from slipping.

pi-las-ter (pĭ-lăs'tẽr), *n.* a rectangular column, with a base and a capital, inserted in a wall.

Pi-late (pī'lȧt), *n.* the Roman governor of Judea under whom Christ was crucified: called in full *Pontius Pilate.*

pil-chard (pĭl'chȧrd), *n.* **1**, a sea fish resembling the herring, found chiefly on the coasts of Devon and Cornwall, England; **2**, in some places, the sardine.

1pile (pīl), *n.* **1**, a mass or heap; as, a *pile* of sand; **2**, a large building; **3**, a mass of inflammable material for burning a body; a pyre; as, a funeral *pile;* **4**, in electricity, a series of plates of unlike metals laid alternately one upon another so as to produce an electric current; **5**, *Colloq.*, a great quantity; a collection; **6**, *Slang,* a fortune:—*v.t.* [*p.t.* and *p.p.* piled (pīld), *p.pr.* pil'ing], **1**, to throw into a heap; as, to *pile* stone; **2**, to collect and arrange; as, to *pile* bricks; **3**, to accumulate:—*v.i.* to form a mass or heap.

2pile (pīl), *n.* **1**, a timber driven into the ground, as for a wharf, foundation for a building, or the like; also, metal or concrete columns similarly used; **2**, a pointed stake or post: **pile driver,** a machine for driving piles into the ground:—*v.t.* [*p.t.* and *p.p.* piled (pīld), *p.pr.* pil'ing], to drive piles into.

3pile (pīl), *n.* **1**, nap of cloth; **2**, hair, esp. soft hair or fur; **3**, a fiber or filament, as of cotton.—*adj.* **piled.**

pi-le-at-ed (pī'lē-āt''ĕd; pĭl'ē-), *adj.* having a crest on the head, as a bird.

piles (pīlz), *n.pl.* hemorrhoids, a swelling of the veins within the anus.

pil-fer (pĭl'fẽr), *v.t.* and *v.i.* to steal in small amounts.—*n.* **pil'fer-er.**

pil-grim (pĭl'grĭm), *n.* **1**, one who travels from a distance to visit some sacred place or shrine; **2**, a traveler: **Pilgrims,** the Puritan settlers of the first colony in Massachusetts in 1620: also called *Pilgrim Fathers:* **Pilgrim's Progress,** an allegory by John Bunyan, symbolizing the trials and temptations of Christians in attaining salvation.

pil-grim-age (pĭl'grĭ-māj), *n.* **1**, a long journey, esp. to some sacred place; **2**, life considered as a journey.

pill (pĭl), *n.* **1**, medicine prepared in the form of a small ball; **2**, a pellet; **3**, something disagreeable that must be accepted.

pil-lage (pĭl'āj), *n.* **1**, the act of plundering, or robbing openly, esp. in war; **2**, booty; spoil:—*v.t.* and *v.i.* [*p.t.* and *p.p.* -laged (-ājd), *p.pr.* -lag-ing], to plunder, or rob openly; despoil; sack.—*n.* **pil'lag-er.**

pil-lar (pĭl'ȧr), *n.* **1**, a column to support a structure or to serve as a monument; **2**, any firm, slender, upright support; **3**, any support or mainstay.—*adj.* **pil'lared.**

pil-lion (pĭl'yŭn), *n.* a pad put on the back of a horse behind a man's saddle so that a second person may ride: formerly much used by women.

pil-lo-ry (pĭl'ō-rĭ), *n.* [*pl.* pillories (-rĭz)], an old instrument of punishment, consisting of a wooden frame supported by an upright post, and having holes through which the head and hands of a person standing exposed to public disgrace were passed and secured:—*v.t.* [*p.t.* and *p.p.* -ried (-rĭd), *p.pr.* -ry-ing], **1**, to punish by putting in such a framework; **2**, to expose to public disgrace.

pil-low (pĭl'ō), *n.* **1**, a case filled with feathers, etc., to support the head of a person lying down; **2**, any rest for the head:—*v.t.* to place on a rest for the head.

pil-low block a support for a shaft which drives machinery.

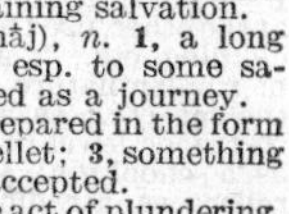

PILLOW BLOCK

pil-low-case (pĭl′ō-kās″), *n.* a covering, as of linen or cotton, for a pillow: also called *pillow slip.*

pi-lose (pī′lōs), *adj.* having abundant hair. Also, **pi′lous.**

pi-lot (pī′lŭt), *n.* **1,** one who steers a vessel; one licensed to conduct a vessel in or out of a port or in waters where sailing is difficult or dangerous; **2,** one who flies a balloon, airship, or flying machine; **3,** the cowcatcher of a locomotive (see *locomotive,* illus.); **4,** a guide of any sort; **5,** a mechanical regulating device:—*v.t.* **1,** to direct the course of, as a vessel or airship; **2,** to guide through difficulties.

pi-lot-age (pī′lŭt-āj), *n.* **1,** the act or business of conducting vessels, esp. in or out of a port or through dangerous waters; **2,** the fee paid for such service.

pi-lot bal-loon a small balloon, sent up unmanned ahead of a larger balloon, to show the direction and strength of the wind.

pi-lot fish a small, bluish, marine fish which accompanies sharks in order to feed on the scraps of their prey.

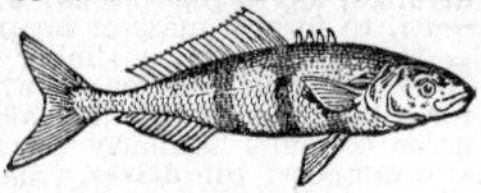

PILOT FISH ($\frac{1}{10}$)

pi-men-to (pĭ-mĕn′tō), *n.* [*pl.* pimentos (-tōz)], the unripe fruit of the allspice tree, dried and used as a flavoring.

***pi-mien-to** (pē-myĕn′tō), [Span.], *n.* [*pl.* pimientos (-tōs)], a variety of sweet pepper, the fruit of which is used as a vegetable, in salads, in flavoring for cheese, etc.: also called, incorrectly, *pimento.*

pim-per-nel (pĭm′pĕr-nĕl), *n.* a plant of the primrose family, with white, purple, or scarlet flowers.

pim-ple (pĭm′pl), *n.* **1,** a small swelling of the skin, containing pus; **2,** any small swelling.—*adj.* **pim′pled.**—*adj.* **pim′ply.**

pin (pĭn), *n.* **1,** a short piece of wire with a sharp point at one end and a round head at the other, used for fastening together papers, clothing, etc.; **2,** a larger, pointed instrument of similar nature, used for holding the hair, the hat, etc.; as, a scarf *pin;* **3,** an ornament, badge, or jewel fitted with a pin and a clasp; as, a school *pin;* **4,** a bolt or peg; **5,** a wooden roller; as, a rolling-*pin;* **6,** anything resembling a pin in shape or use; **7,** *Colloq.,* anything of small value:—*v.t.* [*p.t.* and *p.p.* pinned (pĭnd), *p.pr.* pin′ning], **1,** to fasten with, or as with, a pin; **2,** to inclose; **3,** to seize and hold.

pin-a-fore (pĭn′ȧ-fōr″), *n.* a loose sleeveless apron or covering to protect the clothing of a child or young girl.

***pince–nez** (pȧṅs″-nā′), [Fr.], *n.* [*pl.* pince-nez], eyeglasses kept on the nose by a spring.

pin-cers (pĭn′sĕrz), *n.pl.,* sometimes used as *sing.,* **1,** an instrument with two handles and two jaws working on a pivot, used for gripping things; nippers (see *tool,* illus.); **2,** an organ resembling pincers, as the claw of a lobster. Also, **pinch′ers.**

pinch (pĭnch), *v.t.* **1,** to squeeze or nip between two hard edges, or between the thumb and a finger; as, to *pinch* a hand; **2,** to press on so as to hurt; as, the shoe *pinches* my toe; **3,** to oppress or distress; **4,** to make thin or wan; as, to be *pinched* with hunger; **5,** *Slang:* **a,** to arrest; **b,** to rob; steal:—*v.i.* **1,** to press hard; as, my shoe *pinches;* **2,** to be mean or miserly:—*n.* **1,** a squeeze or nip, as with the fingers and thumb; **2,** painful pressure; as, the *pinch* of poverty; **3,** a sudden difficulty or necessity; as, to do it at a *pinch;* **4,** as much as can be held between the thumb and a finger; as, a *pinch* of salt.

pinch-beck (pĭnch′bĕk), *n.* **1,** a cheap imitation of gold made of copper, zinc, and tin: used in cheap jewelry; **2,** anything cheap or sham.

pinch-ers (pĭn′chĕrz), *n.pl.,* sometimes used as *sing.,* an instrument with two handles and two jaws, used for gripping things; nippers. See **pin′cers,** *Pfd. S.*

pin-cush-ion (pĭn′ko͝osh″ŭn), *n.* a small cushion used for pins.

[1]**pine** (pīn), *n.* **1,** any of a genus (*Pinus*) of cone-bearing trees with needlelike leaves growing in clusters; **2,** the timber of the tree; **3,** a pineapple.

[2]**pine** (pīn), *v.i.* [*p.t.* and *p.p.* pined (pīnd), *p.pr.* pin′ing], **1,** to grow thin and weak from distress, anxiety, or the like; **2,** to long intensely: usually with *for.*

Syn. languish, droop, wither, flag.

pine-ap-ple (pīn′ăp″l), *n.* **1,** a tropical plant with spiny leaves, bearing a large, cone-shaped fruit; **2,** the edible, juicy fruit of this plant.

pine cone the fruit of the pine tree (see *tree,* illus.).

pin-feath-er (pĭn′fĕ*th*″ẽr), *n.* a feather just beginning to grow.

pin-head (pĭn′hĕd″), *n.* the head of a pin; hence, anything small, trifling, and insignificant.

pin-hole (pĭn′hōl″), *n.* a very small hole made by, or as by, a pin.

[1]**pin-ion** (pĭn′yŭn), *n.* a gear wheel, the cogs of which engage with those of a larger toothed wheel or of a rack, so that motion is imparted from one to the other; in a pair or set of gears, the smaller gear (see also *gear,* illus.).

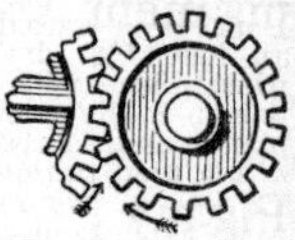

PINION AND GEAR

[2]**pin-ion** (pĭn′yŭn), *n.* **1,** the last group of bones of a bird's wing, corresponding to the human hand and wrist; **2,** a wing; **3,** a feather:—*v.t.* **1,** to bind the wings of, or to clip the last segment of the wings of; as, to *pinion* a bird; **2,** to bind; **3,** to confine.

[1]**pink** (pĭngk), *n.* **1,** a color resulting from a mixture of red and white; a very pale red; **2,** any of various flowering plants, esp. certain garden flowers with sharp-pointed leaves and a sweet, spicy fragrance; **3,** anything of supreme excellence; as, the *pink* of perfection:—*adj.* of a very pale red color.—*adj.* **pink′ish.**

[2]**pink** (pĭngk), *n.* a vessel having a narrow stern.

[3]**pink** (pĭngk), *v.t.* **1,** to stab; pierce or punch with small round holes; **2,** to scallop the edge of, as cloth by cutting; **3,** to prick, as with a sword.

pink eye a contagious inflammation of the eye, marked by redness of the eyeball; acute conjunctivitis.

pin mon-ey money allowed to a wife by her husband for her private expenses: orig. for buying pins.

pin-na (pĭn′ȧ), *n.* [*pl.* pinnæ (-ē); pinnas (-ȧz)], **1,** the cartilaginous part of the ear which projects from the head; **2,** a leaflet of a compound leaf; **3,** a wing, fin, or any similar organ.

pin-nace (pĭn′ās), *n.* **1,** a small, light, schooner-rigged vessel with oars; **2,** an eight-oared man-of-war's boat.

pin-na-cle (pĭn′ȧ-kl), *n.* **1,** a small tower or turret above the rest of a building; **2,** a high point like a spire; **3,** the highest point; as, the *pinnacle* of fame.

pin-nate (pĭn′āt), *adj.* arranged, like a feather, along two sides of an axis: said of the veining of a leaf, or of the leaflet arrangement of a compound leaf: **abruptly pinnate,** having a compound leaf with leaflets on each side of the midrib, with no odd, or terminal, leaflet: **odd-pinnate,** having a compound leaf with leaflets on each side of a midrib, and with a terminal, odd leaflet, as the wistaria (see *leaf,* illus.). Also, **pin'nat-ed.**—*adv.* **pin'nate-ly; pin'nat-ed-ly.**

pi-no-chle (pē'nŏ-kl; pĭn'ŏ-kl), *n.* a game of cards the object of which is the making of certain combinations. Also, **pi'no-cle.**

pint (pīnt), *n.* a measure of capacity: equal to four gills, liquid measure, or one half a quart dry measure.

pin-tle (pĭn'tl), *n.* a pin upon which anything turns, as a hinge.

pin-to (pĭn'tō; pēn'-), *adj.* mottled; pied; as, a *pinto* horse:—*n.* [*pl.* pintos (-tōz)] a mottled animal.

pin-worm (pĭn'wûrm''), *n.* a small, threadlike, parasitic, round worm, infesting the rectum, esp. in children.

pin-y (pīn'ĭ), *adj.* **1,** having many pines; **2,** pertaining to pines. Also, **pin'ey.**

pi-o-neer (pī''ō-nēr') *n.* **1,** one who goes before to prepare the way for another, as a settler in a frontier country; **2,** a soldier in an engineer corps whose special work is road building and repairing:—*v.i.* to prepare a way:—*v.t.* **1,** to take the lead in; **2,** to open up, as a road.

pi-ous (pī'ŭs), *adj.* **1,** showing reverence for God religious; devout; as, *pious* people; **2** done under pretense of religion; as, a *pious* fraud.—*adv.* **pi'ous-ly.**

¹pip (pĭp), *n.* a small seed, as of an apple or an orange.

²pip (pĭp), *n.* **1,** a disease of poultry; **2,** *Slang,* humorously, illness in general.

³pip (pĭp), *n.* one of the distinctive marks or spots on a playing card.

⁴pip (pĭp), *v.i.* [*p.t.* and *p.p.* pipped (pĭpt), *p.pr.* pip'ping], to cry like a chicken or a young bird.

pipe (pīp), *n.* **1,** any long, hollow tube; as, iron *pipe;* **2,** a tube of clay, wood, etc., with a bowl at one end for smoking tobacco, opium, etc.; **3,** as much as the bowl of a pipe will hold: **4,** a wine measure of varying capacity, in England equal to two hogsheads, or 105 imperial gallons, or 126 wine gallons; **5** a high-pitched voice; as, the *pipe* of a child; **6** the note or call of a bird or insect; **7,** a musical wind instrument consisting of a hollow tube, as a flute, **8,** one of the graduated tubes in which the notes of some organs, called *pipe organs,* are produced **9,** in *pl.,* the bagpipe:—*v.t.* [*p.t.* and *p.p.* piped (pīpt), *p.pr.* pip'ing], **1** to play on a musical wind instrument; as, to *pipe* a tune **2** to utter in a high key; as, to *pipe* a song **3** to furnish with pipes, or tubes; as to *pipe* a house for water, **4,** to carry through a tube; as to *pipe* water into a city; **5,** to trim, as a dress, with a fold or cord on certain edges:—*v.i.* **1,** to play on a pipe; **2,** to utter a shrill sound **3,** to whistle.

pipe clay grayish white clay, used for making pipes and in various industrial processes.

pip-er (pīp'ẽr), *n.* one who plays the flute, Panpipe, or the like; esp., one who plays Scottish bagpipes.

pi-pette (pĭ-pĕt'), *n.* a small tube of glass or metal, used for transferring liquids from one vessel to another.

pip-ing (pīp'ĭng), *p.adj.* **1,** feeble; weak; shrill; **2,** playing upon a musical instrument called a pipe; **3,** hissing: used to intensify the adjective *hot:* as, *piping* hot dishes; **4** like the quiet music of the pipe, rather than the loud sounds of brass and drums; as, the *piping* times of peace:—*n.* **1,** the music of a pipe or the act of producing it: **2,** a system of tubes for drainage, gas, etc.; **3** a fold of material used in trimming dresses.

pip-it (pĭp'ĭt), *n.* a small bird, similar to the lark, which sings as it flies.

pip-kin (pĭp'kĭn), *n.* **1,** a small earthen jar or pot; **2,** a small wooden tub.

pip-pin (pĭp'ĭn), *n.* any one of several varieties of apple.

pip-sis-se-wa (pĭp-sĭs'ē-wȧ), *n.* any of various evergreen plants the leaves of which are used as a tonic.

pi-quant (pē'kănt), *adj.* **1,** agreeably sharp to the taste; as, *piquant* fruit; **2,** agreeably keen or clever in manner or speech; humorously charming, as a smile; **3,** sharp or cutting to the feelings; as, *piquant* criticism.—*adv.* **pi'quant-ly.**—*n.* **pi'quan-cy.**
Syn. tart, pungent, spicy.

pique (pēk), *n.* slight anger or resentment; wounded pride:—*v.t.* [*p.t.* and *p.p.* piqued (pēkt), *p.pr.* pi'quing], **1,** to wound the pride of; irritate; displease; **2,** to pride or value (oneself); as, to *pique* oneself on doing something very well; **3,** to stir or prick; as, to *pique* the curiosity.
Syn., n. displeasure, irritation, vexation.

pi-qué (pē-kā'), *n.* a heavy ribbed or figured cotton cloth.

pi-quet (pē-kĕt'; pĭk'ĕt), *n.* a card game for two persons using 32 cards.

pi-ra-cy (pī'rȧ-sĭ), *n.* [*pl.* piracies (-sĭz)], **1,** robbery upon the high seas; **2,** the using, without permission, of another's literary work for profit.

pi-rate (pī'rāt), *n.* **1,** a robber on the high seas; **2,** hence, anyone using lawless methods in gaining something; esp., one who uses another's literary work for profit without permission or claims it as his own product; **3,** a ship engaged in robbery on the high seas:—*v.t.* and *v.i.* [*p.t.* and *p.p.* -rat-ed, *p.pr.* -rat-ing], **1,** to rob at sea; **2,** to take and publish (a literary work) without permission or payment.—*adj.* **pi-rat'ic; pi-rat'i-cal.**—*adv.* **pi-rat'i-cal-ly.**

pi-rogue (pĭ-rōg'), *n.* **1,** a canoe made of a dug-out log; **2,** any boat resembling a canoe in shape.

pir-ou-ette (pĭr''ōō-ĕt'), *n.* a whirling or turning about on the toes: a quick turn of a horse on a given point:—*v.i.* [*p.t.* and *p.p.* -et'ted, *p.pr.* -et'ting], to whirl or turn rapidly in one spot.

pis-ca-to-ry (pĭs'kȧ-tō-rĭ), *adj.* **1,** pertaining to fishes or fishing; **2,** living by fishing. Also, **pis''ca-to'ri-al.**

Pis-ces (pĭs'ēz), *n.pl.* **1,** an equatorial constellation, the Fishes; **2,** the 12th sign of the zodiac, entered by the sun February 19 (see *zodiac,* illus.).

pis-ci-cul-ture (pĭs'ĭ-kŭl''tūr), *n.* the artificial breeding and rearing of fishes.—*adj.* **pis''ci-cul'tur-al.**

pish (pĭsh), *interj.* an exclamation of contempt or disgust:—*v.i.* to scoff.

pis-ta-chi-o (pĭs-tā'shĭ-ō; pĭs-tä'shĭ-ō; -shō), *n.* [*pl.* pistachios (-shĭ-ōz; -shōz)], **1,** a nut, the greenish kernel of which is used for flavoring; **2,** a small tree of Asia and southern Europe that bears the nut.

pis-til (pĭs'tĭl), *n.* in botany, the seed-bearing organ in the center of a flower (see *flower,* ²*style,* illus.).

pis-til-late (pĭs'tĭ-lāt), *adj.* in botany, having pistils; specif., having pistils but no stamens.

pis-tol (pĭs'tŭl), *n.* a small, short gun intended for use with one hand; a revolver (see illus. next page).

pis-tole (pĭs-tōl'), *n.* formerly, a Spanish gold coin of varying value: usually worth about $4.00.

pis-ton (pĭs'tŭn), *n.* a small, solid cylinder of metal or wood, fitting exactly and moving up and down in a tube, such as the barrel of a pump, or the cylinder of an engine: **piston rod,** a rod fastened to the center of the piston in a steam engine or pump, which either transfers the motion of the piston to the driving wheels or other machinery, or itself makes the piston move, as in the pump.

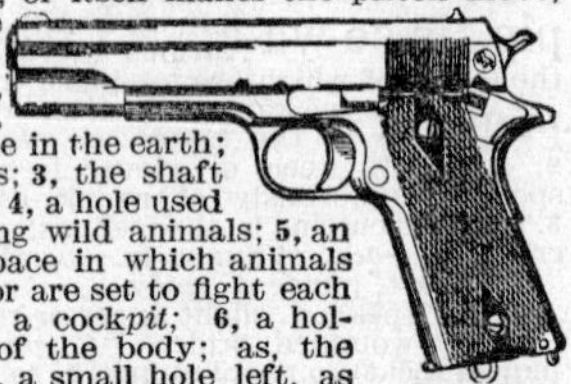

AUTOMATIC PISTOL

¹pit (pĭt), *n.* **1,** a deep hole in the earth; **2,** an abyss; **3,** the shaft of a mine; **4,** a hole used for trapping wild animals; **5,** an inclosed space in which animals are kept, or are set to fight each other; as, a cock*pit;* **6,** a hollow part of the body; as, the arm*pit;* **7,** a small hole left, as by smallpox; **8,** Hades; hell: with *the;* **9,** in England, the ground floor of a theater; also, the people who occupy seats on the ground floor; **10,** any of the special sections in a board of trade, stock exchange, or the like, set aside for trade in corn, wheat, etc.:—*v.t.* [*p.t.* and *p.p.* pit'ted, *p.pr.* pit'ting], **1,** to mark with small hollows or holes; **2,** to match or set to fight against another; as, to *pit* one's strength against an enemy; **3,** to place in a pit.

²pit (pĭt), *n.* in the U. S., the kernel of certain fruits, as the peach.

pit-a-pat (pĭt'ȧ-păt''), *adv.* with quick beating; flutteringly; as, my heart went *pitapat:*—*n.* a succession of light, quick sounds or taps.

¹pitch (pĭch), *n.* a thick, tenacious, black substance, soft when heated, left as a residue of coal tar after the volatile constituents have been driven off by distillation, or obtained as a residue in the distillation of turpentine: used chiefly as a waterproofing material, to fill seams in ships, for roofing, and in medicinal ointments: commonly called *tar:* **pitch dark,** absolutely dark:—*v.t.* to cover or smear with pitch.

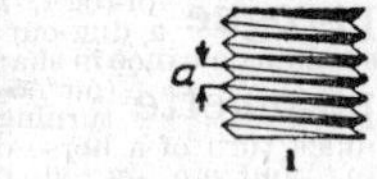

PITCH.—1, thread pitch (*a*).—2, gear pitch; *aa,* pitch circle; *b, c,* centers of gear teeth.—3, roof pitch: measured variously, as by angle *a,* or by ratio $\frac{CB}{AB}$. If rafter length, AB, is three fourths of span, AD, making ABD nearly a right angle, roof is said to have common, or true, pitch.

²pitch (pĭch), *v.t.* **1,** to fix in or on the ground; as, to *pitch* a tent; **2,** to fit, or set in order; arrange: usually in the past participle; as, a *pitched* battle; **3,** to place or fix at a particular level; as, *pitch* your voice low; **4,** to throw or fling; **5,** in music, to determine the key of; start, as a tune, by sounding the keynote:—*v.i.* **1,** to alight; **2,** to fall headlong; as, to *pitch* forward; **3,** to encamp; **4,** to fix the choice with *upon;* **5,** to rise alternately forward and aft, as a ship in heavy seas; to toss; **6,** in baseball, to throw the ball to the batsman; act as pitcher; **7,** in golf, to make an elevated approach stroke to a green: **pitch into,** to attack:—*n.* **1,** a plunging forward or down; as, a headlong *pitch* from a rock; **2,** the act or manner of throwing or tossing; a cast; **3,** a tossing motion, as of a ship in a storm; **4,** that which is thrown or tossed; **5,** degree or rate; as, the highest *pitch* of excitement; **6,** the tone of a voice; **7,** the distance between two successive threads of a screw; **8,** the distance, measured on the pitch line, between the centers of two successive gear teeth; **9,** slope; as, the *pitch* of a roof; **10,** in cricket, the space between the wickets; **11,** in music: **a,** the elevation or depression of a tone in its relation to other tones, dependent upon the number of regular vibrations per second; **b,** the place of a tone in the musical scale; **c,** the standard number of tonal vibrations accepted as a basis for tuning instruments: of two principal grades, *international pitch,* giving middle C 261 vibrations, and *concert pitch,* giving middle C 270 vibrations: **pitch line,** in mechanics, a line on which is measured the distance from center to center of gear teeth (see illus. first column): in a circular gear called *pitch circle.*

pitch-blende (pĭch'blĕnd''), *n.* a lustrous black mineral, a source of radium and uranium.

¹pitch-er (pĭch'ẽr), *n.* one who throws or casts; specif., in baseball, the player who throws the ball to the batter.

²pitch-er (pĭch'ẽr), *n.* a vessel, usually with an open spout and a handle, used to hold or pour liquids.

pitch-er plant any of several plants whose leaves are formed in the shape of a pitcher.

pitch-fork (pĭch'fôrk''), *n.* a pronged fork for tossing hay, straw, etc.:—*v.t.* to toss with, or as with, a pitchfork.

pitch pipe a small pipe, sounded by the mouth, giving a standard musical note: used in tuning instruments, setting a pitch for singers, etc.

pitch wheel one of two toothed wheels that mesh together; a gear wheel (see *gear,* illus.).

pitch-y (pĭch'ĭ), *adj.* **1,** like, or smeared with, the substance called pitch; **2,** dark; black; dismal.—*n.* **pitch'i-ness.**

pit-e-ous (pĭt'ē-ŭs), *adj.* exciting sorrow or sympathy; mournful; sad.—*adv.* **pit'e-ous-ly.**—*n.* **pit'e-ous-ness.**

Syn. miserable, wretched. (See pitiful.)

pit-fall (pĭt'fôl''), *n.* **1,** a hole lightly covered, so that animals may fall into it; a trap; **2,** any unsuspected source of danger or temptation.

pith (pĭth), *n.* **1,** the soft, spongy substance in the center of the stem of some plants; **2,** the marrow in a bone; **3,** energy or force; vigor; as, he lacks *pith;* **4,** gist, substance; as, the *pith* of his speech.—*adj.* **pith'less.**

pith-y (pĭth'ĭ), *adj.* [*comp.* pith'i-er, *superl.* pith'i-est], **1,** of the nature of, or full of, the soft, spongy substance called pith; **2,** forcible; full of meaning; as, a *pithy* saying.—*adv.* **pith'i-ly.**—*n.* **pith'i-ness.**

pit-i-a-ble (pĭt'ĭ-ȧ-bl), *adj.* **1,** deserving sympathy; as, he was in a *pitiable* condition; **2,** contemptible.—*adv.* **pit'i-a-bly.**—*n.* **pit'i-a-ble-ness.**

Syn. sorrowful, sad. (See pitiful.)

pit-i-ful (pĭt'ĭ-fo͝ol), *adj.* **1,** miserable; sad; as, a *pitiful* sight; **2,** compassionate; **3,** insignificant or small; as, a *pitiful* amount; **4,** contemptible; as, a *pitiful* ambition.—*adv.* **pit'i-ful-ly.**—*n.* **pit'i-ful-ness.**

Syn. piteous, pitiable. *Pitiful* is used of something that calls for pity because it is helpless or pathetic; as, a *pitiful* case of neglect; it may also connote contempt; as, a *pitiful* attempt may be inadequate rather than pathetic. That which is *piteous* arouses pity because of need; as, a *piteous* cry. *Pitiable*, like *pitiful*, is sometimes applied to something deserving pity; as, a *pitiable* plight.

pit-i-less (pĭt′ĭ-lĕs), *adj.* without sympathy or mercy; as, war is *pitiless*.—*adv.* **pit′i-less-ly.**—*n.* **pit′i-less-ness.**

Syn. cruel, harsh, relentless.

pit-tance (pĭt′ăns), *n.* a small allowance, esp. of money; a dole.

pit-ted (pĭt′ĕd), *p.adj.* marked with small hollows; as, *pitted* with smallpox.

pit-y (pĭt′ĭ), *n.* [*pl.* pities (-ĭz)], **1**, a feeling of sorrow for the suffering or distress of others; mercy; **2**, a reason for regret or grief:—*v.t.* [*p.t.* and *p.p.* pit′ied (-ĭd), *p.pr.* pit′y-ing], to sympathize with; feel sorry for.

Syn., *n.* compassion. (See sympathy.)

piv-ot (pĭv′ŭt), *n.* **1**, a fixed pin or short shaft on which some object, as a ball or wheel, turns; **2**, some event on which an important happening hinges:—*v.t.* to place on, or supply with, a pivot:—*v.i.* to turn on, or as on, a pivot.

pix (pĭks), *n.* in the Roman Catholic Church, the box in which the Host, or consecrated wafer, is kept. See **pyx**, *Pfd. S.*

pix-y (pĭk′sĭ), *n.* [*pl.* pixies (-sĭz)], in old folk tales, a fairy. Also, **pix′ie.**

pla-ca-ble (plā′kȧ-bl; plăk′ȧ-), *adj.* easily calmed or pacified; willing to forgive; yielding.—*adv.* **pla′ca-bly.**—*n.* **pla″ca-bil′i-ty.**—*n.* **pla′ca-ble-ness.**

plac-ard (plăk′ärd; plȧ-kärd′), *n.* a printed bill or notice posted in a public place, as an advertisement; a poster:—*v.t.* (plȧ-kärd′; plăk′ärd), **1**, to advertise by a bill posted publicly; **2**, to post, as a bill or notice.

pla-cate (plā′kāt; plăk′āt), *v.t.* [*p.t.* and *p.p.* -cat-ed, *p.pr.* -cat-ing], to cause to change from anger to friendliness or kindness; pacify; appease; make friendly.

place (plās), *n.* **1**, orig., an open space, as a public square, in a town or city; sometimes, a part of a street; **2**, a particular location; a special spot or locality, as a town or a residence; **3**, a building devoted to a special purpose; as, a *place* of business; **4**, the location of a given body; as, to get out of *place;* room to stand or sit in; as, a *place* in line; save a *place* for me; **5**, rank; social position; esp., high rank; **6**, duty; rightful responsibility; as, it is your *place* to do it; **7**, a position; job; as, a *place* as a clerk; **8**, in a race, a position among those competitors who have scored, either in money or in points; as, the American runners did not get a *place;* **9**, a passage in writing or in a book; as, I have lost my *place;* **10**, position in order; as, in the first *place;* **11**, in arithmetic, the position occupied by a figure in relation to the other figures of a series: **place kick**, in football, a play in which the ball is kicked after being placed on the ground:—*v.t.* [*p.t.* and *p.p.* placed (plāst), *p.pr.* plac′ing], **1**, to put in a particular spot or position; **2**, to put in office or authority; **3**, to invest; arrange for, as a loan; **4**, in baseball, cricket, tennis, etc., to bat or strike (the ball) to a point out of reach of the opposing players; **5**, to identify by connecting with some place, circumstance, etc.; **6**, to put; repose, as faith or trust; **7**, in a horse race, to state the place of (a horse) at the finish.

pla-cen-ta (plȧ-sĕn′tȧ), *n.* [*pl.* placentas (-tȧz); placentæ (-tē)], **1**, in higher mammals, a disk-shaped, vascular organ developed in the pregnant uterus, its function being to absorb nourishment for the fetus; **2**, that part of the ovary of seed plants that bears the ovules, or rudimentary seeds.

plac-er (plăs′ẽr), *n.* a place where loose surface soil contains gold or other valuable minerals.

plac-id (plăs′ĭd), *adj.* calm; peaceful; mild; as, a *placid* disposition.—*adv.* **plac′id-ly.**—*n.* **pla-cid′i-ty.**—*n.* **plac′id-ness.**

Syn. gentle, serene, tranquil. (See calm.)

plack-et (plăk′ĕt), *n.* an opening or slit in the upper part of a skirt or petticoat to make it easy to put on.

pla-gi-a-rism (plā′jĭ-ȧ-rĭzm; plā′jȧ-rĭzm), *n.* **1**, the act of stealing and using another's ideas, words, etc.; literary theft; **2**, the writing or other matter that is stolen and used.

pla-gi-a-rist (plā′jĭ-ȧ-rĭst; plā′jȧ-rĭst), *n.* one who steals and uses another's ideas, words, etc., as his own.

pla-gi-a-rize (plā′jĭ-ȧ-rīz; plā′jȧ-rīz), *v.t.* and *v.i.* [*p.t.* and *p.p.* -rized (-rīzd), *p.pr.* -riz″ing], to steal and use (another's ideas, words, etc.) as one's own.

pla-gi-a-ry (plā′jĭ-ȧ-rĭ; plā′jȧ-rĭ), *n.* [*pl.* plagiaries (-rĭz)], **1**, a plagiarist; **2**, plagiarism; literary theft.

plague (plāg), *n.* **1**, a deadly disease; **2**, anything very troublesome or causing misery; **3**, *Colloq.*, a nuisance:—*v.t.* [*p.t.* and *p.p.* plagued (plāgd), *p.pr.* pla′guing], **1**, to afflict with disease or evil; **2**, to trouble or annoy greatly.—*adj.* **pla′guy.**

Syn., *v.* harass, torment, vex, disturb.

plaice (plās), *n.* **1**, a European flatfish, or flounder; **2**, in America, any of various flatfishes, esp. the summer flounder.

plaid (plăd; *Scot.* plād), *n.* **1**, a crossbarred or checkered woolen cloth; **2**, a garment made of a large rectangle of such material, worn by the Highlanders of Scotland; **3**, any material with such a pattern:—*adj.* having a pattern of stripes crossing at right angles.

1**plain** (plān), *adj.* **1**, level; flat; even; smooth; plane; **2**, clear; evident; as, in *plain* sight; **3**, easily understood; as, your meaning is *plain;* **4**, unlearned; unpolished; simple in manners; as, a *plain*, blunt man; **5**, frank; sincere; as, I will be *plain* in my criticism; **6**, not luxurious; as, *plain* living; **7**, without ornament; as, *plain* furniture; **8**, all of one color; as, a dress of *plain* material; **9**, without beauty; homely; as, a *plain* but pleasant face: **plain clothes**, the dress of the ordinary civilian, as distinguished from a uniform; as, a police officer in *plain clothes:* **plain dress, plain language**, the sober clothing, and the use of *thou, thy*, and *thee* in common conversation, characteristic of the Society of Friends:—*adv.* clearly:—*n.* **1**, a wide stretch of level land; any flat expanse; **2**, in *pl.*, great tracts of level country without trees: **The Plains**, in North America, the wide stretch of level land extending from the Mississippi and Missouri rivers to the Rocky Mountains.—*adv.* **plain′ly.**—*n.* **plain′ness.**

Syn., *adj.* obvious, apparent, open, intelligible.—*Ant.*, *adj.* obscure, indistinct, vague.

plains-man (plānz′măn), *n.* [*pl.* plainsmen (-mĕn)], a dweller in wide, open, level country.

plain song an ancient setting of the service of the church to a chant in unison without accompaniment.

plaint (plānt), *n.* **1**, the utterance of grief aloud; **2**, a complaint.

plain-tiff (plān′tĭf), *n.* one who begins a suit in a court of law.

plain-tive (plān′tĭv), *adj.* expressing grief or sorrow; mournful; sad.—*adv.* **plain′tive-ly.**—*n.* **plain′tive-ness.**

plait (plāt; plēt; plăt), *n.* **1**, a flattened fold made by doubling cloth over upon itself; a pleat; **2**, (plăt), a braid, as of hair:—*v.t.* **1**, to double over in folds; pleat; **2**, to braid or interweave; **3**, to form by braiding.

plan (plăn), *n.* **1**, a drawing on a flat surface, showing the parts of anything;

as, the *plan* of a building, etc.; **2**, the arrangement of parts according to a fixed design; **3**, a method of procedure; **4**, a scheme or project: —*v.t.* [*p.t.* and *p.p.* planned (plănd), *p.pr.* plan'ning], **1**, to make a sketch of; form in design; outline; **2**, to arrange beforehand:—*v.i.* to scheme; arrange beforehand.—*n.* **plan'ner.**

Syn., *n.* design, purpose, intention, intent. A *plan* is the detailed method by which any scheme is to be carried out. A *design* is an idea of something to be done; it includes the thing itself and the method of accomplishing it with the means at hand. A *purpose* is a thing resolutely and definitely proposed to the mind; its accomplishment depends on the proposer. An *intention* is a purpose, but it may be vague as well as definite, and circumstances as well as character may affect its outcome. *Intent* is a more formal term than *intention*, and is used as a legal and poetical word.

plan-chette (plăn-shĕt'; plăn-chĕt'), *n.* a heart-shaped board resting on three supports, one of them a pencil which traces marks as it moves over a paper when the hands of two persons rest lightly on the board.

1**plane** (plān), *n.* a carpenter's tool for smoothing wood (see *tool*, illus.): —*v.t.* [*p.t.* and *p.p.* planed (plānd), *p.pr.* plan'ing], to make smooth or even with such a tool:—*v.i.* to work with a plane.

2**plane** (plān), *adj.* **1**, flat; level; even; without irregularities of surface; **2**, in geometry, lying wholly in a plane; as, a *plane* curve:—*n.* **1**, a surface such that if any two points in it are joined by a straight line, the line will lie wholly in the surface; **2**, any flat or even surface; **3**, a grade or level; **4**, one of the flat supporting surfaces of an airplane.

3**plane** (plān), *n.* any of several large trees with broad, spreading leaves, including the American sycamore, or buttonwood: also called *plane tree*.

4**plane** (plān), *v.i.* [*p.t.* and *p.p.* planed (plānd), *p.pr.* plan'ing], to rise partly out of the water while moving, in the manner of a hydroplane.

plan-er (plān'ẽr), *n.* a machine for smoothing the surface of wood or metal.

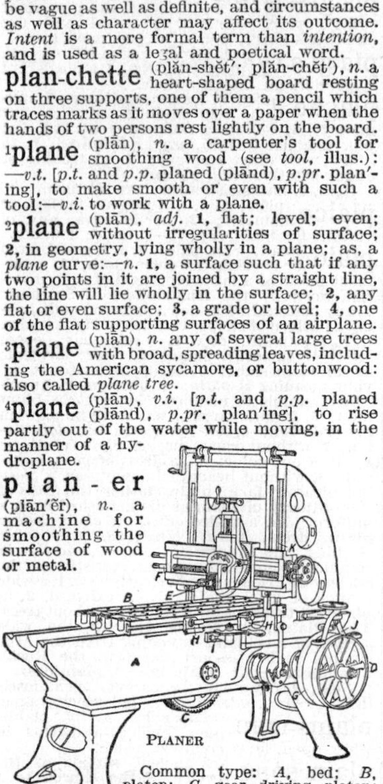

PLANER

Common type: *A*, bed; *B*, platen; *C*, gear driving platen; *D*, driving pulley; *E*, tool head; *F*, cross-feed screw; *G*, return pulley; *H*, *H*, reversing dogs; *I*, belt-shifting lever; *J*, belt shifters; *K*, vertical guide.

plan-et (plăn'ĕt), *n.* any one of the larger celestial bodies of the solar system, revolving round the sun in a nearly circular orbit and shining by reflected light: distinguished from the stars (see *solar system*, illus.).

plan-e-ta-ri-um (plăn''ē-tā'rĭ-ŭm), *n.* [*pl.* planetaria (-ȧ)], a contrivance to show the planets, their motions round the sun, and their relative distances and size; an orrery.

plan-et-a-ry (plăn'ĕt-ā-rĭ), *adj.* **1**, pertaining to a planet or the planets; **2**, moving about like a planet; wandering.

plan-et-oid (plăn'ĕt-oid), *n.* one of the group of small planets whose orbits lie between those of Mars and Jupiter; a minor planet: also called *asteroid*.

pla-nim-e-ter (plȧ-nĭm'ē-tẽr), *n.* an instrument by which the area of a plane surface, regular or irregular, may be measured.

plan-ish (plăn'ĭsh), *v.t.* **1**, in metal working, to polish or smooth by hammering; **2**, in woodworking, to make smooth.

plank (plăngk), *n.* **1**, a long, broad piece of sawed timber thicker than a board; **2**, a support; **3**, an item in the platform of a political party:—*v.t.* **1**, to cover with thick boards; **2**, *Colloq.*, to lay down, as on a plank; hence, to pay; as, to *plank* down money; **3**, to cook on a board; as, to *plank* shad.

plank-ing (plăngk'ĭng), *n.* **1**, sawed timber suitable for floors, walls, etc.; **2**, a bare, rough board floor or structure.

pla-no-con-cave (plā''nō-kŏn'kāv), *adj.* plane or flat on one side, and hollow and curved on the other, as a lens (see *lens*, illus.).

pla-no-con-vex (plā''nō-kŏn'vĕks), *adj.* plane or flat on one side, and convex or bulging on the other, as a lens (see *lens*, illus.).

plant (plănt), *n.* **1**, any vegetable organism; **2**, a sprout or sapling; **3**, the tools, machinery, fixtures, and sometimes buildings, of any trade or business; as, a manufacturing *plant;* **4**, the equipment of an institution, as a college or hospital:—*v.t.* **1**, to put into the ground for growth; as, to *plant* seed; **2**, to provide or prepare with seeds, roots, etc.; as, to *plant* a garden; **3**, to fix firmly, as in the mind; **4**, to establish, as a colony.

Plan-tag-e-net (plăn-tăj'ē-nĕt), *n.* one of the family to which belonged the kings of England from Henry II to Richard III (1154–1485).

1**plan-tain** (plăn'tăn; plăn'tĭn), *n.* a tropical, broad-leaved tree yielding an edible fruit like the banana.

2**plan-tain** (plăn'tăn; plăn'tĭn), *n.* any of several stemless herbs, esp. a common yard or roadside weed, having a rosette of broad leaves (see *inflorescence*, illus.).

plan-ta-tion (plăn-tā'shŭn), *n.* **1**, a place where anything is sowed or set in the ground and cultivated; as, a *plantation* of trees; an oyster *plantation;* **2**, a large estate where cotton, sugar, etc., are cultivated; **3**, a new settlement or colony.

plant-er (plăn'tẽr), *n.* **1**, a settler in a new colony; **2**, the owner or cultivator of a plantation; **3**, one who or that which sows or plants; a planting machine.

plan-ti-grade (plăn'tĭ-grād), *adj.* walking on the entire under part of the foot, as do men and the bears:—*n.* an animal that walks in this manner.

plant louse any of several small, juice-sucking, parasitic insects infesting plants; an aphid.

plaque (plȧk), *n.* a flat, thin piece of metal or earthenware upon which a picture or design is enameled or painted: used chiefly as a wall ornament.

1**plash** (plăsh), *v.t.* to splash or dash with water:—*v.i.* to splash:—*n.* **1**, the sound of splashing water; **2**, a quick fall of rain.—*adj.* 1**plash'y.**

2**plash** (plăsh), *v.t.* to bend down and interweave the branches or twigs of; as, to *plash* a hedge.

3**plash** (plăsh), *n.* a puddle; a small pool of water.—*adj.* 2**plash'y.**

plas-ma (plăz′mȧ), *n.* **1**, the liquid portion of various animal tissues; esp., the colorless watery part of the blood in which the corpuscles float; **2**, a grass-green stone used in jewelry.

plas-ter (plȧs′tẽr), *n.* **1**, a mixture of lime, sand, and water, with or without hair for binding, used for coating walls and partitions of buildings; **2**, a substance with medicinal properties, adhesive when softened by bodily heat, which is spread upon cloth and applied to some part of the body as a remedy; as, a porous *plaster;* **3**, plaster of Paris: **plaster board**, a thin board composed of plaster and paper in alternate layers, used in building: **plaster of Paris**, calcined gypsum or calcium sulphate, used, when mixed with water into a thin paste which soon hardens, for finishing walls, for making moldings, statuettes, casts, etc., and for filling cracks and cavities:—*v.t.* **1**, to overlay or cover with, or as with, a mixture of lime, sand, and water; as, to *plaster* the walls; **2**, to hide, as a defect, with, or as with, such a mixture; **3**, to treat with a cloth coated with a medicinal mixture.—*n.* **plas′ter-er.**

plas-ter-ing (plȧs′tẽr-ĭng), *n.* **1**, the act of putting on plaster or a plaster; **2**, a covering of lime, sand, and water for a wall, ceiling, etc.

plas-tic (plăs′tĭk), *adj.* **1**, capable of being formed or molded; as, clay is *plastic;* **2**, giving form to matter; as, *plastic* art; **3**, quick to receive impressions; as, a *plastic* mind; **4**, of, pertaining to, or characteristic of, molding or modeling: **plastic surgery**, surgery for the restoration of deformed and mutilated parts of the body.—*adv.* **plas′ti-cal-ly.**—*n.* **plas-tic′i-ty.**

plas-tics (plăs′tĭks), *n.* (*sing.*) an article fabricated by chemical synthesis; often molded easily by using heat and pressure, or made infusible and insoluble by chemical action; a group of products resembling and imitating natural ones: substitutes for glass, wood, leather, cloth, rubber, etc. (World War II).—*adj.* as a *plastics* part.

¹plat (plăt), *v.t.* [*p.t.* and *p.p.* plat′ted, *p.pr.* plat′ting], to braid; plait; as to *plat* one's hair:—*n.* a braid.

²plat (plăt), *n.* **1**, a small piece of ground; a plot; **2**, a plan, map, etc:—*v.t.* [*p.t.* and *p.p.* plat′ted, *p.pr.* plat′ting], to map.

plate (plāt), *n.* **1**, a thin piece or sheet of some substance, usually rigid, as metal; as, armor *plate;* **2**, a shallow dish from which food is eaten; also, as much as this dish will hold; **3**, a piece of metal on which something is engraved: as, a door *plate;* **4**, a print made from an engraved metal surface; also, the surface; **5**, in photography, a thin sheet of glass treated with chemicals, on which the picture is taken; **6**, household articles of gold or silver, as teapots, urns, etc.; **7**, metallic ware overlaid with gold or silver; **8**, a thin piece of rubber, metal, or the like, supporting artificial teeth; **9**, in baseball, the home base; **10**, in printing, a reproduction on a single sheet of metal of a section of composed type; **11**, in electricity: **a**, the anode of a vacuum tube; **b**, an electrode in a storage battery; **12**, a cut of beef from the lower part of the side (see *beef*, illus.); **13**, in architecture, a horizontal timber upon which the lower ends of the rafters are set (see *frame house*, illus.):—*v.t.* [*p.t.* and *p.p.* plat′ed, *p.pr.* plat′ing], **1**, to coat with metal; **2**, to cover with sheets of metal; **3**, in printing, to make an electrotype or a stereotype plate of.

pla-teau (plȧ-tō′), n. [*pl.* plateaus; plateaux (-tōz′)], **1**, a broad, elevated tract of flat land; table-land; **2**, on a military map, a flat surface on top of a hill.

plate glass a thick glass, rolled in plates, ground flat, and polished smooth on both sides.

plat-en (plăt′ĕn), *n.* **1**, a flat bed or plate of metal, as the moving part which holds the work in a planer (see *planer*, illus.), or the flat part of a printing press, which presses the paper against the type; **2**, the cylinder, or roller, of a typewriter, around which the paper is placed, and against which the type strikes.

plat-form (plăt′fôrm″), *n.* **1**, a floor raised above the ground or above the main floor; esp., a stage for public speaking; **2**, a political program or policy.

plat-ing (plāt′ĭng), *n.* **1**, the art of overlaying or covering anything with a thin sheet or coating of metal; **2**, a coating of metal or of thin metal sheets.

plat-i-num (plăt′ĭ-nŭm), *n.* a heavy, silver-white, precious metallic element, hard to melt and not affected by oxygen or most acids, but capable of being hammered or pressed thin: much used for chemical utensils and for jewelry. Also, formerly, **plat′i-na** (plăt′ĭ-nȧ; plȧ-tē′nȧ).—*adj.* **plat′i-nous.**

plat-i-tude (plăt′ĭ-tūd), *n.* **1**, commonplaceness, dulness, and flatness of speech; **2**, a stupid and trite remark.

Pla-ton-ic (plȧ-tŏn′ĭk), *adj.* pertaining to, or characteristic of, Plato, the ancient Greek philosopher, or his philosophy; academic: **Platonic love** or **friendship**, an affection between the sexes based solely on mental and spiritual attraction.

pla-toon (plȧ-to͞on′), *n.* a body of soldiers usually consisting of four squads of eight men each.

plat-ter (plăt′ẽr), *n.* a large flat dish for serving meat, poultry, etc.

plau-dit (plô′dĭt), *n.* applause; praise given; the act of praising or applauding, as by shouting or clapping.

plau-si-ble (plô′zĭ-bl), *adj.* **1**, seeming to be true without necessarily being so; having the appearance of truth, as, a *plausible* excuse; **2**, likely to win a confidence not wholly deserved; as, a *plausible* speaker.—*n.* **plau″si-bil′i-ty.**—*adv.* **plau′si-bly.**

Syn. apparent, specious, ostensible.

play (plā), *v.i.* **1**, to move lightly or capriciously; flicker, as a shadow, lightning, or leaves in the wind; **2**, to sport or frolic; exercise actively; **3**, to discharge or operate repeatedly; as, the fountain *plays* continually; **4**, to take part in a game; gamble; **5**, to perform on a musical instrument; **6**, to act on the stage; **7**, to behave; as, to *play* fair or false; **8**, to behave thoughtlessly; dally; trifle:—*v.t.* **1**, to amuse oneself with, as a game; take part in for amusement or as a contestant; also, to compete with in a game; as, he *played* his opponent for a high stake; **2**, to put into action in a game or contest, as by throwing (a ball) or laying (a card) on the table; **3**, to make believe; as, to *play* school; **4**, to perform; as, to *play* a comedy; *play* a waltz on a piano; also, to perform music on; as, to *play* the violin; **5**, to act in the character of; as, to *play* Othello; **6**, to work; set in action; as, to *play* a trick; *play* a hose on; **7**, to trifle with; treat frivolously; **8**, to maneuver; as, to *play* a fish:—*n.* **1**, brisk, lively, sometimes irregular, motion; as, the *play* of light and shade; the *play* of the waves; **2**, freedom or room to act; as, to give one's arm full *play* in throwing a ball; **3**, action or use; as, all their resources were brought into *play;* **4**, exercise, esp. in a contest of strength or skill; as, the *play* of a duelist's sword; also, exercise of mental powers; as, a *play* of fancy; **5**, an athletic or other contest; a game or sport; **6**, recreation; frolic; **7**, gambling; as, to lose money at *play;*

8, any single action in a game; as, with three *plays* more the game ended; also, one's turn to move a piece, lay down a card, etc., in a game; 9, fun; jest; as, she did it in *play;* 10, manner of dealing; as, fair *play;* 11, a drama intended for stage performance; also, the performance of a drama.

Syn., *n.* pastime, diversion. (See game.)

play-bill (plā'bĭl"), *n.* a placard advertising a dramatic performance; also, the program of a drama, with the names of the actors taking part.

play-er (plā'ẽr), *n.* 1, one who takes part in a game; as, a baseball *player;* 2, a musical performer; 3, an actor; 4, a gambler.

play-fel-low (plā'fĕl"ō), *n.* one who plays with another; a playmate.

play-ful (plā'fo͝ol), *adj.* sportive; lively; as, a *playful* kitten.—*adv.* **play'-ful-ly.**—*n.* **play'ful-ness.**

play-go-er (plā'gō"ẽr), *n.* one who habitually goes to the theater.

play-house (plā'hous"), *n.* 1, a theater; 2, a place for children's play.

play-ing card one of the cards of a pack used for playing games; esp., one of a pack of 52 cards divided into four suits: diamonds, hearts, spades, and clubs.

play-mate (plā'māt"), *n.* one who takes part in sports or games with another; a playfellow.

play-thing (plā'thĭng"), *n.* a means of amusement; a toy.

play-wright (plā'rīt"), *n.* a writer of dramas.

pla-za (plä'zȧ), *n.* an open square or market place surrounded by buildings.

plea (plē), *n.* 1, an excuse or apology; 2, an entreaty; as, a *plea* for mercy; 3, the defendant's answer to the charges in a lawsuit.

plead (plēd), *v.i.* [*p.t.* and *p.p.* plead'ed or pled (plĕd), *p.pr.* plead'ing], 1, to argue or reason in support of a cause against another; 2, to argue before a court of law; as, to *plead* for an acquittal; 3, to supplicate or beg earnestly; as, to *plead* for mercy:—*v.t.* 1, to discuss or defend by arguments; as, to *plead* a case; 2, to answer, as to a charge; as, to *plead* not guilty; 3, to offer as an excuse; as, to *plead* poverty.—*n.* **plead'er.**

Syn. urge, beseech, entreat.

plead-ings (plēd'ĭngz), *n.pl.* the written record of the statements made by the two parties in a lawsuit.

pleas-ance (plĕz'ăns), *n.* a quiet nook; a secluded pleasure ground near a large mansion.

pleas-ant (plĕz'ănt), *adj.* 1, grateful to the mind or senses; as, a *pleasant* smell; delightful; as, *pleasant* weather; agreeable; as, a *pleasant* fellow; 2, cheerful; lively; as, a *pleasant* time.—*adv.* **pleas'ant-ly.** —*n.* **pleas'ant-ness.**

Syn. pleasing, comfortable, merry, amiable. —*Ant.* disagreeable, unpleasant, troublesome.

pleas-ant-ry (plĕz'ănt-rĭ), *n.* [*pl.* pleasantries (-rĭz)], 1, merriment; gaiety; 2, a laughable speech or joke.

Syn. raillery, banter, playfulness.

please (plēz), *v.t.* [*p.t.* and *p.p.* pleased (plēzd), *p.pr.* pleas'ing], 1, to gratify; give enjoyment to; 2, to gain approval from; as, to *please* one's parents: —*v.i.* 1, to afford satisfaction or enjoyment; as, we strive to *please;* 2, to like or choose; as, to do as you *please.*

Syn. delight, charm, gladden.—*Ant.* offend, vex, dissatisfy, bore.

pleas-ing (plēz'ĭng), *p.adj.* giving satisfaction.—*adv.* **pleas'ing-ly.**

pleas-ur-a-ble (plĕzh'ûr-ȧ-bl), *adj.* delightful; gratifying; as, a *pleasurable* occasion.—*adv.* **pleas'ur-a-bly.**

pleas-ure (plĕzh'ûr), *n.* 1, that which delights; amusement; enjoyment; as, a day of *pleasure;* 2, a delight; a joy; as, it is a *pleasure* to see you; 3, choice; wish; as, what is your *pleasure?*

Syn. satisfaction, comfort, happiness.

pleat (plēt), *n.* a fold, as of cloth:—*v.t.* to fold, as cloth. See **plait,** *Pfd. S.*

pleb (plĕb), *n. Slang,* a plebeian, or one of the common people.

plebe (plēb), *n. U. S. Colloq.,* a member of the lowest class in the military academy at West Point or in the naval academy at Annapolis.

ple-be-ian (plē-bē'yăn; plē-bē'ăn), *adj.* 1, orig., pertaining to the common people of ancient Rome; 2, hence, common or vulgar:—*n.* 1, one of the common people of ancient Rome: contrasted with *patrician;* 2, any person of common breeding.—*n.* **ple-be'ian-ism.**

pleb-i-scite (plĕb'ĭ-sĭt; plĕb'ĭ-sīt), *n.* a direct vote of all the people on a measure submitted to them, as to determine a form of government.

plec-trum (plĕk'trŭm), *n.* [*pl.* plectra (-trȧ)], a small, flat, triangular piece of shell, ivory, or metal, sometimes used to strike the strings of certain stringed instruments, such as the mandolin and banjo.

pledge (plĕj), *n.* 1, anything placed as a security or guarantee; a pawn; 2, a drinking of a health as an expression of good will or a promise; 3, an agreement or promise to do or not to do something; 4, a token of good will; as, a *pledge* of friendship: —*v.t.* [*p.t.* and *p.p.* pledged (plĕjd), *p.pr.* pledg'ing], 1, to give as security or guarantee; as, to *pledge* one's honor; to put in pawn; as, he *pledged* his watch; 2, to bind by a promise; as, to *pledge* oneself to secrecy; 3, to drink to the health of.—*n.* **pledg'er.**

Ple-ia-des (plē'yȧ-dēz; plē'ȧ-dēz; plī'ȧ-dēz), *n.pl.* a cluster of small stars in the constellation Taurus: named from the seven daughters of Atlas, who were changed after death into stars.

Plei-o-cene (plī'ō-sēn), *adj.* designating, or pertaining to, the next to the last period of the Cenozoic era:—*n.* the Pleiocene period. See **Pli'o-cene,** *Pfd. S.*

Pleis-to-cene (plīs'tō-sēn), *adj.* designating, or pertaining to, the last period of the Cenozoic era, preceding the Recent:—*n.* the Pleistocene period, following the Pliocene, noted for its evidences of ancient human ancestry and for its worldwide glaciation: formerly known as *Quaternary:* also called *glacial period* or *ice age.*

ple-na-ry (plē'nȧ-rĭ; plĕn'ȧ-rĭ), *adj.* full; complete; as, *plenary* authority.

plen-i-po-ten-ti-a-ry (plĕn"ĭ-pō-tĕn'shĭ-ā-rĭ; plĕn"ĭ-pō-tĕn'shȧ-rĭ), *adj.* having full power; unlimited:—*n.* [*pl.* plenipotentiaries (-rĭz)], an ambassador or government agent to a foreign court, given full powers.

plen-i-tude (plĕn'ĭ-tūd), *n.* fulness; abundance.

plen-te-ous (plĕn'tē-ŭs), *adj.* abundant; amply sufficient; fruitful.—*adv.* **plen'te-ous-ly.**—*n.* **plen'te-ous-ness.**

plen-ti-ful (plĕn'tĭ-fo͝ol), *adj.* 1, yielding abundance; as, a *plentiful* harvest; 2, existing in great quantity.—*adv.* **plen'ti-ful-ly.**—*n.* **plen'ti-ful-ness.**

Syn. abundant, ample, bountiful, rich.

plen-ty (plĕn'tĭ), *n.* [*pl.* plenties (-tĭz)], 1, abundance; 2, sufficiency.

ple-o-nasm (plē'ō-năzm), *n.* the use of more words than are necessary; also, an instance of this.—*adj.* **ple"o-nas'tic.**—*adv.* **ple"o-nas'ti-cal-ly.**

pleth-o-ra (plĕth'ō-rȧ), *n.* **1**, the state of being too full; overabundance; excess; **2**, an unhealthy condition marked by an excess of blood.

ple-thor-ic (plē-thŏr'ĭk; plĕth'ō-rĭk), *adj.* **1**, having excess of blood; too full; **2**, hence, bloated; bombastic.

pleu-ra (plōō'rȧ), *n.* [*pl.* pleuræ (-rē)], a delicate membrane covering the inside of the chest and the outside of each lung.—*adj.* **pleu'ral.**

pleu-ri-sy (plōō'rĭ-sĭ), *n.* [*pl.* pleurisies (-sĭz)], inflammation of the pleura, or membrane lining the chest and covering the lungs.—*adj.* **pleu-rit'ic.**

pleu-ro-pneu-mo-ni-a (plōō"rō-nū-mō'nĭ-ȧ), *n.* **1**, inflammation of the pleura and of the lungs; **2**, pleurisy and pneumonia combined.

plex-us (plĕk'sŭs), *n.* [*pl.* plexus; plexuses (-ĕz)], a network, as of veins, nerves, etc.: **solar plexus, a knot of nerve** fibers behind the stomach.

pli-a-ble (plī'ȧ-bl), *adj.* **1**, easily bent; flexible; **2**, easily influenced; as, a *pliable* nature.—*n.* **pli'a-ble-ness.**—*adv.* **pli'a-bly.**—*n.* **pli"a-bil'i-ty.**

pli-ant (plī'ănt), *adj.* **1**, flexible; easily bent; as, a *pliant* twig; **2**, easily influenced.—*adv.* **pli'ant-ly.**—*n.* **pli'an-cy.**

pli-cate (plī'kāt), *adj.* plaited; folded in the form of a fan. Also, **pli'cat-ed.**

pli-ers (plī'ẽrz), *n. pl.* sometimes used as *sing.* small pincers for bending wire, or for holding small objects (see *tool*, illus.).

plight (plīt), *n.* a state or condition, usually an unfavorable or dangerous one; as, a sorry *plight.*

plight (plīt), *n.* a pledge or solemn promise:—*v.t.* **1**, to promise earnestly; pledge, as one's faith; **2**, to engage to marry; betroth.—*n.* **plight'er.**

plinth (plĭnth), *n.* **1**, the lowest, square-shaped part of the base of a column, pedestal, etc.; **2**, the projecting face at the bottom of a wall.

Pli-o-cene (plī'ō-sēn), *adj.* designating, or pertaining to, the next to the last period of the Cenozoic era:—*n.* the Pliocene period, just preceding the Pleistocene; the age of man: the last period in the age formerly called *Tertiary.* Also, **Plei'o-cene.**

plod (plŏd), *v.i.* [*p.t.* and *p.p.* plod'ded, *p.pr.* plod'ding], **1**, to walk slowly and heavily; as, to *plod* along; **2**, to drudge or toil; study laboriously:—*v.t.* to walk over heavily and slowly; as, to *plod* one's way.—*n.* **plod'der.**

plot (plŏt), *n.* **1**, a small area of ground; **2**, a drafted plan of a piece of land, an estate, or the like; a diagram; **3**, a scheme or plan; esp., a conspiracy; an intrigue; **4**, the plan or main story in a play, novel, etc.:—*v.t.* [*p.t.* and *p.p.* plot'ted, *p.pr.* plot'ting], **1**, to lay plans for; scheme; as, to *plot* a crime; **2**, to make a plan or map of; **3**, to locate or show on a map or chart:—*v.i.* to scheme; as, to *plot* against one's enemy.—*n.* **plot'ter.**

Syn., *v.* conspire, plan, contrive.

plov-er (plŭv'ẽr), *n.* a shore bird of various species.

plow (plou), *n.* **1**, a farming implement for turning up the soil in preparation for planting; **2**, any implement that works in a similar way; as, a snow*plow:*—*v.t.* to turn up with a plow; till:—*v.i.* **1**, to break or turn up soil with, or as with, a plow; **2**, to move onward by cutting a way through; as, the ship *plowed* on. Also, **plough.**—*n.* **plow'er.**

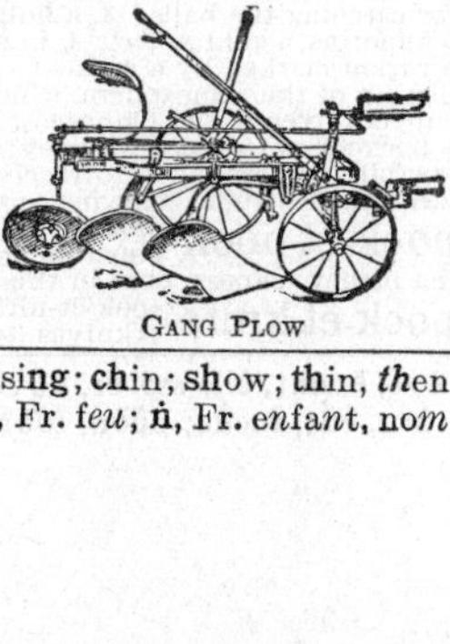

GANG PLOW

plow-boy (plou'boi"), *n.* **1**, a boy who guides the plow; also, a boy who leads the team in plowing; **2**, a country boy. Also, **plough'boy".**

plow-man (plou'măn), *n.* [*pl.* plowmen (-mĕn)], **1**, one who operates a plow; hence, a farmer; **2**, a rustic; countryman. Also, **plough'man.**

plow-share (plou'shâr"), *n.* the strong, steel blade of the plow, which cuts the soil. Also, **plough'share".**

pluck (plŭk), *v.t.* **1**, to pull off, out, or up; as, to *pluck* weeds; **2**, to pick or gather; as, to *pluck* grapes; **3**, to pull or twitch; as, to *pluck* the strings of a banjo; **4**, to strip completely, as of feathers; as, to *pluck* a goose:—*v.i.* to give a sudden pull; tug; as, the child *plucked* at her mother's skirt:—*n.* **1**, a pull; snatch; tug; **2**, that which is pulled or tugged; **3**, the heart, liver, and lungs of an animal; **4**, spirit; courage; as, a man of *pluck.*—*n.* **pluck'er.**

Syn., *n.* resolution, gameness. (See bravery.)

pluck-y (plŭk'ĭ), *adj.* [*comp.* pluck'i-er, *superl.* pluck'i-est], full of spirit; courageous.—*adv.* **pluck'i-ly.**

plug (plŭg), *n.* **1**, a piece of wood, rubber, metal, or the like, used to fill or stop a hole; **2**, a piece of conducting material inserted between conductors to make an electrical connection; **3**, a cake of pressed tobacco; **4**, a point in a water system where a hose may be attached; a fire hydrant:—*v.t.* [*p.t.* and *p.p.* plugged (plŭgd), *p.pr.* plug'ging], to stop or make tight with a piece of wood, cork, etc.

plum (plŭm), *n.* **1**, a tree somewhat like the peach and cherry, or its well-known fruit; **2**, something like this fruit in sweetness or shape; as, a sugar*plum;* **3**, a raisin when used in cooking; **4**, the choice or best part of a thing; a prize.

plum-age (plōōm'āj), *n.* **1**, a bird's feathers collectively; **2**, bright and ornamental costume.

plumb (plŭm), *n.* **1**, a small, heavy weight, fastened to a cord and suspended to indicate a vertical line: used for determining how nearly vertical is a piece of work done: also called *plumb bob;* **2**, a similar weight used to find the depth of water; plummet:—*adj.* **1**, perpendicular to, or at right angles with, the plane of the horizon; upright; **2**, *Colloq.*, out-and-out; absolute:—*adv.* **1**, perpendicularly; **2**, *Slang*, completely; entirely:—*v.t.* **1**, to test the verticalness of with a plumb line; **2**, to straighten; make vertical; as, to *plumb* up a wall; **3**, to sound (the depth of water) by a plummet; **4**, to test; solve; get to the bottom of; as, to *plumb* a mystery.

plum-ba-go (plŭm-bā'gō), *n.* graphite, a form of carbon used for lead pencils, in rubber manufacture, etc.

plumb bob the small, heavy weight that is attached to the end of a plumb line (see *tool*, illus.).

plumb-er (plŭm'ẽr), *n.* one who works in tin, lead, zinc, etc.; esp., one who supplies, repairs, or fits water-closets, water pipes, etc.

plumb-ing (plŭm'ĭng), *n.* **1**, the art or occupation of putting in or repairing the piping and other fittings for the water or gas supply or sewage disposal of a building; **2**, the pipes and fittings so installed.

plumb line **1**, a line from which hangs a weight, often of lead, to show whether something, as a wall, is straight up and down, or to sound the depth of water; **2**, a line straight up and down.

plume (ploo͞m), *n.* **1,** a long and beautiful feather or tuft of feathers; **2,** a feather worn as an ornament; crest; **3,** something like a feather in shape or lightness:—*v.t.* [*p.t.* and *p.p.* plumed (ploo͞md), *p.pr.* plum'ing], **1,** to pick and adjust (the feathers); as, a bird *plumes* its feathers; **2,** to adorn with feathers or with fine clothes: **plume oneself,** to boast; feel proud; as, to *plume* oneself on one's skill.—*adj.* **plum'y.**

plum-met (plŭm'ĕt), *n.* **1,** a weight attached to a plumb line, used for determining a vertical line, etc.; **2,** hence, a test, as of right conduct.

plu-mose (ploo͞'mōs; ploo͞-mōs'), *adj.* covered with feathers; feathery.

[1]**plump** (plŭmp), *adj.* well-filled or rounded out; as, a *plump* figure:—*v.i.* to grow round or full; as, her cheeks *plumped* out:—*v.t.* to cause to fill out or become round.—*adv.* **plump'ly.**—*n.* **plump'ness.**

[2]**plump** (plŭmp), *v.i.* to fall or sink down heavily and abruptly; as, to *plump* down into a chair:—*v.t.* to cause to fall heavily:—*adj.* blunt; direct; as, a *plump* contradiction:—*adv.* heavily; as, he fell *plump* into the water:—*n. Colloq.*, a sudden, heavy fall; also, the sound made by such a fall.

plu-mule (ploo͞'mūl), *n.* **1,** a plant bud which produces the stem and the first true leaves (see *germination,* illus.); **2,** a small or downy feather; a first feather.

plun-der (plŭn'dẽr), *n.* booty; pillage; as, the *plunder* of thieves:—*v.t.* to rob by open force, as in war; despoil:—*v.i.* to commit robbery.—*n.* **plun'der-er.**

plunge (plŭnj), *v.t.* [*p.t.* and *p.p.* plunged (plŭnjd), *p.pr.* plung'ing], **1,** to put suddenly into a liquid or other substance; **2,** hence, to place suddenly in an unexpected condition:—*v.i.* **1,** to sink, fall, or rush, as into water; dive; leap; **2,** to enter suddenly and quickly; as, to *plunge* into the woods; **3,** to move by throwing the body forward:—*n.* **1,** a sudden, abrupt dive, leap, or fall; **2,** motion by a sudden throwing forward of the body; **3,** a diving pool; **4,** in swimming events, a contest in diving for distance.

plung-er (plŭn'jẽr), *n.* **1,** one who takes sudden action; **2,** a diver; **3,** a cylinder used as the piston of a pump, the dasher of a churn, or the like.

plu-per-fect (ploo͞'pûr"fĕkt; ploo͞"pûr'fĕkt), *adj.* designating the tense that represents an event or action as completed before a given past time; past perfect (see *perfect*):—*n.* the pluperfect tense, or a verb form in this tense: formed in English by *had* with the past participle: also called *past perfect.*—*abbr.* **plup.; plupf.**

plu-ral (ploo͞'răl), *adj.* consisting of more than one:—*n.* in grammar, that form of a word expressing more than one.—*abbr.* **pl.; plur.**—*adv.* **plu'ral-ly.**

plu-ral-i-ty (ploo͞-răl'ĭ-tĭ), *n.* [*pl.* pluralities (-tĭz)], **1,** in U. S. politics, the number of votes cast for the leading candidate if he does not receive more than half the votes cast; also, the excess of such a leading candidate's votes over those of his nearest competitor; **2,** the majority.
Syn. (see majority).

plus (plŭs), *n.* **1,** a quantity to be added; **2,** the sign [+] used to denote addition; **3,** a positive quantity: **plus fours,** *Slang,* men's short trousers, of roomy cut, gathered by a band below the knee, well down the leg:—*adj.* **1,** designating the sign used to indicate addition; as, the *plus* sign; **2,** more, or increased (by a certain amount); **3,** above zero; positive, as a quantity; more than nothing.

plush (plŭsh), *n.* a kind of soft cloth with a pile or nap; woolen velvet.

Plu-to (ploo͞'tō), *n.* **1,** in Greek mythology the god of the underworld: usuall called *Hades;* **2,** in astronomy, a remote planet discovered in 1930 (see *solar system,* illus.).

plu-toc-ra-cy (ploo͞-tŏk'rȧ-sĭ), *n.* [*pl.* plutocracies (-sĭz)], **1,** rule o government by the rich; **2,** the wealthy class

plu-to-crat (ploo͞'tō-krăt), *n.* one wh exercises power or influenc because of his wealth.—*adj.* **plu"to-crat'ic.**

Plu-ton-ic (ploo͞-tŏn'ĭk), *adj.* **1,** pertainin to Pluto, or to the lower world **2,** pertaining to the subterranean region of fire **3,** in geology, formed by the action of hea far below the surface of the earth: said o certain igneous rocks. Also, **Plu-to'ni-an.**

plu-vi-al (ploo͞'vĭ-ăl), *adj.* **1,** showery **2,** in geology, resulting from th action of rain; as, a *pluvial* deposit.

plu-vi-om-e-ter (ploo͞"vĭ-ŏm'ē-tẽr), *n.* a instrument for measuring the quantity of rain which falls in a given place during a given time; a rain gauge.—*n* **plu"vi-om'e-try.**

[1]**ply** (plī), *v.t.* [*p.t.* and *p.p.* plied (plīd), *p.pr.* ply'ing], **1,** to work at steadily; as, t *ply* a trade; **2,** to use diligently or earnestly as, to *ply* an oar; **3,** to address insistently; as to *ply* a person with questions; urge; offe something persistently to; as, to *ply* one wit food:—*v.i.* **1,** to keep at work; **2,** to haste forth; **3,** to run regularly on a fixed cours between two ports or places, as does a boat be available for use, as porters, taxicabs, etc. **4,** of a ship, to shape a course to windward.

[2]**ply** (plī), *n.* [*pl.* plies (plīz)], **1,** a web, o layer, as in a carpet; a fold, turn, o twist: generally in composition; as, a three *ply* rug; **2,** a prejudice; bias.

ply-wood (plī'wo͝od"), *n.* two or mor layers, or plies, of wood glued together: used as a construction material.

pneu-mat-ic (nū-măt'ĭk), *adj.* **1,** pertaining to, consisting of, o containing, air; inflated with air, as a tire **2,** made to work by air pressure or vacuum, a a machine; **3,** having pneumatic tires: **pneumatic tire,** a rubber tire inflated with air **pneumatics,** *n.pl.* used as *sing.* the scienc that treats of the physical properties and characteristics of air and other gases. Also, *adj* **pneu-mat'i-cal.**—*adv.* **pneu-mat'i-cal-ly.**

pneu-mo-ni-a (nū-mō'nĭ-ȧ), *n.* inflammation of the tissues o the lungs, esp. in an acute, infectious form.—*adj.* **pneu-mon'ic.**

[1]**poach** (pōch), *v.t.* to cook (an egg) b breaking it into boiling water.

[2]**poach** (pōch), *v.t.* **1,** to catch by stabbing with a spear, as fish; **2,** to capture as game, by trespassing; also, to encroach o trespass on (another's property):—*v.i.* to trespass; obtain game unlawfully; hence, t obtain anything unfairly.—*n.* **poach'er.**

pock (pŏk), *n.* **1,** a slight swelling on th skin filled with pus, as in smallpox **2,** the scar left by such a swelling.

pock-et (pŏk'ĕt), *n.* **1,** a small pouch in garment, for carrying small articles; **2,** a small netted bag in a billiard tabl for catching the balls; **3,** a hole or opening i a mine; as, a gold *pocket;* **4,** in airplane travel a region marked by a sudden variation in th density of the atmosphere, which disturbs th support given to the planes:—*v.t.* **1,** to put int a pocket; as, to *pocket* money; **2,** to take un lawfully, as money; **3,** to receive and let pas (an insult) without showing any feeling.

pock-et-book (pŏk'ĕt-bo͝ok"), *n.* a sma pouch or folder for carry ing money, papers, etc., in the pocket.

pock-et-knife (pŏk'ĕt-nīf"), *n.* [*pl.* pock etknives (-nīvz")], a sma knife with blades that close into the handle, for carrying in the pocket.

pock-et mon-ey a small sum allowed for everyday personal expenses; spending money.

pock-mark (pŏk′märk″), *n.* a scar or small hole left by smallpox.

pod (pŏd), *n.* any seed vessel which dries and opens when ripe; esp., a legume, as that of the bean or pea:—*v.i.* [*p.t.* and *p.p.* pod′ded, *p.pr.* pod′ding], **1,** to swell or fill, as a pod; **2,** to produce pods.

podg-y (pŏj′ĭ), *adj.* [*comp.* podg′i-er, *superl.* podg′i-est], short and fat; dumpy.

po-em (pō′ĕm), *n.* **1,** a composition in verse, marked by beauty of thought and language; a piece of poetry; **2,** any imaginative piece of writing in beautiful language; **3,** something resembling such a composition in beauty; as, the cathedral was a *poem* in stone.

po-e-sy (pō′ē-sĭ), *n.* [*pl.* poesies (-sĭz)], the art of writing verses that express beautiful thoughts in beautiful words.

po-et (pō′ĕt), *n.* **1,** one who writes verses of lasting artistic value, possessing both beauty of thought and grace of language; **2,** any writer gifted with imagination and creative power.—*n.fem.* **po′et-ess.**

po-et-as-ter (pō′ĕt-ăs″tẽr; pō″ĕt-ăs′tẽr), *n.* a writer of inferior verses.

po-et-ic (pō-ĕt′ĭk), *adj.* **1,** pertaining to poetry; as, *poetic* language; **2,** pertaining to, or characteristic of, a poet; as, *poetic* genius; **3,** having the power to express beautiful ideas in beautiful verse or prose; as, a *poetic* writer; **4,** suitable for, or expressed in, poetry; as, a *poetic* scene: **poetics,** *n.pl.* used as *sing.* that branch of literary study which deals with poetry and its technique and criticism. Also, *adj.* **po-et′i-cal.**—*adv.* **po-et′i-cal-ly.**

po-et-ry (pō′ĕt-rĭ), *n.* **1,** that form of literary art which expresses lofty thought, feeling, or action in beautiful language; **2,** composition in verse as opposed to composition in prose.

***po-grom** (pō-grŏm′), [Russ.], *n.* in Russia, an officially organized riot and massacre directed against some special class of the population, often against the Jews.

poign-an-cy (poin′ăn-sĭ; poin′yăn-sĭ), *n.* the state or quality of being keen; sharpness; bitterness.

poign-ant (poin′ănt; poin′yănt), *adj.* **1,** severe; very painful; **2,** sharp and piercing.—*adv.* **poign′ant-ly.**

***poi-lu** (pwȧ″lü′), [Fr.], *n. Slang,* a French private soldier: a term first used in the World War.

poin-set-ti-a (poin-sĕt′ĭ-ȧ), *n.* a Mexican plant with large, handsome, bright red leaves that resemble flowers.

point (point), *n.* **1,** the sharp end of a thing; as, the *point* of a pin; also, something which has a sharp point; **2,** something which projects; esp., a tapering end of land; a cape; **3,** an outstanding physical feature or characteristic, esp. in an animal; **4,** that element in a speech, story, action, etc., which gives it force and application; as, you missed the *point* of the story; also, the essential question in a dispute; **5,** a speck or dot; esp., a mark of punctuation or a certain type of diacritical mark; **6,** a particular spot; exact place, time, or degree; as, to reach a certain *point* on a road; a critical *point* in history; the boiling *point;* **7,** a particular detail or item; as, an important *point* in a lesson; **8,** a particular aim or purpose; as, to gain one's *point;* **9,** lace made with the needle: also called *point lace;* **10,** a railway switch; **11,** in certain games, the unit of scoring: esp. used in athletic meets to give relative credit to winners, those placed second, etc.; **12,** in geometry, that which is considered as having position, but without length, breadth, or thickness; **13,** one of the 32 divisions of a compass, equal to one eighth of a right angle (see *compass card,* illus.); **14,** in printing, a unit of measurement for type, equal to approximately $\frac{1}{72}$ of an inch; **15,** a unit of fluctuation of the price of shares of stock: in the U. S., $1.00, except in certain food staples:—*adj.* made with the needle; as, *point* lace:—*v.t.* **1,** to sharpen; as, to *point* a pencil; **2,** to give liveliness or force to; show the purpose of; as, to *point* a moral; **3,** to show the direction of; as, to *point* the way; **4,** to direct or aim; as, to *point* a gun; **5,** to punctuate; **6,** to fill the joints of (masonry) with mortar and smooth with a trowel; **7,** to show the presence of (game) by assuming a certain position, as do some hunting dogs; **8,** to indicate; designate; direct attention to: usually with *out:*—*v.i.* **1,** to call attention by extending the finger: with *at* or *to;* **2,** to face; tend; be directed; **3,** to indicate the presence of game by assuming a certain position, as do some dogs.

point-blank (point″=blăngk′), *adj.* **1,** straight to the mark; as, a *point-blank* shot; **2,** direct and abrupt; without qualifications; as, a *point-blank* refusal:—*adv.* directly.

point-ed (poin′tĕd), *p.adj.* **1,** sharpened; having a sharp end, as a needle; **2,** direct; telling; personal; as, *pointed* remarks.—*adv.* **point′ed-ly.**—*n.* **point′ed-ness.**

point-er (poin′tẽr), *n.* **1,** one who or that which points, or shows position; **2,** the hand of a watch, etc.; **3,** a kind of dog trained to point, or to stop and show the place where game is hidden; **4,** *Colloq.,* a timely hint: **The Pointers,** two stars in the constellation of the Great Dipper, a line through which points nearly to the North Star.

point-ing (poin′tĭng), *n.* **1,** punctuation; **2,** the act of showing direction; **3,** the operation of filling in the joints of masonry with mortar; also, the finished work.

point-less (point′lĕs), *adj.* **1,** blunt; dull; **2,** having no real meaning.—*adv.* **point′less-ly.**—*n.* **point′less-ness.**
Syn. flat, insipid, inane, irrelevant.

poise (poiz), *n.* **1,** balance; **2,** the manner of carrying the head and body; **3,** mental balance; **4,** the condition of an object which remains in exact balance:—*v.t.* [*p.t.* and *p.p.* poised (poizd), *p.pr.* pois′ing], **1,** to balance; **2,** to weigh; **3,** to consider:—*v.i.* to hang balanced or suspended.

poi-son (poi′zn), *n.* **1,** a substance which, if received into the body, destroys life or health; **2,** a destructive influence:—*v.t.* **1,** to injure or kill by poison **2,** to fill or taint with poison; as, to *poison* food; **3,** to corrupt; as, to *poison* opinion.—*n.* **poi′son-er.**

poi-son i-vy any of several sumacs, esp. a common vine found growing over fences, on trees, and on the ground, bearing bluish white berries and glossy, dark green, compound leaves of three leaflets each, exuding an oil which, on contact, usually causes severe irritation to the human skin.

poi-son oak **1,** poison ivy; **2,** a low, erect species of sumac: also called *poison sumac.*

poi-son-ous (poi′zn-ŭs), *adj.* **1,** having qualities that injure or kill; deadly; **2,** morally corrupting.—*adv.* **poi′son-ous-ly.**—*n.* **poi′son-ous-ness.**

poi-son su-mac an American, swamp-inhabiting shrub with foliage highly poisonous to the skin, resembling the nonpoisonous sumac but bearing greenish white berries: also called *poison elder; poison dogwood.* Also, **poi′son su′mach.**

[1]**poke** (pōk), *n.* **1,** a bag or sack; as, a pig in a *poke;* **2,** formerly, a pocket.

[2]**poke** (pōk), *n.* a tall American herb with white flowers and purple berries: also called *pokeweed.*

[3]**poke** (pōk), *v.t.* [*p.t.* and *p.p.* poked (pōkt), *p.pr.* pok′ing], **1,** to thrust or push against, esp. with a pointed object; prod; **2,** to thrust in or out; as, to *poke* one's head out of the door:—*v.i.* **1,** to thrust or push; as, to *poke* at the fire; **2,** to move lazily; dawdle; **3,** to grope or feel about in the dark:—*n.* **1,** a thrust or push, esp. with something hard or sharp; **2,** a projecting rim on a woman's bonnet; also, the bonnet itself: also called *poke bonnet;* **3,** a wooden collar with a short, projecting pole, to prevent cattle from jumping fences; **4,** *Slang,* a slow, lazy person.

[1]**pok-er** (pōk′ẽr), *n.* a rod of metal used for poking or stirring fires, cleaning grates, and the like.

[2]**pok-er** (pōk′ẽr), *n.* any of several American card games in which the players place bets on their hands, the various combinations of cards having fixed values.

poke-weed (pōk′wēd″), *n.* a common herb; poke (which see).

pok-y (pōk′ĭ), *adj.* [*comp.* pok′i-er, *superl.* pok′i-est], slow; stupid.

po-lar (pō′lȧr), *adj.* **1,** pertaining to, or situated near, either end of the axis of the earth; as, the *polar* regions; **2,** pertaining to either of the poles of a magnet.

Po-la-ris (pō-lā′rĭs), *n.* the polestar, a star of the second magnitude in Ursa Minor, popularly thought of as being at the north pole of the heavens, but in reality about 1¼ degrees from it: also called *North Star.*

po-lar-i-ty (pō-lăr′ĭ-tĭ), *n.* **1,** the quality, possessed by magnets, electromagnets, etc., of having two opposite poles, or centers of attraction, each of which exerts a force opposite to that of the other, one called *positive,* the other *negative;* as, the *polarity* of the earth; **2,** the property possessed by electrified or magnetized bodies, by which they exert directly opposite forces in opposite directions, the positive pole attracting and the negative pole repelling.

po-lar-ize (pō′lȧr-īz), *v.t.* [*p.t.* and *p.p.* -ized (-īzd), *p.pr.* -iz″ing], to give polarity to; provide with two opposite poles.—*n.* **po″lar-i-za′tion.**

[1]**pole** (pōl), *n.* **1,** either of the two ends of the axis of a sphere; esp., either one of the extremities of the earth's axis; also, the territory lying about either of them; **2,** either of two opposed forces or principles of any sort; **3,** a region in a magnet, usually near one of the ends, where the greatest attractive force is manifested; **4,** in electricity, one of the terminals of a voltaic cell or other electrical generator which supply the electrical energy; **5,** one of the two points in which the axis of the earth, produced, pierces the celestial sphere, and about which the stars seem to revolve.

[2]**pole** (pōl), *n.* **1,** a long staff or rod; as, a bean *pole;* a fishing *pole;* **2,** a rod, or linear measure equal to 16½ feet, or 5½ yards: also called *perch;* also, a square rod, or square measure equal to 30¼ square yards; **3,** a measuring instrument:—*v.t.* [*p.t.* and *p.p.* poled (pōld), *p.pr.* pol′ing], to push with a long rod or staff; as, to *pole* a skiff.

Pole (pōl), *n.* a person born in Poland, or a citizen of Poland.

pole-cat (pōl′kăt″), *n.* **1,** a European catlike animal which throws out a strong, offensive odor: valued for its fur; **2,** in the U. S., a skunk.

po-lem-ic (pō-lĕm′ĭk), *n.* **1,** a paper written to support or dispute an opinion or argument; **2,** one who writes to support an opinion against another: **polemics,** *n. pl.* used as *sing.* the art or practice of disputation:—*adj.* supporting or disputing an opinion or argument. Also, *adj.* **po-lem′i-cal.**

pole-star (pōl′stär″), *n.* **1,** Polaris, a star nearly at the northern pole of the heavens: used as a guide by navigators and explorers; the North Star; **2,** hence, a guide; an ideal for action.

po-lice (pō-lēs′), *n.* **1,** in a city, town, or district, that part of the government that enforces the laws and keeps order; **2,** an organized body of officers for keeping order: **police dog,** a breed of dog developed, especially in Europe, by crossing dogs with wolves: often trained to assist police or to serve as watch dog or as playmate for children:—*v.t.* [*p.t.* and *p.p.* -liced′ (-lēst′), *p.pr.* -lic′ing], to watch, protect, or keep in order by means of regular officers.

po-lice-man (pō-lēs′măn), *n.* [*pl.* policemen (-mĕn)], a member of a regular force of officers employed by a state or city, whose duty it is to keep order and enforce the laws.—*n.fem.* **po-lice′-wom″an.**

[1]**pol-i-cy** (pŏl′ĭ-sĭ), *n.* [*pl.* policies (-sĭz)], **1,** management of public affairs; the art or method of government; **2,** a course of conduct; as, it is good *policy* not to meddle; **3,** action based on worldly advantage.

[2]**pol-i-cy** (pŏl′ĭ-sĭ), *n.* [*pl.* policies (-sĭz)], a document containing a contract of insurance; as, a life-insurance *policy.*

pol-i-o-my-e-li-tis (pŏl″ĭ-ō-mī″ĕ-lī′tĭs) *n.* an inflammation and wasting of the gray matter of the spinal cord, esp. an infectious form of this disease, also called *infantile paralysis,* which attacks children, causing a paralysis, sometimes permanent, of the arms and legs.

pol-ish (pŏl′ĭsh), *v.t.* **1,** to make smooth or glossy by rubbing; as, to *polish* silverware; **2,** to make polite or refined:—*v.i.* **1,** to become smooth or glossy; **2,** to become polite and refined:—*n.* **1,** the act of polishing; **2,** a smooth, glossy surface; as, the table has a high *polish;* **3,** a mixture for making a surface smooth and glossy; as, stove *polish;* **4,** elegance of manners.—*n.* **pol′ish-er.**

Syn., v. shine, rub, burnish, furbish.

Pol-ish (pōl′ĭsh), *adj.* pertaining to Poland, its language, or its people:—*n.* the language of the Poles.

po-lite (pō-līt′), *adj.* well-bred; refined in manner; courteous or obliging.—*adv.* **po-lite′ly.**—*n.* **po-lite′ness.**

Syn. courteous, genteel, civil. *Polite* describes a manner characterized not only by good breeding, but by sympathy and tact. *Courteous* is used of a politeness characterized by dignity, consideration, and deference. *Genteel* is now usually sarcastic in serious use; it is used of those who make crude attempts at elegance and refinement. *Civil* implies a mechanical and uninterested observance of the proprieties, which falls short of politeness.

pol-i-tic (pŏl′ĭ-tĭk), *adj.* **1,** prudent; shrewd; **2,** suitable; advisable, as a plan; **3,** crafty; cunning.—*adv.* **pol′i-tic-ly.**

Syn. discreet, diplomatic, cautious, sagacious, judicious.—*Ant.* impolitic, indiscreet.

po-lit-i-cal (pō-lĭt′ĭ-kăl), *adj.* **1,** pertaining to, or treating of, the science of government; as, *political* writers; **2,** relating to, advocating, or having, a particular system of government; **3,** pertaining to, or connected with, the management of public affairs; as, *political* reform; a *political* career; **4,** pertaining to those who engage in politics; as, *political* graft: **political economy,** the science that treats of wealth, its nature, pr duction, distribution, and consumption, and of the laws which regulate and govern these.—*adv.* **po-lit′i-cal-ly.**

pol-i-ti-cian (pŏl″ĭ-tĭsh′ăn), *n.* **1,** one who is skilled in the art of government; **2,** one who is occupied with the management of a system of government, esp. of the affairs of a special political party: often implying self-interest or improper methods.

pol-i-tics (pŏl′ĭ-tĭks), *n.pl.* **1,** used as *sing.*: **a,** the science or art of government; **b,** party management or control; **2,** used as *pl.* one's opinions on political questions.

pol-i-ty (pŏl′ĭ-tĭ), *n.* [*pl.* polities (-tĭz)], **1,** the form or constitution of the government of a state, church, etc.; **2,** any community under an organized government.

pol-ka (pōl′kȧ), *n.* **1,** a dance of Bohemian origin, performed by two persons; **2,** music suitable for such a dance.

poll (pōl), *n.* **1,** the head, esp. the back part of it; **2,** a number resulting from the counting of heads; hence, a list of persons, esp. those entitled to vote at elections; **3,** an election; **4,** the number of votes recorded at an election; **5,** usually in *pl.*, the place where votes are cast; **6,** a tax on each person: also called *poll tax*:—*v.t.* **1,** to lop, clip, or shear; as, to *poll* trees or sheep; **2,** to enroll, as for voting; **3,** to examine or record the votes of; as, to *poll* a jury; **4,** to receive votes; as, he *polled* a large majority; **5,** to cast or drop in a ballot box; as, to *poll* one's vote.—*n.* **poll′er.**

pol-lack (pŏl′ăk), *n.* a food fish of the cod family. Also, **pol′lock.**

pol-lard (pŏl′ẽrd), *n.* **1,** a tree having its upper branches cut off from the trunk, so that it may put out shoots; **2,** an animal that has lost its horns:—*v.t.* to cut off the branches or the horns of.

pol-len (pŏl′ĕn), *n.* the powdery substance produced by the anthers of a flower, which, when carried to the pistil, usually of another flower, acts as a fertilizing element (cf. *flower*, illus.).

pol-li-na-tion (pŏl″ĭ-nā′shŭn), *n.* the carrying of pollen, or dustlike powder, from the anther to the stigma of a flower, in order that seeds may be fertilized.

pol-li-wog (pŏl′ĭ-wŏg), *n.* the larva, or half developed young, of the frog; a tadpole. Also, **pol′ly-wog.**

poll tax a tax on each person, or head: also called *poll.*

pol-lute (pŏ-lūt′), *v.t.* [*p.t.* and *p.p.* -lut′ed, *p.pr.* -lut′ing], **1,** to make unclean; as, to *pollute* water with filth; **2,** to taint with guilt; corrupt.—*n.* **pol-lut′er.**

pol-lu-tion (pŏ-lū′shŭn), *n.* **1,** the act of making unclean; **2,** the state of being unclean; uncleanness; impurity.

Pol-lux (pŏl′ŭks), *n.* **1,** in mythology, son of Zeus and Leda: immortal twin brother of the mortal Castor, with whom he was allowed to share alternate life and death, both being later placed in the sky as the constellation Gemini: also called *Polydeuces;* **2,** in astronomy, the brightest star in the constellation Gemini, or the Twins.

POLO

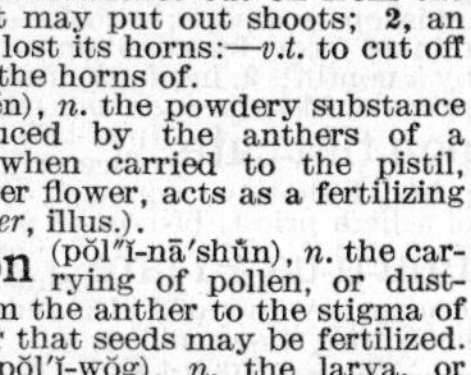

po-lo (pō′lō), *n.* a ball game similar to hockey, played on horseback.

po-lo-naise (pō″lō-nāz′; pŏl″ō-nāz′), *n.* **1,** in the 18th century, a garment consisting of a bodice and a skirt open at the front to show an elaborate petticoat; **2,** a stately Polish dance, or the music for it.

pol-troon (pŏl-trōōn′), *n.* a mean-spirited coward.—*n.* **pol-troon′er-y.**

pol-y- (pŏl′ĭ-), a prefix or combining form from the Greek, meaning many; as, *poly*gon; *poly*syllable.

pol-y-an-dry (pŏl″ĭ-ăn′drĭ; pŏl′ĭ-ăn″drĭ), *n.* the practice of having more than one husband at the same time: contrasted with *polygyny.*—*adj.* **pol″y-an′drous.**

pol-y-chro-mat-ic (pŏl″ĭ-krō-măt′ĭk), *adj.* **1,** many-colored; **2,** showing a play of colors.

po-lyg-a-mist (pō-lĭg′ȧ-mĭst), *n.* one who has more than one wife or husband at the same time.

po-lyg-a-mous (pō-lĭg′ȧ-mŭs), *adj.* pertaining to, or practicing, the custom of having more than one wife or husband at once.—*adv.* **po-lyg′a-mous-ly.**

po-lyg-a-my (pō-lĭg′ȧ-mĭ), *n.* the state or practice of having more than one wife or husband at the same time.

pol-y-glot (pŏl′ĭ-glŏt), *adj.* containing, or knowing, many languages:—*n.* **1,** a book, esp. a Bible, in several languages; **2,** one who speaks several languages.

pol-y-gon (pŏl′ĭ-gŏn), *n.* a closed figure having many sides and angles; specif., such a figure having five or more sides.—*adj.* **po-lyg′o-nal** (pō-lĭg′ō-năl).

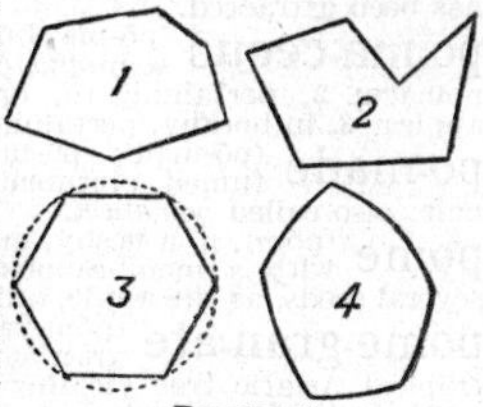

POLYGONS

1, convex; 2, concave; 3, regular; 4, curvilinear.

po-lyg-y-ny (pō-lĭj′ĭ-nĭ), *n.* the practice of having more than one wife at once: one form of polygamy: contrasted with *polyandry.* — *adj.* **po-lyg′y-nous.**

pol-y-he-dral (pŏl″ĭ-hē′drăl), *adj.* having many sides or faces. Also, **pol″y-hed′ric; pol″y-he′drous.**

pol-y-he-dron (pŏl″ĭ-hē′drŏn), *n.* [*pl.* polyhedrons (-drŏnz); polyhedra (-drȧ)], a solid figure bounded by four or more plane faces or surfaces.

Pol-y-hym-ni-a (pŏl″ĭ-hĭm′nĭ-ȧ), *n.* in mythology, the Muse who presided over oratory and sacred poetry, esp. the hymn. Also, **Po-lym′ni-a.**

pol-y-mor-phous (pŏl″ĭ-môr′fŭs), *adj.* **1,** capable of existing in more than one form, esp. in more than one crystalline form, as carbon, which exists as diamond and graphite in different crystalline forms; **2,** in botany and zoölogy, varying much in appearance and structure within the same species.—*adj.* **pol″y-mor′phic.**—*adj.* **pol″y-mor′phe-an.**—*n.* **pol″y-mor′phism.**

Pol-y-ne-sian (pŏl″ĭ-nē′shăn; -zhăn), *adj.* pertaining to the Pacific islands called Oceania, or to their people:—*n.* a member of any of the native races of Oceania; also, the language of Oceania.

pol-y-no-mi-al (pŏl″ĭ-nō′mĭ-ăl), *n.* an expression in algebra containing two or more terms.

pol-yp (pŏl′ĭp), *n.* a simple, invertebrate animal having a mouth surrounded by tentacles at one end, and a means of attachment to some foreign body at the other; as, the coral *polyp.* Also, **pol′ype; pol′y-pus.**

Pol-y-phe-mus (pŏl″ĭ-fē′mŭs), *n.* in mythology, a Cyclops who confined Odysseus and his companions in his cave and devoured two daily until blinded by Odysseus.

pol-y-pus (pŏl′ĭ-pŭs), *n.* [*pl.* polypi (-pī)], **1**, a smooth, stalklike growth from a mucous surface such as that of the nose; **2**, in zoölogy, a polyp.

pol-y-syl-lab-ic (pŏl″ĭ-sĭ-lăb′ĭk), *adj.* having many, but specif., more than three, syllables, as ornithorhyncus. Also, **pol″y-syl-lab′i-cal.**

pol-y-syl-la-ble (pŏl′ĭ-sĭl″*ȧ*-bl), *n.* a word of many, but, specif., of more than three, syllables.

pol-y-tech-nic (pŏl″ĭ-tĕk′nĭk), *adj.* pertaining to many arts and sciences, esp. in their practical application:—*n.* a school for imparting instruction in the arts and sciences, esp. in various branches of engineering and other technical subjects.

pol-y-the-ism (pŏl′ĭ-thē-ĭzm), *n.* the doctrine that there are many gods, sharing in the government of the world.

pol-y-the-ist (pŏl′ĭ-thē-ĭst), *n.* one who holds the belief that the world is governed by many gods.—*adj.* **pol″y-the-is′tic.**

pom-ace (pŭm′ĭs), *n.* **1**, crushed apples from a cider mill; **2**, the crushed pulp of any substance from which juice or oil has been extracted.

po-ma-ceous (pō-mā′shŭs), *adj.* **1**, resembling, or pertaining to, pomace; **2**, pertaining to, or composed of, apples; **3**, in botany, pertaining to a pome.

po-made (pō-măd′; pō-mäd′), *n.* a perfumed ointment used for the hair: also called *pomatum.*

pome (pōm), *n.* a fleshy, many-celled fruit with a membranous core inclosing several seeds, as the apple, quince, or pear.

pome-gran-ate (pŏm-grăn′ăt; pŏm′-grăn″ăt; pŭm′-). *n.* **1**, a tropical Asiatic tree yielding an orangelike, edible fruit with a thick rind and a very seedy, crimson pulp; **2**, the fruit of this tree.

Pom-er-a-ni-an (pŏm″ĕr-ā′nĭ-ăn), *adj.* of or pertaining to Pomerania, a province in Prussia:—*n.* **1**, an inhabitant of Pomerania; **2**, a small dog, having long, thick, black or white, silky hair, and a bushy, curled-up tail: popularly called *pom.*

pom-mel (pŭm′ĕl), *n.* **1**, the knob on a sword hilt (see *saber*, illus.); **2**, the high part of a saddlebow:—*v.t.* to beat.

po-mol-o-gy (pō-mŏl′ō-jĭ), *n.* the science of growing fruit and fruit trees. —*adj.* **po″mo-log′i-cal.**—*n.* **po-mol′o-gist.**

pomp (pŏmp), *n.* showy display; grandeur; splendor.

Syn. ceremony, ostentation, pageantry.

pom-pa-dour (pŏm′p*ȧ*-dōōr; pŏm′p*ȧ*-dôr), *n.* a style of wearing the hair brushed back from the forehead without a part, often over a roll.

Pom-pe-ian (pŏm-pē′yăn; -pē′ăn), *adj.* of or pertaining to Pompeii, an Italian city buried A. D. 79 by an eruption of Vesuvius. Also, **Pom-pei′ian.**

pom–pom (pŏm′=pŏm″), *n.* a machine gun of large size.

pom-pon (pŏm′pŏn), *n.* **1**, an ornamental ball, as of feathers or ribbon, for women's wear; **2**, a round tuft or ball, as on a cap; **3**, a variety of chrysanthemum.

pom-pos-i-ty (pŏm-pŏs′ĭ-tĭ), *n.* the state of being self-important; pretentiousness; ostentation.

pom-pous (pŏm′pŭs), *adj.* **1**, magnificent; splendid; **2**, affectedly stately; self-important; as, a *pompous* individual.—*adv.* **pom′pous-ly.**—*n.* **pom′pous-ness.**

Syn. showy, ostentatious, pretentious.

pon-cho (pŏn′chō), *n.* [*pl.* ponchos (-chōz)], **1**, in Spanish America, a loose cloak consisting of a blanket with a hole in the middle for the head; **2**, a cloak made on the same plan, used chiefly as a raincoat.

pond (pŏnd), *n.* a small body of standing water: **pond lily**, a water lily.

pon-der (pŏn′dẽr), *v.t.* to consider carefully; think about:—*v.i.* to reflect; think deeply.—*n.* **pon′der-er.**

Syn. study, meditate, muse, deliberate.

pon-der-a-ble (pŏn′dẽr-*ȧ*-bl), *adj.* capable of being weighed.

pon-der-ous (pŏn′dẽr-ŭs), *adj.* **1**, very heavy; **2**, labored; dull; as, a *ponderous* style.—*adv.* **pon′der-ous-ly.**—*n.* **pon′der-ous-ness.**—*n.* **pon″der-os′i-ty.**

pone (pōn), *n.* bread made of corn meal, milk, etc.: called in full, *corn pone.*

pon-gee (pŏn-jē′; pŏn′jē″), *n.* a kind of unbleached silk from China or India; also, a dyed silk fabric resembling it.

pon-iard (pŏn′y*ȧ*rd), *n.* a kind of small dagger:—*v.t.* to stab.

***pons a-si-no-rum** (pŏnz ăs″ĭ-nō′-rŭm), [Lat.], literally, the asses' bridge: used as the name of a famous proposition in Euclid, because hard for stupid boys to comprehend.

pon-ti-fex (pŏn′tĭ-fĕks), *n.* [*pl.* pontifices (-tĭf′ĭ-sēz)], **1**, in ancient Rome, a member of the supreme council of priests; **2**, a bishop; esp., a pope.

pon-tiff (pŏn′tĭf), *n.* **1**, a Jewish high priest; **2**, a bishop; **3**, a pope.

pon-tif-i-cal (pŏn-tĭf′ĭ-kăl), *adj.* pertaining to a Jewish high priest, a bishop, or a pope; papal:—*n.* **1**, a book containing forms for ceremonies performed only by a pontiff; **2**, in *pl.*, the full dress worn by a priest or bishop.—*adv.* **pon-tif′i-cal-ly.**

pon-tif-i-cate (pŏn-tĭf′ĭ-kăt), *n.* **1**, the office or dignity of a high priest, bishop, or pope; **2**, the time of office of a high priest, bishop or pope.

Pon-ti-us Pi-late (pŏn′shĭ-ŭs; pŏn′-shŭs; pŏn′tĭ-ŭs), the Roman governor of Judea under whose authority Christ was crucified.

pon-toon (pŏn-tōōn′), *n.* **1**, a lighter or low, flat boat; **2**, a light, floating structure, such as a flat-bottomed boat or a hollow metal cylinder, used as one of the supports of a temporary or floating bridge; sometimes, the bridge so made: **pontoon bridge**, a bridge, often temporary, as when constructed for the use of an army, in which boats or floats are used as supports (see *bridge*, illus.). Also, **pon-ton′.**

po-ny (pō′nĭ), *n.* [*pl.* ponies (-nĭz)], **1**, a horse of certain small breeds; as, a Shetland *pony;* **2**, *U. S. Slang*, a literal translation of a Greek or Latin author.

poo-dle (pōō′dl), *n.* one of a breed of intelligent, black or white, curly-haired dogs.

pooh (pōō; pōōh), *interj.* an exclamation of scorn or contempt; pshaw! nonsense!

pooh–pooh (pōō″=pōō′), *v.t.* to laugh at; treat contemptuously.

[1]pool (pōōl), *n.* **1**, a small body of standing water; a pond; **2**, a short stretch of deep, still water in a small stream.

[2]pool (pōōl), *n.* **1**, a game played on a billiard able; **2**, the money played for in certain gambling games, or the place where it is kept; **3**, in horse racing, athletic contests, etc., the accumulated wagers of a group of persons betting on a certain contestant; **4**, a combination of stockholders for joint speculation; also, a combination of competing industries to control the market, etc.:—*v.t.* to put into a common fund for a joint undertaking or in order to share the profits; as, to *pool* interests:—*v.i.* to form a common fund.

poop (po͞op), *n.* the raised deck in the stern of a vessel; also, the stern itself: also called *poop deck*:—*v.t.* to strike the stern of; break heavily over the stern of: said of waves.

Poop Deck

poor (po͝or), *adj.* 1, having little or no means; lacking riches; 2, lacking in good qualities; inferior in any one of a number of ways, as lacking strength or vigor, beauty or dignity; 3, dejected; spiritless; wretched; as, a *poor* sort of creature; 4, lean; as, a *poor* horse; 5, inferior in skill or execution; as, a *poor* piece of work; 6, without fertility; as, *poor* soil; 7, scanty; as, a *poor* harvest; 8, unimportant; humble; as, in my *poor* opinion; 9, *Colloq.*, calling forth tenderness, compassion, or disdain; as, *poor* child!—*adv.* [1]**poor'ly.**—*n.* **poor'ness.**

poor-house (po͝or'hous"), *n.* an institution for the care of those dependent on public charity; an almshouse.

[2]**poor-ly** (po͝or'lĭ), *adj. Colloq.*, somewhat ill; delicate in health.—*n.* **poor'li-ness.**

pop (pŏp), *n.* 1, a short, sharp, quick sound; 2, the shot from a small firearm; 3, a bubbling, nonintoxicating drink:—*v.t.* [*p.t.* and *p.p.* popped (pŏpt), *p.pr.* pop'ping], 1, to thrust suddenly; as, to *pop* one's head out of a door; 2, to cause to burst open by heat; as, to *pop* corn; 3, to fire, as a gun:—*v.i.* 1, to make a short, sharp, quick sound; as, we could hear the guns *pop;* 2, to move quickly; dart; 3, to come suddenly into view; 4, to burst open with a sound; as, corn *pops* over the fire:—*adv.* suddenly; unexpectedly.

pop corn 1, any of several varieties of Indian corn, having small ears and small, hard grains which, when exposed to heat, burst open with a sharp noise, and become white and puffy; 2, corn so prepared.

pope (pōp), *n.* 1, (usually, *Pope*), the bishop of Rome and head of the Roman Catholic Church; 2, a title of priests of the Greek Catholic Church.

pope-dom (pōp'dŭm), *n.* the office or dignity of a pope; papacy.

pop-er-y (pōp'ẽr-ĭ), *n.* the Roman Catholic system: a scornful term.

pop-gun (pŏp'gŭn"), *n.* a toy which shoots harmless bullets by air pressure.

pop-in-jay (pŏp'ĭn-jā), *n.* 1, formerly, a parrot; 2, a fop or dude who chatters like a parrot.

pop-ish (pōp'ĭsh), *adj.* pertaining to the Roman Catholic Church: a scornful term.—*n.* **pop'ish-ness.**—*adv.* **pop'ish-ly.**

pop-lar (pŏp'lȧr), *n.* a tree with light, soft wood and heart-shaped leaves.

pop-lin (pŏp'lĭn), *n.* a ribbed fabric of silk or silk and worsted.

pop-per (pŏp'ẽr), *n.* one who or that which pops, as a firearm; specif., a utensil, usually made of wire net, in which pop corn is popped.

pop-py (pŏp'ĭ), *n.* [*pl.* poppies (-ĭz)], a plant having bright, showy flowers, from one species of which opium is obtained.

pop-u-lace (pŏp'ū-lās), *n.* the common people; proletariat; often, in contempt, the rabble.
Syn. multitude. (See throng.)

pop-u-lar (pŏp'ū-lȧr), *adj.* 1, pertaining to, or consistin., of, the . mmon people; as, a *popular* form of government; 2, suitable for the common people; having a wide distribution; as, *popular* music; 3, held in favor by many people; as, a *popular* writer; 4, within the means of the ordinary purchaser; as, *popular* prices.—*adv.* **pop'u-lar-ly.**

pop-u-lar-i-ty (pŏp"ū-lăr'ĭ-tĭ), *n.* the state or quality of being pleasing to, or admired or esteemed by, many.

pop-u-lar-ize (pŏp'ū-lȧr-īz), *v.t.* [*p.t.* and *p.p.* -ized (-īzd), *p.pr.* -iz"ing], 1, to make pleasing to many people; 2, to make familiar to, or adapt to the use of, the common people; as, to *popularize* education.—*n.* **pop"u-lar-i-za'tion.**

pop-u-late (pŏp'ū-lāt), *v.t.* [*p.t.* and *p.p.* -lat"ed, *p.pr.* -lat"ing], 1, to furnish with inhabitants or people; as, to *populate* a country; 2, to inhabit.

pop-u-la-tion (pŏp"ū-lā'shŭn), *n.* 1, the total number of people of a country, state, town, etc.; 2, any group of inhabitants separately distinguished; as, the negro *population.*

Pop-u-list (pŏp'ū-lĭst), *n.* in the U. S., a member of the People's party, established in 1891 to advocate government ownership of railways, limitation of land ownership, increase of currency, and other measures of a socialistic nature.—*adj.* **Pop"u-lis'tic.**—*n.* **Pop'u-lism.**

pop-u-lous (pŏp'ū-lŭs), *adj.* containing many inhabitants.—*adv.* **pop'u-lous-ly.**—*n.* **pop'u-lous-ness.**

por-ce-lain (pôr'sē-lĭn; pôrs'lĭn), *n.* 1, a kind of fine, white, glazed earthenware; 2, dishes or ornaments of such ware:—*adj.* made of porcelain: **porcelain crab,** any of a family of crabs with a hard, porcelain-like upper shell (see *crustacean*, illus.).

porch (pōrch), *n.* 1, a covered approach to a doorway, usually extending from the main wall, with a separate roof; 2, *U. S. Colloq.*, a veranda; piazza.

por-cine (pôr'sīn; pôr'sĭn), *adj.* pertaining to swine, or hogs.

por-cu-pine (pôr'kū-pīn), *n.* an animal akin to the squirrel, rat, and beaver, covered with spines or sharp quills.

[1]**pore** (pōr), *n.* a minute hole, as in a leaf; esp., a hole in the skin through which perspiration discharges.

[2]**pore** (pōr), *v.i.* [*p.t.* and *p.p.* pored (pōrd), *p.pr.* por'ing], to study with close attention; be absorbed in thought: with *over.*

por-gy (pôr'gĭ), *n.* [*pl.* porgies (-gĭz)], any of several small salt-water fishes much esteemed for food.

pork (pōrk), *n.* the flesh of swine, or hogs, used for food.—*adj.* **pork'y.**

pork-er (pōr'kẽr), *n.* any fattened hog, esp. a young one fattened for food.

po-ros-i-ty (pō-rŏs'ĭ-tĭ), *n.* [*pl.* porosities (-tĭz)], 1, the state or quality of being porous; 2, a pore.

po-rous (pō'rŭs), *adj.* having tiny holes through which a fluid may pass.—*adv.* **po'rous-ly.**—*n.* **po'rous-ness.**

por-phy-ry (pôr'fĭ-rĭ), *n.* [*pl.* porphyries (-rĭz)], a many-colored, hard stone that takes a high polish.

por-poise (pôr'pŭs), *n.* 1, any of several small, gregarious whales from five to eight feet long; the sea hog; 2, commonly, the dolphin.

por-ridge (pŏr'ĭj), *n.* 1, a food made of oatmeal or other meal boiled slowly in water until it thickens; 2, a broth or stew, as of vegetables or meat.

por-rin-ger (pŏr'ĭn-jẽr), *n.* a small dish or bowl for broth.

[1]**port** (pōrt), *n.* a place where vessels arrive and depart: a harbor; haven.

[2]**port** (pōrt), *n.* **1,** a round opening or window in the side of a ship; esp., such an opening used for ventilation, admittance of light, discharge of cannon, etc.: also called *porthole;* **2,** in mechanics, an outlet, as for steam, water, etc.

[3]**port** (pōrt), *n.* the way in which one carries oneself; bearing:—*v.t.* to carry diagonally, as a rifle, in front of, and close to, the body, holding the upper end to the left.

[4]**port** (pōrt), *n.* the left side of a ship as one faces the bow: formerly called *larboard:* opp. of *starboard:*—*adj.* on the left side of a ship; as, a *port* cabin; a *port* light:—*v.t.* to turn to the port, or left, side of a ship; as, to *port* the helm.

[5]**port** (pōrt), *n.* a strong, sweet wine, usually dark red in color.

port-a-ble (pōr′tȧ-bl), *adj.* capable of being easily carried.—*n.* **port′-a-ble-ness.**—*n.* **port″a-bil′i-ty.**

por-tage (pōr′tāj), *n.* **1,** a break in a chain of waterways over which goods, boats, etc., have to be carried; **2,** the carrying of goods overland from one waterway to another; **3,** any cargo of goods to be carried; **4,** the cost of such carriage.

por-tal (pōr′tăl), *n.* a gate, door, or entrance, esp one that is stately and imposing, as of a cathedral.

port-cul-lis (pōrt-kŭl′ĭs), *n.* a strong grating hung over the gateway of a fortified place and capable of being let down to defend the gate.

Porte (pōrt), *n.* the Turkish government and court: so called from the gate of the Sultan's palace from which justice was formerly administered.

***porte-co-chère** (pōrt′=kō″shâr′), [Fr.], *n.* **1,** a large gateway through which a carriage may drive into a court; **2,** loosely, an extension of a porch roof over a drive for carriages to stop under cover.

***porte-mon-naie** (pôrt″mô″nâ′; pōrt′-mŭn″ĭ), [Fr.], *n.* a small, flat, leather purse or pocketbook.

por-tend (pôr-tĕnd′), *v.t.* to indicate in advance what is to happen; forebode; as, to *portend* a storm.
Syn. prophesy, predict, foretell.

por-tent (pōr′tĕnt; pōr′-; pôr-tĕnt′), *n.* an omen or sign, esp. of ill.

por-ten-tous (pôr-tĕn′tŭs), *adj.* foreshadowing evil; dreadful.—*adv.* **por-ten′tous-ly.**—*n.* **por-ten′tous-ness.**

[1]**por-ter** (pōr′tẽr), *n.* a doorkeeper or gatekeeper.—*n.fem.* **por′tress.**

[2]**por-ter** (pōr′tẽr), *n.* **1,** one who carries baggage, bundles, etc., or runs errands for pay, as at stations and hotels; **2,** in the U. S., one who waits on passengers in the sleeping or parlor cars of trains; **3,** a dark-colored malt beer.

por-ter-age (pōr′tẽr-āj), *n.* the work of one who carries burdens for hire; also, his fee.

port-fo-li-o (pōrt-fō′lĭ-ō; pōrt-fōl′yō), *n.* [*pl.* portfolios (-ōz; -yōz)], **1,** a case for loose papers, drawings, etc., esp. documents of importance to the state; **2,** hence, the office of a minister of state; as, he holds the *portfolio* of war.

port-hole (pōrt′hōl″), *n.* **1,** a round opening, or window, in the side of a ship; **2,** an opening in the wall of a fort, blockhouse, etc., esp. a hole through which to shoot.

Por-ti-a (pōr′shĭ-ȧ; pōr′shȧ), *n.* **1,** in Shakespeare's "The Merchant of Venice," the heiress who, loving Bassanio, disguises herself as a lawyer, contests Shylock's suit against Antonio, Bassanio's friend, and saves Antonio's life; **2,** in Shakespeare's "Julius Cæsar," the wife of Brutus.

por-ti-co (pōr′tĭ-kō), *n.* [*pl.* porticoes; porticos (-kōz)], a walk covered by a roof supported on columns; a columned porch.

PORTICO

***por-tière** (pôr″tyâr′), [Fr.], *n.* a curtain over a door; a drapery hanging in or over a doorway.

por-tion (pōr′shŭn), *n.* **1,** a piece or part of anything; **2,** esp., a share, or a part given; **3,** a part of an estate descending to an heir; **4,** a dower:—*v.t.* **1,** to divide into shares; **2,** to give shares of; **3,** to give part of an estate or fortune to.—*adj.* **por′tion-less.**
Syn., n. allotment, parcel. (See part.)

port-ly (pōrt′lĭ), *adj.* [*comp.* port′li-er, *superl.* port′li-est], **1,** stately in appearance; dignified in bearing; as, a *portly* butler; **2,** stout.—*n.* **port′li-ness.**

port-man-teau (pōrt-măn′tō), *n.* [*pl.* portmanteaus; portmanteaux (-tōz)], a bag or small trunk for carrying clothes or traveling necessities.

por-trait (pōr′trāt), *n.* **1,** a picture of a person, esp. of a person's face, made from life, as a drawing, photograph, or the like: used esp. of a painting in oil; **2,** a vivid or clear description of a person in words.

por-trai-ture (pōr′trā-tūr), *n.* **1,** the art, act, or practice, of drawing or painting pictures of persons; vivid or clear description of persons; **2,** a likeness.

por-tray (pōr-trā′), *v.t.* **1,** to paint or draw the likeness of; **2,** to describe in words; **3,** to represent by acting.

por-tray-al (pōr-trā′ăl), *n.* **1,** the act of making a picture or representation by drawing, painting, or describing in words; **2,** a representation.

Por-tu-guese (pōr′tū-gēz; pōr″tū-gēz′; pōr′tū-gēs), *adj.* relating to Portugal or its people:—*n.* [*pl.* Portuguese], **1,** a native of Portugal; **2,** its language.

por-tu-la-ca (pōr″tū-lā′kȧ; pōr″tū-lăk′ȧ), *n.* any of various fleshy-leaved, chiefly tropical, plants of the purslane family, esp. a low-growing garden plant with showy, many-colored flowers.

[1]**pose** (pōz), *v.t.* [*p.t.* and *p.p.* posed (pōzd), *p.pr.* pos′ing], **1,** to put or set forth, as a proposition or a question; **2,** to place in a suitable attitude; as, to *pose* a person for a portrait:—*v.i.* **1,** to assume and keep an attitude; as, the model *posed* for an hour; **2,** to make a pretense; as, she *poses* as being charitable:—*n.* **1,** attitude or position; **2,** a mental attitude; a manner put on for the sake of effect.

[2]**pose** (pōz), *v.t.* [*p.t.* and *p.p.* posed (pōzd), *p.pr.* pos′ing], to perplex; puzzle.

Po-sei-don (pō-sī′dŏn), *n.* in Greek mythology, the god of the sea: identified with the Roman *Neptune.*

[1]**pos-er** (pōz′ẽr), *n.* one who poses; one who, for the sake of effect, assumes an attitude or style of behavior not natural; an affected person. Also, ***po″seur′** (pō″zûr′).

[2]**pos-er** (pōz′ẽr), *n.* a puzzling question; that which puzzles.

po-sey (pō′zĭ), *n.* [*pl.* poseys (-zĭz)], a flower or bunch of flowers. See **po′sy,** *Pfd.S.*

po-si-tion (pō-zĭsh′ŭn), *n.* **1,** the place where a thing is set or placed; situation; as, the *position* of a house; **2,** standing or rank; as, high *position;* **3,** office or employment; as, to lose one's *position;* **4,** posture; as, a graceful *position;* **5,** mental attitude toward any subject; as, to define one's *position;* **6**, correct or suitable place; as, in *position;* **7**, the laying down of a proposition; affirmation; **8**, a certain way of holding a flag, as in signaling.

pos-i-tive (pŏz′ĭ-tĭv), *adj.* **1**, clearly expressed; **2**, leaving no doubt; actual; direct; as, *positive* proof; a *positive* promise; **3**, confident; as, I am *positive* that this is so; sometimes, strongly or stubbornly assertive; as, a *positive* manner; **4**, affirmative; not negative; as, a *positive* blessing; **5**, designating the simple form of an uncompared adjective or adverb; as, *calm* and *calmly* are in the *positive* degree; **6**, in mathematics, reckoned as more than zero; as, a *positive* quantity; **7**, designating that pole of a magnet which is attracted to that magnetic pole of the earth situated near the geographical north pole; **8**, designating the kind of electricity generated on a glass rod when it is rubbed with silk: opposed to that existing on the silk, which is *negative;* **9**, in photography, corresponding with the object photographed in respect to light and shade; **10**, *Colloq.*, absolute; as, a *positive* bore:—*n.* **1**, that which may be affirmed; reality; **2**, a word which affirms or asserts existence; **3**, a photograph showing natural lights and shades: opp. of *negative;* **4**, in mathematics, electricity, etc., that which is considered as primary: opp. of *negative.*—*adv.* **pos′i-tive-ly.**—*n.* **pos′i-tive-ness.**

Syn., *adj.* certain, sure.

pos-se (pŏs′ē), *n.* a body of men summoned by a sheriff to assist in the carrying out of the law: called in full, *posse comitatus* (kŏm″ĭ-tā′tŭs), (literally, the power of the county).

pos-sess (pŏ-zĕs′), *v.t.* **1**, to be the owner of; own; **2**, to have as a quality; **3**, to hold in control; as, to *possess* one's soul in patience; **4**, to control mentally or morally; as, anger *possessed* him; **5**, to occupy; seize; as, to *possess* a city during war; **6**, to cause to become owner: used reflexively or as a past participle; as, to *possess* oneself of property; *possessed* of great wealth.—*n.* **pos-ses′sor.**—*adj.* **pos-ses′so-ry.**

pos-sessed (pŏ-zĕst′), *p.adj.* mastered, as by evil or passion; mad.

pos-ses-sion (pŏ-zĕsh′ŭn), *n.* **1**, ownership; occupancy; **2**, the thing owned; **3**, self-control; **4**, in *pl.*, property or estate; wealth.

pos-ses-sive (pŏ-zĕs′ĭv), *adj.* **1**, designating ownership or right; **2**, indicative of ownership; as, he treated her with a *possessive* manner; **3**, in grammar, designating that case of nouns or pronouns inflected to show ownership, source, or a similar relation, often equivalent, in English, to the preposition *of* followed by the objective case:—*n.* the possessive case of a noun or pronoun, generally representing a person, or an animal or thing personified.

NOTE.—The possessive case of nouns is regularly formed by adding *'s* to any form, singular or plural, not ending in a sibilant (*man's, men's*), and the apostrophe ['] to a plural in *s* (*boys'*). Nouns ending in a sibilant add *'s* if monosyllabic or bearing any accent on the last syllable (*Burns's, Hortense's*); and also if ending in an unaccented syllable (*Thomas's, Clarence's*) unless the additional sibilant is disagreeable, in which case the apostrophe ['] alone is added (*Ulysses'*).

pos-set (pŏs′ĕt), *n.* a drink made of hot milk curdled with wine, ale, or other liquor, often spiced.

pos-si-bil-i-ty (pŏs″ĭ-bĭl′ĭ-tĭ), *n.* [*pl.* possibilities (-tĭz)], **1**, the fact or state of being able to take place or happen; **2**, that which may take place, or that which may be done; likelihood.

pos-si-ble (pŏs′ĭ-bl), *adj.* **1**, capable of existing or of coming into being; **2**, capable of happening or taking place; **3**, conceivable; **4**, available; deserving consideration; as, a *possible* candidate.—*adv.* **pos′si-bly.**

pos-sum (pŏs′ŭm), *n.* the Southern colloquial form of *opossum.*

[1]**post** (pōst), *n.* **1**, an upright piece of timber, metal, or the like, used to support or fasten that which rests upon, or is attached to, it; **2**, the central part of a lock which fits into the opening in the key: **post light**, a light, as a street lamp, set on a post:—*v.t.* **1**, to fasten, as a notice, to a wall; **2**, to make known by such notices; **3**, to place (a person's name) on a notice; **4**, to fasten notices upon.

[2]**post** (pōst), *n.* **1**, formerly, one of a number of riders, each of whom in turn carried the mail forward one station; a postman; also, formerly, one of the stations where relays of horses were kept for such riders; **2**, a system of carrying and delivering letters; the mail; **3**, in England, any part of the postal system, as a post office, a mail carrier, or a letter box; **4**, a size of writing paper about 20 by 16 inches; **5**, *Obs.*, haste; swiftness:—*v.i.* to travel with speed:—*v.t.* **1**, to send by mail; esp., to drop, as a letter, into a letter box; **2**, in bookkeeping, to transfer (an entry or item) from journal to ledger; **3**, *Colloq.*, to inform fully:—*adv.* speedily.

[3]**post** (pōst), *n.* **1**, a place where a person or thing is stationed; **2**, a position of trust; **3**, a trading settlement or center; **4**, a branch of a veteran soldiers' organization; as, an American Legion *post;* **5**, the position guarded by a sentry; **6**, a military station; also, the soldiers occupying it:—*v.t.* to station; appoint, as to a command or an office.

post- (pōst-), *prefix*, behind; after: opp. of *ante-* and *pre-*.

post-age (pōs′tāj), *n.* the cost of sending letters by mail: **postage stamp**, an official stamp sold by the government to be pasted on mail matter as a sign that the postage has been paid.

post-al (pōs′tăl), *adj.* pertaining to the post office or mail service: **postal card**, **1**, a card for mailing, with a postage stamp officially printed on it: in England, also called *post card;* **2**, a card for mailing, to which a stamp must be attached: officially called *post card.*

post card **1**, in England, an official postal card; **2**, a private postal card for mailing to which a stamp must be attached. Also, *n.* **post′card″.**

post chaise formerly, a carriage with fast horses, in which mail and passengers were carried along regular routes more quickly than by coach.

post-date (pōst″dāt′), *v.t.* [*p.t.* and *p.p.* -dat′ed, *p.pr.* -dat′ing], **1**, to mark with a date later than that of the actual time of writing, as a check; **2**, to follow in time.

post-er (pōs′tẽr), *n.* **1**, a placard or bill put up in a public place, as on a wall, to advertise something; **2**, one who places bills on walls, billboards, etc.

pos-te-ri-or (pŏs-tē′rĭ-ẽr), *adj.* **1**, later; **2**, rear; hinder:—*n.*, often in *pl.*, the hinder part of an animal.

pos-te-ri-or-i-ty (pŏs-tē″rĭ-ŏr′ĭ-tĭ), *n.* the state of being later or subsequent: opp. of *priority.*

pos-ter-i-ty (pŏs-tĕr′ĭ-tĭ), *n.* **1**, future generations collectively; **2**, one's descendants collectively.

pos-tern (pōs′tẽrn), *n.* **1**, formerly, a back door or gate; private entrance; **2**, in fortification, an underground passage, closed by a door, leading inward from the moat:—*adj.* behind; private; rear.

post–free (pōst′=frē″), *adj.* and *adv.* sent through the mail without the payment of postage.

post-grad-u-ate (pōst-grăd′ū-āt), *adj.* pertaining to, or engaging in, studies after graduation from a regular course in a school or college:—*n.* one pursuing such studies.

post-haste (pōst″hāst′), *adj.* instant:—*adv.* quickly; very speedily.

post-hu-mous (pŏs′tū-mŭs; pōst′hū-mŭs), *adj.* **1**, born after the death of the father; **2**, published after the death of an author; **3**, happening or continuing after death.—*adv.* **post′hu-mous-ly.**

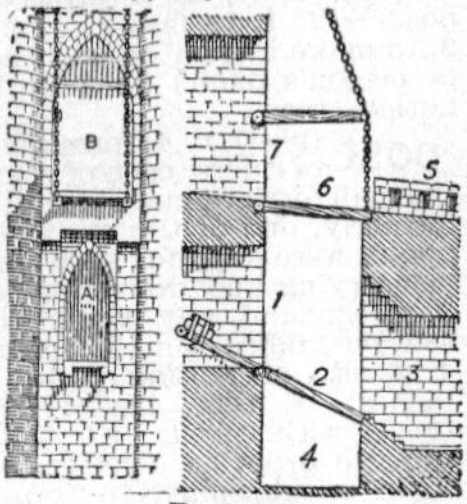

POSTERN

A, B, postern and main entrance, front view; 1, postern, in section; 2, drawbridge; 3, passage to the outer works; 4, moat; 5, bridge; 6, drawbridge; 7, main entrance, in section.

pos-til-ion (pōs-tĭl′yŭn), *n.* one who guides a team by riding one of the horses. Also, **pos-til′-lion.**

post-lude (pōst′lūd), *n.* **1**, organ music played at the end of a church service; **2**, a movement played as a conclusion to a musical composition.

post-man (pōst′măn), *n.* [*pl.* postmen (-mĕn)], a letter carrier.

post-mark (pōst′märk″), *n.* a mark stamped upon mail by a post office, esp. one showing the place and date of mailing:—*v.t.* to stamp with a postmark.

post-mas-ter (pōst′màs″tẽr), *n.* **1**, the superintendent of a post office; **2**, formerly, one who furnished horses for traveling.—*n.fem.* **post′mis″tress.**

post-mas-ter–gen-er-al (pōst′màs-tẽr=jĕn′ẽr-ăl), *n.* the chief officer of the mail-service department of a country or of a state.

post-me-rid-i-an (pōst″mē-rĭd′ĭ-ăn), *adj.* pertaining to the time when the sun has passed the meridian; pertaining to the afternoon.

***post me-ri-di-em** (pōst mē-rĭd′ĭ-ĕm), [Lat.], after noon: used of the hours between midday and midnight.—*abbr.* **P. M.; p. m.**

post–mor-tem (pōst″=môr′tĕm), *adj.* after death; made after death: referring esp. to examination of the internal organs of a dead body:—*n.* an examination made of a body after death.

post-na-tal (pōst-nā′tăl), *adj.* happening after birth.

post of-fice **1**, the department of a government which handles the mail; **2**, any office of this department which receives and distributes mail.

post-paid (pōst′pād″), *adj.* having the postage paid in advance.

post-pone (pōst-pōn′), *v.t.* [*p.t.* and *p.p.* -poned′ (-pōnd′), *p.pr.* -pon′-ing], to delay; defer; put off to another time.—*n.* **post-pone′ment.**

Syn. procrastinate. (See defer.)

post-pran-di-al (pōst-prăn′dĭ-ăl), *adj.* pertaining to the time after dinner; as, a *post-prandial* speaker.

post-script (pōst′skrĭpt), *n.* a written addition to a book, article, etc.; esp., a paragraph added to a letter after the writer's signature.

pos-tu-late (pŏs′tū-lāt), *v.t.* [*p.t.* and *p.p.* -lat″ed, *p.pr.* -lat″ing], **1**, to assume without proof; state as a fact to be taken for granted; **2**, to claim as one's right:—*n.* (pŏs′tū-lāt), **1**, a self-evident statement which may be taken for granted; a proposition accepted without proof; **2**, something that must be assumed in order to account for something else.—*n.* **pos″tu-la′tion.**

pos-ture (pŏs′tūr), *n.* **1**, the placing or position of parts of the body; attitude; pose; **2**, mental attitude; frame of mind:—*v.t.* [*p.t.* and *p.p.* -tured (-tūrd), *p.pr.* -tur-ing], to place in a particular attitude:—*v.i.* to take a certain position.—*n.* **pos′tur-er.**

post-war (pōst′wôr″), *adj.* after any war, as contrasted with *prewar.*

po-sy (pō′zĭ), *n.* [*pl.* posies (-zĭz)], **1**, a flower or a bunch of flowers; **2**, orig., a motto or verse sent with a bouquet or inscribed in a ring. Also, **po′sey.**

pot (pŏt), *n.* **1**, a metal or earthenware vessel for holding or boiling liquids and other substances; **2**, the quantity such a vessel will hold; **3**, a vessel, usually of earthenware, for holding growing plants; **4**, a size of paper 12½ by 15 inches; **5**, *Slang;* **a**, the amount staked, as on a race or a game; **b**, a large sum of money:—*v.t.* [*p.t.* and *p.p.* pot′ted, *p.pr.* pot′-ting], **1**, to preserve in, put into, or plant in, a pot; **2**, to shoot (a bird or animal) for food; **3**, *Colloq.*, to seize.

pot-ash (pŏt′ăsh″), *n.* **1**, any of various potassium salts; **2**, specif., impure potassium carbonate, a powerful white salt obtained from wood ashes and used in making soap, glass, etc. Also, **po-tass′; po-tas′sa.**

po-tas-si-um (pō-tăs′ĭ-ŭm), *n.* a soft, very light, bluish white metal, occurring only in compounds: **potassium carbonate,** a white alkaline salt obtained from ashes of vegetable matter; potash: **potassium cyanide,** a white, crystalline, poisonous compound of potassium and cyanogen, used in photography, electroplating, etc.

po-ta-tion (pō-tā′shŭn), *n.* **1**, the act of drinking; **2**, a drink.

po-ta-to (pō-tā′tō), *n.* [*pl.* potatoes (-tōz)], **1**, a common plant having edible fleshy shoots, or tubers, growing from its roots underground: also called *white potato;* **2**, one of these tubers used as food; **3**, orig., the sweet potato: **potato bug,** a small beetle having yellow and black stripes, which is destructive to the leaves of the potato plant.

pot–bel-lied (pŏt′=bĕl″ĭd), *adj.* having a prominent belly.

pot-boil-er (pŏt′boil″ẽr), *n.* **1**, a piece of work, often inferior, done by an artist or writer merely for the money that it will bring; **2**, one who does such work.

po-teen (pō-tēn′), *n.* in Ireland, whisky manufactured in defiance of the law. Also, **po-theen′** (pō-thēn′).

po-ten-cy (pō′tĕn-sĭ), *n.* [*pl.* potencies (-sĭz)], power, physical or mental; authority. Also, **po′tence.**

¹po-tent (pō′tĕnt), *adj.* **1**, powerful; mighty; **2**, having great authority or influence.—*adv.* **po′tent-ly.**

²po-tent (pō′tĕnt), *n.* a heraldic fur composed of interlocking T-shaped figures, alternately blue and white: **cross potent,** a cross like a plus sign with a short bar across the end of each arm (see *cross,* illus.).

po-ten-tate (pō′tĕn-tāt), *n.* one who has great power; a monarch.

po-ten-tial (pō-tĕn′shăl), *adj.* **1**, capable of being, but not yet in being;

possible, but not actual; **2**, in grammar, expressing power or possibility: said of a mood of verbs; **3**, in physics, existing by reason of position or configuration: said of energy; as, the *potential* energy of a weight that has been raised, or of a spring that has been wound up; **4**, pertaining to, or designating, the electric energy that a body possesses by virtue of the electric charge that it carries:—*n.* **1**, a possibility; **2**, in physics, the condition at a given point in a field of electric, magnetic, or gravitational force, which determines the energy of a body placed there: **difference of potential**, in electricity, a condition determining the tendency of an electric charge to move, or an electric current to flow, from one point to another, as water seeks its level: usually measured in volts.—*adv.* **po-ten'tial-ly.**

po-ten-ti-al-i-ty (pō-tĕn″shĭ-ăl′ĭ-tĭ), *n.* [*pl.* potentialities (-tĭz)], **1**, possibility of development in some particular direction; possibility, but not actuality; **2**, the quality of being able to do; power.

po-ten-ti-om-e-ter (pō-tĕn″shĭ-ŏm′ē-tẽr), *n.* an instrument for finding differences of electric potential.

poth-er (pŏ*th*′ẽr), *n.* confusion; bustle:—*v.i.* to make a stir:—*v.t.* to confuse; worry; bother.

pot-herb (pŏt′ûrb″; pŏt′hûrb″), *n.* any small plant the tops of which are boiled for eating.

pot-hook (pŏt′ho͝ok″), *n.* **1**, an S-shaped iron hook for hanging a pot over an open fire; **2**, formerly, a letter or character used as an exercise in learning to write.

pot-house (pŏt′hous″), *n.* a tavern, esp. one of ill repute.

pot-hunt-er (pŏt′hŭn″tẽr), *n.* **1**, a person who kills game regardless of sportsmanship; **2**, *Slang*, one who engages in competitions more to win prizes than for the sake of sport.—*n.* **pot′hunt″ing.**

po-tion (pō′shŭn), *n.* a drink; dose, esp. of liquid medicine.

Pot-i-phar (pŏt′ĭ-fȧr), *n.* in the Bible, an Egyptian official, who bought Joseph after he had been sold into slavery by his brothers (Genesis 39).

pot-luck (pŏt′lŭk″), *n.* whatever may chance to be on hand to eat.

pot-pie (pŏt′pī″), *n.* **1**, a meat pie; **2**, a meat stew with dumplings.

***pot-pour-ri** (pō″po͞o″rē′), [Fr.], *n.* **1**, a medley or mixture, as of musical airs; **2**, a dish made of various kinds of meats and vegetables; **3**, a mixture of dried, fragrant flower petals used as perfume.

pot roast meat, usually beef, browned in a pot and boiled slowly.

pot-sherd (pŏt′shûrd″), *n.* a piece of broken crockery.

pot shot a hasty shot at an animal, bird, etc., by one who hunts not for sport but to secure food; hence, a hasty shot at an animal within easy reach.

pot-tage (pŏt′ăj), *n.* a stew or thick soup of meat or vegetables, or of both.

¹pot-ter (pŏt′ẽr), *n.* a maker of vessels of earthenware, stoneware, etc.: **potter's field**, a field, or part of a cemetery, for the burial of paupers, criminals, and unknown persons (in allusion to Matthew 27:7): **potter's wheel**, a horizontal rotating disk on which clay is shaped by a potter.

²pot-ter (pŏt′ẽr), *v.i.* to work lazily, fussily, or with little energy. Also, **put′ter.**—*n.* **pot′ter-er.**

pot-ter-y (pŏt′ẽr-ĭ), *n.* [*pl.* potteries (-ĭz)], **1**, ware of various kinds made from clay, or a mixture of clays, molded and hardened by heat; **2**, the place where such ware is manufactured; **3**, the art of making it.

pot-tle (pŏt′l), *n.* **1**, a liquid measure equal to four pints; **2**, a drinking vessel holding this amount, or the liquor it contains.

pot–val-iant (pŏt′=văl″yănt; pŏt=văl′yănt), *adj.* brave and bold from drink.—*n.* **pot′–val″or; pot′–val″our.**

pouch (pouch), *n.* **1**, a small bag; pocket; **2**, a bag or sac of an animal, usually for carrying its young; **3**, a cartridge box.

poult (pōlt), *n.* the young of a domestic fowl, or of the pheasant, partridge, etc.

poul-ter-er (pōl′tẽr-ẽr), *n.* a dealer in fowls, esp. for the table.

poul-tice (pōl′tĭs), *n.* a soft mixture of bread, meal, etc., applied like a plaster to a sore or inflamed part of the body:—*v.t.* [*p.t.* and *p.p.* -ticed (-tĭst), *p.pr.* -tic-ing], to apply such a mixture to.

poul-try (pōl′trĭ), *n.* domestic fowls, as chickens, turkeys, etc.

¹pounce (pouns), *n.* **1**, finely powdered bone, formerly sprinkled on fresh ink to dry it; **2**, a dark-colored powder, as powdered charcoal, sprinkled over paper with a perforated design in order to transfer the pattern, as for embroidery:—*v.t.* [*p.t.* and *p.p.* pounced (pounst), *p.pr.* pounc′ing], to sprinkle or smooth with pounce.

²pounce (pouns), *n.* **1**, the claw of a bird of prey; **2**, a sudden swooping attack:—*v.t.* [*p.t.* and *p.p.* pounced (pounst), *p.pr.* pounc′ing], to swoop upon and seize:—*v.i.* to spring suddenly or unexpectedly: with *on* or *upon*.

¹pound (pound), *n.* **1**, any of several units of weight, esp. one (*avoirdupois* pound) equal to sixteen ounces avoirdupois, or 7,000 grains, or one (*troy* pound) equal to 5,760 grains; **2**, a British money of account, equal to twenty shillings, and having as its par value in U. S. money about $4.86: also called *pound sterling* or *sovereign*.

²pound (pound), *n.* **1**, a place for confining or keeping stray animals; as, a dog *pound;* **2**, a shelter for cattle, sheep, etc.; **3**, a trap for capturing wild animals; **4**, a jail:—*v.t.* to confine in, or as in, a pound.

³pound (pound), *v.t.* **1**, to beat; strike forcibly; **2**, to pulverize, or make fine; **3**, to make solid by blows:—*v.i.* **1**, to deal blows; **2**, hence, to beat heavily or steadily:—*n.* **1**, a blow; **2**, the sound of a blow.

¹pound-er (poun′dẽr), *n.* a person or thing that beats with heavy blows.

²pound-er (poun′dẽr), *n.* a thing that weighs, consists of, or bears some definite relation to, a certain specified number of pounds: usually in composition; as, the fish was a six-*pounder*.

pound–fool-ish (pound′=fo͞ol′ĭsh), *adj.* acting unwisely where large sums of money are concerned.

pour (pōr), *v.t.* **1**, to cause to flow in a stream; as, to *pour* a liquid in or out of a vessel; **2**, to send forth freely; **3**, to utter freely:—*v.i.* to come or flow forth freely in a stream; as, the rain *poured* down.—*n.* **pour′er.**

***pour-par-ler** (po͞or″pȧr″lā′), [Fr.], *n.* a diplomatic conference, as before a treaty is made.

pout (pout), *n.* **1**, a pushing out of the lips; **2**, in *pl.*, a fit of sullenness:—*v.i.* to push out the lips in sullenness, contempt, or displeasure; look sulky:—*v.t.* to push out.

pout-er (pout′ẽr), *n.* **1**, one who pushes out the lips in ill humor; **2**, a kind of pigeon which puffs out its crop.

pov-er-ty (pŏv′ẽr-tĭ), *n.* **1**, the state of being poor; necessity; want; **2**, any lack of richness in quality; scarcity; need.

Syn. destitution, need, indigence. *Poverty* names the state of one who is poor, and hence is relative; it may imply really poor and unable to procure even the necessaries of life, or it may mean an uncomfortable, but not a complete, lack of funds. *Destitution* means a lack of necessities and funds, possibly a sudden deprivation, as by fire or flood; it therefore denotes temporary, but extreme, *poverty*. *Need* may refer to a state of continued *poverty*, or only to the requirement of some particular occasion. *Indigence* is used of the *poverty* of those formerly in better circumstances, and can mean a lack of such necessaries as food and shelter as well as of comforts.

pov-er-ty–strick-en (pŏv′ẽr-tĭ-strĭk″n), *adj.* very poor; in great need; destitute.

pow-der (pou′dẽr), *n.* **1**, any dry substance in fine particles; dust; **2**, an explosive mixture reduced to fine particles: also called *gunpowder;* **3**, a fine, white, often perfumed, dustlike substance used for toilet purposes; **4**, a medicinal substance ground into fine particles; also, a dose of this:—*v.t.* **1**, to reduce to, or sprinkle with, a dustlike substance; **2**, to sprinkle with a seasoning:—*v.i.* **1**, to be reduced to particles; **2**, to use a face preparation called powder.—*adj.* **pow′der-y.**

pow-er (pou′ẽr), *n.* **1**, ability to do or perform something; as, physical or mental *power;* **2**, energy put forth; force; strength; as, the *power* of a man's arm; **3**, rule or authority; as, the *power* of government; **4**, legal authority; as, the *power* to veto a bill; **5**, a ruler or sovereign; **6**, a state or nation, esp. one having international influence; as, the great *powers;* **7**, one who or that which has great effect or influence; **8**, a military or naval force; **9**, the rate at which mechanical energy is put forth, as by an engine, electric motor, etc.; as, ten horse *power;* **10**, the result obtained by multiplying a number by itself: as, four is the second *power* of two:—*v.t.* to equip (a machine, vehicle, etc.) with a power-supplying element, as a motor.

Syn. energy, force. *Power* names the principle which moves, governs, and accomplishes; as, the *power* of a nation to protect its boundaries. *Energy* is the ability to do work or produce an effect; as, *energy* of manner; radiant *energy*. *Force* suggests *power* exerted against resistance; as, *force* of character.

pow-er-ful (pou′ẽr-fŏŏl), *adj.* having great influence; mighty; strong, as a nation.—*adv.* **pow′er-ful-ly.**

Syn. vigorous, sturdy, effectual, influential.

pow-er-less (pou′ẽr-lĕs), *adj.* **1**, weak; **2**, unable to bring about an effect; as, his efforts were *powerless*.—*adv.* **pow′er-less-ly.**—*n.* **pow′er-less-ness.**

Syn. feeble, ineffectual, impotent.

pow-wow (pou′wou″), *n.* **1**, a North American Indian priest or medicine man; **2**, among the Indians, a ceremony in which magic rites are used in trying to bring about things desired, as the cure of disease, success in war, etc.; also, a similar gathering for conference; **3**, *Colloq.*, in the U. S., any meeting resembling this Indian ceremony; esp., a noisy political meeting.

pox (pŏks), *n.* any of various diseases marked by an eruption, or breaking out, on the skin; as, small*pox*.

prac-ti-ca-ble (prăk′tĭ-kȧ-bl), *adj.* capable of being done or used.—*adv.* **prac′ti-ca-bly.**—*n.* **prac″ti-ca-bil′i-ty.**

Syn. usable; possible. (See practical.)

prac-ti-cal (prăk′tĭ-kăl), *adj.* **1**, pertaining to, or obtained through, experience or use; as, *practical* knowledge; **2**, capable of being put to use; **3**, having useful ends in view; useful; as, a *practical* education; **4**, inclined to useful action rather than thought; as, a *practical* disposition; **5**, in effect: **practical joke**, a trick, often carefully planned, in which some particular person is the laughing-stock: **practical science**, applied science.—*n.* **prac″ti-cal′i-ty.**—*n.* **prac′-ti-cal-ness.**

Syn. practicable. To be *practical* is to be capable of being turned to actual or profitable use; as, *practical* knowledge of farming. That which is *practicable* is capable of being done; as, a *practicable* plan or undertaking. The transportation of mail by airplane has proved both *practicable* and *practical*.

prac-ti-cal-ly (prăk′tĭ-kăl-ĭ), *adv.* **1**, in a useful way; **2**, through actual experience; **3**, really; in fact, though not in name; as, he is *practically* the president.

¹prac-tice (prăk′tĭs), *v.t.* [*p.t.* and *p.p.* -ticed (-tĭst), *p.pr.* -tic-ing], **1**, to carry out; **2**, to do frequently or as a rule; **3**, to work at or pursue as a profession; as, to *practice* law; **4**, to perform often in order to learn; as, to *practice* a piece of music; **5**, to teach by frequent repetition; drill:—*v.i.* **1**, to do something as a habit; **2**, to follow a profession; **3**, to do something often in order to learn. Also, **prac′tise.**—*n.* **prac′tic-er.**

²prac-tice (prăk′tĭs), *n.* **1**, custom; habit; as, to make a *practice* of smoking; **2**, the putting to actual use of theoretic knowledge; as, he is skilled in theory, but not in *practice;* **3**, the exercise of any profession; as, the *practice* of medicine; also, a regular clientele in a profession; as, the young doctor bought a *practice;* **4**, regular exercise as a means to learning; as, *practice* in writing; **5**, skill gained by such exercise; **6**, the customary legal procedure in conducting suits at law.

Syn. usage; manner. (See habit).

prac-ti-tion-er (prăk-tĭsh′ŭn-ẽr), *n.* one who is engaged in any profession, esp. medicine or law.

præ- (prē-), *prefix*, before: the Latin form of the prefix *pre-:* now kept as preferred spelling in a few words only; as, *prætor*.

præ-tor (prē′tŏr), *n.* a Roman magistrate ranking next below consul. Also, **pre′tor.**—*n.* **præ′tor-ship.**—*adj.* **præ-to′ri-an.**

prag-mat-ic (prăg-măt′ĭk), *adj.* **1**, practical; businesslike; active; **2**, pertaining to everyday matters; commonplace; **3**, meddlesome; opinionated; **4**, pertaining to affairs of state; **5**, in philosophy, dealing with, based on, or judging from, the actual working out of an idea rather than the theory back of it; as, a *pragmatic* conclusion. Also, **prag-mat′i-cal.**—*adv.* **prag-mat′i-cal-ly.**—*n.* **prag-mat′i-cal-ness.**

prag-ma-tism (prăg′mȧ-tĭzm), *n.* a method of thought in which stress is laid upon practical results as standards in conduct.—*n.* **prag′ma-tist.**

prai-rie (prā′rĭ; prâr′ĭ), *n.* a large, treeless tract of level land covered with tall, coarse grass, esp. in the central U. S.: **prairie chicken**, a grouse found in the Mississippi Valley: **prairie dog**, a small burrowing animal resembling the woodchuck and living on the plains: **prairie schooner**, *U. S. Colloq.*, a large, canvas-covered wagon, used by emigrants to the West: **prairie wolf**, the coyote, a small wolf found on the western prairies.

praise (prāz), *n.* **1**, approval; fame; applause; **2**, glorification of God:—*v.t.* [*p.t.* and *p.p.* praised (prāzd), *p.pr.* prais′ing], **1**, to bestow approval upon; honor; **2**, to worship; glorify.

Syn., v. commend, extol, laud.—*Ant., v.* blame, abuse, defame, upbraid.

praise-wor-thy (prāz′wûr″*th*ĭ), *adj.* deserving approval; commendable.—*adv.* **praise′wor″thi-ly.**—*n.* **praise′wor″thi-ness.**

prance (prȧns), *n.* a springing or high-stepping movement:—*v.i.* [*p.t.* and *p.p.* pranced (prȧnst), *p.pr.* pranc′ing], **1**, to spring or move with high steps, as a horse; **2**, to ride a horse that moves in this way; **3**, to strut about in a lively manner.—*n.* **pranc'er.**

pran-di-al (prăn'dĭ-ăl), *adj.* pertaining to a dinner or a meal.

¹prank (prăngk), *n.* a frolic; a mischievous or playful trick.

²prank (prăngk), *v.t.* to dress showily; decorate: with *up*:—*v.i.* to make a great show; prink.

prate (prāt), *v.i.* [*p.t.* and *p.p.* prat'ed, *p.pr.* prat'ing], to prattle; talk idly:—*v.t.* to utter without sense or meaning:—*n.* trifling talk.—*n.* **prat'er.**

prat-tle (prăt'l), *n.* childish talk:—*v.t.* and *v.i.* [*p.t.* and *p.p.* -tled (-ld), *p.pr.* -tling], to speak much and lightly; chatter. —*n.* **prat'tler.**

prawn (prôn), *n.* a large, shrimplike, edible shellfish (see *crustacean*, illus.).

pray (prā), *v.i.* **1**, to ask earnestly; **2**, to ask with humility and reverence; **3**, to speak to God, in request, confession, or praise; —*v.t.* **1**, to request; **2**, to ask earnestly for.

Syn. entreat, implore, petition, plead.

prayer (prâr), *n.* **1**, the act of entreating earnestly; **2**, thanks and praise given to God, and requests made of him; **3**, a form of words suited to an appeal to God; **4**, the request made; **5**, a form of religious service for public worship.

prayer book a book of forms for use in public and private worship; esp. (usually, *Prayer Book*), the Book of Common Prayer.

prayer-ful (prâr'fo͝ol), *adj.* given to devout appeal to God.—*adv.* **prayer'ful-ly.**—*n.* **prayer'ful-ness.**

pre- (prē-), *prefix*, before in place, time, or standing; as, *pre*cede; *pre*dict.

preach (prēch), *v.i.* **1**, to discourse or speak on a religious subject, esp. from a text of Scripture; **2**, to give advice on religious or moral subjects:—*v.t.* **1**, to declare or teach by public discourse; **2**, to utter with moral or religious purpose, as a sermon.—*n.* **preach'er.**—*n.* **preach'ing.**

preach-ment (prēch'mĕnt), *n.* **1**, the act of discoursing on a religious subject; also, the subject; **2**, a tiresome sermon, speech, or the like.

pre-am-ble (prē'ăm″bl), *n.* **1**, an introduction or preface; **2**, the opening clauses of a statute or law giving the reasons and object of the act: usually commencing with the word *whereas.*

pre-ca-ri-ous (prē-kā'rĭ-ŭs), *adj.* depending upon the will or pleasure of another, or upon a turn of circumstances; uncertain; insecure.—*adv.* **pre-ca'ri-ous-ly.**—*n.* **pre-ca'ri-ous-ness.**

Syn. uncertain. *Precarious* implies an uncertainty dependent on the will of others, dangers, or the unknown; as, changes in political power made his position *precarious. Uncertain* describes that which is not definite, fixed, and sure; as, *uncertain* weather.

pre-cau-tion (prē-kô'shŭn), *n.* **1**, care taken beforehand; **2**, care used to prevent mischief or secure good results.

pre-cau-tion-a-ry (prē-kô'shŭn-ā-rĭ), *adj.* pertaining to, or proceeding from, care taken beforehand; intended to prevent harm or loss.

pre-cede (prē-sēd'), *v.t.* and *v.i.* [*p.t.* and *p.p.* -ced'ed, *p.pr.* -ced'ing], to go before in time, place, rank, or importance.

pre-ced-ence (prē-sēd'ĕns), *n.* **1**, the act or right of going before; **2**, superiority in rank; **3**, a position in advance of others at a ceremony. Also, **pre-ced'en-cy.**

prec-e-dent (prĕs'ē-dĕnt), *n.* something said or done that provides a pattern for similar cases; a rule for action established by previous action; a model.

pre-ced-ing (prē-sēd'ĭng), *p.adj.* existing or happening before.

Syn. previous, prior, antecedent.

pre-cen-tor (prē-sĕn'tŏr), *n.* the leader of a cathedral choir; one who leads the singing of a congregation; also, a singer who leads any audience.

pre-cept (prē'sĕpt), *n.* **1**, a rule of action or of moral conduct; maxim; **2**, in law, a written order issued by a judge.

pre-cep-tor (prē-sĕp'tẽr), *n.* an instructor or teacher.—*n.fem.* **pre-cep'tress.**—*adj.* **pre″cep-to'ri-al.**

pre-cep-to-ry (prē-sĕp'tō-rĭ), *adj.* giving, or containing, precepts; mandatory:—*n.* [*pl.* preceptories (-rĭz)], a college or religious house of the medieval order of Knights Templars.

pre-ces-sion (prē-sĕsh'ŭn), *n.* the act of going before others; a going forward: **precession of the equinoxes**, the slow westward movement of the equinoctial points on the ecliptic, due to a slow change in the direction of the earth's axis in space.—*adj.* **pre-ces'sion-al.**

pre-cinct (prē'sĭngkt), *n.* **1**, a place bounded, or marked off, by fixed lines; **2**, an outward limit or boundary; **3**, a district; a division made for governmental purposes; as, a police *precinct;* **4**, in *pl.*, surrounding regions.

pre-cious (prĕsh'ŭs), *adj.* **1**, of great price or value; costly; **2**, very dear; highly esteemed; **3**, *Colloq.*, thorough; extreme; as, a *precious* nuisance.—*adv.* **pre'cious-ly.**—*n.* **pre'cious-ness.**

prec-i-pice (prĕs'ĭ-pĭs), *n.* a steep descent; an abrupt declivity; an almost vertical cliff, or the edge of it.

pre-cip-i-tant (prē-sĭp'ĭ-tănt), *adj.* **1**, falling headlong; **2**, too hasty or sudden; moving with rash haste, as in flight:—*n.* in chemistry, anything which causes the solid part of a solution to separate from the liquid and fall to the bottom of the vessel containing it.—*adv.* **pre-cip'i-tant-ly.**—*n.* **pre-cip'i-tance; pre-cip'i-tan-cy.**

pre-cip-i-tate (prē-sĭp'ĭ-tāt), *v.t.* [*p.t.* and *p.p.* -tat″ed, *p.pr.* -tat″ing], **1**, to throw headlong; **2**, to urge on violently; hurry on rashly, thoughtlessly, or unexpectedly; bring to a crisis; as, his act *precipitated* the disaster; **3**, to cause to change from vapor to liquid or solid, and fall, as rain or snow; **4**, in chemistry, to cause to separate in solid form from a state of solution:—*v.i.* to separate in solid form from a solution and fall to the bottom of a vessel:—*n.* any substance which separates out as a solid when two solutions are mixed:—*adj.* (prē-sĭp'ĭ-tāt), **1**, rash; **2**, done without deliberation; **3**, falling or rushing headlong; **4**, descending steeply or vertically.—*adv.* **pre-cip'i-tate-ly.**

pre-cip-i-ta-tion (prē-sĭp″ĭ-tā'shŭn), *n.* **1**, a headlong fall; a violent and swift descent; **2**, rashness; rash haste; **3**, in chemistry, the process of causing the solid part of a solution to separate from the liquid and fall; **4**, moisture condensed from the atmosphere and falling upon the earth's surface, as rain, dew, snow, etc.

pre-cip-i-tous (prē-sĭp'ĭ-tŭs), *adj.* **1**, very steep, like a cliff; **2**, descending rapidly and violently.—*adv.* **pre-cip'i-tous-ly.**—*n.* **pre-cip'i-tous-ness.**

Syn. sheer. (See steep.)

***pré-cis** (prā″sē'; prā'sē), [Fr.], *n.* [*pl.* précis], a summing up of the principal parts of a work; a summary; abstract.

pre-cise (prē-sīs'), *adj.* **1**, exact; distinct; accurate; definite, as a report;

2, keeping closely to rule; exact to excess; 3, fastidious; prim; strict, as in conduct or manners.—*adv.* **pre-cise'ly.**—*n.* **pre-cise'ness.**
Syn. particular. (See correct.)

pre-ci-sian (prē-sĭzh'ăn), *n.* one who is very careful to observe rules and forms, esp. in religious matters.

pre-ci-sion (prē-sĭzh'ŭn), *n.* exactness; accuracy; definiteness.

pre-clude (prē-klōōd'), *v.t.* [*p.t.* and *p.p.* -clud'ed, *p.pr.* -clud'ing], 1, to shut out; hinder; 2, to keep from taking place; prevent; as, to *preclude* any action.

pre-clu-sion (prē-klōō'zhŭn), *n.* the act of preventing or excluding.

pre-clu-sive (prē-klōō'sĭv), *adj.* preventive.—*adv.* **pre-clu'sive-ly.**

pre-co-cious (prē-kō'shŭs), *adj.* 1, ripe before the natural time; 2, forward in mental development; developed too early or dangerously early, as a child. —*adv.* **pre-co'cious-ly.**—*n.* **pre-co'cious-ness.**

pre-coc-i-ty (prē-kŏs'ĭ-tĭ), *n.* the state or quality of being ripe or developed before the usual time; too early growth; esp., in a child, remarkably early mental development.

pre-con-ceive (prē"kŏn-sēv'), *v.t.* [*p.t.* and *p.p.* -ceived' (-sēvd'), *p.pr.* -ceiv'ing], to form beforehand, as an impression or opinion, in advance of actual knowledge.—*n.* **pre"con-cep'tion.**

pre-con-cert (prē"kŏn-sûrt'), *v.t.* to arrange together, or agree upon, beforehand.—*p.adj.* **pre"con-cert'ed.**

pre-cur-sor (prē-kûr'sẽr), *n.* one who or that which goes before, to show that a person or an event is about to follow; forerunner; predecessor.

pre-cur-so-ry (prē-kûr'sō-rĭ), *adj.* 1, indicating something that is to happen or follow; 2, preliminary.

pre-da-cious (prē-dā'shŭs), *adj.* 1, killing other animals for food; as, a *predacious* beast; 2, predatory.

pred-a-to-ry (prĕd'ȧ-tō-rĭ), *adj.* 1, plundering; robbing; as, a *predatory* tribe of people; 2, living by preying on other animals; as, a *predatory* beast.

pred-e-ces-sor (prĕd"ē-sĕs'ẽr; prē"dē-), *n.* 1, one who has gone before another, as in the same office, position, etc.: opp of *successor;* 2, an ancestor.

pre-des-ti-nate (prē-dĕs'tĭ-nāt), *v.t.* [*p.t.* and *p.p.* -nat"ed, *p.pr.* -nat"ing], to decree or determine beforehand, or from the very beginning. Also, **pre-des'-tine.**—*n.* **pre-des"ti-na'ri-an.**

pre-des-ti-na-tion (prē-dĕs"tĭ-nā'-shŭn), *n.* 1, the doctrine that God has from all eternity ordered whatever comes to pass; 2, a decree that determines the happiness or misery of men; fate; destiny; foreknowledge.

pre-de-ter-mine (prē"dē-tûr'mĭn), *v.t.* and *v.i.* [*p.t.* and *p.p.* -mined (-mĭnd), *p.pr.* -min-ing], to decide, resolve, or decree beforehand; predestine.—*n.* **pre"de-ter"mi-na'tion.**

pred-i-ca-ble (prĕd'ĭ-kȧ-bl), *adj.* capable of being affirmed or declared.—*n.* **pred"i-ca-bil'i-ty.**

pre-dic-a-ment (prē-dĭk'ȧ-mĕnt), *n.* a situation; esp., an amusing, a trying, or an unfortunate position.

pred-i-cate (prĕd'ĭ-kāt), *v.t.* [*p.t.* and *p.p.* -cat"ed, *p.pr.* -cat"ing], 1, to affirm as belonging to, or characteristic of, something; as, to *predicate* poverty as a result of ignorance; 2, to assert; declare; 3, to signify:—*v.i.* to affirm one thing of another; assert:—*adj.* (prĕd'ĭ-kāt), in grammar, expressing that which is stated about the subject: **predicate adjective,** an adjective in the predicate, following the verb *be, seem, become,* or the like, and modifying the subject; as, lead is *heavy;* he looks *tired:*—*n.* (prĕd'ĭ-kāt), 1, in grammar, the part of a sentence, consisting of the verb and its modifiers and complements, which makes a statement about the subject; 2, in logic, that which is asserted or denied.

pred-i-ca-tion (prĕd"ĭ-kā'shŭn), *n.* assertion; declaration.

pred-i-ca-tive (prĕd'ĭ-kā-tĭv), *adj.* affirmative or declarative. —*adv.* **pred'i-ca-tive-ly.**

pre-dict (prē-dĭkt'), *v.t.* and *v.i.* to tell or make known beforehand; foretell.—*n.* **pre-dic'tor.**—*adj.* **pre-dic'tive.**

pre-dic-tion (prē-dĭk'shŭn), *n.* 1, the foretelling of a future event; 2, that which is foretold; prophecy.

pre-di-lec-tion (prē"dĭ-lĕk'shŭn; prĕd"ĭ-), *n.* a choice made beforehand; preference; partiality.

pre-dis-pose (prē"dĭs-pōz'), *v.t.* [*p.t.* and *p.p.* -posed' (-pōzd'), *p.pr.* -pos'ing], 1, to incline beforehand; as, he was *predisposed* in her favor; 2, to fit or adapt beforehand; make liable to by a previous tendency; as, *predisposed* to contagion.

pre-dis-po-si-tion (prē-dĭs"pō-zĭsh'ŭn), *n.* 1, previous inclination or tendency; 2, bent; bias.

pre-dom-i-nance (prē-dŏm'ĭ-năns), *n.* superiority in strength, power, or influence; prevalence; supremacy. Also, **pre-dom'i-nan-cy.**

pre-dom-i-nant (prē-dŏm'ĭ-nănt), *adj.* having greater influence; controlling.—*adv.* **pre-dom'i-nant-ly.**

pre-dom-i-nate (prē-dŏm'ĭ-nāt), *v.i.* [*p.t.* and *p.p.* -nat"ed, *p.pr.* -nat"ing], to be superior in strength, power, or influence; prevail.—*n.* **pre-dom"i-na'tion.**

pre-ëm-i-nence (prē-ĕm'ĭ-nĕns), *n.* superiority to all others in merit, rank, etc.; distinction.

pre-ëm-i-nent (prē-ĕm'ĭ-nĕnt), *adj.* highly superior to others; distinguished from others who are eminent.—*adv.* **pre-ëm'i-nent-ly.**

pre-ëmpt (prē-ĕmpt'), *v.t.* to appropriate; establish a right or claim to before others; esp., in the U. S., to settle on (public land) so as to have the right to it before others buy:—*v.i.* to establish a claim to public land by settling upon it in advance of others.—*n.* **pre-ëmp'tor.**—*adj.* **pre-ëmp'tive.**

pre-ëmp-tion (prē-ĕmp'shŭn), *n.* the act, right, or privilege of purchasing before others, as public land.

preen (prēn), *v.t.* 1, to cleanse, trim, and smooth with the beak, as a bird its plumage; 2, to dress (oneself) up.

pre-ëx-ist (prē"ĕg-zĭst'), *v.i.* to exist before the present life; have a prior existence.—*n.* **pre"ëx-ist'ence.**—*adj.* **pre"ëx-ist'ent.**

pref-ace (prĕf'ās), *n.* the introduction to a book, speech, etc., preceding the body of the work:—*v.t.* [*p.t.* and *p.p.* -aced (-āst), *p.pr.* -ac-ing], 1, to introduce by some act, statement, or remarks; 2, to act as introduction to:—*v.i.* to offer, or do, something, as an introduction.

pref-a-to-ry (prĕf'ȧ-tō-rĭ), *adj.* pertaining to, or of the nature of, an introduction; introductory.

pre-fect (prē'fĕkt), *n.* 1, in ancient Rome, a civil magistrate or governor; commander; 2, in France, the civil governor of a department; as, the *prefect* of police.

pre-fec-ture (prē'fĕk-tūr), *n.* the office, authority, or official residence of a prefect.

pre-fer (prē-fûr′), *v.t.* [*p.t.* and *p.p.* -ferred′ (-fûrd′), *p.pr.* -fer′ring], **1**, to regard or esteem more than something else; **2**, to offer for consideration; as, to *prefer* a petition.
Syn. choose, elect, favor.

pref-er-a-ble (prĕf′ẽr-*ȧ*-bl), *adj.* more desirable than something else; worthy to be chosen.—*n.* **pref′er-a-ble-ness.**—*adv.* **pref′er-a-bly.**

pref-er-ence (prĕf′ẽr-ĕns), *n.* **1**, choice of one thing more than another; **2**, that which is favored or chosen.

pref-er-en-tial (prĕf″ẽr-ĕn′shăl), *adj.* showing, or receiving, preference; favoring some particular person or thing: **preferential ballot**, a form of ballot on which the voter may indicate first, second, or later choices of candidate, so that if no candidate receives a majority of first choices, the one who receives the greatest number of first and later choices taken together is chosen.—*adv.* **pref″er-en′tial-ly.**

pre-fer-ment (prē-fûr′mĕnt), *n.* promotion to higher rank or office; a high post of honor, dignity, or profit, esp. in the church.

pre-fig-ure (prē-fĭg′ūr), *v.t.* [*p.t.* and *p.p.* -ured (-ūrd), *p.pr.* -ur-ing], **1**, to show or declare beforehand by a type or symbol; **2**, to imagine to oneself beforehand.—*n.* **pre-fig″u-ra′tion.**—*adj.* **pre-fig′ur-a-tive.**

pre-fix (prē′fĭks), *n.* a letter, syllable, or group of syllables placed at the beginning of a word to modify its meaning:—*v.t.* (prē-fĭks′), to place before, or at the beginning of, anything.

preg-nan-cy (prĕg′năn-sĭ), *n.* **1**, in mammals, the condition of being with young, or of carrying unborn young; **2**, significance; suggestiveness; weightiness; as, *pregnancy* of thought.

preg-nant (prĕg′nănt), *adj.* **1**, being with young; carrying unborn young: said of female mammals; **2**, full; heavy; **3**, fruitful; fertile; **4**, full of meaning; weighty.—*adv.* **preg′nant-ly.**

pre-hen-sile (prē-hĕn′sĭl; *Br.* prē-hĕn′-sīl), *adj.* adapted for seizing: usually said of a tail or limb.

pre-hen-sion (prē-hĕn′shŭn), *n.* a taking hold, or grasping, physically or mentally.

pre-his-tor-ic (prē″hĭs-tŏr′ĭk), *adj.* pertaining to a period before the time of which there is a written record.

pre-judge (prē-jŭj′), *v.t.* [*p.t.* and *p.p.* -judged′ (-jŭjd′), *p.pr.* -judg′-ing], **1**, to come to a conclusion concerning, without a full hearing; **2**, to come to a conclusion concerning, beforehand.—*n.* **pre-judg′ment; pre-judge′ment.**

prej-u-dice (prĕj′o͞o-dĭs), *n.* **1**, a bias, favorable or unfavorable; **2**, an opinion formed without due examination of the facts; **3**, injury or harm as a result of hasty or unfair judgment:—*v.t.* [*p.t.* and *p.p.* -diced (-dĭst), *p.pr.* -dic-ing], **1**, to cause to form an opinion, usually unfavorable, before examination of the facts; **2**, to hurt; harm or damage by some opinion or action.
Syn., n. unfairness, partiality.

prej-u-di-cial (prĕj″o͞o-dĭsh′ăl), *adj.* injurious; damaging.

prel-a-cy (prĕl′*ȧ*-sĭ), *n.* [*pl.* prelacies (-sĭz)], **1**, the office or position of a clergyman of high rank, as a bishop; **2**, bishops collectively.

prel-ate (prĕl′ăt), *n.* one of the higher order of clergy, as a bishop or archbishop.—*adj.* **pre-lat′ic** (prē-lăt′ĭk); **pre-lat′i-cal.**—*n.* **prel′ate-ship.**

pre-lim-i-na-ry (prē-lĭm′ĭ-nā-rĭ), *adj.* introductory; preparatory; as, *preliminary* remarks:—*n.* [*pl.* preliminaries (-rĭz)], an introductory act or step.—*adv.* **pre-lim′i-na-ri-ly.**

[1]**prel-ude** (prĕl′ūd; prē′lūd), *n.* **1**, a preface; something done to prepare the way for something more important; **2**, a phrase, section, or short piece of music serving as introduction to the main portion of a composition, as to a suite, an opera, etc.; also, any short piece arbitrarily given this name; as, Rachmaninoff's *Prelude* in C sharp minor.

[2]**pre-lude** (prē-lūd′ or, in reference to music, prĕl′ūd or prē′lūd), *v.t.* [*p.t.* and *p.p.* -lud′ed, *p.pr.* -lud′ing], **1**, to introduce; **2**, in music, to play an introduction to:—*v.i.* to play a prelude.—*n.* **pre-lud′er.**

pre-ma-ture (prē″m*ȧ*-tūr′; prē′m*ȧ*-tūr; *Br.* prĕm′*ȧ*-tūr), *adj.* arriving, occurring, or done, before the usual or proper time; as, a *premature* explosion.—*adv.* **pre″ma-ture′ly.**—*n.* **pre″ma-ture′ness.**

pre-med-i-tate (prē-mĕd′ĭ-tāt), *v.t.* [*p.t.* and *p.p.* -tat″ed, *p.pr.* -tat″ing], to think carefully over or plan beforehand:—*v.i.* to form a plan beforehand.

pre-med-i-ta-tion (prē-mĕd″ĭ-tā′shŭn), *n.* the act of planning or arranging beforehand; forethought.—*adj.* **pre-med′i-ta-tive.**

pre-mi-er (prē′mĭ-ẽr; prĕm′yẽr), *adj.* **1**, foremost; chief; principal; **2**, earliest in time:—*n.* a prime minister or chief officer of the state.

***pre-mière** (prē-myâr′), [Fr.], *n.* **1**, in a theatrical company, the leading lady; **2**, the first performance, as of a play.

pre-mi-er-ship (prē′mĭ-ẽr-shĭp), *n.* the office or position of a prime minister or chief officer of the state.

[1]**prem-ise** (prĕm′ĭs), *n.* **1**, in logic, a statement accepted as true, from which a conclusion is to be drawn; **2**, in *pl.*, in law: **a**, an introductory statement, as in a deed; **b**, real estate.

[2]**pre-mise** (prē-mīz′), *v.t.* [*p.t.* and *p.p.* -mised′ (-mīzd′), *p.pr.* -mis′-ing], to state in advance, as an explanation; offer as an accepted basis from which to draw a conclusion:—*v.i.* to explain beforehand.

pre-mi-um (prē′mĭ-ŭm), *n.* **1**, a reward or prize for excelling, as in a competition; **2**, a free article sometimes offered as an inducement to buy other goods; **3**, a fee paid for instruction, as in a trade; **4**, an amount agreed upon as the price to be paid for a contract of insurance; **5**, the amount by which the market value of stocks, bonds, etc., exceeds their par value; as, the stock sold at a *premium;* **6**, the amount by which the value of one currency exceeds that of another of the same denomination; also, the charge for changing one currency into another of a higher value.

pre-mo-ni-tion (prē″mō-nĭsh′ŭn), *n.* **1**, a warning; **2**, a foreboding, as of danger.—*adj.* **pre-mon′i-to-ry.**

pre-na-tal (prē-nā′tăl), *adj.* occurring, or existing, before birth; also, pertaining to an unborn child; as, *prenatal* care of an expectant mother.

pre-oc-cu-pa-tion (prē-ŏk″ū-pā′shŭn), *n.* **1**, the act of seizing in advance; **2**, the state of being lost in thought or of having the attention centered on one's own affairs; **3**, something that demands all of one's attention.

pre-oc-cu-pied (prē-ŏk′ū-pīd), *p.adj.* **1**, already occupied or in use; **2**, lost in thought; taken up entirely with one's own affairs; absent-minded.

pre-oc-cu-py (prē-ŏk′ū-pī), *v.t.* [*p.t.* and *p.p.* -pied (-pīd), *p.pr.*

-py″ing], **1**, to occupy before another or others; **2**, to absorb; compel the attention of.

prep-a-ra-tion (prĕp″*ȧ*-rā′shŭn), *n.* **1**, the act of making ready or fitting for a particular purpose; **2**, the state of being ready; readiness; **3**, that which is ready or made ready, as a medicine, polish, or the like; **4**, that which fits for a particular purpose, as a course of study.

pre-par-a-tive (prē-păr′*ȧ*-tĭv), *adj.* tending to make ready or fit:—*n.* that which makes ready or fit for something further.—*adv.* **pre-par′a-tive-ly.**

pre-par-a-to-ry (prē-păr′*ȧ*-tō-rĭ), *adj.* **1**, serving to make ready or fit for something further; **2**, being fitted or made ready, as by instruction.

pre-pare (prē-pâr′), *v.t.* [*p.t.* and *p.p.* -pared′ (-pârd′), *p.pr.* -par′ing], **1**, to make ready, fit, or suitable; as, to *prepare* food; **2**, to provide, or fit out; as, to *prepare* an expedition:—*v.i.* to make or get things or oneself ready; as, to *prepare* for a journey or a speech.—*p.adj.* **pre-pared′.**—*adv.* **pre-par′-ed-ly.**—*n.* **pre-par′er.**

pre-par-ed-ness (prē-pâr′ĕd-nĕs), *n.* the state of being ready; specif., readiness for military activity.

pre-pay (prē-pā′), *v.t.* [*p.t.* and *p.p.* -paid′ (-pād′), *p.pr.* -pay′ing], to pay, or pay the cost of, in advance.—*n.* **pre-pay′ment**

pre-pense (prē-pĕns′), *adj.* planned in advance; as, malice *prepense.*

pre-pon-der-ant (prē-pŏn′dẽr-ănt), *adj.* greater in weight, power, or influence; outweighing.—*adv.* **pre-pon′der-ant-ly.**—*n.* **pre-pon′der-ance.**

pre-pon-der-ate (prē-pŏn′dẽr-āt), *v.i.* [*p.t.* and *p.p.* -at″ed, *p.pr.* -at″ing], to outweigh; exceed in power, weight, or influence.

prep-o-si-tion (prĕp″ō-zĭsh′ŭn), *n.* an indeclinable part of speech, as *to, from, by,* used with a noun or pronoun as object, which shows the relation of the object to some other word in the sentence.

prep-o-si-tion-al (prĕp″ō-zĭsh′ŭn-ăl), *adj.* pertaining to a preposition: **prepositional phrase**, a phrase, composed of a preposition and its object, together with modifiers, and used to do the work of a single part of speech, as an adverb or adjective.—*adv.* **prep″o-si′tion-al-ly.**

pre-pos-sess (prē″pŏ-zĕs′), *v.t.* **1**, to occupy beforehand; as, to *prepossess* land; **2**, to fill (the mind) beforehand so as to shut out other thoughts; **3**, hence, to predispose to a favorable opinion.

pre-pos-sess-ing (prē″pŏ-zĕs′ĭng), *p.adj.* tending to win or secure favor; attractive.

pre-pos-ses-sion (prē″pŏ-zĕsh′ŭn), *n.* an opinion, usually favorable, of a person or thing, formed in advance of actual knowledge, and shutting out other ideas from the mind; a bias.

pre-pos-ter-ous (prē-pŏs′tẽr-ŭs), *adj.* contrary to common sense; ridiculous; absurd; unreasonable; as, a *preposterous* statement.—*adv.* **pre-pos′ter-ous-ly.**—*n.* **pre-pos′ter-ous-ness.**

pre-puce (prē′pūs), *n.* the foreskin; the loose fold or sheath of skin covering the end of the penis.

pre-req-ui-site (prē-rĕk′wĭ-zĭt), *adj.* necessary to secure an intended result:—*n.* something necessary to produce a desired result.

pre-rog-a-tive (prē-rŏg′*ȧ*-tĭv), *n.* a right or privilege that has always accompanied a certain office or position; esp., a special right or privilege belonging to kingship:—*adj.* pertaining to such a right.

1**pres-age** (prĕs′āj; prē′sāj), *n.* **1**, a feeling that something is to happen; **2**, an omen or sign; **3**, knowledge of events before they take place; foresight.

2**pre-sage** (prē-sāj′), *v.t.* [*p.t.* and *p.p.* -saged′ (-sājd′), *p.pr.* -sag′ing], **1**, to foretell; predict; give warning of; **2**, to have a foreboding of.

pres-by-ter (prĕz′bĭ-tẽr; prĕs′-), *n.* **1**, in the early church, a priest or elder; **2**, a minister ranking between bishop and deacon; **3**, in the Presbyterian Church, a minister or elder.—*adj.* **pres″by-te′ri-al.**

pres-by-te-ri-an (prĕz″bĭ-tē′rĭ-ăn; prĕs″-), *adj.* pertaining to, or characterized by, government by ministers and elders: **Presbyterian**, *adj.* pertaining to a denomination of Protestant churches governed by ministers and elders, or to its beliefs and institutions:—*n.* a member or supporter of this denomination.—*n.* **Pres″by-te′ri-an-ism.**

pres-by-ter-y (prĕz′bĭ-tẽr-ĭ; prĕs′-), *n.* **1**, in the early church, a body of elders; **2**, in the Presbyterian Church, an organized body, having judicial power, composed of the ministers and ruling elders of the churches in a given district; also, the district so represented.

pre-sci-ence (prē′shĭ-ĕns; prĕsh′ĭ-ĕns), *n.* the knowing of events before they take place; foreknowledge.

pre-sci-ent (prē′shĭ-ĕnt; prĕsh′ĭ-ĕnt), *adj.* foreseeing; foreknowing.

pre-scribe (prē-skrīb′), *v.t.* [*p.t.* and *p.p.* -scribed′ (-skrībd′), *p.pr.* -scrib′ing], **1**, to advise the use of as medicine; **2**, to set down as a guide or rule of action:—*v.i.* **1**, to write medical directions; **2**, to give laws, rules, or directions.—*n.* **pre-scrib′er.**

pre-script (prē-skrĭpt′; prē′skrĭpt), *adj.* laid down authoritatively; ordained:—*n.* (prē′skrĭpt), an order; a rule.

pre-scrip-tion (prē-skrĭp′shŭn), *n.* **1**, the giving of a direction or rule; **2**, the direction or rule given; **3**, a written direction for the preparation and use of a medicine; **4**, in law, the obtaining of a right to property by long-continued use; also, the right thus obtained.—*adj.* **pre-scrip′tive.**

pres-ence (prĕz′ĕns), *n.* **1**, the state or quality of being in a certain place; **2**, nearness; immediate neighborhood; as, in the *presence* of danger; **3**, attendance: opp. of *absence;* **4**, one's appearance or bearing; as, a girl of pleasing *presence;* **5**, all the qualities that make a person what he is: **presence of mind**, quickness in thinking or deciding in time of danger or necessity.

1**pres-ent** (prĕz′ĕnt), *adj.* **1**, being at hand in a given place, in sight, or in attendance: opp. of *absent;* **2**, existing at this time; not past or future; **3**, instant or immediate; **4**, designating a tense of the verb which mainly expresses time that now is, or action now going on, or habitual action:—*n.* **1**, the time or occasion now here; **2**, the present tense; **3**, in *pl.*, in law, a writing or document actually before one, or the words occurring in such a document; as, know all men by these *presents:* **at present**, now.

2**pre-sent** (prē-zĕnt′), *v.t.* **1**, to bring before someone, esp. before a superior; introduce; **2**, to bring to view or notice; display; exhibit; **3**, to offer as a gift; **4**, to furnish (someone) with a gift; **5**, to lay before a person or body for consideration; as, to *present* a petition: **present arms**, to hold a weapon in a vertical position in front of the body (see illus. next page).

3**pres-ent** (prĕz′ĕnt), *n.* a gift; anything given or presented.
Syn., *n.* gratuity. (See gift.)

pre-sent-a-ble (prē-zĕn′tȧ-bl), *adj.* 1, suitable to be offered, given, or introduced; 2, suitable or fit to be seen.—*n.* **pre-sent″a-bil′i-ty.**

pres-en-ta-tion (prĕz″ĕn-tā′shŭn), *n.* 1, the act or state of introducing, offering, or bringing to consideration; as, *presentation* at court; 2, that which is introduced, offered, or brought to consideration.

SOLDIER PRESENTING ARMS

pre-sen-ti-ment (prē-sĕn′tĭ-mĕnt; prē-zĕn′-), *n.* a feeling of fear as to what will occur, usually of coming evil; a foreboding.

pres-ent-ly (prĕz′ĕnt-lĭ), *adv.* 1, *Archaic,* at once; 2, soon; before long.

pre-sent-ment (prē-zĕnt′mĕnt), *n.* 1, the act of setting forth to view; 2, the thing set forth to view; a representation or picture; 3, a report or statement made by a grand jury concerning an offense of which they have personal knowledge without any indictment having been laid before them.

pres-er-va-tion (prĕz″ẽr-vā′shŭn), *n.* 1, the act of keeping from injury or decay; 2, the state of being so kept; as, the *preservation* of fruit.

pre-serv-a-tive (prē-zûr′vȧ-tĭv), *adj.* tending to keep substances from decay or injury:—*n.* a preserving substance or agent.

pre-serve (prē-zûrv′), *v.t.* [*p.t.* and *p.p.* -served′ (-zûrvd′), *p.pr.* -serv′ing], 1, to keep from injury; defend; save; as, to *preserve* life; 2, to keep in a wholesome state; 3, to put up with sugar, salt, etc., for keeping; as, to *preserve* fruit; 4, to keep up; maintain; as, to *preserve* peace:—*v.i.* 1, to prepare fruit, vegetables, etc., so as to keep without spoiling; 2, to protect game:—*n.* 1, usually in *pl.*, fruit kept from spoiling by cooking or by sugar, alcohol, etc.; 2, a place set apart for keeping game, fish, or the like.—*adj.* **pre-serv′a-ble.**—*n.* **pre-serv′er.**—*adj.* and *n.* **pre-serv′a-to-ry.**

pre-side (prē-zīd′), *v.i.* [*p.t.* and *p.p.* -sid′ed, *p.pr.* -sid′ing], 1, to direct or control; act as head; as, to *preside* over one's household; 2, to direct the proceedings of a meeting.—*n.* **pre-sid′er.**

pres-i-den-cy (prĕz′ĭ-dĕn-sĭ), *n.* [*pl.* presidencies (-sĭz)], the function or duty of one who heads an organization, directs a meeting, etc.; also, the office or term of office of such a person: **Presidency,** the office and term of office of the chief executive of the U. S.; as, the *Presidency* of Taft.

pres-i-dent (prĕz′ĭ-dĕnt), *n.* 1, one who directs or acts as head of an organized body; 2, (often, *President*), the highest executive officer of a republic; 3, the chief officer of a college, university, or society.

pres-i-den-tial (prĕz″ĭ-dĕn′shăl), *adj.* pertaining to a president, or to his office; as, a *presidential* election.

¹press (prĕs), *v.t.* 1, to exert considerable force upon; squeeze or crush strongly; 2, to urge; as, they *pressed* him to accept; 3, to compel; 4, to force to hurry; 5, to stress; emphasize; 6, to make smooth by bearing down upon, as cloth; 7, to impose by force; as, to *press* one's opinions upon another:—*v.i.* 1, to bear heavily; 2, to move forward with determination; hasten; as, to *press* on one's way; 3, to be urgent or insistent; call for quick action; as, time *presses:*—*n.* 1, an instrument or machine for compacting, crushing, or stamping anything; 2, a machine for working or forging metal; 3, a printing machine; 4, the product of a printing machine; newspaper and magazine literature; as, the power of the *press;* 5, a crowd; a throng; 6, the act of crowding forward; pressure; 7, urgency of affairs; as, the *press* of business; 8, a closet with shelves.—*n.* **press′er.**

²press (prĕs), *v.t.* to recruit by force; force into service, esp. into naval service.

press a-gent a person who attends to advertising, press notices, and general newspaper or periodical publicity, as for an actor, an organization, or an institution seeking popular support.

press gang a squad of men assigned to capture men for the navy. Also, *n.* **press′gang″.**

press-ing (prĕs′ĭng), *p.adj.* persistent; exacting; urgent; as, a *pressing* engagement.—*adv.* **press′ing-ly.**

press-man (prĕs′măn), *n.* [*pl.* pressmen (-mĕn)], one who manages or operates a press, esp. a printing press.

pres-sure (prĕsh′ŭr), *n.* 1, a heavy bearing down or pushing against something; 2, the exertion of continuous mental or moral force; use of influence or authority; 3, burden; distress; 4, urgent or insistent demand; as, the *pressure* of work.

pres-ti-dig-i-ta-tion (prĕs″tĭ-dĭj″ĭ-tā′shŭn), *n.* 1, sleight of hand, esp. that requiring skill with the fingers; 2, juggling.—*n.* **pres″ti-dig′i-ta″tor.**

pres-tige (prĕs-tēzh′; prĕs′tĭj), *n.* authority or influence due to reputation or achievements.

pres-to (prĕs′tō), *adv.* 1, quickly; suddenly: used as an exclamation by a worker of sleight-of-hand tricks; 2, in music, quickly: a direction for tempo.

pre-sum-a-ble (prē-zūm′ȧ-bl), *adj.* fair to suppose; reasonable.—*adv.* **pre-sum′a-bly.**

pre-sume (prē-zūm′), *v.t.* [*p.t.* and *p.p.* -sumed′ (-zūmd′), *p.pr.* -sum′ing], 1, to take for granted; suppose; 2, to venture; as, to *presume* to offer advice:—*v.i.* 1, to behave with too much confidence or undue boldness; 2, to take liberties; as, to *presume* on one's good nature.—*n.* **pre-sum′er.**

pre-sump-tion (prē-zŭmp′shŭn), *n.* 1, a going beyond due bounds; bold forwardness; 2, acceptance and belief of something not fully proved; as, he acted on the *presumption* that the price would rise; 3, that which is taken for granted.

pre-sump-tive (prē-zŭmp′tĭv), *adj.* affording reasonable ground for belief; probable: **heir presumptive,** an heir whose right may be superseded by the birth of a nearer relative: distinguished from *heir apparent.*—*adv.* **pre-sump′tive-ly.**

pre-sump-tu-ous (prē-zŭmp′tū-ŭs), *adj.* 1, bold; too confident; 2, rash; foolhardy.—*adv.* **pre-sump′tu-ous-ly.**—*n.* **pre-sump′tu-ous-ness.**

pre-sup-pose (prē″sŭ-pōz′), *v.t.* [*p.t.* and *p.p.* -posed′ (-pōzd′), *p.pr.* -pos′ing], to take for granted; assume.

pre-sup-po-si-tion (prē-sŭp″ō-zĭsh′ŭn), *n.* 1, a belief previously formed; 2, that which is taken for granted; an assumption.

pre-tend (prē-tĕnd′), *v.t.* 1, to put forward as an excuse or reason; 2, to make a false show of; as, to *pretend* friendship; 3, to put forward a claim to; as, to *pretend* ownership:—*v.i.* 1, to put forward a claim, true or false; as, to *pretend* to a title; 2, to make a false show; 3, to play at make-believe.
Syn. feign, sham, counterfeit.

pre-tend-ed (prē-tĕn′dĕd), *p.adj.* feigned or imagined; false; as, *pretended* riches.—*adv.* **pre-tend′ed-ly.**

pre-tend-er (prē-tĕn′dẽr), *n.* **1,** one who lays false claim to anything under the appearance of a right; **2,** one who makes a false show of anything: **the Pretender,** James Stuart, son of James II of England, a claimant to the British throne, for whom the Jacobites rebelled in 1715: also called *Old Pretender:* **Young Pretender,** Charles Stuart, his son, who later claimed the throne: also called *Bonnie Prince Charlie.*

pre-tense (prē-tĕns′), *n.* **1,** a putting on of a false appearance in order to hide what is real; deception; **2,** false show; sham; pretext; **3,** a claim. Also, **pre-tence′.**

pre-ten-sion (prē-tĕn′shŭn), *n.* **1,** a claim made, whether true or false; **2,** outward show of importance or excellence.

pre-ten-tious (prē-tĕn′shŭs), *adj.* assuming an air of superiority; making a show.—*adv.* **pre-ten′tious-ly.**—*n.* **pre-ten′tious-ness.**

pre-ter- (prē′tẽr-), *prefix,* past; beyond; outside the range of; more than.

pret-er-it (prĕt′ẽr-ĭt), *adj.* in grammar, past; expressing a past action or state: used generally to designate those tenses in the grammar of foreign languages which correspond to the English past tense:—*n.* the past tense. Also, **pret′er-ite** (prĕt′ẽr-ĭt).

pre-ter-mit (prē″tẽr-mĭt′), *v.t.* [*p.t.* and *p.p.* -mit′ted, *p.pr.* -mit′ting], to pass by; leave out; ignore; neglect, as a duty.—*n.* **pre″ter-mis′sion.**

pre-ter-nat-u-ral (prē″tẽr-năt′ū-răl), *adj.* unlike ordinary occurrences; extraordinary; strange.—*adv.* **pre″ter-nat′u-ral-ly.**

pre-text (prē′tĕkst; prē-tĕkst′), *n.* a pretense or excuse; a false motive put forward to conceal the real one.

pre-tor (prē′tŏr), *n.* the Roman magistrate next below the consul. Also, **præ′tor,** *Pfd. S.*—*adj.* **pre-to′ri-an.**

pret-ty (prĭt′ĭ), *adj.* [*comp.* pret′ti-er, *superl.* pret′ti-est], **1,** pleasing because of grace and daintiness; **2,** moderately large or excellent; as, a *pretty* sum of money; **3,** good; acceptable; fine; as, a *pretty* wit:—*adv.* fairly; moderately; tolerably; as, *pretty* well.—*adv.* **pret′ti-ly.**—*n.* **pret′ti-ness.**

Syn., adj. fair, comely. (See beautiful.)

pret-zel (prĕt′sĕl), *n.* a kind of salted biscuit made in the form of a knot.

pre-vail (prē-vāl′), *v.i.* **1,** to gain the advantage; obtain influence or superiority; as, right will *prevail;* **2,** to be or continue in force, as a custom; **3,** to persuade: with *on.*—*p.adj.* **pre-vail′ing.**

prev-a-lence (prĕv′ȧ-lĕns), *n.* **1,** the state of being widespread or in general use; **2,** superior strength or influence. Also, **prev′a-len-cy.**

prev-a-lent (prĕv′ȧ-lĕnt), *adj.* **1,** powerful; victorious; **2,** most general; common; widespread; as, a *prevalent* belief.—*adv.* **prev′a-lent-ly.**

pre-var-i-cate (prē-văr′ĭ-kāt), *v.i.* [*p.t.* and *p.p.* -cat″ed, *p.pr.* -cat″ing], to stray from the truth; quibble.—*n.* **pre-var′i-ca″tor.**

Syn. evade, equivocate, lie. *Prevaricate* is a milder word than *lie* and means to speak or act so as to deceive; the effect is the same, but is accomplished by using vague statements from which another may draw inaccurate conclusions rather than by downright lying. To *evade* is to avoid giving information and may or may not be deceptive, according as it produces a false impression or is merely noncommittal. To *equivocate* is deliberately to conceal the truth by ambiguity.

pre-var-i-ca-tion (prē-văr″ĭ-kā′shŭn), *n.* a quibbling to avoid the truth; a turning aside from truth or fair dealing; evasion.

pre-vent (prē-vĕnt′), *v.t.* **1,** to stop or keep from happening; **2,** to hinder, obstruct, or impede.—*adj.* **pre-vent′a-ble; pre-vent′i-ble.**—*n.* **pre-vent′er.**

Syn. hinder, obstruct. To *prevent* is to stop or keep from happening; as, caution *prevented* the accident. To *hinder* is to *prevent,* but usually only for a time; the idea of delay is present in this word; as, bad weather *hindered* the builders. *Obstruct* means to place something in the way of accomplishment; it is often applied to the checking of important actions; as, the path of the army was *obstructed* by barricades.

pre-ven-tion (prē-vĕn′shŭn), *n.* **1,** the act of hindering or keeping from happening; **2,** a hindrance or an obstruction; that which hinders.

pre-ven-tive (prē-vĕn′tĭv), *adj.* tending to hinder:—*n.* **1,** that which hinders; **2,** something that wards off disease.—*adv.* **pre-ven′tive-ly.**

pre-vi-ous (prē′vĭ-ŭs), *adj.* going before in time; prior; as, a *previous* action.—*adv.* **pre′vi-ous-ly.**

Syn. former, foregone.—*Ant.* subsequent.

pre-vi-sion (prē-vĭzh′ŭn), *n.* foreknowledge; foresight.

pre-war (prē-wôr′), *adj.* before any war, as opposed to *postwar.*

prey (prā), *n.* **1,** any animal which may be or is seized by a wild beast for food; **2,** hence, anything taken by force or violence; plunder; booty:—*v.i.* **1,** to take booty or plunder; seize and devour an animal as food; **2,** to exert a destructive influence: with *on* or *upon;* as, his guilt *preyed* upon his mind.

Pri-am (prī′ăm), *n.* in mythology, the last king of Troy, father of Hector and Paris: slain in the sack of Troy.

price (prīs), *n.* **1,** worth; value; **2,** something of equal worth, usually money, given or asked in exchange for a thing; the cost of a commodity; **3,** a result, whether good or bad; as, the *price* of honesty:—*v.t.* [*p.t.* and *p.p.* priced (prīst), *p.pr.* pric′ing], **1,** to set a value on; as, to *price* a book at two dollars; **2,** to ask the price of; as, to *price* goods.

Syn., n. expense, outlay, cost.

price-less (prīs′lĕs), *adj.* worth too much to be measured; invaluable.

prick (prĭk), *n.* **1,** a puncture, dot, or point; **2,** a sharp, stinging pain, usually caused by a pointed instrument; **3,** remorse; **4,** a slender, pointed object capable of piercing, as a thorn; **5,** the footprint of a hare or deer:—*v.t.* **1,** to pierce with, or as with, something pointed; **2,** to mark out by puncturing; **3,** to pain or sting; as, his conscience *pricks* him; **4,** to erect or raise; as, a dog *pricks* up its ears; **5,** to spur; urge; as, to *prick* a horse on:—*v.i.* **1,** to feel a sharp, stinging pain; **2,** to press forward; ride at top speed; **3,** to be raised, as the ears of an animal.

prick-er (prĭk′ẽr), *n.* **1,** a sharp point; usually, a tiny point on the stem or leaf of a plant, similar to a thorn; **2,** one who spurs on a horse: also used figuratively.

prick-le (prĭk′l), *n.* a small, slender spine growing from the surface of a plant, as on a nettle:—*v.t.* [*p.t.* and *p.p.* -led (-ld), *p.pr.* -ling], **1,** to give a stinging sensation to (the skin); **2,** to cover with small dots; stipple:—*v.i.* to tingle.

prick-ly (prĭk′lĭ), *adj.* **1,** full of thorns or sharp points; **2,** stinging; as, a *prickly* sensation: **prickly heat,** an inflammation of the sweat glands which causes a rash and itching: **prickly pear,** a cactus bearing a pear-shaped fruit covered with numerous small thorns; also, the fruit.

pride (prīd), *n.* **1,** undue self-esteem; conceit: **2,** haughtiness; disdain; **3,** a sense of personal dignity; high and dignified self-respect; **4,** that of which one is proud; as, his daughter was his *pride;* **5,** the best or highest part of anything; as, he was in the *pride* of his manhood:—*v.t.* [*p.t.* and *p.p.* prid′ed, *p.pr.* prid′ing], to indulge in self-esteem; as, to *pride* oneself.—*adj.* **pride′ful.**
Syn., n. vanity.—*Ant., n.* humility.

priest (prēst), *n.* **1,** one devoted to the service of God or a god, with authority to perform religious rites; **2,** one ordained to the Christian ministry, esp. in liturgical churches.—*n.fem.* **priest′ess.**

priest-craft (prēst′kráft″), *n.* an ambitious and worldly policy practiced by a priest or body of priests.

priest-hood (prēst′ho͝od), *n.* **1,** collectively, the ordained ministers of a religion; **2,** the office of a priest.

priest-ly (prēst′lĭ), *adj.* of or pertaining to a priest.—*n.* **priest′li-ness.**

prig (prĭg), *n.* a conceited person who gives himself airs of wisdom and virtue.

prig-gish (prĭg′ĭsh), *adj.* conceited; affectedly nice.—*adv.* **prig′gish-ly.**—*n.* **prig′gish-ness.**

prim (prĭm), *adj.* [*comp.* prim′mer, *superl.* prim′mest], precise; nice; formally neat:—*v.t.* [*p.t.* and *p.p.* primmed (prĭmd), *p.pr.* prim′ming], to dress or deck with nicety.—*adv.* **prim′ly.**—*n.* **prim′ness.**

pri-ma-cy (prī′mȧ-sĭ), *n.* [*pl.* primacies (-sĭz)], **1,** the state of being first in rank or importance; leadership; **2,** the office or dignity of an archbishop.

pri-ma don-na (prē′mȧ dŏn′ȧ), [*pl.* prima donnas (-ȧz)], the principal female singer in an opera or concert.

***pri-ma fa-ci-e** (prī′mȧ fā′shĭ-ē), [Lat.], at first view; as far as at first appears; as, *prima facie* evidence.

pri-mage (prī′māj), *n.* a small sum of money paid to the owner of a ship for the cost of handling the goods, in addition to the shipping charge.

pri-mal (prī′măl), *adj.* **1,** first; original; **2,** primary; chief.

pri-ma-ri-ly (prī′mā-rĭ-lĭ), *adv.* originally; essentially.

pri-ma-ry (prī′mȧ-rĭ), *adj.* **1,** first in order of origin, time, or place; original; primitive; **2,** fundamental; basic; as, the *primary* pigment colors are red, yellow, blue; **3,** first in order of development; hence, lowest; preparatory; as, a *primary* school; **4,** first thought of; as, the *primary* meaning of a word; **5,** first in rank; chief; principal; as, the *primary* planets; **6,** in music, designating the accent beginning a measure; **7,** in electricity, in an apparatus for mutual induction, designating the inducing current or the circuit designed for it: **primary cell** or **battery,** a battery that is a primary source of electricity, recharged by renewing the electrolyte or positive element: distinguished from *storage battery:* **primary election,** a local meeting of the voters of a political party, at which the nominees, officials, or delegates of that party are chosen:—*n.* [*pl.* primaries (-rĭz)], **1,** that which is first in rank, place, or importance; **2,** a district meeting of voters belonging to one party, held to name candidates to be voted for in a coming election, delegates to a convention, or the like; **3,** one of the large flight feathers in a bird's wing; **4,** in electricity, in an apparatus for mutual induction, as a transformer or induction coil, the inducing current, or the circuit designed for it: **direct primary,** a primary election at which the nominees of a party are chosen directly by the voters, without a nominating convention.

pri-mate (prī′māt), *n.* **1,** a member of the highest order (*Primates*) of mammals, which includes man and the monkeys apes, lemurs, and marmosets; **2** an archbishop.—*n.* **pri′mate-ship.**

¹**prime** (prīm), *adj.* **1,** first in order of rank, time, or importance; original: early; **2,** first in excellence; excellent; **3,** being at the highest point of life; vigorous: **prime meridian,** a meridian by which longitude is measured, usually that passing through Greenwich, England: **prime minister,** in countries with a representative form of government, the chief officer in the cabinet; the premier: not existent in the U. S.: **prime mover, 1,** an original natural force, directed by man, which sets a machine in motion, as steam; **2,** a machine which utilizes power directly from a natural source, as a water wheel: **prime number,** a number not divisible without remainder by any number except itself and unity, as 5, 13, 23, etc.:—*n.* **1,** the first or best part of anything; esp., the beginning of the day or year; **2,** the spring of life: youth; also, full maturity; **3,** a mark [′] placed above and to the right of a figure to indicate a minute, inch, etc., or to distinguish similar but different symbols; **4,** any of the first set of equal subdivisions of a unit, as a degree, itself divisible into seconds: also called *minute;* **5,** a prime number.—*adv.* **prime′ly.**—*n.* **prime′ness.**

²**prime** (prīm), *v.t.* [*p.t.* and *p.p.* primed (prīmd), *p.pr.* prim′ing], **1,** to prepare for firing, as a gun, or for lifting by filling with water, as a pump; **2,** to cover with the first coat of paint or plaster; **3,** to put into good working condition; **4,** to instruct as to what must be said:—*v.i.* to prepare a gun for firing, a pump for lifting, or a surface for painting or plastering.—*n.* ¹**prim′er** (prīm′ẽr).

²**prim-er** (prĭm′ẽr), *n.* **1,** orig., a small book of private devotions; **2,** a small book from which children receive their first lessons in reading; **3,** a textbook containing the first principles of any subject; **4,** in printing, either of two sizes of book type, *long* and *great primer,* nearly equivalent to 10 point and 18 point (see *type*).

pri-me-val (prī-mē′văl), *adj.* pertaining to the earliest age or time; ancient; original.—*adv.* **pri-me′val-ly.**

prim-ing (prīm′ĭng), *n.* **1,** the act of one who primes something; **2,** the first coat of paint; **3,** the powder or other substance used to fire a charge from a gun.

prim-i-tive (prĭm′ĭ-tĭv), *adj.* **1,** pertaining to the beginning; original; **2,** simple or crude; old-fashioned; **3,** serving as a source: used of a word from which another, called a *derivative* word, has come:—*n.* a word in its simplest, original form and not taken from another word or form.—*adv.* **prim′i-tive-ly.**—*n.* **prim′i-tive-ness.**

pri-mo-gen-i-ture (prī″mō-jĕn′ĭ-tūr), *n.* **1,** the state of being born first; **2,** in law, the exclusive right of the eldest son to succeed to real estate.

pri-mor-di-al (prī-môr′dĭ-ăl), *adj.* existing from the beginning; first in order; original.

primp (prĭmp), *v.t.* and *v.i. Colloq.,* to dress (oneself) for show; prink.

prim-rose (prĭm′rōz″), *n.* any of several species of plants bearing pale yellow flowers which blossom in the early spring:—*adj.* **1,** pale yellow; **2,** flowery; gay.

prince (prĭns), *n.* **1,** a ruler or sovereign; **2,** the son of a king or emperor; **3,** a member of a royal family or of a high order of nobility; **4,** a chief or very distinguished member of a class of men; as, a merchant *prince;* **5,** *Slang,* a man of unusually fine character: **Prince Albert coat,** *Colloq.,* a frock coat: **prince consort,** the husband of a queen or princess who reigns in her own right. —*n.* **prince′dom.**

prince-ly (prĭns′lĭ), *adj.* **1,** pertaining to a prince; **2,** like, or worthy of, one who is royal or of very high station; grand; noble; magnificent.—*n.* **prince′li-ness.**

prin-cess (prĭn′sĕs), *n.* **1,** the daughter of a sovereign; **2,** the wife of a prince; **3,** a female member of a royal family: **princess royal,** in England, the eldest daughter of a reigning sovereign.

prin-ci-pal (prĭn′sĭ-păl), *adj.* first or highest in rank, value, character, degree, or importance; most important; main; chief:—*n.* **1,** one who takes the lead; the chief in authority; **2,** the head of an institution; esp., the head of a secondary school in the U. S., or of any of certain colleges in the British Empire; **3,** in commerce: **a,** a sum of money drawing interest; **b,** the main part of an estate or total amount of a bequest: distinguished from *income;* **c,** in a matter of authority and agent, the party who is the source of authority; **d,** in a matter of contracts, any of the parties who sign the contracts; **4,** in law: **a,** the person for whom an agent acts; **b,** the chief perpetrator of a crime; also, one present and abetting him: distinguishedfrom *accessory;* **5,** in a roof, one of the main rafters at either end which support the purlins and, through them, the common rafters, and are themselves supported, usually, by struts: also called *principal rafter.*—*adv.* **prin′ci-pal-ly.**

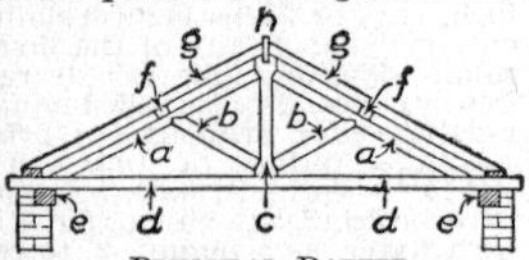

PRINCIPAL RAFTER
a, a, principal rafters; *b, b,* struts; *c,* king-post; *d, d,* tiebeam; *e, e,* wall plate: *f, f,* purlins; *g, g,* common rafters; *h,* ridgepole, or ridgepiece.

Syn., adj. foremost. (See chief.)

prin-ci-pal-i-ty (prĭn″sĭ-păl′ĭ-tĭ), *n.* [*pl.* principalities(-tĭz)], **1,** the territory of a prince or the country from which he obtains his title; **2,** supreme power.

prin-ci-ple (prĭn′sĭ-pl), *n.* **1,** a source or cause from which a thing comes; **2,** a settled rule or law of action or conduct; **3,** a truth which is general and plain and upon which others are founded; as, the *principles* of government; **4,** reason; uprightness; as, a man of *principle.*

Syn. motive, impulse; maxim.

prink (prĭngk), *v.t.* to dress up, or deck out, in a showy fashion; primp:—*v.i.* to dress or deck oneself for show.

print (prĭnt), *n.* **1,** a mark or character made by pressure; as, a foot*print;* **2,** a stamp or die for making an impression; as, a butter *print;* **3,** that which receives the impression; **4,** the letters produced by impression from type; as, large *print;* **5,** material for reading reproduced from type; also, the state of being ready to read; as, the story is in *print;* **6,** anything produced by type or from an engraved plate, as a newspaper, engraving, etc.; **7,** a picture reproduced by impression from a plate, as a photograph, photogravure, lithograph, etc.; **8,** stamped cotton cloth, esp. calico:—*v.t.* **1,** to make an impression on; as, their feet *print* the sand; **2,** to fix or stamp in or on something; as, to *print* footsteps in the sand; **3,** to stamp with letters, patterns, etc.; as, to *print* calico; **4,** to reproduce from type, engraved plates, etc., as books, pictures, newspapers, etc.; **5,** to make in letters, like those of type; as, a child *prints* a letter; **6,** in photography, to produce (a photograph) from a negative, on sensitized paper:—*v.i.* **1,** to make impressions from type, plates, etc.; **2,** to publish books, magazines, etc.; **3,** to make letters like those used in type.

print-er (prĭn′tẽr), *n.* **1,** one whose trade is typesetting or making impressions from type; **2,** one who publishes books, papers, magazines, or the like.

print-ing (prĭnt′ĭng), *n.* the setting of reading matter in type, or the making of printed books, magazines, etc.

print-ing press a machine for making impressions from type, as in newspapers, books, etc.

pri-or (prī′ẽr), *adj.* going before in time, order, or importance; previous:—*n.* the head of a convent or monastery; also, in an abbey, the religious officer next in rank below an abbot.—*n.fem.* **pri′or-ess.**

pri-or-i-ty (prī-ŏr′ĭ-tĭ), *n.* **1,** the state of being first in rank, time, or place; **2,** precedence; superiority.

pri-o-ry (prī′ō-rĭ), *n.* [*pl.* priories (-rĭz)], a monastery or convent ruled by a prior or prioress; a cloister.

prism (prĭzm), *n.* **1,** a solid whose bases are similar, equal, and parallel polygons, and whose sides are parallelograms (see *solid,* illus.); **2,** such a solid, made of glass or other transparent substance, used for separating the colors in a light ray: **prism glass,** glass in flat sheets or panes having one side smooth and the other side formed in parallel, sharp-pointed ridges: used in windows for reflecting light into a room.

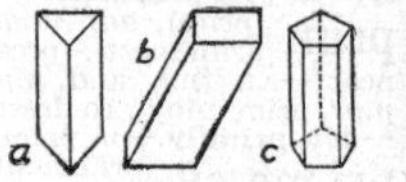

PRISMS
Geometrical prisms, whose bases form (*a*) a triangle, (*b*) a parallelogram, (*c*) a pentagon.

pris-mat-ic (prĭz-măt′ĭk), *adj.* **1,** like, or pertaining to, a prism, esp. a triangular glass prism; **2,** showing the gradation of colors formed by passing a ray of light through a prism; **3,** varied in color like the rainbow: **prismatic colors,** the seven colors (violet, indigo, blue, green, yellow, orange, red), called the solar spectrum, into which a ray of sunlight is dispersed when passed through a refracting substance; the colors of the rainbow: **prismatic lens,** a form of lens, used in correcting errors in vision, in which the two faces are inclined to each other: also called *prism lens.* Also, **pris-mat′i-cal.**

pris-moid (prĭz′moid), *n.* a body somewhat similar in shape to a prism.—*adj.* **pris-moi′dal.**

pris-on (prĭz′n), *n.* **1,** a public building for the confinement of criminals; jail; **2,** any place of confinement or detention.

pris-on-er (prĭz′n-ẽr; prĭz′nẽr), *n.* **1,** one who is under arrest or on trial; **2,** one who is confined in a jail or prison; **3,** anyone held against his will; **4,** a soldier who has been captured by the enemy in war.

pris-tine (prĭs′tĭn; prĭs′tīn), *adj.* pertaining to the earliest time or state; original; primitive.

prith-ee (prĭth′ē), *interj. Archaic,* please; I pray thee.

pri-va-cy (prī′vȧ-sĭ; *Br.* prĭv′ȧ-sĭ), *n.* [*pl.* privacies (-sĭz)], **1,** the state of being away from public view; seclusion; **2,** a place of seclusion or retirement; **3,** secrecy.

pri-vate (prī′văt), *adj.* **1,** concerning or belonging to oneself alone; personal; not public; as, one's *private* affairs; **2,** away from public view; retired; secret; as, *private* information; **3,** not holding a public position; as, a *private* citizen:—*n.* a common soldier.—*adv.* **pri′vate-ly.**—*n.* **pri′vate-ness.**

pri-va-teer (prī″vȧ-tēr′), *n.* **1**, a vessel, not a government warship, licensed or permitted by the government to attack the ships of an enemy; **2**, the commander or one of the crew of such a vessel:—*v.i.* to sail about in such a vessel in search of enemy ships.—*n.* **pri″va-teers′man.**

pri-va-tion (prī-vā′shŭn), *n.* **1**, the state of being without, or of wanting, something; **2**, a lack of the necessaries of life; need; hardship; **3**, absence; the condition of being absent.

priv-a-tive (prĭv′ȧ-tĭv), *adj.* **1**, causing want; **2**, negative; **3**, in grammar, having, or giving, a negative instead of a positive meaning: **alpha privative**, the letter *a*, or alpha, a Greek prefix, signifying negation, as in *a*pathy: written *an-* before a vowel, as in *an*archy:—*n.* **1**, a negative idea; a quality which exists only by virtue of the absence of some other quality, as cold by absence of heat; **2**, in grammar, a syllable attached to a word to change its positive meaning into a negative one, as *in-* or *un-*.—*adv.* **priv′a-tive-ly.**

priv-et (prĭv′ĕt), *n.* any of several ornamental shrubs of the olive family, much used for hedges.

priv-i-lege (prĭv′ĭ-lĕj), *n.* **1**, a special advantage, favor, or right, granted to or enjoyed by some to the exclusion of others; **2**, one of the rights granted to the people by a constitutional form of government; as, the *privilege* of free speech:—*v.t.* [*p.t.* and *p.p.* -leged (-lĕjd), *p.pr.* -leg-ing], **1**, to bestow some particular right or favor on; as, he is *privileged* to speak; **2**, to exempt or set free; as, his position *privileges* him not to be arrested.

Syn., *n.* exemption, immunity, benefit.

priv-i-ty (prĭv′ĭ-tĭ), *n.* [*pl.* privities (-tĭz)], **1**, knowledge shared with another or others about something not publicly known; **2**, privacy; secrecy.

priv-y (prĭv′ĭ), *adj.* **1**, not open to view; retired; as, *privy* chambers; **2**, for private, not public, use; as, the *privy* purse; **3**, secretly informed; as, he was *privy* to everything that went on:—*n.* [*pl.* privies (-ĭz)], an out-of-door toilet.—*adv.* **priv′i-ly.**

[1]**prize** (prīz), *n.* **1**, a reward offered in a contest; **2**, anything of value or worth striving for: **prize fighter**, a professional boxer: **prize ring**, **1**, the roped area within which contestants box; **2**, professional pugilism: used in the abstract:—*v.t.* [*p.t.* and *p.p.* prized (prīzd), *p.pr.* priz′ing], **1**, to value highly, as a gift; **2**, to set a value upon.

[2]**prize** (prīz), *n.* in international law, that which is taken from an enemy in war, esp. a captured vessel:—*v.t.* [*p.t.* and *p.p.* prized (prīzd), *p.pr.* priz′ing], to seize in war, as a thing of value.

[1]**pro** (prō), *adv.* for, in favor of, or on behalf of, a side that affirms a question in debate: opp. of *con*:—*n.* [*pl.* pros (prōz)], usually in *pl.*, a person or argument favoring the affirmative side: opp. of *con*:—*prep.* for; before; in favor of.

[2]**pro** (prō), *n.* [*pl.* pros (prōz)], *Colloq.*, a professional, esp. in golf.

[1]**pro-** (prō-), *prefix*, signifying: **1**, in front of; as, *pro*tection; **2**, motion to the front; as, *pro*ceed; *pro*duce; **3**, in behalf of; favoring; as, *pro*slavery; **4**, instead of; as, *pro*noun; **5**, according to; as, *pro*portion; **6**, forth or forward; as, *pro*pel; *pro*ject.

[2]**pro-** (prō-), *prefix*, before in time, place, rank, etc.; as, *pro*gram; *pro*boscis.

prob-a-bil-i-ty (prŏb″ȧ-bĭl′ĭ-tĭ), *n.* [*pl.* probabilities (-tĭz)], **1**, the quality or state of being likely; **2**, something likely; **3**, in *pl.*, a forecast of the weather.

prob-a-ble (prŏb′ȧ-bl), *adj.* **1**, upheld by evidence, but leaving some room for doubt; as, a *probable* tale; **2**, giving grounds for belief, but not proving absolutely; as, *probable* reasons.—*adv.* **prob′a-bly.**

Syn. (see likely).

pro-bate (prō′bāt), *n.* **1**, official, legal proof, as of wills; **2**, the official copy of a will with the certificate of its having been legally proved.

pro-ba-tion (prō-bā′shŭn), *n.* **1**, the act of proving; proof; **2**, any proceeding intended to put a person to a test as to character, ability, etc.; trial or test; **3**, a period of testing or trial.

pro-ba-tion-a-ry (prō-bā′shŭn-ā-rĭ), *adj.* serving for a test or trial.—*adj.* **pro-ba′tion-al.**

pro-ba-tion-er (prō-bā′shŭn-ẽr), *n.* one who is being subjected to a test or trial, as a nurse in training.

pro-ba-tion of-fi-cer a person appointed by a juvenile court to oversee children who are under court care and observation.

probe (prōb), *n.* **1**, a slender surgical instrument for examining a wound or a cavity; **2**, *Slang*, a searching inquiry:—*v.t.* [*p.t.* and *p.p.* probed (prōbd), *p.pr.* prob′ing], **1**, to examine with a probe, or slender instrument; **2**, to inquire into, or look into closely.

prob-i-ty (prŏb′ĭ-tĭ; prō′bĭ-tĭ), *n.* virtue and honesty tested and proved.

Syn. uprightness, integrity, soundness.

prob-lem (prŏb′lĕm), *n.* **1**, a doubtful question; a difficult matter to be settled; **2**, in mathematics, something that is to be worked out; an example.

prob-lem-at-ic (prŏb″lĕm-ăt′ĭk), *adj.* questionable; doubtful; difficult of solution. Also, **prob″lem-at′i-cal.**—*adv.* **prob″lem-at′i-cal-ly.**

pro-bos-cis (prō-bŏs′ĭs), *n.* [*pl.* proboscides (-ĭ-dēz)], **1**, a long nose or trunk, as that of an elephant; **2**, the long, flexible snout of certain other animals, as the tapir; **3**, the long mouth parts of certain insects.

pro-ce-dure (prō-sē′dūr), *n.* **1**, the manner of carrying on a law case; **2**, the manner of acting; as, parliamentary *procedure;* **3**, a course of action or of conduct.

pro-ceed (prō-sēd′), *v.i.* **1**, to go on or forward; continue; advance; as, *proceed* with your reading; *proceed* on your journey; **2**, to issue or come forth, as from a source; as, all good things *proceed* from God; **3**, to carry on an action in an orderly way; as, to *proceed* with good judgment; **4**, to carry on a legal action:—*n.*, in *pl.* (prō′sēdz), money resulting from a commercial transaction.

pro-ceed-ing (prō-sēd′ĭng), *n.* **1**, the act of going on or forward; **2**, a transaction, as in business; **3**, a course of conduct; **4**, a step in a law case; **5**, in *pl.*: **a**, the course of action in a law case; as, legal *proceedings;* **b**, the records of the business accomplished at a formal meeting.

proc-ess (prŏs′ĕs; prō′sĕs), *n.* **1**, the act of going on; advance; progress; **2**, a series of motions, actions, or events; an act which continues and progresses; an operation, or number of operations, leading to some result; **3**, passage or lapse of time; **4**, any of the modern methods of producing illustrations by photo-engraving: often used as an adjective; as, a *process* cut; **5**, an order of court issued as a part of a legal action; **6**, in anatomy, an outgrowth from, or projecting part of, the body; as, the mastoid *process*.

pro-ces-sion (prō-sĕsh′ŭn), *n.* **1**, orderly progress; **2**, that which moves forward, esp. a train of persons in a formal march; **3**, the act of going on or forward.

pro-ces-sion-al (prō-sĕsh′ŭn-ăl), *adj.* pertaining to a formal march or progress:—*n.* **1,** a hymn sung at the beginning of a church service while clergy and choir pass to their places; **2,** organ music played before a church service, or during a formal march down a church aisle.

pro-claim (prō-klām′), *v.t.* to make known publicly; publish abroad.
Syn. announce. (See declare.)

proc-la-ma-tion (prŏk″lȧ-mā′shŭn), *n.* **1,** a public, official announcement; **2,** that which is announced.

pro-cliv-i-ty (prō-klĭv′ĭ-tĭ), *n.* [*pl.* proclivities (-tĭz)], a natural inclination; tendency.

pro-con-sul (prō-kŏn′sŭl), *n.* a Roman official who performed the duties of a consul, or chief magistrate, esp. outside of Rome, as in governing a province. —*adj.* **pro-con′su-lar.**—*adj.* **pro-con′su-la-ry.**

pro-con-sul-ship (prō-kŏn′sŭl-shĭp), *n.* the office of a proconsul.—*n.* **pro-con′su-late.**

pro-cras-ti-nate (prō-krăs′tĭ-nāt), *v.t.* [*p.t.* and *p.p.* -nat″ed, *p.pr.* -nat″ing], to put off from time to time:—*v.i.* to delay.—*n.* **pro-cras′ti-na″tor.**
Syn. retard, postpone. (See defer.)

pro-cras-ti-na-tion (prō-krăs″tĭ-nā′-shŭn), *n.* the act or habit of putting off from day to day; delay.

pro-cre-ate (prō′krē-āt), *v.t.* [*p.t.* and *p.p.* -at″ed, *p.pr.* -at″ing], to produce, beget, or bring forth.—*n.* **pro′cre-a″tor.** —*n.* **pro″cre-a′tion.**

pro-cre-a-tive (prō′krē-ā″tĭv), *adj.* having power to beget or bring forth; reproductive; as, the *procreative* forms of nature.—*n.* **pro′cre-a″tive-ness.**

Pro-crus-tes (prō-krŭs′tēz), *n.* in mythology, a notorious robber, who laid his victims on an iron bed, stretching them out or cutting them off to make them fit: killed by Theseus.—*adj.* **Pro-crus′te-an.**

proc-tor (prŏk′tẽr), *n.* **1,** one employed to manage the affairs of another, as an attorney or agent; **2,** an officer employed to maintain order in a school or university. —*adj.* **proc-to′ri-al.**—*n.* **proc′tor-ship.**

pro-cur-a-ble (prō-kūr′ȧ-bl), *adj.* capable of being obtained.

proc-u-ra-tion (prŏk″ū-rā′shŭn), *n.* **1,** the managing of affairs for another; **2,** authority to act for another: also called *power of attorney;* **3,** the act of getting or obtaining; procurement.

proc-u-ra-tor (prŏk′ū-rā″tẽr), *n.* **1,** one who manages another's affairs, esp. legal matters; an agent; **2,** a Roman administrator of provincial funds.

pro-cure (prō-kūr′), *v.t.* [*p.t.* and *p.p.* -cured′ (-kūrd′), *p.pr.* -cur′ing], **1,** to get or obtain; **2,** to cause or bring about; as, to *procure* a result.—*n.* **pro-cure′ment.**
Syn. acquire. (See get.)

Pro-cy-on (prō′sĭ-ŏn), *n.* **1,** the principal star of the constellation Canis Minor, conspicuous in the winter sky; **2,** formerly, the constellation Canis Minor.

prod (prŏd), *n.* **1,** a pointed implement for pricking or puncturing, as a goad or pointed stick; **2,** a punch or prick:—*v.t.* [*p.t.* and *p.p.* prod′ded, *p.pr.* prod′ding], **1,** to punch or poke with a pointed instrument; **2,** hence, to goad or urge.—*n.* **prod′der.**

prod-i-gal (prŏd′ĭ-găl), *adj.* reckless in spending money; lavish; wasteful:—*n.* a spendthrift; one who is lavish or wasteful.—*adv.* **prod′i-gal-ly.**

prod-i-gal-i-ty (prŏd″ĭ-găl′ĭ-tĭ), *n.* [*pl.* prodigalities (-tĭz)], the state or quality of being wasteful; improvidence; extravagance; lavishness.

pro-di-gious (prō-dĭj′ŭs), *adj.* unusually great in size, extent, degree, or quantity; vast; immense; enormous.—*adv.* **pro-di′gious-ly.**—*n.* **pro-di′gious-ness.**
Syn. extraordinary, astonishing.

prod-i-gy (prŏd′ĭ-jĭ), *n.* [*pl.* prodigies (-jĭz)], **1,** anything so out of the ordinary as to call forth wonder; a marvel; **2,** a greatly gifted person, esp. a child.

[1]**pro-duce** (prō-dūs′), *v.t.* [*p.t.* and *p.p.* -duced′ (-dūst′), *p.pr.* -duc′ing], **1,** to exhibit or bring to view; as, he *produced* the hidden money; **2,** to yield or bring forth; as, the tree *produces* fruit; **3,** to manufacture; as, a factory *produces* cloth; **4,** to lead to; as, wealth *produces* comfort; **5,** to present upon the stage, as a play:—*v.i.* to yield an increase.

[2]**prod-uce** (prŏd′ūs), *n.* that which is yielded or brought forth; yield, esp. farm products.

pro-duc-er (prō-dūs′ẽr), *n.* **1,** one who manufactures goods or raises crops; **2,** one who presents plays on the stage.

pro-duc-i-ble (prō-dūs′ĭ-bl), *adj.* capable of being grown, made, or brought forth; as, *producible* evidence.

prod-uct (prŏd′ŭkt), *n.* **1,** that which is yielded by nature, or made by labor, thought, etc.; result; **2,** in mathematics, the result obtained by multiplying two or more numbers together.

pro-duc-tion (prō-dŭk′shŭn), *n.* **1,** that which is yielded by nature or made by man's labor, thought, etc.; **2,** a performance on the stage; **3,** the act of bringing forth or making.

pro-duc-tive (prō-dŭk′tĭv), *adj.* **1,** having the quality or power of yielding or bringing forth; fertile; leading to results; **2,** bringing forth in abundance.—*adv.* **pro-duc′tive-ly.**—*n.* **pro-duc′tive-ness.**

pro-em (prō′ĕm), *n.* a preface or introduction; prelude.

prof-a-na-tion (prŏf″ȧ-nā′shŭn), *n.* the act of treating sacred things with disrespect.

pro-fane (prō-fān′), *adj.* **1,** not sacred or holy; hence, having to do with this world; as, *profane* history; **2,** showing disrespect or irreverence toward God or sacred things; unholy; blasphemous; as, *profane* language; **3,** not privileged to take part in the inner mysteries:—*v.t.* [*p.t.* and *p.p.* -faned′ (-fānd′), *p.pr.* -fan′ing], **1,** to treat (something sacred) with irreverence, contempt, or abuse; **2,** to put to an improper or degrading use; debase.—*adv.* **pro-fane′ly.**—*n.* **pro-fane′nesc.**

pro-fan-i-ty (prō-făn′ĭ-tĭ), *n.* [*pl.* profanities (-tĭz)], **1,** contempt for holy things; **2,** blasphemy; swearing.

pro-fess (prō-fĕs′), *v.t.* **1,** to make an open or public statement of, as one's belief, intentions, etc.; avow or acknowledge; **2,** to pretend; as, to *profess* friendship; **3,** to set up a claim of; as, to *profess* ignorance; **4,** to claim to be an authority in.

pro-fessed (prō-fĕst′), *p.adj.* **1,** openly declared; as, a *professed* enemy; **2,** pretended.—*adv.* **pro-fess′ed-ly.**

pro-fes-sion (prō-fĕsh′ŭn), *n.* **1,** the act of declaring; as, *profession* of friendship; **2,** an open declaration or avowal; **3,** something declared or avowed, as religious faith; **4,** a pretense; **5,** a calling or vocation, esp. one that requires learning; as, the *profession* of medicine; **6,** all the persons engaged in any one calling.
Syn. trade, occupation. (See business.)

pro-fes-sion-al (prō-fĕsh′ŭn-ăl), *adj.* **1,** pertaining to a calling or occupation requiring a superior education; **2**, following a calling as a means of livelihood: said esp. of one engaged in sport for the sake of money; as, a *professional* baseball player; **3**, participated in by those who do so for gain; as, a *professional* football match:—*n.* one who makes his living by an occupation, as distinguished from an amateur, or one who practices an occupation occasionally or for pleasure; as, the singer has the air of a *professional.*—*adv.* **pro-fes′sion-al-ly.**—*n.* **pro-fes′sion-al-ism.**

pro-fes-sor (prō-fĕs′ẽr), *n.* **1**, one who makes an open declaration of his opinions, esp. concerning religion; **2**, a teacher of the highest rank in a college or university; **3**, loosely, anyone who teaches.—*adj.* **pro″fes-so′ri-al.**—*adv.* **pro″fes-so′ri-al-ly.**

pro-fes-sor-ship (prō-fĕs′ẽr-shĭp), *n.* the office, duties, or position of a teacher of highest rank in a college or university.

prof-fer (prŏf′ẽr), *v.t.* to offer for acceptance; as, to *proffer* assistance:—*n.* an offer.—*n.* **prof′fer-er.**

pro-fi-cien-cy (prō-fĭsh′ĕn-sĭ), *n.* knowledge, skill, or expertness, in any branch of learning or industry.

pro-fi-cient (prō-fĭsh′ĕnt), *adj.* thoroughly qualified or skilled in any work; expert:—*n.* an expert; one thoroughly skilled.—*adv.* **pro-fi′cient-ly.**

pro-file (prō′fīl; prō′fēl), *n.* **1**, outline or contour; **2**, a side view of a human head or face; **3**, a drawing in outline, as of a vertical section of a building.

prof-it (prŏf′ĭt), *n.* **1**, money gain; the amount by which income exceeds expense in a given time; **2**, benefit or advantage:—*v.t.* to benefit; be of service to:—*v.i.* **1**, to receive benefit; **2**, to be of use.

prof-it-a-ble (prŏf′ĭt-ȧ-bl), *adj.* yielding gain or benefit; useful; paying; as, a *profitable* business.—*n.* **prof′it-a-ble-ness.**—*adv.* **prof′it-a-bly.**

prof-it-eer (prŏf″ĭ-tēr′), *n.* one who takes advantage of an unusual or difficult economic situation, esp. to make undue profits in necessities:—*v.i.* to make excess profits by taking advantage of strained economic conditions.—*n.* **prof″it-eer′ing.**

prof-it-less (prŏf′ĭt-lĕs), *adj.* without gain.—*adv.* **prof′it-less-ly.**

prof-li-ga-cy (prŏf′lĭ-gȧ-sĭ), *n.* **1**, an immoral or wicked course of life; **2**, the state of being immoral.

prof-li-gate (prŏf′lĭ-gāt), *adj.* given up to vice; wicked:—*n.* a depraved or immoral person.—*adv.* **prof′li-gate-ly.**—*n.* **prof′li-gate-ness.**

Syn., adj. abandoned, depraved, corrupt.

pro-found (prō-found′), *adj.* **1**, deep, as to space; as, the *profound* depths of ocean; **2**, deep, as to mental state; thorough; as, *profound* thought; *profound* learning; **3**, deep, as to feeling; intense; as, *profound* sorrow; **4**, bending low; as, a *profound* bow; **5**, coming from the depths; as, a *profound* sigh.—*adv.* **pro-found′ly.**—*n.* **profound′ness.**

Syn. fathomless, penetrating, solemn.

pro-fun-di-ty (prō-fŭn′dĭ-tĭ), *n.* [*pl.* profundities (-tĭz)], **1**, depth of place, thought, knowledge, feeling, or the like; **2**, that which is deep in any sense.

pro-fuse (prō-fūs′), *adj.* **1**, pouring forth freely; giving or given with great liberality; lavish; as, *profuse* kindness; **2**, produced or shown in great abundance, as foliage.—*adv.* **pro-fuse′ly.**—*n.* **pro-fuse′ness.**

Syn. prodigal, excessive, copious, bountiful.

pro-fu-sion (prō-fū′zhŭn), *n.* **1**, a very great plenty or supply; abundance; **2**, lavishness; extreme liberality.

pro-gen-i-tor (prō-jĕn′ĭ-tẽr), *n.* an ancestor in a direct line; forefather; parent.—*n.* **pro-gen′i-tor-ship″.**

prog-e-ny (prŏj′ē-nĭ), *n.* offspring; children; descendants.

prog-na-thous (prŏg′nȧ-thŭs), *adj.* having the jaws projecting forward, as the skull of prehistoric man.

prog-no-sis (prŏg-nō′sĭs), *n.* a forecast of the probable result of a disease from its symptoms or signs; also, an opinion based on such a forecast.

prog-nos-tic (prŏg-nŏs′tĭk), *adj.* showing something that is to come to pass; foreshadowing; foretelling:—*n.* **1**, an omen or sign of what is to come; **2**, a prediction; **3**, a symptom which helps in the forecasting of the result of a disease.

prog-nos-ti-cate (prŏg-nŏs′tĭ-kāt), *v.t.* [*p.t.* and *p.p.* -cat″ed, *p.pr.* -cat″ing], to tell beforehand by means of signs or symptoms.—*n.* **prog-nos′ti-ca″tor.**

prog-nos-ti-ca-tion (prŏg-nŏs″tĭ-kā′shŭn), *n.* **1**, the act of foretelling what is to come to pass; **2**, a sign of something about to happen.

pro-gram (prō′grăm), *n.* **1**, a brief outline giving in order the features that make up a public entertainment, ceremony, etc.; **2**, the features that make up such an entertainment; **3**, a regular plan of action in any undertaking. Also, **pro′gramme.**

[1]**prog-ress** (prŏg′rĕs; *Br.* prō′grĕs), *n.* **1**, a proceeding forward; advancement or improvement in mental, moral, or physical condition; **2**, growth or development; the course taken by something; as, the *progress* of a campaign; **3**, *Rare*, a journey of state, as by a king or queen.

[2]**pro-gress** (prō-grĕs′), *v.i.* **1**, to move forward; advance; **2**, to grow; improve; increase in knowledge or skill.

pro-gres-sion (prō-grĕsh′ŭn), *n.* **1**, the act of going forward; **2**, advancement; passage; also, lapse of time.

pro-gres-sive (prō-grĕs′ĭv), *adj.* **1**, moving forward, esp. by gradations or steps; **2**, developing; improving; **3**, increasingly serious: said of a disease; **4**, making or favoring advancement or improvement: **Progressive Party**, a political party of advanced Republicans which was formed in 1912 and which supported Theodore Roosevelt as presidential candidate:—*n.* one who believes in, and works for, changes and reforms, esp. in political matters.—*adv.* **pro-gres′sive-ly.**—*n.* **pro-gres′sive-ness.**

pro-hib-it (prō-hĭb′ĭt), *v.t.* **1**, to forbid by law; as, to *prohibit* the sale of alcoholic liquors; to *prohibit* drivers from speeding; **2**, to hinder; prevent.

pro-hi-bi-tion (prō″hĭ-bĭsh′ŭn), *n.* **1**, the act of forbidding, esp. by law; specif., the forbidding of the manufacture and sale of intoxicating drinks; **2**, a law or command forbidding something.

pro-hi-bi-tion-ist (prō″hĭ-bĭsh′ŭn-ĭst), *n.* one who is opposed to the manufacture and sale of intoxicating liquors.—*n.* **pro″hi-bi′tion-ism.**

pro-hib-i-tive (prō-hĭb′ĭ-tĭv), *adj.* tending to forbid, prevent, or hinder; as, *prohibitive* prices keep one from buying.—*adj.* **pro-hib′i-to-ry.**

[1]**pro-ject** (prō-jĕkt′), *v.t.* **1**, to throw, shoot, or cast forward; **2**, to plan or scheme; **3**, in geometry, to construct (a figure, line, or the like) on a given surface so that it corresponds point by point with a given figure:—*v.i.* to jut out; extend forward.

[2]**proj-ect** (prŏj′ĕkt), *n.* **1**, a design, scheme, or plan; **2**, in education, a plan voluntarily undertaken by a group of students,

or by a single student, as a practical application of principles learned, or as a means of learning through practice: **project method,** the educational method which teaches by means of such projects.

pro-jec-tile (prō-jĕk'tĭl), *n.* **1,** a body thrown or shot forward; **2,** a ball, shell, torpedo, or the like, intended to be shot from a cannon by the power of gunpowder or other propelling force:—*adj.* forced, or forcing, forward; as, a *projectile* force.

pro-jec-tion (prō-jĕk'shŭn), *n.* **1,** the act or state of extending or jutting out; **2,** that which juts out; **3,** a plan.

pro-jec-tor (prō-jĕk'tẽr), *n.* **1,** one who makes schemes or plans; **2,** an optical instrument for throwing a picture upon a screen by a system of lenses.

pro-late (prō'lāt), *adj.* drawn or stretched out; elongated; of a spheroid, extended lengthwise along the polar axis: opp. of *oblate.*

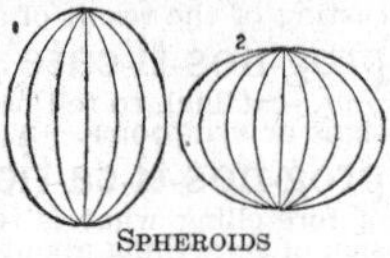

SPHEROIDS
1, prolate spheroid; 2, oblate spheroid.

pro-le-ta-ri-an (prō″lē-tā'rĭ-ăn; prŏl″ē-), *n.* **1,** one of the lowest class of society; **2,** a day laborer:—*adj.* pertaining to the lowest class of society.

pro-le-ta-ri-at (prō″lē-tā'rĭ-ăt; prŏl″ē-), *n.* **1,** the lowest class of society; **2,** the laboring people.

pro-lif-ic (prō-lĭf'ĭk), *adj.* **1,** producing young or fruit abundantly; fertile; fruitful; as, a *prolific* vine; **2,** producing ideas or results abundantly; as, a *prolific* writer.—*adv.* **pro-lif'i-cal-ly.**

pro-lix (prō'lĭks; prō-lĭks'), *adj.* **1,** long drawn out; tedious; **2,** wordy; not concise; as, a *prolix* speaker.
Syn. long, prolonged, tiresome, prosaic.

pro-lix-i-ty (prō-lĭk'sĭ-tĭ), *n.* [*pl.* prolixities (-tĭz)], **1,** the quality of being too long or tedious; **2,** wordiness.

pro-log (prō'lŏg; prŏl'ŏg), *n.* an introduction or preface to a poem, drama, etc.; esp., verses spoken or sung by an actor before the performance of a play, opera, etc., by way of explanation. Also, **pro'logue.**

pro-long (prō-lông'), *v.t.* to lengthen in time or space; draw out; extend; as, to *prolong* a line; *prolong* a visit.

pro-lon-ga-tion (prō″lông-gā'shŭn), *n.* **1,** a lengthening in time or space; **2,** the part added by lengthening.

prom-e-nade (prŏm″ē-näd'), *n.* **1,** a walk for pleasure or exercise; **2,** a public place for walking; **3,** a large ball; now, esp., a college dance:—*v.i.* [*p.t.* and *p.p.* -nad'ed, *p.pr.* -nad'ing], to walk for pleasure.

Pro-me-theus (prō-mē'thūs; prō-mē'thē-ŭs), *n.* in mythology, a Titan who stole fire from heaven for men, and who, as a punishment, passed many years chained to Mt. Caucasus, with a vulture tearing at his liver.—*adj.* **Pro-me'the-an.**

prom-i-nence (prŏm'ĭ-nĕns), *n.* **1,** the state or quality of standing or jutting out beyond a regular line or surface; **2,** the quality of being distinguished or noticeable. Also, **prom'i-nen-cy.**

prom-i-nent (prŏm'ĭ-nĕnt), *adj.* **1,** standing or jutting out beyond a regular line or surface; **2,** conspicuous; noticeable; distinguished.—*adv.* **prom'i-nent-ly.**
Syn. eminent, marked, important, leading.

pro-mis-cu-i-ty (prō″mĭs-kū'ĭ-tĭ; prŏm″ĭs-), *n.* [*pl.* promiscuities (-tĭz)], indiscriminate mixture; a mingling without due regard to person or class.

pro-mis-cu-ous (prō-mĭs'kū-ŭs), *adj.* **1,** confused; mingled: as, a *promiscuous* audience; **2,** not confined to any particular person or class.—*adv.* **pro-mis'cu-ous-ly.**—*n.* **pro-mis'cu-ous-ness.**
Syn. mixed, disarranged, haphazard.

prom-ise (prŏm'ĭs), *n.* **1,** an engagement to do or not to do something; **2,** the thing to be done or left undone; **3,** a cause or ground for hope or expectation of good in the future:—*v.i.* [*p.t.* and *p.p.* -ised (-ĭst), *p.pr.* -is-ing], **1,** to assure, or engage to do, something; **2,** to give reason for hope or expectation; as, the garden *promises* well:—*v.t.* **1,** to engage or pledge (to do or not to do); as, he *promised* to come; agree to give, get, or the like, to or for someone; as, he *promised* her a position; **2,** to give reason to hope for or expect.—*n.* **prom'is-er.**

prom-is-ing (prŏm'ĭs-ĭng), *p.adj.* giving reason to hope for or expect good; as, a *promising* youth; *promising* plans.—*adv.* **prom'is-ing-ly.**

prom-i-sor (prŏm'ĭ-sôr), *n.* one who makes a legal agreement.

prom-is-so-ry (prŏm'ĭ-sō-rĭ), *adj.* containing an agreement to do or not to do something: **promissory note,** a written agreement to pay a certain sum of money at a fixed date, or on demand, to a certain person or to his order, or to bearer.

prom-on-to-ry (prŏm'ŭn-tō-rĭ), *n.* [*pl.* promontories (-rĭz)], a high cape; a point of land jutting into a body of water; a headland.

pro-mote (prō-mōt'), *v.t.* [*p.t.* and *p.p.* -mot'ed, *p.pr.* -mot'ing], **1,** to help the growth or development of; advance; further; as, to *promote* one's interests; **2,** to excite or stir up; encourage; as, to *promote* strife; **3,** to raise to higher rank; advance (a pupil) to higher class.—*adj.* **pro-mo'tive.**

pro-mot-er (prō-mōt'ẽr), *n.* one who encourages or forwards any undertaking; esp., one who makes it his business to start new companies, encourage the sale of stocks or bonds, etc.

pro-mo-tion (prō-mō'shŭn), *n.* **1,** the act of furthering or advancing any cause or course; **2,** the state of being advanced; encouragement; as, *promotion* of industries; **3,** advancement to a better position or higher rank, as in school.

prompt (prŏmpt), *adj.* **1,** ready and quick to act as occasion demands; immediate; **2,** done without delay:—*v.t.* **1,** to rouse to action; **2,** to suggest; as, generosity *prompted* the gift; **3,** to remind (a speaker) when at a loss for words.—*n.* **prompt'er.**—*adv.* **prompt'ly.**—*n.* **prompt'ness.**
Syn., adj. alert, ready, punctual.

promp-ti-tude (prŏmp'tĭ-tūd), *n.* quickness of decision and action; readiness; promptness.

pro-mul-gate (prō-mŭl'gāt), *v.t.* [*p.t.* and *p.p.* -gat-ed, *p.pr.* -gat-ing], **1,** to make known to the public formally and officially; proclaim; **2,** to publish, as a creed, doctrine, etc.—*n.* **pro'mul-ga″tor.**

pro-mul-ga-tion (prō″mŭl-gā'shŭn; prŏm″ŭl-), *n.* **1,** an official declaration; **2,** publication, as of news, doctrine, etc.

prone (prōn), *adj.* **1,** lying face or front downward; **2,** bending forward or downward; hence, humble; cringing; **3,** mentally disposed or inclined; apt; as, *prone* to mischief.—*n.* **prone'ness.**

prong (prông), *n.* a sharp point or sharp-pointed instrument; as, the *prongs* of a pitchfork:—*v.t.* to pierce with a prong.

prong-horn (prông'hôrn″), *n.* **1,** a cud-chewing animal resembling an antelope, found on the western plains of North America; **2**, the white goat of the Rocky Mountains, a goatlike antelope.

pro-nom-i-nal (prō-nŏm'ĭ-năl), *adj.* pertaining to, or like, a pronoun, or word standing for a noun: **pronominal adjective,** a word which modifies a noun (as, *this* man, *that* cat), but which may also be used as a pronoun (as, *this* is what I want).—*adv.* **pro-nom'i-nal-ly.**

pro-noun (prō'noun), *n.* a word which refers to, or is used in the place of, a noun or name, as *he, she, you, it,* etc.

pro-nounce (prō-nouns'), *v.t.* [*p.t.* and *p.p.* -nounced' (-nounst'), *p.pr.* -nounc'ing], **1**, to speak or utter the sound of; as, to *pronounce* words; **2**, to speak or utter with formal effect; as, to *pronounce* a eulogy; **3**, to speak or utter solemnly or formally; as, to *pronounce* a benediction; **4**, to declare positively; as, they *pronounced* him a failure:—*v.i.* **1**, to utter words; **2**, to speak with confidence or authority.—*adj.* **pro-nounce'a-ble.**—*n.* **pro-nounc'er.**

pro-nounced (prō-nounst'), *p.adj.* strongly marked; decided; as, a *pronounced* change in the weather.

pro-nounce-ment (prō-nouns'mĕnt), *n.* a declaration; a formal or public announcement.

pro-nun-ci-a-men-to (prō-nŭn"shĭ-ȧ-mĕn'tō; prō-nŭn"sĭ-ȧ-), *n.* [*pl.* pronunciamentos (-tōz)], a formal or public announcement. Also, ***pro-nun"cia-mien'to** (prō-nōōn"thyä-myĕn'tō).

pro-nun-ci-a-tion (prō-nŭn"sĭ-ā'shŭn; prō-nŭn"shĭ-ā'-), *n.* the act or manner of uttering the sounds which form words.

proof (prōōf), *n.* **1**, the means by which something is found to be true or correct; **2**, the state or quality of having been tested and found worthy; **3**, convincing evidence; **4**, a test or trial; **5**, a standard of strength for distilled liquors; **6**, in printing, a preliminary impression taken from type, as for correction:—*adj.* **1**, capable of resistance; as, the cloth is *proof* against rain; **2**, used in proving or testing; as, a *proof* text; **3**, being of a standard strength or purity; as, *proof* whisky.

Syn., n. evidence. (See trial.)

proof read-er one whose profession, called *proof reading,* is the detection and indication of errors in printers' proof.

prop (prŏp), *n.* a support or stay:—*v.t.* [*p.t.* and *p.p.* propped (prŏpt), *p.pr.* prop'ping], to support by placing something under or against; sustain; stay; hold.

prop-a-gan-da (prŏp"ȧ-găn'dȧ), *n.* **1**, any organization or method for spreading a certain opinion or belief; **2**, the opinion or belief thus spread.

prop-a-gan-dist (prŏp"ȧ-găn'dĭst), *n.* one who devotes himself to the spread of any system of principles, doctrines, opinions, etc.—*n.* **prop"a-gan'dism.**

prop-a-gate (prŏp'ȧ-gāt), *v.t.* [*p.t.* and *p.p.* -gat"ed, *p.pr.* -gat"ing], **1**, to cause to increase or multiply by successive production; as, to *propagate* plants; **2**, to spread from person to person; as, to *propagate* news; **3**, to cause to extend or spread in space; as, to *propagate* light:—*v.i.* **1**, to be produced by generation or other means; **2**, to have offspring.—*n.* **prop'a-ga"tor.**

Syn. circulate, increase, scatter.

prop-a-ga-tion (prŏp"ȧ-gā'shŭn), *n.* the act of producing, reproducing, continuing, or spreading.

pro-pel (prō-pĕl'), *v.t.* [*p.t.* and *p.p.* -pelled' (-pĕld'), *p.pr.* -pel'ling], to drive onward; urge forward; push, as a bicycle.

pro-pel-ler (prō-pĕl'ẽr), *n.* **1**, one who or that which drives forward; **2**, esp., a device with blades for causing an airplane or a ship to progress.

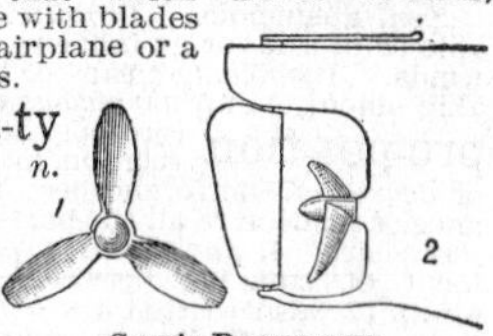

SHIP'S PROPELLER
1 face; 2, profile.

pro-pen-si-ty (prō-pĕn'sĭ-tĭ), *n.* [*pl.* propensities (-tĭz)], natural inclination or tendency.

prop-er (prŏp'ẽr), *adj.* **1**, suitable; fitting; appropriate; **2**, belonging naturally to some person or thing; peculiar; **3**, according to accepted usage; correct; conventional; respectable; **4**, pertaining to a stated, restricted part: usually coming after the noun it modifies; as, Rome *proper;* **5**, in grammar, designating a specific and named individual, place, animal, or the like; as, John is a *proper* name: **proper fraction,** a fraction which, having the numerator less than the denominator, is less than unity, as ½ or ⅞: contrasted with *improper* fraction, as ⁸⁄₃: **proper noun,** or **name,** in grammar, a noun which designates an individual place, person, thing, or the like, as distinct from others of the same general class: opp. of *common noun;* as, *Troy, James, Tower of London.*—*adv.* **prop'er-ly.**—*n.* **prop'er-ness.**

prop-er-ty (prŏp'ẽr-tĭ), *n.* [*pl.* properties (-tĭz)], **1**, any quality or attribute that belongs to a thing, or one that especially marks it; as, sourness is a *property* of vinegar; **2**, ownership; **3**, the thing owned; estate; goods; **4**, in *pl.,* articles required for acting on the stage.

proph-e-cy (prŏf'ē-sĭ), *n.* [*pl.* prophecies (-sĭz)], **1**, a foretelling of future events, esp. under divine influence; as, the Hebrew *prophecies* of the Old Testament; **2**, a book thought of as containing such predictions; as, the *prophecy* of Isaiah.

proph-e-sy (prŏf'ē-sī), *v.t.* [*p.t.* and *p.p.* -sied (-sīd), *p.pr.* -sy"ing], **1**, to foretell, esp. under divine influence; **2**, to predict in any sense; foretell:—*v.i.* **1**, to foretell future events, esp. under divine influence; **2**, to preach, or declare God's will to men.—*n.* **proph'e-si"er.**

proph-et (prŏf'ĕt), *n.* **1**, one inspired by God to teach his will to men and to announce future events; a prophesier; **2**, one who declares what will happen in the future.—*n. fem.* **proph'et-ess.**

pro-phet-ic (prō-fĕt'ĭk), *adj.* **1**, pertaining to the foretelling of future events, or to one who foretells; **2**, containing a prophecy; as, a *prophetic* vision. Also, **pro-phet'i-cal.**—*adv.* **pro-phet'i-cal-ly.**

pro-phy-lac-tic (prō"fĭ-lăk'tĭk; prŏf"ĭ-), *adj.* warding off, or preserving from, disease; as, a *prophylactic* medicine:—*n.* a medicine that prevents disease.

pro-pin-qui-ty (prō-pĭng'kwĭ-tĭ), *n.* nearness in time, place, or blood relationship; proximity.

pro-pi-ti-ate (prō-pĭsh'ĭ-āt), *v.t.* [*p.t.* and *p.p.* -at"ed, *p.pr.* -at"ing], to conciliate or appease; remove displeasure from; make favorable.

pro-pi-ti-a-tion (prō-pĭsh"ĭ-ā'shŭn), *n.* the act of appeasing, or removing displeasure; conciliation.

pro-pi-ti-a-to-ry (prō-pĭsh'ĭ-ȧ-tō-rĭ), *adj.* having the power to appease; conciliatory.

pro-pi-tious (prō-pĭsh'ŭs), *adj.* **1**, favorably inclined; gracious; **2**, favorable; fortunate; as, *propitious* weather or circumstances.—*adv.* **pro-pi'tious-ly.**—*n.* **pro-pi'tious-ness.**

Syn. auspicious. *Propitious* means favorable or of a favoring influence; as, *propitious* winds. *Auspicious* means of happy or favorable omen; as, an *auspicious* occasion.

pro-por-tion (prō-pōr'shŭn), *n.* **1**, the relation in size, quantity, or degree of one to another; **2**, a proper balance or relation to all the parts; **3**, an equal or just share; **4**, any share or part; **5**, a statement of equality between two ratios, as 4:6::8:12 (also written 4:8 = 6:12, or $\frac{4}{8} = \frac{6}{12}$); **6**, the rule for finding the fourth term in such a series when any three are known: also known as the *rule of three;* **7**, in *pl.*, dimensions; size:—*v.t.* **1**, to form symmetrically, or make the parts of suitable to each other; **2**, to cause to be in suitable relation; adapt.

pro-por-tion-al (prō-pōr'shŭn-ăl), *adj.* **1**, having, or being in, due or suitable relation; **2**, in proportion; having a stated ratio to a given quantity; **3**, having a rate invariable under given conditions:—*n.* one of the terms in a proportion.

pro-por-tion-ate (prō-pōr'shŭn-āt), *adj.* adjusted according to a certain relation:—*v.t.* (prō-pōr'shŭn-āt) [*p.t.* and *p.p.* -at″ed, *p.pr.* -at″ing], to adjust according to a settled relation.—*adv.* **pro-por'tion-ate-ly.**—*n.* **pro-por'tion-ate-ness.**

pro-pos-al (prō-pōz'ăl), *n.* **1**, the act of offering something for acceptance; as, a *proposal* of marriage; **2**, that which is offered; an offer, esp. of marriage.

pro-pose (prō-pōz'), *v.t.* [*p.t.* and *p.p.* -posed' (-pōzd'), *p.pr.* -pos'ing], **1**, to bring forward for consideration; suggest; as, he *proposed* that I should go; **2**, to intend; purpose; as, I *propose* to stay at home:—*v.i.* **1**, to make an offer of marriage; **2**, to form a plan; make known a plan.—*n.* **pro-pos'er.**

prop-o-si-tion (prŏp″ō-zĭsh'ŭn) *n.* **1**, that which is offered for consideration; an offer of terms; proposal; **2**, the formal statement of a topic to be discussed in a debate; **3**, in mathematics, the statement of a theorem or problem for solution; **4**, in grammar, an assertion consisting of a subject and predicate.—*adj.* **prop″o-si'tion-al.**

pro-pound (prō-pound'), *v.t.* to offer for consideration; put or set forth, as a question.—*n.* **pro-pound'er.**

pro-pri-e-ta-ry (prō-prī'ē-tā-rĭ), *adj.* pertaining to a proprietor, or owner:—*n.* [*pl.* proprietaries (-rĭz)], **1**, a possessor or owner in his own right; **2**, a body of such possessors or owners.

pro-pri-e-tor (prō-prī'ē-tẽr), *n.* one who has a legal right to something; the sole owner.—*n.fem.* **pro-pri'e-tress; pro-pri'e-trix.**—*n.* **pro-pri'e-tor-ship″.**

pro-pri-e-ty (prō-prī'ē-tĭ), *n.* [*pl.* proprieties (-tĭz)], fitness or suitability, as of conduct; correctness.

prop root a root, as on the mangrove or Indian corn, which serves as a prop or support (see *root*, illus.).

pro-pul-sion (prō-pŭl'shŭn), *n.* the act of driving or pushing along.

pro-pul-sive (prō-pŭl'sĭv), *adj.* having a tendency to push along.

prop-wash (prŏp'wŏsh″), *n.* the backward current of air from the propeller of an airplane.

***pro ra-ta** (prō rā'tȧ), [Lat.], in proportion; according to the interest, right, or obligation of each.

pro-ro-ga-tion (prō″rō-gā'shŭn), *n.* the act of ending a legislative session by royal command.

pro-rogue (prō-rōg'), *v.t.* [*p.t.* and *p.p.* -rogued' (-rōgd'), *p.pr.* -ro'guing], to discontinue for an indefinite time by royal command, as a session of parliament.

pro-sa-ic (prō-zā'ĭk), *adj.* commonplace; dull; as, a *prosaic* person or speech. Also, **pro-sa'i-cal.**—*adv.* **pro-sa'i-cal-ly.**—*n.* **pro-sa'i-cal-ness.**

pro-sce-ni-um (prō-sē'nĭ-ŭm), *n.* [*pl.* proscenia (-ȧ)], that part of the stage in front of the curtain.

pro-scribe (prō-skrīb'), *v.t.* [*p.t.* and *p.p.* -scribed' (-skrībd'), *p.pr.* -scrib'ing], **1**, to punish by declaring to be outside the protection of the law; banish; **2**, to condemn; prohibit.—*n.* **pro-scrib'er.**

pro-scrip-tion (prō-skrĭp'shŭn), *n.* **1**, the act of outlawing, or of declaring outside the protection of the law; outlawry; **2**, the state of being outlawed.

pro-scrip-tive (prō-skrĭp'tĭv), *adj.* pertaining to, or consisting of, proscription, the punishment that outlaws or condemns.—*adv.* **pro-scrip'tive-ly.**

prose (prōz), *n.* **1**, ordinary spoken or written language without meter: opp. of *verse;* **2**, tiresome and commonplace conversation:—*v.i.* and *v.t.* [*p.t.* and *p.p.* prosed (prōzd), *p.pr.* pros'ing], **1**, to write in a form not verse; **2**, to write or speak tediously or uninterestingly:—*adj.* **1**, pertaining to composition that is not verse; **2**, dull; tedious.

pros-e-cute (prŏs'ē-kūt), *v.t.* [*p.t.* and *p.p.* -cut″ed, *p.pr.* -cut″ing], **1**, to follow up or pursue with the view to reach or accomplish; as, to *prosecute* an undertaking; **2**, to bring suit against or carry on a case against in a court of law:—*v.i.* **1**, to carry on a lawsuit; sue; **2**, to conduct the case against an accused person.—*n.* **pros'e-cu″tor.**

pros-e-cu-tion (prŏs″ē-kū'shŭn), *n.* **1**, the act of following up a purpose to accomplish some result; **2**, the starting and carrying on of a lawsuit; **3**, the party starting the suit; **4**, the party, as the state, proceeding against the accused.

pros-e-lyte (prŏs'ē-līt), *n.* a convert, or one won over, as to some religion, belief, or party:—*v.t.* [*p.t.* and *p.p.* -lyt″ed, *p.pr.* -lyt″ing], to try to win over to a different opinion, belief, party, etc.:—*v.i.* to try to obtain followers.

pros-e-ly-tism (prŏs'ē-lĭ-tĭzm; prŏs'ē-līt-ĭzm), *n.* **1**, the act of converting, esp. to some religion; **2**, the state of being so won over.

pros-e-ly-tize (prŏs'ē-lĭ-tīz; prŏs'ē-līt-īz), *v.t.* [*p.t.* and *p.p.* -tized (-tīzd), *p.pr.* -tiz″ing], to make a convert of:—*v.i.* to make converts.

Pro-ser-pi-na (prō-sûr'pĭ-nȧ), *n.* in Roman mythology, the daughter of Jupiter and Ceres, who was carried off to be queen of the lower world: called by the Greeks *Persephone.* Also, **Pros'er-pine** (prŏs'ẽr-pĭn; -pēn).

pro-slav-er-y (prō-slāv'ẽr-ĭ), *adj.* supporting slavery.

pros-o-dy (prŏs'ō-dĭ), *n.* that part of grammar which treats of the quantity of syllables, accent, and the laws of verse making.—*n.* **pros'o-dist.**

pros-pect (prŏs'pĕkt), *n.* **1**, a scene spread out before the sight; view; outlook; **2**, a looking forward; anticipation; expectation:—*v.t.* and *v.i.* to search or explore, esp. for gold, silver, etc.—*n.* **pro-spec'ter.**

pro-spec-tive (prō-spĕk'tĭv), *adj.* **1**, looking forward; showing foresight; **2**, expected.—*adv.* **pro-spec'tive-ly.**

pros-pec-tor (prŏs'pĕk-tẽr), *n.* one who searches for valuable minerals, as gold, silver, etc.

pro-spec-tus (prō-spĕk'tŭs), *n.* **1**, an outline of a proposed undertaking; **2**, a brief sketch, as of a book to be published; **3**, a catalog, as of a school, hotel, etc.

pros-per (prŏs′pẽr), *v.t.* to make successful; favor:—*v.i.* to thrive; make progress; flourish; as, his business *prospers*.

pros-per-i-ty (prŏs-pĕr′ĭ-tĭ), *n.* successful progress in any business or enterprise; good fortune.

pros-per-ous (prŏs′pẽr-ŭs), *adj.* **1**, of good omen; favorable; **2**, successful; thriving, as an undertaking.—*adv.* **pros′per-ous-ly.**

pros-ti-tute (prŏs′tĭ-tūt), *v.t.* [*p.t.* and *p.p.* -tut″ed, *p.pr.* -tut″ing], to use for a low and unworthy purpose for the sake of gaining money or advantage; as, to *prostitute* talent:—*n.* a woman who leads a base and degraded life for pay.—*n.* **pros″ti-tu′tion.**—*n.* **pros′ti-tu″tor.**

pros-trate (prŏs′trāt), *adj.* **1**, lying at full length; extended on the ground; stretched out; **2**, lying at another's mercy; **3**, lying in an entreating or reverent attitude; **4**, exhausted:—*v.t.* [*p.t.* and *p.p.* -trat-ed, *p.pr.* -trat-ing], **1**, to lay flat; throw down from a standing position; **2**, to destroy; ruin; **3**, to bow in humble reverence; **4**, to cause to become weak.—*n.* **pros′tra-tor.**

pros-tra-tion (prŏs-trā′shŭn), *n.* **1**, the act of throwing down, or state of being thrown down; **2**, a falling down in worship; **3**, great depression or exhaustion.

pros-y (prōz′ĭ), *adj.* [*comp.* pros′i-er, *superl.* pros′i-est], **1**, like prose; **2**, tedious; dull; commonplace; as, a *prosy* day.—*adv.* **pros′i-ly.**—*n.* **pros′i-ness.**

pro-tag-o-nist (prō-tăg′ō-nĭst), *n.* **1**, the central figure in a drama; **2**, a prominent figure in, or a chief supporter of, a cause or movement.

prot-a-sis (prŏt′ȧ-sĭs), *n.* **1**, in a conditional sentence, the clause that contains the condition; **2**, in any complex sentence, the introductory or subordinate clause.

pro-te-an (prō′tē-ăn; prō-tē′ăn), *adj.* readily taking on different shapes or forms: from Proteus, the sea god of classic mythology.

pro-tect (prō-tĕkt′), *v.t.* **1**, to keep in safety; guard; shelter; **2**, to foster by a high tariff, as home industries.

Syn. shield, preserve. (See defend.)

pro-tec-tion (prō-tĕk′shŭn), *n.* **1**, the act of keeping in safety; **2**, the state of being kept in safety; **3**, that which keeps safe; defense; shelter; security; **4**, a passport; **5**, the encouragement of home industry by duties on imported goods, produce, etc.: opp. of *free trade*.

pro-tec-tion-ist (prō-tĕk′shŭn-ĭst), *n.* one who believes in and supports the doctrine that imported goods should be taxed to protect home industries; one who opposes free trade.—*n.* **pro-tec′tion-ism.**

pro-tec-tive (prō-tĕk′tĭv), *adj.* **1**, serving to keep safe; defensive; **2**, serving to foster home industries; as, a *protective* tariff.—*adv.* **pro-tec′tive-ly.**

pro-tec-tor (prō-tĕk′tẽr), *n.* one who guards, esp. from injury or oppression; a defender; guardian: **Lord Protector,** the title of Oliver Cromwell as the head of the English Commonwealth, 1653–1658.—*n.fem.* **pro-tec′tress.**

pro-tec-tor-ate (prō-tĕk′tŏr-āt), *n.* **1**, government by a regent, or one appointed to rule in place of a king; also, the rank and office of such a person; **2**, the relation of a great nation to a weak one which it defends and partly controls; **3**, the nation so defended and controlled.

***pro-té-gé** (prō″tā″zhā′), [Fr.], *n.* one who is under the guardianship, patronage, or care of another; as, the young violinist is her *protégé*.—*n.fem.* ***pro″té″gée′.**

pro-te-id (prō′tē-ĭd), *n.* any of a general class of very complex compounds containing nitrogen found in vegetable and animal organisms, formed by combination of a protein with another substance: generally called *protein*.

pro-te-in (prō′tē-ĭn), *n.* any of a general class of very complex compounds containing nitrogen, necessary to form the living tissues of all animals and plants, as muscle tissue and nerve tissue.

pro-test (prō-tĕst′), *v.i.* to make a solemn declaration against some public act or measure; remonstrate:—*v.t.* **1**, to make a solemn declaration or affirmation of; assert; **2**, to declare formally to be dishonored by nonpayment or nonacceptance, as a promissory note, check, or bill of exchange; **3**, to make a formal statement of disapproval with regard to, as a decision, action, or the like:—*n.* (prō′tĕst), **1**, a solemn declaration of opinion against something; **2**, a formal declaration by the holder of a note of its nonpayment or nonacceptance by the drawer.—*n.* **pro-test′er.**

prot-es-tant (prŏt′ĕs-tănt), *n.* one who declares an opinion in advance of, or opposing, those generally accepted: **Protestant,** a member of one of the branches of the Christian church which separated from the Roman Catholic Church during the Reformation in the 16th century:—*adj.* declaring an opposing opinion: **Protestant,** belonging to one of the branches of the Christian church which separated from the Roman Catholic Church in the 16th century: **Protestant Episcopal Church,** the branch of the church which in the U. S. corresponds to the Anglican Church.

Prot-es-tant-ism (prŏt′ĕs-tănt-ĭzm), *n.* the religious system of Protestant Christians; also, Protestant churches collectively.

prot-es-ta-tion (prŏt″ĕs-tā′shŭn), *n.* **1**, the act of declaring solemnly; **2**, a formal declaration of disagreement; **3**, a solemn affirmation.

Pro-teus (prō′tūs; prō′tē-ŭs), *n.* in mythology, a Greek sea god with prophetic power, who, when captured, could change himself at will into any form.

pro-thon-o-ta-ry (prō-thŏn′ō-tȧ-rĭ), *n.* [*pl.* prothonotaries (-rĭz)], **1**, in certain courts, the chief clerk; **2**, in the Roman Catholic Church, one of several high officials who record the important pontifical proceedings.

pro-tho-rax (prō-thō′răks), *n.* the front segment of the thorax of an insect.—*adj.* **pro″tho-rac′ic** (prō″thō-răs′ĭk).

pro-to-col (prō′tō-kŏl), *n.* an original copy or record; esp., the first draft of a treaty, government message, etc.: often a basis for a final treaty or agreement.

pro-to-mar-tyr (prō″tō-mär′tẽr), *n.* a first martyr for any cause: applied esp. to Saint Stephen.

pro-ton (prō′tŏn), *n.* the nucleus of the hydrogen atom, an exceedingly minute particle carrying a unit positive charge, and associated, in the normal hydrogen atom, with one electron, or negatively charged particle.

pro-to-plasm (prō′tō-plăzm), *n.* the vital substance from which develop all forms of animal and plant life: a mixture of extremely complex chemical compounds.—*adj.* **pro″to-plas′mic.**

pro-to-type (prō′tō-tīp), *n.* an original copy or model; a pattern.

Pro-to-zo-a (prō″tō-zō′ȧ), *n.pl.* the first or lowest division of the animal kingdom, containing animals consisting of a single cell.

pro-to-zo-an (prō″tō-zō′ăn), *n.* an animal consisting of a single cell:—*adj.* pertaining to such an animal.

pro-tract (prō-trăkt′), *v.t.* **1,** to draw out or lengthen in time; prolong, as a meeting; **2,** to draw or map by means of a scale; **3,** in animals, to protrude; extend.—*n.* **pro-trac′tion.**—*adj.* **pro-trac′tive.**

pro-trac-tor (prō-trăk′tẽr), *n.* **1,** an instrument for laying down and measuring angles on paper: used in surveying, drawing, etc.; **2,** a muscle that extends a limb.

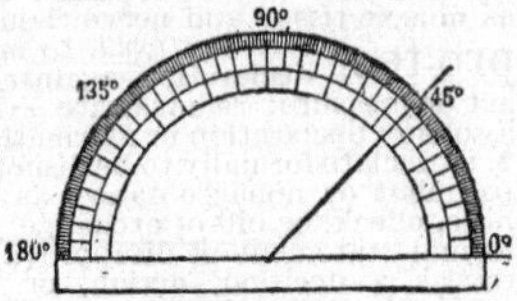

PROTRACTOR

pro-trude (prō-trōōd′), *v.t.* [*p.t.* and *p.p.* -trud′ed, *p.pr.* -trud′ing], to thrust or push forward; cause to project:—*v.i.* to be extended forward; project; jut out.

pro-tru-sile (prō-trōō′sĭl), *adj.* capable of being thrust or pushed forward, as an anteater's tongue.

pro-tru-sion (prō-trōō′zhŭn), *n.* **1,** the act of thrusting out, or the state of being thrust out; **2,** that which is thrust out or pushed forward.

pro-tru-sive (prō-trōō′sĭv), *adj.* **1,** thrusting forward; **2,** projecting.

pro-tu-ber-ance (prō-tū′bẽr-ăns), *n.* **1,** a swelling; a knob; **2,** the quality or state of swelling out.

pro-tu-ber-ant (prō-tū′bẽr-ănt), *adj.* swelling out; prominent; bulging; protruding.

proud (proud), *adj.* **1,** having too great self-esteem; overbearing; haughty; **2,** having worthy self-respect; as, too *proud* to beg; **3,** having a feeling of glad satisfaction; as, *proud* of a friend's success; gratified; **4,** giving just cause for satisfaction or boasting; as, a *proud* castle: **proud flesh,** excessive granulation on an inflamed area in a sore or a healing wound.—*adv.* **proud′ly.**

prove (prōōv), *v.t.* [*p.t.* proved (prōōvd), *p.p.* proved or, *Archaic,* prov′en (prōōv′n), *p.pr.* prov′ing], **1,** to test or try by an experiment; **2,** to demonstrate by argument or evidence; **3,** to cause to be accepted as genuine; as, to *prove* a will; **4,** to learn by experience; as, "we will all the pleasures *prove*":—*v.i.* to turn out to be; be found to be.—*n.* **prov′er.**—*adj.* **prov′a-ble.**

prov-en (prōōv′n), *Archaic* and *Scot.,* past participle of *prove:*—*p.adj.* certified; found to be genuine.

Pro-ven-çal (prō″vän″sȧl′; prō″vĕn-săl′; prō″vĕn-säl′), [Fr.], *adj.* pertaining to Provence, France, its language, or its people:—*n.* **1,** the language of Provence; **2,** a native of Provence.

prov-en-der (prŏv′ĕn-dẽr), *n.* dry feed for live stock, as hay and oats.

prov-erb (prŏv′ẽrb), *n.* a short, familiar saying, expressing some well-known truth or common fact of experience: **Proverbs,** a book of the Old Testament containing the practical philosophy of the wise men of Israel, including Solomon.—*abbr.* **Prov.**

pro-ver-bi-al (prō-vûr′bĭ-ăl), *adj.* **1,** pertaining to, mentioned in, or like, a short, familiar saying; **2,** widely spoken of, or well-known; as, her kindness is *proverbial.*—*adv.* **pro-ver′bi-al-ly.**

pro-vide (prō-vīd′), *v.t.* [*p.t.* and *p.p.* -vid′ed, *p.pr.* -vid′ing], **1,** to make ready beforehand; prepare; **2,** to furnish or supply: followed by *with;* as, *provide* him with funds; **3,** to supply or afford; as, we will *provide* funds for him; **4,** to mention as a condition or requirement; as, the bill *provides* that taxes be raised:—*v.i.* **1,** to procure supplies: with *for;* **2,** to make preparations to avoid: with *for* or *against;* as, to *provide* for emergencies.—*n.* **pro-vid′er.**

pro-vid-ed (prō-vīd′ĕd), *conj.* on condition; if: usually with *that.*

prov-i-dence (prŏv′ĭ-dĕns), *n.* **1,** timely care or preparation; **2,** economy; prudence; **3,** the care of God for mankind; **4,** an event directly showing God's foresight and care: **Providence,** God thought of as watching over mankind.

prov-i-dent (prŏv′ĭ-dĕnt), *adj.* **1,** careful for the future; prudent; **2,** economical; thrifty.—*adv.* **prov′i-dent-ly.**

prov-i-den-tial (prŏv″ĭ-dĕn′shăl), *adj.* **1,** effected by, or showing, divine direction or foresight; **2,** fortunate.—*adv.* **prov″i-den′tial-ly.**

prov-ince (prŏv′ĭns), *n.* **1,** a division of an empire or state; **2,** a country governed by a distant authority; an outlying district; **3,** a proper sphere of action; as, this task is outside your *province;* **4,** a department of knowledge or activity; **5,** in *pl.,* outlying sections remote from the larger cities.

pro-vin-cial (prō-vĭn′shăl), *adj.* **1,** pertaining to, or like, an outlying district or distant dependent country; **2,** countrified; crude and unfinished in appearance or manner; **3,** restricted to the ideas and customs of one special region; hence, narrow; unenlightened:—*n.* an inhabitant of such a country or district.—*adv.* **pro-vin′cial-ly.**

pro-vin-cial-ism (prō-vĭn′shăl-ĭzm), *n.* **1,** a word, expression, mannerism, or way of thinking, peculiar to an outlying district; **2,** devotion to the ideas and customs of one special region; **3,** hence, narrowness of view.

pro-vi-sion (prō-vĭzh′ŭn), *n.* **1,** the act of preparing beforehand; **2,** often in *pl.,* the things supplied, esp. a stock of food; **3,** care taken beforehand; as, to make *provision* for winter; **4,** a condition, requirement, etc.; as, a *provision* of a will:—*v.t.* to supply on a large scale, esp. with food; as, to *provision* an army.

pro-vi-sion-al (prō-vĭzh′ŭn-ăl), *adj.* **1,** serving for present use; temporary; **2,** conditional; as, a *provisional* judgment.—*adv.* **pro-vi′sion-al-ly.**

pro-vi-so (prō-vī′zō), *n.* [*pl.* provisos (-zōz)], a conditional clause or stipulation, as in a deed.

pro-vi-so-ry (prō-vī′zō-rĭ), *adj.* **1,** conditional; **2,** temporary.

prov-o-ca-tion (prŏv″ō-kā′shŭn), *n.* **1,** that which excites to anger or resentment; **2,** the act of so exciting.

pro-voc-a-tive (prō-vŏk′ȧ-tĭv; prō-vō′kȧ-tĭv), *adj.* tending to rouse anger or resentment:—*n.* anything that tends to excite.—*adv.* **pro-voc′a-tive-ly.**—*n.* **pro-voc′a-tive-ness.**

pro-voke (prō-vōk′), *v.t.* [*p.t.* and *p.p.* -voked′ (-vōkt′), *p.pr.* -vok′ing], **1,** to excite or stir up; as, to *provoke* criticism; **2,** to cause; as, to *provoke* a laugh; **3,** to enrage or irritate; as, to *provoke* another to anger.—*n.* **pro-vok′er.**

pro-vok-ing (prō-vōk′ĭng), *p.adj.* tending to annoy or vex; irritating.—*adv.* **pro-vok′ing-ly.**

prov-ost (prŏv′ŭst; prō′vō), *n.* **1,** a chief official or superintendent; **2,** esp., in certain colleges, the president; **3,** the chief magistrate in certain Scotch towns; **4,** a superintending clergyman at the head of a cathedral chapter or collegiate church.

prov-ost mar-shal (prō′vō), a military or naval officer who acts as chief of the military police.

prow (prou), *n.* the bow, or forward part, of a ship.

prow-ess (prou′ĕs), *n.* **1**, daring bravery; valor; **2**, a brave act or feat.

prowl (proul), *v.i.* to wander stealthily, as for prey or plunder:—*v.t.* to roam over, as woods or fields, in search of prey:—*n.* a roving for prey or plunder.—*n.* **prowl′er.**

prox-i-mal (prŏk′sĭ-măl), *adj.* **1**, immediately preceding or following; **2**, nearest; **3**, in anatomy, designating the end of a limb nearer to the body: opp. of *distal.*

prox-i-mate (prŏk′sĭ-māt), *adj.* immediately going before or following; nearest.—*adv.* **prox′i-mate-ly.**

prox-im-i-ty (prŏk-sĭm′ĭ-tĭ), *n.* immediate nearness in place, time, or other relation; vicinity.

prox-i-mo (prŏk′sĭ-mō), *adv.* in or of the coming month.—*abbr.* **prox.**

prox-y (prŏk′sĭ), *n.* [*pl.* proxies (-sĭz)], **1**, the position or powers of one authorized to act for another; **2**, a person who is given authority to represent or act for another; **3**, the document by which one person is authorized to act or vote for another.
Syn. agent, representative, delegate.

prude (pro͞od), *n.* **1**, a woman who affects great reserve, modesty, and virtue; **2**, a squeamishly proper person.

pru-dence (pro͞o′dĕns), *n.* **1**, the quality of being discreet or careful; wisdom put into practice; **2**, economy.
Syn. care, judgment, discretion, wisdom.

pru-dent (pro͞o′dĕnt), *adj.* **1**, practically wise; careful of the result of measures or actions; cautious; discreet; **2**, careful for the future.—*adv.* **pru′dent-ly.**
Syn. frugal, farseeing, forehanded. (See careful.)—*Ant.* careless, heedless, indiscreet.

pru-den-tial (pro͞o-dĕn′shăl), *adj.* **1**, proceeding from, or marked by, careful thought or wisdom; **2**, using sound judgment.—*adv.* **pru-den′tial-ly.**

prud-er-y (pro͞od′ẽr-ĭ), *n.* [*pl.* pruderies (-ĭz)], affected niceness or modesty in conduct; primness.

***prud-homme** (prü″dôm′), [Fr.], *n.* in France, a member of a board to settle trade disputes.

prud-ish (pro͞od′ĭsh), *adj.* affectedly precise and prim.—*adv.* **prud′ish-ly.** —*n.* **prud′ish-ness.**

[1]prune (pro͞on), *v.t.* [*p.t.* and *p.p.* pruned (pro͞ond), *p.pr.* prun′ing], **1**, to cut unnecessary twigs or branches from (a vine, bush, or tree); trim; **2**, to cut out or clear away, as useless parts:—*v.i.* to remove useless branches or parts.—*n.* **prun′er.**

[2]prune (pro͞on), *n.* any of various plums, prepared as a commercial food by being dried without fermentation.

pru-nel-la (pro͞o-nĕl′*ȧ*), *n.* a smooth woolen stuff used for the uppers of shoes and for gaiters. Also, **pru-nel′lo.**

prun-ing hook a pair of shears with one blade hook-shaped, on the end of a pole, for pruning.

pru-ri-ence (pro͞o′rĭ-ĕns), *n.* the state or quality of having impure or lustful desires. Also, **pru′ri-en-cy.**

pru-ri-ent (pro͞o′rĭ-ĕnt), *adj.* impure; lewd; lustful.—*adv.* **pru′ri-ent-ly.**

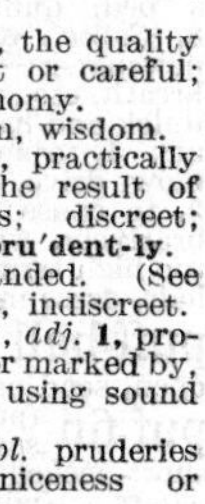

PRUNING HOOK

Prus-sian (prŭsh′ăn), *adj.* pertaining to Prussia, or to its people or language: **Prussian blue,** a rich blue color obtained from iron:—*n.* a native of Prussia.

prus-si-ate (prŭs′ĭ-āt), *n.* a salt of prussic acid.

prus-sic ac-id (prŭs′ĭk), a deadly poisonous acid, formed of hydrogen, carbon, and nitrogen: also called *hydrocyanic acid.*

[1]pry (prī), *v.i.* [*p.t.* and *p.p.* pried (prīd), *p.pr.* pry′ing], to make a close and often inquisitive inspection; peep; peer: with *into.*—*p.adj.* **pry′ing.**

[2]pry (prī), *v.t.* [*p.t.* and *p.p.* pried (prīd), *p.pr.* pry′ing], to raise or open with a lever:—*n.* **1**, a bar used as a lever; **2**, leverage.

psalm (säm), *n.* a sacred song or poem: **Psalms,** a book of the Old Testament containing sacred songs.—*abbr.* **Ps.**

psalm-ist (säm′ĭst), *n.* a composer of psalms, or sacred hymns: **the Psalmist,** any of the authors of the sacred songs in the Bible, esp. David.

psalm-o-dist (säm′ō-dĭst; săl′mō-), *n.* one who sings psalms.

psalm-o-dy (säm′ō-dĭ; săl′mō-dĭ), *n.*[*pl.* psalmodies (-dĭz)], the writing or singing of psalms, or sacred hymns.

Psal-ter (sôl′tẽr), *n.* the Old Testament Book of Psalms, esp. as contained in the Book of Common Prayer.

psal-ter-y (sôl′tẽr-ĭ), *n.* [*pl.* psalteries (-ĭz)], a stringed musical instrument, used by the ancient Hebrews.

pseu-do (sū′dō; psū′dō), *adj.* false; pretended: used freely as a prefix or combining form, usually without hyphen except before a vowel or a capital; as, *pseudo*scholarship; *pseudo*-American.

pseu-do-nym (sū′dō-nĭm), *n.* a fictitious or false name taken by a writer; a pen name.—*adj.* **pseu-don′y-mous.**

pshaw (shô; pshô), *interj.* an expression of contempt, scorn, etc. Also, **psha.**

psi (psī; sī), *n.* the 23d letter of the Greek alphabet [ψ, Ψ], equivalent to *ps.*

Psy-che (sī′kē; psī′kē), *n.* in mythology, a beautiful maiden who represents the soul: **psyche,** the human soul.

psy-chi-a-try (sī-kī′*ȧ*-trĭ; psī-), *n.* the study and treatment of mental disorders; psychotherapy.—*n.* **psy-chi′a-trist.**—*adj.* **psy″chi-at′ric** (sī″kĭ-ăt′rĭk).

psy-chic (sī′kĭk), *n.* a person believed to be susceptible to spiritualistic phenomena; esp., in spiritualism, a medium: —*adj.* pertaining to, or connected with, the soul or mind; spiritual: opp. of *physical.* Also, *adj.* **psy′chi-cal.**—*adv.* **psy′chi-cal-ly.**

psy-cho-a-nal-y-sis (sī″kō-*ȧ*-năl′ĭ-sĭs; psī″-), *n.* **1**, an analysis of the mental life of an individual; a psychological study of personality; **2**, a method of investigating and treating the mental condition of nervous patients.

psy-cho-log-ic (sī″kō-lŏj′ĭk; psī″-), *adj.* pertaining to the science that treats of the mind. Also, **psy″cho-log′i-cal.**—*adv.* **psy″cho-log′i-cal-ly.**

psy-chol-o-gy (sī-kŏl′ō-jĭ; psī-), *n.* [*pl.* psychologies (-jĭz)], the science that treats of the mind; also, a treatise on this science.—*n.* **psy-chol′o-gist.**

psy-cho-pa-thol-o-gy (sī″kō-p*ȧ*-thŏl′ō-jĭ; psī″-), *n.* the science dealing with mental diseases and abnormality.—*adj.* **psy″cho-path″o-log′i-cal.**

psy-chop-a-thy (sī-kŏp′*ȧ*-thĭ; psī-), *n.* disease of the mind, or its treatment.—*adj.* and *n.* **psy″cho-path′ic.**

psy-cho-phys-ics (sī″kō-fĭz′ĭks; psī″-), *n. pl.* used as *sing.*

the science which treats of the mind as affected by, and reacting to, physical conditions.

psy-cho-ther-a-py (sī″kō-thĕr′ȧ-pĭ; psī″-), *n.* the treatment of mental disease; psychiatry.

ptar-mi-gan (tär′mĭ-găn), *n.* any of several grouse of arctic regions.

pter-o-dac-tyl (tĕr″ō-dăk′tĭl; ptĕr″-), *n.* any of several huge flying reptiles no longer in existence.

Ptol-e-ma-ic the-o-ry (tŏl″ē-mā′ĭk), the theory of astronomy held by Ptolemy, a scientist of the second century, which taught that the sun and stars revolved about the earth as a center.

pto-ma-ine (tō′mȧ-ĭn; tō′mȧ-ēn; *Colloq.* tō′mān), *n.* any of a class of substances found in decaying organic matter, and usually poisonous. Also, **pto′ma-in.**

pu-ber-ty (pū′bẽr-tĭ), *n.* the earliest age in human development at which persons can beget or bear children.

pu-bes-cent (pū-bĕs′ĕnt), *adj.* **1,** arrived at the age when a person is able to bear or beget children; **2,** covered with soft, downy hairs, as some leaves.—*n.* **pu-bes′cence.**

pu-bis (pū′bĭs), *n.* one of the principal bones of either half of the pelvis (see *pelvis*, illus.).

pub-lic (pŭb′lĭk), *adj.* **1,** of or pertaining to the people at large; as, *public* property **2,** open; generally known; **3,** common to all; open to general use: with *the:* **public house,** in Great Britain, an inn, tavern, or dramshop: **public school, 1,** in the U. S., a primary, grammar, or high school, provided for all children at public expense; **2,** in Great Britain, a private boarding school for boys, as Eton, which prepares students for the older universities:—*n.* the people in general.—*adv.* **pub′lic-ly.**

pub-li-can (pŭb′lĭ-kăn), *n.* **1,** in Great Britain, one who keeps an inn or public house; **2,** in ancient Rome, a collector of the taxes and public revenues.

pub-li-ca-tion (pŭb″lĭ-kā′shŭn), *n.* **1,** the act of printing and placing on sale or of making generally known; **2,** that which is printed and placed on sale, as a book, magazine, etc.; **3,** that which is proclaimed or made generally known.

pub-li-cist (pŭb′lĭ-sĭst), *n.* one familiar with the laws of nations; also, a writer on politics.

pub-lic-i-ty (pŭb-lĭs′ĭ-tĭ), *n.* **1,** the state of being open to common knowledge; notoriety; **2,** advertising activity.

pub-lic–spir-it-ed (pŭb′lĭk=spĭr″ĭt-ĕd), *adj.* having the interests of the community at heart.

pub-lish (pŭb′lĭsh), *v.t.* **1,** to make known; announce; **2,** to print and offer for sale, as a book, magazine, etc.—*n.* **pub′lish-er.**
Syn. (see declare).

1**puck** (pŭk), *n.* in old folk tales, a fairy: **Puck,** a mischievous fairy or elf, as in Shakespeare's "Midsummer Night's Dream."

2**puck** (pŭk), *n.* a hard rubber disk used in hockey.

puck-er (pŭk′ẽr), *v.t.* and *v.i.* to gather into small folds; wrinkle:—*n.* a small fold or wrinkle.

pud-ding (po͝od′ĭng), *n.* **1,** a kind of soft food, often a dessert, made of flour, milk, eggs, etc.; **2,** a piece of intestine stuffed with ground meat: a kind of sausage.

pud-dle (pŭd′l), *n.* **1,** a small pool of dirty water; **2,** clay, sand, etc., worked together with water:—*v.t.* [*p.t.* and *p.p.* -dled (-ld), *p.pr.* -dling], **1,** to make muddy; **2,** to work water into (clay, sand, etc.) so as to make a mixture through which water will not pass; **3,** to line with such clay in order to make water-tight; **4,** to stir (molten pig iron) so as to produce wrought iron.—*n.* **pud′dler.**

pud-dling (pŭd′lĭng), *n.* the changing of pig iron into wrought iron by intense heat and frequent stirring.

pudg-y (pŭj′ĭ), *adj.* [*comp.* pudg′i-er, *superl.* pudg′i-est], short and fat; dumpy.—*n.* **pudg′i-ness.**

pueb-lo (pwĕb′lō), *n.* [*pl.* pueblos (-lōz)], **1,** a building made of adobe, or sun-dried brick, by the Indians of New Mexico, and serving as the dwelling of the entire village or tribe; **2,** in the U. S. and Spanish America, an Indian or Spanish village: **Pueblo,** a member of one of the tribes of Indians living in pueblos:—*adj.* designating, or pertaining to, such Indians or their villages.

pu-er-i-cul-ture (pū′ẽr-ĭ-kŭl″tûr), *n.* the art or practice of raising and training children.

pu-er-ile (pū′ẽr-ĭl; *Br.* pū′ẽr-īl), *adj.* **1,** pertaining to childhood; **2,** immature; foolish; silly; childish.—*n.* **pu″er-il′i-ty.**

pu-er-per-al (pū-ûr′pẽr-ăl), *adj.* of or pertaining to childbirth.

puff (pŭf), *n.* **1,** a short quick blast; a sudden breath forced out; **2,** any of a number of objects, generally round, soft, light, etc.; **3,** a soft ball or pad used to apply powder to the skin or hair; **4,** a soft roll of hair; **5,** a very light cake or tart filled with cream or custard; **6,** in dressmaking, a piece of material gathered on two sides so as to stand out in the center; **7,** a covering for a bed, quilted and padded with cotton; **8,** *Colloq.*, exaggerated praise printed in a newspaper:—*v.i.* **1,** to send out air, smoke, breath, etc., with sudden force; **2,** to breathe quick and hard, as a runner; **3,** to swell with air; **4,** to swell with importance:—*v.t.* **1,** to blow, drive, etc., with whiffs or little blasts; **2,** to cause to swell, as with wind, or, figuratively, with importance; **3,** to praise in too high terms; **4,** to arrange in puffs, as the hair, dress material, etc.

puff-ball (pŭf′bôl″), *n.* any of various ball-shaped fungi that, when broken open, send out a cloud of dustlike spores.

puf-fin (pŭf′ĭn), *n.* any of various northern sea birds related to the auk, with short-necked bodies and large bills.

puff-y (pŭf′ĭ), *adj.* [*comp.* puff′i-er, *superl.* puff′i-est], **1,** swollen with air or any soft matter; bloated; **2,** inflated in manner; **3,** blowing in little gusts.—*n.* **puff′i-ness.**

1**pug** (pŭg), *n.* one of a breed of lap dogs, with a short, broad nose, wrinkled face, and tightly curled tail: also called *pug dog.*

2**pug** (pŭg), *v.t.* [*p.t.* and *p.p.* pugged (pŭgd), *p.pr.* pug′ging], **1,** in pottery and brick manufacture, to grind, as clay, with water so as to make plastic; **2,** to line with clay so as to make water-tight, or the like:—*n.* clay of such consistency that it may be molded.

pug-ging (pŭg′ĭng), *n.* **1,** the act or operation of working up wet clay for pottery; **2,** clay or mortar used to deaden sound, make waterproof, etc.

pu-gil-ism (pū′jĭ-lĭzm), *n.* professional boxing; prize fighting.

pu-gil-ist (pū′jĭ-lĭst), *n.* a prize fighter; boxer.—*adj.* **pu″gil-is′tic.**

pug-na-cious (pŭg-nā′shŭs), *adj.* inclined to fight; quarrelsome.—*adv.* **pug-na′cious-ly.**—*n.* **pug-na′cious-ness.**

pug-nac-i-ty (pŭg-năs′ĭ-tĭ), *n.* inclination to fight; quarrelsomeness.

pug nose a nose turned up and broadened at the tip; a snub nose.—*adj.* **pug′–nosed″.**

pu-is-sant (pū′ĭ-sănt; pū-ĭs′ănt), *adj.* powerful; strong; forceful; as, *puissant* words.—*n.* **pu′is-sance.**

pul-chri-tude (pŭl'krĭ-tūd), *n.* beauty; comeliness, loveliness.

pule (pūl), *v.i.* [*p.t.* and *p.p.* puled (pūld), *p.pr.* pul'ing], to cry weakly; whine.

pull (po͝ol), *v.t.* **1,** to draw out or toward one by exerting force: as, to *pull* a nail; *pull* a tooth; **2,** to draw in any direction; drag; haul: **3,** to pluck; as, to *pull* grapes; **4,** in golf, to hit (the ball) so as to cause it to fly to the left; **5,** in printing, to make (a proof) by taking an impression of type on paper; as, to *pull* a proof:—*v.i.* to draw forcibly; tug:—*n.* **1,** the act of using force to draw; a tug; **2,** something pulled, as a proof in printing; **3,** a handle by which something is pulled, as of a bell, drawer, etc.; **4,** in golf, a stroke that causes the ball to fly to the left; **5,** *Colloq.*, unfair advantage due to influence.—*n.* **pull'er.**

pul-let (po͝ol'ĕt), *n.* a young hen or one not fully grown.

pul-ley (po͝ol'ĭ), *n.* [*pl.* pulleys (-ĭz)], **1,** a wheel with a flat face, used with a belt drive to transmit power; **2,** a wheel with a grooved rim in which a rope works: used in lifting or directing weights, beams, etc.

Pull-man (po͝ol'măn), *n.* a sleeping car with berths and staterooms, or a day car with comfortable chairs: named from the inventor: also called *Pullman car.*

pul-mo-na-ry (pŭl'mō-nā-rĭ), *adj.* pertaining to the lungs; as, *pulmonary* arteries.—*adj.* **pul-mon'ic.**

pul-mo-tor (pŭl'mō″tẽr), *n.* an instrument for producing artificial breathing by forcing air or oxygen into the lungs in case of suffocation, drowning, etc.

pulp (pŭlp), *n.* **1,** any soft, fleshy part of an animal or vegetable body, as of fruit; specif., the inner, fleshy part of a tooth (see *tooth,* illus.); **2,** any soft, formless mass; esp., the soft mass of ground linen, cotton, or wood, of which paper is made.

pul-pit (po͝ol'pĭt), *n.* **1,** a raised stand or desk in a church, from which the sermon is delivered (see illus. next column); **2,** preachers as a class.

pulp-y (pŭl'pĭ), *adj.* [*comp.* pulp'i-er, *superl.* pulp'i-est], consisting of, or like, a soft, moist mass of matter; soft; fleshy.—*n.* **pulp'i-ness.**

pul-que (po͝ol'kā), *n.* a favorite Mexican fermented drink made from the juice of the century plant.

pul-sate (pŭl'sāt), *v.i.* [*p.t.* and *p.p.* -sat-ed, *p.pr.* -sat-ing], **1,** to throb, as a pulse; **2,** to beat, as the heart.

pul-sa-tion (pŭl-sā'shŭn), *n.* **1,** a single throb or beat, as of the heart; **2,** the act of throbbing or beating.

PULPIT

¹pulse (pŭls), *n.* **1,** a throbbing or beating in an artery, which may be felt with the finger; **2,** a stroke or beat occurring at regular intervals:—*v.i.* [*p.t.* and *p.p.* pulsed (pŭlst), *p.pr.* puls'ing], to beat or throb, as an artery.—*adj.* **pulse'less.**

²pulse (pŭls), *n.* leguminous plants such as peas, beans, or the like: also, their seeds used for food.

pul-som-e-ter (pŭl-sŏm'ē-tẽr), *n.* a pump for raising water by means of steam: also called *vacuum pump.*

pul-ver-ize (pŭl'vẽr-īz), *v.t.* and *v.i.* [*p.t.* and *p.p.* -ized (-īzd), *p.pr.* -iz″ing], to reduce, or be reduced, to powder, by crushing, grinding, etc.—*n.* **pul″ver-i-za'tion.**—*n.* **pul'ver-iz″er.**

pu-ma (pū'mȧ), *n.* a large, tawny, catlike animal of America; the mountain lion; the cougar.

PUMA (1/35)

pum-ice (pŭm'ĭs), *n.* a hard, light, porous, volcanic rock, used for cleaning or rubbing: also called *pumice stone.*

¹pump (pŭmp), *n.* a mechanical device for raising or otherwise moving, or for

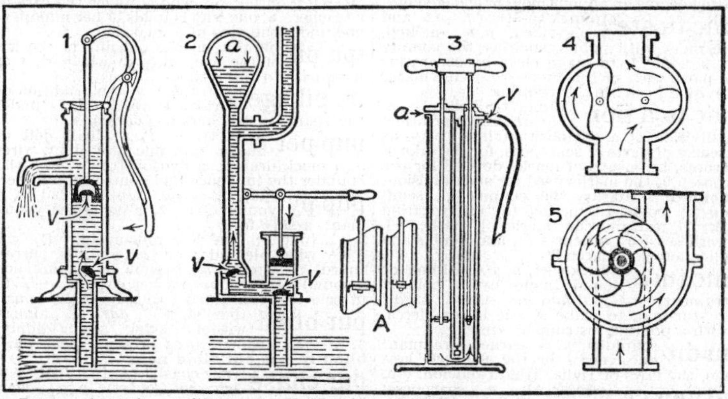

PUMPS.—1, suction, or lift, pump: *V, V,* valves; 2, force pump: *a,* air dome; *V, V,* valves: 3, double-acting tire pump: *a,* intake; *V,* valve at outlet; *A,* detail of the two pistons, showing piston leathers turned in opposite directions; 4, rotary pump; 5, centrifugal pump.

compressing or exhausting, a liquid or gas by means of suction or pressure:—*v.t.* **1**, to raise or draw, as water, by means of a pump; **2**, to draw water or other fluids from; as, to *pump* a well dry; **3**, to draw out by artful questions; as, to *pump* a secret out of a friend; **4**, to question persistently:—*v.i.* **1**, to raise water or other fluids with a pump; **2**, to work a pump.—*n.* **pump'er.**

[2]pump (pŭmp), *n.* a low shoe, usually light in weight, without lacing.

pump-kin (pŭmp'kĭn; *Colloq.* pŭng'kĭn), *n.* a plant of the gourd family; also, its edible fruit.

pun (pŭn), *n.* a play on words similar in sound but different in meaning:—*v.i.* [*p.t.* and *p.p.* punned (pŭnd), *p.pr.* pun'ning], to make puns or a pun.

[1]punch (pŭnch), *n.* **1**, a tool for making dents or holes; **2**, a machine tool for stamping and forming sheet-metal articles; **3**, a blow or thrust, esp. with the closed fist; **4**, *Slang*, force; energy:—*v.t.* **1**, to perforate with a punch; **2**, to make (a hole) with a punch; **3**, to strike with the closed fist.

[2]punch (pŭnch), *n.* a drink made of rum, whisky, or other liquor, with water, lemon juice, sugar, etc.; also, a drink made from fruit juices, sweetened and flavored.

Punch (pŭnch), *n.* a hunchbacked puppet with a hooked nose, the hero in a farcical puppet show, "Punch and Judy."

[1]punch-eon (pŭn'chŭn), *n.* a liquor cask of varying capacity, generally holding 84 wine gallons.

[2]punch-eon (pŭn'chŭn), *n.* **1**, a short, upright supporting timber; **2**, a slab of split timber used for flooring; **3**, a punch or tool used for marking, piercing, etc.

punc-til-i-o (pŭngk-tĭl'ĭ-ō; pŭngk-tĭl'yō), *n.* [*pl.* punctilios (-ōz; -yōz)], a precise point in conduct or ceremony; formal exactness or correctness.

punc-til-i-ous (pŭngk-tĭl'ĭ-ŭs; pŭngk-tĭl'yŭs), *adj.* very nice or precise in conduct; exact to excess.—*adv.* **punc-til'i-ous-ly.**—*n.* **punc-til'i-ous-ness.**

Syn. scrupulous, correct, particular.

punc-tu-al (pŭngk'tū-ăl), *adj.* observing, or done at, the exact time; prompt.—*adv.* **punc'tu-al-ly.**

punc-tu-al-i-ty (pŭngk"tū-ăl'ĭ-tĭ), *n.* the quality of being prompt, esp. in keeping an appointment or engagement.

punc-tu-ate (pŭngk'tū-āt), *v.t.* [*p.t.* and *p.p.* -at"ed, *p.pr.* -at"ing], **1**, to mark with points, such as the comma and period; **2**, to make clear by separating into parts with such points:—*v.i.* to use marks of division in writing or printing.

punc-tu-a-tion (pŭngk"tū-ā'shŭn), *n.* **1**, in writing or printing, the division of a composition into parts, as sentences or parts of sentences, for the sake of clearness, by means of marks devised for the purpose; **2**, the marks used for such division: **punctuation marks,** the comma [,], semicolon [;], colon [:], period [.], interrogation mark [?], exclamation mark [!], dash [—], parentheses [( )], brackets [ ], and double and single quotation marks ["...", '...'].

punc-ture (pŭngk'tūr), *n.* a small hole or wound made by a pointed instrument:—*v.t.* [*p.t.* and *p.p.* -tured (-tūrd), *p.pr.* -tur-ing], to make a hole in, or pierce, as with a pointed instrument; prick.

pun-dit (pŭn'dĭt), *n.* a learned Brahman; one versed in the Sanskrit language, the laws of India, Hindu religion, etc.

pun-gen-cy (pŭn'jĕn-sĭ), *n.* sharpness; tartness; biting quality.

pun-gent (pŭn'jĕnt), *adj.* **1**, stinging, pricking, or biting; as, a *pungent* acid; **2**, piercing; keen; **3**, sarcastic; caustic; as, *pungent* speech.—*adv.* **pun'gent-ly.**

Syn. acrid, sharp, stimulating, bitter.

Pu-nic (pū'nĭk), *adj.* pertaining to, or having the qualities of, the Carthaginians, whom the Romans considered treacherous; hence, deceitful:—*n.* the language of the Carthaginians, akin to Hebrew.

pun-ish (pŭn'ĭsh), *v.t.* **1**, to cause to pay the penalty of a crime or fault, as by fine, imprisonment, pain, or death; chastise; **2**, *Colloq.*, to handle roughly.

Syn. discipline, chastise. (See chasten.)

pun-ish-a-ble (pŭn'ĭsh-ȧ-bl), *adj.* deserving of, or liable to, a penalty; as, a crime *punishable* by death.

pun-ish-ment (pŭn'ĭsh-mĕnt), *n.* **1**, penalty inflicted for a crime or fault; **2**, *Colloq.*, rough treatment.

pu-ni-tive (pū'nĭ-tĭv), *adj.* pertaining to, involving, or inflicting, a penalty. Also, **pu'ni-to-ry.**

punk (pŭngk), *n.* **1**, partly decayed wood: tinder; **2**, a substance that will burn without flame.

pun-kah (pŭng'kȧ), *n.* in British India, a hanging fan moved by a servant to cool a room. Also, **pun'ka.**

pun-ster (pŭn'stẽr), *n.* one given to punning, or playing upon words.

[1]punt (pŭnt), *n.* a flat-bottomed boat, square at the ends, usually propelled with a pole:—*v.t.* to propel, as a boat, by pushing with a pole:—*v.i.* to go fishing, boating, or shooting in a punt.—*n.* **punt'er.**

[2]punt (pŭnt), *n.* in football, the act of kicking the ball, when dropped from the hand, before it touches the ground; also, the kick so made:—*v.t.* and *v.i.* to kick (a football) so dropped before it touches the ground.

pu-ny (pū'nĭ), *adj.* [*comp.* pu'ni-er, *superl.* pu'ni-est], small in strength or size; weak; feeble; as, a *puny* child.—*n.* **pu'ni-ness.**

pup (pŭp), *n.* **1**, a young dog; a puppy; **2**, the young of several other mammals, as of the seal: **pup tent,** a small shelter tent without sides and open at the ends, for soldiers and campers; a dog tent (see *tent*, illus.).

pu-pa (pū'pȧ), *n.* [*pl.* pupæ (-pē)], the resting stage in the life of the higher insects, during which the larva changes to the adult.—*adj.* **pu'pal.**

[1]pu-pil (pū'pĭl), *n.* **1**, a young person of either sex who is under the care of a teacher; **2**, one who is in his or her minority; one under the care of a guardian.

[2]pu-pil (pū'pĭl), *n.* the opening in the iris of the eye, through which rays of light pass to the retina.

pu-pil-age (pū'pĭl-āj), *n.* the condition or period in which one is under the charge of teachers or guardians.

pup-pet (pŭp'ĕt), *n.* **1**, a small doll or image, esp. one moved by wires in a mock drama; a marionette; **2**, one who is under the influence and control of another.

pup-py (pŭp'ĭ), *n.* [*pl.* puppies (-ĭz)], **1**, a young dog; **2**, a conceited young man; a silly fop.

pur (pûr), *n.* the low murmuring of a cat when pleased:—*v.t.* [*p.t.* and *p.p.* purred (pûrd), *p.pr.* pur'ring], to show by making such a sound; as, she *purred* her content:—*v.i.* to utter a low, murmuring sound. *Pfd.S.*, **purr.**

pur-blind (pûr'blīnd"), *adj.* **1**, almost without sight; seeing dimly; **2**, mentally shortsighted or dull.—*adv.* **pur'blind"ly.**—*n.* **pur'blind"ness.**

pur-chase (pûr'chās), *v.t.* [*p.t.* and *p.p.* -chased (-chāst), *p.pr.* -chasing], **1**, to get by paying money or its equivalent, acquire; buy; **2**, to obtain at the expense of some sacrifice, labor, etc.; **3**, to move or raise by the application of some mechanical power:—*n.* **1,** the act of buying; **2,** the thing bought; **3,** a value or worth paid for property, equivalent to the estimated income from the property in a certain number of years; as, land bought at ten years' *purchase;* **4,** a mechanical hold or advantage in raising heavy bodies; as, to get a *purchase* on a thing to be lifted.—*n.* **pur'chas-er.**—*adj.* **pur'chas-a-ble.**

pure (pūr), *adj.* **1,** genuine; real; **2,** free from any foreign or adulterating matter; clear; clean; **3,** free from any defilement; innocent; **4,** sheer; mere; as, *pure* villainy.—*adv.* **pure'ly.**—*n.* **pure'ness.**

Syn. undefiled, chaste, stainless.—*Ant.* polluted, adulterated, impure.

***pu-rée** (pü″rā'), [Fr.], *n.* a thick soup made of meat and vegetables boiled and rubbed through a sieve.

pur-ga-tion (pûr-gā'shŭn), *n.* **1,** the act of cleansing; **2,** the clearing from alleged guilt, as by oath or ordeal.

pur-ga-tive (pûr'gȧ-tĭv), *adj.* having the power of cleansing:—*n.* a medicine for the purpose of cleansing the system of waste and impurities; a cathartic.

pur-ga-to-ri-al (pûr″gȧ-tō'rĭ-ăl), *adj.* pertaining to purgatory, or the place of cleansing after death.

pur-ga-to-ry (pûr'gȧ-tō-rĭ), *n.* **1,** in the Roman Catholic creed, the state after death in which the souls of the faithful are purified from venial sins by suffering; **2,** hence, any place of torment or misery:—*adj.* cleansing.

purge (pûrj), *v.t.* [*p.t.* and *p.p.* purged (pûrjd), *p.pr.* purg'ing], **1,** to cleanse or free from impurities; **2,** to clear of guilt; also, to remove; wash away; as, to *purge* one's sins; **3,** to cleanse by the action of a cathartic medicine:—*v.i.* **1,** to become pure or clean; **2,** to clear the bowels by the use of a cathartic:—*n.* **1,** the act or process of cleansing; **2,** a purgative.—*n.* **purg'er.**

pu-ri-fi-ca-tion (pū″rĭ-fĭ-kā'shŭn), *n.* cleansing from guilt or from moral or physical impurity.

pu-ri-fy (pū'rĭ-fī), *v.t.* [*p.t.* and *p.p.* -fied (-fīd), *p.pr.* -fy″ing], **1,** to make clean; **2,** to free from guilt; **3,** to make ceremonially clean, as by a religious ceremony; **4,** to free from impurities, as food, water, etc.:—*v.i.* to become clean.—*n.* **pu'ri-fi″er.**

Pu-rim (pū'rĭm), *n.* a Jewish feast observed annually to commemorate the deliverance of the Jews in Persia from destruction (Esther 9).

pur-ism (pūr'ĭzm), *n.* **1,** great nicety as to the choice of words; **2,** an example of such nicety.

pur-ist (pūr'ĭst), *n.* one who is very careful and precise in the choice of his language.—*adj.* **pu-ris'tic.**

pu-ri-tan (pū'rĭ-tăn), *n.* one who is very strict in his religious life, or over-strict in morals: **Puritan,** one who in England or her American colonies in the 16th and 17th centuries insisted upon having simpler forms of faith and worship than those established by law, and who emphasized morality and freedom of religious belief:—*adj.* pertaining to the Puritans or their doctrine or practice.

pu-ri-tan-ic (pū″rĭ-tăn'ĭk), *adj.* strict and precise in the matter of religious duties and moral conduct of life; rigid; austere: **Puritanic,** pertaining to the Puritans or to their beliefs, habits, etc. Also, **pu″ri-tan'i-cal.**—*adv.* **pu″ri-tan'i-cal-ly.**—*n.* **pu″ri-tan'i-cal-ness.**

Pu-ri-tan-ism (pū'rĭ-tăn-ĭzm), *n.* the doctrines and practices of the Puritans; hence, great strictness in matters of religion and morals.

pu-ri-ty (pū'rĭ-tĭ), *n.* **1,** the state or quality of being clean; cleanness; freedom from foreign or adulterating matter; **2,** virtue; innocence.

¹purl (pûrl), *n.* a warm spiced ale or gin: so called from the bubbles on the surface.

²purl (pûrl), *n.* **1,** an embroidered or puckered border; **2,** a certain reversed stitch in knitting; **3,** a kind of gilt lace or cord for use on a border:—*v.t.* **1,** to ornament with an embroidered border; **2,** to reverse (stitches) in knitting:—*v.i.* **1,** to reverse knitting stitches; **2,** to embroider a border.

³purl (pûrl), *v.i.* **1,** to ripple or flow with a gentle murmur; **2,** to move in a circular motion; whirl:—*n.* **1,** the continued murmuring sound of a shallow stream; **2,** an eddy; a small whirlpool.

pur-lieus (pûr'lūz), *n.pl.* adjacent districts or those lying near; environs; outskirts.

pur-lin (pûr'lĭn), *n.* in a roof, a horizontal piece of timber supporting the common rafters (see *principal rafter,* illus.). Also, **pur'line** (pûr'lĭn).

pur-loin (pûr-loin'), *v.t.* to steal:—*v.i.* to be guilty of stealing.—*n.* **pur-loin'er.**

pur-ple (pûr'pl), *adj.* **1,** of the color of blended blue and red; of the color of robes of state; **2,** hence, regal; royal:—*n.* **1,** a color resulting from a mixture of red and blue; formerly, a deep crimson; **2,** a robe of this color formerly worn by royalty; **3,** hence, royal power or dignity; also, great wealth or high rank; as, born to the *purple:*—*v.t.* [*p.t.* and *p.p.* -pled (-pld), *p.pr.* -pling], to dye or color a purple color:—*v.i.* to become purple.—*adj.* **pur'plish.**

pur-port (pûr'pōrt), *n.* meaning; design import:—*v.t.* (pûr'pōrt; pûr-pōrt'), to mean; signify; intend.

pur-pose (pûr'pŭs), *n.* **1,** settled intention; design; **2,** the end or aim desired:—*v.t.* [*p.t.* and *p.p.* -posed (-pŭst), *p.pr.* -pos-ing], to intend or resolve; design:—*v.i.* to have an intention.—*adj.* **pur'pose-less.**—*adv.* **pur'pose-ly.**

Syn., n. intent, object. (See plan.)

pur-pose-ful (pûr'pŭs-fo͞ol), *adj.* **1,** having an aim in view; not aimless; **2,** serving an end or aim.—*adv.* **pur'pose-ful-ly.**

purr (pûr), *n.* the low murmuring of a cat when pleased:—*v.t.* to show by making such a sound; as, she *purred* content:—*v.i.* to utter a low, murmuring sound. Also, **pur.**

purse (pûrs), *n.* **1,** a small bag or pouch for money; **2,** a sum of money collected for a purpose; as, they made up a *purse* for the widow; also, such a sum offered as a prize; **3,** treasury; as, the public *purse:*—*v.t.* [*p.t.* and *p.p.* pursed (pûrst), *p.pr.* purs'ing], to pucker or wrinkle; as, to *purse* the lips.

purse-proud (pûrs'-proud″), *adj.* haughty because of the possession of great wealth.

purs-er (pûr'sẽr), *n.* **1,** an officer having charge of the provisions, clothing, and money of a ship; **2,** formerly, a paymaster.

purs-lane (pûrs'lăn), *n.* a species of herb used as a salad or a potherb.

pur-su-ance (pŭr-sū'ăns), *n.* the act of following out, or state of being followed out; as, in *pursuance* of a plan.

pur-su-ant (pŭr-sū'ănt), *adj.* done as a result (of anything); conformable:—*adv.* in accordance; agreeably.—*adv.* **pur-su'ant-ly.**

pur-sue (pŭr-sū'), *v.t.* [*p.t.* and *p.p.* -sued' (-sūd'), *p.pr.* -su'ing], **1,** to follow with the aim of overtaking; chase; as, to *pursue* a thief; **2,** to seek; as, to *pursue* pleasure; **3,** to go on with; continue; as, to

pursue one's studies:—*v.i.* **1**, to follow; **2**, to continue.—*n.* **pur-su'er.**
Syn. hunt. (See follow.)

pur-suit (pûr-sūt'), *n.* **1**, the act of following or seeking; chase; as, the *pursuit* of a thief; **2**, a following up for a purpose; as, in *pursuit* of one's business; **3**, occupation; as, business *pursuits*.

pur-sui-vant (pûr'swĭ-vănt), *n.* **1**, an attendant or follower; retainer; **2**, a state messenger.

pur-sy (pûr'sĭ), *adj.* [*comp.* pur'si-er, *superl.* pur'si-est], fat, thick, and short-winded.—*n.* **pur'si-ness.**

pu-ru-lent (pū'rōō-lĕnt), *adj.* consisting of, or containing, pus; festering.—*n.* **pu'ru-lence; pu'ru-len-cy.**

pur-vey (pûr-vā'), *v.t.* to provide; procure, as provisions:—*v.i.* to purchase provisions or food.—*n.* **pur-vey'or.**

pur-vey-ance (pûr-vā'ăns), *n.* **1**, the act of providing; **2**, provisions supplied; **3**, the right formerly accorded to royalty of buying up provisions without the owner's consent.

pur-view (pûr'vū), *n.* **1**, extent or scope of anything; **2**, the scope or body of a statute; **3**, range of vision; outlook.

pus (pŭs), *n.* the white or yellowish white substance produced by inflammation, in sores, etc.; matter.—*adj.* **¹pus'sy.**

push (pōōsh), *v.t.* **1**, to press against with force, for the purpose of moving; **2**, to urge forward or extend by effort; as, to *push* one's interests; **3**, to drive by pressure; urge; as, to *push* a debtor:—*v.i.* **1**, to make a steady forward effort; as, the army *pushed* on; **2**, to press hard in order to move:—*n.* **1**, a thrust; force applied; **2**, an effort or attempt; **3**, an emergency; **4**, *Colloq.*, enterprise; energy; as, a man with *push*.—*p.adj.* **push'ing.**
Syn., *v.* shove, thrust, force.

push-er (pōōsh'ẽr), *n.* an airplane with the propeller behind the wings.

pu-sil-lan-i-mous (pū″sĭ-lăn'ĭ-mŭs), *adj.* cowardly; mean-spirited; faint-hearted.—*adv.* **pu″sil-lan'i-mous-ly.**—*n.* **pu″sil-la-nim'i-ty.**
Syn. weak, timid, cowardly.—*Ant.* brave.

puss (pōōs), *n.* **1**, a cat: a pet name; **2**, *Colloq.*, a girl or young woman. Also, **²puss'y.**

pus-tu-lar (pŭs'tū-lȧr), *adj.* covered with pimples filled with pus.

pus-tule (pŭs'tūl), *n.* a large pimple full of pus.—*adj.* **pus'tu-lous.**

¹put (pōōt), *v.t.* [*p.t.* and *p.p.* put, *p.pr.* put'-ting], **1**, to push or drive onward; thrust; send; **2**, to throw or hurl with an upward and outward motion of the arm; as, to *put* the shot; **3**, to force or urge; as, to *put* a horse through his paces; **4**, to cause to be in any situation or position; place; lay; as, to *put* a book on the table; **5**, to cause to be in any state or condition; as, to *put* to flight; **6**, to state; propose; as, to *put* a question; **7**, to apply; set; as, to *put* one's mind to a task; **8**, to assign; ascribe; as, to *put* a wrong interpretation on an act; **9**, to express; as, to *put* a thought into words; **10**, to fit; as, to *put* words to music: **put by**, to save, as money: **put off**, **1**, to postpone (an action); **2**, to turn (a person) aside from a purpose: **put on**, to assume, as pretentious airs: **put out**, **1**, to vex; **2**, to inconvenience; **3**, to disconcert; **4**, to send forth, as buds; **5**, to lend, as money at interest; **6**, to extinguish (fire); **7**, to publish: **put over**, *Slang*, to accomplish or bring about: **put through**, **1**, to carry out successfully; **2**, *Colloq.*, to subject to an ordeal; as, to *put* him *through* an examination: **put up**, **1**, to offer for sale, esp. at auction; **2**, to raise (a price); **3**, to can or preserve (fruit); **4**, to offer or advance (funds), as on a bet; **5**, to lodge; **6**, to nominate, as for membership; **7**, to sheathe (a weapon): **put up to**, to incite (a person) to (mischief or daring):—*v.i.* **1**, to go or move; hasten; as, to *put* for school; **2**, to take one's course; as, the ship *put* into port: **put about**, of a ship, to alter the course; esp., to tack: **put in**, to head toward shore; enter a harbor: **put on**, to make a pretense: **put up**, to lodge; take lodgings: **put up with**, to endure; tolerate:—*n.* **1**, a push; throw; thrust; **2**, an agreement to deliver merchandise at a fixed price and date; **3**, (pŭt), a certain game at cards.

pu-ta-tive (pū'tȧ-tĭv), *adj.* supposed; reputed; regarded.

pu-tre-fac-tion (pū″trē-făk'shŭn), *n.* **1**, the act or process of decaying; **2**, decomposition; rottenness.

pu-tre-fac-tive (pū″trē-făk'tĭv), *adj.* pertaining to, or tending to produce, decay or decomposition.

pu-tre-fy (pū'trē-fī), *v.t.* [*p.t.* and *p.p.* -fied (-fīd), *p.pr.* -fy″ing], to rot; corrupt:—*v.i.* to decay or become rotten.

pu-tres-cent (pū-trĕs'ĕnt), *adj.* becoming rotten; decomposed; decayed.—*n.* **pu-tres'cence.**

pu-trid (pū'trĭd), *adj.* **1**, corrupt; rotten; **2**, stinking; as, a *putrid* odor.—*n.* **pu'trid-ness.**—*n.* **pu-trid'i-ty.**

***Putsch** (pōōch), [Ger.], *n.* an unsuccessful uprising or coup d'état.

putt (pŭt), *n.* in golf, a short, careful stroke on the green, to play a ball into a hole:—*v.t.* and *v.i.* to drive (a golf ball) into a hole with a short, careful stroke. Also, **²put.**

put-tee (pŭt'ē), *n.* **1**, a gaiter made of cloth wrapped spirally from ankle to knee: worn by soldiers or sportsmen; **2**, a stiff leather legging. Also, **put'tie; ¹put'ty.**

¹putt-er (pŭt'ẽr), *n.* in golf, a short club, usually with a brass or iron head, used for playing one's ball into the hole.

²put-ter (pŭt'ẽr), *v.i.* to work idly or fussily. Also, **pot'ter,** *Pfd. S.*

putt-ing green (pŭt'ĭng), in golf, a plot of smooth turf around one of the holes into which the ball is played.

²put-ty (pŭt'ĭ), *n.* a cement of whiting and linseed oil used for filling cracks, holding panes in window sashes, etc.:—*v.t.* [*p.t.* and *p.p.* -tied (-ĭd), *p.pr.* -ty-ing], to fill with such cement.

puz-zle (pŭz'l), *n.* **1**, something that perplexes or causes embarrassment; **2**, a toy made to tax one's skill in arranging its parts; **3**, a problem; riddle:—*v.i.* [*p.t.* and *p.p.* -zled (-ld), *p.pr.* -zling], to think in perplexity; as, to *puzzle* over a mystery:—*v.t.* **1**, to perplex; entangle; embarrass; **2**, to solve by clever thinking; as, to *puzzle* out a riddle.—*n.* **puz'zle-ment.**—*n.* **puz'zler.**
Syn., *v.* bewilder, confuse. (See perplex.)

Pyg-ma-li-on (pĭg-mā'lĭ-ŏn), *n.* a king and sculptor of Cyprus, who fell in love with his masterpiece, a statue of a maiden, Galatea, to whom Aphrodite gave life that he might marry her.

Pyg-my (pĭg'mĭ), *n.* [*pl.* Pygmies (-mĭz)], **1**, a member of a race of dwarfs mentioned by classical authors; **2**, one of a dwarf race of Negroes in central Africa: **pygmy**, **1**, a dwarf; **2**, a very insignificant person:—*adj.* very small; dwarfish; as, *pygmy* plants. Also, **Pig'my; pig'my.**

py-ja-ma (pĭ-jä'mȧ; pī-jä'mȧ), *n.* **1**, an Oriental garment, consisting of a pair of loose silk or cotton trousers; **2**, in *pl.*, (usually, in the U. S., *pajamas*), a sleeping suit consisting of a jacket and a pair of loose trousers. Also, **pa-ja'ma** (pȧ-).

py-lon (pī'lŏn), *n.* a gateway in the form of a truncated pyramid; a post or tower used as a marker to indicate the course over which an airplane is to fly.

py-lor-ic (pī-lôr′ĭk; pĭ-), *adj.* pertaining to the pylorus, or opening of the stomach leading to the small intestine.

py-lo-rus (pī-lō′rŭs; pĭ-), *n.* [*pl.* pylori (-rī)], the lower opening of the stomach, leading to the small intestine: also called *pyloric valve.*

py-or-rhe-a (pī″ō-rē′ȧ), *n.* a discharge of pus: used popularly as the name of a disease (*pyorrhea alveolar′s*) of the mouth, characterized by inflammatory infection of the gums and loosening of the teeth.

pyr-a-mid (pĭr′ȧ-mĭd), *n.* **1**, a solid body standing on a triangular, square, or polygonal base, having its triangular sides ending in a point at the apex or top (see *solid*, illus.); **2**, in *pl.:* **a**, a group of Egyptian monuments having a square base and triangular sides sloping to an apex, built by the early kings to serve as their tombs; **b**, a certain game at billiards.

PYRAMIDS OF GIZA, EGYPT

py-ram-i-dal (pĭ-răm′ĭ-dăl), *adj.* shaped like a pyramid.—*adj.* **pyr″-a-mid′ic; pyr″a-mid′i-cal.**

Pyr-a-mus (pĭr′ȧ-mŭs), *n.* in mythology, a Babylonian youth, lover of Thisbe, who, thinking that she had been devoured by a lion, killed himself.

pyre (pīr), *n.* a funeral pile; a pile, as of wood, for burning a dead body.

py-rex (pī′rĕks), *n.* a variety of glassware used in cooking, possessing great strength and resistance to heat: a trade name.

py-rite (pī′rīt; pĭr′īt), *n.* a yellow mineral with a bright luster, formed of iron and sulphur; iron pyrites.

py-ri-tes (pĭ-rī′tēz), *n.* a mixture of sulphur with iron, copper, etc., as pyrite.

py-rog-ra-phy (pī-rŏg′rȧ-fĭ), *n.* the art or process of decorating wood or leather by burning, as with a flame or heated iron.—*n.* **py-rog′ra-pher.**

py-rom-e-ter (pī-rŏm′ē-tẽr), *n.* an instrument for measuring unusually intense heat, as in furnaces.

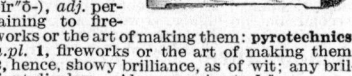

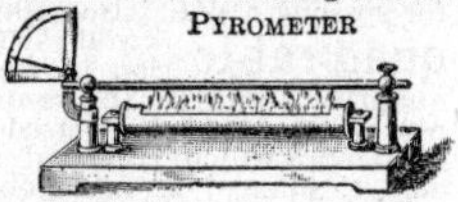
PYROMETER

py-ro-tech-nic (pī″rō-tĕk′nĭk; pĭr″ō-), *adj.* pertaining to fireworks or the art of making them: **pyrotechnics,** *n.pl.* **1**, fireworks or the art of making them; **2**, hence, showy brilliance, as of wit; any brilliant display. Also, *n.* **py′ro-tech″ny.**

py-ro-tech-nist (pī″rō-tĕk′nĭst; pĭr″ō-), *n.* one skilled in the manufacture of fireworks.

Pyr-rha (pĭr′ȧ), *n.* in mythology, the wife of Deucalion, who with him survived the Deluge and repopulated the earth.

Py-thag-o-re-an (pĭ-thăg″ō-rē′ăn; pĭth″-ȧ-gō′rē-ăn), *adj.* pertaining to Pythagoras, a Greek philosopher who lived in the sixth century B. C., or to his system of philosophy, which included the doctrine of the transmigration of souls:—*n.* a disciple of Pythagoras.—*n.* **py-thag″o-re′an-ism.**

Pyth-i-as (pĭth′ĭ-ăs), *n.* in mythology, a youth famed for his faithful friendship with Damon. According to legend, Pythias was condemned to death by Dionysius, tyrant of Syracuse, but was granted leave to visit his home and arrange his affairs if his friend Damon would offer himself as hostage for his return. On the appointed day, Pythias returned to be executed, but was pardoned. Also, rarely but more properly, **Phin′ti-as.**

py-thon (pī′thŏn), *n.* a large serpent closely resembling the boa.

pyth-o-ness (pĭth′ō-nĕs), *n.* any woman supposed to have the power of foretelling events; esp., one of the priestesses of Apollo's temple at Delphi.

pyx (pĭks), *n.* **1**, (also, *pix*), in the Roman Catholic Church, the box or container in which the consecrated wafer or Host is placed; **2**, the box in which coins are tested at the British mint before being circulated.

Q

¹quack (kwăk), *n.* the cry of a duck, or a harsh sound like it:—*v.i.* **1**, of a duck, to utter a quack; **2**, to make a sound like a duck's quack.

²quack (kwăk), *n.* **1**, an ignorant person who claims medical skill and knowledge of marvelous remedies; **2**, hence, a fraudulent pretender to skill of any kind:—*v.i.* **1**, to pretend to medical skill; **2**, to make false claims of any kind; talk noisily and boastfully:—*adj.* making false claims; fraudulent; as, a *quack* doctor.—*n.* **quack′er-y.**

quack-sal-ver (kwăk′săl-vẽr), *n. Rare,* one who boasts of his pretended skill in medicines and salves; a quack doctor.

¹quad (kwŏd), *n.* in printing, a blank type, one-half, one, two, or three ems in width; a quadrat: used for spacing between words or in filling out a line.

²quad (kwŏd), *n. Colloq.*, the quadrangle, or four-sided inclosure, of a college, prison, or like group of buildings.

Quad-ra-ges-i-ma (kwŏd″rȧ-jĕs′ĭ-mȧ), *n.* the first Sunday in Lent: also called *Quadragesima Sunday.*

quad-ra-ges-i-mal (kwŏd″rȧ-jĕs′ĭ-măl), *adj.* consisting of forty: **Quadragesimal,** pertaining to the forty days of Lent.

quad-ran-gle (kwŏd′răng″gl), *n.* **1**, a four-sided court or lawn, surrounded by buildings, esp. on a college campus; **2**, a plane figure with four angles and four straight sides; **3**, a division of land, of varying size. — *adj.* **quad-ran′gu-lar.**

quad-rant (kwŏd′rănt), *n.* **1**, one fourth of a circle, or an arc of 90 degrees; **2**, an instrument containing a scale for measuring angles up to 90 degrees, usually in the form of an arc of 45 degrees, with a movable arm: formerly used in navigation, but now replaced by the sextant; **3**, an instrument for measuring the altitude

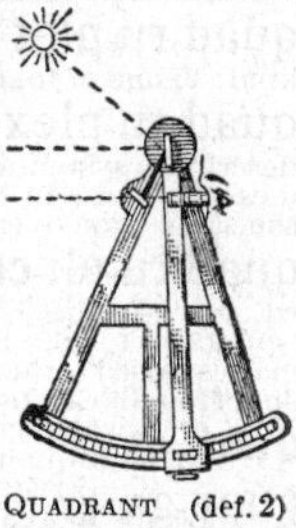
QUADRANT (def. 2)
As formerly used on shipboard.

of heavenly bodies; **4**, an instrument for raising a cannon to give it the desired range.

quad-rat (kwŏd′răt), *n.* in printing, a blank piece of type metal used for spacing a line: also called *quad.*

quad-rat-ic (kwŏd-răt′ĭk), *n.* an equation in which the unknown quantity occurs in the second, but no higher, power: **quadratics,** *pl.* used as *sing.* that part of algebra which treats of such equations:—*adj.* **1**, square; **2**, in algebra, involving the second, but no higher, power of an unknown quantity; as, a *quadratic* equation.

quad-ra-ture (kwŏd′rȧ-tŭr), *n.* **1**, the process of determining the area of a geometrical figure: so called because the result was formerly expressed as a square equal in area to the geometrical figure; **2**, in astronomy, the relative position of two heavenly bodies one of which is 90 degrees east or west of the other; as, the sun and moon are in *quadrature* when halfway between the times of new and full moon (see *syzygy*, illus.).

quad-ren-ni-al (kwŏd-rĕn′ĭ-ăl), *adj.* **1**, lasting through four years; **2**, happening once in four years.—*adv.* **quad-ren′ni-al-ly.**

quad-ri-ga (kwŏd-rī′gȧ), *n.* [*pl.* quadrigæ (-jē)], in ancient Rome, a chariot which was drawn by four horses abreast, as in racing (see *chariot*, illus.).

quad-ri-lat-er-al (kwŏd″rĭ-lăt′ĕr-ăl), *n.* a plane figure bounded by four straight lines:—*adj.* having four sides.

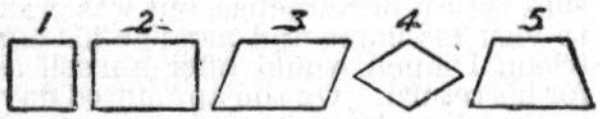

QUADRILATERALS

1–4, parallelograms; 1, 2, rectangles; 1, square; 2, long rectangle; 3, rhomboid, or long parallelogram; 4, rhombus, lozenge, or diamond; 5, trapezoid.

qua-drille (kwȧ-drĭl′), *n.* **1**, an old-fashioned square dance for four couples; **2**, the music for it; **3**, a game of cards played by four persons.

quad-ril-lion (kwŏd-rĭl′yŭn), *n.* in U. S. and French usage, the number denoted by one with 15 ciphers; in Great Britain, one with 24 ciphers.

quad-roon (kwŏd-rōōn′), *n.* a person one fourth of whose blood is Negro; the child of a mulatto and a white.

quad-ru-ma-nous (kwŏd-rōō′mȧ-nŭs), *adj.* having all four feet like hands, as a monkey; four-handed.

quad-ru-ped (kwŏd′rōō-pĕd), *n.* a four-footed animal:—*adj.* four-footed.—*adj.* **quad-ru′pe-dal.**

quad-ru-ple (kwŏd′rōō-pl), *adj.* fourfold:—*n.* a sum or quantity four times as great as another:—*v.t.* [*p.t.* and *p.p.* -pled (-pld), *p.pr.* -pling], to multiply by four:—*v.i.* to increase fourfold.

quad-ru-plet (kwŏd′rōō-plĕt), *n.* **1**, a combination of four of one kind; **2**, one of four children born at one birth.

quad-ru-plex (kwŏd′rōō-plĕks), *adj.* fourfold: used esp. to describe a system of telegraphy in which four messages, two in each direction, are sent at the same time over one wire.

quad-ru-pli-cate (kwŏd-rōō′plĭ-kāt), *v.t.* [*p.t.* and *p.p.* -cat″-ed, *p.pr.* -cat″ing], to multiply by four:—*adj.* (-plĭ-kăt), **1**, four times as great; **2**, in mathematics, raised to the fourth power:—*n.* (-plĭ-kăt), one of four like things.—*n.* **quad-ru″pli-ca′tion.**

quaff (kwȧf), *v.t.* to drink or swallow in large quantities:—*v.i.* to drink deeply.

quag-ga (kwăg′ȧ), *n.* a South African four-footed animal of the zebra family: said to be no longer in existence.

quag-gy (kwăg′ĭ), *adj.* giving under the feet, as soft, wet ground; boggy.

quag-mire (kwăg′mīr″), *n.* soft, miry ground which yields under the feet; a bog; marsh.

qua-hog (kwô′hŏg; kwȧ-hŏg′), *n.* the large, round, hard-shelled, edible clam common along the Atlantic coast of America. Also, **qua′haug.**

¹quail (kwāl), *n.* [*pl.* quail; quails], any of various game birds allied to the partridge, including the bobwhite: in the U. S., locally called *partridge.*

²quail (kwāl), *v.i.* to shrink from pain or danger; lose heart; cower.

quaint (kwānt), *adj.* pleasingly odd or unusual in appearance or manner; esp., attractive because of an old-fashioned daintiness or prettiness.—*adv.* **quaint′ly.**—*n.* **quaint′ness.**

quake (kwāk), *v.i.* [*p.t.* and *p.p.* quaked (kwākt), *p.pr.* quak′ing], **1**, to shake from internal shock or convulsion; as, the earth *quakes;* **2**, to tremble or shake with fear, cold, etc.; quiver:—*n.* a shaking or trembling; esp., an earthquake.

Quak-er (kwāk′ĕr), *n.* one of a religious sect, the Society of Friends, founded about 1650: orig. applied in derision.—*n.fem.* **Quak′er-ess.**—*adj.* **Quak′er-ish.**

Quak-er-ism (kwāk′ĕr-ĭzm), *n.* the principles of religious faith and practice held by the Friends, or Quakers, including the mystical doctrine of the Inner Light, simplicity in worship, dress, and speech, religious toleration, and the belief that judicial oaths, war, slavery, and social injustice are inconsistent with true Christianity.

qual-i-fi-ca-tion (kwŏl″ĭ-fĭ-kā′shŭn), *n.* **1**, the act of making, or state of being, fit; **2**, that which makes a person or thing fitted for or adapted to a special use or circumstance.

qual-i-fied (kwŏl′ĭ-fīd), *p.adj.* **1**, fitted; adapted; as, she is well *qualified* to fill the position; **2**, limited; restricted; as, *qualified* praise.

qual-i-fi-er (kwŏl′ĭ-fī″ĕr), *n.* **1**, that which limits or modifies; **2**, in grammar, a word, as an adjective or adverb, which modifies or limits the meaning of another word.

qual-i-fy (kwŏl′ĭ-fī), *v.t.* [*p.t.* and *p.p.* -fied (-fīd), *p.pr.* -fy″ing], **1**, to make fit for any office, occupation, etc.; **2**, to moderate; lessen; soften; as, to *qualify* censure; **3**, to limit; modify; alter slightly; as, to *qualify* a statement:—*v.i.* to be or become competent or fit for any office or employment.

Syn. modify. To *qualify* is to limit or restrict, usually with a softening effect; as, to *qualify* a statement which is too sweeping. To *modify* is to make partial changes in a thing; as, to *modify* opinions, estimates, decisions, etc.

qual-i-ta-tive (kwŏl′ĭ-tā-tĭv), *adj.* pertaining to quality or kind, as opposed to quantity or amount; as, *qualitative* analysis.—*adv.* **qual′i-ta-tive-ly.**

qual-i-ty (kwŏl′ĭ-tĭ), *n.* [*pl.* qualities (-tĭz)], **1**, that which distinguishes one person or thing from others, as color, weight, skill, etc.; **2**, essential nature; kind; as, the *qualities* of iron; **3**, degree of excellence; as, goods of high *quality;* **4**, trait or characteristic; as, generosity is one of his many fine *qualities;* **5**, special virtue; as, the healing *quality* of an ointment; **6**, rank; as, a lady of *quality;* **7**, of musical sounds, distinctive tone; as, a voice of carrying *quality.*

Syn. attribute, property.

qualm (kwäm), *n.* **1**, a feeling of sickness, esp. of the stomach; **2**, hence, a sudden misgiving; **3**, a twinge of conscience.—*adj.* **qualm′ish.**

quan-da-ry (kwŏn′dȧ-rĭ; *Br.* kwŏn-dā′-rĭ), *n.* [*pl.* quandaries (-rĭz)], a state of hesitation or doubt; dilemma.

quan-ti-ta-tive (kwŏn′tĭ-tā-tĭv), *adj.* pertaining to quantity or amount, as opposed to quality or kind; as, *quantitative* analysis.—*adv.* **quan′ti-ta-tive-ly.**

quan-ti-ty (kwŏn′tĭ-tĭ), *n.* [*pl.* quantities (-tĭz)], **1,** that property of a thing which permits its exact measurement with reference to some fixed standard, as of volume, weight, or the like; size; magnitude; as, this bag contains one bushel in *quantity;* **2,** any uncertain bulk, weight, or number; **3,** a large portion, sum, or mass; as, material in *quantity;* **4,** the sound given to a syllable, as long or short; **5,** in mathematics, anything that can be increased, divided, or measured.

quar-an-tine (kwŏr′ăn-tēn), *n.* **1,** the time during which an incoming vessel suspected of carrying a dangerous disease is not allowed to communicate with the shore; hence, the place where such vessels are held; also, the holding of them or the measures taken to hold them; **2,** any enforced restriction placed on a person, thing, or place because of contagious disease:—*v.t.* (kwŏr′ăn-tēn; kwŏr″ăn-tēn′), [*p.t.* and *p.p.* -tined (-tēnd), *p.pr.* -tin″ing], to place under restraint because of disease.

¹quar-rel (kwŏr′ĕl), *n.* **1,** a heavy bolt or arrow, esp. one with a square head, formerly used with a crossbow; **2,** a small tile or pane of glass, square, diamond-shaped, or lozenge-shaped; a quarry.

²quar-rel (kwŏr′ĕl), *n.* **1,** an angry dispute; petty fight; **2,** a cause for dispute; **3,** a disagreement or falling out; serious breach of friendship:—*v.i.* **1,** to dispute violently; fight: usually with *with;* **2,** to disagree; fall out; **3,** to find fault: with *with.* —*n.* **quar′rel-er; quar′rel-ler.**

Syn., n. controversy, dispute, strife. *Quarrel* names an angry disagreement or act, which may end friendly relations or may be only a trifling matter; as, a children's *quarrel;* it also names the ground for complaint or differences; as, I have no *quarrel* with them. A *controversy* is the oral or written expression of opposition to the opinion of another and is sometimes bitter or angry, sometimes a neutral discussion; as, the *controversy* over states' rights. *Dispute* may be used in a good sense of questioning something asserted by another, or in a bad sense, to suggest a sharp, and usually undignified, *quarrel;* as, a point in *dispute;* a *dispute* over precedence.

quar-rel-some (kwŏr′ĕl-sŭm), *adj.* inclined to dispute, find fault, or fight; easily provoked.—*adv.* **quar′rel-some-ly.**—*n.* **quar′rel-some-ness.**

¹quar-ry (kwŏr′ĭ), *n.* [*pl.* quarries (-ĭz)], a large, open excavation or hole from which stone is obtained by cutting or blasting:—*v.t.* [*p.t.* and *p.p.* -ried (-ĭd), *p.pr.* -ry-ing], **1,** to dig or take from an excavation or hole; **2,** to dig into; excavate.

²quar-ry (kwŏr′ĭ), *n.* [*pl.* quarries (-ĭz)], **1,** a beast or bird when hunted, caught, or killed; **2,** anything hunted, eagerly sought, or killed.

³quar-ry (kwŏr′ĭ), *n.* [*pl.* quarries (-ĭz)], **1,** a square-headed arrow; quarrel; **2,** a small square, lozenge-shaped or diamond-shaped tile or pane of glass.

¹quart (kwôrt), *n.* **1,** a measure of capacity; two pints, or one fourth of a gallon, or, in dry measure, one eighth of a peck; **2,** a vessel containing a quart; also, the contents of such a vessel.—*abbr.* **qt.**

²quart (kärt), *n.* in certain games of cards, a sequence of four cards of the same suit.

quar-tan (kwôr′tăn), *adj.* of or pertaining to the fourth in a series:—*n.* an intermittent fever occurring every fourth day: that is, with two days between attacks.

quar-ter (kwôr′tẽr), *n.* **1,** one of the four equal parts into which a thing may be, or is, divided; **2,** one fourth of a hundredweight; 25 or 28 pounds; **3,** in England, one fourth of a ton, or eight bushels: used esp. in measuring grain; **4,** three months, or a fourth of one year; **5,** one half of a semester at school or college; **6,** fifteen minutes, or a fourth of an hour; also, the moment that marks the end of this period; **7,** a fourth of a dollar, or 25 cents; also, a silver coin of this value; **8,** one of the four cardinal points of the compass; also, one of the four parts of the horizon marked off by these points, or the region under it; hence, any part of the earth; as, men came from all *quarters;* **9,** a particular place or district; as, the Latin *quarter* in Paris; **10,** one of the four limbs of an animal with the parts near it; as, a *quarter* of beef; **11,** the leather of a shoe above the sole and between the back seam and the vamp; **12,** a fourth part of the moon's monthly revolution; **13,** the aspect or phase of the moon when halfway between new and full; **14,** in heraldry, one of the four parts into which a shield is divided; **15,** the after part of a ship's side; **16,** life granted to a captive or enemy; mercy; as, to give no *quarter;* **17,** in *pl.,* lodgings, esp. for soldiers:—*adj.* consisting of, or equal to, a fourth part of something; as, a *quarter* hour: **quarter back,** in football, one of the players behind the line, who generally calls the signals for the plays:—*v.t.* **1,** to divide into four equal parts; also, to divide into parts; dismember, as, formerly, a criminal after execution; **2,** to quarter-saw; **3,** to furnish with food and lodging, as a regiment; **4,** to place different coats of arms on the quarters of one shield:—*v.i.* to be stationed; lodge.

quar-ter day one of the four days of the year, about three months apart, recognized as dates on which rents are due and tenancies begin and end.

quar-ter-deck (kwôr′tẽr-dĕk″), *n.* that part of the upper deck of a ship which is behind the mainmast.

quar-tered (kwôr′tẽrd), *p.adj.* **1,** divided into four equal parts; **2,** furnished with shelter, or quarters: **quartered oak,** oak lumber obtained by sawing the trunk lengthwise into quarters through the center and then sawing these in such a way as to bring out the grain of the marks radiating from the center, called *medullary rays.*

quar-ter-foil (kwôr′tẽr-foil″), *n.* **1,** a flower with four leaves, or a leaf with four leaflets; **2,** an ornament somewhat like a leaf and having four lobes. Also, **quat′re-foil″**, *Pfd. S.*

quar-ter-ing (kwôr′tẽr-ĭng), *n.* **1,** the act of assigning lodging or quarters, as to soldiers; **2,** the placing of more than one coat of arms on a shield to show the different families from which a person is descended; **3,** any one of the four or more quarters of a coat of arms, or the device on it.

quar-ter-ly (kwôr′tẽr-lĭ), *n.* [*pl.* quarterlies (-lĭz)], a publication issued once every three months:—*adj.* **1,** consisting of, or containing, a fourth part; **2,** coming, or falling due, once every three months; as, a *quarterly* meeting:—*adv.* **1,** once in each fourth of the year; **2,** by or in quarters.

quar-ter-mas-ter (kwôr′tẽr-mȧs″tẽr), *n.* **1,** in the army, an officer whose duty it is to provide lodgings, food, clothing, and other supplies for soldiers; **2,** in the navy, a petty officer who attends to the steering, signals, soundings, etc., of ships.

quar-tern (kwôr′tẽrn), *n.* **1**, a quarter; a fourth part; **2**, in Great Britain, a quarter of various weights and measures, as of an ounce, a pint, or a peck; **3**, a loaf of bread weighing four pounds.

quar-ter–saw (kwôr′tẽr=sô″), *v.t.* to saw (a log, esp. an oak log) lengthwise through the center into quarters and then into boards in such a way as to bring out the grain to advantage.

quar-ter-staff (kwôr′tẽr-ståf″), *n.* [*pl.* quarterstaves (-stāvz″; -stävz″)], a stout stick from six to eight feet long, formerly used in England as a weapon.

quar-tet (kwôr-tĕt′), *n.* **1**, a musical composition in four parts for four voices or instruments; **2**, the four performers of such a composition; **3**, anything made up of four. Also, **quar-tette′**.

quar-tile (kwôr′tĭl), *adj.* designating, in a series of values arranged in the order of magnitude, any of the three points which divide the series into four equal parts:—*n.* a quartile point; incorrectly, a quarter.

quar-to (kwôr′tō), *n.* [*pl.* quartos (-tōz)], in printing books, the size of paper or page obtained by folding a sheet twice, so as to form four large leaves, usually nearly square; also, a book of paper so folded:—*adj.* folded four leaves to a sheet; hence, of the size and shape of a quarto.—*abbr.* **4to.**

quartz (kwôrts), *n.* a very common, hard mineral, transparent to opaque,

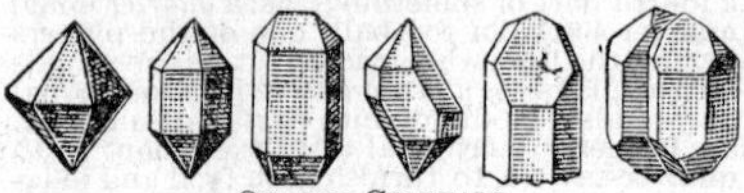

QUARTZ CRYSTALS

found in brilliant crystals or in a massive form and composed of silica.

quartz-ite (kwôrt′sīt), *n.* a compact rock composed of grains of quartz.

[1]**quash** (kwŏsh), *v.t.* to subdue or crush, as a rebellion.

[2]**quash** (kwŏsh), *v.t.* to stop, as a suit; overthrow; set aside, as an indictment, for irregularity in proceedings.

qua-si- (kwā′sī; kwä′sĭ-), *prefix*, used freely with adjectives and nouns, and meaning: **1**, almost; seemingly; as, *quasi-historical*; **2**, apparently; nearly.

quas-si-a (kwŏsh′ĭ-*ȧ*; kwăs′-; kwäsh′-), *n.* a very bitter drug obtained from the wood of any of several tropical American trees, and used as a tonic.

qua-ter-na-ry (kw*ȧ*-tûr′n*ȧ*-rĭ), *adj.* **1**, consisting of four things; **2**, arranged in fours: **Quaternary**, formerly, in geology, designating, or pertaining to, the last period, or ice age, of the Cenozoic era: now called *Pleistocene*:—*n.* [*pl.* quaternaries (-rĭz)], **1**, a group of four things; **2**, the number four: **Quaternary**, the Quaternary period.

qua-ter-ni-on (kw*ȧ*-tûr′nĭ-ŭn), *n.* **1**, a set or group of four persons or things; as, a *quaternion* of soldiers; **2**, in *pl.*, a certain system of mathematical analysis.

quat-rain (kwŏt′rān), *n.* a four-line stanza, in which, usually, the first and third lines rime, and the second and fourth.

qua-tre (kä′tẽr; kȧtr′), *n.* **1**, (also, *cater*), a die, domino, or card bearing a marking of four spots; **2**, the number four; **3**, in *pl.* (usually, *caters* or *quaters*), the changes rung on a set, or ring, of nine bells.

quat-re-foil (kăt′ẽr-foil″), *n.* **1**, a leaf or a flower with four leaflets radiating from a center; **2**, a carved stone ornament, or an opening, resembling a symmetrical leaf with four lobes. Also, **quar′ter-foil″**.

qua-ver (kwā′vẽr), *n.* **1**, a shaking or trembling, as of the voice; **2**, a trill in singing or playing; **3**, in music, an eighth note:—*v.i.* **1**, to shake or tremble; vibrate; **2**, to have a tremulous sound, as a voice or musical instrument:—*v.t.* to utter or sing with trills or a tremulous sound.

quay (kē), *n.* a firmly built wharf for loading or unloading vessels.

quea-sy (kwē′zĭ), *adj.* [*comp.* quea′si-er, *superl.* quea′si-est], **1**, affected with, or causing, nausea or vomiting; **2**, easily nauseated; squeamish; **3**, hence, presenting difficulties; delicate; as, a *queasy* question.

queen (kwēn), *n.* **1**, a female sovereign, or woman who rules in her own right; **2**, the wife of a king; **3**, a gifted woman who is a natural leader in her sphere; as, a social *queen;* **4**, the perfect female of bees, ants, or termites, usually the only female in the group capable of reproduction; **5**, a playing card bearing a conventional drawing of a queen; **6**, the one of a set of chess pieces ranking next to the king; **7**, the best or chief of her kind; as, the *queen* of beauty: **queen consort**, the wife of a reigning king: **queen dowager**, the widow of a king: **queen mother**, a king's widow who is also mother of a reigning sovereign: **queen regent**, **1**, a queen reigning during the childhood, absence, or incapacity of the actual sovereign; **2**, a queen reigning in her own right: also called *queen regnant* (rĕg′nănt):—*v.i.* to rule as, or play the part of, a female sovereign:—*adj.* and *adv.* **queen′ly.**—*n.* **queen′li-ness.**

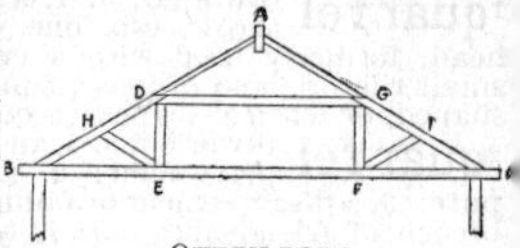

QUEEN-POST

A, ridgepole; BC, tiebeam; AB, AC, rafters; DB, GC, principal rafters; DE, GF, queen-posts; HE, IF, struts; DG, straining piece.

queen–post (kwēn′=pōst″), *n.* one of two upright timbers in a roof truss placed at equal distances from the apex: distinguished from *king-post*, placed at the apex.

queer (kwēr), *adj.* **1**, differing from the ordinary or normal; droll; strange; **2**, giddy; faint; sick; as, a *queer* feeling; **3**, *Colloq.*, mentally unsound; open to question; **4**, *Slang*, counterfeit; sham; as, *queer* money.—*adv.* **queer′ly.**—*n.* **queer′ness.**

Syn. eccentric, erratic, strange, odd, singular. *Queer* describes what differs from the ordinary in some abnormal way; as, a *queer* noise. *Eccentric* applies to anything that deviates from the customary; as, *eccentric* ways. *Erratic* is stronger than *eccentric*, as it implies that such eccentricity is unwise; as, *erratic* conduct. *Strange* means unknown, unusual, and, sometimes, undesirable; as, a *strange* house; *strange* actions. *Odd* means unmatched, uneven, and of persons suggests a failure to adapt oneself; as, an *odd* glove; an *odd* idea. *Singular* of a person means having some distinguishing trait; of things, customs, etc., it means unusual or unconventional.

quell (kwĕl), *v.t.* **1**, to suppress or subdue; put an end to; as, to *quell* a riot; **2**, to calm; as, to *quell* rage.—*n.* **quell′er.**

quench (kwĕnch), *v.t.* **1**, to put out, as a fire; **2**, to cause to cease; stop; as, to *quench* thirst; **3**, to cool suddenly; as, to *quench* hot iron in water.—*adj.* **quench′a-ble.**—*n.* **quench′er.**—*adj.* **quench′less.**

quer-u-lous (kwĕr′o͝o-lŭs), *adj.* **1**, complaining; discontented; fretful; as, a *querulous* old man; **2**, expressing complaint or fretfulness, as a voice.—*adv.* **quer′u-lous-ly.**—*n.* **quer′u-lous-ness.**

que-ry (kwē′rĭ), *n.* [*pl.* queries (-rĭz)], **1,** a question; an inquiry; **2,** a question mark [?]:—*v.t.* [*p.t.* and *p.p.* -ried (-rĭd), *p.pr.* -ry-ing], **1,** to inquire into; ask; **2,** to express a doubt in regard to:—*v.i.* to ask questions.

quest (kwĕst), *n.* **1,** search; as, an animal in *quest* of food; **2,** in medieval romance, an expedition for a particular object, such as the Holy Grail; **3,** those engaged in an adventure or search, collectively:—*v.i.* to go forth seeking adventure; as, the knight *quested* forth.—*n.* **quest′er.**

ques-tion (kwĕs′chŭn), *n.* **1,** the act of asking; inquiry; **2,** that which is asked; interrogation; **3,** the subject under discussion; as, the *question* before the meeting; **4,** dispute or doubt; as, these beyond *question* are the facts; **5,** a matter to be decided; as, that is a *question* for you: **question mark,** an interrogation point [?]:—*v.t.* **1,** to ask; examine by queries; **2,** to consider doubtful: often with *whether;* **3,** to challenge; take exception to:—*v.i.* to make inquiries.—*n.* **ques′tion-er.**—*adv.* **ques′tion-ing-ly.**

Syn., n. query. (See doubt.)

ques-tion-a-ble (kwĕs′chŭn-*ȧ*-bl), *adj.* **1,** open to question or doubt; **2,** arousing suspicion; as, a *questionable* transaction in business.—*adv.* **ques′tion-a-bly.**—*n.* **ques′tion-a-ble-ness.**

ques-tion-naire (kwĕs-chŭn-âr′; *Fr.* kĕs″tyô″nâr′), *n.* a series of questions submitted to a number of persons, whose replies often serve as the basis of a report on the subject of the questions.

quet-zal (kĕt-säl′; kĕt′s*ȧ*l), *n.* **1,** a handsome bird of Central America, the national emblem of Guatemala, with a crest and a long tail; **2,** the monetary unit of Guatemala, equivalent to $1.00. Also, **quezal′** (kĕ-säl′).

queue (kū), *n.* **1,** a pigtail, or the tail of a wig; **2,** a line of people, automobiles, or the like, awaiting their turn to proceed. Also, **cue.**

quib-ble (kwĭb′l), *n.* a turn or shift from the point in question:—*v.i.* [*p.t.* and *p.p.* -bled (-ld), *p.pr.* -bling], to avoid the truth by a skilful but trifling objection; equivocate.—*n.* **quib′bler.**—*n.* **quib′bling.**

quick (kwĭk), *adj.* **1,** rapid; swift; as, *quick* in action; **2,** nimble; as, *quick* on one's feet; **3,** prompt to respond to impressions; alert; as, a *quick* mind; **4,** accurate; unhesitating; ready; as, a *quick* eye; *quick* wit; **5,** easily excited; hasty; as, a *quick* temper; **6,** sensitive; as, a *quick* ear; **7,** sharp, as a curve; **8,** *Archaic,* having life:—*adv.* with haste; rapidly:—*n.* **1,** the living flesh; as, the *quick* under the nails; **2,** the feelings; as, she was hurt to the *quick;* **3,** a hedge of growing shrubs.—*adv.* **quick′ly.**—*n.* **quick′ness.**

Syn., adj. brisk, lively. (See hasty.)

quick-en (kwĭk′n), *v.i.* **1,** to come to life; become alive; **2,** to act or move more rapidly:—*v.t.* **1,** to increase the speed of; hasten; as, to *quicken* one's steps; **2,** to bring to life; **3,** to make keen; give new life to; refresh; cheer.—*n.* **quick′en-er.**

quick-lime (kwĭk′līm″), *n.* lime produced by burning limestone, shells, etc., with intense heat: transformed by the addition of water into slaked lime, and used in cement, mortar, and the like.

quick-sand (kwĭk′sănd″), *n.* sand soaked with water and yielding so easily that a person may readily sink into it.

quick-set (kwĭk′sĕt″), *n.* **1,** a cutting from a living shrub, esp. the hawthorn, set to grow, as for a hedge; **2,** a hedge formed in this manner.

quick-sil-ver (kwĭk′sĭl″vẽr), *n.* **1,** mercury, a silver-white metallic element; **2,** a compound of tin and mercury, formerly used on the backs of mirrors.

quick-step (kwĭk′stĕp″), *n.* a lively march, written in quick time.

[1]quid (kwĭd), *n.* a piece of something to be chewed, esp. of tobacco; a cud.

[2]quid (kwĭd), *n.* [*pl.* quid; *Rare,* quids], *Eng. Slang,* a sovereign, or one pound; formerly, also, a guinea.

quid-di-ty (kwĭd′ĭ-tĭ), *n.* [*pl.* quiddities (-tĭz)], **1,** that which makes a thing what it is and different from other things; **2,** a trifling nicety.

quid-nunc (kwĭd′nŭngk″), *n.* one who is curious to know everything that goes on; a gossip.

qui-es-cent (kwī-ĕs′ĕnt), *adj.* resting; calm; silent; still.—*adv.* **qui-es′-cent-ly.**—*n.* **qui-es′cence; qui-es′cen-cy.**

qui-et (kwī′ĕt), *adj.* **1,** free from motion, disturbance, or noise; as, a *quiet* river; *quiet* life; *quiet* children; **2,** still; calm; as, a *quiet* night; **3,** peaceable; gentle; as, a *quiet* disposition; **4,** subdued and modest; as, *quiet* manners; **5,** not showy; as, *quiet* colors; **6,** informal, as a wedding:—*v.t.* **1,** to calm or make peaceful; **2,** to bring to a state of rest:—*v.i.* to become still or calm:—*n.* **1,** freedom from motion, noise, or disturbance; **2,** gentleness; composure; peace; rest.—*n.* **qui′et-er.**—*adv.* **qui′et-ly.**—*n.* **qui′et-ness.**

Syn., n. tranquillity, repose, serenity, quietude.—*Ant., n.* noise, uproar, disturbance.

qui-et-ism (kwī′ĕt-ĭzm), *n.* **1,** peace; quiet; **2,** (usually, *Quietism*), a form of religious mysticism practiced in France and Spain during the 17th century, having as its chief aim the attainment of spiritual union with God through meditation on divine things rather than through active effort after perfection.—*n.* **qui′et-ist; Qui′et-ist.**

qui-e-tude (kwī′ĕ-tūd), *n.* rest; repose; quietness.

qui-e-tus (kwī-ē′tŭs), *n.* **1,** the final settlement of an account; **2,** anything which puts an end to action, esp. death.

quill (kwĭl), *n.* **1,** one of the large, strong feathers of a bird's wing or tail; also, the hollow shaft of a feather; **2,** a pen made from a feather; **3,** one of the long, sharp spines of the porcupine:—*v.t.* to plait or iron into small fluted ridges.

quill-ing (kwĭl′ĭng), *n.* a strip of material, as silk, net, etc., fluted into ridges.

quilt (kwĭlt), *n.* a bed cover made by stitching a layer of soft cotton or wool between two layers of fabric; hence, any warm bed cover or counterpane:—*v.t.* **1,** to stitch together, as two layers or pieces of cloth, with a soft material between; **2,** to stuff in the manner of a quilt:—*v.i.* to stitch material together with soft material between, as in making a quilt.—*n.* **quilt′er.**

quilt-ing (kwĭlt′ĭng), *n.* **1,** the act or process of making a quilt; **2,** the soft material, usually cotton, for such work.

quince (kwĭns), *n.* **1,** a bushy tree or shrub allied to the apple; **2,** the hard, applelike fruit of this tree, used for preserves.

qui-nine (kwī′nīn; kwĭ-nēn′; kwĭ-nīn′), *n.* a bitter drug obtained from the bark of the cinchona tree.

Quin-qua-ges-i-ma (kwĭn″kw*ȧ*-jĕs′ĭ-m*ȧ*), *n.* the Sunday next before Lent: also called *Quinquagesima Sunday; Shrove Sunday.*

quin-quen-ni-al (kwĭn-kwĕn′ĭ-ăl), *adj.* **1,** occurring once in five years, or at the end of every five years; **2,** lasting five years:—*n.* such an event.

quin-sy (kwĭn′zĭ), *n.* severe inflammation of the tonsils and throat, accompanied by swelling and the formation of pus.

quin-tal (kwĭn′tăl), *n.* a unit of weight varying in different countries from 100 to 220 pounds.

quin-tan (kwĭn′tăn), *adj.* occurring every fifth day; as, a *quintan* fever.

quin-tes-sence (kwĭn-tĕs′ĕns), *n.* **1,** the pure essence, or most characteristic part, of anything; **2,** the most perfect form or embodiment of some quality; as, she is the *quintessence* of neatness.

quin-tet (kwĭn-tĕt′), *n.* **1,** a musical composition in five parts or for five voices or instruments; **2,** the five performers of such a composition; **3,** any set or group of five. Also, **quin-tette′**.

quin-til-lion (kwĭn-tĭl′yŭn), *n.* in U. S. and France, the number denoted by one with eighteen ciphers annexed; in Great Britain, one with thirty ciphers.

quin-tu-ple (kwĭn′tū-pl), *v.t.* and *v.i.* [*p.t.* and *p.p.* -pled (-pld), *p.pr.* -pling], to make or become five times as much:—*adj.* fivefold.

quip (kwĭp), *n.* **1,** a short sarcastic remark; a smart retort; jeer; **2,** a quibble; **3,** an odd or fantastic act or object.

[1]quire (kwīr), *n.* a unit of measure consisting of 24 (sometimes 25) uniform sheets of paper, or the 20th part of a ream: **in quires,** in loose sheets; unbound, as a book.

[2]quire (kwīr), *n.* **1,** a band of singers, esp. in a church; **2,** the place where they sing. Also, **choir,** *Pfd.S.*

Quir-i-nal (kwĭr′ĭ-năl; kwĭ-rī′năl), *n.* **1,** one of the seven hills upon which Rome was built; **2,** the royal palace of the king of Italy, which stands on this hill; **3,** hence, the monarchial government of the Italian king as distinguished from the *Vatican.*

quirk (kwûrk), *n.* **1,** a sudden twist, turn, or curve, as of the pen in writing; a flourish; **2,** a quick turn of fancy; a quip; conceit; **3,** an artful avoidance of the truth in speaking; a quibble; smart answer.

quis-ling (kwĭz′lĭng), *n.* one who traitorously assists an enemy power to invade his country.

quit (kwĭt), *v.t.* [*p.t.* and *p.p.* quit or quit′ted, *p.pr.* quit′ting], **1,** to satisfy or discharge, as an obligation; **2,** to stop; give up; as, to *quit* work; **3,** to resign; abandon; as, to *quit* the path of duty:—*adj.* freed from.
Syn., v. surrender, relinquish, abandon.

quit-claim (kwĭt′klām″), *n.* a deed of release: a legal paper by which a person gives up claim to, or right in, an estate:—*v.t.* to give up claim to, as an estate.

quite (kwīt), *adv.* **1,** wholly; completely; entirely; as, *quite* dead; *quite* certain; **2,** *Colloq.,* very; considerably; as, *quite* cold; *quite* sick.

quit-rent (kwĭt′rĕnt″), *n.* in feudal times, a rent paid by a freeholder or tenant as a substitute for certain services.

quits (kwĭts), *adj.* equal or even (with someone), as when returning or repaying something; as, now we are *quits.*

quit-tance (kwĭt′ăns), *n.* **1,** a discharge or release from a debt, service, or obligation; **2,** recompense; repayment.

quit-ter (kwĭt′ẽr), *n.* **1,** one who shirks or gives up before a task is done; **2,** *Colloq.,* a coward.

[1]quiv-er (kwĭv′ẽr), *n.* a light, portable case, or sheath, for arrows.

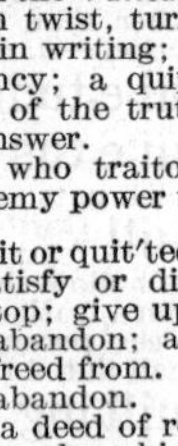
Ancient Quiver

[2]quiv-er (kwĭv′ẽr), *n.* the act of trembling or shivering; a tremor:—*v.i.* to tremble, as from fear; shake; shiver.
Syn., v. (see shake).

***qui vive** (kē″ vēv′), [Fr.], who goes there? the challenge of a sentinel in the French army: **on the qui vive,** on the watch; alert.

quix-ot-ic (kwĭk-sŏt′ĭk), *adj.* chivalrous or romantic to an absurd or extravagant degree: from *Don Quixote,* the hero of Cervantes' romance of that name.—*adv.* **quix-ot′i-cal-ly.**—*n.* **quix′ot-ism.**

quiz (kwĭz), *n.* [*pl.* quizzes (-ĕz)], **1,** an absurd, jesting question, put in pretended seriousness; a joke; **2,** one who jests or asks absurd questions; **3,** *Colloq.,* a questioning of a pupil or class:—*v.t.* [*p.t.* and *p.p.* quizzed (kwĭzd), *p.pr.* quiz′zing], **1,** to make fun of while pretending to be serious; chaff; **2,** to peer at impertinently; **3,** *Colloq.,* to examine (a pupil or class) by questions.—*n.* **quiz′zer.**

quiz-zi-cal (kwĭz′ĭ-kăl), *adj.* comical; humorously serious; queer; odd.—*adv.* **quiz′zi-cal-ly.**

quod (kwŏd), *n. Slang,* a quadrangle, as of a prison; hence, a prison.

quoin (koin; kwoin), *n.* **1,** a large square stone at the corner of a wall; also, the outside angle of a building; **2,** any of several wedge-shaped devices, as for locking type in a chase, for raising a gun barrel, etc.

quoit (kwoit; koit), *n.* **1,** a flat ring of iron to be pitched at a fixed object, as a short peg; **2,** in *pl.,* the game thus played.

quon-dam (kwŏn′dăm), *adj.* having been at some time; former; sometime; as, a *quondam* member of a society.

quo-rum (kwō′rŭm), *n.* the number of regularly assembled members of a body or corporation necessary, by law or constitution, to transact business.

quo-ta (kwō′tȧ), *n.* the part or share which one is entitled to receive from, or bound to contribute to, a total sum.

quo-ta-tion (kwō-tā′shŭn), *n.* **1,** the act of repeating the words of another; **2,** the words repeated; **3,** a passage repeated or referred to as an illustration; **4,** the current market price of a stock or commodity; also, a stating of the current price.

quo-ta-tion mark **1,** one of the marks placed at the beginning and end of a cited or repeated passage or word: two inverted commas [“] at the beginning, and two apostrophes [”] at the end of a quotation; **2,** either of the single marks [‘ or ’] used to show a quotation within a quotation; as, the attorney asked, “Did he approach you and say ‘Good evening’?”

quote (kwōt), *v.t.* [*p.t.* and *p.p.* quot′ed, *p.pr.* quot′ing], **1,** to repeat, as the words of some other person; repeat the words of, as an author or passage; **2,** to name or cite, as an author or passage, as authority or illustration; **3,** to give the present price of; **4,** in printing, to inclose (a passage) in quotation marks:—*v.i.* to repeat the words of another:—*n.* **1,** in printing, a quotation mark, called *single quote* [‘,’], or *double quote* [“,”]; **2,** *Colloq.,* a quotation.—*n.* **quot′er.**—*adj.* **quot′a-ble.**

quoth (kwōth), *v.t. Archaic,* said; spoke; uttered: used only in the first and third persons in the past tense, with the subject always following the verb; as, *quoth* he.

quo-tid-i-an (kwō-tĭd′ĭ-ăn), *n.* an intermittent fever that returns every day:—*adj.* daily.

quo-tient (kwō′shĕnt), *n.* the result of the process of division; esp., the number showing how many times a given number is contained in another.

quo war-ran-to (kwō wŏ-răn′tō), [*pl.* quo warrantos (-tōz)], a judicial writ or order commanding a person to show by what right or authority he exercises an office or certain powers.

R

Ra (rä), *n.* in Egyptian mythology, the sun god; the supreme deity. Also, **Re** (rä).

***raad** (rät; räd), [Du.], *n.* a legislative, or lawmaking, assembly of South Africa.

rab-bet (răb′ĕt), *n.* a groove or cut, made in the edge of one plank so that another may fit into it:—*v.t.* to join, as parts cut or grooved to fit together.

rab-bi (răb′ī; răb′ĭ), *n.* [*pl.* rabbis; rabbies (-īz; -ĭz)], master; teacher; in Jewish usage, a doctor, or interpreter, of the law or ritual. Also, **rab′bin.**

rab-bin-ic (ră-bĭn′ĭk), *adj.* pertaining to rabbis or their doctrines, learning, or language. Also, **rab-bin′i-cal.**

rab-bit (răb′ĭt), *n.* **1,** a well-known small animal of the hare family, esteemed for food and for its fur; **2,** a preparation of melted cheese poured over toasted bread or crackers: also called *Welsh rabbit:*—*v.i.* to hunt and kill rabbits.

rab-ble (răb′l), *n.* a noisy crowd or mob: **the rabble,** the lowest class of people:—*adj.* noisy; disorderly.
Syn., n. populace. (See throng.)

rab-id (răb′ĭd), *adj.* **1,** furious; raging; **2,** extremely unreasonable; excessively zealous; **3,** affected with hydrophobia; mad.—*adv.* **rab′id-ly.**—*n.* **rab′id-ness.**

ra-bi-es (rā′bĭ-ēz), *n.* an infectious and generally fatal disease of such animals as the dog and wolf; hydrophobia.

ra-ca (rā′kȧ; rȧ-kä′), *adj.* worthless: a former Jewish expression of contempt.

rac-coon (ră-kōōn′), *n.* a grayish brown animal of North America with a bushy tail: often called *coon.* Also, **ra-coon′.**

[1]race (rās), *n.* **1,** a swift current of water, or the channel for such a current; as, a mill *race;* **2,** the air current from the screw propeller of an airplane; **3,** course of life; career; as, my *race* is run; **4,** a competitive contest of speed, as in running, swimming, or the like; **5,** a channel or slot along which some part of a machine moves, as the grooves holding the balls in a ball bearing; **race horse,** a horse trained for racing:—*v.i.* [*p.t.* and *p.p.* raced (rāst), *p.pr.* rac′-ing], **1,** to run swiftly; **2,** to compete in speed; **3,** to run too fast, as a machine, because of a lightened load:—*v.t.* **1,** to cause to move swiftly; as, he *raced* me along; **2,** to drive, as horses or cars, at great speed, or in a race; **3,** to contend with in a speed contest.

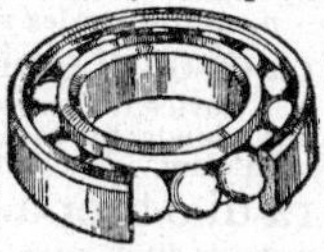
Race (def. 5)

[2]race (rās), *n.* **1,** the descendants of a common ancestor; a family; **2,** a great division of mankind, made up of tribes and nations descended from a common stock, having the same distinguishing characteristics; as, the Negro *race;* **3,** a branch of one such division, forming a tribal or national stock; as, the Latin *race:* **the race,** mankind in general.—*adj.* **ra′cial.**

ra-ceme (rȧ-sēm′; rā-), *n.* a type of bloom in which the flowers grow singly, at almost regular distances, along a stalk, as in the lily of the valley (see *inflorescence,* illus.).—*adj.* **rac′e-mose** (răs′ē-mōs).

rac-er (rās′ẽr), *n.* **1,** one who engages in a speed contest; also, anything that has power to go at great speed; **2,** any of various snakes, esp. the American black snake.

race-way (rās′wā″), *n.* a water channel, as a mill race.

Ra-chel (rā′chĕl), *n.* in the Bible, the wife of Jacob and the mother of Joseph and Benjamin (Genesis 30:25; 35:16–19).

ra-chi-tis (rȧ-kī′tĭs), *n.* a disease of infancy characterized by softening and deformity of the bones: commonly called *rickets.*—*adj.* **ra-chit′ic** (rȧ-kĭt′ĭk).

rac-ism (rās′ĭzm), *n.* racial prejudice; belief that some races are inferior.

[1]rack (răk), *n.* thin, broken, vapory clouds:—*v.i.* to scud before the wind, as clouds. Also, **wrack.**

[2]rack (răk), *n.* **1,** a framework in which articles are held or arranged, as a framework on a wagon for hauling hay; **2,** a wrenching or straining, as by storms; **3,** a bar with teeth that engage the teeth of a gear.

[3]rack (răk), *n.* **1,** an instrument for torturing the body by stretching or straining the limbs; **2,** intense physical or mental anguish:—*v.t.* **1,** to stretch on, or as on, such an instrument of torture; **2,** to subject to great physical or mental anguish; as, remorse *racked* him; **3,** to strain; figuratively, to exert to the utmost; as, to *rack* one's brain.
Syn., v. torture, torment, distort.

[4]rack (răk), *n. Rare,* destruction: used only in *rack and ruin.* Also, **wrack.**

[5]rack (răk), *n.* a gait of a horse in which the two feet on the same side are moved together; a pace; also, a gait like the pace:—*v.i.* to pace.—*n.* **rack′er.**

[1]rack-et (răk′ĕt; răk′ĭt), *n.* **1,** a clattering noise; din; noisy talk or play; **2,** a scene of excitement or gaiety; a carouse; **3,** *Slang,* a trick, scheme, or game; esp., an organized criminal activity of the underworld:—*v.i.* **1,** to make a loud and confused noise; **2,** to carouse.—*adj.* **rack′et-y.**
Syn., n. hubbub, uproar, commotion.

[2]rack-et (răk′ĕt), *n.* **1,** a network bat used in tennis and similar games (see *lacrosse,* illus.); **2,** a broad wooden shoe used in walking over soft ground; also, a snowshoe; **3,** in *pl.,* a game played in a four-walled court. Also, **rac′quet; rac-quette′.**

rack-et-eer (răk″ĕt-ēr′), *n.* **1,** one who makes a din, or carouses; **2,** *Slang,* one who preys upon society in some organized unlawful activity.

***ra-con-teur** (rȧ″kôṅ″tûr′), [Fr.], *n.* [*pl.* raconteurs (-tûrz′; -tûr′)], a clever teller of stories.

rac-y (rās′ĭ), *adj.* [*comp.* rac′i-er, *superl.* rac′i-est], **1,** having a strong flavor that would indicate origin; rich; as, a *racy* wine; **2,** mentally exciting; lively; spirited; as, a *racy* style; **3,** *Colloq.,* suggestive or immodest; as, a *racy* story.—*adv.* **rac′i-ly.**—*n.* **rac′i-ness.**

ra-dar (rā′där), *n.* a device which sends out radio waves of ultra high frequency, and locates a distant object, as a ship, by the radio waves reflected from the ship: (thus used in World War II).

ra-di-al (rā′dĭ-ăl), *adj.* **1,** pertaining to a ray, as of light, or to a radius, as of a circle; shooting out from a center; **2,** pertaining to the radius, or bone on the thumb side of the forearm.—*adv.* **ra′di-al-ly.**

ra-di-an (rā′dĭ-ăn), *n.* the arc of a circle equal in length to the radius; also, the angle at the center which it measures.

ra-di-ance (rā′dĭ-ăns), *n.* brilliancy splendor. Also, **ra′di-an-cy.**

ra-di-ant (rā′dĭ-ănt), *adj.* **1,** sending out rays of light or heat; as, the *radiant* sun; **2,** shining; brilliant; as, *radiant* beauty; **3,** beaming with kindness, joy, etc.;

issuing from a source; as, *radiant* energy.—*adv.* **ra′di-ant-ly.** *Syn.* (see *bright*).

ra-di-ate (rā′dĭ-āt), *v.t.* [*p.t.* and *p.p.* -at″-ed, *p.pr.* -at″ing], to send out in rays; as, the sun *radiates* light and heat:—*v.i.* to issue forth in rays; as, heat and light *radiate* from the sun:—*adj.* having rays.

ra-di-a-tion (rā″dĭ-ā′shŭn), *n.* **1**, the coming forth and spreading, as of rays, in all directions from a common center; as, the *radiation* of light from the sun; **2**, that which is diffused in all directions; **3**, specif., the emission of rays (or atomic particles) by radioactive substances.

ra-di-a-tor (rā′dĭ-ā″tẽr), *n.* **1**, a body from which rays are sent out; **2**, in heating systems, a set of pipes, heated by some medium, as steam, for radiating heat.

rad-i-cal (răd′ĭ-kăl), *n.* **1**, a root; a fundamental part or principle; **2**, a word or root from which other words are formed; **3**, one who cuts at the root of things; an extremist; a member of a group that advocates revolutionary reform; **4**, (also, *radicle*), in chemistry, a group of atoms that acts as a single atom in a compound; **5**, in mathematics, a quantity considered as the root of another quantity; also, a symbol, called *radical sign*, used to indicate that a root is to be extracted:—*adj.* **1**, pertaining to a root or origin; **2**, fundamental; as, *radical* changes; **3**, desiring extreme measures; **4**, in mathematics, pertaining to the root of a quantity: **radical sign,** a symbol [√], orig. the initial *r* of Latin *radix*, root, placed before a quantity to indicate that its root is to be extracted.—*adv.* **rad′i-cal-ly.**

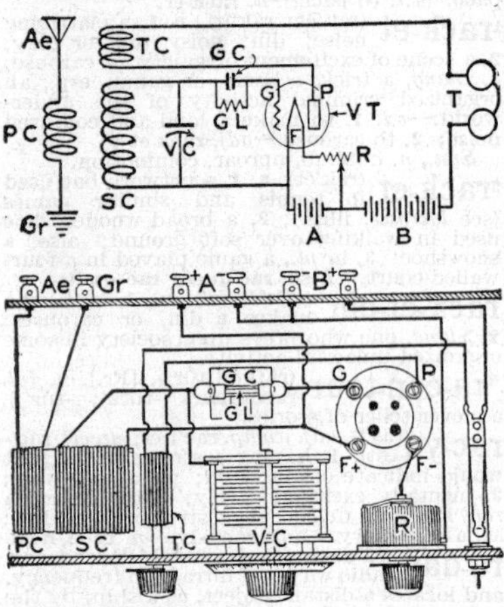

A Simple Vacuum-tube Radio Recieving Set

(Above, diagram; below, diagrammatic plan.)

Alternating current is received from aërial *Ae*, and passes through primary coil *PC* to ground *Gr*, constituting primary circuit. Current of secondary circuit is thereby induced in secondary coil *SC* (tuned to required wave length by variable condenser *VC*) and passes to filament *F* and grid *B* in vacuum tube *VT*, where it is rectified. *F* is heated by a current, regulated by rheostat *R*, from battery *A*, and emits negative electrons through grid *G* to plate *P*, made positive by battery *B*. From *P* current passes through tickler coil *TC*, inducing additional current in *SC*, to telephones *T*, where the electrical vibrations are transformed to audible vibrations. Grid condenser *GC* and grid leak *GL* aid rectifying action of vacuum tube.

rad-i-cle (răd′ĭ-kl), *n.* **1**, in botany, the lower part of an embryo that develops into the primary root (see *germination*, illus.); **2**, (preferably, *radical*), in chemistry, a group of atoms acting as a single atom.

ra-di-o (rā′dĭ-ō), *n.* [*pl.* radios (-ōz)], **1**, anything transmitted or received by means of electromagnetic waves without the agency of intervening wires; **2**, the use of wireless telegraphy or telephony; **3**, equipment for transmitting messages in this way; esp., a radio receiving set (see illus.):—*adj.* **1**, pertaining to radio; as, *radio* supplies; **2**, radioactive; as, *radio* star.

ra-di-o-ac-tive (rā′dĭ-ō-ăk′tĭv), *adj.* having the property of emitting rays or atomic particles as do radium, uranium, etc.—*n.* **ra″di-o-ac-ti′vi-ty.**

ra-di-o-cast (rā′dĭ-ō-kȧst″), *v.t.* to transmit by radio; broadcast.

ra-di-o–fre-quent (rā″dĭ-ō=frē′kwĕnt), *adj.* having a rate of vibration above 10,000 per second: used, esp. in radio, of vibrations too rapid to be perceived by the human ear.—*n.* **ra″di-o–fre′quen-cy.**

ra-di-o-graph (rā′dĭ-ō-grȧf), *n.* a picture obtained by invisible rays, as X rays:—*v.t.* to produce a picture of, by means of X rays, radium rays, etc.—*n.* **ra″di-og′ra-phy.**—*n.* **ra″di-og′ra-pher.**

ra-di-om-e-ter (rā″dĭ-ŏm′ē-tẽr), *n.* an instrument for detecting and measuring radiant energy.

ra-di-on-ics (rā″dĭ-ŏn′ĭks), *n.* that branch of electronics concerned with radio phenomena.

ra-di-o-phone (rā′dĭ-ō-fōn″), *n.* a device for transmitting or receiving sounds by radio.

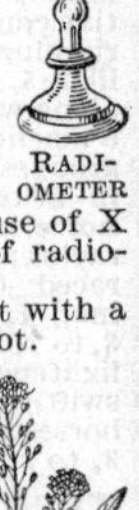

Radiometer

ra-di-o-tel-e-gram (rā″dĭ-ō-tĕl′ē-grăm), *n.* a message sent through space by radio.

ra-di-o-tel-e-graph (rā″dĭ-ō-tĕl′ē-grȧf), *n.* an apparatus for sending messages by radio.—*adj.* **ra″di-o-tel″e-graph′ic.**—*n.* **ra″di-o-te-leg′ra-phy.**

ra-di-o-tel-e-phone (rā″dĭ-ō-tĕl′ē-fōn), *n.* a device for transmitting or receiving sounds by radio.—*n.* **ra″di-o-te-leph′o-ny.**

ra-di-o-ther-a-py (rā″dĭ-ō-thĕr′-ȧ-pĭ), *n.* the use of X rays, radium rays, or other forms of radioactivity, for the treatment of disease.

rad-ish (răd′ĭsh), *n.* a garden plant with a pungent root; also, the root.

ra-di-um (rā′dĭ-ŭm), *n.* a very rare metallic chemical element, which undergoes spontaneous decomposition, giving off several kinds of radiation.

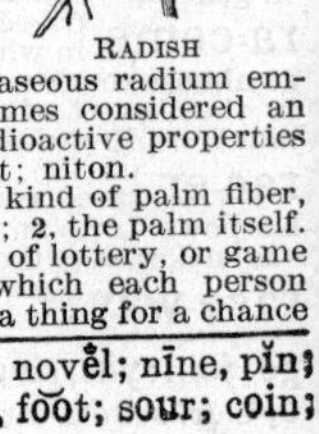

Radish

ra-di-us (rā′dĭ-ŭs), *n.* [*pl.* radii (-ī); radiuses (-ĕz)], **1**, a straight line from the center of a circle or sphere to the circumference or surface; **2**, the shorter bone of the forearm, on the thumb side.

ra-don (rā′dŏn), *n.* a gaseous radium emanation, sometimes considered an element, which confers radioactive properties on substances exposed to it; niton.

raf-fi-a (răf′ĭ-ȧ), *n.* **1**, a kind of palm fiber, used in weaving; **2**, the palm itself.

raf-fle (răf′l), *n.* a kind of lottery, or game of chance, in which each person pays a part of the value of a thing for a chance f winning it:—*v.t.* [*p.t.* and *p.p.* -fled (-ld), ·.*pr.* -fling], to dispose of by selling chances n:—*v.i.* to take part in such a sale.

raft (råft), *n.* a floating framework of logs, boards, etc.:—*v.t.* to carry on, or as on, uch a float.—*n.* **rafts′man.**

raft-er (råf′tẽr), *n.* a sloping beam that supports the roof of a house (see *rincipal,* illus.):—*v.t.* to furnish with rafters.

rag (răg), *n.* **1,** a worn or torn piece of cloth; shred; **2,** a piece of popular music in yncopated time; **3,** in *pl.*, tattered or worn-ut garments:—*v.i.* [*p.t.* and *p.p.* ragged răgd), *p.pr.* rag′ging], **1,** to play music in yncopated time; **2,** *Slang:* **a,** to tease; lay jokes upon; **b,** to scold.

rag-a-muf-fin (răg′ȧ-mŭf″ĭn), *n.* a ragged, disreputable fellow.

rage (rāj), *n.* **1,** uncontrolled anger; **2,** extreme violence; fury; **3,** enthusiasm; reat eagerness; **4,** *Colloq.*, anything eagerly ought because of fashion; as, high heels are he *rage:*—*v.i.* [*p.t.* and *p.p.* raged (rājd), *p.pr.* ag′ing], **1,** to be furious with anger; storm; , to act or speak violently; **3,** to have furious orce or effect; as, a fever *rages.*

rag-ged (răg′ĕd), *adj.* **1,** having holes resulting from wear; torn; as, a *agged* coat; **2,** clothed in tattered garments; s, a *ragged* fellow; **3,** rough; jagged, as a tone.—*adv.* **rag′ged-ly.**—*n.* **rag′ged-ness.**

rag-ged rob-in a common garden flower, having small blossoms with jagged edges.

rag-lan (răg′lăn), *n.* an overcoat with no shoulder seams, the sleeves exending to the collar.

rag-man (răg′măn), *n.* [*pl.* ragmen (-mĕn)], a dealer in rags, bones, and junk.

Rag-na-rok (răg′nȧ-rŏk′), *n.* in Norse mythology, literally, the 'twilight of the gods"; the destruction of the vorld in the conflict of the gods with the owers of the lower world led by Loki: also alled, in German mythology, *Götterdämmerung.* Also, **Rag′na-rök′** (-nä-rûk′).

ra-gout (rȧ-gōō′), *n.* a stew of meat and vegetables highly seasoned.

rag-time (răg′tīm″), *n.* *Colloq.*, **1,** syncopated time in music: a form eculiar to many negro melodies; **2,** popular nusic written in syncopated rhythm.

rag-weed (răg′wēd″), *n.* any of several coarse common herbs of the omposite family, esp. a certain species, the ollen of which is a cause of hay fever.

raid (rād), *n.* **1,** a hostile invasion; a sudden attack; a foray; **2,** *Colloq.*, an attack r forced entrance, as by the police, to make rrests, seize property, or discover stolen oods; **3,** in the World War, an attack by ircraft; also, a night excursion by soldiers to n enemy trench:—*v.t.* **1,** to make a sudden ttack upon; **2,** to enter and seize under uthority of the law.—*n.* **raid′er.**

rail (rāl), *n.* **1,** a bar of wood or metal placed in a horizontal position between wo posts or supports, as n a fence; **2,** a wooden r iron fence, esp. that laced as a guard around he deck of a ship; **3,** one f the two metal bars forming a track for the wheels f a vehicle; **4,** a railroad; s, to travel by *rail:*—*v.t.* o inclose with bars: often vith *in* or *off.*—*n.* **¹rail′er.**

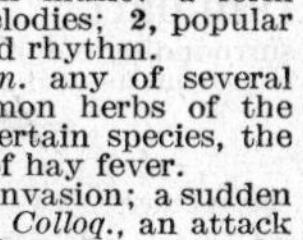

RAILS (def. 3) 1, T-head; 2, double-head.

rail (rāl), *n.* any of several widely distributed birds resembling small cranes.

rail (rāl), *v.i.* to use bitter, scornful, or reproachful language; scoff: with *at* or *gainst.*—*n.* **²rail′er.**—*n.* and *adj.* **¹rail′ing.**

²rail-ing (rāl′ĭng), *n.* **1,** material for rails; **2,** a fence or barrier made of bars or rails upheld by posts.

rail-ler-y (rāl′ẽr-ĭ; răl′-), *n.* [*pl.* railleries (-ĭz)], good-humored ridicule.

rail-road (rāl′rōd″), *n.* **1,** a track formed by two parallel rails, along which cars are propelled by some power, such as steam or electricity; **2,** such a road, with all the land, stations, cars, etc., pertaining to it:—*v.t.* *Colloq.*, to put through rapidly; as, to *railroad* an act through a legislature.

rail-way (rāl′wā″), *n.* **1,** in Great Britain, a railroad; **2,** in the U. S., a railroad for light traffic; as, an electric *railway;* **3,** any track with rails for wheels.

rai-ment (rā′mĕnt), *n.* clothing; garments; wearing apparel.

rain (rān), *n.* **1,** water falling in drops condensed from moisture in the air; **2,** the fall of such drops; a fall or shower of anything in, or as if in, drops; as, a *rain* of bullets:—*v.i.* **1,** to fall in drops of rain; **2,** to fall like rain:—*v.t.* to pour down like rain; as, to *rain* bullets, or favors, on someone.—*adj.* **rain′less.**

rain-bow (rān′bō″), *n.* the bright-colored arc or bow formed in the heavens opposite the sun by the reflection and refraction of the sun's rays from drops of falling rain, spray, or mist:—*adj.* **brilliant,** but passing quickly.

rain-coat (rān′kōt″), *n.* a coat or cloak made of waterproof material.

rain-fall (rān′fôl″), *n.* **1,** a shower of rain; **2,** the amount of rain that falls during a definite period on any given area.

rain gauge an instrument to measure the amount of rainfall at a place during a given time. Also, **rain gage.**

rain-y (rān′ĭ), *adj.* [*comp.* rain′i-er, *superl.* rain′i-est], abounding with rain; showery; wet.—*n.* **rain′i-ness.**

raise (rāz), *v.t.* [*p.t.* and *p.p.* raised (rāzd), *p.pr.* rais′ing], **1,** to set upright; restore to its usual position; lift from the ground; **2,** to restore to life, as the dead; rouse from sleep; rouse from a lair or covert, as game; **3,** to lift by direct effort, as a flag, sail, sunken vessel, minerals from the ground, etc.; **4,** to erect; construct, as a building; **5,** to cause to come into existence; grow; breed, as crops or cattle; **6,** to procure; collect; muster, as money, armies, etc.; **7,** to cause to arise or appear, as a prophet or a ghost; **8,** to originate; give rise to; set going, as strife, rumors, expression of feelings, etc.; **9,** to bring up for consideration, as a question, a claim, an objection, etc.; **10,** to increase in degree, amount, intensity, etc., as prices, the voice, the spirits, etc.; **11,** to increase the height or bulk of; as, to *raise* bread with yeast; **12,** to put an end to; as, to *raise* a blockade; **13,** to utter, as a cry; produce, as sound; **14,** to increase (a number or quantity) by multiplication by itself; **15,** *U. S. Colloq.*, to rear; bring up; as, to *raise* children: **raise a check,** to increase fraudulently the amount for which a check is drawn:—*n.* **1,** an act of raising, or a thing raised; **2,** *Colloq.*, an increase in wages or salary.—*n.* **rais′er.**

rai-sin (rā′zn), *n.* a special variety of grape, containing much sugar and dried in the sun or by artificial means.

***rai-son-né** (râ″zô″nā′), [Fr.], *adj.* arranged in a systematic manner; logical; as, a catalog *raisonné.*

ra-jah (rä′jȧ), *n.* a Hindu prince or chief. Also, **ra′ja.**

Raj-put (räj′pōōt; räj″pōōt′), *n.* a member of the military caste of India. Also, **Raj″poot′.**

¹rake (rāk), *n.* an implement with teeth or tines for gathering together loose matter, or for making soil loose and smooth:—*v.t.* [*p.t.* and *p.p.* raked (rākt), *p.pr.* rak′ing], **1**, to gather, smooth, or loosen with a rake; as, to *rake* up leaves; *rake* a flower bed; **2**, to collect; gather together by diligent effort; as, to *rake* together a few dollars; *rake* up evidence; **3**, to search through carefully; ransack; scour; as, they *raked* the record for proof; **4**, to fire upon, esp. along the length of; as, to *rake* the deck of a ship, or a line of soldiers; **5**, to cut away (the wing tip of an airplane) at an angle, so that the supporting surface has a greater span at the rear than at the front end:—*v.i.* **1**, to work with a rake; **2**, to make a close search; **3**, to gather with great effort; as, they *raked* and scraped to make both ends meet.—*n.* **rak′er.**

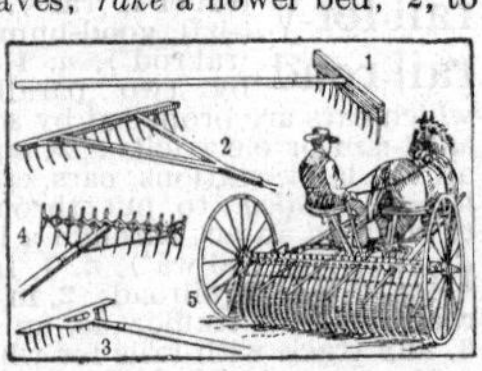

RAKES

1, wooden lawn rake; 2, hay rake; 3, iron rake; 4, adjustable rake; 5, horse-drawn rake.

²rake (rāk), *n.* an immoral or dissipated man; a roué.

³rake (rāk), *v.i.* [*p.t.* and *p.p.* raked (rākt), *p.pr.* rak′ing], to slant or slope, as a ship's mast:—*v.t.* to cause to slant or slope:—*n.* slant or slope, as of a ship's mast or funnel.

¹rak-ish (rāk′ĭsh), *adj.* corrupt; unrestrained.—*adv.* **¹rak′ish-ly.**—*n.* **¹rak′ish-ness.**

²rak-ish (rāk′ĭsh), *adj.* **1**, of a ship, having the mast inclined toward the stern; hence, smart and fast looking; **2**, smart; dashing.—*adv.* **²rak′ish-ly.**—*n.* **²rak′ish-ness.**

¹ral-ly (răl′ĭ), *n.* [*pl.* rallies (-ĭz)], **1**, the act of recovering order or of reassembling; as, the *rally* of the troops; **2**, a quick recovery from depression; as, a *rally* in stocks; **3**, *U. S. Colloq.*, a mass meeting; **4**, in tennis, the repeated return of the ball in play:—*v.t.* [*p.t.* and *p.p.* -lied (-ĭd), *p.pr.* -ly-ing], **1**, to gather and restore to order, as troops in flight; **2**, to call together for any purpose; as, to *rally* voters; **3**, to revive; as, to *rally* a person's spirits:—*v.i.* **1**, to return to order; as, the troops *rallied;* **2**, to come together for action; be aroused to vigorous action; as, *rally* round the flag; **3**, to recover strength; as, to *rally* from fever; **4**, in tennis, to send the ball rapidly back and forth over the net.

²ral-ly (răl′ĭ), *v.t.* [*p.t.* and *p.p.* -lied (-ĭd), *p.pr.* -ly-ing], to tease; banter:—*v.i.* to joke.

ram (răm), *n.* **1**, a male sheep; **2**, a military engine for battering or knocking down by heavy blows; a battering-ram; **3**, an ironclad war vessel with a steel beak for cutting into an enemy ship; also, the beak itself; **4**, a pumping device: more fully called *hydraulic ram;* **5**, the plunger, or piston, of a force pump; **6**, the striking weight, as of a steam hammer; **7**, a heavy piece which moves back and forth between guides, as the piece which holds the cutting tool in a shaper (see *shaper*, illus.): **Ram**, **1**, the constellation Aries; **2**, the first sign of the zodiac (see *zodiac*, illus.):—*v.t.* [*p.t.* and *p.p.* rammed (rămd), *p.pr.* ram′ming], **1**, to strike or butt against in order to damage or crush; **2**, to press or cram (a person or thing) into something.

ram-ble (răm′bl), *n.* an aimless roving or wandering from place to place; a leisurely stroll; as, a *ramble* in the woods:—*v.i.* [*p.t.* and *p.p.* -bled (-bld), *p.pr.* -bling], **1**, to wander or rove aimlessly about, as for pleasure; **2**, to talk or write at length without aim; **3**, to grow or spread at random.—*n.* **ram′bler.**—*p. adj.* and *n.* **ram′bling.**

ram-e-kin (răm′ē-kĭn), *n.* a small, dee dish, as of pottery, in whic food is baked and served. Also, **ram′e-qui**

ram-ie (răm′ē), *n.* **1**, a shrublike plant the East Indies, China, and Japa yielding a valued, soft, woody fiber; **2**, th fiber: now much used in making fine fabric

ram-i-fi-ca-tion (răm″ĭ-fĭ-kā′shŭn), *n* **1**, a division or separa tion into branches; **2**, a division of anythin complex; **3**, the act or manner of producin branches; also, the arrangement of branche **4**, a small branch or offshoot; as, a *ramific tion* of a tree, nerve, etc.

ram-i-fy (răm′ĭ-fī), *v.t.* [*p.t.* and *p.* -fied (-fīd), *p.pr.* -fy″ing], divide into branches, or divisions:—*v.i.* **1**, grow by dividing into branches; **2**, to becom divided or subdivided.

ram-mer (răm′ẽr), *n.* one who or tha which batters or drives wit violence, as a battering-ram.

ra-mose (rā′mōs; rȧ-mōs′), *adj.* pertair ing to, like, or having, branche Also, **ra′mous.**

ramp (rămp), *v.i.* **1**, to rear up; assume threatening position; as, a lio *ramps;* **2**, to rage; rush about wildly:—*n.* slope or incline, as of a road or corridor.

¹ramp-age (răm′pāj; răm″pāj′), *n.* a stat of excitement or rage; angr or violent behavior; as, he is always on th *rampage* about something.

²ram-page (răm-pāj′; răm′pȧj), *v.i.* [*p.* and *p.p.* -paged′ (-pājd′ *p.pr.* -pag′ing], **1**, to dash about wildly; **2**, t storm; rage; as, he *rampaged* for an hour.

ram-pa-geous (răm-pā′jŭs), *adj.* ex tremely noisy or unrul

ramp-ant (răm′pȧnt), *adj.* **1**, climbing c growing unchecked; as, *ramp ant* weeds; **2**, extravagant or aggressive i manner, opinion, etc.; **3**, unchecked or unre strained; as, *rampant* ideas; **4**, in heraldry reared on the hind legs, as a lion, with on foreleg raised above the other (see *lion* illus.).—*adv.* **ramp′ant-ly.**—*n.* **ramp′an-cy.**

ram-part (răm′pärt), *n.* **1**, an embank ment surmounted by a parape surrounding a fortified place; **2**, any protec tion from assault or danger; a defense.

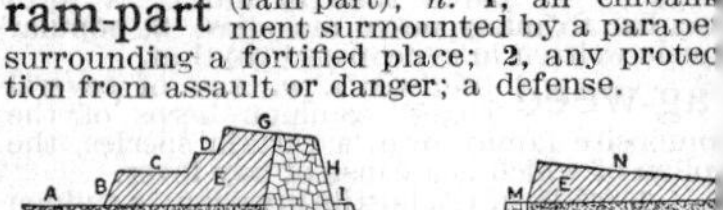

RAMPART

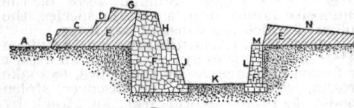

A, boulevard, or parade, on original level; B, i terior slope; C, terreplein; D, banquette; E,E, f from ditch; F, F, masonry; G, parapet; H, face; berm; J, scarp; K, bottom of ditch, or moat; counterscarp; M, covered way; N, glacis, subje to enfilading fire from G.

ram-rod (răm′rŏd″), *n.* a rod used fo ramming down the charge of gun which loads through the muzzle.

ram-shack-le (răm′shăk-l), *adj.* loos out of repair; ricket as, a *ramshackle* cottage.

ran (răn), past tense of the irregular ver *run.*

ranch (rănch), *n.* **1**, in the western U. and Canada, a farm for the rearir of cattle, horses, and sheep in large herds; **2**, large farm for a special crop; as, a fruit *ranc*—*n.* **ranch′er.**—*n.* **ranch′man.**

ran-che-ro (rȧn-chā′rō), *n.* [*pl.* rancher (-rōz)], in the western U.

and Mexico, a worker on, or an owner of, a stock farm; a rancher.

ran-cho (răn′chō), *n.* [*pl.* ranchos(-chōz)], **1**, in Spanish America, a hut or group of huts for workers on a stock farm; **2**, in the southwestern U. S., a ranch.

ran-cid (răn′sĭd), *adj.* not fresh; having a rank, tainted smell or taste of spoiled fat; chemically sour.—*n.* **ran′cid-ness.**

ran-cid-i-ty (răn-sĭd′ĭ-tĭ), *n.* a rank, sour, or tainted condition.

ran-cor (răng′kẽr), *n.* deep spite or malice; a bitter, cherished grudge. Also, **ran′cour.**—*adj.* **ran′cor-ous.**

Syn. hostility, resentment. (See malice.)

ran-dom (răn′dŭm), *n.* want of definite aim or method; chance: **at random,** without direction or method; aimlessly:—*adj.* done without definite aim or purpose; as, a *random* shot.

Syn., adj. haphazard, casual.

rang (răng), past tense of the irregular verb ²*ring.*

range (rānj), *v.t.* [*p.t.* and *p.p.* ranged (rānjd), *p.pr.* rang′ing], **1**, to set or arrange in a row or in order; **2**, to put into a given group; as, to *range* oneself with the minority; **3**, to place in proper order; classify; **4**, to wander over; as, cattle *range* the plains:—*v.i.* **1**, to wander; roam; **2**, to go over or through a place in order to explore it; **3**, to correspond in line or direction; as, the path *ranges* with the brook; **4**, to be capable of sending or of being sent; go; as, the bullet *ranged* wide of the mark; **5**, to vary within certain limits; as, they *range* in height from four to six feet; **6**, to be found or to occur over a certain area: said of plants and animals:—*n.* **1**, a line or row; series; chain, as of buildings or mountains; **2**, line of direction; as, in *range* with my window; **3**, entire space or time taken in or covered; scope; extent; register; as, *range* of voice; the whole *range* of history; **4**, a great tract of land over which cattle graze; **5**, the entire region in which an animal or plant lives; **6**, class or order; as, a *range* of animals; **7**, the limits within which a thing may vary in degree or amount; as, a wide *range* of prices; **8**, the distance to which a missile can be sent; also, the distance of the object aimed at; **9**, a place for shooting at a mark; **10**, a kind of large cooking stove: **range light, 1**, either of two white lights placed on the shore but visible at sea, for guiding a vessel on a given course; **2**, in *pl.*, two white lights, not close together, carried by a vessel at sea to show in what direction she is pointed (see *lantern,* illus.).

range find-er an instrument for determining the distance of an object, as of a target.

rang-er (rān′jẽr), *n.* **1**, in England, the keeper of a royal park or forest; **2**, a rover; **3**, one of a mounted armed band of men; **4**, in America, a forest guard; **5**, a kind of hunting dog; **6**, in *pl.*, mounted troops.

rang-y (rān′jĭ), *adj.* [*comp.* rang′i-er, *superl.* rang′i-est], **1**, having a tendency to roam; able to wander far and wide; **2**, hence, long in limb, lean, and muscular: used mostly of cattle and horses.

¹**rank** (răngk), *n.* **1**, a row or line of objects; also, an orderly formation; **2**, high station or position; as, a man of *rank;* **3**, grade of social position, hereditary or conferred; as, the *ranks* of the British nobility are, in order, duke, marquis, earl, viscount, baron; **4**, grade of official standing or position; as, in the U. S. army, certain officers in the order of their *rank* are general, colonel, major, captain, lieutenant; and in the navy, admiral, captain, commander, lieutenant, ensign; **5**, degree of worth or eminence; as, a poet of the first *rank;* **6**, a line of soldiers, drawn up side by side: opp. of ¹*file;* **7**, in *pl.:* **a**, the army as a whole; **b**, the body of privates as distinguished from the officers: **rank and file,** the body of common soldiers; hence, the common people:—*v.t.* **1**, to place in rows; draw up in line; **2**, to include in a certain class, order, or division; **3**, to be of a higher grade than; take precedence of; as, a captain *ranks* a lieutenant:—*v.i.* **1**, to hold a certain grade or position; as, he *ranks* as captain; his work *ranks* with the best; **2**, to have the highest rank in a given group; as, the *ranking* member.

Syn., n. order, degree. *Rank* denotes the grade of position, esp. social or military. *Order* suggests grading according to some formal or methodical arrangement; as, they were arranged in *order* of height. *Degree* expresses grade of attainment in relation to another person or thing.

²**rank** (răngk), *adj.* **1**, very plentiful and coarse in growth; as, *rank* grass; **2**, very fertile; producing too freely; **3**, coarse; strong in taste or smell; as, *rank* butter; **4**, gross; extreme; as, *rank* deceit.—*adv.* **rank′ly.**—*n.* **rank′ness.**

ran-kle (răng′kl), *v.i.* [*p.t.* and *p.p.* -kled (-kld), *p.pr.* -kling], **1**, to fester or cause to fester; **2**, to cause mental pain or irritation; as, the insult *rankled.*

ran-sack (răn′săk), *v.t.* **1**, to search thoroughly; **2**, to pillage.

ran-som (răn′sŭm), *n.* **1**, the act of securing the return of a captive or seized property by payment of a price demanded as condition of such return; **2**, the sum so paid or demanded:—*v.t.* **1**, to free from prison, slavery, or punishment, by a payment; **2**, to redeem; set free.—*n.* **ran′som-er.**—*adj.* **ran′som-less.**

rant (rănt), *n.* noisy, empty speech; bombast:—*v.i.* to bluster or be noisily wordy; rave in extravagant or violent language.—*n.* **rant′er.**—*adv.* **rant′ing-ly.**

¹**rap** (răp), *n.* **1**, orig., an Irish coin of trifling value; **2**, hence, the least bit.

²**rap** (răp), *v.i.* [*p.t.* and *p.p.* rapped (răpt), *p.pr.* rap′ping], to strike a quick, sharp blow; knock:—*v.t.* **1**, to strike sharply; **2**, to utter sharply; as, she *rapped* out her reply.

ra-pa-cious (rȧ-pā′shŭs), *adj.* **1**, given to plunder; seizing by violence; **2**, greedy; grasping; as, a *rapacious* appetite.—*adv.* **ra-pa′cious-ly.**—*n.* **ra-pa′cious-ness.**

ra-pac-i-ty (rȧ-păs′ĭ-tĭ), *n.* the quality of being extremely greedy or grasping; rapaciousness.

¹**rape** (rāp), *v.t.* [*p.t.* and *p.p.* raped (rāpt), *p.pr.* rap′ing], to assault or ravish (a woman):—*n.* **1**, violation by force; **2**, a seizing and carrying away by force; robbery.

²**rape** (rāp), *n.* a plant of the mustard family, used as forage, from the seeds of which an oil is obtained.

rap-id (răp′ĭd), *adj.* **1**, very quick or swift; **2**, moving with speed; **3**, done quickly; as, a *rapid* decline in health:—*n.*, usually in *pl.*, a place in a river where the water descends swiftly because of a sudden slope in the river bed.—*adv.* **rap′id-ly.**

Syn., adj. fast, fleet. (See hasty.)

ra-pid-i-ty (rȧ-pĭd′ĭ-tĭ), *n.* swiftness; quickness; speed.

ra-pi-er (rā′pĭ-ẽr), *n.* a long, thin sword, used esp. for thrusting.

RAPIER

rap-ine (răp′ĭn), *n.* the act of plundering or of carrying off property by force.

Syn. plunder, pillage, robbery.

rap-port (ră-pōrt′; *Fr.* rȧ″pôr′), *n.* a sympathetic relation; harmony.

***rap-proche-ment** (rȧ″prŏsh″mäṅ′), [Fr.], *n.* **1,** the act or state of agreeing, or of coming to a good understanding; **2,** a state of harmony.

rap-scal-lion (răp-skăl′yŭn), *n.* a rascal; scamp; vagabond.

rapt (răpt), *p.adj.* **1,** carried away with delight or pleasure; enraptured; **2,** deep in thought; as, *rapt* attention; **3,** seized and carried away.

Syn. entranced, charmed, absorbed.

rap-ture (răp′tûr), *n.* **1,** the condition or state of being carried away with joy or delight; extreme pleasure; ecstasy; enthusiasm; **2,** an expression of intense joy or pleasure.

Syn. transport, delight, bliss.

rap-tur-ous (răp′tūr-ŭs), *adj.* showing, or characterized by, joy or delight; ecstatic:—*adv.* **rap′tur-ous-ly.**

[1]**rare** (râr), *adj.* **1,** thin; not dense; as, the *rare* atmosphere on a mountain; **2,** scarce; uncommon; unusual; as, a *rare* plant; **3,** excellent; choice; precious; as, *rare* old lace.—*n.* **rare′ness.**

Syn. extraordinary, incomparable.

[2]**rare** (râr), *adj.* not cooked through; underdone; as, *rare* beefsteak.

rare-bit (râr′bĭt), *n.* a Welsh rabbit: an erroneous form.

rar-e-fac-tion (răr″ē-făk′shŭn; râr″-), *n.* **1,** the act or process of making thin or less dense; **2,** the state of being less dense: opp. of *condensation.*

rar-e-fy (răr′ē-fī; râr′-), *v.t.* [*p.t.* and *p.p.* -fied (-fīd), *p.pr.* -fy″ing], to make thin or less dense:—*v.i.* to become thin or less dense: opp. of *condense.*

rare-ly (râr′lĭ), *adv.* **1,** not often; **2,** splendidly; with great skill; **3,** extremely; remarkably.

rar-i-ty (răr′ĭ-tĭ; râr′-), *n.* [*pl.* rarities (-tĭz)], **1,** thinness; as, the *rarity* of the air at a high altitude; **2,** the state or quality of being uncommon; **3,** a scarce article or occurrence.

ras-cal (răs′kăl), *n.* **1,** a mean fellow; a scoundrel; **2,** in a playful sense, mischievous; roguish.—*adj.* and *adv.* **ras′cal-ly.**

Syn. rogue, vagabond, scamp.

ras-cal-i-ty (răs-kăl′ĭ-tĭ), *n.* [*pl.* rascalities (-tĭz)], **1,** the character or quality of that which is knavish; villainy or dishonesty; **2,** a knavish act.

[1]**rash** (răsh), *n.* an eruption of the skin, showing red patches of large or small extent.

[2]**rash** (răsh), *adj.* **1,** hasty in thought or act; reckless; **2,** done through, or characterized by, lack of caution.—*adv.* **rash′ly.**—*n.* **rash′ness.**

rash-er (răsh′ẽr), *n.* a thin slice of ham or bacon.

rasp (rȧsp), *v.t.* **1,** to rub with, or as with, a file or other rough instrument; **2,** to irritate; as, her voice *rasps* one's nerves:—*v.i.* **1,** to scrape or grate roughly; **2,** to make a harsh, grating noise:—*n.* **1,** a rough file with points instead of lines; **2,** a harsh, grating noise.

rasp-ber-ry (răz′bĕr-ĭ; rȧz′-), *n.* [*pl.* raspberries (-ĭz)], a garden bramble and its edible fruit.

rat (răt), *n.* **1,** any of several rodents somewhat like the mouse, but larger; **2,** in England, one who deserts his party; **3,** *Slang,* a workman who works during a strike, or for less than the usual wages; **4,** a small pad over which the hair is rolled; **5,** in *pl.*, an exclamation implying disbelief or derision:—*v.i.* [*p.t.* and *p.p.* rat′ted, *p.pr.* rat′ting], **1,** to desert one's party for one's own benefit; **2,** to work for less than union wages or to work during a strike; **3,** to catch rats.—*n.* **rat′ter.**

rat-a-ble (rāt′ȧ-bl), *adj.* **1,** capable of being valued; **2,** liable to be taxed; **3,** estimated proportionally. Also, **rate′a-ble.**—*adv.* **rat′a-bly.**

ra-tan (ră-tăn′), *n.* any of several Old World climbing palms, or a product of their long, pliable stems. See **rat-tan′**, *Pfd. S.*

ratch-et (răch′ĕt; răch′ĭt), *n.* **1,** a tooth or tongue, also called a *pawl* or a *click,* which drops into the notches of a toothed wheel and prevents it from turning backward; **2,** the toothed wheel; **3,** the toothed wheel and the pawl, working together: **ratchet wheel,** a toothed wheel which is prevented from moving backward by a pawl, or tooth, which fits into its notches. Also, **ratch.**

[1]**rate** (rāt), *n.* **1,** the amount or number of one thing measured by units of another; as, the death *rate;* a *rate* of ten miles an hour; **2,** a fixed relation of amount, number, or degree between two things; as, the *rate* of income tax; also, a fixed charge for a certain quantity of material, work, etc.; as, wage *rates;* theater *rates;* **3,** relative standard in respect to manner or style; as, to live at a high *rate;* relative quality or condition; rank; class: used esp. of war vessels according to size, armament, etc.; as, first *rate;* **4,** relative speed of working or acting; as, to work at the ordinary *rate;* travel at a fast *rate;* **5,** usually in *pl.*, in England, a public tax or assessment:—*v.t.* [*p.t.* and *p.p.* rat′ed, *p.pr.* rat′ing], **1,** to estimate; appraise; **2,** to settle or fix the value, rank, or degree of; **3,** to consider; regard; as, he is not *rated* among the best authors:—*v.i.* to be estimated; placed in a certain class or rank.

[2]**rate** (rāt), *v.t.* [*p.t.* and *p.p.* rat′ed, *p.pr.* rat′ing], to scold sharply:—*v.i.* to scold a person sharply.

Syn. reprove, upbraid, chide.

rath-er (rȧ*th*′ẽr; rä′*th*ẽr), *adv.* **1,** more willingly; as, I would *rather* read than write; **2,** on the contrary; instead; as, go *rather* to them that sell; **3,** more properly; as, they acted wisely, or *rather* their brother did for them; **4,** somewhat; to a certain extent; as, I *rather* like it that way.

rat-i-fi-ca-tion (răt″ĭ-fĭ-kā′shŭn), *n.* the act of confirming or approving; confirmation; sanction.

rat-i-fy (răt′ĭ-fī), *v.t.* [*p.t.* and *p.p.* -fied (-fīd), *p.pr.* -fy″ing], **1,** to approve of formally; give indorsement to; as, to *ratify* a contract; **2,** to settle or confirm; establish, as a boundary.—*n.* **rat′i-fi″er.**

Syn. accept, indorse, sanction.

[1]**rat-ing** (rāt′ĭng), *n.* **1,** a placing in a class according to relative value or standing; rank; class; **2,** the grade of a man in the navy.

[2]**rat-ing** (rāt′ĭng), *n.* a severe scolding; a sharp reproof.

ra-ti-o (rā′shĭ-ō; rā′shō), *n.* [*pl.* ratios (-ōz)], **1,** relation of number, degree, or quantity; proportion; **2,** the quotient of one quantity divided by another of like kind.

ra-ti-oc-i-na-tion (răsh″ĭ-ŏs″ĭ-nā′shŭn), *n.* reasoning; connected and exact thinking.

ra-tion (rā′shŭn; răsh′ŭn), *n.* **1,** a definite quantity of food or supplies allowed daily to a man or animal in the army or navy; **2,** any fixed or stated share:—*v.t.* to furnish with a fixed allowance of food, supplies, etc., as soldiers or civilians in time of scarcity.

ra-tion-al (răsh′ŭn-ăl), *adj.* **1,** pertaining to reason, **2,** having the power to reason, or think connectedly; as, a *rational* being; **3,** exercising, agreeable to, or in accord with, reason; intelligent; not foolish; as, *rational* conduct; **4,** in mathematics, designating a number or quantity that can be expressed without radical signs: opp. of *surd.*—*adv.* **ra'tion-al-ly.**

Syn. reasonable, sensible, sound.

ra-tion-a-le (răsh"ŭn-ā'lē), *n.* **1,** an explanation of the principles of a science, opinion, or the like; **2,** the fundamental basis or elements of anything.

ra-tion-al-ism (răsh'ŭn-ăl-ĭzm), *n.* a doctrine which makes reason the sole guide in matters of belief or conduct. —*n.* **ra'tion-al-ist.**—*adj.* **ra"tion-al-is'tic.**

ra-tion-al-i-ty (răsh"ŭn-ăl'ĭ-tĭ), *n.* [*pl.* rationalities (-tĭz)], the possession or exercise of the power of reasoning.

ra-tion-al-ize (răsh'ŭn-ăl-īz), *v.t.* [*p.t.* and *p.p.* -ized (-īzd), *p.pr.* -iz"ing], **1,** to explain according to reason; as, to *rationalize* a miracle; **2,** to make, or show to be, reasonable; **3,** to cause to adopt reason as a guide; **4,** in mathematics, to remove radical signs from:—*v.i.* **1,** to rely solely on reason for guidance; **2,** to think, as a philosopher.

rat-line (răt'lĭn), *n.* **1,** one of the small, transverse ropes forming a ladder in a ship's rigging; **2,** light, tarred rope used for ratlines. Also, **rat'lin.**

Ratlines

rats-bane (răts'bān"), *n.* rat poison; esp., white arsenic.

rat-tan (ră-tăn'), *n.* **1,** any of several climbing palms with long, smooth, reedlike stems; **2,** one of the stems of such a palm: used for wickerwork, cordage, etc.; **3,** a walking stick or switch made of such a reedlike stem. Also, **ra-tan'.**

rat-ter (răt'ẽr), *n.* **1,** one who or that which hunts or catches rats; **2,** one who deserts his party.

rat-tle (răt'l), *n.* **1,** a series of short, sharp, clattering sounds following each other quickly; **2,** noisy, rapid, empty talk; **3,** anything for making a clattering sound, as a child's toy:—*v.i.* [*p.t.* and *p.p.* -tled (-ld), *p.pr.* -tling], **1,** to produce short, sharp noises in quick succession; clatter; as, hail *rattles* on a roof; **2,** to talk in a noisy, rapid manner; as, she *rattled* on for an hour; **3,** to move with a clatter; as, the wagon *rattled* along the road: —*v.t.* **1,** to cause to make a succession of rapid, sharp noises; as, the wind *rattles* the shutters; **2,** to utter in a rapid, noisy way; as, he *rattled* off his lesson; **3,** *Colloq.*, to confuse or daze; as, he was completely *rattled.*

rat-tler (răt'lẽr), *n.* **1,** a noisy, rapid talker; **2,** anything that makes a clattering noise; **3,** a rattlesnake.

rat-tle-snake (răt'l-snāk"), *n.* a poisonous snake with hard, bony rings or scales on the tail which make a rattling sound when the tail is shaken.

rat-tle-trap (răt'l-trăp"), *n.* **1,** an old, rickety, worn-out object, such as a wagon; **2,** in *pl.*, trifles; odds and ends.

rat-tling (răt'lĭng), *n.* noise made by the clattering together of small hard objects:—*p.adj.* **1,** making a rapid succession of sharp, noisy sounds; **2,** *Colloq.*, quick; as, they walked at a *rattling* pace:—*adv. Colloq.*, very; as, a *rattling* good story.

rau-cous (rô'kŭs), *adj.* hoarse; harsh; rough; as, a *raucous* voice.—*adv.* **rau'cous-ly.**

rav-age (răv'āj), *n.* destruction by violence; ruin; waste; as, the *ravages* of disease:—*v.t.* [*p.t.* and *p.p.* -aged (-ājd), *p.pr.* -ag-ing], to lay waste; pillage; plunder or sack; as, the army *ravaged* the country:—*v.i.* to work havoc.—*n.* **rav'ag-er.**

Syn., v. overrun, devastate, destroy.

rave (rāv), *v.t.* [*p.t.* and *p.p.* raved (rāvd), *p.pr.* rav'ing], to utter wildly, or in a frenzied manner:—*v.i.* **1,** to act or talk wildly; rage; **2,** to speak enthusiastically.

rav-el (răv'l), *v.t.* **1,** to draw out the threads of, as of a woven or knitted fabric; unmesh; **2,** to disentangle or make less difficult to understand:—*v.i.* **1,** to become unwoven or unknit: often with *out;* as, a stocking *ravels* out; **2,** to become disentangled:—*n.* **1,** a snarl; **2,** raveled material.

rav-el-ings (răv'l-ĭngz), *n.pl.* the threads drawn out of woven or twisted fabrics. Also, **rav'el-lings.**

[1]**ra-ven** (rā'vn), *n.* a large bird of the crow family, noted for its deep, glossy black color:—*adj.* jet black and shining.

[2]**rav-en** (răv'n), *n.* **1,** the act of plundering; **2,** plunder; prey:—*v.t.* **1,** to devour voraciously; **2,** to seize with force:—*v.i.* to seek and devour prey.

rav-en-ing (răv'n-ĭng), *n.* eagerness for plunder:—*p. adj.* seeking eagerly for prey; as, *ravening* wolves.

rav-en-ous (răv'n-ŭs), *adj.* **1,** furiously hungry; **2,** extremely greedy. —*adv.* **rav'en-ous-ly.**—*n.* **rav'en-ous-ness.**

ra-vine (rȧ-vēn'), *n.* a long, deep hollow, worn by the action of a stream or torrent; a mountain gorge; gully.

rav-ing (rāv'ĭng), *n.* furious or wild talk; delirium:—*p.adj.* talking furiously or wildly; delirious; frenzied.

rav-ish (răv'ĭsh), *v.t.* **1,** to seize and remove by force; **2,** to abduct or violate (a woman); **3,** to carry away with delight or rapture.—*n.* **rav'ish-er.**—*p.adj.* **rav'ish-ing.**—*adv.* **rav'ish-ing-ly.**

Syn. enrapture, enchant, delight.

rav-ish-ment (răv'ĭsh-mĕnt), *n.* **1,** violation; **2,** rapture or delight.

raw (rô), *adj.* **1,** uncooked; **2,** without the covering of the skin; as, a *raw* spot; **3,** in the natural state; unprepared; as, *raw* silk; **4,** crude; inexperienced; unpracticed; as, *raw* judgment; *raw* troops; **5,** cold and damp; as, *raw* weather:—*n.* **1,** a sore spot; **2,** something raw, as materials in their natural state.—*adv.* **raw'ly.**—*n.* **raw'ness.**

raw-boned (rô'bōnd"), *adj.* with little flesh on the bones; gaunt.

raw-hide (rô'hīd"), *n.* **1,** untanned skin, as of cattle; **2,** a whip made of a roll or braid of untanned leather.

[1]**ray** (rā), *n.* **1,** a single line of light appearing to stream from a bright center or source; **2,** one of a number of thin lines spreading from a common center; **3,** a beam of mental light; as, a *ray* of intelligence; **4,** in physics: **a,** a line defining the direction of propagation of energy, as of heat, light, etc.; **b,** loosely, a beam of energy of small cross section, propagated through space, in the form either of waves or of projected particles of matter; **5,** the outer flowers of certain composites, as the white florets of the oxeye daisy (see *composite,* illus.); **6,** one of the supporting spines of a fish's fin; one of the radiating arms of a starfish, or the like:—*v.t.* to send forth, as light:—*v.i.* to shine forth; radiate.

[2]**ray** (rā), *n.* any one of various fishes having a broad, flat body and a thin tail, as the skate and torpedo (see illus. next page).

ray-on (rā'ŏn), *n.* a lustrous, elastic cellulose, spun into thread from which are made various fabrics closely resembling silk.

raze (rāz), *v.t.* [*p.t.* and *p.p.* razed (rāzd), *p.pr.* raz'ing], **1,** to level to the ground; as, to *raze* a building; **2,** to blot out; efface.

Syn. demolish, destroy, overthrow, ruin.

ra-zee (rȧ-zē′), *n.* a ship which has been made smaller by the removal of the upper deck:—*v.t.* [*p.t.* and *p.p.* -zeed′ (-zēd′), *p.pr.* -zee′ing], **1,** to make smaller or lower, as a ship, by cutting off the upper deck; **2,** hence, to reduce in size; abridge; as, to *razee* a book.

ra-zor (rā′-zẽr), *n.* a sharp-edged instrument used for shaving hair from the skin.

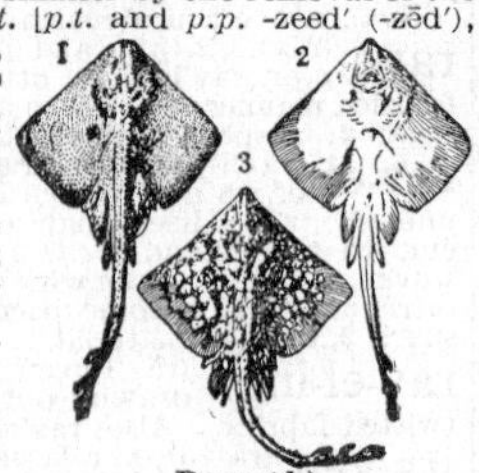

RAYS ($\frac{1}{45}$)
1, skate (top view); 2, same from below; 3, thornback.

ra-zor-back (rā′zẽr-băk″), *n.* **1,** a sharp-backed, long-legged hog of the southern U. S.; **2,** a rorqual: a kind of whale.

¹re (rā), *n.* the second of the syllables used in singing an ascending diatonic scale.

²re (rē), *n.* in the case of; in the matter of: properly, *in re;* as, *in re* Jones.

Re (rā), *n.* the god of the sun; the supreme Egyptian deity. Also, **Ra,** *Pfd. S.*

re- (rē-), *prefix,* used freely with many words to signify: **1,** back; backward; as, *re*call; *re*cline; **2,** again; anew; as, *re*count; *re*pay; **3,** in return; mutually; as, *re*act; *re*ciprocal; **4,** in opposition; as, *re*sist; **5,** used with intensive force; as, *re*splendent; *re*joice.

NOTE.—The prefix *re-,* meaning again, anew, is often set off by a hyphen when it forms a compound having the same spelling as one in which *re-* has some other meaning; as, *re-formation* (distinguished from *reformation*).

reach (rēch), *v.t.* **1,** to stretch out, as the hand; **2,** to touch or grasp, as with the extended hand; **3,** to pass or deliver to another; **4,** to arrive at or come to; gain; **5,** to extend as far as; penetrate to; **6,** to influence; affect; **7,** to hit with an object thrown:—*v.i.* **1,** to extend, as the hand, so as to touch or seize something; **2,** to endeavor to obtain something; **3,** to extend in time, space, amount, etc.; as, the amount will *reach* into the thousands; **4,** to carry, as a gun, sight, sound:—*n.* **1,** the act of stretching out, or the ability to stretch out, touch, grasp, etc.; **2,** the distance within which one can touch, observe, etc.; **3,** the limit of power or influence; **4,** an unbroken stretch, as of water.—*n.* **reach′er.**

re-act (rē-ăkt′), *v.i.* **1,** to act in a manner opposite to some former action; **2,** to respond to an influence or stimulus; **3,** to exert mutual chemical action; **4,** to resist the action of a body by an opposing force.

re-act-ance (rē-ăk′tăns), *n.* in electricity, a choking, or resistance, affecting an alternating current which passes through a coil.

re-ac-tion (rē-ăk′shŭn), *n.* **1,** return action or influence; response to influence or effort exerted; **2,** a tendency to return to a former or opposite state of things; **3,** the response of a living tissue or organism to stimulus or change; **4,** in physics, the opposing force exerted on an agent by the body upon which it acts; **5,** in chemistry, the interaction of chemical substances according to their properties, or the result of such action.

re-ac-tion-a-ry (rē-ăk′shŭn-ā-rĭ), *n.* [*pl.* reactionaries (-rĭz)], **1,** one who favors a return to former conditions; **2,** one who seeks to hinder or undo political progress:—*adj.* **1,** pertaining to, of the nature of, or causing, reverse action; **2,** favoring a return to a former state of affairs.

read (rēd), *v.t.* [*p.t.* and *p.p.* read (rĕd), *p.pr.* read′ing], **1,** to observe and understand the meaning of (something written, printed, or inscribed); peruse; as, to *read* a book; **2,** to utter aloud (something written or printed); as, he *reads* his sermons; **3,** to discover or understand by observation; as, to *read* the stars; **4,** to explain or make clear; as, it is easy to *read* his meaning; **5,** to make a study of; as, to *read* law; **6,** to learn, as from books; as, we *read* that the war has ended; **7,** to impress upon or teach; as, he *read* them a lesson; **8,** to interpret, as riddles; **9,** to show; indicate; as, the meter *reads* twenty miles:—*v.i.* **1,** to peruse written or printed matter; **2,** to learn from written or printed matter: with *of* or *about;* **3,** to utter aloud the words of a book, paper, etc.; as, he *reads* well; **4,** to make a careful study; as, to *read* up on history; **5,** to have a special form; as, the passage *reads* thus; **6,** to reproduce, vocally or on an instrument, written music; as, she *reads* rapidly:—*p.adj.* (rĕd), informed by reading; as, he is well-*read.*

read-a-ble (rēd′ȧ-bl), *adj.* **1,** easy and pleasant to read; interesting; **2,** legible, or plainly written.—*n.* **read′a-ble-ness.**—*n.* **read″a-bil′i-ty.**

read-er (rēd′ẽr), *n.* **1,** one who reads, as a professional reciter or one who reads the lessons in church; **2,** one who criticizes manuscripts offered for publication; **3,** a university lecturer; **4,** a schoolbook for instruction and practice in reading; as, a fifth *reader;* **5,** one who interprets.

read-ing (rēd′ĭng), *n.* **1,** perusal of written or printed matter; **2,** utterance aloud of the words of books, letters, or the like; **3,** the study of books; scholarship; **4,** public recital; as, to give *readings* from the poets; **5,** a version or form of a particular passage in a book; as, various *readings* of a passage in different editions of Shakespeare; **6,** written or printed matter to be perused; **7,** the manner of interpreting something written; as, an actor's *reading* of his lines; **8,** that which is shown by an instrument; as, the *reading* of a gas meter.

re-ad-just (rē″ă-jŭst′), *v.t.* **1,** to set in order again; rearrange; **2,** to settle or regulate again.

read-y (rĕd′ĭ), *adj.* [*comp.* read′i-er, *superl.* read′i-est], **1,** in condition to be used or to act immediately; **2,** quick; prompt; as, *ready* wit; *ready* payment; **3,** mentally fit or prepared; willing; as, *ready* to obey; **4,** on the point of; about to; likely; as, that tree is *ready* to fall; **5,** free to be used; easy to obtain; as, *ready* money.—*adv.* **read′i-ly.**—*n.* **read′i-ness.**

read-y-made (rĕd′ĭ-mād″), *adj.* **1,** not made to individual order or measure; made in standard forms; as, *ready-made* clothing; **2,** prepared beforehand; as, a *ready-made* speech.

re-a-gent (rē-ā′jĕnt), *n.* **1,** that which reacts; **2,** a chemical substance used to test the nature of another substance by observing the effect of one upon the other.

¹re-al (rē′ăl), *adj.* **1,** actually existing; not imaginary; **2,** true; genuine; not counterfeit; **3,** in law, pertaining to things fixed, as lands or tenements: of property, opp. of *personal;* as, *real* estate.

Syn. actual, certain, sure, authentic, veritable.—*Ant.* false, imaginary, untruthful, uncertain.

²re-al (rē′ăl; *Span.* rā-äl′), *n.* a small silver coin used in Spain and other Spanish-speaking countries.

re-al es-tate lands and all belonging to them, as trees, fences, permanent buildings, etc.; all immovable property.

re-al-ism (rē′ăl-ĭzm), *n.* **1,** in art and literature, the practice of presenting people and scenes as they are in real life: opp. of *idealism;* **2,** the doctrine that the objects that can be seen or touched have a real existence.

re-al-ist (rē'ăl-ĭst), *n.* **1,** one who believes in being true to nature in art and literature; **2,** one who believes that objects that can be seen, touched, etc., actually exist.

re-al-is-tic (rē"ăl-ĭs'tĭk), *adj.* presenting people and scenes as they actually exist; true to fact; lifelike.—*adv.* **re"al-is'ti-cal-ly.**

re-al-i-ty (rē-ăl'ĭ-tĭ), *n.* [*pl.* realities (-tĭz)], **1,** the state or quality of being in existence, or of being actual; **2,** that which exists or is actual; fact; truth.

re-al-i-za-tion (rē"ăl-ĭ-zā'shŭn), *n.* **1,** the act of making, or causing to appear, actual or true to nature or fact; **2,** the state of being present to the mind as actual or true to nature or fact; **3,** the act of perceiving the true nature of something, or of feeling fully and vividly; as, a full *realization* of the danger; **4,** the converting or changing of real estate or other property into money.

re-al-ize (rē'ăl-īz), *v.t.* [*p.t.* and *p.p.* -ized (-īzd), *p.pr.* -iz"ing], **1,** to bring into actual existence; hence, to accomplish; **2,** to cause to seem true to nature or fact; bring clearly before the mind; **3,** to feel fully and vividly; **4,** to change, as real estate, into money; **5,** to obtain as a profit; as, he *realized* five dollars from the sale:—*v.i.* to sell property for ready money.—*adj.* **re'al-iz"a-ble.**

Syn. obtain, get, acquire, comprehend.

re-al-ly (rē'ăl-ĭ), *adv.* **1,** actually; as a matter of fact; in truth; **2,** indeed: used for emphasis.

realm (rĕlm), *n.* **1,** a kingdom; an empire; **2,** hence, region, domain, or state; as, the *realm* of dreams.

re-al-tor (rē'ăl-tŏr), *n.* a dealer in real estate who is associated with the National Association of Real Estate Boards: a trade term.

re-al-ty (rē'ăl-tĭ), *n.* [*pl.* realties (-tĭz)], landed property: opp. of *personalty.*

¹ream (rēm), *n.* twenty quires, or 480 sheets, of paper; sometimes 472, 500, or even 516 sheets.

²ream (rēm), *v.t.* **1,** to enlarge or taper (a hole), esp. in metal: often with *out;* **2,** to enlarge (a hole) with a reamer.

ream-er (rēm'ẽr), *n.* any of various tools with sharp edges for enlarging or tapering holes.

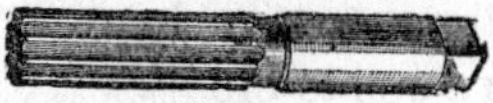

Reamer

re-an-i-mate (rē-ăn'-ĭ-māt), *v.t.* [*p.t.* and *p.p.* -mat"ed, *p.pr.* -mat"-ing], **1,** to bring back to life; **2,** to give new strength to; encourage.

reap (rēp), *v.t.* **1,** to cut down with a scythe, sickle, or machine; gather in; as, to *reap* grain; **2,** to cut a crop from; as, to *reap* a field; **3,** to receive as a reward:—*v.i.* **1,** to cut and gather grain; **2,** to receive the reward of one's actions; gain.—*n.* **reap'er.**

rear (rēr), *n.* **1,** the back or hinder part; as, the *rear* of a building; **2,** a place or position behind; as, the garden is at the *rear* of the house; **3,** that part of a fleet or army behind the rest:—*adj.* pertaining to, or situated at, the back part: **rear guard,** troops stationed behind an army to protect its rear.

rear (rēr), *v.t.* **1,** to raise or lift up; elevate; as, to *rear* a telegraph pole; **2,** to construct or erect, as a tower; **3,** to nurture and train; bring up and educate, as children; **4,** to breed or grow, as cattle or plants:—*v.i.* to rise up on the hind legs, as a horse.

rear ad-mi-ral in the U. S. navy, and in almost all other navies, an officer ranking next above a commodore and next below a vice admiral.

rear-most (rēr'mōst), *adj.* farthest back; hindermost; last.

re-ar-range (rē"ă-rānj'), *v.t.* [*p.t.* and *p.p.* -ranged' (-rāngd'), *p.pr.* -rang'ing], to group or arrange again.

rear-ward (rēr'wẽrd), *adj.* and *adv.* at or toward the rear.

rea-son (rē'zn), *n.* **1,** the power or faculty of understanding and forming conclusions; **2,** the normal exercise of this faculty; sanity; common sense; **3,** a reasonable view of a matter; as, to bring a child to *reason;* **4,** the cause for an opinion or act; **5,** an explanation given for a belief, act, or the like:—*v.i.* **1,** to exercise the power of thinking logically or of drawing conclusions; **2,** to argue:—*v.t.* **1,** to persuade by argument; **2,** to prove or explain by means of the intellect; as, to *reason* out a solution.—*n.* **rea'son-er.**

Syn., n. motive, design. (See cause.)

rea-son-a-ble (rē'zn-ȧ-bl), *adj.* **1,** having the power to think connectedly and reach conclusions; as, a *reasonable* being; **2,** governed by reason; just; as, a *reasonable* employer; **3,** moderate or fair, as a price; **4,** sound or sensible, as a decision.—*adv.* **rea'son-a-bly.**—*n.* **rea'son-a-ble-ness.**

rea-son-ing (rē'zn-ĭng), *n.* **1,** the act of one who reaches conclusions by careful and connected thinking; **2,** a line of argument; presentation of reasons.

re-as-sem-ble (rē"ă-sĕm'bl), *v.t.* and *v.i.* [*p.t.* and *p.p.* -bled (-bld), *p.pr.* -bling], to bring, or come, together again.

re-as-sure (rē"ă-shoor'), *v.t.* [*p.t.* and *p.p.* -sured' (-shoord'), *p.pr.* -sur'ing], to renew the boldness, courage, or certainty of; give new confidence to.—*adv.* **re"-as-sur'ing-ly.**—*n.* **re"as-sur'ance.**

re-bate (rē-bāt'; rē'bāt), *n.* a refund; discount:—*v.t.* (rē-bāt'), [*p.t.* and *p.p.* -bat'ed, *p.pr.* -bat'ing], to make a deduction from; allow a discount to.—*n.* **re-bat'er.**

re-bec (rē'bĕk), *n.* a medieval stringed instrument having a pear-shaped body, played with a bow: the earliest form of violin. Also, **re'beck.**

Rebec

Re-bec-ca (rē-bĕk'ȧ), *n.* in the Bible, the wife of Isaac, and mother of Esau and Jacob (Genesis 25:20–26). Also, **Re-bek'ah.**

¹re-bel (rē-bĕl'), *v.i.* [*p.t.* and *p.p.* -belled' (-bĕld'), *p.pr.* -bel'ling], **1,** to resist, and take up arms against, the law or government; **2,** to revolt against any authority.

²reb-el (rĕb'ĕl), *n.* **1,** one who wars against his government or resists its laws; **2,** one who resists any authority:—*adj.* opposing or resisting authority.

re-bel-lion (rē-bĕl'yŭn), *n.* **1,** the act of taking up arms, or the state of being at war, against the government or its laws; **2,** resistance to, or defiance of, any authority; revolt.

Syn. insurrection, mutiny. (See revolution.)

re-bel-lious (rē-bĕl'yŭs), *adj.* **1,** opposing or resisting lawful authority; **2,** resisting control; mutinous; unmanageable; as, *rebellious* hair.—*adv.* **re-bel'lious-ly.**—*n.* **re-bel'lious-ness.**

re-bound (rē-bound'), *v.i.* **1,** to spring or fly back from that which has been struck; **2,** to spring back repeatedly:—*n.* **1,** the act of springing back; **2,** a flying back from that which has been struck.

re-buff (rē-bŭf'), *n.* **1,** a sudden check; defeat; **2,** a curt refusal; repulse;

3, a driving back:—*v.t.* **1**, to repel curtly; refuse sharply; snub; **2**, to check suddenly; **3**, to drive back.

re-build (rē-bĭld′), *v.t.* [*p.t.* and *p.p.* -built′ (-bĭlt′) or, *Archaic*, -build′ed, *p.pr.* -build′ing], to construct anew; build again.

re-buke (rē-būk′), *n.* a sharp reproof; chiding; reprimand:—*v.t.* [*p.t.* and *p.p.* -buked′ (-būkt′), *p.pr.* -buk′ing], to censure; chide; reprove sharply.

Syn., v. admonish, reprimand. (See scold.)

re-bus (rē′bŭs), *n.* a puzzle in which words, phrases, and sentences are represented by pictures of objects and signs, the names of which, when sounded in sequence, afford the solution.

re-but (rē-bŭt′), *v.t.* [*p.t.* and *p.p.* -but′ted, *p.pr.* -but′ting], to contradict or oppose by argument or proof; refute, as in a debate:—*v.i.* to return an answer in contradiction to evidence already given by an opponent.

re-but-tal (rē-bŭt′ăl), *n.* **1**, the presenting of evidence in contradiction of testimony already given by the opposing side in a trial; **2**, the act of refuting, or contradicting, in general; **3**, the answering of the arguments of one's opponent in a debate.

re-cal-ci-trant (rē-kăl′sĭ-trănt), *adj.* obstinately refusing to submit; refractory.—*n.* **re-cal′ci-trance.**

re-call (rē-kôl′), *n.* **1**, the act of summoning or calling back; **2**, the power by which an unsatisfactory public official may be unseated, or put out of office, by vote of the people; **3**, a signal given by a drum, bugle, flag, or the like, to call back soldiers or boats:—*v.t.* **1**, to order or summon back; as, to *recall* an ambassador; **2**, to remember; recollect; as, to *recall* a name; **3**, to take back; as, to *recall* angry words; **4**, to revoke; annul; as, to *recall* a decision.

re-cant (rē-kănt′), *v.t.* to withdraw or take back formally and publicly (an opinion or belief previously held); renounce:—*v.i.* to renounce formally an opinion or belief previously held.—*n.* **re-cant′er.**

Syn. recall, revoke, abjure.

re-can-ta-tion (rē″kăn-tā′shŭn), *n.* **1**, the act of renouncing or withdrawing that which was previously believed or stated; **2**, the statement made in so doing.

re-ca-pit-u-late (rē″kȧ-pĭt′ū-lāt), *v.t.* [*p.t.* and *p.p.* -lat″ed, *p.pr.* -lat″ing], to sum up the chief points of:—*v.i.* to repeat briefly what has already been said at length.—*adj.* **re″ca-pit′u-la-to-ry.**

re-ca-pit-u-la-tion (rē″kȧ-pĭt″ū-lā′shŭn), *n.* the act of repeating briefly; a summing up.

re-cap-ture (rē-kăp′tūr), *n.* **1**, the act of seizing or taking again; **2**, that which is seized or taken again:—*v.t.* [*p.t.* and *p.p.* -tured (-tūrd), *p.pr.* -tur-ing], to seize or take again.

re-cast (rē-kȧst′), *v.t.* [*p.t.* and *p.p.* -cast′, *p.pr.* -cast′ing], **1**, to plan or lay out anew; **2**, to mold or cast again; **3**, to compute again.

¹re-cede (rē-sēd′), *v.i.* [*p.t.* and *p.p.* -ced′ed, *p.pr.* -ced′ing], **1**, to fall back; retreat; retire; as, the tide *receded;* **2**, to withdraw, as from a claim, proposal, etc.; **3**, to slope or incline backward.

²re-cede (rē-sēd′), *v.t.* [*p.t.* and *p.p.* -ced′ed, *p.pr.* -ced′ing], to give back to a former owner, as property.

re-ceipt (rē-sēt′), *n.* **1**, the act of getting, or state of having, anything that has been given, sent, etc.; as, the *receipt* of a letter; in *receipt* of news; **2**, a direction for making something by mixing certain things together, esp. in cookery; a recipe; as, a *receipt* for cake; **3**, a written acknowledgment of anything, as money or goods, had from another; **4**, usually in *pl.*, that which is taken, in distinction to that which is given out; as, cash *receipts:*—*v.t.* **1**, to sign in acknowledgment of payment; as, to *receipt* a bill; **2**, in the U. S., to give a written acknowledgment of the receipt of:—*v.i.* to give a written acknowledgment of money paid.

re-ceiv-a-ble (rē-sēv′ȧ-bl), *adj.* **1**, capable of, or requiring, acceptance when offered; **2**, of such sort that payment may be expected or demanded; as, bills *receivable.*—*n.* **re-ceiv″a-bil′i-ty.**

re-ceive (rē-sēv′), *v.t.* [*p.t.* and *p.p.* -ceived′ (-sēvd′), *p.pr.* -ceiv′ing], **1**, to take, as a gift, message, payment, or the like, from another; **2**, to get knowledge of; as, to *receive* reports; **3**, to admit to one's company; greet; entertain; as, to *receive* guests; **4**, to serve as a holder for; as, a channel to *receive* the overflow; **5**, to admit as credible; accept; as, they *received* the faith; **6**, to get; experience; be subjected to; as, to *receive* a shock; **7**, to have (a blow, mark, or the like) inflicted upon one; as, to *receive* a sword thrust; **8**, to take from a thief, as stolen goods; **9**, in tennis, to await, or to strike in order to return (a served ball):—*v.i.* **1**, to obtain, or be presented with, something; take what is given or paid; **2**, to take the sacrament; **3**, to entertain; welcome guests; **4**, in tennis, to await the delivery of the ball by the server.

re-ceiv-er (rē-sēv′ẽr), *n.* **1**, one who or that which takes or obtains; **2**, a receptacle; **3**, the part of a telephone which converts the electrical energy into sound waves and imparts them to the ear; **4**, one who knowingly buys or obtains stolen goods; **5**, a person appointed by a court to hold and manage property which is the subject of a lawsuit, or property owned by a person or firm that is bankrupt.—*n.* **re-ceiv′er-ship.**

re-cen-cy (rē′sĕn-sĭ), *n.* lateness of occurrence; newness.

re-cen-sion (rē-sĕn′shŭn), *n.* **1**, a skilled criticism or revision, as of the text of a book; **2**, the text as reviewed or revised; an edited version.

re-cent (rē′sĕnt), *adj.* **1**, pertaining to time not long past; **2**, of origin or occurrence near the present; new; modern; fresh: **Recent**, in geology, designating, or pertaining to, the era extending from the close of the Pleistocene period to the present time.—*adv.* **re′cent-ly.**—*n.* **re′cent-ness.**

Syn. late. (See modern.)

re-cep-ta-cle (rē-sĕp′tȧ-kl), *n.* **1**, anything, as a vessel, used to hold other things; **2**, in a plant, the part of the stalk to which the floral parts are attached: also called *torus* (cf. *flower*, ²*style*, illus.).

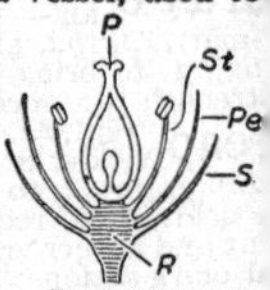

RECEPTACLE
P, pistil; *St*, stamen; *Pe*, petal; *S*, sepal; *R*, receptacle, or torus.

re-cep-tion (rē-sĕp′shŭn), *n.* **1**, the act of receiving, or the state of being received; as, the *reception* of news; **2**, the act or manner of welcoming; as, a cool *reception;* **3**, a social occasion for greeting guests; as, a wedding *reception;* **4**, the formal or official greeting of a person; **5**, acceptance; receptivity; as, the *reception* of new ideas.

re-cep-tive (rē-sĕp′tĭv), *adj.* having the quality or ability of taking in, or holding; esp., quick to take in mental impressions; as, a *receptive* mind.—*adv.* **re-cep′tive-ly.**—*n.* **re-cep′tive-ness.**

re-cep-tiv-i-ty (rē″sĕp-tĭv′ĭ-tĭ; rĕs″ĕp-), *n.* power to take in or hold, as mental impressions.

'e-cess (rē-sĕs'; rē'sĕs), *n.* **1,** a place or space hollowed out, as in a wall; .n alcove or niche; **2,** a quiet or secluded spot r nook; **3,** a brief time during which work eases; an intermission; as, the school *recess.*

re-ces-sion (rē-sĕsh'ŭn), *n.* the act of going back or retiring; ithdrawal; retirement.

re-ces-sion (rē-sĕsh'ŭn), *n.* the act of giving, or granting, back.

'e-ces-sion-al (rē-sĕsh'ŭn-ăl), *n.* **1,** a hymn sung as the clergy nd choir leave the chancel at the close of hurch service; **2,** organ music played at the lose of a church service, or during the passng out of a procession, as at a wedding:—*dj.* **1,** of or pertaining to a withdrawal or etirement; **2,** pertaining to an intermission.

'e-ces-sive (rē-sĕs'ĭv), *adj.* receding; inclined to go back: **recessive haracter,** in biology, a characteristic which oes not appear in the immediate offspring, ut which may, nevertheless, be transmitted: pp. of *dominant character.*

're-cher-ché (rē-shâr"shā'), [Fr.], *adj.* uncommon; rare; choice.

'ec-i-pe (rĕs'ĭ-pē), *n.* **1,** a medical prescription; also, the preparation itself; , a formula for mixing or preparing anything r for accomplishing some result; **3,** a receipt r cooking; as, a good *recipe* for cake.

e-cip-i-ent (rē-sĭp'ĭ-ĕnt), *n.* one who receives; as, a *recipient* of high onors:—*adj.* receiving or ready to receive.

'e-cip-ro-cal (rē-sĭp'rō-kăl), *adj.* **1,** mutual; done, given, or offered y each to the other; as, *reciprocal* affection or enefits; **2,** offered in return for something one or given; **3,** able to be exchanged for ne another; as, *reciprocal* conditions; **4,** in rammar, showing mutual action or relation: sed of certain pronouns, as *each other;* ormerly, of verbs, reflexive:—*n.* **1,** that which given or done by each to the other; **2,** in nathematics, the quotient obtained by dividng unity by any quantity; as, the *reciprocal* f 3 is ⅓.—*adv.* **re-cip'ro-cal-ly.**

e-cip-ro-cate (rē-sĭp'rō-kāt), *v.t.* [*p.t.* and *p.p.* -cat"ed, *p.pr.* :at"ing], **1,** to give and take from one another; s, they *reciprocate* each other's affection; **2,** to ive something in return for; as, to *reciprocate* favor; **3,** in mechanics, to cause to move to nd fro:—*v.i.* **1,** in mechanics, to move to and o; **2,** to interchange; make an exchange ith one another; **3,** to pay back an act or eeling.—*n.* **re-cip"ro-ca'tion.**

'e-cip-ro-cat-ing (rē-sĭp'rō-kāt"ĭng), *p.adj.* designating a o-and-fro motion, as that of a piston.

ec-i-proc-i-ty (rĕs"ĭ-prŏs'ĭ-tĭ), *n.* [*pl.* reciprocities (-tĭz)], **1,** a ondition in which there is mutual action, givng and taking, etc., between two parties; **2,** a elationship or policy existing between two ations in which each grants the other special dvantages in trade.

e-cit-al (rē-sīt'ăl), *n.* **1,** the act of telling the particulars of an event; narition; **2,** the thing told; a story; **3,** a perrmance, vocal or instrumental, by one peron, or a concert consisting of selections from ne works of one composer.

ec-i-ta-tion (rĕs"ĭ-tā'shŭn), *n.* **1,** a public rendering of prose or poetry mmitted to memory; **2,** the selection of rose or poetry so rendered; **3,** the repeating f a lesson by a pupil to a teacher; **4,** the concting of a lesson by a teacher and a class.

ec-i-ta-tive (rĕs"ĭ-tȧ-tēv'), *n.* a kind of singing that imitates the ccents of speech: used in operas and orarios; also, the music for a passage to be sung in such a manner:—*adj.* not conforming to strict musical rhythm; sung with the accents of speech.—*adv.* **rec"i-ta-tive'ly.**

re-cite (rē-sīt'), *v.t.* and *v.i.* [*p.t.* and *p.p.* -cit'ed, *p.pr.* -cit'ing], **1,** to repeat aloud from memory; rehearse; **2,** to tell in detail; relate; **3,** to repeat (a lesson) to a teacher.—*n.* **re-cit'er.**

reck (rĕk), *v.t. Poetic,* to care for; heed:—*v.i. Archaic* or *Poetic,* to care; mind; as, he *recks* not of danger; also, to be of concern matter; as, it *recks* not.

reck-less (rĕk'lĕs), *adj.* **1,** heedless of consequences or danger; rash; **2,** careless; thoughtless.—*adv.* **reck'less-ly.**—*n.* **reck'less-ness.**

Syn. foolhardy, daring, regardless, remiss.

reck-on (rĕk'n), *v.t.* **1,** to count or compute; number; as, to *reckon* the cost; **2,** to look upon as being; consider; as, I *reckon* him among my foes; **3,** to think; suppose: followed by a clause as object; as, I *reckon* it will rain:—*v.i.* **1,** to depend or rely: with *on;* as, he *reckoned* on their friendship; **2,** to calculate; **3,** to settle accounts: with *with;* **4,** *Colloq.,* to guess.—*n.* **reck'on-er.**

reck-on-ing (rĕk'n-ĭng), *n.* **1,** the act of one who counts or computes; also, the result of such calculation; **2,** a statement or settling of accounts between debtor and creditor; **3,** a bill at a hotel or other public house; **4,** the calculation of the position of a ship, or the position so determined: **dead reckoning,** a calculation of the position of a ship based on the distance and direction traversed since the last reckoning, but without astronomical observation.

re-claim (rē-klām'), *v.t.* **1,** to demand or obtain the return of; as, to *reclaim* one's money; **2,** to reform; as, to *reclaim* a drunkard; **3,** to bring under cultivation; as, to *reclaim* land or swamps; **4,** to tame; subdue; as, to *reclaim* a wild animal.—*n.* **re-claim'er.**—*adj.* **re-claim'a-ble.**

rec-la-ma-tion (rĕk"lȧ-mā'shŭn), *n.* **1,** the act of recovering or restoring; restoration; **2,** the making of waste land productive, as through irrigation in the western U. S.

re-cline (rē-klīn'), *v.t.* [*p.t.* and *p.p.* -clined' (-klīnd'), *p.pr.* -clin'ing], to cause to lean or lie back:—*v.i.* to rest or repose; lie down.—*n.* **rec"li-na'tion.**

re-cluse (rē-klo͞os'), *n.* one who lives alone; a hermit:—*adj.* shut up from the world; solitary; secluded.—*n.* **re-clu'sion.**—*adj.* **re-clu'sive.**

rec-og-ni-tion (rĕk"ŏg-nĭsh'ŭn), *n.* **1,** an identifying of something previously known; **2,** formal acknowledgment or commendation; as, *recognition* of a brave deed; **3,** special notice.—*adj.* **re-cog'ni-to-ry.**

re-cog-ni-zance (rē-kŏg'nĭ-zăns; rē-kŏn'ĭ-zăns), *n.* **1,** a legal agreement, entered into before, and recorded by, a magistrate or court, to do, or abstain from doing, some particular act; **2,** the sum of money to be forfeited if such an obligation is not fulfilled.

rec-og-nize (rĕk'ŏg-nīz), *v.t.* [*p.t.* and *p.p.* -nized (-nīzd), *p.pr.* -niz"ing], **1,** to know the identity of; recall as having been previously known; as, to *recognize* an old friend; **2,** to admit acquaintance with; salute; **3,** to take formal notice of; acknowledge; as, to *recognize* the independence of a country; **4,** to appreciate; as, to *recognize* merit; **5,** to concede as true; as, to *recognize* the facts in the case; **6,** in a meeting, to acknowledge as the person who has the floor.—*n.* **rec'og-niz"er.**—*adj.* **rec'og-niz"a-ble.**—*adv.* **rec'og-niz"a-bly.**

re-coil (rē-koil'), *n.* **1,** a shrinking back; **2,** a rebound; **3,** the sudden backward motion, or kick, of a gun after it is fired: —*v.i.* **1**, to start back, as in dismay, fear, etc.; shrink; **2**, to spring back because of some force; rebound; as, a gun *recoils;* **3**, to retreat; **4**, to come back to a starting point.

¹re-col-lect (rē″kō-lĕkt′), *v.t.* **1**, to collect, or gather together again, as things scattered; **2**, to compose (one's thoughts); compose, or regain control of: used with a reflexive pronoun; rally or summon, as courage.

²rec-ol-lect (rĕk″ŏ-lĕkt′), *v.t.* to call back to the mind; remember.

rec-ol-lec-tion (rĕk″ŏ-lĕk′shŭn), *n.* **1**, the recalling of ideas to the mind; **2**, the period of which one has memories; **3**, that which is remembered.

Syn. remembrance. (See memory.)

rec-om-mend (rĕk″ŏ-mĕnd′), *v.t.* **1**, to give in charge or trust, as to God; **2**, to offer to the favor, attention, or use of another; speak in favor of; as, to *recommend* a servant; **3**, to advise; suggest; as, I *recommend* a change of diet; **4**, to make attractive or deserving; as, her gentleness *recommends* her.—*n.* **rec″om-mend′er.**

rec-om-men-da-tion (rĕk″ŏ-mĕn-dā′-shŭn), *n.* **1**, the act of offering a person or thing to favorable notice; **2**, that which procures favorable attention; as, good manners are an excellent *recommendation;* **3**, favorable introduction; as, to present a letter of *recommendation.*

rec-om-mend-a-to-ry (rĕk″ŏ-mĕn′-dȧ-tō-rĭ), *adj.* **1**, attracting favorable attention; **2**, advisory.

rec-om-pense (rĕk′ŏm-pĕns), *n.* something equal given in return for something rendered; reward; compensation:—*v.t.* [*p.t.* and *p.p.* -pensed (-pĕnst), *p.pr.* -pens″ing], **1**, to give an equivalent to (a person); reward; repay; as, to *recompense* him for his devotion; **2**, to make amends for; atone for; as, to *recompense* a loss.

***re-con-cen-tra-do** (rā-kôn″sĕn-trä′-dō), [Span.], *n.* [*pl.* reconcentrados (-dōs)], one whose ordinary residence is in the country, but who, for military reasons, is compelled by the authorities to remain in or near a town.

rec-on-cil-a-ble (rĕk′ŏn-sīl″ȧ-bl), *adj.* **1**, capable of being made friendly or harmonious again; **2**, adjustable; **3**, capable of being made to agree or match; consistent; as, *reconcilable* statements.—*adv.* **rec′on-cil″a-bly.**

rec-on-cile (rĕk′ŏn-sīl), *v.t.* [*p.t.* and *p.p.* -ciled (-sīld), *p.pr.* -cil″ing], **1**, to restore peace or friendship between; as, to *reconcile* brothers who have quarreled; **2**, to adjust; settle; as, to *reconcile* differences; **3**, to make content or submissive; as, to *reconcile* a person to his losses; **4**, to cause to harmonize; make consistent: with *to* or *with;* as, to *reconcile* words with actions.—*n.* **rec′on-cil″er.**—*n.* **rec′on-cile″ment.**

rec-on-cil-i-a-tion (rĕk″ŏn-sĭl″ĭ-ā′-shŭn), *n.* **1**, a renewal of friendship; the making up or settling of a quarrel; **2**, the showing of agreement between things seemingly different.

rec-on-dite (rĕk′ŏn-dīt; rē-kŏn′dīt), *adj.* **1**, too deep or difficult for the ordinary mind to perceive or understand; obscure; **2**, dealing in profound or abstruse things; as, *recondite* studies.—*adv.* **rec′on-dite-ly.**—*n.* **rec′on-dite-ness.**

Syn. hidden, secret, mysterious.

re-con-nais-sance (rē-kŏn′ȧ-săns), *n.* **1**, the making of a preliminary investigation or survey, as for military or scientific purposes; **2**, a party of men sent on such a survey or examination. Also, **re-con′nois-sance** (rē-kŏn′ĭ-săns).

rec-on-noi-ter (rĕk″ŏ-noi′tẽr), *v.t.* to ex plore and investigat with a view to action, as for military or scien tific purposes:—*v.i.* to make examinatio before taking action. Also, **rec″on-noi′tre** [*p.t* and *p.p.* -tred (-tẽrd), *p.pr.* -tring].

re-con-sid-er (rē″kŏn-sĭd′ẽr), *v.t.* **1**, t think over or ponde again; **2**, in a legislative body, to bring up fo further deliberation, as a bill or a motion.— *n.* **re″con-sid″er-a′tion.**

re-con-struct (rē″kŏn-strŭkt′), *v.t.* to re build; remodel; as, to *re construct* a ship.—*adj.* **re″-con-struc′tive.**

re-con-struc-tion (rē″kŏn-strŭk′shŭn) *n.* **1**, the act of re building; **2**, the state of being rebuilt: **Recon struction**, after the Civil War in the U. S., th process of restoring, to the states that ha seceded, the rights and privileges of the Union

¹re-cord (rē-kôrd′), *v.t.* **1**, to write out o set down, as in a book, a tru account of; as, to *record* events; **2**, to se down in some permanent form, as in writing as, to *record* one's opinions; *record* a voic by a phonograph; **3**, to register; enroll; **4**, t mark or indicate; as, the clock *records* time

²rec-ord (rĕk′ŏrd; rĕk′ôrd), *n.* **1**, th writing or printing of facts o events for the purpose of keeping them i memory, or as evidence; also, that on whic the writing is done, as a memorial tablet, register, or the like; **2**, an official written c printed report of public acts; **3**, the body c facts, known and preserved, giving the histor of anything; **4**, the cylinder, disk, or pape roll for reproducing sounds in phonograph piano players, or the like; **5**, in law, an officia copy of all documents presented in a case **6**, an official contemporaneous report of a proceedings in a case before a court, togethe with the judgment given; **7**, in sports, th best performance so far achieved officially a any given time; **8**, the official register of bes performances; **9**, in *pl.*, public documents:— *adj.* best of its kind up to a given time; as, *record* crop.

Syn., *n.* chronicle, annals. (See history.)

re-cord-er (rē-kôr′dẽr), *n.* **1**, a publ officer who registers writing or transactions; as, a *recorder* of deeds; **2**, judicial officer in a city or borough; **3**, an of various devices that register mechanically as, a telegraph *recorder.*

¹re-count (rē-kount′), *v.t.* to tell or repea in full the particulars of; re cite; enumerate.

Syn. relate, describe, narrate, rehearse.

²re-count (rē-kount′), *v.t.* to count agai —*n.* (rē-kount′; rē′kount), new enumeration; a counting again.

re-coup (rē-ko͞op′), *v.t.* **1**, to make goo regain; as, to *recoup* a loss; **2**, t indemnify; as, to *recoup* oneself for a los **3**, in law, to keep back (a part of somethin to be paid) in order to make good a counte claim.—*n.* **re-coup′ment.**

re-course (rē-kōrs′), *n.* **1**, an appeal fo aid or protection; as, to hav *recourse* to the law; **2**, the person or thing t which one turns for aid; as, his purse was *recourse* for all the needy.

re-cov-er (rē-kŭv′ẽr), *v.t.* **1**, to get bac the possession of; regain, one's health or lost property; **2**, to obtain b judgment in a court of law; as, to *recov* damages; **3**, to make up for; make good th loss or damage of; as, to *recover* lost tim **4**, to rescue or save from danger:—*v.i.* **1**, regain health, strength, or any former stat **2**, to succeed in a lawsuit; **3**, in boxin fencing, etc., to regain one's position for new movement.—*adj.* **re-cov′er-a-ble.**

re-cov-er-y (rē-kŭv′ẽr-ĭ), *n.* [*pl.* recoveries (-ĭz)], **1**, the act of regaining; **2**, restoration to health or some other former state; **3**, the obtaining of one's right to something by judgment of a court.

rec-re-ant (rĕk′rē-ănt), *n.* **1**, a faithless person; a deserter; **2**, a coward:—*adj.* **1**, cowardly; craven; **2**, unfaithful to a cause; false.—*n.* **rec′re-an-cy.**

re–cre-ate (rē″-krē-āt′), *v.t.* [*p.t.* and *p.p.* -at′ed, *p.pr.* -at′ing], to make anew.—*n.* **re″–cre-a′tion.**

rec-re-ate (rĕk′rē-āt), *v.t.* [*p.t.* and *p.p.* -at″ed, *p.pr.* -at″ing], to refresh, esp. after toil; amuse:—*v.i.* to take refreshment or amusement.—*adj.* **rec′re-a-tive.**

rec-re-a-tion (rĕk″rē-ā′shŭn), *n.* **1**, refreshment of mind or body after toil or weariness; **2**, any exercise or occupation that diverts.

Syn. sport, pastime, play, amusement.

re-crim-i-nate (rē-krĭm′ĭ-nāt), *v.i.* [*p.t.* and *p.p.* -nat″ed, *p.pr.* -nat″ing], to answer one accusation or charge with another:—*v.t.* to accuse in return.

re-crim-i-na-tion (rē-krĭm″ĭ-nā′shŭn), *n.* **1**, the act of accusing in return; **2**, the accusation made.

re-crim-i-na-to-ry (rē-krĭm′ĭ-nȧ-tō-rĭ), *adj.* retorting, or returning, an accusation or charge with another. Also, **re-crim′i-na-tive.**

re-cru-des-cent (rē″kro͞o-dĕs′ĕnt), *adj.* becoming raw or sore again; breaking out afresh, as a disease.—*n.* **re″cru-des′cence.**

re-cruit (rē-kro͞ot′), *n.* **1**, a man newly enlisted in an army or navy; **2**, one who has just joined any cause:—*v.t.* **1**, to add to, or keep up the numbers of, as an army, a party, a society; **2**, to enlist; **3**, to fill up gaps or weak places in; **4**, to build up; restore; as, to *recruit* health and strength:—*v.i.* **1**, to obtain fresh supplies; **2**, to recover health and strength; **3**, to enlist new men for an army, or new members for any organization.—*n.* **re-cruit′er.**—*n.* **re-cruit′ment.**

rec-tan-gle (rĕk′tăng″gl), *n.* a four-sided figure with four right angles (see *quadrilateral*, illus.).

rec-tan-gu-lar (rĕk-tăng′gū-lȧr), *adj.* **1**, having four sides and four right angles; **2**, having right angles.

rec-ti-fi-ca-tion (rĕk″tĭ-fĭ-kā′shŭn), *n.* **1**, the act of correcting or setting right; **2**, in chemistry, the process of refining or purifying by distillation or other means; **3**, in electricity, the process of changing alternating into direct current.

rec-ti-fy (rĕk′tĭ-fī), *v.t.* [*p.t.* and *p.p.* -fied (-fīd), *p.pr.* -fy″ing], **1**, to correct the faults in; remove mistakes from; set right; **2**, to refine or purify, as liquids, by distillation; **3**, in electricity, to change from alternating to direct, as an electric current.—*n.* **rec′ti-fi″er.**

Syn. correct. To *rectify* is to set right something that is wrong; as, to *rectify* a mistake or a false judgment. To *correct* is to set right according to some standard such as accuracy, convention, etc. These words are used interchangeably, but *correct* is a more definite term than *rectify;* as, printer's proof is *corrected*, not *rectified*.

rec-ti-lin-e-ar (rĕk″tĭ-lĭn′ē-ȧr), *adj.* **1**, straight; **2**, bounded by straight lines. Also, **rec″ti-lin′e-al.**

rec-ti-tude (rĕk′tĭ-tūd), *n.* **1**, rightness of intention and action; honesty; uprightness; **2**, freedom from inaccuracy; correctness of judgment.

Syn. justice, integrity, goodness.—*Ant.* dishonesty, iniquity, partiality.

rec-tor (rĕk′tẽr), *n.* **1**, in the Protestant Episcopal Church, a clergyman in charge of a parish; **2**, the head of a university, college, school, etc.—*adj.* **rec-to′ri-al.**—*n.* **rec′tor-ate.**—*n.* **rec′tor-ship.**

rec-to-ry (rĕk′tō-rĭ), *n.* [*pl.* rectories (-rĭz)], **1**, the house of a rector, or clergyman of the Episcopal Church; **2**, in England, a rector's benefice, including the church, parsonage, lands, etc.

rec-tum (rĕk′tŭm), *n.* [*pl.* recta (-tȧ)], the six or eight inches at the lower end of the large intestine.—*adj.* **rec′tal.**

re-cum-ben-cy (rē-kŭm′bĕn-sĭ), *n.* the act or state of reclining; a reclining position. Also, **re-cum′bence.**

re-cum-bent (rē-kŭm′bĕnt), *adj.* leaning; lying; reclining; as, a *recumbent* position.—*adv.* **re-cum′bent-ly.**

re-cu-per-ate (rē-kū′pẽr-āt), *v.t.* [*p.t.* and *p.p.* -at″ed, *p.pr.* -at″ing], to restore to former strength; regain (health, wealth, etc.):—*v.i.* to regain health; recover, as from loss of health or money.

re-cu-per-a-tion (rē-kū″pẽr-ā′shŭn), *n.* recovery, esp. of health.

re-cu-per-a-tive (rē-kū′pẽr-ā-tĭv), *adj.* pertaining or tending to recovery, esp. of health; as, *recuperative* powers.—*adj.* **re-cu′per-a-to-ry.**

re-cur (rē-kûr′), *v.i.* [*p.t.* and *p.p.* -curred′ (-kûrd′), *p.pr.* -cur′ring], **1**, to go back, as in memory or in speech; as, to *recur* to a former opinion; **2**, to come back or return; as, a thought *recurs* to the mind; **3**, to happen again, or at intervals, as a fever.

re-cur-rence (rē-kŭr′ĕns), *n.* **1**, the act or fact of returning; **2**, a return; as, a *recurrence* of a fever; **3**, recourse.

re-cur-rent (rē-kŭr′ĕnt), *adj.* **1**, coming back at intervals, as a fever; **2**, running or turning back: said of certain nerves and arteries.—*adv.* **re-cur′rent-ly.**

re-curve (rē-kûrv′), *v.t.* [*p.t.* and *p.p.* -curved′ (-kûrvd′), *p.pr.* -curv′ing], to bend back or downward:—*v.i.* to be bent back.—*adj.* **re-cur′vate.**

rec-u-sant (rĕk′ū-zănt; rē-kū′-), *n.* one who refuses to conform to authority, as to a state or church; a dissenter or noncomformist:—*adj.* refusing to conform to authority.—*n.* **rec′u-san-cy.**

red (rĕd), *n.* **1**, the color of blood, or that part of the visible spectrum having the longest wave length; **2**, any coloring matter that produces this color; **3**, a revolutionary socialist.—*adj.* [*comp.* red′der, *superl.* red′dest], **1**, of the color of blood, specif. of arterial blood: opp. of *blue*, or venous.—*n.* **red′ness.**

red- (rĕd-), *prefix*, back; again: a form of *re-* used before vowels; as, *red*olent.

re-dact (rē-dăkt′), *v.t.* to edit; revise and prepare for publication.—*n.* **re-dac′tor; re-dac′tion.**

re-dan (rē-dăn′), *n.* in fortification, a work formed by two parapets meeting at an angle projecting outwards.

red-breast (rĕd′brĕst″), *n.* the American or the European robin.

red cross a red Greek cross on a white ground, adopted by the Geneva Convention, in 1864, as the sign of neutrality in war: **Red Cross**, a society for helping the sick and wounded in war, and for other relief purposes, its emblem being a red cross on a white ground.

red-den (rĕd′n), *v.t.* to make red:—*v.i.* to become red; blush; flush.

red-dish (rĕd′ĭsh), *adj.* somewhat red.—*n.* **red′dish-ness.**

re-deem (rē-dēm′), *v.t.* **1**, to buy back (something formerly possessed); **2**, to free from bondage or a claim of any kind, by paying a price; **3**, to ransom or free from sin and its consequences; **4**, to make good; as, to *redeem* a promise; **5**, to make up for; as, to *redeem* a fault; **6**, to pay off, as a promissory note; **7**, to recover, as mortgaged property, by paying a price.—*adj.* **re-deem′a-ble.**

Syn. rescue, deliver, save, free.

re-deem-er (rē-dēm′ẽr), *n.* one who frees, buys back, or atones for: **the Redeemer**, Jesus Christ.

re-demp-tion (rē-dĕmp′shŭn), *n.* **1**, the act of freeing or buying back; **2**, the state of being freed; **3**, the salvation of mankind by Jesus Christ.

re-demp-tive (rē-dĕmp′tĭv), *adj.* **1**, ransoming or saving; as, *redemptive* work; **2**, serving or tending to fulfil, as a promise, or to recover, as property.

re-demp-to-ry (rē-dĕmp′tō-rĭ), *adj.* **1**, paid for ransom; **2**, serving to set free, buy back, or atone for; **3**, serving to fulfil.

red–hot (rĕd′=hŏt″), *adj.* **1**, heated to redness; **2**, greatly excited; extreme.

re-din-te-grate (rē-dĭn′tē-grāt), *v.t.* [*p.t.* and *p.p.* -grat″ed, *p.pr.* -grat″ing], to make complete or perfect again; put together again.—*n.* **re-din″te-gra′tion.**

re-di-rect (rē″dĭ-rĕkt′), *v.t.* to direct anew:—*adj.* designating the examination of a witness after cross-examination by the opposing attorney.

red–let-ter day a happy or lucky day: so called because the saints' days were printed in red letters in the church calendars.

red-o-lent (rĕd′ō-lĕnt), *adj.* giving off a pleasing odor; fragrant; as, the air was *redolent* of roses.—*n.* **red′o-lence.**

Syn. odorous, scented, aromatic.

re-dou-ble (rē-dŭb′l), *v.t.* [*p.t.* and *p.p.* -bled (-ld), *p.pr.* -bling], to make twice as great; multiply greatly; increase by repeated additions:—*v.i.* to become twice as great.

re-doubt (rē-dout′), *n.* **1**, a small inclosed fortification, often temporary, for defending a pass, the top of a hill, or the like; **2**, a central work inside a fortification, to be used as a retreat for the defenders.

re-doubt-a-ble (rē-dout′ȧ-bl), *adj.* causing fear or dread; formidable or valiant: often ironical.—*adv.* **re-doubt′a-bly.**—*n.* **re-doubt′a-ble-ness.**

re-dound (rē-dound′), *v.i.* to flow back as a consequence; contribute; as, all of his acts *redound* to his glory.

red-poll (rĕd′pōl″), *n.* any of several small finches, the males of which have a red or crimson crown.

re-dress (rē-drĕs′), *n.* **1**, compensation for, or reparation of, a wrong; as, to get no *redress* for dishonest treatment; **2**, the act of redressing a wrong:—*v.t.* **1**, to make right, as a wrong; **2**, to correct or do away with, as abuses; **3**, to make amends to; give relief to; as, to *redress* those who suffer from wrongs.—*n.* **re-dress′er.**

red-skin (rĕd′skĭn″), *n.* a North American Indian.

red-start (rĕd′stärt″), *n.* **1**, a small European bird of the thrush family; **2**, an American warbler.

red tape official conduct of business marked by formality and rigid adherence to regulations: so called from the custom of tying official papers with red tape.—*adj.* **red′–tape″.**—*n.* **red″–tap′ism.**

red-top (rĕd′tŏp″), *n.* a grass valuable for pasturage and hay.

re-duce (rē-dūs′), *v.t.* [*p.t.* and *p.p.* -duced′ (-dūst′), *p.pr.* -duc′ing], **1**, to make less in value, size, etc.; lessen; lower; as, to *reduce* the cost; *reduce* flesh; **2**, to bring from a higher to a lower position; degrade as, to *reduce* an officer to the ranks; **3**, to subdue; conquer; as, to *reduce* an enemy to subjection; **4**, to bring into a class, group, or order; as, to *reduce* mankind to races; **5**, to bring into a particular form or condition; as, to *reduce* sugar to a sirup; **6**, to bring to a specified condition, esp. one that is inferior or disagreeable; as, to *reduce* one to despair; **7**, in arithmetic, to change (numbers or quantities) from one name or form to another without change of value; as, to *reduce* gallons to pints; **8**, in chemistry, to take all nonmetallic elements out of (an ore); specif., to deoxidize; **9**, in surgery, to restore (a displaced part) to its right position; as, to *reduce* a fracture.—*n.* **re-duc′er.**—*adj.* **re-duc′i-ble.**

Syn. decrease, diminish, minimize.

re-duc-tion (rē-dŭk′shŭn), *n.* **1**, the act of lessening, degrading, or changing the form of; **2**, the state of being lessened, degraded, or changed in form; **3**, conquest; as, the *reduction* of a fort; **4**, in surgery, restoration of a part to its normal position, as a dislocated bone; **5**, in chemistry, separation of a metal from substances combined with it; **6**, in arithmetic, the change of a number or quantity in form but not in value

re-dun-dan-cy (rē-dŭn′dăn-sĭ), *n.* **1**, the quality or state of being more than is required; **2**, that which is more than enough; excess; surplus; as, *redundancy* in writing. Also, **re-dun′dance.**

re-dun-dant (rē-dŭn′dănt), *adj.* **1**, exceeding what is needed; superabundant; **2**, in writing or speaking, too full, or too wordy; unnecessary to the sense; superfluous.—*adv.* **re-dun′dant-ly.**

re-du-pli-cate (rē-dū′plĭ-kāt), *v.t.* [*p.t.* and *p.p.* -cat″ed, *p.pr.* -cat″ing], to make double; repeat; multiply:—*adj.* (rē-dū′plĭ-kăt), repeated; doubled; multiplied.—*adj.* **re-du′pli-ca-tive.**

re-du-pli-ca-tion (rē-dū″plĭ-kā′shŭn), *n.* **1**, the act of doubling, or state of being doubled; **2**, the formation of a word element by slight variation of another, as in *clink—clank, hum—drum.*

red-wing (rĕd′wĭng″), *n.* **1**, in Europe, a red-winged thrush; **2**, in America, the red-winged blackbird: **red–winged blackbird**, a common American bird related to the orioles and bobolinks, the adult male of which is black with patches of crimson edged with buff on the wings.

red-wood (rĕd′wo͝od″), *n.* **1**, any of various trees having a reddish wood or yielding a red dye; **2**, a very large California tree of the pine family; also, its wood.

re-ëch-o (rē-ĕk′ō), *v.t.* to echo or repeat the sound of again:—*v.i.* to resound; reverberate:—*n.* [*pl.* reëchoes (-ōz)], a repeated echo; second echo.

reed (rēd), *n.* **1**, any of certain tall, coarse grasses that grow in wet places; also, their jointed hollow stems; **2**, a mass of such grasses; **3**, a musical pipe made of a hollow stem of a plant; **4**, a thin, elastic tongue at the opening of a pipe in a musical instrument; **5**, any reed instrument, as a clarinet; **6**, *Poetic*, an arrow.—*adj.* **reed′y.**—*n.* **reed′i-ness.**

reed-bird (rēd′bûrd″), *n.* in the U. S., the bobolink.

¹reef (rēf), *n.* that part of a sail which can be drawn in and secured by small ropes, or reef points, in shortening sail: **reef knot**, a certain kind of knot: the common square knot, used in reefing a sail (see *knot*, illus.): **reef point**, one of the short ropes by means of which the sail is tied into folds or reefs (see *rigging*, illus.):—*v.t.* to reduce (a sail) by drawing in or folding up part of it.

reef (rēf), *n.* a sand bar or shelf of rock lying level with, or just below, the ırface of the water.

eef-er (rēf′ẽr), *n.* **1,** familiarly, a midshipman; **2,** a short, rough, double-reasted jacket.

eek (rēk), *n.* **1,** vapor; steam; a disagreeable odor; **2,** in Scotland, smoke:—*v.i.* to nd out vapor or fumes, usually with a disgreeable odor; as, to *reek* with filth.

reel (rēl), *n.* **1,** any of various devices consisting of a revolving frame for windıg yarn, rope, or the like; **2,** a bobbin; **3,** in ıotion pictures, the amount of film held by ne spool: usually about 1,000 feet:—*v.t.* **1,** to ind on a frame or bobbin; **2,** to draw in by inding; as, to *reel* in fish; **3,** to tell rapidly nd easily: with *off;* as, to *reel* off a long story.

reel (rēl), *v.i.* **1,** to stagger or sway from side to side in walking; **2,** to turn und and round; feel dizzy; as, his head *eled;* **3,** to give way; waver; as, the whole ne of soldiers *reeled:*—*n.* the act of staggering r swaying from side to side.

reel (rēl), *n.* **1,** a lively country or folk dance; **2,** the music for such a dance.

e-ë-lect (rē″ē-lĕkt′), *v.t.* to elect again, as to another term of office.— . **re″ë-lec′tion.**

e-ën-force (rē″ĕn-fōrs′), *v.t.* [*p.t.* and *p.p.* -forced′ (-fōrst′), *p.pr.* orc′ing], **1,** to give new strength to; esp., to rengthen (an army) by bringing up new oops; **2,** to add a strengthening part to: **ëenforced concrete,** artificial stone, or conete, strengthened by bars of steel or steel esh bedded in it. Also, **re″in-force′.**

e-ën-force-ment (rē″ĕn-fōrs′mĕnt), *n.* **1,** the act of rengthening; **2,** the state of being strengthned; **3,** that which strengthens; **4,** in *pl.,* ore troops or ships sent to strengthen a osition. Also, **re″in-force′ment.**

e-ën-ter (rē-ĕn′tẽr), *v.t.* to go or come into again:—*v.i.* to enter a place gain: **reëntering polygon,** a polygon with at ast one side which, if produced, will enter ne surface of the polygon.—*n.* **re-ën′try.**

e-ës-tab-lish (rē″ĕs-tăb′lĭsh), *v.t.* to fix firmly again; settle again; stablish anew.—*n.* **re″ës-tab′lish-ment.**

reeve (rēv), *v.t.* [*p.t.* and *p.p.* rove (rōv) or reeved (rēvd), *p.pr.* reev′ing], , to pass the end of (a rope) through a hole, lock, or ring; **2,** to make fast (a rope), as y reeving; **3,** to run a rope through (a hole), s in a pulley block.

reeve (rēv), *n.* the female of the ruff, a kind of sandpiper.

reeve (rēv), *n.* formerly, in England, a steward; an overseer of an estate.

e-ëx-port (rē″ĕks-pōrt′), *v.t.* to export again, as in the case of somening that has already been imported.—*n.* **:-ëx′port.**—*n.* **re-ëx″por-ta′tion.**

e-fec-tion (rē-fĕk′shŭn), *n.* a light repast or lunch; refreshment.

e-fec-to-ry (rē-fĕk′tō-rĭ), *n.* [*pl.* refectories (-rĭz)], **1,** orig., a dining all in a convent; **2,** a room for refreshments.

e-fer (rē-fûr′), *v.t.* [*p.t.* and *p.p.* -ferred′ (-fûrd′), *p.pr.* -fer′ring], **1,** to submit another person or authority for information r decision; as, they *referred* the question to ne president; **2,** to direct or send for informaon, authority, etc.; as, to *refer* one to the ictionary; **3,** to explain as due to a certain ause; as, to *refer* his actions to ignorance:— *i.* **1,** to direct attention; allude; as, he did ot *refer* to the war; **2,** to appeal; apply; as, e *referred* frequently to his notes; **3,** to point y marks; as, that sign *refers* to a footnote; , to direct one person to another for information or recommendation; as, to *refer* to a former employer.

Syn. attribute, ascribe, point.

ref-er-a-ble (rĕf′ẽr-ȧ-bl), *adj.* capable of being considered as a result of, or related to, something else; assignable. Also, **re-fer′ri-ble** (rē-fûr′ĭ-bl).

ref-er-ee (rĕf″ẽr-ē′), *n.* **1,** one to whom a matter is handed over for decision and settlement; an umpire; **2,** a person before whom a case is tried or to whom a problem is sent by a court to be investigated and decided, or reported to the court:—*v.t.* [*p.t.* and *p.p.* -eed′ (-ēd′), *p.pr.* -ee′ing], to umpire, as a game:—*v.i.* to act as umpire.

ref-er-ence (rĕf′ẽr-ĕns), *n.* **1,** the act of submitting a matter to another to settle, or of consulting an authority for information; **2,** a directing of attention to something; **3,** a passing allusion; **4,** a passage or note in a book or writing directing attention to some other book or passage; also, the book or passage to which attention is directed; **5,** a person to whom inquiries may be directed regarding another person; **6,** a written statement of the ability of a person given by another; **7,** relation; respect; as, with *reference* to your request:—*adj.* suitable to be used in securing information; as, a *reference* library.

ref-er-en-dum (rĕf″ẽr-ĕn′dŭm), *n.* [*pl.* referendums (-dŭmz); referenda (-dȧ)], **1,** the submission of a legislative act to the decision of a vote of the people; **2,** the right possessed by a people so to vote upon a legislative act; **3,** a direct popular vote on a proposed measure.

re-fine (rē-fīn′), *v.t.* [*p.t.* and *p.p.* -fined′ (-fīnd′), *p.pr.* -fīn′ing], **1,** to make pure; cleanse; as, to *refine* sugar; **2,** to clear from dross or worthless matter; as, to *refine* gold; **3,** to free from coarseness or rudeness; educate or improve; as, to *refine* manners or language:—*v.i.* **1,** to become fine or pure; improve in quality; **2,** to grow in delicacy; **3,** to employ fine distinctions, subtleties, or the like, in thought or language.—*n.* **re-fin′er.**

re-fined (rē-fīnd′), *p.adj.* **1,** made pure; **2,** without coarseness; **3,** cultivated; polished; elegant.

re-fine-ment (rē-fīn′mĕnt), *n.* **1,** the act of making pure or free from coarseness; **2,** the state of being pure or free from coarseness; **3,** elegance; finish; also, an instance of these; **4,** purity of taste, mind, morals, style, or the like.

re-fin-er-y (rē-fīn′ẽr-ĭ), *n.* [*pl.* refineries (-ĭz)], a place where anything, as ore, oil, sugar, etc., is refined or made pure.

re-fit (rē-fĭt′), *v.t.* [*p.t.* and *p.p.* -fit′ted, *p.pr.* -fit′ting], **1,** to make ready for use again; **2,** to equip or furnish anew:—*v.i.* **1,** to obtain repairs or fresh supplies: often said of ships; **2,** to be newly equipped.

re-flect (rē-flĕkt′), *v.t.* **1,** to throw back, as rays of light, heat, or sound; **2,** to give back an image of, as does a mirror; as, the brook *reflects* the sky; conduct *reflects* environment; **3,** to give back as a result; as, his act *reflects* honor upon him:—*v.i.* **1,** to throw back rays of light, sound, or the like; **2,** to give back an image; **3,** to consider carefully in the mind; think; **4,** to cast reproach, blame, etc.; as, bad behavior in school *reflects* upon home training.—*n.* **re-flect′er.**

Syn. ponder, muse, meditate, contemplate.

re-flec-tion (rē-flĕk′shŭn), *n.* **1,** the act of returning or throwing back; also, the state of being returned or thrown back; as, the *reflection* of light or sound; **2,** that which is returned or thrown back, as light, heat, or an image; as, your *reflection* in a mirror; **3,** the turning of thought back upon past experiences or ideas; atten-

tive consideration; thought; **4**, the result of meditation; a thought; remark; **5**, criticism; reproach; as, a *reflection* on one's character; **6**, in anatomy and zoölogy, the bending, turning, or folding of a part back on itself: **angle of reflection**, the angle between the direction at which a ray, as of light, is reflected from a surface at a given point, and the perpendicular to the surface at that point: equal to the angle of incidence (see *incidence*, illus.).
Syn. deliberation, meditation, musing.

re-flec-tive (rē-flĕk'tĭv), *adj.* **1**, throwing back light, images, etc., as a mirror; **2**, thoughtful; given to meditation; as, a *reflective* mind.—*adv.* **re-flec'tive-ly.**—*n.* **re-flec'tive-ness.**

re-flec-tor (rē-flĕk'tẽr), *n.* **1**, anything that sends back, or reflects, light, sound, heat, etc.; specif., a polished, usually concave, surface, as of metal; **2**, a reflecting telescope.

re-flex (rē'flĕks), *n.* **1**, reflection, as of light, sound, or color; **2**, an image of an object, as a reflection in a mirror; **3**, an involuntary movement of some part of the body due to a stimulus:—*adj.* **1**, reflected, as light or color; **2**, coming by way of return or reflection; as, a *reflex* influence; **3**, of thought, tending to turn back upon the mind or its operations; **4**, in physiology, pertaining to, or caused by, some stimulus independent of consciousness or will; as, *reflex* action: **reflex action**, involuntary action of certain muscles, organs, etc., occurring when the excitation of a sensory nerve is transmitted to a nerve center, and thence reflected along an efferent nerve to the muscle or organ in question, the response of which is often unconscious: **reflex angle**, an angle greater than 180 degrees (see [1]*angle*, illus.):—*v.t.* (rē-flĕks'), to bend or fold back.—*p.adj.* **re-flexed'.**

re-flex-ive (rē-flĕk'sĭv), *adj.* in grammar, pertaining to action of a subject upon itself; as, a *reflexive* construction: **reflexive pronoun**, a pronoun that, when used as an object, denotes the same person or thing as the subject: in English, ending in *-self* or *-selves:* **reflexive verb**, a verb whose object denotes the same person or thing as its subject, as in *he seated himself.*—*adv.* **re-flex'ive-ly.**

ref-lu-ent (rĕf'lo͞o-ĕnt), *adj.* returning, as the tide to the sea; ebbing; surging back.—*n.* **ref'lu-ence.**

re-flux (rē'flŭks), *n.* a flowing back; ebb, as of the tide:—*adj.* flowing back.

re-for-est (rē-fŏr'ĕst), *v.t.* to plant anew (deforested land) with trees:—*v.i.* to set out trees again.—*n.* **re-for"est-a'tion.**

re-form (rē-fôrm'), *n.* **1**, a change for the better; the removal of some evil or abuse; also, an instance of this; **2**, a change from an evil to an upright character:—*v.t.* **1**, to change into another and better form; as, Gregory *reformed* the calendar; **2**, to make better by the removal of faults or abuses; as, to *reform* the courts; **3**, to correct or put an end to, as abuses; **4**, to induce (a person) to abandon an evil course of conduct:—*v.i.* to give up evil for that which is good.
Syn., v. reclaim, rectify, mend.

ref-or-ma-tion (rĕf"ŏr-mā'shŭn), *n.* **1**, alteration to a better form; **2**, a radical change for the better in social, political, or religious affairs: **Reformation**, the great religious movement begun by Martin Luther in the 16th century, resulting in the formation of the Protestant churches.

re-form-a-tive (rē-fôr'mȧ-tĭv), *adj.* **1**, having the power of forming again; **2**, tending to improve.

re-form-a-to-ry (rē-fôr'mȧ-tō-rĭ), *n.* [*pl.* reformatories (-rĭz)], an institution or school for correcting and improving the habits and conduct, esp. of youn offenders:—*adj.* tending to correct.

re-formed (rē-fôrmd'), *p.adj.* amended c changed for the better; im proved in character or morals: **Reforme Churches**, those Protestant churches whic originated in the 16th century.

re-form-er (rē-fôr'mẽr), *n.* **1**, one wh carries out or urges a chang for the better; **2**, one of the leaders of th great religious movement of the 16th century

re-fract (rē-frăkt'), *v.t.* to bend from straight line; as, to *refract* ray of light.—*adj.* **re-frac'tive.**—*n.* **re-frac'tor.**

re-frac-tion (rē-frăk'shŭn), *n.* the chang of direction of a ray of ligh in passing obliquely from one medium to ar other of different density, as from air into glas

re-frac-to-ry (rē-frăk'tō-rĭ), *adj.* **1**, dis obedient; stubborn; har to manage; as, a *refractory* boy; **2**, resistin heat; hard to work or fuse; as, *refractory* ore —*adv.* **re-frac'to-ri-ly.**—*n.* **re-frac'to-ri-ness.**

[1]**re-frain** (rē-frān'), *n.* a phrase or vers repeated at intervals, esp. at th end of each stanza of a poem or song; also, th musical setting for these words.

[2]**re-frain** (rē-frān'), *v.i.* to hold onese back; forbear: usually with *from*
Syn. abstain, withhold, cease.—*Ant.* con tinue, persist, persevere.

re-fran-gi-ble (rē-frăn'jĭ-bl), *adj.* capa ble of being bent from straight line, as rays of light.—*n.* **re-fran'gi ble-ness.**—*n.* **re-fran"gi-bil'i-ty.**

re-fresh (rē-frĕsh'), *v.t.* **1**, to make fres again; **2**, to revive after fatigue **3**, to quicken; as, to *refresh* the memory.
Syn. invigorate, recreate, enliven, strengther

re-fresh-ing (rē-frĕsh'ĭng), *p.adj.* **1**, reviv ing or making fresh again as, a *refreshing* nap; **2**, cooling; as, a *refresh ing* drink.—*adv.* **re-fresh'ing-ly.**

re-fresh-ment (rē-frĕsh'mĕnt), *n.* **1**, th act of reviving, or sta of being revived; restoration of strength, live liness, etc.; **2**, that which restores or revive esp. food, drink, or rest; **3**, in *pl.*, food an drink served to guests, as at a reception.

re-frig-er-ant (rē-frĭj'ẽr-ănt), *n.* **1**, any thing that makes cool, a cooling drink or a medicine that lessen fever; **2**, a substance, as liquid air, tha reduces the temperature below freezing:—*adj.* cooling; reducing fever or heat.

re-frig-er-ate (rē-frĭj'ẽr-āt), *v.t.* [*p.t.* an *p.p.* -at"ed, *p.pr.* -at"ing to cool or keep cool, as in an ice box.—*adj.* **re frig'er-a-tive.**—*adj.* and *n.* **re-frig'er-a-to-ry.**

re-frig-er-a-tion (rē-frĭj"ẽr-ā'shŭn), *n* the act of cooling, c the state of being cooled, to a low temperature

re-frig-er-a-tor (rē-frĭj'ẽr-ā"tẽr), *n.* a re ceptacle, a chest, c a room, where food and other perishabl things are kept cool by ice, cold air, c other means.

ref-uge (rĕf'ūj), *n.* **1**, a place of safety fron trouble or danger; a shelter c secure retreat; **2**, one who or that which pr tects or defends from danger or misfortune.
Syn. protection, harbor, cover.

ref-u-gee (rĕf"ū-jē'), *n.* **1**, one who flee for protection, esp. from poli ical or religious persecution, to a foreign lanc **2**, one who escapes from an invading army.

re-ful-gence (rē-fŭl'jĕns), *n.* brightness flood of light; radiance splendor. Also, **re-ful'gen-cy.**

re-ful-gent (rē-fŭl'jĕnt), *adj.* casting brilliant light; splendid.—*adv.* **re-ful'gent-ly.**—*n.* **re-ful'gent-ness.**
Syn. flashing, bright, radiant.

re-fund (rē-fŭnd'), *v.t.* to give back or pay back, as a loan or debt:—*v.i.* to ve back or pay back money.

re-fund (rē-fŭnd'), *v.t.* to discharge, as a loan, through credit secured by a ew loan; as, to *refund* a national debt.

e-fus-al (rē-fūz'ăl), *n.* **1**, the act of rejecting or denying; rejection or enial of anything offered or asked; **2**, the ght to refuse or take before others; as, to ave the *refusal* of an office.

re-fuse (rē-fūz'), *v.t.* [*p.t.* and *p.p.* -fused' (-fūzd'), *p.pr.* -fus'ing], **1**, to deine to take; be unwilling to accept; **2**, to ecline to do or grant; deny; as, to *refuse* aid; , to decline to undergo; as, to *refuse* a responbility:—*v.i.* to decline to take an offer, or the ke, or to do or grant a thing.—*n.* **re-fus'er.**
Syn. reject, renounce, repel.—*Ant.* accept, ssent, admit, acknowledge.

ref-use (rĕf'ūs), *n.* waste material; trash; rubbish:—*adj.* worthless.
Syn., *n.* dregs, sediment, scum, leavings.

ef-u-ta-tion (rĕf"ū-tā'shŭn), *n.* **1**, the act of proving false; **2**, that hich is proved false; **3**, the act of disproving; conclusive answer to an argument.

e-fute (rē-fūt'), *v.t.* [*p.t.* and *p.p.* -fut'ed, *p.pr.* -fut'ing], **1**, to prove to be lse or wrong; **2**, to overthrow by argument : proof; disprove.—*adj.* **re-fut'a-ble.**—*adv.* **e-fut'a-bly.**

'e-gain (rē-gān'), *v.t.* **1**, to get back; as, to *regain* lost health; **2**, to reach gain; as, they at last *regained* the shore.

'e-gal (rē'găl), *adj.* **1**, fit for, or like, a king; royal; **2**, hence, splendid or stately. —*adv.* **re'gal-ly.**

'e-gale (rē-gāl'), *v.t.* [*p.t.* and *p.p.* -galed' (-gāld'), *p.pr.* -gal'ing], to enterain in a regal manner; feast:—*v.i.* to feast.

e-ga-li-a (rē-gā'lĭ-ȧ), *n.pl.* **1**, the emblems of royalty, as the crown, scepter, tc.; **2**, personal decorations of an order or ffice, as of the Freemasons.

e-gal-i-ty (rē-găl'ĭ-tĭ), *n.* [*pl.* regalities (-tĭz)], **1**, sovereignty; royalty; , a country subject to royal authority.

'e-gard (rē-gärd'), *n.* **1**, affection; respect; **2**, consideration; care; **3**, close ttention or notice; a look or gaze; **4**, refernce; **5**, in *pl.*, good wishes:—*v.t.* **1**, to observe losely; look upon attentively; as, she *rearded* him with a frown; **2**, to consider; as, I *egard* her as an enemy; **3**, to heed; respect; s, *regard* my words; **4**, to esteem; care for; s, I *regard* him highly; **5**, to relate to; conern; as, the matter *regards* your happiness; , to take into account:—*v.i.* **1**, to look at a hing with care; **2**, to give heed; take notice.
Syn., *n.* esteem, respect. *Regard* denotes igh opinion deepened by affection. *Esteem* uggests good opinion, based on mental valuaion, and tinged with interest or approval. *Respect* means deference given without any eeling of personal favor.

'e-gard-ful (rē-gärd'fōōl), *adj.* **1**, taking notice; heedful; **2**, respectul.—*adv.* **re-gard'ful-ly.**—*n.* **re-gard'ful-ness.**

'e-gard-ing (rē-gärd'ĭng), *prep.* concerning; about; in respect to.

'e-gard-less (rē-gärd'lĕs), *adj.* heedless; careless; negligent.

'e-gat-ta (rē-găt'ȧ), *n.* a boat race or series of boat races.

'e-gen-cy (rē'jĕn-sĭ), *n.* [*pl.* regencies (-sĭz)], **1**, the office of a ruler; uthority; **2**, the office, government, or authorty of a ruler or body of rulers, acting for a ime in the name and place of another; **3**, a body of rulers acting for another; **4**, the eriod of government of, or territory govrned by, a ruler who acts for another.

re-gen-er-a-cy (rē-jĕn'ẽr-ȧ-sĭ), *n.* the state of being reformed, restored, or renewed; moral improvement.

re-gen-er-ate (rē-jĕn'ẽr-āt), *v.t.* [*p.t.* and *p.p.* -at"ed, *p.pr.* -at"ing], **1**, in theology, to renew spiritually; **2**, to make a change for the better in; **3**, to produce anew; fill with new life or power:—*adj.* (rē-jĕn'ẽr-ât), **1**, having new life; **2**, in theology, born again spiritually.—*adj.* **re-gen'er-a-tive.**

re-gen-er-a-tion (rē-jĕn"ẽr-ā'shŭn), *n.* **1**, the act of renewing or reforming; **2**, the state of being renewed or reformed; **3**, in theology, the new birth of spiritual life; **4**, in biology, the forming of new tissue to replace that which has been lost; **5**, in radio, the building up of the strength of a radio signal in a three-tube radio receiver.

re-gen-er-a-tor (rē-jĕn'ẽr-ā"tẽr), *n.* **1**, one who reforms or renews; **2**, a device, as in a furnace, to save the heat of escaping gases; **3**, a furnace with this device.

re-gent (rē'jĕnt), *n.* **1**, one who governs during the youth, absence, or unfitness of the rightful ruler; **2**, in certain universities, a member of a controlling board; **3**, in some states of the U. S., a member of a board of directors who establish requirements and maintain standards in education:—*adj.* ruling in place of another; as, prince *regent.*—*n.* **re'gent-ship.**

reg-i-cide (rĕj'ĭ-sīd), *n.* the murder or murderer of a king; as, the *regicide* of Charles I.—*adj.* **reg'i-cid"al.**

***ré-gime** (rā"zhēm'), [Fr.], *n.* mode, system, or rule of management or government, social or political. Also, **regime'** (rā-zhēm').

reg-i-men (rĕj'ĭ-mĕn), *n.* **1**, orderly government; control; **2**, a systematic course of diet, exercise, sleep, and general habits, prescribed for some special purpose; **3**, in grammar, the influencing of the form of one word by another.

reg-i-ment (rĕj'ĭ-mĕnt), *n.* an organized body of soldiers under the command of a colonel.

reg-i-men-tal (rĕj"ĭ-mĕn'tăl), *adj.* pertaining to a regiment, or the body of troops under a colonel; as, *regimental* quarters:—*n.*, in *pl.*, the uniforms worn by the troops of a regiment.

re-gion (rē'jŭn), *n.* **1**, an indefinitely large section of land; a country or district; **2**, a division or part of the body; as, in the *region* of the heart.—*adj.* **re'gion-al.**

reg-is-ter (rĕj'ĭs-tẽr), *n.* **1**, an official written record; also, the book containing such record, or an entry in it; **2**, one who or that which records; **3**, a device for regulating the entrance of heated air to an apartment; **4**, the compass or range of a voice or of an instrument; **5**, in printing: **a**, the correct placing of one color upon another, or the correct relative spacing of colors; **b**, the placing of the type pages exactly opposite each other on both sides of a sheet:—*v.t.* **1**, to enter in a list or formal record; enroll; record; as, to *register* securities; **2**, to mark a record of; as, the thermostat *registers* 60 degrees; **3**, in motion pictures, to indicate by facial expression; as, to *register* surprise:—*v.i.* **1**, to write one's name in a list or record; **2**, in printing, to be in correct alignment; be in register; **3**, *Colloq.*, to make an impression.

reg-is-trar (rĕj'ĭs-trär), *n.* **1**, an official who keeps records; **2**, esp., a secretary or official who keeps the records in a college or university.

reg-is-tra-tion (rĕj"ĭs-trā'shŭn), *n.* **1**, the act of entering in a record; as, the *registration* of a mortgage; **2**, enrollment; as, a large *registration* of voters.

reg-is-try (rĕj′ĭs-trĭ), *n.* [*pl.* registries (-trĭz)], **1**, the act of entering on a record; **2**, a written account or record, as of births, deaths, etc.; **3**, the place where such a record is kept.

reg-nant (rĕg′nănt), *adj.* **1**, reigning; exercising royal authority; as, a queen *regnant;* **2**, prevailing, as a fashion.

re-gress (rē′grĕs), *n.* **1**, a passage back; way of return; as, a place which offers no *regress;* **2**, the power or privilege of returning; as, the right of free egress and *regress:*—*v.i.* (rē-grĕs′), to go back; return.—*n.* **re-gres′sion.**—*adj.* **re-gres′sive.**

re-gret (rē-grĕt′), *n.* **1**, sorrow for the loss or want of something; as, *regret* for vanished youth; **2**, moral distress; mild remorse; as, *regret* for harsh words; **3**, uneasiness; vexation; as, I hear with *regret* that you will not come; **4**, in *pl.*, *Colloq.*, a polite expression of refusal, as in answer to an invitation:—*v.t.* [*p.t.* and *p.p.* -gret′ted, *p.pr.* -gret′ting], **1**, to remember with distress; wish to amend (something past); **2**, to feel sorry for the want of; as, what we lose, we *regret.*

re-gret-ful (rē-grĕt′fo͝ol), *adj.* **1**, remembering with distress; feeling sorry for the loss or want of; **2**, discontented.—*adv.* **re-gret′ful-ly.**—*n.* **re-gret′ful-ness.**

re-gret-ta-ble (rē-grĕt′ȧ-bl), *adj.* fit to cause distress or sorrow; as, a *regrettable* accident.—*adv.* **re-gret′ta-bly.**

reg-u-lar (rĕg′ū-lȧr), *adj.* **1**, according to rule, order, or established custom; as, *regular* habits; a *regular* meeting; **2**, following a certain law, plan, type, etc.; as, *regular* features; **3**, pertaining to the standing army; permanent; as, *regular* troops; **4**, belonging to a religious order; as, *regular* clergy; **5**, *Colloq.*, thorough; genuine; as, she is a *regular* bookworm; **6**, in grammar, following the usual form of declension, comparison, or conjugation; **7**, in geometry, of a polygon, having all sides equal and all angles equal: **regular army,** the standing army of a nation, as distinguished from the militia, volunteers, etc.:—*n.* **1**, a soldier belonging to a standing army; **2**, a member of the clergy who belongs to a religious order.—*adv.* **reg′u-lar-ly.**—*n.* **reg′u-lar-ness.**

Syn., adj. normal, typical, customary, ordinary.—*Ant., adj.* irregular, abnormal.

reg-u-lar-i-ty (rĕg″ū-lăr′ĭ-tĭ), *n.* **1**, the state or quality of complying with an established order or custom; **2**, conformity to a law, plan, type, etc.; as, the engine runs with great *regularity.*

reg-u-late (rĕg′ū-lāt), *v.t.* [*p.t.* and *p.p.* -lat″ed, *p.pr.* -lat″ing], **1**, to keep in proper order; **2**, to adapt to, or govern by, rule, method, or certain standard laws; as, to *regulate* one's conduct; **3**, to adjust to some standard condition; as, to *regulate* a clock.—*adj.* **reg′u-la-tive.**

Syn. direct, manage, rule.

reg-u-la-tion (rĕg″ū-lā′shŭn), *n.* **1**, the act of adjusting, or the state of being adjusted, according to a rule, method, or law; **2**, a rule, direction, or law by which to govern or manage; as, government *regulation* of the railroads.

reg-u-la-tor (rĕg′ū-lā″tẽr), *n.* **1**, one who or that which controls or governs in accordance with rules; **2**, a device for controlling motion; as, the *regulator* of a clock or watch (see illus. next column); **3**, a clock of finest mechanism and accuracy, used as a standard of time.

Reg-u-lus (rĕg′ū-lŭs), *n.* a brilliant white star in the constellation Leo.

re-gur-gi-tate (rē-gûr′jĭ-tāt), *v.t.* and *v.i.* [*p.t.* and *p.p.* -tat″ed, *p.pr.* -tat″ing], to pour, gush, or throw forth or out again, esp. from the stomach; as, t*o* *regurgitate* food; blood *regurgitates* to th*e* heart.—*n.* **re-gur″gi-ta′tion.**

re-ha-bil-i-tate (rē″hȧ-bĭl′ĭ-tāt), *v.t.* [*p.*t. and *p.p.* -tat′ed, *p.p*r. -tat″ing], **1**, to restore to a former state, rank or privilege; reinstate; **2**, to clear the char acter or reputation of.—*n.* **re″ha-bil″i-ta′tion**

re-hash (rē-hăsh′; rē′hăsh″), *n.* somethin*g* made over into a new form; as a *rehash* of an old story:—*v.t.* (rē-hăsh′), t*o* prepare or use again; work over into a ne*w* form, as the plot of a story.

re-hears-al (rē-hûr′săl), *n.* **1**, a privat*e* recital or practice before a public performance; as, the *rehearsal* of a play; **2**, a telling over, as of one's experiences.

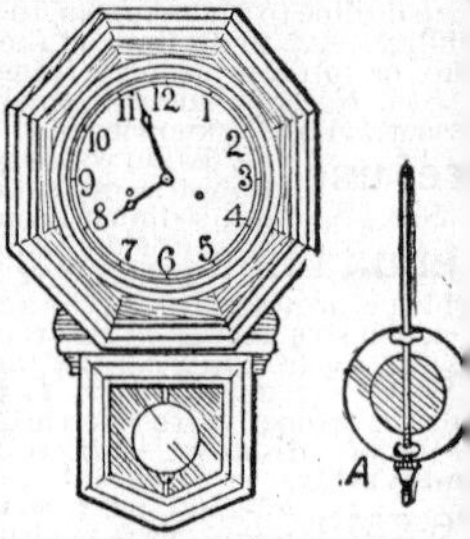

REGULATOR

Showing back view (A) o*f* weight and mechanism for ad*-*justing length of pendulum.

re-hearse (ré-hûrs′), *v.t.* [*p.t.* and *p.p.* -hearsed′ (-hûrst′), *p.pr.* -hears′ing], **1**, to repeat, as what has already been said or written; tell over; **2**, to go over item by item; enumerate; **3**, to practice in private before a public performance; as, to *rehearse* a play:—*v.i.* to repeat something for practice.

Re-ho-bo-am (rē″hō-bō′ăm), *n.* a Hebre*w* king, son of Solomon.

rei (rā; rē), *n.* **1**, in Portugal, a money o*f* account worth about $\frac{1}{10}$ of a cent; **2**, i*n* Brazil, a money of account worth about $\frac{1}{8}$ o*f* a cent. Also, **ree.**

***Reichs-mark** (rīkhs′märk″), [Ger.], *n* a coin and the monetar*y* unit of Germany, established in 1924, equiva lent to about 23.8 cents.

***Reichs-rath** (rīkhs′rät″), [Ger.], *n.* th*e* legislature, or chief law making body, of Austria, under the dua*l* monarchy of Austria-Hungary.

***Reichs-tag** (rīkhs′täkh″), [Ger.], *n* **1**, an imperial parliament the chief deliberative body in certain coun tries of Europe; **2**, the lower house of th*e* German legislature before 1918; **3**, since 1918 the national parliament of Germany; **4**, th*e* national parliament of Hungary under th*e* dual monarchy of Austria-Hungary.

reign (rān), *n.* **1**, supreme rule; roya*l* power; **2**, the time during which a ruler holds sway; **3**, prevailing control o*r* influence; as, the *reign* of law: **Reign o*f* Terror,** the fourth year of the French Revolu tion, characterized by wholesale slaughter o*f* all opponents of the extreme revolutionar*y* party:—*v.i.* **1**, to exercise royal authority rule; **2**, to hold sway; hence, to prevail, as a plague, fear, or the like.

re-im-burse (rē″ĭm-bûrs′), *v.t.* [*p.t.* an*d* *p.p.* -bursed′ (-bûrst′), *p.p*r. -burs′ing], **1**, to refund or pay back, as int*o* the treasury of a country; **2**, to cause to re ceive an amount equal to something spent; re pay (a person); as, to *reimburse* him for his los*s* of time.—*n.* **re″im-burse′ment.**

Syn. repay, compensate, indemnify.

rein (rān), *n.* **1**, usually in *pl.*, a leathe*r* strap fastened to the side of the bit o*f* a horse or other animal as a means of guidin*g* and controlling it; **2**, usually in *pl.*, any means of restraint or control; as, the *reins* of government:—*v.t.* to hold in, direct, or stop, by means of reins; restrain; control.

re-in-car-nate (rē″ĭn-kär′nāt), *v.t.* [*p.t.* and *p.p.* -nat″ed, *p.pr.* -nat″ing], to cause to take a new form or embodiment in flesh; invest anew in bodily form.—*n.* **re-in″car-na′tion.**

rein-deer (rān′dēr″), *n.* [*pl.* reindeer], any of several kinds of large deer found in the northern parts of America, Europe, and Asia.

REINDEER

re-in-force (rē″ĭn-fōrs′), *v.t.* [*p.t.* and *p.p.* -forced′ (-fōrst′), *p.pr.* -forc′ing], to give new strength to; support; strengthen, as an army with more troops. See **re″ën-force′**, *Pfd. S.*—*n.* **re″in-force′ment.**

reins (rānz), *n.pl. Archaic*, **1**, the kidneys; also, the loins: formerly supposed to be the seat of the affections and feelings; **2**, hence, the emotions and affections themselves; as, try my *reins* and my heart.

re-in-state (rē″ĭn-stāt′), *v.t.* [*p.t.* and *p.p.* -stat′ed, *p.pr.* -stat′ing], **1**, to restore to a former state, station, or authority; **2**, to repair; replace, as damaged property, instead of paying its value: used esp. in fire insurance.—*n.* **re″in-state′ment.**

re-is-sue (rē-ĭsh′ū), *v.t.* [*p.t.* and *p.p.* -sued (-ūd), *p.pr.* -su-ing], to send or give out again officially or publicly; republish; as, to *reissue* an edict:—*v.i.* to go forth again:—*n.* **1**, a second publication; **2**, another issue; as, a *reissue* of paper money.

re-it-er-ate (rē-ĭt′ẽr-āt), *v.t.* [*p.t.* and *p.p.* -at″ed, *p.pr.* -at″ing], to do or say again and again.—*n.* **re-it″er-a′tion.**

re-it-er-a-tive (rē-ĭt′ẽr-ā-tĭv), *n.* **1**, a word formed by reduplication, or repeating all or part of another word, as *pell-mell;* **2**, in Latin grammar, a word, esp. a verb, which by its form expresses repetition of action.

re-ject (rē-jĕkt′), *v.t.* **1**, to throw away as worthless; discard; as, to *reject* waste matter; **2**, to refuse to take; decline; as, to *reject* a gift; **3**, to refuse to grant or agree to; as, to *reject* a suggestion; **4**, to refuse to receive (a person); also, to refuse to marry.—*n.* **re-ject′er; re-jec′tor.**

re-jec-tion (rē-jĕk′shŭn), *n.* **1**, the act of refusing; **2**, the state of being refused; **3**, that which is rejected.

re-joice (rē-jois′), *v.i.* [*p.t.* and *p.p.* -joiced′ (-joist′), *p.pr.* -joic′ing], to feel or express joy or gladness; exult: often followed by *at* or *in:*—*v.t.* to make joyful; gladden.

re-joic-ing (rē-jois′ĭng), *n.* **1**, a feeling of joy or gladness, or its expression in words or actions; festivity; **2**, *Rare*, the reason for joy or gladness.

re-join (rē-join′), *v.t.* **1**, to return to after separation; as, to *rejoin* friends; **2**, to answer:—*v.i.* to answer to a reply.

re-join-der (rē-join′dẽr), *n.* **1**, an answer, esp. one made to a reply; **2**, a retort; **3**, in law, the defendant's reply to the plaintiff's statements.

re-ju-ve-nate (rē-jōō′vē-nāt), *v.t.* [*p.t.* and *p.p.* -nat″ed, *p.pr.* -nat″ing], to renew the youth of; cause to feel young again.—*n.* **re-ju″ve-na′tion.**

re-ju-ve-nes-cence (rē-jōō″vē-nĕs′-ĕns), *n.* a state of feeling or seeming young again; renewal of youth.—*adj.* **re-ju″ve-nes′cent.**

re-lapse (rē-lăps′), *n.* **1**, a slipping or sliding back; **2**, a falling into a former bad state or habit; **3**, the return of a disease after partial recovery:—*v.i.* [*p.t.* and *p.p.* -lapsed′ (-lăpst′), *p.pr.* -laps′ing], **1**, to slip or slide back; **2**, to return to a former bad state or habit; **3**, to fall back into illness after a state of partial recovery.

re-late (rē-lāt′), *v.t.* [*p.t.* and *p.p.* -lat′ed, *p.pr.* -lat′ing], **1**, to tell, as a story; recite; narrate; **2**, to show a connection between; as, to *relate* poetry and art; **3**, to establish a relation between, as by blood or marriage:—*v.i.* to refer: with *to.*—*p.adj.* **re-lat′ed.**—*n.* **re-lat′er.**

re-la-tion (rē-lā′shŭn), *n.* **1**, the act of narrating or telling; **2**, the thing narrated or told; **3**, mutual connection between two or more things; interdependence; as, the *relation* between production cost and selling price; **4**, the basis of association in business or social matters; as, a pleasant *relation* between partners; strained *relations;* **5**, reference; respect; as, in *relation* to; **6**, a proportion or ratio; **7**, connection by birth or marriage; **8**, a relative; kinsman or kinswoman; **9**, in *pl.*, dealings; affairs; as, foreign *relations.*—*adj.* **re-la′tion-al.**

re-la-tion-ship (rē-lā′shŭn-shĭp), *n.* the state of being connected by blood or otherwise.

rel-a-tive (rĕl′ȧ-tĭv), *n.* **1**, that which refers to, or is thought of in its connection with, something else; **2**, a person connected with another by blood or marriage; a kinsman; **3**, in grammar, a word which refers to an antecedent; as, the pronouns *who, which, that*, are *relatives:*—*adj.* **1**, having or expressing connection with, or reference to, something; as, their conversation was *relative* to business; **2**, comparative; as, the *relative* value of two things; **3**, having meaning only in connection with something else; as, *large* and *small* are *relative* terms; **4**, in grammar, referring to an antecedent, as a pronoun. —*adv.* **rel′a-tive-ly.**—*n.* **rel′a-tive-ness.**

rel-a-tiv-i-ty (rĕl″ȧ-tĭv′ĭ-tĭ), *n.* **1**, the state or quality of being connected with, or of having reference to, something else; **2**, in physics, relationship to other objects or systems; specif., a theory elaborated by Einstein, which maintains that all statements of physical laws take exactly the same form in all systems of reference in whatever way such systems may be moving relatively to one another.

re-la-tor (rē-lā′tẽr), *n.* one who tells or recounts; a relater.

re-lax (rē-lăks′), *v.t.* **1**, to slacken; make less tight or firm; as, to *relax* one's hold; **2**, to render less strict, harsh, or severe; as, to *relax* punishment; **3**, to relieve from strain; ease, as the mind; **4**, to loosen, as the bowels:—*v.i.* **1**, to become less tight or firm; as, his hold *relaxed;* **2**, to become less severe, as, to *relax* in discipline; **3**, to cease effort; unbend; lessen tension; rest; as, to *relax* after the day's labor.

re-lax-a-tion (rē″lăk-sā′shŭn; rĕl″ăk-), *n.* **1**, the act of loosening, easing, or making less severe; **2**, the state of being loosened, eased, or made less severe; **3**, a lessening of tension or restraint; **4**, diversion or recreation.

[1]**re-lay** (rē-lā′; rē′lā), *n.* **1**, a supply of fresh men, horses, or the like, held ready to replace or relieve others, usually at a given time or place; **2**, the place at which such a relief is to be found; **3**, in general, a supply of anything laid up or kept in store for relief or fresh supply from time to time; **4**, in

electricity, a device by which the opening or closing of one circuit opens or closes another; **5**, in the army, a small detachment of automobiles or of men who carry messages between distant places: **relay race**, a race in which a series of contestants succeed one another, each covering a definite part of the course:—*v.t.* **1**, to send by relay; as, to *relay* a message across the border; **2**, to provide with relays:—*v.i.* to obtain a fresh supply, as of horses or men.

²re-lay (rē-lā′), *v.t.* [*p.t.* and *p.p.* -laid′ (-lād′), *p.pr.* -lay′ing], to lay again; as, to *relay* a wall.

re-lease (rē-lēs′), *n.* **1**, the act of setting free; **2**, the state of being set free; **3**, deliverance from pain, anxiety, distress, etc.; **4**, a freeing from an obligation or penalty; as, *release* from debt:—*v.t.* [*p.t.* and *p.p.* -leased′ (-lēst′), *p.pr.* -leas′ing], **1**, to set free; as, to *release* a man from prison; **2**, to free from obligation or penalty; as, to *release* a person from debt; **3**, to deliver from pain, care, etc.; **4**, to permit the showing or sale of, as a film; **5**, in law, to give up title to.

Syn., *v.* discharge, liberate, acquit.

rel-e-gate (rĕl′ē-gāt), *v.t.* [*p.t.* and *p.p.* -gat″ed, *p.pr.* -gat″ing], **1**, to send away; **2**, to remove, usually to a worse or less desirable place or situation; as, to *relegate* furniture to the attic.

rel-e-ga-tion (rĕl″ē-gā′shŭn), *n.* **1**, the act of banishing or of removing to a worse position; **2**, the state of being banished or removed; removal; exile.

re-lent (rē-lĕnt′), *v.i.* to become less hard, severe, or cruel; become more gentle; feel pity; yield.

re-lent-less (rē-lĕnt′lĕs), *adj.* without sympathy; indifferent to the pain of others; pitiless.—*adv.* **re-lent′less-ly.**—*n.* **re-lent′less-ness.**

Syn. austere, grim, harsh, merciless.

rel-e-vance (rĕl′ē-văns), *n.* the quality or state of bearing upon, or properly applying to, the case in hand; fitness. Also, **rel′e-van-cy.**

rel-e-vant (rĕl′ē-vănt), *adj.* having to do with, or relating to, the case in hand; pertinent; as, a *relevant* question.—*adv.* **rel′e-vant-ly.**

Syn. fit, proper, suitable, appropriate.

re-li-a-bil-i-ty (rē-lī″ȧ-bĭl′ĭ-tĭ), *n.* the state or quality of being trustworthy or fit to be depended upon.

re-li-a-ble (rē-lī′ȧ-bl), *adj.* trustworthy; fit to be depended upon.—*adv.* **re-li′a-bly.**—*n.* **re-li′a-ble-ness.**

re-li-ance (rē-lī′ăns), *n.* **1**, the act of trusting or depending; **2**, the state of being confident or dependent; confidence; trust; dependence; **3**, that on which one depends; foundation for trust.

re-li-ant (rē-lī′ănt), *adj.* trusting; having confidence; dependent.

rel-ic (rĕl′ĭk), *n.* **1**, that which is left after the loss or decay of the rest; a trace or memorial, as of a custom, period, people, etc.; as, the weapon was a *relic* of the stone age; **2**, anything held in religious reverence, as the remains of a martyr or saint; **3**, a keepsake; souvenir.

rel-ict (rĕl′ĭkt), *n.* a widow or widower; esp., a widow.

re-lief (rē-lēf′), *n.* **1**, the removal in whole or in part of pain, grief, want, etc.; also, the feeling caused by such removal; **2**, that which aids or relieves; **3**, release from some post of duty; **4**, charitable help given to the poor; also, help given in time of danger or difficulty; **5**, fresh supplies of men, animals, food, etc., esp. fresh troops, coming to take the place of those tired out in action; **6**, the elevation of a sculptured design from a plane surface; as, the figures carved in *relief* on old furniture; **7**, in painting and drawing, the effect of standing out from the surface, given to objects in the picture by shadows, colors, etc.; hence, a vivid contrast between a figure and its background; **8**, in physical geography, the elevations and depressions of land surface.

Syn. succor, aid, assistance; redress.

re-lieve (rē-lēv′), *v.t.* [*p.t.* and *p.p.* -lieved′ (-lēvd′), *p.pr.* -liev′ing], **1**, to remove; reduce in severity; lessen, as pain; **2**, to free from suffering, distress, or the like, as, to *relieve* an anxious mind; **3**, to release from a post, duty, or from action, as a patrol; **4**, to set off; bring out by contrast; as, a touch of red will *relieve* the black; **5**, to break the monotony of; vary; as, her visit *relieved* the lonely hours.—*adj.* **re-liev′a-ble.**

Syn. ease, assuage, allay, lighten.

re-li-gion (rē-lĭj′ŭn), *n.* **1**, the recognition of man's relation to a divine or supernatural power to whom obedience and honor are due; **2**, the acts and practices of life that grow out of the recognition of such a relation; **3**, any system of faith and worship; as, the *religion* of the Greeks; **4**, specif., conformity to the teachings of the Bible; Christian faith and practice.

re-li-gion-ist (rē-lĭj′ŭn-ĭst), *n.* **1**, one devoted to a religion; **2**, a religious zealot or fanatic: usually unfavorable.—*n.* **re-li′gion-ism.**

re-li-gious (rē-lĭj′ŭs), *adj.* **1**, feeling, and living in accordance with, a belief in a divine power to whom honor and obedience are due; devout; pious; **2**, pertaining to, or set apart for, religion, as a school; teaching religion, as a book; **3**, bound by monastic vows; **4**, strict; conscientious; as, with *religious* care:—*n.* one who is bound by monastic vows.—*adv.* **re-li′gious-ly.**—*n.* **re-li′gious-ness.**

re-lin-quish (rē-lĭng′kwĭsh), *v.t.* **1**, to retire from; give up using or having; leave; as, to *relinquish* one's position; **2**, to cease to demand; surrender, as a claim. —*n.* **re-lin′quish-er.**—*n.* **re-lin′quish-ment.**

Syn. resign, forsake, forgo, abandon.

rel-i-qua-ry (rĕl′ĭ-kwā-rĭ), *n.* [*pl.* reliquaries (-rĭz)], a casket or shrine in which relics are kept.

rel-ish (rĕl′ĭsh), *n.* **1**, a taste or preference; fondness; eager appreciation: usually with *for;* as, a *relish* for food; **2**, flavor, esp. when pleasing; as, that wine has a delightful *relish;* **3**, the quality that makes a thing pleasurable; as, novelty gave *relish* to the journey; **4**, something taken with food to make it more enjoyable, as a sauce; **5**, a slight amount; a dash; as, his act had a *relish* of treason:—*v.t.* **1**, to give flavor to; as, salt *relishes* meat; **2**, to like the taste of; enjoy; as, he *relishes* his dinner:—*v.i.* to have a pleasing taste.

re-load (rē-lōd′), *v.t.* **1**, to load again, as a wagon; **2**, to charge anew or repeatedly, as a gun.

re-luc-tance (rē-lŭk′tăns), *n.* unwillingness; disinclination; aversion. Also, **re-luc′tan-cy.**

re-luc-tant (rē-lŭk′tănt), *adj.* **1**, unwilling; disinclined; as, *reluctant* to leave; **2**, marked by unwillingness; as, a *reluctant* acceptance.—*adv.* **re-luc′tant-ly.**

Syn. averse, loath, indisposed.—*Ant.* eager, willing, inclined, disposed.

re-ly (rē-lī′), *v.i.* [*p.t.* and *p.p.* -lied′ (-līd′), *p.pr.* -ly′ing], to trust; have confidence in someone or something: with *on* or *upon.*

re-main (rē-mān′), *v.i.* **1**, to stay behind when others go; as, only he *remained* in the room; **2**, to stay alive; endure; last; as, the memory of that day *remains;* **3**, to be left after a part has been used, taken away, lost, or destroyed; as, little of his wealth *remains;* **4**, to be left for future consideration or use; as, that *remains* to be seen; **5**, to continue in the same given state; as, he *remains* a bachelor:—*n.* **1**, usually in *pl.*: **a**, the portion left, as of a meal; **b**, ruins, as of a temple; **c**, a relic or relics; **2**, in *pl.*: **a**, a dead body; **b**, works published after an author's death; as, literary *remains.*

Syn., *n.* corpse, carcass. (See body.)

re-main-der (rē-mān′dẽr), *n.* the portion or number left after anything is taken away; remnant; balance; surplus.

Syn. remnant, residue, balance. *Remainder* is the general term for that which is left when the other part is taken away; as, the *remainder* of our life. *Remnant* names a fragment or a scattered few; as, a *remnant* of cloth; the *remnant* of a great army. *Residue* means that which is left after separation, removal, or the like; as, the *residue* of an estate. *Balance* is incorrectly used in the sense of *remainder;* the difference between one's debits and credits is a *balance.* It is correct to call a deficiency in an account a *balance* due; it is incorrect to speak of the *balance* of the day.

re-mand (rē-månd′), *v.t.* **1**, to call, order, or send back; as, to *remand* an officer to his post; **2**, to commit to custody again; as, to *remand* an accused person to prison:—*n.* **1**, the sending back of an accused person to custody after a hearing; **2**, the judicial order sending him back.

re-mark (rē-märk′), *n.* **1**, the act of noticing or observing attentively; **2**, a brief, casual comment or statement; **3**, noticeable appearance; as, his dress made him an object of *remark;* **4**, in *pl.*, conversational speech in general; as, his *remarks* were interesting:—*v.t.* and *v.i.* **1**, to take note of; observe; **2**, to utter briefly and casually.

re-mark-a-ble (rē-mär′kȧ-bl), *adj.* **1**, worthy of observation or comment; noteworthy; **2**, unusual; uncommon. —*adv.* **re-mark′a-bly.**—*n.* **re-mark′a-ble-ness.**

Syn. famous, extraordinary, wonderful.—*Ant.* common, usual, ordinary.

re-me-di-a-ble (rē-mē′dĭ-ȧ-bl), *adj.* capable of being cured; as, a *remediable* disease.

re-me-di-al (rē-mē′dĭ-ăl), *adj.* affording, or intended to be used as, a cure; as, *remedial* treatment.

rem-e-di-less (rĕm′ē-dĭ-lĕs; rē-mĕd′ĭ-), *adj.* **1**, past cure or help; incurable; **2**, irretrievable, as a loss.

rem-e-dy (rĕm′ē-dĭ), *n.* [*pl.* remedies (-dĭz)], **1**, anything which cures or relieves sickness; a helpful medicine; **2**, that which removes or corrects an evil; a relief:—*v.t.* [*p.t.* and *p.p.* -died (-dĭd), *p.pr.* -dy-ing], **1**, to cure or heal, as with medicine; **2**, to repair; make right; correct, as an evil.

Syn., *n.* help, corrective, redress, cure.

re-mem-ber (rē-mĕm′bẽr), *v.t.* **1**, to retain or keep in the mind; think of anew; as, an old man *remembers* the days of his youth; **2**, to keep in mind carefully; know by heart; as, to *remember* a poem; **3**, to hold in mind with gratitude, regard, or reverence; as, to *remember* the soldiers on Memorial Day; **4**, to carry greetings from; remind someone of; as, *remember* me to her; **5**, to do for, out of kindness; **6**, to give a present or fee to; as, *remember* the porter:—*v.i.* to possess or use the faculty of memory.

re-mem-brance (rē-mĕm′brăns), *n.* **1**, the act or power of recalling to, or keeping in, the mind; recollecting; **2**, the state of being held in, or recalled to, mind; recollection; memory; **3**, the length of time within which one has memories; as, the coldest winter in my *remembrance;* **4**, anything that recalls or keeps in mind a particular memory; a memento or keepsake; a gift; **5**, in *pl.*, greetings showing regard; as, give her my *remembrances.*

Syn. reminiscence. (See memory.)

re-mind (rē-mīnd′), *v.t.* to bring to the mind of; cause to recollect; as, *remind* me to go.—*n.* **re-mind′er.**

rem-i-nis-cence (rĕm″ĭ-nĭs′ĕns), *n.* **1**, the calling back to mind of past experiences; **2**, that which is recalled and told; a memory.

Syn. recollection. (See memory.)

rem-i-nis-cent (rĕm″ĭ-nĭs′ĕnt), *adj.* **1**, pertaining to, of the nature of, or having, memory of past experiences; **2**, recalling, or dwelling on, the past; **3**, suggestive; as, a poem *reminiscent* of Burns.

re-miss (rē-mĭs′), *adj.* **1**, careless in matters of duty, business, etc.; neglectful; **2**, lacking energy and earnestness; **3**, not prompt.—*adv.* **re-miss′ly.**—*n.* **re-miss′ness.**

Syn. slack, slothful, negligent.

re-mis-sion (rē-mĭsh′ŭn), *n.* **1**, the canceling of a debt; discharge from a penalty; as, the *remission* of a fine; **2**, forgiveness; pardon; as, *remission* of sins.

re-mit (rē-mĭt′), *v.t.* [*p.t.* and *p.p.* -mit′ted, *p.pr.* -mit′ting], **1**, to forgive; pardon; as, to *remit* sins; **2**, to send, as money in payment of debts or bills due; **3**, to refrain from demanding or insisting upon; as, to *remit* a fine; **4**, to make less severe; relax; as, to *remit* one's watchfulness:—*v.i.* **1**, to moderate; lessen in force; **2**, to send money, as in payment of goods.—*n.* **re-mit′ter.**

re-mit-tal (rē-mĭt′ăl), *n.* **1**, a canceling; **2**, discharge; remission; as, the *remittal* of a penalty.

re-mit-tance (rē-mĭt′ăns), *n.* **1**, the sending of money, bills, etc., esp. to a distant place; **2**, the sum so sent: **remittance man**, a person, usually a younger son of an English family, who lives in the colonies on an allowance sent from home.

re-mit-tent (rē-mĭt′ĕnt), *adj.* growing less temporarily, or at irregular intervals; abating; as, a *remittent* fever:—*n.* a fever that abates irregularly.

rem-nant (rĕm′nănt), *n.* **1**, that which is left after a part has been removed; remainder; **2**, a short length of fabric left when most of the piece has been sold; **3**, a trace; as, not a *remnant* of pity.

Syn. residue, portion. (See remainder.)

re-mod-el (rē-mŏd′ĕl), *v.t.* to put into new shape; arrange again.

re-mon-e-tize (rē-mŏn′ē-tīz; rē-mŭn′-), *v.t.* [*p.t.* and *p.p.* -tized (-tīzd), *p.pr.* -tiz″ing], to restore to use as lawful money; as, to *remonetize* silver.

re-mon-strance (rē-mŏn′străns), *n.* a strong objection or protest against something; reproof.

re-mon-strant (rē-mŏn′strănt), *adj.* protesting, or urging reasons against, something:—*n.* one who signs or presents a protest against something.

re-mon-strate (rē-mŏn′strāt), *v.i.* [*p.t.* and *p.p.* -strat-ed, *p.pr.* -strat-ing], **1**, to urge or put forward strong reasons against some act or course complained of; as, to *remonstrate* against a wrong; **2**, to plead in protest.

Syn. protest, complain, expostulate.

re-morse (rē-môrs′), *n.* great pain or anguish of mind caused by a sense of guilt; keen reproach of oneself.

re-morse-ful (rē-môrs′fo͝ol), *adj.* full of anguish caused by a sense of guilt; keenly reproachful of oneself.—*adv.* **re-morse'ful-ly.**—*n.* **re-morse'ful-ness.**

re-morse-less (rē-môrs'lĕs), *adj.* cruel; merciless; pitiless.—*adv.* **re-morse'less-ly.**—*n.* **re-morse'less-ness.**

re-mote (rē-mōt'), *adj.* **1,** far off in time; as, *remote* centuries; **2,** distant in place; far removed from others; as, a *remote* village in the hills; **3,** having slight connection or relation; as, his remarks were *remote* from the subject; **4,** slight; not plainly seen; as, a *remote* likeness.—*adv.* **re-mote'ly.** —*n.* **re-mote'ness.**

Syn. irrelevant, foreign, alien.—*Ant.* relevant, immediate, near.

re-mount (rē-mount'), *v.t.* **1,** to get upon again, as on a wall; **2,** to set again, as a jewel; **3,** to put on horseback again; **4,** to give a fresh horse to:—*v.i.* **1,** to mount a horse again; **2,** to be furnished with fresh horses, as cavalry:—*n.* **1,** a new frame or setting; **2,** a fresh horse to replace one killed or hurt.

re-mov-a-ble (rē-mo͞ov'ȧ-bl), *adj.* **1,** capable of being taken away, or of being transferred from one place to another; **2,** subject to removal, as from office.

re-mov-al (rē-mo͞ov'ăl), *n.* **1,** the act of taking away; **2,** the state of being removed; **3,** dismissal, as from office.

re-move (rē-mo͞ov'), *v.t.* [*p.t.* and *p.p.* -moved' (-mo͞ovd'), *p.pr.* -mov'-ing], **1,** to put from its place; transfer from one place to another; **2,** to take out of the way; as, to *remove* a hindrance; **3,** to dismiss; displace; as, to *remove* a man from office:—*v.i.* to go from one place to another; change residence:—*n.* **1,** a transfer from one place to another; a change of place; **2,** the space passed over in changing a thing from one place to another; hence, a step or interval.—*n.* **re-mov'er.**

re-moved (rē-mo͞ovd'), *p.adj.* separated by degrees in relationship; as, a first cousin once *removed* is a cousin's child.

re-mu-ner-ate (rē-mū'nẽr-āt), *v.t.* [*p.t.* and *p.p.* -at"ed, *p.pr.* -at"ing], **1,** to pay (someone) in return for service, for time spent, or for loss sustained on one's account; **2,** to pay in return for; compensate; reward; as, to *remunerate* a service.—*adj.* **re-mu'ner-a-tive.**

Syn. recompense, reimburse, satisfy.

re-mu-ner-a-tion (rē-mū"nẽr-ā'shŭn), *n.* payment for loss or for service; compensation.

Re-mus (rē'mŭs), *n.* in mythology, one of the legendary founders of Rome, slain by his twin brother Romulus for leaping scornfully over the walls of the newly built city.

ren-ais-sance (rĕn"ĕ-säns'; rē-nā'säns; *Fr.* rē-nâ"säns'), *n.* (also, *renascence*), **1,** a new birth; a coming to life again, esp. in art; **2,** a revival of, awakened interest and effort in, or a marked improvement along any line, esp. in art: **Renaissance, 1,** (also, *Renascence*), the period of a great revival of learning and classical art in Europe from the 14th to the 16th centuries, beginning in Italy and spreading gradually to other countries and marking the transition from medieval to modern history; **2,** the style of art and architecture, based on the classic, of that period.

re-nal (rē'năl), *adj.* of or pertaining to the kidneys; as, *renal* colic.

re-nas-cence (rē-năs'ĕns), *n.* the fact or state of being born anew; a coming into fresh life: **Renascence,** the revival of learning and the arts in Europe from the 14th to the 16th centuries; the Renaissance.

re-nas-cent (rē-năs'ĕnt), *adj.* coming to life again; being born again; reviving; as, a *renascent* interest in art.

ren-coun-ter (rĕn-koun'tẽr), *n.* **1,** a combat; battle; **2,** an unexpected meeting, as with a friend; **3,** a debate or argument between individuals. Also, **ren-con'tre** (rĕn-kŏn'tẽr; *Fr.* räṅ"kôṅtr').

rend (rĕnd), *v.t.* [*p.t.* and *p.p.* rent (rĕnt), *p.pr.* rend'ing], **1,** to tear apart with violence; split; as, the wind *rends* the sail; **2,** to take away by force; as, to *rend* colonies from a mother country:—*v.i.* to become torn; split apart.—*n.* [1]**rend'er.**

Syn. break, sever, sunder.

[2]**ren-der** (rĕn'dẽr), *v.t.* **1,** to give in return; pay back; as, to *render* blow for blow; **2,** to pay as something owed; as, to *render* tribute; **3,** to present for consideration; as, to *render* a bill; **4,** to utter as final; as, to *render* a decision; **5,** to yield; as, to *render* homage; **6,** to furnish; give; as, to *render* aid; **7,** to cause to be; as, to *render* anything fit for use; **8,** to translate; as, to *render* French into English; **9,** to express or interpret; as, to *render* music; **10,** to clear or separate by melting; as, to *render* lard.

ren-dez-vous (räṅ'dȧ-vo͞o; rŏn'dē-), *n.* [*pl.* rendezvous (-vo͞oz)], **1,** an appointed place of meeting, esp. for warships or troops; **2,** a meeting by appointment:—*v.t.* and *v.i.* [*p.t.* and *p.p.* -voused (-vo͞od), *p.pr.* -vous"ing (-vo͞o"ĭng)], to meet or cause to meet at a certain place, as troops.

ren-di-tion (rĕn-dĭsh'ŭn), *n.* **1,** a yielding or a surrender, as of troops in war; **2,** a version; translation; **3,** the act or style of performing, representing, or interpreting; as, the *rendition* of a piece of music.

ren-e-gade (rĕn'ē-gād), *n.* **1,** one who denies or gives up his faith; **2,** a turncoat; **3,** a deserter from army or navy.

re-nege (rē-nĕg'; *Dial.* rē-năg'), *v.i.* [*p.t.* and *p.p.* -neged' (-nĕgd'), *p.pr.* -neg'ing], **1,** in cards, to fail to follow suit when able to do so; **2,** *Slang,* to back out; fail to come up to expectations:—*n.* the act of failing to follow suit when able to do so. Also, *U.S. Colloq.,* **re-nig'.**—*n.* **re-neg'er.**

re-new (rē-nū'), *v.t.* **1,** to cause to become new once more; bring back the youth and strength of; revive; as, spring *renews* the earth; **2,** to begin again; as, to *renew* the fighting along a battle front; **3,** to rebuild; restore to an original state; **4,** to grant or obtain an extension of, as a loan; **5,** to supply; restore to fulness or sufficiency, as the water in a tank:—*v.i.* **1,** to become new; grow again; **2,** to begin afresh.—*adj.* **re-new'a-ble.**

re-new-al (rē-nū'ăl), *n.* **1,** the act of beginning again, or of making new; **2,** the state of being begun again or made new.

ren-net (rĕn'ĕt), *n.* the lining membrane of the stomach of certain animals, or the contents of the stomach of a calf, lamb, etc., not yet weaned: used to curdle milk.

re-nounce (rē-nouns'), *v.t.* [*p.t.* and *p.p.* -nounced' (-nounst'), *p.pr.* -nounc'ing], **1,** to disown; cast off; as, to *renounce* one's heir; **2,** to give up; abandon: —*v.i.* in card playing, not to follow suit:—*n.* in cards, failure to follow suit.—*n.* **re-nounce'-ment.**—*n.* **re-nounc'er.**

Syn., v. abandon, discard, disclaim.

ren-o-vate (rĕn'ō-vāt), *v.t.* [*p.t.* and *p.p.* -vat"ed, *p.pr.* -vat"ing], to make as good as new; restore to a former or better condition of freshness.—*n.* **ren'o-va"tor.**

Syn. renew, revive, regenerate, refresh.

ren-o-va-tion (rĕn"ō-vā'shŭn), *n.* the act of making, or state of being made, as good as new; a renewal; cleansing.

re-nown (rē-noun'), *n.* fame; celebrity; exalted reputation.

re-nowned (rē-nound'), *adj.* having a widely spread and honorable reputation; famous.

Syn. celebrated, distinguished, honored.

rent (rĕnt), past tense and past participle of the irregular verb *rend:*—*n.* **1,** a ear; a hole or slit made by tearing or splitting apart, as in fabrics, clouds, rocks, or the ike; **2,** a split or division of opinion or belief.
Syn., n. breach, fissure, separation.

rent (rĕnt), *n.* **1,** a fixed amount payable at a stated time or times for the use of property; **2,** in economics, that portion of the eturn on a piece of land which is due to its uperiority in location, productivity, etc., over and which is barely good enough to bring in a eturn to labor (wages) and capital invested in t (interest): also called *economic rent;* **3,** *U. S. Colloq.*, a place rented:—*v.t.* **1,** to lease; hire; hold or use without ownership, in consideration of payments made at stated times; as, to *rent* a house from an owner; **2,** to give possession of, in return for rent; lease; as, to *rent* a house to a tenant:—*v.i.* to be leased or to let; as, the house *rents* for $1,000.—*adj.* **rent'a-ble.**—*n.* **rent'er.**

rent-al (rĕn'tăl), *n.* **1,** the amount of money paid at stated times for possession and use of property; **2,** the entire income obtained from leased property.

re-nun-ci-a-tion (rē-nŭn″sĭ-ā'shŭn; rē-nŭn″shĭ-), *n.* the act of disowning, casting off, or giving up; as, the *renunciation* of dower rights.
Syn. disavowal, abandonment, relinquishment, rejection, repudiation.

re-o-pen (rē-ō'pn), *v.t.* and *v.i.* **1,** to open again, as a flower; **2,** to begin again; resume; as, he *reopened* the argument.

re-or-gan-i-za-tion (rē-ôr″găn-ĭ-zā'shŭn), *n.* **1,** the act of arranging or systematizing anew; **2,** the state of being arranged or systematized anew.

re-or-gan-ize (rē-ôr'găn-īz), *v.t.* and *v.i.* [*p.t.* and *p.p.* -ized (-īzd), *p.pr.* -iz″ing], **1,** to arrange or systematize anew; **2,** to change to a more satisfactory form or system.—*n.* **re-or'gan-iz″er.**

rep (rĕp), *n.* a silk, wool, or silk and wool, fabric having a fine, corded surface.

¹re-pair (rē-pâr'), *v.i.* to go; resort; as, to *repair* to one's home.

²re-pair (rē-pâr'), *v.t.* **1,** to put in good condition again after decay, injury, or the like; mend; renovate; as, to *repair* a garment; **2,** to remedy; set right; heal; mend; as, to *repair* a mistake; **3,** to make amends for; indemnify for; as, to *repair* a loss; *repair* an unkindness:—*n.* **1,** the act of restoring to a sound condition, or the state of being thus restored; **2,** usually in *pl.*, the results of such restoration; as, he made many *repairs* on the barn; **3,** the general state in respect to sound condition; as, the house is in good *repair.*—*adj.* **re-pair'a-ble.**—*n.* **re-pair'er.**

rep-a-ra-ble (rĕp'ȧ-rȧ-bl), *adj.* capable of being mended or made good.

rep-a-ra-tion (rĕp″ȧ-rā'shŭn), *n.* **1,** the act of making amends for a wrong, injury, etc.; as, he made *reparation* for his neglect; **2,** that which is done by way of amends; compensation.
Syn. recompense, satisfaction, redress.

rep-ar-tee (rĕp″är-tē'), *n.* **1,** a quick-witted, bright reply; **2,** quick, clever replies in general; **3,** ability or expertness in making such replies.

re-past (rē-păst'), *n.* a meal; feast; food taken at one time.

re-pa-tri-ate (rē-pā'trĭ-āt), *v.t.* and *v.i.* [*p.t.* and *p.p.* -at″ed, *p.pr.* -at″ing], **1,** to give back citizenship to, as to an exile; **2,** to bring back to one's own country, as prisoners of war after peace is concluded.—*n.* **re-pa″tri-a'tion.**

re-pay (rē-pā'), *v.t.* [*p.t.* and *p.p.* -paid' (-pād'), *p.pr.* -pay'ing], **1,** to pay back; as, to *repay* borrowed money; **2,** to pay back to; as, to *repay* a creditor; **3,** to make a gift to, or do a service for, in return; as, to *repay* a friend for kindness; **4,** to give a return for; as, to *repay* a favor.—*adj.* **re-pay'a-ble.**—*n.* **re-pay'ment.**

re-peal (rē-pēl'), *v.t.* to cancel, or make of no further effect, by recalling; as, to *repeal* a law:—*n.* the recalling, with purpose to cancel, or make of no further effect; as, the *repeal* of a law.—*adj.* **re-peal'a-ble.**
Syn., v. annul, revoke, rescind.

re-peat (rē-pēt'), *v.t.* **1,** to do or speak a second time; **2,** to say over from memory; recite; **3,** to say after another:—*v.i.* to say or do anything over or again:—*n.* **1,** anything said or done over or again; **2,** a sign in music, directing a part to be given again.

re-peat-ed (rē-pēt'ĕd), *p.adj.* done or said again and again or over and over; frequent.—*adv.* **re-peat'ed-ly.**

re-peat-er (rē-pēt'ẽr), *n.* **1,** one who or that which says or does a thing over; **2,** a revolver or rifle which fires several shots without being loaded again; **3,** a watch that strikes the hours when a spring is pressed; **4,** in the U. S., one who votes at an election more than once, in violation of the law; **5,** a kind of telegraph instrument; **6,** in mathematics, a digit or group of digits occurring uninterruptedly in the same order in a repeating decimal: also called *repetend,* which see.

re-peat-ing dec-i-mal **1,** a decimal in which a figure is repeated continuously, as .66666+, .16666+: also called *pure repeater;* **2,** more loosely, a decimal in which a sequence of figures, rather than a single figure, is so repeated, as 1.232323+: generally called *circulating decimal.*

re-pel (rē-pĕl'), *v.t.* [*p.t.* and *p.p.* -pelled' (-pĕld'), *p.pr.* -pel'ling], **1,** to drive back; check the advance of; keep at a distance; as, to *repel* an enemy; his manner *repels* everyone; **2,** to reject, as an offer; **3,** in physics, to drive, or tend to drive, apart; influence by a force tending to drive away: opp. of *attract;* **4,** to cause aversion in; as, the idea *repels* me:—*v.i.* **1,** to act with force against force; **2,** to cause dislike.

re-pel-lent (rē-pĕl'ĕnt), *adj.* **1,** driving back; as, a *repellent* force; **2,** causing aversion; **3,** tending or able to keep at a distance; forbidding; as, a *repellent* manner.—*n.* **re-pel'lence; re-pel'len-cy.**

re-pent (rē-pĕnt'), *v.i.* **1,** to feel regret or sorrow on account of something done or left undone; **2,** to change from past evil:—*v.t.* to feel regret or sorrow for; as, to *repent* a crime.—*n.* **re-pent'er.**

re-pent-ance (rē-pĕn'tăns), *n.* the act of regretting, or the state of one who regrets, wrongdoing; sorrow for wrongdoing, with desire to undo the wrong.
Syn. regret, remorse, contrition.

re-pent-ant (rē-pĕn'tănt), *adj.* feeling or showing sorrow because of wrongdoing; penitent.—*adv.* **re-pent'ant-ly.**

re-per-cus-sion (rē″pẽr-kŭsh'ŭn), *n.* **1,** the act of driving or throwing back; **2,** the state of being forced or thrown back; **3,** reflection; rebound; reverberation, as of sound.—*adj.* **re″per-cus'sive.**

rep-er-toire (rĕp'ẽr-twär), *n.* a list of plays, operas, etc., that a performer or a company has ready to render; a repertory. Also, ***rē″per″toire'** (rā″pâr″twȧr').

rep-er-to-ry (rĕp'ẽr-tō-rĭ), *n.* [*pl.* repertories (-rĭz)], **1,** a place where things are stored; **2,** the things stored; a collection; **3,** a list of dramas, operas, etc., ready for performance; a repertoire.

rep-e-tend (rĕp'ē-tĕnd; rĕp″ē-tĕnd'), *n.* a group of digits in a decimal fraction which recur indefinitely and without interruption, as 6 in the decimal .666+: also called *repeater;* or 32 in 1.03232+: also called *circulating decimal.*

rep-e-ti-tion (rĕp″ē-tĭsh′ŭn), *n.* **1**, the doing, making, or saying of something more than once; **2**, that which is done, said, etc., more than once; **3**, recital from memory.—*adj.* **rep″e-ti′tious.**

re-pine (rē-pīn′), *v.i.* [*p.t.* and *p.p.* -pined′ (-pīnd′), *p.pr.* -pin′ing], to fret oneself; complain; feel discontent.—*n.* **re-pin′er.**

re-place (rē-plās′), *v.t.* [*p.t.* and *p.p.* -placed′ (-plāst′), *p.pr.* -plac′ing], **1**, to put back in place; as, to *replace* a book on a shelf; **2**, to take or fill the place of; as, a new house *replaces* the old one; **3**, to supply an equivalent in place of; as, to *replace* goods which one has lost; **4**, to put in a new place. —*n.* **re-plac′er.**—*adj.* **re-place′a-ble.**

re-place-ment (rē-plās′mĕnt), *n.* **1**, the putting of something back in place; **2**, the putting of something in place of another or in a new place.

re-plen-ish (rē-plĕn′ĭsh), *v.t.* to fill up again; stock in abundance. —*n.* **re-plen′ish-er.**—*n.* **re-plen′ish-ment.**

re-plete (rē-plēt′), *adj.* completely filled; abounding: often with *with.*

re-ple-tion (rē-plē′shŭn), *n.* the act of making, or the state of being, full to excess; surfeit.

re-plev-in (rē-plĕv′ĭn), *n.* **1**, the recovery by a person of goods claimed to have been wrongfully seized, on giving security to try the matter in court and accept the judgment; **2**, the writ or order issued by the court making such return:—*v.t.* to take or get back by a writ, or order of court; replevy.

re-plev-y (rē-plĕv′ĭ), *v.t.* [*p.t.* and *p.p.* -plev′ied (-ĭd), *p.pr.* -plev′y-ing], to regain possession of (goods which have been replevined), by giving security to try at law the right to the goods:—*n.* the recovery by a person of goods which have been replevined, by giving security pending trial of the cause; replevin.—*adj.* **re-plev′i-a-ble.**

rep-li-ca (rĕp′lĭ-kȧ), *n.* **1**, a copy of an original picture or statue, esp. one made by the artist or sculptor himself; **2**, an exact copy or duplicate.

re-ply (rē-plī′), *n.* [*pl.* replies (-plīz′)], **1**, something spoken, written, or done in return for something that calls for it; an answer; a response; **2**, ability in making answer; as, clever in *reply:*—*v.i.* [*p.t.* and *p.p.* -plied′ (-plīd′), *p.pr.* -ply′ing], **1**, to say or write something in answer; rejoin; **2**, to make answer in action; as, to *reply* to the enemy's attack: —*v.t.* to say in answer.—*n.* **re-pli′er.**

Syn., n. rejoinder, repartee, retort.

re-port (rē-pōrt′), *v.t.* **1**, to bring back or prepare a verbal or written account of; as, to *report* the work of a committee; **2**, to bring back, as an answer; also, to relate; as, to *report* the results of an investigation; **3**, to take down; write a description of for publication; as, to *report* a law case; **4**, to state as an ascertained fact; as, he *reports* the enemy's troops close at hand; **5**, to make or present a formal or official statement of; as, to *report* a balance; **6**, to make a charge, or inform against, to a superior; as, to *report* an offender; **7**, to announce the conclusions reached concerning (a matter officially referred); as, the committee *reported* the bill to the House:—*v.i.* **1**, to make, prepare, or present, a written or verbal formal statement; **2**, to give an account or description; **3**, to present oneself at a given place; as, *report* at my office at once:—*n.* **1**, an official or authorized presentation of facts; as, a government *report;* **2**, a written or verbal statement; an account, esp. for publication; as, the *report* of a law case; **3**, something widely talked of; rumor; hearsay; **4**, hence, fame; reputation; as, a man of good *report;* **5**, a loud and sudden noise; sound of explosion; as, the *report* of a pistol; **6**, a record of the proceedings of a court, a judge's decisions, or the like; **7**, in *pl.*, the books containing these proceedings and decisions.

re-port-er (rē-pōr′tẽr), *n.* one who bears or gathers news; esp., one who gathers news and writes accounts of matters and events for a newspaper.

¹re-pose (rē-pōz′), *v.t.* [*p.t.* and *p.p.* -posed′ (-pōzd′), *p.pr.* -pos′ing], **1**, to lay or place; base: with *in* or *on;* as, to *repose* one's faith in God; **2**, *Rare*, to put, as a trust, in the care of another.—*n.* **¹re-pos′al.**

²re-pose (rē-pōz′), *v.t.* [*p.t.* and *p.p.* -posed′ (-pōzd′), *p.pr.* -pos′ing], **1**, to place in a position to rest; lay (oneself) down in a posture of rest: generally reflexive; **2**, *Rare*, to give rest to; refresh by rest; as, to *repose* the weary soldiers:—*v.i.* **1**, to lie at rest; be calm or peaceful; hence, to sleep; **2**, to rest in peace or confidence; place one's trust: with *in, on,* or *upon;* as, to *repose* in God; **3**, to lie or rest on a support; as, the statue *reposes* on a pedestal:—*n.* **1**, the act of resting; **2**, the state of being at rest; sleep; **3**, freedom from anxiety or uneasiness; calmness; hence, composure; **4**, that which gives or causes rest; **5**, in art, moderation or restraint of color and treatment.—*n.* **²re-pos′al.**

Syn., n. ease, peace, relaxation.

re-pose-ful (rē-pōz′fo͞ol), *adj.* tending to quiet or calm; restful: peaceful; tranquilizing.—*adv.* **re-pose′ful-ly.** —*n.* **re-pose′ful-ness.**

re-pos-i-to-ry (rē-pŏz′ĭ-tō-rĭ), *n.* [*pl.* repositories (-rĭz)], a place for the storing and safe-keeping of goods, as a bank, warehouse, etc.; a depository.

***re-pous-sé** (rē-po͞o″sā′), [Fr.], *adj.* **1**, beaten or pressed up from the under side so as to show ornamental figures in relief, as a design on thin metal; **2**, shaped or ornamented with such designs; as, a *repoussé* vase of brass:—*n.* **1**, a pattern formed in such relief; **2**, a surface adorned with a design so made.

rep-re-hend (rĕp″rē-hĕnd′), *v.t.* **1**, to blame; reprove sharply; charge with a fault; **2**, to find fault with; censure; as, to *reprehend* conduct.

Syn. reprimand, rebuke, reproach.—*Ant.* approve, praise, commend, exculpate.

rep-re-hen-si-ble (rĕp″rē-hĕn′sĭ-bl), *adj.* blamable; deserving reproof or rebuke.—*adv.* **rep″re-hen′si-bly.**—*n.* **rep″re-hen′si-ble-ness.**

rep-re-hen-sion (rĕp″rē-hĕn′shŭn), *n.* the act of finding fault; blame; rebuke; censure.

rep-re-hen-sive (rĕp″rē-hĕn′sĭv), *adj.* conveying, or intended as, reproof or blame; as, a *reprehensive* manner. —*adv.* **rep″re-hen′sive-ly.**

rep-re-sent (rĕp″rē-zĕnt′), *v.t.* **1**, to place vividly before the mind or senses; as, that story *represents* a great truth; **2**, to make or show a likeness of; portray; depict; as, the picture *represents* a moonlit sea; **3**, to state one's own impressions or account of; make a statement about in order to influence opinion or to give a desired effect; as, he *represented* himself to be in want; **4**, to act or speak in place of; as, he *represents* his father in the business; **5**, to take or act the part of; as, he *represented* a clown in the play; **6**, to stand for; as, letters *represent* sounds.

rep-re-sen-ta-tion (rĕp″rē-zĕn-tā′shŭn), *n.* **1**, the act of making statements in order to influence opinion; portrayal by words, pictures, or the like: 2, a statement, account, or assertion of fact; 3, that which stands for or symbolizes something; as, Greek myths were *representations* of facts in nature; 4, an image, model, or picture; likeness; reproduction; 5, a dramatic performance; 6, a person, or body of persons, acting for others; as, the *representation* of a district in the legislature; 7, the acting for, or standing in the place of, another or others; 8, the state or right of having persons to speak or act in one's behalf; as, no taxation without *representation*.

Syn. delineation, portraiture, emblem.

rep-re-sent-a-tive (rĕp″rē-zĕn′tȧ-tĭv), *n.* 1, one who or that which stands as a type, or shows the marked features of a group; 2, one who has power to act for another or others; 3, a member of any legislative body, elected by the people: **Representative,** in the U. S., a member of the lower house in Congress, or in a state legislature:—*adj.* 1, acting, or having power to act, for another or others; 2, composed of those so acting; as, a *representative* assembly; 3, based or founded on representation by delegates; as, *representative* government; 4, presenting ideas clearly to the mind; 5, having the marked features of a group; typical; as, a *representative* gathering.

re-press (rē-prĕs′), *v.t.* 1, to keep under control; check; as, to *repress* a wish; 2, to crush; overpower; subdue; as, to *repress* a rebellion.—*n.* **re-press′er.**

Syn. restrain, curb, suppress.—*Ant.* agitate, enliven, arouse, stimulate.

re-pres-sion (rē-prĕsh′ŭn), *n.* 1, the act of checking or keeping in control; 2, the state of being kept in control; 3, that which checks; a restraint.

re-pres-sive (rē-prĕs′ĭv), *adj.* having power, or tending, to control or check; as, a *repressive* law.

re-prieve (rē-prēv′), *n.* 1, a temporary delay in carrying out the sentence of a judge; 2, a temporary relief from pain or escape from danger:—*v.t.* [*p.t.* and *p.p.* -prieved′ (-prēvd′), *p.pr.* -priev′ing], 1, to grant a delay of punishment to; 2, to free for a time from pain or danger.

rep-ri-mand (rĕp′rĭ-mȧnd), *n.* a severe reproof or rebuke:—*v.t.* (rĕp′rĭ-mȧnd; rĕp″rĭ-mȧnd′), to rebuke severely for a fault; esp., to reprove publicly and officially.

Syn., v. censure, upbraid. (See scold.)

re-print (rē′prĭnt″; rē-prĭnt′), *n.* 1, an exact copy of any printed work; 2, a reproduction of printed matter, as from some other publication:—*v.t.* (rē-prĭnt′), to print again; print a new copy or edition of.

re-pris-al (rē-prīz′ăl), *n.* 1, in war, something done to, or taken from, an enemy by way of satisfaction or payment for an injury or wrong suffered; 2, any repayment of injury with injury.

re-proach (rē-prōch′), *n.* 1, rebuke or blame expressed with sorrow or anger; 2, the state of being disgraced or dishonored; 3, the cause or object of blame or scorn:—*v.t.* to charge with something wrong or disgraceful; rebuke or blame.—*adj.* **re-proach′a-ble.**—*n.* **re-proach′er.**

re-proach-ful (rē-prōch′fo͝ol), *adj.* containing, or expressing, rebuke or blame.—*adv.* **re-proach′ful-ly.**—*n.* **re-proach′ful-ness.**

rep-ro-bate (rĕp′rō-bāt), *n.* a sinful or wicked person; a scoundrel:—*v.t.* [*p.t.* and *p.p.* -bat″ed, *p.pr.* -bat″ing], to disapprove of strongly; condemn; reject:—*adj.* given up to sin; depraved.

rep-ro-ba-tion (rĕp″rō-bā′shŭn), *n.* 1, the act of strongly disapproving or censuring; strong condemnation; 2, the state of being so condemned.

re-pro-duce (rē″prō-dūs′), *v.t.* [*p.t.* and *p.p.* -duced′ (-dūst′), *p.pr.* -duc′ing], 1, to bring forward or show again; repeat; as, to *reproduce* a play, sound, or gesture; 2, to bear, yield, or bring forth; as, an animal *reproduces* its kind; 3, to renew (a lost part), as do some animals; 4, to copy; make an image of; as, to *reproduce* a person's features in marble.—*n.* **re″pro-duc′er.**

re-pro-duc-tion (rē″prō-dŭk′shŭn), *n.* 1, the act, power, or process, of producing again or anew; revival; 2, that which is so produced; a copy; 3, the process by which animals and plants bring forth their own kind; 4, the process of recalling previously known objects to memory.

re-pro-duc-tive (rē″prō-dŭk′tĭv), *adj.* pertaining to, or employed in, the process of bringing forth anew, physically or mentally.—*adv.* **re″pro-duc′tive-ly.**—*n.* **re″pro-duc′tive-ness.**

re-proof (rē-pro͞of′), *n.* 1, censure; blame; 2, just and kindly rebuke.

re-prov-a-ble (rē-pro͞ov′ȧ-bl), *adj.* deserving rebuke or blame.

re-prov-al (rē-pro͞ov′ăl), *n.* 1, the act of blaming; 2, a rebuke.

re-prove (rē-pro͞ov′), *v.t.* [*p.t.* and *p.p.* -proved′ (-pro͞ovd′), *p.pr.* -prov′ing], to rebuke with kindness and justice; blame.—*n.* **re-prov′er.**—*adv.* **re-prov′ing-ly.**

Syn. chide, censure. (See scold.)

rep-tile (rĕp′tĭl; rĕp′tīl), *n.* 1, any of a class (*Reptilia*) of cold-blooded animals that crawl on the belly, as a snake, or creep on short legs, as a lizard, turtle, or alligator; 2, a mean, groveling person:—*adj.* 1, creeping; crawling; 2, groveling or cringing; low; base.—*adj.* **rep-til′i-an.**—*adj.* **rep-til′i-ous.**

re-pub-lic (rē-pŭb′lĭk), *n.* a state or country in which the supreme power is held by the people, who elect their own representatives and executive officers, responsible directly to the people; a commonwealth.

re-pub-lic-an (rē-pŭb′lĭ-kăn), *n.* one who favors government by the chosen representatives of the people: **Republican,** a member of the Republican party:—*adj.* pertaining to, characteristic of, or believing in, government by chosen representatives of the people: **Republican,** designating, or pertaining to, the Republican party: **Republican party,** one of the two major political parties in the U. S., established in 1854.

re-pub-lic-an-ism (rē-pŭb′lĭ-kăn-ĭzm), *n.* 1, the system or principles of government by chosen representatives of the people; 2, belief in, or support of, such principles.

re-pub-li-ca-tion (rē-pŭb″lĭ-kā′shŭn), *n.* 1, the act of reprinting, or issuing anew; as, the *republication* of a book; 2, a reprint, as of a book.

re-pub-lish (rē-pŭb′lĭsh), *v.t.* to put forth or issue anew, as a book; print a new edition of.—*n.* **re-pub′lish-er.**

re-pu-di-ate (rē-pū′dĭ-āt), *v.t.* [*p.t.* and *p.p.* -at″ed, *p.pr.* -at″ing], 1, to divorce (a wife); 2, to refuse to own; cast off; as, to *repudiate* an old friend; 3, to decline to be responsible or liable for; as, to *repudiate* a debt; 4, to refuse to admit the truth, justice, or authority of, as a statement.—*n.* **re-pu″di-a′tion.**—*n.* **re-pu′di-a″tor.**

Syn. discard, renounce, disavow.—*Ant.* acknowledge, admit, keep, own.

re-pug-nance (rē-pŭg′năns), *n.* extreme dislike; disgust; aversion. Also, **re-pug′nan-cy.**

re-pug-nant (rē-pŭg′nănt), *adj.* 1, highly distasteful or disagreeable;

repulsive; as, a *repugnant* expression; **2**, contradictory; contrary: often followed by *to;* as, *repugnant* to one's principles; **3**, hostile; as, a *repugnant* attitude.—*adv.* **re-pug′nant-ly.**
Syn. antagonistic, opposite, opposed.

re-pulse (rē-pŭls′), *v.t.* [*p.t.* and *p.p.* -pulsed′ (-pŭlst′), *p.pr.* -puls′ing], **1**, to drive back; beat off; as, to *repulse* the enemy; **2**, to drive away by coldness, lack of sympathy, etc.; **3**, to refuse to accept or meet; as, to *repulse* the advances of a friend:—*n.* **1**, the act of driving back; **2**, the state of being driven back; **3**, a decided refusal.

re-pul-sion (rē-pŭl′shŭn), *n.* **1**, the act of driving back; **2**, the state of being driven back; **3**, a feeling of aversion; strong dislike; **4**, in physics, the action of two bodies upon each other which drives them apart: opp. of *attraction.*

re-pul-sive (rē-pŭl′sĭv), *adj.* **1**, able to drive back; repellent; as, a *repulsive* movement; **2**, *Rare*, cold; forbidding; as, a *repulsive* manner; **3**, offensive; disgusting; as, a *repulsive* sight.—*adv.* **re-pul′sive-ly.** —*n.* **re-pul′sive-ness.**
Syn. disagreeable, revolting, repellent.—*Ant.* attractive, alluring.

rep-u-ta-ble (rĕp′ū-tȧ-bl), *adj.* worthy of esteem; honorable; respectable; creditable.—*adv.* **rep′u-ta-bly.**

rep-u-ta-tion (rĕp″ū-tā′shŭn), *n.* **1**, good name or standing; honor; credit; as, a citizen of *reputation;* **2**, the general opinion, good or bad, held of a person or thing; as, a *reputation* for meanness.

re-pute (rē-pūt′), *n.* the estimation, good or bad, in which a person is held; esp., good character:—*v.t.* [*p.t.* and *p.p.* -put′ed, *p.pr.* -put′ing], to hold in general opinion; consider: usually in a passive sense; as, he is *reputed* rich.

re-put-ed (rē-pūt′ĕd), *p.adj.* **1**, considered as being; having the reputation of being; as, a *reputed* scholar; **2**, supposed to be but probably not existing; as, his *reputed* fortune.—*adv.* **re-put′ed-ly.**

re-quest (rē-kwĕst′), *n.* **1**, the act of asking for something; **2**, that which is asked for; **3**, the state of being asked for or in demand; as, he is in great *request* as a public speaker:—*v.t.* **1**, to ask for with politeness; as, to *request* a favor; **2**, to ask (someone) for something; as, to *request* a person for a loan; also, to ask (something) from someone; as, to *request* a loan from a person.

re-qui-em (rē′kwĭ-ĕm; rĕk′wĭ-ĕm), *n.* **1**, a Mass sung for the repose of the souls of, or in honor of, the dead; **2**, the music for such a Mass; **3**, any hymn or solemn musical service in honor of the dead.

re-quire (rē-kwīr′), *v.t.* [*p.t.* and *p.p.* -quired′ (-kwīrd′), *p.pr.* -quir′ing], **1**, to claim as one's right; as, I *require* your attention; **2**, to demand or insist upon; as, to *require* promptness at school; **3**, to have need of; call for; as, a singular subject *requires* a singular verb; this will *require* haste.

re-quire-ment (rē-kwīr′mĕnt), *n.* **1**, the act of insisting upon or claiming, as by right or authority; demand; **2**, necessity; need; **3**, that which is demanded or necessary; **4**, in *pl.*, the conditions of entrance to a club, institution, or the like; as, college entrance *requirements.*

req-ui-site (rĕk′wĭ-zĭt), *n.* anything that cannot be done without; a necessity:—*adj.* so needful that it cannot be done without; necessary; as, a *requisite* amount of food.—*n.* **req′ui-site-ness.**
Syn., adj. required, essential, needed.

req-ui-si-tion (rĕk″wĭ-zĭsh′ŭn), *n.* **1**, a formal demand or claim made by right or authority; as, a *requisition* for troops or supplies; **2**, the state of being demanded or put to use; as, horses were in *requisition:*—*v.t.* **1**, to demand; claim by authority; as, to *requisition* food for troops; **2**, to make a demand upon (esp. a country invaded in war) for supplies or the like.

re-quit-al (rē-kwīt′ăl), *n.* **1**, the act of repaying or making return for good or evil; **2**, just return for good or evil; reward or punishment; **3**, compensation.
Syn. retribution, redress, recompense.

re-quite (rē-kwīt′), *v.t.* [*p.t.* and *p.p.* -quit′ed, *p.pr.* -quit′ing], **1**, to repay or return good or evil to; as, to *requite* one for a kindness; **2**, to repay or return good or evil for; as, to *requite* kindness with ingratitude; **3**, to compensate.—*n.* **re-quit′er.**
Syn. remunerate, recompense.

rere-brace (rēr′brās″), *n.* in the equipment of the medieval knight, plate armor protecting the arm from shoulder to elbow (see illus. below; see also *armor*, illus.).

rere-dos (rēr′dŏs), *n.* **1**, in church architecture, an ornamental screen or a decorated part of a wall behind an altar; **2**, in medieval armor, a plate protecting the back (see illus.).

re-scind (rē-sĭnd′), *v.t.* to repeal; annul or cancel; as, to *rescind* a law.—*n.* **re-scind′er.**—*n.* **re-scis′sion** (rē-sĭzh′ŭn).

re-script (rē′skrĭpt), *n.* **1**, a written reply from a Roman emperor or a Pope in answer to some question officially submitted to him; **2**, hence, any official order of a ruler or government.

res-cue (rĕs′kū), *n.* **1**, deliverance from danger, imprisonment, or violence; **2**, the forcible taking of persons or goods held by legal authority:—*v.t.* [*p.t.* and *p.p.* -cued (-kūd), *p.pr.* -cu-ing], to set free from danger or imprisonment; liberate; save.—*n.* **res′cu-er.**

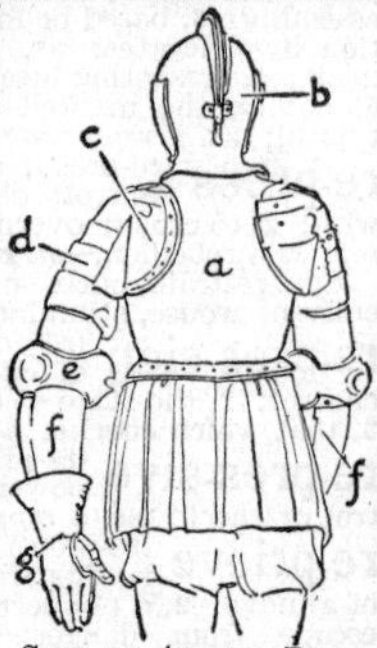

Suit of Armor, Rear View
a, reredos; *b*, helmet; *c*, pauldron, or shoulder piece; *d-e-f*, brassart; *d*, rerebrace; *e*, elbow piece; *f*, vambrace; *g*, gauntlet.

re-search (rē-sûrch′), *n.* **1**, a careful inquiry or investigation; **2**, the effort to find fresh information in history, science, literature, etc., by experiment or by a thorough investigation of sources; as, literary *research.*—*n.* **re-search′er.**

re-sem-blance (rē-zĕm′blăns), *n.* likeness; similarity of outward appearance or of qualities.

re-sem-ble (rē-zĕm′bl), *v.t.* [*p.t.* and *p.p.* -bled (-bld), *p.pr.* -bling], to be like in appearance or character; as, the brothers *resemble* each other.

re-sent (rē-zĕnt′), *v.t.* **1**, to consider as an injury or insult; **2**, to be angry because of; be indignant at.

re-sent-ful (rē-zĕnt′fo͝ol), *adj.* **1**, disposed to consider oneself insulted; **2**, caused or marked by temper; as, a *resentful* look; **3**, full of displeasure because of a wrong.—*adv.* **re-sent′ful-ly.**—*n.* **re-sent′ful-ness.**

re-sent-ment (rē-zĕnt′mĕnt), *n.* strong anger or displeasure because of a real or fancied wrong; a deep sense of injury with a feeling of ill will; indignant feeling accompanied by ill will.
Syn. bitterness, animosity. (See malice.)

res-er-va-tion (rĕz″ẽr-vā′shŭn), *n.* **1,** a holding back or hiding; **2,** anything held back or concealed; **3,** a keeping back for oneself of a right or interest; as, the *reservation* of all rights in a published work; **4,** a limiting of full acceptance or agreement; as, to make a mental *reservation;* **5,** public land kept for some special use; as, an Indian *reservation.*

re-serve (rē-zûrv′), *n.* **1,** that which is kept in store for future use or for a particular purpose; **2,** a tract of land set apart for a special purpose; **3,** the act of suppressing or holding back; as, to state without *reserve;* **4,** restraint in speech and manner; the keeping of one's own counsel; **5,** funds kept on hand by a bank as a basis for credit; also, a portion of profits kept for emergencies; **6,** a body of troops withheld from action and ready as reënforcements; **7,** usually in *pl.*, the militia:—*v.t.* [*p.t.* and *p.p.* -served′ (-zûrvd′), *p.pr.* -serv′ing], **1,** to set aside and keep for future use; **2,** to keep as one's own; hold; as, to *reserve* all rights in a book; **3,** to except from something granted.

re-served (rē-zûrvd′), *p.adj.* **1,** keeping one's thoughts to oneself; showing little feeling; as, a *reserved* manner; **2,** kept back for future or special use; as, *reserved* seats.—*adv.* **re-serv′ed-ly.**

res-er-voir (rĕz′ẽr-vwôr; rĕz′ẽr-vwär), *n.* **1,** a place where anything, esp. water, is collected and stored up for use; **2,** a reserve; a store.

re-side (rē-zīd′), *v.i.* [*p.t.* and *p.p.* -sid′ed, *p.pr.* -sid′ing], **1,** to dwell for a length of time; live; **2,** to exist as an attribute or element; be inherent, as certain qualities or characteristics.

res-i-dence (rĕz′ĭ-dĕns), *n.* **1,** the place where one lives; a settled or permanent home; **2,** the state of living in a place more or less permanently.

res-i-den-cy (rĕz′ĭ-dĕn-sĭ), *n.* [*pl.* residencies (-sĭz)], **1,** the official home of a diplomatic agent or governor at a foreign court; **2,** an administrative division in the Dutch East Indies.

res-i-dent (rĕz′ĭ-dĕnt), *n.* **1,** one who lives in a place; **2,** a government agent at a foreign court:—*adj.* living in a place; as, a *resident* physician of a hospital.

res-i-den-tial (rĕz″ĭ-dĕn′shăl), *adj.* pertaining to, connected with, or fitted for, dwelling places.

re-sid-u-a-ry (rē-zĭd′ū-ā-rĭ), *adj.* pertaining to, or consisting of, the remainder: **residuary legatee,** a person to whom is left the remainder of an estate, after deducting particular bequests, debts, and legal expenses.—*adj.* **re-sid′u-al.**

res-i-due (rĕz′ĭ-dū), *n.* **1,** that which remains after a part has been removed; remainder; **2,** that part of an estate that remains after all debts, charges, and particular bequests have been paid.

Syn. remnant, leavings. (See remainder.)

re-sid-u-um (rē-zĭd′ū-ŭm), *n.* [*pl.* residua (-ȧ)], that which is left after any process of subtraction, purification, etc.

re-sign (rē-zīn′), *v.t.* **1,** to yield to another; give up, as a task; **2,** to submit calmly; as, to *resign* oneself to a loss:—*v.i.* to withdraw from a position or office.

Syn. abdicate. *Resign* and *abdicate* mean to give up a position, but they differ in their application. To *resign* is to give up an unexpired office or dignity; as, the elected officer *resigned.* To *abdicate* is to give up an authority which is inherent, not elective; as, a king *abdicates* his throne.

res-ig-na-tion (rĕz″ĭg-nā′shŭn), *n.* **1,** the act of giving up or yielding; surrender, as of an office; also, the document stating such surrender; **2,** patient submission; a bowing to misfortune.

re-signed (rē-zīnd′), *p.adj.* submissive; yielding; patiently uncomplaining.—*adv.* **re-sign′ed-ly.**—*n.* **re-sign′ed-ness.**

re-sil-i-ence (rē-zĭl′ĭ-ĕns), *n.* the act or power of springing back to an original position; elasticity; as, the *resilience* of a rubber band. Also, **re-sil′i-en-cy.**

re-sil-i-ent (rē-zĭl′ĭ-ĕnt), *adj.* **1,** springing back to a former position; elastic; **2,** having power of recovery; buoyant.

res-in (rĕz′ĭn), *n.* any of various hardened or dried secretions from certain trees, dissolving in alcohol but not in water: **common resin,** rosin (which see).—*adj.* **res′in-ous.**—*adj.* and *n.* **res′in-oid.**

re-sist (rē-zĭst′), *v.t.* **1,** to oppose; set oneself against; check, as progress; **2,** to strive against; defeat:—*v.i.* to offer opposition; refuse to obey or agree.—*n.* **re-sist′er.**

re-sist-ance (rē-zĭs′tăns), *n.* **1,** the act of opposing; a striving against; **2,** a force that acts to prevent or retard motion; as, the *resistance* of the air to bodies passing through it; **3,** the opposition offered by a conductor to the passage of an electrical current: **resistance coil,** a coil of wire used to vary or measure the resistance of a circuit.

re-sist-ant (rē-zĭs′tănt), *n.* one who or that which strives against an opposing force:—*adj.* opposing.

re-sist-i-ble (rē-zĭs′tĭ-bl), *adj.* capable of being opposed, as a force.

re-sist-less (rē-zĭst′lĕs), *adj.* **1,** having no power to oppose or withstand; powerless; **2,** not to be withstood.—*adv.* **re-sist′less-ly.**—*n.* **re-sist′less-ness.**

res-o-lute (rĕz′ō-lūt), *adj.* determined; firm; as, a *resolute* will.—*adv.* **res′o-lute-ly.**—*n.* **res′o-lute-ness.**

Syn. steady, steadfast, inflexible, constant. —*Ant.* indecisive, flexible.

res-o-lu-tion (rĕz″ō-lū′shŭn), *n.* **1,** the act of bringing something, as a chemical compound, into a simpler form or of dividing it into the parts of which it is made up; analysis; **2,** fixed determination; firmness of purpose; **3,** the purpose decided upon; **4,** a formal proposal or statement of opinion voted on and adopted in a legislative assembly or public meeting.

re-solve (rē-zŏlv′), *v.t.* [*p.t.* and *p.p.* -solved′ (-zŏlvd′), *p.pr.* -solv′ing], **1,** to change in form by formal vote; as, the board *resolved* itself into a committee; **2,** to reduce to simpler form; as, the matter *resolves* itself into a question of right and wrong; **3,** to separate into the parts of which the whole is made up; as, to *resolve* a word into its elements; **4,** to explain; clear up; as, to *resolve* a mystery; **5,** to work out or solve, as a problem; **6,** to make up one's mind to; decide; determine; as, he *resolved* to do better; **7,** to adopt by vote:—*v.i.* **1,** to separate into elements or parts; **2,** to come to a determination; decide firmly; **3,** to pass a formal resolution: —*n.* **1,** fixed purpose; determination; **2,** that which has been determined on; a resolution. —*n.* **re-solv′er.**—*adj.* **re-solv′a-ble.**

re-solved (rē-zŏlvd′), *p.adj.* firm in purpose; determined.—*adv.* **re-solv′ed-ly.**—*n.* **re-solv′ed-ness.**

res-o-nance (rĕz′ō-năns), *n.* **1,** the ability to send back or prolong sound; also, a round, full, vibrating quality of sound; as, the *resonance* of an organ; **2,** in physics, the lengthening or strengthening of a sound owing to sympathetic vibrations of a body set in motion by the waves of sound.

res-o-nant (rĕz′ō-nănt), *adj.* **1,** having the ability to return or prolong sound; echoing back; as, the *resonant* walls of a cave; 2, round, full, and vibrant in sound; 3, reënforcing a sound by vibrations of nearly the same frequency.—*adv.* **res'o-nant-ly.**

res-o-na-tor (rĕz'ō-nā"tẽr), *n.* 1, a device for reënforcing or analyzing sounds, consisting usually of a hollow vessel adjusted to respond by resonance to a note of definite pitch; 2, in radio, the high-frequency circuits of a receiving apparatus.

re-sort (rē-zôrt'), *n.* 1, the act of visiting a place frequently; 2, a place much visited; as, a summer *resort;* 3, that to which, or a person to whom, one applies for aid; refuge; as, charity is his final *resort;* 4, the act of going for aid, advantage, etc.:—*v.i.* 1, to go often, habitually, or in numbers; betake oneself; 2, to apply for assistance or for the gaining of an end; as, to *resort* to law.

¹re-sound (rē-zound'), *v.i.* 1, to sound loudly; as, his voice *resounded* far; 2, to be full of sound, as, the woods *resound* with song:—*v.t.* to cause to sound loudly or to reëcho.

²re-sound (rē-sound'), *v.i.* and *v.t.* to sound, or cause to sound, again.

re-source (rē-sōrs'), *n.* 1, that on which one depends for help or supply; an expedient; 2, knowledge of what to do in an emergency or difficulty; as, a man of *resource;* 3, in *pl.:* **a**, practical ingenuity; as, a man of unlimited *resources;* **b**, money or means of any kind which can be used or converted into money; as, a country's natural *resources;* **c**, the assets of an individual or a corporation.

Syn. means, contrivance, ingenuity, resort.

re-source-ful (rē-sōrs'fo͝ol), *adj.* having the ability necessary to meet unusual demands or sudden needs.—*n.* **re-source'ful-ness.**

re-spect (rē-spĕkt'), *n.* 1, regard for worth; honor and esteem; as, the world's *respect* for a great man; 2, thoughtful and attentive notice; as, have *respect* for my words; 3, undue favor or bias; as, to show *respect* for wealth; 4, a courteous manner of treating others; 5, a special point or particular; as, in certain *respects;* 6, relation, reference, or regard; as, with *respect* to a position; 7, in *pl.*, expression of good will or regard; as, to pay one's *respects:*—*v.t.* 1, to honor or esteem; 2, to regard as important; heed; as, to *respect* the advice of parents; 3, to avoid intrusion upon; as, to *respect* private property; 4, to have relation to; as, the matter *respects* our welfare.—*p.adj.* **re-spect'ed.**—*n.* **re-spect'er.**

Syn., *n.* deference. (See regard.)

re-spect-a-bil-i-ty (rē-spĕk"tȧ-bĭl'ĭ-tĭ), *n.* [*pl.* respectabilities (-tĭz)], the state or quality of being of good reputation, or good name; fair social standing.

re-spect-a-ble (rē-spĕk'tȧ-bl), *adj.* 1, worthy of regard or esteem; being of good name or repute; as, a *respectable* woman; 2, of moderate excellence or size; as, a *respectable* performance; a *respectable* number; 3, fairly good; presentable, as a suit; 4, *Colloq.*, proper; decent.—*adv.* **re-spect'a-bly.**—*n.* **re-spect'a-ble-ness.**

re-spect-ful (rē-spĕkt'fo͝ol), *adj.* showing, or marked by, proper regard, esteem, or courtesy, as manners.—*adv.* **re-spect'ful-ly.**—*n.* **re-spect'ful-ness.**

re-spect-ing (rē-spĕk'tĭng), *prep.* 1, considering; in view of; 2, with regard or relation to; as, *respecting* his conduct there is but one opinion.

re-spec-tive (rē-spĕk'tĭv), *adj.* relating to each of several persons or things; particular; as, their *respective* positions; the *respective* merits of two dogs.

re-spec-tive-ly (rē-spĕk'tĭv-lĭ), *adv.* as relating to each; as singly considered in the order named; as, the red, blue, and green ties are for James, George, and William, *respectively.*

re-spir-a-ble (rē-spīr'ȧ-bl; rĕs'pĭ-rȧ-bl), *adj.* that may be, or is fit to be, breathed; as, *respirable* air.

res-pi-ra-tion (rĕs"pĭ-rā'shŭn), *n.* 1, the act or process of breathing; 2, in animals, the inhaling of oxygen and the exhaling of carbon dioxide.

res-pi-ra-tor (rĕs'pĭ-rā"tẽr), *n.* 1, a helmet of cloth or other material, usually chemically treated, with glass eyepieces, worn, as in time of war, as a protection against poison gas, smoke, etc.; 2, any of various devices, similar in form or purpose, used in certain medical treatments.

re-spir-a-to-ry (rē-spīr'ȧ-tō-rĭ; rĕs'pĭ-rȧ-), *adj.* pertaining to, serving for, or caused by, breathing.

re-spire (rē-spīr'), *v.i.* [*p.t.* and *p.p.* -spired' (-spīrd'), *p.pr.* -spir'ing], to breathe:—*v.t.* to breathe in and out, as air.

res-pite (rĕs'pĭt), *n.* 1, a temporary putting off of the carrying out of a sentence; as, the murderer was granted a *respite;* 2, postponement; delay, as in the payment of a debt; 3, a brief period of rest; as, a *respite* from labor:—*v.t.* [*p.t.* and *p.p.* -pit-ed, *p.pr.* -pit-ing], 1, to grant a delay in the carrying out of a sentence upon; 2, to postpone; 3, to relieve by a short period of rest.

Syn., *n.* pause, interval, reprieve, stay.

re-splend-ence (rē-splĕn'dĕns), *n.* brilliant luster; intense light; splendor. Also, **re-splend'en-cy.**

re-splend-ent (rē-splĕn'dĕnt), *adj.* shining brilliantly; intensely bright; splendid.—*adv* **re-splend'ent-ly.**

re-spond (rē-spŏnd'), *v.i.* 1, to return an answer; make a reply; 2, to act in answer or sympathy; as, to *respond* to a friend's need; 3, to be liable; as, the defendant is held to *respond* in damages.—*n.* **re-spond'er.**

re-spond-ent (rē-spŏn'dĕnt), *n.* 1, one who answers or replies; 2, one who answers to a suit at law; a defendant:—*adj.* 1, giving, or given as, reply; answering; 2, defending.

re-sponse (rē-spŏns'), *n.* 1, the act of answering; answer; reply; 2, in a religious service, words said or sung by the congregation or choir in reply to the priest; 3, an act or feeling called forth by something; as, a *response* to an appeal for the Red Cross.

re-spon-si-bil-i-ty (rē-spŏn"sĭ-bĭl'ĭ-tĭ), *n.* [*pl.* responsibilities (-tĭz)], 1, the state of being answerable or accountable; 2, a charge, duty, or obligation; 3, ability to fulfil contracts.

re-spon-si-ble (rē-spŏn'sĭ-bl), *adj.* 1, involving trust, duty, or obligation; as, a *responsible* position; 2, answerable; liable to answer; as, a guardian is *responsible* to the law; 3, able to answer for one's conduct; trustworthy.—*adv.* **re-spon'si-bly.**—*n.* **re-spon'si-ble-ness.**

re-spon-sive (rē-spŏn'sĭv), *adj.* 1, pertaining to an answer or response; 2, containing responses, as a church service; 3, ready or inclined to answer; 4, easily moved to action or feeling; as, a *responsive* audience.—*adv.* **re-spon'sive-ly.**—*n.* **re-spon'sive-ness.**

¹rest (rĕst), *n.* 1, the act or condition of being quiet or at peace; freedom from disturbance; tranquillity; security; 2, sleep; slumber; 3, hence, death; 4, cessation of motion, effort, labor, or exertion; repose; quiet; 5, a place of quiet or repose; a shelter or lodging place, as for sailors; 6, that on which anything leans for support; foundation; 7, in music, a sign indicating a rhythmic silence of definite length; **8**, a short pause in the voice in reading; a cæsura in verse:—*v.i.* **1**, to stop moving or acting; pause; stop; **2**, to be satisfied; remain confident; **3**, to be fixed in any state or opinion; as, to *rest* content; **4**, to take repose; sleep; **5**, hence, to be dead; **6**, to be quiet or still; be at peace; **7**, to trust; depend; as, to *rest* on a man's word; **8**, to stand; lie; lean; also, to be founded or established: usually with *on;* **9**, to remain in one place; abide; **10**, to submit one's case, upon the evidence, to the tribunal for decision; also, to terminate voluntarily one's evidence so that the adversary's evidence may be given:—*v.t.* **1**, to place at rest or in repose; cause to take repose: often reflexive; **2**, to place on a support; base or ground; **3**, in law, to terminate the introduction of evidence on; as, the state *rests* its case.

²rest (rĕst), *n.* **1**, that which remains or is left; remainder: with *the;* **2**, those who remain; the others: preceded by *the* and used as a collective noun followed by a plural verb; as, the *rest* are not going:—*v.i.* to be and to continue to be; stay; as, we *rest* satisfied.

res-tau-rant (rĕs′tō-rănt; rĕs′tô-), *n.* a house where meals or refreshments are served to the public.

***res-tau-ra-teur** (rĕs″tō″rȧ″tûr′), [Fr.], *n.* the keeper of a restaurant, or public eating house.

rest-ful (rĕst′fo͞ol), *adj.* **1**, full of, or giving, repose; as, *restful* sleep; **2**, quiet.—*adv.* **rest′ful-ly.**—*n.* **rest′ful-ness.**

res-ti-tu-tion (rĕs″tĭ-tū′shŭn), *n.* **1**, the act of giving back to the rightful owner that which has been taken away or lost; **2**, the act of making good any loss, injury, or damage.

Syn. return, restoration, compensation, amends, redress, reparation.

res-tive (rĕs′tĭv), *adj.* **1**, unwilling to go forward; stubborn: said of horses; **2**, hence, restless under control; **3**, uneasy.—*adv.* **res′tive-ly.**—*n.* **res′tive-ness.**

Syn. fidgety, nervous.

rest-less (rĕst′lĕs), *adj.* **1**, without repose; uneasy; as, a *restless* manner; **2**, always active or in motion; never quiet; as, a *restless* child; *restless* waves; **3**, discontented; eager for change; as, a *restless* spirit; **4**, affording no repose; as, a *restless* night.—*adv.* **rest′less-ly.**—*n.* **rest′less-ness.**

Syn. wandering, roving, unsettled.—*Ant.* steady, calm, quiet, restful, composed.

res-to-ra-tion (rĕs″tō-rā′shŭn), *n.* the act of bringing back, or the state of being brought back, to a former condition or place; renewal; repair; return; as, *restoration* to health; *restoration* to office: **Restoration,** the return of Charles II to the throne of England in 1660.

re-stor-a-tive (rē-stōr′ȧ-tĭv), *n.* that which has power to bring back to a former state; esp., a food or medicine used to bring back health or to restore to consciousness:—*adj.* having power to bring back to a former state.

re-store (rē-stōr′), *v.t.* [*p.t.* and *p.p.* -stored′ (-stōrd′), *p.pr.* -stor′ing], **1**, to bring back to a former state; repair; **2**, to bring back to the owner.—*n.* **re-stor′er.**

re-strain (rē-strān′), *v.t.* **1**, to check; hold back; as, to *restrain* one's feelings; **2**, to limit; set bounds to; as, to *restrain* a people's liberty.—*adj.* **re-strain′a-ble.**—*adv.* **re-strain′ed-ly.**—*n.* **re-strain′er.**

Syn. bridle, confine, curb.

re-straint (rē-strānt′), *n.* **1**, the act of holding back or hindering from action of any kind; **2**, the state of being held back or hindered; confinement; **3**, that which limits or hinders; **4**, reserve.

Syn. constraint. *Restraint* implies force that prevents action and even feeling; it may be voluntary, or imposed by conditions or by physical force; as, *restraint* of temper under trying conditions is good sportsmanship; they placed the madman under *restraint*. *Constraint* implies force that compels a disagreeable course of action, or that restricts; as, lawless men know no *constraint*.

re-strict (rē-strĭkt′), *v.t.* to keep within bounds; confine or limit; as, to *restrict* a patient to a certain diet.—*p.adj.* **re-strict′ed.**—*adv.* **re-strict′ed-ly.**

re-stric-tion (rē-strĭk′shŭn), *n.* **1**, the act of limiting; **2**, the state of being limited; confinement within bounds; **3**, anything that prevents entire freedom of action; a limitation; as, building *restrictions.*

re-stric-tive (rē-strĭk′tĭv), *adj.* serving or tending to limit; as, *restrictive* laws of trade.—*adv.* **re-stric′tive-ly.**

re-sult (rē-zŭlt′), *n.* conclusion or end to which any course or condition of things leads; consequence; effect; as, the *result* of hard work:—*v.i.* **1**, to follow as a consequence or effect; as, good will *result* from this law; **2**, to conclude; end: with *in.*

Syn., n. consequence, event, issue. *Result* names the specific effect or outcome of an action or an effort as a whole; as, the *result* of an experiment. *Consequences* are *results,* often indirect, which naturally and logically follow a given act, often an act which the speaker condemns; as, the *consequences* of fast living; if you are late, you will have to take the *consequences. Issue* and *event* both denote the final outcome of a set of circumstances; as, the *issue* of a battle; in any *event,* the expedition will be of value.

re-sult-ant (rē-zŭl′tănt), *n.* that which follows as a consequence:—*adj.* following as a consequence.

re-sume (rē-zūm′), *v.t.* [*p.t.* and *p.p.* -sumed′ (-zūmd′), *p.pr.* -sum′ing], **1**, to take up again after interruption; begin again; as, to *resume* work; **2**, to take or occupy again; as, he *resumed* his seat; **3**, to go back to using; as, she *resumed* her needle.—*adj.* **re-sum′a-ble.**—*n.* **re-sum′er.**

***ré-su-mé** (rā″zü″mā′), [Fr.], *n.* a summary; as, a *résumé* of a book.

re-sump-tion (rē-zŭmp′shŭn), *n.* the act of taking up again after interruption, or of beginning again.

re-surge (rē-sûrj′), *v.i.* [*p.t.* and *p.p.* -surged′ (-sûrjd′), *p.pr.* -surg′ing], **1**, to rise again; **2**, to roll back, as the tide.

re-sur-gent (rē-sûr′jĕnt), *adj.* rising, or tending to rise, again:—*n.* one who rises again, as from the dead.

res-ur-rect (rĕz″ŭ-rĕkt′), *v.t.* **1**, to raise from the dead; **2**, *Colloq.*, to bring again to notice or use.

res-ur-rec-tion (rĕz″ŭ-rĕk′shŭn), *n.* **1**, a rising again; esp., the rising again from the dead; **2**, a springing into new life and freshness: **the Resurrection,** the rising of Christ from the dead.

res-ur-rec-tion-ist (rĕz″ŭ-rĕk′shŭn-ĭst), *n.* **1**, one who steals bodies from graves and sells them for dissection; **2**, one who revives or brings to light from obscurity again.

re-sus-ci-tate (rē-sŭs′ĭ-tāt), *v.t.* [*p.t.* and *p.p.*-tat″ed, *p.pr.*-tat″ing], to restore from apparent death; as, to *resuscitate* a drowned person:—*v.i.* to revive.

re-sus-ci-ta-tion (rē-sŭs″ĭ-tā′shŭn), *n.* **1**, the act of restoring to consciousness or life; **2**, restoration; revival.

re-sus-ci-ta-tive (rē-sŭs′ĭ-tā-tĭv), *adj.* having power to bring back to consciousness or life; restorative.

ret (rĕt), *v.t.* [*p.t.* and *p.p.* ret'ted, *p.pr.* ret'ting], to soak, as flax, hemp, etc., so as to remove natural juices or to loosen the fibers:—*v.i.* to rot by exposure to moisture.

re-tail (rē'tāl), *n.* the sale of goods in small quantities: opp. of *wholesale:* —*adj.* pertaining to, or engaged in, the sale of goods in small quantities:—*v.t.* (rē-tāl'; rē'tāl), **1**, to sell in small quantities, or directly to the consumer; **2**, to tell here and there; as, to *retail* gossip:—*v.i.* to sell goods in small quantities.—*n.* **re-tail'er.**

re-tain (rē-tān'), *v.t.* **1**, to hold or keep in possession, practice, control, use, etc.; **2**, to engage by a fee prepaid; hire; as, to *retain* a lawyer; **3**, to keep in mind.

re-tain-er (rē-tān'ēr), *n.* **1**, one kept in the service of a person of high rank or position; an adherent; **2**, one who keeps possession; **3**, a fee paid to a lawyer; also, the agreement made to employ a lawyer.

re-tain-ing wall a wall to prevent a bank of earth from sliding; sometimes, a revetment.

re-tal-i-ate (rē-tăl'ĭ-āt), *v.t.* [*p.t.* and *p.p.* -at″ed, *p.pr.* -at″ing], to return something of the same kind for; as, to *retaliate* a wrong:—*v.i.* to give like for like, esp. evil for evil; as, to *retaliate* for a wrong.—*adj.* **re-tal'i-a-tive.**—*adj.* **re-tal'i-a-to-ry.**

re-tal-i-a-tion (rē-tăl″ĭ-ā'shŭn), *n.* the act of returning like for like, esp. evil for evil; revenge.

re-tard (rē-tärd'), *v.t.* **1**, to cause to move more slowly; **2**, to hinder; delay; defer; put off:—*n.* delay.—*n.* **re-tard'er.**

re-tar-da-tion (rē″tär-dā'shŭn), *n.* **1**, the act of holding back or hindering; a lessening of speed or progress; delay; hindrance; **2**, the amount of delay or hindrance; **3**, that which retards or hinders.

retch (rĕch; *Br.* rēch), *v.i.* to try to vomit; strain, as in vomiting.

re-ten-tion (rē-tĕn'shŭn), *n.* **1**, the act of keeping in one's power or possession; **2**, the state of being kept in possession; **3**, the act or power of keeping things in mind; memory.

re-ten-tive (rē-tĕn'tĭv), *adj.* tending, or having the power, to keep; as, a *retentive* memory.—*adv.* **re-ten'tive-ly.**—*n.* **re-ten'tive-ness.**

ret-i-cence (rĕt'ĭ-sĕns), *n.* the characteristic, act, or habit of keeping silence; reserve in speech. Also, **ret'i-cen-cy.**

ret-i-cent (rĕt'ĭ-sĕnt), *adj.* disposed not to tell one's thoughts or feelings; silent; reserved in speech; as, a *reticent* man. —*adv.* **ret'i-cent-ly.**

re-tic-u-lar (rē-tĭk'ū-lȧr), *adj.* like a network.

re-tic-u-late (rē-tĭk'ū-lāt), *v.t.* [*p.t.* and *p.p.* -lat″ed, *p.pr.* -lat″ing], to make or mark like a network:—*v.i.* to form a network:—*adj.* (rē-tĭk'ū-lăt), **1**, marked or veined like network, as leaves; **2**, formed of fibers woven like network.—*n.* **re-tic″u-la'tion.**

ret-i-cule (rĕt'ĭ-kūl), *n.* a small hand bag or workbag, orig. made of network, carried by women.

re-ti-form (rē'tĭ-fôrm; rĕt'ĭ-), *adj.* arranged like a network.

ret-i-na (rĕt'ĭ-nȧ), *n.* the inner, sensitive coating of the eye, containing the ends of the nerves of sight; that part of the eye which receives the images of objects.

ret-i-nue (rĕt'ĭ-nū), *n.* the body of persons who attend a prince or person of distinction; a train of attendants.

re-tire (rē-tīr'), *v.i.* [*p.t.* and *p.p.* -tired' (-tīrd'), *p.pr.* -tir'ing], **1**, to go to a place of privacy; **2**, to withdraw; retreat; **3**, to withdraw from business, official, or active life; **4**, to go to bed:—*v.t.* **1**, to withdraw; as, to *retire* forces; **2**, to withdraw from circulation, or from the market, as stocks or currency; **3**, to cause to give up active service; as, to *retire* a naval officer.

re-tired (rē-tīrd'), *p.adj.* **1**, away or withdrawn from society; as, a *retired* life; **2**, having given up business or active life.

re-tire-ment (rē-tīr'mĕnt), *n.* **1**, the act of retreating or withdrawing from business or public life; **2**, the state of being withdrawn; privacy; solitude; **3**, a place removed from public notice.

re-tir-ing (rē-tīr'ĭng), *p.adj.* **1**, modest; not forward; quiet; shy; as, a *retiring* manner; **2**, pertaining to withdrawal from active service.

¹re-tort (rē-tôrt'), *n.* a quick, witty, or pointed reply to an argument, charge, taunt, or witticism:—*v.t.* **1**, to say as a retort; **2**, to return or fling back; as, to *retort* the charge of vanity:—*v.i.* to make a retort.

²re-tort (rē-tôrt'), *n.* a vessel or container made of glass, earthenware, metal, or the like, in which substances are subjected to a high temperature for purposes of distillation or decomposition (see *oxygen*, illus.):—*v.t.* to treat, as sulphur, by heating in a retort.

re-touch (rē-tŭch'), *v.t.* to touch again; improve by going over; as, to *retouch* a work of art.—*n.* **re-touch'er.**

re-trace (rē-trās'), *v.t.* [*p.t.* and *p.p.* -traced' (-trāst'), *p.pr.* -trac'ing], **1**, to follow back toward the place of beginning; **2**, to follow again from the beginning.

re-tract (rē-trăkt'), *v.t.* **1**, to draw back; **2**, to draw up or shorten; as, the cat can *retract* its claws; **3**, to recall or withdraw, as an accusation:—*v.i.* **1**, to withdraw something said or written; **2**, to draw back or up; as, muscles *retract* after being cut.
Syn. disavow, recant, repudiate.

re-trac-tile (rē-trăk'tĭl), *adj.* capable of being withdrawn, drawn up, or drawn in, as the feelers of a snail.

re-trac-tion (rē-trăk'shŭn), *n.* **1**, the act of taking back something said or written, or of drawing in or back; **2**, the state of being withdrawn.

re-trac-tive (rē-trăk'tĭv), *adj.* **1**, capable of withdrawing or taking back; **2**, like a withdrawal.

re-trac-tor (rē-trăk'tēr), *n.* one who or that which draws in or back; specif., a muscle or an instrument, as certain devices in surgery, for drawing back.

re-treat (rē-trēt'), *n.* **1**, the act of withdrawing or retiring; **2**, retirement or seclusion; **3**, a place of privacy; shelter; asylum; **4**, a shelter for nervous or insane persons, inebriates, etc.; **5**, the retiring of troops before an enemy or from an advanced position; **6**, a bugle call, the signal for retiring from an engagement or to quarters:—*v.i.* **1**, to go back or backward; **2**, to withdraw to seclusion or safety; **3**, to retire before an enemy.

re-trench (rē-trĕnch'), *v.t.* **1**, to reduce; **2**, to take away; as, to *retrench* certain rights:—*v.i.* to cut down expenses.
Syn. abridge, decrease, diminish, curtail.—*Ant.* expand, enlarge, increase.

re-trench-ment (rē-trĕnch'mĕnt), *n.* **1**, the act of reducing or lessening; **2**, reduction of expenses; **3**, a military work constructed inside another to resist an enemy should the outer line be taken.

re-tri-al (rē-trī'ăl), *n.* another trial or test; a second court trial.

ret-ri-bu-tion (rĕt″rĭ-bū'shŭn), *n.* reward or punishment suitable to a good or bad action; esp., loss or suffering considered as inflicted by way of recompense or just punishment for one's sins.

re-trib-u-tive (rē-trĭb′ū-tĭv), *adj.* rewarding good deeds and punishing offenses; as, the operation of *retributive* justice.—*adv.* **re-trib′u-tive-ly.**

re-trib-u-to-ry (rē-trĭb′ū-tō-rĭ), *adj.* serving as, or making, just reward or punishment.

re-trieve (rē-trēv′), *v.t.* [*p.t.* and *p.p.* -trieved′ (-trēvd′), *p.pr.* -triev′ing], **1**, to recover; regain; as, to *retrieve* a lost advantage; **2**, to restore; revive; as, to *retrieve* one's good name; **3**, to repair the harm done by; as, to *retrieve* a misfortune; **4**, in hunting, to fetch (wounded or killed game):—*v.i.* to find and bring in game.—*adj.* **re-triev′a-ble.**—*n.* **re-triev′al.**

re-triev-er (rē-trēv′ẽr), *n.* one who or that which retrieves; esp., a dog trained to find and bring in game.

re-tro- (rē′trō-; rĕt′rō-), *prefix*, **1**, backward; as, *retro*spect; *retro*grade; **2**, back; hinder: used esp. in scientific words.

re-tro-act (rē″trō-ăkt′; rĕt″rō-), *v.i.* **1**, to act backward or in opposition; **2**, to influence or alter what has been done.—*n.* **re″tro-ac′tion.**—*adj.* **re″tro-ac′tive.**

¹re-tro-cede (rē″trō-sēd′; rĕt″rō-), *v.t.* [*p.t.* and *p.p.* -ced′ed, *p.pr.* -ced′ing], to cede back.—*n.* **¹re″tro-ces′sion.**

²ret-ro-cede (rĕt′rō-sēd; rē′trō-), *v.i.* [*p.t.* and *p.p.* -ced′ed, *p.pr.* -ced′ing], to move back; recede; withdraw; retreat.—*n.* **²re″tro-ces′sion.**

ret-ro-grade (rĕt′rō-grād; rē′trō-), *adj.* **1**, directed or moving backward; reversed; retreating; **2**, going from a better to a worse state or character; as, a *retrograde* people:—*v.i.* [*p.t.* and *p.p.* -grad″ed, *p.pr.* -grad″ing], **1**, to go, or appear to go, backward; **2**, to go from better to worse.

re-tro-gres-sion (rē″trō-grĕsh′ŭn; rĕt″rō-), *n.* **1**, the act of going or moving backward; **2**, degeneration.

re-tro-gres-sive (rē″trō-grĕs′ĭv; rĕt″rō-), *adj.* **1**, going or moving backward; **2**, passing from a better to a worse state; declining.

ret-ro-spect (rĕt′rō-spĕkt; rē′trō-), *n.* a looking back on things past; a review of the past.

ret-ro-spec-tion (rĕt″rō-spĕk′shŭn; rē″trō-), *n.* **1**, the act of meditating upon things past; **2**, a calling to remembrance; a reviewing of the past.

ret-ro-spec-tive (rĕt″rō-spĕk′tĭv; rē″trō-), *adj.* **1**, looking back on things past; **2**, pertaining to the past.—*adv.* **ret″ro-spec′-tive-ly.**

***re-trous-sé** (rē-trōō″sā′), [Fr.], *adj.* turned up, as a nose.

re-tro-ver-sion (rē″trō-vûr′shŭn; rĕt″rō-), *n.* **1**, a turning or bending backward; **2**, the state of being turned or bent backward.

re-turn (rē-tûrn′), *v.i.* **1**, to come or go back again to the same place or state; as, to *return* to one's home; **2**, to begin or appear again; as, spring *returns;* **3**, to come or go back in thought or consideration; as, to *return* to the subject; **4**, to pass back into possession, as an estate; revert; **5**, to reply; make answer:—*v.t.* **1**, to send, carry, or put back; restore; as, to *return* a borrowed book; **2**, to repay, as a call; **3**, to produce or yield; as, the garden will *return* a profit; **4**, to send in reply; as, to *return* an answer; **5**, to report officially; render or give in, as a report; **6**, to elect; as, to *return* a man to Parliament; **7**, to throw back, as light; reflect; **8**, in various games, to strike or play (the ball) back:—*n.* **1**, a coming or going back to or from a place, condition, or the like; as, a *return* from a vacation; a *return* to health; **2**, a restoring or giving back, as of something lost; **3**, that which is restored or given back; **4**, repayment; **5**, that which is received from labor, investment, or the like; profit; advantage; **6**, a formal report or statement of results; as, election *returns;* **7**, election, generally as member of Parliament; **8**, a response or answer; **9**, in *pl.:* **a**, results; **b**, proceeds.

re-turn-a-ble (rē-tûr′nȧ-bl), *adj.* **1**, capable of being given or sent back; **2**, due, or required, to be given back at a certain time and place; as, a book *returnable* within seven days.

Reu-ben (rōō′bĕn), *n.* in the Bible, the eldest son of Jacob; also, the tribe of Israel that bore his name.

re-un-ion (rē-ūn′yŭn), *n.* **1**, the act of joining again; **2**, the state of being joined again; **3**, a gathering of persons, as of members of a family or of a college, who have been separated.—*n.* **re-un′ion-ist.**

re-u-nite (rē″ū-nīt′), *v.t.* [*p.t.* and *p.p.* -nit′ed, *p.pr.* -nit′ing], **1**, to bring together or join again; **2**, to reconcile after disagreement:—*v.i.* to become joined again.

re-vamp (rē-vămp′), *v.t.* **1**, to supply (a shoe) with a new vamp, or upper; **2**, hence, to patch; make over.

re-veal (rē-vēl′), *v.t.* **1**, to make known; disclose; unveil; **2**, to communicate, or make known, by divine or supernatural means.—*n.* **re-veal′er.**

re-veil-le (rē-vāl′yȧ; rĕv″ē-lē′; rĕv′ē-lē″), *n.* in the early morning, the beat of a drum, or the bugle call, that rouses the soldier or sailor for his day's duty.

rev-el (rĕv′ĕl), *n.* a noisy or riotous feast; wild merrymaking:—*v.i.* **1**, to take part in wild merrymaking; **2**, to take great delight: with *in;* as, to *revel* in music.—*n.* **rev′el-er; rev′el-ler.**

rev-e-la-tion (rĕv″ē-lā′shŭn), *n.* **1**, the act of making known that which before was secret or private; **2**, the state of being made known; **3**, that which is made known: **Revelation** (*abbr.* **Rev.**), the last book of the New Testament, ascribed to the apostle John, and containing mystic prophecies; the Apocalypse.

rev-el-ry (rĕv′ĕl-rĭ), *n.* [*pl.* revelries (-rĭz)], uproarious merrymaking.

re-venge (rē-vĕnj′), *n.* **1**, the act of returning an injury; **2**, malicious injury in return for an offense received; **3**, a desire to return evil for evil; **4**, a chance to obtain satisfaction; as, to give a card player his *revenge:*—*v.t.* [*p.t.* and *p.p.* -venged′ (-vĕnjd′), *p.pr.* -veng′ing], to inflict pain or punishment in return for; avenge; as, to *revenge* an insult.—*n.* **re-veng′er.**

Syn., v. retaliate, requite. (See avenge.)

re-venge-ful (rē-vĕnj′fōōl), *adj.* full of the desire to inflict harm or injury in return for injury received.—*adv.* **re-venge′ful-ly.**—*n.* **re-venge′ful-ness.**

Syn. vindictive, resentful, malicious.—*Ant.* forgiving, humane, merciful, kindly.

rev-e-nue (rĕv′ē-nū), *n.* **1**, that which returns from, or is yielded by, an investment; income from any property; **2**, the general income of a state, city, etc., as from taxes or customs.

re-ver-ber-ant (rē-vûr′bẽr-ănt), *adj.* echoing; resonant.

re-ver-ber-ate (rē-vûr′bẽr-āt), *v.t.* [*p.t.* and *p.p.* -at″ed, *p.pr.* -at″ing], **1**, to send back; cause to echo, as sound; **2**, to reflect, as heat or light:—*v.i.* **1**, to be driven back, or reflected, as heat or light; **2**, to resound.—*adj.* **re-ver′ber-a-tive.**

re-ver-ber-a-tion (rē-vûr″bẽr-ā′shŭn), *n.* **1**, the reflection of light or heat; **2**, the echoing of sound.

re-ver-ber-a-to-ry (rē-vûr′bẽr-ȧ-tō-rĭ), *adj.* **1**, pertaining to reverberation; **2**, acting so as to send back or reflect flame or heat; as, a *reverberatory* furnace; **3**, reflected or forced back, as flame.

re-vere (rē-vēr′), *v.t.* [*p.t.* and *p.p.* -vered′ (-vērd′), *p.pr.* -ver′ing], to regard with respectful and affectionate awe; honor.

rev-er-ence (rĕv′ẽr-ĕns), *n.* **1**, deep respect mingled with awe and affection; veneration; **2**, any act or sign of respect, as a low bow; **3**, the state of being respected: **Reverence**, a title given to the clergy: with *his* or *your:*—*v.t.* [*p.t.* and *p.p.* -enced (-ĕnst), *p.pr.* -enc-ing], **1**, to regard with affectionate respect; hold in high esteem; **2**, to bow to with great respect.
Syn., *n.* deference, homage, honor.

rev-er-end (rĕv′ẽr-ĕnd), *adj.* **1**, worthy of reverence, or deep respect; **2**, pertaining to the clergy: **Reverend**, a title of respect given to clergymen.

rev-er-ent (rĕv′ẽr-ĕnt), *adj.* showing, or expressive of, respect and affection mingled with awe or fear; humble; submissive.—*adv.* **rev′er-ent-ly.**

rev-er-en-tial (rĕv″ẽr-ĕn′shăl), *adj.* proceeding from, or showing, deep respect mingled with awe and affection; reverent.—*adv.* **rev″er-en′tial-ly.**

rev-er-ie (rĕv′ẽr-ĭ), *n.* **1**, deep musing; dreaminess; **2**, the state of being lost in thought or dreams. Also, **rev′er-y.**

re-ver-sal (rē-vûr′săl), *n.* **1**, the act of causing to turn back or move in an opposite direction; as, the *reversal* of a rotating wheel; **2**, a causing to be, or appearing to be, upside down or turned around; **3**, a change to an opposite or to a former state; **4**, a setting aside or annulling.

re-verse (rē-vûrs′), *n.* **1**, the direct contrary or opposite; **2**, the back or less important side, as of a coin or medal: opp. of *obverse;* **3**, a change for the worse; misfortune; as, business *reverses;* **4**, check; defeat; as, the enemy met with a *reverse:*—*v.t.* [*p.t.* and *p.p.* -versed′ (-vûrst′), *p.pr.* -vers′ing], **1**, to turn back or upside down; **2**, to cause to move in an opposite direction; **3**, to exchange; transpose; as, to *reverse* positions; **4**, to set aside or annul; as, to *reverse* a judgment:—*v.i.* **1**, to move in an opposite direction; **2**, to change to a former state:—*adj.* **1**, turned backward; opposite; **2**, causing an opposite motion; as, the *reverse* gear in an automobile.—*adv.* **re-verse′ly.**

re-vers-i-ble (rē-vûr′sĭ-bl), *adj.* **1**, capable of being turned back or of being put each in the place of the other; **2**, capable of being used on both sides; as, *reversible* cloth; **3**, liable to be, or capable of being, set aside; as, a *reversible* judgment.

re-ver-sion (rē-vûr′shŭn), *n.* **1**, the right to future enjoyment or possession; as, the *reversion* of a title; **2**, the act of turning, or the condition of being turned, in an opposite direction; **3**, in biology, the tendency of the descendants of variants to return to their original type.

re-ver-sion-a-ry (rē-vûr′shŭn-ā-rĭ), *adj.* **1**, pertaining to the right of future possession; **2**, in law, pertaining to, of the nature of, or involving, the returning of an estate to the grantor or his heirs, after the grant has terminated.

re-vert (rē-vûrt′), *v.i.* **1**, to return or go back; recur; **2**, to return to the original owner or his heirs; **3**, in biology, to return to an earlier type.

re-vert-i-ble (rē-vûr′tĭ-bl), *adj.* **1**, capable of being turned back; **2**, capable of being, or deserving to be, returned to the original owner or his heirs.

rev-er-y (rĕv′ẽr-ĭ), *n.* [*pl.* reveries (-ĭz)], **1**, deep musing; **2**, the state of being lost in thought. Also, **rev′er-ie,** *Pfd. S.*

re-vet-ment (rē-vĕt′mĕnt), *n.* **1**, a covering of stone, cement, etc., to hold in place a sloping embankment; **2**, a retaining wall; **3**, a veneer of stone or other hard substance over less durable material.

re-view (rē-vū′), *n.* **1**, a going over anything again to consider or examine it; **2**, examination by a higher court of the decision of a lower court; **3**, a lesson studied or recited again; **4**, a survey of the past; **5**, a criticism, esp. of a new publication or a work of art; **6**, a magazine or newspaper with criticisms on new books, essays or the like; **7**, inspection of troops under arms, by a higher officer, for the purpose of ascertaining the state of their discipline, equipment, etc.:—*v.t.* **1**, to study or examine again; **2**, to go over in order to make corrections; revise; examine critically; also, to write a critical notice of; **3**, to look back on; **4**, to inspect, as troops; **5**, of a court, to examine (a decision of a lower court):—*v.i.* to write criticisms of books, art, essays, or the like.—*n.* **re-view′er.**

re-vile (rē-vīl′), *v.t.* and *v.i.* [*p.t.* and *p.p.* -viled′ (-vīld′), *p.pr.* -vil′ing], to address with abusive or vile language; treat with abuse.—*n.* **re-vile′ment.**—*n.* **re-vil′er.**
Syn. abuse, slander, malign, vilify.—*Ant.* extol, honor, praise.

re-vise (rē-vīz′), *v.t.* [*p.t.* and *p.p.* -vised′ (-vīzd′), *p.pr.* -vis′ing], **1**, to go over and examine for correction; change and correct; as, to *revise* a manuscript; **2**, to improve:—*n.* a revision.—*n.* **re-vis′er; re-vi′sor.**

re-vi-sion (rē-vĭzh′ŭn), *n.* **1**, the act of examining for correction, as a manuscript; **2**, that which has been examined and corrected; a corrected edition.

re-viv-al (rē-vīv′ăl), *n.* **1**, the act of bringing back to life; also, a return to consciousness; **2**, a new awakening of spirits or energy; **3**, renewed public attention to, or interest in, something, as art, literature, or religion, after a period of indifference; **4**, esp., a meeting or series of meetings to arouse and stimulate interest in religion; **5**, a reproduction; as, the *revival* of an old play.

re-viv-al-ist (rē-vīv′ăl-ĭst), *n.* one who conducts meetings or uses other means to arouse interest in religion.

re-vive (rē-vīv′), *v.i.* [*p.t.* and *p.p.* -vived′ (-vīvd′), *p.pr.* -viv′ing], **1**, to come back to life; as, hope *revived* in him; **2**, to return to consciousness, as after fainting; **3**, to return to vigor or activity, esp. from a state of languor, neglect, or the like; as, learning *revived* in the 15th century:—*v.t.* **1**, to restore to life again; **2**, to give new vigor to; refresh; **3**, to bring back from a state of neglect; **4**, to recall to the mind.—*n.* **re-viv′er.**

re-viv-i-fy (rē-vĭv′ĭ-fī), *v.t.* [*p.t.* and *p.p.* -fied (-fīd), *p.pr.* -fy″ing], **1**, to renew life or interest in; **2**, to restore life to; quicken.—*n.* **re-viv″i-fi-ca′tion.**

rev-o-ca-ble (rĕv′ō-kȧ-bl), *adj.* capable of being called back.—*n.* **rev′o-ca-ble-ness.**—*n.* **rev″o-ca-bil′i-ty.**

rev-o-ca-tion (rĕv″ō-kā′shŭn), *n.* the act of annulling or repealing; reversal; repeal; as, the *revocation* of a law.

re-voke (rē-vōk′), *v.t.* [*p.t.* and *p.p.* -voked′ (-vōkt′), *p.pr.* -vok′ing], to make of no effect by recalling; repeal; annul, as a law or license:—*v.i.* in card playing, to fail to follow suit when able:—*n.* the act of thus failing to follow suit at cards.

re-volt (rē-vōlt′; rē-vŏlt′), *n.* an outbreak or uprising against authority; rebellion:—*v.i.* **1**, to turn away in disgust; be shocked; **2**, to rebel:—*v.t.* to cause to turn

away or shrink with disgust or loathing; shock.—*n.* **re-volt′er.**
Syn., n. insurrection. (See **revolution.**)

re-volt-ing (rē-vōlt′ĭng; rē-vŏlt′ĭng), *p.adj.* **1,** disgusting; loathsome; as, *revolting* cruelty; **2,** rebelling.

rev-o-lu-tion (rĕv″ō-lū′shŭn), *n.* **1,** the course of a body, esp. a heavenly body, in a closed curve around a point considered as fixed, or the complete turn of the body made in such a course; as, the *revolution* of the earth in its orbit; **2,** the round-and-round motion of a body that is spinning about an axis outside itself: distinguished from *rotation;* **3,** the space measured by the regular return of some one point on a turning body; **4,** a succession of changes or events happening in a cycle; as, the *revolution* of the months; **5,** the time occupied by such a cycle; circuit; **6,** a sudden change in the government of a country; the overthrow of one form of government and the setting up of another; **7,** any sudden change, as in ideas: **the Revolution,** in the U. S., the revolt of the American colonies against Great Britain (1775–83).—*n.* **rev″o-lu′tion-ism.**—*n.* **rev″o-lu′tion-ist.**
Syn. rebellion, revolt, mutiny, sedition, insurrection. *Revolution* suggests a fundamental change of government brought about by those governed, and may or may not be accompanied by bloodshed. *Rebellion* means organized resistance to established government, and implies fighting. *Revolt* names an uprising against authority which lacks the scope of *rebellion* in its early stages, and is applied to uprisings of downtrodden peoples. *Mutiny* implies *revolt* against authority, usually on the part of soldiers or sailors against officers. *Sedition* suggests rebellious plotting that, if successful, will be treason.

rev-o-lu-tion-a-ry (rĕv″ō-lū′shŭn-ā-rĭ), *adj.* pertaining to a sudden and complete change, esp. in the government of a country:—*n.* [*pl.* revolutionaries (-rĭz)], one who takes part in such a change.

rev-o-lu-tion-ist (rĕv″ō-lū′shŭn-ĭst), *n.* one who favors or takes part in a sudden and complete change, esp. in the government of a country.

rev-o-lu-tion-ize (rĕv″ō-lū′shŭn-īz), *v.t.* [*p.t.* and *p.p.* -ized (-īzd), *p.pr.* -iz″ing], to cause an entire change in the government, affairs, or character of.

re-volve (rē-vŏlv′), *v.i.* [*p.t.* and *p.p.* -volved′ (-vŏlvd′), *p.pr.* -volv′-ing], **1,** to turn round, as on an axis or in a curving path; rotate; **2,** to move in cycles; occur regularly:—*v.t.* **1,** to cause to turn or roll around; **2,** to turn over and over in the mind.—*adj.* **re-volv′a-ble.**—*p.adj.* **re-volv′ing.**

re-volv-er (rē-vŏl′vẽr), *n.* **1,** that which turns around; **2,** a pistol having chambers in a cylinder that turns around, so that it may be fired several times in succession without loading between shots.

re-vul-sion (rē-vŭl′shŭn), *n.* **1,** a sudden and violent change, esp. of feeling; **2,** the act of holding or drawing back from something; a strong reaction; a violent recoil.—*adj.* **re-vul′sive.**—*adv.* **re-vul′sive-ly.**

re-ward (rē-wôrd′), *n.* **1,** something given as a return for good or ill received, esp. in appreciation of praiseworthy conduct; **2,** money offered for service or for the return of something lost; **3,** profit; return:—*v.t.* **1,** to give in return for (good or ill received); **2,** to show appreciation of by giving something; **3,** to make a return to (somebody) or for (something); requite; recompense.
Syn., n. pay, remuneration, compensation.

Rey-nard (rā′nȧrd; rĕn′ȧrd), *n.* the fox in legend, fable, poetry, etc.: **reynard,** a fox.

rhap-sod-ic (răp-sŏd′ĭk), *adj.* **1,** extravagant, emotional, and disconnected: used of literary or musical composition; as, a book of *rhapsodic* verses; **2,** too enthusiastic; gushing. Also, **rhap-sod′i-cal.**

rhap-so-dist (răp′sō-dĭst), *n.* **1,** among the ancient Greeks, one whose profession it was to recite the Homeric or other epics; **2,** one who recites extempore verses for a livelihood; **3,** one who composes highly emotional, irregular music; **4,** one who writes or speaks with great show of feeling.

rhap-so-dize (răp′sō-dīz), *v.t.* and *v.i.* [*p.t.* and *p.p.* -dized (-dīzd), *p.pr.* -diz″ing], to write or speak in a rapturous, emotional, and disconnected way.

rhap-so-dy (răp′sō-dĭ), *n.* [*pl.* rhapsodies (-dĭz)], **1,** a disconnected, extravagant piece of literature, composed under the influence of excitement and marked by exaggerated feeling; **2,** any rapturous utterance; **3,** a part of an epic poem suitable for recitation at one time; **4,** a highly emotional instrumental composition.

rhe-a (rē′ȧ), *n.* the South American ostrich: **Rhea,** in mythology, the mother of many of the gods.

Rhein-gold (rīn′gōld″; *Ger.* rīn′gôlt″), *n.* in Teutonic mythology, a magic hoard of gold which was guarded by the Rhine maidens for its owner, a dwarf, but which was seized by Loki, and finally passed into the possession of the Nibelungs: told of in the "Volsunga Saga" and in the "Nibelungenlied." Also, **Rhine′gold″.**

Rhen-ish (rĕn′ĭsh), *adj.* of or pertaining to the river Rhine, or to the country near it:—*n.* wine from this section.

rhe-o-stat (rē′ō-stăt), *n.* an instrument for varying the strength of an electric current by varying the resistance in the circuit.

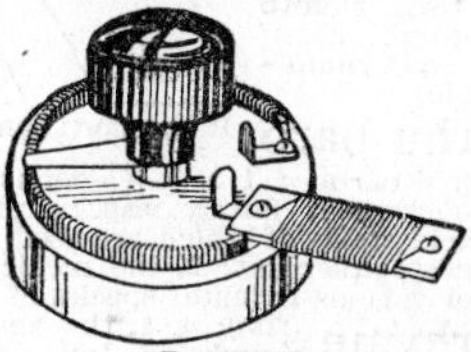
RHEOSTAT

rhet-o-ric (rĕt′ō-rĭk), *n.* **1,** the art of speaking or writing with elegance and force; also, a textbook dealing with this subject; **2,** skilful discourse; esp., fine speech without conviction or feeling; **3,** figuratively, the power of charming and influencing.

rhe-tor-i-cal (rē-tŏr′ĭ-kăl), *adj.* **1,** pertaining to the rules governing literary composition or fine speaking; **2,** oratorical.—*adv.* **rhe-tor′i-cal-ly.**

rhet-o-ri-cian (rĕt″ō-rĭsh′ăn), *n.* **1,** a master or teacher of the rules governing literary composition; **2,** a showy writer or speaker.

rheu-mat-ic (ro͞o-măt′ĭk), *adj.* pertaining to, affected with, or caused by, rheumatism. Also, **rheu-mat′i-cal.**

rheu-ma-tism (ro͞o′mȧ-tĭzm), *n.* **1,** loosely, any painful condition of joints and muscles; **2,** an acute, infectious disease of unknown origin, characterized by fever, inflammation and swelling of joints, and a tendency to heart disease: also called *rheumatic fever.*

rhine-stone (rīn′stōn″), *n.* a colorless, paste gem, made in imitation of a diamond, and used in cheap jewelry.

rhi-noc-er-os (rī-nŏs′ẽr-ŏs), *n.* any of a family of massive, thick-skinned, herb-eating animals of tropical Asia and Africa, having one or two horns on the snout (see illus. next page).

rhi-zome (rī'zōm), *n.* a rootstock; a stem in the ground, which produces roots below and leaves above.

rho (rō), *n.* the 17th letter [ρ, P] of the Greek alphabet, approximately equivalent to English *r*, or to *rh* when initial.

rho-di-um (rō'dĭ-ŭm), *n.* a rare, grayish white, lustrous metallic element, found in platinum ores.

RHINOCEROS
1, African; 2, Asiatic.

rho-do-den-dron (rō″dō-dĕn'drŏn), *n.* any of various shrubs with large flowers of white, pink, or lavender.

rhom-bo-he-dron (rŏm″bō-hē'drŏn), *n.* a prism whose six faces are oblique parallelograms (see *solid*, illus.).—*adj.* **rhom″bo-he'dral.**

rhom-boid (rŏm'boid), *n.* a parallelogram whose sides are unequal and whose angles are oblique:—*adj.* shaped like, or nearly like, such a figure.—*adj.* **rhom-boi'dal.**—*adv.* **rhom-boi'dal-ly.**

rhom-bus (rŏm'bŭs), *n.* a parallelogram whose sides are equal and whose angles are oblique. Also, **rhomb** (rŏmb; rŏm).—*adj.* **rhom'-bic.**

RHOMBUS (1) and RHOMBOID (2)

rhu-barb (rōō'bärb), *n.* **1,** any of a genus of plants of the buckwheat family, esp. a plant, the fleshy, acid stalks of which are used for cooking purposes; pieplant; **2,** the medicinal root of any of various Oriental species of this plant.

rhyme (rīm), *n.* **1,** the agreement in final sounds of two or more words; **2,** a word agreeing in final sound with another; **3,** a verse or line in such agreement; **4,** verse, or poetry, in which the last words of some of the lines correspond in sound:—*v.i.* [*p.t.* and *p.p.* rhymed (rīmd), *p.pr.* rhym'ing], **1,** to accord in sound; **2,** to end in the same sound; **3,** to make verses:—*v.t.* **1,** to make to correspond in sound; **2,** to express in verse. See ²**rime,** *Pfd. S.*—*n.* **rhym'er; rhyme'ster.**

rhythm (rĭthm; rĭthm), *n.* **1,** the regular recurrence, as in poetry or music, of stress, accent, or quantity; **2,** movement marked by a regular, measured recurrence.

rhyth-mi-cal (rĭth'mĭ-kăl; rĭth'mĭ-kăl), *adj.* marked by regularly recurring movement or accent; periodic; metrical. Also, **rhyth'mic.**—*adv.* **rhyth'mi-cal-ly.**

ri-al (rē-äl'), *n.* the monetary unit of Persia, equivalent to about five cents: replacing the reyal in March, 1932.

Ri-al-to (rē-äl'tō; rĭ-ăl'tō), *n.* **1,** in Venice, the ancient business district: with *the;* **2,** a bridge across the Grand Canal, in Venice: **rialto,** [*pl.* rialtos (-tōz)], **1,** a market; **2,** in New York City, the theatrical district.

rib (rĭb), *n.* **1,** one of the set of long, flat, curved bones attached to the spine, and encircling and offering protection for the cavity of the chest; in man, one of the twelve pairs of bones so placed; **2,** anything like a rib in shape or function, as a ridge in fabrics or knitted work, or a rod in an umbrella frame; **3,** a piece of timber to shape and strengthen the side of a ship; **4,** a fore-and-aft member of the wing structure of an airplane, used to give the wing section its form, and to transmit the load from the fabric to the spars (see *airplane*, illus.); **5,** the main vein of a leaf: **false ribs,** the five pairs of ribs not attached to the sternum:—*v.t.* [*p.t.* and *p.p.* ribbed (rĭbd), *p.pr.* rib'bing], to inclose, strengthen, or mark with, or as with, ribs.

rib-ald (rĭb'ăld), *adj.* indecent; low; filthy; as, a *ribald* song.

rib-ald-ry (rĭb'ăld-rĭ), *n.* [*pl.* ribaldries (-rĭz)], indecency.

rib-bon (rĭb'ŭn), *n.* **1,** a fine fabric woven in a narrow strip with two selvages; **2,** a strip or shred; as, a curtain torn to *ribbons:*—*v.t.* to ornament with ribbons. Also, *Archaic,* **rib'and; rib'band.**

rice (rīs), *n.* **1,** a valuable cereal grain, produced extensively in warm countries; **2,** the grass bearing this grain.

rice-bird (rīs'bûrd″), *n.* the bobolink: so called in the southern U. S. because it feeds on rice in the autumn.

rice pa-per **1,** a thin paper made from rice straw; **2,** a delicate paper made in China and used in art.

rich (rĭch), *adj.* **1,** having much money or many possessions; wealthy; **2,** expensive; valuable; as, *rich* clothing; **3,** great in amount; abundant; as, *rich* crops; **4,** fertile; as, *rich* soil; **5,** abounding in pleasing, desirable, or valuable qualities; as, *rich* perfumes or food; **6,** vivid; as, *rich* colors; **7,** sweet and full in sound; **8,** *Colloq.*, full of humor:—*n.* **1,** wealthy people collectively: with *the;* **2,** in *pl.*, wealth.—*adv.* **rich'ly.**—*n.* **rich'ness.**

Syn., *adj.* opulent, affluent; fruitful.

rick (rĭk), *n.* a stack, or rounded pile, as of hay or straw, in the open air:—*v.t.* to pile or heap in a stack.

rick-ets (rĭk'ĕts), *n.* a constitutional disease of children, marked by malnutrition and by softness and curving of the bones: also called *rachitis.*

rick-et-y (rĭk'ĕt-ĭ), *adj.* **1,** affected with rickets, a child's disease; **2,** feeble; shaky; as, a *rickety* chair.

ric-o-chet (rĭk″ō-shā'; rĭk″ō-shĕt'), *n.* the rebounding or skipping of anything along the ground or over the surface of the water:—*v.i.* [*p.t.* and *p.p.* -cheted' (-shād') or -chet'ted (-shĕt'ĕd), *p.pr.* -chet'ing (-shā'ĭng) or -chet'ting (-shĕt'ĭng)], to rebound by touching the earth or the surface of water and glancing off, as a cannon ball; skip; skim:—*v.t.* to cause to rebound or skip.

rid (rĭd), *v.t.* [*p.t.* and *p.p.* rid or rid'ded, *p.pr.* rid'ding], to free; deliver; as, to *rid* one of a nuisance: **be rid of** or **get rid of,** to be, or become, free from; as, to *get rid of* a cold.

rid-dance (rĭd'ăns), *n.* **1,** the act of freeing from something unpleasant; **2,** the state of being released from something unpleasant; as, his going was a good *riddance.*

rid-den (rĭd'n), past participle of the irregular verb *ride.*

¹**rid-dle** (rĭd'l), *n.* **1,** a puzzling or perplexing question; **2,** a person or thing that is difficult to understand; an enigma; a mystery:—*v.t.* [*p.t.* and *p.p.* -dled (-ld), *p.pr.* -dling], to explain; solve:—*v.i.* to speak with doubtful meaning.

Syn., *n.* conundrum, paradox, puzzle.

²**rid-dle** (rĭd'l), *n.* a coarse sieve, as for sifting sand or ashes:—*v.t.* [*p.t.* and *p.p.* -dled (-ld), *p.pr.* -dling], **1,** to sift through a coarse sieve; **2,** to pierce with holes in many places; as, to *riddle* the board with shot:—*v.i.* to use a sieve.

ride (rīd), *n.* **1,** a journey on horseback or in a vehicle; **2,** a road intended for horseback travel:—*v.i.* [*p.t.* rode (rōd) or, *Archaic,* rid (rĭd), *p.p.* rid'den (rĭd'n) or, *Archaic,* rid, *p.pr.* rid'ing], **1,** to be carried on the back of a horse or other animal; **2,** to be borne along in or on a vehicle; **3,** of a vessel, to lie at anchor; **4,** to serve as a means of travel; as, the horse *rides* well:—*v.t.* **1,** to sit upon and manage, as a moving horse; **2,** to be carried on; as, to *ride* the waves; **3,** to traverse; perform, as a race; **4,** to cause to ride; as, he *rode* the baby on his back; **5,** to domineer.

rid-er (rīd'ẽr), *n.* **1,** a horseman; **2,** a section or clause added to a legislative bill.—*adj.* **rid'er-less.**

ridge (rĭj), *n.* **1,** the back, or projecting part of the back, of an animal; **2,** a range of hills or mountains; **3,** the extended projection where two slopes meet; as, the *ridge* of a roof; **4,** any raised strip or line, as of earth, in cloth, etc.:—*v.t.* [*p.t.* and *p.p.* ridged (rĭjd), *p.pr.* ridg'ing], to cover with ridges, or raised lines:—*v.i.* to become marked with raised lines.

ridge-pole (rĭj'pōl''), *n.* **1,** the horizontal timber at the top of a roof, to which the upper ends of the rafters are secured: also called *ridgepiece, ridgeboard,* and *ridgeplate* (see *queen-post, frame house,* illus.); **2,** the horizontal pole at the top of a tent.

ridg-y (rĭj'ĭ), *adj.* [*comp.* ridg'i-er, *superl.* ridg'i-est], having raised lines or strips; as, *ridgy* sand.

rid-i-cule (rĭd'ĭ-kūl), *n.* words, looks, or acts intended to cause the subject of them to be laughed at contemptuously; sarcasm; mockery; satire:—*v.t.* [*p.t.* and *p.p.* -culed (-kūld), *p.pr.* -cul''ing], to make fun of; treat with derision or contempt.

Syn., n. irony, derision, jeer.

ri-dic-u-lous (rĭ-dĭk'ū-lŭs), *adj.* deserving or exciting mockery or contempt; absurd and laughable.—*adv.* **ri-dic'u-lous-ly.**—*n.* **ri-dic'u-lous-ness.**

Syn. comical, funny. (See ludicrous.)

[1]**rid-ing** (rīd'ĭng), *n.* a road for horseback travel, esp. one through woods.

[2]**rid-ing** (rīd'ĭng), *n.* **1,** one of the three administrative divisions (North, East, or West Riding) of Yorkshire and, formerly, of Lincolnshire, England; **2,** any similar division of a county, as formerly in Pennsylvania and Long Island.

rid-ing light a white light, visible from all directions, carried by vessels riding at anchor (see *lantern,* illus.).

rife (rīf), *adj.* **1,** prevalent; common; existing generally; as, the opinion was everywhere *rife;* **2,** abounding; full of: with *with;* as, the town is *rife* with tales of war.

riff-raff (rĭf'răf''), *n.* **1,** scraps; **2,** the rabble; as, the *riffraff* of society.

[1]**ri-fle** (rī'fl), *v.t.* [*p.t.* and *p.p.* -fled (-fld), *p.pr.* -fling], **1,** to search thoroughly with intent to rob; plunder; **2,** to carry off, as booty.—*n.* **ri'fler.**

[2]**ri-fle** (rī'fl), *n.* **1,** a firearm with the barrel spirally grooved inside; **2,** in *pl.,* troops armed with such firearms:—*v.t.* [*p.t.* and *p.p.* -fled (-fld), *p.pr.* -fling], to groove (the barrel of a gun) spirally.

ri-fle-man (rī'fl-măn), *n.* [*pl.* riflemen (-mĕn)], a man armed with, or skilled in using, a rifle.

ri-fle pit a short trench behind a bank of earth, to protect riflemen.

rift (rĭft), *n.* an opening made by splitting; cleft; as, a *rift* in a cloud:—*v.t.* to cleave or split:—*v.i.* to burst open.

rig (rĭg), *n.* **1,** the arrangement of sails, masts, etc., of a vessel; **2,** *Colloq.,* an odd style of dress; **3,** an outfit:—*v.t.* [*p.t.* and *p.p.* rigged (rĭgd), *p.pr.* rig'ging], **1,** to furnish (a ship) with the equipment necessary for service; **2,** to fit; equip; **3,** *Colloq.,* to dress: with *out* or *up;* as, to *rig* oneself out for a party.

rig-a-doon (rĭg''ȧ-dōōn'), *n.* **1,** an old-fashioned lively dance performed by one couple; **2,** the music for it.

Ri-gel (rī'jĕl; rī'gĕl), *n.* a brilliant, bluish white star in the constellation Orion.

rig-ger (rĭg'ẽr), *n.* one whose occupation is to fit the shrouds, stays, etc., of a ship to its masts and yards.

rig-ging (rĭg'ĭng), *n.* **1,** the ropes by which the masts of a vessel are supported and the sails set or furled (see illus. page 613); **2,** any gear or tackle.

right (rīt), *adj.* **1,** straight; as, a *right* line; **2,** not oblique; as, a *right* angle; also, having its axis perpendicular to its base, as a cone or prism (see *solid,* illus.); **3,** in accordance with truth, justice, or law; ethically good; righteous; **4,** correct in views or judgment; not mistaken; **5,** fit; suitable; as, the *right* man for the position; **6,** pertaining to the side, esp. to the arm and hand, normally and traditionally more used for grasping, handling, etc.: opp. of *left;* **7,** in good condition; well; healthy; as, to be all *right;* **8,** most finished or ornamental; exposed to the eye in use; as, the *right* side of a carpet; **9,** most convenient; satisfactory; as, that will be all *right:* **right whale,** any of several whalebone whales, esp. one species which has an exceptionally large amount of whalebone and oil: so called because whalers considered it the "right" kind to take:—*adv.* **1,** in a straight line; directly; as, he went *right* to the place; **2,** justly; righteously; truthfully; as, to act *right;* **3,** suitably; in the proper way; as, nothing has been done *right;* **4,** correctly; as, to get the facts *right;* **5,** precisely; just; exactly; as, *right* there; *right* now; **6,** to the right hand; **7,** very; as, *right* honorable:—*n.* **1,** that which is correct or conforms to some rule; **2,** that which accords with truth, justice, propriety, virtue, or the like: opp. of *wrong;* as, to fight for the *right;* **3,** that to which one has a moral or legal claim; as, to defend one's *right;* **4,** the right-hand side: **Right,** in certain European legislative bodies, the Conservative party:—*v.t.* **1,** to restore to proper condition; correct; as, to *right* a room; *right* a wrong; **2,** to make straight or upright; **3,** to restore rights to, do justice to:—*v.i.* to recover the natural, generally the upright, position.—*n.* **right'ness.**

Syn., adj. lawful, honest, true, fair.

right an-gle an angle of 90 degrees on a plane surface, formed by two straight lines meeting perpendicularly at a point (see [1]*angle,* illus.).—*adj.* **right'-an''gled.**

right-eous (rī'chŭs), *adj.* **1,** living according to, or ruled by, the law of God; upright; as, a *righteous* man; **2,** justifiable; as, *righteous* anger; **3,** just; as, a *righteous* cause.—*adv.* **right'eous-ly.**

right-eous-ness (rī'chŭs-nĕs), *n.* **1,** the quality or state of being blameless or just; **2,** justice.

right-ful (rīt'fōōl), *adj.* **1,** having a just claim according to law; as, the *rightful* heir; **2,** just; as, a *rightful* claim; **3,** held by just claim; as, a *rightful* throne.—*adv.* **right'ful-ly.**—*n.* **right'ful-ness.**

right–hand (rīt'=hănd''), *adj.* **1,** pertaining to, or situated on, the side opposite the left; **2,** chiefly depended upon; as, my *right-hand* man.

right–hand-ed (rīt'=hăn''dĕd; -ĭd), *adj.* **1,** done or used with the right hand; **2,** able to use the right hand more easily than the left; **3,** rotating from left to right, as the hands of a clock; as, a *right-handed* screw.

right-ly (rīt′lĭ), *adv.* **1**, honestly; uprightly; as, duty *rightly* performed; **2**, properly; suitably; as, he is *rightly* called our benefactor; **3**, correctly; as, *rightly* informed.

rig-id (rĭj′ĭd), *adj.* **1**, unyielding; stiff; inflexible; **2**, strict; severe; as, *rigid* discipline.—*adv.* **rig′id-ly.**—*n.* **rig′id-ness.**

Syn. firm, stern, harsh, austere.

ri-gid-i-ty (rĭ-jĭd′ĭ-tĭ), *n.* **1**, stiffness; inflexibility; **2**, sternness; strictness in observing rules.

rig-ma-role (rĭg′mȧ-rōl), *n.* foolish, disconnected talk; nonsense.

rig-or (rĭg′ẽr), *n.* **1**, stiffness; rigidity; **2**, strictness; sternness; harshness; severity; as, to enforce a law with *rigor;* **3**, an act of cruelty or severity; **4**, (rī′gŏr; rĭg′ŏr), a violent chill or shivering caused by cold or nervous shock. Also, **rig′our.**

Syn. exactness, austerity, inclemency.—*Ant.* softness, gentleness, tenderness.

***ri-gor mor-tis** (rī′gŏr môr′tĭs), [Lat.], stiffness of the body occurring shortly after death.

rig-or-ous (rĭg′ẽr-ŭs), *adj.* **1**, marked by sternness or severity; as, *rigorous* discipline; **2**, exact; strict; as, *rigorous* honesty; **3**, harsh; bitter; as, a *rigorous* climate.—*adv.* **rig′or-ous-ly.**—*n.* **rig′or-ous-ness.**

Syn. austere, relentless. (See stern.)

Rigs-dag (rĭgz′dăg), *n.* the Danish parliament, or chief lawmaking body.

rile (rīl), *v.t.* [*p.t.* and *p.p.* riled (rīld), *p.pr.* ril′ing], *Colloq.*, **1**, to vex; irritate; **2**, to make muddy by stirring.

rill (rĭl), *n.* a small stream or rivulet; a brooklet.

rim (rĭm), *n.* a border, edge, or margin of an object, esp. when bound or raised:—*v.t.* [*p.t.* and *p.p.* rimmed (rĭmd), *p.pr.* rim′ming], **1**, to furnish with a border or edge; **2**, to serve as a border around.

Syn., *n.* brim, verge. (See border.)

¹rime (rīm), *n.* hoarfrost; white frost; congealed vapor.

²rime (rīm), *n.* **1**, the agreement in final sounds of two or more words; as, *rime* is found in the words *name* and *flame;* esp., such agreement at the end of related lines of verse; **2**, one of two or more words in which the final sounds are similar; as, *name* and *flame* are *rimes;* **3**, a verse or line in such agreement; **4**, verse, or poetry, in which all or parts of the last words of some of the lines correspond in sound:—*v.i.* [*p.t.* and *p.p.* rimed (rīmd), *p.pr.* rim′ing], **1**, to accord in terminal sounds; **2**, loosely, to harmonize or correspond in sound; **3**, to compose verses:—*v.t.* **1**, to make to agree in final sounds, as the lines of a poem; **2**, to put into verse. Also, **rhyme.**—*n.* **rim′er; rime′ster.**

rim-y (rīm′ĭ), *adj.* [*comp.* rim′i-er, *superl.* rim′i-est], frosty; covered with, or resembling, hoarfrost.

rind (rīnd), *n.* the outer skin or coat, as of fruit, or the bark of a tree.

rin-der-pest (rĭn′dẽr-pĕst), *n.* an infectious disease in cattle.

¹ring (rĭng), *n.* **1**, any circular band, or hoop; **2**, a small ornamental hoop, as of gold or silver, worn as an adornment, usually on the finger or in the ear; **3**, an arena, or space set off for contests or displays, as at a circus, fair, or prize fight; **4**, a combination of men, usually for a selfish aim, as to control the sale of some commodity, to guide public opinion or politics, or the like:—*v.t.* **1**, to put a ring around; encircle; hem in; **2**, to fit or decorate with a ring or rings.

²ring (rĭng), *v.i.* [*p.t.* rang (răng), *p.p.* rung (rŭng), *p.pr.* ring′ing], **1**, to sound musically or resound, as a bell when struck; **2**, to cause a bell to sound; as, *ring* for breakfast; **3**, to sound loudly and clearly; as, his voice *rang* out; **4**, to have a sensation of a buzzing sound; as, my ears *ring;* **5**, to resound; echo; as, the woods *ring* with song; **6**, to be known far and wide; be famous; as, his deeds *ring* through the country:—*v.t.* **1**, to cause (particularly a bell or other metal object) to give forth a resonant sound by a blow; **2**, to announce or proclaim by a bell; as, to *ring* the hours; **3**, to summon, control, or otherwise affect by a bell; as, to *ring* up a servant, a person on the telephone, or a theater curtain; **4**, to utter again and again; repeat:—*n.* **1**, the sound given out by metals or other substances when they are made to vibrate; as, the *ring* of fine glass; **2**, a characteristic sound or quality of utterance; as, a *ring* of sincerity.—*n.* **ring′er.**

ring-dove (rĭng′dŭv″), *n.* a European pigeon with a whitish patch on each side of the throat.

ring-lead-er (rĭng′lēd″ẽr), *n.* the head of a number of persons acting together, generally in some unlawful act.

ring-let (rĭng′lĕt), *n.* **1**, a little circle; a small ring; **2**, a curl of hair.

ring ou-zel a song bird of the British Isles, allied to the thrushes.

ring-worm (rĭng′wûrm″), *n.* a contagious skin disease marked by distinct, circular patches covered with scales.

rink (rĭngk), *n.* **1**, a clear space on the ice marked off for games; **2**, an inclosed sheet of ice or a floor for skating; also, the building in which such sports are held.

rinse (rĭns), *v.t.* [*p.t.* and *p.p.* rinsed (rĭnst), *p.pr.* rins′ing], to wash lightly; esp., to wash with clean water to remove soap:—*n.* a light wash, esp. to remove soap.—*n.* **rins′er.**

rins-ing (rĭn′sĭng), *n.* **1**, the liquid in which anything is rinsed; hence, the dregs; **2**, a rinse.

ri-ot (rī′ŭt), *n.* **1**, disorderly or uproarious behavior; **2**, in law, disturbance of the public peace by a number of persons who are unlawfully assembled; **3**, boisterous festivity; revelry; **4**, unrestrained behavior, display, or growth:—*v.i.* **1**, to raise an uproar; engage in a public disturbance; **2**, to eat and drink without restraint; revel; **3**, to act without restraint.—*n.* **ri′ot-er.**

ri-ot-ous (rī′ŭt-ŭs), *adj.* **1**, engaging in tumultuous disorder; **2**, indulging in revelry; wanton.—*adv.* **ri′ot-ous-ly.**—*n.* **ri′ot-ous-ness.**

Syn. noisy, clamorous.—*Ant.* quiet, orderly.

rip (rĭp), *v.t.* [*p.t.* and *p.p.* ripped (rĭpt), *p.pr.* rip′ping], **1**, to divide by tearing or cutting; tear or cut apart with violence: often with *up*, *off*, or *open;* **2**, to undo the seam of, by cutting the stitches; **3**, to saw (wood) with the grain; **4**, *Colloq.*, to utter violently; as, to *rip* out an oath:—*v.i.* to become torn apart:—*n.* a rent made by the breaking of stitches; tear.

ri-pa-ri-an (rĭ-pā′rĭ-ăn; rī-pā′rĭ-ăn), *adj.* pertaining to the banks of a river or a lake; as, *riparian* rights.

ripe (rīp), *adj.* **1**, grown to maturity or perfection; ready for harvest; as, *ripe* grain or fruit; **2**, brought to a state most fit for use; mellow; as, *ripe* cheese; **3**, advanced to a high degree; matured; as, *ripe* wisdom; **4**, ready to act; prepared; as, *ripe* for trouble.—*adv.* **ripe′ly.**—*n.* **ripe′ness.**

Syn. (see mellow).

rip-en (rīp′n), *v.t.* **1**, to make mature or bring into fit condition for use; **2**, to bring to full growth or perfection:—*v.i.* **1**, to become matured or fit for use; **2**, to come to perfection.

ri-poste (rē-pōst′), *n.* **1**, a return thrust in fencing; **2**, a quick, clever reply:

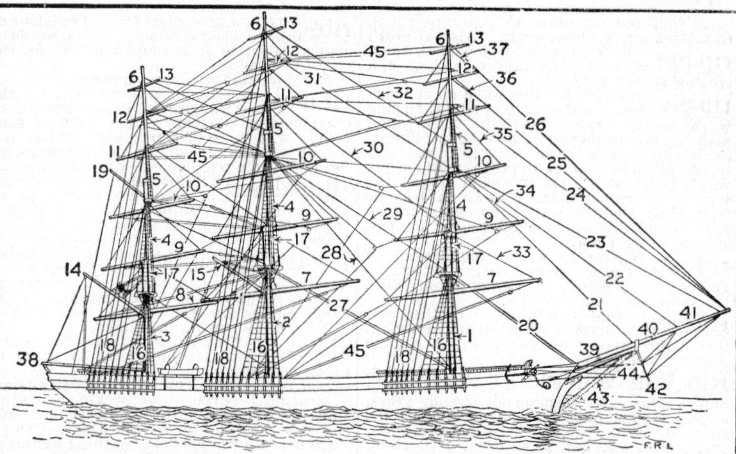

Standing and Running Rigging of a Full-rigged Ship

Explanation.—An asterisk [*] indicates that the part named is shown and numbered in the drawing on fore-, main-, and mizzenmast. A dagger [†] indicates that the part named is shown on fore-, main-, and mizzenmast, but is numbered only on the foremast. A double dagger [‡] indicates that the part named is shown in several places, not always all numbered.

1, foremast; 2, mainmast; 3, mizzenmast; *4, topmast; *5, topgallant mast; *6, royal and skysail masts; 7, yards (fore and main); 8, crossjack yard; *9, lower-topsail yards; *10, upper-topsail yards; *11, topgallant yards; *12, royal yards; *13, skysail yards; 14, spanker gaff; 15, try-sail gaff; *16, lower shrouds; *17, topmast shrouds; *18, backstays; 19, monkey gaff; 20, forestay; 21, fore-topmast stay; 22, jib stay; 23, outer-jib stay; 24, fore-topgallant stay; 25, fore-royal stay; 26, fore-skysail stay; 27, mainstay; 28, main-topmast lower stay; 29, main-topmast upper stay; 30, main-topgallant stay; 31, main-royal stay; 32, main-skysail stay; †33, lift; †34, lower-topsail lift; †35, upper-topsail lift; †36, topgallant lift; †37, royal lift; 38, spanker boom; 39, bowsprit; 40, jib boom; 41, flying-jib boom; 42, dolphin striker, with martingales running to jib boom and flying-jib boom; 43, bobstays; 44, back ropes; ‡45, braces for adjusting sails to wind, named for yards to which they belong.

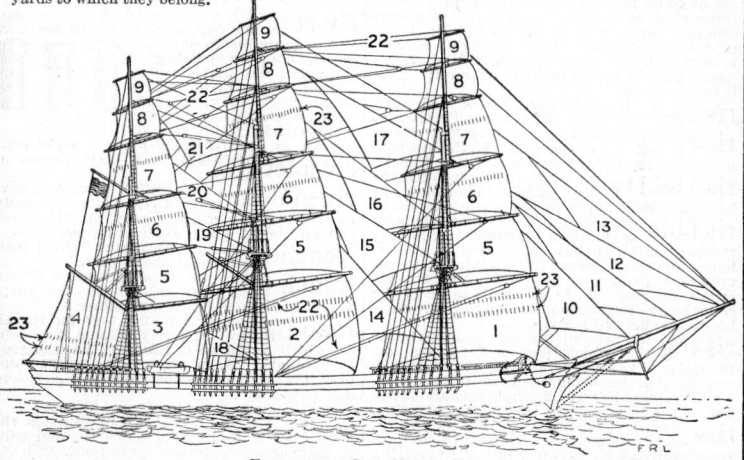

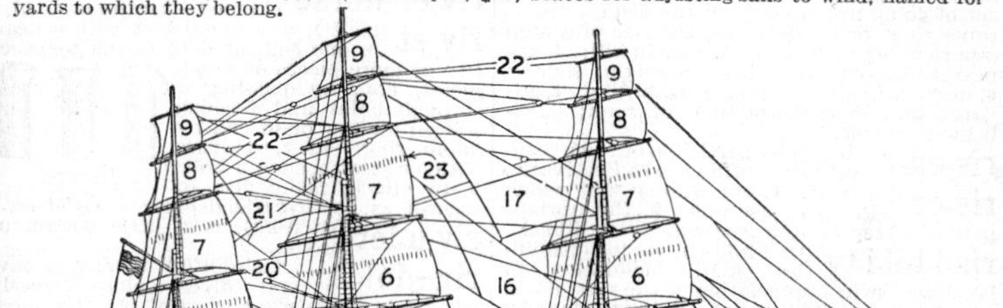

Full-rigged Ship Under Sail

Explanation.—An asterisk [*] indicates that the part named is shown and numbered in the drawing on fore-, main-, and mizzenmast. A double dagger [‡] indicates that the part named is shown in several places, not always all numbered.

1, foresail; 2, mainsail; 3, crossjack; 4, spanker; *5, lower topsail; *6, upper topsail; *7, topgallant sail; *8, royal; *9, skysail; 10, fore-topmast staysail; 11, jib; 12, outer jib; 13, flying jib; 14, main-topmast lower staysail; 15, main-topmast upper staysail; 16, main-topgallant staysail; 17, main-royal staysail; 18, mizzen staysail; 19, mizzen-topmast staysail; 20, mizzen-topgallant staysail; 21, mizzen-royal staysail; ‡22, braces for adjusting sails to wind, named for yard to which they belong; ‡23, reef points on sails.

RIGGING AND SAILS OF A FULL-RIGGED SAILING SHIP

—*v.i.* [*p.t.* and *p.p.* -post′ed, *p.pr.* -post′ing], to make a quick, clever reply. Also, **ri-post′**.

rip-per (rĭp′ẽr), *n.* **1**, one who or that which divides by cutting or tearing; **2**, a tool for such a purpose.

rip-ple (rĭp′l), *n.* **1**, a tiny wave on the surface of water; **2**, any slight, curling wave; as, the *ripples* of her hair; **3**, the sound made by waves of water, or a sound like it; as, a *ripple* of laughter:—*v.t.* [*p.t.* and *p.p.* -pled (-ld), *p.pr.* -pling], to make small curling waves upon or in; as, the wind *ripples* the water; to *ripple* hair:—*v.i.* **1**, to become fretted or slightly waved on the surface; **2**, to sound like water running over a rough surface.—*adj.* **rip′ply.**

rip-rap (rĭp′răp″), *n.* a foundation of broken stones loosely thrown together in deep water, on a soft bottom; also, the stones so used.

rip-saw (rĭp′sô″), *n.* a coarse-toothed saw with teeth raking slightly forward, for cutting wood with the grain; a ripping saw (see *tool*, illus.).

Rip Van Win-kle (rĭp″ văn wĭng′kl), in Irving's story, a hunter who, after sleeping for twenty years, awakens to find himself forgotten and customs changed; hence, one who is behind the times.

rise (rīz), *v.i.* [*p.t.* rose (rōz), *p.p.* ris′en (rĭz′n), *p.pr.* ris′ing], **1**, to go from a lower position to a higher; mount; ascend; **2**, to extend upward; stand in height; as, the building *rises* to a height of 80 feet; **3**, to slope upward; as, *rising* ground; **4**, to get up from kneeling, sitting, or lying down; stand up; **5**, to appear above the horizon, as the sun; **6**, to come into view or existence; **7**, to swell up, as bread dough in fermentation; **8**, to increase in value, force, intensity, or the like; as, his fears *rose*; **9**, to thrive; prosper; also, to be promoted in rank; **10**, to revolt; rebel; **11**, to come back to life; as, to *rise* from the dead; **12**, to originate, as a stream:—*n.* **1**, the act of going up; ascent; **2**, the distance anything rises, or ascends; as, the *rise* of a step (see *step*, [1]*arch*, illus.); **3**, a small hill; **4**, appearance above the horizon; **5**, origin; source; **6**, increase in value, amount, or the like; **7**, advance in power, distinction, or rank; **8**, rebellion; revolt.

ris-en (rĭz′n), past participle of the irregular verb *rise:* often used adjectivally.

ris-er (rīz′ẽr), *n.* **1**, one who or that which gets up or ascends; **2**, the upright part of a step or stair (see *newel*, *step*, illus.).

ris-i-bil-i-ty (rĭz″ĭ-bĭl′ĭ-tĭ), *n.* [*pl.* risibilities (-tĭz)], inclination to laughter; swift appreciation of the ridiculous.

ris-i-ble (rĭz′ĭ-bl), *adj.* **1**, having the faculty or power of laughing; as, man is the only *risible* animal; **2**, laughable; ridiculous; as, *risible* jokes; **3**, pertaining to, or used in, laughing; as, he could not control his *risible* muscles:—*n.*, in *pl.*, one's sense of the ridiculous; inclination to laugh.—*n.* **ris′i-ble-ness.**—*adv.* **ris′i-bly.**

ris-ing (rīz′ĭng), *n.* the act of one who or that which rises, in any sense; as, the *rising* of the moon; a *rising* of the people: —*p.adj.* **1**, increasing in wealth or influence; as, a *rising* young lawyer; **2**, appearing above the horizon; **3**, growing; as, the *rising* generation.

risk (rĭsk), *n.* possibility of loss or injury; peril; danger:—*v.t.* **1**, to expose to danger or peril; as, to *risk* one's life; **2**, to take the chances on; as, to *risk* a battle.—*n.* **risk′er.**

Syn., *n.* hazard. (See danger.)

risk-y (rĭs′kĭ), *adj.* [*comp.* risk′i-er, *superl.* risk′i-est], dangerous; perilous; full of uncertainty.

ris-qué (rēs″kā′), *adj.* suggestive of what is improper; as, a *risqué* remark.

rite (rīt), *n.* a prescribed form of religious or other solemn ceremony, or the words or acts constituting or accompanying it; as, the *rite* of marriage.

Syn. observance. (See ceremony.)

rit-u-al (rĭt′ū-ăl), *n.* **1**, a set form for the performance of divine service or other solemn ceremony; **2**, a book of such forms; **3**, a body of ceremonies used in any church or order:—*adj.* of or pertaining to formal, solemn ceremonies.—*adv.* **rit′u-al-ly.**

rit-u-al-ism (rĭt′ū-ăl-ĭzm), *n.* **1**, a system of prescribed forms to be used in religious worship; **2**, an insistence upon the strict observance of forms in church service.—*n.* **rit′u-al-ist.**—*adj.* **rit″u-al-is′tic.**

ri-val (rī′văl), *n.* one who strives to equal or surpass another in the pursuit of the same object; a competitor:—*v.t.* to try to equal or surpass; engage in competition with: —*adj.* having the same claims; competing.

Syn., *n.* opponent, antagonist.

ri-val-ry (rī′văl-rĭ), *n.* [*pl.* rivalries (-rĭz)], the act of trying to equal or excel; competition.

Syn. competition, emulation. *Rivalry* names a struggle between those seeking the same thing, as in love, politics, influence, etc., and suggests unfriendliness and hostility. *Competition* names a contest between those seeking to gain the same object at the same time; the result is usually tangible, and the feeling may be good-natured. *Emulation* names a commendable striving to equal or outdo others, inspired by the example of another's greatness.

rive (rīv), *v.t.* [*p.t.* rived (rīvd), *p.p.* rived or riv′en (rĭv′n), *p.pr.* riv′ing], to split or tear apart; cleave:—*v.i.* to be split apart.

riv-en (rĭv′n), past participle of the irregular verb *rive*.

riv-er (rĭv′ẽr), *n.* a large stream of water flowing, in a definite channel, into another stream, a lake, or the sea.

riv-er horse the hippopotamus, a thick-skinned African mammal.

riv-et (rĭv′ĕt), *n.* a metal bolt with a head on one end, used to fasten together two or more pieces of wood, metal, etc., by passing it through holes and forming a head on the plain end by hammering:—*v.t.* **1**, to secure with, or as with, such a bolt; **2**, to clinch; make firm or secure; as, to *rivet* friendship.—*n.* **riv′et-er.**

RIVETS

riv-u-let (rĭv′ū-lĕt), *n.* a little stream or brook.

rix–dol-lar (rĭks′=dŏl″ẽr), *n.* any of several silver coins formerly current in Denmark, Germany, etc., the most common being worth about a dollar.

[1]**roach** (rōch), *n.* a cockroach (which see): a household insect pest.

[2]**roach** (rōch), *n.* **1**, a European fresh-water fish related to the carp; **2**, any of various fishes resembling it.

road (rōd), *n.* **1**, a public way for travel; highway; **2**, a way, course, or means by which anything is reached; as, the *road* to happiness; **3**, in *pl.*, a place where ships may ride safely at anchor; roadstead.—*n.* and *adj.* **road′side″.**

Syn. passage, thoroughfare. (See way.)

road-bed (rōd′bĕd″), *n.* **1**, in railroads, the foundation for the ties and rails; **2**, in general, materials for a road.

road house an inn or tavern located on a rural or suburban road and catering especially to automobilists.

road roll-er a heavy cylinder or series of rollers, for pressing smooth the surface of roads: when driven by steam, called *steam roller* (see illus. next page).

road-stead (rōd′stĕd), *n.* an anchorage, not a harbor, for ships at some distance from the shore.

road-ster (rōd′stẽr), *n.* **1,** a horse suited for light driving; **2,** any vehicle built for use on ordinary roads; esp., an open automobile, usually for two passengers.

road-way (rōd′wā″), *n.* a road, esp. the beaten, traveled part.

roam (rōm), *v.i.* to wander about without any definite object; ramble; stroll:—*v.t.* to wander over; rove.—*n.* **roam′er.**

¹roan (rōn), *adj.* of a horse, having a coat whose main color of bay, sorrel, or chestnut is thickly sprinkled with gray or white:—*n.* **1,** a roan color; **2,** an animal of roan color, esp. a horse.

²roan (rōn), *n.* a soft leather of sheepskin, a substitute for morocco.

Steam Road Roller

roar (rōr), *n.* **1,** the deep, full cry of a large animal; as, the *roar* of a lion; **2,** a cry, as of distress; **3,** any loud, confused noise; as, the *roar* of battle; **4,** loudly expressed mirth; as, a *roar* of laughter:—*v.i.* **1,** to cry with a loud, full, deep sound; as, a lion *roars;* **2,** to cry loudly, as in pain, distress, or anger; **3,** to laugh loudly; **4,** to make a loud, confused noise, as wind, waves, passing vehicles, etc.:—*v.t.* to utter boisterously; cry aloud.

roar-ing (rōr′ĭng), *n.* **1,** a loud, deep, prolonged sound, as of a lion, the winds, etc.; **2,** a disease of horses marked by noisy breathing:—*p.adj.* noisy; disorderly.

roast (rōst), *v.t.* **1,** to cook before a fire or in a closed oven, as meat; **2,** to heat to excess; **3,** to dry and parch under the action of heat; **4,** to heat, as an ore, with access of air, to remove sulphur or other constituents; **5,** *Slang,* to joke, criticize, or ridicule severely:—*v.i.* to be cooked by heat, as before a fire or in an oven:—*n.* **1,** the act of cooking before a fire or in an oven; **2,** a piece of meat cooked, or suitable to be cooked, before a fire or in an oven; **3,** *Slang,* merciless criticism or ridicule:—*adj.* cooked before a fire or in an oven.—*n.* **roast′er.**

rob (rŏb), *v.t.* [*p.t.* and *p.p.* robbed (rŏbd), *p.pr.* rob′bing], **1,** to deprive (a person) of something by force or intimidation; **2,** to pillage, as a house; **3,** to deprive unjustly; defraud; as, to *rob* people of their rights:—*v.i.* to commit theft.

rob-ber (rŏb′ẽr), *n.* one who takes what is not his; a thief; bandit; burglar.

rob-ber-y (rŏb′ẽr-ĭ), *n.* [*pl.* robberies (-iz)], the unlawful and forcible taking away of the money or goods of another.

Syn. piracy, plunder, larceny, spoliation.

robe (rōb), *n.* **1,** a long, loose, outer garment, often indicating rank or honor; **2,** an elegant gown, often made in a single piece; **3,** in *pl.,* state or ceremonial costume; **4,** the dressed skin of an animal used for a carriage covering:—*v.t.* and *v.i.* [*p.t.* and *p.p.* robed (rōbd), *p.pr.* rob′ing], to dress in, or put on, a garment, esp. a garment of state.

rob-in (rŏb′ĭn), *n.* **1,** a small European bird of the thrush family: also called *robin redbreast;* **2,** an American thrush somewhat like the English robin, but larger: **Robin,** a familiar form of *Robert:* **Robin Goodfellow,** in folklore, a mischievous and good-natured elf or goblin; Hobgoblin: **Robin Hood,** a merry outlaw of England, head of a band of chivalrous robbers in Sherwood Forest.

ro-bot (rō′bŏt; rŭb′ŭt), *n.* an automaton, often imitating human form and actions; hence, a person who does routine work mechanically; an unimaginative plodder: **robot bomb,** a winged bomb, somewhat like an airplane, controlled mechanically and by radio.

ro-bust (rō-bŭst′), *adj.* strong; vigorous; muscular.—*n.* **ro-bust′ness.**

roc (rŏk), *n.* a fabled bird of prey, imagined to be of enormous size and strength.

¹rock (rŏk), *n.* **1,** a large mass of stone or of stony matter; cliff; crag; **2,** that which resembles such a mass in firmness; a firm support; a defense; **3,** that on which, or by which, one may be ruined or brought to disaster; **4,** the striped bass; **5,** any mineral matter; a bed or mass of one mineral.

²rock (rŏk), *v.t.* **1,** to move alternately to and fro, or backward and forward, as a cradle, chair, or small boat; also, to move, as a baby, in a cradle or the like; **2,** to lull to sleep; quiet; **3,** to cause to sway or reel:—*v.i.* **1,** to move backward and forward, as in a cradle; **2,** to sway or reel:—*n.* a movement backward and forward.

rock can-dy pure sugar obtained in large clear crystals by the process of slow evaporation.

rock crys-tal a transparent, usually colorless, variety of quartz.

rock drill a tool driven by steam, compressed air, or electricity, to bore holes in stone.

rock-er (rŏk′ẽr), *n.* **1,** one who quiets or lulls to sleep; **2,** one of the curved pieces upon which a rocking-chair, cradle, etc., balances; also, a rocking-chair; **3,** any of several devices that operate by swaying.

rock-et (rŏk′ĕt), *n.* a jet propulsion device, unlike the jet engine in that it contains the oxygen needed for combustion of its fuel: used for signaling and display, as fireworks, and in warfare, as missiles released from ships, airplanes, and land-based launching platforms, or fired from recoilless rifles.

rock-ing–chair (rŏk′ĭng-châr″), *n.* a chair having the legs set on curving pieces, or rockers.

rock-ing–horse (rŏk′ĭng-hôrs″), *n.* a toy horse set on rockers, or curving pieces.

rock oil a mineral oil obtained by boring into certain rocks; petroleum.

rock-y (rŏk′ĭ), *adj.* [*comp.* rock′i-er, *superl.* rock′i-est], **1,** full of, or like, stony or mineral masses; hard; **2,** inflexible; without feeling; **3,** *Slang,* weak; shaky.

ro-co-co (rō-kō′kō), *n.* **1,** a showy style of decoration, representing shells, leaves, scrolls, etc., massed together: popular in the 17th and 18th centuries; **2,** hence, anything odd or in bad taste in art or literature:—*adj.* **1,** pertaining to this showy style; **2,** hence, showing bad taste in art or literature.

rod (rŏd), *n.* **1,** a straight, slender stick of wood or metal; **2,** a fishing pole; **3,** a switch or whip; hence, correction or discipline: with *the;* **4,** a scepter; hence, power; **5,** a measure of length containing 5½ yards, or a surface measure equal to 30¼ square yards.

rode (rōd), past tense of the transitive and intransitive verb *ride.*

ro-dent (rō′dĕnt), *n.* any of an order of gnawing mammals, as rats, mice, squirrels, beavers, etc.:—*adj.* **1,** gnawing; biting; **2,** like a gnawing animal; **3,** pertaining to the order of gnawing mammals.

ro-de-o (rō′dē-ō; rō-dā′ō), *n.* **1,** an inclosure for cattle; **2,** an assemblage of ranchmen or cowboys for a round-up; **3,** a contest in horsemanship, cattle roping, etc.

rod-o-mon-tade (rŏd″ō-mŏn-tād′; rŏd″ō-mŏn-täd′), *n.* vain boasting; bluster; brag:—*v.i.* [*p.t.* and *p.p.* -tad'ed, *p.pr.* -tad'ing], to bluster or brag.

[1]roe (rō), *n.* **1**, a small deer of Europe and Asia: also called *roe deer;* **2**, sometimes, a doe of the red deer.

[2]roe (rō), *n.* **1**, the eggs of fishes; **2**, a streak seen in some woods, esp. mahogany.

roe-buck (rō'bŭk″), *n.* the male of the roe; also, any roe deer.

Roent-gen rays (rönt'gĕn; rĕnt'-), a form of radiating energy; X rays. See **Rönt'gen rays**, *Pfd. S.*

ro-ga-tion (rō-gā'shŭn), *n.* in the Episcopal and Roman Catholic churches, a litany or solemn supplication used on the Monday, Tuesday, and Wednesday before Ascension Day, called *rogation days.*

rogue (rōg), *n.* **1**, a dishonest person; cheat; scoundrel; **2**, playfully, a mischievous, frolicsome person.

ro-guer-y (rō'gẽr-ĭ), *n.* [*pl.* rogueries (-ĭz)], **1**, dishonest practices; cheating; **2**, playfully mischievous conduct.

ro-guish (rō'gĭsh), *adj.* **1**, dishonest; knavish; **2**, playfully mischievous.—*adv.* **ro'guish-ly.**—*n.* **ro'guish-ness.**

roil (roil), *v.t.* **1**, to make muddy by stirring; as, to *roil* a spring; **2**, to vex or irritate; disturb, as the temper.—*adj.* **roil'y.**

roist-er (rois'tẽr), *v.i.* to swagger; bluster:—*n. Archaic,* a bold, blustering, disorderly fellow.—*n.* **roist'er-er.**

Ro-land (rō'lănd), *n.* Charlemagne's nephew and the hero of the Old French epic, the "Chanson de Roland."

rôle (rōl), *n.* **1**, a part or character taken by an actor in a play; **2**, a part or character taken, or assumed, by anyone.

roll (rōl), *v.t.* **1**, to cause to move onward by turning over and over; as, to *roll* a ball; **2**, to move or push along on casters or wheels, as a chair; move along easily as if on wheels; **3**, to wrap upon itself or some other object; make into the form of a ball or a cylinder; as, to *roll* a cigarette; *roll* a rug; **4**, to wrap up; as, to *roll* oneself in a blanket; **5**, to move with a gentle up-and-down or side-to-side motion; as, the waves *roll* the ship; *roll* the eyes; **6**, to utter or express with a deep, vibrating sound; as, the organ *rolls* forth its music; **7**, to spread flat with some kind of roller; as, to *roll* a lawn; **8**, to beat in a quick manner, as a drum; **9**, to pronounce with a prolonged trilling sound:—*v.i.* **1**, to move onward by turning over and over; as, a ball *rolls;* **2**, to run on wheels; as, the wagon *rolls* along; also, to travel in a wheeled vehicle; **3**, to turn or toss from side to side; rock, as a ship; **4**, to sweep along, as do waves; go smoothly; **5**, to give forth a long, deep, rumbling sound; as, the thunder *rolls;* **6**, to take, through winding, the form of a ball or a cylinder; as, the cloth *rolls* easily; **7**, to undulate, as land; **8**, to flatten under some kind of roller; as, dough *rolls* easily:—*n.* **1**, the act of turning over and over, or tossing from side to side; **2**, the state of being rolled; **3**, that which rolls; a roller; **4**, anything wrapped upon itself in the form, or nearly the form, of a cylinder, as a scroll, a jelly cake, a strip of fabric or carpet rolled up, or the like; **5**, a list or register, generally official in character; **6**, a kind of raised biscuit or bread, often doubled over; **7**, a continued, deep sound, as of a drum beaten, thunder, or the like; **8**, a swell or unevenness on a surface, as the ground or the sea: **roll call**, the act or time of calling out a list of names of those belonging to an organization, as soldiers or pupils.

roll-er (rōl'ẽr), *n.* **1**, anything that turns round and round, or over and over; **2**, a cylinder used for grinding, smoothing, etc.; **3**, a small wheel; **4**, a heavy wave; **5**, a long, broad bandage; **6**, a tumbler pigeon.

roll-er coast-er an amusement railway, on which cars on rollers run along sharply inclined tracks.

roll-er skate a skate with wheels instead of a runner.

rol-lic (rŏl'ĭk), *v.i.* [*p.t.* and *p.p.* -licked (-ĭkt), *p.pr.* -lick-ing], to move or act with a careless, swaggering air; frolic; revel boisterously. Also, **rol'lick.**

roll-ing (rōl'ĭng), *p.adj.* **1**, moving on by turning over and over; as, a *rolling* ball; **2**, moving on, or as on, wheels; as, a *rolling* chair; **3**, undulating; as, *rolling* country; **4**, turned back or down on itself; as, a *rolling* collar; **5**, reverberating; rumbling: **rolling stock**, the cars and other wheeled equipment of a railway:—*n.* **1**, the act of one who or that which rolls, or of one who uses a rolling tool; **2**, a deep, full, reverberating sound.

roll-ing-pin (rōl'ĭng-pĭn″), *n.* a long, smooth cylinder, made of wood, glass, etc., for rolling out dough or paste.

ro-ly-po-ly (rō'lĭ-pō″lĭ), *n.* [*pl.* roly-polies (-lĭz)], **1**, a game consisting of rolling a ball at a mark or into a hole; **2**, a boiled or steamed pudding made of light dough spread with fruit and rolled up:—*adj.* short and fat; dumpy; as, a *roly-poly* little girl.

Ro-ma-ic (rō-mā'ĭk), *n.* the modern Greek language, esp. the form spoken by uneducated Greeks:—*adj.* pertaining to modern Greece, or, esp., to its language.

Ro-man (rō'măn), *adj.* **1**, pertaining to Rome, ancient or modern; **2**, pertaining to the Roman Catholic Church: **Roman nose**, an aquiline nose; one with a high bridge: **Roman numerals**, the letters I, V, X, L, C, D, M, sometimes used for numbers: distinguished from 1, 2, 3, etc., called *Arabic numerals:*—*n.* **1**, a native or citizen of ancient or modern Rome; **2**, *Rare,* a member of the Roman Catholic Church; **3**, in *pl.*, a book of the New Testament, containing the Epistle of Paul to the Christians at Rome: **roman**, *adj.* designating the form of ordinary type: distinguished from *italic:*—*n.* roman type.

Ro-man Cath-o-lic pertaining to the church of which the Pope in Rome is the head; also, one belonging to this church.

ro-mance (rō-măns'), *n.* **1**, a prose or poetical tale of adventure, chivalry, etc., such as the tales of King Arthur: so called because written originally in the Romance dialects; **2**, a form of prose fiction full of imagination and adventure; **3**, a series of acts or happenings that are strange and charming; **4**, a disposition to ignore what is real and to delight in what is fanciful or mysterious; as, a soul full of *romance;* **5**, falsehood:—*v.i.* [*p.t.* and *p.p.* -manced' (-mănst'), *p.pr.* -manc'ing], **1**, to invent fanciful or extravagant stories; **2**, to indulge in dreamy imaginings.—*n.* **ro-manc'er.**

Ro-mance (rō-măns'), *adj.* of or pertaining to the languages which developed from popular Latin, as Italian, Rumanian, French, Portuguese, and Spanish.

Ro-man-esque (rō″măn-ĕsk'), *n.* a style of architecture and ornamentation developed from the Roman principles during the period from the eighth to the twelfth century:—*adj.* designating, or pertaining to, this style of architecture.

Ro-man-ic (rō-măn'ĭk), *adj.* pertaining to the Romance languages, or to the peoples that speak them.

ro-man-tic (rō-măn'tĭk), *adj.* **1**, pertaining to, or like, what is imaginary, sentimental, or extravagantly ideal; hence, fanciful; visionary; as, *romantic* ideas; **2**, pertaining to, or suggesting, what is strange, marvelous, or heroic; **3**, of a disposition to ignore what is real and delight in what is fanciful and mysterious; as, a *romantic* girl; **4,** strangely wild and picturesque; as, *romantic* scenery; **5,** pertaining to the art and literature of the Middle Ages; picturesque or free in treatment.—*adv.* **ro-man'ti-cal-ly.**

Syn. fictitious, chimerical, dreamy, poetic. —*Ant.* exact, precise, literal.

ro-man-ti-cism (rō-măn'tĭ-sĭzm), *n.* **1,** the quality or characteristic of being imaginative, sentimental, or extravagantly ideal; **2,** in literature, strangeness and improbability; **3,** the movement in Germany, France, and England in the late 18th century, to restore imagination and sentiment to literature and art.—*n.* **ro-man'ti-cist.**

Rom-a-ny (rŏm'ȧ-nĭ), *n.* [*pl.* Romanies (-nĭz)], **1,** one of a wandering race of Eastern origin; a gypsy; **2,** the language spoken by the gypsies. Also, **Rom'ma-ny.**

Ro-me-o (rō'mē-ō), *n.* in Shakespeare's "Romeo and Juliet," a young man who is in love with Juliet, the daughter of his father's hated rival, and whose passion results in the death of the lovers and the reconciliation of their families.

Rom-ish (rōm'ĭsh), *adj.* pertaining to Rome or the Roman Catholic Church: usually derogatory.

romp (rŏmp), *n.* **1,** one who plays boisterously, esp. a girl; **2,** rough, noisy play or frolic:—*v.i.* **1,** to play in a rough, boisterous manner; **2,** to frisk about in play; **3,** in racing, to win easily.—*n.* **romp'ing.**—*adj.* **romp'ish.**—*adv.* **romp'ish-ly.**

romp-ers (rŏm'pẽrz), *n.pl.* an outer garment consisting of a waist with loose trousers: worn by small children.

Rom-u-lus (rŏm'ū-lŭs), *n.* in mythology, the son of Mars, thrown into the Tiber with his twin brother Remus, but rescued and reared by a female wolf, later becoming the founder and first king of Rome.

ron-deau (rŏn'dō; rŏn-dō'), *n.* [*pl.* rondeaux (-dōz)], **1,** a lyric poem of thirteen or, sometimes, ten lines, with two recurring rimes, and with a special kind of refrain; **2,** a rondel; **3,** in music, a simple song of six or eight lines constructed so that the first and last lines are the same.

ron-del (rŏn'dĕl), *n.* orig., a rondeau; later, a lyric of 14 lines, with two rimes, and two recurring refrain lines.

ron-do (rŏn'dō), *n.* [*pl.* rondos (-dōz)], an instrumental composition with one main theme repeated at intervals, with contrasting episodes between repetitions, but always closing with the theme: often used as the last movement in a sonata or symphony.

Rönt-gen rays (rönt'gĕn; rĕnt'-) a form of radiation produced by an electric discharge in a vacuum tube, and capable of passing through many substances opaque to ordinary light rays: called *X rays* by their discoverer because their nature was unknown, but now understood to be similar to light waves but of extremely short wave length. Also, **Roent'gen rays.**

rood (rōōd), *n.* **1,** a cross with the figure of Christ upon it; a crucifix, esp. one placed over an altar; **2,** a square measure equal to one fourth of an acre, or forty square rods.

roof (rōōf), *n.* [*pl.* roofs (rōōfs)], **1,** the top covering of a building; **2,** any similar top covering, as of a car or a cave: **roof garden,** a garden on a roof, esp. one as part of a restaurant or entertainment hall:—*v.t.* to cover with, or as with, a roof.—*n.* **roof'er.**—*p.adj.* and *n.* **roof'ing.**

roof-less (rōōf'lĕs), *adj.* **1,** having no top covering; **2,** having no shelter.

roof-tree (rōōf'trē"), *n.* **1,** the ridgepole, or highest horizontal timber of a roof, against which the rafters rest; **2,** hence, a roof; also, figuratively, home.

[1]**rook** (rŏŏk), *n.* **1,** a European bird similar to the crow; **2,** a swindler; **3,** *Slang,* one easily duped:—*v.t.* to swindle; cheat.

[2]**rook** (rŏŏk), *n.* one of the pieces used in chess, capable of being moved forward, backward, or sideways: also called *castle.*

rook-er-y (rŏŏk'ẽr-ĭ), *n.* [*pl.* rookeries (-ĭz)], **1,** a place where rooks gather and build their nests; **2,** a colony of these birds; **3,** a place where other birds or animals, as gulls or seals, gather and breed; **4,** a mean tenement, or group of tenements, in a slum district, holding many people.

room (rōōm), *n.* **1,** space occupied or vacant; **2,** a free or vacant place or space; **3,** a chamber in a building; **4,** freedom to act:—*v.i. Colloq.,* to lodge.

room-er (rōōm'ẽr), *n.* a lodger; one who rents a room, esp. temporarily.

room-ful (rōōm'fŏŏl), *n.* [*pl.* roomfuls (-fŏŏlz)], **1,** all the people or things, collectively, in a room or chamber; **2,** as many as a room can contain.

room-mate (rōōm'māt"), *n.* a person who shares one's room.

room-y (rōōm'ĭ), *adj.* [*comp.* room'i-er, *superl.* room'i-est], having plenty of room or space; not contracted; spacious. —*adv.* **room'i-ly.**—*n.* **room'i-ness.**

roor-back (rōōr'băk), *n.* in U. S. politics, a political lie; an untrue report defaming a candidate.

roost (rōōst), *n.* **1,** the pole, perch, etc., upon which a bird rests at night; **2,** a number of fowls resting together:—*v.i.* **1,** to sit or sleep upon a perch or pole; **2,** *Dial.,* to rest, esp. temporarily.

roost-er (rōōs'tẽr), *n.* the domestic cock; a male fowl.

[1]**root** (rōōt), *n.* **1,** the underground part of a plant, serving to fix it in the earth, to

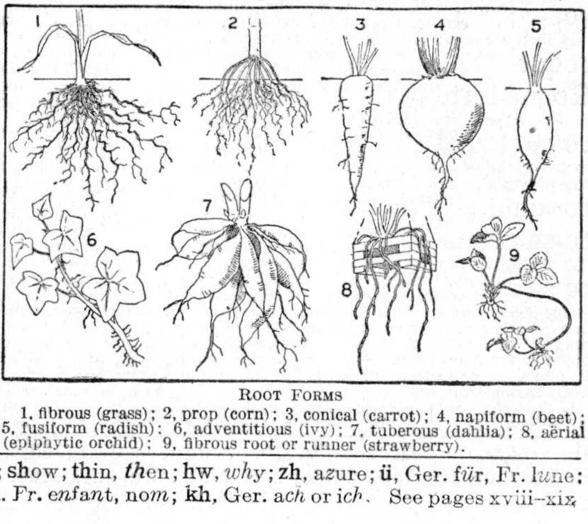

ROOT FORMS

1, fibrous (grass); 2, prop (corn); 3, conical (carrot); 4, napiform (beet); 5, fusiform (radish); 6, adventitious (ivy); 7, tuberous (dahlia); 8, aërial (epiphytic orchid); 9, fibrous root or runner (strawberry).

absorb moisture, and to store nourishment; also, a small plant, as for transplanting; **2,** an edible, underground part of a plant, as a beet; **3,** the part of an organ that is most deeply embedded; as, the *root* of a finger nail; **4,** that from which anything has its origin; an ancestor; a cause or source; as, laziness is the *root* of his poverty; **5,** the lower part of a thing; foundation; **6,** in mathematics: **a,** a value which, if substituted for the unknown quantity in an equation, will satisfy the equation; **b,** the quantity which, multiplied by itself a given number of times, produces a given quantity; as, 2 is the second or square *root* of 4; **7,** the first or lowest member of a common chord or triad; **8,** the basic part of a word, considered apart from prefixes, suffixes, and inflectional forms, which expresses its primary or essential meaning; also, the earliest known form of a word from which later forms, in all of the languages of a given family of languages, are derived; **9,** that part of a gear tooth immediately next the body of the wheel:—*v.t.* **1,** to plant and fix in the earth; **2,** to implant deeply; as, honor *rooted* in dishonor; **3,** to tear or dig up by the roots; figuratively, to eradicate: with *up* or *out;* as, to *root* out vice: —*v.i.* **1,** to take root; **2,** to become firmly fixed or settled; be permanently established. —*n.* **¹root′er.**—*adj.* **root′y.**

²root (rōōt), *v.t.* **1,** to dig with the snout: with *out* or *up;* **2,** *Dial.,* to search; hunt: with *out* or *up:*—*v.i.* **1,** to turn up the earth with the snout; **2,** *Dial.,* to rummage.—*n.* **²root′er.**

³root (rōōt), *v.i. U. S. Slang,* to give aid or encouragement by cheering, as for a team at a football game: with *for.*—*n.* **³root′er.**

root-let (rōōt′lĕt), *n.* a little root; a secondary root.

root-stock (rōōt′stŏk″), *n.* a rootlike stem of a plant running horizontally underground, and sending leaves upward and roots downward; a rhizome.

rope (rōp), *n.* **1,** a thick, stout cord made of several strands of hemp, cotton, flax, etc., twisted together; **2,** a collection of things braided or twined together in a line or string; as, a *rope* of pearls; **3,** any glutinous or slimy thread formed in a liquid; **4,** *Colloq.,* death by hanging:—*v.t.* [*p.t.* and *p.p.* roped (rōpt), *p.pr.* rop′ing], **1,** to fasten, bind, or tie with a rope; **2,** to divide or inclose, as with a rope; as, to *rope* off a field; **3,** *Colloq.,* to lasso; **4,** *Slang,* to deceive: with *in:*—*v.i.* to become drawn out into threads.

rop-y (rōp′ĭ), *adj.* [*comp.* rop′i-er, *superl.* rop′i-est], **1,** capable of being drawn out into threads; **2,** stringy.—*n.* **rop′i-ness.**

roque (rōk), *n.* a kind of croquet as played on a special court by experts.

Roque-fort (rôk″fôr′; rōk′fērt), [Fr.], *n.* a kind of moldy cheese made in Roquefort, France, from the milk of ewes.

ro-quet (rō-kā′), *v.t.* [*p.t.* and *p.p.* -queted′ (-kād′), *p.pr.* -quet′ing (-kā′ĭng)], in the game of croquet, to strike (a ball) with the player's ball:—*n.* the act of so striking.

ror-qual (rôr′kwăl), *n.* a large whalebone whale with a fin on its back.

ro-sa-ceous (rō-zā′shŭs), *adj.* **1,** of or pertaining to the rose family; **2,** like a rose, as in color or shape.

ro-sa-ry (rō′zȧ-rĭ), *n.* [*pl.* rosaries (-rĭz)], **1,** a string of beads for counting a series of prayers to be said one after the other in a certain recurring order; also, the series of prayers thus recited; **2,** a bed of roses or a place where roses grow; **3,** a garland of roses; **4,** hence, a collection of beautiful thoughts from various authors.

¹rose (rōz), *n.* **1,** any of numerous thorny shrubs, erect or climbing, bearing showy, fragrant flowers; also, the flower; **2,** the most typical color of a rose; light crimson; **3,** a fancy knot of ribbon or lace; a rosette: **under the rose,** secretly.

²rose (rōz), past tense of the irregular verb *rise,* which see.

ro-se-ate (rō′zē-āt), *adj.* **1,** rose-colored; **2,** consisting of roses; blooming.

rose-bud (rōz′bŭd″), *n.* the bud of a rose.

rose-ma-ry (rōz′mâ-rĭ), *n.* [*pl.* rosemaries (-rĭz)], an evergreen shrub with pungent leaves and blue flowers.

ro-sette (rō-zĕt′), *n.* **1,** a knot or bunch of ribbon or other fabric made in the shape of a rose; **2,** a painted or sculptured circular ornament, as leaves arranged in a circle around a bud; **3,** a thick cluster of leaves about a short stem.

rose win-dow a circular, stained-glass window with elaborate divisions branching from, or arranged around, its center.

Rose Window

rose-wood (rōz′wŏŏd″), *n.* a valuable, dark red, hard wood, yielded by various tropical trees and used for furniture.

ros-in (rŏz′ĭn), *n.* the resin, or solid substance, that remains after distilling, or driving off, as by heat, the oil of turpentine from crude turpentine:—*v.t.* to rub with rosin.

ros-ter (rŏs′tẽr), *n.* **1,** a list of officers and men enrolled for duty; **2,** a list showing the order in which officers, enlisted men, and companies or regiments of soldiers are called on to serve; **3,** hence, any roll or list; as, the *roster* of a school or college class.

ros-trum (rŏs′trŭm), *n.* [*pl.* rostrums (-trŭmz); rostra (-trȧ)], **1,** a pulpit, platform, or stage for public speaking; **2,** hence, public orators or lecturers collectively.

ros-y (rōz′ĭ), *adj.* [*comp.* ros′i-er, *superl.* ros′i-est], **1,** like a rose; red; blooming; blushing; **2,** made of roses; **3,** favorable; hopeful.—*adv.* **ros′i-ly.**—*n.* **ros′i-ness.**

rot (rŏt), *v.i.* [*p.t.* and *p.p.* rot′ted, *p.pr.* rot′ting], to become corrupt; decay:—*v.t.* to cause to decay; as, to *rot* vegetable fiber:—*n.* **1,** the process of decay; **2,** the state of being decayed; **3,** that which is decayed; **4,** decay, as of plant tissues; **5,** *Slang,* nonsense.

Ro-ta-ri-an (rō-tā′rĭ-ăn), *n.* a member of a local club (*Rotary club*) affiliated with the International Association of Rotary Clubs, and composed of business and professional men meeting regularly to promote good fellowship and improve business and civic conditions.

ro-ta-ry (rō′tȧ-rĭ), *adj.* **1,** turning around, as a wheel on an axis; **2,** having parts that turn around; as, a *rotary* engine.

ro-tate (rō′tāt; *Br.* rō-tāt′), *v.t.* [*p.t.* and *p.p.* -tat-ed, *p.pr.* -tat-ing], **1,** to cause to turn on, or as on, an axis; **2,** to cause to alternate or change about, as crops:—*v.i.* **1,** to turn around its own center or axis; revolve; **2,** to alternate, or do any act, in turn.

ro-ta-tion (rō-tā′shŭn), *n.* **1,** the act of turning around on an axis, like a wheel: distinguished from *revolution;* **2,** a single turn; **3,** recurrence; **4,** regular succession; as, *rotation* in office.

ro-ta-tive (rō′tȧ-tĭv), *adj.* connected with, or causing a movement on, or as on, an axis; rotating.

ro-ta-to-ry (rō′tȧ-tō-rĭ), *adj.* **1,** having, pertaining to, or causing movement on an axis; **2**, alternating, or following one after another.

[1]**rote** (rōt), *n.* the repeating of words or sounds over and over in order to learn them, with little attention to their meaning; as, to learn rules by *rote.*

[2]**rote** (rōt), *n.* a medieval stringed instrument somewhat like a guitar.

ro-to-gra-vure (rō″tō-grȧ-vūr′; rō″tō-grā′vūr), *n.* **1**, a photogravure process for the rapid printing of illustrations from plates etched on copper cylinders; **2**, an illustration so printed.

ro-tor (rō′tẽr), *n.* in an electrical machine, the part which revolves in or around the stationary part, or stator: **rotor ship**, a ship propelled by the effect of the wind on one or more vertical, mastlike cylinders standing on the deck and rotated by power.

rot-ten (rŏt′n), *adj.* **1**, decayed; putrid; as, *rotten* eggs; **2**, liable to break; not firm; as, a *rotten* plank; **3**, corrupt, as politics; **4**, *Slang,* vile; disgusting.—*n.* **rot′ten-ness.**

rot-ten-stone (rŏt′n-stōn″), *n.* a soft, easily crumbled, siliceous limestone used as a polishing powder.

ro-tund (rō-tŭnd′), *adj.* **1**, round from plumpness; rounded out; as, a *rotund* figure; **2**, full in sound; as, a *rotund* voice; **3**, pompous; as, a *rotund* style.

ro-tun-da (rō-tŭn′dȧ), *n.* **1**, a circular building, esp. one with a dome; **2**, a large round room; as, the *rotunda* of the Capitol at Washington.

ro-tun-di-ty (rō-tŭn′dĭ-tĭ), *n.* [*pl.* rotundities (-tĭz)], **1**, the state of being round; **2**, fulness, as of tone.

rou-ble (ro͞o′bl), *n.* a former Russian silver coin with a par value of about 51.5 cents. Also, **ru′ble**, *Pfd. S.*

rouche (ro͞osh), *n.* a frill of plaited material. See **ruche**, *Pfd. S.*

rou-é (ro͞o″ā′), *n.* an evil, dissipated man; a rake.

rouge (ro͞ozh), *n.* **1**, a red substance used for coloring the cheeks and lips; **2**, a red powder used for polishing glass, metals, etc.:—*v.t.* and *v.i.* [*p.t.* and *p.p.* rouged (ro͞ozhd), *p.pr.* roug′ing], to color (the cheeks) with rouge.

rough (rŭf), *adj.* **1**, having an uneven surface; rugged; not smooth or plane; as, a *rough* board; a *rough* road; *rough* cloth; **2**, not polished; crude; unfinished; as, a *rough* diamond; a *rough* sketch; **3**, harsh to the ear; as, a *rough* sound; **4**, uncivil; harsh; unfeeling; as, *rough* treatment; **5**, severe; violent; as, *rough* sports; **6**, boisterous; windy; stormy; as, *rough* weather; **7**, not refined; rude in character; as, *rough* people:—*n.* **1**, a low, coarse fellow; a rowdy; **2**, a crude or unfinished condition; as, diamonds in the *rough;* **3**, in golf, long grass on the side of the course:—*v.t.* **1**, to produce an uneven surface on; destroy the smoothness of; **2**, to shape or make imperfectly: **rough it**, to do without comforts and conveniences, as on a camping trip.—*adv.* **rough′ly.**—*n.* **rough′ness.**

Syn., adj. jagged, abrupt; rustic.

rough-cast (rŭf′kȧst″), *n.* **1**, very coarse plaster for the outside of buildings; **2**, a rude form of anything:—*v.t.* **1**, to coat with coarse plaster, as a wall; **2**, to make a rude plan of.

rough-en (rŭf′n), *v.t.* to produce an uneven surface on; destroy the smoothness of:—*v.i.* to become uneven or coarse on the surface.

rough-hew (rŭf′hū″), *v.t.* to cut or shape roughly, as timber.

rough-rid-er (rŭf′rĭd″ẽr), *n.* one who breaks horses for riding, or who is a skilled rider of untrained horses: **Roughrider**, *Colloq.*, a member of the First U.S. Volunteer Cavalry, organized by Theodore Roosevelt, in the Spanish-American War.

rough-shod (rŭf′shŏd″), *adj.* shod, as a horse, with shoes having calks to prevent slipping: **to ride roughshod**, to domineer: with *over.*

rou-lade (ro͞o″lȧd′), *n.* **1**, an ornamental passage in music; **2**, a dish made of meat rolled with bacon and steamed.

rou-lette (ro͞o-lĕt′), *n.* **1**, a game of chance played with a rotating bowl-like disk which is marked off into numbered sections colored red and black; **2**, an instrument with a toothed wheel used for making dotted lines; also, a cylinder for making perforations, as on a sheet of postage stamps.

Rou-ma-ni-an (ro͞o-mā′nĭ-ăn), *adj.* pertaining to Roumania, its people, or its language:—*n.* **1**, a native or inhabitant of Roumania; **2**, the language of Roumania, one of the Romance languages. Also, **Ru-ma′ni-an**, *Pfd. S.*

round (round), *adj.* **1**, like, or nearly like, in shape to a circle, sphere, or cylinder; as, a *round* pencil; **2**, having a curved contour or surface; as, a *round* cheek; **3**, exact; whole; complete; as, a *round* dozen; **4**, going from, and returning to, the same place; as, a *round* trip; **5**, large; considerable; as, a good *round* price; **6**, easy and brisk in motion; as, a *round* trot; **7**, full in sound; not jarring; as, the *round* tones of a voice; **8**, periodic; well constructed; well balanced; polished; as, a *round* sentence; **9**, open; frank; outspoken; as, a *round* rebuke; **10**, in phonetics, formed by the protruding lips, as *o͞o;* **11**, semicircular, as opposed to pointed; as, a *round* arch: **in round numbers**, approximately: used when a number is given approximately, as in tens, dozens, or the like:—*n.* **1**, a circle, cylinder, or globe; **2**, a fixed course or route: generally one beginning and ending in the same place; a beat; as, a policeman's *round;* **3**, routine; as, the day's *round* of duties; **4**, a series of events or acts; as, a *round* of gaiety; **5**, a circular dance; **6**, some action in which a number of persons take part at one time; as, a *round* of cheers; **7**, one of a series of repeated actions, esp. in a game or contest; as, a *round* of whist; the third *round* in a prize fight; **8**, the rung of a ladder; **9**, a cut of beef between the rump and the leg (see *beef,* illus.); **10**, the state of being perfectly circular; **11**, a simultaneous discharge of shots in a company or detail, each soldier firing once; also, the ammunition needed for such a discharge, or enough for a single shot; **12**, a song sung by several persons or groups starting one after the other at regular intervals:—*v.t.* **1**, to give a curved or rounded form to; **2**, to travel or pass around; double; as, in sailing, to *round* a cape; **3**, to bring to complete perfection or finish: generally with *off* or *out;* as, to *round* out a plan, a sentence, or a story; **4**, to surround; encircle; **5**, to drive in, or gather together, as cattle: with *up;* **6**, in phonetics, to pronounce (a vowel) with the lips formed into a circle; **7**, to form (the lips) in a circle, as when uttering the sound of *o͞o* or of *ō:*—*v.i.* **1**, to become curved, spherical, or circular in form; **2**, to wheel about; **3**, to grow full, complete, or perfect; develop: often with *into:*—*adv.* **1**, on all sides, so as to encircle; as, the people gathered *round;* **2**, with a rotating motion; as, the wheel goes *round;* **3**, from one side or party to another; as, he came *round* to their belief; **4**, in a complete circuit from person to person, or point to point; as, not food enough to go *round;* the summer comes *round* once more; **5**, in outside measure; as, an apple eight inches *round:*—*prep.* **1**, about; on every side of; as, a scarf *round* her shoulders; **2**, passing about in a curved course; as, *round* the corner. —*adv.* **round'ly.**—*n.* **round'ness.**

round-a-bout (round'ȧ-bout″), *adj.* indirect; circuitous:—*n.* **1,** a merry-go-round; **2,** a short coat or jacket.

roun-de-lay (roun'dĕ-lā), *n.* **1,** a song with a simple melody often repeated; **2,** a dance done in a circle.

Round-head (round'hĕd″), *n.* in England in the 17th century, a Puritan: so called in derision because wearing the hair cut close round the head.

round-house (round'hous″), *n.* **1,** the cabin on the after part of a ship's quarter-deck; **2,** a circular building for storing and repairing locomotives in stalls entered by means of a turntable.

round-ish (round'ĭsh), *adj.* tending to be round; nearly round.

round rob-in a document, as a protest or petition, having the signatures written in a circle so as not to show who was the first to sign.

round-shoul-dered (round'=shōl″dẽrd), *adj.* not erect; having stooping shoulders.

rounds-man (roundz'măn), *n.* [*pl.* roundsmen (-mĕn)], a police inspector who visits officers on their beats.

Round Ta-ble **1,** in medieval legend, a table at which King Arthur and his knights sat: made circular so that none might claim precedence; **2,** hence, the knights of King Arthur's court.

round-up (round'=ŭp″), *n.* **1,** the gathering together and driving in of herds of cattle; **2,** the herd so collected; **3,** the men and horses that collect them; **4,** the driving of animals together in hunting.

rouse (rouz), *v.t.* [*p.t.* and *p.p.* roused (rouzd), *p.pr.* rous'ing], **1,** to awaken; **2,** to stir to thought or action; **3,** to drive (game) from a covert or hiding place:—*v.i.* **1,** to start from sleep; **2,** to show signs of activity; **3,** to be stirred to action:—*n.* a signal for action; reveille.—*n.* **rous'er.**

roust-a-bout (roust'ȧ-bout″), *n.* a wharf laborer; esp., a deck hand on a river steamboat.

¹rout (rout), *n.* **1,** total defeat and flight, as of an army; **2,** disorder resulting from such defeat; **3,** a noisy crowd; a rabble; mob; **4,** *Archaic,* a large evening party:—*v.t.* to defeat and put to disorder.

Syn., *v.* overpower, conquer, repulse.

²rout (rout), *v.t.* **1,** to root up, as with the snout; **2,** to dig out, as with a gouging tool; **3,** to bring to view: with *out;* **4,** *Colloq.,* to drag by force: generally with *out;* as, to *rout* him out of bed:—*v.i.* to root about.

route (rōōt), *n.* a way or road traveled; course; journey; march:—*v.t.* [*p.t.* and *p.p.* rout'ed, *p.pr.* rout'ing], to send or forward, as freight, by a certain road or way.

rou-tine (rōō-tēn'), *n.* **1,** a customary course of action in business, pleasure, or duty; **2,** regular habit or practice.

Syn. system. (See habit.)

¹rove (rōv), *v.t.* and *v.i.* [*p.t.* and *p.p.* roved (rōvd), *p.pr.* rov'ing], to wander aimlessly; ramble:—*n.* a walk or ramble.

²rove (rōv), *v.t.* [*p.t.* and *p.p.* roved (rōvd), *p.pr.* rov'ing], **1,** to draw out and twist lightly together, as fibers of cotton, before spinning; **2,** to prepare, as wool, by carding.

rov-er (rōv'ẽr), *n.* **1,** a pirate; **2,** a wanderer; **3,** a fickle person.

¹row (rō), *n.* **1,** a series of persons or things in a line; a file; **2,** a line of houses side by side in a street; also, the street.

²row (rō), *v.i.* **1,** to employ oars in propelling a boat; **2,** to be moved forward by oars:—*v.t.* **1,** to propel, by means of oars; **2,** to carry in a rowboat:—*n.* the act of propelling a boat by oars; also, a ride taken in a rowboat. —*n.* **row'er.**

³row (rou), *n.* *Colloq.,* a noisy quarrel; brawl; fight:—*v.i.* *Colloq.,* to quarrel.

row-boat (rō'bōt″), *n.* a boat equipped with oars for rowing.

row-dy (rou'dĭ), *n.* [*pl.* rowdies (-dĭz)], a rough, riotous fellow:—*adj.* rough and riotous; noisy and rude.—*adj.* **row'dy-ish.**—*n.* **row'dy-ism.**—*n.* **row'di-ness.**

row-el (rou'ĕl), *n.* the small, sharp-pointed wheel of a spur:—*v.t.* to prick with the wheel of a spur, as a horse.

row-en (rou'ĕn), *n.* a second crop, as of hay, on a field during one season.

row-lock (rō'lŏk; rŭl'ŭk), *n.* a notch in the gunwale of a boat, or a piece of metal with a U-shaped top, in which the oar rests in rowing: also called *oarlock.*

roy-al (roi'ăl), *adj.* **1,** pertaining to, or belonging to, a king; kingly; as, a *royal* household; **2,** pertaining to, or connected with, the government of a monarchy; as, the *royal* navy; **3,** befitting or like a king; regal; **4,** specially patronized, founded, or chartered by a king; as, the *Royal* Academy; **5,** unusually fine or superior in some way; as, a *royal* good time: **royal water lily,** a gigantic South American water lily: also called *victoria* or *Victoria regia* (which see for illus.):—*n.* **1,** a size of paper, 20 × 25 for printing or 19 × 24 for writing; **2,** an old English coin; **3,** a small sail above the topgallant sail and under the skysail (see *rigging,* illus.).—*adv.* **roy'al-ly.**

roy-al-ism (roi'ăl-ĭsm), *n.* belief in, and support of, the principles or cause of government by a king; also, the principles of such government.—*n.* **roy'al-ist.**

roy-al-ty (roi'ăl-tĭ), *n.* [*pl.* royalties (-tĭz)], **1,** the state, station, birth, etc., of a king; **2,** the person of a king or of one of sovereign rank; **3,** persons of sovereign rank collectively; **4,** kingly nature or quality; **5,** a tax paid to the crown, as a percentage of gold or silver mined or minted; **6,** hence, a share of the product or profit, as of a mine, claimed by the owner for permitting another to use the property; **7,** a percentage paid to an inventor or author for the use of a patent or copyright; as, a *royalty* from the sale of a book.

rub (rŭb), *v.t.* [*p.t.* and *p.p.* rubbed (rŭbd), *p.pr.* rub'bing], **1,** to cause (a surface) to undergo friction and pressure; as, to *rub* one's face with a towel; **2,** to pass over with a scraping or brushing movement; as, the wheel *rubbed* my dress; **3,** to cause to move over with pressure; as, to *rub* one's hand over one's arm; **4,** to clean or scour by moving something over with pressure; polish; as, to *rub* up the silver; **5,** to remove by moving something over; erase; as, to *rub* out a black mark; **6,** *Colloq.,* to renew one's knowledge of: with *up;* as, to *rub* up one's history; **7,** to affect one's feelings; as, to *rub* one the wrong way: —*v.i.* **1,** to move along a surface with pressure; scrape; as, two things *rub* together; **2,** to get along with difficulty; as, to manage to *rub* along:—*n.* **1,** the use of friction and pressure upon a surface; a rubbing; as, give the table a good *rub;* **2,** that which makes progress difficult; a hindrance; **3,** something that is harsh to the feelings, as a sneer or gibe.

¹rub-ber (rŭb'ẽr), *n.* **1,** one who polishes, erases, massages, or rubs in any way; **2,** anything used for erasing, polishing, or the like; **3,** the prepared, solidified sap from various tropical trees, used for waterproofing, insulating, etc.; caoutchouc: also called *India rubber;* **4,** an article made of this, as an overshoe or an elastic band:—*adj.* made of, or pertaining to, rubber: **rubber plant,** any of various plants which yield rubber; esp., a tree of India and Malaya, often grown for ornament:—*v.i. Slang*, to peer; crane one's neck.

²**rub-ber** (rŭb'ẽr), *n.* in certain games, the winning of two games out of three; also, the two or three games played until one side has won two; sometimes, the third, decisive game played after one game has been won by each side.

rub-bish (rŭb'ĭsh), *n.* anything of no value; trash.—*adj.* **rub'bish-y.**

rub-ble (rŭb'l), *n.* **1,** rough, broken stones or bricks; **2,** masonry built of such fragments; **3,** hence, trash.

Ru-bi-con (rōō'bĭ-kŏn), *n.* the river dividing the province of Cæsar from that of Pompey, the crossing of which by Cæsar led to war: **to cross the Rubicon,** to perform any act that commits one irrevocably to some course or undertaking.

ru-bi-cund (rōō'bĭ-kŭnd), *adj.* inclined to redness; flushed, as a face.

ru-ble (rōō'bl), *n.* formerly, a Russian silver coin, with a par value of about 51.5 cents. Also, **rou'ble.**

ru-bric (rōō'brĭk), *n.* **1,** the directions in prayer books, formerly printed in red; **2,** hence, any rule of conduct; **3,** the title of a law, formerly printed in red:—*adj.* **1,** made prominent by being marked in red; **2,** red.

ru-bri-cate (rōō'brĭ-kāt), *v.t.* [*p.t.* and *p.p.* -cat″ed, *p.pr.* -cat″ing], to mark or distinguish with red, as a book.

ru-by (rōō'bĭ), *n.* [*pl.* rubies (-bĭz)], **1,** a precious stone, usually a variety of corundum, varying in color from carmine red to crimson; **2,** the color of the stone.

ruche (rōōsh), *n.* a frilled or plaited strip of fine dress trimming, used for edging at the neck or wrist. Also, **rouche.**

ruch-ing (rōōsh'ĭng), *n.* **1,** material, such as lace, silk, etc., for making plaited or frilled edgings; **2,** ruches collectively.

ruck (rŭk), *n. Colloq.*, the multitude of common persons or things; throng; crowd.

rud-der (rŭd'ẽr), *n.* **1,** a broad, flat piece of wood or metal, hinged vertically to the stern of a vessel and used for steering; **2,** a similar, hinged or pivoted part, used to steer an aircraft (see *airplane*, illus.).—*adj.* **rud'der-less.**

RUDDER
a, rudder; *b*, tiller.

rud-dy (rŭd'ĭ), *adj.*[*comp.* rud'di-er, *superl.* rud'di-est], **1,** red or approaching to redness; **2,** having a healthy glow, as the skin.—*adv.* **rud'di-ly.**—*n.* **rud'di-ness.**

rude (rōōd), *adj.* **1,** barbarous; not cultivated; ignorant; as, a *rude* people; **2,** impolite; uncivil; impudent; as, *rude* behavior; **3,** robust; strong; rugged; as, *rude* health; **4,** crude; unskilful; as, a *rude* carving; **5,** harsh; rough; severe; as, a *rude* awakening.—*adv.* **rude'ly.**—*n.* **rude'ness.**

Syn. uncouth; discourteous; sturdy, vigorous.—*Ant.* polite, civil, gentle.

ru-di-ment (rōō'dĭ-mĕnt), *n.* **1,** usually in *pl.*, the first or introductory principle of an art, science, etc.; as, the *rudiments* of composition; **2,** anything in the first state of development; a beginning.—*adj.* **ru″di-men'tal.**—*adj.* **ru″di-men'ta-ry.**

¹**rue** (rōō), *n.* an Old World, yellow-flowered, medicinal plant with strong odor and bitter taste, often grown in gardens.

²**rue** (rōō), *v.t.* [*p.t.* and *p.p.* rued (rōōd), *p.pr.* ru'ing], to be sorry for; wish undone:—*n. Obs.*, remorse.

rue-ful (rōō'fŏŏl), *adj.* **1,** showing sorrow or pity; sad; as, a *rueful* smile; **2,** arousing sorrow or regret; pitiable; as, a *rueful* sight.—*adv.* **rue'ful-ly.**—*n.* **rue'ful-ness.**

¹**ruff** (rŭf), *n.* **1,** a large plaited or fluted collar; **2,** anything like such a collar, as a prominent growth of feathers around the neck of a bird or of hair around the neck of an animal; **3,** an Old World sandpiper, the male having at the breeding season an enormous frill of feathers about his neck: the female being called *reeve;* **4,** a kind of pigeon with a neck ruff.

²**ruff** (rŭf), *n.* **1,** formerly, a game like whist; **2,** the act of trumping:—*v.t.* and *v.i.* to trump when one has no card of the suit led.

³**ruff** (rŭf), *n.* a small fish of the perch family.

ruf-fi-an (rŭf'ĭ-ăn; rŭf'yăn), *n.* a brutal, lawless fellow; one given to cruel deeds:—*adj.* brutal; cruel.—*n.* **ruf'fi-an-ism.**—*adj.* **ruf'fi-an-ly.**

ruf-fle (rŭf'l), *n.* **1,** a plaited or gathered strip of material, used as a trimming; **2,** a slight vexation:—*v.t.* [*p.t.* and *p.p.* -fled (-ld), *p.pr.* -fling], **1,** to draw into folds or gathers; **2,** to furnish or adorn with plaited or gathered strips; **3,** to cause to stand up or out; as, a bird *ruffles* its feathers; **4,** to disturb slightly or make ripples upon; as, the wind *ruffles* the water; **5,** to disarrange; disorder, as the hair; **6,** to annoy or vex; as, to *ruffle* one's temper:—*v.i.* **1,** to be rumpled or disordered; **2,** to become vexed or annoyed.

ru-fous (rōō'fŭs), *adj.* yellowish red or brownish red.

rug (rŭg), *n.* **1,** a heavy floor covering, usually made in one piece and of a size to cover only part of the floor; **2,** a mat made of animal skin with the hair or wool left on; **3,** a coarse, warm fabric or skin used as a coverlet or traveling wrap.

Rug-by (rŭg'bĭ), *n.* a kind of football of which American football is a modified form, first played at Rugby school.

rug-ged (rŭg'ĕd), *adj.* **1,** having an uneven surface; rough; **2,** steep and rocky; as, *rugged* country; **3,** disordered; untidy; unkempt; **4,** uncouth; crude; plain; as, a *rugged* countryman; **5,** wrinkled; furrowed; as, a *rugged* brow; **6,** harsh; stern; as, a *rugged* character; **7,** *Colloq.*, healthy; robust.—*adv.* **rug'ged-ly.**—*n.* **rug'ged-ness.**

ru-in (rōō'ĭn), *n.* **1,** overthrow; destruction; downfall; **2,** that which causes destruction or decay; **3,** often in *pl.*, that which remains of something destroyed or fallen into decay; **4,** the state of decay or desolation:—*v.t.* to pull down, destroy, overthrow, or make poor:—*v.i.* **1,** to decay; perish; **2,** to do harm beyond repair.—*n.* **ru″in-a'tion.**

Syn., v. deface, demolish. (See destroy.)

ru-in-ous (rōō'ĭ-nŭs), *adj.* **1,** fallen into decay; dilapidated; as, a house in a *ruinous* state; **2,** destructive; hurtful; as, *ruinous* conduct.—*adv.* **ru'in-ous-ly.**—*n.* **ru'in-ous-ness.**

rule (rōōl), *n.* **1,** a standard or principle of conduct; as, honesty should be the *rule* for all; a regulation; as, a *rule* of the game; an established usage or law, as in arithmetic or grammar; **2,** government; authority; as, a democratic *rule;* **3,** usual course of action; as, I walk there as a *rule;* **4,** that which is true or may be expected in the majority of cases; as, in some countries, ignorance is the *rule;* **5,** a straight-edged, graduated strip, as of wood or metal, for drawing lines; **6,** in printing, a thin strip of metal used for printing lines: **rule of three,** in mathematics, a method of finding a number that has the same ratio to a given number as exists between two other given numbers:—*v.t.* [*p.t.* and *p.p.* ruled (rōōld), *p.pr.* rul'ing], **1,** to govern or control; **2,** to settle, as by a rule; **3,** to manage, control, influence, or restrain; **4**, to establish by a decision, as of a court; **5**, to mark with lines with the aid of a straight strip:—*v.i.* **1**, in law, to decide a point; **2**, to exercise superior authority.

Syn., *v.* guide. (See govern.)

rul-er (rōōl′ēr), *n.* **1**, one who governs; **2**, a strip of wood, metal, etc., used as a guide in drawing lines.

rul-ing (rōōl′ĭng), *p.adj.* governing or having control; predominant:—*n.* **1**, the act of one governing; **2**, a decision laid down by a judge or court; **3**, the act of making lines, or the lines so made.

[1]rum (rŭm), *n.* **1**, a strong, alcoholic liquor made from molasses or the juice of the sugar cane; **2**, *U. S. Colloq.*, any intoxicating drink: **rum runner**, a boat engaged in the trade of smuggling intoxicating liquors into the U. S.: **rum row**, a line of ships stationed off the coast of the U. S., but beyond its jurisdiction, for the purpose of smuggling intoxicating liquors: also called *rum fleet.*

[2]rum (rŭm), *adj. Slang*, queer; peculiar; strange. Also, **rum′my.**

[3]rum (rŭm), *n.* a card game in which each player attempts to clear his hand by discarding and by appropriating discards.

Ru-ma-ni-an (rōō-mā′nĭ-ăn), *adj.* pertaining to Rumania, its people, or their language:—*n.* **1**, a native or inhabitant of Rumania; **2**, the language of Rumania, one of the Romance languages. Also, **Rou-ma′ni-an.**

rum-ble (rŭm′bl), *n.* **1**, a low, heavy, rolling sound; as, the *rumble* of thunder; **2**, a seat for servants at the back of a carriage; also, a small seat behind the body of an automobile, esp. a roadster: also called *rumble seat:*—*v.i.* and *v.t.* [*p.t.* and *p.p.* -bled (-bld), *p.pr.* -bling], to make, or cause to make, a low, heavy, rolling sound.

ru-mi-nant (rōō′mĭ-nănt), *n.* any of a division of animals comprising the hoofed mammals that chew the cud, as oxen, sheep, goats, deer, camels:—*adj.* **1**, chewing the cud; **2**, hence, meditative; thoughtful.

ru-mi-nate (rōō′mĭ-nāt), *v.i.* [*p.t.* and *p.p.* -nat″ed, *p.pr.* -nat″ing], **1**, to chew the cud; **2**, to meditate or muse; reflect; as, to *ruminate* on the future:—*v.t.* **1**, to chew again; **2**, to ponder.—*n.* **ru″mi-na′tion.**—*adj.* **ru′mi-na-tive.**

rum-mage (rŭm′ăj), *n.* a thorough search made by turning things over in a disorderly way:—*v.t.* [*p.t.* and *p.p.* -maged (-ăjd), *p.pr.* -mag-ing], to search thoroughly by turning over the contents of; ransack:—*v.i.* to make a thorough but disorderly search.

ru-mor (rōō′mēr), *n.* **1**, common talk; popular report; **2**, a current story that has not been verified; as, a *rumor* of war:—*v.t.* to spread by report: usually in the passive. Also, **ru′mour.**

rump (rŭmp), *n.* **1**, the hinder parts of an animal; buttocks: used specif. of a cut of beef (see *beef*, illus.); **2**, a remnant.

rum-ple (rŭm′pl), *n.* a wrinkle or disorderly crease:—*v.t.* and *v.i.* [*p.t.* and *p.p.* -pled (-pld), *p.pr.* -pling], to wrinkle; crumple; muss.

rum-pus (rŭm′pŭs), *n.* a disturbance; a row.

run (rŭn), *v.i.* [*p.t.* ran (răn) or run, *p.p.* run, *p.pr.* run′ning], **1**, to move or go on the feet at a pace swifter than a walk; of a man, to move so rapidly that at each step there is an instant when both feet are off the ground; **2**, to act in a way to suggest such motion; hurry; rush; flee; depart suddenly; as, he *ran* away from home; **3**, to travel; proceed; as, the express *runs* forty miles an hour; **4**, to make regular trips; ply; as, the boat *runs* between Boston and New York; **5**, to move in a stream; flow; also, to melt and flow, as butter or tallow; **6**, to give passage to, or discharge, a fluid, as pus or tears; **7**, to act; be in action; operate; as, the engine will not *run;* **8**, to extend from place to place; lie in a certain direction; as, the railroad *runs* through his land; **9**, to continue in time; be kept in action; keep going; as, the play *ran* a year; **10**, to pass into a different state or condition; as, to *run* into luck; *run* to seed; **11**, to slip; become unfastened; ravel; as, a thread *runs* in a stocking; **12**, to engage in a contest; be a competitor; as, to *run* for office; **13**, to follow a line of descent; as, laziness *runs* in the family; **14**, to climb, creep; trail; as, the vine *runs* up the wall; **15**, to expatiate continuously: with *on;* **16**, to be written, expressed, or related; as, the story *runs* that . . . ; **17**, to remain not paid; become payable; **18**, to have a certain value or quality; average; as, the potatoes *run* large; **19**, of a law, to continue in efficacy or force:—*v.t.* **1**, to cause to move, operate, or act, as an engine; cause to take part in a contest; **2**, to chase after; hunt; **3**, to thrust; stick; push; as, to *run* a pin into one's finger; **4**, to drive or dash forcibly; as, to *run* one's head against a wall; **5**, to do by running, or as if by running; as, to *run* errands; **6**, to flow with; pour forth; as, the earth *ran* blood; **7**, to fuse; melt; cast; **8**, to go through (something dangerous or full of risks) with success; as, to *run* a blockade; **9**, to expose oneself to; submit to; as, to *run* a risk; **10**, to take (goods) from one country to another secretly, to avoid paying duties; smuggle; **11**, to discharge, as pus; **12**, to sew in a continuous row; as, to *run* a seam; **13**, to go over and mark out, as a dividing line, boundary, or the like; **14**, to manage; direct; as, to *run* a theater:—*n.* **1**, the act or power of going at a pace swifter than a walk; specif., one of the four gaits of a horse; **2**, a trip or journey; progress; as, the boat made its usual *run;* **3**, the act of flowing or that which flows; as, a *run* of maple sap; **4**, a course or succession; continued operation; as, a *run* of ill luck; **5**, sudden, continuous, pressing demand; as, a *run* on silks; a *run* on a bank; **6**, the average kind; as, the ordinary *run* of people; **7**, a place passed over frequently, esp. by animals; **8**, an inclosed place in which to confine and feed animals; **9**, a brook; **10**, contour or character, as of land; **11**, a period of operation, or the work turned out during the period; as, the mill has had a long *run;* **12**, the horizontal distance between two consecutive risers in a flight of steps (see *step*, illus.); **13**, in some games, as billiards, a series of successful shots, or the resulting score; as, a *run* of 50; **14**, in baseball, cricket, etc., the unit of scoring, made by running once over a specified course; **15**, in music, a quick succession of notes; a roulade; **16**, *Colloq.*, free use or enjoyment; as, the *run* of a friend's house.

run-a-bout (rŭn′ȧ-bout″), *n.* **1**, a light, open automobile; also, an uncovered carriage; **2**, a light motor boat.

run-a-gate (rŭn′ȧ-gāt), *n.* **1**, a fugitive; **2**, a wanderer; vagabond.

run–a-round (rŭn′=ȧ-round″), *n. Colloq.*, a felon; a painful inflammation around a finger nail; Also, **run′round″.**

run-a-way (rŭn′ȧ-wā″), *n.* **1**, one who escapes or runs away; a fugitive; **2**, the act of running away: said esp. of horses; also, a horse of which the driver has lost control:—*adj.* **1**, escaping from control; as, a *runaway* engine; **2**, brought about by running away; as, a *runaway* match.

run-dle (rŭn′dl), *n.* **1**, a rung, as of a ladder; **2**, anything that revolves about an axis, as a driving wheel.

āte, senăte, râre, căt, ȧsk, fär, ȧllow, sofȧ; ēve, ēvent, ĕll, writẽr, novĕl; nīne, pĭn; gō, ōbey, ôr, dôg, tŏp, cŏllide; ūnit, ūnite, ûrn, cŭt, focŭs; nōōn, fŏŏt; sour; coin;

rune (rōōn), *n.* **1**, a character in the alphabet used by the ancient Teutonic peoples; **2**, in *pl.*, poetry expressed in runes.

GOTHIC RUNIC ALPHABET, OR FUTHORC

¹rung (rŭng), past participle of the irregular verb *ring*, which see.

²rung (rŭng), a round of a ladder; also, a bar connecting the legs of a chair.

ru-nic (rōō′nĭk), *adj.* pertaining to, or consisting of, runes, or the characters of the alphabets of the earliest Teutonic nations.

run-let (rŭn′lĕt), *n.* a little stream; a rivulet. Also, **run′nel.**

run-ner (rŭn′ẽr), *n.* **1**, one who runs, as a racer, a messenger, or the like; **2**, one of the pieces on which a sleigh, skate, or sled moves; **3**, a slender trailing branch that takes root at the end or joints (see *root*, illus.); **4**, a plant that spreads in this way; **5**, a soldier acting as messenger in the trenches.

run-ning (rŭn′ĭng), *p.adj.* **1**, moving swiftly; **2**, being in motion; **3**, successive; continuous; **4**, discharging pus; as, a *running* sore: **running board,** a narrow step along the side of a vehicle, esp. an automobile:—*n.* **1**, the act of moving swiftly; **2**, contest; as, out of the *running.*

runt (rŭnt), *n.* **1**, a dwarf animal, as a small pig; **2**, a person stunted in growth.

run-way (rŭn′wā″), *n.* a beaten way or path over which something runs, as a trail followed by animals.

ru-pee (rōō-pē′), *n.* a coin of British India worth about 32.4 cents.

rup-ture (rŭp′tūr), *n.* **1**, the act of bursting or breaking apart; **2**, the state of being broken or violently burst apart; **3**, a breach or an interruption of friendly relations; **4**, a hernia:—*v.t.* [*p.t.* and *p.p.* -tured (-tūrd), *p.pr.* -tur-ing], **1**, to burst or break violently apart; **2**, to affect with hernia; **3**, to bring about a breach of; as, to *rupture* friendship:—*v.i.* to suffer a breach or break.

ru-ral (rōō′răl), *adj.* pertaining to, or like, the country, or country life: **rural free delivery,** free delivery of mail by government carriers to homes in the country districts.—*n.* **ru′ral-ism.**—*n.* **ru′ral-ist.**—*adv.* **ru′ral-ly.**

ruse (rōōz), *n.* a trick; stratagem; fraud or deceit.

¹rush (rŭsh), *n.* **1**, any of many plants, having long, easily twisted stems and growing in wet ground: valuable for seating chairs, making baskets, or the like; **2**, anything of little value; a trifle.—*adj.* **rush′y.**

²rush (rŭsh), *v.i.* **1**, to move with great speed; press forward with violent haste; **2**, to do with extraordinary haste or eagerness:—*v.t.* **1**, to cause to move or act with great speed; hurry; **2**, to make an attack on and occupy; as, to *rush* a fortification; **3**, in football, to advance (the ball) by carrying (it); **4**, *Slang*, to pay marked attention to, as to a girl or a desirable candidate for a fraternity:—*n.* **1**, a driving forward with eagerness and haste; **2**, a sudden migration; as, a *rush* to the gold fields; **3**, *Colloq.:* **a**, an extraordinary demand for activity and haste; as, the Christmas *rush;* **b**, an unusual demand; a run; as, a *rush* on bonds; **4**, *U. S. College Slang*, a rough-and-tumble contest, as between classes; **5**, in football, a play in which the ball is carried toward the goal.—*n.* **rush′er.**

rush-light (rŭsh′līt″), *n.* a candle made of the pith of rushes dipped in tallow: also called *rush candle.*

rusk (rŭsk), *n.* **1**, a kind of cake or sweetened biscuit; **2**, a kind of bread, baked until crisp; also, such bread pulverized.

rus-set (rŭs′ĕt), *n.* **1**, a reddish brown color; **2**, a cloth or clothing of such a color; esp., homespun; **3**, a kind of winter apple:—*adj.* **1**, reddish or yellowish brown; **2**, homespun; coarse.—*adj.* **rus′set-y.**

Rus-sia leath-er (rŭsh′ȧ), a strong, soft leather prepared from hides soaked in birch oil.

Rus-sian (rŭsh′ăn), *adj.* of or pertaining to Russia:—*n.* **1**, a native or inhabitant of Russia; **2**, the language of Russia.

rust (rŭst), *n.* **1**, the reddish matter formed on iron and steel through exposure to dampness; red oxide of iron; **2**, a similar formation from corrosion on other metals; **3**, anything like rust; mildew on wheat, corn, etc.:—*v.i.* **1**, to form rust; **2**, to grow worthless because of idleness:—*v.t.* **1**, to cause to contract rust; **2**, to impair by time or inaction.

rus-tic (rŭs′tĭk), *n.* **1**, a countryman; a peasant; **2**, a person of simple or uncouth manner:—*adj.* **1**, pertaining to, or like, the country; rural; **2**, simple; artless; **3**, crude; without ornamentation. Also, **rus′ti-cal.**—*adv.* **rus′ti-cal-ly.**

Syn., *adj.* rude, plain, uncouth, coarse.

rus-ti-cate (rŭs′tĭ-kāt), *v.i.* [*p.t.* and *p.p.* -cat″ed, *p.pr.* -cat″ing], to reside in, or go into, the country:—*v.t.* **1**, to compel to reside in the country; **2**, to banish or dismiss for a time from college.

rus-ti-ca-tion (rŭs″tĭ-kā′shŭn), *n.* **1**, residence in the country; **2**, temporary dismissal from a college.

rus-tic-i-ty (rŭs-tĭs′ĭ-tĭ), *n.* [*pl.* rusticities (-tĭz)], homely or countrylike manners or simplicity; awkwardness.

rus-tle (rŭs′l), *n.* a soft, crackling sound, such as that made by leaves:—*v.i.* [*p.t.* and *p.p.* -tled (-ld), *p.pr.* -tling], to make a soft, crackling sound, as that made by the rubbing together of silk or dry leaves:—*v.t.* **1**, to cause to make such a sound; **2**, *Slang:* **a**, to get or obtain by energetic action; **b**, to steal (cattle).—*n.* and *p.adj.* **rus′tling.**

rus-tler (rŭs′lẽr), *n. Slang*, **1**, one who hustles; an enterprising, successful man; **2**, a cattle thief.

rust-y (rŭs′tĭ), *adj.* [*comp.* rust′i-er, *superl.* rust′i-est], **1**, covered with rust; **2**, impaired or harmed by inactivity or idleness, as an engine; hence, out of practice.

rut (rŭt), *n.* **1**, the track of a wheel; **2**, a groove or hollow:—*v.t.* [*p.t.* and *p.p.* rut′ted, *p.pr.* rut′ting], to cut into grooves or hollows; make wheel tracks in.—*adj.* **rut′ty.**

ru-ta-ba-ga (rōō″tȧ-bā′gȧ), *n.* a turnip larger than the common turnip and of a yellowish color.

ruth (rōōth), *n. Archaic*, **1**, pity; compassion; **2**, repentance.—*adj.* **ruth′ful.**

Ruth (rōōth), *n.* in the Bible, a book of the Old Testament; also, the heroine of the book, who became the great-grandmother of David: remembered as an example of devotion to her mother-in-law, Naomi.

ruth-less (rōōth′lĕs), *adj.* cruel; pitiless; savage; barbarous.—*adv.* **ruth′less-ly.**—*n.* **ruth′less-ness.**

-ry (-rĭ), *n. suffix*, a shortened form of *-ery*, which see; as, revel*ry*.

rye (rī), *n.* **1**, a hardy cereal plant closely related to wheat; also, its seed: used in making bread, in distilling whisky, and as fodder; **2**, *Colloq.*, whisky distilled from rye grain.

ry-ot (rī′ŏt), *n.* in India, a cultivator; field laborer; peasant.

S

Sab-a-oth (săb'ā-ŏth; sȧ-bā'ŏth), *n.pl.* **1**, in the Bible, armies; hosts: used in the expression *Lord of Sabaoth* (Romans 9:29); **2**, erroneously, the Sabbath.

Sab-ba-ta-ri-an (săb"ȧ-tā'rĭ-ăn), *adj.* pertaining to the Sabbath, or to the keeping of the Sabbath:—*n.* **1**, a rigid observer of the Sabbath; **2**, one who keeps the Sabbath on the seventh day.—*n.* **Sab"ba-ta'ri-an-ism.**

Sab-bath (săb'ȧth), *n.* **1**, the seventh day of the week, observed by the Jews and certain others as a day of rest, commencing at sunset on Friday and ending at sunset on Saturday; **2**, the Christian Sunday, or first day of the week, esp. when observed as a day of rest and worship: **Sabbath school**, a school for religious instruction, held on the Sabbath: also called *Sunday school.*

sab-bat-i-cal (să-băt'ĭ-kăl), *adj.* pertaining to, or like, the Sabbath; as, *sabbatical* peace: **sabbatical year**, **1**, among the ancient Jews, every seventh year, in which the lands and vineyards of the Israelites were allowed to remain fallow; **2**, every seventh year, sometimes granted to a college professor for study or rest. Also, **sab-bat'ic.**

sa-ber (sā'bẽr), *n.* a cavalry sword, having a curved blade:—*v.t.* to cut, wound, or kill with, or as with, such a sword. Also, **sa'bre** [*p.t.* and *p.p.* -bred (-bẽrd), *p.pr.* -bring].

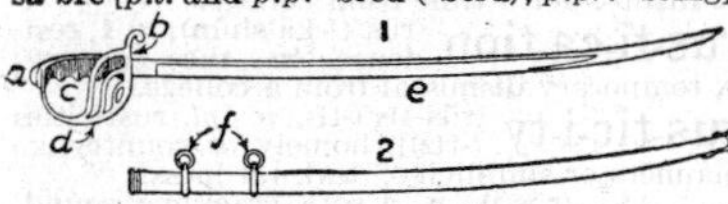

CAVALRY SABER AND SCABBARD

1, saber: *a*, pommel; *b*, plate; *c*, grip; *d*, guard; *e*, blade.—2, scabbard: *f*, slings.

Sa-bine (sā'bīn), *n.* **1**, a member of an ancient central Italian race, which was conquered and absorbed by Rome in 290 B. C.; **2**, its language:—*adj.* pertaining to the Sabines or their language.

sa-ble (sā'bl), *n.* **1**, a kind of weasel valued for its handsome, dark, glossy fur; **2**, the fur of this animal; **3**, in heraldry or coats of arms, black; **4**, in *pl.*, mourning dress:—*adj.* dark-colored; black.

***sa-bot** (sȧ"bō'), [Fr.], *n.* [*pl.* sabots (-bō')], **1**, a wooden shoe worn by peasants; **2**, a shoe with a leather top and a wooden sole.

SABOTS

1, wood; 2, leather.

sa-bo-tage (săb'ō-tāj; *Fr.* sȧ"bō"tȧzh'), *n.* **1**, the wilful injury to, or destruction of, machinery or materials by workmen, as during labor troubles; **2**, similar interference with government activities in time of emergency; **3**, wilful restriction of labor or production.

sac (săk), *n.* a baglike part of a plant or animal, sometimes containing a special fluid.

Sac (săk; sôk), *n.* one of a tribe of American Indians, who at one time lived along the upper Mississippi.

sac-cha-rin (săk'ȧ-rĭn), *n.* a white crystalline product of coal tar, very much sweeter than cane sugar.

sac-cha-rine (săk'ȧ-rīn; săk'ȧ-rĭn), *adj.* pertaining to sugar; sweet.

sac-er-do-tal (săs"ẽr-dō'tăl), *adj.* pertaining to priests; priestly.

sac-er-do-tal-ism (săs"ẽr-dō'tăl-ĭzm), *n.* **1**, a priestly spirit or system; **2**, a tendency to emphasize the priestly office or its sanctity; **3**, priestcraft.

sa-chem (sā'chĕm), *n.* a North American Indian chief.

sa-chet (sȧ"shā'), *n.* a small bag or cushion filled with a perfume in the form of powder; also, the powder itself.

[1]**sack** (săk), *n.* **1**, a bag; esp., a large, coarse bag open at one end, for holding grain, potatoes, etc.; **2**, a quantity of varying size; as, sugar at 30 cents a *sack;* **3**, a loose upper garment or cloak worn by women and children: often written *sacque;* also, a man's short, loose coat; **4**, a sac (which see): **to give** (one) **the sack**, *Colloq.*, to dismiss:—*v.t.* **1**, to put into a bag; **2**, *Colloq.*, to dismiss; **3**, *Slang*, to defeat in a match.—*n.* **sack'ful.**

[2]**sack** (săk), *n.* **1**, the plundering by soldiers of a town taken in war; **2**, loot; booty:—*v.t.* **1**, to plunder or pillage; ravage; **2**, to despoil; rob, as a house.—*n.* **sack'er.**

[3]**sack** (săk), *n.* any of several dry, light-colored wines.

sack-but (săk'bŭt), *n.* **1**, an ancient musical instrument resembling the lyre; **2**, in medieval times, a kind of trombone.

sack-cloth (săk'klôth"), *n.* **1**, a coarse material of which sacks are made; **2**, a coarse, rough cloth worn in ancient times as a token of mourning or repentance.

sack-ing (săk'ĭng), *n.* coarse materials used for making sacks or bags.

sacque (săk), *n.* a short, loose garment or cloak. See [1]**sack**, *Pfd. S.*

sac-ra-ment (săk'rȧ-mĕnt), *n.* **1**, a holy or sacred ceremony, as baptism and the Eucharist, or Lord's Supper; **2**, (also, *Sacrament*), the consecrated elements of the Eucharist.—*adj.* **sac"ra-men'tal.**—*adj.* **sac"ra-men'ta-ry.**

sa-cred (sā'krĕd), *adj.* **1**, set apart for religious uses; consecrated; holy; as, a *sacred* edifice; **2**, pertaining to religion; as, *sacred* literature; **3**, not to be treated irreverently or put to unworthy use.—*adv.* **sa'cred-ly.**—*n.* **sa'cred-ness.**

Syn. hallowed, divine, inviolable.

sac-ri-fice (săk'rĭ-fīs; săk'rĭ-fīz), *n.* **1**, the act of presenting to God, or to a deity, some offering, as a slaughtered animal or incense; **2**, that which is offered; anything offered or consecrated to God; **3**, the destroying, losing, or giving up of something for another's sake; **4**, the thing so destroyed or given up; **5**, goods sold at a loss:—*v.t.* (săk'rĭ-fīz; săk'rĭ-fīs), [*p.t.* and *p.p.* -ficed (-fīzd; -fīst), *p.pr.* -fic"ing], **1**, to offer to a god in worship; **2**, to destroy or give up for the sake of some other person or object; as, to *sacrifice* health for riches; **3**, to sell at a loss:—*v.i.* to offer up a sacrifice.—*n.* **sac'ri-fic"er.**

sac-ri-fi-cial (săk"rĭ-fĭsh'ăl), *adj.* pertaining to, consisting in, or offering, sacrifice.—*adv.* **sac"ri-fi'cial-ly.**

sac-ri-lege (săk'rĭ-lĕj), *n.* the crime or sin of desecrating or profaning sacred persons or things.

sac-ri-le-gious (săk"rĭ-lē'jŭs), *adj.* treating sacred things irreverently; profane.—*adv.* **sac"ri-le'gious-ly.**—*n.* **sac"ri-le'gious-ness.**

sac-ris-tan (săk'rĭs-tăn), *n.* **1**, one who has the care of church vessels, vestments, etc.; **2**, one who takes care of the church in general; a sexton.

sac-ris-ty (săk′rĭs-tĭ), *n.* [*pl.* sacristies (-tĭz)], an apartment in a church where the sacred vessels, minister's vestments or robes, etc., are kept; vestry.

sac-ro-sanct (săk′rō-săngkt), *adj.* most sacred or holy; consecrated; inviolable:—*n.* that which is sacred.

sa-crum (sā′krŭm), *n.* [*pl.* sacra (-krȧ)], a composite, triangular, bony structure forming the back of the pelvis, made of five vertebræ joined together (see *pelvis*, illus.).

sad (săd), *adj.* [*comp.* sad′der, *superl.* sad′dest], **1**, full of grief; mournful; sorrowful; **2**, causing mournfulness; **3**, dark; said of colors.—*adv.* **sad′ly.**—*n.* **sad′ness.**
Syn. downcast, depressed, melancholy.—*Ant.* gay, merry, cheerful, glad.

sad-den (săd′n), *v.t.* to make mournful or sorrowful:—*v.i.* to become depressed or cheerless.

sad-dle (săd′l), *n.* **1**, a padded leather seat for a rider on a horse's back, a bicycle, etc.; **2**, anything shaped like a saddle, as a cut of meat consisting of the two loins; **3**, in geology, a ridge between two hills or summits; **4**, a part of a horse's harness, which rests where the saddle is placed (see *harness*, illus.); **5**, a block over which a cord or cable passes, as in a violin (see *violin*, illus.), or at the top of the piers of a suspension bridge:—*v.t.* [*p.t.* and *p.p.* -dled (-ld), *p.pr.* -dling], **1**, to equip with a seat for a rider; **2**, to burden or embarrass, as with debt.—*n.* **sad′dle-cloth″.**

sad-dle-bag (săd′l-băg″), *n.* one of a pair of pouches attached to a saddle, for carrying articles.

sad-dle-bow (săd′l-bō″), *n.* the pieces which form the pommel, or arched front part, of a saddle.

sad-dler (săd′lẽr), *n.* one who makes or repairs saddles, harness, etc.

sad-dler-y (săd′lẽr-ĭ), *n.* [*pl.* saddleries (-ĭz)], **1**, the business of a saddler or harness maker; **2**, articles made by a harness maker, or the materials he uses; **3**, the shop where these articles are made.

sad-dle-tree (săd′l-trē″), *n.* the frame of a saddle.

Sad-du-cee (săd′ū-sē), *n.* one of an ancient, aristocratic Jewish sect that denied resurrection and personal immortality.—*n.* **Sad′du-cee″ism.**

sad-i-ron (săd′ī″ûrn), an iron for smoothing clothes; a flatiron.

sa-dism (sā′dĭzm; săd′ĭzm; sä′dĭzm), *n.* any abnormal tendency to inflict extreme cruelty.—*n.* **sa′dist.**—*adj.* **sa-dis′tic.**

***Saeng-er-fest** (zĕng′ẽr-fĕst″), [Ger.], *n.* [*pl.* Saengerfeste (-fĕs″tĕ)], a song festival at which various singing societies compete; a musical competition.

[1]**safe** (sāf), *adj.* **1**, free from danger, evil, or damage; **2**, out of danger; secure; not hurt; **3**, incapable of doing injury or harm; securely kept, as a prisoner; **4**, reliable; trustworthy; involving no risk or loss; as, a *safe* investment; **5**, cautious; prudent; as, a *safe* investor.—*adv.* **safe′ly.**—*n.* **safe′ness.**

[2]**safe** (sāf), *n.* **1**, an iron or steel chest for valuables, as jewels and money; **2**, any place, as a room or chest, specially designed for preserving or safe-keeping; as, a butcher's *safe* for meats.

safe–con-duct (sāf″-kŏn′dŭkt), *n.* a guard or passport which guarantees a safe passage, esp. through an enemy's country in war time; a pass:—*v.t.* (sāf″-kŏn-dŭkt′; -kŏn′dŭkt), to provide with a safe-conduct; also, to conduct safely.

safe-guard (sāf′gärd″), *n.* **1**, one who or that which guards or protects; a means of security; defense; **2**, a safe-conduct; protective papers granted to a foreigner:—*v.t.* to protect or watch over.

safe–keep-ing (sāf″-kēp′ĭng), *n.* care; secure guardianship.

safe-ty (sāf′tĭ), *n.* freedom from danger, injury, or damage; safe-keeping.

safe-ty lamp a form of lamp used by miners, designed to prevent explosions by protecting the flame.

safe-ty match a match that will not ignite unless struck on a specially prepared surface.

safe-ty pin a pin made so that the point is held behind a guard, protecting the wearer from being pricked.

safe-ty valve **1**, an automatic valve in a boiler, which opens when the steam exceeds a certain pressure; **2**, hence, a means of relief from worry, or an outlet for strong feeling.

saf-fron (săf′rŭn), *n.* **1**, a crocus bearing purple flowers in the fall; **2**, one of the dried orange-colored stigmas of this plant, which yield a deep yellow dye, and are also used in medicine; **3**, a deep yellow color:—*adj.* deep yellow.

sag (săg), *v.i.* [*p.t.* and *p.p.* sagged (săgd), *p.pr.* sag′ging], **1**, to sink or droop by weight, or under pressure; as, the rope *sags*; **2**, to lean to one side, as an old door; **3**, to lose firmness; weaken, as under disaster:—*n.* the fact or the extent of sinking or drooping under weight; as, the *sag* of a skirt.

sa-ga (sä′gȧ; sā′gȧ), *n.* a medieval Scandinavian narrative of heroic deeds.

sa-ga-cious (sȧ-gā′shŭs), *adj.* having good judgment; shrewd.—*adv.* **sa-ga′cious-ly.**—*n.* **sa-ga′cious-ness.**

sa-gac-i-ty (sȧ-găs′ĭ-tĭ), *n.* readiness of understanding; keen, practical, shrewd judgment.

sag-a-more (săg′ȧ-mōr), *n.* among certain North American tribes, an Indian chief.

[1]**sage** (sāj), *adj.* **1**, wise; discerning; **2**, indicating profound wisdom; keenly judged; shrewd; as, *sage* counsel:—*n.* a profoundly wise and venerable man.—*adv.* **sage′ly.**—*n.* **sage′ness.**

[2]**sage** (sāj), *n.* **1**, any of several plants of the mint family, esp. a plant the spicy, dull green leaves of which are used for flavoring meats, soups, etc.; **2**, scarlet sage, a garden flower; **3**, the American sagebrush.

sage-brush (sāj′brŭsh″), *n.* any of various low, grayish green shrubs of the plains of the western U. S.

Sag-it-ta-ri-us (săj″ĭ-tā′rĭ-ŭs), *n.* **1**, a southern constellation, the Archer; **2**, the ninth sign of the zodiac, entered by the sun on or about November 23 (see *zodiac*, illus.).

SAGO (much reduced)
A, fruit.

sag-it-tate (săj′ĭ-tāt), *adj.* shaped like an arrowhead, as a leaf (see *leaf*, illus.).—*adj.* **sag′it-tal.**

sa-go (sā′gō), *n.* a starch obtained from the pith of certain East Indian palms.

sa-hib (sä′ĭb), *n.* a term of address used by the natives of India, meaning: **1**, when referring to a European gentleman, master; **2**, in direct address, Mister; Sir: placed after the name.

said (sĕd), past tense and past participle of *say*:—*p.adj.* already referred to; mentioned before: used chiefly in legal documents.

sail (sāl), *n.* **1**, a sheet of canvas by means of which the wind is made to drive a vessel forward in the water (see *rigging*, illus.); **2**, a ship or vessel propelled by such a method; **3**, vessels collectively; **4**, an excursion in a sailboat; as, we went for a *sail*:—*v.i.* **1**, to be moved by the action of the wind upon spread canvas; **2**, hence, to be moved through water, as by the force of steam; **3**, to go by water; as, we *sailed* to Liverpool; **4**, to begin a voyage; as, the ship *sailed* at noon; **5**, to glide like a boat, or as an eagle through the air; pass smoothly along:—*v.t.* **1**, to pass over in a ship; as, to *sail* the Atlantic; **2**, to direct, steer, or manage the motion of; as, to *sail* a ship.

sail-boat (sāl'bōt''), *n.* a boat provided with a sail or sails: generally applied to small craft.

sail-er (sāl'ẽr), *n.* a vessel moved by the wind, with special reference to its speed or manner of motion; as, a swift *sailer*.

sail-or (sāl'ẽr), *n.* **1**, one who makes a voyage in a sailing vessel, or in any vessel; **2**, esp., one who acts as member of the crew; a mariner; seaman; **3**, a straw hat with a flat brim and crown.—*adj.* **sail'or-ly.**

saint (sānt), *n.* **1**, a person of holy life; **2**, one dead and among the blessed in heaven; **3**, in the Roman Catholic Church, an exceptionally godly person, who, after death, is officially recognized as being capable of interceding with God for sinners, and is canonized by the church: **Saint, 1**, one canonized by the church: a title prefixed to the name; as, *Saint* Joan of Arc; **2**, an archangel: a title prefixed to the name; as, *Saint* Michael: **St. Andrew's cross,** a cross in the form of the letter X (see *cross*, illus.): **St. Elmo's fire** or **light,** a bright light sometimes seen in severe storms at sea, as at the head of a mast: **St. George's cross,** a red Greek cross, used on many British flags, esp. in combination with a St. Andrew's cross, on the British union jack: **St. Valentine's Day,** February 14, dedicated to the memory of St. Valentine, an early Christian martyr, who was beheaded on that date: the day on which sweethearts are chosen, and letters or tokens are sent to a person of the opposite sex: **St. Vitus's dance,** chorea, a nervous affection accompanied by involuntary muscular twitchings:—*v.t.* to canonize; declare officially to be a saint.

Saint Ber-nard (bẽr-närd'), one of a breed of large dogs formerly bred for the purpose of rescuing travelers, as in the Alps.

saint-ed (sān'tĕd), *p.adj.* **1**, canonized; **2**, pious; holy; **3**, blessed in heaven; dead.

saint-ly (sānt'lĭ), *adj.* [*comp.* saint'li-er, *superl.* saint'li-est], **1**, saintlike; pious; **2**, befitting a saint.—*n.* **saint'li-ness.**

Saint Nich-o-las (nĭk'ō-lȧs), the patron saint of Russia, and of children, seafarers, and virgins; the legendary bringer of Christmas gifts: in this sense known as *Santa Claus*.

saith (sĕth), *Archaic*, third person singular, present indicative, of the verb *say*.

sake (sāk), *n.* **1**, end; purpose; cause; as, for the *sake* of argument; **2**, account; regard; reason; as, for my *sake*.

sal (săl), *n.* formerly, in chemistry, a salt: still used in some commercial names: **sal ammoniac,** a white crystalline salt used in soldering, in wet batteries, etc.

sa-laam (sȧ-läm'), *n.* a certain form of deep bow: an Oriental form of salutation or of showing respect:—*v.i.* to make such a salutation:—*v.t.* to greet with such a salutation.

sal-a-ble (sāl'ȧ-bl), *adj.* capable of being sold; marketable.—*n.* **sal'a-ble-ness.**—*adv.* **sal'a-bly.**—*n.* **sal''a-bil'i-ty.**

sa-la-cious (sȧ-lā'shŭs), *adj.* impure; lustful.—*adv.* **sa-la'cious-ly.**—*n.* **sa-la'cious-ness.**

sal-ad (săl'ȧd), *n.* a cold preparation, as of lettuce with vegetables, fruit, etc., mixed with, or covered by, dressing.

sal-a-man-der (săl'ȧ-măn''dẽr), *n.* **1**, any of many amphibious animals resembling lizards, formerly supposed to be able to live in fire (see *amphibian*, illus.); **2**, *Colloq.*, one who can stand intense heat.—*adj.* **sal''a-man'drine.**

sal-a-ry (săl'ȧ-rĭ), *n.* [*pl.* salaries (-rĭz)], a regular payment for services rendered; recompense:—*v.t.* [*p.t.* and *p.p.* -ried (-rĭd), *p.pr.* -ry-ing], to pay a regular recompense to.—*p.adj.* **sal'a-ried.**

Syn., *n.* wage, pay, fee. *Salary* names a fixed periodical payment made to those who do professional or mental work. A *wage* is payment for mechanical or manual work; it is also fixed and periodical, but it is considered less stable, and is usually paid at shorter intervals than a *salary*. *Pay* is used in the sense of *wage* and *salary*; it suggests actual money given for goods, services, or debts. *Fee* denotes the sum asked by a professional man for his services; as, a lawyer's or a notary's *fee*.

sale (sāl), *n.* **1**, the act of selling; exchange of a commodity or goods for an agreed price; **2**, a disposal of goods at a low price, or in some other special way; as, a cake *sale* for charity; **3**, a chance to dispose of goods; a demand for goods; as, a ready *sale* for meat.

sal-e-ra-tus (săl''ē-rā'tŭs), *n.* sodium bicarbonate; baking soda.

sales-man (sālz'măn), *n.* [*pl.* salesmen (-mĕn)], one whose business it is to sell goods.—*n.fem.* **sales'wom''an.**

sales-man-ship (sālz'măn-shĭp), *n.* skill in the art of selling.

Sa-li-an (sā'lĭ-ăn), *adj.* designating, or pertaining to, a tribe of Franks who settled in the lower Rhine district early in the fourth century; Salic:—*n.* a member of this tribe; also, the German dialect which they spoke.

Sal-ic (săl'ĭk), *adj.* pertaining to the Salian tribe of Franks: **Salic law,** the law of the Salic Franks, later interpreted in France and Spain as excluding women from the succession to the throne.

sal-i-cyl-ic (săl''ĭ-sĭl'ĭk), *adj.* designating, or pertaining to, salicylic acid: **salicylic acid,** a white crystalline substance, used as an antiseptic and as a drug.

sa-li-ence (sā'lĭ-ĕns), *n.* **1**, the state of being conspicuous or prominent; **2**, that which challenges attention because of its prominence. Also, **sa'li-en-cy.**

sa-li-ent (sā'lĭ-ĕnt), *adj.* **1**, outstanding; noticeable; as, *salient* traits; **2**, projecting outward; as, a *salient* angle; **3**, leaping or dancing; also, of liquids, spurting forth; **4**, in heraldry, springing (see *lion*, illus.):—*n.* **1**, a projecting angle; **2**, in trench warfare, a part of a trench system which projects farther than the rest into the enemy's territory; an outward bending of the line of battle.—*adv.* **sa'li-ent-ly.**

sa-line (sā'līn), *adj.* **1**, consisting of, or containing, salt or a salt; **2**, salty; as, a *saline* substance:—*n.* **1**, a salt spring; **2**, any of several mineral salts, as of magnesium, sodium, etc., often used as purgatives.—*n.* **sa-lin'i-ty.**

sa-li-va (sȧ-lī'vȧ), *n.* the watery fluid secreted by the salivary glands and passed into the mouth.

sal-i-va-ry (săl′ĭ-vâ-rĭ), *adj.* of or pertaining to saliva, or the glands which secrete it.

sal-i-vate (săl′ĭ-vāt), *v.t.* [*p.t.* and *p.p.* -vat″ed, *p.pr.* -vat″ing], to produce an abnormal flow of saliva in.

¹sal-low (săl′ō), *adj.* of a pale, sickly yellow color: said of the complexion:—*v.t.* to render a pale, sickly yellow color, as the skin.—*adj.* **sal′low-ish.**—*n.* **sal′low-ness.**

²sal-low (săl′ō), *n.* **1**, a small tree of Europe and Asia, some varieties of which have drooping branches; **2**, a shoot of willow; an osier.—*adj.* **sal′low-y.**

sal-ly (săl′ĭ), *n.* [*pl.* sallies (-ĭz)], **1**, a sudden rushing forth of troops from a fortified place to attack a besieging enemy; **2**, a sudden outburst of wit or fancy; **3**, an excursion:—*v.i.* [*p.t.* and *p.p.* -lied (-ĭd), *p.pr.* -lying], **1**, to rush out, as troops from a besieged town; **2**, to set out, as on a journey, esp. joyfully.

sal-ma-gun-di (săl″mȧ-gŭn′dĭ), *n.* **1**, a dish made of chopped meats mixed with other ingredients; **2**, a mixed collection of things; medley.

salm-on (săm′ŭn), *n.* [*pl.* salmon], **1**, a gamy fish, found in northern waters, which ascends rivers to lay its eggs; **2**, the yellowish pink color of salmon flesh:—*adj.* of the yellowish pink color of salmon flesh.

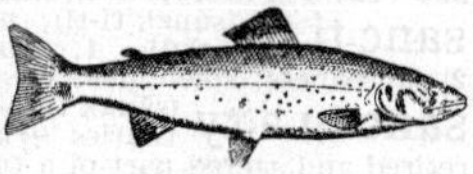

SALMON (1/35)

salm-on-ber-ry (săm′ŭn-bĕr″ĭ), *n.* [*pl.* salmonberries (-ĭz)], **1**, a large raspberry plant; **2**, its fruit.

***sa-lon** (sȧ″lôṅ′), [Fr.], *n.* [*pl.* salons (-lôṅ′)], **1**, an apartment for the reception of guests; **2**, a periodic gathering of distinguished persons; **3**, a fine-arts gallery; **4**, the paintings or sculpture exhibited there.

sa-loon (sȧ-lo͞on′), *n.* **1**, a hall or state apartment; large reception room; **2**, a public hall for special uses; as, a dancing *saloon;* **3**, the main cabin on a steamship; **4**, a drawing-room on a railway train; **5**, in the U. S., formerly, a tavern or barroom.

sal-si-fy (săl′sĭ-fĭ), *n.* a European plant, the root of which is used for food: also called *oyster plant* from its flavor.

sal so-da crystallized sodium carbonate; washing soda. Also, *n.* **sal″so′da.**

salt (sôlt), *n.* **1**, chloride of sodium, used for seasoning, for the preservation of meat, etc.: obtained from the earth or by the evaporation of sea water; **2**, anything which, like salt, gives flavor or character; **3**, dry humor; **4**, in chemistry, the compound formed by the action of an acid on a base, or by other means, containing a metal and a nonmetal; **5**, *Colloq.*, a sailor; **6**, in *pl.*, any salt used as a cathartic; as, Epsom *salts:* **with a grain of salt,** with reserve or allowance, as for exaggeration:—*v.t.* **1**, to preserve with salt; **2**, to sprinkle or season with salt; **3**, to furnish with salt; as, to *salt* cattle:—*adj.* **1**, flavored or seasoned with salt; **2**, preserved with salt, as meats; **3**, growing in salt water.—*adj.* **salt′ish.**—*adj.* **salt′less.**—*n.* **salt′ness.**

sal-ta-to-ry (săl′tȧ-tō-rĭ), *adj.* **1**, pertaining, or adapted, to jumping; **2**, dancing, jumping, or leaping.—*n.* **sal-ta′tion.**—*adj.* **sal″ta-to′ri-al.**

salt-cel-lar (sôlt′sĕl-ẽr), *n.* a dish or shaker to hold salt.

salt lick a place where natural salt is found on the surface of the earth, and where animals go to lick it.

salt-pe-ter (sôlt″pē′tẽr), *n.* **1**, niter, or potassium nitrate: used in explosives, matches, and as a food preservative; **2**, sodium nitrate: often called *Chile saltpeter.* Also, **salt″pe′tre.**

salt rheum (ro͞om), any of various diseases of the skin.

salt-y (sôl′tĭ), *adj.* [*comp.* salt′i-er, *superl.* salt′i-est], tasting of salt; somewhat salt.—*n.* **salt′i-ness.**

sa-lu-bri-ous (sȧ-lū′brĭ-ŭs), *adj.* healthful; promoting health; as, a *salubrious* climate.—*adv.* **sa-lu′bri-ous-ly.**—*n.* **sa-lu′bri-ous-ness.**—*n.* **sa-lu′bri-ty.**

sal-u-ta-ry (săl′ū-tā-rĭ), *adj.* **1**, producing health; as, *salutary* exercises; **2**, wholesome; resulting in benefit, as reforms.—*adv.* **sal′u-ta-ri-ly.**—*n.* **sal′u-ta-ri-ness.**

sal-u-ta-tion (săl″ū-tā′shŭn), *n.* the act or manner of addressing or greeting another; a greeting.

sa-lu-ta-to-ri-an (sȧ-lū″tȧ-tō′rĭ-ăn), *n.* one who delivers a salutatory oration or address, esp. at commencement exercises, as of certain schools.

sa-lu-ta-to-ry (sȧ-lū′tȧ-tō-rĭ), *adj.* **1**, greeting; **2**, opening or introducing: applied to the opening oration at the commencement exercises of certain schools and colleges, usually made by the student second highest in rank:—*n.* [*pl.* salutatories (-rĭz)], a salutatory oration or address.

sa-lute (sȧ-lūt′), *n.* **1**, a greeting; **2**, a gesture or bow expressing welcome, respect, or the like; **3**, a kiss; **4**, in the army and navy, a mark of respect shown by taking a certain prescribed position; as, the officers exchanged *salutes* as they passed; **5**, in the army and navy, the discharge of cannon, the lowering of a flag, etc., as a mark of honor:—*v.t.* [*p.t.* and *p.p.* -lut′ed, *p.pr.* -lut′ing], **1**, to address with kind wishes; welcome; **2**, to greet with a kiss or bow; **3**, in the army and navy, to honor by a discharge of guns, the lowering of a flag, etc.:—*v.i.* in the army and navy, to make the prescribed gesture of respect.—*n.* **sa-lut′er.**

sal-vage (săl′vāj), *n.* **1**, the act of saving a ship or goods from the dangers of the sea, from a wreck, or from other grave danger; **2**, payment given to those who help to save property under such circumstances; **3**, the goods or vessel so saved:—*v.t.* [*p.t.* and *p.p.* -vaged (-vājd), *p.pr.* -vag-ing], to save, as goods or a ship, from a wreck, fire, or other danger.—*n.* **sal′vag-er.**

sal-va-tion (săl-vā′shŭn), *n.* **1**, the act of saving; rescue; **2**, the setting free of the soul from sin and death; **3**, that which saves: **Salvation Army,** a religious body organized on a military basis for the purpose of renewing religious faith among the masses, relieving poverty, and giving spiritual comfort.

¹salve (säv), *n.* **1**, an ointment or greasy mixture, used on sores, inflammatory swellings, skin eruptions, etc.; **2**, anything that calms, soothes, or pacifies:—*v.t.* [*p.t.* and *p.p.* salved (sävd), *p.pr.* salv′ing], **1**, to apply a healing ointment to; heal with an ointment; **2**, to soothe; palliate, esp. temporarily, as a grievance: usually with *over.*

²salve (sălv), *v.t.* and *v.i.* [*p.t.* and *p.p.* salved (sălvd), *p.pr.* salv′ing], to save; salvage.

³sal-ve (săl′vē), *interj.* hail! a form of address or greeting.

sal-ver (săl′vẽr), *n.* a tray, usually of metal, on which anything is presented.

sal-vi-a (săl′vĭ-ȧ), *n.* any of various plants of the mint family; the sages; esp., the scarlet sage.

sal-vo (săl′vō), *n.* [*pl.* salvos (-vōz)], **1**, the discharge all at once of a certain number of guns, intended as a salute; **2**, the loud cheers of a crowd.

sal vo-la-ti-le (vō-lăt'ĭ-lē), an alcoholic solution of ammonium carbonate, used as a restorative in fainting.

sam-a-ra (săm'ȧ-rȧ; sȧ-mā'rȧ), *n.* a dry, single-seeded, winged fruit, as that of the elm, ash, or maple.

Sa-mar-i-tan (sȧ-măr'ĭ-tăn), *adj.* pertaining to, or like, Samaria, or the Samaritans:—*n.* **1,** a native of Samaria; **2,** the language spoken by these people: **Good Samaritan, 1,** in the Bible, a character in one of the parables of the New Testament (Luke 10:30–37); **2,** hence, one willing to aid those in distress.

Sam Browne belt a leather belt supported by a strap over the right shoulder, worn by army officers.

sam-buke (săm'būk), *n.* an ancient stringed instrument resembling a triangular harp.

same (sām), *adj.* **1,** identical; as, this is the *same* picture; **2,** alike in kind or degree; equal; as, the *same* distance; **3,** just mentioned; as, these *same* words.

same-ness (sām'nĕs), *n.* **1,** the state of being exactly alike; identity; **2,** lack of difference; similarity; **3,** monotony.

sa-mite (sā'mīt), *n.* a rich silk, generally interwoven with gold.

Sa-mo-an (sȧ-mō'ăn), *adj.* pertaining to the Samoan Islands, or to their inhabitants:—*n.* **1,** a native of Samoa; **2,** the language of the people of Samoa.

sam-o-var (săm'ō-vär), *n.* a metal vessel of Russian origin, with a heating tube through the center, used to heat water for making tea.

samp (sămp), *n.* hulled Indian corn or coarse hominy.

sam-pan (săm'păn), *n.* a flat-bottomed river boat, propelled by sails or oars, used in China and Japan: sometimes used as a house boat.

SAMPAN

sam-ple (săm'pl), *n.* a specimen; model; pattern; also, a part shown to prove the quality of the whole:—*v.t.* [*p.t.* and *p.p.* -pled (-pld), *p.pr.* -pling], to test or examine; as, to *sample* sugar, butter, or tea.

sam-pler (săm'plẽr), *n.* **1,** one who prepares specimens of goods for inspection; **2,** one who examines goods by means of specimens; **3,** a piece of ornamental needlework made as an exhibition of skill.

Sam-son (săm'sŭn), *n.* in the Bible, one of the judges of Israel, noted for his great strength.

Sam-u-el (săm'ū-ĕl), *n.* **1,** in the Bible, a Hebrew prophet, the last of the judges; **2,** either of two books of the Old Testament which give his story.—*abbr.* **Sam.**

sa-mu-rai (sä'mo͞o-rī''), *n.* [*pl.* samurai], under the ancient feudal system of Japan, the military class, or lesser nobility; also, a member of this class.

san-a-tive (săn'ȧ-tĭv), *adj.* healing; health-giving.

san-a-to-ri-um (săn''ȧ-tō'rĭ-ŭm), *n.* [*pl.* sanatoria (-ȧ); sanatoriums (-ŭmz)], **1,** a health resort; a locality conducive to the restoration of health; **2,** an institution for the care of invalids or the treatment of certain diseases; a sanitarium.

san-a-to-ry (săn'ȧ-tō-rĭ), *adj.* health-giving; tending to cure or to preserve health; healing.

San-cho Pan-za (săng'kō păn'zȧ; sän'chō pän'thä), in Cervantes's "Don Quixote," Don Quixote's squire, an ignorant, but shrewd, peasant.

sanc-ti-fi-ca-tion (săngk''tĭ-fĭ-kā'shŭn), *n.* **1,** the act of making holy; **2,** the state of being made holy; **3,** the act of setting apart for a sacred purpose.

sanc-ti-fied (săngk'tĭ-fīd) *p.adj.* **1,** made holy; **2,** insincerely pious.

sanc-ti-fy (săngk'tĭ-fī), *v.t.* [*p.t.* and *p.p.* -fied (-fīd), *p.pr.* -fy''ing], **1,** to make holy; set apart for some sacred use; hallow; **2,** to purify; **3,** to lend sanctity to; justify.—*n.* **sanc'ti-fi''er.**

sanc-ti-mo-ni-ous (săngk''tĭ-mō'nĭ-ŭs), *adj.* having the appearance of, or making a show of, piety or holiness; hypocritical.—*adv.* **sanc''ti-mo'ni-ous-ly.**—*n.* **sanc''ti-mo'ni-ous-ness.**

sanc-ti-mo-ny (săngk'tĭ-mō-nĭ), *n.* pretended or assumed devoutness; hypocritical show of piety.

sanc-tion (săngk'shŭn), *n.* **1,** the act of giving authority to; **2,** authority; **3,** a formal law or decree:—*v.t.* to give indorsement to; confirm; approve; as, to *sanction* a marriage.

Syn., v. encourage, support, ratify, authorize.—*Ant., v.* disapprove, disavow, deny.

sanc-ti-ty (săngk'tĭ-tĭ), *n.* [*pl.* sanctities (-tĭz)], **1,** holiness; purity; **2,** sacredness; solemnity.

sanc-tu-a-ry (săngk'tū-ā-rĭ), *n.* [*pl.* sanctuaries (-rĭz)], **1,** the most retired and sacred part of a temple; **2,** a consecrated place; church or temple; **3,** the part of a Christian church nearest the altar; **4,** a place of shelter and protection; refuge; hence, immunity; shelter.

sanc-tum (săngk'tŭm), *n.* **1,** a sacred place; **2,** *Colloq.*, a private room; as, an editor's *sanctum.*

sanc-tum sanc-to-rum (săngk-tō'rŭm), **1,** a most holy or sacred place; **2,** a place of the utmost privacy: often used in jest.

Sanc-tus (săngk'tŭs), *n.* a part of the Mass, or Communion service, which begins with the words, *Sanctus, sanctus, sanctus,* meaning Holy, holy, holy.

sand (sănd), *n.* **1,** dry soil composed of fine particles of crushed or worn rock; **2,** sometimes in *pl.*, a stretch of such soil; a beach; **3,** in *pl.*, moments; time: from the use of sand in an hourglass; as, the *sands* of life:—*v.t.* to sprinkle, mix, or rub, with sand; as, to *sand* the floor.—*p.adj.* **sand'ed.**

[1]san-dal (săn'dăl), *n.* **1,** a kind of shoe, consisting of a sole without the upper, fastened by straps over the instep and around the ankle; **2,** a loose slipper; **3,** a low rubber overshoe.—*adj.* **san'daled; san'dalled.**

ROMAN SANDAL

[2]san-dal (săn'dăl), *n.* a kind of hard, sweet-scented wood; also, any of several trees furnishing this wood: also called *sandalwood.*

san-dal-wood (săn'dăl-wo͝od''), *n.* **1,** any of several trees of the tropics; **2,** the close-grained, fragrant wood of these trees, valued as fine material for carving and for the perfume which can be obtained from it; **3,** any of a number of similar woods. Also called *sandal.*

sand-bag (sănd'băg''), *n.* a bag filled with sand: used for ballast, trench parapets, etc.:—*v.t.* [*p.t.* and *p.p.* -bagged'' (-băgd''), *p.pr.* -bag''ging], to give a blow to, or stun with, such a bag.—*n.* **sand'bag''ger.**

sand blast **1,** sand driven by a blast of air or steam: used to cut, polish, or decorate glass and other hard substances, or to clean the outside walls of buildings; **2**, the machine used in this work.

sand-blind (sănd′-blīnd″), *adj. Archaic*, of dim sight; nearly blind.

sand-er-ling (săn′dẽr-lĭng), *n.* a small, three-toed sandpiper.

sand-glass (sănd′glȧs″), *n.* a reversible instrument which measures time by the running of sand: also called, when an hour is measured, *hourglass*.

sand-man (sănd′măn″), *n.* a nursery character, supposed to make children sleepy by putting sand into their eyes.

sand-pa-per (sănd′pā″pẽr), *n.* stout paper with a coating of sand on one side: used for smoothing and polishing:—*v.t.* to smooth or polish with sandpaper.

sand-pip-er (sănd′pīp″ẽr), *n.* any of several small wading birds with long legs and bills.

sand-stone (sănd′stōn″), *n.* a rock composed of hardened sand.

sand-wich (sănd′wĭch), *n.* **1**, two thin slices of bread with meat, cheese, or the like, between; **2**, anything like a sandwich:—*v.t.* to place between two other persons, things, or events.

sand-y (săn′dĭ), *adj.* [*comp.* sand′i-er, *superl.* sand′i-est], **1**, composed of, abounding in, or covered with, sand; **2**, like sand; hence, shifting; not firm underfoot; **3**, of a yellowish red color.—*n.* **sand′i-ness.**

sane (sān), *adj.* **1**, mentally sound or healthy; **2**, coming from a rational mind; as, a *sane* suggestion.—*adv.* **sane′ly.** —*n.* **sane′ness.**

sang (săng), past tense of the transitive and intransitive verb *sing*.

san-ga-ree (săng″gȧ-rē′), *n.* a cold, spiced beverage made of wine and sweetened water.

***sang-froid** (säṅ″-frwä′), [Fr.], *n.* cool indifference or composure; coolness under trying circumstances.

san-gui-na-ry (săng′gwĭ-nā-rĭ), *adj.* **1**, formed of blood; **2**, attended with much bloodshed; as, a *sanguinary* battle; **3**, bloodthirsty; murderous; cruel.—*adv.* **san′gui-na-ri-ly.**—*n.* **san′gui-na-ri-ness.**
Syn. inhuman, savage.—*Ant.* kind, humane.

san-guine (săng′gwĭn), *adj.* **1**, having the color of blood; ruddy; **2**, having an active circulation of blood; hence, warm and ardent in temper; **3**, hopeful; confident; as, *sanguine* of success.—*adv.* **san′guine-ly.**
Syn. optimistic, buoyant, cheerful.

San-he-drin (săn′hē-drĭn), *n.* the great council or court of the ancient Jews, composed of 71 priests, scribes, and elders, presided over by the high priest: also called *Great Sanhedrin*. Also, **San′he-drim.**

san-i-ta-ri-um (săn″ĭ-tā′rĭ-ŭm), *n.* [*pl.* sanitariums (-ŭmz); sanitaria (-*ȧ*)], a place for the care of invalids or the treatment of certain diseases; loosely, a sanatorium; health resort.

san-i-ta-ry (săn′ĭ-tā-rĭ), *adj.* **1**, pertaining to health; as, *sanitary* laws; **2**, producing or preserving health; hygienic.—*adj.* and *n.* **san″i-ta′ri-an.**

san-i-ta-tion (săn″ĭ-tā′shŭn), *n.* **1**, the science of bringing about healthful conditions; **2**, the application of the science to the protection of health; hygiene.

san-i-ty (săn′ĭ-tĭ), *n.* **1**, soundness or health of mind; the state of being in sound mind: opp. of *insanity;* **2**, reasonableness in thought or action.

San Jo-sé scale (săn hō-sā′), a scale insect very destructive to many varieties of fruit trees: first found in the U. S. at San José, California.

sank (săngk), the past tense of the irregular verb *sink*.

sans (sănz; *Fr.* säṅ), *prep.* without; deprived of: chiefly literary or poetic.

sans-cu-lotte (sănz″-kū-lŏt′; *Fr.* säṅ″-kü″lôt′), *n.* **1**, literally, "without breeches": a term of contempt applied by the aristocrats to the French Revolutionists, who wore long trousers instead of short breeches; **2**, hence, a revolutionist.

San-skrit (săn′skrĭt), *n.* the ancient sacred language of the Hindus of India, the oldest known Indo-European language:—*adj.* pertaining to this language. Also, **San′scrit.**—*adj.* **San-skrit′ic.**

San-ta Claus (săn′t*ȧ* klôz), a chubby, white-bearded old man who, according to nursery lore, brings gifts to children on Christmas Eve in a sleigh drawn through the air by reindeer; Saint Nicholas: used esp. in the U. S. Also, **San′ta Klaus.**

¹sap (săp), *n.* **1**, the watery, circulating juice of a plant; **2**, any vital or health-promoting liquid constituent; **3**, hence, vigor; vitality; **4**, *Slang*, a saphead; a stupid person.

²sap (săp), *n.* a deep, narrow trench, extending, often in a zigzag course, toward an enemy's lines:—*v.t.* [*p.t.* and *p.p.* sapped (săpt), *p.pr.* sap′ping], **1**, to dig beneath; undermine, as a wall; **2**, to weaken, as strength: often confused with ¹*sap*.

sap-head (săp′hĕd″), *n. Colloq.*, a stupid fellow; simpleton.

sa-pi-ent (sā′pĭ-ĕnt), *adj.* wise; full of knowledge: often used ironically.—*adv.* **sa′pi-ent-ly.**—*n.* **sa′pi-ence.**

sap-less (săp′lĕs), *adj.* **1**, without sap; dry; **2**, without vitality or energy.

sap-ling (săp′lĭng), *n.* **1**, a flexible young tree; **2**, hence, a youth.

sap-o-na-ceous (săp″ō-nā′shŭs), *adj.* **1**, pertaining to, or like, soap; soapy; **2**, hence, smooth; oily.

sa-pon-i-fy (s*ȧ*-pŏn′ĭ-fī), *v.t.* and *v.i.* [*p.t.* and *p.p.* -fied (-fīd), *p.pr.* -fy″ing], to make into, or become, soap.—*n.* **sa-pon″i-fi-ca′tion.**

sap-per (săp′ẽr), *n.* a soldier employed in digging saps, or hidden trenches, or in building fortifications.

Sap-phic (săf′ĭk), *adj.* pertaining to the Greek lyric poetess Sappho.

Sap-phi-ra (s*ă*-fī′r*ȧ*), *n.* in the Bible, the wife of Ananias, who, with her husband, was struck dead for lying (Acts 5).

sap-phire (săf′īr), *n.* **1**, a precious stone of a bright blue color; **2**, the bright blue color of this gem.

sap-py (săp′ĭ), *adj.* [*comp.* sap′pi-er, *superl.* sap′pi-est], **1**, full of juice, as a plant; **2**, *Colloq.*, weak; silly.—*n.* **sap′pi-ness.**

sap-ro-phyte (săp′rō-fīt), *n.* any of various plants living on dead organic matter, as some bacteria, mushrooms, etc.—*adj.* **sap″ro-phyt′ic** (săp″rō-fĭt′ĭk).

sap-suck-er (săp′sŭk″ẽr), *n.* any of several small American woodpeckers which feed in part on sap.

sap-wood (săp′wŏŏd″), *n.* the soft, living wood between the bark and the hard, inner wood of most trees.

sar-a-band (săr′*ȧ*-bănd), *n.* **1**, a slow Spanish dance; **2**, the music characteristic of this dance.

Sar-a-cen (săr′*ȧ*-sĕn), *n.* **1**, in ancient times, an Arab; **2**, during the Crusades, a Moslem.—*adj.* **Sar″a-cen′ic.**

Sa-rah (sā′r*ȧ*), *n.* in the Bible, the wife of Abraham and mother of Isaac. Also, **Sa′rai** (sā′rī; săr′ā-ī).

sar-casm (sär′kăzm), *n.* a bitter, cutting remark, usually ironical, expressing scorn or contempt.

sar-cas-tic (sär-kăs′tĭk), *adj.* **1**, bitterly scornful or contemptuous; cutting; unkindly ironical; **2**, given to the use of bitter or scornful irony; as, a *sarcastic* teacher.—*adv.* **sar-cas′ti-cal-ly.**

sarce-net (särs′nĕt), *n.* a soft, thin silk, used for ribbons, dress linings, etc. Also, **sarse′net.**

sar-co-ma (sär-kō′mȧ), *n.* a fleshy tumor, often fatal.

sar-coph-a-gus (sär-kŏf′ȧ-gŭs), *n.* [*pl.* sarcophagi (-jī); sarcophaguses (-ĕz)], **1**, a limestone coffin or tomb, generally ornamented, used by the Greeks; **2**, any stone coffin or tomb.

SARCOPHAGUS

sard (särd), *n.* a reddish yellow or brownish red stone of the quartz variety: also called *carnelian.* Also, [1]**sar′dine.**

[2]**sar-dine** (sär-dēn′; sär′dēn), *n.* a small fish of the herring family, good for food when preserved in oil.

sar-di-us (sär′dĭ-ŭs), *n.* **1**, a sard; **2**, in the Bible, one of the gems in the breastplate of the Jewish high priest.

sar-don-ic (sär-dŏn′ĭk), *adj.* forced, bitter, or heartless; sneering; as, a *sardonic* smile.—*adv.* **sar-don′i-cal-ly.**

sar-do-nyx (sär′dō-nĭks), *n.* a kind of onyx made up of alternating layers of light chalcedony and sard.

sar-gas-so (sär-găs′ō), *n.* the floating gulfweed found in various parts of the Atlantic. Also, **sar-gas′sum.**

sar-sa-pa-ril-la (sär″sȧ-pȧ-rĭl′ȧ), *n.* **1**, any of various tropical American plants, the roots of which are used as medicine; **2**, also, a cooling drink made from these roots.

sar-to-ri-al (sär-tō′rĭ-ăl), *adj.* pertaining to a tailor or to his work.

[1]**sash** (săsh), *n.* **1**, orig., a long strip of gauze, silk, linen, etc., worn by Orientals like a turban; **2**, now, a band, ribbon, or scarf, worn round the waist or over the shoulder; a girdle:—*v.t.* to provide with a sash.

[2]**sash** (săsh), *n.* [*pl.* sashes (-ĕz); collectively, sash], a window frame, or a part of a door, made to hold panes of glass.

sas-sa-fras (săs′ȧ-frăs), *n.* a tree of the laurel family, whose root, wood, and flowers have a spicy smell and a pungent taste.

sat (săt), past tense and past participle of the irregular verb *sit.*

Sa-tan (sā′tăn), *n.* the chief of the fallen angels; the Devil, or Prince of Darkness: **satan**, a wicked person.

sa-tan-ic (sȧ-tăn′ĭk), *adj.* pertaining to, or like, Satan; devilish; infernal; wicked.—*adv.* **sa-tan′i-cal-ly.**

satch-el (săch′ĕl), *n.* a small bag in which to carry small personal belongings, papers, etc.

[1]**sate** (sāt), *v.t.* [*p.t.* and *p.p.* sat′ed, *p.pr.* sat′ing], **1**, to satisfy the appetites or desires of; glut; **2**, hence, to weary with an excessive amount of something; surfeit.

[2]**sate** (săt; sāt), *Archaic*, past tense of the irregular verb *sit.*

sa-teen (să-tēn′), *n.* a woolen or cotton fabric made in imitation of satin.

sat-el-lite (săt′ĕ-līt), *n.* **1**, a small planet revolving round a larger one; as, the moon is a *satellite* of the earth; **2**, an attentive follower; **3**, a fawning dependent.

sa-ti-a-ble (sā′shĭ-ȧ-bl), *adj.* capable of being satisfied or filled; as, man's *satiable* desires.

sa-ti-ate (sā′shĭ-āt), *v.t.* [*p.t.* and *p.p.* -at″ed, *p.pr.* -at″ing], **1**, to fill or satisfy fully; **2**, to surfeit; gratify beyond wish or appetite; as, to *satiate* one with sweets:—*adj.* (sā′shĭ-āt), glutted; filled beyond need or requirement.—*n.* **sa″ti-a′tion.**

sa-ti-e-ty (sȧ-tī′ĕ-tĭ), *n.* the state of being filled or satisfied beyond desire.

sat-in (săt′ĭn), *n.* a closely woven, glossy silk:—*adj.* made of, or like, this silk.—*adj.* **sat′in-y.**

sat-i-net (săt″ĭ-nĕt′), *n.* **1**, a kind of thin satin; **2**, a glossy cloth woven of wool and cotton, made to resemble satin.

sat-in-wood (săt′ĭn-wŏŏd″), *n.* **1**, an East Indian tree; **2**, the wood of this tree, which has a satiny sheen.

sat-ire (săt′īr), *n.* **1**, a form of literature, usually in verse, in which vice and folly are held up to ridicule; **2**, a single work of literature of this sort; **3**, sarcasm; ridicule.

sa-tir-ic (sȧ-tĭr′ĭk), *adj.* **1**, pertaining to, or containing, sarcasm or ridicule; **2**, given to the use of sarcasm or ridicule. Also, **sa-tir′i-cal.**—*adv.* **sa-tir′i-cal-ly.**

sat-i-rize (săt′ĭ-rīz; săt′ẽr-īz), *v.t.* [*p.t.* and *p.p.* -rized (-rīzd), *p.pr.* -riz″ing], to attack by ridiculing; hold up to ridicule; subject to biting wit.—*n.* **sat′i-rist.**

sat-is-fac-tion (săt″ĭs-făk′shŭn), *n.* **1**, the act of gratifying a want or of supplying enough of something; **2**, the act of paying off, compensating, contenting, etc.; **3**, the state of having one's wishes filled, or of being gratified, paid off, contented, etc.; contentment; **4**, that which fills one's wishes, compensates, contents, or gratifies.

Syn. enjoyment, comfort, gratification.

sat-is-fac-to-ry (săt″ĭs-făk′tō-rĭ), *adj.* **1**, sufficient; **2**, making redress; **3**, relieving the mind from doubt or uncertainty; as, a *satisfactory* state of affairs; **4**, filling the wishes.—*adv.* **sat″is-fac′to-ri-ly.**—*n.* **sat″is-fac′to-ri-ness.**

sat-is-fy (săt′ĭs-fī), *v.t.* [*p.t.* and *p.p.* -fied (-fīd), *p.pr.* -fy″ing], **1**, to make content; give enough to; fill the wishes of; gratify to the highest degree; as, to *satisfy* hunger; **2**, to free from doubt or uncertainty; convince; as, to *satisfy* oneself of the truth of a report; **3**, to pay in full; as, to *satisfy* a creditor; **4**, to expiate:—*v.i.* **1**, to give gratification; **2**, to make atonement or payment.

Syn. suffice, cloy, surfeit, glut. To *satisfy* is to fill a demand, to please a taste, or to provide contentment. To *suffice* is to be barely adequate. To *cloy* is to sicken with sameness, esp. with sweetness or luxury. To *surfeit* is to get too much, or to cause to take too much, esp. of food. To *glut* is to fill disgustingly full, expressing the extreme of repletion.—*Ant.* deny, restrain, stint, check.

sa-trap (sā′trăp; săt′răp), *n.* the governor of a province in ancient Persia.

sa-trapy (sā′tră-pĭ; săt′ră-pĭ), *n.* [*pl.* satrapies (-pĭz)], the office or position of a satrap.

sat-u-rate (săt′ū-rāt), *v.t.* [*p.t.* and *p.p.* -rat″ed, *p.pr.* -rat″ing], **1**, to cause to become soaked; as, to *saturate* a sponge with water; **2**, to fill to the limit of the capacity for absorbing; as, to *saturate* water with sugar.

sat-u-ra-tion (săt″ū-rā′shŭn), *n.* **1**, the act of soaking; **2**, the state of being thoroughly soaked; **3**, the condition of a substance when it has absorbed as much as it can hold of another substance.

Sat-ur-day (săt′ûr-dā), *n.* the seventh day of the week.—*abbr.* **Sat.**

Sat-urn (săt′ûrn), *n.* **1**, the second largest planet, notable for its rings, which may be seen through a telescope (cf.

solar system, illus.); **2**, the ancient Roman god of seedtime and harvest; father of Jupiter: identified with the Greek *Cronus*.

RINGS OF SATURN

Sat-ur-na-li-a (săt″ûr-nā′lĭ-*à*), *n. pl.* an ancient Roman festival in honor of the god Saturn, a time of disorder and debauch: **saturnalia,** often used as *sing.*, a time of license or disorder.—*adj.* **Sat″ur-na′li-an; sat″ur-na′li-an.**

Sa-tur-ni-an (s*à*-tûr′nĭ-ăn), *adj.* **1**, pertaining to Saturn, esp. to his reign, celebrated as the golden age; **2**, hence, characterized by great happiness, plenty, and purity of life; **3**, pertaining to the ringed planet Saturn.

Sat-ur-nine (săt′ûr-nīn), *adj.* born under, or under the influence of, the planet Saturn: **saturnine**, dull; gloomy; grave; heavy; as, a *saturnine* temper.

sat-yr (săt′ẽr; sā′tẽr), *n.* **1**, a forest god, represented with long, pointed ears, short horns, and the tail of a horse or goat, who indulged in riotous merriment and lust; **2**, a man inclined to free indulgence of base passions.—*adj.* **sa-tyr′ic; sa-tyr′i-cal.**

sauce (sôs), *n.* **1**, a dressing or seasoning for food; any highly seasoned mixture of ingredients, used as a relish; **2**, stewed or canned fruit; **3**, *Colloq.*, insolence; pertness:—*v.t.* [*p.t.* and *p.p.* sauced (sôst), *p.pr.* sauc′ing], **1**, to put seasoning into; add flavor to; **2**, *Colloq.*, to treat with pertness or sauciness.

sauce-box (sôs′bŏks″), *n. Colloq.*, an impudent person, esp. a child.

sauce-pan (sôs′păn″), *n.* a small vessel, usually of metal, having a handle, and used for stewing or boiling.

sau-cer (sô′sẽr), *n.* a shallow china dish, esp. one designed to hold a cup.

sau-cy (sô′sĭ), *adj.* [*comp.* sau′ci-er, *superl.* sau′ci-est], pert; impudent; bold; uncivil.—*adv.* **sau′ci-ly.**—*n.* **sau′ci-ness.**

Syn. impertinent, rude, insolent.

sauer-kraut (sour′krout″), *n.* chopped cabbage, fermented in a brine made of its own juice with salt.

Saul (sôl), *n.* **1**, the first king of Israel (1 Samuel 10); **2**, the apostle Paul: called, before his conversion, by his Hebrew name, *Saul of Tarsus* (Acts 9:11; 13:9).

saun-ter (sän′tẽr; sôn′tẽr), *v.i.* to wander idly; stroll:—*n.* **1**, a strolling gait; a leisurely manner of walking; **2**, an idle walk or ramble.—*n.* **saun′ter-er.**

sau-ri-an (sô′rĭ-ăn), *n.* any one of the order (*Sauria*) of reptiles which includes lizards:—*adj.* pertaining to the lizards.

sau-sage (sô′sāj), *n.* meat, usually pork, ground fine and highly seasoned, inclosed in a skin or made into small cakes.

***sau-té** (sō″tā′), [Fr.], *adj.* fried quickly and lightly in a pan containing little grease: said of food, esp. meat or fish.

sau-terne (sō″târn′; sō-tûrn′), *n.* a variety of white Bordeaux wine. Also, **Sau″terne′.**

sav-age (săv′āj), *adj.* **1**, pertaining to the forest or wilderness; as, *savage* country; **2**, ferocious; as, *savage* beasts; **3**, uncivilized; barbaric; as, *savage* tribes; **4**, hence, barbarous; cruel; fierce; **5**, crude; uncouth; as, *savage* manners:—*n.* **1**, a human being in a rude, uncivilized state; a barbarian; **2**, a fierce, brutal person.—*adv.* **sav′age-ly.**

sav-age-ry (săv′āj-rĭ), *n.* [*pl.* savageries (-rĭz)], **1**, the state of being wild or uncivilized; **2**, brutal roughness.

sa-van-na (s*à*-văn′*à*), *n.* an open plain or meadow having no trees.

sa-vant (s*å*″vänt′; *Fr.* s*å*″väṅ′), *n.* [*pl.* savants (-vänts′; *Fr.* -väṅ′)], a learned man; a scholar.

[1]**save** (sāv), *v.t.* [*p.t.* and *p.p.* saved (sāvd), *p.pr.* sav′ing], **1**, to bring out of danger; deliver; preserve from injury, loss, destruction, etc.; rescue; **2**, to spare; as, to *save* trouble; prevent the waste of; as, to *save* time; **3**, to refrain from expending; hoard; as, to *save* money; **4**, to take advantage of; utilize; as, to *save* the tide; **5**, in theology, to free from the power and results of sin; as, to *save* souls:—*v.i.* **1**, to refrain from spending or wasting; **2**, to lay by money a little at a time.—*adj.* **sav′a-ble; save′a-ble.**—*n.* **sav′er.**

[2]**save** (sāv), *prep.* except; not including; as, all *save* one:—*conj. Archaic*, except; unless: usually with *that;* as, *save* that he were the swine thou speakest of.

sav-ing (sāv′ĭng), *p.adj.* **1**, preserving or redeeming; as, a *saving* grace; **2**, frugal; **3**, reserving or qualifying; as, a *saving* clause:—*n.* **1**, economy; **2**, rescue; **3**, in *pl.*, money saved:—*prep.* and *conj.* with the exception of; except.—*adv.* **sav′ing-ly.**

Syn., adj. thrifty, sparing. (See economical.)

sav-ings bank a bank where small sums may be deposited.

sav-ior (sāv′yẽr), *n.* one who brings out of danger or rescues: **Savior,** Jesus Christ, the Redeemer. Also, **sav′iour; Sav′iour.**

***sa-voir-faire** (s*å*″vwȧr″-fâr′), [Fr.], *n.* tact; knowledge of what to do and of the right time to do it.

sa-vor (sā′vẽr), *n.* **1**, flavor; taste; relish; scent; **2**, essential quality; **3**, reputation; as, he has an evil *savor* in his town:—*v.i.* **1**, to have a certain flavor or smell: with *of;* **2**, to partake of the quality or nature (of); as, to *savor* of disobedience:—*v.t.* **1**, to season; flavor; **2**, to taste or smell with delight. Also, **sa′vour.**—*adj.* **sa′vor-less.**

[1]**sa-vor-y** (sā′vẽr-ĭ), *adj.* **1**, pleasing to taste or smell; palatable; **2**, respected; reputable. Also, **sa′vour-y.**—*adv.* **sa′vor-i-ly.**—*n.* **sa′vor-i-ness.**

[2]**sa-vor-y** (sā′vẽr-ĭ), *n.* a fragrant herb of the mint family, used in cooking: also called *summer savory.*

sa-voy (s*à*-voi′), *n.* any of several varieties of winter cabbage with curled, wrinkled leaves.

[1]**saw** (sô), *n.* a cutting tool with a thin blade and a toothed edge, worked mechanically or by hand; also, a cutting machine having one or more such blades:—*v.t.* [*p.t.* sawed (sôd), *p.p.* sawed or sawn (sôn), *p.pr.* saw′ing], **1**, to cut with, or as with, a saw; **2**, to form or fashion with such a tool; as, to *saw* a rectangular piece from a board:—*v.i.* **1**, to be cut with a saw; as, the wood *saws* easily; **2**, to use a saw; also, to make motions as if using a saw; **3**, to perform the function of a saw.—*n.* **saw′er.**

[2]**saw** (sô), *n.* a proverb; an old and wise saying; adage.

[3]**saw** (sô), past tense of the irregular verb [1]*see.*

saw-buck (sô′bŭk″), *n.* a rack on which sticks of wood are placed while being sawed.

saw-dust (sô′dŭst″), *n.* the fine dust produced in sawing, esp. wood.

saw-fish (sô′fĭsh″), *n.* any of various large fishes of the ray group, with a long, flat snout edged with toothlike spines.

saw-fly (sô′flī″), *n.* [*pl.* sawflies (-flīz″)], any of numerous insects, the female of which has a special sawlike organ for making holes in plants or soft wood so that she may deposit her eggs in them.

saw-horse (sô'hôrs"), *n.* a rack or frame on which sticks of wood are placed when being sawed.

saw-mill (sô'mĭl"), *n.* a mill where logs are sawed into lumber.

sawn (sôn), one of the past participles of the irregular verb *saw.*

saw-yer (sô'yẽr), *n.* one who cuts logs into boards, or cuts wood with a saw.

sax-horn (săks'hôrn"), *n.* any of a group of brass-wind instruments fitted with valves, as the tuba.

sax-i-frage (săk'sĭ-frāj), *n.* any of various white, pink, purple, or yellow flowers, either annuals or perennials, growing in rocky places.

Sax-on (săk'sŭn; săk'sn), *n.* **1,** a member of a Teutonic tribe, which, in the fifth and sixth centuries, together with the Angles and the Jutes, conquered and settled England; **2,** an Anglo-Saxon; **3,** the language of the Saxons; **4,** an inhabitant of modern Saxony:—*adj.* **1,** of or pertaining to the Saxons, or their language; **2,** Anglo-Saxon.

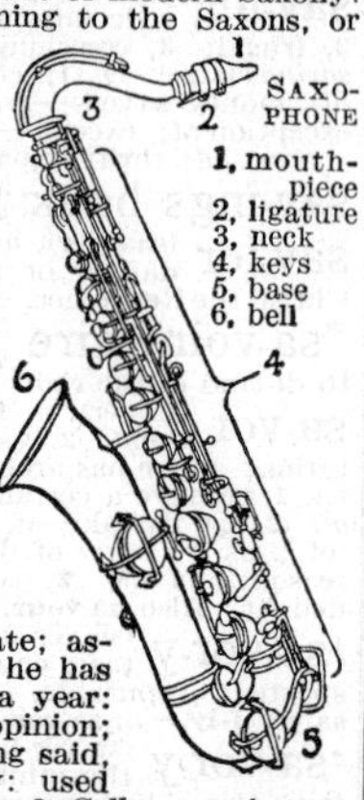

SAXOPHONE
1, mouthpiece
2, ligature
3, neck
4, keys
5, base
6, bell

sax-o-phone (săk'sō-fōn), *n.* a keyed wind instrument consisting of a metal tube and a reed mouthpiece like that of a clarinet (cf. *musical instrument,* illus.).

say (sā), *v.t.* [*p.t.* and *p.p.* said (sĕd), *p.pr.* say'ing, third person sing., pres. indicative, says (sĕz), *Archaic,* saith (sĕth)], **1,** to utter in words; speak; **2,** to declare; state as a decision; assert; as, I *say* he shall go; **3,** to estimate; assume; as, we will *say* he has ten thousand dollars a year:—*v.i.* to express an opinion; assert:—*n.* **1,** something said, or what one has to say: used as in *to have one's say;* **2,** *Colloq.,* one's turn or right to express an opinion.—*n.* **say'er.**

say-ing (sā'ĭng), *n.* **1,** a statement; that which is said; **2,** an adage; maxim. *Syn.* saw, byword, truism, proverb.

scab (skăb), *n.* **1,** a crust formed over a wound or sore; **2,** a disease of sheep; **3,** a disease of plants in which dark-colored spots of mold appear; **4,** *Slang,* a workman who refuses to join a strike, or who takes the place abandoned by a striker.

scab-bard (skăb'ẽrd), *n.* the case in which the blade of a sword or bayonet is kept (see *saber,* illus.):—*v.t.* to put into such a case.

scab-by (skăb'ĭ), *adj.* [*comp.* scab'bi-er, *superl.* scab'bi-est], **1,** covered with, or full of, sores; **2,** affected with the disease called scab; **3,** mean.—*adv.* **scab'bi-ly.**—*n.* **scab'bi-ness.**

sca-bi-es (skā'bĭ-ēz), *n.* a contagious skin disease; the itch.

sca-brous (skā'brŭs), *adj.* scabby; rough; covered with scales; as, the *scabrous* skin of a shark.

scaf-fold (skăf'ōld), *n.* **1,** a temporary timber structure for support, as for workmen and their materials while building; **2,** an elevated platform for the execution of a criminal:—*v.t.* to furnish with a scaffold.

scaf-fold-ing (skăf'ōld-ĭng), *n.* **1,** a scaffold or series of scaffolds; **2,** the materials used in erecting scaffolds.

scal-a-wag (skăl'ȧ-wăg), *n.* **1,** *Colloq.,* a scamp or rascal; **2,** *Slang,* in the South after the Civil War, a white who was a Republican: used contemptuously by southern Democrats. Also, **scal'la-wag.**

[1]**scald** (skôld), *v.t.* **1,** to burn or injure with hot liquid or vapor; expose to heat over a fire or hot liquid; **2,** to bring near to the boiling point, as milk; **3,** to sterilize by the use of boiling water; **4,** to loosen the skin of, by the use of boiling water; as, to *scald* beets:—*n.* a burn or injury from hot liquid or steam.

[2]**scald** (skôld; skäld), *n.* any of the old Norse poets, who recited or sang heroic verses. Also, **skald.**—*adj.* **scald'ic.**

[3]**scald** (skôld), *n. Colloq.,* a hard, dry, scabby formation, esp. on the head.

[1]**scale** (skāl), *n.* **1,** one of the pans or scoops of a balance; **2,** usually in *pl.,* the balance itself; **3,** any instrument or machine for weighing: **Scales, 1,** the constellation Libra: also called *Balance;* **2,** the seventh sign of the zodiac (see *zodiac,* illus.):—*v.t.* [*p.t.* and *p.p.* scaled (skāld), *p.pr.* scal'ing], **1,** to weigh by means of scales; measure; **2,** to compare; estimate; **3,** hence, to come to in weight; as, the package *scales* four pounds.

[2]**scale** (skāl), *n.* **1,** one of the thin, bony or horny plates forming the outer covering of many fishes, lizards, and snakes; **2,** any thin plate resembling such a covering, as the furry spots on a moth's wings; **3,** a scale insect or bark louse, very destructive to fruit trees; **4,** one of the thick leaves which protect the bud of a plant in winter; **5,** the film or layer of oxide which forms on metals when heated below their melting points; **6,** the incrustation on the inside of a boiler; **7,** a loose flake of skin; a scab; **8,** *Rare,* the husk or pod of a seed or fruit:—*v.t.* [*p.t.* and *p.p.* scaled (skāld), *p.pr.* scal'ing], **1,** to strip of scales, as a fish; peel; husk; as, to *scale* almonds; **2,** to pare down; reduce by shaving:—*v.i.* **1,** to form, or drop, scales; separate and come off in thin layers; **2,** to become rough and hard; become crusted.—*adj.* **scale'less.**

[3]**scale** (skāl), *n.* **1,** a graduated measure; esp., a series of marks, laid down at definite distances along a line, used in measurement and computation; as, the *scale* on a medicine glass; also, the rule or system upon which such a series is laid down; **2,** basis for a system of numbering; as, the decimal *scale;* **3,** any progressive series or graded system; as, the social *scale;* **4,** the relative dimensions or proportion between a representation and what it represents; as, a drawing on the *scale* of an inch to a foot; **5,** in music: **a,** a series of tones in consecutive order, ascending or descending generally within the interval of an octave; **b,** any specific succession of tones based upon a given keynote; as, the *scale* of F:—*v.t.* [*p.t.* and *p.p.* scaled (skāld), *p.pr.* scal'ing], **1,** to climb up, as by a ladder; **2,** to reduce in accordance with a settled ratio: often with *down;* as, to *scale* down expenses; **3,** to execute, draw, or make in accordance with a determined scale; **4,** to estimate in the rough, as lumber or timber:—*v.i.* **1,** to go up; **2,** to afford steps for ascent.—*adj.* **scal'a-ble.**

scale in-sect any of various minute, sucking insects which feed on the juices of plants, esp. fruit trees.

sca-lene (skā-lēn'), *adj.* **1,** of a triangle, having three unequal sides and angles; **2,** of a cone, having the axis oblique to the base (see *cone,* illus.). Also, **sca-le'nous.**

scal-ing lad-der a ladder for climbing walls, as of a fort.

scal-lion (skăl'yŭn), *n.* **1,** a kind of onion with a long, thick stem and almost no bulb; **2,** the shallot; **3,** the leek. Also, **scul'lion.**

scal-lop (skŏl'ŭp; skăl'-), *n.* **1**, a marine shellfish having a ribbed shell; also, the shell; **2**, the muscle which closes the shell: in certain of these shellfish, valued as food; **3**, a curve, or one of a series of curves, joined together, to form an ornamental edge, as on lace, linens, etc.:—*v.t.* **1**, to cut the edge or border of in scallops or curves, as for ornament; **2**, to bake in scallop shells; **3**, to mix with bread or cracker crumbs, season, and bake, as oysters. Also, **scol'lop; es-cal'op.**

scalp (skălp), *n.* **1**, the skin on the top of the head, from which the hair grows; **2**, the skin and hair of the head torn off a victim's head by the North American Indians in token of victory:—*v.t.* **1**, to deprive of the skin and hair of the head; **2**, *Colloq.*: **a**, to buy and sell at a small, quick profit, as stocks or bonds; **b**, to buy and sell (railway tickets) at a reduced rate; **c**, to buy (theater tickets) and sell at exorbitant prices.—*n.* **scalp'er.**

scal-pel (skăl'pĕl), *n.* a small, straight, keen-edged knife used by surgeons.

scal-y (skāl'ĭ), *adj.* [*comp.* scal'i-er, *superl.* scal'i-est], **1**, covered, or provided, with scales; also, flaky; scabby; **2**, like scales; **3**, incrusted, as the inside of a kettle.

[1]**scamp** (skămp), *n.* a rascal; a good-for-nothing fellow.—*adj.* **scamp'ish.**

[2]**scamp** (skămp), *v.t.* to perform, as work, carelessly and with bad material.

scam-per (skăm'pẽr), *v.i.* **1**, to run with haste, as in fright; **2**, to frolic around:—*n.* a hasty flight.—*n.* **scam'per-er.**

scan (skăn), *v.t.* [*p.t.* and *p.p.* scanned (skănd), *p.pr.* scan'ning], **1**, to examine and divide, as a verse, into the metrical feet or syllables of which it is made up; **2**, to look closely at or into; examine carefully:—*v.i.* to follow metrical rules: said of a verse.

scan-dal (skăn'dăl), *n.* **1**, careless or malicious gossip injurious to reputation; backbiting; repetition or spreading of evil reports; **2**, reproach caused by shameful actions; **3**, a cause of reproach; as, his conduct was a *scandal* to the community.

Syn. slander. *Scandal* denotes gossip, true or false, repeated maliciously or thoughtlessly, and spread abroad. *Slander* means lies or false reports, circulated maliciously with the intention of injuring the character or reputation of the person concerned.

scan-dal-ize (skăn'dăl-īz), *v.t.* [*p.t.* and *p.p.* -ized (-īzd), *p.pr.* -iz"-ing], **1**, to offend or shock by some action considered immoral, unconventional, or improper; **2**, *Rare*, to disgrace or bring reproach upon.

scan-dal-ous (skăn'dăl-ŭs), *adj.* **1**, tending to harm the good name or reputation of someone; **2**, consisting of evil reports; disgraceful; defamatory.—*adv.* **scan'dal-ous-ly.**—*n.* **scan'dal-ous-ness.**

scan-dent (skăn'dĕnt), *adj.* **1**, climbing by attaching itself to supports, as a vine; **2**, climbing, as certain birds.

Scan-di-na-vi-an (skăn"dĭ-nā'vĭ-ăn), *adj.* pertaining to Scandinavia (Sweden, Norway, and Denmark, and adjacent islands), its languages, literature, or people:—*n.* **1**, a native of Scandinavia; **2**, the languages of the Scandinavians.

scan-sion (skăn'shŭn), *n.* the act or art of dividing verses into the metrical elements of which they are composed.

scan-so-ri-al (skăn-sō'rĭ-ăl), *adj.* **1**, habitually climbing, as a bird with feet adapted for climbing; **2**, pertaining to, or fitted for, climbing.

scant (skănt), *adj.* **1**, having only a small amount: with *of;* as, *scant* of material; **2**, scarcely enough; as, a *scant* supply of food:—*v.t.* **1**, to stint; limit the supply of; **2**, to be stingy with.—*adv.* **scant'ly.**—*n.* **scant'ness.**

scant-ling (skănt'lĭng), *n.* **1**, a piece of lumber of small dimensions, used for a joist or an upright in a lath-and-plaster partition; **2**, such material taken collectively; **3**, the prescribed size of a piece of building stone or lumber.

scant-y (skăn'tĭ), *adj.* [*comp.* scant'i-er, *superl.* scant'i-est], **1**, narrow; **2**, barely sufficient; scarcely enough for necessity; **3**, meager; sparing; as, *scanty* of praise.—*adv.* **scant'i-ly.**—*n.* **scant'i-ness.**

Syn. bare, sparse, insufficient.—*Ant.* plenty, ample, sufficient, abundant.

scape (skāp), *n.* **1**, in architecture, the shaft of a column; **2**, in botany, a long, naked stalk rising directly from the ground or from underneath the ground, as in the daffodil; **3**, the shaft of a feather.

scape-goat (skāp'gōt"), *n.* **1**, among the ancient Jews, a goat selected by lot, over whose head the high priest confessed the sins of the people, after which it was driven into the wilderness; **2**, hence, one who bears the blame for others.

scape-grace (skāp'grās"), *n.* an irresponsible, unprincipled fellow.

scaph-oid (skăf'oid), *adj.* boat-shaped; esp., designating a boat-shaped bone in the wrist and in the ankle:—*n.* **a** scaphoid bone: also called *navicular.*

scap-u-la (skăp'ū-lȧ), *n.* [*pl.* scapulæ (-lē); scapulas (-lȧz)], the shoulder blade.—*adj.* [1]**scap'u-lar.**

[2]**scap-u-lar** (skăp'ū-lȧr), *n.* **1**, in the Roman Catholic Church, a loose, sleeveless garment worn by certain priests; **2**, in the Roman Catholic Church, two pieces of cloth worn over the shoulders, beneath the other garments, from motives of devotion; **3**, the bundle of feathers growing from the shoulder part of a bird.

[1]**scar** (skär), *n.* **1**, a mark left on the skin after the healing of a wound, burn, or ulcer; **2**, any mark or blemish; also, figuratively, any mark left by grief, anguish, or the like; **3**, a mark on a branch where a leaf has been detached:—*v.t.* [*p.t.* and *p.p.* scarred (skärd), *p.pr.* scar'ring], to mark with, or as with, a scar; hence, to wound or injure:—*v.i.* to form a scar.

[2]**scar** (skär), *n.* **1**, bare, broken cliffs on a mountain side; **2**, a bare, detached rock. Also, **scaur** (skär).

scar-ab (skăr'ăb), *n.* **1**, a kind of beetle; esp., one of the tumblebugs, held sacred by the ancient Egyptians; **2**, a gem or seal cut in the form of a beetle and worn as a charm by the ancient Egyptians.

scarce (skârs), *adj.* **1**, not common; **2**, not plentiful; not equal to the demand; rare.—*adv.* **scarce'ly.**—*n.* **scarce'ness.**

scar-ci-ty (skâr'sĭ-tĭ), *n.* **1**, lack; insufficiency; dearth; **2**, rareness.

scare (skâr), *v.t.* [*p.t.* and *p.p.* scared (skârd), *p.pr.* scar'ing], to strike with sudden terror, usually without cause; frighten:—*v.i.* to take fright:—*n.* a sudden panic.

scare-crow (skâr'krō"), *n.* **1**, a figure, usually a crude representation of a man, set up to frighten birds away from crops; **2**, that which terrifies or frightens without real cause; **3**, a person dressed in rags.

[1]**scarf** (skärf), *n.* [*pl.* scarfs (skärfs); scarves (skärvz)], **1**, a neckerchief or necktie; **2**, a strip of fabric worn loosely, for ornament or warmth, about the neck, head, shoulders, or waist; a sash.

[2]**scarf** (skärf), *n.* **1**, a groove made by cutting; **2**, either of two pieces notched or grooved so as to fit into each other in an overlapping joint; **3**, a scarf joint: **scarf joint,** a joint in which the ends of two timbers are cut or grooved so as to overlap each

other:—*v.t.* **1**, to cut a scarf into; **2**, to unite by means of a scarf joint.

scarf-skin (skärf'skĭn"), *n.* the epidermis, or outer layer of skin; cuticle.

scar-i-fy (skăr'ĭ-fī), *v.t.* [*p.t.* and *p.p.* -fied (-fīd), *p.pr.* -fy"ing], **1**, to scratch; cut; **2**, in surgery, to make small cuts in with a lancet; as, to *scarify* the skin; **3**, to stir up on the surface; as, to *scarify* the soil; **4**, to criticize severely; wound.—*n.* **scar"i-fi-ca'-tion.**—*n.* **scar'i-fi"er.**

scar-la-ti-na (skär"lȧ-tē'nȧ), *n.* scarlet fever; also, popularly, a mild form of scarlet fever.

scar-let (skär'lĕt), *n.* **1**, a bright red color, tinged with orange; **2**, cloth of such a color:—*adj.* of a bright red color: **scarlet fever**, a contagious disease marked by fever and a scarlet rash: **scarlet runner**, a kind of kidney bean with brilliant red flowers: **scarlet sage**, a plant of the mint family, cultivated for its showy red flowers; salvia.

scarp (skärp), *n.* **1**, in a system of fortifications, an escarp, or the inner slope of the protecting ditch which surrounds the wall or parapet (see *terreplein, rampart,* illus.); **2**, hence, any sharp, steep slope or incline:—*v.t.* to cut straight up and down, or almost so; as, to *scarp* the face of a rock.

scathe (skāth), *v.t.* [*p.t.* and *p.p.* scathed (skāthd), *p.pr.* scath'ing], to injure; hurt; blast:—*n.* extreme injury; damage.—*adj.* **scathe'less.**

scath-ing (skāth'ĭng), *p.adj.* **1**, injurious; hurtful; blasting; **2**, severe or bitter; as, *scathing* remarks.—*adv.* **scath'ing-ly.**

scat-ter (skăt'ẽr), *v.t.* **1**, to strew carelessly; throw loosely about; **2**, to disperse; drive in several directions; **3**, to use wastefully; as, to *scatter* one's energies:—*v.i.* **1**, to separate and go in different directions, as a crowd; **2**, to send a charge of shot with little or no concentration.—*n.* **scat'ter-er.**

scat-ter-brain (skăt'ẽr-brān"), *n. Colloq.*, a frivolous person, incapable of concentrated thought. Also, **scat'-ter-brains".**—*adj.* **scat'ter-brained".**

scaup duck (skôp), any of various northern salt-water ducks akin to the canvasbacks, esp. a species the male of which has a glossy black head and neck and white belly.

scav-en-ger (skăv'ĕn-jẽr), *n.* **1**, a man employed to clean the streets; **2**, any animal that devours refuse.

sce-na-ri-o (sē-nä'rĭ-ō; shā-nä'-), *n.* [*pl.* scenarios (-ōz); scenari (-rē)], the sketch of a plot; an outline of the chief incidents to be represented in a motion-picture play.

scene (sēn), *n.* **1**, the time, place, or circumstance in which anything occurs, either in real life or in literature; as, the *scene* of his adventure; the *scene* of a story; **2**, one of the painted screens used on a stage; **3**, a division of a play; **4**, an episode; **5**, a spectacle; exhibition; esp., a display of feeling or passion between two or more persons; **6**, a landscape; view; **7**, in *pl.*, the decorations and fittings of a stage.

scen-er-y (sēn'ẽr-ĭ), *n.* **1**, the appearance of a locality presented to the vision; general character of a landscape; the appearance of nature in a given locality; as, mountain *scenery;* **2**, painted screens, hangings, etc., on a stage.

sce-nic (sē'nĭk; sĕn'ĭk), *adj.* **1**, pertaining to the stage; dramatic; artistic; **2**, pertaining to a landscape or view of nature; **3**, offering fine views of nature. Also, **scen'i-cal.**

scent (sĕnt), *n.* **1**, odor; **2**, sense of smell; **3**, the odor which an animal leaves as it moves; **4**, hence, a track followed by means of this odor; **5**, a perfume; **6**, any clue by which pursuit may be guided:—*v.t.* **1**, to smell; **2**, hence, to get a hint of; as, to *scent* trouble; **3**, to perfume:—*v.i.* to hunt animals by the sense of smell.—*adj.* **scent'less.**

scep-ter (sĕp'tẽr), *n.* a ruler's staff, an emblem of authority or power. Also, **scep'tre.**

scep-tic (skĕp'tĭk), *n.* one who doubts; one who is unbelieving:—*adj.* inclined to doubt; incredulous. See **skep'tic,** *Pfd. S.*—*adj.* **scep'ti-cal.**—*n.* **scep'ti-cism.**

sched-ule (skĕd'ūl; *Br.* shĕd'ūl), *n.* **1**, a written or printed paper containing a list or inventory; as, a railroad *schedule;* **2**, a list or document attached to a more important paper, as a will:—*v.t.* [*p.t.* and *p.p.* -uled (-ūld), *p.pr.* -ul-ing], **1**, to place in such a list; **2**, to make a list of, as of trains.

scheme (skēm), *n.* **1**, a carefully arranged and systematic plan; **2**, a plan or theory of action; **3**, an underhand plot or device:—*v.t.* [*p.t.* and *p.p.* schemed (skēmd), *p.pr.* schem'ing], to design or plan; plot:—*v.i.* to form a plot or plan.—*n.* **schem'er.**

***scher-zo** (skẽr'tsō), [It.], *n.* [*pl.* scherzos (-tsōz); scherzi (-tsē)], in music, a sprightly movement, often used in the place of the minuet in a sonata or symphony.

Schick test (shĭk), a test for determining susceptibility to, or immunity from, diphtheria infection.

schil-ling (shĭl'ĭng), *n.* **1**, the monetary unit of Austria, replacing the krone in 1924, and equivalent to about fourteen cents; **2**, formerly, any of various German and Dutch coins of small value.

schism (sĭzm), *n.* **1**, a split or division esp., a division or separation in the Christian church; **2**, the offense of causing such a division; **3**, a body that has so separated from the main body of the church.

schis-mat-ic (sĭz-măt'ĭk), *adj.* pertaining to, or characteristic of, division in a church; as, *schismatic* opinions:—*n.* one who causes or takes part in a division of a church. Also, *adj.* **schis-mat'i-cal.**

schist (shĭst), *n.* a crystalline rock that readily splits into slates or slabs.—*adj.* **schist'ose; schist'ous.**

schnapps (shnăps), *n.* Holland gin; Hollands.

schol-ar (skŏl'ẽr), *n.* **1**, one who attends a school or learns of a teacher; a student; **2**, a learned man or woman; **3**, one who holds a scholarship.—*adj.* **schol'ar-ly.**

schol-ar-ship (skŏl'ẽr-shĭp), *n.* **1**, the quality of work done by a student; as, his *scholarship* is satisfactory; **2**, the quality of knowledge and attainment of a learned man; learning; **3**, financial support for a student, supplied by an educational institution or by an individual.

scho-las-tic (skō-lăs'tĭk), *adj.* **1**, pertaining to learned men, students, or institutions of learning; **2**, characteristic of the schoolmen of the Middle Ages; **3**, hence, pedantic, or devoted to book learning:—*n.* **1**, a student; **2**, a schoolman; a pedantic philosopher of the Middle Ages.

scho-las-ti-cism (skō-lăs'tĭ-sĭzm), *n.* **1**, the system of philosophy and theology of the schoolmen in the Middle Ages whose knowledge was based on books rather than on life; **2**, hence, pedantry or devotion to book learning.

[1]**school** (skōōl), *n.* **1**, a place where instruction is given; institution for learning; schoolhouse; schoolroom; **2**, the body of pupils collectively, with their teachers, in any educational institution; **3**, in the Middle Ages, a seminary or college for teaching theology, logic, etc.; **4**, the followers, imitators, or dis-

ciples of any teacher or leader; those held together by common bonds of doctrine, principles, methods, etc.; **5**, figuratively, any channel through which knowledge, training, or discipline is gained; as, the *school* of experience:—*v.t.* **1**, to train or instruct in a school; educate; **2**, to bring under control, as the will:—*adj.* pertaining to a school.

[2]**school** (skōōl), *n.* a great number of fish feeding or swimming together:—*v.i.* to swim together in great numbers.

Syn., *n.* company, shoal. (See herd.)

school-book (skōōl′bŏŏk″), *n.* a book used in schools; a textbook.

school-boy (skōōl′boi″), *n.* a boy who attends school.

school-fel-low (skōōl′fĕl″ō), *n.* a companion at school.

school-girl (skōōl′gûrl″), *n.* a girl who attends school.

school-house (skōōl′hous″), *n.* a building where school is held.

school-ing (skōōl′ĭng), *n.* **1**, instruction in school; education; **2**, discipline; reproof; **3**, pay given for instruction.

school-man (skōōl′măn), *n.* [*pl.* schoolmen (-mĕn)], one of the divines or philosophers in the Middle Ages.

school-mas-ter (skōōl′mȧs″tẽr), *n.* **1**, a man who teaches a school; **2**, the head or principal of a school.—*n.fem.* **school′mis″tress.**

school-mate (skōōl′māt″), *n.* a companion or associate at school.

school-room (skōōl′rōōm″), *n.* a room in which pupils are taught.

school–teach-er (skōōl′-tēch″ẽr), *n.* one who teaches school.—*n.* **school′–teach″ing.**

schoon-er (skōōn′ẽr), *n.* **1**, a vessel with two or more masts, rigged fore and aft (cf. *ship*, illus.); **2**, *U. S. Colloq.:* **a**, a covered emigrant wagon formerly used on the western prairies; a prairie schooner; **b**, a tall drinking glass for beer, holding about a pint.

SEVEN-MASTED SCHOONER

schot-tische (shŏt′ĭsh), *n.* **1**, a kind of dance, similar to the polka; **2**, the music for such a dance. Also, **schot′tish.**

sci-a-graph (sī′ȧ-grȧf), *n.* a shadow picture. See **ski′a-graph,** *Pfd.S.*

sci-at-ic (sī-ăt′ĭk), *adj.* pertaining to, or affecting, the hip: **sciatic nerve,** either of two nerves arising in the pelvis, esp. one which runs down the back of the thigh.

sci-at-i-ca (sī-ăt′ĭ-kȧ), *n.* neuralgia of the sciatic nerve in the hip or thigh; also, loosely, any painful condition in the region of the hip.

sci-ence (sī′ĕns), *n.* **1**, knowledge, as of general truths or particular facts, obtained and shown to be correct by accurate observation and thinking; **2**, knowledge arranged or classified with reference to general truths or laws; esp., classified knowledge in reference to the physical world; **3**, expert ability or skill, as a result of knowledge; **4**, systematized knowledge of some one subject.

sci-en-tif-ic (sī″ĕn-tĭf′ĭk), *adj.* **1**, pertaining to, or used in, the obtaining of knowledge by experiment and observation; as, *scientific* instruments; **2**, in accordance with the rules or methods of systematized knowledge; systematic; exact; **3**, skilled in some branch of classified knowledge.—*adv.* **sci″en-tif′i-cal-ly.**

sci-en-tist (sī′ĕn-tĭst), *n.* one devoted to systematized knowledge; one whose profession is scientific research.

scim-i-tar (sĭm′ĭ-tẽr), *n.* an Oriental sword with a curved blade. Also, **scim′i-ter.**

SCIMITAR

scin-til-la (sĭn-tĭl′ȧ), *n.* a spark; particle; as, not a *scintilla* of truth in his statement.

scin-til-late (sĭn′tĭ-lāt), *v.i.* [*p.t.* and *p.p.* -lat″ed, *p.pr.* -lat″ing], **1**, to give forth sparks or firelike particles; **2**, to twinkle, as stars; **3**, to flash, as wit.

scin-til-la-tion (sĭn″tĭ-lā′shŭn), *n.* **1**, the act of twinkling or sparkling; **2**, a spark or flash; twinkle; **3**, a brilliant display of wit.

sci-o-list (sī′ō-lĭst), *n.* a person whose knowledge or learning is of a shallow character; a pretender to scholarship and scientific knowledge; charlatan.—*n.* **sci′o-lism.**—*adj.* **sci″o-lis′tic.**

sci-on (sī′ŭn), *n.* **1**, the sprout or vigorous shoot of a plant, cut off, or suitable, for grafting; **2**, a descendant; heir, esp. of a noble family. Also, **ci′on.**

scis-sion (sĭzh′ŭn; sĭsh′ŭn), *n.* the act of cutting; a splitting; division.

scis-sors (sĭz′ẽrz), *n.pl.* a cutting instrument having two opposite sharp edges which meet when moved on a pivot: frequently called *pair of scissors.*

scle-ro-sis (sklē-rō′sĭs), *n.* [*pl.* scleroses (-sēz)], the hardening of a tissue of the body, caused by inflammation and certain diseases.

scle-rot-ic (sklē-rŏt′ĭk), *adj.* **1**, denoting the firm, white, outermost membrane of the eyeball; **2**, affected with hardening of a tissue of the body.

scoff (skŏf), *n.* **1**, an expression of scorn or contempt; ridicule; **2**, an object of scorn or contempt; laughingstock:—*v.i.* to show scorn or contempt by mocking acts or language: followed by *at:*—*v.t.* to mock at; treat with scorn or contempt.—*n.* **scoff′er.**—*adv.* **scoff′ing-ly.**

Syn., *v.* taunt, deride. (See jeer.)

scoff-law (skôf′lô″), *n.* *U. S. Slang,* one who disregards the law prohibiting the manufacture or sale of intoxicants.

scold (skōld), *v.i.* **1**, to chide sharply or rudely; **2**, to speak in a loud or violent manner:—*v.t.* to find fault with; rebuke severely:—*n.* one who habitually finds fault; esp., a rude, quarrelsome woman.

Syn., *v.* reprove, rebuke, reprimand. To *scold* is to find fault and to blame, often noisily and with violence. To *reprove* is to blame for some fault or irregularity; it may be gentle reproof, as from a mother, or stern, as from a judge. *Rebuke* implies more severity than *reprove.* To *reprimand* is to *rebuke* with authority; as, an officer is *reprimanded* by his superior.

scol-lop (skŏl′ŭp), *n.* **1**, any of several mollusks having ribbed shells; **2**, the muscle which closes the shell; **3**, one of a series of semicircular curves forming an ornamental edge:—*v.t.* **1**, to trim (an edge) with ornamental curves, or scallops; **2**, to bake in scallop shells; **3**, to prepare, as oysters, with bread crumbs, etc., and bake. See **scal′lop,** *Pfd. S.*

sconce (skŏns), *n.* **1**, a small fort; **2**, protection; shelter; **3**, an ornamental bracket, fastened to a wall, holding one or more candlesticks; **4**, *Colloq.*, the head:—*v.t.* [*p.t.* and *p.p.* sconced (skŏnst), *p.pr.* sconc′ing], **1**, to shelter; **2**, to settle cosily.

scone (skōn), *n.* a cake of barley, oatmeal, or wheat, often baked on a griddle.

scoop (sko͞op), *n.* **1,** a large ladle; **2,** a deep shovel, as for dipping flour, sugar, etc.; **3,** a hollow; **4,** the act of making hollow or dipping out; **5,** *Colloq.*, large profit made in speculation; **6,** *Slang*, the securing and publishing of a piece of news before a rival; also, the article printed:—*v.t.* **1,** to take out or up with a large ladle; **2,** to make hollow; **3,** *Colloq.*: **a,** to get a news story before (a rival); **b,** to procure (a profit), as by luck.

scoot (sko͞ot), *v.t. Colloq.*, to walk or run hastily; dart:—*n. Colloq.*, a scurrying.

[1]**scoot-er** (sko͞ot'ẽr), *n.* **1,** a flat-bottomed sailboat with runners, for sailing through water or over ice; **2,** a child's toy vehicle, hung low on two wheels.

scope (skōp), *n.* **1,** extent or range of view, intent, or action; **2,** room for free action; liberty; as, ample *scope* for his ability.

scor-bu-tic (skôr-bū'tĭk), *adj.* pertaining to, or affected with, scurvy.

scorch (skôrch), *v.t.* **1,** to burn slightly, as linen; **2,** to parch, as grass; **3,** to affect painfully; attack with caustic criticism:—*v.i.* **1,** to be burned slightly; **2,** figuratively, to be painful; as, wit that *scorches.*—*n.* **scorch'er.**—*adv.* **scorch'ing-ly.**

Syn. singe. (See burn.)

score (skōr), *n.* **1,** a notch or cut, esp. one made for keeping tally or account; **2,** a tally or an account so kept; **3,** a debt; bill; also, a grudge; as, to pay off old *scores;* **4,** a motive; **5,** the number of points, runs, etc., made in a game or contest; **6,** the number twenty; **7,** in *pl.*, a large number; as, *scores* of people came; **8,** in music, the copy of a composition showing all the parts for all the instruments or voices:—*v.t.* [*p.t.* and *p.p.* scored (skōrd), *p.pr.* scor'ing], **1,** to notch or mark furrows in; **2,** to keep record or account of; charge, as a debt; **3,** to win for oneself, as runs, points, etc., in a game; **4,** to remove by marking out; as, to *score* out certain paragraphs; **5,** to blame or find fault with; **6,** in music, to adapt for an instrument:—*v.i.* **1,** to keep the tally in a game; **2,** to win points in a game; also, to win the advantage.—*n.* **scor'er.**

sco-ri-a (skō'rĭ-ȧ), *n.* [*pl.* scoriæ (-ē)], **1,** refuse from the melting of metals or metallic ores; slag; **2,** spongy, slaglike lava.—*adj.* **sco"ri-a'ceous.**

scorn (skôrn), *n.* **1,** extreme contempt; haughty disdain; ridicule; **2,** an object of contempt:—*v.t.* **1,** to hold in extreme contempt or disdain; reject with contempt; **2,** to despise as unworthy; as, to *scorn* cheating.—*n.* **scorn'er.**

Syn., *v.* abhor, detest, mock, deride.—*Ant.*, *v.* admire, honor, respect.

scorn-ful (skôrn'fo͝ol), *adj.* expressing contempt; contemptuous; disdainful: often with *of.*—*adv.* **scorn'ful-ly.**—*n.* **scorn'ful-ness.**

Scor-pi-o (skôr'pĭ-ō), *n.* **1,** a southern constellation; the Scorpion; **2,** the eighth sign of the zodiac, entered by the sun about October 23 (see *zodiac*, illus.). Also, esp. in technical writing, **Scor'pi-us.**

scor-pi-on (skôr'pĭ-ŭn), *n.* **1,** any of an order of arachnids armed with a poisonous sting at the tip of the abdomen; **2,** in the Bible, a whip or scourge: **Scorpion, 1,** the constellation Scorpio; **2,** the eighth sign of the zodiac (see *zodiac*, illus.).

scot (skŏt), *n.* a tax; contribution; assessment; fine.

Scot (skŏt), *n.* a native or inhabitant of Scotland.

Scotch (skŏch), *adj.* pertaining to Scotland, its inhabitants, language, or literature; Scottish:—*n.* **1,** *sing.* any of the dialects of English spoken by the people of North Britain; **2,** *pl.* the people of Scotland.

scotch (skŏch), *n.* **1,** to scratch; score; notch; **2,** to wound without killing; as, to *scotch* a snake:—*n.* a slight scratch.

Scotch-man (skŏch'măn), *n.* [*pl.* Scotchmen (-mĕn)], a native of Scotland, or a person of Scottish ancestry.

sco-ter (skō'tẽr), *n.* any of several northern sea ducks, having the bill swollen at the base. Also, [2]**scoot'er.**

scot-free (skŏt'-frē'), *adj.* **1,** free from scot; **2,** hence, unpunished; safe.

Scots (skŏts), *adj.* pertaining to the Scottish people:—*n.* the Scotch dialect.

Scots-man (skŏts'măn), *n.* [*pl.* Scotsmen (-mĕn)], a Scotchman.

Scot-ti-cism (skŏt'ĭ-sĭzm), *n.* a form of expression peculiar to the Scotch; a Scotch word or idiom.

Scot-tish (skŏt'ĭsh), *adj.* pertaining to the people of Scotland, their language, country, or literature; Scotch.

scoun-drel (skoun'drĕl), *n.* a man without honor or virtue; a low, worthless rascal.—*adj.* low; mean.—*adj.* **scoun'drel-ly.**—*n.* **scoun'drel-dom.**—*n.* **scoun'drel-ism.**

[1]**scour** (skour), *v.t.* **1,** to clean, as by hard rubbing with some rough material, as sand; make bright and shiny; **2,** to cleanse from grease or dirt, as by rubbing and washing with soap, water, etc.; **3,** to wash or clear out by flooding or flushing, as a channel or pipe; **4,** in medicine, to purge thoroughly:—*v.i.* **1,** to scrub anything thoroughly; **2,** to become clean and bright through rubbing; **3,** to be purged; have diarrhea:—*n.* **1,** the action of a strong current, as in clearing out a channel in a stream; **2,** dysentery among cattle and other animals.—*n.* **scour'er.**

[2]**scour** (skour), *v.i.* **1,** to move, run, or pass swiftly; **2,** to go along carefully, as in pursuit or in search of something:—*v.t.* **1,** to pass over swiftly; **2,** to go through thoroughly, as on a search.

scourge (skûrj), *n.* **1,** a whip used to inflict pain or punishment; **2,** a means of inflicting punishment; cause of suffering; **3,** hence, severe punishment; **4,** a cause of affliction; as, the *scourge* of war; hence, any disease that affects a large number of people; as, the *scourge* of Spanish influenza:—*v.t.* [*p.t.* and *p.p.* scourged (skûrjd), *p.pr.* scourg'ing], **1,** to whip severely; **2,** to grieve or torment greatly.—*n.* **scourg'er.**

scour-ing rush the common horsetail plant, formerly used in scouring woods and metals.

[1]**scout** (skout), *n.* **1,** a person sent out to obtain and bring in information; esp., a soldier or vessel sent out in war to gain information of the movements, strength, position, etc., of an enemy; **2,** the act of looking out or watching; a reconnoitering; lookout; watch; **3,** in cricket, a fielder: applied esp. to one who fields at a distance in practice; **4,** *Slang*, a fellow; chap: in expressions of approbation; as, a good *scout:* **Boy Scouts,** an organization founded by General Baden-Powell in England in 1908, having as its aim the development of character, resourcefulness, and public spirit in boys, by a program of constructive recreational training not of a military character: **boy scout,** a member of that or of any similar organization now existing in most countries: **girl scout,** a member of any of several organizations, patterned after the Boy Scouts, for the development of woodcraft and general outdoor training for girls:—*v.i.* to go about for purposes of observation or in search of information, esp. of the movements, position, strength, etc., of an enemy:—*v.t.* **1,** to follow closely; spy upon; **2,** to make a preliminary examination or survey of, as for military purposes; reconnoiter.

²scout (skout), *v.i.* to mock; scorn; scoff; jibe: with *at*:—*v.t.* to treat with contempt; reject with disdain or derision.

scout-mas-ter (skout'mȧs"tẽr), *n.* the leader of a troop of boy scouts consisting of three or more patrols of eight scouts each.

scow (skou), *n.* a large flat-bottomed boat with square ends.

scowl (skoul), *v.i.* **1,** to wrinkle the brows in displeasure; look sullen or angry; **2,** to have a threatening aspect; lower, as clouds:—*n.* **1,** the wrinkling of the brows in displeasure or anger; a frown; **2,** a threatening or gloomy aspect.

scrab-ble (skrăb'l), *v.i.* [*p.t.* and *p.p.* -bled (-ld), *p.pr.* -bling], to scramble; clamber; scrape, scratch, or paw with the hands:—*v.t.* to gather hurriedly; scrape together: with *up, together*, etc.; as, he *scrabbled* his belongings together:—*n.* a scramble; a hasty gathering up.

scrag (skrăg), *n.* anything thin, lean, or rough, as the back of a sheep's neck.

scrag-gly (skrăg'lĭ), *adj.* [*comp.* scrag'gli-er, *superl.* scrag'gli-est], **1,** unkempt, as a beard; **2,** jagged, as broken rocks; **3,** bare and splintered, as dead trees.

scrag-gy (skrăg'ĭ), *adj.* [*comp.* scrag'gi-er, *superl.* scrag'gi-est], **1,** lean, thin, and rough; scrawny; **2,** rough, with uneven points; broken; jagged.—*adv.* **scrag'gi-ly.**—*n.* **scrag'gi-ness.**

scram-ble (skrăm'bl), *v.i.* [*p.t.* and *p.p.* -bled (-bld), *p.pr.* -bling], **1,** to clamber or move on the hands and feet; **2,** to struggle or scrabble for, or as if for, something on the ground; **3,** to struggle eagerly or rudely for something; as, to *scramble* for honors or office:—*v.t.* **1,** to toss together at random; **2,** to prepare (eggs) by stirring the whites and yolks together while they are cooking; **3,** to scale, as a cliff: with *up, along*, etc.:—*n.* **1,** a rude, disorderly struggle; **2,** the act of so struggling.—*n.* **scram'bler.**

¹scrap (skrăp), *n.* **1,** something scraped off; a small piece, cut or broken off; a fragment; **2,** a brief extract from something printed; **3,** discarded iron or other metal in the shape of machinery, broken or whole; trimmings, fragments, etc.; junk metal; **4,** in *pl.*: **a,** crisp pieces of fat tissue left after trying out animal fat; **b,** remnants; odds and ends:—*adj.* in pieces; fragmentary; as, *scrap* iron:—*v.t.* [*p.t.* and *p.p.* scrapped (skrăpt), *p.pr.* scrap'ping], **1,** to break up; destroy; as, to *scrap* a vessel; **2,** to discard, as broken machinery, trimmings, etc.

²scrap (skrăp), *n. Slang,* a boxing match; scrimmage; a fight, either with blows or with words:—*v.i.* [*p.t.* and *p.p.* scrapped (skrăpt), *p.pr.* scrap'ping], *Slang,* to engage in a fight; quarrel; also, to box.—*n.* **scrap'per.**

scrap-book (skrăp'bo͝ok"), *n.* a blank book in which to paste clippings from books, magazines, etc.

scrape (skrāp), *v.t.* [*p.t.* and *p.p.* scraped (skrāpt), *p.pr.* scrap'ing], **1,** to draw over harshly or gratingly; **2,** to rub or file with something sharp; **3,** to clean or remove by rubbing with something sharp or rough: with *out, from*, etc.; **4,** to gather or accumulate in small amounts, with effort, as savings:—*v.i.* **1,** to rub something gratingly; **2,** to play awkwardly, as on the violin; **3,** to save money by being extremely economical; **4,** to bow awkwardly by drawing back the foot:—*n.* **1,** the act, noise, or effect of harsh rubbing or grating; **2,** a difficulty; a perplexity.—*n.* **scrap'er.**

scrap-ple (skrăp'l), *n.* a food made by boiling together seasoned, chopped meat, usually pork, and corn meal.

scrap-py (skrăp'ĭ), *adj.* [*comp.* scrap'pi-er, *superl.* scrap'pi-est], made of fragments or small bits; consisting of scraps.

scratch (skrăch), *v.t.* **1,** to mark, or tear the surface of, with something rough or pointed, as with a pin; wound slightly on the surface, as with a thorn; **2,** to tear or dig with the claws or nails; **3,** to cancel, erase, or strike out, as by drawing a line through; **4,** to scrape or rub lightly, as with the nails, to relieve itching; **5,** to gather by hard work or parsimony: with *up* or *together;* as, to *scratch* up a little money:—*v.i.* **1,** to use the nails or claws in rubbing, tearing, or digging; **2,** to rub the head or body with something rough; **3,** to cause irritation or pain by rubbing; as, the collar *scratches;* **4,** to save money by great effort or parsimony:—*n.* **1,** a mark or tear made by something pointed or rough; **2,** a slight wound or cut, as that made by a pin; **3,** formerly, in pugilism, a line across the prize ring, up to which boxers were brought in order to join fight; **4,** hence, a test or proof of courage; as, he came up to the *scratch;* **5,** the starting line in a race:—*adj.* **1,** in sports, made or done by chance; accidental; as, a *scratch* hit; **2,** taken at random; haphazard; as, a *scratch* team.—*n.* **scratch'er.** —*adj.* **scratch'y.**

scrawl (skrôl), *v.t.* and *v.i.* to write or draw irregularly or hastily, or in badly formed characters:—*n.* careless or irregular writing; a scribble.—*n.* **scrawl'er.**

scraw-ny (skrô'nĭ), *adj.* [*comp.* scraw'ni-er, *superl.* scraw'ni-est], lean; skinny; scraggy.—*n.* **scraw'ni-ness.**

screak (skrēk), *v.i.* to utter a shrill sound or cry; screech; creak:—*n.* a creaking; shriek.

scream (skrēm), *n.* a sharp, shrill cry, as of fear or pain:—*v.i.* **1,** to utter such a cry; **2,** to cry, as certain birds:—*v.t.* to utter in a loud, piercing voice.

scream-er (skrēm'ẽr), *n.* **1,** one who or that which cries out or screams; **2,** a South American wading bird.

scream-ing (skrēm'ĭng), *p.adj.* **1,** uttering cries or screams; **2,** resembling a scream; **3,** calling forth screams, as of laughter; as, a *screaming* comedy.

screech (skrēch), *n.* a harsh, shrill cry, as of fright or pain:—*v.i.* to utter a harsh, shrill cry:—*v.t.* to cry out in a shrill, harsh voice; shriek.—*n.* **screech'er.**

screech owl any owl that utters a shrill, screeching cry instead of hooting.

screed (skrēd), *n.* **1,** a long, noisy, ranting speech on any subject; **2,** an emphatic piece of argumentative writing.

screen (skrēn), *n.* **1,** a light, movable partition for protection, as from observation; a shield; as, a door *screen;* **2,** anything in the nature of a protective curtain; as, concealed behind a *screen* of trees; **3,** a coarse sieve; **4,** a surface on which images are projected by a motion-picture machine or a magic lantern:—*v.t.* **1,** to shut off from danger, observation, etc.; shelter or conceal; protect; **2,** to sift through a coarse sieve; **3,** to project (a picture) upon a screen with a motion-picture machine or magic lantern.—*n.* **screen'er.**

screen-ings (skrēn'ĭngz), *n.pl.* siftings; refuse remaining after anything has been passed through a screen or coarse sieve.

screw (skro͞o), *n.* **1,** a cylinder of metal or wood threaded in an advancing spiral on its external surface; **2,** anything resembling such a device; **3,** a hollow cylinder having a spiral thread or groove on its inner surface; **4,** a turn of a screw; **5,** a device for propelling steamships, motor boats, etc.; **6**, *Slang*, a grasping person; extortioner:—*v.t.* **1**, to tighten or fasten with a screw; **2**, to twist; force; as, to *screw* one's courage to the sticking point; **3**, to turn, as with a screw; **4**, to twist or distort; as, to *screw* up one's eyes; **5**, to extort: with *out*, *of*, or *from*:—*v.i.* **1**, to turn with a motion like a screw; **2**, to practice oppressive extortion.

screw driv-er a tool with a blunt blade, used for driving screws into place, or for withdrawing them (see *tool*, illus.). Also, *n.* **screw′driv″er.**

screw pro-pel-ler a rotating device consisting of several spirally pointed blades attached to a hub, and used to propel steamships, motor boats, etc.

scrib-ble (skrĭb′l), *v.t.* [*p.t.* and *p.p.* -bled (-ld), *p.pr.* -bling], **1**, to write hastily and carelessly; **2**, to cover (paper) with careless writing:—*v.i.* to scrawl:—*n.* hasty, careless writing.—*n.* **scrib′bler.**

scribe (skrīb), *n.* **1**, a writer; esp., a skilled penman; **2**, an official or public writer; a clerk; secretary; **3**, in ancient times, a teacher of the Jewish law.

scrim (skrĭm), *n.* thin, loosely woven, but strong, fabric of cotton or linen, used esp. in making curtains.

scrim-mage (skrĭm′ȧj), *n.* **1**, a general quarrel or fight; a confused struggle; **2**, in football, any play begun by snapping the ball back from the ground.

scrimp (skrĭmp), *v.t.* **1**, to make too small, as a garment; **2**, to be sparing of; be niggardly to; stint:—*v.i.* to be sparing or niggardly:—*adj.* short; narrow; scanty:—*n.* *Colloq.*, a miser.

scrimp-y (skrĭm′pĭ), *adj.* [*comp.* scrimp′i-er, *superl.* scrimp′i-est], *Colloq.*, **1**, scanty; insufficient; **2**, stingy; miserly; niggardly.—*n.* **scrimp′i-ness.**

¹scrip (skrĭp), *n.* *Archaic*, a small pouch or wallet, such as that used by a beggar.

²scrip (skrĭp), *n.* **1**, an original document, esp. one in handwriting; **2**, a written list, schedule, certificate, or the like; **3**, in finance: **a**, a certificate of a right to a fraction of a share of stock, issued generally upon payment of the first instalment and convertible into a share certificate upon completion of the payments, or, sometimes, issued as a dividend; **b**, a certificate issued by a clearing house, esp. in times of shortage of currency, in any of various denominations, intended to be used as currency, and redeemable at any member bank of the issuing clearing house; also, a similar certificate issued to any group within which it will be honored by common consent.

script (skrĭpt), *n.* **1**, ordinary handwriting; **2**, style of writing; **3**, type in imitation of writing; **4**, in English law, the original of a document, as a will.

Scrip-tur-al (skrĭp′tūr-ăl), *adj.* pertaining to, found in, or based upon, the Scriptures; Biblical.

Scrip-ture (skrĭp′tūr), *n.*, usually in *pl.* with *the*, the Bible; the books of the Old and New Testaments, or of either of them: **scripture**, any sacred writing.

scrive-ner (skrĭv′nẽr; skrĭv′n-ẽr), *n.* *Archaic*, a clerk; one who copies documents, draws up contracts, etc.

scrof-u-la (skrŏf′ū-lȧ), *n.* a disease marked by tuberculous enlargement and abscesses of the lymphatic glands, usually those of the neck.—*adj.* **scrof′u-lous.**

scroll (skrōl), *n.* **1**, a roll of paper or parchment; **2**, a spiral ornament, as on a violin (see *violin*, illus.); **3**, an ornamental flourish to a signature.

scroll saw a saw for sawing curved outlines.

scro-tum (skrō′tŭm), *n.* [*pl.* scrota (-tȧ)], in most mammals, the pouch which contains the testicles.—*adj.* **scro′tal.**

¹scrub (skrŭb), *v.t.* [*p.t.* and *p.p.* scrubbed (skrŭbd), *p.pr.* scrub′bing], **1**, to wash by hard rubbing on a board, as clothes; **2**, to rub hard with a wet cloth or brush, as a floor:—*v.i.* to clean or scour something by hard rubbing:—*n.* **1**, the act or process of cleaning by hard rubbing; **2**, one who toils hard for a meager living.—*n.* **scrub′ber.**

²scrub (skrŭb), *n.* **1**, a shrub or tree of inferior grade; also, brushwood; a thicket; as, an oak *scrub;* **2**, in the U. S., anything, as a person, plant, or animal, that is inferior in size, quality, or breed:—*adj.* **1**, mean or small; also, below normal size; stunted; as, a *scrub* oak; **2**, consisting of, or pertaining to, players who are not members of a regular team; as, a *scrub* team.

scrub-by (skrŭb′ĭ), *adj.* [*comp.* scrub′bi-er, *superl.* scrub′bi-est], **1**, mean and small; stunted in growth; **2**, covered with brushwood.

scruff (skrŭf), *n.* the nape or back (of the neck), as of a dog.

scrump-tious (skrŭmp′shŭs), *adj. Slang*, splendid; first-rate; fine.

scrunch (skrŭnch), *v.t.* and *v.i.* to crunch; break with the teeth; chew noisily:—*n.* the act or sound of crunching.

scru-ple (skrōō′pl), *n.* **1**, in apothecaries' weight, a weight of one third of a dram, or twenty grains; **2**, a very small quantity; **3**, hesitation, esp. from difficulty in deciding what is right; unwillingness to do something because of a sense that it is wrong; as, conscientious *scruples* against an act:—*v.i.* and *v.t.* [*p.t.* and *p.p.* -pled (-pld), *p.pr.* -pling], to hesitate from conscientious motives.

scru-pu-los-i-ty (skrōō″pū-lŏs′ĭ-tĭ), *n.* [*pl.* scrupulosities (-tĭz)], the state or quality of being very conscientious or exact; punctiliousness.

scru-pu-lous (skrōō′pū-lŭs), *adj.* **1**, inclined to be conscientious; as, a *scrupulous* person; **2**, exact; careful; strict; as, *scrupulous* methods.—*adv.* **scru′pu-lous-ly.**—*n.* **scru′pu-lous-ness.**

scru-ti-nize (skrōō′tĭ-nīz), *v.t.* and *v.i.* [*p.t.* and *p.p.* -nized (-nīzd), *p.pr.* -niz″ing], to inspect or examine closely.

scru-ti-ny (skrōō′tĭ-nĭ), *n.* [*pl.* scrutinies (-nĭz)], inspection; examination.

scud (skŭd), *v.i.* [*p.t.* and *p.p.* scud′ded, *p.pr.* scud′ding], **1**, to run or move swiftly; **2**, of a ship, to run before a gale of wind with little or no sail spread:—*n.* **1**, the act of so moving or sailing; **2**, loose, vapory clouds or spray driven by the wind.

scuff (skŭf), *v.i.* and *v.t.* **1**, to wear a rough place on, as new shoes; **2**, to shuffle; move (the feet) with a dragging motion.

scuf-fle (skŭf′l), *v.i.* [*p.t.* and *p.p.* -fled (-ld), *p.pr.* -fling], **1**, to fight or struggle confusedly, esp. hand to hand; **2**, to drag the feet in a slovenly manner; scuff:—*n.* a struggle for mastery with close grappling; confused conflict; fight.—*n.* **scuf′fler.**

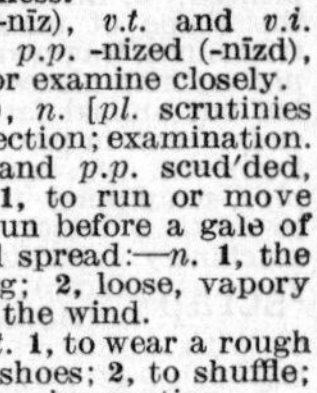
SCULL (def. 2)

scull (skŭl), *n.* **1**, one of a pair of short oars; **2**, an oar used at the stern, or rear end, of a boat to push it forward:—*v.i.* and *v.t.* to propel or move (a boat) with one or more short oars, or with one long oar at the stern.—*n.* **scull′er.**

scul-ler-y (skŭl′ẽr-ĭ), *n.* [*pl.* sculleries (-ĭz)], 1, a room where cooking utensils are kept and cleansed; 2, a back kitchen for rough work.

¹scul-lion (skŭl′yŭn), *n.* 1, a servant who cleans cooking utensils and does other menial service in the kitchen; 2, a low, disreputable wretch.

²scul-lion (skŭl′yŭn), *n.* 1, an onion with a long, thick stem and almost no bulb; 2, the shallot; 3, the leek. Also, **scal′-lion**, *Pfd. S.*

scul-pin (skŭl′pĭn), *n.* any of numerous spiny fish with broad mouths.

sculp-tor (skŭlp′tẽr), *n.* 1, one who practices the art of carving, cutting, or hewing wood, stone, etc., into statues; 2, one who designs models for works of sculpture.—*n.fem.* **sculp′tress.**

sculp-tur-al (skŭlp′tūr-ăl), *adj.* pertaining to sculpture, or the art of carving wood, chiseling stone, etc., into statues.—*adv.* **sculp′tur-al-ly.**

sculp-ture (skŭlp′tūr), *n.* 1, the art of carving, cutting, or hewing wood, stone, etc., into figures or other objects; 2, a carved work or figure:—*v.t.* [*p.t.* and *p.p.* -tured (-tūrd), *p.pr.* -tur-ing], 1, to carve, as with the chisel, on, in, or from wood, stone, etc.; 2, to portray by carving; 3, to ornament by carving; 4, in physical geography, to change in form by gradually wearing away.

scum (skŭm), *n.* 1, a layer of impurities formed on the surface of a liquid; 2, the refuse or dross of metals in a melted state; 3, anything worthless or vile; worthless people; as, the *scum* of the cities.

scup (skŭp), *n.* a common but valuable food fish, found on the eastern coast of the U. S.: also called *porgy.*

scup-per (skŭp′ẽr), *n.* a hole, tube, or gutter at the side of a ship to carry off water from the deck.

scup-per-nong (skŭp′ẽr-nŏng), *n.* a kind of fox grape of the southeastern U. S., or wine made from it.

scurf (skûrf), *n.* 1, white, flaky scales on the skin, esp. on the scalp; dandruff; 2, anything like flakes or scales sticking to a surface.—*adj.* **scurf′y.**

scur-ril-i-ty (skŭ-rĭl′ĭ-tĭ) *n.* [*pl.* scurrilities (-tĭz)], vulgar, vile, or indecent joking or jesting.—*adj.* **scur′rile.**

scur-ril-ous (skŭr′ĭ-lŭs), *adj.* 1, using the low, indecent language of the vulgar; vile; 2, containing abuse.—*adv.* **scur′ril-ous-ly.**—*n.* **scur′ril-ous-ness.**

scur-ry (skŭr′ĭ), *v.i.* [*p.t.* and *p.p.* -ried (-ĭd), *p.pr.* -ry-ing], to hasten or move rapidly along:—*n.* a scampering.

scur-vy (skûr′vĭ), *n.* a disease caused by lack of fresh vegetable food, and marked by great weakness, emaciation, bleeding gums, etc.:—*adj.* [*comp.* scur′vi-er, *superl.* scur′vi-est], contemptible; mean; as, a *scurvy* trick.—*adv.* **scur′vi-ly.**—*n.* **scur′vi-ness.**

scut (skŭt), *n.* the short tail of an animal, as of a rabbit or deer.

scu-tate (skū′tāt), *adj.* 1, shield-shaped; 2, in zoölogy, covered with large, horny scales or plates.

scutch-eon (skŭch′ŭn), *n.* 1, a shield bearing a coat of arms; 2, any metal plate, as that around a keyhole. Also, **es-cutch′eon**, *Pfd. S.*

scu-tel-lum (skū-tĕl′ŭm), *n.* [*pl.* scutella (-*ȧ*)], 1, in botany, a shield-shaped part or organ; 2, in zoölogy, a small shield or plate; scale.—*adj.* **scu-tel′lar.**

scu-ti-form (skū′tĭ-fôrm), *adj.* shaped like a shield.

¹scut-tle (skŭt′l), *v.i.* [*p.t.* and *p.p.* -tled (-ld), *p.pr.* -tling], to hasten; scurry:—*n.* a scampering; hurried flight.

²scut-tle (skŭt′l), *n.* 1, a small opening with a lid, as in the roof of a house; also, its lid; 2, a small opening or hatchway in a ship's deck, bottom, or side; also, its lid:—*v.t.* [*p.t.* and *p.p.* -tled (-ld), *p.pr.* -tling], to sink, or attempt to sink (a vessel), by means of holes cut through the bottom or sides below the water line.

³scut-tle (skŭt′l), *n.* a deep metal vessel or hod for holding a small quantity of coal; a hod: also called *coal scuttle.*

scu-tum (skū′tŭm), *n.* [*pl.* scuta (-t*ȧ*)], 1, in ancient times, a Roman soldier's oblong leather shield; 2, in zoölogy, a shieldlike plate, as on a crocodile.

Scyl-la (sĭl′*ȧ*), *n.* a dangerous rock on the Italian coast, represented in classic mythology as a monster with six fierce heads: closely opposite to Charybdis, a whirlpool on the coast of Sicily: **between Scylla and Charybdis,** between two evils, one of which must be accepted.

scythe (sīth), *n.* a curved cutting instrument used for hand mowing.

Scyth-i-an (sĭth′ĭ-ăn), *adj.* of or pertaining to Scythia, its people, or language:—*n.* 1, one of an ancient, wandering, savage people who inhabited what is now southern Russia and the regions east of the Aral Sea; 2, their language.

se- (sē-), *prefix,* [before vowels, *sed-*], apart or away; as, *se*cede; *sed*ition.

sea (sē), *n.* 1, a body of salt water, smaller than an ocean; as, the Caribbean *Sea;* 2, an inland body of water; as, the *Sea* of Galilee; 3, the ocean as a whole; 4, a billow or large wave; the swell of the ocean in a storm; as, there was a high *sea* after the storm; 5, a large quantity; anything like the sea in vastness; as, a *sea* of troubles: **at sea,** 1, on a sea voyage; 2, figuratively, bewildered.

sea a-nem-o-ne any of several polyps, usually large, beautifully colored, and growing singly.

Sea-bee (sē′bē″), *n.* a member of the Navy's construction battalion, or engineers.

sea-board (sē′bōrd″), *n.* the seacoast:—*adj.* near or on the border of the sea; as, *seaboard* towns.

sea bread ship biscuit; hard-tack; a kind of cracker.

sea calf the common seal, hunted for its fur, hide, and oil.

sea-coast (sē′kōst″), *n.* the coast of the sea or ocean; seashore.

sea cow any of several varieties of large water animals, such as the manatee, dugong, walrus, etc.

sea cu-cum-ber any of a class of cucumber-shaped sea animals, often spiny, as the trepang.

sea dog 1, any of various seals; 2, *Colloq.,* an old sailor.

sea el-e-phant a very large seal of the Southern Hemisphere.

sea-far-ing (sē′fâr″ĭng), *adj.* following the life of a sailor; following the sea as a calling.—*n.* **sea′far″er.**

sea-go-ing (sē′gō″ĭng), *adj.* 1, seafaring; 2, suitable or fitted for use on the open sea; as, a *seagoing* yacht.

sea–green (sē′=grēn″), *adj.* of the bluish green color of the sea.

sea gull any bird of the gull family that habitually stays near the sea.

sea hog the porpoise, a marine mammal from five to eight feet long.

sea horse 1, in mythology, a fabulous creature, half horse and half fish; 2, any of various small fish with a head resembling that of a horse; 3, the walrus; 4, the hippopotamus.

sea king a viking; a chieftain of Scandinavian pirates

[1]seal (sēl), *n.* any of various flesh-eating sea animals valuable for their skin and oil:—*v.i.* to hunt seals.

SEALS ($\frac{1}{15}$)

[2]seal (sēl), *n.* **1**, a stamp or die engraved with some device, motto, or image, used for making an impression in wax; **2**, wax or other soft substance fixed upon a letter, document, etc., and marked with such a stamp; hence, anything that confines or secures; as, the *seal* of silence on his lips; **3**, anything that approves or confirms; **4**, anything that seals or fastens; **5**, specif., in plumbing, a device, as a U-bend in a pipe partly filled with water, for preventing the return of air or other gases:—*v.t.* **1**, to fasten with a device so that it cannot be tampered with; **2**, to set or affix a seal to; **3**, to ratify or confirm; **4**, keep secure or secret; **5**, to settle beyond question; as, to *seal* his fate; **6**, to fill up the cracks or crevices of.

seal brown the dark brown color of the fur of the seal after dyeing.

sea legs *Colloq.*, the ability to adapt oneself to the pitching and rolling motion of a vessel.

[1]seal-er (sēl′ẽr), *n.* one who or that which seals; esp., in the U. S., an officer who inspects weights and measures.

[2]seal-er (sēl′ẽr), *n.* a sailor or vessel engaged in the trade of hunting seals.

seal-er-y (sēl′ẽr-ĭ), *n.* [*pl.* sealeries (-ĭz)], **1**, a place frequented by seals; **2**, a seal-fishing station.

sea let-tuce any of a genus of seaweeds, sometimes used as food.

sea lev-el the level exactly continuous with that of the surface of the sea halfway between high and low water.

seal-ing wax a mixture of shellac, resin, and turpentine, that softens when heated and hardens quickly on cooling: used for sealing letters, legal documents, and the like

sea li-on any of several large seals found in the Pacific Ocean.

seal ring a ring engraved with a crest, or the like; a signet ring.

seal-skin (sēl′skĭn″), *n.* the skin of a fur seal, or a garment made from it.

seam (sēm), *n.* **1**, the line formed by the sewing of two pieces of material together; **2**, a visible line of junction or union, as between two boards; **3**, a scar; **4**, in geology, a layer or bed of mineral or rock; as, a *seam* of coal:—*v.t.* **1**, to form a junction or union upon or of; join or sew together, as a garment; **2**, to scar; line; **3**, to knit with a certain kind of stitch:—*v.i.* **1**, to crack open; **2**, to knit so as to make an apparent seam; purl.

sea-man (sē′măn), *n.* [*pl.* seamen (-mĕn)], one who shares in the actual work of navigating a vessel; a sailor.

sea-man-ship (sē′măn-shĭp), *n.* knowledge of the management of a vessel; the skill of an expert sailor.

sea mew a sea gull; esp., one of the European sea gulls.

seam-less (sēm′lĕs), *adj.* without seams; having no seams.

seam-stress (sēm′strĕs), *n.* a woman whose occupation is sewing; needlewoman. Also, **semp′stress.**

seam-y (sēm′ĭ), *adj.* [*comp.* seam′i-er, *superl.* seam′i-est], **1**, showing, or having, seams, esp. roughly finished seams; **2**, hence, of low character; rough; hard and unpleasant; as, the *seamy* side of life.

sé-ance (sā′äns; *Fr.* sā″äṅs′), *n.* **1**, a meeting or session; **2**, a meeting of spiritualists to receive spirit messages.

sea nettle any water animal that stings like a nettle; esp., a jellyfish.

sea-plane (sē′plān″), *n.* an airplane so made that it can alight or travel upon the water: also called *hydroairplane* and, erroneously, *hydroplane.*

sea-port (sē′pōrt″), *n.* a town, harbor, or port on the seashore, or at a point easy of access to seagoing vessels.

sea purse the horny envelope inclosing the eggs of the skate and of certain sharks and rays.

[1]sear (sēr), *v.t.* **1**, to dry up; wither; scorch; **2**, to burn to dryness and hardness on the surface; brand; cauterize; **3**, to render callous or unfeeling; harden; as, to *sear* one's conscience:—*adj.* (also, *sere*), withered; dried; blasted, as vegetation.

[2]sear (sēr), *n.* a small catch or check in the lock of a gun to hold the hammer at full or half cock (see *trigger*, illus.).

search (sûrch), *v.t.* **1**, to seek for; look for; **2**, to go over and examine; explore; as, to *search* a house; **3**, to probe, as a wound; **4**, to examine; test; as, to *search* men's hearts:—*v.i.* **1**, to seek; **2**, to make careful inquiry:—*n.* **1**, the act of seeking or looking for something; **2**, scrutiny; careful investigation; examination.—*adj.* **search′a-ble.**—*n.* **search′er.**

search-ing (sûr′chĭng), *p.adj.* penetrating; sharp; keen; as, a *searching* glance.—*adv.* **search′ing-ly.**

search-light (sûrch′līt″), *n.* an electric light arranged to revolve so that a powerful beam of light can be thrown in any direction.

search war-rant a warrant or written order giving a police officer authority to search a specified house.

sea room the space at sea needed for maneuvering a ship.

sea-scape (sē′skāp), *n.* a picture showing a scene at sea.

sea ser-pent an enormous snakelike sea monster said to live in the ocean, and occasionally reported as seen, but never proved to exist.

sea-shore (sē′shōr″), *n.* the land bordering the sea.

sea-sick-ness (sē′sĭk″nĕs), *n.* nausea and dizziness caused by the motion of a ship.—*adj.* **sea′sick″.**

sea-side (sē′sīd″), *n.* the shore along the sea; the seashore.

sea-son (sē′zn), *n.* **1**, any particular time as distinguished from others; as, the holiday *season;* **2**, one of the four divisions of the year, as spring, summer, autumn, and winter; **3**, a suitable or convenient time; as, the *season* for shooting; **4**, a short time:—*v.t.* **1**, to habituate, as to a climate; **2**, to bring to the best state for using; as, to *season* timber; **3**, to make more palatable, as with salt or spices; render more agreeable; **4**, to moderate:—*v.i.* **1**, to grow fit for use; become acclimated; **2**, to become dry and hard, as timber.

sea-son-a-ble (sē′zn-ȧ-bl), *adj.* **1**, occurring or done in good or proper time; opportune; **2**, in keeping with the time of year; as, *seasonable* weather.—*adv.* **sea′son-a-bly.**—*n.* **sea′son-a-ble-ness.**

sea-son-al (sē′zn-ăl), *adj.* of, pertaining to, or changing with, the seasons; as, *seasonal* trades.

sea-son-ing (sē′zn-ĭng), *n.* **1**, that which is added to give relish to food, as salt, pepper, etc.; also, something added to give increased pleasure; as, humor serves as a *seasoning;* 2, the act or process of adding relish to food; 3, the act or process of rendering a material fit for use.

seat (sēt), *n.* 1, the place, part, or object on which one sits; a bench, chair, stool, etc.; 2, the part of the body on which one sits; the buttocks; breech; also, the part of a garment which covers the breech; as, the *seat* of the trousers; 3, the place where anything is carried on or flourishes, or is settled or established; location; site; as, the brain is the *seat* of the intellect; 4, residence; as, a country *seat;* 5, the right to sit; membership, as in a legislative body or in a stock exchange; 6, the sitting accommodation for one person; as, to have a *seat* for a play; 7, the manner of sitting, as in riding a horse; 8, a part supporting another part, as in a valve (see *valve*, illus.):—*v.t.* 1, to place on a chair or bench; cause to sit down; 2, to cause to occupy a post, position, or site; 3, to furnish with places to sit; 4, to repair the bottom of, as a chair; 5, to adjust on a seat, as a valve:—*v.i.* to fit well on its seat: said of a valve.

sea ur-chin any of various small sea animals, esp. a globe-shaped one having a thin, prickly shell.

sea wall an embankment for checking the encroachments of the sea or for breaking the force of the waves.

sea-ward (sē'wẽrd), *adj.* going toward, or situated in the direction of, the sea:—*adv.* in the direction of the sea. Also, *adv.* **sea'wards.**

sea-way (sē'wā″), *n.* 1, the forward motion of a ship; headway; 2, a rough sea: used in the expression *in a seaway.*

sea-weed (sē'wēd″), *n.* any plant growing in the sea, as kelp or sea lettuce.

sea-wor-thy (sē'wûr″thĭ), *adj.* fit for a voyage on the open sea: said of a vessel.—*n.* **sea'wor″thi-ness.**

se-ba-ceous (sē-bā'shŭs), *adj.* 1, pertaining to, or resembling, fat; 2, containing or secreting fat; oily.

se-cant (sē'kănt), *adj.* cutting, esp. in two:—*n.* 1, in geometry, a straight line which cuts a curve in two points; 2, in a right-angled triangle, the ratio of the hypotenuse to the side adjacent to the acute angle: one of the trigonometric functions.

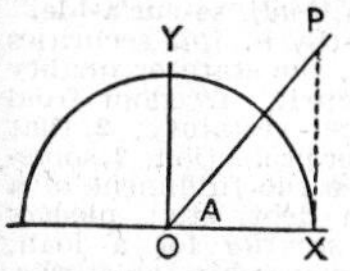

SECANT

$\frac{OP}{OX}$ = secant of angle A.
If OX = 1, the secant is equal to the line OP.

se-cede (sē-sēd'), *v.i.* [*p.t.* and *p.p.* -ced'ed, *p.pr.* -ced'ing], to withdraw from fellowship, union, or association, esp. from a political or religious body.—*n.* **se-ced'er.**

se-ces-sion (sē-sĕsh'ŭn), *n.* 1, the formal withdrawal or separation from the communion or association of others; 2, the withdrawal of a State from the Federal Union; as, the *secession* of the Southern States during the Civil War.—*n.* **se-ces'sion-ism.**

se-ces-sion-ist (sē-sĕsh'ŭn-ĭst), *n.* an upholder of the right of withdrawal, as from membership in a political or religious body; specif., in the U. S., one who upheld the principle that a State has the right to separate from the Union, as in 1860–61.

seck-el (sĕk'l), *n.* a small reddish brown pear: also called *seckel pear.*

se-clude (sē-klōōd'), *v.t.* [*p.t.* and *p.p.* -clud'ed, *p.pr.* -clud'ing], 1, to withdraw or keep apart from others; 2, to place in solitude; keep, or shut, out.

se-clud-ed (sē-klōōd'ĕd), *p.adj.* 1, withdrawn or separated from the society of others; 2, remote; as, a *secluded* spot.—*n.* **se-clud'ed-ness.**

se-clu-sion (sē-klōō'zhŭn), *n.* separation or withdrawal from the society of others; privacy; retirement.

se-clu-sive (sē-klōō'sĭv), *adj.* keeping or living apart from others.

sec-ond (sĕk'ŭnd), *adj.* 1, immediately following the first: the ordinal of *two;* next to the first in order of place or time; 2, next to the first in value, excellence, merit, dignity, or importance; inferior; subordinate; as, *second* choice; 3, being of the same kind as another that has gone before; as, a *second* Brutus; 4, in music, rendering a part that is lower in pitch than the main one; as, a *second* violin: **Second day,** Monday: so named by the Quakers:—*n.* 1, one who or that which is next to the first in place, rank, excellence, or power; 2, one who attends a person who fights a duel; a backer; 3, the 60th part of a minute or of a degree; 4, an article of merchandise of a grade inferior to the best; 5, in music, a part pitched below another, whether of instrument or voice:—*v.t.* 1, to act as an assistant or supporter of; assist; 2, in parliamentary practice, to support, as a motion; 3, to encourage.—*n.* **sec'ond-er.**

sec-ond-a-ry (sĕk'ŭn-dā-rĭ), *adj.* 1, following next in order after the first; of second place, origin, rank, etc.; subordinate; inferior; 2, resultant; derived from something else as its source; as, *secondary* authority; 3, in astronomy, revolving round a primary planet; 4, in electrical usage, of, pertaining to, or denoting, an induced current or its circuit: **secondary cell,** a cell that may be recharged by an electric current when exhausted: **secondary school,** a high school, or any school of high-school grade:—*n.* [*pl.* secondaries (-rĭz)], 1, a delegate or deputy; 2, a person or thing of inferior size, importance, or rank; 3, in astronomy, a planet revolving around another planet; 4, in zoölogy, any of the quill feathers that grow on the second joint of a bird's wing: **Secondary,** *adj.* formerly, in geology, designating, or pertaining to, the Mesozoic era, in which appeared the earliest birds and the great reptiles:—*n.* the Secondary era or its strata.—*adv.* **sec'ond-a-ri-ly.**

sec-ond–class (sĕk'ŭnd=klȧs″), *adj.* 1, ranking in, or belonging to, the class next below the first, the highest, or the best; 2, inferior; second-rate.

sec-ond-hand (sĕk'ŭnd-hănd″), *adj.* 1, taken on another's authority; as, a *secondhand* report; 2, not new; taken or bought from another; as, a *secondhand* car; 3, dealing in goods that are not new; as, he keeps a *secondhand* store.

sec-ond lieu-ten-ant the lowest commissioned officer in the U. S. army.

sec-ond-ly (sĕk'ŭnd-lĭ), *adj.* in the next place; in the second place.

sec-ond–rate (sĕk'ŭnd=rāt″), *adj.* not first-class; second in size, rank, or quality; as, a *second-rate* hotel.

sec-ond–sight (sĕk'ŭnd=sīt″), *n.* ability to foresee events or to see that which is not visible; clairvoyance.

se-cre-cy (sē'krē-sĭ), *n.* [*pl.* secrecies (-sĭz)], 1, the state or quality of being hidden; concealment; retirement; 2, the ability to keep things to oneself; 3, secretive habits; closeness.

se-cret (sē'krĕt), *adj.* 1, not revealed; withdrawn from public view; as, a *secret* treaty; **2**, secluded; retired; as, a *secret* place; **3**, mysterious; occult; as, the *secret* operations of nature: **secret service**, government detective service:—*n.* **1**, that which is purposely concealed or left untold; **2**, something not known; as, the *secrets* of nature; **3**, that which, when made known, makes something clear; as, generosity was the *secret* of his happiness.—*adv.* **se′cret-ly.**

Syn., adj. clandestine, sly, underhand.

sec-re-ta-ry (sĕk′rē-tā-rĭ), *n.* [*pl.* secretaries (-rĭz)], **1**, one who does writing for another; esp., one who attends to correspondence and business for a company or an individual; **2**, an executive who transacts the business of a government department; **3**, a writing desk.—*adj.* **sec″re-ta′ri-al.**—*n.* **sec′re-ta-ry-ship″.**

sec-re-ta-ry bird a large bird of prey of South Africa, with a crest of feathers resembling a number of old-fashioned quill pens.

se-crete (sē-krēt′), *v.t.* [*p.t.* and *p.p.* -cret′ed, *p.pr.* -cret′ing], **1**, to hide or conceal; **2**, in physiology and biology, to separate from the blood or sap and make into a new substance; as, the liver *secretes* bile.

Syn. mask, cloak. (See conceal.)

se-cre-tion (sē-krē′shŭn), *n.* **1**, in physiology, the act or process of separating from a circulating fluid materials out of which a new substance is made; **2**, any such substance, as saliva; **3**, the act of hiding.

se-cre-tive (sē-krē′tĭv), *adj.* **1**, given to reserve or concealment; inclined to be close-mouthed; **2**, in physiology, causing, or pertaining to, secretion; as, a *secretive* gland.—*n.* **se-cre′tive-ness.**

se-cre-to-ry (sē-krē′tō-rĭ), *adj.* in physiology, pertaining to, or causing, secretion.

sect (sĕkt), *n.* **1**, a number of persons who, following a teacher or leader, hold certain opinions; a following; party; **2**, a religious denomination.

sec-ta-ri-an (sĕk-tā′rĭ-ăn), *adj.* **1**, pertaining to, or like, a certain denomination or party; **2**, devoted to a certain party or religious denomination, **3**, hence, narrow-minded; bigoted:—*n.* a member of a denomination or party.

sec-ta-ri-an-ism (sĕk-tā′rĭ-ăn-ĭzm), *n.* **1**, the spirit, tendency, or principles of a party, esp. of a religious denomination; **2**, devotion to some particular religious denomination.

sec-ta-ry (sĕk′tȧ-rĭ), *n.* [*pl.* sectaries (-rĭz)], **1**, a member or supporter of a religious denomination or a party; **2**, one who separates from an established church.

sec-tile (sĕk′tĭl), *adj.* capable of being cut smoothly with a knife.

sec-tion (sĕk′shŭn), *n.* **1**, the act of cutting; separation by cutting; **2**, a part or portion cut off; **3**, a representation of an object as if cut in two crosswise or lengthwise by a plane; as, a transverse *section* of a steam radiator; **4**, a division or subdivision of a chapter; also, the character [§] marking it; **5**, a distinct part of a country, people, community, or class; **6**, in the U. S., one of the portions of one square mile into which public lands are divided; **7**, a division of a genus or class; **8**, a certain length of railway track for whose condition a certain gang of men is responsible; **9**, in a sleeping car, a compartment including an upper and a lower berth:—*v.t.* to divide or cut into sections.

sec-tion-al (sĕk′shŭn-ăl), *adj.* **1**, pertaining to a certain district or part of a country, local; **2**, consisting of parts.

sec-tion-al-ism (sĕk′shŭn-ăl-ĭzm), *n.* prejudice in favor of local interests; devotion to the affairs and interests of a certain district.

sec-tor (sĕk′tẽr; sĕk′tôr), *n.* **1**, an instrument. consisting of two rules hinged together at one end, and bearing various scales, used in making diagrams, maps, etc.; **2**, in geometry, a figure bounded by the arc of a plane curve and the radii drawn from the extremities of the arc: **spherical sector**, the solid generated by the revolution of a plane sector about a line, esp. one of the bounding radii, in the plane of the sector and passing through its vertex (see *solid*, illus.).

SECTOR OF A CIRCLE

sec-u-lar (sĕk′ū-lȧr), *adj.* **1**, pertaining to this present world, or to things not sacred; as, *secular* music; **2**, not bound by monastic vows, as certain priests; **3**, coming or observed once in an age or a century; as, *secular* games; **4**, extending over, or occurring in, a long period of time; as, *secular* changes; **5**, living for an age; as, *secular* trees.—*n.* **sec″-u-lar′i-ty.**—*adv.* **sec′u-lar-ly.**

sec-u-lar-ism (sĕk′ū-lȧr-ĭzm), *n.* **1**, the principles or beliefs of those opposed to religious faith; **2**, the quality or state of being devoted to worldly, rather than to sacred, matters.

sec-u-lar-ist (sĕk′ū-lȧr-ĭst), *n.* **1**, one who objects to religious teaching in schools or to church control of schools or of state affairs; **2**, one who, rejecting all forms of religion, maintains that the duties and problems of this present life should be the principal objects of man's concern.

sec-u-lar-ize (sĕk′ū-lȧr-īz), *v.t.* [*p.t.* and *p.p.* -ized (-īzd), *p.pr.* -iz″-ing], **1**, to convert from sacred to secular or common use, as a building; **2**, to render worldly; as, to *secularize* the Sabbath; **3**, to release from sacred or monastic vows, as a priest.—*n.* **sec″u-lar-i-za′tion.**

se-cure (sē-kūr′), *adj.* **1**, free from fear or danger; protected; **2**, affording safety; **3**, confident; certain; assured: with *of:* **4**, firm; steady; as, a *secure* foundation:—*v.t.* [*p.t.* and *p.p.* -cured′ (-kūrd′), *p.pr.* -cur′ing], **1**, to make safe; protect; **2**, to guarantee; **3**, to make fast; **4**, to gain possession of; **5**, to put beyond chance of losing; as, to *secure* oneself against loss.—*adv.* **se-cure′ly.**—*n.* **se-cure′ness.**—*adj.* **se-cur′a-ble.**

se-cu-ri-ty (sē-kū′rĭ-tĭ), *n.* [*pl.* securities (-tĭz)], **1**, the state or quality of being safe or protected; freedom from fear or danger; assurance; certainty; **2**, that which guarantees safety or protection; **3**, something given to guarantee the fulfilment of a contract, payment of a debt, etc.; pledge; surety; backing; as, *security* for a loan; **4**, evidence of debt or ownership, as stocks, notes, bonds, etc.; **5**, one who becomes responsible for another; **6**, in *pl.*, shares or bonds that may be bought and sold in the money market.

se-dan (sē-dăn′), *n.* **1**, formerly, a portable covered chair, used as a vehicle for carrying one passenger, borne by two men by means of a pole on either side: also called *sedan chair;* **2**, a closed automobile for five or more passengers, with a single compartment for driver and passengers.

se-date (sē-dāt′), *adj.* calm; composed; quiet; serious; habitually staid.—*adv.* **se-date′ly.**—*n.* **se-date′ness.**

Syn. decorous, demure, serene.

sed-a-tive (sĕd′ȧ-tĭv), *adj.* tending to calm or soothe; quieting:—*n.* something having a calming, soothing effect.

sed-en-ta-ry (sĕd′ĕn-tā-rĭ), *adj.* **1**, accustomed to pass much time in a sitting posture; **2,** marked by, or requiring, much sitting; as, *sedentary* work; **3,** sluggish; inactive; **4,** remaining in one place.—*adv.* **sed′en-ta-ri-ly.**—*n.* **sed′en-ta-ri-ness.**

sedge (sĕj), *n.* any of many grasslike herbs growing in wet places.

sed-i-ment (sĕd′ĭ-mĕnt), *n.* **1,** the solid substance which settles at the bottom of a liquid; dregs; lees; settlings; **2,** in geology, matter deposited, as by water.—*adj.* **sed″i-men′tal.**—*n.* **sed″i-men-ta′tion.**

sed-i-men-ta-ry (sĕd″ĭ-mĕn′tȧ-rĭ), *adj.* **1,** pertaining to, or composed of, dregs or lees; **2,** in geology, designating rocks formed of material deposited by water or, sometimes, by wind.

se-di-tion (sē-dĭsh′ŭn), *n.* any offense against the state not actually reaching the point of insurrection or treason; the stirring up of discontent or rebellious feeling against lawful authority.
Syn. disorder. (See revolution.)

se-di-tious (sē-dĭsh′ŭs), *adj.* **1,** pertaining to, like, or tending to excite, rebellion against lawful authority; as, *seditious* behavior; **2,** guilty of rebellion, or of exciting rebellion, against lawful authority; as, a *seditious* person.—*adv.* **se-di′tious-ly.**
Syn. rebellious, turbulent, mutinous.

se-duce (sē-dūs′), *v.t.* [*p.t.* and *p.p.* -duced′ (-dūst′), *p.pr.* -duc′ing], **1,** to draw away from the paths of right, duty, or virtue, by flattery, promises, etc.; lead astray; **2,** specif., to persuade (a woman) to give up her chastity.—*n.* **se-duc′er.**

se-duc-tion (sē-dŭk′shŭn), *n.* **1,** the act of leading astray; **2,** the act of persuading a woman to give up her chastity; **3,** that which leads astray or entices.

se-duc-tive (sē-dŭk′tĭv), *adj.* tending to lead astray; enticing; alluring.—*adv.* **se-duc′tive-ly.**—*n.* **se-duc′tive-ness.**

sed-u-lous (sĕd′ū-lŭs), *adj.* steadily industrious and persevering in business and endeavor; diligent, tireless.—*adv.* **sed′u-lous-ly.**—*n.* **sed′u-lous-ness.**

se-dum (sē′dŭm), *n.* any of a large genus (*Sedum*) of smooth, thick-leaved herbs, including the stonecrop.

¹see (sē), *v.t.* [*p.t.* saw (sô), *p.p.* seen (sēn), *p.pr.* see′ing], **1,** to perceive by the eye; behold; **2,** to discern mentally; as, to *see* a joke; **3,** to escort; as, he *saw* the visitor to the door; **4,** to find out by observation or experience; as, he wished to *see* the result; **5,** to take care of or make sure: with *that;* as, *see* that you address him properly; **6,** to visit or secure an interview with; as, we went to *see* her; **7,** to admit to one's presence; receive; meet; as, she refused to *see* us:—*v.i.* **1,** to possess or use the power of sight; **2,** to comprehend; perceive mentally; discern: often with *into* or *through;* **3,** to find out something by inquiry; **4,** to consider; reflect; as, will you do it? I will *see;* **5,** to take care; attend; as, *see* to the dinner; **6,** to look: obsolete except as an imperative or interjection.

²see (sē), *n.* **1,** the official local seat of a bishop, or of the Pope, from which ecclesiastical authority is exercised; **2,** hence, the episcopal or papal rank, office, authority, or jurisdiction; **3,** the territory embraced within such jurisdiction; the diocese: **Holy See,** the Pope's jurisdiction, court, or office: also called *See of Rome.*

seed (sēd), *n.* [*pl.* seeds (sēdz); collectively, seed], **1,** that part of a plant, the ovule, which holds the embryo, or life-containing germ of the future plant; **2,** popularly, any small, seedlike fruit; **3,** first principle or source; that from which anything springs; as, *seeds* of discord; **4,** offspring; descendants:—*v.i.* **1,** to sow, or shed, the seed; **2,** to go to seed:—*v.t.* **1,** to sprinkle with seed, as a lawn; sow; **2,** to remove the seeds from, as raisins.—*n.* **seed′er.**—*adj.* **seed′less.**

seed bud 1, the ovule, or sac which contains the germ of the future plant; **2,** the plumule, or primary bud of a sprouting plant (see *germination,* illus.).

seed leaf a cotyledon, or leaflike part, first pushed up from a seed: not a true leaf (see *germination,* illus.).

seed-ling (sēd′lĭng), *n.* **1,** a plant grown from a seed; **2,** a very small or young plant or tree.

seeds-man (sēdz′măn), *n.* [*pl.* seedsmen (-mĕn)], **1,** one who sows seeds; **2,** one whose business it is to sell seed.

seed-time (sēd′tīm″), *n.* the proper season for sowing seed.

seed ves-sel any dry, hollow fruit, as a pod, which holds seeds.

seed-y (sēd′ĭ), *adj.* [*comp.* seed′i-er, *superl.* seed′i-est], **1,** full of seed; having run to seed; **2,** *Colloq.:* **a,** shabby; threadbare; worn-out; as, a *seedy* suit; **b,** looking or feeling wretched.—*n.* **seed′i-ness.**

see-ing (sē′ĭng), *n.* the act or power of sight; vision:—*conj.* inasmuch as; considering; since: followed by *that.*

seek (sēk), *v.t.* [*p.t.* and *p.p.* sought (sôt), *p.pr.* seek′ing], **1,** to go in search of; **2,** to aim at; as, to *seek* wealth; **3,** to ask or appeal for; as, to *seek* aid; **4,** to resort to; as, he *sought* the theater for recreation; **5,** to attempt or try; as, he *sought* to go back:—*v.i.* to make search; inquire; make effort to find someone or something.—*n.* **seek′er.**

seem (sēm), *v.i.* **1,** to appear; look; have the semblance of; as, the sky *seems* blue; **2,** to appear to exist; as, there *seems* no need of hurry; **3,** to appear to one's own mind; as, I *seemed* to be floating in space.

seem-ing (sēm′ĭng), *p.adj.* apparent; often, having appearance without reality; as, *seeming* truth:—*n.* appearance; show, esp. false show.—*adv.* **seem′ing-ly.**

seem-ly (sēm′lĭ), *adj.* [*comp.* seem′li-er, *superl.* seem′li-est], fit or becoming; decent; proper; suited to the circumstances, character, or end desired; as, *seemly* behavior; a *seemly* answer.—*n.* **seem′li-ness.**

seen (sēn), past participle of the irregular verb ¹*see.*

seep (sēp), *v.i.* to leak out slowly, as a liquid through pores; ooze; trickle.

seep-age (sēp′āj), *n.* the act or process of leaking out slowly; oozing; also, that which leaks out.

se-er (sē′ẽr; sēr), *n.* **1,** one who sees; **2,** one who foresees future events; a prophet.

seer-suck-er (sēr′sŭk″ẽr), *n.* a thin, linen or cotton fabric with alternating, usually crinkly, stripes.

see-saw (sē′sô″), *n.* **1,** motion to and fro, or up and down, as on a balanced plank; **2,** a plank balanced on a support or pivot, enabling those who sit at the ends to move up and down alternately:—*v.i.* to move up and down or backward and forward.

seethe (sē*th*), *v.t.* [*p.t.* and *p.p.* seethed (sē*th*d), *p.pr.* seeth′ing], to boil; prepare, as food in a hot liquid:—*v.i.* to be cooked in boiling water; also, to boil.

seg-ment (sĕg′mĕnt), *n.* **1,** any of the divisions into which an object naturally separates or is divided; a portion; part; section; as, a *segment* of an orange; **2,** in plane geometry, a part of a line cut off from a figure by another line or lines; also, a part of a circle included between an arc and its chord; **3,** in solid geometry, that portion of the volume of a sphere

SEGMENT OF A CIRCLE

included between a plane and the convex surface, or between two parallel planes (see *solid*, illus.); **4**, a part of an animal naturally marked off as a unit structure or group, as a vertebra of a backbone:—*v.t.* to divide into sections:—*v.i.* **1**, to separate into sections; **2**, to undergo the process of cleavage, whereby the single original cell is converted into a mass of cells; **3**, to reproduce by the process of budding.—*adj.* **seg-men'tal.**—*adj.* **seg'men-ta-ry.**

seg-men-ta-tion (sĕg″mĕn-tā'shŭn), *n.* the act of dividing, or state of being divided, into sections.

seg-re-gate (sĕg'rē-gāt), *v.t.* [*p.t.* and *p.p.* -gat″ed, *p.pr.* -gat″ing], to separate from others; cut off from the main body; set apart; isolate.

seg-re-ga-tion (sĕg″rē-gā'shŭn), *n.* **1**, the act of separating from others; **2**, the state of being separated from others; as, the *segregation* of lepers.

Seid-litz (sĕd'lĭts), *n.* a sparkling mineral water: **Seidlitz powder,** a gentle laxative medicine.

seign-ior (sēn'yẽr), *n.* **1**, a lord; gentleman; **2**, in law, a lord of a manor.—*adj.* **seign-io'ri-al.**

seign-ior-age (sēn'yẽr-ĭj), *n.* **1**, something claimed or taken by sovereign right or authority; as, *seigniorage* is charged on metal brought by private persons to the royal mint to be coined; **2**, a charge or payment for the use of a right, as a copyright or patent; a royalty.

seign-ior-y (sēn'yẽr-ĭ), *n.* [*pl.* seigniories (-ĭz)], **1**, the power or authority of a sovereign lord, extending to fealty and rent service; **2**, the territory of a seignior, or lord of the manor; a principality or province.

seine (sān; sēn), *n.* a large fishing net, equipped with sinkers and floats:—*v.t.* [*p.t.* and *p.p.* seined (sānd; sēnd), *p.pr.* sein'ing], to catch (fish) with such a net:—*v.i.* to fish with a seine.

seise (sēz), *v.t.* [*p.t.* and *p.p.* seised (sēzd), *p.pr.* seis'ing], in law, orig., to put into possession; later, to put into possession of a freehold estate: chiefly passive and followed by *of;* as, to be *seised* of a farm:—*v.i.* to take or lay hold: with *on* or *upon.*

seis-mic (sīs'mĭk; sīz'mĭk), *adj.* pertaining to, or produced by, an earthquake. Also, **seis'mi-cal.**—*adj.* **seis'mal.**

seis-mo-graph (sīs'mō-grȧf; sīz'-), *n.* an instrument for making an automatic record of the time of occurrence, duration, direction, and intensity of an earthquake.—*adj.* **seis″mo-graph'ic.**—*n.* **seis-mog'ra-phy** (sīs-mŏg'rȧ-fĭ; sīz-).

seis-mol-o-gy (sīs-mŏl'ō-jĭ; sīz-), *n.* the scientific study of earthquakes, their causes and results.—*n.* **seis-mol'o-gist.**—*adj.* **seis″mo-log'i-cal.**

seis-mom-e-ter (sīs-mŏm'ē-tẽr; sīz-), *n.* an instrument for measuring the intensity, direction, and duration of earthquakes.—*adj.* **seis″mo-met'ric** (sīs″mō-mĕt'rĭk; sīz-).

seize (sēz), *v.t.* [*p.t.* and *p.p.* seized (sēzd), *p.pr.* seiz'ing], **1**, to take possession of forcibly or suddenly; **2**, to grasp; snatch; take hold of; **3**, to comprehend or understand; as, to *seize* an idea; **4**, (preferably, *seise*), in law, to put in possession; have in legal possession: usually passive; as, to be *seized* of an estate.—*adj.* **seiz'a-ble.**—*n.* **seiz'er.**

sei-zin (sē'zĭn), *n.* possession of land under a claim of freehold. Also, **sei'sin.**

seiz-ing (sēz'ĭng), *n.* **1**, the act of taking possession forcibly and suddenly; **2**, the act of binding or making fast with several turns of a small rope or cord; **3**, the small rope used for this purpose.

sei-zor (sē'zẽr; sē'zôr), *n.* one who takes possession of land as a freehold.

sei-zure (sē'zhūr), *n.* **1**, the act of taking possession of; **2**, a sudden attack, as of a disease; as, a *seizure* of pneumonia.

se-lah (sē'lȧ), *n.* in the Bible, a Hebrew word probably indicating a pause.

sel-dom (sĕl'dŭm), *adv.* rarely; not often; at long intervals of time.

se-lect (sē-lĕkt'), *adj.* **1**, chosen or picked out as more valuable than others; **2**, hence, of great excellence; **3**, *Colloq.*, exclusive; made up of chosen persons; as, a *select* club:—*v.t.* to take by choice from among others; choose.—*n.* **se-lec'tor.**

Syn., *v.* pick, cull. (See elect.)

se-lec-tion (sē-lĕk'shŭn), *n.* **1**, the act of choosing; **2**, the thing or things chosen; **3**, the state of being chosen.

se-lec-tive (sē-lĕk'tĭv), *adj.* **1**, pertaining to, or resulting from, choice; **2**, in electricity, having the property of discriminating or separating oscillations of slightly different frequency: said esp. of a radio receiving set.—*n.* **se″lec-tiv'i-ty.**

se-lect-man (sē-lĕkt'măn), *n.* [*pl.* selectmen (-mĕn)], one of a board of officials chosen annually in most New England towns, to transact the general public business of the town.

Se-le-ne (sē-lē'nē), *n.* in Greek mythology, the goddess of the moon: also called *Phœbe* and identified with the Roman *Luna.* Also, **Se-le'na.**

sel-e-nite (sĕl'ē-nīt), *n.* a crystallized and transparent variety of gypsum, sometimes occurring in large flakes like mica.

se-le-ni-um (sē-lē'nĭ-ŭm), *n.* a nonmetallic element, chemically resembling sulphur and tellurium: valuable in making glass, as a bleaching agent, etc.

self (sĕlf), *n.* [*pl.* selves (sĕlvz)], **1**, one's own person or character; personality; as, "to thine own *self* be true"; **2**, personification; as, she was beauty's *self;* **3**, one's own private interest; as, a person who lives for *self* is unhappy:—*adj.* same or very: used in composition; as, *self*same.—*adj.* **self'less.**

self- (sĕlf-), *prefix*, **1**, the subject of the action named in the word to which it is attached; as, *self*-made; **2**, denoting the object of the action; as, *self*-respect.

-self (-sĕlf), *suffix*, [*pl.* -selves (-sĕlvz)], added to personal pronouns to give emphatic or reflexive force; as, she did it her*self;* she cut her*self*; dress your*self.*

self-a-buse (sĕlf″-ȧ-būs'), *n.* **1**, abuse or misuse of oneself; **2**, specif., sexual misuse of oneself.

self-act-ing (sĕlf″-ăk'tĭng), *adj.* having the power to act or move of itself; automatic.—*n.* **self″-ac'tion.**

self-as-ser-tion (sĕlf″-ȧ-sûr'shŭn), *n.* **1**, insistence on one's own opinions, rights, or claims; **2**, a putting oneself forward in an arrogant or presumptuous manner.—*adj.* **self″-as-ser'tive.**

self-col-ored (sĕlf″-kŭl'ẽrd), *adj.* **1**, all of one color; **2**, of the natural color. Also, **self″-col'oured.**

self-com-mand (sĕlf″-kō-mȧnd'), *n.* poise; self-possession.

self-com-pla-cent (sĕlf″-kŏm-plā'sĕnt), *adj.* pleased with oneself or with one's opinions or conduct; self-satisfied.—*n.* **self″-com-pla'cen-cy.**

self-con-ceit (sĕlf″-kŏn-sēt'), *n.* an exaggerated estimate of one's own abilities or powers; vanity; egotism; self-esteem.—*adj.* **self″-con-ceit'ed.**

self-con-fi-dence (sĕlf″-kŏn'fĭ-dĕns), *n.* **1**, a state of feeling sure of one's own ability; **2**, sometimes, conceited assurance.—*adj.* **self″-con′fi-dent.** —*adv.* **self″-con′fi-dent-ly.**

self-con-scious (sĕlf″=kŏn′shŭs), *adj.* 1, aware of one's own actions, manner, feeling, etc.; 2, embarrassed by the observation of others.—*adv.* **self″-con′scious-ly.**—*n.* **self″-con′scious-ness.**

self-con-tained (sĕlf″=kŏn-tānd′), *adj.* 1, in control of one's own actions; 2, keeping one's affairs to oneself.

self-con-trol (sĕlf″=kŏn-trōl′), *n.* the act, power, or habit of controlling one's desires, acts, and emotions.

self-de-fense (sĕlf″=dē-fĕns′), *n.* 1, the act of protecting one's own person, property, or name; 2, in law, the act of resisting with force an unlawful attack upon one's own person or property, or upon the persons or property of those whom one has a legal right to defend. Also, **self″-de-fence′.**

self-de-ny-ing (sĕlf″=dē-nī′ĭng), *adj.* refusing to consider one's own wishes; setting aside one's own desires for the sake of others.—*n.* **self″-de-ni′al.**

self-dis-ci-pline (sĕlf″=dĭs′ĭ-plĭn), *n.* strict mental or moral training of oneself; self-denial; asceticism.

self-dis-trust (sĕlf″=dĭs-trŭst′), *n.* want of confidence or faith in oneself or one's ability.

self-es-teem (sĕlf″=ĕs-tēm′), *n.* 1, proper respect for oneself; 2, often, an unjustly high opinion of oneself.

self-ev-i-dent (sĕlf″=ĕv′ĭ-dĕnt), *adj.* appearing clearly without need of proof.—*adv.* **self″-ev′i-dent-ly.**

self-gov-ern-ment (sĕlf″=gŭv′ẽrn-mĕnt), *n.* 1, government by the joint action of the people of a nation rather than by a sovereign; specif., a democracy or republic based on the principle of popular representation; 2, a form of organization modeled on the national one, existing in a state, town, school, etc.; 3, self-control; self-command.—*adj.* **self″-gov′ern-ing.**

self-im-por-tant (sĕlf″=ĭm-pôr′tănt), *adj.* valuing oneself too highly; conceited.—*n.* **self″-im-por′tance.**

self in-ter-est (sĕlf″=ĭn′tẽr-ĕst), *n.* 1, private interest or advantage; 2, undue regard for one's own interest, regardless of the rights of others; selfishness.—*adj.* **self″-in′ter-est-ed.**

self-ish (sĕl′fĭsh), *adj.* 1, putting one's own wishes and advantage before the wishes and advantage of others; centered in self, as a person; 2, caused or marked by undue regard for oneself; as, a *selfish* act.—*adv.* **self′ish-ly.**—*n.* **self′ish-ness.**

self-love (sĕlf″=lŭv′), *n.* fondness of oneself; the tendency to put one's own happiness, desires, and advantage first. —*adj.* **self″-lov′ing.**

self-made (sĕlf′=mād″), *adj.* having risen by one's own effort from poverty and low position to wealth and power.

self-mo-tion (sĕlf″=mō′shŭn), *n.* the power of spontaneous or automatic movement.

self-mov-ing (sĕlf″=mōōv′ĭng), *adj.* having the power of moving itself; automobile; automatic.

self-pos-sessed (sĕlf″=pō-zĕst′), *adj.* having or showing composure and calmness; not embarrassed or confused.—*n.* **self″-pos-ses′sion.**

self-reg-is-ter-ing (sĕlf″=rĕj′ĭs-tẽr-ĭng), *adj.* recording of itself, as a barometer.

self-re-li-ance (sĕlf″=rē-lī′ăns), *n.* reliance on, or confidence in, one's own ability, efforts, or judgment.—*adj.* **self″-re-li′ant.**

self-re-spect (sĕlf″=rē-spĕkt′), *n.* a proper regard for one's own person and character; commendable self-esteem.—*adj.* **self″-re-spect′ing.**

self-right-eous (sĕlf″=rī′chŭs) *adj.* upright in one's own eyes. —*n.* **self″-right′eous-ness.**

self-sac-ri-fice (sĕlf″=săk′rĭ-fīs; -fīz), *n.* the sacrifice of one's own self or one's personal interests or welfare, for the sake of duty or other high motive.

self-same (sĕlf′sām″), *adj.* exactly the same; not different; identical.

self-sat-is-fied (sĕlf″=săt′ĭs-fīd), *adj.* entirely pleased with oneself or with one's opinions or conduct.—*n.* **self″-sat″is-fac′tion.**

self-seek-ing (sĕlf″=sēk′ĭng), *adj.* seeking one's own happiness or interests unduly; selfish:—*n.* the act or habit of seeking one's own happiness; self-interest.—*n.* **self″-seek′er.**

self-start-er (sĕlf″=stär′tẽr), *n.* 1, an automatic or partly automatic device for starting an internal-combustion engine; 2, an internal-combustion engine equipped with such a mechanism.

self-styled (sĕlf″=stīld′), *adj.* said or claimed by oneself; would-be.

self-suf-fi-cient (sĕlf″=sŭ-fĭsh′ĕnt), *adj.* 1, needing no aid from another; 2, having undue confidence in oneself; haughty.—*n.* **self″-suf-fi′cien-cy.**

self-will (sĕlf″=wĭl′), *n.* obstinacy: stubbornness; desire to have one's own way.—*adj.* **self″-willed′.**

sell (sĕl), *v.t.* [*p.t.* and *p.p.* sold (sōld), *p.pr.* sell′ing], 1, to give in return for a price, esp. for money; 2, to barter away, esp. in violation of duty or trust; betray for a reward, as one's country:—*v.i.* to dispose of goods for a price.—*n.* **sell′er.**

Selt-zer wa-ter (sĕlt′sẽr), a sparkling, alkaline, mineral water with medicinal properties.

sel-vage (sĕl′vĕj), *n.* the edge of cloth so woven as to prevent raveling. Also, **sel′vedge.**

se-man-tics (sē-măn′tĭks), *n.pl.* used as *sing.*, the science of the meaning and sense development of words.—*adj.* se-man′tic.

sem-a-phore (sĕm′ȧ-fōr), *n.* 1, an apparatus for signaling by

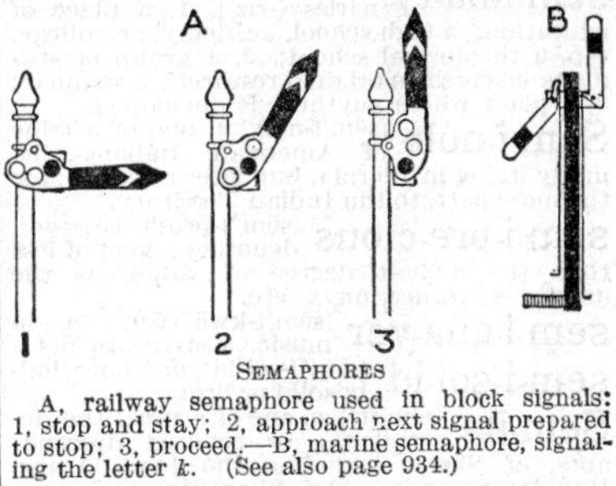

SEMAPHORES

A, railway semaphore used in block signals: 1, stop and stay; 2, approach next signal prepared to stop; 3, proceed.—B, marine semaphore, signaling the letter *k*. (See also page 934.)

means of mechanical arms, lanterns, flags, etc.; 2, in the army, a system of signaling in which letters are represented by various positions of the arms in relation to the body.

sem-blance (sĕm′blăns), *n.* 1, image; representation; 2, resemblance; 3, outside appearance; hence, pretense; as, the *semblance* of truth.

Sem-e-le (sĕm'ē-lē), *n.* in mythology, an earth goddess, who, upon being granted her request to see Zeus in his divine splendor, was consumed by his lightnings.

se-men (sē'mĕn), *n.* [*pl.* semina (sĕm'ĭ-nȧ)], the fertilizing fluid produced in the male reproductive organs; sperm.

se-mes-ter (sē-mĕs'tẽr), *n.* **1**, a period of six months; **2**, specif., one of the two terms of a college or university year.

sem-i- (sĕm'ĭ-), *prefix*, attached freely, usually without hyphen except before capitalized words or words beginning with *i*, and meaning: **1**, half; as, *semi*circle; **2**, partial; imperfect; as, *semi*solid.

sem-i-an-nu-al (sĕm″ĭ-ăn'ū-ăl), *adj.* occurring, published, etc., each half year, or twice a year; as, *semiannual* interest payments.—*adv.* **sem″i-an'nu-al-ly.**

sem-i-breve (sĕm'ĭ-brēv″), *n.* in music, a whole note.

sem-i-cir-cle (sĕm'ĭ-sûr″kl), *n.* a half circle.—*adj.* **sem″i-cir'cu-lar.**

sem-i-cir-cum-fer-ence (sĕm″ĭ-sẽr-kŭm'fẽr-ĕns), *n.* an arc of 180°; half of a circumference.

sem-i-civ-i-lized (sĕm″ĭ-sĭv'ĭ-līzd), *adj.* only partly reclaimed from a savage state; partly civilized.

sem-i-co-lon (sĕm'ĭ-kō″lŏn), *n.* a mark of punctuation [;] in English, marking a pause somewhat greater than that marked by a comma.

sem-i-lu-nar (sĕm″ĭ-lū'nȧr), *adj.* **1**, resembling, or shaped like, a half-moon; **2**, loosely, crescent-shaped: **semilunar bone**, a certain bone of the wrist: **semilunar cartilage**, a large cartilage in the knee joint (see *knee joint*, illus.).

sem-i-month-ly (sĕm″ĭ-mŭnth'lĭ), *adj.* occurring or done every half month, or twice a month:—*n.* a thing appearing or made twice a month, as a periodical:—*adv.* at intervals of half a month.

sem-i-nal (sĕm'ĭ-năl), *adj.* **1**, pertaining to, containing, or consisting of, seed; as, *seminal* fluid; **2**, primary; radical; original; as, *seminal* principles; **3**, rudimentary.

sem-i-nar (sĕm″ĭ-när'), *n.* a group of advanced students, as in a college, pursuing, under the guidance of an instructor, an advanced course of study, esp. original research in a particular line; seminary.

sem-i-na-ry (sĕm'ĭ-nȧ-rĭ), *n.* [*pl.* seminaries (-rĭz)], **1**, a place of education; a high school, academy, or college, esp. a theological school; **2**, a group of students engaged in original research; a seminar; **3**, a place where anything is developed.

Sem-i-nole (sĕm'ĭ-nōl), *n.* one of a tribe of American Indians formerly living in Florida, but later removed, for the most part, to the Indian Territory.

sem-i-pre-cious (sĕm″ĭ-prĕsh'ŭs), *adj.* denoting a gem of less than the highest degree of value, as the amethyst, garnet, onyx, etc.

sem-i-qua-ver (sĕm'ĭ-kwā″vẽr), *n.* in music, a sixteenth note.

sem-i-sol-id (sĕm″ĭ-sŏl'ĭd), *adj.* not wholly solid or firm.

Sem-ite (sĕm'īt), *n.* one of a race, the descendants, or reputed descendants, of Shem, including the Jews, Arabs, Babylonians, etc. Also, **Shem'ite.**

Sem-it-ic (sē-mĭt'ĭk), *adj.* **1**, pertaining to Shem or his descendants; pertaining to the Hebrew race or any of the races akin to it, as the Phœnicians, Assyrians, Arabs, etc.; **2**, designating, or pertaining to, the family of languages spoken by the Semites, as Hebrew and Arabic:—*n.* the Semitic languages collectively. Also, **Shem-it'ic.**

sem-i-tone (sĕm'ĭ-tōn″), *n.* in music properly, a tone at an interval of half a step from a given tone; also commonly, the interval: preferably called *half step*.—*adj.* **sem″i-ton'ic** (sĕm″ĭ-tŏn'ĭk).

sem-i-vow-el (sĕm'ĭ-vou″ĕl), *n.* **1**, sound intermediate between a vowel and a consonant, or having the character of both, as *w* or *y* and, sometimes, and *r* and the nasals *m*, *ng*, and *n*; **2**, the letter or letters representing such a sound.

sem-i-week-ly (sĕm″ĭ-wēk'lĭ), *adj.* occurring, coming, or made twice a week:—*n.* that which comes or occurs twice a week; specif., a periodical so issued.

sem-pi-ter-nal (sĕm″pĭ-tûr'năl), *adj.* everlasting; immortal.

semp-stress (sĕmp'strĕs; sĕm'-), *n.* woman who earns a living by sewing. Also, **seam'stress,** *Pfd. S.*

sen (sĕn), *n.* a Japanese copper coin worth about half a cent.

sen-a-ry (sĕn'ȧ-rĭ), *adj.* containing or pertaining to six; on the basis of six

sen-ate (sĕn'āt), *n.* **1**, a council of state; **2**, in ancient Rome, an assembly of elders, chosen from the nobility, at first an advisory body and later as the supreme council of state; **3**, an assembly or council of citizens invested with governmental powers; a legislative body: **Senate**, the upper and smaller branch of various legislatures, as in the U. S., France, and Italy.

sen-a-tor (sĕn'ȧ-tẽr), *n.* a member of the upper house, or senate, of certain legislatures.—*n.* **sen'a-tor-ship″.**

sen-a-to-ri-al (sĕn″ȧ-tō'rĭ-ăl), *adj.* pertaining to, or befitting, a senator or a senate; as, *senatorial* duties; *senatorial* dignity; a *senatorial* district.

send (sĕnd), *v.t.* [*p.t.* and *p.p.* sent (sĕnt), *p.pr.* send'ing], **1**, to throw, cast, or drive; as, to *send* a ball; **2**, to cause to go; dispatch; as, to *send* a messenger; **3**, to inflict; bestow; **4**, to drive; as, grief *sent* him to ruin; **5**, to cause to be conveyed or transmitted, as greetings:—*v.i.* to dispatch a messenger, agent, or the like:—*n.* the motion of a wave which carries a vessel forward.—*n.* **send'er.**

sen-dal (sĕn'dăl), *n. Archaic*, a light, thin, silk fabric.

Sen-e-ca (sĕn'ē-kȧ), *n.* a member of the largest, most warlike Indian tribe of the Iroquois confederacy of the Five Nations, formerly residing in New York.

se-nes-cent (sē-nĕs'ĕnt), *adj.* **1**, growing old; **2**, having the traits or appearance of old age.—*n.* **se-nes'cence.**

sen-es-chal (sĕn'ĕ-shăl), *n.* an official in the castle of a noble of the Middle Ages, whose duties were those of a steward with military authority.

se-nile (sē'nīl; sē'nĭl), *adj.* pertaining to old age or its weaknesses.

sen-ior (sēn'yẽr), *adj.* **1**, before others in age, dignity, rank, or office; as, the *senior* member of the firm; **2**, elder; **3**, in the U. S., pertaining to the last year of a high-school or college course:—*n.* **1**, one who is before others in age, dignity, rank, or office; **2**, a student in the final year of his high-school or college course.—*n.* **sen-ior'i-ty.**

sen-na (sĕn'ȧ), *n.* the dried leaves of the cassia plant, used as a medicine.

***se-ñor** (sā-nyōr'), [Span.], *n.* [*pl.* señores (sā-nyō'rās)], **1**, a Spanish title of courtesy meaning *Mr.* or *Sir;* **2**, a gentleman.—*n.fem.* ***se-ño'ra.**

***se-ño-ri-ta** (sā″nyō-rē'tä), [Span.], *n.* **1**, Miss: a Spanish title of courtesy given to a young lady; **2**, a young lady.

sen-sa-tion (sĕn-sā'shŭn), *n.* **1**, a state of feeling produced by the action of an outside force upon the body; 2, a mental impression resulting from a bodily feeling; as, a *sensation* of heaviness; 3, an emotion; as, a *sensation* of triumph; 4, a state of excited feeling or interest; 5, the cause of such a state; as, he was the *sensation* of the day.

sen-sa-tion-al (sĕn-sā′shŭn-ăl), *adj.* 1, pertaining to bodily sensation; 2, having the power of feeling; 3, exciting great interest; as, a *sensational* escape; 4, intended to work on the feelings; as, a *sensational* novel.—*adv.* **sen-sa′tion-al-ly.**

sen-sa-tion-al-ism (sĕn-sā′shŭn-ăl-ĭzm), *n.* 1, writing or language intended to work on the feelings; 2, the philosophical doctrine that our ideas consist merely of sense perceptions transformed.—*n.* **sen-sa′tion-al-ist.**

sense (sĕns), *n.* 1, the power by which objects are seen or felt physically or mentally through certain bodily organs; 2, the power to see or feel through one special organ; as, the *sense* of sight, of smell, etc.; 3, bodily feeling in general; as, a *sense* of pleasure; 4, the power of perceiving relations of a particular kind; as, her *sense* of propriety; his *sense* of justice; 5, normal understanding; as, a man of no *sense;* 6, sound or clear mind; good judgment; 7, meaning; as, the *sense* of a remark; 8, that which is wise or sound; as, talk *sense:*—*v.t.* [*p.t.* and *p.p.* sensed (sĕnst), *p.pr.* sens′ing], 1, to perceive by the senses; 2, *Colloq.*, to grasp the meaning of.

sense-less (sĕns′lĕs), *adj.* 1, without feeling; unconscious; 2, foolish; stupid; nonsensical; opposed to reason or sound judgment; as, a *senseless* argument.—*adv.* **sense′less-ly.**—*n.* **sense′less-ness.**

sen-si-bil-i-ty (sĕn″sĭ-bĭl′ĭ-tĭ), *n.* [*pl.* sensibilities (-tĭz)], 1, the state or quality of being capable of feeling, as, weakness made him lose his *sensibility; sensibility* to pain; 2, mental discernment, 3, fineness of feeling; as, *sensibility* to beauty; 4, the property, as of an instrument, to respond quickly to slight changes in condition.

sen-si-ble (sĕn′sĭ-bl), *adj.* 1, capable of affecting the senses, or of making an impression on the mind through the bodily organs; as, *sensible* heat; 2, capable of receiving impressions from external objects, as, the ear is *sensible* to sound; 3, having some particular feeling; aware; as, *sensible* of being tired; 4, marked by good judgment; reasonable; 5, great enough to be perceived; as, a *sensible* difference; 6, mentally or emotionally sensitive.—*adv.* **sen′si-bly.**

sen-si-tive (sĕn′sĭ-tĭv), *adj.* 1, having sense, sensibility, or feeling; capable of receiving impressions from external objects; 2, having keen power to feel; quickly and acutely alive to impressions from external objects or influences; as, a nature *sensitive* to beauty, 3, easily affected or changed by certain outside agents; as, a camera has a *sensitive* plate. **sensitive plant,** a tropical plant with pinnately compound leaves which close, or fold tightly together, at night or when touched also called *humble plant.*—*adv.* **sen′si-tive-ly.**—*n.* **sen′si-tive-ness.**

sen-si-tize (sĕn′sĭ-tīz), *v.t.* [*p.t.* and *p.p.* -tized (-tīzd), *p.pr.* -tiz″ing], 1, to make alive to outside impressions; cause to feel quickly and keenly; 2, to make capable of being acted upon by rays of the sun, X rays, etc., as a photographic plate or film.—*n.* **sen′si-tiz″er.**—*n.* **sen″si-ti-za′tion.**

sen-so-ri-um (sĕn-sō′rĭ-ŭm), *n.* [*pl.* sensoriums (-ŭmz); sensoria (-*ȧ*)], the whole sensory apparatus of the body; the brain, or the brain and the spinal cord.

sen-so-ry (sĕn′sō-rĭ), *adj.* 1, pertaining to feeling; as, *sensory* impulses; 2, conveying impulses which result in sensation: applied to nerves.—*adj.* **sen-so′ri-al.**

sen-su-al (sĕn′shōō-ăl), *adj.* 1, pertaining to, consisting in, or affecting, the senses; 2, not spiritual or mental; basely material; gross; 3, controlled by the passions or appetites.—*adv.* **sen′su-al-ly.**

sen-su-al-ism (sĕn′shōō-ăl-ĭzm), *n.* 1, a state of being controlled by the passions and appetites instead of by mental or spiritual forces; 2, the philosophy that all ideas have their origin in sensation.—*n.* **sen′su-al-ist.**—*adj.* **sen″su-al-is′tic.**

sen-su-al-i-ty (sĕn″shōō-ăl′ĭ-tĭ), *n.* [*pl.* sensualities (-tĭz)], the state or quality of being controlled by appetites and passions; grossness.

sen-su-al-ize (sĕn′shōō-ăl-īz), *v.t.* [*p.t.* and *p.p.* -ized (-īzd), *p.pr.* -iz″ing], to debase by gratification of the appetite and passions.—*n.* **sen″su-al-i-za′tion.**

sen-su-ous (sĕn′shōō-ŭs), *adj.* 1, pertaining or appealing to the senses; as, *sensuous* music; 2, easily affected through the senses; quickly responsive to the pleasures to be received through the senses.—*adv.* **sen′su-ous-ly.**—*n.* **sen′su-ous-ness.**

sent (sĕnt), past tense and past participle of the irregular verb *send.*

sen-tence (sĕn′tĕns), *n.* 1, way of thinking; judgment; opinion; 2, in law, judgment pronounced by a court; 3, in grammar, a series of words containing a subject and a predicate, and expressing a complete thought:—*v.t.* [*p.t.* and *p.p.* -tenced (-tĕnst), *p.pr.* -tenc-ing], to condemn by judgment of a court.—*n.* **sen′tenc-er.**—*adj.* **sen-ten′tial.**

sen-ten-tious (sĕn-tĕn′shŭs), *adj.* 1, terse; 2, given to pithy sayings, wise maxims, etc.—*adv.* **sen-ten′tious-ly.**—*n.* **sen-ten′tious-ness.**

sen-ti-ent (sĕn′shĭ-ĕnt; sĕn′shĕnt), *adj.* 1, able to feel or perceive; 2, having sensation or feeling.—*adv.* **sen′ti-ent-ly.**—*n.* **sen′ti-ence.**

sen-ti-ment (sĕn′tĭ-mĕnt), *n.* 1, an opinion or state of mind based on feeling rather than on reason; 2, refinement of feeling; quickness to feel; hence, a tendency to form emotional judgments; 3, a thought or opinion expressed in words but considered as distinct from them; as, I like the *sentiment* but dislike the language; 4, a sentence expressing some important or agreeable thought; esp., a toast; 5, an emotional attitude toward some particular matter; as, the prevailing *sentiment* toward prohibition.

sen-ti-men-tal (sĕn″tĭ-mĕn′tăl), *adj.* 1, having, expressing, or given to, feeling or emotion; 2, appealing to, or based on, feeling rather than reason, 3, artificially or affectedly tender; having an excessive capacity for feeling or emotion; weakly affectionate.—*adv.* **sen″ti-men′tal-ly.**

sen-ti-men-tal-ism (sĕn″tĭ-mĕn′tăl-ĭzm), *n.* 1, an excessive display of overwrought feeling; 2, the tendency to be swayed by sentiment rather than by reason.—*n.* **sen″ti-men′tal-ist.**

sen-ti-men-tal-i-ty (sĕn″tĭ-mĕn-tăl′ĭ-tĭ), *n.* 1, the state or quality of being guided by feeling rather than reason; 2, weak emotionalism.

sen-ti-nel (sĕn′tĭ-nĕl), *n.* one who watches or guards, esp. a soldier at a camp or fort, on guard against surprise.

sen-try (sĕn′trĭ), *n.* [*pl.* sentries (-trĭz)], a sentinel, guard, or watch.

se-pal (sē′păl; sĕp′ăl), *n.* a leaf or section of the calyx of a flower (see *flower, receptacle,* illus.).—*adj.* **sep′al-ous.**

sep-a-ra-ble (sĕp′*ȧ*-r*ȧ*-bl), *adj.* capable of being divided or distinguished.—*adv.* **sep'a-ra-bly.**—*n.* **sep'a-ra-ble-ness.**—*n.* **sep"a-ra-bil'i-ty.**

sep-a-rate (sĕp'ȧ-rāt), *v.t.* [*p.t.* and *p.p.* -rat"ed, *p.pr.* -rat"ing], **1,** to part or divide; disunite; disconnect; **2,** to come in between; keep apart; **3,** to set apart from a number for a particular purpose:—*v.i.* **1,** to part; withdraw from each other; **2,** to disperse:—*adj.* (sĕp'ȧ-rāt), **1,** divided; not united: said of things once connected; **2,** distinct: said of things that have not been connected; as, every *separate* detail.—*adv.* **sep'a-rate-ly.**—*n.* **sep'a-rate-ness.**

Syn., *v.* sever, detach, estrange, split.—*Ant.*, *v.* unite, connect, join.

sep-a-ra-tion (sĕp"ȧ-rā'shŭn), *n.* **1,** the act of parting, dividing, or disconnecting one thing from another; **2,** the state of being divided or apart; disconnection; **3,** a limited or partial divorce.

sep-a-ra-tist (sĕp'ȧ-rā-tĭst), *n.* one who divides himself from others; esp., one who withdraws from an established church; a dissenter.—*n.* **sep'a-ra-tism.**

sep-a-ra-tive (sĕp'ȧ-rā-tĭv), *adj.* apt to cause parting or dividing; inducing division into parts.

sep-a-ra-tor (sĕp'ȧ-rā"tẽr), *n.* one who or that which divides; specif., any mechanical device for sorting or separating one thing from another; as, a cream *separator.*—*adj.* **sep'a-ra-to-ry.**

se-pi-a (sē'pĭ-ȧ), *n.* **1,** the European cuttlefish; **2,** a dark brown pigment prepared from the black secretion of the cuttlefish; also, the secretion.

se-poy (sē'poi), *n.* an Indian native employed as a soldier by a European government, esp. by Great Britain.

sep-sis (sĕp'sĭs), *n.* poisoning caused by putrefaction or decomposed matter, or by the presence of disease germs in the blood; septicæmia; blood poisoning.

sept (sĕpt), *n.* **1,** formerly, in Ireland, a tribe or clan under a hereditary chief owing allegiance to a king or superior chief; **2,** hence, any similar group or social unit.

sept- (sĕpt-), *prefix,* seven; as, *sept*enary. Also, **sep'tem-; sep'ti-.**

Sep-tem-ber (sĕp-tĕm'bẽr), *n.* the ninth month.—*abbr.* **Sept.**

sep-te-na-ry (sĕp'tē-nȧ-rĭ), *adj.* **1,** consisting of, or relating to, the number seven; **2,** lasting seven years; **3,** occurring once in seven years.

sep-ten-ni-al (sĕp-tĕn'ĭ-ăl), *adj.* **1,** occurring once in seven years; **2,** lasting seven years.—*adv.* **sep-ten'ni-al-ly.**

sep-tet (sĕp-tĕt'), *n.* **1,** a set of seven persons or objects; **2,** a musical composition for seven voices or instruments; **3,** a group of seven performers or instruments. Also, **sep-tette'.**

sep-tic (sĕp'tĭk), *adj.* pertaining to, causing, or caused by, decay.

sep-ti-cæ-mi-a (sĕp"tĭ-sē'mĭ-ȧ), *n.* blood poisoning, caused by poisonous matter taken into the circulation. Also, **sep"ti-ce'mi-a; sep-te'mi-a.**—*adj.* **sep"ti-cæ'mic.**

sep-til-lion (sĕp-tĭl'yŭn), *n.* in the U. S. and France, a number expressed by a unit with 24 ciphers; in the English system, a number expressed by a unit with 42 ciphers.—*adj.* and *n.* **sep-til'lionth.**

sep-tu-a-ge-na-ri-an (sĕp"tū-ȧ-jē-nā'rĭ-ăn), *n.* a person between 70 and 80 years old.

sep-tu-ag-e-na-ry (sĕp"tū-ăj'ē-nȧ-rĭ), *adj.* **1,** consisting of 70; **2,** 70 years old:—*n.* [*pl.* septuagenaries (-rĭz)], a person between 70 and 80 years old; a septuagenarian.

sep-tu-a-ges-i-ma (sĕp"tū-ȧ-jĕs'ĭ-mȧ), *n.* 70 days: **Septuagesima Sunday,** the third Sunday before Lent.—*adj.* **sep"tu-a-ges'i-mal.**

Sep-tu-a-gint (sĕp'tū-ȧ-jĭnt), *n.* a version of the Old Testament in Greek: so called because formerly considered the work of 70 translators.

sep-tum (sĕp'tŭm), *n.* [*pl.* septa (-tȧ)], any dividing wall, as in the nose or between the segments of an earthworm.

sep-tu-ple (sĕp'tū-pl), *adj.* sevenfold; seven times as much.

sep-ul-cher (sĕp'ŭl-kẽr), *n.* a grave or tomb; a place of burial:—*v.t.* to bury; entomb. Also, **sep'ul-chre** [*p.t.* and *p.p.* -chred (-kẽrd), *p.pr.* -chring].

se-pul-chral (sē-pŭl'krăl), *adj.* **1,** pertaining to a tomb or to the burial of the dead; as, a *sepulchral* stone; **2,** gloomy or funereal; **3,** deep, grave, or hollow in tone; as, a *sepulchral* voice.

sep-ul-ture (sĕp'ŭl-tūr), *n.* the act of burying the dead.

se-quel (sē'kwĕl), *n.* **1,** a succeeding part; as, the *sequel* to a book; **2,** result; as, the *sequel* to his address was a riot.

se-quence (sē'kwĕns), *n.* **1,** the state of following in orderly series; succession; **2,** order of events in time; **3,** result.—*adj.* **se-quen'tial.**—*adv.* **se-quen'tial-ly.**

se-quent (sē'kwĕnt), *adj.* following; succeeding:—*n.* a result; sequel.

se-ques-ter (sē-kwĕs'tẽr), *v.t.* **1,** in law, to separate from the owner for a time; take possession of (the property of another) until some claim is paid or established; **2,** to cause to withdraw or retire; seclude:—*v.i.* to renounce, as a widow may, any interest in the estate of her husband.

se-ques-tered (sē-kwĕs'tẽrd), *p.adj.* secluded; retired; quiet.

se-ques-trate (sē-kwĕs'trāt), *v.t.* [*p.t.* and *p.p.* -trat-ed, *p.pr.* -trat-ing], in law, to seize; hold as security for the claims of creditors.—*n.* **se"ques-tra'tion.**—*n.* **se'ques-tra"tor.**

se-quin (sē'kwĭn; sĕk'ĭn), *n.* **1,** a former gold coin of the republic of Venice, worth about $2.25; **2,** a small spangle of jet, silver, or the like.

se-quoi-a (sē-kwoi'ȧ), *n.* either of two evergreen trees of California, called *big tree* and *redwood,* respectively, which grow to immense size.

se-ragl-io (sē-răl'yō; sē-räl'yō), *n.* [*pl.* seragli (-yē); seraglios (-yōz)], the palace of the sultan of Turkey, esp. that part where the women are kept; a harem.

ser-aph (sĕr'ăf), *n.* [*pl.* seraphs (-ăfs); seraphim (-ȧ-fĭm)], an angel of the highest order; hence, any celestial being.

se-raph-ic (sē-răf'ĭk), *adj.* pertaining to, or like, a seraph; sublime; angelic.—*adv.* **se-raph'i-cal-ly.**

Serb (sûrb), *n.* **1,** a Slavic inhabitant of Serbia (Servia) or of the adjoining Slavonic territories included in Yugoslavia; **2,** the language of Serbia and the adjoining Slavonic territories.

Ser-bi-an (sûr'bĭ-ăn), *adj.* pertaining to Serbia, its language, or its inhabitants, or to the neighboring Slavonic territories and peoples:—*n.* **1,** a native or an inhabitant of Serbia; **2,** the language of the Serbians. Also, **Ser'vi-an.**

Ser-bo-Cro-a-tian (sûr"bō-krō-ā'shăn), *n.* **1,** a member of that branch of the South Slavic race which inhabits most of the Serb-Croat-Slovene State, or Yugoslavia, a new state of the Balkans; **2,** the Slavonic language spoken by the inhabitants of Yugoslavia:—*adj.* of or pertaining to these peoples or their language. Also, **Ser″vo–Cro-a′tian.**

sere (sēr), *adj. Poetic,* dry; withered; as, a *sere* leaf. Also, **sear,** *Pfd. S.*

ser-e-nade (sĕr″ē-nād′), *n.* **1,** music sung or played by a lover under the window of a lady; **2,** a piece of music fitted to such an occasion:—*v.t.* and *v.i.* [*p.t.* and *p.p.* -nad′ed, *p.pr.* -nad′ing], to entertain by singing beneath a window.—*n.* **ser″e-nad′er.**

se-rene (sē-rēn′), *adj.* **1,** clear and calm; **2,** placid; composed; as, a *serene* mind.—*adv.* **se-rene′ly.**—*n.* **se-rene′ness.**
Syn. quiet, tranquil, peaceful.—*Ant.* disturbed, ruffled, agitated.

se-ren-i-ty (sē-rĕn′ĭ-tĭ), *n.* [*pl.* serenities (-tĭz)], **1,** the state or quality of being placid or calm; **2,** balance of mind; evenness of temper; coolness; composure.

serf (sûrf), *n.* **1,** orig., a slave; **2,** in medieval Europe, one attached to the land and transferred with it.—*n.* **serf′age.**—*n.* **serf′dom.**
Syn. (see slave).

serge (sûrj), *n.* a ribbed fabric of wool or silk, used as a material for clothing.

ser-gean-cy (sär′jĕn-sĭ), *n.* [*pl.* sergeancies (-sĭz)], the position, rank, or office of a sergeant. Also, **ser′geant-cy; ser′jean-cy.**

ser-geant (sär′jĕnt), *n.* **1,** a sergeant at arms; **2,** a police officer of minor rank; **3,** a noncommissioned army or marine officer ranking next above a corporal: **sergeant at arms,** an officer in any judicial, legislative, or deliberative body, whose duty it is to preserve order, etc. Also, **ser′jeant.**

se-ri-al (sē′rĭ-ăl), *adj.* **1,** pertaining to, or consisting of, a succession of parts; occurring in regular succession; **2,** published in successive parts or numbers; as, a *serial* story:—*n.* **1,** a tale, photoplay, etc., issued in successive parts; **2,** in England, a periodical.—*adv.* **se′ri-al-ly.**

se-ri-a-tim (sē″rĭ-ā′tĭm), *adv.* in regular order.

se-ries (sē′rēz; sē′rĭ-ēz), *n.* [*pl.* series], **1,** a number of things or events succeeding one another in order, and similarly related; **2,** in mathematics, a succession of terms each of which has a fixed relation to one or more of the preceding terms: **series circuit,** an electric circuit in which the parts are placed end to end and form a single continuous conductor: opp. of *parallel circuit.*

ser-if (sĕr′ĭf), *n.* a light line; esp., in printing, a light cross stroke at the top or bottom of a letter, or across the end of a stroke (see *type,* illus.).

se-ri-o–com-ic (sē″rĭ-ō-kŏm′ĭk), *adj.* having a mixture of gravity and humor. Also, **se″ri-o–com′i-cal.**

se-ri-ous (sē′rĭ-ŭs), *adj.* **1,** grave in character or conduct; **2,** sincere; in earnest; **3,** not to be trifled with; important; weighty; **4,** disastrous; as, *serious* consequences.—*adv.* **se′ri-ous-ly.**—*n.* **se′ri-ous-ness.**
Syn. solemn, sober.—*Ant.* flippant, gay.

ser-mon (sûr′mŭn), *n.* **1,** a formal talk or lecture on a moral or religious subject, often based on Scripture; **2,** any serious address.—*adj.* **ser-mon′ic.**
Syn. discourse, exhortation. (See speech.)

ser-mon-ize (sûr′mŭn-īz), *v.i.* [*p.t.* and *p.p.* -ized (-īzd), *p.pr.* -iz″ing], **1,** to compose a sermon; **2,** to preach:—*v.t.* to preach to.—*n.* **ser′mon-iz″er.**

se-rous (sē′rŭs), *adj.* **1,** pertaining to, producing, or containing, serum, as membranes or cavities; **2,** thin and watery, like serum; as, *serous* fluid.

ser-pent (sûr′pĕnt), *n.* **1,** a snake, esp. a large snake; **2,** a kind of firework; **3,** a sly, treacherous person; **4,** the devil.

ser-pen-tine (sûr′pĕn-tīn; sûr′pĕn-tĭn), *adj.* **1,** pertaining to, or like, a snake; moving or winding in coils or curves; **2,** sly and crafty.

ser-rate (sĕr′āt), *adj.* having tooth-shaped projections on the edge, like a saw; as, a *serrate* leaf (see *leaf,* illus.). Also, **ser′rat-ed.**—*n.* **ser-ra′tion.**

ser-ried (sĕr′ĭd), *adj.* crowded; pressed together; as, *serried* ranks.

se-rum (sē′rŭm), *n.* [*pl.* serums (-rŭmz); sera (-rȧ)], **1,** the yellowish, clear, watery fluid left after the blood has coagulated and the clot has been removed; **2,** any serous secretion, as lymph; **3,** the thin part of milk separated from the curd; whey.

ser-val (sûr′văl), *n.* the African wild cat, having a valuable fur.

serv-ant (sûr′vănt), *n.* one who works for another, esp. for wages; one who holds a menial position.

serve (sûrv), *v.t.* [*p.t.* and *p.p.* served (sûrvd), *p.pr.* serv′ing], **1,** to attend or wait upon; work for; **2,** to render spiritual obedience to; worship; **3,** to put on the table and distribute, as food; also, to wait upon at table, or in a shop; **4,** to be of use to, esp. as a substitute: often with *for;* as, this will *serve* him for an excuse; **5,** to meet the needs of; suffice; as, this amount will *serve* my purpose; **6,** to aid by good offices; as, to *serve* one's country; **7,** to treat; deal with; act toward; as, he *served* me shamefully; **8,** to undergo; pass or spend, as a term of imprisonment; **9,** to supply at regular or stated times; provide; as, a farmer *serves* us with fresh eggs; **10,** to handle; work; as, to *serve* a gun; **11,** to deliver, as a legal writ or summons; **12,** to deliver a summons or writ to; make legal service on; **13,** in games, as tennis, to put (the ball) into play by means of a delivery to an opponent:—*v.i.* **1,** to be employed by another; be a servant, slave, or employee; esp., to do domestic work; prepare and dish up food; **2,** to be in subjection or servitude; **3,** to discharge the duties of any office or employment, as in the army or navy; **4,** to be sufficient; act as substitute; answer the purpose: with *for;* as, this will *serve* for an excuse; **5,** to suit; be favorable: said esp. of a wind or current; **6,** in games, as tennis, to put the ball in play by sending it to an opponent in the first stroke:—*n.* in games, as tennis, the act of serving the ball; also, the ball as served or the turn for serving.—*n.* **serv′er.**

Ser-vi-an (sûr′vĭ-ăn), *adj.* of or pertaining to the inhabitants or language of Serbia (Servia) or, loosely, to the inhabitants or language of the adjoining Slavonic territories included in Yugoslavia:—*n.* **1,** an inhabitant of Serbia (Servia) or, by extension, of any territory in Yugoslavia; **2,** the language spoken by the Serbians or Yugoslavians. Also, **Ser′bi-an,** *Pfd. S.*

[1]**serv-ice** (sûr′vĭs), *n.* **1,** the act or occupation of working for another; the rendering of any labor, office, or duty to another; **2,** often in *pl.,* the work done for another; duty required or performed in any office; employment, aid, or kindness rendered to another; **3,** the manner of performing work, serving food, or the like; as, the hotel *service* is poor; **4,** that which is served, as a course at dinner; also, an individual portion; **5,** that which is required for use; a set of implements for some special purpose; as, a silver coffee *service;* **6,** public exercises of worship; as, a Sabbath *service;* **7,** a liturgical form prescribed for public worship or for some special ceremonial; as, the marriage *service;* **8,** the official duty or work required of a person, or appropriate to any office or charge; official function; specif., military or naval duty;

9, the operation of some system of employment or public benefit with an organization of its own, esp. when under government control; as, the civil *service;* **10,** often in *pl.*, profession of respect, spoken or sent; **11,** benefit; advantage; as, your act is of *service* to none; **12,** the means by which some general demand is met; that which is supplied or furnished to meet a general demand: said, usually, of transportation; as, railway *service;* **13,** the legal notification, to the person concerned, of the action of a court; the legal delivery of a writ; **14,** in games, as tennis, that stroke of the ball which puts it in play.

²serv-ice (sûr′vĭs), *n.* **1,** any of a genus of tall shrubs or small trees of the rose family, bearing a red, fleshy, edible fruit; the shadbush: also called *service tree;* **2,** a tree of the rose family, akin to the mountain ash; **3,** the fruit of any service tree.

serv-ice-a-ble (sûr′vĭs-ȧ-bl), *adj.* **1,** fit for work or use; useful; **2,** beneficial; helpful; **3,** having good wearing qualities; durable.—*adv.* **serv′ice-a-bly.**—*n.* **serv′ice-a-ble-ness.**

serv-ice flag a flag with a white field bordered by red, bearing a blue star signifying service, or a gold star signifying death in service, displayed in the U. S. during World Wars I and II, by families or organizations which had members in the military or naval forces, each member being represented by a star.

ser-vi-ette (sûr″vĭ-ĕt′; *Fr.* sȧr″vyĕt′), *n.* [*pl.* serviettes (-ĕts′: *Fr.* -vyĕt′)], a table napkin.

ser-vile (sûr′vĭl; *Br.* sûr′vīl), *adj.* **1,** pertaining to, or like, a slave or menial; **2,** slavishly humble; cringing; fawning; as, *servile* fear; **3,** living in a state of slavish dependence; **4,** obedient; subject to: with *to.*—*adv.* **ser′vile-ly.**—*n.* **ser′vile-ness.**

ser-vil-i-ty (sẽr-vĭl′ĭ-tĭ), *n.* **1,** mean submission; baseness; slavishness; fawning humility; **2,** the state, character, or condition of being a slave or menial.

ser-vi-tor (sûr′vĭ-tẽr), *n.* one who attends upon or serves another; a follower; adherent; specif., a male servant.

ser-vi-tude (sûr′vĭ-tūd), *n.* **1,** the condition of a slave; a state of slavish dependence; bondage; slavery; **2,** menial employment; voluntary subjection to a master; **3,** labor enforced as a punishment; as, penal *servitude.*

ses-a-me (sĕs′ȧ-mē), *n.* any of several East Asian and South African herbs, bearing seeds from which an oil is obtained; also, the seeds: **open sesame,** magical or mysterious means used to obtain admission to what is usually inaccessible; orig., admission to the robbers' cave in the story of Ali Baba in the "Arabian Nights."

ses-qui- (sĕs′kwĭ-), *prefix,* **1,** one and one half; **2,** in chemistry, expressing a proportion of three to two between constituents, as three atoms of the constituent denoted by the word and two of another.

ses-qui-pe-da-li-an (sĕs″kwĭ-pē-dā′lĭ-ăn), *adj.* measuring 1½ feet, as some pygmies: often used humorously of very long words. Also, **sesquip′e-dal** (sĕs-kwĭp′ē-dăl; sĕs″kwĭ-pē′dăl).

ses-sile (sĕs′ĭl), *adj.* attached directly at its base; having no stalk, as a leaf or a flower:—*n.* an animal permanently attached to a base of support, as the oyster.

ses-sion (sĕsh′ŭn), *n.* **1,** the time during which any school, court, council, or lawmaking body holds its sittings; **2,** the sitting of such a body; **3,** the governing body of a single congregation in the Presbyterian Church.—*adj.* **ses′sion-al.**

ses-terce (sĕs′tẽrs), *n.* **1,** in the Roman Republic, a silver coin equal in value to one fourth of a denarius; **2,** in the Roman Empire, a copper coin. Also, **ses-ter′ti-us** (sĕs-tûr′shĭ-ŭs).

ses-tet (sĕs-tĕt′; sĕs′tĕt), *n.* **1,** the last six lines of a sonnet; **2,** a musical composition for six performers; also, the six players or singers rendering such a composition: also called *sextet; sextette.*

set (sĕt), *v.t.* [*p.t.* and *p.p.* set, *p.pr.* set′ting], **1,** to put into a sitting, or upright, position; also, to put in any spot, position, or direction; adjust; establish; fix; plant firmly; **2,** to put upon a nest of eggs; as, to *set* a hen; also, to place (eggs) under a broody hen or other bird; **3,** to cause to be in a certain condition; dispose; as, to *set* a room to rights; **4,** to render rigid or motionless; make firm, as jelly; make permanent, as a color; **5,** to adjust in accordance with some standard; regulate; as, to *set* a clock; **6,** to reduce from a state of fracture or dislocation, as a bone; **7,** to value; regard; as, to *set* a person high in esteem; also, to fix or determine in advance; as, to *set* a price on something; **8,** to assign or prescribe; as, to *set* a time for a meeting; **9,** to mount or frame, as a gem; also, to adorn with, or as with, gems; as, to *set* a crown with jewels; **10,** to fix with settled purpose; as, to *set* one's heart on going; **11,** to spread, as sails; **12,** to fit or adapt, as music to words or words to music; **13,** in printing: **a,** to arrange in the proper order for reading; as, to *set* type; **b,** to put into type, as a manuscript:—*v.i.* **1,** to sink down below the horizon, as the sun; **2,** to plant cuttings or sprouts in the ground; **3,** to become fixed; harden; become firm, as jelly or cement; **4,** to apply oneself; as, to *set* to work; **5,** to flow or tend; as, the current *sets* to the north; **6,** to begin a journey; start: with *out;* as, to *set* out upon a journey; **7,** to begin to develop after fertilization; begin the fruit growth; 8, *Colloq.* (not considered good literary usage): **a,** to fit; as, the coat *sets* well; **b,** to sit; hatch eggs: said of a brooding hen or other fowl:—*p.adj.* **1,** fixed or established; stationary; **2,** regular; deliberate; formal; as, a *set* speech; **3,** determined; firm; immovable; obstinate; as, *set* in her views; **4,** established; prescribed; as, a *set* form of prayer; **5,** formed; constructed; as, thick*set:*—*n.* **1,** the sinking of a heavenly body from sight; **2,** the close, as of day or life; **3,** flow or direction; tendency; current; **4,** a number of persons customarily associated or drawn together by some common interest; as, the younger *set* in society; **5,** a number of things of the same kind intended to be used together; as, a *set* of china; **6,** a series of games played together, as in tennis; **7,** a formal setting, as for a scene in a play or photoplay; 8, carriage; build; pose; **9,** a number of persons necessary to execute a quadrille or other square dance; also, the dance performed; **10,** a young plant ready to set out; a slip; shoot; esp., an onion bulb; **11,** *Colloq.*, fit; way of shaping to the lines of the body; as, the *set* of a skirt.

se-ta-ceous (sē-tā′shŭs), *adj.* covered with, or resembling, bristles.

set-back (sĕt′băk″), *n.* a forcing back to a point previously passed; relapse.

Seth (sĕth), *n.* in the Bible, the third son of Adam (Genesis 4:25).

set-off (sĕt′-ôf″), *n.* **1,** a thing set off against another thing; **2,** in law, the discharge of a debt by setting against it a claim of the debtor; **3,** the claim itself; **4,** an ornament; **5,** the projecting part of a wall.

se-ton (sē′tŭn), *n.* in medicine, a number of small strands of silk or linen inserted under the true skin, in order to produce an artificial sore; also, the running sore.

se-tose (sē′tōs; sē-tōs′), *adj.* covered with bristles; bristly; setaceous.

[1]**set-tee** (sĕ-tē′), *n.* a long bench with a back, seating more than one person.

[2]**set-tee** (sĕ-tē′), *n.* a sailing vessel with a very long, sharp prow: used in the Mediterranean.

set-ter (sĕt′ẽr), *n.* **1**, one who or that which sets; as, a type*setter;* **2**, a kind of long-haired hunting dog trained to stand and point at game.

set-ting (sĕt′ĭng), *n.* **1**, the act of one who or that which sets; **2**, an insertion; that which is set in; **3**, the direction of flow, as of a current; **4**, that in which something is fastened, as the mounting of a jewel; **5**, a background for a play or story; **6**, the eggs placed under a hen for hatching.

[1]**set-tle** (sĕt′l), *v.t.* [*p.t.* and *p.p.* -tled (-ld), *p.pr.* -tling], **1**, to place in a fixed state, as in a business; establish in life or in a home; **2**, to free from doubt or uncertainty; quiet; compose; as, to *settle* one's nerves; **3**, to adjust; as, to *settle* one's dress; **4**, to make up, as a quarrel; pacify; **5**, to make pure or clear of dregs by causing them to sink; clarify; as, to *settle* coffee; **6**, to colonize; as, the Quakers *settled* Philadelphia; **7**, to cause to sink; shake down; **8**, to make compact, firm, solid, or passable, as a roadway; **9**, to determine, decide, or conclude, as a dispute; **10**, to dispose of; set in order; as, to *settle* an estate; **11**, to adjust the balance of; liquidate; pay (a bill):—*v.i.* **1**, to become fixed; **2**, to descend or stop; come to rest; alight, as a bird; also, to establish a residence; make one's home; as, they *settled* in Virginia; **3**, to grow calm or clear; **4**, to sink down gradually, as dregs; become clarified, as a liquid; **5**, to adjust differences or accounts; come to an agreement; **6**, to be established in any employment, profession, or way of life; specif., to marry and establish a home: often with *down;* **7**, to become firm, compact, or solid, as a roadway; sink, as a building's foundations; **8**, to resolve or determine; as, to *settle* on a course of conduct; **9**, *Colloq.*, to pay one's bill.
Syn. regulate, fix.—*Ant.* confuse, disturb.

[2]**set-tle** (sĕt′l), *n.* a long, high-backed bench with arms and, sometimes, in the early types, with a chest under the seat.

set-tle-ment (sĕt′l-mĕnt), *n.* **1**, the act of establishing, fixing, etc.; **2**, the state of being established or fixed; **3**, a disposition of money or other property for the benefit of someone; **4**, payment or adjustment of an account, dispute, etc.; **5**, a colony newly settled.

set-tler (sĕt′lẽr), *n.* **1**, a colonist; **2**, *Slang*, something that decides a contest, as a decisive blow or argument.

set-tlings (sĕt′lĭngz), *n.pl.* the matter which settles to the bottom of a liquid; dregs; lees; sediment.

set–to (sĕt′=tōō″), *n.* [*pl.* set-tos; set-to's (=tōōz″)], *Colloq.*, a contest in boxing, in an argument, or the like; esp., a fist fight.

sev-en (sĕv′n), *adj.* composed of one more than six: **the Seven Wonders of the World,** seven notable objects of ancient times, comprising the Egyptian pyramids, the Pharos, or lighthouse at Alexandria, the walls and hanging gardens of Babylon, the temple of Artemis (Diana) at Ephesus, the Colossus of Rhodes, the statue of Zeus (Jupiter) by Phidias, at Olympia, and the Mausoleum erected by Artemisia at Halicarnassus:—*n.* **1**, the sum of one and six; **2**, the sign representing seven units, as 7 or vii.

sev-en-fold (sĕv′n-fōld″), *adv.* seven times as much or as often:—*adj.* **1**, multiplied seven times; **2**, having seven folds, layers, or parts.

sev-en-teen (sĕv′n-tēn″; sĕv″n-tēn′), *adj.* composed of one more than sixteen:—*n.* **1**, the sum of ten and seven, or sixteen and one; **2**, the sign used to represent seventeen units, as 17 or xvii: **seventeen–year locust,** any of several cicadas, commonly called *locusts*, which require several years to mature from egg to adult.—*adj.* and *n.* **sev′en-teenth″.**

sev-enth (sĕv′nth), *adj.* **1**, next in order after the sixth: the ordinal of seven; **2**, designating one of seven equal parts into which anything is divided: **Seventh day,** Saturday: so called by the Quakers:—*n.* **1**, the quotient of one divided by seven; **2**, one of seven equal parts of anything; **3**, in music, the interval between any degree of a scale and the one preceding its octave above.

sev-en-ty (sĕv′n-tĭ), *adj.* composed of one more than sixty-nine, or ten times seven:—*n.* [*pl.* seventies (-tĭz)], **1**, the sum of ten times seven; **2**, the sign representing seventy units, as 70 or lxx.—*adj.* and *n.* **sev′en-ti-eth.**

sev-er (sĕv′ẽr), *v.t.* **1**, to divide or separate with violence; **2**, to separate from the rest, as the head from the body; **3**, to keep distinct or apart:—*v.i.* to separate; part; be torn apart.—*adj.* **sev′er-a-ble.**
Syn. detach, disjoin, break, rend.

sev-er-al (sĕv′ẽr-ăl), *adj.* **1**, distinct; separate; as, they went their *several* ways; **2**, consisting of more than two, but not many; **3**, different; various; diverse.—*adv.* **sev′er-al-ly.**

sev-er-al-ty (sĕv′ẽr-ăl-tĭ), *n.* the holding of land by individual right.

sev-er-ance (sĕv′ẽr-ăns), *n.* **1**, the act of separating, dividing, or cutting open or through; **2**, the state of being separated, divided, or cut open or through; separation; division.

se-vere (sē-vēr′), *adj.* **1**, strictly adhering to rule; **2**, grave in manner; forbidding in appearance; **3**, strict; harsh; as, *severe* methods of discipline; **4**, extremely plain; as, a gown of a *severe* style; **5**, extreme; sharp; distressing; as, *severe* pain; **6**, hard to bear or undergo; trying; as, a *severe* test.—*adv.* **se-vere′ly.**—*n.* **se-vere′ness.**
Syn. stern, austere.—*Ant.* gentle.

se-ver-i-ty (sē-vĕr′ĭ-tĭ), *n.* [*pl.* severities (-tĭz)], **1**, the quality of being stern or strict; harshness; sharpness; **2**, seriousness; sedateness; gravity; **3**, plainness; lack of ornament, as in dress.

sew (sō), *v.t.* [*p.t.* sewed (sōd), *p.p.* sewed or sewn (sōn), *p.pr.* sew′ing], **1**, to join or fasten together with stitches; **2**, to produce an effect upon by sewing: often with *up;* as, to *sew* up a tear:—*v.i.* **1**, to make stitches; **2**, to work with needle and thread.—*n.* [1]**sew′er.**

sew-age (sū′ăj), *n.* the contents of a sewer or drain; foul liquids or waste matter carried off by a sewer.

[2]**sew-er** (sū′ẽr), *n.* an underground pipe or channel to carry off water, waste material, etc.; public drain.

sew-er-age (sū′ẽr-ăj), *n.* **1**, drainage by underground pipes; **2**, the system of drainage of a town, city, etc.; **3**, refuse matter carried off by a sewer.

sewn (sōn), a past participle of the irregular verb *sew*, which see.

sex (sĕks), *n.* **1**, the physical characteristics that make a human being, animal, or plant, male or female; **2**, one of the two divisions into which the higher forms of life are grouped, as being distinctly male or female.
Syn. (see gender).

sex- (sĕks-), *prefix*, six: in words derived from Latin compounds, and in modern words similarly compounded; as, *sex*ennial; *sex*agenary. Also, **sex′i-.**

sex-a-ge-na-ri-an (sĕk″sȧ-jē-nā′rĭ-ăn), *n.* one who is between 60 and 70 years old:—*adj.* between 60 and 70 years old.

sex-ag-e-na-ry (sĕk-săj′ē-nȧ-rĭ), *adj.* **1**, pertaining to the number 60; **2**, progressing by sixties; **3**, 60 years old:—*n.* [*pl.* sexagenaries (-rĭz)], a sexagenarian.

Sex-a-ges-i-ma (sĕk″sȧ-jĕs′ĭ-mȧ), *n.* the second Sunday before Lent: also called *Sexagesima Sunday.*

sex-en-ni-al (sĕks-ĕn′ĭ-ăl), *adj.* extending over, or occurring once in, six years:—*n.* **1**, a thing that lasts over, or occurs once in, six years; **2**, a sixth anniversary.—*adv.* **sex-en′ni-al-ly.**

sex-less (sĕks′lĕs), *adj.* neither male nor female.—*n.* **sex′less-ness.**

sex-tant (sĕks′tănt), *n.* **1**, in mathematics, the sixth part of a circle; **2**, a device for measuring angular distances, used esp. at sea for finding latitude and longitude.

sex-tet (sĕks-tĕt′), *n.* a musical composition for six performers; also, the six players or singers rendering such a composition. Also, **sex-tette′.**

sex-til-lion (sĕks-tĭl′yŭn), *n.* in the U. S. and France, a number expressed by a unit followed by 21 ciphers: in Great Britain, a unit followed by 36 ciphers.

sex-to-dec-i-mo (sĕks″tō-dĕs′ĭ-mō), *adj.* folded into 16 leaves, or 32 pages: said of a sheet of paper or of a book made of sheets thus folded:—*n.* [*pl.* sextodecimos (-mōz)], **1**, a sheet of paper folded into sixteen leaves; **2**, a book, pamphlet, or the like, made up of sheets folded in this way; **3**, the size of a book so made: usually written *16mo:* also called *sixteenmo.*

sex-ton (sĕks′tŭn), *n.* an under official, or janitor, of a church, whose duty it is to take care of the church building, attend to burials, etc.—*n.* **sex′ton-ship.**

sex-tu-ple (sĕks′tū-pl), *adj.* sixfold; multiplied by six.

sex-u-al (sĕk′shū-ăl), *adj.* **1**, pertaining to sex or the sexes; **2**, in biology, having sex.—*adv.* **sex′u-al-ly.**—*n.* **sex″u-al′i-ty.**

shab-by (shăb′ĭ), *adj.* [*comp.* shab′bi-er, *superl.* shab′bi-est], **1**, threadbare or worn, as clothes; **2**, poorly dressed; **3**, dilapidated; **4**, petty or unworthy; as, *shabby* behavior.—*adv.* **shab′bi-ly.**—*n.* **shab′bi-ness.**

shack (shăk), *n. Colloq.*, **1**, a shabby old house; hut; **2**, a log cabin.

shack-le (shăk′l), *n.* **1**, usually in *pl.*, anything that confines the arms or legs so as to prevent free action, as a strap or chain; a fetter; handcuff; **2**, hence, anything which restrains or prevents free action; **3**, any of various fastenings, as the U-shaped bow of a padlock:—*v.t.* [*p.t.* and *p.p.* -led (-ld), *p.pr.* -ling], **1**, to tie or confine so as to prevent free action; fetter; **2**, to embarrass or hinder; **3**, to unite or fasten, as with a strap or chain.

shad (shăd), *n.* a fish of the herring family, highly valued as food.

shad-bush (shăd′bo͝osh″), *n.* an American, white-flowered, tall shrub or small tree, bearing a red, edible, berrylike fruit: also called *service berry.*

shad-dock (shăd′ŭk), *n.* **1**, the fruit of a tropical citrus tree, characterized by a light yellow, bitter rind and an agreeable, acid pulp, as the grapefruit; **2**, any tree bearing such fruit.

shade (shād), *n.* **1**, partial darkness caused by cutting off rays of light; **2**, often in *pl.*, darkness; dimness; as, the *shades* of night; **3**, a spot not exposed to the sun; **4**, something which cuts off or softens the rays of light; specif., an adjustable screen or curtain fitting close to a window pane to regulate the light admitted; **5**, a special degree of color; as, this *shade* of blue is difficult to match; **6**, a slight degree of difference, as in meaning; **7**, a ghost or phantom:—*v.t.* [*p.t.* and *p.p.* shad′ed, *p.pr.* shad′ing], **1**, to screen from light or heat; **2**, to darken or make dim; **3**, to mark or paint with varying degrees of light or color; **4**, *Colloq.*, to slightly lower (the price):—*v.i.* to change by slight degrees; as, the sunset clouds *shade* from pale pink to deep purple.—*adj.* **shade′less.**

Syn., *n.* tint, hue. (See color.)

shad-ow (shăd′ō), *n.* **1**, partial darkness within certain limits; a darkened portion of space, representing in its outline the form of the body which intercepts or cuts off from it the rays of light; as, the *shadow* of a tree; **2**, hence, that which follows inseparably; a constant companion; **3**, often in *pl.*, the dark part of a picture; **4**, obscurity or darkness; **5**, protection or security; **6**, a reflected image; faint representation; **7**, small degree; as, not the *shadow* of a doubt:—*v.t.* **1**, to darken; cloud; **2**, to mark with degrees of light or color; **3**, to represent faintly; **4**, to attend closely; follow and watch, as a detective.—*n.* **shad′ow-er.**—*adj.* **shad′ow-less.**

shad-ow-y (shăd′ō-ĭ), *adj.* full of spots of darkness; obscure; sheltered from light or heat; dim; unreal; as, the *shadowy* past.—*n.* **shad′ow-i-ness.**

Sha-drach (shā′drăk), *n.* in the Bible, a Jewish captive in Babylon who, with Meshach and Abednego, survived the fiery furnace (Daniel 3).

shad-y (shād′ĭ), *adj.* [*comp.* shad′i-er, *superl.* shad′i-est], **1**, dim; obscure; partially darkened; **2**, sheltered from the glare of light or heat; **3**, pertaining to darkness; hence, *Colloq.*, unable to bear the light; questionable; of doubtful honesty; as, the deal was a *shady* transaction.—*adv.* **shad′i-ly.**—*n.* **shad′i-ness.**

shaft (shȧft), *n.* **1**, an arrow or its stem; **2**, anything shaped like an arrow, as the stalk of a plant or the handle of a golf club; **3**, the long, narrow entrance to a mine; **4**, the pole of a wagon or carriage; **5**, the narrow, vertical open space inside of a chimney; **6**, in an engine or machine, a bar to hold wheels or other rotating parts; **7**, a well-like space through which air and light reach the windows of a tenement or factory building; **8**, the body of a column between base and top; **9**, the open vertical space in which an elevator runs.

shag (shăg), *n.* **1**, a kind of tobacco; **2**, rough, woolly hair; **3**, a kind of cloth having a long, coarse nap; also, the nap itself:—*v.t.* [*p.t.* and *p.p.* shagged (shăgd), *p.pr.* shag′ging], to make shaggy; roughen:—*v.i.* to fall or hang in shaggy masses.

shag-bark (shăg′bärk″), *n.* a kind of white hickory, yielding the best commercial hickory nuts; the shellbark.

shag-gy (shăg′ĭ), *adj.* [*comp.* shag′gi-er, *superl.* shag′gi-est], **1**, rough with long hair or wool; as, a *shaggy* dog; **2**, unkempt; tangled, as hair; **3**, hence, overgrown with wild vegetation; scrubby.—*adv.* **shag′gi-ly.**—*n.* **shag′gi-ness.**

sha-green (shȧ-grēn′), *n.* **1**, a kind of grained leather, prepared without tanning from the skins of horses, camels, etc., and usually dyed green; **2**, a pressed leather imitating this; **3**, the rough skin of sharks and dogfishes, used for rasping and polishing:—*adj.* made of shagreen.

shah (shä), *n.* the title of the ruler of Persia, and of other Eastern countries.

shake (shāk), *v.t.* [*p.t.* shook (sho͝ok), *p.p.* shak′en (shāk′n), *p.pr.* shak′ing] **1**, to cause to shiver; move with a quick short motion; **2**, to move from a firm position; as, to *shake* one's faith; **3**, in music, to

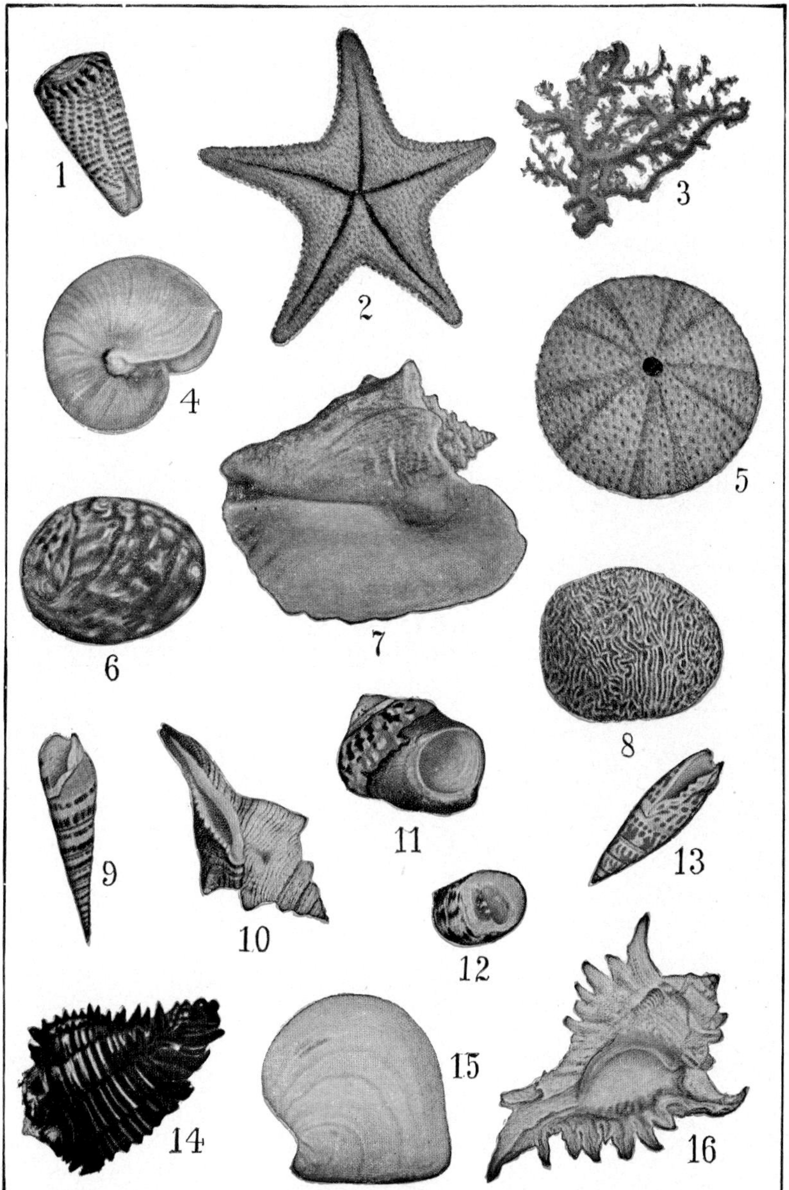

COMMON SEA SHELLS AND SKELETONS OF SEA ANIMALS

1. Spotted cone. 2. Giant sea star. 3. Rosy coral. 4. Pearly nautilus. 5. Sea urchin. 6. Red ear. 7. Giant conch. 8 Brain coral. 9. Marlin spike. 10. Trapeze shell. 11. Turk's cap. 12. Bleeding tooth. 13. Red spotted mitre. 14. Black rock shell. 15. Pearl oyster. 16. White rock shell.

give a quivering note to; trill; **4**, to loosen; remove: with *down*, *out*, etc.; as, to *shake* out a sail:—*v.i.* **1**, to tremble; quake; **2**, in music, to make a trill:—*n.* **1**, a shiver; **2**, a trill.

Syn., *v.* quiver, shiver, shudder. To *shake* is to move violently up and down, back and forth, or from side to side, with rapid, short motions. To *quiver* is to be stirred by a rapid, vibrating motion, as leaves in the breeze, flames in a draft. *Shiver* suggests a trembling, vibrating, momentary emotion, such as runs over the body from cold or terror. To *shudder* is to experience a kind of shivering, and implies loathing or repugnance; as, to *shudder* at the sight of a poisonous snake.

shake-down (shāk′doun″), *n.* **1**, a bed of straw, hay, or the like, shaken loosely on the ground; **2**, hence, any makeshift place for sleeping.

shak-er (shāk′ẽr), *n.* **1**, one who shakes; **2**, that with which, or from which, something is shaken; as, a salt *shaker*: **Shaker**, one of a religious celibate sect living in community settlements in the U. S.: so called from the motions of a religious dance in their worship.—*n.* **Shak′er-ism.**

Shake-spear-e-an (shāk-spēr′ē-ăn), *adj.* pertaining to, or like, William Shakespeare, or his works; as, a *Shakespearean* play. Also, **Shak-sper′e-an.**

shak-ing piece the cut of beef which is taken from the under side of the neck (see *beef*, illus.).

shak-o (shăk′ō), *n.* [*pl.* shakoes; shakos (-ōz)], a kind of high military cap.

shak-y (shāk′ĭ), *adj.* [*comp.* shak′i-er, *superl.* shak′i-est], **1**, not firmly supported; easily made to tremble; **2**, feeble; unsound; **3**, *Colloq.*: **a**, wavering; uncertain; embarrassed; **b**, of questionable solvency.—*adv.* **shak′i-ly.**—*n.* **shak′i-ness.**

shale (shāl), *n.* a rock of clayey origin, easily split into sheets.—*adj.* **shal′y.**

shall (shăl), *v.aux.* [*p.t.* should (shŏŏd); participles, imperative, and infinitive lacking: an auxiliary followed by the infinitive without *to*], **1**, am to, are to, etc.: used in the first person to express simple futurity, the second and third persons using *will*; as, I *shall* be 21 years old tomorrow; **2**, is to, are to; must: used in the second and third persons to express command, determination, threat, promise, permission, etc., on the part of the speaker; as, "Curfew *shall* not ring tonight."

shal-lop (shăl′ŭp), *n.* a small, light, open boat with sails or oars, or both.

shal-lot (shă-lŏt′), *n.* **1**, a small, onion-like vegetable; **2**, a small onion.

shal-low (shăl′ō), *adj.* **1**, not deep; **2**, having no mental depth; superficial; as, a *shallow* mind:—*n.* a place where the water is not deep; a shoal.—*adv.* **shal′low-ly.**—*n.* **shal′low-ness.**

shalt (shălt), the second person singular, present indicative, of *shall*: with *thou*.

sham (shăm), *n.* **1**, one who or that which deceives; a trick, fraud, or make-believe; **2**, a trimmed cover for the pillow of a bed, etc.:—*adj.* feigned; false; unreal:—*v.i.* [*p.t.* and *p.p.* shammed (shămd), *p.pr.* sham′ming], **1**, to make false pretenses; **2**, to trick; cheat:—*v.t.* **1**, to make a pretense of in order to deceive; feign; as, to *sham* death; **2**, to trick; delude; cheat.—*n.* **sham′mer.**

sham-ble (shăm′bl), *v.i.* [*p.t.* and *p.p.* -bled (-bld), *p.pr.* -bling], to walk awkwardly and waveringly; shuffle:—*n.* a shuffling gait.—*p.adj.* **sham′bling.**

sham-bles (shăm′blz), *n.pl.*, often used as *sing.*, **1**, a meat market; **2**, a slaughterhouse; **3**, any scene of carnage.

shame (shām), *n.* **1**, a painful feeling caused by the consciousness of wrongdoing, immodesty, or dishonor; **2**, that which causes a feeling of guilt; dishonor; disgrace; **3**, a reproof incurred because of wrongdoing; **4**, a restraining sense of modesty or decency:—*v.t.* [*p.t.* and *p.p.* shamed (shāmd), *p.pr.* sham′ing], **1**, to mortify; cause to blush; **2**, to disgrace, as one's family; **3**, to make (a person) do a thing through the sense of shame or disgrace: with *into* or *out of*.

Syn., *n.* humiliation, distress, chagrin.

shame-faced (shām′făst″), *adj.* bashful; showing embarrassment or shame.—*adv.* **shame′faced″ly** (shām′făst″lĭ; shām″fās′ĕd-lĭ).—*n.* **shame′faced″ness** (shām′făst″nĕs; shām″fās′ĕd-nĕs).

shame-ful (shām′fŏŏl), *adj.* **1**, causing disgrace; disgraceful; **2**, offensive to modesty; indecent.—*adv.* **shame′ful-ly.**—*n.* **shame′ful-ness.**

Syn. infamous, scandalous, outrageous.—*Ant.* praiseworthy, honorable, commendable.

shame-less (shām′lĕs), *adj.* **1**, without decency; brazen; **2**, marked by want of shame.—*adv.* **shame′less-ly.**—*n.* **shame′less-ness.**

sham-my (shăm′ĭ), *n.* [*pl.* shammies (-ĭz)], soft, flexible leather made from the skin of the chamois. Also, **cham′my** (shăm′ĭ); *Pfd. S.*, **cham′ois.**

sham-poo (shăm-pōō′), *v.t.* **1**, to cleanse and rub (the head), as with soap and water; **2**, to wash the head and hair of (a person):—*n.* **1**, the act of washing the head; **2**, a preparation used in washing the head.

sham-rock (shăm′rŏk), *n.* any one of several three-leaved plants, as the white clover, wood sorrel, etc.: the national emblem of Ireland.

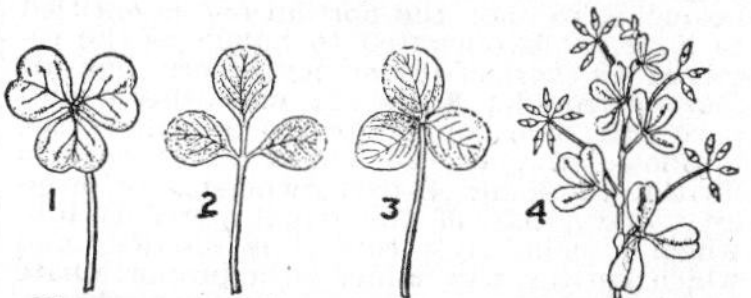

VARIETIES of SHAMROCK: 1, wood sorrel; 2, black medic; 3, white clover; 4, hop clover.

shang-hai (shăng-hī′), *v.t. Slang*, to drug and kidnap for service as a sailor, usually for money.

shank (shăngk), *n.* **1**, the leg; esp., the leg from the knee to the ankle in man, or a corresponding part in animals; **2**, in butchering, the lower part of the hind leg of beef cattle; **3**, the portion of a tool, implement, etc., between the cutting, or acting, part, and the part by which it is held, as the stem of a key, bit, or drill, or the central part of an anchor.

shan't (shânt; shănt), *Colloq.*, a contraction for *shall not*.

shan-ty (shăn′tĭ), *n.* [*pl.* shanties (-tĭz)], a rude shack.

shape (shāp), *n.* **1**, the form or figure of a person or thing; outline; contour; guise; external appearance; **2**, that which has form or figure, whether real or imaginary; a person or object indistinctly seen or imagined; a ghost; apparition; **3**, a pattern, as to guide a cutter; a mold; **4**, concrete or definite embodiment or form; as, to whip an idea into *shape*; **5**, way; description; manner; fashion; as, in no way, *shape*, or form; **6**, *Colloq.*, condition or state of being; as, his affairs were in bad *shape*:—*v.t.* [*p.t.* and *p.p.* shaped (shāpt), *p.pr.* shap′ing], **1**, to make into a certain form; mold; fashion; cut to certain specified measurements, as a garment; **2**, to adapt to a particular end; regulate; adjust: usually with *to*; **3**, to plan; devise; direct; **4**, to aim;

direct; as, to *shape* one's course east; **5,** to imagine; form a mental image of:—*v.i.* to develop; give signs of future form or fate.

shape-less (shāp′lĕs), *adj.* without definite contour; formless.—*adv.* **shape′less-ly.**—*n.* **shape′less-ness.**

shape-ly (shāp′lĭ), *adj.* [*comp.* shape′li-er, *superl.* shape′li-est], **1,** well-formed; pleasing in shape; **2,** symmetrical.—*n.* **shape′li-ness.**

shap-er (shāp′ẽr), *n.* one who or that which shapes; specif., a machine for planing metals, in which the work is stationary while the tool moves: **pillar shaper,** a shaping machine that is mounted on a pedestal.

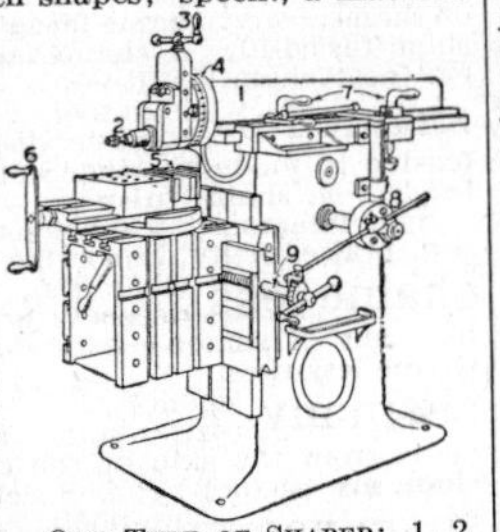

ONE TYPE OF SHAPER: 1, 2, ram, moving parallel to its length, and tool holder; 3, vertical feed; 4, head scale; 5, 6, chuck and handle; 7, stroke stops; 8, 9, cross-feed mechanism.

shard (shärd), *n.* **1,** a piece or fragment of brittle material, as earthenware; **2,** any hard, thin covering, as a shell; **3,** a wing cover, as of a beetle. Also, **sherd.**

[1]**share** (shâr), *n.* **1,** a certain portion or part allotted to an individual from a common lot; **2,** an equitable part given or belonging to one; the portion one is entitled to have, or is obligated to have; as, he received his *share* of the money; more than his *share* of trouble; **3,** the aid, enthusiasm, support, etc., one contributes to an enterprise, business, etc.; as, he had a large *share* in floating the loan; **4,** part ownership of property; esp., one of the equal portions into which a company's capital is divided, and which entitles the holder to a proportionate fraction of the earnings: **common shares,** shares which are entitled to dividends only in case there are profits left after payments to bondholders and on preferred shares: also called *common stock:* **deferred shares,** stocks on which a lower dividend or none will be paid until a specified date, or until some future requirements have been met: **preferred shares,** shares upon which a dividend must be paid before a dividend can be paid on common shares, and which, in case of bankruptcy, sometimes have a first claim on the assets of the concern: also called *preferred stock:*—*v.t.* [*p.t.* and *p.p.* shared (shârd), *p.pr.* shar′ing], **1,** to give away a part of; divide and distribute; apportion; **2,** to possess in common; partake of, experience, enjoy, or suffer, with others:—*v.i.* to participate in something: often with *in.*—*n.* **shar′er.**

[2]**share** (shâr), *n.* **1,** the part of a plow which turns over the earth and makes the furrows and ridges; the blade: also called *plowshare;* **2,** the blade of any of various other agricultural machines.

share-hold-er (shâr′hōl″dẽr), *n.* one who owns one or more parts, or shares, of a property, as a railway.

shark (shärk), *n.* **1,** any of various large, voracious fishes with sharp teeth; **2,** *Colloq.,* a dishonest, swindling fellow; a cheat.

sharp (shärp), *adj.* **1,** having a very thin, fine edge, as a knife; **2,** ending in a fine point; not blunt, as a needle; **3,** well-defined; distinct; as, *sharp* features; **4,** angular; abrupt; making an acute angle; as, a *sharp* bend in the road; **5,** quick; keen; alert; as, a *sharp* eye; also, clever; shrewd; intelligent; **6,** close in dealing; hence, dishonest; unscrupulous; as, a *sharp* dealer; **7,** severe; intense; as, a *sharp* pain; also, violent; fierce; as, a *sharp* struggle; **8,** piercing; shrill; penetrating; as, a *sharp* sound; **9,** acid; sour; tart; as, a *sharp* taste; **10,** sarcastic; caustic; bitter; as, a *sharp* reproof; **11,** in music: **a,** raised a half step in pitch; **b,** above true pitch; **12,** in phonetics, uttered without voice; hard; surd: said of the voiceless consonants, *f, h, k, p, s,* and *t:*—*adv.* **1,** in music, slightly above true pitch; **2,** *Colloq.,* promptly; precisely; as, six o'clock *sharp:*—*n.* **1,** in music: **a,** a tone or note raised a half step in pitch; **b,** a character [♯] on a degree of the staff, indicating that the notes on that degree represent tones a half step higher than those normally indicated thereon; **2,** in phonetics, a voiceless consonant: **double sharp,** in music, a sign [✕ or ※] placed before a note to indicate that the tone desired is a whole step higher than the note itself:—*v.t.* **1,** to sharpen; **2,** in music: **a,** to make higher in pitch by a half step; **b,** to mark with a sharp [♯]:—*v.i.* in music, to sing or play above the correct pitch.—*adv.* **sharp′ly.**—*n.* **sharp′ness.**

sharp-en (shär′pn), *v.t.* to make sharp or sharper; give point or keenness to:—*v.i.* to become sharp.—*n.* **sharp′en-er.**

sharp-er (shär′pẽr), *n.* **1,** one who drives a close bargain; **2,** hence, a cheat.

sharp-shoot-er (shärp′shōōt″ẽr), *n.* one expert in shooting, esp. with a rifle; a skilled marksman.

sharp–sight-ed (shärp′=sīt″ĕd), *adj.* having keen sight.

sharp–wit-ted (shärp′=wĭt″ĕd), *adj.* mentally alert; discerning; intelligent; as, a *sharp-witted* lawyer.

shat-ter (shăt′ẽr), *v.t.* **1,** to break at once into many pieces; smash; **2,** to derange or disorder, as the mind; destroy the health or power of, as the body; **3,** to defeat; ruin; as, to *shatter* hopes:—*v.i.* to fly into splinters or pieces.—*adj.* **shat′ter-y.**

shave (shāv), *v.t.* [*p.t.* shaved (shāvd), *p.p.* shaved or shav′en (shāv′n), *p.pr.* shav′ing], **1,** to cut or pare off with a razor or other instrument having a sharp edge; remove (hair) from the face or head with a razor; **2,** to cut in thin slices; **3,** to skim along the surface of; **4,** to plunder or fleece:—*v.i.* **1,** to use the razor to remove hair; **2,** to cut closely; pare the surface of anything; **3,** hence, to practice cheating; drive a hard bargain:—*n.* **1,** a thin slice; **2,** the act or operation of removing hair with a razor; **3,** any of various woodworking instruments for paring or smoothing the surface of wood; **4,** *Colloq.,* a short time or distance; also, a narrow escape; as, a close *shave*

shave-ling (shāv′lĭng), *n. Archaic,* **1,** a shaven person; **2,** esp., a priest or monk: often used contemptuously.

shav-er (shāv′ẽr), *n.* **1,** one who or that which shaves; a barber; **2,** one who is close in bargains; **3,** *Colloq.,* a boy; lad

shav-ing (shāv′ĭng), *n.* **1,** the act of one who pares, cuts off, etc.; **2,** a thin slice pared off, as from a plank or board

shawl (shôl), *n.* a wrap or scarf made of a square or oblong piece of cloth, used as a loose outer covering for the shoulders.

Shaw-nee (shô-nē′), *n.* one of a tribe of American Indians, former[ly] living in what is now Georgia.

shay (shā), *n. Dial.* or *Colloq.,* a chaise as, the one-horse *shay.*

she (shē), *fem. pron.* of third person [*no* she, *poss.* her (hûr), hers (hûrz), *obj.* h[er] *pl. nom.* they (*th*ā), *poss.* their (*th*âr), the[irs] (*th*ârz), *obj.* them (*th*ĕm)], a previously des[ignated]

nated female, or object thought of as female: —*n.* [*pl.* often shes (shēz)], any girl or woman.

sheaf (shēf), *n.* [*pl.* sheaves (shēvz)], **1,** a quantity of cut grain bound together; **2,** any bundle, as of enough arrows to fill a quiver:—*v.t.* to gather and bind into bundles, as grain or straw.

shear (shēr), *v.t.* [*p.t.* sheared (shērd) or, *Archaic*, shore (shōr), *p.p.* sheared or shorn (shōrn), *p.pr.* shear′ing], **1,** to cut, esp. with large scissors, shears, or the like: clip; as, to *shear* a fleece; **2,** to cut or clip something from; as, to *shear* sheep; **3,** hence, to fleece; strip bare; cheat:—*v.i.* to use cutting or clipping scissors, shears, or the like: —*n.* a machine for cutting or clipping metal.—*n.* **shear′er.**

shears (shērz), *n.pl.* **1,** any of various large cutting instruments or machines working in a way similar to scissors, by the crossing of opposed cutting blades or edges; **2,** anything resembling large scissors; **3,** the ways or tracks of a lathe; **4,** a kind of hoisting appliance provided with tackle blocks.

shear-wa-ter (shēr′wô″tēr), *n.* any of various long-winged sea birds related to the petrels.

sheath (shēth), *n.* [*pl.* sheaths (shēthz)], **1,** a case for a sword or knife; a scabbard; **2,** any covering inclosing a part or organ.

sheathe (shēth), *v.t.* [*p.t.* and *p.p.* sheathed (shēthd), *p.pr.* sheath′ing], **1,** to put into, furnish, or cover with, a case, as a sword; **2,** incase with a protecting covering; as, to *sheathe* a ship's hull with copper; **3,** to conceal, as in a case or sheath.

sheath-ing (shēth′ĭng), *n.* **1,** that which incases, covers, or protects; esp., the copper casing on a ship's hull or the protective boarding on the outside of a frame house (see *frame house*, illus.); **2,** the act of one who sheathes.

[1]**sheave** (shēv), *n.* a grooved wheel turning in a frame and used, with a rope, for raising weights: also called *pulley*.

[2]**sheave** (shēv), *v.t.* [*p.t.* and *p.p.* sheaved (shēvd), *p.pr.* sheav′ing], to gather and bind into bundles, as grain; make into sheaves.

[1]**shed** (shĕd), *v.t.* [*p.t.* and *p.p.* shed, *p.pr.* shed′ding], **1,** to pour out; pour forth; as, to *shed* tears; the sun *sheds* light; **2,** to cause to flow; as, to *shed* blood; **3,** to cause to flow off without sinking in; as, oilskins *shed* water; **4,** to cast away; let fall; as, birds *shed* their feathers; trees *shed* leaves:—*v.i.* **1,** to cast, part with, or let fall, a covering, seed, etc.; **2,** to throw off a natural covering, as scales, hair, etc.:—*n.* **1,** that which turns off or sheds: used chiefly in composition; as, a water*shed;* **2,** the act of pouring forth: used only in composition; as, blood*shed*.

[2]**shed** (shĕd), *n.* **1,** a small building used for sheltering animals, farm implements, etc., or for storing supplies, as wood; **2,** a small, rude cabin.

sheen (shēn), *n.* brightness; splendor; luster.—*adj.* **sheen′y.**

sheep (shēp), *n.* [*pl.* sheep], **1,** any of various timid, cud-chewing animals valued for their wool and edible flesh; **2,** a bashful fellow; **3,** leather made of sheepskin.

sheep-fold (shēp′fōld″), *n.* a pen or place where sheep are kept.

sheep-ish (shēp′ĭsh), *adj.* **1,** shrinking; awkwardly bashful; **2,** foolish. —*adv.* **sheep′ish-ly.**—*n.* **sheep′ish-ness.**

sheep's eye usually in *pl.*, a bashful or, more commonly, a loving glance. Also, **sheep's-eye″.**

sheep-shank (shēp′shăngk″), *n.* a kind of knot for temporarily shortening a rope (see *knot*, illus.).

sheeps-head (shēps′hĕd″), *n.* a valued food fish of the Atlantic coast of the United States.

sheep-skin (shēp′skĭn″), *n.* **1,** the skin of a sheep, or anything, as leather or parchment, made from it; **2,** *Slang*, a graduation diploma.

[1]**sheer** (shēr), *adj.* **1,** pure; utter; absolute; as, *sheer* folly; **2,** very thin or transparent: said of fabrics; as, *sheer* lace; **3,** straight up and down; vertical; steep; as, a *sheer* precipice:—*adv.* **1,** perpendicularly; straight; **2,** quite; completely.—*adv.* **sheer′ly.** —*n.* **sheer′ness.**

[2]**sheer** (shēr), *v.i.* to turn from the proper course, as a ship; slope away in another direction, as a road:—*n.* **1,** a curving course; **2,** a deviation or change in the course of a vessel; **3,** the upward slope of the deck and lines of a ship toward the bow and stern.

sheet (shēt), *n.* **1,** a large, broad, thin piece of any substance, as paper, cloth, etc.; **2,** a broad piece of linen or cotton to cover a bed; **3,** a single piece of paper of any of various sizes; **4,** a newspaper; **5,** a broad expanse or surface; as, a *sheet* of water; **6,** a rope attached to a sail to regulate it; **7,** in *pl.*, the leaves of a book before binding.

sheet an-chor **1,** a large, very heavy anchor, for use in emergency; **2,** hence, a sure reliance or refuge.

sheet-ing (shēt′ĭng), *n.* **1,** the act of spreading out or forming into sheets; **2,** material for making sheets for beds.

sheik (shēk; shāk), *n.* **1,** the chief, or head, of an Arab family, tribe, or clan; **2,** the chief magistrate of an Arab village; **3,** *U. S. Slang:* **a,** a masterful lover; **b,** a ladies' man. Also, **sheikh.**

shek-el (shĕk′l), *n.* **1,** an ancient Hebrew coin; **2,** in *pl.*, *Slang*, money.

She-ki-nah (shē-kī′nȧ), *n.* the Jewish name for the Divine Presence, or a symbol of the Divine Presence, as the light which rested on the tabernacle.

shel-drake (shĕl′drāk″), *n.* **1,** any of several fish-eating birds of the Old World which resemble geese; **2,** any of several American fish-eating ducks.

shelf (shĕlf), *n.* [*pl.* shelves (shĕlvz)], **1,** a flat ledge or board for holding things, usually long and narrow and set horizontally, as into a wall, bookcase, or cupboard; **2,** something resembling a shelf, as a sand bank; **3,** a flat, projecting ledge of rock.

shell (shĕl), *n.* **1,** a hard outside case or covering, as on a fruit, egg, nut, seed, crab, etc.; a husk, as on corn; **2,** the covering of a tortoise, used for manufacturing various articles; **3,** a framework; skeleton; **4,** a very light, long, narrow racing boat; **5,** a cartridge case to hold ammunition for breech-loading small arms; **6,** [*pl.* shell], a metal projectile filled with explosive, for use in a cannon or mortar:—*v.t.* **1,** to take out of the outside covering, as peas from the pod; **2,** to separate from the cob, as corn; **3,** to bombard, as a stronghold:—*v.i.* **1,** to cast or throw off the husk; **2,** to fall off, as a crust or shell.

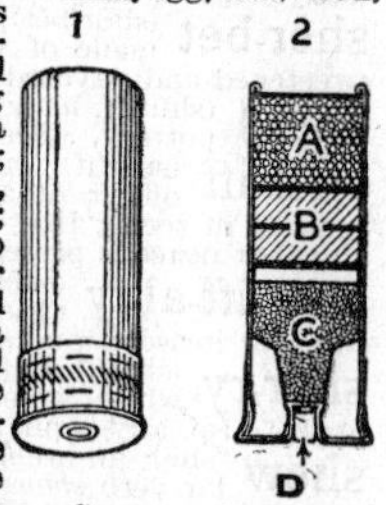

SHOTGUN SHELL

1, outside view; 2, cross section: A, shot; B, wads; C, powder charge; D, firing cap.

shel-lac (shĕ-lăk′; shĕl′ăk), *n.* **1,** a sticky substance secreted by certain scale insects, and used in making sealing wax, varnish, etc.: called *lac* in the crude form; **2**, a solution of dry shellac, esp. in alcohol, used as a varnish:—*v.t.* [*p.t.* and *p.p.* -lacked′ (-lăkt′), *p.pr.* -lack′ing], to coat or treat with this substance. Also, *n.* **shel-lack′; shell″-lac′.**

shell-bark (shĕl′bärk″), *n.* any of several kinds of rough-barked hickory; the shagbark.

shell-fish (shĕl′fĭsh″), *n.* an invertebrate water animal having a shell, as a clam, lobster, mollusk, etc.

shell shock mental disorder caused by the violent sights and sounds, and other horrors, of war.

shell-y (shĕl′ĭ), *adj.* **1**, of, pertaining to, or like, a shell; **2**, full of, abounding in, or consisting of, shells; as, a *shelly* beach.

shel-ter (shĕl′tẽr), *n.* **1**, a place which protects, covers, or shields; refuge; place of protection, esp. from the weather; house; cabin; **2**, the state of being protected, covered, or shielded; safety:—*v.t.* to protect or shield from injury or violence; place in safety; conceal:—*v.i.* to take refuge; cover oneself.—*n.* **shel′ter-er.**—*adj.* **shel′ter-less.**

[1]**shelve** (shĕlv), *v.t.* [*p.t.* and *p.p.* shelved (shĕlvd), *p.pr.* shelv′ing], **1**, to place on a shelf; **2**, hence, to dismiss from service; as, to *shelve* an officer; also, to postpone indefinitely; **3**, to furnish with shelves.

[2]**shelve** (shĕlv), *v.i.* [*p.t.* and *p.p.* shelved (shĕlvd), *p.pr.* shelv′ing], to incline gradually; slope; as, the bottom *shelves* from the shore.—*adj.* **shelv′y.**

Shem (shĕm), *n.* in the Bible, Noah's eldest son.

Shem-ite (shĕm′īt), *n.* a member of a race including the Jews, Arabs, ancient Assyrians, Babylonians, etc. Also, **Sem′ite,** *Pfd.S.*—*adj.* **Shem-it′ic.**

She-ol (shē′ōl), *n.* **1**, among the Hebrews, the place of departed spirits; Hades; **2**, the grave.

shep-herd (shĕp′ẽrd), *n.* **1**, one who tends sheep; **2**, a pastor:—*v.t.* to tend, as sheep; lead.—*n.fem.* **shep′herd-ess.**

shep-herd's–purse (shĕp′ẽrdz-pûrs″), *n.* an annual weed akin to mustard and cress, bearing white flowers and notched triangular pods.

Sher-a-ton (shĕr′ȧ-tŏn), *adj.* designating a style of English furniture of the 18th century, designed chiefly by Thomas Sheraton (1751–1806), and characterized by straight lines and light, simple construction (see *furniture*, illus.).—*adj.* **Sher″a-to′ni-an.**

sher-bet (shûr′bĕt), *n.* **1**, a cooling drink made of water and fruit juices sweetened and flavored; **2**, a water ice.

sherd (shûrd), *n.* a fragment or piece of pottery. See **shard,** *Pfd. S.*

sher-iff (shĕr′ĭf), *n.* the chief executive officer of a county, whose duty consists in seeing that the law is carried out and that peace is preserved.

sher-iff-al-ty (shĕr′ĭf-ăl-tĭ), *n.* [*pl.* sheriffalties (-tĭz)], the office, term, or jurisdiction, of a sheriff.

sher-ry (shĕr′ĭ), *n.* [*pl.* sherries (-ĭz)], a dry white wine, made in Andalusia, Spain; also, any similar wine.

shew (shō), an archaic form of the irregular verb *show*.

shew-bread (shō′brĕd″), *n.* in the ancient Jewish ritual, the unleavened bread placed in the sanctuary (Exodus 25:30). Also, **show′bread″.**

shib-bo-leth (shĭb′ō-lĕth), *n.* **1**, in the Bible, a Hebrew word used by Jephthah to distinguish his own men from the fleeing enemies who were not able to pronounce *sh* (Judges 12); **2**, hence, the password of a secret society, or the test or watchword of a party; a party phrase or slogan.

shied (shīd), past tense and past participle of the verb *shy*.

shield (shēld), *n.* **1**, one who or anything which defends or protects; a defender; defense; protection; **2**, a broad piece of armor, usually carried on the left arm to protect the body in fighting; a large buckler; **3**, in heraldry, the field upon which emblems or coats of arms are represented; **4**, a screen of steel to protect guns and the men who operate them:—*v.t.* to protect with, or as with, a protecting or sheltering screen; defend.

shift (shĭft), *n.* **1**, a turning from one thing to another; change; substitution; **2**, an expedient; as, to make one's way by *shifts;* **3**, hence, a trick, dodge, or evasion; **4**, the change of one set of workmen for another; also, either set of workmen, or its working time; as, the night *shift;* **5**, a change of clothes; hence, formerly, a chemise: —*v.t.* **1**, to change the place of; transfer; as, to *shift* the blame; **2**, to exchange; substitute; **3**, to vary in form:—*v.i.* **1**, to change position, as the wind; **2**, to manage; to live; contrive; as, to *shift* for oneself; **3**, to practice evasions.—*n.* **shift′er.**

shift-less (shĭft′lĕs), *adj.* **1**, lacking in energy; without resource; **2**, lazy; thriftless; taking no thought for the future; **3**, badly done; as, *shiftless* work.—*adv.* **shift′-less-ly.**—*n.* **shift′less-ness.**

shift-y (shĭf′tĭ), *adj.* [*comp.* shift′i-er, *superl.* shift′i-est], **1**, capable of turning things or circumstances to good advantage; **2**, hence, tricky; evasive.—*n.* **shift′i-ness.**

shil-la-lah (shĭ-lā′lȧ), *n.* a stout, oaken cudgel; a heavy club. Also, **shil-le′lah; shil-le′lagh.**

shil-ling (shĭl′ĭng), *n.* a British silver coin, worth about 24 cents.

shil-ly–shal-ly (shĭl′ĭ-shăl″ĭ), *adv.* in a hesitating manner; irresolutely:—*v.i.* [*p.t.* and *p.p.* -lied (-ĭd), *p.pr.* -ly-ing], to hesitate; trifle; be irresolute:—*n.* trifling; weak indecision:—*adj.* irresolute.

shi-ly (shī′lĭ), *adv.* timidly; bashfully; watchfully. Also, **shy′ly,** *Pfd. S.*

shim-mer (shĭm′ẽr), *v.i.* to shine waveringly; flicker:—*n.* **1**, a tremulous gleam; flicker; **2**, gloss; sheen.

shim-my (shĭm′ĭ), *v.i.* [*p.t.* and *p.p.* -mied (-mĭd), *p.pr.* -my-ing], to shake:—*n.* a shaking motion, esp. from side to side.

shin (shĭn), *n.* the front part of the leg between the ankle and knee; shank:—*v.i.* [*p.t.* and *p.p.* shinned (shĭnd), *p.pr.* shin′-ning], to climb a tree by alternately gripping the trunk with the arms and legs: usually with *up:*—*v.t.* to climb, as a tree, with alternate movements of the arms and legs.

shin-dy (shĭn′dĭ), *n.* [*pl.* shindies (-dĭz)], *Slang,* an uproar; a spree; row.

shine (shīn), *v.i.* [*p.t.* and *p.p.* shone (shōn; shŏn), *p.pr.* shin′ing], **1**, to emit or give out rays of light; beam; be bright; **2**, to be noted or prominent:—*v.t.* [*p.t.* and *p.p.* shined (shīnd)], *Colloq.,* to cause to glisten; polish:—*n.* **1**, luster; sheen; **2**, illumination; **3**, sunshine; bright weather; as, rain or *shine;* **4**, *Colloq.,* a polish given to shoes; **5**, *Slang:* **a**, a liking; **b**, a caper.

shin-er (shīn′ẽr), *n.* **1**, one who or that which shows or causes brightness; **2**, a kind of small fish.

[1]**shin-gle** (shĭng′gl), *n.* **1**, one of the thin oblong pieces of wood, slate, or the like, used in overlapping rows for roofing and siding; **2**, a style of hair cut in which the hair at the back of the head lies in overlapping rows; **3**, *Humorous* and *Colloq.,* a signboard as of a doctor's office:—*v.t.* [*p.t.* and *p.p.* -gled (-gld), *p.pr.* -gling], **1**, to cover, as a roof, with

thin overlapping pieces of wood or other material; **2**, to cut (the hair) short in overlapping rows along the back of the head.—*n.* **shin′gler.**

[2]**shin-gle** (shĭng′gl), *n.* **1**, pebbles worn smooth by water; rounded seashore pebbles; **2**, a beach.—*adj.* **shin′gly.**

shin-gles (shĭng′glz), *n. pl.* used as *sing.* an acute inflammatory disease of the skin, characterized by groups of small blisters and accompanied by severe pain or intense itching.

shin-ing (shīn′ĭng), *p.adj.* **1**, giving light; radiant; **2**, distinguished; as, a *shining* instance of bravery.—*adv.* **shin′ing-ly.**
Syn. luminous, brilliant. (See bright.)

shin-ny (shĭn′ĭ), *n.* [*pl.* shinnies (-ĭz)], **1**, the game of hockey; **2**, the stick used in playing hockey.

shin-plas-ter (shĭn′plȧs″tẽr), *n.* **1**, a medicated fabric for use on a sore or injured shin; **2**, *U. S. Slang*, formerly, a piece of paper money of a denomination less than a dollar; also, a piece of paper money so depreciated in value as to be practically worthless.

Shin-to (shĭn′tō″), *n.* the primitive religion of the Japanese, having as its important features sacrifice to, and worship of, dead heroes and ancestors.—*n.* **Shin′to-ism.**—*n.* **Shin′to-ist.**

shin-y (shīn′ĭ), *adj.* [*comp.* shin′i-er, *superl.* shin′i-est], **1**, diffusing, or giving off, light; bright; cloudless; **2**, polished; glossy.

ship (shĭp), *n.* **1**, any large seagoing vessel; **2**, esp., a sailing vessel with three, four, or five square-rigged masts (see illus. page 659):—*v.t.* [*p.t.* and *p.p.* shipped (shĭpt), *p.pr.* ship′ping], **1**, to place on board a vessel; **2**, to carry or transport by water; **3**, to send through any regular channel of transportation, as by rail; **4**, to put in the proper place or position, as oars; **5**, to hire for service on a ship, as sailors; **6**, *Colloq.*, to get rid of: **ship a sea**, to have the waves break over the decks:—*v.i.* **1**, to engage oneself for service on a vessel, as a sailor; **2**, to embark on a ship.

-ship (-shĭp), *n. suffix*, **1**, state or quality of being: attached to adjectives; as, hard*ship;* or to nouns; as, friend*ship;* **2**, office, dignity, or profession; as, governor*ship;* **3**, art or skill; as, horseman*ship.*

ship bis-cuit coarse, hard biscuit made for use on shipboard.

ship-board (shĭp′bōrd″), *n.* the side or deck of a ship; hence, a ship.

ship-build-er (shĭp′bĭl″dẽr), *n.* one who designs or constructs ships.—*n.* **ship′build″ing.**

ship-mas-ter (shĭp′mȧs″tẽr), *n.* the master of a merchant ship, or of any ship other than a war vessel.

ship-ment (shĭp′mĕnt), *n.* **1**, the act of sending goods for transportation; **2**, the consignment of goods.

ship-per (shĭp′ẽr), *n.* one who sends goods to be transported.

ship-ping (shĭp′ĭng), *n.* **1**, the act or business of one who sends goods to be moved; **2**, ships collectively; tonnage.

ship-shape (shĭp′shāp″), *adj.* in good order:—*adv.* neatly.

ship-worm (shĭp′wûrm″), *n.* any of several wormlike mollusks that bore into ship timbers, wharf piles, etc.

ship-wreck (shĭp′rĕk″), *n.* **1**, the destruction of a ship by disaster at sea, or by grounding; **2**, a wrecked ship; **3**, utter ruin; as, the *shipwreck* of hopes:—*v.t.* **1**, to cause to suffer shipwreck; **2**, to ruin.

ship-wright (shĭp′rīt″), *n.* one who builds or repairs vessels.

ship-yard (shĭp′yärd″), *n.* a place where ships are built or repaired.

shire (shīr; shēr), *n.* **1**, in England, a district, province, or county; **2**, esp., a division of English territory for governmental purposes, usually the same as a county.

shirk (shûrk), *v.t.* and *v.i.* **1**, to neglect purposely; **2**, to get out of the doing of; avoid:—*n.* one who purposely neglects or evades work or obligation.—*n.* **shirk′er.**

shirr (shûr), *n.* **1**, a puckering produced in a fabric by means of parallel gathers; **2**, the series of parallel running stitches by which the material can be fulled:—*v.t.* **1**, to draw up (cloth) by gathering on such stitches; **2**, in cooking, to bake (eggs), as in cream.

shirt (shûrt), *n.* **1**, a man's sleeved blouse, usually worn under a coat; **2**, a woman's mannish blouse; **3**, an undergarment.

shirt-ing (shûrt′ĭng), *n.* any of various materials suitable for making outer shirts and blouses.

shit-tim wood (shĭt′ĭm), in the Bible, a hard, tough wood susceptible of a fine polish, of which the ark, altars, etc., of the Jewish tabernacle were constructed (Exodus 37: 4, 10, 25): also called *shittim.* Also, *n.* **shit′tim-wood″.**

Shi-va (shē′vȧ), *n.* the third member of the Hindu trinity. See **Si′va**, *Pfd. S.*

[1]**shiv-er** (shĭv′ẽr), *v.i.* to tremble, as from cold or fright; quiver; shake:—*n.* **1**, the act of trembling or shaking from cold, fear, or the like; **2**, a shake or quiver.
Syn., v. shudder. (See shake.)

[2]**shiv-er** (shĭv′ẽr), *v.i.* and *v.t.* to break, or cause to break, into small pieces; shatter; splinter:—*n.* a small fragment splintered off by a fall or blow; a sliver.

shiv-er-y (shĭv′ẽr-ĭ), *adj.* **1**, tremulous; shaking; **2**, causing shivers; **3**, given to shivering; **4**, slightly cold or chilly.

[1]**shoal** (shōl), *n.* a large company; multitude, esp. of fishes; school:—*v.i.* to throng or run together in a school, as fish.
Syn., n. crowd. (See herd.)

[2]**shoal** (shōl), *adj.* of little depth; shallow; as, *shoal* water:—*n.* **1**, a shallow place in any body of water; a shallow; **2**, a sand bank or bar which shows only at low tide; **3**, hence, a hidden or unexpected danger:—*v.i.* to grow shallow; as, the water *shoals:*—*v.t.* to make shallow.—*adj.* **shoal′y.**—*n.* **shoal′i-ness.**

shoat (shōt), *n.* **1**, a young hog; **2**, a lazy, shiftless fellow. Also, **shote**, *Pfd. S.*

[1]**shock** (shŏk), *n.* **1**, a forcible blow; impact; violent jar; as, the *shock* of an earthquake; **2**, an unexpected and violent jarring of the feelings, mind, etc.; **3**, the passage of an electric current through the body; also, the involuntary contractions and other nervous phenomena accompanying such passage; **4**, a sudden depression in vitality, or a state of prostration following a severe physical or mental strain; **5**, a sudden and unexpected disturbance in a business, caused by unusual conditions; **6**, *Colloq.*, a stroke of paralysis: **shock absorber**, **1**, in an automobile, a device to check the rebound of the springs caused by rough places on the road; **2**, in an airplane, a device to lessen the jar when alighting:—*v.t.* **1**, to cause to shake; jar; strike against suddenly and violently; **2**, to strike with surprise, horror, disgust, etc.; **3**, to subject (a human or animal body) to the passage of an electric current:—*v.i.* to receive a shock, either mental or physical; as, she *shocks* easily.—*n.* [1]**shock′er.**

[2]**shock** (shŏk), *n.* a stack of sheaves of grain set upright together in a field:—*v.t.* to collect, as sheaves of grain, and stack:—*v.i.* to place in shocks.—*n.* [2]**shock′er.**

[3]**shock** (shŏk), *n.* **1**, a bushy, tangled mass, as of hair; **2**, a kind of long-haired dog; poodle.

shock-ing (shŏk′ĭng), *p.adj.* **1**, causing to shake or tremble, as by a blow; **2**, causing disturbance of the feelings; as, *shocking* news; **3**, extremely offensive or disgusting; as, he used *shocking* language.—*adv.* **shock′ing-ly.**—*n.* **shock′ing-ness.**

shod (shŏd), past tense and past participle of the irregular verb *shoe.*

shod-dy (shŏd′ĭ), *n.* [*pl.* shoddies (-ĭz)], **1**, the refuse fibers from carding or weaving wool; **2**, an inferior material made by picking apart waste cotton or woolen fabrics, with or without other materials; **3**, rubbish; waste:—*adj.* [*comp.* shod′di-er, *superl.* shod′di-est], **1**, made of such inferior material; inferior in grade; **2**, *Colloq.*, not genuine; sham.

shoe (shōō), *n.* [*pl.* shoes (shōōz) or, *Obs.*, *Archaic,* or *Dial.*, shoon (shōōn)], **1**, the ordinary outer covering for the human foot, made of leather, suède, satin, etc.; **2**, a U-shaped metal bar nailed on an animal's hoof; **3**, something resembling a shoe in form, use, or position, as the strip of steel fastened on the runners of a sleigh, the part of a brake that presses against a wheel (see *locomotive,* illus.), or the outer covering of a pneumatic automobile tire:—*v.t.* [*p.t.* and *p.p.* shod (shŏd), *p.pr.* shoe′ing], **1**, to furnish with a shoe or shoes, as a horse; **2**, to protect, strengthen, or ornament, by adding harder material; as, to *shoe* a wooden pole with iron.

shoe-horn (shōō′hôrn″), *n.* a curved, smooth piece of metal or other material, to aid in putting on a shoe.

shoe-mak-er (shōō′māk″ẽr), *n.* one whose business it is to make or mend shoes.—*n.* **shoe′mak″ing.**

sho-er (shōō′ẽr), *n.* one who supplies or puts on shoes; as, a *shoer* of horses.

sho-gun (shō′gōōn″), *n.* the hereditary military governor of Japan, who usurped many of the powers of the Mikado until the revolution of 1867–68, when the Mikado was restored to power.

shone (shōn; shŏn), past tense and past participle of the verb *shine.*

shoo (shōō), *v.t.* and *v.i.* to scare away (fowls); drive by a cry of "shoo":—*interj.* be off! used esp. to fowls.

¹shook (shŏŏk), the past tense of the irregular verb *shake,* which see.

²shook (shŏŏk), *n.* **1**, a set of barrel staves and headings sufficient in number for one cask, barrel, etc.; **2**, a set of boards, rails, rods, or the like, ready to be assembled to make some object, as a box or a chair.

shoot (shōōt), *v.t.* [*p.t.* and *p.p.* shot (shŏt), *p.pr.* shoot′ing], **1**, to let fly, send out, or discharge with sudden force, as an arrow; emit, as rays; **2**, to strike, kill, or wound with a missile discharged from a gun; **3**, to fire off or discharge (a weapon); **4**, to cause to grow forth; as, the trees *shot* forth their leaves; **5**, to stick out: usually with *out;* **6**, to pass rapidly through, over, or under; as, to *shoot* a rapid; **7**, to variegate with different colors or tints; as, a sky *shot* with crimson:—*v.i.* **1**, to protrude or project; **2**, to rush or flash along swiftly; as, the meteor *shot* through the sky; **3**, to bud; sprout; **4**, to grow or develop; **5**, to dart or pierce, as a pain; **6**, to discharge a missile from a gun; cause a gun, bow, etc., to discharge a missile; **7**, to be emitted in flashes, as light:—*n.* **1**, a young branch or growth; **2**, a passage or trough through which things are carried by gravity; **3**, a shooting match; a hunt.—*n.* **shoot′er.**

shoot-ing star a small body of the solar system heated to incandescence by friction in passing through the earth's atmosphere; meteor.

shop (shŏp), *n.* **1**, a room or building where goods are sold at retail; a store; **2**, a place where mechanics carry on their trade; also, usually in *pl.*, a factory; **3**, *Colloq.*, one's own business as a subject of conversation; as, to talk *shop:*—*v.i.* [*p.t.* and *p.p.* shopped (shŏpt), *p.pr.* shop′ping], to visit stores to look over or purchase goods.—*n.* **shop′per.**—*n.* and *p.adj.* **shop′ping.**

shop-keep-er (shŏp′kēp″ẽr), *n.* one who sells goods at retail in a store; a retailer; tradesman.

shop-lift-ing (shŏp′lĭf″tĭng), *n.* the theft of goods from a shop or store under pretense of inspection or purchase.—*n.* **shop′lift″er.**

shop-worn (shŏp′wōrn″), *adj.* soiled or worn from having been kept a long time in stock in a shop.

¹shore (shōr), *n.* the land bordering on a large body of water, as on the sea, a lake, or a river:—*v.t.* [*p.t.* and *p.p.* shored (shōrd), *p.pr.* shor′ing], to set on shore, as goods.

Syn., n. (see border).

²shore (shōr), *n.* a prop or support set obliquely as a temporary support against or beneath a ship, wall, etc.:—*v.t.* [*p.t.* and *p.p.* shored (shōrd), *p.pr.* shor′ing], to support, steady, or hold by a prop, as a ship; usually with *up.*

shore-less (shōr′lĕs), *adj.* having no shore; boundless.

shorn (shōrn), past participle of the irregular verb *shear.*

short (shôrt), *adj.* **1**, brief in time; as, a *short* vacation; **2**, not long; limited from end to end; as, a *short* piece of string; **3**, not measuring up to the average stature; not tall; as, a *short* man; **4**, scant; deficient; as, a *short* supply of food; *short* measure; **5**, faulty; as, a *short* memory; **6**, curt; abrupt; uncivil; as, a *short* answer; **7**, crisp; crumbly; as, *short* pie crust; **8**, as applied to any of the English vowels *a, e, i, o, u,* sounded as in h*a*t, m*e*t, s*i*t, h*o*t, b*u*t; **9**, in finance, not possessing at the time of sale the goods or property that one has contracted to deliver: **short ton,** a weight of 2,000 pounds avoirdupois, used in the U. S. and Canada: often called *ton:*—*n.*, in *pl.:* **a,** milled grain somewhat finer than bran; **b,** short, loose trousers, worn by oarsmen, runners, and other athletes; trunks; **c,** in finance, the goods, stocks, etc., sold on short sales:—*adv.* abruptly; suddenly; curtly; as, to stop *short.*—*n.* **short′ness.**

Syn., adj. brief, concise, terse, curt. *Short* describes something of limited duration and may also suggest incompleteness or be used in the sense of abrupt; as, a *short* vacation, *short* measure; to be *short* with an inquisitive person. *Brief* and *short* are interchangeable when used to refer to duration; as, a *brief* interval. *Concise* and *terse* refer to manner or style in speech or writing. *Concise* describes something decisively brief; *concise* writing has no unnecessary words. *Terse* adds to *concise* the idea of smoothness and polish. *Curt* may denote *concise* or it may mean *short* in the sense of rudely abrupt.

short-age (shôr′tāj), *n.* the quantity needed to make up the whole amount; a deficit; as, his accounts at the end of each year showed a *shortage.*

short-cake (shôrt′kāk″), *n.* **1**, a cake resembling biscuit in texture made crisp by butter or lard; **2**, such a cake split and served with fruit between the layers; as, strawberry *shortcake;* **3**, a sweetened layer cake or sponge cake served with fruit between the layers or over the cake.

short cir-cuit **1**, an electrical conductor of low resistance connecting two points electrically charged; **2**, an accidental contact of the mains of an electric system, resulting in an excessive current.

TYPES OF SAILING BOATS AND SHIPS

1, sailing dinghy; 2, catboat; 3, knockabout; 4, Chesapeake Bay bugeye; 5, sloop; 6, yawl; 7, ketch; schooner; 9, topsail schooner; 10, brig; 11, bark; 12, hermaphrodite brig; 13, barkentine. (See also full ge illus. oi *Rigging and Sails*, page 613.)

short-cir-cuit (shôrt′=sûr″kĭt), *v.t.* to connect by an electrical conductor of low resistance:—*v.i.* **1,** to connect two points electrically charged, by means of a conductor of low resistance; **2,** to cause an excessive current by accidental contact of the mains of an electrical system.

short-com-ing (shôrt′kŭm″ĭng; shôrt″-kŭm′ĭng), *n.* **1,** a failing; fault; **2,** failure or neglect in doing one's duty.

short-en (shôr′tn), *v.t.* **1,** to make short or shorter in time, extent, or measure; **2,** to lessen; **3,** to contract; take in, as a sail; **4,** to make crisp or brittle, as pastry, by using butter, lard, etc.:—*v.i.* to grow or become shorter or briefer.—*n.* **short′en-er.**

short-en-ing (shôr′tn-ĭng; shôrt′nĭng), *n.* **1,** the act of making short or shorter; **2,** that which makes pastry crisp and brittle, as lard, butter, cooking oils, etc.

short-hand (shôrt′hănd″), *n.* a system of rapid writing in which characters, symbols, etc., are used for letters, words, phrases, etc.; stenography.

short-lived (shôrt′=līvd″), *adj.* of short duration; not of long life.

short-ly (shôrt′lĭ), *adv.* **1,** soon; **2,** quickly; curtly; **3,** in a few words.

short-sight-ed (shôrt′sīt″ĕd), *adj.* **1,** unable to see far; **2,** due to, or marked by, lack of foresight.—*adv.* **short″sight′ed-ly.**—*n.* **short″sight′ed-ness.**

short-stop (shôrt′stŏp″), *n.* in baseball, an infielder stationed between the second and third bases.

short-wind-ed (shôrt′=wĭn″dĕd), *adj.* affected with shortness of breath; liable to be so affected under the strain of exertion.

¹shot (shŏt), past tense and past participle of the verb *shoot:*—*p.adj.* variegated in color; as, rose silk *shot* with silver.

²shot (shŏt), *n.* **1,** the act of shooting; the discharge, as of a firearm; **2,** a projectile or missile, esp. for firearms; also, such missiles collectively; **3,** [*pl.* shot], a small ball or pellet of lead, or a number of such pellets combined in one charge, and used in a shotgun for killing birds and small quadrupeds; **4,** the range or distance which is or can be covered by a missile; **5,** figuratively, reach or range in general; the distance to or at which a thing will carry; as, within ear*shot;* **6,** in certain games, a stroke or blow; **7,** a marksman; as, he is a good *shot;* **8,** in mining, a blast; **9,** in sports, a spherical weight to be put, or thrown, in competition for distance; **10,** *Slang,* an attempt; as, take a *shot* at it.

shote (shōt), *n.* **1,** a young hog; pig; **2,** a lazy, shiftless fellow. Also, **shoat.**

shot-gun (shŏt′gŭn″), *n.* a smoothbore gun, for firing at short range.

should (shŏŏd), *v.aux.* past tense of *shall,* followed by the infinitive without *to* and used: **1,** in indirect discourse, to express simple futurity or determination from the standpoint of past time, following the rule for the use of *shall* in direct discourse; as, expressing simple futurity, he said he *should* go; expressing determination, I said he *should* go; **2,** to express condition, supposition, hesitation, etc., on the speaker's part; as, if it *should* rain, do not go; **3,** to express moral obligation or duty; as, you *should* try to do better.
Syn. (see ought).

shoul-der (shōl′dẽr), *n.* **1,** either of the two projecting parts of the human body between the neck and the place where the arm joins the trunk; **2,** in animals, the fore quarter; **3,** that which resembles a shoulder; a prominence; **4,** a support to keep something in place or to keep it from moving beyond a certain point:—*v.t.* **1,** to take upon the shoulder; **2,** hence, to assume the responsibility of; as, to *shoulder* a wrong; **3,** to push with, or as with, the shoulders; as, to *shoulder* one's way:—*v.i.* to push with the shoulders.

shoul-der blade the flat bone of the shoulder; the scapula.

shoul-der strap **1,** a strap worn over the shoulders to support something; **2,** a narrow strap bearing insignia of rank, worn on the shoulder by commissioned officers of the army and navy.

shout (shout), *n.* a loud and sudden cry, as of joy, command, encouragement, etc.; a burst of a voice or voices:—*v.i.* to utter a loud and sudden cry:—*v.t.* to utter with a loud, resonant voice: usually with *out;* as, he *shouted* out his orders and ran.

shove (shŭv), *n.* **1,** the act of pushing; **2,** a forcible push:—*v.t.* [*p.t.* and *p.p.* shoved (shŭvd), *p.pr.* shov′ing], **1,** to push along; **2,** to jostle; crowd; **3,** to thrust:—*v.i.* **1,** to move along; crowd against others; **2,** to push something along.—*n.* **shov′er.**

shov-el (shŭv′l), *n.* a tool made of a broad, flat scoop with a handle, for lifting and throwing coal, grain, etc., or for digging:—*v.t.* **1,** to take and throw up with such a tool; **2,** to gather up with, or as with, a shovel; as, to *shovel* food; **3,** to clear or clean with this tool.

shov-el-board (shŭv′l-bōrd″), *n.* a game played with weights or metal disks shoved toward a certain line on a specially prepared board; also, the board: now generally called *shuffleboard.*

shov-el-er (shŭv′l-ẽr), *n.* **1,** one who uses a shovel; **2,** a widely distributed species of river duck. Also, **shov′el-ler.**

show (shō), *v.t.* [*p.t.* showed (shōd), *p.p.* shown (shōn) or showed, *p.pr.* show′ing], **1,** to present to view; exhibit; display; **2,** to tell, reveal, or make known; **3,** to make clear; make (a person) understand; **4,** to prove by a process of reasoning; **5,** to direct; as, to *show* one to his seat; **6,** to bestow; as, to *show* favor:—*v.i.* **1,** to present an appearance; **2,** to be visible or noticeable; as, the stain *shows;* **3,** *Colloq.,* to make a display: with *off:*—*n.* **1,** the act of exhibiting or displaying; **2,** an exhibition or display; **3,** a public parade or spectacle; **4,** pomp; **5,** a deceitful appearance or pretense; as, a *show* of wealth; a *show* of wisdom; **6,** a sign or promise, as of metal in a mine; **7,** *Colloq.,* a theatrical performance; **8,** *Slang,* a fair opportunity.—*n.* **¹show′er.**

show bill a large printed poster containing advertisements.

show-bread (shō′brĕd″), *n.* in the ancient Jewish ritual, the unleavened bread placed in the sanctuary (Exodus 25:30). Also, **shew′bread″**, *Pfd. S.*

show case a glass case for displaying and protecting goods or wares in stores, articles or exhibits in museums, etc.

²show-er (shou′ẽr), *n.* **1,** a brief fall of rain sleet, or hail; **2,** figuratively a copious fall of drops of any liquid or of solid objects in considerable number; as, a *shower* of bricks; also, a number of gifts given together; as, a bride's kitchen *shower;* **3,** an abundant supply of anything; as, a *shower* of suggestions:—*v.t.* **1,** to water abundantly with rain or any other liquid; **2,** to pour out also, to bestow liberally upon:—*v.i.* **1,** to rain for a short time; **2,** to fall in a shower.

show-er bath a device constructed to send a spray of water over the entire body, for bathing purposes also, a bath taken by the use of this device.

show-er-y (shou′ẽr-ĭ), *adj.* **1,** raining for brief intervals or abounding in short, rainy periods; **2,** resembling a shower—*n.* **show′er-i-ness.**

show-ing (shō′ĭng), *n.* a display; an exhibition of something; a presentation of a fact, condition, or the like.

show-man (shō′măn), *n.* [*pl.* showmen (-mĕn)], **1,** one who exhibits; sp., the proprietor of a traveling exhibition; , one who takes part in exhibiting a show.

shown (shōn), the past participle of the irregular verb *show.*

show-room (shō′rōōm″), *n.* a room where goods are displayed.

show-y (shō′ĭ), *adj.* [*comp.* show′i-er, *superl.* show′i-est], **1,** attracting attention; gorgeous; as, a *showy* flower; **2,** gaudy; narked by pretentious parade; as, *showy* ewelry.—*adv.* **show′i-ly.**—*n.* **show′i-ness.**

shrank (shrăngk), the past tense of the irregular verb *shrink.*

shrap-nel (shrăp′nĕl), *n.* bullets or pieces of iron in a shell timed to xplode and scatter its contents over a deired point; also, shells so charged.

shred (shrĕd), *n.* **1,** a long, narrow strip torn or cut off: a rag; scrap; **2,** the iniest bit; fragment:—*v.t.* [*p.t.* and *p.p.* hred or shred′ded, *p.pr.* shred′ding], to tear r cut into small pieces.—*n.* **shred′der.**

shrew (shrōō), *n.* **1,** a scolding, brawling woman; **2,** any of several mouselike nimals feeding chiefly on insects and worms.

shrewd (shrōōd), *adj.* **1,** sharp-witted or clever in practical affairs; keen; s, a *shrewd* business man; **2,** cunning; as, a *hrewd* planner; **3,** *Archaic,* biting; harsh.—*dv.* **shrewd′ly.**—*n.* **shrewd′ness.**
Syn. astute, sagacious, farsighted.

shrew-ish (shrōō′ĭsh), *adj.* scolding; habitually nagging; peevish. —*adv.* **shrew′ish-ly.**—*n.* **shrew′ish-ness.**

shriek (shrēk), *v.t.* to cry out sharply; utter with a sharp, shrill cry:—*v.i.* o utter a sharp, shrill cry; scream:—*n.* a iercing scream; a shrill outcry.—*n.* **shriek′er.**

shriev-al-ty (shrēv′ăl-tĭ), *n.* [*pl.* shrievalties (-tĭz)], the office, term, r authority of a sheriff.

shrift (shrĭft), *n. Archaic,* **1,** confession to a priest, and absolution; **2,** the act of earing a confession and of giving absolution.

shrike (shrīk), *n.* any of various birds which feed chiefly on insects, but hich sometimes kill smaller birds, mice, etc.

shrill (shrĭl), *adj.* sharp and piercing in tone:—*v.i. Poetic,* to utter a sharp, iercing sound:—*v.t. Poetic,* to utter in a sharp, iercing tone.—*adv.* **shril′ly.**—*n.* **shrill′ness.**

shrimp (shrĭmp), *n.* **1,** any of various crustaceans, of salt or fresh water, elated to the lobster (see *crustacean,* illus.); , contemptuously, a puny person.

shrine (shrīn), *n.* **1,** a case or box in which sacred relics are kept; **2,** the tomb f a saint; **3,** any sacred place or hallowed bject, as an altar:—*v.t.* [*p.t.* and *p.p.* shrined hrīnd), *p.pr.* shrin′ing], to cherish as sacred; ut in a sacred place; enshrine.

hrink (shrĭngk), *v.i.* [*p.t.* shrank (shrăngk) or shrunk (shrŭngk), *p.p.* shrunk or, sp. as *p.adj.,* shrunken (shrŭngk′n), *p.pr.* nrink′ing], **1,** to contract; become smaller or horter; **2,** to draw back, as from a danger or reat: often with *from;* **3,** to draw back, as om something repellent or disagreeable: ith *from:*—*v.t.* to cause to contract or grow maller:—*n.* the act or amount of shrinking. -*adj.* **shrink′a-ble.**—*n.* **shrink′er.**
Syn., v. shrivel, wither, blight, fade.

hrink-age (shrĭngk′āj), *n.* **1,** the act of contracting or making small- ; contraction; **2,** amount lost by contracon or shrinking; **3,** decrease in value.

hrive (shrīv), *v.t.* [*p.t.* shrived (shrīvd) or shrove (shrōv), *p.p.* shriv′en (shrĭv′n) or shrived, *p.pr.* shriv′ing], **1,** to hear or receive the confession of and give absolution to; **2,** to cause (oneself) to be confessed and absolved:—*v.i.* to hear confession and give absolution.

shriv-el (shrĭv′l), *v.i.* to be drawn into wrinkles; contract; shrink; dry up:—*v.t.* to cause to wrinkle, shrink, wither, or dry up; as, heat will *shrivel* the leaves.

shroud (shroud), *n.* **1,** a winding sheet; a dress or covering for the dead; **2,** anything that envelops and conceals; as, a *shroud* of mystery; **3,** in *pl.,* a set of ropes, usually in pairs, supporting the masts of a vessel (see *rigging,* illus.):—*v.t.* **1,** to dress in a shroud, as a corpse; **2,** to hide or conceal with a covering; veil.

shrove (shrōv), the past tense of the irregular verb *shrive.*

Shrove Sun-day the Sunday before Shrove Tuesday; Quinquagesima Sunday.

Shrove-tide (shrōv′tīd″), *n.* a period of penitence and confession, covering sometimes only Shrove Tuesday, and sometimes including the three days preceding Ash Wednesday.

Shrove Tues-day the Tuesday before Ash Wednesday.

[1]**shrub** (shrŭb), *n.* a drink or cordial made of sweetened raspberry or other acid fruit juice, usually with spirits.

[2]**shrub** (shrŭb), *n.* a woody, perennial plant less in stature than a tree, and usually divided into several or many primary stems at or near the ground; a bush.

shrub-ber-y (shrŭb′ẽr-ĭ), *n.* [*pl.* shrubberies (-ĭz)], **1,** shrubs collectively; **2,** a place where shrubs or bushes are planted or where they abound.

shrub-by (shrŭb′ĭ), *adj.* [*comp.* shrub′bi-er, *superl.* shrub′bi-est], **1,** full of, or covered with, bushes or shrubs; **2,** of the nature of a bush or shrub; stunted.—*n.* **shrub′bi-ness.**

shrug (shrŭg), *v.t.* [*p.t.* and *p.p.* shrugged (shrŭgd), *p.pr.* shrug′ging], to contract or draw up (the shoulders) to express some emotion, as doubt, contempt, surprise, etc.:—*v.i.* to raise the shoulders to express disagreement, contempt, displeasure, etc.:—*n.* a raising or contracting of the shoulders to express some emotion.

shrunk-en (shrŭngk′n), *p.adj.* shriveled up; contracted; dried up.

shuck (shŭk), *n.* a shell; husk or pod; esp., the outer covering of a nut:—*v.t.* to shell, as peanuts; husk, as corn.

shud-der (shŭd′ẽr), *n.* a convulsive trembling, as from fear, horror, aversion, cold, or excitement:—*v.i.* to tremble or shake, as with fear or horror; quake; shiver. —*p.adj.* **shud′der-ing.**—*adv.* **shud′der-ing-ly.**
Syn., v. quiver. (See shake.)

shuf-fle (shŭf′l), *v.t.* [*p.t.* and *p.p.* -fled (-ld), *p.pr.* -fling], **1,** to shift from one position or person to another; **2,** to rearrange, as cards in a pack; **3,** to move with a dragging motion, as the feet in walking or dancing; **4,** to slip off carelessly; as, to *shuffle* off a burden; **5,** to make up with haste or fraud; as, to *shuffle* up a makeshift; **6,** to intermingle; mix up:—*v.i.* **1,** to shift from one position to another; **2,** to rearrange the cards in a pack; **3,** to shift one's ground; evade questions or issues; **4,** to do a task listlessly or awkwardly; as, she *shuffled* through the cleaning; **5,** to drag the feet in a slovenly manner; as, he *shuffled* along in his big slippers:—*n.* **1,** the act of shifting, rearranging, etc.; **2,** a rearranging of cards in a pack; **3,** a trick or evasion; **4,** a careless scuffle; also, a dance characterized by a dragging motion of the feet.—*n.* **shuf′fler.**—*n.* and *p.adj.* **shuf′fling.**

shuf-fle-board (shŭf′l-bōrd″), *n.* **1**, a game played with counters or weights, by shoving or sliding them toward a line or goal, on a specially prepared board; **2**, the long, narrow board, often spread with a thin layer of sand, on which the game is played. Also called *shovelboard.*

shun (shŭn), *v.t.* [*p.t.* and *p.p.* shunned (shŭnd), *p.pr.* shun′ning], **1**, to avoid; keep clear of; as, to *shun* evil companions; **2**, to refrain from, as evil ways.

shunt (shŭnt), *v.t.* **1**, to turn off or switch, as a car or train; **2**, to supply another path for (an electric current); **3**, to put off upon someone else, as a task or duty:—*v.i.* to turn aside or off:—*n.* **1**, the act of turning off; **2**, a turning off, as of a car, to a side rail; a switch; **3**, in electricity, a conductor joining two points of an electric circuit over which part of the current may be diverted: **shunt circuit**, in electricity, a circuit provided to divert a part of the current.—*n.* **shunt′er.**

shut (shŭt), *v.t.* [*p.t.* and *p.p.* shut, *p.pr.* shut′ting], **1**, to close so as to prevent entrance or exit, as a door; **2**, to bar; as, to *shut* the ports of a country; **3**, to exclude; as, to *shut* out certain imports; **4**, to close over; as, to *shut* the hand; fold together, as an umbrella; bring the parts of together, as a book; **5**, to imprison, confine, or hold within the parts of something; as, to *shut* up a convict; **6**, to close or pinch; as, to *shut* one's finger in the door; **7**, to hide from sight; as, to *shut* out the view:—*v.i.* **1**, to become closed; **2**, to cease working, as a factory: with *down.*

shut-ter (shŭt′ẽr), *n.* **1**, one who or that which closes; **2**, a movable solid cover for a window; **3**, any of various devices for covering an opening; **4**, in photography, a device for regulating the exposure of a sensitive plate to light:—*v.t.* to close, cover, or supply, with shutters.

shut-tle (shŭt′l), *n.* **1**, an instrument used in weaving to carry the thread of the weft, or woof, back and forth through the warp; **2**, in a sewing machine, the sliding holder inclosing the bobbin; **3**, any similar device, as one used in tatting.

shut-tle-cock (shŭt′l-kŏk″), *n.* **1**, a cork stuck with feathers and driven with a battledore, or bat; **2**, the game played with such implements.

[1]**shy** (shī), *adj.* [*comp.* shi′er or shy′er, *superl.* shi′est or shy′est], **1**, easily scared away; timid, as an animal; **2**, bashful; sensitive; as, a *shy* girl; **3**, cautious; wary; as, the stranger was *shy* of questions; **4**, disposed to avoid: with *of;* as, *shy* of bad roads; **5**, *Slang,* short; lacking; as, one card *shy:*—*v.i.* [*p.t.* and *p.p.* shied (shīd), *p.pr.* shy′ing], **1**, to start suddenly aside from fear: said usually of a horse; **2**, to turn away; as, the people *shied* at his new plan:—*n.* [*pl.* shies (shīz)], the act of starting aside from fear; a sudden start, esp. one made by a horse.—*adv.* **shy′ly.**—*n.* **shy′ness.**

Syn., adj. diffident, bashful, modest. To be *shy* is to be reserved and uneasy in the company of others, and to conceal one's real personality behind a manner often entirely different from the natural one. To be *diffident* is to suffer so much from distrust of oneself as to lack confidence to undertake work within one's ability to perform. To be *bashful* is to shrink from the notice of others in an awkward or timid manner. To be *modest* is to have suitable self-confidence, and to be at ease, although not obtrusive, with others.

[2]**shy** (shī), *v.t.* [*p.t.* and *p.p.* shied (shīd), *p.pr.* shy′ing], to throw with a jerk; fling, as a stone:—*v.i.* to throw a stone, brick, or the like, with a jerk:—*n.* [*pl.* shies (shīz)], **1**, a throw; a fling; **2**, *Slang,* a try; an attempt.

Shy-lock (shī′lŏk), *n.* in Shakespeare' "Merchant of Venice," a re vengeful Jewish money lender who requires pound of flesh as pledge for a loan to hi enemy, Antonio.

shy-ster (shī′stẽr), *n. Colloq.,* one wh carries on business in a mean an tricky manner; esp., a rascally lawyer.

si (sē), *n.* in music, **1**, the seventh of th syllables used in singing the tones of diatonic scale: now superseded by *ti,* as th syllable *si* is used for the sharp of *so;* **2**, th seventh tone of a diatonic scale.

Si-a-mese (sī″ȧ-mēz′; sī″ȧ-mēs′), *adj.* o or pertaining to Siam, it natives, or its language:—*n.* [*pl.* Siamese **1**, one of the inhabitants of Siam; **2**, th natives of Siam collectively; **3**, the languag of the Siamese people.

Si-be-ri-an (sī-bē′rĭ-ăn), *adj.* of or per taining to Siberia or its peopl —*n.* one of the inhabitants of Siberia.

sib-i-lant (sĭb′ĭ-lănt), *adj.* making, o uttering, a hissing sound; a *s* has a *sibilant* sound:—*n.* a hissing sound o a symbol standing for such a sound; as, *s, sh* *z,* and *zh* are *sibilants.*—*n.* **sib′i-lance.**

sib-i-la-tion (sĭb″ĭ-lā′shŭn), *n.* utteranc with a hissing sound.

sib-yl (sĭb′ĭl), *n.* **1**, a woman supposed t have the power to foretell the futur prophetess; **2**, a witch.

sib-yl-line (sĭb′ĭ-līn; sĭb′ĭ-lĭn), *adj.* **1**, pe taining to, or coming from, prophetess; **2**, mysterious; prophetic.

***sic** (sĭk), [Lat.], *adv.* so; thus: frequentl inserted in italics in brackets after word in a quoted passage, to indicate that, i spite of apparent absurdity or misspelling, is quoted correctly.

Si-cil-i-an (sĭ-sĭl′ĭ-ăn; sĭ-sĭl′yăn), *adj.* pe taining to the island of Sicil to its people or their language:—*n.* **1**, a nati or inhabitant of Sicily; **2**, the language of Sicil

sick (sĭk) *adj.* **1**, ill in health; indispose **2**, affected with nausea, or vomitin inclined to vomit; **3**, disgusted; surfeited; a *sick* of flattery; **4**, longing or pining: with *fo* as, *sick* for recognition; **5**, used by, or s apart for the use of, a person who is ill; as, *sick* bed; a *sick* benefit: **sick leave**, a leave absence granted to officers or privates becau of illness or disability.

Syn. diseased, sickly, **unhealthy.**—*An* sound, well, healthy.

sick-en (sĭk′n), *v.i.* **1**, to become ill; **2**, be filled with disgust; **3**, to dec or languish; as, the flower *sickened* and die —*v.t.* **1**, to make ill; **2**, to disgust.

sick-en-ing (sĭk′n-ĭng), *p.adj.* **1**, maki sick; nauseating; as, a *sic ening* odor; **2**, repulsive; as, a *sickening* sigh

sick-ish (sĭk′ĭsh), *adj.* **1**, somewhat slightly nauseated; **2**, apt nauseate one; as, *sickish* sweets.—*adv.* **sick ish-ly.**—*n.* **sick′ish-ness.**

sick-le (sĭk′l), *n.* a reaping instrume consisting of a curved steel bla with a handle.

sick-ly (sĭk′lĭ), *adj.* [*comp.* sick′li-er, *supe* sick′li-est], **1**, ailing; weak; nev well; **2**, characteristic of illness; as, a *sick* look; **3**, apt to make one ill; as, *sickly* weath **4**, weak; pale; as, a *sickly* color; **5**, marked mawkishness; sickening; as, *sickly* sen ments.—*n.* **sick′li-ness.**

sick-ness (sĭk′nĕs), *n.* **1**, the state of bei ill or in bad health; diseas condition; **2**, a particular malady; **3**, naus

Syn. (see disease).

side (sīd), *n.* **1**, an edge or bounding line a surface, esp., in a rectangle, one the longer lines as distinguished from the en

2, one of the surfaces or faces that limit a solid; 3, the right or left part of an object or of the body; as, the right *side* of a barn; 4, a contrasted part or surface; as, the upper *side;* the lower *side;* the in*side;* 5, either longitudinal half of a person or animal; as, a *side* of beef; 6, a party of men upholding a cause against another group; faction; also, the cause that is upheld; as, he is on our *side;* 7, a line of descent through a parent; as, a cousin on the mother's *side:*—*adj.* 1, pertaining to a side or sides; 2, viewed from or toward one side; 3, laterally placed or situated; as, a *side* door; 4, minor; incidental:—*v.i.* [*p.t.* and *p.p.* sid'ed, *p.pr.* sid'ing], to take the part of one against another: followed by *with;* as, he *sided* with the Unionists.

side-board (sīd'bōrd"), *n.* a piece of dining-room furniture for holding articles used on the table.

side drum a kind of small military drum: also called *snare drum* (see *drum*, illus.).

side light 1, a window on one side, as of a door; 2, a light placed on, or falling from, one side; 3, hence, an incidental revelation or illustration.

side-ling (sīd'lĭng), *adj.* oblique; having a sidewise motion; directed toward the side:—*adv.* laterally; obliquely.

side-long (sīd'lông"), *adv.* 1, on the side; 2, obliquely:—*adj.* lateral; having an oblique direction; as, a *sidelong* glance.

si-de-re-al (sī-dē'rē-ăl), *adj.* 1, pertaining to the stars; starry; astral; 2, measured by the apparent motion of the stars; as, a *sidereal* hour.

sid-er-ite (sĭd'ẽr-īt), *n.* an iron ore, usually yellowish brown in color.

side-sad-dle (sīd'săd"l), *n.* a woman's saddle having but one stirrup, so that both feet of the rider rest on the same side of the horse.

side-track (sīd'trăk"), *v.t.* 1, to transfer (a car or train) from the main track to a siding; 2, to lead away from the main subject or issue; postpone; as, to *sidetrack* a legislative bill:—*v.i.* to run a train upon a siding:—*n.* a siding.

side-walk (sīd'wôk"), *n.* a path beside a road or street for foot travel; a foot pavement.

side-ways (sīd'wāz"), *adv.* toward or from the side. Also, **side'way"**.

side wheel one of two paddle wheels at the side of a steamboat.—*adj.* **side'-wheel"**.—*n.* **side"-wheel'er**.

side-wise (sīd'wīz"), *adv.* and *adj.* toward or from the side.

sid-ing (sīd'ĭng), *n.* 1, a railroad track by the side of the main track, on to which cars may be switched; a short track connected with the main track; 2, the boarding that forms the sides of a wooden house.

si-dle (sī'dl), *v.i.* [*p.t.* and *p.p.* -dled (-dld), *p.pr.* -dling], to move sidewise, as from shyness or fear; as, he *sidled* up to us.

siege (sēj), *n.* 1, the surrounding of a fortified place by an army to compel its surrender; investment of a town or fortified place; 2, a prolonged or persistent attempt to gain possession of something; as, he laid *siege* to her heart: **siege gun**, a heavy field gun designed to hurl projectiles with sufficient force to break through strong fortifications: **siege mortar**, a short cannon used to attack by high-angle fire parts not capable of being reached by horizontal fire.

Sieg-fried (sēg'frēd; *Ger.* zēkh'frēt), *n.* in the "Nibelungenlied," and, under the name *Sigurd*, in the Volsunga Saga, a hero who, having slain a dragon and won a cursed treasure, marries Kriemhild (Gudrun), sister of the Burgundian king Gunther, and is treacherously slain by the latter's vassal Hagen.

si-en-na (sī-ĕn'ȧ), *n.* 1, a brownish yellow clay pigment, or coloring matter; 2, the color of this pigment; brownish orange.

si-er-ra (sĭ-ĕr'ȧ), *n.* a mountain chain or range rising in irregular peaks.

si-es-ta (sĭ-ĕs'tȧ), *n.* a midday nap; an after-dinner nap.

sieve (sĭv), *n.* a utensil provided with meshes, as of wire, for separating the finer from the coarser parts of a substance.

sift (sĭft), *v.t.* 1, to separate, as the fine parts from the coarser, with, or as with, a sieve; 2, to pass through a sieve; 3, hence, to examine critically; scrutinize; as, he *sifted* out the secret.—*n.* **sift'er**.

sigh (sī), *v.i.* 1, to breathe deeply and audibly as a result of fatigue, sorrow, etc.; 2, to long; yearn; grieve: with *for;* as, the boy *sighed* for his mother; 3, to make a sound like sighing; as, the winds *sigh:*—*v.t.* to express by sighs:—*n.* a deep, audible respiration, expressing sorrow, anxiety, etc.—*n.* **sigh'er**.

sight (sīt), *n.* 1, the power of seeing; vision; 2, the act of seeing or being seen; as, she caught *sight* of him; 3, that which is seen; a view; 4, something remarkable or worth seeing; a spectacle; 5, the limit of the power of the eyesight; the visibility of something; as, in *sight;* out of *sight;* 6, opinion; as, in his *sight*, she did well; 7, insight; opportunity for study; as, to get a *sight* into the great man's methods; 8, any of several devices to help in guiding the eye or aim, as on a gun, optical instrument, etc.; 9, the aim or observation so taken:—*v.t.* 1, to see with the eye; find by looking; as, to *sight* a distant object; 2, to look at closely or critically; 3, to direct by means of an aiming device; as, to *sight* a gun; 4, to furnish with sights, or adjust the sights of, as an instrument or gun:—*v.i.* to aim a gun by a sight.

sight-less (sīt'lĕs), *adj.* incapable of seeing; blind.—*n.* **sight'less-ness**.

sight-ly (sīt'lĭ), *adj.* pleasing to the eye: comely.—*n.* **sight'li-ness**.

sight-see-ing (sīt'-sē"ĭng), *adj.* engaged in visiting objects or places of interest:—*n.* the act of visiting objects or places of interest.—*n.* **sight'-se"er**.

sig-ma (sĭg'mȧ), *n.* the 18th letter of the Greek alphabet [Σ; at an early period *S*, and in uncial writing *C;* and σ, ς], approximately equivalent to English *s*.

sign (sīn), *n.* 1, a symbol or emblem typifying or representing an idea; as, the *sign* of the cross; 2, any written word, character, or the like, conventionally used to express a familiar meaning; 3, any representation of something; that by which anything is made known; a mark; token; proof; as, his gift was a *sign* of his love; 4, an omen; portent; esp., an unusual event considered as representing the will of God; 5, a gesture or motion used instead of words to express some thought, command, or wish; as, she gave him a *sign* to go; 6, a lettered board or plate which displays the name of the person or firm conducting an office or business; 7, one of the twelve equal divisions of the zodiac, or the symbol representing it, named for the constellations which they formerly represented (see *zodiac*, illus.); 8, in mathematics, a character or symbol indicating a relation between quantities or an operation to be performed; as, the *signs* +, −, ×, and ÷, indicating the four fundamental operations; also, a symbol used as an abbreviation; as, the radical *sign* [√] for the expression, "the square root of": —*v.t.* 1, to affix a signature to; as, to *sign* a letter; 2, to transfer, as a right or property, by affixing the signature to a deed or the like: with *off* or *away;* **3**, to acknowledge or guarantee the genuineness of (a document, work of art, etc.), by affixing one's signature, initials, or recognized mark; **4**, to hire by getting the signature of; as, to *sign* a person for a particular position:—*v.i.* **1**, to write one's signature, as indicating assent, responsibility, or obligation; **2**, to signal; as, he *signed* for them to approach; **3**, in law, to assent to, or acknowledge, the terms of a document by subscribing one's name: **sign off**, in radio, to announce a cessation of broadcasting and the name of the station.—*n.* **sign'er.**

Syn., n. (see emblem).

sig-nal (sĭg'năl), *n.* a sign agreed upon, or intended to be understood, for giving notice, as of danger, esp. at a distance; a token:—*adj.* memorable; extraordinary; distinguished from the commonplace by some mark or sign; remarkable; as, a *signal* success:—*v.t.* to communicate with by means of flags, lights, etc.; make signs to:—*v.i.* to make signs; communicate with someone by means of flags, lights, etc.—*n.* **sig'nal-er; sig'nal-ler.**—*adv.* **sig'nal-ly.**—*n.* **sig'nal-man.**

sig-nal-ize (sĭg'năl-īz), *v.t.* [*p.t.* and *p.p.* -ized (-īzd), *p.pr.* -iz"ing], **1**, to make especially conspicuous or prominent; **2**, to point out with care.

sig-na-to-ry (sĭg'nȧ-tō-rĭ), *adj.* having signed an agreement, esp. a treaty:—*n.* [*pl.* signatories (-rĭz)], one who signs, or subscribes to, a treaty, esp. a state or power bound in this way.

sig-na-ture (sĭg'nȧ-tūr), *n.* **1**, the name of a person written by himself; autograph; also, a mark or stamp affixed in place of the written name; **2**, in music: **a**, one or more flats or sharps placed after the clef to indicate the key; **b**, a sign placed after the key designation to indicate the time; **c**, all the signs at the beginning of the staff; **3**, in printing, a distinguishing mark at the bottom of the first page of each sheet of a book, magazine, etc., to guide in assembling the sheets; also, the sheet so marked.

sign-board (sīn'bōrd"), *n.* a board bearing, or designed for, a notice.

sig-net (sĭg'nĕt), *n.* **1**, a seal; **2**, the imprint made by, or as by, a seal.

sig-nif-i-cance (sĭg-nĭf'ĭ-kăns), *n.* **1**, meaning; often, the hidden or underlying meaning; import; **2**, importance; consequence. Also, **sig-nif'i-can-cy.**

sig-nif-i-cant (sĭg-nĭf'ĭ-kănt), *adj.* **1**, full of, or having, meaning; **2**, expressive; as, a *significant* look; **3**, important, as an event.—*adv.* **sig-nif'i-cant-ly.**

sig-ni-fi-ca-tion (sĭg"nĭ-fĭ-kā'shŭn), *n.* that which is suggested or expressed; the meaning of a sign, character, etc.; implication.—*adj.* **sig-nif'i-ca-tive.**

Syn. sense, import, significance.

sig-ni-fy (sĭg'nĭ-fī), *v.t.* [*p.t.* and *p.p.* -fied (-fīd), *p.pr.* -fy"ing], **1**, to show by a sign, mark, or token; make known; declare; as, to *signify* one's consent; **2**, to denote; mean:—*v.i.* to be of consequence; matter.

si-gnior (sēn'yẽr), *n.* **1**, Mr.; Sir: the English form of the Italian *signore* and the Spanish *señor;* **2**, a lord or gentleman.

***si-gnor** (sē-nyōr'), [It.], *n.* **1**, Master; Mister (Mr.); Sir: a title of address or respect among the Italians, used before a person's name; as, *Signor* Marconi; **2**, a lord.

***si-gno-ra** (sē-nyō'rä), [It.], *n.* [*pl.* signore (-rā)], **1**, a title of respectful address to an Italian lady, corresponding to *Mrs.* or *madam;* **2**, a lady.

***si-gno-re** (sē-nyō'rā), [It.], *n.* [*pl.* signori (-rē)], **1**, a title of address or respect among the Italians, corresponding to *Mr.* or *sir:* spelled, when used before a person's name, *signor;* **2**, a gentleman.

***si-gno-ri-na** (sē"nyō-rē'nä), [It.], *n.* [*pl.* signorine (-nā)], **1**, a title of address to a young lady, corresponding to *Miss;* **2**, a young lady.

sign-post (sīn'pōst"), *n.* **1**, a guidepost; **2**, a pole which bears signs.

Si-gurd (zē'gŏŏrt), *n.* in Norse mythology, the hero of the Volsunga Saga: the counterpart of Siegfried (which see), the hero of the "Nibelungenlied."

si-lage (sī'lȧj), *n.* a fermentation product used as a cattle food, made from green fodder cut up and partially fermented in a silo; ensilage.

si-lence (sī'lĕns), *n.* **1**, the state of being still or mute; **2**, entire absence of sound or noise; general stillness; **3**, forbearance from, or absence of, mention; secrecy; oblivion:—*v.t.* [*p.t.* and *p.p.* -lenced (-lĕnst), *p.pr.* -lenc-ing], **1**, to cause to be still; as, *silence* the dogs; **2**, to quiet; put to rest; as, to *silence* one's conscience; **3**, to cause to cease firing, as hostile guns in an engagement.

si-lenc-er (sī'lĕn-sẽr), *n.* that which muffles or dulls; specif., the muffler of a gas engine: **Maxim silencer**, a device which may be attached to a rifle to reduce the sound when the gun is fired.

si-lent (sī'lĕnt), *adj.* **1**, saying nothing; mute; **2**, not given to speech; as, a *silent* man; **3**, quiet; still; free from noise; as, a *silent* place; **4**, not expressed; not spoken; as, a *silent* command; **5**, calm; free from disturbance; as, a *silent* nook; **6**, having a share, not publicly acknowledged, in a business; as, a *silent* partner; **7**, written, but not pronounced: said of a letter; as, the *b* in *doubt* is *silent.*—*adv.* **si'lent-ly.**—*n.* **si'lent-ness.**

Syn. dumb, speechless.

Si-le-nus (sī-lē'nŭs), *n.* in mythology, a Greek woodland god, son of Hermes, or of Pan, and companion and tutor to Dionysus (Bacchus): usually represented as a fat, drunken, bald-headed old man with pointed ears, full beard, and flat nose, bestriding a donkey: **silenus**, [*pl.* sileni (-nī)], any of various woodland deities related to the centaurs and satyrs.

si-le-si-a (sĭ-lē'shĭ-ȧ; sī-lē'shȧ), *n.* **1**, a twilled cotton fabric, used for dress linings; **2**, a kind of linen cloth.

si-lex (sī'lĕks), *n.* silicon dioxide: an archaic term, used as a synonym for quartz, flint, or silica.

sil-hou-ette (sĭl"ōō-ĕt'), *n.* **1**, an outline drawing, esp. a profile portrait, filled in with a uniform color, usually black; **2**, the figure cast by a shadow, as on a wall or screen:—*v.t.* [*p.t.* and *p.p.* -et'ted, *p.pr.* -et'ting], to cause to appear in outline; as, the light *silhouetted* his form on the wall.

sil-i-ca (sĭl'ĭ-kȧ), *n.* in chemistry, silicon dioxide; quartz; opal.

sil-i-cate (sĭl'ĭ-kāt), *n.* in chemistry, a salt of silicic acid.

si-li-ceous (sĭ-lĭsh'ŭs), *adj.* pertaining to, containing, or like, silica.

si-lic-ic (sĭ-lĭs'ĭk), *adj.* in chemistry, pertaining to silica or silicon.

sil-i-con (sĭl'ĭ-kŏn), *n.* an element found abundantly in rocks and sand.

sil-i-co-sis (sĭl"ĭ-kō'sĭs), *n.* a disease of the lungs caused by inhaling silica dust, as from sand, quartz, or granite.

si-lique (sĭ-lēk'; sĭl'ĭk), *n.* a narrow pod or fruit containing many seeds and having two valves.

silk (sĭlk), *n.* **1**, a fine, soft, lustrous fabric made from threads spun by various insect larvæ, esp. by the larvæ of silkworms, to form their nests or cocoons; **2**, the thread or fiber produced by these larvæ; **3**, any similar thread, as that spun by certain spiders; **4**, anything like silk, as the silky down of the milkweed pod: **artificial silk**, a preparation of wood cellulose which, spun into threads and woven, is used as a substitute for silk: also called *rayon.*

silk-en (sĭl′kn), *adj.* **1**, made of, or like, silk; soft; lustrous; smooth; **2**, dressed in silk; **3**, luxurious.

silk-worm (sĭlk′wûrm″), *n.* the larva of any of certain moths, commercially cultivated, that make a strong silk fiber in spinning their cocoons.

silk-y (sĭl′kĭ), *adj.* [*comp.* silk′i-er, *superl.* silk′i-est], of, pertaining to, or like, silk: soft; smooth; lustrous.—*n.* **silk′i-ness.**

sill (sĭl), *n.* **1**, a horizontal piece forming the foundation, or part of the foundation, of a structure (see *frame house,* illus.); **2**, a threshold; **3**, the bottom or lowest piece in a window frame.

sil-la-bub (sĭl′ȧ-bŭb), *n.* a dish made by mixing milk or cream, often whipped, with wine or cider, to form a soft curd. Also, **syl′la-bub.**

sil-ly (sĭl′ĭ), *adj.* [*comp.* sil′li-er, *superl.* sil′li-est], **1**, weak in intellect; lacking good sense; foolish; simple, as a person; **2**, unwise; stupid; absurd; as, a *silly* answer. —*adv.* **sil′li-ly.**—*n.* **sil′li-ness.**

si-lo (sī′lō), *n.* [*pl.* silos (-lōz)], a pit or tower for preserving green fodder for winter use by excluding air and water.

silt (sĭlt), *n.* mud or fine earth carried in, or deposited by, water; also, a deposit of such mud or fine earth:—*v.t.* to choke or block up by such a deposit:—*v.i.* to become obstructed by such a deposit.—*adj.* **silt′y.**

sil-va (sĭl′vȧ), *n.* [*pl.* silvas (-vȧz); silvæ (-vē)], the forest trees of a region, taken collectively. Also, **syl′va.**

sil-van (sĭl′văn), *adj.* of or pertaining to forests, woods, or trees; rustic; shady; as, a *silvan* retreat. Also, **syl′van.**

sil-ver (sĭl′vẽr), *n.* **1**, a soft, lustrous, white, malleable and ductile metallic element, found native in the metallic state and also in compounds: in its metallic state capable of a high polish, and used for table implements, dishes, jewelry, etc., its compounds being used in medicine and photography: one of the precious metals; **2**, anything made of this metal, as silverware or money; **3**, anything like silver; the luster or color of silver; as, cloth of *silver:*—*adj.* **1**, pertaining to silver; **2**, made of silver; **3**, resembling, or like, silver; esp., glistening, lustrous white; as, *silver* dew; **4**, soft and clear, as the tones of a silver bell; hence, eloquent; **5**, *Colloq.,* second best; next best to gold; as, the *silver* age of literature: **silver nitrate,** a white crystalline salt formed by the action of nitric acid on metallic silver: used in electroplating, looking-glass manufacture, and as a caustic: —*v.t.* **1**, to cover or coat with silver, or with something resembling it; **2**, to give a silverlike polish to; **3**, to make white, or hoary, like silver; as, the moonbeams *silver* the lake:—*v.i.* to turn silvery white or gray; as, her hair *silvered* at a very early age.

sil-ver-ing (sĭl′vẽr-ĭng), *n.* **1**, the act, art, or process of covering with silver, or with a substance resembling silver; **2**, the film or coating thus laid on.

sil-vern (sĭl′vẽrn), *adj. Poetic,* silvery; as, the *silvern* moon.

sil-ver-smith (sĭl′vẽr-smĭth″), *n.* a worker in silver; one who makes articles of silver.

sil-ver-ware (sĭl′vẽr-wâr″), *n.* silver plate; vessels, dishes, vases, table implements, etc., made of silver.

sil-ver-y (sĭl′vẽr-ĭ), *adj.* **1**, resembling silver; lustrous; as, *silvery* hair; **2**, covered with, containing, or like, silver; **3**, soft and clear in tone; as, a *silvery* voice.

sim-i-an (sĭm′ĭ-ăn), *adj.* pertaining to, or like, an ape:—*n.* an ape.

sim-i-lar (sĭm′ĭ-lȧr), *adj.* **1**, having a general likeness or correspondence; analogous; **2**, like, but not the same or exactly alike; **3**, of like nature, scope, etc.; **4**, in geometry, shaped alike, but not of the same size, position, etc.—*adv.* **sim′i-lar-ly.**

Syn. corresponding. (See alike.)

sim-i-lar-i-ty (sĭm″ĭ-lăr′ĭ-tĭ), *n.* [*pl.* similarities (-tĭz)], **1**, the quality or state of bearing a strong resemblance to one another or to something else; likeness; **2**, the point or points of likeness.

sim-i-le (sĭm′ĭ-lē), *n.* a figure of speech in which two different things having some accidental likeness are compared by the use of such words as *like, so,* etc.; as, the girl is *like* a flower.

si-mil-i-tude (sĭ-mĭl′ĭ-tūd), *n.* **1**, similarity; likeness; **2**, a simile.

sim-mer (sĭm′ẽr), *v.t.* and *v.i.* **1**, to boil gently; **2**, to cook in liquid just at or below the boiling point:—*n.* **1**, the state of boiling gently; **2**, a state of suppressed emotion or excitement.

Si-mon (sī′mŏn), *n.* in the Bible, **1**, one of the Twelve Apostles, considered as the author of the two Epistles of Peter in the New Testament: usually called *Simon Peter* or *Peter* (Luke 6:14); **2**, one of the Twelve Apostles: usually called *Simon Zelotes,* or *the Zealot* (Luke 6:15); **3**, a sorcerer rebuked by Simon Peter for offering to buy the power of the Holy Ghost: also called *Simon Magus* (Acts 8:9–24).

sim-o-ny (sĭm′ō-nĭ), *n.* the act or crime of buying or selling church offices, or positions of honor.

si-moom (sĭ-mo͞om′), *n.* a hot, suffocating, dust-laden wind which blows from the deserts of Arabia. Also, **si-moon′.**

sim-per (sĭm′pẽr), *v.i.* to smile in an affected, silly, or self-conscious manner; smirk:—*n.* an affected smile; a smirk.—*adv.* **sim′per-ing-ly.**

sim-ple (sĭm′pl), *adj.* **1**, single; elementary; not mixed or compounded; **2**, mere; without qualification; as, a *simple* fact; **3**, plain; unadorned; as, *simple* clothes; **4**, sincere; straightforward; ingenuous; **5**, having a taste for the plain, natural methods of living; as, *simple* people; **6**, humble; of low rank or degree; **7**, unlearned; hence, weak in intellect; foolish; **8**, resulting from ignorance or foolishness; as, a *simple* answer: **simple fraction,** a fraction whose terms are whole numbers, as $\frac{3}{4}$: **simple interest,** interest paid only on a fixed principal: distinguished from *compound interest:* **simple sentence,** a sentence containing only one subject and one predicate:—*n.* **1**, an element; that which is not mixed; **2**, a plant, or herb, from which medicine is extracted; also, the medicine.—*n.* **sim′ple-ness.**

sim-ple-ton (sĭm′pl-tŭn), *n.* one who is foolish or weak-minded.

sim-plex (sĭm′plĕks), *adj.* in telegraphy, naming, or pertaining to, a system by which only one message at a time can be sent over the wire.

sim-plic-i-ty (sĭm-plĭs′ĭ-tĭ), *n.* [*pl.* simplicities (-tĭz)], **1**, the state or quality of being clear, plain, unaffected, etc.; **2**, lack of cunning; **3**, lack of common sense, or of average ability to judge.

sim-pli-fi-ca-tion (sĭm″plĭ-fĭ-kā′shŭn), *n.* **1**, the act of making plainer or easier to make or do, as a task;

2, the process of making a thing easier to understand; as, the *simplification* of spelling.

sim-pli-fy (sĭm′plĭ-fī), *v.t.* [*p.t.* and *p.p.* -fied (-fīd), *p.pr.* -fy″ing], to make easier; render less complex; make plainer to the understanding.

sim-ply (sĭm′plĭ), *adv.* **1**, clearly; plainly; **2**, without elaborate show; **3**, only; merely; **4**, hence, absolutely; **5**, artlessly; **6**, foolishly; weakly.

sim-u-late (sĭm′ū-lāt), *v.t.* [*p.t.* and *p.p.* -lat″ed, *p.pr.* -lat″ing], to pretend; assume the character or semblance of; as, to *simulate* goodness:—*adj.* (sĭm′ū-lȧt), pretended; imitated.—*n.* **sim′u-la″tor.**

Syn., *v.* dissimulate, dissemble, feign.

sim-u-la-tion (sĭm″ū-lā′shŭn), *n.* the act of pretending that which is not true; feigning; pretense.

si-mul-ta-ne-ous (sī″mŭl-tā′nē-ŭs; sĭm″ŭl-), *adj.* happening, done, or existing, at the same time; as, *simultaneous* events.—*adv.* **si″mul-ta′ne-ous-ly.**—*n.* **si″mul-ta′ne-ous-ness.**

sin (sĭn), *n.* **1**, wilful breaking of the divine law; violation of the principles of morality and religion; **2**, a special case or instance of such violation; **3**, the state of one who has thus transgressed; **4**, loosely, any fault:—*v.i.* [*p.t.* and *p.p.* sinned (sĭnd), *p.pr.* sin′ning], **1**, to transgress, offend, or neglect the law of God or any duty; commit evil deeds; **2**, to violate human rights; transgress against an accepted standard:—*v.t.* **1**, to bring about by sin; as, he *sinned* his way to destruction; **2**, to commit (a sin).

since (sĭns), *adv.* **1**, from a certain past time until now; as, he left six years ago and has not been seen *since;* **2**, at some time after a certain past event and before now; as, he was then treasurer, but has *since* been elected president; **3**, before this; ago; as, not long *since:*—*prep.* from the time of; during the time after; ever after; as, *since* that time, I have never seen him:—*conj.* **1**, from and after a time when; as, I have never seen him *since* that happened; **2**, seeing that; because; as, *since* that is the case, I shall go.

sin-cere (sĭn-sēr′), *adj.* **1**, true; honest; honorable; genuine; **2**, without hypocrisy.—*adv.* **sin-cere′ly.**—*n.* **sin-cere′ness.**

Syn. candid, hearty, straightforward.

sin-cer-i-ty (sĭn-sĕr′ĭ-tĭ), *n.* **1**, the state or quality of being true or genuine; **2**, honesty; integrity.

Sind-bad (sĭnd′băd; sĭn′-), *n.* in the "Arabian Nights' Entertainments," a wealthy merchant of Baghdad, often called *Sindbad the Sailor*, who tells many tales of his extraordinary voyages. Also, **Sin′bad.**

sine (sīn), *n.* in a right-angled triangle, the ratio of the side opposite an acute angle to the hypotenuse: one of the trigonometric functions.

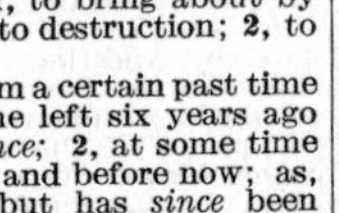

SINE

$\frac{CP}{OP}$ = sine of angle XOP.
If OP = 1, the sine is equal to CP.

si-ne-cure (sī′nē-kūr), *n.* **1**, an office or position having a salary or fees but carrying with it little work or responsibility; **2**, in England, the benefice of a clergyman who, though receiving a salary, has no spiritual duties.

***si-ne di-e** (sī′nē dī′ē), [Lat.], without day; without setting a day for reassembling: said of the adjournment of a meeting; as, Congress adjourned *sine die.*

sin-ew (sĭn′ū), *n.* **1**, a tendon; **2**, strength; **3**, anything supplying strength; as, the *sinews* of war.—*adj.* **sin′ew-less.**

sin-ew-y (sĭn′ū-ĭ), *adj.* **1**, pertaining to, or like, a sinew; **2**, vigorous; tough.

sin-ful (sĭn′fo͝ol), *adj.* full of wickedness; unholy; tainted with sin.—*adv.* **sin′ful-ly.**—*n.* **sin′ful-ness.**

sing (sĭng), *v.i.* [*p.t.* sang (săng) or, *Archaic,* sung (sŭng), *p.p.* sung, *p.pr.* sing′ing], **1**, to lift the voice in song; utter musical rhythmical sounds; **2**, to make a shrill or humming noise; as, a flying arrow *sings;* **3**, to celebrate some event in verse or poetry; as, he *sang* of the deeds of Æneas; **4**, to make pleasant, musical sounds; as, the brook *sings* merrily; **5**, to ring with a buzzing sound; as, my ears are *singing:*—*v.t.* **1**, to utter with musical inflections of the voice; **2**, to celebrate in song or poetry; **3**, to lull by singing; as, to *sing* a child to sleep; **4**, to express warmly; as, he *sang* our praises.—*n.* [1]**sing′er.**

singe (sĭnj), *v.t.* [*p.t.* and *p.p.* singed (sĭnjd), *p.pr.* singe′ing], **1**, to burn slightly or on the surface; scorch; **2**, to burn so as to remove down, as a fowl:—*n.* a slight burn; a surface burn.—*n.* [2]**sing′er.**

Syn., *v.* sear, char. (See [2]burn.)

Sin-gha-lese (sĭng″gȧ-lēz′; sĭng″gȧ-lēs′), *adj.* of or pertaining to Ceylon, its chief race, or their language:—*n.* [*pl.* Singhalese], **1**, a member of this race; **2**, their language. Also, **Sin″ha-lese′.**

sin-gle (sĭng′gl), *adj.* **1**, consisting of one only; separate; **2**, alone; without aid; **3**, not married; **4**, performed by one person; having only one on each side; as, *single* combat; **5**, straightforward; sincere; artless; honest; **6**, in botany, having only one row of petals; as, a *single* tulip: opp. of *double:* **single file**, a line of men one behind the other; also, any line so formed:—*v.t.* [*p.t.* and *p.p.* -gled (-gld), *p.pr.* -gling], to select (one person or thing) from others; choose from others: with *out* or *from:*—*n.* a unit; one.

sin-gle–foot (sĭng′gl=fo͝ot″), *n.* a horse's gait in which each foot strikes the ground singly.

sin-gle–hand-ed (sĭng′gl=hănd″ĕd), *adj.* **1**, done with one hand; **2**, done without aid or assistance.

sin-gle–heart-ed (sĭng′gl=härt″ĕd), *adj.* sincere; inclined to be free from deceitfulness.

sin-gle–mind-ed (sĭng′gl=mīnd″ĕd), *adj.* having but one purpose; hence, without guile; single-hearted.

sin-gle-ness (sĭng′gl-nĕs), *n.* **1**, the state or quality of being separate or alone; the state of being single; **2**, sincerity; **3**, constancy, as of purpose.

sin-gle-stick (sĭng′gl-stĭk″), *n.* **1**, a long stick or cudgel used for fencing or fighting; **2**, the sport of so fencing.

sin-gle-tree (sĭng′gl-trē″), *n.* the pivoted bar to which the traces of a harness are fastened; a swingletree.

sin-gly (sĭng′glĭ), *adv.* **1**, individually; one by one; **2**, without others; alone.

sing-song (sĭng′sông″), *n.* **1**, singing or poetry marked by an unvaried, monotonous rhythm; **2**, a monotonous or drawling tone:—*adj.* monotonous in rhythm.

sin-gu-lar (sĭng′gū-lȧr), *adj.* **1**, in grammar, denoting one person or thing; **2**, being the only one of its kind; unique; **3**, peculiar; strange; **4**, remarkable; extraordinary; **5**, exceptional; as, a woman of *singular* charm:—*n.* **1**, in grammar, the number denoting one person or thing; **2**, the form of a word denoting this number; **3**, a word in the form of this number.—*adv.* **sin′gu-lar-ly.**

Syn., *adj.* uncommon. (See queer.)

sin-gu-lar-i-ty (sĭng″gū-lăr′ĭ-tĭ), *n.* [*pl.* singularities (-tĭz)], **1**, the state or quality of being uncommon, strange, or separated from others; **2**, the state of being of the singular grammatical number; **3**, peculiarity; oddity; **4**, a person or thing that is uncommon, odd, or peculiar.

sin-is-ter (sĭn'ĭs-tẽr), *adj.* **1**, left; as, the *sinister* side: applied in heraldry to the side of an escutcheon on the bearer's left, the beholder's right: opp. of *dexter;* **2**, observed on the left; hence, unlucky; ill-omened; evil; as, a *sinister* look; **3**, corrupt; dishonest; as, *sinister* intentions.—*adv.* **sin'-is-ter-ly.**—*adj.* **sin'is-trous.**

sin-is-tral (sĭn'ĭs-trăl), *adj.* pertaining to the left side or hand; bent or slanted toward the left: opp. of *dextral.*—*adv.* **sin'is-tral-ly.**

sink (sĭngk), *v.i.* [*p.t.* sank (săngk) or sunk (sŭngk), *p.p.* sunk or, obsolete except as *p.adj.*, sunk'en (sŭngk'n), *p.pr.* sink'ing], **1**, to fall or go downward; fall to the bottom; descend lower and lower; **2**, to decline gradually, as in strength; **3**, hence, to degenerate; **4**, to become hollow: often said of the cheeks; **5**, to enter deeply; as, to *sink* into the mind; **6**, to subside; as, a flood soon *sinks:*—*v.t.* **1**, to cause to go to the bottom; as, to *sink* ships; **2**, to make by digging downward; as, to *sink* a well; **3**, to place in the excavation made; as, to *sink* a pipe; **4**, to lower in value or amount; **5**, to reduce or extinguish by payment; as, to *sink* the national debt; **6**, to degrade; debase:—*n.* **1**, a kind of basin, as in a kitchen, with a drain to carry off dirty or superfluous water; **2**, in geology, any slight depression of the land, esp. one that has no water outlet, or an underground outlet.

sink-er (sĭngk'ẽr), *n.* that which sinks or causes to sink, as a small weight attached to a fishing line.

sink-ing fund the total amount of sums of money set aside for investment, to be used, with its accumulated interest, to pay off a debt.

sin-less (sĭn'lĕs), *adj.* without guilt; blameless; as, a *sinless* thought.—*adv.* **sin'less-ly.**—*n.* **sin'less-ness.**

sin-ner (sĭn'ẽr), *n.* one who offends against the law of God; an offender.

Sinn Fein (shĭn fān), an Irish movement organized in 1905 for the purpose of promoting home industries and developing nationalism; also, the society thus formed.

sin-u-ate (sĭn'ū-āt), *adj.* **1**, wavy; winding; **2**, having a strongly indented margin; as, a *sinuate* leaf.—*adv.* **sin'u-ate-ly.**—*n.* **sin"u-a'tion.**

sin-u-os-i-ty (sĭn"ū-ŏs'ĭ-tĭ), *n.* [*pl.* sinuosities (-tĭz)], **1**, a wavy line; **2**, the quality or state of that which curves or winds in and out.

sin-u-ous (sĭn'ū-ŭs), *adj.* **1**, curving in and out; winding; **2**, crooked; twisting; **3**, having a strongly waved margin; sinuate, as leaves.—*adv.* **sin'u-ous-ly.**—*n.* **sin'u-ous-ness.**

si-nus (sī'nŭs), *n.* [*pl.* sinuses (-ĕz); sinus], **1**, an opening; a hollow or depression; **2**, a curving arm of the sea, as a bay; **3**, a natural cavity or hollow, as in some bones of the face; esp., a cavity leading to the nose.

Si-on (sī'ŏn), *n.* **1**, a certain hill in Jerusalem; **2**, the Church; **3**, the new Jerusalem. See **Zi'on,** *Pfd. S.*

-sion (-shŭn; -zhŭn), *n. suffix,* indicating: **1**, act, state, or quality; as, expul*sion;* fu*sion;* **2**, the result of an act; as, pen*sion;* posses*sion.* Also, **-tion.**

Sioux (sōō), *n.* [*pl.* Sioux], one of an important and warlike tribe of American Indians of the upper Mississippi valley.

sip (sĭp), *v.t.* [*p.t.* and *p.p.* sipped (sĭpt), *p.pr.* sip'ping], to drink by taking a small portion, as a teaspoonful, at a time; taste:—*v.i.* to drink a liquid by taking a little at a time with the lips:—*n.* **1**, the act of drinking a little at a time; **2**, a small taste.

si-phon (sī'fŏn), *n.* **1**, a pipe or tube bent like an inverted **U** having one leg longer than the other, used for drawing off liquids from a higher to a lower level; **2**, a bottle fitted with such a tube:—*v.t.* to draw off by such a tube.—*n.* **si'phon-age.**

Sir (sûr), *n.* the title of respect used before the Christian name of a baronet or knight: **sir,** a term of respect in addressing a man without using his name.

sire (sīr), *n.* **1**, a title of respect used in addressing a sovereign or king; **2**, a father; the head of a family; **3**, the male progenitor of a beast:—*v.t.* [*p.t.* and *p.p.* sired (sīrd), *p.pr.* sir'ing], to procreate, or beget: used esp. of male beasts.

si-ren (sī'rĕn), *n.* **1**, in mythology, any of several sea nymphs said to inhabit an island off the coast of Italy, and to lure sailors to destruction by their beauty and sweet singing; **2**, hence, a woman dangerous because of her fascinating, enticing wiles; **3**, a device for producing a tone of varying pitch by interruption of a blast of air or steam: often used as a foghorn:—*adj.* **1**, pertaining to, or like, a siren; **2**, bewitching.

Sir-i-us (sĭr'ĭ-ŭs), *n.* the Dog Star, the most brilliant fixed star in the sky.

sir-loin (sûr'loin"), *n.* a choice cut of beef, taken from the upper part of the loin. Also, **sur'loin".**

si-roc-co (sĭ-rŏk'ō), *n.* [*pl.* siroccos (-ōz)], **1**, a hot, dusty wind blowing north from the Sahara; **2**, any hot wind.

sir-rah (sĭr'ȧ), *n.* fellow: a term used in addressing a man or boy, implying inferiority, contempt, displeasure, etc.

sir-up (sĭr'ŭp), *n.* **1**, a thick, sticky liquid made from the juice of fruits, herbs, etc., boiled with sugar; **2**, any concentrated solution of sugar. Also, **syr'up.**—*adj.* **sir'up-y.**

Sis-er-a (sĭs'ẽr-ȧ), *n.* in the Bible, a commander of the Canaanites against the Israelites (Judges 4 : 4–24).

sis-ter (sĭs'tẽr), *n.* **1**, a female thought of in relation to another person born of the same parents; **2**, a woman of the same religious society, order, or community as others; a nun: **half sister,** a female having one parent in common with another person:—*adj.* of the same kind or condition; as, *sister* republics.—*adj.* **sis'ter-ly.**—*n.* **sis'ter-li-ness.**

sis-ter-hood (sĭs'tẽr-hŏŏd), *n.* **1**, the relationship between sisters; **2**, the state of being a sister; **3**, a group of things thought of as sisters; as, a *sisterhood* of churches; **4**, a number of women united by a common interest, as in a religious society; **5**, the office or duty of a sister.

sis-ter–in–law (sĭs'tẽr=ĭn=lô"), *n.* [*pl.* sisters-in-law (-tẽrz=)], **1**, a husband's or wife's sister; **2**, a brother's wife.

Sis-tine (sĭs'tēn; sĭs'tĭn), *adj.* pertaining to, or made for, any of the Popes named Sixtus: **Sistine Madonna,** a famous representation of the Madonna, painted by Raphael for the church of St. Sixtus at Piacenza, Italy, but now at Dresden.

Sis-y-phus (sĭs'ĭ-fŭs), *n.* in mythology, a greedy king of Corinth who was condemned in Hades to roll uphill a huge stone, which always fell back again.—*adj.* **Sis"y-phe'an.**

sit (sĭt), *v.i.* [*p.t.* sat (săt) or, *Archaic,* sate (săt; sāt), *p.p.* sat or, *Obs.*, sitten (sĭt'n), *p.pr.* sit'ting], **1**, to rest with the weight of the body on the lower part of the trunk; take a seat after standing; **2**, to perch; also, to rest on the ground, as birds; **3**, to have place or position; be situated: with *on;* **4**, to fit; suit; as, the dress *sits* well; **5,** to occupy a seat officially; be a member of a council or assembly; as, to *sit* in Parliament; **6,** to convene or hold a session, as a court; **7,** to cover eggs to be hatched, as a fowl; **8,** to pose; as, to *sit* for a portrait:—*v.t.* **1,** to have, or keep, a seat upon, as a horse; **2,** to seat: generally reflexive; as, he *sat* him down by the well.—*n.* **sit'ter.**

site (sīt), *n.* **1,** position or situation; **2,** a plot of land suitable for a building.

sith (sĭth), *prep.* *Archaic,* since:—*adv.* *Archaic,* then:—*conj.* *Archaic,* since.

sit-ting (sĭt'ĭng), *p.adj.* **1,** resting on the haunches; perching; **2,** pertaining to, or used for, sitting:—*n.* **1,** the position or act of one who sits; **2,** a seat, as in a church; **3,** a session or meeting; **4,** time during which one sits, as for a portrait; **5,** a set of eggs for hatching.

sit-u-ate (sĭt'ū-āt), *adj.* placed; situated; located.

sit-u-at-ed (sĭt'ū-āt″ĕd), *adj.* having a position; located.

sit-u-a-tion (sĭt″ū-ā'shŭn), *n.* **1,** position; locality; **2,** circumstances; **3,** office; employment; **4,** the temporary state of affairs at any given moment.

Syn. condition, plight, predicament, state.

sitz bath (sĭts), a tub for bathing in a sitting posture; also, such a bath.

Si-va (sē'vȧ; shē'vȧ), *n.* in the Hindu religion, the god of destruction and reproduction, forming, with Brahma and Vishnu, the supreme trinity. Also, **Shi'va.**

six (sĭks), *adj.* composed of one more than five:—*n.* **1,** the number consisting of five plus one; **2,** a sign which is used to represent six units, as 6 or vi.

six-fold (sĭks'fōld″), *adj.* **1,** taken six times; **2,** consisting of six parts.

six-pence (sĭks'pĕns), *n.* a small British silver coin, of the value of six English pence, or about twelve cents; also, this sum of money.

six-teen (sĭks'tēn″; sĭks″tēn'), *adj.* composed of one more than fifteen:—*n.* **1,** the number consisting of fifteen plus one, **2,** a sign used to represent sixteen units, as 16 or xvi.

six-teen-mo (sĭks-tēn'mō), *n.* [*pl.* sixteenmos (-mōz)], a book whose sheets are folded into sixteen leaves; sextodecimo (which see): often written *16mo.*

six-teenth (sĭks'tēnth″; sĭks″tēnth'), *adj.* **1,** next in order after the fifteenth: the ordinal of *sixteen;* **2,** designating one of the sixteen equal parts of anything:—*n.* (sĭks″tēnth'; sĭks'tēnth″), **1,** the quotient of one divided by sixteen; **2,** one of the sixteen equal parts of anything; **3,** in music, a note whose time value is half that of an eighth; a semiquaver.

sixth (sĭksth), *adj.* **1,** next in order after the fifth: the ordinal of *six;* **2,** designating one of six equal parts: **Sixth day,** Friday so called by the Quakers:—*n.* **1,** the quotient of one divided by six; **2,** one of the six equal parts of anything; **3,** in music: **a,** the sixth tone of a diatonic scale, counting upward; **b,** an interval of six diatonic degrees; **c,** a tone at this interval.—*adv.* **sixth'ly.**

six-ty (sĭks'tĭ), *adj.* composed of six times ten, or threescore:—*n.* [*pl.* sixties (-tĭz)], **1,** the sum of six times ten; sixty units or objects; **2,** a sign representing sixty units, as 60 or lx.—*adj.* and *n.* **six'ti-eth.**

siz-a-ble (sīz'ȧ-bl), *adj.* of considerable bulk; fairly large. Also, **size'a-ble.**—*adv.* **siz'a-bly.**—*n.* **siz'a-ble-ness.**

siz-ar (sīz'ẽr), *n.* in some British universities, an undergraduate who is granted a reduction in his college fees. Also, **siz'er.**—*n.* **si'zar-ship.**

¹size (sīz), *n.* any of various thin, glutinous washes, used by painters, paper makers, etc., for glazing the surface of various materials:—*v.t.* [*p.t.* and *p.p.* sized (sīzd), *p.pr.* siz'ing], to prepare, stiffen, or cover with thin glue, as cloth or fabric.—*n.* **siz'ing.**

²size (sīz), *n.* **1,** the dimensions, magnitude, or bulk of anything; **2,** a relative measure showing how large something is, as a hat or a glove; **3,** *Slang,* actual fact; truth of the matter:—*v.t.* [*p.t.* and *p.p.* sized (sīzd), *p.pr.* siz'ing], **1,** to arrange in order of bulk, height, volume, or extent; **2,** *Colloq.,* to form a conclusion about: with *up;* as, to *size* up a situation.

sized (sīzd), *p.adj.* being of a particular bulk, volume, or dimension.

siz-zle (sĭz'l), *v.i.* [*p.t.* and *p.p.* -zled (-ld), *p.pr.* -zling], *Colloq.,* to make a hissing sound, as in frying; be intensely hot:—*n.* *Colloq.,* a hissing sound.

skald (skôld; skäld), *n.* any of the old Norse poets, who recited or sang heroic verses. Also, **scald.** *Pfd. S.*

skat (skät), *n.* a three-handed card game played with 32 cards.

¹skate (skāt), *n.* any of various broad, flat-bodied fishes (see ²*ray,* illus.).

²skate (skāt), *n.* **1,** a metallic runner attached to a frame shaped to fit a shoe and used for gliding rapidly over ice; **2,** a device consisting of small wheels attached to a frame which clamps to the sole of the shoe; a roller skate:—*v.i.* [*p.t.* and *p.p.* skat'ed, *p.pr.* skat'ing], to move or glide along on skates.—*n.* **skat'er.**

skein (skān), *n.* a quantity of thread, yarn, or the like, coiled together.

skel-e-ton (skĕl'ē-tŭn), *n.* **1,** the bony framework of an animal; **2,** the supporting framework of anything; **3,** an outline sketch; as, the *skeleton* of a play:—*adj.* consisting of, or like, a framework: **skeleton key,** a key which has part of the bit filed away so that it can be used as a master key to open a number of locks.—*adj.* **skel'e-tal.**

skep-tic (skĕp'tĭk), *n.* **1,** a person of a doubting state of mind; **2,** one who doubts whether ultimate truth can be certainly known; **3,** one who doubts the truth of the religious belief of his associates:—*adj.* inclined to doubt. Also, **scep'tic.**

Syn. doubter, infidel, unbeliever.

skep-ti-cal (skĕp'tĭ-kăl), *adj.* **1,** pertaining to, or like, a doubter or skeptic; **2,** doubting everything; unbelieving; critically searching; **3,** doubting the truth of the religious belief of one's associates. Also, **scep'ti-cal.**—*adv.* **skep'ti-cal-ly.**

skep-ti-cism (skĕp'tĭ-sĭzm), *n.* **1,** an incredulous, doubting, or critical state of mind, active rather than passive; **2,** doubt or denial of Christianity; **3,** the doctrine that ultimate truth is not attainable by man. Also, **scep'ti-cism.**

sketch (skĕch), *n.* **1,** a simple, quickly made drawing; as, a crayon *sketch;* **2,** an outline; a rough draft; preliminary study; **3,** a short, simple piece of literature or music; **4,** a short, simple, dramatic performance:—*v.t.* to draw the outline or give the principal features of; make a draft of; outline the plan of:—*v.i.* to make an outline or preliminary draft.—*n.* **sketch'er.**

sketch-book (skĕch'bo͝ok″), *n.* a book of drawings, or for drawings.

sketch-y (skĕch'ĭ), *adj.* [*comp.* sketch'i-er, *superl.* sketch'i-est], **1,** of the nature of a sketch; given in outline only; **2,** giving the main features in a rapid, incomplete fashion.—*adv.* **sketch'i-ly.**—*n.* **sketch'i-ness.**

skew (skū), *adj.* **1,** twisted or turned to one side; **2,** not symmetrical:—*n.* a twisted movement; distortion:—*v.i.* **1**, to move in a sidelong way; **2**, to glance obliquely: —*v.t.* to shape obliquely; hence, to pervert.

skew-er (skū'ẽr), *n.* a pin of wood or metal for keeping meat in shape while roasting:—*v.t.* to fasten with, or as with, a skewer or pin.

ski (skē), *n.* [*pl.* skis (skēz); ski], one of a pair of long, narrow pieces of wood, to be fastened one on each foot and used with a sliding motion in traversing snow:—*v.i.* to slide or travel on skis.—*n.* **ski'er.**

ski-a-graph (skī'ȧ-grȧf), *n.* a shadow picture, esp. one produced by X rays, which pass through the object and fall upon a sensitive film. Also, **sci'a-graph.**—*n.* **ski-ag'ra-phy** (skī-ăg'rȧ-fĭ).

skid (skĭd), *n.* **1**, a wedge or drag used on the wheel of a vehicle to check its motion; **2**, one of a pair or set of logs, rails, etc., used to form a track down which heavy objects roll or slide; **3**, a piece of timber on which something rests; **4**, in an airplane, a projecting frame on the under side of the fuselage near the rear end (*tail skid*) or of each end of the lower wing (*wing skid*), intended to drag or slide along the ground and protect the airplane from damage (see *airplane*, illus.):—*v.t.* [*p.t.* and *p.p.* skid'ded, *p.pr.* skid'ding], **1**, to cause to move on skids; **2**, to protect or check with a drag or skid:—*v.i.* **1**, to slip sideways on the road: said of an automobile; **2**, to slide without turning around: said of a locked wheel.—*n.* **skid'der.**

skiff (skĭf), *n.* a small, light boat for rowing.

skil-ful (skĭl'fo͝ol), *adj.* **1**, having or showing deftness or practical ability; expert; clever; **2**, showing or requiring expertness. Also, **skill'ful.**—*adv.* **skil'ful-ly.**—*n.* **skil'ful-ness.**

Syn. adroit, apt, deft. (See clever.)—*Ant.* awkward, clumsy, inexpert.

skill (skĭl), *n.* knowledge of any art or science, together with expert ability to put that knowledge to use; cleverness; dexterity.

skilled (skĭld), *adj.* **1**, having the knowledge and ability which come from experience; dexterous; clever; trained in some art, craft, or science; **2**, demanding technical training of a specialized type, as some trades.

skil-let (skĭl'ĕt), *n.* a small metal vessel with a handle, used for cooking.

skim (skĭm), *v.t.* [*p.t.* and *p.p.* skimmed (skĭmd), *p.pr.* skim'ming], **1**, to remove the scum or floating substances from the top of; as, to *skim* milk; **2**, to take from the surface of a liquid, as with a ladle or spoon; as, to *skim* cream; **3**, to brush or touch the surface of lightly; as, the boat *skims* the water; **4**, to read or glance at hurriedly; as, to *skim* a book; **5**, to cause to skip, as a stone on the water:—*v.i.* **1**, to pass lightly over a surface or very near a surface; also, to glide, as through the air; **2**, to read without thoroughness; **3**, to skip over a surface, as a stone on water: **skim milk,** milk from which the cream has been taken.

skim-mer (skĭm'ẽr), *n.* **1**, one who or that which skims; **2**, any of several long-winged marine birds.

skim-ming (skĭm'ĭng), *n.*, usually in *pl.*, anything skimmed from the top of a liquid; scum.

skimp (skĭmp), *v.t. Colloq.*, **1**, to do badly or carelessly; slight; **2**, to make insufficient allowance for:—*v.i. Colloq.*, to save; be miserly.

skimp-y (skĭm'pĭ), *adj.* [*comp.* skimp'i-er, *superl.* skimp'i-est], *Colloq.*, **1**, stingy; miserly; **2**, narrow, as a skirt.

skin (skĭn), *n.* **1**, the outer covering of the body of an animal; **2**, the pelt of an animal after removal from the body; **3**, rind, as of an orange; **4**, a vessel made of an animal's skin: used to hold liquids:—*v.t.* [*p.t.* and *p.p.* skinned (skĭnd), *p.pr.* skin'ning], **1**, to remove or strip the outer membrane from; flay; peel; **2**, *Slang*, to defraud; get the better of:—*v.i.* to become covered over with skin, as a wound.—*n.* **skin'ner.**—*adj.* **skin'less.**

skin-deep (skĭn'=dēp'), *adj.* shallow; lacking depth; not profound:—*adv.* superficially.

skin-flint (skĭn'flĭnt''), *n.* a miser; a niggardly person.

skin-ny (skĭn'ĭ), *adj.* [*comp.* skin'ni-er, *superl.* skin'ni-est], **1**, like skin in appearance or texture; **2**, lean; emaciated. —*adv.* **skin'ni-ly.**—*n.* **skin'ni-ness.**

skip (skĭp), *v.t.* [*p.t.* and *p.p.* skipped (skĭpt), *p.pr.* skip'ping], **1**, to leap lightly over; **2**, to pass over or omit; **3**, to cause to rebound; as, to *skip* stones:—*v.i.* **1**, to leap or bound lightly; move with light trips and hops; caper; **2**, to pass along rapidly; hurry along, omitting portions, as in reading:—*n.* **1**, a light leap or bound; **2**, an omission; a passing over.

[1]**skip-per** (skĭp'ẽr), *n.* **1**, one who or that which moves with a light leaping or tripping gait; **2**, a maggot found in cheese; **3**, any of a family of butterflies with small, but stout, bodies, and swift, jerky flight.

[2]**skip-per** (skĭp'ẽr), *n.* **1**, the master of a small merchant or fishing vessel; **2**, *Colloq.*, the master or captain of a ship.

skir-mish (skûr'mĭsh), *n.* **1**, a brisk fight on a small scale in war, usually in connection with a greater conflict; **2**, any slight encounter:—*v.i.* **1**, to fight in small parties; **2**, to take part in a brisk, short engagement.—*n.* **skir'mish-er.**

Syn., *n.* attack, engagement. (See battle.)

skirt (skûrt), *n.* **1**, the lower and loose part of a coat, dress, or other garment; **2**, an outer garment for women and girls, covering the body below the waist; also, a petticoat; **3**, an edge or border; **4**, on a saddle, one of the side flaps:—*v.t.* to border; run or pass along the edge of; as, to *skirt* a forest:—*v.i.* to be on, or move along, a border.

skit (skĭt), *n.* a short literary composition, esp. one that is simply constructed: usually humorous or satirical.

skit-tish (skĭt'ĭsh), *adj.* **1**, shy; easily frightened; as, a *skittish* horse; **2**, capricious; fickle.—*adv.* **skit'tish-ly.**—*n.* **skit'tish-ness.**

skit-tles (skĭt'lz), *n. pl.* used as *sing.* a game resembling ninepins.

skive (skīv), *v.t.* [*p.t.* and *p.p.* skived (skīvd), *p.pr.* skiv'ing], to cut or split (leather) into thin layers or strips; also, to pare.

skiv-er (skĭv'ẽr), *n.* a leather made from the outside portion of a split sheepskin.

sku-a (skū'ȧ), *n.* any of several large, fierce, gull-like birds, one species being found along the coasts of the North Atlantic; a jaeger.

skulk (skŭlk), *v.i.* to hide or get out of the way in a sneaking or underhand manner:—*n.* an idle, good-for-nothing fellow.—*n.* **skulk'er.**

skull (skŭl), *n.* the bony case inclosing the brain of an animal; the bones which form the head and the face.

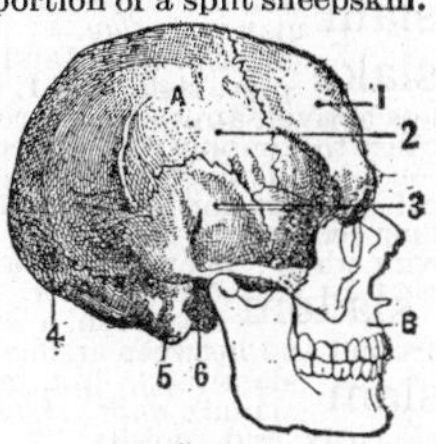

SKULL
A, cranium, or brainpan; B, face.—1, frontal bone; 2, parietal; 3, temporal; 4, occipital; 5, mastoid process of temporal; 6, external auditory meatus.

skull-cap (skŭl′kăp″), *n.* a soft, brimless cap for use indoors; also, any small, tight-fitting cap.

skunk (skŭngk), *n.* an American mammal which, when pursued, ejects an offensive liquid: in the U. S., also called *polecat:* **skunk cabbage,** a swamp plant of the arum family, which comes up in early spring and emits a fetid odor like that of a skunk.

sky (skī), *n.* [*pl.* skies (skīz)], **1,** the heavens or upper atmosphere; the region of clouds and winds; **2,** often in *pl.*, the climate or weather; **3,** the celestial regions; heaven.

¹sky-lark (skī′lärk″), *n.* a small, Old World lark that sings continuously as it soars high in the air.

²sky-lark (skī′lärk″), *v.i.* to frolic boisterously.

sky-light (skī′līt″), *n.* a window in a roof, or in the ceiling of a room, for letting in light from above.

sky pi-lot **1,** *Slang,* a clergyman, as in the navy, lumber camps, etc.; **2,** a licensed aviator.

sky-rock-et (skī′rŏk″ĕt), *n.* a kind of firework that explodes high in the air: sometime used in signaling.

sky-sail (skī′sāl″; skī′sl), *n.* the sail set at the top of a mast, next above the royal (see *rigging,* illus.).

sky-scrap-er (skī′skrāp″ẽr), *n.* a very tall building.

sky-ward (skī′wẽrd), *adj.* and *adv.* toward the sky. Also, *adv.* **sky′wards.**

slab (slăb), *n.* **1,** a thick piece of anything, as of marble or stone; **2,** the outside piece, with or without the bark, removed from a log in sawing it into boards.

slab-ber (slăb′ẽr; slŏb′ẽr), *v.i.* to dribble from the mouth; slobber:—*v.t.* to wet and foul by slobbering:—*n.* moisture running from the mouth; slaver.

¹slack (slăk), *adj.* **1,** slow; **2,** sluggish, as water; **3,** relaxed; not taut; **4,** weak; unstrung; **5,** careless; remiss; **6,** not brisk; dull, as business:—*n.* that part of anything, as a rope, that is not taut:—*adv.* slowly; insufficiently.—*adv.* **slack′ly.**—*n.* **slack′ness.**

²slack (slăk), *adj.* fine coal with more or less dirt.

slack-en (slăk′n), *v.i.* **1,** to become less firm, tense, or rigid; **2,** to be remiss or less diligent; **3,** to languish; become slower; **4,** to slake:—*v.t.* **1,** to cause to decline or become less vigorous; **2,** to slake, as lime; **3,** to loosen; reduce the tension of.

slack-er (slăk′ẽr), *n.* *Slang,* one who is negligent or careless in duty.

slag (slăg), *n.* **1,** the dross or dregs of a melted metal; **2,** lava from a volcano.

slain (slān), the past participle of the irregular verb *slay.*

slake (slāk), *v.t.* [*p.t.* and *p.p.* slaked (slākt), *p.pr.* slak′ing], **1,** to quench; render less active; appease; as, to *slake* thirst; **2,** to cause to combine with water; as, to *slake* lime:—*v.i.* to be mixed with water, so that a chemical combination occurs: **slaked lime,** quicklime reduced to a crumbly mass by mixing it with water; chemically, calcium hydroxide.

***sla-lom** (slä′lŏm), *n.* a skiing race for speed on a steep zigzag course around and between artificial obstacles.

slam (slăm), *v.t.* [*p.t.* and *p.p.* slammed (slămd), *p.pr.* slam′ming], **1,** to shut violently and noisily; **2,** to put or throw with force and loud noise:—*v.i.* to bang; as, the door *slams:*—*n.* **1,** a violent and noisy banging; **2,** the act of banging.

slan-der (slăn′dẽr), *n.* the utterance of a false or malicious report tending to injure the reputation of another; also, the report itself:—*v.t.* to injure the reputation of by telling malicious falsehoods; malign; revile; calumniate.—*n.* **slan′der-er.**

Syn., n. aspersion. (See scandal.)

slan-der-ous (slăn′dẽr-ŭs), *adj.* **1,** given to uttering false reports about a person; **2,** of the nature of, or containing, malicious reports about a person's character.—*adv.* **slan′der-ous-ly.**—*n.* **slan′der-ous-ness.**

slang (slăng), *n.* **1,** orig., the special vocabulary of vagrants, thieves, etc.; **2,** popular but inelegant language; **3,** the language of some particular calling or class of people; as, the *slang* of the theater.

slang-y (slăng′ĭ), *adj.* [*comp.* slang′i-er, *superl.* slang′i-est], **1,** of the nature of, or containing, words that are in common use, but are not considered strictly proper; **2,** given to the use of such words.—*adv.* **slang′i-ly.**—*n.* **slang′i-ness.**

slant (slånt), *n.* an inclined plane; a slope:—*v.t.* to give a sloping direction to:—*v.i.* to slope; incline from a certain line or level:—*adj.* inclined from a straight line; oblique; sloping.—*p.adj.* **slant′ing.**—*adv.* **slant′ing-ly.**

slant-wise (slånt′wīz″), *adv.* slantingly; obliquely.

slap (slăp), *n.* **1,** a blow, esp. one given with the open hand; **2,** an insult; a repulse:—*v.t.* [*p.t.* and *p.p.* slapped (slăpt), *p.pr.* slap′ping], **1,** to strike, as with the open hand; **2,** *Colloq.,* to throw down with careless force.

slap-dash (slăp′dăsh″), *adv.* *Colloq.,* in a bold, careless manner:—*adj.* *Colloq.,* **1,** reckless; boldly careless of consequences; **2,** done in a heedless, hurried way.

slash (slăsh), *n.* **1,** a long cut; **2,** a stroke of a whip; **3,** a random cut; slit; gash:—*v.t.* **1,** to cut by striking violently and at random; **2,** to cut into strips or panels, as a garment; **3,** to cut with a whip:—*v.i.* to strike violently and at random.—*n.* **slash′er.**

slash-ing (slăsh′ĭng), *p.adj.* **1,** cutting violently or at random; **2,** hence, severe; as, *slashing* remarks:—*n.* the act of cutting recklessly or at random.—*adv.* **slash′ing-ly.**

slat (slăt), *n.* a thin, narrow strip of wood or metal; as, bed *slats.*

slate (slāt), *n.* **1,** a kind of rock that splits into thin plates; **2,** the dark gray color of this rock; **3,** a thin plate of this rock prepared for use as a roof covering, writing tablet, etc.; **4,** in the U. S., a list of proposed candidates for nomination or election:—*v.t.* [*p.t.* and *p.p.* slat′ed, *p.pr.* slat′ing], **1,** to cover with slate; **2,** in the U. S., to register or book (a person) for something, as an office, a rôle, or a political appointment.—*n.* **slat′er.**—*n.* **slat′ing.**—*adj.* **slat′y.**

slat-tern (slăt′ẽrn), *n.* a slovenly woman.—*adj.* and *adv.* **slat′tern-ly.**

slaugh-ter (slô′tẽr), *n.* **1,** the act of killing; **2,** wanton destruction of life; carnage; **3,** the killing of animals for food:—*v.t.* **1,** to kill with violence; **2,** to butcher (beasts) for the market.—*n.* **slaugh′ter-er.**

Syn., n. butchery, bloodshed, massacre.

slaugh-ter-house (slô′tẽr-hous″), *n.* a place where animals are butchered for the market; an abattoir.

Slav (släv; slăv), *n.* a member of one of the great divisions of the Aryan family, which is spread over southeastern and eastern Europe and includes Russians, Poles, Czechs, and natives of the Balkan states.

slave (slāv), *n.* **1,** a human being held in bondage; a bondsman; serf; **2,** a drudge; **3,** one under the power of a habit or vice; as, a *slave* to drink:—*v.i.* [*p.t.* and *p.p.* slaved (slāvd), *p.pr.* slav′ing], to work like a drudge; toil.

Syn., n. vassal, serf. A *slave* is the actual legal property of another, and is entirely subject to his owner. A *vassal* was one who held land under feudal tenure; the word is now in literary usage interchangeable with *slave.* A *serf* is one who is attached to the estate on which he lives, and, like the land itself, may be transferred to a new owner.

slave-hold-er (slāv′hōl″dẽr), *n.* one who owns or keeps human beings as slaves.—*adj.* **slave′hold″ing.**

[1]**slav-er** (slăv′ẽr), *v.i.* to let saliva run from the mouth:—*v.t.* to cover or dribble with saliva:—*n.* saliva running from the mouth.—*n.* **slav′er-er.**

[2]**slav-er** (slāv′ẽr), *n.* a vessel or person engaged in the slave trade.

slav-er-y (slāv′ẽr-ĭ), *n.* [*pl.* slaveries (-ĭz)], **1**, the condition of being a slave, or bondsman; **2**, the business of holding human beings in bondage; **3**, bondage; involuntary servitude; complete submission to the will of another, or to some influence or vice; **4**, drudgery.

Syn. thraldom, captivity, vassalage.

Slav-ic (släv′ĭk; slăv′ĭk), *adj.* of or pertaining to the Slavs, or the peoples that inhabit eastern Europe, including the Russians, Bulgarians, Serbians, etc., or their language: —*n.* the language of any of the Slavs.

slav-ish (slāv′ĭsh), *adj.* pertaining to, or like, a bond servant or drudge. —*adv.* **slav′ish-ly.**—*n.* **slav′ish-ness.**

Sla-vo-ni-an (slȧ-vō′nĭ-ăn), *adj.* **1**, pertaining to the Slavs of Serbia, Croatia, Slavonia, Montenegro, etc., or to their language; **2**, pertaining to Slavonia, a state of the Yugoslav group, or to its people:—*n.* **1**, a native of Slavonia; **2**, a Slav; **3**, the Slavic language.—*abbr.* **Slav.**

Sla-von-ic (slȧ-vŏn′ĭk), *adj.* **1**, pertaining to the Slavs of Serbia, Croatia, Slavonia, Montenegro, etc., or to their language; **2**, pertaining to Slavonia, in South Hungary, a state of the Yugoslav group, or to its people.

slaw (slô), *n.* sliced cabbage served, usually raw, as a salad.

slay (slā), *v.t.* [*p.t.* slew (slōō), *p.p.* slain (slān), *p.pr.* slay′ing], to kill or put to death by violence; destroy.—*n.* **slay′er.**

sleave (slēv), *n.* **1**, anything matted or tangled, as silk or thread; **2**, floss.

slea-zy (slē′zĭ; slā′zĭ), *adj.* [*comp.* slea′zi-er, *superl.* slea′zi-est], lacking firmness; thin; flimsy; as, *sleazy* silk; *sleazy* muslin.—*adv.* **slea′zi-ly.**—*n.* **slea′zi-ness.**

sled (slĕd), *n.* **1**, a conveyance on runners, used for carrying loads, esp. over ice and snow; a sledge; **2**, a light frame on runners, used in coasting:—*v.t.* [*p.t.* and *p.p.* sled′ded, *p.pr.* sled′ding], to carry on a sled or sledge.—*n.* **sled′ding.**

[1]**sledge** (slĕj), *n.* a vehicle, usually on runners, designed for carrying heavy loads, as over snow:—*v.i.* and *v.t.* [*p.t.* and *p.p.* sledged (slĕjd), *p.pr.* sledg′ing], to travel or carry on a sledge.

[2]**sledge** (slĕj), *n.* a large, heavy hammer, used by blacksmiths: also called *sledge hammer.*

sleek (slēk), *adj.* smooth; glossy:—*v.t.* to make smooth.—*adv.* **sleek′ly.**—*n.* **sleek′ness.**

sleep (slēp), *n.* **1**, a temporary, normal suspension of consciousness, occurring at regular intervals; slumber; **2**, rest; **3**, figuratively, death:—*v.i.* [*p.t.* and *p.p.* slept (slĕpt), *p.pr.* sleep′ing], **1**, to take rest in sleep; **2**, to be motionless or inactive; **3**, to be dead: —*v.t.* **1**, to make go away by sleep; as, he *slept* away his pain; **2**, to make pass through sleep; as, she *slept* the day away.

sleep-er (slēp′ẽr), *n.* **1**, one who slumbers; hence, a lazy person; a dead person; **2**, a horizontal beam that serves as support for some structure above, as for the rails of a railroad; **3**, *Colloq.*, a sleeping car.

sleep-ing car a car in use on railways, equipped with compartments and berths for sleeping.

sleep-ing part-ner one who has a share, not publicly acknowledged, in a business; sometimes, one without voice in a business.

sleep-ing sick-ness a disease, usually fatal, prevalent in West Africa, marked by increasing inertia and extreme drowsiness.

sleep-less (slēp′lĕs), *adj.* **1**, having no rest; wakeful; **2**, alert.—*adv.* **sleep′less-ly.**—*n.* **sleep′less-ness.**

sleep-walk-ing (slēp′wôk″ĭng), *n.* the act or habit of walking in one's sleep.—*n.* **sleep′walk″er.**

sleep-y (slēp′ĭ), *adj.* [*comp.* sleep′i-er, *superl.* sleep′i-est], **1**, inclined to, or ready for, slumber; **2**, causing drowsiness or heaviness; as, a *sleepy* day; **3**, drowsy; sluggish.—*adv.* **sleep′i-ly.**—*n.* **sleep′i-ness.**

sleet (slēt), *n.* driving rain partly frozen:—*v.i.* to shower frozen rain.

sleet-y (slēt′ĭ), *adj.* [*comp.* sleet′i-er, *superl.* sleet′i-est], consisting of half-frozen rain.—*n.* **sleet′i-ness.**

sleeve (slēv), *n.* **1**, the part of a garment that covers the arm; **2**, in mechanics, a part, usually shaped like a tube, to cover or protect some other part: **sleeve nut,** a nut the opposite ends of which are threaded in opposite directions: used to draw together two stays, rods, or the like:—*v.t.* [*p.t.* and *p.p.* sleeved (slēvd), *p.pr.* sleev′ing], to furnish with sleeves.—*adj.* **sleeve′less.**

sleigh (slā), *n.* a vehicle equipped with runners, used for conveying loads over snow or ice.

sleigh-ing (slā′ĭng), *n.* **1**, the act of riding or traveling in a sleigh; **2**, the condition of the snow which permits this kind of traveling.

sleight (slīt), *n.* **1**, skill; expertness; **2**, a scheme; artful trick; as, the juggler's *sleight:* **sleight of hand,** a trick or set of tricks requiring expert handling of the articles employed to produce the effect: **sleight-of-hand,** *adj.* pertaining to, or performed with, the skill of a juggler.

slen-der (slĕn′dẽr), *adj.* **1**, narrow in proportion to the length or height; slim; as, a *slender* figure; **2**, feeble; as, *slender* hope; **3**, moderate; relatively small; as, *slender* means of support; **4**, spare; as, *slender* meals.—*adv.* **slen′der-ly.**—*n.* **slen′der-ness.**

slept (slĕpt), past tense and past participle of the irregular verb *sleep.*

sleuth (slōōth), *n.* **1**, formerly, the track of a man or animal as known by the scent; **2**, *Colloq.*, a detective.

sleuth-hound (slōōth′hound″), *n.* a dog that follows the scent of men or animals; a bloodhound.

[1]**slew** (slōō), the past tense of the irregular verb *slay,* which see.

[2]**slew** (slōō), *n. Slang,* a great number or amount; a lot. Also, **slue.**

[3]**slew** (slōō), *v.t.* to turn about a fixed point: —*v.i.* to turn or twist about; swing round. See [1]**slue,** *Pfd. S.*

slice (slīs), *n.* a thin, broad piece cut from something; as, a *slice* of bread:—*v.i.* [*p.t.* and *p.p.* sliced (slīst), *p.pr.* slic′ing] in golf, to hit the ball with a stroke which causes it to curve, for a right-hand player, to the right:—*v.t.* **1**, to cut into thin pieces or layers; **2**, to cut (a layer or layers) from; divide or cut off; **3**, in golf, to hit (a ball) with a slicing stroke: opp. of *hook.*—*n.* **slic′er.**

slick (slĭk), *adj.* smooth; sleek; clever:—*adv.* smoothly; cleverly; smartly:—*v.t.* to make sleek:—*n.* a smooth surface, as one on water made by oil.

slick-er (slĭk'ẽr), *n.* in the U. S., an oilskin raincoat; a loose waterproof.

slid (slĭd), past tense and past participle of the irregular verb *slide.*

slide (slīd), *v.i.* [*p.t.* slid (slĭd), *p.p.* slid or slid'den (slĭd'n), *p.pr.* slid'ing], **1,** to move along a surface without leaving it; glide; **2,** to pass gradually or without being noticed; as, time *slides* by; **3,** to move quietly or secretly: with *away, out of, into;* as, he *slid* into a seat:—*v.t.* **1,** to push along; cause to slip into place; **2,** to put quietly; slip; as, he *slid* his hand into his pocket:—*n.* **1,** the act of sliding; **2,** a surface of ice for sliding; **3,** any smooth incline; **4,** a glass plate upon which is a picture for projection on a screen or an object for examination through a microscope; **5,** a fall of a mass of rock or snow down a mountain; **6,** that part of a device upon which anything moves by sliding; also, the part that slides; **7,** a cover, door, partition, or other part, that operates by sliding, as a slide valve: **slide rule,** a rule graduated in two or more scales, used for making mathematical calculations: **slide valve,** a valve with a D-shaped lengthwise section, controlling the steam supply in an engine (see *cylinder,* illus.).—*n.* **slid'er.**

slid-ing (slīd'ĭng), *p.adj.* **1,** varying according to certain conditions; as, a *sliding* scale of wages; **2,** slipping along in, or as in, a groove; as, a *sliding* door.

slight (slīt), *adj.* **1,** lacking in force or strength; as, *slight* resistance; **2,** frail; slender; as, a *slight* figure; **3,** not important; trivial; as, a *slight* difference in color; **4,** small in amount, degree, or quantity:—*n.* an action showing intentional neglect or discourtesy:—*v.t.* **1,** to treat with incivility; as, she *slighted* her guests; **2,** to neglect or perform carelessly; as, he habitually *slights* his work.—*n.* **slight'ness.**

slight-ing (slīt'ĭng), *p.adj.* containing or conveying the intention of discourtesy; detracting.—*adv.* **slight'ing-ly.**

slight-ly (slīt'lĭ), *adv.* to a small or trifling extent; partially.

sli-ly (slī'lĭ), *adv.* in a crafty or mischievous manner. Also, **sly'ly,** *Pfd. S.*

slim (slĭm), *adj.* [*comp.* slim'mer, *superl.* slim'mest], **1,** of small diameter; slender; as, a *slim* person; **2,** frail; slight; weak or insufficient; as, a *slim* excuse.—*adv.* **slim'ly.**—*n.* **slim'ness.**

slime (slīm), *n.* **1,** soft, moist earth or clay; **2,** any moist, sticky substance, esp. one that is dirty; **3,** a sticky substance, such as the mucous secretion upon certain snails.

slim-y (slīm'ĭ), *adj.* [*comp.* slim'i-er, *superl.* slim'i-est], **1,** pertaining to, or consisting of, slime; hence, repulsive; **2,** covered with, or giving off, slime.—*adv.* **slim'i-ly.**—*n.* **slim'i-ness.**

sling (slĭng), *n.* **1,** an implement for hurling a missile, as a stone; **2,** the act of hurling or flinging; a throw; also, figuratively, a stroke; **3,** any of various devices for hoisting or lowering heavy articles, or for suspending a gun, pack, or the like, from the shoulder; **4,** a supporting bandage, as for a wounded arm, or the like:—*v.t.* [*p.t.* slung (slŭng) or, *Archaic,* slang (slăng), *p.p.* slung, *p.pr.* sling'ing], **1,** to hurl with, or as if with, a sling; cast; fling; **2,** to hang so as to swing, as a hammock, or so as to be carried easily, as a camera; **3,** to place or suspend in a device for hoisting or lowering.—*n.* **sling'er.**

slink (slĭngk), *v.i.* [*p.t.* slunk (slŭngk) or, *Archaic,* slank (slăngk), *p.p.* slunk, *p.pr.* slink'ing], to go furtively; sneak off.

slip (slĭp), *v.i.* [*p.t.* and *p.p.* slipped (slĭpt), *p.pr.* slip'ping], **1,** to glide or slide; **2,** to miss one's foothold; lose one's balance; **3,** to pass without being seen; as, to *slip* into the room; **4,** to move, often unexpectedly, out of place; as, the chair *slipped;* **5,** to escape; as, the address has *slipped* from my mind; **6,** to blunder; err:—*v.t.* **1,** to put on or off with ease, as a ring or a garment; **2,** to cause to slide, as a door or panel; **3,** to let loose, as hounds; **4,** to cause to slide off; as, the horse *slips* his bridle; **5,** to carry secretly; **6,** to escape; as, the address has *slipped* my mind; **7,** to cut a part from (a plant) for planting; cut from a plant; **8,** to fail to seize or use:—*n.* **1,** the act of sliding or missing one's foothold; a sudden mischance; **2,** a fault; an error; a blunder; as, a *slip* of the tongue; **3,** a cutting from a plant; hence, an offshoot; **4,** a space between wharves for vessels; a dock; **5,** something that may be put on or off with ease, as a kind of undergarment, a pillowcase, etc.; **6,** a long, narrow piece of something; a strip; as, a *slip* of paper; **7,** a slim person; as, a mere *slip* of a girl.

slip-knot (slĭp'nŏt''), *n.* a knot which slips along the string, rope, or cord around which it is formed.

slip-per (slĭp'ẽr), *n.* a low, comfortable shoe, intended for indoor wear.

slip-pered (slĭp'ẽrd), *adj.* wearing or having slippers.

slip-per-y (slĭp'ẽr-ĭ), *adj.* **1,** having a surface so smooth or slimy as to yield no firm hold or footing; as, a *slippery* pavement; **2,** not easily caught, as a person; also, shifty; not trustworthy.—*n.* **slip'per-i-ness.**

slip-per-y elm **1,** a North American tree having a sticky inner bark; **2,** the bark, used to make a soothing medicine.

slip-shod (slĭp'shŏd''), *adj.* **1,** wearing shoes or slippers down at the heel; **2,** hence, slovenly; careless.

slit (slĭt), *v.t.* [*p.t.* and *p.p.* slit or slit'ted, *p.pr.* slit'ting], **1,** to cut lengthwise or into long strips; **2,** to cut or tear a lengthwise opening in; split:—*n.* **1,** a long cut; a lengthwise tear; **2,** a narrow opening.—*n.* **slit'ter.**

sliv-er (slĭv'ẽr), *v.t.* and *v.i.* **1,** to break off or split into long, thin, or very small pieces; **2,** to cut or break off:—*n.* **1,** a splinter; a sharp, thin, pointed piece, as of wood; **2,** a loose strand of fiber, as of cotton.

slob-ber (slŏb'ẽr), *v.i.* to let saliva dribble:—*v.t.* to wet by letting liquid run from the mouth.—*n.* **slob'ber-er.**

sloe (slō), *n.* **1,** a small, bitter plum of the blackthorn tree; also, the tree; **2,** in the U. S., any of various small, wild plums.

slo-gan (slō'găn), *n.* **1,** the war cry or gathering cry of a Highland clan; **2,** any rallying cry; as, the *slogan* of a party.

sloop (sloo͞p), *n.* a one-masted vessel with a fore-and-aft rig (see *ship,* illus.).

¹slop (slŏp), *n.* **1,** water, or other liquid, carelessly spilled; also, the spot made by spilled liquid; **2,** poor or weak liquid food: used contemptuously; **3,** in *pl.:* **a,** dirty or refuse water; **b,** distillery mash after removal of the alcohol: used as food for animals:—*v.t.* [*p.t.* and *p.p.* slopped (slŏpt), *p.pr.* slop'ping], **1,** to soil by letting liquid fall upon; **2,** to spill:—*v.i.* to be spilled: often with *out* or *over.*

²slop (slŏp), *n.* **1,** in *pl.,* cheap, ready-made clothes; also, among sailors, bedding, clothing, etc.; **2,** usually in *pl.,* wide trousers.

slope (slōp), *n.* **1,** an inclined line; a slant; **2,** any extent of rising or falling ground; specif., the land that descends toward the ocean:—*v.i.* and *v.t.* [*p.t.* and *p.p.* sloped (slōpt), *p.pr.* slop'ing], to incline; slant.—*p.adj.* **slop'ing.**—*adv.* **slop'ing-ly.**

slop-py (slŏp'ĭ), *adj.* [*comp.* slop'pi-er, *superl.* slop'pi-est], **1**, wet or splashy; muddy; **2**, soiled with liquids; dirty; **3**, *Colloq.*, untidy.—*adv.* **slop'pi-ly.**—*n.* **slop'pi-ness.**

slop-shop (slŏp'shŏp"), *n.* a store selling cheap, ready-made clothes.

slop-work (slŏp'wûrk"), *n.* **1**, the manufacture of cheap clothing, or slops; **2**, clothing of such a sort.

[1]**slot** (slŏt), *n.* **1**, a broad, flat wooden bar; **2**, *Eng. Dial.*, a door bolt.

[2]**slot** (slŏt), *n.* **1**, a narrow crack or groove; **2**, a small opening to receive the coin in a slot machine: **slot machine,** a device or machine released for operation by the insertion of a coin, as for selling candy:—*v.t.* [*p.t.* and *p.p.* slot'ted, *p.pr.* slot'ting], to cut a narrow crack or groove in.

[3]**slot** (slŏt), *n.* a deer's track; hence, any trail or trace.

sloth (slōth; slôth), *n.* **1**, laziness; indolence; **2**, any of various animals of South and Central America, which cling upside down to branches: so called from their slow movements.

Two-toed Sloth ($\frac{1}{20}$)

sloth-ful (slōth'fōōl; slôth'-), *adj.* lazy; slow; idle; sluggish; indolent.—*adv.* **sloth'ful-ly.**—*n.* **sloth'ful-ness.**

slouch (slouch), *n.* **1**, a stooping or droop, as of the head or shoulders; an ungainly carriage; **2**, hence, an ungainly, clownish fellow: **slouch hat,** a soft hat with a flexible brim:—*v.t.* **1**, to cause to droop; **2**, to pull down at the side, as a hat:—*v.i.* **1**, to walk in a clumsy, heavy, awkward manner; **2**, to droop or hang the head.

slouch-y (slouch'ĭ), *adj.* [*comp.* slouch'i-er, *superl.* slouch'i-est], awkward in manner or gait; ungainly; drooping.—*adv.* **slouch'i-ly.**—*n.* **slouch'i-ness.**

[1]**slough** (slou), *n.* **1**, a place full of deep mud; a bog; **2**, hence, a place or situation from which it is difficult to get out; **3**, (slōō), a backwater or inlet.—*adj.* [1]**slough'y.**

[2]**slough** (slŭf), *n.* **1**, the cast-off skin of a snake or other animal; **2**, in medicine, a mass of dead tissue cast off from living tissue: also used figuratively; as, to cast off the *slough* of ignorance:—*v.i.* **1**, to come off or be shed, as the skin of an animal; shed or cast the skin; **2**, in medicine, to come away in the form of dead tissue from living tissue:—*v.t.* to cast off, as the skin; hence, to discard.—*adj.* [2]**slough'y.**

Slo-vak (slō-văk'; slō'văk), *n.* **1**, a member of a race of Slavs living in central Europe, closely akin to the Czechs of Bohemia, with whom they form the Republic of Czechoslovakia; **2**, the language of these people.

slov-en (slŭv'n), *n.* one, esp. a man, who is untidy, careless, slipshod, or lazy.

Slo-vene (slō-vēn'), *n.* **1**, a member of a Slavic people native to the inland territory east of the Adriatic Sea, and now forming the northern part of the kingdom of the Serbs, Croats, and Slovenes, or Yugoslavia; **2**, their native language:—*adj.* pertaining to the Slovenes, or their language. Also, **Slo-ve'ni-an.**

slov-en-ly (slŭv'n-lĭ), *adj.* untidy in appearance; careless; not neat.—*n.* **slov'en-li-ness.**

slow (slō), *adj.* **1**, not rapid in motion; as, a *slow* step; **2**, not prompt; as, *slow* in arriving; **3**, occupying a long time; as, *slow* progress; **4**, not rash or hasty; as, *slow* to anger; **5**, dull or stupid; as, a *slow* pupil; a *slow* party; **6**, behind time; as, the clock is *slow*:—*v.i.* to move with less speed; as, the train *slowed* down:—*v.t.* **1**, to cause to move with less speed; **2**, to delay.—*adv.* **slow'ly.**—*n.* **slow'ness.**

Syn., adj. sluggish, tardy. To be *slow* is not to be rapid in motion, action, thought, etc.; as, *slow* trains arrive later than fast ones; *slow* growth is gradual. To be *sluggish* is to be *slow* to move or rouse; as, *sluggish* circulation; a *sluggish* stream. To be *tardy* is to be *slow* or behind time in putting in an appearance; as, *tardy* pupils; *tardy* recognition.

slow match a fuse made to burn slowly and regularly: used for firing a blast, mine, etc.

slow-worm (slō'wûrm"), *n.* a small, harmless, burrowing lizard, like a snake in appearance; the blindworm.

sloyd (sloid), *n.* a system of manual training whereby a practical knowledge of tools and materials is acquired. Also, **sloid.**

sludge (slŭj), *n.* **1**, slush; mire; sticky mud; **2**, anything resembling slush; **3**, floating ice.—*adj.* **sludg'y.**

[1]**slue** (slōō), *v.t.* [*p.t.* and *p.p.* slued (slōōd), *p.pr.* slu'ing], to cause to turn around a fixed point or pivot:—*v.i.* **1**, to slide around, as on a slippery surface; **2**, *Colloq.*, to twist or turn about. Also, **slew.**

[2]**slue** (slōō), *n.* *Slang*, a large amount; a lot. Also, **slew,** *Pfd. S.*

[1]**slug** (slŭg), *n.* **1**, any of various land snails without external shells; **2**, any of various shell-less marine mollusks; **3**, the creeping larva of certain insects; **4**, *Archaic*, a sluggard.

[2]**slug** (slŭg), *n.* **1**, a small, rough piece of metal; specif., a kind of rough, small bullet; **2**, in printing: **a**, a piece of metal thicker than a type but not so high, used for spacing; also, a thick piece of metal of the same height as type, used by printers as a marker; **b**, a line of type in one piece.

[3]**slug** (slŭg), *v.t.* [*p.t.* and *p.p.* slugged (slŭgd), *p.pr.* slug'ging], *Slang*, to strike hard, esp. with the fist, as in boxing; also, to throw heavily:—*n.* *Slang*, a hard blow, as with the fist or a club.—*n.* **slug'ger.**

slug-gard (slŭg'ȧrd), *n.* one who is always lazy and idle:—*adj.* lazy.

slug-gish (slŭg'ĭsh), *adj.* **1**, always lazy and idle: dull; slothful; **2**, inactive; slow; torpid; as, a *sluggish* river.—*adv.* **slug'gish-ly.**—*n.* **slug'gish-ness.**

Syn. indolent, languid. (See slow.)

sluice (slōōs), *n.* **1**, an artificial channel for conducting water, having a gate to regulate the flow; **2**, hence, an opening or channel through which anything flows; **3**, a stream of water issuing through a floodgate; **4**, an inclined trough for washing gold ore, carrying down logs, or the like:—*v.t.* [*p.t.* and *p.p.* sluiced (slōōst), *p.pr.* sluic'ing], **1**, to wash with water from, or as from, a sluice; as, to *sluice* gold; **2**, to draw off by a sluice, as water; **3**, to transport by a sluice, as

Sluice Gates

logs: **sluice gate**, an apparatus for holding in or letting out water, as from a canal; a floodgate (see illus. preceding page).

slum (slŭm), *n.* **1**, a foul, dirty street or district, or a city or town inhabited by the very poor or criminal classes; **2**, in *pl.*, a neighborhood composed of such streets: —*v.i.* [*p.t.* and *p.p.* slummed (slŭmd), *p.pr.* slum'ming], to visit such neighborhoods for the purpose of study or charity, or out of curiosity.—*n.* **slum'mer.**—*n.* **slum'ming.**

slum-ber (slŭm'bẽr), *v.i.* **1**, to sleep; esp., to sleep lightly; doze; **2**, to be in a state of rest or inactivity:—*n.* sleep; a doze.—*n.* **slum'ber-er.**—*adj.* **slum'ber-less.**

slum-ber-ous (slŭm'bẽr-ŭs), *adj.* **1**, bringing on, or inducing, sleep; **2**, heavy with sleep; drowsy. Also, **slum'brous.**—*adv.* **slum'ber-ous-ly.**

slump (slŭmp), *n.* **1**, the act of falling through a surface, as through weak ice; **2**, *Colloq.*, a sudden falling off; as, a *slump* in price:—*v.i.* **1**, to fall or sink suddenly, as into a marsh; **2**, to sink down heavily; as, he *slumped* in his chair; **3**, *Colloq.*, to fall or decline suddenly, as prices.

slung (slŭng), past tense and past participle of the irregular verb *sling.*

slung shot a weight attached to a cord or strap, used as a weapon.

slunk (slŭngk), past tense and past participle of the irregular verb *slink.*

slur (slûr), *v.t.* [*p.t.* and *p.p.* slurred (slûrd), *p.pr.* slur'ring], **1**, to soil; **2**, to pass over in a slighting manner, without proper consideration; **3**, to make obscure; **4**, to speak slightingly of; **5**, to pronounce indistinctly; **6**, in music: **a**, to sing or execute without breaks between two or more tones; **b**, to mark so as to indicate that the passage is to be sung or executed in this manner:—*n.* **1**, a stain; **2**, a slight reproach, or remark implying reproach; stigma; **3**, in music: **a**, a mark (⌒ or ‿), connecting notes that are to be sung or played without a break; **b**, the effect of singing or playing in this manner.

slush (slŭsh), *n.* **1**, partly melted snow; **2**, a greasy mixture for oiling machinery; **3**, *Rare*, soft mud.—*adj.* **slush'y.**

slut (slŭt), *n.* **1**, a dirty, untidy woman; **2**, a female dog.—*adj.* **slut'tish.**—*adv.* **slut'tish-ly.**—*n.* **slut'tish-ness.**

sly (slī), *adj.* [*comp.* sli'er or sly'er, *superl.* sli'est or sly'est], **1**, secretly mischievous; underhand; deceitful; **2**, playfully mischievous; roguish.—*adv.* **sly'ly.**—*n.* **sly'ness.**

Syn. artful, subtle. (See wily.)

[1]**smack** (smăk), *n.* **1**, a slight taste or flavor; **2**, a smattering; small amount; tinge:—*v.i.* to have a suggestion: usually with *of;* as, this *smacks* of treason.

[2]**smack** (smăk), *n.* **1**, a quick, sharp noise, as one made with the lips in kissing or in tasting; **2**, a loud, hearty kiss; **3**, a quick, resounding blow; slap:—*v.t.* **1**, to kiss with a quick, sharp noise; **2**, to make a loud noise with (the mouth, lips, or the like); **3**, *Colloq.*, to strike with a sharp blow:—*v.i.* to make a noise with the lips.

[3]**smack** (smăk), *n.* a small sailing vessel used in fishing; fishing sloop.

smack-ing (smăk'ĭng), *p.adj.* **1**, making a sharp noise; **2**, lively; brisk.

small (smôl), *adj.* **1**, comparatively little in size, quantity, degree, or the like; as, a *small* school; a *small* amount; **2**, not important; insignificant; as, his opinion is of *small* value; this is a *small* matter; **3**, not powerful: said of the voice; **4**, weak: said of diluted liquors, as beer; **5**, doing business in a limited way; as, a *small* farmer; **6**, petty; not generous; narrow: **small arms**, firearms that can be carried on the person, such as muskets, rifles, pistols, etc.: **small hours**, the early morning hours after midnight: with *the:* **small pica**, a size of type, now called 11 point (see *type*): **small talk**, light, trifling conversation.—*adj.* **small'ish.**—*n.* **small'ness.**

small-pox (smôl'pŏks''), *n.* a contagious disease marked by vomiting, fever, and an eruption of pustules.

smart (smärt), *adj.* **1**, causing a stinging, sharp sensation; severe; sharp; as, a *smart* punishment; **2**, brisk; fresh: said of a breeze; **3**, clever; shrewd; **4**, pertly witty; **5**, showy; fashionable; as, a *smart* gown:—*n.* **1**, a quick, lively pain; **2**, keen grief:—*v.i.* **1**, to feel a stinging sensation; be the seat of a stinging sensation; **2**, to cause a stinging sensation; **3**, to suffer; have one's feelings wounded.—*adv.* **smart'ly.**—*n.* **smart'ness.**

smart-en (smär'tn), *v.t.* to make stylish or spruce: often with *up.*

smash (smăsh), *v.t.* to break in pieces by violence; shatter; destroy utterly: —*v.i.* **1**, to break into many pieces, as from a blow or pressure; **2**, *Colloq.*, to go into bankruptcy suddenly, as a business; **3**, to be thrown violently against something; as, the machine *smashed* against the wall:—*n.* **1**, a breaking to pieces; **2**, utter destruction; **3**, *Colloq.*, bankruptcy.—*n.* **smash'er.**

smat-ter (smăt'ẽr), *n.* a slight knowledge of anything.—*n.* **smat'ter-er.**

smat-ter-ing (smăt'ẽr-ĭng), *n.* slight, superficial knowledge.

smear (smēr), *v.t.* **1**, to spread with anything greasy, oily, or sticky; daub; **2**, to soil in any way:—*n.* a blot or stain.

smell (smĕl), *v.t.* [*p.t.* and *p.p.* smelled (smĕld) or smelt (smĕlt), *p.pr.* smell'ing], **1**, to perceive by means of the nerves in the nose; obtain the scent of; **2**, to inhale the odor of; **3**, to seek or detect by, or as by, the odor; as, to *smell* trouble:—*v.i.* **1**, to have an odor; as, this room *smells* of sulphur; **2**, *Colloq.*, to use the power of perceiving by the sense of smell: with *of;* as, *smell* of this flower:—*n.* **1**, that quality of things which is perceived by the olfactory nerves; odor; **2**, the sense by which such qualities are perceived; **3**, an act of smelling.—*n.* **smell'er.**—*adj.* **smell'y.**

Syn., *n.* fragrance, scent, perfume.

smell-ing salts aromatic carbonate of ammonia, used to relieve faintness, headache, etc.

[1]**smelt** (smĕlt), *n.* any of certain small fishes found in northern waters.

[2]**smelt** (smĕlt), past tense and past participle of the verb *smell.*

[3]**smelt** (smĕlt), *v.t.* to fuse or melt (ore) in a furnace for the purpose of extracting the metallic contents; also, to obtain (metal) by this process:—*v.i.* to melt or fuse.

smelt-er (smĕl'tẽr), *n.* **1**, one who melts or refines ore; **2**, an establishment or furnace for reducing ore; also, its owner.

smelt-ing fur-nace a furnace in which ore is melted to obtain the metal in it.

smi-lax (smī'lăks), *n.* **1**, a delicate, trailing, foliage plant of the lily family, much used for decoration; **2**, any of several prickly vines or herbs of the same family.

smile (smīl), *v.i.* [*p.t.* and *p.p.* smiled (smīld), *p.pr.* smil'ing], **1**, to show pleasure, amusement, contempt, disdain, or the like, by an expression of the face; **2**, to look gay or cheerful, as a landscape; **3**, to look with favor; as, to *smile* on one's labors:—*v.t.* to express by a look of pleasure, kindness, etc.: —*n.* **1**, an expression of the face showing amusement, pleasure, or affection, irony, contempt, or the like; **2**, an agreeable or pleasing appearance; **3**, good will; favor.—*n.* **smil'er.**—*adv.* **smil'ing-ly.**

smirch (smûrch), *v.t.* **1,** to smear; soil; stain; **2,** to bring disgrace upon; as, to *smirch* her name:—*n.* a smear or stain.

smirk (smûrk), *v.i.* to smile affectedly or conceitedly:—*n.* an affected smile.

smite (smīt), *v.t.* [*p.t.* smote (smōt), *p.p.* smit'ten (smĭt'n), *p.pr.* smit'ing], **1,** to hit; strike with, or as with, the hand; **2,** to destroy; **3,** to cast down; punish; trouble; **4,** to touch with any strong feeling, as love, grief, fear, or the like; **5,** to strike with; cause to strike; as, to *smite* a staff upon the ground; **6,** to affect with the abruptness of a blow; as, an idea *smote* him:—*v.i.* to give or deal a blow.—*n.* **smit'er.**

smith (smĭth), *n.* one who works or shapes metal with forge, anvil, and hammer; a worker in metals.

smith-er-y (smĭth'ẽr-ĭ), *n.* [*pl.* smitheries (-ĭz)], **1,** the shop of a smith; smithy; **2,** the trade or art of a smith.

smith-y (smĭth'ĭ), *n.* [*pl.* smithies (-ĭz)], a forge.

smit-ten (smĭt'n), past participle of the irregular verb *smite:*—*p.adj.* **1,** grievously afflicted; **2,** deeply affected.

smock (smŏk), *n.* **1,** a long, loose, outer blouse; **2,** a similar blouse worn by women; **3,** *Archaic,* a chemise:—*v.t.* **1,** to dress in a smock; **2,** to trim with smocking.

smock frock a coarse, long, loose blouse, worn as a working garment over other clothes, as by painters, European peasants, etc.

smock-ing (smŏk'ĭng), *n.* a kind of decorative needlework used for holding gathers in place.

smoke (smōk), *n.* **1,** the visible, finely divided material that is formed or escapes when a substance is burned; **2,** anything resembling smoke, as vapor; **3,** the act of smoking tobacco, opium, etc.; **4,** something transitory and unsubstantial, as careless talk:—*v.t.* [*p.t.* and *p.p.* smoked (smōkt), *p.pr.* smok'ing], **1,** to apply smoke to, as meat; blacken, dry, scent, or medicate by the action of smoke; **2,** to inhale and puff out the smoke of, as of burning tobacco; **3,** to force out by smoke; as, to *smoke* an animal from its hole; **4,** *Archaic,* to detect or search out:—*v.i.* **1,** to emit or give out smoke; **2,** to inhale and puff out the smoke of smoldering tobacco, or the like: **smoke consumer,** a device used by coal-burning industries to do away with the black smoke from their chimneys; **smoke screen,** an extremely dense smoke cloud, formed by various devices and used to conceal the movements of ships or troops.

smoke-jack (smōk'jăk"), *n.* a device for turning a roasting spit in a fireplace, consisting of a wheel rotated in a chimney by the passage of the heated gases.

smoke-less (smōk'lĕs), *adj.* burning with little or no visible gas: **smokeless powder,** an explosive powder that burns with but little smoke.

smok-er (smōk'ẽr), *n.* **1,** one who or that which smokes; esp., one who smokes tobacco; **2,** a railway car in which passengers may smoke; **3,** *Colloq.,* a social gathering at which smoking is permitted.

smoke-stack (smōk'stăk"), *n.* a chimney, esp. the smoke pipe on a factory or a locomotive.

smok-ing (smōk'ĭng), *p.adj.* **1,** giving out smoke; **2,** connected with the smoking of tobacco; as, a *smoking* room.

smok-y (smōk'ĭ), *adj.* [*comp.* smok'i-er, *superl.* smok'i-est], **1,** giving out, or filled with, smoke; as, a *smoky* stove; **2,** soiled with smoke; **3,** hazy in atmosphere; as, a *smoky* day; **4,** grayish black in color, like smoke.—*adv.* **smok'i-ly.**—*n.* **smok'i-ness.**

smol-der (smōl'dẽr), *v.i.* **1,** to burn slowly, giving forth smoke without flame; **2,** to burn beneath the surface; exist in a stifled condition; as, their discontent *smolders.* Also, **smoul'der.**

smolt (smōlt), *n.* a young salmon that has acquired its silver scales.

smooth (smōōth), *adj.* **1,** not rough; even in surface or texture; **2,** perfectly blended; free from lumps; **3,** gently flowing; as, a *smooth* river; hence, placid; serene; calm; pleasant; mild; **4,** flattering; as, *smooth* words; **5,** easy and polished, as diction; **6,** steady in motion; **7,** without hair, esp. on the face; **8,** free from sharpness; pleasant, as wine:—*n.* **1,** the act of making smooth; **2,** that part of anything that is not rough:—*v.t.* **1,** to remove roughness from; **2,** to make even, steady, or calm; take away harshness from; **3,** to make light of; as, to *smooth* over an offense; **4,** to make pleasant by soft words; **5,** to remove, as difficulties or hindrances: with *away;* **6,** to soothe, as the feelings.—*n.* **smooth'er.**—*adv.* **smooth'ly.**—*n.* **smooth'ness.**

smooth-bore (smōōth'bōr"), *adj.* having a tube, or bore, with a smooth inner surface: said of a gun:—*n.* a gun with such a bore. Also, **smooth'-bore".**

smooth-faced (smōōth'=fāst"), *adj.* **1,** without beard or mustache; **2,** blank; hence, deceptive.

smote (smōt), past tense of the irregular verb *smite.*

smoth-er (smŭth'ẽr), *v.t.* **1,** to destroy the life of by depriving of air; stifle; also, to suffocate, as a fire; **2,** to suppress or conceal; as, to *smother* one's anger:—*v.i.* **1,** to be suffocated or deprived of air; **2,** to be subdued, restrained, or concealed:—*n.* **1,** that which is dense, as stifling smoke or thick dust; **2,** a suppressed or smoldering state; also, a smoldering fire.—*adj.* **smoth'er-y.**

smudge (smŭj), *n.* **1,** a smear or stain; **2,** suffocating smoke; also, a smoldering fire of damp wood giving forth dense smoke: used to prevent frost or to keep off insects:—*v.t.* [*p.t.* and *p.p.* smudged (smŭjd), *p.pr.* smudg'ing], **1,** to smear or stain; **2,** to keep away by a smudge.—*adj.* **smudg'y.**—*adv.* **smudg'i-ly.**—*n.* **smudg'i-ness.**

smug (smŭg), *adj.* [*comp.* smug'ger, *superl.* smug'gest], **1,** affectedly precise or prim; **2,** self-satisfied; conceited.—*adv.* **smug'-ly.**—*n.* **smug'ness.**

smug-gle (smŭg'l), *v.t.* and *v.i.* [*p.t.* and *p.p.* -gled (-ld), *p.pr.* -gling], **1,** to bring or send (goods) to or from a country, without paying duties; **2,** to carry or introduce secretly.—*n.* **smug'gler.**—*n.* **smug'gling.**

smut (smŭt), *n.* **1,** a spot or stain made by soot or dirt; **2,** a poor quality of soft coal; **3,** a disease affecting corn, wheat, etc.; **4,** foul language:—*v.t.* [*p.t.* and *p.p.* smut'ted, *p.pr.* smut'ting], to soil or blacken with, or as with, soot:—*v.i.* **1,** to become blackened by soot, or affected by mildew or smut; **2,** to give off soot or dirt.

smutch (smŭch), *v.t.* to soil with smoke, soot, or coal:—*n.* a dirty spot.—*adj.* **smutch'y.**

smut-ty (smŭt'ĭ), *adj.* [*comp.* smut'ti-er, *superl.* smut'ti-est], **1,** soiled or stained with dirt or soot; **2,** indecent or foul in talk.—*adv.* **smut'ti-ly.**—*n.* **smut'ti-ness.**

snack (snăk), *n.* *Colloq.,* a slight, hurried repast, or meal.

snaf-fle (snăf'l), *n.* a horse's bit having a joint in the middle and no curb:—*v.t.* [*p.t.* and *p.p.* -fled (-ld), *p.pr.* -fling], to put such a bit in the mouth of.

snag (snăg), *n.* **1,** the stump of a branch projecting from the trunk; **2,** a broken tree sticking up from the bottom of a river or lake and dangerous to boats; **3,** a tooth projecting beyond the rest; also, a broken or decayed tooth; **4,** *Colloq.*, any unexpected obstacle or difficulty:—*v.t.* [*p.t.* and *p.p.* snagged (snăgd), *p.pr.* snag′ging], to injure or destroy by contact with a broken, jagged stump.—*adj.* **snag′gy.**

snail (snāl), *n.* **1,** any of numerous land or water mollusks having a spiral shell; **2,** hence, any slow-moving person; a sluggard. —*adj.* **snail′-paced″.**

snake (snāk), *n.* any of various limbless reptiles having long, slim bodies, a few species of which have a poisonous bite:—*v.t.* [*p.t.* and *p.p.* snaked (snākt), *p.pr.* snak′-ing], *Slang,* to drag; jerk: often with *out.*

snake-root (snāk′ro͞ot″), *n.* any of various plants supposed to cure the bite of a snake; also, the root of such a plant.

snak-y (snāk′ĭ), *adj.* [*comp.* snak′i-er, *superl.* snak′i-est], **1,** pertaining to, or like, a snake; **2,** infested with snakes; **3,** deceitful.

snap (snăp), *v.i.* [*p.t.* and *p.p.* snapped (snăpt), *p.pr.* snap′ping], **1,** to break suddenly; **2,** to snatch at something suddenly, esp. with the teeth; **3,** to produce a sharp, sudden sound; crackle; **4,** to speak crossly or angrily; **5,** to miss fire: said of a gun; **6,** to flash or sparkle; as, her eyes *snapped:*—*v.t.* **1,** to break off short; crack; **2,** to seize suddenly and unexpectedly, as with the teeth; **3,** to speak to sharply and angrily: followed by *up;* **4,** to cause to make a sudden, sharp sound; as, to *snap* the fingers; **5,** to close with a sudden sharp sound; **6,** to throw with a jerk, as a baseball; **7,** to take an instantaneous photograph of:—*n.* **1,** the act of seizing or breaking suddenly; **2,** the sudden breaking of something stiff or tightly stretched; **3,** a sudden, sharp sound; as, the *snap* of a whip; **4,** a spring lock or catch; **5,** a kind of small, thin, crisp cooky; **6,** *Colloq.*, a sudden short period of severe weather; as, a cold *snap;* **7,** *Colloq.*, energy or vim:—*adj. Colloq.*, receiving or requiring little thought; as, a *snap* judgment; a *snap* course of study.

snap-drag-on (snăp′drăg″ŭn), *n.* **1,** a plant with a showy flower of curious shape; **2,** a game in which raisins are snatched from a bowl of burning brandy.

snap-per (snăp′ẽr), *n.* **1,** one that snaps; **2,** any of various flesh-eating, edible fishes of tropical seas.

snap-ping tur-tle either of two fresh-water turtles that seize their prey by a snap of the jaws.

snap-pish (snăp′ĭsh), *adj.* **1,** likely to snatch with the jaws; eager to bite; as, a *snappish* dog; **2,** sharp in speech; easily irritated.—*adv.* **snap′pish-ly.** —*n.* **snap′pish-ness.**

snap-py (snăp′ĭ), *adj.* [*comp.* snap′pi-er, *superl.* snap′pi-est], *Colloq.*, **1,** sharp and irritable in speech; **2,** full of energy; brisk; as, a *snappy* talk.

snap-shot (snăp′shŏt″), *n.* **1,** an instantaneous photograph; **2,** a quick shot made without careful aim. Also, **snap shot.**

snare (snâr), *n.* **1,** a running noose or loop of cord or wire, for catching an animal or a bird; **2,** anything that entangles or entraps; **3,** usually in *pl.*, a catgut string stretched across the lower head of a snare drum:—*v.t.* [*p.t.* and *p.p.* snared (snârd), *p.pr.* snar′ing], to catch or entangle with, or as with, a noose or net.—*n.* **snar′er.**

snare drum a small drum, with catgut strings across one head to add to its resonance (see *drum,* illus.).

¹snarl (snärl), *v.i.* **1,** to make a growling noise, as an angry dog; **2,** to speak in harsh, surly tones; quarrel:—*v.t.* to utter in a growl or a harsh, surly tone:—*n.* **1,** the act of growling; **2,** a surly tone; **3,** an angry quarrel.—*n.* **snarl′er.**—*adj.* **snarl′y.**

²snarl (snärl), *v.t.* **1,** to knot or entangle, as thread or hair; **2,** to ornament, as hollow silverware, with raised work or hammered work:—*v.i.* to become tangled or knotted:—*n.* an entanglement or knot, as of thread or hair; hence, a perplexity; a complicated situation.

snarl-ing (snärl′ĭng), *n.* the decorating of hollow metal with raised work by hammering on the inner surface.

snatch (snăch), *v.t.* to seize suddenly or rudely: often used figuratively; as, to *snatch* an hour of sleep:—*v.i.* to attempt to seize anything suddenly: with *at:*—*n.* **1,** a hasty catch or seizing; **2,** a small fragment; as, a *snatch* of music; **3,** a brief period.—*n.* **snatch′er.**—*adj.* **snatch′y.**

snath (snăth), *n.* the handle or curved shaft of a scythe. Also, **snathe** (snā*th*).

sneak (snēk), *v.i.* **1,** to creep or steal away privately or meanly; slink; **2,** to act in a cowardly or mean way:—*n.* **1,** a mean, cowardly fellow; **2,** a petty thief.—*p.adj.* **sneak′ing.**—*adj.* **sneak′y.**—*n.* **sneak′er.**

sneer (snēr), *v.i.* **1,** to show contempt by an expression of the face, as by curling the lips; **2,** to speak contemptuously or with ridicule: often followed by *at;* as, to *sneer* at religion:—*v.t.* to utter in a scornful manner:—*n.* **1,** contempt or scorn shown in speech or manner; **2,** a contemptuous smile. —*n.* **sneer′er.**—*adv.* **sneer′ing-ly.**

Syn., v. taunt, scoff. (See jeer.)

sneeze (snēz), *n.* a sudden and brief spasm of the breathing organs, causing a violent and audible rush of air through the mouth and nostrils:—*v.i.* [*p.t.* and *p.p.* sneezed (snēzd), *p.pr.* sneez′ing], to be seized with such a violent and brief spasm.

snell (snĕl), *n.* a short piece of gut or other strong material by which a fishhook is attached to the line; snood.

snick-er (snĭk′ẽr), *n.* a half suppressed laugh; giggle:—*v.i.* to laugh slyly; giggle. Also, **snig′ger.**

sniff (snĭf), *v.i.* to draw in the breath audibly through the nose, often as an expression of contempt:—*v.t.* **1,** to smell or scent; as, a dog will *sniff* an enemy; to *sniff* danger; **2,** to draw in through the nose:—*n.* **1,** the act of smelling; **2,** an audible, often scornful, inhaling through the nose.

snip (snĭp), *v.t.* [*p.t.* and *p.p.* snipped (snĭpt), *p.pr.* snip′ping], to cut into or clip, as with scissors or shears; nip: often with *off:*—*n.* **1,** a single cut with scissors; clip; **2,** a small piece; bit; **3,** *Colloq.*, a small person or a thing of no importance.

snipe (snīp), *n.* [*pl.* snipe], any of several long-billed shore birds akin to the woodcock:—*v.i.* [*p.t.* and *p.p.* sniped (snīpt), *p.pr.* snip′ing], **1,** to hunt such birds; **2,** to shoot from a hidden position, as do sharpshooters:—*v.t.* to shoot, or shoot at, from a hidden position.

snip-er (snīp′ẽr), *n.* **1,** a hidden shooter; **2,** a sharpshooter expert in using the periscope, telescope, etc., and in determining enemy positions from the return fire.

snip-py (snĭp′ĭ), *adj.* [*comp.* snip′pi-er, *superl.* snip′pi-est], **1,** cut short; fragmentary; **2,** *Slang,* curt; disdainful, as remarks.—*adv.* **snip′pi-ly.**—*n.* **snip′pi-ness.**

sniv-el (snĭv′l), *v.i.* **1,** to run at the nose; **2,** to cry or fret in a complaining or affected manner.—*n.* **sniv′el-er; sniv′el-ler.**

snob (snŏb), *n.* one who is servile to persons of wealth or position and supercilious to those whom he considers inferior; one who judges by externals.—*n.* **snob′ber-y.**

snob-bish (snŏb'ĭsh), *adj.* pertaining to, or like, a snob; overbearing; supercilious; arrogant.—*adv.* **snob'bish-ly.**—*n.* **snob'bish-ness.**

snood (snōōd), *n.* **1**, a band or ribbon worn around the hair of a young woman; **2**, a short line, as of gut, to connect a fishing line with the hook.

snoop (snōōp), *v.i. U. S. Colloq.*, to pry into other persons' affairs; look about in a furtive or sneaking way:—*n. U. S. Colloq.*, one who pries.—*n.* **snoop'er.**

snooze (snōōz), *v.i.* [*p.t.* and *p.p.* snoozed (snōōzd), *p.pr.* snooz'ing], *Colloq.*, to take a nap; doze:—*n. Colloq.*, a nap.

snore (snōr), *v.i.* [*p.t.* and *p.p.* snored (snōrd), *p.pr.* snor'ing], to breathe audibly through the nose in sleep:—*n.* a noisy breathing in sleep.—*n.* **snor'er.**

snort (snôrt), *v.i.* **1**, to force the air through the nose with a loud sound; **2**, to express feeling by such a sound; as, to *snort* with anger:—*v.t.* to utter with such a sound:—*n.* a loud, abrupt sound so made; as, a *snort* of rage.—*n.* **snort'er.**

snout (snout), *n.* **1**, the projecting nose of a beast, as of swine; **2**, the nozzle of a pipe, hose, etc: **snout beetle**, any of several weevils, with a well-defined beak.

snow (snō), *n.* frozen vapor in the form of white, feathery flakes, or crystals, falling through the air or lying upon the earth: **snow line**, the lowest limit of perpetual snow:—*v.i.* to fall in frozen crystals: used impersonally; as, it *snows*:—*v.t.* **1**, to pour out thickly, like falling snow; **2**, to obstruct or shut in with masses of snow: with *in* or *up*; as, the farm was *snowed* in for three days.

snow-ball (snō'bôl"), *n.* **1**, a mass of snow pressed together in the form of a ball; **2**, any of various shrubs or trees of the honeysuckle family, bearing ball-like clusters of white flowers:—*v.i.* to throw snowballs:—*v.t.* to storm or attack with snowballs.

snow-bird (snō'bûrd"), *n.* either of two small American finches, common in time of heavy snow.

snow-blind (snō'=blīnd"), *adj.* having the sight affected by the glare of snow.—*n.* **snow'-blind"ness.**

snow-bound (snō'=bound"), *adj.* shut in by a heavy snowfall.

snow-drift (snō'drĭft"), *n.* a mass of snow heaped up by the wind.

snow-drop (snō'drŏp"), *n.* **1**, a plant with white flowers, which blooms in very early spring; **2**, its flower or bulb.

snow-fall (snō'fôl"), *n.* **1**, the quantity of snow which falls during a given time or a single storm; **2**, a light snowstorm.

snow-flake (snō'flāk"), *n.* a white feathery crystal of frozen vapor.

snow-plow (snō'plou"), *n.* a machine or engine used to clear roads of heavy snow. Also, **snow'plough".**

snow-shed (snō'shĕd"), *n.* a roof or shelter to keep off snow, as from a railroad track in the mountains.

snow-shoe (snō'shōō"), *n.* a network of rawhide stretched upon a racket-shaped wooden frame, and fastened on by thongs: worn for traveling over deep snow.

snow-slide (snō'slīd"), *n.* the sudden sliding of a mass of snow, as down a mountain slope; an avalanche.

snow-storm (snō'stôrm"), *n.* a heavy downfall of snow, usually accompanied by a strong wind.

snow-y (snō'ĭ), *adj.* [*comp.* snow'i-er, *superl.* snow'i-est], **1**, white like fresh snow; as, *snowy* linen; **2**, covered with, or full of, snow; **3**, pure.—*adv.* **snow'i-ly.**—*n.* **snow'i-ness.**

snub (snŭb), *v.t.* [*p.t.* and *p.p.* snubbed (snŭbd), *p.pr.* snub'bing], **1**, to answer or interrupt with rude or scornful words; **2**, to treat with scorn; slight intentionally:—*n.* **1**, an intentional slight; **2**, a check.

snub-nosed (snŭb'=nōzd"), *adj.* having a short, broad, tilted nose.

[1]**snuff** (snŭf), *v.t.* **1**, to draw in through the nose; **2**, to smell; examine by the scent; as, the dog *snuffed* him all over:—*v.i.* to snort or sniff:—*n.* **1**, the act of drawing in through the nose; **2**, powdered tobacco to be inhaled through the nose.—*n.* **snuff'er.**

[2]**snuff** (snŭf), *n.* the burned part of the wick of a candle or lamp:—*v.t.* **1**, to cut the charred part from; as, to *snuff* a candle; **2**, to extinguish: generally with *out;* **3**, hence, to end suddenly; as, his life was *snuffed* out.

snuff-box (snŭf'bŏks"), *n.* a small, often ornamental, holder for snuff.

snuff-ers (snŭf'ẽrz), *n.pl.* an instrument for trimming the wick of a candle and holding the charred end.

CANDLE SNUFFERS

snuf-fle (snŭf'l), *v.i.* [*p.t.* and *p.p.* -fled (-ld), *p.pr.* -fling], to speak or breathe noisily through the nose, esp. when it is obstructed:—*n.* **1**, a noisy breathing through the nose, esp. when it is obstructed; **2**, an affected nasal twang; **3**, in *pl.*, *Colloq.*, obstruction of the nostrils; a cold in the head.

snuff-y (snŭf'ĭ), *adj.* **1**, soiled with snuff; **2**, of a dull brownish color.

snug (snŭg), *adj.* [*comp.* snug'ger, *superl.* snug'gest], **1**, lying comfortable and warm; **2**, compact and convenient; as, a *snug* house; **3**, sheltered and safe; cozy and comfortable; **4**, fitting tightly but easily; as, a *snug* jacket:—*v.i.* [*p.t.* and *p.p.* snugged (snŭgd), *p.pr.* snug'ging], to lie close and warm; snuggle: with *up* or *together.*—*adv.* **snug'ly.**—*n.* **snug'ness.**

snug-ger-y (snŭg'ẽr-ĭ), *n.* [*pl.* snuggeries (-ĭz)], *Colloq.*, a cozy room.

snug-gle (snŭg'l), *v.i.* [*p.t.* and *p.p.* -gled (-ld), *p.pr.* -gling], to cuddle or nestle close for warmth and comfort: often with *up* or *together:*—*v.t.* to hold close and make comfortable: often with *up*.

[1]**so** (sō), *adv.* **1**, in like manner or degree: correlative with *as*, in negative expressions; as, she is not *so* tall as he; **2**, to such a degree; in such manner: correlative with *that;* as, it is *so* hot that it burns; **3**, just as stated; as, it may be *so:* used also to gather up and repeat an idea with emphasis; as, we have a gray cat, and *so* have they; **4**, for this or that reason; such being the case; accordingly; therefore; as, the door opened, *so* he went in: in this use equivalent to a conjunction; **5**, thereabouts; more or less; as, I shall be gone an hour or *so;* **6**, well: used as an expletive expressing mild surprise; as, *so* you are back, are you? **7**, too: used in emphatic contradiction; as, you can't do that. I can *so;* **8**, *Colloq.:* **a**, to a degree that needs emphasis; as, *so* much to do; *so* beautiful; **b**, to such an extent; as, I long *so* to go; **c**, indeed: used for *is it so?* as, *so?* **9**, *Archaic*, ever: usually used in compounds; as, who*so:* **so help me God**, a form of oath used when bearing witness or making a statement:—*conj.* **1**, therefore; as a consequence of which; so that; as, it is raining, *so* we cannot go; **2**, on condition that; as, many things are forgiven a man, *so* he be rich:—*interj.* keep still! stay as you are!

[2]**so** (sō), *n.* the fifth in the series of syllables used, for convenience, in singing the degrees of a diatonic scale. Also, formerly, **sol.**

soak (sōk), *v.t.* **1**, to cause to absorb moisture; steep in a fluid; **2**, to wet thoroughly; **3**, to draw in by the pores or openings; as, a sponge will *soak* up water:—*v.i.* **1**, to become thoroughly wet; **2**, to be steeped in fluid; **3**, to enter by pores or small openings; as, water *soaks* into the earth:—*n.* **1**, the act or process of wetting thoroughly; **2**, the fluid in which anything steeps.—*n.* **soak'er.**—*n.* **soak'age.**

soap (sōp), *n.* a substance for cleansing, made by combining fats or oils with an alkali:—*v.t.* to cover or wash with soap.

soap bub-ble **1**, a frail, iridescent bubble, formed of strong soapsuds inflated by being blown from a pipe; **2**, anything of an attractive but fleeting and unsubstantial nature.

soap-stone (sōp'stōn''), *n.* a massive, rock form of talc; also, the same substance when powdered.

soap-suds (sōp'sŭdz''), *n.pl.* soapy water whipped into a froth or foam.

soap-y (sōp'ĭ), *adj.* [*comp.* soap'i-er, *superl.* soap'i-est], **1**, covered with, or like, soap; **2**, smooth.—*n.* **soap'i-ness.**

soar (sōr), *v.i.* **1**, to fly high in the air, as a bird; mount upward with wings; **2**, to rise above what is usual or common in thought or life; as, prices *soar;* hope *soars;* **3**, to move along without the aid of the motor, as an airplane:—*n.* a lofty flight; high flying.

sob (sŏb), *v.i.* [*p.t.* and *p.p.* sobbed (sŏbd), *p.pr.* sob'bing], **1**, to sigh by catching the breath convulsively; **2**, to weep with a convulsive heaving of the breast; **3**, to make a sound like a catch of the breath:—*v.t.* to utter with a catch of the breath:—*n.* **1**, a convulsive sigh; a sudden catching of the breath; **2**, any similar sound.

so-ber (sō'bẽr), *adj.* **1**, temperate by habit, esp. in the use of intoxicating liquors; **2**, not under the influence of liquor; **3**, self-possessed; calm; steady; sedate; **4**, solemn; grave; **5**, plain; subdued; as, *sober* colors:—*v.t.* and *v.i.* **1**, to make free, or recover, from drunkenness; **2**, to make, or become, calm.—*adv.* **so'ber-ly.**—*n.* **so'ber-ness.**

so-ber–mind-ed (sō'bẽr=mīnd''ĕd), *adj.* of grave and serious disposition; sedate.—*n.* **so''ber–mind'ed-ness.**

so-bri-e-ty (sō-brī'ĕ-tĭ), *n.* **1**, the state or quality of being moderate or temperate in all ways; **2**, calmness; seriousness; gravity of manner.

so-bri-quet (sō''brĕ''kā'; sō'brĭ-kā), [Fr.], *n.* a nickname; fanciful name.

so–called (sō'=kōld''), *adj.* usually thus named or termed: often implying a want of accuracy.

soc-cer (sŏk'ẽr), *n.* a kind of football game in which the ball is driven by the feet, legs, body, or head, the use of hands or arms being prohibited.

so-cia-ble (sō'shȧ-bl), *adj.* **1**, disposed to associate and talk with others; companionable; **2**, giving opportunity for friendly companionship; as, a *sociable* neighborhood; **3**, marked by friendliness.—*n. U. S. Colloq.*, an informal friendly party.—*adv.* **so'cia-bly.**—*n.* **so'cia-ble-ness.**—*n.* **so''cia-bil'i-ty.**

so-cial (sō'shăl), *adj.* **1**. pertaining to men as living in association with one another; **2**, relating to general conditions of human life; as, *social* welfare; **3**, inclined to friendly relationship and conversation; as, a *social* disposition; **4**, pertaining to the life of people of wealth and fashion; as, the *social* whirl; **5**, of plants, in groups; **6**, of insects, in organized communities, as ants or bees.—*adv.* **so'cial-ly.**—*n.* **so''ci-al'i-ty.**

Syn. sociable, communicative.

so-cial-ism (sō'shăl-ĭzm), *n.* **1**, the economic doctrine that there should be public ownership and operation of the principal means of production and distribution of wealth, and a fair division of opportunity and of rewards of labor; **2**, the political movement associated with this doctrine.

so-cial-ist (sō'shăl-ĭst), *n.* one who believes in socialism:—*adj.* pertaining to the economic doctrine of socialism, or to its advocates.—*adj.* **so''cial-is'tic.**

so-cial-ize (sō'shăl-īz), *v.t.* [*p.t.* and *p.p.* -ized (-īzd), *p.pr.* -iz''ing], **1**, to bring into friendly relations with others; **2**, to arouse interest in the welfare of humanity; **3**, to put into control of a group, rather than of an individual; **4**, to subject, as an industry, to the principles of ownership, operation, and distribution laid down by socialism.

So-cial Se-cur-it-y Act an act of Congress, creating a Federal system of old-age insurance, providing Federal cooperation in the establishment and regulation of state unemployment compensation laws, and making Federal grants to aid states in the public assistance of the blind, the aged in need, and dependent children.—(Administered by a Social Security Board of three members, appointed by the President.)

so-cial work **1**, any of several kinds of organized work aiming at improvement of physical, mental, or moral conditions of persons as members of a community, as welfare work in stores and factories, vocational guidance, and organized recreation; **2**, educational or preventive work for the improvement of social and economic conditions, including propaganda for social legislation and reform: **social worker**, a person professionally engaged in social work.

so-ci-e-ty (sō-sī'ĕ-tĭ), *n.* [*pl.* societies (-tĭz)], **1**, people in general, considered as living in relationship with one another; also, a group of people bound together by some common interest or relationship; **2**, companionship; **3**, people of culture and of good standing in any community: sometimes applied exclusively to people of wealth and fashion; **4**, an organized body of persons united by a common interest and purpose.

so-ci-o-log-i-cal (sō''shĭ-ō-lŏj'ĭ-kăl), *adj.* pertaining to sociology, or the science of human association. Also, **so''ci-o-log'ic.**—*adv.* **so''ci-o-log'i-cal-ly.**

so-ci-ol-o-gy (sō''shĭ-ŏl'ō-jĭ), *n.* the science of human relationships and conditions.—*n.* **so''ci-ol'o-gist.**

[1]**sock** (sŏk), *n.* **1**, a light shoe worn by the ancient actors of comedy; **2**, a short stocking not reaching the knee.

[2]**sock** (sŏk), *v.t. Slang*, to hit or strike with, or as with, a missile or the fist:—*n. Slang*, a violent blow.

sock-et (sŏk'ĕt), *n.* a hollow into which something is fitted; as, the *socket* of the eye; the *socket* of an electric light.

So-crat-ic (sō-krăt'ĭk), *adj.* relating to Socrates (469–399 B. C.), the Athenian philosopher, his method of teaching, or his belief: **socratic irony**, pretended ignorance in argument.

sod (sŏd), *n.* **1**, the grassy top layer of the soil; turf; **2**, a piece of turf, usually cut square:—*v.t.* [*p.t.* and *p.p.* sod'ded, *p.pr.* sod'ding], to cover with turf or pieces of turf.

so-da (sō'dȧ), *n.* **1**, sodium carbonate, a white powdery salt, one of the most largely used and important of chemical compounds, used in manufacture of glass, soap, paper, etc.: when crystalline, called *washing soda;* **2**, sodium bicarbonate or acid sodium carbonate, a white powdery salt used in baking powders and in various industries: also called *baking* or *cooking soda;* **3,** any of several compounds of sodium, as sodium hydroxide; **4,** *Colloq.*, soda water; also, a soft drink made from soda water: **baking** or **cooking soda,** acid sodium carbonate, or sodium bicarbonate: **washing soda,** sodium carbonate: **soda ash,** crude sodium carbonate.

so-dal-i-ty (sō-dăl′ĭ-tĭ), *n.* [*pl.* sodalities (-tĭz)], a brotherhood for religious or charitable purposes.

so-da wa-ter **1,** an effervescent solution of bicarbonate of soda with an acid; **2,** water charged with carbon dioxide gas, to which fruit sirups, ice cream, etc., are usually added: a popular drink.

sod-den (sŏd′n), *adj.* **1,** soaked; heavy with moisture; **2,** half cooked or baked, as cake; **3,** looking as if boiled or soaked; hence, stupid; dull.—*n.* **sod′den-ness.**

so-di-um (sō′dĭ-ŭm), *n.* a silvery white, alkaline, metallic element always occurring in nature in combination, as in common salt, rock salt, borax, or the like: **sodium bicarbonate,** a substance in the form of crystals or a white powder, commonly called *baking soda,* or, incorrectly, *saleratus:* **sodium carbonate,** a white powdery salt manufactured from common salt, widely used in manufactures: **sodium chloride,** common salt.

¹soil (soil), *n.* **1,** the loose top layer of the earth's surface, as distinguished from solid rock; **2,** land; the country.

²soil (soil), *v.t.* **1,** to make dirty; stain; as, to *soil* the hands; **2,** to mar or sully; as, to *soil* a reputation; **3,** to make rich, as land, with manure:—*v.i.* to become stained or dirty:—*n.* **1,** dirt; stain; **2,** manure.

soil-ure (soil′ūr), *n. Archaic,* **1,** the act of dirtying; **2,** a stain; **3,** impurity.

soi-rée (swȧ′rā′; swŏ-rā′), [Fr.], *n.* an evening party, as a reception or ball.

so-journ (sō′jûrn; sō-jûrn′), *v.i.* to dwell for a time:—*n.* a temporary dwelling; short stay.—*n.* **so′journ-er.**

Sol (sŏl), *n.* the sun: so called from the Roman god of the sun.

sol (sōl), *n.* the fifth of the series of syllables used, for convenience, in singing the degrees of a diatonic scale. See ²**so,** *Pfd. S.*

sol-ace (sŏl′ās), *n.* comfort in sorrow; lessening of pain or grief; consolation:—*v.t.* [*p.t.* and *p.p.* -aced (-āst), *p.pr.* -ac-ing], **1,** to comfort in sorrow; **2,** to cheer.

so-lar (sō′lȧr), *adj.* pertaining to, measured by, or proceeding from, the sun; as, *solar* rays; *solar* light: **solar system,** the sun together with the planets and the other bodies that circle round it: **solar year,** the period during which the earth makes one complete journey round the sun, about 365 days, 5 hours, 48 minutes, 46 seconds.

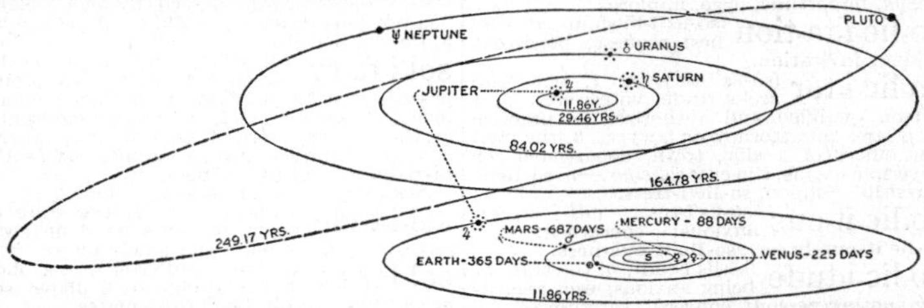

SOLAR SYSTEM, showing orbits, and lengths of solar year, of nine planets, and moons about each planet. The orbits of the four inner planets cannot be clearly shown to scale in the upper diagram; hence Jupiter's orbit, the inmost ring above, is repeated, enlarged, below, inclosing the orbits of the four inner planets. Pluto's orbit south of the ecliptic is shown with a broken line. S (in lower diagram), sun.

Sod-om (sŏd′ŏm), *n.* in the Bible, a wicked city destroyed with Gomorrah by fire from heaven (Genesis 19:24).

-so-ev-er (-sō-ĕv′ẽr), *suffix,* added to *who, what, where, when, how,* etc., to make them more general or indefinite; as, whosoever: often separable; as, in what place *soever.*

so-fa (sō′fȧ), *n.* a long, upholstered seat, usually having a back and arms.

soft (sôft), *adj.* **1,** easily yielding to pressure: opp. of *hard;* **2,** easily molded or shaped; as, *soft* wax; **3,** smooth to the touch; as, *soft* fur; **4,** not glaring; as, a *soft* light; **5,** not loud; as, *soft* music; **6,** kind; courteous; mild or gentle; as, a *soft* answer; **7,** having feelings easily moved; as, a *soft* heart; **8,** of the weather, moist or mild; **9,** not sharp or abrupt, as outlines; **10,** making a lather easily with soap: used of water; **11,** *Colloq.:* **a,** not in good physical condition; **b,** weak or foolish; **c,** containing no alcohol; as, *soft* drinks: **soft coal,** bituminous coal:—*adv.* quietly:—*interj.* gently! stop!—*adv.* **soft′ly.**—*n.* **soft′ness.**

Syn., adj. (see mellow).

sof-ten (sôf′n), *v.t.* and *v.i.* **1,** to make, or become, less hard, loud, glaring, severe, rude, or the like; tone down; **2,** to melt.

sog-gy (sŏg′ĭ), *adj.* [*comp.* sog′gi-er, *superl.* sog′gi-est], soaked; wet; heavy with dampness.—*n.* **sog′gi-ness.**

***soi-di-sant** (swȧ′=dē″zäṅ′), [Fr.], *adj.* self-styled: would-be.

so-la-ri-um (sō-lā′rĭ-ŭm), *n.* [*pl.* solaria (-ȧ)], a sun parlor, usually for invalids or convalescents.

so-lar plex-us (plĕk′sŭs), the great network of nerves and sympathetic ganglia lying back of the stomach.

sold (sōld), past tense and past participle of the irregular verb *sell.*

sol-der (sŏd′ẽr), *n.* a metal or metallic alloy used, when melted, to join metal surfaces, or to mend breaks in metal:—*v.t.* **1,** to join with such an alloy; **2,** to patch.

sol-dier (sōl′jẽr), *n.* **1,** a man engaged in military service; **2,** a private as distinguished from a commissioned officer; **3,** a man of military experience: **soldier of fortune,** an adventurer; esp., a military adventurer, ready to take service under any state or person that will hire him:—*v.i.* **1,** to serve in the army; **2,** *Colloq.,* (sō′jẽr), to make a pretense of work.—*adj.* **sol′dier-ly.**

sol-dier-y (sōl′jẽr-ĭ), *n.* military forces collectively; troops.

¹sole (sōl), *n.* any of several flatfishes, some of which are used as food.

²sole (sōl), *n.* **1,** the under side of the foot; **2,** the bottom of a shoe or slipper; **3,** any flat surface on which something rests, as of a plow:—*v.t.* [*p.t.* and *p.p.* soled (sōld), *p.pr.* sol′ing], to furnish with a sole.

[3]sole (sōl), *adj.* being or acting alone; only; single.—*adv.* **sole′ly.**

sol-e-cism (sŏl′ē-sĭzm; sō′lē-sĭzm), *n.* **1,** a mistake in the use of words or in the structure of a sentence; an error of grammar or idiom; **2,** any rude or ridiculous breach of manners or taste.

sol-emn (sŏl′ĕm), *adj.* **1,** attended with sacred rites or ceremonies; as, a *solemn* feast day; **2,** inspiring awe or fear; **3,** serious; devout; grave.—*adv.* **sol′emn-ly.** —*n.* **sol′emn-ness.**

so-lem-ni-ty (sō-lĕm′nĭ-tĭ), *n.* [*pl.* solemnities (-tĭz)], **1,** a sacred rite or ceremony; **2,** a formal and grave celebration; **3,** gravity; impressiveness; **4,** seriousness of manner or expression.

sol-em-nize (sŏl′ĕm-nīz), *v.t.* [*p.t.* and *p.p.* -nized (-nīzd), *p.pr.* -niz″ing], to perform in a ceremonious or legally formal manner, or according to ritual. —*n.* **sol′em-niz″er.**—*n.* **sol″em-ni-za′tion.**

Syn. honor, observe, dignify.

sol–fa (sōl″=fä′), *v.i.* [*p.t.* and *p.p.* -faed′ (=fäd′), *p.pr.* -fa′ing], to sing the scale to the syllables *do, re, mi, fa,* etc.

so-lic-it (sō-lĭs′ĭt), *v.t.* **1,** to ask for with earnestness; entreat; as, to *solicit* a favor; **2,** to endeavor to obtain; as, to *solicit* trade:—*v.i.* to seek orders, support, votes, etc.

Syn. importune, urge, implore.

so-lic-i-ta-tion (sō-lĭs″ĭ-tā′shŭn), *n.* earnest request; persistent asking; invitation.

so-lic-i-tor (sō-lĭs′ĭ-tẽr), *n.* **1,** one who seeks trade, votes, etc.; **2,** a person qualified and authorized to practice civil law; an attorney or lawyer; **3,** the civil law officer of a city, town, department, or government; as, the city *solicitor.*—*n.* **so-lic′i-tor-ship″.**—*n.fem.* **so-lic′i-tress.**

so-lic-it-ous (sō-lĭs′ĭ-tŭs), *adj.* eager; anxious; concerned.—*adv.* **so-lic′it-ous-ly.**—*n.* **so-lic′it-ous-ness.**

so-lic-i-tude (sō-lĭs′ĭ-tūd), *n.* the state of being anxious, esp. regarding another person; concern; carefulness.

Syn. uneasiness, anxiety. (See care.)

sol-id (sŏl′ĭd), *adj.* **1,** capable of withstanding pressure: opp. of *fluid;* **2,** cubic; as, the *solid* contents of a mass; **3,** not hollow; compact; dense; **4,** weighty; as, a *solid* argument; **5,** *Colloq.,* continuous; as, a *solid* hour; **6,** unbroken; as, a *solid* line of defense; **7,** firm or reliable; as, a *solid* foundation; **8,** in printing, having no leads between the lines of type; **9,** not hyphenated; as, a *solid* word:—*n.* **1,** a body capable of resisting pressure; a substance not fluid; **2,** in geometry, a body having length, breadth, and thickness.—*adv.* **sol′id-ly.**—*n.* **sol′id-ness.**

Syn., adj. rigid, stable. (See [1]firm.)

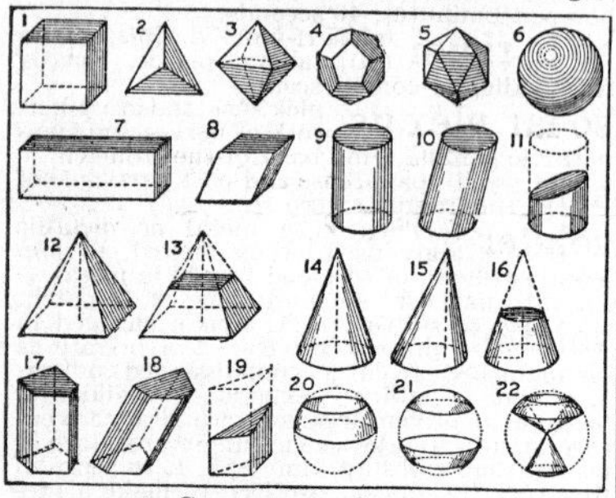

GEOMETRICAL SOLIDS

1, cube, or hexahedron; 2, tetrahedron; 3, octahedron; 4, dodecahedron; 5, icosahedron; 6, sphere; 7, rectangular parallelepiped; 8, rhombohedron; 9, right cylinder; 10, oblique cylinder; 11, truncated cylinder; 12, pyramid; 13, truncated pyramid; 14, right cone; 15, oblique cone; 16, truncated cone; 17, right prism; 18, oblique prism; 19, truncated prism; 20, 21, spherical segments; 22, spherical sectors.

sol-i-dar-i-ty (sŏl″ĭ-dăr′ĭ-tĭ), *n.* **1,** a state of being united in opinion and effort; as, the *solidarity* of a nation; **2,** firmness; singleness of purpose.

so-lid-i-fy (sō-lĭd′ĭ-fī), *v.t.* and *v.i.* [*p.t.* and *p.p.* -fied (-fīd), *p.pr.* -fy″ing], **1,** to make or become hard or firm; change from a fluid to a solid state; **2,** to unite.—*n.* **so-lid″i-fi-ca′tion.**

so-lid-i-ty (sō-lĭd′ĭ-tĭ), *n.* [*pl.* solidities (-tĭz)], **1,** hardness; firmness; **2,** the cubic contents of a body; volume; **3,** moral soundness.

so-lil-o-quize (sō-lĭl′ō-kwīz), *v.i.* [*p.t.* and *p.p.* -quized (-kwīzd), *p.pr.* -quiz″ing], to talk to oneself.

so-lil-o-quy (sō-lĭl′ō-kwĭ), *n.* [*pl.* soliloquies (-kwĭz)], a talk to oneself; an utterance in solitude; a monolog.

sol-i-taire (sŏl″ĭ-târ′), *n.* **1,** a game of cards played by one person; **2,** a precious stone, esp. a diamond, set singly; **3,** *Rare,* a hermit.

sol-i-ta-ry (sŏl′ĭ-tā-rĭ), *adj.* **1,** living by oneself; **2,** lonely; **3,** done, passed, or suffered alone; as, *solitary* confinement; **4,** far removed; without inhabitants; as, the *solitary* desert; **5,** separate from others: —*n.* [*pl.* solitaries (-rĭz)], a hermit.—*adv.* **sol′i-ta-ri-ly.**—*n.* **sol′i-ta-ri-ness.**

Syn., adj. deserted, desolate, alone.

sol-i-tude (sŏl′ĭ-tūd), *n.* **1,** the state of being by oneself; loneliness; seclusion; **2,** a remote and lonely place.

sol-ler-et (sŏl′ẽr-ĕt; sŏl″ẽr-ĕt′), *n.* a shoe of overlapping steel plates (see *armor,* illus.); also, one of the plates.

sol-mi-za-tion (sŏl″mĭ-zā′shŭn), *n.* the method or practice of using the syllables *do, re, mi, fa, so, la, ti* (or *si*), *do,* in singing the tones of a diatonic scale.

so-lo (sō′lō), *n.* [*pl.* solos (-lōz); soli (-lē)], the whole or part of a musical selection played or sung by one person, usually with an accompaniment.—*n.* **so′lo-ist.**

Sol-o-mon (sŏl′ō-mŭn), *n.* in the Bible, the son of David, king of Israel in the tenth century B. C., and builder of the first temple in Jerusalem: noted for his wisdom; hence, any very wise person.

Sol-o-mon's–seal (sŏl′ō-mŭnz=sēl′), *n.* an herb of the lily family, having yellowish green flowers.

So-lon (sō′lŏn), *n.* **1,** an Athenian lawgiver of the sixth century B. C.; **2,** hence, a wise man; a skilled legislator.

sol-stice (sŏl′stĭs), *n.* that point in the sun's path at which the sun is farthest from the equator, north in summer, south in winter: **summer solstice,** June 21 or 22, the longest day in the northern year: **winter solstice,** December 21 or 22, the shortest day in the northern year.—*adj.* **sol-sti′tial.**

sol-u-bil-i-ty (sŏl″ū-bĭl′ĭ-tĭ), *n.* [*pl.* solubilities (-tĭz)], capability of being dissolved in a fluid; as, the *solubility* of salt.

sol-u-ble (sŏl′ū-bl), *adj.* **1,** capable of being dissolved in a fluid; as, sugar is *soluble* in water; **2,** capable of being solved or explained; as, a *soluble* mystery: **soluble glass,** a solution of silicate of sodium in water: also called *water glass.*—*adv.* **sol′u-bly.**—*n.* **sol′u-ble-ness.**

o-lu-tion (sō-lū′shŭn), *n.* **1,** the division of a body into its component arts; a breaking up into parts; **2,** the state f being so divided; as, a substance in *solution;* the process of causing any substance to be bsorbed into a liquid; also, the liquid which esults from such a process; as, a salt *solution;* a solving; an explanation; as, the *solution* f a mystery; also, the result of solving or xplaining; **5,** the act or method of finding he answer to a problem.

olv-a-ble (sŏl′và-bl), *adj.* **1,** capable of being dissolved; **2,** allowing xplanation or solution.—*n.* **solv′a-ble-ness.**—. **solv″a-bil′i-ty.**

solve (sŏlv), *v.t.* [*p.t.* and *p.p.* solved (sŏlvd), *p.pr.* solv′ing], **1,** to explain; reason ut to a conclusion or result, as a problem; , to make clear, as a mystery.—*n.* **solv′er.**

sol-ven-cy (sŏl′vĕn-sĭ), *n.* **1,** capability of being dissolved; **2,** the state of eing able to pay just debts.

sol-vent (sŏl′vĕnt), *n.* any liquid in or by which a substance can be disolved:—*adj.* **1,** able to pay just claims or lebts; **2,** having the power of dissolving.

so-mat-ic (sō-măt′ĭk), *adj.* **1,** pertaining to the body; physical; **2,** of or ertaining to the walls of the body, as distinuished from the organs: **somatic cell,** a body ell: distinguished from *germ cell.*

so-ma-tol-o-gy (sō″mà-tŏl′ō-jĭ), *n.* in anthropology, the science and study of the human body regarded physically.—*n.* **so″ma-tol′o-gist.**

som-ber (sŏm′bẽr), *adj.* **1,** dull; dark; **2,** melancholy; gloomy; as, *somber* thoughts. Also, **som′bre.**—*adv.* **som′ber-ly.**—*n.* **som′ber-ness.**

som-bre-ro (sŏm-brā′rō), *n.* [*pl.* sombreros (-rōz)], a broad-brimmed hat, orig. of Spain and Spanish America, but now also worn in the southwestern U. S.

some (sŭm), *adj.* **1,** a certain; particular, but not specified; as, I know *some* boy did it· often used as a correlative of *other;* as, *some* people came, other people left; **2,** of a certain amount or number, either small or large; as, I have *some* money; he went *some* distance to get it:—*pron.* a partial number or quantity; a portion: usually indefinite, and often used as a correlative of *others;* as, *some* came, others went:—*adv.* **1,** about; approximately; as, *some* ten men came; **2,** *Colloq.*, somewhat; as, *some* colder.

-some (-sŭm), *adj. suffix,* **1,** joined to nouns, meaning pertaining to, producing; as, quarrel*some;* **2,** joined to adjectives, meaning to a considerable degree; as, lithe*some;* **3,** joined to verbs, meaning likely to; as, win*some;* tire*some.*

some-bod-y (sŭm′bŏd-ĭ), *n.* [*pl.* somebodies (-ĭz)], **1,** a person unknown or not placed; **2,** a notable person.

some-how (sŭm′hou″), *adv.* in one way or another; by some means.

som-er-sault (sŭm′ẽr-sôlt), *n.* an acrobatic feat in which one turns over by throwing the heels over the head. Also, **som′er-set.**

some-thing (sŭm′thĭng), *n.* **1,** a thing not definitely known, or not specified; **2,** a part or portion of indefinite size; **3,** a person or thing of importance:—*adv.* in an indefinite degree.

some-time (sŭm′tīm″), *adv.* **1,** at a past time, not known or not definitely stated; formerly; once; **2,** at a time in the future, not yet decided upon; **3,** once in a while; sometimes:—*adj.* former.

some-times (sŭm′tīmz″), *adv.* once in a while; now and then; on certain occasions; as, I go there *sometimes.*

some-what (sŭm′hwŏt″), *n.* an indefinite amount:—*adv.* to an indefinite degree or extent; rather.

some-where (sŭm′hwâr″), *adv.* **1,** in one place or another; **2,** in, at, or to, a place not named or not known.

som-nam-bu-lism (sŏm-năm′bū-lĭzm), *n.* a state in which a sleeping person walks, or otherwise acts as if awake.—*n.* **som-nam′bu-list.**

som-nif-er-ous (sŏm-nĭf′ẽr-ŭs), *adj.* causing sleep.

som-no-lent (sŏm′nō-lĕnt), *adj.* inclined to sleep; drowsy.—*adv.* **som′no-lent-ly.**—*n.* **som′no-lence.**

son (sŭn), *n.* **1,** a human male child; a boy or man spoken of in relation to his parent or parents; **2,** a male descendant; **3,** a native of a particular country; **4,** a graduate of a certain college; as, *sons* of Harvard: **the Son,** Jesus Christ: also called *Son of God; Son of Man.*—*n.* **son′ship.**

so-nant (sō′nănt), *adj.* **1,** of or pertaining to sound; **2,** having sound; **3,** voiced, or pronounced with vibration of the vocal cords, as *b, d, g, z:* opp. of *surd* or *voiceless:*—*n.* a voiced sound or the letter representing it.—*n.* **so′nan-cy.**—*n.* **so′nance.**

so-na-ta (sō-nä′tà), *n.* a musical composition in three or four related but varied movements, usually for one instrument, esp. the piano.

song (sông), *n.* **1,** a rhythmic and tuneful musical sound uttered vocally, as by a bird or an insect; **2,** music produced by the human voice; **3,** a lyric or ballad; poetry; esp., a poem which can be set to music; **4,** a musical composition to be rendered by the voice; **5,** *Colloq.*, a mere trifle; as, he sold it for a *song:* **Song of Solomon,** a poetical book of the Old Testament, consisting of a symbolic love poem: also called *Song of Songs.*

song-ster (sông′stẽr), *n.* a good singer, esp. a bird.—*n. fem.* **song′stress.**

so-nif-er-ous (sō-nĭf′ẽr-ŭs), *adj.* producing, or carrying, sound.

son-in-law (sŭn′-ĭn-lô″), *n.* [*pl.* sons-in-law (sŭnz′-)], the husband of one's daughter.

son-net (sŏn′ĕt), *n.* a poem of fourteen lines, arranged according to any of several rime schemes.

son-net-eer (sŏn″ĕt-ēr′), *n.* a writer of sonnets; a dabbler in poetry:—*v.i.* to write sonnets.

so-no-rous (sō-nō′rŭs), *adj.* **1,** giving sound when struck; resonant; **2,** giving a full or loud sound; deep-toned; as, a *sonorous* voice.—*adv.* **so-no′rous-ly.**—*n.* **so-no′rous-ness.**

soon (so͞on), *adv.* **1,** in a short time; in the near or immediate future; **2,** early; without delay; **3,** willingly; as, as *soon* as not.

soot (so͝ot; so͞ot), *n.* the fine black powder, consisting chiefly of carbon, formed by burning substances; the particles of carbon which color smoke.

sooth (so͞oth), *adj. Obs.*, according to truth:—*n. Archaic,* truth; as, in *sooth.*

soothe (so͞oth), *v.t.* [*p.t.* and *p.p.* soothed (so͞othd), *p.pr.* sooth′ing], **1,** to make quiet or calm; comfort or console; **2,** to make less severe, as pain.—*n.* **sooth′er.**

Syn. assuage, mitigate, pacify.

sooth-say-er (so͞oth′sā″ẽr), *n.* one who claims power to foretell the future; a fortune teller.—*n.* **sooth′say″ing.**

soot-y (so͝ot′ĭ; so͞ot′ĭ), *adj.* [*comp.* soot′i-er, *superl.* soot′i-est], **1,** pertaining to, causing, or covered with, the carbon from smoke; **2,** dusky; black.—*n.* **soot′i-ness.**

sop (sŏp), *n.* **1,** anything steeped, dipped, or softened in a liquid, esp. in broth;

2, something given to calm or soothe the feelings:—*v.t.* [*p.t.* and *p.p.* sopped (sŏpt), *p.pr.* sop′ping], 1, to dip or soak; 2, to mop up.

soph-ism (sŏf′ĭzm), *n.* a plausible, but unsound, argument; also, any argument intended to make the worse appear the better cause.

Soph-ist (sŏf′ĭst), *n.* one of a body of philosophers and teachers in ancient Greece, famous for their clever, plausible, but unsound reasoning: **sophist,** one whose reasoning is clever but unsound.

so-phis-ti-cal (sō-fĭs′tĭ-kăl), *adj.* pertaining to, or like, an unsound reasoner or unsound reasoning; falsely clever; plausible but not sound, as an argument. Also, **so-phis′tic.**—*adv.* **so-phis′ti-cal-ly.**

so-phis-ti-cate (sō-fĭs′tĭ-kāt), *v.t.* [*p.t.* and *p.p.* -cat″ed, *p.pr.* -cat″ing], 1, to mislead, as by false argument; 2, to adulterate; 3, to give worldly knowledge to; deprive of simplicity: **sophisticated,** worldly-wise:—*v.i.* to argue or reason falsely. —*n.* **so-phis″ti-ca′tion.**—*n.* **so-phis′ti-ca″tor.**

soph-ist-ry (sŏf′ĭs-trĭ), *n.* [*pl.* sophistries (-trĭz)], plausible or clever, but unsound, reasoning.

soph-o-more (sŏf′ō-mōr″), *n.* in American universities, colleges, and high schools, a student in the second year.—*adj.* **soph″o-mor′ic.**

Soph-o-ni-as (sŏf″ō-nī′ăs), *n.* in the Bible, Zephaniah: so called in the Douay Bible.

so-por (sō′pŏr), *n.* a deep sleep, occurring in illness, from which a patient is aroused with difficulty.

so-po-rif-ic (sō″pō-rĭf′ĭk; sŏp″ō-), *adj.* causing, or tending to induce, sleep:—*n.* a medicine, drug, plant, or the like, that causes sleep.

sop-py (sŏp′ĭ), *adj.* [*comp.* sop′pi-er, *superl.* sop′pi-est], soaked; very wet.

so-pra-no (sō-prä′nō), *n.* [*pl.* sopranos, (-nōz); soprani (-nē)], 1, the highest singing voice; 2, a singer with such a voice; 3, a musical part for such a voice.

sor-cer-er (sôr′sẽr-ẽr), *n.* a magician; conjurer.—*n.fem.* **sor′cer-ess.**

sor-cer-y (sôr′sẽr-ĭ), *n.* [*pl.* sorceries (-ĭz)], a foreseeing or foretelling of future events by the aid of evil spirits; witchcraft; magic; enchantment.—*adj.* **sor′cer-ous.**

sor-did (sôr′dĭd), *adj.* 1, without noble ideals; vile; base; as, a *sordid* purpose; 2, greedy of gain; miserly; as, a *sordid* wretch.—*adv.* **sor′did-ly.**—*n.* **sor′did-ness.**

sore (sōr), *adj.* 1, tender or painful to the touch; inflamed; 2, afflicted; grieved; as, her heart was *sore;* 3, severe; hence, distressing; as, a *sore* disappointment; 4, resentful; as, he was *sore* at this unkind treatment: **sore throat,** soreness and inflammation in the throat, as from pharyngitis:—*adv.* grievously; severely; deeply:—*n.* 1, a painful or diseased spot in an animal body; ulcer; wound; a bruise or break in the skin; 2, a cause of annoyance.—*adv.* **sore′ly.**—*n.* **sore′ness.**

sor-ghum (sôr′gŭm), *n.* a canelike grass resembling broom corn, yielding sugar; molasses or sirup prepared from the juice of this grass.

so-ror-i-cide (sō-rŏr′ĭ-sīd), *n.* 1, one who slays his sister; 2, the act of committing this crime.

so-ror-i-ty (sō-rŏr′ĭ-tĭ), *n.* [*pl.* sororities (-tĭz)], a sisterhood; a women's or girls' club.

¹so-ro-sis (sō-rō′sĭs), *n.* a fleshy fruit, as a pineapple, formed by the union of many flowers.

²so-ro-sis (sō-rō′sĭs), *n.* in the U. S., a women's club or society.

¹sor-rel (sŏr′ĕl), *n.* 1, any of several ere perennial herbs having lon spear-shaped leaves, small, reddish flower and a sour juice: also called *garden* and *shee sorrel;* 2, any of several delicate herbs havin white, yellow, or violet flowers, and a sou juice; the wood sorrel (see *shamrock,* illus.).

²sor-rel (sŏr′ĕl), *adj.* reddish brown:—*n* 1, a reddish brown color; 2, a animal, esp. a horse, of this color.

sor-row (sŏr′ō), *n.* 1, mental pain or un easiness caused by loss, regret disappointment, etc.; grief; distress; 2, tha which causes unhappiness; 3, contrition:—*v.i* to feel mental pain or uneasiness; grieve lament; be sad.—*n.* **sor′row-er.**

Syn., n. remorse, lamentation, tribulation —*Ant., n.* glee, mirth, happiness.

sor-row-ful (sŏr′ō-fōōl), *adj.* full of, show ing, or causing, sadness o grief; unhappy; regretful; grievous.—*adv* **sor′row-ful-ly.**—*n.* **sor′row-ful-ness.**

Syn. sad, mournful, doleful, disconsolate.—*Ant.* joyous, merry, happy, gay.

sor-ry (sŏr′ĭ), *adj.* [*comp.* sor′ri-er, *superl.* sor′ri-est], 1, feeling regret for loss disappointment, wrongdoing, etc.; pained 2, feeling pity, as for a cripple; 3, mournful dismal; as, a *sorry* sight; 4, mean; worthless, as an excuse.—*adv.* **sor′ri-ly.**—*n.* **sor′ri-ness.**

sort (sôrt), *n.* 1, a kind or species; 2, way; manner; 3, quality; nature; as, that *sort* of material:—*v.t.* to separate and place in different divisions according to classes, kind, etc.; classify.—*adj.* **sort′a-ble.**—*n.* **sort′er.**

Syn., n. group. (See kind.)

sor-tie (sôr′tē), *n.* a sudden issuing of a body of troops from a besieged place to attack the besiegers.

S O S (ĕs′ ō′ ĕs′), *n.* in radio, a signal call of distress consisting of the letters *sos* (- - - — — — - - -) of the international Morse alphabet: used because these letters are easily and quickly transmitted: a code signal, not an abbreviation.

so-so (sō′sō″), *adj. Colloq.,* neither very good nor very bad; passable; tolerable:—*adv. Colloq.,* passably. Also, **so′-so″.**

sot (sŏt), *n.* a person whose powers have become weakened by the constant use of alcoholic liquors; a confirmed drunkard.

sot-tish (sŏt′ĭsh), *adj.* like a drunkard; stupid; drunken.—*adv.* **sot′tish-ly.**—*n.* **sot′tish-ness.**

***sot-to vo-ce** (sōt′tō vō′chā), [It.], in an undertone, as if to oneself; with a moderate or low tone of voice.

sou (sōō), *n.* [*pl.* sous (sōōz; *Fr.* sōō)], 1, an old French coin; 2, the modern five-centime piece, the 20th part of a franc.

sou-brette (sōō-brĕt′), *n.* 1, a theatrical term for an attractive, scheming lady's maid, or a lively young woman; 2, an actress who plays such parts.

Sou-da-nese (sōō″dȧ-nēz′; sōō″dȧ-nēs′), of or pertaining to the Sudan or its inhabitants:—*n.* [*pl.* Soudanese], a native of the Sudan. See **Su″da-nese′,** *Pfd. S.*

***souf-flé** (sōō″flā′; sōō′flā), [Fr.], *adj.* made light and puffy, as with well-beaten whites of eggs:—*n.* a light, delicate dish of eggs and milk, mixed with cheese, fish, etc., well beaten and baked.

sough (sŭf; sou), *n.* a hollow murmur or whistling, as of the wind:—*v.i.* to murmur or sigh, as the wind.

sought (sôt), past tense and past participle of the irregular verb *seek.*

soul (sōl), *n.* 1, the spiritual and immortal part in man, as distinguished from the body; 2, the essential part of a person's identity; that part of man's nature where feelings, ideals, and morals center; 3, the necessary or central part of anything; as, the *soul* of art; **4,** a person who leads and inspires; as, the *soul* of the company; **5,** any trait which indicates a noble nature, such as courage; **6,** a person; as, not a *soul* was there; **7,** a spirit separated from the body; as, the *souls* of the departed; **8,** fine feelings or ideals collectively.

soul-ful (sōl′fo͝ol), *adj.* **1,** full of, or appealing to, fine ideas or feelings; **2,** showing a noble nature.—*adv.* **soul′ful-ly.** —*n.* **soul′ful-ness.**

soul-less (sōl′lĕs), *adj.* **1,** without a soul; lacking nobility of nature; **2,** spiritless; dull; mean.—*adv.* **soul′less-ly.**—*n.* **soul′less-ness.**

¹sound (sound), *adj.* **1,** whole; not hurt; in prime condition; as, safe and *sound;* **2,** continued; profound and unbroken; as, a *sound* slumber; **3,** healthy; not decayed; free from defects; as, a *sound* tooth; **4,** founded on truth or right; free from error; as, *sound* doctrine; **5,** morally good or honorable; as, a *sound* business man; **6,** firm; safe; strong; as, a *sound* floor; **7,** legal; valid; as, a *sound* title; **8,** in the best financial condition; trustworthy; solvent; as, a *sound* banking establishment; **9,** thorough; hearty; as, a *sound* thrashing:—*adv.* deeply; thoroughly; as, *sound* asleep.—*adv.* **sound′ly.**—*n.* **sound′ness.**

²sound (sound), *n.* **1,** the sensation perceived through the ear; noise; **2,** the physical phenomena which, normally, are the cause of this sensation, consisting usually of vibrations or waves, usually in the air; **3,** any distinctive or characteristic noise; tone; as, a *sound* of exultation; **4,** the distance to which a sound is audible; as, within *sound* of the bell; **5,** meaningless noise; **6,** in phonetics, any of the series of articulate utterances of which speech is made up:—*v.t.* **1,** to cause to make a noise; as, to *sound* a bell; **2,** to cause to be heard; express; as, to *sound* a high note; **3,** to order or announce by sound; as, to *sound* an alarm; **4,** to play upon, as an instrument; **5,** to examine or test by causing to give forth sound; as, to *sound* the walls of a building; **6,** to publish abroad by, or as by, sounds; honor or celebrate:—*v.i.* **1,** to make a noise or sound; **2,** to be played upon, as an instrument; make music; **3,** to be spread or published audibly; **4,** to give a certain impression, when heard; as, her voice *sounds* sad.

Syn., n. (see noise).

³sound (sound), *v.t.* **1,** to measure the depth of; fathom; **2,** to examine; try to find out the opinions or attitude of; probe; **3,** in medicine, to search or examine with a sound, or instrument for probing or exploring:—*v.i.* **1,** to measure the depth of water by any of various devices; **2,** to dive deeply, as whales:—*n.* in surgery, an instrument introduced into a cavity to dilate it or to detect a foreign substance.—*n.* **sound′er.**

⁴sound (sound), *n.* **1,** a long stretch of water, wider than a strait, connecting two large bodies of water, or lying between a mainland and an island; **2,** the air bladder of a fish: also called *swimming bladder.*

¹sound-ing (sound′ĭng), *p.adj.* **1,** resounding; resonant or ringing; as, *sounding* brass; **2,** giving forth much noise.

²sound-ing (sound′ĭng), *n.* **1,** the act of measuring the depth of water or of using a probe; **2,** the result obtained by measuring the depth of water; **3,** in *pl.,* a place where the water is shallow enough to permit depth measurements to be taken: **sounding line,** a weighted line for sounding, the depth in fathoms being shown, in a hand line, by distinguishing marks.

sound-less (sound′lĕs), *adj.* silent; making no noise; without sound. —*adv.* **sound′less-ly.**—*n.* **sound′less-ness.**

sound-proof (sound′pro͞of″), *adj.* not admitting sound; as, *soundproof* walls.

soup (so͞op), *n.* a liquid food made by boiling meat or vegetables, or both together, in water, with seasoning.

***soup-çon** (so͞op″sôṅ′), [Fr.], *n.* [*pl.* **soupçons** (so͞op″sôṅ′)], **1,** a suspicion; intimation; **2,** hence, a small portion; trace.

sour (sour), *adj.* **1,** having an acid or sharp, biting taste, as vinegar or green fruit; **2,** acid; rancid or musty; **3,** disagreeable; cross; as, a *sour* disposition:—*v.t.* **1,** to cause to become acid; **2,** to turn, as milk; **3,** to make cross:—*v.i.* **1,** to become cross; **2,** to turn from sweet to acid; **3,** to ferment; spoil.—*adv.* **sour′ly.**—*n.* **sour′ness.**—*adj.* **sour′ish.**

Syn., adj. tart, acrid. (See bitter.)

source (sōrs), *n.* **1,** that from which anything rises or originates; **2,** a spring or fountain, esp. as the origin of a stream.

souse (sous), *n.* **1,** the act of steeping in brine, or of plunging into water or other liquid; **2,** brine, or salt pickle, for preserving food; **3,** anything soaked or preserved in pickle, as pigs' feet or fish:—*v.t.* [*p.t.* and *p.p.* soused (soust), *p.pr.* sous′ing], **1,** to steep in brine; **2,** to plunge into water; **3,** to dash; splash; as, to *souse* water.

south (south), *n.* **1,** that one of the principal points of the compass which is directly opposite the north; **2,** a region lying to the south of another: **the South, 1,** the section of the U. S. lying below the southern boundary of Pennsylvania; **2,** the states that seceded from the Union in 1861:—*adj.* **1,** lying in the direction of the point of the compass opposite the north; **2,** going to, or coming from, any point in that direction: **south pole,** the southern end of the earth's axis:—*adv.* away from the north.—*adj.* and *adv.* **south′er-ly** (sŭth′ẽr-lĭ).

south-east (south″ēst′; sou″ēst′), *n.* **1,** the point of the compass halfway between south and east; **2,** land lying in that direction:—*adj.* lying in, going to, or coming from, the southeast:—*adv.* to or from the southeast.—*adj.* **south″east′ern.**—*adj.* and *adv.* **south″east′er-ly.**—*adv.* **south″east′ward.**

south-east-er (south″ēs′tẽr; sou″-), *n.* a storm or gale coming from the southeast. Also, **sou′-east′er.**

south-ern (sŭth′ẽrn), *adj.* pertaining to, situated in, or proceeding from or toward, the south: **Southern,** pertaining to that part of the U. S. lying south of Mason and Dixon's line: **Southern Cross,** a southern constellation with four bright stars forming a cross: **Southern Hemisphere,** that part of the earth's surface between the equator and the south pole.—*adj.* and *adv.* **south′ern-ly.**

south-ern-er (sŭth′ẽr-nẽr), *n.* a native of a southern land: **Southerner,** a native of the southern part of the U. S.: opp. of *Northerner.*

south-ern-most (sŭth′ẽrn-mōst), *adj.* lying farthest south.

south-ing (south′ĭng), *n.* inclination or movement toward the south.

south-ron (sŭth′rŭn), *n. Rare,* a native of a southern land: **Southron,** *Scot.,* an Englishman: often used in contempt.

south-ward (south′wẽrd), *adv.* toward the south:—*adj.* lying in, or toward, the south.—*adv.* **south′wards.**—*adv.* **south′ward-ly.**

south-west (south″wĕst′; sou″-), *n.* **1,** the point of the compass halfway between south and west; **2,** land lying in that direction:—*adj.* lying in, going to, or coming from, the southwest:—*adv.* to or from the southwest.—*adj.* **south″west′ern.**—*adj.* and *adv.* **south″west′er-ly.**—*adv.* **south″west′ward.**

south-west-er (south″wĕs′tẽr; sou″-), *n.* **1**, a storm or gale from the southwest; **2**, a painted canvas or oilskin hat with a flap at the back, worn in bad weather by sailors and fishermen. Also, **sou′-west′er.**

sou-ve-nir (sōō″vē-nēr′; sōō′vē-nēr), *n.* a thing by which to remember a person or event; a memento or keepsake.

sov-er-eign (sŏv′ẽr-ĭn; sŭv′-), *adj.* **1**, royal; supreme in power; possessing supreme dominion or authority; not restricted; as, *sovereign* rights; **2**, hence, supreme; chief; **3**, effectual; as, a *sovereign* remedy:—*n.* **1**, a ruler, as a king, emperor, or queen; **2**, a British gold coin equal to twenty shillings, or $4.8665: also called *pound.*

sov-er-eign-ty (sŏv′ẽr-ĭn-tĭ; sŭv′-), *n.* [*pl.* sovereignties (-tĭz)], supreme power or dominion.

so-viet (sō″vyĕt′), *n.* a representative council set up in a country that has adopted communism; any of the governing bodies which perform the political functions in a communistic society, and which correspond to boards of aldermen or county officials, state legislatures, and Congress in the United States: used particularly with reference to political organization in Russia under communism, after the World War.—*n.* **so″viet′ism.**—*v.t.* **so″viet′ize.**

[1]**sow** (sou), *n.* **1**, the full-grown female of the swine; **2**, a sow bug.

[2]**sow** (sō), *v.t.* [*p.t.* sowed (sōd), *p.p.* sown (sōn) or sowed, *p.pr.* sow′ing], **1**, to strew, as seed, upon the earth; **2**, to strew seed in, on, or over; as, to *sow* a lawn; **3**, to disseminate; as, to *sow* revolutionary ideas:—*v.i.* to strew seed for growth.—*n.* **sow′er.**

sow bug (sou), any of various small, terrestrial crustaceans often found in damp places and under boards lying on the ground; the wood louse (see *crustacean*, illus.).

soy (soi), *n.* a kind of bean sauce used with fish in China and Japan: **soy bean,** a small, erect plant, cultivated for forage.

spa (spä), *n.* **1**, a mineral spring; **2**, a resort or place containing such springs.

space (spās), *n.* **1**, that which has length, breadth, and height, and is unlimited in extension; the medium in which objects can exist and move; **2**, the quality of unlimited extensiveness; **3**, room; distance between things; **4**, a length of time; **5**, in music, one of the open places between the lines of the staff; **6**, in printing, a blank piece of type metal:—*v.t.* [*p.t.* and *p.p.* spaced (spāst), *p.pr.* spac′ing], to arrange with open places between; separate, as letters or words, by means of such spaces.—*n.* **spac′er.**

spa-cious (spā′shŭs), *adj.* **1**, extending far and wide; roomy; as, a *spacious* house; **2**, great in expanse; comprehensive.—*adv.* **spa′cious-ly.**—*n.* **spa′cious-ness.**

Syn. large, vast, expansive.

[1]**spade** (spād), *n.* **1**, a tool for digging, or cutting the ground, consisting of a broad, flat blade of iron with a handle; **2**, any tool of similar shape: **to call a spade a spade,** to call a thing by its right name:—*v.t.* [*p.t.* and *p.p.* spad′ed, *p.pr.* spad′ing], to dig or work with a spade.—*n.* **spad′er.**

[2]**spade** (spād), *n.* **1**, any of that suit of cards bearing one or more black figures resembling a pointed spade; also, the figure itself; **2**, in *pl.*, the suit.

spa-dix (spā′dĭks), *n.* [*pl.* spadices (spȧ-dī′sēz)], a spikelike flower head on a fleshy axis, often inclosed in a spathe, as in the jack-in-the-pulpit (see *inflorescence*, illus.).

spa-ghet-ti (spȧ-gĕt′ĭ), *n.* round dried sticks of flour paste, used, when cooked, for food: like macaroni, but solid and smaller.

spake (spāk), *Archaic*, the past tense of the irregular verb *speak.*

span (spăn), *n.* **1**, the distance from the end of the thumb to the tip of the little finger when extended; as a measure, nine inches; **2**, a short space of time; **3**, any extent having two definite ends; **4**, horizontal distance between the two supports of an arch (see [1]*arch*, illus.), or between any two supports, as of a roof truss (see [2]*pitch*, illus.) or of a bridge; **5**, a yoke of oxen; **6**, a pair of horses similar in color harnessed together:—*v.t.* [*p.t.* and *p.p.* spanned (spănd), *p.pr.* span′ning], **1**, to measure by the width of the extended fingers; **2**, to reach from one side of to the other.

span-gle (spăng′gl), *n.* **1**, a small disk, triangle, etc., of shining metallic substance; **2**, any glittering ornament, esp. for a dress:—*v.t.* [*p.t.* and *p.p.* -gled (-gld), *p.pr.* -gling], to set or adorn with, or as with, small, shining metal disks, or any bits of shining stuff; as, stars *spangle* the heavens.

Span-iard (spăn′yȧrd), *n.* a native or inhabitant of Spain.

span-iel (spăn′yĕl), *n.* **1**, a breed of small dogs with hanging ears and long, silky hair; **2**, a cringing, fawning person.

SPANIELS

Span-ish (spăn′ĭsh), *adj.* pertaining to Spain, its language, or its people:—*n.* the people of Spain; also, their language, esp. Castilian.

Span-ish fly a bright green beetle of southern Europe, used in making a medicine called *cantharides.*

Span-ish Main orig., the northeastern coast of South America: later incorrectly used of the southern part of the Caribbean Sea and the coasts of the West Indies.

spank (spăngk), *v.t.* to strike or slap; punish by striking the buttocks with the open hand:—*n.* a slap.

spank-er (spăngk′ẽr), *n.* **1**, one who or that which spanks; **2**, the after sail of a ship (see *rigging*, illus.).

spank-ing (spăngk′ĭng), *p.adj.* **1**, moving with a quick, lively step; dashing; as, a *spanking* gray horse; **2**, fresh; brisk; as, a *spanking* breeze:—*n.* a punishment given to a child, by striking him upon the buttocks, as with the open hand.

span-ner (spăn′ẽr), *n.* a wrench for tightening or loosening nuts.

[1]**spar** (spär), *n.* any of certain crystalline minerals with a shiny luster, as calcite.

[2]**spar** (spär), *n.* in general, any stout, round pole, as for a mast, yard, boom, or the like:—*v.t.* [*p.t.* and *p.p.* sparred (spärd), *p.pr.* spar′ring], to fit with spars.

[3]**spar** (spär), *v.i.* [*p.t.* and *p.p.* sparred (spärd), *p.pr.* spar′ring], **1**, to fight with the feet or spurs, as a cock; **2**, to fight with the hands or fists; box, esp. without striking decisive blows; **3**, to engage in a contest of words:—*n.* a contest, either at boxing or in words.

spare (spâr), *v.t.* [*p.t.* and *p.p.* spared (spârd), *p.pr.* spar′ing], **1**, to use in a frugal or saving manner; use rarely; as, *spare* the rod; **2**, to part with conveniently; as, to *spare* a book; **3**, to refuse to punish; treat leniently; as, to *spare* the feelings; **4**, to withhold or refrain from; omit; as, to *spare* no expense:—*v.i.* **1**, to live frugally or cheaply; **2**, to forbear or forgive:—*adj.* **1**, thin or lean; scanty; **2**, additional; extra; held in reserve;

as, *spare* cash; a *spare* tire:—*n.* **1**, in bowling, the act of knocking over all the pins in two attempts; **2**, an extra tire carried on an automobile, to be used in case any of the tires in use goes flat.—*adv.* **spare'ly.**—*n.* **spare'ness.**
Syn., adj. gaunt, lank, meager.

spare-rib (spâr'rĭb″), *n.* ribs of pork with the meat closely trimmed.

spar-ing (spâr'ĭng), *p.adj.* **1**, frugal or saving; economical; **2**, little in amount; limited; as, a *sparing* use of salt.—*adv.* **spar'ing-ly.**—*n.* **spar'ing-ness.**
Syn. (see economical).

¹spark (spärk), *n.* **1**, a tiny, burning particle thrown off, esp. by a body that is on fire; **2**, any bright, small flash of light; **3**, hence, any sudden flash; as, a *spark* of genius; **4**, a small sign or particle; as, not a *spark* of life remained; **5**, a disruptive electric discharge through a gas, accompanied by a flash of light and a snapping sound; specif., in an internal-combustion engine, the electric discharge which ignites the fuel (see *gas engine*, illus.); **6**, a mechanism which controls such a spark; as, to advance the *spark*:—*v.i.* **1**, to emit sparks; **2**, to produce an electric spark:—*v.t.* in electricity, to act upon or affect by sparks.—*n.* **¹spark'er.**

²spark (spärk), *n.* a gay, dashing, young fellow; a beau; gallant:—*v.i.* to play the gallant or suitor; court.—*n.* **²spark'er.**—*adj.* **spark'ish.**

spar-kle (spär'kl), *v.i.* [*p.t.* and *p.p.* -kled (-kld), *p.pr.* -kling], **1**, to give off light in small flashes; glisten; gleam; **2**, to effervesce:—*n.* **1**, a gleam of light; **2**, the quality of effervescing or of flashing.—*n.* **spar'kler.**

spar-kling (spär'klĭng), *p.adj.* **1**, glittering; flashing; **2**, effervescing; **3**, brilliant in speech or manner.

spark plug a device in an internal-combustion engine for making an electric spark to ignite the gaseous fuel.

spar-row (spăr'ō), *n.* any of numerous, widely distributed, small gray and brown birds of the finch family.

spar-row hawk **1**, any of several small hawks or falcons that prey on sparrows and other small birds; **2**, in America, a small falcon akin to the kestrel.

sparse (spärs), *adj.* thinly scattered; few and thinly distributed; as, a *sparse* population.—*adv.* **sparse'ly.**—*n.* **sparse'ness.**

Spar-tan (spär'tăn), *adj.* **1**, pertaining to Sparta in ancient Greece, whose people were noted for their bravery and stern military discipline; **2**, hence, unwavering in courage and endurance:—*n.* **1**, a native or inhabitant of Sparta; **2**, an unusually courageous and resolute person.—*n.* **Spar'tan-ism.**

spasm (spăzm), *n.* **1**, a sudden, violent, involuntary contraction, or shortening, of the muscles; **2**, a sudden, violent movement or emotion that lasts but a short time; as, a *spasm* of anger.

spas-mod-ic (spăz-mŏd'ĭk), *adj.* **1**, pertaining to, or of the nature of, a spasm, or sudden, involuntary shortening of muscles; convulsive; as, a *spasmodic* cough; **2**, violent but short-lived; acting by fits and starts; as, *spasmodic* efforts. Also, **spas-mod'i-cal.**—*adv.* **spas-mod'i-cal-ly.**
Syn. fitful, jerky, intermittent.

¹spat (spăt), *n.* the eggs or spawn of some mollusks, esp. of the oyster:—*v.i.* [*p.t.* and *p.p.* spat'ted, *p.pr.* spat'ting], to spawn: said of oysters.

²spat (spăt), *n. Colloq.*, **1**, a slight blow with the open hand; a slap; **2**, a dash or spatter, as of rain; **3**, in the U. S., a little quarrel or dispute:—*v.i.* [*p.t.* and *p.p.* spat'ted, *p.pr.* spat'ting], *U. S. Colloq.*, to engage in a petty quarrel or dispute:—*v.t.* to slap.

³spat (spăt), *n.*, usually in *pl.*, a kind of short cloth gaiter covering the ankle.

⁴spat (spăt), *Archaic*, past tense of the irregular verb ²*spit*.

spathe (spāth), *n.* the large enveloping bract, or leaflike appendage, or a pair of bracts, inclosing a group of flowers, as in the skunk cabbage and jack-in-the-pulpit.

spa-tial (spā'shăl), *adj.* pertaining to distance or area. Also, **spa'cial.**—*adv.* **spa'tial-ly.**

spat-ter (spăt'ẽr), *v.t.* **1**, to splash a liquid upon; soil by splashing; as, to *spatter* a table cover with ink; **2**, to scatter in drops or by splashing; as, to *spatter* milk over the floor; **3**, to injure by slander; as, to *spatter* a man's good name:—*v.i.* to scatter or splash in drops:—*n.* **1**, a splashing; sprinkling; **2**, the spot or splash made, or the substance splashed.

spat-u-la (spăt'ū-lȧ), *n.* an instrument with a thin, flat blade, used in cooking, for mixing ointments, etc.

spat-u-late (spăt'ū-lāt), *adj.* resembling a spatula, as a leaf (see *leaf*, illus.): opp. of *lanceolate*, or lance-shaped.

spav-in (spăv'ĭn), *n.* a disease of horses: a deposit of bony matter in the hock joint, causing lameness.—*adj.* **spav'ined.**

spawn (spôn), *n.* **1**, the eggs of fish, oysters, etc.; **2**, contemptuously, human offspring:—*v.i.* **1**, to lay or produce eggs: said of fish, oysters, etc.; **2**, to bring forth offspring; used in contempt of human beings:—*v.t.* **1**, to lay or produce (eggs or spawn), as do fish; **2**, to bring forth: used in contempt.

spay (spā), *v.t.* to remove the ovaries: used only of animals.

speak (spēk), *v.i.* [*p.t.* spoke (spōk) or *Archaic*, spake (spāk), *p.p.* spo'ken (spō'kn) or, *Obs.*, spoke, *p.pr.* speak'ing], **1**, to utter words; as, to *speak* distinctly; **2**, to talk; tell; mention; as, do not *speak* of this; **3**, to make an address; as, he *spoke* for an hour; **4**, to convey ideas; as, our actions *speak* for us:—*v.t.* **1**, to utter, as a word; pronounce; **2**, to express in words; as, to *speak* the truth **3**, to use, or be able to use, in conversation; as, he *speaks* four languages; **4**, to address; hail; as, ships *speak* each other in passing; **5**, to cause to be known; show; reveal; as, his actions *speak* what he is.—*adj.* **speak'a-ble.**

speak-er (spēk'ẽr), *n.* **1**, one who utters words; esp., one who delivers an address in public; **2**, in the U. S., a book of selections for declamation in school: **Speaker**, the presiding officer of the popular branch of a lawmaking body, as of Congress.—*n.* **speak'er-ship.**

speak-ing (spēk'ĭng), *p.adj.* **1**, uttering words; **2**, very expressive; vivid; lifelike; as, a *speaking* likeness:—*n* **1**, the act of uttering words; **2**, the making of addresses in public.—*adv.* **speak'ing-ly.**

spear (spēr), *n.* **1**, a weapon to be thrust or thrown, having a sharp, pointed head at the end of a long shaft; a lance; **2**, an instrument with barbed prongs for catching fish; **3**, a shoot, as of grass:—*v.t.* to pierce or kill with a long, pointed weapon:—*v.i.* to shoot up into a long stem, as some plants.

spear grass any of various grasses having stiff, spear-shaped leaves, as meadow grass.

spear-head (spēr'hĕd″), *n.* the pointed head of a spear.

spear-man (spēr'măn), *n.* [*pl.* spearmen (-mĕn)], a person armed with a spear, generally a soldier.

spear-mint (spēr'mĭnt″), *n.* a pungent, spicy herb similar to peppermint; the common garden mint.

spe-cial (spĕsh'ăl), *adj.* **1**, pertaining to, or forming, a species or sort; as, the *special* characteristics of man; **2,** designed for a particular purpose; as, a *special* course of study; hence, limited in range, extent, aim, or purpose; as, a *special* train; **3,** different from others; uncommon; particular; as, a *special* favor:—*n.* a person or thing used for a particular purpose.—*adv.* **spe′cial-ly.**

spe-cial-ist (spĕsh′ăl-ĭst), *n.* one who limits his work and his study to a particular branch; as, an eye *specialist.* —*n.* **spe′cial-ism.**

spe-ci-al-i-ty (spĕsh″ĭ-ăl′ĭ-tĭ), *n.* [*pl.* specialities (-tĭz)], **1,** the special or distinctive mark of a person or thing; as, the *speciality* of an author's style; **2,** an object or occupation possessing a distinctive quality that marks it off from others; as, *specialities* of arts and crafts.

spe-cial-ize (spĕsh′ăl-īz), *v.t.* [*p.t.* and *p.p.* -ized (-īzd), *p.pr.* -iz″ing], to apply, modify, or adapt, for a particular use; as, *specialized* knowledge:—*v.i.* to pursue a particular line of action or course of study; as, to *specialize* in science.—*n.* **spe′cial-iz″er.** —*n.* **spe″cial-i-za′tion.**

spe-cial-ty (spĕsh′ăl-tĭ), *n.* [*pl.* specialties (-tĭz)], **1,** a line of study or work to which one is particularly devoted; as, his *specialty* is music; **2,** an article dealt in exclusively, or receiving particular attention; as, the *specialty* of the store was fruit; **3,** an article of particular character or use; as, *specialties* in silver; **4,** a mark of particular or individual character in a person or thing; **5,** the state or quality of being individual.

spe-cie (spē′shĭ), *n.* coin; gold or silver money, as opposed to paper money.

spe-cies (spē′shēz; spē′shĭ-ēz), *n.* [*pl.* species], **1,** a kind; variety; **2,** a group of animals or plants, usually making up a subdivision next smaller than a genus, having certain common characteristics which clearly distinguish it from other groups and which are ordinarily inherited.

spe-cif-ic (spē-sĭf′ĭk), *adj.* **1,** of or pertaining to a species, or group, of which the members have common characteristics and are called by a common name; **2,** definite or particular; precise; as, *specific* information; **3,** having some particular curing or healing quality; as, a *specific* medicine; **4,** causing a definite disease; as, the *specific* germ of diphtheria: **specific duty,** a tax on goods, esp. on imports, definitely fixed, and not calculated in proportion to the value of the goods: distinguished from *ad valorem duty:* **specific gravity,** the relative weight of a given volume of any kind of matter as compared with the weight of an equal volume of a standard substance, as water or air:—*n.* **1,** anything specially suited to a particular use or purpose; **2,** a remedy for a particular disease. Also, *adj.* **spe-cif′i-cal.**—*adv.* **spe-cif′i-cal-ly.**

spec-i-fi-ca-tion (spĕs″ĭ-fĭ-kā′shŭn), *n.* **1,** the act of particularizing, or naming in detail; **2,** a definite and full statement of particulars; as, the *specification* of a charge against an officer; **3,** one detail in such a statement; **4,** in *pl.*, a detailed statement of requirements for carrying out a contract; as, the *specifications* for a building.

spec-i-fy (spĕs′ĭ-fī), *v.t.* [*p.t.* and *p.p.* -fied (-fīd), *p.pr.* -fy″ing], to mention or name particularly; state in full, so as to distinguish from other things; as, to *specify* the uses of a plant.

spec-i-men (spĕs′ĭ-mĕn), *n.* **1,** a sample; a part which shows the quality and character of the whole; as, a *specimen* of stone; **2,** one of several things, which represents all.

Syn. example, instance. A *specimen* is a part that represents the whole or a class; as, a *specimen* of ore; a *specimen* of manhood. *Example* is a more general term; it may often be used interchangeably with *specimen* or *instance;* as, an *example* of good conduct. An *instance* is an *example* that confirms a certain point; the word is applied only to actions or cases; as, *instances* of loyalty and of treason.

spe-cious (spē′shŭs), *adj.* appearing right at first sight but not really so; apparently, but not actually, fair or right; as, a *specious* argument.—*adv.* **spe′cious-ly.**—*n.* **spe′cious-ness.**—*n.* **spe″ci-os′i-ty** (spē″shĭ-ŏs′ĭ-tĭ).

speck (spĕk), *n.* **1,** a spot; flaw; blemish; spot of decay, as in fruit; **2,** a very small thing; particle:—*v.t.* to spot, or stain with small spots; speckle.

speck-le (spĕk′l), *n.* a small spot in or on anything, different in substance or color from the thing itself:—*v.t.* [*p.t.* and *p.p.* -led (-ld), *p.pr.* -ling], to mark with spots of a color different from that of the thing itself.

spec-ta-cle (spĕk′tȧ-kl), *n.* **1,** something displayed to view, esp. something unusual or worthy of notice; **2,** a pageant or parade; a grand exhibition; **3,** in *pl.*, a device for assisting the sight, consisting of two lenses in a frame, with a bridge to fit over the nose and bows to pass over the ears.

Syn. exhibition, display, show.

spec-tac-u-lar (spĕk-tăk′ū-lȧr), *adj.* **1,** pertaining to a show or exhibition; **2,** marked by grand display; designed to excite wonder by scenic or dramatic effect; imposing.—*adv.* **spec-tac′u-lar-ly.**

spec-ta-tor (spĕk-tā′tẽr), *n.* one who looks on; an observer.

spec-ter (spĕk′tẽr), *n.* a ghost or apparition. Also, **spec′tre.**

spec-tral (spĕk′trăl), *adj.* **1,** pertaining to, or like, a ghost; ghostly; **2,** pertaining to a spectrum; **3,** pertaining to the division of light into its several colors; as, *spectral* analysis.—*adv.* **spec′tral-ly.**

spec-tro-scope (spĕk′trō-skōp), *n.* an optical instrument for dividing light into the rays of which it is composed, and for examining the image so produced.—*adj.* **spec″tro-scop′ic; spec″tro-scop′i-cal.**—*adv.* **spec″tro-scop′i-cal-ly.**

spec-tros-co-py (spĕk-trŏs′kō-pĭ; spĕk′-trō-skō″pĭ), *n.* the science of the phenomena seen by the spectroscope; also, the science of using such an instrument.—*n.* **spec-tros′co-pist.**

spec-trum (spĕk′trŭm), *n.* [*pl.* spectra (-trȧ)], an image formed by the dividing of a ray of light into parts arranged according to their different wave lengths, as in the rainbow or in the passing of light through a prism.

spec-u-lar (spĕk′ū-lȧr), *adj.* of or pertaining to a mirror or reflector.

spec-u-late (spĕk′ū-lāt), *v.i.* [*p.t.* and *p.p.* -lat″ed, *p.pr.* -lat″ing], **1,** to consider a subject from all sides; meditate upon a topic and form opinions upon it; **2,** to purchase stock, land, goods, etc., at a risk, with the idea of selling them at a higher market value.—*n.* **spec′u-la″tor.**

spec-u-la-tion (spĕk″ū-lā′shŭn), *n.* **1,** mental examination or theorizing; reflective, inquiring consideration; **2,** the purchase of stock, goods, etc., at a risk, for future sale at a profit.

spec-u-la-tive (spĕk′ū-lā-tĭv), *adj.* **1,** pertaining to, or given to, contemplation, reflection, or theorizing; **2,** pertaining to ventures which involve a risk and which hold out a hope of profit to offset a possibility of loss.—*adv.* **spec′u-la-tive-ly.**—*n.* **spec′u-la-tive-ness.**

spec-u-lum (spĕk′ū-lŭm), *n.* [*pl.* specula (-lȧ); speculums (-lŭmz)],

1, a reflector of polished metal, esp. one used in an optical instrument; 2, a surgical instrument used to expand certain passages of the body for purposes of examination.

sped (spĕd), past tense and past participle of the irregular verb *speed.*

speech (spēch), *n.* 1, the power of uttering articulate sounds or words; 2, expression of thought in words; act of speaking; 3, manner of speaking; as, his *speech* is indistinct; 4, that which is spoken; conversation; 5, a language or dialect; as, Italian is a musical *speech;* 6, a formal discourse in public, or the published report of it; as, to make a *speech.*

Syn. oration, harangue, sermon. *Speech* is the general term for the public utterance of thoughts or sentiments; a *speech* may be formal or informal. An *oration* is a formal and elaborate *speech,* often delivered for some ceremony, always carefully prepared and composed in polished style; as, the *orations* of Cicero. A *harangue* is a vehement appeal, often argumentative; as, a *harangue* on government ownership. A *sermon* is a discourse usually delivered by a clergyman, but it may be any informal talk of an improving nature given by anyone. (See language.)

speech-less (spēch′lĕs), *adj.* 1, being without the power to speak; 2, dumb; silent; 3, not expressed in words; as, a *speechless* entreaty.—*adv.* **speech′less-ly.** —*n.* **speech′less-ness.**

speed (spēd), *n.* 1, the act or state of moving rapidly; swiftness; quickness; 2, rate of motion, or velocity; 3, *Archaic,* good fortune; as, he wished her all *speed:*—*v.i.* [*p.t.* and *p.p.* sped (spĕd), *p.pr.* speed′ing], to move quickly; as, the bullet *sped* through the air: —*v.t.* 1, to prosper; 2, to send away with good wishes; as, to *speed* the parting guest; 3, to cause to move faster; as, to *speed* an engine; to *speed* the work.—*n.* **speed′er.**

speed-ing (spēd′ĭng), *n.* the act of driving a motor vehicle at a greater speed than that permitted by law.

speed-om-e-ter (spēd-ŏm′ē-tẽr), *n.* an instrument for indicating speed, as the miles per hour that an automobile is traveling.

speed-ster (spēd′stẽr), *n.* an automobile, esp. a two-seated roadster, built to make great speed.

speed-way (spēd′wā″), *n.* a track where fast driving or racing, as of horses or automobiles, is permitted.

speed-y (spēd′ĭ), *adj.* [*comp.* speed′i-er, *superl.* speed′i-est], 1, swift; quick; hasty; 2, prompt; without delay.—*adv.* **speed′i-ly.**—*n.* **speed′i-ness.**

Syn. fast, rapid. (See hasty.)

speiss (spīs), *n.* a mixture of metallic chemical compounds of arsenic and antimony, formed in the smelting of certain ores, as copper, iron, nickel, etc.

[1]**spell** (spĕl), *n.* 1, an incantation; a spoken word, or words, supposed to act as a charm; 2, hence, fascination:—*v.i.* [*p.t.* and *p.p.* spelled (spĕld) or spelt (spĕlt), *p.pr.* spell′ing], to form words with letters, esp. with the correct letters, either orally or in writing; as, he *spells* accurately:—*v.t.* 1, to write, repeat, or point out in order, the proper letters of (a word); 2, to make out or decipher with difficulty; as, to *spell* out an inscription; 3, to make up or form: said of letters; as, d o g *spells* dog; 4, hence, to indicate or mean; involve; as, war *spells* hardship; 5, to bewitch; fascinate.

[2]**spell** (spĕl), *n.* 1, a turn at work to relieve another; as, a *spell* at the oars; 2, time during which a person works; 3, *Colloq.:* a, any short, continuous, or particular period of time; as, he visited us for a *spell;* a hot *spell;* b, an attack of sickness:—*v.t.* to take the place of (another) for a time.

spell-bind (spĕl′bīnd″), *v.t.* [*p.t.* and *p.p.* -bound″ (-bound″), *p.pr.* -bind″ing], to hold as by a spell; fascinate; esp., to interest others intensely by an oration. —*p.adj.* **spell′bound″.**—*n.* **spell′bind″er.**

spell-er (spĕl′ẽr), *n.* 1, one who spells; one apt in spelling; 2, a book containing exercises and drills for training pupils in correct spelling.

spell-ing (spĕl′ĭng), *n.* 1, the act or art of forming words by letters; orthography; 2, the way in which a word is spelled; 3, *Colloq.,* a lesson or exercise in spelling: **spelling book,** a book containing exercises for training students to spell.

[1]**spelt** (spĕlt), one form of the past tense and past participle of [1]*spell.*

[2]**spelt** (spĕlt), *n.* a variety of wheat, common in early times.

spel-ter (spĕl′tẽr), *n.* zinc: used in commercial parlance only.

spend (spĕnd), *v.t.* [*p.t.* and *p.p.* spent (spĕnt), *p.pr.* spend′ing], 1, to pay out, as money; expend; 2, to give freely; 3, to squander; 4, to exhaust by using; as, his violence soon *spent* itself; 5, to consume; pass: —*v.i.* 1, to incur expense; as, he *spends* unwisely; 2, to waste away.—*n.* **spend′er.**

spend-thrift (spĕnd′thrĭft″), *adj.* wasteful; extravagant:—*n.* one who spends foolishly or wastefully.

spent (spĕnt), *p.adj.* exhausted; worn out; without energy or force.

[1]**sperm** (spûrm), *n.* 1, the fertilizing fluid of male animals, which enables them to reproduce their kind: also called *semen;* 2, a spermatozoön.—*adj.* **sperm′ic.** —*adj.* **sper-mat′ic.**

[2]**sperm** (spûrm), *n.* a white, waxy solid; spermaceti; also, an oil called *sperm oil,* found in the head of the sperm whale.

sper-ma-ce-ti (spûr″mȧ-sē′tĭ; spûr″mȧ-sĕt′ĭ), *n.* a white, waxy substance obtained from the head of the sperm whale: used in making ointments and candles.

sper-ma-to-zo-ön (spûr″mȧ-tō-zō′ŏn), *n.* [*pl.* spermatozoa (-ȧ)], the male germ cell, which fertilizes the female cell by uniting with it; a sperm cell.

sperm oil a yellowish oil obtained from the sperm whale, esp. from the head: distinguished from *train oil.*

sperm whale a large whale found in warm seas, valued for the sperm oil and a waxlike substance, spermaceti, obtained from its head.

spew (spū), *v.t.* and *v.i.* 1, to vomit; 2, to cast forth; eject.

sphe-noid (sfē′noid), *adj.* 1, wedge-shaped; as, a *sphenoid* crystal; 2, designating, or pertaining to, an irregular, wedge-shaped, compound bone forming the lower front part of the cranium, or brainpan: —*n.* the sphenoid bone.—*adj.* **sphe-noi′dal.**

sphere (sfẽr), *n.* 1, a solid body bounded by a single surface, whose every point is equally distant from a point within called its center; also, the surface of such a solid; 2, a globe or globelike body; a ball; also, a planet; 3, extent or range of knowledge, influence, action, etc.; as, to seek a wider *sphere* for one's abilities; 4, province; place of existence; social position; 5, the spherical dome of the heavens:—*v.t.* [*p.t.* and *p.p.* sphered (sfẽrd), *p.pr.* spher′ing], 1, to place in a sphere; 2, to make round like a sphere.—*adj.* **spher′al.**

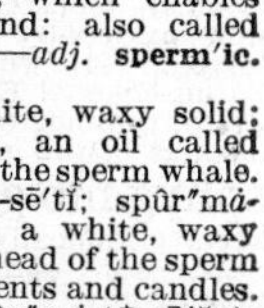

SPHERE

spher-i-cal (sfĕr′ĭ-kăl), *adj.* like, or pertaining to, a sphere, or globe. Also, **spher′ic.**—*adv.* **spher′i-cal-ly.**—*n.* **spher′i-cal-ness.**

sphe-ric-i-ty (sfē-rĭs′ĭ-tĭ), *n.* the state or fact of being a sphere, or globe; roundness.

sphe-roid (sfē′roid), *n.* **1,** a body that is nearly a sphere in shape; as, the earth is an oblate *spheroid;* **2,** in geometry, a solid or surface generated by the revolution of an ellipse about either its major (*prolate spheroid*) or its minor (*oblate spheroid*) axis (see *prolate,* illus.).—*adj.* **sphe-roi′dal.**

spher-ule (sfĕr′ōōl), *n.* a little sphere; a globule.—*adj.* **spher′u-lar.**

sphinc-ter (sfĭngk′tẽr), *n.* a ringlike muscle that surrounds a natural opening in the body, contracting to close it and expanding to open it.

sphinx (sfĭngks), *n.* [*pl.* sphinxes (sfĭngk′-sĕz); sphinges (sfĭn′jēz)], **1,** in Greek myth, a monster having the body of a winged lion and a woman's head and breasts; in Egyptian art, a creature represented as having a lion's body with a hawk's, ram's, or man's head; **2,** a reticent person; a person with an inscrutable character: **Sphinx, 1,** a mythological monster at Thebes, Greece, who slew passers-by when they were unable to solve a riddle which she propounded to them; **2,** the colossal Egyptian statue at Giza, near Cairo, the face of which is supposed to be a likeness of the god Harmachis.

EGYPTIAN SPHINX

sphyg-mo-graph (sfĭg′mō-grȧf), *n.* an instrument that registers graphically the character of the pulse beat.—*adj.* **sphyg″mo-graph′ic.**—*n.* **sphyg-mog′ra-phy.**

Spi-ca (spī′kȧ), *n.* the brightest star in the constellation Virgo.

spice (spīs), *n.* **1,** any of various aromatic vegetable substances, sometimes ground or powdered, used for seasoning, as cinnamon, nutmeg, or pepper; **2,** that which gives flavor or zest; a relish; smack; as, a *spice* of mischief:—*v.t.* [*p.t.* and *p.p.* spiced (spīst), *p.pr.* spic′ing], to season or flavor, with, or as with, condiments.—*n.* **spic′er-y.**

spic-ule (spĭk′ūl), *n.* a slender, sharp-pointed, hard body.—*adj.* **spic′u-lar.**—*adj.* **spic′u-late.**

spic-y (spīs′ĭ), *adj.* [*comp.* spic′i-er, *superl.* spic′i-est], **1,** flavored with, containing, or having the qualities of, spice; fragrant; aromatic; **2,** full of life and point; as, a *spicy* discussion.—*adv.* **spic′i-ly.**—*n.* **spic′i-ness.**

Syn. lively, piquant, pungent.

spi-der (spī′dẽr), *n.* **1,** any of various arachnids capable of spinning silken fibers, with which some varieties construct webs for catching prey (see illus. page 171); **2,** anything suggestive of a spider in form; **3,** a kind of frying pan: **spider crab,** any of various spiderlike crabs (see illus. page 171).

spied (spīd), past tense and past participle of the verb *spy.*

spig-ot (spĭg′ŭt), *n.* **1,** a pointed piece of wood used to stop the opening in a cask; **2,** the plug of a faucet or cock; sometimes, the faucet or cock itself.

¹spike (spīk), *n.* **1,** a sharp point or projection; **2,** any sharp, slender object, as a kind of large nail:—*v.t.* [*p.t.* and *p.p.* spiked (spīkt), *p.pr.* spik′ing], **1,** to fasten or equip with large nails or sharp points; **2,** to run through with a sharp point; **3,** to close the vent of (cannon) by plugging with a spike.

²spike (spīk), *n.* **1,** an ear of grain; **2,** in botany, a mode of inflorescence, or arrangement of flowers on a stalk, in which the flowers are attached directly, without stems, along the end of the stalk, as in the plantain (see *inflorescence,* illus.).

spike-let (spīk′lĕt), *n.* in botany, a very small or secondary spike, as the flower cluster of certain grasses.

spike-nard (spīk′nȧrd), *n.* **1,** a fragrant oil or ointment used by the ancients; **2,** an aromatic herb of the East Indies, supposed to yield this oil.

spile (spīl), *n.* **1,** a large timber driven into the ground as a foundation; a pile; **2,** a wooden plug or spigot; **3,** in the U. S., a spout driven into a sugar-maple tree to drain off the sap:—*v.t.* [*p.t.* and *p.p.* spiled (spīld), *p.pr.* spil′ing], **1,** to provide with a spigot; **2,** to drive piles into; **3,** to set up supporting timbers under.

¹spill (spĭl), *n.* **1,** a slender piece of anything, as a splinter, wooden pin, metal rod, or the like; **2,** a thin strip of wood or small roll of paper for lighting a lamp, etc.

²spill (spĭl), *v.t.* [*p.t.* and *p.p.* spilled (spĭld) or spilt (spĭlt), *p.pr.* spill′ing], **1,** to cause or permit to run over, or fall out of, a vessel or other container; **2,** to cause to be scattered, wasted, lost, or the like; as, to *spill* blood; **3,** *Colloq.,* to throw or overthrow, as a rider from his horse:—*v.i.* to flow over, fall out, be scattered, or the like:—*n.* **1,** the act or state of overflowing, scattering, falling out, or running over; **2,** the overflow of a dam; **3,** *Colloq.,* a throw or tumble.

spin (spĭn), *v.t.* [*p.t.* spun (spŭn) or, *Archaic,* span (spăn), *p.p.* spun, *p.pr.* spin′ning], **1,** to draw out and twist into threads; as, to *spin* cotton; **2,** to draw out tediously; as, to *spin* a long story; **3,** to form (a web or cocoon) by drawing out threads of fluid from a gland; **4,** to cause to whirl rapidly, as a top:—*v.i.* **1,** to draw out and twist fiber into threads; **2,** to whirl; **3,** *Colloq.,* to move swiftly; as, to *spin* along the road on a bicycle; **4,** to make and expel a thread, as a spider:—*n.* **1,** the act of spinning; esp., a rapid whirling; **2,** *Colloq.,* a short drive, as in an automobile.

spin-ach (spĭn′ăj; spĭn′ĕch), *n.* a common garden herb, the leaves of which are eaten as a vegetable. Also, **spin′age.**

spi-nal (spī′năl), *adj.* **1,** pertaining to the backbone, or spinal column; as, *spinal* disease; **2,** pertaining to a spine, or thornlike, spinous process: **spinal column,** the backbone, a series of similar bones joined by cartilage, extending from the base of the skull to the pelvis, and affording a strong, flexible support for the body: **spinal cord,** a cord of nervous tissue running lengthwise through the spinal column.

spin-dle (spĭn′dl), *n.* **1,** in a spinning wheel or machine, the long, thin rod used for twisting and winding the thread; in spinning by hand, a round stick tapering at each end, on which the thread is twisted and held; **2,** a slender rod or pin on which anything turns:—*v.i.* [*p.t.* and *p.p.* -dled (-dld), *p.pr.* -dling], to grow into long, slim stalks.

spin-dle–leg-ged (spĭn′dl-lĕg″ĕd; spĭn′dl-lĕgd″), *adj.* having long, slender legs, as a table.

spin-dle-shanks (spĭn′dl-shăngks″), *n.* **1,** in *pl.* used as *sing.,* a tall person with long, thin legs; **2,** in *pl.,* long, thin legs.—*adj.* **spin′dle–shanked″.**

spin-dling (spĭn′dlĭng), *p.adj.* long and thin; esp., too thin in proportion to height.

spin-drift (spĭn′drĭft), *n.* foam or spray blown up from the surface of a stormy sea; spoondrift.

spine (spīn), *n.* **1,** the backbone, or spinal column; **2,** something like the backbone; **3,** a thorn-shaped or pointed stiff growth on a plant or animal.

spin-el (spĭn′ĕl; spĭ-nĕl′), *n.* any of various colored crystalline minerals, valuable as ores: **spinel ruby,** a deep red variety of spinel, valued as a gem.

spine-less (spīn′lĕs), *adj.* **1,** having no backbone; invertebrate; **2,** without courage; without the will to resist; **3,** without spines; as, the *spineless* cactus.

spin-et (spĭn′ĕt; spĭ-nĕt′), *n.* an obsolete keyed instrument like the harpsichord, but smaller: an early form of piano.

spin-na-ker (spĭn′ȧ-kẽr), *n.* a large sail, triangular in shape, used when a vessel is running before the wind.

spin-ner (spĭn′ẽr), *n.* **1,** one who or that which spins; **2,** a conical cap over the hub of the propeller of an airplane (see *airplane,* illus.); **3,** a spider.

spin-ner-et (spĭn′ẽr-ĕt), *n.* an organ that spins silk, as in spiders.

spin-ney (spĭn′ĭ), *n.* [*pl.* spinneys (-ĭz)], a thicket; a small wood.

spin-ning jen-ny a machine having several spindles, so as to spin a number of threads at a time.

spin-ning wheel a machine with a spindle which is turned by a large wheel operated by hand or foot power, on which fibers, as cotton, wool, etc., are twisted into thread or yarn.

spi-nous (spī′nŭs), *adj.* **1,** (also, *spinose*), full of, or covered with, sharp, pointed thorns or quills, as the porcupine; thorny; **2,** like a spine; as, a *spinous* process.

spin-ster (spĭn′stẽr), *n.* a woman who has not married; esp., in popular use, an elderly single woman.

spin-y (spīn′ĭ), *adj.* [*comp.* spin′i-er, *superl.* spin′i-est], full of, or covered with, thorny spines; thorny: **spiny anteater,** an egg-laying anteater of Australia, with spines mixed with its fur (see *anteater,* illus.): **spiny lobster,** a crustacean resembling the lobster but without the large claws; a sea crawfish (see *crustacean,* illus.).

spir-a-cle (spĭr′ȧ-kl; spī′rȧ-kl), *n.* one of the small openings through which many aquatic mammals, including whales, porpoises, etc., breathe.

spi-ræ-a (spī-rē′ȧ), *n.* any of several shrubs of the rose family, both cultivated and wild. Also, **spi-re′a.**

spi-ral (spī′răl), *adj.* **1,** winding around a center and gradually receding from it, like a watch spring; **2,** winding and going forward, like the thread of a screw; **3,** winding in a cone:—*n.* a curve or curved line moving continually from or toward the center about which it revolves.—*adv.* **spi′ral-ly.**

spi-rant (spī′rănt), *n.* a consonant produced by forcing the breath through a narrow opening, as *f, s, sh, v.*

[1]**spire** (spīr), *n.* a spiral, or single turn of a spiral; specif., the upper part of a spiral shell.—*adj.* **spired.**

[2]**spire** (spīr), *n.* **1,** a slender leaf or blade, as of grass; **2,** a body that tapers to a point; esp., a slender, tapering top of a tower or steeple; also, a steeple:—*v.i.* [*p.t.* and *p.p.* spired (spīrd), *p.pr.* spir′ing], to shoot forth, or point up, in, or as in, a spire.

spir-it (spĭr′ĭt), *n.* **1,** life; the principle of life regarded as a mysterious entity separable from the body; **2,** the soul; the immortal, spiritual part of man; **3,** a supernatural being, as a ghost or fairy; **4,** a person, considered with reference to qualities of mind or temper; as, a noble *spirit;* **5,** usually in *pl.,* temper; mood; disposition; also, lively or courageous mood; courage, energy, and vim; **6,** power of mind, moral or intellectual; as, "the *spirit* is willing"; **7,** condition of mind, temper, or disposition; as, the *spirit* of the army was loyal; **8,** enthusiasm for an object; as, school *spirit;* **9,** real meaning; as, the tone of the words contradicted their *spirit;* **10,** usually in *pl.,* any strong, distilled alcoholic liquor, as brandy, whisky, etc.; **11,** often in *pl.,* a solution in alcohol of certain drugs; as, *spirit* of camphor: **Spirit,** the third person of the Trinity: also called *Holy Spirit; Holy Ghost:* —*v.t.* to carry suddenly or secretly: often with *off* or *away*; as, they *spirited* her away.

spir-it-ed (spĭr′ĭt-ĕd), *adj.* **1,** full of vigor or life; animated; lively; as, a *spirited* horse; **2,** showing disposition of a certain kind: in composition; as, a mean-*spirited* fellow.—*adv.* **spir′it-ed-ly.**—*n.* **spir′it-ed-ness.**
Syn. bold, vivacious.—*Ant.* lifeless, dull.

spir-it-ism (spĭr′ĭ-tĭzm), *n.* the belief that the souls of the dead communicate with the living, either directly or through mediums; spiritualism.—*n.* **spir′it-ist.**—*adj.* **spir″it-is′tic.**

spir-it-less (spĭr′ĭt-lĕs), *adj.* without vigor or animation; as, a *spiritless* address or speaker.—*adv.* **spir′it-less-ly.**

spir-it lev-el an instrument for determining a horizontal plane by the position of a bubble in a glass tube of alcohol or other liquid: often called *level* (see *tool,* illus.).

spir-it-u-al (spĭr′ĭt-ū-ăl), *adj.* **1,** not material; of or pertaining to the mind or soul, as distinguished from matter: opp. of *physical;* **2,** pertaining to the soul or higher nature of man; **3,** pure; holy; heavenly minded; **4,** pertaining to sacred or religious things; not lay or temporal; ecclesiastical: opp. of *carnal.*—*adv.* **spir′it-u-al-ly.**

spir-it-u-al-ism (spĭr′ĭt-ū-ăl-ĭzm), *n.* **1,** the belief that nothing is real except soul, or spirit; **2,** the belief that the souls of the dead communicate with the living, esp. through a medium.—*n.* **spir′-it-u-al-ist.**—*adj.* **spir″it-u-al-is′tic.**

spir-it-u-al-i-ty (spĭr″ĭt-ū-ăl′ĭ-tĭ), *n.* [*pl.* spiritualities (-tĭz)], **1,** the state or quality of being neither physical nor material; soul as apart from matter; **2,** unworldliness; elevation of mind; as, the *spirituality* of an author; **3,** that which belongs to the church, as tithes.

spir-it-u-al-ize (spĭr′ĭt-ū-ăl-īz), *v.t.* [*p.t.* and *p.p.* -ized (-īzd), *p.pr.* -iz″ing], **1,** to make spiritual; purify; **2,** to animate; breathe life into; **3,** to give a pure or religious meaning to.—*n.* **spir″it-u-al-i-za′tion.**

spi-ri-tu-el (spĭr′ĭt-ū-ĕl′; *Fr.* spē″rē″tü″ĕl′), *adj.* having the higher and finer qualities of mind; also, having the appearance of grace or delicacy.—*fem. adj.* ***spi″ri″tu″elle′.**

spir-it-u-ous (spĭr′ĭt-ū-ŭs), *adj.* containing, or of the nature of, alcohol; intoxicating; as, *spirituous* liquors.

spi-rom-e-ter (spī-rŏm′ē-tẽr), *n.* any of various instruments for measuring the amount of air that can be breathed out of the lungs.—*n.* **spi-rom′e-try.**

[1]**spirt** (spûrt), *v.i.* to gush forth in a sudden jet:—*v.t.* to force out in a sudden jet: —*n.* a sudden gush, as of steam or a liquid. See [1]**spurt,** *Pfd. S.*

[2]**spirt** (spûrt), *v.i.* to make a sudden, brief, extreme effort:—*n.* a sudden, increased exertion. Also, **spurt,** *Pfd. S.*

[1]**spit** (spĭt), *n.* **1,** a long, pointed rod which is used to hold meat for roasting before an open fire; **2,** a small point of land, or a

long, narrow shoal, extending out into the sea:—*v.t.* [*p.t.* and *p.p.* spit'ted, *p.pr.* spit'ting], to pierce with a spit; impale.

[2]**spit** (spĭt), *v.t.* [*p.t.* and *p.p.* spit or, *Archaic,* spat (spăt), *p.pr.* spit'ting], **1,** to eject from the mouth, as blood or saliva; **2,** to eject or throw out in scattering drops from an opening; **3,** to send down in drops or flakes, as rain or snow:—*v.i.* **1,** to eject saliva from the mouth; expectorate; **2,** to rain or snow lightly; **3,** to make a hissing noise like that of expectorating: said esp. of cats:—*n.* **1,** saliva; **2,** the act of ejecting saliva; **3,** a light fall of rain or snow.—*n.* **spit'ter.**

spite (spīt), *n.* ill will or hatred toward another, with the desire to irritate, annoy, or injure; petty malice; grudge; **in spite of,** or **spite of,** formerly, in contempt of; now, notwithstanding:—*v.t.* [*p.t.* and *p.p.* spit'ed, *p.pr.* spit'ing], to try to injure or baffle; annoy; thwart.

Syn., n. enmity, rancor. (See malice.)

spite-ful (spīt'fo͝ol), *adj.* full of ill will; malicious; having a desire to injure.—*adv.* **spite'ful-ly.**—*n.* **spite'ful-ness.**

spit-fire (spĭt'fīr''), *n. Colloq.,* a very quick-tempered person.

spit-tle (spĭt'l), *n.* saliva, esp. as ejected from the mouth; spit.

spit-toon (spĭ-to͞on'), *n.* a vessel for spittle, or spit; a cuspidor.

spitz dog (spĭts), a variety of Pomeranian dog, usually white, with a sharp muzzle, long, silky hair, and bushy tail: also called *spitz.*

splash (splăsh), *v.t.* **1,** to spatter or toss about; as, to *splash* water; **2,** to spatter or soil with water, mud, etc.; as, the automobile *splashed* her dress; **3,** to cause to look as if splashed; decorate with spots; as, a robe *splashed* with gold:—*v.i.* **1,** to dash or spatter a liquid about in drops; **2,** to fall or proceed with a dash or splatter; as, to *splash* into, or through, a puddle; **3,** to fall or fly about in drops; as, paint *splashes:*—*n.* **1,** a spot or daub, esp. one made by a liquid thrown upon anything; **2,** a noise as from water dashed up, or by anything striking in or upon a liquid; **3,** an irregular spot of color; a blotch.—*n.* **splash'er.**—*adj.* **splash'y.**

splat (splăt), *n.* in joinery, a wide, flat piece of wood, as in a chair back.

splat-ter (splăt'ẽr), *v.t.* and *v.i.* to splash; spatter:—*n.* a splashing sound.

splay (splā), *v.t.* **1,** to dislocate, or throw out of joint, as the shoulder bone of a horse; **2,** to slope or slant, as a window opening:—*n.* a sloped surface:—*adj.* spread out; broad and flat; hence, clumsy.

splay-foot (splā'fo͝ot''), *n.* [*pl.* splayfeet (-fēt'')], **1,** unnatural flatness and turning outward of a foot; **2,** a foot so deformed:—*adj.* having such a deformity.—*adj.* **splay'foot''ed.**

spleen (splēn), *n.* **1,** one of the ductless glands near the stomach, supposed by the ancients to be the seat of anger, melancholy, or vexation; **2,** hence, ill temper, melancholy, or spite.—*adj.* **spleen'y.**

splen-did (splĕn'dĭd), *adj.* **1,** magnificent; gorgeous; as, a *splendid* spectacle; **2,** very bright; brilliant; lustrous; as, *splendid* diamonds; **3,** heroic; grand; glorious; as, a *splendid* triumph; **4,** *Colloq.,* very good; excellent.—*adv.* **splen'did-ly.**

splen-dor (splĕn'dẽr), *n.* **1,** great brightness; **2,** richness; magnificence; pomp. Also, **splen'dour.**—*adj.* **splen'dor-ous.**

Syn. luster, grandeur, brilliance.

sple-net-ic (splē-nĕt'ĭk; splĕn'ē-tĭk), *adj.* **1,** affected with splenic disorder; **2,** fretful; peevish; melancholy.

Syn. morose, sullen, gloomy.

splen-ic (splĕn'ĭk; splē'nĭk), *adj.* pertaining to, connected with, or supplying, the spleen; as, the *splenic* artery.

splice (splīs), *v.t.* [*p.t.* and *p.p.* spliced (splīst), *p.pr.* splic'ing], **1,** to unite without knots, as two ropes, by interweaving or otherwise joining the ends of the strands; **2,** to connect, as pieces of wood or metal, by overlapping parts and making them fast:—*n.* the union, or place of union, of ropes, timbers, etc., by splicing.—*n.* **splic'er.**

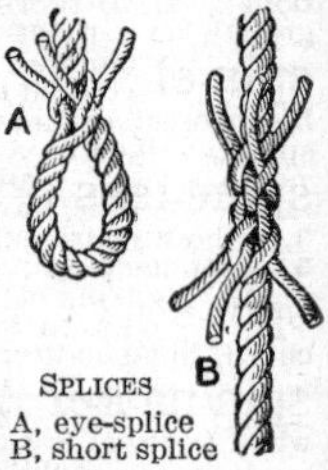

SPLICES
A, eye-splice
B, short splice

splint (splĭnt), *n.* **1,** a splinter; **2,** a thin strip of wood for chair seats, baskets, etc.; **3,** something to hold in place an injured part, as a broken bone; **4,** in medieval armor, any of a number of thin, narrow metal plates, overlapping but permitting motion.

splint bone in the leg of the horse and similar animals, one of the small bones on either side of the leg bone between the knee and the fetlock.

splin-ter (splĭn'tẽr), *n.* a thin piece of wood, split or torn off lengthwise; fragment:—*v.t.* to split into long thin pieces; sliver:—*v.i.* to be torn into slivers or fragments.—*adj.* **splin'ter-y.**

split (splĭt), *v.t.* [*p.t.* and *p.p.* split or, *Rare,* split'ted, *p.pr.* split'ting], **1,** to divide or cut lengthwise, as wood with the grain; **2,** to rend or tear apart violently; **3,** to divide or break up into parts or layers; also, to break up into factions or sides, as a political party; **4,** to divide between candidates; as, to *split* a vote: **split infinitive,** an infinitive with *to,* having a qualifier between the *to* and the verb, as in the expression *to really know:* **to split hairs,** to make fussy and unnecessary distinctions:—*v.i.* **1,** to burst; break apart; **2,** to divide lengthwise, or with the grain; **3,** to separate into parties or factions:—*n.* **1,** a rent or crack; **2,** division or separation, as in an organization; rupture; **3,** a splint for weaving baskets; also, a splinter; **4,** any of the layers into which a hide may be divided (see *leather,* illus.).—*n.* **split'ter.**

splotch (splŏch), *n.* a stain; daub; blotch; spot:—*v.t.* to soil with a stain or blotch.—*adj.* **splotch'y.**

splurge (splûrj), *n. Colloq.,* a showy display; a conceited personal demonstration:—*v.i.* [*p.t.* and *p.p.* splurged (splûrjd), *p.pr.* splurg'ing], to make a conceited or offensive display.

splut-ter (splŭt'ẽr), *v.t. Colloq.,* to utter hastily and confusedly:—*v.i. Colloq.,* **1,** to speak hastily and confusedly; **2,** to make a hissing or confused noise:—*n. Colloq.,* a confused noise; stir.—*n.* **splut'ter-er.**

spoil (spoil), *v.t.* [*p.t.* and *p.p.* spoiled (spoild) or spoilt (spoilt), *p.pr.* spoil'ing], **1,** to rob; despoil: often with *of;* **2,** to corrupt; ruin; **3,** to indulge, with harmful effects on character; as, to *spoil* a child:—*v.i.* **1,** to become corrupted; decay; lose freshness or other good qualities; **2,** to practice plunder or robbery:—*n.* **1,** pillage; plunder; booty; **2,** an object or article of pillage; prey; **3,** in *pl.,* public offices and the gain derived from them, appropriated as plunder by the successful party in an election: **spoils system,** in the U. S., the distribution of public official positions among the members of the winning party.—*n.* **spoil'age.**—*n.* **spoil'er.**

[1]**spoke** (spōk), the past tense of the irregular verb *speak,* which see.

[2]spoke (spōk), *n.* **1,** one of the bars of a wheel connecting the center with the rim; **2,** a round, or rung, of a ladder; **3,** a bar to keep a wheel from turning.

spo-ken (spō'kn), past participle of the irregular verb *speak:*—*p.adj.* **1,** uttered in speech; oral; **2,** speaking: used in combination; as, pleasant-*spoken.*

spoke-shave (spōk'shāv"), *n.* a carpenter's tool having a handle on either end of a short blade, used in dressing the curved surfaces of woodwork: orig. used in making spokes (see *tool,* illus.).

spokes-man (spōks'măn), *n.* [*pl.* spokesmen (-mĕn)], one who speaks for another; an agent or representative.

spo-li-ate (spō'lĭ-āt), *v.t.* and *v.i.* [*p.t.* and *p.p.* -at"ed, *p.pr.* -at"ing], to rob; plunder.—*n.* **spo'li-a"tor.**

spo-li-a-tion (spō"lĭ-ā'shŭn), *n.* **1,** the act of plundering or robbing, esp. in time of war; **2,** in law, injury done to a document to impair its value as evidence.

Syn. robbery, piracy, plunder, larceny.

spon-dee (spŏn'dē), *n.* a poetic foot of two long or stressed syllables, as the word *backbone.*—*adj.* **spon-da'ic** (spŏn-dā'ĭk).

sponge (spŭnj), *n.* **1,** the porous, elastic skeleton of certain salt-water animals; **2,** the animal producing it; **3,** any substance resembling sponge, as raised dough; **4,** a mop for cleansing a gun after its discharge; **5,** one who or that which sucks in anything as a sponge does water, as a parasite, or one who lives upon others:—*v.i.* [*p.t.* and *p.p.* sponged (spŭnjd), *p.pr.* spong'ing], **1,** to suck in like a sponge; **2,** to live upon others; **3,** to gather sponges:—*v.t.* **1,** to cleanse, wipe out, or dampen, with a sponge; **2,** to take up or absorb, as with a sponge: usually with *up;* **3,** to obtain by mean methods without cost.—*n.* **spong'er.**

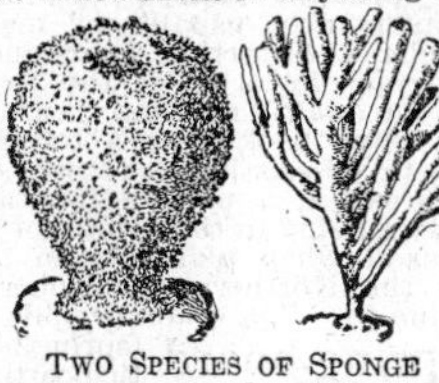

TWO SPECIES OF SPONGE

spon-gy (spŭn'jĭ), *adj.* [*comp.* spon'gi-er, *superl.* spon'gi-est], **1,** full of small holes and easily compressed; **2,** having the quality of sucking in fluids.—*n.* **spon'gi-ness.**

spon-son (spŏn'sŭn), *n.* a part projecting from the side of a vessel to protect or support some part; also, a hollow, water-tight, projecting ridge along the gunwale of a canoe, to keep it from sinking.

spon-sor (spŏn'sẽr), *n.* **1,** one who binds himself to be responsible for another's obligations in case of default; **2,** a godfather or godmother; **3,** one who indorses or stands behind a person or a movement:—*v.t.* **1,** to be surety for; **2,** to stand behind; indorse.—*adj.* **spon-so'ri-al.**—*n.* **spon'sor-ship.**

spon-ta-ne-i-ty (spŏn"tȧ-nē'ĭ-tĭ), *n.* [*pl.* spontaneities (-tĭz)], the quality or state of acting from quick, natural feeling or impulse; fresh naturalness.

spon-ta-ne-ous (spŏn-tā'nē-ŭs), *adj.* **1,** done or acting from natural impulse, prompting, temperament, or desire; as, *spontaneous* applause; **2,** produced naturally by internal causes rather than by external influences; as, *spontaneous* combustion; **3,** produced without human labor; natural to the soil; as, weeds are a *spontaneous* growth.—*adv.* **spon-ta'ne-ous-ly.**—*n.* **spon-ta'ne-ous-ness.**

spook (spo͞ok), *n.* a ghost or spirit; an apparition: now used humorously.—*adj.* **spook'ish.**—*adj.* **spook'y.**

spool (spo͞ol), *n.* **1,** a hollow cylinder, usually of wood, with a ridge at each end, on which thread, wire, etc., is wound; **2,** any similar device, as the revolving shaft of an angler's reel:—*v.t.* to wind on a spool.

[1]spoon (spo͞on), *n.* **1,** a small utensil having a round or oval shallow bowl at the end of a handle, used in preparing, serving, or eating food; **2,** something resembling a spoon, as an oar with a broad, curved blade (see *oar,* illus.); **3,** in golf, a wooden club, having the face so pitched as to loft the ball:—*v.t.* to take with, or as with, a spoon.

[2]spoon (spo͞on), *v.i. Colloq.,* to act with sentimental fondness.—*adj.* **spoon'y.**

spoon-bill (spo͞on'bĭl"), *n.* a wading bird with a broad, flat bill, somewhat like a spoon.

spoon-drift (spo͞on'drĭft), *n.* the foam or spray blown from the waves in a stormy sea; spindrift.

spoon-ful (spo͞on'fo͝ol), *n.* [*pl.* spoonfuls (-fo͝olz)], **1,** as much as a spoon will hold; **2,** a small quantity.

spoor (spo͞or), *n.* the track, trail, or scent of any wild animal:—*v.t.* to follow by a track:—*v.i.* to follow a track.

spo-rad-ic (spō-răd'ĭk), *adj.* occurring here and there in a scattered manner; as, a *sporadic* case of disease. Also, **spo-rad'i-cal.**—*adv.* **spo-rad'i-cal-ly.**

spore (spōr), *n.* **1,** a very small cell, as in fungi, capable of growing into a new plant: distinguished from *seed;* **2,** a unicellular plant or animal in the quiescent stage.

spor-ran (spŏr'ăn), *n.* the furry pouch worn in the Highland costume in front of the kilt.

sport (spōrt), *n.* **1,** pastime; amusement; **2,** jest or pleasantry; as, he said it in *sport;* **3,** mockery or derision; as, they made *sport* of him; **4,** a toy or plaything; as, to be the *sport* of chance; **5,** outdoor play or recreation, as hunting, shooting, etc.; **6,** an athletic game or other game of skill for which prizes are given or money staked; **7,** an animal or plant, or a part of either, which exhibits a sudden and spontaneous variation from the usual or normal type; **8,** *Colloq.:* **a,** one interested in sports; esp., a gambler; **b,** a cheap, flashy person; **c,** a person willing to take a chance, and cheerful when he loses: often called *good sport:*—*v.i.* **1,** to play or frolic; **2,** to trifle; **3,** to practice field diversions, such as athletic contests:—*v.t. Colloq.,* to show off, or wear, in public; as, to *sport* a diamond ring.

Syn., n. diversion. (See game.)

sport-ful (spōrt'fo͝ol), *adj.* **1,** full of sport; merry; frolicsome; **2,** done in, or tending to cause, mirth.—*adv.* **sport'ful-ly.**

sport-ing (spōr'tĭng), *p.adj.* **1,** pertaining to amusements, esp. athletic games; as, *sporting* goods; **2,** inclined to make the best of defeat or difficulty; as, a *sporting* spirit; **3,** engaged in, or devoted to, sports, chiefly for gambling ends; as, a *sporting* man.

spor-tive (spōr'tĭv), *adj.* frolicsome; playful; merry; lively.—*adv.* **spor'tive-ly.**—*n.* **spor'tive-ness.**

sports-man (spōrts'măn), *n.* [*pl.* sportsmen (-mĕn)], **1,** one who patronizes or engages in field sports, as hunting, racing, fishing, etc.; **2,** one who is fair and honorable in sports; **3,** in a bad sense, one who gambles.—*adj.* **sports'man-like.**—*adj.* **sports'man-ly.**—*n.* **sports'man-ship.**

spot (spŏt), *n.* **1,** a blot or mark; discolored place or stain; **2,** a blemish; disgrace or reproach; as, a *spot* on his reputation; **3,** locality; place; as, the exact *spot* where he fell; **4,** a small part of a surface, having a different color from the whole:—*v.t.* [*p.t.* and *p.p.* spot'ted, *p.pr.* spot'ting], **1,** to mark with spots; discolor; stain; **2**, to disgrace or blemish; **3**, *Slang*, to mark or note so as to recognize; as, to *spot* the guilty man:—*v.i.* **1**, to become marked or stained; as, this silk *spots* with water; **2**, to make a mark or stain; as, fruit juices *spot*.—*p.adj.* **spot'ted.**—*adj.* **spot'ty.**—*n.* **spot'ti-ness.**

spot-less (spŏt'lĕs), *adj.* **1**, without a stain or flaw; **2**, pure; blameless.—*adv.* **spot'less-ly.**—*n.* **spot'less-ness.**

spot-light (spŏt'līt"), *n.* **1**, *Colloq.*, a brilliant, concentrated light directed upon some object or person, as upon an actor on the stage; **2**, *Colloq.*, publicity; notoriety; prominence.

spot-ter (spŏt'ẽr), *n.* one who keeps watch on suspicious persons; specif., one who secretly keeps tally of the fares received and registered by conductors.

spouse (spouz), *n.* either one of a married couple.—*n.* and *adj.* **spous'al.**

spout (spout), *n.* **1**, the projecting tube, nozzle, or the like, through which a liquid is poured; **2**, a stream or jet of liquid:—*v.t.* **1**, to throw out forcibly in a jet or stream, as from a pipe; **2**, *Colloq.*, to utter pompously; as, to *spout* poetry:—*v.i.* **1**, to come forth with violence in a jet or stream, as liquid from a pipe; **2**, to force out a fluid in a jet or stream, as from a nozzle; **3**, *Colloq.*, to speak in a pompous manner.—*n.* **spout'er.**

sprain (sprān), *n.* a severe twisting or straining of the muscles or ligaments around a joint:—*v.t.* to strain or twist severely, as muscles or ligaments.

sprang (sprăng), the past tense of the irregular verb *spring*.

sprat (sprăt), *n.* a small fish, similar to the herring.

sprawl (sprôl), *v.i.* **1**, to lie with the body and limbs carelessly stretched out; stretch or toss out the limbs or move awkwardly; **2**, to spread in an irregular manner, as a plant:—*v.t.* to cause to lie or move with the limbs awkwardly stretched out:—*n.* an awkward spreading position, or movement.

¹spray (sprā), *n.* a small branch of a tree or plant, bearing leaves or flowers.

²spray (sprā), *n.* **1**, water or other liquid driven in small particles; **2**, an instrument for throwing fine drops of liquid or vapor; atomizer:—*v.t.* **1**, to throw fine drops of liquid upon; as, to *spray* shrubbery; **2**, to disperse, as a liquid, in fine drops:—*v.i.* **1**, to throw or scatter a liquid in fine particles; **2**, to scatter in fine particles.—*n.* **spray'er.**

spread (sprĕd), *v.t.* [*p.t.* and *p.p.* spread, *p.pr.* spread'ing], **1**, to scatter or extend evenly over a surface; as, to *spread* butter on bread; **2**, to cover with a thin layer; as, to *spread* bread with butter; **3**, to publish or make widely known; as, to *spread* a report; **4**, to unfold; open; as, a plant *spreads* its leaves; **5**, to diffuse, as a fragrance; **6**, to propagate; as, to *spread* a disease; **7**, to display before the eye; as, to *spread* out goods; **8**, to place food upon; as, to *spread* the table; **9**, to push apart, as rails:—*v.i.* **1**, to be extended or scattered over a larger surface; expand, as plants; **2**, to be dispersed or scattered; **3**, to become circulated or widely known, as rumors; **4**, to be propagated, as disease; **5**, to diffuse, as an odor; **6**, to become, or be forced, apart, as rails:—*n.* **1**, extension; as, the *spread* of education; **2**, extent; as, a fine *spread* of land; **3**, a covering for a bed, table, etc.; **4**, *Colloq.*, a table set with provisions; a feast.—*n.* **spread'er.**

Syn., *v.* disperse, circulate, expand.

spread ea-gle the figure of an eagle with wings spread, as in the arms of the U. S.: **spread-eagle**, *adj.* pretentious; boastful; as, *spread-eagle* oratory.

spree (sprē), *n.* **1**, a merry frolic; **2**, a drunken debauch:—*v.i.* [*p.t.* and *p.p.* spreed (sprēd), *p.pr.* spree'ing], **1**, to go on a gay party; **2**, to carouse.

sprig (sprĭg), *n.* **1**, a small twig or shoot; **2**, a headless nail or brad; **3**, an ornament in the form of a spray; as, muslin with a pattern of *sprigs*:—*v.t.* [*p.t.* and *p.p.* sprigged (sprĭgd), *p.pr.* sprig'ging], **1**, to work or adorn with sprigs; **2**, to drive brads into.

spright-ly (sprīt'lĭ), *adj.* [*comp.* spright'li-er, *superl.* spright'li-est], brisk; animated; gay.—*n.* **spright'li-ness.**

Syn. vivacious, lively, cheerful.

spring (sprĭng), *v.i.* [*p.t.* sprang (sprăng) or sprung (sprŭng), *p.p.* sprung, *p.pr.* spring'ing], **1**, to leap; bound; **2**, to rise suddenly; dart, as an animal from a covert; **3**, to arise; appear; as, a breeze has *sprung* up; **4**, to escape from, or as from, restraint; recoil; rebound; **5**, to become warped or bent, as a board; **6**, to issue; proceed; result, as from a course or principle; as, his actions *spring* from real conviction:—*v.t.* **1**, to start or rouse (game) from a covert; **2**, to reveal or produce with unexpected suddenness, as a surprise; **3**, to release the spring of, as a trap; **4**, to explode or discharge, as a mine; **5**, to weaken by a crack or strain; as, I have *sprung* the baseball bat; **6**, to insert in a tight-fitting place by bending or straining; as, to *spring* a tire into a rim; **7**, to leap over:—*n.* **1**, the act of springing; a leap; bound; **2**, an elastic contrivance, usually of metal, that yields under a distorting force and returns to its original form when the force is removed; **3**, the quality of being elastic; also, the act of shooting back from a tense condition as a result of elasticity; recoil; **4**, cause; origin; source; **5**, a natural fountain or supply of water rising to the surface of the earth; **6**, the season when plants begin to grow; specif., in the Northern Hemisphere, March 21 to June 21; **7**, a crack or split, as in a mast.

spring-board (sprĭng'bōrd"), *n.* an elastic board used by acrobats and others in leaping, or by swimmers in diving.

spring-bok (sprĭng'bŏk"), *n.* the South African gazelle, noted for its agility. Also, **spring'buck".**

springe (sprĭnj), *n.* a snare or noose fastened to an elastic body, as a sapling, for catching small game.

spring-er (sprĭng'ẽr), *n.* **1**, one that springs; **2**, the top stone of a pillar which supports an arch; **3**, also, the bottom stone of an arch (see ¹*arch*, illus.).

spring tide **1**, a tide of unusually great range occurring at or near the new and the full moon: opp. of *neap tide* (see *tide*, illus.); **2**, hence, any great flood, as of feeling or emotion.

spring-tide (sprĭng'tīd"), *n.* the spring season: also called *springtime*.

spring-y (sprĭng'ĭ), *adj.* [*comp.* spring'i-er, *superl.* spring'i-est], **1**, elastic; as, a *springy* gait; **2**, having springs of water; spongy.—*n.* **spring'i-ness.**

sprin-kle (sprĭng'kl), *v.t.* [*p.t.* and *p.p.* -kled (-kld), *p.pr.* -kling], **1**, to scatter in small drops or particles; **2**, to cover with small drops or particles; as, to *sprinkle* the lawn; **3**, to baptize with a few drops of water:—*v.i.* **1**, to rain lightly; **2**, to scatter something in small particles:—*n.* **1**, a light shower; **2**, a small quantity.—*n.* **sprin'kler.**

sprin-kling (sprĭng'klĭng), *n.* **1**, a small, scattered quantity or number; as, a mere *sprinkling* of people; **2**, a light shower; **3**, the act of scattering drops of liquid.

sprint (sprĭnt), *n.* a short run at full speed:—*v.i.* and *v.t.* to run (a specified distance) at full speed.—*n.* **sprint'er.**

sprit (sprĭt), *n.* a small spar running from the bottom of the mast to the top outside corner of the sail of a boat.

sprite (sprīt), *n.* **1**, an elf, goblin, or fairy; **2**, a ghost or spirit.

sprit-sail (sprĭt′sāl″; sprĭt′sl), *n.* a gaff sail extended by a small spar, or sprit, attached near the bottom of the mast and crossing the sail diagonally.

sprock-et (sprŏk′ĕt), *n.* **1**, a tooth, as on a wheel, shaped so as to engage with the links of a chain; **2**, a wheel having such teeth on its rim.

sprout (sprout), *v.i.* **1**, to begin to grow; **2**, to put forth shoots, as the seed of a plant:—*v.t.* **1**, to cause to put forth shoots and begin to grow; **2**, to take the sprouts from:—*n.* **1**, a shoot; bud; **2**, in *pl.*, the edible buds of a kind of cabbage: commonly called *Brussels sprouts*.

[1]**spruce** (sprōōs), *adj.* **1**, smart; trim; neat; **2**, finicking:—*v.t.* [*p.t.* and *p.p.* spruced (sprōōst), *p.pr.* spruc′ing], *Colloq.*, to dress smartly; arrange in a neat and tidy manner: often with *up*:—*v.i. Colloq.*, to dress smartly; to become smart or trim: often with *up*.—*adv.* **spruce′ly**.—*n.* **spruce′ness**.

[2]**spruce** (sprōōs), *n.* any of several related evergreen trees bearing cones and needle-shaped leaves; also, their wood:—*adj.* pertaining to, or made of, any part of a spruce; as, *spruce* gum; *spruce* beer.

sprung (sprŭng), past tense and past participle of the irregular verb *spring*.

spry (sprī), *adj.* [*comp.* spri′er or spry′er, *superl.* spri′est or spry′est], *Colloq.*, nimble; active; agile.

spud (spŭd), *n.* **1**, a sharp, narrow spade, esp. for digging up large-rooted weeds; **2**, *Colloq.*, a potato.

spume (spūm), *n.* froth; foam; scum:—*v.i.* [*p.t.* and *p.p.* spumed (spūmd), *p.pr.* spum′ing], to foam.

spu-mous (spū′mŭs), *adj.* frothy; foamy. Also, **spum′y**.

spun (spŭn), past tense and past participle of the irregular verb *spin*.

spunk (spŭngk), *n.* **1**, touchwood, or wood that instantly takes fire; punk; **2**, *Colloq.*, mettle, spirit, or pluck; also, anger:—*v.i.* **1**, to flame up; **2**, *Colloq.*, to show spirit or quick temper: with *up*.

spunk-y (spŭngk′ĭ), *adj.* [*comp.* spunk′i-er, *superl.* spunk′i-est], *Colloq.*, **1**, mettlesome; plucky; **2**, touchy; peevish; **3**, not tractable; obstinate; as, a *spunky*, disobedient child.

spur (spûr), *n.* **1**, a small wheel with sharp points, worn on the heel by a horseman to urge on a horse; **2**, anything that urges to action; as, the challenge was a *spur* to his ambition; **3**, anything resembling a spur, as the projecting part of a flower, or a projecting root of a tree; **4**, a mountain ridge running out to the side from a range of mountains; **5**, the stiff, sharp spine on a rooster's leg:—*v.t.* [*p.t.* and *p.p.* spurred (spûrd), *p.pr.* spur′ring], **1**, to prick with a spur; as, to *spur* a horse; **2**, to excite to action; as, to *spur* one to greater effort; **3**, to attach spurs to:—*v.i.* **1**, to travel with haste; as, to *spur* rapidly along the road; **2**, to hasten or press onward in any plan.—*p.adj.* **spurred**.

spu-ri-ous (spū′rĭ-ŭs), *adj.* not genuine; counterfeit; as, *spurious* coin.—*adv.* **spu′ri-ous-ly**.—*n.* **spu′ri-ous-ness**.
Syn. artificial, fraudulent, sham.

spurn (spûrn), *v.t.* **1**, to drive away, as by kicking; **2**, to reject with contempt; treat with disdain:—*v.i.* to reject anything with contempt.

[1]**spurt** (spûrt), *v.i.* to gush forth suddenly in a stream or jet:—*v.t.* to throw out, as a liquid, in a stream or jet; squirt:—*n.* **1**, a sudden, forcible pouring out of liquid; **2**, any brief and sudden outbreak, as of passion or anger. Also, **spirt**.

[2]**spurt** (spûrt), *v.i.* to put forth one's utmost energy for a short time, as in a race:—*n.* a sudden and extraordinary effort for a brief period. Also, **spirt**.

spur wheel the simplest form of gear wheel, having external radial teeth lying at right angles to the rims.

sput-ter (spŭt′ẽr), *v.i.* **1**, to throw out small particles, as sparks from burning wood; **2**, to spit small, scattered drops of saliva, as in rapid or excited speech; **3**, hence, to speak rapidly and indistinctly:—*v.t.* **1**, to throw out in small particles with a crackling or spluttering noise, as jets of steam; **2**, to utter in an excited or confused way:—*n.* **1**, matter thrown out in small particles or drops; **2**, excited and indistinct talk; **3**, fuss; bustle.—*n.* **sput′ter-er**.

spu-tum (spū′tŭm), *n.* [*pl.* sputa (-tȧ)], saliva; spittle; spit.

spy (spī), *n.* [*pl.* spies (spīz)], **1**, a person who in time of war enters the enemy's camp secretly to gain information; **2**, one who keeps watch on others; a secret agent:—*v.t.* [*p.t.* and *p.p.* spied (spīd), *p.pr.* spy′ing], **1**, to discover, esp. at a distance; gain sight of; **2**, to discover by looking carefully; detect; **3**, to examine or explore secretly:—*v.i.* **1**, to examine narrowly; **2**, to keep watch secretly: with *on* or *upon*.

spy-glass (spī′glȧs″), *n.* a small telescope for looking at distant objects.

squab (skwŏb), *n.* **1**, a young pigeon, esp. one still in the nest; **2**, a short, fat person; **3**, a cushioned sofa; also, a cushion:—*adj.* **1**, short and fat; **2**, recently hatched.

squab-ble (skwŏb′l), *n.* a noisy quarrel; wrangle; dispute:—*v.i.* [*p.t.* and *p.p.* -bled (-ld), *p.pr.* -bling], to wrangle or dispute in a noisy manner.—*n.* **squab′bler**.

squad (skwŏd), *n.* **1**, a small party of soldiers assembled for drill, inspection, etc.; **2**, the smallest of the organized groups into which a regiment is divided; **3**, any small group of persons engaged in a common effort; as, a *squad* of police.

squad-ron (skwŏd′rŭn), *n.* **1**, any group of men in regular formation; **2**, a division of a cavalry regiment containing two troops; **3**, a group of war vessels employed on some particular service.

squal-id (skwŏl′ĭd), *adj.* extremely dirty through neglect; foul; as, a *squalid* tenement.—*adv.* **squal′id-ly**.—*n.* **squal′id-ness**.

[1]**squall** (skwôl), *n.* **1**, a sudden and violent gust of wind, often accompanied by rain, sleet, or snow; **2**, hence, trouble or danger of any sort:—*v.i.* to blow a sudden gust of wind accompanied by rain or snow.

[2]**squall** (skwôl), *v.i.* to weep, scream, or cry out violently, as a child in pain:—*v.t.* to scream in a harsh, strident voice:—*n.* a loud, harsh scream.—*n.* **squall′er**.

squall-y (skwôl′ĭ), *adj.* [*comp.* squall′i-er, *superl.* squall′i-est], gusty; stormy; blustering.

squal-or (skwŏl′ŏr; skwā′lôr), *n.* a wretched and filthy condition; also, foulness; dirt.

squa-ma (skwā′mȧ), *n.* [*pl.* squamæ (-mē)], a scale or scalelike part, as a leaflike scale on a plant or the wing cover of an insect.—*adj.* **squa′mate**.—*n.* **squa-ma′tion**.—*adj.* **squa′mous**; **squa′mose**.

squan-der (skwŏn′dẽr), *v.t.* to spend lavishly or wastefully:—*v.i.* to be very wasteful.—*n.* **squan′der-er**.

square (skwâr), *n.* **1**, a plane figure having four right angles and four equal sides; an equilateral rectangle; **2**, anything of, or resembling, this form; as, the *squares* on a checkerboard; **3**, in the U. S., a town or city block, consisting of a four-sided space on each side of which is a street; **4**, the distance along one of these sides; a block; the distance between two consecutive streets; as, it is three *squares* from First Street to Fourth; **5**, an open space or area, as formed by two or more intersecting streets, often used as a small park; as, Union *Square;* **6**, a body, as of troops, drawn up in a four-sided array; **7**, any of various instruments, consisting usually of two straight edges at right angles to each other, used for measuring or laying out right angles; **8**, conformity to the shape of a square; as, out of *square;* **9**, in mathematics, the product obtained by multiplying a number or quantity by itself; as, 4 is the *square* of 2:—*v.t.* [*p.t.* and *p.p.* squared (skwârd), *p.pr.* squar′ing], **1**, to form with four equal sides and four right angles; **2**, to form into a right angle; cause to make a right angle with another line, side, or part; also, to bring into a position suggesting such an angle; as, to *square* one's shoulders; **3**, to balance; make even; as, to *square* accounts; **4**, to cause to conform to a given standard; adjust to a given measure; as, to *square* one's conduct to a certain rule; **5**, in mathematics, to multiply (a number or quantity) by itself:—*v.i.* **1**, to be cut or formed so as to make a right angle with another line, side, or part; **2**, to accord or agree; coincide; fit: with *with;* as, his story does not *square* with mine:—*adj.* **1**, having four equal sides and four right angles; loosely, approximating a square in form; **2**, forming a right angle; rectangular; as, a *square* edge; **3**, straight and angular, rather than curved, in outline; as, a *square* jaw; **4**, true; upright; honest; just; as, a *square* deal; **5**, balanced; settled; as, our account is *square;* **6**, absolute; complete; unmistakable; as, a *square* refusal; **7**, stated in terms of square measure; as, *square* feet; **8**, *Colloq.*, full or satisfying; as, a *square* meal: **square dance**, a dance consisting of a series of set figures, or steps, performed by an even number of couples: **square knot**, a common knot used to tie together two pieces of string or rope (see *knot*, illus.): **square measure**, two-dimensional measure, or measure of area, the units of which, as the *square* inch and *square* foot, are the areas of squares with sides equal to the given unit of length: **square root**, one of two equal factors of a number or quantity; as, 3 is the *square root* of 9:—*adv.* squarely; directly; as, he hit the nail *square.*—*adv.* **square′ly.**—*n.* **square′ness.**

square–rigged (skwâr′=rĭgd″), *adj.* having rectangular sails stretched on yards suspended horizontally at the middle, as a brig.

¹squash (skwŏsh), *n.* any of various vines of the gourd or cucumber family, bearing an edible fruit; also, the fruit.

²squash (skwŏsh), *v.t.* **1**, *Colloq.*, to beat, crush, or squeeze into a flat mass or pulp; **2**, *Slang*, to silence (a person) by a crushing argument or retort:—*v.i. Colloq.*, **1**, to fall in a soft mass; be crushed into a mass or pulp, as from a fall; **2**, to make a noise like that of a sodden mass falling:—*n.* **1**, something soft and easily crushed, as too ripe fruit; **2**, a crushed object or mass; **3**, the sudden fall of a soft, heavy body; also, the noise made when such a body falls; **4**, a game similar to tennis, played in a walled court with a racket and ball.

squash-y (skwŏsh′ĭ), *adj.* [*comp.* squash′i-er, *superl.* squash′i-est], **1**, easily crushed; mushy; **2**, miry; soft and wet.—*n.* **squash′i-ness.**

squat (skwŏt), *v.i.* [*p.t.* and *p.p.* squat′ted or squat, *p.pr.* squat′ting], **1**, to sit down on the heels, or with the knees drawn up; **2**, to lie close to the ground, as an animal; crouch; **3**, to settle on public land with a view to gaining title to it; **4**, to settle on the land, esp. new or unoccupied land, without permission or right:—*adj.* **1**, sitting on the heels, or with the knees drawn up; crouching; **2**, short and thick:—*n.* the position of one who or that which squats.

squat-ter (skwŏt′ẽr), *n.* **1**, one who settles on public or unimproved land without right or permission; **2**, in Australia, one who leases government land for pasturing.

squat-ty (skwŏt′ĭ), *adj.* [*comp.* squat′ti-er, *superl.* squat′ti-est], short and thick; dumpy.

squaw (skwô), *n.* a North American Indian woman or wife: **squaw man**, a white man married to an Indian woman and, therefore, having the rights of one of her tribe.

squawk (skwôk), *n.* a loud, harsh cry, as of a duck or hen:—*v.i.* to utter a loud, harsh cry.—*n.* **squawk′er.**

squeak (skwēk), *n.* a short, shrill, sharp sound; as, the *squeak* of a mouse:—*v.i.* **1**, to utter a short, shrill, sharp cry; **2**, to make a sharp, disagreeable noise; **3**, *Slang*, to break silence; betray a secret; confess.—*n.* **squeak′er.**—*adj.* **squeak′y.**—*adv.* **squeak′i-ly.**—*n.* **squeak′i-ness.**

squeal (skwēl), *n.* a shrill, prolonged cry, as of a pig:—*v.i.* **1**, to utter a shrill, prolonged cry; **2**, *Slang*, to betray a plot or a companion in a crime or fault.—*n.* **squeal′er.**

squeam-ish (skwēm′ĭsh), *adj.* **1**, inclined to feel sick at the stomach; **2**, prudish; easily disgusted; **3**, fastidious; too careful about trifles.—*adv.* **squeam′ish-ly.**—*n.* **squeam′ish-ness.**

squee-gee (skwē′jē; skwē-jē′), *n.* **1**, a hoe-shaped tool with a rubber edge or plate, for cleaning windows, removing water from a vessel's deck, etc.; **2**, a similar instrument used in photography.

squeeze (skwēz), *v.t.* [*p.t.* and *p.p.* squeezed (skwēzd), *p.pr.* squeez′ing], **1**, to press between two bodies; compress; **2**, to draw forth by pressure; extract; as, to *squeeze* juice out of a lemon; **3**, to force into place by pressure; as, to *squeeze* people into a car; **4**, to oppress; burden, as the people by taxation:—*v.i.* to press; force one's way; push; as, to *squeeze* through a crowd:—*n.* **1**, pressure; a crowding together; **2**, the act of squeezing.—*n.* **squeez′er.**

squelch (skwĕlch), *v.t. Colloq.*, to crush; silence; disconcert.

squib (skwĭb), *n.* **1**, a broken firecracker which burns with a hissing sound; **2**, a paper roll or case filled with gunpowder: used as a safety fuse in blasting; **3**, a short, sarcastic speech or writing; a lampoon.

squid (skwĭd), *n.* **1**, a name for various ten-armed cuttlefish; **2**, any of various kinds of artificial fish bait.

squill (skwĭl), *n.* **1**, a plant of the lily family, the bulb of which is used as a medicine; **2**, this bulb.

squil-la (skwĭl′ȧ), *n.* [*pl.* squillas (-ȧz); squillæ (-ē)], any of a genus of burrowing crustaceans, somewhat resembling a praying mantis (see *crustacean*, illus.).

squint (skwĭnt), *n.* **1**, the act or habit of looking obliquely or through half-closed eyes; **2**, strabismus:—*v.i.* **1**, to see or look obliquely; **2**, to look with eyes half closed; **3**, to be cross-eyed:—*v.t.* **1**, to cause to look obliquely; **2**, to half close (the eyes):—*adj.* **1**, looking obliquely; **2**, cross-eyed.

squint–eyed (skwĭnt′=īd″), *adj.* **1**, having eyes that look in different directions; cross-eyed; **2,** hence, prejudiced; malicious; evil.

squire (skwīr), *n.* **1,** formerly, a shield bearer of a knight; **2,** a devoted gallant; **3,** in the U. S., any prominent citizen; esp., a justice of the peace; **4,** an English landholder; esp., the important man of a district.

squirm (skwûrm), *v.i.* to twist about like an eel or a snake; wriggle; writhe.

squir-rel (skwŭr′ĕl; skwĭr′ĕl), *n.* any of various small, active, gray, black, or reddish brown animals, living mostly in trees and feeding largely on grains and nuts.

squirt (skwûrt), *v.i.* to gush forth in a stream or jet from a small opening; spurt:—*v.t.* to force out in a quick jet:—*n.* **1,** a small stream or jet squirted forth; **2,** an instrument for squirting water or other liquid.

stab (stăb), *v.t.* [*p.t.* and *p.p.* stabbed (stăbd), *p.pr.* stab′bing], **1,** to pierce with, or as with, a pointed weapon; **2,** to wound, as a person's feelings or conscience:—*v.i.* **1,** to pierce something with a pointed weapon; **2,** to wound a person's feelings:—*n.* **1,** a thrust with a sharp-pointed weapon; **2,** a wound so made; **3,** a wound inflicted on a person's feelings, reputation, etc.—*n.* **stab′ber.**

sta-bil-i-ty (stȧ-bĭl′ĭ-tĭ), *n.* **1,** the state or quality of being stable, or firm; **2,** firmness of character; **3,** strength of purpose or resolution; **4,** that property of a body by virtue of which it tends to regain its original position after slight displacement.

sta-bi-lize (stā′bĭ-līz; stăb′ĭ-), *v.t.* [*p.t.* and *p.p.* -lized (-līzd), *p.pr.* -liz″ing], **1,** to make stable, or firm; **2,** to produce or maintain the balance of (a floating body) by some device.—*n.* **sta″bi-li-za′tion.**

sta-bi-liz-er (stā′bĭ-līz″ẽr; stăb′ĭ-), *n.* a device variously constructed, for maintaining the balance of floating bodies, as ships and airplanes, or for keeping them level (see *airplane, empennage,* illus.).

¹sta-ble (stā′bl), *adj.* **1,** firmly established; not easily moved or destroyed; **2,** having permanence; continuing without any radical change; **3,** firm in purpose; steadfast; constant.—*adv.* **sta′bly.**—*n.* **sta′ble-ness.**
Syn. inflexible, steady. (See ¹firm.)

²sta-ble (stā′bl), *n.* a building, usually divided into stalls, in which horses, cows, etc., are housed:—*v.t.* [*p.t.* and *p.p.* -bled (-bld), *p.pr.* -bling], to put or keep in such a building:—*v.i.* to be so lodged.—*n.* **sta′ble-man.**

stac-ca-to (stȧ-kä′tō; *It.* stäk-kä′tō), *adj.* **1,** in music, played, or to be played, in an abrupt, disconnected way, with breaks between notes; **2,** marked by abrupt, sharp emphasis.

stack (stăk), *n.* **1,** a large quantity of hay, corn, wood, etc., piled up in orderly fashion; **2,** a somewhat orderly mass or heap; as, a *stack* of letters; **3,** a number of chimneys standing together; also, any chimney; **4,** a rack or a set of racks with shelves for books; **5,** *Colloq.,* a large amount:—*v.t.* to pile up: **stack arms,** to set up rifles in a cone-shaped pile with the butts on the ground: **stack cards,** to arrange playing cards secretly in order to cheat.

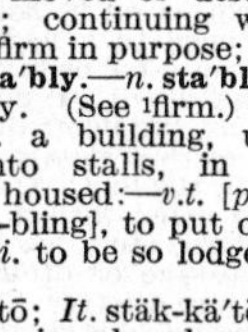

STACKED ARMS

stad-hold-er (stăd′hōl″dẽr), *n.* the chief magistrate of Holland. Also, **stadt′hold″er** (stăt′-).

sta-di-um (stā′dĭ-ŭm), *n.* [*pl.* stadia (-ȧ); stadiums (-ŭmz)], **1,** a Greek linear measure equal to about 600 feet; **2,** in ancient Greece, the course for foot races, surrounded by tiers of seats for spectators; **3,** in modern times, a similar structure, with its inclosed space, for athletic games, etc.

¹staff (ståf), *n.* plaster work in sheets: much used for temporary buildings.

²staff (ståf), *n.* [*pl.* staves (stāvz; stävz); staffs (ståfs)], **1,** a pole or heavy stick for support in walking or climbing, for a weapon of defense, or as an emblem of authority; **2,** a long, slender shaft or pole serving as a support; as, a flag*staff;* **3,** a handle, as of a spear, battle-ax, or the like, **4,** [*pl.* staffs], a body of assistants serving to carry out the plans of a leader or manager; as, the *staff* of a newspaper; **5,** [*pl.* staffs], a body of officers, not commanding troops, but assisting a commander in his executive and administrative duties; **6,** [*pl.* staffs; staves], in music, the set of five horizontal lines and four spaces on which the notes are written or printed to indicate the pitch of the intended tones: also called *stave.*

stag (stăg), *n.* **1,** the full-grown male of various large deer; **2,** *Colloq.:* **a,** at a social function, a man who does not escort a lady; **b,** a social gathering where only men are present: often used adjectively; as, a *stag* party: **stag beetle,** any of various beetles, the males of which have jaws like a stag's horns.

stage (stāj), *n.* **1,** a raised platform, as in a theater or concert hall, for a play or spectacle, for public speakers or performers, or for convenience of use, access, or view; also, a scaffold used by workmen in building; **2,** the drama, as acted or exhibited on such a platform; the theater; **3,** the theatrical profession; **4,** a place or field of action; the scene of any celebrated event or career; **5,** a place of rest on a journey; station; **6,** hence, the distance between any two such stations; **7,** a degree of progress in any journey, business, process, or the like; a point or period of development; as, the first *stage* of a disease; **8,** a stagecoach; also, in the U. S., an omnibus; **9,** in a microscope, the part which supports the object to be examined (see *microscope,* illus.); **10,** in biology, each of the several periods in the development and growth of animals and plants: **stage whisper,** a loud whisper, as by an actor on the stage, heard by the audience, but not supposed to be heard by one or more of the actors:—*v.t.* [*p.t.* and *p.p.* staged (stājd), *p.pr.* stag′ing], **1,** to represent in a play or on the stage; **2,** to put on the stage; mount, as a play; **3,** to exhibit or display in a theatrical manner:—*v.i.* **1,** to travel by stagecoach; **2,** to be adaptable to dramatic representation; as, Barrie's plays invariably *stage* well.

stage-coach (stāj′kōch″), *n.* a four-wheeled coach, having seats within and, usually, on top, plying regularly and carrying passengers and mail.

stag-er (stāj′ẽr), *n.* **1,** *Colloq.,* a horse for drawing a stagecoach; **2,** one who has had long experience; as, an old *stager.*

stag-ger (stăg′ẽr), *v.i.* **1,** to totter or reel; **2,** to begin to doubt; waver; hesitate:—*v.t.* **1,** to cause to totter or reel; **2,** to shock; **3,** to make less confident:—*n.* **1,** a sudden reeling or tottering; **2,** in *pl.* used as *sing.,* a disease of horses and cattle, marked by staggering and falling: often termed *blind staggers.*—*n.* **stag′ger-er.**—*adv.* **stag′ger-ing-ly.**

stag-ing (stāj′ĭng), *n.* **1,** a temporary structure of boards and posts; scaffolding; **2,** the business of running and managing stagecoaches; **3,** the act of putting on a play.

stag-nant (stăg′nănt), *adj.* **1.** not flowing; stale or foul from standing; **2,** not brisk; dull; sluggish.—*n.* **stag′nan-cy.**

stag-nate (stăg′nāt), *v.i.* [*p.t.* and *p.p.* -nat-ed, *p.pr.* -nat-ing], **1**, to cease to flow or run; be motionless; **2**, to be or become inactive or dull.

stag-na-tion (stăg-nā′shŭn), *n.* **1**, the state or quality of being inactive, dull, or sluggish; **2**, staleness or foulness from long standing.

stag-y (stāj′ĭ), *adj.* [*comp.* stag′i-er, *superl.* stag′i-est], theatrical in manner: generally used in contempt.—*n.* **stag′i-ness.**

staid (stād), past tense and past participle of the verb *stay:*—*adj.* sober in character; sedate; steady.—*adv.* **staid′ly.**—*n.* **staid′ness.**

stain (stān), *n.* **1**, a discoloration; spot or blot; **2**, a dye; **3**, taint of guilt or crime; cause of reproach:—*v.t.* **1**, to blot; spot; **2**, to soil with guilt; **3**, to tinge with a coloring matter that penetrates, or that combines with, the substance:—*v.i.* to take or make a stain.—*n.* **stain′er.**—*adj.* **stain′less.**

stair (stâr), *n.* **1**, any one of a set of steps connecting different levels; **2**, usually in *pl.*, a flight of steps.

stair-case (stâr′kās″), *n.* a flight of steps with handrail, balusters, etc.

stair-way (stâr′wā″), *n.* a flight of steps; staircase.

stake (stāk), *n.* **1**, a post or strong stick sharpened at one end and fixed in the ground; **2**, a post to which a person condemned to be burned is bound; hence, death by burning; **3**, often in *pl.*, money or the like, wagered or risked on an event, as on a horse race; **4**, often in *pl.*, the prize in any contest: **at stake**, involved; hence, in danger:—*v.t.* [*p.t.* and *p.p.* staked (stākt), *p.pr.* stak′ing], **1**, to fasten, support, or provide with stakes; **2**, to mark out the limits of; as, to *stake* a claim; **3**, to wager or pledge.

stake-hold-er (stāk′hōl″dẽr), *n.* one who holds an amount wagered, until the matter is settled.

sta-lac-tite (stȧ-lăk′tīt), *n.* an iciclelike formation of carbonate of lime, hanging from the roof of a cave.—*adj.* **stal″ac-tit′ic** (stăl″ăk-tĭt′ĭk).

sta-lag-mite (stȧ-lăg′mīt), *n.* a cone of carbonate of lime deposited by water containing lime carbonate dripping on the floor of a cave.—*adj.* **stal″ag-mit′ic** (stăl″ăg-mĭt′ĭk).

stale (stāl), *adj.* **1**, not fresh or new; tasteless; beginning to decay: used esp. of food; **2**, worn out by use or familiarity; trite; **3**, having vigor or ability impaired, as an athlete from too long or too rigorous training:—*v.t.* [*p.t.* and *p.p.* staled (stāld), *p.pr.* stal′ing], to make stale, destroy the freshness or charm of:—*v.i.* to lose newness or freshness; wear out.—*n.* **stale′ness.**

stale-mate (stāl′māt″), *n.* the situation in chess when the king, though not in check, cannot move without being placed in check:—*v.t.* [*p.t.* and *p.p.* -mat″ed, *p.pr.* -mat″ing], to put in the position of stalemate; hence, to bring to a standstill.

[1]**stalk** (stôk), *n.* **1**, the stem or main axis of a plant; also, the stem of a leaf, flower, or fruit; **2**, in zoölogy, any stem or part resembling the stalk of a plant; **3**, any slender stem, as of a goblet.—*adj.* **stalk′y.**

[2]**stalk** (stôk), *v.t.* to approach (game) cautiously and under cover, as in hunting:—*v.i.* **1**, to walk in a stately and haughty manner; **2**, to creep toward game stealthily:—*n.* **1**, a proud and haughty step; **2**, the act of stalking game.—*n.* **stalk′er.**

stalk-ing–horse (stôk′ĭng-hôrs″), *n.* **1**, a horse, or figure of a horse, behind which a hunter hides in stalking game; **2**, a pretense; blind.

stall (stôl), *n.* **1**, a stable or cattle shed; also, an inclosed space in a stable, as for a horse; **2**, a booth where goods are sold; also, a bench or table where goods are exposed for sale; **3**, a seat in the choir of a church; **4**, in Great Britain, an orchestra seat in the theater:—*v.t.* **1**, to place or keep in a stall; **2**, to cause to stick fast, as in sand or mud; as, to *stall* a cart; **3**, to stop because of an obstruction or unskilful management; as, to *stall* an engine:—*v.i.* **1**, to stick fast, as in mud; **2**, to come to an undesired standstill.

stall–feed (stôl′-fēd″), *v.t.* [*p.t.* and *p.p.* -fed″ (-fĕd″), *p.pr.* -feed″ing], to fatten (cattle) in a stall or on dry fodder.—*p.adj.* **stall′–fed″.**

stal-lion (stăl′yŭn), *n.* an uncastrated male horse.

stal-wart (stôl′wẽrt; stŏl′-), *adj.* **1**, sturdy; strong; tall and stout; **2**, brave; daring:—*n.* a firm, loyal partisan.—*adv.* **stal′wart-ly.**—*n.* **stal′wart-ness.**

sta-men (stā′mĕn), *n.* the pollen-bearing part of a flower, consisting of the filament and the anther (see *flower*, *receptacle*, [2]*style*, illus.).—*adj.* **stam′i-nate.**

stam-i-na (stăm′ĭ-nȧ), *n.pl.* **1**, the firm, supporting part of a body, as an animal's bones; **2**, used as *sing.*, vigor; power of endurance.

stam-i-nal (stăm′ĭ-năl), *adj.* **1**, pertaining to a stamen or stamens: also, *stamineal* (stȧ-mĭn′ē-ăl); **2**, showing strength or power of endurance; relating to vitality.

stam-mer (stăm′ẽr), *v.i.* to hesitate or falter in speaking; stutter:—*v.t.* to pronounce with difficulty or hesitation:—*n.* **1**, hesitating or faltering speech due to nervousness; **2**, any difficulty in pronouncing; a stutter.—*n.* **stam′mer-er.**

stamp (stămp), *n.* **1**, a mark or design impressed upon a surface; as, the *stamp* on a coin; **2**, an implement or machine for making such a mark; a die; **3**, a small piece of paper, having a certain device and value printed on it, sold by the government, and fastened to a letter, document, etc., as payment of a fee or tax; as, a postage *stamp;* a revenue *stamp;* **4**, characteristic quality or nature; as, the *stamp* of genius; **5**, sort; kind; as, men of that *stamp;* **6**, a heavy downward blow with the foot; **7**, sanction; authority:—*v.t.* **1**, to mark with a design by means of a die, pattern, etc.; as, to *stamp* a coin; **2**, to put a postage or other official stamp upon; as, to *stamp* a letter; **3**, to label; brand; as, our acts *stamp* our characters; **4**, to fix deeply; as, to *stamp* a scene on the memory; **5**, to set (the foot) down heavily; **6**, to beat by such a motion; **7**, to crush or grind into powder; **8**, to shape or cut out, as by pressure of a die or stamp: **stamp out**, to destroy or end by, or as if by, setting the foot heavily upon; as, to *stamp out* an epidemic:—*v.i.* to strike or beat the foot forcibly downward.—*n.* **stamp′er.**

stam-pede (stăm-pēd′), *n.* **1**, a sudden, wild running away of a herd of animals, caused by fear or panic; hence, any sudden flight or rush, as of an army; **2**, any sudden, impulsive movement or action on the part of a crowd; as, a *stampede* in a political convention:—*v.t.* [*p.t.* and *p.p.* -ped′ed, *p.pr.* -ped′ing], to cause to take to sudden flight:—*v.i.* **1**, to start off in a panic; **2**, to act together from a sudden impulse.

stanch (stănch; stänch), *v.t.* **1**, to stop the flow of; as, to *stanch* blood; **2**, to stop a flowing from; as, to *stanch* a wound:—*v.i.* to stop flowing:—*adj.* **1**, seaworthy, as a ship; **2**, loyal; as, a *stanch* friend. Also, **staunch.**—*adv.* **stanch′ly.**—*n.* **stanch′ness.**

stan-chion (stăn′shŭn), *n.* an upright, supporting bar, post, or pillar.

stand (stănd), *v.i.* [*p.t.* and *p.p.* stood (stŏŏd), *p.pr.* stand'ing], **1,** to be stationary on the feet in an erect position: said of persons and animals; **2,** to be upright; rest on the end or base: said of things; **3,** to cease to move; pause; **4,** to be at rest or lie stagnant; as, water *stands* in the pond; **5,** to be placed or situated in a specified condition, attitude, or position; as, he *stands* acquitted; he *stands* high in his classes; also, to rest or be; as, I *stand* ready to pay; **6,** to be a substitute: with *for;* as, Esq. *stands* for Esquire; **7,** to become a candidate; as, to *stand* for office; **8,** to remain firm or in force; as, the agreement *stands;* **9,** to remain in existence, esp. without injury or change; endure; last; as, the house still *stands;* **10,** to accord; agree: usually with *with;* **11,** to step or move; as, *stand* out of the path; **12,** to be of a certain height or measure when erect; **13,** to maintain a certain attitude, as toward a question or a principle; as, to *stand* for prohibition: **stand by, 1,** to support; help; **2,** to abide by; live up to; as, to *stand by* one's word; **3,** at sea, to be at hand and ready to attend to something: **stand pat,** *Colloq.*, to stick to the existing plan, situation, etc.:—*v.t.* **1,** to set on the feet, or on end, in an upright position; put in place; **2,** to put up with; endure; undergo; bear; as, to *stand* insult; also, to undergo successfully; as, to *stand* a test; **3,** *Colloq.*, to pay for; as, to *stand* treat: **stand off,** to repel:—*n.* **1,** a stop or halt, as to maintain a position or to offer resistance; **2,** hesitation; standstill; as, to be at a *stand* what to do; **3,** position; place of standing; **4,** an outdoor platform for spectators, often with seats in tiers; **5,** any habitual booth or station for business; as, a cab *stand;* **6,** any of several pieces of furniture on which things may be placed or kept; as, a plant *stand;* **7,** a standing growth, as of grain or grass; **8,** a town where a company halts for a performance.

Syn., *v.* suffer. (See [2]bear.)

stand-ard (stăn'dȧrd), *n.* **1,** a figure, flag, etc., used as an emblem, as of a regiment; **2,** an established measure of weight, length, quality, or the like, esp. one serving as a model by which the accuracy of others may be determined; **3,** any type, example, or model generally accepted as correct; **4,** an upright support:—*adj.* **1,** serving as an accepted model for comparison, basis for measurement, etc.; as, *standard* time; **2,** having a recognized value; as, a *standard* novel.

Syn., *n.* test, ideal, criterion.

stand-ard-ize (stăn'dȧr-dīz), *v.t.* [*p.t.* and *p.p.* -ized (-īzd), *p.pr.* -iz''ing], to regulate by, or make to conform to, an established rule, model, value, authority, etc.—*n.* **stand''ard-i-za'tion.**

stand-ing (stăn'dĭng), *n.* **1,** the act of stopping or of being erect on the feet, or the state of being in an upright position; **2,** a station; **3,** duration; as, a habit of long *standing;* **4,** reputation; rank; as, he is in good *standing:*—*adj.* **1,** erect, or in an upright position; **2,** stagnant or not flowing, as water; **3,** lasting; established or settled; fixed; as, a *standing* rule; **4,** performed from an upright position; as, a *standing* jump.

stand-pipe (stănd'pīp''), *n.* a high pipe or reservoir, into which water is pumped to secure pressure in a water system.

stand-point (stănd'point''), *n.* a position from which things are looked at, considered, or judged.

stand-still (stănd'stĭl''), *n.* a ceasing of action; a halt or stop; rest.

stan-hope (stăn'hōp; stăn'ŏp), *n.* a light, two-wheeled, one-seated carriage without a top.

stank (stăngk), a past tense of the irregular verb *stink.*

stan-nic (stăn'ĭk), *adj.* of or pertaining to tin: specif. applied to compounds of tin in its higher valence.

stan-nous (stăn'ŭs), *adj.* of or pertaining to tin: specif. applied to compounds of tin in its lower valence.

stan-za (stăn'zȧ), *n.* a group of lines, or verses, varying in number, forming a section of a poem.

sta-pes (stā'pēz), *n.* the stirrup-shaped bone of the middle ear.

[1]**sta-ple** (stā'pl), *n.* **1,** the chief commodity produced in a district; **2,** a settled market or place for wholesale traffic; **3,** the principal element of something; chief item; **4,** raw material for manufacture; **5,** the fiber of cotton, flax, or wool; as, wool of a fine *staple:*—*adj.* **1,** chief; regularly produced; as, *staple* goods; **2,** fixed in commerce; as, *staple* demand; **3,** marketable:—*v.t.* [*p.t.* and *p.p.* -pled (-pld), *p.pr.* -pling], to sort according to the quality of its fiber; as, to *staple* wool.

[2]**sta-ple** (stā'pl), *n.* a small, U-shaped piece of metal, to be driven into wood to hold or fasten something; also, a piece of wire similarly bent to hold papers together: —*v.t.* [*p.t.* and *p.p.* -pled (-pld), *p.pr.* -pling], to fasten or attach by such a device.

sta-pler (stā'plẽr), *n.* **1,** one who deals in the regular products of a country; **2,** a sorter of wool, cotton, etc.; **3,** a machine for fastening papers together with staples.

star (stär), *n.* **1,** any celestial body visible as a point of light; **2,** specif., one of those luminous bodies, or suns, at such a great distance from the earth that it appears as a point of light; **3,** any mark or figure with radiating points resembling a star, as an asterisk or a policeman's badge; **4,** in astrology, a planet supposed to influence a person's life; **5,** a brilliant or prominent person, esp. in the theatrical profession:—*v.t.* [*p.t.* and *p.p.* starred (stärd), *p.pr.* star'ring], **1,** to set or adorn with stars; **2,** to mark with an asterisk; **3,** to put forward as the principal actor in a play:—*v.i.* **1,** to shine, as a star; be brilliant or prominent; **2,** to appear as principal actor in a play; as, she *starred* for a week.—*adj.* **star'less.**—*adj.* **star'like.**—*p.adj.* **starred.**

star-board (stär'bōrd; stär'bẽrd), *n.* the side of a vessel at the right of a person on deck looking toward the bow: opp. of *port:*—*adj.* pertaining to, or lying on, the right side:—*v.t.* to steer a boat to the right.

starch (stärch), *n.* **1,** a white, odorless, tasteless substance obtained commercially from grain and potatoes, but found in nearly all plants; **2,** a commercial preparation of this substance used to stiffen fabrics; **3,** hence, a stiff, formal manner; **4,** *Colloq.*, courage; backbone:—*v.t.* to stiffen with starch; make stiff.—*p.adj.* **starched.**—*adj.* **starch'y.**

Star Cham-ber in England, a court of civil and criminal jurisdiction, dealing chiefly with offenses such as conspiracy and riots: notorious for its harshness and tyrannical methods, and abolished in 1641.

stare (stâr), *n.* a fixed, steady look with wide-open eyes, as suggesting curiosity, wonder, boldness, or the like:—*v.i.* [*p.t.* and *p.p.* stared (stârd), *p.pr.* star'ing], **1,** to look with eyes wide open; gaze fixedly in one direction; **2,** to be very conspicuous or prominent, as colors:—*v.t.* to gaze at.—*n.* **star'er.**

Syn., *v.* glare. (See gape.)

star-fish (stär'fĭsh''), *n.* any of various marine animals, having a star-shaped body with five or more rays, or arms.

star-gaz-ing (stär'gāz''ĭng), *n.* **1,** the act or practice of gazing at the stars; 2, hence, astrology; sometimes, astronomy; esp., popular astronomy; 3, absent-mindedness: often used contemptuously; 4, impractical idealism.—*n.* **star'gaz"er.**

stark (stärk), *adj.* 1, stiff; rigid, as in death; 2, utter; complete; as, *stark* nonsense:—*adv.* wholly; completely; as, *stark* naked.—*adv.* **stark'ly.**

star-light (stär'līt"), *n.* the light given by the stars:—*adj.* lighted by the stars.—*adj.* **star'lit".**

[1]**star-ling** (stär'lĭng), *n.* a bird about nine inches long with black plumage, in parts iridescent and in parts spotted with buff, which nests about houses or towers.

[2]**star-ling** (stär'lĭng), *n.* a breakwater of piles, as those driven in front of the piers of a bridge; also, a pile so used.

star-ry (stär'ĭ), *adj.* [*comp.* star'ri-er, *superl.* star'ri-est], 1, set with stars; as, a *starry* crown; 2, lighted by stars; as, a *starry* night; 3, shining like stars.—*n.* **star'ri-ness.**

Stars and Stripes a popular name for the U. S. flag.

Star-Span-gled Ban-ner a patriotic anthem of the U. S., the words of which were written by Francis Scott Key during the War of 1812: **star-spangled banner,** the U. S. flag.

start (stärt), *v.i.* 1, to spring suddenly; leap; bound; 2, to make a sudden involuntary movement, as of surprise, pain, or the like; 3, to begin; set out; as, to *start* on a journey; to *start* in business; 4, to become loosened:—*v.t.* 1, to originate action in, or set going; as, to *start* a clock; 2, to rouse suddenly, as game; 3, to originate or begin; as, to *start* a quarrel; 4, to draw from a cask; 5, to loosen; 6, to cause, or help, to begin; as, to *start* a man in business:—*n.* 1, a sudden leap or bound; 2, an involuntary twitch or jerk, as of fear or joy; 3, a brief, spasmodic effort; as, to work by fits and *starts;* 4, a beginning; as, a *start* in business; 5, a lead or advantage; as, he had the *start* of them; 6, a sudden outburst, as of wit.—*n.* **start'er.**

Syn., *v.* jerk, twitch. (See flinch.)

star-tle (stär'tl), *v.i.* [*p.t.* and *p.p.* -tled (-tld), *p.pr.* -tling], to move suddenly, as in alarm:—*v.t.* to cause to move suddenly; scare; shock:—*n.* a scare; a shock, as of surprise.—*n.* **star'tler.**—*p.adj.* **star'tling.** —*adv.* **star'tling-ly.**

star-va-tion (stär-vā'shŭn), *n.* 1, the condition of suffering or dying from lack of food; 2, the state of extreme hunger or of death from lack of food.

starve (stärv), *v.i.* [*p.t.* and *p.p.* starved (stärvd), *p.pr.* starv'ing], 1, to suffer or die from extreme hunger; 2, to suffer from lack of mental or spiritual food:—*v.t.* to cause to suffer or die from hunger.

starve-ling (stärv'lĭng), *n.* one who is weak from lack of food; a thin, weak animal or plant:—*adj.* hungry; weak.

state (stāt), *n.* 1, the condition in which a person or thing is; 2, political or social standing; rank; style of living; 3, ceremonious style or formal dignity; as, to receive in *state;* 4, a body of people united under one government; a commonwealth; 5, the civil powers of such a community; 6, the territory occupied by it; 7, one of several such communities forming a federation. often written *State:*—*adj.* 1, pertaining to the body politic; as, *state* papers; 2, used upon formal or ceremonious occasions: **State,** pertaining to one of the United States:—*v.t.* [*p.t.* and *p.p.* stat'ed, *p.pr.* stat'ing], to set forth clearly and formally; tell; declare; as, to *state* the facts.

state-craft (stāt'krȧft"), *n.* the art of managing the political affairs of a commonwealth or state.

stat-ed (stāt'ĕd), *p.adj.* fixed; regular; as *stated* business hours.

state-house (stāt'hous"), *n.* in the U. S. a building in which the State legislature meets; a State capitol. Also **state house.**

state-ly (stāt'lĭ), *adj.* [*comp.* state'li-er *superl.* state'li-est], having a grand or imposing appearance or manner; noble majestic; dignified:—*adv.* imposingly; majestically.—*n.* **state'li-ness.**

state-ment (stāt'mĕnt), *n.* 1, the act of presenting or expressing formally in words; 2, that which is so expressed 3, a report, as of a bank account.

state pris-on a prison maintained by a state, esp. for political offenders: **State prison,** in the U. S., a prison maintained by a State, for felons sentenced to imprisonment. Also, **state's pris'on.**

State rights the rights and powers not given to the Federal government of the U. S. by the Constitution, but reserved to each of the individual States. Also, **States' rights.**

state-room (stāt'ro͞om"), *n.* a private sleeping room on a passenger vessel or in a railway sleeper.

state's ev-i-dence testimony presented by the government, or prosecution, in a criminal case; esp., testimony given by a participant in the crime, confessing his own guilt and giving evidence against his accomplices.

states-gen-er-al (stāts'-jĕn'ẽr-ăl), *n.* a legislative assembly composed of representatives of the governing classes of citizens: **States-General,** the Dutch parliament, or legislative body.

states-man (stāts'măn), *n.* [*pl.* states-men (-mĕn)], one skilled in public affairs and the art of government; a person of great ability and prominence in politics.—*adj.* **states'man-like";** **states'man-ly.**—*n.* **states'man-ship.**

stat-ic (stăt'ĭk), *adj.* 1, pertaining to bodies at rest, or to forces in equilibrium: opp. of *dynamic;* 2, acting without motion; as, *static* pressure; 3, pertaining to electrical charges in equilibrium, as distinguished from an electric current:—*n.* in radio, irregular electrical discharges interfering with the reception of radio signals: also called *strays:* **statics,** *pl.* used as *sing.* the division of dynamics treating of the relations between forces when in equilibrium: distinguished from *kinetics.* Also, *adj.* **stat'i-cal.**—*adv.* **stat'i-cal-ly.**

sta-tion (stā'shŭn), *n.* 1, a place where a person or thing usually remains; position; 2, the place to which a person or force is appointed for duty; as, a fire *station;* 3, a regular stopping place on a railway; also, the buildings there; 4, rank; standing:—*v.t.* to place in a certain position; assign.

Syn., *n.* depot. A *station* is a regular stopping place on a railroad. *Depot* in this sense is not in good usage, and is gradually being replaced by *station.*

sta-tion-a-ry (stā'shŭn-ā-rĭ), *adj.* 1, not moving, as machinery when at rest; fixed; 2, unchanging in state or condition; as, *stationary* in size.

sta-tion-er (stā'shŭn-ẽr), *n.* one who deals in writing materials.

sta-tion-er-y (stā'shŭn-ẽr-ĭ), *n.* paper, and other writing materials:—*adj.* pertaining to such materials.

stat-is-ti-cian (stăt"ĭs-tĭsh'ăn), *n.* one skilled in collecting and arranging for general use facts about a given country, industry, etc.

sta-tis-tics (stȧ-tĭs'tĭks), *n.pl.* 1, numerical facts, collected and classified, relating to a large body of people, as a nation or state, or to some special industry, interest, or the like; **2,** in *pl.* used as *sing.*, the art or science of collecting and arranging such facts.—*adj.* **sta-tis'ti-cal; sta-tis'tic.**—*adv.* **sta-tis'ti-cal-ly.**

sta-tor (stā'tŏr; stăt'ẽr), *n.* in some types of electrical apparatus, a stationary part which influences or reacts upon a rotating part, as in a dynamo: opp. of *rotor.*

stat-u-a-ry (stăt'ū-ā-rĭ), *n.* [*pl.* statuaries (-rĭz)], **1,** the art of making statues; **2,** one who makes statues; **3,** a number, or collection, of statues.

stat-ue (stăt'ū), *n.* the sculptured or cast figure of a person or animal, as in marble or bronze, esp. when about life-size.

stat-u-esque (stăt"ū-ĕsk'), *adj.* having the beauty or formal dignity of a statue or modeled figure; as, a *statuesque* beauty.—*n.* **stat"u-esque'ly.**

stat-u-ette (stăt"ū-ĕt'), *n.* a little statue or modeled figure.

stat-ure (stăt'ūr), *n.* the normal height of an animal, esp. man.

sta-tus (stā'tŭs), *n.* **1,** the legal condition of a person; as, the *status* of a married woman; **2,** relative social standing; rank; **3,** state; condition; position of affairs.

***sta-tus quo** (kwō), [Lat.], the condition in which (something has been or is); the existing condition.

stat-ute (stăt'ūt), *n.* **1,** an ordinance or law passed by a duly authorized lawmaking body; **2,** any rule regarded as established by authority, as divine law: **statute mile,** 5,280 feet.

stat-u-to-ry (stăt'ū-tō-rĭ), *adj.* enacted or imposed by statute, or law.

staunch (stänch), *v.t.* **1,** to stop the flow of; **2,** to stop a flowing from:—*v.i.* to stop flowing:—*adj.* **1,** water-tight; sound; firm; **2,** constant; loyal; steadfast. Also, **stanch,** *Pfd. S.*—*adv.* **staunch'ly.**—*n.* **staunch'ness.**

stave (stāv), *n.* **1,** one of the thin narrow strips of wood forming the sides of a cask or barrel; **2,** a pole or piece of wood of some length; **3,** a verse or stanza; **4,** in music, the five parallel lines on and between which the notes and rests are written; a staff:—*v.t.* [*p.t.* and *p.p.* staved (stāvd) or stove (stōv), *p.pr.* stav'ing], **1,** to break a hole in: with *in;* as, to *stave* in a boat; **2,** to make by breaking in the staves; as, to *stave* a hole in a boat; **3,** to furnish with staves; **4,** to keep or drive away: with *off;* as, to *stave* off an illness.

staves (stāvz; stävz), *n.* plural of [2]*staff* in some meanings, and of *stave.*

[1]**stay** (stā), *v.t.* [*p.t.* and *p.p.* stayed or staid (stād), *p.pr.* stay'ing], **1,** to hold up; prop; **2,** to check; hold back; put off; postpone; **3,** to fasten or secure; **4,** to satisfy or appease for a time, as the stomach with food:—*v.i.* **1,** to remain; sojourn; abide; as, to *stay* at the seashore; **2,** to stop; delay; linger; **3,** *Colloq.*, to hold out or last; as, a horse *stays* well:—*n.* **1,** a prop or support; **2,** a stop; halt; sojourn; **3,** that which delays; specif., a suspension of judicial proceedings; **4,** in *pl.*, formerly, a vest stiffened so as to support the figure; now, a corset: also called *pair of stays.*

[2]**stay** (stā), *n.* a strong rope, wire, or the like, used to steady or support a mast, spar, or funnel; also, any rope used to steady or guy (see *airplane, rigging,* illus.):—*v.t.* **1,** to hold (a mast) in position with ropes; **2,** to put (a ship) from one tack to another:—*v.i.* to tack; go about.

stay-sail (stā'sāl"; stā'sl), *n.* a sail set on a stay (see *rigging,* illus.).

stead (stĕd), *n.* **1,** the place which another had or might have; as, to go to war in another's *stead;* **2,** use; service; advantage; as, it will stand you in good *stead.*

stead-fast (stĕd'fȧst), *adj.* **1,** firmly fixed or settled; **2,** steady; constant; as, *steadfast* faith. Also, **sted'fast.**—*adv.* **stead'fast-ly.**—*n.* **stead'fast-ness.**

stead-y (stĕd'ĭ), *adj.* [*comp.* stead'i-er, *superl.* stead'i-est], **1,** firm in position or support; as, a *steady* foundation; **2,** constant in feeling or purpose; resolute; unwavering; as, *steady* devotion to a cause; **3,** regular; uniform; as, the *steady* beat of the pulse; **4,** *Colloq.*, sober; industrious; as, a *steady* young man; **5,** of a ship, keeping its direction unchanged:—*v.t.* [*p.t.* and *p.p.* stead'ied (-ĭd), *p.pr.* stead'y-ing], **1,** to make or keep steady or firm; **2,** to make sober or resolute:—*v.i.* to become balanced or firm.—*adv.* **stead'i-ly.**—*n.* **stead'i-ness.**

steak (stāk), *n.* a slice of beef or other meat, cut for broiling or frying.

steal (stēl), *v.t.* [*p.t.* stole (stōl), *p.p.* sto'len (stō'ln), *p.pr.* steal'ing], **1,** to take by theft; take without leave or right; **2,** to take or get by craft or surprise; as, to *steal* a kiss; **3,** to move in a secret or stealthy manner; as, to *steal* a hand into a pocket; **4,** to gain gradually; as, time *steals* away one's youth:—*v.i.* **1,** to commit theft; **2,** to move or act stealthily or secretly:—*n. Colloq.*, a theft.—*n.* **steal'er.**

stealth (stĕlth), *n.* **1,** theft; **2,** a secret or unseen going or coming.

stealth-y (stĕl'thĭ), *adj.* [*comp.* stealth'i-er, *superl.* stealth'i-est], acting or done slyly, or by stealth; furtive; as, a *stealthy* tread.—*adv.* **stealth'i-ly.**—*n.* **stealth'-i-ness.**

steam (stēm), *n.* **1,** the invisible vapor into which water is changed by boiling; **2,** loosely, the visible mist of condensed water; vapor, esp. when rising from heated water; **3,** *Colloq.*, force; energy:—*v.i.* **1,** to throw off visible vapor; as, the soup *steams* in the kettle; **2,** to rise or pass off in visible vapor; as, moisture *steams* from the earth; **3,** to move under the power of steam; as, the vessel *steamed* away:—*v.t.* to expose to, or treat by, steam; as, to *steam* a pudding.—*adj.* **steam'y.**

steam-boat (stēm'bōt"), *n.* a steam-propelled boat.

steam en-gine an engine operated by the power of steam.

steam-er (stēm'ẽr), *n.* **1,** a vessel or vehicle moved by steam; **2,** an apparatus for steaming articles.

steam roll-er a heavy roller driven by steam and used to smooth the surface of roads; a road roller.

steam-ship (stēm'shĭp"), *n.* a vessel moved by steam power.

steam tur-bine an engine in which the steam acts upon a rotor wheel fitted with vanes or buckets, instead of upon a piston.

ste-ar-ic (stē-ăr'ĭk), *adj.* **1,** pertaining to suet or fat; **2,** obtained from stearin: **stearic acid,** a solid, white, fatty acid present in most animal and vegetable fats and oils: used for soaps and candles.

ste-a-rin (stē'ȧ-rĭn), *n.* **1,** a glycerin compound of stearic acid; a white substance forming the chief constituent of many fats; **2,** popularly, stearic acid.

ste-a-tite (stē'ȧ-tīt), *n.* an impure form of talc: also called *soapstone.*

steed (stēd), *n.* a horse, esp. one which is spirited or high-strung.

steel (stēl), *n.* **1,** an alloy of iron and carbon, capable of being hardened, toughened, or otherwise altered by suitable heat treatment, and of being made serviceable for special purposes by the addition of various elements; **2,** any instrument or weapon made of steel:—*adj.* **1,** made of, or like, steel;

2, hence, hard; unfeeling:—*v.t.* 1, to fit or furnish with steel; 2, to make hard, strong, or unfeeling; as, to *steel* one's heart.

steel-y (stēl'ĭ), *adj.* [*comp.* steel'i-er, *superl.* steel'i-est], 1, made of steel; 2, like steel, as in hardness or color.

steel-yard (stēl'yärd; *Colloq.* stĭl'yẽrd), *n.* a weighing apparatus consisting of a movable weight on a graduated arm, which balances the object to be weighed suspended from a shorter arm.

[1]**steep** (stēp), *adj.* 1, having a sharp pitch or slope; nearly vertical; precipitous; 2, *Colloq.*, exorbitant:—*n.* a steep place; cliff.—*adv.* **steep'ly.**—*n.* **steep'ness.**

Syn., *adj.* abrupt, precipitous. *Steep* is used of a very sharp ascent; as, a *steep* hill. *Abrupt* describes a sharp irregularity of surface, and is applied to an ascent or a descent; as, the *abrupt* pitch of the highway. *Precipitous* suggests a sheer, vertical drop; as, a *precipitous* descent over the cliff.

[2]**steep** (stēp), *v.t.* 1, to soak, usually in a liquid below the boiling point, in order to clean, soften, extract some element, or the like; 2, figuratively, to imbue or saturate with; as, to *steep* him in crime:—*v.i.* to be bathed or soaked in a liquid.—*n.* **steep'er.**

stee-ple (stē'pl), *n.* a tapering tower, esp. on a church, often with a spire: **steeple jack,** a workman who climbs high structures, as for the purpose of making repairs.

stee-ple-chase (stē'pl-chās"), *n.* a cross-country race on horseback; hence, a race over a prescribed course in which obstructions have to be leaped.

[1]**steer** (stēr), *n.* a young castrated male ox; also, in the U. S., any ox.

[2]**steer** (stēr), *v.t.* to control the direction or course of:—*v.i.* 1, to direct something in its course, as a ship; 2, to go in a given direction; 3, to obey the helm.

steer-age (stēr'āj), *n.* 1, the act of steering or guiding; 2, the effect of the helm on a vessel; 3, that part of a ship set apart for those passengers who pay the lowest rates; 4, in a warship, the quarters of junior officers, clerks, etc.

steer-age-way (stēr'āj-wā"), *n.* the headway necessary to make a vessel governable by the helm.

steers-man (stērz'măn), *n.* [*pl.* steersmen (-mĕn)], a helmsman.

stein (stīn; *Ger.* shtīn), *n.* a mug, generally of earthenware: used esp. for beer.

stel-lar (stĕl'ȧr), *adj.* pertaining to stars; as, *stellar* photography.

stel-late (stĕl'āt), *adj.* like a star; as, *stellate* leaves. Also, **stel'lat-ed.**

stel-li-form (stĕl'ĭ-fôrm), *adj.* shaped like a star.

stel-lu-lar (stĕl'ū-lȧr), *adj.* 1, spangled with, or as if with, little stars; 2, shaped like a little star.

[1]**stem** (stĕm), *n.* 1, the main stalk of a tree or any other plant; 2, the slender stalk that bears a leaf, flower, or fruit; 3, any shaft, support, handle, or the like, resembling the stalk of a plant; as, the *stem* of a tobacco pipe; 4, the main line of descent of a family; also, a branch of a family; 5, the upright wooden or metal piece to which the two sides of a vessel are united at the prow; the forward part of a vessel; 6, in a printed letter, the main stroke, or the part of the type face that prints it (see *type*, illus.); 7, in music, the vertical line joined to the head of certain notes (see *note*, illus.); 8, the part of a word to which inflectional endings are attached:—*v.t.*[*p.t.* and *p.p.* stemmed (stĕmd), *p.pr.* stem'ming], 1, to pluck stems from; 2, to strike with the prow; hence, to make headway against.—*n.* **stem'mer.**—*adj.* **stem'less.**

[2]**stem** (stĕm), *v.t.* [*p.t.* and *p.p.* stemmed (stĕmd), *p.pr.* stem'ming], to stop; check; dam up, as a stream.

stem-wind-ing (stĕm'=wīn"dĭng), *adj.* designating a mechanism, as a watch, wound by a milled head on a stem.—*n.* **stem'-wind"er.**

stench (stĕnch), *n.* a strong, offensive odor; disgusting smell; stink.

sten-cil (stĕn'sĭl), *n.* 1, a thin sheet of metal, paper, or the like, cut with an open pattern, so that when it is placed on a surface and color is laid on, a certain figure or design is made; 2, a design or decoration so made:—*v.t.* to mark or color with a stencil.—*n.* **sten'cil-er; sten'cil-ler.**

sten-o-graph (stĕn'ō-grȧf), *n.* writing in shorthand:—*v.t.* to write or report in shorthand.

ste-nog-ra-pher (stē-nŏg'rȧ-fẽr), *n.* a shorthand writer. Also, **ste-nog'ra-phist.**

sten-o-graph-ic (stĕn"ō-grăf'ĭk), *adj.* pertaining to, or written in, shorthand. Also, **sten"o-graph'i-cal.**—*adv.* **sten"o-graph'i-cal-ly.**

ste-nog-ra-phy (stē-nŏg'rȧ-fĭ), *n.* a rapid method of writing by using abbreviations or symbols for words, phrases, etc.; shorthand.

Sten-tor (stĕn'tŏr), *n.* in Homer's "Iliad," a Greek herald with a very loud voice: **stentor,** any person having a resonant and powerful voice.

sten-to-ri-an (stĕn-tō'rĭ-ăn), *adj.* extremely loud or powerful; as, *stentorian* tones.

step (stĕp), *v.i.* [*p.t.* and *p.p.* stepped (stĕpt), *p.pr.* step'ping], 1, to move the foot, or the feet alternately, as in walking forward, backward, or sidewise; 2, to walk, esp. a short distance; as, to *step* around the corner; 3, to walk slowly or with dignity:—*v.t.* 1, to set or place, as the foot; 2, to measure by steps; as, to *step* off a rod; 3, to place the heel or foot of (a mast) in a socket:—*n.* 1, the complete movement made in raising and setting down the foot, as in walking or dancing; a pace; 2, the distance gained in one such movement; hence, any short distance; 3, a degree of progress; promotion: generally part of a series; 4, a footprint; 5, sound or manner of walking; gait; 6, a support or rest for the foot in ascending or descending, such as a tread in a stairway or a rung of a ladder; 7, one of a series of actions or measures; as, the first *step* in an undertaking; 8, a platform or framework in which the foot of a mast rests; 9, in music, the interval between two successive degrees on a scale or staff: called *whole step* (or, loosely, *tone* or *whole tone*) if equivalent to one of the five larger intervals, as from C to D, or *half step* (or, loosely, *half tone* or *semitone*) if equivalent to one of the two smaller intervals, as from E to F.—*n.* **step'per.**

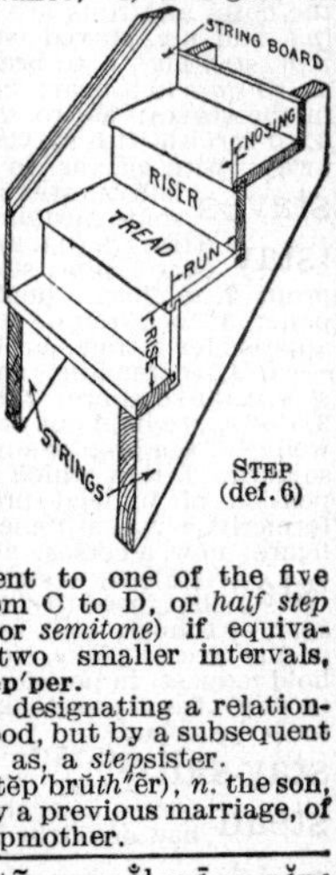

STEP (def. 6)

step- (stĕp-), *prefix,* designating a relationship not by blood, but by a subsequent marriage of a parent; as, a *step*sister.

step-broth-er (stĕp'brŭ*th*"ẽr), *n.* the son, by a previous marriage, of one's stepfather or stepmother.

step-child (stĕp′chīld″), *n.* the child, by a previous marriage, of one's husband or wife; as, the *stepchild* Cinderella.

step-daugh-ter (stĕp′dô″tẽr), *n.* the daughter, by a previous marriage, of one's husband or wife.

step-fa-ther (stĕp′fä″*th*ẽr), *n.* the husband of one's mother by a marriage subsequent to her marriage with one's own father.

Ste-phen (stē′vn), *n.* in the Bible, the first Christian to suffer a martyr's death (Acts 7:59).

step-lad-der (stĕp′lăd″ẽr), *n.* a short, portable set of steps, supported at the back by a hinged prop.

step-moth-er (stĕp′mŭ*th*″ẽr), *n.* the wife of one's father by a marriage subsequent to that with one's mother.

step–par-ent (stĕp′=pâr″ĕnt), *n.* a stepfather or stepmother.

steppe (stĕp), *n.* a vast level plain without forests, as in Siberia.

step-ping–stone (stĕp′ĭng=stōn″), *n.* **1**, a stone that serves as a foothold, as in crossing a stream; **2**, hence, any means by which one may advance.

step-sis-ter (stĕp′sĭs″tẽr), *n.* a daughter, by a previous marriage, of one's stepfather or stepmother.

step-son (stĕp′sŭn″), *n.* a son, by a previous marriage, of one's husband or of one's wife.

-ster (-stẽr), *n. suffix,* denoting an agent or the holder of an occupation or profession; as, team*ster:* sometimes in a disparaging sense; as, rime*ster:* orig. a feminine suffix; as, spin*ster*.

stere (stēr), *n.* in the metric system, a cubic meter, equal to 35.31 cubic feet.

ster-e-om-e-ter (stẽr″ē-ŏm′ē-tẽr; stē″rē-), *n.* an instrument for measuring volume, and, indirectly, for determining specific gravity.

ster-e-op-ti-con (stẽr″ē-ŏp′tĭ-kŏn; stē″rē-), *n.* a form of magic lantern for magnifying and projecting pictures, usually photographs, on a screen.

ster-e-o-scope (stẽr′ē-ō-skōp″; stē′rē-), *n.* an optical instrument with two lenses, through which photographs taken in pairs from slightly different angles appear to stand out and have solidity.—*adj.* **ster″e-o-scop′ic;** **ster″e-o-scop′i-cal.**—*adv.* **ster″e-o-scop′i-cal-ly.**

ster-e-o-type (stẽr′ē-ō-tīp″; stē′rē-), *n.* a plate made by casting type metal into a papier-mâché mold made from the original type:—*v.t.* [*p.t.* and *p.p.* -typed″ (-tīpt″), *p.pr.* -typ″ing], **1**, to make or cast such plates of; **2**, figuratively, to fix in permanent form.—*n.* **ster′e-o-typ″er.**—*n.* **ster′e-o-typ″ist.**

ster-ile (stẽr′ĭl; *Br.* stẽr′īl), *adj.* **1**, not fertile or fruitful; producing little; as, *sterile* land; **2**, without power to reproduce; barren; as, *sterile* seed; **3**, free from living germs; **4**, figuratively, barren mentally or spiritually; as, a *sterile* writer.—*n.* **ste-ril′i-ty.**

ster-i-lize (stẽr′ĭ-līz), *v.t.* [*p.t.* and *p.p.* -lized (-līzd), *p.pr.* -liz″ing], **1**, to make fruitless or barren; deprive of the power of reproduction; **2**, to free from germs.—*n.* **ster′i-liz″er.**—*n.* **ster″i-li-za′tion.**

ster-ling (stûr′lĭng), *adj.* **1**, of standard weight or purity: said esp. of English money; as, two pounds *sterling;* **2**, pure; genuine; of acknowledged worth; as, a *sterling* character:—*n.* English money of standard weight.

[1]stern (stûrn), *adj.* **1**, severe; rigorous; strict; as, *stern* discipline; **2**, forbidding; repelling; as, a *stern* look.—*adv.* **stern′ly.**—*n.* **stern′ness.**

Syn. strict, rigorous. *Stern* denotes harsh and unyielding; as, a *stern* parent; *stern* necessity. *Strict* is applied to the rigid observance of requirements or conditions; as, *strict* rules. *Rigorous* suggests extreme severity, often verging on harshness; as, *rigorous* methods.

[2]stern (stûrn), *n.* **1**, the aft or rear part of a vessel; **2**, the rear of anything.

stern chase a pursuit in which the attacking vessel follows in the wake of the one being attacked.

ster-num (stûr′nŭm), *n.* [*pl.* sterna (-nȧ); sternums (-nŭmz)], the breastbone (which see).—*adj.* **ster′nal.**

ster-nu-ta-tion (stûr″nū-tā′shŭn), *n.* the act of sneezing.—*adj.* **ster-nu′ta-tive** (stẽr-nū′tȧ-tĭv).—*adj.* **ster-nu′ta-to-ry** (-tō-rĭ).

stern-way (stûrn′wā″), *n.* backward movement of a vessel.

ster-to-rous (stûr′tō-rŭs), *adj.* making, or characterized by, a heavy snoring sound; as, *stertorous* breathing.—*adv.* **ster′to-rous-ly.**—*n.* **ster′to-rous-ness.**

stet (stĕt), *v.t.* [*p.t.* and *p.p.* stet′ted, *p.pr.* stet′ting], let (it) stand: used in proof reading as a mark to indicate that something marked for omission or change is to remain.

steth-o-scope (stĕth′ō-skōp), *n.* an instrument for examining the heart, lungs, or like organs of the body, by listening to the sounds which they make.

ste-ve-dore (stē′vē-dōr″), *n.* one who loads or unloads ship cargoes.

stew (stū), *v.t.* and *v.i.* **1**, to boil slowly; simmer; **2**, *Colloq.*, to worry:—*n.* **1**, a dish of food prepared by boiling slowly; **2**, *Colloq.*, nervous anxiety; worry.

stew-ard (stū′ẽrd), *n.* **1**, one who manages the household affairs of a family or institution; the manager of a large estate or farm; **2**, a person employed at a hotel, club, or on board ship, to superintend the buying and distribution of food; also, on board ship, a waiter or an attendant in staterooms; **3**, one who controls financial affairs, as of a church. —*n.fem.* **stew′ard-ess.**—*n.* **stew′ard-ship.**

[1]stick (stĭk), *n.* **1**, a piece of wood, generally long and slender; a small branch or shoot broken or cut from a tree or shrub; **2**, something long and slender like a rod of wood, as a long piece of candy, a mast, a cane, the baton of a musical director, etc.; **3**, the tendency to adhere; **4**, in printing: **a**, a hand tray in which the loose type is assembled into words and lines; **b**, the amount of type a stick will hold; **5**, *Colloq.*, a stiff or dull person; **6**, *Colloq.*, alcoholic liquor mixed with a nonalcoholic drink, or used as flavoring in cookery: —*v.t.* [*p.t.* and *p.p.* sticked (stĭkt), *p.pr.* stick′ing], **1**, to furnish with sticks, as a row of peas; **2**, in printing, to compose; as, to *stick* type.

[2]stick (stĭk), *v.t.* [*p.t.* and *p.p.* stuck (stŭk) or, *Obs.*, sticked (stĭkt), *p.pr.* stick′ing], **1**, to puncture with a pointed instrument; also, to impale on something pointed; **2**, to cause to enter or pierce; as, he *stuck* the spurs in; **3**, to put in a specified position; as, to *stick* a hat on; **4**, to put; push; thrust without piercing; as, to *stick* one's head out of the window; **5**, to cause to adhere, as by an adhesive substance; as, to *stick* a stamp on an envelope; **6**, *Slang*, to puzzle; pose:—*v.i.* **1**, to persist; persevere; **2**, to protrude: with *in, out, up,* etc.; **3**, to adhere closely; as, dough *sticks* to the hands; **4**, to be checked by some obstacle; lose power of motion; as, to *stick* in a rut; **5**, to be puzzled; **6**, to have misgivings: with *at;* as, to *stick* at nothing.—*n.* **stick′er.**

stick-ing plas-ter fabric covered with an adhesive substance; court-plaster: used for small wounds.

stick-le-back (stĭk′l-băk″), *n.* any of several small, scaleless fish with sharp spines on their bodies.

stick-ler (stĭk′lẽr), *n.* one who stubbornly argues or insists, esp. about something of little importance.

stick-y (stĭk′ĭ), *adj.* [*comp.* stick′i-er, *superl.* stick′i-est], adhesive; gluey.—*adv.* **stick′i-ly.**—*n.* **stick′i-ness.**

stiff (stĭf), *adj.* **1,** not easily bent; rigid; firm; inflexible; as, *stiff* cardboard; **2,** not easily moved or operated; not working smoothly, as an engine; **3,** fluid; as, a *stiff* paste; **4,** strong; violent; as, a *stiff* breeze; **5,** not natural or easy; formal; as, a *stiff* manner; **6,** difficult; as, a *stiff* climb or examination; **7,** taut; drawn tight; **8,** stubborn; obstinate; **9,** *Slang,* high; dear; as, a *stiff* charge; **10,** in sailing, standing nearly upright under a large spread of sail: opp. of [3]*crank.*—*adv.* **stiff′ly.**—*n.* **stiff′ness.**

stiff-en (stĭf′n), *v.t.* to make rigid, more unbending, thicker, more stubborn, or the like:—*v.i.* to become stiff.

stiff–necked (stĭf′=nĕkt″), *adj.* stubborn; obstinate.

[1]**sti-fle** (stī′fl), *v.t.* [*p.t.* and *p.p.* -fled (-fld), *p.pr.* -fling], **1,** to suffocate; smother; **2,** to put out; stop; check, as a sound or a fire; **3,** to hide or conceal; suppress, as a yawn, tears, or the truth:—*v.i.* to be suffocated or suppressed.—*p.adj.* **sti′fling.**

[2]**sti-fle** (stī′fl), *n.* the joint above the hock in the hind leg of certain animals, as the dog: corresponding to the knee in man.

stig-ma (stĭg′mȧ), *n.* [*pl.* stigmas (-mȧz); stigmata (-tȧ)], **1,** a mark of disgrace or dishonor; a reproach or slur; **2,** the upper part of the pistil of a flower, on which the pollen falls (see *flower,* [2]*style,* illus.); **3,** a defect or blemish, as a birthmark; **4,** [*pl.* stigmata], a small red spot on the skin.

stig-mat-ic (stĭg-măt′ĭk), *adj.* **1,** of or pertaining to a stigma or stigmas; **2,** marked with, or as if with, a brand.

stig-ma-tize (stĭg′mȧ-tīz), *v.t.* [*p.t.* and *p.p.* -tized (-tīzd), *p.pr.* -tiz″ing], to hold up to disgrace, reproach, or dishonor; brand with infamy; denounce.—*n.* **stig″ma-ti-za′tion.**

stile (stīl), *n.* **1,** a set of steps leading over a fence or wall; **2,** an upright piece in framing or paneling, as one of the vertical side pieces of a paneled door.

sti-let-to (stĭ-lĕt′ō), *n.* [*pl.* stilettos (-ōz)], **1,** a small sharp dagger having a slender blade; **2,** a pointed instrument for making holes in needlework.

[1]**still** (stĭl), *adj.* **1,** characterized by little or no motion; motionless; **2,** characterized by peace and calm; tranquil; **3,** characterized by little or no sound; silent; **4,** not sparkling, as wine: **still hunt,** a stealthy, silent, or cautious hunt or pursuit after anything: **still life,** inanimate objects, as bowls, fruit, dead game, etc., used as the subject matter of a picture:—*adv.* **1,** till then or till now, as previously; **2,** for all that; nevertheless; **3,** always; continually; **4,** even; yet: used with comparatives; as, louder *still:*—*v.t.* to check motion, disturbance, or sound in; calm; put at rest.—*n.* **still′ness.**

Syn., v. lull, allay, subdue, pacify.—*Ant., v.* arouse, agitate, excite, disturb, incite.

Still

[2]**still** (stĭl), *n.* **1,** an apparatus for distilling liquids, esp. to obtain alcoholic liquors; **2,** a place in which alcoholic liquors are made; a distillery:—*v.t.* to obtain by heating, evaporating, and condensing; distil.

still-born (stĭl′bôrn″), *adj.* dead at the time of birth.

still-y (stĭl′ĭ), *adj. Poetic,* calm; quiet:—*adv. Poetic,* calmly; quietly.

stilt (stĭlt), *n.* **1,** a pole of wood with a rest for the foot: used in pairs in walking; **2,** any of several wading shore birds having very long legs with three toes: also called *stiltbird:*—*v.t.* to set or raise on stilts.

Stilt (1/18)

stilt-ed (stĭlt′ĕd), *p.adj.* **1,** elevated or raised, as if on stilts; **2,** hence, pompous; formal, as a speech.—*n.* **stilt′ed-ness.**

stim-u-lant (stĭm′ū-lȧnt), *n.* **1,** that which excites or spurs on; **2,** any remedy or agent that produces an increase of energy or activity; **3,** in *pl.,* intoxicants:—*adj.* **1,** serving to excite or spur on; **2,** producing, temporarily, greater vitality or energy.

stim-u-late (stĭm′ū-lāt), *v.t.* [*p.t.* and *p.p.* -lat″ed, *p.pr.* -lat″ing], **1,** to rouse to activity; animate; encourage; **2,** to produce greater activity in; affect, as by an intoxicant:—*v.i.* to act as a goad or stimulant in rousing to action.—*n.* **stim′u-la″tor.**

stim-u-la-tion (stĭm″ū-lā′shŭn), *n.* **1,** the act of exciting or of producing a temporary increase of vitality or energy; **2,** the condition of being so excited.

stim-u-la-tive (stĭm′ū-lā-tĭv), *adj.* having the power of exciting or spurring on:—*n.* anything that spurs on.

stim-u-lus (stĭm′ū-lŭs), *n.* [*pl.* stimuli (-lī)], something that rouses the mind or senses.

sting (stĭng), *n.* **1,** the sharp, often poisonous, organ with which certain animals, as the scorpion and bee, are furnished; **2,** one of the stiff, sharp, piercing hairs of certain plants; **3,** the thrust of such an organ or hair; also, the wound made by it; **4,** keen, smarting, mental or physical pain; **5,** that which goads to action; as, the *sting* of conscience:—*v.t.* [*p.t.* and *p.p.* stung (stŭng), *p.pr.* sting′ing], **1,** to prick or wound with, or as with, a sharp point; cause a sharp, smarting pain to; as, cold *stings* the face; **2,** to incite to action, as by taunts or reproaches; **3,** to cause to suffer keenly:—*v.i.* **1,** to inflict a sharp, smarting wound; as, the wasp *stings;* **2,** to be sharply painful.—*n.* **sting′er.**—*adj.* [1]**sting′y.**

sting ray any of several large, tropical fish, with bony spines in the tail that inflict severe wounds. Also, *n.* **sting′ray″.**

[2]**stin-gy** (stĭn′jĭ), *adj.* [*comp.* stin′gi-er, *superl.* stin′gi-est], **1,** meanly saving of money; miserly; **2,** scanty; meager.—*adv.* **stin′gi-ly.**—*n.* **stin′gi-ness.**

stink (stĭngk), *n.* an offensive odor; disgusting smell:—*v.i.* [*p.t.* stank (stăngk) or stunk (stŭngk), *p.p.* stunk, *p.pr.* stink′ing], to throw off a strong, offensive odor:—*v.t.* to cause to have an offensive smell: with *up.*

stint (stĭnt), *v.t.* to keep within certain limits; limit to a scant allowance; as, to *stint* the food:—*v.i.* to be sparing or frugal:—*n.* **1,** a limit or bound; **2,** an amount fixed or task assigned.—*p.adj.* **stint′ed.**

stipe (stīp), *n.* a stem or stalk; esp., the supporting stem of a mushroom, a fern leaf, or a pistil.

sti-pend (stī′pĕnd), *n.* fixed pay or salary for services.

sti-pen-di-a-ry (stī-pĕn′dĭ-ā-rĭ), *adj.* receiving salary:—*n.* [*pl.*

stipendiaries (-rĭz)], one who performs services for a salary.

stip-ple (stĭp'l), *v.t.* [*p.t.* and *p.p.* -pled (-ld), *p.pr.* -pling], to draw or paint by means of light touches or dots; engrave by means of dots:—*n.* the art or method of drawing, painting, or engraving by means of dots; also, the effect so produced.—*n.* **stip'pler.**—*n.* **stip'pling.**

[1]**stip-u-late** (stĭp'ū-lāt), *v.i.* [*p.t.* and *p.p.* -lat″ed, *p.pr.* -lat″ing], to make an agreement or bargain; insist: often with *for*:—*v.t.* to arrange or settle definitely; specify, as part of an agreement.—*n.* **stip'u-la″tor.**

stip-u-la-tion (stĭp″ū-lā'shŭn), *n.* **1**, the act of agreeing or insisting on something; **2**, a contract, agreement, or bargain; also, a special condition in a contract.

stip-ule (stĭp'ūl), *n.* one of two small leaflike appendages at the base of some leaves, as in the rose.—*adj.* [2]**stip'u-late.**

stir (stûr), *v.t.* [*p.t.* and *p.p.* stirred (stûrd), *p.pr.* stir'ring], **1**, to change the position of; move; **2**, to put into motion; agitate, as a leaf; **3**, to change the relative position of the particles of, as a liquid; **4**, to incite; rouse; as, to *stir* men to devotion:—*v.i.* **1**, to move or be moved; change position; **2**, to be in motion; be active or busy; **3**, to be incited or roused:—*n.* **1**, bustle; activity; **2**, agitation; tumult; excitement.—*n.* **stir'rer.**

Syn., *v.* actuate, stimulate, provoke.—*Ant.*, *v.* calm, soothe, still, quiet.

stir-ring (stûr'ĭng), *n.* the act of moving:—*p.adj.* **1**, busy; bustling; **2**, exciting; stimulating; as, *stirring* events.

stir-rup (stĭr'ŭp; stûr'-), *n.* **1**, a loop-shaped rest or support for a rider's foot: usually made of metal and hung from the saddle by a strap; **2**, any device resembling such a foot rest in shape or use, as a metal loop for supporting a beam: **stirrup cup**, **1**, a cup of liquor, presented to a rider ready to depart; **2**, a farewell drink.

stitch (stĭch), *n.* **1**, in sewing, a single pass of a threaded needle in and out of the material; also, the section of thread left in the fabric; **2**, in knitting, crocheting, and such work, a single complete movement of the needle or hook; also, the link or loop so formed; **3**, a particular arrangement of threads in needlework; **4**, a sudden, sharp pain; as, a *stitch* in the side; **5**, *Colloq.*, the least portion, as of work or of clothing; as, he had not a clean *stitch*:—*v.t.* **1**, to sew; **2**, to ornament by stitches:—*v.i.* to practice stitching or sewing.—*n.* **stitch'er.**

stith-y (stĭth'ĭ; stĭth'ĭ), *n.* [*pl.* stithies (-ĭz)], **1**, a blacksmith's shop or forge; smithy; **2**, an anvil.

sti-ver (stī'vẽr), *n.* **1**, a small Dutch coin; **2**, hence, anything of little value.

stoat (stōt), *n.* the European ermine or weasel, esp. in its summer coat of reddish brown; also, any ermine or weasel.

stock (stŏk), *n.* **1**, the trunk or principal stem of a tree or plant; **2**, a log or post; block; hence, something lifeless and senseless; **3**, a trunk or plant in which a graft is placed; also, the plant from which cuttings are taken; **4**, race, family, or relationship; also, an origin or source, as the founder of a family; **5**, domestic animals kept on a farm (see *live stock*, illus.); **6**, that part of an implement or machine that serves as the body or main support for other parts, as the part of a gun that is put against the shoulder, and to which the barrel, lock, etc., are attached; **7**, a metal frame with two long, straight handles for holding dies used in cutting threads (see [2]*die*, illus.), etc.; **8**, a fund or debt due to persons for money loaned, or the securities for such a fund; **9**, the capital of a company or corporation, in the form of shares: as, common or preferred *stock*; **10**, the capital or goods employed in a business; **11**, hence, any accumulation or supply; **12**, a wide, close-fitting band of silk, or the like, worn about the neck; **13**, any raw material for manufacture; **14**, in *pl.*, a wooden frame with holes in which to confine the legs, and sometimes the hands, of those guilty of minor offenses; **15**, in *pl.*, a frame on which a ship rests while it is being built; **16**, the foundation of soups, consisting of extracts of meat, vegetables, etc.; **17**, a commonly cultivated herb bearing showy, single or double flowers: also called *gillyflower*: **to take stock, 1**, to make an inventory of goods on hand; **2**, hence, to estimate on the value, as of a business: **to take stock in, 1**, to invest money in by taking shares: **2**, hence, to be interested in or, esp., to have confidence in: —*v.t.* **1**, to store away; set by for the future; **2**, to fill; fit out or supply with something.

stock-ade (stŏk-ād'), *n.* **1**, a line of posts or trunks of trees set firmly in the earth and close together, used as a barrier for defense or an inclosure for cattle; **2**, the space so inclosed:—*v.t.* [*p.t.* and *p.p.* -ad'ed, *p.pr.* -ad'ing], to surround with, or defend by, such a barrier.

stock-bro-ker (stŏk'brō″kẽr), *n.* one who buys and sells shares of stock.—*n.* **stock'bro″king.**

stock com-pa-ny **1**, a corporation, the capital of which is divided into shares of stock; **2**, a group of actors more or less permanently associated under one management and playing a repertoire.

stock ex-change **1**, an association of dealers in shares of stock companies, who meet and conduct their business according to settled rules; **2**, a place where such securities are bought and sold.

stock-hold-er (stŏk'hōl″dẽr), *n.* one who holds shares, or stock, as in a stock company or corporation.

stock-i-net (stŏk″ĭ-nĕt'), *n.* an elastic, knitted fabric used chiefly for making underwear.

stock-ing (stŏk'ĭng), *n.* a close-fitting, woven or knitted covering for the foot and leg: made of silk, wool, or cotton.

stock-job-ber (stŏk'jŏb″ẽr), *n.* one who deals or speculates in shares of corporations.—*n.* **stock'job″bing.**

stock-man (stŏk'măn), *n.* [*pl.* stockmen (-mĕn)], one who owns, or has charge of, live stock or cattle; a ranchman.

stock–still (stŏk'=stĭl'), *adj.* still as a post; motionless.

stock-y (stŏk'ĭ), *adj.* [*comp.* stock'i-er, *superl.* stock'i-est], short and stoutly built; thickset of body.—*adv.* **stock'i-ly.**—*n.* **stock'i-ness.**

stock-yard (stŏk'yärd″), *n.* a large inclosure for domestic animals, as in connection with an abattoir or a market.

stodg-y (stŏj'ĭ), *adj.* [*comp.* stodg'i-er, *superl.* stodg'i-est], *Colloq.*, **1**, thick and heavy, as food; **2**, dull, as a book or person; **3**, bulky; distended.

sto-gy (stō'gĭ), *n.* [*pl.* stogies (-gĭz)], **1**, a long, coarse cigar; **2**, *Colloq.*, a coarse boot or shoe:—*adj.* [*comp.* sto'gi-er, *superl.* sto'gi-est], *Colloq.*, rough; coarse.

Sto-ic (stō'ĭk), *n.* a follower of the Greek philosopher Zeno, who taught that a wise man should be governed by the reason, subdue all passions, and be indifferent to pleasure or pain:—*adj.* (also, *Stoical*), pertaining to the Stoics: **stoic**, *n.* a person practicing great self-control; one indifferent to pleasure or pain:—*adj.* (also, *stoical*), indifferent to pleasure or pain; enduring without complaint.—*adv.* **sto'i-cal-ly.**—*n.* **sto'i-cal-ness.**

Sto-i-cism (stō′ĭ-sĭzm), *n.* the beliefs and teachings of the Stoics: **stoicism**, indifference to pleasure or pain; endurance without complaint.

stoke (stōk), *v.t.* [*p.t.* and *p.p.* stoked (stōkt), *p.pr.* stok′ing], to tend (a fire or furnace); supply with fuel:—*v.i.* to tend a fire or furnace.—*n.* **stok′er.**

stoke-hold (stōk′hōld″), *n.* in a steamship, the space in front of the boilers, from which the fires are fed by the stokers. Also, **stoke′hole″.**

1**stole** (stōl), *n.* **1,** a long, loose, outer garment worn by Roman matrons in ancient times; **2,** a long, narrow scarf fringed at the ends and worn over the shoulders by the clergy during services.

2**stole** (stōl), past tense of *steal,* which see: **stolen,** past participle of *steal.*

stol-id (stŏl′ĭd), *adj.* not easily aroused or excited; stupid; dull.—*adv.* **stol′id-ly.**—*n.* **stol′id-ness.**

sto-lid-i-ty (stō-lĭd′ĭ-tĭ), *n.* impassiveness; mental dulness.

stom-ach (stŭm′ŭk), *n.* **1,** a part of the digestive tract; in man, a pear-shaped sac at the end of the gullet; **2,** desire for food; appetite; **3,** hence, inclination; liking; desire; as, he had no *stomach* for revenge:—*v.t.* to put up with; bear without resistance.

stom-ach-er (stŭm′ŭk-ẽr; stŭm′*ȧ*-chẽr), *n.* an ornamental breast covering, formerly worn by women.

sto-mach-ic (stō-măk′ĭk), *adj.* pertaining to the stomach:—*n.* a tonic for improving the appetite or digestion.

stone (stōn), *n.* **1,** a small piece of rock; **2,** the hard, nonmetallic mineral matter of which rock consists; **3,** a piece of rock cut and shaped for a special use; as, hearth*stone;* **4,** a gem: as, a precious *stone;* **5,** something resembling a small stone in hardness or shape; as, a hail*stone;* a gall*stone;* **6,** in Europe, a varying measure of weight; in Great Britain, usually fourteen pounds avoirdupois:—*v.t.* [*p.t.* and *p.p.* stoned (stōnd), *p.pr.* ston′ing], **1,** to pelt with pieces of rock; kill by hurling pieces of rock at; **2,** to remove the stones, or pits, from; as, to *stone* cherries:—*adj.* made of stone or earthenware; as, a *stone* jar: **stone age,** the age in which weapons, tools, etc., were made of stone.

stone bruise a bruise made by a stone, esp. on the bare foot.

stone-crop (stōn′krŏp″), *n.* a mosslike herb with thick, fleshy leaves and yellow flowers.

stone-cut-ter (stōn′kŭt″ẽr), *n.* a person or machine that cuts and dresses stone.—*n.* **stone′cut″ting.**

stone-ware (stōn′wâr″), *n.* a kind of coarse pottery, made from siliceous clay, baked hard and glazed.

stone-work (stōn′wûrk″), *n.* **1,** any piece of work built of stone; **2,** the process of working in stone.

ston-y (stōn′ĭ), *adj.* [*comp.* ston′i-er, *superl.* ston′i-est], **1,** full of, or containing many, stones; as, a *stony* road; **2,** pertaining to, or like, stone; **3,** fixed; rigid; also, cruel; pitiless; as, a *stony* heart.—*adv.* **ston′i-ly.**—*n.* **ston′i-ness.**

stood (stŏŏd), past tense and past participle of the irregular verb *stand.*

stool (stōōl), *n.* **1,** a seat without a back, often having three legs; **2,** a bench for the feet, or for the knees in kneeling; **3,** the seat used in emptying the bowels; also, an emptying of the bowels, or the matter discharged; **4,** a pole to which a bird, as a pigeon, is fastened to lure other birds within range: **stool pigeon, 1,** a pigeon used as a decoy; **2,** a person used to decoy, or to spy on, others.

1**stoop** (stōōp), *v.i.* **1,** to bend the body down and, usually, forward; incline; also, to carry the head and shoulders habitually bowed forward; **2,** to condescend or deign: with *to;* **3,** to submit; yield; **4,** to pounce; swoop down, as on prey:—*v.t.* to bend down:—*n.* **1,** a bending down and forward, as of the head and shoulders; **2,** condescension; **3,** the swoop of a bird upon its prey.

2**stoop** (stōōp), *n.* any porch, veranda, or the like, at the entrance to a house.

stop (stŏp), *v.t.* [*p.t.* and *p.p.* stopped (stŏpt), *p.pr.* stop′ping], **1,** to close, as a hole or opening, by stuffing, covering, or the like; hence, to stanch (a wound); **2,** to obstruct or make impassable, as a road; **3,** to check the progress or motion of; cause to come to a state of rest; cause to cease; **4,** to desist from:—*v.i.* **1,** to cease; discontinue; desist; halt; **2,** *Colloq.,* to tarry; stay; lodge:—*n.* **1,** an obstruction, check, or hindrance; **2,** a pause or delay; **3,** a halt; also, a halting place; **4,** a punctuation mark; **5,** any of several devices, as a block, peg, or pin, to regulate or check motion or to keep a movable part in place; as, a window *stop;* **6,** any device to regulate the pitch of a musical instrument; **7,** in an organ, a set of pipes producing tones of the same quality; **8,** a consonant sound formed by momentary, but complete, closure of the vocal passage, as *k, g, t, d, p, b;* **9,** in a camera, an aperture, or its size, by which light is permitted to pass through the lens to the sensitive plate.

stop-cock (stŏp′kŏk″), *n.* a faucet or tap with a valve to regulate the flow of a liquid or gas.

stope (stōp), *n.* an excavation from which ore is extracted in a series of ledges.

stop–gap (stŏp′=găp″), *n.* **1,** that which closes or fills an opening or gap; **2,** hence, a temporary expedient or makeshift; substitute.

stop-page (stŏp′ȧj), *n.* the act of arresting motion or action; also, the state of being so stopped; as, the *stoppage* of circulation.

stop-per (stŏp′ẽr), *n.* **1,** one who or that which plugs up or closes; **2,** a plug, as of glass, wood, or cork, that closes a vent or hole, as in a bottle or cask.

stop-ple (stŏp′l), *n.* a cork or plug; a stopper:—*v.t.* [*p.t.* and *p.p.*-pled (-ld), *p.pr.* -pling], to close with a cork or bung.

stop watch a watch with a hand showing seconds and fractions of a second, that can be instantly started or stopped by pressing a spring or catch: used for timing races, contests, etc.

stor-age (stōr′ȧj), *n.* the placing of goods, as in a warehouse, for protection; also, the space thus occupied or the price charged for the service: **storage battery,** a unit consisting of a number of connected storage cells; also, loosely, one such cell:

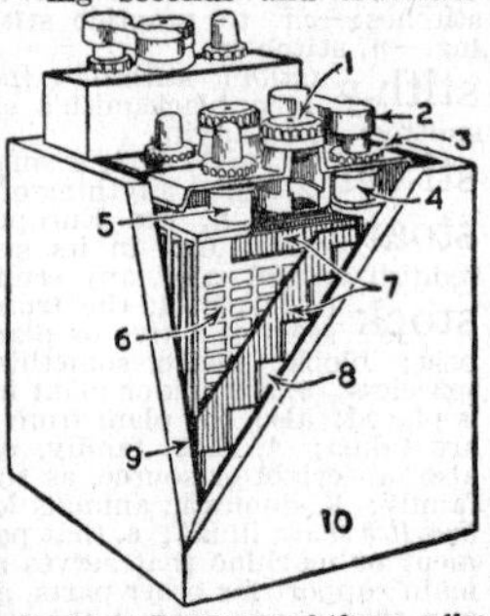

STORAGE BATTERY of three cells, one raised slightly out of place: 1, filling plug; 2, cell connection; 3, sealing nut; 4, 5, negative and positive posts; 6, positive plate; 7, wood separators; 8, negative plate; 9, rubber jar; 10, case.

storage cell, a type of voltaic cell, usually composed of plates of lead and lead peroxide immersed in sulphuric acid, which, after exhaustion of the charge, is charged anew by passing through it an electric current in the reverse direction, thus storing up the electrical energy of the current as chemical energy.

store (stōr), *n.* **1,** a great quantity or number; **2,** often in *pl.*, an accumulation or supply kept in reserve or ready for use; as, naval *stores;* **3,** a warehouse; shop where goods are kept for sale: **department store,** a large store with general supplies, which are sold from special departments: **in store,** in waiting; as, pleasures are *in store* for you: **to set store by** or **upon,** to value or esteem:—*v.t.* [*p.t.* and *p.p.* stored (stōrd), *p.pr.* stor′ing], **1,** to furnish or stock; equip; as, to *store* a building with coal; **2,** to collect; hoard; **3,** to put, as in a warehouse for safe-keeping.

store-house (stōr′hous″), *n.* a building where goods, esp. foods, are stored; a warehouse.

store-keep-er (stōr′kēp″ẽr), *n.* in the U. S., one who keeps a shop, or retail store; a retailer.

store-room (stōr′ro͞om″), *n.* **1,** a room for storage, as of reserve supplies; **2,** a room where goods are stored.

[1]**sto-ried** (stō′rĭd), *adj.* **1,** told in, or associated with, story, legend, or history; **2,** decorated, as a frieze, with historical or legendary scenes.

stork (stôrk), *n.* any of a family of wading birds with long legs, neck, and bill.

storm (stôrm), *n.* **1,** a violent disturbance of the atmosphere, often with a heavy fall of rain, snow, or hail; hence, anything like a violent shower; as, a *storm* of applause; **2,** an outburst of passion or excitement; a violent commotion; **3,** a violent assault on a fortified place:—*v.t.* to attack suddenly with violence; as, to *storm* a fort:—*v.i.* **1,** to blow violently, or to rain, hail, snow, etc.: used impersonally; **2,** to rage.

storm-ing (stôr′mĭng), *n.* the taking of a fortified place by a violent and open assault:—*p.adj.* violently angry or raging.

storm-y (stôr′mĭ), *adj.* [*comp.* storm′i-er, *superl.* storm′i-est], **1,** marked by, or accompanied with, tempests or furious winds; boisterous; tempestuous; as, *stormy* weather; **2,** marked by passion or fury; turbulent; violent; as, a *stormy* life.—*adv.* **storm′i-ly.**—*n.* **storm′i-ness.**

Stor-thing (stôr′tĭng″), *n.* the parliament, or chief lawmaking body, of Norway. Also, **Stor′ting″.**

[1]**sto-ry** (stō′rĭ), *n.* [*pl.* stories (-rĭz)], the set of rooms between two floors of a building. Also, **sto′rey.**—*adj.* [2]**sto′ried.**

[2]**sto-ry** (stō′rĭ), *n.* [*pl.* stories (-rĭz)], **1,** a connected account of the past; history; **2,** the narration of real or imagined events in prose or verse; a short tale or romance; also, an anecdote; **3,** a report or statement; rumor; **4,** *Colloq.*, a fib; falsehood: **story-teller, 1,** one who relates tales or anecdotes; **2,** *Colloq.*, a liar; a person who tells falsehoods.—*n.* **sto′ry-tell″ing.**

Syn. (see anecdote).

stoup (sto͞op), *n.* **1,** a small vessel or a cup for holding liquors; as, a *stoup* of wine; **2,** a basin for holy water at the entrance of a church. Also, **stoop.**

stout (stout), *adj.* **1,** bold; brave; resolute; as, a *stout* heart; **2,** firm; tough; strong; as, a *stout* vessel; **3,** large; bulky; fat; as, a *stout* girl:—*n.* strong, dark porter, ale, or beer.—*adv.* **stout′ly.**—*n.* **stout′ness.**

Syn., adj. portly, corpulent, stocky.

stout–heart-ed (stout′=härt″ĕd), *adj.* brave; courageous; undaunted. — *adv.* **stout″–heart′ed-ly.** — *n.* **stout″–heart′ed-ness.**

sto-va-in (stō′vȧ-ĭn), *n.* a solution of a crystalline compound that is injected into the spinal canal to produce insensibility during surgical operations. Also, **sto′va-ine.**

[1]**stove** (stōv), *n.* an apparatus, constructed generally of iron, to burn fuel and so generate heat, as for cooking.

[2]**stove** (stōv), past tense and past participle of the irregular verb *stave.*

stow (stō), *v.t.* **1,** to fill by packing anything closely in; as, to *stow* the hold of a ship with goods; **2,** to put away compactly; pack; as, to *stow* cargo in a ship's hold.

stow-age (stō′āj), *n.* **1,** the act of storing or packing away; also, the state of being packed; **2,** room in which things may be packed; **3,** things packed away; **4,** money paid for storing things.

stow-a-way (stō′ȧ-wā″), *n.* one who hides on a vessel or railway train to avoid paying his fare.

stra-bis-mus (strȧ-bĭz′mŭs), *n.* cross-eye.—*adj.* **stra-bis′mic.**

strad-dle (străd′l), *v.t.* [*p.t.* and *p.p.* -dled (-ld), *p.pr.* -dling], to stand or sit astride of:—*v.i.* to sit, stand, or walk with the legs wide apart:—*n.* **1,** the act of standing, sitting, or walking with the legs wide apart; **2,** the space between the legs when wide apart.

strag-gle (străg′l), *v.i.* [*p.t.* and *p.p.* -gled (-ld), *p.pr.* -gling], **1,** to wander out of the direct course; stray; ramble; **2,** to roam idly about; wander; **3,** to spread about; occur here and there; grow unevenly, as vines.—*n.* **strag′gler.**—*adj.* **strag′gly.**

straight (strāt), *adj.* **1,** not crooked or curved; extending evenly without change in direction; **2,** conforming to truth, honesty, or justice; accurate; upright; as, a *straight* life; *straight* thinking; *straight* accounts; **3,** properly placed or arranged; **4,** *Slang:* **a,** direct from the source; reliable; as, a *straight* tip; **b,** out-and-out; unreserved; as, a *straight* Democrat: **straight angle,** an angle whose sides lie in the same straight line, but extend in opposite directions from the vertex; equal to two right angles, or 180° (see [1]*angle*, illus.): **straight line,** a line that extends without change of direction:—*adv.* **1,** directly; in a direct course; **2,** at once.—*adv.* **straight′ly.**—*n.* **straight′ness.**

straight-edge (strāt′ĕj″), *n.* a strip of wood or metal having a perfectly straight edge with which to test lines or surfaces or to draw straight lines.

straight-en (strāt′n), *v.t.* **1,** to make free of turns or curves; **2,** to put in order; **3,** to make clear; disentangle; as, to *straighten* out a mystery:—*v.i.* to become straight.—*n.* **straight′en-er.**

straight-for-ward (strāt″fôr′wẽrd), *adj.* **1,** proceeding in a direct course; **2,** honest.—*adv.* **straight″-for′ward-ly.**—*n.* **straight″for′ward-ness.**

Syn. frank, open, candid.

straight-way (strāt′wā″), *adv.* at once; immediately.

[1]**strain** (strān), *n.* **1,** stock; race; line of descent; hence, family blood; breed; **2,** inborn disposition; tendency; **3,** character; tenor; tone; as, to speak in a lofty *strain;* **4,** a trace or streak; as, a *strain* of madness in her family; **5,** a flight or burst of the imagination, as a poem or verse; **6,** a tune or melody; esp., a definite section in a piece of music.

[2]**strain** (strān), *v.t.* **1,** to put to its utmost strength; exert as much as possible; as, to *strain* every muscle; stretch even beyond proper limits; as, to *strain* the law;

2, to weaken or injure by excessive use; sprain; as, the load *strained* his back; 3, hence, to force or constrain; as, to *strain* a welcome; 4, to press or squeeze: hence, to embrace: 5, to filter; also, to remove by, or as if by, filtering; 6, to alter in form or size, as by bending, twisting, stretching, etc.:—*v.i.* 1, to make violent efforts; strive; 2, to pass through, or as if through, a filter; be filtered; 3, to become injured by excessive use or exertion:—*n.* 1, extreme stretching; tension; constrained state or condition; 2, a violent effort; 3, injury due to violent effort or to overwork; a sprain; 4, an alteration in the size or form of a body, or in both, usually regarded as due to the application of a force or stress.

strain-er (strān′ẽr), *n.* 1, one who or that which stretches or exerts great tension; 2, a device through which any liquid is passed to make it pure or to separate it from solid matter; as, a coffee *strainer*.

strain-ing piece a short, horizontal timber in a truss with queen-posts, serving to hold in place the upper ends of the queen-posts (see *queen-post*, illus.).

strait (strāt), *n.* 1, often in *pl.*, a narrow passage of water connecting two larger bodies of water; 2, often in *pl.*, perplexity; difficulty; as, to be in financial *straits*:—*adj.* 1, narrow; as, a *strait* gate; 2, confined, as a space; 3, confining; tight; as, a *strait*-jacket; 4, restricted; hampered; as, *strait* circumstances; 5, strict; exacting; scrupulous.—*adv.* **strait′ly.**—*n.* **strait′ness.**

strait-en (strāt′n), *v.t.* 1, to make narrow; contract; 2, to confine; 3, to put into difficulties; embarrass.

strait–jack-et (strāt′-jăk″ĕt), *n.* a strong, tight coat so made as to prevent the use of the arms: used to restrain criminals and the violently insane: also called *strait-waistcoat*.

strait–laced (strāt′-lāst″), *adj.* 1, laced tightly, as corsets; 2, very strict in manners or morals.

strake (strāk), *n.* a continuous line of planks or plates from stem to stern along the bottom or sides of a vessel.

¹strand (strănd), *n.* the shore, as of an ocean:—*v.t.* 1, to drive ashore; run aground; 2, to leave in a state of embarrassment or difficulty:—*v.i.* to run aground.

²strand (strănd), *n.* one of a number of flexible strings, as of wire, hemp, or other fiber, twisted together into a rope; also, any similar string, as of pearls, beads, or hair:—*v.t.* 1, to break one of the twists in (a rope); 2, to make, as a rope, by twisting the parts together.

strange (strānj), *adj.* 1, of or belonging to others; not one's own; belonging to some other place; as, a *strange* cat; 2, not before known or seen; not familiar; as, the writing is *strange* to me; 3, odd; queer; unusual; as, *strange* jewelry; 4, reserved; shy; timid; as, to feel *strange* in company; 5, inexperienced; as, she is *strange* to that work.—*adv.* **strange′ly.**—*n.* **strange′ness.**

Syn. peculiar, singular. (See queer.)

stran-ger (strān′jẽr), *n.* 1, a foreigner; 2, a guest or visitor; 3, one who is unknown or who is not an acquaintance; 4, one who is not familiar with a certain thing; as, he is a *stranger* to Greek.

stran-gle (străng′gl), *v.t.* [*p.t.* and *p.p.* -gled (-gld), *p.pr.* -gling], 1, to choke; kill by squeezing the throat; 2, to suppress or stifle, as one's desires:—*v.i.* to be choked or suffocated:—*n.*, in *pl.*, a disease of horses: also called *distemper*.—*n.* **stran′gler.**

stran-gu-late (străng′gū-lāt), *v.t.* [*p.t.* and *p.p.* -lat″ed, *p.pr.* -lat″ing], 1, to obstruct or compress so as to stop the function of; as, to *strangulate* a blood vessel; 2, to strangle.—*n.* **stran″gu-la′tion.**

strap (străp), *n.* 1, a narrow strip, as of leather or cloth, used to fasten about objects; 2, any narrow strip or band, as of metal, to hold a frame together, a loop of leather for pulling on a boot, a band of cloth used as a shoulder ornament, etc.; 3, a razor strop:—*v.t.* [*p.t.* and *p.p.* strapped (străpt), *p.pr.* strap′ping], 1, to fasten or bind with a strap; 2, to beat with a strap; 3, to sharpen, as a razor, by rubbing on a strap.

strap-ping (străp′ĭng), *adj. Colloq.*, tall; robust; as, a *strapping* fellow.

strass (stràs), *n.* a kind of lustrous glass used in making imitation gems.

stra-ta (strā′tȧ), *n.* plural of *stratum*; layers, as of rock.

strat-a-gem (străt′ȧ-jĕm), *n.* 1, a trick for deceiving an enemy, esp. in war; 2, any trick or deceptive plan.

stra-te-gic (strȧ-tē′jĭk; strȧ-tĕj′ĭk), *adj.* 1, pertaining to, or serving the ends of, strategy; 2, skilfully adapted to the end in view; advantageous: **strategics,** *n.pl.* used as *sing.* the science of directing a military campaign; generalship. Also, *adj.* **stra-te′gi-cal.**—*adv.* **stra-te′gi-cal-ly.**

strat-e-gy (străt′ē-jĭ), *n.* 1, the art of maneuvering troops or ships on a broad scale; 2, skill in managing any affair; 3, the use of artifice.—*n.* **strat′e-gist.**

strat-i-fi-ca-tion (străt″ĭ-fĭ-kā′shŭn), *n.* 1, formation in layers; 2, rock structure in which the several layers can be clearly distinguished.

strat-i-fy (străt′ĭ-fī), *v.t.* and *v.i.* [*p.t.* and *p.p.* -fied (-fīd), *p.pr.* -fy″ing], to form in strata, or layers.—*p. adj.* **strat′i-fied.**

stra-to-sphere (strā′tō-sfẽr; străt′ō-), *n.* the upper portion of the atmosphere, more than four miles above the earth at the poles, or nine miles at the equator.

stra-tum (strā′tŭm), *n.* [*pl.* strata (-tȧ); stratums (-tŭmz)], a layer of material of any kind; as, a *stratum* of rock.

stra-tus (strā′tŭs), *n.* a continuous, horizontal layer of cloud, usually at a low altitude.

straw (strô), *n.* 1, the stalk of grain; 2, such stalks when cut and threshed; 3, anything practically worthless; as, he is not worth a *straw*:—*adj.* made of, or stuffed with, straw.

straw-ber-ry (strô′bĕr-ĭ), *n.* [*pl.* strawberries (-ĭz)], any of several low-growing plants, much cultivated for their delicious, red, acid fruit; also, the fruit.

straw-board (strô′bōrd″), *n.* a coarse cardboard made of straw and used for boxes, box covers, and the like.

straw vote an unofficial vote, as for testing the chances of election.

stray (strā), *v.i.* 1, to wander from the path or beyond limits; 2, to roam; rove freely; 3, to wander from the path of right or duty; err:—*adj.* 1, wandering beyond limits; lost; 2, incidental; occasional; as, a *stray* remark:—*n.* 1, a domestic animal or a person that has wandered beyond limits or is lost; 2, usually in *pl.*, in radio, an electrical disturbance interfering with reception; static.

Syn., *v.* (see wander).

streak (strēk), *n.* 1, a line of color; stripe; 2, a trait of character; 3, a layer, as in bacon:—*v.t.* to mark with streaks; stripe.

streak-y (strēk′ĭ), *adj.* [*comp.* streak′i-er, *superl.* streak′i-est], marked with streaks or stripes.—*adv.* **streak′i-ly.**—*n.* **streak′i-ness.**

stream (strēm), *n.* 1, a current of water or other fluid; 2, anything flowing out of a source; as, a *stream* of words; 3, a continued current or course; drift or tendency;

—*v.i.* **1**, to issue or flow in a stream; run in a current; as, the crowd *streamed* from the hall; **2**, to float, or stretch out with a waving movement; as, banners *streamed* in the air; **3**, to move with a trail of light, as a meteor:—*v.t.* **1**, to cause to flow; **2**, to cause to float out; wave.

stream-er (strēm′ẽr), *n.* anything that floats or streams out, as a pennant, or a shaft of light, as in the aurora.

stream-let (strēm′lĕt), *n.* a little stream; rivulet; rill.

stream-line (strēm′līn″), *n.* the path of a moving particle of fluid when flowing without eddy past a solid:—*adj.* shaped in long smooth curves so as to offer the least possible resistance to air or water; as, *streamline* design:—*v.t.* **1**, to make or remodel in such form; **2**, hence, to modernize or reorganize for efficiency.—*adj.* **stream′lined.**

street (strēt), *n.* **1**, a public way in a city or town, usually lined with houses on one or both sides; **2**, that part of the way reserved for vehicles, as distinguished from the sidewalk: **the street**, *Colloq.*, the vicinity or street in a city where most of the financial business is done; also, those doing business there.
Syn. thoroughfare, avenue. (See way.)

street Ar-ab a homeless child of the streets; an outcast child.

street car in the U. S., an electric passenger car, usually run on surface tracks on the streets.

strength (strĕngth), *n.* **1**, the state or quality of being strong; muscular force; also, the ability to do or bear; **2**, in material substances, the power of resistance to a rending force; toughness; as, the *strength* of a rope; **3**, power, vigor, or ability of any kind; violence; resistance; vehemence; potency; **4**, force in numbers; as, the *strength* of an army; **5**, one who is a support or stay.—*v.t.* & *v.i.* **strength′en.**—*n.* **strength′en-er.**

stren-u-ous (strĕn′ū-ŭs), *adj.* **1**, urgent; zealous; ardent; as, a *strenuous* reformer; **2**, marked by, or calling for, strong effort or exertion; as, a *strenuous* life. —*adv.* **stren′u-ous-ly.**—*n.* **stren′u-ous-ness.** —*n.* **stren″u-os′i-ty.**

strep-to-coc-cus (strĕp″tō-kŏk′ŭs), *n.* [*pl.* -cocci (kŏk′sī)], one of a certain genus of bacteria, some of which cause serious diseases, as scarlet fever, sepsis, pneumonia.—*adj.* **strep″to-coc′cic** (-sĭk).

strep-to-my-cin (strĕp″tō-mī′sĭn), *n.* an antibiotic extracted from a bacterium found in the soil.

stress (strĕs), *n.* **1**, constraining or impelling force; compulsion; pressure; as, under the *stress* of work; **2**, importance; significance; emphasis; as, to lay *stress* on a particular fact; **3**, in physics, a force, esp. one causing deformation or change of volume:—*v.t.* **1**, to emphasize; **2**, to accent; **3**, to subject to mechanical pressure.

-stress (-strĕs), *fem. n. suffix*, meaning a woman who does (a certain thing) with skill or as an occupation; as, seam*stress*.

stretch (strĕch), *v.t.* **1**, to draw out to a greater length or width; as, to *stretch* rubber; hence, to draw tight; as, to *stretch* a tent; **2**, to extend or reach out; as, to *stretch* out the arm; **3**, to extend between two points; as, to *stretch* a rope across a street; **4**, to strain; as, to *stretch* every nerve; **5**, to exaggerate; as, to *stretch* the truth:—*v.i.* **1**, to spread; reach; as, the rope *stretches* across the street; **2**, to admit of being extended; as, that cloth *stretches;* **3**, to extend or spread the body or limbs:—*n.* **1**, the act of straining or extending; **2**, reach; scope; extent; **3**, a continuous line, space, or time; as, a *stretch* of road.

stretch-er (strĕch′ẽr), *n.* **1**, one that extends or draws out; **2**, a frame, usually covered with canvas, for carrying the disabled; **3**, a beam used as a tie in the frame of a building; **4**, a brick laid lengthwise in a wall: opp. of *header*.

strew (strōō; *Br.* strō), *v.t.* [*p.t.* strewed (strōōd; strōd), *p.p.* strewed or strewn (strōōn; strōn), *p.pr.* strew′ing], **1**, to scatter, or let fall loosely; as, to *strew* flowers on a path; **2**, to cover in spots, as a path.

stri-a (strī′ȧ), *n.* [*pl.* striæ (-ē)], **1**, a narrow stripe, streak, or line, whether of structure or of color; **2**, a fine ridge or groove; esp., one of a series of parallel ridges.

stri-ate (strī′āt), *adj.* marked with very small grooves or fine lines of color. Also, **stria′at-ed.**—*n.* **stri-a′tion.**

strict (strĭkt), *adj.* **1**, exacting; severe; as, *strict* laws; **2**, extremely careful and thorough; as, *strict* honesty; **3**, accurate; precise; as, the *strict* sense of a word; **4**, stretched tight; as, *strict* bandages.—*adv.* **strict′ly.**—*n.* **strict′ness.**
Syn. rigid, harsh, austere. (See stern.)— *Ant.* lenient, lax, indulgent.

stric-ture (strĭk′tūr), *n.* **1**, the abnormal narrowing of a passage of the body; **2**, severe censure or blame.

stride (strīd), *n.* **1**, the act or manner of striding; **2**, a long step:—*v.i.* [*p.t.* strode (strōd), *p.p.* stridden (strĭd′n), *p.pr.* strid′ing], to walk with long steps:—*v.t.* **1**, to pass over with one step; **2**, to straddle.

stri-dent (strī′dĕnt), *adj.* harsh; as, a *strident* voice.—*adv.* **stri′dent-ly.**

strid-u-late (strĭd′ū-lāt), *v.i.* [*p.t.* and *p.p.* -lat″ed, *p.pr.* -lat″ing], to make a shrill, creaking noise, as locusts, crickets, etc.—*n.* **strid″u-la′tion.**

strife (strīf), *n.* **1**, contention for superiority; competition; **2**, discord; conflict.

strike (strīk), *v.t.* [*p.t.* struck (strŭk), *p.p.* struck or, *Poetic*, strick′en (strĭk′n), *p.pr.* strik′ing], **1**, to hit; smite; dash against; attack; **2**, to give or deal, as a blow; **3**, to come into sudden and forcible contact with; also, to bring thus into contact with something; as, to *strike* the table; to *strike* the hand against a table; **4**, to lower, as a flag; also, to take down and pack, as a tent; **5**, to cause to sound; as, to *strike* a bell; also, to announce by sound; as, the clock *strikes* twelve; **6**, to produce by friction, as a light; also, to cause to ignite, as a match; **7**, to stamp with a die, as coins; **8**, to come to the mind of; occur to; **9**, to impress or affect strongly, as with emotion; as, to be *struck* with pity; **10**, to come upon suddenly; as, to *strike* the track; **11**, to conclude, as a bargain; **12**, to level or shape with a special tool, as in measuring grain or molding sand; **13**, to obliterate, as by a stroke of a pen: with *off* or *out;* **14**, to assume, as an attitude:—*v.i.* **1**, to deal a quick blow or thrust; make an attack; fight; **2**, to hit; collide; become stranded, as a ship; **3**, to proceed; as, they *struck* into the woods; **4**, to sound, as a bell or a clock; **5**, to lower a flag or sail, as a sign of respect or submission; **6**, to cease from work in order to secure or prevent a change in conditions; **7**, *Colloq.*, to come or happen suddenly: with *upon;* **8**, in gardening, to become rooted:—*n.* **1**, a blow; **2**, a stopping of work in order to secure or prevent a change in conditions of labor; **3**, an instrument for leveling or shaping, as in measuring grain or molding sand; **4**, a fortunate discovery of ore or oil; hence, any sudden success; **5**, in baseball, an unsuccessful attempt by the batter to hit the ball, or a ball so pitched that the batter should have struck at it; **6**, in bowling, the upsetting, by a player, of all the pins with the first ball bowled; also, the score so made.

strike break-er **1**, a workman who takes the place of one who has left his work in order to force his employer to agree to some demand; **2,** a person who supplies such workmen.

strik-er (strīk'ẽr), *n.* one who or that which strikes; esp., one who stops work in an effort to gain better conditions.

strik-ing (strīk'ĭng), *p.adj.* **1,** very noticeable; as, a *striking* resemblance; **2,** remarkable; surprising; as, a *striking* fact. —*adv.* **strik'ing-ly.**—*n.* **strik'ing-ness.**

string (strĭng), *n.* **1,** a small cord; thick thread; twine; also, a narrow strip of cloth; as, an apron *string;* **2,** in a musical instrument, a tightly stretched cord whose vibration produces a musical tone; **3,** a set of things, as beads, arranged on a cord; hence, a series of things in, or as in, a line; as, a *string* of cars; a *string* of oaths; **4,** a fiber, as of a vegetable body; **5,** in *pl.*, stringed musical instruments; also, those who play on them; **6,** one of the notched, inclined timbers of a stair, supporting the treads and risers (see *newel, step,* illus.):—*v.t.* [*p.t.* strung (strŭng), *p.p.* strung or, *Rare,* stringed (strĭngd), *p.pr.* string'ing], **1,** to furnish with a fine cord or cords, as a bow or violin; **2,** to tighten, or put in tune, the cords of; **3,** hence, to brace; make as if tense; as, danger *strings* his nerves; **4,** to thread on a cord; **5,** to extend or stretch like a cord; also, to extend in a line or series; **6,** to fasten or hang, as with a cord: with *up;* **7,** to take strings from, as beans; **8,** *U. S. Slang,* to jolly; take in:—*v.i.* **1,** to form into strings; **2,** to stretch out into a series.

stringed (strĭngd), *p.adj.* **1,** furnished with strings, as certain musical instruments; **2,** fastened with strings.

strin-gen-cy (strĭn'jĕn-sĭ), *n.* **1,** severity or strictness; as, the *stringency* of the law; **2,** tightness; scarcity of funds, as in the money market.

strin-gent (strĭn'jĕnt), *adj.* **1,** strict; rigid; as, *stringent* rules; **2,** having little ready money; tight; as, the money market is *stringent.*—*adv.* **strin'gent-ly.**

string-er (strĭng'ẽr), *n.* **1,** one who furnishes strings to an instrument or bow; **2,** in building, a heavy horizontal timber connecting uprights and supporting other members; also, a board supporting the ends of steps in a staircase (see *step,* illus.).

string-halt (strĭng'hôlt″), *n.* a jerky affection of a horse's hind legs.

string-piece (strĭng'pēs″), *n.* a main timber supporting the edge of a framework, as of a floor or a staircase.

string-y (strĭng'ĭ), *adj.* [*comp.* string'i-er, *superl.* string'i-est], **1,** full of, consisting of, or like, fibers, or threads; as, *stringy* meat; **2,** gluey; ropy.—*n.* **string'i-ness.**

strip (strĭp), *v.t.* [*p.t.* and *p.p.* stripped (strĭpt) or, *Rare,* stript (strĭpt), *p.pr.* strip'ping], **1,** to make naked; deprive of a covering; hence, to rob; deprive; as, to *strip* a man of his riches; **2,** to pull off; as, to *strip* bark from a tree; hence, to snatch away; as, to *strip* riches from a man; **3,** to milk dry, as a cow:—*v.i.* to undress:—*n.* a long, narrow piece, as of cloth or wood.—*n.* **strip'per.**

stripe (strīp), *n.* **1,** a line, band, or streak; a long, narrow division of a surface; **2,** a strip of different color or material attached to anything; **3,** a discolored line or streak on the skin made by a blow of a whip; also, a blow made by a whip; **4,** distinctive color; hence, particular sort; kind; as, they are persons of the same *stripe:*—*v.t.* [*p.t.* and *p.p.* striped (strīpt), *p.pr.* strip'ing], to mark with lines or bands.—*p.adj.* **striped** (strīpt; strīp'ĕd).

strip-ling (strĭp'lĭng), *n.* a mere youth; lad; boy.

strive (strīv), *v.i.* [*p.t.* strove (strōv), *p.p.* striv'en (strĭv'n) or, *Rare,* strove, *p.pr.* striv'ing], **1,** to make strenuous efforts; labor hard or earnestly; as, to *strive* for success; **2,** to struggle in opposition; compete; as, to *strive* in a race.—*n.* **striv'er.**

strob-ile (strŏb'ĭl), *n.* a cone-shaped fruit, as that of the pine (see *inflorescence,* illus.). Also, **strob'i-lus.**

strode (strōd), the past tense of the irregular verb *stride.*

stroke (strōk), *n.* **1,** the act of making a blow, or the blow made; as, the *stroke* of a hammer; **2,** a powerful or sudden action or ill effect suggesting a blow; as, a *stroke* of lightning; a *stroke* of paralysis; **3,** a strong effort to bring about a result, or the result brought about; as, a *stroke* of business; **4,** a gently moving touch; as, a soft *stroke* of the hand; **5,** a movement with an instrument, as a pencil or pen, or the mark made; **6,** the sound of a clock in marking the time, or the time marked; as, on the *stroke* of nine; **7,** in rowing, a complete movement of the oars, or manner of moving them; also, the principal oarsman in a boat, who sets the time for the rowers:—*v.t.* [*p.t.* and *p.p.* stroked (strōkt), *p.pr.* strok'ing], **1,** to rub gently with the hand, as a cat; **2,** to set the time for (rowers). (See [3]blow.)

Syn., n. knock, lash.

stroll (strōl), *n.* a ramble; wandering:—*v.i.* **1,** to wander on foot from place to place; **2,** to ramble or rove idly.—*n.* **stroll'er.**

strong (strông), *adj.* **1,** physically powerful; muscular; robust; healthy; **2,** morally vigorous; energetic; firm; efficient; capable; as, a *strong* character; **3,** powerful in wealth, numbers, or other resources; as, a *strong* party; also, of a specified numerical force; as, 9,000 *strong;* **4,** impetuous or violent, as wind; **5,** ardent or warm, as the affections; **6,** vigorous or forceful, as an argument; **7,** deeply rooted; firm; as, a *strong* belief; **8,** stable or settled, as a government; **9,** solid, tough, or resistant, as a plank or fort; **10,** intense or concentrated, as tea or light; **11,** too intense, as an odor; **12,** tending to higher prices; firm, as the stock market; **13,** in grammar: **a,** designating, or pertaining to, certain verbs in English, German, and other Teutonic languages, which show tense form by a vowel change in the stem, as in *sing, sang, sung;* **b,** designating, or pertaining to, the declension of certain nouns in these languages, which have relatively full and varied inflectional endings and do not form the plural in *-n;* also, in modern German, designating, or pertaining to, the declension of adjectives in which relatively fuller inflectional endings are used, instead of the *-n* inflection of the weak declension: **strong drink,** intoxicating liquor:—*adv.* **1,** *Colloq.,* firmly; vigorously; greatly; **2,** strongly: used in combinations; as, *strong*-built.—*adv.* **strong'ly.**

strong-hold (strông'hōld″), *n.* a fort or fortress; a place of refuge.

stron-ti-um (strŏn'shĭ-ŭm), *n.* a soft, white, alkaline metallic element resembling calcium, the salts of which are used in fireworks to color flames red.

strop (strŏp), *n.* a strip of leather, as for sharpening a razor:—*v.t.* [*p.t.* and *p.p.* stropped (strŏpt), *p.pr.* strop'ping], to sharpen on a strop, as a razor.

stro-phe (strō'fē), *n.* **1,** in the ancient Greek choral dance, a movement of the chorus, while singing, to one side of the stage; **2,** hence, the part of the choral ode sung during this movement; **3,** sometimes, a stanza of modern verse.

strove (strōv), the past tense of the irregular verb *strive.*

strow (strō), *v.t.* [*p.t.* strowed (strōd), *p.p.* strown (strōn) or strowed, *p.pr.* strow'ing], *Archaic,* to scatter; strew.

struck (strŭk), past tense and past participle of the verb *strike*.

struc-tur-al (strŭk'tūr-ăl), *adj.* of or pertaining to construction or formation.—*adv.* **struc'tur-al-ly.**

struc-ture (strŭk'tūr), *n.* **1,** that which is built, as a bridge or building; **2,** the manner or form of building; **3,** the form or arrangement of parts or elements in a natural organism, as of a rock or mineral.
Syn. edifice. (See building.)

strug-gle (strŭg'l), *n.* **1,** a violent effort or great endeavor; **2,** contest; strife:—*v.i.* [*p.t.* and *p.p.* -gled (-ld), *p.pr.* -gling], **1,** to put forth great effort, as in trying to escape from a grasp; **2,** to labor; strive.—*n.* **strug'gler.**

strum (strŭm), *v.t.* and *v.i.* [*p.t.* and *p.p.* strummed (strŭmd), *p.pr.* strum'ming], to play badly and noisily on a stringed instrument; as, to *strum* a waltz; to *strum* on a piano:—*n.* the act of so playing, or the sound produced.

strum-pet (strŭm'pĕt), *n.* a woman of low moral character.

strung (strŭng), past tense and past participle of the verb *string.*

¹strut (strŭt), *v.i.* [*p.t.* and *p.p.* strut'ted, *p.pr.* strut'ting], to walk stiffly with a pompous or conceited air, or with affected dignity:—*n.* a proud or affected step or walk with the head erect.

²strut (strŭt), *n.* in construction, a brace or bar to support weight or pressure, or to receive weight or pressure in the direction of its length (see *airplane, king truss,* illus.):—*v.t.* [*p.t.* and *p.p.* strut'ted, *p.pr.* strut'ting], to brace with a strut.

strych-nine (strĭk'nĭn; strĭk'nēn), *n.* a very powerful poison obtained from certain plants and used in medicine to stimulate the nerves and the action of the heart. Also, **strych'nin; strych'ni-a.**

stub (stŭb), *n.* **1,** the stump of a tree; also, any projection resembling a stump; as, the *stub* of a tail; **2,** the short, blunt, remaining part of anything; as, the *stub* of a pencil; **3,** the part of a leaf left in a check book after a check is torn out, serving as a memorandum of the check; **4,** a pen with a short, blunt point:—*v.t.* [*p.t.* and *p.p.* stubbed (stŭbd), *p.pr.* stub'bing], **1,** to dig up, as roots; **2,** to dig roots from; **3,** to strike against some fixed object; as, to *stub* one's toe.

stub-bed (stŭb'ĕd, stŭbd), *p.adj.* **1,** cut off short, like a stump; **2,** full of stumps or roots; **3,** hardy; rugged.—*n.* **stub'bed-ness.**

stub-ble (stŭb'l), *n.* **1,** the stumps of grain left in the ground after mowing; **2,** anything resembling stubble, as a beard of several days' growth.—*adj.* **stub'bly.**

stub-born (stŭb'ērn), *adj.* **1,** fixed in opinion; resolute in purpose; esp., unreasonably obstinate; as, a *stubborn* child; **2,** persistently or obstinately followed or held to; as, a *stubborn* attempt; **3,** hard to handle or treat, as a cold.—*adv.* **stub'born-ly.** —*n.* **stub'born-ness.**
Syn. headstrong, perverse. (See obstinate.)

stub-by (stŭb'ĭ), *adj.* [*comp.* stub'bi-er, *superl.* stub'bi-est], **1,** full of stumps or roots; as, a *stubby* field; **2,** short and dense, as a beard; also, short and thickset, as a person.—*adv.* **stub'bi-ly.**—*n.* **stub'bi-ness.**

stuc-co (stŭk'ō), *n.* [*pl.* stuccoes; stuccos (-ōz)], a fine plaster used on outside and inside walls, and for decorations such as cornices and moldings; also, work made of such plaster:—*v.t.* to overlay, or decorate, with stucco.

stuck (stŭk), past tense and past participle of the irregular verb *stick.*

stuck-up (stŭk'=ŭp'), *adj. Colloq.*, arrogant; conceited.

¹stud (stŭd), *n.* **1,** in building, an upright timber in walls, often two by four inches, to which the laths are nailed; **2,** an ornamental boss or knob projecting from a surface; a carved disk; **3,** a device resembling a two-headed button and used as a fastener, esp. in a shirt front; **4,** in mechanics, a projecting pin serving as a support, stop, or the like:—*v.t.* [*p.t.* and *p.p.* stud'ded, *p.pr.* stud'ding], **1,** to furnish with upright props; **2,** to adorn or set with bosses or bright knobs; **3,** to be set thickly in; as, stars *stud* the sky.

²stud (stŭd), *n.* **1,** a collection of horses, as for breeding; also, the place where they are kept; **2,** a number of horses kept for racing, hunting, etc.; **3,** *Colloq.*, a stallion.

stud-ding (stŭd'ĭng), *n.* in building, the studs, or upright beams, in walls, collectively; also, the material of which they are made (see *frame house,* illus.).

stud-ding sail (stŭd'ĭng săl; stŭn'sl), a light sail set beside a square sail of a vessel and used in light winds.

stu-dent (stū'dĕnt), *n.* **1,** one who attends school; **2,** hence, one devoted to books or learning; any close observer; as, a *student* of human nature.

stud-horse (stŭd'hôrs″), *n.* a stallion kept for breeding.

stud-ied (stŭd'ĭd), *p.adj.* designed; deliberate; as, a *studied* compliment.—*adv.* **stud'ied-ly.**—*n.* **stud'ied-ness.**

stu-di-o (stū'dĭ-ō), *n.* [*pl.* studios (-ōz)], the workroom of an artist.

stu-di-ous (stū'dĭ-ŭs), *adj.* **1,** given to study, or to the gaining of knowledge; **2,** heedful; thoughtful; earnest; as, *studious* endeavor to please.—*adv.* **stu'di-ous-ly.**—*n.* **stu'di-ous-ness.**

stud-y (stŭd'ĭ), *n.* [*pl.* studies (-ĭz)], **1,** the application of the mind to the gaining of knowledge; **2,** any particular object of careful thought; any branch of learning; **3,** earnest and careful examination of a particular question; as, a *study* of trade conditions; **4,** deep meditation; reverie; **5,** in painting, a preliminary sketch for a picture; **6,** in music, a piece for a special kind of practice; **7,** a room set apart for mental work:—*v.i.* [*p.t.* and *p.p.* stud'ied (-ĭd), *p.pr.* stud'y-ing], **1,** to devote oneself closely to books and learning, or to any subject of inquiry; **2,** to use thoughtful care in planning; **3,** to reflect:—*v.t.* **1,** to examine closely in order to learn thoroughly; devote one's thoughts to; look at closely and thoughtfully; **2,** to learn, or memorize the details of; as, to *study* Latin.

stuff (stŭf), *n.* **1,** the material of which anything is composed or may be made; **2,** any immaterial principle or essence; as, the *stuff* of which brave men are made; **3,** woven fabrics or cloth; **4,** household goods; **5,** refuse or waste matter; hence, nonsense:—*v.t.* **1,** to crowd, cram, or pack; as, to *stuff* clothes into a suitcase; also, to fill by crowding something into; as, to *stuff* one's pockets; **2,** to fill with specially prepared material; as, to *stuff* a chicken; **3,** to fill (the skin of a dead animal) so as to preserve its natural form; **4,** to put dishonest votes into, as a ballot box:—*v.i.* to eat more than enough.—*n.* **stuff'ing.**

stuff-y (stŭf'ĭ), *adj.* [*comp.* stuff'i-er, *superl.* stuff'i-est], **1,** close or badly ventilated; as, a *stuffy* room; **2,** *Slang,* sulky; cross.—*n.* **stuff'i-ness.**

stul-ti-fy (stŭl'tĭ-fī), *v.t.* [*p.t.* and *p.p.* -fied (-fīd), *p.pr.* -fy″ing], to make foolish; reduce to absurdity.—*n.* **stul″ti-fi-ca'tion.**

stum-ble (stŭm'bl), *n.* **1,** a trip in walking or running; **2,** a failure or blunder:—*v.i.* [*p.t.* and *p.p.* -bled (-bld), *p.pr.*

-bling], **1**, to trip or fall in walking; **2**, to walk in an unsteady manner; **3**, to fall into error; **4**, to come by chance: with *on*, *upon*, or *against*.—*n.* **stum′bler.**—*adv.* **stum′bling-ly.**

stum-bling-block (stŭm′blĭng-blŏk″), *n.* an obstacle or hindrance, moral or physical.

stump (stŭmp), *n.* **1**, that part of a tree which remains in the ground after the trunk is cut down; **2**, the part, as of an arm or leg, remaining after a portion has been cut off; **3**, an artist's rubbing implement; **4**, in cricket, any of the three posts of a wicket; **5**, a place for political speaking: formerly a tree stump; hence, political speaking; **6**, a dare; challenge:—*v.t.* **1**, to lop; reduce to a stump; **2**, *Colloq.*, to strike, as the toes, against a stone or something fixed; **3**, to canvass (a district) making political speeches:—*v.i.* to walk heavily and stiffly.

stump-y (stŭm′pĭ), *adj.* [*comp.* stump′i-er, *superl.* stump′i-est], **1**, full of stumps, as a field; **2**, *Colloq.*, short and thick; as, *stumpy* fingers.

stun (stŭn), *v.t.* [*p.t.* and *p.p.* stunned (stŭnd), *p.pr.* stun′ning], **1**, to make senseless by, or as by, a blow; **2**, to confuse or daze with noise; **3**, to overpower with astonishment; astound:—*n.* **1**, an overpowering blow or shock; **2**, the condition of being dazed, bewildered, or unconscious.—*n.* **stun′ner.**

stung (stŭng), past tense and past participle of the irregular verb *sting.*

stunk (stŭngk), a form of the past tense, and the past participle, of the verb *stink.*

stun-ning (stŭn′ĭng), *p.adj.* **1**, overpowering the senses, as a blow; **2**, *Slang*, very handsome; as, a *stunning* dress.

[1]**stunt** (stŭnt), *v.t.* to check the growth or development of; dwarf:—*n.* **1**, a check in growth; **2**, something of which the growth has been checked.

[2]**stunt** (stŭnt), *n. Colloq.*, a striking act or feat, as of strength or skill.

stupe (stūp), *n.* a piece of flannel or similar material wrung out of hot water or some healing liquid, and applied to a hurt.

stu-pe-fac-tion (stū″pē-făk′shŭn), *n.* **1**, the act of dulling the senses; **2**, the state of having the senses dulled.

stu-pe-fy (stū′pē-fī), *v.t.* [*p.t.* and *p.p.* -fied (-fīd), *p.pr.* -fy″ing], to dull the senses of; make stupid.—*n.* **stu′pe-fi″er.**

stu-pen-dous (stū-pĕn′dŭs), *adj.* overcoming the senses by enormous size or greatness; astonishing; wonderful; amazing.—*adv.* **stu-pen′dous-ly.** —*n.* **stu-pen′dous-ness.**

stu-pid (stū′pĭd), *adj.* **1**, wanting in understanding; foolish; **2**, benumbed; incapable of feeling; **3**, foolish; as, a *stupid* error.—*adv.* **stu′pid-ly.**—*n.* **stu′pid-ness.**

Syn. dull. *Stupid* is applied to those of such sluggish intelligence that they seem unable to grasp an idea. *Dull* describes a slow and heavy mind, lacking all quickness of wit, but not *stupid.*

stu-pid-i-ty (stū-pĭd′ĭ-tĭ), *n.* great dulness of mind; slowness.

stu-por (stū′pŏr), *n.* **1**, suspension or great lessening of the senses and faculties; **2**, great moral or intellectual stupidity.

stur-dy (stûr′dĭ), *adj.* [*comp.* stur′di-er, *superl.* stur′di-est], **1**, hardy; robust; stout; as, a *sturdy* countryman; **2**, resolute; firm and unyielding; as, a man of *sturdy* faith.—*adv.* **stur′di-ly.**—*n.* **stur′di-ness.**

stur-geon (stûr′jŭn), *n.* any of a family of large fishes found in the north temperate zone: an important source of caviar and isinglass.

stut-ter (stŭt′ẽr), *n.* a form of stammering in which the initial sounds are repeated; a stammer:—*v.i.* and *v.t.* to speak, or utter, with hesitation or stammering.—*n.* **stut′ter-er.**—*n.* **stut′ter-ing.**

[1]**sty** (stī), *n.* [*pl.* sties (stīz)], **1**, a pen for swine; **2**, a filthy or vile place.

[2]**sty** (stī), *n.* [*pl.* sties (stīz)], an inflamed swelling on the eyelid. Also, **stye.**

Styg-i-an (stĭj′ĭ-ăn), *adj.* in mythology, pertaining to the Styx, the river of Hades, over which the dead were ferried by the boatman Charon; hence, infernal or hellish; gloomy; dark.

[1]**style** (stīl), *n.* **1**, a pointed instrument used by the ancients for writing upon wax tablets; also, any of various similar instruments, as an engraver's tool; **2**, a characteristic manner of writing or speaking; as, a florid *style;* also, suitable or appropriate diction; as the speech lacked *style;* **3**, mode of expression or execution in any art; as, the Renaissance *style;* **4**, manner of conduct or action; as, a graceful *style* of dancing; **5**, fashion; as, a coat of the latest *style;* also, fine or dashing appearance; **6**, form of address; title; as, he is entitled to the *style* of Colonel; **7**, in chronology, mode of expressing dates: New Style [*abbr.* N. S.] being according to the Gregorian calendar as reformed in 1582, and Old Style [*abbr.* O. S.], according to the old Julian calendar, now thirteen days behind the New Style:—*v.t.* [*p.t.* and *p.p.* styled (stīld), *p.pr.* styl′ing], to term, name, or call; dub.

Syn., *n.* (see diction, mode).

[2]**style** (stīl), *n.* **1**, the pin, marker, or gnomon of a sundial; **2**, the stemlike part of the pistil of a flower which, when present, bears the stigma at its end (see also *flower*, illus.).

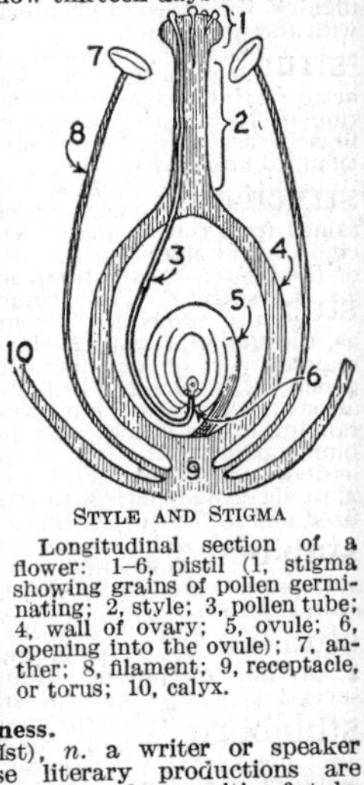

STYLE AND STIGMA

Longitudinal section of a flower: 1–6, pistil (1, stigma showing grains of pollen germinating; 2, style; 3, pollen tube; 4, wall of ovary; 5, ovule; 6, opening into the ovule); 7, anther; 8, filament; 9, receptacle, or torus; 10, calyx.

sty-let (stī′lĕt), *n.* any slender, pointed instrument.

styl-ish (stīl′ĭsh), *adj.* very fashionable; modern. —*adv.* **styl′ish-ly.**—*n.* **styl′ish-ness.**

styl-ist (stīl′ĭst), *n.* a writer or speaker whose literary productions are marked by high quality; also, a critic of style.

sty-lo-graph (stī′lō-grăf), *n.* a variety of fountain pen fitted with a conical writing point which controls the flow of the ink stored in a reservoir in the handle: also called *stylographic pen.*

sty-log-ra-phy (stī-lŏg′rȧ-fĭ), *n.* the manner or process of drawing or writing with a style, as on a waxed tablet. —*adj.* **sty″lo-graph′ic.**

sty-lus (stī′lŭs), *n.* a style, or sharp-pointed instrument or process.

sty-mie (stī′mĭ), *n.* the position of the ball lying directly between the ball of an opponent and the hole which he is playing —*v.t.* [*p.t.* and *p.p.* -mied (-mĭd), *p.pr.* -mying], to impede or obstruct by playing a ball into this position.

styp-tic (stĭp′tĭk), *adj.* able to stop bleeding; as, a *styptic* pencil used by barbers:—*n.* a substance that stops bleeding.

Styx (stĭks), *n.* in mythology, the river which encircled the lower regions, or Hades, seven times, and over which Charon ferried the shades of the dead.

sua-sion (swā′zhŭn), *n.* persuasion.—*adj.* **sua′sive.**—*adv.* **sua′sive-ly.**

suave (swāv; swäv), *adj.* pleasant in manner; bland.—*adv.* **suave′ly.**

suav-i-ty (swăv′ĭ-tĭ; swä′vĭ-tĭ), *n.* [*pl.* suavities (-tĭz)], agreeableness; pleasantness; blandness; urbanity.

sub- (sŭb-), *prefix,* [often appearing as *suc-, suf-, sug-, sum-, sup-, sur-, sus-,* before *c, f, g, m, p, r, s,* respectively], **1,** under; beneath; below; near; next to; as, *sub*marine; *sub*urb; **2,** slightly or somewhat; as, *sub*acid; **3,** inferior or subordinate in rank, classification, etc.; as, *sub*lieutenant; in verbs, indicating division into subordinate parts; as, *sub*divide; **4,** low; lower of two; as, *sub*way; *sub*maxillary; **5,** in chemistry, indicating presence in a less than the normal amount; as, *sub*carbide.

sub-ac-id (sŭb-ăs′ĭd), *adj.* slightly sour, as fruit:—*n.* a mild acid.

sub-al-tern (sŭb-ôl′tẽrn), *n.* a military officer under the rank of captain:—*adj.* **1,** of inferior, or lower, rank; **2,** ranking below a captain.

sub-a-que-ous (sŭb-ā′kwē-ŭs), *adj.* **1,** being or formed under water; **2,** intended for use under water.

sub-base (sŭb′-bās″), *n.* the lowest part of a pedestal, or of a base when it is divided into layers.

sub-car-bide (sŭb″kär′bīd; -bĭd), *n.* a carbide containing less than the normal proportion of carbon.

sub-class (sŭb′klȧs″), *n.* a classification of plants or animals above the order but below the class.

sub-con-scious (sŭb-kŏn′shŭs), *adj.* designating, or pertaining to, mental functioning of which one is not conscious:—*n.* mental functioning of which one is not conscious.—*adv.* **sub-con′scious-ly.**—*n.* **sub-con′scious-ness.**

sub-con-tract (sŭb″kŏn′trăkt), *n.* a contract made after, and subordinate to, another contract, as for one part of the work in building a house.

sub-cu-ta-ne-ous (sŭb″kū-tā′nē-ŭs), *adj.* **1,** situated under the skin; **2,** intended for use under the skin.

sub-di-vide (sŭb″dĭ-vīd′), *v.t.* [*p.t.* and *p.p.* -vid′ed, *p.pr.* -vid′ing], to separate the parts of into other parts:—*v.i.* to divide or separate again.

sub-di-vi-sion (sŭb″dĭ-vĭzh′ŭn), *n.* **1,** the separation of parts into smaller parts; **2,** a part of a larger part.

sub-dom-i-nant (sŭb-dŏm′ĭ-nănt), *n.* the fourth degree of an ascending diatonic scale.

sub-due (sŭb-dū′), *v.t.* [*p.t.* and *p.p.* -dued′ (-dūd′), *p.pr.* -du′ing], **1,** to conquer; vanquish; as, to *subdue* an enemy; **2,** to overcome; control, as a disease; **3,** to master; control, as the passions; **4,** to tone down; soften, as a color.—*n.* **sub-du′er.**

sub-fam-i-ly (sŭb″făm′ĭ-lĭ), *n.* [*pl.* subfamilies (-lĭz)], a classification of plants or animals, above the genus but below the family.

sub-floor (sŭb′flōr″), *n.* a layer of boards on the floor joists, upon which the flooring is nailed (see *frame house,* illus.).

sub-ge-nus (sŭb″jē′nŭs), *n.* a classification of plants or animals, above the species but below the genus.

sub-ja-cent (sŭb-jā′sĕnt), *adj.* **1,** lying directly under or below; **2,** situated lower, but not directly beneath; as, hills and *subjacent* valleys.

sub-ject (sŭb′jĕkt), *n.* **1,** one who is under the power or control of another; one who owes allegiance to a sovereign; as, the rights of *subjects;* **2,** one who or that which is subjected to an operation or treatment, esp. a dead body for the use of medical students; **3,** that which is treated in writing, speaking, etc., or concerning which anything is said or done; topic; **4,** the word or word group in a sentence, denoting that of which anything is affirmed: distinguished from *predicate,* the thing affirmed; **5,** the thinking and feeling entity; the mind; **6,** in music, the theme of a movement:—*adj.* **1,** under the power or control of another; as, to be *subject* to a king; **2,** disposed; exposed; liable: with *to;* as, *subject* to temptation; **3,** conditional (upon): with *to;* as, *subject* to your approval:—*v.t.* (sŭb-jĕkt′), **1,** to bring under control; **2,** to make liable; expose; as, to *subject* a person to unpleasantness; **3,** to cause to undergo; as, to *subject* a substance to heat.

sub-jec-tion (sŭb-jĕk′shŭn), *n.* **1,** the act of bringing under the rule of another; **2,** the state of being under the power or control of another.

sub-jec-tive (sŭb-jĕk′tĭv), *adj.* **1,** based upon one's own feelings; introspective; as, a *subjective* view of life, **2,** in literature and art, affected by the personality of the author or artist; **3,** in psychology, having reference to the self rather than to one's environment.—*adv.* **sub-jec′tive-ly.**—*n.* **sub-jec′tive-ness.**

sub-jec-tiv-i-ty (sŭb″jĕk-tĭv′ĭ-tĭ), *n.* **1,** the character of existing merely as a mental representation; the absence of objective reality apart from the mind; illusion; **2,** the revelation by an artist in his art of his personal qualities; **3,** in psychology, reference to oneself rather than to one's environment.

sub-join (sŭb-join′), *v.t.* to add to the end of what has been said or written.

sub-ju-gate (sŭb′jo͞o-gāt), *v.t.* [*p.t.* and *p.p.* -gat″ed, *p.pr.* -gat″ing], to conquer; vanquish; subdue.—*n.* **sub″ju-ga′tion.**—*n.* **sub′ju-ga″tor.**

Syn. overcome, defeat, enslave.

sub-junc-tive (sŭb-jŭngk′tĭv), *adj.* designating, or pertaining to, that mood of a verb which expresses state or action as provisional or dependent, rather than as a fact:—*n.* the subjunctive mood.

sub-let (sŭb-lĕt′), *v.t.* [*p.t.* and *p.p.* -let′, *p.pr.* -let′ting], to let or lease to another (that which has already been let or leased to oneself, as a contract or property).

sub-lieu-ten-ant (sŭb″lū-tĕn′ănt; *Br.* sŭb″lĕf-), *n.* a subordinate, or second, lieutenant.

sub-li-mate (sŭb′lĭ-māt), *v.t.* [*p.t.* and *p.p.* -mat″ed, *p.pr.* -mat″-ing], **1,** to cause (a solid) to pass directly into vapor, and back again directly to the solid state; as, to *sublimate* sulphur; **2,** to refine or purify:—*adj.* **1,** having been changed by heat into vapor, and again become solid; **2,** refined:—*n.* (sŭb′lĭ-măt), a deposit of a substance obtained by sublimating.—*n.* **sub″li-ma′tion.**

sub-lime (sŭb-līm′), *adj.* **1,** causing a feeling of awe and reverence; filling the mind with a sense of greatness, power, or grandeur; as, a *sublime* sacrifice; *sublime* music; **2,** exalted; noble; elevated; as, *sublime* faith or trust in another:—*n.* that which is grand or awe-inspiring: sometimes distinguished from the merely beautiful: with *the:*—*v.t.* [*p.t.* and *p.p.* -limed′ (-līmd′), *p.pr.*

-lim'ing], 1, to dignify; exalt; make noble; 2, to cause to pass from solid to gaseous or from gaseous to solid form, without becoming liquid:—*v.i.* to pass from solid to gaseous or from gaseous to solid form, without becoming liquid.—*adv.* **sub-lime'ly.**—*n.* **sub-lime'ness.**

sub-lim-i-ty (sŭb-lĭm'ĭ-tĭ), *n.* [*pl.* sublimities (-tĭz), 1, the state or quality of being exalted; loftiness or majesty of character; 2, that which is exalted.
Syn. splendor, magnificence, grandeur.

sub-lu-nar (sŭb-lū'nȧr), *adj.* 1, situated beneath the moon; 2, pertaining to this world. Also, **sub'lu-na-ry.**

sub-ma-rine (sŭb"mȧ-rēn'), *adj.* living, situated, or used, beneath the surface of the sea; as, a *submarine* diving bell:—*n.* a vessel, usually a war vessel, which can be operated under water.

SUBMARINE DIVING BELL

sub-max-il-la-ry (sŭb-măk'-sĭ-lā-rĭ), *adj.* designating, pertaining to, or situated beneath, the lower jaw; as, the *submaxillary* gland or bone.

sub-merge (sŭb-mûrj'), *v.t.* [*p.t.* and *p.p.* -merged' (-mûrjd'), *p.pr.* -merg'ing], 1, to put under water; 2, to cover with water; flood; overwhelm:—*v.i.* to sink under water or out of sight; be covered or buried.—*n.* **sub-mer'-gence.**—*adj.* **sub-mer'gi-ble.**

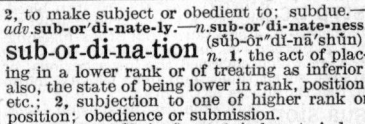

sub-mers-i-ble (sŭb-mûr'sĭ-bl), *adj.* capable of being submerged, or put under water:—*n.* a submarine.

sub-mer-sion (sŭb-mûr'shŭn), *n.* 1, the act of submerging or of causing to be overflowed; 2, the state of being submerged or of being overflowed.

sub-mis-sion (sŭb-mĭsh'ŭn), *n.* 1, the act of referring to the judgment or consideration of another; 2, the act of yielding to power or authority; obedience; 3, humility or meekness.

sub-mis-sive (sŭb-mĭs'ĭv), *adj.* 1, yielding to authority; obedient; as, a *submissive* child; 2, humble.—*adv.* **sub-mis'sive-ly.**—*n.* **sub-mis'sive-ness.**
Syn. compliant, docile, passive.—*Ant.* independent, disobedient, unyielding.

sub-mit (sŭb-mĭt'), *v.t.* [*p.t.* and *p.p.* -mit'-ted, *p.pr.* -mit'ting], 1, to yield to the authority or will of another; surrender; 2, to present for, or refer to, the judgment of another; as, to *submit* a question to others; 3, to offer as an opinion:—*v.i.* 1, to be obedient; 2, to yield or surrender.

sub-nor-mal (sŭb-nôr'măl), *adj.* below the normal or usual.

sub-or-der (sŭb"ôr'dẽr), *n.* in biology, the division in classification next above a family and below an order.

sub-or-di-nate (sŭb-ôr'dĭ-nȧt), *adj.* 1, lower in rank, value, power, or importance; 2, subject to another; 3, in grammar, designating the less important clause of a complex sentence, or the conjunction which introduces it; dependent:—*n.* one who is below another in rank, power, or the like:—*v.t.* (sŭb-ôr'dĭ-nāt), [*p.t.* and *p.p.* -nat"ed, *p.pr.* -nat"ing], 1, to place in a lower order; 2, to make subject or obedient to; subdue.—*adv.* **sub-or'di-nate-ly.**—*n.* **sub-or'di-nate-ness.**

sub-or-di-na-tion (sŭb-ôr"dĭ-nā'shŭn), *n.* 1, the act of placing in a lower rank or of treating as inferior; also, the state of being lower in rank, position, etc.; 2, subjection to one of higher rank or position; obedience or submission.

sub-orn (sŭb-ôrn'), *v.t.* 1, in law, to induce (another) to give false testimony; 2, to induce to do an evil act.—*n.* **sub-orn'er.**—*n.* **sub"or-na'tion.**

sub-pœ-na (sŭb-pē'nȧ), *n.* a written order commanding the attendance of a person in court, under a penalty for failure to obey:—*v.t.* to serve or summon with such a written order. Also, **sub-pe'na.**

sub-ro-gate (sŭb'rō-gāt), *v.t.* [*p.t.* and *p.p.* -gat"ed, *p.pr.* -gat"ing], to substitute (a person) in the place of another, esp. as a creditor.—*n.* **sub"ro-ga'tion.**

sub-scribe (sŭb-skrīb'), *v.t.* [*p.t.* and *p.p.* -scribed' (-skrībd'), *p.pr.* -scrib'ing], 1, to write or put (one's name) to a paper or document; 2, to give or promise (a sum of money) for some object, by writing one's name; 3, to give consent to; 4, to bear witness to by signing:—*v.i.* 1, to sign one's name to a letter or other document; 2, to give consent by signing something; hence, to agree; 3, to sign a paper in token of promise to give a certain sum, or to take and pay for something, as a book.—*n.* **sub-scrib'er.**

sub-scrip-tion (sŭb-skrĭp'shŭn), *n.* 1, the act of putting one's name to by way of agreement; 2, that which is agreed to; also, a signature; 3, a formal agreement entered into by signing one's name; 4, an order for a book or periodical; 5, an amount pledged by the signing of one's name.

sub-se-quent (sŭb'sē-kwĕnt), *adj.* 1, following, or coming after, in time or order; as, *subsequent* events; 2, following as a result.—*adv.* **sub'se-quent-ly.**—*n.* **sub'se-quence; sub'se-quen-cy.**

sub-serve (sŭb-sûrv'), *v.t.* [*p.t.* and *p.p.* -served' (-sûrvd'), *p.pr.* -serv'-ing], to serve; advance or promote; as, to *subserve* another's interests.

sub-ser-vi-ence (sŭb-sûr'vĭ-ĕns), *n.* 1, the quality or state of being subordinate; 2, fitness to promote some end; 3, servility. Also, **sub-ser'vi-en-cy.**

sub-ser-vi-ent (sŭb-sûr'vĭ-ĕnt), *adj.* 1, fitted to promote some end; being of service; 2, servile.—*adv.* **sub-ser'vi-ent-ly.**—*n.* **sub-ser'vi-ent-ness.**

sub-side (sŭb-sīd'), *v.i.* [*p.t.* and *p.p.* -sid'ed, *p.pr.* -sid'ing], 1, to sink or fall to the bottom; settle; 2, to sink to a lower level; as, the swollen river will *subside;* 3, to become quiet or calm; abate, as a storm.—*n.* **sub-sid'ence** (sŭb-sīd'ĕns; sŭb'sĭ-dĕns).

sub-sid-i-a-ry (sŭb-sĭd'ĭ-ā-rĭ), *adj.* 1, furnishing aid or help; supplementary; 2, of or pertaining to a subsidy or grant of money:—*n.* [*pl.* subsidiaries (-rĭz)], one that gives aid or supplies; a helper.

sub-si-dize (sŭb'sĭ-dīz), *v.t.* [*p.t.* and *p.p.* -dized (-dīzd), *p.pr.* -diz"ing], 1, to furnish with financial help; 2, to purchase the assistance of by money.

sub-si-dy (sŭb'sĭ-dĭ), *n.* [*pl.* subsidies (-dĭz)], 1, any gift made to aid another financially; money granted by one government to another for war purposes; 2, a government grant of money to aid a private enterprise which serves to benefit the public.

sub-sist (sŭb-sĭst'), *v.i.* 1, to remain in existence or keep a certain state; continue; 2, to exist or be; 3, to be supported; live:—*v.t.* to maintain; support, esp. with food and clothing.—*adj.* **sub-sist'ent.**

sub-sist-ence (sŭb-sĭs′tĕns), *n.* **1**, the act or state of existing; **2**, means of support, as food and clothing; maintenance; **3**, inherence in something else.

sub-soil (sŭb′soil″), *n.* the bed of earth and stones just beneath the surface soil:—*v.t.* to break up the under soil of.

sub-spe-cies (sŭb″spē′shēz; sŭb″spē′shĭ-ēz), *n.* [*pl.* subspecies], a group of animals or plants forming a subdivision of a species.

sub-stage (sŭb′stāj″), *n.* in a microscope, an attachment beneath the stage, or platform upon which rests the object to be examined, for holding reflectors, prisms, or other parts (see *microscope*, illus.).

sub-stance (sŭb′stăns), *n.* **1**, the real or essential part of anything; **2**, hence, the stuff, matter, or material of anything; **3**, the real meaning of a speech, writing, or action; as, give me the *substance* of his address; **4**, wealth; property; as, a man of *substance*.

sub-stan-tial (sŭb-stăn′shăl), *adj.* **1**, having real existence; actual; true; not imaginary; **2**, solid; strong; firm; as, a *substantial* building; *substantial* cloth; **3**, of real worth or considerable amount; valuable; as, a *substantial* gift to charity; **4**, wealthy; prosperous; **5**, real or true for the most part; as, *substantial* justice:—*n.* **1**, that which is real or material, or which is of value; **2**, a necessary part; an essential.—*adv.* **sub-stan′tial-ly.**—*n.* **sub-stan′tial-ness.**

sub-stan-ti-al-i-ty (sŭb-stăn″shĭ-ăl′ĭ-tĭ), *n.* [*pl.* substantialities (-tĭz)], the state or quality of being real or material, or of being strong or valuable.

sub-stan-ti-ate (sŭb-stăn′shĭ-āt), *v.t.* [*p.t.* and *p.p.* -at″ed, *p.pr.* -at″ing], to establish, as a claim or charge, by proof or evidence.—*n.* **sub-stan″ti-a′tion.**

Syn. confirm, ratify, sustain.

sub-stan-tive (sŭb′stăn-tĭv), *adj.* **1**, independent; existing independently and separately; as, France is a *substantive* state; **2**, real; permanent; substantial; **3**, in grammar: **a**, expressing existence; as, "to be" is the *substantive* verb; **b**, of the nature of, or used as, a noun; as, a *substantive* clause:—*n.* a noun, or group of words used as a noun.—*adv.* **sub′stan-tive-ly.**

sub-sti-tute (sŭb′stĭ-tūt), *n.* **1**, one who or that which is put in, or takes, the place of another; **2**, a man who, for a certain sum, enlists in the army to take the place of a drafted man:—*v.t.* [*p.t.* and *p.p.* -tut″ed, *p.pr.* -tut″ing], to put in the place of someone or something else; exchange.

sub-sti-tu-tion (sŭb″stĭ-tū′shŭn), *n.* **1**, the act of putting in the place of another; **2**, the state of being exchanged, or put in the place of another.

sub-stra-tum (sŭb-strā′tŭm), *n.* [*pl.* substrata (-tȧ); substratums (-tŭmz)], **1**, an under layer, as of soil or rock; **2**, hence, that which forms the groundwork or support of some other structure.

sub-sume (sŭb-sūm′), *v.t.* [*p.t.* and *p.p.* -sumed′ (-sūmd′), *p.pr.* -sum′ing], in logic, to include in some particular class, or under some particular rule; classify.—*n.* **sub-sump′tion.**—*adj.* **sub-sump′tive.**

sub-tend (sŭb-tĕnd′), *v.t.* to lie opposite to; as, the hypotenuse of a right triangle *subtends* the right angle.

sub-ter-fuge (sŭb′tẽr-fūj), *n.* anything, as a trick, pretext, or evasion, by which one seeks to escape from a difficulty; a false excuse.

sub-ter-ra-ne-an (sŭb″tĕr-ā′nē-ăn), *adj.* **1**, below the surface of the earth, as a cave; **2**, hence, hidden; secret. Also, **sub″ter-ra′ne-ous.**

sub-tile (sŭb′tĭl; sŭt′l), *adj.* *Rare* or *Archaic*, subtle.—*adv.* **sub′tile-ly.**—*n.* **sub′tile-ness.**

sub-ti-tle (sŭb″tī′tl), *n.* a secondary, usually explanatory, title; sometimes, a main title repeated in a secondary place.

sub-tle (sŭt′l), *adj.* **1**, thin; delicately formed; fine, as a spider's web; **2**, artful; crafty; cunning; as, a *subtle* scheme; **3**, keen; nicely discriminating; as, a *subtle* mind; **4**, delicate; elusive; as, a *subtle* odor; **5**, clever; ingeniously devised or wrought; **6**, intricate; hard to follow; as, *subtle* reasoning; **7**, skilful; clever or handy, as a workman.—*n.* **sub′tle-ness.**—*adv.* **sub′tly.**

Syn. clever, handy. (See wily.)

sub-tle-ty (sŭt′l-tĭ), *n.* [*pl.* subtleties (-tĭz)], **1**, keenness of mind; **2**, cunning; artifice; **3**, elusiveness; **4**, obscurity of meaning.

sub-tract (sŭb-trăkt′), *v.t.* to withdraw or take away, as a part from a whole; as, to *subtract* five from ten.—*n.* **sub-tract′er.**—*adj.* **sub-trac′tive.**

sub-trac-tion (sŭb-trăk′shŭn), *n.* the act or process of taking away, as a part from a whole.

sub-tra-hend (sŭb′trȧ-hĕnd″), *n.* the quantity or number to be taken from another.

sub-trop-i-cal (sŭb-trŏp′ĭ-kăl), *adj.* of or pertaining to the regions bordering the tropical zone; as, *subtropical* plants. Also, **sub-trop′ic.**—*n.pl.* **sub-trop′ics.**

sub-urb (sŭb′ûrb), *n.* an outlying district of a city or town; outer part; as, the *suburbs* of New York.

sub-ur-ban (sŭb-ûr′băn), *adj.* pertaining to, in, or living within, the outlying districts of a city or town; as, *suburban* residents.

sub-vene (sŭb-vēn′), *v.i.* [*p.t.* and *p.p.* -vened′ (-vēnd′), *p.pr.* -ven′ing], to come as an aid; occur so as to help, esp. by preventing something.

sub-ven-tion (sŭb-vĕn′shŭn), *n.* **1**, the coming to the help of someone; support; assistance; **2**, a grant, as of money, from a government: used esp. of literary or scientific grants.

sub-ver-sion (sŭb-vûr′shŭn), *n.* the act of overturning; overthrow, as of a government.—*adj.* **sub-ver′sive.**

sub-vert (sŭb-vûrt′), *v.t.* to turn upside down; overthrow or ruin completely; as, to *subvert* a government.—*n.* **sub-vert′er.**—*adj.* **sub-vert′i-ble.**

sub-way (sŭb′wā″), *n.* an underground passage, used for a railway or other purpose.

suc- (sŭk-), *prefix*, under or below: used in Latin compounds of *sub-* with words beginning with *c*; as, *suc*ceed. See **sub-.**

suc-ceed (sŭk-sēd′), *v.t.* **1**, to take the place of; **2**, to follow:—*v.i.* **1**, to come next in the possession of anything: with *to;* as, to *succeed* to a throne; **2**, to accomplish something attempted; as, he *succeeded* in whatever he did; **3**, to meet with success; as, all his plans *succeed*.—*n.* **suc-ceed′er.**

Syn. (see follow).

suc-cess (sŭk-sĕs′), *n.* **1**, a favorable end or result of any undertaking; **2**, *Colloq.*, a person or thing that prospers or turns out well; as, the book was a *success*.

suc-cess-ful (sŭk-sĕs′fo͝ol), *adj.* resulting in the attainment of what is desired or intended; doing what is proposed; prosperous; fortunate.—*adv.* **suc-cess′ful-ly.**—*n.* **suc-cess′ful-ness.**

suc-ces-sion (sŭk-sĕsh′ŭn), *n.* **1**, a following in order; a series of persons or things following in order, as letters or kings; **2**, the act or right of coming into the place, office, duty, possessions, or rights of another; **3**, esp., the act or right of succeeding to a throne; **4**, a series of descendants.—*adj.* **suc-ces′sion-al.**—*adv.* **suc-ces′sion-al-ly.**

suc-ces-sive (sŭk-sĕs′ĭv), *adj.* following in a series without omission, or in regular order; consecutive.—*adv.* **suc-ces′sive-ly.**—*n.* **suc-ces′sive-ness.**

suc-ces-sor (sŭk-sĕs′ẽr), *n.* one who follows, or takes the place of, another, as in office: opp. of *predecessor.*

suc-cinct (sŭk-sĭngkt′), *adj.* clear but briefly expressed; concise; terse.—*adv.* **suc-cinct′ly.**—*n.* **suc-cinct′ness.**

suc-cor (sŭk′ẽr), *v.t.* to help or relieve when in difficulty or distress; aid:—*n.* **1**, relief; aid; help; **2**, one who or that which brings help. Also, **suc′cour.**

Syn., v. assist, sustain. (See help.)

suc-co-tash (sŭk′ō-tăsh), *n.* green corn and beans boiled together.

suc-cu-lent (sŭk′ū-lĕnt), *adj.* juicy: said of fruit, plants, etc.—*n.* **suc′cu-lence; suc′cu-len-cy.**

suc-cumb (sŭ-kŭm′), *v.i.* to yield; submit, as to a disease.

such (sŭch), *adj.* **1**, of that, or the like, kind; as, pens, pencils, and *such* things; **2**, having the particular quality or character named; of the class; as, avoid *such* things; **3**, the same as previously mentioned or referred to; not different; as, I have described the house; *such* it remained for a century; **4**, indicating a certain person or thing: used instead of a specific term; as, on *such* a date: sometimes *such and such* or *such or such;* as, he inquired where *such and such* men lived; **5**, the same: used correlatively with *as;* as, this flour is *such* as I have always used:—*adv.* so; in so great degree: used for special emphasis; as, *such* a weak rope that it broke:—*pron.*, used as *sing.* or *pl.*, such a person or thing; as, I may have offended him, but *such* was not my intention.

suck (sŭk), *v.t.* **1**, to draw in (a liquid) with the mouth; **2**, to draw a liquid from with the mouth; **3**, to drink in or absorb; as, a sponge *sucks* up water; **4**, to draw in; engulf, as does a quicksand:—*v.i.* **1**, to draw milk from the breast or udder; **2**, to draw air instead of water, as does a pump:—*n.* **1**, the act of drawing into the mouth, or of absorbing or engulfing; **2**, that which is drawn into the mouth; **3**, *Colloq.*, a taste; sip.

suck-er (sŭk′ẽr), *n.* **1**, one that sucks, or draws in with the mouth, as a young pig or whale; **2**, a sprout of a plant from the roots or from the lower part of the stem; **3**, any of certain fishes with thick lips for sucking in food; **4**, a special organ of some animals by which they can stick to other bodies.

suck-le (sŭk′l), *v.t.* and *v.i.* [*p.t.* and *p.p.* -led (-ld), *p.pr.* -ling], to nurse at the breast; give suck (to).

suck-ling (sŭk′lĭng), *n.* an unweaned child or animal.

su-cre (so͞o′krā), *n.* the monetary unit of Ecuador, equivalent to 34 cents.

suc-tion (sŭk′shŭn), *n.* **1**, the act or process of drawing a fluid into an empty space by removing the air; **2**, the sticking together of bodies due to the pressure of the air: **suction pump**, a common type of pump, in which the liquid is sucked (that is, forced by atmospheric pressure when a partial vacuum is made) into the chamber beneath the rising piston, and, being prevented on the return stroke from flowing back by a valve, flows through a valve in the piston: distinguished from *force pump* (see *pump*, illus.).

suc-to-ri-al (sŭk-tō′rĭ-ăl), *adj.* adapted for, or capable of, sucking.

Su-da-nese (so͞o″dȧ-nēz; -nēs′), *n.* [*pl.* Sudanese], an inhabitant or native of the Sudan, a region south of the Sahara in Africa:—*adj.* pertaining to the Sudan. Also, **Sou″da-nese′.**

su-da-to-ry (sū′dȧ-tō″rĭ), *adj.* causing perspiration or sweat; as, a *sudatory* bath:—*n.* [*pl.* sudatories (-rĭz)], anything that causes sweating; a sweating bath.

sudd (sŭd), *n.* a mass of water plants, tree limbs, and decayed vegetation floating on the surface of the Upper Nile.

sud-den (sŭd′n; sŭd′ĕn), *adj.* **1**, happening unexpectedly; as, a *sudden* death; **2**, quickly done; hasty; as, a *sudden* change.—*adv.* **sud′den-ly.**—*n.* **sud′den-ness.**

Su-de-ten (so͞o-dā′tĕn), *n.* [*pl.* -tens or -ten], a German resident of Bohemia living near the German boundary.

su-dor-if-er-ous (sū″dŏr-ĭf′ẽr-ŭs), *adj.* secreting or producing sweat; as, *sudoriferous* glands.

su-dor-if-ic (sū″dŏr-ĭf′ĭk), *adj.* causing sweat:—*n.* a medicine producing such an effect.

suds (sŭdz), *n.pl.* soapy water; also, the froth or bubbles on it.—*adj.* **suds′y.**

sue (sū), *v.t.* [*p.t.* and *p.p.* sued (sūd), *p.pr.* su′ing], to seek justice from (a court) through legal proceedings; also, to start action in law against (a person); prosecute; as, to *sue* a man for debt:—*v.i.* **1**, to entreat, beg, or petition: with *for;* as, to *sue* for peace; **2**, to pay court; as, to *sue* for her hand; **3**, to begin a lawsuit; as, to *sue* for damages.

suède (swād; *Fr.* swâd), *n.* undressed kid, used for gloves, shoes, etc.:—*adj.* made of undressed kid.

su-et (sū′ĕt), *n.* the hard fat around the kidneys and loins of mutton and beef: used for cooking and for making tallow.

suf- (sŭf-), *prefix*, under, a form of *sub-* used before *f;* as, *suf*fuse. See **sub-.**

suf-fer (sŭf′ẽr), *v.t.* **1**, to feel with pain; undergo; bear; as, to *suffer* a wrong; **2**, to feel or endure; as, to *suffer* pain; **3**, to be affected by; experience; undergo; as, his manners *suffered* a change for the better; **4**, to permit; as, he *suffered* his horse to rest:—*v.i.* **1**, to feel pain, distress, loss, etc.; **2**, to endure loss or injury.—*n.* **suf′fer-er.**

Syn. support, allow. (See [2]bear.)

suf-fer-a-ble (sŭf′ẽr-ȧ-bl), *adj.* tolerable; endurable; allowable.

suf-fer-ance (sŭf′ẽr-ăns), *n.* **1**, *Archaic*, patience under pain; endurance; **2**, toleration; permission; leave.

suf-fer-ing (sŭf′ẽr-ĭng), *n.* **1**, the bearing of physical or mental pain; **2**, the pain borne; the loss or injury endured.

suf-fice (sŭ-fīs′; sŭ-fīz′), *v.i.* [*p.t.* and *p.p.* -ficed′ (-fīst′; -fīzd′), *p.pr.* -fic′ing], to be enough or sufficient:—*v.t.* to satisfy.

Syn. content, gratify. (See satisfy.)

suf-fi-cien-cy (sŭ-fĭsh′ĕn-sĭ), *n.* **1**, the state or quality of being sufficient or enough; **2**, skill or ability; **3**, enough substance or means; supply equal to wants; **4**, self-confidence; conceit.

suf-fi-cient (sŭ-fĭsh′ĕnt), *adj.* equal to any end or purpose; equal to the need; enough.—*adv.* **suf-fi′cient-ly.**

suf-fix (sŭf′ĭks), *n.* a letter or letters, syllable or syllables, added to the end of a word or root to modify the meaning; as, *-ant* is the *suffix* in defend*ant:*—*v.t.* (sŭ-fĭks′), to add, as a letter or syllable, to the end of a word to modify its meaning.

suf-fo-cate (sŭf′ō-kāt), *v.t.* [*p.t.* and *p.p.* -cat″ed, *p.pr.* -cat″ing], **1**, to kill by stopping the breath; smother; stifle; **2**, to extinguish; as, to *suffocate* a fire:—*v.i.* to be choked or stifled.—*adj.* **suf′fo-ca-tive.**

suf-fo-ca-tion (sŭf″ō-kā′shŭn), *n.* **1**, the act of choking, or stopping the breath; **2**, the state of being choked or stifled; **3**, death due to smothering.

suf-fra-gan (sŭf′rȧ-găn), *n.* an assistant bishop:—*adj.* **1**, assisting; assistant; auxiliary; **2**, of or pertaining to an assistant bishop.

suf-frage (sŭf′rāj), *n.* **1**, a vote upon a measure or candidate; hence, approval or assent; **2**, the right or act of voting, esp. in political matters.

suf-fra-gette (sŭf″rā-jĕt′), *n. Colloq.*, a woman who believes in, and works for, the right of women to vote.

suf-fra-gist (sŭf′rā-jĭst), *n.* **1**, a voter; **2**, one interested in some special cause of suffrage, esp. one who favors voting by women.

suf-fuse (sŭ-fūz′), *v.t.* [*p.t.* and *p.p.* -fused′ (-fūzd′), *p.pr.* -fus′ing], to overspread, as does a fluid or a color; as, tears *suffused* her eyes.

suf-fu-sion (sŭ-fū′zhŭn), *n.* **1**, the act of spreading, as color over the cheeks, or the state of being overspread; **2**, that which spreads over a surface.

sug-ar (shŏŏg′ẽr), *n.* **1**, a sweet crystalline substance obtained from sugar cane, sugar beets, etc.; **2**, any sweet substance like sugar, as glucose; **3**, *Colloq.*, flattering words: **sugar of lead**, a crystalline salt used in medicine: **sugar of milk**, a white crystalline powder with a sweetish taste, used in infants' food:—*adj.* like, made of, or yielding, sugar:—*v.t.* **1**, to sprinkle or cover with sugar; **2**, to make less disagreeable by flattery:—*v.i.* to become like sugar; as, sirup *sugars* if boiled too long.

sug-ar beet a variety of the common garden beet, with large, white roots from which sugar is obtained.

sug-ar cane a tall, jointed, maizelike grass growing in tropical and subtropical regions, and having a sap from which sugar is obtained.

sug-ar loaf **1**, a cone-shaped loaf or mass of hard, refined sugar; **2**, something resembling such a mass in shape, as a conical hat or hill: **sugar-loaf**, *adj.* similar in shape to a sugar loaf; conical.

sug-ar ma-ple the hard maple of the eastern U. S., from the sap of which maple sugar is made.

sug-ar-plum (shŏŏg′ẽr-plŭm″), *n.* **1**, a bonbon; sweetmeat; **2**, anything pleasant; flattery.

sug-ar-y (shŏŏg′ẽr-ĭ), *adj.* **1**, like, made of, or containing, sugar; sweet; also, granular; **2**, flattering; **3**, fond of sweets.

sug-gest (sŭg-jĕst′), *v.t.* **1**, to present or introduce indirectly to the mind or thoughts; hint; **2**, to propose, as a plan, for another's acceptance or rejection:—*v.i.* to give rise to thoughts.—*n.* **sug-gest′er.**

sug-ges-tion (sŭg-jĕs′chŭn), *n.* **1**, the act of presenting an idea indirectly to the mind; also, a hint so presented; **2**, the act of proposing something; also, the thing proposed; **3**, the mental process by which one idea brings to mind another idea.

sug-ges-tive (sŭg-jĕs′tĭv), *adj.* **1**, tending to excite thought; as, a *suggestive* criticism; **2**, tending to bring into the mind what is improper.—*adv.* **sug-ges′tive-ly.**—*n.* **sug-ges′tive-ness.**

su-i-cid-al (sū′ĭ-sīd″ăl), *adj.* **1**, pertaining to, or suggestive of, suicide; **2**, fatal to one's own interests; as, *suicidal* plans.—*adv.* **su′i-cid″al-ly.**

su-i-cide (sū′ĭ-sīd), *n.* **1**, the act of intentionally taking one's own life; **2**, a person who kills himself intentionally; **3**, ruin of one's own interests.

suit (sūt), *n.* **1**, the act of seeking favor or justice; the process by which one tries to gain an end; petition or prayer; **2**, courtship; **3**, an action or process at law for the protection or recovery of a right or claim; **4**, a number of things used together; as, a *suit* of clothes; **5**, things that follow in a series or succession, making a set; as, a *suit* (or suite) of rooms; **6**, any of the four sets of thirteen cards each, which together make up a deck:—*v.t.* **1**, to fit; adapt; as, *suit* your words to the occasion; **2**, to be proper or suitable to; become; befit; as, puns do not *suit* your position; **3**, to please; satisfy; as, this hat *suits* me:—*v.i.* **1**, to correspond or accord; agree: with *with* or *to*; **2**, to please.

suit-a-ble (sūt′ȧ-bl), *adj.* fitting; becoming; appropriate.—*n.* **suit′a-ble-ness.**—*adv.* **suit′a-bly.**—*n.* **suit″a-bil′i-ty.**
Syn. accordant, adequate.—*Ant.* unfit, unbecoming, inappropriate.

suit-case (sūt′kās″), *n.* a flat, rectangular hand bag, usually of stiffened leather. Also, **suit case.**

suite (swēt), *n.* **1**, a company of attendants or servants; as, a king and his *suite;* **2**, a series or set, as of rooms; **3**, in music: **a**, a set of dances written in the same or related keys: popular in the 17th and 18th centuries; **b**, a modern form of instrumental composition, usually of less scope than a symphony.

suit-or (sūt′ẽr), *n.* **1**, one who sues or entreats; **2**, a man who seeks to marry a woman; **3**, a party to a lawsuit.

sul-fa (sŭl′fȧ), *adj.* designating, or pertaining to, certain compounds of sulphur and ammonia, as sulfanilamide, sulfathiazole, etc., used in medicine.

sulk (sŭlk), *v.i.* to be sullen or silently obstinate:—*n.*, often in *pl.*, a sullen mood or humor.

sulk-y (sŭl′kĭ), *adj.* [*comp.* sulk′i-er, *superl.* sulk′i-est], moody; sullen; unsociable:—*n.* [*pl.* sulkies (-kĭz)], a light, two-wheeled vehicle, seating but one person.—*adv.* **sulk′i-ly.**—*n.* **sulk′i-ness.**

RACING SULKY

sul-len (sŭl′ĕn), *adj.* **1**, morose; sulky; gloomy; unsociable; as, a *sullen* disposition; **2**, dismal; heavy; gloomy; as, a *sullen* sky; **3**, dull; slow; as, a *sullen* current.—*adv.* **sul′len-ly.**—*n.* **sul′len-ness.**
Syn. surly, morose, sulky, grim.

sul-ly (sŭl′ĭ), *v.t.* [*p.t.* and *p.p.* -lied (-lĭd), *p.pr.* -ly-ing], **1**, to tarnish or soil; dirty or stain; as, to *sully* a mirror; **2**, hence, to lessen in purity or reputation; as, to *sully* one's fame:—*v.i.* to become tarnished or soiled:—*n.* soil; stain; disgrace.

sul-phate (sŭl′fāt), *n.* a salt of sulphuric acid, used in medicine and chemistry. Also, **sul′fate.**

sul-phide (sŭl′fīd; sŭl′fĭd), *n.* a compound of sulphur with another element. Also, **sul′fide; sul′phid; sul′fid.**

sul-phite (sŭl′fīt), *n.* any of several salts of sulphurous acid: used for commercial purposes. Also, **sul′fite.**

sul-phur (sŭl′fẽr), *n.* **1**, a yellow, brittle, crystalline element found in various parts of the world: used in the manufacture of gunpowder and matches, as a disinfectant, in medicine, etc.; **2**, a pale, greenish yellow color. Also, **sul′fur.**—*adj.* **sul′phur-y.**

sul-phu-rate (sŭl′fū-rāt), *v.t.* [*p.t.* and *p.p.* -rat″ed, *p.pr.* -rat″ing], **1**, to treat or combine with sulphur; **2**, to subject to the action of sulphur:—*adj.* (sŭl′fū-rāt), mixed with, consisting of, or like, sulphur. Also, **sul′fu-rate.**—*n.* **sul″phu-ra′tion.**

sul-phur–bot-tom (sŭl′fūr=bŏt″ŭm), *n.* a species of finback whale, the largest of all the whales, sometimes 85 feet long: found in the North Atlantic.

sul-phu-re-ous (sŭl-fū′rē-ŭs), *adj.* consisting of, saturated with, or having the qualities of, sulphur. Also, **sul-fu′re-ous.**

sul-phu-ret (sŭl′fū-rĕt), *n.* a compound of sulphur with another element: now called *sulphide.* Also, **sul′fu-ret.**

sul-phu-ric (sŭl-fū′rĭk), *adj.* of, pertaining to, or obtained from, sulphur: **sulphuric acid,** a dense, oily, colorless, highly acid liquid, prepared in several strengths for commercial use, and extensively used in manufacturing processes: commercially known as *oil of vitriol.* Also, **sul-fu′ric.**

sul-phur-ous (sŭl′fūr-ŭs; sŭl-fū′rŭs), *adj.* **1**, of, pertaining to, or containing, sulphur; **2**, hence, fiery; heated: **sulphurous acid,** an acid formed by the solution of sulphur dioxide in water, forming a series of salts called *sulphites.* Also, **sul′fur-ous.**

sul-tan (sŭl′tăn; so͞ol-tän′), *n.* a Mohammedan ruler: **Sultan,** formerly, the emperor of Turkey.—*n.* **sul′tan-ship″.**

sul-ta-na (sŭl-tä′nȧ; sŭl-tā′nȧ), *n.* **1**, the wife, or often the daughter, mother, or sister, of a sultan; **2**, a kind of seedless raisin grown in and near Smyrna.

sul-tan-ate (sŭl′tăn-āt), *n.* the authority or territory of a sultan.

sul-try (sŭl′trĭ), *adj.* [*comp.* sul′tri-er, *superl.* sul′tri-est], **1**, giving out oppressive heat; burning; as, a *sultry* sun; **2**, very hot, close, moist, and oppressive; as, a *sultry* day.—*adv.* **sul′tri-ly.**—*n.* **sul′tri-ness.**

sum (sŭm), *n.* **1**, the total of two or more things; the whole; all; **2**, a quantity, as of money; **3**, summary; substance; as, the *sum* of the evidence; **4**, utmost degree; highest point; hence, fulfilment; as, the *sum* of happiness; **5**, in arithmetic, a problem:—*v.t.* [*p.t.* and *p.p.* summed (sŭmd), *p.pr.* sum′ming], **1**, to add into one amount: usually with *up;* **2**, to condense into few words: usually with *up;* as, to *sum* up a case:—*v.i.* to make a brief restatement of all the facts: usually with *up;* as, and now, let us *sum* up.

su-mac (sū′măk; sho͞o′măk), *n.* **1**, any of a genus of plants of the cashew family, of which some species produce a severe skin rash; **2**, the dried leaves and roots of certain species, used in tanning and dyeing.

sum-ma-rize (sŭm′ȧ-rīz), *v.t.* [*p.t.* and *p.p.* -rized (-rīzd), *p.pr.* -riz″ing], to state briefly or concisely; sum up.

sum-ma-ry (sŭm′ȧ-rĭ), *n.* [*pl.* summaries (-rĭz)], a brief account containing the sum or substance of a fuller account; an abridgment; as, a *summary* of a law case:—*adj.* **1**, giving the general idea; brief; concise; **2**, quickly performed; as, the crime deserves *summary* punishment.—*adv.* **sum′ma-ri-ly.**—*n.* **sum′ma-ri-ness.**

sum-ma-tion (sŭm-ā′shŭn), *n.* **1**, the act of adding, or finding a total amount; **2**, that which is added up.

[1]**sum-mer** (sŭm′ẽr), *n.* **1**, the hottest season of the year, varying with the climate: in the Northern Hemisphere, June 21 to September 21; **2**, *Poetic:* **a**, a year of life; as, a maid of three *summers;* **b**, a happy and prosperous period:—*v.i.* to pass or spend the summer; as, to *summer* at the shore:—*v.t.* to care for during the summer:—*adj.* of, pertaining to, or happening in, the summer season.—*adj.* **sum′mer-y.**

[2]**sum-mer** (sŭm′ẽr), *n.* **1**, the stone of a column which supports an arch or lintel; **2**, formerly, a horizontal beam supporting the floor joists: now called *girder.*

sum-mer-house (sŭm′ẽr-hous″), *n.* a small, rustic, open building in a garden or park.

sum-mit (sŭm′ĭt), *n.* **1**, the top or highest point, as of a mountain; **2**, the highest degree; as, the *summit* of one's hopes.

sum-mon (sŭm′ŭn), *v.t.* **1**, to call by authority; command to appear, as in court; **2**, to send for; invite; **3**, to rouse to exertion; as, to *summon* all one's strength.

sum-mons (sŭm′ŭnz), *n.* [*pl.* summonses (-ŭn-zĕz)], **1**, an order or notice to appear in court on a certain day; **2**, a paper or document containing such a notice.

sump-ter (sŭmp′tẽr), *n.* an animal, usually a horse or mule, for carrying packs or burdens.

sump-tu-a-ry (sŭmp′tū-ā-rĭ), *adj.* pertaining to, or regulating, expenses, or the spending of money: **sumptuary laws,** formerly, laws to limit the amount of money spent on dress or other luxuries, and to regulate prices, wages, etc.

sump-tu-ous (sŭmp′tū-ŭs), *adj.* **1**, expensive; costly; **2**, hence, luxurious; magnificent; as, a *sumptuous* feast.—*adv.* **sump′tu-ous-ly.**—*n.* **sump′tu-ous-ness.**

sun (sŭn), *n.* **1**, the central body of the solar system, round which the earth and other planets revolve (see *solar system,* illus.); **2**, a heavenly body like our sun, that is the center of a system of planets; **3**, anything like the sun in brightness or as a source of warmth, animation, etc.; **4**, sunshine; hence, a day:—*v.t.* [*p.t.* and *p.p.* sunned (sŭnd), *p.pr.* sun′ning] to expose to the sun's rays; as, to *sun* oneself.

sun-beam (sŭn′bēm″), *n.* a ray of sunlight.

sun-bon-net (sŭn′bŏn″ĕt), *n.* a bonnet of light material, having a projecting brim for protection from the sun.

sun-burn (sŭn′bûrn″), *n.* an inflammation of the skin caused by exposure to the sun:—*v.t.* and *v.i.* to discolor by the sun.

Sun-day (sŭn′dā), *n.* the first day of the week; the Christian Sabbath, or Lord's Day:—*adj.* pertaining to, or happening on, Sunday; as, a *Sunday* school.—*abbr.* **Sun.**

sun-der (sŭn′dẽr), *v.t.* to divide or rend break; separate:—*v.i.* to become separated or broken apart:—*n.* separation into parts: used chiefly in the phrase *in sunder.*

sun-dew (sŭn′dū″), *n.* any of a genus of bog plants, whose leaves secrete a dewlike sticky fluid by which they capture small insects for food.

sun-di-al (sŭn′dī″ăl), *n.* a device to show the time of day by the shadow of a pointer, usually called a style or gnomon, on a dial or diagram.

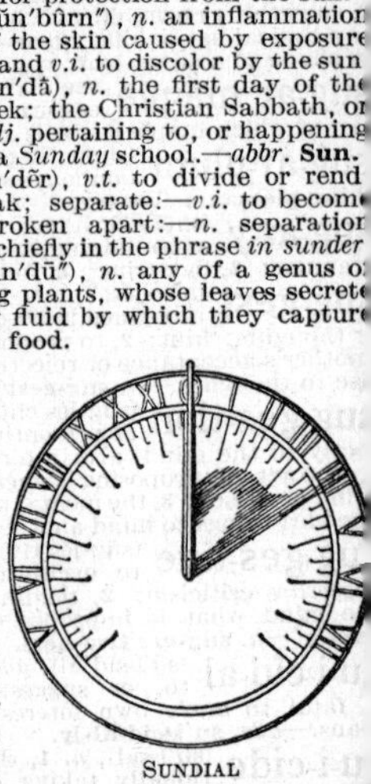

SUNDIAL

sun dog **1**, a mock sun, or parhelion, a bright spot of light near the sun, sometimes colored, caused by refraction; **2**, a small or fragmentar rainbow near the horizon. Also, *n.* **sun′dog′**

sun-down (sŭn′doun″), *n.* **1,** sunset; **2,** the time of sunset.

sun-dry (sŭn′drĭ), *adj.* various; several; as, *sundry* reasons: **sundries,** *n.pl.* various articles or matters too small or numerous to be mentioned separately.

sun-fish (sŭn′fĭsh″), *n.* **1,** a stubby, almost tailless fish, one of the largest of all fishes, found in most warm seas; **2,** any of various small, American fresh-water fishes resembling the perch.

sun-flow-er (sŭn′flou″ẽr), *n.* any of various plants of the composite family, esp. the tall, straight-stemmed garden species, having large leaves and round, flat heads with yellow ray flowers.

sung (sŭng), past participle and archaic past tense of the verb *sing.*

sunk (sŭngk), past tense and past participle of the irregular verb *sink.*

sunk-en (sŭngk′n), *adj.* **1,** lying beneath the surface, esp. on the bottom of the sea or other body of water; **2,** fallen or pressed down; on a lower level or pitch; as, *sunken* gardens; **3,** hollow; as, *sunken* eyes.

sun-less (sŭn′lĕs), *adj.* **1,** without light and heat from the sun; **2,** dark; cheerless.—*adv.* **sun′less-ly.**—*n.* **sun′less-ness.**

sun-light (sŭn′līt″), *n.* the light of the sun.

sunn (sŭn), *n.* **1,** an East Indian plant, the fiber of which is used as a substitute for hemp; **2,** the fiber of this plant.

sun-ny (sŭn′ĭ), *adj.* [*comp.* sun′ni-er, *superl.* sun′ni-est], **1,** pertaining to, or like, the sun; cheerful; as, a *sunny* disposition; **2,** filled with, or exposed to, the warmth and light of the sun; as, the *sunny* side of the street.—*adv.* **sun′ni-ly.**—*n.* **sun′ni-ness.**

sun-rise (sŭn′rīz″), *n.* **1,** the daily appearance of the sun above the horizon; **2,** the brightening of the sky at that time; **3,** the time at which the sun appears; **4,** the east; the region where the sun rises.

sun-set (sŭn′sĕt″), *n.* **1,** the disappearance of the sun below the horizon; **2,** the brightness of the sky at that time; **3,** the time at which the sun disappears; **4,** the west.

sun-shade (sŭn′shād″), *n.* **1,** anything used as a protection from the light or heat of the sun, as an awning; **2,** a parasol or sun umbrella.

sun-shine (sŭn′shīn″), *n.* **1,** the light or rays of the sun; also, the place where they fall; **2,** warmth.—*adj.* **sun′shin″y.**

sun spot one of the dark, irregular patches or spots visible on the sun's disk. Also, *n.* **sun′spot″.**

sun-stroke (sŭn′strōk″), *n.* a prostration, often fatal, due to exposure to the sun or to other intense heat.

sun-ward (sŭn′wẽrd), *adj.* facing, or looking toward, the sun:—*adv.* toward the sun. Also, *adv.* **sun′wards.**

sup (sŭp), *v.t.* [*p.t.* and *p.p.* supped (sŭpt), *p.pr.* sup′ping], to take into the mouth little at a time, with the lips or in spoonfuls; sip:—*v.i.* **1,** to take the evening meal, or supper; **2,** to sip:—*n.* a small mouthful of liquid.

su-per- (sū′pẽr-), *prefix,* over; beyond; above; in excess: used: **1,** in reference to place, to give the idea of above, over, on; as, *super*position; **2,** in reference to rank, authority, etc., to give the idea of above, over, superior to; as, *super*intendent; **3,** in reference to degree, to give the idea of beyond, in addition to, more than, in excess of; as, *super*man; **4,** in reference to quantity or amount, to give the idea of unusually large, a great quantity; as, *super*abundance.

su-per-a-bound (sū″pẽr-*ȧ*-bound′), *v.i.* to be unusually abundant; be much greater than is sufficient.

su-per-a-bun-dance (sū″pẽr-*ȧ*-bŭn′dăns), *n.* an amount much greater than is sufficient; excess; surplus.—*adj.* **su″per-a-bun′dant.**—*adv.* **su″per-a-bun′dant-ly.**

su-per-add (sū″pẽr-ăd′), *v.t.* to add over and above something else.

su-per-an-nu-ate (sū″pẽr-ăn′ū-āt), *v.i.* [*p.t.* and *p.p.* -at″ed, *p.pr.* -at″ing], **1,** to impair or render unfit by age; **2,** to retire or pension on account of old age or weakness, as a teacher.

su-per-an-nu-a-tion (sū″pẽr-ăn″ū-ā′shŭn), *n.* **1,** disqualification for service on account of old age, infirmity, or arrival at a certain age; **2,** discharge from service with a pension granted because of long service, old age, or infirmity.

su-perb (sū-pûrb′), *adj.* **1,** grand; proud; stately; as, a *superb* residence; **2,** rich; elegant; as, *superb* attire.—*adv.* **su-perb′ly.**—*n.* **su-perb′ness.**

su-per-car-go (sū″pẽr-kär′gō), *n.* [*pl.* supercargoes (-gōz)], an officer of a merchant ship who has charge of its cargo and business affairs during the voyage.

su-per-cil-i-ous (sū″pẽr-sĭl′ĭ-ŭs), *adj.* contemptuously haughty; proud; overbearing; as, a *supercilious* air or manner.—*adv.* **su″per-cil′i-ous-ly.**—*n.* **su″per-cil′i-ous-ness.**

su-per-er-o-ga-tion (sū″pẽr-ẽr″ō-gā′shŭn), *n.* the performance of more than is required by duty.

su-per-e-rog-a-to-ry (sū″pẽr-ĕ-rŏg′*ȧ*-tō-rĭ), *adj.* **1,** performed beyond what is required by duty; **2,** hence, superfluous.

su-per-fi-cial (sū″pẽr-fĭsh′ăl), *adj.* **1,** pertaining to, or being on, the surface; not deep; shallow; **2,** reaching or understanding only what is apparent or on the surface; lacking depth of understanding or wisdom; as, a *superficial* mind.—*adv.* **su″per-fi′cial-ly.**—*n.* **su″per-fi′cial-ness.**

su-per-fi-ci-al-i-ty (sū″pẽr-fĭsh″ĭ-ăl′ĭ-tĭ), *n.* [*pl.* superficialities (-tĭz)], **1,** the state or quality of being shallow, or on the surface only; shallowness; **2,** that which is shallow.

su-per-fi-ci-es (sū″pẽr-fĭsh′ĭ-ēz; -fĭsh′ēz) *n.* the surface, or outside part, of anything; exterior.

su-per-fine (sū′pẽr-fīn), *adj.* **1,** of the very choicest quality; very fine or good; **2,** very subtle.—*n.* **su″per-fine′ness.**

su-per-flu-i-ty (sū″pẽr-flōō′ĭ-tĭ), *n.* [*pl.* superfluities (-tĭz)], **1,** the state of being more than is needed or wanted; **2,** something beyond what is needed or wanted.

su-per-flu-ous (sū-pûr′flōō-ŭs), *adj.* being more than is needed or wanted; excessive; needless.—*adv.* **su-per′flu-ous-ly.**—*n.* **su-per′flu-ous-ness.**

su-per-heat (sū″pẽr-hēt′), *v.t.* **1,** to heat to an extreme degree; **2,** to heat (steam) until it resembles a perfect gas.

su-per-heat-er (sū″pẽr-hēt′ẽr), *n.* a device in a steam engin for heating the steam to a higher temperature than it would maintain while in contact with the boiling water (see *locomotive,* illus.).

su-per-het-er-o-dyne (sū″pẽr-hĕt′ẽr-ō-dīn), *n.* a type of radio receiving apparatus involving the production of a beat note of frequency above the limits of perception by the ear.

su-per-hu-man (sū″pẽr-hū′măn), *adj.* **1,** above or beyond what is human, or like the nature of man; **2,** miraculous.—*adv.* **su″per-hu′man-ly.**

su-per-im-pose (sū″pẽr-ĭm-pōz′), *v.t.* [*p.t.* and *p.p.* -posed′

(-pōzd′), *p.pr.* -pos′ing], to lay (something) on something else.—*n.* **su″per-im″po-si′tion.**

su-per-in-cum-bent (sōō″pẽr-ĭn-kŭm′bĕnt), *adj.* lying or resting on something else.—*n.* **su″per-in-cum′bence; su″per-in-cum′ben-cy.**

su-per-in-duce (sōō″pẽr-ĭn′dūs′), *v.t.* [*p.t.* and *p.p.* -duced′ (-dūst′), *p.pr.* -duc′ing], to bring in, as an addition to something else; give rise to in addition to something else.—*n.* **su″per-in-duc′tion.**

su-per-in-tend (sōō″pẽr-ĭn-tĕnd′), *v.t.* to have, or exercise, the charge or oversight of; direct or control.

su-per-in-tend-ence (sōō″pẽr-ĭn-tĕn′dĕns), *n.* the act of managing or directing; supervision; control.—*n.* **su″per-in-ten′den-cy.**

su-per-in-tend-ent (sōō″pẽr-ĭn-tĕn′dĕnt), *n.* one who manages or controls; an overseer, director:—*adj.* managing; directing; overseeing.

su-pe-ri-or (sōō-pē′rĭ-ẽr), *adj.* **1**, higher or above in place, position, rank, dignity, or office; **2**, of higher or better quality; preferable; **3**, exceeding others in number; **4**, too fine or great to be influenced: with *to;* as, he is *superior* to petty jealousies:—*n.* **1**, one who surpasses another, as in rank or ability; one of higher rank or position; **2**, the head of a religious house: as, a Mother *Superior.*—*n.* **su-pe″ri-or′i-ty.**—*adv.* **su-pe′ri-or-ly.**

Syn., adj. dominant, principal, foremost.

su-per-la-tive (sū-pûr′lȧ-tĭv), *adj.* **1**, superior to all others; highest in degree; as, a man of *superlative* wisdom; **2**, in grammar, expressing the highest degree or amount: said of a form of adjectives and adverbs, as *greatest, best:*—*n.* **1**, the highest degree of excellence; **2**, the highest degree of comparison of an adjective or adverb; also, a word expressing the highest degree.—*adv.* **su-per′la-tive-ly.**—*n.* **su-per′la-tive-ness.**

su-per-man (sōō′pẽr-măn″), *n.* [*pl.* supermen (-mĕn″)], **1**, a hypothetical, superior human being; **2**, a man of unusual strength or ability, or with more than human powers.

su-per-mar-ket (sōō′pẽr-mär″kĕt), *n.* a large food store with most articles so arranged that customers can wait on themselves. Also **su-per mar-ket.**

su-per-nal (sū-pûr′năl), *adj.* **1**, pertaining to, or situated in, a higher place or region; **2**, celestial; heavenly.

su-per-nat-u-ral (sōō″pẽr-năt′ū-răl), *adj.* being outside, or exceeding, the laws of nature; miraculous:—*n.* that which exceeds the usual course of nature.—*adv.* **su″per-nat′u-ral-ly.**—*n.* **su″per-nat′u-ral-ness.**—*n.* **su″per-nat′u-ral-ism.**

su-per-nu-mer-a-ry (sōō″pẽr-nū′mẽr-ā-rĭ), *n.* [*pl.* supernumeraries (-rĭz)], **1**, a person or thing beyond the stated number, or beyond what is necessary or usual; **2**, esp., a person employed not for regular service, but merely to fill the place of another or to meet a need:—*adj.* exceeding the number stated or required.

su-per-pose (sōō″pẽr-pōz′), *v.t.* [*p.t.* and *p.p.* -posed′ (-pōzd′), *p.pr.* -pos′ing], to lay or place above or on something.—*n.* **su″per-po-si′tion.**

su-per-scribe (sōō″pẽr-skrīb′), *v.t.* [*p.t.* and *p.p.*-scribed′(-skrībd′), *p.pr.* -scrib′ing], **1**, to write or engrave on the outside or top; **2**, to direct or address, as an envelope containing a letter.

su-per-scrip-tion (sōō″pẽr-skrĭp′shŭn), *n.* **1**, the act of writing or engraving on the outside or top of something; **2**, that which is so written or engraved; esp., the address on a letter.

su-per-sede (sōō″pẽr-sēd′), *v.t.* [*p.t.* an *p.p.* -sed′ed, *p.pr.* -sed ing], **1**, to come into or take the place of, as b superior right or worth; **2**, to remove and pu another in place of; as, to *supersede* an officer **3**, to make void, as a law.—*n.* **su″per-sed′er** —*n.* **su″per-se′dure.**—*n.* **su″per-ses′sion.**

su-per-son-ic (sōō″pẽr-sŏn′ĭk), *adj.* o sound, having a frequenc higher than can be heard by the human ear; o speed, faster than the speed of sound in ai (about 738 m.p.h.).

su-per-sti-tion (sōō″pẽr-stĭsh′ŭn), *n* **1**, fear of, reverence fo or belief in, the unknown or mysterious; **2**, belief, or practice, or a system of these, ofte religious, based on fear or credulity.

su-per-sti-tious (sōō″pẽr-stĭsh′ŭs), *ad* pertaining to, marke by, or disposed to, belief in that which is un known or mysterious.—*adv.* **su″per-sti′tious ly.**—*n.* **su″per-sti′tious-ness.**

su-per-struc-ture (sōō′pẽr-strŭk″tūr *n.* **1**, anything bui or founded on something else; **2**, that part o a building which is above the basement.

su-per-vene (sōō″pẽr-vēn′), *v.i.* [*p.t.* an *p.p.* -vened′ (-vēnd′), *p.p* ven′ing], **1**, to come as something additiona **2**, to happen as an interruption; follow closel upon something else.—*adj.* **su″per-ven′ient.**— *n.* **su″per-ven′tion.**

su-per-vise (sōō′pẽr-vīz″), *v.t.* [*p.t.* an *p.p.* -vised″ (-vīzd″), *p.p* -vis″ing], to oversee; superintend.

su-per-vi-sion (sōō″pẽr-vĭzh′ŭn), *n.* **1**, th act of inspecting with au thority; **2**, the authority to oversee and direc

su-per-vi-sor (sōō′pẽr-vī″zẽr), *n.* an ove seer or superintendent.— *adj.* **su″per-vi′so-ry.**

[1]**su-pine** (sū-pīn′; sū′pīn), *adj.* **1**, lying o the back; **2**, inclining backwar sloping; **3**, careless; indifferent; listless.—*ad* **su-pine′ly.**—*n.* **su-pine′ness.**

[2]**su-pine** (sū′pīn), *n.* a part of the Lat verb, in reality a verbal nou formed from the stem of the past participle.

sup-per (sŭp′ẽr), *n.* the evening meal; th last meal of the day, sometim following dinner, sometimes taking the pla of it: **Last Supper**, the last meal eaten b Christ with his disciples.—*adj.* **sup′per-less.**

sup-plant (sŭ-plănt′), *v.t.* to displace an take the place of, as by craft o cunning.—*n.* **sup-plant′er.**

sup-ple (sŭp′l), *adj.* **1**, easily bent; flexibl as, *supple* joints; **2**, submissiv yielding; as, a *supple* nature; **3**, meanly ben ing to the humor of others; flattering:—*v.* [*p.t.* and *p.p.* -pled (-ld), *p.pr.* -pling], **1**, to mak soft and flexible; **2**, to make obedient:—*v.* to grow soft and flexible.—*n.* **sup′ple-ness.**

Syn., adj. limber, pliant, elastic.

sup-ple-ment (sŭp′lē-mĕnt), *n.* **1**, th which completes, or ad something to, something already made; esp a part added to a book or paper to complete or to correct its mistakes; **2**, in mathemati the amount by which an arc or angle must increased to make 180°:—*v.t.* (sŭp′lē-mĕnt to complete by supplying what is lacking.- *adj.* **sup″ple-men′tal.**

sup-ple-men-ta-ry (sŭp″lē-mĕn′tȧ-r *adj.* **1**, additiona supplemental; as, *supplementary* evidenc **2**, in mathematics, equal in sum to 180 degree said of two angles or arcs; also, equal to th difference between a given angle or arc an 180°; as, 60° and 120° are *supplementary* angle 60° is *supplementary* to 120° (see [1]*angle*, illus.

sup-pli-ant (sŭp′lĭ-ănt), *n.* one who e treats or asks earnestly a humbly:—*adj.* asking earnestly and humbly; beseeching; entreating; suing.—*n.* **sup′pli-ance.**—*adv.* **sup′pli-ant-ly.**

sup-pli-cant (sŭp′lĭ-kănt), *n.* one who entreats or asks earnestly and humbly:—*adj.* asking humbly; beseeching.

sup-pli-cate (sŭp′lĭ-kāt), *v.t.* [*p.t.* and *p.p.* -cat″ed, *p.pr.* -cat″ing], **1**, to ask or beg for humbly and earnestly; **2**, to address in prayer; beseech; implore:—*v.i.* to pray or beseech humbly and earnestly.

sup-pli-ca-tion (sŭp″lĭ-kā′shŭn), *n.* **1**, the act of entreating or asking humbly and earnestly; **2**, humble and earnest prayer or entreaty.

sup-pli-ca-to-ry (sŭp′lĭ-kȧ-tō-rĭ), *adj.* expressing earnest and humble entreaty; as, a *supplicatory* letter.

sup-ply (sŭ-plī′), *v.t.* [*p.t.* and *p.p.* -plied′ (-plīd′), *p.pr.* -ply′ing], **1**, to furnish with what is required; provide; as, to *supply* a people with food; **2**, to give; furnish; as, to *supply* food for a people; **3**, to fill temporarily; as, to *supply* a pulpit; **4**, to make up for; as, to *supply* a loss:—*n.* [*pl.* supplies (-plīz′)], **1**, the act of providing or furnishing; **2**, that which is needed or furnished; **3**, the amount of any article on hand to meet a demand; stock; store; **4**, one who serves for another for a time, as in a pulpit; **5**, in *pl.*, daily necessities, as water or food, ready for use, as for an army.—*n.* **sup-pli′er.**

sup-port (sŭ-pōrt′), *v.t.* **1**, to bear the weight of; bear up; uphold; as, columns *support* the roof; **2**, to endure; bear; suffer: as, to *support* pain; **3**, to keep from sinking; encourage; as, to *support* the spirits or courage; **4**, to act with; as, to *support* a star; **5**, to verify; make good; as, to *support* an accusation of theft; **6**, to aid, favor, or defend; as, to *support* a political party; **7**, to carry on; as, to *support* a conversation; **8**, to provide for; as, to *support* a family:—*n.* **1**, the act of maintaining or upholding; **2**, one who or that which maintains or upholds; a prop; pillar; **3**, maintenance; livelihood; aid; **4**, one who furnishes means of support, as to a family; **5**, one person or a company acting with a star.—*n.* **sup-port′er.**

sup-port-a-ble (sŭ-pōr′tȧ-bl), *adj.* **1**, bearable; endurable; **2**, maintainable, as a theory.—*adv.* **sup-port′a-bly.**—*n.* **sup-port′a-ble-ness.**

sup-pos-a-ble (sŭ-pōz′ȧ-bl), *adj.* capable of being assumed; not altogether unlikely.—*adv.* **sup-pos′a-bly.**

sup-pose (sŭ-pōz′), *v.t.* [*p.t.* and *p.p.* -posed′ (-pōzd′), *p.pr.* -pos′ing], **1**, to represent to oneself or another to be true or real; **2**, to imagine; believe; think; assume as true; **3**, to imply; involve:—*v.i.* to think; imagine.—*n.* **sup-pos′er.**

sup-posed (sŭ-pōzd′), *p.adj.* thought to be true; imagined: often implying false belief.—*adv.* **sup-pos′ed-ly.**

sup-po-si-tion (sŭp″ō-zĭsh′ŭn), *n.* **1**, the act of assuming a probability, or the probability which is accepted as true, esp. for the purposes of argument; **2**, hence, opinion or belief without proof.—*adj.* **sup″po-si′tion-al.**—*adv.* **sup″po-si′tion-al-ly.**

sup-pos-i-ti-tious (sŭ-pŏz″ĭ-tĭsh′ŭs), *adj.* **1**, assumed or imagined; **2**, not genuine; counterfeit.—*adv.* **sup-pos″i-ti′tious-ly.**—*n.* **sup-pos″i-ti′tious-ness.**

sup-pos-i-to-ry (sŭ-pŏz′ĭ-tō-rĭ), *n.* [*pl.* suppositories (-rĭz)], a conelike mass, containing medicine, for putting into some cavity or passage of the body, where it dissolves.

sup-press (sŭ-prĕs′), *v.t.* **1**, to subdue; crush; as, to *suppress* a rebellion; **2**, to keep in; restrain; as, to *suppress* a smile; **3**, to conceal; as, to *suppress* the facts in a case; also, to stop the publication of; as, to *suppress* a magazine; **4**, to cause to cease; check; as, to *suppress* a hemorrhage.—*n.* **sup-press′er; sup-pres′sor.**

sup-pres-sion (sŭ-prĕsh′ŭn), *n.* **1**, the act of crushing, checking, or concealing; **2**, the state of being crushed, checked, or concealed; restraint; **3**, a withholding from publication; **4**, stoppage or obstruction, as of a hemorrhage.

sup-pres-sive (sŭ-prĕs′ĭv), *adj.* tending to crush, check, or conceal; subduing; concealing.

sup-pu-rate (sŭp′ū-rāt), *v.i.* [*p.t.* and *p.p.* -rat″ed, *p.pr.* -rat″ing], to form pus; fester.—*n.* **sup″pu-ra′tion.**—*adj.* **sup′pu-ra-tive.**

su-pra- (sū′prȧ-), *prefix*, **1**, over; above; as, *supra*renal; **2**, beyond; superior to; as, *supra*mundane: opp. of *infra-*.

su-pra-mun-dane (sū″prȧ-mŭn′dān), *adj.* **1**, superior to the world or worldly things; **2**, supernatural.

su-pra-re-nal (sū″prȧ-rē′năl), *adj.* above the kidneys: **suprarenal gland**, a small, ductless gland situated, in mammals, near each kidney: used, esp. those from sheep, as a source of adrenaline.

su-prem-a-cy (sŭ-prĕm′ȧ-sĭ), *n.* **1**, the state of being supreme, or in the highest position of power; **2**, the supreme or highest authority.

su-preme (sŭ-prēm′), *adj.* **1**, highest in power or authority; as, a *supreme* ruler or court; **2**, highest in degree; greatest possible; utmost; as, *supreme* sacrifice: **the Supreme Being**, God: **Supreme Court**, in the U. S., any of several appellate courts having supervisory jurisdiction over inferior courts; esp., the highest national court of appeal.—*adv.* **su-preme′ly.**—*n.* **su-preme′ness.**

[1]**sur-** (sûr-), *prefix*, a form of *super-*, meaning over; as, *sur*charge. See **su′per-.**

[2]**sur-** (sûr-), *prefix*, a form of *sub-*, meaning under, used before initial *r*; as, *sur*reptitious. See **sub-.**

su-rah (sōō′rȧ; sū′rȧ), *n.* a soft, twilled silk material for women's garments: also called *surah silk.*

sur-base (sûr′bās″), *n.* the molding around the top of a pedestal or along the top of a wainscot or a baseboard.

sur-cease (sŭr-sēs′), *n.* final end; stop; discontinuance.

sur-charge (sŭr-chärj′), *n.* **1**, an excessive charge, load, or burden; a charge beyond what is just and right; **2**, an additional or secondary printing on a stamp or document:—*v.t.* [*p.t.* and *p.p.* -charged′ (-chärjd′), *p.pr.* -charg′ing], to charge more than is due; overburden.—*n.* **sur-charg′er.**

sur-cin-gle (sûr′sĭng″gl), *n.* a girth, belt, or girdle for passing around the body of a horse or other animal to secure the saddle, blanket, etc.

sur-coat (sûr′kōt″), *n.* **1**, a coat worn over another coat or garment; **2**, esp., the long, loose garment worn by medieval knights over their armor.

surd (sûrd), *n.* **1**, a quantity that cannot be expressed by rational numbers, as the square root of 2; **2**, a consonant sound made with the breath but without voice, as *f, p, s*: opp. of *voiced* or *sonant:*—*adj.* **1**, not capable of being expressed in rational numbers; involving surds: opp. of *rational;* **2**, uttered, as certain consonants, without voice or tone.

sure (shŏŏr), *adj.* **1**, knowing and believing; confident beyond doubt; certain; as, I am *sure* it is true; **2**, certain to find or retain; as, he is *sure* to succeed; **3**, fit to be depended upon; reliable, as an investment; 4, firmly fixed; not likely to change or fail: —*adv. Colloq.*, certainly.—*n.* **sure'ness.**

sure–foot-ed (shōōr'=fŏŏt"ĕd), *adj.* not likely to fall or stumble.—*adv.* **sure"–foot'ed-ly.**—*n.* **sure"–foot'ed-ness.**

sure-ly (shōōr'lĭ), *adv.* **1,** certainly; without risk or doubt; **2,** firmly; securely.

sure-ty (shōōr'tĭ), *n.* [*pl.* sureties (-tĭz)], **1,** the state of being certain; certainty; **2,** that which makes sure; esp., security or guaranty against loss or damage; **3,** security for the payment of a debt or for the performance of some act; bail; **4,** one who becomes bound, or agrees to be responsible, for another, as for payment of a debt.

sure-ty-ship (shōōr'tĭ-shĭp), *n.* responsibility for the fulfilment of another's obligation, as for paying a debt.

surf (sûrf), *n.* the waves of the sea as they break and foam upon the shore.

sur-face (sûr'fās), *n.* **1,** the outside or face of a body; the upper face of a body of liquid; **2,** outward appearance:—*v.i.* [*p.t.* and *p.p.* -faced (-fāst), *p.pr.* -facing], to rise to the surface, as a submarine.

surf-boat (sûrf'bōt"), *n.* a strong, light boat for riding through the surf.

sur-feit (sûr'fĭt), *n.* **1,** indulgence to excess, esp. in eating or drinking; **2,** fulness or sickness caused by such excess:—*v.t.* to feed to excess; cloy:—*v.i.* to indulge in anything to excess, esp. in eating.—*n.* **sur'feit-er.**

Syn., v. glut, satiate. (See satisfy.)

surge (sûrj), *n.* **1,** a large wave or billow; a great roll of water; swell; **2,** a great rolling motion; sweep; rush; as, the *surge* of a mob:—*v.i.* [*p.t.* and *p.p.* surged (sûrjd), *p.pr.* surg'ing], to rise high and roll; swell.

sur-geon (sûr'jŭn), *n.* **1,** one who treats injuries, deformities, or diseases by manual operation, or the use of the knife; **2,** a staff officer of the Medical Department of the army or navy: **surgeon-general, 1,** the chief medical officer of the U. S. army or navy; **2,** the chief of the U. S. Public Health Service.

sur-ger-y (sûr'jĕr-ĭ), *n.* [*pl.* surgeries (-ĭz)], **1,** that branch of medical science dealing with the treatment of injuries, deformities, or diseases by manual operations, or the use of the knife; **2,** the place where a surgeon operates or experiments.

sur-gi-cal (sûr'jĭ-kăl), *adj.* **1,** pertaining to surgery, or the art of healing by the use of the knife, **2,** pertaining to surgeons.—*adv.* **sur'gi-cal-ly.**

sur-loin (sûr'loin"), *n.* the upper part of a loin of beef. Also, **sir'loin"**, *Pfd. S.*

sur-ly (sûr'lĭ), *adj.* [*comp.* sur'li-er, *superl.* sur'li-est], **1,** gloomily ill-humored; morose; rough; **2,** uncivil; ill-natured; rudely abrupt.—*adv.* **sur'li-ly.**—*n.* **sur'li-ness.**

Syn. rude, gruff, sullen, gloomy.

sur-mise (sŭr-mīz'), *n.* a thought or supposition based upon little evidence; a guess:—*v.t.* and *v.i.* [*p.t.* and *p.p.* -mised' (-mīzd'), *p.pr.* -mis'ing], to imagine without certain knowledge; suppose; guess.

sur-mount (sŭr-mount'), *v.t.* **1,** to rise above; **2,** to overcome; conquer; vanquish; as, to *surmount* one's difficulties.—*adj.* **sur-mount'a-ble.**—*n.* **sur-mount'er.**

sur-name (sûr'nām"), *n.* orig., a name, often descriptive, added to the Christian name, as in Charles *the Bold;* now, the last, or family name, shared by all the members of the same family:—*v.t.* (sûr'nām"; sŭr-nām'), [*p.t.* and *p.p.* -named" (-nāmd"), *p.pr.* -nam"ing], to give a family name to; call by a family name.

sur-pass (sŭr-pȧs'), *v.t.* **1,** to exceed; **2,** to excel; go beyond in excellence.—*adj.* **sur-pass'a-ble.**—*p.adj.* **sur-pass'ing.**

sur-plice (sûr'plĭs), *n.* an outer linen garment with wide sleeves, worn esp. by the priests and choir members of ritualistic churches during the service.

sur-plus (sûr'plŭs), *n.* that which remains over and above what is required; excess:—*adj.* exceeding what is used or needed; as, *surplus* supplies.—*n.* **sur'plus-age.**

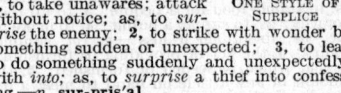

One Style of Surplice

sur-prise (sŭr-prīz'), *n.* **1,** the act of coming upon or attacking unexpectedly; **2,** the feeling excited by what is sudden and strange; wonder; astonishment; **3,** a sudden or unexpected event or fact:—*v.t.* [*p.t.* and *p.p.* -prised' (-prīzd'), *p.pr.* -pris'ing], **1,** to take unawares; attack without notice; as, to *surprise* the enemy; **2,** to strike with wonder by something sudden or unexpected; **3,** to lead to do something suddenly and unexpectedly with *into;* as, to *surprise* a thief into confessing.—*n.* **sur-pris'al.**

sur-pris-ing (sŭr-prīz'ĭng), *p.adj.* causing wonder or astonishment unexpected; extraordinary; as, *surprising* news—*adv.* **sur-pris'ing-ly.**—*n.* **sur-pris'ing-ness.**

sur-ren-der (sŭ-rĕn'dẽr), *n.* the act of yielding, or giving up, oneself or a thing into the power or possession of another:—*v.t.* **1,** to yield, under pressure, to the power of another; give up possession of on compulsion or demand; as, to *surrender* an army or arms; **2,** to resign possession of; give up; as, to *surrender* one's claim to property **3,** to yield to any influence, emotion, or power as, to *surrender* oneself to sorrow:—*v.i.* to yield; give up oneself or a thing into the power of another.

Syn., v. abandon, relinquish, quit.

sur-rep-ti-tious (sŭr"ĕp-tĭsh'ŭs), *adj* done by stealth or fraud, or without proper authority; as, a *surreptitious* entry.—*adv.* **sur"rep-ti'tious-ly.**

Syn. sly, secret.—*Ant.* open, undisguised.

sur-rey (sŭr'ĭ), *n.* [*pl.* surreys (-ĭz)], a light four-wheeled pleasure carriage with two seats, both facing forward.

sur-ro-gate (sŭr'ō-gāt), *n.* **1,** a person appointed to act for another a deputy or substitute; **2,** one appointed by a bishop to act in his place; **3,** a court officer who deals with the probating, or proving, of wills, and the settlement of estates.

sur-round (sŭ-round'), *v.t.* **1,** to inclose on all sides; **2,** to besiege.

sur-round-ings (sŭ-round'ĭngz), *n. pl* the things or conditions that make up an environment.

sur-tax (sûr'tăks"), *n.* an extra tax:—*v.t* (sûr'tăks"; sŭr-tăks'), to impose or add, an extra tax on, as in railroad rates.

sur-tout (sŭr-tōōt'; sŭr-tōō'), *n.* a man's wide-skirted overcoat with tight fitting waist, reaching below the knees.

sur-veil-lance (sŭr-vāl'yăns; sŭr-vāl'ăns), *n.* close watch oversight; inspection; as, police *surveillance*

sur-vey (sûr'vā; sŭr-vā'), *n.* **1,** the act of examining carefully, or of determining the features of, as of land; **2,** a careful view or examination; **3,** a measured plan and description of any portion of country, made by means of such an examination:—*v.t.* (sŭr-vā'), **1,** to inspect, or take a view of; as to *survey* the landscape; **2,** to examine closely as, to *survey* a subject or a building; **3,** to measure and determine the features of, as land

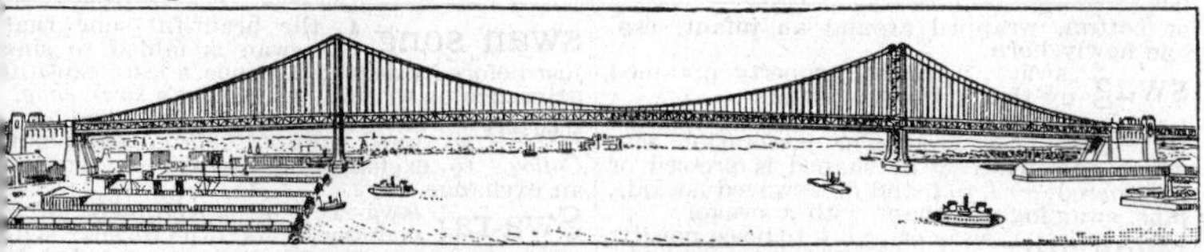

Suspension Bridge over the Delaware River

sur-vey-ing (sûr-vā'ĭng), *n.* the science, art, or business, of measuring and determining the various features of land.

sur-vey-or (sûr-vā'ẽr), *n.* **1**, one whose business is to measure land; **2**, any official inspector of a particular office, business, etc.; as, *surveyor* of weights; **3**, an inspector of customs.

sur-viv-al (sûr-vīv'ăl), *n.* **1**, the act or fact of living or continuing longer than, or beyond the life of, another person, thing, or event; **2**, any ancient use, custom, or belief continuing to the present day.

sur-vive (sûr-vīv'), *v.t.* [*p.t.* and *p.p.* -vived' (-vīvd'), *p.pr.* -viv'ing], to live longer than (another); to outlive; outlast; live beyond or through (an event, state, etc.):—*v.i.* to remain alive or in existence.

sur-viv-or (sûr-vīv'ẽr), *n.* **1**, one who outlives another person, or any time, event, or thing; as, a *survivor* of a wreck; **2**, in law, the one of two or more designated persons having a common interest who outlives the other or others.

sus-cep-ti-bil-i-ty (sŭ-sĕp"tĭ-bĭl'ĭ-tĭ), *n.* [*pl.* susceptibilities (-tĭz)], the state or quality of receiving impressions, or of being easily affected; capacity for emotion; sensitiveness.

sus-cep-ti-ble (sŭ-sĕp'tĭ-bl), *adj.* **1**, capable of being changed, influenced, or easily affected: with *of* or *to;* **2**, tender; sensitive to emotional impressions; easily acted upon.—*n.* **sus-cep'ti-ble-ness.**—*adv.* **sus-cep'ti-bly.**—*adj.* **sus-cep'tive.**

sus-pect (sŭs-pĕkt'), *v.t.* **1**, to imagine to exist; surmise; **2**, to believe in the possible guilt of, without having proof; **3**, to doubt; mistrust:—*v.i.* to imagine something as possible, esp. evil; be suspicious:—*n.* a person believed, but not proved, to be guilty of some crime.

sus-pend (sŭs-pĕnd'), *v.t.* **1**, to fasten to something above so as to hang down; **2**, to hang, or to hold as if by hanging, as particles of dust in the air; **3**, to delay; hold undecided; as, to *suspend* judgment; **4**, to cause to cease for a time; as, to *suspend* a rule; **5**, to debar, or keep out, for a time; as, to *suspend* a pupil from school.

sus-pend-er (sŭs-pĕn'dẽr), *n.* **1**, one who or that which holds, holds back, or upholds; **2**, in *pl.*, two bands, worn over the shoulders, to support the trousers.

sus-pense (sŭs-pĕns'), *n.* **1**, a state of uncertainty, doubt, or anxiety; indecision; **2**, the act of delaying, as judgment.

sus-pen-sion (sŭs-pĕn'shŭn), *n.* **1**, the act of hanging, or state of being hung, from a support; **2**, the act of stopping, delaying, or interrupting for a time; esp., a brief stop, delay, or interruption; **3**, a stopping of payments in business; **4**, a floating, as of particles, in a fluid; also, the mixture of the fluid and the suspended particles.

sus-pen-sion bridge a bridge having a roadway hung, without support from below, from cables stretched across the interval to be bridged.

sus-pen-so-ry (sŭs-pĕn'sō-rĭ), *adj.* **1**, fitting or serving to sustain or suspend; as, a *suspensory* muscle; **2**, serving to delay:—*n.* [*pl.* suspensories (-rĭz)], that which supports, as a truss.

sus-pi-cion (sŭs-pĭsh'ŭn), *n.* **1**, the act of feeling, or of imagining on slight evidence, that something is wrong; mistrust; doubt; **2**, a very small quantity; hint; as, just a *suspicion* of humor.

Syn. misgiving. (See doubt.)—*Ant.* belief, confidence, assurance.

sus-pi-cious (sŭs-pĭsh'ŭs), *adj.* **1**, inclined to imagine without proof; doubtful; distrustful; **2**, showing, or suggesting, doubt; **3**, open to, or exciting, mistrust; questionable.—*adv.* **sus-pi'cious-ly.**—*n.* **sus-pi'cious-ness.**

sus-pire (sŭs-pīr'), *v.i.* [*p.t.* and *p.p.* -pired' (-pīrd'), *p.pr.* -pir'ing], *Obs.* or *Poetic*, to breathe deeply and audibly; sigh.

sus-tain (sŭs-tān'), *v.t.* **1**, to hold up or support; as, to *sustain* a weight; **2**, to maintain or keep up; as, to *sustain* an argument; **3**, to support, or keep alive; as, food *sustains* life; **4**, to undergo; as, to *sustain* a money loss; **5**, to bear up under; stand up against; as, to *sustain* a blow; **6**, to keep up the courage or spirits of; encourage; as, his faith *sustained* him; **7**, to prove; **8**, to confirm, as an accusation with proof; **9**, to support or admit as just and true, as a decision.—*adj.* **sus-tain'a-ble.**—*n.* **sus-tain'er.**

sus-tained (sŭs-tānd'), *p.adj.* held up to, or kept at, a certain pitch or level; uniform; as, *sustained* efforts.

sus-te-nance (sŭs'tē-năns), *n.* **1**, the act of maintaining; support; **2**, that which supports life; food.

sut-ler (sŭt'lẽr), *n.* a person who follows an army and sells food, liquor, etc., to the troops.

sut-tee (sŭ-tē'), *n.* formerly, a Hindu widow burned to death on the funeral pyre of her husband; also, such cremation.

su-ture (sū'tūr), *n.* **1**, the act of sewing; **2**, a seam, or that which resembles a seam; **3**, the drawing together of the edges of a wound by stitches; **4**, the lines or seams where bones, as those of the skull, are united.

su-ze-rain (sū'zē-rān), *n.* **1**, formerly, a feudal lord with authority over vassals who owed him loyalty and service in return for the use of land; **2**, a person or state holding sovereign power over a semi-independent state.

su-ze-rain-ty (sū'zē-rān-tĭ), *n.* **1**, the office or dignity of a suzerain, or feudal lord; **2**, the relation of a sovereign state to another under its control.

swab (swŏb), *n.* **1**, a mop for cleaning decks, floors, etc.; **2**, a sponge attached to a handle, as for cleaning the barrel of a gun; **3**, a bit of sponge or cotton fastened to a handle to clean, or apply medicine to, the mouth, throat, etc.:—*v.t.* [*p.t.* and *p.p.* swabbed (swŏbd), *p.pr.* swab'bing], to clean, or apply medicine to, with a swab.—*n.* **swab'ber.**

swad-dle (swŏd'l), *v.t.* [*p.t.* and *p.p.* -dled (-ld), *p.pr.* -dling], to swathe or wrap closely with cloths or bandages; as, to *swaddle* a baby: **swaddling band** or **swaddling cloth**, a bandage, or long strip of linen or cotton, wrapped around an infant, esp. one newly born.

swag (swăg), *n. Slang*, property obtained by theft; booty; plunder.

swage (swāj), *n.* a metal-shaping tool having a groove or perforation into which the metal to be shaped is pressed or hammered:—*v.t.* [*p.t.* and *p.p.* swaged (swājd), *p.pr.* swag′ing], to shape with a swage.

swag-ger (swăg′ẽr), *v.i.* **1**, to boast noisily; bluster; bully; **2**, to strut or walk with affected superiority:—*n.* **1**, noisy boastfulness; **2**, an affected or insolent manner of walking: **swagger stick**, a light hand stick carried esp. by British military men when off duty.—*n.* **swag′ger-er.**

swain (swān), *n.* **1**, a young man living in the country; **2**, hence, a country gallant or lover.—*adj.* **swain′ish.**

swale (swāl), *n.* a slight depression of the ground, usually swampy.

¹swal-low (swŏl′ō), *n.* **1**, any of a widely distributed family of small perching birds, with forked tail, long, pointed wings, and weak legs, noted for their graceful, swift flight; **2**, any of a class of swifts resembling the swallow, as the chimney swift.

²swal-low (swŏl′ō), *v.t.* **1**, to transfer, by a specific muscular act, from the mouth to the stomach through the esophagus, or gullet; **2**, to absorb or take in, in any manner; **3**, to cause to disappear; make away with: usually with *up;* as, the crowd *swallowed* him up; **4**, to retract or take back; as, to *swallow* one's boasts; **5**, to put up with; bear submissively; as, to *swallow* an insult; **6**, *Colloq.*, to believe easily and without proof:—*v.i.* to perform the muscular act of taking food, drink, etc., through the gullet:—*n.* **1**, the passage between the mouth and the stomach; **2**, as much as is taken through this passage by swallowing once; hence, a small amount; a mere taste; **3**, the muscular act of swallowing.—*n.* **swal′low-er.**

swal-low–tailed (swŏl′ō-tāld″), *adj.* **1**, forked, like a swallow's tail; **2**, having tapering or forked skirts; as, a *swallow-tailed* coat.

swam (swăm), the past tense of the irregular verb *swim.*

swa-mi (swä′mĭ), *n.* [*pl.* swamis (-mĭz)], **1**, lord: a Hindu title of address; **2**, a Hindu teacher, esp. of religion: often used humorously or contemptuously. Also, **swa′my.**

swamp (swŏmp), *n.* wet, spongy land; land soaked with water:—*v.t.* **1**, to plunge or sink in spongy or marshy land; **2**, to cause to fill, or to sink by filling, with water; as, to *swamp* a boat; **3**, to overwhelm; ruin, as with difficulties or numbers:—*v.i.* **1**, to fill with water and sink, as a boat; **2**, to stick or sink in spongy or marshy land; **3**, to be overwhelmed by difficulties.—*adj.* **swamp′y.**

swan (swŏn), *n.* **1**, any of several large, web-footed, aquatic, gooselike birds, with very long necks, noted for their grace on the water; **2**, a poet or singer noted for beauty of song or voice: in allusion to the myth that the swan sang sweetly, esp. just before death; as, Shakespeare, the *Swan* of Avon: **Swan,** in astronomy, a northern constellation along the Milky Way: also called *Cygnus.*

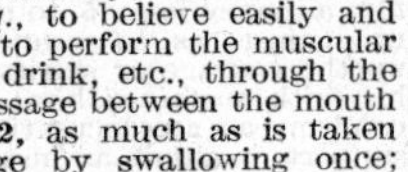
SWAN (1/38)

swan's–down (swŏnz′-doun″), *n.* **1**, the soft, fine feathers of the swan, often used as trimming, as on a baby's hood; **2**, a very soft, thick cloth of fine wool; **3**, cotton flannel. Also, **swans′down″.**

swan song **1**, the beautiful song that the swan is fabled to sing just before its death; **2**, hence, a last beautiful utterance or writing; as, a poet's *swan song.*

swap (swŏp), *v.t.* and *v.i.* [*p.t.* and *p.p.* swapped (swŏpt), *p.pr.* swap′ping], *Colloq.*, to exchange or barter:—*n. Colloq.*, an exchange.

Swa-raj (swȧ-räj′), *n.* government of a country by its own citizens; self-government; home rule: a term applied in British India to a movement for native home rule. Also, **Sva-raj′.**

sward (swôrd), *n.* a stretch of land covered thickly with short grass; turf.—*adj.* **sward′ed.**

sware (swâr), *Archaic*, a past tense of the irregular verb *swear.*

¹swarm (swôrm), *n.* **1**, a large number of moving birds, animals, insects, etc.; esp., a throng of tiny insects in motion; as, a *swarm* of ants; **2**, a large number of honeybees, accompanied by a queen, leaving one hive to establish a new home in another; also, a colony of bees settled in a hive; **3**, a great number; a crowd, esp. in motion; as, a *swarm* of people:—*v.i.* **1**, to move about in great numbers; as, people *swarmed* everywhere; **2**, to be crowded; as, the street *swarms* with people; **3**, to leave a hive in a body and make a new colony: said of bees:—*v.t.* to throng or crowd; as, people *swarmed* the streets.

Syn., *n.* crowd, collection. (See herd.)

²swarm (swôrm), *v.i. Colloq.*, **1**, to climb up a tree, pole, etc., by grasping with the arms and legs; **2**, to scramble up any steep surface:—*v.t.* to shin up, as a tree.

swarth-y (swôr′thĭ; swôr′*th*ĭ), *adj.* [*comp.* swarth′i-er, *superl.* swarth′i-est], of a dark or dusky color; dark-skinned. Also, **swart.**—*adv.* **swarth′i-ly.**—*n.* **swarth′i-ness.**

swash (swŏsh), *n.* **1**, a dashing or splashing, as of water; also, the water so dashing; **2**, a narrow channel between sand banks:—*v.i.* **1**, to dash or wash with a splashing sound, as water against rocks; **2**, to make a noise as of swords clashing; hence, to bluster or brag:—*v.t.* to dash or splash about, as water.

swash-buck-ler (swŏsh′bŭk″lẽr), *n.* a noisy, blustering bully or ruffian; swaggerer.—*adj.* **swash′buck″ler-ing.**—*adj.* and *n.* **swash′buck″ling.**

swas-ti-ka (swȧs′tĭ-kȧ), *n.* a religious symbol or ornament, dating from ancient times, shaped like four capital L's or gammas joined: used in modern Europe as a symbol of anti-Semitic feeling: also called *fylfot; gammadion* (cf. *cross,* illus.). Also, **swas′ti-ca.**

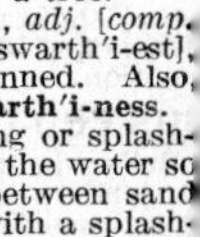
SWASTIKA

swath (swôth; swŏth), *n.* **1**, a line or row of grass or grain as cut down by the mower; **2**, the whole reach of a mowing machine or scythe; **3**, the space cut in one course.

swathe (swā*th*), *v.t.* [*p.t.* and *p.p.* swathed (swā*th*d), *p.pr.* swath′ing], **1**, to bind with a band or bandage; **2**, to bind about or inclose; as, to *swathe* oneself in furs:—*n.* a band or bandage.—*n.* **swath′er.**

sway (swā), *v.t.* **1**, to cause to bend or to move backward and forward, or from side to side; as, the wind *sways* the trees; also, to wield, as a sword; **2**, to influence by power or moral force; direct; rule; as, to *sway* the lives of a people; **3**, to cause to lean to one side; as, to *sway* opinion:—*v.i.* **1**, to incline to one side; **2**, to move or swing from side to side; **3**, to have weight or influence:—*n.* **1**, the act of leaning or of swinging back and forth; **2**, controlling influence; as, under the *sway* of anger; **3**, hence, rule or control.

sway-backed (swā′=băkt″), *adj.* having an abnormally sagging back, as a horse.

swear (swâr), *v.i.* [*p.t.* swore (swōr) or, *Archaic*, sware (swâr), *p.p.* sworn (swōrn), *p.pr.* swear′ing], **1,** to make a solemn declaration, with an appeal to God or the Bible, as to the truth of what is affirmed; **2,** to make a solemn vow or promise; **3,** to give evidence on oath; **4,** to use profane language:—*v.t.* **1,** to declare solemnly, with an appeal to God or some sacred object; **2,** to vow or promise solemnly; **3,** in law, to cause to take, or bind by, an oath; as, to *swear* witnesses; **4,** to utter profanely.—*n.* **swear′er.**

sweat (swĕt), *n.* **1,** the moisture which is given off through the pores of the skin; perspiration; **2,** moisture given off by any substance; **3,** the act of perspiring; **4,** the state of one who gives off perspiration; **5,** *Colloq.*, toil; drudgery:—*v.i.* [*p.t.* and *p.p.* sweat or sweat′ed, *p.pr.* sweat′ing], **1,** to give off moisture through the pores of the skin; perspire; **2,** to give off moisture, as plants; **3,** to form moisture in drops on the outside, as a glass of water; **4,** *Colloq.*, to labor hard; drudge:—*v.t.* **1,** to cause to perspire freely; **2,** to send forth (moisture) through the pores; **3,** to wet with perspiration; **4,** to force the moisture out of by heat; **5,** to force moisture out of by fermentation, as tobacco; **6,** *Colloq.*, to employ at hard work for very low and unfair wages.—*adj.* **sweat′y.**

sweat-er (swĕt′ẽr), *n.* **1,** a person who overworks and underpays those who work for him; **2,** an outside knitted coat or jersey, made of silk or wool; **3,** a medicine that induces perspiration; a sudorific.

sweat-ing sys-tem a system of garment manufacture in which unskilled laborers are forced to work very hard at low wages.

sweat-shop (swĕt′shŏp″), *n.* a shop where persons work very hard for very low wages.

Swede (swēd), *n.* a native of Sweden: **swede,** a rutabaga, or kind of large turnip with yellow flesh: also called *Swedish turnip.*—*adj.* **Swed′ish.**

Swe-den-bor-gi-an (swē″dĕn-bôr′jĭ-ăn), *adj.* pertaining to the doctrines of Swedenborg (1688–1772), a Swedish philosopher and founder of the New Jerusalem Church:—*n.* a member of this church or a believer in its doctrines.—*n.* **Swe″den-bor′gi-an-ism.**

sweep (swēp), *v.t.* [*p.t.* and *p.p.* swept (swĕpt), *p.pr.* sweep′ing], **1,** to brush, pass over, or clean, as with a broom; as, to *sweep* a carpet; **2,** to remove or clear away, as dirt, with a broom, brush, or the like; **3,** to drive, flow over, or carry along or off with force; as, waves *swept* the deck; the epidemic *swept* off people by thousands; **4,** to brush against or over; as, to *sweep* the strings of a violin; **5,** to carry away, as with enthusiasm; **6,** to scan; search thoroughly; as, to *sweep* the sea:—*v.i.* **1,** to clean or clear away dirt with a brush, broom, etc.; **2,** to pass with speed or force; **3,** to move with stateliness or dignity; **4,** to lie or extend for a long distance; as, the lawn *sweeps* away to the right:—*n.* **1,** the act of sweeping; a clearing out or away; as, to make a clean *sweep;* **2,** a sweeping motion, as of the arm; **3,** the compass or range of such a motion; as, the *sweep* of a scythe; hence, range; extent; as, the *sweep* of a storm or an epidemic; **4,** a bend or curve; as, the *sweep* of a drive; **5,** one who makes a business of cleaning chimneys; as, a chimney *sweep;* **6,** a long pole, attached to a post, used in drawing a bucket from a well: also called *well sweep;* **7,** a long oar.—*n.* **sweep′er.**

sweep-ing (swēp′ĭng), *p.adj.* **1,** carrying off, or clearing away, as with a broom or by force; as, a *sweeping* wind; **2,** inclusive; comprehensive; as, a *sweeping* assertion:—*n.*, in *pl.*, a collection of dirt and particles swept up; refuse.—*adv.* **sweep′ing-ly.**

sweep-stakes (swēp′stāks″), *n. pl.* used as *sing.* or *pl.* a form of gambling, as on a horse race, in which the entire stakes are divided among those who draw first, second, etc.

sweet (swēt), *adj.* **1,** tasting like sugar, **2,** not stale or sour; as, *sweet* butter or milk; **3,** fresh; not salt; as, *sweet* water; **4,** fragrant; as, *sweet* honeysuckle; **5,** pleasing in sound; soft; as, a *sweet* voice; **6,** charming or attractive in manner or appearance; **7,** gentle; mild; as, a *sweet* disposition; **8,** beloved; **9,** containing sugar:—*n.* **1,** the quality of being sweet; **2,** one dearly loved; a darling; **3,** a tart, pudding, or the like; dessert; **4,** in *pl.*, confectionery or candy.—*adj.* **sweet′ish.**—*adv.* **sweet′ly.**—*n.* **sweet′ness.**

sweet a-lys-sum a low-growing plant of the mustard family, with small, white, fragrant flowers.

sweet bay **1,** the true laurel; the laurel of the ancients and the poets; **2,** a handsome shrub of the magnolia family, with thick leaves and very fragrant, white flowers, common in the southern U. S.: also called *magnolia.*

sweet-bread (swēt′brĕd″), *n.*, often in *pl.*, the pancreas, or gland lying behind the stomach of an animal, esp. that of a calf or a lamb, when used as food.

sweet-bri-er (swēt′brī″ẽr), *n.* a thorny shrub of the rose family, bearing single pink flowers.

sweet corn a kind of maize, or corn, of a sweet, delicate taste, much used as a vegetable.

sweet-en (swēt′n), *v.t.* **1,** to make sweet or pleasant; **2,** to make mild or kind; **3,** to make grateful to the mind or feeling; **4,** to render less painful, difficult, or laborious; **5,** to make pure; as, to *sweeten* the air of a room:—*v.i.* to become sweet.—*n.* **sweet′en-er.**—*n.* **sweet′en-ing.**

sweet fern a low shrub with long, fragrant, fernlike leaves

sweet flag a fragrant plant with sword-shaped leaves.

sweet-heart (swēt′härt″), *n.* **1,** a lover; **2,** one who is beloved.

sweet-meat (swēt′mēt″), *n.*, usually in *pl.*, fruit or nuts preserved with sugar; candy, preserve, or the like.

sweet po-ta-to a tropical American vine with a sweet, starchy root; also, the edible root.

sweet Wil-liam a flowering plant of the pink family.

swell (swĕl), *v.i.* [*p.t.* swelled (swĕld), *p.p.* swelled or swoll′en (swōl′n), *p.pr.* swell′ing], **1,** to expand or enlarge; increase in size, volume, or force; hence, to increase in importance, value, or the like; **2,** to be inflated, or bulge out, as sails in the wind; **3,** to be puffed up; as, to *swell* with importance; **4,** to rise above a given level; as, the ground *swells:*—*v.t.* **1,** to cause to rise or increase; inflate or fill; puff up; **2,** to inflate with pride; **3,** in music, to play or sing, as a note, with gradual increase and decrease of volume:—*n.* **1,** the act or state of swelling; increase in volume, force, or value; **2,** in music, gradual increase and decrease of sound; **3,** a long continuous wave or billow; **4,** a gradual elevation of land; **5,** *Slang*, a very fashionable person; one in high society.

swell-ing (swĕl′ĭng), *n.* **1,** the act of expanding, or increasing in size or bulk; also, the state of being so increased; **2**, a prominence; **3**, an abnormally enlarged part of the body, as from inflammation.

swel-ter (swĕl′tẽr), *v.i.* to perspire, or sweat, very freely; be faint from heat.—*p.adj.* **swel′ter-ing.**—*adj.* **swel′try.**

swept (swĕpt), past tense and past participle of the irregular verb *sweep.*

swerve (swûrv), *v.i.* [*p.t.* and *p.p.* swerved (swûrvd), *p.pr.* swerv′ing], to turn aside from any certain line, or any course or rule of duty:—*v.t.* to turn aside:—*n.* a sudden turning aside.

swift (swĭft), *adj.* **1**, moving far in a short time; rapid; speedy; fleet; as, a *swift* train or horse; **2**, passing quickly; as, the *swift* hours; **3**, acting quickly; prompt; as, *swift* to answer:—*n.* **1**, a bird of the humming-bird family, but resembling the swallow; **2**, a kind of moth.—*adv.* **swift′ly.**—*n.* **swift′ness.**

swig (swĭg), *v.t.* and *v.i.* [*p.t.* and *p.p.* swigged (swĭgd), *p.pr.* swig′ging], *Colloq.*, to drink in deep drafts; gulp:—*n.* *Colloq.*, a deep drink, as of liquor.

swill (swĭl), *v.t.* and *v.i.* to drink or swallow greedily in large quantity; guzzle; also, to fill with drink:—*n.* **1**, drink taken in large quantities; **2**, liquid food for animals, particularly kitchen refuse given to swine.

swim (swĭm), *v.i.* [*p.t.* swam (swăm) or, *Archaic*, swum (swŭm), *p.p.* swum, *p.pr.* swim′ming], **1**, to float, as on water or other liquid; **2**, to propel or push oneself forward in the water with the hands and feet, or fins and tail; **3**, to be carried along by, or as by, a current; glide smoothly; **4**, to overflow; as, the eyes *swim* in tears; **5**, to have great abundance; as, to *swim* in luxury; **6**, to be dizzy; as, the head *swims*:—*v.t.* **1**, to cause to swim or float; **2**, to pass over or through by swimming; as, to *swim* a river:—*n.* **1**, the act of swimming; **2**, the process of swimming as a sport; as, he went for a *swim;* **3**, dizziness; faintness.—*n.* **swim′mer.**—*n.* and *p.adj.* **swim′ming.**—*adv.* **swim′ming-ly.**

swim-ming blad-der the air bladder of a fish, by which the fish maintains equilibrium or adjustment to depth: also called *sound.*

swin-dle (swĭn′dl), *v.t.* and *v.i.* [*p.t.* and *p.p.* -dled (-dld), *p.pr.* -dling], to cheat deliberately; defraud:—*n.* the act of cheating or defrauding; also, a fraudulent scheme.—*n.* **swin′dler.**
Syn., *v.* steal, trick, delude.

swin-dling (swĭn′dlĭng), *n.* the act of one who defrauds or cheats.

swine (swīn), *n.* [*pl.* swine], any animal of the hog family, with bristly skin and long snout: usually used collectively.—*adj.* **swin′ish.**—*adv.* **swin′ish-ly.**—*n.* **swin′ish-ness.**

swine-herd (swīn′hûrd″), *n.* a tender or keeper of swine, or hogs.

swing (swĭng), *v.i.* [*p.t.* and *p.p.* swung (swŭng), *p.pr.* swing′ing], **1**, to move to and fro regularly, as the pendulum of a clock; **2**, to turn on, or as on, a hinge, or axis; as, the gate *swings* open; **3**, to go along with a loose, free, swaying gait; as, the soldiers *swung* down the road; **4**, to use a swing; **5**, to turn or wheel round, as a ship; **6**, *Colloq.*, to be hanged; as, to *swing* on the gallows:—*v.t.* **1**, to cause to move to and fro; as, to *swing* a pendulum; **2**, to wave to and fro; brandish; as, to *swing* a cane; **3**, to cause to turn or wheel about, as, to *swing* a ship about; **4**, to put up so as to hang freely; as, to *swing* a hammock; hang on hinges; as, to *swing* a gate; **5**, to manage or handle; as, to *swing* a business:—*n.* **1**, the act of swinging; a swaying motion from side to side; also, the distance through which an object swings; **2**, a loose, free gait; **3**, an apparatus, usually a rope bearing a seat, for swinging to and fro; **4**, full course or freedom; as, to give full *swing* to imagination; **5**, the rhythmic movement of a passage in prose or poetry.—*n.* **swing′er.**

swinge (swĭnj), *v.t.* [*p.t.* and *p.p.* swinged (swĭnjd), *p.pr.* swinge′ing], to whip or thrash; strike hard.

swin-gle (swĭng′gl), *n.* **1**, a wooden instrument for beating flax; **2**, the striking end of a flail:—*v.t.* [*p.t.* and *p.p.* -gled (-gld), *p.pr.* -gling], to clean (flax) with a swingle.

swin-gle-tree (swĭng′gl-trē″), *n.* a swinging or pivoted crossbar on a wagon, plow, or the like, to the ends of which the traces of a harness are attached: also called *swinglebar; swingtree; singletree; whippletree; whiffletree.*

swipe (swīp), *n.* a vigorous blow, as with a club:—*v.t.* [*p.t.* and *p.p.* swiped (swīpt), *p.pr.* swip′ing], **1**, to hit with force; **2**, *Slang*, to steal.

swirl (swûrl), *v.i.* to rush along with a circular or whirling motion:—*v.t.* to cause to eddy or whirl:—*n.* **1**, a whirling or eddying motion; **2**, a curve or twist.

swish (swĭsh), *n.* a rustling or whistling sound, or the movement that makes it; as, the *swish* of skirts:—*v.t.* to brandish or flourish, as a cane; switch:—*v.i.* to move with a rustling sound.

Swiss (swĭs), *adj.* pertaining to Switzerland, its language, or its people:—*n.* [*pl.* Swiss], a native or inhabitant of Switzerland; also, in *pl.*, collectively, the people of Switzerland.

switch (swĭch), *n.* **1**, a small, thin, flexible rod, esp. one suitable for whipping; **2**, a movable section of rail for shifting cars from one track to another; **3**, a device for making, breaking, or shifting electric circuits; **4**, a tress of false hair, used by women in hair dressing:—*v.t.* **1**, to whip or lash with a thin flexible rod; **2**, to swing or jerk; as, to *switch* a cane; **3**, to shift to another track; as, to *switch* a train; **4**, in electricity, to shift to another circuit, or on or off a circuit; as, to *switch* off the electric light.—*n.* **switch′er.**

switch-back (swĭch′băk″), *n.* **1**, a railway for going up and down a steep incline on zigzag tracks; **2**, an amusement railway with steep ascents and descents.

switch-board (swĭch′bōrd″), *n.* **1**, a board for controlling electric circuits; **2**, such a board for connecting telephone lines, as at an exchange.

switch-man (swĭch′măn), *n.* [*pl.* switchmen (-mĕn)], one who operates and guards railway switches.

Switz-er (swĭt′sẽr), *n.* a Swiss; esp., a Swiss mercenary soldier.

swiv-el (swĭv′l), *n.* **1**, anything that turns on a headed bolt or pin; as, the *swivel* of a watch chain; **2**, a link in two parts, connected by such a bolt or pin, so that each part can rotate independently: **swivel gun**, a gun mounted on a swivel to allow firing in any direction:—*v.* and *v.i.* to turn on a swivel, or pivots.

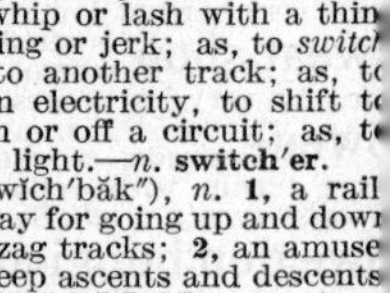

Swivel

swoll-en (swōl′n), the past participle of the irregular verb *swell.*

swoon (swōōn), *v.i.* to faint:—*n.* the act of fainting; also, a faint.

swoop (swōōp), *v.t.* to fall upon and seize, as, the eagle *swoops* up its prey:—*v.i.* to sweep down swiftly and suddenly; as, the eagle *swoops* down on its prey:—*n.* a sudden sweeping down and seizing.

sword (sōrd), *n.* **1**, a weapon consisting of a long, pointed blade, with one two sharp edges, set in a handle, or hilt; a rapier; saber; scimitar; **2,** hence, symbolically, military power, justice, or vengeance; **3,** conflict or war; as, an appeal to the *sword:* **sword arm,** the right arm, as symbolic of strength: **sword cane,** a hollow cane which conceals within it the blade of a sword or dagger.

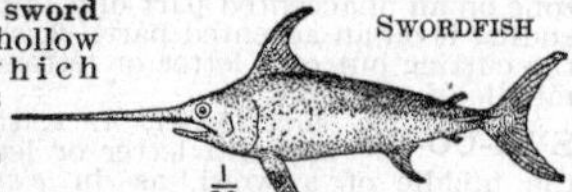

SWORDFISH 1/80

sword-fish (sōrd′fĭsh″), *n.* a large, edible sea fish, having the upper jaw formed into a swordlike beak.

sword grass any of various sedges or grasses the leaves of which have sharp or toothed edges.

sword-play (sōrd′plā″), *n.* fencing; the act or art of fighting with the sword or foil; swordsmanship.

swords-man (sōrdz′măn), *n.* [*pl.* swordsmen (-mĕn)], one skilled in the use of the sword; a fencer.

swords-man-ship (sōrdz′măn-shĭp), *n.* the art or skill of a swordsman; swordplay; fencing.

swore (swōr), past tense of *swear:* **sworn, 1,** past participle of *swear;* **2,** as *p.adj.*, bound by an oath; as, a *sworn* enemy.

swum (swŭm), past participle and one of the past tenses of *swim.*

swung (swŭng), past tense and past participle of the irregular verb *swing.*

Syb-a-rite (sĭb′ȧ-rīt), *n.* an inhabitant of Sybaris, an ancient Greek city in Italy, noted for its luxury and wealth: **sybarite,** a person devoted to luxury and pleasure.—*adj.* **Syb″a-rit′ic; syb″a-rit′ic.**

syc-a-mine (sĭk′ȧ-mīn), *n.* the black mulberry (Luke 17:6).

syc-a-more (sĭk′ȧ-mōr), *n.* **1,** a fig tree of Syria; **2,** in England, a kind of maple; **3,** the American buttonwood.

syc-o-phan-cy (sĭk′ō-făn-sĭ), *n.* [*pl.* sycophancies (-sĭz)], the character or practices of a servile flatterer; fawning.

syc-o-phant (sĭk′ō-fănt), *n.* a servile flatterer; toady; parasite. —*adj.* **syc″o-phan′tic.**

sy-e-nite (sī′ĕ-nīt), *n.* a granular, gray rock, consisting of feldspar with very little quartz.—*adj.* **sy″e-nit′ic.**

syl-la-ba-ry (sĭl′ȧ-bă-rĭ), *n.* [*pl.* syllabaries (-rĭz)], a list of characters, analogous to the letters of an alphabet, but representing syllables instead of letters, as in the Japanese language.

syl-lab-ic (sĭ-lăb′ĭk), *adj.* pertaining to, or consisting of, a syllable or syllables. Also, **syl-lab′i-cal.**—*adv.* **syl-lab′i-cal-ly.**

syl-lab-i-cate (sĭ-lăb′ĭ-kāt), *v.t.* [*p.t.* and *p.p.* -cat″ed, *p.pr.* -cat″ing], to syllabify (which see).—*n.* **syl-lab″i-ca′tion.**

syl-lab-i-fy (sĭ-lăb′ĭ-fī), *v.t.* [*p.t.* and *p.p.* -fied (-fīd), *p.pr.* -fy″ing], to divide into syllables.—*n.* **syl-lab″i-fi-ca′tion.**

syl-la-ble (sĭl′ȧ-bl), *n.* **1,** that part of a word which can be clearly spoken by a single effort of the voice; **2,** such a part separated from the rest of the word.

syl-la-bub (sĭl′ȧ-bŭb), *n.* a dish made by mixing milk or cream, often whipped, with wine or cider, to form a soft curd. Also, **sil′la-bub,** *Pfd. S.*

syl-la-bus (sĭl′ȧ-bŭs), *n.* [*pl.* syllabuses (-ĕz); syllabi (-bī)], a brief statement of the main points of a subject, book, course of study, or the like.

syl-lo-gism (sĭl′ō-jĭzm), *n.* an argument stated in a logical form, consisting of three propositions, the first two being called the premises, and the last the conclusion, containing the matter to be proved. —*adj.* **syl″lo-gis′tic; syl″lo-gis′ti-cal.**—*adv.* **syl″lo-gis′ti-cal-ly.**

sylph (sĭlf), *n.* **1,** an imaginary being living in the air; a fairy; **2,** a slender, graceful young woman.—*adj.* **sylph′like″.**

sylph-id (sĭl′fĭd), *n.* a young or diminutive sylph.—*adj.* **sylph′id-ine.**

syl-va (sĭl′vȧ), *n.* [*pl.* sylvas (-vȧz); sylvæ (-vē)], the forest trees of a region, considered collectively. Also, **sil′va,** *Pfd. S.*

syl-van (sĭl′văn), *adj.* pertaining to woods or groves; rustic; woody; shady; as, a *sylvan* retreat. Also, **sil′van,** *Pfd. S.*

sym- (sĭm-), *prefix,* a form of *syn-*, which see, used before initial *p, b,* and *m.*

sym-bol (sĭm′bŏl), *n.* **1,** something, not a likeness, that stands for something else, and in some way brings it to mind, as by resemblance; esp., an emblem, or object that represents an idea, quality, or another thing; as, the cross is the *symbol* of Christianity; **2,** a mark, character, or letter representing something; as, a *symbol* in mathematics.
Syn. token, figure. (See emblem.)

sym-bol-ic (sĭm-bŏl′ĭk), *adj.* **1,** pertaining to a symbol, or sign, or to symbols; **2,** serving as a sign; expressing by signs. Also, **sym-bol′i-cal.**—*adv.* **sym-bol′i-cal-ly.**—*n.* **sym-bol′i-cal-ness.**

sym-bol-ics (sĭm-bŏl′ĭks), *n.pl.* used as *sing.* the study of creeds, or of ancient symbolic rites.

sym-bol-ism (sĭm′bŏl-ĭzm), *n.* representation by symbols or signs.—*n.* **sym′bol-ist.**—*adj.* **sym″bol-is′tic.**

sym-bol-ize (sĭm′bŏl-īz), *v.t.* [*p.t.* and *p.p.* -ized (-īzd), *p.pr.* -iz″ing], **1,** to represent or show by symbols, or signs; **2,** to be representative of; as, the lion *symbolizes* courage:—*v.i.* to use symbols, or signs, as in decoration.—*n.* **sym″bol-i-za′tion.**

sym-met-ri-cal (sĭ-mĕt′rĭ-kăl), *adj.* regular or even; having harmonious parts; well-balanced; as, a *symmetrical* design. Also, **sym-met′ric.**—*adv.* **sym-met′ri-cal-ly.**—*n.* **sym-met′ri-cal-ness.**

sym-me-try (sĭm′ĕ-trĭ), *n.* [*pl.* symmetries (-trĭz)], **1,** harmony, balance, or right proportion of the several parts of a body; **2,** similarity of parts on opposite sides of a dividing line.

sym-pa-thet-ic (sĭm″pȧ-thĕt′ĭk), *adj.* **1,** sharing, or affected by, the feelings of another; as, a *sympathetic* friend; **2,** hence, compassionate; **3,** congenial; harmonious: **sympathetic ink,** an ink that remains invisible on the paper until treated with some agent, as heat, strong light, acid, etc.: also called *invisible ink.* Also, **sym″pa-thet′i-cal.**—*adv.* **sym″pa-thet′i-cal-ly.**

sym-pa-thize (sĭm′pȧ-thīz), *v.i.* [*p.t.* and *p.p.* -thized (-thīzd), *p.pr.* -thiz″ing], **1,** to understand and share the sentiments, emotions, etc., of another; **2,** to feel compassion; **3,** to agree; harmonize, as colors. —*n.* **sym′pa-thiz″er.**

sym-pa-thy (sĭm′pȧ-thĭ), *n.* [*pl.* sympathies (-thĭz)], **1,** the quality of sharing another's emotions; as, in *sympathy* with her anger; **2,** compassion for another's trouble: with *for;* **3,** harmony or agreement of affections or tastes; congeniality.
Syn. pity, condolence. *Sympathy* means the sharing of another's feelings, esp. of trouble or sorrow, and implies equality. *Pity* suggests a feeling of tenderness and helpfulness for the unfortunate or needy. *Condolence* denotes a formal expression of *sympathy,* for some serious or terrible occurrence.

sym-phon-ic (sĭm-fŏn′ĭk), *adj.* **1,** agreeing in sound; harmonious;

2, relating to, or in the manner of, a musical composition called a *symphony*.

sym-pho-ni-ous (sĭm-fō′nĭ-ŭs), *adj.* agreeing in sound; harmonious.—*adv.* **sym-pho′ni-ous-ly.**

sym-pho-ny (sĭm′fō-nĭ), *n.* [*pl.* symphonies (-nĭz)], 1, harmony of sound; 2, an agreeable blending of any kind; 3, an elaborate musical composition, consisting of three or four movements, for a full orchestra; 4, an instrumental introduction or ending in a vocal composition.

sym-po-si-um (sĭm-pō′zĭ-ŭm), *n.* [*pl.* symposia (-*ȧ*)], 1, a drinking together, or a banquet at which there is brilliant and entertaining conversation; 2, a collection of essays in which various writers express their views on some given topic.

symp-tom (sĭmp′tŭm), *n.* 1, that which shows the existence of something else of which it is the effect; a token or sign; as, *symptoms* of unrest in a country; 2, any noticeable change in the body or its functions, as indicating disease.

symp-tom-at-ic (sĭmp″tŭm-ăt′ĭk), *adj.* 1, according to symptoms, or noticeable changes in the body; 2, indicative; pointing out. Also, **symp″tom-at′i-cal.**—*adv.* **symp″tom-at′i-cal-ly.**

syn- (sĭn-), *prefix*, [appearing also in the forms *sym-* before *b*, *p*, and *m; syl-* before *l; sys-* before *s* not followed by a consonant; *sy-* before *z* or *s* followed by a consonant], forming compounds with Greek words, and having the following meanings: 1, with, along with, together; as, *sym*posium; *syn*tax; *sym*pathy; 2, the same, at the same time; as, *syn*onymous; *sym*metrical; *syn*opsis; 3, a general meaning of together, the exact force having been lost; as, *sym*ptom.

syn-ær-e-sis (sĭn-ĕr′ē-sĭs), *n.* the drawing together into one syllable of two vowels that are ordinarily in two syllables, as *e′er* for *ever*. Also, **syn-er′e-sis.**

syn-a-gogue (sĭn′*ȧ*-gŏg), *n.* 1, an assembly or gathering of Jews for worship; 2, the place used for such worship.

syn-chro-nism (sĭng′krō-nĭzm), *n.* 1, sameness in time of two or more events; 2, arrangement of events and personages, according to dates, in a table.

syn-chro-nize (sĭng′krō-nīz), *v.t.* [*p.t.* and *p.p.* -nized (-nīzd), *p.pr.* -niz″ing], 1, to assign to the same date or period of time; 2, to make to agree in time or speed:—*v.i.* to happen at the same time; agree in time.—*n.* **syn′chro-niz″er.**

syn-chro-nous (sĭng′krō-nŭs), *adj.* 1, happening at the same time rate; having the same rate of vibration; 2, happening at the same time; simultaneous.—*adj.* **syn′chro-nal.**—*adj.* **syn-chron′ic.**—*adv.* **syn′chro-nous-ly.**

syn-cli-nal (sĭn-klī′năl; sĭng′klĭ-năl), *adj.* 1, sloping downward from opposite directions so as to meet; 2, dipping downward on each side toward a common line, as some rock strata: opp. of *anticlinal*. Also, *n.* **syn′cline** (sĭng′klīn; sĭn-klīn′).

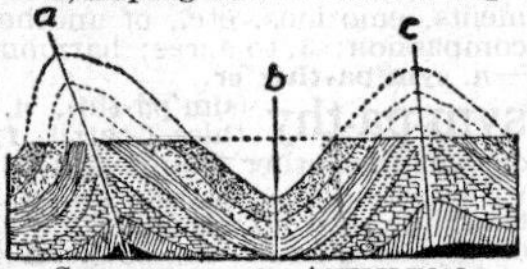

SYNCLINAL AND ANTICLINAL STRATA
Strata on opposite sides of axis *b* are synclinal; strata on opposite sides of axis *a* or *c* are anticlinal.

syn-co-pate (sĭng′kō-pāt), *v.t.* [*p.t.* and *p.p.* -pat″ed, *p.pr.* -pat″ing], 1, to contract by omitting a letter or letters from the middle of (a word); 2, in music, to begin (a tone) on an unaccented beat of a measure and end on an accented beat; as, to *syncopate* a waltz.

syn-co-pa-tion (sĭng″kō-pā′shŭn), *n.* 1, the beginning of a tone on an unaccented part of a measure, and ending it on an accented part; 2, syncope, or the cutting out of a letter or letters from the middle of a word.

syn-co-pe (sĭng′kō-pē), *n.* 1, the cutting out of a letter or letters from the middle of a word, as in *e′er* for *ever;* 2, fainting, or a fainting fit.

syn-dic (sĭn′dĭk), *n.* 1, a government officer having varying powers in different countries; 2, a business agent of a corporation, university, or body of men.

syn-di-cal-ism (sĭn′dĭ-kăl-ĭzm), *n.* a plan or theory in accordance with which workers in all trades should attempt to gain control of production by a general strike.—*n.* **syn′di-cal-ist.**

syn-di-cate (sĭn′dĭ-kāt), *n.* 1, an association or company of persons who combine to carry out some special business project or plan, often requiring large capital; as, a newspaper or motion-picture *syndicate;* 2, the office of a syndic:—*v.t.* (sĭn′-dĭ-kāt), [*p.t.* and *p.p.* -cat″ed, *p.pr.* -cat″ing], 1, to form into a syndicate; 2, to manage, control, or issue, by a syndicate; as, to *syndicate* cartoons.

syne (sīn), *adv. Scot.*, 1, since; ago; 2, immediately afterward; 3, since that time:—*n.* time: **auld lang syne**, bygone days.

syn-er-e-sis (sĭn-ĕr′ē-sĭs), *n.* the uniting into one syllable of two vowels that are ordinarily in two syllables, as *e′er* for *ever*. Also, **syn-ær′e-sis,** *Pfd. S.*

syn-od (sĭn′ŭd), *n.* 1, a church council, or meeting, to consult on religious matters; 2, any assembly or council.

syn-od-ic (sĭ-nŏd′ĭk), *adj.* of or pertaining to a synod, or church council. Also, **syn-od′i-cal.**—*adv.* **syn-od′i-cal-ly.**

syn-o-nym (sĭn′ō-nĭm), *n.* a word having the same or nearly the same meaning as another, as *sharp* and *keen:* opp. of *antonym*. Also, **syn′o-nyme** (-nĭm).

syn-on-y-mous (sĭ-nŏn′ĭ-mŭs), *adj.* having the same or nearly the same meaning.—*adv.* **syn-on′y-mous-ly.**

syn-on-y-my (sĭ-nŏn′ĭ-mĭ), *n.* [*pl.* synonymies (-mĭz)], 1, identity of meaning; 2, the study of the use and nice discrimination of synonymous words; 3, a collection or list of synonyms.

syn-op-sis (sĭ-nŏp′sĭs), *n.* [*pl.* synopses (-sēz)], a general view, as of any subject; a summary or abstract; as, the *synopsis* of a book or play.

syn-op-tic (sĭ-nŏp′tĭk), *adj.* 1, giving a general view of a whole or of its principal parts; 2, having the same or a similar point of view: **Synoptic Gospels,** Matthew, Mark, and Luke: so called because of their many agreements in subject, order, and language. Also, **syn-op′ti-cal.**—*adv.* **syn-op′ti-cal-ly.**

syn-o-vi-a (sĭ-nō′vĭ-*ȧ*), *n.* the oily fluid in the joints of the body: also called *synovial fluid*.—*adj.* **syn-o′vi-al.**

syn-tac-tic (sĭn-tăk′tĭk), *adj.* pertaining to the rules of syntax, or that part of grammar that treats of sentences. Also, **syn-tac′ti-cal.**—*adv.* **syn-tac′ti-cal-ly.**

syn-tax (sĭn′tăks), *n.* that part of grammar which treats of the proper construction of sentences; sentence structure.

syn-the-sis (sĭn′thē-sĭs), *n.* [*pl.* syntheses (-sēz)], 1, the putting of things together to form a whole; 2, in chemistry, the building up of substances into a compound;

3, a process of reasoning from a general law to a specific case; deduction.

syn-thet-ic (sĭn-thĕt′ĭk), *adj.* **1**, pertaining to the putting of elements together in a new form; **2**, in chemistry, made or combined by artificial means; as, *synthetic* rubber. Also, **syn-thet′i-cal.**—*adv.* **syn-thet′i-cal-ly.**—*n.* **syn-thet′ics.**

syph-i-lis (sĭf′ĭ-lĭs), *n.* a contagious, venereal disease, often fatal.—*adj.* and *n.* **syph″i-lit′ic.**

Syr-i-ac (sĭr′ĭ-ăk), *adj.* pertaining to Syria, or to its language:—*n.* the language of Syria.

Syr-i-an (sĭr′ĭ-ăn), *adj.* pertaining to Syria, or to its people:—*n.* a native of Syria, esp. of the native Semitic race.

sy-rin-ga (sĭ-rĭng′gȧ), *n.* any of a genus of garden shrubs with white or cream-colored flowers; esp., the mock orange.

syr-inge (sĭr′ĭnj), *n.* **1**, an instrument for injecting a liquid in a jet or stream into the body; **2**, any of various devices for this purpose, as a bulb with a nozzle:—*v.t.* [*p.t.* and *p.p.* -inged (-ĭnjd), *p.pr.* -ing-ing], to inject or cleanse by means of a syringe.

syr-inx (sĭr′ĭngks), *n.* [*pl.* syringes (sĭ-rĭn′jēz)], **1**, the song organ of birds, located at the lower end of the trachea; **2**, the Eustachian tube; **3**, a primitive wind instrument made of reeds or pipes.

syr-up (sĭr′ŭp), *n.* **1**, a thick, sticky liquid made from the juice of fruits, herbs, etc., boiled with sugar; **2**, any concentrated solution of sugar. Also, **sir′up,** *Pfd. S.*

sys-tem (sĭs′tĕm), *n.* **1**, the orderly combination of parts into a whole; **2**, a group or assemblage of objects forming a natural whole and arranged or acting according to some common law; as, the solar *system;* a school *system;* **3**, an orderly collection of rules and principles; as, a *system* of laws; **4**, an orderly grouping of facts and objects; as, a *system* of classification or of filing; **5**, any specified method of procedure; as, a shorthand *system;* **6**, regularity or method in transacting business; orderliness.—*adj.* **sys-tem′ic.**

sys-tem-at-ic (sĭs″tĕm-ăt′ĭk), *adj.* **1**, of or pertaining to, or of the nature of, a system, or orderly whole; acting according to a regular method or plan; **2**, methodical; as, *systematic* study. Also, **sys″tem-at′i-cal.**—*adv.* **sys″tem-at′i-cal-ly.**

sys-tem-a-tize (sĭs′tĕm-ȧ-tīz), *v.t.* [*p.t.* and *p.p.* -tized (-tīzd), *p.pr.* -tiz″ing], to reduce to a system, or regular method.—*n.* **sys″tem-a-ti-za′tion.**

sys-tem-ize (sĭs′tĕm-īz), *v.t.* [*p.t.* and *p.p.* -ized (-īzd), *p.pr.* -iz″ing], to reduce to a system; arrange in order.—*n.* **sys″tem-i-za′tion.**

sys-to-le (sĭs′tō-lē), *n.* **1**, the rhythmical contraction of the heart, esp. of the ventricles, alternating with the diastole, or expansion, with which it forms the pulse, or heart beat; **2**, the shortening of a syllable naturally long: opp. of *diastole.*—*adj.* **sys-tol′ic.**

syz-y-gy (sĭz′ĭ-jĭ), *n.* [*pl.* syzygies

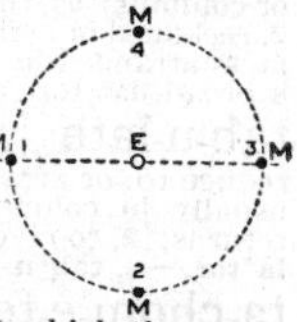

SYZYGY

S, sun; E, earth; M, moon in four positions: 1, 3, syzygies; 2, 4, quadratures.

(-jĭz)], either of the points at which the moon is most nearly in line with the earth and the sun, as when the moon is new or full.

T

tab (tăb), *n.* **1**, a small flap or tag attached to the edge of something, as a garment; a loop for pulling or lifting something; **2**, *Colloq.*, reckoning; account; as, to keep *tab.*

tab-ard (tăb′ȧrd), *n.* **1**, formerly, a short, coarse, outer coat worn by the poorer classes; **2**, a loose garment worn over armor, esp. such a coat worn by a herald and blazoned with the arms of his sovereign.

ta-bas-co (tȧ-băs′kō), *n.* a very peppery Mexican sauce.

tab-by (tăb′ĭ), *n.* [*pl.* tabbies (-ĭz)], **1**, a taffeta silk or moreen, with a wavy marking: often called *watered silk;* **2**, a very hard substance, made by mixing lime, water, and stone or shell; **3**, a striped or brindled cat; hence, any domestic cat, esp. a female cat; **4**, *Colloq.*, an old maid or a gossip:—*v.t.* [*p.t.* and *p.p.* -bied (-ĭd), *p.pr.* -by-ing], to put a wavy marking into:—*adj.* **1**, having a wavy marking; **2**, brindled.

tab-er-na-cle (tăb′ẽr-nȧ-kl;-nă-), *n.* **1**, a temporary dwelling; a movable residence, or tent; hence, the human body as the temporary dwelling of the soul; **2**, the movable tent used as a place of worship by the Israelites in the wilderness (Exodus 26–27); later, the Jewish temple; **3**, a place of worship, esp. one erected temporarily for special services; **4**, in the church communion, a small receptacle to hold the sacred elements.

ta-ble (tā′bl), *n.* **1**, a thin piece of wood, stone, metal, etc., with a flat surface, esp. one on which an inscription may be written or carved; **2**, a piece of furniture consisting of a flat, smooth top supported by legs; **3**, the persons sitting around a table, as to eat, play games, etc.; **4**, food; fare in general; as, the *table* at the hotel is good; **5**, an arrangement of words, facts, figures, etc., in systematic order for reference; as, the multiplication *table;* a *table* of statistics:—*v.t.* [*p.t.* and *p.p.* -bled (-bld), *p.pr.* -bling], **1**, to lay aside, as a report, for future consideration; **2**, to lay on a table, as a card or money.

tab-leau (tăb′lō; *Fr.* tȧ″blō′), *n.* [*pl.* tableaux (tăb′lōz; *Fr.* tȧ″blō′), tableaus (tăb′lōz)], a striking and lifelike representation; esp., a scene representing a picture, showing persons appropriately dressed and grouped, and remaining silent and motionless.

ta-ble-cloth (tā′bl-klôth″), *n.* a cover of linen, cotton, etc., spread upon a table, usually during a meal.

***ta-ble d'hôte** (tȧbl′ dōt′), [Fr.], [*pl.* tables d'hôte (tȧbl′)], **1**, designating a complete meal served at a fixed price: opp. of *à la carte;* **2**, formerly, a common table for guests at a hotel or café.

ta-ble–land (tā′bl=lănd″), *n.* a plateau, or broad, elevated piece of land.

ta-ble-spoon (tā′bl-spo͞on″), *n.* a large spoon for use in preparing and serving meals, holding four times as much as a teaspoon.—*n.* **ta′ble-spoon″ful.**

tab-let (tăb′lĕt), *n.* **1**, a small flat surface, esp. one used for drawing or writing; **2**, a set of blank sheets of paper fastened together at one end and used for writing upon; a writing pad; **3**, in classic antiquity, one of a number of thin, flat pieces of wax-coated wood, ivory, etc., fastened together and used for memoranda; **4**, a flat panel, often of stone, brass, or bronze, fastened in a wall and containing an inscription; **5**, medicine in the form of a small, flat disk; **6**, a small, flat cake, as of soap, candy, or the like.

ta-ble-ware (tā′bl-wâr″), *n.* articles put upon a table for use at meals.

tab-loid (tăb′loid), *n.* **1**, a small tablet of highly concentrated drugs, etc.: a trade name; **2**, hence, anything small or compact:—*adj.* condensed; brief; as, *tabloid* news.

ta-boo (tȧ-bōō′), *n.* **1**, a religious system and practice, among the Polynesians and other savage races, in which certain things are made sacred and contact with them forbidden; **2**, ban; prohibition:—*v.t.* to place under a ban; forbid; prohibit:—*adj.* **1**, set apart; made untouchable or sacred by religious custom; **2**, prohibited by social custom, law, or prejudice. Also, **ta-bu′**.

ta-bor (tā′bẽr), *n.* a small drum, shaped like a tambourine. Also, **ta′bour.**

tab-o-ret (tăb′ō-rĕt), *n.* **1**, a small tabor, or drum; **2**, a small stand or stool. Also, **tab′ou-ret.**

tab-u-lar (tăb′ū-lȧr), *adj.* **1**, arranged in the form of a table, or systematic outline; set down or arranged in schedules or columns; as, the report was in *tabular* form; **2**, reckoned or arrived at from sets of figures or facts arranged in systematic order; **3**, having a broad flat top, as a mountain.

tab-u-late (tăb′ū-lāt), *v.t.* [*p.t.* and *p.p.* -lat″ed, *p.pr.* -lat″ing], **1**, to reduce to, or arrange in, a systematic outline, usually in columns; as, to *tabulate* election returns; **2**, to give a flat surface to.—*n.* **tab′u-la″tor.**—*n.* **tab″u-la′tion.**

ta-chom-e-ter (tȧ-kŏm′ē-tẽr), *n.* a device for measuring speed; esp., a device for indicating the revolutions per minute of an engine: used to show the engine speed in airplanes.

tac-it (tăs′ĭt), *adj.* given or existing in silence; implied, but not stated outright; as, *tacit* consent.—*adv.* **tac′it-ly.**

tac-i-turn (tăs′ĭ-tûrn), *adj.* not apt to speak; disinclined to talk.—*adv.* **tac′i-turn-ly.**

Syn. silent, reticent.—*Ant.* talkative.

tac-i-tur-ni-ty (tăs″ĭ-tûr′nĭ-tĭ), *n.* the habit or state of speaking little; reserve.

tack (tăk), *n.* **1**, a small, broad-headed nail; **2**, a rope for holding down the lower corner of certain sails; **3**, the corner of the sail so held down; **4**, the direction of a ship in regard to the trim, or position, of her sails; **5**, a change in a ship's direction; **6**, hence, any course or policy of action:—*v.t.* **1**, to fasten with small nails; as, to *tack* down matting; **2**, to fasten slightly; attach; as, to *tack* a bow on a dress; **3**, to change the course of (a vessel) by using the helm and shifting the sails:—*v.i.* to change the course of a vessel by shifting her helm and the position of her sails.—*n.* **tack′er.**

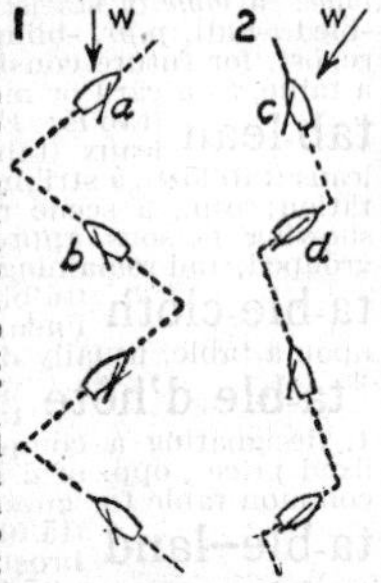

TACK (def. 4)
1: *a*, port tack; *b*, starboard tack.—2: *c*, starboard tack; *d*, port tack.—W,W, direction of wind.

tack-le (tăk′l), *n.* **1**, the ropes, pulleys, etc., of a vessel; **2**, equipment; gear; as, hunting and fishing *tackle;* **3**, the act of seizing or grappling; **4**, in football: **a**, the act of seizing and holding an opponent who is running with the ball, or an attempt to do so; **b**, a player in the line next to either end player, or the position next to either end position: **block and tackle**, an apparatus for raising or lowering heavy weights, consisting of pulleys and the ropes operating them (see [1]*block*, illus.):—*v.t.* [*p.t.* and *p.p.* -led (-ld), *p.pr.* -ling], **1**, to grapple with; endeavor to overcome, as a problem; **2**, to fasten with ropes and pulleys; **3**, in football, to seize and hold, or attempt to seize and hold (an opponent running with the ball).—*n.* **tack′ling.**

tact (tăkt), *n.* sympathetic understanding; delicate skill in saying and doing exactly what is best or most suitable in given circumstances; intuitive ability to deal wisely with others.

tact-ful (tăkt′fŏŏl), *adj.* **1**, skilful in saying and doing what is most proper; **2**, suitable in given circumstances, as a remark.—*adv.* **tact′ful-ly.**—*n.* **tact′ful-ness.**

tac-ti-cal (tăk′tĭ-kăl), *adj.* **1**, having to do with military or naval science; **2**, marked by adroitness or clever management.

tac-ti-cian (tăk-tĭsh′ăn), *n.* **1**, one skilled in military tactics; **2**, a skilful manager or organizer.

tac-tics (tăk′tĭks), *n. pl.* **1**, used as *sing.*, the science or practice of disposing and handling military or naval forces in the presence of an enemy; **2**, any procedure requiring skilful maneuvering to gain an end.

tac-tile (tăk′tĭl; *Br.* tăk′tīl), **1**, pertaining to the sense of touch; **2**, capable of being touched.—*n.* **tac-til′i-ty.**

tact-less (tăkt′lĕs), *adj.* **1**, lacking in discernment; blunt; **2**, not suitable; as, a *tactless* remark.—*adv.* **tact′less-ly.**—*n.* **tact′less-ness.**

tac-tu-al (tăk′tū-ăl), *adj.* **1**, pertaining to touch or the organs of touch; **2**, giving the sensation of, or caused by, touch.

tad-pole (tăd′pōl″), *n.* the larva of certain animals, as the frog, which has gills and a long tail (see *amphibian*, illus.).

tael (tāl), *n.* **1**, a Chinese monetary unit; **2**, a Chinese weight of from one to two and a half ounces.

taf-fe-ta (tăf′ē-tȧ), *n.* a lustrous silk of a fine, plain texture. Also, **taf′fe-ty.**

taff-rail (tăf′rāl), *n.* the rail round a ship's stern. Also, **taf′fa-rel.**

taf-fy (tăf′ĭ), *n.* **1**, candy made of brown sugar or molasses and butter, often with nuts added; **2**, *Colloq.*, flattery.

tag (tăg), *n.* **1**, a card or label to be attached to a box, package, etc.; **2**, a loose end or rag, as of clothing; **3**, a metal binding at the end of a string or lace to give stiffness; **4**, a children's game in which one chases the others in order to touch, or "tag," them:—*v.t.* [*p.t.* and *p.p.* tagged (tăgd), *p.pr.* tag′ging], **1**, to fix a tag to; append or tack on; **2**, in the game of tag, to catch by touching; **3**, *Colloq.*, to follow closely and persistently:—*v.i. Colloq.*, to follow another closely: with *after.*

Ta-ga-log (tä-gä′lŏg), *n.* **1**, a member of one of the chief native tribes of the Philippines; **2**, their language. Also, **Ta-gal′** (tä-gäl′).

Ta-hi-ti-an (tä-hē′tĭ-ăn), *adj.* pertaining to the island of Tahiti, or to its inhabitants or language:—*n.* **1**, one of a Polynesian race inhabiting Tahiti; **2**, the native language of Tahiti.

[1]**tail** (tāl), *n.* **1**, the hindmost part of an animal's body; esp., the appendage formed by the prolongation of the end of the backbone, hanging loose; hence, any of various things resembling this appendage in any of a number of ways; as, the *tail* of a parade; the *tail* of a coat, kite, or the like; **2**, usually in *pl.*, the reverse of a coin; **3**, in music, the vertical line running up or down

·rom a note on a staff: also called *stem* (see ·ote, illus.); **4,** a plane or planes at the rear ·f an airplane to give it balance: **tail skid,** runner at the rear of an airplane to keep ·he tail off the ground while the airplane · on the ground (see *airplane*, illus.):—*v.t.* to ·urnish with a tail:—*v.i.* to follow close behind; ·ag: with *after.*—*adj.* **tail'less.**

tail (tāl), *n.* in law, limitation of ownership; entailment:—*adj.* restricted in ·wnership and succession; entailed.

ail-ing (tāl'ĭng), *n.* **1,** the part of a projecting stone or brick inserted in a ·vall; **2,** in *pl.*, refuse, as stamped ore thrown ·rom the washing apparatus; chaff.

ai-lor (tā'lẽr), *n.* one whose business it is to make, and sometimes to repair, ·uter garments for men and women: **tailor ·ird,** any of several small African and Asiatic ·irds which strengthen their nests by stitching ·eaves together:—*v.i.* to follow the trade of a ·ailor.—*n.fem.* **tai'lor-ess.**

:ail-piece (tāl'pēs''), *n.* **1,** something added at the end; **2,** the piece to ·hich the strings of certain instruments, as ·he violin, are attached; **3,** a decorative design ·elow the print on an incompletely filled page.

:ail-stock (tāl'stŏk''), *n.* in a lathe, one of the adjustable, sliding parts ·olding the work (see *lathe*, illus.).

:aint (tānt), *n.* a spot; tinge; trace, as of decay or corruption; also, a corrupt ·r infected condition:—*v.t.* **1,** to fill with some·hing unpleasant or poisonous, as a disease; ·nfect; poison; **2,** to defile; render morally ·orrupt:—*v.i.* to become spoiled, as meat.

take (tāk), *v.t.* [*p.t.* took (to͝ok), *p.p.* tak'en (tāk'n), *p.pr.* tak'ing], **1,** to lay hold of, ·s with the hands; as, to *take* a man by the ·hroat; **2,** to seize; capture; as, the general *·ook* the fort by storm; **3,** to seize the interest ·of; captivate; as, the hat *took* her fancy; **4,** to ·ssume possession of; receive voluntarily; ·cquire; avail oneself of; as, to *take* a holiday; **5,** to engage, as seats in a theater; also, to buy ·regularly; subscribe to, as periodicals; **6,** to ·conduct or carry; convey; also, to escort; as, ·to *take* a guest home; **7,** to abstract; filch; ·steal; as, he *took* the gems; **8,** to use; make ·use of; as, to *take* medicine; **9,** to obtain as ·result of a process; as, to *take* a photograph; **10,** to submit to; endure; as, to *take* punish·ment; **11,** to come upon (suddenly); as, to *take* ·him by surprise; **12,** to retract or recant: used ·with *back;* as, to *take* back a statement; **13,** to ·be infected with; catch, as a contagious ·disease; **14,** to require: often impersonal; as, ·it *takes* two to do this; **15,** to perform; do, as ·an action; as, to *take* exercise; **16,** to pass; ·clear; go over; as, the horse *took* the obstacle; **17,** to conceive; experience; feel; as, to *take* ·offense, pride, joy, or the like; **18,** to under·stand; infer; as, I *take* you to be joking; **19,** to treat or regard in a specific manner; as, I *took* him for a fool; **20,** to remove by death; **21,** to choose; select; as, *take* the left-hand ·trail; **22,** to assume; take the shape or im·pression of; absorb; as, silk *takes* dye easily; **23,** to observe; find out; as, to *take* the depth ·of the water:—*v.i.* **1,** to have the intended ·effect; operate; act; as, the inoculation *took;* **2,** to proceed; go; as, to *take* to one's heels; **3,** to prove attractive; be acceptable; **4,** in ·law, to become possessed of property: **take ·after,** to resemble: **take off,** to jump, spring, ·or start: with *from:* **take to, 1,** to begin; fall ·into the habit of; **2,** to form a liking for:—*n.* ·the amount or quantity received or caught: ·said esp. of fish.—*n.* **tak'er.**

take–off (tāk'-ôf''), *n.* **1,** a caricature, parody, or imitation; **2,** a place from which one makes a start in running, or from which one jumps; also, the manner of starting.

tak-ing (tāk'ĭng), *p.adj.* **1,** attractive; alluring; pleasing; as, *taking* manners; **2,** infectious; contagious:—*n.* **1,** the act of gaining possession; seizure; **2,** in *pl.*, that which is accepted or received; receipts.—*adv.* **tak'ing-ly.**—*n.* **tak'ing-ness.**

talc (tălk), *n.* a silicate of magnesium, very soft and slippery, used in rubber manufacture, toilet powders, etc.: also called *soapstone* and *steatite.*—*adj.* **talc'ose; talc'ous.**

tale (tāl), *n.* **1,** that which is told; a narrative or story; fable; anecdote; **2,** a false report or piece of gossip; **3,** a count; reckoning; as, the *tale* of bricks made in a day.
Syn. account. (See anecdote.)

tale-bear-er (tāl'bâr''ẽr), *n.* one who maliciously spreads gossip, scandal, etc.; a gossip.—*n.* **tale'bear''ing.**

tal-ent (tăl'ĕnt), *n.* **1,** among the ancients, a weight or a coin of varying value, the Hebrew *talent* of gold being valued at $32,640; **2,** mental capacity or ability; skill; cleverness; **3,** a special gift, fitting one for a particular business, art, or profession; as, he has a *talent* for painting; **4,** collectively, persons of ability: often with *the.*—*adj.* **tal'ent-ed.**
Syn. genius. *Talent* implies unusual mental ability, capable of development by training, but not usually marked by much originality. *Genius* suggests great intellectual capacity but, unlike *talent*, implies originality and creative power of a high order. (See ability.)

ta-ler (tä'lẽr), *n.* an old German silver coin. See **tha'ler,** *Pfd. S.*

ta-les (tā'lēz), *n. pl.* **1,** used as *sing.*, a writ, or court order, for summoning additional jurors; **2,** persons who are so summoned to fill the vacant places in a jury.

tales-man (tālz'măn), *n.* [*pl.* talesmen (-mĕn)], a person summoned to fill a jury when the regular panel, or group of persons from which the jury is chosen, is used up before the jury is complete.

tale-tell-er (tāl'tĕl''ẽr), *n.* one who tells stories or tales; esp., one who maliciously spreads gossip; a talebearer; telltale.—*n.* **tale'tell''ing.**

tal-is-man (tăl'ĭs-măn; tăl'ĭz-măn), *n.* [*pl.* talismans (-mănz)], a figure cut in metal or stone, supposed to possess magical powers in averting evil or bringing good luck; a charm; an amulet; hence, something that produces an extraordinary effect.—*adj.* **tal''is-man'ic; tal''is-man'i-cal.**

talk (tôk), *v.i.* **1,** to utter words; express and try to communicate thoughts in speech; **2,** to speak familiarly; converse; **3,** to confer; consult; as, to *talk* with a teacher about one's progress; **4,** to prattle:—*v.t.* **1,** to utter; make a subject of conversation; as, to *talk* business; esp., to discuss favorably; as, to *talk* socialism; **2,** to speak (a language) freely; as, to *talk* French; **3,** to affect by talking; as, they *talked* him over to their side; **4,** to use or spend in talking: with *away;* as, to *talk* away an evening:—*n.* **1,** the act of expressing thoughts in words; speech; familiar conversation; as, an evening of friendly *talk;* **2,** a subject of discourse; as, the *talk* of the town; **3,** rumor; as, there is *talk* of a strike; **4,** meaningless speech; as, idle *talk;* **5,** a conference; as, *talk* about future plans; **6,** an informal address.—*n.* **talk'er.**

talk-a-tive (tôk'ȧ-tĭv), *adj.* given to much speaking; loquacious.—*adv.* **talk'a-tive-ly.**—*n.* **talk'a-tive-ness.**
Syn. communicative, voluble, fluent, glib.

talk-ie (tôk'ĭ), *n.* [*pl.* talkies (-ĭz)], a motion picture in which the words of the actors, and other sounds, are mechanically reproduced along with the picture.

talk-ing (tôk'ĭng), *n.* conversation or speech:—*p.adj.* **1,** given to speaking; 2, able to speak, or to imitate speech; as, a *talking* machine.

tall (tôl), *adj.* 1, high in stature; 2, of a certain height.—*n.* **tall'ness.**

tall-boy (tôl'boi″), *n.* a chest of drawers standing five or six feet high, mounted on legs about 18 inches long; a highboy (see *furniture*, illus.).

tal-low (tăl'ō), *n.* the harder fat of animals, as beef or mutton suet, separated from membranous tissues by melting, and used for making candles, soap, or the like:—*v.t.* 1, to cover with tallow; 2, to fatten, as sheep.—*adj.* **tal'low-y.**

tal-ly (tăl'ĭ), *n.* [*pl.* tallies (-ĭz)], 1, orig., a stick on which scores were recorded by notches; 2, anything on which a reckoning is kept; 3, an account or score; 4, one of a series of marks for recording a number of objects; also, the number of objects so recorded; 5, anything corresponding to another, as a duplicate: **tally sheet,** a sheet on which a score or account is kept; esp., a record of votes:—*v.t.* [*p.t.* and *p.p.* -lied (-ĭd), *p.pr.* -ly-ing], to keep score of with marks, notches, etc.:—*v.i.* to match; correspond; as, make your account *tally* with mine.

tal-ly-ho (tăl'ĭ-hō″), *interj.* the huntsman's cry to urge on his hounds:—*n.* [*pl.* tallyhos (-hōz″)], a four-in-hand coach.

Tal-mud (tăl'mŭd), *n.* the collection of Jewish civil and canonical laws not included in the Pentateuch.

tal-on (tăl'ŭn), *n.* the claw of a bird of prey; as, the *talon* of an eagle.

ta-lus (tā'lŭs), *n.* [*pl.* tali (-lī)], 1, the ankle or ankle bone; 2, a sloping heap of broken rocks at the foot of a cliff; 3, the front slope of a fortification.

tam-a-ble (tām'ȧ-bl), *adj.* capable of being subdued, made gentle, or rescued from wildness. Also, **tame'a-ble.**

ta-ma-le (tȧ-mä'lē), *n.* a Mexican dish of chopped meat and corn meal, seasoned with red pepper, wrapped in corn husks, and boiled or steamed.

tam-a-rack (tăm'ȧ-răk), *n.* any of several American larches; esp., the hackmatack: found in the eastern U. S.

tam-a-rin (tăm'ȧ-rĭn), *n.* any of several South American marmosets, or monkeys about the size of a squirrel.

tam-a-rind (tăm'ȧ-rĭnd), *n.* a tall tropical tree having yellow flowers striped with red; also, its podlike fruit, from which preserves and a cooling drink are made.

tam-a-risk (tăm'ȧ-rĭsk), *n.* any of a genus of Old World tropical shrubs or small trees; esp., a species having scalelike leaves of feathery appearance.

tam-bour (tăm'bo͝or; tăm'bẽr), *n.* 1, a small military drum; 2, a drumlike embroidery frame, usually consisting of two closely fitting hoops, between which the material is stretched; 3, embroidery made on such a frame:—*v.t.* and *v.i.* to embroider on a frame, or tambour.

tam-bou-rine (tăm″bo͞o-rēn'), *n.* 1, a small hand drum, having little metallic disks or jingles fastened in the hoop or rim, and played by striking, as with the knuckles (see *musical instrument*, illus.); 2, an old French dance.

tame (tām), *adj.* 1, altered from native wildness; made useful to man; 2, subdued; harmless; gentle; 3, lacking in spirit; dull:—*v.t.* [*p.t.* and *p.p.* tamed (tāmd), *p.pr.* tam'ing], 1, to bring from a wild to a gentle state; subdue; as, to *tame* a wild animal; 2, to remove spirit or courage from; make quiet.—*adv.* **tame'ly.**—*n.* **tame'ness.**

tame-less (tām'lĕs), *adj.* wild; not capable of being subdued.

Tam o' Shan-ter (tăm″ ō shăn'tẽr) the hero of Robert Burns's poem of the same name, a drunken farmer who is chased by witches: **tam-o'-shanter,** *n.* a Scotch cap with a tight band and a loose, round top: popularly called *tam*.

tamp (tămp), *v.t.* 1, to block up (the blast hole in a rock) with clay or similar material, in order to direct the force of the explosion; 2, to drive in or down by repeated gentle strokes.—*n.* [1]**tamp'er.**

[2]**tam-per** (tăm'pẽr), *v.i.* 1, to make meddlesome alterations in anything; experiment foolishly: followed by *with;* as, to *tamper* with a lock; 2, to use unfair influence; esp., to bribe; as, to *tamper* with a jury.

tam-pon (tăm'pŏn), *n.* a plug, as of cotton, inserted into a wound or cavity to stop bleeding, absorb secretions, or keep a part in position.

tam–tam (tŭm'=tŭm″), *n.* a drum or a gong used in eastern countries. Also, **tom'–tom″**, *Pfd. S.*

tan (tăn), *n.* 1, oak bark, or other bark containing tannic acid, broken into small bits and used in making leather; 2, a yellowish brown color, like that of such bark; 3, a brown color given to the skin by exposure to the sun:—*v.t.* [*p.t.* and *p.p.* tanned (tănd), *p.pr.* tan'ning], 1, to prepare, as skins of animals, by treating with tannic acid; convert into leather by the use of mineral salts; 2, to make brown by exposure to the sun:—*v.i.* 1, to be converted into leather; 2, to become brown in the sun:—*adj.* yellowish brown.

tan-a-ger (tăn'ȧ-jẽr), *n.* any of a family of American song birds closely related to the finches, usually of brilliant plumage, as the scarlet tanager.

tan-bark (tăn'bärk″), *n.* oak or other bark containing tannic acid, used in making leather, and, when the acid is exhausted, used as a soft surface on race tracks.

tan-dem (tăn'dĕm), *adv.* one behind another:—*adj.* of seats on a bicycle or of horses, arranged one behind another:—*n.* 1, a pair of horses harnessed one before the other; 2, a bicycle for two or more, with seats placed one before the other.

TANDEM

[1]**tang** (tăng), *n.* 1, of a knife, fork, or similar tool, the part which goes into the handle; 2, a strong, sharp taste or flavor; esp., a taste that does not belong to the thing itself; as, the air has the *tang* of the sea; 3, a sharp, characteristic flavor or tinge:—*v.t.* to furnish with a tang.

[2]**tang** (tăng), *n.* a sharp, twanging sound; twang:—*v.t.* to cause to sound with a vibrant, twanging noise; twang.

tan-gent (tăn'jĕnt), *adj.* 1, touching; 2, in geometry, meeting a line or surface only at one point, but not cutting it:—*n.* 1, a tangent line or surface; 2, any line or course leading abruptly away from the usual course; 3, in a right-angled triangle, the ratio between the side opposite and the side adjacent to an acute angle: one of the trigonometric functions.—*n.* **tan'gen-cy.**

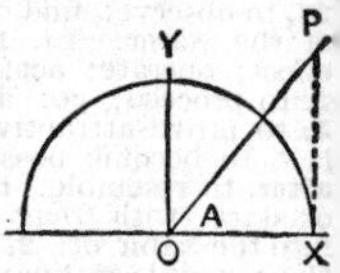

TANGENT

$\frac{XP}{OX}$ = tangent of angle A.
If OX = 1, the tangent is equal to the line XP.

tan-gen-tial (tăn-jĕn'shăl), *adj.* pertaining to, or in the direction of, a tangent.—*adv.* **tan-gen'tial-ly.**

tan-ger-ine (tăn'jẽr-ēn; tăn″jẽr-ēn'), *n.* a small orange with a sweet, spicy flavor and a thin, deep-colored skin.

tan-gi-ble (tăn'jĭ-bl), *adj.* **1**, capable of being touched; perceptible to the touch; **2**, capable of being demonstrated; evident; real; as, *tangible* proof.—*n.* **tan'gi-ble-ness.**—*adv.* **tan'gi-bly.**—*n.* **tan″gi-bil'i-ty.**

tan-gle (tăng'gl), *v.t.* [*p.t.* and *p.p.* -gled (-gld), *p.pr.* -gling], **1**, to knot or snarl so as to make difficult to unravel; **2**, to involve or implicate; as, to *tangle* oneself in excuses:—*v.i.* to be or become entangled or involved:—*n.* **1**, a snarl; a confused mass, as of string; **2**, a puzzling situation; as, his affairs were in a *tangle.*—*adj.* **tan'gly.**

tan-go (tăng'gō), *n.* [*pl.* tangos (-gōz)], a dance in two-four time, with a great variety of steps.

tank (tăngk), *n.* **1**, a large cistern or basin built to hold water or other liquid; as, a swimming *tank;* **2**, a large, often circular, receptacle or building for storing a fluid, as gas, gasoline, etc.; **3**, a kind of armored motor car, adapted from the caterpillar tractor and equipped with guns: used in modern warfare.

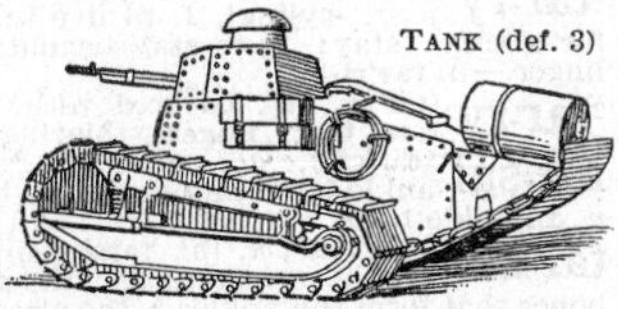
TANK (def. 3)

tank-age (tăngk'āj), *n.* **1**, the contents or capacity of a receptacle for liquid; **2**, the price for storing liquid in a tank.

tank-ard (tăngk'ȧrd), *n.* a large drinking vessel, usually with a lid.

tan-nate (tăn'āt), *n.* a salt of tannic acid, or tannin.

tan-ner (tăn'ẽr), *n.* one who tans hides into leather.

tan-ner-y (tăn'ẽr-ĭ), *n.* [*pl.* tanneries (-ĭz)], a place where hides are tanned.

Tann-häu-ser (tän'hoi-zẽr), *n.* a German knight and minnesinger, identified with a legendary knight who dwelt for a time under the spell of Venus in the enchanted caves: hero of an old ballad, and of a music drama of the same name by Wagner.

tan-nic (tăn'ĭk), *adj.* pertaining to, or obtained from, any bark, as oak or hemlock, which produces tan: **tannic acid,** a strong acid obtained from tea, sumac, gallnuts, etc., and used in tanning, dyeing, medicine, etc.: also called *tannin.*

tan-ning (tăn'ĭng), *n.* **1**, the process of converting hides into leather; **2**, a browning of the skin by exposure to the sun or weather; **3**, *Slang,* a flogging.

tan-sy (tăn'zĭ), *n.* [*pl.* tansies (-zĭz)], any of a genus of herbs of the composite family, with small heads of yellow flowers.

tan-ta-lize (tăn'tȧ-līz), *v.t.* [*p.t.* and *p.p.* -lized (-līzd), *p.pr.* -liz″ing], to tease or torment by exciting hopes or fears which will not be realized; provoke.—*n.* **tan″-ta-li-za'tion.**—*n.* **tan'ta-liz″er.**

Syn. harass, vex, irritate, plague.—*Ant.* satisfy, appease, pacify.

tan-ta-liz-ing (tăn'tȧ-līz″ĭng), *p.adj.* teasing or tormenting; provoking.—*adv.* **tan'ta-liz″ing-ly.**

Tan-ta-lus (tăn'tȧ-lŭs), *n.* in mythology, a son of Zeus, who, because of various crimes, was punished in the lower world by being placed up to his neck in water which receded when he stooped to drink, and under fruit-laden branches which retreated when he reached for them.

tan-ta-mount (tăn'tȧ-mount″), *adj.* equivalent or equal to in effect, value, or importance; as, your wish is *tantamount* to a command.

tan-trum (tăn'trŭm), *n. Colloq.,* a sudden outburst of temper or passion.

Tao-ism (tou'ĭzm), *n.* a Chinese religious system, whose greatest exponent, Lao-tse, in the sixth century B. C., prescribed a life of contemplation and reason and avoidance of force as the means of regeneration.—*n.* and *adj.* **Tao'ist.**—*adj.* **Tao-is'tic.**

[1]**tap** (tăp), *n.* **1**, a pipe or cock through which liquor is drawn from a cask; also, a faucet or spigot for drawing water; **2**, a place where liquor is drawn and retailed; **3**, liquor of a particular brewing or quality; **4**, a tool for cutting screw threads on an inner surface, as in a nut; **5**, in electricity, a device for making connection with a wire: **on tap,** ready to be drawn, as beer in a cask; ready for use:—*v.t.* [*p.t.* and *p.p.* tapped (tăpt), *p.pr.* tap'ping], **1**, to furnish, as a cask, with a cock or spigot; pierce, as a cask or the bark of a tree, in order to draw out liquid; **2**, to draw or let out liquid from; **3**, to make connections so as to draw or extract something from; as, to *tap* sources of information; **4**, to cut screw threads on the inner surface of, as a nut; **5**, in electricity, to make connection with (a wire) so as to draw off current:—*v.i.* to act as a tapster.—*n.* [1]**tap'per.**

TAP (def. 4)

[2]**tap** (tăp), *v.t.* [*p.t.* and *p.p.* tapped (tăpt), *p.pr.* tap'ping], **1**, to strike or touch lightly; **2**, to cause to strike or touch lightly; as, to *tap* a pencil on a desk; **3**, to apply a new piece of leather to (the sole or heel of a shoe) for the purpose of mending:—*v.i.* to strike light blows:—*n.* **1**, a gentle blow or touch; pat; rap; **2**, a piece of leather nailed or sewed on the sole of a boot or shoe to repair it; **3**, in *pl.,* in the U. S. army and navy, the last signal of the day, ordering lights out.—*n.* [2]**tap'per.**

tape (tāp), *n.* **1**, a narrow woven band of linen or cotton; **2**, the narrow strip of paper used on a printing telegraph or stock ticker; **3**, the line held to mark the finish of a race; **4**, a narrow strip of cloth, paper, or steel, marked with dimensions so as to be used for measuring length: **red tape,** needless formality in official business.

tape-line (tāp'līn″), *n.* a strip of fabric or of metal, marked with inches, feet, etc., used for measuring.

ta-per (tā'pẽr), *n.* **1**, a small wax candle; **2**, a gradual lessening of thickness toward a point; as, the *taper* of a cone:—*adj.* growing smaller toward the point, or toward one end:—*v.i.* and *v.t.* to narrow to a point.

tap-es-try (tăp'ĕs-trĭ), *n.* [*pl.* tapestries (-trĭz)], a picture made of hand-woven fabric, used as a wall hanging; also, a similar fabric, often machine-made, with similar or simpler designs, used for upholstered furniture: **tapestry carpet,** a kind of carpet somewhat resembling Brussels:—*v.t.* [*p.t.* and *p.p.* -tried (-trĭd), *p.pr.* -try-ing], to hang, or adorn, with tapestry.

tape-worm (tāp'wûrm″), *n.* any of several worms often found in the intestines of man and other animals.

tap-i-o-ca (tăp″ĭ-ō'kȧ), *n.* the starch prepared from the fleshy roots of the bitter cassava, and used in cookery.

ta-pir (tā'pẽr), *n.* any of a family of hoofed animals having short, stout legs and a long, flexible snout: found chiefly in South and Central America (see illus. next page).

ta-pis (tā'pĭs; tăp'ĭs; *Fr.* tȧ"pē'), *n.* tapestry, or similar material, used for wall hangings or floor covering: orig. the cover of a council table: **on the tapis,** up for, or under, consideration.

tap-pet (tăp'ĕt), *n.* in a machine, a small lever or projection, as a cam, touching, or touched by, some other part of the machine, and used to regulate motion, as in some valve gears.

SOUTH AMERICAN TAPIR (1/70)

tap-room (tăp'rōōm"), *n.* a place where liquors are kept ready to be drawn and sold; a barroom.

tap-root (tăp'rōōt"), *n.* the main root of certain plants, growing nearly straight downward and having few or many small branches, as in the radish or dandelion.

tap-ster (tăp'stẽr), *n.* one whose business it is to draw liquor at a bar.

[1]**tar** (tär), *n.* a thick, brownish black, oily substance obtained by the distillation of wood, coal, peat, etc.: used chiefly as a preservative or an antiseptic, and as the source of many chemical products: **tar camphor,** a chemical used as a moth preventive:—*v.t.* [*p.t.* and *p.p.* tarred (tärd), *p.pr.* tar'ring], to cover with, or as with, tar.

[2]**tar** (tär), *n. Colloq.,* a sailor; seaman; as, Jack's a jolly *tar.*

ta-ran-tel-la (tȧ"răn-tĕl'ȧ), *n.* **1,** a whirling, rapid, Italian dance; **2,** the music for such a dance.

ta-ran-tu-la (tȧ-răn'tū-lȧ), *n.* **1,** a large, hairy spider of southern Europe; **2,** any of several similar spiders of the warmer regions of America, whose bite is painful, but not fatal.

tar-boosh (tär-bōōsh'), *n.* a brimless, tasseled, fezlike cap, usually red, worn by men in Moslem countries.

tar-dy (tär'dĭ), *adj.* [*comp.* tar'di-er, *superl.* tar'di-est], **1,** moving with a slow pace or motion; **2,** not swift; not prompt; late.—*adv.* **tar'di-ly.**—*n.* **tar'di-ness.**

Syn. sluggish. (See slow.)

[1]**tare** (târ), *n.* an allowance of weight made to a purchaser by deducting the weight of the container:—*v.t.* [*p.t.* and *p.p.* tared (târd), *p.pr.* tar'ing], to weigh (a container) in order to ascertain the allowance of weight to be deducted.

[2]**tare** (târ), *n.* **1,** any of a genus of herbs of the pea family, mostly climbing; **2,** in the Bible, an unidentified weed, generally understood to be darnel (Matthew 13:25, 36).

tar-get (tär'gĕt), *n.* **1,** formerly, a small shield or buckler; **2,** a mark set up for archery, rifle, or artillery practice; **3,** one who or that which is an object of criticism, remark, etc.

tar-iff (tăr'ĭf), *n.* **1,** a schedule or table of duties or taxes placed by a government on goods coming into, or going out of, the country; **2,** such duties collectively; also, the principle of levying such duties; **3,** a tax or duty levied according to such a schedule; **4,** any schedule of rates, charges, etc.

tar-la-tan (tär'lȧ-tăn), *n.* a thin, stiff muslin with open mesh.

tarn (tärn), *n.* a small lake or pool in the mountains.

tar-nish (tär'nĭsh), *v.t.* to dull the brightness of; sully or stain:—*v.i.* to lose luster or brightness; become dull:—*n.* dulness; lack of polish; stain.

ta-ro (tä'rō), *n.* [*pl.* taros (-rōz)], a tropical plant grown especially on the islands of the Pacific Ocean, where its root is much used for food; also, the root of this plant.

tar-pau-lin (tär-pô'lĭn), *n.* **1,** stout waterproof canvas used for covering a ship's hatches, boats, etc.; **2,** a hat or coat of waterproof canvas.

tar-pon (tär'pŏn), *n.* a large sea fish found in West Indian waters and along the coasts of Georgia and Florida.

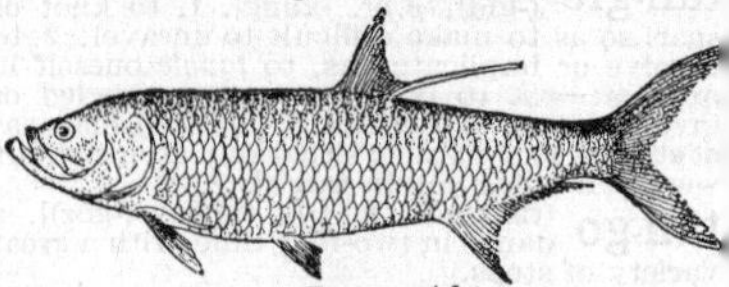

TARPON (1/30)

[1]**tar-ry** (tăr'ĭ), *v.i.* [*p.t.* and *p.p.* -ried (-ĭd), *p.pr.* -ry-ing], **1,** to live in a place for a time; stay; **2,** to stay behind; delay; linger.—*n.* **tar'ri-er.**

[2]**tar-ry** (tär'ĭ), *adj.* covered with, or like, tar: **tarry fingers,** thieving fingers.

tar-sal (tär'săl), *adj.* pertaining to the ankle or to any one of its bones:—*n.* an ankle bone.

tar-sus (tär'sŭs), *n.* [*pl.* tarsi (-sī)], **1,** the ankle, or instep; also, the group of bones that form the ankle; **2,** the plate of cartilage which stiffens the eyelids of man and certain other animals: also called *tarsal plate.*

[1]**tart** (tärt), *adj.* sharp to the taste; acid; hence, severe; cutting; as, a *tart* rejoinder.—*adv.* **tart'ly.**—*n.* **tart'ness.**

Syn. piquant, sour. (See bitter.)

[2]**tart** (tärt), *n.* a small piece of pastry filled with fruit or jam and without a top crust; sometimes, any fruit pie.

tar-tan (tär'tăn), *n.* **1,** woolen cloth, woven with a checkered or crossbarred pattern of narrow bands of various colors; **2,** any material, as gingham, of such a pattern:—*adj.* made from, or in the pattern of, tartan.

tar-tar (tär'tȧr), *n.* **1,** a white substance often found incrusting the teeth; **2,** the salt of tartaric acid, esp. when crude and forming a crust on the inside of wine casks: **tartar emetic,** a poisonous white substance used to induce sweating or vomiting.—*adj.* **tar'tar-ous.**—*v.t.* **tar'tar-ize.**

Tar-tar (tär'tȧr), *n.* a member of one of the nomadic Mongol tribes of central Asia: more correctly written *Tatar:*—*adj.* of or pertaining to the Tartars: **tartar,** *n.* an overbearing, irritable, or violent person.

tar-tar-ic (tär-tăr'ĭk), *adj.* pertaining to, or derived from, tartar: **tartaric acid,** an acid found in the juice of grapes, oranges, etc.: used in dyeing, medicine, etc.

Tar-ta-rus (tär'tȧ-rŭs), *n.* in mythology, the infernal regions; a place of punishment for wicked spirits; Hades.

task (tȧsk), *n.* **1,** labor, work, or study imposed by another: usually a certain amount; a lesson to be learned; **2,** duty; undertaking: **task force,** a force sent out, as by the Army or Navy, to perform a specific task:—*v.t.* **1,** to impose a certain amount of work upon; **2,** to burden with work.

Syn., n. undertaking, toil, drudgery.

task-mas-ter (tȧsk'mȧs"tẽr), *n.* one who sets work for another and oversees it; hence, an exacting employer.

task-work (tȧsk'wûrk"), *n.* a definite piece of work set to be done; also, work paid for by the piece.

tas-sel (tăs'l), *n.* **1,** a hanging ornament consisting of a bunch of threads or cords of silk, wool, or the like; 2, the hanging flower or head of certain plants; as, corn *tassels*:—*v.i.* to put forth hanging flowery heads:—*v.t.* to trim with, or make into, tassels.

tas-set (tăs′ĕt), *n.* one of a set of steel plates attached to the cuirass and protecting the thighs (see *armor*, illus.).

taste (tāst), *v.t.* [*p.t.* and *p.p.* tast′ed, *p.pr.* tast′ing], 1, to perceive or know by the tongue and palate; 2, to test the flavor of by eating or drinking a little; 3, to eat or drink a small portion of; hence, to experience slightly; 4, to participate in or experience; as, to *taste* remorse; 5, to enjoy; relish:—*v.i.* 1, to try food by the tongue or palate; 2, to have a certain flavor; 3, to eat or drink sparingly; partake; 4, to have experience or enjoyment: with *of*:—*n.* 1, the flavor of a substance as perceived by the tongue and palate; 2, the act of taking into the mouth to find out the quality or flavor; 3, a little bit or piece; esp., a small quantity tasted; 4, the one of the five senses which perceives the flavor of substances by the tongue and palate; 5, liking or inclination: with *for*; as, he had from his youth a *taste* for reading; 6, ability to see and admire what is beautiful; critical judgment; 7, habit or manner in relation to that which is refined or elegant; as, she dresses in good *taste*.—*n.* **tast′er.**

taste-ful (tāst′fo͝ol), *adj.* marked by, or showing, refinement, good judgment, or a sense of the beautiful; as, a *tasteful* arrangement of pictures on a wall.—*adv.* **taste′ful-ly.**—*n.* **taste′ful-ness.**

taste-less (tāst′lĕs), *adj.* 1, without flavor; flat; insipid, as food; 2, lacking refinement.—*n.* **taste′less-ness.**

tast-y (tās′tĭ), *adj.* [*comp.* tast′i-er, *superl.* tast′i-est], 1, having a fine flavor; savory; as, a *tasty* dish of food; 2, *Colloq.*, showing artistic refinement.—*adv.* **tast′i-ly.**—*n.* **tast′i-ness.**

tat (tăt), *v.t.* and *v.i.* [*p.t.* and *p.p.* tat′ted, *p.pr.* tat′ting], to make (trimming or lace) by looping and knotting thread wound on a shuttle. Also, **tatt.**

Ta-tar (tä′tȧr), *n.* a member of one of the nomadic Mongol races inhabiting central Asia. Also, **Tar′tar.**—*adj.* **Ta-ta′ri-an.**—*adj.* **Ta-tar′ic.**

tat-ter (tăt′ẽr), *n.* 1, a loose-hanging rag; 2, in *pl.*, rags.

tat-ter-de-mal-ion (tăt″ẽr-dē-māl′-yŭn; tăt″ẽr-dē-măl′yŭn), *n.* a ragged fellow; ragamuffin.

tat-tered (tăt′ẽrd), *adj.* 1, ragged; torn to pieces; 2, raggedly dressed.

tat-ting (tăt′ĭng), *n.* a kind of narrow lace for edging, made with a small hand shuttle; also, the art of making such lace.

tat-tle (tăt′l), *v.i.* [*p.t.* and *p.p.* -tled (-ld), *p.pr.* -tling], to chatter; talk idly or triflingly; tell tales or secrets:—*n.* trifling or idle talk; gossip.—*n.* **tat′tler.**—*n.* **tat′tling.**

¹tat-too (tă-to͞o′), *n.* a drum or other signal to call soldiers to quarters; also, a continuous beating of, or as of, a drum.

²tat-too (tă-to͞o′), *v.t.* to produce a permanent design on (the skin) by searing it or by puncturing a design on it and filling the punctures with indelible ink:—*n.* a mark or figure made by puncturing the skin and rubbing indelible stain or dye into the punctures.—*n.* **tat-too′er.**

tat-too-ing (tă-to͞o′ĭng), *n.* 1, the operation or practice of puncturing the skin and rubbing a stain or dye into the wounds; 2, the designs so made on skin.

tau (tou), *n.* the 19th letter of the Greek alphabet [τ, T], equivalent to English *t*: **tau cross,** a cross shaped like the Greek capital tau, or T (see *cross*, illus.).

taught (tôt), past tense and past participle of the irregular verb *teach*.

taunt (tänt; tônt), *n.* a bitter or sarcastic reproach:—*v.t.* to reproach with bitter, sarcastic, or insulting language; revile or jeer at.—*n.* **taunt′er.**—*adv.* **taunt′ing-ly.**

Syn., *v.* deride, mock. (See jeer.)

tau-rine (tô′rīn; tô′rĭn), *adj.* 1, pertaining to, or like, a bull; 2, pertaining to the constellation Taurus.

Tau-rus (tô′rŭs), *n.* 1, a northern constellation containing the Pleiades and the bright star Aldebaran; the Bull; 2, the second sign of the zodiac, entered by the sun about April 20 (see *zodiac*, illus.).

taut (tôt), *adj.* 1, tight; stretched; as, a *taut* rope; 2, snug; secure, as a ship.

tau-tog (tô-tŏg′), *n.* a medium-sized food fish found off the Atlantic coast of North America, particularly of New England.

tau-to-log-i-cal (tô″tō-lŏj′ĭ-kăl), *adj.* needlessly repeating the same idea in different words.

tau-tol-o-gy (tô-tŏl′ō-jĭ), *n.* [*pl.* tautologies (-jĭz)], a useless repeating of the same idea in different words; repetition which adds nothing to the sense, as "a panacea for all ills."—*n.* **tau-tol′o-gist.**

tav-ern (tăv′ẽrn), *n.* an inn or public house; a hotel; esp., a house licensed to sell liquor in small quantities.

¹taw (tô), *v.t.* to convert (hides or skins) into leather by treating with metallic salts.—*n.* **taw′er.**—*n.* **taw′ing.**

²taw (tô), *n.* 1, a mark or line from which players shoot in playing marbles; 2, a type of game played with marbles; 3, a marble, esp. one with which a player shoots.

taw-dry (tô′drĭ), *adj.* [*comp.* taw′dri-er, *superl.* taw′dri-est], showy without elegance; cheap; gaudy; as, a *tawdry* dress.—*adv.* **taw′dri-ly.**—*n.* **taw′dri-ness.**

taw-ny (tô′nĭ), *adj.* [*comp.* taw′ni-er, *superl.* taw′ni-est], of a yellowish brown color; as, the *tawny* lion.—*n.* **taw′ni-ness.**

tax (tăks), *n.* 1, a charge or duty on income or property, imposed by a government for its support; 2, a heavy or oppressive burden; as, a *tax* on one's strength:—*v.t.* 1, to impose a rate or duty upon for the support of a government; 2, to burden or oppress; as, to *tax* one's memory; 3, to accuse; as, to *tax* a man with crime.—*n.* **tax′er.**

Syn., *n.* custom, toll, assessment.

tax-a-ble (tăk′sȧ-bl), *adj.* subject or liable to a duty, charge, or tax.—*adv.* **tax′a-bly.**—*n.* **tax″a-bil′i-ty.**

tax-a-tion (tăk-sā′shŭn), *n.* 1, the act of imposing a charge or duty on persons or property; 2, the rate or sum imposed; 3, a system of raising money for public use by means of duties, or taxes.

tax-i (tăk′sĭ), *n. Colloq.*, a taxicab:—*v.i.* [*p.t.* and *p.p.* tax′ied (-sĭd), *p.pr.* tax′i-ing or tax′y-ing], 1, of an airplane, to skim along on water or land, as when preparing to rise or after landing; 2, *Colloq.*, to ride in a taxicab.

tax-i-cab (tăk′sĭ-kăb″), *n.* a motor cab provided with a taximeter; hence, any motor cab: generally shortened to *taxi*.

tax-i-der-my (tăk′sĭ-dûr″mĭ), *n.* the art of preparing, stuffing, and mounting the skins of animals so as to keep a lifelike appearance.—*n.* **tax′i-der″mist.**

tax-im-e-ter (tăk-sĭm′ē-tẽr), *n.* 1, an automatic device for measuring the distance traveled by a cab and recording the fare; 2, a taxicab.

tax-on-o-my (tăk-sŏn′ō-mĭ), *n.* the science of classification, esp. of animals and plants.—*adj.* **tax″o-nom′ic.**

tcher-vo-netz (chȧr-vô′nĕts), *n.* [*pl.* tchervontsi (-vônt′sĭ)], the monetary unit of Russia, normally worth ten gold rubles and equivalent to $5.14½. See **cher'vo-netz**, *Pfd. S.*

tea (tē), *n.* **1,** a shrub of eastern Asia, cultivated for its leaves; **2,** the dried leaves of the tea plant; **3,** the drink obtained by pouring boiling water on these leaves; **4,** any of various mild beverages resembling tea; as, beef *tea;* **5,** a light afternoon meal at which tea is served; **6,** hence, an evening meal, when dinner has been eaten in the middle of the day; **7,** a social affair at which tea is served.

teach (tēch), *v.t.* [*p.t.* and *p.p.* taught (tôt), *p.pr.* teach'ing], **1,** to show or instruct how to perform some action; as, to *teach* a boy to swim; **2,** to give instruction to; educate, as a pupil; **3,** to give lessons in, as a subject of study; **4,** to explain; show in the course of instruction; as, they *teach* that two and two make four:—*v.i.* to give instruction; engage in teaching.—*n.* **teach'er.**

teach-a-ble (tēch'ȧ-bl), *adj.* **1,** quick or apt to learn; **2,** of such a nature as to be easily taught.—*n.* **teach'a-ble-ness.**—*adv.* **teach'a-bly.**—*n.* **teach"a-bil'i-ty.**

teach-ing (tēch'ĭng), *n.* **1,** the profession of instructing or educating; **2,** usually in *pl.*, that which is taught.

tea-cup (tē'kŭp"), *n.* **1,** a cup in which tea is served; also, any cup of this size; **2,** a teacupful.

tea-cup-ful (tē'kŭp"fo͝ol), *n.* [*pl.* teacupfuls (-fo͝olz)], the amount that a teacup will hold.

teak (tēk), *n.* **1,** a tall East Indian tree whose leaves yield a red dye; **2,** the hard, durable timber of this tree, used for shipbuilding and furniture.

tea-ket-tle (tē'kĕt"l), *n.* a covered kettle with a spout and handle, in which water is heated.

teal (tēl), *n.* any of certain small, short-necked, fresh-water ducks.

team (tēm), *n.* **1,** two or more horses or other beasts in one harness; also, the animals with their harness and the vehicle that they draw; often, a single animal in harness and the vehicle; **2,** a group or brood of young, esp. of ducks; **3,** a number of persons working or playing together, as to form a side in a game, to raise a sum of money, etc.

team-ster (tēm'stẽr), *n.* **1,** the driver of a team of horses or other animals; **2,** one whose business is hauling.

team-work (tēm'wûrk"), *n.* **1,** work done by several persons together, as distinguished from work done by a single person; **2,** efficient work done in harmony by a group of persons for a common cause.

tea-pot (tē'pŏt"), *n.* a vessel with a spout, handle, and cover, in which tea is made and from which it is served.

[1]**tear** (târ), *v.t.* [*p.t.* tore (tōr), *p.p.* torn (tōrn), *p.pr.* tear'ing], **1,** to pull apart; rend; **2,** to lacerate; scratch, as the skin or flesh; **3,** to produce or cause by the action of rending; as, to *tear* a hole in a paper; **4,** to wrench or sever with force: with *from, away,* etc.; **5,** hence, to disrupt; distress greatly; as, a mind *torn* by doubts:—*v.i.* **1,** to part on being pulled or roughly handled; **2,** to move or act with force or agitated haste:—*n.* **1,** a rent; a hole made by pulling apart; **2,** *Slang,* a carouse; spree.—*n.* **tear'er.**

[2]**tear** (tēr), *n.* **1,** a small drop of salty liquid secreted by a gland of the eye; **2,** any similar drop, as of resin; **3,** in *pl.*, figuratively, sorrow.—*adj.* **tear'y.**

tear bomb a projectile which, when exploded, gives out a gas very irritating to the eyes: also called *tear shell.*

tear-drop (tēr'drŏp"), *n.* a drop of watery fluid from the eye; a tear.

tear-ful (tēr'fo͝ol), *adj.* **1,** full of tears; given to weeping; **2,** causing tears.—*adv.* **tear'ful-ly.**—*n.* **tear'ful-ness.**

tear gas an irritating gas which causes a profuse flow of tears.

tear-less (tēr'lĕs), *adj.* **1,** not given to weeping; **2,** unable to weep; dry-eyed.—*adv.* **tear'less-ly.**—*n.* **tear'less-ness.**

tease (tēz), *v.t.* [*p.t.* and *p.p.* teased (tēzd), *p.pr.* teas'ing], **1,** to comb or unravel, as wool or flax; separate the fibers of; **2,** to roughen, as cloth, with a teasel; **3,** to annoy by petty requests or by good-natured ridicule:—*n. Colloq.*, one who annoys by petty requests or by ridicule.—*n.* **teas'er.**

tea-sel (tē'zl), *n.* **1,** any of a large family of herbs with oblong flower heads bearing stiff, hooked spines; **2,** the dried flower heads of one species, used to raise the nap on woolen cloth; **3,** any mechanical device substituted for the flower heads of this plant. Also, **tea'zel.**—*n.* **tea'sel-er; tea'sel-ler.**

tea-spoon (tē'spo͞on"), *n.* a small spoon, the ordinary size for table use.—*n.* **tea'spoon"ful.**

teat (tēt), *n.* the nipple on the breast or udder, through which milk passes.

tech-nic (tĕk'nĭk), *adj. Rare,* pertaining to the mechanical arts; relating to art, science, or to a profession:—*n.* **1,** (usually, *technique*), manner of performance in an art; **2,** in *pl.*, details or methods of mechanical arts.

tech-ni-cal (tĕk'nĭ-kăl), *adj.* **1,** relating to the mechanical arts, or to any art or science; **2,** having to do with the exact or mechanical part of any art or science; as, a *technical* term.—*adv.* **tech'ni-cal-ly.**

tech-ni-cal-i-ty (tĕk"nĭ-kăl'ĭ-tĭ), *n.* [*pl.* technicalities (-tĭz)], **1,** the state or quality of pertaining to the mechanical or exact side of any art or science; **2,** anything pertaining or peculiar to any profession, trade, art, or science; **3,** a small point, formally exact but often of a trifling or quibbling nature; as, acquitted on a *technicality.*

tech-nique (tĕk"nēk'), *n.* the method of performance in any fine art: also, skill in executing the details in any performance. Also, **tech'nic.**—*n.* **tech-ni'cian.**

tech-noc-ra-cy (tĕk-nŏk'rȧ-sĭ), *n.* [*pl.* technocracies (-sĭz)], a social and economic system so planned and administered that technological knowledge may be fully utilized.

tech-nol-o-gy (tĕk-nŏl'ō-jĭ), *n.* the science of industrial arts and manufactures.—*adj.* **tech"no-log'ic; tech"no-log'i-cal.**—*n.* **tech-nol'o-gist.**

tech-y (tĕch'ĭ), *adj.* [*comp.* tech'i-er, *superl.* tech'i-est], fretful; peevish; irritable; easily offended. Also, **tetch'y.**

tec-ton-ic (tĕk-tŏn'ĭk), *adj.* pertaining to construction or building: **tectonics,** *n.pl.* used as *sing.* the science or art of producing beautiful buildings, furniture, etc.

ted (tĕd), *v.t.* [*p.t.* and *p.p.* ted'ded, *p.pr.* ted'ding], to turn or spread (hay) to dry.

ted-der (tĕd'ẽr), *n.* **1,** a machine for spreading hay; **2,** one who spreads something for drying.

Te De-um (tē dē'ŭm), **1,** a hymn of praise or thanksgiving beginning, "We praise thee, O God"; **2,** a musical setting of this hymn.

te-di-ous (tē'dĭ-ŭs; tēd'yŭs), *adj.* wearisome; tiresome; as, *tedious* work.—*adv.* **te'di-ous-ly.**—*n.* **te'di-ous-ness.**

te-di-um (tē'dĭ-ŭm), *n.* tediousness; tiresomeness; monotony.

tee (tē), *n.* **1,** in golf, a small cone, as of sand, from which the ball may first be driven; also, the area of turf at the beginning of each hole within which such mounds must be placed; **2,** the mark aimed at in certain games, as quoits:—*v.t.* [*p.t.* and *p.p.* teed (tēd), *p.pr.* tee'ing], in golf, to place (the ball) on a tee.

teem (tēm), *v.i.* to be very productive; be full; be stocked to overflowing; as, the river *teems* with fish.

teem-ing (tēm'ĭng), *p.adj.* **1,** producing freely, as young; fruitful; **2,** full; overflowing; as, a brook *teeming* with trout.

-teen (-tēn), *suffix,* meaning plus ten: used in numbers from 13 to 19; as, six*teen.*

teens (tēnz), *n.pl.* the years of one's age marked by numbers ending in *-teen;* as, a girl in her *teens.*

tee-pee (tē'pē), *n.* the cone-shaped tent of the Indians. See **te'pee,** *Pfd. S.*

tee-ter (tē'tẽr), *v.t.* and *v.i.* to seesaw:—*n.* a seesaw.

teethe (tēth), *v.i.* [*p.t.* and *p.p.* teethed (tēthd), *p.pr.* teeth'ing], to cut teeth; also, to grow or develop teeth.

teeth-ing (tēth'ĭng), *n.* the process of cutting teeth, esp. milk teeth.

tee-to-tal (tē-tō'tăl), *adj.* **1,** *Colloq.,* entire or total; **2,** pertaining to those who do not drink intoxicating liquors.—*n.* **tee-to'tal-er.**—*n.* **tee-to'tal-ism.**

tee-to-tum (tē-tō'tŭm), *n.* a kind of top used for gaming; also, any of various children's tops spun with the fingers.

teg-u-ment (tĕg'ū-mĕnt), *n.* a natural covering or envelope; skin.—*adj.* **teg″u-men'ta-ry.**

teil (tēl), *n.* the linden, or lime, a large tree of Europe.

Tel-a-mon (tĕl'ȧ-mŏn), *n.* in mythology, a Greek hero, father of Ajax and co panion of Hercules in many of his exploits: fabled to have taken part in the expedition of the Argonauts and other exploits: **telamon,** [*pl.* telamones (tĕl″ȧ-mō'nēz)], a supporting column or pilaster in the form of a male figure: used like a caryatid.

tel-au-to-graph (tĕl-ô'tō-grȧf), *n.* a device that will transmit handwriting, drawing, etc., in facsimile, by telegraphy.—*n.* **tel-au'to-gram.**

tel-e-gram (tĕl'ē-grăm), *n.* a written message sent by telegraph.

tel-e-graph (tĕl'ē-grȧf), *n.* an instrument or system for sending and receiving written messages at a distance by means of electricity:—*v.t.* **1,** to send, as a message, by means of electricity passing through wires; **2,** to send such a message to, as a person or place:—*v.i.* to send a message by means oi electric current passing through wires.

te-leg-ra-pher (tē-lĕg'rȧ-fẽr; tĕl'ē-grȧf″ẽr), *n.* one skilled or employed in sending and receiving messages by telegraph; a telegraph operator.

tel-e-graph-ic (tĕl″ē-grăf'ĭk), *adj.* pertaining to the instrument or system for sending and receiving written messages at a distance by means of electricity.

te-leg-ra-phist (tē-lĕg'rȧ-fĭst; tĕl'ē-grȧf″ĭst), *n.* one skilled in the art of operating a telegraph instrument; a telegrapher.

te-leg-ra-phone (tē-lĕg'rȧ-fōn), *n.* an instrument electrically connected with a telephone receiver, which records messages on a metal disk, ribbon, or the like, for reproduction.

te-leg-ra-phy (tē-lĕg'rȧ-fĭ), *n.* the science, art, or process of transmitting messages by electricity.

Te-lem-a-chus (tē-lĕm'ȧ-kŭs), *n.* in mythology, in Homer's "Odyssey," the son of Odysseus and Penelope.

tel-e-ol-o-gy (tĕl″ē-ŏl'ō-jĭ; tē″lē-ŏl'ō-jĭ), *n.* **1,** the idea or doctrine that the existence of everything in nature can be explained in terms of purpose; **2,** the philosophical study of evidence of a creator's design in nature.—*adj.* **tel″e-o-log'ic; tel″e-o-log'i-cal.**—*n.* **tel″e-ol'o-gist.**

te-lep-a-thy (tē-lĕp'ȧ-thĭ), *n.* the transference of thought from one person to another, without conscious communication through the senses; thought transference.—*adj.* **tel″e-path'ic.**

tel-e-phone (tĕl'ē-fōn), *n.* an instrument for transmitting speech over a distance by means of electricity:—*v.t.* and *v.i.* [*p.t.* and *p.p.* -phoned (-fōnd), *p.pr.* -phon″ing], to communicate or talk by such an instrument.—*n.* **tel'e-phon″er.**

tel-e-phon-ic (tĕl″ē-fŏn'ĭk), *adj.* **1,** of, pertaining to, or carried by, the telephone; as, a *telephonic* communication; **2,** carrying sound to a distance.—*adv.* **tel″e-phon'i-cal-ly.**—*n.* **tel'e-phon″ist.**

te-leph-o-ny (tē-lĕf'ō-nĭ; tĕl'ē-fō″nĭ), *n.* the science, art, or process of sending sounds to a distance by telephone.

tel-e-pho-tog-ra-phy (tĕl″ē-fō-tŏg'rȧ-fĭ), *n.* **1,** the sending and reproducing of photographs at a distance by means of a method like that used in the electric telegraph; **2,** the art of photographing distant objects so as to make them appear near by.

tel-e-scope (tĕl'ē-skōp), *n.* **1,** an optical instrument used for viewing objects at a distance, esp. the moon, stars, etc.: called *refracting* if the rays are brought to a focus by a lens, and *reflecting* if by a concave mirror; **2,** any of several articles, as a certain type of valise, made of parts sliding within one another as do the sections of small telescopes:—*v.t.* [*p.t.* and *p.p.* -scoped (-skōpt), *p.pr.* -scop″ing], to drive together so that one part slides into another, like a section of a collapsible telescope, as a valise:—*v.i.* to slide together like a telescope, as sections of a valise, or railway cars in collision.

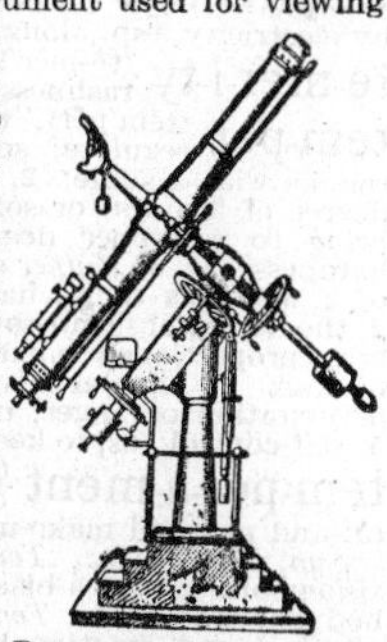

REFRACTING TELESCOPE

tel-e-scop-ic (tĕl″ē-skŏp'ĭk), *adj.* **1,** pertaining to, or made by, the telescope; **2,** visible only by means of the telescope; **3,** farseeing; as, a *telescopic* eye; **4,** having the power to extend or close up, by means of parts sliding one into another. Also, **tel″e-scop'i-cal.**—*adv.* **tel″e-scop'i-cal-ly.**

te-les-co-py (tē-lĕs'kō-pĭ; tĕl'ē-skō″pĭ), *n.* the art or science of making or of using telescopes—*n.* **te-les'co-pist.**

tel-e-vi-sion (tĕl″ē-vĭzh'ŭn), *n.* projection to a far distant point, and reproduction on a screen, esp. by electricity, of images of a motion picture or of actual objects; also, the act of seeing such reproduction.

tell (tĕl), *v.t.* [*p.t.* and *p.p.* told (tōld), *p.pr.* tell'ing], **1,** to count; mention one by one, as beads; **2,** to relate in words; narrate; **3,** to express or make known by words; disclose; confess; **4,** to explain; communicate to; **5,** to decide; as, I cannot *tell* what is best to do; **6,** to order; as, I *told* the officer to report; **7,** to recognize; as, I cannot *tell* who she is; **8,** to assure with emphasis; as, I *tell* you it is so:—*v.i.* **1,** to give an account; report; **2,** to play the informer; **3,** to take effect; as, the continued attacks began to *tell* upon the enemy's line of defense.

Tell, Wil-liam a legendary Swiss peasant who, because of his refusal to salute the hat of an oppressive governor, was ordered to shoot an apple from the head of his son, and who is credited with starting the revolt of the 14th century, which freed Switzerland from Austria.

tell-er (tĕl′ẽr), *n.* **1,** one who discloses, narrates, communicates, etc.; **2,** a bank clerk who receives and pays money over the counter; **3,** one who counts the votes in a legislative body, meeting, etc.

tell-ing (tĕl′ĭng), *n.* the act of relating or making known:—*p.adj.* effective; as, his words had a *telling* effect.

tell-tale (tĕl′tāl″), *n.* **1,** a talebearer; an informer; esp., one who betrays secrets or makes known private affairs; **2,** a device that gives information or warning:—*adj.* betraying; giving information of what should be kept secret; as, a *telltale* blush.

tel-lu-ri-um (tĕ-lū′rĭ-ŭm), *n.* a white metallic element resembling sulphur and selenium.

Tel-lus (tĕl′ŭs), *n.* in Roman mythology, a goddess personifying the earth: also called *Tellus Mater*, and identified with the Greek goddess *Gæa*.

tel-pher-age (tĕl′fẽr-āj), *n.* a system of automatic transportation by electricity, esp. along a suspended cable.

te-mer-i-ty (tē-mĕr′ĭ-tĭ), *n.* foolhardiness; rashness.

tem-per (tĕm′pẽr), *v.t.* **1,** to change or regulate; soften; as, to *temper* a rebuke with a smile; **2,** to mix to the proper degree of firmness or softness, as clay; **3,** to bring to a proper degree of toughness or hardness; as, to *temper* steel:—*n.* **1,** the state of a metal as to its hardness or toughness; **2,** the degree of firmness or softness in a properly proportioned mixture, as of clay or mortar; **3,** mental disposition; **4,** a state of irritation or anger, or readiness to anger; **5,** self-control; as, to keep one's *temper*.

tem-per-a-ment (tĕm′pẽr-ȧ-mĕnt), *n.* disposition; the mental and physical make-up of a person.

Syn. disposition. *Temperament* and *disposition* both suggest a bias or tendency of mind, body, or character. *Temperament* emphasizes physical and emotional bias, as shown in action and thought; as, the artistic, the placid, or the nervous, *temperament*. *Disposition* refers rather to a bias of mind or of character; as, a *disposition* to doubt; a bad *disposition*.

tem-per-a-men-tal (tĕm″pẽr-ȧ-mĕn′tăl), *adj.* **1,** arising from, or pertaining to, a person's mental or physical make-up; as, a *temperamental* peculiarity; **2,** sensitive; easily irritated; as, she is so *temperamental* that she is hard to get along with.—*adv.* **tem″per-a-men′tal-ly.**

tem-per-ance (tĕm′pẽr-ăns), *n.* **1,** moderation; avoidance of extremes; **2,** moderation in, or abstinence from, the use of alcoholic liquors.

tem-per-ate (tĕm′pẽr-ăt), *adj.* **1,** not inclined to eat or drink to excess; moderate; **2,** calm; **3,** not liable to excess of heat or cold; as, *temperate* weather: **temperate zone,** one of the two zones of mild climate, lying between the torrid and frigid zones of the earth's surface.—*adv.* **tem′per-ate-ly.**—*n.* **tem′per-ate-ness.**

tem-per-a-ture (tĕm′pẽr-ȧ-tūr), *n.* the degree or amount of heat or cold as measured by the thermometer.

tem-pered (tĕm′pẽrd), *adj.* **1,** having some special kind of disposition: usually in compounds; as, sweet-*tempered* or ill-*tempered;* **2,** having the proper toughness and elasticity; as, a *tempered* tool.

tem-pest (tĕm′pĕst), *n.* **1,** a violent storm, characterized by strong wind and usually accompanied by rain, hail, etc.; a hurricane; **2,** any violent tumult.

tem-pes-tu-ous (tĕm-pĕs′tū-ŭs), *adj.* stormy; agitated; turbulent.—*adv.* **tem-pes′tu-ous-ly.**—*n.* **tem-pes′tu-ous-ness.**

Tem-plar (tĕm′plȧr), *n.* **1,** one of a former religious and military order; **2,** a member of an order of Freemasons: also called *Knight Templar*.

tem-plate (tĕm′plăt), *n.* **1,** a flat pattern made of wood or metal, used to show the shape of a piece of work; **2,** a stone or timber for distributing weight in a building; **3,** (usually, *templet*), a wedge under a ship's keel. Also, **tem′plet.**

[1]**tem-ple** (tĕm′pl), *n.* **1,** an edifice dedicated to the worship of a deity; **2,** a building for Christian public worship: **the Temple,** any of three successive edifices built in Jerusalem for the worship of Jehovah.

[2]**tem-ple** (tĕm′pl), *n.* the flat part of the head at each side, between the eye and the ear.

tem-po (tĕm′pō), *n.* [*pl.* tempi (-pē)], in music, the rate of speed at which a composition is rendered; time.

[1]**tem-po-ral** (tĕm′pō-răl), *adj.* **1,** pertaining to time; not eternal or everlasting; transitory; **2,** pertaining to the present life; secular; of the world; **3,** relating to civil or political matters; **4,** in grammar, expressing time; as, *temporal* clauses.—*adv.* **tem′po-ral-ly.**—*n.* **tem′po-ral-ness.**

Syn. worldly.—*Ant.* spiritual, heavenly.

[2]**tem-po-ral** (tĕm′pō-răl), *adj.* pertaining to the temples: **temporal bone,** a compound bone at the side of the human skull (see *skull*, illus.).

tem-po-ra-ry (tĕm′pō-rā-rĭ), *adj.* transient; passing; not permanent; as, *temporary* relief.—*adv.* **tem′po-ra-ri-ly.**—*n.* **tem′po-ra-ri-ness.**

tem-po-rize (tĕm′pō-rīz), *v.i.* [*p.t.* and *p.p.* -rized (-rīzd), *p.pr.* -riz″ing], **1,** to yield temporarily to current opinion or circumstances; delay; **2,** to avoid committing oneself; try to please both parties.—*n.* **tem′po-riz″er.**

tempt (tĕmpt), *v.t.* **1,** to try to persuade; lead, or try to lead, into evil ways; entice; allure; **2,** to defy; as, to *tempt* fate or fortune.—*adj.* **tempt′a-ble.**

temp-ta-tion (tĕmp-tā′shŭn), *n.* **1,** the act of leading, or the state of being led, into evil; persuasion, esp. to evil; **2,** an enticement; that which allures.

tempt-er (tĕmp′tẽr), *n.* one who seeks to lead others into evil: **the Tempter,** Satan; the Devil.—*n.fem.* **tempt′ress.**

tempt-ing (tĕmp′tĭng), *p. adj.* alluring; attractive; as, a *tempting* meal.—*adv.* **tempt′ing-ly.**—*n.* **tempt′ing-ness.**

ten (tĕn), *adj.* composed of one more than nine, or twice five:—*n.* **1,** the number consisting of five and five; **2,** a sign representing ten units, as 10 or x: **Ten Commandments,** the precepts of God, given to Moses; the Decalog (Exodus 20:1–17).—*adj.* and *n.* **tenth.**

ten-a-ble (tĕn′ȧ-bl), *adj.* capable of being held, maintained, or defended; as, a *tenable* argument or position.—*n.* **ten′a-ble-ness.**—*adv.* **ten′a-bly.**—*n.* **ten″a-bil′i-ty.**

te-na-cious (tē-nā′shŭs), *adj.* **1,** holding fast or firmly; as, the *tenacious* grip of a bulldog's jaw; **2,** sticky, as glue; **3,** tough, as steel; **4,** capable of holding or retaining; as, a *tenacious* memory.—*adv.* **te-na′cious-ly.**—*n.* **te-na′cious-ness.**

te-nac-i-ty (tē-năs′ĭ-tĭ), *n.* **1**, the state or quality of being able or inclined to hold fast; as, *tenacity* of memory or purpose; **2**, that quality of a substance by which it resists being pulled apart.

ten-an-cy (tĕn′ăn-sĭ), *n.* [*pl.* tenancies (-sĭz)], **1**, the temporary holding of land or houses; **2**, the period of possession of one who rents property; **3**, in law, a holding of lands and houses by any title; occupancy; tenure.

ten-ant (tĕn′ănt), *n.* one who holds possession of real estate by any sort of title or right; esp., one who holds lands or houses from another; an occupant:—*v.t.* to hold by rent from another.—*adj.* **ten′ant-a-ble.**—*adj.* **ten′ant-less.**

ten-ant-ry (tĕn′ănt-rĭ), *n.* [*pl.* tenantries (-rĭz)], **1**, the entire group of tenants occupying land and houses on one estate; **2**, tenancy.

¹tend (tĕnd), *v.i.* **1**, to move or go in a certain direction: usually with *to* or *toward;* **2**, to serve as a means; have a tendency: with *to;* as, cleanliness *tends* to godliness.

²tend (tĕnd), *v.t.* to care for; attend to; watch over or protect; as, to *tend* sheep; to *tend* an invalid:—*v.i.* **1**, to attend or serve: with *on* or *upon;* **2**, to pay attention.

tend-ance (tĕn′dăns), *n.* the act of caring for; attention.

tend-en-cy (tĕn′dĕn-sĭ), *n.* [*pl.* tendencies (-sĭz)], **1**, inclination; as, no *tendency* to study; **2**, aim; direction or course.

¹tend-er (tĕn′dẽr), *n.* **1**, one who takes care of or guards a person or thing; **2**, a small car containing coal and water, attached behind a locomotive; **3**, a small vessel attending and supplying a larger one, as with fuel, provisions, etc.; **4**, a rowboat or launch used to land passengers from a ship.

²ten-der (tĕn′dẽr), *v.t.* to offer for acceptance; make an offer of; present:—*v.i.* to make an offer:—*n.* **1**, an offer, bid, or proposal for acceptance; **2**, the thing offered: **legal tender,** currency that is legally adequate to discharge a debt.—*n.* **ten′der-er.**

³ten-der (tĕn′dẽr), *adj.* **1**, easily cut or chewed, as meat; **2**, soft; not hardy or tough; weak in body; **3**, easily hurt or injured; sensitive physically; as, a *tender* skin; **4**, easily touched by pain, grief, love, or kindness; sympathetic; **5**, gentle; kind; loving; **6**, immature; youthful; **7**, delicate: said of colors or sounds; **8**, requiring careful handling; as, a *tender* subject of debate; **9**, considerate; having solicitude; careful: with *of.*—*adv.* **ten′der-ly.**—*n.* **ten′der-ness.**

ten-der-foot (tĕn′dẽr-fo͝ot″), *n.* [*pl.* tenderfeet (-fēt″)], *Colloq.*, new to the life in a mining camp, the plains, etc.; a newcomer; a greenhorn, as on a ranch.

ten-der-heart-ed (tĕn′dẽr=härt″ĕd), *adj.* readily touched by the pain or grief of others; sympathetic.

ten-der-loin (tĕn′dẽr-loin″), *n.* the tenderest part of the loin of beef or other meat; a strip of tender meat under the short ribs, in beef, pork, etc.

ten-don (tĕn′dŭn), *n.* a tough cord or band of inelastic fibrous tissue attaching a muscle to a bone, another muscle, or an organ of the body.—*adj.* **ten′di-nous.**

ten-dril (tĕn′drĭl), *n.* a slender, twining, modified leaf of a plant, which attaches itself to a support, thus enabling the plant to climb or to hold itself up.

ten-e-ment (tĕn′ē-mĕnt), *n.* **1**, in law, any kind of permanent property held by one person of another; **2**, a dwelling house; **3**, an apartment, or suite of rooms, usually of inferior grade: **tenement house,** a large building containing suites of rooms, each occupied by a family: used commonly of buildings occupied by families of small means.

ten-et (tĕn′ĕt), *n.* a doctrine, dogma, opinion, or belief, maintained as true.

ten-fold (tĕn′fōld″), *adj.* and *adv.* ten times as much or as many.

ten-nis (tĕn′ĭs), *n.* either of two games played by batting a ball with rackets, back and forth over a net across a specially marked floor called a court; strictly, court tennis; popularly, lawn tennis: **court tennis,** a variety of tennis played indoors in a walled and covered court: **lawn tennis,** tennis played outdoors on turf, clay, etc.

ten-on (tĕn′ŭn), *n.* a projection at the end of a timber cut so as to fit into a hole in another timber (see *mortise*, illus.):—*v.t.* **1**, to cut a projection at the end of (a timber); **2**, to fit such a projection into.

ten-or (tĕn′ẽr), *n.* **1**, settled tendency, direction, or course; **2**, general character; nature; **3**, general tendency or drift; purport; as, the *tenor* of his conversation; **4**, the highest of adult male voices; also, a part written for this voice; **5**, one who sings the part written for the highest adult male voice, or an instrument, as the viola, that plays it:—*adj.* pertaining to, or adapted for, the highest adult male voice; as, the *tenor* part in a choir.

ten-pins (tĕn′pĭnz″), *n.* a bowling game played with ten pins set up at the farther end of a bowling alley.

¹tense (tĕns), *adj.* stretched tight; rigid; not lax; hence, severely strained, as nerves.—*adv.* **tense′ly.**—*n.* **tense′ness.**

²tense (tĕns), *n.* **1**, the form a verb takes to indicate the time of an action or state of being; as, *went* serves as the past *tense* of *go;* **2**, the time thus indicated; **3**, a complete set of the forms used in inflecting a verb to express any given time of action or state of being.

ten-sile (tĕn′sĭl), *adj.* **1**, pertaining to tension or the act of stretching; as, the *tensile* strength of wire; **2**, capable of being stretched or strained.—*n.* **ten-sil′i-ty.**

ten-sion (tĕn′shŭn), *n.* **1**, the act of stretching or straining; **2**, the state of being stretched or strained; **3**, mental strain; intensity of feeling; **4**, strained relations, as between nations; **5**, in machinery: **a**, a device to loosen or tighten as in a sewing machine; **b**, the stress due to pulling; **6**, in electricity: **a**, a condition, due to local attraction or repulsion, such that an electrical charge tends to discharge itself; **b**, potential.

ten-sor (tĕn′sŏr), *n.* a muscle that stretches or tightens some part of the body.

ten-strike (tĕn′=strīk″), *n.* **1**, in bowling, a knocking down of all the pins with one throw of the ball; **2**, *Colloq.*, a successful performance.

¹tent (tĕnt), *n.* a portable shelter, usually made of canvas, supported by poles and ropes (see illus. next page): **tent caterpillar,** any of numerous species of destructive, leaf-eating caterpillars which make large, silky webs, or tents, to which they retire when not feeding:—*v.i.* **1**, to camp out; **2**, to pitch a tent:—*v.t.* to cover with, or as with, a tent.

²tent (tĕnt), *n.* a small plug or roll of gauze, lint, or cotton, placed in a wound, or in some natural opening, to keep it open:—*v.t.* to keep open or probe with such a plug.

ten-ta-cle (tĕn′tȧ-kl), *n.* **1**, a feeding, motor, or sense organ of certain insects, fish, etc.; a feeler: usually attached to the mouth parts or to the head; **2**, a feeler on the leaf of a plant.—*adj.* **ten-tac′u-lar.**

ten-ta-tive (tĕn′tȧ-tĭv), *adj.* pertaining to an experiment or trial; used in experimenting; provisional; as, a *tentative* offer.—*adv.* **ten′ta-tive-ly.**

tent-ed (tĕnt′ĕd), *p.adj.* **1,** covered with, sheltered by, or furnished with, a tent; **2,** like a tent.

ten-ter (tĕn′tẽr), *n.* a frame on which to stretch cloth by hooks to prevent shrinking in drying:—*v.t.* to hang or stretch on such a frame, as cloth.

ten-ter-hook (tĕn′tẽr-hŏŏk″), *n.* one of the sharp, hooked nails set on a tenter: **on tenterhooks**, under a strain; in suspense or an anxious state.

te-nu-i-ty (tē-nū′ĭ-tĭ), *n.* **1,** thinness; slenderness, as of a leaf; **2,** rareness; rarity; lack of substance, as of the air.

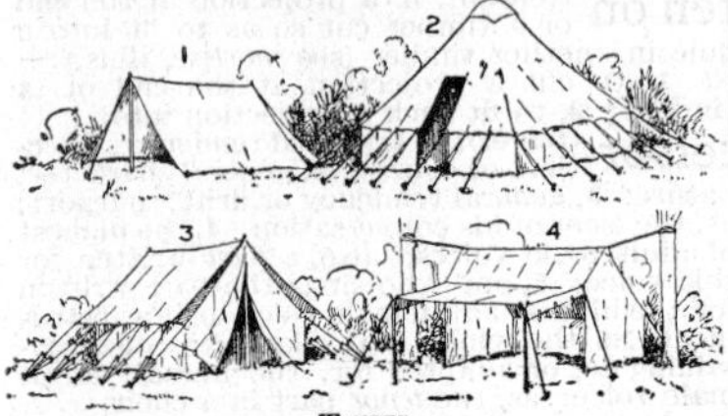

TENTS

1, soldiers' dog tent; 2, army squad tent; 3, wall tent, with fly; 4, one type of outing tent, with front flap raised as an awning.

ten-u-ous (tĕn′ū-ŭs), *adj.* **1,** slender; thin; as, *tenuous* wire; **2,** rare; not dense or heavy; as, *tenuous* air; **3,** simple; unpretentious; plain.—*adv.* **ten′u-ous-ly.**—*n.* **ten′u-ous-ness.**

ten-ure (tĕn′ūr), *n.* **1,** the conditions under which a house or real estate is held; **2,** the right or manner of holding real estate; **3,** the period during which anything is held and enjoyed.—*adj.* **te-nu′ri-al.**

te-pee (tē′pē; tĕp′ē), *n.* the cone-shaped tent, or wigwam, of the North American Indians. Also, **tee′pee.**

tep-id (tĕp′ĭd), *adj.* moderately warm; lukewarm, as water.—*n.* **tep′id-ness.**

te-pid-i-ty (tē-pĭd′ĭ-tĭ), *n.* moderate warmth; a lukewarm condition.

ter-cen-te-na-ry (tûr-sĕn′tē-nā-rĭ), *adj.* comprising or including 300 years:—*n.* [*pl.* tercentenaries (-rĭz)], the 300th anniversary of an event. Also, **tri-cen′te-na-ry.**

te-re-do (tē-rē′dō), *n.* [*pl.* teredos (-dōz); teredines (-rĕd′ĭ-nēz)], the shipworm, which bores into ship timbers.

ter-gi-ver-sate (tûr′jĭ-vẽr-sāt″), *v.i.* [*p.t.* and *p.p.* -sat″ed, *p.pr.* -sat″ing], to evade; shift; change sides.—*n.* **ter′gi-ver-sa″tor.**—*n.* **ter″gi-ver-sa′tion.**

term (tûrm), *n.* **1,** a limit or boundary; **2,** a limited time; as, a *term* of five years; **3,** a division of a school year; **4,** the time of a court's session; **5,** a word or expression, esp. one belonging to a specific art, business, etc.; as, a legal *term;* **6,** in *pl.:* **a,** conditions or arrangements; as, *terms* of a sale; **b,** relationship; footing; as, I am on good *terms* with him; **7,** in mathematics: **a,** any of the members in a proportion or ratio; **b,** a member, consisting of one or more factors, of an algebraic expression, standing alone or connected with others by plus or minus signs; **8,** in logic, one of the three parts of a syllogism:—*v.t.* to name, point out, or call; denominate.

ter-ma-gant (tûr′mȧ-gănt), *n.* a noisy, quarrelsome woman:—*adj.* noisy and quarrelsome.—*n.* **ter′ma-gan-cy.**

ter-mi-na-ble (tûr′mĭ-nȧ-bl), *adj.* capable of being limited or ended; ending at a given time.

ter-mi-nal (tûr′mĭ-năl), *adj.* **1,** pertaining to the end or boundary; **2,** forming the end; as, a *terminal* station; **3,** pertaining to a fixed length of time; **4,** pertaining to the delivery of freight; as, *terminal* charges:—*n.* **1,** a limit or boundary; an end; **2,** the end of a railroad line, including the station, switches, etc.; **3,** one end of an electrical circuit; **4,** usually in *pl.*, charges for handling freight at terminals.

ter-mi-nate (tûr′mĭ-nāt), *v.t.* [*p.t.* and *p.p.* -nat″ed, *p.pr.* -nat″ing], **1,** to limit or bound; as, a wall *terminates* the garden; **2,** to bring to an end; finish; as, to *terminate* a war:—*v.i.* **1,** to be limited or bounded; as, his property *terminates* at the river; **2,** to come to an end; as, his career *terminated* in disaster.—*adj.* **ter′mi-na-tive.**

Syn. end, cease. (See [1]close.)

ter-mi-na-tion (tûr″mĭ-nā′shŭn), *n.* **1,** the act of limiting or ending; **2,** a bound or limit; end; **3,** conclusion or result; **4,** the final syllable or letter of a word.

ter-mi-nol-o-gy (tûr″mĭ-nŏl′ō-jĭ), *n.* [*pl.* terminologies (-jĭz)], the special or technical expressions used in a science, art, or business.—*adj.* **ter″mi-no-log′i-cal.**—*adv.* **ter″mi-no-log′i-cal-ly.**

ter-mi-nus (tûr′mĭ-nŭs), *n.* [*pl.* termini (-nī)], **1,** a limit or boundary; **2,** an end of a railway line; also, the town and station at that place.

ter-mite (tûr′mīt), *n.* any of numerous species of destructive, pale-colored, social insects found especially in the tropics; the white ant.

tern (tûrn), *n.* any of a family of swimming sea birds resembling gulls, having long wings and a slim, straight bill.

ter-na-ry (tûr′nȧ-rĭ), *adj.* **1,** proceeding by, or consisting of, threes; **2,** in chemistry, consisting of three (elements, atoms, or the like):—*n.* [*pl.* ternaries (-rĭz)], **1,** the number three; **2,** three things together.

ter-nate (tûr′nāt), *adj.* arranged in threes, or consisting of threes, as leaves.

Terp-sich-o-re (tûrp-sĭk′ō-rē), *n.* in mythology, one of the nine Muses, the Muse of dancing.

terp-si-cho-re-an (tûrp″sĭ-kō-rē′ăn), *adj.* of or pertaining to dancing; as, the *terpsichorean* art.

ter-race (tĕr′ās), *n.* **1,** a raised level space or platform of earth with sloping sides; **2,** one of the sides of such a space and the raised space collectively; **3,** the flat roof of an Oriental or Spanish house; **4,** a row of houses set along the top of a bank or slope: often used in naming a short street or row of houses:—*v.t.* [*p.t.* and *p.p.* -raced (-āst), *p.pr.* -rac-ing], to form into, or supply with, a terrace or terraces, as a lawn.

ter-ra cot-ta (tĕr′ȧ kŏt′ȧ), **1,** pottery of baked clay or earth, esp. that of a reddish or yellowish brown; **2,** hence, a reddish or yellowish brown color.

***ter-ra fir-ma** (fûr′mȧ), [Lat.], **1,** dry land; mainland; solid earth; **2,** land, as opposed to water.

ter-rain (tĕ-rān′; tĕr′ān), *n.* **1,** (usually, *terrane*), a geological formation or group of formations; **2,** ground considered for its fitness for some special purpose, as for a fortification, the landing of airplanes, etc.

ter-ra-pin (tĕr′ȧ-pĭn), *n.* **1,** any of several North American fresh-water turtles used as food; **2,** the flesh of these turtles as a table dish.

ter-ra-que-ous (tĕr-ā′kwē-ŭs), *adj.* consisting of land and water; as, the earth is a *terraqueous* globe.

ter-rene (tĕ-rēn′), *adj.* **1,** of or pertaining to the earth; earthy; **2,** mundane.

terre-plein (târ′plān″), *n.* **1**, an embankment having a wide, level top; **2**, the main upper level of a rampart,

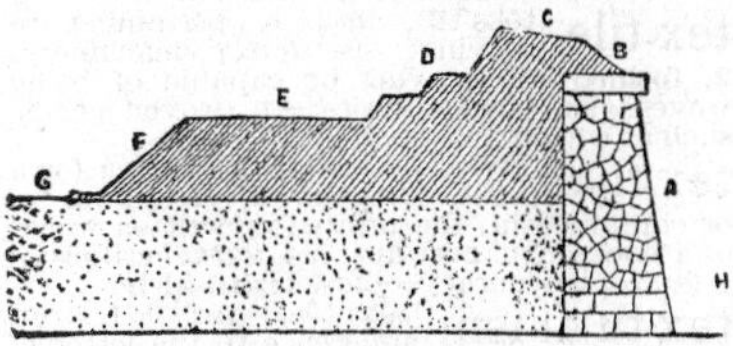

TERREPLEIN, SHOWN IN SECTION OF PARAPET

A, wall, or scarp; B, exterior slope; C, parapet; D, banquette; E, terreplein; F, interior slope; G, boulevard, or parade; H, ditch, or moat.

where guns, shielded by the parapet, are mounted (cf. *rampart*, illus.).

ter-res-tri-al (tē-rĕs′trĭ-ăl), *adj.* **1**, pertaining to, or consisting of, earth or land, in distinction to water; **2**, belonging to the earth; not celestial; **3**, existing on land.—*adv.* **ter-res′tri-al-ly.**

ter-ret (tĕr′ĕt), *n.* one of the rings on a harness pad, through which the driving reins pass (see *harness*, illus.).

ter-ri-ble (tĕr′ĭ-bl), *adj.* exciting or causing fear or awe; dreadful; appalling.—*n.* **ter′ri-ble-ness.**—*adv.* **ter′ri-bly.**
Syn. shocking, grim, horrible.

ter-ri-er (tĕr′ĭ-ĕr), *n.* any of several breeds of small, intelligent dogs, used as pets, for killing rats, etc.

ter-rif-ic (tē-rĭf′ĭk), *adj.* such as to cause fear or terror; alarming; dreadful; as, a *terrific* explosion.—*adv.* **ter-rif′i-cal-ly.**

ter-ri-fy (tĕr′ĭ-fī), *v.t.* [*p.t.* and *p.p.* -fied (-fīd), *p.pr.* -fy″ing], to fill with terror; frighten thoroughly.

ter-ri-to-ri-al (tĕr″ĭ-tō′rĭ-ăl), *adj.* **1**, pertaining to a given region of land, esp. to a division of a national domain; as, *territorial* disputes; **2**, limited to a particular district; as, *territorial* laws: **Territorial**, pertaining to the Territories of the U. S.:—*n.* a soldier enrolled in the territorial defense, or home reserves.—*adv.* **ter″ri-to′ri-al-ly.**—*n.* **ter″ri-to″ri-al′i-ty.**

ter-ri-to-ry (tĕr′ĭ-tō-rĭ), *n.* [*pl.* territories (-rĭz)], **1**, a large tract of land; region; district; as, the unexplored *territory* in South America; **2**, the entire extent of land and water under the control of one ruler or government; as, British *territory*: **Territory**, in the U. S., a region or portion of the country not yet admitted into the Union as a State, but having a temporary government.

ter-ror (tĕr′ĕr), *n.* **1**, extreme fear; fright; **2**, one who or that which causes extreme fear.
Syn. consternation. (See horror.)

ter-ror-ism (tĕr′ĕr-ĭzm), *n.* **1**, a system of government or opposition to government by methods which excite fear; **2**, any series of deeds which arouse fear.

ter-ror-ist (tĕr′ĕr-ĭst), *n.* one who governs by violent methods which arouse fear; esp., one of the revolutionary party during the Reign of Terror in France.—*adj.* **ter″ror-is′tic.**

ter-ror-ize (tĕr′ĕr-īz), *v.t.* [*p.t.* and *p.p.* -ized (-īzd), *p.pr.* -iz″ing], **1**, to make timid by fear; put into a state of extreme fear; **2**, to force by intimidation.—*n.* **ter″ror-i-za′tion.**—*n.* **ter′ror-iz″er.**

ter-ry (tĕr′ĭ), *n.* [*pl.* terries (-ĭz)], **1**, a cloth of silk or wool, woven like velvet, but with the loops uncut; **2**, one of the loops.

terse (tûrs), *adj.* concise or brief; short; exactly to the point; as, a *terse* style of writing.—*adv.* **terse′ly.**—*n.* **terse′ness.**
Syn. pointed, succinct. (See short.)

ter-tian (tûr′shăn), *adj.* occurring every other day, as certain fevers:—*n.* fever returning every other day.

Ter-ti-a-ry (tûr′shĭ-ā-rĭ; tûr′shȧ-rĭ), *adj.* in geology, designating, or pertaining to, the earlier periods of the Cenozoic era, or their characteristic formations, between the Mesozoic era and the Quaternary period of the Cenozoic, in which the great reptiles had disappeared, the mammals were beginning, and various great ranges, as the Alps, Andes, etc., were forming:—*n.* in geology, the Tertiary period: **tertiary**, *adj.* third in order of time or rank.

tes-sel-late (tĕs′ĕ-lāt), *v.t.* [*p.t.* and *p.p.* -lat″ed, *p.pr.* -lat″ing], to lay off in, or inlay with, squares or checkers, as a tiled floor.—*n.* **tes″sel-la′tion.**

¹test (tĕst), *n.* **1**, a close examination or a decisive trial; as, he stood the *test*; also, the means or method used in such an examination; **2**, a touchstone; a standard by which a thing or person may be gauged, as for use, ability, etc.; as, self-control is the *test* of a man's power; **3**, in chemistry, an experiment for discovering the presence of any particular substance in a compound:—*v.t.* **1**, to put to the proof; **2**, in chemistry, to try to find a particular substance in; as, to *test* rice for starch; **3**, to refine; as, to *test* gold in a furnace.—*n.* **¹test′er.**
Syn., *n.* experiment, ordeal. (See trial.)

²test (tĕst), *n.* the hard outside covering, or shell, of many invertebrates, as the crab, oyster, or snail.

tes-ta-ceous (tĕs-tā′shŭs), *adj.* pertaining to, or having, a shell.

tes-ta-ment (tĕs′tȧ-mĕnt), *n.* a written document in which a person provides for the disposing of his property after his death: usually in the phrase *last will and testament:* **Testament**, **1**, either of the two main parts of the Bible; as, the Old *Testament*; **2**, a book containing the New Testament.

tes-ta-men-ta-ry (tĕs″tȧ-mĕn′tȧ-rĭ), *adj.* **1**, of or pertaining to a will, or the administration or settlement of a will; as, letters *testamentary*; **2**, provided or appointed by a will; as, a *testamentary* guardian.

tes-tate (tĕs′tāt), *adj.* having left a will; as, he died *testate*.

tes-ta-tor (tĕs-tā′tŏr), *n.* a man who leaves a valid will at his death.—*n. fem.* **tes-ta′trix.**

²tes-ter (tĕs′tĕr), *n.* a flat canopy or covering, as over a pulpit or tomb; esp., a canopy on a bed.

tes-ti-cle (tĕs′tĭ-kl), *n.* either of the two male genital glands which secrete the spermatozoa; a testis.

tes-ti-fy (tĕs′tĭ-fī), *v.i.* [*p.t.* and *p.p.* -fied (-fīd), *p.pr.* -fy″ing], **1**, to bear witness; make a formal declaration; **2**, to declare under oath before a court of law; **3**, to make a charge or a protest: with *against*; **4**, to serve as evidence; as, his works *testify* to his industry:—*v.t.* to declare solemnly on oath; bear witness to.—*n.* **tes′ti-fi″er.**

tes-ti-mo-ni-al (tĕs″tĭ-mō′nĭ-ăl), *n.* **1**, a writing or certificate regarding one's character, ability, etc.; **2**, a token of respect, of acknowledgment of services, or the like, presented to, or established in memory of, a person:—*adj.* pertaining to, or containing, recognition or acknowledgment of worth or services.

tes-ti-mo-ny (tĕs′tĭ-mō-nĭ), *n.* [*pl.* testimonies (-nĭz)], **1**, a statement made to establish or prove some fact; **2**, in law, a spoken or written declaration furnished by a witness under oath; **3**, often in *pl.*, the Scriptures.

tes-tis (tĕs′tĭs), *n.* [*pl.* testes (-tēz)], either of the two male genital glands in which spermatozoa are produced; a testicle.

test tube a tube of thin glass, closed at one end and used for making certain chemical tests.

tes-tu-di-nal (tĕs-tū′dĭ-năl), *adj.* **1**, pertaining to, or like, a tortoise or its shell; **2**, hence, arched or vaulted.

tes-ty (tĕs′tĭ), *adj.* [*comp.* tes′ti-er, *superl.* tes′ti-est], peevish; techy; easily angered.—*adv.* **tes′ti-ly.**—*n.* **tes′ti-ness.**
Syn. fretful, impatient, touchy.

tet-a-nus (tĕt′*ȧ*-nŭs), *n.* an acute and usually fatal disease causing muscular spasms: called *lockjaw* when confined to the muscles of the lower jaw.

tetch-y (tĕch′ĭ), *adj.* [*comp.* tetch′i-er, *superl.* tetch′i-est], fretful; peevish; irritable; cross. Also, **tech′y,** *Pfd. S.*

tête-à-tête (tāt″=ȧ=tāt′; tĕ″=tȧ=tât′), *n.* [*pl.* tête-à-têtes (=tāts′)], **1**, a private conversation between two persons; **2**, a short sofa or couch with an S-shaped back, on which two persons can sit facing each other: —*adj.* face to face; confidential: **tête à tête,** **1**, face to face; **2**, privately; confidentially.

teth-er (tĕ*th*′ẽr), *n.* **1**, a rope to fasten an animal; **2**, hence, scope; authority: —*v.t.* to tie with a rope or chain.

tet-ra- (tĕt′r*ȧ*-), a prefix or combining form from the Greek, meaning four; as, *tetra*gon; *tetra*hedron; *tetra*meter.

tet-ra-eth-yl lead (tĕt″r*ȧ*-ĕth′ĭl), a colorless, heavy liquid, a compound of lead, sometimes added to gasoline to prevent knocking.

tet-ra-gon (tĕt′r*a*-gŏn), *n.* a plane figure with four sides and four angles. —*adj.* **tet-rag′o-nal.**

tet-ra-he-dron (tĕt″r*ȧ*-hē′drŏn), *n.* [*pl.* tetrahedrons (-drŏnz); tetrahedra (-dr*ȧ*)], a solid figure bounded by four triangular plane surfaces, as a three-sided pyramid.—*adj.* **tet″ra-he′dral.**

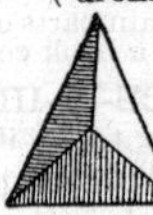

TETRAHEDRON

tet-ram-e-ter (tĕt-răm′ē-tẽr), *n.* a verse consisting of four measures.

te-trarch (tē′trärk; tĕt′rärk), *n.* **1**, a Roman governor whose authority extended over the fourth part of a province; **2**, an inferior prince or king; **3**, in ancient Greece, an inferior officer in the army.—*n.* **tet′rarch-y.**

tet-ter (tĕt′ẽr), *n.* a skin disease marked by itching and redness; eczema.

Teu-ton (tū′tŏn), *n.* **1**, a member of any Teutonic nation, ancient or modern; **2**, loosely, a German.

Teu-ton-ic (tū-tŏn′ĭk), *adj.* **1**, designating, or pertaining to, a group of peoples including the ancient Goths, Scandinavians, Anglo-Saxons, Germans, etc., inhabiting central and northern Europe, or the modern descendants of these peoples; **2**, designating, or pertaining to, the group of languages spoken by these peoples, as German, Dutch, English, etc.:—*n.* the group of languages spoken by these peoples.

text (tĕkst), *n.* **1**, the printed or written words of a book, treatise, poem, play, etc., used as a basis for notes or critical discussion; as, to comment on the *text* of a play by Shakespeare; the original words of an author; **2**, a verse of Scripture forming the subject of a sermon; **3**, a theme; topic, as of an argument; **4**, the main body of any piece of written or printed matter; the printed part of a book in distinction from the illustrations, notes, etc.; **5**, black-letter or Old English type.

text-book (tĕkst′bo͝ok″), *n.* a standard book of instruction.

tex-tile (tĕks′tĭl), *adj.* **1**, pertaining to weaving; as, *textile* machinery; **2**, formed by weaving or capable of being woven; as, *textile* fabrics:—*n.* woven goods, such as cotton and wool.

tex-tu-al (tĕks′tū-ăl), *adj.* **1**, serving for a text, or topic; **2**, pertaining to, or contained in, the printed or written words of a book or manuscript; as, *textual* criticism; a *textual* inaccuracy.—*adv.* **tex′tu-al-ly.**

tex-tu-al-ism (tĕks′tū-ăl-ĭzm), *n.* **1**, strict adherence to the letter of the text; **2**, the art or methods of textual criticism, as of the Bible.—*n.* **tex′tu-al-ist.**

tex-ture (tĕks′tŭr), *n.* **1**, any woven fabric; hence, the structure of a woven fabric; the arrangement of threads making up a fabric; as, a cloth of close *texture;* **2**, the way in which the small particles of a substance are united; as, the granular *texture* of granite.

-th (-th), *suffix,* **1**, forming abstract nouns of quality, state, etc.; as, tru*th;* steal*th;* weal*th;* **2**, forming ordinal numbers; as, six*th;* ten*th:* after a vowel, *-eth;* as, forti*eth;* **3**, *Archaic,* forming the third person singular of the present indicative of some verbs; as, ha*th;* do*th:* also written *-eth.*

tha-ler (tä′lẽr), *n.* [*pl.* thaler], a German silver coin equal to three marks, formerly worth about 72 cents. Also, **ta′ler.**

Tha-li-a (th*ȧ*-lī′a), *n.* in mythology, **1**, the Muse presiding over comedy and pastoral poetry; **2**, one of the three Graces; **3**, a Nereid.

thal-lus (thăl′ŭs), *n.* [*pl.* thalli (-ī)], the simple plant body characteristic of the algæ, fungi, lichens, and liverworts, usually having no differentiation into leaves, stems, or true roots.—*adj.* **thal′loid.**

than (*th*ăn), *conj.* a particle used before the second member of a comparison and after certain adjectives and adverbs which express comparison or diversity.

thane (thān), *n.* **1**, orig., a servant; **2**, hence, among the Anglo-Saxons, a freeman attached to the service of a lord: corresponding to a knight or baron in later times. Also, **thegn.**—*n.* **thane′ship.**

thank (thăngk), *v.t.* to express gratitude or obligation to.

thank-ful (thăngk′fo͝ol), *adj.* **1**, feeling gratitude; esp., feeling conscious of blessings received from God; **2**, expressing gratitude; grateful; as, *thankful* hearts.—*adv.* **thank′ful-ly.**—*n.* **thank′ful-ness.**

thank-less (thăngk′lĕs), *adj.* **1**, ungrateful; not appreciative of favors; as, a *thankless* child; **2**, not gaining gratitude; unprofitable; as, a *thankless* task. —*adv.* **thank′less-ly.**—*n.* **thank′less-ness.**

thanks (thăngks), *n.pl.* an expression of gratitude or obligation.

thanks-giv-ing (thăngks″gĭv′ĭng; thăngks′gĭv″ĭng), *n.* **1**, the act of expressing gratitude for favors and mercies; **2**, a public celebration of divine goodness; **3**, a day set apart for such a celebration; **4**, a form of worship acknowledging the blessings received from God.

Thanks-giv-ing Day in the U. S., a day set apart each year, usually the last Thursday in November, for gratitude and praise to God for his blessings: also called *Thanksgiving.*

that (*th*ăt), *adj.* [*pl.* those (*th*ōz)], **1**, designating something more or less distant; yon; as, *that* house across the street; **2**, indicating something already spoken of or considered as known; as, with *that* deep voice of his; **3,** the other, or second, of two: correlative of *this;* as, on this side and on *that* side:—*pron.* **1,** something more or less distant; as, do you see *that* over there? **2,** something already spoken of or considered as known; as, so *that* is what he said; **3,** the thing, the one, etc., characterized in a specified way by a modifier; as, hold fast to *that* which is good:—*relative pron.* **1,** who; which: used of persons or things, usually in restrictive clauses only; **2,** *Colloq.*, in, for, on, or at, which; as, the time *that* he arrived:—*conj.* **1,** introducing a noun clause serving as object, subject, or predicate nominative of a verb; as, he said *that* he would come; **2,** introducing a clause of purpose or result; as, work *that* you may succeed; a sound so loud *that* he was deafened; **3,** introducing an exclamation; as, oh, *that* you were here! **4,** *Colloq.*, introducing a reason: equivalent to *because;* as, I am surprised *that* he did it:—*adv. Colloq.*, to such a degree; so; as, he is about *that* high.

thatch (thăch), *n.* a roof or covering made of straw, reeds, or the like:—*v.t.* to cover with, or as with, a roof of straw, reeds, or the like.—*n.* **thatch'er.**—*adj.* **thatch'y.**

thaw (thô), *v.i.* **1,** to melt or become liquid, as ice or snow; **2,** impersonally, of weather, to become warm enough to melt ice and snow; as, if it *thaws*, we shall go; **3,** to have frozen contents change to a liquid; as, the pipes will soon *thaw;* **4,** to become milder or more genial:—*v.t.* to cause to melt or dissolve:—*n.* **1,** the melting of ice or snow by temperature above the freezing point; **2,** a state of weather when ice and snow melt.

[1]**the** (*thĕ* when unaccented before a consonant, as in *the cat;* *th*ē or *th*ĭ before a vowel, as in *the ear;* *th*ē when emphatic or alone), *definite article*, used: **1,** before a noun naming something already mentioned or known; as, I saw *the* man yesterday; also, to limit the application of a noun; as, hand me *the* book you were reading: distinguished from the indefinite force of *a* or *an;* **2,** before a noun, to emphasize a person or thing as the best known or most distinguished of a class or group; as, he is *the* man for the position; **3,** before a noun naming something well known; as, *the* Hudson; **4,** before a singular noun standing for a class; as, *the* horse is a useful animal; **5,** before an adjective used as a noun; as, *the* brave deserve *the* fair.

[2]**the** (*th*ĕ), *adv.* by however much; also, by so much: the two meanings often being used correlatively before comparatives; as, *the* sooner, *the* better.

the-ar-chy (thē'är-kĭ), *n.* [*pl.* thearchies (-kĭz)], **1,** government under the immediate direction of God; also, divine rule or sovereignty; **2,** a group of, or government by, ecclesiastics as the personal representatives of God.

the-a-ter (thē'*ȧ*-tẽr), *n.* **1,** a public building where plays or dramatic performances are given; **2,** a place resembling a theater, as a music hall; **3,** the field of dramatic art; **4,** a place where events or things of importance take place; as, the *theater* of war. Also, **the'a-tre.**

the-at-ri-cal (thē-ăt'rĭ-kăl), *adj.* **1,** of or pertaining to a theater, a dramatic performance, or actors; **2,** suitable in style or manner for the stage; **3,** resembling the manner of actors; **4,** hence, affectedly emotional:—*n.*, in *pl.*, a dramatic performance, esp. by amateurs. Also, *adj.* **the-at'ric.**—*adv.* **the-at'ri-cal-ly.**—*n.* **the-at'ri-cal-ness.**

The-ban (thē'băn), *adj.* of or pertaining to Thebes, the ancient capital of Upper Egypt, or Thebes, the most important city of ancient Bœotia, in Greece:—*n.* an inhabitant of Thebes.

***thé dan-sant** (tā' däṅ"säṅ'), [Fr.], a tea, or social gathering, with light refreshments and dancing.

thee (*th*ē), *pron. Archaic*, **1,** the objective singular of the personal pronoun of the second person, used mainly in prayer, poetry, or in poetic prose; **2,** in some Quaker usage and in some English dialects, the nominative or the objective singular of the personal pronoun of the second person.

theft (thĕft), *n.* **1,** the act of stealing; robbery; **2,** the property stolen.

thegn (thān), *n.* a freeman under an Anglo-Saxon lord. See **thane,** *Pfd. S.*

the-ine (thē'ĭn; thē'ēn), *n.* a bitter alkaloid, identical with caffeine: found in tea, coffee, and other plants. Also, **the'in; the-i'na** (thē-ī'n*ȧ*).

their (*th*âr), the possessive case of the personal pronoun *they:* used as a possessive adjective.

theirs (*th*ârz), a possessive form of the personal pronoun *they*, used alone: **1,** as *adj.*, in the predicate; as, whose book is it? it is *theirs;* **2,** as *pron.;* as, whose book have you? I have *theirs.*

the-ism (thē'ĭzm), *n.* **1,** the belief in the existence of a god or gods; **2,** belief in the personal nature and immanence of one righteous god.—*n.* **the'ist.**—*adj.* **the-is'tic; the-is'ti-cal.**

them (*th*ĕm), *pron.* the objective case of *they*, the plural form of the third person *he*, *she*, and *it.*

the-mat-ic (thē-măt'ĭk), *adj.* **1,** pertaining to the melodic subject of a composition or movement; **2,** in grammar, pertaining to a stem or root.

theme (thēm), *n.* **1,** the subject or topic of a conversation, speech, essay, etc.; **2,** a short essay or composition on a given subject; **3,** in music, a series of notes forming the subject of a composition or movement.

The-mis (thē'mĭs), *n.* in mythology, a female Titan, mother of Prometheus, an earth goddess personifying physical law, custom, and divine justice.

them-selves (*th*ĕm-sĕlvz'), *pron.* the plural form of *himself*, *herself*, and *itself;* the emphatic or reflexive form of *they* or *them.*

then (*th*ĕn), *conj.* in consequence; therefore; in that case:—*adv.* **1,** next; immediately after; **2,** at that time; **3,** later; at another time:—*adj.* existing at the time mentioned:—*n.* a time specifically mentioned; as, by *then* he was ready.

thence (*th*ĕns), *adv.* **1,** from that place; as, he departed *thence;* **2,** from or after that time; as, a week *thence.*

thence-forth (*th*ĕns"fōrth'; *th*ĕns'fōrth), from that time on.

thence-for-ward (*th*ĕns"fôr'wẽrd), *adv.* **1,** forward from that time; thenceforth; **2,** forward from that place.

the-oc-ra-cy (thē-ŏk'r*ȧ*-sĭ), *n.* [*pl.* theocracies (-sĭz)], **1,** the government of a state by the immediate direction of God; **2,** hence, government by an organized church; **3,** the state thus governed.

the-o-crat-ic (thē"ō-krăt'ĭk), *adj.* pertaining to a theocracy, or a government by the direction of God; as, the *theocratic* government of the ancient Hebrews. Also, **the"o-crat'i-cal.**

the-od-o-lite (thē-ŏd'ō-līt), *n.* a surveying instrument used for measuring horizontal and vertical angles, and heights (see illus. next page).

the-og-o-ny (thē-ŏg'ō-nĭ), *n.* [*pl.* theogonies (-nĭz)], **1,** that branch of mythology which treats of the origin of the gods; **2,** a poem treating of such histories.

the-o-lo-gi-an (thē″ō-lō′jĭ-ăn), *n.* one skilled in theology, or the science of religion; a professor of theology.

the-o-log-i-cal (thē″ō-lŏj′ĭ-kăl), *adj.* pertaining to theology, or the science of religion.—*adv.* **the″o-log′i-cal-ly.**

the-ol-o-gy (thē-ŏl′ō-jĭ), *n.* [*pl.* theologies (-jĭz)], the study of the existence, nature, and powers of God, esp. as affecting man; divinity; the science of religion.

the-o-rem (thē′ō-rĕm), *n.* **1,** that which can be shown to be true, and has been established as a principle or law; **2,** in mathematics, a proposition to be proved.

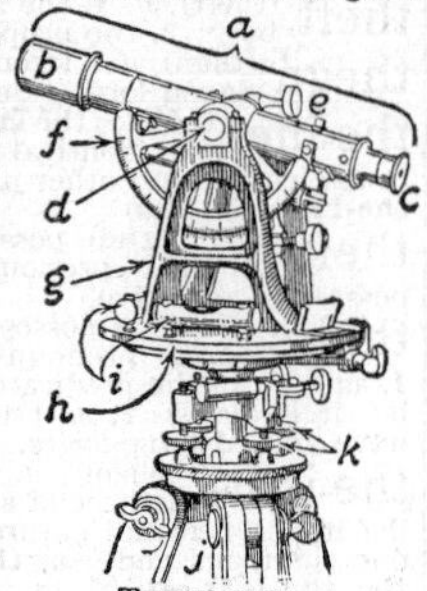

THEODOLITE

a, telescope; *b,* sunshade; *c,* eyepiece cap; *d,* trunnion, or supporting pivot; *e,* trunnion clamp screw; *f,* vertical half circle (quadrant, or limb); *g,* standard; *h,* horizontal circle; *i,* levels; *j,* tripod; *k,* leveling screws.

the-o-ret-i-cal (thē″ō-rĕt′ĭ-kăl), *adj.* **1,** pertaining to, or depending on, an abstract principle; ideal; **2,** based on ideas rather than on fact or experience; not practical; speculative; uncertain. Also, **the″o-ret′ic.**—*adv.* **the″o-ret′i-cal-ly.**

the-o-rist (thē′ō-rĭst), *n.* one who draws conclusions from abstract principles rather than from facts; a dreamer; an impractical person.

the-o-rize (thē′ō-rīz), *v.i.* [*p.t.* and *p.p.* -rized (-rīzd), *p.pr.* -riz″ing], to form theories or offer speculative explanations; draw conclusions from abstract principles. —*n.* **the′o-riz″er.**

the-o-ry (thē′ō-rĭ), *n.* [*pl.* theories (-rĭz)], **1,** a collection of principles giving a more or less complete and rounded view of an art or science; as, the *theory* of architecture; **2,** a statement of a supposed principle intended to explain observed facts; a hypothesis, esp. one that has been verified to some extent; as, the *theory* of the solar system; **3,** the sphere of speculation as opposed to practice; as, it sounds good in *theory*, but how will it work? **4,** a speculative view or opinion.
Syn. speculation, scheme, conjecture.

the-os-o-phy (thē-ŏs′ō-fĭ), *n.* [*pl.* theosophies (-fĭz)], a philosophy which claims to put man into direct touch with God and the spiritual world by physical processes and extreme spiritual inspiration; esp., a modern belief embodying many doctrines found in Brahmanism and Buddhism, including that of reincarnation.—*n.* **the-os′o-phist.**—*adj.* **the″o-soph′ic; the″o-soph′i-cal.**

ther-a-peu-tic (thĕr″ȧ-pū′tĭk), *adj.* **1,** pertaining to healing; **2,** curative; remedial: **therapeutics,** *n.pl.* used as *sing.* the science of curing diseases; therapy.

ther-a-py (thĕr′ȧ-pĭ), *n.* a division of medical science concerned with the treatment of diseases; therapeutics.

there (*thâr*), *adv.* **1,** in that place: opp. of *here;* as, I went *there;* **2,** in that direction; **3,** at that point or stage; as, he came to decimals and stopped *there;* **4,** in that matter, relation, etc.; as, you're right *there;* **5,** (*th*ẽr), used preceding, or, in questions, following, a verb to introduce a sentence; as, *there* is time; is *there* time?

there- (*th*âr-), *prefix,* that: forming combinations with prepositions; as, *there*on; *there*for; *there*from.

there-a-bout (*th*âr′ȧ-bout″), *adv.* near that place, time, number, etc.; nearly. Also, **there′a-bouts″.**

there-aft-er (*th*âr-ȧf′tẽr), *adv.* **1,** after that; **2,** accordingly.

there-at (*th*âr-ăt′), *adv.* **1,** at that place; **2,** on that account; at that; as, *thereat* he ceased.

there-by (*th*âr-bī′), *adv.* **1,** by that means; **2,** connected with that; **3,** near by.

there-for (*th*âr-fôr′), *adv.* for that or this; as, we give thanks *therefor.*

there-fore (*th*âr′fōr; *th*ûr′fōr), *adv.* and *conj.* for that or this reason; for that reason or purpose; as a result of that.
Syn. accordingly, hence.

there-from (*th*âr-frŏm′), *adv.* from this or that place, time, cause, etc.

there-in (*th*âr-ĭn′), *adv.* **1,** in or into this or that place, time, etc.; **2,** in this or that respect; as, *therein* you are to blame.

there-of (*th*âr-ŏv′; *th*âr-ŏf′), *adv.* **1,** of or concerning that or this; **2,** from this or that cause.

there-on (*th*âr-ŏn′), *adv.* on that, this, or it; as, rely *thereon.*

there-to (*th*âr-tōō′), *adv.* **1,** to that, this, or it; **2,** in proof of this; also.

there-to-fore (*th*âr″tōō-fōr′), *adv.* up to that time; until then; previously to a given date.

there-un-to (*th*âr″ŭn-tōō′), *adv.* thereto; to that or this.

there-up-on (*th*âr″ŭ-pŏn′), *adv.* **1,** thereon; upon that; **2,** therefore; by reason of that; **3,** immediately.

there-with (*th*âr-wĭ*th*′; *th*âr-wĭth′), *adv.* **1,** with that or this; **2,** at the same time; immediately. Also, *Archaic,* **there″with-al′** (-ôl′).

ther-mal (thûr′măl), *adj.* **1,** of or pertaining to heat; as, *thermal* units; **2,** hot; as, *thermal* baths:—*n.* a vertical current of air: **thermal soaring,** soaring on thermals in a glider.—*adj.* **ther′mic.**

ther-mo- (thûr′mō-), a combining form from the Greek, meaning heat; as, *thermo*meter; *thermo*stat.

ther-mo-dy-nam-ics (thûr″mō-dī-năm′ĭks), *n.pl.* used as *sing.* the science of the relations coexisting between heat and mechanical action. —*adj.* **ther″mo-dy-nam′ic.**

ther-mo-e-lec-tric-i-ty (thûr″mō-ē-lĕk-trĭs′ĭ-tĭ), *n.* electricity generated, or produced, by the action of heat.—*adj.* **ther″mo-e-lec′tric.**

ther-mom-e-ter (thẽr-mŏm′ē-tẽr), *n.* an instrument for measuring temperature changes, esp. one consisting of a glass tube of capillary bore partly filled with mercury or colored alcohol, the degree of the expansion or contraction of which, due to heat changes, is read on a graduated scale: **Fahrenheit thermometer,** one in which the freezing point of water is 32 degrees and the boiling point 212 degrees: **centigrade thermometer,** one in which the corresponding

THERMOMETERS

1, house; 2, bath; 3, air; 4, maximum and minimum; 5, horticultural, for soil.

points are 0 and 100 degrees: **Réaumur thermometer**, one in which the corresponding points are 0 and 80 degrees.—*adj.* **ther″mo-met′ric; ther″mo-met′ri-cal.**

ther-mo-pile (thûr′mō-pīl), *n.* an instrument used for detecting very slight variations in temperature.

ther-mos bot-tle (thûr′mŏs), an air-tight receptacle for liquids, so prepared as to keep them at the same degree of heat or cold as when they are put into it: a trade name.

ther-mo-scope (thûr′mō-skōp), *n.* an instrument for showing differences in temperature without exact measurement in degrees.

ther-mo-stat (thûr′mō-stăt), *n.* an automatic apparatus for regulating temperature.

ther-mot-ic (thẽr-mŏt′ĭk), *adj.* pertaining to heat: **thermotics,** *n.pl.* used as *sing.* the science of heat.

the-sau-rus (thē-sô′rŭs), *n.* [*pl.* thesauri (-rī)], **1,** a place where treasure is kept; **2,** hence, a lexicon or dictionary; as, a *thesaurus* of English words.

these (thēz), plural of the demonstrative adjective and pronoun *this;* as, *these* girls are pretty; give me *these:* opp. of *those.*

The-seus (thē′sūs; thē′sē-ŭs), *n.* in mythology, the leading legendary hero of Attica, famed for many exploits, such as slaying the Minotaur in Crete.

the-sis (thē′sĭs), *n.* [*pl.* theses (-sēz)], **1,** something laid down or stated; esp., a proposition advanced by a person who undertakes to support it by argument; **2,** a long essay, based on original research work, and offered by a candidate for an advanced degree; **3,** in logic, a statement which is to be maintained and proved by argument.

Thes-pi-an (thĕs′pĭ-ăn), *adj.* **1,** pertaining to Thespis, the founder of Greek drama; **2,** hence, dramatic.

Thes-sa-li-an (thĕ-sā′lĭ-ăn), *adj.* pertaining to Thessaly, a district of Greece:—*n.* **1,** an inhabitant of Thessaly; **2,** the language of Thessaly.

Thes-sa-lo-ni-an (thĕs″ȧ-lō′nĭ-ăn), *n.* **1,** a native or resident of Thessalonica; **2** in *pl.,* (*abbr.* **Thess.**), either of two books of the New Testament, consisting of letters written by the apostle Paul to the church at Thessalonica.

the-ta (thē′tȧ; thā′tȧ), *n.* the eighth letter of the Greek alphabet [θ, Θ], nearly equivalent to the English *th.*

The-tis (thē′tĭs), *n.* a Nereid, wife of Peleus, who, by dipping her son Achilles in the Styx, made him invulnerable, except for the heel by which she held him.

thews (thūz), *n.pl.* muscles; sinews; hence, muscular power or strength.

they (thā), *personal pron.* **1,** the nominative plural of the pronouns *he, she,* or *it;* **2,** people in general; men; as, *they* say.

Thi-bet-an (tĭ-bĕt′ăn), *adj.* pertaining to Tibet, a country of central Asia, or to its inhabitants:—*n.* **1,** a member of the native race of this country; **2,** the language of its people. Also, **Ti-bet′an,** *Pfd. S.*

thick (thĭk), *adj.* **1,** large in diameter; coarse, as a wire or stem; **2,** relatively deep or extensive from one surface to its opposite; as, a *thick* book; **3,** of compact or dense texture, consistency, or the like; as, *thick* glue; **4,** close together; abundant; as, the weeds are *thick;* also, closely set or occupied; **5,** frequent; **6,** stupid; dull; as, a *thick* mind; **7,** not clear; muddy; foggy; as, the air was *thick* with smoke; **8,** muffled; dull, as sounds: opp. of *thin;* **9,** *Colloq.,* extremely friendly or intimate; as, she's too *thick* with Mary:—*adv.* close together; following closely or quickly; as, the blows came *thick* and fast:—*n.* **1,** the thickest part of anything; as, the *thick* of the thumb; **2,** the most intense moment; the place where action is liveliest; as, the *thick* of the combat: **through thick and thin,** under all sorts of conditions; resolutely; in spite of difficulties:—*adv.* **thick′ly.** —*n.* **thick′ness.**—*adj.* **thick′ish.**

thick-en (thĭk′n), *v.t.* **1,** to make less thin or slender; **2,** to make dense; as, to *thicken* gravy with flour; **3,** to set more closely:—*v.i.* **1,** to become more dense or closer together, as trees; **2,** to become dark; as, night *thickens;* **3,** to lose thinness.

thick-en-ing (thĭk′n-ĭng), *n.* something added to a liquid mass to make it more dense; as, flour or cornstarch is used as *thickening* for soups, sauces, etc.

thick-et (thĭk′ĕt), *n.* a dense growth of tangled underbrush, trees, etc.

thick-set (thĭk′sĕt″), *adj.* **1,** closely planted; **2,** having a short, stout body; as, a *thickset* man:—*n.* **1,** a close, thick hedge; **2,** a dense growth of trees and bushes.

thick-skinned (thĭk′=skĭnd″), *adj.* **1,** having thick skin; **2,** hence, not sensitive; not affected by criticism, insult, or the like.

thief (thēf), *n.* [*pl.* thieves (thēvz)], one who steals or robs, esp. by stealth.

thieve (thēv), *v.t.* [*p.t.* and *p.p.* thieved (thēvd), *p.pr.* thiev′ing], to steal; rob by stealth:—*v.i.* to practice stealing.

thiev-er-y (thēv′ẽr-ĭ), *n.* [*pl.* thieveries (-ĭz)], act or habit of stealing.

thiev-ish (thēv′ĭsh), *adj.* **1,** given to stealing; dishonest; **2,** like a thief; stealthy.—*adv.* **thiev′ish-ly.**—*n.* **thiev′ish-ness.**

thigh (thī), *n.* the muscular part of the leg between the knee and the body.

thill (thĭl), *n.* either of the two shafts of a cart or carriage.

thim-ble (thĭm′bl), *n.* **1,** a metal cap to protect the finger in sewing; **2,** anything shaped like a thimble; **3,** an iron ring belonging to a sail, fitted to receive a rope.

thim-ble-ber-ry (thĭm′bl-bĕr″ĭ), *n.* [*pl.* thimbleberries (-ĭz)], an American raspberry with thimble-shaped fruit.

thim-ble-rig (thĭm′bl-rĭg″), *n.* a sleight-of-hand trick in which a pea is supposed to be hidden under one of three thimbles: also known as the *shell game:* —*v.t.* [*p.t.* and *p.p.* -rigged″ (-rĭgd″), *p.pr.* -rig″-ging], to swindle by means of this trick; hence, to cheat by any trick.—*n.* **thim′ble-rig″ger.**

thin (thĭn), *adj.* [*comp.* thin′ner, *superl.* thin′nest], **1,** small in diameter; fine; slim; slender, as a wire or stem; **2,** having little extent between two opposite surfaces; of little thickness; as, a *thin* board; **3,** transparent; sheer; as, *thin* muslin; **4,** hence, easily seen through; slight; shallow; as, his excuses are too *thin;* **5,** lacking density; rarefied; as, *thin* air; **6,** high-pitched; shrill; faint; as, a *thin* voice; **7,** lacking roundness or plumpness of figure; gaunt; **8,** scanty; lacking substance or vigor; as, *thin* blood; *thin* humor; **9,** clear, as sound: opp. of *thick:*—*v.t.* [*p.t.* and *p.p.* thinned (thĭnd), *p.pr.* thin′ning], **1,** to make thin or less dense; **2,** to reduce in numbers:—*v.i.* to become less dense or numerous; as, the forest *thins* daily.—*adv.* **thin′ly.**—*n.* **thin′ness.**

Syn., adj. (see lean).

thine (thīn), *Archaic* or *Poetic* (except in the speech of Friends), a possessive form of the personal pronoun *thou,* used: **1,** alone: **a,** as *adj.,* in the predicate; as, whose hat is this? it is *thine;* **b,** as *pron.;* as, whose hat hast thou? I have *thine;* **2,** as *adj.,* used attributively before an initial vowel or *h;* as, *thine* own self.

[1]**thing** (thĭng), *n.* **1,** that which has physical, concrete existence and may be perceived through the senses, as a book, cloud, etc.; **2,** that which is, or may be made, an object of thought; that which exists as an abstract conception or ideal, or in the imagination, as virtue, a fairy, etc.; **3,** a particular event, fact, or affair; as, this *thing* must not occur again; **4,** a person or animal: often a term of pity, sympathy, affection, or contempt; as, he, poor *thing;* **5,** *Rare,* bit; degree; whit: usually compounded, with an adverbial force, with *any, no,* or *some;* as, she was some*thing* better today; **6,** in *pl.,* wraps; personal baggage.

[2]**thing** (tĭng), *n.* a Scandinavian legislative or judicial body: often in compounds; as, the Stor*thing.* Also, ***ting.**

[1]**think** (thĭngk), *v.i.* [*p.t.* and *p.p.* thought (thôt), *p.pr.* think′ing], **1,** to exercise the mind with ideas, conceptions, inferences, judgments, etc.; **2,** to meditate; muse; ponder; as, I am *thinking* of my boyhood; **3,** to bring something before the mind: often with *of;* as, I can *think* of no alternative; **4,** to have an opinion or judgment; as, he *thinks* well of you; **5,** to purpose, plan, or intend; as, I had not *thought* of going until tomorrow:—*v.t.* **1,** to occupy the mind with; imagine; conceive; as, *think* nothing evil of her; **2,** to review or examine mentally; as, I *thought* the matter over; **3,** to hold as an opinion: used with an object clause; as, I *think* that you are right.—*adj.* **think′a-ble.**—*n.* **think′er.**

[2]**think** (thĭngk), *v.i.* [*p.t.* and *p.p.* thought (thôt), *p.pr.* think′ing], to seem; appear: an impersonal verb, rare except in me*thinks,* me*thought* (it seems, seemed, to me).

think-ing (thĭngk′ĭng), *p.adj.* having the power of thought:—*n.* meditation; judgment.—*adv.* **think′ing-ly.**

thin–skinned (thĭn′=skĭnd″), *adj.* **1,** having thin skin; **2,** hence, sensitive; easily hurt by criticism.

third (thûrd), *adj.* **1,** next in order after the second: the ordinal of *three;* **2,** designating one of the three equal parts of anything: **Third day,** Tuesday: so called by the Friends, or Quakers: **third degree,** in Freemasonry, the ceremony by which the degree of Master Mason is conferred; hence, *Colloq.,* the grilling examination of a prisoner by the police, to obtain information or force a confession: **third person,** in grammar: **1,** the person or thing spoken of; **2,** the special grammatical form indicating such a person or thing: **third rail,** a rail running parallel to the two rails of an electric railway, carrying the electric current which is utilized as motive power by the cars:—*n.* **1,** the quotient of one divided by three; **2,** one of the three equal parts of anything; **3,** in music: **a,** the interval between any tone in a diatonic scale and the tone next but one above it; **b,** the second number of a common chord or triad.—*adv.* **third′ly.**

thirst (thûrst), *n.* **1,** the desire for drink; **2,** a great craving, as for liquor; **3,** hence, eager wish; as, a *thirst* for knowledge:—*v.i.* **1,** to desire drink; **2,** hence, to be eager; as, to *thirst* for revenge.

thirst-y (thûrs′tĭ), *adj.* [*comp.* thirst′i-er, *superl.* thirst′i-est], **1,** feeling desire for drink; **2,** eager; **3,** without moisture; parched.—*adv.* **thirst′i-ly.**—*n.* **thirst′i-ness.**

thir-teen (thûr′tēn″; thûr″tēn′), *adj.* composed of ten plus three:—*n.* **1,** the number consisting of ten and three; **2,** a sign representing thirteen units, as 13 or xiii.—*adj.* and *n.* **thir′teenth″.**

thir-ty (thûr′tĭ), *adj.* composed of three times ten, or of twenty-nine plus one:—*n.* [*pl.* thirties (-tĭz)], **1,** the number consisting of three tens; **2,** a sign representing thirty units, as 30 or xxx.—*adj.* and *n.* **thir′ti-eth.**

this (*th*ĭs), *adj.* [*pl.* these (*th*ēz)], **1,** designating that which is near in space, time, or the like; as, take *this* letter; **2,** indicating something just mentioned or about to be mentioned; as, *this* little problem; **3,** the first of two. correlative of *that;* as, *this* girl and that boy:—*pron.* **1,** the thing present or near; as, *this* is my house; **2,** the thing just mentioned or to be mentioned; as, *this* is what I think: **this and that,** a variety of things.

This-be (thĭz′bē), *n.* in mythology, a Babylonian maiden who, upon discovering that her lover, Pyramus, had ended his life because he believed she had been killed by a lioness, killed herself.

this-tle (thĭs′l), *n.* any of various plants of the aster family, with a prickly stem and leaves.—*adj.* **this′tly.**

thith-er (*th*ĭ*th*′ẽr), *adv.* **1,** to that place; in that direction; **2,** to that end.

thith-er-ward (*th*ĭ*th*′ẽr-wẽrd), *adv.* in that direction; toward that place. Also, **thith′er-wards.**

tho (*th*ō), *conj.* a short form of *though.* See **though,** *Pfd. S.*

thole (thōl), *n.* a pin used in a boat as a rowlock to keep the oar in place: commonly called *tholepin.*

Thom-as (tŏm′*a*s), *n.* the one of the twelve apostles who doubted the resurrection of Jesus until he had seen him, and who, therefore, is often called "doubting Thomas" (John 20: 24–29).

thong (thông), *n.* **1,** a thin leather strap or string for fastening something; **2,** the lash of a whip.

Thor (thôr), *n.* in Norse mythology, the god of thunder, who always carried the magic hammer, the thunderbolt, and for whom Thursday is named.

tho-rac-ic (thō-răs′ĭk), *adj.* pertaining to the thorax, or part of the body between the neck and the abdomen: **thoracic duct,** in anatomy, the main vessel of the lymphatic system, situated along the front of the spinal column.

tho-rax (thō′răks), *n.* **1,** in the human body, the chest, containing the heart, lungs, etc.; **2,** in insects, the middle of the three main sections of the body.

tho-ri-um (thō′rĭ-ŭm), *n.* a rare, grayish, metallic element: **thorium oxide,** a white, earthy compound used in manufacturing gas mantles.

thorn (thôrn), *n.* **1,** a prickle, spine, or sharp point, as on a plant or an animal; **2,** any tree or shrub bearing thorns; **3,** hence, anything that annoys; worry.—*adj.* **thorn′y.**—*n.* **thorn′i-ness.**

thorn ap-ple a poisonous weed belonging to the nightshade family; the Jimson weed.

thorn-back (thôrn′băk″), *n.* a kind of ray having short, strong spines on the back and tail (see [2]*ray,* illus.).

thor-ough (thŭr′ō), *adj.* **1,** going on to the end; finished; complete; **2,** accurate; as, *thorough* scholarship. Also, **thor′o.**—*adv.* **thor′ough-ly.**—*n.* **thor′ough-ness.**

Syn. accurate, trustworthy, reliable.

thor-ough bass loosely, the science of harmony; also, a system, formerly used, of writing a bass voice part with one or more numerals under the notes, to show the general nature of the harmony.

thor-ough–brace (thŭr′ō=brās″), *n.* a heavy leather strap under the body of a vehicle, serving both as a support and as a spring.

thor-ough-bred (thŭr′ō-brĕd″), *adj.* **1,** of pure and unmixed breed; as, a *thoroughbred* horse; **2,** well brought up; accomplished; polished; **3,** high-spirited:—*n.* **1**, an animal of pure breed; **2**, *Colloq.*, a person of fine breeding.

thor-ough-fare (thŭr′ō-fâr″), *n.* **1**, a street, road, or passage open at both ends; **2**, the right or possibility of using such a route; as, no *thoroughfare*.

Syn. highway, street. (See way.)

thor-ough-go-ing (thŭr′ō-gō″ĭng), *adj.* going to all lengths; complete; as, a *thoroughgoing* search.

thor-ough-paced (thŭr′ō-pāst″), *adj.* **1**, thoroughly trained in all gaits, or paces, as a horse; **2**, hence, thoroughgoing; as, a *thoroughpaced* rogue.

thor-ough-wort (thŭr′ō-wûrt″), *n.* a coarse, white-flowered American herb of the composite family, used as medicine; boneset.

thorp (thôrp), *n.* a small cluster of houses; a hamlet or village. Also, **thorpe.**

those (*th*ōz), plural of the demonstrative pronoun and adjective *that;* as, *those* books are hers: opp. of *these.*

thou (*th*ou), *pron.* [*nom.* thou, *poss.* thy (*th*ī) or thine (*th*īn), *obj.* thee (*th*ē); *pl.* ye (yē) or you (yōō)], *Archaic* or *Poetic*, nominative singular of the personal pronoun of the second person; you.

though (*th*ō), *conj.* **1**, granting that; notwithstanding the fact that; as, I shall go, *though* it is late; **2**, even if; as, *though* he go, I will stay; **3**, and yet; still; as, I will go, *though* I am not well:—*adv.* nevertheless; however. Also, **tho.**

[1]**thought** (thôt), *n.* **1**, the act or process of mental activity; meditation; reflection; **2**, that which the mind conceives, considers, remembers, or imagines; an idea; conception; memory; recollection; intention; **3**, the capacity or function of conceiving and reasoning; intellect; as, man is endowed with the power of *thought;* **4**, concern; care; worry; as, take *thought* for the morrow; **5**, a way of thinking, or group of ideas or beliefs, characteristic of a period, nation, class, society, or the like; as, modern *thought;* **6**, *Colloq.*, a little; a shade; as, she was a *thought* more kindly.

Syn. contemplation, deliberation; solicitude.

[2]**thought** (thôt), past tense and past participle of the verb *think.*

thought-ful (thôt′fōōl), *adj.* **1**, given to contemplation; **2**, attentive; careful; **3**, considerate of others.—*adv.* **thought′ful-ly.**—*n.* **thought′ful-ness.**

Syn. reflective, cautious, heedful.—*Ant.* heedless, careless, inconsiderate.

thought-less (thôt′lĕs), *adj.* **1**, unthinking; **2**, heedless; careless.—*adv.* **thought′less-ly.**—*n.* **thought′less-ness.**

thought read-ing the act, art, or science of perceiving another's thought without ordinary intercourse; mind reading; **thought read′er.**

thou-sand (thou′zănd), *adj.* **1**, consisting of ten times one hundred; **2**, indefinitely great in number:—*n.* **1**, the number consisting of ten hundreds; **2**, a sign representing one thousand units, as 1000 or M; **3**, indefinitely, a large number; as, *thousands* of people.—*adj.* and *n.* **thou′sandth.**

Thra-cian (thrā′shăn), *adj.* pertaining to the country or inhabitants of ancient Thrace, in the eastern part of the Balkan Peninsula.

thral-dom (thrôl′dŭm), *n.* serfdom or slavery; a condition of bondage. Also, **thrall′dom.**

thrall (thrôl), *n.* **1**, a slave or serf; **2**, thraldom or bondage; as, held in *thrall.*

thrash (thrăsh), *v.t.* **1**, (preferably, *thresh*), to beat out (grain) from the hull or husk; **2**, to arrive at by repeated effort; as, to *thrash* out a problem; **3**, to beat or flog soundly:—*v.i.* **1**, (preferably, *thresh*), to beat out grain; **2**, *Colloq.*, to move violently: often with *about.* Also, **thresh.**

thrash-er (thrăsh′ẽr), *n.* **1**, (usually, *thresher*), one who or that which beats out grain; a threshing machine; **2**, (also, *thresher*), a large shark with the upper lobe of the tail as long as the rest of the body.

thread (thrĕd), *n.* **1**, a thin, twisted cord of flax, cotton, silk, or other fibrous substance; **2**, a filament, as of glass or metal; a fiber; **3**, something running through and connecting the parts of anything; as, the *thread* of a story; **4**, the spiral ridge of a screw or nut:—*v.t.* **1**, to provide with a thread, or something like a thread; **2**, to put a thread through, as a needle; **3**, to string, as beads; **4**, to pass or pierce through; make (one's way) with difficulty; as, to *thread* a narrow street.

thread-bare (thrĕd′bâr″), *adj.* **1**, worn to the threads; as, a *threadbare* garment; **2**, poverty-stricken; shabby; as, a *threadbare* appearance; **3**, hackneyed or worn-out; dull; as, a *threadbare* story.

thread-worm (thrĕd′wûrm″), *n.* any of various small, threadlike worms, esp. those parasitic in man.

threat (thrĕt), *n.* **1**, a menace; **2**, a warning of coming evil or danger.

threat-en (thrĕt′n), *v.i.* to be a menace; give notice of coming evil or danger:—*v.t.* **1**, to declare evil intentions against; **2**, to give evidence of, as a coming calamity.—*n.* **threat′en-er.**—*p.adj.* **threat′en-ing.**—*adv.* **threat′en-ing-ly.**

Syn. menace. *Threaten* is more commonly used than *menace.* Things or persons may *threaten;* only persons or things personified *menace.* Large or small misfortunes may *threaten;* only great ones *menace;* as, clouds *threaten* the earth with a downpour, but floods *menace* dwellers in valleys with destruction.

three (thrē), *n.* **1**, the number consisting of two plus one; **2**, a sign representing three units, as 3 or iii: **three times three,** three cheers repeated three times: **rule of three,** proportion; the rule for finding the fourth term of a proportion when three are given:—*adj.* consisting of one more than two: **the three R's,** reading, writing, and arithmetic, considered as the basis of education.

three–deck-er (thrē′=dĕk″ẽr), *n.* **1**, a vessel having three decks; **2**, any structure having three floors.

three-fold (thrē′fōld″), *adj.* triple; in three layers, forms, etc.; consisting of three; repeated three times:—*adv.* in a threefold manner; triply.

three-pence (thrĭp′ĕns; thrĕp′ĕns), *n.* a small British silver coin worth about six cents.

three–ply (thrē′=plī″), *adj.* consisting of three parts combined.

three-score (thrē′skōr″), *adj.* three times twenty; sixty.

three-some (thrē′sŭm), *adj.* performed by three persons or with three taking part:—*n.* a game played by three persons; specif., a golf match in which one plays his ball against a ball played by two others, who play alternate strokes.

thren-o-dy (thrĕn′ō-dĭ), *n.* [*pl.* threnodies (-dĭz)], a dirge or funeral song; a lament in verse or music.

thresh (thrĕsh), *v.t.* **1**, to beat out grain from; **2**, (usually, *thrash*), to arrive at by repeated effort; **3**, (usually, *thrash*), to beat soundly:—*v.i.* to beat out grain. Also, **thrash.**

thresh-er (thrĕsh′ẽr), *n.* **1**, (also, *thrasher*), one who or that which beats out grain; esp., a machine for beating out grain; **2**, (usually, *thrasher*), a shark of tropical seas, with a very long tail used as a weapon.

thresh-old (thrĕsh'ōld), *n.* **1**, the stone, plank, or piece of timber under a door; a door sill; **2**, an entrance; a door; place or point of entrance.

threw (thrōō), the past tense of the irregular verb *throw.*

thrice (thrīs), *adv.* **1**, three times; **2**, in a threefold manner; **3**, extremely.

thrift (thrĭft), *n.* **1**, economical or careful management; frugality; economy; **2**, any of certain plants growing on mountains and the seashore, esp. those bearing heads of pink or white flowers.—*adj.* **thrift'less.**—*adv.* **thrift'less-ly.**—*n.* **thrift'less-ness.**

thrift-y (thrĭf'tĭ), *adj.* [*comp.* thrift'i-er, *superl.* thrift'i-est], **1**, economical; frugal; saving; as, the *thrifty* housekeeper; **2**, prosperous; thriving; as, a *thrifty* village; **3**, growing quickly and vigorously; as, *thrifty* trees.—*adv.* **thrift'i-ly.**—*n.* **thrift'i-ness.**

Syn. (see economical).

thrill (thrĭl), *v.t.* **1**, to fill with intense emotion; stir deeply; **2**, to cause to have a shivering, tingling sensation:—*v.i.* **1**, to feel deeply; **2**, to experience a sharp tingling or quivering sensation; **3**, to quiver:—*n.* a tingling, vibrating sensation; tremor.

thrips (thrĭps), *n.* **1**, any of several minute winged or wingless insects which feed upon the juices of plants; as, the onion *thrips;* **2**, also, popularly, any of various other small insects injurious to grapevines.

thrive (thrīv), *v.i.* [*p.t.* throve (thrōv) or thrived (thrīvd), *p.p.* thrived or thriv'en (thrĭv'n), *p.pr.* thriv'ing], **1**, to prosper by industry, economy, and good management; **2**, to increase or prosper in any way; succeed; **3**, to grow vigorously; increase or flourish.—*n.* **thriv'er.**—*p.adj.* **thriv'ing.**

throat (thrōt), *n.* **1**, the front part of the neck; also, the passage through it; **2**, hence, a narrow entrance or passage; as, the *throat* of a cannon.

throat-latch (thrōt'lăch"), *n.* the part of a horse's bridle that passes under the throat (see *harness,* illus.).

throat-y (thrōt'ĭ), *adj.* [*comp.* throat'i-er, *superl.* throat'i-est], guttural, as sounds made by the throat; harsh.

throb (thrŏb), *v.i.* [*p.t.* and *p.p.* throbbed (thrŏbd), *p.pr.* throb'bing], **1**, to beat, as the pulse, with more than usual force; palpitate; **2**, hence, to thrill, as with joy:—*n.* **1**, a strong pulsation or beat; **2**, a thrill; as, a *throb* of joy.

throe (thrō), *n.* agony; extreme pain; the keenest anguish.

throne (thrōn), *n.* **1**, the chair of state of a king, bishop, or other high dignitary; **2**, sovereign or kingly power and dignity; **3**, hence, the one invested with sovereign power:—*v.t.* [*p.t.* and *p.p.* throned (thrōnd), *p.pr.* thron'ing], to place in a position of kingly power; exalt or elevate.

throng (thrông), *n.* a multitude or great number; crowd:—*v.t.* **1**, to crowd or press upon; **2**, to crowd into; fill:—*v.i.* to come in multitudes or great numbers.

Syn., n. crowd, mob, rabble, populace. *Throng* denotes a large number of people thickly packed together and moving. A *crowd* has too many people for comfort in the space at its disposal; its mood depends on circumstances. A *mob* is a *crowd* under the influence of excitement or inflamed to some purpose. The *rabble* is always the lowest class of people. *Populace* means the common people; sometimes the term is used contemptuously in reference to the ignorance and vulgarity associated with the great uneducated masses.

thros-tle (thrŏs'l), *n.* **1**, the song thrush; **2**, a spinning machine.

throt-tle (thrŏt'l), *v.t.* [*p.t.* and *p.p.* -tled (-ld), *p.pr.* -tling], **1**, to strangle or choke by pressure on the windpipe; **2**, to shut off, as steam from an engine:—*v.i.* to choke; strangle:—*n.* **1**, *Rare,* the throat or windpipe; **2**, a valve to control the supply, as of steam or gas, to an engine: also called *throttle valve.*—*n.* **throt'tler.**

through (thrōō), *prep.* **1**, in general, from end to end of: used of time, space, or degree; as, *through* life; *through* a tunnel; *through* thick and thin; **2**, into at one place and out of at another; as, to bore *through* a plank; **3**, in the midst of; as, to walk *through* the woods; **4**, by means of; as, *through* the influence of a friend; **5**, on account of; by reason of; as, he departed *through* fear of being discovered:—*adv.* **1**, from end to end, or from side to side; as, to drive a nail *through;* **2**, from the beginning to the end; as, he played the music *through;* **3**, at an end; to the end or to a conclusion; as, we will put the job *through;* **4**, *Colloq.*, finished; as, I'm *through:*—*adj.* **1**, extending from one place or surface to another; as, a *through* passage; a *through* bolt; **2**, specif., transporting passengers or freight from one place to another without change of cars; as, a *through* train. Also, **thru; thro'.**

through-out (thrōō-out'), *adv.* everywhere; in every part; as, the jewelry is gold *throughout:*—*prep.* during; in every part of; as, *throughout* the year. Also, **thru-out'.**

throve (thrōv), past tense of the irregular intransitive verb *thrive.*

throw (thrō), *v.t.* [*p.t.* threw (thrōō), *p.p.* thrown (thrōn), *p.pr.* throw'ing], **1**, to fling or hurl to a considerable distance; pitch; toss; as, to *throw* a ball; **2**, to push over violently; upset; as, the wrestler *threw* his opponent; unseat; unhorse; as, his horse *threw* him; **3**, to put on, as clothes, hastily or carelessly; **4**, to put in place or spread with a quick, casting motion; **5**, to shed; cast off; molt; as, the snake *threw* its skin; **6**, to cause to move rapidly forward, as troops; as, he *threw* a detachment into the gap; **7**, to bear (young); produce: usually of animals; **8**, to direct; cast, as a glance; **9**, to cast, as dice; also, to make (a specified cast) with the dice; as, to *throw* sixes; **10**, to turn, twirl, or twist, as two or more strands into one thread; specif., to spin, as filaments of silk, into threads; **11**, in mechanics, to move (a pivoted bar) into a new position; also, to connect or disconnect (a gear, electric switch, etc.) by such a motion: with *in, out, over,* etc.: **throw over,** *Colloq.*, to desert in favor of another; jilt: **throw up,** *Colloq.*, **1**, to resign; give up; as, to *throw up* a job; **2**, to recall tauntingly; **3**, to vomit:—*v.i.* to cast an object through the air to a distance; fling; hurl:—*n.* **1**, the act of twirling, casting, or flinging; **2**, a cast of dice; **3**, hence, a venture; risk; **4**, the distance something may be thrown; as, a stone's *throw;* **5**, the extent of movement made by a movable part of a machine, as by one connecting with a crank; length of stroke; **6**, the motion or path of a lever, switch, etc.—*n.* **throw'er.**

[1]**thrum** (thrŭm), *n.* **1**, in weaving, the end or fringe of warp threads left on the loom after the web has been cut off; also, one of such threads; **2**, hence, any short, loose thread, fringe, or tassel; **3**, in *pl.*, coarse, loose yarn waste.

[2]**thrum** (thrŭm), *v.t.* [*p.t.* and *p.p.* thrummed (thrŭmd), *p.pr.* thrum'ming], **1**, to play on or finger (a stringed instrument) idly, monotonously, or listlessly; strum; **2**, to drum on or tap, as a table, board, or the like:—*v.i.* **1**, to play idly on a stringed instrument; strum; **2**, to drum or tap on a table,

board, or the like:—*n.* a monotonous tapping or drumming.

[1]**thrush** (thrŭsh), *n.* any of a large family of small and medium-sized perching birds, often brown with light-colored, spotted throat and breast: noted for their rich, flutelike song.

[2]**thrush** (thrŭsh), *n.* **1,** an inflammatory infection of the feet in certain animals, esp. the horse; **2,** a mouth disease of infants, marked by small, pearl-colored spots.

thrust (thrŭst), *v.t.* [*p.t.* and *p.p.* thrust, *p.pr.* thrust'ing], **1,** to push or shove with force; as, to *thrust* a person off the sidewalk; drive or impel; **2,** to pierce; as, their swords *thrust* him through:—*v.i.* to attack someone or something with a pointed weapon; as, to *thrust* with a dagger:—*n.* **1,** a violent or sudden push; **2,** a stab; as, the *thrust* of a sword; **3,** hence, a short, pointed, verbal attack; **4,** a strain tending to push a part of a structure outward; as, the *thrust* of a roof.

thud (thŭd), *n.* a dull sound produced by a body falling; a thump.

thug (thŭg; t'hŭg), *n.* **1,** formerly, one of a band of religious robbers and assassins in India; **2,** hence, any assassin or ruffian. —*n.* **thug'ger-y.**—*n.* **thug'gism.**

Thu-le (thū'lē), *n.* the region which the ancients regarded as farthest north.

thumb (thŭm), *n.* **1,** the shortest and thickest digit of the human hand; **2,** the part of a glove which covers this digit:—*v.t.* **1,** to play, as a musical instrument, awkwardly; **2,** to rub, press, soil, or wear, with the thumb; as, to *thumb* the leaves of a book: —*v.i.* to play a musical instrument awkwardly.

thumb-screw (thŭm'skrōō''), *n.* **1,** a screw made to turn by means of the forefinger and thumb; **2,** an old instrument of torture for squeezing the thumb.

thumb-stall (thŭm'stôl''), *n.* a covering, as of leather, for the thumb.

thump (thŭmp), *n.* **1,** a hard, heavy blow; **2,** a heavy fall, or the sound of it: —*v.t.* to pound; strike or beat with dull, heavy blows:—*v.i.* to pound or throb, as the heart.—*n.* **thump'er.**

thun-der (thŭn'dẽr), *n.* **1,** the noise following a flash of lightning; **2,** any similar loud noise; as, the *thunder* of the guns; **3,** any impressive utterance:—*v.i.* **1,** to produce thunder; **2,** to send forth a similar sound; **3,** to utter violent threats:—*v.t.* to utter in a loud and threatening voice.—*n.* **thun'der-er.**

thun-der-bolt (thŭn'dẽr-bōlt''), *n.* **1,** a shaft of lightning and the thunder accompanying it; **2,** something swift and terrible, like lightning and thunder.

thun-der-clap (thŭn'dẽr-klăp''), *n.* the quick, sharp, crashing noise accompanying a flash of lightning.

thun-der-cloud (thŭn'dẽr-kloud''), *n.* a dark, heavy, storm cloud which accompanies a thunderstorm.

thun-der-ing (thŭn'dẽr-ĭng), *adj. Colloq.,* big; astonishing; extraordinary; as, a *thundering* idiot.

thun-der-ous (thŭn'dẽr-ŭs), *adj.* **1,** likely to produce thunder; **2,** exceedingly loud and heavy in sound; as, *thunderous* applause.—*adv.* **thun'der-ous-ly.**

thun-der-storm (thŭn'dẽr-stôrm''), *n.* a storm accompanied by lightning and thunder.

thun-der-struck (thŭn'dẽr-strŭk''), *adj.* astonished or struck dumb, as by sudden amazement.

thu-ri-ble (thū'rĭ-bl), *n.* a vessel for burning incense; a censer.

Thurs-day (thûrz'dā), *n.* the fifth day of the week: named for the god Thor.—*abbr.* **Th.; Thur.; Thurs.**

thus (thŭs), *adv.* **1,** in this or that manner; as, write it *thus;* **2,** to this degree or extent; **3,** so; therefore.

thwack (thwăk), *v.t.* to strike with something flat and heavy; thump:—*n.* a heavy blow with something flat; thump.

thwart (thwôrt), *adj.* situated or placed across something:—*adv.* from side to side; obliquely:—*n.* a rower's seat in a boat, extending from side to side:—*v.t.* **1,** to oppose or baffle; run counter to; **2,** hence, to outwit or defeat; as, to *thwart* an enemy.

Syn., v. frustrate, hinder, circumvent, foil.

thy (thī), *Archaic* or *Poetic,* your: the singular possessive case of *thou:* used as a possessive adjective; as, Love *thy* neighbor.

thyme (tīm), *n.* any of a genus of herbs of the mint family, esp. the common species used for seasoning.—*adj.* **thym'ic.**

thy-roid (thī'roid), *adj.* literally, shield-shaped: **thyroid cartilage,** the chief cartilage forming the outer wall of the larynx: **thyroid gland,** a ductless gland lying on either side of the windpipe below the pharynx.

thy-self (*thī*-sĕlf'), *pron.* an emphatic or reflexive form of *thou* and *thee.*

ti (tē), *n.* the seventh of the syllables used in singing the diatonic scale. Also, **si** (sē).

ti-a-ra (tī-ā'rȧ; tē-ä'rȧ), *n.* **1,** the triple crown worn by the Pope; **2,** a form of headdress worn by the ancient Persians; **3,** a crownlike ornament for the head; diadem or coronet; as, a *tiara* of diamonds.

Ti-bet-an (tĭ-bĕt'ăn; tĭb'ĕt-ăn), *adj.* pertaining to Tibet, a country of central Asia:—*n.* **1,** an inhabitant of Tibet, esp. one of the native race; **2,** the language of Tibet. Also, **Thi-bet'an** (tĭ-bĕt'ăn).

tib-i-a (tĭb'ĭ-ȧ), *n.* [*pl.* tibiæ (-ē); tibias (-ȧz)], the inner and larger of the two bones of the leg or hind limb, extending from knee to ankle; the shin bone.—*adj.* **tib'i-al.**

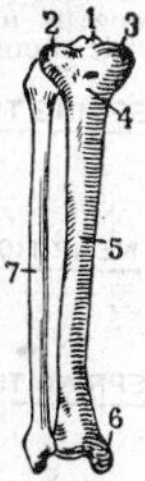

HUMAN TIBIA AND FIBULA
1, spine of tibia
2, external tuberosity
3, inner tuberosity
4, tubercle
5, shaft
6, inner malleolus
7, fibula

tic (tĭk), *n.* a recurring, involuntary, convulsive twitching of the muscles.

ti-cal (tĭ-käl'; -kôl'; tē'kŭl), *n.* the monetary unit of Siam, equivalent to about 44 cents.

[1]**tick** (tĭk), *v.i.* to make a slight, quick, repeated sound, like that of a clock:—*v.t.* **1,** to mark or check off with dots or other small marks, as those used to check items or numbers on a list; score; **2,** to mark off (time) by repeated clicking sounds, as does a clock:—*n.* **1,** a light, recurring sound, as that made by a watch or clock; **2,** a tiny mark like a dot, a √, etc., used in checking off, or in marking something for attention.

[2]**tick** (tĭk), *n.* any of numerous tiny, parasitic, blood-sucking animals, some insects and some arachnids, which attach themselves to the skin of various animals; as, the horse *tick;* cattle *tick* (see illus. page 171).

[3]**tick** (tĭk), *n.* **1,** the cloth case or cover which contains the feathers or other filling of a mattress; **2,** the material of which the case is made; ticking.

[4]**tick** (tĭk), *n. Colloq.* or *Slang,* credit; trust; as, to buy goods on *tick.*

tick-er (tĭk'ẽr), *n.* one who or that which makes a slight, quick, clicking sound; specif., a telegraphic instrument used to receive and print stock quotations or general news on a paper strip, or tape.

tick-et (tĭk'ĕt), *n.* **1,** a certificate which entitles the holder to certain specified privileges, such as admission, a reserved seat, transportation by rail or boat, etc.; as, a theater *ticket;* **2,** a card or label stating price, size, etc., of goods; **3,** a printed list of candidates to be voted for; as, an election *ticket:*—*v.t.* to mark by a label.

tick-ing (tĭk′ĭng), *n.* a strong, closely woven cloth, usually striped, used for mattresses and pillow covers.

tick-le (tĭk′l), *v.t.* [*p.t.* and *p.p.* -led (-ld), *p.pr.* -ling], **1,** to touch lightly so as to produce a peculiar thrill or tingle; **2,** to please or amuse:—*v.i.* **1,** to produce a peculiar thrill or tingle by a light touch; **2,** to feel this sensation:—*n.* a peculiar thrill or tingle or the touch causing it.

tick-ler (tĭk′lẽr), *n.* **1,** one who or that which tickles; **2,** any of various devices for bringing details, as of office administration, to notice on a specified day; an automatic reminder; **3,** a coil used to intensify the electrical oscillations in a receiving circuit: also called *tickler coil.*

tick-lish (tĭk′lĭsh), *adj.* **1,** easily tickled; **2,** delicate to handle or achieve.—*adv.* **tick′lish-ly.**—*n.* **tick′lish-ness.**

tick-tack-too (tĭk″tăk-to͞o′), *n.* a child's game played on crossed parallel lines: also called *crisscross.*

tid-al (tīd′ăl), *adj.* pertaining to, having, or affected by, the tide; as, a *tidal* river; *tidal* flats: **tidal wave,** popularly, an extraordinarily large ocean wave or swell, attributed to an earthquake or other unusual natural cause.

tid-bit (tĭd′bĭt″), *n.* **1,** a small bit or choice morsel, as of food; **2,** hence, a choice bit, as of gossip. Also, **tit′bit″**, *Pfd. S.*

tide (tīd), *n.* **1,** time or season: rare except in combination; as, Easter*tide;* spring*tide;* **2,** the regular rise and fall twice every day of the oceans and the bodies of water connected with them; **3,** anything which in-

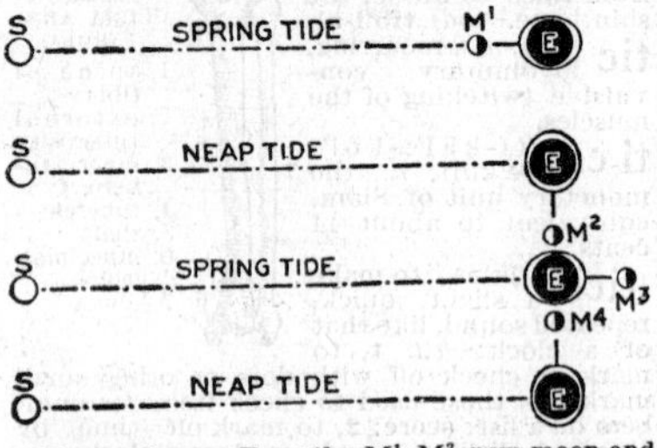

TIDE.—S, sun; E, earth; M^1, M^3, new moon and full moon, causing spring tides; M^2, M^4, moon in first and third quarters, causing neap tides.

creases and decreases, like the tide; **4,** a stream or flood; **5,** the natural tendency of events:—*v.t.* [*p.t.* and *p.p.* tid′ed, *p.pr.* tid′ing], **1,** to carry along with the current or tide; **2,** to help (another) along; assist when needed: with *over;* as, his gift *tided* me over the winter.

tide-wait-er (tīd′wāt″ẽr), *n.* an officer who boards vessels to enforce customs regulations.

tide-wa-ter (tīd′wô″tẽr), *n.* **1,** water affected by the rise and fall of the tide; **2,** land bordered by such water.

ti-dings (tī′dĭngz), *n.pl.* news; information; a message; as, glad *tidings.*
Syn. intelligence. (See news.)

ti-dy (tī′dĭ), *adj.* [*comp.* ti′di-er, *superl.* ti′di-est], **1,** trim; neat; orderly; **2,** *Colloq.,* considerable; as, a *tidy* sum of money:—*v.t.* [*p.t.* and *p.p.* -died (-dĭd), *p.pr.* -dy-ing], to make neat; put in proper order; as, to *tidy* a room:—*v.i.* to put things in order:—*n.* an ornamental cover for the back of a chair.—*adv.* **ti′di-ly.**—*n.* **ti′di-ness.**
Syn., adj. cleanly, prim, dapper.

tie (tī), *v.t.* [*p.t.* and *p.p.* tied (tīd), *p.pr.* ty′ing], **1,** to draw together, fasten, bind, or attach, by a cord or other bond; as, to *tie* two pieces of rope together; **2,** to fasten by means of a loop or knot; as, he *tied* the scarf about his neck; **3,** to make (a loop, knot, or bow) by fastening the ends or parts of a string together; as, to *tie* a bowline knot; **4,** to make a knot in; as, to *tie* bonnet strings; **5,** to restrict or limit; as, his business *ties* him down; **6,** to equal in score; make the same score as; as, we *tied* the other team at football; **7,** in music, to unite, as two notes, with a tie or bind, indicating that they are to be sung or played as one continuous note: **tie up,** to obstruct, restrain, or otherwise interfere with the operation of:—*v.i.* **1,** to form a bow or knot; **2,** to equal a score, as in a contest:—*n.* **1,** something, as a band, rope, or ribbon, used to bind, draw, or fasten together; **2,** a plank or rod used to hold parts together and to receive tensile stress; as, a railroad *tie;* **3,** something tied, as a ribbon, and used as a fastening or ornament; esp., a necktie; **4,** a restriction or limitation; as, business *ties;* **5,** a common interest which unites; as, a strong family *tie;* **6,** equality of numbers, as of votes; equality in a contest, as in a race: **7,** in music, a curved line [⌒] connecting two notes of the same pitch, indicating that they are to be sung or played as one.

tie-beam (tī′bēm″), *n.* a beam which acts as a tie in connecting the lower ends of rafters, as in a house (see *king truss, mansard, principal,* illus.). Also, **tie beam.**

¹ti-er (tī′ẽr), *n.* one who or that which binds or draws together.

²tier (tēr), *n.* a row or rank, as of seats; esp., one of a set of such rows in an ascending arrangement, as in a theater.

tierce (tērs), *n.* **1,** a cask between a barrel and a hogshead in size; **2,** a sequence of three playing cards in the same suit; as, a *tierce* of ace, king, and queen; **3,** in music, a third; **4,** in fencing, a certain thrust or position.

tie-up (tī′-ŭp″), *n. Colloq.,* a temporary cessation of business brought about by an accident, storm, strike, or the like.

tiff (tĭf), *n.* **1,** a fit of anger; **2,** a slight quarrel; disagreement.

tif-fin (tĭf′ĭn), *n.* in India, luncheon, esp. at midday.

ti-ger (tī′gẽr), *n.* **1,** a large, fierce beast of prey of the cat family, having tawny yellow fur with black stripes; **2,** a servant boy in livery; **3,** an added and louder cheer after three cheers.—*n.fem.* **ti′gress.**

ti-ger cat any of various wild cats, similar to the tiger, but smaller.

ti-ger-ish (tī′gẽr-ĭsh), *adj.* savage; fierce; cruel. Also, **ti′grish.**

ti-ger lil-y a handsome lily having orange flowers spotted with black.

tight (tīt), *adj.* **1,** not loose; fastened firmly together; close; as, a *tight* knot **2,** closely built; as, a *tight* barrel; **3,** fitting close to the body; as, a *tight* shoe; **4,** taut or stretched; as, a *tight* rope; **5,** not easily obtained: said of money; **6,** *Colloq.,* stingy; as, he is *tight* with his money; **7,** *Slang,* intoxicated: **tight rope,** a taut rope or cable on which acrobats balance themselves while performing:—*n.,* in *pl.,* closely fitting garments for the lower limbs, worn by actors, acrobats, dancers, etc.—*adv.* **tight′ly.**—*n.* **tight′ness.**

tight-en (tīt′n), *v.t.* and *v.i.* to make or become close or firm.

tike (tīk), *n.* **1,** a dog or cur; **2,** *Colloq.,* a mischievous child; playfully, any child.

il-bu-ry (tĭl′bĕr-ĭ), *n.* [*pl.* tilburies (-ĭz)], a two-wheeled carriage without a over or top.

il-de (tĭl′dĕ; *Span.* tēl′dā), *n.* the diacritical mark [~] used in *señor, cañon,* etc.

ile (tīl), *n.* **1,** a thin slab of baked clay, stone, etc., used for roofing, floors, wall ecoration, etc.; **2,** tiles collectively; **3,** *Colq.,* a stiff hat:—*v.t.* [*p.t.* and *p.p.* tiled (tīld), *.pr.* til′ing], **1,** to cover with tiles; **2,** to drain y means of tiles; **3,** to guard (the door of a Iasonic lodge).

il-er (tīl′ĕr), *n.* **1,** one who roofs houses, lays floors, etc., with tiles; **2,** the oorkeeper of a Masonic lodge.

il-ing (tīl′ĭng), *n.* tiles collectively; also, work made of tiles.

till (tĭl), *n.* **1,** a money drawer in a desk or counter; **2,** the tray of a trunk.

till (tĭl), *prep.* to the time of; as far as: used only of time; as, wait *till* one 'clock:—*conj.* until; as, wait *till* I return.

till (tĭl), *v.t.* to prepare for seed, as by plowing; sow and produce crops from; ultivate, as the soil:—*v.i.* to cultivate the soil.

ill-a-ble (tĭl′ȧ-bl), *adj.* capable of being cultivated, as a field.

ill-age (tĭl′āj), *n.* **1,** the act or art of tilling land; **2,** land under cultivation.

till-er (tĭl′ĕr), *n.* one who cultivates land; a farmer; husbandman.

till-er (tĭl′ĕr), *n.* a lever for turning the rudder of a vessel (see *rudder,* illus.); ence, any means of guidance.

till-er (tĭl′ĕr), *n.* the shoot of a plant; esp., a sucker.

tilt (tĭlt), *n.* the cloth covering of a cart, wagon, boat, or the like; a canopy; wning; tent: **tilt roof,** a rounded roof, esembling a wagon canopy:—*v.t.* to cover, provide, with an awning or canopy.

tilt (tĭlt), *v.i.* **1,** to lean or tip; fall partly to one side; keel over; **2,** to contend on orseback, armed with a lance; **3,** hence, to rgue; **4,** *Colloq.,* to rush pell-mell, as into a lace:—*v.t.* **1,** to raise at one end; tip; as, to *lt* a stone; lean; incline; as, to *tilt* a ladder; to forge or work (metal) with a heavy, ivoted tilt hammer; **3,** to point or thrust, as lance:—*n.* **1,** an incline; **2,** an ancient mock ilitary contest with lances or spears; a ournament; **3,** hence, any contest, as of wits.

ilth (tĭlth), *n.* **1,** cultivated land or land upon which good crops can be raised; the act or science of preparing land for crops.

ilt ham-mer a heavy hammer at the end of a lever, used in rging or working metal, raised by a cam and lowed to fall by gravity.

im-ber (tĭm′bĕr), *n.* **1,** the body or stem of a tree; **2,** wood suitable for carentry, buildings, shipbuilding, etc.; **3,** a large iece of wood prepared for use in building or ready in place; **4,** wooded land, as forests: **mber hitch,** a kind of knot or hitch used to sten a rope end to a spar (see *knot,* illus.): -*v.t.* to furnish or construct with wood.

im-ber-land (tĭm′bĕr-lănd″), *n.* land covered with trees whose ood is suitable for use in building.

im-bre (tĭm′bĕr; *Fr.* tăṅbr′), *n.* the quality, or tone character, of usical sound; as, the *timbre* of a violin.

im-brel (tĭm′brĕl), *n.* **1,** a small drum used by the ancient Hebrews; a tambourine.

ime (tīm), *n.* **1,** measured or measurable duration; present life as contrasted ith immortality; finite duration as distinuished from infinite duration; **2,** a definite ortion of duration, whether past, present, or ture; the period, or amount, of duration, quired or consumed in performing an action; as, the winner's *time* was 3.01; also, a period; season; as, summer *time;* **3,** often in *pl.,* an era; epoch; age; as, in the *time* of Julius Cæsar; in ancient *times;* **4,** a definite period for some specific purpose, event, or the like; an allotted period, as the duration of human life; **5,** a date; occasion, as the hour of death, hour of travail, etc.; as, I fear his *time* has come; also, a definite or precise moment; as, the *time* was set as twelve o'clock noon; **6,** a portion of duration characterized by some special qualities or experiences of its own; as, to have a good *time;* also, often in *pl.,* prevailing state of circumstances; as, hard *times;* **7,** a portion of duration available for some special purpose; leisure; as, *time* for golf; *time* for reading; **8,** a system of reckoning or measuring duration; as, solar *time;* also, a system of specifying an exact moment; as, standard *time;* mountain *time* (see phrases below); **9,** often in *pl.,* a case of recurrence or repetition; renewal of an action, or addition of a number to itself; as, ten is five *times* two; I see her three *times* a week; **10,** indefinite duration; lapse of time; as, such building will not stand the test of *time;* **11,** a measured interval in verse: an important element in classical verse; **12,** in music: **a,** the arrangement of the rhythmic beats of a composition into equal measures included between successive bars; as, two-four *time:* preferably called *meter* or *rhythm;* **b,** the metrical duration or time value of a note or rest; **c,** the rate of speed at which a passage or composition is rendered: preferably called *tempo;* **d,** loosely, the characteristic rhythm or tempo of a composition; as, waltz *time;* **13,** *Colloq.,* a term of imprisonment: **solar time,** time measured by the rotation of the earth with reference to the sun: **Greenwich time,** the time of the meridian of Greenwich in England, used as a standard of reference in most countries throughout the world: **civil time,** the accepted time of any given region, used for regulating ordinary business, and having the beginning of the day at midnight: **standard time,** the time established by law or custom for general observance over a country or a given section of a country, each of the five standard times in the U. S. and Canada being an exact number of hours slower than Greenwich time: **Atlantic, Eastern, Central, Mountain,** and **Pacific time,** the standard times in use in Canada and the U. S., respectively four, five, six, seven, and eight hours slower than Greenwich time, the corresponding meridians at which local and standard times coincide being 60°, 75°, 90°, 105°, and 120° west of Greenwich, each of which is nearly in the middle of the region concerned: **daylight-saving time,** a temporary standard of time in many localities during the summer months, obtained by setting timepieces ahead, generally by an even hour:—*interj.* in sports, a command to suspend play temporarily or to indicate that the time of play is finished:—*v.t.* [*p.t.* and *p.p.* timed (tīmd), *p.pr.* tim′ing], **1,** to adapt to the occasion; as, I will *time* my visit to suit your convenience; begin or do at a particular season; **2,** to regulate or measure; as, to *time* the speed of a machine; **3,** to measure, as in music or harmony; **4,** to find out or record the speed of, as a sprinter.

time clock a clock at the entrance of a factory, office, etc., with a mechanism by means of which employees record the time of their coming and going.

time draft a draft payable at some specified future date.

time fuse a fuse which fires its charge a fixed time after being lighted.

time–hon-ored (tīm′=ŏn″ĕrd), *adj.* respected or reverenced because of age or long usage; as, a *time-honored* ceremony. Also, **time′–hon″oured.**

time-keep-er (tīm′kēp″ẽr), *n.* **1**, one who or that which keeps time, as a watch; **2**, one who records the working time of employees; **3**, one who notes and gives the time in any sport or game.

time-ly (tīm′lĭ), *adj.* [*comp.* time′li-er, *superl.* time′li-est], seasonable; opportune; suitable to the moment or occasion. —*n.* **time′li-ness.**

Syn. fortunate, favorable.—*Ant.* unseasonable, unlucky, inopportune.

time note a note payable at some specified future time.

time-piece (tīm′pēs″), *n.* any instrument that measures or records the time; esp., a clock or watch.

time-serv-er (tīm′sûr″vẽr), *n.* one who basely suits his action to a special occasion.—*adj.* and *n.* **time′serv″ing.**

time–ta-ble (tīm′-tā″bl), *n.* a systematically arranged list of the dates and hours for events; esp., a list of trains with their times of arriving at and leaving various stations.

time-work (tīm′wûrk″), *n.* work paid for by the hour, day, or week at a fixed rate: distinguished from *piecework.*

tim-id (tĭm′ĭd), *adj.* shy; wanting in courage; faint-hearted; fearful.—*adv.* **tim′id-ly.**—*n.* **tim′id-ness.**

Syn. afraid, diffident, timorous.

ti-mid-i-ty (tĭ-mĭd′ĭ-tĭ), *n.* want of courage; shyness.

tim-or-ous (tĭm′ẽr-ŭs), *adj.* **1**, fearful of danger; lacking in courage; timid; **2**, indicating alarm; as, a *timorous* look. —*adv.* **tim′or-ous-ly.**—*n.* **tim′or-ous-ness.**

Syn. shy, afraid, diffident.

tim-o-thy (tĭm′ō-thĭ), *n.* a valuable grass with long, round flower spikes, used for hay: also called *timothy grass.*

Tim-o-thy (tĭm′ō-thĭ), *n.* **1**, in the Bible, a companion and follower of St. Paul; the person to whom were written two epistles, known as First and Second Timothy; **2**, either of these two epistles.—*abbr.* **Tim.**

tin (tĭn), *n.* **1**, a silvery white, soft metal from which many useful articles are made, as boxes, cans, pans, etc.; **2**, thin plates of iron covered with this metal; **3**, wares made of tin plate:—*v.t.* [*p.t.* and *p.p.* tinned (tĭnd), *p.pr.* tin′ning], **1**, to cover with tin, or with tinned iron; **2**, in Great Britain, to put into tins, as food.—*n.* **tin′ner.**

tin-a-mou (tĭn′ȧ-mōō), *n.* any of a family of slender-billed, short-tailed birds similar to the partridge, chiefly found in South America.

tinc-ture (tĭngk′tūr), *n.* **1**, a tinge of color; **2**, an alcoholic solution of a drug:—*v.t.* [*p.t.* and *p.p.* -tured (-tūrd), *p.pr.* -tur-ing], **1**, to color; tinge; **2**, to imbue.

tin-der (tĭn′dẽr), *n.* any inflammable material, as rotten wood or scorched linen, used to kindle a fire from a spark.

tin-der box a metal box for holding tinder, usually equipped with a flint and steel for lighting it.

tine (tīn), *n.* a tooth or spike; prong; as, the *tine* of a fork.

tin foil tin beaten into thin leaf: used for wrapping many small articles and in electric apparatus.

[1]**ting** (tĭng), *n.* a sharp, bell-like sound:—*v.t.* and *v.i.* to sound or ring sharply.

*[2]**ting** (tĭng), *n.* a Scandinavian legislative or judicial body: often in compounds. Also, **thing** (tĭng).

tinge (tĭnj), *v.t.* [*p.t.* and *p.p.* tinged (tĭnjd), *p.pr.* tinge′ing or ting′ing], **1**, to stain; dye faintly; **2**, to give a slight flavo or touch of something else to:—*n.* **1**, a sligh degree of some color; tint; **2**, a touch; trace.

tin-gle (tĭng′gl), *v.i.* [*p.t.* and *p.p.* -gle (-gld), *p.pr.* -gling], to feel or have stinging sensation or pricking pain; as, h fingers *tingled* with the cold:—*n.* a stinging se sation or pain, as from cold or a slap.

tink-er (tĭngk′ẽr), *n.* a mender of met pots, kettles, etc.:—*v.t.* **1**, to men in a bungling way; **2**, to patch:—*v.i.* **1**, mend metal ware; **2**, to work at anything in bungling or careless manner.

tin-kle (tĭng′kl), *n.* a small, quick, shar ringing sound; as, the *tinkle* of small bell:—*v.i.* [*p.t.* and *p.p.* -kled (-kld *p.pr.* -kling], to make such a sound:—*v.t.* t cause to give out a sharp, ringing sound.

tin-man (tĭn′măn), *n.* [*pl.* tinmen (-mĕn) **1**, a worker in tin; tinsmith; **2**, dealer in tinware.

tinned (tĭnd), *p.adj.* **1**, covered with ti as a roof; **2**, packed or put up i tins; as, *tinned* vegetables.

tin-ny (tĭn′ĭ), *adj.* [*comp.* tin′ni-er, *super* tin′ni-est], **1**, pertaining to, or cor taining, tin; **2**, having a flat taste, as of tin **3**, sounding like tin; as, a *tinny* piano.

tin plate thin sheet iron or steel coate with tin.

tin-sel (tĭn′sĕl), *n.* **1**, a kind of gauzy clot covered or woven with gold an silver threads; **2**, thin, glittering, metall material in strips or sheets, used for inexpe sive but showy decoration, as of a Christma tree; **3**, something showy but of little valu **4**, hence, exterior show; pretense:—*ad* **1**, made of, or like, tinsel; **2**, superficial; chea —*v.t.* to decorate with, or as with, cheap im tation gold or silver trimming; make gaudy.

tin-smith (tĭn′smĭth″), *n.* one who wor with tin or tin plate; a tinma

tint (tĭnt), *n.* **1**, a slight coloring; tinge; **2**, delicate hue of a color; as, a *tint* c green:—*v.t.* to give a slight coloring to.

Syn., n. dye, stain. (See color.)

tin-tin-nab-u-la-tion (tĭn″tĭ-năb″ū lā′shŭn), *n.* tinkling sound, as of bells.

tin-type (tĭn′tīp″), *n.* a photograph take on a thin iron plate.

tin-ware (tĭn′wâr″), *n.* household articl made of tin or tinned iron.

ti-ny (tī′nĭ), *adj.* [*comp.* ti′ni-er, *super* ti′ni-est], very small; puny; wee.

-tion (-shŭn), *n. suffix,* indicating: **1**, act o as, inven*tion;* **2**, state of being; a deject*ion;* **3**, result or product of an act; a planta*tion.* Also, **-sion.**

-tious (-shŭs), *adj. suffix,* used to for adjectives usually corresponding t a noun ending in *-tion;* as, superstition, supe sti*tious;* ambition, ambi*tious.*

[1]**tip** (tĭp), *n.* **1**, the point or end of anythi small or tapering; as, the *tip* of a finge **2**, a small piece or part attached to the end of thing; cap; ferrule:—*v.t.* [*p.t.* and *p.p.* tippe (tĭpt) or, *Rare,* tipt (tĭpt), *p.pr.* tip′ping **1**, to form a point on; **2**, to cover the end o

[2]**tip** (tĭp), *v.t.* [*p.t.* and *p.p.* tipped (tĭpt *p.pr.* tip′ping], **1**, to slant or tilt; rai at one end or side; as, to *tip* a chair; **2**, t overturn; cause to lose balance; as, to *tip* person into a lake; **3**, to strike lightly; ta **4**, *Colloq.:* **a**, to give a private hint or inform tion to; as, to *tip* one off on the race; **b**, give a small fee or present to; as, to *tip* waiter:—*v.i.* **1**, to lean, slant, or fall over; a the boat *tipped* dangerously; **2**, *Colloq.*, give a fee or present, as to a servant:—*n.* **1**, light tap or blow; **2**, a fee or present, as to servant; **3**, *Colloq.*, a friendly hint; secret advance information, as in speculation.

tip-pet (tĭp′ĕt), *n.* a neck scarf or small shoulder cape made of fur or other warm material; a muffler of wool or silk.

tip-ping (tĭp′ĭng), *n.* a piece of thin metal reënforcing the outer ends of an airplane propeller (see *airplane*, illus.).

tip-ple (tĭp′l), *v.i.* [*p.t.* and *p.p.* -pled (-ld), *p.pr.* -pling], to drink alcoholic liquors habitually but in small amounts:—*v.t.* to take (strong drink) in sips; drink, as liquor, often but in small amounts:—*n.* liquor in small amounts.—*n.* **tip′pler.**

tip-staff (tĭp′ståf″),*n.*[*pl.*tipstaves(-stāvz″; -stävz″); tipstaffs (-ståfs″)], **1**, a staff with a metal top; **2**, an officer whose badge of office this is; a constable or bailiff.

tip-ster (tĭp′stẽr), *n. Colloq.*, one who supplies private information about race horses, stock markets, etc.

tip-sy (tĭp′sĭ), *adj.* [*comp.* tip′si-er, *superl.* tip′si-est], intoxicated or drunk; weak or foolish from the effect of liquor.—*adv.* **tip′si-ly.**—*n.* **tip′si-ness.**

tip-toe (tĭp′tō″), *n.* the end or point of a toe or the toes:—*adj.* **1**, being on the ends of the toes; hence, stretched to full height; **2**, stepping softly; hence, cautious:—*adv.* on the ends of the toes; hence, cautiously; eagerly:—*v.i.* [*p.t.* and *p.p.* -toed″ (-tōd″), *p.pr.* -toe″ing], **1**, to walk or stand on the ends of the toes; **2**, to step softly; **3**, to strain upward; hence, to be on the alert.

tip-top (tĭp′tŏp′), *n.* the highest point or degree; the best of anything:—*adj.* (tĭp′tŏp″), *Colloq.*, fine; without equal.

ti-rade (tĭ-rād′; tī′rād), *n.* a long, violent speech, esp. of blame or abuse.

¹tire (tīr), *n.* (also, *Br.*, *tyre*), a band or hoop of iron or rubber, on the rim of a vehicle wheel, used to strengthen it; also, a flexible tube, as of inflated rubber, fitted into a rim, as on the wheel of a bicycle or automobile, to reduce vibration or shock:—*v.t.* [*p.t.* and *p.p.* tired (tīrd), *p.pr.* tir′ing], to furnish (a wheel) with a rim of iron or of rubber.—*adj.* **¹tired.**—*adj.* **¹tire′less.**

²tire (tīr), *n. Archaic*, dress; also, a headdress.

³tire (tīr), *v.t.* [*p.t.* and *p.p.* tired (tīrd), *p.pr.* tir′ing], to exhaust or wear out the strength, interest, or patience of; fatigue:—*v.i.* to become physically weary; become jaded, as from boredom or tediousness.

²tired (tīrd), *adj.* weary; exhausted; fatigued.—*adv.* **tired′ly.**—*n.* **tired′ness.**

²tire-less (tīr′lĕs), *adj.* unwearying; not to be wearied; as, *tireless* efforts.—*adv.* **tire′less-ly.**—*n.* **tire′less-ness.**

tire-some (tīr′sŭm), *adj.* **1**, wearisome; tedious; fatiguing; as, a *tiresome* journey; **2**, annoying; as, *tiresome* talk.—*adv.* **tire′some-ly.**—*n.* **tire′some-ness.**

tire-wom-an (tīr′wŏŏm″ăn), *n.* [*pl.* tire-women (-wĭm″ĕn)], *Archaic*, a lady's maid; also, a dressmaker.

tir-ing-room (tīr′ĭng=rōōm″), *n.* formerly, a dressing room, esp. one in a theater.

tis-sue (tĭsh′ū), *n.* **1**, a woven fabric or cloth, esp. thin, transparent silk used for veiling; **2**, that which forms the structure and substance of any organ or plant; as, muscular *tissue;* **3**, any thin or delicate texture or fabric; as, *tissue* paper; **4**, a closely woven network, as of deceit: **tissue paper**, very thin, gauzelike paper used to wrap up delicate articles, protect engravings, etc.

¹tit (tĭt), *n.* any of various small birds, esp. the titmouse.

²tit (tĭt), *n.* a blow; tap: only in the phrase *tit for tat*, a fair return; blow for blow.

³tit (tĭt), *n. Dial.*, a teat or teatlike protuberance; nipple.

Ti-tan (tī′tăn), *n.* **1**, one of the fabled giants who fought against Jupiter; **2**, hence, a man of enormous strength.—*n.fem.* **Ti′tan-ess.**

Ti-ta-ni-a (tĭ-tā′nĭ-ȧ; -tä′nĭ-ȧ), *n.* the queen of fairyland in Shakespeare's "A Midsummer Night's Dream."

Ti-tan-ic (tī-tăn′ĭk), *adj.* **1**, pertaining to, or like, the Titans; **2**, (also, *titanic*), huge; of enormous strength.

ti-ta-ni-um (tī-tā′nĭ-ŭm), *n.* a metallic element found in small amounts in many minerals and ores.

tit-bit (tĭt′bĭt″), *n.* **1**, a small bit or choice morsel, as of food; **2**, hence, a choice bit, as of gossip. Also, **tid′bit″.**

tithe (tīth), *n.* **1**, the tenth part of anything; esp., the tenth part of one's income given to the church or to charity; **2**, a small part:—*v.t.* [*p.t.* and *p.p.* tithed (tīthd), *p.pr.* tith′ing], **1**, to grant or pay a tenth of; **2**, to impose tithes upon.—*n.* **tith′ing.**

tit-il-late (tĭt′ĭ-lāt), *v.t.* and *v.i.* [*p.t.* and *p.p.* -lat″ed, *p.pr.* -lat″ing], to tickle.—*n.* **tit″il-la′tion.**

tit-i-vate (tĭt′ĭ-vāt), *v.t.* [*p.t.* and *p.p.* -vat″ed, *p.pr.* -vat″ing], *Colloq.* to dress smartly:—*v.i. Colloq.*, to dress oneself up. Also, **tit′ti-vate.**—*n.* **tit″i-va′tion.**

tit-lark (tĭt′lärk″), *n.* any of several small birds resembling the lark; a pipit.

ti-tle (tī′tl), *n.* **1**, the inscription or name of a book, poem, etc.; also, a title-page; **2**, a name of dignity, rank, or distinction; **3**, a claim or right; as, a *title* to respect; **4**, the legal right to property, esp. real estate; as, a *title* to land; **5**, the paper giving such right: **title rôle**, the part or character in a play for which it is named:—*v.t.* [*p.t.* and *p.p.* -tled (-tld), *p.pr.* -tling], to entitle; give a name to.

ti-tled (tī′tld), *p.adj.* having an honorary term attached to one's name; esp., belonging to the nobility.

ti-tle-page (tī′tl=pāj″), *n.* that page at the beginning of a book, giving its name, author, publisher, etc.

ti-tlist (tī′tlĭst), *n.*, the holder of the championship, as the *titlist* in a tennis tournament.

tit-mouse (tĭt′mous″), *n.* [*pl.* titmice (-mīs″)], any of a large family of small song birds, including the chickadee, the tufted titmouse, etc.

tit-ter (tĭt′ẽr), *v.i.* to laugh or giggle in a silly, restrained, or hysterical fashion:—*n.* a foolish, hysterical giggle.

tit-tle (tĭt′l), *n.* **1**, a very small particle; an iota or jot; **2**, a mark over a letter to distinguish it in form or pronunciation.

tit-tle-tat-tle (tĭt′l=tăt″l), *n.* trifling talk; senseless chatter; gossip:—*v.i.* [*p.t.* and *p.p.* -tled (-ld), *p.pr.* -tling], to talk foolishly; gossip.

tit-u-lar (tĭt′ū-lȧr), *adj.* **1**, pertaining to, having, or resulting from, a title; **2**, existing in name or title only; nominal; as, a *titular* duke:—*n.* one who holds the title of an office, but does not possess the power and authority belonging to it.—*adj.* **tit′u-la-ry.**

Ti-tus (tī′tŭs), *n.* a short book of the New Testament, consisting of the epistle written by Paul to Titus.—*abbr.* **Tit.**

T. N. T. *abbr.* trinitrotoluene, or trinitrotoluol: a high explosive.

to (tōō; when unemphatic, tŏŏ), *prep.* expressing: **1**, direction toward; as, the earth turns from west *to* east; **2**, approach and arrival; as, to go *to* town; **3**, progress, development, continuance, or duration as far as stated limit; as, wet *to* the skin; from four *to* six o'clock; **4**, correlation; agreement; as, to set words *to* music; seasoned *to* taste; **5**, comparison; ratio; as, true *to* life; drawn *to* scale; I have two dollars *to* your one: often used after such words as *superior*, *inferior*, *preferable*, etc.; **6**, belonging; as, there is no point *to* that; **7**, relationship, esp. personal relationship; as, kind *to* animals; it seems *to* me; **8**, result; consequence; as, he learned *to* his cost that bees sting; **9**, opposition; antithesis; as, face *to* face; they fought man *to* man; **10**, the condition of serving as substitute or equivalent; as, we have Abraham *to* our father; **11**, introducing a person or thing indirectly affected by the action of an intransitive verb; as, apply *to* the cashier; **12**, introducing an indirect object, generally in some relation to a transitive verb and a direct object; as, give it *to* me; apply heat *to* the mixture; **13**, introducing an infinitive in a noun construction; as, *to* err is human; I want *to* go; or expressing purpose; as, we eat *to* live; or defining or limiting the application of an adjective; as, fit *to* eat; or as the equivalent of a finite verb after a verb of knowing, thinking, or the like; as, we believe him *to* be reliable; **14**, used as a substitute for an infinitive; as, wait if you want *to:*—*adv.* **1**, into the usual or desired condition or position; as, the wind blows the door *to;* he fell *to* and worked; **2**, in a certain direction; as, they stood wrong end *to.*

toad (tōd), *n.* **1**, a tailless, leaping animal resembling the frog, which breeds in water, but in the later stages of its development lives for the most part on land and eats worms, flies, etc.; **2**, a disgusting person: often one despised for currying favor by flattery.

toad-eat-er (tōd′ēt″ẽr), *n.* a mean flatterer; one who curries favor.

toad-stool (tōd′sto͞ol″), *n.* an umbrella-shaped poisonous mushroom.

toad-y (tōd′ĭ), *n.* [*pl.* toadies (-ĭz)], a mean flatterer; one who caters to the rich or powerful for the sake of gain or favor; a toadeater:—*v.t.* and *v.i.* [*p.t.* and *p.p.* toad′ied (-ĭd), *p.pr.* toad′y-ing], to flatter for selfish reasons.—*adj.* **toad′y-ish.**—*n.* **toad′y-ism.**

toast (tōst), *n.* **1**, sliced bread browned by the heat of the fire; **2**, the act of drinking the health of some person or thing; **3**, one who or that which is named when a health is drunk:—*v.t.* **1**, to brown or heat at the fire; as, to *toast* bread; **2**, to name when a health is drunk.—*n.* **toast′er.**

toast-mas-ter (tōst′mȧs″tẽr), *n.* one who presides over the drinking of healths after dinner, or who introduces after-dinner speakers.

to-bac-co (tō-băk′ō), *n.* [*pl.* tobaccos (-ōz)], **1**, an American plant of the nightshade family; **2**, the dried leaves of this plant prepared for smoking and chewing, or as snuff: **tobacco heart,** a disease marked by irregular action of the heart, caused by too constant use of tobacco.

to-bac-co-nist (tō-băk′ō-nĭst), *n.* a dealer in tobacco, cigars, etc.

to-bog-gan (tō-bŏg′ăn), *n.* a kind of long, flat sled, without runners, curving up at the front and holding one or more persons: **toboggan slide,** a hill or inclined track prepared for coasting on a toboggan:—*v.i.* **1**, to slide downhill by means of such a sled; **2**, to slide rapidly, as if coasting.

to-by (tō′bĭ), *n.* [*pl.* tobies (-bĭz)], a small jug or mug in the form of a fat old man with a three-cornered hat.

toc-sin (tŏk′sĭn), *n.* **1**, a bell for sounding an alarm; **2**, the sound made by it; **3**, any warning signal.

to-day (to͞o-dā′), *adv.* **1**, on the present day; **2**, at the present time:—*n.* **1**, the present day; **2**, this present time or age. Also, **to-day′.**

tod-dle (tŏd′l), *v.i.* [*p.t.* and *p.p.* -dled (-ld), *p.pr.* -dling], to walk with short, uncertain steps like a child:—*n.* a walk marked by short, uncertain steps.—*n.* **tod′dler.**

tod-dy (tŏd′ĭ), *n.* [*pl.* toddies (-ĭz)], **1**, a sweet juice obtained from certain palm trees of East India; **2**, a sweetened mixture of liquor and hot water.

to-do (to͞o-do͞o′), *n. Colloq.*, bustle; stir; fuss; as, a great *to-do* about nothing.

toe (tō), *n.* **1**, one of the digits of the foot of a man, an animal, or a bird; **2**, the front of the foot, or of a stocking or other foot covering; **3**, the fore part of a horse's hoof; **4**, anything resembling a toe:—*v.t.* [*p.t.* and *p.p.* toed (tōd), *p.pr.* toe′ing], **1**, to touch, reach, or strike with the tip of the foot; as, to *toe* the mark in a race; **2**, to attach the foot of (an upright timber) to a beam by nails driven slantwise.

toe-nail (tō′nāl″), *n.* **1**, the horny scale that grows at the end of the toe; **2**, a nail driven obliquely through the edge of a timber into another timber:—*v.t.* to fasten by toed nails.

tof-fee (tŏf′ĭ), *n.* a sweetmeat; molasses taffy. Also, **tof′fy.**

tog (tŏg), *v.t.* and *v.i.* [*p.t.* and *p.p.* togged (tŏgd), *p.pr.* tog′ging], *Slang*, to dress, esp. in one's finery: often with *out* or *up;* as, he was all *togged* up.

to-ga (tō′gȧ), *n.* [*pl.* togas (-gȧz); togæ (-jē)], the loose outer garment worn by the ancient Romans.

to-geth-er (to͞o-gĕth′ẽr), *adv.* **1**, in company or association; as, to live *together;* **2**, mutually; as, to weep *together;* **3**, in union or combination; as, the houses were joined *together;* **4**, without interruption; as, we talked for hours *together;* **5**, at the same time; as, the guns were fired *together.*

tog-ger-y (tŏg′ẽr-ĭ), *n. Slang*, clothes; articles of dress or finery.

tog-gle (tŏg′l), *n.* **1**, on clothing, an oblong button or frog; **2**, on shipboard, a bolt or pin with a groove around the middle, intended to be inserted between the strands of a rope or through a link of a chain; **3**, in mechanics: **a**, a short bar or pin, attached in the middle, as to a rope, intended to hold by being inserted through a ring and turned crosswise; **b**, a toggle joint: **toggle joint,** a joint like an elbow, connecting two rods in such way that force applied at the joint to straighten it forces the ends of the rods apart.

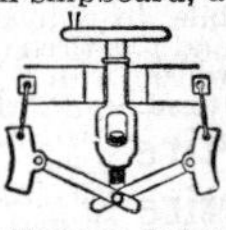

TOGGLE JOINT

togs (tŏgz), *n.pl. Slang*, toggery; clothes, esp. new or showy ones.

[1]**toil** (toil), *v.i.* **1**, to work or labor with fatigue or distress; **2**, to move with difficulty; trudge; plod:—*n.* work or effort that exhausts the mind or body.—*n.* **toil′er.**

Syn., n. drudgery, exertion. (See labor.)

[2]**toil** (toil), *n.* a trap, as a net or cord, for insnaring game; hence, usually in *pl.*, snares or difficulties.

toi-let (toi′lĕt), *n.* **1**, a dressing table; **2**, the act of dressing, arranging the hair, etc.; **3**, style of dress; also, a particular costume; **4**, a lavatory, esp. one with a water-closet. Also, **toi-lette′** (toi-lĕt′; *Fr.* twȧ″lĕt′).

toi-let wa-ter a fragrant liquid, milder than a perfume.

toil-some (toil′sŭm), *adj.* **1**, laborious or tiresome; wearisome; **2**, working hard; as, the *toilsome* oxen.—*adv.* **toil′some-ly.**—*n.* **toil′some-ness.**

To-kay (tō-kā′), *n.* **1**, a kind of large, sweet, white or purple grape; **2**, a sweet wine, orig. from Tokay.

to-ken (tō′kn), *n.* **1**, something representing something else; a sign, symbol, or indication; **2**, a memento; keepsake; as, a *token* of affection; **3**, a symbol or sign of authority, right, pledge, etc.; **4**, a piece of money whose face value is more than its real value; hence, any piece of currency, as a bill or note, similarly issued.

Syn. (see emblem).

told (tōld), past tense and past participle of the irregular verb *tell.*

To-le-do (tō-lē′dō), *n.* [*pl.* Toledos; Toledoes (-dōz)], a sword or blade of the finest temper, made in Toledo, Spain.

tol-er-a-ble (tŏl′ẽr-ȧ-bl), *adj.* **1**, capable of being borne or endured; supportable; as, his conduct was scarcely *tolerable;* **2**, passable; fairly good.—*n.* **tol′er-a-ble-ness.**—*adv.* **tol′er-a-bly.**

tol-er-ance (tŏl′ẽr-ȧns), *n.* willingness to bear with others, esp. those whose views differ from one's own.

tol-er-ant (tŏl′ẽr-ȧnt), *adj.* **1**, willing or inclined to put up with views different from one's own; forbearing; **2**, able to take without harm large doses of dangerous drugs.—*adv.* **tol′er-ant-ly.**

tol-er-ate (tŏl′ẽr-āt), *v.t.* [*p.t.* and *p.p.* -at″ed, *p.pr.* -at″ing], **1**, to suffer; put up with; permit to exist or continue without interference; **2**, to withstand the effects or action of, as a drug.

tol-er-a-tion (tŏl″ẽr-ā′shŭn), *n.* the act of putting up with, or permitting to go on, without interference; the allowance of something not wholly approved, esp. of religious doctrines or practices.

[1]**toll** (tōl), *n.* **1**, a tax or compensation paid for some special use, privilege, or the like, as for using a bridge, highway, or canal; **2**, the right to collect a tax or compensation for such special uses or privileges; **3**, a compensation for services rendered, as a portion of grain retained by a miller in payment for grinding; **4**, in telephoning, the charge made for a long-distance call: **toll board**, a telephone switchboard for connecting subscribers to toll lines: **toll line**, a long-distance telephone line:—*v.t.* to exact, as a tax or claim.

Syn., n. custom, impost, assessment, duty.

[2]**toll** (tōl), *v.t.* **1**, to cause to sound with slow, regular strokes; as, the sexton *tolls* the bell; **2**, to announce, as by the slow, regular ringing of a bell; as, "the curfew *tolls* the knell of parting day"; **3**, to ring slowly and solemnly for or on account of:—*v.i.* to emit a slow, regular, ringing sound, as a bell in announcing a death:—*n.* a slow ringing of a bell.

toll-gate (tōl′gāt″), *n.* a gate, as on a bridge, where toll is paid.

Tol-tec (tŏl′tĕk), *n.* an individual of an early, cultured Mexican race antedating the Aztecs, to whom, according to Aztec tradition, they gave their culture:—*adj.* pertaining to this race.—*adj.* **Tol′tec-an.**

to-lu (tō-lōō′), *n.* a fragrant, medicinal resin obtained from a South American tree: also called *tolu balsam.*

tol-u-ene (tŏl′ū-ēn), *n.* a colorless liquid derivative of benzene, obtained from balsam or coal tar, and used in manufacturing dyes, explosives, etc. Also, **tol′u-ol** (tŏl′ū-ōl; -ŏl); **tol′u-ole.**

Tom (tŏm), *n.* a shortened form of *Thomas:* **tom**, the male of certain animals, esp. the cat when full-grown.

tom-a-hawk (tŏm′ȧ-hôk), *n.* a hatchet used by the North American Indians in war and the chase:—*v.t.* to strike, or kill, with such a hatchet.

to-ma-to (tō-mā′tō; tō-mä′tō), *n.* [*pl.* tomatoes (-tōz)], **1**, a garden plant of the nightshade family; **2**, the red or yellow edible fruit of this plant.

tomb (tōōm), *n.* **1**, a grave or vault for the dead; hence, death; **2**, a monument erected to the memory of the dead:—*v.t.* to put in a grave or vault.

tom-boy (tŏm′boi″), *n.* a girl with boyish ways; a hoyden.

tomb-stone (tōōm′stōn″), *n.* a stone marking a grave.

tom-cat (tŏm′kăt″), *n.* a full-grown domestic cat of the male sex.

tom-cod (tŏm′kŏd″), *n.* a small, edible fish of the cod family.

tome (tōm), *n.* **1**, a large, heavy book; **2**, one volume of a work.

tom-fool (tŏm′fōōl″), *n. Colloq.*, a very foolish or silly person.

tom-fool-er-y (tŏm″fōōl′ẽr-ĭ), *n.* [*pl.* tomfooleries (-ĭz)], nonsense; ridiculous trifling; silliness.

Tom-my At-kins (tŏm′ĭ ăt′kĭnz), popularly, a British private soldier: often shortened to *Tommy.*

to-mor-row (tōō-mŏr′ō), *n.* the day after the present day; the next coming day:—*adv.* on or for the day after today; on the morrow. Also, **to-mor′row.**

Tom Thumb a person of very small size often mentioned in English fables and fairy tales; hence, a dwarf of any kind, as of flowers or vegetables.

tom-tit (tŏm′tĭt″; tŏm″tĭt′), *n.* any of the family of small song birds including the titmice, as the chickadee.

tom–tom (tŏm′-tŏm″), *n.* a drum used by jugglers or musicians in some Oriental countries. Also, **tam′-tam″.**

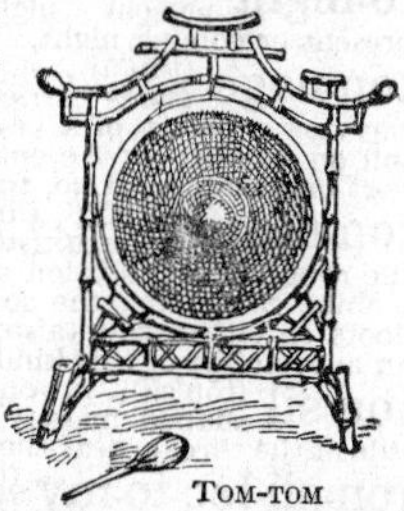

TOM-TOM

ton (tŭn), *n.* **1**, any of various relatively large measures of weight; esp., 2,240 pounds, used in Great Britain, commonly called *long ton*, or 2,000 pounds, used in America, called *short ton*, or 2,204.6 pounds, called *metric ton;* **2**, a unit of volume of cargo space in ships, equal to 100 cubic feet: called *register ton;* also, a unit of volume equal to that of a long ton of sea water, or 35 cubic feet: also called *displacement ton.*

ton-al (tōn′ăl), *adj.* pertaining to the character or quality of sound.

to-nal-i-ty (tō-năl′ĭ-tĭ), *n.* **1**, the quality of sound in a musical composition; **2**, the principle of key relationship in music; **3**, the relation to one another of the shades of color in a picture or design.

tone (tōn), *n.* **1**, a sound or the quality of a sound; **2**, the quality of a voice; **3**, one of the larger intervals in a diatonic scale, as that from C to D: preferably called *step;* **4**, the normal or healthy condition of the body; **5**, the quality and harmony of the colors of a painting; **6**, a hue, tint, or shade of color; as, a brown *tone;* **7**, the general character or tendency; as, the *tone* of the rebuke made it acceptable; **8**, the sound of the voice as expressive of feeling; as, there was contempt in her *tone;* **9**, a condition of temper, mood, or the like; as, a reflective *tone:*—*v.t.* [*p.t.* and *p.p.* toned (tōnd), *p.pr.* ton′ing], **1**, to bring to a required shade or color, as a photographic print, a painting, etc.; **2**, to give a particular sound to: **tone down**, to modify or make less extreme, as lights, colors, musical sounds, feelings, etc.: **tone up**, to heighten or intensify, as lights, colors, sounds, feelings, etc.:—*v.i.* to harmonize in color; as, the wall paper *tones* with the curtains.—*adj.* **tone′less.**

tongs (tôngz), *n.pl.* any of various devices with two legs joined by a hinge, used for grasping anything; as, fire *tongs*.

tongue (tŭng), *n.* **1**, the muscular organ in the mouth of mammals, used in tasting, and also, in man, for speech; **2**, a language; as, the French *tongue;* **3**, manner of speaking; discourse; as, he spoke with halting *tongue;* **4**, anything resembling a tongue, as the clapper or hammer of a bell, the strip of leather under the lacing of a shoe, the pole of a two-horse vehicle, the pin of a buckle, the point of a flame, a point of land, etc.—*adj.* **tongued.**—*adj.* **tongue'less.**

Syn. speech. (See language.)

tongue–tied (tŭng'-tīd''), *adj.* **1**, unable to speak clearly because the connecting membrane beneath the tongue is too short; **2**, silent, as from embarrassment. —*v.t.* and *n.* **tongue'–tie''.**

ton-ic (tŏn'ĭk), *adj.* **1**, pertaining to sounds; **2**, tending to strengthen; bracing; **3**, stiff; rigid; as, a *tonic* spasm:—*n.* **1**, the keynote of a scale or composition in music; **2**, a strengthening medicine.

to-nic-i-ty (tō-nĭs'ĭ-tĭ), *n.* the state of being normal or healthy in tone or tension: said of muscles; vigor.

ton-ic sol–fa in music, a system of notation for the scale, in which the syllables *do*, *re*, *mi*, etc., replace the usual staff symbols and the letters *C*, *D*, *E*, etc.

to-night (tōō-nīt'), *n.* the coming or present night:—*adv.* on the present or coming night. Also, **to–night'.**

ton-nage (tŭn'āj), *n.* **1**, the weight of goods carried in a ship; **2**, the carrying capacity of a vessel; **3**, the duty or toll on vessels; **4**, the entire shipping of any port or country. Also, **tun'nage.**

ton-neau (tô''nō'; tŭn-ō'), [Fr.], *n.* [*pl.* tonneaux (-nō'); tonneaus (-ōz')], the rounded rear section of a passenger automobile, containing the seats and entered by doors on either side; also, the entire body of an automobile of this kind.

ton-sil (tŏn'sĭl), *n.* one of two almond-shaped masses of tissue on either side of the throat, near the base of the tongue.

ton-sil-lec-to-my (tŏn''sĭ-lĕk'tō-mĭ), *n.* [*pl.* tonsillectomies (-mĭz)], the operation of cutting out the tonsils.

ton-sil-li-tis (tŏn''sĭ-lī'tĭs), *n.* inflammation of the tonsils: a form of sore throat. Also, **ton''sil-i'tis.**

ton-so-ri-al (tŏn-sō'rĭ-ăl), *adj.* pertaining to a barber or his trade.

ton-sure (tŏn'shŭr), *n.* **1**, the act of cutting the hair, or of shaving the crown of the head, as by persons entering the priesthood; **2**, hence, the priesthood; **3**, the part of a priest's head left bare by such shaving.—*adj.* **ton'sured.**

ton-tine (tŏn'tēn; tŏn-tēn'), *n.* **1**, a financial scheme whereby an annuity is shared by a number of persons on such a plan that the shares of those dying are divided among the survivors until all goes to the last survivor; **2**, the subscribers collectively.

too (tōō), *adv.* **1**, more than enough; as, *too* long; **2**, also; likewise; as, he *too*.

took (tŏŏk), the past tense of the transitive and intransitive irregular verb *take*.

tool (tōōl), *n.* **1**, an instrument used in doing work, esp. one used by the hand, as a chisel, hammer, saw, etc.; **2**, a machine for shaping; **3**, one used as the agent of another: —*v.t.* **1**, to shape with a chisel, saw, file, etc.; **2**, to ornament, as leather, by impressing a design with tools.

Syn., n. utensil, implement.

toot (tōōt), *v.t.* to cause to sound, as a horn or flute:—*v.i.* to sound shortly and rapidly:—*n.* **1**, a blast on a horn; **2**, a short, repeated sound, as from a horn.—*n.* **toot'er.**

tooth (tōōth), *n.* [*pl.* teeth (tēth)], **1**, one of the hard, bony projections growing in the jaws of most vertebrates and used for biting and chewing; **2**, any projection resembling such a bone; as, a gear *tooth;* **3**, a taste or fondness for a certain kind of food; as, she has a sweet *tooth:*—*v.t.* to indent or form into jagged points; notch, as a saw.—*adj.* **tooth'less.**

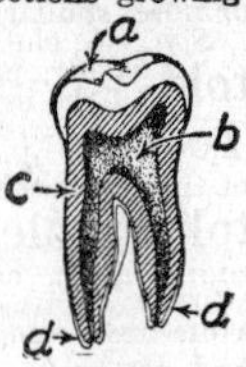

TOOTH

a, enamel, covering crown; *b*, pulp; *c*, dentine; *d*, *d*, cement, covering the fangs, or roots.

tooth-ache (tōōth'āk''), *n.* pain in a tooth or in the teeth.

tooth-brush (tōōth'-brŭsh''), *n.* a small brush with a handle, used for cleaning the teeth.

toothed (tōōtht), *adj.* having teeth of a given sort; as, sharp-*toothed*.

tooth-pick (tōōth'pĭk''), *n.* a pointed piece of wood, a quill, or the like, used to clear the spaces between the teeth.

tooth-some (tōōth'sŭm), *adj.* palatable or pleasing to the taste.—*adv.* **tooth'some-ly.**—*n.* **tooth'some-ness.**

[1]**top** (tŏp), *n.* **1**, the highest part; summit; as, the *top* of a mountain; **2**, the upper surface, side, or part, as of a table, a carriage, a shoe, or a page; **3**, the most important person, place, or rank; as, the *top* of his profession; **4**, the crown of the head; **5**, the part of a plant above the ground: used of plants with edible roots; **6**, utmost degree; as, the *top* of his ambition; **7**, in golf: **a**, a stroke in which a player hits the ball above its center; **b**, a forward spin given to the ball by such a stroke; **8**, a small platform at the upper end of the lower mast of a ship:—*v.t.* [*p.t.* and *p.p.* topped (tŏpt), *p.pr.* top'ping], **1**, to put a cover over; cap; as, the mountain was *topped* with snow; **2**, to surmount; **3**, to excel or surpass; as, that *tops* his other achievements; **4**, to cut off the upper part of, as a plant:—*v.i.* **1**, to rise to a height; tower; **2**, to excel; surpass: —*adj.* **1**, pertaining to the highest part; highest; as, the *top* shelf; **2**, highest in degree; greatest; as, at *top* speed; *top* prices.

[2]**top** (tŏp), *n.* a child's cone-shaped toy with a point on which it can be made to spin.

to-paz (tō'păz), *n.* **1**, a mineral often used as a gem, varying in color from yellow to blue or green; **2**, the yellow sapphire.

top–boots (tŏp'-bōōts''), *n.pl.* high boots generally having a band of leather of a lighter color around the top.

top-coat (tŏp'kōt''), *n.* a coat for outside wear; an overcoat.

top-er (tōp'ẽr), *n.* one who drinks intoxicants to excess; a drunkard.

top-gal-lant (tŏp''găl'ănt; tō-găl'ănt), *adj.* situated next above the topmast of a vessel; as, a *topgallant* sail:—*n.* such a mast or sail (see *rigging*, illus.).

top–heav-y (tŏp'-hĕv''ĭ), *adj.* **1**, heavier at the top than at the bottom; **2**, hence, unwieldy.—*n.* **top'–heav''i-ness.**

To-phet (tō'fĕt), *n.* **1**, a place in the Valley of Hinnom, near Jerusalem, where human sacrifices by fire were made; **2**, hence, a place of torment by fire; hell. Also, **To'pheth** (tō'fĕt).

top-ic (tŏp'ĭk), *n.* the subject of a discourse, argument, literary composition, paragraph, etc.—*adj.* **top'i-cal.**—*adv.* **top'i-cal-ly.**

Syn. theme, question, issue.

top-knot (tŏp'nŏt''), *n.* a decorative arrangement of ribbons, flowers, feathers, wool, or hair, on the head.

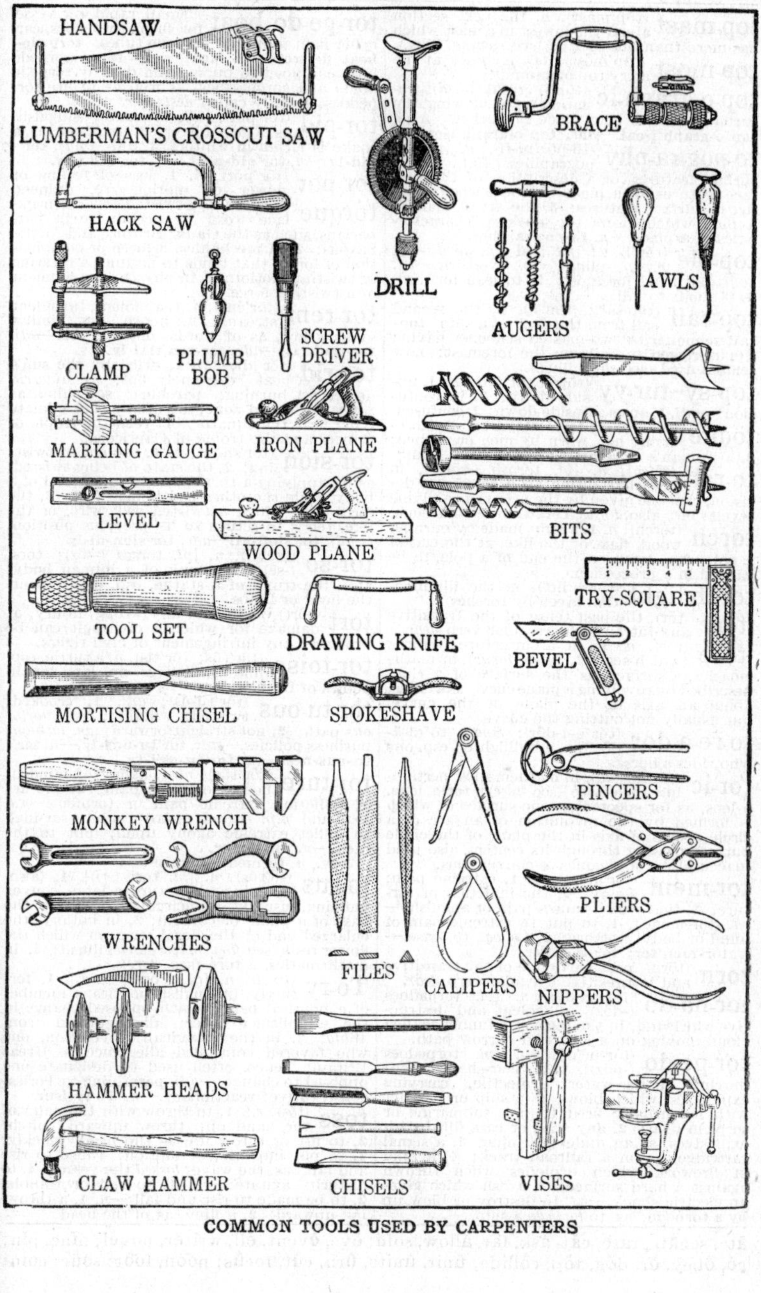

COMMON TOOLS USED BY CARPENTERS

top-mast (tŏp′mȧst), *n.* the next section above the lowest in a mast which has more than one section (see *rigging*, illus.).

top-most (tŏp′mōst), *adj.* highest; at the very top or summit.

top-o-graph-ic (tŏp″ō-grăf′ĭk), *adj.* relating to, or showing, the surface features of a place or region. Also, **top″o-graph′i-cal.**—*adv.* **top″o-graph′i-cal-ly.**

to-pog-ra-phy (tō-pŏg′rȧ-fĭ), *n.* [*pl.* topographies (-fĭz)], **1,** the surface features, or a description of the surface features, of a place; **2,** the science treating of surface features; **3,** the art of making a map which shows the physical characteristics of a place.—*n.* **to-pog′ra-pher.**

top-ple (tŏp′l), *v.t.* [*p.t.* and *p.p.* -pled (-ld), *p.pr.* -pling], to overturn:—*v.i.* **1,** to fall head foremost; **2,** to lean forward, as if about to fall.

top-sail (tŏp′săl″; tŏp′sl), *n.* the second sail from the deck of a ship: **topsail schooner,** a two-masted schooner having square-rigged topsails on the foremast: now seldom used (see *ship*, illus.).

top-sy–tur-vy (tŏp′sĭ-tûr′vĭ), *adv.* **1,** upside down; **2,** in confusion:—*adj.* **1,** upset; upside down; **2,** confused.

toque (tōk), *n.* **1,** formerly, a small, close-fitting hat, worn by men or women; **2,** a woman's close-fitting hat with no brim.

to-rah (tō′rä), *n.* [*pl.* toroth (-rōth)], in Jewish tradition, an instruction or decision, esp. one given by the priests as a divine revelation: also, *tora:* **Torah,** the Pentateuch.

torch (tôrch), *n.* **1,** a light made by burning wood, flax, or the like, at the end of a pole; **2,** a lamp on the end of a pole, to be carried in a procession.

torch-light (tôrch′līt″), *n.* the illumination given by torches.

¹tore (tōr), the past tense of the transitive and intransitive irregular verb ¹*tear.*

²tore (tōr), *n.* **1,** in architecture, a torus (which see); **2,** (also, *torus*), in mathematics, a surface, as the surface of a ring, described by revolving a plane curve, as a circle, about an axis in the plane of the curve, but usually not cutting the curve.

to-re-a-dor (tŏr″ē-ȧ-dôr′; *Span.* tō″rā-ä-dōr′), *n.* a bullfighter, esp. one who rides a horse.

tor-ic (tŏr′ĭk), *adj.* in mathematics, pertaining to a tore (see ²*tore*): **toric lens,** a lens, as for spectacles, one surface of which is formed by the revolution of an arc of a circle about an axis in the plane of the circle but not passing through its center: also used inaccurately of a concavo-convex lens.

tor-ment (tôr′mĕnt), *n.* **1,** extreme pain; agony; **2,** the infliction of torture; **3,** that which causes pain or anguish:—*v.t.* (tôr-mĕnt′), **1,** to put to extreme pain of mind or body; torture; **2,** *Colloq.*, to tease.—*n.* **tor-men′tor; tor-ment′er.**

torn (tōrn), past participle of the transitive and intransitive irregular verb ¹*tear.*

tor-na-do (tôr-nā′dō), *n.* [*pl.* tornadoes (-dōz)], a violent and destructive whirlwind, in the form of a funnel-shaped cloud moving on a long and narrow path.

tor-pe-do (tôr-pē′dō), *n.* [*pl.* torpedoes (-dōz)], **1,** a cigar-shaped, self-moving, under-water projectile, carrying explosives, which blows up a ship on contact with it: usually fired from a submarine or torpedo boat; **2,** any shell or case filled with explosives, as an under-sea mine; **3,** a signal cartridge, as on a railroad track; **4,** a kind of firework which explodes when thrown against a hard surface; **5,** a fish which gives an electric shock:—*v.t.* to destroy or blow up by a torpedo; as, to *torpedo* a ship.

tor-pe-do boat a small, rapid war vessel for firing torpedoes, carrying light guns and torpedo tubes: **torpedo-boat destroyer,** a large, very rapid torpedo boat equipped to pursue and destroy torpedo boats and submarines, as well as to fire torpedoes: usually called *destroyer.*

tor-pid (tôr′pĭd), *adj.* **1,** numb; sluggish; as, a *torpid* liver; **2,** dormant; as, a snake is *torpid* in winter; **3,** dull.—*adv.* **tor′pid-ly.**—*n.* **tor′pid-ness.**—*n.* **tor-pid′i-ty.**

tor-por (tôr′pŏr), *n.* **1,** loss of feeling or power of motion; **2,** dulness.

torque (tôrk), *n.* **1,** a twisted collar or necklace worn by certain early barbarians, such as the Gauls, Britons, and Anglo-Saxons; **2,** in mechanics, a force or combination of forces that tends to produce a rotating or twisting motion; **3,** in physics, the moment of a twisting force.

tor-rent (tŏr′ĕnt), *n.* **1,** a violent, turbulent stream; **2,** hence, any similar violent flow, as of words, objects, etc.—*adj.* **tor-ren′tial.**—*adv.* **tor-ren′tial-ly.**

tor-rid (tŏr′ĭd), *adj.* **1,** dried by the sun's heat; extremely hot; as, a *torrid* desert; **2,** burning; parching; scorching, as the sun: **torrid zone,** the area of hot climate lying near the equator, between the tropic of Cancer and the tropic of Capricorn.

tor-sion (tôr′shŭn), *n.* **1,** the act of twisting; **2,** the state of being twisted, as by applying a turning force to one end of a body while the other end is held fast; **3,** the force with which a twisted rod, wire, or the like, tends to return to its previous position. —*adj.* **tor′sion-al.**—*adv.* **tor′sion-al-ly.**

tor-so (tôr′sō), *n.* [*pl.* torsos (-sōz); torsi (-sē), the trunk of a human body; also, the trunk of a statue, esp. one without the head or limbs.

tort (tôrt), *n.* in law, any wrong, injury, or damage for which a civil suit can be brought; any infringement of civil rights.

tor-toise (tôr′tŭs; tôr′tĭs), *n.* a turtle, esp. one that lives on land or in bodies of fresh water.

tor-tu-ous (tôr′tū-ŭs), *adj.* **1,** crooked; twisted; winding; as, a *tortuous* path; **2,** not straightforward; as, *tortuous* business policies.—*adv.* **tor′tu-ous-ly.**—*n.* **tor′tu-ous-ness.**—*n.* **tor″tu-os′i-ty.**

tor-ture (tôr′tūr), *n.* **1,** agony of mind or body; extreme pain; **2,** the act of inflicting extreme pain or torment:—*v.t.* [*p.t.* and *p.p.* -tured (-tūrd), *p.pr.* -tur-ing], to inflict extreme agony upon; put to the rack.—*n.* **tor′tur-er.**

Syn., *n.* torment, anguish.

to-rus (tō′rŭs), *n.* [*pl.* tori (-rī)], **1,** (also, *tore*), in architecture, a large, convex molding, usually semicircular, used at the base of a pillar or column; **2,** in botany, the enlarged end of the floral stem on which the flower rests (see *flower*, *receptacle*, illus.); **3,** in mathematics, a tore (see ²*tore*).

To-ry (tō′rĭ), *n.* [*pl.* Tories (-rĭz)], **1,** formerly, in English politics, a member of a political party which opposed change in the established order: distinguished from *Whig;* **2,** in the American Revolution, one who favored continued allegiance to Great Britain; hence, often used to designate one opposed to change:—*adj.* pertaining to Tories; conservative; reactionary.—*n.* **To′ry-ism.**

toss (tôs), *v.t.* **1,** to throw with the palm of the hand up; throw upward; pitch; **2,** to lift or throw up, as the head, quickly; **3,** to put into violent motion; cause to rise and fall; as, the waves *tossed* the vessel; **4,** to disturb; agitate:—*v.i.* **1,** to roll or tumble; **2,** to be made to rise and fall:—*n.* **1,** a throwing upward; **2,** a fling, as of the head.

tot (tŏt), *n.* anything very small, esp. a little child.

to-tal (tō′tăl), *adj.* **1**, whole; not divided; as, the *total* amount; **2**, complete; utter; as, *total* darkness:—*n.* the whole sum or amount:—*v.t.* to find the sum of; add; as, to *total* a column of figures:—*v.i.* to amount to a certain sum, number, etc.—*adv.* **to′tal-ly.**
Syn., n. aggregate, entirety, mass.

to-tal-i-ty (tō-tăl′ĭ-tĭ), *n.* [*pl.* totalities (-tĭz)], **1**, the state or quality of being whole; **2**, the entire quantity or sum.

tote (tōt), *v.t.* [*p.t.* and *p.p.* tot′ed, *p.pr.* tot′-ing], *U. S. Dial.*, **1**, to carry; transport; esp., to carry on the person; as, to *tote* an armful of wood; **2**, to haul, as by wagon or sled:—*adj. U. S. Dial.*, pertaining to carrying or transportation; as, a *tote* road.—*n.* **tot′er.**

to-tem (tō′tĕm), *n.* **1**, an animal or object conceived among some peoples, as American Indians, as being closely related to a tribe or clan; **2**, a carved or painted representation of this relationship, as a pole or post.—*adj.* **to-tem′ic.**—*n.* **to′tem-ism.**

tot-ter (tŏt′ẽr), *v.i.* **1**, to be unsteady on one's feet; stagger; **2**, to shake as if about to collapse; lose strength and firmness, as a building.—*adj.* **tot′ter-y.**

tou-can (tōō-kăn′; tōō′kăn), *n.* any of several noisy, fruit-eating birds with large, pointed beaks and bright plumage: found in Central and South America.

touch (tŭch), *v.t.* **1**, to come into contact with; strike lightly; extend the hand or an object so as to come into contact with; **2**, to perceive or know by feeling; **3**, to bring into contact; as, to *touch* his hand to his hat; **4**, to concern; affect; **5**, to refer to in a light manner; as, in conversation, to *touch* a subject briefly; **6**, to add a light stroke to; also, to improve: with *up;* as, he *touched* up the drawing; **7**, to reach; attain; **8**, to affect the senses or feelings of; melt; soften; also, to hurt or wound in feelings; irritate; **9**, to meddle with; disturb; **10**, to affect to a slight extent; as, plants *touched* by frost; also, to make weak in mind; as, *touched* by illness; **11**, to take a portion of; taste; as, he has not *touched* food for days; **12**, to impress; affect; as, water won't *touch* this stain; **13**, to have to do with; as, he dare not *touch* wine; **14**, in geometry, to be tangent to; **15**, *U. S. Slang*, to borrow from:—*v.i.* **1**, to be in contact; as, the two benches *touch;* **2**, to speak of a subject lightly: with *on* or *upon;* **3**, to call at a port: with *at:*—*n.* **1**, the act or state of coming into, or being in, contact; contact; **2**, the sense of feeling; sensation; **3**, the peculiar manner of execution, as in a painting; as, the *touch* of a master; **4**, a single delicate stroke on a painting, drawing, or the like; **5**, a close understanding or sympathy; harmony; as, in close *touch* with a friend; **6**, communication, as between troops; **7**, a very slight amount; dash; as, a *touch* of pepper; **8**, a light attack, as of a disease; as, a *touch* of gout; **9**, in music, the manner of manipulating the keys or strings; **10**, in football, that part of the field outside the side lines.—*adj.* **touch′a-ble.**—*n.* **touch′er.**

touch-down (tŭch′doun″), *n.* in football, the forcing of the ball through the opponents' goal.

touch-hole (tŭch′hōl″), *n.* a hole at the breech of old-time cannons and other firearms, through which fire was applied to the charge of powder; a vent.

touch-ing (tŭch′ĭng), *p.adj.* affecting; pathetic; as, a *touching* scene in a play:—*n.* the act of coming in contact with:—*prep.* with respect to; concerning; as, *touching* the matter referred to in your letter.—*adv.* **touch′ing-ly.**—*n.* **touch′ing-ness.**

touch-me-not (tŭch′=mē=nŏt″), *n.* **1**, a plant of the balsam family, whose ripe fruit bursts, if touched, and scatters the seeds; **2**, the squirting cucumber.

touch-stone (tŭch′stōn″), *n.* **1**, a kind of black stone by means of which gold and silver are tested, the streak left on the stone indicating the purity of the metal; **2**, a standard or test.

touch-wood (tŭch′wŏŏd″), *n.* decayed wood which easily catches fire and burns slowly; tinder.

touch-y (tŭch′ĭ), *adj.* [*comp.* touch′i-er, *superl.* touch′i-est], irritable; peevish; easily offended.—*n.* **touch′i-ness.**

tough (tŭf), *adj.* **1**, standing great strain without breaking; not easily broken or separated; as, *tough* wood; *tough* meat; **2**, able to endure hardship or strain; **3**, strong; firm; sticky; as, *tough* pitch; **4**, hard to influence; stubborn; **5**, *Colloq.:* **a**, difficult; as, a *tough* problem; **b**, rough and bad:—*n. U. S. Colloq.*, a rough fellow; a rowdy.—*adv.* **tough′ly.**—*n.* **tough′ness.**

tough-en (tŭf′n), *v.t.* and *v.i.* **1**, to make or become hard to break or divide; **2**, to make or become strong, stubborn, etc.

tou-pee (tōō-pē′), *n.* a small wig; a false front of curled hair.

tour (tōōr), *n.* **1**, a journey, esp. one that begins and ends in the same place; an excursion or trip; **2**, a long journey; **3**, a circuit, as in inspecting all parts of a building:—*v.i.* to make a journey:—*v.t.* to make a circuit of; as, to *tour* the country.

tour-ing car a large, open, passenger automobile, suitable for long trips (see *automobile*, illus.).

tour-ist (tōōr′ĭst), *n.* one who makes a journey, usually for sightseeing; an excursionist; a traveler.

tour-ma-line (tōōr′mȧ-lĭn), *n.* a mineral that is usually black, but sometimes red, blue, green, or, rarely, colorless: often used as a gem. Also, **tur′ma-line.**

tour-na-ment (tōōr′nȧ-mĕnt; tûr′-), *n.* **1**, in the Middle Ages, a contest, or series of contests, with blunt lances and swords, by knights on horseback; **2**, in modern times, any trial of skill in sports.

tour-ney (tōōr′nĭ; tûr′nĭ), *n.* [*pl.* tourneys (-nĭz)], a tournament or trial of skill:—*v.i.* to take part in a tournament.

tour-ni-quet (tōōr′nĭ-kĕt), *n.* a device for stopping the flow of blood when an artery, as in the arm, is cut.

tou-sle (tou′zl), *v.t.* [*p.t.* and *p.p.* -sled (-zld), *p.pr.* -sling], **1**, *Dial.*, to pull about roughly; **2**, *Colloq.*, to put in disorder; tumble. Also, **tou′zle.**

tout (tout; tōōt), *v.i. Colloq.*, **1**, to look out for customers, as for a hotel; **2**, in England, to watch race horses in training, secretly, in order to give private information to customers to guide them in betting:—*n. Colloq.*, **1**, one who looks out for customers; **2**, in England, one who gives tips on horses.

***tout en-sem-ble** (tōō″ täṅ″säṅbl′), [Fr.], the general effect when all parts of something are considered together.

¹tow (tō), *v.t.* to pull or drag by a rope or line: used esp. of pulling vessels along through the water, or of pulling wheeled vehicles or sleds behind other vehicles:—*n.* **1**, the act of pulling, or the condition of being pulled; as, a boat in *tow;* **2**, anything pulled along by, or as by, a towline; **3**, a towline.

²tow (tō), *n.* the short, coarse part of flax or hemp.

tow-age (tō′ăj), *n.* **1**, the act of pulling through the water by a chain or rope; **2**, the price paid for such towing.

¹to-ward (tō'ẽrd; tōrd), *prep.* **1,** in the direction of: used with verbs of motion and of rest; as, to go *toward* the city; to point *toward* the west; **2,** tending to, as a condition, situation, result, or the like; as, man's efforts *toward* perfection; **3,** with respect to; regarding; as, his attitude *toward* free trade; **4,** near to; close upon: used of time; as, he came *toward* evening; **5,** with a view to; for; contributing to; as, take this *toward* your supper. Also, **to'wards.**

²to-ward (tō'ẽrd; tōrd), *adj.* **1,** ready to do or learn; tractable; promising; **2,** *Archaic:* **a,** at hand; imminent; **b,** accommodating; favorable.—*n.* **to'ward-ness.**

tow-boat (tō'bōt''), *n.* a boat, esp. a powerful steam vessel, used for pulling other vessels; a tug.

tow-el (tou'ĕl), *n.* a cloth for drying anything wet, as the body or dishes.

tow-el-ing (tou'ĕl-ĭng), *n.* material from which drying cloths are made.

tow-er (tou'ẽr), *n.* **1,** a high structure, variously shaped, rising above its surroundings, and either standing alone or attached to a building; as, a church *tower;* **2,** a citadel or fortress:—*v.i.* to rise to a great height; overtop other objects; soar, as do some birds.

Leaning Tower of Pisa

tow-er-ing (tou'ẽr-ĭng), *p.adj.* **1,** very high; lofty; as, a *towering* tree; **2,** extreme; violent; as, a *towering* rage.

tow-head (tō'hĕd''), *n.* a person, usually a child, having pale yellow, or very light, hair.—*adj.* **tow'-head''ed.**

tow-line (tō'līn''), *n.* a line or rope used for pulling or towing something.

town (toun), *n.* **1,** any collection of houses, making a distinct place with a name, larger than a village but not organized as a city; **2,** the citizens or voters of such a place; **3,** in New England, a unit of local government of comparatively simple organization; in other states, a unit of local government more or less similar to the town government in New England; **4,** a collection of buildings, as contrasted with more or less open country: **down town,** in or to the business district of any city or town.

town clerk an official who acts as secretary for a town organization.

town hall a public building belonging to a community, containing public offices and a hall or halls for public meetings: also called *townhouse.*

towns-folk (tounz'fōk''), *n.* the people of a town or community.

town-ship (toun'shĭp), *n.* **1,** a district, or unit of local government; **2,** a rural community organized as a unit of government; **3,** a land unit six miles square divided into 36 sections, of one square mile each.

towns-man (tounz'măn), *n.* [*pl.* townsmen (-mĕn)], a citizen of a town; a fellow citizen.

towns-peo-ple (tounz'pē''pl), *n.* the people of a town or community; townsfolk.

tow-path (tō'path''), *n.* a path beside a canal or other stream along which men or animals walk when towing boats.

tow-rope (tō'rōp''), *n.* a rope or chain used for pulling something along, esp. for pulling a vessel through the water.

tox-æ-mi-a (tŏk-sē'mĭ-*ȧ*), *n.* a poisoned condition of the blood; blood poisoning. Also, **tox-e'mi-a.**—*adj.* **tox-æ'mic.**

tox-ic (tŏk'sĭk), *adj.* of, pertaining to, or produced by, poison; poisonous.—*adj* and *n.* **tox'i-cant.**—*n.* **tox-ic'i-ty** (tŏk-sĭs'ĭ-tĭ).

tox-i-col-o-gy (tŏk''sĭ-kŏl'ō-jĭ), *n.* the science of poisons, their sources, effects, etc.—*n.* **tox''i-col'o-gist.**—*adj.* **tox''i-co-log'i-cal.**—*adv.* **tox''i-co-log'i-cal-ly.**

tox-in (tŏk'sĭn), *n.* a poison produced by secretion in animal or vegetable tissue. Also, **tox'ine** (tŏk'sĭn; -sēn).

toy (toi), *n.* **1,** a child's plaything; **2,** something of no real value; a bauble:—*v.i.* to trifle; as, to *toy* with another's affections; to play or amuse oneself by light or playful handling; as, to *toy* with a spoon.

¹trace (trās), *n.* either of the side straps connecting the collar or breastplate of a harness with the vehicle (see *harness,* illus.).

²trace (trās), *v.t.* [*p.t.* and *p.p.* traced (trāst), *p.pr.* trac'ing], **1,** to draw or sketch by means of lines; delineate; specif., to copy by following the lines of, as with a pencil on transparent paper placed over the original; hence, to chart; map out; plan; **2,** to form, as characters in writing, laboriously or with extreme care; **3,** to follow up to origins, developments, or other details; pursue; as, to *trace* a family record; **4,** to look for the remains or relics of; as, to *trace* the course of a glacier; **5,** to follow, as by tracks or vestiges, esp. something lost; as, to *trace* a fox; **6,** to pursue one's way over or along; as, to *trace* a path:—*v.i.* to make one's way; follow a trail:—*n.* **1,** a mark, indication, or sign left by something that has passed away, or disappeared; a vestige; footprint; **2,** the mark or record made by a recording instrument; **3,** a small quantity or portion of something; as, a *trace* of poison.—*adj.* **trace'a-ble.**—*n.* **trac'er.**

trac-er-y (trās'ẽr-ĭ), *n.* [*pl.* traceries (-ĭz)], a fine, delicately executed design, as in carved stone.

tra-che-a (trā'kē-*ȧ*; tr*ȧ*-kē'*ȧ*), *n.* [*pl.* tracheæ (-ē)], the windpipe; the air tube leading to the lungs.

tra-che-ot-o-my (trā''kē-ŏt'ō-mĭ), *n.* [*pl.* tracheotomies (-mĭz)], the process of cutting an opening into the windpipe from the side.

tra-cho-ma (tr*ȧ*-kō'm*ȧ*), *n.* a contagious inflammation or soreness of the eyelids; granular conjunctivitis.

trac-ing (trās'ĭng), *n.* **1,** the act of one who follows up or copies; **2,** that which is traced, or copied, as a drawing made by marking on thin paper over the original.

track (trăk), *n.* **1,** a mark or impression left by the foot; trace; **2,** a beaten path; road; **3,** a course or way; as, a race *track;* **4,** a set of metal rails supported by ties, for cars or trains to run upon:—*v.t.* **1,** to seek or follow by means of traces or signs left by someone; **2,** to journey across, as a wilderness; **3,** to make footprints upon or with; as, to *track* mud into the house; **4,** to wear into a path or beaten road.—*n.* **track'er.**

track-age (trăk'āj), *n.* **1,** the extent or amount of railroad tracks; **2,** the right to use the tracks of another railroad.

track-less (trăk'lĕs), *adj.* pathless; without a road; without footprints; as, the *trackless* desert or forest.

¹tract (trăkt), *n.* a short pamphlet, usually on some moral or religious subject.

²tract (trăkt), *n.* **1,** a region or area of land, large or small; **2,** *Archaic,* a period, as of time; extent; duration; **3,** in anatomy, an entire system of related organs, or their location; as, the digestive *tract*.

trac-ta-ble (trăk′tȧ-bl), *adj.* **1**, docile; easily led or managed; as, a *tractable* child; **2**, easily handled or worked, as some metals.—*adv.* **trac′ta-bly.**—*n.* **trac′ta-ble-ness.**—*n.* **trac″ta-bil′i-ty.**

trac-tate (trăk′tāt), *n.* a small book or treatise; a tract.

trac-tile (trăk′tĭl), *adj. Rare*, capable of being drawn out or lengthened; as, *tractile* metal.—*n.* **trac-til′i-ty.**

trac-tion (trăk′shŭn), *n.* the act of drawing, or power to draw, a body along a surface; as, electric *traction*: **traction engine**, a locomotive which runs on a road or field, not on a track.—*adj.* **trac′tion-al.**

trac-tor (trăk′tŏr), *n.* **1**, that which draws, or is used in drawing; as, a farm *tractor* is used for drawing farm machinery; **2**, a small motor-driven truck used to draw loads about stores, railway stations, etc.; **3**, an airplane of the usual type, in which the propeller is ahead of the wings: opp. of *pusher*.

trade (trād), *n.* **1**, an occupation; business; **2**, a particular means of livelihood learned and engaged in, esp. along mechanical lines; **3**, buying and selling for money; commerce; as, *trade* in wheat or cotton; **4**, collectively, the persons engaged in a particular business; **5**, the total amount of business transacted at one place; **6**, a deal; bargain: often in a corrupt sense; **7**, an exchange; as, a horse *trade;* **8**, *Obs.*, a way; course; **9**, hence, in *pl.*, the trade winds, blowing steadily toward the equator: **trade acceptance**, a draft drawn by the seller directly on the purchaser of goods, and accepted by the purchaser for payment at a definite time: **trade name**, **1**, the term generally used in commerce for some article; **2**, a name, generally descriptive, adopted or invented for some article to distinguish it from others of a similar character; **3**, the official name of a firm: **trade school**, an institution, often public, where the various trades are taught:—*adj.* pertaining to, or carried on by, a special business or firm; commercial:—*v.i.* [*p.t.* and *p.p.* trad′ed, *p.pr.* trad′ing], **1**, to conduct a trading business; buy and sell goods; **2**, to have dealings; carry on commerce: followed by *with*:—*v.t.* to exchange.
Syn., *n.* pursuit, calling. (See business.)

trade-mark (trād′=märk″), *n.* a mark used by a merchant or manufacturer on his goods to distinguish them from the goods made or sold by other merchants or manufacturers.

trad-er (trād′ẽr), *n.* **1**, one engaged in commerce; a merchant or storekeeper; **2**, a vessel engaged in commerce; **3**, one who barters or exchanges goods; as, a fur *trader*.

trades-man (trādz′măn), *n.* [*pl.* tradesmen (-mĕn)], one who engages in buying and selling; a shopkeeper.

trades-peo-ple (trādz′pē″pl), *n.pl.* the employees in a store; also, people engaged in buying and selling.

trade-un-ion (trād′=ūn″yŭn; trād″=ūn′yŭn), *n.* a society of workmen in any particular branch of industry, organized to better the wages, hours, and working conditions of labor. Also, **trades′-un″ion.**—*n.* **trade″-un′ion-ism.**

trade wind a wind in or near the torrid zone, which blows steadily in the same course, or *trade*, toward the equator, from an easterly direction.

tra-di-tion (trȧ-dĭsh′ŭn), *n.* **1**, the oral handing down of information, opinions, doctrines, practices, etc., through successive generations, as from father to son; **2**, that which is so handed down; as, the *tradition* of King Arthur and the Round Table; **3**, an ancient custom so established as to be almost like a law; **4**, a story, often relating to historical characters, but not itself based on fact; hence, any belief which owes its acceptance to habit rather than to reason.

tra-di-tion-al (trȧ-dĭsh′ŭn-ăl), *adj.* **1**, of or pertaining to a custom, story, belief, etc., handed down from father to son; as, it is *traditional* to have fireworks on July 4th; **2**, not historically reliable; as, many Robin Hood stories are only *traditional*.—*adv.* **tra-di′tion-al-ly.**—*adj.* **tra-di′tion-a-ry.**

tra-duce (trȧ-dūs′), *v.t.* [*p.t.* and *p.p.* -duced′ (-dūst′), *p.pr.* -duc′ing], to defame or slander; expose unjustly to shame.—*n.* **tra-duc′er.**

traf-fic (trăf′ĭk), *n.* **1**, business or trade; commerce; **2**, the business done by a railway, steamship line, etc., in carrying persons or goods; **3**, the passing of vehicles, persons, or animals, in a city street; as, to drive through *traffic*:—*v.i.* [*p.t.* and *p.p.* -ficked (-ĭkt), *p.pr.* -fick-ing], **1**, to barter; buy or sell goods: with *in;* **2**, to do business in a mean spirit.—*n.* **traf′fick-er.**

trag-a-canth (trăg′ȧ-kănth), *n.* a gum obtained from certain Asiatic or European trees: used in making medicines and mucilage.

tra-ge-di-an (trȧ-jē′dĭ-ăn), *n.* **1**, a writer of drama that presents the sad, solemn, or terrible aspects of life; **2**, an actor of such a type of play.

***tra-gé-dienne** (trȧ″zhā″dyĕn′; trȧ-jē′dĭ-ĕn″; trȧ-jē″dĭ-ĕn′), [Fr.], *n.* [*pl.* tragédiennes (-dyĕn′; -dĭ-ĕnz″; -dĭ-ĕnz′)], an actress who plays in tragic drama.

trag-e-dy (trăj′ē-dĭ), *n.* [*pl.* tragedies (-dĭz)], **1**, a drama of which the outcome is bad, often fatal, for the hero or heroine; **2**, any work of literature of a similar character; **3**, a melancholy or fatal event; **4**, that quality of life or art which places catastrophe on a plane commanding deep sympathy and respect.

trag-ic (trăj′ĭk), *adj.* **1**, pertaining to, or like, tragedy; as, a *tragic* play; a *tragic* death; **2**, fatal; terrible. Also, **trag′i-cal.**—*adv.* **trag′i-cal-ly.**—*n.* **trag′i-cal-ness.**

trag-i-com-e-dy (trăj″ĭ=kŏm′ē-dĭ), *n.* [*pl.* tragi-comedies (-dĭz)], a play combining tragic and comic scenes and not having a fatal end.—*adj.* **trag″i-com′ic; trag″i-com′i-cal.**

trail (trāl), *v.t.* **1**, to draw or drag along behind; as, to *trail* oars in the water; **2**, to hunt or follow by tracking; as, to *trail* a rabbit; **3**, to trample down into a path, as grass; **4**, in the army, to carry (a rifle) grasped near the middle by the right hand, with the barrel tilted upward and forward:—*v.i.* **1**, to fall or hang down, or extend behind; as, her dress *trails* on the floor; **2**, to grow at some length; as, the vine *trails* along the fence; **3**, to follow; esp., to follow in a long and straggling line; **4**, to go along in a leisurely fashion:—*n.* **1**, a track left by a person or an animal; as, a bear's *trail;* **2**, a footpath or track through a wilderness; as, a blazed *trail;* **3**, figuratively, a trace or clew; **4**, anything drawn out in the wake of something; also, the track left by something moving; **5**, the part of a gun carriage which slants backward to the ground when the piece is unlimbered and in firing position.

trail-er (trāl′ẽr), *n.* **1**, one who or that which trails, drags, or is drawn along; **2**, a light vehicle, sledge, or the like, having no motive power of its own, pulled along behind a motor car, wagon, trolley, or the like; **3**, a short pole attached to a rear wagon axle, one end of which drags on the ground to keep the wagon from sliding back.

train (trān), *n.* **1**, a connected line of railroad cars; **2**, something drawn or dragged behind; as, the *train* of a dress; **3**, a retinue or body of servants; a company or procession; **4**, the line of motor trucks, army wagons, etc., which carry supplies for an army; **5**, a series of connected things; as, a *train* of ideas; **6**, a line of gunpowder laid to fire a charge; **7**, a heavy kind of Canadian sledge drawn by dogs; **8**, in radio, a series of wave disturbances in the ether; as, a wave *train*:—*v.t.* **1**, to instruct by practice; drill; discipline; educate; **2**, to aim or point at an object; as, to *train* a cannon upon the enemy; **3**, to discipline or tame for use; as, to *train* a wild animal; **4**, to prepare for athletic contests or horse racing; **5**, to direct the growth of, as a plant:—*v.i.* **1**, to prepare oneself for a contest of strength or skill; drill; **2**, to instruct or discipline.—*n.* **train'man.**

train-band (trān'bănd"), *n.* one of the companies of citizen soldiers formerly organized and drilled in London and other places.

train-er (trān'ẽr), *n.* an instructor; esp., one who prepares men or animals for the exercise of skill, races, etc.

train-ing (trān'ĭng), *n.* **1**, the process or state of being guided, drilled, or prepared; as, the *training* of plants on a trellis; the *training* of athletes for a game; **2**, thorough instruction and ability along some special line; as, his *training* as an engineer was excellent.

Syn. discipline. (See education.)

train oil oil obtained from the blubber of whales and other sea animals: distinguished from *sperm oil.*

trait (trāt; *Br.* trā), *n.* **1**, a stroke or touch; **2**, a peculiar feature or characteristic; as, a *trait* of character.

Syn. quality. (See characteristic.)

trai-tor (trā'tẽr), *n.* **1**, one who is guilty of treason, or the betrayal of his country to an enemy; one who in time of war gives aid and comfort to the enemy; **2**, one who betrays a confidence or is false to a friend. —*n.fem.* **trai'tress.**

trai-tor-ous (trā'tẽr-ŭs), *adj.* **1**, capable or guilty of treason or of the betrayal of trust; faithless; treacherous; **2**, characterized by treason, as plans.—*adv.* **trai'tor-ous-ly.**—*n.* **trai'tor-ous-ness.**

tra-jec-to-ry (trȧ-jĕk'tō-rĭ), *n.* [*pl.* trajectories (-rĭz)], the curve described by a body moving through space, as the path of a bullet discharged from a gun.

tram (trăm), *n.* **1**, a kind of coal wagon used in mines; **2**, a railway; **3**, in England, a street railway car.

tram-car (trăm'kär"), *n.* **1**, in England, a street car that runs on tracks; **2**, a four-wheeled car on tracks in a mine.

tram-mel (trăm'ĕl), *n.* **1**, a net used for catching birds, fish, etc.; **2**, a kind of shackle for controlling the motions of a horse; **3**, anything that hinders progress, action, or freedom, as a net or shackle:—*v.t.* to hamper or hinder; shackle or bind.—*n.* **tram'mel-er; tram'mel-ler.**

Syn., n. fetter, bond, chain, impediment.

tra-mon-tane (trȧ-mŏn'tān; trăm'ŏn-tān), *adj.* **1**, beyond the mountains; coming from the other side of the mountains; **2**, hence, foreign or savage:—*n.* a foreigner or barbarian.

tramp (trămp), *v.t.* **1**, to step upon forcibly and repeatedly; **2**, *Colloq.*, to travel over on foot; as, to *tramp* the highway:—*v.i.* **1**, to wander on foot; **2**, to walk with a heavy step:—*n.* **1**, a penniless foot traveler; vagrant; **2**, a journey on foot; **3**, the sound of heavy footsteps.—*n.* **tramp'er.**

tram-ple (trăm'pl), *v.t.* [*p.t.* and *p.p.* -pled (-pld), *p.pr.* -pling], to tread under the feet; tread down, as dirt into a hole:—*v.i.* to tread heavily; hence, to tread roughly, so as to hurt or crush: with *on* or *upon;* as, to *trample* on one.—*n.* **tram'pler.**

tram-road (trăm'rōd"), *n.* a roadway equipped with rails for wheeled vehicles; esp., a railway in a mine.

tram-way (trăm'wā"), *n.* in England, a street railway; also, a road or track for heavy hauling.

trance (trȧns), *n.* **1**, a state in which the soul appears to be absent from the body or to be in a state of ecstatic rapture; **2**, a deep, abnormal sleep from which the patient cannot readily be aroused, usually due to hysteria or hypnotism; **3**, a state of mental vacancy due to shock; bewilderment.

tran-quil (trăng'kwĭl), *adj.* calm; quiet; serene; as, a *tranquil* mind; a *tranquil* lake.—*adv.* **tran'quil-ly.**

Syn. serene, peaceful. (See calm.)

tran-quil-ize (trăng'kwĭl-īz), *v.t.* [*p.t.* and *p.p.* -ized (-īzd), *p.pr.* -iz"ing], to make peaceful or calm.

Syn. soothe, allay, appease, pacify.—*Ant.* arouse, excite, disturb, alarm.

tran-quil-li-ty (trăn-kwĭl'ĭ-tĭ; trăng-), *n.* calmness; quiet; peace.

trans- (trăns-), *prefix,* [occasionally shortened to *tra-;* as, *tra*dition; *tra*verse usually written *tran-* before a word beginning with *s;* as, *tran*scribe; *tran*sept], **1**, across; over; beyond; through; as, *trans*port; *trans*fix: opp. of *cis-;* **2**, completely; thoroughly: compounded with verbs signifying a change of form; as, *trans*form; *trans*figure.

trans-act (trăns-ăkt'; trăn-zăkt'), *v.t.* to conduct or manage; as, to *transact* business; also, to carry through; perform or do.—*n.* **trans-ac'tor.**

trans-ac-tion (trăns-ăk'shŭn; trăn-zăk'-), *n.* **1**, the management of any business or affair; **2**, that which is done or performed; a proceeding; affair; as, a dangerous *transaction;* **3**, in *pl.*, the report of the proceedings of a society, etc.

Syn. negotiation, occurrence.

trans-al-pine (trăns-ăl'pĭn; -pīn), *adj.* beyond the Alps, from the point of view of Rome: opp. of *cisalpine.*

trans-at-lan-tic (trăns"ăt-lăn'tĭk), *adj.* beyond, or crossing, the Atlantic; as, a *transatlantic* flight.

tran-scend (trăn-sĕnd'), *v.t.* **1**, to rise above; exceed; as, to *transcend* belief; **2**, to surpass; excel.

tran-scend-ent (trăn-sĕn'dĕnt), *adj.* of surpassing excellence; superior or supreme; as, *transcendent* worth or ability.—*adv.* **tran-scend'ent-ly.**—*n.* **tran-scend'ence; tran-scend'en-cy.**

tran-scen-den-tal (trăn"sĕn-dĕn'tăl), *adj.* **1**, superior; supreme; **2**, in philosophy, pertaining to that which lies beyond the limits of human experience; **3**, vague; unknown; imaginary; fantastic; speculative.—*adv.* **tran"scen-den'tal-ly.**

tran-scen-den-tal-ism (trăn"sĕn-dĕn'tăl-ĭzm), *n.* **1**, the philosophical doctrine that final reality lies outside the realm of sense experience; **2**, any philosophy, as that of Emerson, which bases knowledge on a spiritual intuition of reality outside of sense experience.—*n.* **tran"scen-den'tal-ist.**

tran-scribe (trăn-skrīb'), *v.t.* [*p.t.* and *p.p.* -scribed' (-skrībd'), *p.pr.* -scrib'ing], **1**, to copy or make a copy of, as shorthand notes on a typewriter; **2**, in music to arrange for a voice or instrument other than that originally planned.—*n.* **tran-scrib'er.**

tran-script (trăn′skrĭpt), *n.* **1**, a written copy; **2**, any copy; imitation.

tran-scrip-tion (trăn-skrĭp′shŭn), *n.* **1**, a copy; **2**, the act of copying; **3**, in music, an arrangement of a composition to suit a voice or instrument other than that for which it was written.

tran-sept (trăn′sĕpt), *n.* that part of a cruciform church crossing at right angles the main body of the building.

trans-fer (trăns-fûr′), *v.t.* [*p.t.* and *p.p.* -ferred′ (-fûrd′), *p.pr.* -fer′ring], **1**, to convey or carry from one person or place to another; **2**, in law, to convey, as a right, title, etc.; as, to *transfer* a piece of land; **3**, to copy from one surface to another:—*v.i.* to proceed on a journey by changing from one conveyance to another:—*n.* (trăns′fûr), **1**, the conveyance or making over of a right, title, property, etc., from one person to another; **2**, the writing or deed by which such an exchange is made; **3**, a removal; **4**, the exchange of a soldier from one troop or company to another; **5**, a drawing or writing copied off from one surface to another; **6**, a ticket allowing a passenger to continue his passage by another route.—*n.* **trans-fer′rer; trans-fer′or.**

Syn., v. change, move, shift, transport.

trans-fer-a-ble (trăns-fûr′ȧ-bl), *adj.* **1**, capable of being carried from one person or place to another; **2**, capable of being made over to another person; as, the ticket is *transferable.*

trans-fer-ence (trăns′fĕr-ĕns; trăns-fûr′ĕns), *n.* **1**, the act of carrying, or state of being carried, from one place to another; **2**, a making over of a right or property to another person.

trans-fig-u-ra-tion (trăns-fĭg″ū-rā′shŭn), *n.* a change of form or appearance: **Transfiguration, 1**, the wonderful change in the personal appearance of Jesus Christ on the mount (Matthew 17:2); **2**, the festival, August 6, celebrating this change.

trans-fig-ure (trăns-fĭg′ūr), *v.t.* [*p.t.* and *p.p.* -ured (-ūrd), *p.pr.* -uring], **1**, to change the outward form or appearance of; **2**, to change or transform to something high and glorious.

trans-fix (trăns-fĭks′), *v.t.* **1**, to pierce through with a pointed weapon; as, to *transfix* a body with a spear; **2**, to make stop as if pierced; as, he stood *transfixed.*

trans-form (trăns-fôrm′), *v.t.* **1**, to change the shape or appearance of; **2**, to change the character of; as, to *transform* water into wine; **3**, to change the heart or mind of; convert; as, to *transform* the nature of a child by kindness; **4**, to change (a mathematical expression) into another of different form without altering its value; **5**, to change (a current) from higher to lower voltage, or vice versa; also, to change (one form of energy) into another of a different type:—*v.i.* to be or become changed.

trans-for-ma-tion (trăns″fŏr-mā′shŭn), *n.* **1**, the act of changing, or the state of being changed, in shape, appearance, or nature; **2**, change of character, heart, etc.; **3**, a kind of woman's wig.

trans-form-er (trăns-fôr′mẽr), *n.* **1**, one who or that which changes the shape, appearance, or nature of something; **2**, a device for raising or lowering the potential of an alternating current.

trans-fuse (trăns-fūz′), *v.t.* [*p.t.* and *p.p.* -fused′ (-fūzd′), *p.pr.* -fus′ing], **1**, to pour out of one vessel into another; **2**, to transfer, as blood from the veins of one person or animal to those of another.

trans-fu-sion (trăns-fū′zhŭn), *n.* **1**, the act of transferring blood from the veins of one body to those of another; **2**, the transference of a liquid from one vessel to another; **3**, a mingling, as of liquids.

trans-gress (trăns-grĕs′), *v.i.* to break a law, rule, etc.; sin:—*v.t.* **1**, to break, sin against, or violate; as, to *transgress* a law; **2**, to pass, or go beyond, as a limit.—*n.* **trans-gres′sor.**

trans-gres-sion (trăns-grĕsh′ŭn), *n.* **1**, the act of breaking any law or rule of moral duty; an offense; sin; **2**, a passing beyond a limit.

Syn. crime, misdeed, delinquency.

tran-ship (trăn-shĭp′), *v.t.* [*p.t.* and *p.p.* -shipped′ (-shĭpt′), *p.pr.* -ship′ping], to transfer from one car, ship, or other carrier, to another. Also, **trans-ship′**, *Pfd. S.* —*n.* **tran-ship′ment.**

tran-sient (trăn′shĕnt), *adj.* **1**, fleeting; brief; passing; as, *transient* hopes; **2**, having the power to effect a passing from one place, condition, or the like, to another; transitive; as, a *transient* force; **3**, *Colloq.*, temporary, as lodgers.—*adv.* **tran′sient-ly.**—*n.* **tran′sience; tran′sien-cy.**

trans-it (trăn′sĭt), *n.* **1**, a passage through or over; as, the *transit* of goods through a state; **2**, the act or process of carrying over or through; **3**, the passage of a celestial body across the meridian of a given place; **4**, the apparent passage of a smaller celestial body across the disk of a larger one, as of Venus across the sun; **5**, in surveying, an instrument used to measure horizontal angles: also called *transit theodolite.*

tran-si-tion (trăn-sĭzh′ŭn), *n.* **1**, the passage from one place, period, or state, to another; as, the *transition* from youth to old age; **2**, a change, as of a key in music, or of the subject of a speech.

tran-si-tion-al (trăn-sĭzh′ŭn-ăl), *adj.* pertaining to the passage or change from one state, time, or place, to another; as, a *transitional* movement; a *transitional* period.—*adv.* **tran-si′tion-al-ly.**

tran-si-tive (trăn′sĭ-tĭv), *adj.* **1**, able to make a passage across; **2**, in grammar, taking, or used with, a direct object: said of certain verbs.—*adv.* **tran′si-tive-ly.**—*n.* **tran′si-tive-ness.**

tran-si-to-ry (trăn′sĭ-tō-rĭ), *adj.* brief; continuing but a short time; fleeting; passing.—*adv.* **tran′si-to-ri-ly.** —*n.* **tran′si-to-ri-ness.**

trans-late (trăns-lāt′), *v.t.* [*p.t.* and *p.p.* -lat′ed, *p.pr.* -lat′ing], **1**, to change from one language into another; as, to *translate* French into English; **2**, to interpret, or make plain, in different words; as, to *translate* one's remarks; **3**, to remove to another place or position; **4**, to remove to heaven without death; as, Enoch was *translated;* **5**, to remove (a churchman) to another field. —*adj.* **trans-lat′a-ble.**—*n.* **trans-la′tor.**

trans-la-tion (trăns-lā′shŭn), *n.* **1**, the act of changing or removing; **2**, the act of changing from one language to another; **3**, a book, article, or the like, changed from one language into another; **4**, the removal of a person to heaven without death; **5**, a change or removal, as of a bishop from one see to another.

trans-lit-er-ate (trăns-lĭt′ẽr-āt), *v.t.* [*p.t.* and *p.p.* -at″ed, *p.pr.* -at″ing], to express or spell (a letter or word) in the letters or characters of a language having a different alphabet; as, to *transliterate* Greek into English.—*n.* **trans-lit″er-a′tion.**

trans-lu-cent (trăns-lū′sĕnt), *adj.* semitransparent or capable of letting light through so as to allow objects to be indistinctly visible; as, *translucent* glass.—*n.* **trans-lu′cence; trans-lu′cen-cy.**

Syn. lucid, lucent. (See transparent.)

trans-mi-gra-tion (trăns″mī-grā′shŭn), *n.* **1**, the going from one place to another; **2**, the passing of the soul at death from one body to another.

trans-mis-si-ble (trăns-mĭs′ĭ-bl), *adj.* capable of being passed from one to another, or through a body or substance; as, electricity is *transmissible* through copper wire.

trans-mis-sion (trăns-mĭsh′ŭn), *n.* **1**, the act of passing, or the state of being passed, through or over something; as, the *transmission* of a telegram; **2**, that part of the mechanism of an automobile which transfers the power from the engine to the driving shaft.—*adj.* **trans-mis′sive.**

trans-mit (trăns-mĭt′), *v.t.* [*p.t.* and *p.p.* -mit′ted, *p.pr.* -mit′ting], **1**, to cause or allow to pass over or through; as, to *transmit* news by wire; **2**, to conduct; as, air *transmits* heat; **3**, to send down from one place or person to another; transfer; pass on, as a title.—*n.* **trans-mit′tal.**—*adj.* **trans-mit′ti-ble.**

trans-mit-ter (trăns-mĭt′ẽr), *n.* a person or thing through which, or by which, something is sent; esp., the mouthpiece of a telephone or the sending instrument of a telegraph.

trans-mu-ta-tion (trăns″mū-tā′shŭn), *n.* a change from one form, nature, substance, or class, into another.

trans-mute (trăns-mūt′), *v.t.* [*p.t.* and *p.p.* -mut′ed, *p.pr.* -mut′ing], to change from one form, nature, substance, or class, into another; as, the alchemist's dream was to *transmute* base metals into gold.—*adj.* **trans-mut′a-ble.**—*n.* **trans-mut′er.**

tran-som (trăn′sŭm), *n.* **1**, a crossbar in a window or over a door; **2**, a window over a door or other window, set on hinges so as to swing horizontally.

trans-par-en-cy (trăns-pâr′ĕn-sĭ), *n.* [*pl.* transparencies (-sĭz)], **1**, the state or quality of being seen through clearly; **2**, that which is seen through, as a picture, placard, etc., shown by light shining through it from behind; **3**, figuratively, simplicity; as, the *transparency* of one's nature.

trans-par-ent (trăns-pâr′ĕnt), *adj.* **1**, allowing light to pass through so readily that objects behind can be seen distinctly; loosely, capable of being easily seen through; as, *transparent* glass; **2**, easy to understand; evident; as, a *transparent* attempt to deceive.—*adv.* **trans-par′ent-ly.**—*n.* **trans-par′ent-ness.**

Syn. translucent. That is *transparent* which allows objects to be seen through it, as plain window glass. That is *translucent* which transmits light, but does not allow objects to be seen through it, except in blurred form, as ground glass, or thin white paper.—*Ant.* cloudy, vague, obscure, opaque.

tran-spire (trăn-spīr′), *v.i.* [*p.t.* and *p.p.* -spired′(-spīrd′), *p.pr.*-spir′ing], **1**, to pass off as vapor; **2**, to send out as vapor or moisture, as through the skin; **3**, to become known or leak out; **4**, popularly, to happen; come about; occur:—*v.t.* to throw off, as vapor; exhale or breathe out.—*n.* **tran″spi-ra′tion.**

trans-plant (trăns-plănt′), *v.t.* to remove and establish in another place, as trees or people.—*n.* **trans-plant′er.**

trans-plan-ta-tion (trăns″plăn-tā′shŭn), *n.* **1**, the act of removing and settling in another place; **2**, the state of being thus removed and settled.

trans-port (trăns-pōrt′), *v.t.* **1**, to carry from one place to another; as, to *transport* goods or soldiers; **2**, to carry away emotionally; as, he was *transported* by the music; **3**, to banish from a country; deport, as across the ocean:—*n.* (trăns′pōrt), **1**, the act of conveying or of being conveyed; **2**, a means of conveyance; esp., a vessel employed for carrying troops, stores, etc., from one place to another; **3**, a violent display of anger, rapture, etc.; as, a *transport* of joy.—*adj.* **trans-port′a-ble.**—*n.* **trans-port′er.**

trans-por-ta-tion (trăns″pōr-tā′shŭn), *n.* **1**, the act of carrying, or state of being carried, from one place to another; as, the *transportation* of goods, soldiers, etc.; **2**, the act of banishing, or sending to another place, for crime; as, the criminal was sentenced to *transportation;* **3**, means of conveyance; also, the charge for conveyance.

trans-pose (trăns-pōz′), *v.t.* [*p.t.* and *p.p.* -posed′ (-pōzd′), *p.pr.* -pos′ing], **1**, to change the place or order of by putting one in the place of the other; as, to *transpose* letters; **2**, in music, to change the key of; **3**, in algebra, to change (a term) from one side of an equation to the other, with change of algebraic sign.—*n.* **trans-pos′al.**

trans-po-si-tion (trăns″pō-zĭsh′ŭn), *n.* **1**, the act of changing the place or order of something; **2**, the state of being so changed; **3**, in music, the act of setting a composition in a different key; **4**, a composition so changed.—*adj.* **trans″po-si′tion-al.**

trans-ship (trăns-shĭp′), *v.t.* [*p.t.* and *p.p.* -shipped′ (-shĭpt′), *p.pr.* -ship′ping], to transfer from one ship, car, or other carrier, to another; as, to *transship* freight. Also, **tran-ship′.**—*n.* **trans-ship′ment.**

tran-sub-stan-ti-ate (trăn″sŭb-stăn′shĭ-āt), *v.t.* [*p.t.* and *p.p.* -at″ed, *p.pr.* -at″ing], to change into another substance, usually of a higher type.

tran-sub-stan-ti-a-tion (trăn″sŭb-stăn″shĭ-ā′shŭn), *n.* **1**, a changing into another substance; a transformation; **2**, the doctrine held by the Roman Catholic Church that the bread and wine of the Eucharist, or Holy Communion, are changed into the body and blood of Christ upon being consecrated.

trans-ver-sal (trăns-vûr′săl), *adj.* lying or being across, or crosswise:—*n.* a line, generally straight, that intersects, or cuts, a system of lines.

trans-verse (trăns-vûrs′), *adj.* lying or being across, or crosswise; as, *transverse* lines:—*n.* anything that lies crosswise.—*adv.* **trans-verse′ly.**

[1]**trap** (trăp), *n.* **1**, a device, as a snare, pitfall, or spring mechanism, to catch animals, such as game; **2**, an ambush; also, a trick contrivance for betraying people; **3**, a device, as an S-shaped or U-shaped bend, to seal a drain pipe with water against the return of sewer gas; **4**, any of various straining or separating devices; **5**, a device for throwing into the air clay disks, called pigeons, balls, etc., to be shot at; **6**, a trapdoor; **7**, *Colloq.*, a light, two-wheeled carriage:—*v.t.* [*p.t.* and *p.p.* trapped (trăpt), *p.pr.* trap′ping], **1**, to catch in, or as in, a snare or spring; **2**, to ambush or insnare, as an enemy; take by trick or stratagem; as, to *trap* a thief; **3**, to furnish with a trap, as a drain:—*v.i.* to set traps for game.

[2]**trap** (trăp), *n.* a kind of fine-grained, dark, igneous rock occurring in seams through other rocks: also called *trap rock.*

[3]**trap** (trăp), *v.t.* [*p.t.* and *p.p.* trapped (trăpt), *p.pr.* trap′ping], to adorn; bedeck: said esp. of horses or other beasts of burden:—*n.*, in *pl.*, *Colloq.*, baggage; belongings.

trap-door (trăp′dōr″), *n.* a door which lifts up, as in a roof or floor.

tra-peze (trȧ-pēz′), *n.* a swinging horizontal bar suspended by a rope at each end, used in gymnasiums.

tra-pe-zi-um (trȧ-pē′zĭ-ŭm), *n.* [*pl.* trapeziums (-ŭmz); trapezia

(-*ȧ*)], **1**, a plane figure bounded by four straight lines, of which no two are parallel; **2**, one of the bones of the wrist below the thumb.

trap-e-zoid (trăp'ē-zoid), *n.* **1**, a plane figure with four straight sides, only two of which are parallel; **2**, one of the small bones of the wrist.—*adj.* **trap"-e-zoi'dal.**

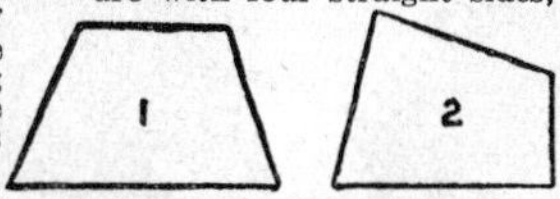

1, Trapezoid; 2, Trapezium

trap-per (trăp'ẽr), *n.* one who catches animals, esp. fur-bearing animals, to obtain their pelts.

trap-pings (trăp'ĭngz), *n.pl.* **1**, ornamental coverings or harness for a horse; **2**, hence, any ornaments in dress.

trash (trăsh), *n.* **1**, that which is worthless or useless; refuse or rubbish; **2**, parts broken off, as leaves, twigs, corn husks, etc.; **3**, a worthless person.

trash-y (trăsh'ĭ), *adj.* [*comp.* trash'i-er, *superl.* trash'i-est], worthless; useless; as, a *trashy* novel.—*adv.* **trash'i-ly.**—*n.* **trash'i-ness.**

trau-ma (trô'mȧ), *n.* [*pl.* traumata (-tȧ)], a bodily injury; a wound; bruise.—*n.* **trau'ma-tism.**

trau-mat-ic (trô-măt'ĭk), *adj.* **1**, pertaining to, or resulting from, an injury or wound; **2**, used for curing wounds, as a remedy.

trav-ail (trăv'āl), *n.* **1**, the suffering endured in childbirth; **2**, physical or mental agony or severe pain; as, a mind in *travail:*—*v.i.* to suffer in childbirth.

trav-el (trăv'ĕl), *v.i.* **1**, to pass; move; go; **2**, to journey, esp. as a salesman; **3**, to move onward or proceed:—*v.t.* to journey over or through; as, to *travel* a hard road:—*n.* **1**, the act of journeying; **2**, a journey; **3**, progression of any kind; **4**, the number of persons, vehicles, etc., passing over a certain road; as, heavy *travel;* **5**, in mechanics, movement or stroke, as of a piston; **6**, in *pl.*, an account of a journey.—*p.adj.* **trav'eled.**

trav-el-er (trăv'ĕl-ẽr), *n.* **1**, one who or that which journeys; **2**, one who goes from place to place, as a salesman; as, a commercial *traveler.* Also, **trav'el-ler.**

trav-e-log (trăv'ē-lŏg), *n.* a lecture, usually illustrated by views, on a journey or journeys. Also, **trav'e-logue.**

trav-erse (trăv'ẽrs), *adj.* lying or being across:—*adv.* (trăv'ẽrs; trȧ-vûrs'), athwart or crosswise:—*n.* **1**, something lying or placed across something else, as a communicating gallery across a building; **2**, in military use, a parapet across an exposed place, or a part of a trench at right angles to the main line of trenches:—*v.t.* [*p.t.* and *p.p.* -ersed (-ẽrst), *p.pr.* -ers-ing], **1**, to lay or place crosswise; **2**, to thwart or cross in opposition; **3**, to cross in traveling; travel or pass over; as, to *traverse* Pennsylvania:—*v.i.* **1**, to turn, as on a pivot; **2**, to walk or move across.

trav-er-tine (trăv'ẽr-tĭn), *n.* a porous, cream-colored limestone of the same structure as a stalactite.

trav-es-ty (trăv'ĕs-tĭ), *n.* [*pl.* travesties (-tĭz)], **1**, a burlesque or parody; **2**, a burlesque translation or imitation of an originally serious literary work; also, any absurd or grotesque likeness:—*v.t.* [*p.t.* and *p.p.* -tied (-tĭd), *p.pr.* -ty-ing], to burlesque or parody; represent in a ludicrous light.

trawl (trôl), *n.* **1**, a large, bag-shaped net used in sea fishing; **2**, a very long fishing line to which are attached many short lines with hooks:—*v.t.* and *v.i.* to catch or fish with such a net or line.—*n.* **trawl'ing.**

trawl-er (trôl'ẽr), *n.* **1**, one who fishes in the ocean with a trawl; **2**, a vessel used in trawling.

tray (trā), *n.* a flat or shallow receptacle of wood, metal, etc., with a raised rim.

treach-er-ous (trĕch'ẽr-ŭs), *adj.* **1**, betraying a trust or a pledge; **2**, apparently good, strong, sound, honest, or the like, but in reality the opposite; as, a *treacherous* friend; a *treacherous* smile; *treacherous* ice.—*adv.* **treach'er-ous-ly.**—*n.* **treach'er-ous-ness.**

Syn. traitorous, disloyal, false, untrue.—*Ant.* faithful, loyal, honest, true.

treach-er-y (trĕch'ẽr-ĭ), *n.* [*pl.* treacheries (-ĭz)], treasonable or disloyal conduct; betrayal of faith or confidence; falseness to one's friends or country.

trea-cle (trē'kl), *n.* **1**, the sirup obtained in refining crude sugar; **2**, loosely, molasses.—*adj.* **trea'cly.**

tread (trĕd), *v.i.* [*p.t.* trod (trŏd), *p.p.* trod'-den (trŏd'n) or trod, *p.pr.* tread'ing], **1**, to step or walk; **2**, to press something beneath the foot; trample: usually with *upon* or *on:*—*v.t.* **1**, to walk on; **2**, to press or crush under the feet; **3**, to subdue or overcome; **4**, to dance; as, to *tread* a minuet:—*n.* **1**, a walking or stepping; **2**, manner of stepping; style of walking; as, a heavy *tread;* **3**, in a flight of stairs, the horizontal upper surface of a step (see *newel, step*, illus.); **4**, the part of a wheel or tire that touches the road or rail; also, the parts of the road or rail touched by the wheel or tire; **5**, of an automobile, the gauge, or distance between opposite wheels; **6**, the point in the yolk of an egg at which germination begins.—*n.* **tread'er.**

trea-dle (trĕd'l), *n.* a flat piece attached to a crank and worked by the foot, by which a lathe, sewing machine, or the like, is run:—*v.i.* [*p.t.* and *p.p.* -dled (-ld), *p.pr.* -dling], to operate such a device.

tread-mill (trĕd'mĭl"), *n.* a mill kept in motion by persons or animals walking on a wheel or endless belt.

trea-son (trē'zn), *n.* **1**, the crime of betraying or attacking the state or the government of the state to which the offender belongs; esp., in the U. S., levying war against the government or aiding an enemy in time of war: sometimes called *high treason;* **2**, treachery; betrayal of faith; falseness to any trust or pledge.—*adj.* **trea'son-ous.**

trea-son-a-ble (trē'zn-ȧ-bl), *adj.* tending to, or characterized by, falseness to pledges, friends, or country; as, *treasonable* speech.—*adv.* **trea'son-a-bly.**—*n.* **trea'son-a-ble-ness.**

Syn. treacherous, disloyal, traitorous.

treas-ure (trĕzh'ũr), *n.* **1**, a hoard or store, as of money or jewels; abundance or wealth; **2**, something highly valued, or of great value:—.*pt.* [*p.t.* and *p.p.* -ured (-ũrd), *p.pr.* -ur-ing], **1**, to lay up or collect for future use; hoard; **2**, to value highly.

treas-ur-er (trĕzh'ũr-ẽr), *n.* one who has charge of receiving and expending collected funds.—*n.* **treas'ur-er-ship.**

treas-ure-trove (trĕzh'ũr-trōv"), *n.* gold, silver, jewels, or like valuables, found hidden in the earth and not claimed by an owner.

treas-ur-y (trĕzh'ũr-ĭ), *n.* [*pl.* treasuries (-ĭz)], **1**, a place where wealth is stored; esp., a place where public funds are kept and paid out; **2**, (also, *Treasury*): **a**, that department of a government which has charge of the public funds; **b**, the officials of such a department: **treasury note**, any of various kinds of paper money issued by the U. S.

treat (trēt), *v.t.* **1**, to handle, deal with, or manage; as, the speaker *treated* his

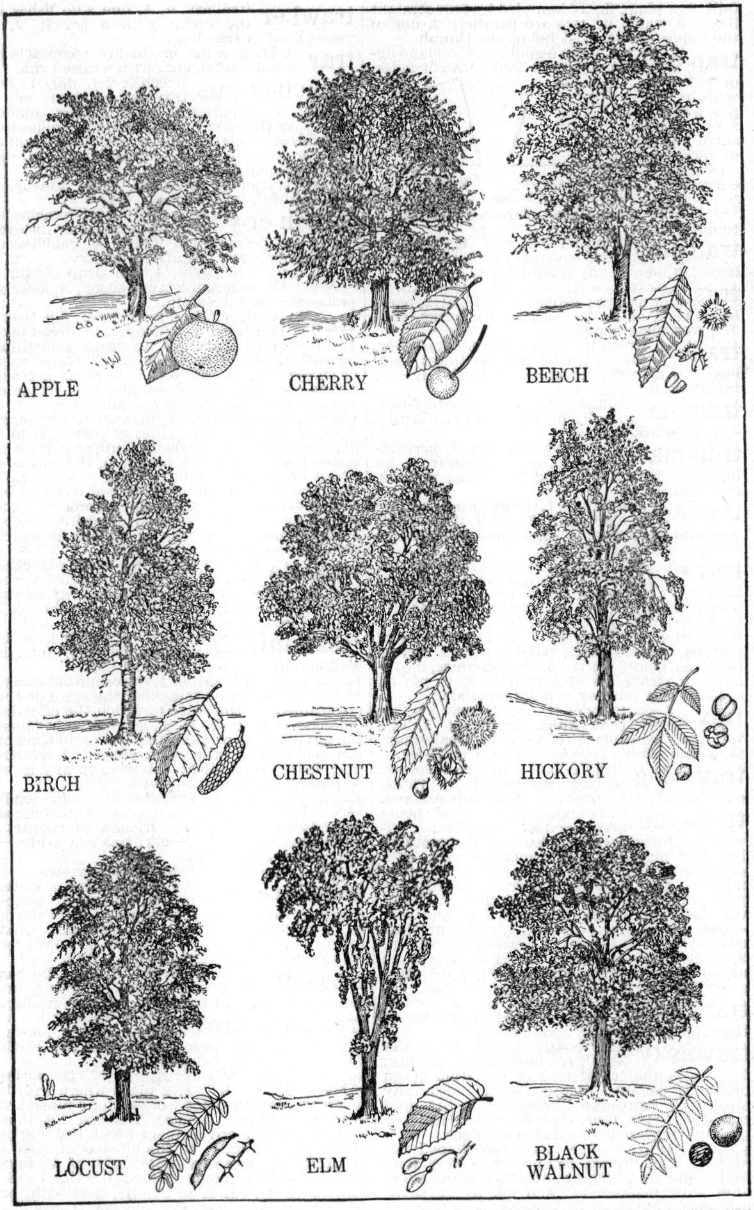

TYPICAL NORTH AMERICAN DECIDUOUS TREES, WITH THEIR LEAVES AND FRUITS

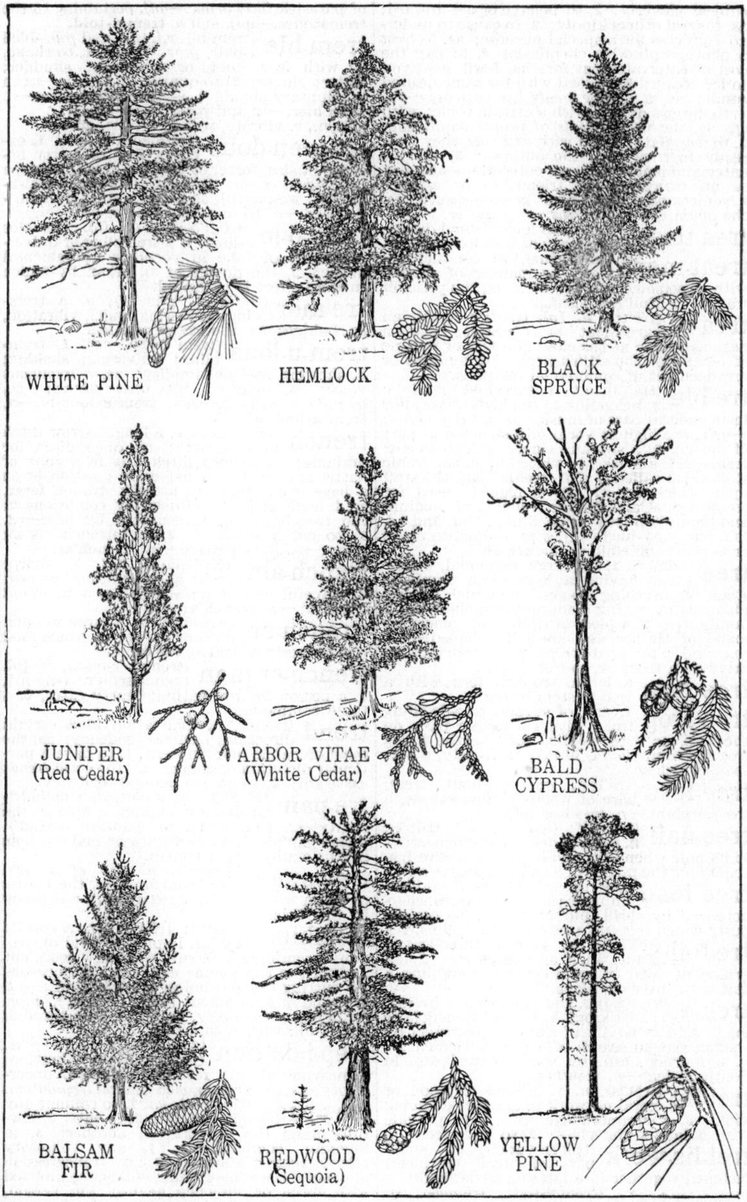

TYPICAL NORTH AMERICAN EVERGREEN TREES, WITH THEIR LEAVES AND FRUITS

subject cleverly; 2, to behave or act toward; as, to *treat* others kindly; 3, to cause to undergo a process for a special purpose; as, to *treat* a photograph with chemicals; 4, to pay the cost of entertainment for; as, I will *treat* you to ice cream; 5, to deal with for some desired result; as, a doctor *treats* his patients:—*v.i.* 1, to discuss or deal with a certain topic: with *of;* as, the paper *treats* of proper sanitation; 2, to negotiate: often with *with;* as, they were ready to *treat* with the outlaws; 3, to give entertainment:—*n.* 1, an entertainment given as an expression of friendship or esteem; 2, something which affords great pleasure; as, the opera is a great *treat.*—*n.* **treat'er.**

trea-tise (trē'tĭs), *n.* a long, formal discussion or essay on a serious subject.

treat-ment (trēt'mĕnt), *n.* conduct toward, or manner of dealing with, a person, problem, etc.; as, the prisoner was given kind *treatment.*

trea-ty (trē'tĭ), *n.* [*pl.* treaties (-tĭz)], an agreement or contract between nations, either at the close of a war or in time of peace, for the adjustment of differences or arrangement of commercial relations.

tre-ble (trĕb'l), *adj.* 1, threefold or triple; 2, belonging to the highest vocal or instrumental part of music; as, a *treble* violin:—*n.* 1, the highest vocal or instrumental part of music; 2, a soprano singer or instrument: **treble clef,** a mark [𝄞] placed upon the treble staff: also called *G clef:* **treble staff,** the staff upon which the G clef is placed: used for treble voices and for instruments of medium and high pitch (see *degree,* illus.):—*v.t.* and *v.i.* [*p.t.* and *p.p.* -bled (-ld), *p.pr.* -bling], to make or become threefold.—*adv.* **tre'bly.**

tree (trē), *n.* 1, any large, perennial, woody plant having a high main trunk or stem; 2, anything suggestive of such a large plant, as in having stem and branches; as, a family *tree;* 3, a piece of timber, or something made of timber and specially shaped:—*v.t.* [*p.t.* and *p.p.* treed (trēd), *p.pr.* tree'ing], to drive up a tree; as, to *tree* a cat.

tree fern a large, tropical fern with a woody stem or trunk.

tree frog 1, any of several tree-dwelling frogs with suckerlike pads on the toes, or with webbed feet, as the flying frog (see *amphibian,* illus.); 2, loosely, a tree toad (which see).

tree-less (trē'lĕs), *adj.* without trees; bare of woods or forests; as, a *treeless* plain.—*n.* **tree'less-ness.**

tree-nail (trē'nāl"; *Colloq.* trĕn'l; trŭn'l), *n.* a pin of dry wood which swells in its hole when wet, and is thus a secure fastening for the planks of a ship. Also, **tre'nail".**

tree toad any of several small, tailless animals that live in trees, characterized by shrill, piping calls: also erroneously called *tree frog* (see *amphibian,* illus.).

tre-foil (trē'foil), *n.* 1, any three-leaved plant, such as the clover; 2, an ornament used in architecture, resembling a leaf with three divisions.

trek (trĕk), *v.i.* [*p.t.* and *p.p.* trekked (trĕkt), *p.pr.* trek'king], 1, to pull a vehicle or load: said generally of oxen; 2, to travel by wagon, esp. in search of a new settlement:—*n.* a journey, esp. by wagon: used esp. in South Africa.—*n.* **trek'ker.**

trel-lis (trĕl'ĭs), *n.* 1, a kind of wood or metal network to support climbing vines; 2, a summerhouse:—*v.t.* 1, to provide with a lattice for vines; 2, to interlace.

trel-lis-work (trĕl'ĭs-wûrk"), *n.* small bars of wood or metal fastened together in a lattice; latticework.

trem-a-tode (trĕm'ȧ-tōd; trē'mȧ-), *n.* any of a class (*Trematoda*) of parasitic flatworms:—*adj.* pertaining to the trematodes.—*adj.* and *n.* **trem'a-toid.**

trem-ble (trĕm'bl), *v.i.* [*p.t.* and *p.p.* -bled (-bld), *p.pr.* -bling], 1, to shake, as with fear, cold, or weakness; shudder; totter; shiver; 2, to quaver, as sound:—*n.* an involuntary shaking; a shiver; shudder.—*n.* **trem'bler.**—*n.* and *p.adj.* **trem'bling.**

Syn., v. vibrate, waver, flutter, quiver.

tre-men-dous (trē-mĕn'dŭs), *adj.* 1, exciting fear or terror because of size, force, or effect; dreadful; as, a *tremendous* crash; 2, causing awe or astonishment; wonderful, as a feat.—*adv.* **tre-men'dous-ly.**—*n.* **tre-men'dous-ness.**

trem-o-lo (trĕm'ō-lō), *n.* [*pl.* tremolos (-lōz)], 1, a trembling or quivering effect of tone in vocal or instrumental music; 2, the device in an organ by which such an effect is produced.

tre-mor (trē'mŏr; trĕm'ŏr), *n.* a trembling; quivering; quick vibration, or shaking; as, the *tremor* of a leaf.

trem-u-lous (trĕm'ū-lŭs), *adj.* 1, trembling; quivering; shaking; 2, showing fear or timidity; as, a *tremulous* voice; 3, marked by unsteadiness; as, *tremulous* writing.—*adv.* **trem'u-lous-ly.**—*n.* **trem'u-lous-ness.**

trench (trĕnch), *n.* 1, a long, narrow ditch in the earth; an open ditch for draining; 2, a deep ditch dug in a zone of battle and held as a defensive position or as a base from which to attack: **trench fever,** an infectious fever induced by conditions in the trenches, and transmitted by lice:—*v.t.* 1, to cut a ditch in; 2, to intrench, as an army:—*v.i.* to encroach.—*n.* [1]**trench'er.**

trench-ant (trĕn'chănt), *adj.* 1, sharp; keen; as, a *trenchant* sword; 2, forceful and clear; sharp; as, a *trenchant* criticism.—*n.* **trench'an-cy.**

[2]**trench-er** (trĕn'chẽr), *n.* a large wooden plate or platter on which food was formerly served at the table.

trench-er-man (trĕn'chẽr-măn), *n.* [*pl.* trenchermen (-mĕn)], 1, a person fond of eating; hearty eater; 2, a table companion.

trend (trĕnd), *n.* inclination in a certain direction; general tendency; as, the *trend* of public opinion:—*v.i.* 1, to have a particular direction or course; as, the coast *trends* eastward; 2, to have a general tendency.

tre-pan (trē-păn'), *n.* a surgeon's cylindrical saw for making a hole in the skull:—*v.t.* [*p.t.* and *p.p.* -panned' (-pănd'), *p.pr.* -pan'ning], to perforate or make a hole in (the skull) with a trepan.

tre-pang (trē-păng'), *n.* any of several large sea cucumbers, the bodies of which when dried are regarded as a delicacy by the Chinese.

tre-phine (trē-fīn'; trē-fēn'), *n.* a special saw, an improved kind of trepan, resembling a ferrule with saw teeth cut around the rim at one end, used by surgeons for cutting circular holes, as in the skull:—*v.t.* [*p.t.* and *p.p.* -phined' (-fīnd'; -fēnd'), *p.pr.* -phin'ing], in surgery, to cut a hole through (the skull) with such a saw.

trep-i-da-tion (trĕp"ĭ-dā'shŭn), *n.* 1, trembling or vibration; 2, nervous alarm; fear mingled with uncertainty; as, the news caused general *trepidation.*

tres-pass (trĕs'pȧs), *v.i.* 1, to commit any offense; sin; 2, to enter unlawfully upon the property of another; 3, to intrude; encroach:—*n.* 1, any voluntary offense against another; 2, any transgression of a moral law; 3, any unlawful act committed with force or violence against the person, rights, or property of another.—*n.* **tres'pass-er.**

tress (trĕs), *n.* a braid, curl, lock, or ringlet of human, esp. a woman's, hair.

tres-tle (trĕs'l), *n.* **1,** a movable frame, or horse, made of a horizontal beam and spreading legs, as for supporting a table; **2,** a strong framework of timbers or steel over which a bridge is built across a ravine or gully.

tres-tle board a draftsman's drawing or designing board.

tres-tle-tree (trĕs'l-trē"), *n.,* usually in *pl.,* one of two stout bars of timber fastened horizontally to a masthead to support the crosstrees.

tres-tle-work (trĕs'l-wûrk"), *n.* a series of trestles built to support a bridge, railroad, or the like.

tret (trĕt), *n.* an allowance to purchasers to cover waste in transporting goods.

trey (trā), *n.* a three at cards or dice; a card with three spots.

tri- (trī-), *prefix,* **1,** three; threefold; as, *tri*color; **2,** in chemistry, containing three atoms or radical groups; as, *tri*oxide.

tri-ad (trī'ăd), *n.* **1,** a group or union of three; three similar things; as, a *triad* of virtues; **2,** in music, a chord of three tones, consisting of a fundamental tone together with its third and fifth.

tri-al (trī'ăl), *n.* **1,** the act of testing or putting to proof; examination; **2,** the state of being tested; **3,** an endeavor; experiment; **4,** hardship; suffering or temptation; that which puts to the test faith, mercy, patience, etc.; **5,** a judicial examination; as, a *trial* in court: **trial by battle,** the settlement of a dispute by personal combat: a legal form of trial in England until 1819.

Syn. test, proof, experiment. *Trial* suggests the idea of attempting to verify something that is uncertain; as, a *trial* of skill in shooting at a target. A *test* is a *trial* that proves and is therefore decisive; as, to put a new machine through a careful *test.* A *proof,* like a *test,* is final; it is a definite discovery in the intellectual or the practical field. An *experiment* may be merely an attempt to confirm an opinion, or, if it does prove something, it may be a *test* or *proof* of great value.

tri-al bal-ance in double-entry bookkeeping, the statement of the totals of the columns of a ledger, which tests whether the two sides balance.

tri-al ju-ry a jury called to try a case in court: also called *petit jury,* and distinguished from *grand jury.*

tri-an-gle (trī'ăng"gl), *n.* **1,** a plane figure bounded by three straight lines and having three angles; **2,** a musical instrument consisting of a steel rod bent in the form of a triangle, sounded by being struck by a metallic rod.

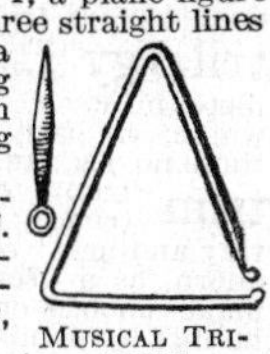

Musical Triangle

tri-an-gu-lar (trī-ăng'gū-lår), *adj.* **1,** having three angles; three-sided; three-cornered; **2,** concerned with, or comprising, three persons or things.

tri-an-gu-late (trī-ăng'gū-lāt), *v.t.* [*p.t.* and *p.p.* -lat"ed, *p.pr.* -lat"ing], **1,** to divide into triangles; survey by so dividing; **2,** to make three-cornered, or triangular.

tri-an-gu-la-tion (trī-ăng"gū-lā'shŭn), *n.* the process of dividing into triangles, esp. for surveying purposes.

trib-al (trīb'ăl), *adj.* pertaining to, or like, a clan or group of related families; as, *tribal* customs or characteristics.

tribe (trīb), *n.* **1,** a family or clan descended from a common ancestor; as, the *tribe* of Judah; **2,** a group of uncivilized people under one chief; as, a Tatar *tribe;* **3,** *Colloq.,* a group of people made akin to each other by some common trait.

Syn. class, division. (See nation.)

tribes-man (trībz'măn), *n.* [*pl.* tribesmen (-mĕn)], a member of a clan, tribe, or racial group.

trib-u-la-tion (trĭb"ū-lā'shŭn), *n.* **1,** severe affliction or distress; deep sorrow; **2,** an acute trial; a source of grief.

Syn. suffering, trouble, grief.

tri-bu-nal (trī-bū'năl), *n.* **1,** the seat of a judge; **2,** a court of justice.

[1]**trib-une** (trĭb'ūn), *n.* **1,** a Roman magistrate elected by the people to protect their liberties; **2,** hence, one who champions the rights of the people: often used as the title of a newspaper.—*n.* **trib'une-ship.**

[2]**trib-une** (trĭb'ūn), *n.* **1,** in ancient Rome, a raised stand for public speakers; **2,** hence, a platform, as in a hall.

trib-u-ta-ry (trĭb'ū-tā-rĭ), *adj.* **1,** paying tribute or taxes to another; **2,** contributory; subordinate:—*n.* [*pl.* tributaries (-rĭz)], **1,** a state or government which pays taxes to, or is under control of, a superior government; **2,** a stream or river flowing into a larger body of water.

trib-ute (trĭb'ūt), *n.* **1,** an annual or stated sum of money paid by one state or ruler to another to obtain protection, or by the terms of a treaty; **2,** a personal tax or payment; **3,** an acknowledgment of worth, service rendered, or the like.

[1]**trice** (trīs), *v.t.* [*p.t.* and *p.p.* triced (trīst), *p.pr.* tric'ing], to pull and tie with a small rope, as a sail: usually with *up.*

[2]**trice** (trīs), *n.* a very short space of time: used only in the phrase *in a trice.*

tri-cen-te-na-ry (trī-sĕn'tē-nā-rĭ), *adj.* including or relating to a period of 300 years:—*n.* [*pl.* tricentenaries (-rĭz)], the 300th anniversary of any event. Also, **ter-cen'te-na-ry,** *Pfd. S.*

tri-ceps (trī'sĕps), *n.* the great extensor muscle having three heads, at the back of the upper arm.

tri-chi-na (trī-kī'nȧ), *n.* [*pl.* trichinæ (-nē)], a microscopic worm, parasitic in the muscles of human beings, swine, and other animals.—*adj.* **trich'i-nous.**

trich-i-no-sis (trĭk"ĭ-nō'sĭs), *n.* the disease produced by the presence of trichinæ in the muscles and intestines. Also, **trich"i-ni'a-sis** (trĭk"ĭ-nī'ȧ-sĭs).

trick (trĭk), *n.* **1,** an artifice or fraud; a crafty or deceitful device or action; as, a *trick* in trade; **2,** a puzzle to amuse or annoy; a petty, deceptive device; **3,** a juggler's feat; a sleight-of-hand feat; **4,** a mischievous, sometimes annoying, prank; **5,** a peculiarity of manner; habit; as, a *trick* of raising the eyebrows; **6,** a particular skill; knack; the best way of doing something; as, he soon learned the *trick;* **7,** all the cards played in one round of a game; **8,** a sailor's turn at the helm; a spell:—*v.t.* **1,** to cheat; impose upon; **2,** to adorn fantastically: usually with *up* or *out:*—*v.i.* to play tricks; juggle.

trick-er-y (trĭk'ẽr-ĭ), *n.* [*pl.* trickeries (-ĭz)], the act or practice of deception; cheating; fraud; imposture.

trick-ish (trĭk'ĭsh), *adj.* full of craft, deceit, artifice, mischief, etc.—*adv.* **trick'ish-ly.**—*n.* **trick'ish-ness.**

trick-le (trĭk'l), *v.i.* [*p.t.* and *p.p.* -led (-ld), *p.pr.* -ling], to flow gently down or in a small stream; drip; run down in drops; as, moisture *trickles* through the walls of a cave:—*n.* a small amount of liquid dropping or flowing gently.—*adj.* **trick'ly.**

trick-ster (trĭk'stẽr), *n.* a cunning or crafty cheat or deceiver.

trick-sy (trĭk′sĭ), *adj.* full of mischief; given to pranks; playful.

trick-y (trĭk′ĭ), *adj.* [*comp.* trick′i-er, *superl.* trick′i-est], given to deceit; not to be trusted.—*adv.* **trick′i-ly.**—*n.* **trick′i-ness.**

tric-o-lette (trĭk″ō-lĕt′), *n.* a soft, elastic dress material of silk or cotton, woven with a knitting stitch.

tri-col-or (trī′kŭl″ẽr), *n.* a flag of three colors arranged in equal stripes; esp., the national flag of France, of blue, white, and red vertical stripes. Also, **tri′col″our.**—*adj.* **tri′col″ored.**

tri-cot (trē′kō), *n.* **1,** material of wool, silk, or cotton, resembling a knitted fabric; **2,** a soft, ribbed dress goods.

tri-co-tine (trē″kō″tēn′), *n.* a woolen dress material, like a light twill.

tri-cus-pid (trī-kŭs′pĭd), *adj.* **1,** having three cusps, or points, as certain teeth, or as one of the valves of the heart; **2,** pertaining to this valve.

tri-cy-cle (trī′sĭ-kl), *n.* **1,** a light, three-wheeled vehicle, with a single seat and usually operated by pedals; **2,** a three-wheeled motor cycle:—*v.i.* [*p.t.* and *p.p.* -cled (-kld), *p.pr.* -cling], to ride in a three-wheeled vehicle.

tri-dent (trī′dĕnt), *n.* **1,** a weapon with three points or prongs, esp. that carried by the god of the sea, Neptune; **2,** a three-pronged fish spear.

tri-den-tate (trī-dĕn′tāt), *adj.* having three points, prongs, or teeth. Also, **tri-den′tat-ed.**

tried (trīd), past tense and past participle of the verb *try:*—*p.adj.* proved; trustworthy; as, a *tried* and true friend.

tri-en-ni-al (trī-ĕn′ĭ-ăl), *adj.* **1,** continuing three years; **2,** happening every three years; as, a *triennial* meeting:—*n.* **1,** an event occurring every three years; **2,** the third anniversary of an event.—*adv.* **tri-en′ni-al-ly.**

tri-er (trī′ẽr), *n.* **1,** one who makes experiments or tests; **2,** a judge.

tri-fid (trī′fĭd), *adj.* partly or entirely divided into three, as a leaf or as the tail of a bird.

tri-fle (trī′fl), *n.* **1,** anything of little value or importance; **2,** a dessert made of sponge cake covered with jam, cream, etc.: **a trifle,** a little; slightly:—*v.i.* [*p.t.* and *p.p.* -fled (-fld), *p.pr.* -fling], **1,** to act or talk without seriousness; **2,** to dally; as, she *trifled* with her necklace as she talked:—*v.t.* to waste; as, to *trifle* away one's money.—*n.* **tri′fler.**

tri-fling (trī′flĭng), *adj.* **1,** of small value or importance; as, a *trifling* matter; **2,** thoughtless or shallow; as, a *trifling* character.—*adv.* **tri′fling-ly.**

tri-fo-li-ate (trī-fō′lĭ-āt), *adj.* having three leaves or leaflets growing from the same point, as the clover.

tri-fo-li-o-late (trī-fō′lĭ-ō-lāt), *adj.* having three leaflets growing from the same point, as the clover leaf. more generally, *trifoliate.*

[1]**trig** (trĭg), *adj.* [*comp.* trig′ger, *superl.* trig′gest], trim; neat; as, a *trig* ship.—*adv.* **trig′ly.**—*n.* **trig′ness.**

[2]**trig** (trĭg), *v.t.* [*p.t.* and *p.p.* trigged (trĭgd), *p.pr.* trig′ging], *Dial.*, to stop; obstruct; as, to *trig* a wheel by putting a stone in the way:—*n. Dial.*, anything used as a stop, as a stone or block.

trig-ger (trĭg′ẽr), *n.* a lever which, when pulled by the finger, releases the hammer of a gun; also, a catch doing similar work, as on a trap or other device.

tri-glyph (trī′glĭf), *n.* in a Doric frieze, a rectangular tablet having two vertical grooves, with a half groove at each side.

trig-o-nom-e-try (trĭg″ō-nŏm′ē-trĭ), *n.* [*pl.* trigonometries (-trĭz)], **1,** the branch of mathematics which treats of the relations between the sides and angles of triangles; **2,** a text treating of this science.—*adj.* **trig″o-no-met′ric; trig″o-no-met′ri-cal.**—*adv.* **trig″o-no-met′ri-cal-ly.**

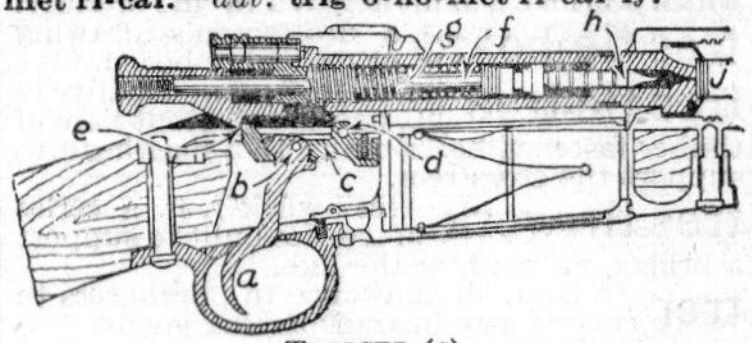

TRIGGER (*a*)

a is pivoted at *b* to sear *c*, which is pivoted to frame at *d*. Pulling trigger depresses sear at *e*, releases firing pin *f*, so that mainspring *g* drives striker *h* into percussion cap in cartridge at *j*.

tri-graph (trī′grăf), *n.* a group of three letters representing one sound, as *eau* in beauty.

tri-he-dron (trī-hē′drŏn), *n.* [*pl.* trihedrons (-drŭnz); trihedra (-drȧ)], a figure having three plane sides or faces.—*adj.* **tri-he′dral.**

tri-lat-er-al (trī-lăt′ẽr-ăl), *adj.* three-sided, or having three sides, as a triangle.—*adv.* **tri-lat′er-al-ly.**

tri-lit-er-al (trī-lĭt′ẽr-ăl), *adj.* consisting of three letters, as a syllable:—*n.* a word or syllable of three letters.

trill (trĭl), *n.* **1,** a shake or vibration of the voice on a letter or musical tone; as, the *trill* of a bird; **2,** in music, the quick alternation of two notes:—*v.t.* to utter with a vibration; as, to *trill* one's *r's:*—*v.i.* to make the voice vibrate.

tril-lion (trĭl′yŭn), *n.* **1,** in the French system of numbering, followed in the U. S., a unit followed by twelve ciphers; **2,** in the English system, a unit followed by eighteen ciphers.—*adj.* and *n.* **tril′lionth.**

tril-li-um (trĭl′ĭ-ŭm), *n.* any of several plants having three leaves surrounding one large flower.

tri-lo-bate (trī-lō′bāt; trī′lō-bāt), *adj.* having three lobes.

tri-lo-bite (trī′lō-bīt), *n.* any of many extinct, marine crustaceans, having the body divided into three more or less distinct lobes, the head, thorax, and abdomen.—*adj.* **tri″lo-bit′ic** (-bĭt′ĭk).

tril-o-gy (trĭl′ō-jĭ), *n.* [*pl.* trilogies (-jĭz)], a series of three dramas, each complete in itself, but forming one connected whole; similarly, three musical compositions, three novels, etc.

trim (trĭm), *v.t.* [*p.t.* and *p.p.* trimmed (trĭmd), *p.pr.* trim′ming], **1,** to make tidy and neat; set in order; **2,** to decorate or adorn, as a dress with beads or lace; **3,** to make smooth or ready for use; as, to *trim* lumber by planing it; **4,** to make neat, as the hair or a plant, by cutting or clipping; hence, to cut or clip (superfluous parts), as from a plant; **5,** to adjust or balance, as a ship, by proper distribution of cargo; **6,** to adjust for sailing; as, to *trim* the sails; **7,** *Colloq.:* **a,** to lecture or reprove; chastise; **b,** to beat, as in a game; **8,** *Slang,* to defraud:—*v.i.* **1,** to try to please two sides or parties at the same time; compromise; **2,** to take a certain position in the water: said of a vessel:—*n.* **1,** order; adjustment; suitable condition; **2,** dress; style; gear; **3,** the inside woodwork of a building around the windows, doors, or the like; **4,** fitness for sailing: said of a ship; **5,** of a ship, position in the water relative to the horizontal plane:—*adj.* [*comp.* trim'mer, *superl.* trim'mest], **1**, neat; as, a *trim* ship; **2**, in good order; as, her hair was *trim.*—*adv.* **trim'ly.**—*n.* **trim'mer.**—*n.* **trim'ness.**

trim-e-ter (trĭm'ē-tẽr), *n.* a verse, or line of poetry, having three metrical feet:—*adj.* having three metrical feet.—*adj.* **tri-met'ric** (trī-mĕt'rĭk); **tri-met'ri-cal.**

trim-ming (trĭm'ĭng), *n.* **1**, the act of one who arranges, decorates, or the like; **2**, adornment, esp. for articles of dress; **3**, in *pl.*, parts removed by cutting off the edges; as, the *trimmings* of a piece of meat; **4**, in *pl.*, *Colloq.*, the garnishings of a dish; as, boiled mutton with *trimmings.*

trine (trīn), *adj.* triple; threefold.—*adj.* **tri'nal.**—*adj.* **tri'na-ry.**

Trin-i-ta-ri-an (trĭn"ĭ-tā'rĭ-ăn), *adj.* pertaining to the Trinity, or the doctrine of the Trinity:—*n.* one who believes in the doctrine of the Trinity. Also, **trin"i-ta'ri-an.**—*n.* **Trin"i-ta'ri-an-ism.**

tri-ni-tro-tol-u-ene (trī-nī"trō-tŏl'ū-ēn), *n.* a chemical substance widely used as a bursting charge for high explosive shells. Also, **tri-ni"tro-tol'-u-ol** (trī-nī"trō-tŏl'ū-ōl; -ŏl).—*abbr.* **T.N.T.**

Trin-i-ty (trĭn'ĭ-tĭ), *n.* [*pl.* Trinities (-tĭz)], the union of the Father, the Son, and the Holy Ghost in one Godhead: **Trinity Sunday,** the Sunday next after Pentecost: **trinity,** any union of three in one; a trio.

trin-ket (trĭng'kĕt), *n.* **1**, a small ornament or jewel; **2**, a trifle; toy; gewgaw.

tri-no-mi-al (trī-nō'mĭ-ăl), *n.* a mathematical expression consisting of three terms, connected by the sign plus [+] or minus [−]; as, $x^2-2xy+y^2$ is a *trinomial:*—*adj.* composed of three terms.

tri-o (trē'ō; trī'ō), *n.* [*pl.* trios (-ōz)], **1**, a set of three; three united; **2**, in music, a composition for three voices or instruments.

tri-ode (trī'ōd), *n.* an electric tube containing three electrodes, a filament, grid, and plate: used for producing, detecting, or amplifying radio signals.

tri-o-let (trī'ō-lĕt), *n.* a stanza consisting of eight lines with two rimes, the first line being repeated as the fourth and seventh, and the second line as the eighth.

tri-ox-ide (trī-ŏk'sīd; trī-ŏk'sĭd), *n.* a compound composed of three atoms of oxygen with another compound. Also, **tri-ox'id.**

trip (trĭp), *v.i.* [*p.t.* and *p.p.* tripped (trĭpt), *p.pr.* trip'ping], **1**, to run or step lightly or nimbly; take short, quick steps; skip; **2**, to stumble; **3**, to make a mistake or error, mentally or morally; err:—*v.t.* **1**, to execute with light, agile steps, as a dance; **2**, to cause to stumble or halt by getting in the way of: often with *up;* **3**, to catch in a mistake or deception: often with *up;* **4**, to release or set free, as by pulling a catch, trigger, or the like:—*n.* **1**, a brisk, short step; **2**, a false step; mistake; **3**, a journey or excursion; **4**, a kind of grip or catch used by wrestlers to overturn an opponent; **5**, a device that unfastens or releases a mechanism.—*n.* **trip'per.**

tri-par-tite (trī-pär'tīt; trĭp'ȧr-tīt), *adj.* **1**, divided into three parts; **2**, made or existing among three persons or groups of persons; as, a *tripartite* agreement.—*adv.* **tri-par'tite-ly.**—*n.* **tri"par-ti'tion.**

tripe (trīp), *n.* the greater part of the stomach of the ox, prepared for food.

tri-pet-al-ous (trī-pĕt'ăl-ŭs), *adj.* in botany, having three petals.

trip ham-mer a heavy power hammer, raised by a tripping device and then allowed to drop by gravity.

triph-thong (trĭf'thŏng), *n.* **1**, a combination of three vowel sounds in a single syllable, as in the word *wye* (o͞o+ă+ē); **2**, commonly, but incorrectly, a trigraph: three vowels used to represent a single vowel sound or diphthong, as in *beauty.*—*adj.* **triph-thon'gal** (trĭf-thŏng'găl).

tri-plane (trī'plān"), *n.* an airplane having three main planes.

tri-ple (trĭp'l), *adj.* **1**, threefold; consisting of three joined; as, a *triple* window; **2**, thrice repeated; as, a *triple* knock: **Triple Alliance,** any of several historic alliances involving three European powers; specif., the Dreibund, an alliance of Germany, Austria, and Italy, contracted in 1882: **Triple Entente,** (äṅ"täṅt'), an understanding with respect to common and conflicting interests, developed gradually after 1890, between France, Russia, and Great Britain, resulting in a virtual alliance between them during the first three years of the World War:—*v.t.* and *v.i.* [*p.t.* and *p.p.* -pled (-ld), *p.pr.* -pling], to increase threefold.—*adv.* **tri'ply.**—*n.* **tri-plic'i-ty.**

trip-let (trĭp'lĕt), *n.* **1**, a set of three of a kind or three united; **2**, in poetry, three lines riming together; **3**, in music, three notes sounded in the time of two; **4**, one of three children at one birth.

tri-plex (trī'plĕks; trĭp'lĕks), *adj.* having three parts; threefold:—*n.* in music, triple time or measure.

trip-li-cate (trĭp'lĭ-kăt), *n.* something which matches two others of the same kind:—*adj.* threefold; made in three copies; as, a *triplicate* agreement:—*v.t.* (trĭp'lĭ-kāt), [*p.t.* and *p.p.* -cat"ed, *p.pr.* -cat"-ing], to triple.—*n.* **trip"li-ca'tion.**

tri-pod (trī'pŏd), *n.* **1**, a three-legged stand or support, as for a camera; **2**, an article with three legs, as a stool, vase, etc.

trip-ping (trĭp'ĭng), *p.adj.* stepping lightly or gracefully.—*adv.* **trip'ping-ly.**

trip-tych (trĭp'tĭk), *n.* **1**, a picture, design, or carving on three panels, often an altar piece; also, three separate pictures of related subjects, arranged side by side; **2**, in classical antiquity, a set of three writing tablets joined together.

tri-reme (trī'rēm), *n.* in ancient times, a ship with three banks of oars.

TRIREME

tri-sect (trī-sĕkt'), *v.t.* **1**, to divide into three parts; **2**, in geometry, to divide into three equal parts, as an angle.

tri-sec-tion (trī-sĕk'shŭn), *n.* the division of anything into three, esp. the division of an angle into three equal parts.

Tris-tram (trĭs'trăm), *n.* in many medieval romances and lays, the unfortunate lover of Iseult (Isolde), wife of King Mark of Cornwall, celebrated in modern times by Wagner in his "Tristan und Isolde." Also, **Tris'tan; Tris'tam; Tris'trem.**

tri-syl-la-ble (trī-sĭl′ȧ-bl; trĭ-), *n.* a word of three syllables.—*adj.* **tris″yl-lab′ic; tris″yl-lab′i-cal.**

trite (trīt), *adj.* worn out; stale; commonplace; as, a *trite* remark.—*adv.* **trite′ly.** —*n.* **trite′ness.**

Syn. old, ordinary, hackneyed, banal.—*Ant.* fresh, vivid, striking, new.

Tri-ton (trī′tŏn), *n.* in mythology, a demigod of the sea, the son of Poseidon: **triton,** any of certain marine mollusks having highly colored, elongated, spiral shells: also, its elongated, spiral shell.

trit-u-rate (trĭt′ū-rāt), *v.t.* [*p.t.* and *p.p.* -rat″ed, *p.pr.* -rat″ing], **1,** to rub or grind to a fine powder; **2,** to masticate thoroughly:—*n.* a medicine in which the active substance has been thoroughly ground and mixed with something inert.—*n.* **trit″u-ra′tion.**

tri-umph (trī′ŭmf), *n.* **1,** great joy over success; exultation; **2,** in ancient Rome, a grand parade in honor of a victorious general; **3,** conquest or victory; as, the *triumph* of knowledge:—*v.i.* **1,** to rejoice in success; **2,** to be successful or victorious.

Syn., n. achievement. (See victory.)

tri-um-phal (trī-ŭm′făl), *adj.* of or pertaining to a victory or its celebration; as, a *triumphal* procession.

tri-um-phant (trī-ŭm′fănt), *adj.* **1,** rejoicing for victory; exultant; **2,** victorious; successful; as, a *triumphant* cause.—*adv.* **tri-um′phant-ly.**

tri-um-vir (trī-ŭm′vẽr), *n.* [*pl.* triumviri (-vĭ-rī); triumvirs (-vẽrz)], in ancient Rome, one of three men equally sharing public authority and rule.

tri-um-vi-rate (trī-ŭm′vĭ-rȧt), *n.* **1,** a government by three men having equal authority; **2,** the office or authority of three men sharing the control of a government; **3,** a group of three.

tri-une (trī′ūn), *adj.* being three in one; as, the *triune* God.—*n.* **tri-u′ni-ty.**

triv-et (trĭv′ĕt), *n.* **1,** a three-legged stand for holding a kettle near or over an open fire; **2,** a short-legged metal plate on which to set hot dishes; **3,** anything supported by three legs; a tripod: **right as a trivet,** in first-class condition; all right.

triv-i-al (trĭv′ĭ-ăl), *adj.* **1,** trifling; **2,** common; ordinary; of little worth or importance; as, the *trivial* affairs of everyday work.—*adv.* **triv′i-al-ly.**—*n.* **triv′i-al-ness.**

triv-i-al-i-ty (trĭv″ĭ-ăl′ĭ-tĭ), *n.* [*pl.* trivialities (-tĭz)], **1,** the state or quality of being of little worth; **2,** a matter of little importance.

tri-week-ly (trī″wēk′lĭ), *adj.* coming three times a week or every third week:—*adv.* thrice a week or every third week.

-trix (-trĭks), *n. suffix,* one who: feminine form corresponding to *-tor;* as, administra*trix;* testa*trix.*

tro-cha-ic (trō-kā′ĭk), *adj.* pertaining to a metrical foot called *trochee.*

tro-chan-ter (trō-kăn′tẽr), *n.* any of several rough prominences of bone on the upper part of the thigh bone (see *femur,* illus.).

tro-che (trō′kē), *n.* a tablet or small round cake containing medicine.

tro-chee (trō′kē), *n.* a metrical foot of two syllables, the first long or accented and the second short or unaccented, as in "Art is long and time is fleeting."

trod (trŏd), past tense and archaic past participle of *tread:* **trodden,** past participle of *tread.*

trog-lo-dyte (trŏg′lō-dīt), *n.* **1,** a prehistoric cave man; **2,** an anthropoid, or manlike ape, such as the chimpanzee.—*adj.* **trog″lo-dyt′ic** (trŏg″lō-dĭt′ĭk).

tro-gon (trō′gŏn), *n.* any of a large family of tropical small birds having brilliant plumage and short bills.

Tro-i-lus (trō′ĭ-lŭs), *n.* **1,** in mythology, a son of Priam, slain by Achilles; **2,** in medieval romance, in Chaucer's "Troilus and Criseyde," and in Shakespeare's "Troilus and Cressida," the lover of Cressida.

Tro-jan (trō′jăn), *adj.* of or pertaining to the ancient city of Troy, in Asia Minor, or its inhabitants: **Trojan War,** the ten-year conflict between the Greeks and the Trojans to avenge the carrying off of Helen, wife of King Menelaus of Sparta:—*n.* **1,** an industrious and fearless person; as, he worked like a *Trojan;* **2,** an inhabitant of Troy.

¹troll (trōl), *v.t.* **1,** to sing the parts of, in succession; also, to carol lustily; as, to *troll* a song; **2,** to fish for, or in, by dragging a line from a boat:—*v.i.* **1,** to share in a round, or part song; also, to sing a song lustily or casually; **2,** to fish, as for pike, with a hook and line drawn along through the water:—*n.* **1,** a round, or part song; **2,** a reel on a fishing rod.—*n.* **troll′er.**—*n.* and *p.adj.* **troll′ing.**

²troll (trōl), *n.* in folk tales, a giant or, later, a dwarf, supposed to live in caves.

trol-ley (trŏl′ĭ), *n.* [*pl.* trolleys (-ĭz)], **1,** a kind of truck running on an overhead track and carrying a suspended load; as, the money-carrying *trolleys* in large stores; **2,** a grooved metal wheel traveling in contact with a live electric wire; as, the car stopped because the *trolley* was off the wire; **3,** in America, an electric car; **4,** in England, a small car, or truck: **trolley car,** a car moved by means of a trolley and an electric motor; street car: **trolley line, 1,** a system of electric cars; **2,** a route taken by an electric car: **trolley pole,** the metal pole on the roof of an electric car, having the trolley at its top, touching the wire. Also, **trol′ly** [*pl.* trollies (-ĭz)].

trol-lop (trŏl′ŭp), *n.* **1,** a careless, slovenly woman; **2,** a prostitute.

trom-bone (trŏm′bōn), *n.* a large brass instrument of the trumpet kind, able to produce the complete chromatic scale (cf. *musical instrument,* illus.).

TROMBONES
1, slide; 2, key.

troop (trōōp), *n.* **1,** a collection of people; a company; number; as, a *troop* of children going to school; **2,** in the Boy Scouts, a formation consisting of a certain number of patrols; **3,** the unit of cavalry formation, commanded by a captain; **4,** in *pl.,* armed forces; soldiers collectively:—*v.i.* **1,** to march in a body; **2,** to collect or move in crowds; **3,** to depart hastily.

troop-er (trōōp′ẽr), *n.* **1,** a cavalryman; **2,** his horse, or charger.

troop-ship (trōōp′shĭp″), *n.* a vessel carrying soldiers; a military transport.

trope (trōp), *n.* a figure of speech; a word or expression figuratively used; as, in the sentence, the wise man is a fox, the use of the word *fox* is a *trope.*

tro-phy (trō′fĭ), *n.* [*pl.* trophies (-fĭz)], **1,** anything kept in memory of a victory, as arms, flags, etc.; **2,** a memento of deeds, achievements, etc.; as, a *trophy* of the hunt; **3,** in ancient Greece and Rome, a monument or other memorial raised in celebration of a victory; **4,** a prize in a contest; as, a silver cup was the *trophy.*

trop-ic (trŏp′ĭk) *n.* **1,** either of the two imaginary circles around the earth parallel to the equator, at a distance of 23° 27′ north and south of it, called *tropic of Cancer* and *tropic of Capricorn* respectively, marking the limits of the torrid zone; **2,** in *pl.*, the region on the earth lying between these two circles:—*adj.* pertaining to the region between the tropics of Cancer and Capricorn.

trop-i-cal (trŏp′ĭ-kăl), *adj.* **1,** produced in, or situated within, the tropics; as, *tropical* fruit; **2,** used in a figurative sense; metaphorical.—*adv.* **trop′i-cal-ly.**

trot (trŏt), *n.* **1,** that gait of a horse by which it moves faster than at a walk, and in which the right forefoot moves with the left hind foot; **2,** a jogging gait; **3,** a brisk walk or run with short steps; **4,** *Slang*, a translation used in the study of a foreign language:—*v.i.* [*p.t.* and *p.p.* trot′ted, *p.pr.* trot′ting], **1,** to move faster than at a walk; **2,** to run with a jogging pace:—*v.t.* **1,** to cause to move faster than a walk; **2,** to jog on one's knee, as a child.

troth (trôth; trōth), *n.* **1,** faith or fidelity; **2,** truth to one's word; as, I pledge my *troth;* **3,** betrothal:—*v.t.* to pledge; betroth.

trot-ter (trŏt′ẽr), *n.* **1,** a trotting horse; **2,** the foot of an animal used for food; as, pigs' *trotters* or sheep's *trotters*.

trou-ba-dour (trōō′bȧ-dōōr), *n.* one of a class of French or Italian poets and singers of love songs, who flourished during the 11th, 12th, and 13th centuries.

trou-ble (trŭb′l), *n.* **1,** mental excitement, distress, or worry; **2,** that which causes such distress; **3,** inconvenience; exertion; pains; as, to take a great deal of *trouble;* **4,** illness; as, stomach *trouble:*—*v.t.* [*p.t.* and *p.p.* -bled (-ld), *p.pr.* -bling], **1,** to excite, distress, or worry; **2,** to cause inconvenience to; **3,** to stir up, as water:—*v.i.* to take pains.—*n.* **trou′bler.**

Syn., n. misfortune, calamity, disaster.

trou-ble-some (trŭb′l-sŭm), *adj.* causing distress, annoyance, or worry; disturbing; as, a *troublesome* child.—*adv.* **trou′ble-some-ly.**—*n.* **trou′ble-some-ness.**

Syn. irksome, laborious, painful.—*Ant.* pleasant, light, easy, helpful.

trou-blous (trŭb′lŭs), *adj.* disturbed; full of distress or annoyance; as, *troublous* times followed the war.

trough (trôf), *n.* **1,** a long, shallow vessel, as one for holding liquid or food for animals; **2,** anything hollowed out; any long channel; as, the *trough* between ocean waves.

trounce (trouns), *v.t.* [*p.t.* and *p.p.* trounced (trounst), *p.pr.* trounc′ing], to beat soundly; whip or flog.—*n.* **trounc′ing.**

troupe (trōōp), *n.* a company, as of actors or acrobats.

trou-sers (trou′zẽrz), *n.pl.* an outer garment worn by men and boys, covering the body from the waist to the knee or ankle, each leg being covered separately.

trous-seau (trōō″sō′), *n.* [*pl.* trousseaux (-sōz′)], a bride's outfit, such as clothes, jewelry, etc.

trout (trout), *n.* [*pl.* usually, trout], **1,** any of several species of medium-sized, fresh-water game fishes of the salmon family; **2,** any of various fishes resembling the trout.

tro-ver (trō′vẽr), *n.* an action at law to recover damages for goods wrongfully withheld or used by another.

trow (trō), *v.t.* and *v.i. Archaic,* **1,** to think; suppose; **2,** to believe.

trow-el (trou′ĕl), *n.* **1,** a flat implement or hand tool, as one used for spreading mortar; **2,** a gardener's tool for digging up or setting out small plants.

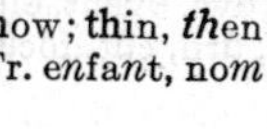

TROWEL (def. 2)

troy weight (troi), a system of weights with twelve ounces to the pound, used for gold, silver, etc.: distinguished from *avoirdupois weight* (see page 939).

tru-an-cy (trōō′ăn-sĭ), *n.* [*pl.* truancies (-sĭz)], the act or habit of staying away from work or duty, esp. of staying out of school without permission.

tru-ant (trōō′ănt), *n.* **1,** one who stays out of school without permission; **2,** one who remains away from any work or duty; a loafer:—*adj.* **1,** pertaining to, or like, a truant; **2,** idle; loafing.—*adv.* **tru′ant-ly.**

truce (trōōs), *n.* **1,** a temporary peace or stopping of war by agreement; an armistice; **2,** a brief cessation or pause; temporary respite.

[1]truck (trŭk), *v.t.* to give in exchange; rarely, to peddle:—*v.i.* to barter or exchange goods; bargain:—*n.* **1,** articles of commerce; **2,** the system of paying wages in commodities, not in money; **3,** in the U. S., fresh vegetables cultivated for sale; as, garden *truck;* **4,** *Colloq.*, useless articles or rubbish; belongings; also, dealings; intercourse.—*n.* **[1]truck′er.**

[2]truck (trŭk), *n.* **1,** orig., a strong, small wheel; **2,** a wheeled vehicle for carrying heavy loads; esp., a large motor vehicle for such a purpose; **3,** a strong frame or platform on wheels, as a sort of barrow used for carrying baggage in railroad stations; **4,** a set of wheels, or a frame mounted on wheels, to support one end of a locomotive, railroad car, etc.; **5,** a small wooden cap on the top of a flagpole or mast: usually fitted with holes for ropes or halyards:—*v.t.* to carry by means of a truck.—*n.* **[2]truck′er.**

truck-age (trŭk′ȧj), *n.* **1,** the transportation of goods by truck; **2,** the charge made for such transportation.

truck-le (trŭk′l), *n.* a trundle-bed:—*v.t.* [*p.t.* and *p.p.* -led (-ld), *p.pr.* -ling], to cause to move on rollers:—*v.i.* to yield submissively to another's will; as, to *truckle* to a lord.—*n.* **truck′ler.**

truck-le-bed (trŭk′l-bĕd″), *n.* a low bed on rollers, which may be rolled under a high bed: also called *trundle-bed.*

[1]truck-man (trŭk′măn), *n.* [*pl.* truckmen (-mĕn)], one who deals in fresh vegetables or raises them for sale.

[2]truck-man (trŭk′măn), *n.* [*pl.* truckmen (-mĕn)], one who drives a truck; one who transports goods by truck.

truc-u-lence (trŭk′ū-lĕns; trōō′kū-lĕns), *n.* ferocity; cruelty or fierceness; quarrelsomeness. Also, **truc′u-len-cy.**

truc-u-lent (trŭk′ū-lĕnt; trōō′kū-lĕnt), *adj.* **1,** fierce; savage; cruel; **2,** violent; rude; harsh.—*adv.* **truc′u-lent-ly.**

Syn. ferocious.—*Ant.* gentle, kind.

trudge (trŭj), *v.i.* [*p.t.* and *p.p.* trudged (trŭjd), *p.pr.* trudg′ing], to travel on foot, esp. with labor or fatigue; as, he *trudged* along through the woods.

trudg-en stroke (trŭj′ĕn), in swimming, a racing stroke having a double over-arm motion.

true (trōō), *adj.* **1,** in accord with fact or reality; not false; **2,** faithful or loyal; reliable; **3,** genuine; being what it seems to be; **4,** rightful; legitimate; as, the *true* heir; **5,** corresponding to a standard; correct; exact:—*adv.* **1,** in truth; **2,** accurately:—*n.* the condition of being accurate; as, the wall is out of *true.*—*n.* **true′ness.**

truf-fle (trŭf′l; trōōf′l; trōō′fl), *n.* any of various potato-shaped edible fungi that grow underground.

tru-ism (trōō′ĭzm), *n.* an old and accepted truth; also, a hackneyed truth.

Syn. adage, maxim, proverb, axiom.

tru-ly (trōō'lĭ), *adv.* **1**, in agreement with truth or fact; precisely; **2**, sincerely; honestly; as, *truly* spoken; **3**, in fact; indeed.

¹trump (trŭmp), *n. Archaic* or *Poetic*, a horn or trumpet:—*v.t.* to devise unfairly; fabricate, as an excuse: with *up*.

²trump (trŭmp), *n.* **1**, usually in *pl.*, in cards, the suit which temporarily outranks the other suits; also, any card of this suit; **2**, *Slang*, an admirable fellow; a person always to be depended upon:—*adj.* pertaining to the suit designated as trump:—*v.t.* in cards, to play a trump card on (a trick):—*v.i.* in cards, to play a trump card.

trump-er-y (trŭm'pẽr-ĭ), *n.* [*pl.* trumperies (-ĭz)], worthless finery; rubbish:—*adj.* **1**, having a showy appearance, but worthless; **2**, hence, deceiving or delusive.

trump-et (trŭm'pĕt), *n.* **1**, a metal wind instrument formed of a single curved tube with a flare at the end (see *musical instrument*, illus.); **2**, something resembling this instrument in sound or shape, as the cry of an elephant, or an instrument which helps the deaf to hear:—*v.t.* **1**, to publish by, or as by, the sound of such an instrument; noise abroad; **2**, to praise highly:—*v.i.* to utter a sound like that of a trumpet.

trump-et-er (trŭm'pĕt-ẽr), *n.* **1**, one who sounds a trumpet; one who proclaims or noises abroad; **2**, a kind of pigeon; **3**, a wild swan of North America; **4**, a large South American bird.

trun-cate (trŭng'kāt), *v.t.* [*p.t.* and *p.p.* -cat-ed, *p.pr.* -cat-ing], to lop or cut the top or end from; cut down:—*adj.* appearing as if cut squarely off (see *leaf*, illus.); having a top plane as if cut off evenly, or lacking an apex, as certain spiral shells or the tails of some birds.—*n.* **trun-ca'tion**.

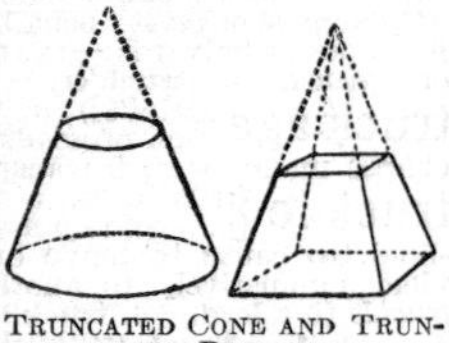

TRUNCATED CONE AND TRUNCATED PYRAMID

trun-cat-ed (trŭng'kāt-ĕd), *p.adj.* cut off squarely; as, a *truncated* cone or pyramid.

trun-cheon (trŭn'shŭn; trŭn'chŭn), *n.* **1**, a stout club or cudgel; **2**, a baton, or staff of authority.

trun-dle (trŭn'dl), *v.t.* and *v.i.* [*p.t.* and *p.p.* -dled (-dld), *p.pr.* -dling], to roll along; roll on small wheels:—*n.* **1**, a kind of low-wheeled truck; **2**, a small, wide wheel, like that in a caster; **3**, a kind of low bed.

trun-dle-bed (trŭn'dl=bĕd″), *n.* a low bed that runs on rollers, so that, when not in use, it may be rolled under a high bed: also called *truckle-bed.*

trunk (trŭngk), *n.* **1**, the upright stem, body, or stock of a tree; **2**, the body of an animal, not including the head and limbs; **3**, the most important part of anything which has branches or projections; **4**, an elephant's proboscis; **5**, a large box or chest to hold personal belongings, as for a journey; **6**, a boxlike shaft or conduit for the passage of air, water, etc.; **7**, in *pl.*, short, tight breeches reaching about half way to the knee: also called *trunk hose:*—*adj.* pertaining to a chief line; as, *trunk* lines of a railroad.

trun-nion (trŭn'yŭn), *n.* one of the two pivots or axles that support a cannon or other device.

truss (trŭs), *n.* **1**, a bandage or support for rupture; **2**, a measured mass of hay, straw, etc.; **3**, timbers or bars fastened together to form a framework for any structure:—*v.t.* **1**, to bind or fasten with skewers or string; as, to *truss* a chicken; **2**, to support by a brace, framework, or the like.

trust (trŭst), *n.* **1**, confidence; faith; belief in someone's goodness; **2**, expectation or hope; **3**, one who or that which is confided in; one who has an important duty committed to him; **4**, credit granted because of belief in one's honesty; as, he lent money on *trust;* **5**, a duty or responsibility; something given over to one's custody or care; **6**, a particular form of big business combination, whereby the stockholders of the constituent companies turn over control to a board of trustees; popularly, any combination of business men designed to create a large corporation with a view to restricting competition or developing a monopoly; **7**, a right or property, real or personal, held and managed by one party (the trustee) for the benefit of another; **8**, the responsibility or guardianship of such an estate:—*v.t.* **1**, to place confidence in; rely upon; **2**, to believe; **3**, to intrust to someone's care; place in someone's charge; confide to; **4**, to sell to on credit; **5**, to hope with confidence; as, I *trust* that all will be well:—*v.i.* **1**, to have confidence: with *in* or *on;* **2**, to hope:—*adj.* held in charge for someone else; as, a *trust* fund.—*n.* **trust'er.**—*adv.* **trust'ing-ly.**

trus-tee (trŭs-tē'), *n.* a person to whom property, or the management of property, is committed.—*n.* **trus-tee'ship.**

trust-ful (trŭst'fōōl), *adj.* full of hope and confidence; ready to believe in others.—*adv.* **trust'ful-ly.**—*n.* **trust'ful-ness.**

trust-wor-thy (trŭst'wûr″thĭ), *adj.* reliable; meriting trust and confidence.—*adv.* **trust'wor″thi-ly.**—*n.* **trust'wor″thi-ness.**

trust-y (trŭs'tĭ), *adj.* [*comp.* trust'i-er, *superl.* trust'i-est], worthy to receive confidence; faithful; reliable; as, a *trusty* servant:—*n.* a person to be trusted; esp., a convict found worthy of special privileges.—*adv.* **trust'i-ly.**—*n.* **trust'i-ness.**

truth (trōōth), *n.* **1**, the quality of being according to fact; veracity; sincerity; also, faithfulness; loyalty; **2**, correctness; accuracy or exactness; **3**, something real and actual; a fact; **4**, a general statement of something proved to be always the case; **5**, righteousness; godliness.

Syn. verity.—*Ant.* falsehood, untruth.

truth-ful (trōōth'fōōl), *adj.* **1**, according to facts; as, a *truthful* statement; **2**, given to saying only what is the fact; veracious.—*adv.* **truth'ful-ly.**—*n.* **truth'ful-ness.**

try (trī), *v.t.* [*p.t.* and *p.p.* tried (trīd), *p.pr.* try'ing], **1**, to put to a trial or experiment; test; **2**, to gain acquaintance with, by experience; experiment with; as, to *try* a new brand of coffee; **3**, to subject to trouble or affliction; as, a sorely *tried* people; **4**, to subject to strain; as, the light *tries* the eyes; **5**, to test the strength or endurance of; as, to *try* the patience; **6**, to decide by argument or contest; as, a question to be *tried* by war; **7**, to attempt; endeavor; **8**, to purify or refine; as, to *try* silver; **9**, to melt out or render, as fat: generally with *out;* **10**, in law: **a**, to examine into the guilt of, before a court; as, to *try* a prisoner; **b**, to act as judge at the trial of (a case):—*v.i.* to endeavor; make an effort: with *to* and an infinitive:—*n.* [*pl.* tries (trīz)], an attempt; effort; test.

try-ing (trī'ĭng), *p.adj.* annoying; hard to bear; difficult; severe.

try-out (trī'out″), *n.* a test or trial of fitness or qualities, as of an athlete.

try-sail (trī'sāl″; trī'sl), *n.* a fore-and-aft sail set suspended from a gaff and generally placed on the foremast or mainmast of a sailing vessel (see *rigging*, illus.).

try–square (trī′=skwâr″), *n.* a carpenter's tool for laying off right angles and testing the accuracy of square work.

TRY-SQUARE

tryst (trĭst; trīst), *n.* **1**, an engagement to meet at a certain place and time; **2**, a meeting; also, the place of meeting; as, a lovers' *tryst:* also called *trysting place.*

tsar (tsär), *n.* formerly, the emperor of Russia. Also, **tzar.** See **czar**, *Pfd. S.*

tsar-e-vitch (tsär′ē-vĭch), *n.* formerly, the eldest son and heir of the emperor of Russia.—Also, **tzar′e-vitch;** *Pfd. S.*, **czar′e-vitch.**

tsa-rev-na (tsä-rĕv′nȧ), *n.* formerly, a daughter of a czar. Also, **tza-rev′na;** *Pfd. S.*, **cza-rev′na.**

tsa-ri-na (tsä-rē′nȧ), *n.* formerly, an empress of Russia; also, the wife of an emperor of Russia. Also, **tza-ri′na;** *Pfd. S.*, **cza-ri′na.**

tset-se (tsĕt′sē), *n.* any of several species of small African fly.

T square a ruler having a crossbar at one end which serves as a guide, as in making parallel lines.

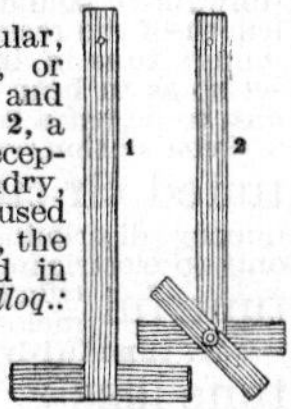

T SQUARES
1, fixed; 2, adjustable.

tub (tŭb), *n.* **1**, a circular, open, wooden vessel, or low cask, used for washing and other household purposes; **2**, a large, deep, stationary receptacle placed in a laundry, kitchen, or bathroom, and used for washing, bathing, etc.; **3**, the amount of anything held in such a receptacle; **4**, *Colloq.:* **a**, a bath; **b**, a very slow, clumsy boat:—*adj.* washable; as, *tub* silk:—*v.t.* [*p.t.* and *p.p.* tubbed (tŭbd), *p.pr.* tub′bing], to place, or wash, in a tub:—*v.i. Colloq.*, to take a bath in a tub.

tu-ba (tū′bȧ), *n.* a large, brass-wind instrument of the trumpet family.

Tu-bal–cain (tū′băl=kān″), *n.* in the Bible, traditionally, the first artificer and instructor in the art of working in brass and iron (Genesis 4:22).

tube (tūb), *n.* **1**, a hollow cylinder of glass, rubber, metal, or other material; as, a *tube* of paint; **2**, an instrument, or part of an instrument, that is cylindrical, or even conical, in shape, as of a wind instrument, telescope, gun, or the like; **3**, an underground passage for a railway; a subway; also, the underground railway; **4**, a sealed glass vessel containing a more or less perfect vacuum and usually provided with one or more electrodes: used for studying the electrical discharge in gases, for producing X rays, in radio, etc.: also called *vacuum tube* or, in radio, *electron tube:*—*v.t.* [*p.t.* and *p.p.* tubed (tūbd), *p.pr.* tub′ing], to put into, or furnish with, a cylinder or tunnel.—*adj.* **tub′al.**—*adj.* **tub′ate.**

tu-ber (tū′bẽr), *n.* **1**, a thick, roundish, often edible, underground stem bearing small buds or "eyes," as the potato; **2**, an edible fungus, or truffle.

tu-ber-cle (tū′bẽr-kl), *n.* **1**, a growth like a small knob, as on a bone or on the root of a plant; **2**, a nodule or small lump appearing on the skin, on a bone (see *tibia*, illus.), or in the soft tissues of the body; esp., one found in lungs affected by pulmonary tuberculosis, or consumption.

tu-ber-cu-lar (tū-bûr′kū-lȧr), *adj.* full of, like, or pertaining to, the small growths called tubercles; less correctly, affected with tuberculosis.

tu-ber-cu-lin (tū-bûr′kū-lĭn), *n.* a liquid preparation made from cultures of the bacilli of tuberculosis: used in treating tuberculosis, and, esp. in cattle, in testing for the existence of the disease.

tu-ber-cu-lo-sis (tū-bûr″kū-lō′sĭs), *n.* an infectious disease characterized by the growth of tubercles in the tissues of the body; esp., this disease affecting the lungs, commonly called *consumption.*

tu-ber-cu-lous (tū-bûr′kū-lŭs), *adj.* **1**, affected with, or pertaining to, tuberculosis; **2**, full of tubercles, or small unhealthy growths.

[1]**tube-rose** (tūb′rōz″; tū′bẽr-ōs″), *n.* a perennial, cultivated plant bearing a spike of fragrant, white flowers.

tu-ber-os-i-ty (tū″bẽr-ŏs′ĭ-tĭ), *n.* [*pl.* tuberosities (-tĭz)], **1**, the state of being covered with swellings; **2**, a knoblike swelling, as on a bone (see *tibia*, illus.).

tu-ber-ous (tū′bẽr-ŭs), *adj.* **1**, covered with knobs or swellings resembling warts; **2**, consisting of, or like, a tuber, as the potato (see *root*, illus.). Also, [2]**tu′ber-ose** (tū′bẽr-ōs).

tub-ing (tūb′ĭng), *n.* **1**, a piece of tube; **2**, cylindrical material for tubes; a number of tubes; **3**, the act of making tubes.

tu-bu-lar (tū′bū-lȧr), *adj.* pertaining to, shaped like, or consisting of, a hollow cylinder or pipe.

tu-bu-late (tū′bū-lāt), *adj.* **1**, having a tube, or hollow cylinder; **2**, shaped like a tube. Also, **tu′bu-lat″ed.**—*n.* **tu″bu-la′tion.**

tuck (tŭk), *n.* **1**, a sewed fold, as in a dress; **2**, *Slang*, things to eat, esp. sweetmeats:—*v.t.* **1**, to thrust or press into a small, compact space; as, to *tuck* a book into one's pocket; **2**, to gather or turn up, as sleeves or bed coverings; **3**, to make and sew folds in; as, to *tuck* a dress; **4**, to cover snugly; as, to *tuck* a child into bed:—*v.i.* to make tucks.

Tuck, Fri-ar in the Robin Hood legend, a jolly and corpulent friar.

tuck-a-hoe (tŭk′ȧ-hō), *n.* either of two American plants whose roots, when cooked, were formerly used by the Indians of Virginia as food.

tuck-er (tŭk′ẽr), *n.* **1**, a piece of lace, linen, or other thin material, folded across the front, or fastened into the neck, of a woman's dress; **2**, a machine for stitching folds into cloth:—*v.t. U. S. Colloq.*, to tire; as, the long march has *tuckered* him out.

-tude (-tūd), *n. suffix*, quality or state of being; as, servi*tude;* grati*tude.*

Tu-dor (tū′dŏr), *adj.* designating, or pertaining to, the royal house of England from 1485 to 1603, whose reigning members were Henry VII, Henry VIII, Edward VI, Mary, and Elizabeth:—*n.* a member of this family.

Tues-day (tūz′dā), *n.* the third day of the week; the day after Monday.—*abbr.* **Tu.; Tues.**

tu-fa (tōō′fȧ), *n.* **1**, soft or porous stone usually deposited from springs or streams; **2**, sometimes, a porous, volcanic rock: properly called *tuff.*—*adj.* **tu-fa′ceous.**

tuff (tŭf), *n.* **1**, a light, varicolored rock formed naturally of compacted volcanic dust and ash; **2**, sometimes, a porous limestone deposited by water: more properly called *travertine* or *tufa.*—*adj.* **tuff-a′ceous.**

tuft (tŭft), *n.* **1**, a knot or bunch of long, slender parts; as, a *tuft* of grass; **2**, a cluster or clump; as, a *tuft* of plants:—*v.t.* to divide into tufts; divide (upholstery) with depressions marked by tufts or buttons.

tuft-hunt-er (tŭft′hŭn″tẽr), *n.* one who courts or invites the acquaintance of persons of rank; a toady.—*n.* **tuft′hunt″ing.**

tug (tŭg), *n.* **1**, a pull with great effort; **2**, a steam towing vessel; **3**, a rope or chain used for pulling; esp., the trace of a harness: **tug of war,** a contest in which two groups of persons pull on a rope against each other:—*v.t.* [*p.t.* and *p.p.* tugged (tŭgd), *p.pr.* tug′ging], to pull or draw with great effort; tow:—*v.i.* to use great effort in pulling; also, to struggle; exert oneself.—*n.* **tug′ger.**

tuille (twēl), *n.* a steel plate attached below the tasset (see *armor*, illus.), to protect the thigh.

tu-i-tion (tū̇-ĭsh′ŭn), *n.* **1**, instruction; teaching; **2**, the charge for instruction.—*adj.* **tu-i′tion-al.**

tu-lip (tū′lĭp), *n.* a plant of the lily family, bearing brilliant flowers in spring; also, its bulb or flower (see *inflorescence*, illus.).

tu-lip tree **1**, an American tree of the magnolia family, having greenish yellow flowers resembling the tulip; **2**, any of several other trees with tuliplike blossoms.

tulle (tōōl; *Fr.* tül), *n.* a delicate silk netlike material, used for veils, scarfs, etc.

tum-ble (tŭm′bl), *v.i.* [*p.t.* and *p.p.* -bled (-bld), *p.pr.* -bling], **1**, to fall suddenly and hard; as, to *tumble* downstairs; **2**, to roll about; **3**, to execute gymnastic feats, such as springs, somersaults, etc.; **4**, to move in a disorderly fashion; as, the children *tumbled* into the room:—*v.t.* **1**, to throw down; **2**, to turn over and over; **3**, to rumple; disorder:—*n.* **1**, a fall; **2**, a rolling over; **3**, a state of confusion.

tum-ble-bug (tŭm′bl-bŭg″), *n.* any of certain beetles which roll up balls of dung and use them as places in which to deposit their eggs.

tum-bler (tŭm′blẽr), *n.* **1**, one who performs feats of rolling, somersaulting, or the like, as on mats; an acrobat; **2**, a drinking glass with straight sides, but without a stem: orig. made with round or pointed bottom; also, the contents of such a glass; **3**, a part of a lock that must be put in a certain position, generally by the key, before the bolt can be moved; **4**, a child's toy weighted so that it will rock about but not fall over; **5**, a kind of pigeon which, when flying, turns somersaults in the air: also called *tumbler pigeon;* **6**, in a firearm, a part of the lock against which the mainspring acts; **7**, a kind of greyhound, formerly used in hunting rabbits; **8**, *Scot.*, a porpoise.

tum-ble-weed (tŭm′bl-wēd″), *n.* any of certain weeds, common on the prairies of the U. S., which, in the fall, break loose and blow about in the wind.

tum-brel (tŭm′brĕl), *n.* **1**, a rude cart that may be tilted up; **2**, such a cart used in the French Revolution to take prisoners to the guillotine; **3**, in the army, a kind of two-wheeled, covered cart for hauling tools, ammunition, etc. Also, **tum′bril.**

tu-me-fac-tion (tū″mē-făk′shŭn), *n.* a swelling; tumor.

tu-me-fy (tū′mē-fī), *v.t.* and *v.i.* [*p.t.* and *p.p.* -fied (-fīd), *p.pr.* -fy″ing], to inflate; puff up; swell.

tu-mid (tū′mĭd), *adj.* **1**, bulging; swollen; **2**, full of high-sounding words.—*adv.* **tu′mid-ly.**—*n.* **tu′mid-ness.**—*n.* **tu-mid′i-ty.**

tu-mor (tū′mẽr), *n.* an abnormal swelling or growth within or upon the body. Also, **tu′mour.**

tu-mult (tū′mŭlt), *n.* **1**, the noise and confusion made by a number of excited people; **2**, any violent agitation.

Syn. uproar, turbulence. (See noise.)

tu-mul-tu-ous (tū̇-mŭl′tū̇-ŭs), *adj.* **1**, marked by, or full of, noisy confusion; disorderly; **2**, agitated, as the feelings; **3**, rough, as a sea.—*adv.* **tu-mul′tu-ous-ly.**—*n.* **tu-mul′tu-ous-ness.**

Syn. turbulent, riotous, boisterous.

tu-mu-lus (tū′mū̇-lŭs), *n.* [*pl.* tumuli (-lī)], a hill or mound artificially built; esp., one over a grave.

tun (tŭn), *n.* **1**, a large cask; **2**, a measure of wine formerly equal to 252 gallons.

tun-dra (tōōn′drȧ), *n.* a stretch of mossy, marshy, flat land in northern Siberia or the arctics.

tune (tūn), *n.* **1**, a series of musical tones having rhythm and melody and forming a complete theme; air; melody; **2**, the condition of giving forth tones of the proper pitch; as, the piano is in *tune;* **3**, agreement in respect to musical sounds; as, the violins are in *tune;* **4**, state of harmonious adjustment; fitting mood; as, to be in *tune* with one's friends:—*v.t.* [*p.t.* and *p.p.* tuned (tūnd), *p.pr.* tun′ing], **1**, to cause to produce the proper sounds; adjust (a voice or instrument) to a correct musical pitch; **2**, to utter or express in a musical manner; **3**, to put in harmony or agreement with; **4**, in radio, to adjust (a receiver or transmitter) to a certain wave length or frequency: **tune out,** in radio, to eliminate (unwanted sounds) by adjusting the wave length of the receiving set:—*v.i.* to be in harmony: **tune in,** in radio, to adjust a receiving set so as to hear from a given station: **tune out,** to adjust a receiving set so as to exclude a given station.—*adj.* **tun′a-ble.**

tuned cir-cuit in radio, a circuit which has the property of frequency discrimination, adjusted to respond only to electric impulses of a given frequency.

tune-ful (tūn′fŏŏl), *adj.* full of music or melody; musical; harmonious.—*adv.* **tune′ful-ly.**—*n.* **tune′ful-ness.**

tune-less (tūn′lĕs), *adj.* **1**, without harmony; without melody; hence, sometimes, monotonous; **2**, not producing music; silent; as, a *tuneless* lyre.—*adv.* **tune′less-ly.**—*n.* **tune′less-ness.**

tun-er (tūn′ẽr), *n.* **1**, one who adjusts musical instruments to their proper pitch; as, a piano *tuner;* **2**, in radio, a device for adjusting a receiver or transmitter to a given wave length or frequency.

tung-sten (tŭng′stĕn), *n.* a heavy, hard, brittle, grayish white metallic element, much used in making filaments for electric lamps.

tu-nic (tū′nĭk), *n.* **1**, an undergarment worn by both the men and women in ancient Greece and Rome; **2**, as a modern garment, a loose outside blouse of varying length; **3**, a kind of military coat.

tu-ni-cate (tū′nĭ-kāt), *adj.* (also, *tunicated*), having a natural covering membrane:—*n.* any of certain small, saclike, marine animals characterized by a leathery enveloping tunic.

tun-ing coil in radio, a coil of insulated wire forming an inductance for tuning; a receiving or transmitting set.

tun-ing fork in music, a fork-shaped piece of steel with two equal prongs which, when struck, vibrate at a certain rate so as to give a fixed tone: used to establish or test the pitch of tones and of musical instruments.

tun-nage (tŭn′ĭj), *n.* **1**, the weight of a ship's cargo; **2**, the carrying capacity of a ship; **3**, a toll on vessels. See **ton′nage,** *Pfd. S.*

tun-nel (tŭn′ĕl), *n.* **1**, an underground passage cut through a hill or under a river; as, a railroad *tunnel;* **2**, the shaft of a chimney:—*v.t.* to form an underground passage through or under; as, to *tunnel* a rock:—*v.i.* to make a tunnel.—*n.* **tun'nel-er; tun'nel-ler.**

tun-ny (tŭn'ĭ), *n.* [*pl.* tunnies (-ĭz)], any of various large salt-water fishes of the mackerel family.

tu-pe-lo (tū'pē-lō), *n.* [*pl.* tupelos (-lōz)], any of various North American gum trees with blue-black berries and hard, close-grained wood.

tuque (tūk), *n.* a cap shaped like a long bag tapering at both ends, and worn with one end tucked inside the other: worn in Canada as part of a winter sport costume.

Tu-ra-ni-an (tū-rā'nĭ-ăn), *adj.* pertaining to, or denoting, those languages and peoples of Europe and Asia not included in the Aryan and Semitic families, as Chinese.

tur-ban (tûr'băn), *n.* **1**, the men's headdress worn by Orientals, consisting of a cap around which a scarf or sash is wrapped; **2**, any similar headdress, as the bandanna sometimes worn by negro women; **3**, a small, close-fitting hat, either brimless or with a closely turned-up brim, worn by women and children.—*adj.* **tur'baned.**

tur-bid (tûr'bĭd), *adj.* **1**, having the sediment stirred up; hence, muddy; impure; thick; as, *turbid* waters; **2**, unsettled; confused.—*adv.* **tur'bid-ly.**—*n.* **tur'bid-ness.**—*n.* **tur-bid'i-ty.**

tur-bi-nal (tûr'bĭ-năl), *adj.* in zoölogy, shaped like a spiral; rolled in a spiral-shaped coil.

tur-bi-nate (tûr'bĭ-nāt), *adj.* **1**, whirling like a top; **2**, in botany and zoölogy, having the shape of a top, as some shells; **3**, in anatomy, shaped like a spiral; rolled in a coil:—*n.* a turbinate bone. Also, *adj.* **tur'bi-nat"ed.**—*n.* **tur"bi-na'tion.**

tur-bine (tûr'bĭn; tûr'bīn), *n.* a form of motor in which the power is derived from water or steam driven against curved vanes or cups on the rim of a wheel (cf. *hydraulic*, illus.).

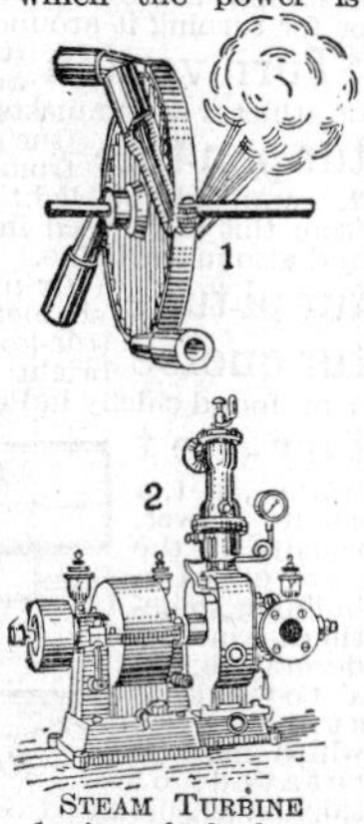

STEAM TURBINE
1, view of wheel
2, complete machine

tur-bot (tûr'bŏt), *n.* any of various flounders; esp., a large European fish greatly valued as food.

tur-bu-lence (tûr'bū-lĕns), *n.* a state of disturbance; disorder; noisy agitation. Also, **tur'bu-len-cy.**

tur-bu-lent (tûr'bū-lĕnt), *adj.* **1**, disorderly; uncontrollable; as a *turbulent* nature; **2**, agitated; wild; as, a *turbulent* stream; **3**, restless; noisy; riotous; as, a *turbulent* crowd.—*adv.* **tur'bu-lent-ly.**

tu-reen (tū-rēn'), *n.* a deep, covered dish, as for soup.

turf (tûrf), *n.* **1**, the grassy surface of ground; sod; **2**, peat: **the turf**, **1**, the race course; **2**, horse racing:—*v.t.* to cover with grassy sod.

turf-man (tûrf'măn), *n.* [*pl.* turfmen (-mĕn)], one who is interested in horses and horse racing.

turf-y (tûr'fĭ), *adj.* [*comp.* turf'i-er, *superl.* turf'i-est], having a grassy surface; well-sodded.—*n.* **turf'i-ness.**

tur-ges-cent (tûr-jĕs'ĕnt), *adj.* swelling; becoming unnaturally distended.—*n.* **tur-ges'cence; tur-ges'cen-cy.**

tur-gid (tûr'jĭd), *adj.* **1**, swollen beyond the natural size; bloated; as, a *turgid* stream of water; *turgid* veins; **2**, bombastic; pompous; as, a *turgid* style in writing.—*adv.* **tur'gid-ly.**—*n.* **tur'gid-ness.**—*n.* **tur-gid'i-ty.**

Turk (tûrk), *n.* **1**, a native of Turkey; **2**, any member of the race from which the Ottomans are descended; **3**, loosely, a Mohammedan, esp. one dwelling in Turkey.

tur-key (tûr'kĭ), *n.* [*pl.* turkeys (-kĭz)], a large, wild or domestic American bird of the pheasant family, used as food.

TURKEYS: A, domestic; B, wild.

tur-key buz-zard a large, glossy, black and brown carrion-eating vulture found in South America and the southern U. S.: also called *turkey vulture.*

Tur-key red **1**, a very bright red coloring matter; also, the color; **2**, cotton cloth colored with this red.

Turk-ic (tûr'kĭk), *adj.* **1**, pertaining to a group of Ural-Altaic peoples, such as the Turks and Cossacks, or to their language; **2**, loosely, Turkish.

Turk-ish (tûr'kĭsh), *adj.* pertaining to Turkey or the Turks; as, the *Turkish* empire; *Turkish* customs: **Turkish bath**, a kind of bath in which the bather is made to perspire freely in a highly heated room, and is then washed and rubbed down:—*n.* the language of the Turks.

Tur-ko-man (tûr'kō-măn), *n.* [*pl.* Turkomans (-mănz)], a member of any one of various Turkish tribes, chiefly nomadic, in Afghanistan and Turkestan. Also, **Tur'co-man.**

tur-ma-line (tûr'mȧ-lĭn), *n.* a semiprecious mineral, usually colored. See **tour'ma-line**, *Pfd. S.*

tur-mer-ic (tûr'mẽr-ĭk), *n.* **1**, an East Indian plant or its aromatic rootstock, used as a yellow dye and as a condiment, particularly in curry powder; **2**, any of several other plants with colored juices.

tur-moil (tûr'moil), *n.* confused movement; disturbance; agitation.

turn (tûrn), *v.t.* **1**, to make to revolve or go round, as a wheel; hence, to revolve in the mind or ponder: often with *over;* **2**, to do or perform by means of a revolving motion; as, to *turn* a somersault; **3**, to give a circular shape to, by revolving against a sharp edge, as in a lathe; **4**, figuratively, to fashion or mold; as, to *turn* a delicate compliment; **5**, to change the direction, attitude, or position of; as, to *turn* an automobile; to *turn* one's attention; **6**, figuratively, to unsettle or upset; as, to *turn* one's stomach; praise *turned* his head; **7**, to change from one state or form to another; as, to *turn* cream into butter; **8**, to translate; as, to *turn* English into Latin; **9**, to cause to be in a certain position, state, or condition; as, joy *turned* her faint; **10**, to cause to go; send: with *out, in, away, back;* as, to *turn* the cows out; to *turn* in a report; **11**, to move to the other side of; go around; as, to *turn* a corner; **12**, to apply to a particular purpose; convert; as, to *turn* the room into a library; **13**, to invert; reverse; as, to *turn* a coat: **turn down**, *Colloq.*, **1**, to snub; reject; **2**, to decline, as an offer:—*v.i.* **1**, to have a circular motion; revolve; rotate; **2**, to depend; hinge; as, my action *turns* on yours; **3**, to change in direction, attitude, or position; as, the tides *turn;* **4**, figuratively, to become unsettled or upset; as, my stomach *turns* at the very thought; my head *turns;* **5**, to change one's attitude or course of action; as, my friend *turned* against me; **6**, to change in condition; change to any stated condition; as, the milk *turned* during the night; the cream *turned* sour; **7**, to change in form: usually with *to* or *into;* as, the cider *turned* to vinegar; **8**, to direct the attention and efforts (to something); as, to *turn* to farming: **turn in**, *Colloq.*, to go to bed: **turn out**, **1**, to result; **2**, to prove to be; show itself; as, it *turned out* worthless; **3**, to come out, as to a meeting; as, few *turned out* to greet him: **turn up**, **1**, to happen; develop; **2**, to put in an appearance; be found; as, he *turned up* yesterday:—*n.* **1**, the act of revolving; circular motion, as of a wheel; also, a single revolution or twisting; as, a *turn* of the rope about the post; **2**, a change of direction; also, the point where change of direction occurs; a bend or curve; as, a *turn* in the road; **3**, a short promenade for exercise; as, a *turn* in the park; **4**, a deed or act; as, to do a good *turn;* **5**, the time for some act which one does in rotation with others; as, it is your *turn* to sing; **6**, a special purpose or occasion; as, this will not serve your *turn;* **7**, a change in condition, as in the progress of a disease; **8**, tendency; bent; as, he has a *turn* for engineering; **9**, a particular cast of mind, thought, or the like; inclination; bent; as, a man of his *turn* of mind; **10**, a short piece or act on the stage; **11**, in music, an embellishment consisting of four notes played or sung rapidly in the following order: the major or minor tone above a given tone, the main tone, the tone immediately below, and the main tone; also, the sign [~] indicating it; **12**, *Colloq.*, a startling surprise or shock; as, the news gave him a *turn:* **in turn**, in proper sequence.

turn-buck-le (tûrn'bŭk″l), *n.* **1**, a kind of catch to hold a window shutter; **2**, a metal loop which can be turned, by means of a swivel and a screw, so as to tighten a rod, stay, or the like.

turn-coat (tûrn'kōt″), *n.* one who forsakes his principles; one who goes over to an opposite party; a deserter.

turn-down (tûrn'doun″), *adj.* intended to have the upper part folded down; as, a *turndown* collar.

turn-er (tûr'nẽr), *n.* **1**, one who or that which turns; as, a pancake *turner;* **2**, one who shapes articles with a lathe; **3**, a kind of tumbler pigeon.

turn-ing (tûr'nĭng), *n.* **1**, the act of one who or that which revolves, shapes, etc.; **2**, an angle or corner: **turning point**, a critical or decisive moment.

tur-nip (tûr'nĭp), *n.* **1**, a green-leaved plant of the mustard family, having an edible root; **2**, the root itself.

turn-key (tûrn'kē″), *n.* [*pl.* turnkeys (-kēz″)], one who has charge of the keys of a prison or penitentiary; a warden.

turn-out (tûrn'out″), *n.* **1**, a coming forth; **2**, a railroad siding; **3**, *Colloq.:* **a**, a public gathering of persons, or attendance at a meeting; **b**, in England, a labor strike; **c**, a carriage and horses.

turn-o-ver (tûrn'ō″vẽr), *n.* **1**, the act or result of going round, upsetting, reversing position, or the like; an upset; **2**, a pie or tart made semicircular by folding one half of the crust over the other half and the filling; **3**, in commerce: **a**, the act or process of getting back invested money; **b**, of money, the number of times in a given period that a sum invested in a business is returned by the business for reinvestment; **c**, hence, the amount of business done in a specified period, usually a year:—*adj.* **1**, capable of being bent over or under; **2**, made with a part folded over; as, a *turnover* collar.

turn-pike (tûrn'pīk″), *n.* **1**, a gate or bar to stop wagons, carriages, etc., until toll is paid; tollgate; **2**, a road having tollgates; **3**, loosely, a main highway: also called *turnpike road; pike.*

turn-sole (tûrn'sōl″), *n.* any of several plants whose flowers and stems seem to turn with the sun, as the sunflower.

turn-spit (tûrn'spĭt″), *n.* **1**, one who turns a spit, or slender, pointed rod for holding roasting meat; **2**, a dog of a breed trained to turn a spit by means of a treadmill.

turn-stile (tûrn'stīl″), *n.* **1**, formerly, a gate at the entrance of a path or passage, made of four arms pivoted on the top of a post and turning to let a person through; **2**, a similar but more complicated device, as at a doorway, to regulate or record the number of persons passing through.

turn-stone (tûrn'stōn″), *n.* either of two species of ploverlike shore birds, which turn over stones in seeking food.

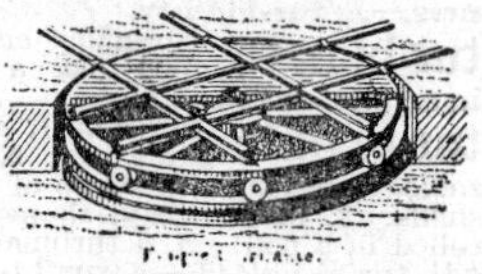

RAILROAD TURNTABLE

turn-ta-ble (tûrn'tā″bl), *n.* a circular platform that may be revolved, as for switching a locomotive on to another track or for turning it around.

***Turn-ver-ein** (tōōrn'fẽr-īn″), [Ger.], *n.* an association, or club, of athletes or gymnasts.

tur-pen-tine (tûr'pĕn-tīn), *n.* **1**, the sap from pine and fir trees; **2**, commonly, a light-colored fluid distilled from this sap: used in paints and varnishes, and also in medicine.

tur-pi-tude (tûr'pĭ-tūd), *n.* baseness; shameful wickedness.

tur-quoise (tŭr-koiz'; tûr'kwoiz), *n.* a bright blue or greenish blue gem: found chiefly in Persia. Also, **tur-quois'.**

NAVAL GUN TURRET

tur-ret (tŭr'ĕt), *n.* **1**, a small tower, usually at the corner of a building, sometimes merely decorative; **2**, a towerlike structure, which may be rotated, of thick steel, mounted on battleships or in fortifications, and containing heavy guns.

tur-ret-ed (tŭr'ĕt-ĕd), *adj.* **1**, furnished with, or shaped like, a small tower; **2**, having, or forming, a high, conelike spiral, as some shells.

tur-tle (tûr'tl), *n.* a reptile whose body is inclosed in a bony shell covered with horny shields; tortoise (see illus. next page).

tur-tle-dove (tûr'tl-dŭv″), *n.* any of several Old World doves, noted for their gentleness and their soft cooing.

Tus-can (tŭs′kăn), *adj.* **1**, pertaining to Tuscany, in Italy; **2**, designating a certain type of architecture, most clearly seen in the column (see *column*, illus.):—*n.* **1**, a native of Tuscany; **2**, the Tuscan dialect, considered the purest form of Italian.

Tus-ca-ro-ra (tŭs″kȧ-rō′rȧ), *n.* one of a tribe of Indians of Iroquoian stock, formerly living in the region which is now the state of North Carolina, but migrating north in the early 18th century to join the Iroquois Confederacy.

TURTLE

¹tush (tŭsh), *interj.* an expression of contempt, reproof, or restraint.

²tush (tŭsh), *n.* **1**, a tusk; **2**, a horse's canine tooth.

tusk (tŭsk), *n.* **1**, the long, pointed tooth on each side of the upper jaw of certain animals; as, the *tusk* of an elephant; **2**, hence, any very long tooth.

tus-sle (tŭs′l), *n.* a scuffle, usually in sport:—*v.i.* [*p.t.* and *p.p.* -sled (-ld), *p.pr.* -sling], to struggle, as in sport.

tus-sock (tŭs′ŭk), *n.* a tuft or hummock of grass, twigs, etc.

tus-sock moth any of numerous moths whose caterpillars are covered with tufts of hair, as the gypsy moth.

tut (tŭt), *interj.* hush! be quiet! an expression of rebuke, impatience, etc.

tu-te-lage (tū′tē-lāj), *n.* **1**, the act of teaching or acting as guardian for someone; protection; **2**, the state of being under a tutor or guardian.

tu-te-lar (tū′tē-lẽr), *adj.* **1**, acting as guardian; protecting; **2**, pertaining to a guardian or tutor. Also, **tu′te-la-ry.**

tu-tor (tū′tẽr), *n.* **1**, one who instructs another; **2**, a private teacher; **3**, formerly, in the U. S., a college instructor, or assistant, with disciplinary duties:—*v.t.* to instruct or teach privately:—*v.i.* **1**, to do the work of a tutor; **2**, *Colloq.*, to be taught privately.—*adj.* **tu-to′ri-al.**—*n.* **tu′tor-ship.**

tut-ti–frut-ti (to͞ot′tē=fro͞ot′tē), *n.* a flavoring or confection made of different kinds of preserved fruits:—*adj.* made with, or flavored by, preserved fruits.

tux-e-do (tŭk-sē′dō), *n.* in the U. S., a man's dinner jacket, less formal than a full-dress coat. Also, **Tux-e′do.**

twad-dle (twŏd′l), *n.* silly talk:—*v.t.* and *v.i.* [*p.t.* and *p.p.* -dled (-ld), *p.pr.* -dling], to talk in a silly or foolish manner.—*n.* **twad′dler.**

twain (twān), *adj. Poetic* or *Archaic*, two:—*n. Poetic*, a pair.

twang (twăng), *n.* **1**, a sharp, quick, vibrating sound; **2**, a sharp nasal tone in speech; as, a Yankee *twang:*—*v.t.* and *v.i.* to sound or speak with a twang.

tweak (twēk), *v.t.* to pinch or twist with a jerk:—*n.* a sudden, sharp pull or pinch; twitch; twist.

tweed (twēd), *n.* a twilled fabric, usually woolen, of two or more colors.

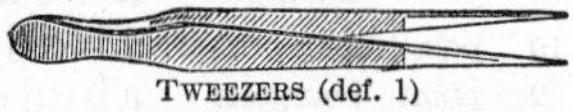
TWEEZERS (def. 1)

tweez-ers (twēz′ẽrz), *n.pl.* **1**, a small instrument for taking hold of, or pulling out, something tiny, as a hair; a tool used for grasping something; **2**, (also, *n. sing.*, *tweeze*,), a case of surgeon's instruments.

twelfth (twĕlfth), *adj.* next in order after eleventh: the ordinal of *twelve:*—*n.* **1**, one of twelve equal parts; **2**, in music, an interval of an octave and a fifth.

Twelfth–night (twĕlfth′=nīt″), *n.* the evening before Epiphany, the twelfth day after Christmas.

twelve (twĕlv), *adj.* composed of one more than eleven:—*n.* **1**, the number consisting of eleven plus one; a dozen; **2**, a sign representing twelve units, as 12 or xii: **the Twelve**, the twelve apostles, Christ's original disciples.

twelve-mo (twĕlv′mō), *n.* [*pl.* twelvemos (-mōz)], a book having the sheet folded into twelve leaves; also, a sheet so folded; duodecimo: also written *12mo:*—*adj.* having twelve leaves to a sheet.

twelve-month (twĕlv′mŭnth″), *n.* a year of twelve calendar months:—*adv.* a year hence or a year ago.

twen-ty (twĕn′tĭ), *adj.* composed of one more than nineteen: also used indefinitely; as, I told him *twenty* times not to go:—*n.* [*pl.* twenties (-tĭz)], **1**, the number consisting of nineteen plus one; a score; **2**, a sign representing twenty units, as 20 or **xx.**—*adj.* and *n.* **twen′ti-eth.**

twi- (twī-), a prefix meaning two; double; as, *twi*light; *twi*bil.

twi-bil (twī′bĭl″), *n.* **1**, formerly, a double-bladed battle-ax; **2**, an axlike garden tool.

twice (twīs), *adv.* **1**, two times; **2**, doubly; in twofold measure or degree.

twid-dle (twĭd′l), *v.t.* [*p.t.* and *p.p.* -dled (-ld), *p.pr.* -dling], to twirl in a light manner; as, to *twiddle* one's thumbs:—*v.i.* to play or trifle.

twig (twĭg), *n.* a small shoot or branch of a tree.—*adj.* **twigged.**

twi-light (twī′līt″), *n.* **1**, the faint light before sunrise and after sunset; **2**, partial light; dimness; obscurity: **Twilight of the Gods**, in Teutonic mythology, the final destruction in the conflict of the gods and the powers of the underworld: also called *Götterdämmerung* and *Ragnarok:*—*adj.* **1**, pertaining to the time before sunrise or after sunset; **2**, dim; obscure.

twill (twĭl), *n.* **1**, a weave of cloth which shows diagonal lines or ribs on the surface; **2**, a fabric so woven, as serge;—*v.t.* to weave, as a fabric, with diagonal lines or ribs.

twin (twĭn), *adj.* **1**, made of two separate, but equal, parts; double; as, *twin* towers; **2**, very like each other; **3**, born at the same birth with another; as, a *twin* brother:—*n.* **1**, one of two born at one birth; **2**, a person or thing very like another: **the Twins, 1**, Gemini, a northern zodiacal constellation; also, its two brightest stars, Castor and Pollux; **2**, the third sign of the zodiac (see *zodiac*, illus.).

twine (twīn), *v.t.* [*p.t.* and *p.p.* twined (twīnd), *p.pr.* twin′ing], **1**, to twist; **2**, to wind; encircle; as, to *twine* ribbons around a pole; to *twine* a pole with ribbons; **3**, to make by twisting or coiling; as, to *twine* a garland:—*v.i.* **1**, to twist; **2**, to wind or coil; as, the vine *twines* over the porch:—*n.* **1**, a kind of strong cord made of twisted strands; **2**, an entwining.—*n.* **twin′er.**

twinge (twĭnj), *v.i.* [*p.t.* and *p.p.* twinged (twĭnjd), *p.pr.* twing′ing], to feel a sudden, darting or stinging pain:—*v.t.* to cause to feel a sudden, sharp, stinging pain:—*n.* a sudden, stinging or darting pain.

twin-kle (twĭng′kl), *n.* **1**, a quick motion of the eye, as a wink; **2**, a flash or sparkle, as of the eye or a star; **3**, the time occupied by a wink; a moment:—*v.i.* [*p.t.* and *p.p.* -kled (-kld), *p.pr.* -kling], **1**, to open and shut rapidly; wink: said of the eyelids; **2**, to shine with a gleam that comes and goes in flashes, as a star; hence, to sparkle, as the eyes; **3**, to flash in and out rapidly, as the feet in dancing:—*v.t.* **1**, to blink, as the eyelids; **2**, to give out in quick flashes, as beams.

twin-kling (twĭng′klĭng), *n.* **1**, the time occupied by a wink or a brief flash; a moment; as, in the *twinkling* of an eye; **2**, a wink or flash, as of light.

twirl (twûrl), *v.t.* to move or turn around rapidly, as with the hand; whirl; as, to *twirl* a cane:—*v.i.* to rotate rapidly:—*n.* **1**, a quick, circular motion; **2**, a coil; twist; curl.

twist (twĭst), *v.t.* and *v.i.* **1**, to unite or form by twisting two or more strands together; **2**, to contort; distort; **3**, to wreathe; twine or wind, as hair into a knot; **4**, to wrench or turn; as, to *twist* one's wrist; **5**, to turn from a direct line; as, the path *twists* in and out:—*n.* **1**, the act or manner of winding or twining; **2**, something made by winding strands together, as certain kinds of silk or cotton thread; as, buttonhole *twist;* **3**, tobacco in a twisted roll; **4**, a long, rolled loaf of bread; **5**, a wrench, as of a muscle; **6**, in cattle, the back part of the hind leg where the direction of the hair changes: **twist drill**, a drill or bit cut with deep spiral grooves along its body to carry out the chips (see [1]*drill*, illus.).—*n.* **twist′er.**

twit (twĭt), *v.t.* [*p.t.* and *p.p.* twit′ted, *p.pr.* twit′ting], to annoy or tease by reminding of a mistake, weakness, etc.

twitch (twĭch), *v.t.* to pull with a sudden jerk:—*v.i.* to move jerkily:—*n.* **1**, a sudden jerk or pull; **2**, a short, jerky contraction of a muscle.

twit-ter (twĭt′ẽr), *v.i.* **1**, to utter in repetition small, sharp, broken sounds, as does a bird; **2**, *Dial.*, to feel a slight nervous excitement or tremor:—*v.t.* to utter in short, broken sounds:—*n.* **1**, a series of short, broken sounds; **2**, a nervous trembling.

'twixt (twĭkst), *prep. Poetic* or *Dial.*, between; betwixt.

two (to͞o), *adj.* composed of one added to one:—*n.* [*pl.* twos (to͞oz)], **1**, the number consisting of one plus one; **2**, a sign representing two units, as 2 or ii.

two–edged (to͞o′=ĕjd″; to͞o′=ĕj″ĕd), *adj.* having two edges, or one edge on each side; as, a *two-edged* saw.

two-fold (to͞o′fōld″), *adj.* double; made of two:—*adv.* doubly.

two–hand-ed (to͞o′=hănd″ĕd), *adj.* **1**, having two hands; **2**, used with two hands; **3**, able to use either hand with equal ease; ambidextrous.

two-pence (tŭp′ĕns; when used as two words, to͞o pĕns), *n.* **1**, the sum of two English pennies; **2**, a coin worth that amount of money.

two-pen-ny (tŭp′ĕn-ĭ), *adj.* **1**, of the value of two pence; **2**, hence, cheap, worthless, or commonplace.

two–ply (to͞o′=plī″), *adj.* **1**, having two thicknesses, strands, etc.; **2**, woven double, as a carpet or other fabric.

two-some (to͞o′sŭm), *adj.* **1**, performed, or taken part in, by two persons, as a game or dance; **2**, making a pair:—*n.* a game, dance, or the like, by two persons.

two–step (to͞o′=stĕp″), *n.* **1**, a kind of round dance in march or two-four time; **2**, the music for such a dance.

[1]**-ty** (-tĭ), *n. suffix*, forming abstract nouns denoting quality, state, or condition; as, pie*ty;* loyal*ty.*

[2]**-ty** (-tĭ), *suffix*, times ten: a termination of numerals; as, thir*ty;* six*ty.*

ty-coon (tī-ko͞on′), *n.* the shogun, or commander in chief of the Japanese army, till 1868, the military governor of the nation: the title given by foreigners.—*Colloq., U. S.* a prominent financier or industrialist.

tym-pan (tĭm′păn), *n.* in a printing press, a sheet of paper stretched under the paper to be printed: used as a cushion to equalize pressure.

tym-pa-num (tĭm′pȧ-nŭm), *n.* [*pl.* tympanums (-nŭmz); tympana (-nȧ)], **1**, in anatomy: **a**, the middle ear; **b**, the thin membrane dividing the outer from the middle ear: also called *tympanic membrane;* **2**, in architecture, a surface usually decorated, inclosed between the slanting sides of a pediment or within an arch over a window or door.—*adj.* **tym-pan′ic.**

type (tīp), *n.* **1**, a person or thing representative of a group because of characteristics possessed in common with the individuals of the group; a specimen; example; model; standard; as, he is the *type* of the modern athlete; **2**, in biology, a form of structure common to a group, or the ideal exemplification of it; as, an animal of the cat *type;* **3**, something that represents or stands for something else; an emblem; symbol; **4**, the first form of something to be followed or copied; a pattern; **5**, the mark or impress of something; stamp; sign; **6**, the figure or design on either side of a coin or medal; **7**, in printing: **a**, a metal or wooden block bearing on one end a raised letter, figure, or other character, an impression of which may be transferred, after inking, to paper; **b**, such blocks taken collectively:—*v.t.* [*p.t.* and *p.p.* typed (tīpt), *p.pr.* typ′ing], **1**, to be a symbol of; typify; represent; **2**, to reproduce in type, or to make a plate impression of, from such blocks; **3**, *Colloq.*, to write or copy on a typewriter.

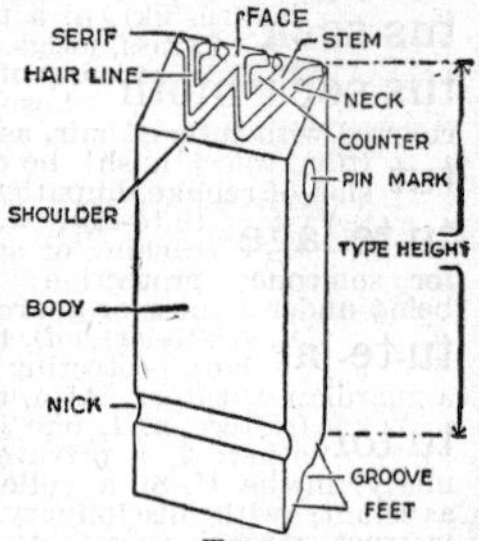

TYPE

NOTE.—The size of type was formerly given by name, and in England this system is still often followed. In America, the point system is used, with approximately 72 points to the inch, meaning that in 72-point the type is one inch high. Types may be cut in any size; below are given the commonly used point sizes from 18 point to 5 point, with the name of the nearest equivalent named size.

18	point	great primer	abcdef
14	point	English	abcdefg
12	point	pica	abcdefg
11	point	small pica	abcdefgh
10	point	long primer	abcdefghi
9	point	bourgeois	abcdefghij
8	point	brevier	abcdefghijk
7	point	minion	abcdefghijkl
6	point	nonpareil	abcdefghijkl
5½	point	agate	abcdefghijklm
5	point	pearl	abcdefghijklm

type met-al an alloy of lead and antimony, used to make type.

type-set-ter (tīp′sĕt″ẽr), *n.* **1**, one who arranges type to form words, by hand or by machine; a compositor; **2**, a machine for setting type, as a linotype.—*n.* **type′set″ting.**

type-write (tīp′rīt″), *v.t.* and *v.i.* [*p.t.* -wrote″ (-rōt″), *p.pr.* -writ″ten (-rĭt″n), *p.pr.* -writ″ing], to write with a machine; type.—*n.* **type′writ″ing.**

type-writ-er (tīp′rīt″ẽr), *n.* **1**, an instrument or machine for writing, by means of a keyboard, in letters similar to those used in print; **2**, one who operates such a machine; a typist.

ty-phoid (tī′foid), *adj.* pertaining to, or like, typhus, a contagious fever:—*n.* typhoid fever: **typhoid fever**, an infectious, often fatal, disease, usually acquired through drinking infected milk or water, but often carried by other foods.—*adj.* **ty-phoi′dal.**

ty-phoon (tī-fōōn′), *n.* a violent tornado or whirlwind.

ty-phus (tī′fŭs), *n.* a dangerous contagious fever marked by great weakness, delirium, and a characteristic eruption of red spots on the body.—*adj.* **ty′phous.**

typ-i-cal (tĭp′ĭ-kăl), *adj.* **1**, symbolic; representative of a class; **2**, in botany and zoölogy, showing the characteristics of its group; **3**, like others of its kind; as, a *typical* case; a *typical* Yankee.—*adv.* **typ′i-cal-ly.**—*n.* **typ′i-cal-ness.**

typ-i-fy (tĭp′ĭ-fī), *v.t.* [*p.t.* and *p.p.* -fied (-fīd), *p.pr.* -fy″ing], **1**, to represent or show by an image or emblem; **2**, to show the qualities of (one's class or group).

typ-ing (tīp′ĭng), *n.* the act of making impressions from type; esp., the act of writing or copying on a typewriter: also, the resulting impression.

typ-ist (tīp′ĭst), *n.* one who operates a typewriting machine; a typewriter.

ty-po-graph-i-cal (tī″pō-grăf′ĭ-kăl; tĭp″ō-), *adj.* of the nature of, or pertaining to the art of, printing; as, a *typographical* error. Also, **ty″po-graph′ic.**—*adv.* **ty″po-graph′i-cal-ly.**

ty-pog-ra-phy (tī-pŏg′rȧ-fĭ; tĭ-), *n.* [*pl.* typographies (-fĭz)], the art of printing with type.—*n.* **ty-pog′ra-pher.**

Tyr (tēr), *n.* in Norse mythology, the son of Odin and god of war and the sky, after whom Tuesday is named. Also, **Tyrr.**

ty-ran-ni-cal (tī-răn′ĭ-kăl), *adj.* **1**, pertaining to, or like, a tyrant; as, a *tyrannical* master; **2**, despotic; cruel; overbearing.—*adv.* **ty-ran′ni-cal-ly.**

ty-ran-ni-cide (tī-răn′ĭ-sīd), *n.* **1**, one who kills a tyrant, or despot; **2**, the killing of a tyrant.

tyr-an-nize (tĭr′ȧ-nīz), *v.i.* [*p.t.* and *p.p.* -nized (-nīzd), *p.pr.* -niz″ing], to act like a despot; rule severely and cruelly:—*v.t.* to treat oppressively and unjustly.

tyr-an-nous (tĭr′ȧ-nŭs), *adj.* arbitrary; unjustly severe; despotic.—*adv.* **tyr′an-nous-ly.**—*n.* **tyr′an-nous-ness.**

tyr-an-ny (tĭr′ȧ-nĭ), *n.* [*pl.* tyrannies (-nĭz)], **1**, the government or conduct of a despot, or cruel and unjust ruler; **2**, cruel or oppressive government; **3**, undue severity; as, the *tyranny* of the majority.

ty-rant (tī′rănt), *n.* **1**, an absolute monarch; a despot; **2**, a ruler or master who uses his great power to oppress those under him, as Nero of Rome.

tyre (tīr), *n.* a band of iron or rubber on the rim of a wheel. See [1]**tire**, *Pfd. S.*

Tyr-i-an (tĭr′ĭ-ăn), *adj.* pertaining to ancient Tyre in Phœnicia, or its people: **Tyrian purple**, a famous dye, properly a crimson, obtained by the ancient Greeks and Romans from a fluid secreted by certain mollusks, which turns purple upon exposure to the light:—*n.* a native of Tyre.

ty-ro (tī′rō), *n.* [*pl.* tyros (-rōz)], a beginner; novice or learner.

Tyr-o-lese (tĭr″ō-lēz′; tĭr″ō-lēs′), *adj.* pertaining to the Tyrol, a former Austrian province, or to its natives:—*n.* a native of the Tyrol.

tzar (tsär), *n.* formerly, an emperor of Russia. Also, **tsar.** See **czar**, *Pfd. S.*

tzar-e-vitch (tsär′ĕ-vĭch), *n.* formerly, the eldest son of a czar. Also, **tsar′e-vitch;** *Pfd. S.*, **czar′e-vitch.**

tza-rev-na (tsä-rĕv′nȧ), *n.* formerly, a daughter of a czar. Also, **tsa-rev′na;** *Pfd. S.*, **cza-rev′na.**

tza-ri-na (tsä-rē′nȧ), *n.* formerly, an empress of Russia; also, the wife of a czar. Also, **tsa-ri′na;** *Pfd. S.*, **cza-ri′na.**

U

u-biq-ui-tous (ū-bĭk′wĭ-tŭs), *adj.* being, or seeming to be, everywhere at the same time.—*adv.* **u-biq′ui-tous-ly.**—*n.* **u-biq′ui-tous-ness.**

u-biq-ui-ty (ū-bĭk′wĭ-tĭ), *n.* omnipresence, or existence everywhere at one and the same time.

U–boat (ū′=bōt″), *n.* a German or Austrian submarine.

U bolt a bolt shaped like the letter U and having threads and a nut at each end. Also, *n.* **U′–bolt.**

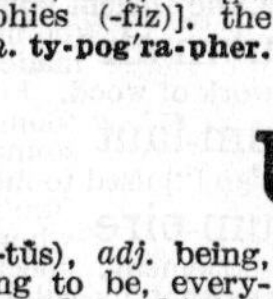

U Bolt

ud-der (ŭd′ẽr), *n.* the milk gland of a mammal, esp. when baglike and having two or more teats, as in the cow (see *beef*, illus.).

u-dom-e-ter (ū-dŏm′ē-tẽr), *n.* an instrument for measuring rain; a rain gauge.

ugh (ōō; ŭ; ŭkh), *interj.* an exclamation of disgust or horror.

ug-ly (ŭg′lĭ), *adj.* [*comp.* ug′li-er, *superl.* ug′li-est], **1**, displeasing to the eye; hideous; **2**, morally repulsive; **3**, suggesting trouble; as, an *ugly* rumor.—*n.* **ug′li-ness.**
Syn. plain, homely, repulsive.

U-gri-an (ōō′grĭ-ăn; ū′grĭ-ăn), *n.* a member of the eastern division of the Finno-Ugric peoples, found in Siberia, northern Europe, Hungary, etc., including the Magyars, Finns, Lapps, and others.

uh-lan (ōō′län; ōō-län′; ū′lȧn), *n.* a Prussian cavalryman. Also, **u-lan′.**

u-kase (ū-kās′), *n.* **1**, formerly, a decree of the czar of Russia, taking effect as law; **2**, hence, any official decree.

U-krain-i-an (ū-krān′ĭ-ăn), *adj.* pertaining to the Ukraine, a political state in southeastern Europe, one of the six states of the Union of Soviet Socialist Republics:—*n.* an inhabitant of this state.

u-ku-le-le (ōō″kōō-lā′lā; ū″kōō-lā′lā), *n.* a stringed instrument, of Hawaiian origin, shaped like a small guitar.

ul-cer (ŭl′sẽr), *n.* **1**, an open sore on the surface of the body, often discharging pus; **2**, hence, a corrupt influence; a public evil.—*adj.* **ul′cer-ous.**

ul-cer-ate (ŭl′sẽr-āt), *v.t.* [*p.t.* and *p.p.* -at″ed, *p.pr.* -at″ing], to affect with an ulcer, or surface sore:—*v.i.* to be affected by an ulcer.—*n.* **ul″cer-a′tion.**

-ule (-ūl), *n. suffix,* forming diminutives from Latin stems; as, glob*ule;* gran*ule.*

ul-na (ŭl′nȧ), *n.* [*pl.* ulnæ (-nē)], the inner and larger of the two bones of the forearm.—*adj.* **ul′nar.**

ul-ster (ŭl′stẽr), *n.* a long, loose overcoat of woolen cloth.

ul-te-ri-or (ŭl-tē′rĭ-ẽr), *adj.* **1,** lying beyond; more distant; **2,** beyond what is expressed or implied; as, an *ulterior* motive.—*adv.* **ul-te′ri-or-ly.**

ul-ti-ma (ŭl′tĭ-mȧ), *n.* the last syllable of a word.

ul-ti-mate (ŭl′tĭ-mȧt), *adj.* **1,** last; final; **2,** fundamental; admitting of no discussion; as, *ultimate* facts of nature.—*adv.* **ul′ti-mate-ly.**—*n.* **ul′ti-mate-ness.**

ul-ti-ma Thu-le (thū′lē), **1,** in ancient times, the most northern land known; **2,** hence, any far distant or mythical region.

ul-ti-ma-tum (ŭl″tĭ-mā′tŭm), *n.* [*pl.* ultimatums (-tŭmz); ultimata (-tȧ)], **1,** the statement of a final proposition; **2,** a last offer of terms of agreement, refusal of which means an end of friendly relations.

***ul-ti-mo** (ŭl′tĭ-mō), [Lat.], *adv.* in the month before the present.

ul-tra (ŭl′trȧ), *adj.* extreme; extravagant; immoderate in opinion or action; as, an *ultra* conservative.

ul-tra- (ŭl′trȧ-), *prefix,* used rather freely, generally without a hyphen, and meaning: **1,** beyond; as, *ultra*montane: opp. of *cis-;* **2,** excessively; beyond the usual; as, *ultra*conservative; *ultra*modern.

ul-tra-ma-rine (ŭl″trȧ-mȧ-rēn′), *n.* a beautiful blue coloring matter made by pulverizing the gem lapis lazuli; also, an artificial pigment.

ul-tra-mon-tane (ŭl″trȧ-mŏn′tān), *adj.* on the other side of the mountains, esp. the Alps:—*n.* **1,** one who lives beyond the mountains, esp., south of the Alps; **2,** a supporter of the Pope.

ul-tra-mun-dane (ŭl″trȧ-mŭn′dān), *adj.* beyond the world, or beyond the limits of the solar system; also, beyond the present life.

ul-tra–vi-o-let (ŭl″trȧ-vī′ō-lĕt), *adj.* beyond the violet end of the spectrum: said of certain invisible radiations which are of shorter wave length than the visible violet rays.

ul-u-late (ŭl′ū-lāt), *v.i.* [*p.t.* and *p.p.* -lat″ed, *p.pr.* -lat″ing], to wail; howl, as a dog; hoot, as an owl.—*adj.* **ul′u-lant.**—*n.* **ul″u-la′tion.**

U-lys-ses (ū-lĭs′ēz), *n.* in mythology, the Roman name for Odysseus, king of Ithaca: the wisest and craftiest of the Greek chiefs in the Trojan War.

um-bel (ŭm′bĕl), *n.* a flower cluster in which a number of pedicels, or flower stalks, of nearly equal length spread or radiate from a common center, as in the cherry blossom (see *inflorescence,* illus.).

um-bel-late (ŭm′bĕl-āt), *adj.* arranged in, bearing, or like, umbels.

um-bel-lif-er-ous (ŭm″bĕ-lĭf′ẽr-ŭs), *adj.* bearing or producing umbels, as a plant.

um-ber (ŭm′bẽr), *n.* a brown earth, used as coloring matter, containing iron and manganese:—*adj.* of an olive-brown color; dark brown; dusky.—*adj.* **um′ber-y.**

um-bil-i-cal (ŭm-bĭl′ĭ-kăl), *adj.* of or pertaining to the umbilicus, or navel: **umbilical cord,** a tubelike structure connecting the unborn young of a mammal, at the navel, with the placenta of the mother.

um-bi-li-cus (ŭm″bĭ-lī′kŭs; ŭm-bĭl′ĭ-kŭs), *n.* [*pl.* umbilici (-sī)], the navel; the scar on the abdomen indicating the place of former attachment of the umbilical cord to the unborn young.

um-bra (ŭm′brȧ), *n.* [*pl.* umbræ (-brē)], a shade or shadow; esp., the dark cone of shadow cast by a planet or satellite on

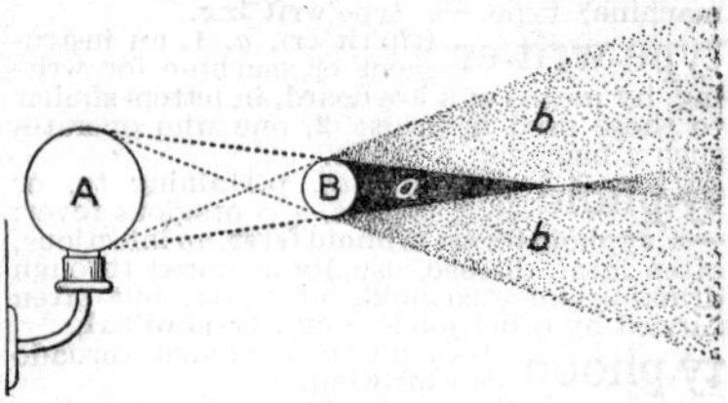

UMBRA

A, light; B, opaque object.—*a,* umbra; *b, b,* penumbra.

the side opposite to the sun, in whose limits the sun's disk is invisible; also, the dark central portion of a sun spot.

um-brage (ŭm′brȧj), *n.* **1,** formerly, shade or obscurity; **2,** a sense of being put in the shade; hence, hurt pride.

Syn. dissatisfaction, displeasure, offense.

um-bra-geous (ŭm-brā′jŭs), *adj.* shady; as, *umbrageous* trees.—*adv.* **um-bra′geous-ly.**—*n.* **um-bra′geous-ness.**

um-brel-la (ŭm-brĕl′ȧ), *n.* a device for protection against rain, sun, etc., consisting of a folding frame, covered with silk, cotton, or other waterproof fabric, and carried in the hand: **umbrella tree,** an American magnolia, with leaves so arranged as to suggest an open umbrella.

Um-bri-an (ŭm′brĭ-ăn), *adj.* pertaining to Umbria, an inland district of central Italy, to its inhabitants, ancient or modern, or to the language spoken there, esp. in ancient times:—*n.* **1,** a native of Umbria; **2,** the ancient language spoken there.

u-mi-ak (ōō′mĭ-ăk), *n.* an Eskimo boat made of skins drawn over a framework of wood. For illus. see **oo′mi-ak,** *Pfd.S.*

um-laut (ŏŏm′lout), *n.* **1,** a modified vowel sound, esp. in German; **2,** the sign [¨] used to indicate such a sound.

um-pire (ŭm′pīr), *n.* a third party to whom a dispute is referred for settlement; specif., one chosen in a game to see that its rules are observed and to decide disputes:—*v.t.* and *v.i.* [*p.t.* and *p.p.* -pired (-pīrd), *p.pr.* -pir-ing], **1,** to settle, as a dispute; **2,** to decide as judge on the plays of a game; as, to *umpire* a game of baseball.

Syn., n. referee, arbitrator, judge.

[1]un- (ŭn-), *prefix,* **1,** not; the reverse of: freely used with adjectives and their derivative nouns and adverbs; as, *un*fair; *un*fairness; *un*fairly; also, with participles; as, *un*seen; **2,** lack of: used with nouns; as, *un*concern.

[2]un- (ŭn-), *prefix,* used: **1,** with verbs or nouns, to express reversal or annulment (of an action) or deprivation (of a thing); as, *un*twist; **2,** with a few verbs felt as negatives, with intensive effect; as, *un*ravel.

NOTE.—The prefix [1]*un-,* and to a less extent [2]*un-,* can be attached to a very large number of words, forming compounds of which the meaning is usually self-evident. Only the more important compounds, or those presenting special difficulty, are listed.

un-a-ble (ŭn-ā′bl), *adj.* **1**, incapable; **2**, without sufficient power; incompetent; as, *unable* to reach the top.

Syn. incapable. *Unable* means not able, and may refer to permanent lack of ability or merely a temporary state; as, an idiot is *unable* to reason; an invalid is *unable* to take solid food. *Incapable* always refers to an innate or permanent lack of ability; as, *incapable* of reason.—*Ant.* able, competent.

un-a-bridged (ŭn″ȧ-brĭjd′), *adj.* not shortened; having nothing omitted; as, an *unabridged* dictionary.

un-ac-cent-ed (ŭn″ăk-sĕnt′ĕd), *adj.* **1**, not stressed, as a syllable; **2**, in music, not emphasized.

un-ac-count-a-ble (ŭn″ă-koun′tȧ-bl), *adj.* **1**, not to be explained; **2**, not responsible.—*n.* **un″ac-count′a-ble-ness.**—*adv.* **un″ac-count′a-bly.**

un-ac-cus-tomed (ŭn″ă-kŭs′tŭmd), *adj.* **1**, not usual or customary; **2**, not familiar: with *to;* as, *unaccustomed* to the work.

un-ad-vised (ŭn″ăd-vīzd′), *adj.* **1**, not discreet or prudent, as a person; **2**, done, or carried out, without careful consideration; as, an *unadvised* policy; **3**, without counsel or advice.—*adv.* **un″ad-vis′ed-ly.**—*n.* **un″ad-vis′ed-ness.**

un-af-fect-ed (ŭn″ă-fĕk′tĕd), *adj.* without pretense; natural.—*adv.* **un″af-fect′ed-ly.**—*n.* **un″af-fect′ed-ness.**

un-al-loyed (ŭn″ă-loid′), *adj.* **1**, pure; without inferior part, as metal; **2**, unmixed; as, *unalloyed* pleasure.

u-na-nim-i-ty (ū″nȧ-nĭm′ĭ-tĭ), *n.* agreement in opinion; accord.

u-nan-i-mous (ū-năn′ĭ-mŭs), *adj.* **1**, united in a single opinion; agreeing; **2**, showing that all agree; as, a *unanimous* vote.—*adv.* **u-nan′i-mous-ly.**—*n.* **u-nan′i-mous-ness.**

un-apt (ŭn-ăpt′), *adj.* **1**, not suitable, as a remark; **2**, not inclined; not likely; as, *unapt* to resent; **3**, dull; as, an *unapt* pupil.—*adv.* **un-apt′ly.**—*n.* **un-apt′ness.**

un-armed (ŭn-ärmd′), *adj.* without weapons; defenseless.

un-as-sum-ing (ŭn″ă-sūm′ĭng), *adj.* retiring; modest.

un-a-void-a-ble (ŭn″ȧ-void′ȧ-bl), *adj.* not to be escaped; inevitable.—*adv.* **un″a-void′a-bly.**

un-a-wares (ŭn″ȧ-wârz′), *adv.* **1**, without previous planning; **2**, by surprise; as, they caught the enemy *unawares.*—*adj.* and *adv.* **un″a-ware′.**

un-backed (ŭn-băkt′), *adj.* **1**, unsupported; **2**, not broken; not taught to bear a rider, as a horse.

un-bal-anced (ŭn-băl′ănst), *adj.* **1**, of unequal weight; out of equilibrium; **2**, hence, mentally disordered; slightly insane.

un-bar (ŭn-bär′), *v.t.* [*p.t.* and *p.p.* -barred′ (-bärd′), *p.pr.* -bar′ring], to remove a bar from, as a door; unlock.

un-bear-a-ble (ŭn-bâr′ȧ-bl), *adj.* not to be endured; intolerable.—*adv.* **un-bear′a-bly.**—*n.* **un-bear′a-ble-ness.**

un-be-com-ing (ŭn″bē-kŭm′ĭng), *adj.* **1**, not suitable or fit; improper; as, conduct *unbecoming* a lady; **2**, not suited to one's appearance; as, an *unbecoming* hat.—*adv.* **un″be-com′ing-ly.**—*n.* **un″be-com′ing-ness.**

un-be-lief (ŭn″bē-lēf′), *n.* lack of positive faith or belief; esp., refusal to accept the teachings of revealed religion.

Syn. incredulity. (See disbelief.)

un-be-liev-er (ŭn″bē-lēv′ẽr), *n.* one who lacks faith; a doubter; esp., one who refuses to accept the teachings of revealed religion.—*adj.* **un″be-liev′ing.**

un-bend (ŭn-bĕnd′), *v.t.* [*p.t.* and *p.p.* -bent′ (-bĕnt′), *p.pr.* -bend′ing], **1**, to straighten; **2**, to free from strain, as a bow; **3**, to unfasten (a sail) from a spar:—*v.i.* **1**, to become straight; **2**, to become less severe or stiff; become gracious.

un-bend-ing (ŭn-bĕnd′ĭng), *p.adj.* **1**, stiff; inflexible; **2**, of determined and unyielding temper.—*adv.* **un-bend′ing-ly.**—*n.* **un-bend′ing-ness.**

un-bi-ased (ŭn-bī′ăst), *adj.* not favoring any party. Also, **un-bi′assed.**—*adv.* **un-bi′ased-ly.**—*n.* **un-bi′ased-ness.**

un-bid-den (ŭn-bĭd′n), *adj.* **1**, not ordered; **2**, not invited.

un-bind (ŭn-bīnd′), *v.t.* [*p.t.* and *p.p.* -bound′ (-bound′), *p.pr.* -bind′ing], **1**, to make loose; untie; **2**, to release; free, as from bonds.

un-blessed (ŭn-blĕst′), *adj.* **1**, without a blessing; **2**, hence, unhappy; wretched. Also, **un-blest′.**

un-bolt (ŭn-bōlt′), *v.t.* to draw back a bolt from; unfasten; open.—*p.adj.* [1]**un-bolt′ed.**

[2]**un-bolt-ed** (ŭn-bōl′tĕd), *adj.* coarse; not sifted; as, *unbolted* flour.

un-born (ŭn-bôrn′), *adj.* not yet born; pertaining to the future.

un-bos-om (ŭn-bo͝oz′ŭm), *v.t.* **1**, to free oneself from, as a secret; **2**, to relieve (oneself) by disclosing:—*v.i.* to free one's mind by telling one's thoughts.

un-bound-ed (ŭn-boun′dĕd), *adj.* unlimited; great beyond measure; as, *unbounded* goodness.—*adv.* **un-bound′ed-ly.**—*n.* **un-bound′ed-ness.**

[1]**un-bowed** (ŭn-bōd′), *adj.* not arched or bent.

[2]**un-bowed** (ŭn-boud′), *adj.* not conquered; uncrushed.

un-braid (ŭn-brād′), *v.t.* to take apart the strands of, as a plait of hair.

un-bri-dled (ŭn-brī′dld), *adj.* **1**, not fastened with a bridle; **2**, free; not restrained; as, an *unbridled* tongue.

un-bro-ken (ŭn-brō′kn), *adj.* **1**, whole; **2**, not interrupted; as, an *unbroken* silence; **3**, not tamed; as, an *unbroken* horse; **4**, not surpassed, as a record.—*adv.* **un-bro′ken-ly.**—*n.* **un-bro′ken-ness.**

un-build (ŭn-bĭld′), *v.t.* [*p.t.* and *p.p.* -built′ (-bĭlt′), *p.pr.* -build′ing], to tear down, as a house; demolish.

un-bur-den (ŭn-bûr′dn), *v.t.* **1**, to rid of a load; ease; **2**, hence, to relieve (oneself), as of an oppressive secret; **3**, to throw off as being burdensome. Also, **un-bur′then** (ŭn-bûr′*th*n).

un-called–for (ŭn-kôld′-fôr″), *adj.* not needed; undemanded; out of place; superfluous.

un-can-ny (ŭn-kăn′ĭ), *adj.* weird; not to be explained reasonably; vaguely mysterious; unearthly.—*adv.* **un-can′ni-ly.**—*n.* **un-can′ni-ness.**

un-ceas-ing (ŭn-sēs′ĭng), *adj.* never stopping; continuous; without interruption.—*adv.* **un-ceas′ing-ly.**

Syn. endless, incessant, continual, ceaseless.

un-cer-tain (ŭn-sûr′tĭn), *adj.* **1**, not sure; doubtful; as, the result is *uncertain;* **2**, not positive; doubting; **3**, not steady; as, the shaky platform gave an *uncertain* support; **4**, not reliable.—*adv.* **un-cer′tain-ly.**—*n.* **un-cer′tain-ness.**

Syn. variable, fitful. (See precarious.)

un-cer-tain-ty (ŭn-sûr′tĭn-tĭ), *n.* [*pl.* uncertainties (-tĭz)], the state of being doubtful; lack of positiveness; indefiniteness; unreliability.

un-change-a-ble (ŭn-chān′jȧ-bl), *adj.* not alterable.—*n.* **un-change′a-ble-ness.**—*adv.* **un-change′a-bly.**

un-char-i-ta-ble (ŭn-chăr′ĭ-tȧ-bl), *adj.* **1,** not generous toward the needy; **2,** unkind; harsh in judging others; as, *uncharitable* criticism.—*n.* **un-char′i-ta-ble-ness.**—*adv.* **un-char′i-ta-bly.**

un-chris-tian (ŭn-krĭs′chăn), *adj.* **1,** heathen; **2,** not suitable for, or like, a Christian; as, *unchristian* conduct; **3,** not in accordance with the customs of the so-called Christian nations.

un-ci-al (ŭn′shĭ-ăl; ŭn′shăl), *adj.* designating, or pertaining to, a variety of characters, or letters, found in manuscripts from the fourth to about the ninth century, resembling modern capitals, but with more rounded forms:—*n.* a character of this kind; also, a document written in such characters.

un-cir-cum-cised (ŭn-sûr′kŭm-sīzd), *adj.* not circumcised; hence, not of the Israelites; Gentile.

un-civ-il (ŭn-sĭv′ĭl), *adj.* rude; without courtesy.—*adv.* **un-civ′il-ly.**

un-civ-i-lized (ŭn-sĭv′ĭ-līzd), *adj.* savage; barbarous.

un-cle (ŭng′kl), *n.* **1,** the brother of one's father or mother; **2,** one's aunt's husband; **3,** *Colloq.*, an old man, usually in an inferior position; **4,** *Slang*, a pawnbroker.

un-clean (ŭn-klēn′), *adj.* **1,** soiled; foul; filthy; **2,** morally impure; evil. —*n.* **un-clean′ness.**

un-clean-ly (ŭn-klĕn′lĭ), *adj.* **1,** habitually dirty; foul; **2,** not chaste. —*n.* **un-clean′li-ness.**

Un-cle Sam (săm), *Colloq.*, the U. S. government personified.

un-clothe (ŭn-klōth′), *v.t.* [*p.t.* and *p.p.* -clothed′ (-klōthd′), *p.pr.* -cloth′ing], to remove the clothes or covering from; hence, to deprive of anything.

un-coil (ŭn-koil′), *v.t.* and *v.i.* to make or become loose; unwind, as a spring.

un-coined (ŭn-koind′), *adj.* **1,** not minted; not made into coins, as gold; **2,** not manufactured or artificial.

un-com-fort-a-ble (ŭn-kŭm′fẽr-tȧ-bl), *adj.* **1,** not at ease, physically or mentally; **2,** causing uneasiness. —*adv.* **un-com′fort-a-bly.**

un-com-mon (ŭn-kŏm′ŭn), *adj.* unusual; rare; strange.

un-com-mu-ni-ca-tive (ŭn″kŏ-mū′nĭ-kā-tĭv), *adj.* not given to talking; reticent; shy.

un-com-pro-mis-ing (ŭn-kŏm′prō-mīz″ĭng), *adj.* not willing to make concessions; unyielding; also, showing such an attitude.—*adv.* **un-com′pro-mis″ing-ly.**—*n.* **un-com′pro-mis″ing-ness.**

un-con-cern (ŭn″kŏn-sûrn′), *n.* lack of interest or anxiety.—*adj.* **un″con-cerned′.**—*adv.* **un″con-cern′ed-ly.**

un-con-di-tion-al (ŭn″kŏn-dĭsh′ŭn-ăl), *adj.* without any limitations; absolute; as, an *unconditional* surrender.—*adv.* **un″con-di′tion-al-ly.**

un-con-firmed (ŭn″kŏn-fûrmd′), *adj.* not based on official information; not authoritative, as a report.

un-con-scion-a-ble (ŭn-kŏn′shŭn-ȧ-bl), *adj.* **1,** unreasonable; **2,** not influenced by the conscience. —*adv.* **un-con′scion-a-bly.**

un-con-scious (ŭn-kŏn′shŭs), *adj.* **1,** not mentally awake; without apparent feeling or life; **2,** not aware: with *of;* as, *unconscious* of error; **3,** not done knowingly.—*n.* **un-con′scious-ness.**

un-con-sti-tu-tion-al (ŭn-kŏn″stĭ-tū′shŭn-ăl), *adj.* not in accordance with the constitution of a country.—*n.* **un-con″sti-tu″tion-al′i-ty.**

un-con-trolled (ŭn″kŏn-trōld′), *adj.* without control or restraint; as, *uncontrolled* anger.

un-couth (ŭn-kōōth′), *adj.* awkward; ungainly; odd; boorish.—*adv.* **un-couth′ly.**—*n.* **un-couth′ness.**

un-cov-er (ŭn-kŭv′ẽr), *v.t.* **1,** to remove a cover from; **2,** to take the hat or cap from; **3,** to make known:—*v.i.* to take off the hat or cap; as, *uncover* for the flag.
Syn. divulge, reveal, expose, disclose.

unc-tion (ŭngk′shŭn), *n.* **1,** the act of anointing in sign of consecration; **2,** an ointment; hence, anything soothing; **3,** a manner which indicates or arouses emotion, esp. religious fervor.

unc-tu-ous (ŭngk′tū-ŭs), *adj.* **1,** oily; smooth; **2,** bland; fervid; **3,** esp., insincerely gushing; as, an *unctuous* speech.—*adv.* **unc′tu-ous-ly.**—*n.* **unc′tu-ous-ness.**—*n.* **unc″tu-os′i-ty.**

un-curl (ŭn-kûrl′), *v.t.* and *v.i.* to straighten out, as hair, feathers, etc.

un-daunt-ed (ŭn-dän′tĕd; ŭn-dôn′tĕd), *adj.* not dismayed; fearless.—*adv.* **un-daunt′ed-ly.**

un-dec-a-gon (ŭn-dĕk′ȧ-gŏn), *n.* a plane figure having eleven sides and eleven angles.

un-de-ceive (ŭn″dē-sēv′), *v.t.* [*p.t.* and *p.p.* -ceived′ (-sēvd′), *p.pr.* -ceiv′ing], to set free from error or mistake.

un-de-ni-a-ble (ŭn″dē-nī′ȧ-bl), *adj.* **1,** not to be contradicted; compelling admission; **2,** *Colloq.*, decidedly good.—*adv.* **un″de-ni′a-bly.**

un-der (ŭn′dẽr), *prep.* **1,** below or beneath in position, authority, dignity, excellence, or value; **2,** less than, as in height, weight, age, or number; as, *under* six feet; *under* six years; for less than; as, sold *under* cost; below a certain average or standard of; as, *under* age, size, or weight; **3,** subject to the action or effect of; as, *under* treatment for illness; *under* a burden or strain; *under* orders; **4,** because of; as, *under* the circumstances; **5,** in conformity with; as, *under* a rule of the firm; classified beneath; as, *under* this head:—*adj.* **1,** lower in position; as, the *under* surface; **2,** lower in rank; as, the *under* secretary:—*adv.* in or to a lower place or subordinate position.

un-der- (ŭn′dẽr-), *prefix*, meaning: **1,** below; as, *under*ground; *under*foot; **2,** insufficient(ly); as, *under*done; **3,** subordinate; as, *under*graduate.

un-der-bid (ŭn″dẽr-bĭd′), *v.t.* [*p.t.* -bid′, *p.p.* -bid′den (-bĭd′n), *p.pr.* -bid′ding], to offer to sell or do for a lower price than (another bidder).

un-der-bred (ŭn′dẽr-brĕd″), *adj.* **1,** lacking good manners; showing careless training; **2,** not of pure breed.

un-der-brush (ŭn′dẽr-brŭsh″), *n.* bushes, shrubs, and small trees growing thickly in a forest.

un-der-clothes (ŭn′dẽr-klōthz″), *n.pl.* garments worn beneath other clothes. Also, **un′der-cloth″ing.**

un-der-cur-rent (ŭn′dẽr-kŭr″ĕnt), *n.* **1,** a current below the surface of air, water, etc.; **2,** a concealed tendency of thought or feeling.

un-der-done (ŭn′dẽr-dŭn″; ŭn″dẽr-dŭn′), *adj.* cooked too little; rare: said esp. of meat.

un-der-foot (ŭn″dẽr-fŏŏt′), *adv.* beneath the feet; underneath.

un-der-gar-ment (ŭn′dẽr-gär″mĕnt), *n.* a garment worn under the outer clothing.

ın-der-go (ŭn″dẽr-gō′), *v.t.* [*p.t.* -went′ (-wĕnt′), *p.p.* -gone′ (-gôn′), ›.pr. -go′ing], to pass through or experience; ›uffer; endure; as, to *undergo* an operation.

ın-der-grad-u-ate (ŭn″dẽr-grăd′ū-āt), *n.* **1**, a college or ıniversity student who has not taken his first, ›r bachelor's, degree; **2**, any student who has ıot received his diploma.

ın-der-ground (ŭn′dẽr-ground″), *adj.* **1**, below the surface of he earth; **2**, *Colloq.*, maintained or acting in ecret: **underground railroad, 1**, a railroad ›uilt below the surface of the earth: in the ·. S., usually called *subway;* **2**, in American ıistory, before the abolition of slavery, a sysem maintained by white abolitionists, which ›assed runaway slaves northward through a eries of hiding places:—*n.* a space, place, or onstruction beneath the earth:—*adv.* **1**, beıeath the earth's surface; **2**, *Colloq.*, secretly.

ın-der-growth (ŭn′dẽr-grōth″), *n.* underbrush; low shrubs nd bushes growing in a forest.

ın-der-hand (ŭn′dẽr-hănd″), *adj.* **1**, done by meanness or fraud; , deceitful; sly; as, *underhand* business; **3**, of ball, thrown with an upward swing of the rm, with the palm turned up:—*adv.* unfairly.

ın-der-hand-ed (ŭn′dẽr-hănd″ĕd), *adj.* deceptive; secretive; 'ealing crookedly; sly.—*adv.* **un″der-hand′-d-ly.**—*n.* **un″der-hand′ed-ness.**

ın-der-lay (ŭn″dẽr-lā′), *v.t.* [*p.t.* and *p.p.* -laid′ (-lād′), *p.pr.* -lay′ing], to ›ut something beneath or spread something ınder:—*n.* (ŭn′dẽr-lā″), a layer of paper put ınder type to raise it to the necessary level.

ın-der-let (ŭn″dẽr-lĕt′), *v.t.* [*p.t.* and *p.p.* -let′, *p.pr.* -let′ting], **1**, to rent a rented property) to another; sublet; **2**, to ›t or lease at a price below the real value.

ın-der-lie (ŭn″dẽr-lī′), *v.t.* [*p.t.* -lay′ (-lā′), *p.p.* -lain′ (-lān′), *p.pr.* -ly′ing], ., to lie or be beneath; **2**, to be at the bottom ›f; serve as the basis of, as of an argument or heory; support.—*p.adj.* **un′der-ly″ing.**

ın-der-line (ŭn″dẽr-līn′), *v.t.* [*p.t.* and *p.p.* -lined′ (-līnd′), *p.pr.* lin′ing], to draw a line beneath, as in a manucript to indicate italics.

ın-der-ling (ŭn′dẽr-lĭng), *n.* a person occupying a low, esp. a ıenial, position; a servile person.

ın-der-mine (ŭn″dẽr-mīn′), *v.t.* [*p.t.* and *p.p.* -mined′ (-mīnd′), *p.pr.* min′ing], **1**, to dig beneath; form a tunnel ınder; **2**, to weaken; as, to *undermine* one's ealth; work against secretly; as, to *underıine* someone's influence.—*n.* **un″der-min′er.**

ın-der-most (ŭn′dẽr-mōst), *adj.* lowest in place, position, or rank.

ın-der-neath (ŭn″dẽr-nēth′; ŭn″dẽr-nēth′), *adv.* and *prep.* ›eneath; below; under.

ın-der-pay (ŭn″dẽr-pā′), *v.t.* [*p.t.* and *p.p.* -paid′ (-pād′), *p.pr.* -pay′ing], o pay insufficiently.

ın-der-pin (ŭn″dẽr-pĭn′), *v.t.* [*p.t.* and *p.p.* -pinned′ (-pĭnd′), *p.pr.* pin′ning], **1**, to lay bricks, stones, etc., under, s for a foundation; **2**, to support by a foundaıon; **3**, hence, to prop.

ın-der-pin-ning (ŭn′dẽr-pĭn″ĭng), *n.* **1**, the foundation maerial of a building; **2**, in *pl.*, *Colloq.*, the legs.

ın-der-rate (ŭn″dẽr-rāt′), *v.t.* [*p.t.* and *p.p.* -rat′ed, *p.pr.* -rat′ing], › rate too low; undervalue.

ın-der-score (ŭn″dẽr-skōr′), *v.t.* [*p.t.* and *p.p.* -scored′ (-skōrd′), .pr. -scor′ing], to draw a line under; as, to *nderscore* a word:—*n.* a line so drawn.

un-der–sea (ŭn′dẽr-sē″), *adj.* beneath the surface of the ocean; submarine.—*adv.* **un′der-sea″; un′der-seas″.**

un-der-sell (ŭn″dẽr-sĕl′), *v.t.* [*p.t.* and *p.p.* -sold′ (-sōld′), *p.pr.* -sell′-ing], to sell at a lower price.

un-der-shirt (ŭn′dẽr-shûrt″), *n.* a garment for the upper half of the body, worn next the skin.

un-der-shot (ŭn′dẽr-shŏt″), *adj.* **1**, driven by water passing underneath: said of a water wheel (see *hydraulic*, illus.); **2**, having a prominent lower jaw.

un-der-sign (ŭn″dẽr-sīn′), *v.t.* to write one's name at the end of, or at the foot of, as a legal paper or petition: **the undersigned**, the person or persons subscribing to, or signing, a document.

un-der-skirt (ŭn′dẽr-skûrt″), *n.* a skirt worn beneath a dress or outside skirt; petticoat.

un-der-slung (ŭn′dẽr-slŭng″), *adj.* of an automobile, having the supporting springs of the chassis attached to the under side of the axle.

un-der-stand (ŭn″dẽr-stănd′), *v.t.* [*p.t.* and *p.p.* -stood′ (-stŏŏd′), *p.pr.* -stand′ing], **1**, to perceive or know; **2**, to be informed of; as, I *understand* he will accept; **3**, to know the meaning of; as, to *understand* the proof of a theorem; **4**, to assume or infer; **5**, to know by experience; as, to *understand* the folly of resisting:—*v.i.* **1**, to comprehend; **2**, to be made aware.

un-der-stand-ing (ŭn″dẽr-stănd′ĭng), *p.adj.* intelligent:—*n.* **1**, the reasoning faculties; **2**, a state of knowing, or power to know, the meaning of anything; **3**, the agreement of two or more minds; as, the *understanding* between them was complete.

Syn., *n.* reason, discernment, judgment.

un-der-state (ŭn″dẽr-stāt′), *v.t.* [*p.t.* and *p.p.* -stat′ed, *p.pr.* -stat′-ing], **1**, to tell less than the truth about; as, to *understate* the facts; **2**, to represent (a matter) as less important than it really is.—*n.* **un″der-state′ment.**

un-der-stood (ŭn″dẽr-stŏŏd′), past tense and past participle of *understand:*—*p.adj.* in grammar, implied but not expressed; as, the subject is *understood.*

un-der-strap-per (ŭn′dẽr-străp″ẽr), *n.* one who holds an inferior position; a petty official.

un-der-stud-y (ŭn′dẽr-stŭd″ĭ), *v.t.* and *v.i.* [*p.t.* and *p.p.* -stud″ied (-stŭd″ĭd), *p.pr.* -stud″y-ing], to learn another actor's part in a play, in order to take his place if necessary:—*n.* [*pl.* understudies (-ĭz)], **1**, an actor trained to serve as substitute; **2**, any person trained to take another's place.

un-der-take (ŭn″dẽr-tāk′), *v.t.* [*p.t.* -took′ (-tŏŏk′), *p.p.* -tak′en (-tāk′n), *p.pr.* -tak′ing], **1**, to take upon oneself; as, to *undertake* a mission; **2**, to attempt or try; **3**, to promise; as, I will *undertake* that the work shall be finished:—*v.i.* to promise.

un-der-tak-er (ŭn″dẽr-tāk′ẽr), *n.* **1**, one who assumes any task or agrees to perform any service; specif., in economics, one who assumes the management of a business: also called *entrepreneur;* **2**, (ŭn′dẽr-tāk″ẽr), one who makes a business of preparing the dead for burial, and of conducting funerals; a mortician.

un-der-tak-ing (ŭn″dẽr-tāk′ĭng), *n.* **1**, the taking upon oneself of a task or responsibility; **2**, an enterprise; a task; **3**, (ŭn′dẽr-tāk″ĭng), the business of managing funerals.

un-der-tone (ŭn′dẽr-tōn″), *n.* **1**, a low or subdued pitch of voice or sound; **2**, a dull or quiet color.

un-der-took (ŭn″dẽr-to͝ok′), past tense of the irregular verb *undertake*.

un-der-tow (ŭn′dẽr-tō″), *n.* a current below the surface of water, esp. on the seashore, which moves in the opposite direction from the surface movement.

un-der-val-ue (ŭn″dẽr-văl′ū), *v.t.* [*p.t.* and *p.p.* -ued (-ūd), *p.pr.* -u-ing], to rate, estimate, or value, below actual worth; regard as unimportant; underrate.—*n.* **un″der-val″u-a′tion.**

un-der-vest (ŭn′dẽr-vĕst″), *n.* an undershirt, usually sleeveless.

un-der-wa-ter (ŭn′dẽr-wô″tẽr), *adj.* and *adv.* beneath the surface of the water:—*n.* underground water.

un-der-wear (ŭn′dẽr-wâr″), *n.* garments worn under the ordinary outer clothing; underclothing collectively.

un-der-went (ŭn″dẽr-wĕnt′), past tense of the verb *undergo*.

un-der-work (ŭn″dẽr-wûrk′), *v.t.* **1**, to do the same work for less than another; as, the carpenter *underworks* his rival; **2**, to exact too little work from:—*v.i.* to do less than is expected in a given task.

un-der-world (ŭn′dẽr-wûrld″), *n.* **1**, Hades, or the place of departed souls; **2**, that part of the globe beneath the horizon; **3**, the degraded and criminal classes; as, the *underworld* of New York.

un-der-write (ŭn″dẽr-rīt′), *v.t.* [*p.t.* -wrote′ (-rōt′), *p.p.* -writ′ten (-rĭt′n), *p.pr.* -writ′ing], **1**, to write underneath; **2**, to write one's name under or sign (an insurance policy), as a guarantee that in case of loss one will be responsible for the amount specified; **3**, to sign an agreement to buy on a given date at a specified price (bonds or shares not yet issued); **4**, loosely, to subscribe to, as a project which requires capital:—*v.i.* to carry on an insurance business.

un-der-writ-er (ŭn′dẽr-rīt″ẽr), *n.* one whose business it is to underwrite insurance, issues of stock, etc.

un-dine (ŭn-dēn′; ŭn′dēn), *n.* in medieval legend, a water nymph who acquired a soul by marrying a mortal.

un-di-rect-ed (ŭn″dĭ-rĕk′tĕd), *adj.* **1**, not directed; without leadership or guidance; **2**, lacking an address, as mail.

un-do (ŭn-do͞o′), *v.t.* [*p.t.* -did′ (-dĭd′), *p.p.* -done′ (-dŭn′), *p.pr.* -do′ing], **1**, to make null and void; do away with the result of; as, to *undo* the man's good influence; **2**, to destroy; ruin; as, to *undo* one's morals; **3**, to loosen; as, to *undo* a knot.—*n.* **un-do′er.**

un-do-ing (ŭn-do͞o′ĭng), *n.* **1**, the act of making something of no effect; **2**, ruin; as, gambling was his *undoing;* **3**, the act of unfastening.

un-done (ŭn-dŭn′), past participle of *undo:*—*p.adj.* **1**, made of no effect; altered to an opposite condition; **2**, ruined; **3**, not accomplished, as a task.

un-doubt-ed (ŭn-dout′ĕd), *adj.* certain; not to be questioned; sure.—*adv.* **un-doubt′ed-ly.**

un-dress (ŭn-drĕs′), *v.t.* **1**, to take clothes from; strip; **2**, to remove decorations, bandages, etc., from:—*v.i.* to take off one's clothes:—*n.* (ŭn′drĕs″; ŭn-drĕs′), informal, everyday costume:—*adj.* (ŭn′drĕs), informal; as, an *undress* uniform.

un-due (ŭn-dū′; ŭn′dū), *adj.* **1**, not requiring payment as yet; as, the bill was *undue;* **2**, wrong or illegal; **3**, more than proper or suitable; unreasonable; as, *undue* attention to details.—*adv.* **un-du′ly.**

un-du-late (ŭn′dū-lāt), *v.t.* and *v.i.* [*p.t.* and *p.p.* -lat″ed, *p.pr.* -lat″ing], to wave up and down or back and forth; move with a wavy motion:—*adj.* (ŭn′dū-lāt), **1**, having a wavy margin (see *leaf*, illus.); **2**, vibrating; wavering.—*n.* **un″du-la′tion.**

un-du-la-to-ry (ŭn′dū-lȧ-tō-rĭ), *adj.* wavelike; having a wav[y] motion: **undulatory theory**, the theory tha[t] light and other kinds of radiant energy ar[e] transmitted through space in the form o[f] vibrations or waves.

un-dy-ing (ŭn-dī′ĭng), *adj.* **1**, never ceas[ing]; without end; **2**, immortal; imperishable.—*adv.* **un-dy′ing-ly.**

un-earned (ŭn-ûrnd′), *adj.* not earned o[r] deserved: **unearned incre[ment]**, any natural increase in the value o[f] land or property occurring without labor o[r] effort on the part of the owner, as from in[]creased demand through larger population o[r] other natural causes.

un-earth (ŭn-ûrth′), *v.t.* **1**, to take fro[m] the earth; dig from under[]ground; uncover; **2**, hence, to bring to know[l]edge; discover; as, to *unearth* a crime.

un-earth-ly (ŭn-ûrth′lĭ), *adj.* **1**, not ac[]cording to, or like, natur[e]; supernatural; **2**, hence, weird; uncanny; as an *unearthly* sound.—*n.* **un-earth′li-ness.**

un-eas-y (ŭn-ēz′ĭ), *adj.* **1**, not at ease i[n] mind or body; restless; uncom[]fortable; anxious; **2**, awkward in manne[r]; constrained; **3**, causing discomfort.—*ad[v].* **un-eas′i-ly.**—*n.* **un-eas′i-ness.**

un-ed-u-cat-ed (ŭn-ĕd′ū-kāt″ĕd), *ad[j].* **1**, lacking the advan[]tages of education; illiterate; **2**, not properl[y] trained; as, *uneducated* taste.

Syn. (see ignorant).

un-em-ployed (ŭn″ĕm-ploid′), *ad[j].* **1**, without occupation; out of work; **2**, not in use; idle; as, *unem[]ployed* funds.—*n.* **un″em-ploy′ment.**

un-e-qual (ŭn-ē′kwăl), *adj.* **1**, not of th[e] same size, strength, amoun[t], ability, weight, etc.; **2**, not well balanced o[r] matched; **3**, not sufficiently large, strong, etc.: with *to;* as, he was *unequal* to the task; **4**, irregular; uneven.—*adv.* **un-e′qual-ly.**

un-e-qualed (ŭn-ē′kwăld), *adj.* no[t] matched; without a paral[]lel, peer, or rival. Also, **un-e′qualled.**

un-e-quiv-o-cal (ŭn″ē-kwĭv′ō-kăl), *ad[j].* not doubtful or uncer[]tain; unmistakable as to meaning.

un-err-ing (ŭn-ûr′ĭng; ŭn-ĕr′ĭng), *ad[j].* without error, as a judgment; accurate; as, *unerring* aim.—*adv.* **un-err′ing-l[y].**

un-es-sen-tial (ŭn″ĕ-sĕn′shăl), *adj.* no[t] indispensable or neces[]sary; hence, of minor importance.

un-e-ven (ŭn-ē′vn), *adj.* **1**, not regular; not smooth or flat, as a surfac[e]; **2**, not uniform, as pressure; **3**, not equal; odd: used of a number not exactly divisible by tw[o].—*adv.* **un-e′ven-ly.**—*n.* **un-e′ven-ness.**

un-ex-am-pled (ŭn″ĕg-zăm′pld; ŭn″ĕg[]zȧm′pld), *adj.* so unusu[]al as to be without a parallel; unprecedented.

un-ex-cep-tion-a-ble (ŭn″ĕk-sĕp′shŭn-ȧ-bl), *ad[j].* not open to blame or criticism; irreproach[]able.—*n.* **un″ex-cep′tion-a-ble-ness.**—*ad[v].* **un″ex-cep′tion-a-bly.**

un-ex-pect-ed (ŭn″ĕks-pĕk′tĕd), *adj.* no[t] looked for; sudden.—*adv.* **un″ex-pect′ed-ly.**—*n.* **un″ex-pect′ed-ness.**

un-fail-ing (ŭn-fāl′ĭng), *adj.* **1**, not liabl[e] to fall short, as a supply; no[t] growing less or weaker; **2**, reliable; sure, as [a] friend.—*adv.* **un-fail′ing-ly.**

un-fair (ŭn-fâr′), *adj.* **1**, not just; **2**, dis[]honest; tricky.—*adv.* **un-fair′ly.**—*n.* **un-fair′ness.**

un-faith-ful (ŭn-fāth′fo͝ol), *adj.* **1**, no[t] trustworthy; **2**, false; no[t] loyal; 3, not holding to duty, promise, vows, etc. —*adv.* **un-faith′ful-ly.**—*n.* **un-faith′ful-ness.**

un-fas-ten (ŭn-fȧs′n), *v.t.* to untie; loosen; —*v.i.* to become loose.

un-fa-vor-a-ble (ŭn-fā′vẽr-ȧ-bl), *adj.* 1, not favorable; discouraging; adverse; as, an *unfavorable* opinion; 2, not contributing to success; as, the weather was *unfavorable.* Also, **un-fa′vour-a-ble.**—*adv.* **un-fa′vor-a-bly.**

un-feel-ing (ŭn-fēl′ĭng), *adj.* 1, cruel; brutal; 2, without impulses or emotions; insensible.—*adv.* **un-feel′ing-ly.** —*n.* **un-feel′ing-ness.**

un-feigned (ŭn-fānd′), *adj.* genuine; sincere; without pretense.

un-fin-ished (ŭn-fĭn′ĭsht), *adj.* 1, not complete; imperfect; 2, not polished, as in style or finish.

un-fit (ŭn-fĭt′), *v.t.* [*p.t.* and *p.p.* -fit′ted, *p.pr.* -fit′ting], 1, to make unsuitable; 2, to deprive of ability, appropriateness, etc.: —*adj.* not suitable; inappropriate; improper. —*adv.* **un-fit′ly.**—*n.* **un-fit′ness.**

un-fledged (ŭn-flĕjd′), *adj.* 1, without feathers: said of a young bird; 2, hence, undeveloped; immature.

un-fold (ŭn-fōld′), *v.t.* 1, to spread open, as a pocket map; 2, to reveal by degrees:—*v.i.* 1, to open, as a flower; 2, to be revealed, esp. gradually.

un-formed (ŭn-fôrmd′), *adj.* 1, not fully developed; 2, shapeless.

un-for-tu-nate (ŭn-fôr′tū-nāt), *adj.* 1, not lucky; not prosperous; 2, badly chosen; regrettable; as, an *unfortunate* speech:—*n.* an unlucky or unsuccessful person.—*adv.* **un-for′tu-nate-ly.**

un-found-ed (ŭn-foun′dĕd), *adj.* 1, without basis; not established; 2, hence, doubtful, as a rumor.

un-fre-quent-ed (ŭn″frē-kwĕn′tĕd), *adj.* rarely visited by people; solitary; lonely.

un-friend-ly (ŭn-frĕnd′lĭ), *adj.* 1, not like a friend; lacking cordiality; 2, antagonistic.—*n.* **un-friend′li-ness.**

un-frock (ŭn-frŏk′), *v.t.* 1, to divest of a frock; 2, hence, to deprive (a priest, clergyman, etc.) of ecclesiastical rank or authority.

un-furl (ŭn-fûrl′), *v.t.* 1, to loose from its fastenings and spread out, as a flag, a sail, etc.; 2, to display; show:—*v.i.* to be spread out or displayed.

un-gain-ly (ŭn-gān′lĭ), *adj.* awkward; clumsy; uncouth:—*adv.* in an awkward manner.—*n.* **un-gain′li-ness.**

un-gen-er-ous (ŭn-jĕn′ẽr-ŭs), *adj.* 1, stingy or mean; 2, narrow in judgment of others; uncharitable.—*adv.* **un-gen′er-ous-ly.**

un-god-ly (ŭn-gŏd′lĭ), *adj.* 1, wicked; having no likeness to God; 2, *Slang*, outrageous.—*n.* **un-god′li-ness.**

un-gov-ern-a-ble (ŭn-gŭv′ẽr-nȧ-bl), *adj.* not to be controlled; unruly; rebellious.

un-gra-cious (ŭn-grā′shŭs), *adj.* 1, rude; uncivil; 2, disagreeable; offensive.—*adv.* **un-gra′cious-ly.**

un-grate-ful (ŭn-grāt′fo͝ol), *adj.* not thankful; not appreciating favors received.—*adv.* **un-grate′ful-ly.**—*n.* **un-grate′ful-ness.**

un-gual (ŭng′gwăl), *adj.* pertaining to, or bearing, a nail, claw, or hoof.

un-guent (ŭng′gwĕnt), *n.* an oil or salve for burns, sores, etc.; an ointment.

un-gu-la (ŭng′gū-lȧ), *n.* [*pl.* ungulæ (-lē)], 1, a hoof, or a nail or claw, slightly hooked; 2, the part of a cylinder, cone, or other solid remaining after the top has been cut off by a plane oblique to the base.—*adj.* **un′gu-lar.**

un-gu-late (ŭng′gū-lāt), *adj.* hooflike or hoofed:—*n.* a hoofed animal.

un-hal-lowed (ŭn-hăl′ōd), *adj.* 1, not made or kept for sacred uses; 2, profane; unholy.

un-hand (ŭn-hănd′), *v.t.* to let go of; release from a grasp.

un-hand-y (ŭn-hăn′dĭ), *adj.* 1, clumsy; awkward; 2, inconvenient.

un-hap-py (ŭn-hăp′ĭ), *adj.* 1, not glad; sorrowful; wretched; 2, unfortunate; unsuccessful, as a venture.—*adv.* **un-hap′pi-ly.**—*n.* **un-hap′pi-ness.**

un-health-y (ŭn-hĕl′thĭ), *adj.* 1, lacking health; unwell; 2, not conducive to health; 3, morally injurious.

un-heard (ŭn-hûrd′), *adj.* 1, not heard; as, an *unheard* cry; 2, not given a hearing: **unheard-of,** unprecedented.

un-hinge (ŭn-hĭnj′), *v.t.* [*p.t.* and *p.p.* -hinged′ (-hĭnjd′), *p.pr.* -hing′-ing], 1, to remove from its hinges; 2, to take from its place; 3, to unsettle; as, his trouble *unhinged* his mind.

un-ho-ly (ŭn-hō′lĭ), *adj.* not sacred; unhallowed; hence, profane; wicked.—*adv.* **un-ho′li-ly.**—*n.* **un-ho′li-ness.**

un-horse (ŭn-hôrs′), *v.t.* [*p.t.* and *p.p.* -horsed′ (-hôrst′), *p.pr.* -hors′-ing], to throw or drag from the back of a horse.

u-ni- (ū′nĭ-), a prefix or combining form from the Latin, meaning one; as, *uni*cellular; *uni*form; *uni*corn.

u-ni-cam-er-al (ū″nĭ-kăm′ẽr-ăl), *adj.* consisting of, or pertaining to, one chamber only: said of a legislative body: distinguished from *bicameral.*

u-ni-cel-lu-lar (ū″nĭ-sĕl′ū-lȧr), *adj.* having one cell only.

u-ni-corn (ū′nĭ-kôrn), *n.* a fabled animal resembling the horse, with one straight horn projecting from its forehead.

u-ni-form (ū′nĭ-fôrm), *adj.* 1, not changing in form, manner, or character; unvarying; 2, like one another:—*n.* an official or regulation dress belonging to a particular class or profession.—*adv.* **u′ni-form″ly.**—*n.* **u′ni-form″ness.**

u-ni-form-i-ty (ū″nĭ-fôr′mĭ-tĭ), *n.* the quality or state of having one unchanging form, or of being of the same form as others; resemblance.

u-ni-fy (ū′nĭ-fī), *v.t.* [*p.t.* and *p.p.* -fied (-fīd), *p.pr.* -fy″ing], 1, to form into one; 2, to make alike in form.—*n.* **u″ni-fi-ca′tion.**—*n.* **u′ni-fi″er.**

u-ni-lat-er-al (ū″nĭ-lăt′ẽr-ăl), *adj.* having one side or surface.

un-im-peach-a-ble (ŭn″ĭm-pēch′ȧ-bl), *adj.* 1, irreproachable; 2, not to be doubted as regards honesty.

un-im-proved (ŭn″ĭm-pro͞ovd′), *adj.* 1, not made better; 2, of land, not developed.

un-in-formed (ŭn″ĭn-fôrmd′), *adj.* 1, not knowing the facts; 2, lacking knowledge; ignorant.

un-ion (ŭn′yŭn), *n.* 1, the act of joining two or more things into one; also, the state of being so joined; combination; 2, a league; mutual agreement; 3, matrimony; 4, a confederation; a whole made by combining parts previously under individual organization; as, the *union* of states into the United States; 5, a flag or part of a flag emblematic of union, as the starry canton on the U. S. flag; 6, an association of individuals or groups; specif., an association of workers formed for mutual benefit and protection by means of collective bargaining, legislation, etc.: often called *labor union* or *trade-union*;

7, any of various kinds of coupling for connecting pipes or rods; **8**, a fabric consisting of two or more materials combined: **union jack**, a jack, or small flag, emblematic of union: applied esp. to the canton of the flag of the U. S., or to the British union flag, when flown as a jack (see *flag*, colored illus.): **the Union**, the United States of America:—*adj.* of or pertaining to union or unions; as, *union* principles; *union* labor: **union suit**, a one-piece undergarment combining undershirt and drawers.

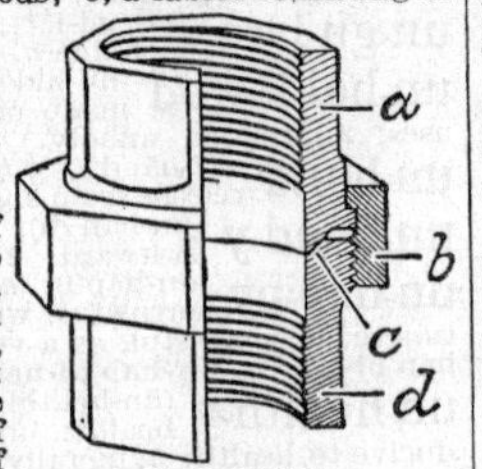

PIPE UNION

Section *a*, with nut *b* on it, is screwed on a pipe end, and section *d* on the end of the pipe to be coupled. Sections *a* and *d* are then drawn together in a tight joint at the fitted seat, *c*, by screwing nut *b*, swiveled on *a*, to *d*.

Syn., *n.* unity. *Union* means the act of bringing together to make one, or the state or product of such an act; as, the *union* of several brooks to make a river; a labor *union*. *Unity* means a state of oneness; as, *unity* of purpose.—*Ant.*, *n.* separation, division.

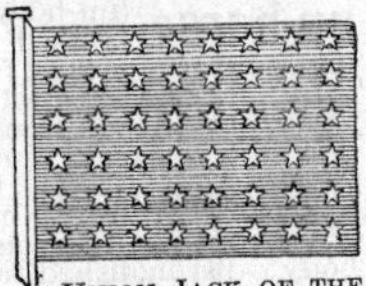

UNION JACK OF THE UNITED STATES

un-ion-ist (ūn′yŭn-ĭst), *n.* **1**, a believer in labor unions; **2**, a member of a labor union; **3**, one who supported the national government in the American Civil War: **Unionist**, in Great Britain, formerly, a member of a party opposing home rule for Ireland.—*n.* **un′ion-ism.**

un-ion-ize (ūn′yŭn-īz), *v.t.* [*p.t.* and *p.p.* -ized (-īzd), *p.pr.* -iz″ing], to cause to form, or to become a part of, a labor union.

u-nique (ū-nēk′), *adj.* **1**, unlike anything else; without an equal; **2**, loosely, unusual; as, a *unique* design.—*adv.* **u-nique′ly.** —*n.* **u-nique′ness.**

u-ni-son (ū′nĭ-sŭn; ū′nĭ-zŭn), *n.* **1**, oneness; agreement; concord; **2**, in music: **a**, sameness of pitch; **b**, the sounding at once of two tones an octave apart; **c**, the singing of the same series of tones by all the voices at once: distinguished from *harmony*.

u-nit (ū′nĭt), *n.* **1**, one person or thing of a number which make up a group; as, each citizen is a *unit* in the national body; also, a single group in an association made up of groups; **2**, in mathematics: **a**, the least whole number; one; **b**, one undivided number or amount, as opposed to a fractional one; **3**, a fixed amount, quantity, distance, etc., taken as a standard of measurement; as, a pound is a *unit* of measurement for weight.

U-ni-ta-ri-an (ū″nĭ-tā′rĭ-ăn), *n.* **1**, one who does not believe in the doctrine of the Trinity, and who believes that God is only one person; **2**, a member of the church body founded upon such a belief:—*adj.* of or pertaining to Unitarians or their beliefs.—*n.* **U″ni-ta′ri-an-ism.**

u-ni-ta-ry (ū′nĭ-tā-rĭ), *adj.* **1**, of or relating to a unit; characterized by, or relating to, unity; **2**, of the nature of, or like, a unit; not divided.

u-nite (ū-nīt′), *v.t.* [*p.t.* and *p.p.* u-nit′ed, *p.pr.* u-nit′ing], **1**, to join together; combine so as to make one; **2**, to bind together legally or otherwise, as in marriage.—*v.i.* **1**, to be joined together; **2**, to grow into one: **3**, to act together.

Syn. merge, join. (See combine, mix.)

u-nit-ed (ū-nīt′ĕd), *p.adj.* joined together; in agreement.—*adv.* **u-nit′ed-ly.**

U-nit-ed Breth-ren a Protestant sect formed in Moravia about 1450: often called *Moravians*.

u-ni-ty (ū′nĭ-tĭ), *n.* [*pl.* unities (-tĭz)], **1**, the state of being one; **2**, harmony; agreement; **3**, the number one; **4**, in literary or artistic creations, the quality of having all the parts centered about one theme, design, or effect; also, the symmetry so produced.

Syn. accord, harmony. (See union.)

u-ni-va-lent (ū″nĭ-vā′lĕnt; ū-nĭv′ȧ-lĕnt), *adj.* in chemistry, having the degree of combining power of one; capable of replacing, or combining with, a single hydrogen atom.—*n.* **u″ni-va′lence; u″ni-va′len-cy.**

u-ni-valve (ū′nĭ-vălv), *n.* **1**, a mollusk having one valve only, as the snail; a gastropod; **2**, a shell consisting of but one piece:—*adj.* having but one valve.—*adj.* **u′ni-valved″.**—*adj.* **u″ni-val′vu-lar.**

u-ni-ver-sal (ū″nĭ-vûr′săl), *adj.* **1**, pertaining to the whole system of created things; as, the *universal* law of gravitation; hence, embracing or including the whole; general; prevailing everywhere; as, *universal* peace; **2**, entire; whole: **universal joint**, a coupling or joint that permits the turning of two connected parts in any direction; esp., a coupling joining two shafts, so made as to permit angular motion in any direction, and at the same time transmit rotary motion from one shaft to the other (see *automobile*, illus.).—*adv.* **u″ni-ver′sal-ly.**

Syn. catholic. (See general.)

U-ni-ver-sal-ism (ū″nĭ-vûr′săl-ĭzm), *n.* the doctrine or belief that all mankind will finally be saved and that good will triumph.—*n.* **U″ni-ver′sal-ist.**

u-ni-ver-sal-i-ty (ū″nĭ-vẽr-săl′ĭ-tĭ), *n.* [*pl.* universalities (-tĭz)], the state or quality of being general; the state of prevailing everywhere; limitless extent.

u-ni-verse (ū′nĭ-vûrs), *n.* **1**, the whole system of existing material things; **2**, loosely, the world.

u-ni-ver-si-ty (ū″nĭ-vûr′sĭ-tĭ), *n.* [*pl.* universities (-tĭz)], **1**, an institution organized to provide instruction, study, or examination in the higher branches of learning, and conferring degrees in its various departments, as of the arts, medicine, law, or engineering; **2**, all the students of such an institution: **university extension**, educational courses given by a university, esp. in places remote from its center.

un-just (ŭn-jŭst′), *adj.* **1**, unfair, as an act; **2**, unrighteous, as a person; **3**, not in accordance with legal justice.—*adv.* **un-just′ly.**—*n.* **un-just′ness.**

un-kempt (ŭn-kĕmpt′), *adj.* **1**, not combed; disheveled; neglected; as, *unkempt* hair; **2**, slovenly; unpolished; **3**, rough.—*n.* **un-kempt′ness.**

un-kind (ŭn-kīnd′), *adj.* not gentle or sympathetic; harsh; wounding the feelings of others; as, *unkind* words.—*adv.* **un-kind′ly.**—*n.* **un-kind′ness.**

un-known (ŭn-nōn′), *adj.* not apprehended; not recognized or discovered:—*n.* a strange person or thing.

un-lace (ŭn-lās′), *v.t.* [*p.t.* and *p.p.* -laced′ (-lāst′), *p.pr.* -lac′ing], to undo the lacing of, as a shoe.

un-law-ful (ŭn-lô′fo͞ol), *adj.* **1**, contrary to law; **2**, illegitimate; illegal —*adv.* **un-law′ful-ly.**—*n.* **un-law′ful-ness.**

un-learn-ed (ŭn-lûr′nĕd), *adj.* **1**, ignorant; without schooling; **2**, not giving evidence of knowledge; **3**, (ŭn-lûrnd′), not acquired by study, as lessons.

un-less (ŭn-lĕs′), *conj.* if not; were it not the fact that; except when.

un-let-tered (ŭn-lĕt′ẽrd), *adj.* untaught; not educated; also, not able to read and write.
Syn. ignorant, untutored, illiterate.

un-like (ŭn-līk′), *adj.* having no resemblance; different.—*n.* **un-like′ness.**

un-like-ly (ŭn-līk′lĭ), *adj.* **1**, not probable; **2**, not giving prospects of success; as, an *unlikely* plan.—*n.* **un-like′li-hood.**—*n.* **un-like′li-ness.**

un-lim-ber (ŭn-lĭm′bẽr), *v.t.* to detach from (a gun) the limber, or front part of a gun carriage:—*v.i.* to detach or unfasten the limber from a gun.

un-lim-it-ed (ŭn-lĭm′ĭ-tĕd), *adj.* **1**, boundless; without restrictions; as, an *unlimited* area; **2**, not restricted or restrained; as, *unlimited* power; **3**, indefinite; as, a note which runs for an *unlimited* term.

un-load (ŭn-lōd′), *v.t.* **1**, to remove a burden from; as, to *unload* a wagon; **2**, to remove from a car, wagon, ship, etc.; as, to *unload* freight; **3**, to relieve from anything troublesome:—*v.i.* to discharge a burden or cargo.

un-lock (ŭn-lŏk′), *v.t.* **1**, to unfasten; open, as something that has been fastened; **2**, hence, to make open or clear; as, to *unlock* a mystery.

un-looked–for (ŭn-lo͝okt′=fôr″), *adj.* not expected or foreseen.

un-loose (ŭn-lo͞os′), *v.t.* [*p.t.* and *p.p.* -loosed′ (-lo͞ost′), *p.pr.* -loos′ing], **1**, to unfasten; untie; undo; **2**, to unbind; set at liberty:—*v.i.* to become unfastened; fall in pieces. Also, **un-loos′en.**

un-love-ly (ŭn-lŭv′lĭ), *adj.* without charm; unattractive.

un-luck-y (ŭn-lŭk′ĭ), *adj.* **1**, not fortunate; as, an *unlucky* speech; **2**, tending to bring bad luck; as, an *unlucky* day.—*adv.* **un-luck′i-ly.**—*n.* **un-luck′i-ness.**

un-man (ŭn-măn′), *v.t.* [*p.t.* and *p.p.* -manned′ (-mănd′), *p.pr.* -man′ning], to rob of courage and strength; unnerve.

un-man-ly (ŭn-măn′lĭ), *adj.* lacking the qualities of a man; without courage; cowardly; weak.

un-man-ner-ly (ŭn-măn′ẽr-lĭ), *adj.* rude; without courtesy; impolite.—*n.* **un-man′ner-li-ness.**

un-mask (ŭn-mȧsk′), *v.t.* **1**, to remove a disguise from; **2**, to show the true nature of:—*v.i.* **1**, to lay aside a mask; **2**, to take off a disguise.

un-mean-ing (ŭn-mēn′ĭng), *adj.* senseless; signifying nothing.

un-mer-ci-ful (ŭn-mûr′sĭ-fo͝ol), *adj.* **1**, without kindness or pity; cruel; **2**, *Colloq.*, extremely severe; unreasonable; as, an *unmerciful* delay.—*adv.* **un-mer′ci-ful-ly.**—*n.* **un-mer′ci-ful-ness.**

un-mis-tak-a-ble (ŭn″mĭs-tāk′ȧ-bl), *adj.* incapable of being mistaken or misunderstood; clear; obvious.—*adv.* **un″mis-tak′a-bly.**

un-mit-i-gat-ed (ŭn-mĭt′ĭ-gāt″ĕd), *adj.* not lessened; not softened; hence, very bad.

un-mor-al (ŭn-mŏr′ăl), *adj.* **1**, having no sense of right and wrong; **2**, not involving a question of morality.

un-nat-u-ral (ŭn-năt′ū-răl), *adj.* **1**, not like or representing nature; artificial; **2**, abnormal; **3**, without the common impulses of humanity; monstrous.—*adv.* **un-nat′u-ral-ly.**—*n.* **un-nat′u-ral-ness.**

un-nec-es-sa-ry (ŭn-nĕs′ĕ-sĕr″ĭ), *adj.* not needed; of no use.—*adv.* **un-nec′es-sar″i-ly.**

un-nerve (ŭn-nûrv′), *v.t.* [*p.t.* and *p.p.* -nerved′ (-nûrvd′), *p.pr.* -nerv′ing], to rob of nerve control; weaken, as by misfortune or a shock.

un-num-bered (ŭn-nŭm′bẽrd), *adj.* **1**, not counted; **2**, countless; hence, exceedingly numerous.

un-oc-cu-pied (ŭn-ŏk′ū-pīd), *adj.* **1**, not occupied; not inhabited; **2**, unemployed; not busy.

un-or-gan-ized (ŭn-ôr′găn-īzd), *adj.* **1**, not arranged in systematic form; **2**, inorganic; not living.

un-pack (ŭn-păk′), *v.t.* **1**, to take out, as goods, from a receptacle; **2**, to remove the contents of; as, to *unpack* a trunk.

un-par-al-leled (ŭn-păr′ă-lĕld), *adj.* not matched; without an equal; having nothing similar.

un-par-lia-men-ta-ry (ŭn-pär″lĭ-mĕn′tȧ-rĭ), *adj.* not conforming to the rules of parliamentary bodies.

un-pin (ŭn-pĭn′), *v.t.* [*p.t.* and *p.p.* -pinned′ (-pĭnd′), *p.pr.* -pin′ning], to unfasten by taking out a pin or pins.

un-pleas-ant (ŭn-plĕz′ănt), *adj.* **1**, not amiable; disagreeable; **2**, distasteful; offensive.—*adv.* **un-pleas′ant-ly.**—*n.* **un-pleas′ant-ness.**

un-prec-e-dent-ed (ŭn-prĕs′ē-dĕn-tĕd), *adj.* having no precedent; unusual; novel.

un-prej-u-diced (ŭn-prĕj′o͞o-dĭst), *adj.* **1**, not influenced by hastily formed opinions; impartial; fair; **2**, not encroached upon, as privileges.

un-pre-med-i-tat-ed (ŭn″prē-mĕd′ĭ-tāt″ĕd), *adj.* not planned or considered beforehand.

un-prin-ci-pled (ŭn-prĭn′sĭ-pld), *adj.* without right moral ideals; careless of right and wrong.

un-pro-fes-sion-al (ŭn″prō-fĕsh′ŭn-ăl), *adj.* **1**, not consistent with the rules or ethics of a given profession; as, *unprofessional* conduct; **2**, not belonging to a profession; **3**, spoken or performed by one outside a profession; as, *unprofessional* advice.

un-qual-i-fied (ŭn-kwŏl′ĭ-fīd), *adj.* **1**, lacking the proper qualifications; unfit; **2**, not legally fitted; lacking legal authority; **3**, unrestricted.

un-ques-tion-a-ble (ŭn-kwĕs′chŭn-ȧ-bl), *adj.* not to be doubted or disputed; indisputable.—*adv.* **un-ques′tion-a-bly.**

un-qui-et (ŭn-kwī′ĕt), *adj.* **1**, noisy; disturbed; not at peace; **2**, causing discomfort; disturbing.—*adv.* **un-qui′et-ly.**

un-rav-el (ŭn-răv′l), *v.t.* **1**, to pull apart the threads of; pull out, as knitting; **2**, to free from complication; solve, as a mystery:—*v.i.* to be pulled apart or out.

un-read-y (ŭn-rĕd′ĭ), *adj.* **1**, not prepared; tardy or slow; **2**, not quick to act.—*adv.* **un-read′i-ly.**—*n.* **un-read′i-ness.**

un-re-al (ŭn-rē′ăl), *adj.* not actual; imaginary; fanciful.—*n.* **un″re-al′i-ty.**

un-rea-son-a-ble (ŭn-rē′zn-ȧ-bl), *adj.* **1**, not based upon reason; **2**, demanding too much; exorbitant; as, *unreasonable* prices.—*n.* **un-rea′son-a-ble-ness.**—*adv.* **un-rea′son-a-bly.**

un-re-mit-ting (ŭn″rē-mĭt′ĭng), *adj.* never ceasing or relaxing; as, *unremitting* toil.

un-re-served (ŭn″rē-zûrvd′), *adj.* **1**, given without restriction; not held back; as, all the seats are *unreserved;* **2,** holding nothing back; outspoken; as, *unreserved* confidence.—*adv.* **un″re-serv′ed-ly.**—*n.* **un″re-serv′ed-ness.**

un-rest (ŭn-rĕst′), *n.* lack of ease and quiet; anxiety; mental worry.

un-right-eous (ŭn-rī′chŭs), *adj.* **1,** not just; **2,** wicked.—*adv.* **un-right′eous-ly.**—*n.* **un-right′eous-ness.**

un-ripe (ŭn-rīp′), *adj.* not ripe; immature; hence, not fully ready.

un-ri-valed (ŭn-rī′vȧld), *adj.* unequaled; peerless. Also, **un-ri′valled.**

un-roll (ŭn-rōl′), *v.t.* **1,** to open by unwrapping (something which is rolled); **2,** to display:—*v.i.* to become straight, as from a rolled condition.

un-ruf-fled (ŭn-rŭf′ld), *adj.* not ruffled; hence, peaceful; serene.

un-rul-y (ŭn-rōōl′ĭ), *adj.* paying no attention to rules or commands; hard to manage; ungovernable.—*n.* **un-rul′i-ness.**

un-sad-dle (ŭn-săd′l), *v.t.* [*p.t.* and *p.p.* -dled (-ld), *p.pr.* -dling], **1,** to take off a saddle from; **2,** to unhorse.

un-sa-vor-y (ŭn-sā′vĕr-ĭ), *adj.* **1,** lacking taste or seasoning; **2,** disagreeable to taste or smell; **3,** morally offensive, as a story. Also, **un-sa′vour-y.**

un-screw (ŭn-skrōō′), *v.t.* **1,** to loosen by taking out a screw or screws; **2,** to draw out or off by turning, as a nut.

un-scru-pu-lous (ŭn-skrōō′pū-lŭs), *adj.* lacking in moral qualities; careless of right and wrong; as, *unscrupulous* business methods.—*adv.* **un-scru′pu-lous-ly.**—*n.* **un-scru′pu-lous-ness.**

un-seal (ŭn-sēl′), *v.t.* to open by breaking or removing a seal.

un-search-a-ble (ŭn-sûr′chȧ-bl), *adj.* incapable of being traced; hidden; mysterious; as, an *unsearchable* motive for such a crime.

un-sea-son-a-ble (ŭn-sē′zn-ȧ-bl), *adj.* **1,** not at a well-chosen time; untimely; **2,** taking place out of season.—*n.* **un-sea′son-a-ble-ness.**—*adv.* **un-sea′son-a-bly.**

un-seat (ŭn-sēt′), *v.t.* **1,** to remove from a seat; **2,** to depose; deprive of the right to sit as representative, as in a legislature.

un-seem-ly (ŭn-sēm′lĭ), *adj.* improper; not fitting:—*adv.* in an unsuitable manner.—*n.* **un-seem′li-ness.**

un-seen (ŭn-sēn′), *adj.* **1,** not seen; beyond the range of vision; **2,** invisible.

un-set-tle (ŭn-sĕt′l), *v.t.* [*p.t.* and *p.p.* -tled (-ld), *p.pr.* -tling], **1,** to loosen from a firm position; disturb; **2,** to derange, as one's opinions or sense of security:—*v.i.* to be disturbed.

un-sex (ŭn-sĕks′), *v.t.* to deprive of sex characteristics or organs.

un-sheathe (ŭn-shēth′), *v.t.* [*p.t.* and *p.p.* -sheathed′ (-shēthd′), *p.pr.* -sheath′ing], to take from its scabbard, as a dagger or sword.

un-ship (ŭn-shĭp′), *v.t.* [*p.t.* and *p.p.* -shipped′ (-shĭpt′), *p.pr.* -ship′ping], **1,** to take out of a ship, as a cargo; **2,** to remove or take out of position, as an oar, a mast, or a rudder.

un-sift-ed (ŭn-sĭf′tĕd), *adj.* **1,** not having been passed through a sieve; **2,** not having been closely examined.

un-sight-ly (ŭn-sīt′lĭ), *adj.* ugly; unpleasant to look upon.

un-skil-ful (ŭn-skĭl′fōōl), *adj.* without expertness; inapt; not clever in performance of work, esp. work with the hands. Also, **un-skill′ful.**—*adv.* **un-skil′ful-ly.**—*n.* **un-skil′ful-ness.**

un-so-cia-ble (ŭn-sō′shȧ-bl), *adj.* not friendly; not disposed to seek the companionship of others.—*adv.* **un-so′cia-bly.**—*n.* **un-so″cia-bil′i-ty.**

un-so-phis-ti-cat-ed (ŭn″sō-fĭs′tĭ-kāt″ĕd), *adj.* not experienced in the ways of the world; simple.—*n.* **un″so-phis′ti-cat″ed-ness.**
Syn. naïve, artless, innocent.

un-sound (ŭn-sound′), *adj.* **1,** not safe or reliable; **2,** not founded on truth; as, *unsound* doctrine; **3,** diseased.—*adv.* **un-sound′ly.**—*n.* **un-sound′ness.**

un-speak-a-ble (ŭn-spēk′ȧ-bl), *adj.* **1,** not to be expressed in words; **2,** *Colloq.*, too bad to be talked of.—*n.* **un-speak′a-ble-ness.**—*adv.* **un-speak′a-bly.**

un-spot-ted (ŭn-spŏt′ĕd), *adj.* without stain; flawless; immaculate.

un-sta-ble (ŭn-stā′bl), *adj.* **1,** not steady; **2,** easily thrown over or upset.

un-stop (ŭn-stŏp′), *v.t.* [*p.t.* and *p.p.* -stopped′ (-stŏpt′), *p.pr.* -stop′ping], to remove the cork, stopper, or other obstruction, from, as a bottle or pipe.

un-strung (ŭn-strŭng′), *adj.* **1,** having a string or strings loosened or missing, as a banjo or a violin; **2,** nervously upset; unnerved; relaxed, as from a shock.

un-sub-stan-tial (ŭn″sŭb-stăn′shăl), *adj.* **1,** without material form or body; **2,** fanciful; imaginary; **3,** not strong or solid, as a structure.—*adv.* **un″sub-stan′tial-ly.**

un-think-ing (ŭn-thĭngk′ĭng), *adj.* **1,** not showing thought; **2,** careless; inconsiderate.—*adv.* **un-think′ing-ly.**

un-ti-dy (ŭn-tī′dĭ), *adj.* not neat; disorderly; slovenly.—*adv.* **un-ti′di-ly.**—*n.* **un-ti′di-ness.**

un-tie (ŭn-tī′), *v.t.* [*p.t.* and *p.p.* -tied′ (-tīd′), *p.pr.* -ty′ing], to unfasten by loosening (a knot or an object bound by a knot); hence, to set free from any restraint:—*v.i.* to become unfastened.

un-til (ŭn-tĭl′), *prep.* to or up to: used in relation to time:—*conj.* to the degree or place that; to the time when.

un-time-ly (ŭn-tīm′lĭ), *adj.* not at the right moment or on the right occasion; happening too soon:—*adv.* inopportunely; too soon.—*n.* **un-time′li-ness.**

un-to (ŭn′tōō), *prep. Archaic* or *Poetic*, to:—*conj. Obs.*, until; till.

un-told (ŭn-tōld′), *adj.* **1,** not expressed or revealed; **2,** not counted; hence, very great; as, *untold* riches.

un-touch-a-ble (ŭn-tŭch′ȧ-bl), *adj.* not to be touched:—*n.* in India, a member of the lowest caste, whose touch or presence is thought by higher castes to bring pollution.

un-to-ward (ŭn-tō′ẽrd; ŭn-tôrd′), *adj.* **1,** wayward; stubborn; **2,** unfortunate; inconvenient; as, *untoward* fate.—*adv.* **un-to′ward-ly.**—*n.* **un-to′ward-ness.**

un-tried (ŭn-trīd′), *adj.* **1,** not put to the test; not yet demonstrated; **2,** not yet brought to trial, as a case.

un-true (ŭn-trōō′), *adj.* **1,** false; contrary to the truth; **2,** not faithful to one's duty; disloyal; faithless; **3,** varying from a standard; out of tune or alignment.

un-truth (ŭn-trōōth′), *n.* **1,** falseness; incorrectness; **2,** a lie.
Syn. falsity, mendacity. (See lie.)

un-truth-ful (ŭn-trōōth′fōōl), *adj.* **1,** wanting in veracity; lying; **2,** contrary to the truth.—*adv.* **un-truth′ful-ly.**—*n.* **un-truth′ful-ness.**

un-tu-tored (ŭn-tū′tẽrd), *adj.* not taught; having little learning.

un-twist (ŭn-twĭst′), *v.t.* and *v.i.* to make or become unloosed, as the strands of a rope.

un-used (ŭn-ūzd′), *adj.* **1**, not put to use; **2**, not accustomed; not in the habit of: with *to;* as, *unused* to hard labor.

un-u-su-al (ŭn-ū′zhū-ăl), *adj.* not customary; uncommon; strange; remarkable.—*adv.* **un-u′su-al-ly.**

un-ut-ter-a-ble (ŭn-ŭt′ẽr-ȧ-bl), *adj.* inexpressible; beyond description.—*adv.* **un-ut′ter-a-bly.**

un-val-ued (ŭn-văl′ūd), *adj.* **1**, not considered of much worth; neglected; **2**, not appraised, as property.

un-var-nished (ŭn-vär′nĭsht), *adj.* **1**, not coated with varnish; not polished; **2**, without embellishments; plain; as, the *unvarnished* truth.

un-veil (ŭn-vāl′), *v.t.* to disclose by taking off a veil or covering; uncover; reveal clearly:—*v.i.* **1**, to take off a veil; **2**, to show one's own true nature.

un-war-rant-a-ble (ŭn-wŏr′ăn-tȧ-bl), *adj.* **1**, without authority; **2**, not to be justified, or proved right; unjust; as, he took an *unwarrantable* liberty with my property.—*adv.* **un-war′rant-a-bly.**

un-wa-ry (ŭn-wā′rĭ), *adj.* off one's guard; heedless; incautious.—*adv.* **un-wa′ri-ly.**—*n.* **un-wa′ri-ness.**

un-wea-ried (ŭn-wē′rĭd), *adj.* **1**, not tired; **2**, tireless; still strong.

un-well (ŭn-wĕl′), *adj.* not in good health; indisposed; ailing.

un-wield-y (ŭn-wēl′dĭ), *adj.* difficult to move or manage because of size, shape, or weight; bulky; clumsy.—*adv.* **un-wield′i-ly.**—*n.* **un-wield′i-ness.**

un-will-ing (ŭn-wĭl′ĭng), *adj.* reluctant; disinclined.—*adv.* **un-will′ing-ly.**—*n.* **un-will′ing-ness.**

un-wind (ŭn-wīnd′), *v.t.* [*p.t.* and *p.p.* -wound′ (-wound′), *p.pr.* -wind′ing], to loosen by uncoiling:—*v.i.* to uncoil.

un-wise (ŭn-wīz′), *adj.* not showing good judgment; rash; foolish; imprudent.—*adv.* **un-wise′ly.**

un-wit-ting (ŭn-wĭt′ĭng), *adj.* **1**, unintentional; **2**, unaware; not knowing.—*adv.* **un-wit′ting-ly.**

un-wont-ed (ŭn-wŭn′tĕd), *adj.* **1**, unusual; uncommon; infrequent; rare; **2**, unaccustomed; not habitual.—*adv.* **un-wont′ed-ly.**—*n.* **un-wont′ed-ness.**

un-world-ly (ŭn-wûrld′lĭ), *adj.* free from sordid or worldly motives; spiritually minded.—*n.* **un-world′li-ness.**

un-wor-thy (ŭn-wûr′*th*ĭ), *adj.* **1**, lacking merit, value, soundness, etc.; **2**, not deserving; **3**, not suitable or becoming: with *of;* as, such conduct is *unworthy* of you.—*adv.* **un-wor′thi-ly.**—*n.* **un-wor′thi-ness.**

un-wrap (ŭn-răp′), *v.t* and *v.i.* [*p.t.* and *p.p.* -wrapped′ or -wrapt′ (-răpt′), *p.pr.* -wrap′ping], to make, or become, loose or open; as, he *unwrapped* the package.

un-writ-ten (ŭn-rĭt′n), *p.adj.* **1**, not expressed or recorded in writing; **2**, blank; without writing: **unwritten law, 1**, a legal code developed from customs and precedents, as the English and American common law; **2**, the public sentiment that justifies leniency to those who commit criminal acts in avenging **injury to their own or** their family honor.

up (ŭp), *adv.* **1**, toward or in a higher position or degree; as, to go *up* in the world: opp. of *down;* **2**, into being or action; as, *up* in arms; **3**, into notice or consideration; as, to bring *up* a question; **4**, completely; in or to a finished state; as, to tear *up* a report; a stream dries *up;* **5**, away; in a safe place; as, to store *up* wealth; **6**, to a higher scale, price, or volume; as, potatoes are *up;* to swell *up;* **7**, even with in time, degree, space, amount, etc.; as, to catch *up* in a race; keep *up* with the times; **8**, in the state of being well informed or skilful; as, *up* on science; **9**, in an erect position; on one's feet; out of bed: hence, in an active condition: **up to, 1**, capable of; competent for; as, he is *up to* the job; **2**, on the point of or engaged in; as, *up to* mischief; **3**, *Slang,* incumbent upon; as, it is *up to* you to make good:—*prep.* **1**, from a lower to a higher place on or along; as, to walk *up* the hill; **2**, toward the source of; as, *up* the river; also, toward the interior of, as of a country or region; **3**, at or near the top of; as, *up* a tree:—*adj.* **1**, leading, moving, or sloping toward a higher place; upward; as, on the *up* grade; **2**, in golf, ahead of an opponent; as, two *up:* **ups and downs**, alternate states of good and bad fortune.

up- (ŭp-), *prefix,* placed before verbs and nouns, meaning up or upward; as, *up*heave; *up*growth.

u-pas (ū′păs), *n.* **1**, a tree, common in Java, with a poisonous juice used as arrow poison; **2**, the juice of this tree.

up-braid (ŭp-brād′), *v.t.* **1**, to accuse of a wrong or shameful act; **2**, to chide or blame:—*v.i.* to utter reproach.
Syn. censure, reprove, rebuke, berate.

up-grade (ŭp′grād″), *n.* **1**, an ascent, as in a road; **2**, *Colloq.*, an improvement, as on the *upgrade.*—Also *adj.* and *adv.*

up-growth (ŭp′grōth″), *n.* **1**, the process of growing up; development; **2**, that which grows up or has grown up.

up-heav-al (ŭp-hēv′ăl), *n.* **1**, a lifting from below; esp., a lifting of some part of the earth's crust by an internal force; **2**, hence, a political or social disturbance, as a revolution.

up-heave (ŭp-hēv′), *v.t.* [*p.t.* and *p.p.* -heaved′ (-hēvd′), *p. pr.* -heav′ing], to lift, as something heavy, by force from beneath:—*v.i.* to rise by such pressure.

up-hill (ŭp-hĭl′), *adv.* **1**, to a higher level or point on a slope; **2**, in an upward direction:—*adj.* (ŭp′hĭl″), **1**, sloping upward; ascending; **2**, hence, toilsome; as, study is *uphill* work for him.

up-hold (ŭp-hōld′), *v.t.* [*p.t.* and *p.p.* -held′ (-hĕld′), *p.pr.* -hold′ing], **1**, to support; as, pillars *uphold* the roof; **2**, to encourage or give aid to; as, the council *upheld* the mayor; **3**, to maintain or confirm, as a decision.—*n.* **up-hold′er.**

up-hol-ster (ŭp-hōl′stẽr), *v.t.* **1**, to fit out with curtains, hangings, etc., as rooms; **2**, to provide with cushions, springs, etc., as furniture.—*n.* **up-hol′ster-er.**

up-hol-ster-y (ŭp-hōl′stẽr-ĭ), *n.* [*pl.* upholsteries (-ĭz)], **1**, the business of fitting out rooms and furniture with coverings, draperies, etc.; **2**, curtains, cushions, and like interior fittings of a house.

up-keep (ŭp′kēp″), *n.* **1**, the maintaining of a house, store, etc.; also, the state of being kept up, or in repair; **2**, the means or cost of maintenance.

up-land (ŭp′lănd), *n.* high ground; an elevated region bordering a low shore, valley, etc.:—*adj.* pertaining to an elevated region.

up-lift (ŭp-lĭft′), *v.t.* to raise; elevate; lift up:—*n.* (ŭp′lĭft″), **1**, an elevation; **2**, hence, a tendency or move toward a higher standard; as, a moral *uplift;* **3**, in geology, an upheaval.—*p.adj.* **up-lift′ed.**—*n.* **up-lift′er.**

up-on (ŭ-pŏn′), *prep.* **1**, on; resting on the top or surface of; as, *upon* the shelf; **2**, against; as, *upon* the wall; **3**, situated on; as, *upon* the coast; **4**, judging from; as, *upon* the evidence; **5**, chosen for or belonging to; as, *upon* the committee; **6**, in a state or condition of; as, *upon* sale; **7**, at the moment of;

as, *upon* arrival; **8,** to or toward; as, we came *upon* them suddenly; **9,** relating to; as, a speech *upon* prohibition.

up-per (ŭp′ẽr), *adj.* **1,** higher in place; as, the *upper* story of a house; **2,** superior in rank; as, the *upper* classes: **the upper hand,** the advantage:—*n.* the part of a shoe above the sole: **on one's uppers,** in need of money or necessities.

up-per-most (ŭp′ẽr-mōst), *adj.* highest in place, rank, or authority.

up-pish (ŭp′ĭsh), *adj. Colloq.*, arrogant; snobbish; supercilious; haughty. —*adv.* **up′pish-ly.**—*n.* **up′pish-ness.**

up-right (ŭp′rīt″), *adj.* **1,** standing erect; as, an *upright* piano; **2,** just; honest; as, a man of *upright* character:—*adv.* in an erect position:—*n.* something standing straight up, as a timber supporting a beam.—*adv.* **up′right″ly.**—*n.* **up′right″ness.**

up-ris-ing (ŭp-rīz′ĭng), *n.* a rebellion against authority; revolt.

up-roar (ŭp′rōr″), *n.* a noisy disturbance; confusion and clamor.
Syn. racket, commotion. (See noise.)

up-roar-i-ous (ŭp-rōr′ĭ-ŭs), *adj.* making or accompanied by noise and disturbance; loud and boisterous.—*adv.* **up-roar′i-ous-ly.**—*n.* **up-roar′i-ous-ness.**

up-root (ŭp-rōōt′), *v.t.* to pull up by the roots; hence, to remove; eradicate.

up-set (ŭp-sĕt′), *v.t.* [*p.t.* and *p.p.* -set′, *p.pr.* -set′ting], **1,** to overthrow; overturn, as a glass of water; also, to interfere with; as, to *upset* plans; **2,** to shorten and thicken, as a piece of red-hot iron, by striking on the end; **3,** *Colloq.*, to put out of normal mental or physical condition; as, to have one's nerves *upset*:—*n.* (ŭp′sĕt), **1,** the act of overturning or disturbing; **2,** the state of being overturned; **3,** *Colloq.*, mental or physical disturbance.

up-shot (ŭp′shŏt″), *n.* final result; conclusion; outcome.

up-side (ŭp′sīd″), *n.* the upper part: **upside down,** having the top part at the bottom; hence, in disorder.

up-si-lon (ūp′sĭ-lŏn), *n.* the 20th letter of the Greek alphabet [υ, Υ], approximately equivalent to the English *u* or German *ü*: often appearing as *y* in English words derived from the Greek.

up-stairs (ŭp-stârz′), *adv.* toward or on an upper floor:—*adj.* (ŭp′stârz″), pertaining to, or on, an upper floor; as, an *upstairs* room:—*n.* (ŭp′stârz″), the part of a building above the first floor.

up-start (ŭp′stärt″), *n.* **1,** one who springs up or rises suddenly; esp., one who has suddenly risen from humbleness to wealth; a parvenu; **2,** one who is arrogant:—*adj.* **1,** suddenly raised to a position of wealth and influence; **2,** arrogant; pretentious.

up–to–date (ŭp′=tōō=dāt′), *adj.* **1,** up to the present time; **2,** in the latest style; as, an *up-to-date* hat.

up-turn (ŭp-tûrn′), *v.t.* and *v.i.* to turn up; as, to *upturn* sod.

up-ward (ŭp′wẽrd), *adv.* **1,** in an ascending direction; from lower to higher; **2,** toward a higher rank or position; as, to climb *upward* in a profession; **3,** toward the direction of origin; as, they followed the river *upward;* **4,** indefinitely more; as, children of three years and *upward:* **upward of** or **upwards of,** more than; as, they collected *upward of* a million dollars for the Red Cross: —*adj.* directed from lower to higher; as, an *upward* slope. Also, *adv.* **up′wards.**

u-ræ-mi-a (ū-rē′mĭ-*ȧ*), *n.* a poisoned condition of the blood caused by suppression, or deficient secretion, of urine. Also, **u-re′mi-a.**—*adj.* **u-ræ′mic.**

u-ræ-us (ū-rē′ŭs), *n.* the representation of a serpent appearing in the headdress of Egyptian divinities and kings, symbolizing sovereignty.

URÆUS

U-ral–Al-ta-ic (ū′răl=ăl-tā′ĭk), *adj.* designating, or pertaining to, a large linguistic family, scattered over northern and central Asia and Europe, comprising the Turkish, Mongolian, Finno-Ugric, and other languages.

U-ra-ni-a (ū-rā′nĭ-*ȧ*), *n.* in mythology, the Muse of astronomy.—*adj.* **U-ra′ni-an.**

u-ra-ni-um (ū-rā′nĭ-ŭm), *n.* a hard, heavy, white metallic element which possesses radioactive properties: found chiefly in pitchblende.

U-ra-nus (ū′r*ȧ*-nŭs), *n.* **1,** in mythology, the son of Gæa (Earth), and the father of the Titans and the Cyclopes; **2,** the most remote, excepting Neptune and Pluto, of the planets (see *solar system*, illus.).

ur-ban (ûr′băn), *adj.* of or pertaining to a city or town; as, *urban* residents.

ur-bane (ûr-bān′), *adj.* courteous; polite; affable; suave.—*adv.* **ur-bane′ly.**

ur-ban-i-ty (ûr-băn′ĭ-tĭ), *n.* politeness; refinement; suavity.
Syn. courtesy, civility, affability.

ur-chin (ûr′chĭn), *n.* **1,** a small boy; **esp.,** a pert or mischievous little fellow; **2,** a sea urchin.

Ur-du (ōōr′dōō), *n.* Hindustani, the common language of the Mohammedans of India.

-ure (-ūr), *n.* a suffix denoting action, state or result: usually attached to a past participle stem; as, text*ure;* fiss*ure;* junct*ure.*

u-re-a (ū′rē-*ȧ*), *n.* a white, highly soluble, crystalline substance, one of the final products of oxidation of the nitrogenous compounds of the body, found abundantly in the urine of mammals.—*adj.* **u′re-al.**

u-re-ter (ū-rē′tẽr), *n.* the duct or tube through which urine passes from a kidney to the bladder.

u-re-thra (ū-rē′thr*ȧ*), *n.* the duct or canal through which urine is discharged from the bladder.—*adj.* **u-re′thral.**

urge (ûrj), *v.t.* [*p.t.* and *p.p.* urged (ûrjd), *p.pr.* urg′ing], **1,** to force onward; drive; **2,** to seek to influence the will of; as, to *urge* one to action; **3,** to present insistently; as, to *urge* a point in an argument:—*v.i.* to insist upon a statement, argument, etc.
Syn. push, encourage, promote.

ur-gent (ûr′jĕnt), *adj.* **1,** calling for immediate attention; important; pressing; as, an *urgent* message; **2,** insistent; eager. —*n.* **ur′gen-cy.**—*adv.* **ur′gent-ly.**

U-ri-ah (ū-rī′*ȧ*), *n.* in the Bible, a Hittite captain in the army of Israel, slain by being placed at David's order in the hottest part of the battle (2 Samuel 11:3–24).

u-ric (ū′rĭk), *adj.* pertaining to, or derived from, urine: **uric acid,** a white, almost insoluble, compound, found in small quantities in the urine of mammals.

u-ri-nal (ū′rĭ-năl), *n.* **1,** a vessel for urine; **2,** a place for urinating.

u-ri-na-ry (ū′rĭ-nā-rĭ), *adj.* pertaining to urine, or to the organs that secrete and discharge it.

u-ri-nate (ū′rĭ-nāt), *v.i.* [*p.t.* and *p.p.* -nat″ed, *p.pr.* -nat″ing], to void urine.—*n.* **u″ri-na′tion.**

u-rine (ū′rĭn), *n.* the fluid secreted by the kidneys, cast off as waste.

urn (ûrn), *n.* **1,** a vase, usually with a base or pedestal; **2,** a receptacle for the ashes of the dead; **3,** hence, the grave.

Ur-sa Ma-jor (ûr′sȧ), the Great Bear, the most prominent of the northern constellations, containing the seven stars that form the Great Dipper, two of which, the *Pointers*, are nearly in line with the North Star: also called *Charles's Wain*.

Ur-sa Mi-nor the Little Bear, a constellation in the northern heavens, in the shape of a small dipper, the end star of the handle being the North Star, Polaris: also called *Little Dipper*.

ur-sine (ûr′sīn; ûr′sĭn), *adj.* pertaining to, or like, a bear.

u-rus (ū′rŭs), *n.* a now extinct European wild ox described by Cæsar.

us (ŭs), *pron.* the objective case of *we*, the plural of the first person *I*.

us-a-ble (ūz′ȧ-bl), *adj.* fit to be employed or made use of. Also, **use′a-ble.** —*n.* **us′a-ble-ness.**

us-age (ūz′āj; ūs′āj), *n.* **1,** the act or mode of using; treatment; **2,** settled habit or custom; habitual employment by people at large; as, the *usage* of certain words.
Syn. use, fashion, practice.

[1]**use** (ūs), *n.* **1,** the act of employing; the application of anything to a particular purpose; as, the *use* of steel for rails; **2,** familiarity; custom; continued practice; **3,** practical worth; utility; as, it is of no *use;* **4,** reason for employing; necessity; as, we have no *use* for the goods; **5,** right or power of employing; as, to lose the *use* of an eye:—*v.t.* (ūz), [*p.t.* and *p.p.* used (ūzd), *p.pr.* us′ing], **1,** to make use of; employ; **2,** to avail oneself of; as, to *use* a friend's library; **3,** to practice or make habitual use of; as, to *use* economy; **4,** to treat, act, or behave toward; as, to *use* one's servants kindly; **5,** to make accustomed: chiefly in the passive voice and followed by *to;* as, the man is *used* to ease:—*v.i.* to be accustomed: now only in the past tense; as, they *used* to work together.—*n.* **us′er.**
Syn., n. (see utility); *v.* (see employ).

[2]**use** (ūs), *n.* in law, the right which one has to the enjoyment of the rents of lands, etc., belonging to another.

use-ful (ūs′fool), *adj.* full of practical worth; adapted to a purpose; as, *useful* work.—*adv.* **use′ful-ly.**—*n.* **use′ful-ness.**

use-less (ūs′lĕs), *adj.* **1,** having, or being of, no practical worth; as, *useless* material; **2,** without results; as, *useless* efforts. —*adv.* **use′less-ly.**—*n.* **use′less-ness.**

ush-er (ŭsh′ẽr), *n.* **1,** a doorkeeper; hence, one who escorts or directs persons to seats in a church, theater, etc.; **2,** in England, an assistant teacher:—*v.t.* **1,** to announce; **2,** to escort or accompany.

u-su-al (ū′zhŭ-ăl), *adj.* ordinary; habitual. —*adv.* **u′su-al-ly.**—*n.* **u′su-al-ness.**
Syn. customary, habitual, regular.

u-su-fruct (ū′zū-frŭkt), *n.* in law, the right to enjoyment of profits from another's property.

u-su-ri-ous (ū-zū′rĭ-ŭs; ū-zhōō′-), *adj.* **1,** practicing usury, or lending money at an unlawful rate of interest; **2,** like, or involving, usury.

u-surp (ū-zûrp′), *v.t.* to take possession of by force, or unjustly; as, to *usurp* the office, functions, powers, or rights of another, esp. of a king or ruler:—*v.i.* to take possession of the office, functions, powers, or rights of another by force.—*n.* **u-surp′er.** —*n.* **u″sur-pa′tion.**

u-su-ry (ū′zhŭ-rĭ), *n.* **1,** the practice of lending money at a rate higher than the lawful rate; **2,** very high interest.—*n.* **u′su-rer.**

Ute (ūt; ū′tē), *n.* a member of a western Indian tribe, formerly found in Colorado, Utah, New Mexico, and Arizona.

u-ten-sil (ū-tĕn′sĭl), *n.* an implement or vessel for use in practical work, esp. one used in a kitchen.

u-ter-us (ū′tẽr-ŭs), *n.* [*pl.* uteri (-ī)], the womb, or organ in a female mammal in which the young are carried and nourished before birth.—*adj.* **u′ter-ine.**

U-ther (ū′thẽr), *n.* a legendary king of Britain, the father of King Arthur.

u-til-i-ta-ri-an (ū-tĭl″ĭ-tā′rĭ-ăn), *adj.* **1,** pertaining to utility or usefulness; **2,** valuing things by their practical, rather than spiritual, usefulness:—*n.* **1,** one who regards too highly mere material utility; **2,** one who believes that the greatest good of the greatest number should be the goal of all human effort.—*n.* **u-til″i-ta′ri-an-ism.**

u-til-i-ty (ū-tĭl′ĭ-tĭ), *n.* [*pl.* utilities (-tĭz)], **1,** the quality or state of being suitable for use; general usefulness; **2,** something serviceable, as mails, railroads, etc.
Syn. usefulness, use. *Utility* is an abstract term applied to the quality of being useful for some desired end; as, the *utility* of scientific research. *Usefulness* is ordinarily applied to that which has proved its practical quality; as, the *usefulness* of radio to ships at sea. *Use* implies the actual employment of a thing, or the end secured by that employment; as, the *use* of good materials; what is the *use* of complaining?

u-ti-lize (ū′tĭ-līz), *v.t.* [*p.t.* and *p.p.* -lized (-līzd), *p.pr.* -liz″ing], to make useful or profitable; make use of.—*adj.* **u′ti-liz″a-ble.**—*n.* **u″ti-li-za′tion.**

ut-most (ŭt′mōst), *adj.* **1,** greatest; **2,** most removed in space or time; farthest; extreme:—*n.* **1,** the extreme limit; as, he can be trusted to the *utmost;* **2,** all that is possible; as, I will do my *utmost* to help you.

U-to-pi-a (ū-tō′pĭ-ȧ), *n.* **1,** an imaginary island, described in Sir Thomas More's "Utopia" (1516), where perfection existed in government, social life, and politics; **2,** (often, *utopia*), any conception of an ideal state; a visionary plan for social reform.

U-to-pi-an (ū-tō′pĭ-ăn), *adj.* **1,** pertaining to Utopia; **2,** (also, *utopian*), ideal; visionary; impossible to be made actual:—*n.* a dweller in Utopia: **utopian,** a person who dreams of ideal social perfection.

[1]**ut-ter** (ŭt′ẽr), *adj.* entire; absolute; complete; as, *utter* denial; *utter* gloom.

[2]**ut-ter** (ŭt′ẽr), *v.t.* **1,** to speak; sound; make vocal; as, to *utter* a groan; **2,** to express in words; **3,** to put into circulation, as stamps or money; also, to offer as genuine (a forged document) with intent to defraud.—*adj.* **ut′ter-a-ble.**—*n.* **ut′ter-er.**

ut-ter-ance (ŭt′ẽr-ăns), *n.* **1,** expression by the voice; speech; style of speaking; as, indistinct *utterance;* **2,** something, usually of weight, expressed in words.

ut-ter-ly (ŭt′ẽr-lĭ), *adv.* fully; totally; altogether; as, *utterly* useless.

ut-ter-most (ŭt′ẽr-mōst), *adj.* extreme; utmost; in the furthest, greatest, or highest degree:—*n.* the furthest extent or degree.

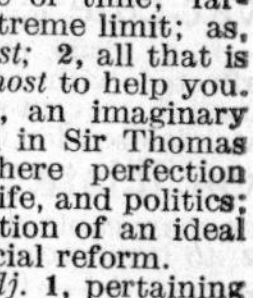
U TUBE

U tube a U-shaped tube used by chemists to hold liquids or solids through which gases may be passed for absorption or cleaning.

u-vu-la (ū′vū-lȧ), *n.* the small, fleshy projection in the mouth, hanging from the soft palate above the back part of the tongue.—*adj.* **u′vu-lar.**

ux-o-ri-ous (ŭk-sō′rĭ-ŭs; ŭg-zō′-), *adj.* foolishly fond of one's wife. —*adv.* **ux-o′ri-ous-ly.**—*n.* **ux-o′ri-ous-ness.**

V

va-can-cy (vā'kăn-sĭ), *n.* [*pl.* vacancies (-sĭz)], **1**, the state of being empty; **2**, emptiness of mind; idleness; lack of mental power; **3**, an empty space; **4**, an office or a position open to applicants; **5**, a room or rooms offered for rent.

va-cant (vā'kănt), *adj.* **1**, empty; **2**, lacking thought or expression; as, a *vacant* stare; **3**, not occupied; as, a *vacant* building; a *vacant* position; **4**, free from duties, as time; **5**, *Poetic*, free from care.
Syn. void. (See empty.)

va-cate (vā'kāt), *v.t.* [*p.t.* and *p.p.* -cat-ed, *p.pr.* -cat-ing], **1**, to make empty; give up the possession of; as, to *vacate* a house; **2**, to nullify or make void:—*v.i.* **1**, to give up a house, office, etc.; **2**, *Colloq.*, to go away.

va-ca-tion (vȧ-kā'shŭn), *n.* **1**, the act of making empty or leaving without an occupant; **2**, a making void; **3**, a period of interruption in work or business; time of rest or recreation.—*n.* **va-ca'tion-ist.**

vac-ci-nate (văk'sĭ-nāt), *v.t.* [*p.t.* and *p.p.* -nat″ed, *p.pr.* -nat″ing], **1**, to inoculate, or give a mild form of a disease to, in order to prevent a severe attack of the same or a similar disease; **2**, esp., to make immune from smallpox, by injecting into the body the virus from the disease of cowpox.—*n.* **vac″ci-na'tion.**—*n.* **vac'ci-na″tor.**

vac-cine (văk'sĭn; văk'sēn), *adj.* pertaining to, or obtained from, cows:—*n.* **1**, virus, or poison, obtained from cows affected with a disease called cowpox, and used to prevent smallpox; **2**, loosely, any substance used for inoculation against disease.

vac-il-late (văs'ĭ-lāt), *v.i.* [*p.t.* and *p.p.* -lat″ed, *p.pr.* -lat″ing], **1**, to be changeable or uncertain in mind or opinion; **2**, to be unsteady; stagger.—*n.* **vac″il-la'tion.**

va-cu-i-ty (vȧ-kū'ĭ-tĭ), *n.* [*pl.* vacuities (-tĭz)], **1**, space not filled or occupied; **2**, mental inactivity; **3**, lack of intelligence in mind or expression.

vac-u-ous (văk'ū-ŭs), *adj.* **1**, empty; vacant; **2**, without expression.

vac-u-um (văk'ū-ŭm), *n.* [*pl.* vacuums (-ŭmz); vacua (-ȧ)], **1**, a space entirely empty of matter; **2**, hence, a space, such as the inside of a bottle, nearly emptied of air by artificial means: **vacuum cleaner**, a machine for cleaning the interior of a house by means of suction which draws the dust into a bag or other receptacle: **vacuum pump**, a pump in which, by forming a partial vacuum, or empty space, water is forced through a pipe: **vacuum tube**, (also called *electron tube*), **1**, in electricity, a sealed glass tube containing highly rarefied gas, used esp. for investigating the properties of the electric discharge in gases, for producing X rays by such a discharge, etc.; **2**, in radio, such a tube used for producing, detecting, or amplifying electrical oscillations or for rectifying an alternating current.

***va-de me-cum** (vā″dē mē'kŭm), [Lat.], something, esp. a book, to be kept constantly with one.

vag-a-bond (văg'ȧ-bŏnd), *n.* **1**, one who roams about with no permanent abode; **2**, esp., an idle fellow without honest means of support; a vagrant or tramp; **3**, *Colloq.*, a rascal; scamp:—*adj.* **1**, wandering about without a fixed dwelling place; roaming; **2**, idle and vicious.—*n.* **vag'a-bond″age.**

va-ga-ry (vȧ-gā'rĭ), *n.* [*pl.* vagaries (-rĭz)], a mental wandering; irresponsible dreaming; freak of fancy; whim.

va-gi-na (vȧ-jī'nȧ), *n.* [*pl.* vaginæ (-nē); vaginas (-nȧz)], in female mammals, the passage leading out from the womb.

va-grant (vā'grănt), *adj.* wandering from place to place without purpose and without a settled home:—*n.* one who wanders about without honest means of support; a tramp.—*adj.* **va'grant-ly.**—*n.* **va'gran-cy.**
Syn., *n.* beggar, vagabond.

vague (vāg), *adj.* **1**, not clearly outlined, stated, or understood; hazy; as, a *vague* idea; **2**, not sure; doubtful; as, a *vague* rumor; **3**, not seeing or thinking clearly.—*adv.* **vague'ly.**—*n.* **vague'ness.**
Syn. indistinct, obscure, indefinite.—*Ant.* clear, distinct, definite.

vail (vāl), *n. Archaic*, **1**, a thin, diaphanous covering for the face; **2**, a drapery; curtain:—*v.t.* to cover; hide. See **veil**, *Pfd. S.*

vain (vān), *adj.* **1**, valueless; empty; trifling; as, *vain* words; **2**, without force or effect; useless; as, *vain* efforts; **3**, proud of small accomplishments or of personal appearance; conceited: **in vain**, without success; to no purpose.—*adv.* **vain'ly.**

vain-glo-ri-ous (vān″glō'rĭ-ŭs), *adj.* boastful; full of excessive pride or vanity.—*adv.* **vain″glo'ri-ous-ly.**—*n.* **vain″glo'ri-ous-ness.**

vain-glo-ry (vān″glō'rĭ), *n.* **1**, excessive vanity or pride over one's own accomplishments; **2**, vain pomp or show.

vair (vâr), *n.* a kind of squirrel fur much in vogue in the 14th century for the trimming of expensive dresses.

val-ance (văl'ăns), *n.* **1**, a kind of damask used for upholstering; **2**, a short, full curtain above a window, or around a bedstead from the mattress to the floor.

[1]**vale** (vāl), *n. Poetic*, low land between hills; a valley.

[2]**va-le** (vā'lē), *interj.* farewell! adieu! used only in formal or lofty style.

val-e-dic-tion (văl″ē-dĭk'shŭn), *n.* a farewell utterance.

val-e-dic-to-ri-an (văl″ē-dĭk-tō'rĭ-ăn), *n.* a person who makes a farewell address; esp., a member of a graduating class in a school or college, usually the one with highest standing, who makes the farewell oration at commencement.

val-e-dic-to-ry (văl″ē-dĭk'tō-rĭ), *n.* [*pl.* valedictories (-rĭz)], a farewell speech; esp., a farewell address at a school or college commencement:—*adj.* pertaining, or suited, to a farewell.

va-lence (vā'lĕns), *n.* in chemistry, the combining power of an element, measured by the number of hydrogen atoms with which an atom of the element will combine or which it will replace in a chemical reaction. Also, **va'len-cy.**

Va-len-ciennes (vȧ-lĕn″sĭ-ĕnz'; *Fr.* vȧ″-läṅ″syĕn'), *n.* **1**, a kind of fine pillow lace originally made at Valenciennes, France; **2**, an imitation of this lace.

val-en-tine (văl'ĕn-tīn), *n.* **1**, a sweetheart chosen on St. Valentine's Day; **2**, a love message, real, sentimental, or burlesque, sent on February 14.

va-le-ri-an (vȧ-lē'rĭ-ăn), *n.* **1**, any of certain perennial herbs with a peculiarly pungent odor, esp. a plant with roots of medicinal value; **2**, a drug of a strong and unpleasant odor obtained from the dried root of this plant.

val-et (văl′ĕt; văl′ā), *n.* a manservant who personally attends a man, taking care of his apartment, clothes, etc.: ***valet de chambre,** (và″lâ′ dē shäṅbr″), a valet.

val-e-tu-di-na-ri-an (văl″ē-tū″dĭ-nā′-rĭ-ăn), *n.* **1**, an invalid or sickly person; **2**, a person whose chief interest is health:—*adj.* **1**, in poor health; seeking for health; **2**, too anxious about one's own health and that of others.—*n.* **val″e-tu″di-na′ri-an-ism.**—*adj.* and *n.* **val″e-tu′di-na-ry.**

Val-hal-la (văl-hăl′ȧ), *n.* in Norse mythology, the palace of Odin, in which dwell the souls of heroes slain in battle.

val-iant (văl′yănt), *adj.* **1**, brave; courageous; as, *valiant* soldiers; **2**, done with bravery; heroic; as, *valiant* deeds.—*adv.* **val′iant-ly.**—*n.* **val′iant-ness.**

val-id (văl′ĭd), *adj.* **1**, based on fact; sound; well-grounded; as, a *valid* argument; **2**, executed with all formalities required by law, as a contract.—*adv.* **val′id-ly.**—*n.* **val′id-ness.**—*n.* **va-lid′i-ty.**

val-i-date (văl′ĭ-dāt), *v.t.* [*p.t.* and *p.p.* -dat″ed, *p.pr.* -dat″ing], to ratify; confirm; give legal force to.

va-lise (vȧ-lēs′), *n.* a traveling bag of leather, wicker, or the like.

Val-kyr-ie (văl-kĭr′ĭ; văl-kī′rĭ), *n.* in Norse mythology, one of Odin's handmaidens who watched over the battlefields, chose those who were to be slain, and conducted to Valhalla the souls of the favored heroes. Also, **Val′kyr; Val-kyr′i-a; Wal-kyr′ie.**—*adj.* **Val-kyr′i-an.**

val-la-tion (vă-lā′shŭn), *n.* a military defensive work, in the form of trenches or ramparts.

val-ley (văl′ĭ), *n.* [*pl.* valleys (-ĭz)], low land between hills or mountains.

val-or (văl′ẽr), *n.* fearlessness in facing danger; bravery. Also, **val′our.**
Syn. heroism, gallantry. (See bravery.)

val-or-i-za-tion (văl″ẽr-ĭ-zā′shŭn), *n.* the maintenance of an arbitrary market price of a commodity, usually by government action.

val-u-a-ble (văl′ū-ȧ-bl), *adj.* **1**, costly or worth a good price; as, a *valuable* ring; **2**, of high worth; of great importance; as, *valuable* news:—*n.*, in *pl.*, costly possessions, esp. small personal things.

val-u-a-tion (văl″ū-ā′shŭn), *n.* **1**, the act of putting a price (on a commodity); **2**, an estimated worth or price; as, a *valuation* of property.

val-ue (văl′ū), *n.* **1**, worth; that which makes anything worth possessing; **2**, precise import; exact meaning; as, the *value* of a word, quality, or symbol; **3**, valuation; estimated worth; **4**, purchasing power; **5**, fair price; **6**, in music, the relative duration of a tone or silence as indicated by a note or rest: **face value,** the principal sum named in contracts of indebtedness, as in promissory notes, checks, drafts, or acceptances: **par value,** the nominal value given to shares of capital stock or other securities, but not giving any indication of the market value of the securities:—*v.t.* [*p.t.* and *p.p.* -ued (-ūd), *p.pr.* -u-ing], **1**, to estimate the worth of; put a price on; as, to *value* an estate; **2**, to esteem highly; hold dear; as, to *value* one's friendship.—*n.* **val′u-er.**—*adj.* **val′ue-less.**

val-ued (văl′ūd), *p.adj.* highly appreciated; dearly prized, as a friend.

valve (vălv), *n.* **1**, a door; esp., one of a pair of folding doors; **2**, any of various mechanical devices for opening and closing a conduit, and thus regulating or directing the movement through it of a gas, liquid, etc.; **3**, a fold in the wall of a blood vessel, canal, or other organ, which allows the contents to flow through it in one direction only; **4**, either of the two separable pieces, as of the shell of a clam, the seed pod of the pea, etc.; **5**, a device permitting the passage of an electric current in one direction only; esp., an exhausted tube with two or more electrodes, one of which may be rendered incandescent: used in radio: **gate valve,** a valve in a pipe line, with an opening the size of the pipe, in which a plate intercepts the flow like a sluice gate: **globe valve,** a valve in which the checking mechanism, usually a disk which closes against a seat, is surrounded by a globelike housing or case.—*adj.* **valv′ate.**

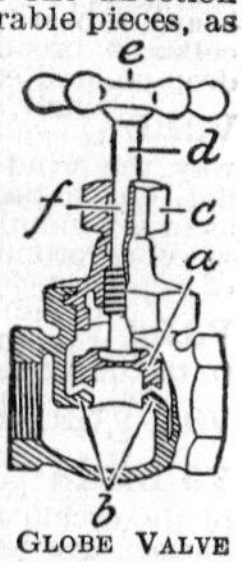

GLOBE VALVE

a, disk, which fits upon *b*, seat; *c*, packing nut; *d*, spindle, passing through packing at *f*; *e*, wheel.

val-vu-lar (văl′vū-lȧr), *adj.* **1**, pertaining to, serving as, or of the nature of, a valve; **2**, specif., pertaining to the valves of the heart.

vam-brace (văm′brās), *n.* the piece of armor protecting the arm from the elbow to the wrist (see *reredos*, illus.).

[1]**vamp** (vămp), *n.* **1**, the part of a shoe just above the sole, covering the toes and extending to the sides; **2**, a piece added to something old to give it a new appearance:—*v.t.* **1**, to furnish with an upper leather; **2**, to patch with new material: often with *up;* **3**, in music, to improvise; as, to *vamp* an accompaniment or part.—*n.* **vamp′er.**

[2]**vamp** (vămp), *n. U. S. Slang*, in novels or plays, a seductive adventuress; a flirt:—*v.t. Slang*, to charm seductively.

vam-pire (văm′pīr), *n.* **1**, in superstition, a ghost supposed to suck the blood of sleeping persons; **2**, one who preys on, or makes a living at the expense of, others, esp. a woman of this sort; **3**, any of various South American bats which suck the blood of animals; **4**, any of various other bats incorrectly supposed to suck blood.

VAMPIRE (def. 3)

[1]**van** (văn), *n.* **1**, the front, as of an army or fleet; **2**, the people who lead any movement; also, the place of those who so lead; as, he was in the *van* of all reform.

[2]**van** (văn), *n.* **1**, a large covered truck for moving household goods, circus animals, etc.; **2**, in England, a light wagon for carrying goods; also, a railway baggage car.

Van (văn), *n.* [*pl.* Vans (vănz); Vanir (vä′nẽr)], one of the three Norse gods, Njorth, Frey, and Freya, patrons of commerce and trade: often in *pl.*, *Vanir*, which see.

va-na-di-um (vȧ-nā′dĭ-ŭm), *n.* a somewhat rare, silver-white metallic element, chiefly used as an alloying element in steel, to which it adds strength.

Va-na-heim (vä′nä-hām″), *n.* the home of the Vanir, the three wealthy gods of trade and commerce.

Van-dal (văn′dăl), *n.* one of a Teutonic race once inhabiting the south shores of the Baltic, and ravaging Gaul, Spain, Northern Africa, and Rome, in the fourth and fifth centuries: **vandal,** one who wilfully destroys or injures anything beautiful, esp. a work of art.—*adj.* **Van-dal′ic; van-dal′ic.**—*n.* **Van′dal-ism; van′dal-ism.**

Van-dyke (văn-dīk′), *adj.* pertaining to, or in the style of, Van Dyck, or

Vandyke, the Flemish painter: **Vandyke beard**, a beard trimmed to a point: **Vandyke collar**, a broad linen and lace collar with a deep pointed edge.

vane (vān), *n.* **1**, a movable device fastened to an elevated object to show which way the wind blows; a weathercock; **2**, a flat, fan-shaped arm projecting from an axis, as in a windmill; **3**, a similar part of a water wheel or propeller; **4**, the flat spreading part of a feather.

vang (văng), *n.* either of two stay ropes running from the end of a ship's gaff to the deck: used to steady the gaff.

van-guard (văn′gärd″), *n.* the first line or advance guard of an army.

va-nil-la (vȧ-nĭl′ȧ), *n.* **1**, any of a genus of tropical American climbing plants of the orchid family; **2**, the pod or bean of various species of this plant, used to make a flavoring extract for confectionery, cakes, etc.; **3**, the flavoring so obtained.

Va-nir (vä′nẽr; wä′nẽr), *n.pl.* in Norse mythology, Njorth, Frey, and Freya, gods of trade and commerce, who lived in Vanaheim: at first enemies, later allies, of the Æsir in Asgard.

van-ish (văn′ĭsh), *v.i.* **1**, to disappear; fade from sight; **2**, to pass out of existence; be lost; as, hopes *vanish*.

van-i-ty (văn′ĭ-tĭ), *n.* [*pl.* vanities (-tĭz)], **1**, the state or quality of being vain or futile; **2**, shallow pride, as in one's appearance or attainments; conceit; **3**, a trivial or worthless thing; a frivolous trifle: **vanity bag** or **case**, a woman's small bag or box containing powder, rouge, and mirror.

Van-i-ty Fair **1**, in Bunyan's "Pilgrim's Progress," a town fair where all the wares were vanities, and the buyers lovers of vanity; **2**, hence, worldly social life devoted to emptiness and show.

van-quish (văng′kwĭsh), *v.t.* **1**, to conquer; subdue; as, Cæsar *vanquished* Gaul; **2**, to get the better of; defeat, as in an argument or debate.—*adj.* **van′quish-a-ble.**—*n.* **van′quish-er.**

van-tage (vȧn′tȧj), *n.* **1**, a superior position or opportunity; advantage; **2**, in tennis, advantage; the first point scored following deuce: **vantage ground**, a position which gives its holder an advantage.

vap-id (văp′ĭd), *adj.* lacking life or spirit; flat; pointless; as, *vapid* talk.—*adv.* **vap′id-ly.**—*n.* **vap′id-ness.**—*n.* **va-pid′i-ty.**

Syn. dull, insipid, stale, stupid.—*Ant.* effective, spirited, substantial.

va-por (vā′pẽr), *n.* **1**, in physics, the gaseous form of any substance: used esp. of such substances as may exist in the liquid or solid state under ordinary conditions; **2**, a cloudlike substance floating in the air and robbing it of clearness, as fog, smoke, etc.; **3**, anything impossible to seize and hold; something that vanishes like smoke or mist; **vapor density**, strictly, the mass (weight) of a gas per unit volume; as, the *vapor density* of air is 1.293 grams per liter; commonly, the relative mass of a gas compared with that of air or hydrogen at the same temperature and pressure:—*v.i.* **1**, to pass off in the form of gas, steam, etc.; **2**, to send out gas, steam, etc.; **3**, to indulge in idle talk. Also, **va′pour.**—*n.* **va′por-er.**—*adj.* **va′por-ish.**

va-por-ize (vā′pẽr-īz), *v.t.* and *v.i.* [*p.t.* and *p.p.* -ized (-īzd), *p.pr.* -iz″ing], to change, or be changed, into steam, gas, etc., as by means of heat.—*n.* **va″por-i-za′tion.**—*n.* **va′por-iz″er.**

va-por-ous (vā′pẽr-ŭs), *adj.* **1**, full of, or like, vapor, gas, etc.; **2**, producing gas; flatulent; **3**, unreal; unsubstantial.—*adv.* **va′por-ous-ly.**—*n.* **va′por-ous-ness.**

va-por-y (vā′pẽr-ĭ), *adj.* **1**, full of, or like, vapors, gas, etc.; **2**, peevish or melancholy; hysterical. Also, **va′pour-y.**

***va-que-ro** (vä-kā′rō), [Span.], *n.* [*pl.* vaqueros (-rōz; *Span.* -rōs)], in Spanish America, New Mexico, etc., one who raises or cares for cattle; a cowboy.

va-ri-a-bil-i-ty (vā″rĭ-ȧ-bĭl′ĭ-tĭ), *n.* **1**, ability to alter or change; **2**, tendency to alter or change; fickleness.

va-ri-a-ble (vā′rĭ-ȧ-bl), *adj.* **1**, changeable; as, a *variable* wind; **2**, inconstant; fickle; as, *variable* love; **3**, in mathematics, capable of taking on different numerical values:—*n.* **1**, that which is subject to change; **2**, in mathematics, a quantity that may have a number of different values under given conditions: opp. of *constant*.—*n.* **va′ri-a-ble-ness.**—*adv.* **va′ri-a-bly.**

va-ri-ance (vā′rĭ-ăns), *n.* **1**, the state of being changeable; also, the act of changing or differing; **2**, degree of alteration or change; **3**, a difference of opinion; disagreement.

va-ri-ant (vā′rĭ-ănt), *adj.* differing from others in the same general class; as, a *variant* form of a word:—*n.* something that differs from another thing in form, though essentially the same.

va-ri-a-tion (vā″rĭ-ā′shŭn), *n.* **1**, the act of altering or changing; a modification or change; departure from a regular rule or course; **2**, the extent to which a thing alters; as, there is little *variation* in the temperature; **3**, in grammar, inflection, as in the declension of a noun; **4**, in music, the repeating of a single melody with changes and elaborations in tune, harmony, tempo, etc.; **5**, a deviation from the mean orbit or motion of a heavenly body, caused by the attraction of another heavenly body.—*adj.* **va″ri-a′tion-al.**

var-i-col-ored (vā′rĭ-kŭl″ẽrd), *adj.* streaked, spotted, or marked with various colors, as a flower.

va-ri-cose (văr′ĭ-kōs), *adj.* irregularly swollen; as, *varicose* veins.

va-ried (vā′rĭd), *p.adj.* **1**, altered; **2**, of different sorts; diversified.

va-ri-e-gate (vā′rĭ-ē-gāt), *v.t.* [*p.t.* and *p.p.* -gat″ed, *p.pr.* -gat″ing], to change the appearance of by marking with different colors; streak; spot.—*n.* **va″ri-e-ga′tion.**—*p.adj.* **va′ri-e-gat″ed.**

va-ri-e-ty (vȧ-rī′ē-tĭ), *n.* [*pl.* varieties (-tĭz)], **1**, the state of being different; diversity; **2**, a collection of unlike objects; medley; **3**, an individual differing in some details from others of the same general class or kind; a sort; as, one *variety* of palm bears dates, another coconuts; **4**, in biology, the group of next lower rank than a species; **5**, lack of sameness.—*adj.* **va-ri′e-tal.**

va-ri-o-coup-ler (vā″rĭ-ō-kŭp′lẽr), *n.* a device for tuning a radio receiving set, consisting of a fixed, primary coil, the inductance of which can be varied in steps by a switch, and a secondary coil, not variable and not connected with the primary, but rotating within it.

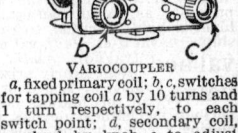

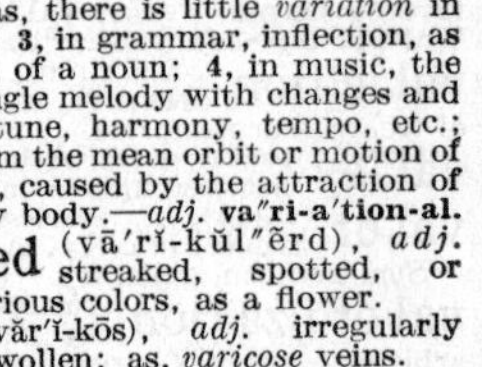

VARIOCOUPLER

a, fixed primary coil; *b*, *c*, switches for tapping coil *a* by 10 turns and 1 turn respectively, to each switch point; *d*, secondary coil, revolved by knob *e* to adjust coupling with coil *a*.

va-ri-o-la (vȧ-rī′ō-lȧ), *n.* smallpox, a contagious eruptive disease.

va-ri-o-loid (vā′rĭ-ō-loid; văr′ĭ-), *n.* a mild form of smallpox.

va-ri-om-e-ter (vā″rĭ-ŏm′ē-tẽr), *n.* **1**, an instrument for determining changes in magnetism, esp. changes in the earth's magnetic field; **2**, a device for regulating the amount of inductance in an electrical circuit: used in radio and in wireless telegraphy.

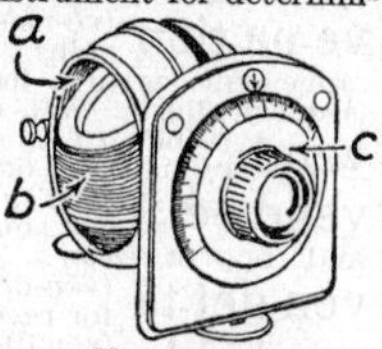

VARIOMETER
a, revolving primary coil; *b*, stationary secondary coil; *c*, dial on shaft of *b*.

va-ri-o-rum (vā″rĭ-ō′rŭm), *adj.* containing comments and explanations by different critics, editors, etc.: said of an edition of a book in which such comments are correlated, as in an edition of Shakespeare.

va-ri-ous (vā′rĭ-ŭs), *adj.* **1**, different; diverse; of several sorts; as, *various* plants; **2**, several; **3**, changeable; uncertain; **4**, having several different characteristics; many-sided.—*adv.* **va′ri-ous-ly.**

var-let (vär′lĕt), *n.* **1**, formerly, a servant, footman, or page; **2**, a scoundrel.

var-nish (vär′nĭsh), *n.* **1**, a liquid preparation of resin used for giving gloss to the surface of wood or metal work; **2**, outside smoothness or gloss, as of politeness:—*v.t.* **1**, to cover with such a liquid; give a gloss to; **2**, to give a good appearance to.

va-ry (vā′rĭ), *v.t.* [*p.t.* and *p.p.* -ried (-rĭd), *p.pr.* -ry-ing], **1**, to alter in appearance, shape, substance, etc.; **2**, to make unlike one another; as, to *vary* the lessons; **3**, in music, to adorn with variations:—*v.i.* **1**, to alter or change; undergo a change; **2**, to differ; **3**, to depart from a rule or course; **4**, to alternate.

vas-cu-lar (văs′kū-lȧr), *adj.* **1**, relating to the vessels of an animal or vegetable body which carry or convey fluids, as blood in animals and sap in plants; **2**, having, or made up of, vessels or ducts: **vascular bundle,** in stems, roots, and leaves of higher plants, the unit combination of tissues which forms the basis of growth, consisting of the cambium, or actively growing cells, the woody tissue, or xylem, and the food-conducting tissue, or phloëm, into which it is differentiated.

vase (vās; vāz; *Br.* väz), *n.* a vessel of glass, pottery, or the like, usually circular in shape and of a height greater than its width, intended for ornament or use.

Vas-e-line (văs′ē-lĭn; văs′ē-lēn), *n.* a trade-mark name for various products, the chief of which is petroleum jelly, a semisolid product of petroleum used as an ointment and lubricant; also, a product bearing this trade-mark name.

Vash-ti (văsh′tī), *n.* in the Bible, a wife of King Ahasuerus, replaced by Esther (Esther 1:9).

vas-sal (văs′ăl), *n.* **1**, in the feudal system, one who placed himself under the protection of another as his lord or master, and in return rendered homage and service; one who held land under feudal tenure; **2**, a retainer; servant; **3**, a bondsman; slave:—*adj.* under the control of a superior power; dependent; as, a *vassal* state.
Syn., n. (see slave).

vas-sal-age (văs′ăl-āj), *n.* **1**, the state of one who renders service to a feudal lord in return for his protection; **2**, services so rendered; **3**, slavery or servitude; **4**, lands held under control of a superior state.

vast (vȧst), *adj.* **1**, immense; extensive; **2**, very great in quantity or amount; **3**, very great in degree, intensity, etc. Also, *Archaic,* **vast′y.**—*adv.* **vast′ly.**—*n.* **vast′ness.**
Syn. (see enormous).

vat (văt), *n.* a large tank, tub, or vessel, esp. one for holding liquors, dyes, etc., in process of manufacture.

Vat-i-can (văt′ĭ-kăn), *n.* **1**, the palace of the Pope at Rome; **2**, the papal authority, as distinguished from the *Quirinal,* or monarchial government of Italy.

va-tic-i-nate (vȧ-tĭs′ĭ-nāt), *v.i.* and *v.t.* [*p.t.* and *p.p.* -nat″ed, *p.pr.* -nat″ing], to prophesy or foretell.—*n.* **va-tic″i-na′tion.**—*n.* **va-tic′i-na″tor.**

vaude-ville (vōd′vĭl; *Fr.* vōd″vēl′), *n.* a kind of theatrical performance consisting of a series of songs, dances, acrobatic feats, short dramatic sketches, etc.; a variety show.

[1]**vault** (vôlt), *n.* **1**, a light, low leap or bound; a curvet, as by a horse; **2**, a leap over a high barrier, by the aid of the hands or a pole:—*v.t.* to leap over; as, to *vault* a fence:—*v.i.* **1**, to leap over a high barrier, esp. by aid of the hands or a pole; **2**, to curvet, as a horse.—*n.* **vault′er.**

[2]**vault** (vôlt), *n.* **1**, an arched roof or ceiling; **2**, storage space, usually in a cellar; **3**, any subterranean chamber; **4**, a prison; **5**, a cavern; tomb; **6**, a steel room, as in a bank, in which valuables, such as jewels or money, are kept; **7**, the arch of heaven:—*v.t.* to shape like a vault; provide with an arched ceiling.—*n.* **vault′ing.**

vault-ed (vôl′tĕd), *p.adj.* **1**, arched and lofty, as a roof; also, covered with a vault; **2**, having a vault or vaults.

vaunt (vänt; vônt), *v.i.* to brag:—*v.t.* to boast of; display boastfully; as, to *vaunt* one's courage:—*n.* a boast; brag; vain display.—*n.* **vaunt′er.**—*adv.* **vaunt′ing-ly.**

veal (vēl), *n.* the flesh of the calf used as meat.

Ve-da (vā′dȧ; vē′dȧ), *n.* **1**, the ancient sacred scriptures of the Hindus, comprising about 100 books and forming the basis of Brahmanism; **2**, any of these books; **3**, any of the four groups into which these books are arranged.—*adj.* **Ve′dic.**

ve-dette (vē-dĕt′), *n.* a mounted sentinel or soldier stationed in front of the regular pickets or guards of an army to give the signal of danger. Also, **vi-dette′.**

veer (vēr), *v.t.* and *v.i.* to change in direction; shift, as the wind: opp. of *back.*

veer-y (vēr′ĭ), *n.* [*pl.* veeries (-ĭz)], a variety of American thrush.

Ve-ga (vē′gȧ), *n.* a bluish white star of the first magnitude, the brightest in the constellation Lyra.

veg-e-ta-ble (vĕj′ē-tȧ-bl), *n.* **1**, a plant, esp. one cultivated for food; **2**, the edible portion of such a plant, gathered and prepared for market or for the table:—*adj.* **1**, of or pertaining to plants; **2**, having the nature of, or produced by, plants; as, *vegetable* fiber.

veg-e-tal (vĕj′ē-tăl), *adj.* pertaining to plants or vegetables; vegetable.

veg-e-ta-ri-an (vĕj″ē-tā′rĭ-ăn), *n.* **1**, one who avoids meat as an element of diet; **2**, one who claims that plants are the only proper source of food for man:—*adj.* **1**, pertaining to those opposed to eating meat; **2**, consisting of vegetables; as, a *vegetarian* diet.—*n.* **veg″e-ta′ri-an-ism.**

veg-e-tate (vĕj′ē-tāt), *v.i.* [*p.t.* and *p.p.* -tat″ed, *p.pr.* -tat″ing], **1**, to fulfil the vegetable functions of growth, nutrition, etc.; **2**, to grow with no more effort than a plant; **3**, to allow mind and body to become inactive; lead a passive or monotonous existence.—*adj.* **veg′e-ta-tive.**—*adv.* **veg′e-ta-tive-ly.**—*n.* **veg′e-ta-tive-ness.**

veg-e-ta-tion (vĕj″ē-tā′shŭn), *n.* **1,** the growth of vegetables or plants; **2,** plant life; plants in general.

ve-he-mence (vē′hē-mĕns; vē′ē-), *n.* **1,** passionate earnestness; **2,** fury; violence; **3,** eagerness; urgency.

ve-he-ment (vē′hē-mĕnt; vē′ē-), *adj.* **1,** very violent; furious; as, a *vehement* wind; **2,** passionate; earnest; as, a *vehement* speech.—*adv.* **ve′he-ment-ly.**

Syn. fiery, impetuous, ardent, furious.

ve-hi-cle (vē′hĭ-kl; vē′ĭ-kl), *n.* **1,** any kind of conveyance, esp. one used on land; **2,** anything which may be used as a medium for communicating thought, feeling, etc.; as, the press is the *vehicle* for public opinion; **3,** a substance in which medicine is taken; **4,** in painting, a liquid, as oil, which is mixed with a colored pigment to render its application easier.—*adj.* **ve-hic′u-lar.**

veil (vāl), *n.* **1,** a thin, gauzy covering for the face; **2,** a piece of fabric hanging from the head, over the shoulders, as worn by a nun; **3,** a curtain or covering to conceal something; **4,** a disguise: **to take the veil,** to become a nun:—*v.t.* **1,** to cover with a veil or curtain; **2,** to hide; as, to *veil* one's intentions. Also, *Archaic,* **vail.**—*p.adj.* **veiled.**

veil-ing (vāl′ĭng), *n.* thin, gauzy material, as for veils.

vein (vān), *n.* **1,** one of the tubelike vessels which carry the blood to or toward the heart; **2,** one of the branching ribs of a plant or of the wing of an insect; **3,** a crack or seam in rock filled by foreign mineral matter; as, a *vein* of gold; **4,** ore, or other material, filling a fissure in rock; **5,** a streak, as in wood or marble; **6,** a particular strain or disposition; peculiarity of mood, speech, etc.; as, he spoke in a solemn *vein:*—*v.t.* to cover, fill, or form with veins.—*p.adj.* **veined.**—*n.* **vein′ing.**—*adj.* **vein′less.**—*adj.* **vein′y.**

vein-let (vān′lĕt), *n.* a small or secondary vein.

veldt (fĕlt; vĕlt), *n.* in South Africa, open or thinly wooded country.

vel-lum (vĕl′ŭm), *n.* **1,** a fine parchment, usually made of calfskin, intended for binding books, writing upon, etc.; **2,** a manuscript written upon vellum; **3,** a kind of paper or cotton cloth made in imitation of fine parchment.

ve-loc-i-pede (vē-lŏs′ĭ-pēd), *n.* a light, two- or three-wheeled vehicle, generally moved by pedals: the form from which the bicycle and tricycle have developed.

ve-loc-i-ty (vē-lŏs′ĭ-tĭ), *n.* [*pl.* velocities (-tĭz)], the rate of movement of a moving object; speed; swiftness.

ve-lours (vē-lo͞or′), *n.* [*pl.* velours (-lo͞orz′)], any of various woven fabrics having a pile like that of velvet.

ve-lum (vē′lŭm), *n.* [*pl.* vela (-lȧ)], any membranous or veil-like organ or partition, esp. the soft palate.

vel-ure (vĕl′ūr), *n.* velvet, or similar material; esp., a heavy linen or silk fabric with a velvety finish, used for drapery.

vel-vet (vĕl′vĕt), *n.* **1,** a closely woven silk material with a short, thick pile, or surface of upright cut threads; **2,** the soft skin on the horns of young deer; **3,** *Slang,* money or funds secured without effort, as by speculation:—*adj.* **1,** made of velvet; **2,** soft like velvet; velvety; as, a *velvet* touch; a *velvet* paw.—*adj.* **vel′vet-y.**

vel-vet-een (vĕl″vē-tēn′), *n.* **1,** a velvety material of mixed silk and cotton; **2,** a cotton material resembling velvet; imitation velvet.

ve-nal (vē′năl), *adj.* **1,** ready or willing to be bought or bribed; mercenary: said of a person; **2,** to be obtained by purchase or hire; as, *venal* talents: used esp. of a base or degrading transaction.—*adv.* **ve′nal-ly.**—*n.* **ve-nal′i-ty.**

ve-na-tion (vē-nā′shŭn), *n.* a system of veins, or their peculiar arrangement, as in a leaf or an insect's wing (see *leaf,* illus.).—*adj.* **ve-na′tion-al.**

vend (vĕnd), *v.t.* to sell; offer for sale, esp. by hawking or peddling.—*n.* **vend′er.**

vend-ee (vĕn-dē′), *n.* in law, one to whom something, esp. land, is sold: opp. of *vendor.*

ven-det-ta (vĕn-dĕt′ȧ), *n.* a private feud for revenge by bloodshed.

vend-i-ble (vĕn′dĭ-bl), *adj.* marketable or salable:—*n.,* usually in *pl.,* a marketable or salable article.

ven-di-tion (vĕn-dĭsh′ŭn), *n.* the act of peddling or selling; sale.

vend-or (vĕn′dŏr; vĕn-dôr′), *n.* in law, one who sells: opp. of *vendee.*

ven-due (vĕn-dū′), *n.* a public sale by bidding; an auction.

ve-neer (vē-nēr′), *v.t.* **1,** to overlay with a thin surface of more valuable or beautiful material, as a piece of furniture with better wood; **2,** hence, to cover or conceal (something bad or common) with a surface polish; give a gloss to:—*n.* **1,** a thin surface of fine wood overlaying wood of a poorer quality; **2,** outside show; pretense; surface elegance.—*n.* **ve-neer′ing.**

ven-er-a-ble (vĕn′ẽr-ȧ-bl), *adj.* **1,** so old and wise as to be worthy of reverence; as, a *venerable* old man; **2,** sacred by reason of associations of a religious or historic nature, as a cathedral.—*adv.* **ven′er-a-bly.**—*n.* **ven″er-a-bil′i-ty.**

ven-er-ate (vĕn′ẽr-āt), *v.t.* [*p.t.* and *p.p.* -at″ed, *p.pr.* -at″ing], **1,** to regard as sacred; regard with the highest respect; **2,** to revere because of age or wisdom; reverence.—*n.* **ven′er-a″tor.**

ven-er-a-tion (vĕn″ẽr-ā′shŭn), *n.* **1,** respectful awe; **2,** the act of veneration; worship.

ve-ne-re-al (vē-nē′rē-ăl), *adj.* **1,** pertaining to sexual intercourse; **2,** pertaining to the venereal diseases: **venereal diseases,** certain diseases, as gonorrhea and syphilis, frequently contracted as a result of sexual intercourse with infected persons.

ven-er-y (vĕn′ẽr-ĭ), *n. Archaic,* **1,** the art of hunting; **2,** the pleasures or sports of the chase.

ve-ne-sec-tion (vē″nē-sĕk′shŭn), *n.* the art or practice of opening a vein to let blood; phlebotomy.

Ve-ne-tian (vē-nē′shăn), *adj.* **1,** pertaining to Venice, in Italy, or its people; as, *Venetian* lace; **2,** pertaining to the medieval style of Italian architecture prevailing in Venice between the 12th and early 16th centuries:—*n.* **1,** a native of Venice; **2,** in *pl.,* tape or cord used on Venetian blinds: **Venetian blind,** a window shade, or blind, made of horizontal slats of wood on cords, adjustable so as to admit or exclude light and air.

venge-ance (vĕn′jăns), *n.* punishment inflicted for a wrong endured; retribution.

venge-ful (vĕnj′fo͝ol), *adj.* inclined to inflict stern punishment for an offense; revengeful; as, a *vengeful* spirit.—*adv.* **venge′ful-ly.**—*n.* **venge′ful-ness.**

ve-ni-al (vē′nĭ-ăl), *adj.* not beyond forgiveness; pardonable: **venial sin,** in the Roman Catholic Church, a fault that may be forgiven.—*adv.* **ve′ni-al-ly.**—*n.* **ve′ni-al-ness.**—*n.* **ve″ni-al′i-ty.**

ve-ni-re (vē-nī'rē), *n.* a legal writ or judge's order to a sheriff or coroner for the summoning of a jury for a court trial: called in full *venire facias* (fā'shĭ-ăs).

ven-i-son (vĕn'ĭ-zn; *Br.* vĕn'zn), *n.* deer's flesh used for meat.

ven-om (vĕn'ŭm), *n.* **1**, the poison of certain animals and insects, which makes their bite or sting injurious and sometimes fatal; **2**, hence, injurious influence; spite.

ven-om-ous (vĕn'ŭm-ŭs), *adj.* **1**, full of poison; poisonous; as, a *venomous* sting; **2**, having poison glands; as, a *venomous* snake; **3**, baneful; spiteful; as, *venomous* speech.—*adv.* **ven'om-ous-ly.**—*n.* **ven'om-ous-ness.**

ve-nous (vē'nŭs), *adj.* **1**, pertaining to veins; **2**, designating blood, for the most part carried in veins, which has lost its oxygen and become charged with carbon dioxide: distinguished from *arterial*.

vent (vĕnt), *n.* **1**, a small opening for the passage of air, liquid, etc.; **2**, an outlet; passage; hence, utterance; as, to give *vent* to one's thoughts; **3**, the opening at the breech of a firearm, through which fire is communicated to the powder of the charge:—*v.t.* **1**, to let out through a hole, as steam; **2**, to utter publicly; as, to *vent* one's opinion; **3**, to furnish with an outlet; relieve by speech; as, to *vent* one's anger.—*n.* **vent'er.**

ven-ti-late (vĕn'tĭ-lāt), *v.t.* [*p.t.* and *p.p.* -lat"ed, *p.pr.* -lat"ing], **1**, to supply with fresh air; as, to *ventilate* a room; **2**, to bring out (a subject) for public discussion.—*n.* **ven"ti-la'tion.**

ven-ti-la-tor (vĕn'tĭ-lā"tẽr), *n.* a contrivance for admitting fresh air and letting out foul air.

ven-tral (vĕn'trăl), *adj.* of, pertaining to, or situated on or near, the abdomen, or belly; as, the *ventral* fins of a fish.—*adv.* **ven'tral-ly.**

ven-tri-cle (vĕn'trĭ-kl), *n.* any small cavity of the body or of an organ; esp., either of the two lower chambers of the heart.—*adj.* **ven-tric'u-lar.**

ven-tril-o-quism (vĕn-trĭl'ō-kwĭzm), *n.* the art of speaking in such a way that the voice appears to come from another person or place.—*n.* **ven-tril'o-quist.**—*n.* **ven-tril'o-quy.**

ven-tril-o-quize (vĕn-trĭl'ō-kwīz), *v.i.* [*p.t.* and *p.p.* -quized (-kwīzd), *p.pr.* -quiz"ing], to perform as a ventriloquist; practice ventriloquism.

ven-ture (vĕn'tūr), *n.* **1**, a dangerous or daring undertaking; **2**, an enterprise involving risk; as, a business *venture;* **3**, something risked; a hazard:—*v.t.* [*p.t.* and *p.p.* -tured (-tûrd), *p.pr.* -tur-ing], **1**, to risk; expose to danger; **2**, to chance; as, to *venture* money in a business scheme; **3**, to assume the risk of; dare:—*v.i.* **1**, to dare; **2**, to take a chance; run a risk.—*n.* **ven'tur-er.**

Syn., n. chance, peril, stake.

ven-ture-some (vĕn'tûr-sŭm), *adj.* **1**, daring; rash; **2**, dangerous, as a journey.—*adv.* **ven'ture-some-ly.**—*n.* **ven'ture-some-ness.**

Ven-tu-ri tube (vĕn-tōō'rē), a tube with a narrowing or constriction, which utilizes the principle that the velocity of a fluid flowing through is increased, and its pressure against the tube walls decreased, in the constricted portion.

ven-tur-ous (vĕn'tūr-ŭs), *adj.* rash; bold; daring.—*adv.* **ven'tur-ous-ly.**—*n.* **ven'tur-ous-ness.**

ven-ue (vĕn'ū), *n.* **1**, in a lawsuit, the locality where the alleged events occurred that caused the suit; **2**, the locality where the jury must be drawn and the case tried.

Ve-nus (vē'nŭs), *n.* **1**, in Roman mythology, the goddess of beauty, spring, and love, and the wife of Vulcan: identified with the Greek *Aphrodite;* **2**, the second planet in order of distance from the sun, and, as seen from the earth, the most brilliant (see *solar system*, illus.): called *Lucifer* by the ancients, when the morning star, and *Hesperus*, when the evening star.

Ve-nus-berg (vē'nŭs-bûrg; *Ger.* vā'nōōs-bĕrkh), *n.* any of several mountains, esp. the Hörselberg, in Germany, where, according to a medieval legend, Venus lived with her court, luring persons into it by music, dancing, etc.: known through Wagner's music drama, "Tannhäuser."

Ve-nus's-fly-trap (vē'nŭs-ĭz-flī'trăp"), *n.* a wild herb having leaves ending in two plates which fold together and so entrap insects: native only in a small area about Wilmington, North Carolina.

ve-ra-cious (vē-rā'shŭs), *adj.* **1**, habitually telling the truth; truthful; as, a *veracious* person; **2**, marked by truth; reliable, as a report.—*adv.* **ve-ra'cious-ly.**

ve-rac-i-ty (vē-răs'ĭ-tĭ), *n.* [*pl.* veracities (-tĭz)], **1**, habitual regard for the truth; truthfulness; **2**, accordance with truth; **3**, exactness; as, *veracity* of hearing.

ve-ran-da (vē-răn'dȧ), *n.* **1**, an open balcony, attached to the outside of a house and having a roof supported by light pillars or posts; **2**, in the U. S., a piazza or porch. Also, **ve-ran'dah.**

verb (vûrb), *n.* that part of speech which expresses action, existence, or condition; as, the *verb* "run."

ver-bal (vûr'băl), *adj.* **1**, of or pertaining to words; consisting merely of words; as, his sympathy was only *verbal;* **2**, stated or expressed in words, commonly, spoken words; **3**, hence, spoken; not written; as, a *verbal* agreement; **4**, literal; word for word, as a translation; **5**, of or pertaining to a verb; as, a *verbal* prefix; the *verbal* sense of a word: **verbal noun**, a word derived directly from a verb, and having in some degree the sense and construction of both noun and verb; esp., the English nouns formed by adding *-ing*, as in *seeing* is *believing:*—*n.* a verbal noun.—*adv.* **ver'bal-ly.**

ver-bal-ism (vûr'băl-ĭzm), *n.* **1**, expression in words without attention to thought; **2**, wordiness.

ver-ba-tim (vẽr-bā'tĭm), *adv.* word for word; using the same words; as, to report a speech *verbatim.*

ver-be-na (vẽr-bē'nȧ), *n.* any of several garden plants, with large flowers of various colors and spicy fragrance.

ver-bi-age (vûr'bĭ-āj), *n.* wordiness; the use of too many words.

ver-bose (vẽr-bōs'), *adj.* wordy; full of words; using too many words.—*adv.* **ver-bose'ly.**—*n.* **ver-bose'ness.**

ver-bos-i-ty (vẽr-bŏs'ĭ-tĭ), *n.* [*pl.* verbosities (-tĭz)], the use of too many words; wordiness; verbiage.

ver-dant (vûr'dănt), *adj.* **1**, covered with fresh green grass or foliage, as a landscape; having the freshness of spring; **2**, *Colloq.*, fresh and untried in knowledge or judgment; inexperienced; as, *verdant* youth.—*adv.* **ver'dant-ly.**—*n.* **ver'dan-cy.**

verd an-tique (vûrd), **1**, a kind of green mottled or veined building stone, employed extensively for indoor decoration; serpentine; **2**, an incrustation of green found on ancient bronzes.

ver-dict (vûr'dĭkt), *n.* **1**, the decision of a jury on a case in court; as, the jury's *verdict* was "Not guilty"; **2**, the expression of any important decision.

ver-di-gris (vûr'dĭ-grēs), *n.* **1,** a green or bluish green pigment, produced by acetic acid acting on copper; **2,** *Colloq.*, a greenish or bluish rust on copper, bronze, brass, etc.

ver-dure (vûr'dûr), *n.* **1,** greenness or freshness, esp. of grass and growing plants; **2,** green grass, growing plants, etc.; as, the meadows were clad with *verdure.* —*adj.* **ver'dur-ous.**—*adj.* **ver'dure-less.**

[1]verge (vûrj), *n.* **1,** a rod or staff carried before a bishop, dean, etc., as a sign of authority or of office; **2,** boundary; brink; an extreme edge, as of a precipice; **3,** that which incloses or encircles, as a ring. *Syn.* margin, border, limit.

[2]verge (vûrj), *v.i.* [*p.t.* and *p.p.* verged (vûrjd), *p.pr.* verg'ing], **1,** to approach closely; be on the border: with *on;* as, to *verge* on treason; **2,** to tend; incline.

ver-ger (vûr'jẽr), *n.* **1,** an officer who carries a rod as a sign of authority; **2,** in the English Church, an attendant on a bishop, dean, etc.; **3,** in the Protestant Episcopal Church, one who takes care of a church building or property; a sexton.

ve-rid-i-cal (vē-rĭd'ĭ-kăl), *adj.* speaking or telling the truth; veracious; truthful.—*adv.* **ve-rid'i-cal-ly.**

ver-i-fi-a-ble (vĕr'ĭ-fī"ȧ-bl), *adj.* capable of being proved true.

ver-i-fi-ca-tion (vĕr"ĭ-fĭ-kā'shŭn), *n.* **1,** the act of proving to be true; **2,** the state of being proved true.

ver-i-fy (vĕr'ĭ-fī), *v.t.* [*p.t.* and *p.p.* -fied (-fīd), *p.pr.* -fy"ing], **1,** to prove the correctness of; examine so as to prove; **2,** to confirm or substantiate, as a statement.

ver-i-ly (vĕr'ĭ-lĭ), *adv.* **1,** in truth; certainly; as, *verily* I say unto you; **2,** really; truly; as, I *verily* believe.

ver-i-sim-i-lar (vĕr"ĭ-sĭm'ĭ-lȧr), *adj.* with likeness to truth; likely; probable.—*adv.* **ver"i-sim'i-lar-ly.**

ver-i-si-mil-i-tude (vĕr"ĭ-sĭ-mĭl'ĭ-tūd), *n.* **1,** the appearance of truth; probability; likelihood; **2,** likeness to things as they actually are.

ver-i-ta-ble (vĕr'ĭ-tȧ-bl), *adj.* actual; genuine; true; as, the rain was a *veritable* godsend.—*adv.* **ver'i-ta-bly.**

ver-i-ty (vĕr'ĭ-tĭ), *n.* [*pl.* verities (-tĭz)], **1,** that which is true; a truth; fact; **2,** the quality of being true or correct; truthfulness; reality.

ver-juice (vûr'jōōs"), *n.* **1,** the sour juice of unripe fruits, as grapes, apples, etc.; **2,** an acid liquor, used chiefly in cooking, made from this; **3,** tartness; acerbity; **4,** sharpness of manner.

ver-mi-cel-li (vûr"mē-sĕl'ĭ; vûr"mē-chĕl'ĭ), *n.* a paste made of fine flour dried in slender, solid, round sticks, smaller than either macaroni or spaghetti.

ver-mic-u-lar (vẽr-mĭk'ū-lȧr), *adj.* **1,** like a worm in shape or motion; vermiform; **2,** like worm tracks; **3,** worm-eaten.—*adj.* **ver-mic'u-lose.**

ver-mic-u-late (vẽr-mĭk'ū-lāt), *v.t.* [*p.t.* and *p.p.* -lat"ed, *p.pr.* -lat"ing], to ornament or inlay with wavy lines resembling worm tracks:—*adj.* (-lāt), **1,** shaped like a worm; **2,** ornamented with markings like the tracks of worms; **3,** similar to a worm in motion; wriggling; **4,** insinuating; suggestive; **5,** full of holes made by worms.

ver-mic-u-la-tion (vẽr-mĭk"ū-lā'shŭn), *n.* **1,** wormlike motion; specif., peristalsis, or the wavelike contraction of the intestines; **2,** the state of being worm-eaten; **3,** ornamentation resembling worm tracks, or the act or art of making it; **4,** markings of wavy lines, as on a bird.

ver-mi-form (vûr'mĭ-fôrm), *adj.* shaped like a worm; **vermiform appendix,** a small, closed tube, now without function, attached to the large intestine in the lower right-hand part of the abdomen: the seat of the disease appendicitis.

ver-mi-fuge (vûr'mĭ-fūj), *n.* a medicine that expels or forces parasitic worms from animal bodies.

ver-mil-ion (vẽr-mĭl'yŭn), *n.* **1,** a brilliant red pigment made from sulphide of mercury; **2,** a vivid red color.

ver-min (vûr'mĭn), *n.* [*pl.* vermin], **1,** usually in *pl.*, harmful and offensive insects or small animals, as bedbugs, flies, lice, fleas, mice, rats, etc.; **2,** an unwholesome person.—*adj.* **ver'min-ous.**

ver-muth (vûr'mōōth), *n.* a kind of bitter alcoholic cordial flavored with wormwood. Also, **ver'mouth.**

ver-nac-u-lar (vẽr-năk'ū-lȧr), *adj.* pertaining to one's native country: used esp. of a language:—*n.* **1,** one's native tongue; **2,** the prevailing fashion of speech among the people in general in any locality; as, he could converse in the *vernacular* with his mountaineer friends; **3,** the vocabulary peculiar to a business, profession, etc.; as, the *vernacular* of the motion-picture studios.

ver-nal (vûr'năl), *adj.* **1,** pertaining to, or appearing in, the spring; as, the *vernal* equinox; **2,** springlike; **3,** hence, youthful; as, the *vernal* fires of enthusiasm: **vernal equinox,** the time of the sun's northward passage across the equator, about March 21.

ver-ni-er (vûr'nĭ-ẽr), *n.* a scale made to slide along the divisions of another scale in order to obtain accurate fractional parts of its subdivisions.

ver-sa-tile (vûr'sȧ-tĭl; vûr'sȧ-tīl), *adj.* turning easily from one action, style, subject, etc., to another; able to do many things well; as, a *versatile* writer.—*n.* **ver"sa-til'i-ty.**

verse (vûrs), *n.* **1,** a line of poetry; **2,** a form of composition possessing rhythm; poetry: opp. of *prose;* **3,** loosely, a group of metrical lines; stanza; **4,** any of the short divisions of a chapter in the Bible.

versed (vûrst), *adj.* thoroughly trained; taught by experience, practice, study, etc.; skilled; learned; informed.

ver-si-cle (vûr'sĭ-kl), *n.* any of a series of short verses or sentences, said or sung by a minister, priest, or other leader, alternating with the congregation.

ver-si-fi-ca-tion (vûr"sĭ-fĭ-kā'shŭn), *n.* **1,** the art or practice of composing verses, as of poetry; **2,** the science of metrical construction.

ver-si-fy (vûr'sĭ-fī), *v.i.* [*p.t.* and *p.p.* -fied (-fīd), *p.pr.* -fy"ing], to express thought or feeling in verse form; make verses:—*v.t.* to express in verse; put into verse.—*n.* **ver'si-fi"er.**

ver-sion (vûr'shŭn), *n.* **1,** a translation from one language into another; as, a revised *version* of the Bible; **2,** an individual report of an occurrence or form of a story peculiar to some individual or group; as, his *version* of the accident.

verst (vûrst), *n.* the Russian mile, equal to 3,500 English feet, or about two thirds of a mile.

ver-sus (vûr'sŭs), *prep.* against: used chiefly in a legal or sporting sense.—*abbr.* **v.; vs.**

ver-te-bra (vûr'tē-brȧ), *n.* [*pl.* vertebræ (-brē)], a single bone of the spinal column, or backbone.—*adj.* **ver'te-bral.**

ver-te-brate (vûr'tē-brāt), *adj.* **1,** belonging to a great subdivision (*Vertebrata*) of the animal kingdom, comprising all animals with a backbone, and including mammals, birds, amphibians, fishes, etc.; **2,** having a backbone, or spinal column:—*n.* an animal with a spinal column.—*adj.* **ver'te-brat"ed.**

ver-tex (vûr'tĕks), *n.* [*pl.* vertices (-tĭ-sēz); vertexes (-tĕk-sĕz)], **1,** the highest point; top; apex; as, the *vertex* of a pyramid; **2,** in geometry, the point where the sides of an angle meet (see [1]*angle*, illus.).

ver-ti-cal (vûr'tĭ-kăl), *adj.* **1,** pertaining to the apex or top; at or in the zenith; straight overhead; **2,** at right angles with the horizon; upright: opp. of *horizontal;* **3,** of or pertaining to a vertex: **vertical angles,** the opposite angles made by two intersecting straight lines:—*n.* a line, plane, or circle at right angles with the horizon.—*adv.* **ver'ti-cal-ly.**—*n.* **ver'ti-cal-ness.**—*n.* **ver"ti-cal'i-ty.**

ver-ti-cil (vûr'tĭ-sĭl), *n.* **1,** a circular arrangement of leaves, petals, etc., around a common center; a whorl; **2,** one of the turns of a spiral shell.

ver-tig-i-nous (vẽr-tĭj'ĭ-nŭs), *adj.* **1,** affected with dizziness; giddy; **2,** making dizzy; **3,** turning around; whirling; reeling.—*adv.* **ver-tig'i-nous-ly.**—*n.* **ver-tig'i-nous-ness.**

ver-ti-go (vûr'tĭ-gō), *n.* [*pl.* vertigoes (-gōz); vertigines (vẽr-tĭj'ĭ-nēz)], giddiness; extreme dizziness.

ver-tu (vĭr-tōō'; vûr'tōō), *n.* **1,** the character or quality of being rare, artistic, beautiful, or curious; as, objects of *vertu;* also, objects of art collectively; **2,** a taste for, or love of, such objects. Also, **vir-tu'**, *Pfd. S.*

verve (vûrv), *n.* **1,** the enthusiasm which inspires a poet or an artist; quickness of imagination; **2,** energy; vigor.

ver-y (vĕr'ĭ), *adj.* [*comp., Rare,* ver'i-er, *superl.* ver'i-est], **1,** absolute; complete; utter; as, that is the *very* truth; **2,** identical; the same; as, that is the *very* one; **3,** even; even the: used for emphasis; as, the *very* thought frightens me:—*adv.* **1,** truly; exactly; absolutely; as, the *very* last thing I expected; **2,** in a high degree; extremely; as, she does *very* good work.

ves-i-cant (vĕs'ĭ-kănt), *adj.* producing blisters:—*n.* anything which produces blisters.

ves-i-cate (vĕs'ĭ-kāt), *v.t.* [*p.t.* and *p.p.* -cat"ed, *p.pr.* -cat"ing], to blister, as the skin.—*n.* **ves"i-ca'tion.**

ves-i-ca-to-ry (vĕs'ĭ-kȧ-tō-rĭ), *adj.* causing, or capable of raising, a blister:—*n.* [*pl.* vesicatories (-rĭz)], a blister-forming dressing or plaster.

ves-i-cle (vĕs'ĭ-kl), *n.* a small bladder, or sac, in the body, containing fluid; a blister; cyst.—*adj.* **ve-sic'u-lar.**

ves-per (vĕs'pẽr), *adj.* pertaining to the evening:—*n.* **1,** *Poetic,* evening; **2,** an evening hymn, prayer, etc.: **Vesper,** the evening star, or Hesperus; esp., the planet Venus as an evening star.—*adj.* **ves'per-al.**

ves-pers (vĕs'pẽrz), *n.pl.* **1,** in the Protestant Episcopal Church, evening prayer; **2,** in certain other churches, a late Sunday afternoon service, often musical.

ves-per-tine (vĕs'pẽr-tĭn; vĕs'pẽr-tīn), *adj.* relating to, or happening in, the evening.

ves-sel (vĕs'ĕl), *n.* **1,** a hollow receptacle or container, usually for liquids, as a barrel, bottle, cup, etc.; **2,** a tube or canal in the body through which a fluid passes; as, a blood *vessel;* **3,** a hollow, floating structure for conveying people and goods by water; any boat larger than a rowboat; a ship.

vest (vĕst), *n.* **1,** a waistcoat; a man's sleeveless garment, worn beneath the coat; **2,** a woven or knitted undershirt; **3,** an ornamental insertion in the front of a woman's waist:—*v.t.* **1,** to dress in, or as in, a garment; hence, to encircle or surround; **2,** to clothe, as with authority or power: followed by *with;* **3,** to put into the care of another: with *in;* as, the control of the city is *vested* in its officials:—*v.i.* to be fixed; pass or take effect, as title to property: with *in.*

Ves-ta (vĕs'tȧ), *n.* in mythology, the Roman virgin goddess of the hearth and home, in whose temple the sacred fire was kept by the Vestal Virgins: **vesta, 1,** a short wax match or taper, ignited by friction; **2,** a short wooden match.

ves-tal (vĕs'tăl), *adj.* **1,** pertaining to, or sacred to, Vesta; **2,** designating the virgins who served in her temple:—*n.* **1,** in the Roman religion, a virgin vowed to the service of Vesta; **2,** hence, a virgin; also, a nun: **Vestal Virgins,** the six virgin priestesses who tended the sacred fire on the altar of the temple of Vesta in ancient Rome.

vest-ed (vĕs'tĕd), *adj.* **1,** clothed, esp. in priestly or other ceremonial garments; **2,** fixed; having rights established by law; as, *vested* interests.

ves-ti-bule (vĕs'tĭ-būl), *n.* **1,** a small entry or lobby between an outer and an inner door of a house; **2,** an inclosed porch or entrance hall outside the main door of a building; as, the *vestibule* of a church; **3,** an inclosed entrance to a railway passenger car; **4,** in anatomy, any of various channels opening into others; as, the *vestibule* of the inner ear.—*adj.* **ves'ti-buled.**

ves-tige (vĕs'tĭj), *n.* **1,** a mark left in passing; **2,** a visible sign or trace of something that is gone or has disappeared or ceased; as, not a *vestige* of the house remained.

vest-ment (vĕst'mĕnt), *n.* **1,** a robe; garment; esp., an official dress or robe of ceremony; **2,** in *pl.,* garments or robes worn over the ordinary dress by priests, ministers, choir, etc., in church services.

ves-try (vĕs'trĭ), *n.* [*pl.* vestries (-trĭz)], **1,** a room in a church where the clergy put on their vestments or robes; **2,** in some Protestant churches, a room or building attached to a church, and used as a chapel, Sunday-school room, etc.; **3,** in the Protestant Episcopal Church, a body of men who direct the affairs of a parish.

ves-try-man (vĕs'trĭ-măn), *n.* [*pl.* vestrymen (-mĕn)], one of a group that directs or manages the affairs of a church or parish.

ves-ture (vĕs'tūr), *n.* **1,** clothing; garments taken collectively; **2,** the external covering of a plant or an animal.

vetch (vĕch), *n.* any of several plants of the pea family, often used as fodder.

vet-er-an (vĕt'ẽr-ăn), *adj.* **1,** possessing experience due to age; **2,** long trained or practiced, esp. as a soldier:—*n.* **1,** a person of age and experience; **2,** one grown old in service; **3,** a soldier of any age who has seen active service in war.

vet-er-i-na-ri-an (vĕt"ẽr-ĭ-nā'rĭ-ăn), *n.* one who practices the healing of diseases and injuries of animals.

vet-er-i-na-ry (vĕt'ẽr-ĭ-nā-rĭ), *adj.* pertaining to the healing of diseases of domestic animals, as horses, cattle, etc.; as, a *veterinary* surgeon:—*n.* [*pl.* veterinaries (-rĭz)], one who treats the diseases of domestic animals.

ve-to (vē'tō), *n.* [*pl.* vetoes (-tōz)], **1,** the right to stop or prevent the enactment of a measure as law; **2,** the act of exercising this right; **3,** a prohibition by one in authority; **4,** the constitutional right of a chief executive to refuse his approval to a legislative enactment; **5,** chiefly in the U. S., the official document giving the executive's reason for refusing his approval:—*v.t.* **1**, to exercise the right of veto against, as a bill; **2**, to forbid with authority.—*n.* **ve'to-er.**

vex (vĕks), *v.t.* **1**, to irritate by small annoyances; harass; tease; make angry; **2**, to agitate; disquiet; **3**, to subject to argument; as, a *vexed* question.—*adv.* **vex'ed-ly.**
Syn. provoke, annoy, exasperate.

vex-a-tion (vĕk-sā'shŭn), *n.* **1**, the act of annoying; **2**, the state of being irritated; **3**, annoyance; displeasure.
Syn. chagrin, mortification, humiliation.

vex-a-tious (vĕk-sā'shŭs), *adj.* **1**, causing irritation or annoyance; **2**, full of disquiet; disturbed.—*adv.* **vex-a'tious-ly.**—*n.* **vex-a'tious-ness.**

vi-a (vī'ȧ), *prep.* by the way of; as, he traveled *via* the Panama Canal.

vi-a-ble (vī'ȧ-bl), *adj.* capable of living or maintaining life, as a newly born infant or a transplanted plant.

vi-a-duct (vī'ȧ-dŭkt), *n.* a bridge, generally built of arched masonry

VIADUCT

or of steel, for carrying a roadway over a valley or ravine.

vi-al (vī'ăl), *n.* a small glass bottle; phial; as, a *vial* for medicine.

vi-ands (vī'ăndz), *n.pl.* food or provisions; eatables.

vi-at-ic (vī-ăt'ĭk), *adj.* pertaining to a journey or travel.

vi-at-i-cum (vī-ăt'ĭ-kŭm), *n.* [*pl.* viatica (-kȧ)], the Eucharist, or Communion, as given to one supposedly on the verge of death.

vi-brant (vī'brănt), *adj.* vibrating; thrilling; tremulous; resonant or resounding; as, a *vibrant* voice.

vi-brate (vī'brāt), *v.i.* [*p.t.* and *p.p.* -brated, *p.pr.* -brat-ing], **1**, to move back and forth periodically, as a pendulum; **2**, to quiver, as the voice; make a tremulous sound:—*v.t.* to cause to quiver; set in motion to and fro; oscillate.

vi-bra-tile (vī'brȧ-tĭl), *adj.* employed in, or capable of, vibration.

vi-bra-tion (vī-brā'shŭn), *n.* **1**, the act of swinging back and forth; **2**, a quivering or throbbing, as of the voice; **3**, periodic motion to and fro, as of a pendulum.—*adj.* **vi-bra'tion-al.**

vi-bra-tor (vī'brā-tẽr), *n.* that which moves rapidly back and forth, or oscillates, or which causes such movements. —*adj.* **vi'bra-to-ry.**

vi-bur-num (vī-bûr'nŭm), *n.* any of a large genus (*Viburnum*) of shrubs or, rarely, small trees, with simple leaves and white, or sometimes pink, flowers.

vic-ar (vĭk'ẽr), *n.* **1**, in the Roman Catholic Church, a member of the clergy representing one higher up, as an archbishop or the Pope; **2**, in England, the priest of a parish in which the tithes are in lay hands; **3**, in the Protestant Episcopal Church, a minister who is the head of one chapel in a large parish; also, a bishop's representative in charge of a church or mission.

vic-ar-age (vĭk'ẽr-āj), *n.* in England, the office, position, or residence of a vicar, or minister of a parish, the tithes of which are in charge of laymen.

vic-ar-gen-er-al (vĭk'ẽr=jĕn'ẽr-ăl), *n.* [*pl.* vicars-general (-ẽrz"=)], **1**, in the Anglican Church, a lay legal officer who represents an archbishop in certain matters; **2**, in the Roman Catholic Church, a deputy acting for a bishop in matters requiring legal power or jurisdiction.

vi-ca-ri-ate (vī-kā'rĭ-āt), *n.* **1**, the authority, office, or jurisdiction, of a vicar; **2**, a power or an office delegated or intrusted to another.—*adj.* **vi-ca'ri-al.**

vi-ca-ri-ous (vī-kā'rĭ-ŭs), *adj.* **1**, delegated; as, *vicarious* power; **2**, acting for another; as, a *vicarious* agent; **3**, performed or suffered in place of another; as, *vicarious* suffering.— *adv.* **vi-ca'ri-ous-ly.**—*n.* **vi-ca'ri-ous-ness.**

[1]**vice** (vīs), *n.* **1**, a fault; defect; blemish; **2**, a habitual departure from moral rectitude; any debasing practice or habit; as, the *vice* of intemperance; **3**, depravity; wickedness; corruption; **4**, a bad trick or habit, as of a horse, dog, or the like.

[2]**vice** (vīs), *n.* a device consisting of two jaws tightened by a screw: used to hold objects firmly. See [1]**vise,** *Pfd. S.*

[3]**vice** (vīs), *adj.* **1**, designating one next in rank to, or acting or qualified to act in place of, a specified official; as, *vice* president; **2**, designating the office of such a one; as, *vice* presidency. Also, **vice-.**

[4]**vi-ce** (vī'sē), *prep.* in the place of; as, he became chief, *vice* John, resigned.

vice-ge-rent (vīs-jē'rĕnt), *adj.* holding power from another; acting in the place of another:—*n.* an officer authorized to exercise the powers of another: an agent or lieutenant.

vice-re-gal (vīs"rē'găl), *adj.* pertaining to a viceroy.

vice-roy (vīs'roi), *n.* a ruler of a colony or province, acting with royal authority in the place of a king; as, the *viceroy* of India.—*n.* **vice"roy'al-ty.**

***vi-ce ver-sa** (vī'sē vûr'sȧ), [Lat.], the relation or order of terms being reversed; conversely.

vic-i-nage (vĭs'ĭ-nāj), *n.* neighborhood; vicinity; locality.

vi-cin-i-ty (vĭ-sĭn'ĭ-tĭ), *n.* [*pl.* vicinities (-tĭz)], **1**, nearness; closeness; **2**, a region about or near; neighborhood; as, he lives in our *vicinity.*

vi-cious (vĭsh'ŭs), *adj.* **1**, faulty; as, *vicious* reasoning; **2**, corrupt; depraved; wicked; as, he led a *vicious* life; **3**, unruly; not well tamed or broken; as, a *vicious* horse; **4**, impure, as air; **5**, malicious.—*adv.* **vi'cious-ly.**—*n.* **vi'cious-ness.**

vi-cis-si-tude (vĭ-sĭs'ĭ-tūd), *n.* a complete, unexpected change of circumstances; as, the *vicissitudes* of war.

vic-tim (vĭk'tĭm), *n.* **1**, a living being sacrificed in a religious ceremony; **2**, a person or thing destroyed or hurt in the pursuit of some object, or in an accident.

vic-tim-ize (vĭk'tĭm-īz), *v.t.* [*p.t.* and *p.p.* -ized (-īzd), *p.pr.* -iz"ing], **1**, to injure, destroy, or sacrifice; **2**, to swindle.

vic-tor (vĭk'tẽr), *n.* **1**, a conqueror; **2**, one who wins in a contest:—*adj.* conquering; as, the *victor* flag.

vic-to-ri-a (vĭk-tō′rĭ-*a*), *n.* **1,** a kind of low four-wheeled carriage with a top that may be lowered and a high seat for the coachman; **2,** a very large South American water lily; the Victoria regia (which see).

Vic-to-ri-a Cross a bronze Maltese cross, bearing the legend "For Valour," awarded to members of the British army and navy for conspicuous bravery: instituted by Queen Victoria in 1856.

Vic-to-ri-an (vĭk-tō′rĭ-ăn), *adj.* pertaining to the reign of Queen Victoria of England (1837–1901):—*n.* **1,** a person living during that time, esp. a writer; as, Dickens, Thackeray, Tennyson, and Carlyle were among the greatest *Victorians;* **2,** a person whose thoughts and habits are like those common during Queen Victoria's reign.

Vic-to-ri-a re-gi-a (rē′jĭ-*ȧ*), a water lily native to Guiana and Brazil, in South America, remarkable for its immense rose-white flowers, twelve to eighteen inches in diameter, and for its large, floating leaves, three to six feet across, with rims two to six inches high: also called *victoria; royal water lily.*

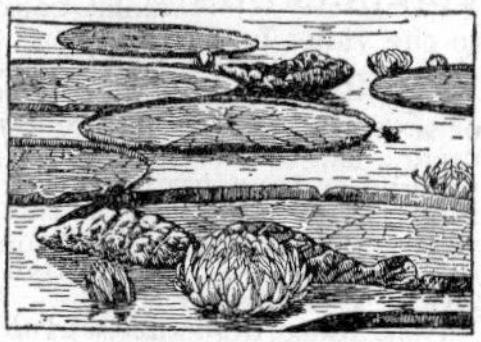

VICTORIA REGIA

vic-to-ri-ous (vĭk-tō′rĭ-ŭs), *adj.* **1,** having conquered in battle or contest; triumphant; as, a *victorious* army; **2,** marked by, or ending in, conquest or triumph; as, a *victorious* fight; **3,** pertaining to, or symbolizing, victory; as, *victorious* laurel wreaths.—*adj.* **vic-to′ri-ous-ly.**—*n.* **vic-to′ri-ous-ness.**

vic-to-ry (vĭk′tō-rĭ), *n.* [*pl.* victories (-rĭz)], **1,** the defeat of an enemy; triumph; conquest; **2,** the gaining of superiority in any contest.

Syn. conquest, triumph. A *victory* is a decisive winning of any contest. A *conquest* is a *victory* with the idea of permanent advantage. A *triumph* is a brilliant *victory* characterized by open, and often public, rejoicing.

vict-ual (vĭt′l), *v.t.* to supply or stock with food:—*n.,* in *pl.,* food for human beings; esp., such food when ready for eating.

vict-ual-er (vĭt′l-ẽr, vĭt′lẽr), *n.* one who provides victuals or food, esp. a hotel keeper. Also, **vict′ual-ler.**

vi-cu-ña (vĭ-kōōn′y*ȧ*), *n.* an animal of the high Andes, belonging to the llama and alpaca family, and furnishing a fine, long, reddish wool: **vicuña cloth,** soft cloth made of this wool; also, an imitation of such cloth.

VICUÑA ($\frac{1}{28}$)

***vi-de** (vī′dē) [Lat.], *v.* see: a term used to direct attention; as, *vide* page 40.

***vi-del-i-cet** (vĭ-dĕl′ĭ-sĕt), [Lat.], *adv.* to wit or namely: often abbreviated to *viz.*

vi-dette (vĭ-dĕt′), *n.* a mounted sentinel stationed in front of the regular pickets of an army. Also, **ve-dette′**, *Pfd. S.*

vie (vī), *v.i.* [*p.t.* and *p.p.* vied (vīd), *p.pr.* vy′ing], to strive for superiority; compete, as in games, school, etc.

view (vū), *n.* **1,** the act of seeing; **2,** that which is seen; spectacle; as, a splendid *view;* **3,** range of mental perception; as, to take a broad *view* of the matter; **4,** range of vision; outlook, physical or mental; as, he passed from *view;* **5,** a picture of a scene, object, or person; as, a fine *view* of Mount Washington; **6,** a way of looking at anything mentally; opinion; as, he held advanced *views;* **7,** regard or consideration; as, make your plans with a *view* to success:—*v.t.* **1,** to see; gaze at; look upon; **2,** to survey mentally; form an opinion.—*n.* **view′er.**

view-less (vū′lĕs), *adj. Archaic,* unseen; invisible.—*adv.* **view′less-ly.**—*n.* **view′less-ness.**

view-point (vū′point″), *n.* **1,** the position or place from which one looks at something; **2,** mentally, a way of regarding or judging events; the attitude of mind lying at the basis of an opinion; as, our judgment depends on our *viewpoint.*

vig-il (vĭj′ĭl), *n.* **1,** a purposeful keeping awake during a time usually devoted to sleep; **2,** usually in *pl.,* religious devotions in the evening or night; **3,** formerly, devotional watch kept on the eve of a feast day.

vig-i-lance (vĭj′ĭ-lăns), *n.* watchfulness; caution; alertness to avoid danger: **vigilance committee,** a body of citizens self-organized or unofficially appointed to preserve law and order or to administer justice, as in newly settled or poorly policed districts.

vig-i-lant (vĭj′ĭ-lănt), *adj.* keenly watchful; alert; wary.—*adv.* **vig′i-lant-ly.**—*n.* **vig′i-lant-ness.**

Syn. wakeful, circumspect, observant.

vig-i-lan-te (vĭj″ĭ-lăn′tē), *n.* a person belonging to a vigilance committee (which see).

vi-gnette (vĭn-yĕt′), *n.* **1,** a small design decorating the blank space left at the beginning or end of a magazine article, a chapter in a book, etc.; **2,** any engraving or picture which shades off gradually without definite border; **3,** a portrait of the head and shoulders only:—*v.t.* [*p.t.* and *p.p.* -gnet′ted (-yĕt′ĕd), *p.pr.* -gnet′ting], **1,** to ornament with a vignette; **2,** to make a vignette of.—*n.* **vi-gnet′ter.**—*n.* **vi-gnet′tist.**

vig-or (vĭg′ẽr), *n.* **1,** physical or mental strength or energy; **2,** any effective strength; as, *vigor* of literary style; *vigor* of attack. Also, **vig′our.**

vig-or-ous (vĭg′ẽr-ŭs), *adj.* **1,** full of physical and mental strength and energy; **2,** powerful; energetic; as, a *vigorous* constitution; a *vigorous* speech.—*adv.* **vig′or-ous-ly.**—*n.* **vig′or-ous-ness.**

vi-king (vī′kĭng; vē′-), *n.* one of the Scandinavian pirates, or Northmen, who plundered the coasts of Europe from the eighth to the tenth century.

vil-a-yet (vē″lä-yĕt′), *n.* one of the main administrative divisions or provinces into which Turkey is divided.

vile (vīl), *adj.* **1,** worthless; mean; ignoble; **2,** morally base or impure; as, *vile* language; **3,** foul or offensive; as, *vile* odors.—*adv.* **vile′ly.**—*n.* **vile′ness.**

vil-i-fy (vĭl′ĭ-fī), *v.t.* [*p.t.* and *p.p.* -fied (-fīd), *p.pr.* -fy″ing], to make low and base by report; slander; asperse.—*n.* **vil′i-fi″er.**—*n.* **vil″i-fi-ca′tion.**

Syn. debase, revile, defame, asperse.—*Ant.* extol, honor, praise, acclaim.

vil-la (vĭl′*ȧ*), *n.* a pretentious residence in the country or suburbs, usually set in extensive grounds.

vil-lage (vĭl′āj), *n.* a small collection of houses in a country district, larger than a hamlet and yet smaller than a town.—*n.* **vil′lag-er.**

vil-lain (vĭl′ĭn), *n.* **1**, one capable of great wickedness; a rascal; **2**, *Archaic:* **a**, a rustic; **b**, (usually, *villein*), a feudal serf; **3**, in a play or novel, the character who opposes the hero or otherwise makes difficulties.

vil-lain-ous (vĭl′ĭn-ŭs), *adj.* marked by extreme wickedness; evil; base; as, a *villainous* character. Also, **vil′lan-ous.**—*adv.* **vil′lain-ous-ly.**
Syn. infamous, heinous, detestable.—*Ant.* honorable, good, noble.

vil-lain-y (vĭl′ĭn-ĭ), *n.* [*pl.* villainies (-ĭz)], **1**, the quality or state of being very evil; great wickedness; **2**, a very wicked act; a crime.

vil-lein (vĭl′ĭn), *n.* under the feudal system, a serf. Also, **vil′lain.**

vil-len-age (vĭl′ĕn-āj), *n.* **1**, under the feudal system, the position of a serf; **2**, the holding of land by a serf from his lord. Also, **vil′lein-age; vil′lan-age.**

vil-lous (vĭl′ŭs), *adj.* covered with fine, soft hairs; downy.

vil-lus (vĭl′ŭs), *n.* [*pl.* villi (-ī)], **1**, one of the short, threadlike processes on some membranes, esp. the mucous membrane on the inside of the small intestine; **2**, in *pl.*, fine, straight, soft hairs on plants.—*n.* **vil-los′i-ty.**

vim (vĭm), *n. Colloq.*, force; energy; spirit; vitality.

***vin** (văṅ), [Fr.], *n.* wine: ***vin ordinaire** (vâ″ nôr″dē″nâr′), a cheap grade of claret: the common table wine of France.

vi-na-ceous (vī-nā′shŭs), *adj.* **1**, of or pertaining to wine or grapes; **2**, like red wine in color.

vin-ai-grette (vĭn″ā-grĕt′), *n.* **1**, a small, usually ornamented, bottle for holding smelling salts; **2**, a vinegar sauce for cold meats or salads.

vin-ci-ble (vĭn′sĭ-bl), *adj.* capable of being vanquished; conquerable.—*n.* **vin′ci-ble-ness.**—*n.* **vin″ci-bil′i-ty.**

vin-cu-lum (vĭng′kū-lŭm), *n.* [*pl.* vincula (-lȧ)], **1**, a bond of union; tie; **2**, a horizontal mark placed over two or more algebraic quantities to indicate that they are to be treated as one, as in $x + \overline{a - 1} = b$.

vin-di-cate (vĭn′dĭ-kāt), *v.t.* [*p.t.* and *p.p.* -cat″ed, *p.pr.* -cat″ing], to defend successfully against denial, objection, or accusation; clear from suspicion of wrong, dishonor, or invalidity; as, to *vindicate* one's courage, claim, or assertion.—*adj.* **vin-dic′a-tive.**—*n.* **vin′di-ca″tor.**

vin-di-ca-tion (vĭn″dĭ-kā′shŭn), *n.* **1**, the act of proving something right or true against blame or accusation; **2**, the state of being so proved right or true; defense; support by proof.

vin-di-ca-to-ry (vĭn′dĭ-kȧ-tō-rĭ), *adj.* serving to justify.

vin-dic-tive (vĭn-dĭk′tĭv), *adj.* given to, or prompted by, revenge; inclined to hold a grudge; as, a *vindictive* man.—*adv.* **vin-dic′tive-ly.**—*n.* **vin-dic′tive-ness.**

vine (vīn), *n.* **1**, any climbing or trailing plant; **2**, a grapevine.—*adj.* **vin′y.**

vin-e-gar (vĭn′ē-gẽr), *n.* **1**, a sour liquid obtained by fermenting cider, wine, etc., and used to season or preserve food; **2**, hence, anything sour.—*adj.* **vin′e-gar-y.**

vin-er-y (vīn′ẽr-ĭ), *n.* [*pl.* vineries (-ĭz)], **1**, a greenhouse for cultivating grapes; **2**, a dense mass of vines.

vine-yard (vĭn′yẽrd), *n.* a grape plantation.

vi-nous (vī′nŭs), *adj.* pertaining to, or like, wine; as, *vinous* spirits.

vin-tage (vĭn′tāj), *n.* **1**, the act of, or the season for, gathering grapes and making wine; **2**, the yearly produce of a vineyard, or of the vineyards of a country; **3**, the wine produced in a given season; as, the *vintage* of 1872.—*n.* **vin′tag-er.**

vint-ner (vĭnt′nẽr), *n.* one who sells wine, esp. at wholesale.

vi-ol (vī′ŏl), *n.* a medieval musical instrument from which the violin was developed: now used only in *bass viol*, which see.

vi-o-la (vē-ō′lȧ; vī-ō′lȧ), *n.* a stringed instrument of the violin class, between the violin and violoncello in size and range, and tuned below the violin (see *musical instrument*, illus.).

vi-o-la-ble (vī′ō-lȧ-bl), *adj.* capable of being broken; as, a *violable* pledge or agreement.

vi-o-la-ceous (vī″ō-lā′shŭs), *adj.* **1**, of violet color; **2**, belonging to the violet family.

vi-o-late (vī′ō-lāt), *v.t.* [*p.t.* and *p.p.* -lat″ed, *p.pr.* -lat″ing], **1**, to treat roughly or severely; use ill; **2**, to encroach or trespass upon; as, to *violate* another's rights; **3**, to profane or treat irreverently; as, to *violate* a tomb; **4**, to transgress, as the law; disregard, as a treaty; break, as a promise; **5**, to outrage or dishonor.—*n.* **vi″o-la′tion.**—*adj.* **vi′o-la-tive.**—*n.* **vi′o-la″tor.**
Syn. abuse, desecrate.—*Ant.* respect, regard.

vi-o-lence (vī′ō-lĕns), *n.* **1**, great strength or energy, physical or emotional, forcibly exerted or expressed; fury; as, the *violence* of a storm; the *violence* of grief; **2**, profanation; outrage; as, he did *violence* to his better nature.
Syn. severity, intensity, rage, vehemence.

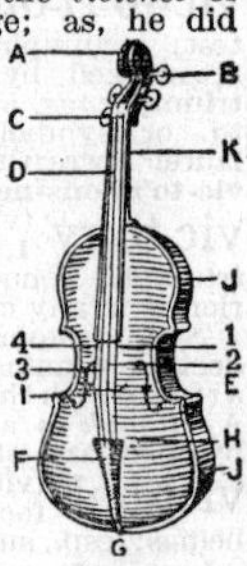

VIOLIN

A, scroll; B, pegs; C, upper saddle; D, finger board; E, bridge; F, tailpiece; G, tailpiece button; H, front or belly; I, sound holes; J, back; K, neck; 1, 2, 3, 4, first, second, third, and fourth strings.

vi-o-lent (vī′ō-lĕnt), *adj.* **1**, marked by, or acting with, great physical force, esp. when unlawfully exercised; as, to lay *violent* hands on one; **2**, characterized by, or due to, strong feeling; passionate; as, a *violent* dislike; **3**, resulting from the use of force; as, a *violent* death; **4**, extreme; as, a *violent* shock.—*adv.* **vi′o-lent-ly.**
Syn. boisterous, vehement.

vi-o-let (vī′ō-lĕt), *n.* **1**, any of a large genus (*Viola*) of low-growing, flowering plants; also, its flower, purple, white, yellow, or, as in the pansy, variegated; **2**, the color at the end of the spectrum opposite to the red:—*adj.* of a bluish purple color.

vi-o-lin (vī″ō-lĭn′), *n.* **1**, the smallest and highest tuned of the group of four-string musical instruments played with a bow (cf. *musical instrument*, illus.); **2**, a violin player.—*n.* **vi″o-lin′ist.**

vi-o-lon-cel-lo (vē″ō-lŏn-chĕl′ō; vī″ō-lŏn-sĕl′ō), *n.* [*pl.* violoncellos (-ōz)], a large four-string instrument of the violin class, tuned below the viola: often shortened to *'cello* or *cello* (see *musical instrument*, illus.).—*n.* **vi″o-lon-cel′list.**

vi-per (vī′pẽr), *n.* **1**, any of various Old World poisonous snakes; an adder (see illus. next page); **2**, hence, a baleful or evil person.—*adj.* **vi′per-ine.**—*adj.* **vi′per-ish.**—*adj.* **vi′per-ous.**

vi-ra-go (vĭ-rā′gō; vī-), *n.* [*pl.* viragoes (-gōz)], a bold, quarrelsome woman; a scold; termagant.

vir-e-o (vĭr′ē-ō), *n.* [*pl.* vireos (-ōz)], any of a family of small American song birds, olive-green or gray in color.

vi-res-cent (vĭ-rĕs′ĕnt), *adj.* **1**, beginning to be green, as trees in spring; **2**, slightly green; greenish.—*n.* **vi-res′cence.**

European Viper (1/8)

vir-gin (vûr′jĭn), *n.* a maid; a person, esp. a woman, who has had no sexual intercourse: **Virgin, 1**, a constellation, Virgo (which see); **2**, the sixth sign of the zodiac (see *zodiac*, illus.): **the Virgin**, the Virgin Mary, mother of Christ:—*adj.* **1**, chaste; modest; maidenly; **2**, pure; spotless; as, *virgin* white; **3**, new; fresh; untouched; as, *virgin* soil: **the Virgin Queen**, Queen Elizabeth of England.—*n.* **vir′gin-hood.**—*n.* **vir-gin′i-ty.**

vir-gin-al (vûr′jĭ-năl), *adj.* of, pertaining to, or like, a virgin; maidenly; chaste:—*n.* a musical instrument of the 16th century, like a small spinet without legs.

Vir-gin-i-a (vẽr-jĭn′ĭ-*ȧ*), *n.* **1**, in Roman legend, the daughter of the centurion Virginius, who slew her to save her from falling a prey to the decemvir Appius Claudius; **2**, one of the States of the U. S.: **Virginia creeper**, a North American woody vine, having bluish black berries: also called *woodbine* or *American ivy*: **Virginia reel**, a dance in which the partners, facing each other in opposite lines, perform a set series of figures.—*adj.* and *n.* **Vir-gin′i-an.**

Vir-gin Ma-ry in the Bible, the mother of Jesus of Nazareth (Matthew 1:18; Luke 2:5–7).

Vir-go (vûr′gō), *n.* **1**, a large constellation, the Virgin, near the ecliptic, containing the bright star Spica; **2**, the sixth sign of the zodiac, entered by the sun about August 22 (see *zodiac*, illus.).

vir-i-des-cent (vĭr″ĭ-dĕs′ĕnt), *adj.* **1**, tending to become green; **2**, slightly green; greenish.—*n.* **vir″i-des′cence.**

vi-rid-i-ty (vĭ-rĭd′ĭ-tĭ), *n.* greenness; freshness; verdure.

vir-ile (vĭr′ĭl; vī′rĭl), *adj.* **1**, characteristic of, or befitting, a man; manly; masculine; as, *virile* strength; **2**, forceful; masterful.—*n.* **vi-ril′i-ty.**

vir-tu (vĭr-to͞o′; vûr′to͞o), *n.* **1**, the character or quality of being artistic, rare, or beautiful: generally used in the phrases *objects of virtu, articles of virtu;* also, objects of art collectively; **2**, a taste for, or a love of, such objects. Also, **ver-tu′.**

vir-tu-al (vûr′tū-ăl), *adj.* in essence or effect, though not in fact; as, his words amounted to a *virtual* confession of guilt.—*n.* **vir″tu-al′i-ty.**—*adv.* **vir′tu-al-ly.**

vir-tue (vûr′tū), *n.* **1**, strength or effectiveness; worth; as, the *virtue* of exercise; **2**, excellence or merit, as of a material or object; **3**, general moral excellence; uprightness; rectitude; **4**, a specific kind of goodness; as, patience is a *virtue;* **5**, chastity; purity.—*adj.* **vir′tu-ous.**—*adv.* **vir′tu-ous-ly.**—*n.* **vir′tu-ous-ness.**

vir-tu-o-so (vĭr″to͞o-ō′sō; vûr″-), *n.* [*pl.* virtuosos (-sōz); virtuosi (-sē)], **1**, one with a special knowledge of, or taste for, objects of art, curios, or the like; a collector; **2**, one skilled in the technique of an art, esp. the art of music.—*n.* **vir″tu-os′i-ty.**

vir-u-lence (vĭr′o͞o-lĕns), *n.* **1**, the state or quality of being very poisonous or deadly; **2**, extreme bitterness; malignity. Also, **vir′u-len-cy.**

vir-u-lent (vĭr′o͞o-lĕnt), *adj.* **1**, very poisonous; venomous; **2**, deadly; malignant, as a disease; **3**, bitter and malicious, as a speech.—*adv.* **vir′u-lent-ly.**

vi-rus (vī′rŭs), *n.* **1**, the poison produced by, and containing the germs that cause, a disease; **2**, hence, moral contamination.

vi-sa (vē′z*ȧ*; vē-zä′), *n.* **1**, an official indorsement on a passport, giving permission to proceed; **2**, an official signature approving a document:—*v.t.* [*p.t.* and *p.p.* vi′saed (-z*ȧ*d; -zäd), *p.pr.* vi′sa-ing], to examine and mark as approved. Also, **vi-sé′** (vē-zā′).

vis-age (vĭz′ĭj), *n.* the face or countenance; appearance; also, aspect: chiefly in literary usage.—*adj.* **vis′aged.**

***vis-à-vis** (vē″=zä=vē′), [Fr.], *adj.* and *adv.* face to face:—*n.* **1**, one who is face to face with another; **2**, a kind of chair or carriage in which persons may sit facing each other.

Vi-sa-yan (vē-sä′yăn), *n.* **1**, a member of the chief native race of the Philippine Islands; **2**, the language of this race.

vis-cer-a (vĭs′ẽr-*ȧ*), *n.pl.* [*sing. Rare*, viscus (-kŭs)], the organs in the great cavities of the body, as the heart, liver, intestines, etc.—*adj.* **vis′cer-al.**

vis-cid (vĭs′ĭd), *adj.* sticky or gluelike; as, *viscid* gum.—*n.* **vis-cid′i-ty.**

vis-count (vī′kount″), *n.* a nobleman next in rank below an earl or count and next above a baron.—*n.fem.* **vis′count″ess.**

vis-count-y (vī′koun″tĭ), *n.* the rank or office of a viscount. Also, **vis′count″cy.**

vis-cous (vĭs′kŭs), *adj.* thick and sticky, as liquid.—*n.* **vis-cos′i-ty.**

[1]**vise** (vīs), *n.* a device having two jaws made to be drawn together by means of a screw, lever, or the like, for holding objects firmly: usually attached to a work bench or table. Also, **vice.**

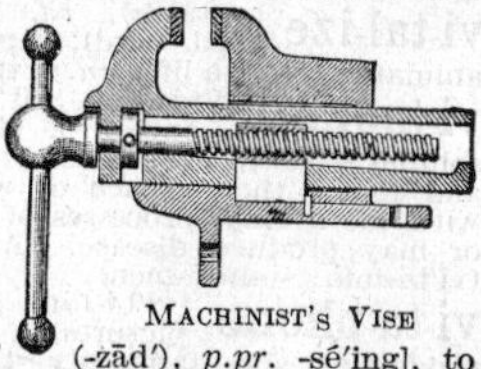

Machinist's Vise

[2]**vi-sé** (vē-zā′), *n.* an official indorsement on a document:—*v.t.* [*p.t.* and *p.p.* -séed′ (-zād′), *p.pr.* -sé′ing], to mark as approved. See **vi′sa**, *Pfd. S.*

Vish-nu (vĭsh′no͞o), *n.* the second god of the Hindu trinity, called the Preserver: associated with Brahma and Siva, Creator and Destroyer respectively.

vis-i-ble (vĭz′ĭ-bl), *adj.* **1**, capable of being seen; in sight; **2**, obvious; apparent; as, *visible* signs of grief.—*n.* **vis′i-ble-ness.**—*adv.* **vis′i-bly.**—*n.* **vis″i-bil′i-ty.**

Vis-i-goth (vĭz′ĭ-gŏth), *n.* one of the West Goths, an ancient Teutonic race that in the fifth and sixth centuries overran Europe and finally settled in Spain and southern France: distinguished from *Ostrogoth.*—*adj.* **Vis″i-goth′ic.**

vi-sion (vĭzh′ŭn), *n.* **1**, the act of seeing; **2**, the sense of sight; **3**, that which is seen; **4**, perception, esp. with the mind's eye; **5**, a supernatural appearance.

vi-sion-a-ry (vĭzh′ŭn-ā-rĭ), *adj.* **1**, pertaining to, or favorable for, visions; **2**, dreamy; imaginative, as a person; **3**, impracticable, as a plan:—*n.* [*pl.* visionaries (-rĭz)], **1**, a person given to fancies or reveries; a dreamer; **2**, one who is not practical.

vis-it (vĭz′ĭt), *n.* **1**, the act of going to see a person, place, or thing; a brief stay; **2**, the act of going to inspect, attend, or view:—*v.t.* **1**, to go or come to see; **2**, to come upon, as with good or evil; as, *visit* us with thy salvation:—*v.i.* to be a guest.—*adj.* **vis'it-a-ble.**—*n.* **vis'i-tor; vis'it-er.**

vis-it-ant (vĭz'ĭ-tănt), *n.* one who or that which makes a short stay; a visitor:—*adj.* visiting.

vis-it-a-tion (vĭz"ĭ-tā'shŭn), *n.* **1,** the act of going or coming to see; a visit; **2,** a special dispensation of divine favor or wrath; hence, any unusual event resembling such dispensation; judgment; **3,** an official inspection, as by a bishop.

vis-or (vĭz'ẽr; vī'zẽr), *n.* **1,** the movable front of a helmet, which, when lowered, protected the upper part of the face; **2,** the projecting brim of a cap. Also, **viz'or.**

vis-ta (vĭs'tȧ), *n.* **1,** a view down a long, narrow passage, as a street; hence, the trees, buildings, etc., forming such an avenue; **2,** a mental view of a series of remembered or anticipated events.

vis-u-al (vĭzh'ū-ăl), *adj.* **1,** pertaining to, or used in, sight; **2,** capable of being seen; visible.—*adv.* **vis'u-al-ly.**

vis-u-al-ize (vĭzh'ū-ăl-īz), *v.t.* and *v.i.* [*p.t.* and *p.p.* -ized (-īzd), *p.pr.* -iz"ing], **1,** to make visible; **2,** to make a picture of in the mind; see in fancy.—*n.* **vis'u-al-iz"er.**—*n.* **vis"u-al-i-za'tion.**

vi-tal (vī'tăl), *adj.* **1,** pertaining to, supporting, or necessary to, life; as, *vital* functions; air and food are *vital* necessities; **2,** living; full of life; **3,** essential; as, things of *vital* importance:—*n.*, in *pl.*, **1,** the parts of animal bodies necessary to life; **2,** the parts necessary to the health, soundness, etc., of anything.—*adv.* **vi'tal-ly.**

vi-tal-i-ty (vī-tăl'ĭ-tĭ), *n.* **1,** life force; ability to sustain life; vital power; **2,** capacity for enduring, as in resisting disease, old age, etc.

vi-tal-ize (vī'tăl-īz), *v.t.* [*p.t.* and *p.p.* -ized (-īzd), *p.pr.* -iz"ing], to animate; fill with life.—*n.* **vi'tal-iz"er.**

vi-ta-min (vī'tȧ-mĭn; vĭt'ȧ-; vī-tăm'ĭn), *n.* one of a class of obscure soluble substances present in living tissues and foods, the absence of which interferes with the normal processes of animal growth or may produce disease. Also, **vi'ta-mine** (vī'tȧ-mĭn; -mīn; -mēn).

vi-ta-phone (vī'tȧ-fōn), *n.* in motion pictures, a device for reproducing simultaneously the action and appropriate accompanying sounds, as instrumental music, singing, or the words spoken by the actors shown on the screen.

vi-ta-scope (vī'tȧ-skōp), *n.* a machine for projecting motion pictures upon a screen; cinematograph.

vi-ti-ate (vĭsh'ĭ-āt), *v.t.* [*p.t.* and *p.p.* -at"ed, *p.pr.* -at"ing], **1,** to corrupt; debase; contaminate; as, escaping gas *vitiates* the air; **2,** to make worthless; as, to *vitiate* a contract.—*n.* **vi"ti-a'tion.**—*n.* **vi'ti-a"tor.**

vit-i-cul-ture (vĭt'ĭ-kŭl"tūr), *n.* the cultivation of grapes.—*adj.* **vit"i-cul'tur-al.**—*n.* **vit"i-cul'tur-ist.**

vit-re-ous (vĭt'rē-ŭs), *adj.* of, pertaining to, or similar to, glass; as, *vitreous* rocks: **vitreous humor,** the jellylike substance filling the eyeball.—*n.* **vit're-ous-ness.**

vi-tres-cent (vĭ-trĕs'ĕnt), *adj.* tending to become, or capable of being made into, glass.—*n.* **vi-tres'cence.**

vit-ric (vĭt'rĭk), *adj.* of or like glass: **vitrics,** *n.pl.* **1,** glassware in general; **2,** used as *sing.*, the art or study of glass manufacture: contrasted with *ceramics.*

vit-ri-form (vĭt'rĭ-fôrm), *n.* having the composition or form of glass.

vit-ri-fy (vĭt'rĭ-fī), *v.t.* [*p.t.* and *p.p.* -fied (-fīd), *p.pr.* -fy"ing], to convert by heat into glass or a glassy substance:—*v.i.* to become glass, or like glass.—*adj.* **vit'ri-fi"a-ble.**—*p.adj.* **vit'ri-fied.**—*n.* **vit"ri-fi-ca'tion.**—*n.* **vit"ri-fac'tion.**

vit-ri-ol (vĭt'rĭ-ŭl), *n.* **1,** sulphuric acid: also called *oil of vitriol;* **2,** any of several of the salts of this acid, differentiated by adjectives indicating their color; as, blue *vitriol*, or copper sulphate; **3,** anything sharp or biting, as sarcasm.

vit-ri-ol-ic (vĭt"rĭ-ŏl'ĭk), *adj.* **1,** pertaining to, or derived from, sulphuric acid; **2,** hence, sarcastic; biting; caustic.

vi-tu-per-ate (vī-tū'pẽr-āt), *v.t.* [*p.t.* and *p.p.* -at"ed, *p.pr.* -at"ing], to blame; berate; revile abusively.—*n.* **vi-tu"per-a'tion.**—*adj.* **vi-tu'per-a"tive.**

***vi-va** (vē'vä), [It.], *interj.* long live! an expression of well wishing.

***vi-va-ce** (vē-vä'chā), [It.], *adj.* in music, lively; brisk; spirited:—*adv.* in music, in a lively or spirited manner; vivaciously: a direction to a performer.

vi-va-cious (vī-vā'shŭs; vĭ-), *adj.* lively; gay; animated; full of spirit.—*adv.* **vi-va'cious-ly.**—*n.* **vi-va'cious-ness.**
Syn. sportive, merry, jocose, mirthful.

vi-vac-i-ty (vī-văs'ĭ-tĭ; vĭ-), *n.* [*pl.* vivacities (-tĭz)], animation; high spirits; sprightliness.

vi-va-ri-um (vī-vā'rĭ-ŭm), *n.* [*pl.* vivariums (-ŭmz); vivaria (-ȧ)], a place, as a zoölogical garden, for keeping live animals, esp. land animals.

***vi-va vo-ce** (vī'vȧ vō'sē), [Lat.], by spoken word; expressed orally; as, a *viva voce* vote.

***vive** (vēv), [Fr.], *interj.* long live! an expression of acclamation.

Viv-i-an (vĭv'ĭ-ăn), *n.* in Arthurian legend, a beautiful woman who chained the magician Merlin by magic to a tree or rock after wheedling from him the secret of his sorcery: also called *the Lady of the Lake:* the subject of one of Tennyson's "Idylls of the King." Also, **Viv'i-en.**

viv-id (vĭv'ĭd), *adj.* **1,** animated; fresh; vigorous; esp., of colors, brilliant; intense; as, a *vivid* purple; **2,** active; lively; as, a *vivid* imagination; **3,** producing, or tending to produce, lifelike images in the mind; as, a *vivid* description.—*adv.* **viv'id-ly.**—*n.* **viv'id-ness.**

viv-i-fy (vĭv'ĭ-fī), *v.t.* [*p.t.* and *p.p.* -fied (-fīd), *p.pr.* -fy"ing], to invest with life; animate; quicken.—*n.* **viv'i-fi"er.**

vi-vip-a-rous (vī-vĭp'ȧ-rŭs), *adj.* producing living young (instead of eggs): opp. of *oviparous.*

viv-i-sect (vĭv"ĭ-sĕkt'; vĭv'ĭ-sĕkt), *v.t.* to dissect or experiment upon (the living body of an animal), for scientific study:—*v.i.* to operate or experiment upon a living animal.—*n.* **viv"i-sec'tor.**

viv-i-sec-tion (vĭv"ĭ-sĕk'shŭn), *n.* the dissection, or cutting, of a living animal for scientific study.—*n.* **viv"i-sec'tion-ist.**

vix-en (vĭk'sn), *n.* **1,** a female fox; **2,** a quarrelsome, ill-tempered woman.—*adj.* **vix'en-ish.**—*adj.* **vix'en-ly.**

viz. (vĭz), *adv.* namely: abbreviation of *videlicet.*

vi-zier (vĭ-zēr'; vĭz'yẽr), *n.* a high officer of various Mohammedan countries, esp. of Turkey; minister of state; councillor. Also, **vi-zir'.**—*n.* **vi-zier'ship.**

viz-or (vĭz'ẽr; vī'zẽr), *n.* **1,** the movable, face-protecting part of certain helmets; **2,** the projecting brim of a cap. Also, **vis'or,** *Pfd. S.*

vo-ca-ble (vō'kȧ-bl; vŏk'ȧ-bl), *n.* a word, term, or name, thought of merely for the sounds which compose it.

vo-cab-u-la-ry (vō-kăb′ū-lā-rĭ), *n.* [*pl.* vocabularies (-rĭz)], **1**, a list or collection of words arranged alphabetically and explained; **2**, the stock of words employed by a language, class, or individual; as, his *vocabulary* was limited.
Syn. (see diction).

vo-cal (vō′kăl), *adj.* **1**, pertaining to the voice or speech; having voice; full of voices; **2**, uttered or produced by the voice, as music; **3**, voiced: used of sounds uttered by vocal cords, as the vowels and *m*, *d*, etc., as distinguished from mere breath sounds, as *p*, *t*, *s*, etc.; **4**, pertaining to a vowel: **vocal cords**, either of two pairs of bands of fibrous tissue, called the *false* and the *true* vocal cords respectively, situated in the larynx: **vocal organs**, those parts of the mouth, nose, throat, and larynx used in the production of speech:—*n.* **1**, a vowel sound or diphthong; **2**, a vowel-like consonant or liquid, like *n* or *l*.—*adv.* **vo′cal-ly**. —*n.* **vo-cal′i-ty**.

vo-cal-ic (vō-kăl′ĭk), *adj.* pertaining, or relating, to vowel sounds.

vo-cal-ist (vō′kăl-ĭst), *n.* a singer; esp., a trained singer.

vo-cal-ize (vō′kăl-īz), *v.t.* [*p.t.* and *p.p.* -ized (-īzd), *p.pr.* -iz″ing], **1**, to utter with the voice; **2**, to use (a consonant) as a vowel; as, to *vocalize* y:—*v.i.* to produce sound with the voice, as in singing.—*n.* **vo″cal-i-za′tion**.

vo-ca-tion (vō-kā′shŭn), *n.* regular employment; calling; occupation; trade; profession; as, his *vocation* is law.—*adj.* **vo-ca′tion-al**.

voc-a-tive (vŏk′ȧ-tĭv), *adj.* **1**, relating to the act of calling or addressing by name; **2**, in grammar, pertaining to the case denoting a person or thing directly addressed:—*n.* a noun which names a person or thing addressed.

vo-cif-er-ate (vō-sĭf′ẽr-āt), *v.i.* [*p.t.* and *p.p.* -at″ed, *p.pr.* -at″ing], to cry out or exclaim noisily; shout; bawl; clamor.—*n.* **vo-cif″er-a′tion**.

vo-cif-er-ous (vō-sĭf′ẽr-ŭs), *adj.* making a loud outcry; clamorous; noisy; as, *vociferous* applause.—*adv.* **vo-cif′er-ous-ly**.—*n.* **vo-cif′er-ous-ness**.

vod-ka (vŏd′kȧ), *n.* in Russia, a spirituous liquor containing from 40 to 60 per cent alcohol, distilled from fermenting rye, potatoes, or maize.

vogue (vōg), *n.* the prevailing fashion or mode; also, popularity for a short time only; as, the author's works had a great *vogue* in his own time.

voice (vois), *n.* **1**, sound proceeding from the mouth, esp. human utterances in speech, a cry, song, etc.; **2**, the power of utterance; speech; as, he lost his *voice*; **3**, any sound suggesting speech, or likened to human utterance; as, the *voices* of the birds; **4**, expressed choice, wish, or opinion; also, the right to express a choice or opinion; as, he had no *voice* in the matter; **5**, admonition; teaching; as, the *voice* of conscience; **6**, sound produced by the vocal organs, as in pronouncing all vowels and such consonants as *b*, *d*, *v*, *m*, etc.; **7**, in grammar, the form of the verb indicating whether the subject acts or is acted upon:—*v.t.* [*p.t.* and *p.p.* voiced (voist), *p.pr.* voic′ing], **1**, to give expression to; put into speech; also, to divulge; rumor; **2**, to utter with vocal tone.

voiced (voist), *p.adj.* **1**, having a voice; also, expressed by the voice; **2**, uttered with a vocal tone, as the vowels and *b*, *d*, *m*, and such consonants: opp. of *voiceless* or *surd*.

voice-less (vois′lĕs), *adj.* **1**, having no voice or vote; as, in some states women are *voiceless* in the government; **2**, soundless; silent; as, the *voiceless* desert; **3**, not sounded vocally; surd: opp. of *voiced* or *sonant*.—*adv.* **voice′less-ly**.—*n.* **voice′less-ness**.

void (void), *adj.* **1**, empty; vacant; **2**, lacking: with *of*; **3**, without result; in vain; useless; as, all their efforts were *void*; **4**, unfilled, as an office; **5**, in law, having no force; null:—*v.t.* **1**, to cause to be empty; vacate; **2**, to send or throw out; discharge; **3**, to annul or cancel, as a law:—*n.* a vacuum; an empty space.—*adj.* **void′a-ble**.

vo-lant (vō′lȧnt), *adj.* **1**, flying; **2**, capable of flying; **3**, light; nimble; quick.

Vo-la-pük (vō″lȧ-pük′), *n.* an artificial language intended to be universal, invented in Germany about 1879.

vol-a-tile (vŏl′ȧ-tĭl), *adj.* **1**, easily evaporating or changing into vapor; as, ether is a *volatile* liquid; **2**, hence, lighthearted; lively; gay; also, changeable; fickle. —*n.* **vol′a-tile-ness**.

vol-a-til-i-ty (vŏl″ȧ-tĭl′ĭ-tĭ), *n.* [*pl.* volatilities (-tĭz)], **1**, the state or quality of anything readily evaporating; **2**, airiness; changeableness; fickleness.

vol-a-til-ize (vŏl′ȧ-tĭl-īz), *v.t.* and *v.i.* [*p.t.* and *p.p.* -ized (-īzd), *p.pr.* -iz″ing], **1**, to make, or become, volatile; **2**, to evaporate, or change into vapor.—*adj.* **vol′a-til-iz″a-ble**.—*n.* **vol″a-til-i-za′tion**.

vol-can-ic (vŏl-kăn′ĭk), *adj.* **1**, pertaining to a volcano; **2**, influenced or produced by, or like, a volcano, or its action; **3**, violent; powerful; explosive.

vol-ca-no (vŏl-kā′nō), *n.* [*pl.* volcanoes; volcanos (-nōz)], an opening in the earth's surface, usually surrounded by a mass of ejected material forming a conical hill or mountain, from which molten rock, fire, and steam are, or have been, expelled: said to be *active* when frequently in process of eruption; *dormant* during a long cessation of activity; *extinct* when eruptions are believed to have ceased permanently.

[1]**vole** (vōl), *n.* any of a genus of mouselike or ratlike rodents, including certain field and meadow mice.

[2]**vole** (vōl), *n.* **1**, in some card games, the winning of all the tricks in a deal; **2**, hence, the whole range or gamut.

vo-li-tion (vō-lĭsh′ŭn), *n.* **1**, the act or power of using the will to decide, choose, etc.; **2**, the state of determination or decision; **3**, that which is particularly determined upon.—*adj.* **vo-li′tion-al**.—*adv.* **vo-li′tion-al-ly**.
Syn. desire, preference, choice.

***Volks-lied** (fōlks′lēt″), [Ger.], *n.* [*pl.* Volkslieder (-lē″dẽr)], a folk song; a song sung by the common people.

vol-ley (vŏl′ĭ), *n.* [*pl.* volleys (-ĭz)], **1**, the throwing of many missiles at the same time; also, the missiles so thrown; **2**, a sudden burst of any sort; as, a *volley* of words; **3**, in tennis, the return of a ball before it reaches the ground: **volley ball**, a game in which two groups of players attempt with the hands to keep a large ball moving from side to side over a net without letting the ball touch the ground:—*v.t.* and *v.i.* to discharge, or be discharged, suddenly and all together; as, the cannon *volleyed* and thundered.

vol-plane (vŏl′plān″), *n.* a glide in an airplane with little or no engine power:—*v.i.* [*p.t.* and *p.p.* -planed″ (-plānd″), *p.pr.* -plan″ing], to execute such a glide.

Vol-stead Act (vŏl′stĕd), an act of Congress, passed October 28, 1919, providing for the enforcement of the eighteenth amendment to the Constitution of the U. S. (which amendment prohibited the manufacture, sale, or transportation of intoxicating liquors for beverage purposes within territory subject to the jurisdiction of the U. S.), and defining intoxicating liquor as a liquor, fit for beverage purposes, which contains more than one half of one per cent of alcohol by volume.

Vol-sun-ga Sa-ga (vŏl′so͝ong-gä), in mythology, the Old Norse version of the famous medieval legend of Sigurd the Volsung and the Nibelungs.

volt (vōlt), *n.* the practical unit of electromotive force, which will cause a current of one ampere to flow through a conductor against a resistance of one ohm.

volt-age (vōl′tāj), *n.* electromotive force, or difference in potential, in terms of volts.

vol-ta-ic (vŏl-tā′ĭk), *adj.* pertaining to the process of producing electricity by chemical action; galvanic: **voltaic arc,** the curved band of light between two electrodes, caused by the passage of an electric current: used as the source of heat, and hence of light, in an arc light: **voltaic battery,** a combination of several voltaic cells, or, less correctly, a single cell: **voltaic cell,** a device for producing electrical energy by chemical action, consisting of two electrodes of different materials in contact with one or more electrolytes.

volt-me-ter (vōlt′mē″tẽr), *n.* in electricity, an instrument for measuring an electromotive force, or difference in potential, in volts.

vol-u-bil-i-ty (vŏl″ū-bĭl′ĭ-tĭ), *n.* too great fluency in speech; talkativeness; glibness.

vol-u-ble (vŏl′ū-bl), *adj.* smooth or fluent in speech; talkative; glib.—*n.* **vol′u-ble-ness.**—*adv.* **vol′u-bly.**

vol-ume (vŏl′ūm), *n.* **1,** a number of printed sheets bound together; a book; **2,** one of several parts of a large work, each of which is bound separately; **3,** the amount of space filled; as, the *volume* of water in a vessel; **4,** fulness of voice or tone.

vo-lu-mi-nous (vō-lū′mĭ-nŭs), *adj.* **1,** consisting of many books or volumes; as, a *voluminous* library; **2,** having produced many books; as, Balzac was a *voluminous* writer; **3,** filling much space; swelling; as, in old times ladies wore *voluminous* hoop skirts.—*adv.* **vo-lu′mi-nous-ly.**—*n.* **vo-lu′mi-nous-ness.**

vol-un-ta-ry (vŏl′ŭn-tā-rĭ), *adj.* **1,** coming from the will; **2,** intentional; as, the man's offense was *voluntary,* not accidental; **3,** free; not constrained; spontaneous; as, his confession was *voluntary;* **4,** regulated by the will; as, the *voluntary* muscles; **5,** able to act by one's own will; as, a *voluntary* agent:—*n.* [*pl.* voluntaries (-rĭz)], **1,** any free act or task; **2,** an organ solo played before, during, or after, a church service.—*adv.* **vol′un-ta-ri-ly.**—*n.* **vol′un-ta-ri-ness.**

vol-un-teer (vŏl″ŭn-tēr′), *n.* one who enters into any service of his own free will; esp., one who offers himself for military or naval service: **Volunteers of America,** an organization for religious and philanthropic work, somewhat resembling the Salvation Army:—*v.i.* to offer one's services freely:—*v.t.* to offer or bestow without constraint or compulsion:—*adj.* pertaining to volunteers; voluntary.

vo-lup-tu-a-ry (vō-lŭp′tū-ā-rĭ), *n.* [*pl.* voluptuaries (-rĭz)], one who is devoted to the pleasures that appeal to the senses:—*adj.* pertaining to, or promoting, the gratification of sensual appetites.

vo-lup-tu-ous (vō-lŭp′tū-ŭs), *adj.* **1,** producing, or arising from, the pleasures of the senses; sensuous; **2,** devoted to luxurious pleasures or the gratification of the senses; sensual; as, a *voluptuous* existence.—*adv.* **vo-lup′tu-ous-ly.**—*n.* **vo-lup′tu-ous-ness.**

vo-lute (vō-lūt′), *n.* **1,** a spiral, scroll-shaped, architectural ornament, such as appears in the Ionic capital; **2,** a whorl, or single turn, of a spiral shell:—*adj.* having a spiral scroll.—*adj.* **vo-lut′ed.**

vom-it (vŏm′ĭt), *v.i.* **1,** to throw up the contents of the stomach; **2,** to come forth, or be sent out, with violence:—*v.t.* **1,** to throw up from the stomach; spew; **2,** to discharge with violence; belch forth:—*n.* **1,** matter thrown up by the stomach; **2,** an emetic; a substance that causes vomiting.

voo-doo (vo͞o′do͞o; vo͞o-do͞o′), *n.* **1,** a degraded form of sorcery, found among certain Negroes, esp. in Haiti: also called *voodooism;* **2,** one who practices such sorcery:—*adj.* of or pertaining to voodooism or a voodoo; as, a *voodoo* doctor.

voo-doo-ism (vo͞o′do͞o-ĭzm), *n.* a belief in, or the practice of, sorcery, as found among certain Negroes; voodoo.

vo-ra-cious (vō-rā′shŭs), *adj.* greedy in eating; ravenous; also, figuratively, insatiable; as, a *voracious* reader.—*adv.* **vo-ra′cious-ly.**—*n.* **vo-ra′cious-ness.**

vo-rac-i-ty (vō-răs′ĭ-tĭ), *n.* ravenous hunger; greediness in eating.

vor-tex (vôr′tĕks), *n.* [*pl.* vortexes (-tĕk-sĕz); vortices (-tĭ-sēz)], air or water with a rotary motion tending to suck bodies caught in it into a depression or partial vacuum at the center; an eddy or whirlpool.—*adj.* **vor′ti-cal.**—*adj.* **vor′ti-cose.**

vo-ta-ry (vō′tȧ-rĭ), *adj.* promised; devoted:—*n.* [*pl.* votaries (-rĭz)], one consecrated by a vow or promise to some service; also, one devoted to any pursuit; as, a *votary* of music.—*n.fem.* **vo′ta-ress.**

vote (vōt), *n.* **1,** a formally stated choice, judgment, or wish, of one or more persons, as in an election; also, that which is so expressed; something resolved by the decision of a majority; as, a *vote* of thanks; **2,** the right to express such a choice or wish; as, women were given the *vote;* **3,** something by which such a choice or wish is expressed, as the voice or a ballot; **4,** the entire number of ballots or expressions of opinion; as, a presidential *vote:*—*v.t.* [*p.t.* and *p.p.* vot′ed, *p.pr.* vot′ing], **1,** to declare or authorize by a formal expression of a wish; as, to *vote* a reform; **2,** to grant; as, to *vote* money; **3,** *Colloq.,* to pronounce by general consent; as, we *voted* the meeting a failure:—*v.i.* to cast a ballot: often with *for* or *against.*

vot-er (vōt′ẽr), *n.* one who casts a ballot; also, one who has a right to vote.

vo-tive (vō′tĭv), *adj.* given, or consecrated, by a vow; as, a *votive* offering to the church.—*adv.* **vo′tive-ly.**—*n.* **vo′tive-ness.**

vouch (vouch), *v.t.* to confirm; bear witness to; as, to *vouch* a statement:—*v.i.* to bear witness; guarantee: with *for;* as, to *vouch* for a man's honesty.

vouch-er (vouch′ẽr), *n.* **1,** one who bears witness; **2,** a paper or the like, which bears witness to something; specif., a receipt for payment.

vouch-safe (vouch-sāf′), *v.t.* [*p.t.* and *p.p.* -safed′ (-sāft′), *p.pr.* -saf′ing], to deign to grant; concede; as, to *vouchsafe* an opinion:—*v.i.* to deign.

vous-soir (vo͞o″swär′), *n.* any one of the wedge-shaped sections of an arch (see [1]arch, illus.).

vow (vou), *n.* **1,** a solemn promise or pledge, esp. one made to God or before God; **2,** a pledge of love and faithfulness:—*v.t.* **1,** to promise solemnly; **2,** to assert solemnly; swear:—*v.i.* **1,** to make a solemn promise; **2,** to declare with emphasis.

vow-el (vou'ĕl), *n.* **1**, a simple vocal sound: distinguished from *consonant;* **2**, a letter representing such a sound, as *a, e, i, o, u:*—*adj.* of or pertaining to a vowel; as, a *vowel* sound.

voy-age (voi'āj), *n.* a journey by water, esp. a long one; as, a *voyage* to Europe:—*v.i.* [*p.t.* and *p.p.* -aged (-ājd), *p.pr.* -ag-ing], to make a journey by water:—*v.t.* to sail, or travel, over; traverse.—*n.* **voy'ag-er.**

***voy-a-geur** (vwȧ"yȧ"zhûr'), [Fr.], *n.* [*pl.* voyageurs (-zhûr')], **1**, a traveler; **2**, in Canada, an employee of a fur company, engaged in furnishing transportation for men and goods; also, a trapper.

***vrai-sem-blance** (vrâ"säṅ"bläṅs'), [Fr.], *n.* an appearance of truth; probability; likelihood.

***vrille** (vrĭl), [Fr.], *n.* a feat in which an airplane is made to descend with a spinning motion:—*v.i.* [*p.t.* and *p.p.* vrilled (vrĭld), *p.pr.* vrill'ing], to do a vrille.

Vul-can (vŭl'kăn), *n.* in Roman mythology, the god of fire and of metal working: identified with the Greek *Hephæstus.*

vul-can-ite (vŭl'kăn-īt), *n.* a hardened compound of India rubber; hard rubber, made by heating with sulphur or oxides, or by soaking in a sulphur chloride solution: widely used in making tubing, chemical and electrical apparatus, etc.

vul-can-ize (vŭl'kăn-īz), *v.t.* [*p.t.* and *p.p.* -ized (-īzd), *p.pr.* -iz"ing], to harden (India rubber) by heating, under pressure, with sulphur.—*n.* **vul"can-i-za'tion.**—*n.* **vul'can-iz"er.**

vul-gar (vŭl'gȧr), *adj.* **1**, of or pertaining to the common people; plebeian; common; general; **2**, unrefined; in bad taste; **3**, low; mean: **vulgar fraction**, a common fraction, expressed by placing the numerator above the denominator, with a horizontal or oblique line between: distinguished from *decimal fraction* (see *fraction*).—*adv.* **vul'gar-ly.**
Syn. coarse, base, gross, offensive, vile.—*Ant.* refined, cultured, elegant, dainty.

vul-ga-ri-an (vŭl-gā'rĭ-ăn), *n.* an unrefined person; esp., a rich person with coarse or low ideas and tastes.

vul-gar-ism (vŭl'gȧr-ĭzm), *n.* **1**, rudeness; lack of refinement; **2**, a phrase or expression not in use by cultivated speakers.
Syn. vulgarity. A *vulgarism* is a phrase or expression in common but not standard usage, not necessarily coarse but always incorrect; the use of "party" for "person" is a *vulgarism.* A *vulgarity* is an instance of coarseness in manners or speech; the use of profanity or unrefined expressions is a *vulgarity.*

vul-gar-i-ty (vŭl-găr'ĭ-tĭ), *n.* [*pl.* vulgarities (-tĭz)], **1**, the state or quality of being coarse or common; **2**, coarseness of manners or language.
Syn. (see vulgarism).

vul-gar-ize (vŭl'gȧr-īz), *v.t.* and *v.i.* [*p.t.* and *p.p.* -ized (-īzd), *p.pr.* -iz"ing], to make, or become, common, coarse, or low.—*n.* **vul"gar-i-za'tion.**

Vul-gate (vŭl'gāt), *n.* a Latin translation of the Bible in use in the Roman Catholic Church, made originally by St. Jerome in the fourth century:—*adj.* pertaining to this translation.

vul-ner-a-ble (vŭl'nẽr-ȧ-bl), *adj.* **1**, capable of being wounded or hurt; **2**, liable to injury or criticism, as a reputation, record, etc.—*n.* **vul'ner-a-ble-ness.**—*n.* **vul"ner-a-bil'i-ty.**

vul-ner-a-ry (vŭl'nẽr-ā-rĭ), *adj.* pertaining to the healing of wounds:—*n.* a remedy for the healing of wounds.

vul-pine (vŭl'pīn; vŭl'pĭn), *adj.* pertaining to, or like, a fox; cunning.

vul-ture (vŭl'tūr), *n.* any member of either of two families, one found in Europe, the other in America, of large, carrion-eating birds of prey allied to the hawks and eagles.—*adj.* **vul'tur-ine** (vŭl'tūr-īn; -ĭn).—*adj.* **vul'tur-ous.**

vy-ing (vī'ĭng), *n.* a competing or contending, as in a race.—*adv.* **vy'ing-ly.**

W

wab-ble (wŏb'l), *v.i.* [*p.t.* and *p.p.* -bled (-ld), *p.pr.* -bling], **1**, to move unsteadily from side to side, or back and forth; totter; **2**, to lack firmness in opinion or action; waver:—*v.t.* to cause to move unsteadily from side to side:—*n.* a swaying motion. Also, **wob'ble.**—*n.* **wab'bler.**—*adj.* **wab'bly.**

[1]**wad** (wŏd), *n.* **1**, a small mass or little bundle of soft material; **2**, a soft bunch of cotton, wool, rope, etc., used to stop an opening, pad a garment, etc.; **3**, a plug to hold a charge of powder or shot in position in a gun or in a cartridge; **4**, *Slang:* **a**, a roll of paper money for personal use; **b**, often in *pl.*, a large amount, as of money:—*v.t.* [*p.t.* and *p.p.* wad'ded, *p.pr.* wad'ding], **1**, to form, as some soft material, into a compact mass or bunch; **2**, to insert a wad into; close, as an opening, with a small, compact mass; **3**, to provide with a pad.

[2]**wad** (wȧd), *Scot.* and *Dial.* form for *would,* past tense of the irregular verb *will.*

wad-ding (wŏd'ĭng), *n.* soft material used for gun wads, plugs, or for stuffing or lining garments; cotton prepared in sheets for padding.

wad-dle (wŏd'l), *v.i.* [*p.t.* and *p.p.* -dled (-ld), *p.pr.* -dling], to sway from side to side in walking; walk with short, clumsy steps, as a duck; toddle:—*n.* a clumsy, rocking gait.—*n.* **wad'dler.**

wade (wād), *v.i.* [*p.t.* and *p.p.* wad'ed, *p.pr.* wad'ing], **1**, to walk through water, mud, snow, or other substance that hinders progress; **2**, hence, to proceed with difficulty or against hindrances; as, to *wade* through a tiresome lesson:—*v.t.* to cross by passing through water, mud, etc.—*n.* **wad'er.**

wa-di (wä'dĭ), *n.* [*pl.* wadies (-dĭz)], in the Near East, a valley or ravine which becomes a watercourse in the rainy season. Also, **wa'dy.**

wa-fer (wā'fẽr), *n.* **1**, a thin cake or biscuit; **2**, a thin cake of unleavened, or unraised, bread used in the communion service in certain churches: in the Roman Catholic Church often called *Host;* **3**, a small, colored disk of adhesive paper, paste, etc., for fastening letters, sealing documents, etc.; **4**, in medicine, a flat capsule.

waf-fle (wŏf'l), *n.* a flat batter cake baked in a waffle iron: **waffle iron**, often in *pl.*, a device for baking waffles, consisting of a pair of iron plates, hinged together so as to close over batter poured upon one of them.

waft (wȧft), *v.i.* and *v.t.* to float, or cause to float, along through the air or on the water:—*n.* **1**, the act of floating, or causing to float along; **2**, a current or wave, as of water; a gust or puff, as of wind.

[1]**wag** (wăg), *v.t.* [*p.t.* and *p.p.* wagged (wăgd), *p.pr.* wag'ging], **1**, to move,

or cause to swing, usually from side to side, as an object having one end fast; **2**, to turn from side to side, as the head: expressing disapproval or the like:—*v.i.* **1**, to move, as from side to side; **2**, *Colloq.*, to move, as in idle chatter: said of the tongue:—*n.* a turning movement, as from side to side.

2**wag** (wăg), *n.* **1**, a practical joker; **2**, a witty person.—*adj.* **wag′gish.**—*adv.* **wag′gish-ly.**—*n.* **wag′gish-ness.**

wage (wāj), *v.t.* [*p.t.* and *p.p.* waged (wājd), *p.pr.* wag′ing], to engage in vigorously; carry on, as a war, conflict, or campaign:—*n.* **1**, usually in *pl.*, that which is paid or received for services: usually, payments made by the hour, day, or week: distinguished from *salary;* **2**, requital: often in *pl.* used as *sing.*; as, "the *wages* of sin is death."
Syn., *n.* (see salary).

wa-ger (wā′jẽr), *n.* something risked on an uncertainty; a bet: **wager of battle**, formerly, in English law, a mode of trial by which the defendant was privileged to challenge the plaintiff to single combat, and, if successful, was declared innocent:—*v.t.* and *v.i.* to bet.—*n.* **wa′ger-er.**

wag-ger-y (wăg′ẽr-ĭ), *n.* [*pl.* waggeries (-ĭz)], sport; jesting; humorous mischievousness.

wag-gle (wăg′l), *v.i.* and *v.t.* [*p.t.* and *p.p.* -gled (-ld), *p.pr.* -gling], to move from side to side; wag:—*n.* a movement from side to side.

wag-on (wăg′ŭn), *n.* a four-wheeled conveyance for goods or freight, drawn by horses, mules, etc. Also, **wag′gon.**—*n.* **wag′on-er.**—*n.* **wag′on-ful.**

wag-on-ette (wăg″ŭn-ĕt′), *n.* a light, open, four-wheeled pleasure carriage, with two side seats facing each other.

wag-tail (wăg′tāl″), *n.* a small bird with a long tail which is constantly jerked up and down.

waif (wāf), *n.* **1**, anything found that is unclaimed; **2**, a homeless wanderer; esp., a foundling, or deserted child.

wail (wāl), *v.t.* to mourn or lament aloud:—*v.i.* to utter a loud cry:—*n.* a lamentation or mournful cry; a sound like such a cry; as, the *wail* of the wind.—*n.* **wail′er.**

wain (wān), *n. Poetic*, a wagon: **Charles's Wain**, the seven principal stars in the constellation Ursa Major, or the Great Bear: also called *Dipper*.

wain-scot (wān′skŏt; wān′skŏt), *n.* a wooden lining around the walls of a room, hall, etc.:—*v.t.* to line or face, as the walls of a room, with wood.

wain-scot-ing (wān′skŏt-ĭng; wān′-skŏt-), *n.* **1**, wooden facing or paneling surrounding the inner walls of a house; **2**, the material of which this paneling is made. Also, **wain′scot-ting.**

wain-wright (wān′rīt″), *n.* one who makes or repairs wagons.

waist (wāst), *n.* **1**, the narrowest part of the body, just below the ribs; **2**, the slender middle part of anything, as of an hourglass; **3**, a garment, or that section of a garment, which covers the body from shoulders to belt; **4**, the middle part of a vessel's deck, between the forecastle and quarter-deck.

waist-band (wāst′bănd″; wāst′bănd), *n.* the band, as of a skirt or trousers, which encircles the waist.

waist-coat (wāst′kōt″; *Colloq.* wĕs′kŭt), *n.* a short, sleeveless, formerly ornamental, man's garment, worn under the coat; a vest.

wait (wāt), *v.i.* **1**, to linger or tarry; remain; as, we *waited* there until it snowed; **2**, to continue in a state of expecting: with *for;* as, we *waited* an hour for her; **3**, to attend or serve: with *on;* as, to *wait* on a table:—*v.t.* **1**, to expect or tarry for; **2**, *Colloq.*, to delay; as, to *wait* dinner:—*n.* **1**, the act of delaying or lingering; **2**, the length of time during which one lingers in expectation; delay; as, a long *wait;* **3**, ambush; **4**, usually in *pl.*, one of a group of carol singers who sing in the streets at Christmas time.

wait-er (wāt′ẽr), *n.* **1**, one who stays, as if expecting something; **2**, a man who serves at table; **3**, a serving tray for dishes: **dumb waiter**, a kind of small elevator for conveying food, dishes, etc., from one part of the house to another.—*n.fem.* **wait′ress.**

wait-ing (wāt′ĭng), *n.* **1**, the act or state of delaying, lingering, etc.; **2**, service; attendance: **in waiting**, in attendance; as, ladies *in waiting:*—*p.adj.* attendant; serving: **waiting room**, a room for the convenience of persons waiting, as for a train.

waive (wāv), *v.t.* [*p.t.* and *p.p.* waived (wāvd), *p.pr.* waiv′ing], to give up a claim to; forego.—*n.* **waiv′er.**

1**wake** (wāk), *v.i.* [*p.t.* and *p.p.* waked (wākt) or woke (wōk), *p.pr.* wak′ing], **1**, to be awake; **2**, to cease to sleep: usually with *up;* also, to be roused from sleep; **3**, to be aroused, excited, or made active: usually with *up;* **4**, to experience new birth or resurrection; as, at the Last Judgment the dead will *wake;* **5**, to keep a watch or vigil at night:—*v.t.* **1**, to rouse from sleep; awake: often with *up;* **2**, to make active; excite; arouse: often with *up;* **3**, to revive; resurrect; **4**, to keep a watch or vigil over, as a dead body:—*n.* the act or state of being awake; a vigil; esp., keeping awake to watch over a dead body prior to burial.—*n.* **wak′er.**

2**wake** (wāk), *n.* a trail left behind some moving object, as a vessel, a storm, etc.: **in the wake of**, behind; after the example of; following.

wake-ful (wāk′fo͝ol), *adj.* **1**, free from sleepiness; unable to sleep; **2**, watchful; as, a *wakeful* sentinel.—*adv.* **wake′ful-ly.**—*n.* **wake′ful-ness.**
Syn. vigilant, heedful.

wak-en (wāk′n), *v.t.* and *v.i.* to rouse, or be roused, from sleep.—*n.* **wak′en-er.**

wake-rob-in (wāk′=rŏb″ĭn), *n.* **1**, in America, any one of a number of trilliums; also, the jack-in-the-pulpit; **2**, in England, a plant of the arum family.

Wal-den-ses (wŏl-dĕn′sēz), *n.pl.* a sect of dissenters from the Roman Catholic Church, numerous in the valleys of Piedmont in Italy, and Dauphiné and Provence in France: founded about 1170, and much persecuted in the 16th and 17th centuries.—*adj.* and *n.* **Wal-den′sian.**

1**wale** (wāl), *n.* **1**, (also, *wheal*), a ridge or mark produced on flesh by flogging; **2**, a ridge on the surface, as of cloth; hence, texture; **3**, a heavy plank along the side of a vessel; **4**, a timber fastened to a row of piles, to hold them in position; **5**, a strengthening ridge on a basket:—*v.t.* [*p.t.* and *p.p.* waled (wāld), *p.pr.* wal′ing], **1**, (also, *whale*), *U. S. Colloq.*, to mark with a ridge or stripes, as the body by flogging; **2**, to secure or protect, as with a wale. Also, **weal.**

2**wale** (wāl), *v.t.* [*p.t.* and *p.p.* waled (wāld), *p.pr.* wal′ing], *Obs.* or *Dial.*, to choose; hence, to woo:—*n. Obs.* or *Dial.*, a choice; hence, the choicest; the pick.

walk (wôk), *v.i.* **1**, to go on foot; move by steps; **2**, to take a stroll or ramble for exercise or pleasure; **3**, to be restless, as a ghost; **4**, to live in a regular manner; hence, to behave:—*v.t.* **1**, to traverse on foot; as, he *walked* the floor in anxiety; **2**, to cause to go on foot or at a moderate pace; as, *walk* your horses across the bridge:—*n.* **1**, the act of going on foot without running, esp. for exercise or recreation; **2**, manner of walking; gait; esp., one of the gaits of a horse; **3**, a place for people on foot; as, the side*walk;* also, pasture land for grazing; **4**, the circle of life in which one moves; as, his *walk* in life was a humble one; **5**, conduct or deportment; as, let your *walk* and conversation be holy.—*n.* **walk'er.**

walk-out (wôk'out″), *n. Colloq.*, in the U. S., a labor strike.

walk-o-ver (wôk'-ō″vẽr), *n. Colloq.*, a success or victory easily won.

Wal-kyr-ie (wäl-kĭr'ĭ; wäl-kī'rĭ), *n.* in Norse mythology, one of the handmaidens of Odin, who conducted the souls of slain heroes to Valhalla. Also, **Wal'kyr.** See **Val-kyr'ie,** *Pfd. S.*

wall (wôl), *n.* **1**, a solid fence of stone, brick, etc.; **2**, the solid, vertical structure which forms any one of the sides of a building; **3**, a partition forming the side of a room; **4**, a structure for defense; **5**, the side or inside surface of any cavity, vessel, or receptacle; **6**, in *pl.*, fortifications:—*v.t.* **1**, to surround with, or as with, a structure for inclosure, security, or defense; **2**, to fill in, as an opening.

wal-la-by (wŏl'ȧ-bĭ), *n.* [*pl.* wallabies (-bĭz)], any of several of the smaller Australian kangaroos: **rock wallaby,** any of certain wallabies found in rocky regions.

wal-let (wŏl'ĕt), *n.* **1**, a bag or knapsack for carrying about the person the necessaries for a march or journey; **2**, a folding pocketbook.

wall-eye (wôl'-ī″), *n.* **1**, an eye, the iris of which is white, as of horses; **2**, a condition in which the two eyes point in divergent directions: opp. of *cross-eye;* **3**, any of various kinds of fish with prominent eyes.

wall-eyed (wôl'-īd″), *adj.* **1**, having a whitish, staring, or fierce eye; **2**, having wall-eyes: opp. of *cross-eyed.*

wall-flow-er (wôl'flou″ẽr), *n.* **1**, a plant of the mustard family, with sweet-scented yellow, orange, or red flowers; **2**, *Colloq.*, at a dance, one who, for lack of partners, sits idle.

Wal-loon (wŏ-lo͞on'), *n.* **1**, a member of a mixed race of southern Belgium; **2**, their language, a French dialect.

wal-lop (wŏl'ŭp), *v.t. Colloq.*, to flog or beat soundly:—*n. Colloq.*, a blow.

wal-low (wŏl'ō), *v.i.* **1**, to roll about, flounder, or welter, in, or as in, mud, as a hog; **2**, to live in vice or filth; as, to *wallow* in dirt:—*n.* **1**, the act of weltering, as in mud or vice; **2**, a muddy place in which an animal rolls about.

wall pa-per paper for covering the inner walls of houses.

wall plate a horizontal timber along the top of a wall, as of a house, upon which the lower ends of the rafters are set (see *principal*, illus.).

Wall Street **1**, a narrow street in lower Manhattan, New York City, which is the most important financial center of the U. S.; **2**, hence, high finance; **3**, the financial interests, considered collectively.

wal-nut (wôl'nŭt; wŏl'-), *n.* **1**, any of various trees bearing edible nuts, esp. the black walnut and the English walnut; **2**, the nut of such a tree; **3**, the wood of the tree.

wal-rus (wôl'rŭs; wŏl'-), *n.* a large sea animal allied to the seal, found in the Arctic Ocean, and valuable for blubber, skin, and tusks.

waltz (wôlts), *n.* **1**, a round dance in triple time; **2**, music for such a dance:—*v.i.* to dance such a round dance.—*n.* **waltz'er.**

wam-pum (wŏm'pŭm; wôm'-), *n.* beads of shell, used by the North American Indians as money and for ornament.

wan (wŏn), *adj.* pale; sickly; looking worn or exhausted; as, a *wan* child; a *wan* smile.—*adv.* **wan'ly.**—*n.* **wan'ness.**

wand (wŏnd), *n.* **1**, a slender rod or stick; **2**, a staff of authority; also, a baton; often, a staff with supposedly magic power; as, a conjurer's *wand.*

wan-der (wŏn'dẽr), *v.i.* **1**, to rove; ramble; stroll; **2**, to stray; **3**, to be delirious or out of one's mind; **4**, to digress or turn aside; as, the speaker *wandered* from his subject:—*n.* **1**, the act of roaming aimlessly; **2**, a stroll.—*n.* **wan'der-er.**

Syn., v. digress, deviate, stray. To *wander* is to move here and there without a purpose; as, to *wander* from room to room. To *digress* is to leave, temporarily, the main theme of a speech or writing; as, the author *digressed* from his subject. *Deviate* and *stray* mean to turn aside from a predetermined course or rule; as, to *deviate* from routine; to *stray* from the accustomed paths.

Wan-der-ing Jew in a medieval legend, a Jew who drove Christ, on the way to the crucifixion, from his door, and was condemned to wander, undying, until Christ's second coming: **wandering jew,** any of several wild or cultivated creeping plants; esp., in the U. S., an ornamental, trailing house plant.

***Wan-der-lust** (vän'dẽr-lo͞ost″), [Ger.], *n.* an impulse toward wandering; love of travel.

wan-der-oo (wŏn″dẽr-o͞o'), *n.* a large, black monkey of western India, notable for its heavy, whitish mane.

wane (wān), *v.i.* [*p.t.* and *p.p.* waned (wānd), *p.pr.* wan'ing], **1**, to grow less; decrease: applied esp. to the moon; **2**, to decline in power or importance; fail:—*n.* **1**, the decrease of the visible bright part of the moon from full to new; **2**, decrease in power or importance; gradual failure.

want (wônt; wŏnt), *n.* **1**, lack; need; **2**, poverty; as, a family in *want;* **3**, a thing greatly desired; necessity:—*v.t.* **1**, to be without; **2**, to have need of; **3**, to desire:—*v.i.* **1**, to be deficient or lacking; **2**, to come short; **3**, to be in poverty.

Syn., n. destitution, penury. (See need.)

want-ing (wôn'tĭng; wŏn'-), *p.adj.* **1**, lacking; short of; **2**, missing; hence, not present.

wan-ton (wŏn'tŭn), *adj.* **1**, capricious; playful; sportive; as, the *wanton* wind; **2**, loose in morals; **3**, careless; reckless; malicious; as, *wanton* destruction of property:—*n.* a man or woman of loose, immoral habits:—*v.i.* to pass the time in reckless pleasure; revel:—*v.t.* to spend or waste recklessly.—*adv.* **wan'ton-ly.**—*n.* **wan'ton-ness.**

wap-i-ti (wŏp'ĭ-tĭ; wăp'-), *n.* a variety of large American deer: often called *elk*, but distinct from the European elk.

WAPITI, OR AMERICAN ELK ($\frac{1}{80}$)

war (wôr), *n.* **1**, a conflict by force of arms between political bodies, as nations; also, the condition created by such a conflict; **2**, the science or art of the profession of arms; **3**, any contest or contention; as, a *war of* words; **4**, hostility or enmity: **Wars of the**

Roses, in English history, a series of wars extending from 1455 to 1485, between the House of York and the House of Lancaster, whose emblems were a white and a red rose, respectively:—*v.i.* [*p.t.* and *p.p.* warred (wôrd), *p.pr.* war′ring], **1**, to engage in an armed conflict; **2**, to contend.

war-ble (wôr′bl), *v.t.* and *v.i.* [*p.t.* and *p.p.* -bled (-bld), *p.pr.* -bling], **1**, to trill; carol; **2**, to make a melodious sound:—*n.* a soft, sweet flow of sounds; carol.

war-bler (wôr′blẽr), *n.* **1**, one who carols; a singer; **2**, any of various small, singing birds, often brightly colored.

war cry **1**, a battle shout; **2**, a party or national slogan in any contest.

ward (wôrd), *v.t.* **1**, *Archaic*, to guard; **2**, to turn aside: with *off;* as, to *ward* off an attack:—*n.* **1**, a political division of a city or town; as, the fifth *ward;* **2**, the act of guarding or watching; **3**, a person under guard or protection; as, the *ward* of a court or state; **4**, one section of a hospital; as, a surgical *ward;* **5**, a projection or ridge in a lock, to obstruct any but the proper key; also, the notch made in a key to correspond (see [1]*key*, illus.).

-ward (-wẽrd), *adj.* and *adv. suffix*, toward; in the direction of: added to adverbs, prepositions, and nouns; as, up*ward:* **-wards**, *adv. suffix*, toward; as, home*wards.*

war dance a dance of savage tribes before going to war.

ward-en (wôr′dn), *n.* **1**, a guardian; keeper; **2**, a head keeper; as, a prison *warden;* **3**, a trustee; as, a church*warden;* **4**, in England, the chief officer of government in a college.—*n.* **ward′en-ship.**—*n.* **ward′en-ry.**

ward-er (wôr′dẽr), *n.* one who watches or keeps; a guard or keeper; as, the *warder* of an English prison.

ward-robe (wôrd′rōb″), *n.* **1**, a room or closet for clothes; **2**, one's stock of wearing apparel.

ward-room (wôrd′rōōm″), *n.* in a war vessel, the living quarters of the officers above the rank of ensign, not including the captain.

ward-ship (wôrd′shĭp), *n.* **1**, the office of keeper; guardianship; care and protection of a ward; **2**, the state of being a ward, or a person under the care of a guardian.

[1]**ware** (wâr), *n.* **1**, an article of merchandise; **2**, articles of the same class: usually in *pl.*, except in its compounds; as, hard*ware.*

[2]**ware** (wâr), *v.t.* [*p.t.* and *p.p.* wared (wârd), *p.pr.* war′ing], *Archaic*, to beware of: used in such phrases as *ware hounds.*

ware-house (wâr′hous″), *n.* a building for storing goods: **warehouse receipt**, a receipt given to the owner of goods so stored:—*v.t.* (wâr′houz″), [*p.t.* and *p.p.* -housed″ (-houzd″), *p.pr.* -hous″ing], to store in a warehouse.—*n.* **ware′house″man.**

war-fare (wôr′fâr″), *n.* **1**, a condition of armed conflict; **2**, military operations between enemies; **3**, hence, any strife, contest, or struggle.

war-like (wôr′līk″), *adj.* **1**, fit for, or fond of, military life or fighting; **2**, threatening conflict in arms; **3**, of or for war; as, *warlike* preparations.

war-lock (wôr′lŏk), *n.* formerly, a wizard; necromancer.

warm (wôrm), *adj.* **1**, moderately heated; not cold; giving out moderate heat; as, the October sun is pleasantly *warm;* **2**, serving to keep heat in; as, a *warm* coat; **3**, having little cold weather; as, a *warm* climate; **4**, passionate; earnest or eager; hence, kindly; as, she has a *warm* heart; **5**, in painting, having tones of red, yellow, or orange:—*v.t.* **1**, to impart moderate heat to; **2**, to fill with interest or excitement:—*v.i.* **1**, to become moderately heated; **2**, to become interested or excited; as, the audience *warmed* to the speaker.—*n.* **warm′er.**—*adv.* **warm′ly.**

warm-blood-ed (wôrm′=blŭd″ĕd), *adj* **1**, having blood like that of mammals and birds, which remains at an almost uniform temperature; **2**, having an ardent, enthusiastic temperament.

warm-ing pan a covered pan, often highly ornamented, for holding live coals: formerly used to warm beds by passing between the sheets.

warmth (wôrmth), *n.* **1**, the sensation, state, or quality of being moderately heated; **2**, the power to give heat; **3**, earnestness; zeal; ardor.

warn (wôrn), *v.t.* **1**, to put on guard; make aware of possible danger; foretell a risk to; **2**, to advise against something; **3**, to notify in advance; summon.—*n.* **warn′er.**

warn-ing (wôrn′ĭng), *n.* **1**, previous notice, esp. against danger; **2**, a summons; **3**, notice to quit.

warp (wôrp), *n.* **1**, the lengthwise thread in weaving: distinguished from *woof;* **2**, the tow rope of a boat; **3**, a twist, as of a board:—*v.t.* **1**, to turn or twist out of shape; **2**, to turn from the proper course; **3**, to tow (a vessel); **4**, to change the form of (an airplane wing) by twisting, usually by changing the angle of inclination of the rear spar relative to the front spar, so as to maintain stability:—*v.i.* **1**, to become twisted; **2**, to swerve.

war paint **1**, ceremonial paint, applied to the face and body by savages when about to go to war; **2**, *Slang*, ceremonial dress; regalia

war-path (wôr′pȧth″), *n.* the route taken by Indians going to war.

war-rant (wŏr′ănt), *n.* **1**, an official paper giving authority to receive money, to carry out an arrest, or to represent a principal in a lawsuit; **2**, that which vouches for or guarantees anything; **3**, just ground; as, he acted without *warrant;* **4**, in the army, a certificate of rank or appointment issued to one of lower rank than a commissioned officer:—*v.t.* **1**, to guarantee; answer for the genuineness of; **2**, to authorize (a person) to do something; **3**, to declare as certain; as, I *warrant* that this will happen; **4**, in law: **a**, to give assurance to (a purchaser) of the quality of goods sold; **b**, to give assurance of (the quality of goods sold, the validity of a title, etc.); **5**, to make secure; **6**, to give just ground for or to; as, the state of affairs *warrants* decided action.—*n.* **war′rant-er; war′ran-tor″.**

war-rant-a-ble (wŏr′ăn-tȧ-bl), *adj.* capable of being authorized; justifiable.—*adv.* **war′rant-a-bly.**

war-rant of-fi-cer in the navy, an officer of subordinate rank, appointed by the President.

war-ran-ty (wŏr′ăn-tĭ), *n.* [*pl.* warranties (-tĭz)], **1**, *Archaic*, authority; **2**, legal guarantee; security; as, a *warranty* that certain property is as it is represented.

war-ren (wŏr′ĕn), *n.* **1**, an inclosure for protecting game or breeding animals; **2**, a place where rabbits live and breed.

war-rior (wôr′yẽr; wôr′ĭ-ẽr; wŏr′ĭ-ẽr), *n.* **1**, a soldier; a man in military life; **2**, an Indian brave.

war-ship (wôr′shĭp″), *n.* a government ship equipped for war.

wart (wôrt), *n.* a small, usually hard, lump on the skin.—*adj.* **wart′y.**

wart hog a large-headed wild hog of Africa, having two pairs of warty protuberances on the face.

wa-ry (wā′rĭ), *adj.* [*comp.* wa′ri-er, *superl.* wa′ri-est], **1**, careful in the face of

danger; as, a *wary* foe; **2,** marked by caution; as, a *wary* step.—*adv.* **wa'ri-ly.**—*n.* **wa'ri-ness.**
Syn. watchful, prudent, circumspect.

was (wŏz), the first and third persons singular, past tense, of the verb *be.*

wash (wŏsh), *v.t.* **1,** to cleanse by means of a liquid, usually water; **2,** to cover with water; as, the shores are *washed* by breakers; **3,** to flow against; as, the sea *washes* the rocks; **4,** to take away by the action of water; as, many houses were *washed* away in the flood; **5,** to overlay with thin metal; **6,** in painting, to cover with a thin coat of color:—*v.i.* **1,** to become clean by the use of water; **2,** to cleanse something by rubbing it in water; **3,** *Colloq.,* to endure without harm being rubbed in water; as, some kinds of silk *wash;* **4,** to move with a flowing, lapping sound; **5,** to be worn away by action of water:—*n.* **1,** the act of becoming or making clean with water; **2,** a collection of articles to be washed; **3,** the dash or sound of a body of water; **4,** material deposited by water, as wreckage on a beach; **5,** a liquid for cleansing, healing, or treating something; as, a *wash* for sunburn; **6,** disturbed air behind a moving airplane; disturbed water behind the propellers, oars, paddles, etc., of a boat.—*adj.* **wash'a-ble.**—*n.* **wash'a-ble-ness.**—*n.* **wash'ing.**

wash-board (wŏsh'bōrd"), *n.* a board with a ribbed surface on which clothes are rubbed in being washed.

wash-er (wŏsh'ẽr), *n.* **1,** one who or that which washes; specif., a machine for washing dishes, clothes, etc.; **2,** a flat ring of metal, leather, or other material, used to secure the tightness of a joint, screw, etc.

wash-er-wom-an (wŏsh'ẽr-wŏŏm"ăn), *n.* [*pl.* washerwomen (-wĭm"ĕn)], a woman who earns a living by washing clothes; laundress.

wash-out (wŏsh'out"), *n.* **1,** the carrying away of earth, rocks, etc., as by heavy rain; **2,** a place where earth, rocks, etc., have been so carried away.

wash-stand (wŏsh'stănd"), *n.* a table or cabinet equipped with conveniences for washing the face and hands.

wasp (wŏsp), *n.* **1,** any of numerous insects with a sharp sting; **2,** an irritable, peevish person.—*adj.* **wasp'y.**

wasp-ish (wŏs'pĭsh), *adj.* **1,** slender of waist; **2,** irritable; peevish.—*adv.* **wasp'ish-ly.**—*n.* **wasp'ish-ness.**

was-sail (wŏs'ĭl; wŏs'āl; wăs'-), *n.* **1,** an old form of merrymaking accompanied with drinking, esp. at Christmas time; **2,** liquor made of ale, spices, apples, and sugar; **3,** an ancient expression used in drinking a health.—*n.* **was'sail-er.**

wast (wŏst), *Archaic* or *Poetic,* the second person singular, past indicative, of *be.*

wast-age (wās'tĭj), *n.* loss through use, wear and tear, deterioration, evaporation, etc.

waste (wāst), *v.t.* [*p.t.* and *p.p.* wast'ed, *p.pr.* wast'ing], **1,** to lay in ruins; devastate or destroy; **2,** to wear away gradually; as, the fever *wasted* his strength; **3,** to spend or use recklessly or unprofitably, as time, money, etc.:—*v.i.* to lose vigor, substance, or strength gradually; as, to *waste* away with disease:—*adj.* **1,** lying unused; unproductive; as, *waste* land; **2,** desolate; dreary; desert:—*n.* **1,** the act or process of spending carelessly, of wearing gradually away, etc.; **2,** that which is of no value; refuse; **3,** something thrown aside in a manufacturing process; as, cotton *waste;* **4,** that which is devastated, desolate, or unproductive; a desert.—*n.* **wast'er.**

waste-ful (wāst'fo͝ol), *adj.* **1,** spending or consuming extravagantly or uselessly, as in cooking; **2,** destructive.—*adv.* **waste'ful-ly.**—*n.* **waste'ful-ness.**
Syn. lavish, prodigal, profuse.—*Ant.* economical, frugal, saving.

watch (wŏch), *n.* **1,** wakefulness and close observation for the purpose of guarding or protecting; **2,** close observation; vigilance; **3,** a watchman; guard or sentry; **4,** the time a guard is on duty; **5,** on shipboard: **a,** one of the periods during which a given part of a ship's crew is on duty; **b,** the section of a crew on duty during this period; **6,** a pocket timepiece:—*v.i.* **1,** to be or keep awake; **2,** to keep guard; **3,** to be on the lookout; **4,** to be expectant; wait:—*v.t.* **1,** to tend; guard; **2,** to keep in sight.—*n.* **watch'er.**

watch-dog (wŏch'dŏg"), *n.* a dog quick to detect the approach of, and hostile toward, strangers: kept to protect property and guard those placed in his charge.

watch-ful (wŏch'fo͝ol), *adj.* cautious; alert and attentive.—*adv.* **watch'ful-ly.**—*n.* **watch'ful-ness.**

watch-mak-er (wŏch'māk"ẽr), *n.* one who makes watches and repairs them.—*n.* **watch'mak"ing.**

watch-man (wŏch'măn), *n.* [*pl.* watchmen (-mĕn)], a guard; esp., one who guards a locality or building at night.

watch-tow-er (wŏch'tou"ẽr), *n.* **1,** an ancient or medieval tower or high structure upon which a sentinel was placed; **2,** any tower or high platform used as a lookout.

WATCHTOWER

watch-word (wŏch'wûrd"), *n.* **1,** a password; secret word used as a countersign; as, the *watchword* is "Mary"; **2,** a rallying cry; slogan.

wa-ter (wô'tẽr), *n.* **1,** the fluid which forms lakes, rivers, etc., and which comes from the clouds as rain: a colorless compound of two parts hydrogen and one part oxygen (H_2O); **2,** a body of water, as a sea, river, lake, etc.; **3,** the luster or brilliance of a precious stone; as, a diamond of the first *water;* **4,** any of various liquids secreted by animals, made up chiefly of water, as tears; **5,** a kind of wavy, shiny pattern, as in silk: **water of crystallization,** water which is present in certain crystalline combinations but which is not an inherent part of the molecules themselves:—*v.t.* **1,** to moisten or sprinkle with water; as, to *water* plants; **2,** to provide with water; **3,** to produce a wavy, shiny pattern upon, as silk; **4,** to flow through; irrigate; **5,** to lessen the quality or strength of by diluting; as, to *water* milk:—*v.i.* **1,** to obtain, or take in, water; **2,** to secrete or discharge liquid; as, her eyes *watered.*—*p.adj.* **wa'tered.**—*n.* **wa'ter-er.**

Wa-ter Bear-er **1,** the constellation Aquarius; **2,** the 11th sign of the zodiac (see *zodiac,* illus.).

wa-ter–clos-et (wô'tẽr-klŏz"ĕt), *n.* **1,** a small room or compartment fitted with a hopper that can be flushed with water, to receive waste matter from the body; **2,** also, the hopper.

wa-ter col-or **1,** a paint prepared for use by moistening with water; **2,** a picture made with paints of this kind, as distinguished from one painted with oil colors.

wa-ter-course (wô'tẽr-kōrs"), *n.* **1,** a stream of water; **2,** a channel for water; **3,** in map reading, a line showing where water would or does flow.

wa-ter cress a plant with pungent leaves, usually growing in running water: used for salad and for garnishing. Also, *n.* **wa'ter-cress″**.

wa-ter cure the treatment of diseases by use of water, either as baths or taken internally.

wa-ter dog 1, a dog used to the water, or one that takes readily to water; esp., a dog taught to retrieve ducks and the like; 2, *Colloq.*, an experienced sailor.

wa-ter-fall (wô'tẽr-fôl″), *n.* a very steep descent, or fall, of the water of a stream or river; a cascade; cataract.

wa-ter-fowl (wô'tẽr-foul″), *n.* a bird which lives on or close to a body of water, such as a wild duck or goose: used also as *pl.*

wa-ter gas a highly poisonous mixture produced by passing steam over red-hot coal.

wa-ter glass a substance made of silicates of sodium or potassium, or of both in combination, in solution in water: often used in preserving eggs.

wa-ter ice 1, ice formed by the freezing of water: distinguished from ice formed by the freezing of wet snow; 2, a frozen dessert made of water flavored with fruit juice and sugar; sherbet.

wa-ter-ing place 1, a place for getting water; 2, a pleasure resort, esp. one noted for mineral springs.

wa-ter jack-et a case for holding water, or through which water may circulate for cooling or heating purposes.

wa-ter lil-y a plant which grows in the water, bearing a fragrant, beautiful flower and broad, flat, floating leaves; also, the flower itself.

wa-ter–logged (wô'tẽr=lŏgd″), *adj.* soaked or filled with water, so as to be unmanageable or heavy like a log; as, a *water-logged* ship.

Wa-ter-loo (wô″tẽr-lōō'; wô'tẽr-lōō″), *n.* *Colloq.*, a complete defeat or failure: so called from Napoleon's final defeat at Waterloo, Belgium, in 1815.

wa-ter-man (wô'tẽr-măn), *n.* [*pl.* watermen (-mĕn)], 1, a man who runs or manages a boat for hire; 2, one experienced in boats and boating.

wa-ter-mark (wô'tẽr-märk″), *n.* 1, a mark showing the limit of the rise of water; 2, a faintly visible marking or design in some kinds of paper, due to variation in texture, indicating the maker or brand:—*v.t.* to mark with a watermark.

wa-ter-mel-on (wô'tẽr-mĕl″ŭn), *n.* a trailing plant cultivated for its large, edible fruit with green rind and red, sweet, juicy pulp; also, the fruit.

wa-ter ou-zel any of certain song birds akin to the thrush: often called *dipper:* distinguished from the *ring ouzel.* Also, **wa'ter ou'sel.**

wa-ter po-lo a game resembling basket ball, played by swimmers.

wa-ter pow-er 1, power from falling or running water, used to run machinery; 2, a fall of water which may be used for such a purpose.

wa-ter-proof (wô'tẽr-prōōf″), *adj.* shedding moisture; not admitting water:—*n.* any material treated so as to shed water; esp., a garment, as a raincoat, made of such material:—*v.t.* to make secure against water, as a garment or a roof.

wa-ter-shed (wô'tẽr-shĕd″), *n.* 1, a ridge or height of land lying between areas drained by different river systems; a divide; 2, an area drained by a single river or lake system.

wa-ter-side (wô'tẽr-sīd″), *n.* the shore or edge of a body of water.

wa-ter–soak (wô'tẽr=sōk″), *v.t.* to soak or saturate with water.

wa-ter-spout (wô'tẽr-spout″), *n.* 1, a column of water drawn up by a whirlwind at sea to meet a descending funnel-shaped cloud; 2, a spout for the discharge of water, esp. of rain water.

wa-ter–tight (wô'tẽr=tīt″), *adj.* so closely or compactly made as to permit no water to leak out or enter.

wa-ter tow-er 1, a tower serving as a reservoir or tank for holding water; 2, a fire-fighting apparatus provided with a pipe which may be raised to deliver a jet of water at a great height.

wa-ter-way (wô'tẽr-wā″), *n.* 1, a channel for water; 2, a body of water permitting navigation.

wa-ter wheel a wheel turned by the direct action of flowing or falling water (see *hydraulic*, illus.).

wa-ter-works (wô'tẽr-wûrks″), *n. pl.,* sometimes used as *sing.,* a pumping station; a system for supplying water to a city, town, etc.

wa-ter-y (wô'tẽr-ĭ), *adj.* 1, pertaining to, or like, water; 2, soggy; tasteless; 3, tearful; moist.—*n.* **wa'ter-i-ness.**

watt (wŏt), *n.* the electrical unit of power, or rate of work done by a current of one ampere with a potential of one volt.

wat-tle (wŏt'l), *n.* 1, a twig; a rod easily bent; also, a hurdle of pliant rods, 2, the loose red flesh under the throat of certain birds, as the cock:—*v.t.* [*p.t.* and *p.p.* -tled (-ld), *p.pr.* -tling], 1, to twist or interweave (twigs or rods) one with another; 2, to fence in with rods.—*p.adj.* **wat'tled.**

wat-tle-bird (wŏt'l-bûrd″), *n.* an Australasian honey-eating bird.

watt-me-ter (wŏt'mē″tẽr), *n.* an instrument for measuring the power delivered by an electric current.

wave (wāv), *n.* 1, a swell on the surface of water; billow; 2, the wavelike motion by which sound, light, and electrical radiations are transmitted; 3, a curving ridge on any surface; 4, an up-and-down or back-and-forth motion, as with the hand: **wave length,** the distance between successive waves:—*v.i.* [*p.t.* and *p.p.* waved (wāvd), *p.pr.* wav'ing], 1, to be moved up and down or back and forth; 2, to signal by such a motion; 3, to have undulations, or curves; as, her hair *waves* beautifully: —*v.t.* 1, to cause to move or swing back and forth; brandish; 2, to signal by such a movement; 3, to give an undulating, or curved, surface or form to.—*adj.* **wave'less.**—*n.* [1]**wav'er.**

[2]**wa-ver** (wā'vẽr), *v.i.* 1, to tremble to and fro or back and forth; reel or stagger; 2, to hesitate, as in opinion.—*n.* **wa'ver-er.**—*p.adj.* **wa'ver-ing.**—*adv.* **wa'ver-ing-ly.**

wav-y (wāv'ĭ), *adj.* [*comp.* wav'i-er, *superl.* wav'i-est], 1, rising and swelling in waves; 2, full of waves; as, *wavy* hair.—*adv.* **wav'i-ly.**—*n.* **wav'i-ness.**

[1]**wax** (wăks), *v.i.* 1, to increase in size, power, degree, etc.; grow: often used of the moon; 2, to pass gradually into a specified condition; become; as, to *wax* merry.

[2]**wax** (wăks), *n.* 1, a sticky, yellowish secretion of bees from which the honeycomb is built; beeswax; 2, any of several similar substances:—*v.t.* to smear, polish, or treat the surface of, with wax:—*adj.* made of wax; as, a *wax* candle: **wax bean,** a variety of bean with rich yellow pods.—*adj.* **wax'en.**

wax myr-tle any of certain slender, evergreen shrubs or trees from the waxy berries of which candles are made: also called *bayberry.*

NORTH AMERICAN WILD FLOWERS

1. Violet. 2. Wake robin. 3. Fringed gentian. 4. Day lily. 5. Smooth rose. 6. Lady's slipper. 7. Marsh marigold. 8. Jack in the pulpit. 9. Phlox.

wax-wing (wăks′wĭng″), *n.* any of several crested birds with seed-shaped, red tips, resembling sealing wax, on certain wing feathers, as the cedar bird.

wax-work (wăks′wûrk″), *n.* **1**, figures formed of wax in imitation of animals, flowers, people, etc.; **2**, in *pl.*, a collection of wax figures, often life-size representations of historical characters.

wax-y (wăk′sĭ), *adj.* [*comp.* wax′i-er, *superl.* wax′i-est], like, or full of, wax; adhesive or sticky; pliable.—*n.* **wax′i-ness.**

way (wā), *n.* **1**, a road, street, path, or passage; hence, room for passing; as, make *way* for the procession; **2**, the route from one place to another; the direction; as, tell me the *way;* also, distance in general; as, it is a long *way* to China; **3**, advance; headway; as, the ship gathers *way;* **4**, manner; as, she has a winning *way;* also, method or means; as, find a *way* to accomplish it; **5**, mode of life; custom; as, he was set in his *ways;* **6**, aspect; respect; as, in some *ways* it proved a success; **7**, the ordinary range or field of one's action or notice; as, he did it in the *way* of business; **8**, condition; state; as, we're in a bad *way;* **9**, in *pl.*, a structure of timbers on which a ship is built and down which it slides when being launched: **by way of, 1**, passing through on the way; as, he went to Boston *by way of* New York: also written *via;* **2**, as a substitute for; as serving for; as, he took an umbrella *by way of* a cane; he said that *by way of* an apology: **out of the way, 1**, off the road; **2**, secluded; retired; **3**, out of the right course; hence, improper; wrong: **to give way**, to give passage; hence, to yield or break down, as under pressure: **under way**, in motion or progress, as a ship or a project: **ways and means**, methods and means of accomplishing some end, esp. of meeting expenses, as of a government.

Syn. road, highway, street, avenue, thoroughfare. *Way* is the general term used to name a place which provides room for passing along. A *road* is a route, a *way* for getting to a place, and may be private or public. A *highway* is a public, and often a main, *road;* it may be a water or a land route. A *street* is a *road* in a town, village, or city, with houses on one or both sides. An *avenue* may be a wide *street*, but usually names a *street* marked by trees. A *thoroughfare* is a way through; it is a public *road*, esp. one open at both ends.

way-bill (wā′bĭl″), *n.* a document, or paper, describing and containing shipping instructions for goods carried by train or steamer.

way-far-er (wā′fâr″ẽr), *n.* a traveler. esp. one who goes on foot.

way-far-ing (wā′fâr″ĭng), *adj.* traveling or journeying, esp. on foot; as, a *wayfaring* man.

way-lay (wā″lā′; wā′lā″), *v.t.* [*p.t.* and *p.p.* -laid′ (-lād′), *p.pr.* -lay′ing], **1**, to lie in wait for; **2**, to beset by the road, esp. in order to rob.—*n.* **way″lay′er.**

-ways (-wāz), *adv. suffix*, indicating position, direction, manner, etc.; as, length*ways;* side*ways;* al*ways:* often interchangeable with *-wise.*

way-side (wā′sīd″), *n.* the edge of the road:—*adj.* on or pertaining to the edge of the road; as, *wayside* flowers.

way sta-tion a small station between larger ones on a railroad.

way train a train which stops at nearly all stations along the road.

way-ward (wā′wẽrd), *adj.* **1**, perverse or disobedient; **2**, freakish; unaccountable; unsteady.—*adv.* **way′ward-ly.**—*n.* **way′ward-ness.**

Syn. obstinate, headstrong, wilful.

way-worn (wā′wōrn″), *adj.* tired out by travel or by events.

we (wē), *personal pron.* the nominative plural of the pronoun *I*, used as follows: **1**, by the speaker or writer to mean himself and others; also, people in general; **2**, by sovereigns, as a sign of distinction, to mean *I;* **3**, by editors and other formal writers to denote the class of which they represent themselves as spokesmen.

weak (wēk), *adj.* **1**, lacking in strength of body or in endurance; as, a *weak* back; easily overcome; as, a *weak* crew; **2**, wanting in mental or moral strength; easily influenced; as, a *weak* will; **3**, faulty; defective; below standard; as, she is *weak* in algebra; a *weak* point; **4**, faint in sound; feeble; as, a *weak* voice; also, diluted; thin; watery; as, *weak* tea; **5**, in grammar: **a**, regular: applied to verbs which form the past tense and past participle with a consonant suffix, in English *-ed, -d,* or *-t;* **b**, in German grammar, designating, or pertaining to, a certain declension of nouns and adjectives, distinguished from the declension called *strong* (which see) by inflectional endings in *-n*, still seen in a few English forms, as ox-*en.*

weak-en (wēk′n), *v.t.* to reduce in quality or strength:—*v.i.* to become less strong or resolute..

weak-fish (wēk′fĭsh″), *n.* any of several kinds of edible sea fish with a very tender mouth.

weak-ling (wēk′lĭng), *n.* a person lacking strength of body or character.

weak-ly (wēk′lĭ), *adj.* [*comp.* weak′li-er, *superl.* weak′li-est], feeble; sickly; not strong:—*adv.* in a faint manner; feebly.

weak-ness (wēk′nĕs), *n.* **1**, the state or quality of lacking strength; **2**, a fault; defect, as in a plan.

¹weal (wēl), *n.* **1**, (also, *wheal*), a mark made on flesh by flogging; **2**, a ridge on a surface, as of cloth; hence, texture; **3**, a plank along the edge of a vessel; **4**, a timber fastened to a row of piles; **5**, a strengthening ridge on a basket:—*v.t.* **1**, to mark with a ridge or stripes; **2**, to secure, as with a weal. Also, **wale**, *Pfd. S.*

²weal (wēl), *n.* **1**, happiness; prosperity; welfare; **2**, *Archaic:* **a**, the people at large; the body politic; **b**, wealth; riches.

weald (wēld), *n.* a region without woods; open, wild country; wold.

wealth (wĕlth), *n.* **1**, riches; large amounts of money or worldly possessions; **2**, abundance, profusion, or display of anything.—*adj.* **wealth′y.**—*adv.* **wealth′i-ly.**

wean (wēn), *v.t.* **1**, to accustom (a child or any young animal) to substitute other food for the mother's milk; **2**, to draw away the affections or interests of (a person or animal) from any object or habit.

wean-ling (wēn′lĭng), *n.* a child or animal recently weaned:—*adj.* recently weaned.

weap-on (wĕp′ŭn), *n.* any instrument for fighting or for defense, as a gun; hence, any means of contest; as, his tongue was his best *weapon.*—*adj.* **weap′on-less.**

¹wear (wâr), *v.t.* [*p.t.* wore (wōr), *p.p.* worn (wōrn), *p.pr.* wear′ing], **1**, to carry on or about the body; as, to *wear* a coat; **2**, to bear or maintain about one, or to show habitually; as, to *wear* a careless manner; **3**, to use up or consume, wholly or in part, esp. by personal use: often with *out;* as, he *wears* his shoes out rapidly; **4**, to diminish the quality or value of by use, esp. when rubbing, scraping, or friction is involved; hence, to weaken; weary; fatigue; as, anxiety *wore* her out; **5**, to reproduce or bring about by use, friction, attrition, erosive action, or the like; as, to *wear* a hole in the carpet; the wheel *wore* a groove:—*v.i.* **1**, to go through, or endure, the process of being used; as, these gloves *wear* like iron: also used figuratively, as regarding adaptability or personality; as, the girl *wears* well; **2**, to become used up; be diminished in value as a result of use, friction, etc.: often with *out, off,* or *down;* as, cheap clothes *wear* out soon; **3**, to pass gradually or painfully; as, the night *wore* on:—*n.* **1**, the state of being used, or act of using; **2**, garments worn; as, women's *wear;* **3**, that which is customarily worn; the fashion; as, this hue is not the *wear* just now; **4**, damage caused by use; as, to show *wear:* **wear and tear**, the damage to which an object is subject in the course of ordinary use.—*adj.* **wear'a-ble.**—*n.* **wear'er.**

²wear (wâr), *v.i.* [*p.t.* and *p.p.* wore (wōr), *p.pr.* wear'ing], of a ship, to go about by swinging bow to leeward; veer:—*v.t.* to turn (a ship) about by swinging bow to leeward.

³wear (wâr), *n.* **1**, a dam in a stream or river; **2**, a fence set in a stream for catching fish. See **weir**, *Pfd. S.*

wea-ri-some (wē'rĭ-sŭm), *adj.* causing fatigue; tedious; irksome; as, a *wearisome* journey.—*adv.* **wea'ri-some-ly.** —*n.* **wea'ri-some-ness.**

wea-ry (wē'rĭ), *adj.* [*comp.* wea'ri-er, *superl.* wea'ri-est], **1**, fatigued; tired; worn out physically or mentally; **2**, exhausted, as in patience, by continuance of something tiresome; as, *weary* of routine; **3**, characteristic of, or showing, fatigue; as, a *weary* sigh; **4**, causing, or accompanied by, fatigue; as, we walked many *weary* miles:—*v.t.* [*p.t.* and *p.p.* -ried (-rĭd), *p.pr.* -ry-ing], **1**, to wear out or make tired; **2**, to harass or worry by something irksome:—*v.i.* **1**, to become tired or fatigued; **2**, to become impatient.—*adv.* **wea'-ri-ly.**—*n.* **wea'ri-ness.**

wea-sand (wē'zănd), *n.* *Archaic,* the windpipe; hence, loosely, the throat in general.

wea-sel (wē'zl), *n.* a small animal of the same family as the mink and skunk, with a pointed face and a long, thin body: destructive to poultry, mice, etc.

weath-er (wĕth'ẽr), *n.* the state of the atmosphere as to cold, heat, wetness, dryness, etc.:—*v.t.* **1**, to expose to the air; season, alter, or injure by exposure to the air; **2**, to sail to the windward of; **3**, to endure or resist; as, to *weather* a gale at sea: —*v.i.* to undergo change by the action of the air, sun, rain, etc., as shingles or paint.

weath-er–beat-en (wĕth'ẽr-bēt″n), *adj.* **1**, defaced or worn by the action of air, sun, rain, etc.; as, a *weather-beaten* house; **2**, toughened; as, a *weather-beaten* countenance.

weath-er-board (wĕth'ẽr-bōrd″), *n.* a board cut and fitted to form lapped joints with boards above and below, so as to make a waterproof outer wall; clapboard (see *frame house,* illus.):—*v.t.* to nail boards on (a building) so as to overlap one another.—*n.* **weath'er-board″ing.**

Weath-er Bu-reau an office in the U. S. Department of Agriculture which keeps statistics of weather reports and forecasts the weather.

weath-er-cock (wĕth'ẽr-kŏk″), *n.* **1**, a figure, often shaped like a cock, fastened to a high spire, roof, pole, etc., and turning with the wind to show which way it blows; a weather vane; **2**, a fickle person.

weath-er-glass (wĕth'ẽr-glȧs″), *n.* an instrument, as a barometer, for predicting the weather.

weath-er vane a thin strip of wood or metal, often shaped like a bird, fish, etc., and fastened to a high spire, roof, or pole, where it turns with the wind and shows which way it blows; a weathercock: also called *vane.*

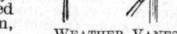

WEATHER VANES

weath-er-wise (wĕth'ẽr-wīz″), *adj.* skilful in foretelling weather changes, as by observing the clouds, winds, etc.

weath-er-worn (wĕth'ẽr-wōrn″), *adj.* damaged or altered by exposure to sun, rain, wind, etc.

weave (wēv), *v.t.* [*p.t.* wove (wōv), *p.p.* wo'ven (wō'vn) or wove, *p.pr.* weav'ing], **1**, to twist or interlace, as threads; **2**, to form by interlacing or twisting, as cloth on a loom; **3**, to compose or fabricate; as, to *weave* a thrilling story:—*v.i.* **1**, to make cloth on a loom; **2**, to become twisted together or interlaced; **3**, to wind in and out:—*n.* a specified texture or pattern in weaving.

weav-er (wēv'ẽr), *n.* one whose trade is making cloth on a loom.

weav-er bird any of various Old World birds that make their nests by interlacing twigs, grass, etc.

web (wĕb), *n.* **1**, anything woven; tissue; texture; fabric; **2**, a substance or piece of material resembling woven cloth; specif., a cobweb; **3**, anything carefully contrived, as a plan or scheme; **4**, the skin between the toes of many water birds, as in the duck; **5**, a large roll of paper for printing:—*v.t.* [*p.t.* and *p.p.* webbed (wĕbd), *p.pr.* web'bing], to unite or surround with, or as with, a web; entangle.—*p.adj.* **webbed.**—*adj.* **web'by.**

web-bing (wĕb'ĭng), *n.* **1**, a heavy woven strip of cotton or linen; **2**, skin joining the toes, as of a bird's foot.

web-foot (wĕb'fo͝ot″), *n.* [*pl.* webfeet (-fēt″)], **1**, a foot with the toes joined by a membrane; **2**, any animal with feet of this kind.—*adj.* **web'-foot″ed.**

wed (wĕd), *v.t.* [*p.t.* and *p.p.* wed'ded or wed, *p.pr.* wed'ding], **1**, to marry; unite with in wedlock; **2**, to join in marriage; **3**, to attach (oneself) devotedly; as, he was *wedded* to his hobbies:—*v.i.* to marry.

wed-ding (wĕd'ĭng), *n.* **1**, a marriage; a marriage ceremony and festivities; **2**, a marriage anniversary or its celebration; as, a golden *wedding.*
Syn. (see marriage).

wedge (wĕj), *n.* **1**, a piece of wood or metal, thick at one end and thin at the other, used for splitting wood or rocks, raising heavy objects, etc.; **2**, anything of a similar shape:—*v.t.* [*p.t.* and *p.p.* wedged (wĕjd), *p.pr.* wedg'-ing], **1**, to cleave, force, drive, or fasten, with a wedge; **2**, to press in closely; **3**, to fasten with a wedge, as a door or wheel.—*adj.* **wedg'y.**

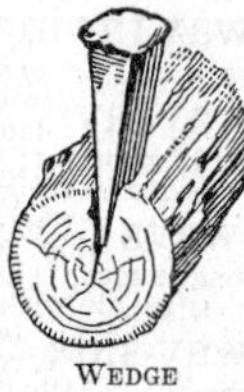

WEDGE

wed-lock (wĕd'lŏk), *n.* the state of being married; matrimony.
Syn. (see marriage).

Wednes-day (wĕnz'dȧ), *n.* the fourth day of the week.—*abbr.* **Wed.**

wee (wē), *adj.* very small; little; as, a *wee* bit of anything; a *wee* baby.

¹weed (wēd), *n.* **1**, a wild plant growing in cultivated fields and injurious to the cultivated plants; **2**, any unsightly or useless plant; **3**, anything useless or troublesome; **4**, *Colloq.*, tobacco, esp. when prepared for use;

a cigar:—*v.t.* **1**, to root out or remove, as undesirable plants: usually with *out;* **2**, to free from wild and useless plants; as, to *weed* a garden; **3**, to remove from a group, as inferior, useless, and harmful parts; as, to *weed* out the drones:—*v.i.* to take out weeds or anything obnoxious.—*n.* **weed'er.**—*adj.* **weed'less.**

²**weed** (wēd), *n.* **1**, *Archaic*, a garment; **2**, in *pl.*, *Colloq.*, a widow's mourning garments: usually in the phrase *widow's weeds.*

weed-y (wēd'ĭ), *adj.* [*comp.* weed'i-er, *superl.* weed'i-est], **1**, pertaining to, consisting of, or abounding with, weeds; as, a *weedy* garden; **2**, hence, ill-kept.—*n.* **weed'i-ness.**

week (wēk), *n.* **1**, a period of seven days, usually counted as beginning with Sunday; **2**, the six working days as a unit.

week day any day of the week except Sunday.

week-end (wēk'=ĕnd'), *n.* **1**, the time from Friday night or Saturday noon to Monday morning, usually free from business; **2**, a holiday or house party at this time.—*n.* **week'-end"er.**

week-ly (wēk'lĭ), *adj.* **1**, continuing for, or produced within, a week; **2**, happening or coming every seven days:—*adv.* once a week:—*n.* [*pl.* weeklies (-lĭz)], a paper or magazine issued once every seven days.

ween (wēn), *v.i. Archaic*, to suppose; think; as, I *ween.*

weep (wēp), *v.i.* [*p.t.* and *p.p.* wept (wĕpt), *p.pr.* weep'ing], **1**, to shed tears; cry; **2**, to droop:—*v.t.* **1**, to shed, as tears; **2**, to shed tears for; hence, to lament or mourn; bewail.—*n.* **weep'er.**

weep-ing (wēp'ĭng), *n.* the act of shedding tears:—*p.adj.* **1**, crying; **2**, having drooping branches, as a willow.

wee-vil (wē'vl), *n.* a small beetle, whose larvæ are injurious to fruit and grain.

weft (wĕft), *n.* **1**, in weaving, the threads that cross the warp, or lengthwise threads; woof; **2**, a web; a woven fabric.

weigh (wā), *v.t.* **1**, to find the heaviness of; examine by a scale or balance; **2**, to ponder; reflect on carefully; **3**, to press heavily upon: with *down;* **4**, to raise: used only in *to weigh anchor:*—*v.i.* **1**, to have (a given) heaviness; **2**, to bear heavily; as, the burden of anxiety *weighs* on his mind; **3**, to be considered important; as, the common good should *weigh* heaviest.—*n.* **weigh'er.**

weight (wāt), *n.* **1**, heaviness; the property by which bodies tend toward the earth; **2**, the force with which a body is attracted toward the earth; **3**, a system of units used in finding the heaviness or quantity of objects or substances; as, apothecaries' *weight;* **4**, a piece of metal used as a balance in finding the heaviness of other bodies; **5**, a heavy mass; a load; **6**, something oppressive; as, a *weight* on the mind; **7**, power; importance:—*v.t.* to put weight upon; load down.

weight-y (wāt'ĭ), *adj.* [*comp.* weight'i-er, *superl.* weight'i-est], **1**, heavy; **2**, important; serious; as, a *weighty* matter. —*adv.* **weight'i-ly.**—*n.* **weight'i-ness.**

weir (wēr), *n.* **1**, a dam in a stream, esp. a dam which forms a mill pond; **2**, a fence of brush or stakes set in a stream for catching fish. Also, **wear.**

weird (wērd), *adj.* **1**, pertaining to fate or to witchcraft; hence, uncanny or unearthly; as, a *weird* sound; **2**, *Colloq.*, strange and mysterious.—*adv.* **weird'ly.**—*n.* **weird'ness.**

wel-come (wĕl'kŭm), *adj.* **1**, received with gladness or hospitality; as, a *welcome* guest; producing gladness; as, *welcome* news; **2**, permitted gladly; as, you are *welcome* to keep it:—*n.* a greeting, usually kindly; the reception of a guest or newcomer: —*v.t.* [*p.t.* and *p.p.* -comed (-kŭmd), *p.pr.* -com-ing], to salute with kindness; receive with hospitality.—*n.* **wel'com-er.**

weld (wĕld), *v.t.* **1**, to unite by heating and hammering; press together, as two pieces of heated iron; **2**, hence, to unite closely:—*v.i.* to become melted, or firmly joined, together:—*n.* **1**, the state of being heated and pressed together; **2**, a joint made by heating and hammering.—*n.* **weld'er.**

wel-fare (wĕl'fâr"), *n.* **1**, the state or condition of having good health, happiness, or prosperity; also, state or condition in general: **welfare work, 1**, social work for the improvement of the condition of the less-favored part of a population, esp. of the poor; **2**, work done among employees to improve conditions of labor and morale: often called *personnel work.*

wel-kin (wĕl'kĭn), *n. Archaic*, the expanse of the heavens; the sky.

¹**well** (wĕl), *n.* **1**, a spring or fountain; **2**, a shaft sunk in the earth, and lined with stone, etc., for obtaining subterranean fluid, as water; a round opening drilled or bored into rock, often very deep, for water, gas, or oil; **3**, a source of steady or continuous supply; **4**, an inclosed, sunken space resembling a well: applied to many such formations; as, an ink-*well;* the *well* of a staircase; **5**, an eddy or whirlpool in the sea:—*v.i.* to flow, as from a spring.

²**well** (wĕl), *adv.* [*comp.* bet'ter, *superl.* best], **1**, in a right, just, or praiseworthy manner; **2**, satisfactorily or suitably; with reason; as, I can *well* spare it; you may *well* say; **3**, favorably; fortunately; prosperously; **4**, to a considerable extent or degree; as, he is *well* on in life:—*adj.* **1**, in good health; as, I am *well;* **2**, in a satisfactory state; as, all is *well:*—*interj.* used to reënforce any of several different shades of feeling indicated by the context, such as: **1**, wonder; as, *well!* what do you think of that? **2**, relief; as, *well,* here we are at last; **3**, resignation; as, *well,* I suppose I shall have to stand it; **4**, expectation of continuation; as, *well,* what next?

well-be-ing (wĕl'=bē'ĭng), *n.* the state of general health and welfare.

well-born (wĕl'=bôrn"), *adj.* born of a good family.

well-bred (wĕl'=brĕd"), *adj.* **1**, refined in manners; cultivated; **2**, of good breed, as an animal.

well-do-er (wĕl'=dōō'ẽr), *n.* one who does good deeds and lives uprightly.—*adj.* and *n.* **well'-do'ing.**

well-nigh (wĕl'=nī"), *adv.* very nearly; almost; as, *well-nigh* sick.

well-spring (wĕl'sprĭng"), *n.* a source of never-failing supply; as, a *wellspring* of inspiration.

well-to-do (wĕl'=tōō=dōō'), *adj.* prosperous; fairly wealthy.

Wels-bach burn-er (wĕlz'băk; wĕlz'-bäk), a gas burner for illuminating purposes, in which a noncombustible mantle becomes incandescent in the flame of a Bunsen burner.

Welsh (wĕlsh), *adj.* pertaining to Wales, its people, or their language:—*n.* **1**, the people of Wales; **2**, the language of Wales: **Welsh rabbit**, a dish of melted cheese, cooked with milk, seasoned, and spread upon toasted bread or crackers: sometimes erroneously called *Welsh rarebit.*

welt (wĕlt), *n.* **1**, an edge or border fastened around something, as the narrow strip of leather around a shoe between the upper and the sole; **2**, a red, swollen mark raised on the skin by a blow:—*v.t.* **1**, to secure or ornament with a welt; **2**, to flog.

wel-ter (wĕl'tẽr), *v.i.* **1**, to roll; wallow, as a pig in mire; hence, to indulge to excess, as in vice; **2**, to rise and fall with violent tossing, as waves:—*n.* **1**, a rolling, as of waves; **2**, a state of confusion; **3**, a wallow.

wen (wĕn), *n.* a painless tumor inclosed in a cyst, or closed sac.

wench (wĕnch), *n.* **1**, formerly, a young girl; **2**, a female servant.

wend (wĕnd), *v.i. Archaic*, to direct one's course; journey:—*v.t.* to direct or continue; as, to *wend* one's way.

Wend (wĕnd), *n.* a member of a race of eastern Germany, distinct in the Middle Ages as a Slavic race, but now mixed with Germanic elements.—*adj.* **Wend′ish.**

went (wĕnt), formerly, past tense of *wend*, now used as past tense of *go*.

wept (wĕpt), the past tense and past participle of the verb *weep*.

were (wûr; *Br.* wâr), **1**, past indicative, plural, of *be*; **2**, past subjunctive, singular and plural, of *be*.

were-wolf (wēr′wo͝olf″; wēr′wo͝olf″), *n.* [*pl.* werewolves (-wo͝olvz″)], in folklore, a person turned into a wolf, or one who could assume a wolf's shape at will. Also, **wer′wolf″.**

wert (wûrt), *Archaic* or *Poetic*, second person singular, past indicative and subjunctive, of the verb *be*.

Wes-ley-an (wĕs′lĭ-ăn), *adj.* pertaining to John Wesley (1703–91), or to Methodism, the religion which he founded:—*n.* **1**, a follower of John Wesley; **2**, a Methodist.—*n.* **Wes′ley-an-ism.**

west (wĕst), *n.* **1**, that part of the heavens where the sun is seen to set; **2**, one of the four points of the compass; **3**, the part of the earth lying toward the sunset: **West**, **1**, the Western Hemisphere; **2**, the part of the U. S. between the Mississippi River and the Pacific Ocean:—*adj.* pertaining to, or coming from, the direction of the sunset; lying on the left hand when one faces the north:—*adv.* in the direction of the sunset.

west-er-ly (wĕs′tẽr-lĭ), *adj.* **1**, toward the west; **2**, from the west, as a wind:—*adv.* in the direction of the west:—*n.* [*pl.* westerlies (-lĭz)], a wind from the west.

west-ern (wĕs′tẽrn), *adj.* pertaining to, situated toward, or lying in, the part of the earth toward the sunset; occidental: **Western**, designating, or pertaining to, the hemisphere which includes North and South America.—*n.* **west′ern-er; West′ern-er.**

West Goth one of the Visigoths, a Teutonic race which, after wandering over Europe, settled in Spain early in the Christian era.

west-ward (wĕst′wẽrd), *adj.* and *adv.* toward, or in the direction of, the sunset. Also, *adv.* **west′wards**

wet (wĕt), *v.t.* [*p.t.* and *p.p.* wet′ted or wet, *p.pr.* wet′ting], to cover, moisten, or soak with water or some other liquid:—*n.* water; moisture; also, rainy or misty weather:—*adj.* [*comp.* wet′ter, *superl.* wet′test], **1**, containing, or soaked with, water or some other liquid; **2**, rainy or misty; as, *wet* weather; **3**, *Slang*, permitting, or opposed to prohibiting, the manufacture and sale of alcoholic beverages; as, a *wet* state.—*n.* **wet′ness.**

Syn., adj. (see moist).

weth-er (wĕth′ẽr), *n.* a male sheep that has been castrated.

wet nurse a woman employed to give suck to the child of another.

whack (hwăk), *n. Colloq.*, a smart, resounding blow:—*v.t. Colloq.*, to strike with a smart, resounding blow.

[1]**whale** (hwāl), *n.* **1**, any of several species of large, warm-blooded, air-breathing sea mammals having finlike fore limbs, no external hind limbs, and a fishlike tail; loosely, the dolphin or porpoise; **2**, *Colloq.*, anything big or impressive; as, a *whale* of a story; esp., in angling, a big fish; as, a *whale* of a trout:—*v.i.* [*p.t.* and *p.p.* whaled (hwāld), *p.pr.* whal′ing], to engage in the occupation of catching whales, and preparing and selling the products obtained from them, as blubber, whalebone, etc.—*n.* **whal′er.**—*n.* [1]**whal′ing.**

WHALE AND CALF

[2]**whale** (hwāl), *v.t.* [*p.t.* and *p.p.* whaled (hwāld), *p.pr.* whal′ing], to flog or beat soundly. Also, **wale**, *Pfd. S.*—*n.*[2]**whal′ing.**

whale-back (hwāl′băk″), *n.* a long, low freight steamer having a convexly curved deck.

whale-boat (hwāl′bōt″), *n.* a long, narrow boat, sharp and slanting at both ends, first used in whaling.

whale-bone (hwāl′bōn″), *n.* a stiff, springy substance found in the upper jaw of certain whales.

whap (hwŏp), *v.t.* [*p.t.* and *p.p.* whapped (hwŏpt), *p.pr.* whap′ping], *Obs.* or *Dial.*, to thrash or beat:—*v.i. Archaic*, to flop down suddenly:—*n. Obs.* or *Dial.*, **1**, a blow; stroke; **2**, a bump; **3**, noise made by a blow. Also, **whop**, *Pfd. S.*

whap-per (hwŏp′ẽr), *n. Colloq.*, **1**, something unusually large; **2**, a big lie. Also, **whop′per**, *Pfd. S.*

whap-ping (hwŏp′ĭng), *p.adj.* unusually large; startling; daring. Also, **whop′ping**, *Pfd. S.*

wharf (hwôrf), *n.* [*pl.* wharves (hwôrvz); wharfs (hwôrfs)], a structure built at the water's edge, for loading or unloading ships; a pier or quay.

wharf-age (hwôr′fāj), *n.* **1**, the fee collected for the use of a wharf or pier; **2**, the entire wharf space at a port.

wharf-in-ger (hwôr′fĭn-jẽr), *n.* the owner of a wharf.

what (hwŏt), *adj.* **1**, in interrogative use, asking for selection from an indefinite number or amount; as, *what* trade does he follow? *what* money have you? **2**, in exclamatory use, how strange or unusual; as, *what* recklessness! **3**, that or those which: having the force of a demonstrative adjective plus a relative pronoun; as, give me *what* books you have:—*pron.* **1**, a neuter compound relative, that or those which; the thing or things that; as, give him *what* he wants; **2**, the neuter interrogative pronoun, singular and plural, with the meaning what thing or things, asking for selection from an indefinite number; as, *what* is wrong? *what* are you doing? **3**, in exclamatory use, what things; how much; as, *what* he has suffered!—*adv.* **1**, with exclamatory force, how; as, *what* bright colors! **2**, with interrogative force, how much; in what way; as, *what* does it profit a man? **3**, partly: often followed by *with*; as, *what* with the cold and *what* with the darkness, we could go no farther:—*conj. Obs.*, as far as: **but what**, *Colloq.* and *Dial.*, but that; as, I do not know *but what* it is true: **what though**, even supposing that; even though:—*interj.* indicating astonishment, dismay, indignation, etc., used: **1**, alone; as, *what!* the boat stolen? **2**, in certain expressions; as, *what* the deuce!

what-ev-er (hwŏt-ĕv′ẽr), *pron.* **1**, all that; anything that; as, give *whatever* you can; **2**, no matter what; as, we must have sugar, *whatever* its cost:—*adj.* **1**, of any kind; as, no truth *whatever* in it; **2**, no matter what kind of; as, *whatever* property he has, sell it.

what-not (hwŏt′nŏt″), *n.* an article of furniture consisting of shelves for books, ornaments, etc.

what-so-ev-er (hwŏt″sō-ĕv′ẽr), *pron.* and *adj.* the formal or emphatic form of *whatever*.

wheal (hwēl), *n.* a discolored swelling on the flesh, as from the stroke of a whip. Also, **weal**; *Pfd. S.*, **wale**.

wheat (hwēt), *n.* **1**, any of several varieties of a cultivated grass, the most important of the cereals; **2**, the seed of this grass, used in the making of flour and cereals. —*adj.* **wheat′en**.

whee-dle (hwē′dl), *v.t.* [*p.t.* and *p.p.* -dled (-dld), *p.pr.* -dling], **1**, to flatter; cajole; coax; as, she *wheedled* her father into consenting; **2**, to get by coaxing or flattery; as, she *wheedled* permission out of her father: —*v.i.* to coax.—*n.* **whee′dling**.

wheel (hwēl), *n.* **1**, a circular frame or body capable of turning on a central axis or axle; **2**, a circular frame for steering, as in a boat or an automobile; **3**, a bicycle; **4**, an old instrument of torture; **5**, a circular revolving firework; **6**, a complete turning around; **7**, in *pl.*, the inner workings of anything; as, he soon had the *wheels* of the business running smoothly; **8**, a maneuver in drill in which troops in line change direction without destroying their alignment: **wheel base**, the distance between the front and rear axles of a vehicle, as an automobile:—*v.t.* **1**, to move on wheels; **2**, to cause to turn, as a line of troops:—*v.i.* **1**, to turn on, or as if on, an axis; as, to *wheel* about; **2**, to move on wheels, as a vehicle.—*p.adj.* **wheeled**.

wheel-bar-row (hwēl′băr″ō), *n.* a light vehicle with two handles and usually one wheel, used to carry small loads: also called *barrow*.

wheel-er (hwēl′ẽr), *n.* **1**, one who moves a wheeled vehicle; **2**, a wheel horse.

wheel horse **1**, the horse nearest to the vehicle drawn, when there is a leader; **2**, hence, the person who bears the brunt of the hard work in an undertaking.

wheel-house (hwēl′hous″), *n.* a small structure on the forward deck of a ship, to shelter the helmsman.

wheel-man (hwēl′măn), *n.* [*pl.* wheelmen (-mĕn)], **1**, one who rides a bicycle; **2**, the steersman of a boat.

wheel-wright (hwēl′rīt″), *n.* one who makes or repairs wheels and vehicles with wheels.

wheeze (hwēz), *v.i.* [*p.t.* and *p.p.* wheezed (hwēzd), *p.pr.* wheez′ing], **1**, to breathe noisily and with difficulty; **2**, to make a whistling noise; as, the pump *wheezes*:—*n.* a whistling or gasping breath, as in asthma.

wheez-y (hwēz′ĭ), *adj.* [*comp.* wheez′i-er, *superl.* wheez′i-est], affected with difficult breathing.—*n.* **wheez′i-ness**.

whelk (hwĕlk), *n.* any of a number of large, spiral-shelled, marine gastropods, some of which are edible.

whelm (hwĕlm), *v.t.* to overpower, as with a mass of water; engulf.

whelp (hwĕlp), *n.* **1**, the young of a dog, lion, fox, etc.; a cub; **2**, a worthless child or youth: used contemptuously:—*v.t.* to give birth to (a whelp):—*v.i.* to bring forth whelps, or cubs.

when (hwĕn), *adv.* **1**, in interrogative use, at or during what time; as, *when* are you coming? how soon; as, *when* shall you see him? how long ago; as, *when* did you see him last? **2**, in relative use, at which: used of time; as, the hour *when* he arrived; at or after the time at which; as, *when* he came, it was too late; on any occasion that; whenever; at whatever time; as, "*when* Greek meets Greek"; as soon as; as, *when* the war is over:—*conj.* whereas; while on the contrary, etc.; as, he gave me ten dollars *when* he owed me only five:—*n.* what time; as, since *when* have you been here?

whence (hwĕns), *adv.* **1**, in interrogative use, from what place, source, or origin; hence, for what reason; **2**, in relative use, from which; as, the place *whence* I came.

whence-so-ev-er (hwĕns″sō-ĕv′ẽr), *adv.* and *conj.* from no matter what place or origin; also, because of; for whatever reason.

when-ev-er (hwĕn-ĕv′ẽr), *adv.* and *conj.* at whatever time. Also, *Poetic*, **when-e′er** (hwĕn-âr′; -ār′).

when-so-ev-er (hwĕn″sō-ĕv′ẽr), *adv.* and *conj.* at no matter what time; whenever.

where (hwâr), *adv.* **1**, in interrogative use, at or in what place or places; as, *where* do we live? hence, in what part; in what respect; as, *where* am I wrong? to what place; whither; as, *where* are you going? **2**, in relative use, in, at, or to which: used of place; as, the house *where* I lived; to the place in, at, or to which; wherever; as, go *where* you are called:—*conj.* whereas; as, he did much, *where* we expected little:—*n.* the place at or in which something occurs; situation.

-where (-hwâr), *adv. suffix*, indicating a place or direction: compounded with adjectives such as *some* or *any*; as, some*where*; any*where*; no*where*.

where- (hwâr-), *prefix*, used in combination with a preposition, in place of a relative or interrogative, as *which* or *whom*; as, *where*of; *where*by; *where*fore.

where-a-bouts (hwâr′ȧ-bouts″), *adv.* about where; near what place:—*n. pl.*, commonly used as *sing.*, the place where a person or thing is; as, her *whereabouts* is unknown. Also, **where′a-bout″**.

where-as (hwâr-ăz′), *conj.* **1**, considering that; since; it being the case that; **2**, while on the contrary; the case being that; as, he said he was late, *whereas* in reality he was early.

where-at (hwâr-ăt′), *adv.* **1**, in relative use, at which, or upon which; whereupon; **2**, in interrogative use, at what; as, *whereat* did he take offense?

where-by (hwâr-bī′), *adv.* **1**, in relative use, by which; as, means *whereby* to help; **2**, in interrogative use, by what; how; as, *whereby* shall we be saved?

where-fore (hwâr′fōr), *adv.* **1**, in relative use, for which reason; therefore; **2**, in interrogative use, why:—*n.* a cause or reason; as, the whys and *wherefores*.

where-in (hwâr-ĭn′), *adv.* **1**, in relative use, in which; in which time, place, respect, etc.; **2**, in interrogative use, in what; as, *wherein* am I mistaken?

where-of (hwâr-ŏv′; hwâr-ŏf′), *adv.* **1**, in relative use, of which; of whom; **2**, in interrogative use, of what.

where-on (hwâr-ŏn′), *adv.* **1**, in relative use, on which; **2**, in interrogative use, on what; as, *whereon* do you rely?

where-so-ev-er (hwâr″sō-ĕv′ẽr), *adv.* in or to whatsoever place; wherever; as, *wheresoever* thou goest.

where-to (hwâr-tōō′), *adv.* **1**, in relative use, to which; **2**, in interrogative use, to what, or to what end or place.

where-up-on (hwâr″ŭ-pŏn′), *adv.* **1**, in relative use, upon which;

as the result of, or after, which; as, *whereupon* he rose to speak; **2,** in interrogative use, upon what; upon what grounds.

wher-ev-er (hwâr-ĕv′ẽr), *adv.* at, to, or in, whatever place.

where-with (hwâr-wĭ*th*′; hwâr-wĭth′), *adv.* **1,** in relative use, with which; **2,** in interrogative use, with what.

where-with-al (hwâr″wĭ*th*-ôl′), *adv.* **1,** in relative use, with which; **2,** in interrogative use, with what:—*n.* that with which a thing can be bought or done; as, he has the *wherewithal.* Also, *adv.* **where-with′.**

wher-ry (hwĕr′ĭ), *n.* [*pl.* wherries (-ĭz)], **1,** a light, shallow rowboat; **2,** a light barge or fishing vessel.

whet (hwĕt), *v.t.* [*p.t.* and *p.p.* whet′ted, *p.pr.* whet′ting], **1,** to sharpen by rubbing, as a knife; **2,** to make keen or eager; as, sea air *whets* the appetite:—*n.* **1,** anything which, taken in a small amount, stimulates an appetite for more; **2,** the act of grinding or sharpening a tool or the like.

wheth-er (hwĕ*th*′ẽr), *pron.* and *adj. Archaic,* which (of two) or which one (of two):—*conj.* used to introduce the first of two or more alternatives, having *or,* or *or whether,* as its correlative; as, I do not know *whether* this or that is the true reason.

whet-stone (hwĕt′stōn″), *n.* a stone for sharpening edged tools.

whew (hwū; hū), *interj.* an exclamation of surprise, disgust, or dismay; as, *whew!* how the wind blows.

whey (hwā), *n.* the thin, sweet, watery part of milk, separated from the curds, as in cheese making.—*adj.* **whey′ey.**

which (hwĭch), *pron.* **1,** used as an interrogative, asking for selection from a definite, limited number; as, *which* of these men is your friend? **2,** used as a relative, introducing a subordinate clause when the antecedent is not a person; **3,** used as a compound relative, the one that; as, point out *which* is yours; **4,** *Archaic,* in relative use, who or whom; as, Our Father *which* art in heaven:—*adj.* in interrogative use, asking for selection from a limited, definite number; as, *which* house is yours?

which-ev-er (hwĭch-ĕv′ẽr), *pron.* whether one or the other; whether one or another. Also, **which″so-ev′er.**

whid-ah bird (hwĭd′*à*), any of a number of West African weaver birds of which the male is distinguished by drooping tail feathers which, in the breeding season, attain to twice the body length. Also, **wid′ow bird.**

whiff (hwĭf), *n.* **1,** a sudden breath or blast, as of air or smoke; a light puff; **2,** a faint odor; a trace:—*v.t.* and *v.i.* to puff or blow out in sudden breaths.—*n.* **whiff′er.**

whif-fle (hwĭf′l), *v.i.* [*p.t.* and *p.p.* -fled (-ld), *p.pr.* -fling], **1,** to blow unsteadily or in gusts, as the wind; **2,** hence, to be fickle or unsteady.—*n.* **whif′fler.**

whif-fle-tree (hwĭf′l-trē″), *n.* a swinging, crosswise bar at the front of a carriage or wagon to which the traces of the harness are fastened. Also, **whip′ple-tree″,** *Pfd. S.*

Whig (hwĭg), *n.* **1,** a member of a former political party in the U. S. that favored a protective tariff, and was succeeded by the present Republican party; **2,** a supporter of the American Revolution; **3,** a member of a liberal political party which originated in England in the 17th century, and developed into the Liberal party: distinguished from *Tory:*—*adj.* pertaining to Whigs.—*adj.* **Whig′gish.**—*adv.* **Whig′gish-ly.**—*n.* **Whig′ger-y.**

while (hwīl), *n.* **1,** a period of time; **2,** time or pains required to do something: used in the expressions *worth while* and *worth one's while:*—*conj.* **1,** as long as; during the time that; at the same time that; **2,** although; whereas:—*v.t.* [*p.t.* and *p.p.* whiled (hwīld), *p.pr.* whil′ing], to cause to pass; spend; as, to *while* away time.

whiles (hwīlz), *adv. Scot.,* sometimes:—*conj. Archaic,* while.

whi-lom (hwī′lŭm), *adv. Archaic,* formerly; once:—*adj.* former; sometime; as, his *whilom* friends deserted him.

whilst (hwīlst), *conj.* while: an old variant, still widely used in England.

whim (hwĭm), *n.* a fancy; caprice; notion; a sudden, often unreasonable, wish.

whim-per (hwĭm′pẽr), *v.i.* to weep with a low, whining, broken voice:—*n.* a low, broken complaint; fretful whining.—*n.* **whim′per-er.**

whim-sey (hwĭm′zĭ), *n.* [*pl.* whimseys (-zĭz)], a caprice; a sudden freak; an unreasonable notion. Also, **whim′sy.**

whim-si-cal (hwĭm′zĭ-kăl), *adj.* freakish; full of odd notions; capricious; queerly humorous.—*adv.* **whim′si-cal-ly.**—*n.* **whim′si-cal-ness.**—*n.* **whim″si-cal′i-ty.**

whin (hwĭn), *n.* in England, the common gorse, or furze.

whine (hwīn), *v.i.* [*p.t.* and *p.p.* whined (hwīnd), *p.pr.* whin′ing], **1,** to show distress by a plaintive, nasal cry; **2,** to murmur in a mean or childish manner; complain; talk in a plaintive, nasal tone:—*v.t.* to utter in a fretful or complaining way:—*n.* **1,** a plaintive tone; **2,** the act or sound of weak, fretful complaining.—*n.* **whin′er.**

whin-ny (hwĭn′ĭ), *v.i.* [*p.t.* and *p.p.* -nied (-ĭd), *p.pr.* -ny-ing], to neigh: said of a horse:—*n.* [*pl.* whinnies (-ĭz)], the usual call of a horse; a neigh, esp. a gentle neigh.

whin-stone (hwĭn′stōn″), *n.* locally in England, any of various kinds of unusually hard, resistant, basaltic rock.

whip (hwĭp), *v.t.* [*p.t.* and *p.p.* whipped or whipt (hwĭpt), *p.pr.* whip′ping], **1,** to strike, as with a lash or rod; beat; **2,** to beat into froth, as cream; **3,** to beat out; separate, as grain from chaff; **4,** to fish (a body of water) with a rod and line, making repeated, lashing casts; **5,** to take forcibly; snatch; jerk: usually with *off, out,* or the like; as, she *whipped* off her cape; **6,** to sew with an overcasting stitch, as a seam in a fabric; **7,** to overlay, or wrap, as a cord or rope, with a cord or thread going round and round it; **8,** *Colloq.,* to defeat in a contest; conquer:—*v.i.* **1,** to thrash about, as a loose sail; **2,** to move quickly; whisk; as, the fox *whipped* out of sight:—*n.* **1,** a flexible rod, often tapering to a lash; **2,** anyone who makes use of a whip, as a driver; **3,** a hoist, as in coal mines; **4,** a member of a legislature whose duty it is to keep the members of his party together: **whip hand,** in driving, the hand used to hold the whip; hence, advantage of position; mastery.—*n.* **whip′per.**

Whipped End of Rope

whip-cord (hwĭp′kôrd″), *n.* a hard cord, often used for whiplashes.

whip-lash (hwĭp′lăsh″), *n.* the striking part of a whip.

whip-per–in (hwĭp′ẽr=ĭn′), *n.* [*pl.* whippers-in (-ẽrz=)], **1,** a huntsman who has charge of the hounds; **2,** one who serves as a whip in a legislature.

whip-per-snap-per (hwĭp′ẽr-snăp″ẽr), *n. Colloq.,* a small, insignificant person who feels important.

whip-pet (hwĭp′ĕt), *n.* **1,** a very fleet kind of dog resembling a greyhound, but smaller: used for racing; **2,** a small tank or armored caterpillar tractor, used in war.

whip-ple-tree (hwĭp'l-trē"), *n.* a swinging crosswise bar at the front of a carriage or wagon to the ends of which the traces of the harness are fastened; a swingletree. Also, **whif'fle-tree"**.

whip-poor-will (hwĭp'pōōr-wĭl"), *n.* a small American bird, named from its cry, heard only at night.

whip-saw (hwĭp'sô"), *n.* a long, narrow saw set in a frame.

whip-stock (hwĭp'stŏk"), *n.* the handle of a whip.

whir (hwûr), *v.i.* [*p.t.* and *p.p.* whirred (hwûrd), *p.pr.* whir'ring], to fly, revolve, or otherwise move quickly with a buzzing noise:—*n.* a buzzing or whizzing noise caused by rapid motion; as, the *whir* of machinery.

whirl (hwûrl), *v.t.* **1**, to cause to revolve rapidly; **2**, to cause to move rapidly, with a revolving motion; as, the wind *whirled* the leaves away:—*v.i.* **1**, to revolve with great speed; as, the earth *whirls* on its axis; **2**, to move along swiftly, esp. on wheels:—*n.* **1**, a rapid rotation or circular motion; **2**, something revolving rapidly; as, a *whirl* of dust; the *whirl* of the dance.—*n.* **whirl'er**.

whirl-i-gig (hwûr'lĭ-gĭg"), *n.* **1**, anything that turns around rapidly; **2**, a child's toy that spins or whirls round; **3**, a merry-go-round.

whirl-pool (hwûrl'pōōl"), *n.* an eddy in water, sometimes with a central depression into which floating objects are drawn by suction.

whirl-wind (hwûrl'wĭnd"), *n.* **1**, a violent wind moving with a circular current, or with a whirling, spiral motion; a tornado; cyclone; **2**, a sudden, violent rush.

whisk (hwĭsk), *v.t.* **1**, to sweep or brush rapidly; **2**, to move or carry off with a quick, sweeping motion:—*v.i.* to move rapidly and nimbly; as, the squirrel *whisked* up the tree:—*n.* **1**, the act of brushing with a quick motion; **2**, a quick, nimble movement; **3**, a small bunch or bundle of hair, grass, or straw, used as a brush; **4**, hence, a small broom or brush.—*n.* ¹**whisk'er**.

²**whisk-er** (hwĭsk'ẽr), *n.* **1**, usually in *pl.*, a hair growing on the side of a man's face, or on his upper lip or his chin; **2**, a long, bristly hair growing near the mouth of a cat, rat, or other animal.—*adj.* **whisk'ered**.

whis-ky (hwĭs'kĭ), *n.* [*pl.* whiskies (-kĭz)], a strong alcoholic liquor distilled from grain or potatoes. Also, **whis'key**.

whis-per (hwĭs'pẽr), *v.i.* **1**, to speak in a low voice; **2**, to speak softly or under the breath; **3**, to make a hissing sound:—*v.t.* to say under the breath; speak privately:—*n.* **1**, a low, soft tone of voice; toneless speech; **2**, a private disclosure; **3**, a hint or suggestion; **4**, a soft, rustling sound; as, the *whisper* of the trees.—*n.* **whis'per-er**.

¹**whist** (hwĭst), *n.* a card game for four persons, opposite pairs being partners, in which the trump suit is that of the last card dealt, and the object is to take the greatest possible number of tricks.

²**whist** (hwĭst), *interj. Archaic,* hush! be silent!—*adj. Archaic,* hushed or quiet; as, the winds are *whist*.

whis-tle (hwĭs'l), *v.i.* [*p.t.* and *p.p.* -tled (-ld), *p.pr.* -tling], **1**, to make a shrill sound by forcing the breath through the teeth or puckered lips, or by forcing air, steam, or the like, through a small aperture; **2**, to make any similar shrill sound; **3**, to go or pass with a sharp, shrill sound; as, the wind *whistled* through the woods:—*v.t.* **1**, to utter by whistling; as, to *whistle* a tune; **2**, to call or signal by whistling; as, the hunter *whistled* his dog home:—*n.* **1**, the shrill noise made by forcing air, steam, etc., through an opening; **2**, an instrument to produce such a sound.—*n.* **whis'tler**.

whit (hwĭt), *n.* the smallest particle; speck; jot; as, not a *whit*.

white (hwīt), *adj.* **1**, of the color of clean snow: opp. of *black;* **2**, hence, pure; innocent; **3**, silvery; gray: said of the hair; **4**, pale; bloodless; **5**, fair-skinned; of the Caucasian race: **white elephant,** *Colloq.*, anything difficult or costly to keep; a burdensome possession: **to show the white feather,** to betray cowardice: **white flag,** a flag of truce: **white lie,** a trivial falsehood, told to save the feelings of another:—*n.* **1**, the color of clean snow: opp. of *black;* **2**, a white pigment; **3**, a Caucasian, or white man; **4**, the albumen of an egg; **5**, the white part of an eyeball.—*n.* **white'ness.**—*adj.* **whit'ish.**

white ant any of a family of pale-colored, soft-bodied, social insects, most abundant in Africa, and destructive to wooden structures, books, etc.

white-bait (hwīt'bāt"), *n.* [*pl.* whitebait], the young of the herring, and of several other fishes: caught while small and considered a delicacy as food.

white-cap (hwīt'kăp"), *n.* a wave crest breaking into foam.

white-fish (hwīt'fĭsh"), *n.* **1**, any of several edible, fresh-water fishes of the salmon family; **2**, locally, any of several other fishes of fresh or salt water.

White Fri-ar a Carmelite monk: so called from the robe worn.

White House the residence, at Washington, of the President of the U. S.: officially called *Executive Mansion.*

white lead **1**, a heavy white substance having lead carbonate as a base, used in the manufacture of paints; **2**, natural lead carbonate.

white–liv-ered (hwīt'=lĭv"ẽrd), *adj.* **1**, of a pallid, feeble appearance; **2**, timid; cowardly.

whit-en (hwīt'n), *v.t.* to make white, blanch:—*v.i.* to become white.

white plague tuberculosis, esp. of the lungs.

white slave a woman held in prostitution against her will, for the gain of another.—**white slav'er-y.**

white-throat (hwīt'thrōt"), *n.* any of several European singing birds of the warbler family.

white-wash (hwīt'wŏsh"), *n.* a white mixture of lime and water, for coating walls, ceilings, fences, etc.:—*v.t.* **1**, to cover with a coat of lime and water; **2**, hence, to gloss over in order to hide faults.—*n.* **white'wash"er.**

white-wings (hwīt'wĭngz"), *n.pl. Slang,* street cleaners.

white-wood (hwīt'wōōd"), *n.* **1**, any of a number of trees having light-colored wood, as the tulip tree; **2**, the timber of such a tree.

whith-er (hwĭ*th*'ẽr), *adv.* **1**, to what place; as, *whither* goest thou? **2**, wherever; as, go *whither* you will; **3**, to which (place): used relatively; as, the place *whither* you sent me: **no whither,** to no place.

whith-er-so-ev-er (hwĭ*th*"ẽr-sō-ĕv'ẽr), *adv.* wherever; to whatever place; as, I go *whithersoever* you go.

whit-ing (hwīt'ĭng), *n.* **1**, any of various marine food fishes; **2**, a powdered preparation of chalk used in the manufacture of putty, in polishing silverware, etc.

whit-low (hwĭt'lō), *n.* **1**, a felon; **2**, a certain foot disease in animals.

Whit-sun (hwĭt'sŭn), *adj.* pertaining to, or observed at, Whitsuntide.

Whit-sun-day (hwĭt′sn-dā; hwĭt″sŭn′-dā), *n.* the seventh Sunday after Easter, commemorating the day of Pentecost. Also, **Whit″-Sun′day.**

Whit-sun-tide (hwĭt′sn-tīd″), *n.* the week following Whitsunday; the eighth week after Easter. Also, **Whit′sun Tide.**

whit-tle (hwĭt′l), *v.t.* [*p.t.* and *p.p.* -tled (-ld), *p.pr.* -tling], **1,** to cut, shape, or sharpen with a knife; as, to *whittle* a stick; **2,** to reduce bit by bit by cutting away:—*v.i.* to cut aimlessly, as at a piece of wood.

whiz (hwĭz), *v.i.* [*p.t.* and *p.p.* whizzed (hwĭzd), *p.pr.* whiz′zing], **1,** to make a humming or hissing noise, as from rapid motion; **2,** to move rapidly with a humming or hissing sound:—*v.t.* to cause to whiz:—*n.* a humming noise accompanying rapid motion; as, the *whiz* of a bullet: **whiz bang,** *Slang,* a high-explosive shell. Also, **whizz.**

who (ho͞o), *pron.* [*nom.* who, *poss.* whose (ho͞oz), *obj.* whom (ho͞om)], **1,** in interrogative use, what person or persons; as, *who* was at the theater with you? I know *who* was there; also, what sort of person or persons; as, *who* am I to be so honored? **2,** in relative use, that; as, Mr. Smith, *who* lives near me; **3,** whoever: used as a compound or indefinite relative, with its antecedent implied; as, *who* heard and saw, immediately believed.

whoa (hwō), *interj.* stop! hold! a call to a horse. Also, **ho,** *Pfd. S.*

who-ev-er (ho͞o-ĕv′ẽr), *pron.* anyone or everyone who; whatever person or persons; as, *whoever* wishes it.

whole (hōl), *adj.* **1,** *Archaic,* in good health; hale and sound in body; **2,** not defective or broken; intact; **3,** complete; containing all the parts: **whole note,** in music, a note written ○, taking up a whole measure in four-four time: also called *semibreve:* **whole number,** an integer; a number expressed without the use of a fraction: distinguished from *fraction:*—*n.* **1,** all the parts of something taken together; a total; **2,** a unity formed from an organization of parts; as, the body is an organic *whole.*—*n.* **whole′ness.**

whole–heart-ed (hōl′-härt″ĕd), *adj.* **1,** sincere; having one single purpose; **2,** earnest; energetic; hearty, as applause.—*adv.* **whole″–heart′ed-ly.** —*n.* **whole″–heart′ed-ness.**

whole-sale (hōl′sāl″), *n.* the sale of goods in large quantities: opp. of *retail:*—*adj.* **1,** buying or selling in large quantities; **2,** widely spread; indiscriminate.

whole-some (hōl′sŭm), *adj.* **1,** tending to promote health of body or mind, or good morals; as, *wholesome* food or books; **2,** characteristic of, or suggesting, health; as, a *wholesome* appearance.—*adv.* **whole′some-ly.**—*n.* **whole′some-ness.**

whol-ly (hōl′lĭ; hōl′ĭ), *adv.* completely; entirely; totally; as, he is not *wholly* satisfied; he is not *wholly* bad.

whom (ho͞om), *pron.* objective case, singular and plural, of the pronoun *who.*

whom-so-ev-er (ho͞om″sō-ĕv′ẽr), *pron.* the objective case of the pronoun *whosoever.*

whoop (ho͞op), *v.i.* **1,** to utter a loud, shrill, and prolonged cry; shout; halloo; **2,** to make the gasping sound produced after a fit of coughing, as in whooping cough:—*v.t.* to drive, call, or mock with loud cries or shouts:—*n.* **1,** a loud shout, as of pursuit, attack, triumph, etc.; **2,** a gasping sound following a paroxysm of coughing; **3,** the hoot of an owl: **war whoop,** an Indian battle cry; also, any horrible yell.—*n.* **whoop′er.**

whoop-ing cough an infectious disease to which children are particularly susceptible: characterized by spasmodic coughing followed by a long, shrill inspiration.

whop (hwŏp), *v.t.* [*p.t.* and *p.p.* whopped (hwŏpt), *p.pr.* whop′ping], *Obs.* or *Dial.,* to thrash or beat:—*v.i. Archaic,* to flop down suddenly:—*n. Obs.* or *Dial.,* **1,** a blow; stroke; **2,** a bump; **3,** noise made by a blow. Also, **whap** (hwŏp).

whop-per (hwŏp′ẽr), *n. Colloq.,* **1,** something unusually large; **2,** a big lie. Also, **whap′per.**

whop-ping (hwŏp′ĭng), *p.adj.* unusually large; startling; daring; as, a *whopping* story. Also, **whap′ping.**

whore (hōr), *n.* a prostitute; harlot: not in polite usage.—*n.* **whore′dom.**

whorl (hwûrl; hwôrl), *n.* **1,** a circular arrangement of leaves, petals, etc., around a common center; **2,** one of the turns of a spiral shell.—*adj.* **whorled.**

whor-tle-ber-ry (hwûr′tl-bĕr″ĭ), *n.* [*pl.* whortleberries (-ĭz)], **1,** any of several low-growing shrubs bearing small, firm, glossy black berries; the huckleberry; **2,** the fruit of this plant; **3,** in Europe, any of several blueberry plants; the bilberry; also, its fruit.

whose (ho͞oz), *pron.* of whom; sometimes, of which; possessive case, singular and plural, of *who* and *which.*

whose-so-ev-er (ho͞oz″sō-ĕv′ẽr), *pron.* possessive case of *whosoever;* as, *whosesoever* it may be.

who-so (ho͞o′sō), *pron.* any person who; whoever.

who-so-ev-er (ho͞o″sō-ĕv′ẽr), *pron.* any person who; whoever.

why (hwī), *adv.* **1,** used interrogatively, for what cause, with what motive, or for what purpose; on what account; wherefore; as, *why* did you do this? tell me *why* you did this; **2,** used relatively, on account of which; for which; as, tell me the reason *why* he did this:—*n.* [*pl.* whys (hwīz)], a reason; as, the *whys* and wherefores.

wick (wĭk), *n.* the cotton cord, tape, etc., through which oil in a lamp or candle passes, and which is lighted at the top.

wick-ed (wĭk′ĕd), *adj.* **1,** evil; sinful; immoral; as, a *wicked* heart; **2,** *Colloq.,* in a playful sense, mischievous.—*adv.* **wick′ed-ly.**—*n.* **wick′ed-ness.**

Syn. infamous, vicious. (See bad.)

wick-er (wĭk′ẽr), *n.* **1,** a pliant twig; esp., a pliant willow rod; **2,** such twigs woven into baskets, furniture, etc.:—*adj.* made of wicker; as, a *wicker* table.

wick-er-work (wĭk′ẽr-wûrk″), *n.* **1,** a fabric made of woven or plaited twigs, esp. of osier; **2,** collectively, articles made of wicker.

wick-et (wĭk′ĕt), *n.* **1,** a small door; a gate, esp. one in a larger gate or door; **2,** in cricket, either of the two frames at which the ball is bowled; **3,** an arch in a croquet set.

wide (wīd), *adj.* **1,** of considerable extent from side to side; broad; as, a *wide* road; also, stretching for a given space at right angles to length; **2,** vast; spacious; as, a *wide* domain; **3,** inclusive of much; comprehensive; as, a *wide* acquaintance; **4,** far from a point aimed at; as, *wide* of the mark; **5,** open; expanded; as, *wide* eyes:—*adv.* **1,** widely; far; as, the news spread *wide;* **2,** to a great extent; as, *wide* open; fully open; as, fling the gate *wide;* **3,** far from the point aimed at:—*n.* in cricket, a ball bowled so as to be out of the reach of the batsman on either side of the wicket.—*adv.* **wide′ly.**—*n.* **wide′ness.**

wid-en (wīd′n), *v.t.* to make broader; spread open:—*v.i.* to become broader or larger; as, here the river *widens.*

wide-spread (wīd′sprĕd″), *adj.* scattered far and wide; extensive.

widg-eon (wĭj′ŭn), *n.* any of several fresh-water ducks.

wid-ow (wĭd′ō), *n.* **1**, a woman who has lost her husband by death and has not married again; **2**, in cards, an extra hand dealt on the table: **grass widow,** *Colloq.*, a woman whose husband is divorced or otherwise separated from her: **widow's weeds,** black clothing worn by a widow:—*v.t.* to bereave of a husband or wife; as, a *widowed* mother.

wid-ow bird any of a number of small West African weaver birds, named from their somber coloring. See **whid′ah bird,** *Pfd. S.*

wid-ow-er (wĭd′ō-ẽr), *n.* a man whose wife has died and who has not married again.

wid-ow-hood (wĭd′ō-ho͝od), *n.* **1**, the state of having lost a husband by death; **2**, the time during which a woman is a widow.

width (wĭdth), *n.* the extent of a thing from side to side; breadth.

wield (wēld), *v.t.* **1**, to use with the hands; as, to *wield* a hammer; **2**, to exercise, as influence.—*n.* **wield′er.**

wife (wīf), *n.* [*pl.* wives (wīvz)], a woman joined to a man in marriage; a married woman: correlative of *husband.*—*n.* **wife′hood.** —*adj.* **wife′ly.**

¹wig (wĭg), *n.* an artificial covering of hair for the head, to conceal baldness, to adorn, or to form part of official dress.—*adj.* **wigged.**—*adj.* **wig′less.**

²wig (wĭg), *v.t.* [*p.t.* and *p.p.* wigged (wĭgd), *p.pr.* wig′ging], *Colloq.*, to scold; censure sharply.—*n.* **wig′ging.**

wig-an (wĭg′ăn), *n.* a kind of cotton canvas, used to stiffen parts of garments, as lapels.

wig-gle (wĭg′l), *v.t.* and *v.i.* [*p.t.* and *p.p.* -gled (-ld), *p.pr.* -gling], *Colloq.*, to move from side to side with a quick, jerky, shaky motion; wriggle.

wig-gler (wĭg′lẽr), *n.* **1**, one who or that which moves jerkily from side to side; **2**, the larva, or young, of the mosquito.

wight (wīt), *n.* a human being: archaic, except in jest.

wig-wag (wĭg′wăg″), *v.t.* and *v.i.* [*p.t.* and *p.p.* -wagged″ (-wăgd″), *p.pr.* -wag″ging], **1**, to move back and forth; **2**, to signal with flags or movable lights, moved or flashed according to a code, as in the army or navy.—*n.* **wig′wag″ger.**

wig-wam (wĭg′wôm; wĭg′wŏm), *n.* a hut made of poles covered with bark or skins of animals, used by the eastern American Indians.

wik-i-up (wĭk′ĭ-ŭp″), *n.* among certain North American Indians of the west and southwest, a hut loosely constructed of boughs, reed mats, etc. Also, **wick′i-up″.**

wild (wīld), *adj.* **1**, living in its natural state; untamed; as, a *wild* animal; **2**, uncultivated; as, *wild* flowers; **3**, not civilized; savage; as, the *wild* men of Borneo; **4**, violent; turbulent; uncontrolled; passionate; as, a *wild* wind; *wild* youth; **5**, fantastic; unreasonable; as, a *wild* scheme; **6**, disorderly; reckless; as, a *wild* life; **7**, wide of the mark; as, a *wild* shot; **8**, *Colloq.*, eager; as, I am *wild* to see you:—*n.*, usually in *pl.*, a desert or wilderness; as, the *wilds* of Africa.—*adv.* **wild′ly.**—*n.* **wild′ness.**

wild boar an untamed, savage European hog, from which the domestic hog has been developed.

wild cat any of numerous species of the smaller savage cats, widely spread over the world, as the lynx and the Texas wild cat: also written *wildcat:* **wildcat,** *adj.* **1**, out of control: used of a runaway locomotive or one running contrary to orders; **2**, *Colloq.*, risky; highly speculative or fraudulent, as a stock promotion.

wilde-beest (wīld′bēst″; *Du.* vĭl′dĕ-bāst″), *n.* a Dutch name for the African antelope, or gnu.

wil-der-ness (wĭl′dẽr-nĕs), *n.* **1**, a region neither cultivated nor inhabited; a desert or waste; **2**, a large, confused mass; as, a *wilderness* of flowers.

wild-fire (wīld′fīr″), *n.* **1**, any fire hard to quench; **2**, a skin disease of sheep.

wild-goose chase a useless pursuit or foolish attempt.

wild-ing (wīl′dĭng), *n.* a wild plant or its fruit:—*adj. Poetic*, uncultivated.

wild-wood (wīld′wo͝od), *n.* a primeval or unfrequented wood.

wile (wīl), *n.* a sly trick; a subtle or crafty maneuver:—*v.t.* [*p.t.* and *p.p.* wiled (wīld), *p.pr.* wil′ing], **1**, to wheedle; beguile; as, to *wile* the secret from him; **2**, to pass (time): with *away:* incorrect for *while.*

wil-ful (wĭl′fo͝ol), *adj.* **1**, bent on having one's own way; stubborn; obstinate; as, a *wilful* child; **2**, intentional; deliberate; as, *wilful* murder. Also, **will′ful.**—*adv.* **wil′ful-ly.**—*n.* **wil′ful-ness.**

will (wĭl), *n.* **1**, the power by which the mind decides upon, and directs its energies to carry out, an action; **2**, control over impulse; as, a strong *will;* **3**, choice; desire; determination upon a special end or purpose; as, where there's a *will* there's a way; **4**, determination by an authority; hence, a command; decree; **5**, a legal document disposing of one's property at death:—*v.aux.* [*p.t.* would (wo͝od); no other parts], followed by the infinitive without *to* and used: **1**, to form the simple future tense in the second and third persons; **2**, to express promise or determination in the first person; as, I *will* do it, whether you approve or not; **3**, to express a polite command; as, you *will* please take this report to the colonel; **4**, in questions, in the second and third persons, when expected in the answer; as, *will* you go with me? yes, I *will:*—*v.t.* [*p.t.* and *p.p.* willed (wĭld), *p.pr.* will′ing], **1**, to decide; determine: often with *to* and an infinitive; as, he recovered because he *willed* to do so; **2**, to give at death; bequeath; as, to *will* an estate; **3**, to influence by exerting the power of will or by hypnotic power; as, she *willed* him to turn around:—*v.i.* to wish; desire; prefer.

will-ing (wĭl′ĭng), *p.adj.* **1**, cheerfully ready; as, *willing* to serve; **2**, given or done freely or gladly; as, a *willing* service.—*adv.* **will′ing-ly.**—*n.* **will′ing-ness.**

will-o'-the-wisp (wĭl′=ō=*th*ē=wĭsp′), *n.* **1**, a light that flits above marshy ground; a jack-o'-lantern; an ignis fatuus; **2**, hence, anything that misleads, or that escapes one's grasp.

wil-low (wĭl′ō), *n.* **1**, any of several trees and shrubs usually growing near water and having slender branches which are easily bent and twisted; **2**, the wood of this tree: **weeping willow,** a willow, native in Asia, having slender, drooping branches: **pussy willow,** a small American willow bearing silver-gray catkins: **willow pattern,** a certain pattern, done in blue on white English chinaware, representing a Chinese romantic legend (see illus. next page).

wil-low-herb (wĭl′ō=ûrb″), *n.* an herb with willowlike leaves and racemes of pinkish purple flowers. Also, **wil′low herb.**

wil-low-y (wĭl′ō-ĭ), *adj.* **1**, abounding in willow trees; **2**, like a willow tree; **3**, hence, swaying; slender; graceful.

wil-ly–nil-ly (wĭl′ĭ-nĭl′ĭ), *adv.* willingly or unwillingly; by force of outside influence or authority.

[1]**wilt** (wĭlt), *v.i.* **1**, to wither or droop, as a flower; **2**, to lose strength; become faint or weak:—*v.t.* to cause to wither or droop.

[2]**wilt** (wĭlt), *Archaic*, second person singular of the verb *will;* as, if thou *wilt.*

WILLOW PATTERN

wil-y (wīl′ĭ), *adj.* [*comp.* wil′i-er, *superl.* wil′i-est], cunning; crafty; as, the *wily* fox.—*adv.* **wil′i-ly.**—*n.* **wil′i-ness.**

Syn. cunning, crafty, artful, sly, subtle. To be *wily* is to trap and deceive others by stratagems and tricks; as, a *wily* detective. To be *cunning* is to be shrewd enough to gain one's ends and clever enough to conceal the means used; as, a *cunning* plotter. To be *crafty* requires more alertness and more ability than to be *cunning;* as, a *crafty* statesman. *Artful* people are tricky and indirect, and conceal their purposes behind their words and actions; a child may be *artful. Sly* suggests smooth, wary, and silent *cunning;* a *sly* trick is mean as well as underhand. *Subtle* implies higher mental ability; as, a *subtle* mind.

wim-ble (wĭm′bl), *n.* a gimlet; an auger; any of several boring tools.

wim-ple (wĭm′pl), *n.* a covering of linen, silk, etc., for the neck, chin, and sides of the face, worn by some orders of nuns:—*v.t.* [*p.t.* and *p.p.* -pled (-pld), *p.pr.* -pling], **1**, to clothe with such a covering; **2**, to lay in folds or plaits:—*v.i.* **1**, to lie in folds; **2**, to ripple, as a stream.

WIMPLE (*a*)

win (wĭn), *v.i.* [*p.t.* and *p.p.* won (wŭn), *p.pr.* win′ning], to gain a victory; prevail; as, to *win* in a battle:—*v.t.* **1**, to get by labor; obtain; as, to *win* promotion; earn, as a living; **2**, to gain in a contest; as, he *won* the prize; **3**, to effect, as by perseverance; as, to *win* one's way; **4**, to reach by effort, as a point on a journey; **5**, to persuade; as, try to *win* him over to our side.—*n.* **win′ner.**

Syn. acquire, achieve, attain. (See get.)

wince (wĭns), *v.i.* [*p.t.* and *p.p.* winced (wĭnst), *p.pr.* winc′ing], to shrink or draw back suddenly, as from a blow; flinch:—*n.* the act of flinching.—*n.* **winc′er.**

Syn., *v.* (see flinch).

winch (wĭnch), *n.* **1**, a projecting handle or crank for turning a revolving machine such as the common grindstone; **2**, a hoisting machine in which a rope or chain is wound up on a drum turned by a crank handle.

Win-ches-ter (wĭn′chĕs-tẽr), *n.* a kind of repeating rifle.

[1]**wind** (wĭnd; *Poetic* wīnd), *n.* **1**, a natural current of air; breeze; **2**, an artificial current of air, as that caused by bellows; **3**, breath; ability to breathe; **4**, anything as light as the wind; hence, idle words or threats; **5**, in an orchestra, the brass and wood instruments sounded by blowing; **6**, scent; as, to get *wind* of game; **7**, news; as, to get *wind* of a plot; **8**, gas formed in the digestive organs: **second wind**, a state of regular respiration following the lack of breath that comes shortly after the beginning of continued exertion: **to sail close to the wind**, to sail as closely as possible in the direction from which the wind blows; hence, *Colloq.*, to pursue a course dangerously near to disaster, dishonesty, or the like:—*v.t.* (wĭnd), **1**, to follow by scent; **2**, to expose to the wind; winnow; **3**, to put out of breath; **4**, to rest, as a horse, so as to permit recovery of breath.

[2]**wind** (wīnd; wĭnd), *v.t.* [*p.t.* and *p.p.* wound (wound) or, *Rare*, wind′ed (wīn′dĕd; wĭn′dĕd), *p.pr.* wind′ing], to blow, as a horn, or to cause by blowing, as a blast.

[3]**wind** (wīnd), *v.i.* [*p.t.* and *p.p.* wound (wound) or, *Rare*, wind′ed (wīn′dĕd), *p.pr.* wind′ing], **1**, to turn; keep changing direction; as, the stream *winds* through the valley; **2**, to twine round and round; as, the vine *winds* around the post; **3**, *Colloq.*, to come to an end or conclusion: with *up:*—*v.t.* **1**, to turn; twist; coil: often with *up;* as, to *wind* up a watch; **2**, to twist round and round on something; as, to *wind* a bandage around the arm; **3**, to introduce by artful means; as, he *wound* himself into favor; **4**, to entwine; as, to *wind* a pole with a vine; **5**, to accomplish by turning; as, to *wind* one's course; **6**, *Colloq.*, to conclude; bring to an end: with *up;* as, to *wind* up a business successfully:—*n.* a bend; coil; twist.—*n.* **wind′er.**

wind-age (wĭn′dāj), *n.* **1**, the space between the inside surface of the bore of a gun and the shot or shell loaded in it; **2**, the stir of the air caused by a moving shell or bullet; **3**, the force of the wind in turning aside a shell or bullet, or the distance it is turned aside; **4**, the surface of a ship exposed to the wind.

wind-bag (wĭnd′băg″), *n.* **1**, a bag to hold wind, as in the bagpipes; **2**, *Slang*, a wordy orator; blusterer.

wind-break (wĭnd′brāk″), *n.* a shelter or protection from the wind.

wind–bro-ken (wĭnd′-brō″kn), *adj.* afflicted with the heaves, a disease marked by difficulty in breathing: said of horses.

wind-fall (wĭnd′fôl″), *n.* **1**, something brought down by the wind, as ripe fruit; **2**, an unexpected piece of good fortune, as a legacy.

wind-flow-er (wĭnd′flou″ẽr), *n.* the wood anemone.

wind-gall (wĭnd′gôl″), *n.* in horses, a soft swelling on the fetlock joint.

wind gauge a graduated attachment to the sights of a firearm or cannon, by which allowance may be made, in aiming, for the effect of the wind upon the projectile. Also, **wind gage.**

wind-ing sheet a garment to cover the dead.

wind in-stru-ment any of several instruments sounded by a current of air, including the organ.

wind-jam-mer (wĭnd′jăm″ẽr), *n. Colloq.*, a sailing vessel: orig., a scornful term applied to sailing ships by sailors on newly invented steam vessels.

wind-lass (wĭnd′lȧs), *n.* a machine for hoisting by winding a rope or chain on a cylinder turned either by hand or by machinery.

WINDLASS

wind-mill (wĭnd′-mĭl″), *n.* a mill operated by a wheel whose oblique sails or vanes turn as they catch the wind.

win-dow (wĭn′dō), *n.* **1**, an opening in the side of a building to let in light and air; **2**, the sash, shutter, or other framework which fills such a space.

wind-pipe (wĭnd′pīp″), *n.* the trachea, or breathing tube, leading from the larynx to the lungs.

wind-row (wĭnd′rō″; wĭn′-), *n.* **1**, a long, low ridge of raked hay, or a row of sheaves of grain stacked in a line and left to dry before being piled; **2**, dust, dry leaves, etc., swept by the wind into ridges.

wind-shield (wĭnd′shēld″), *n.* a glass shield in front of the front seat of a motor vehicle, to shield the occupants from wind, rain, dust, etc.

Wind-sor (wĭn′zẽr), *n.* a town in Berkshire, England: **Windsor chair,** a style of wooden chair with a back made of rods (see *furniture*, illus.): **Windsor tie,** a wide necktie made in a double bow.

wind-storm (wĭnd′stôrm″), *n.* a storm characterized by violent wind and little or no rain.

wind–up (wīnd′=ŭp″), *n. Colloq.*, the end of an affair; a conclusion; as, the *wind-up* of a meeting.

wind-ward (wĭnd′wẽrd), *n.* the direction from which the wind blows:—*adj.* being on the side from which the wind blows:—*adv.* toward the wind.

wind-y (wĭn′dĭ), *adj.* [*comp.* wind′i-er, *superl.* wind′i-est], **1**, pertaining to, like, or consisting of, air in motion; breezy; exposed to the wind; **2**, *Colloq.*, noisy or boastful.—*adv.* **wind′i-ly.**—*n.* **wind′i-ness.**

wine (wīn), *n.* **1**, the fermented juice of grapes, used as a drink; **2**, the fermented juice of other fruits or plants, such as currants or dandelions, used similarly: **wine gallon,** a liquid measure containing 231 cubic inches: the standard gallon in the U. S.:—*v.t.* [*p.t.* and *p.p.* wined (wīnd), *p.pr.* win′ing], to furnish with wine:—*v.i. Colloq.*, to drink wine.—*adj.* **wine′less.**—*adj.* **win′y.**

wine-bib-ber (wīn′bĭb″ẽr), *n.* one who is continually drinking wine.

wine-glass (wīn′glȧs″), *n.* a small glass, holding about two ounces.

wine press **1**, a vat in which grapes were formerly trodden upon to press out the juice; **2**, a machine for pressing the juice from grapes.

win-er-y (wīn′ẽr-ĭ), *n.* [*pl.* wineries (-ĭz)], an establishment for making wine.

wine-sap (wīn′săp″), *n.* a large, deep red, fall and winter apple, extensively grown in America.

wine skin the skin of an animal made into a vessel for wine.

wing (wĭng), *n.* **1**, a broad, flat organ or part, used for flight through the air; **2**, the fore limb of a vertebrate, corresponding to the human arm, developed for flying, as in the bird; also, a structure on a bat, similar in appearance but consisting of a fold of skin extending from the body between the hind and the fore limb; **3**, an appendage on the back of an insect, used for flying; **4**, one of the main supporting surfaces of an airplane; **5**, a building projecting from the main body of a structure; **6**, in a theater, the stage platform extended at either side, or a room at the side of the stage; **7**, in the army or navy, a force at the extreme right or left of the main force: **wing rib,** any of the rigid parts of an airplane wing frame running in a fore-and-aft direction (see *airplane*, illus.): **wing skid,** a brace or skid projecting downward from the lower wing of an airplane, near the outer end, to keep the wing from touching the ground (see *airplane*, illus.):—*v.t.* **1**, to equip with means of flight; specif., to feather; as, to *wing* an arrow; **2**, to accomplish by flying; **3**, to wound in the wing; as, to *wing* a bird:—*v.i.* to fly.—*adj.* **wing′less.**

winged (wĭngd; wĭng′ĕd), *p.adj.* having wings, or projections like wings.

wing-tip (wĭng′tĭp), *n.* **1**, the point of a wing; **2**, the outer extremity of a wing of an airplane, provided with hinged parts which are moved to control the horizontal position of the plane.

wink (wĭngk), *v.i.* **1**, to close and open quickly one or both eyelids; **2**, to convey a hint by the motion of the eyelid; **3**, to close the eyes, feigning ignorance: with *at;* as, to *wink* at a wrong; **4**, to twinkle; gleam, as the light of a lighthouse:—*v.t.* **1**, to close and open quickly, as the eyelids; **2**, to remove by winking, as tears:—*n.* **1**, the act of opening and shutting the eyelids, esp. one eyelid; **2**, a hint thus given; **3**, the time required for one such act; an instant; **4**, a gleam; sparkle.

wink-er (wĭngk′ẽr), *n.* **1**, one who winks; **2**, a blinder for a horse; blinker; **3**, *Colloq.*, an eyelash.

win-ning (wĭn′ĭng), *p.adj.* **1**, successful; **2**, attractive; charming; as, *winning* manners:—*n.* **1**, the act of gaining or conquering; **2**, in *pl.*, that which one gains.—*adv.* **win′ning-ly.**

win-now (wĭn′ō), *v.t.* **1**, to blow chaff and refuse from (grain) by a current of air; **2**, to separate; as, to *winnow* truth from falsehood; **3**, to disperse by blowing:—*v.i.* to separate chaff from grain by the wind.—*n.* **win′now-er.**

win-some (wĭn′sŭm), *adj.* attractive; pretty; gay; charming.—*adv.* **win′some-ly.**—*n.* **win′some-ness.**

win-ter (wĭn′tẽr), *n.* **1**, the coldest season of the year, varying with the climate; specif., in the Northern Hemisphere, December 21 to March 21; cold weather; **2**, any time, as of gloom or sorrow, suggesting winter: **winter quarters,** the quarters, or settled station, of an army during the winter:—*v.i.* to pass the months of the cold season; as, snakes *winter* in the ground:—*v.t.* to keep during the cold season.

win-ter-green (wĭn′tẽr-grēn″), *n.* a woody, low, evergreen plant that bears white blossoms and edible red berries, and whose leaves yield an aromatic oil: also called *checkerberry*.

win-ter-kill (wĭn′tẽr-kĭl″), *v.t.* to kill by exposure to cold weather.

win-try (wĭn′trĭ), *adj.* [*comp.* win′tri-er, *superl.* win′tri-est], pertaining to, or like, the cold season. Also, **win′ter-y.**—*n.* **win′tri-ness.**

wipe (wīp), *v.t.* [*p.t.* and *p.p.* wiped (wīpt), *p.pr.* wip′ing], **1**, to dry or cleanse by rubbing with something soft; as, to *wipe* dishes; to *wipe* furniture; **2**, to remove by rubbing: usually with *away* or *off;* as, to *wipe* away tears:—*n.* the act of cleansing by rubbing.—*n.* **wip′er.**

wire (wīr), *n.* **1**, a metal rod of comparatively small, often minute, diameter: usually flexible and of great length; **2**, a telegraph wire or cable; **3**, *Colloq.*, a telegram: **to**

pull wires, to use influence in order to gain an end:—*v.t.* [*p.t.* and *p.p.* wired (wīrd), *p.pr.* wir'ing], **1,** to bind, fit, or provide with wire; as, to *wire* a house for electricity; **2,** *Colloq.*, to send a message to by telegraph.

wire-draw (wīr'drô″), *v.t.* [*p.t.* -drew″ (-droo″), *p.p.* -drawn″ (-drôn″), *p.pr.* -draw″ing], **1,** to make into wire, as metal; **2,** to draw out very long and very fine: also used figuratively; as, a *wiredrawn* argument.

wire gauge an instrument for measuring the diameter of wire, thickness of sheet metal, etc.: usually a metal plate with a series of notches of various widths on its edge. Also, **wire gage.**

wire glass glass strengthened by a netting of wire inclosed within it in manufacture.

wire-less (wīr'lĕs), *adj.* without the use of wires: used esp. of a system of telegraphing, telephoning, etc., by means of electric waves in space without connecting wires: **wireless telegraphy** or **telephony,** telegraphic or telephonic communication without the use of wires: distinguished from *line telegraphy*, etc.:—*n.* telegraphy, or a telegraphic system, without connecting wires; as, to inform by *wireless:*—*v.t.* to transmit (a message) by wireless:—*v.i.* to communicate by wireless.

wire-pull-ing (wīr'pool″ĭng), *n.* the use of underhand or secret influence to control a person or an organization, esp. a political body.—*n.* **wire'pull″er.**

wire tap-ping the act of making a secret connection with any message-carrying wire in order to obtain desired information.—**wire tap'per.**

wire-worm (wīr'wûrm″), *n.* the slender, hard-bodied larva of any of various beetles, often injurious to crops.

wir-y (wīr'ĭ), *adj.* [*comp.* wir'i-er, *superl.* wir'i-est], **1,** like wire; stiff; **2,** lean and slight, but strong and sinewy; as, a *wiry* horse.—*adv.* **wir'i-ly.**—*n.* **wir'i-ness.**

wis-dom (wĭz'dŭm), *n.* **1,** the faculty of forming a sound judgment in a matter; discernment based on experience of men and things; discretion; **2,** hence, learning; knowledge: **wisdom tooth,** the third molar, or extreme back tooth, on each side in each jaw, usually appearing between the ages of 17 and 22.

Syn. (see knowledge).

¹wise (wīz), *adj.* **1,** having the faculty of forming a true judgment; discerning; **2,** having knowledge or experience; learned; skilled.—*adv.* **wise'ly.**

²wise (wīz), *n.* way; manner; mode: esp. in the expression *in such wise.*

-wise (-wīz), *adv. suffix,* in the way or manner of; as, clock*wise;* other*wise.*

wise-a-cre (wīz'ā-kẽr), *n.* **1,** a knowing person: usually used humorously; **2,** a stupid person who affects wisdom.

wish (wĭsh), *v.i.* to have a strong desire: usually with *for:*—*v.t.* **1,** to desire or long for; crave; **2,** to desire for someone else; as, to *wish* her good fortune:—*n.* **1,** a strong or eager desire; **2,** the object or thing desired; **3,** a request.—*n.* **wish'er.**

Syn., n. longing. (See desire.)

wish-bone (wĭsh'bōn″), *n.* the forked bone in front of the breastbone in most birds.

wish-ful (wĭsh'fool), *adj.* full of longing; wistful; desirous.—*adv.* **wish'ful-ly.**—*n.* **wish'ful-ness.**

wish-y-wash-y (wĭsh'ĭ-wŏsh″ĭ), *adj.* [*comp.* -wash″i-er, *superl.* -wash″i-est], *Colloq.*, **1,** pale; thin; **2,** weak; diluted: said of liquids.

wisp (wĭsp), *n.* a handful or small bundle, as of straw or hay.

wist (wĭst), *Archaic,* past tense and past participle of the irregular verb *wit.*

wis-ta-ri-a (wĭs-tā'rĭ-ȧ), *n.* a climbing shrub of the pea family, with drooping purple flowers. Also, **wis-te'ri-a.**

wist-ful (wĭst'fool), *adj.* **1,** earnestly thoughtful; pensive; **2,** longing; wishful; as, a *wistful* expression of the face.—*adv.* **wist'ful-ly.**—*n.* **wist'ful-ness.**

¹wit (wĭt), *v.t.* and *v.i.* [*pres.* I wot, thou wot'test, he wot, we, you, they wit'en or wite; *p.t.* and *p.p.* wist, *p.pr.* wit'ting], to know; be aware: archaic except in the phrase *to wit,* namely: used in legal documents.

²wit (wĭt), *n.* **1,** intellect; wisdom; sagacity; **2,** often in *pl.*, mental faculty or power; as, keep your *wits* about you; **3,** the power quickly to perceive an odd situation and to phrase it in an unexpected and amusing way; also, the written or spoken words of persons having this power; **4,** a person who has this power; also, a quick or clever person: **at one's wit's end,** confused; at a loss.

Syn. humor. *Wit* names a flashing perception of unexpected and amusing ideas or situations, expressed keenly and sometimes cuttingly. *Humor* means a tendency to see the amusing or absurd side of anything, expressing itself usually in a sympathetic and kindly way.

witch (wĭch), *n.* **1,** one supposed to have supernatural powers from a compact with the Devil: now used only of a woman; **2,** a hag; **3,** an attractive young woman:—*v.t.* to bewitch or charm.

witch-craft (wĭch'kraft″), *n.* dealings with evil spirits; sorcery.

witch-er-y (wĭch'ẽr-ĭ), *n.* [*pl.* witcheries (-ĭz)], fascination; compelling charm or influence.

witch-ha-zel (wĭch'-hā″zl), *n.* **1,** a shrub having small yellow flowers which appear after the leaves are dead; **2,** an extract from the bark of this shrub, used as a soothing lotion.

witch-ing (wĭch'ĭng), *p.adj.* fascinating; enchanting.

wit-e-na-ge-mot (wĭt'ē-nȧ-gĕ-mōt″), *n.* the Anglo-Saxon national council, which decided matters of war, taxes, and the like. Also, **wit'e-na-ge-mote″.**

with (wĭth), *prep.* indicating: **1,** proximity or companionship; as, put the glove *with* its mate; come *with* me; **2,** association, connection, or intercourse; as, he has been *with* the firm for years; **3,** agreement or harmony; as, blue does not go *with* green; **4,** possession, endowment, or combination; as, the boy came *with* the milk; New York *with* its skyscrapers; **5,** keeping, care, or guardianship; as, leave the child *with* me; **6,** the instrument of an action; as, slain *with* a dagger; **7,** manner or circumstances; as, *with* ease; **8,** cause; as, perish *with* hunger; **9,** estimation or opinion; as, his excuses had no weight *with* his employer; **10,** proportion, relation, or simultaneousness; as, the river rose higher *with* every minute; **11,** in spite of; notwithstanding; as, *with* all his learning, he was modest; **12,** separation or difference; as, he parted *with* me; I differ *with* you; **13,** antagonism; as, to fight *with* the Romans.

with- (wĭth-), *prefix,* **1,** against; as, *with*stand; **2,** back; as, *with*draw.

with-al (wĭth-ôl'), *adv. Archaic,* moreover; likewise:—*prep. Archaic,* with: used after its object.

with-draw (wĭth-drô'), *v.t.* [*p.t.* -drew' (-droo'), *p.p.* -drawn' (-drôn'), *p.pr.* -draw'ing], **1,** to remove; take back; **2,** to recall; as, to *withdraw* a charge in court:—*v.i.* to retire; as, to *withdraw* from a room.—*n.* **with-draw'al.**—*n.* **with-draw'ment.**

withe (wĭth; wĭth), *n.* a tough, flexible twig used as a binding material, as for fagots and the like; a withy.

with-er (wĭth'ẽr), *v.t.* to cause to shrink, fade, droop, or decay:—*v.i.* to lose sap or juice; dry up or fade; hence, to languish.

with-ers (wĭth'ẽrz), *n.pl.* the part of the body lying between the shoulder blades, as of the horse.

with-hold (wĭth-hōld'), *v.t.* [*p.t.* and *p.p.* -held' (-hĕld'), *p.pr.* -hold'ing], **1**, to hold back, as from action; restrain; **2**, to keep back; as, to *withhold* payment.

with-in (wĭth-ĭn'), *adv.* in the inner part; inside; in the house:—*prep.* **1**, inside of; **2**, in the limits or space of; as, *within* an hour; *within* hail.

with-out (wĭth-out'), *adv.* outside; outwardly; outdoors; as, clean within and *without*:—*prep.* **1**, outside of; **2**, beyond; as, *without* question; **3**, in the absence of; lacking; as, *without* hope.

with-stand (wĭth-stănd'), *v.t.* [*p.t.* and *p.p.* -stood' (-stŏŏd'), *p.pr.* -stand'ing], to stand against; oppose; resist; as, to *withstand* temptation.

with-y (wĭth'ĭ; wĭth'ĭ), *n.* [*pl.* withies (-ĭz)], a tough, flexible twig, esp. of willow, used as a binding material; a withe:—*adj.* flexible and tough.

wit-less (wĭt'lĕs), *adj.* without understanding; hence, foolish; unwise.

wit-ness (wĭt'nĕs), *n.* **1**, declaration of personal knowledge of the truth of a stated fact or event; testimony; evidence; **2**, a person or thing that gives evidence; **3**, a person who tells in court under oath what he knows of a fact or event; **4**, one who puts his signature to a document to show that he has seen it signed; **5**, one who from actual presence knows of an occurrence: also called *eyewitness*:—*v.t.* **1**, to give evidence of, as in court; **2**, to show by behavior or appearance; as, her face *witnessed* her fear; **3**, to sign (a document) to indicate knowledge of another's signing; **4**, to see or know personally; as, to *witness* a performance of a play:—*v.i.* to testify.

wit-ti-cism (wĭt'ĭ-sĭzm), *n.* a witty remark; a clever saying.

wit-ting-ly (wĭt'ĭng-lĭ), *adv.* with knowledge; intentionally.

wit-ty (wĭt'ĭ), *adj.* [*comp.* wit'ti-er, *superl.* wit'ti-est], **1**, having the faculty of arousing laughter by a bright or unusual way of expressing ideas; as, a *witty* person; **2**, marked by quickness and cleverness; as, *witty* remarks.—*adv.* **wit'ti-ly.**—*n.* **wit'ti-ness.**

wive (wīv), *v.i.* [*p.t.* and *p.p.* wived (wīvd), *p.pr.* wiv'ing], to marry a woman.

wives (wīvz), *n.* plural of *wife;* as, old *wives'* tales.

wiz-ard (wĭz'ărd), *n.* **1**, one supposed to possess magical powers from alliance with evil spirits: now used only of a man; a magician; conjurer; sorcerer; **2**, a wonder worker; **3**, *Colloq.*, a very clever person.—*adv.* **wiz'ard-ly.**—*n.* **wiz'ard-ry.**

wiz-en (wĭz'n), *adj.* dried up; shriveled:—*v.i.* and *v.t.* to dry up or shrivel.—*p. adj.* **wiz'ened.**

woad (wōd), *n.* **1**, a plant of the cabbage family, formerly cultivated for a blue dye obtained from its leaves; **2**, the dye obtained from its leaves.

wob-ble (wŏb'l), *v.i.* [*p.t.* and *p.p.* -bled (-ld), *p.pr.* -bling], **1**, to move unsteadily from side to side; **2**, to vacillate:—*v.t.* to cause to move unsteadily from side to side:—*n.* a swaying motion. Also, **wab'ble,** *Pfd. S.*—*n.* **wob'bler.**—*adj.* **wob'bly.**

Wo-den (wō'dĕn), *n.* in Teutonic mythology, the chief god: called by the Norse *Odin*. Also, **Wo'dan.**

woe (wō), *n.* **1**, deep sorrow; inconsolable grief; **2**, the cause of sorrow or grief; an affliction. Also, **wo.**

woe-be-gone (wō'bē-gôn"), *adj.* overwhelmed with woe; showing grief; as, a *woebegone* appearance. Also, **wo'be-gone".**

woe-ful (wō'fŏŏl), *adj.* **1**, sorrowful; miserable; **2**, mean; paltry; wretched. Also, **wo'ful.**—*adv.* **woe'ful-ly.**

wold (wōld), *n.* in England, a wild, treeless tract of land; a down or moor.

wolf (wŏŏlf), *n.* [*pl.* wolves (wŏŏlvz)], **1**, any of various fierce, carnivorous wild animals of wide distribution over the world; **2**, hence, a fierce, greedy, or destructive person; **3**, a discordant sound in certain musical instruments, as the piano and violin, due to the system of tuning or to defective vibration: **to keep the wolf from the door,** to keep away want; support oneself or one's family.

wolf-hound (wŏŏlf'hound"), *n.* a large, long-haired dog of a breed formerly used for hunting wolves.

wolf-ish (wŏŏl'fĭsh), *adj.* **1**, like a wolf; savage: **2**, *Colloq.*, very hungry.—*adv.* **wolf'ish-ly.**—*n.* **wolf'ish-ness.**

wolf-ram (wŏŏl'frăm; wŏl'frăm), *n.* a hard, heavy, grayish white metallic element used for hardening steel and in the manufacture of electric lamps: also called *tungsten*.

wolfs-bane (wŏŏlfs'bān"), *n.* monkshood, a European plant of the crowfoot family, yielding the drug aconite.

wol-ver-ene (wŏŏl"vẽr-ēn'), *n.* a wary, voracious, carnivorous mammal of Canada and the northern U. S., related to the sable and the marten, thickset, and between two and three feet long: also called *glutton:* **Wolverene,** *Colloq.*, a resident of Michigan. Also, **wol"ver-ine'.**

wolves (wŏŏlvz), *n.* plural of *wolf;* as, a pack of *wolves*.

wom-an (wŏŏm'ăn), *n.* [*pl.* women (wĭm'ĕn)], **1**, an adult female of the human race; **2**, the female sex; **3**, a female servant: **woman suffrage,** the franchise, or right of voting in political matters, possessed or exercised by women.

wom-an-hood (wŏŏm'ăn-hŏŏd), *n.* **1**, the state of being a woman; **2**, the character or qualities of a woman; **3**, women collectively.

wom-an-ish (wŏŏm'ăn-ĭsh), *adj.* like a woman; effeminate or weak: usually contemptuous.

Syn. feminine. (See female.)

wom-an-kind (wŏŏm'ăn-kīnd"), *n.* women collectively.

wom-an-ly (wŏŏm'ăn-lĭ), *adj.* **1**, suitable for a woman; **2**, having the noble qualities of feminine character:—*adv.* in the manner of a woman.—*adj.* **wom'an-like".**—*n.* **wom'an-li-ness.**

Syn., adj. (see female).

womb (wōōm), *n.* **1**, the uterus; the organ which holds the young of mammals before birth; **2**, hence, a place where anything is concealed; as, the *womb* of the earth.

wom-bat (wŏm'băt), *n.* any of several Australian mammals, related to the kangaroo, and resembling a small bear.

wom-en (wĭm'ĕn), *n.* plural of *woman:* often in compounds; as, gentle*women;* sales*women*.

won (wŭn), past tense and past participle of the irregular verb *win*.

won-der (wŭn'dẽr), *n.* **1**, the state of mind produced by anything new, strange, unexpected, or surprising; astonishment; **2**, a cause of surprise; marvel; miracle:—*v.i.* **1**, to feel surprise; be astonished; **2**, to feel doubt and curiosity:—*v.t.* to be doubtful about; have a desire to know; as, I *wonder* what I ought to do.

won-der-ful (wŭn′dẽr-fo͝ol), *adj.* exciting surprise; strange; marvelous.—*adv.* **won′der-ful-ly.**

won-der-land (wŭn′dẽr-lănd″), *n.* a land of strange surprises.

won-der-ment (wŭn′dẽr-mĕnt), *n.* **1,** astonishment; **2,** a cause for wonder; a marvel.

won-drous (wŭn′drŭs), *adj.* marvelous; strange.—*adv.* **won′drous-ly.** —*n.* **won′drous-ness.**

poisonous liquid, obtained synthetically or by the distillation of wood: used esp. as a solvent for shellacs, gums, etc., and as a fuel: also called *methyl alcohol.*

wood-bine (wo͝od′bīn″), *n.* **1,** any of several vines of the honeysuckle family, esp. one bearing fragrant, white or purplish flowers; **2,** the Virginia creeper, a climbing shrub supported by tendrils and bearing clusters of bluish black, autumn berries.

wood-chuck (wo͝od′chŭk″), *n.* a coarse-furred, American burrowing rodent about eighteen inches long: also called *ground hog.*

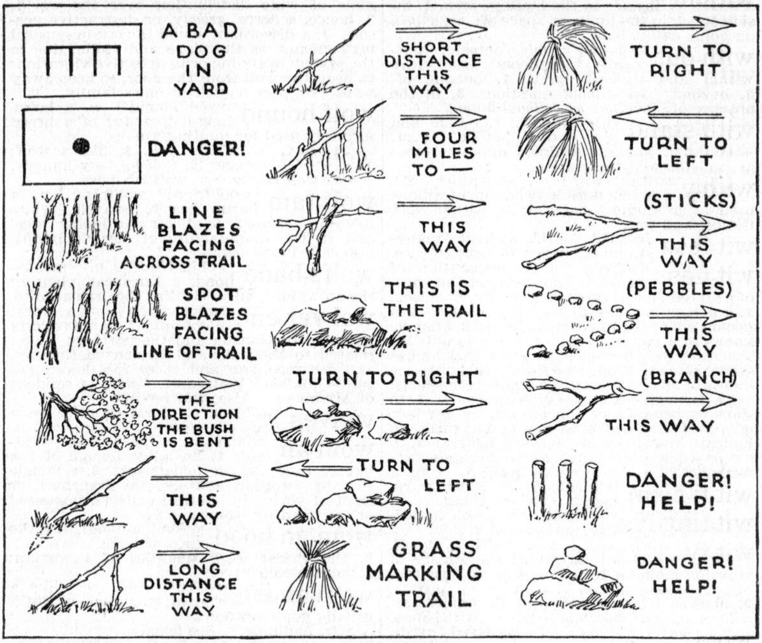

WOODCRAFT SIGNS AND SYMBOLS

The signs shown above are widely used by woodsmen and campers. They are adapted, with permission, from the chapter on Signs, Signals, and Symbols, by Daniel Carter Beard, in the official handbook of the Boy Scouts of America

wont (wŭnt; wōnt), *adj.* used or accustomed; as, she is *wont* to give much to charity:—*n.* habit or custom:—*v.t.* and *v.i. Rare,* to accustom or be accustomed.

won't (wōnt; wŭnt), a contraction of *woll not,* archaic variant of *will not.*

wont-ed (wŭn′tĕd; wōn′-), *p.adj.* **1,** accustomed; **2,** usual; customary.

woo (wo͞o), *v.t.* **1,** to court or make love to; **2,** to ask earnestly; **3,** to seek; as, to *woo* success:—*v.i.* to go courting.—*n.* **woo′er.**

wood (wo͝od), *n.* **1,** a thick growth of trees; grove or forest; **2,** the hard part of a tree between the pith and the bark; **3,** sticks for making a fire; also, lumber; timber; **4,** anything made of wood, as a cask:—*v.t.* **1,** to supply with wood; **2,** to make into a forest.—*p.adj.* **wood′ed.**

wood al-co-hol a colorless, light, volatile, inflammable, and

wood-cock (wo͝od′kŏk″), *n.* a small European game bird allied to the snipe and plover; also, a related American bird.

wood-craft (wo͝od′krȧft″), *n.* knowledge of the woods and how to live in them; esp., knowledge of camping, hunting, trapping, etc.

wood-cut (wo͝od′kŭt″), *n.* an engraving on wood; also, a print from such an engraving: also called *wood engraving.*

wood-en (wo͝od′n), *adj.* **1,** made, or consisting, of wood; as, a *wooden* bucket; **2,** hence, stiff; awkward; without expression; **3,** dull; spiritless.

wood-land (wo͝od′lănd; wo͝od′lănd″), *n.* land covered with trees; a forest:—*adj.* of or pertaining to the woods; silvan.—*n.* **wood′land-er.**

wood louse **1,** any of several small animals akin to the crabs, found under old logs: also called *sow bug* (see *crustacean*, illus.); **2**, any of several insects that eat wood, books, etc.

wood-man (wŏŏd′măn), *n.* [*pl.* woodmen (-mĕn)], **1**, a forest officer; forester; **2**, one who cuts down trees; **3**, one who lives in a forest.

wood–note (wŏŏd′-nōt″), *n.* a musical sound of the forest, as the call of a bird or the chirp of an insect.

wood nymph **1**, in mythology, one of the maiden deities supposed to inhabit the trees; a dryad; **2**, any of several moths, butterflies, or humming birds.

wood-peck-er (wŏŏd′pĕk″ẽr), *n.* any of several birds with tail feathers and feet adapted for climbing, and a strong beak for piercing the bark of trees for insects.

RED-HEADED WOODPECKER

wood pulp pulp made from wood fiber: used in making certain kinds of paper, esp. the cheaper grades.

wood-ruff (wŏŏd′rŭf″), *n.* a small, sweet-scented European herb of the madder family, with an aromatic fragrance.

woods-man (wŏŏdz′măn), *n.* [*pl.* woodsmen (-mĕn)], one who lives or works in the woods, as a hunter.

wood sor-rel any of several plants native to the north temperate zone and having three-parted leaves, delicate white, purple, or yellow flowers, and acid juice (see *shamrock*, illus.).

wood thrush **1**, a migratory North American thrush with a bell-like note: also called *wood robin;* **2**, any of several other thrushes, as the hermit thrush.

wood war-bler in the U. S., any of a family of small, insect-eating, singing birds, including the Kentucky warbler, ovenbird, water thrush, etc.

wood winds in an orchestra, the wooden wind instruments collectively, including oboe, English horn, bassoon, clarinet, flute, and piccolo: also called *wood-wind instruments* (see *musical instrument*, illus.).—*adj.* **wood′-wind″**.

wood-work (wŏŏd′wûrk″), *n.* objects, or parts of objects, made of wood; esp., the wooden finishings of a house, as stairways, doors, etc.—*n.* **wood′work″er.**

wood-work-ing (wŏŏd′wûrk″ĭng), *adj.* the act or process of working with, or shaping things in, wood.

wood-y (wŏŏd′ĭ), *adj.* [*comp.* wood′i-er, *superl.* wood′i-est], **1**, covered with, or abounding in, woods; **2**, like, or characteristic of, woods or forests; silvan; **3**, like, or characteristic of, wood; as, a *woody* consistency.—*n.* **wood′i-ness.**

woof (wŏŏf), *n.* **1**, in weaving, the threads carried back and forth by the shuttle: distinguished from *warp;* **2**, the texture of a fabric; cloth.

wool (wŏŏl), *n.* **1**, the soft, fine, curly hair which covers the sheep and some other animals; **2**, anything resembling the hair of sheep; as, steel or cotton *wool.*

wool-en (wŏŏl′ĕn), *adj.* made in part, or wholly, of wool; as, a *woolen* blanket:—*n.*, often in *pl.*, cloth made in part, or wholly, of wool. Also, **wool′len.**

wool-gath-er-ing (wŏŏl′găth″ẽr-ĭng), *adj.* given to idle fancies:—*n.* indulgence in idle dreaming.

wool-grow-er (wŏŏl′grō″ẽr), *n.* one who raises sheep for their wool.

wool-ly (wŏŏl′ĭ), *adj.* [*comp.* wool′li-er, *superl.* wool′li-est], consisting of, like, or clothed with, wool; as, a *woolly* head. —*n.* **wool′li-ness.**

wool-pack (wŏŏl′păk″), *n.* **1**, a bale of wool, weighing 240 pounds; **2**, a wrapping or covering for such a bale; **3**, a fleecy, rounded cloud.

wool-sack (wŏŏl′săk″), *n.* **1**, a sack of wool; **2**, a cushion stuffed with wool on which the Lord Chancellor sits in the British House of Lords.

word (wûrd), *n.* **1**, a group of letters representing one or more sounds and expressing an idea; **2**, that which is said or spoken, esp. a brief expression; **3**, a statement; tidings; information; a message or communication; as, he received *word* today; **4**, a password; **5**, a command; **6**, a promise; as, to keep one's *word;* **7**, in *pl.:* **a**, talk or discourse; **b**, a dispute; as, to have *words:* **Word, 1**, the second person of the Trinity; as, the *Word* was made flesh; **2**, the Scriptures: —*v.t.* to express in words.

word-book (wûrd′bŏŏk″), *n.* a vocabulary or dictionary.

word-play (wûrd′plā″), *n.* using words in a subtle way, as in a pun.

word build-ing the formation of words, as by adding prefixes, suffixes, inflections, etc., or by combining or modifying roots.

word-ing (wûrd′ĭng), *n.* the manner in which anything is expressed in words; as, the *wording* of a letter.

word-y (wûrd′ĭ), *adj.* [*comp.* word′i-er, *superl.* word′i-est], full of words; verbose; as, a *wordy* argument.—*adv.* **word′i-ly.**—*n.* **word′i-ness.**

wore (wōr), past tense of [1]*wear;* past tense and past participle of [2]*wear.*

work (wûrk), *v.i.* [*p.t.* and *p.p.* worked (wûrkt) or, in certain meanings, wrought (rôt), *p.pr.* work′ing], **1**, to put forth physical or mental effort; labor; toil; **2**, to be occupied in business; be employed; as, he *works* in the steel mill; **3**, to act, operate, or run; esp., to act effectively; accomplish the end desired, as a scheme; **4**, to ferment, as liquors; **5**, to be moved through agitation; as, his features *worked;* **6**, to progress slowly or laboriously: with *through, loose, out,* etc.; as, the rain *worked* through the roof: **work out,** to materialize, as a plan; develop into a practicable or working method, or a satisfactory situation:—*v.t.* **1**, to operate, manage, or set in motion, as a quarry or a scheme; **2**, to prepare for use; manipulate; as, to *work* the soil; **3**, to win by labor, or achieve gradually or with difficulty; as, to *work* one's way; **4**, to bring or move gradually or laboriously, as into a given position, situation, or the like: with *into, through,* etc.; as, he *worked* the stone into position; **5**, to perform, produce, or cause; as, he *wrought* marvelous cures; **6**, to make or fashion; esp., to embroider; **7**, to exact labor from; cause to labor, as horses; **8**, to solve: sometimes with *out;* as, to *work* out a problem; **9**, to influence or control; as, to *work* a committee; **10**, to ply a trade in (a district), esp. temporarily or as part of an itinerary; cover; as, a salesman *works* a town; **11**, to cause to ferment; **12**, *Slang,* to utilize or exploit (a person), esp. through deceit; as, he was only *working* you for your money: **work off, 1**, to dispel gradually and by effort, as anger or a cold; **2**, to discharge (a scholastic requirement): **work out, 1**, to pay for with labor; as, to *work out* one's board; **2**, to secure (a solution); also, to solve (a problem); **3**, to achieve through effort, as one's salvation; **4**, to exhaust, as a mine: **work over**, to make over or revise, as a sermon: **work up**, **1**, to fashion or elaborate; put into proper shape; **2**, to incite or excite by degrees; as, to *work* one *up* to a state of anger:—*n.* **1**, physical or mental effort directed to some end or purpose; toil; labor; **2**, occupation; employment; job; **3**, a task; an undertaking; **4**, a product of mental or physical effort, or both; as, a *work* of art; **5**, in *pl.*: **a**, the moving parts of any machinery; as, the *works* of a watch; **b**, structures connected with civil or mechanical engineering, as bridges, docks, or dams; as, public *works;* **c**, often used as *sing.*, an establishment for manufacturing, or the like, with its contents, outbuildings, etc.—*n.* **work'er.**

Syn., *n.* (see labor).

work-a-day (wûr'kȧ-dā"), *adj.* everyday; commonplace; prosaic.

work-bag (wûrk'băg"), *n.* a bag for holding tools or materials for work; esp., a bag for needlework.

work-day (wûrk'dā"), *n.* a day for employment, as distinguished from Sunday, festivals, holidays, etc.

work-house (wûrk'hous"), *n.* **1**, a house in which work is carried on; a shop; **2**, a house of correction in which convicts are confined at labor; **3**, in England, a public institution where the poor are supported, the able-bodied among them being made to work; a poorhouse.

work-ing day a day for work.—*adj.* **work'ing-day".**

work-ing-man (wûr'kĭng-măn), *n.* [*pl.* workingmen (-mĕn)], a man who works with his hands; laboring man; common laborer.—*n.fem.* **work'ing-wom"an.**

work-man (wûrk'măn), *n.* [*pl.* workmen (-mĕn)], a man who is employed in manual labor; esp., a skilled laborer.

work-man-like (wûrk'măn-līk"), *adj.* worthy of a skilled workman.—*adj.* and *adv.* **work'man-ly.**

work-man-ship (wûrk'măn-shĭp), *n.* **1**, the skill and methods of a workman; **2**, the finish or peculiar quality of anything made; as, the delicate *workmanship* of a carving; **3**, the product of skill and labor; work.

work-room (wûrk'rōōm"), *n.* a room in which work is done.

work-shop (wûrk'shŏp"), *n.* a room or building where manufacturing is carried on or handicraft taught.

work-wom-an (wûrk'wŏŏm"ăn), *n.* [*pl.* workwomen (-wĭm"ĕn)], a woman who is employed, esp. at labor with her hands.

world (wûrld), *n.* **1**, the earth with all living things and the traces of them, esp. man and his works; **2**, any one of the planets or stars imagined as similar to the earth; **3**, the material universe; **4**, a part of the earth distinguished from the rest in some way; as, the New *World;* the Roman *world;* **5**, any separate system, state, or sphere of existence, conceived as a whole; a separate group of persons and their affairs; as, the present *world;* the literary *world;* **6**, the inhabitants of the earth and their affairs; esp., people in general as the bearers of public opinion; as, the *world* disapproves of polygamy; **7**, those people who are esp. devoted to pleasure; also, material affairs as opposed to spiritual; **8**, fashionable society or life; **9**, the social habits, manners, and motives of mankind; as, to know the *world;* **10**, the current of events; the course of human affairs; as, how goes the *world* with you? **11**, a great number or amount; as, his father's coat is a *world* too big for the boy: **World War**, the great war of 1914–18, which involved nearly all the important nations of the earth: also called *Great War.*

world-ling (wûrld'lĭng), *n.* one who is devoted to the pleasures and advantages of the present life.

world-ly (wûrld'lĭ), *adj.* pertaining to, or devoted to, this life and its enjoyment and advantages.—*n.* **world'li-ness.**

world-ly-wise (wûrld'lĭ-wīz"), *adj.* wise in the affairs of this life.

world-wide (wûrld'-wīd"), *adj.* universal; extending to every part of the earth; as, *world-wide* interests.

worm (wûrm), *n.* **1**, any small, slender, creeping or crawling, limbless animal, usually having a soft, naked body; **2**, any device resembling such an animal, as a short rotating screw, made to mesh with a worm wheel, or a condensing coil in a still; **3**, an insignificant or contemptible person: used in scorn or disgust; **4**, something conceived of as stealthily gnawing the mind, as remorse, melancholy, or the like; **5**, in *pl.*, a disorder of the intestines due to the presence of parasitic worms: **worm gear**, **1**, a gear wheel, the teeth of which engage with the threads of a rotating worm or short screw; a worm wheel; **2**, a worm wheel and worm screw geared to each other: **worm wheel**, a wheel fitted with teeth which can be acted on by a short rotating screw, or worm: also called *worm gear:*—*v.t.* to elicit by devious or insidious means; as, to *worm* his secret from him; also, reflexively, to insinuate (oneself); as, he *wormed* himself into favor: **worm one's way**, to progress slowly by wormlike, devious means:—*v.i.* to accomplish or proceed by devious methods.

worm-eat-en (wûrm'-ēt"n), *adj.* eaten, or bored into, by a worm or worms; as, a *worm-eaten* board.

worm-wood (wûrm'wŏŏd"), *n.* **1**, a bitter plant of the aster family, formerly used as a remedy for the disorder of worms, now used as a tonic and in making absinth; **2**, hence, a source of bitterness; as, ridicule is *wormwood* to a man.

worm-y (wûr'mĭ), *adj.* [*comp.* worm'i-er, *superl.* worm'i-est], **1**, infested with worms; **2**, mean; groveling, like a worm.

worn (wōrn), past participle of the irregular verb *wear.*

worn-out (wōrn'-out"), *adj.* **1**, past repair; spoiled by constant use; **2**, exhausted or tired out from exertion; **3**, past or departed; as, a *worn-out* age.

wor-ri-ment (wŭr'ĭ-mĕnt), *n.* anxiety; disturbance of mind.

wor-ri-some (wŭr'ĭ-sŭm), *adj.* **1**, causing trouble or anxiety; annoying; **2**, fretful.

wor-ry (wŭr'ĭ), *v.t.* [*p.t.* and *p.p.* -ried (-ĭd), *p.pr.* -ry-ing], **1**, to shake, tear, or mangle with the teeth; **2**, to trouble; tease; harass:—*v.i.* to feel or express undue anxiety; be fretful:—*n.* anxiety; disturbance of mind. —*p.adj.* **wor'ried.**—*n.* **wor'ri-er.**

Syn., *n.* (see care).

worse (wûrs), *adj.* comparative of *bad;* **1**, bad or ill to a larger extent; more evil or corrupt; **2**, less good; more sick; as, the patient is *worse:*—*adv.* comparative of *badly* or *ill:* in a less good manner or degree: —*n.* that which is less good.

wors-en (wûr'sn), *v.i. Rare,* to become worse:—*v.t. Rare,* to make worse.

wor-ship (wûr'shĭp), *n.* **1**, the act of paying reverence, adoration, or homage to God, a god, or a sacred object; as, the *worship* of an idol; **2**, devotion; adoration; excessive admiration; **3**, a title of honor used, esp. in England, in addressing magistrates: preceded by *your:*—*v.t.* **1**, to pay divine honors, or religious service, to; **2**, to admire excessively; idolize:—*v.i.* **1**, to perform acts of homage or adoration, such as religious services; **2**, to feel excessive admiration.—*n.* **wor'ship-er; wor'ship-per.**

wor-ship-ful (wûr'shĭp-fo͝ol), *adj.* **1**, worthy of respect or honor; honorable; **2**, a term of respect used of magistrates, and, in Freemasonry, of certain officials. —*adv.* **wor'ship-ful-ly.**—*n.* **wor'ship-ful-ness.**

worst (wûrst), *adj.* superlative of *bad:* bad or evil in the highest degree; most severe or dangerous:—*adv.* superlative of *badly* or *ill:* in the most evil way possible:—*n.* that which is most bad or evil:—*v.t.* to defeat; as, to *worst* an enemy.

wor-sted (wo͝os'tĕd; wo͝or'stĕd), *n.* **1**, a twisted yarn spun out of wool; also, the cloth made from such yarn; **2**, a softer woolen yarn, twisted or untwisted, used in knitting and embroidery:—*adj.* consisting of worsted yarn.

[1]**wort** (wûrt), *n.* a plant; an herb: usually used as a suffix in old botanical names; as, liver*wort.*

[2]**wort** (wûrt), *n.* in brewing, the liquid which, at a certain stage before fermenting, is separated from the solid part of the grain mash, and which, after fermentation, becomes beer, ale, or other drink.

[1]**worth** (wûrth), *v.i. Obs.*, to become; happen; come to pass; betide: surviving only in the phrase *woe worth the day.*

[2]**worth** (wûrth), *n.* **1**, excellence or desirable qualities; merit: used of persons or things; **2**, value as expressed in a standard of exchange; **3**, of a person, extent of possessions; riches:—*adj.* **1**, deserving of; meriting; as, *worth* attention; **2**, having the actual value of; as, *worth* the price asked; **3**, priced at; as, *worth* twenty dollars; **4**, possessed of; as, the man is *worth* a million dollars.

worth-less (wûrth'lĕs), *adj.* having no value, merit, or excellence; useless; contemptible.—*adv.* **worth'less-ly.**—*n.* **worth'less-ness.**

wor-thy (wûr'*th*ĭ), *adj.* [*comp.* wor'thi-er, *superl.* wor'thi-est], **1**, having value or excellence; estimable; **2**, meriting; deserving:—*n.* **1**, a local celebrity: used in jest; **2**, in *pl.*, persons of importance.—*adv.* **wor'thi-ly.**—*n.* **wor'thi-ness.**

wot (wŏt), *Archaic*, first and second person singular, present, of the verb *wit.*

would (wo͝od), *v. aux.* past tense of *will*, followed by the infinitive without *to* and used: **1**, in a dependent clause following a past tense, to express determination in the first person; as, I resolved that I *would* go; **2**, in such a clause, to express simple future action in the second and third persons; as, he said he *would* return soon; **3**, in an independent clause, to express determination in all three persons; as, he *would* try it, in spite of all we could do; **4**, to express a customary action in the past; as, every day he *would* come to call; **5**, to express a wish; as, *would* that I could go; **6**, in the conclusion of a sentence expressing a present condition contrary to fact; as, if he were here, he *would* defend me.

would–be (wo͝od'=bē″), *adj.* pretending to be; wishing to be thought to be; as, a *would-be* nobleman.

[1]**wound** (wo͞ond; *Archaic* wound), *n.* **1**, a hurt or injury caused by violence, esp. one in which the skin is broken; a cut; stab; **2**, an injury to the feelings or reputation:—*v.t.* to hurt by violence; cut; slash; hurt the feelings of:—*v.i.* to inflict injury.

[2]**wound** (wound), past tense and past participle of the irregular verbs [2]*wind* and [3]*wind.*

wove (wōv), past tense of *weave:* **woven,** past participle of *weave.*

[1]**wrack** (răk), *n.* **1**, *Rare*, a wreck; **2**, that which is cast ashore, as seaweed and wreckage; **3**, *Archaic*, (usually, *rack*), destruction; ruin.

[2]**wrack** (răk), *n.* thin, broken, flying clouds: —*v.i.* to scud before the wind, as clouds. Also, **rack**, *Pfd. S.*

wraith (rāth), *n.* the ghost of a living person, supposedly seen just before or just after death; hence, an apparition

wran-gle (răng'gl), *v.i.* [*p.t.* and *p.p.* -**gled** (-gld), *p.pr.* -**gling**], **1**, to argue or dispute angrily or noisily; **2**, to engage in discussion; debate:—*n.* a noisy dispute.

wran-gler (răng'glẽr), *n.* **1**, a debater; esp., an angry or noisy disputer; **2**, at Cambridge University, England, one who is in the highest of the three classes of honor men in mathematics.

wrap (răp), *v.t.* [*p.t.* and *p.p.* wrapped or wrapt (răpt), *p.pr.* wrap'ping], **1**, to roll, fold, or wind together; **2**, to cover by folding or winding; infold; **3**, to do up in a package:—*n.* **1**, an article of dress to be folded round the person, as a fur, cloak, shawl, etc.; **2**, in *pl.*, outside garments.

wrap-per (răp'ẽr), *n.* **1**, one who or that which folds or winds; **2**, that in which anything is inclosed or folded; **3**, a dressing gown.

wrath (räth; råth; *Br.* often rôth), *n.* **1**, deep, determined, and violent anger; rage; **2**, punishment; vengeance; as, the *wrath* of God.—*adj. Colloq.*, **wrath'y.**

wrath-ful (räth'fo͝ol; råth'fo͝ol), *adj.* **1**, very angry; furious; **2**, expressing great anger.—*adv.* **wrath'ful-ly.**—*n.* **wrath'ful-ness.**

wreak (rēk), *v.t.* to execute; inflict; as, he *wreaked* his fury on the dog.

wreath (rēth), *n.* **1**, a circular band of flowers or leaves; garland; **2**, anything curled or twisted into circular shape; as, a *wreath* of smoke.

wreathe (rē*th*), *v.t.* and *v.i.* [*p.t.* and *p.p.* wreathed (rē*th*d), *p.pr.* wreath'ing], **1**, to make by twisting and twining, as a garland; **2**, to entwine or infold.

wreck (rĕk), *n.* **1**, (also, *Rare, wrack*), the act or process of destruction by violence or misuse; esp., the destruction of a vessel afloat; shipwreck; **2**, anything that has been thus ruined or disabled; **3**, (also, *Rare, wrack*), a vessel that has been wholly or partly destroyed while afloat; **4**, goods, or fragments of ships, cast ashore by the sea:—*v.t.* **1**, to ruin or disable by violence; **2**, to involve in ruin, esp. in a shipwreck; as, a *wrecked* cargo; **3**, to dismantle or raze, as a building:—*v.i.* to engage in wrecking.

wreck-age (rĕk'ȧj), *n.* **1**, the remains of a destroyed ship, train, building, etc.; **2**, the act of destroying or ruining; the state of being destroyed or ruined.

wreck-er (rĕk'ẽr), *n.* **1**, one who causes destruction or ruin; as, a train *wrecker;* **2**, a person or vessel employed to recover wrecked vessels or wrecked goods; **3**, *Colloq.*, a train or car for clearing away railroad wreckage.

wren (rĕn), *n.* any of several kinds of small singing birds, having short wings and a short tail that stands up.

wrench (rĕnch), *v.t.* **1**, to twist; wring or pull sidewise or obliquely with effort or violence; **2**, to distort; pervert:—*n.* **1**, a violent twist; **2**, a sprain; **3**, a tool for turning nuts, bolts, etc.; as, a monkey *wrench* (see *tool*, illus.).

wrest (rĕst), *v.t.* **1**, to wrench or turn, esp. from its normal state; pull or take away by force or violence; **2**, to distort; pervert:—*n.* a key for tuning a harp or piano.

wres-tle (rĕs'l), *v.i.* [*p.t.* and *p.p.* -tled (-ld), *p.pr.* -tling], **1**, to grapple with an opponent in an effort to force him to the ground; **2**, to struggle; strive earnestly; as, to *wrestle* with a problem:—*n.* a contest in which each of two contestants strives to force his opponent to the ground.—*n.* **wres'tler.**—*n.* **wres'tling.**

wretch (rĕch), *n.* **1**, an unfortunate or miserable person; **2**, a mean, contemptible person: often used in playful abuse.

wretch-ed (rĕch'ĕd), *adj.* **1**, miserable; unhappy; **2**, causing misery; **3**, mean; inadequate; unsatisfactory; **4**, poor.—*adv.* **wretch'ed-ly.**—*n.* **wretch'ed-ness.**

wrig-gle (rĭg'l), *v.t.* and *v.i.* [*p.t.* and *p.p.* -gled (-ld), *p.pr.* -gling], to move by twisting and turning; squirm:—*n.* the act of twisting or squirming; a squirming motion.

wrig-gler (rĭg'lẽr), *n.* **1**, one who or that which squirms; **2**, the larva of the mosquito, often seen in stagnant water.

wright (rīt), *n.* a workman, esp. one who works in wood; as, a ship*wright.*

wring (rĭng), *v.t.* [*p.t.* and *p.p.* wrung (rŭng), *p.pr.* wring'ing], **1**, to twist and strain, as wet clothes; **2**, to force out by twisting or pressure; extort; as, to *wring* water from clothes; to *wring* a confession from a criminal; **3**, to give pain to, as if by twisting; as, her sad story *wrings* my heart.

wring-er (rĭng'ẽr) *n.* **1**, one who or that which twists, strains, etc.; **2**, specif., a machine for pressing the water out of clothes after washing.

[1]**wrin-kle** (rĭng'kl), *n.* a slight ridge caused by folding, puckering, or rumpling; a crease:—*v.t.* [*p.t.* and *p.p.* -kled (-kld), *p.pr.* -kling], to form small ridges or creases in; pucker:—*v.i.* to become creased.—*adj.* **wrin'kly.**

[2]**wrin-kle** (rĭng'kl), *n.* *Colloq.*, a valuable hint; clever device; good idea.

wrist (rĭst), *n.* **1**, the joint between the hand and forearm; **2**, in mechanics, a wrist pin (which see).

wrist-band (rĭst'bănd; *Colloq.* rĭz'bănd), *n.* the part of a sleeve, esp. of a shirt sleeve, that covers the wrist.

wrist-let (rĭst'lĕt), *n.* a band worn around the wrist as a protection from cold, or as an ornament.

wrist pin in mechanics, a stud or pin serving to attach a crank, wheel, or other moving part to a connecting rod: also called *wrist.*

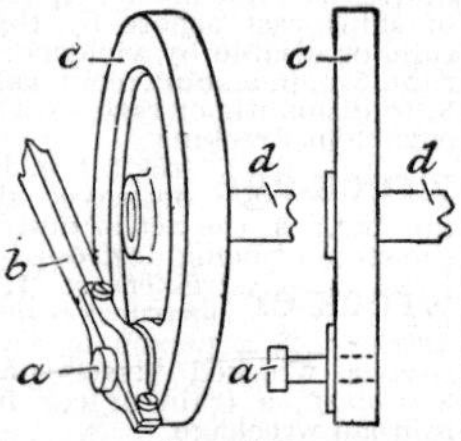

WRIST PIN

Two views of wrist pin and wheel: *a*, wrist pin; *b*, connecting rod; *c*, rim of wheel; *d*, axle.

writ (rĭt), *n.* **1**, anything written: mainly applied to Scripture; as, Holy *Writ;* **2**, a written order of a court of justice.

write (rīt), *v.t.* [*p.t.* wrote (rōt) or, *Archaic*, writ (rĭt), *p.p.* writ'ten (rĭt'n) or, *Archaic*, writ, *p.pr.* writ'ing], **1**, to trace (symbols representing words or sounds) on a surface with an instrument; **2**, to express in words or characters on paper with a pen or pencil; as, to *write* one's name; **3**, to cover with writing; as, the sheet is *written* on both sides; **4**, to produce as author; compose; **5**, to leave traces on; engrave; as, trouble is *written* on his face; **6**, to address a letter to: **write down, 1**, to describe; call; style; as, *write* me *down* an idiot; **2**, to set down a record of; **3**, to disparage: **write off**, to remove (an item, as a bad debt) from an open account; acknowledge in the accounts the annulment of: **write up, 1**, to write an account of; **2**, to praise; extol:—*v.i.* **1**, to form letters, as with a pen; **2**, to compose; **3**, to communicate by letter.

writ-er (rīt'ẽr), *n.* **1**, one who or that which sets down words on paper; as, a rapid *writer;* **2**, a correspondent; **3**, an author.

write-up (rīt'-ŭp"), *n.* **1**, a written account or record, as of an event; **2**, *Colloq.*, a written narrative, description, criticism, or the like, esp. in a newspaper.

writhe (rīth), *v.i.* [*p.t.* and *p.p.* writhed (rīthd), *p.pr.* writh'ing], to squirm or twist about, as from pain or distress:—*v.t.* *Rare*, to contort; distort by twisting.

writ-ing (rīt'ĭng), *n.* **1**, the act of forming letters with a pen or pencil, as on paper; **2**, that which is so set down, as an autograph; **3**, the art of literary production; **4**, a product of literary work, as a book or poem; in *pl.*, literary works.

writ-ten (rĭt'n), past participle of the irregular verb *write.*

wrong (rông), *adj.* **1**, deviating from what is morally right or just; unjust; unlawful; immoral; as, lying is *wrong;* **2**, deviating from fact; false; erroneous; incorrect; as, that addition is *wrong;* **3**, unsuitable; not according to intention or requirement; amiss; out of order; as, the clock is *wrong;* **4**, contrary to law; illegal; **5**, not well-finished; meant to be turned away from view or wear: used of that side of a piece of cloth, or the like, which is opposite to the *right* side:—*n.* **1**, that which is contrary to moral right, fact, intention, or purpose, etc.; evil; injury; crime: opp. of *right;* **2**, in law, an invasion of a legal right; a tort: **in the wrong**, mistaken, unjust, or unfair:—*adv.* in a manner not right morally; also, incorrectly:—*v.t.* **1**, to treat unjustly; injure; harm; **2**, to have a false opinion of; as, I *wronged* you when I thought you intended to insult me.—*n.* **wrong'er.**—*adv.* **wrong'ly.**—*n.* **wrong'ness.**

wrong-do-er (rông'dōō"ẽr; rông"dōō'ẽr), *n.* one who does evil; an offender against the law.—*n.* **wrong'do"ing.**

wrong-ful (rông'fōōl), *adj.* full of evil, injury, or injustice; unfair; as, a *wrongful* accusation.—*adv.* **wrong'ful-ly.**—*n.* **wrong'ful-ness.**

wrote (rōt), past tense of the irregular verb *write.*

wroth (rôth; *Br.* rōth), *adj.* angry; full of wrath; furious.

wrought (rôt), *Archaic*, past tense and past participle of *work:*—*p.adj.* worked; fashioned or molded from the rough: **wrought iron**, iron of low carbon content, produced in a puddling furnace: useful because of its toughness, ductility, and malleability.

wrung (rŭng), past tense and past participle of the irregular verb *wring.*

wry (rī), *adj.* [*comp.* wri'er, *superl.* wri'est], **1**, twisted; askew; as, to make a *wry* face; **2**, distorted or changed in meaning; perverted.—*adv.* **wry'ly.**—*n.* **wry'ness.**

wry-neck (rī'nĕk"), *n.* **1**, a bird of the woodpecker family: so called from its habit of twisting the head; **2**, a contraction of the neck muscles, causing an unnatural position of the head.

wych-elm (wĭch'-ĕlm"), *n.* an elm of Europe and northern Asia.

wye (wī), *n.* the letter Y, or something shaped like a Y.

wynd (wīnd), *n.* *Scot.*, a lane, alley, or small court.

X

xan-the-in (zăn'thē-ĭn), *n.* that part of the yellow coloring matter in flowers that is soluble in water: distinguished from *xanthin.*

xan-thic (zăn'thĭk), *adj.* having, or inclined to, a yellow color.

xan-thin (zăn'thĭn), *n.* **1,** that part of the yellow coloring matter in flowers that is insoluble in water: distinguished from *xanthein;* **2,** (preferably, *xanthine*), a white, amorphous substance, a derivative of carbonic acid, allied to urea, caffeine, etc.: found in the organs and secretions of the body.

xan-thous (zăn'thŭs), *adj.* pertaining to the yellow-skinned races, esp. the Mongolian, or to those races with yellowish, auburn, red, or brown hair.

xe-bec (zē'bĕk), *n.* a small, three-masted ship of the Mediterranean Sea: formerly used by the pirates of Algeria. Also, **ze'bec.**

XEBEC

xen-on (zĕn'ŏn; zē'nŏn), *n.* a heavy, inert, gaseous element occurring in the atmosphere in very minute quantities.

xi (zī; ksē), *n.* the 14th letter of the Greek alphabet [ξ, Ξ], corresponding approximately to English *x.*

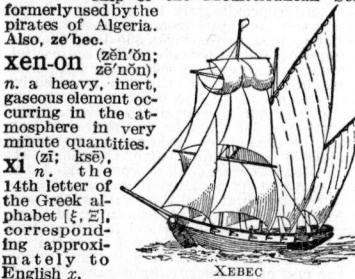

X ray **1,** usually in *pl.*, a Röntgen ray: a ray or radiation produced by an electric discharge in a vacuum tube, now known to be similar to a light ray, but of very short wave length, capable of penetrating many substances ordinarily opaque, and used in medical diagnosis to locate fractures, malformations, and pathological conditions of tissue, and in the treatment of certain morbid tissue conditions, as in cancer; **2,** a photograph made with the aid of such rays; a radiograph, or skiagraph. Also, **X'-ray'; x ray; x'-ray'.**

X-ray (ĕks'=rā'), *adj.* pertaining to X rays; as, an *X-ray* apparatus or photograph:—*v.t.* to examine or photograph with X rays:—*v.i.* to use an X-ray machine. Also, **x'-ray'.**

xy-lem (zī'lĕm), *n.* the woody tissue of plants; esp., in higher plants, the supporting and water-conducting, thick-walled cells of the vascular bundle: distinguished from *phloëm.*

xy-lene (zī'lēn), *n.* a colorless oily liquid in coal and wood tar.

xy-lo- (zī'lō-), a combining form from the Greek, meaning wood; as, *xylo*phone.

xy-lo-gen (zī'lō-jĕn), *n.* the substance which forms xylem.

xy-lo-graph (zī'lō-grăf), *n.* an engraving on a wooden block; also, an impression from such an engraving.

xy-log-ra-phy (zī-lŏg'rȧ-fĭ), *n.* the art or process of making prints from engravings on wood.—*adj.* **xy"lo-graph'ic.**

xy-loid (zī'loid), *adj.* **1,** like wood; **2,** composed of woody tissue.

xy-loi-din (zī-loi'dĭn), *n.* an explosive compound produced by the action of nitric acid on starch or wood fiber.

xy-lon-ite (zī'lŏn-īt), *n.* celluloid, an artificial material like ivory.

xy-lo-phone (zī'lō-fōn), *n.* a musical instrument made of parallel wooden bars, and played with small, flexible mallets.

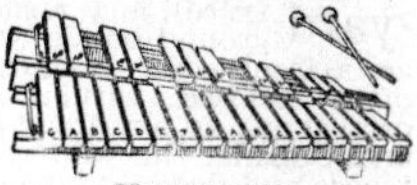

XYLOPHONE

xys-ter (zĭs'tĕr), *n.* a surgical instrument for scraping bones.

Y

y- (ĭ-), *prefix,* used in Middle English as a sign of the past participle, and still found in a few archaic words; as, *y*-cleped.

1-y (-ĭ), *n. suffix,* forming diminutives, appearing chiefly in childish names of animals and familiar forms of personal names; as, dogg*y:* also written *-ie;* as, lass*ie.*

2-y (-ĭ), *adj. suffix,* **1,** of; pertaining to; having; full of: added to nouns; as, ston*y;* guilt*y:* often spelled *-ey,* esp. when attached to words ending in *y;* as, clay*ey;* **2,** inclined toward; shading into: added to adjectives of color; as, gold*y*-brown; **3,** with intensive force but no change of meaning: added to adjectives: chiefly poetical; as, still*y.*

yac-ca (yăk'ȧ), *n.* either of two West Indian evergreens, the wood of which is used for furniture and other purposes.

yacht (yŏt), *n.* a light and quick sailing or steam vessel, used privately for pleasure or racing (see illus. next column):—*v.i.* to sail in a yacht.—*n.* **yacht'ing.**

yachts-man (yŏts'măn), *n.* [*pl.* yachtsmen (-mĕn)], one who owns or sails a yacht.—*n.fem.* **yachts'wom"an.**

Ya-hoo (yä'hōō), *n.* in Swift's "Gulliver's Travels," one of a race of brutes in human form, subject to a race of beings in the form of horses, but of superior intelligence, called *Houyhnhnms,* which see: **yahoo,** a person of bestial habits; also, a bumpkin.

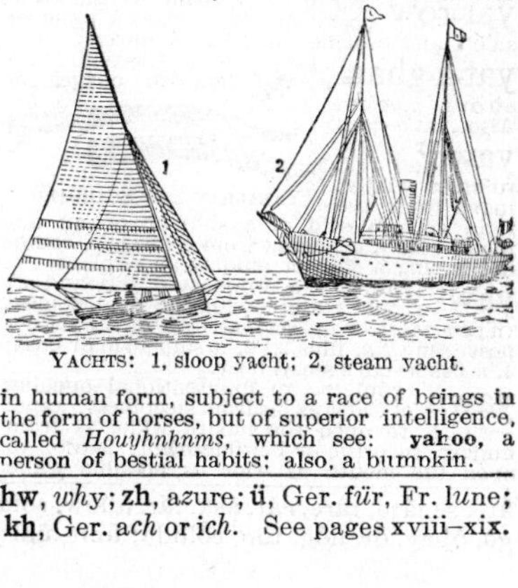

YACHTS: 1, sloop yacht; 2, steam yacht.

Yah-weh (yä'wĕ), *n.* Jehovah: a modern reconstruction of the supposed original name of the God of the ancient Hebrews, called *Jehovah* in the Bible. Also, **Yah'we; Yah've; Yah'veh; Jah'weh; Jah'veh.**

yak (yăk), *n.* a wild or domesticated ox of central Asia, with long hair hanging from its shoulders and sides.

YAK ($\frac{1}{68}$)

yam (yăm), *n.* **1,** a tropical vine with edible potatolike roots; also, the root; **2,** a kind of sweet potato.

yank (yăngk), *v.t. Colloq.,* to jerk or pull quickly:—*n. Colloq.,* a jerk or twist.

Yan-kee (yăng'kē), *n.* **1,** a citizen of New England; **2,** a native of the U. S.: chiefly a foreign usage; **3,** a soldier of the Federal armies, or any Northerner: so used in the South, esp. during the Civil War:—*adj.* pertaining to, or like, Yankees.

yap (yăp; yȧp), *v.i.* [*p.t.* and *p.p.* yapped (yăpt; yȧpt), *p.pr.* yap'ping], **1,** to bark or yelp: usually said of a small dog; **2,** *Slang,* to chatter:—*n.* **1,** a bark or yelp; **2,** a worthless cur; **3,** *Slang,* a noisy, ill-bred person.

[1]**yard** (yärd), *n* **1,** the standard unit of English lineal measure, equal to three feet, or 36 inches; **2,** a measuring rod of 36 inches; yardstick; **3,** a comparatively slender spar slung crosswise to a mast: used to support a sail (see *rigging,* illus.).

[2]**yard** (yärd), *n.* **1,** a small piece of inclosed ground beside or around a building; as, a front *yard;* a church*yard;* **2,** a space, often inclosed, within which any work is carried on; as, a railroad *yard;* **3,** in the U. S. and Canada, the winter browsing ground of moose and deer:—*v.t.* to collect within, or to gather into, an inclosure:—*v.i.* **1,** in the U. S. and Canada, to resort to winter pastures: said of deer and moose; **2,** to shoot game in their winter yard.

yard-arm (yärd'ärm''), *n.* either end of the yard that supports a sail.

yard-stick (yärd'stĭk''), *n.* a measuring stick three feet in length.

yarn (yärn), *n.* **1,** heavy spun thread, esp. of wool; **2,** *Colloq.,* an exaggerated story:—*v.i.* to tell an unlikely story.

yar-row (yăr'ō), *n.* a plant of the composite family, having a pungent smell, and bearing small white flowers.

yat-a-ghan (yăt'ȧ-găn; yä''tä-gän'), *n.* a curved Turkish dagger or short saber. Also, **yat'a-gan.**

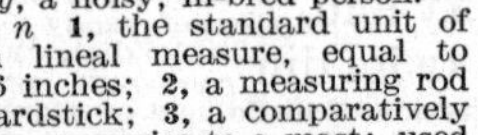

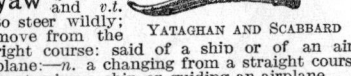

YATAGHAN AND SCABBARD

yaw (yô), *v.i.* and *v.t.* to steer wildly; move from the right course: said of a ship or of an airplane:—*n.* a changing from a straight course in steering a ship or guiding an airplane.

yawl (yôl), *n.* **1,** a two-masted, fore-and-aft rigged vessel having the smaller mast (jigger mast or mizzenmast) aft of the rudder post (see *ship,* illus.); **2,** a ship's small boat; **3,** a fisherman's small boat.

yawn (yôn), *n.* an unintentional opening of the jaws, as from sleepiness; gape:—*v.i.* **1,** to open the mouth wide, as from hunger, surprise, or bewilderment; **2,** esp., to open the mouth as wide as possible while inhaling deeply, as from drowsiness; **3,** to open wide; as, the chasm *yawned* beneath him.

y-cleped (ĭ-klĕpt'), *p.p. Obs.* or *Archaic,* called; named. Also, **y-clept'.**

[1]**ye** (yē), *pron. Archaic* and *Poetic,* you: plural of *thou:* strictly used for nominative plural only, but sometimes used for the nominative and objective of both singular and plural.

[2]**ye** (thē), *definite article,* the: an archaic form of writing or printing *the,* in which the *y* represents the Anglo-Saxon and Middle English character *thorn* [þ], equivalent to modern English *th:* generally incorrectly pronounced *yē:* also written *ye.*

yea (yā), *adv.* **1,** yes; indeed; **2,** truly; **3,** not only this, but more:—*n.* an affirmative vote; also, an affirmative voter.

yean (yēn), *v.i.* and *v.t.* of sheep or goats, to give birth to (young).

yean-ling (yēn'lĭng), *n.* the young of the sheep or goat.

year (yēr), *n.* **1,** the length of time required by the earth to make one complete revolution around the sun, or by the sun to complete approximately its apparent circuit among the fixed stars from vernal equinox to vernal equinox, consisting of 365 days, 5 hours, 48 minutes, and 46 seconds: called *equinoctial, astronomical, natural,* or *solar, year;* **2,** a period approximately equal to the time required by the earth to make one complete revolution around the sun; a period of twelve months, consisting of 365 days, or, in the case of leap year, 366 days, now reckoned as beginning January 1 and ending with December 31: also called *calendar, civil,* or *legal year;* **3,** the time required by a planet to make one complete revolution around the sun; as, the *year* of Mars or of Saturn; **4,** usually in *pl.,* age; time of life; as, well stricken in *years:* **leap year,** a year of 366 days, or one more than in a common year, the extra day being added at the end of February: **light year,** the distance traversed in a year by a light wave traveling at the rate of about 186,000 miles a second: used as a unit in stating stellar distances: **lunar year,** a year of twelve lunar months that contains 354 days: **year of grace,** any year of the Christian Era: designated by *A. D.:* also called *year of our Lord.*

year-book (yēr'bo͝ok''), *n.* **1,** a book giving facts about the current year, such as its seasons, dates, etc.; **2,** a book either published or revised annually.

year-ling (yēr'lĭng), *n.* an animal between one and two years old:—*adj.* one year old; of a year's duration.

year-ly (yēr'lĭ), *adj.* **1,** pertaining to a year; as, *yearly* rent; **2,** lasting, or accomplished in, a year; **3,** happening or coming once a year:—*adv.* once a year.

yearn (yûrn), *v.i.* to be filled with longing, compassion, or tenderness.

yeast (yēst), *n.* **1,** a fungus consisting of minute cells, causing fermentation in sugar solutions and starchy substances: used in making beer, bread, etc.; **2,** froth.

yeast-y (yēs'tĭ), *adj.* [*comp.* yeast'i-er, *superl.* yeast'i-est], **1,** tending to ferment or rise; **2,** light; **3,** frothy.

yegg-man (yĕg'măn), *n.* [*pl.* yeggmen (-mĕn)], *Slang,* a criminal; esp., a burglar: also called *yegg.*

yelk (yĕlk), *n. Rare,* the yellow part of an egg. See **yolk,** *Pfd. S.*

yell (yĕl), *n.* **1,** a loud cry, as of pain, rage, or terror; a shriek; **2,** a characteristic shout, as used in warfare or by a group of persons; as, a college *yell:*—*v.t.* to shout or utter noisily:—*v.i.* to utter a sharp cry.

yel-low (yĕl'ō), *adj.* **1,** of the color of gold, butter, etc.; **2,** *Slang,* cowardly or

āte, senāte, râre, căt, ȧsk, fär, ållow, sofȧ; ēve, ēvent, ĕll, writẽr, novẹl; nīne, pĭn; gō, ōbey, ôr, dôg, tŏp, cŏllide; ūnit, ūnite, ûrn, cŭt, focus; no͞on, fo͝ot; sour; coin;

dishonorable; as, a *yellow* streak; 3, *Colloq.*, sensational: said of some newspapers:—*n.* **1**, an elementary color, between orange and green in the spectrum; **2**, any dye or paint that gives this color; **3**, the yolk of an egg:—*v.t.* and *v.i.* to make, or become, yellow.—*adj.* **yel'low-ish.**—*n.* **yel'low-ness.**

yel-low-bird (yĕl'ō-bûrd''), *n.* **1**, the American goldfinch; **2**, the yellow warbler; **3**, in England, the golden oriole.

yel-low fe-ver a dangerous, infectious fever of the tropics, marked by a yellow skin, vomiting, etc., and carried by certain mosquitoes; yellow jack.

yel-low-ham-mer (yĕl'ō-hăm''ẽr), *n.* **1**, in the U. S., the flicker; **2**, an Old World finch, the male of which has bright yellow markings.

yel-low jack **1**, yellow fever; **2**, the quarantine flag; **3**, a West Indian golden and silvery food fish.

yel-low jack-et an American wasp, having a black abdomen marked with yellow.

yel-low spot a small yellowish area on the retina of the eye, on which are formed the images of objects directly viewed and most distinctly seen.

yelp (yĕlp), *v.i.* to utter a sharp bark, as a dog when hurt:—*n.* a sharp, quick bark, as of a dog.—*n.* **yelp'er.**—*n.* **yelp'ing.**

yen (yĕn), *n.* [*pl.* yen], the Japanese unit of coinage, worth, at par, about 50 cents.

yeo-man (yō'măn), *n.* [*pl.* yeomen (-mĕn)], **1**, formerly, a retainer of a member of the English nobility; **2**, in England, a commoner; a small landowner; **3**, in the U. S. navy, a petty officer who does clerical work: **yeoman of the guard**, one of the bodyguard of the English sovereign, consisting of one hundred yeomen, armed with partisans, or pikes.—*adj.* and *adv.* **yeo'man-ly.**

yeo-man-ry (yō'măn-rĭ), *n.* **1**, yeomen collectively; **2**, the common people of England, esp. the farming class.

yes (yĕs), *adv.* aye; yea; it is so: opp. of *no.*

yes-ter (yĕs'tẽr), *adj.* pertaining to a period of time just past: usually in compounds; as, *yester*year.

yes-ter-day (yĕs'tẽr-dā), *n.* **1**, the day just past; **2**, hence, a recent day:—*adv.* on the day before today.

yes-ter-year (yĕs'tẽr-yẽr''), *n.* the preceding year; last year.

yet (yĕt), *adv.* **1**, up until now; as, he has not come *yet;* **2**, still: in relation to time; as, I have your present *yet;* **3**, in addition; besides; still; as, greater *yet;* **4**, finally; **5**, even though this is so; still; as, *yet* I cannot do it: **as yet**, up till now:—*conj.* **1**, nevertheless; however; **2**, although; though.

yew (yōō), *n.* **1**, a large, cone-bearing, evergreen tree of the Old World, with dark green foliage; also, the fine-grained wood of this tree, formerly used for making bows; **2**, a small evergreen tree of Pacific North America; **3**, a dwarf evergreen shrub of the eastern U. S., often called *ground hemlock;* **4**, *Archaic*, a bow of wood of the yew.

Y-gerne (ē-gĕrn'), *n.* in the Arthurian legend, the beautiful mother of King Arthur. Also, **I-graine'**, *Pfd. S.*

Ygg-dra-sill (ĭg'drȧ-sĭl), *n.* in Norse mythology, the great ash tree whose roots embrace and support heaven, earth, and hell, destined to live until the end of the world. Also, **Yg'dra-sil; Yg'dra-syl.**

Yid-dish (yĭd'ĭsh), *n.* a kind of mixed German and Hebrew language spoken by Jews.

yield (yēld), *v.t.* **1**, to produce; as, the land *yields* wheat; **2**, to concede; as, I *yield* the point; **3**, to surrender; **4**, to afford; as, to *yield* space; **5**, to give as return for labor, money invested, etc.:—*v.i.* **1**, to assent; comply; **2**, to give way; submit; **3**, to give a return; produce:—*n.* the return for labor expended or for capital invested.—*n.* **yield'er.**

yield-ing (yēld'ĭng), *p.adj.* **1**, inclined to give way; flexible; **2**, compliant; obedient.—*adv.* **yield'ing-ly.**

-yl (-ĭl), *suffix*, a termination used to designate a radical, or group of atoms which act as a single atom; as, eth*yl*.

yo-del (yō'dl), *v.t.* and *v.i.* to sing or call with sudden changes in the voice from chest tones to falsetto:—*n.* a call or song so executed: a form of music common among Swiss shepherds. Also, **yo'dle.**—*n.* **yo'del-er.**

yo-ga (yō'gȧ), *n.* a form of Hindu mystical and ascetic philosophy which enjoins withdrawal from worldly things, and a concentration of thought upon the Supreme Spirit. Also, **Yo'ga.**

yo-gi (yō'gē), *n.* [*pl.* yogis (-gēz)], one who follows the yoga; an ascetic. Also, **yo'gin** (yō'gĕn).—*n.* **yo'gism.**

yoke (yōk), *n.* **1**, a wooden frame to couple draft animals, as oxen, together for work; **2**, a frame of wood fitted to a person's shoulders for carrying a bucket, or the like, hanging from each end; **3**, a band or piece of cloth cut to fit the shoulders or hips, to support a gathered or plaited part, as of a skirt; **4**, that which binds or connects; a bond or tie; **5**, a mark or sign of slavery; **6**, hence, bondage; **7**, two animals coupled together; as, a *yoke* of oxen:—*v.t.* [*p.t.* and *p.p.* yoked (yōkt), *p.pr.* yok'ing], **1**, to put a yoke on; as, to *yoke* oxen; **2**, to tie together; couple; **3**, to enslave or confine.

yoke-fel-low (yōk'fĕl''ō), *n.* **1**, a person bound to another by some tie; **2**, an associate in work.

yo-kel (yō'kl), *n.* a plowboy; rustic; country fellow.

yolk (yōk; yōlk), *n.* **1**, the yellow part of an egg; **2**, an oily secretion found in sheep's wool. Also, *Rare*, **yelk.**—*adj.* **yolk'y.**

Yom Kip-pur (yŏm kĭp'ōōr), the Hebrew "Day of Atonement," observed by 24 hours of fasting (Leviticus 16) on the 10th day of the first month of the Jewish civil year.

yon (yŏn), *adj.* and *adv.* *Poetic*, yonder:—*pron.* *Rare*, that; those: used of persons or things at a distance, yet within view.

yon-der (yŏn'dẽr), *adj.* situated at a distance, but still visible:—*adv.* at that place; there.

yore (yōr), *n.* old time; long ago: used only in *of yore.*

York (yôrk), *n.* an English royal house which occupied the throne from 1461 to 1485, and was opposed to the house of Lancaster in the Wars of the Roses.—*adj.* and *n.* **York'ist.**

you (yōō), *pron.* of the second person (used as *sing.* or *pl.* but always taking a plural verb), [*nom.* you, *poss.* your (yōōr), yours (yōōrz), *obj.* you], **1**, the person or persons addressed; **2**, one; anyone; a person; people: used as an indefinite pronoun.

young (yŭng), *adj.* **1**, being in the early part of life or growth; **2**, inexperienced; **3**, vigorous in body or mind; **4**, pertaining to youth; **5**, of youthful appearance:—*n.* the offspring of animals.—*adj.* **young'ish.**

young-ling (yŭng'lĭng), *n.* a person in early years; also, a young animal or plant:—*adj.* young; immature.

young-ster (yŭng'stẽr), *n.* **1**, a person in early years; a child or youth; lad; **2**, *Slang*, a subaltern recently assigned to a regiment or other organization.

your (yo͝or), *poss. adj.* belonging to you: possessive case of the personal pronoun *you:* used before the noun; as, *your* coat.

yours (yo͝orz), a possessive form of the personal pronoun *you*, used alone: **1**, as *adj.*, in the predicate; as, whose hat is it? it is *yours;* **2**, as *pron.;* as, which hat have you? I have *yours*.

your-self (yo͝or-sĕlf′), *pron.* [*pl.* your-selves (-sĕlvz′)], you in your own person: used as a reflexive and as an emphatic form of *you*.

youth (yo͞oth), *n.* **1**, the state or quality of being young; **2**, a young person, esp. a young man; **3**, young people; **4**, the part of life between childhood and maturity.

youth-ful (yo͞oth′fo͝ol), *adj.* **1**, pertaining to the early part of life; **2**, fresh; vigorous; **3**, immature.—*adv.* **youth′ful-ly.**—*n.* **youth′ful-ness.**

yowl (youl), *n.* a howl; a long, wailing cry, as of a cat:—*v.i.* to howl or yell.

yuc-ca (yŭk′ȧ), *n.* a plant of the lily family, having long, pointed leaves, and bearing white blossoms.

YUCCA (1/70)

Yu-go-slav (yo͞o′gō-slăv″ -slăv″), *n.* a citizen of Yugoslavia, or, officially, the Serb-Croat-Slovene state, located south of Austria and Hungary and east of the Adriatic:—*adj.* pertaining to the Yugoslavs. Also, **Yu′go-Slav″; Ju′go-slav″.**—*adj.* **Yu″go-slav′i-an.**—*adj.* **Yu″go-slav′ic.**

yule (yo͞ol), *n.* Christmas or Christmas time; also, the Christmas feast: **yule log,** a huge log for the Christmas fire.

yule-tide (yo͞ol′tīd″), *n.* Christmas time; the holiday season.

Z

Zac-chæ-us (ză-kē′ŭs; *Colloq.* zăk′ē-ŭs), *n.* in the Bible, a rich publican with whom Jesus dined in Jericho (Luke 19:2-10). Also, **Zac-che′us.**

Zach-a-ri-as (zăk″ȧ-rī′ȧs), *n.* in the Bible, **1**, the father of John the Baptist (Luke 1:5); **2**, a certain martyr (Matthew 23:35); **3**, Zechariah: so called in the Douay Bible.—*abbr.* **Zach.**

za-ny (zā′nĭ), *n.* [*pl.* zanies (-nĭz)], **1**, a clown; buffoon; **2**, a stupid person.

zeal (zēl), *n.* ardor in a cause, or in promoting some end; great earnestness.

zeal-ot (zĕl′ŭt), *n.* an enthusiast; a fanatic; one who is zealous.—*n.* **zeal′ot-ry.**

zeal-ous (zĕl′ŭs), *adj.* eager in the pursuit of an object; enthusiastic.—*adv.* **zeal′ous-ly.**—*n.* **zeal′ous-ness.**

ze-bec (zē′bĕk), *n.* a small, three-masted ship, sometimes seen in the Mediterranean. See **xe′bec,** *Pfd. S.*

Zeb-e-dee (zĕb′ē-dē), *n.* in the Bible, father of the disciples James and John (Matthew 4:21).

ZEBRA (1/80)

ze-bra (zē′brȧ), *n.* any of several African wild animals of the horse family, esp. one with dark stripes on a white or tawny body.

ze-bu (zē′bū), *n.* the Indian ox or cow, with long ears, and a large hump on the shoulders.

ZEBU (1/24)

Zeb-u-lun (zĕb′ū-lŭn), *n.* in the Bible, **1**, a son of Jacob (Genesis 30:20); **2**, the tribe descended from him: one of the twelve tribes of Israel.

Zech-a-ri-ah (zĕk″ȧ-rī′ȧ), *n.* **1**, an ancient Hebrew prophet; **2**, a short book of the Old Testament, containing his prophecies. Also, in the Douay Bible, **Zach″a-ri′as.**—*abbr.* **Zech.**

zed (zĕd), *n.* the English name for Z, the last letter of the alphabet.

zem-stvo (zĕmst′fō), *n.* [*pl.* zemstvos (-fōz)], a local Russian elective body, administering local affairs, such as roads, schools, and charity.

ze-na-na (zē-nä′nȧ), *n.* in India, the part of the house set apart for the women; the harem. Also, **za-na′na** (zȧ-).

Zend (zĕnd), *n.* **1**, a translation of, and commentary on, the Avesta, or sacred writings of ancient Persia by Zoroaster; **2**, sometimes, the language of the Avesta: **Zend-Avesta,** (ȧ-vĕs′tȧ), commonly, the sacred writings of ancient Persia; more properly, the sacred writings, or *Avesta*, along with the commentary, or *Zend*.

zen-dik (zĕn-dēk′), *n.* in the East, an unbeliever, or atheist.

ze-nith (zē′nĭth; *Br.* zĕn′ĭth), *n.* the point in the heavens directly overhead: opp. of *nadir;* **2**, the greatest height; summit.

Zeph-a-ni-ah (zĕf″ȧ-nī′ȧ), *n.* in the Bible, **1**, an ancient Hebrew prophet; **2**, a book of the Old Testament giving his message. Also, in the Douay Bible, **Soph″o-ni′as** (sŏf″ō-nī′ăs).—*abbr.* **Zeph.**

zeph-yr (zĕf′ẽr), *n.* **1**, the west wind; **2**, a soft, gentle breeze; **3**, a kind of soft, fine woolen yarn.

Zep-pe-lin (zĕp′ē-lĭn; *Ger.* tsĕp″ē-lēn′), *n.* a large, cigar-shaped, dirigible balloon, able to fly long distances.

ze-ro (zē′rō), *n.* [*pl.* zeros; zeroes (-rōz)], **1**, a cipher; **2**, nothing; **3**, the point on a scale from which reckoning begins, as on a thermometer; **4**, the lowest point: **absolute zero,** the lowest temperature that the nature of matter admits, about 273.1° below zero centigrade: **zero hour,** the hour fixed for beginning an attack.

zest (zĕst), *n.* **1**, a spicy flavor; something that gives a pleasant taste or relish; **2**, keen enjoyment; eager enthusiasm; as, he went at his work with *zest*.

ze-ta (zē′tȧ; zā′tȧ), *n.* the sixth letter of the Greek alphabet [ζ, Z], corresponding in general to English *z* and *dz*.

zeug-ma (zūg′mȧ), *n.* a figure of speech in which a word, esp. a verb or an adjective, serves a double purpose, as by governing or referring to two words, its sense and application usually changing; as, his *fair* hair and play attracted the ladies; we *ate* a bun and a glass of milk.

Zeus (zūs), *n.* in Greek mythology, the supreme god, ruler of Olympus: identified with Roman *Jupiter*.

zig-zag (zĭg′zăg″), *n.* **1**, one of a number of short, sharp angles or turns in a course; **2**, something with quick turns, as a path:—*adj.* having short, sharp turns:—*adv.* crookedly; with sharp turns:—*v.t.* and *v.i.* [*p.t.* and *p.p.* -zagged″ (-zăgd″), *p.pr.* -zag″-ging], to move, form, or be in zigzags.

zinc (zĭngk), *n.* an important, bluish white metal, which can stand exposure to air and moisture: **zinc blende**, native sulphide of zinc, an important zinc ore:—*v.t.* [*p.t.* and *p.p.* zincked or zinced (zĭngkt), *p.pr.* zinck′ing or zinc′ing], to coat or cover with zinc.—*adj.* **zinck′y; zink′y.**—*adj* **zinc′ous.**

zin-cog-ra-phy (zĭng-kŏg′rȧ-fĭ), *n.* the art of drawing upon, or printing from, zinc plates.

zinc-oid (zĭngk′oid), *adj.* pertaining to zinc; zinclike, as in color.

zin-ni-a (zĭn′ĭ-ȧ), *n.* any of several plants, often cultivated, bearing bright-colored, asterlike flowers.

Zi-on (zī′ŏn), *n.* **1**, a hill in Jerusalem, the royal residence of King David and his successors and the seat of the temple; **2**, the chosen people; the Jewish race; **3**, the Church of God; **4**, the new Jerusalem, or heaven. Also, **Si′on.**

Zi-on-ism (zī′ŏn-ĭzm), *n.* a plan for, or belief in, the return of the Jews as a nation to Palestine.—*n.* **Zi′on-ist.**

zir-con (zûr′kŏn), *n.* zirconium silicate, an important ore of zirconium.

zir-co-ni-a (zẽr-kō′nĭ-ȧ), *n.* zirconium dioxide: notable for hardness and resistance to heat: much used for furnace linings.

zir-co-ni-um (zẽr-kō′nĭ-ŭm), *n.* a lustrous, blackish gray metallic element found widely distributed in nature: useful in various alloys, and in compounds for resisting heat and acids.

zith-er (zĭth′ẽr), *n.* a modern musical instrument of the lyre class, with about 36 strings over a shallow sounding box, played by plucking with a plectrum: distinguished from *cittern*. Also, **zith′ern.**

zit-tern (zĭt′ẽrn), *n.* a guitarlike stringed instrument. See **cit′tern,** *Pfd. S.*

zlo-ty (zlō′tĭ), *n.* [*pl.* zlotys (-tĭz)], the monetary unit of Poland, equivalent to 11.22 cents by a decree of 1927.

zo-di-ac (zō′dĭ-ăk), *n.* **1**, a belt of twelve constellations, extending eight degrees on each side of the ecliptic, containing the paths of the moon, planets, and most of the asteroids, and divided into twelve equal parts, called *signs;* **2**, a figure or diagram of the heavens, showing the relation of the parts of the zodiac to the sun and the earth: **signs of the zodiac,** the twelve divisions of the zodiac, each with a specific name, as Leo, the Lion, and each represented by a symbolic design.

A REPRESENTATION OF THE SIGNS OF THE ZODIAC

[The figures **1**, 2, etc., represent the months (January, February, etc.) during which the sun enters the respective signs. As commonly numbered, Aries (3) is the first sign of the zodiac, Taurus (4) the second, etc.]

1, Aquarius, *Water Bearer;* 2, Pisces, *Fishes;* 3, Aries, *Ram;* 4, Taurus, *Bull;* 5, Gemini, *Twins;* 6, Cancer, *Crab;* 7, Leo, *Lion;* 8, Virgo, *Virgin;* 9, Libra, *Balance;* 10, Scorpio, *Scorpion;* 11, Sagittarius, *Archer;* 12, Capricornus, *Goat.*

zo-di-a-cal (zō-dī′ȧ-kăl), *adj.* pertaining to, or situated within or along, the zodiac: **zodiacal light,** a faint radiance in the sky, best seen in tropical latitudes, lying along the zodiac in the east before dawn and in the west after evening twilight.

zo-ic (zō′ĭk), *adj.* **1**, pertaining to, or connected with, animal life; **2**, containing fossils: said of rocks.

***Zoll-ver-ein** (tsôl′fẽr-īn″), [Ger.], *n.* **1**, the German customs union, formed in the first half of the 19th century and gradually extended, with the aim of establishing uniform rates throughout the German Confederation; **2**, any customs union.

zone (zōn), *n.* **1**, any encircling belt, band, stripe, or path; as, a *zone* of color; **2**, any of the five sections into which the earth's surface is divided by imaginary lines on the parallels of latitude at 23° 27′ and

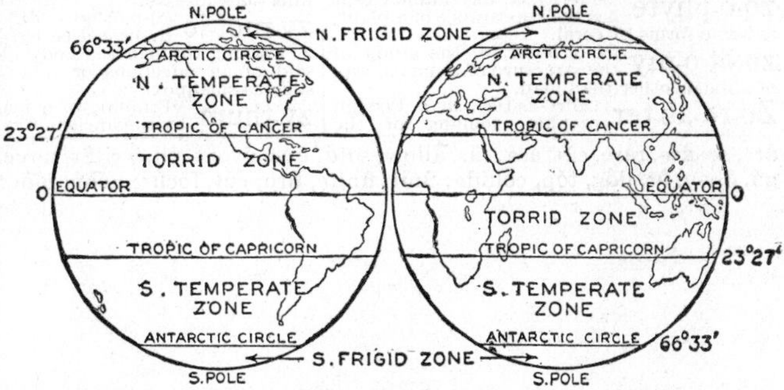

THE ZONES OF THE EARTH

66° 33′ north and south of the equator: called *torrid zone* (about the equator), *frigid zones* (about the poles), and *temperate zones* (lying between); **3**, in the U. S. parcel-post system, an area including all post offices between two specified radial distances from a given mailing point: used in determining postal rates for parcels; as, points in the third *zone* lie between 150 and 300 miles from the mailing point; **4**, an area or region distinct because of its use, its natural characteristics, or the like; as, a safety *zone;* a cotton *zone;* **5**, in mathematics, the part of the surface of a sphere included between two parallel planes:—*v.t.* [*p.t.* and *p.p.* zoned (zōnd), *p.pr.* zon′ing], to divide into areas, or zones.—*adj.* **zon′al.**—*p.adj.* **zoned** (zōnd).

ZONE OF A SPHERE

zoo (zōō), *n. Colloq.*, a park or other large inclosure in which live animals are kept for public exhibition; a zoölogical garden.

zo-ö- (zō′ō-), a combining form from the Greek, meaning life; as, *zoö*graphy; *zoö*logy; *zoö*tomy. Also, **zo-.**

zo-ö-ge-og-ra-phy (zō″ō-jē-ŏg′rȧ-fĭ), *n.* the study or description of the distribution of animals in different parts of the earth; animal geography. —*adj.* **zo″ö-ge″o-graph′ic; zo″ö-ge″o-graph′i-cal.**—*n.* **zo″ö-ge-og′ra-pher.**

zo-ög-ra-phy (zō-ŏg′rȧ-fĭ), *n.* [*pl.* zoögraphies (-fĭz)], the technical description of animals, their habits, etc.—*adj.* **zo″ö-graph′ic; zo″ö-graph′i-cal.**

zo-oid (zō′oid), *n.* **1**, a unit in a colonial animal, as one individual in a coral colony; **2**, an organism that resembles an animal; **3**, a free-swimming sperm of plant or animal:—*adj.* pertaining to, or resembling, an animal.—*adj.* **zo-oi′dal.**

zo-öl-a-try (zō-ŏl′ȧ-trĭ), *n.* animal worship, as the crocodile worship of Egypt.—*n.* **zo-öl′a-ter.**

zo-ö-log-i-cal (zō″ō-lŏj′ĭ-kăl), *adj.* pertaining to zoölogy, or the science of animal life.—*adv.* **zo″ö-log′i-cal-ly.**

zo-öl-o-gist (zō-ŏl′ō-jĭst), *n.* one skilled in the science of animal life.

zo-öl-o-gy (zō-ŏl′ō-jĭ), *n.* [*pl.* zoölogies (-jĭz)], the branch of biology dealing with animal life; also, a textbook on this subject.

zoom (zōōm), *n.* in aëronautics, the maneuver executed when a pilot turns his airplane suddenly upward, utilizing its speed in climbing for a time at a steeper angle than can be maintained:—*v.i.* to execute such a maneuver.

zo-ö-phyte (zō′ō-fīt), *n.* any animal that has the appearance of a plant, as some forms of coral.

zo-öt-o-my (zō-ŏt′ō-mĭ), *n.* the study of the structure of animals, esp. of animals other than man.

Zo-ro-as-ter (zō″rō-ăs′tẽr), *n.* a Persian prophet, founder of the ancient religion that preceded Mohammedanism. Also, **Za″ra-thus′tra** (zä″rȧ-thōōs′trȧ).

Zo-ro-as-tri-an (zō″rō-ăs′trĭ-ăn), *adj.* pertaining to Zoroaster, the founder of the ancient Persian religion, or to his doctrines:—*n.* a follower of Zoroaster.—*n.* **Zo″ro-as′tri-an-ism.**

Zou-ave (zōō-äv′), *n.* **1**, in the French army until 1914, an infantryman wearing a brightly colored uniform similar to that worn in Algeria; **2**, one of a body of soldiers in the American Civil War, which adopted a similar dress and drill.

zounds (zoundz), *interj. Archaic*, an oath expressing anger or wonder.

Zu-lu (zōō′lōō), *n.* one of a warlike native tribe of Natal, South Africa.

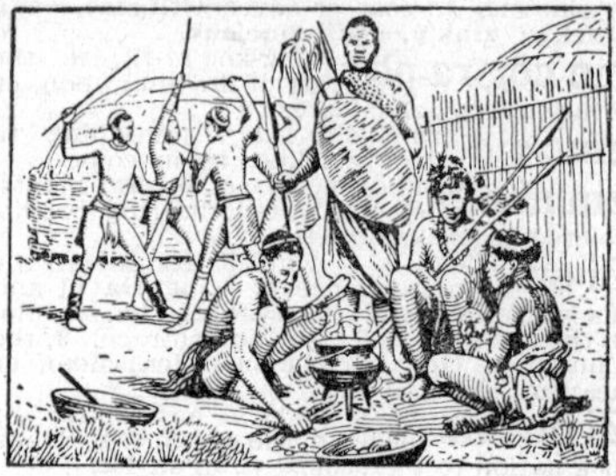

ZULUS

Zu-ñi (zōō′nyē; sōō′-), *n.* [*pl.* Zuñis (-nyēz); Zuñi], one of a tribe of Pueblo Indians of New Mexico.

zwie-back (zwē′băk″; *Ger.* tsvē′-), *n.* a kind of biscuit or roll first baked in a loaf and then sliced and browned.

Zwing-li-an (tsvĭng′lĭ-ăn; zwĭng′glĭ-ăn), *adj.* pertaining to Ulrich Zwingli (1484–1531), leader of the Swiss Protestant Reformation, or to his doctrines: —*n.* a follower of Zwingli.

zyme (zīm), *n.* **1**, that which causes fermentation; **2**, a virus or ferment supposed to be the cause of diseases that result from the multiplication of disease germs in the body.—*adj.* **zym′ic** (zīm′ĭk; zĭm′ĭk).

zy-mol-o-gy (zī-mŏl′ō-jĭ), *n.* [*pl.* zymologies (-jĭz)], the science or study of fermentation.—*n.* **zy-mol′o-gist.**

zy-mo-sis (zī-mō′sĭs), *n.* **1**, a fermentation; **2**, any contagious or infectious disease.

zy-mot-ic (zī-mŏt′ĭk), *adj.* **1**, pertaining to, or caused by, fermentation; **2**, working through the body like a ferment: said of an infectious or contagious disease, such as smallpox.

zy-thum (zī′thŭm), *n.* a malt beer made by the ancient Egyptians.

MYTHOLOGICAL, BIBLICAL, AND LITERARY NAMES

These names are in addition to those contained in the main section of the dictionary. Fictitious literary characters and book titles are listed as they appear in the original text: that is, Adam Bede is in the "A" section. This is true, except where a character's title designates his occupation (Bligh, Captain). Under mythological names, the abbreviation Cl. (Classical) indicates that the name is associated with both Greek and Roman mythology.

MYTHOLOGICAL NAMES

Achates (ȧ-kā′tēz), [Cl.], the companion of Æneas in Vergil's "Æneid."

Acheron (ăk′ēr-ŏn), [Cl.], the "river of woe," one of the five rivers of Hades. Over this river (or the Styx) the aged boatman, Charon, ferried the souls of the dead.

Achilles (ȧ-kĭl′ēz), [Cl.], the greatest Greek hero of the Trojan War; son of Peleus and Thetis; hero of Homer's "Iliad"; Greek type of youthful strength, beauty, and valor. In anger at Agamemnon for having taken Briseis, he withdrew from combat at the siege of Troy, but soon returned to avenge the death of his friend Patroclus. He was killed by Paris, who treacherously shot him in the heel, his one vulnerable spot.

Actæon (ăk-tē′ŏn), [Cl.], a Greek hunter who came upon Artemis (Diana) bathing. In anger, she turned him into a stag. His own hounds killed him.

Admetus (ăd-mē′tŭs), [Cl.], king of Thessaly, saved from death by Alcestis, his wife, who voluntarily died in his stead. His old friend, Heracles (Hercules), however, restored her to life.

Adonis (ȧ-dō′nĭs), [Cl.], a beautiful youth beloved by Venus. He was killed by a wild boar. The tears which Venus shed at his death became anemones and the drops of his blood became red roses.

Æacus (ē′ȧ-kŭs), [Cl.], a king of Ægina famous for his justice and piety; grandfather of Achilles. After his death, he was associated with Rhadamanthus and Minos, in judging the spirits of the dead.

Æëtes (ē-ē′tēz), [Cl.], father of Medea and king of Colchis, where the Golden Fleece was kept.

Ægir (ē′jĭr; â′gĭr), [Teut.], god of the sea, who entertained the gods every harvest time. Also, **Æger; Egir.**

ægis (ē′jĭs), breastplate of Athena (Minerva), bordered with serpents and set with the Gorgon's head. Also, **egis.**

Ægisthus (ē-jĭs′thŭs), [Cl.], a nephew of Atreus, and lover of Clytemnestra, with whom he murdered her husband Agamemnon upon the latter's return from the Trojan War, and was himself slain by Orestes.

Æneas (ē-nē′ăs), [Cl.], a Trojan prince, son of Anchises and the goddess Aphrodite (Venus); the hero of Vergil's "Æneid."

Æneid (ē-nē′ĭd), Vergil's Latin epic poem, of which Æneas is the hero.

Æolus (ē′ō-lŭs), [Cl.], the god of the winds, which he kept imprisoned in a cavern.

Æsculapius (ĕs″kū-lā′pĭ-ŭs), [Rom.], the god of medicine, and the son of Apollo, killed by Jupiter with a thunderbolt on account of his skill, and particularly for having restored Hippolytus to life: identified with the Greek Asclepius.

Æsir (ē′sĭr; â′sĭr), *pl.*, [*sing.* As (äs)], [Teut.], the chief gods, including Odin or Woden, Thor or Donar, Tyr or Tiu, Balder, Forseti, Heimdall, Loki, and others. Loki later became leader of the forces of Hel, in conflict with whom most of the Æsir were to be destroyed on the last day (Ragnarok). Associated with these gods were eighteen goddesses.

Æson (ē′sŏn), [Cl.], the father of Jason, the Argonaut; restored to youth by Medea, the enchantress.

Agamemnon (ăg″ȧ-mĕm′nŏn), [Cl.], king of Mycenæ, brother of Menelaus, and commander in chief of the Greeks at Troy.

Aglaia (ȧ-glā′yȧ), [Cl.], brilliance, one of the three Graces.

Agni (ăg′nē), [Hindu], the Vedic god of fire: similar to Hephæstus (Vulcan).

Ajax (ā′jăks), [Cl.], **1**, in Homer's "Iliad," the son of Telamon, and next to Achilles the bravest of all the Greeks in the Trojan War; **2**, the son of Oïleus, king of Locris, second only to Achilles in fleetness.

Albion (ăl′bĭ-ŏn), [Cl.], a son of Poseidon (Neptune), founder of a kingdom in Britain, slain by Hercules (Heracles).

Alcestis (ăl-sĕs′tĭs), [Cl.], wife of Admetus, king of Thessaly, and permitted by the Fates to die in his place, but later restored to life by Hercules (Heracles).

Alcides (ăl-sī′dēz), [Cl.], Hercules (Heracles): so called because Alcæus was the father of his mother's husband.

Alecto (ȧ-lĕk′tō), [Cl.], one of the three Furies.

Alpheus (ăl-fē′ŭs), [Cl.], a river god who loved and pursued the nymph Arethusa until Artemis (Diana) changed her into a stream, whereupon their waters united in the fountain of Arethusa on the island of Ortygia, Sicily.

Amazons (ăm′ȧ-zŏnz), [Cl.], a warlike race of women from Asia Minor, who helped the Trojans in the Trojan War.

ambrosia (ăm-brō′zhĭ-ȧ; -zĭ-ȧ), the substance which with nectar formed the food and drink of the Greek gods.

Ammon (ăm′ŏn), [Egypt.], the supreme god in Thebes, upper Egypt: identified by the Romans with Jupiter in *Jupiter Ammon.* Also, **Amon** (ä′mŏn); **Amen** (ä′mĕn).

Amphion (ăm-fī′ŏn), [Cl.], the son of Zeus (Jupiter) and Antiope; husband of Niobe. He built the walls of Thebes by charming each stone into position with a lyre given him by Hermes (Mercury).

Amphitrite (ăm″fĭ-trī′tē), [Cl.], a Nereid; the wife of Poseidon (Neptune), and the goddess of the sea.

Anchises (ăn-kī′sēz), [Cl.], the father of Æneas, whom Æneas carried on his shoulders from the burning city of Troy.

Andromache (ăn-drŏm′ȧ-kē), [Cl.], the loving and beloved wife of Hector. At his death she was carried off and married by Neoptolemus, son of Achilles. Later she married Helenus, a brother of Hector.

Andromeda (ăn-drŏm′ē-dȧ), [Cl.], a daughter of Cepheus and Cassiopeia, rulers of Ethiopia in Africa: exposed to a sea monster that she might save her country from destruction, but rescued and married by Perseus.

Andvari (än′dwä-rē), [Teut.], the dwarf whom Loki robbed of his treasure and of his cursed magic ring.

Antæus (ăn-tē′ŭs), [Cl.], a Libyan giant, invincible as long as he touched the earth, his mother. Heracles (Hercules) lifted him from the ground and then strangled him.

Antigone (ăn-tĭg′ō-nē), [Cl.], a faithful daughter of Œdipus and Jocasta of Thebes. In defiance of her uncle, Creon, she performed the funeral rites over the body of her brother, Polynices.

Antiope (ăn-tī′ō-pē), [Cl.], a Theban princess, mother, by Zeus, of Amphion and Zethus. Antiope's husband divorced her and married Dirce, who treated her cruelly; and her sons, in revenge, fastened Dirce to the horns of a wild bull.

Anubis (ȧ-nū′bĭs), [Egypt.], a jackal god, who conducted the spirits of the dead to the judgment hall.

Aphrodite (ăf″rō-dī′tē), [Gk.], the goddess of love: identified with the Roman Venus.

Apis (ā′pĭs), [Egypt.], the sacred white bull, supposed to embody the god Ptah, and hence treated like a god.

Apollo (ȧ-pŏl′ō), [Cl.], the son of Zeus (Jupiter) and Leto (Latona): the god of the sun, music, poetry, eloquence, medicine, and the fine arts. Also called *Helios*.

Arachne (ȧ-răk′nē), [Cl.], a Lydian maiden, turned into a spider for competing with Athena (Minerva) at weaving.

Ares (ā′rēz), [Gk.], god of war, son of Zeus and Hera: identified with the Roman Mars.

Arethusa (ăr″ē-thū′sȧ), [Cl.], a wood nymph, beloved of the river god Alpheus. To escape him, she was changed by Artemis (Diana) into a stream. Alpheus merged with her, and they became a fountain in Sicily.

Argo (är′gō), [Cl.], the ship which carried the Argonauts in search of the Golden Fleece.

Argonauts (är′gō-nôts), [Cl.], the Greek heroes who sailed with Jason in the *Argo*.

Argus (är′gŭs), [Cl.], the hundred-eyed son of Zeus (Jupiter) and Niobe, founder of Argos. After his murder by Hermes (Mercury), Hera (Juno) placed his eyes in the tail of the peacock.

Ariadne (ăr″ĭ-ăd′nē), [Cl.], daughter of King Minos of Crete. She loved Theseus and gave him the thread to guide him out of the Labyrinth. Later, deserted by Theseus, she married Dionysus (Bacchus).

Arion (ȧ-rī′ŏn), [Cl.], a Greek poet and musician from Lesbos, who was robbed by sailors and thrown overboard. He was saved and carried to shore by a dolphin, which his music had drawn to the ship.

Artemis (är′tē-mĭs), [Gk.], the virgin goddess of wild nature, the moon, and maidenhood, twin sister of Apollo: identified by the Romans with Diana.

Ascanius (ăs-kā′nĭ-ŭs), [Cl.], the son and companion of Æneas on his wanderings after the fall of Troy; founder of Alba Longa and supposed ancestor of Julius Cæsar. Also called *Iulus*.

Asclepius (ăs-klē′pĭ-ŭs), [Gk.], the god of medicine, and son of Apollo, slain by Zeus because he had acquired the skill to raise the dead: identified with the Roman Æsculapius.

Asgard (ăs′gärd), [Teut.], the residence of the chief gods, or Æsir.

Ask (äsk), [Teut.], the first man, created by Odin, Hœnir, and Loki from an ash tree. Also, **Askr** (äs′kr).

Astyanax (ăs-tī′ȧ-năks), [Cl.], the infant son of Hector, dashed by the Greeks from the walls of Troy.

Atalanta (ăt″ȧ-lăn′tȧ), [Cl.], a beautiful Greek heroine, beloved of Meleager, who took part in the Calydonian boar hunt and in the Argonautic Expedition. In another legend she challenged her suitors to a race, offering death to the vanquished, her hand to the victor. All lost save Hippomenes, who threw down on the course three golden apples, which Atalanta stooped to pick up.

Athena (ȧ-thē′nȧ), [Gk.], the goddess of wisdom: identified with the Roman Minerva. Also called *Pallas Athena*. Also, **Athene** (-nē).

Atlas (ăt′lăs), [Cl.], in Homer, a deity in charge of the pillars of heaven; later, a Titan who supported the earth, or the heavens, on his shoulders: in some stories changed to a mountain.

Atli (ät′lē), [Norse], Attila, king of the Huns. He treacherously slew his wife Gudrun's brothers to get the treasure left them by Sigurd. In revenge, Gudrun slew her own and Atli's children. In the German version called *Etzel*.

Atreus (ā′trōōs; ā′trē-ŭs), [Cl.], father of Menelaus and Agamemnon, famous heroes in the Trojan War.

Atropos (ăt′rō-pŏs), [Cl.], one of the three Fates, who cut off the thread of life after Clotho has spun it, and Lachesis had measured it off.

Audhumla (ou′thōōm-lä), [Teut.], the cow whose milk fed the giant Ymir.

Augean stables (ô-jē′ăn), [Cl.], the great stables of Augeas, king of Elis, which contained 3,000 oxen, but remained uncleaned for 30 years. Hercules cleaned them in a day by turning two rivers, the Alpheus and the Peneus, through them.

Aurora (ô-rō′rȧ), [Rom.], the goddess of the morning: identified with the Greek Eos.

Avernus (ȧ-vûr′nŭs), [Cl.], a lake in the crater of an extinct volcano in Italy, supposed to have been connected with the infernal regions; hence, the infernal regions.

bacchante (bȧ-kănt′; băk′ănt; bȧ-kăn′tē), [Cl.], a woman follower of Bacchus.

Bacchus (băk′ŭs), [Rom.], the son of Jupiter and Semele, the god of wine and drunkards: identified with the Greek Dionysus. Also called *Liber*.

Balder (bôl′dẽr), [Teut.], the god of the summer sunlight, peace, of the good, beautiful, eloquent, and wise, the son of Odin and Frigg. He was innocently slain by the blind god Hoder, whose arrow was guided by Loki. His dwelling was Breidablik.

Bast (bȧst), [Egypt.], a lion- or cat-headed goddess; the "lady of life."

Baucis (bô′sĭs), [Cl.], an aged Phrygian woman, wife of Philemon (which see).

Bellerophon (bĕ-lĕr′ō-fŏn), [Cl.], a Greek hero, who killed the monster Chimera with the aid of his winged horse Pegasus.

Bellona (bĕ-lō′nȧ), [Rom.], the goddess of war, closely associated with Mars.

Belus (bē′lŭs), [Cl.], the son of Poseidon (Neptune), and Libya; an early king of Babylon or Assyria, ancestor of many heroes.

Bifrost (bēf′rŏst), [Teut.], the rainbow bridge between Asgard, the home of the Æsir, or chief gods, and the world below.

Boreas (bō′rē-ăs), [Cl.], the North Wind, son of Æolus and Eos (Aurora), brother of Hesperus, Zephyrus, and Notus.

PRINCIPAL MYTHOLOGICAL CHARACTERS

1, Achilles; 2, Ammon; 3, Amphitrite; 4, Anubis; 5, Apollo; 6, Arion; 7, Atlas; 8, Atropos; 9, Bacchus; 10, Castor and Pollux; 11, Clio; 12, Euterpe; 13, Ganymede; 14, Hercules; 15, Hermes; 16, Horus; 17, Iris; 18, Jupiter; 19, Laocoön and his sons; 20, Mars and Venus; 21, Minerva; 22, Minotaur; 23, Neptune; 24, Nereid; 25, Proserpina.

Bragi (brä′gē), [Teut.], god of poetry and eloquence. Also, **Brage.**

Brahma (brä′mȧ), [Hindu], the creator; first member of the trinity, or Trimurti.

Briareus (brī-ā′rē-ŭs), [Cl.], a Greek hundred-handed giant.

Briseis (brī-sē′ĭs), [Cl.], a beautiful girl, captured by Achilles in the Trojan War, whom Agamemnon took to replace Chryseis.

Brynhild (brün′hĭlt), [Teut.], a Valkyrie, whom Sigurd found asleep in an enchanted castle and waked. When he became married to Gudrun, Brynhild procured his murder and killed herself.

Buri (bōō′rē), [Teut.], a being licked out of salty frost stones by the cow Audhumla: the ancestor of the Teutonic gods.

Busiris (bū-sī′rĭs), [Cl.], an Egyptian king, who sacrificed strangers to Zeus to end a famine: killed by Heracles (Hercules).

Buto (bū′tō), [Egypt.], the goddess of the North, nurse of Horus and Bast: identified with the Greek Leto (Latona).

Cacus (kā′kŭs), [Cl.], a crafty Italian giant, slain by Hercules (Heracles) for stealing the cattle of Geryon.

Cadmus (kăd′mŭs), [Cl.], son of Agenor, king of Phœnicia, who killed a dragon and sowed its teeth. From these grew soldiers, who fought together until only five were left. These helped Cadmus to found Thebes.

caduceus (kȧ-dū′sē-ŭs), the winged staff of Hermes (Mercury), entwined with two serpents.

Calchas (kăl′kăs), [Cl.], the wisest prophet among the Greeks at Troy, surpassed only by Mopsus at Claros.

Calliope (kă-lī′ŏ-pē), [Cl.], the Muse of eloquence and epic poetry.

Callisto (kă-lĭs′tō), [Cl.], an Arcadian nymph, attendant of Artemis (Diana), beloved by Zeus (Jupiter); therefore changed into a bear by Hera (Juno). She narrowly escaped being hunted to death by her own son, but was then, with him, placed in the sky as the Great and the Little Bear.

Calydonian Hunt (kăl″ĭ-dō′nĭ-ăn), [Cl.], the pursuit of a destructive wild boar sent by Artemis (Diana) to punish King Œneus for neglected sacrifices. The boar was killed by the hero Meleager, who gave the spoils to Atalanta.

Calypso (kȧ-lĭp′sō), [Cl.], a sea nymph, who kept Odysseus (Ulysses) seven years on her island of Ogygia.

Camilla (kȧ-mĭl′ȧ), [Rom.], the swift-footed maiden queen of the Volsci, an Italian tribe, who opposed Æneas on his landing in Italy.

Capaneus (kăp′ȧ-nūs; kȧ-pā′nē-ŭs), [Cl.], one of the seven Greek heroes who marched against Thebes to help Polynices gain the throne. As he was scaling the walls, he was struck by lightning and killed.

Cassandra (kă-săn′drȧ), [Cl.], a daughter of Priam and Hecuba of Troy: inspired by Apollo to prophesy, but later condemned never to be believed.

Castor (kȧs′tẽr), [Cl.], a son of Zeus (Jupiter) and Leda; champion horse tamer. At his death in the Argonautic Expedition, his immortal twin brother Pollux also asked for death. Zeus decreed that the brothers should live in the upper and lower world on alternate days. Later, they were placed in the sky as the constellation Gemini.

Cecrops (sē′krŏps), [Cl.], a hero represented as half snake, first king of Attica, founder of Athens.

centaur (sĕn′tôr), [Cl.], one of a mythical Thessalian tribe, half man and half horse.

Cephalus (sĕf′ȧ-lŭs), [Cl.], a Greek hunter, whose devotion to his wife Procris (Procne) was so determined, that Eos (Aurora), who sought his love, caused him accidentally to kill Procris with his javelin.

Cerberus (sûr′bẽr-ŭs), [Cl.], the three-headed dog of Hades, which guarded the gates to the lower world; carried away by Heracles.

Ceres (sē′rēz), [Rom.], daughter of Saturn and Ops; goddess of the growing vegetation, later of corn, harvest, and flowers: identified with the Greek Demeter.

Charon (kā′rŏn), [Cl.], the boatman who ferried souls across the Acheron (or the Styx) in the lower world. A coin for his fare was always placed in the mouth of a dead man.

Charites (kăr′ĭ-tēz), [Cl.], *pl.* [*sing.* Charis (kăr′ĭs)], the three Graces, goddesses of grace and beauty.

Charybdis (kȧ-rĭb′dĭs), [Cl.], a very dangerous whirlpool on the Sicilian coast opposite Scylla, a rock on the Italian shore.

chimera (kĭ-mē′rȧ; kī-mē′rȧ), [Cl.], a fire-breathing monster with a lion's head, a goat's body, and a dragon's tail: killed by Bellerophon. Also, **chimæra.**

Chiron (kī′rŏn), [Cl.], a Greek centaur, son of Cronos (Saturn) and Philyra, teacher of Achilles, Asclepius (Æsculapius), and Heracles (Hercules).

Chryseis (krī-sē′ĭs), [Cl.], a beautiful captive in the Trojan War, whom Agamemnon was forced to restore to her father, Chryses; to replace her, he took Briseis from Achilles.

Circe (sûr′sē), [Cl.], the noted enchantress of Ææa, who changed some of the companions of Odysseus (Ulysses) into animals. Odysseus, protected by an herb, the gift of Hermes (Mercury), restored them.

Clio (klī′ō), [Cl.], the Muse of history.

Clotho (klō′thō), [Cl.], the youngest of the three Fates, who spun the thread of life.

Clytemnestra (klī″tĕm-nĕs′trȧ), [Cl.], the faithless wife of Agamemnon, who, with her lover Ægisthus, murdered Agamemnon upon his return from the Trojan War, and was killed by her son Orestes.

Cocytus (kō-sī′tŭs), [Cl.], the "river of wailing," one of the five rivers of Hades.

Colchis (kŏl′kĭs), [Cl.], the country east of the Black Sea, where the Golden Fleece was kept: the home of Medea.

Comus (kō′mŭs), [Rom.], the youthful god of revelry, feasting, and jollity.

Corybantes (kŏr″ĭ-băn′tēz), [Cl.], *pl.* attendants and priests of Cybele in Phrygia, accompanying her in the mountains with wild music and dances.

Creüsa (krē-ū′sȧ), [Cl.], a daughter of Priam, first wife of Æneas, separated from her husband and lost during the flight from Troy on the night of its capture.

Crocus (krō′kŭs), [Cl.], the beloved friend of the nymph Smilax, changed into a crocus.

Crœsus (krē′sŭs), a wealthy king of Lydia in Asia Minor of the sixth century B. C.

Cronus (krō′nŭs), [Gk.], a Titan, father of Zeus (Jupiter), Poseidon (Neptune), and Hades (Pluto): identified with the Roman Saturn.

Cumæ (kū′mē), [Cl.], an ancient Italian city near Naples, the home of the Sibyl who helped Æneas and sold the Sibylline Books to King Tarquin of Rome.

Cupid (kū′pĭd), [Rom.], the god of love: identified with the Greek Eros.

Cybele (sĭb′ē-lē), [Cl.], a nature goddess introduced to Greece and Rome from Asia Minor: identified with the Greek Rhea and with the Roman Ops.

Cyclops (sī′klŏps), [*pl.* Cyclopes (sī-klō′pēz)], [Cl.], one of a race of one-eyed Sicilian shepherd giants, who may also have worked at the forges of Hephæstus (Vulcan) under Mount Etna.

Cynthia (sĭn′thĭ-ȧ), [Cl.], the hunting goddess Artemis (Diana): so called because born on Mount Cynthus, on the island Delos.

Cytherea (sĭth″ẽr-ē′ȧ), [Cl.], Aphrodite (Venus): so called because she rose from the sea foam on the island of Cythera.

Dædalus (dĕd′ȧ-lŭs; dē′dȧ-lŭs), [Cl.], an Athenian artist, artificer, and architect, inventor of the saw, ax, gimlet: exiled for murder to Crete, where he built the Labyrinth. Later, he and his son Icarus were forced to escape by flight on wings. Dædalus reached Sicily; the son flew too near the sun, the wax melted and he was drowned in the sea, named Icarian for him.

Damon (dā′mŏn), [Cl.], a youth of Syracuse, famed for his friendship with Pythias (or, more properly, *Phintias*). According to legend, Pythias was condemned to death by Dionysius, tyrant of Syracuse, but was granted leave to visit his home and arrange his affairs if his friend Damon would offer himself as hostage for his return. On the appointed day, Pythias returned to release his friend and be executed, but was pardoned by Dionysius.

Danaë (dăn′ā-ē), [Cl.], a princess of Argos, mother of Perseus by Zeus (Jupiter), who visited her in the form of a golden shower.

Danaïd (dăn′ā-ĭd), [*pl.* Danaïdes (dȧ-nā′ĭ-dēz)], any of the fifty daughters of King Danaüs of Argos, all of whom, except Hypermnestra, killed their husbands on their wedding night. They were doomed in Tartarus to pour water into a broken cistern, or, as some say, to draw it with a sieve.

Daphne (dăf′nē), [Cl.], the lovely daughter of the river god Peneus, beloved by Apollo; to escape him, she was changed into a laurel tree.

Deianira (dē″yȧ-nī′rȧ), [Cl.], the deserted wife of Heracles (Hercules), whose death she unwittingly caused by a poisoned magic shirt, the gift of Nessus; in despair she killed herself.

Delphi (dĕl′fī), [Cl.], a sacred city of Greece, famous for a cleft in the rock, out of which came poisonous vapors. These affected a priestess of Apollo seated there on a golden tripod, so that she uttered wild words, interpreted as expressing the will of Apollo.

Demeter (dē-mē′tẽr), [Gk.], the goddess of agriculture and fruitfulness: identified with the Roman Ceres.

Deucalion (dū-kā′lĭ-ŏn), [Cl.], the son of Prometheus; like Noah, he with his wife Pyrrha was saved from a flood. They repeopled the world by throwing stones behind them, as directed by an oracle.

Diana (dī-ăn′ȧ; dī-ā′nȧ), [Rom.], the daughter of Jupiter and Latona; goddess of the moon and chase: identified with the Greek Artemis. Also called *Cynthia; Phœbe; Selene.*

Dido (dī′dō), [Cl.], a Tyrian princess, founder and queen of Carthage in Africa, who entertained Æneas on his wanderings from Troy and later killed herself when he was ordered by the gods to depart.

Diomedes (dī″ō-mē′dēz), [Cl.], a brave Greek warrior in the Trojan War, the opponent of Hector and Æneas, and companion of Odysseus (Ulysses) in carrying off the horses of Rhesus and the Palladium. Also, **Diomed** (dī′ō-mĕd).

Dionysus (dī″ō-nī′sŭs), [Gk.], the god of vegetation and wine, known commonly among the Romans as Bacchus, or Liber.

Dioscuri (dī″ŏs-kū′rī), [Cl.], *pl.* Castor and Pollux, the twin sons of Zeus (Jupiter): patrons of warriors and travelers and, in Rome, of the order of knights and of chariot races.

Dirce (dûr′sē), [Cl.], a wicked queen of Thebes, fastened to a wild bull by the sons of Antiope (which see).

Dis (dĭs), [Rom.], god of the underworld; Pluto: identified with the Greek Hades.

Discordia (dĭs-kôr′dĭ-ȧ), [Rom.], the goddess of strife and disagreement: identified with the Greek Eris.

Dodona (dŏ-dō′nȧ), [Cl.], an ancient Greek oracle of Zeus (Jupiter), where priests interpreted the rustling of the oak leaves.

dryad (drī′ăd), [Cl.], one of the nymphs who lived and died with the trees which were their abode. Also, **dryas** [*pl.* dryades].

Dyaus (dyous), [Hindu], in Vedic mythology, Heaven, the father of the gods.

Echo (ĕk′ō), [Cl.], a Greek nymph, who pined away for unrequited love of Narcissus, until only her voice was left.

Edda (ĕd′ȧ), either of two old Norse books: **a**, the Elder Edda, a collection of 33 mythological songs composed between 900 and 1200; **b**, the Younger Edda, a prose mythology from about 1200.

Electra (ē-lĕk′trȧ), [Cl.], a daughter of Agamemnon, who induced her brother Orestes to kill their mother Clytemnestra for having murdered their father.

elf (ĕlf), [*pl.* elves (ĕlvz)], [Teut.], fairies of light and of darkness. The god Frey was king of the light fairies; Alfheim, their home.

Elysium (ē-lĭzh′ĭ-ŭm; ē-lĭz′ĭ-ŭm), [Cl.], the eternal dwelling place of the happy souls after death. Also called *Elysian Fields.*

Embla (ĕm′blä), [Teut.], the first woman, created by the gods from an elm.

Enceladus (ĕn-sĕl′ȧ-dŭs), [Cl.], a Greek hundred-armed giant buried under Mount Etna.

Endymion (ĕn-dĭm′ĭ-ŏn), [Cl.], a beautiful Greek youth beloved by the moon goddess Selene (Diana), who caressed him nightly with her moonbeams.

Eos (ē′ŏs), [Gk.], the goddess of dawn: identified with the Roman Aurora.

Epeus (ē-pē′ŭs), [Cl.], a Greek who built the wooden horse left as a decoy outside the walls of Troy.

Epimetheus (ĕp″ĭ-mē′thūs; -mē′thē-ŭs), [Cl.], brother of Prometheus and husband of Pandora, the first woman.

Erato (ĕr′ȧ-tō), [Cl.], the Muse of lyric and love poetry.

Erebus (ĕr′ē-bŭs), [Cl.], the dark space through which spirits pass into Hades.

Erinyes (ē-rĭn′ĭ-ēz), *pl.* [*sing.* Erinys (ē-rĭn′ĭs; ē-rī′nĭs; ĕr-)], [Gk.], the Furies, Alecto, Tisiphone, and Megæra, who relentlessly pursued with secret stings unpunished criminals: called by the Romans *Furiæ.* Also called *Eumenides.*

Eris (ē′rĭs; ĕr′ĭs), [Gk.], goddess of discord: identified with the Roman Discordia.

Eros (ē′rŏs), [Gk.], god of love, son of Aphrodite: identified with the Roman Cupid.

Erymanthus (ĕr″ĭ-măn′thŭs), [Cl.], a mountain in Arcadia, where the devastating boar killed by Heracles (Hercules) lived.

Eteocles (ē-tē′ō-klēz), [Cl.], son of Œdipus and Jocasta of Thebes. He and his brother Polynices were to reign in alternate years, but Eteocles broke the agreement and provoked the expedition of the Seven against Thebes; here the brothers killed each other.

Eumenides (ū-mĕn′ĭ-dēz), [Cl.], the "gracious goddesses," a flattering name for the avenging Furies.

Euphrosyne (ū-frŏs′ĭ-nē), [Cl.], joy, one of the three Graces.

Europa (ū-rō′pȧ), [Cl.], a Phœnician princess, loved by Zeus (Jupiter), who wooed her as a white bull. On his back she rode to Crete, where she became the mother of Minos, Rhadamanthus, and Sarpedon.

Eurydice (ū-rĭd′ĭ-sē), [Cl.], beloved wife of Orpheus, the Greek poet and musician. Killed by a poisonous snake bite, she was in Hades only until Orpheus could by his persuasive strains gain permission to lead her out. When almost in the upper world, Orpheus looked back at her, against the divine command, and Eurydice vanished.

Euterpe (ū-tûr′pē), [Cl.], the Muse of music.

Fafnir (fäv′nĕr), [Teut.], a giant who, in the form of a dragon, guarded a golden treasure, until killed by Sigurd.

Fama (fā′mȧ), [Rom.], goddess of rumor and slander.

Fates (fāts), [Cl.], the three goddesses who determined the course of each life. Clotho spun the thread of life, Lachesis measured it, Atropos cut it off: identified with the Roman Parcæ. Also called *Mœræ;* cf. *Norns.*

faun (fôn), [Cl.], a rural deity with pointed ears, small horns and tail, and, sometimes, the legs of a goat.

Fenrir (fĕn′rĕr), [Teut.], a monster wolf, son of Loki, bound by the Æsir and thrown into Niflheim but loosed for the final combat at Ragnarok. Also called *Fenris-wolf.*

Flora (flō′rȧ), [Rom.], the goddess of flowers and gardens.

Forseti (fŏr-sĕt′ē), [Teut.], the god of justice, son of Balder and Nanna.

Frey (frā), [Teut.], the god of rain, sunshine, and fruits. Also, **Freyr** (frā′r).

Freya (frā′ȧ), [Teut.], the goddess of love and beauty, presiding also over the regions of the dead; daughter of Njorth, and, in later mythology, wife of Odin: eventually superseding Frigg. Also, **Freyja** (frā′yä).

Frigg (frĭg), [Teut.], queen of the gods, wife of Odin, and mother of Balder and other gods. Similar to the Greek Hera and the Roman Juno. Also, **Frigga.**

Furies (fū′rĭz), [Cl.], the Greek goddesses of vengeance, or Erinyes (which see).

Gæa (jē′ȧ), [Gk.], the goddess Earth: identified with the Roman Terra, or Tellus. Also, **Gaia** (gā′ȧ); **Ge** (jē).

Galatea (găl″ȧ-tē′ȧ), [Cl.], **1,** a sea nymph beloved by Polyphemus, a Cyclops, who in jealousy murdered her preferred lover, Acis; **2,** an ivory statue of a maiden, the work of Pygmalion, a king of Cyprus, to which Aphrodite (Venus), in answer to his prayer, gave life that he might make her his wife.

Ganymede (găn′ĭ-mēd), [Cl.], a handsome Trojan lad carried off by Zeus (Jupiter) in the form of an eagle, to be his cupbearer.

Gerd (gĕrd), [Teut.], a beautiful young giantess, whose union with Frey probably symbolized the new life of spring. Also, **Gerdh; Gerth** (gĕr*th*); **Gerthr** (gĕr*th*′r).

Geryon (jē′rĭ-ŏn), [Cl.], a winged three-bodied being, killed by Heracles (Hercules), one of whose twelve labors was to steal Geryon's red oxen.

Giants (jī′ănts), mythical beings of great size and strength. In classic myth they were the enemies of the gods and were defeated by them. In Teutonic myth there was less hostility, for some of them represented kindly natural forces.

Ginnungagap (gĭn′nōōng-gä-gäp″; yĭn′-), [Teut.], the formless void before creation.

Gladsheim (gläts′hām″), [Teut.], Odin's dwelling in Asgard, containing the thrones of the Æsir. Also, **Glathsheim.**

Glaucus (glô′kŭs), [Cl.], a Greek fisherman, lover of Scylla, changed into a sea deity as a result of eating magic grass.

Golden Fleece, [Cl.], the wool of gold covering the ram that bore Phrixus through the air to Colchis, where it was hung up in a sacred grove by King Æëtes and guarded by a dragon until it was carried off by Jason.

Gordius (gôr′dĭ-ŭs), [Cl.], king of Phrygia, maker of a most intricate knot. Alexander the Great was told that, according to an oracle, the master of the knot should be master of Asia; he straightway cut the knot with his sword.

Gorgon (gôr′gŏn), [Cl.], any of the three hideous sister monsters with snaky locks, Stheno, Euryale, Medusa, the last-named of whom turned the beholder to stone.

Graces [Cl.], three beautiful sister goddesses, Aglaia (Brilliance), Euphrosyne (Joy), and Thalia (Bloom): attendants on Eros (Cupid), Aphrodite (Venus), and Dionysus (Bacchus): called *Gratiæ* by the Romans, *Charites* by the Greeks.

Grææ (grē′ē), [Cl.], three sisters, hoary, misshapen, and hideous from birth, with but one eye and one tooth among them: watchers for the Gorgons. Also, **Graiæ** (grā′yē; grī′ē).

Gudrun (gŏŏd′rōōn), [Norse], wife of Sigurd (in the German version *Siegfried*) whom she won from Brynhild by a magic drink; later, wife of the Hun king Atli (Etzel). In the German version called *Kriemhild.*

Gunnar (gōōn′när), [Norse], a Burgundian king, whose sister Gudrun (in German version called *Kriemhild*) married Sigurd (Siegfried). In the German version, *Gunther.*

Hades (hā′dēz), [Gk.], Pluto, god of the lower world, or the lower world itself: as a god, also called *Pluto,* and identified with the Roman Dis.

hamadryad (hăm′ȧ-drī″ăd), [*pl.* hamadryads (-ădz); hamadryades (-ȧ-dēz)], a tree nymph.

Harmonia (här-mō′nĭ-ȧ), [Cl.], the wife of the Greek king Cadmus, famous for her wedding gift from Hephæstus (Vulcan) of an ill-omened necklace.

Harpy (här′pĭ), [*pl.* Harpies (-pĭz)], an evil, defiling monster having the head and body of a maiden, the wings and claws of a bird.

Hathor (hä′thŏr), [Egypt.], goddess of love, represented with a cow's head: similar to the Greek Aphrodite (Venus).

Hebe (hē′bē), [Cl.], the Greek goddess of youth, cupbearer to the gods before Ganymede; later, the wife of the deified Hercules, with the power of restoring youth.

Hecate (hĕk′ȧ-tē; formerly often hĕk′ăt), [Cl.], an ancient Greek goddess of the moon, earth, and lower world, and esp. of magic: often merged with Artemis and Selene.

Hector (hĕk′tĕr), [Cl.], son of Priam and Hecuba of Troy, husband of Andromache; bravest of Trojan warriors in the Trojan War, slain by Achilles to avenge Patroclus.

Hecuba (hĕk′ū-bȧ), [Cl.], the wife of Priam, king of Troy, and mother of Hector, Paris, Helenus, and many other heroes.

Heimdall (hām′däl), [Teut.], the vigilant watchman of Asgard. His horn Gjallarhorn was to summon the gods on the last day (Ragnarok). Also, **Heimdal.**

Hel (hĕl), [Teut.], daughter of Loki, and queen of Hel, the lower world: similar to the Greek Persephone (Proserpina).

Helen (hĕl′ĕn), [Cl.], the daughter of Zeus (Jupiter) and Leda, wife of Menelaus, king of Sparta: the most beautiful woman in the world. Her elopement with Paris to Troy caused the Trojan War.

Helenus (hĕl′ē-nŭs), [Cl.], a son of Priam and Hecuba of Troy, spared by the Greeks for his prophetic gift; later, husband of Andromache and ruler of Epirus.

Helios (hē′lĭ-ŏs), [Gk.], the sun god, who drove his four-horse chariot through the sky.

Helle (hĕl′ē), [Cl.], sister of Phrixus, with whom she was fleeing when she fell from the ram with the golden fleece into the sea named for her the Hellespont (Sea of Helle).

Hephæstus (hē-fĕs′tŭs), [Gk.], god of fire and master of the forge: identified with the Roman Vulcan. Also, **Hephaistos** (-fĭs′tŏs).
Hera (hē′rȧ), [Gk.], queen of the Greek gods, sister and wife of Zeus (Jupiter), goddess of women and marriage: identified with the Roman Juno. Also, **Here** (hē′rē).
Hercules (hûr′kū-lēz), [Cl.], a famous hero, called by the Greeks *Heracles*, son of Zeus (Jupiter) and Alcmene. His remarkable physical strength was shown in the achievement of twelve great "labors": the killing of the Nemean lion; the killing of the Lernean hydra; the capture of the Arcadian hind; the capture of the Erymanthian boar; the cleaning of the Augean stables; the capture of the mad Cretan bull; the taking of the man-eating mares of Diomed; the procuring of Hippolyte's girdle; the slaughter of the Stymphalian birds; the capture of the red cattle of Geryon; the securing of the golden apples of the Hesperides; the bringing up of Cerberus from Hades.
Hermes (hûr′mēz), [Gk.], son of Zeus and Maia, messenger of the gods, god of eloquence, commerce, and travelers, and conductor of the dead to the lower world: identified with the Roman Mercury.
Hermione (hẽr-mī′ō-nē), [Cl.], the daughter of Menelaus and Helen, wife of Neoptolemus (Pyrrhus), and later, of Orestes.
Hero (hē′rō), [Cl.], a priestess of Aphrodite (Venus) at Sestos in Thrace, beloved by Leander, who swam the Hellespont nightly to see her. Leander was finally drowned and Hero threw herself into the sea.
Hesione (hē-sī′ō-nē), [Cl.], the daughter of Laomedon, king of Troy, exposed on a rock to a sea monster to avert disaster from her country, but rescued by Heracles (Hercules), who slew the monster.
Hesperides (hĕs-pĕr′ĭ-dēz), *pl.* [Cl.], three nymphs, daughters of Hesperus, the evening star. With the help of a dragon, they guarded the golden apples which Hera (Juno) received as a wedding gift from Gæa.
Hestia (hĕs′tĭ-ȧ), [Gk.], goddess of the hearth and of intimate family relations, daughter of Cronus (Saturn) and Rhea (Ops): identified with the Roman Vesta.
Hippodamia (hĭp″ō-dȧ-mī′ȧ), [Cl.], **1**, a Greek princess, daughter of Œnomaus of Elis, won by Pelops with the aid of winged horses from Neptune; **2**, wife of Pirithoüs, friend of Theseus: the cause of the famous battle of the Centaurs and Lapithæ.
Hippolyte (hĭ-pŏl′ĭ-tē), [Cl.], a queen of the Amazons, wife of Theseus: possessor of a famous girdle. Also, **Hippolyta** (-ĭ-tȧ).
Hippolytus (hĭ-pŏl′ĭ-tŭs), [Cl.], the noble son of Theseus and Hippolyta, falsely accused and killed through the efforts of his young stepmother, Phædra, whose love for him was not returned.
Hippomenes (hĭ-pŏm′ē-nēz), [Cl.], the Greek hero who outran Atalanta (which see).
Hlithskjalf (hlĭth′skyälf″), [Teut.], the seat of Odin, above Asgard, from which he looked out over all the worlds.
Hœnir (hû′nẽr), [Teut.], a god, strong but dull, who helped create Ask and Embla, the first mortals: one of the few survivors of Ragnarok, the last day.
Horus (hō′rŭs), [Egypt.], the hawk-headed god of day: similar to the Greek Apollo.
Hoder (hō′dẽr), [Teut.], the blind god who unwittingly slew Balder.
Hyacinthus (hī″ȧ-sĭn′thŭs), [Cl.], a beautiful Greek youth beloved by Apollo and Zephyrus, the west wind. As Hyacinthus was playing quoits with Apollo, Zephyrus out of jealousy caused a quoit of Apollo to kill him, and Apollo caused the hyacinth to grow from his blood.
Hydra (hī′drȧ), [Cl.], a many-headed monster in the swamp of Lerna: killed by Heracles (Hercules).
Hylas (hī′las), [Cl.], a handsome Greek lad beloved by Heracles (Hercules). While drawing water at a spring for his master, he was drawn in by the amorous nymphs.
Hymen (hī′mĕn), [Cl.], god of marriage.
Hymir (hü′mẽr), [Teut.], a giant personifying the unfriendly sea. Also, **Hymer.**
Hyperboreans (hī″pẽr-bō′rē-ănz), [Cl.], a mythical people dwelling beyond the north wind (Boreas) in everlasting bliss, free from disease and old age.
Hypermnestra (hī″pẽrm-nĕs′trȧ), [Cl.], the only one of the fifty daughters of Danaüs who did not kill her husband. Her descendants ruled in Argos.
Icarus (ĭk′ȧ-rŭs), [Cl.], the young son of Dædalus (which see).
Iliad (ĭl′ĭ-ăd), a Greek epic poem in 24 books, by Homer, giving the events of part of the last year of the Trojan War, from the quarrel of Achilles and Agamemnon to the burial of Hector.
Ilium (ĭl′ĭ-ŭm), a poetical name for Troy.
Indra (ĭn′drȧ), [Hindu], greatest of the Vedic gods, wielder of the thunderbolt, dispenser of rain.
Io (ī′ō), [Cl.], daughter of the river god Inachus, beloved by Zeus (Jupiter), who changed her into a heifer to escape the wrath of Hera (Juno). Then Io, tormented by a gadfly sent by Hera, wandered through many lands, swam through the sea named Ionian for her, and came to Egypt, where she regained her form and freedom.
Iphigenia (ĭf″ĭ-jē-nī′ȧ), [Cl.], a daughter of Agamemnon, sacrificed to secure favorable winds for the Greeks in the expedition against Troy. At the fatal moment, Artemis (Diana) rescued her and made her a priestess in Tauris, where Orestes found her.
Iris (ī′rĭs), [Cl.], goddess of the rainbow, messenger of Zeus (Jupiter) and Hera (Juno).
Ishtar (ĭsh′tär), the Assyrian supreme goddess, the goddess of love and fertility: identified with Aphrodite and Isis.
Isis (ī′sĭs), [Egypt.], goddess of fruitfulness, wife of Osiris: identified with Ishtar.
Ismene (ĭs-mē′nē), [Cl.], the timid, practical sister of Antigone, daughter of Œdipus.
Ithaca (ĭth′ȧ-kȧ), [Cl.], the island home of Odysseus (Ulysses), off the coast of Greece.
Ithunn (ē′thōōn), [Teut.], the wife of Bragi and goddess of early spring, possessor of the golden apples of youth, which kept the gods young. Also, **Ithun; Idun.**
Iulus (ī-ōō′lŭs), son of Æneas and Creusa; reputed ancestor of Julius Cæsar. Also called *Ascanius*.
Ixion (ĭk-sī′ŏn), [Cl.], father of the centaurs. For wickedly aspiring to the love of Hera (Juno), he was bound in Tartarus to a perpetually revolving wheel.
Janus (jā′nŭs), [Rom.], god of all beginnings. His temple in the Roman Forum was closed only in times of peace; January is named for him.
Jason (jā′sŭn), [Cl.], the leader of the Greek Argonauts in the successful expedition to Colchis for the Golden Fleece.
jotunn (yō′tōōn), [Teut.], any giant. The giants lived in Jotunnheim (yō′tōōn-hām), on the outermost edge of the world.
Jove (jōv), [Rom.], Jupiter, the chief of the gods: identified with the Greek Zeus.
Juno (jōō′nō), [Rom.], the daughter of Saturn and Ops, sister and wife of Jupiter: queen of the Roman gods, goddess of marriage and births: identified with the Greek Hera

Jupiter (jōō′pĭ-tẽr), [Rom.], an ancient Italian god of the heavens, supreme ruler over all things, son of Saturn and Ops: identified with the Greek Zeus.

Kriemhild (krēm′hĭlt), [Teut.], in the "Nibelungenlied," the sister of the Burgundian king Gunther (in the Norse "Volsunga Saga" called *Gunnar*), wife of Siegfried (Sigurd), and later of Etzel (Atli), king of the Huns. In the Norse version called *Gudrun*.

Labyrinth (lăb′ĭ-rĭnth), [Cl.], the maze constructed for King Minos of Crete by Dædalus, to hold the Minotaur.

Lachesis (lăk′ĕ-sĭs), [Cl.], that one of the three Fates who measured off the thread of life (see *Fates*).

Lakshmi (lăksh′mē), [Hindu], goddess of fortune and beauty, wife of Vishnu.

Laocoön (lā-ŏk′ō-ŏn), a faithful priest of Apollo at Troy, who mistrusted the wooden horse left on the shore by the Greeks. The Greek gods then sent two serpents out of the sea to kill him and his two sons.

Laodamia (lā-ŏd″ȧ-mī′ȧ), [Cl.], the wife of Protesilaus, a Greek hero killed before Troy. In answer to her prayer, Protesilaus was restored to her for three hours; then she went to the lower world with him.

Laomedon (lā-ŏm′ĕ-dŏn), [Cl.], a king of Troy, father of Priam and Hesione: killed by Heracles (Hercules) for denying him Hesione to wife, after he had rescued her from a sea monster.

lares and penates (lā′rēz, pē-nā′tēz), [Rom.], household gods, comprising the *lares*, or spirits of the ancestors, and *penates*, or spirits of the storeroom.

Latinus (lȧ-tī′nŭs), [Rom.], king of Latium when Æneas came to Italy, father of Lavinia, the second wife of Æneas.

Latona (lȧ-tō′nȧ), [Rom.], mother of Apollo and Diana: called *Leto* by the Greeks.

Lavinia (lȧ-vĭn′ĭ-ȧ), [Rom.], daughter of King Latinus of Latium, engaged to Turnus, but finally married to Æneas.

Leander (lē-ăn′dẽr), [Cl.], a youth who swam the Hellespont nightly to visit Hero, priestess of Aphrodite at Sestos, until drowned in a storm.

Leda (lē′dȧ), [Cl.], beloved by Zeus (Jupiter) in the form of a swan, mother of Castor, Pollux, Helen, and Clytemnestra.

Lethe (lē′thē), [Cl.], the "river of forgetfulness" in Hades.

Leto (lē′tō), [Gk.], a beautiful maiden beloved by Zeus, persecuted by Hera in her wanderings to the island Delos in the Ægean Sea, where Apollo and Artemis were born: called *Latona* by the Romans.

Loki (lō′kē), [Teut.], the god of evil, contriver of constant discord and mischief, even to the death of Balder; father of the Fenriswolf, the Midgard serpent, and the goddess Hel: finally bound by Thor and placed by Skathi beneath a venom-dripping serpent, where he was deserted by all save his wife Signy. On the last day (Ragnarok) Loki was to lead forth the forces of Hel.

mænad (mē′năd), [*pl.* mænads (-nădz); mænades (mĕn′ȧ-dēz)], [Cl.], one of the women devotees of Dionysus (Bacchus).

Maia (mā′yȧ; mī′ȧ), [Cl.], eldest and most beautiful of the Pleiades, mother of Hermes.

manes (mā′nēz), [Rom.], the spirits of the ancestors of the Romans, worshiped as gods.

Mars (märz), [Rom.], the god of war: identified with the Greek god Ares.

Marsyas (mär′sĭ-ăs), [Cl.], a Phrygian satyr, punished, for competing with Apollo on the flute, by being flayed alive.

Medea (mē-dē′ȧ), [Cl.], a sorceress, daughter of King Æëtes of Colchis. For love of Jason she helped him win the Golden Fleece.

Medusa (mē-dū′sȧ), [Cl.], orig., a maiden whose pride in her glorious hair caused it to be changed into snakes: one of the three Gorgons, slain by Perseus.

Megæra (mē-jē′rȧ), [Cl.], one of the three Furies, or Erinyes (which see).

Meleager (mĕl″ē-ā′jẽr), [Cl.], son of Althæa, queen of Calydon; lover of Atalanta, and one of the Argonauts. At his birth it was foretold that his life would be only as long as that of the brand then burning on the hearth. His mother quenched it and hid it. Years later, after his success in the Calydonian boar hunt, Althæa decided to avenge the death of her brothers at Meleager's hands; she threw the fatal brand on the fire and Meleager soon died. In remorse, his mother killed herself.

Melpomene (mĕl-pŏm′ē-nē), [Cl.], the Muse of tragedy.

Menelaus (mĕn″ē-lā′ŭs), [Cl.], king of Sparta, husband of Helen.

Mentor (mĕn′tŏr), [Cl.], the faithful friend of Odysseus (Ulysses), and the guide and teacher of Telemachus.

Mercury (mûr′kū-rĭ), [Rom.], the son of Jupiter and Maia, messenger of the gods, god of eloquence, commerce, and travelers: identified with the Greek Hermes.

Midas (mī′dȧs), [Cl.], a king of Phrygia, in answer to whose prayer Dionysus (Bacchus) turned everything he touched to gold. When even his food became gold, he prayed for help and was freed of the curse by bathing in the river Pactolus. King Midas had ass's ears, inflicted on him for giving the preference in a musical contest to Pan, rather than to Apollo.

Midgard (mĭd′gärd), [Teut.], the earth. The Midgard serpent was a horrible sea monster, offspring of Loki, destined to slay, and be slain by, Thor, on the last day (Ragnarok).

Mimir (mē′mẽr), [Teut.], god of wisdom.

Minerva (mĭ-nûr′vȧ), [Rom.], goddess of wisdom, thought, and invention: identified with the Greek Athena.

Minos (mī′nŏs), [Cl.], **1**, a king and lawgiver of Crete; after death, a judge in the lower world; **2**, grandson of the preceding, also a king of Crete, husband of Pasiphaë, father of Ariadne, owner of the Labyrinth and the Minotaur, and oppressor of Athens.

Minotaur (mĭn′ō-tôr), [Cl.], a monster, half man and half bull, which fed on Athenian maidens and lads, until slain by Theseus in its lair, the Labyrinth in Crete.

Mnemosyne (nē-mŏs′ĭ-nē), [Cl.], the Greek goddess of memory, mother of the Muses.

Mœræ (mē′rē), [Gk.], goddesses of destiny: the Fates (which see).

Morpheus (môr′fūs; môr′fē-ŭs), [Cl.], the Greek god of dreams.

Mors (môrz), [Rom.], the personification of death: called *Thanatos* by the Greeks.

Muses (mū′zĕz), the nine Greek goddesses who presided over the arts and sciences: Calliope (the chief, Muse of poetic inspiration, eloquence, and epic poetry), Clio (history), Erato (erotic poetry), Euterpe (music and lyric poetry), Melpomene (tragedy), Polyhymnia (the stately hymn), Terpsichore (choral dancing), Thalia (comedy), and Urania (astronomy).

Muspellsheim (mōōs′pĕls-hām″), [Teut.], one of the Nine Worlds, the region of warmth and sunlight south of Ginnungagap. Also called *Muspel*.

Mut (mōōt), [Egypt.], the Theban goddess of womanhood: similar to the Greek Demeter.

naiad (nā′yăd; nī′ăd), [*pl.* naiads; also, naiades (nā′yȧ-dēz; nī′ȧ-)], [Cl.], any of the nymphs who lived in springs, rivers, lakes, and fountains; a water nymph.

Nanna (nän′nä), [Teut.], the devoted wife of Balder, at whose loss she grieved to death.

Narcissus (när-sĭs′ŭs), [Cl.], a handsome Greek youth, for vain love of whom Echo pined away. Narcissus was punished, for he fell in love with his own reflection and also pined away, until he was changed into the flower narcissus.

Nastrond (nä′strŏnd), [Teut.], the place of punishment in Niflheim: similar to the Greek Tartarus.

Nausicaä (nô-sĭk′ā-*ȧ*; nou-), [Cl.], the Phæacian princess who found Odysseus (Ulysses) after his shipwreck and brought him to the court of her father, Alcinoüs.

nectar (nĕk′t*ȧ*r), the substance which with ambrosia formed the food and drink of the Greek gods.

Neith (nā′ĭth), [Egypt.], the Theban goddess of the upper heaven, of wisdom and the arts of peace and war: likened by the Greeks to Athena.

Nemesis (nĕm′ē-sĭs), [Cl.], the Greek goddess of righteous vengeance.

Neoptolemus (nē″ŏp-tŏl′ē-mŭs), [Cl.], son of Achilles, a Greek hero in the Trojan War. At the fall of Troy, he cruelly killed the aged Priam and hurled the infant son of Hector from the walls; later, he married Hermione, daughter of Menelaus and Helen. Also called *Pyrrhus.*

Nephthys (nĕf′thĭs), [Egypt.], goddess of the dead.

Neptune (nĕp′tūn), [Rom.], god of the sea, son of Saturn and Ops, represented with a trident in his hand: identified with the Greek Poseidon.

Nereid (nē′rē-ĭd), [Cl.], any of the 50 sea nymphs, daughters of Nereus and Doris, attendants of Poseidon (Neptune).

Nereus (nē′rūs), [Cl.], a Greek sea god, father of the Nereids.

Nessus (nĕs′ŭs), [Cl.], a centaur who tried to carry off Deianira, and was shot through the heart with a poisoned arrow by Heracles (Hercules), her husband. Nessus bequeathed his blood-stained shirt to Deianira, but when she used it to regain the love of her husband, it fatally poisoned him.

Nestor (nĕs′tŏr), [Cl.], a Greek king of Pylus, noted for his wisdom, who fought in his old age with the Greeks in the Trojan War.

Niflheim (nĕv′l-hām), [Teut.], the northern region of cold and mist; also, the underworld, or abode of the dead; Hel.

Nine Worlds the Teutonic divisions of the universe, supported by the tree Yggdrasill, comprising Asgard, the abode of the gods; Midgard, the abode of men; Jotunnheim, the abode of the giants; Muspellsheim, the realm of fire and warmth; Niflheim, the cold world of fog; and others, sometimes including Hel, the abode of the dead.

Niobe (nī′ō-bē), [Cl.], daughter of Tantalus and Amphion, bereft of her fourteen children by the arrows of Apollo and Artemis (Diana), because she dared to compare herself with their mother Leto (Latona), who had but the two. Niobe herself was changed to stone by Zeus (Jupiter).

Njorth (nyôrth), [Teut.], god of the sea and winds, protector of sailors: the hostage given by the Vanir to the Æsir to insure peace.

Norns (nôrnz), [Teut.], three sister demigoddesses, Urth (Past), Verthandi (Present), Skuld (Future), possessing absolute power over the lives of gods and men: similar to the Greek Fates.

Nox (nŏks), [Rom.], the goddess of night: identified with the Greek Nyx.

Nut (no͞ot), [Egypt.], the Heavens: similar to the Greek Rhea.

nymph (nĭmf), one of the lesser Greek divinities of nature in the form of beautiful maidens, variously called according to residence: in trees (dryad), mountains (oread), streams (naiad), seas (Nereid), or the ocean (Oceanid).

Oceanid (ō-sē′*ȧ*-nĭd), [Cl.], an ocean nymph.

Oceanus (ō-sē′*ȧ*-nŭs), [Cl.], a Greek Titan, the first sea god, father of the Oceanids: succeeded by Poseidon (Neptune).

Odin (ō′dĭn), [Teut.], the chief of the Teutonic gods, husband of Frigg and, in later mythology, of Freya. With Vili and Ve, he constructed the world out of Ymir's body; with Hœnir and Loki, he created the first man (Ask) and woman (Embla). He was the progenitor of kings, and the lord of battle. Also, **Woden.**

Odysseus (ō-dĭs′ūs; ō-dĭs′ē-ŭs), [Cl.], a famous king of Ithaca, the wisest, shrewdest, and most eloquent of the Greek chiefs who fought against Troy, the hero of Homer's "Odyssey": called by the Romans *Ulixes; Ulysses.*

Odyssey (ŏd′ĭ-sĭ), Homer's Greek epic poem describing the ten years' wanderings of Odysseus (Ulysses) from Troy to Ithaca.

Œdipus (ĕd′ĭ-pŭs; ē′dĭ-pŭs), the son of Laius and Jocasta of Thebes in Greece. At his birth an oracle foretold that he would kill his father and marry his mother. He was exposed, but rescued, adopted by the king of Corinth, and brought up in ignorance of his parentage. Later, while on a journey, he unwittingly did kill his own father Laius. Then at Thebes he answered the riddle of the Sphinx, was made king of Thebes and given the hand of his mother Jocasta. Plagues and persecutions followed; and at the revelation of his identity, he blinded himself, and Jocasta hanged herself. Of four children, Eteocles, Polynices, Antigone, and Ismene, Antigone alone remained with him until his sad death in exile.

Œnone (ē-nō′nē), a nymph of Mount Ida, the loving, but deserted, wife of Paris.

Oïleus (ō-ī′lūs), [Cl.], king of Locris, father of Ajax, and one of the Argonauts.

Olympic games, a great Panhellenic festival held in northwest Greece every fourth summer, beginning 776 B. C.

Olympus (ō-lĭm′pŭs), [Cl.], a mountain in Thessaly, where the Greek gods lived.

Ops (ŏps), [Rom.], goddess of the harvest: identified with the Greek Rhea.

oread (ō′rē-ăd), [Cl.], a mountain nymph.

Orestes (ō-rĕs′tēz), the son of Agamemnon and Clytemnestra of Argos in Greece. In obedience to Apollo, he avenged the murder of his father by slaying his mother and her lover Ægisthus. Persecution by the Furies followed this crime until his purification by bringing from Tauris, with the help of his friend Pylades, his sister Iphigenia and the Tauric cult of Artemis (Diana).

Orion (ō-rī′ŏn), [Cl.], a Greek hunter beloved by Artemis (Diana), who accidentally killed him. In sorrow she placed him and his dog Sirius in the sky as a constellation.

Orpheus (ôr′fūs; ôr′fē-ŭs), [Cl.], a Thracian poet and musician, son of Apollo and Calliope, who, with his lyre, could draw to himself beasts, rocks, and trees. He descended into Hades and so charmed Pluto with his music that he was permitted to bring his dead wife Eurydice back to earth, if only he should not look back at her. He did look back and she vanished.

Osiris (ō-sī′rĭs), [Egypt.], the chief god of the underworld, brother and husband of Isis and father of Horus, opposed and treacherously slain by his brother Set, a god of evil. He has many characteristics of the Greek Apollo and Dionysus (Bacchus).

Ossa (ŏs'ȧ), [Cl.], a mountain in Greece. The Titans piled Ossa on Pelion (or, in some stories, Pelion on Ossa) in a vain attempt to scale heaven (Olympus).
Ossian (ŏsh'ăn), a legendary Gallic bard and hero of the third century.
Palinurus (păl″ĭ-nū'rŭs), [Rom.], the pilot of Æneas. While asleep at the helm, he fell overboard and was murdered by natives on the shore of Italy.
Palladium (pȧ-lā'dĭ-ŭm), [Cl.], a famous statue of Athena (Minerva), which fell from heaven to Troy. On it depended the safety of Troy, which fell only after the Palladium had been stolen by the Greeks Odysseus (Ulysses) and Diomed.
Pallas (păl'ȧs), [Gk.], an epithet of Athena.
Pan (păn), [Gk.], the son of Hermes, and god of flocks and herds: identified with the Roman Faunus.
Pandora (păn-dō'rȧ), a beautiful woman, created by the gods and married to Epimetheus as a means of punishing mortals for Prometheus's theft of fire from heaven. Her curiosity led her to open a certain box and let out into the world all the mortal ills and diseases. Hope alone remained.
Parcæ (pär'sē), [Rom.], the Fates: identified with the Mœræ.
Paris (păr'ĭs), [Cl.], the handsome son of Priam of Troy, brought up as a shepherd and married to Œnone: judge in the famous beauty contest between Hera (Juno), Athena (Minerva), and Aphrodite (Venus). (See *Trojan War.*) Paris was fatally shot by Philoctetes with one of the arrows of Hercules.
Parnassus (pär-năs'ŭs), a mountain in Greece sacred to Apollo and the Muses.
Pasiphaë (pȧ-sĭf'ā-ē), [Cl.], wife of King Minos of Crete, mother of Ariadne and Phædra, and also of the Minotaur.
Patroclus (pȧ-trō'klŭs), [Cl.], a Greek hero of the Trojan War, the devoted friend of Achilles, who lent him his armor and who later avenged his death.
Pegasus (pĕg'ȧ-sŭs), [Cl.], a winged horse belonging to Apollo and the Muses.
Peleus (pē'lūs), [Cl.], king of the Myrmidons; father by Thetis of Achilles.
Pelias (pē'lĭ-ăs; pĕl'ĭ-ăs), [Cl.], a Greek king for whom Jason secured the Golden Fleece. In vain hope of restoring his youth, as Medea had done that of her father-in-law, his own daughters killed and boiled him.
Pelion (pē'lĭ-ŏn), [Cl.], a mountain in Greece. (See *Ossa.*)
penates (pē-nā'tēz), *pl.* [Rom.], household gods of the ancient Romans. (See *lares.*)
Penelope (pē-nĕl'ō-pē), [Cl.], the wife of Odysseus (Ulysses) of Ithaca, noted for her persistent faithfulness to him during his long absence in the Trojan War.
Penthesilea (pĕn″thē-sĭ-lē'ȧ), [Cl.], the brave queen of the Amazons, slain before Troy by Achilles.
Persephone (pẽr-sĕf'ō-nē), [Gk.], queen of the lower world, daughter of Zeus and Demeter, wife of Hades: symbol of the changing seasons: called by the Romans *Proserpina.*
Perseus (pûr'sūs; pûr'sē-ŭs), [Cl.], a Greek hero who slew the Gorgon Medusa, giving her head to Athena (Minerva), and who delivered Andromeda from the sea monster.
Phædra (fē'drȧ), [Cl.], the daughter of King Minos of Crete, wife of Theseus: a suicide for vain love of Hippolytus, her stepson.
Phaëthon (fā'ē-thŏn), [Cl.], the son of Apollo, the sun god. Attempting to drive the sun chariot one day, he lost control of the horses, which drove too low, and, lest he burn up the earth, was struck down by a thunderbolt of Zeus (Jupiter).
Philemon (fĭ-lē'mŏn), [Cl.], a hospitable old Phrygian, who with Baucis, his wife, entertained Zeus (Jupiter) and Hermes (Mercury) unawares. When their country was destroyed by a flood, their house was changed to a temple, the couple being made priest and priestess, and changed at death into two trees.
Philomela (fĭl″ō-mē'lȧ), [Cl.], the daughter of Pandion of Athens, and sister of Procne: changed into a nightingale (or swallow).
Phlegethon (flĕg'ē-thŏn; flĕj'-), [Cl.], the "river of fire" in the lower world.
Phœbe (fē'bē), [Gk.], another name for Artemis, goddess of the chase.
Phœbus (fē'bŭs), [Gk.], Apollo, the sun god.
Pleiades (plē'yȧ-dēz; plē'ȧ-dēz; plī'ȧ-dēz), [Cl.], seven beautiful nymphs of Artemis (Diana), beloved and pursued by Orion, and changed by Zeus (Jupiter), in answer to prayer, into pigeons and then into stars. Six are still visible; one left her place that she might not behold the fall of Troy, or, perhaps, became invisible from shame at having loved a mortal.
Pluto (plōō'tō), the son of Cronus (Saturn) and Rhea (Ops), Greek god of the lower world: also called *Hades*, and, by the Romans, *Dis.*
Plutus (plōō'tŭs), the blind god of riches.
Pollux (pŏl'ŭks), [Cl.], champion boxer, son of Zeus (Jupiter), and immortal twin brother of the mortal Castor (which see): also called *Polydeuces.*
Polyhymnia (pŏl″ĭ-hĭm'nĭ-ȧ), [Cl.], the Muse of oratory and sacred poetry. Also, **Polymnia.**
Polynices (pŏl″ĭ-nī'sēz), [Cl.], a son of Œdipus, slain in the expedition of the Seven against Thebes by his brother Eteocles, from whom he sought to gain the throne.
Polyphemus (pŏl″ĭ-fē'mŭs), [Cl.], a Cyclops who, confining Odysseus (Ulysses) and his companions in his cave, devoured two daily, until Odysseus bored out his one eye, as he lay in drunken sleep. The Greeks escaped by clinging to the stomachs of his sheep as they passed between the giant's legs to go out of the cave to pasture.
Polyxena (pō-lĭk'sē-nȧ), [Cl.], a daughter of Priam and Hecuba of Troy, the affianced wife of Achilles. After his tragic death, she killed herself at his tomb (or was sacrificed to his shade).
Pomona (pō-mō'nȧ), [Rom.], the ancient Italian goddess of gardens and fruit trees.
Poseidon (pō-sī'dŏn), [Gk.], god of the sea, horses, and chivalry: identified with the Roman Neptune.
Priam (prī'ăm), [Cl.], king of Troy during the Trojan War, and father of Hector and Paris.
Procris (prŏk'rĭs; prō'krĭs), the jealous wife of Cephalus, who accidentally slew her.
Procrustes (prō-krŭs'tēz), [Cl.], a notorious robber, slain by Theseus, who laid his victims on an iron bed, stretching them out or cutting them off to make them fit.
Prometheus (prō-mē'thūs; prō-mē'thē-ŭs), [Cl.], a Titan who stole fire from heaven for mortals, and taught them all useful arts. In punishment he passed many years chained to Mount Caucasus, with a vulture gnawing at his liver. His name means "forethought"; he was a brother of Epimetheus, or "afterthought."
Proserpina (prō-sûr'pĭ-nȧ), [Rom.], daughter of Jupiter and Ceres, carried off to the lower world by Pluto and made his queen: symbol of the changing seasons: called *Persephone* by the Greeks. Also, **Proserpine.**
Protesilaus (prō-tĕs″ĭ-lā'ŭs), [Cl.], a Greek hero who, by being the first to meet death in the Trojan War, assured an ultimate

Greek victory. His wife, Laodamia, begged the gods to allow him to return from death for three hours, and when he died the second time, she died with him.

Proteus (prō′tūs; prō′tē-ŭs), [Cl.], a Greek sea god and prophet, who could change himself into any form at will.

Psyche (sī′kē; psī′kē), [Cl.], a lovely Greek maiden personifying the human soul, wooed and won by Eros (Cupid).

Ptah (ptä), [Egypt.], the chief god of Memphis in Egypt, father of gods and men.

Pygmalion (pĭg-mā′lĭ-ŏn), [Cl.], a king and sculptor of Cyprus, who fell in love with his ivory statue of Galatea, a beautiful maiden. In answer to his ardent prayer, Aphrodite (Venus) gave the statue life and she became his wife.

Pylades (pĭl′ȧ-dēz), [Cl.], cousin and friend of the Greek hero Orestes.

Pyramus (pĭr′ȧ-mŭs), [Cl.], a secret lover of Thisbe in ancient Babylon. When he arrived one day at their tryst outside the walls, he saw only her blood-stained veil, which she had left behind in her flight from a lion. Pyramus supposed that she was dead, however, and killed himself. Thisbe presently returned, saw that she had lost him forever and then killed herself.

Pyrrha (pĭr′ȧ), [Cl.], wife of Deucalion. These two, like Noah and his wife, were saved from a great flood, and repeopled the earth.

Pyrrhus (pĭr′ŭs), [Cl.], a Greek hero of the Trojan War, son of Achilles. Also called *Neoptolemus*.

Pythias (pĭth′ĭ-ăs), [Cl.], friend of Damon (which see). Also, more properly, **Phintias**.

Python (pī′thŏn), [Cl.], an enormous serpent which crept forth after the flood subsided: killed by Apollo.

Quirinus (kwĭ-rī′nŭs), [Rom.], the deified Romulus: a god of armed peace.

Ra (rä), [Egypt.], the great god of the sun, life, and right, from whom most of the Pharaohs claimed descent: similar to the Greek god Helios. Also, **Re** (rā).

Ragnarok (răg′nȧ-rŏk′), [Teut.], the Twilight of the Gods (called, in German, *Götterdämmerung*), or the last day for gods and men. Also, **Ragnarök** (-rûk′).

Ran (rän), [Teut.], goddess of the sea, wife of Ægir.

Reginn (rā′yĭn), [Teut.], the treacherous dwarf who taught Sigurd and forged his sword. Also, **Regin.**

Remus (rē′mŭs), [Rom.], the twin brother of Romulus, the founder of Rome: slain for ridiculing the walls of the new city.

Rhadamanthus (răd″ȧ-măn′thŭs), [Cl.], son of Zeus (Jupiter) and Europa. Because of his justice in life he became one of the three judges of the lower world.

Rhea (rē′ȧ), [Gk.], wife of Cronus, and mother of many of the gods: identified with Cybele and the Roman Ops.

Romulus (rŏm′ū-lŭs), [Rom.], the son of Mars and Ilia, thrown into the Tiber, as an infant, with his twin brother Remus, but rescued and adopted by a shepherd; later, the founder and first king of Rome.

Saga (sä′gȧ; sā′gȧ), [Teut.], goddess of history. Her home was Sokkvabekk.

Saturn (săt′ûrn), [Rom.], the ancient god of the seed sowing, son of Uranus, and father of Jupiter: identified with the Greek Cronus.

satyr (săt′ēr; sā′tēr), a Greek sylvan deity, represented as a youth with the ears, horns, and hind legs of a goat.

Savitar (săv′ĭ-tȧr), [Hindu], the Vedic golden-handed sun in his daily course.

Scylla (sĭl′ȧ), [Cl.], a Greek sea nymph beloved by Glaucus, changed into a ravenous monster by the jealous Circe. From a cliff on the Italian coast, opposite the whirlpool of Charybdis on the Sicilian coast, she thrust forth her long neck and seized sailors as they passed.

Seb (sĕb), [Egypt.], god of earth and its vegetation: similar to the Greek Cronus.

Selene (sē-lē′nē), [Gk.], goddess of the moon: often identified with Artemis and Hecate.

Semele (sĕm′ē-lē), [Cl.], mother of Dionysus (Bacchus) by Zeus (Jupiter): consumed by lightning when Zeus appeared to her, at her request, in all his glory.

Serapis (sē-rā′pĭs), [Egypt.], a deity representing Osiris in the lower world.

Set (sĕt), [Egypt.], the personification of evil.

Seven against Thebes (thēbz), the expedition, against the Greek city of Thebes, of seven heroes, Adrastus, Amphiaraüs, Capaneus, Hippomedon, Polynices, Parthenopæus, and Tydeus, in an unsuccessful effort to wrest the throne for Polynices, son of Œdipus, from his brother Eteocles. All save Adrastus were killed.

Seven Wonders of the World, seven noted objects of antiquity, usually listed as the pyramids of Egypt, the temple of Diana at Ephesus, the hanging gardens of Babylon, the Colossus of Rhodes, the mausoleum built by Artemisia at Halicarnassus, the statue of Zeus by Phidias at Olympia, the Pharos (lighthouse) of Alexandria in Egypt.

Sibyl (sĭb′ĭl), [Rom.], a prophetess who lived in a cave at Cumæ near Naples and guided Æneas through Hades: the authoress of the inspired Sibylline Books.

Sif (sēf), [Teut.], wife of Thor, and goddess of the sanctity of the family and of wedlock.

Sigmund (sĭg′mŭnd; zēkh′mo͝ont), [Teut.], the Volsung hero, father of Sigurd.

Sigurd (zē′go͞ort), [Norse], the hero of the "Volsunga Saga," who delivered Brynhild, but deserted her for Gudrun (in the German version, *Kriemhild*), sister of Gunnar (Gunther). He was treacherously slain, through the instigation of Brynhild, by Gunnar's brother.

Sigyn (sē′gün), [Teut.], the faithful wife of Loki, who went with him to his place of punishment and tried to keep the drops of venom of the serpent from falling on his face by catching it in a cup. Each time the cup becomes full, she turns to empty it, and a drop falls on Loki's face, so that he trembles in agony, causing earthquakes.

Silenus (sī-lē′nŭs), [Cl.], a Greek woodland god, tutor of Dionysus (Bacchus).

Sinon (sī′nŏn), [Cl.], a wily Greek of the Trojan War, whose false tale persuaded the Trojans to take the wooden horse into the city, that he might free the Greek warriors concealed within.

sirens (sī′rĕnz), [Cl.], nymphs on an island near Italy, where they sang so sweetly that they lured many sailors to their destruction.

Sirius (sĭr′ĭ-ŭs), [Cl.], the faithful hunting dog of Orion, with whom he was translated to the skies as a constellation.

Sisyphus (sĭs′ĭ-fŭs), [Cl.], a greedy king of Corinth in Greece, condemned in Tartarus to roll uphill a large stone, which constantly fell back again.

Siva (sē′vȧ; shē′vȧ), [Hindu], the god of destruction and reproduction, forming, with Brahma and Vishnu, the supreme trinity.

Skathi (skä′*thē*), [Teut.], goddess of winter, wife of Njorth, whose home was Thrymheim.

Skuld (sko͞old), [Teut.], one of the Norns, who correspond to the Greek Fates.

Sleipnir (slāp′nēr), [Teut.], Odin's eight-footed horse.

Somnus (sŏm′nŭs), [Rom.], god of sleep: identified with the Greek god Hypnos.

Stentor (stĕn'tôr), [Cl.,] a Greek herald, whose voice had the strength of fifty men.
Styx (stĭks), [Cl.], the river in Hades by which the gods swore their most irrevocable oaths.
Tantalus (tăn'tȧ-lŭs), [Cl.], a wicked Greek king punished in Tartarus by being placed in water up to his neck, with fruit hanging just above his head. If he stooped to drink, the water receded; if he reached for food, the wind snatched it away.
Tartarus (tär'tȧ-rŭs), [Cl.], the place of punishment in the lower world.
Telamon (tĕl'ȧ-mŏn), [Cl.], father of Ajax, companion of Hercules in many exploits.
Telemachus (tē-lĕm'ȧ-kŭs), [Cl.], son of Odysseus (Ulysses) and Penelope. He tried unsuccessfully to find his father after the Trojan War, but returned in time to greet him and help him avenge Penelope.
Terpsichore (tûrp-sĭk'ō-rē), [Cl.], the Muse of dancing.
Thalia (thȧ-lī'ȧ), **1**, the Muse of comedy; **2**, one of the three Graces.
Thanatos (thăn'ȧ-tŏs), [Gk.], death personified: identified with the Roman Mors.
Themis (thē'mĭs), [Cl.], a Greek Titaness of justice.
Theseus (thē'sūs; thē'sē-ŭs), [Cl.], the great Attic hero, king of Athens. He killed Procrustes; slew the Minotaur and eloped with Ariadne; conquered the Amazons, carrying off their queen, Hippolyte (or Antilope); went on the Argonautic expedition; hunted the Calydonian boar; and tried to help Pirithoüs abduct Persephone.
Thetis (thē'tĭs), [Cl.], a Nereid, wife of Peleus; mother of Achilles.
Thisbe (thĭz'bē), [Cl.], a beautiful maiden of Babylon, lover of Pyramus (which see).
Thor (thôr), [Teut.], son of Odin, god of thunder and might: keeper of the hammer and defender of the earth, the heavens, and the gods.
Thyestes (thī-ĕs'tēz), [Cl.], a wicked Greek hero, who wronged his brother Atreus, the latter, in revenge, serving up Thyestes' sons to him at a banquet. For this deed the gods cursed the house of Atreus forever.
Tisiphone (tĭ-sĭf'ō-nē), [Cl.], one of the Furies, or Erinyes (which see).
Titans (tī'tănz), [Cl.], Greek giants who warred unsuccessfully against the gods of Olympus.
Tithonus (tĭ-thō'nŭs), [Cl.], son of Laomedon, king of Troy, beloved by Eos (Aurora), who secured immortality for him, but forgot to ask for immortal youth. Tithonus grew old and feeble, and was finally changed into a grasshopper.
Tityus (tĭt'ĭ-ŭs), [Cl.], a Greek giant so large that he covered nine acres in Tartarus, where vultures continually gnawed his liver.
Trimurti (trē-mōōr'tē), [Hindu], the trinity, consisting of Brahma (the Creator), Vishnu (the Preserver), and Siva (the Destroyer).
Triton (trī'tŏn), [Cl.], a Greek sea demigod, provided with a conch trumpet to raise or calm the waves.
Trojan War (trō'jăn), [Cl.], the famous ten-year siege of Troy, an ancient city of Asia Minor, subject of Homer's "Iliad." At the wedding of Peleus and Thetis, Eris, goddess of discord, threw among the guests a golden apple, inscribed "For the Fairest." The decision was left to Paris, son of Priam, King of Troy. Hera (Juno) thereupon offered him power and riches; Athena (Minerva), martial glory; Aphrodite (Venus), the most beautiful woman in the world. Paris awarded the prize to Aphrodite, who helped him to carry off Helen to Troy; and the Trojan War resulted.
Turnus (tûr'nŭs), [Rom.], the chief of the Rutuli, an Italian tribe; the unsuccessful rival of Æneas for the hand of Lavinia: slain by Æneas.
Tyr (tēr), [Teut.], god of war and the sky; son of Odin. Also, **Tyrr.**
Ull (ōōl), [Teut.], god of the chase.
Ulysses (ū-lĭs'ēz), [Rom.], a hero, called by the Greeks Odysseus: king of Ithaca, and the wisest, shrewdest, and subtlest of the Greek chiefs in the Trojan War.
Urania (ū-rā'nĭ-ȧ), [Cl.], the Muse of astronomy.
Uranus (ū'rȧ-nŭs), [Cl.], heaven personified.
Urth (ōōr*th*), [Teut.], one of the Norns, corresponding to the Greek Fates.
Ushas (ōō'shȧs; ōō-shȧs'), [Hindu], goddess of dawn: similar to the Roman Aurora.
Valhalla (văl-hăl'ȧ), [Teut.], the hall of the slain, where fallen warriors were fêted.
Vali (vä'lē), [Teut.], Odin's precocious son, who, as soon as born, avenged the death of Balder. He was to rule with Vitharr after Ragnarok.
Valkyrie (văl-kĭr'ĭ; -kī'rĭ), [Teut.], one of a troop of goddesses, handmaids of Odin. Hovering over the field of battle, they woke up heroes with a kiss, and led away their souls to Valhalla, there to fight and to drink ale, as of old.
Vanaheim (vä'nä-hām"), [Teut.], the home of the Vanir, gods of trade: one of the nine worlds told of in the Eddas.
Vanir (vä'nēr; wä'nēr), [Teut.], Njorth, Frey, and Freya, gods of trade and commerce, who lived in Vanaheim; at first enemies, later allies, of the Æsir in Asgard.
Vayu (vä'yōō; wä'yōō), [Hindu], god of the winds: similar to the Greek god Æolus.
Ve (vē), [Teut.], brother of Odin and Vili, whom he helped slay the giant Ymir.
Venus (vē'nŭs), [Rom.], goddess of beauty and love; wife of Vulcan: identified with the Greek goddess Aphrodite.
Verthandi (vĕr'*th*ăn-dē), [Teut.], one of the Norns, corresponding to the Greek Fates.
Vesta (vĕs'tȧ), [Rom.], goddess of virginity, fire, and the domestic hearth: similar to the Greek goddess Hestia.
Vili (vē'lē), [Teut.], brother of Odin and Ve, whom he helped slay the giant Ymir.
Vishnu (vĭsh'nōō), [Hindu], the Preserver, the second god of the trinity.
Vitharr (vē'*th*är), [Teut.], son of Odin and Grid; destined to slay the Fenris-wolf at Ragnarok and then to rule with Vali.
Vulcan (vŭl'kăn), [Rom.], god of fire and the working of metals: identified with the Greek god Hephæstus.
Woden (wō'dĕn), [Teut.], another name for Odin. Also, **Wodan.**
Yama (yăm'ȧ), [Hindu], the first man; after death he and Yami, the first woman, became king and queen of the other world: similar to Pluto and Proserpina.
Yggdrasill (ĭg'drȧ-sĭl), [Teut.], the ash tree which embraces and supports the world.
Ymir (ü'mēr; ē'mēr), [Teut.], the ancestor of the giants, formed of the frost and fire in Ginnungagap, from whose body the present world was created. His flesh became earth; his blood, the sea; his bones, the mountains; his teeth, the cliffs; his skull, the heavens, wherein his brains float in the form of clouds. Also, **Ymer.**
Zephyrus (zĕf'ĭ-rŭs), [Cl.], the West Wind.
Zethus (zē'thŭs), [Cl.], twin brother of Amphion and son of Antiope (which see).
Zeus (zūs), [Gk.], the supreme deity of the Greeks; god of nature, giver of victory, god of law and order, of social virtues; the beginning and end of all things: identified by the Romans with Jupiter (Jove).

FOREIGN WORDS AND PHRASES

Including Proverbs and Quotations found in English Literature, Colloquial Expressions, Mottoes of States and Nations, and Law Terms

The pronunciation indicated is, except in the case of phrases from the Latin, that of the language from which the phrase is taken. For a discussion of certain points in the pronunciation of foreign words, see page xix.

There are in use two methods of pronouncing Latin: one, the so-called English method, follows in general the principles of English pronunciation; the other, the so-called Roman or Continental method, follows more or less closely the pronunciation of the ancient Romans themselves. The English pronunciation is still generally used for Latin scientific terms, and for names, phrases, and quotations in English context. All listings in this Appendix are syllabified according to the method of the language from which they are taken; but in the case of Latin words and phrases, the pronunciation is given according to the English method; as, **e-di-ti-o** (ē-dĭsh'ĭ-ō). A Latin grammar should be consulted for further details as to the Roman pronunciation.

A

à bas *Fr.* (à bä'), down; down with.

ab-e-unt stu-di-a in mo-res *Lat.* (ăb'ē-ŭnt stū'dĭ-*à* ĭn mō'rēz), studies become habits; pursuits influence character.

ab ex-tra *Lat.* (ăb ĕks'tr*à*), from without.

ab in-con-ve-ni-en-ti *Lat.* (ăb ĭn″kŏn-vē″-nĭ-ĕn'tī), lit., from (the resulting) inconvenience: of an argument, employed only in a case in which the law on the subject is doubtful, in favor of a given construction of the law based on the fact that the opposite construction would create a degree of inconvenience or hardship which would be unreasonable.

ab in-i-ti-o *Lat.* (ăb ĭn-ĭsh'ĭ-ō), from the beginning; from the very first.

ab in-tra *Lat.* (ăb ĭn'tr*à*), from within.

ab in-vi-to *Lat.* (ăb ĭn-vī'tō), unwillingly.

à bon chat, bon rat *Fr.* (à bôṅ″ shà', bôṅ″ rà'), lit., to a good cat, a good rat; it takes a thief to catch a thief; things should be well matched. [good bargain; cheap.

à bon mar-ché *Fr.* (à bôṅ″ màr″shā'), at a

ab o-ri-gi-ne *Lat.* (ăb ō-rĭj'ĭ-nē), from the beginning; from the origin.

ab o-vo us-que ad ma-la *Lat.* (ăb ō'vō ŭs'-kwē ăd mā'l*à*), lit., from the egg to the apples; of a dinner, from beginning to end.

ab-sit in-vi-di-a *Lat.* (ăb'sĭt ĭn-vĭd'ĭ-*à*), let there be no ill will; no slight intended.

ab (or **ex**) **u-no dis-ce om-nes** *Lat.* (ăb (ĕks) ū'nō dĭs'ē ŏm'nēz), from one learn all.

ab ur-be con-di-ta *Lat.* (ăb ûr'bē kŏn'dĭ-t*à*), from the founding of the city (Rome, founded 753 B. C.): used by the Romans in giving dates.

à che-val *Fr.* (à shē-vàl'), lit., on horseback; hence, astraddle; on both sides. [payment.

à compte *Fr.* (à kôṅt'), on account; in part

ad ar-bi-tri-um *Lat.* (ăd är-bĭt'rĭ-ŭm), at will.

ad as-tra per as-pe-ra *Lat.* (ăd ăs'tr*à* pûr ăs'pē-r*à*), to the stars through hardships: motto of Kansas.

ad cap-tan-dum vul-gus *Lat.* (ăd kăp-tăn'-dŭm vŭl'gŭs), to catch the crowd; in order to please.

à de-mi *Fr.* (à dē-mē'), half; incompletely.

ad fi-nem *Lat.* (ăd fī'nĕm), at the end; to the end. [specially.

ad hoc *Lat.* (ăd hŏk), with respect to this;

ad ho-mi-nem *Lat.* (ăd hŏm'ĭ-nĕm), lit., to the man: of an argument, appealing to one's prejudices or special interest.

a-dieu *Fr.* (a″dyö'), farewell (cf. **au revoir**).

ad in-fi-ni-tum *Lat.* (ăd ĭn″fĭ-nī'tŭm), to infinity; endlessly. [beginning.

ad in-i-ti-um *Lat.* (ăd ĭn-ĭsh'ĭ-ŭm), at the

ad in-te-rim *Lat.* (ăd ĭn'tē-rĭm), meanwhile; temporarily.

ad ka-len-das Græ-cas *Lat.* (ăd k*à*-lĕn'dăs grē'kăs), lit., at the Greek calends; that is, never (the Greek calendar had no calends).

ad li-bi-tum *Lat.* (ăd lĭb'ĭ-tŭm), at pleasure.

ad nau-se-am *Lat.* (ăd nô'zhē-ăm), lit., to nausea; to (the point of causing) disgust.

ad pa-tres *Lat.* (ăd pā'trēz), (gone) to his fathers; dead. [opp. of *a quo*.

ad quem *Lat.* (ăd kwĕm), at, or to, which:

ad rem *Lat.* (ăd rĕm), to the purpose; pertaining to the matter in hand. [right.

à droite *Fr.* (à drwät'), to the right; on the

ad va-lo-rem *Lat.* (ăd v*à*-lō'rĕm), according to value; proportional to value.

ad vi-vum *Lat.* (ăd vī'vŭm), lit., to that which is alive; to the quick; to the life.

æ-quam me-men-to re-bus in ar-du-is ser-va-re men-tem *Lat.* (ē'kwăm mē-mĕn'tō rē'bŭs ĭn är'dū-ĭs sûr-vā'rē mĕn'-tĕm), remember to keep an unruffled mind in difficulties.

æ-quo a-ni-mo *Lat.* (ē'kwō ăn'ĭ-mō), lit., with equal mind; calmly; with equanimity.

af-faire d'a-mour *Fr.* (à″fâr' dà″mōōr'), an amour; a love affair.

af-faire d'hon-neur *Fr.* (à″fâr' dô″nûr'), an affair of honor; a duel.

af-faire du cœur *Fr.* (à″fâr' dü kûr'), an affair of the heart; a love affair. [ly; fully.

à fond *Fr.* (à fôṅ'), to the bottom; thorough-

a for-ti-o-ri *Lat.* (ā fôr″shĭ-ō'rī; fôr″-), with the greater force; all the more.

à gauche *Fr.* (à gōsh'), to the left; on the left.

à grands frais *Fr.* (à gräṅ' frâ'), at great expense. [voice; aloud; loudly.

à haute voix *Fr.* (à ōt' vwà'), at the top of the

al-ki (ȧ″ĭ-kē′), by and by: motto of the State of Washington.

à la bonne heure *Fr.* (á lȧ bôn″ ûr′), just in time: as an exclamation, good; fine.

à la carte *Fr.* (á lȧ kȧrt′), lit., by the card, or bill of fare: used to designate a meal in which each dish is paid for at a specified price: opp. of *table d'hôte*.

à la fran-çaise *Fr.* (á lȧ fräṅ″sâz′), in the French fashion; in cookery, applied to various dishes, some not typically French.

à la mode *Fr.* (á lȧ môd′), in fashion; in cookery, served in some special manner.

à l'an-glaise *Fr.* (á läṅ″glâz′), in the English style; specif., in cookery, roasted or boiled.

a-lis vo-lat pro-pri-is *Lat.* (ā′lĭs vō′lăt prō′-prē-ĭs), she flies with her own wings: motto of Oregon.

al-ter e-go *Lat.* (ăl′tẽr ē′gō), another, or second, I; an intimate, or bosom, friend.

a-mende ho-no-ra-ble *Fr.* (ȧ″mäṅd′ ô″nô″-rȧbl′′), in the Middle Ages, satisfaction given or reparation made, publicly, to the injured party.

a men-sa et tho-ro *Lat.* (ā mĕn′sȧ ĕt thō′rō), lit., from table and bed; from bed and board: a legal phrase applied to separation by divorce.

a-mor pa-tri-æ *Lat.* (ā′môr păt′rĭ-ē), love of one's country or native land. [esteem.

a-mour pro-pre *Fr.* (ȧ″mōōr′ prôpr′′), self-

an-cien ré-gime *Fr.* (äṅ″syăṅ′ rā″zhēm′), the former order (of things); specif., the state of government in France before the Revolution.

an-guis in her-ba *Lat.* (ăng′gwĭs ĭn hûr′bȧ), lit., a snake in the grass; insidious danger.

a-ni-mis o-pi-bus-que pa-ra-ti *Lat.* (ăn′ĭ-mĭs ŏp″ĭ-bŭs′kwē pȧ-rā′tī), prepared in minds and resources: one of the mottoes of South Carolina.

an-no æ-ta-tis su-æ *Lat.* (ăn′ō ē-tā′tĭs sū′ē), in the (designated) year of his, or her, life.

an-no Do-mi-ni *Lat.* (ăn′ō dŏm′ĭ-nī), in the (given) year of our Lord.

an-no ur-bis con-di-tæ *Lat.* (ăn′ō ûr′bĭs kŏn′dĭ-tē), in the (designated) year of the founded city (Rome, founded about 753 B. C.): used in giving dates: similar to *anno Domini*.

an-nus mi-ra-bi-lis *Lat.* (ăn′ŭs mĭ-răb′ĭ-lĭs), lit., wonderful year: said of various years, esp. 1666, the year of the great London fire.

an-te bel-lum *Lat.* (ăn′tē bĕl′ŭm), lit., before the war; usually, before the American Civil War. [before noon.

an-te me-ri-di-em *Lat.* (ăn′tē mē-rĭd′ĭ-ĕm),

an-te vic-to-ri-am ne ca-nas tri-um-phum *Lat.* (ăn′tē vĭk-tō′rĭ-ăm nē kā′năs trī-ŭm′fŭm), do not sing your triumph before you have conquered; do not shout before you are out of the woods.

à ou-trance *Fr.* (á ōō″träṅs′), to the bitter end; to the utmost.

à peu près *Fr.* (á pö″ prâ′), nearly; almost.

à pied *Fr.* (á pyā′), on foot.

à plomb *Fr.* (á plôṅ′), plumb; in the perpendicular; hence, with assurance.

a po-ste-ri-o-ri *Lat.* (ā pŏs-tē″rĭ-ō′rī), from that which follows: opp. of *a priori*.

a-près moi (or **nous**) **le dé-luge** *Fr.* (ȧ″prâ″ mwȧ′ (nōō′) lē dā″lüzh′), after me (us) the deluge: an alleged remark of Louis XV to Madame de Pompadour.

a pri-o-ri *Lat.* (ā prĭ-ō′rī), from that which precedes: from cause to effect: opp. of *a posteriori*; hence, self-evidently.

à pro-pos de bottes *Fr.* (á prō″pō′ dē bôt′), lit., apropos of boots; by the way: used jocularly in suddenly changing the subject.

à pro-pos de rien *Fr.* (ȧ″ prō″pō′ dē ryăṅ), apropos of nothing; by the way. [*quem.*

a quo *Lat.* (ā kwō), from which: opp. of *ad*

ar-bi-ter e-le-gan-ti-æ *Lat.* (är′bĭ-tẽr ĕl″ē-găn′shĭ-ē), judge of elegance; authority in matters of taste: said of Caius Petronius, of Nero's court.

a ri-ve-der-ci *It.* (ä rē″vā-dâr′chē), until our next meeting; good-by; au revoir.

ar-rec-tis au-ri-bus *Lat.* (ȧ-rĕk′tĭs ô′rĭ-bŭs), with ears pricked up; attentively.

ar-rière pen-sée *Fr.* (ȧ″ryâr′ päṅ″sā′), a thought kept back; mental reservation.

ars est ce-la-re ar-tem *Lat.* (ärz ĕst sē-lā′rē är′tĕm), it is true art to conceal art.

ars lon-ga, tem-pus fu-git *Lat.* (ärz lông′gȧ, tĕm′pŭs fū′jĭt), art (is) lasting, time is fleeting.

ars lon-ga, vi-ta bre-vis *Lat.* (ärz lông′gȧ, vī′tȧ brĕv′ĭs), art (is) lasting, life (is) brief.

a-te-lier *Fr.* (ȧ″tē-lyā′), a workshop; studio.

a tem-po *It.* (ä tĕm′pō), in music, in time: used after a change in movement to direct a return to the original time. [trary.

au con-traire *Fr.* (ō kôṅ″trâr′), on the con-

au cou-rant *Fr.* (ō kōō″räṅ′), lit., with the current; up-to-date; informed. [expert.

au fait *Fr.* (ō fâ′), well acquainted; skilful;

au fond *Fr.* (ō fôṅ′), at bottom; fundamentally; in the main.

auf Wie-der-seh-en *Ger.* (ouf vē′dẽr-zā″ĕn), till we meet again; good-by; au revoir.

au gra-tin *Fr.* (ō″ grȧ′tăṅ′), in cookery, dressed with bread crumbs.

au pied de la let-tre *Fr.* (ō pyā′ dē lȧ lĕtr′′), lit., to the foot of the letter; literally.

au reste *Fr.* (ō rĕst′), as for the rest; besides.

au re-voir *Fr.* (ō″ rē-vwȧr′), till we meet again; good-by: implying that the separation is to be temporary: distinguished from *adieu*, which implies a final farewell.

au-ri sa-cra fa-mes *Lat.* (ô′rī sā′krȧ fā′mēz), the accursed greed for gold.

aut vin-ce-re, aut mo-ri *Lat.* (ôt vĭn′sē-rē, ôt mō′rī), either to conquer or to die: motto of the Duke of Kent.

aux armes *Fr.* (ō zȧrm′), to arms.

aux grands maux les grands re-mèdes *Fr.* (ō gräṅ″ mō′ lā gräṅ″ rē-mâd′), for great ills great remedies. [syôṅ′), with permission.

a-vec per-mis-sion *Fr.* (ȧ″vĕk″ pâr″mē″-

a-vec plai-sir *Fr.* (ȧ″vĕk″ plâ″zēr′), with pleasure. [vûr′bē-rȧ), from words to blows.

a ver-bis ad ver-be-ra *Lat.* (ā vûr′bĭs ăd

a vin-cu-lo ma-tri-mo-ni-i *Lat.* (ā vĭng′-kū-lō măt″rĭ-mō′nē-ī), lit., from the marriage bond; of divorce, absolute: a legal phrase.

à vo-tre san-té *Fr.* (á vôtr′″ säṅ″tā′), to your health: sometimes given as a toast.

B

bas bleu *Fr.* (bä″ blö′), a bluestocking.

be-a-tæ me-mo-ri-æ *Lat.* (bē-ā′tē mē-mō′-rĭ-ē), of blessed memory; revered.

beau monde *Fr.* (bō″ môṅd′), lit., the fine world; fashionable society. [good looks.

beaux yeux *Fr.* (bō″ zyö′), beautiful eyes;

bel-es-prit *Fr.* (bĕl″=ĕs″prē′), a man of wit; a genius. [well invented; well discovered.

ben tro-va-to *It.* (bĕn trō-vä′tō), well found;

bête noire *Fr.* (bât″ nwȧr′), lit., black beast; a bugbear; an object of aversion.

bis dat qui ci-to dat *Lat.* (bĭs dăt kwī sī′tō dăt), he gives twice who gives quickly.

bo-na fi-de *Lat.* (bō′nȧ fī′dē), in good faith.

bon gré, mal gré *Fr.* (bôṅ′ grā″, mȧl′ grā″), (with) good grace, (or with) bad grace; willy-nilly. [morning.

bon jour *Fr.* (bôṅ″ zhōōr′), good day; good

bon mot *Fr.* (bôṅ″ mō′), lit., a good word; a witty saying.

bonne foi *Fr.* (bôn″ fwä′), good faith. [night.

bon soir *Fr.* (bôṅ″ swȧr′), good evening; good

bon ton *Fr.* (bôṅ″ tôṅ′), lit., good tone; the height of fashion; fashionable society.

bon vi-vant *Fr.* (bôṅ″ vē″väṅ′), lit., a good

liver; hence, a lover of good living; an epicure.

bon voy-age *Fr.* (bôṅ" vwȧ"yȧzh'), a good [voyage (or journey) to you.

bru-tum ful-men *Lat.* (bro͞o'tŭm fŭl'mĕn), a thunderbolt striking blindly; a wasted display of force.

C

car-pe di-em *Lat.* (kär'pē dī'ĕm), make use of the day; enjoy the present.

carte blanche *Fr.* (kȧrt bläṅsh), lit., white paper; hence, unlimited authority; absolute freedom of action and judgment.

ca-sus bel-li *Lat.* (kā'sŭs bĕl'ī), an occasion for war: that is, an act which justifies, or might cause, war.

cau-sa si-ne qua non *Lat.* (kô'zȧ sī'nē kwā nŏn), lit., a cause without which not; an indispensable condition. Also, **si-ne qua non.**

ca-ve-at emp-tor *Lat.* (kā'vē-ăt ĕmp'tŏr), lit., let the buyer beware; sold without guarantee.

ca-ve ca-nem *Lat.* (kā'vē kā'nĕm), beware [the dog.

ce-dant ar-ma to-gæ *Lat.* (sē'dȧnt är'mȧ tō'jē), let arms yield to the gown (the costume of peace): that is, let military power yield to civil authority.

c'est à dire *Fr.* (sĕ" tȧ" dēr'), that is to say; [namely.

c'est plus qu'un crime, c'est une faute *Fr.* (sĕ plü" kŭṅ krēm', sĕ tün fōt'), it is worse than a crime, it is a blunder.

c'est se-lon *Fr.* (sĕ" sē-lôṅ'), that depends.

ce-te-ra de-sunt *Lat.* (sĕt'ē-rȧ dē'sŭnt), the rest are wanting; the others are lacking.

ce-te-ris pa-ri-bus *Lat.* (sĕt'ē-rĭs păr'ĭ-bŭs), other things being equal.

cha-cun à son goût *Fr.* (shȧ"kŭṅ' ȧ" sôṅ" go͞o'), every one to his taste.

châ-teau en Es-pagne *Fr.* (shä"tō' ä" nĕs"-pȧny''), lit., a castle in Spain; a visionary hope; a castle in the air: because the French regarded Spain as a land of romance.

chef de cui-sine *Fr.* (shĕf' dē küē"zēn'), head cook: usually contracted to *chef*.

chef-d'œu-vre *Fr.* (shā "=dûvr''), a masterpiece; one's greatest achievement.

che-min de fer *Fr.* (shē-măṅ" dē fâr'), railroad.

cher a-mi *Fr.* (shâr" ȧ"mē'), dear friend [(masc.).

cher-chez la femme *Fr.* (shâr"shā' lȧ fȧm'), lit., look for the woman; there's a woman in the case.

chère a-mie *Fr.* (shâr" ȧ"mē'), dear friend [(fem.).

che-va-lier d'in-dus-trie *Fr.* (shē-vȧ"lyā' dăṅ"düs"trē'), a swindler.

ci-gît *Fr.* (sē"=zhē'), here lies.

cir-ca *Lat.* (sûr'kȧ), around; round about; [about.

co-gi-to, er-go sum *Lat.* (kŏj'ĭ-tō, ûr'gō sŭm), I think, therefore I am: a fundamental principle in Descartes's philosophy.

comme il faut *Fr.* (kô" mēl" fō'), as it should be; proper.

compte ren-du *Fr.* (kôṅt' räṅ"dü'), an account given; a report. [count given; a report.

con a-mo-re *It.* (kŏn ä-mō'rā), with love; hence, earnestly; enthusiastically.

con do-lo-re *It.* (kŏn dō-lō'rā), with grief; [sadly.

con-sue-tu-do pro le-ge ser-va-tur *Lat.* (kŏn"swē-tū'dō prō lē'jē sûr-vā'tŭr), custom serves as law: a legal phrase.

con-tra bo-nos mo-res *Lat.* (kŏn'trȧ bō'nōs mō'rēz), contrary to good manners (or practices).

con-tre-temps *Fr.* (kôṅtr'"täṅ'), an untoward accident; an embarrassing event.

co-pain *Fr.* (kô"păṅ'), comrade.

co-ram po-pu-lo *Lat.* (kō'răm pŏp'ū-lō), [publicly.

cor-pus de-lic-ti *Lat.* (kôr'pŭs dē-lĭk'tī), the body, or substantial and essential facts, of a crime.

cor-ri-gen-da *Lat.* (kŏr"ĭ-jĕn'dȧ), things to [be corrected.

cor-tège *Fr.* (kôr"tâzh'), a procession, as of attendants.

coup de grâce *Fr.* (ko͞o" dē gräs'), lit., a stroke [of mercy; a finishing stroke.

coup de main *Fr.* (ko͞o" dē măṅ'), a sudden military movement.

coup de maî-tre *Fr.* (ko͞o" dē mâtr''), a master stroke; an act showing ability.

coup de pied *Fr.* (ko͞o" dē pyā'), a kick.

coup de so-leil *Fr.* (ko͞o" dē sô"lāy''), a sunstroke.

coup d'é-tat *Fr.* (ko͞o" dā"tȧ'), a sudden act in politics, as the overthrow of an existing government.

coup de thé-â-tre *Fr.* (ko͞o" dē tā"ätr''), a sudden action in a play; hence, a theatrical effect.

coup d'œil *Fr.* (ko͞o" dûy''), a rapid glance.

coûte que coûte *Fr.* (ko͞ot" kē ko͞ot'), cost what it may.

cre-du-la res a-mor est *Lat.* (krĕd'ū-lȧ rēz ā'môr ĕst), love is a credulous thing.

cres-ci-te et mul-ti-pli-ca-mi-ni *Lat.* (krĕs'ĭ-tē ĕt mŭl"tĭ-plĭ-kăm'ĭ-nī), increase and multiply: a motto of Maryland.

cres-cit e-un-do *Lat.* (krĕs'ĭt ē-ŭn'dō), it grows by going (or, as it goes): motto of New Mexico.

croix de guerre *Fr.* (krwä" dē gâr'), war cross: the French war cross, given to men of all ranks, for bravery under fire.

cui bo-no *Lat.* (kwī bō'nō), lit., to whom (is it) for a benefit? of what use is it?

cul-de-sac *Fr.* (kü"=dē=sȧk'; kŭl"=dē=săk'), lit., bottom of a bag; hence, a passage with only one outlet; a blind alley; trap.

cum gra-no sa-lis *Lat.* (kŭm grā'nō sā'lĭs), lit., with a grain of salt; making allowance.

cur-ren-te ca-la-mo *Lat.* (kŭ-rĕn'tē kăl'ȧ-mō), with a running (or ready) pen; without hesitation.

D

d'ac-cord *Fr.* (dȧ"kôr'), in accord; in harmony.

dame d'hon-neur *Fr.* (dȧm" dô"nûr'), maid [of honor.

de bonne grâce *Fr.* (dē bôn" gräs'), with good grace; willingly.

de fac-to *Lat.* (dē făk'tō), in fact; actually; in reality: distinguished from *de jure*.

de gus-ti-bus non (est) dis-pu-tan-dum *Lat.* (dē gŭs'tĭ-bŭs nŏn (ĕst) dĭs"pū-tăn'-dŭm), there is no disputing about tastes.

De-i gra-ti-a *Lat.* (dē'ī grā'shĭ-ȧ), by the grace of God.

de ju-re *Lat.* (dē jo͞o'rē), by right or lawful [title: opp. of *de facto*.

de-len-da est Car-tha-go *Lat.* (dē-lĕn'dȧ ĕst kär-thā'gō), Carthage must be destroyed: words of Cato the Elder.

de luxe *Fr.* (dē lüks'), of unusually fine qual- [ity; sumptuous.

de mor-tu-is nil ni-si bo-num *Lat.* (dē môr'tū-ĭs nĭl nī'sī bō'nŭm), of the dead (say) nothing but good.

de ni-hi-lo ni-hil *Lat.* (dē nī'hĭ-lō nī'hĭl), from nothing nothing (can come).

de no-vo *Lat.* (dē nō'vō), anew.

De-o ad-ju-van-te, non ti-men-dum *Lat.* (dē'ō ăd"jū-văn'tē, nŏn tĭ-mĕn'dŭm), God helping, nothing is to be feared.

De-o fa-ven-te *Lat.* (dē'ō fȧ-vĕn'tē), lit., God favoring; with God's favor.

De-o gra-ti-as *Lat.* (dē'ō grā'shĭ-ăs), thanks [to God.

De-o vo-len-te *Lat.* (dē'ō vō-lĕn'tē), God willing.

de pro-fun-dis *Lat.* (dē prō-fŭn'dĭs), out of [the depths.

de ri-gueur *Fr.* (dē rē"gûr'), obligatory; indispensable.

der-nier res-sort *Fr.* (dâr"nyā' rē-sôr'), a [last resort.

de trop *Fr.* (dē trō'), too much; hence, in the way; unwelcome.

de-us ex ma-chi-na *Lat.* (dē'ŭs ĕks măk'ĭ-nȧ), lit., a god (let down) from a machine (as in ancient theaters); an unexpected occurrence (which settles some problem); a superhuman agency.

di-es faus-tus *Lat.* (dī'ēz fôs'tŭs), lucky day.

Di-es I-ræ *Lat.* (dī'ēz ī'rē), Day of Wrath:

the opening words of a celebrated Latin hymn on the Day of Judgment.

Dieu a-vec nous *Fr.* (dyö′ ȧ″vĕk″ nōō′), God with us.

Dieu dé-fend le droit *Fr.* (dyö′ dā″fäṅ′ lē drwä′), God defends the right.

Dieu et mon droit *Fr.* (dyö′ ā môṅ drwä′), God and my right: motto in the British royal arms.

Dieu vous garde *Fr.* (dyö′ vōō gȧrd′), God protect you.

Dios y fe-de-ra-ción *Span.* (dyôs′ ē fā″dā-rä-thyôn′), God and federation: motto of Venezuela.

di-ri-go *Lat.* (dĭr′ĭ-gō), I direct (or guide): motto of the State of Maine.

dis a-li-ter vi-sum *Lat.* (dĭs ăl′ĭ-tẽr vī′sŭm), the gods have willed otherwise.

dis-jec-ta mem-bra *Lat.* (dĭs-jĕk′tȧ mĕm′-brȧ), scattered parts.

di-tat De-us *Lat.* (dī′tăt dē′ŭs), God enriches: motto of the State of Arizona.

di-vi-de et im-pe-ra *Lat.* (dĭv′ĭ-dē ĕt ĭm′pē-rȧ), divide and rule: sometimes given **di-vi-de ut reg-nes** (dĭv′ĭ-dē ŭt rĕg′nēz), divide that you may govern.

do-cen-do dis-ci-mus *Lat.* (dō-sĕn′dō dĭs′ĭ-mŭs), we learn by teaching.

dol-ce far nien-te *It.* (dōl′chā fär nyĕn′tā), lit., sweet to do nothing; it is charming to be idle.

Do-mi-ne, di-ri-ge nos *Lat.* (dŏm′ĭ-nē, dĭr′ĭ-jē nōs), Lord, direct us: motto of the city of London.

Do-mi-nus vo-bis-cum *Lat.* (dŏm′ĭ-nŭs vō-bĭs′kŭm), the Lord (be) with you.

do-mus su-a cui-que est tu-tis-si-mum re-fu-gi-um *Lat.* (dō′mŭs sū′ȧ kwī′kwē ĕst tū-tĭs′ĭ-mŭm rē-fū′jĭ-ŭm), lit., each one's own home is his safest refuge; every man's house is his castle.

dra-ma-tis per-so-næ *Lat.* (drăm′ȧ-tĭs pẽr-sō′nē), the characters or persons in a play.

Drei-bund *Ger.* (drī′bŏŏnt″), a triple alliance; specif., the alliance formed in 1882 by Germany, Austria-Hungary, and Italy.

du-cit a-mor pa-tri-æ *Lat.* (dū′sĭt ā′môr păt′rĭ-ē), love of country leads (us).

dul-ce et de-co-rum est pro pa-tri-a mo-ri *Lat.* (dŭl′sē ĕt dē-kō′rŭm ĕst prō păt′rĭ-ȧ mō′rī), it is sweet and fitting to die for one's country.

dum spi-ro, spe-ro *Lat.* (dŭm spī′rō, spē′rō), while I breathe, I hope: a motto of South Carolina.

dum vi-vi-mus, vi-va-mus *Lat.* (dŭm vĭv′ĭ-mŭs, vī-vā′mŭs), lit., while we live, let us live; let us make the most of life.

E

eau de vie *Fr.* (ō″ dē vē′), lit., water of life; brandy.

ec-ce ho-mo *Lat.* (ĕk′sē hō′mō), behold the man: words of Pilate at Christ's trial; hence, a picture or statue of Christ crowned with thorns.

ec-ce sig-num *Lat.* (ĕk′sē sĭg′nŭm), behold the sign; look at the proof.

e con-tra-ri-o *Lat.* (ē kŏn-trā′rĭ-ō), on the contrary; on the other hand.

é-di-tion de luxe *Fr.* (ā″dē″syôṅ′ dē lüks′), an expensive edition (of a book).

e-di-ti-o prin-ceps *Lat.* (ē-dĭsh′ĭ-ō prĭn′sĕps), the first edition.

é-ga-li-té *Fr.* (ā″gȧ″lē″tā′), equality.

en a-mi *Fr.* (ä″ nȧ″mē′), as a friend.

en ar-rière *Fr.* (ä″ nȧ″ryâr′), in the rear; in arrears.

en a-vant *Fr.* (ä″ nȧ″väṅ′), forward.

en con-gé *Fr.* (äṅ″ kôṅ″zhā′), on leave; on furlough.

en dés-ha-bil-lé *Fr.* (äṅ″ dā″zȧ″bē″yā′), in undress; in negligee.

en ef-fet *Fr.* (ä″ nē″fā′), in effect; in fact; indeed.

en fa-mille *Fr.* (äṅ″ fȧ″mēy′′), with one's family.

en-fant gâ-té *Fr.* (äṅ″fäṅ′ gä″tā′), a spoiled child.

en-fants per-dus *Fr.* (äṅ″fäṅ′ pâr″dü′), lit., lost children; a forlorn hope: a military expression.

en-fant ter-ri-ble *Fr.* (äṅ″fäṅ′ tâ″rēbl′′), lit., a terrible child; one who makes embarrassing remarks.

en-fin *Fr.* (äṅ″fâṅ′), at last; finally; in short.

en masse *Fr.* (äṅ″ mäs′), in a body; all together.

en pas-sant *Fr.* (äṅ″ pä″säṅ′), in passing; by the way.

en rap-port *Fr.* (äṅ″ rȧ″pôr′), in agreement; in sympathy; in harmony.

en re-gle *Fr.* (äṅ″ râgl′′), according to rule; in proper order.

en route *Fr.* (äṅ″ rōōt′), on the way.

en-se pe-tit pla-ci-dam sub li-ber-ta-te qui-e-tem *Lat.* (ĕn′sē pĕt′ĭt plăs′ĭ-dăm sŭb lĭb″ẽr-tā′tē kwī-ē′tĕm), with the sword she seeks calm repose under liberty: motto of Massachusetts.

en suite *Fr.* (äṅ″ süēt′), in a series, succession, or set; connecting or adjoining, as rooms in an apartment or hotel.

en-tente cor-diale *Fr.* (äṅ″täṅt′ kôr″dyȧl′), a cordial understanding: used esp. of relations existing between governments.

en-tou-rage *Fr.* (äṅ″tōō″rȧzh′), surroundings; hence, associates; retinue of attendants.

en-tre nous *Fr.* (äṅtr′′ nōō′), between ourselves.

e plu-ri-bus u-num *Lat.* (ē plōō′rĭ-bŭs ū′nŭm), one out of many: meaning, one government made of many states: motto of the United States of America.

er-ra-re hu-ma-num est *Lat.* (ĕ-rā′rē hū-mā′nŭm ĕst), to err is human.

es-prit de corps *Fr.* (ĕs″prē′ dē kôr′), lit., spirit of the body; a spirit cementing the members of an organization; comradeship.

es-se quam vi-de-ri *Lat.* (ĕs′ē kwăm vĭ-dē′-rī), to be rather than to seem: motto of North Carolina.

est mo-dus in re-bus *Lat.* (ĕst mō′dŭs ĭn rē′bŭs), there is a limit in (all) things.

es-to per-pe-tu-a *Lat.* (ĕs′tō pûr-pĕt′ū-ȧ), may she endure forever: motto of Idaho.

é-toile du nord *Fr.* (ā″twȧl′ dü nôr′), the star of the North: motto of Minnesota.

et tu, Bru-te *Lat.* (ĕt tū, brōō′tē), thou, too, Brutus: the cry of Julius Cæsar when he saw his friend among his (Cæsar's) assassins.

ex ab-u-su non ar-gu-i-tur in u-sum *Lat.* (ĕks ȧ-bū′sū nŏn är-gū′ĭ-tŭr ĭn ū′sŭm), the abuse of a thing is no argument against its use: a legal phrase.

ex a-ni-mo *Lat.* (ĕks ăn′ĭ-mō), from the heart; sincerely; willingly.

ex ca-the-dra *Lat.* (ĕks kȧ-thē′drȧ; kăth′ē-drȧ), lit., from the chair; with authority: used esp. of papal utterances.

ex-cep-ti-o pro-bat re-gu-lam *Lat.* (ĕk-sĕp′shĭ-ō prō′băt rĕg′ū-lăm), the exception proves the rule.

ex-em-pli gra-ti-a *Lat.* (ĕg-zĕm′plī grā′-shĭ-ȧ), for the sake of example; for instance.

ex-e-unt om-nes *Lat.* (ĕk′sē-ŭnt ŏm′nēz), all go out.

ex-i-tus ac-ta pro-bat *Lat.* (ĕk′sĭ-tŭs ăk′tȧ prō′băt), the result justifies the deeds; the end justifies the means: motto of George Washington.

ex li-bris *Lat.* (ĕks lī′brĭs), from the books (of): an inscription used with the owner's name in a book; also, a bookplate.

ex ne-ces-si-ta-te re-i *Lat.* (ĕks nē-sĕs″ĭ-tā′tē rē′ī), from the necessity of the case.

ex ni-hi-lo ni-hil fit *Lat.* (ĕks nī′hĭ-lō nī′hĭl fĭt), from nothing comes nothing.

ex of-fi-ci-o *Lat.* (ĕks ŏ-fĭsh′ĭ-ō), lit., from office; by right of office and without other special authority.

ex par-te *Lat.* (ĕks pär′tē), lit., of the one part; hence, with only one party (to a dispute) represented; biased.

ex-per-to cre-di-te *Lat.* (ĕks-pûr′tō krĕd′ĭ-tē), believe a person of experience.

ex post fac-to *Lat.* (ĕks pōst făk'tō), from what is done afterward; judging a former state of facts from a later point of view.

ex (or **ab**) **u-no dis-ce om-nes** *Lat.* (ĕks (ăb) ū'nō dĭs'ē ŏm'nēz), from one learn all.

F

fa-ci-le prin-ceps *Lat.* (făs'ĭ-lē prĭn'sĕps), easily chief; by far the best.

fa-ci-lis de-scen-sus A-ver-ni *Lat.* (făs'ĭ-lĭs dē-sĕn'sŭs ȧ-vûr'nī), the descent to Avernus is easy; the road to evil is easy to follow.

faire sui-vre *Fr.* (fâr″ süēvr''), please forward; to be forwarded: a postal instruction.

fait ac-com-pli *Fr.* (fâ″ tȧ″kôṅ″plē'), a thing already done; something accomplished.

Fa-ta ob-stant *Lat.* (fā'tȧ ŏb'stănt), the Fates oppose.

fat-ti ma-schi-i, pa-ro-le fe-mi-ne *It.* (fät'tē mä'skē-ē, pä-rō'lā fĕm'ē-nā), deeds (are) manly, words (are) womanly: a motto of Maryland.

fau-teuil *Fr.* (fō″tûy''), armchair.

faux pas *Fr.* (fō″ pä'), a false step; esp., an offense against convention.

femme de cham-bre *Fr.* (fȧm″ dē shäṅbr''), a chambermaid; lady's maid.

fe-ræ na-tu-ræ *Lat.* (fĕr'ē nȧ-tū'rē), of a wild nature: referring in law to animals living free and wild.

fer-vet o-pus *Lat.* (fûr'vĕt ō'pŭs), lit., the work boils; there is great activity.

fes-ti-na len-te *Lat.* (fĕs-tī'nȧ lĕn'tē), make haste slowly. [rural or open-air festival.

fête cham-pê-tre *Fr.* (fât' shäṅ″pâtr''), a

feu de joie *Fr.* (fö″ dē zhwȧ'), a bonfire; also, a firing of rifles in token of joy.

fi-at jus-ti-ti-a, ru-at cæ-lum *Lat.* (fī'ăt jŭs-tĭsh'ĭ-ȧ, rōō'ăt sē'lŭm), let justice be done, even though the heavens should fall.

fi-at lux *Lat.* (fī'ăt lŭks'), let there be light.

fi-de-i de-fen-sor *Lat.* (fī-dē'ī dē-fĕn'sôr), defender of the faith: a title of the sovereigns of England, first bestowed upon Henry VIII. [faith; hence, treachery.

fi-des Pu-ni-ca *Lat.* (fī'dēz pū'nĭ-kȧ), Punic

fi-dus A-cha-tes *Lat.* (fī'dŭs ȧ-kā'tēz), faithful Achates; hence, a loyal friend: in allusion to the companion of Æneas in Virgil's "Æneid."

fi-nis co-ro-nat o-pus *Lat.* (fī'nĭs kō-rō'năt ō'pŭs), the end crowns the work.

fla-gran-te bel-lo *Lat.* (flȧ-grăn'tē bĕl'ō), while war is raging; during actual warfare.

fla-gran-te de-lic-to *Lat.* (flȧ-grăn'tē dē-lĭk'tō), during the commission of the crime; in the very act.

for-tes for-tu-na ju-vat *Lat.* (fôr'tēz fôr-tū'nȧ jōō'văt), fortune favors the brave.

for-ti-ter in re, sua-vi-ter in mo-do *Lat.* (fôr'tĭ-tĕr ĭn rē', swăv'ĭ-tĕr ĭn mō'dō), mightily in deed, gently in manner.

fou qui se tait, passe pour sage *Fr.* (fōō' kē″ sē tâ', päs' pōōr sȧzh'), the fool who keeps silent passes for a wise man.

four-ra-gère *Fr.* (fōō″rȧ″zhâr'), a decoration granted for bravery to an entire body of troops, consisting of a braided cord, to be worn individually on the left shoulder of the coat. [privileged.

fran-co *It.* (frän'kō), free; hence, franked;

frap-pé *Fr.* (frȧ″pā'), beaten; as a noun, a mixture, generally frozen and flavored, as a water ice.

fu-git ho-ra *Lat.* (fū'jĭt hō'rȧ), the hour flies; time flies. Cf. **tempus fugit.**

fu-it I-li-um *Lat.* (fū'ĭt ĭl'ĭ-ŭm), Troy has been: that is, Troy is no more.

func-tus of-fi-ci-o *Lat.* (fŭngk'tŭs ŏ-fĭsh'ĭ-ō), having fulfilled his office; out of office.

fu-ror po-e-ti-cus *Lat.* (fū'rôr pō-ĕt'ĭ-kŭs), poetic frenzy. [a mania for writing.

fu-ror scri-ben-di *Lat.* (fū'rôr skrī-bĕn'dī),

G

Gal-li-ce *Lat.* (găl'ĭ-sē), in French; in the French way. [guard.

garde du corps *Fr.* (gȧrd″ dü kôr'), a body-

gauche *Fr.* (gōsh), left-handed; hence, clumsy. [the place.

ge-ni-us lo-ci *Lat.* (jē'nĭ-ŭs lō'sī), spirit of

gen-re *Fr.* (zhäṅr'), a kind, sort, or class of anything; specif., a style of painting or sculpture representing everyday life in a realistic way.

Ger-ma-ni-ce *Lat.* (jûr-măn'ĭ-sē), in German; after the German manner.

gno-thi se-au-ton *Gk.* (gnō'thĭ sē-ou-tŏn'), know thyself: inscription on the temple of Apollo at Delphi.

Gott mit uns *Ger.* (gôt mĭt ōōns), God with us: motto of the Order of the Crown, Prussia. [to God.

grâce à Dieu *Fr.* (gräs' ȧ dyö'), thanks (be)

grande pas-sion *Fr.* (gräṅd″ pä″syôṅ'), great passion; great love.

grand monde *Fr.* (gräṅ″ môṅd'), lit., the great world; high society.

guerre à ou-trance *Fr.* (gâr' ȧ ōō″träṅs'), war to the uttermost; implacable war.

H

han-gar *Fr.* (häng'gär″; äṅ″gȧr'), a building or shed for aircraft. [seasoning.

haut goût *Fr.* (ō″ gōō'), high flavor: used of

hic et u-bi-que *Lat.* (hĭk ĕt ū-bī'kwē), here and everywhere. [epitaphs.

hic ja-cet *Lat.* (hĭk jā'sĕt), here lies: used in

hinc il-læ la-cri-mæ *Lat.* (hĭngk ĭl'ē lăk'rĭ-mē), hence those tears.

hoc o-pus, hic la-bor est *Lat.* (hŏk ō'pŭs, hĭk lā'bôr ĕst), this (is) the work, this is the labor; here lies the great difficulty.

hoc tem-po-re *Lat.* (hŏk tĕm'pō-rē), at this time. [populace; the masses.

hoi pol-loi *Gk.* (hoi″ pô-loi'), the many; the

ho-mi-nem quæ-ro *Lat.* (hŏm'ĭ-nĕm kwē'rō), I am looking for a man.

ho-mi-nis est er-ra-re *Lat.* (hŏm'ĭ-nĭs ĕst ĕ-rā'rē), to err is human.

homme d'af-faires *Fr.* (ôm″ dȧ'fâr'), a business man; an agent. [of wit.

homme d'es-prit *Fr.* (ôm″ dĕs″prē'), a man

ho-ni soit qui mal y pense *Fr.* (ō″nē″ swȧ' kē mȧl″ ē päṅs'), lit., shamed be he who thinks evil of it; usually translated, evil be (it) to him who evil thinks: the motto of the Order of the Garter.

hon-neur et pa-trie *Fr.* (ō″nûr' ā pȧ″trē'), honor and country: motto of the French Legion of Honor.

ho-ra fu-git *Lat.* (hō'rȧ fū'jĭt), the hour flies; time flies. Cf. **tempus fugit.**

hor-ri-bi-le dic-tu *Lat.* (hŏ-rĭb'ĭ-lē dĭk'tū), horrible to relate. [the combat; disabled.

hors de com-bat *Fr.* (ôr″ dē kôṅ″bȧ'), out of

hors d'œu-vre *Fr.* (ôr″ dûvr''), a relish.

hô-tel de ville *Fr.* (ō″tĕl' dē vēl'), a town hall.

hu-ma-num est er-ra-re *Lat.* (hū-mā'nŭm ĕst ĕ-rā'rē), to err is human.

I

i-bi-dem *Lat.* (ĭ-bī'dĕm), in the same place.

ich dien *Ger.* (ĭkh″ dēn'), I serve: motto of the Prince of Wales.

i-ci on parle fran-çais *Fr.* (ē″sē' ôṅ pȧrl' fräṅ″sā'), French is spoken here.

id est *Lat.* (ĭd ĕst), that is. [sive (man).

il pen-se-ro-so *It.* (ēl pĕn″sĕ-rō'sō), the pen-

ils ne pas-se-ront pas *Fr.* (ēl nē pä″sē-rôṅ' pä'), they shall not pass: a motto of the French in the World War.

im-me-di-ca-bi-le vul-nus *Lat.* (ĭ-mĕd'ĭ-kăb'ĭ-lē vŭl'nŭs), an incurable wound.

im-pe-ri-um in im-pe-ri-o *Lat.* (ĭm-pē'rĭ-ŭm ĭn ĭm-pē'rĭ-ō), lit., an empire in an empire; a government within a government.

im-pri-ma-tur *Lat.* (ĭm″prĭ-mā′tŭr), let (it) be printed.

im-pri-mis *Lat.* (ĭm-prī′mĭs), in the first place; especially; particularly. [always.

in æ-ter-num *Lat.* (ĭn ē-tûr′nŭm), forever;

in ar-ti-cu-lo mor-tis *Lat.* (ĭn är-tĭk′ū-lō môr′tĭs), at the point of death.

in es-se *Lat.* (ĭn ĕs′ē), in existence; in actuality: opp. of *in posse.* [length; in full.

in ex-ten-so *Lat.* (ĭn ĕks-tĕn′sō), at full

in ex-tre-mis *Lat.* (ĭn ĕks-trē′mĭs), at the point of death; in the last extremity.

in-fra dig-ni-ta-tem *Lat.* (ĭn′frȧ dĭg″nĭ-tā′tĕm), beneath one's dignity; undignified: often abbreviated to *infra dig.*

in hoc sig-no vin-ces *Lat.* (ĭn hŏk sĭg′nō vĭn′sēz), in (or by) this sign thou wilt conquer: motto of Constantine the Great, referring to the fiery cross which he claimed to have seen in the sky.

in li-mi-ne *Lat.* (ĭn lĭm′ĭ-nē), on the threshold; at the beginning. [place.

in lo-co *Lat.* (ĭn lō′kō), in place; in the proper

in lo-co pa-ren-tis *Lat.* (ĭn lō′kō pȧ-rĕn′tĭs), in the place of a parent.

in me-di-as res *Lat.* (ĭn mē′dĭ-ăs rēz), into the midst of things; into full activity.

in me-mo-ri-am *Lat.* (ĭn mē̆-mō′rĭ-ăm), in memory (of): used upon memorials to the dead. [rā′tŭs), ready for all things.

in om-ni-a pa-ra-tus *Lat.* (ĭn ŏm′nĭ-ȧ pȧ-

in per-pe-tu-um *Lat.* (ĭn pûr-pĕt′ū-ŭm), forever; always; in perpetuity.

in pos-se *Lat.* (ĭn pŏs′ē), in possibility; potentially: opp. of *in esse.*

in pro-pri-a per-so-na *Lat.* (ĭn prō′prĭ-ȧ pûr-sō′nȧ), in one's own person; personally.

in pu-ris na-tu-ra-li-bus *Lat.* (ĭn pū′rĭs năt″ū-răl′ĭ-bŭs), in a purely natural state; entirely naked. [to; concerning.

in re *Lat.* (ĭn rē), in the matter of; in regard

in sæ-cu-la sæ-cu-lo-rum *Lat.* (ĭn sĕk′ū-lȧ sĕk″ū-lō′rŭm), for ages of ages; for ever and ever; eternally. [engraved (it).

in-sculp-sit *Lat.* (ĭn-skŭlp′sĭt), (he or she)

in si-tu *Lat.* (ĭn sī′tū), in place; in its original position. [state in which (it is or was).

in sta-tu quo *Lat.* (ĭn stā′tū kwō), in the

in-ter a-li-a *Lat.* (ĭn′tẽr ā′lĭ-ȧ), among other things. [other persons.

in-ter a-li-os *Lat.* (ĭn′tẽr ā′lĭ-ōs), among

in-ter nos *Lat.* (ĭn′tẽr nōs), between us; between (or among) ourselves; mutually.

in ter-ro-rem *Lat.* (ĭn tĕ-rō′rĕm), as a warning. Also, **ad** (ăd) **ter-ro-rem.**

in-ter se *Lat.* (ĭn′tẽr sē), among (or between) themselves; mutually. [entirety, in general.

in to-to *Lat.* (ĭn tō′tō), in the whole; in (its)

in u-trum-que pa-ra-tus *Lat.* (ĭn ū-trŭm′kwē pȧ-rā′tŭs), prepared for either (event or outcome); ready for either (alternative).

in va-cu-o *Lat.* (ĭn văk′ū-ō), in a vacuum.

ip-se dix-it *Lat.* (ĭp′sē dĭk′sĭt), lit., he himself said it; a statement, apparently weighty, but unsupported; a dictum.

ip-so fac-to *Lat.* (ĭp′sō făk′tō), by the act (or fact) itself; (obvious) from the very facts of the case. [itself; legally.

ip-so ju-re *Lat.* (ĭp′sō jo͞o′rē), by the law

I-ta-lia ir-re-den-ta *It.* (ē-tä′lyä ĕr″rā-dĕn′tä), unredeemed Italy; regions adjacent to Italy, with a population partly Italian.

J

jac-ta est a-le-a *Lat.* (jăk′tȧ ĕst ā′lē-ȧ), the die is cast. Also, **jac-ta a-le-a est.**

je main-tien-drai *Fr.* (zhē mâṅ″tyâṅ″drā′), I will maintain: motto of The Netherlands.

je ne sais quoi *Fr.* (zhē nē sā″ kwȧ′), lit., I know not what; something inexpressible.

jeu de mots *Fr.* (zhö″ dē mō′), a play on words; a pun. [of mind; something witty.

jeu d'es-prit *Fr.* (zhö″ dĕs″prē′), lit., a play

jeu-nesse do-rée *Fr.* (zhû″nĕs′ dô″rā′), lit., gilded youth; rich and gay young people.

Jo-an-nes est no-men e-jus *Lat.* (jō-ăn′ēz ĕst nō′mĕn ē′jŭs), his name is John: motto of Porto Rico. [joice in the Lord.

ju-bi-la-te De-o *Lat.* (jo͞o″bĭ-lā′tē dē′ō), re-

Ju-pi-ter To-nans *Lat.* (jo͞o′pĭ-tẽr tō′nănz), Jupiter, the Thunderer.

jus ci-vi-le *Lat.* (jŭs sĭv′ĭ-lē), civil law. [law.

jus di-vi-num *Lat.* (jŭs dĭ-vī′nŭm), divine

jus gen-ti-um *Lat.* (jŭs jĕn′shĭ-ŭm), formerly, the (Roman) law for aliens; now, international law.

juste mi-lieu *Fr.* (zhüst″ mē″lyö′), the golden mean: used of a course pursued by an impartial and equable government.

jus-ti-ti-a om-ni-bus *Lat.* (jŭs-tĭsh′ĭ-ȧ ŏm′nĭ-bŭs), justice to all: motto of the District of Columbia.

K

ka-kou ko-ra-kos ka-kon o-on *Gk.* (kä-ko͞o′ kôr′ȧ-kōs kä-kôn′ ō-ōn′), from a bad crow a bad egg; like produces like.

ka-los k'a-ga-thos *Gk.* (kä-lōs′ kä-gä-thōs′), a beautiful and good (man); gentleman.

Kul-tur *Ger.* (ko͞ol-to͞or′), civilization.

L

la-bo-ra-re est o-ra-re *Lat.* (lā″bō-rā′rē ĕst ō-rā′rē), to work is to pray; work is prayer.

la-bor ip-se vo-lup-tas *Lat.* (lā′bôr ĭp′sē vō-lŭp′tăs), work itself (is) a pleasure.

la-bor om-ni-a vin-cit *Lat.* (lā′bôr ŏm′nĭ-ȧ vĭn′sĭt), work conquers all things: motto of Oklahoma.

lais-sez faire *Fr.* (lâ″sā″ fâr′), lit., let (people) do (what they choose); hence, as a noun, noninterference, as of a government in matters of trade or industry. [(person).

l'al-le-gro *It.* (läl-lā′grō), the cheerful

Land-sturm *Ger.* (länt′sto͝orm″; -shto͝orm″), a levy, or mustering, in time of war, of all men fit for military duty and not already under arms, or the forces called under such a levy: for use only in case of a great emergency.

Land-tag *Ger.* (länt′täkh″), the lawmaking body of a German state, esp. of Prussia.

lap-sus ca-la-mi *Lat.* (lăp′sŭs kăl′ȧ-mī), a slip of the pen. [of the tongue.

lap-sus lin-guæ *Lat.* (lăp′sŭs lĭng′gwē), a slip

lap-sus me-mo-ri-æ *Lat.* (lăp′sŭs mē-mō′rĭ-ē), a slip of the memory.

la-res et pe-na-tes *Lat.* (lā′rēz ĕt pē-nā′tēz), in Roman times, household gods, comprising the *lares*, or spirits of ancestors, and *penates*, or spirits of the storeroom: now used of one's treasured possessions.

lau-da-tor tem-po-ris ac-ti *Lat.* (lô-dā′tôr tĕm′pō-rĭs ăk′tī), a praiser of the past.

laus De-o *Lat.* (lôs′ dē′ō), praise (be) to God.

leb' wohl *Ger.* (lāp″ vōl′), farewell; good-by.

le grand Mo-narque *Fr.* (lē grāṅ″ mō″nărk′), the Great Monarch (Louis XIV).

le pas *Fr.* (lē pä′), lit., the step; precedence.

le roi le veut *Fr.* (lē rwä′ lē vö′), the king wills it.

l'é-tat, c'est moi *Fr.* (lā″tȧ′, sâ mwȧ′), it is I who am the state: a saying attributed to Louis XIV.

l'é-toile du nord *Fr.* (lā″twȧl′ dü nôr′), the star of the north: motto of Minnesota.

le tout en-sem-ble *Fr.* (lē to͞o″ täṅ″säṅbl′), the whole (taken) together.

let-tre de ca-chet *Fr.* (lĕtr′ dē kȧ″shā′), a sealed letter, esp. an order issued by a sovereign.

lex lo-ci *Lat.* (lĕks lō′sī), the law of the place.

lex non scrip-ta *Lat.* (lĕks nŏn skrĭp′tȧ), unwritten law; common law. [statute, law.

lex scrip-ta *Lat.* (lĕks skrĭp′tȧ), written, or

l'homme pro-pose et Dieu dis-pose *Fr.*

(lôm′ prō″pōz′ ā dyö′ dĕs″pōz′), man proposes and God disposes.

li-ber-tad y or-den *Span.* (lē-bâr-täth′ ē ôr′-dān), liberty and order: motto of Colombia.

li-cen-ti-a va-tum *Lat.* (lī-sĕn′shĭ-ȧ vā′-tŭm), lit., freedom of seers; poetic license.

li-te-ra-ti *Lat.* (lĭt″ĕr-ā′tī), men of letters; scholars.

li-te-ra-tim *Late Lat.* (lĭt″ĕr-ā′tĭm), literally.

lit-te-ra scrip-ta ma-net *Lat.* (lĭt′ĕr-ȧ skrĭp′tȧ mā′nĕt), the written letter remains; it is in black and white.

lo-co ci-ta-to *Lat.* (lō′kō sī-tā′tō), in the place quoted; in the cited passage.

lo-cum te-nens *Lat.* (lō′kŭm tē′nĕnz), a substitute; esp., an acting pastor of a church.

lo-cus si-gil-li *Lat.* (lō′kŭs sĭ-jĭl′ī), the place of the seal.

lon-go in-ter-val-lo *Lat.* (lông′gō ĭn-tĕr-văl′ō), with, by, or after, a long interval: used either of time or space.

lu-cus a non lu-cen-do *Lat.* (lū′kŭs ā nŏn lū-sĕn′dō), lit., (called) a grove from its not being bright: as if *lucus*, a grove, had been derived from *lucēre*, to shine, because a grove does not shine; hence, an absurd sequence; illogical conclusion.

l'u-nion fait la force *Fr.* (lü″nyôṅ′ fâ″ lȧ fôrs′), union makes strength: motto of Belgium.

lu-sus na-tu-ræ *Lat.* (lū′sŭs nȧ-tū′rē), a sport of nature; freak of nature.

M

ma chère *Fr.* (mȧ″ shâr′), my dear (fem.).

mac-te (or **mac-te es-to**) **vir-tu-te** *Lat.* (măk′tē ĕs′tō vûr-tū′tē), lit., be of increased courage; keep up your courage; good luck to you.

ma foi *Fr.* (mȧ″ fwä′), lit., my faith: good gracious; my word: an interjection.

mag-na est ve-ri-tas, et præ-va-le-bit *Lat.* (măg′nȧ ĕst vĕr′ĭ-tăs ĕt prēv″ȧ-lē′bĭt), great is truth and it will prevail.

mag-num o-pus *Lat.* (măg′nŭm ō′pŭs), a great work.

ma-la fi-de *Lat.* (mā′lȧ fī′dē), in bad faith: opp. of *bona fide.*

mal de mer *Fr.* (mȧl″ dē mâr′), seasickness.

ma-ña-na *Span.* (mä-nyä′nä), tomorrow.

ma-re clau-sum *Lat.* (mā′rē klô′sŭm), a closed sea; a sea within the separate rule of one state.

ma-ri-age de con-ve-nance *Fr.* (mȧ″ryȧzh′ dē kôṅ″vē-näṅs′), a marriage of convenience.

mau-vais goût *Fr.* (mō″vâ′ gōō′), bad taste.

mehr licht *Ger.* (mār lĭkht), more light.

me ju-di-ce *Lat.* (mē jōō′dĭ-sē), I being judge; in my judgment.

me-men-to mo-ri *Lat.* (mē-mĕn′tō mō′rī), lit., remember to die; hence, a reminder of death.

mens sa-na in cor-po-re sa-no *Lat.* (mĕnz sā′nȧ ĭn kôr′pō-rē sā′nō), a sound mind in a sound body.

me-um et tu-um *Lat.* (mē′ŭm ĕt tū′ŭm), mine and thine.

mi-ra-bi-le dic-tu *Lat.* (mĭ-rā′bĭ-lē dĭk′tū), wonderful to relate.

mi-ra-bi-le vi-su *Lat.* (mĭ-rā′bĭ-lē vī′sū), wonderful to see.

mi-ra-bi-li-a *Lat.* (mĭr″ȧ-bĭl′ĭ-ȧ), miracles.

mise en scène *Fr.* (mē″ zäṅ″ sân′), lit., a setting up theatrically; stage setting.

mo-dus o-pe-ran-di *Lat.* (mō′dŭs ŏp″ē-răn′-dī), method of operating; manner of working.

mon a-mi (masc.); **mon a-mie** (fem.) *Fr.* (mô″ nȧ″mē′), my friend.

mon cher *Fr.* (môṅ″ shâr′), my dear (masc.).

monde *Fr.* (môṅd), world; the world of fashion and leisure; also, the sphere of life in which one moves.

mon-ta-ni sem-per li-be-ri *Lat.* (mŏn-tā′nī sĕm′pĕr lĭ′bĕr-ī), mountaineers (are) always free men: motto of West Virginia.

mo-ri-tu-ri te sa-lu-ta-mus *Lat.* (môr″ĭ-tū′rī tē săl″ū-tā′mŭs), we who are about to die salute thee: the salutation of Roman gladiators made to the emperor as they entered the arena.

moy-en âge *Fr.* (mwȧ″yȁ″ näzh′), the Middle Ages.

mul-tum in par-vo *Lat.* (mŭl′tŭm ĭn pär′-vō), much in little.

mu-ta-tis mu-tan-dis *Lat.* (mū-tā′tĭs mū-tăn′dĭs), the necessary changes having been made.

N

na-tu-ra ab-hor-ret a va-cu-o *Lat.* (nȧ-tū′rȧ ăb-hôr′ĕt ā văk′ū-ō), nature abhors a vacuum.

ne-mo de-bet ju-dex in pro-pri-a su-a cau-sa *Lat.* (nē′mō dē′bĕt jōō′dĕks ĭn prō′prĭ-ȧ sū′ȧ kô′zȧ), no man can be judge in his own case: a legal phrase.

ne-mo me im-pu-ne la-ces-sit *Lat.* (nē′mō mē ĭm-pū′nē lȧ-sĕs′ĭt), no one attacks me with impunity: motto of Scotland.

ne plus ul-tra *Lat.* (nē plŭs ŭl′trȧ), no more beyond; as a noun, the summit of achievement; the highest degree; as a command, no further.

ne quid ni-mis *Lat.* (nē kwĭd nĭm′ĭs), not anything too much; avoid excess.

n'est-ce pas? *Fr.* (nĕs″ pä′), lit., is it not? used after any statement to mean, is it not true?

nicht wahr? *Ger.* (nĭkht″ vär′), lit., not true? used after any statement to mean, isn't that so?

ni-hil ob-stat *Lat.* (nī′hĭl ŏb′stăt), nothing stands in the way.

nil ad-mi-ra-ri *Lat.* (nĭl ăd″mĭ-rā′rī), to wonder at nothing; be surprised, or astonished, at nothing.

nil si-ne nu-mi-ne *Lat.* (nĭl sī′nē nū′mĭ-nē), nothing without the divine will: motto of Colorado.

n'im-porte *Fr.* (nâṅ″pôrt′), no matter; it matters not.

no-blesse o-blige *Fr.* (nō″blĕs′ ō″blēzh′), rank imposes obligation; nobleness of conduct is expected from those who are well-born.

no-lens vo-lens *Lat.* (nō′lĕnz vō′lĕnz), unwilling (or) willing; willy-nilly.

no-li me tan-ge-re *Lat.* (nō′lī mē tăn′jē-rē), touch me not; hence, a person or thing not to be touched.

nol-le pros-e-qui *Lat.* (nŏl′ē prŏs′ē-kwī), to be unwilling to prosecute; hence, notice that a suit at law will be dropped.

nom de guerre *Fr.* (nôṅ″ dē gâr′), lit., a war name; a pen name; pseudonym.

nom de plume *Fr.* (nôṅ″ dē plüm′), a pen name; an author's assumed name.

non com-pos men-tis *Lat.* (nŏn kŏm′pŏs mĕn′tĭs), not of sound mind.

non est vi-ve-re sed va-le-re, vi-ta *Lat.* (nŏn ĕst vĭv′ē-rē sĕd vȧ-lē′rē, vī′tȧ), it is not life just to live, but to be healthy.

non om-ni-a pos-su-mus om-nes *Lat.* (nŏn ŏm′nĭ-ȧ pŏs′ū-mŭs ŏm′nēz), all of us cannot do everything.

non om-nis mo-ri-ar *Lat.* (nŏn ŏm′nĭs mō′rĭ-är), I shall not wholly die.

non pas-si-bus æ-quis *Lat.* (nŏn păs′ĭ-bŭs ē′kwĭs), not with equal steps; out of step.

non pos-su-mus *Lat.* (nŏn pŏs′ū-mŭs), we cannot (do it).

non sans droict *Old Fr.* (nôṅ″ säṅ″ drwät′), not without right: motto of Shakespeare.

nos-ce te ip-sum *Lat.* (nŏs′ē tē ĭp′sŭm), know thyself.

no-ta be-ne *Lat.* (nō′tȧ bē′nē), note well; take notice.

No-tre Dame *Fr.* (nôtr″ dȧm′), Our Lady: a title of the Virgin Mary in the Roman Catholic Church.

nous ver-rons (or **nous ver-rons ce que nous ver-rons**) *Fr.* (nōō″ vâ″rôṅ′ sē kē nōō″ vâ″rôṅ′), we shall see (or, we shall see what we shall see); time will tell.

nou-veau riche *Fr.* (nōō″vō′ rēsh′), newly rich. [kwăm), now or never.
nunc aut nun-quam *Lat.* (nŭngk ôt nŭn′-
nunc di-mit-tis *Lat.* (nŭngk dĭ-mĭt′ĭs), lit., now lettest thou go; permission to depart.

O

ob-i-it *Lat.* (ŏb′ē-ĭt), (he or she) died.
ob-i-ter dic-tum *Lat.* (ŏb′ĭ-tẽr dĭk′tŭm), lit., (something) said by the way; a passing remark; in law, an incidental decision not considered binding. [artistic merit.
ob-jet d'art *Fr.* (ôb″zhȧ″ dȧr′), a work of
o-di-um the-o-lo-gi-cum *Lat.* (ō′dĭ-ŭm thē″ō-lŏj′ĭ-kŭm), the hatred of (opposing) theologians.
oh-ne Hast, a-ber oh-ne Rast *Ger.* (ō′nē häst, ä′bẽr ō′nē räst), without haste, but without rest.
om-ne bo-num de-su-per *Lat.* (ŏm′nē bō′nŭm dē′sū-pẽr), all good (is) from above.
om-ni-a mu-tan-tur et nos mu-ta-mur *Lat.* (ŏm′nĭ-ȧ mū-tăn′tŭr ĕt nōs mū-tā′-mŭr), all things change and we change (with them).
om-ni-a vin-cit a-mor *Lat.* (ŏm′nĭ-ȧ vĭn′sĭt ā′môr), love conquers all things.
om-nis in-no-va-ti-o plus no-vi-ta-te per-tur-bat quam u-ti-li-ta-te pro-dest *Lat.* (ŏm′nĭs ĭn″ō-vā′shĭ-ō plŭs nŏv″ĭ-tā′tē pûr-tûr′băt kwăm ū-tĭl″ĭ-tā′tē prō′dĕst), every innovation disturbs more by its novelty than it benefits by its usefulness.
on dit *Fr.* (ôṅ″ dē′), they say; it is said.
o-nus pro-ban-di *Lat.* (ō′nŭs prō-băn′dī), the burden of proof. [always.
o-ra e sem-pre *It.* (ō′rä ā sĕm′prā), now and
o-ra et la-bo-ra *Lat.* (ō′rȧ ĕt lȧ-bō′rȧ), pray and work. [for us.
o-ra pro no-bis *Lat.* (ō′rȧ prō nō′bĭs), pray
o-ra-tor fit, po-e-ta nas-ci-tur *Lat.* (ō-rā′-tôr fĭt, pō-ē′tȧ năs′ĭ-tŭr), the orator is made, the poet is born.
o-re ro-tun-do *Lat.* (ō′rē rō-tŭn′dō), lit., with round mouth; with full, clear, ringing speech.
o-ro y pla-ta *Span.* (ō′rō ē plä′tä) gold and silver: motto of the State of Montana.
O tem-po-ra, O mo-res *Lat.* (ō tĕm′pō-rȧ, ō mō′rēz), O the times! O the customs!
o-ti-a dant vi-ti-a *Lat.* (ō′shĭ-ȧ dănt vĭsh′-ĭ-ȧ), leisure creates vices.
o-ti-um cum dig-ni-ta-te *Lat.* (ō′shĭ-ŭm kŭm dĭg″nĭ-tā′tē), leisure with dignity.

P

pa-ce *Lat.* (pā′sē), lit., with peace; by leave (of). [death.
pal-li-da mors *Lat.* (păl′ĭ-dȧ môrz), pale
pal-mam qui me-ru-it fe-rat *Lat.* (păl′-măm kwī mĕr′ōō-ĭt fĕr′ăt), let him bear the palm who merits it. [pardon me.
par-don-nez-moi *Fr.* (pȧr″dō″nā′=mwȧ′),
par ex-cel-lence *Fr.* (pȧr ĕk″sĕ″läṅs′), preëminently. [example.
par ex-em-ple *Fr.* (pȧr″ ĕg″zäṅpl′′), for
pa-ri pas-su *Lat.* (pā′rī păs′ū), with equal pace. [burden.
par o-ne-ri *Lat.* (pär ŏn′ẽr-ī), equal to the
par-ti-ceps cri-mi-nis *Lat.* (pär′tĭ-sĕps krĭm′ĭ-nĭs), a participator in crime; an accomplice. opinion.
par-ti pris *Fr.* (pȧr″tē″ prē′), a preconceived
pas-sim *Lat.* (păs′ĭm), everywhere; throughout (a given book or passage).
pa-ter-nos-ter *Lat.* (pā′tẽr-nŏs′tẽr), lit., our Father; the Lord's prayer; also, the 11th bead of the rosary or the entire rosary.
pa-ter Pa-tri-æ, or **pa-ter-pa-tri-æ** *Lat.* (pā′tẽr păt′rĭ-ē), father of his country: a title given to heroes ancient and modern, esp. George Washington. [land.
pa-trie *Fr.* (pȧ″trē′), one's country; native
pax vo-bis-cum *Lat.* (păks vō-bĭs′kŭm), peace be with you. [ing suit.
pen-den-te li-te *Lat.* (pĕn-dĕn′tē lī′tē), pend-
per an-num *Lat.* (pûr ăn′ŭm), by the year; per year.
per ca-pi-ta *Lat.* (pûr kăp′ĭ-tȧ), by heads; for each individual; as individuals.
per con-tra *Lat.* (pûr kŏn′trȧ), on the contrary. [daily.
per di-em *Lat.* (pûr dī′ĕm), by the day;
per men-sem *Lat.* (pûr mĕn′sĕm), by the month; monthly. [intrinsically.
per se *Lat.* (pûr sē), by itself; of itself;
per-so-na non gra-ta *Lat.* (pûr-sō′nȧ nŏn grā′tȧ), an unacceptable person; one who is obnoxious. [gradually.
peu à peu *Fr.* (pö′ ȧ pö′), little by little;
peu de chose *Fr.* (pö′ dē shōz′), a mere trifle.
pièce de ré-sis-tance *Fr.* (pyâs′ dē rā″zēs″-täṅs′), lit., piece of resistance; hence, the main dish of a meal; also, the chief article of any series or collection.
pince-nez *Fr.* (pâṅs″=nā′), eyeglasses.
pinx-it *Lat.* (pĭngk′sĭt), (he or she) painted (it): put after the painter's name.
pis al-ler *Fr.* (pē″ zȧ″lā′), a last shift or resource. [room for the ladies.
place aux dames *Fr.* (plȧs″ ō″ dȧm′), (make)
po-co a po-co *It.* (pō′kō ä pō′kō), little by little; gradually: a musical term.
po-e-ta nas-ci-tur, non fit *Lat.* (pō-ē′tȧ năs′ĭ-tŭr, nŏn fĭt), a poet is born, not made. Cf. **orator fit,** etc. [support; basis.
point d'ap-pui *Fr.* (pwâṅ″ dȧ″püē′), point of
pol-li-ce ver-so *Lat.* (pŏl′ĭ-sē vûr′sō), with thumb turned (downward); with disapproval or condemnation: Roman condemnation of a defeated gladiator.
poste res-tante *Fr.* (pôst″ rĕs″täṅt′), general delivery. [after noon.
post me-ri-di-em *Lat.* (pōst mē-rĭd′ĭ-ĕm),
pour faire rire *Fr.* (pōōr fâr″ rēr′), to create laughter. [pay a visit.
pour faire vi-site *Fr.* (pōōr fâr″ vē″zēt′), to
pour le mé-rite *Fr.* (pōōr lē mā″rēt′), for merit. [täṅ′), to pass away the time.
pour pas-ser le temps *Fr.* (pōōr pä″sā′ lē
pren-dre con-gé *Fr.* (präṅdr′′ kôṅ″zhā′), to take leave from military service.
pri-ma fa-ci-e *Lat.* (prī′mȧ fā′shĭ-ē), at first sight; as far as at first appears.
pri-ma (or **pri-mus**) **in-ter pa-res** *Lat.* (prī′mȧ (prī′mŭs) ĭn′tẽr pā′rēz), first among her (or his) peers.
pro a-ris et fo-cis *Lat.* (prō ā′rĭs ĕt fō′sĭs), for altars and firesides.
pro bo-no pub-li-co *Lat.* (prō bō′nō pŭb′-lĭ-kō), for the public good; for the general welfare.
pro De-o et Ec-cle-si-a *Lat.* (prō dē′ō ĕt ĕ-klē′zhĭ-ȧ), for God and the Church.
pro-fa-num vul-gus *Lat.* (prō-fā′nŭm vŭl′-gŭs), the unhallowed multitude; the rabble.
pro for-ma *Lat.* (prō fôr′mȧ), for the sake of form; as a matter of formal record.
pro me-mo-ri-a *Lat.* (prō mē-mō′rĭ-ȧ), as a memorial. [country.
pro pa-tri-a *Lat.* (prō păt′rĭ-ȧ), for one's
pro ra-ta *Lat.* (prō rā′tȧ), in proportion; according to the interest or share of each.
pro sa-lu-te a-ni-mæ *Lat.* (prō sȧ-lū′tē ăn′ĭ-mē), for the health of the soul.
pro tan-to *Lat.* (prō tăn′tō), for so much; as far as it goes. [rarily.
pro tem-po-re *Lat.* (prō tĕm′pō-rē), tempo-
punc-ta-tim *Lat.* (pŭngk-tā′tĭm), point for point.

Q

quand même *Fr.* (käṅ″ mâm′), even if; whether or not.
quan-tum li-bet *Lat.* (kwăn′tŭm lĭb′ĕt), as much as you please; what you like.

quan-tum suf-fi-cit *Lat.* (kwän'tŭm sŭf'ĭ-sĭt), as much as is sufficient: enough for the time.
quan-tum vis *Lat.* (kwän'tŭm vĭs), as much as you will; what you choose.
quel-que chose *Fr.* (kĕl″kē shōz'), something.
qui do-cet, dis-cit *Lat.* (kwī dō'sĕt, dĭs'ĭt), he who teaches, learns.
quid pro quo *Lat.* (kwĭd prō kwō), lit., something for something; an equivalent; a substitute.
quién sa-be? *Span.* (kyĕn' sä'bā), who knows?
qui s'ex-cuse, s'ac-cuse *Fr.* (kē″ sĕks″küz', sȧ″küz'), he who excuses himself, accuses himself.
qui trans-tu-lit sus-ti-net *Lat.* (kwī trăns'tŭ-lĭt sŭs'tĭ-nĕt), he who transplanted, (still) sustains: motto of Connecticut.
qui va là? *Fr.* (kē″ vȧ″ lȧ'), who goes there?
quo-ad hoc *Lat.* (kwō'ăd hŏk), as to this; to this extent.
quod e-rat de-mon-stran-dum *Lat.* (kwŏd ĕr'ăt dĕm'ŏn-străn'dŭm), which was to be demonstrated; as was to be proved.
quod vi-de *Lat.* (kwŏd vī'dē), which see.
quo ju-re *Lat.* (kwō jo͞o'rē), by what right.
quot ho-mi-nes, tot sen-ten-ti-æ *Lat.* (kwŏt hŏm'ĭ-nēz, tŏt sĕn-tĕn'shĭ-ē), as many opinions as men; many men, many minds.

R

rai-son d'être *Fr.* (râ″zôṅ' dâtr''), reason for existence.
ra-ra a-vis *Lat.* (râ'rȧ ā'vĭs), a rare bird; an unusual person or thing.
re-duc-ti-o ad ab-sur-dum *Lat.* (rē-dŭk'shĭ-ō ăd ăb-sûr'dŭm), a reducing to the absurd: a method of proving a proposition by showing the absurdity of all of its alternatives, or of disproving it by showing the absurdity of its implications.
reg-nat po-pu-lus *Lat.* (rĕg'năt pŏp'ū-lŭs), the people rule: motto of Arkansas.
ré-pon-dez s'il vous plaît *Fr.* (rā″pôṅ″dā' sēl″ vo͞o″ plâ'), please reply.
re-qui-es-cat in pa-ce *Lat.* (rĕk″wĭ-ĕs'kăt ĭn pā'sē), may he (or she) rest in peace.
res an-gus-ta do-mi *Lat.* (rēz ăn-gŭs'tȧ dō'mī), straitened circumstances at home.
re-spi-ce fi-nem *Lat.* (rĕs'pĭ-sē fī'nĕm), look to the end; consider the consequences; look before you leap.
re-sur-gam *Lat.* (rē-sûr'găm), I shall rise again.
re-ve-nons (or **re-tour-nons**) **à nos mou-tons** *Fr.* (rē-vē-nôṅ' (rē-to͞or″nôṅ') zȧ″ nō″ mo͞o″tôṅ'), let us return to our sheep; let us return to our subject.
robe de cham-bre *Fr.* (rôb' dē shäṅbr''), a dressing gown.
ruse de guerre *Fr.* (rüz″ dē gâr'), a stratagem of war.
rus in ur-be *Lat.* (rŭs ĭn ûr'bē), country in city.

S

salle à man-ger *Fr.* (sȧl″ ȧ mäṅ″zhā'), dining room.
sa-lus po-pu-li su-pre-ma lex es-to *Lat.* (sā'lŭs pŏp'ū-lī sū-prē'mȧ lĕks ĕs'tō), let the welfare of the people be the supreme law: motto of Missouri.
sanc-tum sanc-to-rum *Lat.* (săngk-tŭm săngk-tō'rŭm), lit., holy of holies; hence, a most holy place; a place of the utmost privacy.
sans gêne *Fr.* (säṅ″ zhân'), without constraint; unembarrassed; at ease.
sans peur et sans re-proche *Fr.* (säṅ″ pûr' ā säṅ″ rē-prôsh'), without fear and without reproach.
sans rime et sans rai-son *Fr.* (säṅ″ rēm' ā säṅ″ râ″zôṅ'), without rime or reason; unwarranted.
sans sou-ci *Fr.* (säṅ″ so͞o″sē'), without care; gay; happy.
sar-tor re-sar-tus *Lat.* (sär'tôr rē-sär'tŭs), the tailor retailored.
sa-tis ver-bo-rum *Lat.* (sā'tĭs vûr-bō'rŭm), enough of words.
sauve qui peut *Fr.* (sōv' kē″ pö'), save (himself) who can: a cry of rout in battle: **sauve-qui-peut,** a complete rout.
sa-voir-faire *Fr.* (sȧ″vwȧr″-fâr'), the knowing how to do or act; tact; address.
sa-voir-vi-vre *Fr.* (sȧ″vwȧr″-vēvr''), the knowing how to live; good breeding.
scrip-sit *Lat.* (skrĭp'sĭt), (he or she) wrote (it).
sculp-sit *Lat.* (skŭlp'sĭt), (he or she) carved or engraved (it): put after the artist's name.
scu-to bo-næ vo-lun-ta-tis tu-æ co-ro-nas-ti nos *Lat.* (skū'tō bō'nē vŏl″ŭn-tā'tĭs tū'ē kŏr″ō-năs'tī nōs), with the shield of thy good will thou hast encompassed us: a motto of Maryland.
sem-per e-a-dem *Lat.* (sĕm'pĕr ē-ā'dĕm), always the same (fem.): motto of Queen Elizabeth.
sem-per fi-de-lis *Lat.* (sĕm'pĕr fī-dē'lĭs), ever faithful: motto of the United States Marine Corps.
sem-per i-dem *Lat.* (sĕm'pĕr ī'dĕm), always the same (masc. and neut.).
se-ñor *Span.* (sā-nyôr'), a lord or gentleman: also used as a title equivalent to Mr.
se-ño-ra *Span.* (sā-nyō'rä), a lady: also used as a title equivalent to Mrs. or Madam.
se-ño-ri-ta *Span.* (sā″nyō-rē'tä), a young lady: also used as a title equivalent to Miss.
sic pas-sim *Lat.* (sĭk păs'ĭm), so everywhere.
sic sem-per ty-ran-nis *Lat.* (sĭk sĕm'pĕr tĭ-răn'ĭs), ever thus to tyrants: motto of Virginia.
sic trans-it glo-ri-a mun-di *Lat.* (sĭk trăn'sĭt glō'rĭ-ȧ mŭn'dī), so passes away the glory of the world.
sic-ut pa-tri-bus, sit De-us no-bis *Lat.* (sĭk'ŭt păt'rĭ-bŭs, sĭt dē'ŭs nō'bĭs), as with our fathers, may God be with us: motto of Boston.
si-gnor *It.* (sē-nyôr'), a lord or gentleman: also used as a title equivalent to Mr.
si-gno-ra *It.* (sē-nyō'rä), a lady: also used as a title equivalent to Mrs. or Madam.
si-gno-ri-na *It.* (sē″nyō-rē'nä), a young lady: also used as a title equivalent to Miss.
s'il vous plaît *Fr.* (sēl″ vo͞o″ plâ'), lit., if it please you; if you please.
si-mi-li-a si-mi-li-bus cu-ran-tur *Lat.* (sĭ-mĭl'ĭ-ȧ sĭ-mĭl'ĭ-bŭs kū-răn'tŭr), like is cured by like: the principle of homeopathy.
si-ne cu-ra *Lat.* (sī'nē kū'rȧ), without care.
si-ne di-e *Lat.* (sī'nē dī'ē), lit., without day; finally; without appointing a day for reassembling: used with reference to an adjournment.
si-ne qua non *Lat.* (sī'nē kwā nŏn), lit., without which not; an indispensable condition; a necessity.
si quæ-ris pe-nin-su-lam a-mœ-nam, cir-cum-spi-ce *Lat.* (sī kwē'rĭs pē-nĭn'sū-lăm ȧ-mē'năm, sûr″kŭm-spī'sē), if you seek a delightful peninsula, behold it here: motto of Michigan.
sis-te vi-a-tor *Lat.* (sĭs'tē vī-ā'tôr), stop, traveler.
si vis pa-cem, pa-ra bel-lum *Lat.* (sī vĭs pā'sĕm, pā'rȧ bĕl'ŭm), if you wish peace, prepare for war.
splen-di-de men-dax *Lat.* (splĕn'dĭ-dē mĕn'dăks), nobly untruthful.
spur-los ver-senkt *Ger.* (shpo͞or'lōs fâr-zĕngkt'), sunk without a trace; totally lost.
sta-tus (in) quo *Lat.* (stā'tŭs, or stăt'ŭs, (ĭn) kwō), the condition in which (it is).
sua-vi-ter in mo-do, for-ti-ter in re. See **fortiter in re, suaviter in modo.**
sub ju-di-ce *Lat.* (sŭb jo͞o'dĭ-sē), before the judge.
sub ro-sa *Lat.* (sŭb rō'zȧ), lit., under the rose; secretly.
sub vo-ce *Lat.* (sŭb vō'sē), under the (specified) word (as in a dictionary).
su-i ge-ne-ris *Lat.* (sū'ī jĕn'ĕr-ĭs), of its own kind; unique.

go; join; yet; sing; chin; show; thin, *th*en; hw, *why*; zh, azure; ü, Ger. für, Fr. lune; ö, Ger. schön, Fr. feu; ṅ, Fr. enfant, nom; kh, Ger. ach or ich. See pages xviii–xix.

sum-mum bo-num *Lat.* (sŭm'ŭm bō'nŭm), the supreme good; the highest good.

sur-sum cor-da *Lat.* (sûr'sŭm kôr'dȧ), lift up (your) hearts.

T

ta-ble d'hôte *Fr.* (tȧbl'' dōt'), lit., host's table: used to designate a complete meal served at a fixed price: opp. of *à la carte;* formerly, a common table for guests, as at a hotel.

ta-bu-la ra-sa *Lat.* (tăb'ū-lȧ rā'zȧ), lit., a blank tablet: applied to a mind unaffected by experience.

tæ-di-um vi-tæ *Lat.* (tē'dĭ-ŭm vī'tē), weariness of life; ennui.

tant mieux *Fr.* (täṅ'' myö'), so much the better.

tant pis *Fr.* (täṅ'' pē'), so much the worse.

Te De-um *Lat.* (tē dē'ŭm), an ancient Christian hymn of thanksgiving, beginning "Te Deum laudamus" (We praise thee, O God).

tem-po-ra mu-tan-tur, et nos mu-ta-mur in il-lis *Lat.* (tĕm'pō-rȧ mū-tăn'tŭr, ĕt nōs mū-tā'mŭr ĭn ĭl'ĭs), times change and we change with them.

tem-pus e-dax re-rum *Lat.* (tĕm'pŭs ē'dăks rē'rŭm), lit., time, greedy of things; time, devouring things.

tem-pus fu-git *Lat.* (tĕm'pŭs fū'jĭt), time flies.

ter-ræ fi-li-us *Lat.* (tĕr'ē fĭl'ĭ-ŭs), a son of the soil; a man of humble origin.

ter-ra fir-ma *Lat.* (tĕr'ȧ fûr'mȧ), solid earth; dry land, as differentiated from water.

ter-ra in-cog-ni-ta *Lat.* (tĕr'ȧ ĭn-kŏg'nĭ-tȧ), an unknown land; an unexplored region.

ter-ti-um quid *Lat.* (tûr'shĭ-ŭm kwĭd), lit., a third something; something intermediate; generally, a harmonizing medium between two diverse things.

tête-à-tête *Fr.* (tĕ''=tȧ=tât'), lit., head to head; hence, a private conversation between two persons.

tiers é-tat *Fr.* (tyâr'' zā''tȧ'), the third estate, or commonalty, as distinguished from the nobility and clergy.

ti-me-o Da-na-os et do-na fe-ren-tes *Lat.* (tĭm'ē-ō dăn'ā-ōs ĕt dō'nȧ fē-rĕn'tēz), I fear the Greeks even (when they are) bringing gifts: in allusion to the fear of Greek treachery in the bringing of the wooden horse into Troy as a gift to Neptune. (Virgil's "Æneid.")

to-ti-dem ver-bis *Lat.* (tŏ'tĭ-dĕm vûr'bĭs), in so many words.

tour de force *Fr.* (to͞or'' dē fôrs'), a feat of strength; an exhibition of skill.

tout à fait *Fr.* (to͞o'' tȧ'' fā'), quite; wholly; entirely.

tout à l'heure *Fr.* (to͞o'' tȧ'' lûr'), just now; a little while ago; also, very soon; shortly.

tout à vous *Fr.* (to͞o'' tȧ vo͞o'), lit., all for you; wholly yours; at your service.

tout com-pren-dre, c'est tout par-don-ner *Fr.* (to͞o'' kôṅ'' präṅdr'', sâ to͞o'' pȧr''dō''nā'), to understand all is to pardon all.

tout de suite *Fr.* (to͞o'' dē süēt'), immediately.

tout en-sem-ble *Fr.* (to͞o'' täṅ''säṅbl''), all together; hence, the general effect of a work, costume, etc., as a whole.

tu-um est *Lat.* (tū'ŭm ĕst), it is thine.

U

u-bi su-pra *Lat.* (ū'bī sū'prȧ), where (stated) above.

ul-ti-ma ra-ti-o re-gum *Lat.* (ŭl'tĭ-mȧ rā'shĭ-ō rē'gŭm), the final argument of kings: referring to war.

ul-ti-ma Thu-le *Lat.* (ŭl'tĭ-mȧ thū'lē), lit., most distant Thule, in ancient times the most northern land known; hence, any distant region.

u-na vo-ce *Lat.* (ū'nȧ vō'sē), lit., with one voice; unanimously.

und so wei-ter *Ger.* (o͝ont zō vī'tẽr), and so forth.

Un-ter-see-boot *Ger.* (o͝on''tẽr-zā'bōt), a submarine; U-boat.

u-ti-le dul-ci *Lat.* (ū'tĭ-lē dŭl'sī), the useful with the agreeable.

ut su-pra *Lat.* (ŭt sū'prȧ), as above.

V

va-de in pa-ce *Lat.* (vā'dē ĭn pā'sē), go in peace.

va-de me-cum *Lat.* (vā'dē mē'kŭm), lit., go with me: as a noun, a manual or handbook.

væ vic-tis *Lat.* (vē vĭk'tĭs), woe to the conquered.

va-le *Lat.* (vā'lē), farewell.

va-let de cham-bre *Fr.* (vȧ''lâ' dē shäṅbr''), a personal attendant; valet.

va-ri-æ lec-ti-o-nes *Lat.* (vā'rĭ-ē lĕk''shĭ-ō'nēz), various readings; varied readings.

va-ri-o-rum no-tæ *Lat.* (vā''rĭ-ō'rŭm nō'tē), the notes of various (commentators).

ve-ni, vi-di, vi-ci *Lat.* (vē'nī, vī'dī, vī'sī), I came, I saw, I conquered: Julius Cæsar's curt report of a victory, sent to the Roman Senate.

ver-ba-tim et li-te-ra-tim *Lat.* (vẽr-bā'tĭm ĕt lĭt''ẽr-ā'tĭm), word for word and letter for letter; without change in word or letter.

ver-bum sat sa-pi-en-ti *Lat.* (vûr'bŭm săt săp''ĭ-ĕn'tī), a word to the wise (is) sufficient.

vi-a me-di-a *Lat.* (vī'ȧ mē'dĭ-ȧ), a middle way; the golden mean.

vi-ce ver-sa *Lat.* (vī'sē vûr'sȧ), conversely.

vi-de ut su-pra *Lat.* (vī'dē ŭt sū'prȧ), see what is stated above.

vi et ar-mis *Lat.* (vī ĕt är'mĭs), by force and arms; by main force.

vin-cet a-mor pa-tri-æ *Lat.* (vĭn'sĕt ā'môr păt'rĭ-ē), love of country will prevail.

vin-cit om-ni-a ve-ri-tas *Lat.* (vĭn'sĭt ŏm'nĭ-ȧ vĕr'ĭ-tăs), truth conquers all things.

vin-cu-lum ma-tri-mo-ni-i *Lat.* (vĭng'kū-lŭm măt''rĭ-mō'nē-ī), the bond of matrimony; the marriage tie.

vir-gi-ni-bus pu-e-ris-que *Lat.* (vûr-jĭn'ĭ-bŭs pū''ē-rĭs'kwē), for girls and boys.

vis a fron-te (vĭs ā frŭn'tē), force from in front.

vis a ter-go *Lat.* (vĭs ā tûr'gō), force from behind.

vis-à vis *Fr.* (vē''=zȧ''=vē'), face to face; opposite.

vis in-er-ti-æ *Lat.* (vĭs ĭn-ûr'shĭ-ē), power of inertia.

vis vi-tæ *Lat.* (vĭs vī'tē), vital force.

vi-ta bre-vis, ars lon-ga *Lat.* (vī'tȧ brĕv'ĭs, ärz lông'gȧ), life (is) brief, art (is) lasting.

vi-vat rex *Lat.* (vī'văt rĕks), (long) live the king.

vive la ré-pu-blique *Fr.* (vēv' lȧ rā''pü''blēk'), (long) live the republic.

vive le roi *Fr.* (vēv' lē rwä'), (long) live the king.

voi-là tout *Fr.* (vwȧ''lȧ' to͞o'), that is all.

vox, et præ-te-re-a ni-hil *Lat.* (vŏks, ĕt prē-tĕr'ē-ȧ nī'hĭl), a voice, and nothing besides.

vox po-pu-li, vox De-i *Lat.* (vŏks pŏp'ū-lī, vŏks dē'ī), the voice of the people (is) the voice of God; the voice of the people is authoritative.

vrai-sem-blance *Fr.* (vrâ''säṅ''bläṅs'), probability; the appearance of truth.

vul-go *Lat.* (vŭl'gō), commonly.

W

Wan-der-jahr *Ger.* (vän'dẽr-yär''), a year of wandering.

Wan-der-lust *Ger.* (vän'dẽr-lo͝ost''), a passion for wandering or traveling.

Welt-krieg *Ger.* (vĕlt'krēkh''; -krēg''), world war.

Y

y á Ro-ma por to-do *Span.* (ē ä rō'mä pôr tō'thō), and to Rome for everything.

Z

Zeit-geist *Ger.* (tsīt'gīst''), the spirit of the age.

zum Bei-spiel *Ger.* (tso͞om bī'shpēl''), for example.

NAMES OF PERSONS AND PLACES

The following abbreviations, and the official abbreviations of the several States of the United States, not here listed, are used in this Appendix.

abbr. ....abbreviation
abp. ....archbishop
act.; acts ....actor, actress; actors
adm. ....admiral
admin. ..administrator
adven. ....adventurer
Afr. ....Africa(n)
Am. ....America(n)
anc. ....ancient
arch. ....architect
art., arts ....artist(s)
A. S. ......Anglo-Saxon
Assyr. ....Assyrian
astron. ....astronomer
au. ....author
Aus. ....Austrian
b. ....born
bacter. ....bacteriologist
bat., bats. ......battle(s)
bet. ....between
Bib. ....Biblical
biog. ....biographer
biol. ....biologist
bor. ....borough
bp. ....bishop
Br. ....British
Can. ....Canada, Canadian
cap., caps. ....capital(s)
cen. ....center; central
Cen. Am. ....Central America
cent. ....century
Ch. ....Church
Chin. ....Chinese
clergy. ....clergyman, clergymen
co., cos. ....county, counties
col.; cols. ....colony, colonial; colonies
coll. ....college
com. ....commune
comm. ....commander
comp. ....composer
Confed. ....Confederate
confed. ..confederation
conq. ....conqueror
cont. ....continent
d. ....died
Da. ....Danish
depend. .....dependency, dependencies
dept., depts. ......department(s)
dipl. ....diplomat
disc. ....discovered; discoverer
dist. ....district
div. ....division
dram. ....dramatist
Du. ....Dutch
E. ....east
econ. ....economist
ed. ....editor
educ. ....educator
emp.; emps. ...emperor, empress; emperors
Eng. ..England; English
eng. .... engineer
esp. .... especially
essay. ....essayist
est. .... estuary
estab. ...... established
expl. .... explorer
extrem. .... extremity
Fin. ....Finland
for. .... foreign
Fr. ......France; French
fr. ....from
ft. ....feet
gen., gens. ......general(s)
geog. ....geographer
geol. ....geologist
geom. ....geometrician
Ger.; Gers. .....German, Germany; Germans
Gk., Gks. ....Greek(s)
gov. ....governor
govt. .....government(al)
Gt. Br. .....Great Britain
Heb. ....Hebrew
hist. ....historian
Hung. ....Hungarian
illus. ....illustrator
imp. ....important
indep. ....independent
inv., invs. ..inventor(s)
Ir. ....Irish
Ire. ....Ireland
isl., isls ....island(s)
It. ....Italy; Italian
Jap. ....Japan(ese)
jour. ....journalist
Lat. ....Latin
law. ....lawyer
legis. ....legislator
m. ....miles
math. ..mathematician
Medit. ..Mediterranean
Mex. ....Mexico; Mexican
mfg. ....manufacturing
mfr. ....manufacturer
mil. ....military
min. ....mineral
mod. ....modern
Mt. ....Mount
mt.; mts. ....mount, mountain; mountains
mus. ....musical; musician
N. ....north
N. Am. ....North America
natur. ....naturalist
nav. ....naval
navig. ....navigator
Norw. ....Norwegian
nov. ....novelist
oc., ocs. ....ocean(s)
off. ...officer; official(ly)
or. ....orator
orig. ....original(ly)
p. ....population
pen. ....peninsula
Pers. ....Persian
philan. ...philanthropist
philos. ....philosopher
phys. ....physician
P. I. ....Philippine Islands
Pol. ....Polish
pol. ....political; politician
Port. ....Portugal; Portuguese
pres. ....president
prin. ....principal
prof. ....professor
Prot. ....Protestant
protec. ....protectorate
prov., provs. ....province(s)
pseud. ....pseudonym
pt. ....point
repub., repubs. ....republic(s)
Rev. ..Revolution(ary)
riv., rivs ....river(s)
Rom. ....Roman
R.R., R.Rs. railroad(s)
Russ. ....Russia(n)
S. ....south
S. Am. ....South America
sci. ....scientist
Scot. ..Scotch; Scotland
sculp. ....sculptor
sec. ....secretary
sen. ....senator
sol. ....soldier
sop. ....soprano
Sp. ....Spain
Span. ....Spanish
spt. ....seaport
sq. ....square
str. ....strait
stsm. ....statesman
Sw. ..Sweden; Swedish
ter., ters. ....territory, territories
theolog. ....theologian
tn., tns. ....town(s)
trag. ....tragedian, tragedienne; tragic
trav. ....traveler
trib. ....tributary
Turk. ....Turkish
twp. ....township
univ. ....university
U. S. .....United States
vil. ....village
W. ....west

A

Aachen (ä′khĕn), [Fr. **Aix-la-Chapelle**], city, Prussia, p. 155,816: cathedral; cap. of Charlemagne's empire; bat. World War II, 1944.

Aar (är), largest riv. wholly in Switzerland, [175 m. long.

Abbey (ăb′ĭ), Edwin Austin (1852–1911), Am. painter & illus.

Abbott (ăb′ŭt), Lyman (1835–1922), Am. [clergy., au., & ed.

Abd-el-Kadir (äb″-dĕl-kä′dĕr), (1807–83), Arabian chief.

Abd-el-Krim (äb″-dĕl-krĭm′), (1885–), leader of the Riffs in Morocco, 1919–26.

Abdul-Hamid (äb″dōōl-hȧ-mēd′), name of 2 sultans of Turkey: **I** (1725–89); **II** (1842–1918), 1876–1909: deposed.

Abélard (ăb′ĕ-lärd; ȧ″bā″lȧr′), Pierre (1079–1142), Fr. scholastic philos. & theolog.

Abercrombie (ăb′ẽr-krŭm″bĭ), James (1706–81), Br. gen. in Am.

Aberdeen (ăb″ẽr-dēn′), city, Scot., p. 158,969.

Abo (ō′bōō), spt. city, S. W. Finland, p. 63,918: univ.

Abruzzi (ä-brōōt′sē), Prince Luigi Amedeo, Duke of the (1873–1933), It. trav. & expl.

Abydos (ȧ-bī′dŏs), **1**, anc. tn., Asia Minor, on Hellespont; **2**, anc. city, Upper Egypt.

Abyssinia (ăb″ĭ-sĭn′ĭ-ȧ), kingdom, E. Afr., 350,000 sq. m., p. 7,600,000; cap., Addis Ababa. Also called **Ethiopia.**

Acadia (ȧ-kā′dĭ-ȧ). See **Nova Scotia.**

Acarnania (ăk″ȧr-nā′nĭ-ȧ), anc. mountainous div., N. W. Greece.

Achaia (ȧ-kā′yȧ), or **Achæa** (ȧ-kē′ȧ), anc. dist., N. Peloponnesus: **– and Elis,** dept., Greece, 2,028 sq. m., p. 320,623; cap., Patras, p. 61,278.

---

go; join; yet; sing; chin; show; thin, *th*en; hw, *wh*y; zh, azure; ü, Ger. für, Fr. lune; ö, Ger. schön, Fr. feu; n̈, Fr. e*n*fa*n*t, no*m*; kh, Ger. a*ch* or i*ch*. See pages xviii–xix.

Aconcagua (ä″kōn-kä′gwä). See **Andes.**
Actium (ăk′shĭ-ŭm; -tĭ-ŭm), anc. tn. & cape, Greece: nav. bat. 31 B. C.
Adams (ăd′ămz), **1,** Henry (1838–1918), Am. hist. & writer; **2,** John (1735–1826), 2d pres. of U. S.; **3,** John Quincy (1767–1848), 6th pres. of U. S.; **4,** Maude (1872–), Am. act.; **5,** Samuel (1722–1803), a leader in Am. Rev.
Addams (ăd′ămz), Jane (1860–1935), Am. social worker.
Addis Ababa (äd′ĭs ä′bȧ-bȧ), city, cap. of Abyssinia, p. 250,000.
Addison (ăd′ĭ-sŭn), Joseph (1672–1719), Eng. essay.
Ade (ād), George (1866–1944), Am. humorist & playwright.
Adelaide (ăd′ĕ-lād), city, cap. of S. Australia, [p. 330,217.]
Aden (ä′dĕn; ā′dĕn), pen., protec. & tn., Arabia, p. 54,923.
Adige (ä′dē-jā), riv., N. It., to Gulf of Venice: bats. World War I.
Adirondacks (ăd″ĭ-rŏn′dăks), group of mts., N. E. N. Y.: Mt. Marcy, 5,344 ft.
Adler (äd′lĕr), Felix (1851–1933) Am. educ.: founder of Ethical Culture Society.
Admiralty Islands (ăd′mĭ-răl-tĭ), isl. group, in Pac. oc., p. 13,800: Australian mandate.
Adrian (ā′drĭ-ăn), **1,** name of 6 popes, notably **IV** Nicholas Breakspeare (1100–59); **2,** Rom. emp.: see *Hadrian.*
Adrianople (ā″drĭ-ăn-ō′pl; ăd″rĭ-), vilayet and city, European Turkey. See **Edirne.**
Adriatic Sea (ā″drē-ăt′ĭk), arm of Medit., N. E. of It., 500 m. long, 130 m. broad.
Ægean Sea (ē-jē′ăn), bet. Asia Minor and Greece, 400 m. long.
Ægina (ē-jī′nȧ), isl., Greece, in Gulf of Ægina, [33 m. long.]
Ægospotami (ē″gŏs-pŏt′ȧ-mī), or **Ægospotamos** (-mŏs), anc. riv. & tn., coast of Thrace: bat. 405 B. C.
Æmilia (ē-mĭl′ĭ-ȧ), anc. div., N. It.
Æolis (ē′ō-lĭs), anc. dist., N. W. Asia Minor.
Æschylus (ĕs′kĭ-lŭs), (525–456 B. C.), Gk. trag.
Æsop (ē′sŏp), (6th cent. B. C.), Gk. fabulist.
Ætolia (ē-tō′lĭ-ȧ), anc. Gk. dist., N. of Gulf of Corinth.
Afghanistan (ăf-găn′ĭ-stăn″), country, S. Asia, 250,000 sq. mi., p. 12,000,000; cap., Kabul, p. 120,000.
Africa (ăf′rĭ-kȧ), cont., Eastern Hemisphere, 11,596,000 sq. mi., p. 187,494,000.
Agassiz (ăg′ȧ-sē), Jean Louis Rudolphe (1807–73), Swiss-Am. natur.
Agincourt (ȧ″zhăṅ″ko͞or′), vil., N. Fr.: bat. [1415.]
Agra (ä′grä), anc. city, N. India, p. 185,532: Taj Mahal.
Agram (ä′gräm). See **Zagreb.**
Agricola (ȧ-grĭk′ō-lȧ), Cnæus Julius (37–93), Rom. gen.
Agrigentum (ăg″rĭ-jĕn′tŭm), [mod. **Girgenti** (jĕr-jĕn′tē)], anc. tn., S. Sicily.
Aguinaldo (ä″gē-näl′dō; ăg″wĭ-), Emilio (1870–), Filipino leader.
Ahmadabad (ä″mŭd-ä-bäd′), city, presidency of Bombay, India, p. 274,007.
Aiken (ā′kĕn), Conrad (1889–), Am. critic & poet.
Aisne (ân), riv., N. Fr., 170 m.: bats. 1914–18.
Aix-la-Chapelle (āks″-lȧ-shȧ″pĕl), city, Prussia. See **Aachen.**
Ajaccio (ä-yät′chō), spt. tn., cap. of Corsica, p. 20,797: Napoleon's birthplace.
Akron (ăk′rŭn), city, Ohio, p. 273,189.
Alabama (ăl″ȧ-bä′mȧ; -băm′ȧ), **1,** State in U. S., 51,279 sq. m., p. 3,052,754; cap., Montgomery; **2,** riv., Ala., 320 m.
Alamo (ä′lä-mō), **the,** Franciscan mission, San Antonio, Tex.: massacre 1836.
Aland Islands (ō′lȧn; ô′lȧn), archipelago, Gulf of Bothnia, 210 sq. m., p. 27,156.
Alaric (ăl′ȧ-rĭk), (376?–410), chief of the Visigoths: conquered Rome 409.
Alaska (ȧ-lăs′kȧ), ter., U. S., 586,400 sq. m., p. 128,643; cap., Juneau.
Albania (ăl-bā′nĭ-ȧ), state, Balkan pen., 10,629 sq. m., 175,000; cap., Tirana.
Albany (ôl′bȧ-nĭ), city, cap. of N. Y., on Hudson riv., p. 134,382.
Albay (äl-bī), city, Luzon, P. I., p. 52,756.
Albert (ăl′bĕrt), **1, I** (1875–1934), king of Belgians, 1909–34; **2,** Prince of Saxe-Coburg-Gotha (1819–61), husband of Queen Victoria.
Albert (ȧl″bâr′), [formerly **Ancre** (äṅkr′)], tn., Fr., p. 7,000; bats. 1915–18.
Alberta (ăl-bûr′tȧ), prov., Can., 255,285 sq. m., p. 936,566; cap., Edmonton.
Albert Edward Nyanza (nyän′zä), lake, E. cen. Afr., 100 m. S. of Albert Nyanza.
Albert Nyanza (nyän′zä), lake, E. cen. Afr., 130 m. N. W. of Victoria Nyanza.
Albertus Magnus (ăl′bûr′tŭs măg′nŭs), (1193?–1280), Swabian philos.
Albuquerque (ăl′bŭ-kĕrk), Alfonso de [*the Great*] (1453–1515), Port. navig.
Albuquerque (ăl″bŭ-kûr′kē), city, N. Mex., p. 97,012.
Alcibiades (ăl″sĭ-bī′ȧ-dēz), (450–404 B. C.), [Athenian gen. & pol.]
Alcock (ôl′kŏk), Sir John (1892–1919), Eng. aviator: first nonstop transatlantic flight.
Alcott (ôl′kŭt), Louisa May (1832–88), Am. nov.
Alden (ôl′dĕn), John (1599–1687), a Pilgrim [Father.]
Alderney (ôl′dĕr-nĭ), isl., Eng. channel, 3 sq. m., p. 1,598.
Aldrich (ôl′drĭch), Thomas Bailey (1836–[1907), Am. au.]
Aleppo (ȧ-lĕp′ō), city, N. Syria, p. 369,000.
Aleutian Islands (ȧ-lū′shăn; ȧ-lo͞o′-), volcanic isls. extending 800 m. W. of Alaska.
Alexander (ăl″ĕg-zăn′dĕr), **1,** name of 8 popes, notably **VI** Roderigo L. Borgia (1431–1503); **2,** name of 3 emps. of Russ.: **I** (1777–1825); **II** (1818–81); **III** (1845–94); **3, I** (1857–93), prince & ruler of Bulgaria; **4, I** (1893–1920), king of Greece; **5,** [*the Great*] (356–323 B. C.), king of Macedonia: conq. of the eastern world; **6, I** [*the Fierce*] (1078–1124), king of Scot.: **7, I** (1876–1903), king of Serbia; **8, I** (1888–1934), king of Yugoslavia: assassinated.
Alexandria (ăl″ĕg-zăn′drĭ-ȧ), spt. city, Egypt, on Medit., p. 573,063.
Alfieri (äl-fyā′rē), Vittorio, Count (1749–1803), It. poet & dram.
Alfonso XIII (ăl-fŏn′sō), (1886–1941), king of [Sp. 1902–31.]
Alfred (ăl′frĕd), [*the Great*] (849–901), king of Wessex, 871–901.
Alger (ăl′jĕr), Horatio, 2d (1832–99), Am. [juvenile writer.]
Algeria (ăl-jē′rĭ-ȧ), Fr. col., N. Afr., 851,078 sq. m., p. 8,983,100; cap., **Algiers,** p. 360,700.
Ali Pasha (ä′lē pȧ-shä′), [*the Lion of Janina*] (1741–1822), ruler of Albania.
Allahabad (ăl″ȧ-hä-bäd′), div. & city, N. W. India, p. 157,220.
Allegheny (ăl′ē-gā″nĭ), **1,** W. range Appalachian system of mts., Pa., Md., Va., & W. Va.; **2,** riv., Pa., about 350 m.
Allen (ăl′ĕn), **1,** Ethan (1737–89), Am. sol; **2,** James Lane (1849–1925), Am. nov.
Allenby (ăl′ĕn-bĭ), Sir Edmund Henry Hynman (1861–1936), Br. gen.
Allentown (ăl′ĕn-toun), city, Pa., p. 106,233.
Alma-Tadema (ăl′mȧ-tăd′ē-mȧ), Sir Lawrence (1836–1912), Eng. art. of Du. origin.
Alost (ä′lŏst), or **Aalst** (älst), tn., E. Belgium, on Dender riv., p. 37,380.
Alpheus (ăl-fē′ŭs), riv., Peloponnesus, Greece.
Alps (ălps), mt. system, S. cen. Europe: highest peak, Mont Blanc, 15,782 ft.
Alsace (ăl-säs′), anc. Ger. prov.: seized in 1681 by Fr.: ceded to Ger. as part of Alsace-Lorraine in 1871.
Alsace-Lorraine (ăl-säs′-lō″rān′), former imperial state of Ger.: ceded to Fr. 1919; 5,605 sq. m., p. 1,795,100.
Altai (äl-tī′), mts., N. cen. Asia, 11,000 ft.

Altdorf (ält′dôrf), tn., Switzerland: scene of William Tell's exploit.
Altoona (ăl-to͞o′nȧ), city, Pa., p. 76,844.
Alva (äl′vä; ăl′vȧ), or **Alba** (äl′bä; ăl′bȧ), Fernando Álvarez de Toledo, Duke of (1508–82), Span. gen.
Alvarado, de (dā äl″vä-rä′*th*ō), **1,** Alonso (?–1553), Span. conq. in Mex.; **2,** Pedro (1495?–1541), Span. adven. & gov.
Amati (ä-mä′tē), Nicolo (1596–1684), It. violin maker.
Amazon (ăm′ȧ-zŏn), largest riv. in world, 3,900 m. fr. Peruvian Andes to Atlantic oc.
Amboina (ăm-boi′nȧ), Du. isl., Molucca group, 17,372 sq. m., p. 359,181. [Milan.
Ambrose (ăm′brōz), Saint (340–397), bp. of
Amenophis (ăm″ē-nō′fĭs), or **Amenhotep** (ăm″ĕn-hō′tĕp), name of 4 pharaohs of Egypt, notably **IV** [*Akhenaton*, or *Akhnaton*], about 1375–1357 B. C.
America (ȧ-mĕr′ĭ-kȧ), continental mass of Western Hemisphere; New World: often used for the United States of America, which see: **North–,** cont., including land N. of Isthmus of Panama, 9,387,000 sq. m., p. 214,824,000: **Central–,** comprising Guatemala, Honduras, Salvador, Nicaragua, Costa Rica, Br. Honduras, and Panama, 221,000 sq. m., p. 10,270,000: **South–,** cont., including land S. of Central America, 6,863,000 sq. m., p. 105,763,000.
Amiens (ȧ″myăN; ăm′ĭ-ĕnz), city, Fr., p. 91,576; cathedral. [p. 300,000.
Amoy (ȧ-moi′), city, Fukien prov., China,
Ampère (äN″pâr′), André Marie (1775–1836), Fr. physicist & natur.
Amsterdam (ăm′stẽr-dăm), **1,** city, N. Y., p. 32,269; **2,** spt. city, one of the caps. of the Netherlands, on Zuider Zee, p. 769,144.
Amu Daria (ä-mo͞o′ där′yä), riv., Turkestan, cen. Asia, 1,400 m. to Lake Aral.
Amundsen (ä′mŭn-sĕn), Roald (1872–1928), Norw. expl.: disc. S. pole 1911.
Amur (ä-mo͞or′), riv., E. Asia, 2,760 m. to N. Pacific. [Gk. lyric poet.
Anacreon (ȧ-năk′rē-ŏn), (563?–478 B. C.),
Anam (ȧ-năm′), or **Annam** (ăn″näm′), now part of the State Viet-Nam in the Fr. Union, 57,838 sq. m., p. 7,184,000.
Anastasius (ăn″ă-stā′shĭ-ŭs), **I** Saint, bp. of Rome, 398–401; **II** pope, 496–498; **III** pope, 911–913; **IV** pope, 1153–54.
Anatolia (ăn″ȧ-tō′lĭ-ȧ). See **Asia Minor.**
Anaxagoras (ăn″ăk-săg′ō-rȧs), (500–428 B. C.), Ionian philos. & geom.
Anaximander (ăn-ăk″sĭ-măn′dẽr), (611–547 B. C.), Gk. philos., astron., & math. [S. Sp.
Andulasia (ăn″dȧ-lo͞o′shĭ-ȧ), former prov.,
Andersen (ăn′dẽr-sĕn), Hans Christian (1805–75), Da. writer of fairy tales.
Anderson (ăn′dẽr-sŭn), **1,** Alexander (1775–1870), pioneer of wood engraving in U. S.; **2,** Sherwood (1876–1941), Am. au.
Andes (ăn′dēz), mt. system, 4,500 m. long, Panama to Cape Horn, S. Am.: Aconcagua, 23,080 ft.
Andorra (ăn-dŏr′rä), **1,** repub., bet. N. E. Sp. & Fr., 191 sq. m., p. 5,231; **2,** city, its cap., p. 1,000.
Andrassy (ŏn′drä-shĭ), Julius, Count (1823–90), Hung. stsm.: 1st premier of Hungary under dual monarchy.
André (än′drā; ăn′drĭ), John (1751–80), Eng. major in Am. Rev.: executed.
Andros (ăn′drŏs), Sir Edmund (1637–1714), col. gov. of N. Y. & Va.
Androscoggin (ăn″drŏs-kŏg′ĭn), riv., 155 m. to Kennebec riv., near Bath, Me.
Angelico (ăn-jĕl′ē-kō), Fra (1387–1455), Florentine painter. [Am. educ.
Angell (ān′jĕl), James Rowland (1869–1949),
Angola (ăng-gō′lȧ), Port. depend., W. Afr., 1,000 m. of coast, p. 5,000,000.
Angora (ăn-gō′rȧ). See **Ankara.**
Anhalt (än′hält), administrative div., Ger., 888 sq. m., p. 351,045; cap., Dessau, p. 71,272.
Ankara (ăng′kä-rä) [formerly **Angora**], city, Asia Minor, cap. of repub. of Turkey since 1922, p. 74,784.
Ann (ăn), **Cape,** E. end of Essex co., Mass
Annapolis (ă-năp′ō-lĭs), spt. city, cap. of Md., p. 15,016; U. S. Nav. Academy.
Anne (ăn), **1, of Austria** (1601–66), wife of Louis XIII of Fr. & queen regent for Louis XIV; **2, of England** (1665–1714), queen of Gt. Br. & Ire.
Annunzio, d' (dän-no͞on′dzē-ō), Gabriele (1864–1937), It. poet, nov. & patriot.
Anselm (ăn′sĕlm), Saint (1033–1109), abp. of Canterbury, 1093–1109. [**Tananarive.**
Antananarivo (ȧn″tȧ-nä″nȧ-rē′vō). See
Antarctica (ănt-ärk′tĭ-kȧ), cont. around S. pole. [pole.
Antarctic Ocean (ănt-ärk′tĭk), oc. near S.
Anthony (ăn′thō-nĭ), Susan Brownell (1820–1906), Am. woman suffrage leader.
Antietam (ăn-tē′tăm), creek, Pa. & Md., 25 m. to Potomac: bat. in Md. 1862.
Antigua (ăn″tē′gwä), one of Leeward isls., Br. W. Indies, 108 sq. m., p. 29,767.
Antilles (ăn-tĭl′ēz), **Greater** & **Lesser,** two groups of isls., W. Indies: Fr. depend.
Antioch (ăn′tĭ-ŏk), anc. cap. of Syria, on Orontes riv., p. 28,000.
Antiochus (ăn-tī′ō-kŭs), name of 13 kings of Syria, notably **III** [*the Great*] (?–187 B. C.).
Antipodes (ăn-tĭp′ō-dēz), uninhabited isl. group, New Zealand depend., S. Pacific oc.
Antisthenes (ăn-tĭs′thē-nēz), (445?–370? B. C.), Gk. cynic philos. [p. 51,531.
Antofagasta (än″tō-fä-gäs′tä), spt., N. Chile,
Antoninus Pius (ăn-tō-nī′nŭs pī′ŭs), (86–161), Rom. emp.
Antonius (ăn-tō′nĭ-ŭs), Marcus [**Mark Antony**], (83–30 B. C.), Rom. triumvir.
Antwerp (ănt′wẽrp), [Fr. **Anvers** (äN″vâr′)], spt. city, Belgium, p. 300,115; bat. 1944.
Apennines (ăp′ĕ-nīnz), mt. chain, It., 750 m. long: Monte Corno, 9,580 ft.
Appalachian (ăp″ȧ-lăch′ĭ-ăn; -lā′chĭ-ăn), mt. system, eastern N. Am.
Appomattox Court House (ăp-ō-măt′ŭks), vil., Va., p. 992: Gen. Lee's surrender.
Apponyi (ŏp′pō-nyē), Albert, Count (1846–1933), Hung. stsm.
Apremont (ȧ″prē-môN′), tn., dept. of Meuse, Fr. 20 m. fr. Verdun: bats. World War.
Aquinas (ȧ-kwī′nȧs), Thomas, Saint (1225?–74?), It. theolog. [Gaul.
Aquitania (ăk″wĭ-tā′nĭ-ȧ), S. W. div. of anc.
Arabia (ȧ-rā′bĭ-ȧ), country, S. W. Asia, 1,350,000 sq. m., p. 10,000,000.
Arabian Sea (ȧ-rā′bĭ-ăn), part of Indian oc., bet. India and Arabia.
Aral (ăr′ăl; ȧ-räl′), **Lake,** inland sea, Asiatic Russ., 26,166 sq. m.
Ararat (ăr′ȧ-răt), dist. & mt., Armenia: two peaks, highest Great Ararat, 16,969 ft.
Arbil (ȧr-bēl′), or **Erbil** (ẽr-bēl′), [anc. **Arbela** (ȧr-bē′lȧ)], tn. & vilayet of Basra, Iraq. p. 106,000. [(1412–31), Fr. national heroine.
Arc, d', Jeanne (zhän′ dȧrk′), [**Joan of Arc**],
Arcadia (är-kā′dĭ-ȧ), country, anc. Greece.
Archangel (ärk-ān′jĕl), spt. tn., near Arctic oc., cap. Archangel prov. Russ., p. 281,000.
Archimedes (är″kĭ-mē′dēz), (287–212 B. C.), Gk. math. & physicist. [5,600,000 sq. m.
Arctic Ocean (ärk′tĭk), oc. around N. pole,
Arezzo (ä-rĕt′sō), city, It., p. 58,206.
Argentina (är″jĕn-tē′nȧ), [**Argentine Republic**], repub., S. Am., 1,153,418 sq. m., p. 10,622,348; cap., Buenos Aires.
Argolis (är′gō-lĭs), anc. div. & mod. dept., Greece. [Ardennes, Fr.: bats. 1914–18.
Argonne (ȧr″gŏn′), forest, depts. of Meuse &
Argos (är′gŏs), chief city, anc. Argolis, Greece.

Aristides (ăr″ĭs-tī′dēz), [*the Just*] (?–468 B. C.), Athenian stsm. & gen.

Aristippus (ăr″ĭs-tĭp′ŭs), (435?–356? B. C.), Gk. philos.

Aristophanes (ăr″ĭs-tŏf′ȧ-nēz), (448?–380? B. C.), Gk. comic playwright. [philos.

Aristotle (ăr′ĭs-tŏt″l), (384–322 B. C.), Gk.

Arizona (ăr″ĭ-zō′nȧ), State in U. S., 113,810 sq. m., p. 745,259: cap., Phoenix.

Arkansas (är′kăn-sô), **1,** State in U. S., 53,335 sq. m., p. 1,901,631: cap., Little Rock; **2,** riv., 1,500 m. to Miss. riv.

Arkwright (ärk′rīt), Sir Richard (1732–92), Eng. inv. of cotton-spinning machinery.

Arlington (är′lĭng-tŭn), vil., Va.: home of Robert E. Lee; National Cemetery.

Arliss (är′lĭs), George (1868–1946), Anglo-Am. act.

Armenia (är-mē′nĭ-ȧ), soviet socialist repub., S. of Caucasus mts., federated with Russ., 15,240 sq. m., p. 876,557; cap., Erivan.

Armentieres (är″män′tyâr′), tn., N. Fr., on Lys. riv., p. 18,795; bats. 1914–18.

Arminius (är-mĭn′ĭ-ŭs), Jacobus [**Harmensen** (här′mĕn-sĕn)], (1560–1609), Du. theolog.: founder of Arminianism.

Arnold (är′nŭld), **1,** Benedict (1714–1801), sol. Am. Rev., traitor; **2,** Henry H. (1886–1950), gen. of the army, U. S., chief army air force (1942–45); **3,** Matthew (1822–88), Eng. poet.

Aroostook (ȧ-rōōs′tŏŏk), riv., Me., 125 m. to St. John riv. [1917–18.

Arras (ȧ″räs′), city, Fr., p. 25,970: bats.

Arrhenius (ȧr-rā′nĭ-ŭs), Svante (1859–1927), Sw. sci.: Nobel prize 1903.

Arriaga (är-rē-ä′gȧ), Manoel de (1842–1917), Port. revolutionist: 1st constitutional pres., 1911–15. [high.

Arrowrock Dam (ăr′ō-rŏk″), Idaho, 349 ft.

Artaxerxes (är″tăk-sûrk′sēz), name of 3 kings of Persia.

Artemisia (är″tē-mĭsh′ĭ-ȧ), (?351? B. C.), queen of Halicarnassus: builder of the Mausoleum.

Arthur (är′thŭr), **1,** legendary king of Britain, 6th cent.; **2,** Chester Alan (1830–86), 21st pres. of U. S. [Atlantic, 34 sq. m.

Ascension Island (ă-sĕn′shŭn), Br. isl., S.

Ashanti (ȧ-shăn′tē; -shän′-), Br. protec., Gold Coast, W. Afr., 11,000 sq. m., p. 407,000; cap., Kumasi.

Asheville (ăsh′vĭl), city, N. C., in Blue Ridge mts., p. 52,208: health resort.

Ashokan Dam (ä-shō′kăn), N. Y., 252 ft. high.

Asia (ā′shȧ; -zhȧ), cont., N. E. region of Old World, 17,206,000 sq. m., p. 1,280,047,000.

Asia Minor (ā′zhȧ), [formerly **Anatolia**], pen, forming W. extrem. of Asia, div. of Turkey, 200,000 sq. m., p. 13,880,000.

Asquith (ăs′kwĭth), Herbert Henry, Earl of Oxford and Asquith (1852–1928), Eng. stsm.

Assam (ă″săm′), state, repub. of India, 71,455 sq. m., p. 8,510,000.

Assiniboia (ă-sĭn″ĭ-boi′ȧ), former dist., Northwest Territory, Can., now part of Saskatchewan. [Francis.

Assisi (äs-sē′zē), tn., It.: birthplace of St.

Assuan (äs-swän′). See **Aswan.** [Nineveh.

Assyria (ă-sĭr′ĭ-ȧ), anc. empire, W. Asia; cap.,

Astor (ăs′tẽr), Nancy Langhorne, Lady (1879–), b. in Va., U. S.: member of Br. House of Commons. [p. 176,530.

Astrakhan (ăs″trȧ-kăn′), spt. city, Russ.,

Asunción (ä-sōōn″syōn′), city, cap. of Paraguay, S. Am., p. 142,519.

Aswan (ä-swän′), or **Assuan**, or **Assouan, 1,** prov., Upper Egypt; **2,** [anc. **Syene** (sī-ē′nē)], tn., its cap., p. 16,458: great dam.

Athabaska (ăth″ȧ-băs′kȧ), **1,** lake, N. W. Can., 200 m. long; **2,** riv., N. W. Can. about 600 m. long. [of Alexandria.

Athanasius (ăth″ȧ-nā′shĭ-ŭs), (296?–373), bp.

Athens (ăth′ĕnz), city, cap. of Greece, p. 452,919 (many refugees).

Athos (ăth′ŏs), pen., N. E. Greece: Mt. Athos; many monasteries. [327,090.

Atlanta (ăt-lăn′tȧ), city, cap. of Ga., p.

Atlantic City (ăt-lăn′tĭk), city & seaside resort, N. J., p. 61,642; summer p. 350,000.

Atlantic Ocean (ăt-lăn′tĭk), bet. Am. & Europe & Afr., 41,321,000 sq. m., average breadth 3,000 m.

Atlas (ăt′lăs), mts., N. Afr., 1,500 ft.

Attica (ăt′ĭ-kȧ), pen. & anc. country, Greece; anc. cap., Athens: **– and Bœotia,** mod. dept., Greece, p. 1,024,667.

Attila (ăt′ĭ-lȧ), (406?–53), king of the Huns.

Auber (ō″bâr′), Daniel François (1782–1871), Fr. comp.

Auburn (ô′bŭrn), city, N. Y., p. 36,667.

Auckland (ôk′lănd), **1,** dist., New Zealand; **2,** city of same, p. 209,800.

Audubon (ô′dŏŏ-bŏn), John James (1785–1851), Am. ornithologist. [165,522; cathedral.

Augsburg (ouks′bŏŏrkh), city, Bavaria, p.

Augusta (ô-gŭs′tȧ), **1,** city, Ga., p. 71,507; **2,** city, cap. of Me., p. 20,900.

Augustine (ô-gŭs′tĭn), **1,** Saint (354–430), Lat. Ch. father; **2,** Saint [*Apostle of the Anglo-Saxons*] (?–604), 1st abp. of Canterbury.

Augustus (ô-gŭs′tŭs), Octavius (63 B. C.–A. D. 14), 1st Rom. emp. [275), Rom. emp.

Aurelian (ô-rē′lĭ-ăn), Lucius Domitius (212?–

Aurelius (ô-rē′lĭ-ŭs), Marcus (121–180), philos. & Rom. emp.

Aurora (ô-rō′rȧ), city, Ill., p. 50,508.

Austen (ôs′tĕn), Jane (1775–1817), Eng. nov.

Austerlitz (ôs′tẽr-lĭts; ous′-), tn., Moravia, p. 4,231: bat. 1805.

Austin (ôs′tĭn), Alfred (1835–1913), Eng. poet laureate. [riv., p. 131,564: univ.

Austin (ôs′tĭn), city, cap. of Tex., on Colo.

Australasia (ôs″trăl-ā′shȧ), **English,** commonwealth of Australia & additional isls., including New Zealand, Fiji, etc.: **French–,** New Caledonia & depend.

Australia (ôs-trā′lĭ-ȧ; -trāl′yȧ), Br. isl. & cont., S. E. of Asia, 2,948,366 sq. m., p. 5,215,515: **Commonwealth of –,** same with adjacent isls., 2,974,581 sq. m., p. 6,373,219; cap., Canberra.

Austria (ôs′trĭ-ȧ), formerly part of Austria-Hungary in Europe; democratic repub., 1920–39; annexed by Germany 1938, occupied by Allies, 1945: 32,396 sq. m., p. 6,534,481.

Austria-Hungary (ôs′trĭ-ȧ-hŭng′gȧ-rĭ), former dual monarchy, cen. Europe.

Avon (ā′vŏn; ăv′ŏn), name of several rivs. in Eng., esp. one flowing through Stratford, Shakespeare's birthplace.

Ayr (âr), bor., S. W. Scot., p. 38,000.

Azerbaijan (ä″zĕr-bä-ē-jän′; ăz″ĕr-bī-jän′), soviet socialist repub., W. of S. Caspian sea, federated with Russ., 33,640 sq. m., p. 2,313,172; cap., Baku.

Azores (ȧ-zōrz′), isls., Atlantic oc., prov. of Portugal, 922 sq. m., p. 232,012.

Azov (ä′zŏf; ȧ-zôf′), or **Azof, Sea of,** 14,515 sq. m., S. Russ., arm of Black sea.

B

Baalbek (bäl′bĕk; bäl″bĕk′), anc. city, Syria: now in ruins.

Bab el Mandeb (băb″ ĕl män′dĕb), str. bet. Red sea & Indian oc., 14½ m. wide.

Babylon (băb′ĭ-lŏn), anc. city, Babylonia, in mod. Iraq, on Euphrates riv. [Ger. comp.

Bach (bäkh), Johann Sebastian (1685–1750).

Bacon (bā′kn), **1,** Francis, Baron Verulam, Viscount St. Albans (1561–1626), Eng. essay. & philos.; **2,** Henry (1866–1924), Am. arch.: designed Lincoln Memorial; **3,** Roger, Friar (1214–94), Eng. monk & sci.

Badajoz (bä″thä-hōth′), city, Sp., p. 41,982.

Baden (bä'dĕn), administrative div., Ger., 5,819 sq. m., p. 2,312,462; cap., Karlsruhe.

Baden-Powell (bā'dĕn-pō'ĕl), Sir Robert S. S. (1857–1941), 1st Baron, Br. gen.: founder of Boy Scouts. [publisher of guidebooks.

Baedeker (bā'dē-kēr), Karl (1801–59), Ger.

Baffin (băf'ĭn), William (1584?–1622), Eng. navig. [N. Am., 825 m. long.

Baffin Bay (băf'ĭn), or **Sea,** W. of Greenland,

Baffin Island (băf'ĭn), Br. isl., part of Can., 236,000 sq. m. [Eng. au.

Bagehot (băj'ŭt; băg'-), Walter (1826–77),

Baghdad (bȧg-däd'; băg'dăd), or **Bagdad,** city, cap. of Iraq, S. W. Asia, p. 170,000.

Bahama Islands (bȧ-hā'mȧ), isls., Br. W. Indies, 4,404 sq. m., p. 60,367; cap., Nassau.

Bahia (bä-ē'ä), [off. **Sao Salvadore**], spt. Brazil, p. 283,422.

Baiæ (bī'yē), [mod. **Baja** (bä'yä)], anc. tn. & resort, Campania: now watering place & nav. station. [13,500 sq. m.

Baikal Lake (bī-käl'), lake, S. Siberia,

Bainbridge (bān'brĭj), William (1774–1833), Am. nav. off.: comm. *Constitution.*

Baku (bȧ-kōō'), city, cap. of Azerbaijan, Asia, p. 452,808.

Balboa, de (dā bäl-bō'ä), Vasco Núñez (1475–1517), Span. expl. & disc. Pacific oc.

Baldwin (bôld'wĭn), Stanley (1867–1947), Eng. stsm.; premier 1923–24, 1924–29, 1935–1937; created 1st Earl of Bewdley, 1937.

Balearic Islands (băl"ē-ăr'ĭk), isls., off Sp., in Medit. sea, 1,935 sq. m , p. 351,339.

Balfe (bălf), Michael William (1808–70), Ir. comp. [Balfour (1848–1930), Br. stsm.

Balfour (băl'fōōr), Arthur James, 1st Earl of

Balkan Mountains (bôl'kăn; bȧl-kän') range, S. E. Europe.

Balkan Peninsula (bôl'kăn; bȧl-kän') pen. bounded by Adriatic, Black, & Ægean seas, comprising Rumania, Yugoslavia, Bulgaria, Albania, & Greece.

Baltic Provinces (bôl'tĭk), former name of repubs. Estonia, Latvia, & Lithuania.

Baltic Sea (bôl'tĭk), in N. Europe, E. of Denmark, & inclosed by Sw. pen. & main cont., 178,000 sq. m.

Baltimore (bôl'tĭ-mōr), city, Md., p. 940,205.

Baluchistan (bȧ-lōō"chĭ-stän'), or **Beluchistan,** prov., W. Pakistan, 134,002 sq. m., p. 857,835; cap., Khelat.

Balzac, de (dē bȧl"zȧk'), Honoré (1799–1850), Fr. nov. [hist.

Bancroft (băn'krŏft), George (1800–91), Am.

Bangalore (băng"gȧ-lōr'), city, India, p. 237,-496. [Thailand], on Menam riv., p. 450,000.

Bangkok (băng"kŏk'), city, cap. of Siam

Banka (băng'kȧ), isl., Du. E. Indies, 4,549 sq. m., p. 154,141.

Banting (băn'tĭng), Sir Frederick G. (1891–1941), Can. sci.: disc. insulin; Nobel prize 1923. [1871, 1914–18.

Bapaume (bȧ"pōm'), tn., Fr., p. 3,000; bats.

Barbados (bär-bā'dōz), Br. isl., W. Indies, 166 sq. m., p. 167,953; cap., Bridgetown.

Barbary (bär'bȧ-rĭ), undefined region, N. Afr., fr. Egypt to Atlantic oc.

Barcelona (bär"sē-lō'nȧ; bär"thā-lō'nä), city, Sp., on Medit., p. 767,774; univ.

Barfrush (bär-frōōsh'), tn., Persia, near Caspian sea, p. 30,000.

Bari (bä'rĭ), spt. city, S. E. It., p. 174,619.

Baring-Gould (bâr'ĭng-gōōld'), Sabine (1834–1924), Eng. clergy. & hymn writer.

Barnard (bär'nȧrd), **1,** George Grey (1863–1938), Am. sculp.; **2,** Henry (1811–1900), Am. educ. [91), Am. showman.

Barnum (bär'nŭm), Phineas Taylor (1810–

Baroda (bȧ-rō'dȧ), city, India, p. 94,712.

Barotseland (bȧ-rŏt'sē-lănd), former name of region now part of N. W. Rhodesia, in S. Afr. [Scot. nov. & dram.

Barrie (băr'ĭ), Sir James M. (1860–1937),

Barrow (băr'ō), **Cape,** Br. Am., Coronation gulf: **Point –,** headland, N. end Alaska.

Barrymore (băr'ĭ-mōr), **1,** Ethel (1879–), Am. act.; **2,** John (1882–1942), Am. act.

Bartholdi (bär"tôl"dē'), Frédéric A. (1834–1904), Fr. sculp.: "Statue of Liberty."

Bartolommeo (bär"tō-lŏm-mĕ'ō), Fra (1469–1517), It. painter.

Barton (bär'tŭn), Clara (1821–1912), Am. nurse: founded Am. Red. Cross.

Bartram (bär'trăm), John (1699–1777), Am. botanist.

Basel (bä'zĕl), [Fr. **Bâle** (bäl)], city, Switzerland, on Rhine riv., p. 144,550.

Basil (băz'ĭl; bā'zĭl), Saint [*the Great*] (329–379), a father of the Gk. Ch.

Basra (bȧs'rȧ), or **Busrah** (bŭs'rä), or **Bassora** (băs'sō-rä), anc. city, Iraq, S. W. Asia, p. 165,000.

Bass Strait (bȧs), bet. Australia & Tasmania, 185 m. long, 80–150 m. wide.

Basutoland (bȧ-sōō'tō-lănd"), Br. col., S. Afr., 11,716 sq. m., p. 498,781.

Batangas (bä-täng'gäs), spt. tn., Luzon, P. I., p. 41,089: U. S. mil. post.

Batavia (bä-tä'vĭ-ä), city, cap. of Java, Indonesia, 1,200,000.

Bath (bȧth), city, Eng., p. 70,280.

Baton Rouge (băt'ŭn rōōzh'), city, cap. of La., on Miss. riv., p. 123,957: univ.

Battle Creek (băt'l), city, Mich., p. 48,469.

Batum (bȧ-tōōm'), or **Batoum,** free port, repub. of Georgia, on Black sea, p. 45,450.

Bavaria (bȧ-vā'rĭ-ȧ), administrative div., Ger., 29,486 sq. m., p. 7,379,594; cap., Munich.

Bayard, de (dē bȧ"yȧr), Pierre du Terrail, Seigneur [*the Chevalier*] (1473?–1524), Fr. [knight.

Bay City, city, Mich., p. 52,372.

Bayonne (bā"yōn'), city, N. J., p. 76,657.

Bayreuth (bī"roit'), or **Baireuth,** tn., Bavaria, p. 35,306.

Beaconsfield (bē'kŭnz-fēld; bĕk'ŭnz-), Benjamin Disraeli, Earl of (1804–81), Br. stsm. & nov. [Scot. poet & philos.

Beattie (bē'tĭ; bā'tĭ), James (1735–1803),

Beatty (bē'tĭ), Sir David (1871–1936), 1st Earl of the North Sea and of Brooksby, Br. adm.: comm. Grand Fleet 1916–19.

Beauharnais, de (dē bō"ȧr"nâ'), Hortense Eugénie (1783–1837), daughter of Josephine: wife of Louis Bonaparte & queen of Holland.

Beaumarchais, de (dē bō"mȧr"shâ'), (1732–99), Fr. dram.: pseud. of *Pierre Augustin Caron.* [Eng. dram.

Beaumont (bō'mŏnt), Francis (1584–1616,

Beaumont (bō'mŏnt), city, Tex., p. 93,715.

Beauregard (bō'rē-gärd), Pierre G. Toutant (1818–93), Am. Confed. gen.

Bechuanaland (bĕch"ōō-ä'nȧ-lănd"). Br. protec., S. W. Afr., 275,000 sq. m., p. 152,983.

Becket (bĕk'ĕt), Thomas à (1118?–70), Eng. prelate. [monk & writer.

Bede (bēd), [*the Venerable*] (673–735), Eng.

Bedford (bĕd'fērd), bor., Eng., p. 41,780.

Bedloe Island (bĕd'lō), [**Liberty Island**], isl., N. Y. bay: Statue of Liberty.

Beecher (bē'chēr), Henry Ward (1813–87), Am. clergy. [(1770–1827), Ger. comp.

Beethoven, van (vän bā'tō-vĕn), Ludwig

Beirut (ba'rōōt'). See **Beyrouth.**

Belasco (bē-lăs'kō), David (1859–1931), Am. dram. & producer.

Belem (bȧ-lĕṅ'), [**Pará** (pä-rä')], city, cap. of Pará prov., Brazil, p. 236,402.

Belfast (bĕl-fȧst'; bĕl'fȧst), bor., cap. of Northern Ire., p. 415,151.

Belfort (bĕl"fôr'), tn., Fr., p. 36,356.

Belgian Congo (kŏng'gō), country, S. cen. Afr., 909,654 sq. m., p. 8,723,276; cap., Leopoldville.

Belgium (bĕl'jĭ-ŭm; bĕl'jŭm), kingdom, Europe, 11,752 sq. m., 7,465,782; cap., Brussels: bats. 1914–18, 1944.

Belgrade (bĕl″grād′), [Serbian, **Beograd**], city, cap. of Yugoslavia, formerly cap. of Serbia, p. 241,542.
Bell (bĕl), Alexander Graham (1847–1922), Scot.-Am. inv.: telephone.
Belleau Wood (bĕl″ō′), [*Bois de la Brigade de Marine*], in dept. of Aisne, Fr.: bat. 1918.
Belleisle (bĕl″īl′), **Strait of,** bet. Labrador & Newfoundland, 80 m. long, 10–15 m. wide.
Bellini (bĕl-lē′nē), **1,** Venetian painters: Jacopo (1400?–70); Gentile (1427–1507); Giovanni (1426?–1516); **2,** Vincenzo (1802–35), Sicilian comp. [jour., au., & poet.
Belloc (bĕl′ŏk), Hilary (1870–), Eng.
Bellows (bĕl′ōz), George W. (1882–1925), Am. painter. [See **Baluchistan.**
Beluchistan, Beloochistan, dist., W. India.
Benares (bĕn-ä′rĕz), holy city of Hindus, India, on Ganges riv., p. 263,100: univ.
Benavente (bā″nä-vĕn′tā), Jacinto (1866–), Span. playwright: Nobel prize 1922.
Benedict (bĕn′ē-dĭkt), **1,** name of 15 popes, notably: **XIV** Prospero Lambertini (1675–1758); **XV** Giacomo della Chiesa (1854–1922); **2,** Saint (480–543), It. abbot.
Bengal (bĕn-gôl′), prov., India, 76,843 sq. m., p. 46,695,536; cap., Calcutta: **Bay of –,** part of Indian oc. bet. India & E. India.
Benjamin (bĕn′jȧ-mĭn), Judah Philip (1811–84), Am. Law. & stsm.: Confed. leader.
Bennett (bĕn′ĕt), **1,** Arnold (1867–1931), Eng. nov.; **2,** James Gordon (1841–1918), Am. jour.; **3,** Richard Bedford (1870–1947), Can. stsm.
Ben Nevis (nē′vĭs; nĕv′ĭs), highest mt. in Gt. Br., Inverness co., Scot., 4,406 ft.
Benson (bĕn′sŭn), **1,** Arthur Christopher (1862–1925), Eng. poet, au., & educ.; **2,** Edward Frederic (1867–1940); Eng. nov.
Bentham (bĕn′tȧm; bĕn′thȧm), Jeremy (1748–1832), Eng. philos. & jurist.
Beresford (bĕr′ĕs-fẽrd), Charles W. de la Poer, Lord (1846–1919), Br. adm.
Bergerac, de (dē bĕr″zhē-râk′), Cyrano (1619–55), Fr. nov. & dram.
Bergh (bûrg), Henry (1823–88), Am. humanitarian: founder of S. P. C. C. & S. P. C. A.
Bergson (bârg″sôṅ′), Henri Louis (1859–1941), Fr. philos. [Da. navig.
Bering (bē′rĭng; bā′rĭng), Vitus (1680–1741),
Bering Sea (bē′rĭng; bā′rĭng), or **Behring,** bet. Aleutian isls. & Bering str., latter separating Asia and America, 878,000 sq. m.
Berkeley (bûrk′lĭ; bärk′-), Sir William (1610–77), col. gov. of Va.
Berkeley (bûrk′lĭ), city, Calif., p. 113,217: univ.
Berlin (bûr″lĭn′; bĕr-lēn′), city, administrative div., of Prussia & cap. of Ger., on Spree riv., p. 4,024,165: with extensions called *Greater Berlin*; univ. [comp.
Berlioz (bâr″lyōz′), Hector (1803–69), Fr.
Bermejo (bĕr-mā′hō), riv., S. Am., trib. Paraguay riv., 1,000 m.
Bermuda (bẽr-mū′dȧ), Br. isls., W. Atlantic oc., 20 sq. m., p. 30,884; cap. Hamilton.
Bernadotte (bûr″nȧ-dŏt′; bâr″nȧ″dôt′), Jean Baptiste Jules (1764–1844), marshal of Fr.: became king (Charles XIV John) of Sw. & Norway, 1818.
Bernard (bûr′nȧrd; bẽr-närd′; bâr″nȧr′), Saint [*de Clairvaux*] (1091–1153), Fr. priest, mystic, & crusader.
Berne (bĕrn), or **Bern,** city, federal cap. of Switzerland, p. 109,850: univ.
Bernhardt (bĕrn′härt), Sarah (1844–1923), Fr. act. of Fr. & Du. parentage.
Bernini (bĕr-nē′nē), Giovanni Lorenzo (1598–1680), It. sculp. [1,000: bats. 1914–18.
Berry-au-Bac (bâ″rē″-ō″-bȧk′), tn., Fr., p.
Berthelot (bârt′″lō′), Pierre Eugène Marcellin (1827–1907), Fr. chemist.
Bertillon (bâr″tē″yôṅ), Alphonse (1853–1914), Fr. anthropologist: Bertillon system.
Berzelius (bẽr-zē′lĭ-ŭs; bĕr-sā′lē-o͞os), Jöns Jacob, Baron (1779–1848), Sw. chemist.
Besant (bĕs′ănt), **1,** Annie (1847–1933), Eng. theosophist; **2,** (bē-sănt′), Sir Walter (1836–1901), Eng. nov.
Bessarabia (bĕs′ȧ-rā′bĭ-ȧ), div., U.S.S.R., 17,146 sq. m., p. 2,344,800; cap., Kishinev.
Bessemer (bĕs′ē-mẽr), Sir Henry (1813–98), Eng. eng. & inv. [ruins.
Bethel (bĕth′ĕl), anc. tn., Palestine: now in
Bethlehem (bĕth′lē-hĕm), **1,** city, Pa., p. 66,027; **2,** tn., Palestine, 6 m. S. of Jerusalem: birthplace of David & Jesus.
Bethmann-Hollweg, von (fôn bāt′män-hôl′vȧkh), Theobald (1856–1921), Ger. stsm.
Beyrouth (bā″ro͞ot′), spt., Syria, p. 134,655.
Bhutan (bo͞o-tän′), state, bet. Tibet & Br. India, 20,000 sq. m., p. 300,000.
Bienville, de (dē byăṅ″vēl′), Jean Baptiste (1680–1768), col. gov. of La.
Bigelow (bĭg′ē-lō), **1,** John (1817–1911), Am. au. & dipl.; **2,** Poultney (1855–), his son, Am. hist. & trav.
Billings (bĭl′ĭngz), Josh (1818–85), Am. humorist: pseud. of *Henry Wheeler Shaw.*
Binet (bē″nâ′), Alfred (1857–1911), Fr. psychologist: mental tests.
Binghamton (bĭng′ăm-tŭn), city, N. Y., p. 81,132. [159,200.
Birkenhead (bûr′kĕn-hĕd), spt., Eng., p.
Birmingham (bûr′mĭng-ăm; -hăm), **1,** city, Ala., p. 298,720; **2,** bor., Eng., p. 968,600.
Bisayas (bē-sä′yäs). See **Visayan Islands.**
Biscay (bĭs′kā), **Bay of,** part of Atlantic oc., N. of Sp. [p. 18,544.
Bismarck (bĭz′märk), city, cap. of N. Dak.,
Bismarck-Schönhausen, von (fôn bĭs′märk-shön′hou″zĕn), Otto Leopold, Prince (1815–98), Ger. stsm.
Bispham (bĭs′făm; -păm), David Scull (1857–1921), Am. barytone. [Minor.
Bithynia (bĭ-thĭn′ĭ-ȧ), anc. div., N. W. Asia
Bizet (bē″zâ′), Alexandre César Léopold [*Georges*] (1838–75), Fr. comp.: *Carmen.*
Björnsen (byûrn′sŭn), Björnstjerne (1832–1910), Norw. dram. & nov.: Nobel prize 1903. [berg, Ger., 1,900 sq. m.
Black Forest, mt. region, Baden & Württem-
Black Hawk, (1767–1838), Am. Indian chief.
Blackmore (blăk′mōr), Richard Doddridge (1825–1900), Eng. nov.
Black Sea (blăk), sea, S. of Russ., bet. Europe & Asia, 165,000 sq. m.
Blackstone (blăk′stōn), Sir William (1732–80), Eng. jurist & writer on law. [stsm.
Blaine (blān), James Gillespie (1830–93), Am.
Blake (blāk), **1,** Robert (1599–1657), Eng. adm.; **2,** William (757–1827), Eng. engraver & poet.
Blanc, Mont (môṅ blăṅ), highest mt. of Alps, on frontier of Fr. & It., 15,782 ft.
Blarney (blär′nĭ), vil., Ire.: Blarney stone.
Blasco Ibáñez (bläs′kō ē-bän′yāth), Vincente (1867–1928), Span. nov.
Blavatsky (blä-väts′kĭ), Helena Petrovna (1831–91), Russ. theosophist.
Blennerhassett (blĕn″ẽr-hăs′ĕt), Harman (1764?–1831), Eng. conspirator with Aaron Burr in Am. [gen.
Bliss (blĭs), Tasker Howard (1853–1930), Am.
Bloemfontein (blo͞om′fŏn-tān″), city, cap. of Orange Free State, p. 39,034. [p. 34,048.
Bloomington (blo͞om′ĭng-tŭn), city, Ill.,
Blücher, von (fôn blü′kẽr), Gebhard Leberecht (1742–1819), Prussian field marshal at Waterloo. [lachians in Pa., Va., & N. C.
Blue Ridge, easternmost range of Appa-
Boadicea (bō″ȧ-dĭ-sē′ȧ), (?–A. D. 62), Br. queen during Rom. occupation.
Boccaccio (bŏk-kä′chō), Giovanni (1313–75), It. writer of tales: *Decameron.*
Boccherini (bŏk″kā-rē′nē), Luigi (1743–1805), It. comp. & cellist.
Bœotia (bē-ō′shĭ-ȧ), **1,** anc. country, Greece:

cap., Thebes; **2,** with Attica, mod. dept., Greece: see *Attica.*

Boethius (bō-ē′thĭ-ŭs), or **Boetius** (-shĭ-ŭs), Anicius Manlius Torquatus Severinus (475?–524?), Rom. stsm. & philos.

Bogotá (bō″gō-tä′), city, cap. of Colombia, S. Am., p. 166,148.

Bohemia (bō-hē′mĭ-*à*), former crownland, Austria-Hungary; now part of Czechoslovakia, 20,098 sq. m., p. 6,976,909.

Boise (boi′zā), city, cap. of Idaho, p. 34,152.

Boleyn (bo͝ol′ĭn), Anne (1507?–36), 2d wife of Henry VIII of Eng.

Bolingbroke (bŏl′ĭn-bro͝ok; bō′lĭng-), Henry St. John, Viscount (1678–1751), Eng. stsm.

Bolivar (bŏl′ĭ-v*à*r; bō-lē′vär), Simon [*the Liberator*], (1783–1830], S. Am. gen. & stsm.

Bolivia (bō-lĭv′ĭ-*à*; bō-lē′vyä), repub., S. Am., 514,595 sq. m., p. 2,861,212; cap., La Paz.

Bologna (bō-lō′nyä), city, N. It., p. 245,036.

Bolton (bōl′tŭn), tn., Eng., p. 181,200.

Bombay (bŏm-bā′), **1,** prov. India, 111,394 sq. m., p. 32,680,000; **2,** city, cap. of same, p. 1,489,883.

Bonaparte (bō′n*à*-pärt), or **Buonaparte** (bwō″nä″pär′tā), Corsican family: **1, Napoleon I** (1769–1821), emp. of Fr., 1804–14, March–June, 1815; **2,** his brothers: Jerôme (1784–1860), king of Westphalia; Joseph (1768–1844), king of Naples & Sp.; Louis (1778–1846), king of Holland; Lucien (1775–1840), prince of Canino; **3, Napoleon II** Charles Joseph [*L'Aiglon*] (1811–32), his son, duke of Reichstadt; **4, Napoleon III** Charles Louis (1808–73) son of Louis, emp. of Fr., 1852–70.

Bonheur (bô″nûr′), Marie Rosalie [*Rosa*] (1822–99), Fr. painter of animals.

Boniface (bŏn′ĭ-fās), **1,** name of 9 popes, notably **VIII,** Benedict Cajetan, (1228–1303); **2,** Saint [*the Apostle of Germany*] (680?–775).

Bonn (bŏn), city, Prussia; occupied by Br. 1945; cap. W. Ger. 1949; p. 90,249; univ.

Boone (bo͞on), Daniel (1735–1820), Am. pioneer in Ky.

Booth (bo͞oth), **1,** Ballington (1857–1940), Eng.-Am. clergy.: founder of Volunteers of Am.; **2,** Edwin Thomas (1833–93), Am. act.; **3,** John Wilkes (1839–65), Am. act., assassin of Abraham Lincoln; **4,** William [*General*] (1829–1912), Eng. clergy.: founder of Salvation Army; **5,** Evangeline Cory (1866–1950), comm., Salvation Army, 1934.

Borah (bō′r*à*), Wm. E. (1865–1940), Am. stsm.

Borchgrevink (bôrkh′grĕ-vĭngk), Carsten E. (1864–1934), Norw. antarctic expl.

Bordeaux (bôr″dō′), spt. city, Fr., p. 256,026.

Borghese (bŏr-gā′sā), noted It. family in repub. of Siena & in Rome.

Borgia (bôr′jä), powerful It. family: **1,** Cesare (1476–1507), son of pope Alexander VI, cardinal & sol.; **2,** Lucrezia (1480–1519), his sister.

Borglum (bŏr′glŭm), Gutzon (1867–1941), Am. sculp. [garia, 1918–43.

Boris III (bō′rĭs), (1894–1943), king of Bul-

Borneo (bôr′nē-ō), isl., E. Indies: **British** or **N. –,** 31,106 sq. m., p. 257,804; **Dutch-,** S. part of isl., 206,810 sq. m., p. 1,822,426.

Borodin (b*à*″rä-dĭn′), Alexander (1834–87), Russ. comp. [Eng. au. & gypsy scholar.

Borrow (bŏr′ō), George Henry (1803–81),

Bosnia (bŏz′nĭ-*à*), country, S. E. Europe; included, with Herzegovina, in Yugoslavia, 1918; 19,768 sq. m., p. 1,889,929; cap., Sarajevo, p. 64,500.

Bosporus (bŏs′pō-rŭs), str., bet. Black & Marmora seas, 18 m. long. [p. 790,863: univ.

Boston (bŏs′tŭn), spt. city, cap. of Mass.,

Boswell (bŏz′wĕl), James (1740–95), Scot. law.: biographer of Samuel Johnson.

Botha (bō′tä), Louis (1863–1919), Boer gen. & stsm. [bet. Russ. & Sw., 450 m. long.

Bothnia (bŏth′nĭ-*à*), **Gulf of,** N. Baltic sea.

Bothwell (bŏ*th*′wĕl), James Hepburn, Earl of (1536?–78), husband of Mary Stuart.

Botticelli (bŏt″tē-chĕl′lē), Sandro (1447?–1510), It. art. [Ir.-Am. dram. & act.

Boucicault (bo͞o′sē-kō″), Dion (1820–90),

Bougainville, de (dē bo͞o″găṅ″vēl′), Louis Antoine (1729–1811), Fr. navig.

Boulogne (bo͞o″lôny″; bo͞o-lōn′), or **Boulogne-sur-Mer** (bo͞o″lôny″-sür-mâr′), spt. city, N. W., Fr., p. 53,336.

Boulogne (bo͞o″lôny″; bo͞o-lōn′), or **Boulogne-sur-Seine** (bo͞o″lôny″-sür-sân′), tn., suburb of Paris, Fr., p. 75,559.

Bourget (bo͞or″zhâ′), Paul (1852–1935), Fr. poet., nov., & essay. [neer & sol.

Bowie (bō′ĭ), James (1796–1836), Am. pio-

Boyle (boil), Robert (1627–91), Eng. physicist & chemist.

Braddock (brăd′ŭk), Edward (1695–1755), Br. gen. in Am. [2d gov. of Plymouth col.

Bradford (brăd′fẽrd), William (1589–1657),

Bradford (brăd′fẽrd), city, Eng., p. 285,979.

Bradstreet (brăd′strēt), Simon (1603–97), col. gov. of Mass.

Brady (brā′dĭ), Cyrus Townsend (1861–1920), Am. au. & clergy. [astron.

Brahe (brä; brä′ē), Tycho (1546–1601), Da.

Brahmaputra (brä″m*à*-po͞o′tr*à*), riv. W. Tibet & India, 1,800 m. to Bay of Bengal.

Brahms (bräms), Johannes (1833–97), Ger. comp. [system of printing for the blind.

Braille (brāy″), Louis (1806–52), Fr. educ.:

Brandeis (brăn′dĭs), Louis Dembitz (1856–1941), Am. jurist.

Brandenburg (brăn′dĕn-bo͝orkh), prov., cen. Prussia, 15,072 sq. m., p. 2,592,430; cap., Berlin. [au. & literary critic.

Brandes (brăn′dĕs), Georg (1842–1927), Da.

Brandywine (brăn′dĭ-wīn″), creek, Pa. & Del., 45 m. long: bat. Sept. 11, 1777.

Brangwyn (brăng′wĭn), Frank (1867–); Eng. painter & etcher. [p. 36,555.

Brantford (brănt′fẽrd), city, Ontario, Can.,

Branting (brăn′tĭng), Hjalmar (1860–1925), Sw. stsm.: Nobel prize 1921.

Bratislava (brä′tĭ-slä″vȧ), [Hung. **Pozsony** (pô′zhôny′); Ger. **Pressburg**], city, cap. of Slovakia, p. 93,189.

Brazil (br*à*-zĭl′), **United States of,** repub., S. Am., 3,276,358 sq. m., p. 39,103,856; cap., Rio de Janeiro.

Brazos (brä′zōs), riv., Tex., 900 m. to Gulf of Mex.

Bremen (brā′mĕn; brĕm′ĕn), **1,** administrative div., Ger.; **2,** city, its cap., p. 294,966.

Breslau (brĕs′lou), city, Prussia, p. 599,770; univ.: cathedral. [in World Wars I & II.

Brest (brĕst), spt., Fr., p. 67,861: nav. base

Brest-Litovsk (brĕst′-lyĕ-tôfsk′), former cap. of Grodno, Russ., incorporated in Poland 1921, p. 29,100. [N. W. Fr.

Bretagne (brĕ-tȧny″), [Eng. **Brittany**], pen.,

Brewster (bro͞o′stẽr), William (1560?–1644), a Pilgrim Father. [stsm.

Briand (brē″äṅ′), Aristide (1862–1932), Fr.

Bridgeport (brĭj′pōrt), city, Conn., p. 159,352.

Bridges (brĭj′ĭz), Robert (1844–1930), Eng. poet laureate.

Brieux (brē″ö′), Eugène (1858–1932), Fr. dram.

Bright (brīt), John (1811–89), Eng. stsm.

Brighton (brī′tŭn), bor., S. Eng., p. 148,800.

Brindisi (brēn′dē-zē), [anc. **Brundusium** or **Brundisium**], tn., S. It., p. 41,393.

Brisbane (brĭz′băn), spt. city, cap. of Queensland, Australia, p. 308,580.

Bristol (brĭs′tŭl), city, Eng., p. 390,400; univ.: **– Channel,** inlet of Atlantic oc., bet. Wales & S. W. Eng., 80 m. long.

British Columbia (kō-lŭm′bĭ-*à*), maritime prov., Can., on Pacific oc., 366,255 sq. m., p. 1,153,059; cap., Victoria.

British Empire, now **Br. Commonwealth of Nations,** Gt. Br. & Northern Ire., Chan-

go; join; yet; sing; chin; show; thin, *th*en; hw, *why*; zh, azure; ü, Ger. für, Fr. l*u*ne; ö, Ger. schön, Fr. f*eu*; ṅ, Fr. *en*fant, no*m*; kh, Ger. a*ch* or i*ch*. See pages viii–x.

nel isls. & Isle of Man, Canada, India, Pakistan, Ceylon, Australia, New Zealand, Union of S. Afr.; cols.; 13,022,758 sq. m., p. 597,600,479; cap., London, Eng.
British Honduras. See **Honduras.**
Brittany (brĭt'*ȧ*-nĭ). See **Bretagne.**
Brockton (brŏk'tŭn), city, Mass., p. 62,856.
Brontë (brŏn'tē), **1,** Charlotte (1816–55), Eng. au.: pseud., *Currer Bell:* **2,** Emily (1818–48), Eng. au.: pseud., *Ellis Bell.*
Bronx (brŏngks), bor., New York City, p. 1,444,903. [poet.|
Brooke (brŏŏk), Rupert (1887–1915), Eng.|
Brookline (brŏŏk'lĭn), tn., Mass., p. 56,952.
Brooklyn (brŏŏk'lĭn), bor., New York City, p. 2,716,347. [clergy. & bp.|
Brooks (brŏŏks), Phillips (1835–93), Am.|
Brown (broun), John (1800–59), Am. abolitionist.
Browning (broun'ĭng), **1,** Elizabeth Barrett (1806–61), Eng. poet; **2,** Robert (1812–89), Eng. poet. [king of Scot., 1306–29.|
Bruce, de (dē brōōs'), Robert (1274–1329),|
Bruges (brüzh), city, Belgium, p. 51,686.
Brummell (brŭm'ĕl), George Bryan [*Beau Brummel*] (1778–1840), Eng. fop. [**disi.**|
Brundusium (brŭn-dū'zhĭ-ŭm). See **Brin-**|
Brunelleschi (brōō″nĕl-lĕs'kē), Filippo (1377–1446), Florentine arch.
Brünn (brün), [Bohemian **Brno** (bûr'nō)], tn., Moravia, Ger., p. 221,758.
Brunswick (brŭnz'wĭk), [Ger. **Braunschweig** (broun'shvīkh)], **1,** administrative div., Ger., 1,424 sq. m., p. 501,875; **2,** city, its cap., p. 146,725.
Brusa (brōō'sä). See **Bursa.**
Brussels (brŭs'ĕlz), city, cap. of Belgium, p., with suburbs, 815,098: univ.
Brutus (brōō'tŭs), Marcus Junius (85–42 B. C.), Rom. pol.: an assassin of Cæsar.
Bryan (brī'ăn), William Jennings (1860–1925), Am. pol. & lecturer.
Bryant (brī'ănt), William Cullen (1794–1878), Am. poet. [Br. stsm., dipl., & au.|
Bryce (brīs), James, Viscount (1838–1922),|
Buchanan (bŭ-kăn'ăn), James (1791–1868), 15th pres. of U. S. [mania, p. 345,628.|
Bucharest (bōō″k*ȧ*-rĕst'), city, cap. of Ru-|
Buckingham (bŭk'ĭng-ăm), **1,** George Villiers, Duke of (1592–1628), Eng. lord high adm.; **2,** George Villiers, Duke of (1628–87), his son, Eng. courtier.
Budapest (bōō'dȧ-pĕst″), city, cap. of Hungary, p. 1,217,325; univ.
Buddha (bŏŏd'*ȧ*), Gautama, Indian mystic: founder of Buddhism in 5th cent. B. C.
Buenos Aires (bō'nŭs ā'rēz; bwā″nōs ī'rās), city, cap. of Argentina, p. 2,030,765.
Buffalo (bŭf'*ȧ*-lō), city, N. Y., p. 577,393.
Buffon, de (dē bü″fôn'), Georges Louis Leclerc, Count (1707–88), Fr. natur.
Bug (bŏŏg), **1,** riv., Ukraine, 500 m. to Black sea; **2,** riv., cen. Poland, 450 m. to Vistula riv.
Bukhara (bōō-khä'rä), or **Bokhara, 1,** dist., W. Cen. Asia, joined with Khiva to form Uzbek soviet socialist repub.; **2,** city, its cap., p. 75,000.
Bukowina (bōō″kō-vē'nä), dist., Rumania, 4,030 sq. m., p. 811,721; cap., Cernauti.
Bulgaria (bŏŏl-gā'rĭ-*ȧ*; bŭl-), kingdom, Balkans, 40,667 sq. m., p. 5,483,125; cap., Sofia.
Bullard (bŏŏl'ărd), Robert Lee (1861–1947), Am. sol.: comm. 2d army in Fr. 1918–19.
Bull Run, stream in N. E. Va.: bats, 1861–62.
Bülow, von (fôn bü'lō), Bernard, Prince (1849–1921), Ger. stsm.: chancellor, 1900–09.
Bulwer-Lytton (bŏŏl'wēr-lĭt'ŭn), **1,** Edward G. E., Baron Lytton (1803–73), Eng. nov.; **2,** Edward Robert, Earl of Lytton (1831–91), Eng. poet.: pseud., *Owen Meredith.*
Bunker Hill (bŭngk'ēr), mod. name of Breed's Hill, Charlestown, Mass.: bat. of Bunker Hill, June 17, 1775.

Bunsen (bŏŏn'sĕn), Robert W. (1811–99), Ger. chemist. [*Pilgrim's Progress.*|
Bunyan (bŭn'yăn), John (1628–88), Eng. au.:|
Burbank (bûr'băngk), Luther (1849–1926), Am. horticulturist. (Am. humorist.|
Burgess (bûr'jĕs), Frank Gelett (1866–1951),|
Burgoyne (bûr-goin'), John (1722–92), Eng. gen. in Am. Rev.
Burgundy (bûr'gŭn-dĭ), former kingdom, duchy, & later prov. of Fr.
Burke (bûrk), Edmund (1729–97), Br. stsm.
Burma (bûr'm*ȧ*), Republic on Bay of Bengal, 262,732 sq. m., p. 16,823,798; cap., Rangoon.
Burne-Jones (bûrn'-jōnz'), Sir Edward (1833–98), Br. painter.
Burnett (bûr'nĕt), Frances Hodgson (1849–1924), Anglo-Am. nov.
Burns (bûrnz), **1,** John (1858–1943), Eng. labor leader; **2,** Robert (1759–96), Scot. poet.
Burr (bûr), Aaron (1756–1836), Am. pol.
Burroughs (bŭr'ōz), John (1837–1921), Am. natur. [Turkey, p. 61,450.|
Bursa (bŏŏr'sä), or **Brusa** (brōō'sä), city,|
Busrah (bŭs'rä). See **Basra.**
Butler (bŭt'lēr), **1,** Benjamin Franklin (1818–93), Am. gen. & pol.; **2,** Nicholas Murray (1862–1947), Am. educ.; **3,** Samuel (1612–80), Eng. satirist; **4,** Samuel (1835–1902), Eng. satirist.
Butte (būt), city, Mont., p. 32,904.
Buzzard's Bay (bŭz'ărdz), inlet of Atlantic oc., on S. coast of Mass., 30 m. long.
Byng (bĭng), Julian H. G., Viscount Byng of Vimy (1862–1935), Br. gen.: gov.-gen. of Can., 1921–26.
Byrd (bûrd), Richard Evelyn (1888–), Am. nav. aviator: first flight over N. Pole, May 9, 1926; antarctic expeditions, 1928–30, 1933–35, 1939–40, 1947. [1824), Eng. poet.|
Byron (bī'rŭn), George Gordon, Lord (1788–|
Byzantium (bĭ-zăn'shĭ-ŭm), anc. city; founded 658 B. C. on site of Istanbul (Constantinople).

C

Cabell (kăb'ĕl), James Branch (1879–), Am. nov. & essay.
Cable (kā'bl), George W. (1844–1925), Am. nov.
Cabot (kăb'ŭt), **1,** John (1450–98), It. navig.; **2,** Sebastian (1472?–1557), Eng. navig. [78,731.|
Cádiz (kā'dĭz; kä'*th*ēth), spt. city, S. Sp., p.|
Cadorna (kä-dôr'nä), Luigi, Count (1850–1928), It. gen. in World War 1915–17.
Cædmon (kăd'mŭn), A.-S. poet of 7th cent.
Cæsar (sē'z*ȧ*r), Caius Julius (100–44 B. C.), Rom. gen., stsm., & hist.
Cæsarea (sĕs″*ȧ*-rē'*ȧ*; sĕz'-), anc. tn., Palestine, N. W. of Jerusalem. [Fr. stsm.|
Caillaux (kȧ″yō'), Joseph M. (1863–),|
Caine (kān), Sir Thomas Hall (1853–1931), Eng. nov.: pseud., *Hall Caine.*
Cairo (kī'rō), city, cap. of Egypt, p. 1,064,567.
Calabria (k*ȧ*-lā'brĭ-*ȧ*; kä-lä-brē-ä), pen. & dept., S. It., 5,819 sq. m., p. 1,691,259.
Calais (kăl'ā; kȧ″lā'), spt. tn., Fr., on Str. of Dover, p. 71,629.
Calcutta (kăl-kŭt'*ȧ*), city, W. Bengal prov., India, p. 2,108,891: univ.
Caledonia (kăl″ē-dō'nĭ-*ȧ*). See **Scotland.**
Calgary (kăl'g*ȧ*-rĭ), city, Alberta, Can., p. 126,631. [Am. stsm. & or.|
Calhoun (kăl-hōōn'), John C. (1782–1850),|
California (kăl″ĭ-fôr'nĭ-*ȧ*), State in U. S., 158,297 sq. m., p. 10,490,070; cap., Sacramento: **Gulf of –,** arm of Pacific oc., W. coast of N. Am. in Mex., 700 m. long: **Lower –,** ter., Mex., 58,343 sq. m., p. 62,831; prin. city, La Paz.
Caligula (k*ȧ*-lĭg'ū-l*ȧ*), Caius Cæsar Augustus [*Germanicus*] (A. D. 12–41), emp. of Rome.
Calixtus (k*ȧ*-lĭks'tŭs), name of 3 popes.
Callao (käl-yä'ō), spt. tn., Peru, p. 52,843.

Calles (käl′yās), Plutarco Elias (1877–1945), pres. of Mex., 1924–28.
Calvé (kȧl″vā′), Emma (1866–1942), Fr. sop.
Calvert (kăl′vẽrt), **1,** George, Lord Baltimore (1580?–1632), Br. stsm.; **2,** Leonard (1606?–47), his son, 1st gov. of Md.
Calvin (kăl′vĭn), John (1509–64), Fr.-Swiss reformer & theolog. [Greece.
Calydon (kăl′ĭ-dŏn), anc. city, Ætolia,
Cambodia (kăm-bō′dĭ-ȧ), kingdom, indep. state in Fr. Union, Indochina, 67,550 sq. m., p. 3,227,000; cap., Pnompenh., p. 128,950.
Cambrai (käṅ″brâ′), city, Fr., on Scheldt riv., p. 26,047: bats. 1917–18.
Cambridge (kām′brĭj), **1,** city, opposite Boston, Mass., on Charles riv., p. 120,676: univ.; **2,** tn., Eng., p. 60,860: univ.
Cambyses (kăm-bī′sēz), (?–522 B. C.), king of Medes & Persians.
Camden (kăm′dĕn), city, N. J., p. 125,546.
Cameroons (kăm″ẽr-o͞onz′), or **Kamerun,** mandated ter., W. Afr.: **English –,** 33,750 sq. m., p. 700,050; cap., Buëa: **French –,** 267,000 sq. m., p. 1,878,683; cap., Yaoundé.
Camoëns, de (dā kăm′ō-ĕns) Luis (1524–80), Port. poet.
Camp (kămp), Walter (1859–1925), Am. football coach & physical-culture advocate.
Campania (kăm-pā′nĭ-ȧ; käm-pä′nyä), anc. div., S. cen. It.
Campeche (käm-pā′chā), **1,** state, Mex., 18,089 sq. m., p. 76,419; **2,** city, its cap.
Canada (kăn′ȧ-dȧ), **Dominion of,** country, N. Am., member of Br. empire; 3,843,144 sq. m., p. 13,893,208; cap., Ottawa.
Canal Zone (kȧ-năl′), ter. surrounding Panama Canal, owned by U. S.; 47 m. long, 10 m. wide, p. 51,827; cap., Balboa Heights.
Canary Islands (kȧ-nā′rĭ), Span. isls., in Atlantic oc. near Afr., 2,810 sq. m., p. 543,018.
Canberra (kăn′bẽr-ȧ), city in federal ter. (912 sq. m.), cap. of Australia since 1927.
Canea (kä-nē′ä), city, cap. of Crete, p. 26,604.
Canfield (kăn′fēld), Dorothy (1879–), Am. au.: pseud. of *Dorothea Frances Canfield Fisher* (*Mrs. John Redwood Fisher*).
Cannon (kăn′ŭn), Joseph G. [*Uncle Joe*] (1836–1926), Am. pol.
Cano (kä′nō), Alonso [*the Spanish Michelangelo*] (1601–67), Span. arch., painter, & sculp.
Canova (kä-nō′vä), Antonio (1757–1822), It. sculp. [Eng., p. 22,680.
Canterbury (kăn′tẽr-bẽr-ĭ), cathedral city,
Cantigny (käṅ″tē′nyē), vil., N. E. Fr.: 1st Am. bat. in World War I, May 28, 1918.
Canton (kăn′tŏn), **1,** city, Ohio, p. 116,312; **2,** (kăn-tŏn′), city, cap. of Kwantung prov., S. China, p. 811,800.
Canute (kȧ-nūt′), or **Cnut, Knut** (k′no͞ot), (995–1035), king of Eng. & Denmark.
Cape Breton (brĭt′ŭn), isl., Nova Scotia, Can., 3,120 sq. m., p. 119,844.
Cape Cod, pen., Mass., 65 m. long.
Cape Colony. See **Cape of Good Hope** (**2**).
Cape Hatteras (hăt′ẽr-ȧs), pt., on isl. outside Pamlico sound, off coast of N. C.
Cape Horn, S. pt. of Chile, S. Am.
Cape May, S. end of N. J., 5 m. long.
Cape of Good Hope, 1, cape, S. end of Afr.; **2,** prov. [formerly **Cape Colony**], Union of S. Afr.; cap., Cape Town.
Cape St. Vincent (vĭn′sĕnt), S. W. pt. of Port.
Cape Town, city, Union of S. Afr., p. 212,997.
Cape Verde (vûrd), extreme W. pt. of Afr.: **– Islands,** Port. col. in Atlantic oc., W. of Afr., 1,480 sq. m., p. 131,147; cap., Praia.
Cappadocia (kăp″ȧ-dō′shĭ-ȧ), anc. div. & Rom. prov., E. Asia Minor.
Capri (kä′prē), It. isl., Bay of Naples.
Caracalla (kăr″ȧ-kăl′ȧ), (188–217), Rom. emp.
Caracas (kä-rä′käs), city, cap. of Venezuela, p. 135,253. [225,600.
Cardiff (kär′dĭf), spt. tn., cap. of Wales, p.
Carducci (kär-do͞ot′chē), Giosuè (1836–1907), It. poet: Nobel prize 1906.
Caribbean Sea (kăr″ĭ-bē′ăn), arm of Atlantic oc., bet. Cen. & S. Am. & W. Indies.
Carleton (kärl′tŭn), Sir Guy, Baron Dorchester (1724–1808), Br. gen. in N. Am.
Carlisle (kär-līl′; kär′līl), city, Eng., p. 52,710.
Carlyle (kär-līl′), Thomas (1795–1881), Scot. essay. & hist. [1929), Can. poet.
Carman (kär′măn), (William) Bliss (1861–
Carmel (kär′mĕl), mt., N. W. Palestine.
Carmen Sylva. See **Elizabeth** (**2**).
Carnegie (kär-nĕg′ĭ), Andrew (1835–1919), Scot.-Am. ironmaster & philan.
Carol II (kăr′ŭl), (1893–), king of Rumania, 1930–1940.
Caroline Islands (kăr′ō-līn), N. Pacific isls., bet. P. I. & Marshall isls.
Carpathians (kär-pā′thĭ-ănz), mts., N. E. Slovakia & Poland.
Carracci (kär-rät′chē), It. painters: Agostino (1557–1602); Annibale (1560–1609); Ludovico (1555–1619).
Carranza (kär-rän′sä), Venustiano (1859–1920), pres. of Mex., 1917–20.
Carrara (kär-rä′rä), city, N. It., p. 23,951.
Carrel (kȧ″rĕl′), Alexis (1873–1944), Fr.-Am. phys. & biol.: Nobel prize 1912.
Carroll (kăr′ŭl), Lewis: pseud, of *Charles Lutwidge Dodgson*: *Alice in Wonderland*.
Carson (kär′sŭn), **1,** Christopher [*Kit Carson*] (1809–68), Am. frontiersman; **2,** Sir Edward Henry, Baron (1854–1935), Anglo-Ir. stsm.
Carson City (kär′sŭn), cap. of Nev., p. 3,069.
Cartagena (kär″tȧ-jē′nȧ), spt. tn. & nav. station, Murcia prov., Sp., p. 96,981.
Carthage (kär′thāj), anc. region & city, N. Afr.
Cartwright (kärt′rīt), Edmund (1743–1823), Eng. inv. of power loom. [tenor.
Caruso (kä-ro͞o′zō), Enrico (1873–1921), It.
Carver (kär′vẽr), John (1575?–1621), 1st gov. of Plymouth col.
Cary (kâ′rē), name of 2 Am. poets: Alice (1820–71); Phoebe (1824–71).
Casabianca (kä″zä-byäng′kä), Louis (1755?–98), Fr. nav. off.: father of Giacomo Jocante, hero of Mrs. Heman's poem "Casabianca."
Cascade Range (kăs-kād′), mts., N. Am., near Pacific coast, fr. N. Calif. to Br. Columbia: Mt. Rainier, 14,408 ft.
Caspian Sea (kăs′pĭ-ăn), bet. Europe & Asia, 760 m. long, 115–280 m. wide.
Cassius Longinus (kăsh′ĭ-ŭs lŏn-jī′nŭs), Caius [*Cassius*] (?–42 B. C.), Rom. stsm.: an assassin of Julius Cæsar.
Castile (kăs-tēl′), former kingdom, cen. Sp.
Castro (käs′trō), Cipriano (1860–1924), Venezuelan insurgent: pres., 1900–09.
Catania (kä-tä′nyä), city, E. coast Sicily, p. 289,644: cathedral; univ.
Cathay (kȧ-thā′), an old name for China.
Cather (kăth′ẽr), Willa Sibert (1876–1947), Am. nov.
Catherine (kăth′ẽr-ĭn), **1, I** (1684?–1727), emp. of Russ.; **2, II** [*the Great*] (1729–96), emp. of Russ.; **3, of Aragon** (1485–1536), queen of Eng., 1st wife of Henry VIII; **4, de' Medici** (1519–89), queen of Fr.
Catiline (kăt′ĭ-līn), Lucius Sergius (108–62 B. C.), Rom. conspirator.
Cato (kā′tō), **1,** Marcus Porcius [*the Elder*] (234–149 B. C.), Rom. stsm.; **2,** Marcus Porcius [*the Younger*] (95–46 B. C.), Rom. sol. & stsm. [N. Y.: Slide Mt., 4,205 ft.
Catskill Mountains (kăts′kĭl), mts., E. cen.
Catt (kăt), Carrie Chapman (1859–1947), Am. suffragist leader.
Catullus (kȧ-tŭl′ŭs), (87–54 B. C.), Rom. poet.
Caucasus (kô′kȧ-sŭs), mt. group, S. E. Europe, bet. Black & Caspian seas: 18,000 ft.
Cavell (kăv′ĕl), Edith (1865–1915), Eng. nurse: executed by Gers. in Belgium.

Cavour, di (dē kȧ″vo͞or′), Camillo Benso, Count (1810–61), It. stsm.
Cawnpore (kôn″pōr′), city, India, on Ganges riv., p. 216,436.
Caxton (kăks′tŭn), William (1422?–91), [1st Eng. printer.
Cebu (sā-bo͞o′), isl., P. I., 1,695 sq. m.
Cedar Rapids (sē′dẽr), city, Iowa, p. 72,149.
Celebes (sĕl′ē-bēz), isl., Indonesia 76,260 sq. m., p. 2,347,645.
Cellini (chĕl-lē′nē), Benvenuto (1500–71), [It. sculp. & engraver.
Central America. See **America.**
Cernauti (chẽr-nou′tsĭ), [formerly **Czernowitz**], city, cap. of Bukowina, Rumania, p. 87,128: univ.
Cervantes (sẽr-văn′tēz; thĕr-vän′tās) **Saavedra, de** (sä″ä-vā′drä dā), Miguel (1547–1616), Span. writer: "Don Quixote."
Cévennes (sā″vĕn′), mt. range, S. E. Fr.
Ceylon (sē-lŏn′), Br. isl., Indian oc., 60 m. S. E. of India, 25,332 sq. m., p. 4,504,549.
Cézanne (sā″zȧn′), Paul (1839–1906), Fr. painter.
Chæronea (kĕr″ō-nē′ȧ), anc. city, Bœotia, Greece.
Chagres (chä′grĕs), riv., Panama: dammed [to form Gatun Lake.
Chaliapin (shä″lyä′pĭn), Feodor (1873–1938), Russ. basso.
Châlons-sur-Marne (shä″lôn′-sür-mȧrn′), city, Fr., p. 31,367: bats. 1914–18.
Chamberlain (chăm′bẽr-lĭn), **1,** Joseph (1836–1914), Br. stsm.; **2,** Joseph Austen (1863–1937), his son, Br. stsm.; **3,** Arthur Neville (1869–1940), Br. stsm.
Chaminade (shȧ″mē″nȧd′), Cécile (1861–[1944), Fr. comp.
Champagne (shăm-pān′; shäṅ″pȧny″), anc. prov., Fr., now comprising depts. of Aube, Haute-Marne, Marne, & Ardennes.
Champlain (shăm-plān′), lake, U. S., bet. Vt. & N. Y., 110 m. long: nav. bat. 1814.
Champlain, de (shăm″plān′; dē shäṅ″plâṅ′), Samuel (1567–1635), Fr. expl.
Chancellorsville (chȧn′sĕl-ẽrz″vĭl), tn., Va.: [bat. 1863.
Changchowfu (chäng′chō″fo͞o′), city, Fukien prov., China, p. about 900,000.
Changsha (chäng′shä′), city, cap. of Hunan prov., China, p. 535,800.
Channel Islands (chăn′ĕl), Br. isls. in Eng. Channel, 75 sq. m., p. 90,230.
Chantilly (shäṅ″tē″yē′), tn., Fr.: bats. [1914–18.
Chapman (chăp′măn), George (1559–1634), Eng. poet, dram., & translator of Homer.
Chardin (shȧr″dâṅ′), Jean Simeon (1699–1779), Fr. genre painter.
Charlemagne (shär′lē-mān), [*Charles the Great*] (742–814), emp. of the West fr. 800, & king of the Franks fr. 768.
Charles (chärlz), **1,** name of 10 kings of Fr.; **2,** name of 2 kings of Gt. Br. & Ire.: **I** (1600–49); **II** (1630–85); also, **3, – Edward Stuart** [*the Pretender*] (1720–88); **4, V** (1500–58), Holy Rom. emp. & king of Sp. as Charles I; **5, I** (1863–1908), king of Port.; **6, I** (1839–1914), king of Rumania; **7,** name of 15 kings of Sw., notably: **XII** (1682–1718); **XIII** (1748–1818); **XIV John** [*Bernadotte*] (1764–1844); **8, I** (1887–1922), last emp. of Austria-Hungary, 1916–18: abdicated.
Charleston (chärlz′tŭn), **1,** spt. city, S. C., p. 68,243; **2,** city, cap. of W. Va., p. 72,818.
Charlestown (chärlz′toun), city, Mass., now part of Boston: bat. of Bunker Hill 1775.
Charlotte (shär′lŏt), city, N. C., p. 133,219.
Chartres (shȧrtr′), tn., N. Fr.: cathedral.
Chateaubriand, de (dē shȧ″tō″brē″äṅ′), François Auguste, Vicomte (1768–1848), Fr. au. & pol.
Château-Thierry (shȧ″tō′-tyâ″rē′), tn., Fr., on Marne riv.: bats. 1914–18.
Chattanooga (chăt″ȧ-no͞o′gȧ), city, Tenn., p. 130,333: bat. 1863; univ.
Chatterton (chăt′ẽr-tŭn), Thomas (1752–70), [Eng. boy poet.
Chaucer (chô′sẽr), Geoffrey [*Father of Eng. poetry*] (1340?–1400), Eng. poet.

Chautauqua (shȧ-tô-kwȧ), lake, N. Y.: Chautauqua institution near.
Chekiang (chû″kyăng′), prov., China, 36,670 sq. m., p. 22,043,300; cap., Hangchow.
Chelsea (chĕl′sē), **1,** city, Mass., p. 39,038; **2,** bor., London, Eng., p. 63,700.
Cheltenham (chĕlt′năm), city, Gloucestershire, Eng., p. 49,580: coll.
Chemnitz (kĕm′nĭts), city, Ger., p. 331,-[655.
Chengtu (chŭng″to͞o′), city, cap. of Szechwan prov., China, p. 400,000.
Cheops (kē′ŏps), (about 3700 B. C.), Egyptian king, builder of the great pyramid.
Cherbourg (shâr″bo͞or′), spt., Fr., p. 32,030.
Chersonese (kûr′sō-nēz; -nēs), or **Chersonesus** (-ne′sŭs), **The,** pen., anc. Greece.
Cherubini (kā″ro͞o-bē′nē), Maria Luigi (1760–1842), It. comp.
Chesapeake Bay (chĕs′ȧ-pēk), in Md. & Va., 200 m. long, 12–40 m. wide.
Chester (chĕs′tẽr), **1,** city, Pa., on Del. riv., p. 65,824; **2,** city, Eng., p. 42,030.
Chesterfield (chĕs′tẽr-fēld), Philip Dormer Stanhope, Earl of (1694–1773), Eng. stsm. & au.
Chesterton (chĕs′tẽr-tŭn), Gilbert Keith (1874–1936), Eng. au.
Cheyenne (shī-ĕn′), city, cap. of Wyo., p. [31,807.
Chiang Kai-shek (jē-äng′kī′shĕk′), Chin. gen., stsm. Pres. National govt., Oct. 1943.
Chiapas (chē-ä′päs), state, Mex., 27,527 sq. m., p. 421,744.
Chicago (shĭ-kô′gō), city, Ill., on Lake Michigan, p. 3,606,436: univ.
Chickamauga (chĭk-ȧ-mô′gȧ), trib. of Tenn. riv.: bat. 1863.
Chihli (chē′lē″), [formerly **Pechili** (pā′chē-lē″)], prov., China, 115,800 sq. m., p. 34,-186,711; caps., Tientsin & Paotingfu.
Chihuahua (chē-wä′wä″), **1,** state, Mex., 90,036 sq. m., p. 401,622; **2,** city, its cap., p. 37,078.
Chile (chē′lā), or **Chili** (chĭl′ĭ), repub., S. W. S. Am., 289,798 sq. m., p. 3,753,799; cap., Santiago.
China (chī′nȧ), **1,** div. Chinese Repub., 1,534,420 sq. m., p. 302,113,000; **2,** [**Chinese Republic**], repub., E. Asia, 4,279,170 sq. m., p. 439,759,380; cap. Nanking.
Chios (kī′ŏs), isl., off W. coast Asia Minor, in Ægean sea, 318 sq. m., p. 65,000.
Chippendale (chĭp′ĕn-dāl), Thomas, (?–1779), Eng. cabinetmaker.
Choate (chōt), Joseph Hodges (1832–1917), Am. law. & dipl.
Chopin (shô″pâṅ), Frédéric François (1809–[49), Pol. pianist & comp.
Chosen (chō′sĕn″), [now **Korea**], pen., E. Asia, 85,223 sq. m., p. 19,103,900; cap., Seoul: in Jap. empire 1910–46.
Christchurch (krīst′chûrch), city, N. Zealand, p. 123,370.
Christian (krĭs′chăn), name of 10 Da. kings, notably: **II** (1481–1599), king of Denmark, Norway, & Sw.; **IV** (1577–1648), king of Denmark & Norway; **IX** (1818–1906), king of Denmark; **X** (1870–1947), king of Denmark.
Christiana (krĭs-tĭ-ä′nē-ä), former name of [cap. of Norway. See **Oslo.**
Chrysostom (krĭs′ŏs-tŭm), John, Saint (347?–407), Gk. father of the church.
Chungking (cho͝ong″kĭng′), city, Szechwan prov., China, p. 623,300.
Churchill (chûrch′ĭl), **1,** Winston (1871–1947), Am. au.; **2,** Winston Leonard Spencer (1874–), Br. stsm.
Cicero (sĭs′ẽr-ō), Marcus Tullius (106–43 B. C.), [Rom. stsm., or., & philos.
Cicero (sĭs′ẽr-ō), tn., Ill., p. 67,195.
Cienfuegos (syĕn-fwā′gōs), spt., Cuba, p. [73,480.
Cilicia (sĭ-lĭsh′ĭ-ȧ), anc. country, S. E. Asia Minor.
Cimon (sī′mŏn), (510?–449 B. C.), Athenian gen. & stsm.
Cincinnati (sĭn″sĭ-năt′ĭ), city, Ohio, on Ohio, [riv., p. 500,510: univ.

Cincinnatus (sĭn″sĭ-nā′tŭs), Lucius Quintius (519?–439? B. C.), dictator of Rome.
Circassia (sẽr-kăsh′ĭ-*ȧ*), undefined region, S. Russ., E. of Black sea.
Ciudad Trujillo (syōō-*thäth′* trōō-hē′lyō), [formerly **Santo Domingo**], city, cap. of Dominican Republic, p. 71,297.
Clark (klärk), **1,** Champ (1850–1921), Am. pol.; **2,** George Rogers (1752–1818), Am. sol. & frontiersman; **3,** William (1770–1838), Am. sol. & expl.
Claudius (klô′dĭ-ŭs), Tiberius C. Drusus Nero Germanicus (10 B. C.–A. D. 54), Rom. emp.
Clay (klā), Henry (1777–1852), Am. stsm. & or.
Clemenceau (klẽ-mäṅ″sō′), Georges Eugène Benjamin (1841–1929), Fr. jour. & stsm.
Clemens (klĕm′ĕnz), Samuel Langhorne (1835–1910), Am. nov. & humorist: pseud., *Mark Twain.*
Clement (klĕm′ĕnt), name of 14 popes, notably **VII** Giulio de Medici (1480?–1534).
Cleopatra (klē″ō-pā′tr*ȧ*), (69–30 B. C.), queen of Egypt.
Cleveland (klēv′lănd), Stephen Grover (1837–1908), 22d & 24th pres. of U. S.
Cleveland (klēv′lănd), city, Ohio, on Lake Erie, p. 905,636: univ.
Clinton (klĭn′tŭn), **1,** De Witt (1769–1828), Am. stsm.: promoted Erie Canal; **2,** Sir Henry (1738–95), Br. gen. in Am. Rev.
Clive (klīv), Robert, Lord (1725–74), Eng. gen.
Clyde (klīd), riv., S. Scot., 105 m. [& stsm.]
Cnidus (nī′dŭs), anc. tn., Caria, S. W. Asia Minor: bat. 394 B. C.
Cnossus. See **Knossos.**
Cobden (kŏb′dĕn), Richard (1804–65), Eng. pol: apostle of free trade.
Cobh (kōv), [formerly **Queenstown**], spt. tn., Ireland, p. 7,934: oc. steamship port of call.
Coblenz (kō′blĕnts), city, Prussia, p. 58,322.
Cochin China (kō′chĭn), state, Viet-Nam, 26,476 sq. m., p. 5,579,000; cap., Saigon.
Cody (kō′dĭ), William Frederick [*Buffalo Bill*] (1846–1917), Am. scout & showman.
Cohan (kō′ăn), George Michael (1878–1942), Am. dram. & act.
Colchis (kŏl′kĭs), anc. region, coast of Black sea: mod. Georgia & Armenia.
Cold Harbor (kōld), locality, Hanover co., Va.: bats. 1862, 1864. [1834), Eng. poet.]
Coleridge (kōl′rĭj), Samuel Taylor (1772–
Coleridge-Taylor (kōl′rĭj-tā′lẽr), Samuel (1875–1912), Afro-Eng. comp.
Collins (kŏl′ĭnz), **1,** Michael (1891–1922), Ir. stsm.; **2,** William Wilkie (1824–89), Eng. nov.; **3,** William (1721–59), Eng. lyric poet.
Cologne (kō-lōn′), [Ger. **Köln** (köln)], city, Prussia, p. 700,222: cathedral: univ.
Colombia (kō-lōm′bē-ä), repub., S. Am., 440,846 sq. m., p. 7,967,788; cap., Bogotá.
Colombo (kō-lŏm′bō), spt. tn., cap. of Ceylon, p. 244,163. [nillo isl., p. 31,203.]
Colón (kō-lōn′), spt. tn., Panama, on Manza-
Colorado (kŏl-ō-rä′dō), **1,** State in U. S., 103,948 sq. m., p. 1,318,048; cap., Denver; **2,** riv., S. W. U. S., 1,080 m. to Gulf of Calif.; **3,** riv., Tex., 715 m. to Gulf of Mex.; **4,** riv., Argentina, 700 m. to Atlantic oc.
Colorado Springs (kŏl-ō-rä′dō), city & health resort, Colo., p. 45,268. [Ir. poet & dram.]
Colum (kŏl′ŭm), Padraic (păd′rĭk) (1881–),
Columbia (kō-lŭm′bĭ-*ȧ*), city, cap. of S. C., p. 85,949: univ.
Columbia River (kō-lŭm′bĭ-*ȧ*), [orig. **Oregon**], riv., Br. Columbia & N. W. U. S., 1,400 m. to Pacific oc.
Columbus (kō-lŭm′bŭs), Christopher (1446?–1506), Genoese disc. of Am. in 1492.
Columbus (kō-lŭm′bŭs), **1,** city, Ga., p. 75,510; **2,** city, cap. of Ohio, p. 374,770: univ.
Commodus (kŏm′ō-dŭs), Lucius Ælius Aurelius (161–192), Rom. emp.
Como (kō′mō), lake, N. It., 43 m. long.
Comte (kôṅt), Isidore Auguste (1798–1857), Fr. philos.
Concord (kŏng′kŏrd), **1,** tn., Mass., home of Emerson, Hawthorne, & Thoreau, p. 8,676; **2,** city, cap. of N. H., p. 27,984.
Confucius (kŏn-fū′shĭ-ŭs), [**Kung-fu-tze** (kōōng′-fōō″-tsĕ′)], (551–478 B. C.), Chin. philos. and religious teacher.
Congo (kŏng′gō), or **Kongo,** riv., Afr., 3,000 m. to Atlantic oc.: **Belgian –,** see *Belgian Congo*: **French –,** see *French Equatorial Africa.*
Connaught (kŏn′ôt), Arthur William, Duke of (1850–1942), gov.-gen. of Can., 1911–16.
Connecticut (kŏ-nĕt′ĭ-kŭt), State in U. S., 4,965 sq. m., p. 1,995,263; cap., Hartford.
Conrad (kŏn′răd), Joseph (1857–1924), Pol.-Br. nov. & shipmaster. [Eng. art.]
Constable (kŭn′st*ȧ*-bl), John (1776–1837),
Constance (kŏn-stăns), lake, bet. Switzerland & Austria, 208 sq. m. [Fr. painter.]
Constant (kôṅ″stäṅ′), Benjamin (1845–1902),
Constantine (kŏn′stăn-tīn), **1,** Caius Flavius [*the Great*] (272–337), Rom. emp.; **2,** (1868–1923), king of Greece: abdicated.
Constantinople (kŏn-stăn″tĭ-nō′pl), [now **Istanbul**], city, former cap. of Turkey.
Conwell (kŏn′wĕl), Russell H. (1843–1925), Am. sol., Baptist clergy., & lecturer.
Cooch-Behar (kōōch″-bē-här′), **1,** state, N. India, 1,318 sq. m., p. 592,489; **2,** tn., its cap.
Cook (kŏŏk), James (1728–79), Br. navig.
Coolidge (kōōl′ĭj), Calvin (1872–1933), 30th pres. of U. S., 1923–29. [1851), Am. nov.]
Cooper (kōō′pẽr), James Fenimore (1789–
Copenhagen (kō″pĕn-hā′gĕn), city, cap. of Denmark. See **København.**
Copernicus (kō-pûr′nĭ-kŭs), Nicholas (1473–1543), Pol. astron. [Am. portrait painter.]
Copley (kŏp′lĭ), John Singleton (1737–1815),
Coppée (kô″pā′), François Édouard Joachim (1842–1908), Fr. poet & dram.
Coquelin (kôk″lăṅ′), **1,** Benoit Constant (1841–1909), Fr. act.; **2,** Ernest Alexandre Honoré (1848–1909), his brother, Fr. act.
Corcyra (kŏr-sī′r*ȧ*). See **Corfu.**
Corday d'Armans (kôr″dâ′ dȧr″mäṅ′), Marie Charlotte [*Charlotte Corday*] (1768–93), Fr. patriot: assassin of Marat.
Cordoba (kôr′dŏ-vä), [Span. **Córdoba**], **1,** city, Sp., p. 81,125; **2,** city, Argentina, S. Am., p. 221,200: univ. Also, **Cordova.**
Corelli (kō-rĕl′ĭ), Marie (1864–1924), Eng. nov.
Corfu (kôr-fōō′; kôr′fū), [anc. **Corcyra**], **1,** Gk. isl. & dept. in Medit.; **2,** city, cap. of isl., p. 32,221.
Corinth (kŏr′ĭnth), **Gulf of,** inlet of Medit., 75 m. long: **Isthmus of –,** connects the Morea pen. with S. Greece, 20 m. long.
Coriolanus (kō″rĭ-ō-lā′nŭs), Caius Marcius (about 5th cent. B. C.), Rom. hero.
Cork (kôrk), city, Ireland, p. 78,490.
Corneille (kôr″nây′′), Pierre (1606–84), Fr. dram. [(1738–1805), Eng. gen.]
Cornwallis (kôrn-wŏl′ĭs), Charles, Marquis
Corot (kô″rō′), Jean Baptiste Camille (1796–1875), Fr. Painter. [It. painter.]
Correggio, da (dä kō-rĕd′jō), (1494–1534).
Corregidor (kô-rĕg′ĭ-dôr), [Sp. kôr-rĕ″hē-*thôr′*], fortified isl., Manila Bay, P. I., 2 sq. m.: bats. 1942, 1945.
Corsica (kôr′sĭ-k*ȧ*), Fr. isl. in Medit., 3,367 sq. m., p. 289,890; cap., Ajaccio.
Cortés (kŏr-tās′), or **Cortes,** or **Cortez** (kôr′-tĕz), Hernando (1485–1547), Span. conq. of Mex. [rūn′*ȧ*)], city, N. W. Sp., p. 62,000.]
Coruña (kō-rōōn′yä), [Eng. **Corunna** (kō-
Cossacks. See **Don Cossacks.**
Costa Rica (kŏs″t*ȧ* rē′k*ȧ*), repub., Cen. Am 23,000 sq. m., p. 480,326; cap., San José.
Cotopaxi (kō″tō-păk′sē), volcanic mt. of the Andes, Ecuador, 19,613 ft. [theolog.]
Cotton (kŏt′n), John (1584?–1652), Puritan

Coué (kōō″ā′), Emile (1857–1926], Fr. chemist & mental healer. [45,184.

Council Bluffs (koun′sĭl), city, Iowa, p.

Courtrai (kōōr″trâ′), tn., Belgium, on Lys riv., p. 38,251: bats. 1914–18.

Coventry (kŭv′ĕn-trĭ), city, Eng., p. 161,100.

Coverdale (kŭv′ẽr-dāl), Miles (1488–1569), Eng. divine: translated Bible 1535.

Covington (kŭv′ĭng-tŭn), city, Ky., on Ohio riv., p. 64,282. [1800), Eng. poet.

Cowper (kōō′pẽr; kou′pẽr), William (1731–

Cox (kŏks), Palmer (1840–1924), Am. au. & illus.

Cracow (krā′kō), now **Krakow,** city, Poland, p. 183,706. [and illus.

Crane (krān), Walter (1845–1915), Eng. art.

Cranmer (krăn′mẽr), Thomas (1489–1556), Eng. abp. & martyr. [1909), Am. nov.

Crawford (krô′fẽrd), Francis Marion (1854–

Cremona (krĕ-mō′nȧ), city, It., p. 65,305.

Crete (krēt), Gk. isl. in Medit., p. 284,447; cap., Canea.

Crichton (krī′tŭn), James [*the Admirable*] (1560–85?), Scot. scholar & swordsman.

Crimea (krī-mē′ȧ), repub. & pen., S. Russ., on Black sea, 15,060 sq. m., p. 700,027.

Croatia (krō-ā′shĭ-ȧ), div., Yugoslavia, with Slavonia & isls., 16,290 sq. m., p. 2,739,593.

Crockett (krŏk′ĕt), David (1786–1836), Am. frontiersman. [Lydia, 560–546 B. C.

Crœsus (krē′sŭs), (?–546 B. C.), last king of

Croker (krō′kẽr), Richard (1843–1922), Am. Tammany Hall pol. [inv. of spinning mule.

Crompton (krŏmp′tŭn), Samuel (1753–1822),

Cromwell (krŏm′wĕl), Oliver (1599–1658), lord protector of Commonwealth of Eng.

Crookes (krōōks), Sir William (1832–1919), Eng. physicist. [(1915), Am. hymn writer.

Crosby (krôs′bĭ), Frances Jane [*Fanny*] (1820–

Crown Point (kroun), vil., N. Y., p. 1,468: of Rev. fame.

Croydon (kroi′dŭn), city, Eng., p. 212,400.

Cruikshank (krōōk′shăngk), George (1792–1878), Eng. satirical art.

Cuba (kū′bȧ), isl. repub., W. Indies, with isls. 44,164 sq. m., p. 3,579,507; cap., Habana.

Culebra (kōō′lā′brȧ), hill & R. R. station, Canal Zone: **– Cut,** see *Gaillard Cut.*

Cumæ (kū′mē), anc. city, Campania, It.: destroyed A. D. 1203.

Cumberland (kŭm′bẽr-lȧnd), **1,** city, Md., p. 37,632; **2,** mts., Appalachian system, Tenn.; **3,** riv., Ky. & Tenn., 678 m. to Ohio riv.

Cunaxa (kū-năk′sȧ), anc. tn., Mesopotamia (Iraq), on Euphrates riv.

Curaçao (kōō″rä-sä′ō; kū″rȧ-sō′), **1,** Du. prov. & several isls. N. of Venezuela; cap., Willemstad; **2,** one of isls., 210 sq. m., p. 41,014.

Curie (kü″rē′), **1,** Pierre (1859–1906), Fr. sci.: Nobel prize 1903; **2,** Marie (1867–1934), codiscoverer of radium: Nobel prize 1911.

Currie (kûr′ĭ), Sir Arthur (1875–1933), Can. gen.: comm. Can. troops in Fr. 1917–18.

Curtin (kur′tĭn), John (1885–1945), Australian pol.; premier, 1941–45.

Curtis (kûr′tĭs), Charles (1860–1936), U. S. Sen.: vice pres. of U. S., 1929–1933.

Curtiss (kûr′tĭs), Glenn Hammond (1878–1930), Am. inv. & aviator.

Curzon of Kedleston (kûr′zŏn ŏv kĕd′l-stŭn), George Nathaniel (1859–1925), 1st Earl, Br. stsm.: gov.-gen. India.

Custer (kŭs′tẽr), George Armstrong (1839–76), Am. sol.

Cuvier (kü″vyā′), Georges Leopold, Baron (1769–1832); Fr. natur. [Du. art.

Cuyp (koip), or **Kuyp,** Aalbert (1620–91),

Cyclades (sĭk′lȧ-dēz), Gk. isl. group, Ægean sea, 1,040 sq. m., p. 129,702. [Minor.

Cydnus (sĭd′nŭs), riv., anc. Cilicia, Asia

Cyprus (sī′prŭs), Br. isl., in E. Medit., 3,584 sq. m., p. 274,108; cap., Nicosia.

Cyrenaica (sĭr″ē-nā′ĭ-kȧ), dist. Libia, N. Afr., 230,000 sq. m., p. 234,714.

Cyrus (sī′rŭs), **1,** [*the Elder* or *the Great*] (?–529 B. C.), king of Persia; **2,** [*the Younger*] (424?–401 B. C.), led Gks. against his brother Artaxerxes II.

Cyzicus (sĭz′ĭ-kŭs), pen. & anc. city, Sea of Marmora: city now in ruins.

Czechoslovakia (chĕk″ō-slō-vä′kĭ-ȧ), a repub., comprising Bohemia, Moravia, Slovakia, & Ruthenia.

Czernowitz (chĕr′nō-vĭts), now Rumanian **Cernauti,** which see. [comp.

Czerny (chĕr′nē), Karl (1791–1857), Aus.

D

Dacia (dā′shĭ-ȧ), anc. Rom. prov., bet. Danube & Carpathian mts.

Daguerre (dȧ″gâr′), Louis Jacques Mandé (1789–1851), Fr. maker of daguerreotypes.

Dahomey (dä″hō′mā′), Fr. col., W. Afr., 42,460 sq. m., p. 979,602; cap. Porto Novo.

Dairen (dī′rĕn′), [formerly **Dalny** (dȧly′′nĭ)] spt. city, cap. of Kwangtung ter. & pen., China, p. 543,690. [of Va.

Dale (dāl), Sir Thomas (?–1619), col. gov.

Dallas (dăl′ȧs), city, Tex., p. 432,927.

Dalmatia (dăl-mā′shĭ-ȧ), div., Yugoslavia, on Adriatic sea, 4,916 sq. m., p. 621,429.

Dalton (dôl′tŭn), John (1766–1844), Eng. chemist. [p. 188,000.

Damascus (dȧ-măs′kŭs), city, cap. of Syria,

Damrosch (dăm′rŏsh), Walter J. (1862–1950), Am. comp. & orchestra director.

Dana (dā′nȧ), **1,** Charles A. (1819–97), Am. ed.; **2,** Francis (1743–1811), Am. stsm.; **3,** James Dwight (1813–95), Am. geol.

Daniels (dăn′yĕlz), Josephus (1862–1948), Am. jour.: sec. of navy, 1913–21.

d'Annunzio. See **Annunzio, d'.**

Dante Alighieri (dän′tā ä″lē-gyā′rē), [commonly **Dante** (dăn′tē)], (1265–1321), It. poet. [94), leader in Fr. Rev.

Danton (dän″tôn′), Georges Jacques (1759–

Danube (dăn′ūb), riv., S. Europe, 1,750 m. fr. Black forest to Black sea.

Danville (dăn′vĭl), city, Ill., p. 37,892.

Danzig (dän′tsĭkh), **Free State of,** ter. on Baltic sea, 754 sq. m., p. 415,000.

Dardanelles (där′dȧ-nĕlz″), [anc. **Hellespont**], channel bet. Marmora & Ægean seas.

Darien (dā″rĭ-ĕn′), **Gulf of –,** gulf of Caribbean sea: **Isthmus of –,** bet. Gulf of Darien & Pacific oc. [Persia.

Darius I (dȧ-rī′ŭs), (558?–486? B. C.), king of

Darmstadt (därm′shtät), tn., cap. of Hesse, Ger., on Rhine riv., p. 89,465.

Darnley (därn′lĭ), Henry Stuart, Lord (1545–67), 2d husband of Mary, Queen of Scots.

Darwin (där′wĭn), Charles Robert (1809–82), Eng. natur.

Daubigny (dō″bē″nyē′), Charles François (1817–78), Fr. painter.

Daudet (dō″dâ′), Alphonse (1840–97), Fr. nov.

Davenport (dăv′ĕn-pōrt), city, Iowa, p. 73,640.

David (dā′vĭd), **1,** 2d king of Israel, about 1085 B. C.; **2,** name of 2 kings of Scot.; **3,** (dȧ″vēd′), Jacques Louis (1748–1825), Fr. painter.

Davis (dā′vĭs), **1,** Jefferson (1808–89), pres. of Confed. States, 1861–65; **2,** John William (1873–), Am. law. & dipl.; **3.** Richard Harding (1864–1916), Am. nov. & jour.

Davis Strait (dā′vĭs), narrow sea, bet. Greenland & Baffin isl.

Davy (dā′vĭ), Sir Humphry (1778–1829), Eng. chemist: inv. of lamp for miners.

Dawes (dôz), Charles G. (1865–1951), financier & vice pres. of U. S., 1925–29.

Day (dā), William Rufus (1849–1923), Am. stsm. & justice U. S. Supreme Court fr. 1903.

Dayton (dā′tŭn), city, Ohio, p. 243,108.

Dead Sea (dĕd), salt lake, S. Palestine, 1,312 ft. below level of Medit.

Debs (dĕbz), Eugene Victor (1855–1926), Am. socialist & pol. [1918), Fr. comp.

Debussy (dē-bü″sē′), Claude Achille (1862–

Decapolis (dē-kăp′ō-lĭs), anc. confed., N. Palestine. [Am. nav. comm.

Decatur (dē-kā′tŭr), Stephen (1779–1820),

Decatur (dē-kā′tŭr), city, Ill., p. 67,801.

Defoe (dē-fō′), Daniel (1661–?1731), Eng. nov.

De Koven (dē kō′vĕn), Henry Louis Reginald (1861–1920), Am. comp.

Delacroix (dē-lȧ″krwä′), Ferdinand Victor Eugène (1799–1863), Fr. art.

Deland (dē-lănd′), Margaret Wade (1857–1945), Am. nov. [(1797–1856), Fr. art.

Delaroche (dē-lȧ″rōsh′), Hippolyte Paul

Delaware (dĕl′ȧ-wâr), **1,** State in U. S., 2,370 sq. m., p. 316,309; cap., Dover; **2,** riv., U. S., 375 m. to Del. bay; **3,** bay, bet. Del. & N. J., 60 m. long. [Fr. stsm.

Delcassé (dĕl″kȧ″sā′), Théophile (1852–1923),

Delhi (dĕl′ē), city, cap. of India, p. 521,849.

Delos (dē′lŏs), smallest isl. of the Cyclades, Greece, 2 sq. m. [B. C.), Gk. philos.

Democritus (dē-mŏk′rĭ-tŭs), (460?–362?

De Morgan (dē môr′găn), William Frend (1839–1917), Eng. art. & nov. [B. C.), Gk. or.

Demosthenes (dē-mŏs′thē-nēz), (384?–322

Denmark (dĕn′märk), kingdom, N. Europe, 17,144 sq. m., p. 3,434,555; cap., Köbenhavn.

Denver (dĕn′vẽr), city, cap. of Colo., on S. Platte riv., p. 412,856: univ.

Depew (dē-pū′), Chauncey Mitchell (1834–1928), Am. law., or., & stsm.

De Quincey (dē kwĭn′sĭ), Thomas (1785–1859), Eng. au. [142,406.

Derby (där′bĭ; dûr′-), co. bor. Eng., p.

De Reszke (dā rĕsh′kĕ). See **Reszke, de.**

Descartes (dā″kȧrt′), René (1596–1650), Fr. philos. & math.

Deschanel (dā″shȧ″nĕl′), Paul Eugène Louis (1856–1922), pres. of Fr. repub., Jan.–Sept., 1920. [p. 176,954.

Des Moines (dē moin′), city, cap. of Iowa,

De Soto (dē sō′tō), Hernando (1499?–1542), Span. expl.: disc. of Miss. riv., 1541.

Detaille (dē-tȧy″), Jean Baptiste Édouard (1848–1912), Fr. mil. & historical painter.

Detroit (dē-troit′), city, Mich., p. 1,838,517.

De Valera (dā vȧ-lā′rä), Eamon (1882–), Ir. republican leader. [botanist.

De Vries (dē vrēs′), Hugo (1848–1935), Du.

Dewey (dū′ĭ), **1,** George (1837–1917), Am. adm.; **2,** John (1859–), Am. educ.

Diaz (dē′äs), **1,** Armando (1861–1928), It. gen. in World War I; **2,** (dē′äs; dē′äth), Porfirio (1830–1915), pres. of Mex. [nov.

Dickens (dĭk′ĕnz), Charles (1812–70), Eng.

Dickinson (dĭk′ĭn-sŭn), Emily (1830–1886), Am. poet. [philos. & encyclopedist.

Diderot (dē″dē-rō′), Denis (1713–84), Fr.

Diesel (dē′zĕl), Rudolf (1858–1913), Ger. sci.

Dillon (dĭl′ŭn), John (1851–1927), Ir. pol.

Dinwiddie (dĭn-wĭd′ĭ; dĭn′wĭd″ĭ), Robert (1690–1770), col. gov. of Va.

Diocletian (dī″ō-klē′shăn), Caius Valerius (245–313), Rom. emp. [cynic.

Diogenes (dī-ŏj′ē-nēz), (412?–323? B. C.), Gk.

Dionysius (dī″ō-nĭsh′ĭ-ŭs), (430–367 B. C.), tyrant of Syracuse.

Dismal Swamp (dĭz′măl), marsh bet. Chesapeake bay & Albemarle sound, N. C. [**field.**

Disraeli (dĭz-rā′lĭ), Benjamin. See **Beacons-**

District of Columbia (kō-lŭm′bĭ-ȧ), federal ter. of U. S., seat of cap., Washington, 70 sq. m., p. 797,670. [Black sea.

Dnieper (nē′pẽr), riv., W. Russ., 1,330 m. to

Dniester (nēs′tẽr), riv., S. Poland, 850 m. to Black sea. [1921), Eng. poet.

Dobson (dŏb′sŭn), Henry Austin (1840–

Dodgson (dŏj′sŭn), Charles Lutwidge (1832–98), Eng. au.: pseud., *Lewis Carroll.*

Dominic (dŏm′ĭ-nĭk), Saint (1170–1221), Span. friar: founder of Dominican Order.

Dominican Republic (dō-mĭn′ĭ-kăn), [**Santo Domingo**], repub., E. Hispaniola isl., West Indies, 19,332 sq. m., p. 897,405; cap., Ciudad Trujillo.

Domitian (dō-mĭsh′ĭ-ăn), Titus Flavius Augustus (51–96), Rom. emp.

Don (dŏn), riv., S. E. Russ., 1,300 m. long.

Donatello (dŏn″ä-tĕl′lō), or **Donato** (dō-nä′tō) (1386–1466), Florentine sculp.

Don Cossacks (dŏn kŏs′ăks), **Province of the,** undefined region, N. of Black & Caspian seas, p. about 3,591,900.

Donizetti (dō″nē-dzĕt′tē), Gaetano (1797–1848), It. comp. [painter, illus., & sculp.

Doré (dō″rā′), Paul Gustave (1833–83), Fr.

Dortmund (dôrt′mo͝ont), city, Prussia, p. 321,743.

Dostoyevsky (dŏs′tō-yĕf′skē), Fiodor Mikhailovitch (1821–81), Russ. nov.

Dou (dou), or **Dow,** Gerard (1613–75), Du. genre painter. [1914–18.

Douai (do͞o-â′), tn., Fr., p. 25,510: bats.

Douglas (dŭg′lȧs), Stephen Arnold (1813–61), Am. stsm.

Doumergue (do͞o″mârg′), Gaston (1863–1937), pres. of Fr. repub. fr. 1924 to 1931.

Dover (dō′vẽr), **1,** tn., cap. of Del., p. 6,322; **2,** spt. & bor., Eng., p. 39,995: **Strait of –,** bet. Eng. & Fr., 20–27 m. wide.

Doyle (doil), Sir Arthur Conan (1859–1930). Eng. phys., nov., & spiritualist.

Draco (drā′kō), (about 620 B. C.), Athenian legis.: au. of stern code of laws. [navig.

Drake (drāk), Sir Francis (1540?–96), Eng.

Dreiser (drī′sẽr), Theodore (1871–1945), Am. nov. [Elbe riv., p. 619,157.

Dresden (drĕz′dĕn), city, cap. of Saxony, on

Drew (dro͞o), John (1853–1927), Am. act.

Dreyfus (drâ″füs′), Alfred (1859–1935), Jewish artillery off. in Fr. army: convicted of treason: later reinstated.

Drinkwater (drĭngk′wô″tẽr), John (1882–1937), Eng. poet & dram.

Drummond (drŭm′ŭnd), **1,** Henry (1851–97), Scot. theolog.; **2,** William Henry (1854–1907), Can. phys. & poet. [poet & dram.

Dryden (drī′dĕn), John (1631–1700), Eng.

Du Barry (dü bȧ″rē′), Jeanne Bécu, Comtesse (1746–93), mistress of Louis XV.

Dublin (dŭb′lĭn), city, cap. of Repub. of Ire., on Liffey riv., p. 316,693.

Dubuque (do͞o-būk′), city, Iowa, p. 49,528.

Dudevant (dü″dē-väṅ′), Madame (1804–76), Fr. nov.: pseud., *George Sand.* [272,798.

Duisburg (düs′bo͝orkh), tn., Prussia, Ger., p.

Duluth (do͞o-lo͞oth′), city, Minn., p. 104,066.

Dumas (dü″mä′), **1 ,** Alexander (1802–70), Fr. nov. & dram.: *The Three Musketeers;* **2,** Alexandre (1824–95), his son, Fr. dram.

Du Maurier (dü mō″ryā′), George Louis (1834–96), Fr.-Eng. art. & nov.: *Trilby.*

Düna (dü′nä), Russ. riv. See **Dvina.**

Dunbar (dŭn′bär), Paul Laurence (1872–1906), Am. poet & nov. of Afr. race.

Dundee (dŭn-dē′), spt. city, Scot., p. 174,800.

Dunkirk (dŭn-kûrk′), spt. tn., Fr., p. 30,597.

Dunmore (dŭn″mōr′), John Murray, Earl of (1732–1809), col. gov. of N. Y. & Va.

Dunsany (dŭn-sā′nĭ), Edward John, Baron (1878–), Ir. sol., dram. & au.

Durango (do͞o-räng′gō), **1,** state, Mex., 42,272 sq. m., p. 336,766; **2,** city, its cap., p. 39,091.

Durazzo (do͞o-rät′sō), [anc. **Dyrrhachium**], spt. tn., Albania, p. 10,000.

Dürer (dü′rẽr), Albrecht (1471–1528), Ger. painter & engraver.

Durham (dŭr′ăm), city, N. C., p. 70,307.

Duse (do͞o′zā), Eleonora (1861–1924), It. act.

Düsseldorf (düs′ĕl-dôrf), city, Prussia, on Rhine riv., p. 432,633: birthplace of Heine.

Dutch East Indies (ĭn′dĭz) isls., Malay archipelago, now United States of Indonesia, 733,642 sq. m., p. 51,881,8 62.

Dvina (dvē-nä'), or **Dwina** (dwē'nȧ), riv., Russ., 650 m. through Latvia to Gulf of Riga: **North –,** riv., N. Russ., 780 m. to White sea.

Dvorák (dvôr'zhäk), Antonin (1841–1904), Bohemian comp.

Dyrrhachium (dĭ-rā'kĭ-ŭm). See **Durazzo.**

E

East Africa, British, region, Afr., comprising Kenya, Uganda, Zanzibar: **Portuguese –,** see *Mozambique.*

East Chicago, city, Ind., p. 54,124.

East Indies (ĭn'dĭz), S. E. part of Asia: loosely, India, Indochina, & Malay Archipelago; strictly, Du. E. Indies, which see.

Easton (ēs'tŭn), city, Pa., p. 34,410.

East Orange (ŏr'ĕnj), city, N. J., p. 78,057.

East River, str. bet. Long Island sound & New York bay, 16 m. long, 1½–3½ m. wide.

East St. Louis, city, Ill., p. 81,950.

Ebert (ā'bĕrt), Friedrich (1871–1925), 1st pres. of Ger. repub., 1919–25.

Ecbatana (ĕk-băt'ȧ-nȧ), [mod. **Hamadan** (hä"mä-dôn')], anc. city, cap. of Media, Asia.

Echegaray (ā"chā-gä-rī'), José (1832–1916), Span. dram.: Nobel prize 1904.

Ecuador (ĕk'wȧ-dôr"), repub., S. Am., 118,627 sq. m., p. 1,562,500; cap., Quito.

Eddy (ĕd'ĭ), Mrs. Mary B. G. (1821–1910), Am. religious leader: Christian Science.

Edessa (ē-dĕs'ȧ), [mod. **Urfa** (o͞or-fä')], anc. city, Mesopotamia.

Edinburgh (ĕd'ĭn-bŭr"ō), city, cap. of Scot., p. 426,300: univ.

Edirne (ĕ-dĭr'nĕ), [formerly **Adrianople**], **1,** vilayet, Turkey, p. 111,080; **2,** city, its cap., p. 34,169.

Edison (ĕd'ĭ-sŭn), Thomas Alva (1847–1931), Am. inv.

Edmonton (ĕd'mŭn-tŭn), city, cap. of Alberta, Can., p. 158,709: univ.

Edom (ē'dŭm), or **Idumæa,** anc. region, S. E. of Palestine, 2,000 sq. m.

Edward (ĕd'wẽrd), **1,** name of 8 kings of Eng., notably: **VII** (1841–1910); **VIII** (1894–), Jan.–Dec. 1936: abdicated; **2,** [*the Black Prince*] (1330–76), Prince of Wales, son of Edward III.

Edwards (ĕd'wẽrdz), Am. theologs.: Jonathan (1703–58); Jonathan (1745–1801), his son.

Egypt (ē'jĭpt), kingdom, N. E. Afr., 360,000 sq. m., p. 14,186,898; cap., Cairo.

Ehrlich (âr'lĭkh), Paul (1854–1915), Ger. phys. & bacteriologist: Nobel prize 1908.

Eiffel (ĕ"fĕl'), Alexandre Gustave (1832–1924), Fr. eng.: the Eiffel Tower in Paris.

Einstein (īn'stīn), Albert (1879–), Ger.-Swiss sci.: relativity; Nobel prize 1921.

Eire (âr'ē), repub. in southern Ire., formerly Irish Free State, now Ireland (which see).

Eisenhower (ī'zĕn-hou"ẽr'), Dwight D. (1890–), gen. of the army, U.S.: supreme comm. Allied forces on western front in Europe, World War II, (1943–45); Chief of Staff, U.S.A., 1945–48; Pres. Columbia U., 1948– ; comm. NATO mil. forces, 1951– .

Ekaterinburg (yĕ-kȧ"tyĕ-rēn-bo͝orkh'), now **Sverdlovsk,**

Ekaterinoslav (yĕ-kȧ"tyĕ-rē"nō-slȧf'),or **Dnepro-Petrovsk,** city, Ukraine, p. 187,357.

Elam (ē'lăm), [See **Khuzistan**].

Elba (ĕl'bȧ), It. isl. in Medit. sea, 86 sq. m., p. 26,164: Napoleon exiled here, 1814–15.

Elbe (ĕl'bē), riv., cen. Europe, 725 m.

Elbruz (ĕl'bro͞oz; ăl'-), or **Elbrus** (-bro͞os), mt. in Caucasus, 18,526 ft.: highest in Europe.

Eleusis (ē-lū'sĭs), [mod. **Leusina** (lū-sē'nȧ)], anc. Gk. tn. in Attica.

El Frat (ĕl frät). See **Euphrates.**

Elia (ē'lĭ-ȧ), Eng. essay.: pseud. of *Charles Lamb.*

Eliot (ĕl'ĭ-ŭt), **1,** Charles William (1834–1926), Am. educ.; **2,** George (1819–80), Eng. nov.: pseud. of *Mary Ann Evans* (*Lewes*) (*Cross*); **3,** John [*Apostle to the Indians*] (1604–90), Am. clergy & missionary.

Elis (ē'lĭs), anc. city & div. of Greece.

Elizabeth (ē-lĭz'ȧ-bĕth), **1,** name of 2 queens of Eng.: **I** (1533–1603); **II** (1926–), 1952– ; **2,** Pauline Ottilie Luise (1843–1916), queen of Rumania & au.: pseud., *Carmen Sylva.*

Elizabeth (ē-lĭz'ȧ-bĕth), city, N. J., p. 112,675.

Ellis (ĕl'ĭs), Henry Havelock (1859–1939), Eng. phys., sci., & au.

Ellis Island (ĕl'ĭs), in N. Y. harbor: immigrant station.

Elman (ĕl'mȧn), Mischa (1892–), Russ.-Jewish violinist.

Elmira (ĕl-mī'rȧ), city, N. Y., p. 49,690.

El Paso (ĕl păs'ō), city, Tex., p. 130,003.

Emanuele III (ā-mä-no͞o-ā'lā), Vittorio [*Victor Emmanuel*] (1869–1947), king of It. 1900–1947, emp. of Ethiopia 1936–1941.

Emerson (ĕm'ẽr-sŭn), Ralph Waldo (1803–82), Am. essay., philos., & poet.

Emmet (ĕm'ĕt), Robert (1778–1803), Ir. patriot.

Emmett (ĕm'ĕt), Daniel Decatur (1815–1904), writer of negro songs: "Dixie."

Empedocles (ĕm-pĕd'ō-klēz), (5th cent. B. C.), Gk. philos.

Endicott (ĕn'dĭ-kŏt), John (1589?–1665), col. gov. of Mass.

Endor (ĕn'dôr), anc. vil. Palestine.

England (ĭng'glȧnd), div., Gt. Br., S. E. part of isl., 50,874 sq. m., p. 35,681,014; cap., London.

English Channel, inlet of Atlantic oc., bet. Eng. & Fr.

Epaminondas (ē-păm"ĭ-nŏn'dȧs), (418?–362 B. C.), Gk. stsm. & gen.: hero of Thebes.

Epictetus (ĕp"ĭk-tē'tŭs), (50–120?), Gk. stoic philos.

Epicurus (ĕp"ĭ-kū'rŭs), (342?–270 B. C.), Gk. philos.

Epirus (ē-pī'rŭs), anc. country, N. Greece.

Erasmus (ē-răz'mŭs), Desiderius (1466?–1536), Du. scholar.

Ericson (ĕr'ĭk-sŭn), Leif (about 1000), Icelandic disc. of Am.

Ericsson (ĕr'ĭk-sŭn), John (1803–89), Sw. eng. & inv.

Erie (ē'rĭ), **1,** one of the great lakes bet. U. S. & Can., 246 m. long; **2,** city, Pa., p. 130,125: **– Canal,** waterway, 352 m. fr. Buffalo to Troy, connecting Great Lakes with Hudson riv.: now called *New York State Barge Canal.*

Erin (ē'rĭn; ĕ'rĭn), anc. & poetic name for Ire.

Eritrea (ā"rē-trā'ä), It. col., on Red sea, 45,754 sq. m., p. 402,793; cap., Asmara.

Erivan (ĕr"ē-vän'), city, cap., of Armenia, p. 66,413.

Erzerum (ĕrz"ro͞om'), vilayet, Turkey, 19,180 sq. m., p. 270,763.

Esdraelon (ĕs"drā-ē'lŏn), plain in Palestine.

Essen (ĕs'ĕn), city, Prussia, p. 470,524.

Estonia (ĕs"tō'nĭ-ȧ), or **Esthonia** (ĕs"thō'-), repub. in U.S.S.R., 16,955 sq. m., p. 1,117,270; cap., Tallinn.

Ethiopia (ē"thĭ-ō'pĭ-ȧ), anc. country, Afr., S. of Egypt: also called Abyssinia.

Etna (ĕt'nȧ), active volcano, Sicily, 10,884 ft.

Etruria (ē-tro͞o'rĭ-ȧ), anc. country, N. It.

Eubœa (ū-bē'ȧ), [mod. **Evvia** (ĕv-vē'ȧ)], Gk. dept. & isl., in Ægean sea, 2,216 sq. m., p. 133,317; cap., Chalcis.

Eucken (oik'ĕn), Rudolf (1846–1926), Ger. philos.: Nobel prize 1908.

Euclid (ū'klĭd), (about 300 B. C.), Gk. geom.

Eugénie (ū"zhā"nē'), (1826–1920), emp. of the Fr.: wife of Napoleon III.

Euphrates (ū-frā'tēz), riv., Asia, 1,750 m. fr. Armenia to Pers. gulf.

Eurasia (ūr-ā'shȧ; -zhȧ), Europe and Asia combined.

Euripides (ū-rĭp'ĭ-dēz), (480–406 B. C.), Gk. trag.

Europe (ū'rŭp), cont., N. W. region of Old World, 3,872,561 sq. m., p. 494,262,755.

Evans (ĕv'ănz), **1,** Mary Ann: see **Eliot, George; 2,** Robley Dunglison [*Fighting Bob*] (1846–1912), Am. nav. off.

Evanston (ĕv'ănz-tŭn), city, Ill., p. 78,030.

Evansville (ĕv'ănz-vĭl), city, Ind., p. 109,869.

Everest (ĕv'ẽr-ĕst), highest mt. in world, Himalayas, bet. Nepal & Tibet, 29,141 ft.

Everett (ĕv′ẽr-ĕt), city, Mass., p. 45,789.

Eyck, van (vän īk′), Flemish painters: Hubert (1365–1426); Jan (1385–1440).

F

Fabius (fā′bĭ-ŭs), Maximus [*the Delayer*] (about 210 B. C.), Rom. gen.: opponent of Hannibal.

Falkland Islands (fôk′lănd), Br. isls., in S. Atlantic, 6,500 sq. m., p. 2,271.

Fall River (fôl), city, Mass., p. 111,759.

Faraday (făr′*ȧ*-dā), Michael (1791–1867), Eng. physicist.

Farnese (fär-nā′sā), It. family, famous in [15th & 16th cents.

Faroe (fâr′ō; fā′rō), Da. isls., bet. Iceland & the Shetlands, 540 sq. m., p. 22,835.

Farragut (făr′*ȧ*-gŭt), David Glasgow (1801–70), Am. adm.

Fawkes (fôks), Guy (1570–1606), Eng. con- [spirator.

Fayal (fä″yäl′), isl., in Azores, 68 sq. m., p. 26,264.

Feisal (fā′săl), (1887–1933), king of Iraq, [1921–1933.

Fénelon (fā″nẽ-lôn′), François de Salignac de la Mothe (1651–1715), Fr. prelate & au.

Ferdinand (fûr′dĭ-nănd), **1, I** [*the Just*] (1379–1416), king of Aragon; **2,** name of 7 kings of Sp., notably: **V** [*the Catholic*] (1452–1516): patron of Columbus; **VII** (1784–1833); **3, I** (1861–1948), king of Bulgaria, 1908–18: abdicated in favor of Boris; **4, I** (1865–1927), king of Rumania.

Fernández (fẽr-năn′dēz; fẽr-nän′dāth), Juan (1536–1602?), Span. navig.

Ferrara (fĕr-rä-rä), city, N. It., p. 117,221.

Fez (fĕz), a cap. of Morocco, p. 81,172.

Fezzan (fĕz″zän′), div., Libya, N. Afr., 160,000 sq. m., p. 70,000.

Field (fēld), **1,** Cyrus West (1819–92), Am. promoter of 1st Atlantic cable; **2,** Eugene (1850–95), Am. poet & jour.

Fielding (fēl′dĭng), Henry (1707–54), Eng. nov.

Fiji (fē′jē), Br. isls., in S. Pacific, 7,083 sq. m., p. 173,836.

Fillmore (fĭl′mōr), Millard (1800–74), 13th [pres. of U. S.

Finisterre (fĭn″ĭs-târ′), cape, W. end of Sp.

Finland (fĭn′lănd), formerly a grand duchy of Russ.; indep. state, 1918, 149,641 sq. m., p. 3,582,406; cap., Helsingfors: **Gulf of –,** arm of Baltic sea.

Fiske (fĭsk), John (1842–1901), Am. philos. [& hist.

Fitch (fĭch), Clyde (1865–1909), Am. dram.

Fitchburg (fĭch′bûrg), city, Mass., p. 42,671.

Fitzgerald (fĭts-jĕr′ăld), Edward (1809–83), Eng. poet and translator.

Fiume (fyōō′mā), city, N. E. It., free state fr. 1920, annexed to It. 1924, p. 49,199.

Flagg (flăg), James Montgomery (1877–), Am. art. & illus.

Flagstaff (flăg′stăf), tn., Ariz., p. 6,733: Low- [ell observatory.

Flammarion (flȧ″mȧ″ryôn′), Camille (1842–1925), Fr. astron.

Flanders (flăn′dẽrz), Belgian provs.: **East –,** 1,158 sq. m., p. 1,128,720; cap., Ghent: **West –,** 1,248 sq. m., p. 873,087; cap., Bruges.

Flaubert (flō″bâr′), Gustave (1821–80), Fr. [nov.

Fletcher (flĕch′ẽr), John (1579–1625), Eng. dram., with Beaumont.

Flint (flĭnt), city, Mich., p. 162,800.

Florence (flŏr′ĕns), [It. **Firenze** (fē-rĕnt′sä)], city, It., on the Arno, p. 316,806.

Florida (flŏr′ĭ-d*ȧ*), State in U. S., 58,666 sq. m., p. 2,743,736; cap., Tallahassee.

Flotow, von (fôn flō′tō), Friedrich (1812–83), Ger. comp.

Foch (fôsh), Ferdinand (1851–1929), marshal of Fr.: generalissimo Allied armies 1918.

Fontainbleau (fôn″tăn″blō′), tn., S. E. of Paris, Fr.: palace of former Fr. kings.

Foochow (fōō″chō′), city, cap. of Fukien prov., China, p. 314,900: Christian coll.

Forbes-Robertson (fôrbz″-rŏb′ẽrt-sŭn), Sir Johnston (1853–1937), Eng. act. & manager.

Ford (fōrd), Henry (1863–1947), Am. auto [mfr.

Formosa (fŏr-mō′s*ȧ*). See **Taiwan.**

Forrest (fŏr′ĕst), Edwin (1806–72), Am. trag.

Fort Donelson (dŏn′ĕl-sŭn), fortress, N. W. Tenn.: captured by General Grant 1862.

Fort Duquesne (dōō-kān′), Fr. fort, site of Pittsburgh, Pa.: taken by Eng. 1758.

Forth, Firth of (fûrth, fōrth), est. of Forth riv. in cen. Scot.: great cantilever bridge.

Fort Monroe (mŭn-rō′), fortress, Va.: Jefferson Davis imprisoned here, 1865–67.

Fort Sumter (sŭm′tẽr), fort, Charleston harbor: first engagement in Civil War, 1861.

Fort Wayne (wān), city, Ind., p. 132,840.

Fort Worth (wûrth), city, Tex., p. 277,047.

Foucault (fōō″kō′), Jean Bernard Léon (1819–68), Fr. physicist.

Fourier (fōō″ryā′), **1,** François Marie Charles (1772–1837), Fr. socialist; **2,** Jean Baptiste (1768–1830), Fr. math.

Fox (fŏks), **1,** Charles James (1749–1806), Eng. stsm.; **2,** George (1624–91), Eng. founder of Society of Friends, or Quakers.

France (fräns), Anatole (1844–1924), Fr. nov. & critic: pseud. of *Jaques Anatole Thibault.*

France (frȧns), repub., W. Europe, 212,659 sq. m., p. 40, 743,897; cap., Paris.

Francis (frȧn′sĭs), **1,** Saint [*of Assisi*] (1182–1226), It. friar: founder of Franciscans; **2, – Joseph I** (1830–1916), emp. of Austria fr. 1848; king of Hungary fr. 1867; **3,** name of 2 kings of Fr.; **4, – Ferdinand** (1863–1914), archduke of Austria: assassinated at Sarajevo, June 28, 1914.

Franco (frăng′kō), Francisco (1892–), Rightist leader of Sp. rev. of 1936–39.

Frankfort, 1, (frăngk′fûrt), city, cap. of Ky., p. 11,492; **2,** (frängk′fōōrt), city, Prussia, p. 467,520: univ.

Franklin (frăngk′lĭn), **1,** Benjamin (1706–90), Am. writer & stsm.; **2,** Sir John (1786–1847), Eng. arctic expl.

Fraser (frā′zẽr), riv., Br. Columbia, 750 m.

Frederick (frĕd′ẽr-ĭk), **1,** name of 3 Holy Rom. emps., notably: **I** [*Barbarossa*] (1123?–90); **II** (1194–1250); **2,** name of 8 kings of Denmark, notably **VIII** (1843–1912); **3,** name of 3 kings of Prussia: **I** (1657–1713), 1st king of Prussia; **II** [*the Great*] (1712–86); **III** (1831–88), emp. of Ger., 1888; **4, – William,** name of 4 kings of Prussia, notably **I** (1688–1740); **5, – William** [*the Great Elector*] (1620–88).

Fredericton (frĕd′ẽr-ĭk-tŭn), city, cap. of New Brunswick, Can., p. 15,870.

Freiburg (frī-bōōrkh), city, Ger., p. 90,475; cathedral; univ.

Fremont (frē-mŏnt′), John Charles (1813– [90), Am. expl. & sol.

French (frĕnch), **1,** Daniel C. (1850–1931), Am. sculp.; **2,** John Denton Pinkstone, Earl of Ypres (1852–1925), Br. field marshal.

French Equatorial Africa (ăf′rĭ-k*ȧ*), [**French Congo**], Fr. col., W. Afr., 912,049 sq. m., p. 3,127,707; cap., Brazzaville.

French Guiana (gē-ä′n*ȧ*). See **Guiana.**

French Guinea (gĭn′ĭ). See **Guinea.**

French Indochina (ĭn′dō-chī′n*ȧ*), Fr. Un., S. E. Asia, 256,878 sq. m., p. 20,700,000; cap., Hanoi.

French Somaliland (sō-mä′lē-lănd″). See [**Somaliland.**

French Sudan (sōō″dän′). See **Sudan.**

French West Africa (ăf′rĭ-k*ȧ*), Fr. col. on W. coast of Afr., 1,800,566 sq. m., p. 13,541,611; cap., Dakar, p. 40,152.

French West Indies (ĭn′dĭz), Fr. cols., including Martinique, Guadeloupe, & depend., 1,043 sq. m., p. 528,863.

Fresno (frĕz′nō), city, Calif., p. 90,618.

Freud (froid; froit), Sigmund (1856–1939), Aus. phys. & psychoanalyst.

Friendly Islands (frĕnd′lĭ). See **Tonga** [**Islands.**

Froebel (frö′bĕl), Friedrich (1782–1852), Ger. educ.: kindergarten system.

Frohman (frō′măn), Charles (1860–1915), Am. theatrical manager. [Fr. poet & hist.
Froissart (frwä″sȧr′), Jean (1337?–1410?),
Frost (frôst), Robert (1875–), Am. poet.
Froude (frōōd), James A. (1818–94), Eng. hist.
Fujiyama (fōō′jē-yä′mȧ), or **Fujisan** (-sän′), volcanic mt., Honshu, Japan, 12,365 ft.
Fukien (fōō′kĭ-ĕn′), maritime prov., China, 46,320 sq. m., p. 13,157,791; cap., Foochow.
Fulton (fōōl′tŭn), Robert (1765–1815), Am. eng.: inv. of steamboat.
Fundy (fŭn′dĭ), **Bay of,** inlet of Atlantic oc., bet. Nova Scotia & New Brunswick: tides 12 to 70 ft. high. [Am. gen.
Funston (fŭn′stŭn), Frederick (1865–1917),

G

Gaboriau (gȧ″bô″ryō′), Émile (1835–73), Fr. nov. [1936), Russ.-Am. pianist.
Gabrilowitsch (gȧ″brĭ-lŭv′ĭch), Ossip (1878–
Gaillard Cut (găl′ärd), [formerly **Culebra Cut**], cut of Panama canal, about 7 m. long, 300 ft. wide at bottom. [88), Eng. art.
Gainsborough (gānz′brō), Thomas (1727–
Gaius (gā′yŭs), (about 110–180), Rom. jurist.
Galatia (gȧ-lā′shĭ-ȧ), anc. country & Rom. prov., Asia Minor. [A. D. 69), Rom. emp.
Galba (găl′bȧ), Servius Sulpicius (3 B. C.–
Gale (gāl), Zona (1874–1938), Am. nov. & dram.
Galicia (gȧ-lĭsh′ĭ-ȧ), former crownland of Austria: detached 1919; now in Poland, 30,307 sq. m., p. 7,980,477.
Galilee (găl′ĭ-lē), anc. prov., Palestine: **Sea of –,** lake, cen. Palestine, 13 m. long: also called *Sea of Tiberias* or *Lake of Gennesaret.*
Galilei (gä″lē-lā′ē), Galileo (1564–1642), It. astron.: commonly called *Galileo* (găl″ĭ-lē′ō).
Galli-Curci (gäl′lē-kōōr′chē), Amelita (1889–), It.-Span. coloratura sop.
Gallienus (găl″ĭ-ē′nŭs), Publius Lucinius (?–268), Rom. emp.
Gallio (găl′ĭ-ō), Lucius Junius Annæus (1st cent. B. C.), Rom. proconsul: Apostle Paul appeared before him.
Gallipoli (gȧ-lĭp′ō-lē). See **Gelibolu.**
Galsworthy (gôlz′wûr″*thĭ*), John (1867–1933), Br. dram. & nov. [98), It. physicist.
Galvani (gäl-vä′nē), Luigi or Aloisio (1737–
Galveston (găl′vĕs-tŭn), city, Tex., p. 65,898.
Gama, da (dä gä′mä), Vasco (1469?–1524), Port. navig. [to Atlantic oc.
Gambia (găm′bĭ-ȧ), riv., W. Afr., 1,000 m.
Gandhi (gänd′hē; gȧn′dē), Mohandas Karamchand (1869–1948), Hindu law. & reformer. [Bay of Bengal.
Ganges (găn′jēz), riv., N. India, 1,500 m. to
Garden (gär′dn), Mary (1877–), Am. operatic sop.: 1st woman impresario.
Gardinas (gȧr′dĭ-nȧs), [**Grodno**], city, Lithuania, p. 61,600.
Garfield (gär′fēld), James Abram (1831–81), 20th pres. of U. S.: assassinated.
Garibaldi (gä″rē-bäl′dē), Guiseppe [*the Liberator*] (1807–82), It. patriot & gen.
Garner (gär′nẽr), John Nance (1869–), Am. law. & pol.: vice pres. of U. S., 1933–41.
Garonne (gȧ″rôn′), riv., S. W. Fr., 355 m. fr. Pyrenees mts. to Bay of Biscay.
Garrick (găr′ĭk), David (1717–79), Eng. act.
Garrison (găr′ĭ-sŭn), William Lloyd (1805–79), Am. abolitionist & internationalist.
Gary (gâ′rē), city, Ind., p. 132,496.
Gascony (găs′kō-nĭ), [Fr. **Gascogne** (gäs″-kôny″)], anc. duchy, S. W. Fr.
Gates (gāts), Horatio (1728–1806), Am. gen.
Gatun (gä-tōōn′), tn., Canal Zone, p. 7,000: **– Dam,** part of Panama canal, 8,000 ft. long: **– Lake,** 164 sq. m.
Gaul (gôl), [anc. **Gallia** (găl′ĭ-ȧ)], **Hither,** anc. country, now N. It.: **Further –,** mod. France, Belgium, & Switzerland. [poet & nov.
Gautier (gō″tyā′), Théophile (1811–72), Fr.
Geddes (gĕd′ĭs), **1,** Sir Auckland C. (1879–), Scot. stsm. & sci.: Br. ambas. to U. S., 1920–24; **2,** Sir Eric Campbell (1875–1937), Scot. stsm. & admin., 1919–21.
Gelibolu (gē-lĭb′ō-lōō), pen., bet. Dardanelles & Gulf of Saros, 55 m. long: bats. 1915–16.
Gelsenkirchen (gĕl″zĕn-kĭrkh′ĕn), city, Prussia, p. 208,512.
Geneva (jē-nē′vȧ), city, Switzerland, p. 126,700: univ.: **Lake of –,** [**Lake Leman** (lē′măn)], largest Swiss lake, 45 m. long.
Genghis Khan (jĕn′gĭz khän′), (1162?–1227), Mongol conq. [**Galilee.**
Gennesaret (ge-nĕs′ȧ-rĕt), **Lake of.** See
Genoa (jĕn′ō-ȧ), spt. city, It., p. 623,096: univ.
George (jôrj), **1,** Saint, patron saint of Eng.; **2,** name of 6 kings of Eng., notably: **III** (1738–1820); **V** (1865–1936); **VI** (1895–1952), 1936–52; **3,** name of 2 kings of Greece: **I** (1845–1913); **II** (1890–1947).
Georgia (jôr′jĭ-ȧ; jôr′jȧ), **1,** State in U. S., 59,265 sq. m., p. 3,433,190; cap., Atlanta; **2,** soviet socialist repub., Transcaucasia: federated with Russ.; 27,800 sq. m., p. 2,660,963; cap., Tiflis. [**Territory.**
German East Africa. See **Tanganyika**
German Southwest Africa. See **Southwest Africa.** [Philadelphia, Pa.: bat. 1777.
Germantown (jûr′măn-toun), N. part of
Germany (jûr′măn-ĭ), state, cen. Europe, 143,200 sq. m., p. 67,032,242; cap., Berlin: occupied by Allies, 1945; divided into west and east zones.
Gérôme (zhā″rōm′), Jean Léon (1824–1904), Fr. sculp. & painter.
Gershwin (gûrsh′wĭn), George (1898–1937), Am. comp. [bat. July 1–3, 1863.
Gettysburg (gĕt′ĭz-bûrg), city, Pa., p. 7,043;
Ghent (gĕnt), [Fr. **Gand** (gäṅ)], city, Belgium, p. 163,207: univ. [It. sculp.
Ghiberti (gē-bĕr′tē), Lorenzo (1378?–1455),
Ghirlandajo (gēr″län-dä′yō), (1449–94), Florentine painter.
Gibbon (gĭb′ŭn), Edward (1737–94), Eng. hist.
Gibbons (gĭb′ŭnz), James (1834–1921), Am. cardinal.
Gibbs (gĭbz), **1,** Josiah Willard (1839–1903), Am. physicist; **2,** Sir Philip (1877–), Eng. au. & war correspondent.
Gibraltar (jĭ-brôl′tẽr), tn. & fortified rock, S. Sp., 1⅞ sq. m., p. 16,120: annexed by Gt. Br. 1704: **Strait of –,** str. bet. Atlantic oc. & Medit. [Am. illus.
Gibson (gĭb′sŭn), Charles Dana (1867–1944),
Gilbert (gĭl′bẽrt), **1,** Sir Humphrey (1539?–83), Eng. navig. & expl.; **2,** Sir William Schwenck (1836–1911), Eng. librettist with Sullivan: "*Mikado.*" [tine.
Gilead (gĭl′ē-ăd), anc. mt. dist., E. of Pales-
Giotto (jôt′tō), Bondone (1276?–1337?), Florentine painter. [merchant & philan.
Girard (jĭ-rärd′), Stephen (1750–1831), Am.
Giza (gē′zȧ), city, Upper Egypt: sphinx.
Gladstone (glăd′stŭn), William E. (1809–98), Br. stsm. [1,061,900: univ.
Glasgow (glăs′gō; -kō), city, Scot., p.
Gluck, von (fôn glōōk), Christoph Willibald Ritter (1714–87), Ger. comp.
Goa (gō′ȧ), Port. col., S. India, 1,469 sq. m., p. 508,058; cap., Panjin, p. 7,388.
Gobi (gō′bē), desert, cen. Mongolia & N. E. Turkestan, 500,000 sq. m.
Goethals (gō′thălz), George Washington (1858–1928), Am. mil. eng.: Panama canal.
Goethe, von (fôn gö′tē), Johann Wolfgang (1749–1832), Ger. poet, dram., & philos.
Gogh, van (vän kōkh), Vincent (1853–90), Du. painter. [noted for diamond cutting.
Golconda (gŏl-kŏn′dȧ), ruined city, India:
Gold Coast (gōld), Br. col., W. Afr., 80,000 sq. m., p. 2,078,043; cap., Akkra, p. 38,000.
Goldsmith (gōld′smĭth), Oliver (1728–74), Eng. au. & poet. [Am. labor leader.
Gompers (gŏm′pẽrz), Samuel (1850–1924),

Good Hope, Cape of, Br. prov., Union of S. Afr., 276,966 sq. m., p. 2,782,719.
Gordon (gôr'dŭn), **1,** Charles George [*Chinese Gordon*] (1833–85), Br. gen.; **2,** Charles William (1860–1937), Can. clergy. & au.: pseud., *Ralph Connor.*
Gorky (gôr'kē), Maxim (1868–1936), Russ. nov.: pseud. of *A. M. Pyeshkov.* [233,303.
Göteburg (yö″tĕ-bŏry″), city, S. W. Sw., p.
Göttingen (gût'ĭng-ĕn), tn., Prussia, p. 41,240: univ. [93), Fr. comp.
Gounod (goo″nō'), Charles François (1818–
Goya y Lucientes, de (dä gō'yä ē loo″thē-ĕn'tās), Francisco (1746–1828), Span. art.
Gracchus (grăk'ŭs), famous Rom. family: Sempronius (162?–133 B. C.); Caius (153?–121 B. C.). [of Gks., E. coast of S. It.
Græcia Magna (grē'shĭ-ȧ măg'nȧ), anc. col.
Granada (grȧ-nä'dȧ), city, Sp., p. 107,124.
Grand Canyon, [Cañon], gorge of Colo. riv., N. W. Ariz.
Grand Pré (grän″ prā'), **[Lower Horton** (hôr'tŭn)], vil., Nova Scotia, p. 1,000: scene of Longfellow's *Evangeline.*
Grand Rapids, city, Mich., p. 165,674.
Granicus (grȧ-nī'kŭs), anc. riv., Troas, Asia Minor: bats. of Alexander & Lucullus.
Grant (grănt), Ulysses Simpson (1822–85), Am. gen.: 18th pres. of U. S.
Gray (grā), **1,** Asa (1810–88), Am. botanist; **2,** Thomas (1716–71), Eng. poet: *Elegy.*
Graz (gräts) or **Gratz,** city, Austria, p. 152,706.
Great Britain (brĭt'n), kingdom & largest isl. of Europe, comprising Eng., Scot., & Wales, 89,046 sq. m., p. 44,790,485; cap., London.
Great Salt Lake (sôlt), in Utah, 4,200 ft. above sea, 75 m. long, 30 m. wide.
Great Slave Lake (slāv), Connaught prov., N. W. Ters., Can., 300 m. long.
Greece (grēs), [anc. **Hellas**], repub., S. E. Europe, 49,912 sq. m., p. 6,204,684 (many refugees); cap., Athens. [& publicist.
Greeley (grē'lĭ), Horace (1811–72), Am. ed.
Green Bay, city, Wis., p. 52,443.
Greene (grēn), Nathanael (1742–86), Am. gen.
Greenland (grēn'lănd), **1,** Da. isl., N. E. of N. Am.; **2,** Da. col., S. part, 46,740 sq. m., p. 14,355; chief tn., Sydproven, p. 901.
Green Mountains, in N. New Eng. [sculp.
Greenough (grēn'ō), Horatio (1805–52), Am.
Greenwich (grĭn'ĭj), metropolitan bor., Eng., on Thames riv., p. 100,493: observatory.
Greenwich Village (grĕn'ĭch), part of N. Y. City, near Washington Square: residence of arts., writers, & acts.
Gregory (grĕg'ō-rĭ), **1,** name of 16 popes, notably: **I** [*the Great*] (540–604); **VII** Saint [*Hildebrand*] (1020–85); **XIII** (1512–85): reformed the calendar; **2,** Augusta, Lady (1859–1932), Ir. poet & dram.
Grenfell (grĕn'fĕl), Wilfred T. (1865–1940), Eng. au. & medical missionary to Labrador.
Grenoble (grē-nō'bl), city, S. Fr., p. 85,621.
Greuze (gröz), Jean Baptiste (1725–1805), Fr. painter.
Grey (grā), **1,** Charles, Earl (1764–1845), Eng. stsm.; **2,** Lady Jane (1537–54), heir to Eng. throne: beheaded; **3,** Edward, Viscount, of Fallodon (1862–1933), Br. stsm.; **4,** Zane (1875–1939), Am. nov. [Norw. comp.
Grieg (grēg), Edvard Hagerup (1843–1907),
Griffith (grĭf'ĭth), Arthur (1872–1922), Ir. Free State stsm. [cel. Eng. clown.
Grimaldi (grē-mäl'dē), Joseph (1779–1837),
Grimm (grĭm) Wilhelm Karl (1786–1856), & Jacob Ludwig Karl (1785–1863), Ger. philologists & writers of fairy tales.
Grodno (grôd'nŏ), **1,** mil. district., Poland; **2, [Gardinas],** city, Lithuania, p. 61,600.
Grotius (grō'shĭ-ŭs), Hugo (1583–1645), Du. stsm. & jurist. [p. 143,376.
Guadalajara (gwä″thä-lä-hä'rä), city, Mex.
Guadalquivir (gwä″dăl-kwĭv'ĕr; gwä″thäl-kē-bēr'), riv., S. Sp., 360 m. to Cadiz gulf.
Guadeloupe (gô″dĕ-loop'), two isls. & Fr. col. of the Lesser Antilles, W. Indies, 688 sq. m., p. 243,243; chief tn., Basse Terre.
Guadiana (*Span.* gwä-*th*-yä'nä; *Port.* gwä-dyä'nä), riv., Sp. & Port., 515 m. to Atlantic oc.
Guam (gwäm), Am. isl., Mariana archipelago, Pacific oc., 210 sq. m., p. 22,290: bat. 1944.
Guarneri (gwär-nā'rē), Giuseppe Antonio (1683–1745), It. violin maker.
Guatemala (gwä″tä-mä'lȧ), **1,** repub., Cen. Am., 48,290 sq. m., p, 2,004,900; **2,** city, its cap., p. 115,938.
Guernsey (gûrn'zĭ), one of the Channel isls., 25 sq. m., p., with Alderney & Sark, 40,120.
Guest (gĕst), Edgar Albert (1881–), Am. poet & humorist.
Guiana (gē-ä'nȧ), ter., N. E. S. Am.: **British –,** 89,480 sq. m., p. 307,784; cap., Georgetown, p. 55,490: **French –,** 32,000 sq. m., p. 47,341; cap., Cayenne, p. 13,936: **Dutch –, [Surinam],** 54,291 sq. m., p. 148,960; cap., Paramaribo, p. 45,791.
Guido Reni (gwē'dō rā'nē), (1575–1642), painter of Bologna, It. [merly Aquitania.
Guienne (gyĕn), anc. prov., S. W. Fr., for-
Guinea (gĭn'ĭ), coast dist., W. Afr.: **French –,** 92,640 sq. m., p. 2,185,697; cap., Konakry: **Portuguese –,** 13,940 sq. m., p. 350,000; cap., Bolaina: **Spanish –,** 10,810 sq. m., p. 140,000; cap., Santa Isabel: **Gulf of –,** on W. coast of Afr.
Guizot (gē″zō'), François Pierre Guillaume (1787–1874), Fr. hist. & stsm.
Gutenberg (goo'tĕn-bĕrkh), Johannes (1397?–1468), Ger. inv. of printing fr. movable types. [act.: mistress of Charles II.
Gwyn (gwĭn), Eleanor [*Nell*] (1650–87), Eng.

H

Haakon VII (hô'kŏn), (1872–), king of Norway fr. 1905. [Cuba, p. 581,076.
Habana (hȧ-văn'ȧ; hä-vä'nä), city, cap. of
Hadrian (hā'drĭ-ăn), or **Adrian,** Publius Ælius (76–138), Rom. emp.
Haeckel (hĕk'ĕl), Ernst Heinrich (1834–1919), Ger. biol. & philos.
Hague (hāg), **The,** city, seat of govt. of the Netherlands, p. 416,179.
Hahnemann (hä'nē-män), S. C. F. (1755–1843), Ger. phys.: founder of homeopathy.
Haig (hāg), Douglas, Earl of Bemersyde (1861–1928), Br. field marshal.
Haile Selassie (hī'lĕ sē-lás'yĕ) (1890–), emp. Ethiopia, 1930–
Haiti (hā'tĭ), [off. **Hispaniola**], isl., W. Indies, 28,240 sq. m., p. 2,942,000: **Republic of –,** W. part of Haiti isl., 10,204 sq. m., p. 2,300,200; cap., Port au Prince.
Hale (hāl), **1,** Edward Everett (1822–1909), Am. clergy. & au.; **2,** Nathan (1755–76), Am. patriot. [dram.
Halévy (ȧ″lā″vē'), Ludovic (1834–1908), Fr.
Halicarnassus (hăl″ĭ-kär-năs'ŭs), [mod. **Budrum** (boo″droom')], anc. Gk. city, Asia Minor.
Halifax (hăl'ĭ-făks), **1,** city, Eng., p. 96,320; **2,** city, cap. of Nova Scotia, Can., p. 84,433.
Hallam (hăl'ăm), **1,** Henry (1777–1859), Eng. hist.; **2,** Arthur Henry (1811–33), his son, Eng. essay.
Halle (häl'ē), tn., Prussia, p. 194,575: univ.
Halley (hăl'ĭ; hôl'ĭ), Edmund (1656–1742), Eng. astron.: disc. of comet 1682.
Hals (häls), Franz (1581?–1666), Du. painter.
Hamburg (häm'boorkh), **1,** administrative div., Ger., 160 sq. m., p. 1,152,523: univ.; **2,** spt. city of same, p. 1,079,126.
Hamilcar (hä-mĭl'kär), any of several Carthaginian gens. [1804), Am. sol. & stsm.
Hamilton (hăm'ĭl-tŭn), Alexander (1757–

Hamilton (hăm'ĭl-tŭn), **1,** city, Ohio, p. 57,717; **2,** city, Ontario, Can., p. 155,547.
Hammerfest (häm'ẽr-fĕst″), tn., Norway, most northern in Europe, p. 3,470.
Hammond (hăm'ŭnd), John Hays (1855–1936), Am. mining eng.
Hammond (hăm'ŭnd), city, Ind., p. 87,423.
Hammurabi (häm″o͞o-rä'bē), (about 1900 B. C.), king of Babylon: code of laws.
Hampden (hăm'dĕn), **1,** John (1594–1643), Br. stsm.; **2,** Walter (1879–), Am. act.
Hamsun (häm'sŭn), Knut (1859–1952), Norw. nov.: Nobel prize 1920.
Hamtramck (hăm-trăm'ĭk), tn., Mich., near Detroit, p. 43,245.
Hancock (hăn'kŏk), **1,** John (1737–93), Am. stsm.; **2,** Winfield Scott (1824–86), Am. gen.
Handel (hăn'dĕl), George Frederick (1685–1759), Ger.-Eng. comp.
Hangchow (hăng'chō'), city, cap. of Chekiang prov., China, p. 426,900.
Hankow (hän'kō'), city & port, Hupeh prov., China, p. 1,583,900. [thaginian gen.
Hannibal (hăn'ĭ-băl), (247–183 B. C.), Car-
Hanover (hăn'ō-vẽr), city, Prussia, p. 422,745.
Harding (här'dĭng), Warren Gamaliel (1865–1923), 29th pres. of U. S.
Hardy (här'dĭ), Thomas (1840–1928), Eng. nov.: awarded Order of Merit 1910.
Hargreaves (här'grēvz), James (?–1778), Eng. inv. of spinning jenny.
Harlem (här'lĕm), upper section Manhattan isl., part of N. Y. City: **– River,** channel N. E. of Manhattan isl. [1906), Am. educ.
Harper (här'pẽr), William Rainey (1856–
Harper's Ferry (här'pẽrz), vil., W. Va., on Potomac riv., p. 665: notable in Civil War.
Harris (hăr'ĭs), Joel Chandler (1848–1908), Am. au.: "Uncle Remus." [p. 89,091.
Harrisburg (hăr'ĭs-bûrg), city, cap. of Pa.,
Harrison (hăr'ĭ-sŭn), **1,** Benjamin (1833–1901), 23d pres. of U. S.; **2,** Frederic (1831–1923), Eng. essay.; **3,** William Henry (1773–1841), Am. sol.: 9th pres. of U. S.
Harte (härt), Francis Bret (1836–1902), Am. au. & poet. [177,073.
Hartford (härt'fẽrd), city, cap. of Conn., p.
Harun-al-Rashid (hä-ro͞on″-är-rä-shēd'), or **Haroun,** [*Aaron the Just*] (766?–809), caliph of Baghdad. [anat.: disc. blood circulation.
Harvey (här'vĭ), William (1578–1657), Eng.
Hasdrubal (hăz'dro͞o-băl), name of several Carthaginian gens.
Hastings (hās'tĭngz), Warren (1732–1818), Eng. gov.-gen. of India.
Hastings (hās'tĭngz), co. bor., Sussex, Eng., p. 61,560: bat. 1066.
Hathaway (hăth'ȧ-wā), Ann (1556–1623), maiden name of Shakespeare's wife. [N. C.
Hatteras (hăt'ẽr-ȧs), cape on isl. off coast of
Hauptmann (houpt'män), Gerhart (1862–1946), Ger. dram.: Nobel prize 1912.
Haut-Rhin (ō″-răn'), dept., Fr., formerly Upper Alsace, 1,354 sq. m., p. 468,943; cap., Kolmar.
Havana (hȧ-văn'ȧ). See **Habana.** [Br. gen.
Havelock (hăv'lŏk), Sir Henry (1795–1857),
Haverhill (hā'vẽr-ĭl), city, Mass., p. 47,213.
Havre, Le (lē ȧvr'), spt. city, Fr., p. 158,022.
Hawaii (hä-wī'ē), **1,** largest of Hawaiian group; **2,** [**Hawaiian Islands** (hä-wī'yăn), off. **Territory of Hawaii**], isl. ter. of U. S. in Pacific oc., 6,449 sq. m., p. 499,794; cap., Honolulu. [Am. nov.
Hawthorne (hô'thôrn), Nathaniel (1804–64),
Hay (hā), John (1838–1905), Am. stsm. & au.
Haydn (hā'dn; hī'-), Joseph (1732–1809), Aus. comp. [19th pres. of U. S.
Hayes (hāz), Rutherford Birchard (1822–93),
Hazleton (hā'zl-tŭn), city, Pa., p. 35,486.
Hazlitt (hăz'lĭt), William (1778–1830), Eng. writer. [1st gov.-gen. of Ir. Free State.
Healy (hē'lĭ), Timothy Michael (1855–1931),
Hearn (hûrn), Lafcadio (1850–1904), Br.-Jap. au. [2,812 sq. m., p. 70,517.
Hebrides (hĕb'rĭ-dēz), 500 isls. W. of Scot.,
Hegel (hā'gĕl), George Wilhelm Friedrich (1770–1831), Ger. philos.
Heidelberg (hī'dĕl-bûrg; -bĕrkh), city, Baden, Ger., p. 73,034: univ. [Jewish violinist.
Heifetz (hī'fĕts), Jascha (1901–), Russ.-
Heine (hī'nē), Heinrich (1797–1856), Ger. poet.
Hejaz (hĕj-äz'), or **Hedjaz,** kingdom of Arabia, 112,500 sq. m., p. 900,000; cap., Mecca.
Helena (hĕl'ē-nȧ), city, cap. of Mont., p. 17,498.
Helgoland (hĕl'gō-länt″), [Eng. **Heligoland** (hĕl'ĭ-gō-lănd″), Ger. isl., North sea, ¼ sq. m., p. 2,588: fortress dismantled.
Heliopolis (hē″lĭ-ŏp'ō-lĭs), anc. city, Egypt.
Hellas (hĕl'ȧs). See **Greece.**
Hellespont (hĕl'ĕs-pŏnt). See **Dardanelles.**
Helsinki (hĕl'sĕn-kē), [Sw. **Helsingfors** (hĕl″-sĭng-fôrs')], spt. tn., cap. of Finland, p. 220,904.
Helvetia (hĕl-vē'shĭ-ȧ), anc. country of Gaul, now Switzerland. [Eng. poet.
Hemans (hĕm'ănz), Felicia (1793–1835).
Henry (hĕn'rĭ), **1,** name of 8 kings of Eng., notably: **IV** [*Bolingbroke*] (1367–1413); **V** (1387–1422); **VI** [*of Windsor*] (1421–71). **VIII** (1491–1547); **2,** name of 4 kings of France, notably **IV, of Navarre** (1553–1610); **3,** name of 7 Ger. kings & emps. of Holy Rom. Empire; **4, O. –,** pseud. of *Sydney Porter*; **5,** Patrick (1736–99), Am. patriot.
Heraclea (hĕr″ȧ-klē'ȧ), anc. city, It.: bat. 280 B. C. [Gk. philos.
Heraclitus (hĕr″ȧ-klī'tŭs), (about 500 B. C.),
Herbert (hûr'bẽrt), Victor (1859–1924), Am. comp. & conductor.
Herculaneum (hûr″kū-lā'nē-ŭm), anc. city. It.: buried by eruption of Vesuvius, A. D. 79.
Herod (hĕr'ŭd), [*the Great*] (73?–4 B. C.), king of the Jews. [Gk. hist.
Herodotus (hē-rŏd'ō-tŭs), (484?–425? B. C.),
Herrick (hĕr'ĭk), **1,** Myron T. (1854–1929), Am. stsm.; **2,** Robert (1591–1674), Eng. poet.
Herschel (hûr'shĕl), Sir William (1738–1822), Ger.-Eng. astron.
Herzegovina (hĕr″tsĕ-gō-vē'nä). See **Bosnia.**
Hesiod (hē'sĭ-ŏd), (about 776 B. C.), Gk. poet.
Hesse (hĕs), [Ger. **Hessen**], state, Ger., 2,968 sq. m., p. 1,347,279; cap., Darmstadt.
Hewlett (hū'lĕt), Maurice Henry (1861–1923), Eng. nov.
Heyse (hī'zē), Paul J. L. (1830–1914), Ger. nov. & poet: Nobel prize 1910. [46,155.
Highland Park (hī'lănd), city, Mich., p.
Himalaya (hĭ-mä'lȧ-yȧ), mt. system, bet. India & Tibet: Mt. Everest, 29,141 ft.
Hindenburg, von (fôn hĭn'dĕn-bo͝orkh), Paul (1847–1934), Ger. gen. & 2d pres. of Ger.
Hindu Kush (hĭn'do͞o ko͞osh'), mt. range of Afghanistan: Tirach Mir, 25,400 ft.
Hindustan (hĭn″do͞o-stän'), or **Hindostan** (hĭn″dō-stän'), Persian name of India.
Hipparchus (hĭ-pär'kŭs), **1,** (?–514 B. C.). Gk. tyrant; **2,** (about 160–125 B. C.), Gk. [astron.
Hippo (hĭp'ō), anc. city, N. Afr.
Hippocrates (hĭ-pŏk'rȧ-tēz), (460–359? B. C.), Gk. phys. [of Haiti.
Hispaniola (hĭs″păn-yō'lȧ), off. name of isl.
Hissarlik (hĭs-sär'lĭk), [anc. **Troy**], tn., N. W. Asia Minor: excavations of Troy.
Hitler (hĭt'lẽr), Adolf (1889–1945?), Ger. head of National Socialists, chancellor 1933–45.
Hobart (hō'bȧrt), city, cap. of Tasmania. p. 52,600. [philos.
Hobbes (hŏbz), Thomas (1588–1679), Eng.
Hoboken (hō'bō-kĕn), spt. city, N. J., p. 50,510. [1937), Am. nav. off. & legis.
Hobson (hŏb'sn), Richmond Pearson (1870–
Hoe (hō), Richard M. (1812–86), Am. inv.
Hofmann (hôf'män), Josef (1876–), Pol.-Am. pianist. [Eng. satirical painter.
Hogarth (hō'gärth), William (1697–1764),

Hokkaido (hŏk′kī″dō), [formerly, **Yezo**], isl., N. Jap., 30,502 sq. m., p. 843,717.
Holbein (hol′bīn), Ger. artists: Hans [*the Elder*] (1460–1524); Hans [*the Younger*] (1497?–1543), his son.
Holland (hŏl′ănd). See **Netherlands.**
Holmes (hōmz), **1,** Oliver Wendell (1809–94), Am. au.; **2,** Oliver Wendell (1841–1935), his son, Am. jurist.
Holyoke (hōl′yōk), city, Mass., p. 54,441.
Homer (hō′mĕr), **1,** (9th cent. B. C.), Gk. epic poet; **2,** Winslow (1836–1910), Am. art.
Honan (hō″năn′), prov., China, 69,830 sq. m., p. 30,831,909; cap., Kaifeng.
Hondo (hŏn′dō). See **Honshu.**
Honduras (hŏn-dōō′rȧs), repub., Cen. Am., 44,275 sq. m., p. 773,408; cap., Tegucigalpa, p. 40,000: **British –,** crown col. on Caribbean sea, 8,598 sq. m., p. 49,249.
Hong Kong (hŏng′ kŏng), Br. crown col., shore & isl., mouth of Canton riv., China, 391 sq. m., p. 961,400; cap., Victoria.
Honolulu (hō″nō-lōō′lōō), city, cap. of Hawaii ter., on isl. Oahu, p. 137,582. [Rom. emp.
Honorius (hō-nō′rĭ-ŭs), Flavius (384–423),
Honshu (hŏn′shōō), mainland, largest isl. of Jap., 86,953 sq. m., p. 59,736,822.
Hood (hŏŏd), Thomas (1790–1845), Eng. poet.
Hood (hŏŏd), **Mount,** peak of Cascades, Oreg., 11,253 ft.
Hoover (hōō′vĕr), Herbert Clark (1874–), Am. eng. & stsm.: 31st pres. of U. S., 1929–33. [pseud. of *Sir Anthony Hope Hawkins.*
Hope (hōp), Anthony (1863–1933), Eng. nov.:
Horace (hŏr′ās), Quintus [*Horatius*] Flaccus (65–8 B. C), Lat. poet.
Hortense (ȯr″täṅs′), Eugénie (1783–1837), wife of Louis Bonaparte & queen of Holland.
Horthy, von (fon hŏr′tē), Nicholas (1868–), Hung. stsm. & adm.
Hough (hŭf), Emerson (1857–1923), Am. nov.
Houston (hūs′tŭn), Sam (1793–1863), Am. gen.: pres. of repub. of Tex., 1836.
Houston (hūs′tŭn), city, Tex., p. 594,321.
Howe (hou), **1,** Elias (1819–67), Am. inv.: sewing machine; **2,** Julia Ward (1819–1910), Am. poet; **3,** William, Viscount (1729–1814), Br. gen. in Am.
Howells (hou′ĕlz), William Dean (1837–1920), Am. nov. & essay. [of rules of games.
Hoyle (hoil), Edmond (1672–1769), Eng. au.
Hsinking (shĭn′chĭng′), a city in Manchuria, cap. of Manchukuo: formerly, *Changchun.*
Hubbard (hŭb′ērd), (Elbert 1856–1915), Am. business promoter, ed., & au.
Huddersfield (hŭd′ērz-fēld), tn., Yorkshire, Eng., p. 112,100. [navig. in Du. service.
Hudson (hŭd′sn), Henry (1576?–1611), Eng.
Hudson (hŭd′sŭn), riv., 300 m. to N. Y. bay: **– Bay,** 850 m. long, N. E. Can., opens into Arctic & Atlantic ocs. [Mex. gen. & pol.
Huerta (wĕr′tä), Victoriano (1854–1916),
Hughes (hūz), **1,** Charles Evans (1862–1948), Am. jurist & Sec. of State; Chief Justice U. S. Supreme Court, 1930–41; **2,** Thomas (1822–96), Eng. au. [1802–85), Fr. nov.
Hugo (hū′gō; ü″gō′), Victor Marie, Viscount
Hull (hŭl), Cordell (1871–), Am. stsm.: sec'y of state 1933–44.
Humbert I (hŭm′bērt), [It. **Umberto** (ōōm-bĕr′tō)], (1844–1900), king of It.
Humboldt, von (fon hōōm′bolt), Alexander, Baron (1769–1859), Ger. natur. & trav.
Hume (hūm), David (1711–76), Scot. hist. & philos. [(1854–1921), Ger. comp.
Humperdinck (hōōm′pĕr-dĭngk), Engelbert
Hunan (hōō′năn′), prov., cen. China, 83,380 sq. m., p. 28,443,279; cap., Changsha.
Hungary (hŭng′gȧ-rĭ), state, cen. Europe, 35,875 sq. m., p. 8,457,852; cap., Budapest.
Hunt (hŭnt), **1,** (James Henry) Leigh (1784–1859), Eng. poet & essay.: **2,** William Holman (1827–1910), Eng. painter.

Huntington (hŭn′tĭng-tŭn), city, W. Va., p. 86,160. [Hung. gen.
Hunyadi (hōōn′yŏd-ĭ), Janos (?–1456)
Hupeh (hōō′pĕ′), prov., cen. China, 71,410 sq. m., p. 28,616,576; cap., Wuchang.
Huron (hū′rŏn), **Lake,** one of the five Great Lakes of N. Am., 23,010 sq. m.
Hus (hŭs), John (1369–1415), Bohemian reformer. [Eng. biol.
Huxley (hŭks′lĭ), Thomas Henry (1825–95),
Hwang (hwăng), or **Huang Ho** (hō), [**Yellow River** (yĕl′ō)], riv., China, 2,700 m. to Yellow sea. [city, India, p. 404,187.
Hyderabad (hī″dĕr-ä-bäd′), or **Haidarabad**
Hypatia (hī-pā′shĭ-ȧ), (?–415), lady of Alexandria; math. & philos.
Hyslop (hĭs′lŏp), James Hervey (1854–1920), Am. psychologist.

I

Iasi (yä′shē). See **Jassy.**
Ibáñez, Blasco. See **Blasco Ibáñez.** [Port.
Iberia (ī-bē′rĭ-ȧ), anc. name of pen. of Sp. &
Ibsen (ĭb′sĕn; ĭp′-), Henrik (1828–1906), Norw. dram. [Ægean sea.
Icarian Sea (ī-kā′rĭ-ăn), anc. name of S.
Iceland (īs′lănd), Da. isl. & state, N. Atlantic oc., 39,709 sq. m., p. 94,690; cap., Reykjavik.
Ida (ī-dȧ), **1,** mt. range, N. W. Asia Minor; **2,** highest mt. in Crete.
Idaho (ī′dȧ-hō), State in U. S., 83,888 sq. m., p. 585,092; cap., Boise.
Idumæa, Idumea (ĭd″ū-mē′ȧ). See **Edom.**
Ilium (ĭl′ĭ-ŭm), name of anc. Troy.
Illinois (ĭl″ĭ-noi′: -noiz′), **1,** State in U. S., 56,665 sq. m., p. 8,684,513; cap., Springfield; **2,** riv., 500 m. to Miss. riv.
Illyria (ĭ-lĭr′ĭ-ȧ), [ancient **Illyricum**], mod. Yugoslavia.
Illyricum (ĭ-lĭr′ĭ-kŭm), Rom. prov. of Illyria.
India (ĭn′dĭ-ȧ), cen. pen. S. Asia, S. of Himalaya mts., **Repub. of-** Hindu section of former Indian Empire; 1,221,000 sq. m., p. 320,000,000; cap., Delhi. Moslem section of India now called *Pakistan* with capital at Karachi.
Indiana (ĭn″dĭ-ăn′ȧ), State in U. S., 36,354 sq. m., p. 3,921,213; cap., Indianapolis.
Indianapolis (ĭn″dĭ-ăn-ăp′ō-lĭs), city, cap. of Indiana, p. 424,683.
Indian Ocean (ĭn′dĭ-ăn), one of the five great ocs., S. of Asia & E. of Afr., to Antarctic circle, 28,000,000 sq. m.
Indochina (ĭn′dō-chī′nȧ), **Federation of** [**Farther India**], the S. E. pen. of Asia, 274,385 sq. m., p. 20,700,000; cap., Hanoi.
Indonesia (ĭn″dō-nē′zhȧ). See **Du. E. Indies.**
Indus (ĭn′dŭs), riv., S. Asia, 1,800 m. fr. Tibet to Arabian sea.
Ingersoll (ĭng′gĕr-sŏl), Robert G. (1833–99), Am. law., or., & freethinker.
Inness (ĭn′ĕs), George (1825–94), Am. art.
Innocent (ĭn′ō-sĕnt), name of 13 popes, notably **III** (1161–1216). [Minor.
Ionia (ī-ō′nĭ-ȧ), anc. Gk. col., W. coast Asia
Ionian Islands (ī-ō′nĭ-ăn), group, E. Medit., 1,117 sq. m., p. 224,189. [Greece & S. It.
Ionian Sea (ī-ō′nĭ-ăn), part of Medit. bet.
Iowa (ī′ō-wȧ), State in U. S., 56,147 sq. m., p. 2,612,598; cap., Des Moines.
Iran (ī-răn′; ē″rän′), native name of Persia.
Iraq (ē″räk′), [formerly **Mesopotamia**], kingdom, S. W. Asia, 116,600 sq. m., p. 4,794,449; cap., Baghdad.
Ireland (īr′lănd), one of the Br. Isles. See **Ireland, Republic of & Northern Ireland.**
Ireland, Republic of (īr′lănd), formerly called *Irish Free State* then *Erie*, an independent repub. since 1949, comprising three former S. provs. Leinster, Munster, & Connaught, with Cavan, Donegal, & Monaghan cos. of Ulster prov., 26,592 sq. m., p. 2,971,992; cap., Dublin.
Irish Sea, part of Atlantic oc. bet. Eng. & Ire.

Irrawaddy (ĭr″ȧ-wŏd′ĭ), or **Irawadi,** riv. Burma, S. E. Asia, 1,500 m. to Bay of Bengal.
Irving (ûr′vĭng), **1,** Sir Henry (1838–1905), Eng. act.; **2,** Washington (1783–1859), Am. essay. & hist.
Isabella (ĭz″ȧ-bĕl′ȧ), (1451–1504), queen of Castile & León: patroness of Columbus.
Isle of Man (măn), isl., Irish sea, 227 sq. m., p. 60,284; cap., Douglas.
Isocrates (ī-sŏk′rȧ-tēz), (436–338 B. C.), [Athenian or.]
Ispahan (ĭs″pȧ-hän′; ĭs″fȧ-), city, W. Persia.
Israel (ĭz′rā-ĕl), anc. kingdom, Palestine; ind. state in Palestine established 1948.
Israels (ēs″rä-ĕls′), Joseph (1824–1911), Du.-Jewish painter.
Issus (ĭs′ŭs), anc. spt., Asia Minor: victory of [Alexander, 333 B. C.]
Istanbul (ē″stän-bōōl′), [formerly **Constantinople**], city, Turkey, p. 673,029.
Italy (ĭt′ȧ-lĭ), repub., S. Europe, 117,982 sq. m., p. 41,169,000; cap., Rome.
Ithaca (ĭth′ȧ-kȧ), isl. W. of Greece.
Ivan (ē-vȧn′; ī′văn), name of 6 czars of Russ., notably: **III** [*the Great*] (1440–1505): founded Russ. empire; **IV** [*the Terrible*] (1530–84).
Ivory Coast (ī′vō-rĭ), Fr. col., W. Afr., 121,-976 sq. m., p. 1,724,545; cap., Bingerville.
Izmir (ĭz-mēr′), [formerly **Smyrna**], city, Turkey, p. 190,291.

J

Jackson (jăk′sŭn), **1,** Andrew (1767–1845), Am. gen.: 7th pres. of U. S.; **2,** Thomas J. [*Stonewall*] (1824–63), Am. Confed. gen.
Jackson (jăk′sŭn), **1,** city, Mich., p. 50,904; **2,** city, cap. of Miss., p. 97,674.
Jacksonville (jăk′sŭn-vĭl), city, Fla., p. 203,404.
Jaffa (yä′fä; jăf′ȧ), [anc. **Joppa**], spt. tn., [Palestine, p. 47,709.]
Jamaica (jȧ-mā′kȧ), Br. isl., W. Indies, 4,297 sq. m., p. 974,742; cap., Kingston.
James (jāmz), **1,** name of 2 kings of Eng.: **I** (VI of Scot.), (1566–1625), son of Mary, Queen of Scots; **II** (VII of Scot.), (1633–1701): deposed; **2,** name of 5 kings of Scot.; **3,** Henry (1843–1916), Am. nov.; **4,** William (1842–1910), Am. psychologist.
James (jāmz), riv., Va., 450 m. to Chesa-[peake bay.]
Jamestown (jāmz′toun), **1,** city, N. Y., p. 43,250; **2,** ruined vil., Va.: 1st Eng. settlement in present U. S., 1607.
Japan (jȧ-păn′), [Jap. **Nippon; Nihon** (nē′hŏn′)], isl. empire, off E. coast Asia, 147,690 sq. m., p. 80,500,000; cap., Tokyo: **Sea of –,** bet. Honshu & Manchuria.
Jassy (yäs′ē), [**Iasi**], city, former cap. of Moldavia, Rumania, p. 185,000.
Jaurès (zhō″rĕs′), Jean Léon (1859–1914), Fr. socialist & au.
Java (jä′vȧ), isl., Indonesia. 50,745 sq. m., [p., with Madura, 50,000,000.]
Jay (jā), John (1745–1829), Am. law. & stsm.
Jefferson (jĕf′ĕr-sŭn), **1,** Joseph (1829–1905), Am. act.; **2,** Thomas (1743–1826), 3d pres. of U. S.
Jefferson City (jĕf′ĕr-sŭn), city, cap. of Mo., [p. 24,990.]
Jena (yā′nä), tn., Ger., p. 62,649: univ.
Jenner (jĕn′ĕr), Edward (1749–1823), Eng. phys.: disc. vaccination.
Jericho (jĕr′ĭ-kō), anc. city, Palestine.
Jerome (jĕ-rōm′; jĕr′ŏm), **1,** Jerome K. (1859–1927), Eng. humorist & dram.; **2,** Saint (340?–420), Lat. Ch. father: translated Bible into Lat.
Jersey (jûr′zĭ), Channel isl., 45 sq. m., p. 49,494: **– City,** city, N. J., p. 300,447.
Jerusalem (jĕ-rōō′sȧ-lĕm), city, Israel, p. 164,440: former cap. of Palestine.
Joan of Arc (jōn, ärk). See **Arc d', Jeanne.**
Joffre (zhôfr′), Joseph Jacques Césaire (1852–1931), Fr. gen. & comm. in chief.
Johannesburg (yō-hän′ĕs-bûrg), tn., Transvaal, Union of S. Afr., p. 288,131.
John (jŏn), **1,** name of 23 popes of Rome; **2,** [*the Blind*] (1296–1346), king of Bohemia; **3,** [*Lackland*] (1167–1216), king of England; **4,** name of 2 kings of Fr.; **5,** name of 3 kings of Poland, notably **III** [*Sobieski*] (1624–96); **6,** name of 6 kings of Portugal; **7,** [*of Gaunt*] Duke of Lancaster (1340–99), son of Edward III of Eng.
Johnson (jŏn′sŭn), **1,** Andrew (1808–75), 17th pres. of U. S.; **2,** Samuel (1709–84), Eng. lexicographer & writer.
Johnston (jŏn′stŭn), **1,** Albert Sidney (1803–62), Am. Confed. gen.; **2,** Sir Harry Hamilton (1858–1927), Br. expl. & au.; **3,** Joseph Eggleston (1807–91), Am. Confed. gen.
Johnstown (jŏnz′toun), city, Pa., p. 62,723.
Joliet (jō′lĭ-ĕt), city, Ill., p. 52,460.
Jones (jōns), John Paul (1747–92), Am. nav. [comm.]
Jonson (jŏn′sŭn), Ben. (1573?–1637), Eng. poet & dram.
Joplin (jŏp′lĭn), city, Mo., p. 38,515.
Joppa (jŏp′pȧ). See **Jaffa.**
Jordan (jôr′dăn), David Starr (1851–1931), Am. biol. & educ.
Jordan (jôr′dăn), riv., Palestine, 200 m. to [Dead sea.]
Josephine (jō′zĕf-ēn), (1763–1814), emp. of Fr.: 1st wife of Napoleon I.
Josephus (jō-sē′fŭs), Flavius (37?–95?), [Jewish hist.]
Jovian (jō′vĭ-ăn), or **Jovianus** (jō″vĭ-ā′nŭs), Flavius Claudius (331–364), Rom. emp.
Jowett (jou′ĕt), Benjamin (1817–93), Eng. Gk. scholar: translator of Plato.
Juan de Fuca (hwän′ dā fōō′kä; jōō′ăn dē fū′kȧ), str. bet. Vancouver & U. S., 80 m.
Juan Fernandez (hwän′ fĕr-nän′dāth; jōō′ăn fĕr-năn′dĕz), group of isls., Pacific oc., W. of Valparaiso, Chile, 70 sq. m.
Judah (jōō′dȧ), anc. kingdom, Palestine.
Judea (jōō-dē′ȧ), or **Judæa,** Rom. dist., Palestine.
Judith (jōō′dĭth), Heb. heroine, slew Holo-[fernes, Assyr. gen.]
Jugoslovia (yū″gō-slä′vĭ-ȧ). See **Yugoslavia.**
Julian (jōōl′yăn; jōō′lĭ-ăn), Flavius Claudius [*the Apostate*] (331–363), Rom. emp.
Juliana (jōō″lĭ-ăn′ȧ), (1909–), queen of the Netherlands fr. 1948.
Julius (jōōl′yŭs; jōō′lĭ-ŭs), name of 3 popes.
Juneau (jōō′nō), cap. of Alaska, p. 7,000.
Jungfrau (yŏŏng′frou″), [*the Maiden*], mt., Bernese Alps, Switzerland, 13,670 ft.
Justinian I (jŭs-tĭn′ĭ-ăn), Flavius Anicius [*the Great*] (483–565), Byzantine emp.
Jutland (jŭt′lănd), pen., Denmark, 11,443 sq. m., p. 3,434,555: nav. bat. 1916.
Juvenal (jōō′vĕ-năl), Decimus Junius (60?–140?), Lat. satirist.

K

Kabul (kä′bōōl), city, cap. of Afghanistan, p. 100,000.
Kaifeng (kī′fŭng′), city, cap. of Hunan prov., China, p. 200,000.
Kalamazoo (kăl″ȧ-mȧ-zōō′), city, Mich., p. [57,326.]
Kalmyk (kăl′mĭk), autonomous area, S. E., Russ., on Caspian sea, 38,440 sq. m., p. 142,000; cap., Elista.
Kamchatka (kȧm-chȧt′kă), pen., N. E. Siberia, 104,433 sq. m., p. 7,270.
Kamerun. See **Cameroons.**
Kandy (kăn′dē), tn., anc. cap. of Ceylon, p. 32,562: Buddhist temples.
Kansas (kăn′zȧs), State in U. S., 82,158 sq. m., p. 1,884,390; cap., Topeka: **– City, 1,** city, Mo., p. 453,290; **2,** city, Kans., p. 129,583.
Kansu (kăn′sōō′), prov., China, 125,450 sq. m., p. 5,927,997; cap., Lanchow.
Kant (känt; kănt), Immanuel (1724–1804) Ger. metaphysician.
Karachi (kȧ-rä′chē), spt. city, cap. Pakistan, [p. 386,555.]
Karlsruhe (kärls′rōō″ē), tn., cap. of Baden, Ger., p. 145,694.
Karnak (kär′năk), vil., Upper Egypt, site of [anc. Thebes: temples.]
Kashmir (kăsh″mēr′), or **Cashmere,** state N. India, 84,258 sq. m., p. 3,320,518.

Kato (kä′tō″), Takaaki, Viscount (1860–1926), Jap. stsm.

Katrine (kăt′rĭn), **Loch,** lake, Perthshire, Scot.: scene of Scott's *Lady of the Lake.*

Kattegat (kăt′ĕ-găt″), or **Cattegat,** part of North sea, bet. Sw. & Jutland.

Kazan (kȧ-zäny′′), city, Russ., p. 195,300.

Kean (kēn), **1,** Charles John (1811–68), Eng. act.; **2,** Edmund (1787–1833), Eng. trag.

Keats (kēts), John (1795–1821), Eng. poet.

Keble (kē′bl), John (1792–1866), Eng. clergy. & poet. [Am. blind & deaf au.

Keller (kĕl′ẽr), Helen Adams (1880–),

Kelvin (kĕl′vĭn), William Thomson, Baron (1824–1907), Br. physicist. [Eng. acts.

Kemble (kĕm′bl), name of famous family of

Kempis, à (*ȧ* kĕm′pĭs), Thomas (1380–1471), Ger. theolog.

Kenilworth (kĕn′ĭl-wûrth), tn., Eng., p. 6,000: scene of Scott's *Kenilworth.*

Kennebec (kĕn″ĕ-bĕk′), riv., Me., 150 m. long.

Kennedy (kĕn′ĕ-dĭ), Charles Rann (1871–), Anglo-Am. dram.

Kenosha (kē-nō′sh*ȧ*), city, Wis., p. 54,360.

Kentucky (kĕn-tŭk′ĭ), State in U. S., 40,598 sq. m., p. 2,921,708; cap., Frankfort.

Kepler (kĕp′lẽr), Johannes (1571–1630), Ger. math. & astron.

Kerak (kĕ-räk′). See **Transjordan.**

Key (kē), Francis Scott (1780–1843), Am. poet: *Star Spangled Banner.*

Kharkov or **Kharkof** (khär′kôf), city, Russ., p. 417,186.

Khartum (khär″to͞om′), tn., cap. of Anglo-Egyptian Sudan, p. 40,760.

Khuzistan (kho͞o′zĭ-stän), [anc. **Elam**], prov., S. W. Persia, 38,600 sq. m., p. 200,000.

Kiangsu (kyäng′so͞o′), prov., China, 38,600 sq. m., p. 28,378,565; cap., Nanking.

Kiaochow (kyou′chō′), bay, tn., & dist., on E. coast of Shantung, China, p. 192,000.

Kidd (kĭd), William [*Captain Kidd*] (1650?–1701), Scot. navig. & pirate.

Kidron (kĭd′rŏn), or **Cedron** (sē′drŏn), valley & brook, E. of Jerusalem.

Kief (kē′ĕf), or **Kiev,** city, Russ., p. 513,789.

Kiel (kēl), tn., Prussia, p. 213,881: univ.: **– Canal,** connects Kiel with Elbe riv.

Killarney (kĭ-lär′nĭ), **Lakes of,** three lakes, S. W. Ire. [poet, critic, & sol.

Kilmer (kĭl′mẽr), Joyce (1886–1918), Am.

Kimberley (kĭm′bẽr-lĭ), city, Union of S. Afr., p. 39,702: diamond mines.

King (kĭng), **1,** Basil (1859–1928), Can. poet & nov.; **2,** Ernest J. (1878–), adm. of the fleet, U. S.: comm. in chief U. S. fleet; chief of naval operations 1942–1945; **3,** William Lyon Mackenzie (1874–1950), Can. premier 1921–26, 1926–30, 1935–48.

Kingsley (kĭngz′lĭ), Charles (1819–75), Eng. clergy. & nov.

Kingston (kĭngz′tŭn), city, cap. of Jamaica, Br. W. Indies, p. 62,707: **– upon Hull** [formerly **Hull**], city, Eng., p. 460,880.

Kipling (kĭp′lĭng), Rudyard (1865–1936), Anglo-Indian nov. & poet: Nobel prize 1907.

Kirghiz (kĭr-gēz′), autonomous repub., Russ., 843,640 sq. m., p. 5,058,553.

Kishinev (kē-shē-nyôf′), city, cap. of Bessarabia, U.S.S.R., p. 128,200.

Kitchener of Khartum (kĭch′ĕn-ẽr; khär″to͞om′), Horatio Herbert, Earl (1850–1916), Br. gen.

Knossos (nŏs′ŭs), or **Cnossus,** anc. city & cap., N. shore of Crete: fabled birthplace of Zeus; site of labyrinth, etc.

Knox (nŏks), William Franklin (Frank) (1874–1944), Am. publisher, pol.; sec'y navy, 1940–44.

Knoxville (nŏks′vĭl), city, Tenn., p. 124,183.

Kobe (kō′bĕ), spt., Honshu, Jap., p. 644,212.

Koch (kōkh), Robert (1843–1910), Ger. bacter.: Nobel prize 1905.

Konia (kō′nē-ȧ), [anc. **Iconium** (ī-kō′nĭ-ŭm)], vilayet, Turkey, p. 504,384.

Königsberg (kö′nĭkhs-bĕrkh), spt. tn., E. Prussia, p. 279,926: univ.

Korea (kō-rē′*ȧ*). See **Chosen.**

Kosciusko (kŏs″ĭ-ŭs′kō), Thaddeus (1746–1817), Pol. patriot.

Kosice (kō′shĭt-sĕ), tn., Slovakia, p. 52,898.

Krakow (krä′kō), city, Poland, p. 183,706.

Kreisler (krīs′lẽr), Fritz (1875–), Aus.-born Am. violinist & comp.

Kristiania, Christiania. See **Oslo.**

Kruger (krü′gẽr), Stephen J. Paul (1825–1904), pres. of former S. Afr. repub. [mfr.

Krupp (kro͞op), Alfred (1812–87), Ger. gun

Kublai Khan (ko͞o′blī khän′), (1214–94), Chin. emp. & founder of Mongol dynasty.

Kurdistan (ko͞or″dĭ-stän′), region, Asia, E. Turkey, & W. Persia, N. of Syria & Iraq.

Kuyp, Albert. See **Cuyp.**

Kwangchow (kwäng′chō′), or **Kwang-chow-wan** (kwäng′-chō″-wän′), pen., China, in S. China sea, 190 sq. m., p. 250,000.

Kwangtung (kwäng′to͝ong′), pen., S. Manchuria, 1,438 sq. m., p. 1,656,726; cap., Dairen.

Kyoto (kyō′tō), or **Kioto,** city, Honshu, Jap., p. 679,963: cap. of Jap. until 1868.

Kyushu (kyo͞o′sho͞o′), or **Kiushu,** isl., Jap., 13,870 sq. m., p. 7,727,000.

L

Labrador (lăb″r*ȧ*-dôr′; lăb′r*ȧ*-dôr), with Newfoundland, the 10th prov. of Canada, E. Br. N. Am., 110,000 sq. m., p. 7,847.

Lacedæmon (lăs″ē-dē′mŏn). See **Sparta.**

Laconia (l*ȧ*-kō′nĭ-*ȧ*), **1,** anc. country of the Peloponnesus, Greece; **2,** mod. dept., Greece, p. 139,014.

La Crosse (l*ȧ* krôs′), city, Wis., p. 47,396.

Ladd (lăd), George Trumbull (1842–1921), Am. psychologist. [Hungary & Poland.

Ladislas (lăd′ĭs-lȧs), name of several kings of

Ladoga (lȧ′dō-gȧ), lake, N. W. Russ., 7,000 sq. m.: largest in Europe. [**Islands.**

Ladrone Islands (l*ȧ*-drōn′). See **Mariana**

La Farge (lȧ färzh′), John (1835–1910), Am painter. [1834), Fr. gen. & stsm.

Lafayette, de (dẽ lȧ″fā″yĕt′), Marquis (1757–

La Follette (lä fŏl′ĕt), Robert M. (1855–1925), Am. pol. [95), Fr. fabulist & poet.

La Fontaine, de (dẽ lȧ fôɴ″tân′), Jean (1621–

Lagerlöf (lä′gẽr-löf), Selma (1858–1940), Sw. nov.: Nobel prize 1909.

Lagos (lä′gōs; lā′gŏs), spt., W. Afr., p. 60,000.

Lagrange (lȧ″gräɴzh′), Joseph Louis, Comte (1736–1813), Fr. math.

Lahore (l*ȧ*-hōr′), city, India, p. 281,781.

Lakewood (lāk′wo͝od″), city, Ohio, p. 67,878.

Lamarck (lȧ″märk′), Jean de (1744–1829), Fr. natur. [pseud., *Elia.*

Lamb (lăm), Charles (1775–1834), Eng. essay.:

Lancaster (lăng′kăs-tẽr), **1,** city, Pa., p. 63,601; **2,** city, N. W. Eng., p. 41,250.

Lanchow (län′chō′), city, cap. of Kansu prov., China, p. 500,000.

Landor (lăn′dôr), Walter Savage (1775–1864), Eng. poet & writer. [73), Eng. art.

Landseer (lănd′sēr), Sir Edwin Henry (1802–

Lang (lăng), Andrew (1844–1912), Br. au.

Langland (lăng′lănd), or **Langley** (lăng′lĭ), William (1332?–1400?), Eng. poet.

Lanier (lă-nēr′), Sidney (1842–81), Am. poet & mus. [91,694.

Lansing (lăn′sĭng), city, cap. of Mich., p.

Laodicea (lā-ŏd″ĭ-sē′*ȧ*), **1,** anc. city, Phrygia, Asia Minor; **2,** [mod. **Latakia**], anc. spt., Syria. [1914–18.

Laon (läɴ), tn., Fr., p. 13,982: bats. 1814,

Lao-tse (lä′ō-tsŭ′), (about 600 B. C.), Chin. sage: founder of Taoism. [142,549.

La Paz (lä päs′), city, cap. of Bolivia, p.

Laplace, de (dẽ lȧ″plȧs′), Pierre Simon, Marquis (1749–1827), Fr. math. & astron.

Lapland (lăp′lănd), region, N. Europe, 150,000 sq. m., p. 30,000.

La Plata (lä plä′tä), city, Argentina: see **Plata: Rio de –**, est. of Paranā & Uruguay rivs., 200 m. long.

La Rochefoucauld, de (dē lȧ rôsh″fōō″kō′), François, Duc. (1613–80), Fr. essay.

La Salle, de (dē lȧ sȧl′), René Robert Cavelier (1643–87), Fr. expl.

Latakia (lä″tä-kē′ä), [anc. **Laodicea**], spt. tn., Syria, p. 21,404.

Latium (lā′shĭ-ŭm), anc. div., cen. It.

Latvia (lăt′vĭ-ȧ), repub. in U.S.S.R., on Baltic, 24,440 sq. m., p. 1,895,016; cap., Riga.

Lauder (lô′dẽr), Sir Harry M. (1870–1950), Scot. comedian, singer, & comp.

Lausanne (lō″zȧn′), city, Switzerland, p. 78,050.

Lavoisier (lȧ″vwȧ″zyā′), Antoine Laurent (1743–94), Fr. chemist.

Lawrence (lô′rĕns), city, Mass., p. 80,427.

Leacock (lē′kŏk), Stephen Butler (1869–1944), Can. educ. & humorist.

Leahy (lā′hĭ), William D. (1875–), admiral of the fleet, U. S.: chief of staff to the comm. in chief, army and navy 1942–49.

Lebrun (lē-brûṅ′), **1,** Albert (1871–1950), Fr. stsm.; pres. of Fr. 1932–40; **2,** Marie Anne Elizabeth Vigée (1755–1842), Fr. artist.

Lee (lē), **1,** Fitzhugh (1835–1905), Am. Confed. gen. & Span. War off.; **2,** Henry [*Light-Horse Harry*] (1756–1818), Am. Rev. gen.; **3,** Robert E. (1807–70), son of Henry: comm. Confed. army.

Leeds (lēdz), city, Eng., p. 476,500.

Leeward Islands (lē′wẽrd), **1,** Br. isls., W. Indies, 715 sq. m., p. 122,242; **2,** isl. group, Fr. Oceania.

Le Gallienne (lē găl″ĭ-ĕn′), **1,** Eva (1899–), Am. actress born in London; **2,** Richard (1866–1947), Eng. poet & writer in Am.

Leibnitz, von (fôn lĭp′nĭts), Gottfried Wilhelm (1646–1716), Ger. philos.

Leicester (lĕs′tẽr), city, cen. Eng., p. 246,000.

Leighton (lā′tŭn), Frederic, Baron (1830–96), Eng. painter.

Leipzig (līp′tsĭkh), or **Leipsic** (līp′sĭk), city, Ger., p. 679,159: univ.

Lemnos (lĕm′nŏs), or **Limnos** (lĭm′nŏs), Turkish isl., Ægean sea, 160 sq. m., p. 27,000.

Lenin (lĕn′ĭn; lyĕ′nĕn), Nikolai (1870–1924), Russ. Bolshevist leader & pres. of Russ. Soviet Federal Socialist Repub.

Leningrad (lĕn′ĭn-grăd), [formerly **Saint Petersburg** & **Petrograd**], city, former cap. of Russ., p. 1,614,008.

Leo (lē′ō), name of 13 popes, notably: **I** Saint [*the Great*] (390?–461); **III** (750?–816); **X** Giovanni di Medici (1475–1521); **XIII** (1810–1903).

Leonardo da Vinci (lē-ō-är′dō dä vēn′chē), (1452–1519), It. sculp., arch., eng., math., sci. & painter.

Leoncavallo (lā″ōn-kä-väl′lō), Ruggiero (1858–1919), It. comp.

Leonidas (lē-ŏn′ĭ-dȧs), (?–480 B. C.), king of Sparta: killed at Thermopylæ.

Leopold (lē′ō-pōld), name of 3 kings of Belgium: **I** (1790–1865); **II** (1835–1909); **III** (1901–).

Lesseps, de (dē lĕ″sĕps′), Ferdinand, Vicomte (1805–94), Fr. dipl. & eng.

Lessing (lĕs′ĭng), Gotthold Ephraim (1729–81), Ger. dram. & critic.

Lewis (lū′ĭs), **1,** Meriwether (1774–1809), Am. expl.; **2,** Sinclair (1885–1951), Am. nov.: Nobel prize 1930; **3,** John L. (1880–), Am. labor leader.

Lewiston (lū′ĭs-tŭn), city, Me., p. 41,142.

Lexington (lĕk′sĭng-tŭn), **1,** city, Ky., p. 54,449: univ.; **2,** tn., Mass., p. 17,098: 1st bat. Rev. War, April 19, 1775.

Leyden (lī′dĕn), city, Netherlands, p. 70,068: univ.

Lhasa (läs′ä), city, cap. of Tibet, p. 25,000.

Libau (lē′bou), tn., Latvia, N. Europe, p. 60,762.

Liberia (lī-bē′rĭ-ȧ), native repub., W. Afr., 43,000 sq. m., p. 2,000,000.

Libya (lĭb′ĭ-ȧ), **1,** anc. name given Afr. by the Gks.; **2,** mod. state, N. Afr., 679,358 sq. m., p. 1,072,000.

Libyan Desert (lĭb′ĭ-ăn), N. part of the Sahara, Afr., bet. Egypt & Fezzan.

Liebig, von (fôn lē′bĭkh), Justus, Baron (1803–73), Ger. chemist.

Liechtenstein (lĭkh′tĕn-shtīn), indep. principality of Europe bet. Austria & Switzerland, 65 sq. m., p. 10,716; cap., Vaduz.

Liége (lyāzh), tn., Belgium, p. 169,566: univ.; 1st bat. World War I, 1914.

Liggett (lĭg′ĕt), Hunter K. (1857–1937), Am. off. in command 1st army in Fr., 1917–18.

Li Hung Chang (lē′ hōōng′ chȧng′), (1823–1901), Chin. stsm.

Liliuokalani (lē″lē-ōō-ō-kä-lä′nē), Lydia (1838–1917), queen of Hawaii, 1891–93.

Lille (lēl), city, Fr., p. 201,921: univ.

Lima, 1, (lī′mȧ), city, Ohio, p. 49,880; **2,** (lē′mä), cap. of Peru, p. 265,000: univ.

Limerick (lĭm′ẽr-ĭk), bor., repub. of Ire., p. 39,488.

Limoges (lē″mōzh′), tn., S. W. Fr., p. 98,209: famed for porcelain.

Lincoln (lĭng′kŭn), Abraham (1809–65), 16th pres. of U. S.: assassinated by J. W. Booth.

Lincoln (lĭng′kŭn), **1,** city, cap. of Nebr., p. 97,423: univ.; **2,** city, Eng., p. 65,550.

Lind (lĭnd), Jenny (1820–87), Sw. soprano.

Lindbergh (lĭnd′bûrg), Charles Augustus (1902–), Am. aviator.

Lindsay (lĭn′zĭ), (Nicholas) Vachel (1879–1931), Am. poet & lecturer.

Lindsey (lĭn′zĭ), Ben B. (1869–1943), Am. jurist & social reformer: juvenile court.

Linnæus (lĭ-nē′ŭs), Carolus [Sw. *Karl von Linné*] (1707–78), Sw. botanist.

Lippi (lēp′pē), name of 2 It. arts.: Fra Filippo (1406?–69); Filippino (1457–1504).

Lisbon (lĭz′bŭn), city, cap. of Port., p. 529,524: earthquake 1755.

Lister (lĭs′tẽr), Sir Joseph (1827–1912), Eng. surgeon.

Liszt (lĭst), Franz (1811–86), Hung. comp. & pianist.

Lithuania (lĭth″ū-ā′nĭ-ȧ), repub. in U.S.S.R., on Baltic, former grand duchy; 59,633 sq. m., p. 2,316,615; cap., Kovno, p. 96,535.

Little Rock, city, cap. of Ark., p. 101,387.

Liverpool (lĭv′ẽr-pōōl), spt., Eng., p. 872,600.

Livingstone (lĭv′ĭng-stŭn), David (1813–73), Scot. missionary & Afr. expl.

Livonia (lĭ-vō′nĭ-ȧ), [now **Vidzeme** (vĕd′zē-mā)], former Russ. Baltic prov., now prov. of Latvia.

Livy (lĭv′ĭ), [Lat. **Titus Livius**], (59 B. C.–A. D. 17), Rom. hist.

Lloyd George (loid″ jôrj′), David (1863–1945), Br. stsm.: war premier.

Locarno (lō-kär′nō), tn., Switzerland, p. com. 5,630: pact of Locarno, 1925.

Locke (lŏk), **1,** John (1632–1704), Eng. philos.; **2,** Wm. J. (1863–1930), Br. nov.

Lockyer (lŏk′yẽr), Sir Norman (1836–1920) Eng. astron.

Locris (lō′krĭs), name of two small dists., anc. Greece.

Lodge (lŏj), **1,** Henry Cabot (1850–1924), Am. pol. & writer; **2,** Sir Oliver (1851–1940), Eng. sci.

Lodz (lôdz), tn., Poland, p. 451,974.

Lombardy (lŏm′bȧr-dĭ), div., It., 9,160 sq. m., p. 5,400,263; cap., Milan.

Lombroso (lŏm-brō′zō), Cesare (1836–1909), It. criminologist.

Lomond (lō′mŭnd), **Loch,** lake in Scot.

London (lŭn′dŭn), Jack (1876–1916), Am. nov.

London (lŭn′dŭn), **1,** city, Eng., on Thames riv., cap. of Br. empire; p. registration area 4,458,200; "outer ring," 3,390,800; "Greater London," 7,849,000: univ.; **2,** city, Ontario, Can., p. 94,984.

Londonderry (lŭn′dŭn-dẽr″ĭ), city, N. Ire., p. 45,159.

Long (lông), **1,** Crawford W. (1815–78), Am. phys. & surgeon: 1st to use ether; **2,** John L. (1861–1927), Am. nov. & dram.

Long Beach, city, Calif., p. 244,072.
Longfellow (lông'fĕl″ō), Henry Wadsworth (1807–82), Am. poet.
Long Island, isl., S. E. of N. Y., 1,682 sq. m.: **– Sound,** bet. Conn. & N. shore Long Isl.
Lorain (lō-rān') city, Ohio, p. 50,819.
Lorenz (lō'rĕnts), Adolf (1854–1946), Aus. orthopedic surgeon: Nobel prize 1902.
Lorraine (lō-rān'), orig. a duchy; later part of Alsace-Lorraine, Ger.: ceded to Fr. 1918; now Fr. prov. See **Alsace-Lorraine.**
Los Angeles (lŏs ăng'gĕl-ĕs; lŏs ăn'jĕl-ĕs), city, Calif., p. 1,957,692.
Loti (lô″tē'), Pierre (1850–1923), Fr. nov.: pseud. of *Louis Marie Julien Viaud.*
Louis (lo͞o'ĭs; lo͞o'ĭ; lo͞o″ē'), name of 18 kings of Fr., notably: **IX** [*Saint*] (1215–70); **XIII** (1601–43); **XIV** [*le Grand Monarque*] (1638–1715); **XV** (1710–74); **XVI** (1754–93): executed in Fr. Rev.; **XVII** (1785–95), nominally king; **XVIII** [*Monsieur*] (1755–1824).
Louisiana (lo͞o-ē″zē-ăn'ȧ), State in U. S., 48,506 sq. m., p. 2,667,022; cap., Baton Rouge.
Louisville (lo͞o'ĭs-vĭl; lo͞o'ĭ-), city, Ky., p. 367,359.
Lourdes (lo͞ord), tn., S. W. Fr., p. 8,805: pilgrimages to shrine there.
Louvain (lo͞o″văṅ'), city, Belgium, p. 40,021.
Low Countries, the Netherlands & Belgium.
Lowell (lō'ĕl), **1,** Amy (1874–1925), Am. poet, biog., & critic; **2,** James Russell (1819–91), Am. poet, essay., & dram.
Lowell (lō'ĕl), city, Mass., p. 96,523.
Lower California (lō'ẽr kăl″ĭ-fôr'nĭ-ȧ), pen., W. coast, N. Am., ter. of Mex., 58,328 sq. m., p. 62,831; cap., La Paz.
Loyola, de (dā lō-yō'lä), Ignatius (1491–1556), Span. priest, founder of the Jesuits.
Lubbock (lŭb'ŭk), Sir John (1834–1913), Eng. sci.
Lübeck (lü'bĕk), spt. city, Ger., p. 224,427.
Lublin (lyo͞o'blyĕn), city, Poland, p. 94,412.
Lucan (lū'kăn), Marcus Annæus [*Lucanus*] (39–65), Rom. poet.
Lucania (lū-kā'nĭ-ȧ), anc. div. of S. It., or Græcia Magna.
Lucerne (lū-sûrn'), [Ger. **Luzern** (lo͞o-tsĕrn')], city, Switzerland, p. 46,150: **Lake –,** N. cen. Switzerland, 23 m. long.
Lucian (lū'shăn), (120?–200?), Gk. satirist & humorist.
Lucknow (lŭk'nou″), city, India, p. 240,566.
Lucretius (lū-krē'shĭ-ŭs), Titus [*Lucretius*] Carus (96?–55 B. C.), Rom. poet.
Lusitania (lū″sĭ-tā'nĭ-ȧ), anc. name of cen. W. part Iberian pen., nearly coextensive with mod. Portugal.
Luther (lo͞o'thẽr), Martin (1483–1546), leader of Ger. Reformation.
Luxembourg (lük″säṅ″bo͞or'; lŭk'sĕm-bo͞org), or **Luxemburg** (-bûrg), **1,** grand duchy, Europe, 999 sq. m., p. 222,749; **2,** city, its cap., p. 62,440.
Luzon (lo͞o-zŏn'), isl., P. I., 40,814 sq. m., p. 3,900,000.
Lwow (lvo͞of), [formerly **Lemberg**], city, Poland, p. 219,388: univ.
Lycaonia (lĭk″ā-ō'nĭ-ȧ), anc. dist., Asia Minor.
Lycia (lĭsh'ĭ-ȧ), anc. prov., Asia Minor.
Lydia (lĭd'ĭ-ȧ), anc. country, Asia Minor.
Lyell (lī'ĕl), Sir Charles (1797–1875), Scot. geol.
Lynchburg (lĭnch'bûrg), city, Va., p. 47,639.
Lynn (lĭn), city, Mass., p. 99,521.
Lyon (lī'ŭn; lē″ôṅ'), [Eng. **Lyons** (lī'ŭnz)], city, Fr., p. 570,840: univ.
Lys (lēs), riv. Fr. & Belgium, 100 m.
Lysander (lī-săn'dẽr), (?–395 B. C.), Spartan gen.
Lysias (lĭs'ĭ-ăs), (450?–380? B. C.), Athenian or.
Lysippus (lī-sĭp'ŭs), (about 330 B. C.), Gk. sculp.
Lystra (lĭs'trȧ), anc. tn., Lycaonia.
Lytton (lĭt'ŭn). See **Bulwer-Lytton.**

M

Mabie (mā'bē), Hamilton Wright (1846–1916), Am. essay. & ed.
Mabini (mä-bē'nē), Apolinario (?–1903), Filipino patriot & stsm.
McAdoo (măk'ȧ-do͞o), William G. (1863–1941), Am. law.: sec. of treasury, 1913–18.
MacArthur (măk-är'thẽr), Douglas (1880–), gen. of the army, U. S., in supreme comm. of Allied forces in the Pacific 1942; accepted Jap. surrender for Allies, 1945.
Macaulay (mȧ-kô'lĭ), Thomas B., Lord (1800–59), Eng. hist., essay., & stsm.
Macdonald (măk-dŏn'ăld), James Ramsay (1866–1937), Eng. premier, 1924, 1929–35.
MacDowell (măk-dou'ĕl), Edward A. (1861–1908), Am. comp.
Machiavelli (mä″kyä-vĕl'lē; măk″ĭ-ȧ-vĕl'ĭ), Niccolo (1469–1527), It. stsm. & writer.
McKeesport (mȧ-kēz'pōrt), city, Pa., p. 51,223.
Mackenzie River (mȧ-kĕn'zĭ), in N. W. Can., 900 m. to Arctic oc.
Mackinac (măk'ĭ-nô), **Strait of,** bet. Lake Michigan & Lake Huron.
McKinley (mȧ-kĭn'lĭ), William (1843–1901), 25th pres. of U. S.: assassinated.
McKinley (mȧ-kĭn'lĭ), **Mount,** Alaska, highest peak of N. Am., 20,464 ft.
Maclaren (mȧ-klăr'ĕn), Ian (1850–1907), Scot. au.: pseud. of *John Watson.*
MacMonnies (măk-mŭn'ĭz), Frederick William (1863–1937), Am. sculp.
Macon (mā'kŏn), city, Ga., p. 70,106.
Madagascar (măd″ȧ-găs'kȧr), Fr. isl., E. of Afr., 224,721 sq. m., p. 3,621,342; cap., Tananarive.
Madeira Islands (mȧ-dē'rȧ), Port. isls., W. of Morocco, 314 sq. m., p. 179,002.
Madero (mä-*th*ä'rō), Francisco (1873–1913), pres. of Mex., 1911–13: assassinated.
Madison (măd'ĭ-sŭn), James (1751–1836), 4th pres. of U. S.
Madison (măd'ĭ-sŭn), city, cap. of Wis., p. 95,594: univ.
Madras (mȧ-drȧs'), city, India, p. 771,481.
Madrid (mȧ-drĭd'), city, cap. of Sp., p. 816,928.
Mæcenas (mē-sē'năs), Caius Cilnius (73?–8 B. C.), Rom. stsm. & patron of letters.
Maeterlinck (mä'tẽr-lĭngk), Maurice (1862–1949), Belgian dram. & essay.: Nobel prize 1911.
Magdalena Bay (măg″dȧ-lē'nȧ), Lower Calif., Mex., 40 m. long.
Magdeburg (mäg'dĕ-bo͝orkh), tn., Prussia, Ger., p. 293,959.
Magellan (mȧ-jĕl'ăn), Fernando (1480?–1521), Port. navig.
Magellan (mȧ-jĕl'ăn), **Strait of,** bet. S. Am. & Tierra del Fuego.
Main (mān; mīn), riv., Ger., 305 m. long.
Maine (mān), State in U. S., 33,040 sq. m., p. 910,456; cap., Augusta.
Mainz (mīnts), or **Mayence** (mȧ″yäṅs'), city, Ger., p. 108,537.
Majorca (mȧ-jôr'kȧ), Span. isl., Medit., 1,310 sq. m., p. 264,231; cap., Palma.
Malacca (mȧ-lăk'ȧ), or **Malakka,** ter., Malay pen., S. E. Asia, 640 sq. m., p. 236,087; cap., Malacca, p. 43,258.
Malaya (mȧ-lā'ȧ; mā-), **Federation of,** Br. protec., Malay pen., 49,827 sq. m., p. 5,086,405; cap. Kuala Lumpur, p. 176,195.
Malay Archipelago (mȧ-lā'; mā'lā), or **Malaysia** (mȧ-lā'shȧ; -zhȧ), isl. groups, S. E. of Asia, including Indonesia, the Philippines, and New Guinea.
Malay Peninsula (mȧ-lā'; mā'lā), pen., S. Asia, 90,000 sq. m.
Malden (môl'dĕn), city, Mass., p. 59,779.
Malory (măl'ō-rĭ), Sir Thomas (1430?–70?), Eng. au.
Malta (môl'tȧ), Br. isl., Medit., 92 sq. m., p. 230,618.
Man (măn), **Isle of,** isl., Ir. sea, p. 60,284.
Manchester (măn'chĕs-tẽr), **1,** city, N. H., p. 77,685; **2,** bor., Eng., p. 755,900: univ.
Manchukuo (măn'jō'kwō'; often măn'cho͞o'-kwō'), former state; now *Manchuria.*
Manchuria (măn-cho͞o'rĭ-ȧ), div. N. E. China. Called *Manchukuo* under the Japanese.

Mandalay (măn′då-lā; măn″då-lā′), riv. port, Upper Burma, p. 150,000.
Manhattan (măn-hăt′ăn), isl., part of city of N. Y., p. 1,936,540.
Manila (må-nĭl′å), city, Luzon, cap. of P. I., p. 285,306: **– Bay,** inlet of China sea, P. I.
Manitoba (măn″ĭ-tō′bå), prov., Can., 246,512 sq. m., p. 771,818; cap., Winnipeg.
Mann (män), Heinrich (1871–1950), & Thomas (1875–), brothers, Ger. authors.
Mann (măn), Horace (1796–1859), Am. educ.
Mannheim (män′hīm), city, Ger., p. 247,486.
Manning (măn′ĭng), **1,** Henry (1808–92), Eng. cardinal & au.; **2,** William T. (1866–1949), Eng.-Am. Prot. Episcopal bp.
Mansfield (mănz′fēld), Richard (1857–1907), Am. act. [1506), It. painter.
Mantegna (män-tā′nyä), Andrea (1431–
Mantua (măn′tū-å), city, N. It., p. 44,201.
Maracaibo (mä″rä-kī′bō), **Gulf of,** bet. Goajira pen., Colombia, & Venezuela: **– Lake,** N. W. Venezuela. [of Fr. Rev.
Marat (må″rå′), Jean Paul (1744–93), leader
Marathon (măr′å-thŏn), vil., anc. Greece: bat. 490 B. C.
Marconi (mär-kō′nē), Guglielmo (1874–1937), It. electrician: disc. wireless telegraphy; Nobel prize 1909.
Mariana Islands (mä″rē-ä′nä), or **Marianne** (-nē), [**Ladrone** (lå-drōn′)], isls., S. Pacific oc., p. 15,000; cap., Garapan on Saipan isl.
Maria Theresa (må-rī′å tē-rē′så), (1717–80), wife of Francis I, emp. of Ger.
Marie Antoinette (må″rē′ äṅ″twå″nĕt′), (1755–93), consort of Louis XVI of Fr.
Marion (măr′ĭ-ŭn), Francis (1732–95), Am. Rev. gen. [Am. poet.
Markham (mär′kăm), Edwin (1852–1940),
Marlowe (mär′lō), **1,** Christopher (1564–93), Eng. poet & dram.; **2,** Julia (1866–1950), Eng.-Am. act. [sea & Ægean sea.
Marmara (mär′må-rå), **Sea of,** bet. Black
Marne (märn; mårn), riv., Fr., 326 m. long: bats. 1914–18.
Marquesas Islands (mär-kā′sås), Fr. isl. group, in S. Pacific, 480 sq. m., p. 2,300.
Marseilles (mär-sālz′), [Fr. **Marseille** (mår″-sây″)]. spt., S. Fr., p. 652,196.
Marshall (mär′shăl), George C. (1880–), gen. of the army, U. S.: chief of staff U. S. A., 1939–45; sec′y of state, 1947–49; sec′y of defense, 1950–51.
Martha's Vineyard (mär′thåz vĭn′yård), isl., Mass., p. 5,669. [385 sq. m., p. 234,695.
Martinique (mär″tĭ-nēk′), Fr. isl., W. Indies,
Mary (mā′rĭ), **1, I** [*Bloody Mary*] (1516–58), queen of Eng.; **2, II** (1662–94), wife of William III, queen of Gt. Br.; **3, – Stuart** (1542–87), queen of Scots: beheaded; **4, Victoria –,** (1867–), consort of George V, queen of Eng., 1910–1936.
Maryland (mĕr′ĭ-lănd), State in U. S., 12,327 sq. m., p. 2,324,243; cap., Annapolis.
Masaryk (mä′så-rēk), Thomas G. (1850–1937), Czechoslovakian stsm. [It. comp.
Mascagni (mäs-kä′nyē), Pietro (1863–1945),
Masefield (māz′fēld), John (1875–), Eng. poet laureate fr. 1930. [S. Rhodesia, Afr.
Mashonaland (må-shō′nå-lănd″), region of
Massachusetts (măs″å-chōō′sĕts), State in U. S., 8,266 sq. m., p. 4,664,284; cap., Boston.
Massenet (mä″sē-nā′), Jules (1842–1912), Fr. comp. [Am. poet, biog., & nov.
Masters (mås′tẽrz), Edgar Lee (1869–1950),
Matanzas (må-tăn′zås), city, Cuba, p. 39,000.
Matisse (må″tēs′), Henri (1869–), Fr. painter & sculp. [& Switzerland, 14,789 ft.
Matterhorn (măt′ẽr-hôrn), mt., Alps, bet. It.
Maude (môd), **1,** Cyril (1862–1951), Eng. act.; **2,** Sir Frederick S. (1864–1917), Br. gen.
Mauna Kea (mou′nä kā′ä), mt., Hawaii, 13,805 ft.
Mauna Loa (mou′nä lō′ä), volcano, Hawaii.
Maupassant, de (dē mō″pä″säṅ′), Guy (1850–93), Fr. nov. and writer of short stories.
Mauretania (mô″rē-tā′nĭ-å), **1,** anc. country, N. Afr.; **2,** col., Fr. W. Afr., 347,400 sq. m., p. 296,816.
Mauritius (mô-rĭsh′ĭ-ŭs), Br. isl. & col., Indian oc., 720 sq. m., p. 404,802.
Maxim (măk′sĭm), **1,** Hiram S. (1840–1916), Br.-Am. inv.; **2,** Hudson (1853–1927), Am. inv.
Maximilian (măk″sĭ-mĭl′yăn; -ĭ-ăn), **1,** name of 2 Holy Rom. emps.; **2,** Ferdinand Joseph (1832–67), archduke of Austria & emp. of Mex.: executed.
Mayo (mā′ō), Charles Horace (1865–1939), & William James (1861–1939), Am. surgeons.
Mazzini (mät-sē′nē), Giuseppe (1805–72), It. patriot. [Mohammedans, Arabia, p. 85,000.
Mecca (mĕk′å), or **Mekka,** holy city of
Mechlin (mĕk′lĭn), [Fr. **Malines** (må″lēn′)], tn., Belgium, p. 60,440.
Medford (mĕd′fẽrd), city, Mass., p. 66,109.
Media (mē′dĭ-å), anc. kingdom, now N. W. Persia, Asia.
Medici, de' (dā mĕd′ē-chē), Florentine family, statesmen & patrons of art, esp.: **1,** Catherine (1519–89), queen of Henry II of Fr.; **2,** Lorenzo [*the Magnificent*] (1449–92).
Mediterranean Sea (mĕd″ĭ-tẽr-ā′nē-ăn), inland sea, bet. Europe & Afr., 2,330 m. long, 1,007,220 sq. m.
Megara (mĕg′å-rå), tn., Megaris, anc. Greece.
Meissonier (mā″sō″nyā′), Jean L. E. (1815–91), Fr. painter.
Mekong (mā″kŏng′), riv., Tibet, Fr. Indo-china, 2,600 m. to China Sea.
Melanchthon (mē-lăngk′thŭn; -tŭn), Philipp (1497–1560), Ger. reformer.
Melanesia (mĕl″å-nē′shĭ-å; -shå), isl. group, N. E. of Australia. [tralian sop.
Melba (mĕl′bå), Madame (1861?–1931), Aus-
Melbourne (mĕl′bŭrn), city, cap. of Victoria, Australia, p. 1,000,000: univ.
Memphis (mĕm′fĭs), **1,** city, Tenn., p. 394,012; **2,** anc. city, Egypt.
Menai Strait (mĕn′ī), bet. Anglesey isl. & N. Wales, 13 m.: two bridges.
Mencius (mĕn′shĭ-ŭs), [Chin. **Meng-tse** (mĕng″tsŭ′)], (372–289 B. C.), Chin. sage.
Mendel (mĕn′dĕl), Gregor (1822–84), Aus. priest & biol. [1907), Russ. chemist.
Mendeléeff (mĕn″dĕ-lā′yĕf), Dmitri I (1834–
Mendelssohn-Bartholdy (mĕn′dĕl-sōn-bär″-tōl″dē′), Felix (1809–47), Ger. comp.
Mercator (mẽr-kā′tẽr; mẽr-kä′tôr), Gerard (1512–94), Flemish geog.
Mercier (mâr″syā′), Desiré J. (1851–1926) Belgian cardinal & patriot. [Eng. nov.
Meredith (mĕr′ē-dĭth), George (1828–1909),
Meriden (mĕr′ĭ-dĕn), city, Conn., p. 43,747.
Mérimée (mā″rē″mā′), Prosper (1803–70), Fr. nov.
Mesopotamia (mĕs″ō-pō-tā′mĭ-å). See **Iraq.**
Messina (mĕ-sē′nå), city, Sicily, p. 203,609: **Strait of –,** bet. Sicily & It.
Metchnikoff (mĕch′nĭ-kŏf), Elie (1845–1916), Russ. biol.: Nobel prize 1908.
Metternich, von (fŏn mĕt′ẽr-nĭkh), Clemens, Prince (1773–1859), Aus. stsm. & dipl.
Metz (mĕts), city, Lorraine, Fr., p. 69,624.
Meuse (mŏz), riv., Fr., Belgium, & Holland, 498 m. to North Sea: bats. 1914–18, 1944.
Meuse-Argonne (mōz′-âr″gôn′), region, Fr., scene of World War I bats. 1918.
Mexico (mĕk′sĭ-kō), **1,** repub., N. Am., 767,198 sq. m., p. 14,334,780; **2,** city, its cap., p. 906,063. [1864), Ger. comp.
Meyerbeer (mī′ẽr-bār), Giacomo (1791–
Michelangelo (mī″kĕl-ăn′jē-lō), or **– Buonarroti** (mē″kĕl-än′jä-lō bwō″när-rō′tē), (1475–1564), Florentine sculp., painter, poet, & arch.
Michelson (mī′kĕl-sŭn), Albert A. (1852–1931), Ger.-Am. physicist: Nobel prize 1907.

Michigan (mĭsh′ĭ-găn), State in U. S., 57,980 sq. m., p. 6,308,794; cap., Lansing: **Lake –**, one of the great lakes of N. Am., 320 m. long.

Micronesia (mī″krō-nē′shĭ-ȧ; -shȧ), isl. group, Oceania, of the P. I.

Middlesbrough (mĭd′lz-brŭ), tn., Eng., p. 132,000.

Milan (mĭl′ăn; mĭ′lăn′), city, N. It., p. 961,979: univ.; cathedral.

Miles (mīlz), Nelson A. (1839–1925), Am. gen.

Miletus (mī-lē′tŭs), anc. city, Ionia, Asia Minor.

Mill (mĭl), John Stuart (1806–73), Eng. philos. & pol. econ.

Millais (mĭ-lā′), Sir John Everett (1829–96), Eng. painter.

Millerand (mēl″rän′), Alexandre (1859–1943), Fr. stsm.

Millet (mē″yâ′), Jean François (1814–75), Fr. painter.

Millikan (mĭl′ĭ-kăn), Robert Andrews (1868–), Am. physicist: Nobel prize 1923.

Miltiades (mĭl-tī′ȧ-dēz), (about 500 B. C), Gk. gen.: bat. of Marathon.

Milton (mĭl′tŭn), John (1608–74), Eng. poet.

Milwaukee (mĭl-wô′kē), city, Wis., p. 632,651.

Mindanao (mĭn″dä-nä′ō), isl., P. I., 36,906 sq. m., p. 560,000; cap., Zamboanga.

Mindoro (mēn-dō′rō), cen. isl., P. I., 3,794 sq. m., p. 28,362; cap., Calapan.

Minneapolis (mĭn″ē-ăp′ō-lĭs), city, Minn., p. 517,277: univ.

Minnesota (mĭn″ē-sō′tȧ), State in U. S., 84,682 sq. m., p. 2,968,135; cap., St. Paul.

Minorca (mĭ-nôr′kȧ), isl., in Medit., Balearic group, 293 sq. m., p. 41,939; cap., Mahon, or Port Mahon, p. 17,542.

Minsk (mēnsk), city, cap. of White Russ., p. 131,083.

Mirabeau, de (dē mē″rȧ″bō′), Honoré Gabriel Riquetti, Comte (1749–91), Fr. stsm.

Mississippi (mĭs″ĭ-sĭp′ĭ), **1,** State in U. S., 46,865 sq. m., 2,173,373; cap., Jackson; **2,** riv., U. S., 2,486 m. to Gulf of Mex.

Missouri (mĭ-sōō′rĭ; -zōō′-), **1,** State in U. S., 69,420 sq. m., p. 3,933,636; cap., Jefferson City; **2,** riv., U. S., trib. of Miss. riv., 2,945 m.

Mistral (mēs″träl′), Frederic (1830–1914), Provençal poet: Nobel prize 1904.

Mitchell (mĭch′ĕl), **1,** John (1870–1919), Am. labor leader; **2,** S. Weir (1829–1914), Am. nov. & neurologist.

Mithridates VI (mĭth″rĭ-dā′tēz), or **Mithradates** [*the Great*] (132?–63 B. C.), king of Pontus.

Mitylene (mĭt″ĭ-lē′nē), or **Mytiline,** anc. tn., isl. of Lesbos, Ægean sea.

Moab (mō′ăb), anc. kingdom, Syria.

Mobile (mō-bēl′), city, Ala., p. 127,151: **– Bay,** est. of Gulf of Mex.

Modjeska (mō-jĕs′kȧ), Helena (1844–1909), Pol. act. in Poland & Eng.: **Modjeski** (-kĭ), Ralph (1861–1940), her son, Am. eng., designed Del. riv. bridge.

Mœsia (mē′shĭ-ȧ), anc. country, N. of Thrace.

Mohammed (mō-hăm′ĕd), or **Mahomet** (mȧ-hŏm′ĕt), (570?–632), founder of Islamism.

Moldavia (mŏl-dā′vĭ-ȧ), anc. principality joined with Wallachia to form Rumania, 1861; anc. cap., Jassy.

Molière (mô″lyâr′), (1622–73), Fr. dram.: pseud. of *Jean Baptiste Poquelin.*

Moline (mō-lēn′), city, Ill., p. 37,296.

Molokai (mō″lō-kä′ē), isl., Hawaiian group, 261 sq. m., p. 1,800: leper colony.

Molucca Islands (mō-lŭk′ȧ), or **Molukka,** isl. group, Indonesia, 25,000 sq. m., p. 600,000; cap., Ternate, p. 6,374.

Mommsen (mŏm′zĕn), Theodor (1817–1903), Ger. scholar & hist.: Nobel prize 1902.

Monaco (mŏn′ȧ-kō), **1,** smallest indep. state of Europe, bet. Fr. & Medit., 8 sq. m., p. 24,927; **2,** tn., its cap., p. 2,085.

Mongolia (mŏng-gō′lĭ-ȧ), a prin. div. of China, E. Asia, 1,367,600 sq. m., p. 1,800,000; cap., Urga, p. 38,000.

Monroe (mŭn-rō′), James (1758–1831), 5th pres. of U. S.

Mons (môṅs), city, Belgium, p. 28,335: bats.

Montaigne, de (dē môṅ″tȧny′; mŏn-tān′), Michel Eyquem (1533–92), Fr. essay.

Montana (mŏn-tăn′ȧ; -tä′nȧ), State in U. S. 146,997 sq. m., p. 587,337; cap., Helena.

Montcalm, de (dē môṅ″kȧlm′), Louis Joseph, Marquis (1712–59), Fr. gen. in Can.

Montenegro (mŏn″tē-nē′grō), former kingdom, now part of Yugoslavia.

Montessori (mŏn″tĕs-sō′rē), Maria (1870–), It. phys. & educ.

Montevideo (mŏn″tē-vĭd′ē-ō), city, cap. of Uruguay, on La Plata riv., p. 458,784: univ.

Montezuma II (mŏn″tē-zōō′mȧ), (1479?–1520), last Aztec emp. of Mex.

Montgomery (mŏnt-gŭm′ẽr-ĭ), city, cap. of Ala., p. 105,098.

Montpelier (mŏnt-pēl′yẽr), city, cap. of Vt., p. 8,585.

Montpellier (môṅ″pē-lyā′), city, S. Fr., p. 82,819: univ.

Montreal (mŏnt″rē-ôl′), city, Quebec prov., Can., p. 1,002,703; "Greater Montreal," p. 1,370,044: univ.

Moore (mōōr), Thomas (1779–1852), Ir. poet.

Moravia (mō-rā′vĭ-ȧ), protec., Ger., 8,616 sq. m., p. 2,840,167; cap., Brünn.

More (mōr), Sir Thomas (1478–1535), Eng. stsm. & au.: "Utopia."

Morea (mō-rē′ȧ), [anc. **Peloponnesus**], pen., S. Greece.

Morgan (môr′găn), Daniel (1736–82), Am. Rev. sol.

Morley (môr′lĭ), **1,** Christopher (1890–), Am. au. & ed.; **2,** John, Viscount Blackburn (1838–1923), Br. au. & stsm.

Morocco (mō-rŏk′ō), Fr. & Span. protec., N. W. Afr., 231,500 sq. m., p. 6,000,000; caps., Fez, Meknes, Marrakesh, & Rabat.

Morris (mŏr′ĭs), **1,** Charles (1784–1856), Am. nav. off.; **2,** Gouverneur (1752–1816), Am. stsm. & dipl.; **3,** Robert (1734–1806), Am. financier; **4,** William (1834–96), Eng. poet, art., and socialist.

Morse (môrs), Samuel Finley Breese (1791–1872), Am. inv.

Moscow (mŏs′kō), [Russ. **Moskva** (mŏs-kvȧ′)], cap. of Russ. Soviet Federal Socialist Repub., p. 2,025,947: univ.

Moselle (mō-zĕl′), riv., Fr., 314 m. fr. Vosges mts. to Rhine.

Motley (mŏt′lĭ), John Lothrop (1814–77), Am. hist.

Mount Vernon (vûr′nŭn), **1,** city, N. Y., p. 71,837; **2,** estate, Va., on Potomac, 15 m. below Washington, D. C.: homestead & burial place of George Washington.

Mozambique (mō″zăm-bēk′), [**Portuguese East Africa**], Port. col., E. Afr., 426,712 sq. m., p. 3,652,000: **– Channel,** bet. Afr. & Madagascar.

Mozart (mō′zärt; mō′tsärt), Wolfgang Amadeus (1756–91), Aus. comp.

Mukden (mōōk″dĕn′), city, cap. of Manchuria, China, p. 250,000: univ.

Mulhouse (mü″lōōz′), [Ger. **Mülhausen** (mül″hou′zĕn)], city, Fr., p. 99,892.

Muncie (mŭn′sĭ), city, Ind., p. 58,364.

Munich (mū′nĭk), [Ger. **München** (mün′-khĕn)], city, cap. of Bavaria, p. 680,704.

Munkácsy (mōōn′kä-chē), Mihály (1844–1900), Hung. art.: pseud. of *Michael Lieb.*

Münster (mün′stẽr), tn., Prussia, p. 106,418.

Münsterberg (mün′stẽr-bĕrkh), Hugo (1863–1916), Ger.-Am. psychologist & educ.

Murillo (mū-rĭl′ō; mōō-rē′lyō), Bartolome Esteban (1618–82), Span. painter.

Murray (mŭr′ĭ), Sir James A. H. (1837–1915), Scot. philologist & lexicographer.

Murray (mŭr′ĭ), chief riv. of Australia, 1,500 m. long.

Muscle Shoals (mŭs′l), series of rapids in Tenn. riv., near Florence, Ala.

Muscovy (mŭs′kō-vĭ), former name of Russ.

Muskegon (mŭs-kē′gŭn), city, Mich., p. 48,047.

Muskogee (mŭs-kō′gē), city, Okla., p. 37,355.

Mussolini (mōōs″ō-lē′nē), Benito (1883–1945), It. premier & sol.; deposed 1943.

Mustapha Kemal (mōōs'tä-fä kā-mäl'), Ghazi, Pasha (1881–1938), mil. leader & 1st pres. of Turk. repub. fr. 1923. [1400 B. C.

Mycenæ (mī-sē'nē), anc. city, Argolis, Greece,

Myron (mī'rŏn), (about 5th cent.), Gk. sculp.

Mysia (mĭsh'ĭ-*ȧ*), anc. country, N. W. Asia Minor.

Mysore (mī-sōr'), city, S. India, p. 83,921.

Mytiline (mĭt"ĭ-lē'nē). See **Mitylene.**

N

Nagasaki (nä'gȧ-sä'kē), spt. city, Kiushu isl., Jap., p. 189,071. [isl., Jap., p. 768,558.

Nagoya (nä'gō"yȧ), city & fortress, Honshu

Namaland (nä'mä-lănd"). See **Southwest Africa.** [univ.

Nancy (năn'sĭ; näṅ"sē'), city, Fr., p. 114,491:

Nanking (năn"kĭng'), city, cap. of Kiangsu prov., and cap. of China, 1928–37, 1946–50, p. 390,000.

Nansen (nän'sĕn), Fridtjof (1861–1930), Norw. arctic expl., au., natur., & dipl.: Nobel prize 1922. [cathedral.

Nantes (nănts; näṅt), city, Fr., p. 184,509:

Nantucket (năn-tŭk'ĕt), isl., 15 m. long, off S. E. coast Mass., in Atlantic oc., p. 3,417.

Naples (nā'plz), [It. **Napoli** (nä'pō-lē)], city, W. cen. It., p. 966,423.

Napoleon (n*ȧ*-pō'lē-ŭn). See **Bonaparte.**

Nara (nä'rȧ), city, Jap., p. 54,643. [173,359.

Nashville (năsh'vĭl), city, cap. of Tenn., p.

Nassau (năs'ô), city, cap. of Bahama isls., p. 10,000.

Nast (nȧst), Thomas (1840–1902), Am. caricaturist: originated Democratic donkey & Republican elephant. [tine.

Nazareth (năz'*ȧ*-rĕth), small tn., N. Pales-

Nebraska (nē-brăs'k*ȧ*), State in U. S., 77,520 sq. m., p. 1,318,079; cap., Lincoln.

Negros (nā'grōs), isl. of P. I., 4,903 sq. m., p. 612,386. [1805), Br. adm.

Nelson (nĕl'sŭn), Horatio, Viscount (1758–

Nelson (nĕl'sŭn), riv., Manitoba, Can.

Nepâl (nē-pôl'), indep. kingdom, in Himalayas, 54,459 sq. m., p. 5,600,000; cap., Katmandu, p. 80,000. [Rom. hist.

Nepos (nē'pŏs), Cornelius (1st cent. B. C.),

Nero (nē'rō), (37–68), Rom. emp.

Netherlands (nĕ*th*'ẽr-lăndz), [**Holland**], kingdom., N. W. Europe, 12,582 sq. m., p. 7,730,577; off. cap., Amsterdam; seat of govt., The Hague.

Nevada (nĕ-vä'd*ȧ*), State in U. S., 110,690 sq. m., p. 158,283; cap., Carson City.

Nevin (nĕv'ĭn), Ethelbert (1862–1901), Am. comp. [name for the City of New York.

New Amsterdam (ăm'stẽr-dăm), Du. col.

Newark (nū'ẽrk), city, N. J., p. 437,857. [033.

New Bedford (bĕd'fẽrd), city, Mass., p. 109,-

New Britain (brĭt'n), city, Conn., p. 73,663.

New Brunswick (brŭnz'wĭk), **1,** city, N. J., p. 38,768; **2,** prov., Can., 27,985 sq. m., p. 512,186; cap., Fredericton.

Newburgh (nū'bûrg), city, N. Y., p. 31,924.

New Caledonia (kăl"ē-dō'nĭ-*ȧ*), Fr. isl., in Pacific oc., with depend. 8,548 sq. m., p. 47,505; cap., Numea.

Newcastle (nū'kȧs"l), city, Pa., p. 48,563.

Newcastle upon Tyne (nū'kȧs"l ŭ-pŏn' tīn'), city, Eng., p. 281,500.

New England (ĭng'glănd), N. E. portion U. S., comprising Me., N. H., Vt., Mass., R. I., & Conn.

Newfoundland (nū'fŭnd-lănd"; nū"fŭn(d)-lănd'), prov. of Canada., N. Am., 42,734 sq. m., p. 349,915; with Labrador, 154,734 sq. m., p. 357,762; cap., St. John's, p. 52,003.

New Guinea (gĭn'ĭ), **1,** isl., Australasia, W. Pacific; N. E. part formerly Ger., now mandate Australia, 89,550 sq. m., p. 1,010,000; cap., Rabaul; N. W. part, Du. prov., 160,692 sq. m., p. 237,179; cap., Ternate, Moluccas; **2,** Br. protec.: see *Papua.*

New Hampshire (hămp'shĭr), State in U. S. 9,341 sq. m., p. 529,880; cap., Concord.

New Haven (hā'vn), city, Conn., p. 163,344.

New Hebrides (hĕb'rĭ-dēz), Br.-Fr. isl. group, in Pacific oc., 5,700 sq. m.

New Jersey (jûr'zĭ), State in U. S., 8,224 sq. m., p. 4,822,528; cap., Trenton.

Newman (nū'măn), John Henry (1801–90), Eng. au. & cardinal.

New Mexico (mĕk'sĭ-kō), State in U. S., 122,634 sq. m., p. 677,152; cap., Santa Fe.

New Orleans (ôr'lē-ănz), city, La., p. 567,257.

Newport (nū'pōrt), city, R. I., p. 32,090.

Newport News (nū'pōrt nūz'), spt. city, Va., p. 41,571. [59,626.

New Rochelle (rō-shĕl'), city, N. Y., p.

New South Wales (wālz), state in Australia, 310,372 sq. m., p. 2,462,421; cap., Sydney.

Newton (nū'tŭn), Sir Isaac (1642–1727), Eng. math. & sci.

Newton (nū'tŭn), city, Mass., p. 80,996.

New York (yôrk), **1,** State in U. S., 49,204 sq. m., p. 14,741,445; cap., Albany; **2,** city, S. E. N. Y., p. 7,835,099.

New Zealand (zē'lănd), dominion within Br. empire: isls. in S. Pacific, 103,568 sq. m., p. 1,344,469; cap., Wellington, p. 133,770.

Niagara (nī-ăg'*ȧ*-r*ȧ*), riv., 33 m. fr. Lake Erie to Lake Ontario: **– Falls, 1,** falls in Niagara riv.: Am. falls, 167 ft. high, 1,060 ft. wide; Can. falls, 158 ft. high, 3,010 ft. wide; **2,** city, N. Y., p. 90,875.

Nicæa (nī-sē'*ȧ*), [**Nice** (nīs)], anc. city, Asia Minor, cap. of Bithynia.

Nicaragua (nĭk"*ȧ*-rä'gw*ȧ*), repub., Cen. Am., 51,660 sq. m., p. 754,000; cap., Managua.

Nice (nēs), city, S. Fr., p. 184,441.

Nicholas (nĭk'ō-l*ȧ*s), **1,** name of 5 popes; **2,** Saint [*Santa Claus*] (about 326), patron & guardian of children; **3,** name of 2 czars of Russ.: **I** (1796–1855); **II** (1868–1918): executed by Bolshevists.

Nicopolis (nĭ-kŏp'ō-lĭs), name of several ancient cities of Rom. empire: **1,** in Epirus, founded by Augustus: ruins; **2,** in N. Bulgaria, founded by Trajan, mod. Nikopol, p. 5,400. [1900), Ger. philos.

Nietzche (nē'chē), Friedrich Wilhelm (1844–

Nieuport (nē'ōō-pōrt), tn., Belgium: bats. 1488–89, 1600, & 1914–18. [of Guinea.

Niger (nī'jẽr), riv., W. Afr., 2,600 m. to Gulf

Nigeria (nī-jē'rĭ-*ȧ*), Br. col. & protec., W. Afr., 335,700 sq. m., p. 18,966,574; cap., Lagos.

Nightingale (nīt'ĭng-gāl; nīt'ĭn-), Florence (1820–1910), Eng. nurse & philan.

Nile (nīl), riv., E. Afr., 4,000 m. to Medit. sea.

Nîmes (nēm), tn., S. Fr., p. 84,667.

Nimitz (nĭm'ĭts), Chester W. (1885–), adm. of the fleet, U. S.; comm. in chief U. S. Pacific fleet 1941–45.

Nineveh (nĭn'ē-vĕ), anc. cap. of Assyria.

Ningpo (nĭng'pō'), city, Chekiang prov., China, p. 212,400.

Nippur (nĭp-pōōr'), anc. city, Babylonia.

Nobel (nō-bĕl'), Alfred Bernhard (1833–96), Sw. mfr. & philan.: inv. of dynamite; founder of Nobel prizes.

Norfolk (nôr'fŏk), spt., Va., p. 188,601.

North America. See **America.** [p. 94,070.

Northampton (nôr-thămp'tŭn), city, Eng.,

North Cape, promontory, Magerö isl., Norway: most northern pt. of Europe.

North Carolina (kăr"ō-lī'n*ȧ*), State in U. S., 52,426 sq. m., p. 4,038,814; cap., Raleigh.

North Dakota (d*ȧ*-kō't*ȧ*), State in U. S., 70,837 sq. m., p. 587,337; cap., Bismarck.

Northern Ireland (īr'lănd), free state in N. Ire., united with Br. govt.: former prov. of Ulster, except Cavan, Donegal, & Monaghan cos., 5,263 sq. m., p. 1,256,561; cap., Belfast.

North Island, isl., New Zealand, 44,130 sq. m., p. 831,813.

North Sea, branch of Atlantic oc., bet. Gt. Br. & the cont. of Europe, 221,000 sq. m.
Norway (nôr'wā), kingdom, N. Europe, 124,964 sq. m., p. 2,810,592; cap., Oslo.
Norwich (nŏr'ĭj; -ĭch), city, Eng., p. 124,700.
Nottingham (nŏt'ĭng-hăm), bor., Eng., p. 266,600.
Nova Scotia (nō'vȧ skō'shyȧ), [formerly **Acadia**], prov., Can., 21,068 sq. m., p. 638,277; cap., Halifax.
Nova Zembla (nō'vȧ zĕm'blȧ), Russ. isls., Arctic oc., 36,000 sq. m., p. 100.
Noyes (noiz), Alfred (1880–), Eng. poet.
Nubia (nū'bĭ-ȧ), undefined region, S. Egypt.
Numantia (nū-măn'shĭ-ȧ), anc. city, Sp.: taken by the Romans 133 B. C.
Numidia (nū-mĭd'ĭ-ȧ), anc. country, N. Afr., part of mod. Algeria.
Nürnberg (nürn'bĕrkh), or **Nuremberg** nū'rĕm-bûrg), tn., Bavaria, p. 392,494.
Nyasaland (nyä'sä-lănd″), Br. protec., S. E. Afr., 37,890 sq. m., p. 1,329,127; cap., Zomba.

O

Oahu (ō-ä'hōō), one of the Hawaiian isls., 598 sq. m., p. 123,496.
Oakland (ōk'lănd), city, Calif., p. 380,756.
Oak Park (ōk), city, Ill., p. 63,175.
Ob (ôp), riv., W. Siberia, 2,250 m. to Arctic oc.: **Gulf of –,** inlet, Arctic oc., Siberia.
Oberammergau (ō″bĕr-äm'ĕr-gou″), vil., upper Bavaria, p. 1,700: Passion Play.
Obregon (ō″brā-gōn'), Alvaro (1880–1928), Mex. gen.: pres. of Mex., 1920–24.
Oceania (ō″shē-ăn'ĭ-ȧ), or **Oceanica** (-ē-kȧ), isls., Pacific & Malay archipelago, 70,000 sq. m., p. 1,000,000. [Black sea, p. 420,889.
Odessa (ē-dĕs'ȧ), spt. city, Ukraine, Russ., on
Offenbach (ôf'ĕn-bäkh; ô″fäṅ″bȧk'), Jacques (1819–80), Ger.-Fr. comp.
Ogden (ŏg'dĕn), city, Utah, p. 59,910.
Ohio (ō-hī'ō), **1,** State in U. S., 41,040 sq. m., p. 7,899,095; cap., Columbus; **2,** riv., U. S., 963 m. fr. Pittsburgh, Pa., to Miss. riv.
Ohm (ōm), Georg Simon (1787–1854), Ger. physicist: disc. Ohm's law.
Oise (wäz), riv., Belgium & Fr., 186 m. to Seine. [E. Siberia, 1,000 m. long.
Okhotsk (ō-kŏtsk'), **Sea of,** inlet of Pacific,
Oklahoma (ō″klȧ-hō'mȧ), State in U. S., 70,057 sq. m., p. 2,223,650: **– City,** city, cap. of Okla., p. 242,450.
Oldenburg (ôl'dĕn-bŏŏrkh), administrative div., Ger., 2,480 sq. m., p. 545,172.
Oldham (ōld'ăm), bor., Eng., p. 143,200.
Olives (ŏl'ĭvz), **Mount of,** [**Olivet** (ŏl'ĭ-vĕt)], hill, on E. side Jerusalem, 2,700 ft. high.
Olympia (ō-lim'pĭ-ȧ), **1,** city, cap. of Wash., p. 15,711; **2,** vale, near Elis, Greece.
Olympus (ō-lĭm'pŭs), mt. range, anc. Thessaly, Greece, 9,794 ft.
Omaha (ō'mȧ-hô″), city, Nebr., p. 247,408.
Oman (ō-män'), indep. state, S. E. Arabia, 82,000 sq. m., p. 500,000; cap., Muscat.
Omar Khayyâm (ō'mär kī-yäm'), (?–1123?), Pers. poet & astron.: *Rubáiyát.*
Omsk (ômsk), tn., Russ. Soviet Federal Socialist Repub., p. 161,615.
Onega (ō-nē'gȧ), lake, N. W. Russ., 3,763 sq. m.
O'Neill (ō-nēl'), Eugene Gladstone (1888–), Am. dram.
Ontario (ŏn-tā'rĭ-ō), prov., Can., 412,582 sq. m., p. 4,562,354; cap., Toronto: **Lake –,** one of great lakes of N. Am., 7,243 sq. m.
Ophir (ō'fĕr), anc. country identified with Bib. times, location unknown.
Oporto (ō-pōr'tō), city, Port., p. 215,625.
Orange (ŏr'ĕnj), city, N. J., p. 38,413.
Orange Free State (ŏr'ĕnj), prov., Union of S. Afr., 50,389 sq. m., p. 628,827; cap., Bloemfontein. [to Atlantic oc.
Orange River (ŏr'ĕnj), riv., S. Afr., 1,300 m.
Oregon (ŏr'ē-gŏn), State in U. S., 96,699 sq. m., p. 1,512,100; cap., Salem.
Orinoco (ō″rĭ-nō'kō), riv., S. Am., 1,550 m. fr. Venezuela to Atlantic oc.
Orkney (ôrk'nĭ), isl. group & co., off N. Scot., 376 sq. m., p. 21,700; cap., Kirkwall.
Orléans (ôr″lā″äṅ'), city, Fr., p. 70,611.
Osaka (ō'zä″kä), spt. city, W. Honshu, Jap., p. 2,114,804.
Oshkosh (ŏsh'kŏsh″), city, Wis., p. 40,934.
Osler (ŏs'lĕr), Sir William (1849–1919), Can. phys. in U. S. & Eng.
Oslo (ŏs'lō), city, cap. of Norway, p. 258,483.
Ossa (ŏs'ȧ), mt., N. Thessaly, Greece, 5,348 ft.
Ossian (ŏsh'ăn), (3d cent.), legendary Scot. poet.
Ostend (ŏst-ĕnd'), seaside resort, North sea, Belgium, p. 44,241; summer p. 100,000.
Österreich (ös'tĕr-rīkh), Ger. name for Austria. [Ger. chemist: Nobel prize 1909.
Ostwald (ôst'vält), Wilhelm (1853–1932),
Othman (ŏth'măn), or **Osman** (ŏs'măn), [*the Conqueror*] (1259–1326), founded Ottoman Empire. [Ottawa riv., p. 198,773: univ.
Ottawa (ŏt'ȧ-wȧ), city, cap. of Can., on
Otto (ŏt'ō), or **Otho** (ō'thō), **I** [*the Great*] (912–973), emp. of Ger., 936–973: Holy Rom. emp. fr. 962.
Ottoman Empire. See **Turkey.** [Rom. poet.
Ovid (ŏ'vĭd), Publius Naso (43 B. C.–A. D. 17),
Oxford (ŏks'fĕrd), city, Eng., p. 73,660: univ.
Ozark (ō'zärk), mts., Ark. & Mo., 1,400 ft.

P

Pacific Ocean (pȧ-sĭf'ĭk), bet. Am. & Asia & Australia, 55,000,000 sq. m.
Paderewski (pä″dĕ-rĕf'skē; -rĕs'kē), Ignace Jan (1860–1941), Pol. pianist, comp., & stsm.
Padua (păd'ū-ȧ), [It. **Padova** (pä'dō-vä)], city, N. E. It., p. 125,159: univ.
Pæstum (pĕs'tŭm), [mod. **Pesto** (pĕs'tō)], anc. Gk. city, It.: ruins. [Genoese violinist.
Paganini (pä″gä-nē'nē), Niccolo (1782–1840),
Page (pāj), **1,** Thomas Nelson (1853–1922), Am. nov.; **2,** Walter Hines (1855–1918), Am. ed. & dipl. [& writer.
Paine (pān), Thomas (1737–1809), Am. pol.
Pakistan (păk'ĭs-tăn), Dominion of, Moslem section of former Indian Empire; 361,000 sq. m., p. 70,000,000; cap., Karachi.
Palermo (pȧ-lûr'mō), city, N. Sicily, p. 447,335: univ.
Palestine (păl'ĕs-tīn), [Bib. **Canaan**], country, S. W. Syria: former Br. mandate; now divided into Israel and Arab Palestine.
Palestrina, da (dä pä″lās-trē'nä), Giovanni Pierluigi (1526–94), It. comp.
Palisades (păl″ĭ-sādz'), high cliffs, 20 m. long, on W. bank of Hudson riv., N. Y. & N. J.
Palmer (päm'ĕr), Alice Freeman (1855–1902), Am. educ.
Palmerston (päm'ĕr-stŭn), Henry John Temple, Viscount (1784–1865), Eng. stsm.
Palmyra (păl-mī'rȧ), anc. city, Syria: sacked by the Romans, A. D. 273: ruins. [Minor.
Pamphylia (păm-fĭl'ĭ-ȧ), anc. prov., Asia
Panama (păn″ȧ-mä'), **1,** repub., Cen. Am., 32,380 sq. m., p. 442,522, exclusive of Canal zone; **2,** city, its cap., p. 59,458: **– Canal,** across Isthmus of Panama: see *Canal Zone*: **Isthmus of –,** connects N. Am. & S. Am.
Pankhurst (păngk'hûrst), Emmeline (1857–1928), Eng. militant suffragist.
Pannonia (pă-nō'nĭ-ȧ), anc. dist., Europe: now Austria.
Paphlagonia (păf″lȧ-gō'nĭ-ȧ), anc. dist., N. W. Asia Minor. [W. Cyprus.
Paphos (pā'fŏs), name of two anc. cities,
Papini (pä-pē'nē), Giovanni (1881–), It. au. & philos.
Papua (pä'pōō-ä; păp'ū-ȧ), former name of isl. New Guinea; now limited to Br. protec., S. E. New Guinea & near-by isls., 90,540

sq. m., p. 276,523; cap., Port Moresby. See **New Guinea.**
Paracelsus (păr″ȧ-sĕl′sŭs), Philippus Aureolus (1493–1541), Swiss alchemist & phys.
Paraguay (păr′ȧ-gwā), repub., S. Am., 61,647 sq. m., p. 836,360; cap., Asunción.
Paris (păr′ĭs; pȧ″rē′), city, cap. of Fr., on Seine, 30 sq. m., p. 2,871,429: univ.
Parker (pär′kẽr), **1,** Alton B. (1852–1926), Am. jurist & pol.; **2,** Sir Gilbert (1862–1932), Can. nov. in Eng. [Am. hist.
Parkman (pärk′măn), Francis (1823–93),
Parnassus (pär-năs′ŭs), [mod. **Liakoura** (lyä′ko͞o-rȧ)], mt., Greece, 8,070 ft. [Ir. stsm.
Parnell (pär′nĕl), Charles Stewart (1846–91),
Parrish (păr′ĭsh), Maxfield (1870–), Am. painter. [Persia.
Parthia (pär′thĭ-ȧ), small anc. country,
Pasadena (păs″ȧ-dē′nȧ), city, Calif., p. 104,-087. [Fr. philos.
Pascal (păs′kăl; päs″kȧl′), Blaise (1623–62),
Passaic (pȧ-sā′ĭk), **1,** city, N. J., p. 57,851; **2,** riv., N. N. J., 100 m. to Newark bay.
Pasteur (päs″tûr′), Louis (1822–95), Fr. chemist & biol.: pasteurization.
Patagonia (păt″ȧ-gō′nĭ-ȧ), undefined region, S. part Argentine Repub., S. Am., about 320,000 sq. m., p. 45,000. [Eng. essay.
Pater (pā′tẽr), Walter Horatio (1839–94),
Paterson (păt′ẽr-sŭn), city, N. J., p. 139,423.
Patmos (păt′mŏs), It. isl., Ægean sea, 15 sq. m., p. 2,550: St. John exiled here.
Patrick (păt′rĭk), Saint (389?–461?), apostle to, & patron saint of, Ire. [operatic sop.
Patti (păt′ē), Adelina (1843–1919), It.-Span.
Pau (pō), tn., S. W. Fr., p. 37,000: resort.
Paul (pôl), name of 5 popes, notably **V** Camillo Borghese (1552–1621).
Pawtucket (pô-tŭk′ĕt), city, R. I., p. 81,180.
Payne (pān), **1,** John Howard (1792–1852), Am. act. & poet: "Home Sweet Home."
Peace River (pēs), riv., Br. Columbia & Alberta, Can., 1,000 m. to Great Slave riv.
Peary (pē′rĭ), Robert Edwin (1856–1920), Am. arctic expl.: recognized 1911 by Congress as disc. of N. pole in 1909.
Peel (pēl), **1,** Sir Robert (1788–1850), Br. stsm.; **2,** Sir Robert (1822–95), his son, Br. stsm.
Peiping (bā″pĭng′), [formerly **Peking** (pē″-king′)], city, Chihli prov., cap. of Communist China, p. 700,000.
Pelée, Mont (môṅ″ pē-lā′), volcano, N. W. Martinique, W. Indies, 4,500 ft. [5,300 ft.
Pelion (pē′lĭ-ŏn), mt., S. E. Thessaly, Greece,
Peloponnesus (pĕl″ō-pŏ-nē′sŭs), [mod. **Morea**], anc. name of pen., S. Greece.
Penang (pē-năng′), [**Prince of Wales Island**], isl., Malaya, 400 sq. m., p. 446,500.
Penn (pĕn), William (1644–1718), Eng. Quaker: founder of Pa. [etcher & au.
Pennell (pĕn′ĕl), Joseph (1860–1926), Am.
Pennsylvania (pĕn″sĭl-vā′nĭ-ȧ), State in U. S., 45,126 sq. m., p. 10,462,628; cap., Harrisburg.
Penobscot (pē-nŏb′skŏt), riv., Me., 300 m. to Penobscot bay: **– Bay,** inlet of Atlantic oc., Me., 30 m. long, 20 m. wide.
Pensacola (pĕn″sȧ-kō′lȧ), spt., Fla., p. 43,293.
Peoria (pē-ō′rĭ-ȧ), city, Ill., p. 111,523.
Pepys (pēps; pĕp′ĭs; pĕps), Samuel (1633–1703), Eng. diarist.
Pergamum (pûr′gȧ-mŭm), or **Pergamus** (-mŭs), **1,** citadel of Troy; **2,** anc. city. N. W. Asia Minor, cap. of Rom. prov. of Asia: famed for its sculptures.
Periander (pĕr″ĭ-ăn′dẽr), (625?–585? B. C.). tyrant of Corinth: one of the Seven Wise Men of Greece. [stsm.
Pericles (pĕr′ĭ-klēz), (495?–429 B. C.), Gk.
Pernambuco (pĕr″näm-bo͞o′kō), or **Recife** (rā-sē′fā), city, Brazil, p. 268,000.
Perry (pĕr′ĭ), **1,** Matthew C. (1794–1858), Am. nav. off.; **2,** Oliver H. (1785–1819), Am nav. off.
Persepolis (pẽr-sĕp′ō-lĭs), [mod. **Istakhr**], city, cap. of Pers. empire under Darius.
Pershing (pûr′shĭng), John Joseph (1860–1948), Am. gen.
Persia (pûr′shȧ; -zhȧ), kingdom, W. cen. Asia, 628,000 sq. m., p. 9,000,000; cap., Tehran.
Persian Gulf (pûr′shăn; -zhăn), arm of Arabian sea, 75,000 sq. m. [p. 196,251.
Perth (pûrth), city, cap. of W. Australia,
Perth Amboy (pûrth ăm′boi), spt. city, N. J., on Raritan bay, p. 41,291.
Peru (pē-ro͞o′), repub., S. Am., 532,047 sq. m., p. 6,147,000; cap., Lima.
Perugia (pā-ro͞o′jä), [anc. **Perusia** (pā-ro͞o′-shä)], city, It., p. 81,409: univ.
Petain (pā″tăṅ′), Henri Philippe (1856–1951), marshal of Fr.; defender of Verdun 1916; chief of state 1940–44.
Peter (pē′tẽr), **1,** name of 3 czars of Russ., notably: **I** [*the Great*] (1672–1725); **2, – the Hermit,** preacher of the First Crusade; **3, II** (1923–), king of Yugoslavia, 1934–45. [34,948: bats. 1864–65.
Petersburg (pē′tẽrz-bûrg), city, Va., p.
Petersburg (pē′tẽrz-bûrg), **Saint,** city, Russ.: name changed to Petrograd, then to Leningrad, which see. [It. poet.
Petrarch (pē′trärk), Francesco (1304–74),
Petrograd (pĕt′rō-grăd). See **Leningrad.**
Phidias (fĭd′ĭ-ăs), (500?–432 B. C.), Gk. sculp.
Philadelphia (fĭl″ȧ-dĕl′fĭ-ȧ), city & co., Pa., 129 sq. m., p. 2,064,794: univ.
Philip (fĭl′ĭp), **1, II** (382–336 B. C.), king of Macedonia; **2,** name of 6 kings of Fr.; **3,** name of 5 kings of Sp.; **4,** [*King*], (?–1676), Indian chief of New Eng.
Philippi (fĭ-lĭp′ī), anc. city, N. E. Macedonia.
Philippine Islands (fĭl′ĭ-pēn), [**Philippines** (-pēnz)], isl. group, Pacific oc., off coast of China, 115,026 sq. m., p. 12,000,000; cap., Manila: annexed by U. S.; since 1935, an independent commonwealth.
Phillips (fĭl′ĭps), **1,** Stephen (1868–1915), Eng. poet; **2,** Wendell (1811–84), Am. abolitionist.
Phocæa (fō-sē′ȧ), anc. city, Ionia.
Phocis (fō′sĭs), W. div., anc. Greece. [Syria.
Phœnicia (fē-nĭsh′ĭ-ȧ), anc. country, coast of
Phoenix (fē′nĭks), city, cap., Ariz., p. 105,442.
Phrygia (frĭj′ĭ-ȧ), anc. region, Asia Minor.
Piave (pyä′vā), riv., It.: bats. World War I.
Pickett (pĭk′ĕt), George (1825–75), Am. Confed. gen. [of U. S.
Pierce (pērs), Franklin (1804–69), 14th pres.
Pierre (pēr), city, cap. of S. Dak., p. 5,690.
Pike (pīk), Zebulon Montgomery (1779–1813), Am. gen. & expl.
Pikes Peak (pīks), mt., Colo., 14,107 ft.
Pilsen (pĭl′zĕn), [**Plzen**], city, Bohemia, Ger., p. 114,704.
Pindar (pĭn′dȧr), (522?–443? B. C.), Gk. poet.
Pinero (pĭ-nĕr′ō), Sir Arthur Wing (1855–1934), Br. dram. [p. 75,000.
Piræus (pī-rē′ŭs), spt. near Athens, Greece,
Pisa (pē′sä; pē′zä), [anc. **Pisæ**], city, Tuscany, It., p. 77,105: univ.; leaning tower.
Pisano (pē-zä′nō), family of It. sculptors.
Pisgah (pĭz′gȧ), mt., Abarim range, anc. Moab, E. of Dead sea: peak called *Nebo.*
Pitt (pĭt), William, Earl of Chatham (1708–78), Eng. stsm.
Pittsburgh (pĭts′bûrg), city, Pa., p. 673,763.
Pittsfield (pĭts′fēld), city, Mass., p. 53,055.
Pius (pī′ŭs), name of 11 popes, notably: **XI** Achille Ratti (1857–1939), 1922–39; **XII** Eugenio Pacelli (1876–), 1939–
Pizarro (pĭ-zär′rō), Francisco (1475–1541), Span. conq. of Peru. [kings, 1154–1399.
Plantagenet (plăn-tăj′ē-nĕt), family of Eng.
Plata (plä′tä), city, Argentina, p. 165,318.
Platæa (plȧ-tē′ȧ), anc. city, Bœotia: ruins.

Plato (plā'tō), (427–347 B. C.), Gk. philos.
Plautus (plô'tŭs), (254?–184 B. C.), Rom. dram.
Pliny (plĭn'ĭ), **1**, [*the Elder*] (23–79), Rom. natur.; **2**, [*the Younger*], (62–113?), Rom. au. & or. [philos.
Plotinus (plō-tī'nŭs), (205?–270?), Egyptian
Plutarch (plōō'tärk), (46?–120?), Gk. biog.
Plymouth (plĭm'ŭth), **1**, tn., S. E. Mass., p. 10,589: Pilgrims landed here 1620; **2**, nav. station, Devonshire, Eng., p. 194,500.
Plzen (pl'zĕn). See **Pilsen.**
Po (pō), riv., N. It., 418 m. to Adriatic.
Pocahontas (pō″kȧ-hŏn'tȧs), (1595?–1617), daughter of Powhatan, Indian chief.
Poe (pō), Edgar Allan (1809–49), Am. essay., poet, & story-writer.
Poincaré (pwăṅ″kȧ″rā'), Raymond (1860–1934), pres. of Fr. repub., 1913–20.
Pola (pō'lä), spt. tn., Istria, It., p. 54,477.
Poland (pō'lănd), former kingdom, Europe; now repub., 149,359 sq. m., p. 27,176,717; cap., Warsaw.
Polk (pōk), **1**, James Knox (1795–1849), 11th pres. of U. S.; **2**, Leonidas (1806–64), Con. fed. gen. [trav. & au.
Polo (pō'lō), Marco (1254–1323), Venetian
Polycletus (pŏl″ĭ-klē'tŭs), (452?–412? B. C.), Gk. sculp. & arch.
Polynesia (pŏl″ĭ-nē'shĭ-ȧ; -shȧ), isls., E. Oceania, in S. Pacific oc., p. 150,000.
Pompeii (pŏm-pā'yē), anc. city, It., near Naples: buried by volcano A. D. 79.
Pompey (pŏm'pĭ), [*the Great*] (106–48 B. C.), Rom. gen. & triumvir.
Ponce de Leon (pŏns dē lē'ŭn; pōn'thā dā lä-ōn'), Juan (1460?–1521), Span. disc. of Fla.
Poniatowski (pō″nyȧ-tôf'skē; -tôs'kē), Jôzef Anton (1762–1813), Pol. nationalist & marshal of Fr.
Pontiac (pŏn'tĭ-ăk), city, Mich., p. 73,112.
Pontus (pŏn'tŭs), anc. country, S. E. of Black sea, Asia Minor.
Poona (pōō'nȧ), city, India, p. 214,796.
Pope (pōp), Alexander (1688–1744), Eng. poet.
Popocatepetl (pō-pō″kä-tā'pĕt-l), volcano, Puebla state, Mex., 17,782 ft.
Porphyry (pôr'fĭ-rĭ), (233–304?), Gk. philos.: antagonist of Christianity.
Port Arthur (är'thŭr), fortified (Russian) port, Manchuria, China, p. 17,000.
Porter (pōr'tĕr), **1**, David Dixon (1813–91), Am. adm.; **2**, Jane (1776–1850), Eng. nov.; **3**, Sydney (1867–1910), Am. au.: pseud., *O. Henry.* [**2**, city, Oreg., p. 371,011.
Portland (pōrt'lănd), **1**, city, Me., p. 76,926;
Port-of-Spain (spān), tn., cap. of Trinidad isl., p. 66,836.
Port Said (sä-ēd), tn., Egypt, on Medit., at W. end of Suez Canal, p. 100,899.
Portsmouth (pōrts'mŭth), **1**, city, Ohio, p. 36,663; **2**, city, Va., p. 71,294; **3**, spt. co. bor., Eng., p. 240,700: nav. station.
Portugal (pōr'tū-găl), repub., S. W. Europe, on Atlantic oc., 35,490 sq. m., p. 6,032,991: cap., Lisbon. [**bique.**
Portuguese East Africa. See **Mozam-**
Portuguese Guinea (gĭn'ĭ), col., W. coast Afr., 13,940 sq. m., p. 343,961; cap., Bissau.
Portuguese India (ĭn'dĭ-ȧ), col., W. coast India, comprising Goa, Damao, & Diu, 1,638 sq. m., p. 570,426.
Posen (pō'zĕn), [Pol. **Poznan**], city, Poland, p. 184,756: univ.
Potidæa (pŏt″ĭ-dē'ȧ), anc. city, Macedonia.
Potomac (pō-tō'măk), riv., bet. Md. & Va., 550 m. to Chesapeake bay.
Potsdam (pŏts'dăm), city, Prussia, p. 64,203.
Potter (pŏt'ĕr), Paul (1625–54), Du. art.
Poughkeepsie (pō-kĭp'sĭ), city, N. Y., p. 40,975: Vassar coll.
Powhatan (pou″hȧ-tăn'), (1550–1618), Am. Indian chief.
Poznan (poz'näny'). See **Posen.**
Praha (prä'hä), city, cap. Czechoslovakia, p. 676,663: formerly **Prague** (prāg).
Praxiteles (prăk-sĭt'ĕ-lēz), (?–330 B. C.), Gk. sculp. [1859), Am. hist.
Prescott (prĕs'kŭt), William Hickling (1796–
Pressburg (prĕs'bōōrkh). See **Bratislava.**
Preston (prĕs'tŭn), bor., Eng., p. 127,100.
Pretoria (prē-tō'rĭ-ȧ), tn., cap. of Union of S. Afr., p. 74,052. [sci.: produced oxygen.
Priestley (prēst'lĭ), Joseph (1733–1804), Eng.
Prince Edward Island (prĭns ĕd'wĕrd), isl. & prov., Can., in Gulf of St. Lawrence, 2,184 sq. m., p. 97,787; cap., Charlottetown.
Princeton (prĭns'tŭn), bor., N. J., p. 12,160: univ.; bat. 1777.
Proclus (prō'klŭs), (411?–485), Gk. philos.
Protagoras (prō-tăg'ō-răs), (480?–411 B. C.), Gk. philos.
Proudhon (prōō″dôṅ'), Pierre Joseph (1809–65), Fr. socialist. [p. 247,700: univ.
Providence (prŏv'ĭ-dĕns), city, cap. of R. I.,
Prussia (prŭsh'ȧ), administrative div., Ger., 113,149 sq. m., p. 38,175,989; cap., Berlin.
Przemysl (pshĕ'mĭsh-l), tn., S. E. Poland, p. 47,958: bats. 1915.
Ptolemy (tŏl'ē-mĭ), **1**, name of 16 kings of Egypt, fr. 323 B. C. till 47 B. C.; **2**, [*Claudius Ptolemæus*] (2d cent.), Gk.-Egyptian astron., geog. & math. [It. comp.
Puccini (pōōt-chē'nē), Giacomo (1858–1924),
Puebla (pwā'blä), city, Mex., p. 96,121.
Pueblo (pwĕb'lō), city, Colo., p. 63,561.
Puerto Rico (pwĕr'tō rē'kō), Am. isl., W. Ind., 3,435 sq. m., p. 2,210,703.
Puget Sound (pū'jĕt), arm of Pacific oc., N. W. coast of U. S., 2,000 sq. m.
Pulitzer (pū'lĭt-sĕr), Joseph (1847–1911), Hung. jour. in Am.: literary prizes.
Punjab (pŭn-jäb'), prov., N. W. India, 99,846 sq. m., p. 20,685,024; cap., Lahore, p. 281,781; native states, 37,059 sq. m., p. 4,416,036. [Russ. poet.
Pushkin (pōōsh'kĭn), Alexander (1799–1837),
Putnam (pŭt'năm), **1**, Israel (1718–90), Am. sol.; **2**, Rufus (1738–1824), Am. sol.
Pyeshkov (pyĕsh-kôf'), Alexei Maximovitch. See **Gorky, Maxim.**
Pylos (pī'lŏs), anc. region, Greece.
Pyrenees (pĭr'ē-nēz), mts., bet. Fr. & Sp., 280 m. long: highest peak, 11,165 ft.
Pyrrhus (pĭr'ŭs), (318?–272 B. C.), king of Epirus. [Gk. philos.
Pythagoras (pĭ-thăg'ō-răs), (582–507 B. C.),

Q

Quebec (kwē-bĕk'), **1**, prov., Can., 594,534 sq. m., p. 4,010,235; **2**, city, its cap., p. 161,439.
Queensland (kwēnz'lănd), state, N. E. Australia, 670,500 sq. m., p. 927,092; cap., Brisbane.
Quézon y Molina (kā'sôn ē mō-lē'nä), Manuel Louis (1878–1944), pres. the Philippines 1935–1944.
Quiller-Couch (kwĭl'ĕr-kōōch'), Sir Arthur Thomas (1863–1944), Eng. nov. & critic.
Quincy (kwĭn'zĭ), Josiah (1772–1864), Am. stsm. & au.
Quincy, 1, (kwĭn'sĭ), city, Ill., p. 41,402; **2**, (kwĭn'zĭ), city, Mass., p. 83,190.
Quintilian (kwĭn-tĭl'ĭ-ăn), Marcus Favius (35?–100?), Rom. rhetorician.

R

Rabelais (rȧ″bē-lâ'), François (1490?–1553), Fr. satirist.
Rachmaninoff (räkh-mä'nē-nôf), Serge V. (1873–1943), Russ. pianist & comp.
Racine (rȧ″sēn'), Jean Baptiste (1639–99), Fr. dram.
Racine (rȧ-sēn'), city, Wis., p. 70,749.
Raeburn (rā'bŭrn), Sir Henry (1756–1823), Scot. portrait painter.

Rainier (rā-nēr′), **Mount,** extinct volcano, Cascade range, Wash., 14,408 ft.
Rajputana Agency (räj″po͞o-tä′nȧ), collection of former native states, now parts of Repub. of India, 132,559 sq. m., p. 14,000,000.
Raleigh (rô′lĭ; răl′ĭ), Sir Walter (1552–1618), Eng. sol., au., & navig.
Raleigh (rô′lĭ), city, cap. of N. C., p. 65,123.
Rameses (răm′ē-sēz), name of several rulers of anc. Egypt.
Ramôn y Cajal (rä-mōn′ ē kä-häl′), Santiago (1852–1934), Span. phys.: Nobel prize 1906.
Ramsay (răm′zĭ), Sir William (1852–1916), Br. chemist: Nobel prize 1904.
Rangoon (răng-go͞on′), city, cap. of Burma, p. 501,219: univ.
Raphael Sanzio (răf′ā-ĕl, or rä′fä-ĕl, sän′-zyō), (1483–1520), It. painter.
Rasputin (rȧs-po͞o′tĕn), Gregory E. (1871–1916), Russ. monk & fanatic.
Ravenna (rä-vĕn′nä), city, It., p. 78,997.
Rayleigh (rā′lĭ), John W. S., Baron (1842–1919), Eng. physicist: Nobel prize 1904.
Reade (rēd), Charles (1814–84), Eng. nov.
Reading (rĕd′ĭng), **1,** city, Pa., p. 109,062; **2,** city, S. Eng., p. 97,020.
Récamier (rā″kȧ″myā′), Mme. Jeanne Julie (1777–1849), noted Fr. society leader, beauty, & wit: exiled by Napoleon.
Recife (rā-sē′fā), city, Brazil. See **Pernambuco.**
Redmond (rĕd′mŭnd), John Edward (1851–1918), Ir. stsm.
Red River (rĕd), riv., 1,550 m. fr. N. W. Tex. to Miss. riv.
Red Sea (rĕd), branch of Indian oc., bet. Arabia & Egypt, 160,000 sq. m.
Regina (rē-jī′nȧ), city, Can., p. 69,928.
Reims (rēmz; răṅs), or **Rheims,** city, Fr., p. 100,998: cathedral; bats. 1914–18.
Rembrandt van Rijn, or **Ryn** (rĕm′bränt vän rīn′; rĕm′brănt), (1606–69), Du. art.
Renan (rē-näṅ′), Joseph Ernest (1823–92), Fr. hist. & essay.
Rennes (rĕn), city, Fr., p. 83,418: univ.
Reszke, de (dā rĕsh′kē), Edouard (1856–1917), & Jean (1853–1925), Pol. operatic singers.
Reval (rā′väl). See **Tallinn.**
Revere (rē-vēr′), Paul (1735–1818), Am. patriot.
Reykjavik (rā′kyȧ-vēk″), city, cap. of Iceland, p. 25,217: univ.
Reymont (rā″mōnt′), W. Stanislaw (1868–1925), Pol. nov.: Nobel prize 1924.
Reynolds (rĕn′ŭlz; -ŭldz), Sir Joshua (1723–92), Eng. painter.
Rhætia (rē′shĭ-ȧ), anc. prov. of Rome, N. It.
Rhine (rīn), riv., Europe, 810 m. to North sea.
Rhode Island (rōd), State in U. S., 1,248 sq. m., p. 779,931; cap., Providence.
Rhodes (rōdz), Cecil John (1853–1902), Eng. admin. in S. Afr.: Rhodes scholarships.
Rhodes (rōdz), It. isl., Ægean sea, off coast of Asia Minor, 565 sq. m., p. 45,000.
Rhodesia (rō-dē′shĭ-ȧ), **Northern –,** Br. protec., Afr., N. of Zambesi riv., 291,000 sq. m., p. 1,269,508; cap., Livingstone: **Southern –,** region, S. of Zambesi riv., 149,000 sq. m., p. 1,032,703; cap., Salisbury.
Rhone (rōn), riv., Europe, 500 m. to Medit.
Richard (rĭch′ȧrd), name of 3 kings of Eng.: **I** [*Cœur de Lion*] (1157–99); **II** (1367–1400); **III** (1452–85), last of the Plantagenets.
Richardson (rĭch′ȧrd-sŭn), Samuel (1689–1761), Eng. nov.
Richelieu, de (dē rē″shē-lyö′; rĕsh′ē-lo͞o″), Duc (1585–1642), Fr. cardinal & stsm.
Richmond (rĭch′mŭnd), **1,** city, cap. of Va., p. 229,906; **2,** bor., Eng., p. 35,639.
Richter (rĭkh′tēr), Jean Paul Friedrich (1763–1825), Ger. au.
Riga (rē′gȧ), city, cap. of repub. of Latvia, p. 339,324: **Gulf of –,** arm of the Baltic.
Riis (rēs), Jacob August (1849–1914), Da.-Am. social worker & au.
Riley (rī′lĭ), James Whitcomb (1853–1916), Am. poet.
Rimini (rē′mē-nē), [anc. **Ariminum** (ȧ-rĭm′ĭ-nŭm)], tn., N. It., p. 57,672.
Rimski-Korsakof (rĭm′skĭ-kôr′sȧ-kŏf), Nikolay A. (1844–1908), Russ. comp.
Rio de Janeiro (rē′ō dā zhȧ-nā′rō), city, cap. of Brazil, p. 1,157,873: univ.
Rio Grande (rē′ō grän′dā), riv., boundary bet. Mex. & Tex., 1,770 m. to Gulf of Mex.
Riviera (rē-vyā′rä), undefined region, N. W. Medit. coast from Nice to Spezia.
Riza Khan Pahlevi (rē′zä khän pä′lȧ-vē), (1877–1944), shah of Persia, 1925–41: deposed.
Rizal (rē-säl′), José (1861–96), Filipino patriot & writer.
Roanoke (rō′ȧ-nōk″), city, Va., p. 91,089.
Robbia, della (dĕl′lä rŏb′byä), (1400?–82), It. sculp.
Robespierre, de (dē rŏbs″pyâr′), Maximilien (1758–94), Fr. revolutionist.
Robin Hood (rŏb′ĭn ho͝od), legendary Eng. outlaw.
Robinson (rŏb′ĭn-sŭn), **1,** Edwin Arlington (1869–1935), Am. poet; **2,** James Harvey (1863–1936), Am. educ.
Rob Roy (rŏb roi′), (1671–1734), Scot. freebooter: real name, *Robert Macgregor.*
Rochester (rŏch′ĕs-tēr), city, N. Y., p. 331,252: univ.
Rockefeller (rŏk′ē-fĕl″ēr), John Davison (1839–1937), Am. capitalist & philan.
Rockford (rŏk′fērd), city, Ill., p. 92,503.
Rock Island (rŏk), city, Ill., p. 48,594.
Rocky Mountains (rŏk′ĭ), W. range of N. Am., fr. N. Mex. to Arctic oc., 4,000 m. long: Mt. McKinley, Alaska, 20,300 ft.
Rodin (rô″daṅ′), Auguste (1840–1917), Fr. sculp.
Rolland (rô″läṅ′), Romain (1866–1944), Fr. nov.: Nobel prize 1915.
Rome (rōm), city, cap. of It., p. 914,631: univ.
Röntgen (rönt′gĕn; rĕnt′-), Wilhelm K. (1845–1923), Ger. sci.: Nobel prize 1901.
Roosevelt (rōz′vĕlt), **1,** Theodore (1858–1919), 26th pres. of U. S.: Nobel prize 1906; **2,** Franklin Delano (1882–1945), 32d pres. of U. S., 1933–45.
Root (ro͞ot), Elihu (1845–1937), Am. stsm.: Nobel prize 1912.
Rosario (rō-sä′rē-ō), tn., Argentina, S. Am., p. 265,000.
Ross (rŏs), Betsy (1752–1836), maker of 1st Am. flag.
Rossetti (rō-sĕt′ē), **1,** Christina (1830–94), Eng. poet; **2,** Dante Gabriel (1828–82), Eng. poet & Pre-Raphaelite painter.
Rossini (rŏs-sē′nē), Gioachino Antonio (1792–1868), It. comp.
Rostand (rŏs″täṅ′), Edmond (1868–1918), Fr. dram.
Rostov-on-Don (rŏs-tôf′-ŏn-dŏn′), city, Russ., p. 308,284.
Rotterdam (rŏt′ēr-dăm), spt. city, Netherlands, p. 577,694.
Rouen (ro͞o-äṅ′), city, Fr., p. 123,712.
Rouget de Lisle or **l'Isle** (ro͞o″zhâ′ dē lēl′), Claude Joseph (1760–1836), Fr. mil. eng., poet, & mus.: "La Marseillaise," 1792.
Roumania. See **Rumania.**
Rousseau (ro͞o″sō′), Jean Jacques (1712–78), Fr. essay. & philos.
Rowe (rō), Nicholas (1674–1718), Eng. dram. & poet laureate.
Rubens (ro͞o′bĕnz), Peter Paul (1577–1640), Flemish painter.
Rubicon (ro͞o′bĭ-kŏn), riv., N. It.
Rubinstein (ro͞o′bĭn-stīn), Anton (1830–94), Russ. pianist & comp.
Rumania (ro͞o-mā′nĭ-ȧ), kingdom, S. E. Europe, 122,282 sq. m., p. 17,393,149; cap., Bucharest.
Runnymede (rŭn′ĭ-mēd), meadow on bank of Thames riv., Eng.: Magna Charta 1215.
Ruskin (rŭs′kĭn), John (1819–1900), Eng. au.
Russia (rŭsh′ȧ), **1, Union of Soviet Socialist Republics,** a union in E. Europe & N. & W. Asia, of allied & federated socialist repubs., consting of Soviet Russ., White Russ., Ukraine, Uzbek, Turcoman, & Trans-

caucasian Federation, 8,166,144 sq. m., p. 147,013,609; **2, Soviet –,** or **Russian Soviet Federal Socialist Republic** [abbr. **R. S. F. S. R.**], a socialist govt., covering the remainder of the former Russ. empire in Europe & Asia, 7,597,638 sq. m., p. 100,857,985; cap., Moscow.
Ruthenia (ro͞o-thē'nĭ-ȧ), prov., Hungary, 4,886 sq. m., p. 702,846.

S

Saar (zär), riv., in Lorraine & S. Prussia: **– Basin,** region in S. W. Ger. near Fr. border, 751 sq. m., p. 770,030: coal mines.
Saba (sā'bȧ), [mod. **Yemen**], anc. kingdom, S. Arabia, land of Sabæans: Sheba of Bible.
Sacramento (săk″rȧ-mĕn'tō), **1,** city, cap. of Calif., p. 135,761; **2,** riv., Calif., 500 m. to San Francisco bay.
Saginaw (săg'ĭ-nô), city, Mich., p. 92,352.
Saguenay (săg″ē-nā'), riv., Quebec, 100 m. to St. Lawrence.
Sahara (sȧ'hä'rȧ), desert, N. Afr.: **French –,** ter. W. of Nile Basin, exclusive of the Libyan desert, 1,500,000 sq. m., p. 800,000; cap., Timbuctu.
Saint Augustine (sānt ô'gŭs-tēn″), city, Fla., p. 13,418: oldest tn. in U. S.
Saint Christopher (sānt krĭs'tō-fẽr), or **Saint Kitts** (kĭts), Br. isl. of Leeward group, W. Indies, 65 sq. m., p. 38,214; cap., Basseterre.
Sainte Beuve (săṅt″ böv'), Charles Augustin (1804–69), Fr. writer & critic.
Saint-Etienne (săṅ″-tā″tyĕn'), city, S. Fr., p. 193,737: cathedral.
Saint Gaudens (sānt gô'dĕnz), Augustus (1848–1907), Ir.-Am. sculp.
Saint Helena (sānt hĕ-lē'nȧ), Br. isl., Atlantic oc., 47 sq. m., p. 3,747: Napoleon's exile.
Saint Helens (sānt hĕl'ĕnz), tn., Eng., p. 102,640.
Saint John (sānt jŏn'), city, Can., p. 50,023.
Saint John's (sānt jŏnz'), city, cap. of Newfoundland, p. 52,003. [75,572.
Saint Joseph (sānt jō'zĕf), city, Mo., p.
Saint Lawrence (sānt lô'rĕns), riv., Can., 775 m. Lake Ontario to Gulf of St. Lawrence: **Gulf of –,** inlet of Atlantic, 500 m. long. [p. 852,623.
Saint Louis (sānt lo͞o'ĭs; lo͞o'ĭ), city, Mo.,
Saint Lucia (sānt lū'shĭ-ȧ; lo͞o-sē'ȧ), isl., Br. W. Indies, in Windward group, 233 sq. m., p. 56,917; cap., Castries, p. 7,757.
Saint Mihiel (săṅ″ mē″yĕl'), tn., N. E. Fr.: bat. 1918. [p. 309,474.
Saint Paul (sānt pôl'), city, cap. of Minn.,
Saint Petersburg (sānt pē'tẽrz-bûrg), former name of Leningrad (Petrograd).
Saint Quentin (săṅ″ käṅ″täṅ'), city, Fr., p. 48,525: bat. 1918.
Saint-Saens (săṅ″-säṅs'), Charles Camille (1835–1921), Fr. comp.
Saint-Simon, de (dē săṅ″-sē″môṅ'), Claude Henri, Comte (1760–1825), Fr. Socialist.
Saint Thomas (sānt tŏm'ȧs), **1,** one of U. S. Virgin isls., W. Indies, 28 sq. m., p. 8,826; **2,** city, its cap., p. 6,374.
Saint Vincent (sānt vĭn'sĕnt), isl., Br. W. Indies, in Windward group, 150 sq. m., p. 51,426; cap., Kingstown, p. 3,836.
Sakhalin (sȧ″khȧ-lēn'), or **Saghalien** (sä'gä-lyĕn'), [Jap. **Karafuto** (kä'rȧ-fo͞o'tō)], isl., off E. Siberia, N. of Japan, formerly divided bet. U.S.S.R. and Jap., now controlled by U.S.S.R., 28,597 sq. m. [36,350: univ.
Salamanca (säl″ȧ-măng'kȧ), city, Sp., p.
Salamis (săl'ȧ-mĭs), Gk. isl., in gulf of Ægina, 35 sq. m., p. 6,600: bat. 480 B. C.
Salem (sā'lĕm), **1,** spt., Mass., p. 41,842; **2,** city, cap. of Oreg., p. 43,064.
Salerno (sä-lĕr'nō), city, It., p. 63,106.
Salford (sôl'fẽrd), bor., Eng., p. 241,500.
Salust (săl'ŭst), (86–34 B. C.), Rom. hist.
Salonika (sä″lō-nē'kȧ), or **Saloniki** (-kē), [anc. **Thessalonica**], city, N. E. Greece, p. 236,524. [181,718: univ.
Salt Lake City (sôlt), city, cap. of Utah, p.
Salvador (säl″vȧ-dōr'), repub., Cen. Am., 7,225 sq. m., p. 1,722,579; cap., San Salvador. [tine: former cap. of Israel.
Samaria (sȧ-mā'rĭ-ȧ), dist. & anc. tn., Pales-
Samoa (sä-mō'ä), isl. group, S. Pacific.
Samos (sā'mŏs), Gk. isl., W. coast Asia Minor, 180 sq. m., p. 70,497.
Samothrace (săm'ō-thrās), [**Samothraki** (sä'mō-thrä'kē)], Turk. isl., in N. Ægean sea: site of discovery of "Winged Victory."
San Antonio (săn ăn-tō'nĭ-ō), city, Tex., p. 406,811.
Sand (sănd; säṅd), George (1804–76), Fr. nov.: pseud. of *Madame Dudevant.* [321,485.
San Diego (săn dē-ā'gō), city, Calif., p.
Sandwich Islands (sănd'wĭch). See **Hawaii.**
San Francisco (săn frăn-sĭs'kō), spt. city, Calif., p. 760,753.
San José (săn hō-sā'), city, Calif., p. 95,044.
San Jose (sän hō-sā'), city, cap. of Costa Rica, Cen. Am., p. 62,637. [Rico, p. 71,443.
San Juan (săn hwän'), city, cap. of Puerto
San Salvador (sän säl″vȧ-dōr'), city, cap. of Salvador, Cen. Am., p. 89,066.
Santa Cruz (săn'tȧ kro͞oz'), spt. city, cap. of Canary isls., p. 53,309. [p. 27,547.
Santa Fe (săn'tȧ fā'), city, cap. of N. Mex.,
Santiago (sän″tē-ä'gō), city, cap. of Chile, S. Am., p. 739,492: univ.: **– de Cuba,** spt. tn., Cuba, p. 48,500: bat. 1898.
Santo Domingo (sän'tō dō-mĭng'gō). See **Dominican Republic.**
São Francisco (souṅ″ fräṅ-sēsh'ko͞o), riv., E. Brazil, 1,800 m. to Atlantic.
São Paulo (souṅ″ pou'lo͞o), city, Brazil, p. 579,033. [Free State: now called *Ireland.*
Saorstat Eirann (sâr'stôt âr'ăn), the Irish
São Salvadore (souṅ″ säl″vä-dōr'), [**Bahia**], spt., E. Brazil, p. 283,422. [poetess.
Sappho (săf'ō), (about 600 B. C.), Gk. lyric
Sarajevo (sȧ-rä'yā-vō), or **Serajevo** (sĕ-), city, Yugoslavia, p. 78,173.
Saratoga (săr'ȧ-tō'gȧ), **1,** [now **Schuylerville,** which see]; **2,** [off. **Saratoga Springs**], city, N. Y., p. 15,434: mineral springs; races.
Saratov (sȧ-rä'tôf), city, Russ., cap. of Saratov govt., p. 215,369: univ.
Sardinia (sär-dĭn'ĭ-ȧ), It. isl., in Medit., 9,299 sq. m., p. 955,303: cap., Cagliari, p. 94,902.
Sardis (sär'dĭs), anc. cap. of Lydia. [dram.
Sardou (sȧr″do͞o'), Victorien (1831–1908), Fr.
Sargasso Sea (sär-găs'ō), area in Atlantic oc. covered with floating seaweed.
Sargent (sär'jĕnt), John Singer (1856–1925), Am. painter in Eng. [Florentine art.
Sarto, del (dĕl sär'tō), Andrea (1486–1531),
Saskatchewan (săs-kăch'ē-wŏn), **1,** prov., W. Can., 251,700 sq. m., p. 829,175; cap., Regina; **2,** riv., Can., 1,300 m. to Lake Winnipeg.
Savannah (sȧ-văn'ȧ), **1,** city, Ga., p. 119,689; **2,** riv., Ga., 450 m. to Atlantic oc.
Savonarola (săv″ō-nȧ-rō'lȧ), Girolamo (1452–98), It. monk & reformer.
Saxony (săk'sŭn-ĭ), administrative div., Ger., 5,789 sq. m., p. 4,992,320: cap., Dresden.
Scandinavia (skăn″dĭ-nā'vĭ-ȧ), **1,** anc. name of Norway, Sw., Denmark, & Iceland; **2,** pen. comprising Norway & Sw.
Scheldt (skĕlt), riv., Fr. 270 m. to North sea.
Schelling, von (fôn shĕl'ĭng), Friedrich Wilhelm Joseph (1775–1854), Ger. philos.
Schenectady (skĕ-nĕk'tȧ-dĭ), city, N. Y., p. 92,070: univ.
Schiller, von (fôn shĭl'ẽr), Johann Christoph Friedrich (1759–1805), Ger. poet.
Schleswig-Holstein (shlĕs'vĭkh-hôl'shtīn),

prov., N. Prussia, 5,802 sq. m., p. 1,519,365; cap., Schleswig, p. 19,025. [Am. nav. off.|
Schley (slī), Winfield Scott (1839–1911),|
Schopenhauer (shō′pĕn-hou″ẽr), Arthur (1788–1860), Ger. philos. [Aus. comp.|
Schubert (shōō′bẽrt), Franz (1797–1828),|
Schumann (shōō′män), Robert (1810–56), Ger. comp.
Schumann-Heink (shōō′män-hīngk′), Ernestine (1861–1936), Ger.-Am. operatic contralto.
Schurz (shōōrtz), Carl (1829–1906), Ger.-Am. stsm. & or.
Schuylerville (skī′lẽr-vĭl), [formerly **Saratoga**], vil., N. Y., p. 1,319: Burgoyne's surrender 1777. [to Del. riv.|
Schuylkill (skōōl′kĭl), riv., S. E. Pa., 130 m.|
Scilla (shēl′lä), [anc. **Scylla**], headland in str. of Messina: subject of legends.
Scio (sī′ō; shē′ō), [anc. **Chios** (kī′ŏs)], isl., Ægean sea, 320 sq. m., p. 74,000.
Scipio (sĭp′ĭ-ō), **1,** [*the Elder*] (237–183? B. C.), Rom. gen.; **2,** [*the Younger*] (185?–129 B. C.), Rom. gen.
Scotland (skŏt′lånd), N. div. of Gt. Br., 31,510 sq. m., p. 4,896,600; cap., Edinburgh.
Scott (skŏt), **1,** Robert F. (1868–1912), Eng. antarctic expl.: reached S. pole, Jan. 17, 1912; **2,** Sir Walter (1771–1832), Scot. nov. & poet.
Scranton (skrăn′tŭn), city, Pa., p. 124,747.
Scylla (sĭl′ȧ). See **Scilla.**
Scyros (skē′rŏs), [mod. **Skyros**], isl., Ægean sea, E. of Eubœa, Greece.
Scythia (sĭth′ĭ-ȧ), anc. undefined region of S. E. Europe.
Seattle (sē-ăt′l), spt. city, Wash., p. 462,440.
Sebastopol (sē-băs′tō-pōl). See **Sevastopol.**
Sedan (sē-dän′), tn., Fr., p. 16,300: bats.
Seeland (sē′lånd). See **Zealand.**
Seine (sân), riv., Fr., 480 m. to Eng. channel.
Seleucia (sē-lū′shĭ-ȧ), **1,** anc. commercial city on the Tigris; **2,** anc. spt., Cilicia.
Selkirk (sĕl′kûrk), Alexander (1676–1721), Scot. sailor: orig. of Robinson Crusoe.
Seneca (sĕn′ē-kȧ), Lucius Annæis (4? B. C.–A. D. 65), Rom. philos.
Senegal (sĕn″ē-gôl′), **1,** riv., S. W. Sahara, Afr., 1,000 m. to Atlantic oc.; **2,** Fr. col., W. Afr., 74,112 sq. m., p. 1,318,287.
Seoul (sē-ōōl′), [Jap. **Keijo** (kā′jō′)], city, cap. of S. Korea, p. 935,464.
Serb-Croat-Slovene State (sûrb″-krō″ăt-slō-vēn′), former name of the kingdom of Yugoslavia, formed of Serbia, parts of Austria-Hungary, & Montenegro, after World War I. See **Yugoslavia.**
Serbia (sûr′bĭ-ȧ), [formerly, **Servia**], former Balkan state, now part of Yugoslavia.
Service (sûr′vĭs), Robert William (1874–), Can. poet.
Seton (sē′tŭn), Ernest Thompson (1860–1946), Can. au.: pseud., *Seton Thompson.*
Sevastopol (sē-văs′tō-pōl), or **Sebastopol,** tn., S. W. Crimea, S. Russ., p. 74,703.
Severn (sĕv′ẽrn), riv., Wales & Eng., 210 m. long. [211), Rom. emp.|
Severus (sē-vē′rŭs), Lucius Septimius (146–|
Seville (sĕv′ĭl; sē-vĭl′), [Span. **Sevilla** (sä-vē′lyä)], city, S. Sp., p. 216,511: univ.
Shackleton (shăk′l-tŭn), Sir Ernest Henry (1874–1922), Br. antarctic expl.
Shakespeare (shāk′spēr), William (1564–1616), Eng. dram. & poet. [2,677,100.|
Shanghai (shăng″hä′ĭ), spt. city, China, p.|
Shannon (shăn′ŭn), riv., Ire., 240 m. long.
Shantung (shän′tōōng′), prov., N. China, 55,970 sq. m., p. 34,375,849; cap., Tsinan.
Shaw (shô), **1,** Anna Howard (1847–1919), Am. suffragist, minister, & phys.; **2,** George Bernard (1856–1950), Ir. dram.; **3,** Henry Wheeler (1815–85), Am. humorist: pseud., *Josh Billings.*

Sheba (shē′bȧ), or **Saba** (sä′bȧ), [mod. **Yemen**], anc. region, S. Arabia. [42,485.|
Sheboygan (shē-boi′gån), city, Wis., p.|
Sheffield (shĕf′ēld), bor., Eng., p. 515,440.
Shelley (shĕl′ĭ), Percy Bysshe (bĭsh), (1792–1822), Eng. poet. [m. to the Potomac.|
Shenandoah (shĕn″ăn-dō′ȧ), riv., Va., 200|
Sheridan (shĕr′ĭ-dăn), **1,** Philip Henry (1831–88), Am. gen.; **2,** Richard Brinsley (1751–1816), Br. dram. [(1820–91), Am. gen.|
Sherman (shûr′mån), William Tecumseh|
Shetland Islands (shĕt′lånd), isls., N. of Scot., 551 sq. m., p. 22,600.
Shreveport (shrēv′pōrt), city, La., p. 125,426.
Siam (sī-ăm′; sī′ăm), [off. **Thailand**], kingdom, S. E. Asia, 200,148 sq. m., p. 9,207,355; cap., Bangkok.
Siberia (sī-bē′rĭ-ȧ), E., or Asiatic, div. of Soviet Russ., 3,357,450 sq. m., p. 17,000,000.
Sicily (sĭs′ĭ-lĭ), isl., Medit., 9,935 sq. m., p. 4,426,113; cap., Palermo. [1831), Eng. trag.|
Siddons (sĭd′ŭnz), Sarah Kemble (1755–|
Sienkiewicz (shĕn-kyā′vĭch), Henryk (1846–1916), Pol. nov.: Nobel prize 1905.
Sierra Leone (sĭ-ĕr′ȧ lē-ō′nē), **1,** Br. protec., W. Afr., 27,000 sq. m., p. 1,541,311; **2,** Br. col., W. Afr., 4,000 sq. m., p. 85,163; cap., Freetown.
Sierra Nevada (sĭ-ĕr′ȧ nē-vä′dȧ), mt. range, Calif., 500 m.: Mt. Whitney, 14,501 ft.
Silesia (sĭ-lē′shĭ-ȧ; -shȧ), **1,** former dist. of Prussia; E. portion assigned to Poland 1919; remainder divided into provs. of Prussia: **Upper –,** 3,746 sq. m., p. 1,379,228, & **Lower –,** 10,269 sq. m., p. 3,132,328; **2,** former prov. of Czechoslovakia, part of Ger. 1939–45, 1,708 sq. m., p. 735,532.
Simonides (sī-mŏn′ĭ-dēz), (556?–469 B. C.), Gk. poet. [Am. nav. off.|
Sims (sĭmz), William Sowden (1858–1936),|
Singapore (sĭng″gȧ-pōr′), Br. isl., S. of Malay pen., Crown Colony, former cap. of Straits Settlements, 217 sq. m., p. 961,856.
Sinkiang (sĭn″kyäng′), [**New Dominion**], Chin. prov., bet. Mongolia & Tibet, 550,-340 sq. m., p. 2,688,305.
Sioux City (sōō), city, Iowa, p. 84,035.
Skagerrack (skăg′ẽr-råk), arm of North sea, bet. Norway & Denmark.
Skye (skī), isl., largest of the Hebrides, W. of Scot., 535 sq. m., p. 11,301.
Slovakia (slō-vä′kĭ-ȧ), prov., Czechoslovakia, 18,895 sq. m., p. 3,279,795; cap., Bratislava (Pressburg).
Smith (smĭth), **1,** Adam (1723–90), Scot. pol. econ.; **2,** Alfred Emanuel (1873–1944), Am. pol.; **3,** F. Hopkinson (1838–1915), Am. art. & au.; **4,** Joseph (1805–44): founded Mor-|
Smyrna (smûr′nȧ). See **Izmir.** [monism.|
Society Islands (sō-sī′ē-tĭ), isl. group, Fr. Oceania, S. Pacific oc.; prin. isl., Tahiti.
Socrates (sŏk′rȧ-tēz), (469–399 B. C.), Gk. philos. [p. 213,002.|
Sofia (sô′fē-yä; sō-fē′ä), city, cap. of Bulgaria,|
Soissons (swä″sôn′), tn., Fr., p. 15,781: bats. 1914–18. [lawgiver.|
Solon (sō′lŏn), (639?–559 B. C.), Athenian|
Somaliland (sō-mä′lē-lănd″), section E. Afr.: Br. protec., 68,000 sq. m.; Fr. protec., 5,790 sq. m.; It. protec., 154,000 sq. m.
Somerville (sŭm′ẽr-vĭl), city, Mass., p. 102,254.
Somme (sôm), riv., N. Fr., 150 m.: bats. 1916.
Soochow (sōō′chō′), city, Kiamgsu prov., China, p. 350,000.
Sophocles (sŏf′ō-klēz), (496?–406 B. C.), Gk. dram.
Sorolla y Bastida (sō-rō′lyä ē′bäs-tē′dä), Joaquín (1863–1923), Span. art.
Sothern (sŭ*th*′ẽrn), Edward Hugh (1859–1933), Am. act.
Sousa (sōō′zȧ), John Philip [*the March King*] (1854–1932), Am. bandmaster & comp.
South Africa, Union of. See **Union.**

South African Republic. See **Transvaal.**
South America. See **America.**
Southampton (south-ămp′tŭn), city, S. W. Eng., p. 169,900.
South Australia (ôs-trā′lĭ-ȧ), state, Australia, 380,070 sq. m., p. 495,160; cap., Adelaide.
South Bend (bĕnd), city, Ind., p. 115,698.
South Carolina (kăr″ō-lī′nȧ), State in U. S., 30,989 sq. m., p. 2,107,432; cap., Columbia.
South Dakota (dȧ-kō′tȧ), State in U. S., 77,615 sq. m., p. 650,029; cap., Pierre.
Southey (sou*th*′ĭ; sŭ*th*′ĭ), Robert (1774–1843), Eng. poet.
South Island, largest isl. of New Zealand, 58,500 sq. m., p., with Chatham isls., 512,656.
Southwest Africa (ăf′rĭ-kȧ), [**Namaland**], ter. in S. W. Afr., formerly Ger., now Br. protect. under mandate of Union of S. Afr., 322,400 sq. m., p. 258,905; cap., Windhoek.
Spain (spān), monarchy, S. W. Europe, including isls. & cols., 194,800 sq. m., p. 28,154,645; cap., Madrid.
Sparta (spär′tȧ), [**Lacedæmon,** (lăs″ē-dē′mŏn)], anc. cap. of Laconia, Peloponnesus.
Spartacus (spär′tȧ-kŭs), (?–71 B. C.), Thracian gladiator, Rome: leader slave revolt.
Spencer (spĕn′sẽr), Herbert (1820–1903), Eng. philos. [Eng. poet.
Spenser (spĕn′sẽr), Edmund (1552?–99),
Spinoza (spĭ-nō′zȧ), Baruch (1632–77), Du.-Jewish philos. [See **Svalbard.**
Spitsbergen (spĭts′bûr″gĕn), or **Spitzbergen.**
Spokane (spō″kăn′), city, Wash., p. 160,484.
Springfield (sprĭng′fēld), **1,** city, cap. of Ill., p. 80,832; **2,** city, Mass., p. 162,601; **3,** city, Mo., p. 66,302; **4,** city, Ohio, p. 78,029.
Stalin (stä′lĕn), Generalissimo Joseph V. (1879–), Russ. pol. leader, commissar for defence, chairman of Council, supreme director mil. operations.
Stamford (stăm′fẽrd), city, Conn., p. 73,584.
Standish (stăn′dĭsh), Miles (1584?–1656), leader of Plymouth colonists.
Stanley (stăn′lĭ), Sir Henry Morton (1841–1904), Br. expl. in Afr.
Staten Island (stăt′ĕn), isl. in N. Y. bay, 60 sq. m., p. 191,015; coextensive with bor. of Richmond, N. Y. City. [essay.
Steele (stēl), Sir Richard (1672–1729), Eng.
Stefansson (stā′fäns-sŏn), Vilhjalmur (1879–), Can. arctic expl.
Steinmetz (stīn′mĕts, Charles Proteus (1865–1923), Ger.-Am. electrical expert.
Stephenson (stē′vĕn-sŭn), George (1781–1848), Eng. eng. & inv. [humorist & nov.
Sterne (stûrn), Laurence (1713–68), Br.
Stevenson (stē′vĕn-sŭn), Robert Louis Balfour (1850–94), Scot. au.
Stilwell (stĭl′wĕll), Joseph W. (1883–1946), Amer. gen. in Burma campaign. Promoted to full gen. 1944. [474,094).
Stockholm (stŏk′hōlm), city, cap. of Sw., p.
Stoke on Trent (stōk ŏn trĕnt), bor., Eng., p. 279,700. [Am. orchestral conductor.
Stokowski (stō-kŏf′skē), Leopold, (1882–).
Stone (stōn), **1,** Harlan Fiske (1872–1946), Am. jurist: Chief Justice U. S. Supreme Court 1941–46; **2,** Lucy (1818–93), Am. suffragist.
Stowe (stō), Harriet Beecher (1811–96), Am. nov. & abolitionist. [geog.
Strabo (strā′bō), (66? B. C.–A. D. 24?), Gk.
Strachey (strā′chĭ), G. Lytton (1880–1932), Eng. essay. & biog.
Stradivarius (străd″ĭ-vā′rĭ-ŭs), or **Stradivari** (strä″dē-vä′rē), Antonio (1644–1737), violin maker of Cremona, It.
Straits Settlements, former Br. crown col., S. Malay pen. & isls., now Fed. of Malaya, and Crown col. of Singapore.
Strasbourg (strȧs″bo͞or′), [Ger. **Strassburg** (shträs′bo͞orkh)], city, N. E. Fr., p. 164,136.
Stratford on Avon (străt′fẽrd ŏn ā′vŏn), bor. & tn., Warwickshire, Eng., p. 9,392: Shakespeare's birthplace.
Strauss (shtrous), **1,** Johann (1804–49), & his son, Johann (1825–99), Aus. comps.; **2,** Richard (1864–1949), Ger. comp. & conductor. [1912), Sw. nov. & dram.
Strindberg (strĭnd′bĕry′), August (1849–
Stuart (stū′ẽrt), Scot. & Eng. royal family.
Stuttgart (shto͝ot′gärt), city, Ger., p. 341,967.
Stuyvesant (stī′vē-sănt), Peter (1602–82), last Du. col. gov. of New Netherland.
Sudan (so͞o″dän′), region, Afr., S. of Sahara: **Anglo-Egyptian –,** S. of Egypt, 1,014,400 sq. m., p. 5,483,899; cap., Khartum: under Br.-Egyptian rule: **French –,** col., Sahara region S. of Algeria, 356,471 sq. m., p. 2,632,618; cap., Bamako. [1929), Ger. au.
Sudermann (zo͞o′dẽr-män), Hermann (1857–
Sudeten (so͞o-dā′tĕn), mt. range & dist. in Czechoslovakia betw. Silesia and Bohemia, ceded to Germany in 1938, returned 1945.
Suetonius (swē-tō′nĭ-ŭs), Gaius Tranquillus (A. D. 100), Rom. writer.
Suez (so͞o-ĕz′; so͞o′ĕz), **Isthmus of,** strip of land, 100 m. long, joining Afr. & Asia: **– Canal,** canal, 87 m. long, crossing isthmus.
Sullivan (sŭl′ĭ-văn), Sir Arthur Seymour (1842–1900), Eng. comp.
Sully, 1, (sŭl′ĭ), Thomas (1783–1872), Am. painter; **2,** (sü″lē′), Maximilien de Béthune, Duc de (1560–1641), Fr. minister of Henry IV.
Sulu Archipelago (so͞o′lo͞o), group of 245 isls. in the P. I., 1,500 sq. m., p. 172,726.
Sumatra (so͞o-mä′trȧ), one of Sunda Isles, Indonesia, 180,000 sq. m., p. 11,490,000; cap., Padang, p. 42,574. [stsm.
Sumner (sŭm′nẽr), Charles (1811–74), Am.
Sumter (sŭm′tẽr), Thomas (1734–1832), Am. Rev. gen. [archipelago.
Sunda Isles (sŭn′dȧ), isl. group, Malay
Sunderland (sŭn′dẽr-lȧnd), spt. bor., Eng., p. 184,700. [Chin. rev. leader.
Sun Yat-sen (so͞on′ yät″sĕn′), (1865–1925),
Superior (sū-pē′rĭ-ẽr), city, Wis., p. 35,091. **Lake –,** largest of Great Lakes of N. Am. bet. U. S. & Can., 31,200 sq. m.
Suribachi (so͞or″ĭ-bä′chĭ), **Mount,** volcano, Iwo Jima, 546 ft.: bat. 1945. [**Dutch.**
Surinam (so͞o″rĭ-näm′). See **Guiana,**
Susquehanna (sŭs″kwē-hăn′ȧ), riv., E. cen. Pa., 422 m. to Chesapeake bay.
Sutlej (sŭt′lĕj), riv., N. Hindustan, 900 m. fr. Tibet to Indus riv. [to Gulf of Mex.
Suwannee (so͞o-wô′nē), riv., S. Ga., 240 m.
Svalbard (sväl′bärd), arctic archipelago, N. of Norway, including isl. of Spitsbergen, 25,000 sq. m., p. 1,503. [Mts., p. 136,494.
Sverdlovsk (svârd′lŏfsk), tn., Russ., in Ural
Swansea (swŏn′sē), spt., S. Wales, p. 161,700.
Swaziland (swä′zē-lănd″), S. E. dist. Transvaal, S. Afr., 6,678 sq. m., p. 112,838.
Sweden (swē′dĕn), kingdom, N. Europe, 173,105 sq. m., p. 6,105,190; cap., Stockholm. [1772), Sw. sci. & theolog.
Swedenborg (swē′dĕn-bôrg), Emanuel (1688–
Swift (swĭft), Jonathan [*Dean Swift*] (1667–1745, Br. satirist. [(1837–1909), Br. poet.
Swinburne (swĭn′bŭrn), Algernon Charles
Switzerland (swĭt′zẽr-lȧnd), repub., cen. Europe, 15,944 sq. m., p. 4,645,000; cap., Berne.
Sybaris (sĭb′ȧ-rĭs), anc. Gk. city: destroyed 510 B. C. [Wales, p. 1,127,470: univ.
Sydney (sĭd′nĭ), spt., cap. of New South
Symonds (sĭm′ŭnz), John Addington (1840–93), Br. au. [220,067; **2,** anc. city, Sicily.
Syracuse (sĭr′ȧ-kūs″), **1,** city, N. Y., p.
Syria (sĭr′ĭ-ȧ), **1,** anc. country, eastern end Medit. sea; **2,** mod. repub. in Asia, bet. Euphrates & Medit., N. of Palestine, 66,046 sq. m., p. 3,092,203; cap., Damascus.
Szechwan (sä″chwän′), prov., W. China, 218,480 sq. m., p. 82,063,606; cap., Chengtu.

T

Tabriz (tȧ-brēz′), city, Persia, p. 180,000.
Tacitus (tăs′ĭ-tŭs), Publius Cornelius (55–117?), Rom. hist.
Tacoma (tȧ-hō′mȧ), city, Wash., p. 142,975.
Taft (tȧft), **1,** Lorado (1860–1936), Am. sculp.; **2,** William Howard (1857–1930), 27th pres. of U. S.; chief justice U. S. Supreme Court, 1921–30.
Tagore (tȧ-gōr′), Sir Rabindranath (1861–1941), Hindu poet: Nobel prize 1913.
Tagus (tā′gŭs), riv., Sp. & Port., 565 m. long.
Tahiti (tä′hē-tē; tä-hē′tē), [formerly **Otaheite** (ō″tȧ-hē′tē)], Fr. isl., Society isls., 600 sq. m., p. 7,145; cap., Papeete, p. 4,601.
Tahoe (tā′hō; tä′-), largest lake in Sierras, bet. Calif. & Nev., 20 m. by 10 m.
Taihoku (tī-hō′ko͞o), city, cap. of Taiwan isl., p. 195,555.
Tainan (tī′nän′), city, Taiwan isl., p. 53,794.
Taine (tān), Hippolyte Adolphe (1828–93), Fr. hist.
Taiwan (tī″wän′), [**Formosa**], isl., in China sea, 13,944 sq. m., p. 4,241,759; cap., Taihoku. [p. 27,158.
Tallahassee (tăl″ȧ-hăs′ē), city, cap. of Fla.,
Talleyrand-Périgord, de (dē tȧ″lē″räṅ′pā″rē″gôr′), Charles Maurice, Prince Benevent (1754–1838), Fr. stsm. & dipl.
Tallinn (tȧl′lĭn), [**Reval**], cap. of repub. Estonia, p. 127,000.
Tamerlane (tăm″ẽr-lān′). See **Timur.**
Tampa (tăm′pȧ), city, Fla., p. 124,073.
Tampico (täm-pē′kō), port, Mex., p. 24,980.
Tanagra (tăn′ȧ-grȧ), anc. tn., Bœotia, Greece: remains; figurines.
Tananarive (tȧ-nä″nȧ-rē′vē), [**Antananrivo**], tn., cap. of Madagascar, p. 70,847.
Tanganyika (tăn″găn-yē′kä), **Lake,** E. cen. Afr., 13,000 sq. m.: **– Territory** [formerly **German East Africa**], ter., Br. mandate, 365,000 sq. m., p. 4,319,000.
Tangier (tăn-jēr′), spt., Morocco, p. 60,000.
Tarkington (tär′kĭng-tŭn), (Newton) Booth (1869–1946), Am. nov.
Tarquin (täk′kwĭn), Lucius [*Tarquinius*] Superbus, last legendary king of Rome, 534–510 B. C. [Tartessus, near Gibraltar.
Tarshish (tär′shĭsh), anc. place, probably
Tarsus (tär′sŭs), city, Rom. cap. of Cilicia, Asia Minor: birthplace of Apostle Paul.
Tartary (tär′tȧ-rĭ). See **Tatary.**
Tashkent (tȧsh″kĕnt′), city, cap. of Turkestan, Asiatic Russ., p. 323,613: univ.
Tasmania (tăz-mā′nĭ-ȧ), isl. & state, Australia, 26,215 sq. m., p. 213,780; cap., Hobart. [It. poet.
Tasso (tăs′ō; täs′sō), Torquato (1544–95),
Tatary (tä′tȧ-rĭ), or **Tartary,** old name for section of E. Europe and W. Asia. [40,056.
Taunton (tän′tŭn; tôn′-), city, Mass., p.
Taylor (tā′lẽr), **1,** Bayard (1825–78), Am. poet & trav.; **2,** Zachary (1784–1850), 12th pres. of U. S. [350,000.
Tehran (tĕ-rän′), city, cap. of Persia, p.
Tehuantepec (tā-wän″tā-pĕk′), isthmus, S. Mex., bet. Gulf of Mex. & Pacific oc.
Teneriffe (tĕn″ẽr-ĭf′), one of the Canary isls., 782 sq. m., p. 138,008; cap., Santa Cruz de Teneriffe
Teniers (tĕ-nērs′), David [*the Elder*] (1582–1649), & David [*the Younger*] (1610–90), Flemish painters.
Tennessee (tĕn″ĕ-sē′), **1,** State in U. S., 42,022 sq. m., p. 3,291,718; cap., Nashville; **2,** riv., Tenn. & Ala., 1,200 m. to Ohio riv.
Tennyson (tĕn′ĭ-sŭn), Alfred, Baron (1809–92), Eng. poet laureate.
Ter Borch (tĕr bōrkh′), [**Terburg: Terborch**] Gerard (1617–81), Du. painter.
Terence (tĕr′ĕns), Publius [*Terentius*] Afer (190?–159? B. C.), Rom. au.: comedies.
Terre Haute (tĕr′ē-hōt′), city, Ind., p. 64,047.
Territory of Hawaii. See **Hawaii.**
Terry (tĕr′ĭ), Ellen A. (1848–1928), Eng. act.
Tertullian (tẽr-tŭl′ĭ-ăn), (160?–230?), Lat. Ch. father. [Am. electrician: Nobel prize.
Tesla (tĕs′lä), Nikola (1857–1943), Serbian-
Texas (tĕk′sȧs), State in U. S., 265,896 sq. m., p. 7,711,194; cap., Austin.
Thackeray (thăk′ẽr-ĭ), William Makepeace (1811–63), Eng. nov.
Thailand (tī′lănd), off. name for Siam (which see). [Gk. philos.
Thales (thā′lēz), of Miletus (640–546 B. C.),
Thames (tĕmz), **1,** riv., Eng., 250 m. to North sea; **2,** riv., Ontario, Can., 160 m. to Lake St. Clair; **3,** (or thāmz), riv., E. Conn.
Thebes (thēbz), **1,** city, anc. Egypt, on Nile; **2,** city, Bœotia, anc. Greece.
Themistocles (thē-mĭs′tō-klēz), (527?–460? B. C.), Athenian gen. & stsm. [Gk. poet.
Theocritus (thē-ŏk′rĭ-tŭs), (310–245 B. C.),
Theodoric (thē-ŏd′ō-rĭk), [*the Great*] (454?–526), founder of Ostrogothic kingdom in It.
Theodosius (thē″ō-dō′shĭ-ŭs), [*the Great*] (346–395), Rom. emp.
Theophrastus (thē″ō-frăs′tŭs), (?–287 B. C.), Gk. philos. [saly & Greece.
Thermopylæ (thẽr-mŏp′ĭ-lē), pass bet. Thes-
Thespis (thĕs′pĭs), (6th cent. B. C.), father of Gk. drama. [**niki.**
Thessalonica (thĕs″ȧ-lō-nī′kȧ). See **Salo-**
Thessaly (thĕs′ȧ-lĭ), anc. div., N. Greece.
Thomas (tŏm′ȧs), **1,** George Henry [*Rock of Chickamauga*] (1816–70), Am. sol.; **2,** Theodore (1835–1905), Ger.-Am. orchestra conductor; **3,** Norman (1884–), Am. publicist and socialist.
Thomson (tŏm′sŭn), **1,** James (1700–48), Scot. poet; **2,** J. Arthur (1861–1933), Eng. zoölogist; **3,** Sir Joseph John (1856–1940), Eng. physicist; **4,** Sir William: see *Kelvin.*
Thoreau (thō′rō; thō-rō′), Henry David (1817–62), Am. natur. & essay.
Thorwaldsen (tôr′wôld-sĕn), or **Thorvaldsen** (-vȧl-sĕn), Albert Bertel (1770–1844), Da. sculp.: "Lion of Lucerne."
Thousand Islands, about 1,700 isls. in St. Lawrence riv., bet. N. Y. & Ontario, Can.
Thrace (thrās), anc. name of country, E. Balkan pen. [Gk. gen.
Thrasybulus (thrăs″ĭ-bū′lŭs), (411–391 B. C.),
Thucydides (thū-sĭd′ĭ-dēz), (471?–400 B. C.), Gk. hist.
Thuringia (thū-rĭn′jĭ-ȧ), administrative div., Ger., 4,527 sq. m., p. 1,609,300; cap., Weimar.
Tiber (tī′bẽr), riv., It., 260 m. fr. Apennines to Tyrrhenian sea.
Tiberias (tī-bē′rĭ-ȧs), **Sea of.** See **Galilee.**
Tiberius (tī-bē′rĭ-ŭs), (42 B. C.–A. D. 37), Rom. emp.
Tibet (tĭ-bĕt′; tĭb′ĕt), or **Thibet,** prov., cen. Asia, depend. of China, 463,200 sq. m., p. 2,000,000; cap., Lhasa.
Ticonderoga (tī-kŏn″dẽr-ō′gȧ), vil., N. Y., p. 3,510: taken by Ethan Allen 1775.
Tientsin (tĭ-ĕn′tsĕn′), city & treaty port, Chihli prov., China, p. 800,000.
Tierra del Fuego (tyĕr′rä dĕl fwā′gō), isls., S. end S. Am.: belong partly to Argentina, partly to Chile.
Tiflis (tyē-flyēs′), [**Tpilisi** (t′pē′lē-sē)], city, cap. of repub. of Georgia & of Transcaucasian Federation, p. 282,973. [phrates riv.
Tigris (tī′grĭs), riv., Iraq., 1,150 m. to Eu-
Tilsit (tĭl′zĭt), tn., E. Prussia, p. 50,834.
Timur (tī-mo͝or′; tē-), [**Tamerlane**] (1336?–1405), Mongol conq. [Venetian painter.
Tintoretto, Il (ēl tēn″tō-rĕt′tō), (1518–94),
Tippecanoe (tĭp″ē-kȧ-no͞o′), riv., N. W. Ind.: bat. 1811. [1902), Fr. painter.
Tissot (tē″sō′), James Joseph Jacques (1836–
Titian (tĭsh′ăn), (1477–1576), Venetian painter. [(40–81), Rom. emp.
Titus (tī′tŭs), Flavius Sabinus Vespasianus

Tobago (tō-bā'gō), isl., Br. W. Indies, 411 sq. m., p. 23,390; chief tn., Scarborough.
Tobolsk (tō-bŏlsk'), govt., N. W. Siberia, 535,739 sq. m., p. 2,085,700.
Tocqueville, de (dē tôk"vēl'), Alexis Charles Henri (1805–59), Fr. stsm. & writer.
Togo (tō'gō), Heihachiro, Count (1847–1934), Jap. adm.
Togoland (tō'gō-lănd"), [**Togo**], former Ger. ter. in W. Afr., now Fr. & Br. mandates.
Tokyo (tō'kē-ō), city, cap. of Japan, on Honshu isl., p. 1,995,567.
Toledo (tō-lē'dō), **1,** city, Ohio, p. 301,358; **2,** city, N. cen. Sp., p. 25,251.
Tolstoy (tŏl-stoi'), Leo Nicolaevich, Count (1828–1910), Russ. nov. & social reformer.
Tombigbee (tŏm-bĭg'bē), riv., E. Miss. & W. Ala. [p. 92,418: univ.
Tomsk (tômsk), govt. & city, Siberia; city
Tonga (tŏng'gȧ), [**Friendly Islands**], isls., S. Pacific oc., Br. protec., 385 sq. m., p. 25,918.
Tonkin (tŏn"kĭn'), ter., N. Anam., Indochinese Fed., Fr. Union, 40,530 sq. m., p. 9,851,-000; cap., Hanoi, p. 160,000. [77,827.
Topeka (tō-pē'kȧ), city, cap. of Kans., p.
Toronto (to-rŏn'tō), city, cap. of Ontario, Can., p. 670,945; "Greater Toronto," p. 1,108,532: univ.
Torquemada, de (dā tôr"kā-mä'*th*ä), Tomás (1420–98), Span. inquisitor-gen.
Torres Strait (tŏr'ĕz), str. bet. New Guinea & Australia, 80–90 m. wide.
Torricelli (tŏr"rē-chĕl'lē), Evangelista (1608–47), It. physicist. [It. orchestral conductor.
Toscanini (tôs"kä-nē'nē), Arturo (1867–),
Tottenham (tŏt'ĕn-ăm), tn., Eng., p. 146,711.
Toulon (tōō"lôṅ'), spt., Fr., p. 115,120.
Toulouse (tōō"lōōz'), city, S. Fr., p. 180,771.
Tours (tōōr), city, Fr., p. 77,192.
Toussaint L'Ouverture (tōō"săṅ' lōō"vâr"-tür'), François Dominique (1743–1803), Haitian negro sol. & stsm.
Trabzon (trăb'zŏn), city, Turkey, Asia Minor, on Black sea, p. 60,975.
Trafalgar (trăf"ăl-gär'; *Br.* trȧ-făl'gȧr), cape, S. Sp., entrance to Gibraltar str.
Trajan (trā'jăn), Marcus Ulpius Nerva [*Trajanus*] (52–117), Rom. emp.
Transcaucasian Federation (trăns"kô-kā'-shăn; -kăsh'ăn), or **Transcaucasia** (trăns"-kô-kā'shĭ-ȧ), federated repub., lying bet. Black & Caspian seas, S. of Caucasus mts., comprising Georgia, Armenia, & Azerbaijan.
Transjordan (trăns-jôr'dăn), now **Jordan,** kingdom, Arabia, 35,000 sq. m., p. 370,794; cap. Amman, p. 60,000.
Transvaal (trăns-väl'), state, Union of S. Afr., 110,450 sq. m., p. 2,087,636; cap., Pretoria.
Transylvania (trăn"sĭl-vā'nĭ-ȧ), div., Rumania, 22,312 sq. m., p. 2,678,367.
Trebbia (trĕb'byä), [anc. **Trebia**], riv., N. It.: bats. 218 B. C. & 1799. [1917), Eng. act.
Tree (trē), Sir Herbert Beerbohm (1853–
Trent (trĕnt), **1,** [anc. **Tridentum** (trĭ-dĕn'-tŭm)], city, Tyrol, It., p. 31,881; **2,** riv., cen. Eng. [127,867.
Trenton (trĕn'tŭn), city, cap. of N. J., p.
Treves (trēvz), [Fr. **Trèves** (trâv); Ger. **Trier** (trēr)], city, Prussia, p. 58,975.
Tribonian (trĭ-bō'nĭ-ăn), (?–545), Rom. jurist.
Trichinopoly (trĭch"ĭ-nŏp'ō-lĭ), city, Madras, India, p. 120,422.
Trieste (trē-ĕst'; trē-ĕs'tā), [Ger. **Triest** (trē-ĕst')], com., It., p. 252,517.
Trinidad (trĭn'ĭ-dăd"), Br. isl., W. Indies, 1,862 sq. m., p., with Tobago, 391,705; cap., Port-of-Spain.
Tripoli (trĭp'ō-lĭ), **1,** see *Tripolitania*; **2,** city, cap. of Tripolitania, p. 108,240.
Tripolitania (trē"pō-lē-tä'nyä), dist., Libya, N. Afr., 350,000 sq. m.; cap., Tripoli.

Troas (trō'ăs), [**the Troad** (trō'ăd)], ter., anc. Troy, N. W. Asia Minor. [nov.
Trollope (trŏl'ŭp), Anthony (1815–82), Eng.
Trotzky (trôt'skē), Leon (1879–1940), Russ-Soviet minister of war, 1918–25.
Troy (troi), **1,** city, N. Y., p. 71,659; **2,** [**Ilium**], anc. city, N. W. Asia Minor.
Troyes (trwä), city, N. E. Fr., p. 58,321.
Troyon (trwä"yôṅ'), Constant (1810–65), Fr. painter. [33d pres. of U. S., 1945– .
Truman (trōō'măn), Harry S. (1884–),
Tschaikowsky (chĭ-kôf'skē), Peter Ilyitch (1840–1893), Russ. comp.
Tsingtao (tsĭng"tou'), city, Shantung prov., China, Ger. protec., 1898: taken by Jap. 1914; returned to China 1922; p. 308,200.
Tulsa (tŭl'sȧ), city, Okla., p. 180,586.
Tunisia (tū-nĭsh'ĭ-ȧ), Fr. protec., N. Afr., 48,300 sq. m., p. 2,159,708; cap., Tunis, p. 185,996.
Turcoman (tŏŏr"kō-män'), [**Turkmenistan** (tŏŏrk-mĕn"ĭ-stän')], soviet socialist repub., 181,478 sq. m., p. 1,030,540: federated with Soviet Russ.
Turgenev (tŏŏr-gĕn'yĕf), Ivan Sergeyevitch (1818–83), Russ. nov.
Turin (tū'rĭn), city, N. It., p. 570,173: univ.
Turkestan (tŏŏr"kĕ-stän'), formerly autonomous repub., Russ., cen. Asia, 649,644 sq. m., p. 7,201,551; cap., Tashkent: **Chinese** or **East –,** dist. Sinkiang prov.; cap., Kashgar.
Turkey (tûr'kĭ), [formerly **Ottoman Empire**], repub., Europe & Asia, 294,538 sq. m., p. 13,660,275; cap., Ankara.
Turner (tûr'nēr), Joseph Mallord William (1775–1851), Eng. painter.
Tuscany (tŭs'kȧ-nĭ), dept., W. cen. It., 8,883 sq. m., p. 2,766,291.
Tusculum (tŭs'kū-lŭm), anc. tn., It.
Tut-Ankh-Amen (tōōt"-änk-ä'mĕn), (about 1350 B. C.), king of ancient Egypt.
Twain (twān), Mark: pseud. of *Samuel L. Clemens.* [North sea.
Tweed (twēd), riv., S. E. Scot., 96 m. to
Tyler (tī'lēr), **1,** John (1790–1862), 10th pres. of U. S.; **2,** Wat (?–1381), Eng. revolutionist. [martyr: translated Bible.
Tyndale (tĭn'dăl), William (?–1536), Eng.
Tyndall (tĭn'dăl), John (1820–93), Br. physicist.
Tyne (tīn), riv., N. Eng., 80 m. to North sea.
Tyre (tīr), [mod. **Sur** (sōōr)], anc. city & port, cap. of Phœnicia.
Tyrol (tĭr'ŏl), prov., W. Austria, 4,882 sq. m., p. 313,885; cap., Innsbruck, p. 56,401.
Tyrrhenian Sea (tĭ-rē'nĭ-ăn), part of Medit. sea bet. It. & Sardinia & Sicily.
Tz'u Hsi (tsōō shē), (1834?–1908), empress dowager of China.

U

Ucayali (ōō"kä-yä'lē), riv., Peru, 1,500 m. to Amazon riv.
Uganda (ōō-gän'dä; ū-găn'dȧ), Br. protec., E. cen. Afr., 110,300 sq. m., p. 3,157,008; caps., Entebbe & Mengo.
Uinta Mountains (ū-ĭn'tȧ), range, N. E. Utah & N. W. Wyo., U. S.
Ukraine (ū'krān), soviet socialist repub., E. Europe, federated with Russ., 172,311 sq. m., p. 29,020,304; cap., Kharkov. [Goths.
Ulfilas (ŭl'fĭ-lȧs), (311?–381), bp. of the
Ulster (ŭl'stēr), former Ir. prov., nearly identical with mod. Northern Ire. See **Ireland** & **Northern Ireland.**
Umbria (ŭm'brĭ-ȧ), [mod. **Perugia** (pā-rōō'-jä)], anc. dept., cen. It. [**Russia.**
Union of Soviet Socialist Republics. See
Union of South Africa (ăf'rĭ-kȧ), commonwealth within Br. empire, comprising Cape of Good Hope, Transvaal, Natal, & Orange Free State, 472,550 sq. m., p. 11,391,950; caps., Cape Town & Pretoria.

United Kingdom [**British Isles**], a term used until 1927 to designate isl. kingdom comprising Gt. Br. (Eng., Scot., & Wales) & Ire.; with Isle of Man & Channel isls. 95,041 sq. m., p. 50,519,000. See **Northern Ireland.**

United Nations, an international organization for the preservation of world peace, estab. after World War II, permanent headquarters New York City.

United States of America (*ȧ*-mĕr′ĭ-k*ȧ*), federal repub., N. Am., 2,750 m. by 1,680 m., 48 States & District of Columbia, 3,026,789 sq. m., p. 150,555,592; cap., Washington; with Alaska & Hawaii and all depend.,3,620,490sq.m.,totalp.169,507,548.

Ur (ûr), anc. city & dist., Babylonia.

Ural (ū′răl), mts., Russ., bet. Europe & Asia.

Urban (ûr′băn), any of 8 popes. [650 m. long.

Uruguay (ū′rōō-gwā; ōō″rōō-gwī′), **1,** repub., S. Am., 72,153 sq. m., p. 1,808,286; cap., Montevideo; **2,** riv., S. Am., 1,000 m. to La Plata. [See **Russia.**

U.S.S.R., Union of Soviet Socialist Republics.

Utah (ū′tô; ū′tä), State in U. S., 84,990 sq. m., p. 686,797; cap., Salt Lake City.

Utica (ū′tĭ-k*ȧ*), city, N. Y., p. 101,479.

Utrecht (ū′trĕkt; ü′-), city, Netherlands, p. 151,660: univ.

Uzbek (ōōz′bĕk), soviet socialist repub., Union of Bukhara and Khiva, 103,751 sq. m., p. 5,270, 195: federated with Soviet Russ.

V

Vaal (väl), riv., Transvaal, S. Afr., 700 m. to Orange riv.

Valencia (v*ȧ*-lĕn′shĭ-*ȧ*), city, E. Sp., p. 267,346: univ.

Valentine (văl′ĕn-tīn), Saint (3d cent. A. D.), Christian martyr: feast day Feb. 14.

Valentinian (văl″ĕn-tĭn′ĭ-ăn), name of 3 Rom. emps.: **I** (321–375); **II** (371–392); **III** (419–455). [260), Rom. emp.

Valerian (v*ȧ*-lē′rĭ-ăn), Publius Licinius (?–

Valley Forge (fōrj), Pa., N. W. of Philadelphia: Washington's headquarters, 1777–78.

Valparaiso (văl″p*ȧ*-rā′zō), city, Chile, p. 286,947: univ.

Van Buren (văn bū′rĕn), Martin (1782–1862), 8th pres. of U.S.

Vancouver (văn-kōō′vẽr), **1,** city, Can., p. 340,272; **2,** isl., part of Br. Columbia.

Vandegrift (văn′dĕ-grĭft), Alexander A. (1887–), Am. general, commandant Marines, 1944–48.

Van Dyck (văn dīk′), Sir Anthony (1599–1641), Du. portrait painter.

VanDyke (văn dīk′), Henry (1852–1933), Am. au., clergy., & educ.

Van Loon (văn lōn′), Hendrik Willem (1882–1944), Du.-Am. hist. & writer. [& bio.

Vasari (vä-zä-rē), Giorgio (1511–74), It. art.

Vega Carpio, de (dā vā′gä kär′pyō), Lope Felix (1562–1635), Span. dram. & poet.

Velásquez (vā-läs′kāth), or **Velázquez** (vā-läth′kāth), Diego Rodriguez de Silva y (1599–1660), Span. painter.

Venezuela (vĕn″ē-zwē′l*ȧ*), repub., S. Am., 393,874 sq. m., p. 3,026,878; cap., Caracas.

Venice (vĕn′ĭs), city, It., p. 253,608.

Venizelos (vĕn″ĕ-zā′lōs), Eleutherios (1864–1936), Gk. stsm.

Veracruz (vā″r*ȧ*-krōōs′; vẽr″*ȧ*-krōōz′), spt., on Campeche bay, Mex., p. 54,225: occupied by U. S. forces, 1847 & 1914.

Vercingetorix (vẽr″sĭn-jĕt′ō-rĭks), (?–45 B. C.), Gallic chief: defeated by Julius Cæsar.

Verde (vûrd), **Cape,** western extrem. of Afr.

Verdi (vâr′dē), Giuseppi (1813–1901), It. comp. [bats. 1916–18.

Verdun (vâr″dûṅ′), tn. & fortress, N. E. Fr.:

Vereshchagin (vyĕ′rĕ-shchä′gĭn), Vasili Vasilevich (1842–1904), Russ. painter.

Vergil (vûr′jĭl), or **Virgil,** Publius [*Vergilius*] Maro (70–19 B. C.), Rom. poet.

Vermont (vẽr-mŏnt′), State in U. S., 9,564 sq. m., p. 375,833: cap., Montpelier. [nov.

Verne (vûrn; vârn), Jules (1828–1905), Fr.

Veronese (vā″rō-nā′zā), Paul (1528–88), It. painter. [(1435–88), It. sculp. & art.

Verrochio, del (dĕl vĕr-rŏk′kyō), Andrea

Versailles (vâr″sȧy′′; vẽr-sālz′), city, near Paris, Fr., p. 68,575: treaty with Ger. 1919.

Vespasian (vĕs-pā′zhĭ-ăn), Titus Flavius [*Vespasianus*], (9–79), Rom. emp.

Vespucci (vĕs-pōōt′chē), Amerigo (1451–1512), It. navig. and geog.

Vesuvius (vē-sū′vĭ-ŭs), active volcano, 4,000 ft. high, Bay of Naples. [pseud., *Pierre Loti.*

Viaud (vyō), Louis (1850–1923), Fr. nov.:

Vichy (vĭsh′ĭ; vē″shē′), tn., cen. Fr., p. 14,820: hot min. springs; seat of govt. of unoccupied France, 1940–44. [riv., p. 27,344: bat. 1863.

Vicksburg (vĭks′bûrg), city, Miss., on Miss.

Victor Emmanuel III (vĭk′tẽr ĕ-măn′ū-ĕl), (1869–1947), king of It., 1900–46, emp. of Ethiopia, 1936–41.

Victoria (vĭk-tō′rĭ-*ȧ*), Alexandrina (1819–1901), queen of Gt. Br. & Ire. fr. 1837, & emp. of India fr. 1876.

Victoria (vĭk-tō′rĭ-*ȧ*), **1,** city, Can., on Vancouver isl, p. 50,774; **2,** state, Australia; cap., Melbourne.

Victoria Nyanza (vĭk-tō′rĭ-*ȧ* nyän′zä), lake, E. Afr., 32,000 sq. m.

Vidzeme (vēd′zĕ-mā), formerly Livonia, Russ. prov., now div. of Latvia, 8,716 sq. m.

Vienna (vē-ĕn′*ȧ*), [Ger. **Wien** (vēn)], city, Austria, p. 1,865,780: univ.

Viet-Nam (vē′ĕt-näm′), repub., S. E. Asia, indep. state in Fr. Union, 123,979 sq. m., p. 22,614,000; cap., Saigon.

Villa (vē′lyä), Francesco [*Pancho*] (1872–1923), Mex. bandit. [Fr. poet.

Villon (vē′yôṅ′), François (1431–after 1463),

Vilna (vĕl′n*ȧ*), [**Wilno**], anc. and modern cap. of Lithuania, p. 214,600. [1917.

Vimy (vē″mē′), tn., Fr.: **– Ridge,** hill: bat.

Vinci, da (dä vēn′chē). See **Leonardo.**

Virgil (vûr′jĭl). See **Vergil.**

Virginia (vẽr-jĭn′ĭ-*ȧ*), State in U. S., 42,627 sq. m., p. 3,270,322; cap., Richmond.

Virgin Islands (vûr′jĭn), **American** [formerly **Danish West Indies**], isls. in the Leeward group: St. Thomas, St. John, & St. Croix, 132 sq. m., p. 24,889: **British –,** group of 30 isls., bet. Greater & Lesser Antilles, 58 sq. m., p. 5,082.

Visayan Islands (vē-sä′yän), or **Bisayas,** cen. group, P. I., 24,747 sq. m., p. 2,600,000.

Visconti (vēs-kōn′tē), a celebrated family of Lombardy, It., 1208–1447. [to Baltic sea.

Vistula (vĭs′tū-l*ȧ*), riv., cen. Europe, 650 m.

Vladivostok (vlä″dĭ-vōs-tôk′), spt. & nav. base, Siberia, p. 107,977.

Volga (vŏl′g*ȧ*), riv., Russ., 2,310 m. to Caspian sea: largest riv. in Europe. [Am. stsm.

Volstead (vŏl′stĕd), Andrew J. (1860—1947),

Voltaire (vôl″târ′), Jean François Marie Arouet (1694–1778), Fr. philos. & satirist.

Vosges (vōzh), mt. chain, bet. Fr. & Ger.

W

Wabash (wô′băsh), riv., Ohio & Ind., 550 m. to Ohio riv.

Waco (wā′kō), city, Tex., p. 84,300.

Wagner (väg′nẽr), Wilhelm Richard (1813–83), Ger. comp. [Kong.

Wake (wāk), U. S. isl., bet. Hawaii and Hong

Waldemar I (wŏl′dĕ-mär; väl′-), or **Valdemar** (väl′-), (1131–82), king of Denmark.

Wales (wālz), W. div. of Gt. Br., 7,466 sq. m., p. 2,205,680; cap., Cardiff.

Wallace (wŏl′ăs), **1,** Gen. Lew (1827–1905), Am. army off. & au.; **2,** Henry Agard (1888–), vice pres. of U. S. 1941–45.

Wallachia (wŏ-lā'kĭ-*ȧ*), anc. principality, now part of Rumania.
Walpole (wôl'pōl; wŏl'-), **1,** Horace, Earl of Oxford (1717–97), Eng. au.; **2,** Hugh Seymour (1884–1941), Eng. nov.
Walpurgis (väl-po͝or'gĭs), Saint (710?–777?), Eng. nun: missionary to Germany.
Waltham (wôl'thăm), city, Mass., p. 47,198.
Walton (wôl'tŭn), Izaak (1593–1683), Eng. au.
Wanamaker (wŏn'*ȧ*-māk″ẽr), John (1838–1922), Am. merchant.
Ward (wôrd), **1,** Artemus (1834–67), Am. humorist: pseud. of *Charles Farrar Browne*; **2,** Mrs. Humphry (1851–1920), Eng. nov.
Warfield (wôr'fēld), David (1866–1951), Am. act.
Warsaw (wôr'sô), city, cap. of Poland, on Vistula riv., p. 936,713: univ.
Warwick (wŏr'ĭk), Richard Neville, Earl of [*the Kingmaker*] (1428–71), Eng. sol. & stsm.
Washington (wŏsh'ĭng-tŭn), **1,** George [*Father of his Country*] (1732–99), 1st pres. of U. S.; **2,** Booker Taliaferro (1859?–1915), Am. negro educ.
Washington (wŏsh'ĭng-tŭn), **1,** State in U. S., on W. coast, 69,127 sq. m., p. 2,363,289; cap., Olympia; **2,** city, cap. of U. S., coterminous with D. C., on Potomac riv., p. 797,670: 6 univs.
Wassermann, von (fôn väs'ẽr-män), August (1866–1925), Ger. phys. & bacter.
Waterbury (wô'tẽr-bẽr-ĭ), city, Conn., p. 104,242.
Waterloo (wô″tẽr-lo͞o'), **1,** city, Iowa, p. 64,354; **2,** vil., Belgium, p. 5,033: bat. 1815.
Watertown (wô'tẽr-toun), city, N. Y., p. 34,280. [nov.: pseud., *Ian Maclaren*.
Watson (wŏt'sŭn), John (1850–1907), Scot.
Watt (wŏt), James (1736–1819), Scot. inv.
Watteau (wä-tō'), Antoine (1684–1721), Fr. painter.
Watts (wŏts), **1,** George Frederick (1817–1904), Eng. painter & sculp.; **2,** Isaac (1674–1748), Eng. theolog. & hymn writer.
Wayne (wān), Anthony [*Mad Anthony*] (1745–96), Am. Rev. gen.
Weber, von (fôn vā'bẽr), Karl Maria, Baron (1786–1826), Ger. comp.
Webster (wĕb'stẽr), **1,** Daniel (1782–1852), Am. stsm.; **2,** Noah (1758–1843), Am. lexicographer. [Eng. potter.,
Wedgewood (wĕj'wo͝od), Josiah (1730–95),
Weihaiwei (wā'hī″wā'), spt. & treaty port N. Shantung, China, 285 sq. m., p. 154,416
Weimar (vī'mär), city cap. of Thuringia, Ger., p. 45,957.
Weismann (vīs'män), August (1834–1914), Ger. biol.
Wellington (wĕl'ĭng-tŭn), Arthur Wellesley, Duke of (1769–1852), Br. gen.
Wells (wĕlz), Herbert George (1866–1946). Br. nov. [1929), Aus. chemist.
Welsbach (vĕls'bäkh), Carl Auer von (1858–
Wenceslas (wĕn'sĕs-lȧs), or **Wenceslaus** (-lôs), or **Wenzel** (vĕn'tsĕl) (1361–1419), king of Bohemia & Holy Rom. emp.
Wenchow (wŭn'chō'), spt., Chekiang prov., China, p. 202,700.
Weser (vā'zẽr), riv., N. W. Ger., 440 m. long.
Wesley (wĕs'lĭ), **1,** Charles (1707–88), Eng. hymn writer; **2,** John (1703–91), Eng. clergy.: founder of Methodism.
West (wĕst), Benjamin (1738–1820), Am. art.
Western Australia (ôs-trā'lĭ-*ȧ*), state in Australia, 975,920 sq. m., p. 332,732; cap., Perth.
West Indies (ĭn'dĭz), archipelago, several groups of isls. E. of Cen. Am., 100,000 sq. m.. p. 9,000,000.
West Orange (ŏr'ĕnj), tn., N. J., p. 28,624.
West Point, tn., N. Y., on Hudson riv.: U. S. Mil. Academy.
West Virginia (vẽr'jĭn'ĭ-*ȧ*), State in U. S., 24,170 sq. m., p. 1,999,097; cap., formerly Wheeling, now Charleston.
Weyman (wī'măn), Stanley John (1855–1928), Eng. nov. [Am. nov.
Wharton (hwôr'tŭn), Edith (1862–1937),
Wheeling (hwēl'ĭng), city, W. Va., p. 58,447.
Whistler (hwĭs'lẽr), James Abbott M'Neill (1834–1903), Am. painter in Eng.
White (hwīt), **1,** Edward Douglass (1845–1921), chief justice of U. S. Supreme Court fr. 1910; **2,** William Allen (1868–1944), Am. jour. & nov.
White Mountains, mt. range, N. H. & Me.: Mt. Washington, in N. H., 6,293 ft.
White Russia, soviet repub., W. Russ., 32,060 sq. m., p. 154,800,000; cap., Minsk.
White Sea, gulf, arm of Arctic oc., N. Russ., 36,000 sq. m.
Whitlock (hwĭt'lŏk), Brand (1869–1934), Am. dipl.: minister to Belgium, 1913–17.
Whitman (hwĭt'măn), Walt (1819–92), Am. poet.
Whitney (hwĭt'nĭ), Eli (1765–1825), Am. inv.
Whitney (hwĭt'nĭ), **Mount,** peak in Sierra Nevada range, Calif., 14,502 ft.
Whittier (hwĭt'ĭ-ẽr), John Greenleaf (1807–92), Am. poet.
Wichita (wĭch'ĭ-tô), city, Kans., p. 166,306; **– Falls,** city, Tex., p. 67,709.
Wicklif (wĭk'lĭf). See **Wycliffe.** [102,476.
Weisbaden (vēs'bä″dĕn), tn., Prussia, p.
Wigan (wĭg'ăn), tn., Eng., p. 88,690.
Wiggin (wĭg'ĭn), Kate Douglas (1857–1923), Am. nov.
Wight (wīt), **Isle of,** isl., off S. coast of Eng., 147 sq. m., p. 94,697; cap., Newport.
Wilcox (wĭl'kŏks), Ella Wheeler (1855–1919), Am. au. & poet.
Wilde (wīld), Oscar (1856–1900), Br. poet & dram. [queen of Netherlands 1890–1948.
Wilhelmina I (vĭl″hĕl-mē'nä), (1880–),
Wilhelmj (vĭl-hĕl'mē), August (1845–1908), Ger. violinist, conductor, & comp.
Wilkes-Barre (wĭlks'-băr″ĭ), city, Pa., p. 76,638. [social reformer & philan.
Willard (wĭl'ȧrd), Frances E. (1839–98), Am.
William (wĭl'yŭm), **1,** name of 4 kings of Eng., notably: **I** [*the Conqueror*] (1027–87); **III** of Orange (1650–1702); **2,** name of 2 Ger. emps.: **I** (1797–1888), king of Prussia fr. 1861 & Ger. emp. fr. 1871; **II** (1859–1941): abdicated 1918; **3, I** [*the Silent*] (1533–84), Prince of Orange, founder of the Du. repub.
Williams (wĭl'yŭmz), Roger (1604?–83), Eng. theolog.: founder of R. I. [44,964.
Williamsport (wĭl'yămz-pōrt), city, Pa., p.
Wilmington (wĭl'mĭng-tŭn), **1,** city, Del., p. 109,907; **2,** city, N. C., p. 44,975.
Wilno (vĕl'nō). See **Vilna.**
Wilson (wĭl'sŭn), (Thomas) Woodrow (1856–1924), 28th pres. of U. S.: Nobel prize 1918.
Winchester (wĭn'chĕs-tẽr), Oliver F. (1810–90), Am. mfr. of firearms.
Windermere (wĭn'dẽr-mẽr), lake, Westmoreland co., Eng.: largest lake in Eng.
Windsor (wĭn'zẽr), name of royal house of Eng.: adopted 1917 in place of *Hanover*.
Windsor (wĭn'zẽr), city, Can., p. 119,550.
Windward Islands (wĭnd'wẽrd), isl. group, div. of Lesser Antilles in Br. W. Indies.
Winnipeg (wĭn'ĭ-pĕg), **1,** city, cap. of Manitoba, Can., p. 233,617; **2,** lake, W. Can., 275 m. long. [gov. of Plymouth col.
Winslow (wĭnz'lō), Edward (1595–1655),
Winston (wĭn'stŭn), John Clark (1856–1920), Am. publisher.
Winston-Salem (wĭn'stŭn-sā'lĕm), city, N. C., p. 86,816: coll. [poet, essay., & critic.
Winter (wĭn'tẽr), William (1836–1917), Am.
Winthrop (wĭn'thrŭp), **1,** John (1588–1649), gov. of Mass. col.; **2,** John (1606–76), gov. of Conn. col.

Wisconsin (wĭs-kŏn′sĭn), State in U. S., 56,066 sq. m., p. 3,421,316; cap., Madison.
Wise (wīz), Stephen Samuel (1872–1949), Am.-Jewish rabbi: leader of reformed Judaism in U. S.
Wister (wĭs′tẽr), Owen (1860–1940), Am. nov.
Wolfe (wo͝olf), James (1727–59), Eng. gen.
Wolff (vôlf), Kaspar Friedrich (1733–94), Ger. embryologist: 1st to propose cell theory of embryology.
Wolsey (wo͝ol′zĭ), Thomas (1475?–1530), Eng. cardinal & stsm.
Wolverhampton (wo͝ol″vẽr-hămp′tŭn), bor., Eng., p. 135,200.
Wood (wo͝od), Leonard (1860–1927), Am. gen., gov.-gen. of P. I.
Woolsey (wo͝ol′sĭ), Theodore Dwight (1801–89), Am. educ.
Woonsocket (wo͞on″sŏk′ĕt), city, R. I., p. 50,186.
Worcester (wo͝os′tẽr), **1**, city, Mass., p. 201,885; **2**, city, S. W. Eng., p. 50,890.
Wordsworth (wûrdz′wûrth), William (1770–1850), Eng. poet.
Wrangell Mountains (răng′gĕl), mts., Alaska: Mt. Wrangell, 14,005 ft.
Wren (rĕn), Sir Christopher (1632–1723), Eng. arch.
Wright (rīt), Orville (1871–1948), and his brother, Wilbur (1867–1912), Am. perfecters of the airplane.
Wuchang (wo͞o″chäng′), city, cap. of Hupeh prov., China, p. 500,000.
Wundt (vo͝ont), Wilhelm (1832–1920), Ger. physiologist & psychologist.
Württemberg (vür′tĕm-bĕrkh), administrative div., Ger., 7,532 sq. m., p. 2,580,235; cap., Stuttgart.
Würzburg (vürts′bo͝orkh), tn., Bavaria, p. 89,910.
Wycliffe (wĭk′lĭf), or **Wiclif,** John (1320?-1384), Eng. reformer: translated Bible.
Wyoming (wī-ō′mĭng), State in U. S., 97,914 sq. m., p. 290,529; cap., Cheyenne: **– Valley,** Luzerne co., Pa.: massacre 1778.
Wyss (vĭs), Johann Rudolph (1781–1830), Swiss au.: *Swiss Family Robinson.*

X

Xanthippe (zăn-thĭp′ē), or **Xantippe** (-tĭp′ē), shrewish wife of Socrates.
Xanthus (zăn′thŭs), anc. city, Lycia, Asia Minor.
Xenocrates (zē-nŏk′rȧ-tēz), (396–314 B. C.), Gk. philos.
Xenophanes (zē-nŏf′ȧ-nēz), (about 536 B. C.), Gk. philos.
Xenophon (zĕn′ō-fŏn), (435?–355 B. C.), Gk. sol. & au.
Xerxes (zûrk′sēz), (?–465 B. C.), king of Persia.

Y

Yalu (yä″lo͞o′), riv., bet. Manchuria & Korea, 300 m. to Korea bay: nav. bats.
Yangtze (yäng′tsē″), [**Yangtze-kiang** (-kyäng′)], riv., China, 3,500 m. fr. Tibet to Yellow sea.
Yap (yäp), one of the W. Caroline isls., 79 sq. m., p. 7,418; formerly Ger., now Jap.
Yeats (yāts; yēts), William Butler (1865–1939), Ir. au. & poet: Nobel prize 1923.
Yeddo (yĕd′ō), former name of Tokyo, cap. of Jap.
Yellow Sea (yĕl′ō), arm of Pacific oc., N. E. coast of China.
Yellowstone (yĕl′ō-stōn″), riv., Wyo. & Mont., 1,000 m. to Mo. riv.: **– National Park,** in Wyo., Mont., & Idaho, 3,348 sq. m.
Yemen (yĕm′ĕn), [anc. **Sheba**], div., Arabia, 75,000 sq. m., p. 3,000,000; cap., Sana.
Yenisei (yĕ″nē-sĕ′ē), riv., Siberia, 2,650 m. to Arctic oc.
Yezo (yĕz′ō). See **Hokkaido.**
Yokohama (yō′kō-hä′mȧ), spt. city, on S. Honshu isl., Jap., p. 405,888.
Yonkers (yŏng′kẽrz), city, N. Y., p. 152,533.
York (yôrk), **1,** city, Pa., p. 59,704; **2,** city, Eng., p. 83,930: cathedral.
Yorktown (yôrk′toun), tn., S. E. Va.: surrender of Cornwallis 1781.
Yosemite (yō-sĕm′ĭ-tē), national park, cen. Calif., 1,512 sq. m.
Young (yŭng), Brigham (1801–77), leader of the Mormons.
Youngstown (yŭngz′toun), city, Ohio, p. 167,643.
Ypres (ēpr′), city, Belgium: bats. 1914–18.
Ypsilanti (ĭp″sē-län′tē), a distinguished Gk. family, notably Demetrios (1793–1832), Gk. patriot.
Ysaye (ē-zȧ′yē), Eugène (1858–1931), Belgian violinist.
Yucatan (yo͞o″kä-tän′), state, Mex., 15,939 sq. m., p. 358,221; cap., Merida.
Yugoslavia (yo͞o′gō-slä′vĭ-ȧ), [formerly **Serb-Croat-Slovene State**], kingdom, S. E. Europe, 95,558 sq. m., p. 13,934,038; cap., Belgrade.
Yukon (yo͞o′kŏn), **1,** ter., Can., 207,076 sq. m., p. 8,986; cap., Dawson; **2,** riv., Yukon ter., Can., 2,300 m. to Bering sea.
Yunnan (yo͞on″nän′), S. W. prov., China, 146,680 sq. m., p. 11,020,591; cap., Yunnanfu.

Z

Zagreb (zä′grĕb), city, Yugoslavia, p. 185,581.
Zambezi (zăm-bē′zĭ), riv., S. cen. Afr., 1,600 m. fr. Angola to Mozambique channel.
Zangwill (săng′wĭl), Israel (1864–1926), Br. nov. & dram.
Zanzibar (zăn″zĭ-bär′), **1,** Br. isl. & protec., off E. coast of Afr., 640 sq. m., p. 128,099; **2,** city, its cap., p. 38,700.
Zarathustra. See **Zoroaster,** *Pfd. S.*
Zealand (zē′lănd), [**Seeland**], largest Da. isl., bet. Kattegat & Baltic, 2,682 sq. m., p. 1,096,897.
Zeebrugge (zā′bro͝og″ē), spt. tn., W. Flanders, Belgium; before World War I, p. 50,000.
Zenger (zĕng′ẽr), Peter (1680?-1746), Ger.-Am. publisher.
Zeno (zē′nō), (336?–264? B. C.), Gk. philos.
Zenobia (zē-nō′bĭ-ȧ), (?–after 272), queen of Palmyra, 262–272.
Zeppelin, von (fŏn tsĕp″ĕ-lēn′), Ferdinand, Count (1838–1917), Ger. inv.
Zola (zo″lȧ′), Emile (1840–1902), Fr. nov.
Zorn (tsōrn), Anders L. (1860–1920), Sw. art. & etcher.
Zoroaster (zō″rō-ăs′tẽr), or **Zarathustra** (zä″rȧ-tho͞os′trȧ), (about 1000 B. C.), founder of anc. Pers. religion.
Zuider Zee (zī′dẽr zā′), arm of North sea, Netherlands, 2,027 sq. m.
Zuloaga (tho͞o″lō-ä′gä), Ignacio (1870–1945), Span. painter.
Zululand (zo͞o′lo͞o-lănd″), prov., Natal, S. Afr., 10,427 sq. m., p. 250,829.
Zurbarán, de (dā tho͞or″bä-rän′), Francisco (1598–1662), Span. painter.
Zurich (zo͞o′rĭk), city, Switzerland, p. 215,460.
Zwingli (tsvĭng′lē), Ulrich (1484–1531), Prot. reformer in Switzerland.

GLOSSARY OF BUSINESS TERMS

A 1, or **A number 1,** a registry mark given to ships in first-class condition; hence, prime; first-class.
absorbed, having been taken up by the public: said of an issue of stocks or bonds.
accept, to assent to (the terms of a bid, offer, order, or the like); to receive in discharge of another's obligation; to agree to pay, as a draft.
acceptance, 1, an agreement by a person on whom a bill of exchange or draft is drawn, to pay it when due according to the terms of the acceptance: usually made by his writing the word "accepted" and his signature across the face of the draft; **2,** an accepted draft.
acceptor, one who agrees to pay a bill of exchange or draft.
accommodation, a loan of money or credit.
accommodation paper, a promissory note made or indorsed by one person for another, not in payment of a debt or as part of a business transaction, but without consideration, to enable the latter to raise money or obtain credit thereby: distinguished from a note given for value received.
account, a record of business transactions and of the financial relations between two parties, implying a continuous business relation; also, the amount involved in such a record: **on account,** in part payment of a debt.
account and risk, a blank form provided by a broker upon which a customer may write an order for the purchase or sale of stocks, goods, etc., and used as evidence that the broker is merely acting as agent.
accountant, an expert in keeping or adjusting financial records; a person who has charge of such records in a business or public office.
account current, an open or running record of business dealings, showing what is due.
account sales, a statement sent by one person to another, giving details as to sales made by the sender on the other's behalf. It usually shows the amount and rate of sales, expenses of freight, commission, and other charges.
accrual, the act or process of increasing by natural additions, or the amount of such increase: **accrual basis** (of bookkeeping), a method of keeping accounts according to which the net taxable income for a given taxable year is computed from the income earned during that year, whether actually received then or later, and the expenses incurred during that year, whether actually disbursed then or later: distinguished from *cash basis*.
accrued, accumulated, as interest, taxes, rent, etc.; added as increase.
acknowledgment, a declaration made in legal form before a duly qualified public officer; also, the paper officially certifying to such a declaration.
acquittance, a written agreement discharging a person from an obligation to pay a sum of money; a receipt in full.
adjustment, the settlement of a business transaction by the apportionment among the various parties in it of a loss or a payment.
administer, to manage; specif., to settle (the estate of one who dies without a will).
ad valorem duty, a tax, duty, or charge levied upon goods at a certain rate per cent upon their value as stated in their invoice: distinguished from *specific duty*.
advance, *n.* **1,** an increase or rise in price or value; **2,** something furnished before an equivalent is received; that which is supplied or paid beforehand:—*v.* **1,** to increase in price; **2,** to raise (the price, etc.); **3,** to furnish beforehand, as money or credit.
adventure, a consignment of goods to an agent, usually foreign, by a manufacturer who wishes to introduce his goods into a fresh market.
advertising, any form of publicity which has as its object the gaining of public attention to some article or service to be sold, in order to create a demand for it.
affidavit, a sworn statement; esp., a written declaration, made upon oath, before an authorized public officer.
agent, a person authorized to act for, or in the place of, another; a deputy.
allowance, a sum granted as a reimbursement or repayment; a deduction from the gross weight or value of goods.
annuity, a sum of money payable yearly; a grant or gift paid yearly, either in one sum or in instalments; an investment which produces a fixed yearly income.
appraise, to set a value on; to estimate the worth of.
appraisement, the act of setting a value; an estimation of the worth of goods, esp. by persons appointed for the purpose.
appraiser, an expert licensed to estimate the value of goods or estates.
appurtenance, that which belongs to an estate or property, as trees and shrubbery.
arbitrage, traffic in stocks and bonds, etc., with the purpose of deriving profit from the difference in price of the same securities in different markets at the same time.
arbitration of exchange, a calculation of the money values in three or more countries in order to determine the ratios of exchange among them, so that a merchant in one of the countries may determine the proceeds of a business transaction with a party in another country through an agent in a third country.
article, 1, a single piece of goods; **2,** a division or paragraph of a document, agreement, or contract.
articles of partnership, a written agreement setting forth the purposes and conditions of the association of a number of persons for the carrying on of a joint enterprise; esp., such a written agreement duly carried out according to law and filed so as to have the force of a charter.
assessment, 1, the determination of an amount to be paid; **2,** a share of joint expenses; **3,** the valuation of a property or income for the purpose of taxation.
assets, the entire property of a person, association, or corporation, available to pay his or its debts: opp. of *liabilities*.
assignee, one to whom property is made over, either in trust or for his own use and enjoyment; a trustee.
assignment, a transfer of title or interest by writing, as of a note, bond, or lease; esp., a transfer of property in trust or for the bene-

fit of creditors, also, the deed of writing effecting such transfer.
assignor, a person who makes an assignment.
association, a body of persons organized for the prosecution of a business undertaking, usually without a charter, but having the general form and mode of procedure of a corporation, as a stock company.
assortment, a quantity of goods varying in form, color, style, size, and price.
assurance, insurance (which see); specif., life insurance.
attachment, legal seizure, as of goods or property, to compel compliance with a judicial decision; also, the writ effecting it.
auction, a public sale of property or goods at which the price offered for each item is increased by the prospective buyers who bid against one another, the highest bidder becoming the purchaser.
audit, a formal examination and certification of accounts; an official settling of accounts.
auditor, a person authorized to examine and verify accounts and claims.
average, any of several charges or losses connected with marine shipping, as a fee paid by shippers to the master of a ship for the care of goods, fees paid by the master for pilotage, towage, etc., incidental losses, as of an anchor, borne by the ship's owner, etc.
avoid, to invalidate, as a contract.
bail, 1, to turn over (something) in trust, to be used in a specified way, under an agreement that the purpose of the delivery shall be faithfully carried out; as, to *bail* goods to a railroad for transportation; 2, to release (a person under arrest) upon the undertaking of another to be responsible for the appearance of the bailed person at a stated time and place.
bailee, the person to whom goods are committed in trust, and who has a conditional possession of them until the specific purpose for which they were pledged has been accomplished.
bailment, a contract whereby personal property is delivered by one person to another to be held for the benefit of either party or both parties and returned when the purpose of the delivery is accomplished.
balance, the equality between the totals of two sides of an account; also, the excess shown on either side.
balance sheet, a statement made to show the true condition of a business by exhibiting its capital or assets, its liabilities or debts, and its profit or loss.
bank, an establishment for the custody, loan, exchange, or issue of money, and for aiding the settlement of business transactions by the transmission and collection of funds.
bankable, receivable as good at a bank.
bank book, the depositor's book in which his deposits and withdrawals are entered by the bank: also called *pass book*.
banker, a person or corporation engaged in the business of borrowing, lending, exchanging, issuing, or caring for money.
bank discount, a deduction from the principal of a loan, or from the face value of a note, amounting to the interest charge upon it up until the time due, made in favor of one who gives value for it before it is due.
bank draft, a bill of exchange drawn by one bank on another bank.
bankrupt, one legally adjudged unable to pay his debts, and liable to, or under legal procedure for, insolvency.
bargain, an agreement on the terms of a transaction; also, the terms agreed upon.
barrel, the quantity constituting a full barrel. In the U. S., a barrel, liquid measure, is usually 31½ gallons, but a barrel of oil or gasoline is about 55 gallons, and, in dry measure, a barrel of flour is 196 pounds, of beef or pork 200 pounds, of fish 200 pounds, of sugar 350 pounds, etc.: **barrel bulk,** in freight measurement, five cubic feet.
bear, a speculator who sells stocks or other securities for future delivery in expectation of being able to buy the securities for delivery at a price below that of the time of sale.
bearer, one who holds and presents for payment a note, bill of exchange, or check.
bid, a written statement of the amount in money for which one will do a thing, furnish a thing, or render some specific service.
bill, a general term for any negotiable paper; also, an account or statement of money owed for goods sold, services rendered, or work done. The sender of a bill for goods sold or shipped calls the bill an *invoice*.
bill book, a book in which a person keeps a record of his notes and drafts, showing all he issues and receives.
billhead, a printed form with business address at the top, for the issuing of a bill.
bill of exchange, a written order from one person, the drawer, to another, the acceptor, to pay a certain sum at a fixed time; a draft.
bill of lading, a receipt issued by a railroad, shipping company, or other carrier, to the shipper, acknowledging responsibility for the shipment of goods and promising to make delivery to the person or place designated.
bill of sale, a formal paper transferring to a buyer the title to personal property.
bills payable: see *notes payable*.
bills receivable: see *notes receivable*.
black list, a list of the names of persons or firms who have lost their credit by failure to meet financial obligations.
block of stock, a considerable amount of stock purchased or sold at one time or held by one person.
blotter, a daybook, in which are kept accounts of the day's business transactions.
board of trade, an association of business men, organized to protect and promote their business interests.
bond, 1, a promise by a corporation or government to pay an investor, in return for the use of his credit, a principal sum on a certain date, with interest; 2, a guarantee on the part of the owner of imported goods, liable to duty but held in a warehouse pending disposal, that he will pay the duty when the goods are removed for sale; 3, that form of the debt of a corporation or government, which is not due until a given date relatively far in the future, as distinguished from floating or current debts.
bonded goods, goods on which import duties or taxes have been met by bonds instead of cash; also, goods placed in a bonded warehouse.
bonded warehouse, a warehouse in which, under state or federal statute, goods are held in bond awaiting reëxport or the payment of import duties.
bondholder, a creditor whose debt is secured by a bond.
bondsman, one who becomes surety for another's debt, appearance for trial, etc.
bonus, a payment in excess of what is regular or stipulated; also, a dividend or wage in excess of the usual or required amount.
book debts, debts or accounts charged on the books.
bounty, a special payment, premium, or additional allowance given to encourage trade or manufacture.
Bradstreet's, (Bradstreet Company, New York City), a mercantile agency which publishes a reference book containing the credit ratings of manufacturers and traders throughout the U. S. and Canada, and which lends copies of the book to those who subscribe to its credit service.
breach of trust, violation of legal duty by one holding goods or property in trust.

breadstuff, any kind of grain, corn, or meal.
breakage, allowance made by a shipper for loss due to injury or destruction.
breaking bulk, the opening of a package of goods or merchandise in transit or in process of transportation.
broker, one who executes orders from actual buyers or sellers for the transfer of stocks or other property, on commission.
building and loan association, an association organized to enable its members to invest money safely, as by regular monthly payments, and to aid them in buying or improving houses and other real property.
bull, a speculator who buys stocks, bonds, or other securities in expectation of, or in order to bring about, a rise in price.
bullion, gold and silver, considered as so much metal; specif., uncoined silver and gold in the shape of bars or ingots.
call, 1, a formal demand for the payment of money due; **2,** a notice to a stockholder to pay in an instalment of his subscription; **3,** a right to demand an amount of stock or goods, at a definite price, at or within a certain time agreed on; specif., in stock speculation, such a transaction closed by payment of the difference in price in favor of the holder of the call: **on call,** deliverable, or to be delivered, on demand.
call money, funds borrowed subject to repayment on demand.
capital, 1, accumulated wealth; specif., the amount of property owned by an individual or corporation; **2,** the amount of such property used for business purposes.
capitalist, one who has capital invested, or for investment; generally, one of large wealth, which is, or may be, employed in business.
cargo, a general term for all goods or merchandise conveyed in a vessel or boat.
carrier, a person or agency engaged in the business of carrying goods for others.
cash, money; strictly, coin, but also paper money, bank notes, bills of exchange, drafts, notes, checks, and other commercial paper easily convertible into money: **cash basis** (of bookkeeping), a method of keeping accounts according to which the net taxable income for a given taxable year is computed from the income actually received during that year, whether earned then or earlier, and expenses actually disbursed during that year, whether incurred then or earlier. Cf. *accrual basis.*
cashbook, a book in which is kept a record of money received and paid out.
cashier's check, a check drawn by a bank upon its own funds, signed by the cashier.
cash sale, a sale of goods for cash. In mercantile transactions, such a sale usually allows ten or thirty days for payment.
certificate of deposit, a paper issued by a bank to a depositor to the effect that a stated amount is set aside not subject to withdrawal by check, except on surrender of the paper.
certified check, a check guaranteed to be good by the bank upon which it is drawn.
chamber of commerce, 1, an association of merchants or other business men, having as its purpose the furthering and protection of the trade interests of its members; **2,** an association of persons organized to further the commercial, economic, social, and civic interests of their community; a citizens', or civic, association.
charter, 1, a formal official paper from the sovereign power of a state or country, bestowing or guaranteeing certain rights and privileges; **2,** a lease, as of a merchant ship; **3,** a written order from the authorities of a society to established a branch or lodge.
charter party, the contract between the shipowner and the shipper for the letting of the ship and the delivery of the cargo.
chattel, any kind of personal property, movable or immovable, except real estate.
check, a written order on a bank to pay a specified amount of money on demand.
clearance, passage through the clearing house of checks, bills of exchange, drafts, and other similar negotiable paper.
clearance papers, papers issued by a customhouse giving permission for the departure of a ship or vessel, and showing that all formalities have been observed and duties met.
clearing, a method of settling accounts, used by banks and other businesses, by which checks, drafts, etc., are exchanged at a common center and only balances are paid in cash.
clearing house, an institution through which banks, and, to a lesser extent, other businesses, regularly exchange drafts, checks, etc., settling in cash only the balances due.
c. o. d., collect on delivery: a call for immediate payment for goods or merchandise at time of delivery.
collateral, property, as stocks or bonds, offered as security in addition to one's note or other personal obligation: also called *collateral security.*
commerce, the buying and selling of merchandise or commodities; particularly, the exchange of merchandise on a large scale between different places or countries.
commercial paper, bills of exchange, drafts, promissory notes, or other negotiable paper, given and passed in due course of business.
commission, a percentage paid to an agent for transacting business for another.
commission broker, one who buys or sells on commission.
common carrier, a person or organization, as a railroad, trolley system, steamship company, etc., in the business of transporting goods or persons for compensation and without discrimination.
compound interest, interest calculated on the sum obtained by adding to the original principal all interest which has accrued and has not been paid.
consideration, compensation; fee; also, that which is accepted by one contracting party as an equivalent or recompense for an act or promise of another.
consign, to ship or send (goods) to a particular place and person; specif., to send (goods) to another for sale, the consignor retaining ownership until sale is made.
consignee, one to whom something is sent.
consignment, 1, the sending of goods or property to another to be sold or cared for; **2,** the goods or property so sent; **3,** the contract providing for the shipment: **on consignment,** shipped or delivered by one party, the consignor, to another, the consignee, with the condition that the goods so shipped remain the property of the consignor, and are not to be paid for by the consignee, until they are sold to a third party, or accepted for use by the consignee, or otherwise disposed of according to agreement.
consignor, one who sends goods to another.
consul, an agent appointed by a government to represent it in a foreign country, to care for the commercial interests of its citizens, and to protect its seamen.
contraband, goods or merchandise which cannot lawfully be imported or exported.
contract, a formal agreement legally enforceable; also, the document containing it.
contractor, one who contracts to do work, or supply goods or merchandise on a large scale, at a stated price or rate.
conveyance, the act by which the title to property, esp. real estate, is transferred; also, the written document by which title to property is transferred.
copyright, an exclusive right granted by the

government for the multiplication and sale of a literary or artistic work.

corner, a control of the supply of a commodity, stock issue, etc., to such an extent as to enable the one in control to fix the market price.

corporation, an association of persons authorized by law to act as a single body, and endowed by law with the right to provide for its continued existence.

coupon, a certificate of interest due, attached to a transferable bond.

covenant, a mutual agreement under seal, between two or more persons.

credentials, a letter or certificate proving one's right to the exercise of authority or to claims or privileges.

credit, 1, trust in a person's business integrity and in his financial capacity to meet all obligations when due; 2, the rating of a person or firm based upon reputation for paying debts and evidence of resources adequate to future payment; 3, an extension of time allowed a customer to pay; 4, the sum remaining at a customer's disposal or in his favor on the books of a bank; specif., an amount turned over to a person, for his use, by a bank or other business establishment; 5, in bookkeeping, the right-hand page or column showing, in the ledger, payment by, or obligation to, a customer, or, in the cash book, money or its equivalent paid out: opp. of *debit*.

creditor, 1, one to whom money is owing; 2, the title or heading of that side of an account reserved for entering the sums paid.

curb, a stock market for dealing in securities not listed in the formal stock exchange, or, sometimes, for trading in securities outside the regular business hours. The leading curb market is the New York Curb, formerly conducted in the middle of Broad Street, New York City, now housed in a building at 78 Trinity Place. It has become the second largest stock market in the world. Also, esp. in British use, **kerb.**

currency, the accepted medium of exchange: coin, paper money, and bank notes.

customhouse, the government office where customs and duties are paid on exported or imported goods, and where vessels are entered or cleared.

customhouse broker, an agent who acts for an importer or an exporter in handling the business arising from entering and clearing goods and vessels in foreign commerce.

customs, duties or taxes levied by the government of a country on commodities imported or exported.

damages, compensation awarded by law to one injured in his person or property, through the fault of another.

daybook, a book in which transactions are recorded in the order of their occurrence.

debit, the entry of an item in an account showing something charged or due, or the sum of several items so entered; also, the left-hand side of an account on which such entries are made: opp. of *credit*.

debtor, the title or heading put at the head of the debit side of an account.

deed, a written paper, properly made out and under seal, conveying or transferring title to land or other real property.

deficit, a shortage, esp. in money, income, or resources.

demand, 1, the quantity of any commodity that will be bought in the market, esp. at a given price; 2, a formal request for payment: **on demand,** upon presentation (of a note or the like) and request for payment.

demurrage, the holding by a shipper of a vessel or freight car beyond the time allowed for the purpose of loading or unloading it; also, the charge made for such delay.

deposit, 1, funds and money turned over to a bank, subject to withdrawal by order or request; 2, a payment made as a pledge of good faith.

depositary, one to whom something is intrusted; a guardian.

depository, a place where things are deposited for storage or until sold.

deposit slip, a statement which a depositor leaves with a deposit, as a memorandum and evidence that the money, checks, or other funds, have been deposited.

depot, a building for the accommodation, protection, or sale, of goods.

depreciation, a decline in value or market price.

discount, 1, a deduction made as an interest charge in lending money upon a bill of exchange, draft, or promissory note not due; 2, a deduction from the gross amount; 3, an allowance upon a debt, or price asked, usually made to bring about cash payment.

dishonor, to fail to pay a note or draft.

dividend, a share of profits distributed among stockholders.

dividend warrant, a formal order by which a stockholder receives his dividend.

dockage, 1, docking facilities; 2, a payment exacted for the use of a dock.

domestic bill, a draft or bill of exchange payable in the country where drawn.

double-name paper, a note, draft, bill of exchange, or trade acceptance, payment of which is made more sure by the indorsement of someone approved by the bank that accepts or discounts it.

draft, a written order for the payment of money. In its broad sense, *draft* includes the check, by which the writer orders the payment of money which is to be charged against his own account; but it is usually applied to an order written by one person directing another to pay money to a specified person.

draw, 1, to obtain by use of a draft; 2, to take away from a place of deposit.

drawback, an amount of money paid back after having been collected; esp., duties or customs remitted by the government when the imports on which they were levied are exported without being sold.

drawee, the person on whom an order, draft, or bill of exchange is drawn.

drawer, one who draws a bill of exchange, draft, or order for payment.

drayage, the charge or sum paid for hauling or for the use of a dray or truck.

duebill, an informal written acknowledgment of a debt, nonnegotiable in form.

dun, to ask persistently for payment.

Dun's, (R. G. Dun & Company, New York City), a mercantile agency which publishes a reference book containing the credit ratings of manufacturers and traders throughout the U. S. and Canada, and which lends copies of the book to those who subscribe to its credit service.

duty, a tax levied by a government on the importation, exportation, or use and consumption of goods.

earnest, money or a valuable article given to insure the fulfilment of a bargain.

ejectment, a legal action for the recovery of possession of real property, and, usually, to secure damages for wrongful withholding; also, the official authorization, or writ, by which this action is begun.

embargo, an order of a government prohibiting the departure or entry of commercial ships at specified ports within its dominions; also, any government prohibition on commerce.

embezzlement, unlawful appropriation of what is entrusted to one's care.

entry, 1, the act of reporting at a customhouse the arrival of a ship, and procuring permission to land its cargo; 2, the act of taking formal possession of lands and other property; **3**, the act of putting on record in proper form and order; also, the item so written in.

equity, 1, the administration of the law according to its spirit in cases in which its strict administration according to the letter works an obvious injustice; **2**, the value of property in excess of mortgages or other encumbrances that are a lien against it.

escrow, an instrument under seal, placed in the hands of a third person for delivery upon stated conditions, and having no effect until delivered.

estate, the title or interest one has in property; also, property in general, or the amount of property under one ownership.

excess profits, net profits above a percentage considered normal.

exchange, 1, the process involved in carrying on trade and commerce; **2**, the process of settling accounts between parties located at a distance from each other by the use of bills of exchange and drafts, or by a transfer of credits; **3**, the amount paid for the collection of a bill of exchange, draft, check, or other negotiable instrument; **4**, conversion of the money of one country into that of another, with allowance for difference in value; also, the amount of the difference in value between two currencies; **5**, a place where merchants and traders meet to carry on particular business transactions; as, the stock *exchange*.

exchange broker, one who acts as agent for another in executing orders for the buying and selling of bills of exchange, drafts, acceptances, stocks, bonds, etc.

excise, a duty or tax levied upon the manufacture, sale, or consumption of goods within a country; also, a tax upon the pursuit or following of certain trades.

ex-coupon, a term used to indicate that the quotation of coupon bonds does not include the value of coupons due or about to become due.

ex-dividend, a term used to indicate that the purchaser of stock will not be entitled to the next dividend, since a transfer of the stock cannot be made on the company's books in time.

executed, performed; specif., carried out and performed according to law.

execution, a legal warrant or order given to an officer, authorizing him to enforce a judgment; also, the act of executing, or completing, an instrument by signing, sealing, and delivering.

expense, expenditure which is incidental and necessary to the management and prosecution of a business, as distinguished from costs of labor, materials, etc.

exports, commodities sold and sent to a foreign country.

express business, a system of transportation of goods or merchandise, generally managed by express companies, providing special care, security, and quickness of delivery.

express money order, a negotiable order for the payment of money issued by one office of an express company and payable at another. Such orders afford the public a convenient method of sending money to distant points and are purchasable at their face value plus a fee for issuance.

extension, an allowance of additional time by a creditor to a debtor for the payment of a debt.

face, the principal amount of a note or other financial obligation.

facsimile, a copy of anything, so made as to give every part and detail of the original.

factor, an agent; one who transacts business for another.

failure, a becoming insolvent or bankrupt.

fair, average; middling; free from marked merit or defect.

fall, a decline in value or price.

federal reserve bank, any of twelve district banks established under the laws of the U. S. to act as an agent in the maintenance of money reserves, to issue bank currency, to rediscount commercial paper, and otherwise aid the member banks of each respective district.

fee, a charge fixed by law for the services of a public officer.

finance, the science of money, credit, and banking; also, the science of government budgets, revenues, and expenditures.

firm, *n.* a partnership of two or more persons, not a corporation, for doing business; also, the name under which a partnership or company transacts business:—*adj.* steady; not declining in value or price.

fiscal year, the period of one year, beginning on any convenient date, considered by a business or government as a fixed recurring period in keeping accounts, taking inventories, calculating profits and losses, etc.

fixture, an article of furniture attached to a house and considered as a part of it.

flat, without additional charge or interest.

floating indebtedness, unfunded debts, or current liabilities, such as notes payable, book accounts, etc.

flotation, the process of financing a business or undertaking of any kind.

f. o. b., free on board; delivered free of charge to a vessel or train.

footing, the act of adding up a column of figures, or the sum total of such a column.

forced sale, sale of goods under compulsion or foreclosure.

foreclose, to cut off or debar (a person who has defaulted in payments due on a mortgage) from the right of redeeming mortgaged property.

foreclosure, a legal proceeding which cancels a mortgagor's right of redeeming a mortgaged property.

foreign bill, a bill of exchange or draft payable in a foreign country.

forgery, the act of making, with fraudulent intent, a false or counterfeited document; also, the writing so counterfeited.

forwarder, one who accepts goods for transportation and delivery to another carrier.

franchise, a particular right or privilege granted by a sovereign or by a lawmaking body to an individual or business company.

free list, 1, the schedule of goods or merchandise admitted to a country free of duty; **2**, a list of persons who enjoy certain privileges without payment.

free trade, commerce and trade not subjected to duties or tariff regulations.

freight, the compensation paid for the transportation of goods by rail or water; also, the cargo.

frozen assets, assets which can be turned into cash only at a loss or at a future date.

funded debt, that part of a public or corporate debt which runs for a long period of time, and is in the form of bonds bearing a fixed rate of interest.

funds, money or negotiable paper readily convertible into cash; available resources.

futures, commodities bought or sold for future delivery.

good will, the value of an established business over and above its material property, consisting of such assets as reputation, patents, trade-marks, and trade secrets.

grace, a period of delay, usually three days, allowed by law in some states, for payment of a note or draft after the date of maturity.

great gross, twelve gross, or 1,728 articles.

gross, *adj.* whole; entire; total; without any deduction: **gross ton,** 2,240 pounds avoirdupois; a long ton:—*n.* twelve dozen; 144 articles.

guarantee, to become responsible for the

fulfilment of an obligation of another; to be surety for.

guarantor, a person who gives a guaranty.

guaranty, an agreement to pay a debt, or perform a duty, of another, in case of the failure of the latter to fulfil the obligation.

holder, a person in possession of, and legally entitled to payment of, a draft or note.

honor, to accept and pay when due.

house, a business firm or a place of business.

house organ, a magazine or newspaper published by a business house or factory, in which is printed information concerning the house or its personnel of especial interest to employees or customers.

hypothecate, to pledge as security without giving title or ownership; mortgage.

importer, a merchant who brings goods or merchandise into a country from abroad.

imports, goods or merchandise imported, or brought into a country from abroad.

impost, a tax or duty laid by a government on goods imported into a country.

imprest cash fund, a specified amount of cash set aside from the regular cash account and placed in charge of a cashier for petty cash payments.

income, the return from labor, business, or property. The total receipts from any branch of business are called the *gross income;* that portion which remains after paying costs and expenses is known as the *net income.*

income tax, a tax on income or on an excess of income over a certain amount.

indemnify, to secure against loss or damage; to reimburse in case of loss or damage.

indemnification, reimbursement for loss, damage, or injury; indemnity.

indorse, to write upon the back of (a negotiable instrument, as a note or check). The usual purposes of indorsing are: **1,** to order the instrument paid to another, by writing out such an order, over one's signature; **2,** to guarantee payment, as of a note or check, by writing one's name; **3,** to obtain payment of the amount of a check made payable to oneself, by writing one's name, thus in effect giving a receipt for the amount, and binding oneself to repay it in case the check is worthless.

indorsee, the person to whom a negotiable instrument is made payable by indorsement.

indorsement, the act of writing on the back of a check; also, that which is written.

indorser, the person who indorses.

industrials, securities of corporations engaged in production.

injunction, a legal process whereby a person is commanded by a court to do, or is forbidden to do, certain things.

inland bill, a bill of exchange or draft payable in the country where drawn: generally called *domestic bill.*

in re, a Latin phrase meaning in the matter of, in connection with, referring to.

insolvent, not having sufficient assets to meet all debts.

instalment, a portion of a debt that is to be paid in parts at stated intervals.

instalment plan, the system of making sales for a sum to be paid in portions at stated intervals.

instant, present; current: used with a date to indicate the current month; as, the 5th *instant* (the 5th of the present month).

insurable interest, such an interest in the subject insured as carries with it legal damage in the event of the loss insured against.

insurance, 1, a system of protection against the risk of individual loss, by distributing according to the law of averages the burden of losses over a large number of individuals; **2,** a contract whereby, in consideration of a certain payment called a *premium,* one party to the contract agrees, in case of certain eventualities, as loss by fire, accident, death, etc., to idemnify a person or persons designated by the other party, by the payment of a stated sum of money; **3,** the sum paid for the insuring; the premium; **4,** the amount for which anything is insured; the amount of indemnity to be paid: **insurance broker,** a broker who handles or places insurance: **insurance policy,** a written contract of insurance.

interest, a sum paid for the use of money, being a certain per cent of the sum loaned per unit of time, as per year.

internal revenue, a revenue or income derived by a government from licenses, duties, and special taxes levied on personal property or the production and use of domestic goods.

intestate, a person who dies without having made a valid will.

in transit, on the road; not brought to an end or destination.

inventory, a catalog or itemized list, as of books or furniture; specif., the account of stock on hand in a business, or the things that are, or may be, included in such a list.

invest, to apply money or funds to the purchase of property for income or profit.

investment, 1, the act of laying out money for profit; **2,** the money or funds invested; **3,** that in which capital or money is invested.

invoice, 1, an itemized statement of merchandise sent to a purchaser or consignee, with the quantity, prices, and charges; **2,** the goods mentioned in the document, either shipped or received. An invoice (def. 1) and a bill are the same thing. Statements which are sent to others are called *invoices;* statements received are called *bills.*

invoice book, a book for recording or entering copies of invoices.

jobber, one who buys from importers or manufacturers and sells to retailers; a middleman.

joint note, a promissory note signed by several persons, each of whom is liable for a proportional part of the amount.

joint and several note, a promissory note signed by two or more persons, each of whom agrees to hold himself liable for the full amount in case the others are unable to pay.

joint stock, stock or capital held and used in a joint enterprise.

joint stock company, a company like a corporation in that its capital is divided into transferable shares of stock, but like a partnership in that shareholders are individually liable without limit for the debts of the company, except in states in which specific legislation decrees a limited liability.

journal, a book of accounts in which is recorded a condensed statement of daily business transactions arranged according to debit and credit.

judgment, 1, the final order of a court in civil or criminal proceedings; **2,** an obligation created by an order or decree of a court; **3,** the official certificate evidencing such an obligation.

judgment note, a promissory note, containing, in addition to its usual contents, a power of attorney authorizing a confession of judgment against the maker or signer upon default of payment.

leakage, an allowance or deduction made for waste by leaking of casks or barrels.

lease, a contract by which one person conveys to another person the use of lands, buildings, or other real property, usually for a specified rent or compensation and for a specified term; also, the instrument by which such conveyance is made, or the term for which it is made.

ledger, a book in which are recorded the final summaries of debits and credits.

legal tender, coin or currency which a government has declared shall be received in payment of debts; also, a formal proffer of money to pay a debt.
lessee, one to whom a lease is given, or who takes property under a contract of lease; a tenant under a lease.
lessor, one who gives a lease; one who leases.
letter of advice, 1, a written report from an agent to a principal, or from a consignor to a consignee, transmitting special information; **2,** a letter by which the drawer of a bill of exchange, or draft, notifies the drawee that the bill has been drawn.
letter of credit, a letter addressed by a bank or mercantile house to one or more of its correspondents at home or abroad, authorizing the correspondent to honor drafts or bills of exchange drawn upon it by certain designated parties. When such a letter is addressed to several correspondents, it is sometimes called a *circular letter of credit.*
letters of administration, a document issued by a court, granting authority to an administrator to manage and settle the business affairs and estate of a person who has died.
liability, a debt; that which one is under obligation to pay.
license, a document issued by the proper authorities granting permission to do something that would otherwise be contrary to the law; a legal permit.
lien, a legal claim upon real or personal property, for the satisfaction of some debt.
lighterage, the use of large, open barges for transporting goods between the shore and a ship not lying at a dock; also, the charge made for such service.
liquidate, to apportion the assets of a business in settlement of indebtedness.
liquidation, settling the debts of a business.
Lloyd's, a marine insurance association with central offices in London, having for its main objects the carrying on of marine insurance and the dissemination of maritime information, but also dealing in other kinds of insurance.
loan, 1, the act of lending; **2,** that which one lends or borrows; esp., a sum of money lent at interest.
long, in the position of having bought stocks or commodities on the exchanges, in the expectation of a rise in price and a resulting opportunity to sell at a profit.
maintenance, expense incurred in keeping property in good and efficient condition.
manifest, an invoice of a ship's cargo, to be shown at the customhouse.
margin, 1, the difference between the cost and the selling price of an article; **2,** money or other property deposited with a broker by a client to insure the broker against loss, as from a drop in the price of stocks, on transactions for the client's account: **to buy (stock) on margin,** to buy (a specified stock) through a broker, the client depositing a margin, as 10 or 20 per cent of the purchase price, and assuming profits and losses, the broker paying the balance and reserving the right, as a protection against loss, to sell in the open market in case the fall in the market price approaches the amount of the margin deposited.
market, 1, the state of demand as shown by rate or price; **2,** the place in which buyers and sellers transact business; **3,** the economic organization which deals with buying and selling.
maturity, the time at which a note or other obligation becomes due.
memorandum, an informal document, stating terms of a contract, recording a proceeding, or the like: **on memorandum,** (sold) with the privilege of return.
mercantile agency, an organization which collects information as to the credit and reputation of merchants or others doing business, and furnishes this to others for compensation; a commercial agency.
mercantile paper, negotiable paper, as drafts, bills of exchange, etc., given in the course of business.
merchant marine, the ships of a nation which are engaged in commerce.
middleman, an intermediary between producer and consumer; one who buys at wholesale and resells at wholesale or retail.
money, in general usage, paper currency, as well as gold or silver coin, in circulation as a medium of exchange; popularly, any form of bank credit, as checks, promissory notes, etc., which can be exchanged for money.
money market, the state of demand for loans as shown by rates of interest; the whole body of agencies which regulate and direct financial operations and equalize the supply of, and demand for, capital.
money order, an order for the payment of money. See *express money order* and *postal money order.*
monopoly, 1, the exclusive or nearly exclusive right to, or possession of, a given industry, resulting in a power of control over it, whereby prices may be raised through an artificial limitation of supply; **2,** a company possessing such control.
moratorium, an emergency act of legislation authorizing a debtor or bank to suspend payment of obligations for a given period; also, the period of such suspension.
mortgage, a legal document or instrument given by one person (the *mortgagor*), usually a borrower, to another (the *mortgagee*), usually a lender, which conveys to the latter the title to property of the former, with the proviso that the instrument become void under specified conditions, as upon the repayment of a loan; also, the title or claim created by such an instrument.
mortgagee, the person to whom property is mortgaged.
mortgagor, one who gives a mortgage.
negotiable, capable of being transferred by delivery, with or without indorsement, so as to give possession of notes, drafts, or other valuable rights to another party.
negotiable paper, bills of exchange, drafts, promissory notes, checks, or other similar instruments, that are payable to bearer or order; also, under some laws, other business instruments, such as bonds, forms of stock, and bills of lading.
negotiation, the discussion and bargaining which goes on between parties before a contract is settled or an agreement executed.
net, free from all charges, deductions, and allowances; as, *net* profits; *net* weight.
nominal, 1, designating a price that is given for quotation purposes only, it being understood that neither buyer nor seller is obligated to do business at that price; **2,** designating assets that are of doubtful value or entirely worthless; hence, of values, prices, or the like, negligible; **3,** designating values that are fictitious, as face or par values, as distinct from actual or market values.
nonacceptance, refusal of the buyer to accept or receive delivery, for valid reasons.
no protest, a phrase marked on a draft or promissory note to indicate that it is not to be protested.
notary public, a public officer authorized to take acknowledgments, to attest or certify deeds and other business instruments, usually under his official seal, to make them authentic, and to take affidavits, and protests of negotiable paper.
note, a written instrument acknowledging a debt, and promising payment.
notes payable, notes, drafts, and bills of exchange issued by oneself in favor of others.

notes receivable, notes, drafts, and bills of exchange made by others and payable to oneself.
obligation, a written deed or bond by which one binds himself under penalty to do a thing; a contract.
offer, any proposal submitted for acceptance or rejection.
open account, an account not settled or adjusted.
open policy, an insurance policy in which the value is to be proved by the insured, in case of loss.
operative, one who works for another for a wage; a wage-earning employee.
operator, 1 an owner, whether a person or a corporation, engaged in mining: distinguished from a laboring employee, commonly called *miner;* **2,** a professional trader who speculates in the rise and fall of market prices.
option, a privilege, allowed in a time contract, of buying or selling at a specified price within a specified time.
order, 1, an instruction to buy, sell, or supply goods or merchandise; **2,** an indorsement by which the holder of negotiable paper directs to whom payment shall be made.
outlawed, removed from legal enforcement by the statute of limitations, as a debt.
outstanding accounts, accounts unsettled and unpaid.
overdraw, to draw upon (an account) in excess of the amount standing to the credit of the drawer.
overdue, unpaid at the time at which payment is due.
overhead, 1, that part of the expense of a business which does not include the cost of materials, labor, and other direct agents of production, but which includes indirect costs, such as rent, interest, insurance, heating, advertising, etc.; **2,** the general costs of running a business.
panic, a sudden general condition of distress in financial and commercial quarters, marked by a precipitate, widespread attempt to withdraw deposits from banks, the conversion of property into cash, and the demand for immediate payment of loans.
paper, in business and finance, promissory notes, drafts, etc., collectively.
par, 1, full or normal value; as, the stock is below *par;* **2,** the rate of exchange at which the money unit of one country may be exchanged for an equivalent weight of the precious metal of the money unit of another country; as, the *par* of the English gold sovereign is $4.8665 in American money, the sovereign containing 4.8665 times as much gold by weight as the dollar; **3,** the established standard from which to measure quality of goods or value of property.
partner, one who is associated with another or others in business for mutual benefit.
partnership, relation between two or more persons who have contracted to do business together and to share profits.
party, one concerned in an affair, cause, or side; as, a *party* to a contract.
pass book, the depositor's book in which an account of deposits and withdrawals is kept; a bank book.
passport, an official permission to enter or leave a port, or to pass into or through a country.
patent, a government grant which secures to a specified person the exclusive right of manufacture and sale of an invention for a specified time; also, the official paper granting this right.
payable, justly due, as a note or bill: **payable to bearer,** payable to holder with or without indorsement: a phrase used on notes, bills of exchange, checks, or drafts: **payable to order of,** or **pay to the order of,** a phrase making notes, bills of exchange, checks, or drafts negotiable only by indorsement of the person to whose order the instrument was made or previously indorsed.
payee, the one to whom money is, is to be, or has been, paid.
payer, the person who is to pay a financial obligation.
payment, 1, the act of giving money for wages, a debt, etc.; **2,** that which is given in discharge of a debt, duty, penalty, etc.
permit, an authorization for an act or the conduct of a business.
personal property, chattels; any kind of property except real estate.
petty cash, money paid out or received in small amounts.
petty-cash book, a book in which a record is kept of petty cash receipts and payments.
pilotage, the act or business of conducting vessels into or out of a port or through dangerous waters.
plaintiff, one who sues another or brings an action in court.
policy, 1, a contract of insurance; **2,** a definite or settled course of action adopted and followed by a government, individual, or business enterprise.
post, to transfer an entry or entries from a book of original record to one of final classification and summary, as from a journal to a ledger.
postal money order, an order for the payment of money issued by one post office upon another. See *express money order.*
postdate, to place a date upon (a document) which is later than the date of writing.
power of attorney, a written authority issued by one person to another and giving the second person the right and power to act for the first in specified matters.
premium, 1, the amount agreed upon to be paid for a contract of insurance; **2,** the amount by which the market value of stocks, bonds, etc., exceeds their par value.
prime, of first quality.
principal, 1, the sum of money drawing interest; **2,** the main part of an estate; **3,** in a matter of authorizing an agent, the party who is the source of authority; **4,** in a matter of contracts, any of the parties who sign the contract.
proceeds, the financial return that is derived from some possession or transaction; esp., the amount realized from a sale of property.
produce, 1, that which is yielded; **2,** specif., farm products, esp. green vegetables.
producer, one who raises crops or takes any material substance and through labor or the process of manufacture makes it into an article of trade.
profit, the excess of returns over costs and expenses; gain in a business undertaking.
profit sharing, any system in which employees receive a percentage of profits in addition to wages.
promissory note, a written promise to pay a sum of money at a future time to, or to the order of, a specified person or to bearer.
promoter, one whose business it is to start new companies, encourage the sale of stock or bonds, etc.
property, 1, the legal right to a thing; **2,** anything of value that may be owned: generally classified as *personal property* when movable and *real property* when immovable.
pro rata, in proportion; by a proportional distribution.
prospectus, an outline of the constitution and projected plans or operations of any company about to be formed, published as a means of inducing the public to buy shares in the concern.
protest, to declare formally that a promissory note, check, or draft has been dishonored by nonpayment or nonacceptance.

proxy, a person authorized to represent another in specified matters, as in a vote; also, the document authorizing a person so to represent another.
quotation, the current market price of a stock or commodity; also, a statement of the current price.
rate, 1, an established price or charge; **2,** an amount fixed by the government for tariffs and taxes.
rating, an estimate of financial worth. Mercantile agencies compile rating books in which is stated the estimated financial standing of all business houses.
re, in the case of; in the matter of: often written *in re*.
real estate, lands and everything attached, or belonging, to them, as trees, buildings, or the like; all immovable property.
realize, 1, to obtain (a specified amount of profit) from a transaction; **2,** to reduce some form of property to ready cash.
realtor, a dealer in real estate who is associated with the National Association of Real Estate Boards.
realty, real estate or real property.
rebate, 1, a deduction or allowance; **2,** a giving back of part of a sum already paid.
receipt, a written acknowledgment of anything obtained from another.
receipt book, a book of printed receipt forms or one in which receipts are filed.
receiver, an officer appointed by a court to hold in trust, and manage, the property and funds involved in a suit at law, or to wind up the affairs of a bankrupt or insolvent business enterprise.
referee, a person appointed after suit is brought to hear and determine matters in controversy and to report to the court.
register and recorder, an officer charged with recording certain business transactions.
reinsurance, insurance of an underwriter's risk by placing part of it with one or more other insurance companies, thereby distributing the risk and gaining the utmost protection.
release, the surrender of a legal claim.
remittance, the act of sending money, bills, or the like, esp. to a distant place.
rent, 1, a fixed amount payable at a stated time or times for the use of property; specif., in economics, that portion of the return on a piece of land which is due to its superiority in location, productivity, etc., over land which is barely good enough to bring in a return to labor (wages) and capital invested in it (interest): also called *ground rent, economic rent,* or *Ricardian rent;* **2,** the price paid to the owner of land, buildings, or other property, for the use of such material over a given period of time: also called *contract rent.*
reserve, a portion of profits that is set aside for a specific purpose or for meeting unforeseen emergencies.
resources, everything of value which belongs to or is owing to a concern or individual.
retail, to sell in small quantities.
retailer, one who sells in small quantities directly to the consumer.
return, 1, a statement; a report; **2,** that which is received from securities, sales, options, business, etc.; specif., profit.
right of way, the right to pass over the land of another person; also, the way over which one has such right to pass.
royalty, a share of the product or profit, as from a mine, paid to the owner in consideration of his permitting another to use the property; a percentage paid to an inventor or author for the use of a patent or copyright.
run on a bank, a sudden demand for payment of notes and deposits, caused by fears that the bank cannot meet its liabilities.
safe-deposit box, a steel box, generally fitted into the wall of a vault, provided by banks or safe-deposit companies, for containing and safeguarding securities and valuables.
sale, 1, the transfer of property and the title to it, in return for money or its equivalent; the act of selling; **2,** a chance to dispose of goods; a market: **on sale, 1,** for sale; **2,** shipped on consignment, for purposes of sale by the consignee (see *consignment*).
salvage, an allowance for saving a ship, or cargo, or particularly goods.
savings bank, a bank employed in the business of receiving deposits, investing them, and paying interest on them.
security, 1, something given as a pledge to assure the fulfilment of an obligation or the payment of a debt; **2,** a person who becomes responsible as a surety for the performance of another's obligation or the payment of his debts; **3,** any document or evidence of debt or of property, such as a bond or a share of stock.
sell, *v.* to give in return for a consideration, esp. for money; transfer ownership or right of possession of something to another for an equivalent:—*n.* on the stock exchange, a stock that should be sold.
set-off, the discharge of a debt by means of a counterclaim which a debtor has against his creditor; also, the counterclaim itself.
share, part ownership of property; esp., one of the equal portions into which a company's capital is divided, entitling the holder to a proportionate fraction of the earnings.
shipping clerk, one who oversees the forwarding and shipping of merchandise.
short, a dealer who has sold goods, stocks, or the like, which he does not possess, but which he expects to be able to buy at an advantageous price before the date specified for delivery; also, a short sale.
shrinkage, decrease in bulk or measurement; also, a decrease in value.
sight draft, an order directing payment at sight, or on demand or presentation.
sinking fund, a fund set apart from income in regular instalments, with the purpose of accumulating resources to pay a debt, particularly a bond issue.
solvent, able to meet all one's debts.
specie, gold and silver money.
specifications, the detailed statement of requirements for carrying out a contract, as for a building.
specific duty, a tax on goods, esp. on imports, definitely fixed, and not calculated in proportion to the value of the goods: distinguished from *ad valorem duty.*
speculation, the buying and selling of stocks, goods, etc., with the expectation of profiting by a change in market prices.
stale demand, a claim for payment, made long after it should have been made.
standard, the grade and quality of certain kinds of merchandise such as cotton, wool, etc., customary in the trade.
statement, a report, as of a bank account, or of the condition and items of an open account.
statute of limitations, a law assigning a definite time limit after which certain claims cannot be legally enforced.
stock, 1, the capital represented by a given number of shares of a corporate company; also, the assets or funds utilized by a company to carry on its business, represented by a given number of shares; **2,** the goods on hand at a given time in a mercantile house or manufacturing plant.
stockbroker, one who buys and sells stocks on commission.
stock exchange, an association of stockbrokers who meet to buy and sell stocks and bonds; also, the place where they meet.

street, the, the financial district of a city; also, those doing business there.
sundries, unclassified articles or items.
supply, the total quantity of a salable commodity; more narrowly, the quantity of a commodity obtainable at any given time.
surcharge, an additional charge; one to be added to and paid with the fixed charges.
surety, one who makes himself liable to pay money in case another fails to pay, to fill a contract, or to serve with integrity.
surtax, an extra tax levied in addition to the normal tax, as the extra tax on large incomes over and above the normal tax on all incomes.
suspend, of a business, to stop payment temporarily, or fail to meet one's financial obligations.
syndicate, an association of persons or corporations to promote some particular enterprise, esp. one requiring a large amount of capital and controlling the market in a particular commodity.
tare, an allowance in weight made to a purchaser by deducting the weight of the container.
tariff, a schedule of taxes levied by a government on goods going into, or coming out of, a country; any schedule of rates or charges.
tenant, one who leases or rents real property.
tender, an offer of something, as money, in settlement of a debt or claim.
term, the space of time between one time date and another.
testator, the deceased maker of a valid will.
title, the right to exclusive possession of property; also, the legal evidence of one's right of property.
tort, an injury or detriment, not including a breach of contract, for which damages may be obtained.
trade, buying and selling; traffic; commerce: **the trade,** collectively, dealers in a given line of merchandise.
trade acceptance, a draft drawn by the seller on the purchaser of goods, and accepted by the purchaser for payment at a definite time. Trade acceptances are popular with manufacturers, jobbers, wholesalers, etc., because they provide a way, through discount, of obtaining immediate cash on sales, and they are in favor with banks because it is understood that the drawee will pay them when due, and not ask to have the obligation renewed.
trade discount, an allowance made to dealers in the same line of business.
trade-mark, letters, figures, or devices legally registered, used on goods and labels by a manufacturer or merchant to designate his goods.
trade price, the price allowed by wholesalers to retailers.
transfer, the conveyance and delivery of a right, title, property, or the like, from one person to another.
transshipment, removing goods or merchandise from one ship or means of transportation to another.
trust, 1, credit granted because of belief in one's honesty; 2, a particular form of big business combination, whereby the stockholders of the constituent companies turn over their stock to a board of trustees, with the power to vote the stock, to control the management of all the member companies, and to distribute the profits to the holders of trust certificates who turned over their stock to the board; 3, popularly, any combination of business men designed to create a large corporation with the view to restricting competition or developing a monopoly.
trust company, a corporation engaged in the business of acting as a trustee, and carrying on banking according to state laws.
trust deed, a document placing a debtor's property in the hands of a trustee for the benefit of the creditors.
trustee, a person to whom property, or the management of property, is committed.
turnover, 1, the act or process of getting back invested money; 2, of money, the number of times in a given period that a sum invested in a business is returned by the business for reinvestment; 3, hence, the amount of business done in a specified period, usually a year; 4, the annual business as compared with the stock on hand; the ratio of the aggregate value of a year's sales to the value of the average daily stock on hand; 5, of labor, the rate at which employees in a given establishment are replaced by others.
under seal, a term used to show lawful consideration for the promise or agreement made in a contract, and commonly evidenced by the use of the letters "L. S." (for Latin *locus sigilli*, "place of the seal"), or the word "seal" in addition to the signatures of the parties in the contract.
undersell, to sell below the trade price.
usury, interest greater than the lawful rate.
value, the estimated worth of a commodity, expressed in money; market price.
value received, a phrase used to signify that a note has been made or a bill accepted in return for a lawful and valuable consideration.
valued policy, 1, in marine insurance, a policy in which the total value of the thing insured is inserted in the contract and must be paid in case of total loss; 2, in fire insurance, a policy under which the insured receives the full amount of insurance in case of total loss, regardless of the actual value of the property destroyed.
void, not enforceable by law.
voidable, capable of being nullified or made of no effect.
voucher, a receipt, entry, or document which establishes the truth or authenticity of a business transaction or record.
waiver, a voluntary surrender of a legal right.
Wall Street, 1, a narrow street in downtown New York, formerly the most important financial center of the United States, but now equalled in importance by Broad Street, on which are located the Stock Exchange, the curb market, and the Consolidated Exchange; hence, 2, high finance; 3, the financial interests.
warehouse, a storehouse for storing and safeguarding goods or merchandise.
warehouse receipt, a receipt, sometimes negotiable, given at a warehouse to the owner of goods in storage.
warranty, a guarantee of the accurate representation of goods or of title.
warranty deed, a deed carrying with it the assurance of the one who grants it that his title to the property is as represented.
wastage, the loss due to handling of goods.
waybill, a document, or paper, describing and containing shipping instructions for goods carried by train or steamer.
wharfage, charges paid for the use of a wharf.
wholesale, trading in large quantities; selling to retailers or middlemen rather than to consumers.
will, the legal document by which a person makes provision for the settlement or distribution of his estate after his death.
without recourse, a phrase added to an indorsement of a note or bill of exchange to prevent the indorser from liability.
writing off, removing an item, as a bad debt, from an open account; acknowledging in the accounts the annulment of such an item.
yield, the return, as in farm crops, mining products, or the like, for labor expended or for capital invested; also, the return in interest or dividends from money invested in bonds or stocks.

WORD FORMATION

Prefixes and Suffixes, and Latin and Greek Stems and Combining Forms

A simple abbreviation, as Eng., Lat., etc., indicates that the form occurs in, or is immediately derived from, English, Latin, etc. The symbol +, as +Fr., indicates that the form has suffered some little change in coming into English through the language so marked, from an already named earlier source.

The prefixes, suffixes, and combining forms are listed in the form in which they appear in modern English. The stems of the Greek and Latin words show various changes in spelling when they appear in English words, especially those of Latin words which have come into English through the French (as in Latin *brevi-s* 'short,' *cognitu-s* 'known,' appearing in English as a*bridge*, ac*quaint*). Words derived *directly* from the Greek or Latin show fewer changes; but *c*, *ch*, and *y* in English words from the Greek usually stand for Greek *k*, *kh*, and *u* (as in *c*ardiac, *ch*orus, p*y*re), and English *e* may stand for Greek *oi* or Latin *œ* or *æ* (as in *e*conomic, c*e*lestial, *e*qual).

Prefixes, Suffixes, and Combining Forms

[1]a-, *prefix*, **1**, [Eng.]: **a**, up (*a*rise); **b**, of (*a*kin); **c**, [a form of [1]*an-* used before a consonant], in, on, into, to, at (*a*fire, *a*shore); **2**, [a form of *ab-*], from (*a*vert).

[2]a-, [Gk.], *prefix*, [*an-* before vowels (*an*archy)], without, not (*a*pathy, *a*morphous).

-a, [Lat.], *suffix*, forming the plural of Latin neuter nouns in *-um* (dat*a*, memorand*a*).

ab-, [Lat.], *prefix*, [*a-* before *p* and *v* (*a*vert); *abs-* before *c* and *t* (*abs*tain)], **1**, from, away (*ab*duct); **2**, used intensively (*ab*sorb).

-able, [Lat.], *adj. suffix*, [with some stems, *-ible* (poss*ible*, terr*ible*, vis*ible*), or *-ble* (no*ble*)], meaning: **1**, able to (dur*able*, delect*able*); **2**, capable of being (leg*ible*); **3**, fit to be (laud*able*, detest*able*); **4**, inclined to; characterized by (peace*able*, season*able*). Akin to **habēre**.

ac-, *prefix*, a form of *ad-* used before **c** and *q* (*ac*cede, *ac*quire).

-ac, [Gk.], *adj. suffix*, like or affected by, having (elegi*ac*, ammoni*ac*); pertaining to (pericardi*ac*): the adjectives often being used as nouns (mani*ac*, hypochondri*ac*).

-aceous, [Lat.], *adj. suffix*, belonging or pertaining to, or like (herb*aceous*): in botany, belonging to a (given) family (lili*aceous*).

-acious, [Lat.], *adj. suffix*, abounding in or inclined to (mend*acious*, fall*acious*, aud*acious*, pugn*acious*).

-acy, [Lat.], *n. suffix*, meaning quality, state, or office (accur*acy*, magistr*acy*).

ad-, [Lat.], *prefix*, [*a-* before *sc*, *sp*, *st* (*a*scend, *a*spire, *a*stringent), *ad-* before a vowel or *d*, *h*, *j*, *m*, or *v* (*ad*equate, *ad*duce, *ad*here, *ad*jective, *ad*mire, *ad*vent), or changed according to the initial sound of the word to which it is prefixed (*ab*breviate, *ac*cede, *af*fect, *ag*gregate, *al*lusion, *an*notate, *ap*ply, *ac*quiesce, *ar*rogate, *as*sociate, *at*tract)], meaning to, toward, in addition to, etc.; sometimes merely intensifying the meaning of the word to which it is attached.

-ad, [Gk.], *n. suffix*, forming: **1**, collective numerals (tri*ad*); **2**, names of poems (Ili*ad*, Dunci*ad*); **3**, patronymics or names of family groups with a common designation (dry*ad*); **4**, names of some family plant groups; **5**, [see *-ade*], forms shortened from the suffix *-ade* (ball*ad*, sal*ad*).

-ade, [Lat.+Fr.], *n. suffix*, denoting: **1**, something done (escap*ade*); **2**, something going on or taking place (par*ade*); **3**, something made or created (lemon*ade*, masquer*ade*); **4**, [see *-ad*], a group formed of similar units (dec*ade*).

af-, ag-, *prefixes*, forms of *ad-* used before *f* and *g* (*af*filiate, *ag*gregate).

-age, [Lat.+Fr.], *n. suffix*, denoting: **1**, a collection, sum, etc. (foli*age*, mile*age*); **2**, the act or process (pass*age*, mass*age*); **3**, fees for or cost of (cart*age*, post*age*); **4**, condition or rank (bond*age*, peer*age*).

al-, *prefix*, a form of *ad-* used before **l** (*al*leviate).

-al, [Lat.], *adj. suffix*, like or pertaining to (fat*al*, natur*al*):—*n. suffix*, that which is like or pertaining to (recit*al*, withdraw*al*).

ambi-, [Lat.], *prefix*, [in certain combinations *am-* (*am*putate), *amb-* (*amb*ient)], around, about, on both sides (*ambi*dextrous).

amphi-, [Gk.], *prefix*, on both sides, around (*amphi*bious, *amphi*theater).

[1]an-, *prefix*, **1**, [Eng.], on, in (*an*on): also, **a-** (*a*shore); **2**, [Eng.], against (*an*swer).

[2]an-, **1**, a form of [2]*a-* used before a vowel (*an*archy); **2**, a form of *ana-* used before a vowel (*an*ode); **3**, a form of *ad-* used before *n* (*an*notate).

-an, [Lat.], *adj. suffix*, like or pertaining to (Americ*an*): the adjectives often becoming nouns denoting a member of a zoölogical group (crustace*an*), a person of a given characteristic (utilitari*an*) or nationality (Rom*an*), or a language (Itali*an*). Also, **-ane** (mund*ane*).

ana-, [Gk.], *prefix*, [*an-* before a vowel (*an*ode)], up, back, anew, again (*ana*tomy, *ana*basis).

-ana, [Lat.], *n.pl. suffix*, things pertaining to, sayings or anecdotes of or information upon (Americ*ana*).

-ance, [Lat.], *n. suffix*, denoting action, process, quality, or state (assist*ance*, hindr*ance*, brilli*ance*). Also, **-ancy** (hesit*ancy*).

-ane, [a form of *-an*], *adj. suffix*, pertaining to (mund*ane*): often used in differentiation from a similar form ending in *-an* (urb*an*, urb*ane*; hum*an*, hum*ane*).

-ant, [Lat.], *adj. suffix*, attached to Latin verb stems of the first conjugation with the force of the present participle (regn*ant*, reigning; defi*ant*, defying):—*n. suffix*, denoting the doer of the action indicated by the root (claim*ant*).

ante-, [Lat.], *prefix*, [in certain combinations, *anti-* (*anti*cipate), *an-* (*an*cestor)], before in time, place, or position (*ante*date, *ante*room).

anti-, [Gk.], *prefix*, [before a vowel sometimes *ant-* (*ant*acid)], against, preventive of, opposite of (*anti*slavery, *anti*fat, *anti*climax).

apo-, [Gk.], *prefix*, [*aph-* before a rough breathing (*aph*elion), *ap-* before a vowel], **1**, from, off (*apo*stle); **2**, used intensively (*apo*plexy); **3**, used as a negative (*apo*calypse).
ar-, *prefix*, a form of *ad-* used before *r* (*ar*rogate).
-ar, [Lat.], *adj. suffix*, like or pertaining to (famili*ar*, simil*ar*, popul*ar*):—*n. suffix*, **1**, a thing like or pertaining to (alt*ar*, exempl*ar*); **2**, [Eng.: a form of [1]*-er*], a doer or agent (begg*ar*, li*ar*).
arch-, [Gk.], *n.* chief (*arch*bishop).
-ard, [Old High German +Fr.], denoting one with an excess of a quality: often of an adverse meaning (drunk*ard*, lagg*ard*). Also, **-art** (bragg*art*).
-arian, [Lat.], *adj.* and *n. suffix*, expressing: **1**, occupation (veterin*arian*); **2**, religious affiliation; habit of thought (Unit*arian*); **3**, age (nonagen*arian*).
-arium, [Lat.], *n. suffix*, denoting place where (herb*arium*).
-ary, [Lat.], *n. suffix*, forming names of persons, places, or things (not*ary*, libr*ary*, diction*ary*):—*adj. suffix*, pertaining to or characterized by (liter*ary*, honor*ary*).
as-, at-, *prefixes*, forms of *ad-* used before *s*, *t* (*as*sociate, *at*tract).
-ate, [Lat.], *suffix*, in adjectives from the Latin past participle (orn*ate*): the adjectives often being used as nouns (deleg*ate*, reprob*ate*):—*v. suffix*, forming verbs derived from Latin verbs, most often of the first conjugation (nomin*ate*):—*n. suffix*, denoting: **1**, function or station (potent*ate*, pontific*ate*); **2**, in chemistry, a salt from an acid ending in *-ic* (nitr*ate*).
-atic, [Lat.], *adj. suffix*, pertaining to, characterized by (lymph*atic*, err*atic*): the adjectives often becoming nouns (lun*atic*).
-ation, [Lat.], *n. suffix*, indicating: **1**, act or process (cre*ation*); **2**, condition or state (starv*ation*, emaci*ation*); **3**, a thing that is formed or made (plant*ation*). Also, **-sion; -tion; -ion.**
-ative, [Lat.], *adj. suffix*, pertaining to, characterized by (form*ative*, decor*ative*): the adjectives often becoming nouns (nomin*ative*, rel*ative*).
auto-, [Gk.], a prefix or combining form meaning self, oneself, itself (*auto*biography); also, by itself, independent or independently (*auto*crat, *auto*mobile).
be-, [Eng.], *prefix*, **1**, to cause to be, make: forming transitive verbs from adjectives and nouns (*be*foul, *be*friend); **2**, all around, all over, completely, thoroughly (*be*spread, *be*dabble, *be*deck); **3**, to call: used to form transitive verbs from nouns (*be*devil); **4**, to surround with, behave toward as, affect with: used to form transitive verbs from nouns (*be*cloud, *be*dew, *be*witch); **5**, off, away: used with privative force (*be*head, *be*reave); **6**, adding a tone of contempt or jocularity to a participial adjective (*be*wigged).
bi-, [Lat.], *prefix*, two, twice, doubly (*bi*lateral); specif., **1**, lasting two or occurring every two specified intervals (*bi*ennial); **2**, (in this sense preferably *semi-*, to avoid ambiguity), coming or occurring twice (*bi*weekly).
biblio-, [Gk.], a combining form meaning book (*biblio*phile, *biblio*grapher).
-ble, *adj. suffix*, a form of *-able* or of *-ile* (no*ble*, volu*ble*, hum*ble*).
by-, [Eng.], *prefix*, secondary, out of the direct road (*by*path).
cata-, [Gk.], *prefix*, [*cath-* before a rough breathing (*cath*ode), *cat-* before vowels (*cat*ion)], **1**, down (*cat*aract); **2**, under (*cata*comb); **3**, against (*cata*pult). Also, **kata-**.
circum-, [Lat.], *prefix*, around, roundabout (*circum*navigate).
cis-, [Lat.], *prefix*, on this side (*cis*alpine): opp. of *trans-* or *ultra-*.
-cle, [Lat.+Fr.], *n. suffix*, used to form diminutives (corpus*cle*, parti*cle*).
co-, *prefix*, a form of *com-* used esp. before vowels, *w*, *h*, and *gn* (*co*öperate, *co*worker, *co*heir, *co*gnate).
col-, *prefix*, a form of *com-* used before *l* (*col*laborate).
com-, [Lat.], *prefix*, [*com-* before *b*, *m*, *p*, and sometimes *f*; *col-* before *l*; *cor-* before *r*; *co-* before *h*, *w*, *gn*, or a vowel; *con-* before any consonant except *b*, *m*, *p*, *l*, *r*, *h*, *w*, *gn*], **1**, together (*com*pose); **2**, with (*com*pete); **3**, completely, fully: an intensive (*com*pel).
con-, *prefix*, a form of *com-* used before any consonant except *v*, *m*, *p*, *l*, *r*, *h*, *w*.
contra-, [Lat.], *prefix*, against, opposite, opposite to, contrary, contrary to (*contra*dict, *contra*diction).
cor-, a form of *com-* used before *r* (*cor*respond).
counter-, [Lat.], *prefix*, used with nouns, verbs, adverbs, and participial adjectives, with the following senses: **1**, reciprocation (*counter*act); **2**, retaliation, opposition (*counter*claim); **3**, oppositeness of direction, tendency, intent, or the like (*counter*march, *counter*clockwise, *counter*mand); **4**, correspondence, or a complementary thing, state, etc. (*counter*part, *counter*point, *counter*sign); **5**, a duplicate or substitute (*counter*feit, *counter*foil).
-cracy, [Gk.], *n. suffix*, a government or method of ruling (auto*cracy*, demo*cracy*).
-crat, [Gk.], *n. suffix*, a ruler (auto*crat*, demo*crat*).
-cy, [Lat. and Gk.], *n. suffix*, forming abstract nouns (bankrupt*cy*, captain*cy*).
de-, [Lat.], *prefix*, **1**, down (*de*pend, *de*press); **2**, off, away (*de*tract, *de*sist, *de*port); **3**, entirely: used with intensive effect (*de*note, *de*clare, *de*claim); **4**, expressing reversal or negation (*de*capitate, *de*mobilize); **5**, [a form of *dis-*], away, etc. (*de*bar, *de*camp, *de*fer).
deca-, [Gk.], a combining form meaning ten (*deca*gon, *deca*thlon). Also, **deka-**.
deci-, *prefix*, ten or tenth (*deci*mate); esp., in the metric system of weights and measures, the tenth part of (a given unit) (*deci*meter).
demi-, [Lat.], *prefix*, **1**, half (*demi*semiquaver); **2**, less or smaller than usual (*demi*-tasse); inferior (*demi*god).
di-, [Gk.], *prefix*, **1**, two, twofold, double (*di*graph, *di*pterous): used in chemistry to indicate two atoms, radicals, groups, or equivalents (*di*oxide); **2**, [a form of *dia-* used before a vowel], through (*di*optric); **3**, [Lat.: a form of *dis-*], away, etc. (*di*vert, *di*late, *di*rect).
dia-, [Gk.], *prefix*, [*di-* before a vowel (*di*optric)], **1**, through, across (*dia*meter, *dia*phanous); **2**, apart (*dia*lysis); **3**, thoroughly: used intensively (*dia*gnosis).
dis-, [Lat.], *prefix*, [also, in certain combinations, *di-* (*di*rect), *dif-* (*dif*fer), *de-* (*de*camp)], expressing: **1**, removal, separation (*dis*tract, *dis*bar); **2**, negation (*dis*obliging); **3**, reversal: equivalent to [2]*un-* or *not* (*dis*entangle); **4**, used intensively (*dis*annul).
-dom, [Eng.], *n. suffix*, used to form nouns expressing: **1**, rank, domain (duke*dom*); **2**, state or condition (martyr*dom*); **3**, a collection or group (official*dom*).
dys-, [Gk.], *prefix*, bad, difficult, or painful: opp. of *eu-* (*dys*pepsia).
e-, *prefix*, a form of [1]*ex-* used before *b*, *d*, *g*, *h*, *l*, *m*, *n*, *r*, *v*.
ec-, *prefix*, a form of [2]*ex-* sometimes used before a consonant (*ec*centric, *ec*lectic).
-ed, [Eng.], *v. suffix*, ending of the past tense and past participle of regular verbs (trust*ed*):—*adj. suffix*, possessed of, having the characteristics of, etc.: added to nouns (a wall*ed* garden).
-ee, [Lat.+Fr.], *n. suffix*, one who receives, or is affected by, an action (pay*ee*).
ef-, *prefix*, a form of [1]*ex-* used before *f* (*ef*fect).

-eer, [Lat.+Fr.], *n. suffix,* [*-ier* in some words (financ*ier*)], denoting a person connected or concerned with (auction*eer*, engin*eer*): sometimes suggesting contempt (sonnet*eer*, profit*eer*).

electro-, [Gk.], a combining form meaning, in English compounds, electricity (*electro*-magnet, *electro*graph).

em-, *prefix,* a form of [1]*en-* or [2]*en-* used before *b*, *m*, or *p* (*em*bank, *em*ploy).

[1]en-, [Lat.], *prefix,* [*em-* before *b* (*em*brace), *m*, *p* (*em*peror)], **1,** in or into (*en*snare); **2,** on (*en*grave); **3,** to make, make into or like (*en*feeble); **4,** sometimes used intensively (*en*cumber).

[2]en-, [Gk.], *prefix,* [see [1]*en-*], in, on: most often in words of Greek derivation (*en*comium).

-en, [Eng.], *n. suffix,* used to form: **1,** certain plurals (ox*en*); **2,** diminutives (kitt*en*, maid*en*):—*v. suffix,* **1,** used to form the past participle of many irregular verbs (fall*en*, strick*en*); **2,** to make: added to nouns or adjectives (redd*en*, height*en*):—*adj. suffix,* made of, composed of: added to nouns (wood*en*, gold*en*).

-ence, [Lat.], *n. suffix,* denoting, in general, act, quality, or state, or the thing produced (emerg*ence*, emin*ence*). Also, **-ency** (corpul*ency*).

endo-, [Gk.], *prefix,* within (*endo*gen).

-ent, [Lat.], *adj. suffix,* attached to Latin verb stems of the second, third, and fourth conjugations with the force of the present participle (persist*ent*):—*n. suffix,* denoting the doer of the action indicated by the root (superintend*ent*).

epi-, [Gk.], *prefix,* [*ep-* before a vowel (*ep*ode), *eph-* before a rough breathing (*eph*emeral)], used with Greek stems, meaning upon, above, or over (*epi*dermis, *epi*glottis).

[1]-er, [Eng.], *n. suffix,* denoting: **1,** one who occupies himself with, or one interested in, the idea of the word stem (astronom*er*, lawy*er*); **2,** an agent (lov*er*, mow*er*); **3,** an instrument (pok*er*); **4,** one living in (New York*er*). Also, sometimes, **-ar** (li*ar*).

[2]-er, [Eng.], *suffix,* forming the comparative degree of adjectives and adverbs (high*er*).

[3]-er, [Eng.], *suffix,* forming verbs: **1,** denoting repeated action (glimm*er*, wav*er*); **2,** imitating sounds (titt*er*, whisp*er*).

-ery, [Lat.], *n. suffix,* designating: **1,** place of business, storage, breeding, etc. (tann*ery*, hatch*ery*); **2,** qualities, conduct, practices, principles, etc. (snobb*ery*, rogu*ery*, trick*ery*); **3,** a class of goods (millin*ery*); **4,** art or employment (arch*ery*); **5,** state, condition (drudg*ery*). Also, **-ry** (revel*ry*).

es-, *prefix,* a form of [1]*ex-* used in words of French origin (*es*cape).

-esce, [Lat.], *v. suffix,* showing action just begun (efferv*esce*, conval*esce*).

-escent, [Lat.], *adj. suffix,* being or becoming (qui*escent*, efferv*escent*, coal*escent*):—*n. suffix,* **-escence** (rejuven*escence*).

-ess, [Gk.+Lat.+Fr.], *n. suffix,* forming nouns of the feminine gender (prior*ess*).

-est, [Eng.], *adj. suffix,* forming the superlative degree of adjectives and adverbs (warm*est*, soon*est*):—*v. suffix,* forming the archaic second person singular of the present and past tenses indicative (thou sing*est*).

-ette, [Fr.], *n. suffix,* in nouns borrowed from French since 17th century, forming: **1,** diminutives (statu*ette*); **2,** nouns originally diminutive, now not so regarded (etiqu*ette*, coqu*ette*); **3,** names of substances which are imitations (leather*ette*).

eu-, [Gk.], *prefix,* meaning well or good (*eu*logy, *eu*phony): opp. of *dys-*.

[1]ex-, [Lat.], *prefix,* [*e-* before *b*, *d*, *g*, *h*, *l*, *m*, *n*, *r*, and *v*; *ef-* before *f*; *es-* in combining with French words], **1,** out (*ex*tract); **2,** from (*ex*clude); **3,** beyond (*ex*cessive); **4,** thoroughly: used intensively (*ex*asperate); **5,** formerly, but not now (*ex*-president).

[2]ex-, [Gk.], *prefix,* [sometimes *ec-* before consonants], used with Greek words and meaning out, from, away (*ex*odus, *ec*centric).

extra-, [Lat.], *prefix,* forming adjectives meaning beyond, outside of, besides (*extra*-judicial, *extra*mural).

-fold, [Eng.], *suffix,* denoting multiplication, times (four*fold*).

for-, [Eng.], *prefix,* surviving in about a dozen common words, and meaning: **1,** off, apart (*for*get); **2,** prohibition (*for*fend, *for*bid); **3,** abstention or neglect (*for*bear, *for*sake); **4,** thoroughly (*for*lorn, *for*gather).

fore-, [Eng.], *prefix,* **1,** in front (*fore*runner); **2,** before or beforehand (*fore*tell); **3,** front part of (*fore*arm); **4,** near or at the front (*fore*lock).

-ful, [Eng.], *adj. suffix,* **1,** containing, characterized by (spite*ful*, grace*ful*); having the qualities of (master*ful*): added to nouns; **2,** extremely (dire*ful*): added to adjectives; **3,** able to, likely to (forget*ful*, wake*ful*): added to verbs:—*n. suffix,* an amount that would fill (hand*ful*, cup*ful*): added to nouns.

-fy, [Lat.+Fr.], *v. suffix,* to cause to be or form into (paci*fy*, lique*fy*). Often, with connecting vowel, **-ify** (person*ify*).

geo-, [Gk.], a combining form meaning earth (*geo*logy).

-gram, [Gk.], **1,** a suffix or combining form meaning a writing or something written (tele*gram*); **2,** in the metric system, a gram (kilo*gram*).

-graph, [Gk.], a suffix or combining form meaning something that writes or is written (tele*graph*, auto*graph*, seismo*graph*).

-graphy, [Gk.], a suffix or combining form meaning a writing or description: used in the names of sciences (geo*graphy*).

-head, *n. suffix,* used in a few nouns of condition or character formed from nouns or adjectives (god*head*). Also, **-hood** (child*hood*).

hecto-, [Gk.], a combining form meaning 100 (*hecto*gram, *hecto*liter).

helio-, [Gk.], a combining form meaning sun (*helio*centric).

hemi-, [Gk.], *prefix,* half (*hemi*sphere).

hepta-, [Gk.], a prefix or combining form meaning seven (*hepta*gon).

hetero-, [Gk.], a combining form meaning other, different (*hetero*dox): opp. of *homo-*.

hexa-, [Gk.], a prefix or combining form meaning six (*hexa*chord, *hexa*meter).

-hood, [Eng.], *n. suffix,* forming nouns from nouns and adjectives, meaning: **1,** state, quality, condition, or character (child*hood*, likeli*hood*); **2,** collective group or body (brother*hood*); **3,** example of (false*hood*). Also, *Archaic,* **-head** (god*head*).

hydro-, [Gk.], a combining form meaning water (*hydro*gen, *hydro*meter, *hydro*plane).

hyper-, [Gk.], *prefix,* **1,** over, above, beyond (*Hyper*borean); **2,** abnormally great (*hyper*-critical); **3,** in chemistry, indicating the highest in a series of oxygen compounds: generally abbreviated to *per-*.

hypo-, [Gk.], *prefix,* under, below, less than: in physiology, used to signify deficiency in functions of growth or development; in chemistry, indicating a compound lower in a series than another.

-i, [Lat.], *suffix,* forming the plural of some Latin nouns in *-us* (foc*i*).

-ian, *suffix,* a variant of *-an* with euphonic *-i-* (barbar*ian*): **-iana,** a similar variant of *-ana.*

-ible, *adj. suffix,* a form of *-able* (reduc*ible*).

-ic, [Lat. and Gk.], *adj. suffix,* **1,** made up of (trocha*ic*); **2,** like in nature or kind (angel*ic*, hypnot*ic*); **3,** of, pertaining to, or belonging to (Celt*ic*, rust*ic*, trag*ic*); **4,** patterning after or resembling (class*ic*); **5,** having to do with (publ*ic*, poet*ic*, domest*ic*); **6,** in chemistry, indicating a valence higher than that of the same element in a compound ending in *-ous* (ferr*ic*, nitr*ic*):—*n. suffix*, used: **1,** in nouns derived from adjectives in *-ic* (mag*ic*, publ*ic*); **2,** in nouns adopted in English from certain Greek or Latin adjectives (mechan*ic*, log*ic*).

-ical, [Lat.], *adj. suffix*, forming a variant form of many adjectives in *-ic* (class*ical*, poet*ical*).

-ice, [Lat.+Fr.], *n. suffix*, quality or state (serv*ice*, just*ice*, coward*ice*).

-ics, [Gk.], *n. suffix*, used to form a plural noun naming: **1,** (treated grammatically as singular), a science (dynam*ics*, mechan*ics*); **2,** (usually construed as plural), a system, a group of practical matters or methods (tact*ics*).

[1]**-id,** [Gk.], *n. suffix*, **1,** used in names of poems (Æne*id*); **2,** in zoölogy, a member of a (specified) class or family (arachn*id*).

[2]**-id,** [Gk.], *n. suffix*, in chemistry, used in names of compounds (chlor*id*): chiefly in the U. S. Also, **-ide** (ox*ide*).

[3]**-id,** [Lat.], *adj. suffix*, **1,** forming descriptive words from Latin roots (ac*id*, flu*id*).

-ide, [Gk.], *suffix*, in chemistry, used in names of compounds (sulph*ide*, ox*ide*). Also, **-id.**

-ie, *n. dim. suffix*, [a form of [1]*-y* used esp. with Scotch words], implying affection (lass*ie*).

-ier, [Lat.+Fr.], *n. suffix*, denoting an agent or one concerned with (financ*ier*, gondol*ier*). Also, **-eer** (musket*eer*).

il-, *prefix*, a form or [1]*in-* or [2]*in-* used before words beginning with *l* (*il*luminate, *il*literate).

-ile, [Lat.], *adj. suffix*, [sometimes, *-il* (civ*il*), sometimes changed to *-ble* (hum*ble*)], of, like, or pertaining to (juven*ile*).

im-, *prefix*, a form of [1]*in-* or [2]*in-* used before words beginning with *b*, *m*, or *p*. Also, **em-.**

[1]**in-,** [Lat.], *prefix*, [*il-* before *l; ir-* before *r; im-* or *em-* before *b, m, p;* often *en-* in words coming from the French (*il*lusion, *ir*radiate, *im*bibe, *em*bark, *im*mense, *im*part, *en*rich)], in, into, toward, within, on: also used intensively (*in*valuable).

[2]**in-,** [Lat.], *prefix*, [found, like [1]*in-*, as *il-*, *ir*, and *im-* (*il*licit, *ir*regular, *im*mense)], not, without, non-, [1]un- (*in*audible, *in*active, *in*elastic).

-in, [Lat.], *suffix*, **1,** in nouns and adjectives taken directly from Latin nouns and adjectives (orig*in*, mat*in*, Calv*in*); **2,** in names of certain chemical elements and compounds (fibr*in*): in elements, usually *-ine* (chlor*ine*).

-ine, [Lat.], *adj. suffix*, **1,** of or pertaining to (mar*ine*); **2,** in zoölogy, belonging to a (specified) genus (can*ine*):—*n. suffix*, in chemistry, used to form the names of certain compounds and elements (coca*ine*, chlor*ine*).

-ing, [Eng.], *suffix*, used to form: **1,** the present participle (a walk*ing* delegate); **2,** certain types of verbal noun (the writ*ing* of books, or (gerund) writ*ing* books, is hard); **3,** diminutives, patronymics, etc. (geld*ing*, farth*ing*).

inter-, [Lat.], *prefix*, [sometimes *intel-* before *l* (*intel*lect)], **1,** among, between (*inter*cede, *inter*class); **2,** together, mutually (*inter*lock).

intra-, [Lat.], *prefix*, within, inside (*intra*mural).

intro-, [Lat.], *prefix*, in or into (*intro*duce).

-ion, [Lat.], *n. suffix*, denoting: **1,** action or the result of action (suspic*ion*); **2,** state or condition (dejec*tion*, infec*tion*).

ir-, *prefix*, a form of [1]*in-*, [2]*in-*, used before *r* (*ir*ruption, *ir*reducible).

-ise, *v. suffix*, a form of *-ize*, used esp. in Great Britain.

[1]**-ish,** [Eng.], *adj. suffix*, **1,** pertaining to: added to names of places (Rhen*ish*): the adjectives often being used as nouns (Engl*ish*); **2,** like; esp., having the undesirable traits of: added to nouns (woman*ish*); **3,** somewhat: added to adjectives (black*ish*).

[2]**-ish,** [Lat.+Fr.], *suffix*, in some verbs derive from the French (fin*ish*, furn*ish*, garn*ish*)

-ism, [Gk.], *n. suffix*, indicating: **1,** the actic of (bapt*ism*); **2,** the state, condition, quality of (mystic*ism*, hero*ism*); **3,** a sy tem, doctrine, policy, etc., indicated by th first part of the word (liberal*ism*, Presb terian*ism*); **4,** a characteristic or peculia ity, esp. in manner or language (Britic*ism* **5,** a morbid or abnormal condition (alcoho *ism*, cretin*ism*, albin*ism*).

iso-, [Gk.], a combining form meaning equ (*iso*thermal).

-ist, [Gk.], *n. suffix*, meaning: **1,** one wh makes a practice of doing that which expressed in the corresponding verb, usuall ending in *-ize* (plagiar*ist*, moral*ist*); **2,** on who pursues some branch of art or scienc (art*ist*, alchem*ist*, humor*ist*); **3,** an adheren of some system, religion, political creed, et (Buddh*ist*, social*ist*, color*ist*).

[1]**-ite,** [Gk.+Lat.+Fr.], *n. suffix*, used in word naming: **1,** a follower, descendant, or inhabi ant (Roosevelt*ite*, Israel*ite*); **2,** certai commercial products (vulcan*ite*); **3,** foss organisms (trilob*ite*); **4,** explosives (dyna m*ite*); **5,** in zoölogy, a part, segment, o joint of a body; **6,** in chemistry: **a,** a sa of an acid the name of which ends in *-ou* (phosph*ite*); **b,** a saccharine substanc (dulc*ite*); **7,** certain rocks (gran*ite*).

[2]**-ite,** [Lat.], *suffix*, in adjectives, nouns, an verbs from Latin past participles and verba nouns in *-itus* (fin*ite*, erud*ite*, compos*it* appet*ite*, ign*ite*, un*ite*): the adjectives ofte becoming nouns (requis*ite*, oppos*ite*).

-itis, [Gk.], *n. suffix*, used in the names c inflammatory diseases (tonsill*itis*).

-ive, [Lat.], *adj. suffix*, relating to, of th nature of (act*ive*, fest*ive*): the adjective often becoming nouns (nat*ive*, adhes*ive*).

-ize, [Gk.+Lat.+Fr.], *v. suffix*, meaning: **1,** t subject to or treat with the action denote by the root (critic*ize*); **2,** to make or mak like (fossil*ize*, human*ize*); **3,** to act like treat after the manner or method c (Anglic*ize*, macadam*ize*); **4,** to treat o combine with (oxid*ize*, carbon*ize*). Also esp. in Great Britain, **-ise.**

juxta-, [Lat.], *prefix*, near or alongsid (*juxta*position).

kilo-, [Gk.], a combining form meaning 1000 used esp. in the metric system (*kilo*gram)

-kin, [Eng.], *suffix*, used to form diminutiv nouns (lamb*kin*, Peter*kin*).

-lent, [Lat.], *adj. suffix*, full of (fraudu*lent* corpu*lent*).

-less, [Eng.], *adj. suffix*, without, free from not characterized by (home*less*, worth*less* daunt*less*):—*adv. suffix*, without (doubt*less*)

-let, [Fr.], *n. suffix*, forming: **1,** diminutive (eag*let*); **2,** names of pieces of clothin (arm*let*).

-like, [Eng.], *adj. suffix*, similar to, resem bling: added freely to nouns, withou hyphen except after *l* (boy*like*, eel-*like*).

-ling, [Eng.], *n. suffix*, **1,** one connected o related (nurs*ling*); **2,** forming diminutives often contemptuous (duck*ling*, weak*ling*).

-ly, [Eng.], *adj. suffix*, **1,** like or characterist of (man*ly*); **2,** every (week*ly*):—*adv. suffix* in a specified manner or degree (bold*ly* great*ly*).

Mac-, [Gaelic], *prefix*, son of: used in Scotcl or Irish names: often written *Mc* or *M'*.

macro-, [Gk.], a combining form meanin large, long (*macro*cosm): opp. of *micro-*.

mal-, [Lat.], *prefix*, ill, bad, wrong (*mal*treat *mal*administer). Also, **male-** (*male*diction)

-mancy, [Gk.], a combining form meanin divination (necro*mancy*).

mega-, [Gk.], a prefix or combining forn meaning great (*mega*lith, *mega*phone).

-ment, [Lat.], *n. suffix*, signifying: **1,** the ac or fact of doing something (enforce*ment* infringe*ment*); **2,** the condition or stat resulting from an act (excite*ment*, retire*ment*); **3,** means or instrument (adorn*ment*, integu*ment*); **4,** a concrete result or outcome of an action (attach*ment*, entertain*ment*, pave*ment*).

meso-, [Gk.], a combining form meaning middle (*Meso*zoic).

meta-, [Gk.], *prefix*, orig. meaning with, between, after, about, reversely, the orig. force often being weakened or lost: used esp.: **1,** implying change (*meta*morphosis); **2,** implying sequence in time or rank (*meta*physics); **3,** in the names of certain chemical compounds.

-meter, [Gk.], *suffix*, denoting: **1,** a device for measuring (baro*meter*); **2,** a (specified) arrangement of syllables in a verse (hexa*meter*).

micro-, [Gk.], a combining form meaning small, little, insignificant (*micro*cosm): opp. of *macro-*.

milli-, [Lat.], *prefix*, used in the metric system to indicate the 1000th part of a specified unit (*milli*meter).

mis-, [Eng.; in some words, Lat.+Fr.], *prefix*, used with nouns to mean bad or wrong (*mis*conduct), and with verbs and participles to mean wrongly, ill, amiss, etc. (*mis*direct).

mono-, [Gk.], [*mon-* before a vowel (*mon*arch)], a prefix or combining form meaning one, single (*mono*plane, *mono*gamy).

-most, [Eng.], *adj. suffix*, used to form adjectives in the superlative degree (in*most*, fore*most*).

-mony, [Lat.], *n. suffix*, state or quality (acri*mony*); something pertaining to (patri*mony*).

multi-, [Lat.], a prefix or combining form meaning many, much (*multi*form).

necro-, [Gk.], a combining form meaning dead person (*necro*logy, *necro*polis).

neo-, [Gk.], a combining form meaning new or recent (*neo*lithic, *neo*logy).

-ness, [Eng.], *n. suffix*, quality or state of being: used with adjectives (sick*ness*, good*ness*).

non-, [Lat.], *prefix*, used freely, without hyphen: **1,** with the general meaning *not* (*non*combatant, *non*resident); **2,** forming adjectives distinguished from others formed with *in-* or *un-* (*in*human, *non*human; *im*moral, *non*moral).

ob-, [Lat.], *prefix*, [*oc-* before *c* (*oc*cur); *of-* before *f* (*of*fer); *op-* before *p* (*op*press)], in words already compounded in Latin, indicating: **1,** meeting, contact, or direction (*ob*trude); **2,** opposition or hindrance (*ob*stacle); **3,** finality or completeness (*ob*tain); **4,** reverse direction (*ob*ovate).

oc-, *prefix*, a form of *ob-* used before *c* (*oc*cur).

-ock, [Eng.], *n. suffix*, forming diminutives (hill*ock*).

octa-, [Gk.], *prefix*, [*oct-* before a vowel (*oct*angular)], eight (*octa*gon, *octa*hedron). Also, **octo-** (*octo*pus); **octi-.**

-oid, [Gk.], *suffix*, denoting like, in the form of, or resembling (cycl*oid*).

-ol, *suffix*, **1,** [Lat.], denoting an oil or an oil derivative (benz*ol*); **2,** [Eng.], denoting an alcohol or a phenol (methan*ol*).

-ology, [Gk.], *n. suffix*, a science or branch of learning (ge*ology*).

oö-, [Gk.], a combining form meaning egg (*oö*logy).

-or, [Lat.], *n. suffix*, **1,** denoting state or quality (fav*or*, splend*or*, hon*or*): in British usage spelled *-our;* **2,** denoting agent or instrument (doct*or*, sail*or*, extens*or*): sometimes changed to *-er* (labor*er*).

-ory, [Lat.], *n. suffix*, place where, place for: added to Latin roots (fact*ory*, laborat*ory*):—*adj. suffix*, pertaining to, characterized by: added to Latin roots (obligat*ory*).

¹-ose, [Lat.+Fr.], *adj. suffix*, like, full of (verb*ose*).

²-ose, [from ending of gluc*ose*], *n. suffix*, in chemistry, used to form the names of the various carbohydrates related to glucose (cellul*ose*, malt*ose*).

-osis, [Gk.], *n. suffix*, condition, state, process, etc. (metamorph*osis*).

-ous, [Lat.+Fr.], *adj. suffix*, denoting: **1,** full of, like, etc. (poison*ous*, amor*ous*); **2,** in chemistry, used to indicate that the element to which it is attached is in a compound with a relatively lower valence than in compounds ending in *-ic* (chlor*ous* contrasted with chlor*ic*).

out-, [Eng.], *prefix*, meaning: **1,** more than, exceeding (*out*bid); **2,** outside, some distance away (*out*house); **3,** out, away (*out*bound).

over-, [Eng.], *prefix*, meaning: **1,** excess (*over*confident, *over*due); **2,** outer or upper position (*over*coat, *over*lord); **3,** motion from one side to the other, from edge to edge, across the brim, etc. (*over*step, *over*lap); **4,** motion passing beyond (*over*flow, *over*shoot); **5,** completeness (*over*awe, *over*joyed).

paleo-, [Gk.], a combining form meaning old (*paleo*lithic). Also, **palæo-.**

pan-, [Gk.], a combining form meaning all (*pan*acea, *pan*theon). Also, **panto-** (*panto*graph).

para-, [Gk.], *prefix*, [*par-* before a vowel (*par*ody, *par*allel)], orig. meaning beyond, against, near by, alongside (*para*site, *para*dox), but often having a hardly identifiable force (*para*bola).

pen-, [Lat.], *prefix*, almost (*pen*insula).

penta-, [Gk.], a combining form meaning five (*penta*gon, *penta*meter).

per-, [Lat.], *prefix*, [*pel-* before *l* (*pel*lucid); often *par-* in words derived from the French (*par*don, *par*boil, *par*venu, *par*terre)], **1,** through, over the whole extent of (*per*vade); **2,** very, thoroughly, completely (*per*fervid, *per*turb); **3,** to destruction, bad (*per*dition); **4,** in chemistry, denoting the higher degree of valence, or the highest degree of combination in similar compounds (iron *per*oxide).

peri-, [Gk.], *prefix*, around, about, inclosing, surrounding (*peri*meter, *peri*scope).

philo-, [Gk.], a combining form meaning love, loving (*philo*sophy). Also, **phil-** (*phil*anthropy); **-phile** (biblio*phile*).

phono-, [Gk.], a combining form meaning voice, sound (*phono*graph). Also, **-phone** (tele*phone*).

photo-, [Gk.], a combining form meaning light (*photo*graph).

poly-, [Gk.], a prefix or combining form meaning many (*poly*gon, *poly*syllable).

post-, [Lat.], *prefix*, behind, after (*post*graduate, *post*pone): opp. of *ante-* and *pre-*.

præ-, [Lat.], *prefix*, before: the Latin form of *pre-*, now kept as preferred spelling in a few words only (*præ*tor).

pre-, [Lat.], *prefix*, before in place, time, or standing (*pre*cede, *pre*dict).

preter-, [Lat.], *prefix*, past, beyond, outside the range of, more than (*preter*natural).

¹pro-, [Lat.], *prefix*, signifying: **1,** in front of (*pro*tection); **2,** motion to the front (*pro*ceed, *pro*duce); **3,** in behalf of, favoring (*pro*slavery); **4,** instead of (*pro*noun); **5,** according to (*pro*portion); **6,** forth or forward (*pro*pel, *pro*ject).

²pro-, [Gk.], *prefix*, before in time, place, rank, etc. (*pro*gram, *pro*log, *pro*gnosis, *pro*boscis).

proto-, [Gk.], a prefix or combining form meaning first (*proto*type).

pseudo-, [Gk.], *prefix*, false, pretended (*pseudo*scholarship).

quasi-, [Lat.], *prefix*, used freely with adjectives and nouns, and meaning: **1,** seemingly, apparently (*quasi*-historical); **2,** nearly.

re-, [Lat.], *prefix*, [sometimes *red-* before vowels (*red*olent)], **1,** back, backward (*re*call, *re*cline); **2,** again, anew (*re*count, *re*pay); **3,** in return, mutually (*re*act, *re*-

ciprocal); **4,** in opposition (*re*pugnant, *re*sist); **5,** used with intensive force (*re*splendent, *re*joice).

red-, *prefix*, a form of *re-* used before vowels (*red*olent).

retro-, [Lat.], *prefix*, **1,** backward (*retro*spect, *retro*grade); **2,** back, hinder: used esp. in scientific words.

-ry, *n. suffix*, a shortened form of *-ery* (revel*ry*).

-scope, [Gk.], a combining form or suffix meaning one that watches or sees, and hence an instrument for seeing (tele*scope*).

s-, [Lat.], a contracted form of: **1,** *se-* (sure); **2,** *dis-* (spend, spite, splay, stain); **3,** [1]*ex-* (sample); **4,** *sub-* (somber).

se-, [Lat.], *prefix*, [*sed-* before vowels (*sedi*tion)], apart or away (*se*cede, *se*cure).

self-, [Eng.], *prefix*, denoting: **1,** the subject of the action named in the word to which it is attached (*self*-made, *self*-acting); **2,** the object of the action (*self*-respect).

-self, [Eng.], *suffix*, [*pl.* -selves], added to personal pronouns to give emphatic or reflexive force (she did it her*self*, she cut her*self*).

semi-, [Lat.], *prefix*, attached freely, usually without hyphen except before capitalized words or words beginning with *i*, and meaning: **1,** half (*semi*circle); **2,** partial, imperfect (*semi*fluid).

sept-, [Lat.], *prefix*, seven (*sept*enary, *sept*illion).

sesqui-, [Lat.], *prefix*, **1,** one and one half (*sesqui*pedalian); **2,** in chemistry, expressing a proportion of three to two between constituents, as three atoms of the constituent denoted by the word and two of another.

sex-, [Lat.], *prefix*, six: in words derived from Latin compounds, and in modern words similarly compounded (*sex*ennial, *sex*agenary).

-ship, [Eng.], *n. suffix*, **1,** state or quality: attached to adjectives (hard*ship*), or to nouns (friend*ship*); **2,** office, dignity, or profession (governor*ship*); **3,** art or skill (horseman*ship*).

-sion, [Lat.], *n. suffix*, corresponding to Latin stems ending in *s*, and indicating: **1,** act, state, or quality (expul*sion*, fu*sion*); **2,** the result of an act (pen*sion*, posses*sion*). Also, **-tion.**

-soever, [Eng.], *suffix*, added to *who, what, where, when, how*, etc., to make them more general or indefinite (what*soever*): frequently separable (in what place *soever*).

-some, [Eng.], *adj. suffix*, **1,** joined to nouns, meaning pertaining to, producing (quarrel*some*); **2,** joined to adjectives, meaning to a considerable degree (lithe*some*); **3,** joined to verbs, meaning likely to (win*some*, tire*some*).

step-, [Eng.], *prefix*, designating a relationship not by blood, but by a subsequent marriage of a parent (*step*father).

-ster, [Eng.], *n. suffix*, denoting an agent or the holder of an occupation or profession (team*ster*): sometimes in a disparaging sense (rime*ster*): orig. a feminine suffix (spin*ster*).

-stress, [*-ster*+*-ess*], *fem. n. suffix*, meaning a woman who does (a certain thing) with skill or as an occupation (seam*stress*).

su-, *prefix*, a form of *sub-* often used in Latin compounds before initial *s* (*su*spect).

sub-, [Lat.], *prefix*, [often appearing as *suc-, suf-, sug-, sum-, sup-, sur-, su-*, before *c, f, g, m, p, r, s*, respectively (*suc*cess, *suf*fer, *sug*gest, *sum*mon, *sup*port, *sur*reptitious, *sus*pect)], **1,** under, beneath, below, near, next to (*sup*press, *sub*marine, *sub*urb); **2,** slightly or somewhat (*sub*acid); **3,** inferior or subordinate in rank, classification, etc. (*sub*lieutenant); in verbs, indicating division into subordinate parts (*sub*divide); **4,** low, lower of two (*sub*way, *sub*maxillary); **5,** in chemistry, indicating presence in a less than the normal amount (*sub*carbide).

subter-, [Lat.], *prefix*, under (*subter*fuge.)

suc-, suf-, sug-, sum-, sup-, *prefixes*, forms of *sub-* often used in Latin compounds before initial *c, f, g, m*, and *p* respectively (*suc*ceed, *suf*fuse, *sug*gest, *sum*mon, *sup*press).

super-, [Lat.], *prefix*, [*sur-* in many words taken into English through Old French (*sur*face, *sur*prise)], over, beyond, above, in excess: used: **1,** in reference to place, to give the idea of above, over, on (*super*position); **2,** in reference to rank, authority, etc., to give the idea of above, over, superior to (*super*intendent); **3,** in reference to degree, to give the idea of beyond, in addition to, more than, in excess of (*super*man); **4,** in reference to quantity or amount, to give the idea of unusually large, or in great quantity (*super*abundance).

supra-, [Lat.], *prefix*, **1,** over, above (*supra*renal); **2,** beyond, superior to (*supra*mundane): opp. of *infra-*.

[1]**sur-,** *prefix*, a form of *super-* used in many words taken into English through Old French (*sur*charge).

[2]**sur-,** *prefix*, a form of *sub-* often used in Latin compounds before initial *r* (*sur*reptitious).

sy-, syl-, sym-, *prefixes*, forms of *syn-* used before certain initial letters.

syn-, [Gk.], *prefix*, [*sym-* before *b, p*, and *m* (*sym*bol, *sym*pathy, *sym*metry); *syl-* before *l* (*syl*lable); *sys-* before *s* not followed by a consonant; *sy-* before *z* (*sy*zygy), or before *s* followed by a consonant (*sy*stole)]: forming compounds with Greek words, with the following meanings: **1,** with, along with, together (*sym*posium, *syn*tax, *sym*pathy); **2,** the same, at the same time (*syn*onymous, *sym*metrical, *syn*opsis); **3,** a general meaning of together, the exact force having been lost (*sym*ptom).

sys-, *prefix*, a form of *syn-* used before *z*, or *s* followed by a consonant.

-teen, [Eng.], *suffix*, meaning plus ten: used in numbers from 13 to 19 (seven*teen*).

tetra-, [Gk.], a prefix or combining form meaning four (*tetra*hedron).

-th, [Eng.], *suffix*, **1,** forming abstract nouns of quality, state, etc. (tru*th*, steal*th*, weal*th*); **2,** forming ordinal numbers (six*th*, ten*th*): after a vowel, *-eth* (forti*eth*); **3,** *Archaic*, forming the third person singular of the present indicative of some verbs (ha*th*, do*th*).

-tion, [Lat.], *n. suffix*, indicating: **1,** act of (inven*tion*); **2,** state of being (dejec*tion*); **3,** result or product of an act (planta*tion*). Also, **-sion,** corresponding to Latin stems ending in *s* (ten*sion*, scan*sion*).

-tious, [Lat.], *adj. suffix*, used to form adjectives usually corresponding to a noun ending in *-tion* (superstition, supersti*tious*; ambition, ambi*tious*).

trans-, [Lat.], *prefix*, [occasionally shortened to *tra-* (*tra*dition, *tra*verse); usually *tran-* before a word beginning with *s* (*tran*scribe, *tran*sept)], **1,** across, over, beyond, through (*trans*port, *trans*fix); **2,** completely, thoroughly: compounded with verbs signifying a change of form (*trans*form, *trans*figure).

tri-, [Lat.], *prefix*, **1,** three, threefold (*tri*angle, *tri*color); **2,** in chemistry, containing three atoms or radical groups (*tri*oxide).

-trix, [Lat.], *n. suffix*, one who: feminine form corresponding to *-tor* (administra*trix*).

-tude, [Lat.], *n. suffix*, quality or state of being (servi*tude*, grati*tude*).

[1]**-ty,** [Lat.+Fr.], *n. suffix*, forming abstract nouns denoting quality, state, or condition (pie*ty*, loyal*ty*).

[2]**-ty,** [Eng.], *suffix*, times ten: a termination of numerals (thir*ty*, six*ty*).

-ule, [Lat.], *n. suffix*, forming diminutives from Latin stems (glob*ule*, gran*ule*).

ultra-, [Lat.], *prefix*, used rather freely, generally without a hyphen, and meaning: **1,** beyond (*ultra*montane); **2,** excessively, beyond the usual (*ultra*modern).

[1]un-, [Eng.], *prefix,* **1,** not, the opposite of: freely used with adjectives and their derivative nouns and adverbs (*un*fair, *un*fairness, *un*fairly); also, with participles (*un*seen); **2,** lack of: used with nouns (*un*concern).

[2]un-, [Eng.], *prefix,* used: **1,** with verbs or nouns, to express reversal or annulment of an action or deprivation of a thing (*un*twist); **2,** with a few verbs felt as negatives, with intensive effect (*un*ravel).

under-, [Eng.], *prefix,* meaning: **1,** below (*under*ground); **2,** insufficient(ly) (*under*fed); **3,** subordinate (*under*graduate).

uni-, [Lat.], a prefix or combining form meaning one (*uni*cellular, *uni*form, *uni*corn).

up-, [Eng.], *prefix,* placed before verbs and nouns, meaning up or upward (*up*heave, *up*growth).

-ure, [Lat.], *n. suffix,* denoting action, state, or result: usually attached to the past participle stem (text*ure*, fiss*ure*, junct*ure*).

-ward, [Eng.], *adj.* and *adv. suffix,* toward, in the direction of: added to adverbs, prepositions, and nouns (up*ward*); **-wards,** *adv. suffix,* toward (home*wards*).

-ways, [Eng.], *adv. suffix,* indicating position, direction, manner, etc. (length*ways*, side*ways*, al*ways*): often interchangeable with *-wise*.

-wise, [Eng.], *adv. suffix,* in the way or manner of (clock*wise*, other*wise*).

with-, [Eng.], *prefix,* **1,** against (*with*stand); **2,** back (*with*draw, *with*hold).

xylo-, [Gk.], a combining form meaning wood (*xylo*phone).

[1]-y, [Eng.], *n. suffix,* forming diminutives, appearing chiefly in childish names of animals and familiar forms of personal names (dogg*y*): also written *-ie* (lass*ie*).

[2]-y, [Eng.], *adj. suffix,* **1,** of, pertaining to, having, full of: added to nouns (ston*y*, guilt*y*): often spelled *-ey*, esp. when attached to words ending in *y* (clay*ey*); **2,** inclined toward, almost, shading into: added to adjectives of color (gold*y* brown); **3,** with intensive force but no change of meaning: added to adjectives: chiefly poetical (still*y*).

[3]-y, [Lat.+Fr.], *n. suffix,* in words from Latin and French, originally participial adjectives (deput*y*, arm*y*, assembl*y*, ditt*y*, treat*y*, originally meaning deputed, armed, etc.).

[4]-y, [Lat.+Fr., or often Gk.+Lat. (+Fr.)], *n. suffix* forming abstract nouns (glor*y*, victor*y*; antipath*y*, theolog*y*, therap*y*).

zoö-, [Gk.], a combining form meaning life (*zoö*graphy).

Important Latin and Greek Stems Appearing in English Words

acer, [Lat.], sour, **acutu-s,** sharp (*acr*imony, *acute*, *acu*men, *ac*id; +Fr., *acer*bity).

aede-s, [Lat.], a building (*æd*ile; +Fr., *edi*fice, *edi*fy).

aër, [Gk.], air (*aër*ial, *aër*oplane).

aequu-s, [Lat.], equal (*equ*al, *equ*able, *equa*tion, *equa*tor, *equi*librium, *equi*vocal; +Fr., *equ*animity, *equ*inox, *equ*ivalent, *equ*ity, in*iqu*ity).

aestima-re, aestimatu-s, [Lat.], to appraise (*estimate*; +Fr., *estimat*ion, *esteem*, *aim*).

aevu-m, [Lat.], age (co*ev*al, prim*ev*al, long*ev*ity; +Fr., *age*).

ag-ein, [Gk.], to lead (ped*ag*og, dem*ag*og).

ager, [Lat.], field (*agr*iculture, *agr*arian; +Fr., per*egr*ination).

age-re, actu-s, ig-, [Lat.], to work, do (*agent*, *act*, *act*ion, *ag*itate, co*ag*ulate, ex*ig*ency, amb*ig*uous; +Fr., ess*ay*).

agger, [Lat.: *ad*+*gerere*], a heap, pile (ex*ag*ger*a*te).

aither, [Gk.], air (*ether*, *ether*eal).

ale-re, alitu-s or **altu-s,** [Lat.], to feed, nourish (*al*imony, co*al*esce, co*alit*ion; +Fr., *al*imentary).

aliu-s, [Lat.], other (*ali*en, *ali*enate). Akin to **alter.**

alter, [Lat.], other (*alter*, *alter*native; +Fr., *alter*cation). Akin to **alius.**

altu-s, [Lat.], high (+Fr., *alt*itude, ex*alt*). Akin to **alere.**

ama-re, amatu-s, [Lat.], to love (*amat*ory, *am*orous; +Fr., *amat*eur). Akin to **amicus.**

ambula-re, [Lat.], to walk (per*ambulat*or; +Fr., *amble*).

amicu-s, [Lat.], friend (*amic*able; +Fr., *ami*able).

amplu-s, [Lat.], large (+Fr., *ample*, *ampl*ify).

ange-re, anx-, [Lat.], to choke, strangle (*anx*ious; +Fr., *ang*uish).

angulu-s, [Lat.], corner (*angul*ar, equi*angul*ar; +Fr., tri*angle*, rect*angle*).

anima, [Lat.], breath, life, soul (*anim*ate, *anim*adversion, un*anim*ous, *anim*al; +Fr., equ*anim*ity).

annu-s, enn-, [Lat.], year (*annu*al, super*annu*ated, *annu*ity, bi*enn*ial, per*enn*ial, *anni*versary).

antho-s, [Gk.], flower (*antho*logy, peri*anth*, *anth*er).

anthropo-s, [Gk.], man (phil*anthrop*ic, *anthropo*logy, *anthropo*morphic).

aperi-re, apertu-s, [Lat.], to open (*aperi*ent, *apert*ure).

aqua, [Lat.], water (*aqu*atic, *aqu*arium, *aque*duct).

arbor, [Lat.], tree (*arbor*eal, *arbor*iculture). Eng. *arbor* is from Lat. *herbarium*, herb garden.

ardē-re, arsu-s, [Lat.], to burn, **ardor,** a burning (+Fr., *ardor*, *ard*ent, *ars*on).

arithmo-s, [Gk.], number (*arithm*etic, log*arithm*).

arkh-ē, [Gk.], beginning, government (*arch*aic, *arch*eology, an*arch*y, mon*arch*y).

ars, arti-s, [Lat.], skill (+Fr., [2]*art*, *art*ist, *arti*fice, *arti*llery).

asper, [Lat.], rough (ex*asper*ate; +Fr., *asper*ity).

aster, astro-n, [Gk.], star (*aster*, *astro*nomy).

auctor, [Lat.], one who originates or produces (+Fr., *author*, *au*thority). Akin to **augēre.**

audi-re, [Lat.], to hear (*audi*tory, *audi*ble, *audio*-frequency; +Fr., *audi*ence, ob*edi*ence, ob*ey*, ob*eis*ance).

augē-re, auctu-s, aux-, [Lat.], to increase (*auct*ion; +Fr., *aug*ment). Akin to **auxilium.**

auspiciu-m, [Lat.: *avis*+*specere*], a watching of birds (+Fr., *auspice*, *auspici*ous).

auxiliu-m, [Lat.], help (*auxili*ary). Akin to **augēre.**

avi-s, [Lat.], bird (*avi*ary, *au*spice).

ball-ein, bol-, -bl-, [Gk.], to throw (*ball*istics, para*bol*a, em*bl*em).

baro-s, [Gk.], weight (*baro*meter, *bary*tone).

beatu-s, [Lat.], happy (+Fr., *beat*itude).

bellu-m, [Lat.], war (*bell*igerent; +Fr., re*bel*, re*bell*ion).

bibe-re, [Lat.], to drink (im*bibe*, wine*bibb*er, *bib*ulous).

biblio-n, [Gk.], book (*biblio*graphy, *biblio*phile; +Lat.+Fr., *Bible*).

bio-s, [Gk.], life (*bio*logy, *bio*graphy, am*phibi*ous).

bonu-s, [Lat.], good, **bene,** well [comp. and superl. **melior, optimus,** which see], (*bene*factor; +Fr., *boun*ty, *bene*fice, *bene*fit, *bene*volence).

brevi-s, [Lat.], short (*brev*ity, ab*brevi*ate; +Fr., *brief*, a*bridge*).

cade-re, casu-s, cid-, [Lat.], to fall (de*cid*uous, *casu*al; +Fr., *cad*ence, *chance*, *case*, oc*cas*ion, oc*cid*ent, ac*cid*ent, coin*cid*e, de*cay*).

caede-re, caesu-s, cid-, cis-, [Lat.], to cut, kill (suic*ide*, *caes*ura, circum*cise*; +Fr., homi-*cide*, de*cide*, de*cis*ion, pre*cise*, in*cis*ion, *chis*el, *sciss*ors).
caelu-m, heaven, **caelesti-s,** heavenly (+Fr., *ceil*, *ceil*ing, *celesti*al).
calor, [Lat.], heat, **calidu-s,** hot (+Fr., *calor*ie, *cald*ron, *scald*, *chaf*e, *chauf*fer).
calx, calci-s, [Lat.], stone, lime, **calculu-s,** pebble (*calc*ium, *calcul*ate, *calcul*ous, *calcu-lus;* +Fr., *calc*ine).
candē-re, cens-, [Lat.], to shine, **candidu-s,** bright (*cand*le, *cand*idate, [1]in*cense* (*v.*), in-*cend*iary, in*cand*escent; +Fr., [2]in*cense* (*n.*), *cand*or, *cand*id).
cane-re, cantu-s, [Lat.], to sing (*cant*icle, in*cant*ation, [1]*cant*, re*cant;* +Fr., *chant*, en*chant*, ac*cent*, des*cant;* +It., *canto*).
can-is, [Lat.], dog (*can*ine).
cape-re, captu-s, cip-, cup-, cept-, [Lat.], to take, hold (*cap*acity, re*cip*e, in*cip*ient, parti*cip*ate, *capt*or, pre*cept*or; +Fr., *cap*able, *chase*, *capt*ive, *cait*iff, prin*cip*al, con*ceive*, con*cept*ion, de*ceive*, re*ceive*, oc*cupy*, re*ceipt*, sus*cept*ible, ac*cept*).
caput, capit-, cipit-, [Lat.], head ([2]*capit*al, *capit*ol, de*capit*ate, pre*cipit*ate, re*capit*ulate; +Fr., [2]*cape*, *capt*ain, *chapt*er, *chief*, ker*chief*, a*chieve*, pre*cip*ice).
caro, carn-is, [Lat.], flesh (*carn*al, *carn*ivo-rous, in*carn*ate; +Fr., *carn*age, *carn*ation, *charn*el; +Fr.+It., *carn*ival).
carpe-re, carptu-s, [Lat.], to pluck (ex*cerpt*).
castu-s, [Lat.], pure, **castiga-re,** (lit., to keep pure), to punish (*castig*ate; +Fr., *chast*ise, *chaste*, in*cest*; +Port., *caste*).
catena, [Lat.], chain (con*caten*ation, *caten*ary; +Fr., *chain*, *chign*on).
causa, [Lat.], cause (+Fr., *cause*, be*cause*, ac*cuse*, ex*cuse*, re*cus*ant).
cavē-re, cautu-s, [Lat.], to beware (+Fr., *caut*ion, *caut*ious, pre*caut*ion).
cede-re, cessu-s, [Lat.], to go, depart, yield (*cede*, ac*cede*, ac*cess*, ac*cess*ion, ante*ced*ent, con*cede*, in*cess*ant, re*cede*, re*cess*, se*cede*, abs*cess*, etc.; +Fr., *cease*, *cess*ion, an*cest*or, de*cease*, ex*ceed*, ex*cess*ive, inter*cede*, pre*cede*, pre*ced*ent, pro*ced*ure, pro*ceed*, pro*cess*, suc-*ceed*, suc*cess*, suc*cess*ive, etc.).
cela-re, [Lat.], to hide (+Fr., con*ceal*, *cl*andes-tine).
cella, [Lat.], room, storehouse (*cell;* +Fr., *cell*ar). Akin to **celare**.
censē-re, censu-s, [Lat.], to judge, **censor,** a censor: a Roman official (*censor*, *cens*ure, *census*, re*cens*ion).
centu-m, [Lat.], hundred (*cent*, *cent*igrade, *cent*urion, *cent*enarian, per *cent;* +Fr., *cent*ury, *cent*ipede).
cerne-re, cretu-s, [Lat.], to separate, dis-tinguish, discern (dis*cr*imination; +Fr., con*cern*, dis*cern*, dis*creet*, de*cree*, se*cret*, se*cret*ion, se*cret*ary). Akin to **certus**.
certa-re, [Lat.], to strive (+Fr., con*cert*, dis-con*cert*).
certu-s, [Lat.], determined, certain (+Fr., *certain*, *cert*ify, as*certain*). Akin to **cernere**.
ciē-re, citu-s, [Lat.], to rouse, **cita-re, citatu-s,** to summon (resus*cit*ate; +Fr., *cite*, ex*cite*, in*cite*, re*cite*).
cinge-re, cinctu-s, [Lat.], to gird (*cinct*ure, pre*cinct*, suc*cinct*).
cinis, ciner-is, [Lat.], ashes (*ciner*arium, in*ciner*ator). *Cinder* is from A.S. *sinder*.
circu-s, [Lat.], a circle, **circulu-s,** small circle (*circus*, *circul*ate, *circu*itous; +Fr., *circle*, *circu*it, *circul*ar).
civi-s, [Lat.], citizen, **civitas,** state (*civ*ic, *civ*il, *civ*ilian; +Fr., *city*, *citizen*; +Fr.+It., *cit*adel).
clama-re, clamatu-s, [Lat.], to shout, **clamor,** a loud shouting (ac*clamat*ion, de*cla-mat*ion; +Fr., *claim*, ex*claim*, dis*claim*, re-*claim*).
claru-s, [Lat.], bright, clear (+Fr., *clar*ify, de*clare*, *clear*, *clar*ion, *clar*inet).
classi-s, [Lat.], class (+Fr., *class*, *class*ic, *class*ify).
claude-re, clausu-s, clude-re, clusu-s, [Lat.], to shut, close (con*clude*, con*clus*ion, ex*clude*, in*clude*, etc.; +Fr., *close*, *clause*, *clois*ter, re*cluse*, *clos*et).
clina-re, [Lat.], to lean, **clivu-s,** hill (re*cline*, ac*cliv*ity, pro*cliv*ity; +Fr., in*cline*, in*clina*-tion, de*cline*, de*cliv*ity).
cole-re, cultu-s, [Lat.], to cultivate (*culti*-vate, agri*cult*ure, horti*cult*ure; +Fr., *col*ony, *cult*ure).
comes, comit-is, companion (con*comit*ant; +Fr., [2]*count*). [1]*Count* is from Lat. *com-putare*, to reckon.
communi-s, [Lat.], common (*communi*cate, ex*communi*cate; +Fr., *commune*, *common*). Akin to **munus**.
conciliu-m, [Lat.], an assembly called to-gether (*concili*ate; +Fr., *council*, re*concile*).
coque-re, coctu-s, [Lat.], to cook (*cook*, con-*coct*, de*coct*ion).
cor, cord-is, [Lat.], heart (+Fr., *cord*ial, con-*cord*, con*cord*ance, dis*cord*, re*cord*, *cour*age).
corona, [Lat.], crown (*corona*, *coron*ation, *coro*lla, *coro*llary; +Fr., *crown*, *coron*er, *coron*et; +Ger., *krone;* +Persian, *kran*).
cornu, [Lat.], horn (*cornu*copia, *corn*ea; +Fr., [2]*corn*, *corn*et, uni*corn*).
corpus, corpor-is, [Lat.], body (*corpor*ate, *corpor*ation, *corp*uscle, *corpor*eal; +Fr., *corpor*al, *corp*ulent, *corpse*, *corps*, *cors*elet, *cors*et).
costa, [Lat.], rib, side (+Fr., inter*cost*al, *cut*let, ac*cost*, *coast*).
cras, [Lat.], tomorrow (pro*crast*inate).
crea-re, creatu-s, [Lat.], to create (*create;* +Fr., *creat*ure, re*creat*ion).
crede-re, creditu-s, [Lat.], to trust, believe (*credo*, *credit*, *credit*able, *creed*, *cred*ible).
crepa-re, crepitu-s, [Lat.], to rattle, sound (de*crepit;* +Fr., dis*crep*ancy, *crev*ice, *cre-vasse*).
cresce-re, cretu-s, [Lat.], to grow (*cresc*ent, con*crete;* +Fr., ex*cresc*ence, in*crease*, de-*crease*, re*cruit*).
crimen, crimin-is, [Lat.], accusation, crime (in*crimin*ate, re*crimin*ation; +Fr., *crime*, *crimin*al).
crudu-s, [Lat.], raw (*crude;* +Fr., *cru*el).
crux, cruc-is, [Lat.], a gallows or frame for execution or torture; later, a cross (*crux*, ex*cruc*iate, *cross;* +Fr., *cruc*ial, *cruc*ify; +Fr.+Span., *crus*ade; +Du., *cruise*).
cuba-re, [Lat.], to lie, **cumbe-re,** to lie down (in*cub*ate, in*cub*us, in*cumb*ent, suc*cumb*).
culpa, [Lat.], fault, error (ex*culp*ate; +Fr., *culp*able, *culp*rit).
cumulu-s, [Lat.], heap (*cumul*ative, ac*cu-mul*ate).
cura, [Lat.], care (*cur*ate, ac*cur*ate, sine*cure*, se*cure;* +Fr., *cure*, *cur*ious, *sure*, pro*cure*, pro*xy*).
curre-re, cursu-s, [Lat.], to run (*curs*ory, con*cur*, *curs*ive, ex*curs*ion, re*cur*, pre*curs*or; +Fr., *curr*ent, *course*, dis*course*, oc*cur*, re-*course*, suc*cor;* +It.+Fr., *cour*ier, *cors*air, *corr*idor).
curvu-s, [Lat.], crooked (*curve;* +Fr., *curb;* +It., *curv*et).
cuti-s, [Lat.], skin (*cut*icle, *cut*aneous).
damnu-m, [Lat.], injury, loss (+Fr., *damn*, *dam*age, con*demn*, in*demn*ify).
da-re, datu-s, dit-, [Lat.], to give, **donu-m,** gift (*dat*ive, ad*d*, ad*dit*ion, e*dit*, [1]*date*, *data*, con*done;* +Fr., *don*or, *don*ation, par*don*, ren*der*, [2]*rent*, [2]*die;* +Span., *dado*). See **mandare**, **vendere**.
debē-re, debitu-s, [Lat.], to owe (*debit;* +Fr., *debt*, *debt*or).
demo-s, [Gk.], the people (*dem*agog, *demo*-cracy, epi*dem*ic).
dens, denti-s, [Lat.], tooth (*dent*al, *dent*ist, in*dent;* +Fr., in*dent*ure, tri*dent*).
deu-s, [Lat.], god, **divu-s,** divine (+Fr., *de*ity, *div*ine, *div*ination).

exter, [Lat.], right, pertaining to the right hand (*dexter*, *dexter*ity).
ice-re, dictu-s, [Lat.], to say, **dica-re, dicatu-s,** to proclaim, **dicta-re, dictatu-s,** to repeat (*dictate*, *dictat*or, de*dicate*, in*dicate*, ab*dicate*, contra*dict*, e*dict*, pre*dict*, pre*dicate*; +Fr., *dic*tion, *dic*tionary, bene*diction* or benison, male*diction* or malison, in*dict*, in*dite*, ver*dict*, ju*dge* (see **judicare**), aven*ge*, prea*ch*; +It., *ditto*).
ie-s, [Lat.], day, **diurnu-s,** daily (*diary*, *dial*, *Ju*piter, *diurn*al; +Fr., *journ*al, *journey*, ad*journ*, meri*dian*).
igitu-s, [Lat.], a finger (*digit*).
ignu-s, [Lat.], worthy (+Fr., *dign*ity, *dain*ty, *deign*, dis*dain*, con*dign*, in*dign*ant).
isce-re, [Lat.], to learn, **discipulus,** a scholar (+Fr., *disciple*, *discipl*ine).
ivide-re, divisu-s, [Lat.], to divide (*divide*, *divis*ion, *divis*or, in*divid*ual).
ocē-re, doctu-s, [Lat.], to teach (+Fr., *doct*or, *doct*rine, *doc*ile, *docu*ment).
olē-re, [Lat.], to suffer, **dolor,** pain (con*dole*, in*dole*nce; +Fr., *dole*ful, *dolor*ous).
ominu-s, [Lat.], master (*domin*ate, pre*domin*ate, in*dom*itable; +Fr., *daunt*, *domin*ion, *domain*, *demesne*; +Span., ^{2}*don*, *domino*; +Fr.+Du., *domin*eer); **domina,** mistress (*dame*, ^{2}*dam*, ma*dam*, *dam*sel; +It., *donna*, ma*donna*; +Span., *duenna*).
omu-s, [Lat.], house (+Fr., *dome*, *dom*estic, *domi*cile).
ormi-re, dormitu-s, [Lat.], to sleep (*dormit*ory; +Fr., *dorm*ant).
orsu-m, [Lat.], back (+Fr., *dors*al, in*dorse*).
romo-s, [Gk.], a running, race (*drom*edary, hippo*drome*, air*drome*).
ubita-re, [Lat.], to doubt (*dubi*ous; +Fr., in*dubitable*, *doubt*). Akin to **duo.**
uce-re, ductu-s, [Lat.], to draw, lead (*duct*, aque*duct*, e*duc*ate, ad*duce*, con*duce*, in*duce*, re*duce*, etc., con*duct*, pro*duct*, etc., de*duct*ion, intro*duct*ion, etc.; +Fr., *duct*ile, con*duit*, *duke*, *duch*ess, *duc*al; +It., *doge*; +It.+Fr., *duc*at).
unami-s, [Gk.], power (*dynam*ic, *dyn*asty, *dyne*).
u-o, [Lat.], two (*du*al, *du*plicate; +Fr., *dou*ble, *dou*blet, *du*plicity; +It., *du*el, *du*et; +Span.+Fr., *dou*bloon). Akin to **dubitare.**
uru-s, [Lat.], hard (ob*dur*ate; +Fr., *dur*able, *dur*ance, *dur*ess, en*dur*e).
briu-s, [Lat.], drunken (in*ebri*ate; +Fr., *ebri*ety, so*bri*ety, so*ber*).
de-re, [Lat.], to eat (*ed*ible).
go, [Lat.], I (*ego*tist).
me-re, emptu-s, [Lat.], to buy (pre*ëmpt*; +Fr., ex*empt*, per*empt*ory, pro*mpt*, red*eem*, re*demp*tion, ran*som*). Akin to **exemplum.**
nter-a, [Gk.], the bowels (dys*enter*y, *enter*ic).
qui-, [Lat.], a combining form meaning equal. See **aequus.**
quu-s, [Lat.], horse (*equ*ine, *eq*uestrian).
rgo-n, [Gk.], work (*erg*, en*erg*y, metall*urg*y).
rra-re, erratu-s, [Lat.], to wander, **error,** a wandering, error (ab*errat*ion, *errat*um, *err*oneous; +Fr., *err*, *error*).
so, [Gk.], within (*eso*teric).
stima-re, [Lat.], to appraise: see **aestimare.**
tho-s, [Gk.], a custom (*eth*ics).
thno-s, [Gk.], nation (*ethno*logy).
xemplu-m, [Lat.], an example (+Fr., *example*, *exempl*ary, *sample*). Akin to **emere.**
xtra, [Lat.], outside, **exter,** [comp. **exterior,** superl. **extremu-s**], outward (*extra*, *exter*nal, *extra*neous, the prefix *extra*-; +Fr., *exterior*, *strange*, *extreme*, *extr*insic).
ace-re, factu-s, fic-, fect-, [Lat.], to make, do (*fact*, *fact*or, *fact*ory, *fact*itious, *fact*otum, *fac*simile, *fiat*, de*fect*, de*fic*ient, de*fic*it, pro*fic*ient, con*fect*ion, bene*fact*or; +Fr., *fac*ile, *fac*ulty, *fact*ion, manu*fact*ure, af*fect*ion, af*fect*, con*fect*ion, com*fit*, ef*fect*ual, per*fect*, pre*fect*, in*fect*, re*fect*ory, counter*feit*, for*feit*, sur*feit*, suf*fic*ient, ef*fic*ient, dif*fic*ult, of*fice*, of*fic*ious, sacri*fice*, arti*fice*, *feat*, de*feat*, *feat*ure, af*fa*ir, bene*fit*, bene*fice*, *fash*ion, ponti*ff*, the suffix -*fy*).
facie-s, [Lat.], form, figure, face (+Fr., *face*, de*face*, ef*face*, sur*face*, super*fic*ial; +It.+Fr., *façade*).
falle-re, falsu-s, [Lat.], to cause to fall; to deceive (*fall*ible; +Fr., *false*, *fals*ify, *fall*acy, *fail*, *fault*).
fama, [Lat.], a report (+Fr., *fame*, *fam*ous, de*fame*, in*fam*ous). Akin to **fari** and **fatēri.**
familia, [Lat.], family (*family*, *famili*ar).
fanu-m, [Lat.], temple (*fane*, *fan*atic; +Fr., pro*fane*).
fa-ri, fatu-s, [Lat.], to speak (in*fa*nt [lit., not speaking]; +Fr., *fate*, *fat*al, *fa*ble, af*fa*ble, *fay*, *fa*iry, pre*face*). Akin to **fama** and **fatēri.**
farina, [Lat.], meal, flour (*farina*, *farina*ceous).
fatē-ri, fessu-s, fit-, [Lat.], to confess (+Fr., con*fess*, pro*fess*, pro*fess*or). Akin to **fari** and **fama.**
felix, felici-s, [Lat.], fruitful, fortunate (*felic*ity).
femina, [Lat.], woman (ef*femin*ate; +Fr., *femin*ine, *fem*ale).
-fende-re, -fensu-s, [Lat.], to strike (+Fr., *fence*, de*fend*, de*fense*, *fend*, of*fend*, of*fens*ive).
fera, [Lat.], wild beast (+Fr., *fier*ce, *fer*ocious).
fer-re, [Lat.], to bear, [p.p. **latus:** for derivatives, see ^{3}**latus**], (circum*fer*ence, con*fer*, con*fer*ence, trans*fer*, pesti*fer*ous; +Fr., *fer*tile, de*fer*, dif*fer*, in*fer*, pre*fer*, prof*fer*, suf*fer*, voci*fer*ous).
ferru-m, [Lat.], iron (*ferr*ic, *ferr*ous, *ferru*ginous; +Fr., *farr*ier).
fervē-re, [Lat.], to boil, **fervidu-s,** boiling (*ferm*ent, ef*ferv*esce, *fervid*; +Fr., *fervor*, *ferv*ent).
festu-s, [Lat.], sacred, festive (*fest*ive; +Fr., *fest*al, *fest*ival, *feast*, *fête*).
fide-s, [Lat.], faith (con*fide*, con*fid*ent, dif*fid*ence, per*fid*y, af*fid*avit; +Fr., *fid*elity, de*fy*, af*fi*ance, *faith*). Akin to **foedus.**
fige-re, [Lat.], **fixu-s,** [Lat.], to fasten, fix (trans*fix*, suf*fix*; +Fr., pre*fix*, *fix*, *fix*ture, af*fix*, cruci*fix*, trans*fix*).
filiu-s, [Lat.], son (*fil*ial; +Fr., af*fili*ation).
filu-m, [Lat.], thread (+Fr., ^{1}*file*, ^{2}de*file*, *fil*ament, *fil*let, en*fil*ade; +It.+Fr., *fil*igree).
finge-re, fictu-s, fig-, fic-, [Lat.], to form (ef*fig*y, *fig*ment; +Fr., *fict*ion, *fig*ure, *feign*, *feint*).
fini-re, finitu-s, to limit, end (*finite*, in*finite*, in*finit*ive, in*finite*simal; +Fr., *fin*ish, de*fine*, de*finite*, de*finit*ion, *fin*al, con*fine*, af*finity*).
firmu-s, [Lat.], firm (in*firm*; +Fr., ^{1}*firm*, af*firm*, af*firm*ative, *firm*ament, con*firm*, in*firm*ary, in*firm*ity; +Span., ^{2}*firm*).
fiscu-s, [Lat.], basket, purse (con*fisc*ate; +Fr., *fisc*al).
flagra-re, to burn (+Fr., con*flagra*tion, *flagra*nt).
fla-re, flatu-s, [Lat.], to blow (in*flate*; +Fr., *flat*ulence).
flecte-re, flexu-s, [Lat.], to bend (*flex*ure, in*flect*, in*flect*ion, re*flect*, re*flex*, re*flex*ive; +Fr., *flex*ible).
flige-re, flictu-s, [Lat.], to beat (pro*flig*ate, af*flict*, con*flict*, in*flict*).
flos, flor-is, [Lat.], flower (*flor*al, *flor*id, *Flora*; +Fr., *flower*, ef*flor*escence, *flour*, *flour*ish; +It.+Fr., *flor*in).
flue-re, fluxu-s, [Lat.], to flow (*flu*ent, *flu*id, *fluc*tuate, ef*flux*, af*flu*ence, con*flu*ence, ef*flu*via, re*flux*, re*flu*ent, super*flu*ous; +Fr., *flux*, *flue*, in*flu*ence; +It., in*flu*enza).
foedus, foeder-is, feder-, [Lat.], league (con*feder*ate; +Fr., *feder*al). Akin to **fides.**
foliu-m, [Lat.], leaf (*folio*, *foli*ation; +Fr., *foli*age, ^{1}*foil*; +It., port*folio*).
forma, [Lat.], form (*form*ation, *form*al, *form*ula, cruci*form*; +Fr., *form*, con*form*, de*form*, in*form*, etc., uni*form*, *form*at).
fors, forti-s, [Lat.], chance (*fort*uitous; +Fr., *fort*une).

forti-s, [Lat.], strong, brave (+Fr., *force, fort, fortify, fortitude, comfort, effort*).
frange-re, fractu-s, fring-, frag-, [Lat.], to break (*frangible, refract, refractory, infringe;* +Fr., *fraction, fracture, fragment, fragile, frail, irrefragable;* perh. *suffrage*).
frater, [Lat.], brother (+Fr., *fraternal, fratricide*).
frigus, frigor-is, [Lat.], cold, *n.*, **frigidu-s,** cold, *adj.* (*frigid, refrigerator*).
frons, fronti-s, [Lat.], forehead (+Fr., *front, frontlet, frontier, frontispiece,* [1]*flounce* (for *frounce*), *affront, confront, effrontery*).
fru-i, fructu-s, fruitu-s, [Lat.], to enjoy, **frux, frugi-s,** fruit (+Fr., *fruit, frugal, fruition, fructify*).
fuge-re, fugitu-s, [Lat.], to flee (*centrifugal;* +Fr., *fugitive, refuge, subterfuge;* +It.+Fr., *fugue*).
fulgē-re, fulsu-s, [Lat.], to lighten, shine (*effulgent, fulminate*).
fumu-s, [Lat.], smoke (*fumigate;* +Fr., *fume, perfume*).
funde-re, fusu-s, [Lat.], to pour ([1]*fuse, diffuse, profusion, refund, suffuse,* etc.; +Fr., [3]*found,* [2]*font,* [2]*fount, confound, confuse, futile*).
fundu-s, [Lat.], bottom (+Fr., [2]*found, foundation, fund, fundamental,* [2]*founder,* [3]*founder, profound*).
gamo-s, [Gk.], marriage (*monogamy, bigamy, polygamy*).
gastēr, [Gk.], belly (*gastric*).
gen-esis, [Gk.], origin, source (*genesis, genealogy*).
gere-re, gestu-s, [Lat.], to bear, carry on (*gesture, gesticulate, belligerent, gerund, digest, suggest;* +Fr., *gestation, jest, register, congestion, vicegerent*). See **agger.**
(gi)gne-re, genitu-s, [Lat.], to beget, **genus, gener-is,** race, **gens, genti-s,** clan, nation (*genus, genuine, genius, congenial, ingenuous, indigenous, generic, generate, generation, degenerate, regenerate;* +Fr., *genial, gentle, genteel, gentile, general, generous, engender, primogeniture, progenitor, progeny, genital, malign, malignant*).
gladiu-s, [Lat.], sword (*gladiator, gladiolus;* +Fr., *glaive*).
glott-a, gloss-a, [Gk.], tongue, language (*glottis, epiglottis, glossary, polyglot*).
gluti-re, glutitu-s, [Lat.], to swallow, **gula,** throat (+Fr., *deglutition, glut, glutton, gullet, gully*).
gno-mē, [Gk.], reason, judgment, **gno-sis,** knowledge (*physiognomy, diagnosis, gnostic*).
gradi, gressu-s, [Lat.], to step, walk (*gradual, graduate, gradient, retrograde, congress, digress, egress, ingress;* +Fr., *grade, degree, degrade, aggressive, progress, transgress, ingredient*).
grandi-s, [Lat.], great (*grandiloquent;* +Fr., *grand, grandeur, aggrandize, grandfather;* +Span., *grandee*).
granu-m, [Lat.], grain of corn (*granary, granular, granivorous;* +Fr., *grain, grange, gravy* (for *grainy*); +It., *granite*).
gratu-s, [Lat.], pleasing (*gratuitous, congratulate, gratis, ingratiate;* +Fr., *grateful, gratitude, ingrate, gratify, grace, disgrace*).
gravi-s, [Lat.], heavy (*aggravate;* +Fr., [3]*grave, gravity, grief, grieve, aggrieve*).
grex, greg-is, [Lat.], flock (*gregarious, congregate, aggregate, segregate, egregious*).
gun-ē, gunaik-os, [Gk.], woman (*gynecology, misogynist*).
gusta-re, gustatu-s, [Lat.], to taste (+Fr., *disgust;* +It., *gusto*).
habē-re, habitu-s, hib-, [Lat.], to have (*exhibit, inhibit, prohibit, debilitate;* +Fr., *habit, inhabit, habitation, habitual, habiliment, able, dishabille, malady, ability,* the suffix *-able;* +Span., *binnacle*). Akin to **debēre.**
haerē-re, haesu-s, [Lat.], to adhere (*adhere, adhesion, cohere, cohesion, inherent*).
hala-re, [Lat.], to breathe (*inhale;* +Fr. *exhale*).
hauri-re, haustu-s, [Lat.], to draw (*exhaust*).
hedr-a, [Gk.], seat (*cathedral, tetrahedron, sanhedrin*).
helio-s, [Gk.], sun (*Helios, heliotrope, helium, perihelion*).
heres, hered-is, [Lat.], heir (*hereditary;* +Fr., *heritage, heir, heirloom, inherit*).
hetero-s, [Gk.], other (*heterodox, heterogeneous*).
hiero-s, [Gk.], sacred (*hierarchy, hieroglyphic*).
hippo-s, [Gk.], horse (*hippopotamus, hippodrome*).
hodo-s, [Gk.], road, way (*exodus, method, period, synod, odometer, cathode, anode*).
homo, homin-is, [Lat.], man, **humanu-s,** human (*humane;* +Fr., *human, homage, homicide*).
homo-s, [Gk.], alike (*homophone, homologous*).
honor, [Lat.], honor (+Fr., *honor, honest*).
hora, [Lat.], **hōra,** [Gk.], hour (+Fr., *horology, horoscope, hour*).
hortu-s, [Lat.], garden (*horticulture*).
hospes, hospit-is, [Lat.], guest or host (+Fr., *hospitable, hospital, hospice,* [2]*host, hotel, hostel, hostler*).
hosti-s, [Lat.], enemy (+Fr., [1]*host, hostile*).
humē-re, [Lat.], to be moist, **humidu-s,** moist (+Fr., *humid, humor*).
humu-s, [Lat.], earth, ground, **humili-s,** low, humble (*humus, exhume;* +Fr., *humiliate, humble*).
idio-s, [Gk.], belonging or peculiar (to a person), one's own (*idiot, idiom, idiosyncrasy*).
igni-s, [Lat.], fire (*ignite, igneous*).
imago, imagin-is, [Lat.], image (*imago;* +Fr., *image, imagine, imaginary*). Akin to root of *imitate.*
impera-re, [Lat.], to command (+Fr., *imperial, imperative, emperor, empire*).
inferu-s, [Lat.], low [comp. **inferior**], (+Fr., *inferior, infernal*).
insula, [Lat.], island (*insular, insulate, peninsula;* +Fr., *isolate, isle*). Not *island,* though the *s* in English is inserted because of supposed derivation from *insula.*
integer, [Lat.] lit., untouched; whole: see **tangere.**
intus, intra, [Lat.], within, **interior,** inner, **intimu-s,** inmost (*interior, internal, intimate* (*adj.* and *v.*), the prefixes *intra-, intro-;* +Fr., *intern, intrinsic, entrails, denizen*).
ira, [Lat.], anger (+Fr., *ire, irascible*).
i-re, itu-s, [Lat.], to go (*exit, initial, ambient, transient, transit, transitive;* +Fr., *ambition, circuit, obituary, commence, perish, sedition, trance*). Akin to **iter.**
iter, itiner-is, [Lat.], journey (*itinerary, itinerant*). Akin to **ire.**
iterum, [Lat.], again (*iteration, reiterate*).
jace-re, jactu-s, jic-, ject-, [Lat.], to throw (*abject, adjective, dejection, ejaculate, eject, inject, object, objection;* +Fr., *conjecture, interjection, project, reject, subject,* [1]*jet, jetsam,* [1]*jetty, jess,* [1]*amice*). Akin to **jacēre.**
jacē-re, jacitu-s, [Lat.], to lie, recline (*adjacent;* +Fr., *gist, joist*). Akin to **jacere.**
jocu-s, [Lat.], a joke (*joke, jocose, jocular;* +Fr., *juggler*). Not *jocund.*
judica-re, [Lat. *jus dicere*], to judge (*adjudicate;* +Fr., *judicial, judicious, judiciary, judge, adjudge, prejudice*).
junge-re, junctu-s, jug-, [Lat.], to join (*junction, juncture, adjunct, conjunction, disjunctive, injunction, subjunctive, conjugal, subjugate, jugular;* +Fr., *join, joint, adjoin, enjoin, disjointed;* +Span., *junta, junto*).
jus, jur-is, [Lat.], law, **jura-re,** to swear, **justu-s,** just (*abjure, adjure;* +Fr., *conjure, perjure, perjury, injure, jurist, jury,*

*jur*or, [1]*just*, *just*ice, *just*ify, *jur*isdiction, *jur*isprudence).
juveni-s, [Lat.], young [comp. **junior**], (*junior*; +Fr., *juven*ile).
kako-s, [Gk.], bad (*caco*phony).
kardi-a, [Gk.], heart (*cardi*ac, peri*cardi*um).
kephal-ē, [Gk.], head (*cephal*ic).
kheir, [Gk.], hand (*chiro*graphy, surgeon).
khol-ē, [Gk.], bile, anger (*col*ic, *chol*eric, melan*choly*).
khrom-a, [Gk.], color (*chromat*ic, *chrom*ium).
khrono-s, [Gk.], time (*chrono*meter, *chron*icle, ana*chron*ism).
kosmo-s, [Gk.], world (*cosmo*gony, *cosmo*politan, micro*cosm*).
kranio-n, [Gk.], skull (*cranium*, *cranio*logy).
kuklo-s, [Gk.], circle (*cycle*, *cycl*oid, bi*cycle*, en*cyclo*pedia).
kuon, kuno-s, [Gk.], dog (*cyn*ic, *cyno*sure).
lab-i, lapsu-s, [Lat.], to slide, fall down (*lapse*, col*lapse*, e*lapse*, re*lapse*).
labor, [Lat.], work (*labor*atory, e*labor*ate; +Fr., *labor*, *labor*ious).
lapis, lapid-is, [Lat.], stone (*lapid*ary, di*lapid*ate, *lapis* lazuli).
[1]**latu-s,** [Lat.], broad (+Fr., *lat*itude).
[2]**latus, later-is,** [Lat.], side (*later*al, col*later*al, equi*later*al).
[3]**latu-s,** [Lat.], borne (ob*late*, pro*late*, legis*late*; +Fr., col*late*, col*lat*ion, di*late*, di*lat*ory, ob*lat*ion, pre*late*, ab*lat*ive, re*late*, super*lat*ive, trans*late*). Abbreviated form of **tolatus**, obs. p.p. of **tollo** (which see), to raise, and used as p.p. of **ferre** (which see), to bear.
lega-re, legatu-s, [Lat.], to appoint, send, **lex, leg-is,** law (de*legate*, re*legate*, *leg*itimate, *leg*islature; +Fr., *legate*, *legacy*, *lega*tee, *leg*al, *le*al, *lo*yal, privi*lege*). Akin to **legere.**
lege-re, lectu-s, lig-, [Lat.], to collect, select, read (e*lect*, se*lect*, neg*lect*; +Fr., *leg*end, *lect*ure, *lect*ion, *le*sson, col*lect*, cu*ll*, co*il*, col*league*, col*lege*, *leg*ible, e*lig*ible, e*leg*ant, *leg*ion, di*lig*ent, intel*lect*, intel*lig*ence, neg*lig*ence, neg*lig*ee, predi*lect*ion, sacri*lege*).
leni-s, [Lat.], smooth, soft, gentle (*leni*ent; +Fr., *leni*ty).
leva-re, [Lat.], to raise, **levi-s,** light (e*lev*ate, al*levi*ate; +Fr., *lev*ity, *lev*er, *lev*y, *lev*ee, *lea*ven, re*lev*ant, re*lieve*, *leg*erdemain; +Span. +Fr., *lev*ant).
liber, [Lat.], book (+Fr., *libr*ary).
liber, [Lat.], free (*liber*ate, *liber*tine; +Fr., *liber*al, *liber*ty, *libel*).
libra, [Lat.], a balance, a pound weight (*Libra*, de*liber*ate, equi*libr*ium; +Fr., *lev*el).
licē-re, to be permissible (*lic*entiate; +Fr., *lic*ense, *lic*entious, il*lic*it).
liga-re, [Lat.], to tie, bind (+Fr., *liga*ment, *liga*ture, ob*lig*e, [1]*le*ague, *li*able, *li*aison, *li*en, al*ly*, re*ly*, al*loy*, [1]ra*lly*).
limen, limin-is, [Lat.], threshold (e*limin*ate; +Fr., pre*limin*ary).
lingua, [Lat.], tongue, language (*lingu*al, *lingu*ist; +Fr., *langu*age; +Provençal, *lingo*). The *u* of *tongue* is sometimes defended because of a fancied derivation from *lingua*.
linque-re, lictu-s, [Lat.], to leave (de*linqu*ent, dere*lict*ion; +Fr., re*linqu*ish, re*lic*, re*lict*).
linu-m, [Lat.], flax, **linea,** line, stroke, mark (*lin*en, [1]*line* in most meanings, [2]*line*, *lin*ing, *line*ar, *line*al, curvi*line*ar, de*line*ate, *lin*seed, *lin*sey-woolsey; +Fr., [1]*line* meaning verse, rank, row, *lin*t, a*lig*n, *line*age, *lin*net, *linea*ment).
litera, [Lat.], letter (ob*liter*ate, il*liter*ate, al*liter*ation, *liter*ation, *liter*ati; +Fr., *litera*ture, *liter*ary, *liter*al, *letter*).
litho-s, [Gk.], stone (*litho*graph, mono*lith*).
locu-s, [Lat.], place (*locus*, *loc*ate, *loco*motion, *loco*motive, col*loc*ation, dis*loc*ate; +Fr., *loc*al, *loc*ality, al*loc*ate, al*low*).
logo-s, [Gk.], speech, reason (*log*ic, *logo*type, philo*logy*, mono*log*, apo*logy*, syl*log*ism, the suffix -*ology*).
longu-s, [Lat.], long (*long*evity, e*long*ate; +Fr., *long*itude, ob*long*, pro*long*, pur*loin*). Not *long*: [1]*long* and [2]*long* are of A.S. origin.
loqui, locutu-s, [Lat.], to speak (e*locut*ion, ob*loquy*, col*loquy*, col*loqu*ial, circum*locut*ion, grandi*loqu*ent, soli*loquy*, ventri*loqu*ist; +Fr., *loqu*acity, e*loqu*ent).
lude-re, lusu-s, [Lat.], to play (*lud*icrous, al*lude*, al*lus*ion, de*lude*, de*lus*ion, e*lude*, inter*lude*, col*lus*ion; +Fr., pre*lude*).
lue-re, lutu-s, [Lat.], to wash (di*lute*, di*luv*ial, antedi*luv*ian, al*luv*ial; +Fr., ab*lut*ion, de*luge*).
luna, [Lat.], moon (*lun*ar, sub*lunary*; +Fr., *lun*atic, *lun*acy, *lun*ette). Akin to **lux.**
lusi-s, [Gk.], a loosening, dissolving (ana*lysis*, para*lysis*).
lux, luci-s, [Lat.], a light, **lumen, lumin-is,** a light (*luc*id, *luc*ent, *luci*fer, *lumin*ous, *lu*strum, il*lu*strious, il*lu*strate, e*luc*idate, trans*luc*ent; +Fr., *lumin*ary, pel*luc*id, *limn*, *lu*ster). Akin to **luna.**
magister, [Lat.], master (*magister*ial; +Fr., *magist*rate, *master*, *mister*, *mistr*ess). Akin to **magnus.**
magnu-s, [Lat.], great [comp. and superl. **major, maximus,** which see], (*magn*itude, *magn*ate, *magn*animous, *magn*ificent, *magn*iloquent; +Fr., *magn*ify).
major, [Lat.], greater [comp. of **magnus,** which see], (*major* (*adj.* and *n.*); +Fr., *major*ity, *maj*esty, *mayor*; +Span., *major*-domo).
malu-s, [Lat.], bad, **male,** badly [comp. and superl. **pejor, pessimus,** which see], (*male*factor, *male*volent, *mal*ignant; +Fr., *mal*ice, *male*diction, *mal*ign, the prefix *mal*-).
manda-re, mandatu-s, [Lat.: *manus* + *dare*], lit., to give the hand; to commit, entrust; to command (*mandamus*; +Fr., *mandate*, com*mand*, de*mand*, re*mand*, counter*mand*, recom*mend*; +Du.+Fr., com*modore*).
manē-re, mansu-s, [Lat.], to remain (*manse*; +Fr., *mans*ion, *man*or, per*man*ent, rem*n*ant, re*main*der, re*main*, *men*agerie, *men*ial, *mes*suage).
manu-s, [Lat.], hand (*manu*script, *mani*pulate, a*manu*ensis, e*man*cipate, *manu*mission; +Fr., *manu*al, *manu*facture, *man*acle, *maneu*ver, *man*ure, *mani*ple, *main*tain, *mani*fest; +It.+Fr., *man*age).
mare, [Lat.], sea, **marinu-s,** marine (+Fr., *marine*, *mariner*, *mari*time, sub*marine*; +It., ultra*marine*).
mater, [Lat.], mother (*matr*ix, *matr*iculate; +Fr., *mater*nal, *mater*nity, *matr*imony, *matr*icide).
maximu-s, [Lat.], greatest [superl. of **magnus,** which see], (*maximum*; +Fr., *maxim*).
medicu-s, [Lat.], physician, healer (*medic*al, *medic*ate; +Fr., *medic*ine, *medic*inal, re*medy*, re*med*ial).
mediu-s, [Lat.], middle (*medium*, *medi*al, *medi*ate; +Fr., *medi*ation, im*medi*ate, inter*medi*ate, *medi*ocre).
melior, [Lat.], better [comp. of **bonus,** which see], (*melior*ate; +Fr., a*melior*ate).
memin-i, [Lat.], I remember (*memen*to). Akin to **mens;** see **mnēmē.**
memor, [Lat.], mindful (*memor*andum, com*memor*ate; +Fr., *memory*, *memor*ial, im*memor*ial, *memoir*, *memor*able, re*member*).
mens, menti-s, [Lat.], mind (de*ment*ed; +Fr., *ment*al, *ment*ion).
merge-re, mersu-s, [Lat.], to dip, sink (*merge*, *merg*anser, e*merge*, e*merg*ency, im*mers*ion; +Fr., sub*merge*).
meti-ri, mensu-s, [Lat.], to measure (*mens*uration, com*mens*urate; +Fr., *meas*ure, im*meas*urable, im*mense*, di*mens*ion). Not *mete*, which is from an A.S. word.
metro-n, [Gk.], measure (*meter*, dia*meter*, *metr*ical, sym*metry*).
migra-re, migratu-s, [Lat.], to depart,

migrate (*migrate*, *migration*, e*migrate*, e*mi-grant*, im*migration*; +Fr., trans*migration*).

miles, milit-is, [Lat.], soldier (*milit*ary, *milit*ate, *milit*ant, *milit*arist, *milit*ia).

mille, [Lat.], thousand (*mill*ennium, *mille*-pede, the prefix *milli-*).

minimu-s, [Lat.], least [superl. of **parvus,** small; comp. **minor,** which see], (*minimum*, *minim*ize; +Fr., *minim*).

minor, minus, [Lat.], less [comp. of **parvus,** small; superl. **minimus,** which see], **minue-re, minutu-s,** to make small (*minor*, *minus*, *minor*ity, *minute*, *minuti*æ, *minu*end; +Fr., di*min*ish, di*minut*ive, *menu*, *mince*, *minuet*). Akin to **minister.**

minister, [Lat.], servant (+Fr., *minister*, ad*ministr*ation, *minstr*el). Akin to **minor.**

miru-s, [Lat.], strange, **mira-ri, miratu-s,** to wonder at (+Fr., *mir*acle, ad*mire*, *mir*age, *mir*ror).

miscē-re, mixtu-s, [Lat.], to mix (*misc*ellaneous, *mixt*ure, *mix*, pro*misc*uous).

miser, [Lat.], wretched (*miser;* +Fr., *miser*y, *miser*able, com*miser*ate).

miso-s, [Gk.], hatred (*mis*anthrope, *miso*gynist).

mitte-re, missu-s, [Lat.], to send (ad*mit*, ad*miss*ion, com*mit*, com*miss*ary, compro*mise*, dis*miss*, e*mit*, e*miss*ion, e*miss*ary, *miss*ion, *miss*ionary, *miss*ile, o*mit*, per*mit*, per*miss*ion, re*mit*, re*miss*, sub*mit*, trans*mit*, etc.; +Fr., com*miss*ion, com*miss*ioner, com*mit*tee, de*mise*, manu*miss*ion, *miss*ive, pro*mise*, sur*mise*, *mess*age, *mess*enger, *mess*, *Mass*).

mnē-mē, [Gk.], memory (*mne*monic, a*mne*sia, a*mne*sty). Akin to **memini.**

modu-s, [Lat.], measure; manner (*mod*ulate, *mod*erate, *mod*icum, accom*mod*ate; +Fr., *mode*, [1]*mood*, *mod*ify, *mod*est, *mod*ern, com*mod*ious, com*mod*ity; +It.+Fr., *model*).

mole-s, [Lat.], heap; trouble, difficulty (*mole*cule; +Fr., de*mol*ish; +It.+Fr., [3]*mole*).

molli-s, [Lat.], soft (*moll*usc; +Fr., *moll*ify, e*moll*ient, *moil*).

monē-re, monitu-s, [Lat.], to remind, warn (*monit*or, pre*monit*ory; +Fr., *mon*ument, ad*mon*ish, sum*mon*). Akin to **mens, memini.**

mons, monti-s, [Lat.], mountain (*mount* (*n.*), pro*mont*ory; +Fr., *mount* (*v.*), *mount*ain, *mound*, a*mount*, dis*mount*, para*mount*, sur*mount*, tanta*mount*). Akin to root of e*min*ent (lit., jutting out), pro*min*ent.

monstru-m, [Lat.], omen (lit., that which shows or warns); also, a monster (de*monstr*ate, re*monstr*ate; +Fr., *monster*, *monstr*ous, *muster*). Akin to **monēre, mens.**

mordē-re, morsu-s, [Lat.], to bite (+Fr., *mord*ant, *mors*el, re*morse*).

morpho-s, [Gk.], shape, form (*morpho*logy, meta*morpho*sis, a*morph*ous).

mors, morti-s, [Lat.], death (*morti*cian; +Fr., *mort*al, *mort*ify, *mort*gage).

mos, mor-is, [Lat.], custom (+Fr., *mor*al, de*mor*alize, etc.).

movēre, motu-s, [Lat.], to move (*mot*or, *mom*entum, *mob*, e*mot*ion, re*mote;* +Fr., *move*, *move*ment, *mob*ile, *mot*ive, *mot*ion, pro*mot*ion, re*move*, *mut*iny).

multu-s, [Lat.], much (*multi*ple; the prefix *multi-;* +Fr., *multi*ply, *multi*tude, etc.).

mundu-s, [Lat.], earth (+Fr., *mund*ane, demi*monde*).

munus, muner-is, [Lat.], duty, office; gift (re*muner*ate; +Fr., *mun*icipal, *mun*ificent). Akin to **communis.**

muru-s, [Lat.], wall (+Fr., im*mure*, *mur*al).

muta-re, mutatu-s, [Lat.], to move; change (*mut*able, com*mute*, trans*mute*, per*mute;* +Fr., *mut*ation, *mut*ual, *moult*, [2]*mew*).

nasc-i, natu-s, [**n-** for older **gn-**], [Lat.], to be born, **natura,** orig., birth; nature (in*nate*, cog*nate*, preter*natur*al; +Fr., *nat*al, *nat*ive, *naïve*, *nat*ivity, *nat*ion, *nature*, super*natur*al,).

nata-re, natatu-s, [Lat.], to swim (*nata*orium, *nat*atorial).

navi-s, [Lat.], ship (circum*navi*gate; +Fr *navy*, *nav*al, *navi*gable, [1]*nave*). *Nautica* is from Lat. *nauticus*, from Gk. *naus*, ship

necte-re, nexu-s, [Lat.], to tie, bind (con*nect;* +Fr., an*nex*).

nega-re, negatu-s, [Lat.], to deny (ab*negat*e re*nege;* +Fr., *negat*ion, *negat*ive, de*ny* ru*nagate;* +Span., re*negade*).

negotiu-m, [Lat.: *neg*(*are*) + *otium*, leisure] lit., lack of leisure; business (*negot*iate).

neuro-n, [Gk.], cord, nerve (*neuron*, *neurot*ic *neur*algia).

nihil, [Lat.], nothing (an*nihil*ate, *nihil*ist).

nocē-re, nec-, nic-, [Lat.], to harm, **noxius** harmful (*nox*ious, in*noc*uous, ob*nox*ious +Fr., in*noc*ent, *nuis*ance, per*nic*ious).

nomo-s, [Gk.], law (Deutero*nomy*, astro*nomy* a*nom*alous).

norma, [Lat.], a carpenter's rule (*norm* *norm*al; +Fr., e*norm*ous, e*norm*ity). *Ab* *normal* is a corruption, derived from th same source as *anomal-ous*.

nomen, nomin-is, [Lat.], name (*nomina* *nomen*clature, *nomin*ate, de*nomin*ation, de*nomin*ator; +Fr., *noun*, pro*noun*, mis*nomer*)

nosce-re, notu-s, [**n-** for older **gn-**], [Lat.] to know, **co-gnitu-s,** known (*not*ation, an*not*ation, *not*orious, con*note;* +Fr., *note* *not*ice, *not*ion, *not*ify, de*note*, *cognit*ion re*cogn*ize, recon*noit*er, *nob*le, en*nob*le *ign*oble, *ign*ominy).

nox, nocti-s, [Lat.], night (+Fr., *noct*urnal *noct*urn, equi*nox*).

nube-re, nuptu-s, to cover with a veil; to marry (con*nub*ial; +Fr., *nupt*ial).

nullus, [Lat.], no one (*null*ify; +Fr., *null* *null*ity, an*nul*).

numeru-s, [Lat.], number (*numer*al, e*numer*ate; +Fr., *number*, *numer*ous, *numer*ation *numer*ical, super*numer*ary).

nuntia-re, nuntiatu-s, [Lat.], to announce (e*nunci*ate, de*nunci*ate, an*nunci*ation; +Fr., an*nounce*, de*nounce*, re*nounce*, pro*nuncia*tion; +It., *nuncio*).

oculu-s, [Lat.], eye (*ocul*ar, *ocul*ist, in*ocul*ate, bin*ocul*ar; +Fr., in*veig*le).

od-i, [Lat.], I hate (*od*ium; +Fr., *od*ious, an*noy*).

od-ous, odonto-s, [Gk.], tooth (mast*odon*).

oiko-s, [Gk.], house (*eco*nomic, par*och*ial, di*oc*ese).

olē-re, [Lat.], to emit an odor (*ol*factory: +Fr., red*ol*ent). Akin to Lat. **odor, odor.**

oligo-s, [Gk.], few (*olig*archy).

omni-s, [Lat.], all (*omni*scient, *omni*bus, *omni*vorous; +Fr., *omni*potent, *omni*present).

onom-a, onum-a, [Gk.], name (an*onym*ous, syn*onym*).

onus, oner-is, [Lat.], a burden (ex*oner*ate; +Fr., *oner*ous).

opina-ri, [Lat.], to opine, believe (+Fr., *opine*, *opin*ion).

ops-omai, [Gk.], I shall see, **opt-,** to see (*opt*ical, aut*ops*y, syn*ops*is).

opta-re, [Lat.], to wish (ad*opt*, co*öpt;* +Fr., *opt*ative, *opt*ion).

opus, oper-is, [Lat.], a work (*oper*ate, co*öper*ative, *oper*ator; +Fr., man*euver*, man*ure*, in*ure;* +It., *opera*).

ora-re, oratu-s, [Lat.], to pray, **os, or-is,** mouth (*or*al, ad*ore*, ad*orat*ion; +Fr., *orat*ion, *orat*or, *orat*ory, *oris*on, *ori*fice, *orac*le, *orac*ular, inex*or*able, per*orat*ion; +It., *orat*orio).

orbi-s, [Lat.], circle (*orbi*t; +Fr., *orb*, *orbi*cular, ex*orbi*tant).

ordo, ordin-is, [Lat.], order (*ordin*al, in*ordin*ate, extra*ordin*ary, sub*ordin*ate; +Fr. *ordain*, *order*, *ordin*ance, *ord*nance, *ordin*ary, prim*ord*ial).

ori-ri, ortu-s, [Lat.], to rise, **origo, origin-is,** source (ab*ort*ive; +Fr., *origin*, *origin*ate *origin*al, *ori*ent, *ori*ental).

orna-re, ornatu-s, [Lat.], to furnish; to adorn (*ornate, adorn;* +Fr., *orna*ment, sub*orn*).
ornis, ornitho-s, [Gk.], bird (*ornitho*logy, *ornitho*rhynchus).
ortho-s, [Gk.], straight, erect, right (*ortho*dox, *ortho*ëpy, *ortho*graphic, *ortho*pedic).
os, oss-is, [Lat.], bone (*oss*eous; +Fr., *oss*ify, *os*prey).
osteo-n, [Gk.], bone (*osteo*pathy, peri*osteu*m).
ovu-m, [Lat.], egg (*ov*ary, *ov*ule, *ov*iparous, *ov*oid; +Fr., *ov*al).
oxu-s, [Gk.], sharp (*oxy*gen, par*oxys*m).
pagu-s, [Lat.], village (*pag*an; +Fr., *peas*ant, *pay*nim).
pais, paido-s, [Gk.], boy, child, **paidei-a,** education (*ped*agogy, *ped*ant, ortho*ped*ic).
palliu-m, [Lat.], cloak ([1]*pall, palli*ate, *pallia*tion).
pande-re, pansu-s, [Lat.], to lay open (ex*pand*, ex*pans*ion, ex*pans*ive).
pange-re, pactu-s, [Lat.], to drive in, fasten, fix (im*pinge*, im*pact;* +Fr., [2]com*pact*).
par, [Lat.], equal (*par;* +Fr., *pair,* [1]*peer, peer*age, *par*ity, com*pare*, dis*parage*).
para-re, paratu-s, [Lat.], to prepare (ap*paratus*, re*para*tion, se*parate;* +Fr., *pare*, pre*pare*, [2]re*pair*, *sever*, *para*chute, *parry*, ram*part;* +It.+Fr., *para*pet, *para*sol; +Span., *parade*). Akin to **imperare** (em*per*or, etc.).
[1]**pare-re, paritu-s,** [Lat.], to appear (ap*par*ent, ap*parit*ion; +Fr., ap*pear*, disap*pear*, trans*parent*).
[2]**parē-re, partu-s,** [Lat.], to bring forth (*par*ental; +Fr., *par*ent, *part*urition).
pars, parti-s, [Lat.], part (*parti*cipate, *parse*, bi*partite*; +Fr., *part*, a*part*, *parti*cle, *parti*cular, *parti*ciple, *parti*tion, *party*, *parti*al, *part*ner, *par*cel, de*part*, de*part*ment, im*part*, im*parti*al, *part*ake, re*part*ee, *por*tion; +It.+Fr., [1]*parti*san, a*part*ment).
pasce-re, pastu-s, [Lat.], to feed (*past*or, *pab*ulum; +Fr., re*past*, *past*oral, *past*ure, *past*ern).
pater, [Lat.], father, **patria,** one's native land (*patr*ician, ex*patr*iate, *pater*noster, Ju*piter;* +Fr., *pater*nal, *patr*imony, *patr*on, *pat*tern). *Patriarch, patriot* are derived from a kindred Gk. word, **patēr.**
patho-s, [Gk.], feeling, suffering (*path*etic, a*pathy*, sym*pathy*, *path*ology).
pati, passu-s, to suffer, endure (dis*pass*ionate; +Fr., *pati*ent, *pati*ence, *pass*ive, *pass*ion, com*pass*ion, com*pati*ble).
pausa, [Late Lat.], a pause, **pausa-re,** to cease; cause to rest (+Fr., *pause*, [1]*pose*, ap*pose*, com*pose*, de*pose*, discom*pose*, dis*pose*, ex*pose*, im*pose*, inter*pose*, op*pose*, pro*pose*, pur*pose*, re*pose*, sup*pose*, trans*pose*). These compounds are related in sense to *apposition, composition, deposition,* etc., but not in origin, as the latter are derived from *ponere, positus,* to place. See **ponere.**
pax, paci-s, [Lat.], peace (+Fr., *peace*, *paci*fic, *paci*fy, ap*pease*, [1]*pay*).
pecca-re, to sin, err (im*pecc*able; +Span., *pecc*adillo).
pectus, pector-is, [Lat.], breast (ex*pector*ate; +Fr., *pector*al).
pecu, [Lat.], cattle, **pecunia,** money (*pecu*late; +Fr., *pecu*liar, *pecu*niary).
pelle-re, pulsu-s, [Lat.], to drive (dis*pel*, ex*pel*, im*pel*, re*pel*, pro*pel*, re*pell*ent, pro*pell*er, [2]*pelt*, *puls*ate, *puls*ation, ap*pell*ate, ap*pell*ation, com*puls*ion, com*puls*ory, ex*puls*ion, im*puls*e, im*puls*ive, re*puls*e, re*puls*ion, re*puls*ive; +Fr., [1]*pulse*, *push*, com*pel*, re*peal*, ap*peal*).
pendē-re, [Lat.], to hang, **pende-re, pensu-s,** to cause to hang, weigh, pay, **pondus, ponder-is,** weight (*pend*ulum, *pend*ulous, ap*pend*ix, com*pend*ium, im*pend*, s*pend*, ex*pend*, pro*pens*ity, sti*pend*, *ponder*, pre*ponder*ate, indis*pens*able, ex*pens*e, ex*pend*iture; +Fr., *pend*ent, *pend*ant, *pens*ile, *pens*ion, ap*pend*, ap*pend*age, com*pend*ious, de*pend*, dis*pense*, *pend*ing, per*pend*icular, recom*pense*, sus*pend*, sus*pens*ion, sus*pense*, *poise*, avoirdu*pois*, *pansy*, *pent*house, [1]*pound*).
penit-us, [Lat.], within (*pene*trate).
penna, [Lat.], feather (*penn*ate; +Fr., [2]*pen*, *penn*on, *penn*ant).
persona, [Lat.], the mask worn by an actor; hence, an actor's part; a person (+Fr., *person*, *parson*, *person*al, *person*ality).
pes, ped-is, [Lat.], foot (*ped*al, *ped*estrian, bi*ped*, quadru*ped*, im*pede*, im*ped*iment, ex*ped*ite, ex*ped*ition, ex*ped*ient, *ped*igree, *ped*icel, *ped*uncle; +It.+Span., *ped*estal).
pete-re, petitu-s, [Lat.], to fall upon, seek, ask (centri*pet*al, *pet*ulant, com*pete*, im*pet*us; +Fr., ap*pet*ite, com*pet*ent, im*pet*uous, re*peat*, re*petit*ion).
petr-a, [Gk.], rock (*petr*ify, *petr*oleum).
phag-ein, [Gk.], to eat (sarco*phag*us).
phain-ein, phan-, [Gk.], to appear (*phen*omenon, dia*phan*ous, epi*phan*y).
phē-mi, [Gk.], I say, **phasi-s,** a saying (blas*phem*e, pro*phe*t, a*phas*ia).
pher-ein, phor-, [Gk.], to carry (peri*pher*y, Christo*pher*, phos*phor*us, meta*phor*). Akin to **ferre.**
phrēn, [Gk.], mind (*phren*ology, *fren*zy).
pilu-m, [Lat.], spear, **pila-re,** to rob, pillage ([2]*pile;* +Fr., com*pile*, *pil*lage).
pinge-re, pictu-s, pig-, [Lat.], to paint (*pict*ure, *pict*uresque, de*pict;* +Fr., *paint;* +Span.+Fr., *pint;* +Port., *pim*ento).
pisci-s, [Lat.], fish (*Pisc*es, *pisc*atory).
piu-s, [Lat.], dutiful, pious, **pia-re, piatu-s,** to worship, appease by sacrifice (ex*piate;* +Fr., *pious*, *piety*, *pity*, *pit*iful).
placē-re, placitu-s, [Lat.], to please (com*plac*ent; +Fr., com*plais*ant, *pleas*ure, *pleas*ant, *plac*id, im*plac*able, *please*, *plea*, *plead*).
planta, [Lat.], a green twig or spreading leaf; the sole of the foot (*plant*, *plant*ation; +Fr., *plant*ain, im*plant*, sup*plant*, trans*plant*).
planu-s, [Lat.], even, level (*plac*enta; +Fr., [2]*plane*, *plain*, *plan*, ex*plain;* +It., *piano*).
plaude-re, plausu-s, [Lat.], **plod-, plos-,** to clap, applaud (*plaud*it, *plaus*ible, ap*plaud*, ap*plause;* +Fr., ex*plode*, ex*plos*ive).
plenu-s, [Lat.], full, **plē-re, pletu-s,** to fill (*plen*ary, *pleni*potentiary, com*plete*, de*plete*, ex*plet*ive, com*ple*ment, im*ple*ment; +Fr., *pleni*tude, *plenty*, *plent*eous, accom*plish*, re*plen*ish, re*plete*, sup*ply*, sup*ple*ment; +Span.+It.+Fr., com*pli*ment; +Span.+It., com*ply*).
plica-re, plicatu-s, [Lat.], to fold, **plecte-re, plexu-s,** to weave (ap*plica*tion, com*plex*, com*plicat*ed, du*plicate*, ex*plicit*, im*plicate*, im*plicit*, redu*plicate*, sup*plicate;* +Fr., accom*plice*, ap*ply*, ap*pli*ance, com*plex*ion, [1]*ply*, *pli*ant, *pli*able, *pli*ers, *plait*, *pleat*, [1]*plight*, de*ploy*, dis*play*, s*play*, com*plic*ity, du*plic*ity, inex*plic*able, im*ply*, re*ply*, multi*ply*, multi*plica*tion, per*plex*, sim*ple*, sim*plic*ity, sim*pli*fy, sup*ple*).
plumbu-m, [Lat.], lead (*plumb*ago; +Fr., *plumb*, *plumb* bob, *plumb*er, *plumm*et, [2]*plump*, *plunge*).
plus, plur-is, [Lat.], more (*plus*, non*plus;* +Fr., *plur*al, *plur*ality, sur*plus*).
pne-ein, [Gk.], to blow, breathe, **pneuma,** breath, blast (*pneuma*tic).
poinē, [Gk.], penalty (+Lat., sub*pœna;* +Lat.+Fr., *pen*al, *pen*alty).
polemo-s, [Gk.], war (*polem*ic).
poli-s, [Gk.], city, **polit-ēs,** citizen (metro*polis*, *polit*ics).
polu-s, [Gk.], many (*poly*gon, *poly*gamy, the prefix *poly-*).
pomu-m, [Lat.], apple (*pom*ology; +Fr., *pome*, *pom*ace, *pome*granate, *pomm*el; +It.+Fr., *pom*ade).
pone-re, positu-s, [Lat.], to place, lay down (post*pone*, com*pon*ent, de*pon*ent, ex*pon*ent, op*pon*ent, ap*posite*, [1]*post*, pro*vost;* +Fr., *posit*ion, *posit*ive, [2]*post*, [3]*post*, *post*age,

posture, com*post*, com*pote*, [1]com*pound*, com*posit*, com*positor*, de*posit*, de*pot*, de*position*, ex*pound*, ex*positor*, im*post*, im*position*, im*postor*, op*posite*, pre*position*). The forms *appose*, *compose*, *expose*, *dispose*, etc., are related in meaning to the forms given above, though not in origin, being derived from *pausare*, to cease, cause to rest. See **pausare**.

populu-s, [Lat.], a people (*popul*ation, de*popul*ate; +Fr., *people*, *popul*ar, *popul*ous; +It.+Fr., *popul*ace).

porta, [Lat.], gate (+Fr., [2]*port*, *port*al, [1]*port*er, *Porte*, *port*cullis, *port*hole).

porta-re, portatu-s, [Lat.], to carry (ex*port*, [1]im*port*; +Fr., [2]*port*er, *port*able, *port*manteau, com*port*, de*port*, de*port*ment, [2]im*port*, im*port*ant, *port*ly, dis*port*, s*port*, pur*port*, *port*folio, re*port*, sup*port*, trans*port*).

portu-s, [Lat.], harbor ([1]*port*; +Fr., im*port*une, op*port*une, op*port*unity; +Port., [5]*port*).

posse, [Lat.], to be able, [p.pr. **potens, potenti-s,** powerful], **possibili-s,** possible (*potent*, *potent*ial, pleni*potent*iary; +Fr., im*potent*, omni*potent*, *potent*ate, *puiss*ant).

posteru-s, [Lat.], [comp. **posterior**], following (*posterior*, pre*posterous*; +Fr., *poster*ity, *postern*).

pota-re, potatu-s, [Lat.], to drink, **potio, potion-is,** a drink (*pot*ation; +Fr., *pot*able, *potion*, *poison*).

pous, podo-s, [Gk.], foot (anti*podes*, gastro*pod*).

prass-ein, [Gk.], to do, **prakto-s,** done, **pragm-a,** deed (*pract*ice, *pragm*atic).

preca-ri, precatu-s, [Lat.], to entreat (de*precate*, im*precate*, *precar*ious).

prehende-re, prehensus, [Lat.], to seize (ap*prehend*, com*prehend*, *prehens*ile, re*prehens*ible; +Fr., ap*prent*ice, enter*prise*, im*pregn*able, incom*prehens*ible, *prison*, [2]*prize*, re*pris*al, sur*prise*; +It., im*pres*ario).

preme-re, pressu-s, [Lat.], to press (im*press*, im*press*ion, de*press*, sup*press*; +Fr., [1]*press*, *press*ure, com*press*, ex*press*, op*press*ion, *print*, re*press*, re*prim*and).

pretiu-m, [Lat.], price, value (ap*preci*ate, de*preci*ate; +Fr., *price*, *preci*ous).

primu-s, [Lat.], first, **prior,** earlier (*prim*ary, *prim*eval, *prior* (*adj.*); +Fr., [1]*prime*, [2]*prime*, [2]*prim*er, *prem*ier, *prim*ate, *primo*geniture, *prim*rose, *prim*, *prin*ce, *prin*cipal, *prin*ciple, *prior* (*n.*), *prim*itive, *prim*ordial; +It., *prima* donna).

privu-s, [Lat.], single, **priva-re, privatu-s,** to deprive (*private*, *privat*ive; +Fr., *privi*lege, *privat*ion, *priv*y, *privat*eer, de*prive*).

proba-re, probatu-s, [Lat.], to test, try, examine, **probu-s,** honest (*probe*, *prove*, ap*probat*ion, re*probate*; +Fr., *prob*ity, *prob*able, *probat*ion, ap*prove*, *proof*, dis*prove*, re*prove*, re*prieve*).

prope, [Lat.], near, **proximu-s,** nearest, next (*proxim*ate, ap*proxim*ate; +Fr., *prop*inquity, ap*proach*, re*proach*, ap*proxim*ate).

propriu-s, [Lat.], one's own; peculiar (ap*propri*ate; +Fr., *proper*, *proper*ty, *pro*prietor, *propri*ety.

psukh-ē, [Gk.], soul (*Psyche*, *psych*ology, metem*psych*osis).

publicu-s, [Lat.], public (*public*an; +Fr., *public*, *publish*, re*public*, re*public*an). Derived from **populus.**

pugnu-s, [Lat.], fist, **pugna,** battle (*pug*nacious, *pug*ilist; +Fr., im*pugn*, re*pugn*ant, *poni*ard).

punge-re, punctu-s, [Lat.], to prick, sting (*pung*ent, *punct*ure, *punct*uate, ex*punge*; +Fr., *punct*uality, com*punct*ion, *point*, *poign*ant, [2]*pounce*, [1]*punch*, [1]*punch*eon, [2]*punch*eon; +Span., *punct*ilio).

puni-re, punitu-s, [Lat.], to punish, **paenitē-re,** to cause to repent (+Fr., *puni*sh, *punit*ive, im*punity*, *penit*entiary, *penit*ence, *pen*ance, re*pent*).

pur, [Gk.], fire (*pyre*, *pyr*otechnics, em*pyr*ean).

puta-re, putatu-s, [Lat.], to think, **putu-s,** pure (am*putate*, com*pute*; +Fr., [1]*count*, ac*count*, dis*count*, de*pute*, de*puty*, dis*pute*, im*pute*, *putat*ive, re*putat*ion). Akin to Lat. **purus,** pure.

quaere-re, quaesitu-s, [Lat.], to seek, ask (*query*, ac*quire*, ac*quisit*ion, dis*quisit*ion, ex*quisite*, in*quire*, in*quisit*or, per*quisite*; +Fr., *quest*, con*quer*, con*quest*, in*quisit*ive, in*quisit*ion, re*quire*, re*quest*, re*quisite*).

quate-re, quassu-s, cut-, cuss-, [Lat.], to shake (dis*cuss*, per*cuss*ion; +Fr., *quash*, con*cuss*ion; +Span., *cask*; +Span.+Fr., *casque*).

quatuor, [Lat.], four, **quartu-s,** fourth, **quadru-s,** square (*quadr*ant, *quadr*atic, *quadr*ilateral, *quadru*ped, *quart*o, [1]*quad*; +Fr., [1]*quart*, [2]*quart*, *quart*er, *quadru*ple, *square*, [1]*quarr*y, [3]*quarr*y, [1]*quarr*el; +It.+Fr., *squadr*on, *squad*, [2]*quad*, *quar*antine; +Span.+Fr., *quadr*ille; +Span., *quadr*oon).

quer-i, questu-s, [Lat.], to complain (*quer*ulous; +Fr., [2]*quarr*el).

quiesce-re, quietus, [Lat.], to rest, repose, **quies, quiet-is,** quiet (*quietus*, *quiet*; *quiesc*ence, ac*quiesce*, dis*quiet*, re*quiem*; +Fr., *quit*, *quite*, ac*quit*, re*quite*, *coy*).

radiu-s, [Lat.], rod or spoke (*radius*, *radi*an, *radi*ate, *radi*ant; +Fr., *radi*al, [1]*ray*).

radix, radic-is, [Lat.], root (*radix*, e*radic*ate; +Fr., *radic*al, *radish*).

rade-re, rasu-s, [Lat.], to scrape (ab*rade*, ab*ras*ion, e*rase*; +Fr., *raze*, *razor*, [1]*rash*).

ramu-s, [Lat.], branch (+Fr., *ram*ify).

rape-re, raptu-s, [Lat.], to snatch (*rapt*, *rapt*ure, *rapt*orial, *rap*acious, en*rapt*ure; +Fr., *rap*ine, *rap*id, *rav*age, *rav*ish, [2]*rav*en, *rav*ine, sur*rept*itious).

rege-re, rectu-s, [Lat.], to direct, rule, **regna-re,** to reign (*regn*ant, *rect*or, *reg*alia, *rect*ilinear, *reg*imen, *reg*ular, *reg*ulate, cor*rect*, di*rect*, *dirge*, e*rect*, inter*regn*um; +Fr., *reg*al, *roy*al, [2]*re*al, *realm*, *reg*ent, *rect*itude, *reg*icide, *reg*iment, *reign*, *rect*ify, incor*rig*ible, *rect*angle, *reg*ion, *dress*, ad*dress*, a*droit*).

rē-ri, ratu-s, [Lat.], to think, judge, **ratio, ration-is,** calculation, relation (*ratio*; +Fr., [1]*rate*, *rat*ify, *ration*al, *ration*, *reason*, *ratio*cination).

re-s, [Lat.], thing ([1]*re*al; +Fr., *re*alize).

rhe-ein, [Gk.], to flow (cata*rrh*, hemo*rrh*age, dia*rrh*ea).

ridē-re, risu-s, [Lat.], to laugh (*rid*icule, *rid*iculous, de*ride*, de*ris*ion; +Fr., *ris*ible).

rigē-re, [Lat.], to be stiff, **rigor,** stiffness (*rig*id; +Fr., *rigor*, *rigor*ous).

ripa, [Lat.], bank of a stream (*rip*arian, +Fr., *river*, ar*rive*; +It., *Riv*iera).

rivu-s, [Lat.], a stream (*riv*ulet; +Fr., de*rive*, *riv*al).

roga-re, rogatu-s, [Lat.], to ask (ab*rogate*, ar*rog*ant, de*rogat*ory, inter*rogat*ion, sur*rogate*, supere*rogat*ion; +Fr., pre*rogat*ive).

rota, [Lat.], wheel, **rotundu-s,** round (*rot*ary, *rot*ation, *rotunda*; +Fr., *rotund*, *round*, *ron*deau, *round*elay, *roul*et, *row*el, *roué*, *rol*l, cont*rol*, cont*rol*ler). The letters *mp* in the spelling *comptroller* result from the erroneous belief that the word was derived, through French, either from Lat. *co-emptus* (see **emere**) or *com-putare* (see **putare**).

rumpe-re, ruptu-s, [Lat.], to break (ab*rupt*, cor*rupt*, dis*rupt*, e*rupt*ion, inter*rupt*; +Fr., [1]*rote*, *route*, [1]*rout*, *rout*ine, *rut*; +It.+Fr., bank*rupt*).

rus, rur-is, the country (+Fr., *rur*al, *rus*tic, *rus*ticate, *roi*stering).

sanci-re, [Lat.], **sanctu-s,** to make sacred, **sacer,** consecrated (con*secr*ate, de*secr*ate, exe*cr*ate, *sanct*um, *sanct*ity, *sacrosanct*, *sac*rament; +Fr., *sacr*ed, *sacer*dotal, *sacr*istan, *sex*ton, *sanct*uary, *sain*t, *sanct*ion, *sanct*ify, *sanct*imonious, *sacr*ilege, *sacr*ifice).

sal, [Lat.], salt (+F., *sal*ine, *sal*ary, *sau*ce, *sau*sage; +It.+Fr., *sal*ad). Not the word *salt*, which is derived from an A.S. word.

sali-re, saltu-s, [Lat.], to leap (*sali*ent,

*sal*tatory, de*sult*ory, ex*ult* (for ex*sult*); +Fr., in*sult*, re*sult*, as*sail*, *sal*ly, *sal*mon).
salus, salut-is, [Lat.], health, safety, **salvu-s,** safe (*salute*, *salu*brity; +Fr., *salu*tary, *save*, *safe*, *salv*ation, *savi*or, *salv*age, [2]*sage*; +It.+Fr., *salvo*; +Span., *salv*er).
sanu-s, [Lat.], sound, healthy (*sane*, *san*ity, in*sane*, *san*itarium, *san*itation).
sarx, sark-os, [Gk.], flesh (*sarc*asm, *sarc*ophagus).
satis, [Lat.], enough (+Fr., [1]*sate*, *sat*iate, *satis*fy, *sat*urate).
scande-re, scansu-s, [Lat.], to climb (*scan*, a*scend*, tran*scend*; +Fr., de*scend*, conde*scend*).
sci-re, [Lat.], to know; **scientia,** knowledge (con*sci*ous, omni*sci*ent, uncon*sci*onable, *sci*olist; +Fr., *science*, *scien*tific, pre*science*, con*science*).
scribe-re, scriptu-s, [Lat.], to write (*scribe*, *scrib*ble, sub*scribe*, sub*script*, de*scribe*, de*script*ion, a*scribe*, pre*scribe*, pro*scribe*, tran*scribe*, circum*scribe*, in*scribe*, con*scrip*tion, manu*script*, post*script*, nonde*script*, *shrive*, *shrift*, *Shrove*tide; +Fr., *scrip*ture, *scriv*ener, *scrip*).
seca-re, sectu-s, seg-, [Lat.], to cut (*sec*ant, bi*sect*, dis*sect*, inter*sect*, *seg*ment, *sick*le; +Fr., *sect*ion, in*sect*; +It.+Fr., ri*sk*).
sedē-re, sessu-s, [Lat.], to sit (*sed*ate, as*sid*uous, *sess*ile, pos*sess*; +Fr., *sed*entary, *sess*ion, *sed*iment, in*sid*ious, as*sess*, as*size*, *siege*, [2]*see*, [2]*size*, pre*side*, pre*sid*ent, re*side*, re*sid*ent, re*sid*ue, sub*side*, sub*sid*iary, sub*sid*y, super*sede*, sur*cease*; +It., [1]*size*).
senex, [Lat.], old, **senior,** older (*senior*, *sen*ile; +Fr., *sen*ator, *seignor*, *sir*, *sire*; +It., *signor*).
senti-re, sensu-s, [Lat.], to feel, perceive (*sens*ation, *sens*ual, *sens*uous, non*sense*, con*sens*us, dis*sent*; +Fr., *senti*ment, *senti*mental, *senti*ent, *sense*, *scent*, *sent*ence, *sens*itive, *sens*ible, as*sent*, con*sent*, pre*senti*ment, re*sent*).
sequ-i, secutu-s, [Lat.], to follow (con*sequ*ent, sub*sequ*ent, pro*secute*, ob*sequ*ious; +Fr., *sequ*el, *sequ*ence, con*secu*tive, ex*ecute*, ex*equ*ies, ob*sequ*ies, per*secute*, pur*sue*, en*sue*, *sue*, *suit*, *suit*able, *suite*, *sect*, *second*). Akin to **socius.**
servu-s, [Lat.], servant, **serva-re, servatu-s,** to keep, protect, **servi-re,** to serve (*serv*ile, sub*serv*ient; +Fr., *serve*, *serf*, *serv*ant, *serge*ant, *serv*ice, con*serv*ation, de*serve*, [2]de*sert*, ob*serve*, pre*serve*, re*serve*, re*serv*oir).
sidus, sider-is, [Lat.], star (*sider*ial; +Fr., con*sider*).
signu-m, [Lat.], mark, token (*sign*ificant, in*sign*ia; +Fr., *sign*, *sign*al, *sign*ify, as*sign*, con*sign*, de*sign*, en*sign*, re*sign*, *sign*et).
simili-s, [Lat.], like, **simul,** together (*simil*e, as*simil*ate, *simul*ate, fac*simil*e, *simul*taneous; +Fr., *simil*ar, *simil*itude, dis*semble*, dis*simul*ation, dis*simil*ar, re*semble*).
sinu-s, [Lat.], a curve, fold of a garment, the bosom (*sinus*, *sine*, in*sinu*ate; +Fr., *sinu*ous, in*sinu*ation).
sociu-s, [Lat.], companion (*soci*al, as*soci*ate, dis*soci*ate; +Fr., *soci*able, *soci*ety). Akin to **sequi.**
sol, [Lat.], sun (*sol*ar; +Fr., *sol*stice).
solidu-s, [Lat.], solid (con*solid*ate, con*sol*; +Fr., *solid*, *solid*arity, *sold*er, *sold*ier).
solu-s, [Lat.], alone (*sol*iloquy, de*sol*ate; +Fr., [3]*sole*, *sol*itary, *sol*itude; +It., *solo*).
solve-re, solutu-s, [Lat.], to loose, dissolve (*solve*, *solv*ent, ab*solve*, ab*solute*, ab*solut*ion, dis*solve*, dis*solute*, re*solve*; +Fr., *solut*ion).
sona-re, sonitu-s, [Lat.], to resound (*sonor*ous, *son*ant, re*son*ant; +Fr., [2]*sound*, re*sound*, con*son*ant, uni*son*, per*son*, par*son*; +It., *sona*ta; +It.+Fr., *sonn*et).
sopho-s, [Gk.], wise, **soph-ia,** wisdom (*soph*omore, philo*soph*y, *soph*istry).
sors, sorti-s, [Lat.], destiny, chance, condition (con*sort*; +Fr., *sort*, as*sort*, re*sort*, *sorc*ery).
sparge-re, sparsu-s, [Lat.], to strew, scatter (*sparse*, a*sperse*, di*sperse*, inter*sperse*).
spece-re, spectu-s, spic-, [Lat.], to look, see (*spect*ator, *spec*ulate, *spect*rum, *spec*ies, *spec*imen, a*spect*, circum*spect*, con*spic*uous, de*spic*able, ex*pect*, in*spect*, per*spic*uous, pro*spect*, pro*spect*us, retro*spect*, su*spic*ion; +Fr., per*spect*ive, per*spic*acity, pro*spect*ive, re*spect*, re*spite*, re*spect*able, re*spect*ive, *spec*ial, e*spec*ial, *spec*ific, *spec*ious, *spect*acle, *spect*er, su*spect*, fronti*spiece*, au*spice*, *spice*).
spera-re, speratu-s, [Lat.], to hope (de*sper*ate, pro*sper*ous; +Fr., de*spair*, pro*sper*, pro*sper*ity; +Span., de*sper*ado).
spira-re, spiratu-s, [Lat.], to breathe, **spiritu-s,** breath, spirit (tran*spire*; +Fr., *spirit*, *sprite*, *spright*ly, a*spire*, a*spirate*, con*spire*, con*spir*acy, ex*pire*, in*spirat*ion, in*spire*, in*spirit*, per*spire*, per*spirat*ion, re*spire*, re*spirat*ion).
spondē-re, sponsu-s, [Lat.], to promise (*spons*or, de*spond*; +Fr., *spouse*, e*spouse*, re*spond*, corre*spond*, re*sponse*, re*spons*ible).
sta-re, status, stit-, [Lat.], to stand, **siste-re,** to place (*status*, con*stit*ute, con*stit*ution, ex*ist*, ex*tant*, in*sist*, pro*stit*ute, *sta*men; +Fr., *state*, *stat*ion, *stat*ure, *stat*ionary, *stat*ionery, [1]*sta*ble, [2]*sta*ble, armi*stice*, sol*stice*, inter*stice*, arre*st*, as*sist*, con*sist*, con*sist*ent, de*sist*, per*sist*, re*sist*, sub*sist*, con*stit*ute, re*stit*ution, sub*stit*ute, super*stit*ion, sub*stant*ial, circum*stance*, di*stant*, di*stance*, in*stance*, in*stant*, sub*sist*ence, sub*stance*, con*stant*, con*stancy*, *stage*, sub*stant*ive, ob*sta*cle, con*sta*ble, e*sta*blish).
stasi-s, [Gk.], a standing, a placing, **stato-s,** placed (ec*stasy*, apo*stasy*, *stat*ic).
sterne-re, stratu-s, [Lat.], to stretch out, strew about, make smooth (*stratum*, *strat*ify, pro*strate*, *street*; +Fr., *stray*, con*stern*ation).
stringe-re, strictu-s, [Lat.], to bind (a*string*ent, *strict*, *strict*ure, con*strict*, re*strict*; +Fr., con*strain*, con*strain*t, di*strain*, di*strain*t, *stress*, di*stress*, di*strict*, re*strain*).
stroph-ē, [Gk.], a turning (*strophe*, apo*strophe*, cata*strophe*).
strue-re, structu-s, [Lat.], to build, construct (con*struct*, con*struct*ion, con*strue*, in*struct*, ob*struct*; +Fr., *struct*ure, in*stru*ment, de*stroy*, de*struct*ive, de*struct*ion).
suadē-re, suasu-s, [Lat.], to advise (+Fr., per*suade*, dis*suade*, *suas*ion).
sume-re, sumptu-s, [Lat.], to take (as*sume*, as*sumpt*ion, con*sume*, con*sumpt*ion; +Fr., pre*sume*, pre*sumpt*ion, re*sume*, *sumpt*uous).
super, [Lat.], above, **superior,** higher, **supremu-s,** highest (*super*cilious, the prefix *super-*; +Fr., *superior*, *super*lative, *super*b, *super*abundance, *supreme*, the prefix [1]*sur-*).
surge-re, surrectu-s, [Lat.: *sub*+*regere*], to rise (in*surg*ent; +Fr., *surge*, in*surrect*ion, re*surrect*ion, *sort*ie, *source*).
tacē-re, tacitu-s, tic-, [Lat.], to be silent (*tacit*, re*tic*ent; +Fr., *tacit*urn).
tange-re, tactu-s, tig-, teg-, [Lat.], to touch (*tang*ent, *tang*o, *tact*, *tact*ile, in*tact*, con*tact*, con*tig*uous, con*ting*ent, con*tam*inate, in*teg*er, in*teg*ral; +Fr., *tang*ible, con*tag*ion, en*tire*, en*tire*ty, in*teg*rity, *tax* (for *tacs*), task (for *tasc*), *taste*).
taxi-s, [Gk.], order, arrangement, **takto-s,** arranged (syn*tax*, *tact*ical).
tege-re, tectu-s, [Lat.], to cover, **toga,** toga, **tegula,** tile (*teg*ument, in*teg*ument, de*tect*, de*tect*ive, pro*tect*, *toga*, *tile*; +Fr., pro*tegé*).
tempus, tempor-is, [Lat.], time, **tempera-re,** to modify, regulate (*tempor*ary, con*tempor*ary, ex*tempor*aneous, *temper*, *temper*ament; +Fr., *tempor*al, [2]*temple*, *tempera*ture, [2]*tense*, *tamper*, *tempest*, *temper*ance).
tende-re, tensu-s or **tentu-s,** [Lat.], to stretch, extend (*tend*, *tend*ency, [1]*tense*, *tens*ion, dis*tend*, ex*tend*, ex*tent*, ex*tens*ive, ex*tens*ion, in*tense*, os*tens*ible, por*tend*, pre*tense*, pre*tens*ion, sub*tend*; +Fr., at*tend*,

at*tent*ion, con*tend*, con*tent*ious, in*tend*, in*tent*, os*tent*ation, por*tent*ous, pre*tend*, superin*tend*, *tend*on, [1]*tent*, *tent*er, [1]*tend*er, [2]*tend*er).

tenē-re, tentu-s, tin-, [Lat.], to hold (*ten*acious, *tenet*, con*tin*ual; +Fr., *ten*ure, *ten*able, abs*tain*, abs*tin*ence, con*tain*, [1]con*tent*, [2]con*tent*, con*tin*ue, coun*ten*ance, con*ti*nent, de*tain*, de*ten*tion, enter*tain*, lieu*ten*ant, main*tain*, ob*tain*, per*tain*, apper*tain*, appur*ten*ance, per*tin*ent, per*tin*acious, re*tain*, re*ten*tive, re*tin*ue, rein, sus*tain*, sus*ten*ance, *ten*ant, *ten*ement, *ten*on, *ten*or).

tenui-s, [Lat.], slender; **tener,** delicate, soft (at*tenu*ate, ex*tenu*ate; +Fr., *tenu*ous, *tenu*ity, [3]*tend*er, *tend*ril).

tere-re, tritu-s, [Lat.], to wear by rubbing (*trite*, *tritu*rate, de*tritus*; +Fr., con*trite*, de*tri*ment, *tri*bulation, at*trit*ion).

terminu-s, [Lat.], bound, limit (*termin*ate, ex*terminate*; +Fr., *term*, de*termine*).

terra, [Lat.], the earth (*terr*aqueous, sub*ter*ranean, *terr*estrial, *terra* firma; +Fr., in*ter*, *ter*rain, *terr*itory, *tu*reen; +It.+Fr., *terra*ce; +It., *terra* cotta).

terrē-re, territu-s, [Lat.], to frighten (de*ter*, *terr*ific; +Fr., *terr*or, *terr*ible, *terr*ify).

testi-s, [Lat.], a witness (at*test*, *test*ator, *test*imony, in*test*ate; +Fr., con*test*, de*test*, pro*test*, Pro*test*ant, *test*ament, *test*ify).

texe-re, textu-s, [Lat.], to weave (con*text*, *tex*tile; +Fr., *text*, pre*text*, *text*ure, *text*ual, [2]*toil*, *tissue*).

thesi-s, [Gk.], a placing, **them-a,** a thing placed (*thesis*, syn*thesis*, hypo*thesis*, anti*thet*ic, epi*thet*, *the*saurus, *theme*, ana*thema*).

theo-s, [Gk.], god (*theo*logy, *theo*cracy, mono*the*ism, a*the*ism, pan*the*ism).

timē-re, [Lat.], to fear, **timidu-s,** fearful (*tim*orous, in*timid*ate; +Fr., *timid*).

tinge-re, tinctu-s, [Lat.], to wet; to dye (*tinge*, *tint*, *tinct*ure; +Fr., *taint*, *stain*).

tolle-re, latu-s (for obs. **tolatus, tlatus**), [Lat.], to raise (ex*tol*, *tol*erate). For derivatives of *latus*, see [3]**latus**.

tom-ē, [Gk.], a cutting (*tome*, ana*tomy*, tonsillec*tomy*).

torquē-re, tortu-s, [Lat.], to twist (con*tort*ion, dis*tort*, ex*tort*, re*tort*; +Fr., ex*tort*ion, *tor*ment, *tort*ure, *tort*uous, *tort*, *tors*ion).

trade-re, traditu-s, [Lat.], to give over (*tradit*ion; +Fr., *trea*son, *trait*or, be*tray*).

trahe-re, tractu-s, [Lat.], to draw (sub*trah*end, [2]*tract*, *tract*able, abs*tract*, at*tract*, con*tract*, de*tract*, dis*tract*, dis*traught*, ex*tract*, pro*tract*, sub*tract*; +Fr., por*tray*, por*trait*, re*tract*, *trace*, *trail*, *treat*, *trait*, *tract*ion).

treme-re, [Lat.], to shake (*trem*or, *trem*ulous, *trem*endous; +Fr., *trem*ble).

tre-s, [Lat.], three (*tri*ennial, the prefix *tri-*; +Fr., *triple*. *tri*nity, *tri*vial; +It., *trio*).

tribue-re, tributu-s, [Lat.], to assign, pay, give (at*tribute*, con*tribute*, dis*tribute*; +Fr., *tribute*, *tribut*ary, re*tribut*ion).

tropo-s, [Gk.], a turning (*trop*ic, *trope*).

trude-re, trusu-s, [Lat.], to push (in*trude*, ex*trude*, in*trus*ive, ob*trude*, pro*trude*, ab*struse*).

tumē-re, [Lat.], to swell, **tumidu-s,** swollen (*tumid*, *tu*ber; +Fr., *tum*or, con*tum*acy).

turba, [Lat.], crowd, bustle (*turb*id, imper*turb*able; +Fr., *turb*ulent, dis*turb*, per*turba*tion, *trou*ble).

ultra, [Lat.], beyond, **ulterior,** farther, **ultimu-s,** farthest, last (*ulterior*, *ultim*ate, *ultim*atum; +Fr., *out*rage, the prefix *ultra-*).

umbra, [Lat.], shade (*umbel*; +Fr., *umbr*age, *umbr*ageous, *somber*; +It., *umbr*ella; +It. +Fr., *umber*).

unda, [Lat.], wave (in*und*ate, red*und*ant, *und*ulate, +Fr., ab*und*ant, ab*ound*, red*ound*).

ungue-re, unctu-s, [Lat.], to anoint (*ungu*ent; +Fr., *unct*ion, *unct*uous, *oint*ment, an*oint*).

unu-s, [Lat.], one (*uni*te, *un*animous, the prefix *uni-*; +Fr., *uni*ty, *un*ion, *un*ique, *uni*son, *uni*t, *uni*verse).

ut-i, usu-s, [Lat.], to use (+Fr., *use*, *us*age, *us*ual, *us*ury, *ut*ility, *ut*ensil, ab*use*, per*use*).

vade-re, vasu-s, [Lat.], to go (per*vade*, per*vas*ive; +Fr., e*vade*, e*vas*ion, in*vade*).

vaga-re, vagatu-s, [Lat.], to wander (*vag*ary; +Fr., extra*vag*ant, *vag*abond, *vague*). *Vagrant* is from an Old High German source, akin to *walk*.

valē-re, [Lat.], to be strong, **validu-s,** strong (con*val*escent, in*valid*, in*valid*ate, *val*edictory; +Fr., *val*iant, *valid*, *val*ue, *val*or, *val*uation, in*val*uable, *val*entine, equi*val*ent, a*vail*, pre*vail*, pre*val*ent, *val*etudinarian).

vehe-re, vectu-s, [Lat.], to carry (*veh*icle, in*veigh*, con*vex*; +Fr., in*vect*ive).

vende-re, [Lat.: *venum* + *dare*], to sell, **venu-m,** sale (+Fr., *vend*, *vend*er, *ven*al).

veni-re, ventu-s, [Lat.], to come (ad*vent*, circum*vent*, con*vent*, con*veni*ent, e*vent*, e*vent*ual, pre*vent*, super*vene*; +Fr., ad*vent*ure, a*ven*ue, contra*vene*, con*vene*, con*vent*ion, con*vent*ional, co*ven*ant, inter*vene*, in*vent*, *venue*, re*ven*ue, *vent*ure).

ventu-s, [Lat.], wind (*vent*ilate).

verbu-m, [Lat.], word (*verb*ose, *verbatim*; +Fr., *verb*, *verb*al, *verb*iage, ad*verb*, pro*verb*).

vermi-s, [Lat.], worm (*verm*icular, *vermi*form, *vermi*fuge; +Fr., *verm*in, *verm*ilion; +It., *verm*icelli).

verte-re, versu-s, vort-, [Lat.], to turn (*verse*, *vert*ex, *vert*ical, *vort*ex, *vert*ebra ad*vert*, anni*vers*ary, anim*advers*ion, a*vert*, a*vers*ion, contro*vert*, in*vert*, in*vers*ion, trans*verse*, inad*vert*ent, ob*verse*, *vert*igo; +Fr., ad*verse*, ad*vers*ity, ad*vers*ary, ad*vert*ise, contro*vers*y, con*vert*, con*verse*, di*vert*, di*verse*, di*vers*ity, di*vers*ify, di*vers*, di*vorce*, in*verse*, per*vert*, per*verse*, re*vert*, re*verse*, sub*vert*, sub*vers*ive, trans*verse*, *vers*atile, *vers*ion).

veru-s, [Lat.], true (*ver*acious; +Fr., *ver*ity, *ver*ify, *ver*itable, *ver*y, *ver*ily, *ver*isimilitude).

vesti-s, [Lat.], garment (*vest*; +Fr., in*vest*, *vest*ure, *vest*ment, *ves*try).

vetus, veter-is, [Lat.], old (*veter*an, *veter*inary, in*veter*ate).

via, [Lat.], way, road (*via*, *via*duct, *via*ticum, de*vi*ate, ob*vi*ate, ob*vi*ous, imper*vi*ous, pre*vi*ous; +Fr., tri*vi*al, con*vey*, con*voy*, *voy*age, in*voi*ce). *Viable* is from Lat. **vita**.

vic-is, [Lat.], change, alternation (*vic*arious; +Fr., *vic*ar, *vic*issitude, *vic*eroy, [3]*vice*, [4]*vice*).

vidē-re, visu-s, [Lat.], to see (*vide*, *vide*licet, pro*vide*, pro*viso*, super*vis*ion; +Fr., *vis*ion, *vis*ible, *vis*it, *vis*ual, *vis*or, *vis*age, *view*, e*vid*ent, pro*vis*ion, pro*vid*ent, pru*dent*, pur*vey*or, sur*vey*, re*vise*, *vis-à-vis*, ad*vice*).

vince-re, victu-s, [Lat.], to conquer (con*vince*, con*vict*, con*vict*ion, e*vince*, *vict*or; +Fr., in*vinc*ible, pro*vinc*e, *van*quish, *vict*ory).

vindex, vindic-is, [Lat.], defender, avenger (*vindic*ate; +Fr., *vindic*tive, a*venge*, re*venge*).

vinu-m, [Lat.], wine (*vin*ous; +Fr., *vine*, *vine*gar, *vin*tage, *vin*tner). *Wine* is from a kindred A.S. word.

vir, [Lat.], man, **virtus, virtut-is,** manly excellence (*vir*ago; +Fr., *vir*ile, *virtue*, *virtu*al).

vita, [Lat.], life, **vive-re, victu-s,** to live (*vita*min, *vita*scope, con*viv*ial, *viv*id, *viv*iparous, *viv*isection; +Fr., *vi*able, *vita*l, *via*nd, re*vive*, sur*vive*, *vict*uals, *viv*acity, *viv*ify).

vol-o, [Lat.], I wish (male*vol*ent; +Fr., bene*vol*ent, *vol*untary, *vol*unteer, *vol*uptuous).

volve-re, volutu-s, [Lat.], to roll (re*volve*, e*volve*, de*volve*, *vol*uminous, con*volut*ion, con*volv*ulus, in*volute*; +Fr., in*volute*, re*volu*tion, *volu*ble, *vol*ume, *volute*, [1]*vault*, [2]*vault*; +It.+Fr., re*volt*).

vox, voc-is, [Lat.], voice, **voca-re, vocatu-s,** to call (ad*vocate*, a*vocat*ion, con*voke*, con*vocat*ion, equi*vocate*, equi*voc*al, in*vocat*ion; +Fr., *voc*al, *vow*el, *voice*, *vouch*, *voc*ative, *vocat*ion, *voc*able, *voc*abulary, in*voke*, pro*voke*, re*voke*, irre*voc*able, *voc*iferate).

vulgus, [Lat.], the people, **vulgar-is,** common, ordinary (*vulg*ate; +Fr., *vulgar*, di*vulge*).

ABBREVIATIONS USED IN WRITING AND PRINTING

A

a. about; acre; active; adjectival or adjective (also, **adj.**); adjourned; afternoon; are (metric system); at: also written @:—**A** argon:—**A.** Academician; Academy; adulteress; America(n); Artillery.
A. A. Associate of Arts.
A. A. A. Amateur Athletic Association; Agricultural Adjustment Act.
A. A. A. S. American Academy of Arts and Sciences; American Association for the Advancement of Science.
A. A. C. [Lat. *anno ante Christum*], in the (designated) year before Christ.
A. A. G. Assistant Adjutant General.
A. A. of A. Automobile Association of America.
A. A. U. Amateur Athletic Union.
ab. about:—**a. b.** able-bodied (seaman); in baseball, at bat (also, **A.B.**): —**A. B.** [Lat. *artium baccalaureus*], Bachelor of Arts (also, **B. A.**).
abbr., abbrev. abbreviated; abbreviation.
A. B. C. F. M. American Board of Commissioners of Foreign Missions.
A. B. F. M. American Board of Foreign Missions.
abl. ablative.
Abp. Archbishop.
abr. abridged; abridgment.
abs. absent; absolute; abstract:—**A. B. S.** American Bible Society.
Ac actinium:—**A. C.** Archchancellor; Army Corps; alternating current; [Lat. *ante Christum*], before Christ.
acad. academy.
acc. acceptance; account (also, **a/c**); accountant (also, **acct.**); accusative.
accel. [It. *accelerando*], gradually increasing in speed.
ad., adv., advt. advertisement.
a. d. after date; [Lat. *ante diem*], before the (specified) day:—**A. D.** [Lat. *anno Domini*], in the (specified) year of our Lord.
A. D. C. Aid-de-camp; Aide-de-camp.
ad fin. [Lat. *ad finem*], at the end.
ad inf. [Lat. *ad infinitum*], to infinity.
ad init. [Lat. *ad initium*], at the beginning.
ad int. [Lat. *ad interim*], in the meantime; meanwhile.
adj. adjectival or adjective (also, **a.**); adjourned.
Adj., Adjt. Adjutant.
Adj. Gen., A. G., Adjt. Gen. Adjutant General.
ad lib. [Lat. *ad libitum*], at pleasure.
ad loc. [Lat. *ad locum*], at the place.
Adm. Admiral; Admiralty.
admin. administration; administrator (also, **admr.**).
admix., admrx., admx. administratrix.
adv. adverb; adverbial advertisement (also, **ad., advt.**); advocate; [Lat. *ad valorem*], according to value; [Lat. *adversus*], against:—**Adv.** Advent.
æ., æt., ætat. [Lat. *ætatis*], of age; aged.
A. E. F. American Expeditionary Forces.
aëro. aëronautics.
a. f. firkin of ale.
A.–F., A. F. Anglo-French.
A. F. A. M. Ancient Free and Accepted Masons.
A. F. of L., A. F. L. American Federation of Labor.
Afr. Africa; African.
ag., agr., agric. agriculture; agricultural.
Ag [Lat. *argentum*], silver:—**A. G.** Adjutant General; Attorney-General.
agt. against; agent.
A. H. [Lat. *anno hegiræ*], in the year of the hegira.
A. I. American Institute.
Al aluminum:—**A. L.** American Legion.
Ala. Alabama (official):—**A. L. A.** American Library Association; Automobile Legal Association.
Alas. Alaska.
ald., aldm. alderman.
Alex. Alexander.
alg. algebra:—**Alg.** Algerian; Algiers; Algernon.
alt. alternate; altitude; alto.
Alta. Alberta, Canada (official).
Am., A., Amer. America; American.
a. m., A. M. [Lat. *ante meridiem*], before noon.
A. M. [Lat. *anno mundi*], in the year of the world; [Lat. *artium magister*], Master of Arts (also, **M. A.**); [Lat. *Ave Maria*], Hail, Mary.
A. M. A. American Medical Association.
Amer. Ind. American Indian.
amt. amount.
an. anonymous (also, **anon.**); [Lat. *anno*], in the (specified) year.
A.-N. Anglo-Norman.
anal. analogous; analogy; analysis; analytic.
anat. anatomy; anatomist.
anc. ancient; anciently.
Angl. Anglican.
Angl. Ch. Anglican Church.
Ang.–Sax., A. S., A.–S. Anglo-Saxon.
anon., an. anonymous.
ans. answer.
ant. antonym:—**Ant.** Anthony; Antigua.
antiq. antiquarian; antiquities; antiquity.
A. N. Z. A. C., Anzac Australian and New Zealand Army Corps.
A. O. F. Ancient Order of Foresters.
aor. aorist.
Ap., Apl., Apr. April.
Ap. Apostle:—**A. P.** Associated Press; author's proof.
A. P. A. American Philological Association; American Protective Association.
Apoc. Apocalypse; Apocrypha(l).
app. appendix; appointed.
approx. approximately.
Apr., Ap., Apl. April.
aq. [Lat. *aqua*], water.
A. Q. M. G. Assistant Quartermaster-General.
ar. arrival or arrive (also, **arr.**):—**Ar.** Arabia; Arabian; Arabic:—**A. R.** [Lat. *anno regni*], in the (specified) year of the reign.
A. R. A. Associate of the Royal Academy (of Arts, London).
Arab., Ar. Arabian; Arabic.
Aram. Aramaic.
A R C E C All-Russian Central Executive Committee.
arch. archaic; archaism; archery; archipelago; architect; architecture:—**Arch.** Archibald.
archæol. archæology.
Archd. Archdeacon; Archduke.
arith. arithmetic.
Ariz. Arizona (official).
Ark. Arkansas (official).
Arm. Armenian.
arr. arranged; arrival or arrive (also, **ar.**):—**A. R. R.** [Lat. *anno regni regis* (or *reginæ*)], in the year of the king's (or queen's) reign.
art. article; artificial; artillery; artist.
As arsenic:—**As.** Asia; Asiatic:—**A. S.** Academy of Science.
A.–S., A.S., Ang.–Sax. Anglo-Saxon.:—**A.S.A.** American Statistical Association.

A. S. C. E. American Society of Civil Engineers.
A. S. M. E. American Society of Mechanical Engineers.
assist., asst. assistant.
assoc. associate; association (also, **assn.**).
A. S. S. U. American Sunday-School Union.
Assyr. Assyrian.
astr., astron. astronomer; astronomy; astronomical.
astrol. astrologer; astrology.
Atl. Atlantic.
att., atty. attorney.
attrib. attributive.
at. wt. atomic weight.
au. author:—**Au** [Lat. *aurum*], gold.
A. U. C. [Lat. *ab urbe condita*], from the founding of the city (Rome, about 753 B. C.).
Aug. August; Augustan; Augustus.
Aus., Aust. Austria(n).
Aust.-Hung. Austria-Hungary.
Austral. Australasia(n); Australia(n).
Auth. Ver., A. V. Authorized Version (of the Bible).
aux., auxil. auxiliary.
av. avenue (also, **ave.**); average; avoirdupois (also, **avdp., avoir.**):—**a.v.** [Lat. *ad valorem*], according to value; [Lat. *annos vixit*] he (or she) lived (so many) years:—**A. V.** Artillery Volunteers; Authorized Version (of the Bible).
avdp., av., avoir. avoirdupois.
ave., av. avenue.

B

b. base; bass; bay; book; born; brother (also, **br., bro.**):—**B** boron.
Ba barium:—**B. A.** British Academy; British America (also, **Br. Am.**); British Association (for the Advancement of Science); [Lat. *baccalaureus artium*], Bachelor of Arts (also, **A. B.**).
bacter., bacteriol. bacteriologist; bacteriology.
B. Agr. Bachelor of Agriculture.
bal. balance.
Bapt. Baptist.
bar. barometer; barometric; barrel (also, **bbl.**).
Bart., Bt. Baronet.
bat. battle; battalion (also, **batt., bn.**); battery (also, **batt.**).
bbl., bar., bl. barrel.
B. C. before Christ; British Columbia.
B. C. L. Bachelor of Civil Law.
bd. board:— **B. D.** Bachelor of Divinity.
bdl. bundle.
b. e. bill of exchange:—**Be** beryllium:—**B. E.** Bachelor of Engineering.
B. E. F. British Expeditionary Forces.
Bel., Belg. Belgian; Belgium.
Benj. Benjamin.
B. ès L. [Fr. *bachelier ès lettres*], Bachelor of Letters.
bet. between.
b. f. boldface.
bg. bag.
b. h. p. brake horse power.
Bi bismuth:—**B. I.** British India.
Bib. Bible; Biblical.
biog. biographer; biography; biographical.
biol. biologist; biology.
bk. bank; book.
bkg. banking.
bkt. basket.
bl. bale; barrel (also, **bar., bbl.**):—**b. l.** bill of lading:—**B. L.** [Lat. *baccalaureus legis*], Bachelor of Law.
bldg. building.
B. L. E. Brotherhood of Locomotive Engineers.
B. Litt. [Lat. *baccalaureus litterarum*], Bachelor of Literature (or of Letters).
Blvd. boulevard.
B. M. Bachelor of Medicine; Bachelor of Metallurgy; Brigade Major.
B. M., B. Mus. Bachelor of Music (also, **Mus. B.**); British Museum.
Bn. Baron; battalion.
B. O. buyer's option.
Bohem. Bohemia(n).
Bol. Bolivia.
bor. borough.
bot. botanical; botanist; botany; bottle;—**B. O. T.** Board of Trade.
Bp. Bishop:—**b. p.** below proof; bill of parcels; bills payable.
B. Ph. Bachelor of Philosophy.
bpl. birthplace.
B. P. O. E. Benevolent and Protective Order of Elks.
br. brig; brother (also, **b., bro.**); brown:—**Br** bromine.
Br., Brit. Britain; British.
Br. Am., B. A. British America.
Braz. Brazil; Brazilian.
b. rec. bills receivable.
Brig. Brigade; Brigadier.
Brig. Gen. Brigadier General.
Brit., Br. Britain; British.
Brit. Mus., B. M., B. Mus. British Museum.
bro., b., br. brother.
b. s. balance sheet; bill of sale:—**B. S.** Bachelor of Science (also, **B. Sc.**); Bachelor of Surgery.
B. S. E. Bachelor of Science in Education.
Bt., Bart. Baronet.
bu. bushel.
Bulg. Bulgaria; Bulgarian.
B. V. [Lat. *beata virgo*], Blessed Virgin.
B. V. M. [Lat. *beata virgo Maria*], Blessed Virgin Mary.
bx. box.

C

c. carton; cathode; cent; centime; centimeter (also, **cm.**); century (also, **cent.**); chapter (also, **cap., chap.**); child; cost; cubic (also, **cu.**); current; [Lat. *centum*], 100; [Lat. *circa*], about (also, **circ.**):—**C** carbon:—**C.** Cape; Catholic; Centigrade; Chancellor; Congress; Conservative; Consul; Corps; Court.
Ca calcium:—**C. A.** Chartered Accountant; Chief Accountant; Commercial Agent; Confederate Army; Court of Appeals.
Calif. (official), **Cal.** California.
Camb. Cambridge.
Can. Canada; Canadian.
Cant. Canterbury; Canticles.
Cantab. [Lat. *Cantabrigiensis*], of Cambridge; Cantabrigian.
Cantuar. [Lat. *Cantuaria*], (of) Canterbury.
cap. capital; capitalize; captain; [Lat. *capitulum*], chapter (also, **ch., chap.**).
Capt., Cap. Captain.
Card. Cardinal.
Carib. Caribbean.
carp. carpentry.
cash. cashier.
cath. cathedral:—**Cath.** Catherine; Catholic.
Cav. Cavalry.
Cb columbium:—**C. B.** Cape Breton; Cavalry Brigade; Common Bench.
c.c. cubic centimeter (also, **cc.**):—**C. C.** Circuit Court; City Controller; City Councilor; Civil Court; Common Councilman; County Clerk; County Commissioner.
C. C. A. Circuit Court of Appeals.
Cd cadmium.
c. e. [Lat. *caveat emptor*], let the buyer beware; at the buyer's risk:—**Ce** cerium:—**C. E.** Christian Endeavor (Society); Civil Engineer; Church of England; Common Era: used by the Jews for A. D.; Corps of Engineers.
cel. celebrated.
Celt. Celtic.
cen. center; central; century (also, **c.**).
Cen. Am. Central America.
cent. centigrade (also, **C., centig.**); central; century (also, **c.**); [Lat. *centum*], 100 (also, **c.**).
cf. [Lat. *confer*], compare (also, **comp., cp.**).
c. f. & i., c. i. & f., c. i. f. cost, freight, and insurance.
cg. centigram:—**C. G.** Coast Guard; Commanding General; Commissary General; Consul General.
C. G. H. Cape of Good Hope.
C. G. S. centimeter, gram, second (system of units); Chief of General Staff; Commissary General of Subsistence.
ch. chapter (also, **cap., chap.**); chief; child:—**Ch.** Chancery; China; Church:—**C. H.** Clearing House; Courthouse; Customhouse.
chap. chaplain; chapter.
Chas. Charles.
chem. chemical; chemist; chemistry.
Ch. Hist. Church History.
Chin. China; Chinese.

Ch. J., C. J. Chief Justice
Chr. Christ; Christian; Christopher (also, **Chris.**).
chron. chronological; chronology (also, **chronol.**):—**Chron.** Chronicles.
c. i. & f., c. i. f., c. f. & i. cost, insurance, and freight.
circ., c., cir. circumference; circus; [Lat. *circa, circiter, circum*], about.
C. J. Chief Judge; Chief Justice.
cl. centiliter; class; clause; clergyman (also, **clergy.**); cloth:—**Cl** chlorine.
class. classic(al); classification; classified:—**Class. Myth.** Classical Mythology.
clergy., cl. clergyman.
clk. clerk.
C. L. S. C. Chautauqua Literary and Scientific Circle:—**C. L. U.** Chartered Life Underwriter.
cm. centimeter (also, **c.**):—**C. M.** common meter; Corresponding Member; Court-martial; [Lat. *chirurgiæ magister*], Master in Surgery.
cml., com., coml. commercial.
c. o. care of: also written **c/o**; carried over:—**Co** cobalt:—**Co.** company; county:—**C. O.** Commanding Officer; conscientious objector.
cod. codex:—**C. O. D.** cash, or collect, on delivery.
cog. cognate.
col. college; collegiate; colonial; colony; color; column:—**Col.** colonel; Colorado (officially, **Colo.**); Colossians.
coll. colleague; collection; collector; college.
colloq. colloquial(ly).
Colo. (official), **Col.** Colorado.
com. comedy; commentary; commerce; commercial (also, **cml., coml.**); common(ly); commune; communication:—**Com.** Commander; Commission(er); Committee; Commodore.
comb. combination.
Comdg. Commanding.
Comdr., Com. Commander.
Comdt. Commandant.
coml., cml., com. commercial.
comp. compare (also, **cf., cp.**); comparative; composer; compositor; compound; comprising.
Com. Ver. Common Version (of the Bible).
con. [Lat. *contra*], against.
Confed. Confederate; Confederation.
Cong. Congregational; Congregationalist; Congress; Congressional.
conj. conjunction.
Conn. Connecticut (official).
conq. conqueror.
cont. containing; contents; continent; continue(d).
contemp. contemporary.
contr. contract; contracted; contraction; contrary.
cor. corner; cornet:—**cor., corr.** corrected; correction; correlative; correspondent; corresponding; corrupted; corruption.
Cor. Corinthians.
Corp. Corporal.
cos cosine:—**Cos.** Cossack.
cosec, csc cosecant.
cot cotangent.
cp., comp., cf. compare.
c. p. candle power; chemically pure:—**C. P.** Common Pleas; Common Prayer; Court of Probate.
C. P. A. Certified Public Accountant.
C. P. S. Clerk of the Petty Sessions; [Lat. *custos privati sigilli*], Keeper of the Privy Seal.
cr. created; credit; creditor; crown:—**Cr** chromium.
cres., cresc. [It. *crescendo*], with a gradual increase in sound or volume.
Cs cæsium:—**C. S.** Christian Science; Civil Service; Court of Sessions.
C. S. A. Confederate States Army; Confederate States of America.
csc cosecant (also, **cosec**):—**C. S. C.** Conspicuous-Service Cross.
C. S. N. Confederate States Navy.
C. S. O. Chief Signal Officer.
ct. cent (also, **c.**); count:—**Ct.** Connecticut (officially, **Conn.**); Count; Court.
cu., c., cub. cubic.
Cu [Lat. *cuprum*], copper.
C. V. Common Version (of the Bible).
c. w. o. cash with order.
cwt. [Lat. *centum*+weight], hundredweight(s).
cyc., cyclo. cyclopedia; cyclopedic.
C. Z. Canal Zone.

D

d. date; daughter; day; dead; degree; deputy; died; dime; dollar; [Lat. *denarius*, or *denarii*], penny, or pence:—**D.** Democrat; Department (also, **dep., dept., dpt.**); Dutch (also, **Du.**); [Lat. *Deus*], God; [Lat. *Dominus*], Lord.
Dan. Daniel; Danish.
D. A. R. Daughters of the American Revolution.
dat. dative.
dau. daughter.
d. b. daybook.
dbk. drawback.
D. C. direct current; District Court; District of Columbia; Doctor of Chiropractic; [It. *da capo*], from the beginning.
D. C. L. Doctor of Civil Law.
D. C. M. Distinguished-Conduct Medal.
d. d. days after date:—**D. D.** Doctor of Divinity.
D. D. S. Doctor of Dental Surgery.
Dea. Deacon.
dec. deceased; declension (also, **decl.**); declination:—**Dec.** December.
def. defendant (also, **dft.**); defined; definition.
deg. degree.
del. delegate; [Lat. *delineavit*], he (or she) drew it:—**Del.** Delaware (official).
Dem. Democrat(ic).
Den. Denmark (official).
dep. department; departs; deponent; deputy.
depend. dependency.
dept. department (also, **D., dep., dpt.**); deponent.
der., deriv. derivation; derivative; derive; derived.
Deut. Deuteronomy.
D. F. Dean of the Faculty; [Lat. *defensor fidei*], Defender of the Faith.
D. F. C. Distinguished-Flying Cross.
D. F. M. Distinguished-Flying Medal.
dft. defendant (also, **def.**); draft.
dg. decigram:—**D. G.** Director General; [Lat. *Dei gratia*], by the grace of God; [Lat. *Deo gratias*], thanks to God.
Di didymium.
dial. dialect; dialectic.
diam. diameter.
dict. dictator; dictionary.
dim. diminutive; [It. *diminuendo*], gradually growing softer in sound.
disc. discount; discovered; discoverer.
dist. distant; distinct; distinguished; district.
div. divide; divided; dividend; divine; division; divisor.
dl. deciliter.
D. Lit. Doctor of Literature.
D. L. O. Dead Letter Office.
dm. decimeter.
D. M. S. Director of Medical Service.
do. ditto:—**D. O.** Doctor of Osteopathy.
dol. dollar; dollars.
dom. domestic:—**Dom.** Dominion.
doz. dozen(s).
D. Pd. Doctor of Pedagogy (also, **Pd. D.**).
D. P. O. Distributing Post Office.
dpt., dep., dept. deponent; department.
dr. dram; drawer:—**Dr.** debtor; Doctor:—**D. R.** Dutch Reformed.
dram. dramatist.
dram. pers. [Lat. *dramatis personæ*], the characters or persons in a play.
d. s. [It. *dal segno*], from the sign: a musical direction; daylight saving; days after sight:—**D. S.** Dental Surgeon; Director of Supplies.
D. Sc. Doctor of Science:—**D. S. C.** Distinguished-Service Cross.
D. S. M. Distinguished-Service Medal.
D. S. O. Distinguished-Service Order (British Army and Navy).
d. s. p. [Lat. *decessit sine prole*], died without issue.
d. t.'s delirium tremens.
Du., D. Dutch.
D. V. [Lat. *Deo volente*], God willing.
D. V. M. Doctor of Veterinary Medicine.

dwt. [Lat. *denarius* + weight], pennyweight(s) (also, **pwt.**).
Dy dysprosium.

E

E. Earl; earth; east; eastern; engineer; English.
ea. each.
E. & O. E. errors and omissions excepted.
e. c. [Lat. *exempli causa*], for the sake of example:—**E. C.** Eastern Central (postal district of London); Established Church.
eccl., eccles. ecclesiastic; ecclesiastical:—**Eccl., Eccles.** Ecclesiastes.
Ecclus. Ecclesiasticus.
Ecua. Ecuador.
ed., edit. edited; edition; editor:—**E. D.** Eastern Department.
E. D. S. English Dialect Society.
educ. educator.
Edw. Edward.
E. E. Early English; Electrical Engineer; errors excepted.
E. E. & M. P. Envoy Extraordinary and Minister Plenipotentiary.
E. E. T. S. Early English Text Society.
E. F. Expeditionary Forces.
e. g. [Lat. *exempli gratia*], for the sake of example; for example:—**Eg.** Egypt; Egyptian.
E. I. East India; East Indies.
E. I. C. East India Company.
elec., elect. electrical; electrician; electricity.
Eliz. Elizabeth; Elizabethan.
E. long. east longitude.
Em. Emmanuel:—**E. M.** Earl Marshal.
e. m. f., emf. electromotive force.
Emp. Emperor; Empress.
ency., encyc. encyclopedia.
E. N. E. east-northeast.
eng. engineer; engineering (also, **engin.**); engraving:—**Eng.** England; English.
Ens. Ensign.
entom. entomology.
E. O. Engineer Officer.
Eph. Ephesians; Ephraim.
Epiph. Epiphany.
Epis., Episc. Episcopal.
eq. equal; equation; equator; equivalent (also, **equiv.**).
Er erbium.
E. S. E. east-southeast.
esp., espec. especially.
Esp. Esperanto.
Esq., Esqr. Esquire.
est. established (also, **estab.**); estate; estuary.
Esth. Esther.
Et ethyl:—**E. T.** electric telegraph; English translation.
et al. [Lat. *et alibi*], and elsewhere; [Lat. *et alii*], and others.
etc. [Lat. *et cetera*], and other things; and so forth.
et seq., et sq. [Lat. *et sequens*], and the following.
ety., etym., etymol. etymology.
Eu europium.
ex. examined; example; exception; exchange; executive; export; extract.
Ex., Exod. Exodus.
ex div. ex (without) dividend.
exec. executive; executor.
execx., exrx., exx. executrix.
exp. export; exportation; exported; express.
ext. external; extinct; extra; extract.
extrem. extremity.
Ezek. Ezekiel.

F

f. farthing; fathom (also, **fm., fth., fthm.**); feminine (also, **fem.**); folio (also, **fo., fol.**); foot (also, **ft.**); franc (also, **fr.**); [It. *forte*], loud; loudly:—**F** fluorine:—**F.** Fahrenheit; French (also, **Fr.**); Friday (also, **Fr., Fri.**).
Fahr., F. Fahrenheit.
F. A. I. A. Fellow of the American Institute of Architects.
fam. familiar; family.
F. A. M., F. and A. M. Free and Accepted Masons.
F. B. A. Fellow of the British Academy.
F. B. S. Fellow of the Botanical Society.
fcap., fcp. foolscap.
F. C. C. First Class Certificate.
F. D. [Lat. *fidei defensor*], Defender of the Faith.
Fe [Lat. *ferrum*], iron.
Feb. February.
fec. [Lat. *fecit*], he (or she) made it.
fem., f. feminine.
ff. [It. *fortissimo*], very loudly.
F. F. V. First Families of Virginia.
F. G. S. Fellow of the Geological Society (London).
f. i. for instance.
fict. fiction.
fig. figuratively; figure.
Fin., Finn. Finland; Finnish.
fl. florin; flourished; fluid:—**Fl.** Flanders; Flemish (also, **Flem.**).
Fla. Florida (official).
fm. fathom (also, **f., fth., fthm.**); from.
fo., f., fol. folio.
f. o. b. free on board.
fol. folio; following.
for. foreign.
fort. fortification; fortified.
fr. fragment; franc (also, **f.**); from:—**Fr.** France; [Ger.], Frau (Mrs.); French; Friar; Friday (also, **F., Fri.**).
F. R. C. P. Fellow of the Royal College of Physicians (London).
F. R. C. S. Fellow of the Royal College of Surgeons (London).
F. R. Econ. Soc. Fellow of the Royal Economic Society (London).
Fred. Frederick.
freq. frequent(ative).
Fri., F., Fr. Friday.
Frl. [Ger.], Fräulein (Miss).
F. R. S. Fellow of the Royal Society (Scientific, London).
frt. freight.
ft. feet; foot; fort.
fth., f., fm., fthm. fathom.
fur. furlong; furnished; further.
fut. future.

G

g. gauge; genitive (also, **gen.**); gram (also, **gm., gr.**); guide; guinea; gulf:—**G.** German (also, **Ger.**).
Ga gallium:—**Ga.** Georgia (official).
gal. gallon:—**Gal.** Galatians.
galv. galvanic; galvanism.
G. A. R. Grand Army of the Republic.
gaz. gazette; gazetteer.
G. B., Gt. Br., Gt. Brit. Great Britain.
G. B. & I. Great Britain and Ireland.
G. C. Grand Chancellor; Grand Chaplain; Grand Chapter; Grand Council.
g. c. d. greatest common divisor.
g. c. f. greatest common factor.
g. c. m. greatest common measure.
Gd gadolinium.
Ge germanium.
gen. gender; general; generic; genitive (also, **g.**); genus:—**Gen.** Genesis.
gent., gentn. gentleman.
Geo. George.
geog. geographer; geographic(al); geography.
geol. geologic(al); geologist; geology.
geom. geometer; geometric; geometrician; geometry.
ger. gerund.
Ger., Germ. German (also, **G.**); Germanic; Germany.
g. gr. great gross, or 144 dozen (= 1728).
G. H. P. Grand High Priest.
G. H. Q. General Headquarters.
gi. gill(s).
Gk., Gr. Greek.
Gl glucinum:—**G. L.** Grand Lodge.
gm., g., gr. gram.
G. M. Grand Master.
G. O. General Order.
G. O. P. Grand Old Party; the U. S. Republican Party.
gov. government (also, **govt.**); governor (also, **govr.**).
Gov. Gen. Governor-General.
G. P. Graduate in Pharmacy; Grand Prelate; [Lat. *gloria patri*], Glory to the Father.
G. P. O. General Post Office.
gr. grain; gram (also, **g., gm.**); grand; great; gross:—**Gr.** Greece; Greek (also, **Gk.**); Grecian.
gram. grammar.
Gr. Br., G. B., Gr. Brit. Great Britain.
G. S. General Secretary; Grand Scribe; Grand Secretary; General Staff.
gt. [Lat. *gutta*], drop.

H

h. harbor; hard(ness); height (also, **ht.**); high; hour (also, **hr.**); husband:—**H** hydrogen.
ha. hectare.
Hab. Habakkuk.

Hag. Haggai.
H. B. C. Hudson's Bay Company.
H. B. M. His (or Her) Britannic Majesty.
H. C. House of Commons.
h. c. f. highest common factor.
H.C.L. High Cost of Living.
H. D. Hawaiian Department.
hdkf. handkerchief.
hdqrs., hd. qrs., h. q. headquarters.
h. e. [Lat. *hoc est*], that is; [Lat. *hic est*], this is:—**He** helium:—**H. E.** His Eminence; His Excellency; Horizontal Equivalent; Hydraulic Engineer.
Heb. Hebrew; Hebrews.
hectol., hl. hectoliter.
hectom., hm. hectometer.
H. E. I. C. Honorable East India Company.
her. heraldic; heraldry.
hf. half:—**Hf** hafnium.
H. F. C. High-Frequency Current.
hg. hectogram; heliogram:—**Hg** [Lat. *hydrargyrum*], mercury:—**H. G.** High German; His (or Her) Grace; Horse Guards:—**H. G. D. H.** His (or Her) Grand Ducal Highness.
H. H. His (or Her) Highness; His Holiness (the Pope).
hhd. hogshead(s).
H. I. Hawaiian Islands.
H. I. H. His (or Her) Imperial Highness.
H. I. M. His (or Her) Imperial Majesty.
Hind. Hindu; Hinduism; Hindustan; Hindustani.
hist. histology; historian; historical; history.
H. J. [Lat. *hic jacet*], here lies.
hl., hectol. hectoliter.
H. L. House of Lords.
hm., hectom. hectometer:—**H. M.** His (or Her) Majesty.
H. M. S. His (or Her) Majesty's Service; His (or Her) Majesty's Ship (or Steamship).
ho. house:—**Ho** holmium.
Holl. Holland.
Hon. Honorable (also, **honble.**); Honorary.
hor. horizon; horology (also, **horol.**):—**Hor.** Horace.
hort., hortic. horticultural; horticulture.
Hos. Hosea.
h. p. half pay; high pressure (also, **HP**); horse power.
h. q., hdqrs., hd. qrs. headquarters.
hr. hour (also **h.**):—**H. R.** Home Rule; House of Representatives.
H. R. E. Holy Roman Emperor (or Empire).
H. R. H. His (or Her) Royal Highness.
H. S. high school; [Lat. *hic sepultus*], here is buried; [Lat. *hic situs*], here lies.
H. S. H. His (or Her) Serene Highness.
ht. height (also, **h.**):—**H. T.** Hawaiian Territory.
Hun., Hung. Hungarian; Hungary.
H. W. M. high-water mark.
Hy. Henry.
hyp. hypothesis; hypothetical.

I

i. intransitive (also **int., intrans.**); island (also **is., isl.**):—**I** iodine:—**I.** Idaho; [Lat. *imperator*], emperor.
Ia. Iowa (official) (also, **Io.**):—**I. A.** Indian Army.
ib., ibid. [Lat. *ibidem*], in the same place.
I. C. [Lat. *Iesus Christus*], Jesus Christ.
I. C. C. Interstate Commerce Commission.
Ice., Icel. Iceland(ic).
id. [Lat. *idem*], the same.
Id., I., Ida. Idaho.
I. D. Intelligence Department.
i. e. [Lat. *id est*], that is:—**I. E.** Indo-European.
i. h. p. indicated horse power.
I H S a symbol representing ΙΗΣ, for Greek ΙΗΣΟΥΣ, Jesus.
Il illinium.
ill., illus., illust. illustrated; illustration.
Ill. (official), **Ills.** Illinois.
I. M. Isle of Man.
imp. imperative; imperfect; imperial; impersonal; imported; importer; [Lat. *imprimatur*], let it be printed.
in. inch:—**In** indium.
inc. including; inclusive (also, **incl.**); incorporated (also, **incor.**); increase.
inch. inchoative.
incog. incognito.
ind. independent; indicative (also, **indic.**):—**Ind.** India(n); Indiana (official).
inf. infantry; infinitive.
in lim. [Lat. *in limine*], at the outset.
in loc. cit. [Lat. *in loco citato*], in the place cited.
I. N. R. I. [Lat. *Iesus Nazarenus, Rex Iudæorum*], Jesus of Nazareth, King of the Jews.
ins. inscribed; inspector (also, **insp.**); insurance.
inst. instant; institute; institution.
int. interest; interior; interjection (also, **inter., interj.**); internal; international; interpreter; intransitive (also, **i., intrans.**).
intro., introd. introduction; introductory.
inv. invented; inventor; invoice; [Lat. *invenit*], he (or she) invented it.
Io ionium.
Io., Ia. Iowa.
I. O. F. Independent Order of Foresters.
Ion. Ionian; Ionic.
I. O. O. F. Independent Order of Odd Fellows.
I. O. R. M. Improved Order of Red Men.
I O U, I. O. U. I owe you.
i. q. [Lat. *idem quod*], the same as:—**I. Q.** intelligence quotient.
Ir iridium:—**Ir.** Ireland (also, **Ire.**); Irish:—**I. R.** Internal Revenue.
is., i., isl. island; isle.
Is., Isa. Isaiah.
I. S. Irish Society.
it., ital. italic(s):—**It., Ital.** Italian; Italy.
I. W. Isle of Wight.
I. W. W. Industrial Workers of the World.

J

J. Judge; Justice.
J. A. Judge Advocate.
J. A. G. Judge-Advocate-General.
Jam. Jamaica.
Jan. January.
Jap. Japan; Japanese.
Jas. James.
J. C. D. [Lat. *juris civilis doctor*], Doctor of Civil Law.
J. D. [Lat. *jurum doctor*], Doctor of Laws.
Jer. Jeremiah.
jn., jnc., junc. junction.
Jno. John.
Jo. Joel.
Jon., Jona. Jonathan.
Jos. Joseph.
Josh. Joshua.
jour. journal; journalist.
J. P. Justice of the Peace.
Jr., Jun., Junr. Junior.
Jud., Judg. Judges.
Ju., Jun. June.
Ju., Jul. July.
junc., jn., jnc. junction.
jus., just. justice.
J. W. Junior Warden.

K

K [Lat. *kalium*], potassium:—**K.** King; Kings (also, **Ki.**); Knight (also, **Knt.**).
Kans. (official), **Kan., Kas.** Kansas.
K. C., K. of C. Knights of Columbus.
Ken., Ky. (official), Kentucky.
kg. kilogram:—**K. G.** Knight of the Garter.
Ki., K. Kings.
kilom., km. kilometer.
k. k. [Ger. *kaiserlich-königlich*], imperial-royal.
K. K. K. Ku-Klux Klan.
kl. kiloliter.
K. L. H. Knight of the Legion of Honor (France).
km. kilometer; kingdom:—**K. M.** Knight of Malta.
Knt., K. knight.
K. P. kitchen police; Knight of Pythias.
Kr krypton.
K. T. Knight Templar.
Ky. (official), **Ken.** Kentucky.

L

l. lake; land; latitude (also, **lat.**); leaf; league; left; length; line; link; liter; [Lat. *libra*], pound (also, **lb.**):—**L.** Lady; Late; Latin (also, **Lat.**); Law; Liberal; Licentiate; Lord; Low; [Lat. *liber*], book (also, **lib.**).
La lanthanium:—**La.** Louisiana (official):—**L.A.** Legislative Assembly; Library Association; Literate in Arts.
lab. laboratory:—**Lab.** Laborite; Labrador.

Lam. Lamentations.
lat., l. latitude:—**Lat., L.** Latin.
lb., l. [Lat. *libra*], pound.
l. c. letter of credit: also written **L/C.**; lower case; [Lat. *loco citato*], in the place cited (also, **loc. cit.**): —**L. C.** Lower Canada; Lord Chamberlain.
l. c. d. least common denominator.
l. c. f. least common factor.
L. C. J. Lord Chief Justice.
l. c. m. least common multiple.
ld. lead: used in proof reading:—**Ld.** Lord.
Ldp. Lordship.
L. E. left end (in football): —**lea.** league; leave.
leg. legal; legate; legato; legislative; legislature.
Lev. Leviticus.
l. f., lf lightface.
L. F. C. Low-Frequency Current.
L. G. Life Guards; Low German (also, **L. Ger.**); left guard (in football).
L. H. A. Lord High Admiral.
L. H. D. [Lat. *litterarum humaniorum doctor*], Doctor of Humanities.
Li lithium:—**L. I.** Light Infantry; Long Island.
lib. librarian; library; [Lat. *liber*], book (also, **L.**).
Lieut., Lt. Lieutenant.
liq. liquid; liquor.
lit. liter; literal; literally; literary; literature.
Lit. D. [Lat. *literarum doctor*], Doctor of Letters.
Lith. Lithuanian.
Litt. B. [Lat. *litterarum baccalaureus*], Bachelor of Letters.
Litt. D. [Lat. *litterarum doctor*], Doctor of Letters.
l. l. [Lat. *loco laudato*], in the place cited.
L. L., LL. Late Latin; Low Latin.
L. L. A. Lady Literate in Art.
LL. B. [Lat. *legum baccalaureus*], Bachelor of Laws.
LL. D. [Lat. *legum doctor*], Doctor of Laws.
LL. M. [Lat. *legum magister*], Master of Laws.
L. M. long meter.
loc. cit., l. c. [Lat. *loco citato*], in the place cited.
log., log logarithm(ic).
L. O. M. Loyal Order of Moose.
lon., long. longitude.
Lon., Lond. London.
loq. [Lat. *loquitur*], he (or she) speaks.
L. S. D., £. s. d., l. s. d. [Lat. *libræ, solidi, denarii*], pounds, shillings, pence.
L. S. S. Life-Saving Station.
l. t. long ton:—**L. T.** left tackle (in football):—**Lt., Lieut.** Lieutenant:—**ltd.** limited:—**Lu** lutecium.

M

m. male; manual; [Ger.] mark; masculine (also, **mas., masc.**); mass; measure; medicine; medium; meridian; meter; middle (also, **mid.**); mile (also, **mi.**); minute (also, **min.**); month (also, **mo.**); moon; morning; mountain (also, **mt.**); [Lat. *meridiem*], noon; [It. *mezzo*], moderate:—**M.** Majesty; Manitoba (also, **Manit.**); Marquis; Marshal; Master; Member; Militia; Monday (also, **Mon.**); [Fr.] Monsieur.
Ma masurium:—**M. A.** Military Academy; milliammeter; [Lat. *magister artium*], Master of Arts (also, **A. M.**).
Mac. Maccabees.
Maced. Macedonia(n).
mach. machinery.
mag. magazine; magnitude.
Maj. Major.
Maj. Gen. Major General.
Mal. Malachi; Malayan.
Manit., M. Manitoba.
manuf. manufactory; manufacture.
Mar., Mch. March.
March. Marchioness.
Marq. Marquis.
mas., m., masc. masculine.
Mass. Massachusetts (official).
math. mathematician; mathematics.
Matt. Matthew.
max. maximum.
M. B. A. Master of Business Administration.
M. C. Master of Ceremonies; Member of Congress; Member of Council.
Mch., Mar. March.
m. d. months after date:—**Md.** Maryland (official): —**M. D.** [Lat. *medicinæ doctor*], Doctor of Medicine.
mdse. merchandise.
Me. Maine (official):—**M. E.** Mechanical, Military, or Mining, Engineer; Methodist Episcopal; Middle English (also, **ME.**); Most Excellent.
meas. measure.
mech. mechanical; mechanics.
med. medical; medicine; medieval; medium.
Medit. Mediterranean.
mem. memento; memoir; memorandum; memorial.
Messrs., MM Messieurs.
metal. metallurgy.
meteor. meteorology.
Meth. Methodist.
Mex. Mexican; Mexico.
mf., m. f. [It. *mezzo forte*], moderately loud.
mfd. manufactured.
mfg. manufacturing.
mfr. manufacturer.
mg. milligram(s):—**Mg** magnesium.
mgr. manager.
Mgr., Monsig. Monseigneur; Monsignor.
M. H. G., M H G Middle High German.
M. Hon. Most Honorable.
M. H. R. Member of the House of Representatives.
M. H. S. Massachusetts Historical Society.
Mic. Micah.
Mich. Michigan (official).
mid. middle (also, **m.**).
mil. mileage; military (also, **milit.**); militia; million.
min. mineral(ogy); minimum; mining; minister; minor; minute (also, **m.**).
Minn. Minnesota (official).
Min. Plen. Minister Plenipotentiary.
misc. miscellaneous.
Miss. Mississippi (official).
ml. mail; milliliter.
M. L. A. Member of the Legislative Assembly; Modern Language Association.
M. L. C. Member of the Legislative Council; Modern Language Conference.
M. L. G., M L G Middle Low German.
Mlle Mademoiselle.
mm. millimeter:—**MM** Messieurs: commonly, **Messrs** (Fr.), **Messrs.** (Eng.):—**MM.** Their Majesties:—**M. M.** Master Mason.
Mme Madame.
Mn manganese.
M. N. A. S. Member of the National Academy of Sciences.
mo. month (also, **m.**):—**Mo** molybdenum:—**Mo.** Missouri (official):—**M. O.** money order.
mod. moderate; modern; [It. *moderato*], moderate.
Moham. Mohammedan.
mol. wt. molecular weight.
Mon. Monastery; Monday (also, **M.**).
Monsig., Mgr. Monseigneur; Monsignor.
Mont. Montana (official).
Mor. Morocco.
M. P. melting point; Member of Parliament; Mounted Police.
M. P. C. Member of Parliament, Canada.
m. p. g., miles per gallon:—**m. p. h.** miles per hour.
Mr. Mister.
Mrs. Mistress.
ms., MS. manuscript.
M. S. Master of Science (also, **M. Sc.**); Master of Surgery.
m. s. l. mean sea level.
Msth mesothorium.
mt. mount; mountain.
mun. municipal.
mus. museum; music; musician.
Mus. B., B. M., B. Mus. Bachelor of Music.
Mus. D., Mus. Doc. Doctor of Music.
myth. mythology.

N

n. nephew; neuter (also, **neut.**); new; nominative (also, **nom.**); note; noun; number:—**N** nitrogen:—**N.** Navy; Noon; Norse; North (also, **No., Nor.**); Northern; November (also, **Nov.**).
Na [Lat. *natrium*], sodium: —**N. A.** National Academy; National Army; North America(n); North Australia(n).
N. A. A. National Automobile Association.
N. A. D. National Academy of Design.
Nah. Nahum.

N. A. S. National Academy of Sciences. [ural.
nat. national; native; nat-
Nath. Nathanael; Nathaniel.
naut. nautical.
nav. naval; navigable; navigation (also, **navig.**).
Nb niobium:—**N. B.** New Brunswick; North Britain; North British; [Lat. *nota bene*], note well.
N. C. New Church; North Carolina (official).
N. C. O. Noncommissioned Officer. [dymium.
n. d. no date:—**Nd** neo-
N. Dak. (official), **N. D.** North Dakota.
Ne neon:—**N. E.** New England; northeast(ern).
N. E. A. National Education Association. [braska.
Nebr. (official), **Neb.** Ne-
N. E. D. New English Dictionary: also called *Oxford English Dictionary* (see **O.E.D.**).
neg. negative.
Neh. Nehemiah.
nem. con. [Lat. *nemine contradicente*], no one contradicting; unanimously.
Neth. Netherlands.
neut., n. neuter.
Nev. Nevada (official).
N. F. Newfoundland; Norman-French (also, **N.-F.**).
Ng., Nor., Norweg. Norwegian.
N. G. National Guard; New Guinea; Noble Grand; no good (slang). [cial).
N. H. New Hampshire (offi-
N. H. G. New High German.
N. H. P. nominal horse power. [gua.
Ni nickel:—**Nicar.** Nicara-
NIRA National Industrial Recovery Act.
N. J. New Jersey (official).
N. L. New Latin:—**N. Lat.** north latitude.
N. M. (official), **N. Mex.** New Mexico.
N. N. E. north-northeast.
N. N. W. north-northwest.
No. North (also, **N., Nor.**); [Lat. *numero*], number:—**N. O.** natural order; New Orleans.
nol. pros. [Lat. *nolle prosequi*], to be unwilling to prosecute.
nom., n. nominative.
non obst. [Lat. *non obstante*], notwithstanding.
non pros. [Lat. *non prosequitur*], he does not prosecute.
non seq. [Lat. *non sequitur*], it does not follow.
n. o. p. not otherwise provided for.
Nor. Norman; North (also, **N., No.**); Norway; Norwegian (also, **Ng., Norw., Norweg.**):—**nov.** novelist:—**Nov., N.** November.
N. P. New Providence; Notary Public:—**n. p.** no place (of publication of a book):—**nr.** near.
NRA National Recovery Administration.
N. S. National Society; New Series; New Style; Nova Scotia.
N/S. not sufficient (funds).
N. S. W. New South Wales.
Nt niton:—**N. T.** New Testament (also, **NT.**).
n. u. name unknown.
Num. Numbers.
N. W. North Wales; Northwest; Northwestern.
N. W. S. A. National Women's Suffrage Association.
N. W. T. Northwest Territory.
N. Y. New York (official).
N. Y. C. Newport Yacht Club; New York Central Railroad; New York City.
N. Z. New Zealand; Nova Zembla (Russ. *Novaya Zemlya*).

O

O oxygen:—**O.** October (also, **Oct.**); Ohio (official); Old; Ontario (also, **Ont.**); Order.
o/a. on account (of). [died.
ob. [Lat. *obiit*], he (or she)
Obad. Obadiah.
obdt. obedient. [jective.
obj. object; objection; ob-
obl. oblique: oblong.
obs. observation; observatory; obsolete.
oc. ocean:—**O. C.** Officer Commanding.
Oct., O. October.
O. E. Old English; omissions excepted.
O. E. D., Oxf. E. D. Oxford English Dictionary: also called *New English Dictionary* (see **N. E. D.**).
O. F. Old French.
O. H. G. Old High German.
O. H. M. S. On His (or Her) Majesty's Service.
O. K., OK. it is so; all right.
Okla. Oklahoma (official).
O. L. G. Old Low German.
O. M. Order of Merit.
Ont. (official), **O.** Ontario.
op. [Lat. *opus*], work.
opp. opposed; opposite.
Or. Oregon; Oriental.
O. R. C. Order of the Red Cross. [Oregon.
Oreg. (official), **Or., Ore.**
orig. original(ly).
Os osmium:—**O. S.** Old School; Old Series; Old Style; ordinary seaman.
o. t. overtime:—**O. T.** Old Testament; Old Teutonic.
O. T. C. Officers' Training Camp (or Corps).
Oxf. E. D., O. E. D. Oxford English Dictionary.
Oxon. [Lat. *Oxonia*], Oxford; of Oxford; Oxonian.
oz. ounce(s).

P

p. page [*pl.* pp.]; part; participle (also, **part.**); past; penny; pint (also, **pt.**); population (also, **pop.**); [It. *piano*], softly:—**P** phosphorus:—**P.** pastor; post; president (also, **pres.**); priest; prince.
p. a. participial adjective (also, **p. adj.**); [Lat. *per annum*], by the year:—**Pa** proactinium:—**Pa.** Pennsylvania (official).
P/A. power of attorney; private account.
Pac. Pacific. [adjective.
p. adj., p. a. participial
Pan. Panama.
par. paragraph; parallel; parenthesis; parish.
Para. Paraguay.
parl. parliament(ary).
part., p. participle.
pass. passive.
Pat. Off. Patent Office.
payt. payment.
Pb [Lat. *plumbum*], lead:—**P. B.** British Pharmacopœia; Prayer Book.
p. c. per cent (also, **per ct.**); postal card; post card:—**P. C.** Philippines Constabulary; Post Commander; Privy Council (or Councilor).
pd. paid:—**Pd** palladium.
Pd. D. [Lat. *pædagogiæ doctor*], Doctor of Pedagogy.
P. E. Presiding Elder; Protestant Episcopal (also, **Prot. Epis.**). [Island.
P. E. I. Prince Edward
pen. peninsula.
Penn., Pa. (official), **Penna.** Pennsylvania.
Pent. Pentecost.
per. period; person.
Per., Pers. Persia; Persian.
per an. [Lat. *per annum*], by the year.
per ct., p. c. [Lat. *per centum*], per cent.
perf. perfect.
perh. perhaps.
per pro. [Lat. *per procurationem*], by proxy.
pers. person; personal:—**Pers.** Persia; Persian.
pert. pertaining:—**Pet.** Peter:—**pf., pfd.** preferred:—**Pfd. S.** preferred spelling.
Pg., Port. Portugal; Portuguese. [ter.
P. G. M. Past Grand Mas-
Phar. Pharmacopœia; pharmacy. [pharmacy.
Pharm. pharmaceutical;
Ph. B. [Lat. *philosophiæ baccalaureus*], Bachelor of Philosophy.
Ph. D. [Lat. *philosophiæ doctor*], Doctor of Philosophy. [macy.
Ph. G. Graduate in Phar-
phil. philology (also, **philol.**); philosophy (also, **philos.**):—**Phil.** Philemon; Philip; Philippians; Philippine.
Phila. Philadelphia (official).
Philem. Philemon. [ogy.
philol. philologist; philol-
philos. philosopher; philosophical; philosophy.
Phil. Soc. Philological Society.
Ph. M. [Lat. *philosophiæ magister*], Master of Philosophy. [iology.
physiol. physiologist; phys-
P. I. Philippine Islands (official).
pinx., pnxt., pxt. [Lat. *pinxit*], he (or she) painted (it).
P. J. police justice; presiding judge; probate judge.
pk. peck:—**pkg.** package.
pl. place; plate; plural:—**P. L.** Poet Laureate.
plup., plupf. pluperfect.
plur., pl. plural.

p. m. [Lat. *post meridiem*], afternoon (also, **P. M.**); [Lat. *post mortem*], after death:—**P. M.** Past Master; Postmaster.
P. M. G. Paymaster-general; Postmaster-general.
pnxt., pinx., pxt. [Lat. *pinxit*], he (or she) painted (it).
Po polonium:—**P. O.** Postal Order; Post Office; Province of Ontario.
P. O. B. post-office box.
P. O. D. pay on delivery; Post Office Department.
pol., polit. political.
Pol. Poland; Polish.
pol. econ. political economy.
P. O. O. post-office order.
pop., p. popular; population.
Port., Pg. Portugal; Portuguese:—**poss.** possession; possessive:—**pp.** past participle; [It. *pianissimo*], very softly:—**p. p.** past participle; postpaid.
p. p. c. [Fr. *pour prendre congé*], to take leave.
pph. pamphlet. [terest.
p. p. i. policy proof of in-
p. pr., ppr. present participle:—**P.Q.** previous question; Province of Quebec.
pr. pair; present; price; prince; printer:—**Pr** praseodymium:—**Pr.** preferred (stock):—**P. R.** Puerto Rico (official); proportional representation.
pref. preface; preferred; prefix. [tion.
prep. preparatory; preposi-
pres. present; presidency:—**Pres.** President (also, **P.**); Presbyterian (also,
pret. preterit. [**Presb.**).
prin. principal.
prob. probably; problem.
Prof. Professor.
prom. promontory.
pron. pronominal; pronoun; pronounced; pronunciation:—**pros.** prosody.
Prot. Protestant.
protec. protectorate.
pro tem. [Lat. *pro tempore*], for the time being; temporarily.
prov. proverbial(ly); provincial; provisional:—**Prov.** Provençal; Proverbs; Province; Provost.
prox. [Lat. *proximo* (*mense*)], in the next, or coming, month.
Prus. Prussia; Prussian.
Ps. Psalm(s):—**P. S.** Public School; [Lat. *post scriptum*], postscript.
pseud. pseudonym.
psych., psychol. psychologist; psychology.
pt. part; payment; pint (also, **p.**); point; port:—**Pt** platinum.
Pvt. Private. [**dwt.**).
pwt. pennyweight(s) (also,
pxt., pinx., pnxt. [Lat. *pinxit*], he (or she) painted (it).

Q

q. quart (also, **qt., qu.**); queen (also, **qu.**); query; (also, **qu., qy.**); question (also, **qu.**); quintal (also, **ql.**); quire (also, **qr.**); [Lat. *quadrans*], a farthing (also, **qr.**).
Q., Que. Quebec.
Q. E. D. [Lat. *quod erat demonstrandum*], which was to be demonstrated.
Q. E. F. [Lat. *quod erat faciendum*], which was to be
Q. F. quick-firing. [done.
ql., q. quintal.
Q. M. Quartermaster.
Q. M. G. Quartermaster-general.
qr. quarter; quire (also, **q.**); [Lat. *quadrans*], a farthing (also, **q.**).
q. s., quant. suff. [Lat. *quantum sufficit*], a sufficient quantity.
qt. quantity; quart.
qu. quart; quarterly; queen (also, **q.**); query (also, **q., qy.**); question (also, **q.**).
Que., Q. Quebec. [see.
q. v. [Lat. *quod vide*], which
qy., q., qu. query.

R

r. railroad; railway; rare; received (also, **rec., recd., rec'd**); rector; residence; resides; right; river; road; rod; royal; ruble; rupee (also, **re.**):—**R.** Rabbi; Radical; Republican (also, **Rep., Repub.**); [Lat. *regina*] queen; [Lat. *rex*],
℞ [Lat. *recipe*], take. [king.
Ra, Rd radium.
R. A. Rear Royal Admiral; Academy; Royal Artillery.
rall. [It. *rallentando*], gradually decreasing in tempo.
Rb rubidium.
R. B. A. Royal Society of British Artists.
R. C. Red Cross; Roman Catholic (also, **Rom. Cath.**):—**R. C. A.** Reformed Church in America.
R. C. Ch., R. C. C. Roman Catholic Church.
R. C. P. Royal College of Physicians (London).
R. C. S. Royal College of Surgeons (London).
rd. rod:—**Rd.** road; rixdollar:—**R. D.** refer to drawer; Rural Delivery.
re. [*pl.* rs.], rupee (also, **r.**):—**Re** rhenium:—**R. E.** Reformed Episcopal; Right Excellent: Royal Engineers; real estate; in football, right end.
rec. receipt (also, **rect., rec't**); received (also, **r., recd., rec'd**); recipe; record(ed).
rect. receipt; rector; rectory.
ref. referee; reference; referred; reformation; reformed; reformer.
Ref. Ch. Reformed Church.
reg. regent (also, **regt.**); region; register(ed); registry; regular:—**Reg.** Registrar; Reginald; [Lat. *regina*], queen (also, **R.**).
regt. regent; regiment.
rel. relating; relative(ly); religion; religious.
rep. repeat; report; reporter; representative (also, **repr.**):—**Rep.** Republic; Republican (also, **R., Repub.**).
retd. returned.
rev. revenue; reverse; revise(d); revision; revolution; revolutionary:—**Rev.** Revelation; Reverend.
Rev. Ver. Revised Version (of the Bible).
rf. right field (in baseball):—**r. f.** rapid-fire:—**R. F.** radio-frequency; [Fr. *république française*], French Republic.
R. F. C. Royal Flying Corps.
R. F. D. Rural Free Delivery. [ball).
R. G. right guard (in foot-
R. G. S. Royal Geographical Society.
Rh rhodium:—**r. h.** right hand:—**R. H.** Royal Highlanders; Royal Highness.
rhet. rhetoric; rhetorical.
R. I. Rhode Island (official).
R. I. P. [Lat. *requiescat in pace*], may he (or she) rest in peace.
rit., ritard. [It. *ritardando*], gradually retarding.
riten. [It. *ritenuto*], abruptly slackened.
riv. river.
R. M. A. Royal Military Academy. [er.
R. M. S. Royal Mail Steam-
Rn radon:—**R. N.** Registered Nurse; Royal Navy.
R. N. R. Royal Naval Re-
Robt. Robert. [serve.
rom. roman (type):—**Rom.** Roman(s); Romance.
Rom. Cath., R. C. Roman Catholic.
R. O. T. C. Reserve Officers' Training Camp (or Corps).
R. P. Reformed Presbyterian:—**R. P. D.** [Lat. *rerum politicarum doctor*], Doctor of Political Science:—**R. P. E.** Reformed Protestant Episcopal.
r. p. m. revolutions per minute. [Office.
R. P. O. Railroad Post
R. R. railroad; Right Reverend.
rs. [*sing.* r., re.], rupees:—**R. S.** Recording Secretary; Revised Statutes.
R. S. F. S. R. Russian Socialist Federal Soviet Republic.
R. S. V. P. [Fr. *répondez s'il vous plaît*], reply, if you please. [ball).
R. T. right tackle (in foot-
Rt. Hon. Right Honorable.
Rt. Rev. Right Reverend.
Ru ruthenium.
Rus., Russ. Russia(n).
R. V. Revised Version (of the Bible). [Order.
R. V. O. Royal Victorian
R. W. Right Worshipful; Right Worthy.
Ry. railway.

S

s. section (also, **sec.**); see; series; shilling (also, **sh.**); signed; singular (also, **sing.**); son; soprano (also, **sop.**); substantive (also, **sb., subst.**); sun:—**S** sulphur:—**S.** Saint (usually, **St.**); Saturday (also, **St., Sat.**); Saxon (also, **Sax.**); School· Senate (also,

Sen.); September (also, **Sept.**); Signor; Socialist; Society (also, **Soc.**); South (also, **So.**); Southern; Sunday (also, **Sun.**); [Lat. *socius*], Fellow.

sa. sable:—**s. a.** [Lat. *secundum artem*], according to art or rule; [Lat. *sine anno*], without date:—**Sa** samarium (also, **Sm**):—**S. A.** Salvation Army; sex appeal; South Africa(n); South America(n); South Australia(n).

Sab. Sabbath.

S. Afr., S. A. South Africa; South African.

Salv. Salvador (official).

Sam. Samaritan (also, **Samar.**); Samuel (also, **Saml.**).

S. Am., S. A., S. Amer. South America; South American. [Sanskrit.

Sans., Sansk., Skr., Skt.

Sar. Sardinia(n):—**S. A. R.** Sons of the American Revolution; South African Republic. [cial).

Sask. Saskatchewan (offi-

Sat. Saturday (also, **S., St.**); Saturn.

S. A. T. C. Students' Army Training Corps.

Sax. Saxon; Saxony.

sb. substantive (also, **s., subst.**):—**Sb** [Lat. *stibium*], antimony:—**S.B.** Bachelor of Science (also, **B. S.**); South Britain.

sc. scene; science; scruple; [Lat. *scilicet*], namely; to wit (also, **scil., ss.**); [Lat. *sculpsit*], he (or she) carved it (also, **sculp.**):—**s. c.** small capitals (also, **s. caps., sm. c., sm. caps.**):—**Sc** scandium:—**Sc.** Scotch; Scotland; Scottish:—**S. C.** Signal Corps; South Carolina (official); Staff Corps; Supreme Court (also, **Sup. C.**).

Scand., Scan. Scandinavia; Scandinavian.

Sc. D. [Lat. *scientiæ doctor*], Doctor of Science.

sch. scholium; schooner.

sci. science; scientific.

scil., sc., ss. [Lat. *scilicet*], namely.

Scot., Sc. Scotch; Scottish; Scotland:—**scr.** scruple.

Script. Scripture.

sculp. sculptor; sculpture; [Lat. *sculpsit*], he (or she) carved it (also, **sc.**).

s. d. [Lat. *sine die*], without day; indefinitely.

S. Dak. (official), **S. D.** South Dakota.

Se selenium:—**S. E.** southeast; southeastern.

sec secant:—**sec.** second; secretary (also, **secy., sec'y**); section.

sect., sec. section. [tary.

secy., sec., sec'y secre-

sem. semicolon:—**Sem.** Seminary; Semitic.

Sen. Senate; Senator; Senior (also, **Sr.**).

sep. separate. [tuagint.

Sep., Sept. September; Sep-

ser. series; sermon.

serg., sergt., sgt. sergeant.

sfz., sf. [It. *sforzando*], forced. [ity.

s. g., sp. gr. specific grav-

S. G. Solicitor-general; Surgeon-general. [Major.

Sgt. Maj., S. M. Sergeant

sh., s. share; shilling(s).

Sh. Shakespeare.

Si silicon:—**S. I.** Sandwich Islands; Staten Island:—**Sib.** Siberia(n):—**Sic.** Sicilian; Sicily:—**sing., s.** singular.

S. J. Society of Jesus.

S. J. C. Supreme Judicial Court:—**S. J. D.** (Lat. *scientiæ juridicæ doctor*), Doctor of Juridical Science.

Skr., Sans., Sansk, Skt. Sanskrit:—**S. Lat.** south latitude:—**Slav.** Slavic; Slavonic:—**Sm, Sa** samarium:—**S. M.** senior magistrate; Sergeant Major (also, **Sgt. Maj.**); short meter; State Militia· [Fr. *sa majesté*], His (or Her) Majesty.

sm. c., s. c., sm. caps. small capitals.

Sn [Lat. *stannum*], tin.

So. South (also, **S.**):—**S. O.** seller's option; Signal Officer; special order.

soc. society (also, **S.**):—**S. O. C.** Society for Organizing Charity.

S. of Sol. Song of Solomon.

sop., s. soprano.

S O S a signal call of distress consisting of the letters *sos* (--- — — — ---) of the international Morse alphabet: employed because these letters are easily and quickly transmitted and easily recognized.

sov. sovereign.

sp. seaport (also, **spt.**); species; specimen; spelling; spirit:—**s. p.** [Lat. *sine prole*], without issue:—**Sp.** Spain; Spaniard; Spanish (also, **Span.**).

S. P. C. A. Society for Prevention of Cruelty to Animals:—**S. P. C. C.** Society for Prevention of Cruelty to Children.

specif. specifically.

sp. gr., s. g. specific gravity.

S. P. Q. R. small profits, quick returns; [Lat. *senatus populusque romanus*], the Senate and People of Rome.

spt., sp. seaport.

sq. square; [Lat. *sequens*], (the) following (one).

sq. in. square inch.

sq. m. square mile.

Sr strontium:—**Sr.** Senior (also, **Sen.**); Sir:—**S. R. C.** Signal Reserve Corps.

S. R. S. [Lat. *societatis regiæ socius*], Fellow of the Royal Society.

ss. [Lat. *scilicet*], namely (also, **sc., scil.**); [Lat. *semis*], half:—**SS.** [Lat. *sancti*], Saints; [Lat. *sanctissimus*], most holy:—**S. S.** Secretary of State; simplified spelling; Statistical Society; Steamship; Sunday School.

S. S. E. south-southeast.

S. S. W. south-southwest.

st. stanza; state; stone; strait (also, **str.**); street, strophe; [Lat. *stet*], let (it) stand:—**s. t.** short ton:—**St.** Saint; Saturday (also, **S., Sat.**). [utes.

stat. statuary; statue; stat-

S. T. D. [Lat. *sacræ theologiæ doctor*], Doctor of Sacred Theology.

Ste. [Fr. *Sainte*], *fem.* Saint.

ster., stg. sterling. [er.

str. strait (also, **st.**); steam-

stsm. statesman.—**Sub.** Subaltern:—**subj.** subject; subjective; subjunctive.

subst. substantive (also, **sb., sub.**); substitute.

suff. suffix.

Sun., S., Sund. Sunday.

sup. superior (also, **super.**); superlative (also, **superl.**); supine; supplement (also, **supp.**); supreme (also, **supr.**); [Lat. *supra*], above:—**Sup. C.** Superior Court; Supreme Court.

Supt. Superintendent.

surg. surgeon; surgery.

Surg. Gen., S. G. Surgeon-general.

surv. surveying; surveyor.

s. v. [Lat. *sub voce*], under the (specified) word:—[Lat. *sanctitas vestra*], Your Holiness. [ish.

Sw., Swed. Sweden; Swed-

S. W. southwest; southwestern; Senior Warden.

Switz., Swit. Switzerland.

syn. synonym; synonymous.

Syr. Syria; Syriac.

T

t. temperature; tenor; time; tome; ton; town (also, **tn.**); township (also, **tp., twp.**); transitive (also, **tr., trans.**); [Lat. *tempore*], in the time (of):—**T.** Territory (also, **ter., terr.**); Testament; Tuesday (also, **Tu., Tues.**); Turkish; [Lat. *tomus*, or Fr. *tome*], volume.

Ta tantalum:—**tan** tangent.

t. b. tubercle bacillus or tuberculosis:—**Tb** terbium (also, **Tr**):—**Tb.** Tiberius.

T. C. D. Trinity College, Dublin.

Te tellurium:—**T. E.** Topographical Engineer.

tech. technical(ly); technology (also, **technol.**).

tel. telegram; telegraph; telephone:—**Tenn.** Tennessee (official):—**ter.** terrace (also, **terr.**); territory (also, **T., terr.**):—**Ter.** Terence.

Test. Testament.

Teut. Teuton; Teutonic.

Tex. Texan; Texas (official).

Th thorium:—**Th.** Thomas (also, **Tho., Thos.**); Thursday (also, **Thurs.**):—**T. H.** Territory of Hawaii.

Theo. Theodore; Theodosia.

theol. theological; theology.

theolog. theologian.

Thess. Thessalonians.

Tho., Th., Thos. Thomas.

Thurs., Th. Thursday.

Ti titanium.

Tim. Timothy:—**Tit.** Titus.

Tl thallium:—**Tm** thulium.

T. M. trade-mark; true mean:—**tn., t.** town.
T. N. T., TNT trinitrotoluene, or trinitrotoluol.
T. O. turn over; Telegraph Office:—**tp.** township (also, **t., twp.**):—**t. p.** title-page (also, **t.-p.**).
tr. transfer; transitive; translated; translation; translator; transpose; treasurer; trustee:—**Tr** terbium (also, **Tb**).
trans., t., tr. transitive.
trav. travel; traveler. [ury.
treas., tr. treasurer; treas-
trib. tributary.
trig., trigon. trigonometric; trigonometrical; trigo-
Trin. Trinity. [nometry.
trop. tropic; tropical.
T. S. F. S. R. Transcaucasian Socialist Federal Soviet Republic.
T. T. telegraphic transfer.
T. U. Trade Union.
Tues., T., Tu. Tuesday.
Turk. Turkey; Turkish.
typ., typog. typographer; typographical; typography.
TZ. I. K. [Russ. *Tzentralny Ispolnitelny Kommitet*], Central Executive Committee (of the Soviet Union).

U

U uranium:—**U.** Uncle; Union; Unionist; University (also, **Univ.**); upper.
u. c. upper case:—**U. C.** Upper Canada.
U. K. United Kingdom.
ult. ultimate(ly); [Lat. *ultimo*], in the month preceding the current month.
Unit. Unitarian.
univ. universal(ly):—**Univ.** Universalist; university (also, **U.**).
U. of S. A., U. of. S. Afr. Union of South Africa.
U. P. C. United Presbyterian Church:—**Uru.** Uruguay:—**U. S.** United States; also, Uncle Sam.
U. S. A. United States Army; United States of America.
U. S. C. United States of Colombia:—**U. S. C. & G. S.** United States Coast and Geodetic Survey:—**U. S. C. G.** United States Coast Guard.
U. S. G. S. United States Geodetic Survey; United States Geological Survey.
U. S. M. C. United States Marine Corps:—**U. S. M. A.** United States Military Academy.
U. S. N. United States Navy.
U. S. N. A. United States Naval Academy.
U. S. N. G. United States National Guard.
U. S. P., U. S. Pharm. United States Pharmacopœia. [serves.
U. S. R. United States Re-
U. S. S. United States Senate; United States Steamship (also, **U. S. S. S.**).
U. S. S. B. E. F. C. United States Shipping Board Emergency Fleet Corporation
U. S. S. R. Union of Socialist Soviet Republics; Ukrainian Socialist Soviet Republic:—**usu.** usual(ly).
U. S. V. United States Volunteers.
Ut. Utah (official).

V

v. valence; valve; verb (also, **vb.**); verse (also, **ver.**); version; vicar; village (also, **vil.**); violin; vocative (also, **voc.**); volt; volume (also, **vol.**); [Lat. *versus*], against (also, **vs.**); [Lat. *verte*], turn over; [Lat. *vide*], see (also, **vid.**); [Ger. *von*], of:—**V** vanadium:—**V.** Venerable (also, **Ven.**); Vice; Victoria (also, **Vic.**); Viscount (also, **Vis., Visc.**); Volunteer (also, **Vol.**).
v. a. verb active; verbal adjective; [Lat. *vixit annos*], lived (so many) years:—**Va.** Virginia (official):—**V. A.** Vice Admiral.
var. variant; variation; variety; various.
var. lect. [Lat. *varia lectio*], different reading.
Vat. Vatican.
v. aux. verb auxiliary.
vb. verb; verbal (also, **v.**):—**vb. adj.** verbal adjective (also, **v. a.**):—**vb. intr.** verb intransitive (also, **v. i.**):—**vb. n.** verbal noun:—**vb. tr.** verb transitive (also, **v. t.**).
V. C. Vice Chairman; Vice Chancellor; Victoria Cross; Volunteer Corps.
Ven. Venerable (also, **V.**); Venetian; Venice.
Venez. Venezuela.
ver. verse; verses.
Vet., Veter. veterinarian; veterinary (surgeon).
v. g. [Lat. *verbi gratia*], for the sake of example.
v. i., vb. intr. verb intransi-
Vic., V. Victoria. [tive.
vid., v. [Lat. *vide*], see.
vil., v. village.
Vis., Visc., V. Viscount:—**viz.** [Lat. *videlicet*], namely; to wit.
V. M. D. Doctor of Veterinary Medicine:—**v. n.** verb neuter:—**voc., v.** vocative.
vocab. vocabulary.
vol. volcano (also, **v.**); volcanic; volume (also, **v.**); volunteer (also, **v.**).
V. P. Vice President.
v. r. verb reflexive:—**V. R.** [Lat. *Victoria regina*], Queen Victoria.
V. R. et I., V. R. I. [Lat. *Victoria regina* et *imperatrix*], Victoria Queen and Empress.
V. Rev. Very Reverend.
vs. [Lat. *versus*], against (also, **v.**):—**v. s.** [Lat. *vide supra*], see above:—**V. S.** Veterinary Surgeon.
v. t. verb transitive:—**Vt.** Vermont (official).
V. TZ. I. K., VTZIK [Russ. *Vserossiisky Tzentralny Ispolnitelny Kommitet*], All-Russian Central Executive Committee.
vul., vulg. vulgar(ly):—**Vul., Vulg.** Vulgate.
V. V. vice versa.

W

w. wanting; week (also, **wk.**); wide; wife; with:—**W** watt; [Mod. Lat. *wolframium*], tungsten:—**W.** Wales; Warden; Wednesday (also, **Wed.**); Welsh; West; Western.
W. A. West Africa; Western Australia.
W. A. A. C., Waac Women's Army Auxiliary Corps (British Army).
Wash. Washington (official).
W. C. T. U. Women's Christian Temperance Union.
Wed., W. Wednesday.
w. f. wrong font.
w. g. wire gauge:—**W. G.** Worthy Grand. [Master.
W. G. M. Worthy Grand
W. I., W. Ind. West Indies; West Indians. [consin.
Wis. (official), **Wisc.** Wis-
wk., w. week.
w. l. wave length.
W. long. west longitude.
Wm. William:—**W. M.** Worshipful Master.
W. N. W. west-northwest.
W. R. S. S. R. White Russian Socialist Soviet Republic.
W. S. W. west-southwest.
wt. weight.
W. Va. West Virginia (official). [oming.
Wyo. (official), **Wy.** Wy-

X

X xenon (usually, **Xe**); [for Gk. X (*chi*), first letter in *Khristos*], Christ (also, **Xt.**); Christian.
Xe, X xenon.
Xmas. Christmas.
Xn., X. Christian.
Xnty., Xty. Christianity

Y

y. yard (also, **yd.**); year (also, **yr.**):—**Y** yttrium (also, **Yt**):—**Y.** short for Y. M. (or W.) C. A.
Yb ytterbium:—**yd.** yard.
Y. M. C. A. Young Men's Christian Association.
Y. M. Cath. A. Young Men's Catholic Association.
Y. M. C. U. Young Men's Christian Union.
Y. M. H. A. Young Men's Hebrew Association.
Y. P. S. C. E. Young People's Society of Christian Endeavor. [your.
yr. year (also, **y.**); younger;
yt that: also written **yt**:—**Yt** yttrium (also, **Y**).
Y. W. C. A. Young Women's Christian Association.
Y. W. C. T. U. Young Women's Christian Temperance Union.
Y. W. H. A. Young Women's Hebrew Association.

Z

Zach. Zacharias; Zachary.
Zech. Zechariah.
Zeph. Zephaniah:—**Zn** zinc.
zoöl. zoölogical; zoölogist; zoölogy:—**Zr** zirconium.

SIGNS AND SYMBOLS

ALPHABETS OF FOREIGN LANGUAGES

HEBREW[1]

א	aleph	[2] ʼ, 1
ב	beth	b, 2
ג	gimel	g, 3
ד	daleth	d, 4
ה	he	h, 5
ו	vau	w, 6
ז	zayin	z, 7
ח	cheth	kh, 8
ט	teth	t, 9
י	yod	y, 10
כ	caph	k, 20
ל	lamedh	l, 30
מ	mem	m, 40
נ	nun	n, 50
ס	samekh	s, 60
ע	ayin	[3] ʻ, 70
פ	pe	p, 80
צ	sadhe	ss, 90
ק	koph	q, 100
ר	resh	r, 200
שׂ	sin	s, 300
שׁ	shin	sh, 300
ת	tav	t, th, 400

GREEK

Α α	alpha	a, 1
Β β	beta	b, 2
Γ γ	gamma	g, 3
Δ δ	delta	d, 4
Ε ϵ	epsilon	ĕ, 5
Ζ ζ	zeta	z, 7
Η η	eta	ē, 8
Θ θ	theta	th, 0
Ι ι	iota	i, 10
Κ κ	kappa	k, 20
Λ λ	lambda	l, 30
Μ μ	mu	m, 40
Ν ν	nu	n, 50
Ξ ξ	xi	x, 60
Ο ο	omicron	ŏ, 70
Π π	pi	p, 80
Ρ ρ	rho	r, 100
Σ ς, σ[4]	sigma	s, 200
Τ τ	tau	t, 300
Υ υ	upsilon	u, 400
Φ φ	phi	ph, 500
Χ χ	chi	ch, 700
Ψ ψ	psi	ps, 700
Ω ω	omega	ō, 800

ROMAN		GERMAN[12]	
A a	50; 500	𝔄	𝔞
B b	300	𝔅	𝔟
C c	[5]100	ℭ	𝔠
D d	[6]500	𝔇	𝔡
E e	250	𝔈	𝔢
F f	40	𝔉	𝔣
G g	400	𝔊	𝔤
H h	200	ℌ	𝔥
I i	1	ℑ	𝔦
J j	[7]—	𝔍	𝔧
K k	250	𝔎	𝔨
L l	50	𝔏	𝔩
M m	[8]1,000	𝔐	𝔪
N n	90	𝔑	𝔫
O o	11	𝔒	𝔬
P p	400	𝔓	𝔭
Q q	90; 500	𝔔	𝔮
R r	80	ℜ	𝔯
S s	7; 70	𝔖	𝔰, ſ
T t	160	𝔗	𝔱
U u	[9]—	𝔘	𝔲
V v	[10]5	𝔙	𝔳
W w	[11]—	𝔚	𝔴
X x	10	𝔛	𝔵
Y y	150	𝔜	𝔶
Z z	2,000	ℨ	𝔷

RUSSIAN[13]

А	а	a
Б	б	b, p
В	в	v, f
Г	г	g, k
Д	д	d
Е	е	e
Ж	ж	sh, zh
З	з	z
И	и	i
Й,	й.	[14]y
К	к	k
Л	л	l
М	м	m
Н	н	n
О	о	o
П	п	p
Р	р	r
С	с	s
Т	т	t
У	у	u
Ф	ф	f
Х	х	kh
Ц	ц	ts
Ч	ч	ch
Ш	ш	sh
Щ	щ	shch
Ъ	ъ	[15]—
Ы	ы	[16]y
Ь	ь	[17]—
Э	э	e
Ю	ю	yu
Я	я	ya

NOTES.—The figures indicate the values of the letters when used as numerical symbols.—For runic alphabet see cut in main vocabulary under *rune*.—[1] The Hebrew alphabet had originally no symbols for vowel sounds. Later, a set of dots and dashes was devised, called vowel points, to be written over, under, or within the consonant symbols. Hebrew is written from right to left on the page.—[2] Smooth breathing.—[3] Rough breathing, sounded like *h*.—[4] When final, ς; in other positions, σ.—[5] Originally, as a numeral, ⊙, for Greek θ; taken as initial letter of Latin *centum*, and written C.—[6] Originally, as a numeral, half of the symbol ↀ, for 1,000. See note 8.—[7] Formerly same as I.—[8] Originally, as a numeral, ↀ, the ancient Etruscan symbol for 1,000, written CIↃ, (I), then M.—[9] Formerly same as V.—[10] As a letter, a variant form of U. As a numeral, perhaps originally the upper half of X, for 10.—[11] Not used in medieval Latin.—[12] The alphabet in the style of type often used by the Germans. Roman type is also extensively used, especially in scientific works. A script alphabet, corresponding to this type, is used along with the common Roman script.—[13] Developed mainly from the Greek alphabet.—[14] Appears as final element of a diphthong.—[15] Used between a hard consonant and a following front vowel, to indicate syllabic separation.—[16] Represents a vowel sound occurring in most Slavic languages, but not in English, somewhat like ĭ when followed by l, as in *will*.—[17] Silent; indicates palatalized pronunciation of preceding consonant.

SIGNAL CODES

Explanation of Numbered Columns:

I. **International, or Continental, Morse,** also known as the *General Service Code:* used in commercial radio, in the Army and Navy, and for general signaling. Signals can be transmitted electrically; also, by day, with hand flags or sun flashes, or, by night, with torches, lanterns, or other lights. If the distance is not too great, sound can be used by means of a whistle, drum, bugle, or the like.

II. **American Morse:** used in the United States for telegraphic transmission. For numerals in I and II, see below.

III. **Ardois System:** a code for use at sea, in which the International Morse is adapted to transmission by the display of lights hung from a staff, mast, or yard.

Key: ● red = dot (in the International Morse); ○ white = dash.

IV, V. **Semaphore Signals:** two-arm signals, transmitted by hand flags or by a machine. On the machine a short third arm, or indicator, is displayed on the right of the sender. A special signal indicates "Numerals follow," thus:

VI. **International Code of Signals:** hoists of special flags used for marine signaling.

Key: ☐ white; ■ black; ▥ red; ▤ blue; ⬚ yellow. (Compare *heraldry*, illus., for corresponding key.)

	I	II
A	·—	·—
B	—···	—···
C	—·—·	·· ·
D	—··	—··
E	·	·
F	··—·	·—·
G	——·	——·
H	····	····
I	··	··
J	·———	—·—·
K	—·—	—·—
L	·—··	——
M	——	——
N	—·	—·
O	———	· ·
P	·——·	·····
Q	——·—	··—·
R	·—·	· ··
S	···	···
T	—	—
U	··—	··—
V	···—	···—
W	·——	·——
X	—··—	·—··
Y	—·——	·· ··
Z	——··	··· ·

Columns III, IV, V, VI, A–M:

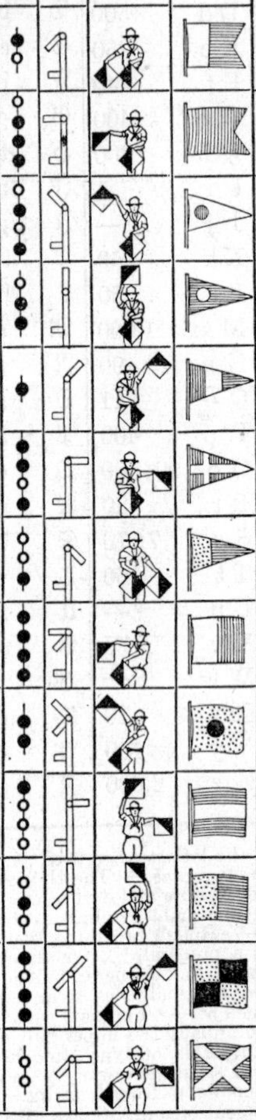

Columns III, IV, V, VI, N–Z:

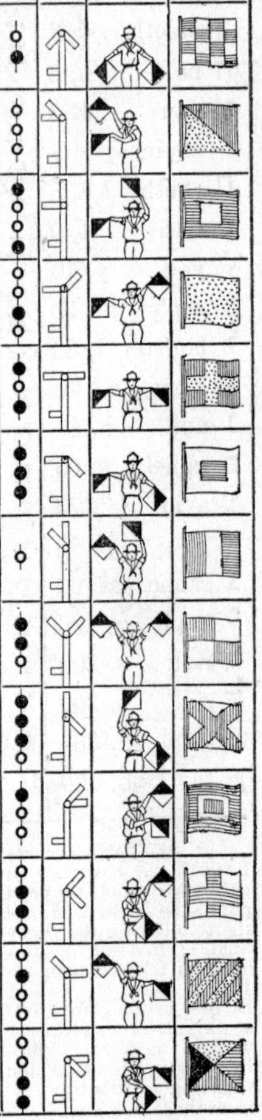

Single Flag, or Wigwag. Four basic signals are employed, messages being sent by International Morse. *Position* is used to call a station; *front* is used once, twice, or three times to indicate end of word, sentence, or message respectively.

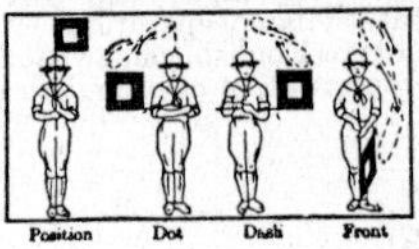

Numerals are given as follows in Morse (I and II):

I: International Morse		II: American Morse	
1. ·————	6. —····	1. ·——·	6. ······
2. ··———	7. ——···	2. ··—··	7. ——··
3. ···——	8. ———··	3. ···—·	8. —····
4. ····—	9. ————·	4. ····—	9. —··—
5. ·····	0. —————	5. ———	0. ——

ASTRONOMY

⊙ the Sun; Sunday. Also, ☉.
☽ or ☾ the Moon; Monday. Also ☾, ☽.
● new moon; ☽, ☽ first quarter.
○, ☺ full moon; ☾, ☾ last quarter.
☿ Mercury; Wednesday.
♀ Venus; Friday.
⊕, ⊖, ♁ the Earth; ♂ Mars; Tuesday.
♃ Jupiter; Thursday; ♄ Saturn; Saturday.
♅, ♁ Uranus.; ♆ Neptune.
☄ comet; ✱, * fixed star.

COMMERCE AND FINANCE

$ dollar; dollars; as, $1; $5.
¢ cent; cents; as, 1¢; 12¢.
/ shilling; shillings; as, 1/6 = 1s. 6d.
£ pound (sterling); pounds: from the initial letter of Lat. *libra*, pound; as, £1; £5.
£E Egyptian pound or pounds.
₱ peso or pesos; as, ₱25.
℔ pound (in weight); pounds; as, 1 ℔; 2 ℔.
@ at; as, gingham @ $.50 per yard; also, to; as, butter, per lb. 45¢ @ 50¢.
% per cent; also, order of; care of.
% account; as, Wm. Jones % with J. Brown.
B/L bill of lading.
* follows stock ticker quotations to denote correctness.

MATHEMATICS

+ plus, and, more; as 3+2=5.
— minus, less; as 6—3=3.
± plus or minus; as the square root of 4 is ±2.
× multiplied by; as 6×2=12.
÷ divided by; as 6÷2=3.
> is greater than; as 6>5.
< is less than; as 5<6.
: is to; as 6:3∷8:4.
∷ as; as 6:3∷8:4.
∠ angle; as, ∠ABC=∠CEF.
√ the square root; as √9=3.
°, ′, ″ degrees, minutes, seconds of arc.

MEDICINE AND PHARMACY

āā [Gk. *ana*], of each.
℞ [Lat. *recipe*, take], take: written on prescriptions.
S [Lat. *signa*], mark preceding directions for taking medicine: often written Sig.
℔ [Lat. *libra*], pound; ℥ ounce.
ʒ dram; a weight of 60 grains or ⅛ ounce; a fluid dram, ⅛ fluid ounce (of water, about a teaspoonful, or 60 drops).
℈ scruple; ♏ or ♍ minim; drop.

PUNCTUATION

, comma.
; semicolon.
: colon.
. period.
? interrogation.
! exclamation.
( ) parentheses.
[ ] brackets.
’ apostrophe.
— dash.
- hyphen.
´ acute accent.
` grave accent.
^ circumflex accent.
~ circumflex; tilde.
¯ long accent; macron.
˘ short; breve.
¨ diæresis.
¸ cedilla.
‸ caret.
* * * ellipsis.
. . . ellipsis.
—— ellipsis.
* asterisk.
† dagger; obelisk.
‡ double dagger.
§ section.
‖ parallel.
¶ paragraph.
☞ index.
⁂, ⁂ asterism.

MISCELLANEOUS

© copyrighted. AP Associated Press (news item).
& ampersand; and; as, Smith & Co
&c and the rest; and so forth; for *etc.* [Lat. *et cetera*.]
′ feet; ″ inches; as, a room 12′ 6″ long.
× by: used in dimensions; as, a room 8′ × 16′.
♣ club; ♦ diamond; ♥ heart; ♠ spade: marks of the suits on playing cards.
number; also, pound.
c/o or ᶜ/ₒ care of.
♂ or ♂, *Zoöl.*, male; ♀, female.
○ *Zoöl.*, of undetermined sex.
† died: used in genealogies.

ELECTRICITY AND RADIO

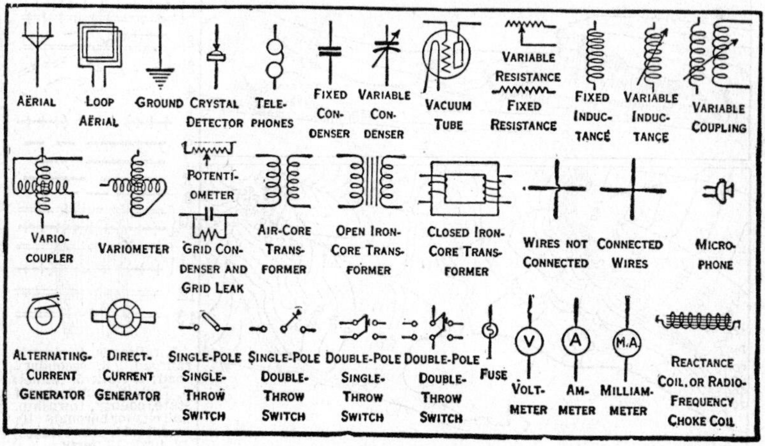

METEOROLOGY

U. S. WEATHER BUREAU SIGNALS

KEY: ☐ white; ▥ red; ■ black; ▤ blue.

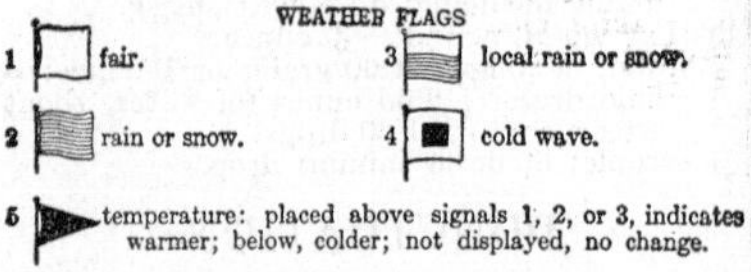

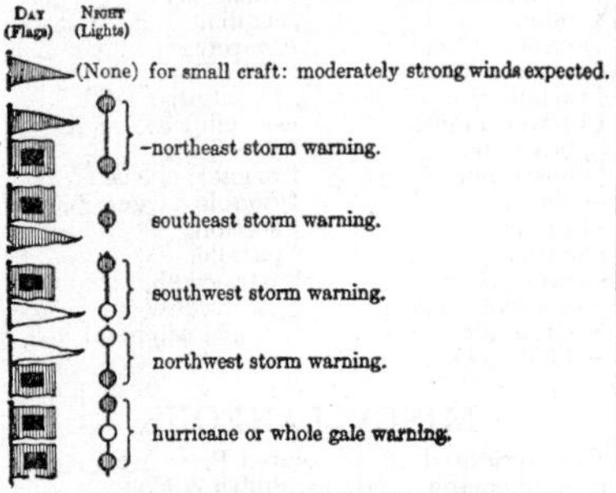

U. S. WEATHER BUREAU SYMBOLS

(Used on Daily Weather Map)

○ clear. Ⓡ rain. ▲ hail.

◑ partly cloudy. Ⓢ snow. △ sleet.

● cloudy. Ⓜ report missing. ⌐K thunderstorm.

⇉○→ storm warning.

○, ●, etc. Arrows attached to other symbols indicate wind direction; arrows fly with the wind.

▤ Shaded area indicates precipitation of 0.01 inch or more during last 24 hours.

TOPOGRAPHY

The following are the principal conventional signs used on maps issued by the United States Coast and Geodetic Survey and by the United States Geologic Survey. The contour map at the lower left would make a much more immediate appeal to the eye if printed in the conventional colors.

RELIEF (printed in brown)

Contours Depression contours Cliffs

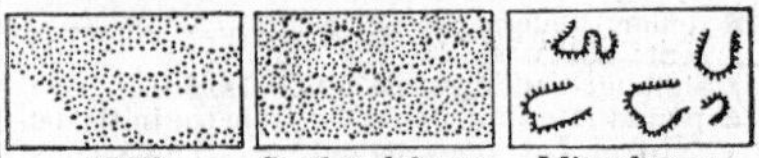

Wash Sand and dunes Mine dumps

WATER (printed in blue)

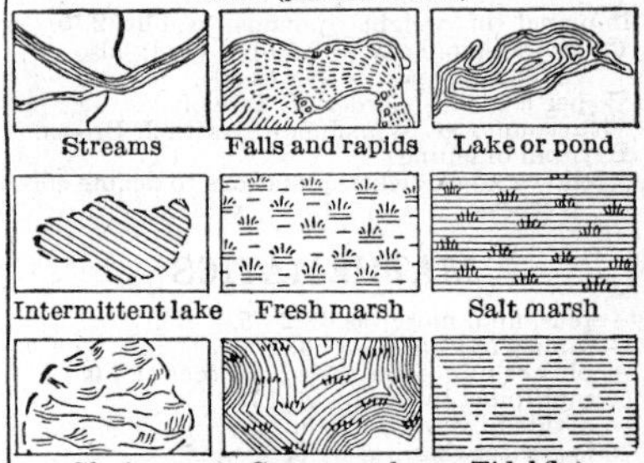

Streams Falls and rapids Lake or pond

Intermittent lake Fresh marsh Salt marsh

Glacier Grassy pond Tidal flat

CULTURE (printed in black)

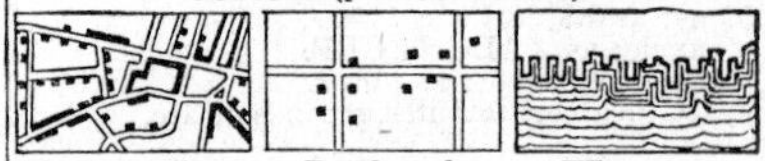

City or village Roads and buildings Wharves

A LANDSCAPE: in perspective (above) and as it would appear on a map (below)

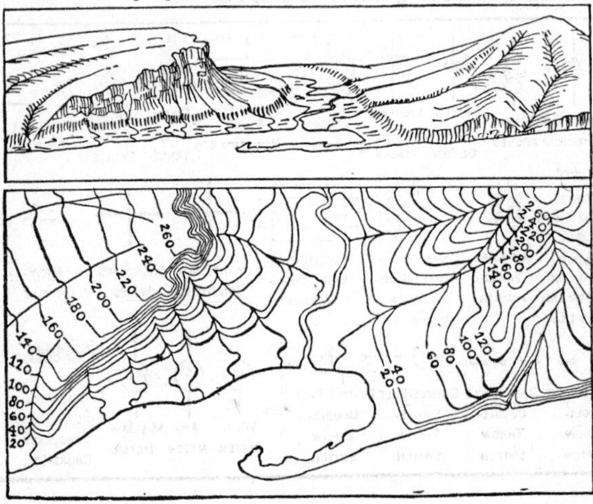

CULTURE (*continued*)

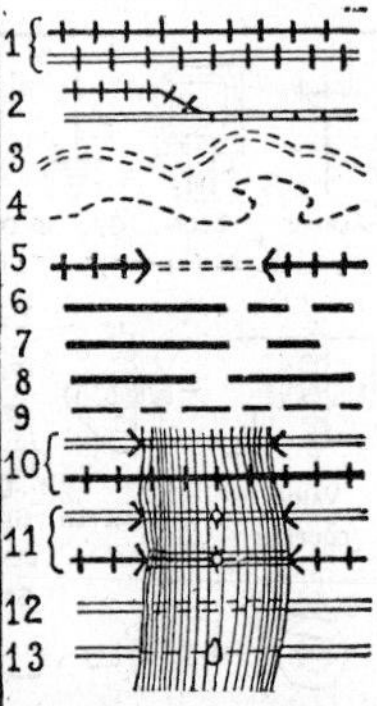

1, railroads; 2, electric railroad: 3, secondary road; 4. trail; 5, tunnel; 6, 7, 8, 9, boundaries of state, county, township, and city (or borough): 10, bridges; 11, drawbridges; 12, ford; 13, ferry.

TABLES OF WEIGHTS, MEASURES, AND STANDARDS

THE METRIC SYSTEM

The meter, unit of length, was originally intended to be, and approximately is, the ten-millionth part of a quadrant of a terrestrial meridian. The International Standard meter is, in practice, the distance between two defining lines on the International Prototype Meter bar at 0° C., at the International Bureau of Weights and Measures, at Sèvres, near Paris, France, accurate copies of which are supplied to the various countries to serve as national standards. The meter is exactly 39.37 United States standard inches long.

The Liter, unit of capacity, is equivalent to the space occupied by one kilogram of pure water at the temperature of its maximum density (4° C., nearly), under standard atmospheric pressure: approximately a cubic decimeter, more exactly 1.000027 cubic decimeters.

The Gram, unit of mass (weight), is one one thousandth of the mass of the International Prototype Kilogram, which was intended to have the same mass as a cubic decimeter of pure water at the temperature of its maximum density (4° C., nearly), under standard atmospheric pressure.

In many of the arts and sciences and in certain branches of commerce and industry, but especially in theoretical physics and in much of the research work in physics and chemistry, lengths are generally stated in centimeters, masses (weights) in grams, and time in mean solar seconds, the system of these units being called the C. G. S. (centimeter-gram-second) system.

The use of the Metric System was legalized in the United States on July 28, 1866.

MEASURES OF LENGTH AND SURFACE

Length

Metric Denominations	*and Values*	*Equivalents*
1 myriameter	10,000 meters	6.2137 miles
1 kilometer	1,000 meters	0.62137 mile, or 3,280 feet 10 inches
1 hectometer	100 meters	328 feet 1 inch
1 decameter	10 meters	393.7 inches
1 meter	1 meter	39.37 inches
1 decimeter	1/10 meter	3.937 inches
1 centimeter	1/100 meter	0.3937 inch
1 millimeter	1/1,000 meter	0.0394 inch
1 micron	1/1,000,000 meter	1/1,000 millimeter
1 millimicron	1/1,000,000,000 meter	1/1,000 micron
1 Angström unit	1/10^{10} meter	1/10,000 micron

Surface

1 square kilometer	1,000,000 square meters	0.3861 square mile
1 hectare	10,000 square meters	2.471 acres: equivalent to a square 328′ 1″ on a side
1 are	100 square meters	119.6 square yards
1 centare	1 square meter	1,550 square inches
1 square decimeter	0.01 square meter	15.50 square inches
1 square centimeter	0.0001 square meter	0.155 square inch
1 square millimeter	0.000001 square meter	0.00155 square inch

MEASURES OF CAPACITY AND VOLUME

Metric Denominations and	*Values*	*Equivalents in Terms of Nonmetric Units* *Cu. In.*	*Dry Measure*	*Liquid Measure*
1 kiloliter[1]	1,000 liters	61025.0	1.308 cubic yards	264.18 gallons
1 hectoliter	100 liters	6102.50	2.8378 bushels	26.418 gallons
1 decaliter	10 liters	610.250	1.1351 pecks	2.6418 gallons
1 liter	1 liter	61.0250	0.9081 quart	1.0567 quarts
1 deciliter	1/10 liter	6.10250	0.18162 pints	0.8454 gill
1 centiliter	1/100 liter	0.610250	0.6102 cubic inch	0.3381 fluid ounce
1 milliliter	1/1000 liter	0.0610250	0.0610 cubic inch	0.2705 fluid dram

[1] 1 kiloliter = 61,025 cubic inches; 1 cubic meter = 61,023.38 cubic inches, or 1.000027 kiloliters. By definition, 1 stere = 1 cubic meter; 1 hectostere = 100 cubic meters.

MEASURES OF MASS (WEIGHTS)

Metric Denominations and Values		Equivalents: Quantity of Water at Standard Pressure and Maximum Density	Equivalents: Avoirdupois Weight	Equivalents: Troy Weight
1 tonne (metric ton)	1,000,000 grams	1 cubic meter (nearly)	1.102311 short tons	
1 quintal	100,000 grams	1 hectoliter	220.46 pounds	
1 myriagram	10,000 grams	10 liters	22.046 pounds	
1 kilogram or kilo	1,000 grams	1 liter	2.2046 pounds	2.6792 pounds
1 hectogram	100 grams	1 deciliter	3.5274 ounces	3.2151 ounces
1 decagram	10 grams	1 milliliter	0.3527 ounce	0.3215 ounce
1 gram	1 gram	1 cubic centimeter	0.0353 ounce	0.0322 ounce
1 decigram	1/10 gram	1/10 cubic centimeter		1.5432 grains
1 centigram	1/100 gram	10 cubic millimeters		0.1543 grain
1 milligram	1/1000 gram	1 cubic millimeter		0.0154 grain

METRIC EQUIVALENTS OF DOMESTIC MEASURES

Length

1 inch	2.54 centimeters
1 foot	0.3048 meter
1 yard	0.9144 meter
1 rod	5.029 meters
1 mile	1,609.35 meters

Surface

1 square inch	6.452 square centimeters
1 square foot	0.0929 square meter
1 square yard	0.8361 square meter
1 square rod	25.293 square meters
1 acre	4046.87 square meters
1 acre	40.469 ares
1 square mile	259.000 hectares

Capacity

1 cubic inch	16.387 cubic centimeters
1 cubic inch	0.0164 liter, cubic decimeter
1 cubic foot	28.316 liters, 28.317 cubic decimeters
1 cubic yard	764.539 liters, 764.559 cubic decimeters
1 cord	3.625 steres
1 quart, dry measure	1.1012 liters
1 peck (U. S.)	8.8096 liters
1 bushel (U. S.)	35.24 liters
1 fluid dram	3.70 cubic centimeter
1 fluid ounce	29.57 cubic centimeters
1 fluid ounce	0.0296 liter
1 gill	0.1183 liter
1 quart, liquid measure	0.9463 liter
1 gallon (231 cubic inches)	3.785 liters

English Measures (used also in Canada)

1 British quart	1.2009 U. S. liquid quarts
1 British quart	1.0320 U. S. dry quarts
1 U. S. dry quart	0.9690 British quart
1 U. S. liquid quart	0.8327 British quart

Weights

1 grain[1]	64.80 milligrams
1 ounce, avoirdupois	28.3495 grams
1 ounce, troy	31.103 grams
1 pound, avoirdupois	0.45359 kilogram
1 pound, troy	0.3732 kilogram
1 short ton (2,000 pounds)	907.2 kilograms
1 short ton (2,000 pounds)	0.9072 metric ton
1 long ton (2,240 pounds)	1.016 metric tons

[1] The troy, avoirdupois, and apothecaries' grain are the same.

THE METRIC SYSTEM SIMPLIFIED

The following tables of the metric system of weights and measures have been simplified as much as possible by omitting such denominations as are not in practical, everyday use in the countries where the system is used.

TABLES OF THE SYSTEM

Length

The denominations in practical use are the millimeter (mm.), centimeter (cm.), meter (m.), and kilometer (km.).

10 millimeters	1 centimeter
10 centimeters	1 decimeter
10 decimeters	1 meter
1,000 meters	1 kilometer

Weight

The denominations in use are the milligram (mg.), gram (g.), kilogram (kg.), and ton (metric ton).

1,000 milligrams	1 gram
1,000 grams	1 kilogram
1,000 kilograms	1 metric ton

Capacity

The denominations in use are cubic centimeter (c.c.) and liter (l.).

1,000 cubic centimeters	1 liter
100 liters	1 hectoliter

Relation of capacity and weight to length: a cubic decimeter is, approximately, a liter, and a liter of water weighs one kilogram.

APPROXIMATE EQUIVALENTS

A meter (39.37 inches) is about a yard.
A kilogram (2.2 pounds) is about two pounds.
A liter (0.91 dry qt. and 1.06 liquid qts.) is about a quart.
A centimeter (0.39 inch) is about one half inch.
A metric ton (2,204.6 pounds) is about a long ton.
A kilometer (0.62 mile, or 3,280 feet) is about 5/8 mile.
A cubic centimeter is about a thimbleful.
A nickel weighs about five grams.

For postal purposes fifteen grams are considered the equivalent of one-half ounce avoirdupois. At the mint a half dollar is considered to weigh 12.5 grams.

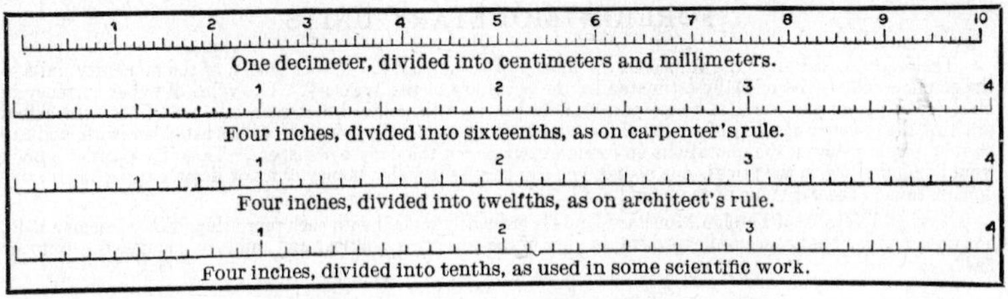
One decimeter, divided into centimeters and millimeters.
Four inches, divided into sixteenths, as on carpenter's rule.
Four inches, divided into twelfths, as on architect's rule.
Four inches, divided into tenths, as used in some scientific work.

THE DECIMETER AND THE INCH

DOMESTIC WEIGHTS AND MEASURES

Long Measure

12 inches	1 foot
3 feet	1 yard
5½ yards	1 rod or pole
40 rods	1 furlong
8 furlongs	1 statute mile (1,760 yards, or 5,280 feet)
3 miles	1 league

Mariners' Measure

6 feet	1 fathom
100 fathoms	1 cable length, or about 1/10 nautical mile
5,280 feet	1 statute mile
6,080.20 feet	1 nautical mile

Surveyors' Measure

1 link	7.92 inches
100 links	1 chain
1 chain	22 yards
10 square chains	1 acre

Square Measure

144 square inches	1 square foot
9 square feet	1 square yard
30¼ square yards	1 square rod
40 square rods	1 rood
4 roods, 160 square rods	1 acre

[An acre contains 43,560 square feet, equivalent to a square approximately 208′ 8½″ on a side.]

640 acres	1 square mile
100 square feet	1 square: used in roofing, etc.

Cubic Measure

1,728 cubic inches	1 cubic foot
27 cubic feet	1 cubic yard
24¾ cubic feet	1 perch

Wood Measure

24¾ cubic feet	1 perch
16 cubic feet	1 cord foot
8 cord feet, or 128 cubic feet	1 cord, a pile of wood 8 feet long, 4 feet wide, and 4 feet high.

Dry Measure

2 pints	1 quart
8 quarts	1 peck
4 pecks	1 bushel
quart, dry measure	67.2 cubic inches
bushel, level	2,150.42 cubic inches

Liquid Measure

4 gills	1 pint
2 pints	1 quart
4 quarts	1 gallon
31½ gallons	1 barrel
2 barrels	1 hogshead

gallon.. 231 cubic inches. [This is the unit of liquid measure; a gallon of water weighs 8⅓ pounds.]

barrel	4 1/5 cubic feet

Apothecaries' Fluid Measure

60 minims	1 fluid dram
8 fluid drams	1 fluid ounce
16 fluid ounces	1 pint
8 pints	1 gallon

Apothecaries' Weight

20 grains	1 scruple
3 scruples	1 dram
8 drams	1 ounce
12 ounces	1 pound

Avoirdupois Weight

16 drams	1 ounce
16 ounces	1 pound (7,000 grains)
25 pounds	1 quarter
4 quarters, or 100 pounds	1 short hundredweight
112 pounds	1 long hundredweight
20 hundredweight	1 ton
2,000 pounds	1 short ton
2,240 pounds	1 long ton

Troy Weight

24 grains	1 pennyweight
20 pennyweights	1 ounce
12 ounces	1 pound
3 1/5 grains	1 carat

[The metric carat, 200 milligrams, is now generally used by jewelers.]

Angular Measure

60 seconds (″)	1 minute (′)
60 minutes	1 degree (°)
90 degrees	1 right angle or quadrant
360 degrees	1 circle or circumference
1 radian	57.296°

Time Measure

60 seconds	1 minute
60 minutes	1 hour
24 hours	1 day
7 days	1 week
28 to 31 solar days	1 month
365 solar days	1 common year
366 solar days	1 leap year

[1 tropical year = 365 days, 5 hours, 48 minutes, 46 seconds; 1 Julian year = 365¼ days.]

FOREIGN MONETARY UNITS

The following list gives the values, in the money of account of the United States, of the monetary units of the countries named, as officially estimated by the Secretary of the Treasury. The value of paper currency in many countries of the world is below par, and fluctuates with political and economic conditions. In actual practice, the *commercial values* of money of foreign countries are usually below the values listed herewith, and can be found by consulting the quotations on foreign exchange in the daily newspapers. Thus if you order a book from London of which the price is one pound, you can pay for it with a money order or draft costing about five dollars, though the par value of the pound is $8.2397.

NOTE.—The table of Foreign Monetary Units is ordinarily revised with each reprinting. Since January 1940, however, revision has not seemed expedient, in view of the unsettled political and military conditions.—October 1943.

COUNTRY	Monetary Unit	Value in Terms of U.S. Money	COUNTRY	Monetary Unit	Value in Terms of U.S. Money
Argentina	Peso[1]	$1.6335	India (British)	Rupee	$0.6180
Austria	See Germany		Indo-China	Piaster[9]	.2250
Belgium	Belga[2]	.1695	Irish Free State	See Eire	
Bolivia	Boliviano	.6180	Italy	Lira [*pl.* lire]	.0526
Brazil	Milreis	.0606	Japan	Yen [*pl.* yen]	.8440
British Colonies in			Latvia	Lat [*pl.* lati]	.3267
Australasia and Africa	Pound Sterling	8.2397	Liberia	Dollar[10]	1.6931
British Honduras	Dollar	1.6931	Lithuania	Litas	.1693
Bulgaria	Lev [*pl.* leva]	.0122	Mexico	Peso[11]	.1675
Canada	Dollar	1.6931	Netherlands	Guilder (florin)[12]	.6806
Chile	Peso	.2060	Newfoundland	Dollar	1.6931
China	Yuan[3]	.2950	Nicaragua	Cordoba	1.6933
	Hong Kong		Norway	Krone [*pl.* kroner]	.4537
	Dollar[3]	.2485	Panama	Balboa[4]	1.0000
Colombia	Peso	.5714	Paraguay	Peso (Argentine)[13]	1.6335
Costa Rica	Colon	.7879	Persia (Iran)	Rial	.0824
Cuba	Peso	1.0000	Peru	Sol	.4740
Czechoslovakia	Koruna		Philippine Islands	Peso	.5000
Denmark	Krone [*pl.* kroner]	.4537	Poland	Zloty	.1899
Dominican Republic	Dollar[4]	1.6931	Portugal	Escudo	.0749
Ecuador	Sucre	.3386	Rumania	Leu [*pl.* lei]	.0101
Egypt	Pound (100 pias-		Russia (Union of Soviet		
	ters)	8.3692	Socialist Republics)	Chervonetz[14]	8.7123
Eire	Irish pound	8.2397	Salvador	Colon	.8466
Estonia	Kroon	.4537	Siam	See Thailand	
Finland	Markka	.0426	Spain	Peseta	
France	Franc[3]	.0225	Straits Settlements	Dollar[15]	.9613
Germany	Reichsmark	.4033	Sweden	Krona [*pl.* kronor]	.4537
	Registered mark[5]	.2300	Switzerland	Franc[5]	.2243
Great Britain	Pound sterling[6]	8.2397	Thailand (Siam)	Baht (tical)	.7491
Greece	Drachma	.0220	Turkey	Piaster[16]	.0744
Guatemala	Quetzal	1.6931	Union of South Africa	Pound Sterling	8.2397
Haiti	Gourde[7]	.2000	Uruguay	Peso	.6583
Honduras	Lempira[8]	.8466	Venezuela	Bolivar	.3267
Hungary	Pengő	.2961	Yugoslavia	Dinar	.0298

[1] Currency, paper nominally convertible at 44% of face value.—[2] 1 belga equals 5 Belgian francs.—[3] No official value assigned; value listed as approximate exchange rate.—[4] U. S. money is principal circulation medium.—[5] No fixed value; price fluctuates. Figure given is an approximate exchange rate.—[6] Obligation to sell gold at legal monetary par suspended September 21, 1931.—[7] Currency, national bank notes redeemable on demand in American dollars.—[8] Lempira circulates as equivalent of half of a U. S. dollar.—[9] Piaster pegged to French franc: 1 piaster = 10 French francs.—[10] U. S. money is principal circulating medium.—[11] A decree of August 28, 1936, left the value of the peso to be later defined by law. Value given is current exchange rate.—[12] Convertibility of notes into gold suspended September 26, 1936.—[13] Currency, depreciated Paraguayan paper currency.—[14] Prewar unit was the ruble, then equivalent to about 51 cents.—[15] British pound sterling also legal tender.—[16] 100 piasters equal to the Turkish pound.

NOTE.—Unsettled conditions throughout the world have made it appear impracticable to keep this table up to date since 1940. It may be remarked, however, that in Liberia (see Note 10 above) U. S. money is now the principal circulating medium.—June 1944.

NOTABLE STATISTICS OF THE WORLD

GATHERED FROM THE LATEST CENSUS REPORTS AND OTHER SOURCES

STATISTICS OF THE COUNTRIES OF THE EARTH

Countries	Population	Sq. Miles	Capitals
NORTH AMERICA			
United States and Possessions	137,008,435	3,738,395	Washington
United States, Continental	122,775,046	3,026,789	Washington
Alaska	59,278	586,400	Juneau
American Samoa	10,055	76	Pago Pago
Guam	18,509	206	Agana
Hawaii	368,336	6,407	Honolulu
Panama Canal Zone	39,467	549	Colon
Philippine Islands	12,082,366	114,400	Manila City
Porto Rico	1,543,913	3,435	San Juan
Virgin Islands	22.012	133	St. Thomas
Canada	10,374,198	3,510,008	Ottawa
Mexico	16,404,030	767,198	Mexico City
British Honduras	51,228	8,598	Belize
Costa Rica	503,856	23,000	San José
Guatemala	2,004,900	42,353	Guatemala City
Honduras	859,761	44,275	Tegucigalpa
Nicaragua	750,000	51,660	Managua
Panama	467,459	32,380	Panama City
Salvador	1,722,579	13,176	San Salvador
Greenland	14,355	46,740	Godthaab
Newfoundland	266,401	42,734	St. John's
Cuba	3,607,919	44,164	Habana
Haiti	2,300,200	10,204	Port-au-Prince
Dominican Republic	1,200,000	19,332	Santo Domingo
SOUTH AMERICA			
Argentine Republic	11,660,000	1,153,119	Buenos Aires
Bolivia	2,974,904	514,155	La Paz
Brazil	40,272,650	3,275,510	Rio de Janeiro
British Guiana	309,676	89,480	Georgetown
Chile	4,264,819	290,119	Santiago
Colombia	7,851,000	447,536	Bogotá
Dutch Guiana (Surinam)	151,350	54,291	Paramaribo
Ecuador	1,785,800	220,502	Quito
Falkland Islands	2,375	5,618	Stanley
French Guiana	47,341	34,740	Cayenne
Paraguay	843,905	61,647	Asunción
Peru	6,147,000	532,047	Lima
Uruguay	2,036,884	72,153	Montevideo
Venezuela	3,053,497	393,874	Caracas
EUROPE			
Albania	1,003,068	10,629	Tirana
Andorra	5,231	191	Andorra

STATISTICS OF THE COUNTRIES OF THE EARTH—Continued

Countries	Population	Sq. Miles	Capitals
Austrian Republic	6,704,467	32,369	Vienna
Belgium	9,060,189	11,755	Brussels
British Empire	449,349,000	13,357,672	London
British Isles	47,307,601	121,633	London
Bulgaria	5,824,900	39,814	Sofia
Czechoslovakia	14,608,412	54,207	Prague (Praha)
Danzig	407,515	754	Danzig
Denmark	3,434,555	16,568	Copenhagen
Estonia	1,114,861	18,353	Tallinn
Finland	3,634,047	132,589	Helsinki
France and Colonies	92,938,418	5,595,694	Paris
France	41,130,000	212,659	Paris
German Republic	63,178,619	181,723	Berlin
Greece	6,204,684	49,912	Athens
Hungary	8,683,740	35,875	Budapest
Iceland	106,350	39,709	Reykjavik
Italy and Possessions	43,000,000	708,976	Rome
Italy	41,173,000	119,710	Rome
Latvia	1,900,450	24,440	Riga
Liechtenstein	10,213	65	Vaduz
Lithuania	2,340,038	21,489	Kaunas
Luxembourg	222,092	999	Luxembourg
Monaco	24,927	8	Monaco
Netherlands and Possessions	56,216,148	746,224	The Hague
Netherlands	7,832,175	12,603	The Hague (Amsterdam)
Norway	2,649,775	125,086	Oslo
Poland	30,737,448	149,958	Warsaw
Portugal and Possessions	14,770,844	971,754	Lisbon
Portugal	6,032,991	35,490	Lisbon
Rumania	17,393,149	122,282	Bucharest
Russia (Soviet Republic)	161,006,200	8,241,910	Moscow
San Marino	13,013	38	San Marino
Spain and Possessions	22,743,147	334,783	Madrid
Spain	21,763,147	194,800	Madrid
Sweden	6,120,080	173,146	Stockholm
Switzerland	4,067,305	15,940	Berne
Republic of Turkey	13,648,270	294,416	Ankara
Ukraine	29,020,304	166,368	Kharkov
Yugoslavia	13,290,000	96,134	Beograd
Asia			
Afghanistan	11,000,000	260,000	Kábul
Arabia	7,000,000	1,000,000	Mecca
Aden	54,923	9,080	Aden
Asir	900,000	20,000	Sabiyah
Hejaz	1,000,000	170,000	Mecca
Nejd	3,000,000	....	Riyadh
Oman	500,000	82,000	Muskat
Yemen	2,500,000	75,000	Sana'
British India	351,500,000	1,805,332	Delhi
French India	288,546	196	Pondicherry

STATISTICS OF THE COUNTRIES OF THE EARTH—Continued

Countries	Population	Sq. Miles	Capitals
Portuguese India	570,426	1,461	Pangin
Chinese Republic	485,508,838	4,279,170	Nanking
Cyprus	310,715	3,584	Nicosia
Dutch East Indies	52,824,569	733,715	Batavia
Japanese Empire	91,792,639	265,129	Tokyo
Japan proper	64,447,724	152,357	Tokyo
Korea (Chösen)	19,189,699	85,228	Seoul
Sakhalin	203,754	13,935	
Formosa (Taiwan)	4,438,084	13,892	Taihoku
Manchukuo	29,606,117	460,383	Hsinking
Iraq (Mesopotamia)	2,849,282	177,148	Baghdad
Nepal	5,600,000	54,000	Katmandu
Palestine	757,182	10,000	Jerusalem
Persia	10,000,000	628,000	Tehran
Siam	11,506,207	200,149	Bangkok
Syria	2,831,622	60,000	Beyrouth
Africa			
Liberia	2,250,000	43,000	Monrovia
Belgian Sphere of Influence—			
Belgian Congo	8,700,000	918,000	Leopoldville
British Sphere of Influence—			
Anglo-Egyptian Sudan	5,579,776	1,008,100	Khartum
Basutoland	498,781	11,716	Maseru
Bechuanaland	152,983	275,000	Mafeking
British East Africa	6,758,904	594,184	
Kenya Colony and Protectorate	3,003,158	224,960	Nairobi
Pemba (Island)	88,691	380	Zanzibar
Tanganyika Territory	4,800,630	374,000	Dar-es-Salaam
Uganda Protectorate	3,410,857	94,204	Entebbe
Zanzibar (Island)	128,099	640	Zanzibar
British Somaliland	344,700	68,000	Berbera
British West Africa	21,772,207	447,500	
Gambia	200,000	4,130	Bathurst
Egypt	14,213,364	383,000	Cairo
Ethiopia	10,000,000	350,000	Addis Ababa
Gold Coast	2,078,043	80,000	Accra
Cameroon (British)	700,050	34,236	Buca
Nigeria	19,409,001	335,700	Lagos
Sierra Leone	85,163	4,000	Freetown
Nyasaland	1,360,098	37,890	Ft. Jamison
Rhodesia	2,401,032	436,950	
Northern Rhodesia	1,308,632	287,950	Livingston
Southern Rhodesia	1,092,400	149,000	Salisbury
Southwest Africa	261,816	322,394	Windhoek
Swaziland	112,838	6,704	Pretoria
Togoland (British)	188,265	12,600	Lome
Union of South Africa	6,928,580	471,917	Pretoria
Cape of Good Hope	2,782,719	276,536	Cape Town
Natal	1,429,398	35,284	Pietermaritzburg
Orange Free State	628,827	49,647	Bloemfontein
Transvaal	2,087,636	110,450	Pretoria

STATISTICS OF THE COUNTRIES OF THE EARTH—Continued

Countries	Population	Sq. Miles	Capitals
French Sphere of Influence—			
Algeria	6,063,496	847,500	Algiers
French Equatorial Africa	3,127,707	912,049	Brazzaville
French Somali Coast	85,778	5,790	Jibuti
French West Africa and Sahara	13,541,611	1,440,191	Dakar
Colony of the Upper Volta	3,240,147	142,820	Ouaga-dougou
Dahomey	979,609	41,302	Porto Noro
French Guinea	2,095,988	89,436	Konakry
French Sudan	2,634,982	360,331	Bamako
Ivory Coast	1,724,545	121,590	Bingerville
Mauretania	289,184	347,400	Morocco
Senegal	1,318,287	74,112	St. Louis
Upper Niger Territory	1,218,717	463,200	Zungeru
Cameroon (French)	1,900,000	166,489	Yaoundé
Madagascar	3,621,342	241,094	Tananarive
Morocco	4,229,146	200,000	Rabat
Togoland (French)	730,504	33,700	Lomé
Tunisia	2,159,708	48,300	Tunis
Italian Sphere of Influence—			
Eritrea	621,776	45,435	Asmara
Italian Somaliland	1,200,000	190,000	Mogadishu
Libya	723,914	420,500	Tripoli
Portuguese Sphere of Influence—			
Angola (Portuguese West Africa)	2,481,956	486,071	Loanda
Mozambique	3,514,602	287,756	Lourenço-Marques
Portuguese Guinea	343,961	22,000	Bolama
Spanish Sphere of Influence—			
Rio de Oro	495	109,200	Villa Cisneros
Spanish Guinea	140,000	10,036	Santa Isabel
Spanish Morocco	600,000	7,700	Tetuan
Australia	6,438,999	74,581	Canberra
New Zealand	1,344,469	103,569	Wellington
Tasmania	213,780	26,215	Hobart

PARTS OF SPEECH AND THEIR USES

HINTS AND HELPS.

The ready use of good language is largely the result of practice in writing and of an abundance of good reading. In the choice of words, the paramount consideration should be exactness. That is, seek to say precisely what the thought requires, neither more nor less. This demands, of course, close scrutiny of meanings, and independence of current fashions in words. Seek to have at command more than one expression for the same thing. Not that several forms are in any case to be employed, but it often happens that if the writer has not thought broadly and deeply enough to have more than one expression for his idea, the one that he has will be meagre. Cultivate the habit of observing the derivation and history of words. A word whose etymology is known defines itself: the writer feels its force intuitively, and need not depend on a dictionary. Enlarge your vocabulary by diligent study of usage in the best writers. The true meaning of words is expressed only when they are interwoven with other words. No fineness of usage can be acquired from the dictionary alone. Do not use technical terms where they are not likely to be understood. Beware of fine writing. By fine writing is meant the use of pretentious terms for trivial ideas.

USES OF THE ARTICLES *A* or *AN*.

1. The article *a* is used before words beginning with a consonant sound, or *y* or *w*; as, a cat, a union, a yew tree, a ewe lamb, a eulogy, such **a** one.

2. The article *an* is used before words beginning with a vowel sound, or silent *h* sound; as. an officer, an aged man, an honor.

USES OF ADJECTIVES.

An adjective describes or limits the noun or pronoun to which it is joined.

Adjectives are usually placed before the noun or pronoun they qualify.

The ascending comparison of adjectives is formed by adding er and est or more and most to the positive form, and the descending comparison by adding less and least.

The comparative degree is used in comparing two objects; the superlative when more than two are compared.

Some adjectives can not be compared, and no adjective will admit of a double comparison.

This and that are singular, these and those are plural.

Two negative forms are not permissible.

THE USES OF THE ADVERB.

An adverb limits or emphasizes a verb, an adjective, or another adverb.

An adverb is often used incorrectly to fulfil the office of another part of speech. A useful rule to follow in the selection of an adverb is to make sure that it answers one of these questions: How? When? Where? In what manner? To what degree? The most common adverbs are the following:

accordingly, afterwards, also, besides, consequently, early, ever, everywhere, hence, here, how, however, late, little, moreover, most, much, nevertheless, now, often, once, rather, so, somewhat, still, then, thence, there, therefore, thus, too, very, well, when, whence, whenever, where, whether, whither, why, yet.

There are many adverbs that are formed from adjectives by adding the letters *ly*, as, *carefully, slowly, swiftly.*

Adverbs should be placed as near the word or words they modify as possible. An adverb should never be placed between to and the infinitive.

USES OF THE PREPOSITION.

A preposition shows the relation between a noun or a pronoun which follows it and some other word. Below are the prepositions most commonly used:

about, above, across, after, against, along, amid, among, around, before, behind, below, beside, between, beyond, but, by, concerning, despite, down, during, ere, except, excepting, for, from, in, into, near, of, off, on, over, save, since, through, throughout, till, to, toward, under, until, unto, up, with, within, without.

USES OF THE CONJUNCTION.

A conjunction is the simplest of the connectives, and is used to join words, phrases, clauses, or sentences. The principal conjunctions are the following:

also, although, and, as, because, both, but, either, except, for, however, if, lest, neither, nevertheless, nor, notwithstanding, or, provided, save, seeing, since, so, still, than, that, then, therefore, though, unless, what, when, whereas, whereat, whereby, wherefor, wherefore, wherein, whereof, whereupon, wherever (where'er), whether, while, without, yet.

Correlative conjunctions are: *although-yet, as-as, as-so, both-and, either-or, if-then, neither-nor, now-now, now-then, so-as, though-yet, whereas-therefore, whether-or.*

THE USES OF PRONOUNS.

The Possessive of Pronouns.—In forming the possessive the letter s only is added to the singular.

Examples.—Yours, hers, theirs. The possessive of who and which is whose. The relatives that and those have no possessive forms.

Singular and Plural Pronouns.—The pronoun should be in the same number as its antecedent.

The relative who is used to refer to persons; which, to inferior animals and things without life: what is used to refer to things, and that to both persons and things. Euphony, as a rule, determines between the uses of who, which and that.

Either refers to "one of the two;" when more than two are referred to "any one" should be used. Neither refers to "no one of the two;" but when more than two are referred to, "no one" should be used. Each refers to numbers separately; all refers to numbers collectively.

THE USES OF NOUNS.

The Possessive Case.—The possessive of nouns in the singular number is formed by adding an apostrophe and the letter s.

Example.—"The girl's bonnet."

Sometimes the possessive is formed by adding the apostrophe only. This is done where the added s makes an unpleasant sound. However, this is a matter of taste.

Examples.—"For goodness' sake;" "John's hat;" "Dickens' Tale of Two Cities."

When the plural of a noun in the nominative case ends in s the possessive is formed by adding the apostrophe (') only, but if the plural does not end in s then the apostrophe (') and an s are added.

Example.—"Men's and boys' hats are for sale."

The possessive of compound nouns is formed by adding the sign of the possessive to the end of the compound.

Example.—"I drove my brother-in-law's horse."

Singular and Plural Number.—The plural of nouns is usually formed by adding s to the singular, but if the sound of s makes an additional syllable then es is added to form the plural.

Examples.—Hand, hands; church, churches.

Nouns ending in o preceded by a vowel form the plural by adding s only to the singular, but when the final o is preceded by a consonant the plural is formed by adding es to the singular

Nouns ending in y form their plurals by adding s to the singular, but if the final y is preceded by a consonant y is changed to i and es is added to form the plural.

Examples.—Money, moneys; lady, ladies.

In forming the plural of compound nouns the sign of the plural is added to the descriptive part of the phase.

Examples.—Aide-de-camp, aides-de-camp.

THE USES OF VERBS.

Verbs and Numbers.—Plural verbs require plural subjects; as, we were, not we was; you were, not you was; they are, not they is; they were, not they was; they have, not they has; they write, not they writes; the men are, not is the children were, not was; the boys have, not has; my sisters write, not writes; they are the boys who were at school. Jennie and Annie were schoolmates.

The Uses of the Auxiliary Verbs.—Shall, Will.—Will expresses the will or pleasure of its own subject. Shall subordinates the will of its subject to that of the speaker. "We will go," means "we are willing to go." "We shall go," means "we have decided upon going." Never say, "Will I do so and so?" The literal meaning of such an expression would be, "Am I willing to do," etc Remember that will always expresses willingness rather than futurity when it has a personal significance.

Should, Would.—Should is the past tense of shall, and would, the past tense of will, and the same rules governing the former govern also the latter. "We should go to town if we were able." "His wife would attend if you should ask her."

Can, Could; May, Might.—Can and could express ability or possibility, while may and might express permission. These words are often confused.

To Do; to See.—These two verbs give considerable trouble. Their principal forms are, do, did, done, and see, saw, seen The second forms, did and saw, should never follow is, are, was, were, have, has, or had. The third forms done and seen, should always follow one of these words expressed or understood; as, I did the work, or I have done the work, or the work is done. I saw the picture, or I have seen the picture, or the picture was seen.

Verbs in General.—The rules given for to do and to see apply alike to all verbs. Such expressions as have came, have sang, was drove, have broke, have began, have knew, is froze, have gave, knowed, has went, has give, has rang, have ran, were took, has stole, throwed, have mistook, etc., are gross errors and should be avoided.

Lie and Lay.—Remember that lie means rest and lay means an action affecting some object.

Examples.—"The watch lies on the piano." "I will lay the watch on the piano." "Mother laid your gloves away for you."

Sit and Set.—Sit means to be in position to rest, to repose. Set is an active, transitive verb and means "to put," "to place," "to plant," to place in a condition, a state, or a posture.

Examples.—"Come sit in the easy chair." "Set the table in the dining room."

Don't (Do Not) Doesn't (Does Not).—These words are often misused. When you are in doubt about their use, compare the full forms with the verb; as, He don't know. If the full form be used, the absurdity is quickly seen; as, He do not know. The correct form should be, He does not know.

Had Rather, Had Better, Had Ought.—These are incorrect forms for would rather, might better, and ought.

Bring, Fetch.—Bring implies motion toward the speaker, not away. Fetch implies motion, first from the speaker, then toward him.

Note the following verb forms:

Present.	Past.	Past Participle.
Alight (to dismount)	Alighted	Alighted
Begin	Began	Begun
Bid	Bade	Bidden or Bid
Bid (at auction)	Bid	Bid
Burst	Burst	Burst
Choose	Chose	Chosen
Do	Did	Done
Eat	Ate	Eaten
Light (to ignite)	Lighted	Lighted
Light (to settle down upon)	Lighted or Lit	Lighted or Lit
Lay	Laid	Laid
Lie	Lay	Lain
Rise	Rose	Risen
Raise	Raised	Raised
See	Saw	Seen
Set	Set	Set
Sit	Sat	Sat
Wake	Woke	Waked

ERRORS TO BE AVOIDED.

Administer.—Blows are dealt. Medicine is administered.
Afraid.—Say I fear it will rain, not I am afraid.
Alike.—Do not couple this word with both.
All over.—Over all the country, not all over the country.
Allow.—Do not say, "He allows he will do it."
Alone.—Distinguish this word from only.
Amateur.—Not necessarily a beginner.
And.—Say try to go, not try and go.
Angry.—Say angry with a person and at a thing.
Answer.—Answer questions; reply to assertions.
Anticipate.—Distinguish from expect.
As.—Say not that I know, instead of not as I know.
At all.—Superfluous in "any at all."
Awful.—A thing cannot be awful pretty.

Balance.—Not to be used for rest or remainder
Beautifully.—Looked beautiful, not beautifully.
Beg.—Say "I beg leave to acknowledge."
Belongs to.—Do not use for is a member of.
Between.—Between two; among more than two
Blacking.—This word is not blackening.
Brakeman.—Not brakesman.
Certain.—Distinguish from sure.
Character.—Distinguish from reputation.
Deal.—Great deal, not good deal.
Die with.—Persons die of, not with disease.
Disremember.—Say forget.
Don't.—Say he doesn't sing, not he don't sing.
Either.—Means the one or the other of two.
Either alternative.—Alternative means choice.
Equally well.—Do not say equally as well.
Every.—Followed by a verb in the singular.
Expect.—Refers to future time.
Fix.—Incorrectly used for arrange or prepare.
Folk.—Folk implies plurality as well as folks.
Gent.—Never use this contraction of gentleman.
Good.—"It looks good." Say well.
Got.—Omit got in "I have got a dollar."
Guess.—Do not use this word for suppose.
Had have.—Never use together.
Hardly.—Do not use with don't and can't.
Healthy.—Distinguish from wholesome.
Hundred.—Use the singular form with numerals.
Just.—Incorrect in the sense of now.
Learn.—To receive instruction. See teach.
Less.—Relates to quantity; fewer to number.
May.—Distinguish from can.
Near.—Do not use in the sense of nearly.
New.—"A pair of new boots;" not "a new pair."
Nice.—See definition of this word.
None.—Contraction of no one, takes singular.
Otherwise than.—Not otherwise but.
Party.—Do not use for person.
Perpetual.—Distinguish from continual.
Portion.—Often incorrectly used for part.
Posted.—Do not use instead of informed.
Prevalent.—Distinguish from prevailing.
Promise.—Distinguish from assure.
Propose.—Distinguish from purpose.
Prudence.—Distinguish from discretion.
Quantity.—Things measured or weighed.
Real.—The adverb is really; as, really good.
Remember.—Distinguish from recollect.
Seem.—Distinguish from appear.
Settle.—To settle does not mean to pay.
So, such.—So long journeys, not such long.
Some better.—Say somewhat better.
Splendid.—Splendid things glitter.
Stop.—We stay at a certain hotel, not stop.
Streamlet.—Do not use with little.
Summon.—Summon is a verb, summons a noun
Teach.—To give instruction. See learn.
Those kind.—Say that kind. Kind is singular.
Transpire.—Do not use for to happen.
Try.—We make an experiment, not try.
Widow woman.—Woman is here superfluous.
Without.—Do not use without for unless.
Year-old.—A two-year-old colt, not a two-years

BUSINESS FORMS AND LAWS

WHAT MONEY IS.

Money is defined as "that which passes freely from hand to hand throughout the community in final discharge of debts and full payment for commodities, being accepted equally without reference to the character or credit of the person who offers it and without the intention of the person who receives it to consume it or enjoy it or apply it to any other use than in turn to tender it to others in discharge of debts or payment for commodities." Currency is the name given to the legal medium of exchange in every country.

Various articles have passed current as money in various communities at different times, but the standard of monetary value of the civilized nations of the world is a fixed amount of gold or of silver, which, taken together, is called bullion.

In the United States the dollar is the unit of value, and is equal to 15.23 grains of gold nine-tenths fine. It was formerly equal to 25.8 grains nine-tenths fine, or 23.22 grains of pure gold; but by the Gold Reserve Act and proclamation of President Roosevelt in January, 1934, the dollar was devalued and stabilized on the basis of 59.06 of its former gold value.

The gold coins of the United States—called in by the government in 1933–34—contain gold in the proportion of 900 parts of gold and 100 parts alloy, and are the only form of money actually worth its face value as a commodity. The gold coins in circulation prior to 1933 included the 20-dollar piece or double eagle, the 10-dollar piece or eagle, the 5-dollar piece or half eagle, and the 2½-dollar piece or quarter eagle. The almost mythical gold dollar had not been coined since 1890.

The silver dollar weighs 412½ grains, of which 371¼ grains is pure silver and 41¼ grains alloy. This amount of pure silver was at one time equal in value with 23.22 grains of pure gold, but it decreased in value and its relative value to gold became determined by commercial conditions. The half dollar, quarter dollar and dime (one-tenth dollar or ten cents), as well as the 5-cent nickel and the bronze cent are in wide circulation as representatives of the fractional parts of a dollar.

PAPER MONEY.

There is another medium of exchange not having any value in itself, but representing the credit of the government. It is, in fact, a form of "promise to pay," and for that reason it is often called "fiat money" or "paper money." Before the United States suspended the gold standard (1933) and called in all the gold, the various types of paper money had very definite significance, but after devaluation of the gold dollar in 1934 these distinctions were of little consequence. First was the gold certificate, or "yellow back," issued against deposits at par of gold and bullion, and redeemable on demand. This was called in and a new form of gold certificate was authorized by Act of January 31, 1934; it was not convertible into gold. Second is the silver certificate, redeemable in silver. Third is the Treasury note, or "greenback," backed by a certain gold reserve but not redeemable; it was called into existence in 1862 and for a time depreciated in value, but today it is on a par with any other paper money. Fourth is the National Bank note, issued by banks holding a charter from the United States, whose circulation is secured by United States bonds deposited with the Treasurer of the United States. Fifth are the Federal Reserve notes, obligations of the twelve Federal Reserve banks and of the national government, formerly convertible into gold, but no longer so convertible. Finally there are the Federal Reserve Bank notes, issued by the Federal Reserve banks themselves; these rest upon U. S. Government obligations pledged as security, also upon certain classes of notes, drafts, bills of exchange, and bankers' acceptances; they are not convertible, and there is no maximum limit placed upon their issue. It should be said that while the dollar bill, and the five- and ten- and twenty-dollar bill are widely used, fully 90 per cent of the country's business is done by the use of bank checks.

BANKS AND BANKING.

Banks, both national and private, offer another means of exchange. Any one having money deposited in a bank to his credit may give to a third party an order on the bank for any number of dollars and cents not exceeding the full amount of his credit. These orders on the banks are called Bank Checks. They differ from paper money, as their acceptance depends upon the credit of the one who draws (or signs) the check. It is usually made payable "to the order of" some one.

The use of checks adds to the circulating medium, and is a benefit to the community at large. It leaves actual money for minor transactions. They are in far more extensive use than any other form of money order. Checks often pass from hand to hand as money before they reach the bank, and then are seldom cashed—usually deposited. Over a hundred million dollars of checks daily in New York alone are not cashed at the paying teller's window, but pass in "exchanges" through the Clearing House, which is an association of the banks of a large city for the purpose of conveniently and quickly transferring checks they hold for collection.

UTILITY OF BANK ACCOUNTS.

Some advantages of keeping an account at bank are:

(1) The bank accepts money on deposit subject to check; (2) it lends money on approved security; (3) it facilitates the sending of money from place to place by allowing the deposits to be drawn out on an order called a check; (4) it provides a safe place to keep valuables and securities; (5) it is very helpful in making collections, such as notes, checks, drafts and trade acceptances; (6) it advises its patrons concerning the advisability of making investments.

HOW TO OPEN A BANK ACCOUNT.

When a patron desires to open an account with a bank, he will usually be required to obtain an introduction to the officer of the bank by some one known to them. After this identification he will be requested to write his name on a signature card in the same way he expects to sign the orders or checks when he desires the bank to deduct money from his account. The object of having this signature on file in the bank is to identify the signature on the check with the one on the card. A plain, neat signature is most difficult to imitate.

The items of the deposit and the amount are entered on a deposit ticket and handed to the receiving teller of the bank, who will enter the amount in a bank book which will be given to the depositor. This bank book serves as a receipt to show the amount you have deposited in the bank.

In listing checks the common practice is to write the name of the local bank on which the check was drawn in the space on the left of the money column on a line with the amount of the check. Each check should be listed separately. If the bank on which the check is drawn is an out-of-town one the name of the city or town should be written instead of the name of the bank.

This practice has been changed to some extent by the numerical system introduced by the Federal Reserve Banks. The United States is divided into twelve districts and each district has located in it a bank which is known as a Federal Reserve Bank. Each reserve bank is assigned a serial number. Other banks located in one of these districts may become members of the Federal Reserve System. Each one of the member banks also will be assigned a serial number. If the member bank is located in one of the twelve cities where a Federal Reserve Bank has been established, the member bank will take as its initial number the one assigned to the Federal Reserve Bank of that city. For instance, the Federal Reserve Bank No. 3 is located in Philadelphia, Pa. Any other member bank located in Philadelphia will have a number assigned to it as follows: 3–56. The figure 3 means that it is located in Philadelphia and it is number 56.

Each state also has an assigned number. If a member bank is located outside of the city in which the Federal Reserve Bank is located the initial number will be the same as assigned to that state. For instance, a member bank located in Reading may have such a number as 60–73. These numbers will be printed on the check of a member bank and should be used in place of the name of the bank or city when listing checks on the deposit ticket.

CHECKS.

A Check is a written demand, which is addressed to a bank by a person who has money deposited therein for the payment of a part or the whole of his money to a third party.

Most business men number their checks in the order they are issued. The number is found in one of the corners which is not occupied by the value of the check written in figures.

HOW TO DRAW A CHECK.

Checks are principally of two kinds: Negotiable and Non-negotiable.

A Negotiable Check is one that may be transferred from one person to another, and a Non-negotiable Check is one that cannot be so transferred.

In drawing a negotiable check the order may be in one of the following forms: Pay to Bearer; Pay to the order of So-and-so; Pay to So-and-so or order. The first makes the money payable to any one that may present the check. The second or third makes the money payable to any person to whom the payee may order it paid.

When the word Bearer is used, the check is negotiable as it stands; but when the word order is used, the payee can neither collect the money himself nor transfer the check to another without writing his name upon the back. This is called indorsing the check. When the payee writes his name only, he is said to indorse the check in blank. By this indorsement he makes the money payable to bearer and the check is still negotiable. When the payee wishes the money paid to a particular person only, he writes on the back "Pay to the order of" So-and-so, and signs his name beneath. With such an indorsement the check is no longer negotiable until signed by the indorsee. If the indorsee wishes to transfer the check to another he either indorses the check in blank, when it again becomes negotiable, or repeats the indorsement to a particular person, and signs his own name beneath. This may be repeated by a third person, and so on. The Holder is the person who is in legal possession of a check.

HOW TO INDORSE CHECKS.

For indorsement, first turn the check so as to bring the left end to the top, and then turn it face downwards and write the indorsement near the top Each successive indorsement should be written under its predecessor.

Checks are usually bound in books. At the left of each check so bound, and on the same piece of paper is a ruled form for a complete description of the check. Between the check and this ruled form there is a line of perforations by means of which the check can be torn off for use. The paper that remains behind is called the stub.

Before depositing the checks they must first be indorsed by the person who is receiving credit for the money. The customary form of indorsement to write or stamp across the back of the check and about one inch from the top:

FOR DEPOSIT TO CREDIT OF
Herbert Smith
or
FOR DEPOSIT ONLY
IN THE HANOVER BANK
FOR CREDIT OF
Herbert Smith

The left end of the face of the check is the top of the back. Any person named for the purpose may sign an indorsement for deposit. Checks thus indorsed can only be deposited, and should they be lost on the way to the bank the finder cannot use them, because as stated the checks are to be deposited, and the bank is not authorized to pay them to any one.

If the holder receives a check in which his name is incorrectly written, he must first indorse the name as it is written and under that write his own name correctly. When the deposit slip has been made out, it is well to keep a copy upon the stub of the check book. The checks, money, deposit slip and pass book are then taken to the receiving teller, who examines the deposit slip to see that it is correct, and enters the amount in the pass book. This entry s his receipt for the amount deposited.

It is of the highest importance that the depositor keep his check book correctly and punctually written up. It is his guide to his bank account and he should be able to tell at once exactly how much money he has in bank at any given time.

RECONCILIATION OF BANK STATEMENT.

The modern bank prepares and sends to its depositors at the end of each month a statement showing the amount of the previous balance, deposits received and checks paid during the month. When this statement is received the depositor should compare the stubs in his check book with the checks listed as paid. If all the checks have been paid the balance should be the same. The statement may show a larger balance than the check book on a certain date. This will be the case if some of the checks which have been written and deducted from the check book have not yet been presented and paid by the bank. In order to prove the bank's statement, the sum of all checks which have not been paid by the bank should be deducted from the balance shown on the bank's statement, and this should equal the balance on the stub of the check book.

If the bank does not send monthly statements, the pass book should be left at the bank for settlement at intervals.

CERTIFIED CHECKS.

In many transactions, involving the transfer of a large amount of valuable property for cash, an ordinary check is not satisfactory to the person who is parting with his property, for he is not sure that his check will be honored when presented, however good the standing of the drawer may be. Therefore the check may be presented to the paying teller or cashier of the bank on which the check has been drawn, who, after finding that the amount is still to drawer's credit, writes or stamps across its face the words "Good when properly indorsed," or "certified," and signs his name. The amount of the check is at once charged to drawer's account, and is the same as cash withdrawn. The certification of checks is largely practiced in large business centers, as in Wall Street, New York, where the daily sales of stocks and bonds run up into the millions, and failures caused by fluctuation in prices often come with startling rapidity. A check which may be good to-day, to-morrow may be worthless.

When a check has been lost in the mails or otherwise, stolen, or given in mistake, the payment of the same may be stopped by the drawer at any time before it is presented at bank. Parties holding such a check honestly, and for value given, may have recourse to law for collection of same.

TRADE ACCEPTANCES.

A trade acceptance must rise out of an actual commercial transaction. It must comply with most of the requirements of negotiable paper. It must possess a definite maturity. It must be an unconditional promise to pay at maturity. It must be signed by the party who has made the purchase of merchandise. All of the above requirements tend toward making the paper self-liquidating. The trade acceptance is given at the time the transaction is made, and carries with it no imputation of inability to pay. When a person sells a bill of merchandise to another he may send with the bill a trade acceptance which the buyer will accept and return. The person selling the merchandise may take the trade acceptance to his bank and discount it and reinvest the money at once. The trade acceptance has a definite specified period of time. The principal thought behind the trade acceptance is to make the financing of transactions easier for all concerned. It tends to make the credit of the country more mobile.

DRAFTS AND BILLS OF EXCHANGE.

A draft, or bill of exchange, is, in fact, a letter written by one person to another living in a different place, requesting him to pay a sum of money to the order of the drawer or to a third person. Commercial usage recognizes particular forms for writing these drafts.

There are two kinds of bills of exchange, Domestic and Foreign.

Domestic Bills of Exchange are payable in the same country in which they are drawn, and are commonly called Drafts.

Foreign Bills of Exchange are payable in another country from that in which they are drawn, and are called Foreign Drafts.

The person who signs a bill of exchange (or draft) is called the Drawer or Maker; the one to whom it is addressed, the Drawee; the one to whom it is made payable, the Payee; and the person who is in legal possession of it, the Holder.

Bills of exchange, like notes and checks, are either negotiable or non-negotiable, according as they are payable to the order of a person or simply to the person himself. The former are the more common.

A Sight Draft is one payable at sight; that is, on presentation.

A Time Draft is one made payable a certain specified length of time after sight or after date.

Foreign bills of exchange are usually made in sets of three, which are alike in all respects except their designations of first, second, and third. The three bills are usually sent by different mails, and whichever arrives first is used. The others are then worthless. These bills differ from ordinary drafts, by the insertion in each, of the condition that it is to be paid if the other two of the set are unpaid.

Drafts are sent through banks, and not through the mails, and are used to avoid the risk, inconvenience, and expense of sending actual money from one place to another. The principal object for which it is used is to collect money due from the drawee to the drawer. For instance, if Jones, of Chicago, owes Smith, of Philadelphia, $750, Smith may draw on Jones for that amount. He will deposit the draft properly drawn with his own bank in Philadelphia, which will forward it to the bank with which Jones does business in Chicago, and which is called its correspondent. The draft when received in Chicago is presented to Jones at his place of business, who pays it by check or cash, or stamps or writes across its face:

ACCEPTED
June 12, 19—
PAYABLE AT
FIRST NATIONAL BANK.
JOHN JONES.

Or, he may write write across the face simply "Accepted" and his name. The draft will then be paid at Jones' office when it falls due.

The draft in the former case becomes a check on Jones' account at the First National Bank when it is charged against his account. The bank in Chicago then credits and advises the bank in Philadelphia, which in turn credits Smith.

By courtesy Smith, when making the draft upon Jones, advises him at once of the fact, that he may be prepared to pay it.

If not paid, the draft is protested—that is, a formal statement of the fact of presentation is made by a notary and served upon drawer and all who have indorsed their names to the draft.

But if the drawer does not wish to incur the expense of protest fees, or to injure the credit of the debtor, there may be pinned to the draft a piece of paper with the words "No protest" upon it. This is to notify the bank presenting the draft that the drawer does not wish it protested if not paid. It is important that this slip of paper be detached before the draft is presented or else the draft would lose its "force."

A check is practically a sight draft upon a bank; but there is a marked difference between a "check" and a "draft." For example: The form and wording are different; a check is drawn upon a bank or banker with whom funds have been deposited; a draft is drawn upon an individual or business house.

Checks are used for paying money to creditors: drafts are used as a means of collecting moneys due to the one drawing.

Checks, when properly drawn and presented, must be paid by the bank if it has funds belonging to the drawer.

The party drawn upon is under no obligation to honor a draft, if for any reason he choses not to do so.

DUE BILLS.

A Due Bill is a formal written acknowledgment that a certain amount is due.

It should in capitalization, punctuation, and arrangement of parts, follow the same rules as are followed for business letters.

Due bills are often given in settling accounts, when it is not convenient to make immediate payment.

Unlike promissory notes, due bills cannot properly be made payable to order. They are therefore non-negotiable.

The amount represented by a due bill should be expressed twice, as in a receipt, check, or note—once in writing, and once in figures.

PROMISSORY NOTES.

A promissory note is a written promise to pay a specified sum of money at a designated time, both of which are stated in the body of the note.

The holder is the person who is in lawful possession of a note, whether he is the original payee or has received the note by indorsement.

Promissory notes are divided, in common usage, into three principal kinds: Individual Notes, Joint Notes, Joint-and-several Notes. Any of these notes may be either negotiable or non-negotiable.

An Individual Note is one signed by a single person.

A Joint Note is one signed by two or more persons who are together responsible for its payment, share and share alike.

A Joint-and-several Note is one signed by two or more persons, all of whom together, or any one of whom separately may be held for the whole amount. The words, "We jointly and severally promise," which are found in this note, are equivalent to "We together and separately promise." Accordingly, when such a note matures, if all the signers are able to pay, they contribute share and share alike; while if one or more cannot pay, the whole amount is paid by the remaining one or more.

A note is made negotiable, that is salable, by making it payable to a person, or his order, or to his assigns, or to bearer, or to the cashier of a bank or incorporated company. A note so drawn may be negotiated, or used in payment to another person by the holder but he must indorse his name on the back of the note. Should the drawer of the note fail to pay it, the holder looks to the person or persons who indorsed it for payment.

A note made payable at a bank and held there for payment until the usual hour for closing, need not be presented to the drawer in person to bind the indorser. It may be protested as in the case of drafts, immediately upon the close of bank-hours. Payment must be immediately demanded of the indorser if he resides in the same place: if he is a non-resident he must be notified at once by letter.

DISCOUNTING NOTE AT BANK.

When notes are offered at bank they are passed upon by its officers or directors, or both, to satisfy themselves that the maker and indorsers are good for payment. If accepted the bank charges interest or discount at an agreed upon rate reckoned upon the face of the note for the time for which the note is to run from the day it is discounted. For instance a note for $500 drawn and dated April 1, 191-, payable in 3 months, would be due and payable July 1st or 4th. If offered at bank for discount on May 1, 19—, the bank would reckon the interest from May 1st to July 1st. It is to be noted that the bank takes its interest in advance and pays to holder of note the proceeds which is the face value less the bank interest or discount. To compute the value of a note which reads "with interest," you add to the face value the interest which will be due at the maturity of note. Upon this value the bank reckons its discount.

INDORSEMENTS, A SUMMARY.

Indorsements are entries written on the back of any paper, whether checks, notes or drafts. They show either a transfer of title, a giving of security, or a receipt for a payment applying on the contract indorsed.

When a paper is written payable to the order of John Smith, and he wishes to transfer his title to Henry Jones, he writes on the back of the paper an order for its payment to Jones.

For the convenience of bank-tellers and others who have large numbers of such indorsed papers to handle daily, it is well to write the indorsement across the left end of the paper.

On negotiable papers that are likely to have several indorsements, care should be taken to write the indorsements as close together as is convenient. If the back of the paper should be covered with indorsements, other indorsements can be written on blank paper attached to the original. We give here, plainly marked, the various forms of indorsements:

1	*(Transfer of Title.)*	Pay to the order of Henry Jones. JOHN SMITH.
2	*(Without Recourse.)*	Pay to Henry Jones, or order, without recourse. JOHN SMITH.
3	*(In Blank.)*	JOHN SMITH.
4	*(Blank—Without Recourse.)*	Without recourse. JOHN SMITH.
5	*(For Money Paid.)*	Oct. 4, 1900, Received on within note Fifty ($50) Dollars.
6	*(For Collection.)*	Pay to the order of the Commercial National Bank of Lansing, Mich., for collection. JOHN SMITH.
7	*(Protest Waived.)*	Notice and protest waived. JOHN SMITH.

No. 1 is the more common and safest form. It transfers the ownership from Smith to Jones, and makes Smith responsible to Jones in case the maker or payer of the paper fails to pay it.

No. 2 transfers ownership, but relieves Smith from any responsibility if the paper is not paid when due. Only under special circumstances is this used.

No. 3 transfers the ownership to any party who may hold the paper, making it in effect payable to the bearer. Such paper should not fall in hands of strangers.

No. 4 transfers the ownership as in No. 3, except that it relieves Smith from further responsibility.

No. 5 is a receipt for money paid to apply on the promise indorsed. Such indorsements need no signature as it might have the effect of a receipt in full.

No. 6 does not transfer the ownership of the paper, but merely gives authority to collect the paper as Smith's agent and to place the amount collected to his account.

No. 7 relieves bank of responsibility of serving notice and protest.

RECEIPTS.

A Receipt is a written acknowledgment, signed by the receiver and delivered to the giver, showing that certain property (money or goods, or both) has been received.

BUSINESS FORMS.

THE CHECK STUB AND CHECK SHOWING HOW RECORD IS KEPT IN CHECK BOOK.

No. 974

Feb. 15, 191–

To P. S. James

Rent for Feb., 191–

94 | 25

No. 974 Wilmington, Del., Feb. 15. 19

First National Bank of Wilmington

Pay to the order of Peter S. James $$94\frac{25}{100}$

Ninety-four $\frac{25}{100}$ Dollars

William G. Pollock

TRADE ACCEPTANCE.

Boston, Mass., Dec. 2, 19 No. 64 a

On December 12, 19 Pay to the order of Ourselves

Eleven hundred seventy-four 50/100 Dollars ($ 1174.50)

The obligation of the acceptor hereof arises out of the purchase of goods from the drawer. The drawee may accept this bill payable at any bank, banker or trust company in the United States which he may designate.

To Thomas B. Miller & Co.
487 State St.,
Philadelphia, Pa.

ACCEPTED

DATE

PAYABLE AT (NAME OF BANK)

LOCATION OF BANK

BY (SIGNATURE OF ACCEPTOR)

Mason Furniture Co
By J. H. Mason

TIME NOTE.

No. 114 Amt. $1300

To Alfred Sidney

For On ac.

Payable Merchants' N. Bank

Time 3 mos.

Due June 13, 191–

$$1300\frac{00}{100}$ Nyack, N.Y., Mch. 13, 19

Three months after date, for value received, I promise to pay to the order of Alfred Sidney at the Merchants' National Bank, Thirteen Hundred $\frac{00}{100}$ Dollars.

Wm. B. White.

No. 114.

A Promissory Note and stub, showing record of note. This record may also be kept in separate book for notes payable and receivable.

DRAFT ON TIME.

$$469\frac{00}{100}$. Mobile, Ala., March 1, 19

Thirty days after date, pay to the order of Sylvester Cutler, Four Hundred Sixty-nine Dollars, and charge to the account of

John G. Cannon.

To J. B. Smith & Co.,
Philadelphia, Pa.

SIGHT DRAFT.

$257\frac{50}{100}$ Savannah, Ga., March 29, 19

At sight, pay to the order of Booker Washington, Two Hundred Fifty-seven Dollars, value received, and charge to our account.

George P. Richards & Co.

To Theodore P. Thomas & Co.,
New York City.

FOREIGN EXCHANGE.

Exchange for £800.

New York, Sept. 3, 19 –.

Ten days after sight of this First of Exchange (second and third unpaid), pay to the order of E. N. Towne, Eight Hundred Pounds sterling, value received, and charge to account of

James H. Moody & Co.

To Drexel, Morgan & Co.,
London, England.

NOTES ON DEMAND.

$300. Toronto, Ont., February 14, 19—.

On demand, I promise to pay Samuel Huestis, or Order, Three Hundred Dollars, value received. James Smith.

$205.50. Winnipeg, Man., July 4, 19—.

For value received, I promise to pay Charles Greene, or Bearer, Two Hundred and Five Dollars and Fifty Cents, on demand, with interest.

Charles P. Huestis.

A JOINT NOTE.

$350.75. New York, June 5, 19—.

Six months after date, we severally and jointly promise to pay George Snyder, or Order, Three Hundred and Fifty Dollars and Seventy-five Cents, value received.

James Bruce,
Philip Cozens.

BANK NOTE.

$800. Reno, Nev., July 10, 19—.

Sixty days from date, I promise to pay S. G. & B. Jones, or Order, at the Chemical Bank, Eight Hundred Dollars, value received.

N. C. Goldsmith.

NOTE NOT NEGOTIABLE.

$700. Regina, Sask., December 8, 19—.

Ten days after date, I promise to pay to Matthew Smith, Seven Hundred Dollars, value received. James Othello Bricks.

NOTE NEGOTIABLE BY INDORSEMENT.

$310. London, June 7, 19—.

Twenty days after date, I promise to pay to the order of John Dee, Three Hundred and Ten Dollars, value received. Richard Third.

NOTE NEGOTIABLE WITHOUT INDORSEMENT.

$1000. New Orleans, September 6, 19—.

Two months after date, I promise to pay to Joseph Suds, or Bearer, One Thousand Dollars, value received. Martin T. Smith.

JOINT NEGOTIABLE NOTE PAYABLE AT A BANK.

$1100. Victoria, B. C., December 20, 19—.

Four months after date, we promise to pay Henry Jones, or Order, Eleven Hundred Dollars, at the Merchants' Bank, Victoria, B. C.

Messrs. Doe, Roe & Co.

NEGOTIABLE NOTE PAYABLE IN MERCHANDISE.

$300. Minneapolis, October 11, 19—.

Thirty days after date, for value received, I promise to pay to Edward Somers, or Order, Three Hundred Dollars in merchantable corn, at the current price.

Alexander Glendening.

FORM OF JUDGMENT NOTE.

$900.

For value received, I promise to pay to Henry Richards, or Order, the sum of Nine Hundred Dollars, ninety days after date; and I hereby nominate, constitute and appoint the said Henry Richards, or any attorney-at-law of this State, my true and lawful attorney irrevocable, for me, and in my name, to appear in any court of record of this State, at any time after the above Promissory Note becomes due, and to waive all process and service thereof, and to confess judgment in favor of the holder hereof for the sum that may be due and owing hereon, with interest and costs, and waiving all errors, etc.

In Witness whereof, I have hereunto set my hand and seal at the City of Cincinnati, State of Ohio, this 10th day of May, one thousand nine hundred and ——.

E. D. Abbott. [seal.]

Sealed and delivered in the presence of
E. Lyon, John Sutherland.

NOTE.—The principal difference between a Sealed Note and one without a Seal is that the former must be first paid in the settlement of a decedent's estate, and is not barred by the Statute of Limitations.

RECEIPT ON ACCOUNT.

Vancouver, B. C., April 27, 19—.

Received from Zachary Taylor, Seventy-five Dollars on account.

Luke F. Cozans.

RECEIPT IN FULL.

New York, May 11, 19—.

Received from Messrs. Sutherland & Abbott, One Hundred Four and $\frac{73}{100}$ Dollars, in full of account to date.

104\frac{73}{100}$. William J. Bunce.

A receipt like the first acknowledges the partial payment of a debt, and one like the second of all claims excepting negotiable notes.

DUE BILL.

$25. Edmonton, Alta., February 6, 19—.

Due John Smith, Twenty-five Dollars on demand, value received.

John Jones.

55\frac{00}{100}$. Chicago, Ill., May 12, 19—.

Due Charles F. Thomas, for work done, Fifty-five $\frac{00}{100}$ Dollars, payable on demand, in merchandise, at my store.

William C. Edwards.

ORDER FOR MONEY.

$75. New York, June 4, 19—.

Mr. George W. Strong:

Please pay Daniel Fanshaw, or Order, Seventy-five Dollars, and place the same to the debt of

Robert H. Elton.

Remarks.—An Order may be written payable to B. C. or Order, or to B. C. or Bearer. If written in the former manner, B. C. can dispose of it, provided he writes his name upon the back. If payable to B. C. or Bearer, it will be good to the holder.

FORM OF A COMMON BILL.

Mr. George Wright, To Stephen Driver, Dr.

March 12, 19—. **To 20 Bushels of Apples, at $1.00 . . . . $20.00**

Rec'd Pay't, George Wright.

BILL OF SALE.

In consideration of Two Hundred Seventy-four Dollars, receipt of which is hereby acknowledged, I, S. D. Haag, of County of Erie, and State of Pennsylvania, do hereby sell and convey unto Peter Cline, of County of Erie, and State of Pennsylvania, the following described personal property:

Dark Bay Horse, "Nepos," 17½ hands high, 1600 lbs. weight, with star on forehead and white on right hind foot:

And I do hereby covenant and agree to warrant and defend the above described personal property against the lawful claims of all persons.

Signed this 5th day of May, A. D. 19—. S. D. Haag.

THE LAW OF NOTES AND CHECKS.

Negotiable instruments, the common forms of which are promissory notes, checks, or other bills of exchange, while having the same general requisites as other contracts, have certain distinct features. The purpose of the law is to facilitate as much as possible their free passing from hand to hand like currency. The assignment of an ordinary contract leaves the assignee in no different position for enforcing his rights than that of his assignor, but one who takes a negotiable instrument from a prior holder, without knowledge of any defenses to it, before its maturity, and gives value for it, holds it free of any defenses which might have been set up against his predecessors, except those defects that were inherent in the instrument itself.

To be negotiable an instrument must be in writing and signed by the maker (of a note) or drawer (of a bill or check).

It must contain an unconditional promise or order to pay a sum certain in money. Must be payable on demand, or at a fixed future time. Must be payable to order or to bearer. In a bill of exchange (check) the party directed to pay must be reasonably certain. Every negotiable instrument is presumed to have been issued for a valuable consideration, and want of consideration in the creation of the instrument is not a defense against a bona-fide holder.

An instrument is negotiated, that is completely transferred, so as to vest title in the purchaser, if payable to bearer, or indorsed simply with the name of the last holder, by mere delivery, if payable to order by the indorsement of the party to whom it is payable and delivery. One who transfers an instrument by indorsement warrants to every subsequent holder that the instrument is genuine, that he has title to it, and that if not paid by the party primarily liable at maturity, he will pay it upon receiving due notice of non-payment.

To hold an indorser liable the holder upon its non-payment at maturity must give prompt notice of such non-payment to the indorser and that the holder looks to the indorser for payment. Such notice should be sent within twenty-four hours.

When an indorser is thus compelled to pay he may hold prior parties through whom he received the instrument liable to him by sending them prompt notice of non-payment upon receiving such notice from the holder.

One who transfers a negotiable instrument by delivery, without indorsing it, simply warrants that the instrument is genuine, that he has title to it, and knows of no defence to it, but does not agree to pay it if unpaid at maturity.

The maker of a note is liable to pay it if unpaid at maturity without any notice from the holder or indorser.

Notice to one of several partners is sufficient notice to all.

When a check is certified by a bank the bank becomes primarily liable to pay it without notice of its non-payment, and when the holder of a check thus obtains its certification by the bank, the drawer of the check and previous indorsers are released from liability, and the holder looks to the bank for payment.

A bona-fide holder of a negotiable instrument, that is, a party who takes an instrument regular on its face, before its maturity, pays value for it and has no knowledge of any defenses to it, is entitled to hold the party primarily liable responsible for its payment, despite any defenses he may have against the party to whom he gave it, except such as rendered the instrument void in its inception. Thus, if the maker of a note received no value for it, or was induced to issue it through fraud or imposition, they do not defeat the right of a bona-fide holder to compel its payment from him.

INTEREST LAWS AND STATUTES OF LIMITATIONS.

States and Territories.	Interest Laws.		Statutes of Limitations		
	Legal Rate, per cent.	Rate Allowed by Contract, per cent.	Judgments, years.	Notes, years.	Open Accounts, years.
Alabama	8	8	20	6	3
Alaska	8	12	10	6	6
Arkansas	6 to 10	6 to 10	10	5	3
Arizona	6	10	4	4	3
California	7	12	5	4	4
Colorado	8	12	20	6	6
Connecticut	6	6	(*k*)	6	6
Delaware	6	6	10(*h*)	6	3
District of Columbia	6	8	12	3	3
Florida	8	10	20	5‡	3
Georgia	7	8	7	6	4†
Hawaii	8	12	20	6	6
Idaho	7	10	6	5	4
Illinois	5	7	7	10	5
Indiana	6	8	20	10	6
Iowa	6	8	20	10	5
Kansas	6	10	5	5	3
Kentucky	6	6	15	15	5
Louisiana	5	8	10	5	3
Maine	6	12	6–20	6–20	6
Maryland	6	6	12	3	3
Massachusetts	6	Any rate.	6(*c*)	6	6
Michigan	5	7	10	6	6
Minnesota	6	10	10	6	6
Mississippi	6	8	7	6	3
Missouri	6	8	10	10	5
Montana	8	10	10	8	5
Nebraska	7	10	5	5	4
Nevada	7	7	6	6	4
New Hampshire	6	6	20	6	6
New Jersey	6	6	20	6	6
New Mexico	10	12	7	6	4
New York	6	6††	20(*j*)	6	6**
North Carolina	6	6	10	3*	3
North Dakota	6	10	10	6	6
Ohio	6	8	21	15	6
Oklahoma	6	10	5	5	3
Oregon	6	10	10	6	6
Pennsylvania	6	6	5(*f*)	6‡	6
Porto Rico	6	12(*e*)	5	3	3
Rhode Island	6†	Any rate.	20	6	6
South Carolina	7	8	10	6	6
South Dakota	7	12	20	6	6
Tennessee	6	6	10	6	6
Texas	6	10	10	4	2–4
Utah	8	12	8	6	4
Vermont	6	(*m*)	6	6(*n*)	6
Virginia	6	6	20	5*	3
Washington	6	12	6	6	3
West Virginia	6	6	10	10	5
Wisconsin	6	10	20(*b*)	6	6
Wyoming	8	12	10	10	8

Key to the Above Table.

* Under seal, 10 years. † Unless a different rate is expressly stipulated. ‡ Under seal, 20 years. †† New York has legalized any rate of interest on call loans of $5,000 or upward, on collateral security. ** Six years from last item on either side. (*a*) Judgments, 6 per cent. (*b*) Justice Court judgments, 6 years. (*c*) Witnessed, 20 years. (*e*) Pawnbrokers, 4 per cent per month. (*f*) Ceases to be a lien after the period unless revived. (*h*) Subject to renewal. (*j*) Not of record, 6 years. (*k*) No limit. (*m*) No statute. (*n*) Except witnessed promissory note, 14 years.

Penalties for usury differ in various States. California, misdemeanor with jail term, $500 fine or both; Colorado, Maine, Massachusetts (except on loans of less than $1,000), have no provisions on the subject. Loss of *principal and interest* is the penalty in Arkansas and New York. Loss of principal in Delaware and Oregon.

Loss of interest in Alabama, Arizona, District of Columbia, Florida, Idaho, Illinois, Iowa, Louisiana, Michigan, Minnesota, Mississippi, Nebraska, New Jersey, North Carolina (double amount if paid), North Dakota (double amount if paid), Porto Rico, South Carolina, South Dakota, Virginia, Washington (double amount if paid), Wisconsin, Hawaii, and Wyoming. In Alaska, Montana, Oklahoma, Texas, Vermont, double the amount of interest collected.

Loss of excess of interest in Connecticut, Georgia, Indiana, Kansas, Kentucky, Maryland, Missouri, Nevada, New Hampshire (three times), Ohio, Pennsylvania, Tennessee, Vermont, and West Virginia. Loss of principal and interest in Rhode Island. also fine or imprisonment. In New Mexico, fine and forfeiture of double amount collected.

BUSINESS LAWS IN DAILY USE.

The following compilation of business law contains the essence of a large amount of legal verbiage:

Ignorance of the law excuses no one.

The law compels no one to do impossibilities.

A contract made with a lunatic is void.

It is a fraud to conceal a fraud.

Signatures made with a lead-pencil are good in law.

If a note is lost or stolen, it does not release the maker; he must pay it if the consideration for which it was given and the amount can be proven.

Notes bear interest only when so stated.

Principals are responsible for the acts of their agents.

Each individual in a partnership is responsible for the whole amount of the debts of the firm, except in cases of special partnership.

An agreement without consideration is void.

A note made on Sunday is void.

Contracts made on Sunday cannot be enforced.

A note by a minor is void.

A contract made with a minor is void.

A note obtained by fraud, or from a person in a state of intoxication, cannot be collected.

A receipt for money is not always conclusive.

The acts of one partner bind all the rest.

The maker of an "accommodation" bill or note (one for which he has received no consideration, having lent his name or credit for the accommodation of the holder) is not bound to the person accommodated, but is bound to all other parties precisely as if there was a good consideration.

Checks or drafts must be presented for payment without unreasonable delay.

If the drawee of a check or draft has changed his residence, the holder must use due or reasonable diligence to find him.

If one who holds a check, as payee or otherwise, transfers it to another, he has a right to insist that the check be presented that day, or, at farthest, on the day following.

A note indorsed in blank (the name of the indorser only written) is transferable by delivery, the same as if made payable to bearer.

If the time of payment of a note is not inserted, it is held payable on demand.

An indorsee has a right of action against all whose names were on the bill when he received it.

If the letter containing a protest of non-payment be put into the post-office, any miscarriage does not affect the party giving notice.

If two or more persons as partners are jointly liable on a note or bill, due notice to one of them is sufficient.

If a note or bill is transferred as security, or even as payment of a pre-existing debt, the debt revives if the bill or note be dishonored.

Claims which do not rest upon a seal or judgment must be sued in most States within six years from the time when they arise.

Part payment of a debt which has passed the time of statutory limitation revives the whole debt, and the claim holds good for another period of six years from the date of such partial payment.

If, when a debt is due, the debtor is out of the State, the "six years" do not begin to run until he returns. If he afterward leave the State, the time forward counts the same as if he remained in the State.

An oral agreement must be proved by evidence. A written agreement proves itself. The law prefers written to oral evidence, because of its precision.

"Value received" is usually written in a note, and should be, but is not necessary. If not written, it is presumed by the law or may be supplied by proof.

No consideration is sufficient in law if it be illegal in its nature.

Checks or drafts should be presented during business hours, but in this country, except in the case of banks, the time extends through the day and evening.

The time of payment of a note must not depend upon a contingency. The promise must be absolute.

A bill may be written upon any paper or substitute for it, either with ink or pencil.

The payee should be distinctly named in the note, unless it is payable to bearer.

Notice of protest may be sent either to the place of business or of residence of the party notified.

The loss of a bill or note is not sufficient excuse for not giving notice of protest.

An indorsement may be written on the face or back.

LAWS OF CONTRACTS.

A contract is an agreement of two or more parties, by which reciprocal rights and obligations are created. One party acquires a right, enforceable at law, to some act or forbearance from the other, who is under a corresponding obligation to thus act or forbear.

Generally speaking, all contracts which are made between two competent parties, for a proper consideration, without fraud and for a lawful purpose, are enforceable at law.

To the creation of a valid contract there must be:

1. Precise agreement. The offer of one party must be met by an acceptance by the other, according to the terms offered.

2. There must be a consideration. Something of value must either be received by one party or given up by the other.

3. The parties must have capacity to contract. The contracts of insane persons are not binding upon them. Married women are now generally permitted to contract as though single, and bind their separate property. The contracts of an infant (minor) are generally not binding upon him, unless ratified after attaining his majority. The contracts of an infant for "necessaries" may be enforced against him to the extent of the reasonable value of the goods furnished. It is incumbent upon one seeking thus to hold an infant to show that the goods furnished were in fact necessary to the infant, and that he was not already supplied by his parents or guardians.

4. The party's consent must not be the result of fraud or imposition, or it may be avoided by the party imposed upon.

5. The purpose of the parties must be lawful. Agreements to defraud others, to violate statutes, or whose aim is against public policy, such as to create monopolies, or for the corrupt procurement of legislative or official action, are void, and cannot be enforced by any party thereto.

Contracts in general are equally valid, whether made orally or in writing, with the exception of certain classes of contracts, which in most of the States are required to be attested by a note or memorandum in writing by the party or his agent sought to be held liable. Some of the provisions, which are adopted from the old **English Statute of Frauds,** vary in some of the States, but the following contracts very generally are required to be thus attested by some writing.

Contracts by their terms not to be performed within a year from the making thereof.

A promise to answer for the debt, default, or miscarriage of another person.

Contracts made in consideration of marriage, except mutual promises to marry.

Promise of an executor, or administrator, to pay debts of deceased out of his own property.

Contracts for the creation of any interest of estate in land, with the exception of leases for a short term, generally one year.

Contracts for the sale of goods above a certain value, unless a portion of the price is paid or part of the goods delivered. The required value of the goods sold varies in different States from $30 to $200. In a number of the States no such provision exists.

In many of the States declarations or conveyances of trust estates.

In many States representations as to the character, credit, or responsibility of another person.

Partial performance of the contract is generally held to dispense with the necessity for a writing.

If the damages liable to result from the breaking of a contract are uncertain, the parties may agree upon a sum to which either may be entitled as compensation of a breach, which will be upheld by the courts, but if the sum so fixed is not designed as a fair compensation to the party injured, but as a penalty to be inflicted, it will be disregarded.

A party is generally excused for the failure to perform what he has agreed only by the act of God or the public enemy, Except in cases involving a personal element in the work to be performed, such as the rendition of services, when the death or sickness of the party contracting to perform them is a valid excuse, or contracts for the performance of work upon a specified object, when its destruction without the fault of the party sought to be held liable is a sufficient excuse.

Written instruments are to be construed and interpreted by law according to the simple, customary and natural meaning of the words used. No evidence can be introduced to contradict or vary a written contract but it may be received in order to explain it, when such explanation is necessary.

POINTS OF CRIMINAL LAW.

Law should be, and is intended to constitute, a rule of right governing the actions of man in his dealings with his fellow-beings.

You cannot lawfully condone an offense by receiving back stolen property.

The exemption of females from arrest applies only in civil not in criminal matters.

Every man is bound to obey the call of a sheriff for assistance in making an arrest.

The rule "Every man's house is his castle" does not hold good when a man is accused of crime.

Embezzlement can be charged only against a clerk or a servant, or the officer or agent of a corporation.

Bigamy cannot be proven in law if one party to a marriage has been absent and not heard from for five years.

Grand larceny is when the value of property stolen exceeds $25.00—when less than that, the offense is petit larceny.

Arson to be in the first degree must have been committed at night, and the buildings fired must have been inhabited.

Drunkenness is not a legal excuse for crime, but delirium tremens is considered by the law as a species of insanity.

In a case of assault it is only necessary to prove an "offer or attempt at assault." Battery presumes physical violence.

Mayhem, although popularly supposed to refer to injury to the face, lip, tongue, eye, or ear, applies to any injury done a limb.

A felony is a crime punishable by imprisonment in a State prison; an "infamous" crime is one punishable with death or State prison.

A police officer is not authorized to make an arrest without a warrant unless he has a personal knowledge of the offense for which the arrest is made.

An accident is not a crime, unless criminal carelessness can be proven. A man shooting at a burglar and killing a member of his family is not a murderer.

Burglary in the first degree can be committed only in the night time. Twilight, if dark enough to prevent distinguishing a man's face, is the same as "night" in law.

Murder to be in the first degree must be wilful, premeditated, and malicious, or committed while the murderer is engaged in a felonious act. The killing of a man in a duel is murder, and it is a misdemeanor to accept or give a challenge.

False swearing is perjury in law only when wilfully done, and when the oath has been legally administered. Such qualifying expressions as "to the best of my belief," "as I am informed," may save an averment from being perjured. The law is that the false statement sworn to must be absolute. Subornation of perjury—that is, inducing another to swear falsely, is a felony.

The penalties which follow the violation of any of the points of criminal

law vary slightly in various places, but all include fines or imprisonment, or both. The penalties are intended to be sufficiently severe to deter those evilly disposed from disturbing the peace and happiness of the community.

PARTNERSHIPS.

Partnerships may be either general or special. In general partnership, money invested ceases to be individual property. Each member is made personally liable for the whole amount of debts incurred by the company. The company is liable for all contracts or obligations made by individual members.

Special partners are not liable beyond the amount contributed.

A person may become a partner by allowing people generally to presume that he is one, as, by having his name on the sign or parcel or in the bills used in the business.

A share or specific interest in the profits or loss of a business, as remuneration for labor may involve one in the liability of a partner.

In case of bankruptcy, the joint estate is first applied to the payment of partnership debts, the surplus only going to the creditors of the individual estate.

A dissolution of partnership may take place under express stipulations in the articles of agreement, by mutual consent, by the death or insanity of one of the firm, by award of arbitrators, or by court of equity in cases of misconduct of some member of the firm.

A partner signing his individual name to negotiable paper, which is for the use of the partnership firm, binds all the partners thereby. Negotiable paper of the firm, even though given on private account by one of the partners, will hold all the partners of the firm, when it passes into the hands of the holders, who are ignorant of the fact attending its creation.

Partnership effects may be bought and sold by a partner; he may make contracts; may receive money; indorse, draw and accept bills and notes, and, while this may be for his own private account, if it apparently be for the use of the firm, his partners will be bound by his action, provided the parties dealing with him were ignorant of the transaction being on his private account; and thus representation or misrepresentation of a partner, having relation to business of the firm, will bind the members in the partnership.

In case of death, the surviving partner must account to the representatives of the deceased.

AGENTS AND ATTORNEYS.

An agent or an attorney is one authorized by a person to act for him and in his stead, in the transaction of business for the person appointing said agent or attorney.

In regard to the subject of an agency, the general rule is, that whatever a man may do in his own right he may also transact through another. Things of a personal nature, implying personal confidence on the part of the person possessing them, cannot be delegated.

Infants, married women, lunatics, idiots, aliens, belligerents, and persons incapable of making legal contracts, cannot act as principals in the appointment of agents. Infants and married women may, however, become principals in certain cases.

The act of the agent always binds his principal. Agents who exceed their authority, become themselves personally responsible to their principals.

One should not consent to act as an agent or attorney in complicated matters, except where the powers of this office be explicitly defined in writing.

Agency may be terminated in two ways: (1) by the act of the principal or agent; (2) by operation of law. In the latter case, the termination of the agency is effected by lapse of time, by completion of the subject-matter of the agency, by the extinction of the subject-matter, or by the insanity, bankruptcy or death of either party.

LANDLORD AND TENANT.

Leases for one year or less need no written agreement. Leases for more than a year must be in writing; if for life, signed, sealed, and witnessed in the same manner as any other important document

Leases for over three years must be recorded. No particular form is necessary.

If no agreement in writing for more than a year can be produced, the tenant holds the property from year to year at the will of the landlord. If there is no agreement as to time, the tenant as a rule holds from year to year.

A tenancy at will may be terminated by giving the tenant one month's notice in writing, requiring him to remove from the premises occupied.

A tenant is not responsible for taxes, unless it be so stated in the lease.

The tenant may underlet as much of the property as he desires, unless it is expressly forbidden in the lease. Tenants at will cannot underlet.

A married woman cannot lease her property under the common law, but this prohibition is removed by statute in most of the States. A husband cannot make a lease which will bind his wife's property after his death.

A lease made by a minor is not binding after the minor has attained his majority. It binds the lessee, however, unless the minor should release him. Should the minor receive rent after attaining his majority, the lease will be therefore ratified. A lease given by a guardian will not extend beyond the majority of the ward.

A new lease renders void a former lease.

In case there are no writings, the tenancy begins from the day possession is taken; where there are writings and the time of commencement is not stated, the tenancy will be held to commence from the date of said writings.

Leases on mortgaged property, whereon the mortgage was given prior to the lease, terminate when the mortgage is foreclosed.

Where a tenant assigns his lease, even with the landlord's consent, he will remain liable for the rent unless his lease is surrendered or cancelled.

A building erected by tenants on foundations sunk into the ground, becomes a part of the realty, and belong to the landlord. Improvements to the building rented, that are nailed or screwed to the building become the property of the landlord. But trade fixtures belong to the tenant, it being presumed when the building is rented for trade purposes that it is permissible to put in the fixtures or make necessary attachments of same to the building.

LAWS GOVERNING LIENS.

In all the States and Canada it is the object of the law to protect the mechanic and laboring man and also the merchant. Hence there are laws in the several States for this purpose. While the general trend is the same, the laws vary in details. It is not difficult to procure a copy of the laws, which every builder and householder should do. Any contractor, sub-contractor or laborer who performs any work, or furnishes any materials, in pursuance of, or in conformity with, any agreement or contract with the owner, lessee, agent or one in possession of the property, toward the erection, altering, improving or repairing of any building, shall have a lien for the value of such labor or materials on the building or land on which it stands to the extent of the right, title and interest of the owner, lessee or person in possession at the time of the claimant's filing his notice with the clerk of the county court. Such lien is called a mechanic's lien.

The notice should be filed within thirty days after completion of the work or the furnishing of the materials, and should state the residence of the claimant, the amount claimed, from whom due, when due, and to whom due, the name of the person against whom claimed, the name of the owner, lessee or person in possession of the premises, with a brief description of the latter.

Liens cease in one year after the filing of the notice, unless an action is begun, or the lien is continued by an order of court.

The following classes of persons are generally entitled to lien: (1) Bailees who may perform labor and services, on the thing bailed, at the request of the bailor. (2) Inn-keepers, upon the baggage of guests they have accommodated. (3) Common carriers, upon goods carried, for the amount of their freight and disbursements. (4) Vendors, on the goods sold for payment of the price where no credit has been expressly promised or implied. (5) Agents, upon goods of their principals, for advancements for the benefit of the latter. (6) All persons are entitled to the right of lien who are compelled by law to receive property and bestow labor or expense on the same.

The right of lien may be waived: (1) By express contract. (2) By neglect. (3) By new agreement. (4) By allowing change of possession. (5) By surrendering possession.

The manner of the enforcement of a lien, whether it be an inn-keeper's, agent's, carrier's, factor's, etc., depends wholly upon the nature and character of the lien.

Perishable property on which a lien is held may be sold, and the lien attaches to the proceeds.

Liens take precedence according to priority, and interest on a judgment on a prior lien must also be satisfied before a subsequent lien may be realized upon.

WILLS.

A Will or Testament is a final disposition of a person's property to take effect after his death. A codicil is an addition or alteration in such disposition. All persons are competent to make a will except idiots, persons of unsound mind, and infants. A nuncupative or unwritten will is one made orally by a soldier in active service, or by a mariner while at sea.

In most instances a will must be in writing, signed by the testator, or by some person in his presence, and by his direction, and attested by witnesses, who must subscribe their names thereto in the presence of the testator. The form of wording a will is immaterial as long as its intent is clear.

A will may be revoked by gifts made by it inconsistent with the earlier will, and generally a will may be revoked by cancellation, tearing or burning by the testator with intention to revoke it, although a part of a will may not be so revoked.

The accidental destruction of a will does not affect its validity or efficacy if its contents can be proved.

FACTS WORTH KNOWING.

STATE FLOWERS.

The following are "State Flowers" as adopted by the schools (marked*), the legislatures (marked †), or the people (marked ‡).

Alabama	*Goldenrod
Arizona	†Sahuaro
Arkansas	†Apple Blossom
California	†Golden Poppy
Colorado	*Columbine
Connecticut	†Mountain Laurel
Delaware	†Peach Blossom
District of Columbia	No choice
Florida	†Orange Blossom
Georgia	†Cherokee Rose
Idaho	‡Syringa
Illinois	†Violet
Indiana	†Carnation
Iowa	‡Wild Rose
Kansas	†Sunflower
Kentucky	‡Trumpet Vine
Louisiana	†Magnolia
Maine	*Pine Cone and Tassel
Maryland	†Black-eyed Susan
Massachusetts	†May Flower
Michigan	†Apple Blossom
Minnesota	†Moccasin Flower
Mississippi	*Magnolia
Missouri	No choice
Montana	†Bitter Root
Nebraska	†Goldenrod
Nevada	‡Sagebrush
New Hampshire	†Purple Lilac
New Jersey	†Violet
New Mexico	*Cactus
New York	*Rose
North Carolina	‡Daisy
North Dakota	†Wild Prairie Rose
Ohio	†Scarlet Carnation
Oklahoma	†Mistletoe
Oregon	†Oregon Grape
Pennsylvania	No choice
Rhode Island	*Violet
South Carolina	No choice
South Dakota	†Pasque Flower
Tennessee	No choice
Texas	†Bluebonnet
Utah	†Sego Lily
Vermont	†Red Clover
Virginia	†Dogwood
Washington	‡Rhododendron
West Virginia	†Rhododendron
Wisconsin	*Violet
Wyoming	†Indian Paintbrush

EUROPEAN FLOWER CUSTOMS.

In England the primrose is worn on the birthday of Lord Beaconsfield. On the anniversary of Parnell's death his followers wear a sprig of ivy. The Jacobites wear white roses on June 10. In France the Orleanists wear white daisies and the Bonapartists the violet.

BIRTHSTONES.

January	Garnet
February	Amethyst
March	Bloodstone and aquamarine
April	Diamond
May	Emerald
June	Pearl and moonstone
July	Ruby
August	Sardonyx and peridot
September	Sapphire
October	Opal and tourmaline
November	Topaz
December	Turquoise and lapis lazuli

WEDDING ANNIVERSARIES.

First	Cotton
Second	Paper
Third	Leather
Fifth	Wooden
Seventh	Woolen
Tenth	Tin
Twelfth	Silk and fine linen
Fifteenth	Crystal
Twentieth	China
Twenty-fifth	Silver
Thirtieth	Pearl
Fortieth	Ruby
Fiftieth	Golden
Seventy-fifth	Diamond

LETTER FORMS, BUSINESS AND SOCIAL

CORRECT ENGLISH

HINTS AND HELPS.

The ready use of good language is largely the result of practice in writing and of an abundance of good reading. In the choice of words, the paramount consideration should be exactness. That is, seek to say precisely what the thought requires, neither more nor less. This demands, of course, close scrutiny of meanings, and independence of current fashions in words. Seek to have at command more than one expression for the same thing. Not that several forms are in any case to be employed, but it often happens that if the writer has not thought broadly and deeply enough to have more than one expression for his idea, the one that he has will be meager. Cultivate the habit of observing the derivation and history of words. A word whose etymology is known defines itself; the writer feels its force intuitively, and need not depend on a dictionary. Enlarge your vocabulary by diligent study of usage in the best writers. The true meaning of words is expressed only when they are interwoven with other words. No fineness of usage can be acquired from the dictionary alone. Do not use technical terms where they are not likely to be understood. Beware of fine writing. By fine writing is meant the use of pretentious terms for trivial ideas.

THE USES OF THE ARTICLES.

A or An, The.—The use of these forms is determined by sound and not by spelling. Before a consonant sound *a* is used; before a vowel sound *an* is used; *the* is used to point out some particular person or thing.
Examples.—A barn, an orchard, the house, etc.

THE USES OF ADJECTIVES.

An adjective describes or limits the noun or pronoun to which it is joined.
Adjectives are usually placed before the noun or pronoun they qualify.
The ascending comparison of adjectives is formed by adding *er* and *est* or *more* and *most* to the positive form, and the descending comparison by adding *less* and *least.*
The comparative degree is used in comparing two objects; the superlative when more than two are compared.
Some adjectives can not be compared, and no adjective will admit of a double comparison.
This and *that* are singular, *these* and *those* are plural.
Two negative forms are not permissible.

THE USES OF THE ADVERB.

An adverb limits or emphasizes a verb, an adjective or another adverb.
Adverbs *soon, often, early, late,* etc., are compared regularly by adding

er, st, est; those ending in *ly* are compared by prefixing *more* and *most.* The following are compared irregularly:

Positive.	Comparative.	Superlative.
Well	Better	Best
Badly	Worse	Worst
Far	Further Farther	Furthest Farthest
Little	Less	Least
Much	More	Most

Some adverbs do not admit of a comparison; as *dead, square,* etc.

Adverbs should be placed as near the word or words they modify as possible. Observe the different uses of the word *only* in the following sentences: "Only John dropped his cane"; "John only dropped his cane"; "John dropped his cane only"; "John dropped only his cane"; "John dropped his only cane."

An adverb should never be placed between *to* and the infinitive.

Good, Well.—*Good* is always an adjective; *well* may be an adjective, but usually it is an adverb; as, "I slept well," "Father looks well."

Most, Almost.—Do not use *most* for *almost.* Say, "He passes here almost every day," not "most every day."

Latest, Last.—Do not say *last* for *latest. Latest* has reference to time, but *last* is a contraction of *latest,* and has not reference to time, but has reference to that which comes in a series.

Here and **There.**—Never use *here* and *there* after the adverbs *this* and *that,* as "This here boy," etc., "That there boy," etc.

Always, Continually.—Do not confuse these two words.

Always refers to what we do at all times. We do continually what we do without intermission.

Further, Farther.—*Further* is comparative and means more, as, "Nothing further was said." *Farther* has reference to distance, as, "He can go farther."

APPROPRIATE PREPOSITIONS.

Good usage requires proper prepositions to express one's meaning well.

At, In, Into.—Usually *in* implies inclosure, as presence inside of; *into* implies movement to the inside of. One cannot live in a house until he has moved into it. *At* implies nearness to the border or to small places or foreign cities.

Beside, Besides.—*Beside* means "at the side of"; as "The house beside the sea." *Besides* means "in addition to"; as, "Besides his farms he has some personal property."

Among, Between.—*Among* should be used when more than two are referred to; *between* when reference is made to two only.

Wait on, Wait for.—*Wait on* means attend to; *wait for* means to tarry, to wait.

CORRELATIVE CONJUNCTIONS.

The correlative conjunctions are as follows:

as....................as
so....................as
neither...............nor
either................or

THE USES OF PRONOUNS.

The Possessive of Pronouns.—In forming the possessive the letter *s* only is added to the singular.

Examples.—Yours, hers, theirs. The possessive of *who* and *which* is *whose.* The relatives *that* and *those* have no possessive forms.

Singular and Plural Pronouns.—The pronoun should be in the same number as its antecedent.

The relative *who* is used to refer to persons; *which,* to inferior animals and things without life; *what* is used to refer to things; and *that* to both persons and things. Euphony, as a rule, determines between the uses of ***who, which*** and ***that.***

Either refers to "one of the two"; when more than two are referred to, "any one" should be used. *Neither* refers to "no one of the two"; but when more than two are referred to, "no one" should be used. *Each* refers to numbers separately; *all* refers to numbers collectively.

THE USES OF NOUNS.

The Possessive Case.—The possessive of nouns in the singular number is formed by adding an apostrophe and the letter *s*.

Example.—"The girl's bonnet."

Sometimes the possessive is formed by adding the apostrophe only. This is done where the added *s* makes an unpleasant sound. However, this is a matter of taste.

Examples.—"For goodness' sake"; "John's hat"; "Dickens' Tale of Two Cities."

When the plural of a noun in the nominative case ends in *s*, the possessive is formed by adding the apostrophe (') only, but if the plural does not end in *s*, then the apostrophe (') and an *s* are added.

Example.—"Men's and boys' hats are for sale."

The possessive of compound nouns is formed by adding the sign of the possessive to the end of the compound.

Example.—"I drove my brother-in-law's horse."

Singular and Plural Number.—The plural of nouns is usually formed by adding *s* to the singular, but if the sound of *s* makes an additional syllable, then *es* is added to form the plural.

Examples.—Hand, hands; church, churches.

Nouns ending in *o* preceded by a vowel form the plural by adding *s* only to the singular, but when the final *o* is preceded by a consonant, the plural is formed by adding *es* to the singular.

Nouns ending in *y* form their plurals by adding *s* to the singular, but if the final *y* is preceded by a consonant, *y* is changed to *i* and *es* is added to form the plural.

Examples.—Money, moneys; lady, ladies.

In forming the plural of compound nouns the sign of the plural is added to the descriptive part of the phase.

Examples.—Aide-de-camp, aides-de-camp.

THE USES OF VERBS.

Verbs and Numbers.—Plural verbs require plural subjects; as, we were, not we was; you were, not you was; they are, not they is; they were, not they was; they have, not they has; they write, not they writes; the men are, not is; the children were, not was; the boys have, not has; my sisters write, not writes; they are the boys who were at school. Jennie and Annie were schoolmates.

The Uses of the Auxiliary Verbs.—Shall, Will.—*Will* expresses the will or pleasure of its own subject. *Shall* subordinates the will of its subject to that of the speaker. "We will go," means "we are willing to go." "We shall go," means "we have decided upon going." Never say, "Will I do so and so?" The literal meaning of such an expression would be, "Am I willing to do," etc. Remember that *will* always expresses willingness rather than futurity when it has a personal significance.

Should, Would.—*Should* is the past tense of *shall*, and *would* the past tense of *will*, and the same rules governing the former also govern the latter. "We should go to town if we were able." "His wife would attend if you should ask her."

Can, Could; May, Might.—*Can* and *could* express ability or possibility, while *may* and *might* express permission. These words are often confused.

To Do; to See.—These two verbs give considerable trouble. Their principal forms are, *do, did, done,* and *see, saw, seen.* The second forms, ***did*** and ***saw,*** should never follow ***is, are, was, were, have, has,*** or ***had.*** The third forms, *done* and *seen*, should always follow one of these words expressed or understood; as, I did the work, or, I have done the work, or, the work is done. I saw the picture. or, I have seen the picture, or, the picture was seen.

Verbs in General.—The rules given for *to do* and *to see* apply alike to all verbs. Such expressions as have came, have sang, was drove, have broke, have began, have knew, is froze, have gave, knowed, has went, has give, has rang, have ran, were took, has stole. throwed, have mistook, etc., are gross errors and should be avoided.

Lie and Lay.—Remember that *lie* means rest and *lay* means an action affecting some object.

Examples.—"The watch lies on the piano." "I will lay the watch on the piano." "Mother laid your gloves away for you."

Sit and Set.—*Sit* means to be in position to rest, to repose. *Set* is an active, transitive verb and means "to put," "to place," "to plant," to place in a condition, a state, or a posture.

Examples.—"Come sit in the easy chair." "Set the table in the dining room."

Don't (Do Not) Doesn't (Does Not).—These words are often misused. When you are in doubt about their use, compare the full forms with the verb; as, He don't know. If the full form be used, the absurdity is quickly seen; as, He do not know. The correct form should be, He does not know.

Had Rather, Had Better, Had Ought.—These are incorrect forms for would rather, might better, and ought.

Bring, Fetch.—*Bring* implies motion toward the speaker, not away. ***Fetch* implies motion, first from the speaker, then toward him.**

Note the following verb forms:

Present.	Past.	Past Participle.
Alight (to dismount)	Alighted	Alighted
Begin	Began	Begun
Bid	Bade	Bidden or Bid
Bid (at auction)	Bid	Bid
Burst	Burst	Burst
Choose	Chose	Chosen
Do	Did	Done
Eat	Ate	Eaten
Light (to ignite)	Lighted	Lighted
Light (to settle down upon)	Lighted or Lit	Lighted or Lit
Lay	Laid	Laid
Lie	Lay	Lain
Rise	Rose	Risen
Raise	Raised	Raised
See	Saw	Seen
Set	Set	Set
Sit	Sat	Sat
Wake	Woke	Waked

ERRORS TO BE AVOIDED.

Administer.—Blows are dealt. Medicine is administered.
Afraid.—Say I fear it will rain, not I am afraid.
Alike.—Do not couple this word with both.
All over.—Over all the country, not all over the country.
Allow.—Do not say, "He allows he will do it."
Alone.—Distinguish this word from only
Amateur.—Not necessarily a beginner.
And.—Say try to go, not try and go.
Angry.—Say angry with a person and at a thing.
Answer.—Answer questions; reply to assertions
Anticipate.—Distinguish from expect.
As.—Say not that I know, instead of not as I know.
At all.—Superfluous in "any at all."
Awful.—A thing cannot be awful pretty.

Balance.—Not to be used for rest or remainder
Beautifully.—Looked beautiful, not beautifully.
Beg.—Say "I beg leave to acknowledge."
Belongs to.—Do not use for is a member of.
Between.—Between two; among more than two
Blacking.—This word is not blackening.
Brakeman.—Not brakesman.
Certain.—Distinguish from sure.
Character.—Distinguish from reputation.
Deal.—Great deal, not good deal.
Die with.—Persons die of, not with disease.
Disremember.—Say forget.
Don't.—Say he doesn't sing, not he don't sing.
Either.—Means the one or the other of two.
Either alternative.—Alternative means choice.
Equally well.—Do not say equally as well.
Every.—Followed by a verb in the singular.
Expect.—Refers to future time.
Fix.—Incorrectly used for arrange or prepare.
Folk.—Folk implies plurality as well as folks.
Gent.—Never use this contraction of gentleman.
Good.—"It looks good" Say well.
Got.—Omit got in "I have got a dollar."
Guess.—Do not use this word for suppose.
Had have.—Never use together.
Hardly.—Do not use with don't and can't.
Healthy.—Distinguish from wholesome.
Hundred.—Use the singular form with numerals.
Just.—Incorrect in the sense of now.
Learn.—To receive instruction. See teach.
Less.—Relates to quantity, fewer to number.
May.—Distinguish from can.
Near.—Do not use in the sense of nearly.
New.—"A pair of new boots;" not "a new pair."
Nice.—See definition of this word.
None.—Contraction of no one, takes singular.
Otherwise than.—Not otherwise but.
Party.—Do not use for person.
Perpetual.—Distinguish from continual.
Portion.—Often incorrectly used for part.
Posted.—Do not use instead of informed.
Prevalent.—Distinguish from prevailing.
Promise.—Distinguish from assure.
Propose.—Distinguish from purpose.
Prudence.—Distinguish from discretion.
Quantity.—Things measured or weighed.
Real.—The adverb is really, as, really good.
Remember.—Distinguish from recollect.
Seem.—Distinguish from appear.
Settle.—To settle does not mean to pay.
So, such.—So long journeys, not such long.
Some better.—Say somewhat better.
Splendid.—Splendid things glitter.
Stop.—We stay at a certain hotel, not stop.
Streamlet.—Do not use with little.
Summon.—Summon is a verb, summons a noun
Teach.—To give instruction. See learn.
Those kind.—Say that kind. Kind is singular.
Transpire.—Do not use for to happen.
Try.—We make an experiment, not try.
Widow woman.—Woman here is superfluous.
Without.—Do not use without for unless.
Year-old.—A two-year-colt, not a two-years.

CORRESPONDENCE.

INTRODUCTION.

The ability to write a neat, legible letter, correct in form and in English, spelling and punctuation, is one of the most valuable achievements a young business man or woman can possess. It is the lack of this ability that causes the failure of more stenographers and clerks than any other one thing. Business men very seldom complain that their stenographers lack speed but there is very bitter complaint that stenographers and clerks are not able to write a perfect letter themselves or correct any error made by the employer.

The following suggestions cover the whole field of ordinary letter writing. Every sentence is short and directly to the point and should be studied with care, lest some fact be overlooked or forgotten.

LETTERS.

The primary idea of a letter is conversation at a distance. If this be kept in mind one can scarcely fail to write appropriately, if one can converse properly; for a letter may be familiar or reserved, jocular or dignified, according to the relations between the writer and the person addressed. Letters of friendship should be simple and natural. It is the littl things, the incidents of every-day life, the home chat, which makes a friendship letter interesting. Letters of courtesy include invitations, acceptances, acknowledgments, letters of congratulation, of condolence, of introduction, and of recommendation. Letters of business include all correspondence relating to business matters. Public letters embrace communications to newspapers regarding public affairs. Frequently a writer publishes a letter addressed to some prominent person criticizing his opinions or actions, or putting to him a number of formal questions with the purpose of receiving a published reply. This is usually called an open letter.

THE HEADING.

The parts of a letter are: (1) Heading; (2) Address; (3) Salutation; (4) Body; (5) Complimentary Close; (6) Signature

The Heading should give the full address, i. e., your post-office, street or box number and the state. The date includes the month, day of the month and the year. The form 13 March, 19—, is occasionally employed in business correspondence. The reason for its use is because it is the natural form of expression. We say the 13th of March, not March the thirteenth. Another reason is that the former is less liable to errors. The following forms are bad and should not be used even by the busiest man: 4-6-19—, or 3-7-'2–, or 6/8/2–. Sometimes the day is written before the month. In such a case it would be difficult to tell the exact date of either one of the above expressions. The contractions 6th, 7th, 2d are never used when the year follows, as April 6, 19—, not April 6th, 19—. Yours of 6th instant is allowable in the body of a letter.

The name of the state should not be omitted when writing letters to the United States, as there are many cities of the same name in the States. There are six Chicagos, thirteen Bostons, sixteen Denvers, etc.

Location.—The heading on letter paper occupies only one line, but on note paper two lines. There are occasions, however, when more than one or two lines are used, but the rule should be to use as few lines as possible. The heading should occupy about two-thirds of the width of the sheet. Study the following models:

1. Media, Pa., April 17, 19—.

2. Box 58, Chicago, Ill.,
April 17, 19—.

3. Starners, Adams Co., Pa., 17 April, 19—.
4. University of Pennsylvania,
Philadelphia, Pa., April 17, 19—.
5. c/o Brown, Robinson Company,
No. 415 Carroll Street,
Atlanta, Ga., 17 April, 19—.

THE ADDRESS.

The address consists of the name, title, and post-office address of your correspondent, and usually occupies two lines; sometimes three are required. The name and title are written on the first line, below the last line of the heading, allowing a margin of one-tenth of the width of the paper at the left The address is written upon the next line below the name and title, allowing a margin of one-fifth the width of the paper. If a third line is used, the margin consists of one-fifteenth of the width of the paper, so that the three lines form a perfect slant of about twenty degrees.

When writing to friends the address may consist of the name only, and with very intimate friends it may be omitted in the superscription of the letter, but, in either case, the address must be given at the end of the letter. The author always gives the address in the superscription, when writing a business letter, and at the end when writing a social letter. The address in the letter should be as full and clear as the address upon the envelope.

Titles.—It is a lack of respect not to add some title to the name of your correspondent. Courtesy demands it. Titles may be classed as follows: Social titles; scholastic titles and official titles.

Mister, abbreviated **Mr.** may be applied to all classes of men, titled or untitled. It always precedes the name, and has many applications, as, Mr. Smith. Mr. Senator. Mr. Chairman. Mr. President, the Rev. Mr. Rogers, etc.

Esquire is abbreviated **Esq.,** and is usually affixed to the name. It applies to men in the legal profession. Mr. and Esq. are never used together.

Messieurs, abbreviated **Messrs.** is always used to supply the plural of Mr. and precedes the firm name, as Messrs. Fink & Fink or Messrs. Group & Co. The title Messrs. is sometimes omitted when the firm name is very long.

Mistress abbreviated **Mrs.** The title precedes the name of a married woman, and if her husband is living, the title Mrs. is prefixed to the name of her husband, as Mrs. Robert S. Williams. But if her husband is dead, then Mrs. is prefixed to her Christian name, as Mrs. Mary Hutchinson.

Mesdames abbreviated **Mmes.** This title is used when addressing more than one married woman. The title is also used with the name of a firm composed of married or unmarried women.

Master.—Not abbreviated, and is prefixed to the name of a boy.

Miss.—This is not an abbreviation It is used as a prefix to the name of an unmarried woman, as Miss Jessie Wood. The plural of Miss is Misses, and is used when more than one person is referred to in the same person or class.

Doctor of Medicine.—Abbreviated **Dr.** or **M. D.** The former precedes the name, and the latter follows it, but they are never used at the same time. The correct forms are as follows: Dr. Edward M. Foose or Edward M. Foose, M. D.

Reverend abbreviated **Rev.** and belongs to the Clergy, as Rev. Upton A. Hankey. When Rev. is used with the official or professional titles The is prefixed; as, The Rev. Prof. Snyder, The Rev. Father Donahue. Rev. is never used immediately before the surname, as Rev. Cross. When no other title can be used, then the Christian name must be used or some other title given, as Rev. Wharton A. Kline or Rev. Mr Kline.

Professor abbreviated **Prof.** and is prefixed to the name of any person who is regularly elected to a chair in some incorporated educational institution conferring degrees under seal. One may be given the honorary title when he has become noted for some special line of learning.

Scholastic Degrees and Official Titles are always abbreviated when used in addresses.

Titles of High Rank such as President, Governor, etc., are never abbreviated.

Two Titles may be used with the same name when one does not include the other.

SALUTATION.

The salutation expresses the respect we pay to our correspondent. It should occupy the next line below the address. When a two line address is used, the salutation may begin as in these examples:

Messrs. Jordan, Williams & Co.,
Hamilton, Ont.
Dear Sirs:—I enclose, etc.

Mr. J. G. Henry,
Ottawa, Ont.
Dear Sir:—Your favor of 10th, etc.

If the address occupies three lines then the salutation should always begin as in these examples:

Messrs. James B. Jerome Company,
714 N. Broad Street,
Philadelphia, Pa.
Dear Sirs:—In reply to your, etc.

Mr. William W. Beckner,
429 Market Street,
San Francisco, Cal.
Dear Sir:—Enclosed you will find, etc.

If only the name is used in the address then the salutation should always begin as in this example:

Mrs. Henry D. Spangler,
Dear Madam:
We extend to you, etc.

If no address is used, then the salutation should begin thus:

My dear Jessie:

The salutation should never be abbreviated. In the use of business salutations Sir and Madam are the most formal: Dear Sir and Dear Madam are less formal and are the most prevalent forms. The more familiar forms are My dear Sir and My dear Madam.

When addressing strangers, use Sir or Madam or Dear Sir or Dear Madam. Although the latter implies some degree of acquaintance, yet the present day etiquette regards it good to use these salutations when addressing strangers. The proper form for a single lady, of whatever age, is Dear Madam in case of a stranger, or Dear Miss Smith in case of an acquaintance.

When addressing an acquaintance use Dear Sir, My dear Sir, Dear Miss Magill, Dear Madam.

When addressing friends, My dear Sir, My dear Gaylord, My dear Friend, My dear Miss James, etc.

When addressing relatives, My dear Brother, My dear Son, etc.

BODY.

The body of a letter is a conversation in writing and one's style should be perfectly natural, i. e., he should write as he would talk. The first and indispensable quality of a good style is clearness. Generally it is enough if the writer devote his efforts simply to being understood. Plainness and clearness are the foundations upon which all other qualities are built. Too exclusive endeavor after precision may make the style stiff and angular. It is always unwise to impair the thought for the sake of the expression. To the quality of clearness must be added the quality of force. In a letter the spirit of the writer should show itself. The strongest thoughts find brief expression. As a rule the language which simply suggests the thought is more interesting than that which gives it full expression.

Penmanship and spelling are two features of a conversation in writing which must receive our careful attention. A misspelled word or an illegible hand are not excusable. Some persons think it is a mark of genius to write so no one can read it, but there are other ways of showing one's genius decidedly more commendable.

The beginning.—When the address consists of two lines and the salutation occupies the third margin space, the body of the letter should begin on the same line with the salutation, as:

Springfield, Mass., Jan. 16, 19 –.

Mr. James M. Group,
Regina, Sask.
Dear Sir:—Your favor of the 14th, etc.

When the address consists of three lines, and the salutation **begins at the first** marginal space, the body should begin on the same line, as:

Edmonton, Alta., Jan. 16, 19—.

Mr. Court F. Wood,
No. 11, East Capitol St.,
Washington, D. C.
Dear Sir:—Your favor of recent date, etc.

Good authorities sometimes drop down on the first line below the salutation when the address consists of but two lines, but this is never allowable when the address consists of more than two lines.

Paragraphs and Margins.—Great care should be taken in paragraphing a letter. Make a new paragraph at every change of subject, or the introduction of a new phase of the same subject.

Paging.—When a letter consists of more than one sheet of single sheet paper, the initials and the number should be written in the upper left-hand corner of each sheet.

Figures.—Amounts of merchandise, as 5 bushels of onions, and dates, as March 2, 191–, are always written in figures. Generally, if numbers contain more than two figures they should be written in figures, but numbers containing one or two figures should be spelled out.

Never abbreviate anything in the body of a letter.

Never write on both sides of the sheet in business correspondence.

In business correspondence always refer to previous correspondence by date or otherwise.

Be prompt in answering letters.

Study how to assort your mail, i. e., how to know what letters need answers and what letters need the waste basket.

Many persons begin to write letters without the least conception of what they want to say. They rattle off something that is about as meaningless as chaff, and will fall short of having the effect intended. Study your correspondent, his character, his habits, his letter, then outline your thought mentally, before attempting to write to him. If business men would make it a rule to put a little more thought into their correspondence they would be surprised to find the wonderful effect it would have upon their business.

Letters should be posted in each departing mail. No firm whose business has reached any magnitude can afford to be negligent in the matter of posting their mail. Often a few minutes will prevent much vexation and trouble.

COMPLIMENTARY CLOSE.

The complimentary close consists of the term of courtesy we use in closing our letter, together with the signature.

The complimentary close should begin on the first line below the body of the letter and at the center of the paper.

In business, Yours truly, Yours very truly, Yours respectfully or Respectfully, Sincerely yours, are some of the most common forms of complimentary closing. Never close a letter with "Yours, etc."

In social correspondence the form of the complimentary close must be determined by the relations existing between the parties.

Complimentary close should not be less formal or more formal than the salutation. Your "good-byes" should always have some consistency with your "how-do-you dos," i. e., if you said "My dear friend," you would not close with "Your friend," That would be a repetition. Nor would you use Respectfully, because that would seem too formal, and would be inconsistent. The complimentary close must be consistent with the salutation used.

Never use "I remain" or "We remain," unless you have had previous correspondence with the person written to.

THE SIGNATURE.

The signature should be written under the complimentary close and should begin at such a point that a margin of about half an inch will be left at the right of the sheet. It should be written plainly, and always in full, i. e., do not sign your name "Tom," "Jack," "E. M. B." or "Your sister." Such letters, if lost, always go the the Dead Letter Office and are destroyed.

Do not write your name at one time, J. W. Smith, then at another time J. William Smith, then John W. Smith, then John William Smith. Have only one way of writing your name.

If you are a woman and do not use your husband's first name, or if you are not married, you should always indicate your relation by using Miss or Mrs either with or without the parenthesis, as (Miss) Gertrude Casey, or (Mrs.) Elizabeth Bailor.

When a secretary signs the letters for his proprietor he should always sign his initials under the signature. Usually the initials are preceded by the prefix per.

FOLDING.

A letter-sheet should be folded from the bottom forward, bringing the lower edge near the top, so as to make the half length a little shorter than the envelope, and then break the fold. Next fold twice the other way. beginning at the left edge, folding towards the right. Measure these folds also, so as to fit

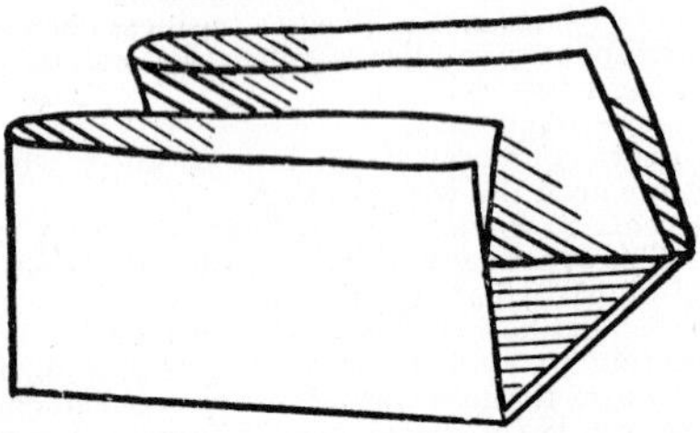

the envelope. A note-sheet should be folded twice, from the bottom forward. When the envelope is nearly square, a single fold of the note-sheet is sufficient. If you want to make a good letter look slovenly, endeavor, by folding down a half inch at each end, to make it fit an envelope an inch too short.

SUPERSCRIPTION.

The Envelope Address.—Many misdirected letters reach the Dead Letter Office daily. The public needs to be educated along this line. In addressing an envelope, write first the name, then the street, then the post-office, then the State or Province. If additional matter, such as box or county, is necessary, put it at the lower left-hand corner. Even in the case of large cities, it is necessary to write the name of the State or Province for there are several cities of the same name both in the United States and Canada.

Be particularly careful in writing the abbreviations of States or Provinces. Thus, N. Y. may easily be taken for N. J.; Pa. for Va.; Cal. for Col.; Md. for Ind.; Me. for Mo.; N. B. for N. S. Mail intended for people who will be in a place only a day or two should have "transient" written in the upper left-hand corner and enclosed in brackets.

Letters to be registered must have the name and address of the sender on the envelope. Do not write the name of the county where the postal employees always look for the name of the post office. Railway mail clerks have to distribute many pieces of mail while the train is running from one station to another, and must decide to what place to send a letter in a fraction of a second. When the county and post office are close together, the clerk is almost as apt to take the name of the county for the post office as the right name. The penmanship should be distinct and legible, and the address neat and elegant, without ornamentation. Non-delivered letters are returned to the writers who have their names and post offices printed on the upper left-hand corner. A little more care in the matter of addressing envelopes would save much labor, and the government much expense.

Postage.—Every letter should have one full rate postage prepaid, otherwise "postage due" is marked upon it, and collected from your correspondent. The stamp should always be placed in the upper right-hand corner of the envelope, leaving a margin of about one-eighth of an inch at the right side and top. Do not put the stamp on any other part of the envelope, as it gives the postal clerks a great deal of trouble and considerable loss of time in stopping to turn the letter to cancel it.

Materials.—Use the best stationery you can afford, and see that your letter paper and envelope correspond in quality and color. The size of the letter sheet ordinarily used in business, is either what is termed note size, about 5 by 8 inches, or letter size, $8\frac{1}{2}$ by 11 inches. Use the best of ink and pens.

Letters Ordering Goods.—Such letters should be clear and to the point. They should state how the goods are to be sent, by what railroad, whether by express or by freight. The goods should be carefully described, so that no mistake will be made in filling the order. If only one or two articles are ordered they may be written in the body of the letter in the proper form. But if a number of articles are ordered, a separate sheet should be used and headed Order No. ——, giving the date and signed by the person ordering. If money is enclosed the amount should be written out in words, sometimes it is written in figures and enclosed in parenthesis. The kind of remittance should be mentioned and for what applied. The remittance should be pinned to the letter.

PARTS OF A LETTER.

Date.

Complimentary Address.

Body of the Letter.

Complimentary closing.

Signature.

Name.

Address.

This form is commonly used in social correspondence.

Date.

Name.

Address.

Salutation.

Body of the Letter.

Complimentary Ending.

Signature.

This form is commonly used in business letters

DICTIONARY OF ENGLISH CHRISTIAN NAMES OF MEN AND WOMEN WITH THEIR DERIVATION AND MEANING

I. NAMES OF MEN.

A

Aaron. [Heb.] Lofty; inspired.
Abel. [Heb.] Breath; transitoriness; vanity.
Abijah. [Heb.] To whom Jehovah is a father.
Abner. [Heb.] Father of light.
Abraham. [Heb.] Father of a multitude.
Abram. [Heb.] Father of elevation.
Adam. [Heb.] Man; earth-man; red earth.
Adolphus. [O. H. Ger.] Noble wolf, i. e., noble hero.
Alan. Variously explained as a hound [Slav.], harmony [Celt.], and a corruption of Hilary, or of Ælianus.
Alaric. [O. H. Ger.] All-rich; or, noble ruler.
Albert. [O. H. Ger.] Nobly bright; illustrious.
Alexander. [Gr.] A defender of men.
Alfred. [O. H. Ger.] Elf in council; i. e., good counselor.
Algernon. [Fr.] With whiskers.
Alonzo. [O. Ger.] The same as ALPHONSO, q. v.
Alphonso. [O. H. Ger.] All-ready; willing.
Amasa. [Heb.] A burden.
Ambrose. [Gr.] Immortal; divine.
Amos. [Heb.] Strong; courageous; otherwise, burden.
Andrew. [Gr.] Strong; manly.
Anselm. [O. H. Ger.] Protection of God.
Anthony, Antony. [Lat.] Priceless; praiseworthy.
Archibald. [Ger.] Extremely bold; otherwise, holy prince.
Arthur. [Celt.] High; noble.
Asa. [Heb.] Healer; physician.
Asaph. [Heb.] A collector.
Asher. [Heb.] Happy; fortunate.
Augustin, Augustine, Austin. [Lat.] Belonging to Augustus.
Augustus. [Lat.] Exalted; imperial.
Azariah. [Heb.] Helped of the Lord.

B

Baldwin. [O. H. Ger.] Bold, courageous friend.
Barnaby. [Heb.] Son of consolation.
Bartholomew. [Heb.] A warlike son.
Basil. [Gr.] Kingly; royal.
Benedict. [Lat.] Blessed.
Benjamin. [Heb.] Son of the right hand.
Beriah. [Heb.] In calamity.
Bernard, Barnard. [O. H. Ger.] Bold as a bear.
Bertram. [O. H. Ger.] Bright raven.
Boniface. [Lat.] A benefactor.
Brian. [Celt.] Strong.
Bruno. [O. H. Ger.] Brown.

C

Cadwallader. [Brit.] Battle-arranger.
Cæsar. [Lat.] Hairy; or blue-eyed.
Caleb. [Heb.] A dog.
Calvin. [Lat.] Bald.
Cecil. [Lat.] Dim-sighted.
Cephas. [Aramaic.] A stone.
Charles. [O. H. Ger.] Strong; manly; noble-spirited.
Christian. [Lat.] Belonging to Christ; a believer in Christ.
Christopher. [Gr.] Bearing Christ.
Clarence. [Lat.] Illustrious.
Claudius, Claude. [Lat.] Lame.
Clement. [Lat.] Mild-tempered; merciful.
Conrad. [O. H. Ger.] Bold in council; resolute.
Constant. [Lat.] Firm; faithful.
Constantine. [Lat.] Resolute; firm.

Cornelius. [Lat.] (Meaning uncertain.)
Cuthbert. [A.-S.] Noted splendor.
Cyril. [Gr.] Lordly.
Cyrus. [Per.] The sun.

D

Daniel. [Heb.] A divine judge.
Darius. [Per.] Preserver.
David. [Heb.] Beloved.
Denis, [Gr.] Same as DIONYSUS.
Dennis, [Fr. form.]
Dionysus. [Gr.] In Greek mythology, the god of wine, corresponding to Bacchus.
Donald. [Celt.] Proud chief.
Duncan. [Celt.] Brown chief.

E

Eben. [Heb.] A stone.
Ebenezer. [Heb.] The stone of help.
Edgar. [A.-S.] A javelin (or protector) of property.
Edmund. [A.-S.] Defender of property.
Edward. [A.-S.] Guardian of property.
Edwin. [A.-S.] Gainer of property.
Egbert. [O. H. Ger.] The sword's brightness; famous with the sword.
Elbert. [O. H. Ger.] The same as ALBERT.
Eldred. [A.-S.] Terrible.
Eleazer. [Heb.] To whom God is a help.
Eli. [Heb.] A foster son.
Elias. [Heb.] The same as ELIJAH.
Elihu. [Heb.] God the Lord.
Elijah. [Heb.] Jehovah is my God.
Elisha. [Heb.] God my salvation.
Ellis. [Heb.] A variation of ELISHA.
Elmer. [A.-S.] Noble; excellent. [A contraction of ETHELMER.]
Emmanuel. [Heb.] God with us.
Emery. [A.-S.] Powerful; rich.
Enoch. [Heb.] Consecrated; dedicated.
Enos. [Heb.] Man.
Ephraim. [Heb.] Very fruitful.
Erasmus. [Gr.] Lovely; worthy to be loved.
Erastus. [Ger.] Lovely; amiable.
Ernest. [Ger.] Earnest.
Ethan. [Heb.] Firmness; strength.
Eugene. [Ger.] Wellborn; noble.
Eustace. [Gr.] Healthy; strong; standing firm.
Evan. [Brit.] The same as JOHN.
Ezekiel. [Heb.] Strength of God.
Ezra. [Heb.] Help.

F

Ferdinand. [O. H. Ger.] Brave; valiant.
Fernando. [O. H. Ger.] Same as FERDINAND.
Francis. [Fr.] Free.
Frank [Fr.] A contraction of FRANCIS.
Frederic,
Frederick. [O. H. Ger.] Abounding in peace; or peaceful ruler.

G

Garret. [O. H. Ger.] Another form of GERALD, or GERARD.
Geoffrey. [O. H. Ger.] The same as GODFREY.
George. [Ger.] A landholder; husbandman.
Gerald,
Gerard. [O. H. Ger.] Strong with the spear.
Gideon. [Heb.] A destroyer.
Gilbert. [O. H. Ger.] Yellow-bright; famous.
Giles. [Gr.] A kid.
Godfrey. [O. H. Ger.] At peace with God.
Gregory. [Ger.] Watchful; vigilant.
Griffith. [Brit.] Having great faith.
Gustavus. [Sw.] A warrior; hero.
Guy. [Fr.] A leader.

H

Hannibal. [Punic.] Grace of Baal.
Harold. [A.-S.] A champion; general of an army.
Henry. [O. H. Ger.] The head or chief of a house.
Herbert. [A.-S.] Glory of the army.
Herman. [O. H. Ger.] A warrior.
Hezekiah. [Heb.] Strength of the Lord.
Hilary. [Lat.] Cheerful; merry.

Hiram. [Heb.] Most noble.
Horace. [Gr.] Same as HORATIO. [Fr. form.]
Horatio. [Gr.] (Meaning uncertain.)
Hosea. [Heb.] Salvation.
Howell. [Brit.] Sound; whole.
Hubert. [O. H. Ger.] Bright in spirit; soul-bright.
Hugh, } **Hugo.** } [D.] Mind; spirit; soul.
Humphrey. [A.-S.] Protector of the home.

I

Ichabod. [Heb.] The glory has departed.
Ignatius. [Gr.] Ardent; fiery.
Immanuel. [Heb.] The same as EMMANUEL.
Ingram. [Teut.] Raven.
Inigo. [Gr.] The same as IGNATIUS. [Sp. form.]
Ira. [Heb.] Watchful.
Isaac. [Heb.] Laughter.
Isaiah. [Heb.] Salvation of the Lord.
Israel. [Heb.] A soldier of God.
Ivan. [Brit.] The same as JOHN.

J

Jabez. [Heb.] He will cause pain.
Jacob. [Heb.] A supplanter.
James. [Heb.] The same as JACOB.
Japheth. [Heb.] Enlargement.
Jason. [Gr.] A healer.
Jasper. [Per.] (Meaning uncertain.)
Jedediah. [Heb.] Beloved of the Lord.
Jeffrey. [O. H. Ger.] The same as GODFREY.
Jeremiah, } **Jeremias,** } **Jeremy.** } [Heb.] Exalted of the Lord.
Jerome. [Gr.] Holy name.
Jesse. [Heb.] Wealth.
Joab. [Heb.] Jehovah is his father.
Job. [Heb.] Afflicted; persecuted.
Joel. [Heb.] The Lord is God.
John. [Heb.] The gracious gift of God.
Jonah, } **Jonas.** } [Heb.] A dove.
Jonathan. [Heb.] Gift of Jehovah.
Joseph. [Heb.] He shall add.
Joshua. [Heb.] God of salvation.
Josiah, } **Josias.** } [Heb.] Given of the Lord.
Judah. [Heb.] Praised.
Julian. [Lat.] Sprung from, or belonging to, Julius.
Julius. [Gr.] Soft-haired.
Justin. [Lat.] Just.
Justus. [Lat.] Just.

K

Kenelm. [A.-S.] A defender of his kindred.
Kenneth. [Gael.] A leader; commander.

L

Lambert. [O. H. Ger.] Illustrious with landed possessions.
Lancelot. [It.] A little angel; otherwise, a little lance or warrior; or a servant.
Laurence, } **Lawrence.** } [Lat.] Crowned with laurel.
Lazarus. [Heb.] God will help.
Leander. [Gr.] Lion-man.
Lemuel. [Heb.] Created by God.
Leonard. [Ger.] Strong; or brave as a lion.
Leopold. [O. H. Ger.] Bold for the people.
Levi. [Heb.] Adhesion.
Lewis. [O. H. Ger.] Bold warrior.
Lionel. [Lat.] Young lion.
Llewellyn. [Celt.] Lightning.
Lorenzo. [Lat.] Same as LAURENCE. [It. & Sp. forms.]
Louis. [O. H. Ger.] The same as LEWIS. [Fr. form.]
Lucian. [Lat.] Belonging to, or sprung from Lucius.
Lucius. [Lat.] Born at break of day.
Luke. [Lat.] Light.
Luther. [Ger.] Illustrious warrior.

M

Malachi. [Heb.] Messenger of the Lord.
Manasseh. [Heb.] Forgetfulness.
Marcus, } **Mark.** } [Lat.] A hammer; otherwise, a male, or sprung from Mars.
Marmaduke. [A.-S.] A mighty noble.
Martin. [Lat.] Of Mars; warlike.

Matthew. [Heb.] Gift of Jehovah.
Maurice. [Lat.] Moorish; dark-colored.
Maximilian. [Lat.] The greatest Æmilianus.
Micah. [Heb.] Who is like the Lord?
Michael. [Heb.] Who is like God?
Miles. [Lat.] A soldier.
Moses. [Egypt.] Drawn out of the water.

N

Napoleon. [Gr.] Lion of the forest-dell.
Nathan. [Heb.] Given; a gift.
Nathanael, Nathaniel. [Heb.] The gift of God.
Neal, Neil. [Lat.] Dark; swarthy; otherwise [Celt.], chief.
Nicholas, Nicolas. [Gr.] Victory of the people.
Noah. [Heb.] Rest; comfort.
Norman. [Ger.] A Northman; a native of Normandy.

O

Obadiah. [Heb.] Servant of the Lord.
Octavius, Octavus. [Lat.] The eighth-born.
Oliver. [Lat.] An olive-tree.
Orlando. [Teut.] Same as ROWLAND. [It. form.]
Oscar. [Celt.] Bounding warrior.
Oswald. [O. H. Ger.] Power of God.
Owen. [Celt.] Lamb; otherwise, young warrior.

P

Patrick. [Lat.] Noble; a patrician.
Paul. [Lat.] Little.
Peleg. [Heb.] Division.
Peregrine. [Lat.] A stranger.
Peter. [Gr.] A rock.
Philander. [Gr.] A lover of men.
Philemon. [Gr.] Loving, friendly.
Philip. [Gr.] A lover of horses.
Phineas. [Heb.] Mouth of brass.
Pius. [Lat.] Pious; dutiful.
Pliny. [Lat.] (Meaning uncertain.)

Q

Quintin. [Lat.] The fifth.

R

Ralph. [O. H. Ger.] Same as RODOLPHUS.
Raphael. [Heb.] The healing of God.
Raymond. [O. H. Ger.] Wise protection.
Reginald. [O. H. Ger.] Strong ruler.
Reuben. [Heb.] Behold, a son.
Reynold. [O. H. Ger.] Same as REGINALD.
Richard. [O. H. Ger.] Rich-hearted; powerful.
Robert. [O. H. Ger.] Bright in fame.
Roderic, Roderick. [O. H. Ger.] Rich in fame.
Rodolph, Rodolphus. [O. H. Ger.] Famous wolf, or hero.
Roger. [O. H. Ger.] Famous with the spear.
Roland. [O. H. Ger.] Same as ROWLAND. [Fr. form.]
Rowland. [O. H. Ger.] Fame of the land.
Rudolph, Rudolphus. [O. H. Ger.] Variations of RODOLPHUS.
Rufus. [Lat.] Red; red-haired.
Rupert. [O. H. Ger.] The same as ROBERT.

S

Samson, Sampson. [Heb.] Splendid sun; i. e., Great joy and felicity.
Samuel. [Heb.] Heard of God; asked for of God.
Saul. [Heb.] Asked for.
Seba. [Heb.] Eminent.
Sebastian. [Gr.] Venerable; reverend.
Seth. [Heb.] Appointed.
Sigismund. [O. H. Ger.] Conquering protection.
Silas. [Lat.] A contraction of SILVANUS.
Silvanus. [Lat.] Living in a wood.
Silvester. [Lat.] Bred in the country; rustic.
Simeon, Simon. [Heb.] Hearing with acceptance.
Solomon. [Heb.] Peaceable.
Stephen. [Gr.] A crown.
Sylvan, Sylvanus. The same as SILVANUS.
Sylvester. The same as SILVESTER.

T

Thaddeus. [Syr.] The wise.
Theobald. [O. H. Ger.] Bold for the people.
Theodore. [Gr.] The gift of God.
Theodoric. [A.-S.] Powerful among the people.
Theophilus. [Gr.] A lover of God.
Thomas. [Heb.] A twin.
Timothy. [Gr.] Fearing God.
Titus. [Gr.] (Meaning uncertain.)
Tobiah, } [Heb.] Distinguished
Tobias. } of the Lord.
Tristam, } [Lat.] Grave; pen-
Tristram. } sive; melancholy; sorrowful; sad.

U

Ulysses. [Gr.] A hater.
Uriah. [Heb.] Light of the Lord.
Uriel. [Heb.] Light of God.

V

Valentine. [Lat.] Strong; healthy; powerful.
Victor. [Lat.] A conqueror.
Vincent. [Lat.] Conquering; victorious.
Vivian. [Lat.] Lively.

W

Walter. [O. H. Ger.] Ruling the host.
William. [O. H. Ger.] Resolute helmet, or helmet of resolution; defense; protector.
Winfred. [A.-S.] Win-peace.

Z

Zabdiel. [Heb.] Gift of God.
Zaccheus. [Heb.] Innocent; pure.
Zachariah, } [Heb.] Remembered
Zachary. } of the Lord.
Zadok. [Heb.] Just.
Zebadiah, } [Heb.] Gift of the
Zebedee. } Lord.
Zechariah. [Heb.] The same as ZACHARIAH.
Zedekiah. [Heb.] Justice of the Lord.
Zephaniah. [Heb.] Hid of the Lord.

II. NAMES OF WOMEN

A

Abigail. [Heb.] My father's joy.
Ada. [O. H. Ger.] Same as EDITH.
Adaline. [O. H. Ger.] Same as ADELINE.
Adela. [O. H. Ger.] Same as ADELINE.
Adelaide. [O. H. Ger.] Same as ADELINE.
Adelina, } [O. H. Ger.] Of noble
Adeline. } birth; a princess.
Agatha. [Gr.] Good; kind.
Agnes. [Gr.] Chaste; pure.
Alberta. [O. H. Ger.] Feminine of ALBERT.
Alexandra, } [Gr.] Feminine of
Alexandrina. } ALEXANDER.
Alice, } [O. H. Ger.] Same as
Alicia. } ADELINE.
Almira. [Ar.] Lofty; a princess.
Amabel. [Lat.] Lovable.
Amanda. [Lat.] Worthy to be loved.
Amelia. [O. H. Ger.] Busy, energetic.—See EMELINE.
Amy. [Lat.] Beloved.
Angelica, } [Gr.] Lovely;
Angelina. } angelic.
Anna, }
Ann, } [Heb.] Grace; same as
Anne. } HANNAH.
Annette. [Heb.] A variation of ANNE. [Fr. form.]
Antoinette. [Gr.] Diminutive of ANTONIA. [Fr. form.]
Antonia. [Lat.] Inestimable.
Arabella. [Lat.] A fair altar; otherwise, an Arabian woman.
Augusta. [Lat.] Feminine of AUGUSTUS.
Aurelia. [Lat.] Feminine of AURELIUS.
Aurora. [Lat.] Morning redness; fresh; brilliant.

B

Barbara. [Gr.] Foreign; strange.

Beatrice, }
Beatrix. } [Lat.] Making happy.
Belinda. (Meaning uncertain.)
Bertha. [O. H. Ger.] Bright; beautiful.
Betsey. [Heb.] A corruption of ELIZABETH.
Blanch, }
Blanche. } [Teut.] White.
Bridget. [Celt.] Strength.

C

Caroline. [O. H. Ger.] Feminine of CAROLUS, the Latin of Charles. [Fr. form.]
Catharina, }
Catharine, } [Gr.] Pure.
Catherine. }
Cecilia, }
Cecily. } [Lat.] Feminine of CECIL.
Celia. [Lat.] Feminine of CŒLIUS. [It. form.]
Charlotte. [O. H. Ger.] Feminine of CHARLES.
Chloe. [Gr.] A green herb; blooming.
Christiana, }
Christina. } [Gr.] Feminine of CHRISTIANUS, Lat. for CHRISTIAN.
Cicely. [Lat.] A corruption of CECILIA.
Clara. [Lat.] Bright; illustrious.
Clarice, }
Clarissa. } [Lat.] A variation of CLARA.
Claudia. [Lat.] Feminine of CLAUDIUS.
Clementina, }
Clementine. } [Lat.] Mild; gentle.
Constance. [Lat.] Firm; constant.
Cora. [Gr.] Maiden; another form of CORINNA.
Cordelia. [Lat.] Warm-hearted.
Corinna. [Gr.] Maiden.
Cornelia. [Lat.] Feminine of CORNELIUS.

D

Deborah. [Heb.] A bee.
Delia. [Gr.] of Delos.
Diana. [Lat.] Goddess.
Dinah. [Heb.] Judged.
Dora. [Gr.] A contraction of DOROTHEA.
Dorcas. [Gr.] A gazelle.
Dorinda. [Gr.] Same as DOROTHEA.
Dorothea, }
Dorothy. } [Gr.] The gift of God.
Drusilla. (Meaning uncertain.)

E

Edith. [O. H. Ger.] Happiness; otherwise, rich gift.
Edna. [Heb.] Pleasure.
Eleanor, }
Elinor. } [Gr.] Light; the same as HELEN.
Elisabeth, }
Elizabeth, } [Heb.] Worshiper of God; consecrated to God.
Eliza. }
Ella. [Gr.] A contraction of ELEANOR.
Ellen. [Gr.] Diminutive of ELEANOR.
Elvira. [Lat.] White.
Emeline, }
Emmeline. } [O. H. Ger.] Energetic; industrious.
Emily. [O. H. Ger.] Same as EMELINE.
Emma. [O. H. Ger.] Same as EMELINE.
Ernestine. [Ger.] Feminine and dim. of ERNEST.
Esther. [Per.] Star; good fortune.
Ethel. [O. H. Ger.] Noble; of noble birth; same as ADELA.
Ethelind, }
Ethelinda. } [Teut.] Noble snake.
Eugenia. [Gr.] Feminine of EUGENE.
Eugenie. [Gr.] Same as EUGENIA. [Fr. form.]
Eunice. [Gr.] Happy victory.
Euphemia. [Gr.] Of good report.
Eva. [Heb.] Life.
Evangeline. [Gr.] Bringing glad news.
Eve. [Heb.] The same as EVA.
Evelina, }
Eveline. } [Heb.] Diminutive of EVA. [It. form.]

F

Fanny. [Ger.] A diminutive of FRANCES.
Faustina. [Lat.] Lucky.
Felicia. [Lat.] Happiness.
Fidelia. [Lat.] Faithful.
Flora. [Lat.] Flowers.
Florence. [Lat.] Blooming; flourishing.
Frances. [Ger.] Feminine of FRANCIS.
Frederica. [O. H. Ger.] Feminine of FREDERICK.

G

Georgiana, }
Georgina. } [Gr.] Feminine of GEORGE.
Geraldine. Feminine of GERALD.
Gertrude. [O. H. Ger.] Spear-maiden.

Grace. [Lat.] Grace, favor.
Griselda. [Teut.] Stone-heroine.

H

Hannah. [Heb.] The same as ANNA.
Harriet. [O. H. Ger.] Feminine diminutive of HENRY. [Eng. form.]
Helen, **Helena.** [Gr.] Light.
Henrietta. [O. H. Ger.] Feminine and diminutive of HENRY. [Fr. form.]
Hephzibah. [Heb.] My delight is in her.
Hester, **Hesther.** [Per.] Same as ESTHER.
Honora, **Honoria.** [Lat.] Honorable.
Hortensia. [Lat.] A lady gardener.
Huldah. [Heb.] A weasel.

I

Ida. [O. H. Ger.] Godlike.
Inez. [Gr.] The same as AGNES.
Irene. [Gr.] Peaceful.
Isabel, **Isabella.** [Heb.] The same as ELIZABETH.

J

Jane. [Heb.] Feminine of JOHN; same as JOANNA.
Janet. [Heb.] Diminutive of JANE.
Jaqueline. [Heb.] Feminine of JAMES. [Fr. form.]
Jean, **Jeanne,** **Jeannette.** [Heb.] The same as JANE or JOAN. [Fr. forms.]
Jemima. [Heb.] A dove.
Jerusha. [Heb.] Possessed; married.
Joan, **Joanna.** [Heb.] Feminine of JOHN.
Josepha, **Josephine.** [Heb.] Feminine of JOSEPH.
Judith. [Heb.] Praised.
Julia. [Lat.] Feminine of JULIUS.
Juliana. [Lat.] Feminine of JULIAN.
Juliet. [Lat.] Diminutive of JULIA. [Fr. form.]

K

Katharine, **Katherine.** [Gr.] Same as CATHARINE.
Keturah. [Heb.] Incense.
Keziah. [Heb.] Cassia.

L

Laura. [Lat.] A laurel.
Lavinia. [Lat.] Of Latium.
Leonora. [Gr.] Same as ELEANOR.
Letitia. [Lat.] Happiness.
Lettice. A corruption of LETITIA.
Lilian. **Lilly.** [Lat.] Lily.
Lois. [Gr.] Good; desirable.
Louisa, **Louise.** [O. H. Ger.] Feminine of LOUIS.
Lucia. [Lat.] Same as LUCY. [It. form.]
Lucinda. [Lat.] The same as LUCY.
Lucretia. [Lat.] Gain; otherwise, light.
Lucy. [Lat.] Feminine of LUCIUS.
Lydia. [Gr.] A native of Lydia, in Asia Minor.

M

Mabel. [Lat.] A contraction of AMABEL.
Madeline. [Heb.] Same as MAGDALENE. [Fr. form.]
Magdalene. [Heb.] Belonging to Magdala.
Marcella. [Lat.] Feminine of MARCELLUS.
Marcia. [Lat.] Feminine of MARCIUS.
Margaret. [Gr.] A pearl.
Maria. [Heb.] The same as MARY. [Lat. form.]
Marianne. [Heb.] A compound of MARY and ANNE.
Marion. [Heb.] A French form of MARY.
Martha. [Heb.] The ruler of the house; otherwise, sorrowful.
Mary. [Heb.] Bitter; otherwise, their rebellion, or star of the sea.
Mathilda, **Matilda.** [O. H. Ger.] Mighty battle-maid; heroine.
Maud. A contraction of MATHILDA, or MAGDALENE.
May. A diminutive of MARY.
Mehetabel, **Mehitable.** [Heb.] Benefited of God.
Melicent. [Lat.] Sweet singer.
Melissa. [Gr.] A bee.
Mildred. [Ger.] Mild threatener.
Miranda. [Lat.] Admirable.
Miriam. [Heb.] The same as MARY.
Myra. [Gr.] She who weeps or laments.

N

Nancy. A familiar form of ANNE.
Nora. A contraction of HONORA.

O

Octavia. [Lat.] Feminine of OCTAVIUS.
Olive, Olivia. [Lat.] An olive.
Ophelia. [Gr.] Serpent.

P

Paula. [Lat.] Feminine of PAUL.
Pauline. [Lat.] Feminine of PAULINUS.
Penelope. [Gr.] A weaver.
Philippa. [Gr.] Feminine of PHILIP.
Phœbe. [Gr.] Pure; radiant.
Phebe. [Gr.] The same as PHŒBE.
Phyllis. [Gr.] A green bough.
Priscilla. [Lat.] Somewhat old.

R

Rachel. [Heb.] A ewe.
Rebecca, Rebekah. [Heb.] Of enchanting beauty.
Rhoda. [Ger.] A rose.
Rosa. [Lat.] A rose.
Rosabel, Rosabella. [Lat.] A fair rose.
Rosalia, Rosalie. [Lat.] Little and blooming rose. [Fr. and It. forms.]
Rosalind. [Lat.] Beautiful as a rose.
Rosamond. [Teut.] Horse-protection, *i. e.*, famous protection.
Roxana. [Per.] Dawn of day.
Ruth. [Heb.] Beauty.

S

Sabina. [Lat.] A Sabine woman.
Salome. [Heb.] Peaceful.
Sara, Sarah. [Heb.] A princess.
Selina. [Gr.] Parsley.
Sibyl, Sibylla. [Gr.] A prophetess.
Sophia. [Gr.] Wisdom.
Sophronia. [Gr.] Of a sound mind.
Stella. [Lat.] A star.
Susan, Susanna, Susannah. [Heb.] A lily.

T

Tabitha. [Syr.] A gazelle.
Theodora. [Gr.] Feminine of THEODORE.
Theodosia. [Gr.] The gift of God.
Theresa. [Gr.] Carrying ears of corn.

U

Ulrica. [O. H. Ger.] Rich.
Urania. [Gr.] Heavenly;—the name of one of the Muses.
Ursula. [Lat.] She-bear.

V

Valeria. [Lat.] Feminine of VALERIUS.
Victoria. [Lat.] Victory. Feminine of VICTOR.
Viola. [Lat.] A violet.
Virginia. [Lat.] Virgin; pure.
Vivian. [Lat.] Lively.

W

Wilhelmina. [O. H. Ger.] Feminine of WILHELM, German of William.
Winifred. [Teut.] Lover of peace.

Z

Zenobia. [Gr.] Having life from Jupiter.

TIME AND DATING.

DIVISIONS OF TIME.

The interval between two consecutive transits of a fixed star over any meridian or the interval during which the earth makes one absolute revolution on its axis is called a Sidereal Day, and is invariable, while the interval between two consecutive transits of the Sun over any meridian is called an Apparent Solar Day, and its length varies from day to day by reason of the variable motion of the earth in its orbit, and the inclination of this orbit to the equator on which time is measured.

A Mean Solar Day is the average or mean of all the apparent solar days in a year. Mean Solar Time is that shown by a well-regulated clock or watch, while Apparent Solar Time is that shown by a well-constructed sun-dial; the difference between the two at any time is the Equation of Time, and may amount to 16 minutes and 21 seconds. The Astronomical Day begins at noon and the Civil Day at the preceding midnight. The Sidereal and Mean Solar Days are both invariable, but one day of the latter is equal to 1 day, 3 minutes and 56.555 seconds of the former.

The interval during which the earth makes one absolute revolution round the Sun is called a Sidereal Year, and consists of 365 days, 6 hours, 9 minutes, and 9.6 seconds, which is invariable.

The Tropical Year is the interval between two consecutive returns of the Sun to the Vernal Equinox. If this were a fixed point, the Sidereal and Tropical Years would be identical; but in consequence of the disturbing influence of the Moon and planets on the spheroidal figure of the earth, the Equinox has a slow, retrograde mean motion of 50″.26 annually, so that the Sun returns to the Equinox sooner every year than he otherwise would by 20 minutes 23.6 seconds; the Tropical Year, therefore, consists of 365 days, 5 hours, 48 minutes, and 46 seconds. The Tropical Year is not of uniform length; it is now slowly decreasing at the rate of .595 second per century, but this variation will not always continue.

Julius Cæsar, in B. C. 45, was the first to reform the calendar by ordering that every year whose date number is exactly divisible by 4 contain 366 days, and all other years 365 days. The intercalary day was introduced by counting the sixth day before the Kalends of March twice; hence the name bissextile, from bis, twice, and sex, six. He also changed the beginning of the year, from 1st of March to the 1st of January, and also changed the name of the fifth month (Quintillis) to July, after himself. The average length of the Julian year is therefore 365¼ days, which, however, is too long by 11 minutes and 14 seconds, and this would accumulate in 400 years, to about three days. The Julian Calendar continued in use until A. D. 1582, when the date of the beginning of the seasons occurred 10 days later than in B. C. 45, when this mode of reckoning time was introduced.

The Gregorian Calendar was introduced by Pope Gregory XIII, with the view of keeping the Equinox to the same day of the month. It consists of 365 days, but every year exactly divisible by 4 and the centurial years which are exactly divisible by 400 contain 366 days; and if in addition to this arbitrary arrangement the centurial years exactly divisible by 4,000 contain 366 days, the error in the Gregorian system will amount to only one day in about 20 centuries. If, however, 31 leap years were intercalated in 128 years, instead of 32 as at present, the calendar would be practically exact and the error would not amount to more than a day in 100,000 years. The length of the mean Gregorian Year may therefore be set down at 365 days, 5 hours, 49 minutes, 12 seconds. The Gregorian Calendar was introduced into England and her colonies in 1752, at which time the Equinox had retrograded 11 days since the Council of Nice in A. D. 325, when the festival of Easter was established and the Equinox occurred on March 21; hence September 3, 1752, was called September 14, and at the same time the commencement of the legal year was changed from March 25 to January 1, so that the year 1751 lost the months of

January and February and the first 24 days of March. The difference between the Julian and Gregorian Calendars is now 13 days. Russia and the Greek Church still employ the Julian Calendar for civil and ecclesiastical purposes.

DIFFERENCE IN TIME BETWEEN PRINCIPAL CITIES.

PLACES.	WHEN IT IS 12 O'CLOCK NOON ACCORDING TO — STANDARD TIME IN THE UNITED STATES			
	Eastern (*a*)	Central (*b*)	Mountain (*c*)	Pacific (*d*)
IT IS AT				
Aden..........Arabia	8.00 P.M.	9.00 P.M.	10.00 P.M.	11.00 P.M.
Amsterdam..........Holland	5.20 P.M.	6.20 P.M.	7.20 P.M.	8.20 P.M.
Athens..........Greece	6.35 P.M.	7.35 P.M.	8.35 P.M.	9.35 P.M.
Berlin..........Germany	5.54 P.M.	6.54 P.M.	7.54 P.M.	8.54 P.M.
Bombay..........India	9.51 P.M.	10.51 P.M.	11.51 P.M.	12.51 A.M.
Bremen..........Germany	5.33 P.M.	6.33 P.M.	7.33 P.M.	8.33 P.M.
Central Time (*b*). United States	11.00 A.M.	....	1.00 P.M.	2.00 P.M.
Constantinople..........Turkey	6.56 P.M.	7.56 P.M.	8.56 P.M.	9.56 P.M.
Copenhagen..........Denmark	5.50 P.M.	6.50 P.M.	7.50 P.M.	8.50 P.M.
Dublin..........Ireland	4.34 P.M.	5.35 P.M.	6.35 P.M.	7.35 P.M.
Eastern Time (*a*) United States	....	1.00 P.M.	2.00 P.M.	3.00 P.M.
Hamburg..........Germany	5.10 P.M.	6.40 P.M.	7.40 P.M.	8.40 P.M.
Havre..........France	5.00 P.M.	6.00 P.M.	7.00 P.M.	8.00 P.M.
Hong Kong..........China	12.37 A.M.*.	1.37 A.M.*	2.37 A.M.*	3.37 A.M.*
Honolulu..........Hawaii	6.29 A.M.	7.29 A.M.	8.29 A.M.	9.29 A.M.
Liverpool..........England	4.48 P.M.	5.48 P.M.	6.48 P.M.	7.48 P.M.
London..........England	5.00 P.M.	6.00 P.M.	7.00 P.M.	8.00 P.M.
Madrid..........Spain	4.45 P.M.	5.45 P.M.	6.45 P.M.	7.45 P.M.
Manila......Philippine Islands	1.04 A.M.*	2.04 A.M.*	3.04 A.M.*	4.04 A.M.*
Melbourne..........Australia	2.40 A.M.*	3.40 A.M.*	4.40 A.M.*	5.40 A.M.*
Mountain Time(*c*) United States	10.00 A.M.	11.00 A.M.	....	1.00 P.M.
Pacific Time (*d*)..United States	9.00 A.M.	10.00 A.M.	11.00 A.M.	....
Paris..........France	5.09 P.M.	6.09 P.M.	7.09 P.M.	8.09 P.M.
Rome..........Italy	5.50 P.M.	6.50 P.M.	7.50 P.M.	8.50 P.M.
Stockholm..........Sweden	6.12 P.M.	7.12 P.M.	8.12 P.M.	9.12 P.M.
St. Petersburg..........Russia	7.01 P.M.	8.01 P.M.	9.01 P.M.	10.01 P.M.
Vienna..........Austria	6.06 P.M.	7.06 P.M.	8.06 P.M.	9.06 P.M.
Yokohama..........Japan	2.19 A.M.*	3.19 A.M.*	4.19 A.M.*	5.19 A.M.*

*** At places marked * the time noted is in the morning of the following day.**

(*a*) "Eastern" includes Montreal, Quebec, Ottawa, Toronto, New York, Boston, Philadelphia, Baltimore, Washington, Richmond, Norfolk, Charleston, Buffalo, Pittsburgh.

(*b*) "Central" includes Winnipeg, Chicago, St. Louis, Minneapolis, St. Paul, Milwaukee, Kansas City, Omaha, Indianapolis, Cincinnati, Cleveland, Detroit, New Orleans, Memphis, Savannah, Pensacola, etc.

(*c*) "Mountain" includes Regina, N. W. T., Denver, Leadville, Colorado Springs, Helena, etc.

(*d*) "Pacific" includes Victoria, Vancouver, San Francisco, Portland (Oregon), Tacoma, Seattle, etc.

STANDARD TIME.

Primarily, for the convenience of the railroads, a standard of time was established by mutual agreement in 1883, by which trains are run and local time regulated. According to this system, the United States, extending from 65° to 125° west longitude, is divided into four time sections, each of 15° of longitude, exactly equivalent to one hour, commencing with the 75th meridian. The first (eastern) section includes all territory between the Atlantic Coast and an irregular line drawn from Detroit to Charleston, S. C., the latter being its most southern point. The second (central) section includes all the territory between the last-named line and an irregular line from Bismarck, N. D., to the mouth of the Rio Grande. The third (mountain) section includes all territory between the last-named line and nearly the western borders of Idaho, Utah, and Arizona. The fourth (Pacific) section covers the rest of the country to the Pacific Coast. Standard time is uniform inside each of these sections, and the time of each section differs from that next to it by exactly one hour. Thus at 12 noon in New York City (eastern time), the time at Chicago (central time) is 11 o'clock A. M.; at Denver (mountain time), 10 o'clock A. M., and at San Francisco (Pacific time), 9 o'clock A. M. Standard time is 16 minutes slower at Boston than true local time, 4 minutes slower at New York, 8 minutes faster at Washington, 19 minutes faster at Charleston, 28 minutes slower at Detroit, 18 minutes faster at Kansas City, 10 minutes slower at Chicago, 1 minute faster at St. Louis, 28 minutes faster at Salt Lake City, and 10 minutes faster at San Francisco.

TABLE OF DAYS BETWEEN TWO DATES.

A Table of the Number of Days between any two Days within Two Years.

Day / Mo.	Jan.	Feb.	Mar.	April	May	June	July	Aug.	Sept.	Oct.	Nov.	Dec.
1	1	32	60	91	121	152	182	213	244	274	305	335
2	2	33	61	92	122	153	183	214	245	275	306	336
3	3	34	62	93	123	154	184	215	246	276	307	337
4	4	35	63	94	124	155	185	216	247	277	308	338
5	5	36	64	95	125	156	186	217	248	278	309	339
6	6	37	65	96	126	157	187	218	249	279	310	340
7	7	38	66	97	127	158	188	219	250	280	311	341
8	8	39	67	98	128	159	189	220	251	281	312	342
9	9	40	68	99	129	160	190	221	252	282	313	343
10	10	41	69	100	130	161	191	222	253	283	314	344
11	11	42	70	101	131	162	192	223	254	284	315	345
12	12	43	71	102	132	163	193	224	255	285	316	346
13	13	44	72	103	133	164	194	225	256	286	317	347
14	14	45	73	104	134	165	195	226	257	287	318	348
15	15	46	74	105	135	166	196	227	258	288	319	349
16	16	47	75	106	136	167	197	228	259	289	320	350
17	17	48	76	107	137	168	198	229	260	290	321	351
18	18	49	77	108	138	169	199	230	261	291	322	352
19	19	50	78	109	139	170	200	231	262	292	323	353
20	20	51	79	110	140	171	201	232	263	293	324	354
21	21	52	80	111	141	172	202	233	264	294	325	355
22	22	53	81	112	142	173	203	234	265	295	326	356
23	23	54	82	113	143	174	204	235	266	296	327	357
24	24	55	83	114	144	175	205	236	267	297	328	358
25	25	56	84	115	145	176	206	237	268	298	329	359
26	26	57	85	116	146	177	207	238	269	299	330	360
27	27	58	86	117	147	178	208	239	270	300	331	361
28	28	59	87	118	148	179	209	240	271	301	332	362
29	29	..	88	119	149	180	210	241	272	302	333	363
30	30	..	89	120	150	181	211	242	273	303	334	364
31	31	..	90	...	151	...	212	243	...	304	...	365

TABLE OF DAYS BETWEEN TWO DATES.—Continued.

Day Mo.	Jan.	Feb.	Mar.	April	May	June	July	Aug.	Sept.	Oct.	Nov.	Dec.
1	366	397	425	456	486	517	547	578	609	639	670	700
2	367	398	426	457	487	518	548	579	610	640	671	701
3	368	399	427	458	488	519	549	580	611	641	672	702
4	369	400	428	459	489	520	550	581	612	642	673	703
5	370	401	429	460	490	521	551	582	613	643	674	704
6	371	402	430	461	491	522	552	583	614	644	675	705
7	372	403	431	462	492	523	553	584	615	645	676	706
8	373	404	432	463	493	524	554	585	616	646	677	707
9	374	405	433	464	494	525	555	586	617	647	678	708
10	375	406	434	465	495	526	556	587	618	648	679	709
11	376	407	435	466	496	527	557	588	619	649	680	710
12	377	408	436	467	497	528	558	589	620	650	681	711
13	378	409	437	468	498	529	559	590	621	651	682	712
14	379	410	438	469	499	530	560	591	622	652	683	713
15	380	411	439	470	500	531	561	592	623	653	684	714
16	381	412	440	471	501	532	562	593	624	654	685	715
17	382	413	441	472	502	533	563	594	625	655	686	716
18	383	414	442	473	503	534	564	595	626	656	687	717
19	384	415	443	474	504	535	565	596	627	657	688	718
20	385	416	444	475	505	536	566	597	628	658	689	719
21	386	417	445	476	506	537	567	598	629	659	690	720
22	387	418	446	477	507	538	568	599	630	660	691	721
23	388	419	447	478	508	539	569	600	631	661	692	722
24	389	420	448	479	509	540	570	601	632	662	693	723
25	390	421	449	480	510	541	571	602	633	663	694	724
26	391	422	450	481	511	542	572	603	634	664	695	725
27	392	423	451	482	512	543	573	604	635	665	696	726
28	393	424	452	483	513	544	574	605	636	666	697	727
29	394	...	453	484	514	545	575	606	637	667	698	728
30	395	...	454	485	515	546	576	607	638	668	699	729
31	396	...	455	...	516	...	577	608	...	669	...	730

The above table applies to ordinary years only. For leap year, one day must be added to each number of days after February 28.

EXAMPLE.—To find the number of days between June 3, 1900, and February 16, 1901: The figures opposite the third day in the first June column are 154; those opposite the sixteenth day in the second February column are 412. Subtract the first from the second product—i. e., 154 from 412, and the result is 258, the number of days between the two dates.

THE ANCIENT AND MODERN YEAR.

The Athenians began the year in June, the Macedonians in September, the Romans first in March and afterward in January, the Persians on August 11, the ancient Mexicans on February 23, the Mohammedans in July The Chinese year, which begins early in February, is similar to the Mohammedan in having 12 months of 29 and 30 days alternately; but in every nineteen years there are seven years which have 13 months. This is not quite correct, and the Chinese have therefore formed a cycle of 60 years, in which period 22 intercalary months occur.

PERPETUAL CALENDAR.—1

For ascertaining any Day of the Week for any given Time within Two Hundred Years from the introduction of the New Style, 1753 to 1952, inclusive.

1753g	1781g	1800e	1828q	1856q	1884q	1900g	1928h
1754d	1782d	1801a	1829a	1857a	1885a	1901d	1929d
1755e	1783e	1802b	1830b	1858b	1886b	1902e	1930e
1756p	1784p	1803c	1831c	1859c	1887c	1903a	1931a
1757c	1785c	1804h	1832h	1860h	1888h	1904k	1932k
1758f	1786f	1805d	1833d	1861d	1889d	1905f	1933f
1759g	1787g	1806e	1834e	1862e	1890e	1906g	1934g
1760q	1788q	1807a	1835a	1863a	1891a	1907d	1935d
1761a	1789a	1808k	1836k	1864k	1892k	1908l	1936l
1762b	1790b	1809f	1837f	1865f	1893f	1909b	1937b
1763c	1791c	1810g	1838g	1866g	1894g	1910c	1938c
1764h	1792h	1811d	1839d	1867d	1895d	1911f	1939f
1765d	1793d	1812l	1840l	1868l	1896l	1912m	1940m
1766e	1794e	1813b	1841b	1869b	1897b	1913e	1941e
1767a	1795a	1814c	1842c	1870c	1898c	1914a	1942a
1768k	1796k	1815f	1843f	1871f	1899f	1915b	1943b
1769f	1797f	1816m	1844m	1872m		1916n	1944n
1770g	1798g	1817e	1845e	1873e		1917g	1945g
1771d	1799d	1818a	1846a	1874a		1918d	1946d
1772l		1819b	1847b	1875b		1919e	1947e
1773b		1820n	1848n	1876n		1920p	1948p
1774c		1821g	1849g	1877g		1921c	1949c
1775f		1822d	1850d	1878d		1922f	1950f
1776m		1823e	1851e	1879e		1923g	1951g
1777e		1824p	1852p	1880p		1924q	1952q
1778a		1825c	1853c	1881c		1925a	
1779b		1826f	1854f	1882f		1926b	
1780n		1827g	1855g	1883g		1927c	

NOTE.—The letters in the list of "Years from 1753 to 1952" refer to the table headed with the Months, the figures in which refer to the same figures at the head of the table of Days. For example—To know on what day July 4, 1910, will fall look for 1910 in the table of Years. The letter "c" attached. Look for the same letter in the table of Months and in a parallel line under July is the figure 5, which directs to column **5 in the table of Days below, in which it will be seen that July 4 falls on Monday.**

	Jan.	Feb.	March.	April.	May.	June.	July.	August.	Sept.	Oct.	Nov.	Dec.
a	4	7	7	3	5	1	3	6	2	4	7	2
b	5	1	1	4	6	2	4	7	3	5	1	3
c	6	2	2	5	7	3	5	1	4	6	2	4
d	2	5	5	1	3	6	1	4	7	2	5	7
e	3	6	6	2	4	7	2	5	1	3	6	1
f	7	3	3	6	1	4	6	2	5	7	3	5
g	1	4	4	7	2	5	7	3	6	1	4	6
h	7	3	4	7	2	5	7	3	6	1	4	6
k	5	1	2	5	7	3	5	1	4	6	2	4
l	3	6	7	3	5	1	3	6	2	4	7	2
m	1	4	5	1	3	6	1	4	7	2	5	7
n	6	2	3	6	1	4	6	2	5	7	3	5
p	4	7	1	4	6	2	4	7	3	5	1	3
q	2	5	6	2	4	7	2	5	1	3	6	1

TABLE OF DAYS.

1	2	3	4	5	6	7
Mond. 1	Tuesd. 1	Wed. 1	Thursd. 1	Frid. 1	Satd. 1	**Sund.** 1
Tuesd. 2	Wed. 2	Thursd. 2	Frid. 2	Satd. 2	**Sund.** 2	Mond. 2
Wed. 3	Thursd. 3	Frid. 3	Satd. 3	**Sund.** 3	Mond. 3	Tuesd. 3
Thursd. 4	Frid. 4	Satd. 4	**Sund.** 4	Mond. 4	Tuesd. 4	Wed. 4
Frid. 5	Satd. 5	**Sund.** 5	Mond. 5	Tuesd. 5	Wed. 5	Thursd. 5
Satd. 6	**Sund.** 6	Mond. 6	Tuesd. 6	Wed. 6	Thursd. 6	Frid. 6
Sund. 7	Mond. 7	Tuesd. 7	Wed. 7	Thursd. 7	Frid. 7	Satd. 7
Mond. 8	Tuesd. 8	Wed. 8	Thursd. 8	Frid. 8	Satd. 8	**Sund.** 8
Tuesd. 9	Wed. 9	Thursd. 9	Frid. 9	Satd. 9	**Sund.** 9	Mond. 9
Wed. 10	Thursd. 10	Frid. 10	Satd. 10	**Sund.** 10	Mond. 10	Tuesd. 10
Thursd. 11	Frid. 11	Satd. 11	**Sund.** 11	Mond. 11	Tuesd. 11	Wed. 11
Frid. 12	Satd. 12	**Sund.** 12	Mond. 12	Tuesd. 12	Wed. 12	Thursd. 12
Satd. 13	**Sund.** 13	Mond. 13	Tuesd. 13	Wed. 13	Thursd. 13	Frid. 13
Sund. 14	Mond. 14	Tuesd. 14	Wed. 14	Thursd. 14	Frid. 14	Satd. 14
Mond. 15	Tuesd. 15	Wed. 15	Thursd. 15	Frid. 15	Satd. 15	**Sund.** 15
Tuesd. 16	Wed. 16	Thursd. 16	Frid. 16	Satd. 16	**Sund.** 16	Mond. 16
Wed. 17	Thursd. 17	Frid. 17	Satd. 17	**Sund.** 17	Mond. 17	Tuesd. 17
Thursd. 18	Frid. 18	Satd. 18	**Sund.** 18	Mond. 18	Tuesd. 18	Wed. 18
Frid. 19	Satd. 19	**Sund.** 19	Mond. 19	Tuesd. 19	Wed. 19	Thursd. 19
Satd. 20	**Sund.** 20	Mond. 20	Tuesd. 20	Wed. 20	Thursd. 20	Frid. 20
Sund. 21	Mond. 21	Tuesd. 21	Wed. 21	Thursd. 21	Frid. 21	Satd. 21
Mond. 22	Tuesd. 22	Wed. 22	Thursd. 22	Frid. 22	Satd. 22	**Sund.** 22
Tuesd. 23	Wed. 23	Thursd. 23	Frid. 23	Satd. 23	**Sund.** 23	Mond. 23
Wed. 24	Thursd. 24	Frid. 24	Satd. 24	**Sund.** 24	Mond. 24	Tuesd. 24
Thursd. 25	Frid. 25	Satd. 25	**Sund.** 25	Mond. 25	Tuesd. 25	Wed. 25
Frid. 26	Satd. 26	**Sund.** 26	Mond. 26	Tuesd. 26	Wed. 26	Thursd. 26
Satd. 27	**Sund.** 27	Mond. 27	Tuesd. 27	Wed. 27	Thursd. 27	Frid. 27
Sund. 28	Mond. 28	Tuesd. 28	Wed. 28	Thursd. 28	Frid. 28	Satd. 28
Mond. 29	Tuesd. 29	Wed. 29	Thursd. 29	Frid. 29	Satd. 29	**Sund.** 29
Tuesd. 30	Wed. 30	Thursd. 30	Frid. 30	Satd. 30	**Sund.** 30	Mond. 30
Wed. 31	Thursd. 31	Frid. 31	Satd. 31	**Sund.** 31	Mond. 31	Tuesd. 31

PERPETUAL CALENDAR.—2.

For Ascertaining the Day of the Week for any given Time from the Beginning of the Christian Era to the Year 2200.

RULE.—To the day of the month, add factors for month, century and year, and divide the total by 7.

If there is no remainder, the day is	Sunday.	Should the total be less than 7, it is to be taken as a remainder.
" 1 is the remainder "	Monday.	
" 2 " "	Tuesday.	
" 3 " "	Wednesday.	
" 4 " "	Thursday.	
" 5 " "	Friday.	
" 6 " "	Saturday.	

EXAMPLE

Week-day of February 22, 1910.
factors for

Day.		Month.		Century		Year.		
22	+	5	+	5	+	5	=	37

37 divided by 7 leaves 2 remainder, therefore the day will be **Tuesday.**

MONTHS.
For leap years figures in heavier type to be taken.

	Jan.	Feb.	Mar.	April	May	June	July	Aug.	Sept.	Oct.	Nov.	Dec.
Factors.	2	5	5	1	3	6	1	4	0	2	5	0
	1	**4**										

CENTURIES (Cardinal Numbers).
The year 00 of centuries in heavier type was, or will be, a leap year.

OLD STYLE, ended Sept. 2, 1752—a Wednesday.	2	1	0	6	5	4	3
	9	8	7	13	12	11	10
	16	15	14				17
NEW STYLE, began Sept. 14, 1752—a Thursday.	18		17		20	19	
	22		21		24	23	
	26		25		28	27	
	and every succeeding fourth century.						
Factors.	0	1	2	3	4	5	6

YEARS.
Leap years in heavier type.

00	1	2	3		**4**	5
6	7		**8**	9	10	11
	12	13	14	15		**16**
17	18	19		**20**	21	22
23		**24**	25	26	27	
28	29	30	31		**32**	33
34	35		**36**	37	38	39
	40	41	42	43		**44**
45	46	47		**48**	49	50
51		**52**	53	54	55	
56	57	58	59		**60**	61
62	63		**64**	65	66	67
	68	69	70	71		**72**
73	74	75		**76**	77	78
79		**80**	81	82	83	
84	85	86	87		**88**	89
90	91		**92**	93	94	95
	96	97	98	99		
0	1	2	3	4	5	6

DICTIONARY OF OBSCURE WORDS USED IN CROSS WORD PUZZLE CONSTRUCTION

A

aa, cooled rough lava: Hawaiian; of each: med. abbr.
aal, the Indian mulberry; morindin dye. Same as **al.**
aam, old Dutch or German liquid measure.
Aar, Swiss river.
Ab, Jewish month.
aba, Arabian garment made of camel's hair cloth.
abb, the woof, or yarn for it; poorest part of a fleece.
abele, the white poplar.
Abi, mother of King Hezekiah.
Abt, German musician.
Abu, Abou, Arabic term for "father."
Adar, Jewish month.
Aden, Arabian seaport.
aes, bronze or copper, esp. money: Roman Antiq.
aet., of the age: Lat. abbr.
Aeta, Negrito of the Philippines.
Afer, the southwest wind.
Ag, symbol for silver.
aga, Turkish commander; also title of respect.
agar, edible substance derived from Ceylon moss.
agio, exchange premium.
agist, pasture or graze for hire.
agora, Greek market place.
aha, sunken fence.
ai, three-toed sloth.
Aino, Ainu, Japanese native.
ait, small island.
ake, forever: Maori. New Zealand tree.
al, the Indian mulberry.
ala, wing: plural, **alae.**
alai, regiment in the Turkish army.
alamo, the poplar; Texas mission.
alan, large hunting dog; wolf hound.
alate, winged.
alb, priest's white vestment.
Alea, appellation of Athena.
alec, fish pickle or sauce; herring.
aline, to place in line; variant of **align.**
alma, alme (h), Egyptian singing girl.
alod, real estate held in absolute independence.
ama, ancient ecclesiastical wine receptacle.
amah, Oriental nurse.
ambo, large pulpit in early churches.
amma, abbess or spiritual mother.
amole, plant used as soap.
ana, collection of facts; literary fragments; of each: med.
anana(s), the pineapple.
anay, anai, white ant or termite: Philippine Islands.
anele, anoint.
anet, the herb dill; dillseed.
ani, tropical black bird of the cuckoo family.
anil, indigo plant.
anile, old-womanish; imbecile.
anoa, small wild ox of Celebes.
ansa, handle.
anta, pier treated as a pilaster: Arch.
Anu, supreme Babylonian god.
Anura, order of amphibians.

Apa, river between Brazil and Paraguay.
Apo, highest mountain in the Philippines.
apod, footless animal.
ar(e), 100 square meters; metric land measure.
Ara, Southern constellation; Greek goddess; Genus of macaws; l.c., Polynesian screw pine.
araba, Oriental wagon.
arar, Moroccan sandarac tree.
arara, Brazilian macaw; Australian palm cockatoo.
aril, accessory seed covering.
areca, Asiatic palm.
arete, sharp, rugged mountain crest.
arna, arnee, the wild buffalo of India.
artel, association of Russian laborers.
as, Roman weight or coin; any Teutonic deity; A-flat: mus.
Ase, character in Ibsen's "Peer Gynt."
Asti, town in Italy.
Asur, Assyrian deity; one of the Munda languages.
at(t), Siamese coin.
Ata, savage of the island of Luzon.
atabal, Moorish kettledrum.
atar, oil of rose petals; variant of **Attar.**
Ate, Character in "The Faerie Queene"; goddess of mischief.
Aten, Egyptian solar disk.
ates, the sweetsop: Philippine Islands.
atle(e), tamarisk salt tree.
atole, corn meal mush: Mex.
att, Siamese coin.
atta, wheaten flour or meal: India.
Atta, Luzon savage; variant of **Ata.**
ava, topaz humming bird.
aviso, information; dispatch boat.
awn, beard of grain.

B

ba, the soul: Egypt. Relig.
Baal, Semitic god; any false god.
barm, yeast formed on brewing liquors.
Bast, Egyptian goddess.
bast, strong woody fiber of trees.
Bel, Babylonian god.
bel, East Indian tree.
ben, Moringa seed or oil.
benne, the sesame or its seeds.
bis, twice; encore.
bleb, blister or bubble.
blet, kind of internal decay in fruit.
bolas, South American missile weapon.
bora, prevalent winter wind over the Adriatic.
Bos, genus of the cow.
bu, Japanese coin or weight.

C

cal, wolframite.
casa, Italian or Spanish house.
cena, principal meal of the ancient Romans.
Ceres, Roman goddess of growing vegetation.
chal, gypsy man.
chai, chi, gypsy woman.
cho, Japanese measure.
Cid, Spanish hero.
cit, inhabitant of a city.
coda, closing musical measures.
col, depression between mountain peaks.
Cola, genus of African trees.
colin, American quail.
cor, brightest star in a constellation.
cos, a race of lettuce.

D

dak, transportation; mail: India.
daman, small mammal of Asia Minor; the cony of the Old Testament.

Danae, mother of Perseus by Zeus.
Danai, the Greeks: Class. Lit.
decad, the number ten; group of ten tones.
dele, erase; take out.
deme, division of ancient Greece.
dene, sand hill: Eng.
deva, a divine being or god: Hinduism.
Devi, Hindu god.
Dis, Roman god of the underworld.
dita, forest tree of eastern Asia and the Philippines.
doge, former Venetian magistrate.
dop, small cup to hold diamonds while cutting them.
dor, kind of beetle; trick; joke; practical joker.
dur, major: mus.

E

Ea, Babylonian god.
eagre, tidal wave.
ean, bring forth young, as sheep.
ebo(e), Central American tree.
ecce, behold: Latin.
ecu, old French coin.
Edam, Dutch pressed cheese; town in Holland.
Edar, Biblical tower.
Edda, either of two works in Old Norse or Icelandic language.
Ede, city in Holland; town in British West Africa.
Eder, German river; same as Edar.
Edom, Esau; Biblical country.
eft, newt; lizard.
egest, excrete.
egis, shield; protection.
Eire, Irish word for Ireland.
ela, highest note in Guido Aretino's scale.
elan, ardor; dash.
elater, click beetle; snapping beetle.
eleme, superior Smyrna figs.
elemi, fragrant gum resin; same as **eleme.**
Elia, Charles Lamb's pen name.
elisor, person appointed to act for a sheriff or coroner.
eloge, funeral oration.
Elon, a judge of Israel.
Elsa, heroine of Wagner's "Lohengrin."
Elul, Jewish month.
eme, uncle: Scotch.
Emesa, genus of long-legged bugs resembling stick insects.
emir, emeer, Arabian chieftain.
enalid, plant growing on the sea bottom.
enate, growing out; related on the mother's side.
Enid, wife of Geraint in Arthurian legend.
ennea-, nine: comb. form.
ennead, the number nine; group of nine.
ente, grafted: heraldry.
eoan, pertaining to the dawn.
Eos, goddess of dawn.
eosin, rose-red dye.
epi, slender finial: Arch.
epode, after song.
epos, epic poem.
Er, Teutonic deity; Son of Judah.
Erato, muse of lyric poetry.
erg(on), unit of work.
ergo, therefore.
ergot, disease of rye and other cereals.
eri(a), Assamese silkworm or its silk.
erica, heather.
ern(e), sea eagle.
Eros, Greek god of love; 433rd asteroid.
ers, the bitter vetch.
Erse, Gaelic; language of the Scottish Highlanders.
Esek, well dug by Isaac's servants.
esne, Anglo-Saxon slave.
esse, to be: Latin; existence.
Este, princely house of Italy.

ester, compound ether; ethereal salt.
Etamin, star in the dragon.
etape, public storehouse; day's march; Russian stockade.
etna, device for heating liquids.
ettle, try: Scotch.
etui, etwee, small toilet case.
Evea, genus of tropical herbs and shrubs; source of ipecac.
evoe, cry of the ancient bacchanals.
ewer, pitcher.
eyas, nestling or unfledged bird; young hawk.

F

faro, gambling game.
Fe, symbol for iron.
feral, untamed; savage; brutal.
ferial, pertaining to a day neither feast nor fast.
fez, Turkish cap.
fob, watch pocket.

G

Ga, linguistic stock of Gold Coast Negroes.
Gaea, Gaia, Greek goddess of earth.
gam, school of whales.
Ge, same as **Gaea.**
ger, stranger received into a Hebrew tribe.
gnu, African antelope.
goa, Tibetan gazelle.

H

hadj, the pilgrimage of a Moslem to Mecca.
haha, sunken fence.
Hebe, goddess of youth; cupbearer of the gods.
Hera, Olympian goddess; sister and wife of Zeus; queen of heaven.
hob, projection in fireplace.

I

ibex, wild goat of the Old World.
ibis, wading bird.
Ibo, Negro of the Niger delta.
ici, here (French).
icon, sacred image.
id, hypothetical structural unit: biology; small European fish.
ide, same as **id,** fish.
Ido, artificial language.
imam, imaum, Mohammedan priest.
impale, to transfix with anything sharp.
impi, body of Kafir warriors of native armed men: So. Afr.
ina, mother: Tagalog.
Inca, Peruvian emperor, chieftain or Indian
inee, African arrow poison.
Inia, genus of dolphin-like cetaceans; fresh-water porpoise.
ion, electrified particle.
Iona, one of the Hebrides Islands.
Ione, character in "The Last Days of Pompeii."
Ioni, Caddoan Indian.
ipil, timber tree of the Pacific Islands.
Ira, one of David's chief rulers; Babylonian war god.
iris, the rainbow; flower; seventh asteroid.
irone, odoriferous principle of violet root and leaves.
Ise, Danish fiord.
Isis, Egyptian goddess.
Ita, Negrito, Variant of **Aeta.**
Itea, genus of shrubs including the Virginia willow.
iter, Roman road.
iva, the yellow bugle, or herb eve.

K

ka, genius of the body: Egypt. Relig.
kat, Arabian shrub used like tea.
kea, sheep-killing parrot of New Zealand.

ker, ghost; disembodied soul: Greek. Relig.

L

labile, unstable; gliding.
Lalo, French composer.
lalo, powdered leaves of the baobab tree.
Lao, one of a branch of the Tai race.
lar, Roman household god (pl. **lares**): gibbon of the Malayan peninsula.
Leda, mother of Castor and Pollux, Clytemnestra, and Helen of Troy.
leet, early English court.
lei, Hawaiian wreath; plural of **leu.**
Lena, Siberian river.
lene, smooth; voiceless and nonaspirate.
leno, light open cotton fabric.
Ler, Gaelic god of the sea.
Leto, mother of Apollo and Artemis.
Lett, one of a people inhabiting the Kurland peninsula.
leu, gold monetary unit of Rumania.
lev, lew, gold monetary unit of Bulgaria.
leveret, young hare.
li, Chinese measure of distance.
liana, liane, any climbing woody perennial.
lin (n), waterfall: Scotch.
lis, fleur-de-lis; circular enclosure or fortification: Irish Antiq.
llano, flat, treeless plain of South America.
Lleu, Cymric sun god.
Loasa, genus of tropical American prickly herbs.
loco, crazy: Spanish; weed poisonous to animals.
loess, peculiar deposit of loam.
loo, card game.
lore, space between the eye and bill in birds; similar space in fishes and reptiles: pl. **lora.**
Lua, Roman goddess to whom were devoted captured arms.

M

malar, pertaining to the cheek.
Mara, bitter: Bib.; Nightmare taken as a demon: Teut. Folklore; Spirit of evil: Hindu Mythol.
melos, continuous melodic outline unbroken by a cadence.
mene, first word of the handwriting on the wall.
mere, small lake.
mesa, tableland or plateau with steep sides.
meta, boundary.
mir, Russian village community.
mo, Japanese money of account.
moa, extinct New Zealand bird.
mora, Italian guessing game; culpable delay: law; South American tree.
moraine, accumulation deposited by a glacier.

N

Nama, African Hottentot.
nare, nostril.
nat, Burmese spirit of the wood or stream; wandering Hindu acrobat.
Nebo, mountain whence Moses saw the promised land, and died.
née, born.
nef, clock or table vessel in the form of a ship.
neo-, new, recent, late: comb. form.
Neri, medieval political faction in Italy.
ness, cape; headland.
neve, glacial snow field; field of granular snow.
nome, province of modern Greece or ancient Egypt.
Nona, one of the Roman Fates.
Nora, character in Ibsen's "A Doll's House."

noria, kind of water wheel.
Nut, mother of Ra.
nye, brood of pheasants.

O

Ob, Siberian river.
obe, sub-division of a clan in ancient Laconia.
obi, West Indian sorcery; Japanese sash.
obol, ancient Greek coin.
oca, South American wood sorrel or its edible tuber.
octo-, eight: comb. form.
od, hypothetical force supposed to produce hypnotism.
oda, room in a harem.
odeon, Greek theater.
oe, whirlwind off the Faroe Islands; grandchild: Scotch.
Og, king of Bashan.
ogee, S-shaped molding.
ola, **ole**, leaf of the palmyra palm.
Olea, genus of the olive tree.
olent, fragrant.
oleo, butter substitute; oil: comb. form.
olio, stewed dish; medley; hodgepodge; part of a minstrel show.
om, mystic Hindu word.
Omar, the Tentmaker (Omar Khayyam).
Ona, Indian of Tierra del Fuego.
oo, Hawaiian bird.
ooaa, Hawaiian bird; the dwarf oo.
oom, Dutch uncle.
opah, large oceanic fish.
Ops, Roman goddess of the harvest.
opus, musical work: abbr., *op.*
ora, Anglo-Saxon money of account; plural of **os**, mouth.
ore, Scandinavian coin; seaweed.
orle, heraldic bearing; wreath bearing a knight's crest.
orlop, lowest deck of a man-of-war.
oro-, mountain: comb. form.
os, mouth; bone; plural, **ossa.**
osar, glacial ridges.
Ossa, Mountain in Greece.
otic, pertaining to the ear.
Oto (e), Siouan Indian.
otto, oil of rose petals: variant of **attar.**
ovi-, **ovo-**, ovum: comb. form.
ovolo, rounded convex molding.
ovum, egg cell.

P

pac, moccasin; lumberman's half-boot.
paca, South and Central American rodent.
pam, card game; highest trump in five-card loo.
para, Turkish coin; New Zealand fish.
parr, young salmon.
pas, dance step; French negative.
pe, Hebrew letter
peba, small armadillo.
pee, part of a turtle attached to the lower shell, esteemed as a delicacy.
pel, stake once used as a dummy in sword practice.
peri, Persian fairy; around: prefix.
pes, footlike part.
pesa, coin of German East Africa.
peso, Central and South American coin.
pina, the pineapple.
plat, interweave; floor for loading in a mine; plot of ground; plan of a town site.
poi, Hawaiian food made from the taro.
Poa, genus of the meadow grasses.
pone, johnnycake: Southern U.S.; player who cuts the cards.
pood, Russian weight.
proa, Malayan outrigger sailing canoe.
Ptah, chief god of Memphis: Egypt. Relig.

R

Ra, Egyptian sun god.
ra, sail yard: Scotch.
rabat, clerical linen collar.
rabi, most important harvest of India.
raca, worthless: Bib.
raggee, ragi, East Indian cereal grass.
rale, adventitious morbid respiratory sound.
Rama, an incarnation of Vishnu; Hindu deity.
ramie, Asiatic plant or its fiber.
ramose, having branches.
Rana, genus of the common frog; East Indian prince.
ranee, rani, Hindu queen.
ras, Oriental ship captain; short-napped fabric.
rata, New Zealand timber tree.
ratel, badgerlike animal; the honey badger.
rea, the turmeric.
rebec, earliest known instrument of the viol class.
redan, kind of fortification.
rede, plan or scheme; interpret: both archaic.
rei, Portuguese or Brazilian money of account.
reina, rena, California rockfish.
rep, corded or ribbed fabric.
res, thing; action at law.
rete, nerve network; plural, **retia.**
Rhea, daughter of Uranus and "Mother of the Gods."
ri, Japanese measure of distance.
ria, long narrow inlet of the sea.
rin, Japanese measure and weight.
Ro, artificial language.
roc, fabulous mythical bird of Arabia so huge that it bore off elephants to feed its young.
rota, list; ecclesiastical court.
rote, meaningless repetition; sound of the surf on the shore.
rugose, wrinkled.
rune, early alphabetic character.

S

Sac, Sauk, Algonquian Indian.
sai, Capuchin monkey.
saic, kind of ketch or sailing vessel common in the Levant.
sake, saki, Japanese fermented liquor.
sala, large front room or hall: Spanish.
sari, principal garment of a Hindu woman.
sec, dry; without sugar: said of wine.
Selene, Greek goddess of the moon.
seme, sown; strewn or scattered over with small bearings: heraldry.
sen, Japanese coin.
Senta, heroine of Wagner's "Flying Dutchman."
seps, Old World lizard.
sept, medieval Irish social unit.
ser, a weight of India.
serac, pinnacle of ice in a glacier.
serin, European finch.
seta, bristle.
seton, surgical thread.
setose, bristly.
shea, African tree.
Shiva, Siva, Hindu deity.
soc, a seeking; jurisdiction: A.-S. and Early Eng. Law.
sora, rail bird.
spile, spout for drawing sap.
stere, cubic meter.
stoa, portico: Greek Arch.

T

taa, Chinese or Japanese pagoda.
tai, Japanese porgy.
Tai, linguistic stock of Indo-China.
taj, pointed cap worn by dervishes.
tal, Hindu religious cymbals: the palmyra palm of India.

tana, Sumatran squirrel shrew; same as **thana.**
tapa, tappa, bark of the paper mulberry or the cloth made from it.
taro, tropical plant; edible tuber from which poi is made.
tarot, 14th century playing card.
tarn, mountain lake.
tass, drinking cup: obs., Scotch, or dial.
ted, Spread loosely.
telial, Pertaining to spores of a fungus.
terete, cylindrical in transverse section, as many plant stems.
terry, upholstery cloth.
thana, police station: India.
tic, habitual convulsive motion of certain muscles; twitching.
til, sesame.
Tinea, genus of the common clothes moth.
tinea, ringworm.
Tiu, Teutonic deity; same as **Tyr.**
tod, bushy clump.
tor, high, pointed hill; rocky pinnacle.
torii, Japanese gateway.
tye, chain or rope used for hoisting a yard or mast.
Tyr, Tyrr, Teutonic sky and war god; god for whom Tuesday is named.

U

Una, character in Spenser's "Faerie Queene."
unau, two-toed sloth.
Urdu, important dialect of India.
Uri, canton in Switzerland.
usee, one for whose use a thing is done or given.
Ute, Shoshonean Indian.
utile, useful.
uva, pulpy fruit, of which the grape is typical.
uve, Philippine yam.
uvea, posterior pigmented portion of the iris; colored portion of the eye.

V

Ve, a brother of Odin.
Veda, most ancient sacred literature of the Hindus.
Vili, a brother of Odin.
vint, make wine.
vis, power.

X

xat, carved memorial post of certain Indians.
xylo-, wood: comb. form.
xyst, long open portico for athletic exercises: Gk. and Rom. Arch.

Y

yad, pointer used in Hebrew synagogues.
Yap, island in the Pacific.
Ymer, primeval giant of Norse mythology.

Z

zax, tool for trimming and puncturing roofing slates.
Zeno, Greek philosopher.